BUSINESS FIRMS
MASTER INDEX

op '94

Related Gale Publications

Business Organizations and Agencies Directory. Covers business organizations, government agencies, commodity and stock exchanges, associations, trade and convention centers, trade fairs, chambers of commerce, and other sources of information about business-related activities. Also available: interedition supplement.

Business Publications Index and Abstracts. An indexing and abstracting service covering over 700 business periodicals and thousands of business books each year. ***Subject-Author Citations*** and ***Abstracts*** are available separately. Each is published in monthly issues with annual cumulations.

Directory of Directories. Thoroughly describes and indexes over 8,000 directories of all kinds. The subject index uses 2,000 headings and many cross references. Also available: interedition supplements.

Encyclopedia of Business Information Sources. Subject-arranged guide to both live and print sources of information on 1,280 topics. With 20,000 citations altogether. Also available: interedition supplement.

Research Services Directory. Provides full details on 2,000 for-profit organizations that offer research services on a contract or fee-for-service basis to a wide range of clients. Also available: interedition supplements.

Small Business Sourcebook. A guide to information services furnished by associations, consultants, educational programs, government agencies, franchisers, trade shows, and venture capital firms for 100 types of small businesses. Also available: interedition supplement.

Trade Shows and Professional Exhibits Directory. Covers a wide range of gatherings in the U.S. and elsewhere that include exhibits—conferences, conventions, trade and industrial shows, expositions, and similar events. Gives dates, locations, attendance, price for display space, exhibits manager, and more. Also available: interedition supplements.

Trade Names Dictionary. A guide to 194,000 consumer-oriented brand names, with addresses of their manufacturers or distributors. Also available: ***Trade Names Dictionary: Company Index.*** In this companion volume to *TND*, each company-and-address entry is followed by an alphabetical listing of its brands. Also available: ***New Trade Names***, interedition supplements.

BUSINESS FIRMS MASTER INDEX

A Guide to Sources of Information on Approximately 110,000 Companies in the United States and Including Canadian and Other Selected Foreign Firms

FIRST EDITION

The first edition covers business firms in the field of communications, and includes advertising agencies, cable networks, computer companies, databases, information systems, newspapers, periodicals, public relations firms, publishers, radio and television stations, telecommunications systems, and other related businesses.

Jennifer Mossman and Donna Wood,
Editors

Gale Research Company • Book Tower • Detroit, Michigan 48226

Editors: Jennifer Mossman, Donna Wood
Assistant Editor: Elwanda Houseworth Smith

Production Director: Carol Blanchard
Senior Production Associate: Mary Beth Trimper
Production Associate: Dorothy Kalleberg
Art Director: Arthur Chartow
Internal Production Supervisor: Laura Bryant
Senior Production Assistant: Louise Gagné
Production Assistants: Sandy Rock, Lord T. Seyon

Editorial Data Systems Director: Dennis LaBeau
Program Design: Donald G. Dillaman
Editorial Data Entry Supervisor: Doris D. Goulart
Editorial Data Entry Associate: Jean Portfolio
Senior Data Entry Assistants: Dorothy Cotter, Sue Lynch, Mildred Sherman, Joyce M. Stone, Anna Marie Woolard
Data Entry Assistants: Ann Blake, William P. Maher, Agnes T. Roland, Patricia Smith, Ann Stockham

Publisher: Frederick G. Ruffner
Executive Vice-President/Editorial: James M. Ethridge
Editorial Director: Dedria Bryfonski
Director, Indexes and Dictionaries Division: Ellen T. Crowley

Library of Congress Cataloging in Publication Data

Main entry under title:

Business firms master index: a guide to sources of information on approximately 110,000 companies in the United States and including Canadian and other selected foreign firms.

Bibliography: p. 11
1. Corporations—United States—Indexes.
2. Corporations—Canada—Indexes. 3. Business enterprises—United States—Indexes. 4. Business enterprises—Canada—Indexes. I. Mossman, Jennifer. II. Wood, Donna, 1949- . III. Gale Research Company.
Z7164.T87B87 1985 016.3387'4'0973 85-1671
ISBN 0-8103-2077-0
[HD2785]

Computerized photocomposition by
Sogitec Incorporated
Lakewood, California

Printed in the United States of America

Contents

Preface to the First Edition 7
Format and Arrangement of Entries 9
List of Sources Cited 11
Business Firms Master Index 21

Preface to
the First Edition

In a world where information proliferates at a rate that is almost unfathomable, the task of finding specific data could be likened to searching for the proverbial needle in the haystack. The types of information needed and the reasons for seeking it are many, but all have one thing in common—the job can be done more efficiently with a point in the right direction.

It is the purpose of *Business Firms Master Index (BFMI)* to provide that starting point for researchers trying to locate specific and often hard-to-find information about companies. The information seekers may be librarians, prospective employees, consumers, journalists, students, businesspeople, career counselors, or others. All too often, the search is time-consuming and nonproductive, because no source with the appropriate information can be found or because there are simply too many sources to examine on an individual basis. Even if the company in question is located, the information provided may not be what is needed, and the search must continue. *BFMI* narrows the focus of these often difficult searches by citing and describing potential sources of information.

First Edition Focuses on Communications Field

The first edition of *BFMI* indexes sources of information on 109,683 public and private business firms located, for the most part, in the United States, but also including Canadian and foreign firms if they are represented in the sources being indexed. When faced with the vast number of businesses in the United States alone, the editors of *Business Firms Master Index* concluded that limiting the companies being indexed to a particular subject area would be a logical approach to the first edition. Therefore, the dynamic and ever-expanding field of communications was chosen as a starting point.

Included within the broad field of communications are publishers, advertising agencies, film production companies, public relations firms, telephone companies, computer companies, databases, newspapers, periodicals, TV and radio stations, cable networks and services, online services, and information systems.

Future editions of *BFMI* will expand coverage into many other subject areas.

Annotated Bibliography Aids Search

Entries in *Business Firms Master Index* include the company name, available divisional and affiliate information, a city and state or country for identification purposes, and one or more citations for sources containing information about that particular company. The citations are limited to a short abbreviation for the title of the source and its edition or year.

The bibliography (List of Sources Cited, page 11) decodes the abbreviation used for each of the 57 sources indexed and provides a full bibliographic citation. The annotation indicates what specific facts are found in a particular source, thus narrowing the search in many cases. Also included may be guidelines concerning the arrangement of the source, if it is unusual or not easily discernible by the user.

Selection of Sources

It is not the purpose of *BFMI* to index sources containing minimal and easily obtainable information. Rather, sources are chosen with particular attention to the amount and quality of information available in them. The kinds of sources indexed include directories, encyclopedias, buying guides, special issues of periodicals, yearbooks, handbooks, factbooks, and almanacs. To be considered for indexing, a source must include the company name, address, phone number, chief executive officer or contact, and, most importantly, information concerning specific aspects of the company's activities, concerns, or structure. It should be noted that the annotated bibliography outlines only the additional information available that is beyond the basic criteria for inclusion just noted.

Scope of Information Available

Although the focus of one indexed source may be to provide financial information about the firms listed within it, another source may provide an entirely different approach and focus on the personnel of a company or the services provided by it or the outlook for its future. *BFMI* selects sources with substantial, current, and varied types of information, often considered to provide an in-depth look at a company. Thus, the user may locate only the specific fact that is needed or, by exploring all the citations listed, may compile a body of facts about the company that is unequaled by an individual sketch.

Acknowledgments

When the concept for *Business Firms Master Index* was being formulated and when editorial approaches and guidelines were being developed, the advice and suggestions of several librarians were of significant help to the editors.

These advisors included Bethia Bamberger, Bloomfield Township (Michigan) Public Library; the late Carol Holbrook, University of Michigan Business Library; Sally Kalin, Fred Lewis Pattee Library, Pennsylvania State University; and Charles Popovich, Ohio State University Commerce Library. They contributed suggestions and ideas about the format of *BFMI,* submitted lists of potential sources on companies in the field of communications, and conveyed the needs of library patrons seeking information on business firms. Their support and interest in this undertaking is greatly appreciated.

Special thanks to the *Trade Names Dictionary* editorial staff—Victoria Dickinson, Lisa Granville, and Cynthia Spomer—whose efforts enabled us to meet a production schedule deadline.

Suggestions Are Welcome

Since subsequent editions of *Business Firms Master Index* are planned, the editors welcome suggestions for additional works that can be indexed, other types of business firms that might be covered, and comments that will increase the usefulness and comprehensiveness of this reference tool.

Format and Arrangement of Entries

Each entry in *Business Firms Master Index* consists of a company name, corporate affiliation (when provided by the source), location, and one or more source-identification codes.

(1) **A & G Research Inc.** [Div. of Michael Amoroso Inc.] (2) -
New York, NY (3) - *IntDirMarRes 83* (4)

(1) Company Name

Company names generally appear in *BFMI* as they are given in the sources being cited. The following exceptions should be noted:

A) English articles ("A," "An," and "The") are transposed if they begin a company name, while foreign articles are left in their original order:

AAA Traveler, The
Bit-Better Software, A
El Arte Tipografico
La Belle Vision Inc.

B) Given names or initials, when used in combination with surnames, are transposed if they begin a company name:

Aaron Associates Inc., Leslie
Abaci, C.

(2) Corporate Affiliation

Corporate or institutional affiliation and divisional information may assist the user in identifying a company. This type of information has been included whenever it was provided by the source:

AAMSI Communication Network [of American Association for Medical Systems & Informatics]
Abbeville Meridional [of Louisiana State Newspapers]
Abernethy Publishing, Ernest H. [Div. of Southeast Advertising Inc.]
Addison-Wesley Publishing Co. Inc. (General Books Div.)
Addison-Wesley Publishing Co. Inc. (Medical/Nursing Div.)
Addison-Wesley Publishing Co. Inc. (School Div.)
Agricultural Online Access [of U.S. Dept. of Agriculture]
Ahsahta Press [of Boise State University]

(3) Location

Because many company names are quite similar, geographic location is helpful in differentiating among them. Location information includes city, state or province, and country (for foreign business firms).

(4) Source Identification

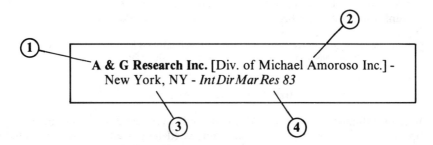

Each entry identifies one or more sources to be consulted by providing the abbreviated title as well as an edition number or year of publication. Page numbers are included for those company names not easily found in the cited source. If a business firm appears in more than one edition of the same reference work, the abbreviated title is listed once and then followed by the appropriate edition information: LitMarPl 83, 84.

The List of Sources Cited should be consulted for complete bibliographic information. Extensive annotations describe the type of information contained in each source as well as any unusual arrangement of which the user should be aware. For quick reference, a list of the abbreviated titles and their full forms can be found on the end sheets.

Cross References Included

All cross references appearing in indexed publications have been retained in *BFMI.* It is not unusual to find a complete listing under a company name, followed by a cross reference that directs the user to a related company (often the parent organization) where further information will be found:

Ambler Gazette - Ambler, PA - Ed&PubIntYB 82
Ambler Gazette - *See* Montgomery Publishing Co.

Alphabetical Arrangement

Companies are listed in one alphabetic sequence. All words and letters are considered, including & ("and") and # ("number"). Spacing affects alphabetizing, and hyphenated names and names separated by a slash mark are treated as separate words. Groups of initials are filed as though they were words. If a company name contains a numeral, it is alphabetized as though the numeral were spelled out. Thus, "1776 Publishing Co." is arranged alphabetically as "Seventeen Seventy Six Publishing Co."

Those companies with the same name are arranged by location—U.S. companies appear first, arranged by state and, then, city within state. They are followed by foreign firms, arranged by country and city (or province) within country:

Advocate - Greenville, AL
Advocate - Julesburg, AL
Advocate - Providence, RI
Advocate - Vancouver, BC, Canada
Advocate - Erin, ON, Canada
Advocate - London, England
Advocate - Manchester, England

Variations in Sources

A great deal of variation exists in the arrangement of names among sources dealing with the same subject area. For example, the editors discovered that some newspaper sources include a city name as the first element of the entry, whereas others routinely omit any reference to a location. Rather than altering these entries in order to standardize *BFMI*, the decision was made to list these and other types of company names as given by the sources being cited. Listings may be found, for instance, under either the "Andalusia Star News," the "Star News," or both.

Further, apparent discrepancies in the locations of newspapers or radio and TV stations may be encountered. These reflect the sources' varied approaches to arrangement: some list such firms under the actual location of the companies' offices, while others list them under the general geographic areas served. In order to facilitate research, *BFMI*'s location listings correspond to those found in the individual sources.

Users are encouraged to consider the possible variations in company name and location to obtain complete citations.

List of Sources Cited

Code	*Publication Indexed*
AdAge	*Advertising Age.* Chicago: Crain Communications. A biweekly periodical that includes in-depth profiles featuring financial and personnel information.
ADAPSO MemDir	*ADAPSO Membership Directory.* Arlington, Va.: Association of Data Processing Service Organizations, 1983. Includes: personnel, founding date, type of ownership, products handled, branch offices, description of services.
ArtMar	*Artist's Market.* Edited by Sally Ann Davis. Cincinnati: Writer's Digest Books, 1983. Includes: type of business, clients, requirements for initial contact, payment schedules, advice on approach, focus of submitted material.
AvMarPl	*Audiovisual Market Place.* New York: R. R. Bowker Co., 1983. Includes: personnel, products handled, catalog availability.
AyerDirPub	*The IMS Ayer Directory of Publications.* Fort Washington, Pa.: IMS Press, 1983. Includes: information on community served (such as population, location, chief industry), founding date, frequency of publication, political affiliation, circulation, specifications, subscription rate.
BaconPub CkMag	*Bacon's Publicity Checker - Magazines.* 32nd ed. Chicago: Bacon's Publishing Co., 1983. Includes: frequency of publication, publication date, circulation, publishing company or sponsoring organization, features within the publication itself, format, requirements for submitted art work, subject focus.
BaconPub CkNews	*Bacon's Publicity Checker - Newspapers.* 32nd ed. Chicago: Bacon's Publishing Co., 1983. Includes: circulation, times and days issued, personnel. Newspapers are arranged by frequency of publication, either daily or weekly. Within these two classifications, entries are arranged geographically. Within the weekly newspaper section, black weekly newspapers and multiple publishers can also be found.
BillIntBG	*Billboard International Buyer's Guide.* New York: Billboard Publications Inc., 1983. Includes: personnel, record labels owned and distributed, cable address, Telex number, branch offices, products supplied, format of products available, products needed.

BoPubDir *Book Publishers Directory.* Edited by Linda S. Hubbard. Detroit: Gale Research Co., 1983, 1984.

BoPubDir 4	4th edition, 1983
BoPubDir 4 Sup	4th edition supplement, 1983
BoPubDir 5	5th edition, 1984

(title changed to: *Publishers Directory* in 5th edition) 2 vols.

Includes: founding date, standard address number (SAN), participation in Cataloging in Publication (CIP), International Standard Book Number (ISBN), subject specialties, discounts, return policy and address, imprints, selected titles, number of titles in print.

Br *Broadcasting.* Washington, D.C.: Broadcasting Publications.

A weekly periodical that includes in-depth profiles featuring financial information.

BrCabYB *Broadcasting Cablecasting Yearbook.* Washington, D.C.: Broadcasting Publications, 1984.

Listings for stations include: date of first appearance, frequency, licensee name and date of acquisition, network affiliations, programming, personnel, advertising rates.

Listings for cable TV systems include: personnel, area served, county of area served, type of TV market, statistics, system summary, access channels, origination, advertising acceptance, services provided, ownership.

Additional information about cable companies listed in the section titled "Multiple System Operators," beginning on page D-296, is found in the section "Cable TV Systems in the United States and Canada," beginning on page D-6, arranged by area served.

Many other companies involved in broadcasting and cablecasting are also represented. The information presented in connection with these companies varies.

CabTVFinDB *The Cable TV Financial Databook.* Carmel, Calif.: Paul Kagan Associates, 1983.

Includes: personnel, subscriber and system statistical data, products/services.

CabTVPrDB *The Cable TV Program Databook.* Carmel, Calif.: Paul Kagan Associates, 1983.

Includes: personnel, launch date, affiliates, subscribers, availability, programming.

CompReadDB *Computer-Readable Databases.* Compiled and edited by Martha E. Williams, Laurence Lannom, and Carolyn G. Robins. White Plains, N.Y.: Knowledge Industry Publications for the American Society for Information Science, 1982.

Includes: acronym, frequency of updates, time coverage, producer, availability and charges, subject matter, elements of entry, user aids.

DataDirOnSer *Datapro Directory of On-Line Services.* 2 vols. Edited by Linda B. Drumheller. Delran, N.J.: Datapro Research Corp., 1984.

Listings for online services include: history, resources and facilities, application-specific services, industry-specific services, networking services, online databases, other services, future plans.

Listings for companies include: principal business, applications emphasis, founding date, personnel, revenues, primary customers, sales concentration, products.

Listings for online databases include: type of organization, scope of coverage, type of database, frequency of update, usage, pricing arrangements, applications emphasis, training and installation services, documentation, services vendors, description.

DataDirSup *Directory of Suppliers.* Delran, N.J.: Datapro Research Corp., 1983.
Includes: founding date, personnel, sales and earnings, services.

Datamation *Datamation.* New York: Technical Publishing Co.
A monthly periodical that includes in-depth profiles.
Arrangement of entries is by ranking within the industry.

DBBus *Data Bases for Business.* By Van Mayros and D. Michael Werner. Radnor, Pa.: Chilton Book Co., 1982.
Includes: type, size, subject coverage, applications, cross references, geographic coverage, time coverage, vendors, description.

DirInfWP *The Directory of Information/Word Processing Equipment and Services.* New York: Information Clearing House for the International Information/Word Processing Association, 1982.
Includes products and services.

DirMarMP *The Direct Marketing Market Place.* Hewlett Harbor, N.Y.: Hilary House Publishers, 1983; distributed by R. R. Bowker Co.
Includes: personnel, clientele, description of services or focus.

DirOnDB *Directory of Online Databases.* Santa Monica, Calif.: Cuadra Associates, 1984.
Includes: type, subject, producer, online service, content, subject coverage, time coverage, updating, conditions, language.

DirPRFirms *O'Dwyer's Directory of Public Relations Firms.* Edited by Jack O'Dwyer. New York: J. R. O'Dwyer Co., 1983.
Includes: type, founding date, personnel, clients.

DirUSTelSta *Directory of U.S. Television Stations.* New York: Television Editorial Corp., March, 1983 ed. (special issue of *Television/Radio Age*)
Includes: channel, network affiliation, ownership, personnel.
Arrangement of entries is geographical.

Ed&PubIntYB *Editor and Publisher International Year Book.* New York: Editor and Publisher Co., 1982.
Listings for American and Canadian newspapers include: population figures for community served, circulation, price, advertising rates, news services, founding date, special editions, personnel, market information, mechanical specifications, equipment used.
Listings for newspaper groups include: newspapers owned and their locations, principal owner or executive of a group.
Also included are listings for related companies such as news, picture, and press services; feature, news, and picture syndicates; comic section networks; art and mat services; and foreign newspaper representatives.

The arrangement for daily, weekly, and black newspapers is geographical. Special-interest newspapers are arranged by subject area and foreign-language newspapers are arranged alphabetically by language.

Other sections in this publication are arranged alphabetically.

EISS *Encyclopedia of Information Systems and Services.* Edited by John Schmittroth, Jr. Detroit: Gale Research Co., 1982, 1983, 1984.

EISS 83	5th edition, 1982
EISS 7-83 Sup	5th edition supplement, 1983
EISS 5-84 Sup	5th edition supplement, 1984

(supplements called: *New Information Systems and Services)*

Includes: founding date, personnel, related organizations, description, scope/ subject matter, input sources, holdings/storage, publications, microform products and services, computer-based products and services, other services, clientele/availability, projected publications and services, remarks and addenda.

ElecNews *Electronic News.* New York: Fairchild Publications.

A weekly periodical that includes products, facilities and activities, personnel, financial information, forecast.

FBInfSer *Fee-Based Information Services.* By Lorig Maranjian and Richard W. Boss. Information Management Series 1. New York: R. R. Bowker Co., 1980.

Includes products and services.

Folio *The Folio 400.* New Canaan, Conn.: Folio Publishing Corp., 1983.

Includes: frequency of publication, personnel, description, membership, rate information, advertising data, Standard Rate and Data classification, market research, subscriber demographics.

Arrangement of entries is by subject area.

HBIndAd &MS *Handbook of Independent Advertising and Marketing Services.* By Sue Fulton. New York: Executive Communications/Ad Day, 1982.

Includes in-depth profiles.

HomeVid& CabYB *The Home Video and Cable Yearbook.* New York: Facts On File, 1982.

Substantial information is available in this source. The content and format of this information varies widely and is unique to the primary business of the company.

InfIndMarPl *Information Industry Market Place.* New York: R. R. Bowker Co., 1982.

Substantial information is available in this source. The content and format of this information varies widely and is unique to the primary business of the company.

InfoS *Information Sources.* By Faye Henderson, Fred Rosenau, and Jennifer Googins. Washington, D.C.: The Information Industry Association, 1983.

Includes in-depth profiles. The information in each profile varies widely and is presented in a textual format.

IntDirMarRes *Green Book: International Directory of Marketing Research Houses and Services.* 21st ed. New York: New York Chapter, American Marketing Association, 1983.

Includes: services, techniques, geographic specializations.

InterCabHB *The Interactive Cable TV Handbook.* 3rd ed. Bethesda, Md.: Phillips Publishing, 1983.

Includes: affiliation, general specifications, subscriber network specifications.

KnowInd *The Knowledge Industry 200.* White Plains, N.Y.: Knowledge Industry Publications, 1983; distributed by Gale Research Co.

Includes in-depth profiles.

LitMag&SmPr *The International Directory of Little Magazines and Small Presses.* 19th ed. Edited by Len Fulton and Ellen Ferber. Paradise, Calif.: Dustbooks, 1983.

Listings for periodicals include: publisher, type of material used, editor comments, publication schedule, subscription and single-copy rates, founding year, physical makeup of the publication, circulation, manuscript contribution guidelines, discounts, back issue information, past and future publication schedules, memberships.

Listings for presses include, in addition to categories mentioned above: magazines published, type of material used.

LitMarPl *Literary Market Place.* New York: R. R. Bowker Co., 1983.

LitMarPl 83 1983 edition
LitMarPl 84 1984 edition

Substantial information is available in this source. The content and format of this information varies widely and is unique to the primary business of the company.

MagDir *The Working Press of the Nation.* Vol. 2, *Magazine Directory.* Chicago: National Research Bureau, 1983.

Includes: founding date, publication frequency and size, subscription rates, publicity material requirements, editorial description, freelance pay scale, printing process, wire services used, circulation, ownership, bureaus, personnel, reader profile, deadlines.

Arrangement of entries is by subject area.

MagIndMarPl *Magazine Industry Market Place.* New York: R. R. Bowker Co., 1982.

Substantial information is available in this source. The content and format of this information varies widely and is unique to the primary business of the company.

MicrocomMPl *Microcomputer Market Place.* New York: Dekotek, 1982, 1983.

MicrocomMPl 83 1983 edition
MicrocomMPl 84 1984 edition

Listings for software publishers include: personnel, number of published and distributed products, applications, special-interest areas, hardware compatibility, freelance contribution requirements, catalog availability and price.

Listings for software distributors and suppliers include: personnel, products distributed/supplied, applications, operating systems, freelance contribution requirements, catalog availability and price.

MicrocomSwDir *Microcomputer Software Directory.* Vol. 1. Princeton, N.J.: Computing Publications, 1983.

Listings for suppliers include: founding date, revenue, personnel, systems, products, agents.

MicroMarPl *Microform Market Place.* Edited by Deborah Ann O'Hara. Westport, Conn.: Meckler Publishing, 1982.

Includes: personnel, microformats offered, micropublication programs.

NatRadPub Dir *National Radio Publicity Directory.* New York: Peter Glenn Publications, 1983, 1984.

NatRadPubDir summer 83	14th edition, summer 1983
NatRadPubDir spring 84	15th edition, spring 1984

Includes: dial position, network affiliation, area coverage, personnel, format, target audience, sister stations, individual shows and pertinent information about them.

Arrangement of entries is geographical.

NewsBur *News Bureaus in the U.S.* 6th ed. Edited by Richard Weiner. New York: Public Relations Publishing Co., 1981.

Includes: location of newspaper and magazine news bureaus, personnel in individual bureaus, circulation.

NewsDir *The Working Press of the Nation.* Vol. 1, *Newspaper Directory.* Chicago: National Research Bureau, 1983.

Includes: county, Standard Metropolitan Statistical Area, and population; founding date; publication frequency; physical size; subscription rates; publicity material accepted; freelance pay scale; printing process; wire services; circulation size/type; owner; bureau information; personnel; reader profile; deadlines; supplements.

Daily, weekly, and black newspapers are arranged geographically. Religious newspapers are arranged alphabetically by affiliation and then, geographically. Foreign-language newspapers are arranged alphabetically by language and then, geographically.

OnBibDB *Online Bibliographic Databases.* 3rd ed. By James L. Hall and Marjorie J. Brown. London: Aslib, 1983; distributed in the U.S. by Gale Research Co.

Includes: supplier, subject area, printed version availability, online version printout sample, online service suppliers, file details, online service suppliers, access charges, available documentation.

ProGuPRSer *Professional's Guide to Public Relations Services.* 4th ed. By Richard Weiner. New York: Richard Weiner, 1980.

Includes in-depth profiles.

StaDirAdAg *Standard Directory of Advertising Agencies.* Wilmette, Ill.: National Register Publishing Co., 1984.

Includes: personnel, founding date, memberships, specialization, financial information, branches, accounts.

TelAl *International Television Almanac.* Edited by Richard Gertner. New York: Quigley Publishing Co., 1983, 1984.

TelAl 83	1983 edition
TelAl 84	1984 edition

Substantial information is available in this source. The content and format of this information varies widely and is unique to the primary business of the company.

'el&CabFB *Television and Cable Factbook.* 52nd ed. 2 vols. Washington, D.C.: Television Digest, 1984.

Tel&CabFB 84C	Cable & Services Volume, 1984
Tel&CabFB 84S	Stations Volume, 1984

Substantial information is available in this source. The content and format of this information varies widely and is unique to the primary business of the company.

Arrangement of entries for television stations and cable companies is geographical while all others are alphabetical within specific categories.

Additional information about cable companies listed in the section titled "Group Ownership of Cable Systems in the United States," beginning on page 1663, is found in the section "Directory of Cable Systems," beginning on page 363, arranged by area served.

TelDir&BG *Telephony's Directory and Buyers' Guide.* 88th ed. Chicago: Telephony Publishing Corp., 1983.

Listings for independent telephone systems include: number of telephones, exchanges, personnel, telephone data, plant data, financial information.

Arrangement of entries is geographical.

Related companies are also presented, and their arrangement is alphabetical within subject area.

TeleSy&Ser Dir *Telecommunications Systems and Services Directory.* Edited by John Schmittroth, Jr., and Martin Connors. Detroit: Gale Research Co., 1983, 1984.

TeleSy&SerDir 7-83	July, 1983 issue
TeleSy&SerDir 2-84	February, 1984 issue

Includes: founding date, related organizations, function/service type, personnel, description, specific applications, access, area served, rates, documentation, clientele/availability, future plans.

Top100Al *Gartner Group Top 100 Almanac.* Stamford, Conn.: Gartner Group, 1983.

Includes: ranking, principal business, financial information, personnel, major functional areas.

TV&RadDir *The Working Press of the Nation.* Vol. 3, *TV and Radio Directory.* Chicago: National Research Bureau, 1983.

Includes: county, Standard Metropolitan Statistical Area, and population; air time; frequency; power; format; publicity materials accepted; wire services; network affiliation; bureaus; personnel; deadlines.

Arrangement of entries is geographical.

VideoDir *Videotex Directory.* Bethesda, Md.: Arlen Communications, 1982.

Includes: personnel, sponsor, description, equipment, services.

WhoW Microcom *Datapro Who's Who in Microcomputing.* Delran, N.J.: Datapro Research Corp., 1983.

Includes: principal businesses, applications emphasis, personnel, founding date, revenues, customers, sales concentration, products.

WritMar *Writer's Market:* By Bernadine Clark. Cincinnati: Writer's Digest Books, 1983.

Listings for publishers include: principal business, titles per year, payment schedules, reporting time, focus, titles published, guidelines for submitting material.

Listings for publications include: sponsoring organization, publication frequency, clientele/major focus, circulation, payment, conditions for submitted manuscripts and photos, advice from editor.

BUSINESS FIRMS
MASTER INDEX

A

A & A Research - Kalispell, MT - *BrCabYB 84*
A & B Interviewing Service - North Bellmore, NY - *IntDirMarRes 83*
A & C Analistas de Empresa y Consultores de Direccion - Buenos Aires, Argentina - *IntDirMarRes 83*
A & F TV Cable - Beech Creek, WV - *Tel&CabFB 84C*
A & G Associates Inc. - Seattle, WA - *AvMarPl 83*
A & G Productions - San Diego, CA - *AvMarPl 83*
A & G Research Inc. [Div. of Michael Amoroso Inc.] - New York, NY - *IntDirMarRes 83*
A & H Cablevision [of Danville Cablevision] - Altavista, VA - *BrCabYB 84*
A & H Cablevision [of The Daily Press Inc.] - Hurt, VA - *Tel&CabFB 84C*
A & J Recording Studios Inc. - New York, NY - *AvMarPl 83*
A & M Associates - Phoenix, AZ - *AdAge 3-28-84; StaDirAdAg 2-84*
A & M CATV - Coal Mountain, WV - *BrCabYB 84*
A & M CATV - Hanover, WV - *Tel&CabFB 84C*
A & M Records Inc. - Hollywood, CA - *BillIntBG 83-84*
A & P Books [Aff. of The Atlantic & Pacific Commerce Co. Inc.] - Oakland, CA - *BoPubDir 4, 5*
A & P Feature Publications [Div. of The Atlantic & Pacific Commerce Co. Inc.] - Oakland, CA - *WritMar 84*
A & R Recording Co. Inc. - New York, NY - *AvMarPl 83*
A & S Press - Chico, CA - *BoPubDir 4 Sup, 5*
A & W Publishers Inc. - New York, NY - *DirMarMP 83; LitMarPl 83, 84; WritMar 84*
A & W TV Inc. - Whitesville, WV - *BrCabYB 84; Tel&CabFB 84C*
A & W Typing Service - Flushing, NY - *LitMarPl 83, 84*
A-Beta Mailing & Shipping Service - Mariner's Harbor, NY - *LitMarPl 84*
A-Beta Mailing & Shipping Service - Staten Island, NY - *LitMarPl 83*
A/C Advertising - Plainville, NY - *StaDirAdAg 2-84*
A-C Book Service - Brooklyn, NY - *BoPubDir 4, 5*
A-E & R Custom Color - Mountain View, CA - *AvMarPl 83*
A/E Systems Report - Thorndale, PA - *BaconPubCkMag 84*
A-H Interviewing Service - Baltimore, MD - *IntDirMarRes 83*
A-K Associates Inc. - Sacramento, CA - *DirPRFirms 83*
A-Lab Records - Enterprise, AL - *BillIntBG 83-84*
A-One Research Inc. - Brooklyn, NY - *IntDirMarRes 83*
A-Plus Inc. - *See* Arista Music Publishing Group
A Plus Rental Center [Subs. of Fairchild Enterprises Inc.] - Springfield, VA - *AvMarPl 83*
A+ Word Processing Service - Bethesda, MD - *LitMarPl 84*
A Publications - Eagle Rock, CA - *BoPubDir 4, 5*
A Publications - York Station, CA - *LitMag&SmPr 83-84*
A-R Telecommunications [of Adams-Russell Co.] - Waltham, MA - *BrCabYB 84 p.D-297; CabTVFinDB 83*
A-Systems Corp. - Salt Lake City, UT - *WhoWMicrocom 83*
A-T Videotext [of Tiffin Publishing Co.] - Tiffin, OH - *EISS 5-84 Sup*
A to Z Images - Chicago, IL - *LitMarPl 83, 84*
A2Devices - Alameda, CA - *MicrocomMPl 84*
A-V Advisor - Atlanta, GA - *BaconPubCkMag 84*
A-V Canada - Toronto, ON, Canada - *BaconPubCkMag 84*
A-V Canada/Business Communications News - Toronto, ON, Canada - *BaconPubCkMag 84*
A-V Sales Center [Div. of Christian Literature Inc.] - Pontiac, MI - *AvMarPl 83*
A-Vidd Electronics Co. - Long Beach, CA - *AvMarPl 83; MicrocomMPl 83*
AA Software - Renton, WA - *WhoWMicrocom 83*
AA Wonderland Records [Div. of Bestway Group] - Mountainside, NJ - *BillIntBG 83-84*
AAA-Anserphone Inc. - Jackson, MS - *Tel&CabFB 84C*
AAA Cablevision Co. [of Western Louisiana Video Co. Inc.] - Arcola, IL - *Tel&CabFB 84C*
AAA Chicago Computer Center - Wheeling, IL - *MicrocomMPl 83, 84*
AAA Hoosier Motorist/Home & Away - Indianapolis, IN - *MagDir 84*
AAA International Printing Co. Inc. - New York, NY - *LitMarPl 83, 84*
AAA Language Services Inc. - Southfield, MI - *MagIndMarPl 82-83*
AAA Motorist of Northeastern Pennsylvania - Scranton, PA - *BaconPubCkMag 84; MagDir 84*
AAA Recording - New York, NY - *AvMarPl 83*
AAA Secretarial Services Inc. - Chicago, IL - *DirInfWP 82*
AAA Travel Topics - Harrisburg, PA - *BaconPubCkMag 84*
AAA Traveler - York, PA - *MagDir 84*
AAA Traveler, The - Columbus, OH - *BaconPubCkMag 84; MagDir 84*
AAA World - Miami, FL - *MagDir 84*
AAA World [of The Webb Co.] - St. Paul, MN - *BaconPubCkMag 84; MagIndMarPl 82-83; WritMar 84*
AAA World - Madison, WI - *MagDir 84*
AAB-Assessoria Administrativa Ltda. - *See* Ogilvy & Mather Public Relations
Aaban News Service - Cleveland, OH - *Ed&PubIntYB 82*
A.A.D. Advertising Inc. - New York, NY - *LitMarPl 83; MagIndMarPl 82-83*
Aag-Aag! - Kendrick, ID - *LitMag&SmPr 83-84*
Aaida - Bronx, NY - *LitMarPl 83*
Aalborg Portland - Aalborg, Denmark - *CompReadDB 82*
Aames-Allen Publishing Co. - Huntington Beach, CA - *BoPubDir 4, 5; LitMag&SmPr 83-84*
Aamodt, Kimball - New York, NY - *LitMarPl 83, 84; MagIndMarPl 82-83*
AAMSI Communication Network [of American Association for Medical Systems & Informatics] - Bethesda, MD - *DirOnDB Spring 84*
AANA Journal - Park Ridge, IL - *BaconPubCkMag 84; MagDir 84*
Aanco Records - Woodland Park, CO - *BillIntBG 83-84*
AANNT Journal - Pitman, NJ - *BaconPubCkMag 84*
AAO Music - Hollywood, CA - *BillIntBG 83-84*

AAPG Bulletin - Tulsa, OK - *BaconPubCkMag 84*
AAPG Explorer - Tulsa, OK - *BaconPubCkMag 84*
AAPG Publications [Aff. of American Association of Petroleum Geologists] - Tulsa, OK - *BoPubDir 4, 5*
AAR/Tantalus Inc. - Austin, TX - *BoPubDir 4, 5*
AAR Times - Dallas, TX - *BaconPubCkMag 84*
Aardvark - New York, NY - *LitMarPl 83, 84*
Aardvark Art Inc. - Bensenville, IL - *ArtMar 84*
Aardvark/McGraw-Hill - Milwaukee, WI - *LitMarPl 84*
Aardvark Software Inc. - Milwaukee, WI - *MicrocomMPl 83, 84; MicrocomSwDir 1*
Aardvark-Vanaheim Inc. - Kitchener, ON, Canada - *BoPubDir 4 Sup, 5*
Aaron Associates Inc., Leslie - Elizabeth, NJ - *StaDirAdAg 2-84*
Aaron/Jenkins Press - Lawndale, CA - *BoPubDir 4, 5*
Aaron Publishers Inc. - Sarasota, FL - *BoPubDir 4, 5; LitMag&SmPr 83-84*
Aaron-Smirnoff Books - Ottawa, ON, Canada - *LitMarPl 84*
AArson Records - Wayne, NJ - *BillIntBG 83-84*
Aasen, Andreas - San Francisco, CA - *BoPubDir 4, 5*
AATEC Publications - Ann Arbor, MI - *BoPubDir 4 Sup, 5*
Aatronics Inc. - Boise, ID - *AvMarPl 83*
AAU News - Indianapolis, IN - *MagDir 84*
Aazunna Publishing - Ventura, CA - *LitMarPl 83*
AB Bookman's Weekly - Clifton, NJ - *ArtMar 84; LitMarPl 83, 84; MagDir 84; WritMar 84*
AB Computers - Colmar, PA - *MicrocomMPl 84*
AB Pressurklipp - Stockholm, Sweden - *ProGuPRSer 4*
ABA Banking Journal [of American Bankers Association] - New York, NY - *BaconPubCkMag 84; MagDir 84; WritMar 84*
Abaci Inc., C. - Raleigh, NC - *MicrocomMPl 83, 84*
Abacus Associates - Bellaire, TX - *MicrocomMPl 84*
Abacus Software - Grand Rapids, MI - *MicrocomMPl 83, 84*
Abadie, M. J. - New York, NY - *MagIndMarPl 82-83*
Abar Business Planning Service - Akron, OH - *EISS 83*
Abaris Books Inc. - New York, NY - *LitMarPl 83, 84*
Abarta Inc. - Bethlehem, PA - *Ed&PubIntYB 82*
ABAS Enterprises Inc. - Summit, NJ - *DirInfWP 82*
Abba Books & Broadsides - Austin, TX - *BoPubDir 4, 5; LitMag&SmPr 83-84*
ABBE Publishers Association of Washington, DC - Annandale, VA - *BoPubDir 5*
Abbeville Cable TV [of TCA Cable TV Inc.] - Abbeville, LA - *BrCabYB 84; Tel&CabFB 84C*
Abbeville Herald - Abbeville, AL - *BaconPubCkNews 84; Ed&PubIntYB 82*
Abbeville Meridional [of Louisiana State Newspapers] - Abbeville, LA - *BaconPubCkNews 84; NewsDir 84*
Abbeville Press & Banner - Abbeville, SC - *BaconPubCkNews 84*
Abbeville Press Inc. - New York, NY - *LitMarPl 83, 84*
Abbey - Columbia, MD - *LitMag&SmPr 83-84*
Abbey Dawn Press - Kingston, ON, Canada - *BoPubDir 4, 5*
Abbey Mailing Service - New York, NY - *LitMarPl 83, 84; MagIndMarPl 82-83*
Abbey Newsletter - New York, NY - *LitMag&SmPr 83-84*
Abbey Press - St. Meinrad, IN - *LitMarPl 83, 84; WritMar 84*
Abbey Tape Duplicators Inc. - North Hollywood, CA - *AvMarPl 83*
Abbot, Elisabeth - New York, NY - *LitMarPl 84*
Abbotsford Tribune-Phonograph - *See* TP Printing Co.
Abbott Advertising Agency - Lexington, KY - *StaDirAdAg 2-84*
Abbott Consultants, Charles G. - New York, NY - *TeleSy&SerDir 7-83*
Abbott, Elisabeth - New York, NY - *LitMarPl 83*
Abbott Laboratories - Abbott Park, IL - *AvMarPl 83*
Abbott, Langer & Associates - Crete, IL - *BoPubDir 5; WritMar 84*
Abbott, Langer & Associates - Park Forest, IL - *BoPubDir 4*
Abbott, Waring - New York, NY - *MagIndMarPl 82-83*
Abbye Printing Co. - New York, NY - *MagIndMarPl 82-83*
ABC - New York, NY - *BrCabYB 84*
ABC Buyers Guide - La Crosse, WI - *AyerDirPub 83*
ABC Circle Music Inc. - *See* American Broadcasting Music Inc.
ABC-Clio Inc. [Subs. of American Bibliographical Center-Clio Press] - Santa Barbara, CA - *DataDirOnSer 84; InfIndMarPl 83; LitMarPl 83, 84; WritMar 84*
ABC-Clio Information Services - Santa Barbara, CA - *InfoS 83-84*
ABC Computers - Austin, TX - *MicrocomMPl 83*
ABC/Data Bank Services [of Audit Bureau of Circulations] - Schaumburg, IL - *EISS 83*
ABC Data Products - San Diego, CA - *MicrocomMPl 84*
ABC Enterprises - Santa Ana, CA - *BoPubDir 4 Sup, 5*
ABC News - New York, NY - *Tel&CabFB 84C*
ABC Pictures International Inc. [Subs. of American Broadcasting Cos. Inc.] - Century City, CA - *Tel&CabFB 84C*
ABC Pictures International Inc. [Subs. of American Broadcasting Cos. Inc.] - New York, NY - *TelAl 84*
ABC Teletraining Inc. - Geneva, IL - *BoPubDir 5*
ABC-TV Television Spot Sales Inc. - New York, NY - *TelAl 83, 84*
ABC Video Enterprises [Subs. of American Broadcasting Cos. Inc.] - New York, NY - *BillIntBG 83-84; Tel&CabFB 84C*
ABC Video Services - *See* Hearst/ABC Video Services
ABDA-Arzneistoffe [of Bundesvereinigung Deutscher Apothekerverbaende] - Frankfurt, West Germany - *DirOnDB Spring 84*
ABDA-Fertigarzneimittel [of Bundesvereinigung Deutscher Apothekerverbaende] - Frankfurt, West Germany - *DirOnDB Spring 84*
ABDA-Interaktionen [of Bundesvereinigung Deutscher Apothekerverbaende] - Frankfurt, West Germany - *DirOnDB Spring 84*
ABDA-Zentral [of Bundesvereinigung Deutscher Apothekerverbaende] - Frankfurt, West Germany - *DirOnDB Spring 84*
Abdominal Surgery - Melrose, MA - *MagDir 84*
Abel Bookmarketing, Marilyn - New York, NY - *LitMarPl 83, 84*
Abel, Carole - New York, NY - *LitMarPl 83, 84*
Abel Literary Agency Inc., Dominick - New York, NY - *LitMarPl 83, 84*
Abel Productions Inc., Ray - Port Chester, NY - *AvMarPl 83*
Abell Communications Corp. - Baltimore, MD - *BrCabYB 84*
Abell Co., A. S. - Baltimore, MD - *AdAge 6-28-84; BrCabYB 84; KnowInd 83*
Abels Advertising Service - Ft. Wayne, IN - *StaDirAdAg 2-84*
Abelson-Taylor - Chicago, IL - *AdAge 3-28-84; StaDirAdAg 2-84*
Abend Post - Detroit, MI - *Ed&PubIntYB 82*
Abendpost - Chicago, IL - *AyerDirPub 83*
Abendpost & Milwaukee Deutsche Zeitung - Chicago, IL - *NewsDir 84*
Abendpost/Sonntagpost - Chicago, IL - *Ed&PubIntYB 82*
Aberdeen American News [of Knight-Ridder Newspapers] - Aberdeen, SD - *BaconPubCkNews 84; Ed&PubIntYB 82; NewsDir 84*
Aberdeen Cable Television [of Midcontinent Cable Systems Inc.] - Aberdeen, SD - *BrCabYB 84; Tel&CabFB 84C*
Aberdeen Daily World [of Donrey Media Group] - Aberdeen, WA - *NewsDir 84*
Aberdeen Examiner - Aberdeen, MS - *BaconPubCkNews 84; Ed&PubIntYB 82; NewsDir 84*
Aberdeen Harford Democrat - Aberdeen, MD - *BaconPubCkNews 84*
Aberdeen Sandhill Citizen - Aberdeen, NC - *BaconPubCkNews 84; NewsDir 84*
Aberdeen Tele-Cable Inc. - Aberdeen, MS - *BrCabYB 84; Tel&CabFB 84C*
Aberdeen Times - Aberdeen, ID - *BaconPubCkNews 84; Ed&PubIntYB 82*
Abernathy Weekly Review - Abernathy, TX - *AyerDirPub 83; BaconPubCkNews 84; Ed&PubIntYB 82*
Abernethy Publishing, Ernest H. [Div. of Southeast Advertising Inc.] - Atlanta, GA - *MagIndMarPl 82-83*
Abersoft - Aberystwyth Dyfed, England - *WritMar 84*
Abert, Newhoff & Burr - Los Angeles, CA - *AdAge 3-28-84; HBIndAd&MS 82-83; StaDirAdAg 2-84*
ABI/Alexander Broude Inc. - New York, NY - *BillIntBG 83-84*
ABI/Inform [of Data Courier Inc.] - Louisville, KY - *CompReadDB 82; DataDirOnSer 84; DBBus 82; DirOnDB Spring 84; EISS 83; OnBibDB 3*
Abileah, Miriam M. - Toronto, ON, Canada - *LitMarPl 83, 84*
Abilene Radio & TV Stations - Abilene, TX - *BrCabYB 84*
Abilene Reflector Chronicle - Abilene, KS - *BaconPubCkNews 84; Ed&PubIntYB 82; NewsDir 84*

Abilene Reporter-News - Abilene, TX - *BaconPubCkNews 84; Ed&PubIntYB 82; LitMarPl 83, 84; NewsDir 84*
Ability Development Associates Inc. [Aff. of Accura Music Inc.] - Athens, OH - *BoPubDir 4, 5*
Abingdon Argus - Abingdon, IL - *Ed&PubIntYB 82*
Abingdon Argus [of Roseville Carlberg Publishing Co.] - Roseville, IL - *AyerDirPub 83; NewsDir 84*
Abingdon Argus - *See* Acklin Newspaper Group
Abingdon Cablesystems of Virginia Inc. [of American Cablesystems Corp.] - Abingdon, VA - *Tel&CabFB 84C*
Abingdon Press [Div. of United Methodist Publishing House] - Nashville, TN - *BillIntBG 83-84; LitMarPl 83, 84; WritMar 84*
Abingdon Virginian - Abingdon, VA - *AyerDirPub 83; BaconPubCkNews 84; Ed&PubIntYB 82; NewsDir 84*
Abingdon Washington County News - Abingdon, VA - *BaconPubCkNews 84; NewsDir 84*
Abington Journal [of Dallas Pennaprint Inc.] - Clarks Summit, PA - *AyerDirPub 83; Ed&PubIntYB 82; NewsDir 84*
Abington Standard - *See* Bulletin Publishing Co.
Abisch-Kaplan - Oceanside, NY - *LitMarPl 83, 84*
ABK Publications - Hanover, NH - *BoPubDir 4, 5*
Abkco Music Inc. - New York, NY - *BillIntBG 83-84*
Abkco Records Inc. - New York, NY - *BillIntBG 83-84*
Able Cablevision Ltd. - Liverpool, NS, Canada - *BrCabYB 84*
Able Music Inc. - *See* Penny Pincher Music
Able Personnel Agency Inc. - New York, NY - *LitMarPl 83, 84; MagIndMarPl 82-83*
Abledata [of National Rehabilitation Information Center] - Washington, DC - *DataDirOnSer 84; DirOnDB Spring 84; EISS 83*
Ablex Publishing Corp. - Norwood, NJ - *LitMarPl 83, 84*
ABM Products - San Diego, CA - *MicrocomMPl 83*
ABN/Associated Broadcast Newsamerica - Washington, DC - *Tel&CabFB 84C*
Abnak Music Enterprises Inc. - Dallas, TX - *BillIntBG 83-84*
ABNewsamerica Satellite NewsNet - Washington, DC - *BrCabYB 84*
Aboard [of North-South Net Inc.] - Coral Gables, FL - *BaconPubCkMag 84; WritMar 84*
Abolins AV Fotografics Inc. - Tacoma, WA - *AvMarPl 83*
Abor State & Cortland News - Wymore, NE - *Ed&PubIntYB 82*
Aborn Advertising - Boston, MA - *StaDirAdAg 2-84*
About Books Inc. - Saguache, CO - *LitMarPl 83, 84*
About Time - Rochester, NY - *BaconPubCkMag 84; WritMar 84*
Above Ground Records - Auburn, AL - *BillIntBG 83-84*
ABP Records - New York, NY - *BillIntBG 83-84*
Abraham & Partners - London, England - *MicrocomSwDir 1*
Abraham-Welch Associates - Chicago, IL - *LitMarPl 84*
Abrahamsen & Co. - Hoboken, NJ - *EISS 5-84 Sup*
Abrams Associates Inc., Sol - New Milford, NJ - *ArtMar 84; DirPRFirms 83*
Abrams Editorial/Design - Emerson, NJ - *LitMarPl 83, 84*
Abrams Inc., Harry N. [Subs. of Times Mirror Co.] - New York, NY - *DirMarMP 83; LitMarPl 83, 84; WritMar 84*
Abramson Associates - Washington, DC - *DirPRFirms 83; StaDirAdAg 2-84*
Abramson, Steven R. - New York, NY - *LitMarPl 83*
Abrasive Engineering Society Magazine - Pittsburgh, PA - *BaconPubCkMag 84*
Abraxas - Madison, WI - *BoPubDir 4, 5; LitMag&SmPr 83-84*
Abraxas Publishing - Kirkland, WA - *BoPubDir 4 Sup, 5*
ABS Multi-Image - Evanston, IL - *AvMarPl 83*
ABS Suppliers - Ann Arbor, MI - *MicrocomSwDir 1; WhoWMicrocom 83*
Absaraka Cooperative Telephone Co. - Absaraka, ND - *TelDir&BG 83-84*
Absarokee Citizen-Sun - Absarokee, MT - *BaconPubCkNews 84*
Absher Direct Marketing - Silver Spring, MD - *DirMarMP 83*
Abstract Bulletin [of The Institute of Paper Chemistry] - Appleton, WI - *CompReadDB 82*
Abstract Dimensioning [Div. of Calle & Co.] - Greenwich, CT - *IntDirMarRes 83*
Abstract Information Digest Service [of Forest Products Research Society] - Madison, WI - *EISS 83*
Abstract Systems Etc. - Chester, MA - *MicrocomMPl 84*
Abstracta Structures Inc. - New York, NY - *DirInfWP 82*
Abstracts of Entomology [of BioSciences Information Service] - Philadelphia, PA - *MagDir 84*
Abstracts of Mycology [of BioSciences Information Service] - Philadelphia, PA - *MagDir 84*
Abstracts on Health Effects of Environmental Pollutants [of BioSciences Information Service] - Philadelphia, PA - *CompReadDB 82; MagDir 84*
Abstracts on Tropical Agriculture [of Royal Tropical Institute] - Amsterdam, Netherlands - *CompReadDB 82; DataDirOnSer 84*
Abstrax Inc. - Boston, MA - *EISS 5-84 Sup*
Abstrax Inc. - Cambridge, MA - *DirOnDB Spring 84*
Abt Books [Subs. of Abt Associates Inc.] - Cambridge, MA - *LitMarPl 83, 84; WritMar 84*
ABT Computer Graphics Corp. - Cambridge, MA - *EISS 83*
Abt Microcomputer Software - Cambridge, MA - *WhoWMicrocom 83*
ABW Corp. - Ann Arbor, MI - *MicrocomMPl 83, 84; MicrocomSwDir 1; WhoWMicrocom 83*
Abwin Corp. - New York, NY - *DirPRFirms 83*
AC & R Advertising [Subs. of Ted Bates & Co.] - New York, NY - *AdAge 3-28-84; StaDirAdAg 2-84*
AC & R Public Relations Inc. [Subs. of AC & R Advertising Inc.] - New York, NY - *DirPRFirms 83*
AC Color Lab Inc. - Cleveland, OH - *AvMarPl 83*
AC Publications - Homer, NY - *BoPubDir 4, 5; LitMag&SmPr 83-84; LitMarPl 83, 84*
ACA Journal of Chiropractic [of American Chiropractic Association] - St. Louis, MO - *MagIndMarPl 82-83*
ACA Journal of Chiropractic [of American Chiropractic Association] - Arlington, VA - *BaconPubCkMag 84; MagDir 84*
Academe - Washington, DC - *BaconPubCkMag 84; MagIndMarPl 82-83*
Academia - Portola Valley, CA - *MagIndMarPl 82-83*
Academia Language Center - Cambridge, MA - *MagIndMarPl 82-83*
Academic American Encyclopedia [of Arete Publishing Co.] - Princeton, NJ - *CompReadDB 82; EISS 83*
Academic American Encyclopedia [of Grolier Electronic Publishing Inc.] - New York, NY - *DataDirOnSer 84; DirOnDB Spring 84; EISS 5-84 Sup*
Academic & Literary Manuscript Preparation - New York, NY - *LitMarPl 83, 84*
Academic Book Center - Portland, OR - *EISS 5-84 Sup; LitMarPl 84*
Academic Book Club - Kingston, ON, Canada - *BoPubDir 4 Sup, 5; LitMarPl 83, 84*
Academic Enterprises Ltd. - Milford, MA - *BoPubDir 4 Sup, 5; LitMarPl 83, 84*
Academic Hallmarks - Durango, CO - *MicrocomMPl 84*
Academic International Press - Gulf Breeze, FL - *BoPubDir 4, 5*
Academic News Service - Madison, WI - *BaconPubCkNews 84; Ed&PubIntYB 82*
Academic Press [Subs. of Harcourt Brace Jovanovich] - New York, NY - *DirMarMP 83; InfoS 83-84; LitMarPl 83, 84; MagIndMarPl 82-83; MicroMarPl 82-83; WritMar 84*
Academic Press Canada [Div. of Harcourt Brace Jovanovich Canada Inc.] - Don Mills, ON, Canada - *LitMarPl 83, 84*
Academic Printing & Publishing - South Edmonton, AB, Canada - *BoPubDir 4 Sup, 5*
Academic Publications - Tulsa, OK - *LitMag&SmPr 83-84*
Academic Publishing Co. - Montreal, PQ, Canada - *BoPubDir 4, 5*
Academic Software - Dumont, NJ - *MicrocomMPl 84*
Academic Therapy Publications - Novato, CA - *BoPubDir 4 Sup, 5; LitMarPl 83, 84; MagDir 84; MagIndMarPl 82-83*
Academic Writers' Service - Healdsburg, CA - *LitMarPl 83; MagIndMarPl 82-83*
Academy Books [Aff. of Sharp Offset Printing Inc.] - Rutland, VT - *BoPubDir 4, 5; LitMarPl 83, 84*
Academy Chicago - Chicago, IL - *LitMag&SmPr 83-84; LitMarPl 83, 84; WritMar 84*
Academy Film Productions Inc. - Lincolnwood, IL - *AvMarPl 83; TelAl 83, 84; Tel&CabFB 84C*
Academy Films - Venice, CA - *AvMarPl 83*
Academy of American Franciscan History - Potomac, MD - *BoPubDir 4, 5*

Academy of General Dentistry - Chicago, IL - *MagDir 84*
Academy of Political Science - New York, NY - *BoPubDir 4 Sup, 5*
Academy of Prison Arts [Aff. of Lion Walk Performing Arts Center Inc.] - Pittsburgh, PA - *BoPubDir 5*
Academy Productions Corp. - North Hollywood, CA - *AvMarPl 83*
Academy Software - San Rafael, CA - *MicrocomMPl 84*
Academy Theatre - Atlanta, GA - *WritMar 84*
Acadia University Institute - Wolfville, NS, Canada - *BoPubDir 4, 5*
Acadian Genealogy Exchange - Covington, KY - *BoPubDir 4, 5*
Acadian Press - Mamou, LA - *AyerDirPub 83*
Acadian Publishing Inc. - Church Point, LA - *BoPubDir 4, 5*
Acadian Tribune - Rayne, LA - *AyerDirPub 83; Ed&PubIntYB 82*
Acadiana MDS Co. - Broussard, LA - *Tel&CabFB 84C*
Acadiana Press - Lafayette, LA - *BoPubDir 4, 5*
Acama Films - Sherman Oaks, CA - *Tel&CabFB 84C*
Acantha - Choteau, MT - *AyerDirPub 83*
ACC Media Services - New York, NY - *StaDirAdAg 2-84*
Accabonac Music - *See* Cherry Lane Music Publishing Co. Inc.
ACCCA Press [Aff. of American Community Cultural Center Association] - Pompton Plains, NJ - *BoPubDir 4, 5; LitMag&SmPr 83-84*
Accelerated Data Systems - Sunnyvale, CA - *DataDirSup 7-83*
Accelerated Development Inc. - Muncie, IN - *BoPubDir 4, 5; LitMarPl 84; WritMar 84*
Accelerated Indexing Systems Inc. - Salt Lake City, UT - *BoPubDir 4, 5*
Accelerated Program Systems - Brooklyn, NY - *MicrocomMPl 84*
Accent - Evanston, IL - *MagDir 84; MagIndMarPl 82-83*
Accent - New York, NY - *NewsBur 6*
Accent - Devon, PA - *BaconPubCkMag 84*
Accent - Radnor, PA - *MagDir 84*
Accent - Ogden, UT - *ArtMar 84; WritMar 84*
Accent Advertising Agency - San Antonio, TX - *StaDirAdAg 2-84*
Accent & Alphabet - Berkeley, CA - *LitMarPl 83, 84; MagIndMarPl 82-83*
Accent Books [Div. of Accent Publications] - Denver, CO - *LitMarPl 83, 84; WritMar 84*
Accent/Midstate Advertising - Johnstown, PA - *StaDirAdAg 2-84*
Accent on Broadcasting Etc. Inc. - New York, NY - *DirPRFirms 83; LitMarPl 83, 84*
Accent on Information [of Accent on Living] - Bloomington, IL - *CompReadDB 82; DataDirOnSer 84; EISS 83; InfIndMarPl 83*
Accent on Language Inc. - New York, NY - *MagIndMarPl 82-83*
Accent on Living - Bloomington, IL - *ArtMar 84; BaconPubCkMag 84; MagDir 84; MagIndMarPl 82-83; WritMar 84*
Accent Records - Rancho Mirage, CA - *BillIntBG 83-84*
Accent Software - Palo Alto, CA - *MicrocomMPl 83, 84*
Accent Special Publications [Aff. of Cheever Publishing] - Bloomington, IL - *BoPubDir 5*
Accent West - Amarillo, TX - *MagDir 84*
Accesory Merchandising - Dallas, TX - *BaconPubCkMag 84*
ACCESS [of Arthur D. Little Inc.] - Cambridge, MA - *InfIndMarPl 83*
Access America [of Tele-Sys Inc.] - Oak Ridge, TN - *TeleSy&SerDir 2-84*
Access Cable of Indiana Inc. - Tipton, IN - *Tel&CabFB 84C*
Access Communicator - Adrian, MI - *Ed&PubIntYB 82*
Access Composition Services [Div. of Electronic Graphics] - Phoenix, AZ - *LitMarPl 83, 84*
Access Corp. - Cincinnati, OH - *DirInfWP 82; EISS 83*
Access Information Center [of Contra Costa County Superintendent of Schools] - Concord, CA - *EISS 83*
Access Innovations Inc. - Albuquerque, NM - *DataDirOnSer 84; EISS 83; InfoS 83-84*
Access Jacksonville [of Associated Computer Consultants Inc.] - Jacksonville, FL - *MicrocomMPl 84*
Access Matrix Corp. - San Jose, CA - *WhoWMicrocom 83*
Access: Microcomputers in Libraries - Oakridge, OR - *BaconPubCkMag 84*
Access Publishing Co. - New York, NY - *EISS 83*
Access Reports/Freedom of Information [of NewsNet Inc.] - Washington, DC - *DirOnDB Spring 84*
Access Reports/Freedom of Information [of NewsNet Inc.] - Bryn Mawr, PA - *DataDirOnSer 84*
Access Service for Profitable Information Resource Exchanges [of Emerald Valley Publishing Co.] - Eugene, OR - *InfIndMarPl 83*
Access Technology Inc. - South Natick, MA - *WhoWMicrocom 83*
Access to Information Inc. - Santa Fe, NM - *FBInfSer 80*
Access Unltd. - Richardson, TX - *MicrocomMPl 83*
Accessing Systems Knowledge - Ben Lomond, CA - *EISS 7-83 Sup*
ACCI Business Systems Inc. - Houston, TX - *MicrocomMPl 84*
Accident/Incident Data System [of Federal Aviation Administration] - Washington, DC - *DBBus 82; DirOnDB Spring 84*
Accident/Incident Data System [of United Information Services Inc.] - Kansas City, MO - *DataDirOnSer 84*
ACCO International Inc. - Wheeling, IL - *DataDirSup 7-83; DirInfWP 82*
Accord Press - San Jose, CA - *BoPubDir 4, 5*
Accord/Townhouse Records - Nashville, TN - *BillIntBG 83-84*
Account-A-Call Corp. - Burbank, CA - *DataDirSup 7-83*
Accountable Advertising Inc. - Garden City, NY - *StaDirAdAg 2-84*
Accountable Marketing Inc. - Paramount, CA - *DirMarMP 83*
Accountants [of SDC Search Service] - Santa Monica, CA - *DataDirOnSer 84*
Accountants' & Controllers' Book Club [of McGraw-Hill Book Co.] - New York, NY - *LitMarPl 83, 84*
Accountants Computer Network Inc. - La Grange, IL - *DataDirOnSer 84*
Accountants' Index [of American Institute of Certified Public Accountants] - New York, NY - *CompReadDB 82; DBBus 82; DirOnDB Spring 84; EISS 83; OnBibDB 3*
Accountants Microsystems Inc. - Bellevue, WA - *MicrocomMPl 83, 84; MicrocomSwDir 1*
Accountemps of NY - New York, NY - *DirInfWP 82*
Accounting Corp. of America - San Diego, CA - *ADAPSOMemDir 83-84*
Accounting Publications Inc. - Gainesville, FL - *BoPubDir 5*
Accounting Review [of American Accounting Association] - Seattle, WA - *MagDir 84*
Accounting Review, The - Sarasota, FL - *MagIndMarPl 82-83*
Accounting Supplies & Systems Inc. - Falls Church, VA - *DirInfWP 82*
Accounts Microsystems Inc. - Bellevue, WA - *WhoWMicrocom 83*
Accounts of Chemical Research - Santa Cruz, CA - *MagIndMarPl 82-83*
Accredited Mailing Lists Inc. - New York, NY - *LitMarPl 83, 84; MagIndMarPl 82-83*
Accu-Data Services - Kent, WA - *IntDirMarRes 83*
Accu-Research Inc. - Cleveland, OH - *IntDirMarRes 83*
Accu-Search Opinion Sampling - Brownsville, TX - *IntDirMarRes 83*
Accu-Weather Graphics/Data System [of Accu-Weather Inc.] - State College, PA - *DataDirOnSer 84*
Accu-Weather Inc. - State College, PA - *DataDirOnSer 84*
Accufax Research [Div. of Network Research Services] - Brooklyn, NY - *IntDirMarRes 83*
Accumulated Copyrights - *See* Moody Music, Doug
Accunet Digital Service [of American Telephone & Telegraph Co.] - Bedminster, NJ - *TeleSy&SerDir 2-84*
Accupipe Corp. - Paoli, PA - *MicrocomMPl 84; MicrocomSwDir 1*
Accuracy in Media - Washington, DC - *Ed&PubIntYB 82*
Accurate Boffer Mail/Marketing Corp. [Subs. of Metro Seliger Corp.] - Long Island City, NY - *LitMarPl 83, 84; MagIndMarPl 82-83*
Accurate Information Service - Bethesda, MD - *EISS 7-83 Sup*
Accurate Literary Services [Div. of Accurate Business Service Inc.] - Seattle, WA - *LitMarPl 83, 84*
Accurate Personnel Agency Inc. - New York, NY - *MagIndMarPl 82-83*
Accurate Personnel Agency Inc. - *See* Moore Agency, William
Accurtone Systems - Arcadia, CA - *DataDirSup 7-83*
Accusystems - New York, NY - *HBIndAd&MS 82-83*
Accutreat Films Inc. - New York, NY - *AvMarPl 83*
Ace - St. Paul, MN - *MagDir 84*
Ace Advertising - Elk Grove Village, IL - *StaDirAdAg 2-84*
Ace-Athletic Club Events - St. Paul, MN - *BaconPubCkMag 84*

Ace Audio-Visual Co. - New York, NY - *AvMarPl 83*
Ace Cable [of Acme Communications & Electronics Inc.] - Camano Island, WA - *BrCabYB 84; Tel&CabFB 84C*
Ace Computer Products of Florida Inc. - Deerfield Beach, FL - *MicrocomMPl 84*
Ace News - Newark, OH - *AyerDirPub 83*
Ace Office Supplies - Woodmere, NY - *DirInfWP 82*
Ace Pix Productions Inc. - North Hollywood, CA - *AvMarPl 83*
Ace Publications [Aff. of Acme Print & Litho] - Stratford, ON, Canada - *BoPubDir 4, 5*
Ace Records Inc. - Jackson, MS - *BillIntBG 83-84*
Ace Science Fiction [of The Berkley Publishing Group] - New York, NY - *WritMar 84*
A.C.E. Systems - Bethlehem, PA - *MicrocomMPl 84*
Ace Telephone Association - Houston, MN - *TelDir&BG 83-84*
Ache Communications - Kingwood, TX - *Tel&CabFB 84C*
Acheron Press - Friendsville, MD - *BoPubDir 4, 5; LitMag&SmPr 83-84; LitMarPl 84*
Aches & Pains - Rockville, MD - *BaconPubCkMag 84; MagIndMarPl 82-83*
Acheson, Alice B. - New York, NY - *LitMarPl 83, 84*
ACI Computer Services - Clayton, Australia - *EISS 83; InfIndMarPl 83*
Acid Rain Information Clearinghouse [of Center for Environmental Information Inc.] - Rochester, NY - *EISS 5-84 Sup*
Acker, Gary L. - *See* Good News Broadcasting Co.
Acker Retail Audits Inc. - Lyndhurst, NJ - *IntDirMarRes 83*
Acker, Worley & Associates Inc. - Odessa, FL - *StaDirAdAg 2-84*
Ackerley Communications Inc. - Seattle, WA - *BrCabYB 84; Tel&CabFB 84S*
Ackerman Advertising Communications - Greenvale, NY - *AdAge 3-28-84; ArtMar 84; StaDirAdAg 2-84*
Ackerman & Associates, Katherine - Chicago, IL - *EISS 5-84 Sup*
Ackerman & McQueen - Oklahoma City, OK - *AdAge 3-28-84; ArtMar 84; DirPRFirms 83; StaDirAdAg 2-84*
Ackerman Cable TV Co. - Ackerman, MS - *BrCabYB 84; Tel&CabFB 84C*
Ackerman Choctaw Plaindealer - Ackerman, MS - *BaconPubCkNews 84*
Ackerman Digital Systems - Elmhurst, IL - *MicrocomMPl 83, 84*
Ackerman, Forrest & Wendayne - Hollywood, CA - *LitMarPl 83*
Ackerman Information Corp. - Ft. Collins, CO - *BoPubDir 5*
Ackerman, James F. - Indianapolis, IN - *BrCabYB 84*
Ackerman, James F. - *See* Cardinal Communications Inc.
Ackerman Telephone Co. - Ackerman, MS - *TelDir&BG 83-84*
Ackerman Translators - Hollywood, CA - *MagIndMarPl 82-83*
Ackley World Journal - Ackley, IA - *BaconPubCkNews 84; Ed&PubIntYB 82*
Acklin Newspaper Group - Abingdon, IL - *BaconPubCkNews 84*
Ackroyd, Hugh S. - Portland, OR - *MagIndMarPl 82-83*
ACL Inc. - Elk Grove Village, IL - *MicrocomMPl 83*
ACM - Chicago, IL - *LitMag&SmPr 83-84*
ACM Northwest - Redmond, WA - *MicrocomMPl 84*
ACM Productions Ltd. - New York, NY - *AvMarPl 83*
Acme-Lite Manufacturing - Skokie, IL - *AvMarPl 83*
Acme Mail Advertising Co. - Omaha, NE - *MagIndMarPl 82-83*
Acme Music Corp. - New York, NY - *BillIntBG 83-84*
Acme Newspapers Inc. - Ardmore, PA - *BaconPubCkNews 84*
Acme Print & Litho - Stratford, ON, Canada - *LitMag&SmPr 83-84*
Acme Recording Studios - Chicago, IL - *BillIntBG 83-84*
Acme Visible Records Inc. - Crozet, VA - *DirInfWP 82*
Acoma Books - Ramona, CA - *BoPubDir 4, 5; LitMarPl 84*
Acomb Inc., Robert - Cincinnati, OH - *StaDirAdAg 2-84*
Acompline [of Greater London Council Research Library] - London, England - *DirOnDB Spring 84; OnBibDB 3*
Acompline [of European Space Agency] - Frascati, Italy - *DataDirOnSer 84*
Acorn - Agoura, CA - *Ed&PubIntYB 82*
Acorn - Canoga Park, CA - *AyerDirPub 83*
Acorn - Oakland, IA - *AyerDirPub 83*
Acorn - Weston, MA - *LitMag&SmPr 83-84*
Acorn - Cleveland, OH - *BoPubDir 4, 5*
Acorn Music Corp. - *See* TRO
Acorn Press - Durham, NC - *BoPubDir 4 Sup, 5*
Acorn Press Inc. - Ridgefield, CT - *BaconPubCkNews 84*
Acorn Software Products Inc. - Washington, DC - *MicrocomMPl 83; WhoWMicrocom 83*
Acorn Software Products Inc. - Falls Church, VA - *MicrocomMPl 84*
Acoustic Music Inc. - Nashville, TN - *BillIntBG 83-84*
Acoustical Screens Corp. - East Longmeadow, MA - *DirInfWP 82*
AcoustoGraphic Records - Edgartown, MA - *BillIntBG 83-84*
Acquire Information - Palo Alto, CA - *FBInfSer 80*
Acquis Data Inc. [Subs. of Acquis Corp.] - Irvine, CA - *WhoWMicrocom 83*
ACR Advertising Agency - Jasper, IN - *StaDirAdAg 2-84*
Acre Press - Endicott, NY - *LitMag&SmPr 83-84*
AcreAge - Ontario, OR - *WritMar 84*
Acree & Associates - Burbank, CA - *DirPRFirms 83*
Acrobat Books - Los Angeles, CA - *BoPubDir 4, 5; LitMag&SmPr 83-84*
Acropac - Atlanta, GA - *DirOnDB Spring 84*
ACROPOL [of Direction de la Documentation Francaise] - Paris, France - *CompReadDB 82*
Acropole Corp. of America - New York, NY - *BillIntBG 83-84*
Acropolis - San Lorenzo, CA - *MicrocomMPl 83; WhoWMicrocom 83*
Acropolis Books Ltd. [Subs. of Colortone Press] - Washington, DC - *ArtMar 84; DirMarMP 83; LitMarPl 83, 84; WritMar 84*
Across the Board - New York, NY - *BaconPubCkMag 84; MagDir 84; MagIndMarPl 82-83*
Across the Miles Music Publishing Co. - Philadelphia, PA - *BillIntBG 83-84*
ACS America Inc. - New York, NY - *DirInfWP 82*
ACS Group [Subs. of Darrin & Associates Ltd.] - Atlanta, GA - *HBIndAd&MS 82-83*
ACS Primary Journal Database [of American Chemical Society] - Washington, DC - *EISS 5-84 Sup*
ACS Publications - San Diego, CA - *BoPubDir 5; LitMarPl 84*
ACS Software - Leeds, England - *MicrocomSwDir 1*
Acseh - Colombes, France - *MicrocomSwDir 1*
ACSM Bulletin - Falls Church, VA - *BaconPubCkMag 84*
ACSN, The Learning Channel - Washington, DC - *CabTVPrDB 83; Tel&CabFB 84C*
Act I [of Marketron Inc.] - Menlo Park, CA - *EISS 83*
Act-Plus [of STSC Inc.] - Rockville, MD - *DataDirOnSer 84; DirOnDB Spring 84*
ACT (Pulsar) Ltd. - Birmingham, England - *MicrocomSwDir 1*
Acta Cytologica - Baltimore, MD - *MagDir 84*
ACTA Foundation [Aff. of Roman Catholic Archdiocese of Chicago] - Chicago, IL - *BoPubDir 4, 5*
Acta Press - Calgary, AB, Canada - *LitMarPl 83, 84*
ACTEO Bookmen - Sarasota, FL - *BoPubDir 5*
Action [of Dept. of Christian Education, Free Methodist Headquarters] - Winona Lake, IN - *ArtMar 84; WritMar 84*
Action [of Action Arabic English Newspapers Inc.] - New York, NY - *AyerDirPub 83; Ed&PubIntYB 82; NewsDir 84*
Action Ads - Hesperia, CA - *AyerDirPub 83*
Action Advertiser - Fond du Lac, WI - *AyerDirPub 83*
Action Advertising - *See* Westchester Communications Inc.
Action Cable Inc. - Bay City, TX - *Tel&CabFB 84C p.1663*
Action Communications Co. Inc. - Greenville, MS - *Tel&CabFB 84C p.1663*
Action Communications Inc. - Wauwatosa, WI - *StaDirAdAg 2-84*
Action Computer Enterprise Inc. - Los Angeles, CA - *MicrocomSwDir 1*
Action Computer Enterprise Inc. - Pasadena, CA - *WhoWMicrocom 83*
Action Data Inc. - Cincinnati, OH - *IntDirMarRes 83*
Action for Children's Television - Newtonville, MA - *BoPubDir 5*
Action/Honeywell - Dallas, TX - *DataDirSup 7-83*
Action Information Resources Management Ltd. - Victoria, BC, Canada - *EISS 83*
Action Letter Inc. - New York, NY - *MagIndMarPl 82-83*
Action Line - Baltimore, MD - *MagDir 84*
Action Marketing Inc. - Darby, PA - *MagIndMarPl 82-83*
Action Merchandising Services Inc. - Greenwich, CT - *IntDirMarRes 83*
Action Newspaper [of American-Arab Relations Committee] - New York, NY - *LitMarPl 83, 84*
Action Oil & Energy Report - Lafayette, LA - *BaconPubCkMag 84*

Action Plus Shopper - De Motte, IN - *AyerDirPub 83*
Action Records - Ft. Worth, TX - *BillIntBG 83-84*
Action Research - Burlington, VT - *IntDirMarRes 83*
Action Research Associates Inc. - Del Mar, CA - *LitMarPl 84*
Action-Research North West - Seattle, WA - *MicrocomMPl 83, 84; WhoWMicrocom 83*
Action Shopper - Gaylord, MI - *AyerDirPub 83*
Action Shopper - Kalkaska, MI - *NewsDir 84*
Action Sports Cable TV, The - New Kensington, PA - *CabTVPrDB 83*
Action Sports Retailer - South Laguna, CA - *BaconPubCkMag 84*
Action Surveys Inc. - Silver Spring, MD - *EISS 83*
Action T.V. - New Kensington, PA - *TelAl 83*
Actioncraft - Anaheim Hills, CA - *MicrocomMPl 84*
Active Translation Bureau - New York, NY - *LitMarPl 83, 84*
Active Well Data On-line [of Petroleum Information Corp.] - Denver, CO - *DataDirOnSer 84*
Active Well Data On-Line - Littleton, CO - *DirOnDB Spring 84*
Active Well Data On-line [of Boeing Computer Services Co.] - Morristown, NJ - *DataDirOnSer 84*
Active Well Information Service [of Petroleum Information Corp.] - Denver, CO - *DataDirOnSer 84*
Activewear Magazine - Denver, CO - *BaconPubCkMag 84*
Activision Inc. - Mountain View, CA - *WritMar 84*
Acton Assabet Valley Beacon - *See* Minute-Man Publications Inc.
Acton CATV Inc. [of Acton Corp.] - Alta Loma, CA - *Tel&CabFB 84C*
Acton CATV Inc. [of Acton Corp.] - Glendora, CA - *BrCabYB 84; Tel&CabFB 84C*
Acton CATV Inc. [of Acton Corp.] - Monrovia, CA - *BrCabYB 84*
Acton CATV Inc. - Pomona, CA - *BrCabYB 84*
Acton CATV Inc. [of Acton Corp.] - Riverside, CA - *Tel&CabFB 84C*
Acton CATV Inc. [of Acton Corp.] - La Junta, CO - *Tel&CabFB 84C*
Acton CATV Inc. [of Acton Corp.] - Brooksville, FL - *BrCabYB 84*
Acton CATV Inc. [of Acton Corp.] - Dade City, FL - *Tel&CabFB 84C*
Acton CATV Inc. [of Acton Corp.] - Deltona, FL - *Tel&CabFB 84C*
Acton CATV Inc. [of Acton Corp.] - Pasco County, FL - *BrCabYB 84; Tel&CabFB 84C*
Acton CATV Inc. [of Acton Corp.] - Spring Hill, FL - *Tel&CabFB 84C*
Acton CATV Inc. [of Acton Corp.] - Wildwood, FL - *Tel&CabFB 84C*
Acton CATV Inc. [of Acton Corp.] - Zephyrhills, FL - *BrCabYB 84; Tel&CabFB 84C*
Acton CATV Inc. [of Acton Corp.] - Eureka, KS - *BrCabYB 84*
Acton CATV Inc. [of Acton Corp.] - Acton, MA - *BrCabYB 84*
Acton CATV Inc. - Benton Harbor, MI - *BrCabYB 84*
Acton CATV Inc. [of Acton Corp.] - Benton Township, MI - *Tel&CabFB 84C*
Acton CATV Inc. [of Acton Corp.] - Beaufort, SC - *BrCabYB 84; Tel&CabFB 84C*
Acton CATV Inc. [of Acton Corp.] - Belton, SC - *Tel&CabFB 84C*
Acton CATV Inc. [of Acton Corp.] - Chester, SC - *Tel&CabFB 84C*
Acton CATV Inc. [of U.S. Cable of Blue Ridge] - Honea Path, SC - *BrCabYB 84*
Acton CATV Inc. [of Acton Corp.] - Whitmire, SC - *Tel&CabFB 84C*
Acton CATV Inc. [of Acton Corp.] - Sandy City, TX - *BrCabYB 84*
Acton CATV Inc. [of Acton Corp.] - Alpine, UT - *BrCabYB 84; Tel&CabFB 84C*
Acton CATV Inc. [of Acton Corp.] - American Fork, UT - *BrCabYB 84*
Acton CATV Inc. [of Acton Corp.] - Brigham City, UT - *BrCabYB 84; Tel&CabFB 84C*
Acton CATV Inc. [of Acton Corp.] - Cedar City, UT - *BrCabYB 84; Tel&CabFB 84C*
Acton CATV Inc. [of Acton Corp.] - Delta, UT - *Tel&CabFB 84C*
Acton CATV Inc. [of Acton Corp.] - Midvale, UT - *Tel&CabFB 84C*
Acton CATV Inc. [of Acton Corp.] - Orem, UT - *BrCabYB 84; Tel&CabFB 84C*
Acton CATV Inc. [of Acton Corp.] - Sandy, UT - *Tel&CabFB 84C*
Acton CATV Inc. [of Acton Corp.] - Springville, UT - *Tel&CabFB 84C*
Acton CATV Inc. [of Acton Corp.] - Vernal, UT - *BrCabYB 84*
Acton CATV Inc. [of Acton Corp.] - West Jordan, UT - *Tel&CabFB 84C*
Acton Corp. - Acton, MA - *BrCabYB 84; CabTVFinDB 83; HomeVid&CabYB 82-83; Tel&CabFB 84C p.1663*
Acton Country News - Acton, MA - *Ed&PubIntYB 82*
Acton Free Press - Acton, ON, Canada - *AyerDirPub 83*
Acton Inc., Edward J. - New York, NY - *LitMarPl 83, 84*
Acton Minute-Man - Acton, MA - *Ed&PubIntYB 82*
Acton Minute-Man - *See* Minute-Man Publications Inc.
Actors Theatre of Louisville - Louisville, KY - *WritMar 84*
Acts - San Francisco, CA - *LitMag&SmPr 83-84*
Acts Books - Caledonia, ON, Canada - *BoPubDir 4, 5; LitMarPl 84*
ACTS Satellite Network - Ft. Worth, TX - *Tel&CabFB 84C*
Acts The Shelflife, The - Madison, WI - *LitMag&SmPr 83-84*
Actuarial Database [of I. P. Sharp Associates] - Toronto, ON, Canada - *DataDirOnSer 84; DBBus 82; DirOnDB Spring 84*
Acuff-Rose Publications Inc. - Nashville, TN - *BillIntBG 83-84*
ACUHO News [of University of Texas] - Austin, TX - *MagIndMarPl 82-83*
Acupinch Outreach Center - Atlanta, GA - *BoPubDir 5*
Acworth Neighbor - Acworth, GA - *Ed&PubIntYB 82*
Acworth Neighbor [of Marietta Neighbor Newspapers Inc.] - Marietta, GA - *AyerDirPub 83; NewsDir 84*
A.D. - New York, NY - *LitMarPl 83; MagDir 84; MagIndMarPl 82-83*
Ad Agency - New York, NY - *AdAge 3-28-84; StaDirAdAg 2-84*
AD & A Records - Hollywood, CA - *BillIntBG 83-84*
Ad Biz [of John K. Adams Publishing Co.] - Oklahoma City, OK - *MagDir 84*
A.D. Book Co. - New York, NY - *ArtMar 84*
Ad-Chart Services [Div. of Chilton Marketing Services] - Radnor, PA - *MagIndMarPl 82-83*
Ad Craft of Arkansas Inc. - Little Rock, AR - *StaDirAdAg 2-84*
Ad Day/USA [of Executive Communications Inc.] - New York, NY - *BaconPubCkMag 84; MagDir 84; MagIndMarPl 82-83*
Ad-Dee Publishers Inc. - Eugene, OR - *BoPubDir 4, 5*
Ad-Delite - Strum, WI - *AyerDirPub 83*
AD Digest-Advertisement Digest - Morton Grove, IL - *BoPubDir 4, 5*
Ad East - Boston, MA - *BaconPubCkMag 84; MagDir 84*
Ad Enterprise Advertising Agency Inc. - Cleveland, OH - *StaDirAdAg 2-84*
Ad-Ex Translations International/USA - Menlo Park, CA - *LitMarPl 84*
Ad-Ex Translations International/USA - Portola Valley, CA - *LitMarPl 83; MagIndMarPl 82-83*
Ad-Ex Translations International/USA - New York, NY - *MagIndMarPl 82-83*
Ad Factors Marketing Research Inc. - Glen Ellyn, IL - *IntDirMarRes 83*
Ad Forum [of MIN Publishing] - New York, NY - *BaconPubCkMag 84; WritMar 84*
Ad-Four Inc. - Baton Rouge, LA - *StaDirAdAg 2-84*
Ad Hoc Committee for Competitive Telecommunications - Washington, DC - *TeleSy&SerDir 7-83*
Ad/Image Advertising - Tampa, FL - *AdAge 3-28-84; StaDirAdAg 2-84*
Ad Infinitum Advertising Services - Mt. Vernon, NY - *MagIndMarPl 82-83*
Ad Infinitum Copy Service - Mt. Vernon, NY - *LitMarPl 83, 84; MagIndMarPl 82-83*
Ad Infinitum Press - Mt. Vernon, NY - *LitMarPl 83, 84; MagIndMarPl 82-83*
Ad Lib Advertising Association - New York, NY - *StaDirAdAg 2-84*
Ad-Lib Publications - Fairfield, IA - *LitMag&SmPr 83-84*

Ad-Link Advertising Pty. Ltd. - West Perth, Australia - *StaDirAdAg 2-84*
Ad/Mag - St. Louis, MO - *BaconPubCkMag 84; MagDir 84*
Ad Masters - Tustin, CA - *StaDirAdAg 2-84*
Ad Methods Advertising Inc. - St. James, NY - *StaDirAdAg 2-84*
Ad-Options - Southport, CT - *HBIndAd&MS 82-83*
Ad-Pak, The - Wilmington, NC - *AyerDirPub 83*
Ad Sack - Corpus Christi, TX - *AyerDirPub 83*
Ad Service Inc. - Worcester, MA - *StaDirAdAg 2-84*
Ad Systems Inc. - Chicago, IL - *Ed&PubIntYB 82*
Ad Trends [of National Research Bureau] - Burlington, IA - *MagDir 84*
Ad Vantage Ad Inc. - Oconomowoc, WI - *Ed&PubIntYB 82*
Ad-Vantage Advertising Inc. - Lubbock, TX - *StaDirAdAg 2-84*
Ad-Vantages - Philadelphia, PA - *LitMarPl 83; MagIndMarPl 82-83*
Ad-Venture Advertising - Chicago, IL - *StaDirAdAg 2-84*
Ad-Viser - Red Deer, AB, Canada - *AyerDirPub 83*
Ad-Visor - Denison, IA - *AyerDirPub 83*
Ad-Visor - Orange City, IA - *AyerDirPub 83*
Ad-Visor - Middletown, NJ - *AyerDirPub 83*
Ad West Co., The - Brea, CA - *MagIndMarPl 82-83*
Ad-Win Display Co. - New York, NY - *LitMarPl 83, 84; MagIndMarPl 82-83*
Ada Cable Associates - Ada, MN - *Tel&CabFB 84C p.1663*
Ada Evening News - Ada, OK - *Ed&PubIntYB 82; LitMarPl 83, 84; NewsDir 84*
Ada Herald - Ada, OH - *BaconPubCkNews 84; Ed&PubIntYB 82*
ADA News - Chicago, IL - *BaconPubCkMag 84; MagDir 84*
Ada News - Ada, OK - *BaconPubCkNews 84*
Ada Norman County Index - Ada, MN - *BaconPubCkNews 84; NewsDir 84*
Ada Report - Ada, MI - *WritMar 84*
Ada Sunday News - Ada, OK - *NewsDir 84*
ADAC Corp. - Wobern, MA - *MicrocomMPl 84*
Adadata Information Services - Ada, MI - *EISS 7-83 Sup*
Adademia Book Exhibits - Fairfax, VA - *MagIndMarPl 82-83*
Adage Inc. - Billerica, MA - *DataDirSup 7-83*
Adagio - Harper Woods, MI - *BoPubDir 4, 5*
Adair Associates/Advertising - Atlanta, GA - *AdAge 3-28-84; StaDirAdAg 2-84*
Adair Co., Devin - Old Greenwich, CT - *DirMarMP 83*
Adair County Free Press - Greenfield, IA - *AyerDirPub 83; Ed&PubIntYB 82; NewsDir 84*
Adair County News - Columbia, KY - *AyerDirPub 83; Ed&PubIntYB 82*
Adair News - Adair, IA - *BaconPubCkNews 84; Ed&PubIntYB 82*
Adairsville Cable TV - Adairsville, GA - *Tel&CabFB 84C*
Adairsville North Bartow News - Adairsville, GA - *BaconPubCkNews 84*
Adairsville-North Bartow News [of Cartersville Daily Tribune News] - Cartersville, GA - *NewsDir 84*
Adam [of Publishers Service Inc.] - Los Angeles, CA - *ArtMar 84; WritMar 84*
Adam, Don A. - Bryan, TX - *BrCabYB 84 p.D-297*
Adam, E. W. - New York, NY - *MagIndMarPl 82-83*
Adam Film World - Los Angeles, CA - *ArtMar 84; MagIndMarPl 82-83; WritMar 84*
Adam Productions Inc. - Hollywood, FL - *BillIntBG 83-84*
Adamant Press - Adamant, VT - *BoPubDir 4, 5*
Adamlock Jamestown Corp. - Jamestown, NY - *DirInfWP 82*
Adams Advertising, A. D. - New York, NY - *StaDirAdAg 2-84; TelAl 83, 84*
Adams Advertising Agency Inc. - Chicago, IL - *StaDirAdAg 2-84*
Adams Advertising, Kelly - York, PA - *AdAge 3-28-84*
Adams & Abbott - Boston, MA - *LitMarPl 83, 84*
Adams & Associates Consultants - Springfield, VA - *TeleSy&SerDir 7-83*
Adams & Co., Moss - Seattle, WA - *DirInfWP 82*
Adams & Longino Advertising - Greenville, NC - *AdAge 3-28-84; StaDirAdAg 2-84*
Adams & Rinehart Inc. - New York, NY - *DirPRFirms 83*
Adams & Roundtree Technology Inc. - Lafayette, LA - *DataDirOnSer 84*
Adams Associates Inc., John - Washington, DC - *DirPRFirms 83; StaDirAdAg 2-84*
Adams Book Co. - Brooklyn, NY - *LitMarPl 83, 84*
Adams Brown Co. - Exeter, NH - *BoPubDir 4*
Adams Brown Co. - Cranbury, NJ - *BoPubDir 5*
Adams CATV Inc., David A. - Carbondale, PA - *Tel&CabFB 84C p.1663*
Adams CATV Inc., David A. - Dundaff, PA - *BrCabYB 84*
Adams CATV Inc., David A. - Harford, PA - *BrCabYB 84; Tel&CabFB 84C*
Adams CATV Inc., David A. - Hop Bottom, PA - *BrCabYB 84*
Adams Communications - Wayzata, MN - *BrCabYB 84; Tel&CabFB 84S*
Adams County Historical Society - Hastings, NE - *BoPubDir 4, 5*
Adams County Leader - Council, ID - *AyerDirPub 83; Ed&PubIntYB 82*
Adams County News - West Union, OH - *Ed&PubIntYB 82*
Adams County Times - Adams, WI - *AyerDirPub 83; BaconPubCkNews 84; Ed&PubIntYB 82*
Adams-Croyle Cable TV [of Eastern Telecom Corp.] - Adams Township, PA - *BrCabYB 84; Tel&CabFB 84C*
Adams, E. M. - Jersey City, NJ - *LitMarPl 84*
Adams-Ethridge Publishing Co. - Galveston, TX - *BillIntBG 83-84*
Adams, Gaffney & Associates Inc. - Cincinnati, OH - *DirPRFirms 83; StaDirAdAg 2-84*
Adams, Golden V. Jr. - Provo, UT - *FBInfSer 80*
Adams Group Inc. - Rockville, MD - *DirPRFirms 83; StaDirAdAg 2-84*
Adams Group Inc., The - New York, NY - *LitMarPl 83, 84*
Adams Inc., Bob - Brighton, MA - *BoPubDir 5; WritMar 84*
Adams Inc., Bob - Brookline, MA - *ArtMar 84; BoPubDir 4*
Adams Inc., Scott - Longwood, FL - *MicrocomMPl 84*
Adams Jefferson County Journal - Adams, NY - *BaconPubCkNews 84*
Adams, Martin & Nelson Inc. - Minneapolis, MN - *StaDirAdAg 2-84*
Adams Music Co., Ace - Bronx, NY - *BillIntBG 83-84*
Adams, Norman Clark - Rutland, VT - *LitMarPl 83, 84; MagIndMarPl 82-83*
Adams Organization Advertising Inc., The - Encino, CA - *StaDirAdAg 2-84*
Adams Press - South Windsor, CT - *BoPubDir 4, 5*
Adams Press - Chicago, IL - *LitMarPl 83, 84; MagIndMarPl 82-83*
Adams, Ray & Rosenberg - Los Angeles, CA - *LitMarPl 83, 84*
Adams, Rickard & Mason - Glastonbury, CT - *AdAge 3-28-84; StaDirAdAg 2-84*
Adams Rite Manufacturing Co. - City of Industry, CA - *DirInfWP 82*
Adams-Russell Cablevision - Lewiston, ME - *BrCabYB 84*
Adams-Russell Cablevision Lexington - Lexington, MA - *BrCabYB 84; Tel&CabFB 84C*
Adams-Russell Cablevision-Middlesex Inc. - Acton, MA - *BrCabYB 84*
Adams-Russell Cablevision-Middlesex Inc. - Maynard, MA - *BrCabYB 84*
Adams-Russell Co. Inc. - Braintree, MA - *BrCabYB 84*
Adams-Russell Co. Inc. - Waltham, MA - *HomeVid&CabYB 82-83; Tel&CabFB 84C p.1663; VideoDir 82-83*
Adams-Russell Co. Inc. - *See* A-R Telecommunications
Adams-Shelton Communications - Amarillo, TX - *BrCabYB 84*
Adams Standard - Adams, ND - *Ed&PubIntYB 82*
Adams Standard - *See* Ness Press Inc.
Adams Station Advertising [Div. of Webcraft] - North Brunswick, NJ - *StaDirAdAg 2-84*
Adams Telephone Cooperative - Golden, IL - *Tel&CabFB 84C p.1663; TelDir&BG 83-84*
Adamson & Associates, W. S. - Salt Lake City, UT - *DirPRFirms 83; StaDirAdAg 2-84*
Adamstahl Associates Ltd. - Edmonton, AB, Canada - *DirPRFirms 83*
Adamsville News - *See* McNairy County Publishing Co.
Adamsville Telephone Co. Inc. [Aff. of Century Telephone Enterprises] - Adamsville, TN - *TelDir&BG 83-84*
ADAP Inc. - McAllen, TX - *DataDirOnSer 84*
Adapt - Nokomis, FL - *MicrocomMPl 84*
Adapt Inc. - San Francisco, CA - *EISS 83*
Adaptec Inc. - Milpitas, CA - *MicrocomMPl 84*

Adastra Press - Easthampton, MA - *BoPubDir 4, 5; LitMag&SmPr 83-84*
ADC Magnetic Controls - Minneapolis, MN - *DataDirSup 7-83*
ADCO Enterprises - Staten Island, NY - *BoPubDir 5*
Adco International Co. - Glendale, NY - *LitMarPl 83, 84*
ADCO Productions - Miami, FL - *AvMarPl 83*
Adcom Communications Inc. - New York, NY - *AvMarPl 83*
Adcom Group, The - *See* Northwoods Communications Inc.
Adcom Inc. [Subs. of The Quaker Oats Co.] - Chicago, IL - *AdAge 3-28-84; StaDirAdAg 2-84*
Adcraft Advertising Agency Inc. - Corpus Christi, TX - *StaDirAdAg 2-84*
Adcrafter [of The Adcraft Club of Detroit] - Detroit, MI - *BaconPubCkMag 84; MagDir 84*
Add Sales Co. Inc. - Manitowoc, WI - *StaDirAdAg 2-84*
Add Subs Associates - Bridgeport, CT - *CabTVFinDB 83*
Addams Peace Association, Jane [Aff. of Women's International League for Peace & Freedom] - Philadelphia, PA - *BoPubDir 4, 5*
Addax Music Corp. - *See* Famous Music Corp.
Added Attractions Inc. - Evansville, IN - *Tel&CabFB 84C*
Addiction Research Foundation - Toronto, ON, Canada - *LitMarPl 83, 84*
Addison Busch Advertising - Buffalo, NY - *ArtMar 84*
Addison County Independent - Middlebury, VT - *AyerDirPub 83*
Addison Home Telephone Co. [Aff. of Armstrong Utilities Inc.] - Addison, NY - *TelDir&BG 83-84*
Addison House [Subs. of American Showcase Inc.] - New York, NY - *LitMarPl 83, 84*
Addison Independent - Middlebury, VT - *Ed&PubIntYB 82*
Addison Leader - Addison, IL - *Ed&PubIntYB 82*
Addison News-Bulletin - Addison, IL - *Ed&PubIntYB 82*
Addison News-Bulletin [of Roselle Copley Record Newspapers] - Schaumburg, IL - *NewsDir 84*
Addison/North Dallas Today Newspaper [of Taylor Communications Inc.] - Carrollton, TX - *NewsDir 84*
Addison Press [of Press Publications] - Elmhurst, IL - *AyerDirPub 83; NewsDir 84*
Addison Press - *See* Press Publications
Addison Press, The - Addison, IL - *Ed&PubIntYB 82*
Addison Today - Addison, TX - *AyerDirPub 83*
Addison-Wesley Publishers Ltd. - Don Mills, ON, Canada - *LitMarPl 83, 84*
Addison-Wesley Publishing Co. Inc. - Reading, MA - *KnowInd 83; LitMarPl 83, 84; MicrocomMPl 83, 84*
Addison-Wesley Publishing Co. Inc. (General Books Div.) - Reading, MA - *WritMar 84*
Addison-Wesley Publishing Co. Inc. (Medical/Nursing Div.) - *See* Benjamin/Cummings Publishing Co., The
Addison-Wesley Publishing Co. Inc. (School Div.) - Menlo Park, CA - *AvMarPl 83; MicrocomSwDir 1*
Addmaster Corp. - San Gabriel, CA - *DataDirSup 7-83; MicrocomMPl 83; WhoWMicrocom 83*
Addmaster Corp. (Peripheral Div.) - San Gabriel, CA - *DirInfWP 82*
Addressograph Farrington - Randolph, MA - *DataDirSup 7-83*
Adel-Compton [of Saatchi & Saatchi Compton Worldwide] - Holargos, Greece - *StaDirAdAg 2-84*
Adel Dallas County News - Adel, IA - *BaconPubCkNews 84*
Adel News - Adel, GA - *BaconPubCkNews 84; Ed&PubIntYB 82; NewsDir 84*
Adelaide Radio & Television Ltd. - St. Mary's, ON, Canada - *BrCabYB 84*
Adelante Advertising - New York, NY - *AdAge 3-28-84; StaDirAdAg 2-84*
Adelanto Cablevision Inc. [of Communications Systems Inc.] - Adelanto, CA - *Tel&CabFB 84C*
Adelantre! The Judezmo Society - New York, NY - *BoPubDir 4, 5*
Adelberg/European Art Color, Peter - New York, NY - *LitMarPl 83, 84*
Adele - Milan, Italy - *DirOnDB Spring 84*
Adelman, Bob - New York, NY - *MagIndMarPl 82-83*
Adelphi Interviewing Service - Forest Hills, NY - *IntDirMarRes 83*
Adelphi Records Inc. - Silver Spring, MD - *BillIntBG 83-84*
Adelphi University Press - Garden City, NY - *BoPubDir 4 Sup, 5*
Adelphi University Waldorf Press - Garden City, NY - *BoPubDir 4, 5*
Adelphia Communications Corp. - Coudersport, PA - *BrCabYB 84 p.D-297; Tel&CabFB 84C p.1663*
Aden Advertising - New York, NY - *StaDirAdAg 2-84*
Adena Cable - Frankfort, OH - *BrCabYB 84; Tel&CabFB 84C*
Adept Consumer Testing - Tarzana, CA - *IntDirMarRes 83*
Adesign Group Inc. - Oak Brook, IL - *StaDirAdAg 2-84*
ADF Research - San Rafael, CA - *IntDirMarRes 83*
Adfilm Producers Inc. - New York, NY - *AvMarPl 83; HBIndAd&MS 82-83*
Adfinity Plus Inc. - Oceanside, NY - *StaDirAdAg 2-84*
Adforce Inc. - New York, NY - *StaDirAdAg 2-84*
Adfosystems Div. [of R. Shriver Associates] - Parsippany, NJ - *DataDirOnSer 84*
Adhesives Age [of Communication Channels Inc.] - Atlanta, GA - *BaconPubCkMag 84; MagDir 84*
ADI - Irvine, CA - *MicrocomMPl 84*
ADI Advertising/Public Relations - Ft. Smith, AR - *ArtMar 84*
ADIGE - Milan, Italy - *DirOnDB Spring 84*
Adirondac - Glens Falls, NY - *ArtMar 84; MagIndMarPl 82-83*
Adirondack Cablevision Inc. - Lewis County, NY - *BrCabYB 84*
Adirondack Echo - Old Forge, NY - *Ed&PubIntYB 82*
Adirondack Enterprise - Saranac Lake, NY - *BaconPubCkNews 84; Ed&PubIntYB 82*
Adirondack Life - Syracuse, NY - *BaconPubCkMag 84; MagDir 84; MagIndMarPl 82-83; WritMar 84*
Adirondack Mountain Club Inc. - Glens Falls, NY - *BoPubDir 4, 5*
Adirondack Record Post - Au Sable Forks, NY - *AyerDirPub 83; Ed&PubIntYB 82*
Adirondack Trail Improvement Society - St. Huberts, NY - *BoPubDir 4, 5*
Adirondack Yesteryears Inc. - Saranac Lake, NY - *BoPubDir 4, 5*
Adis Drug Information Retrieval System [of Adis Press Australasia Pty. Ltd.] - Auckland, New Zealand - *EISS 83*
Adkins, Rose A. - Cincinnati, OH - *LitMarPl 83, 84*
ADL Enterprises [Div. of USCS/ADL] - Denville, NJ - *MicrocomMPl 84; WhoWMicrocom 83*
Adler Associates Syndicated Features - St. John, NB, Canada - *Ed&PubIntYB 82*
Adler Computer Technology - Woodland Hills, CA - *MicrocomMPl 84; MicrocomSwDir 1*
Adler Inc., Roy - New York, NY - *HBIndAd&MS 82-83*
Adler Inc., William Hart - Skokie, IL - *ArtMar 84; DirPRFirms 83; StaDirAdAg 2-84; TelAl 83, 84*
Adler Institute of Chicago, Alfred - Chicago, IL - *BoPubDir 4, 5*
Adler, Larry - New York, NY - *LitMarPl 83*
Adler-Royal Business Machines - Union City, NY - *DirInfWP 82*
Adler, Schwartz - Englewood Cliffs, NJ - *AdAge 3-28-84; ArtMar 84; StaDirAdAg 2-84*
Adlerian Counseling Center - Fair Oaks, CA - *BoPubDir 5*
ADM Technology Inc. - Troy, MI - *AvMarPl 83*
Admar Research Co. - New York, NY - *AdAge 5-17-84 p.36; BrCabYB 84; IntDirMarRes 83; Tel&CabFB 84C*
Admarco Firenze SRL - Florence, Italy - *StaDirAdAg 2-84*
Admark - Mason City, IA - *AdAge 3-28-84; StaDirAdAg 2-84*
Admark Associates - Dallas, TX - *StaDirAdAg 2-84*
Admarketing - Los Angeles, CA - *AdAge 3-28-84; Br 1-23-84; StaDirAdAg 2-84*
Admaster Inc. - New York, NY - *ArtMar 84; AvMarPl 83; LitMarPl 83*
Admin Aid Micro Software - Fairfield, CA - *MicrocomMPl 84*
Administration Laboratory Project File [of University of Alberta] - Edmonton, AB, Canada - *DataDirOnSer 84; EISS 83*
Administration on Aging Data Base [of National Clearinghouse on Aging] - Washington, DC - *CompReadDB 82*
Administrative Compensation Survey [of College & University Personnel Association] - Washington, DC - *EISS 5-84 Sup*
Administrative Digest - Don Mills, ON, Canada - *BaconPubCkMag 84*
Administrative Law Review - Denver, CO - *MagIndMarPl 82-83*
Administrative Management - New York, NY - *MagDir 84; MagIndMarPl 82-83*
Administrative Research Associates - Irvine, CA - *BoPubDir 4, 5*
Administrative Science Quarterly - Ithaca, NY - *MagIndMarPl 82-83*

Admins Inc. - Cambridge, MA - *ADAPSOMemDir 83-84*
Admiral History Book Club - Admiral, SK, Canada - *BoPubDir 4, 5*
Admiration Music Publishing - *See* Brunswick Music Publishing Co.
Admix Advertising - Salt Lake City, UT - *AdAge 3-28-84; StaDirAdAg 2-84*
Admore Publishing Inc. - St. Louis, MO - *BoPubDir 5*
ADN German General News Service - New York, NY - *Ed&PubIntYB 82*
Adnews - Toronto, ON, Canada - *BaconPubCkMag 84*
Adobe House Publications - Tucson, AZ - *BoPubDir 4 Sup, 5*
Adolescence [of Libra Publishers Inc.] - Roslyn Heights, NY - *LitMag&SmPr 83-84*
Adolescent Medicine [of The Lovejoy Press] - Washington, DC - *LitMag&SmPr 83-84*
Adonis Press [Aff. of Rudolf Steiner Educational & Farming Association] - Ghent, NY - *BoPubDir 4 Sup, 5*
Adoption Press [Aff. of Adoption Consultants Inc.] - Brooklyn Center, MN - *BoPubDir 4, 5*
ADP Autonet [Div. of Automatic Data Processing Inc.] - Ann Arbor, MI - *DataDirOnSer 84; TeleSy&SerDir 7-83, 2-84*
ADP Financial System One Quotation Service - Mt. Laurel, NJ - *DirOnDB Spring 84*
ADP-International Trade Service [Subs. of ADP Network Services Inc.] - Salem, NH - *DataDirOnSer 84*
ADP Network Services [Subs. of Automatic Data Processing Inc.] - Ann Arbor, MI - *DataDirOnSer 84; DataDirSup 7-83; EISS 83*
ADP Network Services - London, England - *InfIndMarPl 83; MicrocomSwDir 1*
ADP Salvage Parts Locator - Hayward, CA - *DirOnDB Spring 84*
ADP Telephone Computing Service - Seattle, WA - *DataDirSup 7-83; VideoDir 82-83*
Adplan Associates - Evansville, IN - *StaDirAdAg 2-84*
Adplans - Beaverton, OR - *Ed&PubIntYB 82*
ADPS - San Jose, CA - *MicrocomMPl 84*
ADR Typing Service - Brooklyn, NY - *LitMarPl 83, 84*
Adria Cable Corp. - Bland County, VA - *Tel&CabFB 84C*
Adrian Cablevision Inc. - Adrian, MO - *BrCabYB 84; Tel&CabFB 84C*
Adrian Daily Telegram [of Thomson Newspapers Inc.] - Adrian, MI - *NewsDir 84*
Adrian Journal - Adrian, MO - *BaconPubCkNews 84; Ed&PubIntYB 82*
Adrian Nobles County Review - Adrian, MN - *BaconPubCkNews 84*
Adrian Press - New York, NY - *BoPubDir 4, 5*
Adriatic Stamp Co. - Maitland, FL - *BoPubDir 4, 5*
Adrift - New York, NY - *LitMag&SmPr 83-84*
Adroit Graphic Composition Inc. - New York, NY - *LitMarPl 83, 84*
ADS Audio Visual Productions Inc. - Falls Church, VA - *Tel&CabFB 84C*
Ads Color Lab - Woodbridge, NJ - *AvMarPl 83*
A.D.S. Corp. [Div. of L. E. Walz & Associates Inc.] - Massapequa, NY - *DataDirSup 7-83*
ADS Inc. [Div. of CSW Plastic Types Inc.] - Rocky Hill, CT - *LitMarPl 83, 84; MagIndMarPl 82-83*
Ads Infinitum Inc. - Appleton, WI - *StaDirAdAg 2-84*
ADS Magazine - New York, NY - *BaconPubCkMag 84*
Ads Unltd. - New York, NY - *StaDirAdAg 2-84*
Adsatterwhite Inc. - Nashville, TN - *StaDirAdAg 2-84*
Adserve Computing Ltd. - London, England - *DataDirOnSer 84*
Adsociates Inc. - Oklahoma City, OK - *StaDirAdAg 2-84*
ADT Security Systems - New York, NY - *DirInfWP 82*
Adtech Translations - New York, NY - *LitMarPl 83, 84*
AdTel Inc. [Subs. of Burke Marketing Services Inc.] - Chicago, IL - *IntDirMarRes 83*
Adtrack [of Corporate Intelligence Inc.] - St. Paul, MN - *CompReadDB 82; DataDirOnSer 84; DBBus 82; DirOnDB Spring 84; EISS 83*
Adtrack Trends [of Adtrack Inc.] - Goldendale, WA - *MicrocomMPl 84*
Adtrak Inc. - Mountain View, CA - *EISS 7-83 Sup*
Adtron Inc. - Bloomington, IL - *StaDirAdAg 2-84*
Adult Education - Washington, DC - *MagIndMarPl 82-83*
Advance - Atmore, AL - *AyerDirPub 83*
Advance - Sylacauga, AL - *AyerDirPub 83; Ed&PubIntYB 82*
Advance - Hollister, CA - *AyerDirPub 83*
Advance - Lemoore, CA - *AyerDirPub 83*
Advance - Novato, CA - *AyerDirPub 83*
Advance - Vidalia, GA - *AyerDirPub 83*
Advance - Chetopa, KS - *AyerDirPub 83*
Advance - Bangor, MI - *AyerDirPub 83*
Advance - Blissfield, MI - *AyerDirPub 83*
Advance - St. Edward, NE - *AyerDirPub 83*
Advance - Dover, NJ - *AyerDirPub 83*
Advance - Staten Island, NY - *AyerDirPub 83*
Advance - Elizabeth City, NC - *AyerDirPub 83*
Advance - Leechburg, PA - *AyerDirPub 83*
Advance - Parkston, SD - *AyerDirPub 83*
Advance - Lynchburg, VA - *AyerDirPub 83*
Advance - Randolph, WI - *AyerDirPub 83; Ed&PubIntYB 82*
Advance - Castor, AB, Canada - *AyerDirPub 83*
Advance - Langley, BC, Canada - *AyerDirPub 83; Ed&PubIntYB 82*
Advance - Liverpool, NS, Canada - *Ed&PubIntYB 82*
Advance - Burford, ON, Canada - *AyerDirPub 83; Ed&PubIntYB 82*
Advance - Dutton, ON, Canada - *AyerDirPub 83*
Advance - Flesherton, ON, Canada - *Ed&PubIntYB 82*
Advance - Kemptville, ON, Canada - *AyerDirPub 83*
Advance - Gull Lake, SK, Canada - *AyerDirPub 83*
Advance - Melville, SK, Canada - *AyerDirPub 83; Ed&PubIntYB 82*
Advance - Wynyard, SK, Canada - *AyerDirPub 83; Ed&PubIntYB 82*
Advance Access Group Inc. - Lombard, IL - *WhoWMicrocom 83*
Advance Access Group Inc. - Westchester, IL - *DirInfWP 82*
Advance Advertising & Public Relations - Augusta, GA - *StaDirAdAg 2-84*
Advance Business Computing Corp. - Helena, MT - *DataDirSup 7-83; MicrocomMPl 84*
Advance Business Services - Bedford, OH - *DataDirOnSer 84*
Advance Business Services - Solon, OH - *DataDirOnSer 84*
Advance Communications - Rochester, NY - *DirMarMP 83*
Advance-Guard - Goliad, TX - *Ed&PubIntYB 82*
Advance Inc. - Washington, DC - *BrCabYB 84*
Advance Leader - Ligonier, IN - *AyerDirPub 83; Ed&PubIntYB 82*
Advance-Leader Advertiser - Ligonier, IN - *AyerDirPub 83*
Advance Leader, The [of Dardanell Publications Inc.] - Monroeville, PA - *AyerDirPub 83; NewsDir 84*
Advance Leader, The - Oakmont, PA - *Ed&PubIntYB 82*
Advance Marketing Concepts - Encinitas, CA - *BoPubDir 4, 5*
Advance-Monticellonian [of Times Printing Co.] - Monticello, AR - *AyerDirPub 83; Ed&PubIntYB 82; NewsDir 84*
Advance-News - Nappanee, IN - *AyerDirPub 83*
Advance News - Advance, MO - *AyerDirPub 83; BaconPubCkNews 84; Ed&PubIntYB 82*
Advance News - Lakehurst, NJ - *NewsDir 84*
Advance News - Ocean County, NJ - *Ed&PubIntYB 82*
Advance News [of Park Newspapers of St. Lawrence Inc.] - Ogdensburg, NY - *AyerDirPub 83; Ed&PubIntYB 82; NewsDir 84*
Advance News Service Inc. - Washington, DC - *Ed&PubIntYB 82*
Advance of Bucks County, The - Langhorne, PA - *Ed&PubIntYB 82*
Advance of Bucks County, The - Newtown, PA - *AyerDirPub 83; NewsDir 84*
Advance of Bucks County, The [of Inter County Publishing Co.] - Philadelphia, PA - *NewsDir 84*
Advance Planning Publications - Hudson, WI - *BoPubDir 4, 5*
Advance-Press - Springfield, MN - *AyerDirPub 83*
Advance Process Supply Co. - Chicago, IL - *AvMarPl 83*
Advance Products Co., The - Wichita, KS - *AvMarPl 83*
Advance Publications - New York, NY - *AdAge 6-28-84*
Advance Publishing Systems Inc. - Lavallette, NJ - *LitMarPl 83*
Advance-Register & Times - Tulare, CA - *AyerDirPub 83; Ed&PubIntYB 82*
Advance Sentinel - Jellico, TN - *AyerDirPub 83; Ed&PubIntYB 82*
Advance Star Record - Rotan, TX - *Ed&PubIntYB 82*

Advance-Times - Arthur, ON, Canada - *AyerDirPub 83*
Advance-Times - Wingham, ON, Canada - *AyerDirPub 83; Ed&PubIntYB 82*
Advance-Yeoman - Wickliffe, KY - *AyerDirPub 83*
Advanced Acceptance Program Inc. - Quincy, IL - *BoPubDir 4, 5*
Advanced Analytical Computer Systems - Tarzana, CA - *MicrocomMPl 84*
Advanced Animal Breeder, The - Columbia, MO - *BaconPubCkMag 84; MagDir 84*
Advanced Battery Technology - Dana Point, CA - *BaconPubCkMag 84*
Advanced Business Microsystems - Marina del Rey, CA - *WhoWMicrocom 83*
Advanced Business Technology Inc. - San Jose, CA - *MicrocomMPl 84*
Advanced Business Technology Inc. - Saratoga, CA - *MicrocomMPl 83*
Advanced Century Publishing Corp. - Buffalo Grove, IL - *BoPubDir 5*
Advanced Century Publishing Corp. - Chicago, IL - *BoPubDir 4*
Advanced Communications Inc. [of Progressive Communications Inc.] - Jetmore, KS - *BrCabYB 84; Tel&CabFB 84C*
Advanced Computer Graphics Inc. - Milwaukee, WI - *DataDirSup 7-83*
Advanced Computer Management Corp. - Troy, MI - *ADAPSOMemDir 83-84*
Advanced Computer Management Services Inc. - St. Louis, MO - *DataDirOnSer 84*
Advanced Computer Techniques Corp. - New York, NY - *ADAPSOMemDir 83-84; MicrocomSwDir 1*
Advanced Computing [of NewsNet Inc.] - Bryn Mawr, PA - *DataDirOnSer 84*
Advanced Computing - Lancaster, PA - *DirOnDB Spring 84; EISS 5-84 Sup*
Advanced Data Management - Kingston, NJ - *DataDirSup 7-83*
Advanced Data Systems - Long Beach, CA - *ADAPSOMemDir 83-84; DataDirOnSer 84; MicrocomMPl 84*
Advanced Digital Microsystems - Dayton, OH - *MicrocomMPl 84*
Advanced Digital Products - Nashville, TN - *MicrocomMPl 83*
Advanced Electronics Design Inc. - Sunnyvale, CA - *DataDirSup 7-83; WhoWMicrocom 83*
Advanced Field Research Inc. - Merrick, NY - *IntDirMarRes 83*
Advanced Financial Planning - El Toro, CA - *MicrocomMPl 84*
Advanced Graphic Services Inc. - Long Island City, NY - *LitMarPl 83, 84*
Advanced Industries Inc. - Atlanta, GA - *AvMarPl 83*
Advanced Legal Software - Honolulu, HI - *MicrocomSwDir 1*
Advanced Library Systems Inc. - Andover, MA - *EISS 83; MicroMarPl 82-83*
Advanced Logic Systems - Sunnyvale, CA - *MicrocomMPl 83; WhoWMicrocom 83*
Advanced Management Journal - New York, NY - *MagIndMarPl 82-83*
Advanced Management Strategies Inc. - Atlanta, GA - *WhoWMicrocom 83*
Advanced Marketing - Cambridge, ON, Canada - *BoPubDir 4 Sup, 5*
Advanced Materials Technology - East Orange, NJ - *EISS 7-83 Sup; InfIndMarPl 83*
Advanced Medical Systems [Subs. of LHJ Service Corp.] - Rockville Centre, NY - *DataDirOnSer 84*
Advanced Micro Techniques - Foster City, CA - *MicrocomMPl 83, 84; MicrocomSwDir 1; WhoWMicrocom 83*
Advanced Office Concepts - Bala Cynwyd, PA - *BaconPubCkMag 84; DirInfWP 82; DirOnDB Spring 84; EISS 5-84 Sup; TeleSy&SerDir 7-83*
Advanced Operating Systems - Indianapolis, IN - *MicrocomMPl 84*
Advanced Operating Systems - Michigan City, IN - *MicrocomMPl 83*
Advanced Projects Corp. - Salem, OR - *WhoWMicrocom 83*
Advanced Publishing Systems Inc. - Lavallette, NJ - *LitMarPl 83, 84*
Advanced Software Interface - San Mateo, CA - *MicrocomMPl 84; MicrocomSwDir 1*
Advanced Software Products Inc. - Delray Beach, FL - *WhoWMicrocom 83*
Advanced Software Technology - Overland Park, KS - *BoPubDir 5*
Advanced Systems Inc. - Arlington Heights, IL - *ADAPSOMemDir 83-84*
Advanced Technology Enterprises - Palo Alto, CA - *WhoWMicrocom 83*
Advanced Terminals Inc. - Syracuse, NY - *DataDirSup 7-83*
Advanced Vehicle News [of Porter Corp.] - Westport, CT - *BaconPubCkMag 84; MagDir 84*
Advanced Video Communications - Hinsdale, IL - *AvMarPl 83*
Advances for Medicine [of Hewlett-Packard Medical Products Group] - Waltham, MA - *WritMar 84*
Advanswers Media/Programming Inc. [Subs. of Gardner Advertising Co.] - St. Louis, MO - *Br 1-23-84; HBIndAd&MS 82-83; StaDirAdAg 2-84*
Advant - San Jose, CA - *DirOnDB Spring 84*
Advantage [Div. of Calle & Co.] - Greenwich, CT - *IntDirMarRes 83*
Advantage - Cottage Grove, OR - *AyerDirPub 83*
Advantage Promotion Ltd. - Naperville, IL - *StaDirAdAg 2-84*
Advantage Systems Inc. - Waltham, MA - *ADAPSOMemDir 83-84*
Advantage Typing Service - Hartsdale, NY - *LitMarPl 83, 84*
Advantages - Ridgefield, CT - *BaconPubCkMag 84*
Advantec Systems Ltd. - Birmingham, England - *MicrocomSwDir 1*
Advcom - New York, NY - *MicrocomSwDir 1*
Advent Books Inc. - New York, NY - *BoPubDir 4, 5*
Advent Productions - El Cerrito, CA - *BillIntBG 83-84*
Advent Products Inc. - Orange, CA - *MicrocomMPl 84*
Advent: Publishers Inc. - Chicago, IL - *BoPubDir 4, 5*
Adventure Feature Syndicate - Glendale, CA - *Ed&PubIntYB 82*
Adventure Guides Inc./Farm & Ranch Vacations Inc. - New York, NY - *BoPubDir 4, 5*
Adventure International [Subs. of Scott Adams Inc.] - Longwood, FL - *MicrocomSwDir 1; WhoWMicrocom 83; WritMar 84*
Adventure Music Co. - Nashville, TN - *BillIntBG 83-84*
Adventure Road - Chicago, IL - *MagIndMarPl 82-83*
Adventure Road - New York, NY - *BaconPubCkMag 84; MagDir 84*
Adventure Travel - New York, NY - *MagIndMarPl 82-83*
Adventure Travel - Seattle, WA - *MagDir 84*
Adventures in Living - Lakewood, CO - *BoPubDir 5*
Adventures in Living - Woodland Park, CO - *BoPubDir 4*
Adventures in Poetry Magazine - Junction, TX - *LitMag&SmPr 83-84*
Advernomics Inc. - Newark, NJ - *StaDirAdAg 2-84*
Adverse Drug Reaction Data Base [of U.S. Public Health Service] - Rockville, MD - *EISS 83*
Advert Publishing - Oak Brook, IL - *BoPubDir 5*
Advertiser - Montgomery, AL - *AyerDirPub 83*
Advertiser - Moulton, AL - *AyerDirPub 83*
Advertiser - Fairfield, CA - *AyerDirPub 83*
Advertiser - Sonora, CA - *AyerDirPub 83*
Advertiser - New Canaan, CT - *AyerDirPub 83*
Advertiser [of New Milford Housatonic Valley Publishing Co.] - New Milford, CT - *NewsDir 84*
Advertiser - Inverness, FL - *AyerDirPub 83*
Advertiser - Honolulu, HI - *AyerDirPub 83*
Advertiser - Arco, ID - *AyerDirPub 83*
Advertiser - Lebanon, IL - *AyerDirPub 83*
Advertiser - Alta, IA - *AyerDirPub 83*
Advertiser - Ames, IA - *AyerDirPub 83*
Advertiser [of Mt. Sterling Advocate] - Mt. Sterling, KY - *NewsDir 84*
Advertiser - Baker, LA - *AyerDirPub 83*
Advertiser - Lafayette, LA - *AyerDirPub 83*
Advertiser - Calais, ME - *AyerDirPub 83*
Advertiser - Salisbury, MD - *AyerDirPub 83*
Advertiser - Saugus, MA - *AyerDirPub 83*
Advertiser - Ecorse, MI - *AyerDirPub 83*
Advertiser - Aurora, MO - *AyerDirPub 83; Ed&PubIntYB 82*
Advertiser - Eldon, MO - *AyerDirPub 83*
Advertiser - Fayette, MO - *AyerDirPub 83*
Advertiser - Greenfield, MO - *AyerDirPub 83*
Advertiser - Albion, NY - *AyerDirPub 83*
Advertiser - Alden, NY - *AyerDirPub 83*
Advertiser - Caledonia, NY - *AyerDirPub 83*

Advertiser - East Aurora, NY - *AyerDirPub 83*
Advertiser - Lodi, OH - *AyerDirPub 83*
Advertiser - Milford, OH - *AyerDirPub 83*
Advertiser - Canonsburg, PA - *AyerDirPub 83; NewsDir 84*
Advertiser - Edgefield, SC - *AyerDirPub 83*
Advertiser - Athens, TX - *AyerDirPub 83*
Advertiser [of The Huntington Publishing Co.] - Huntington, WV - *NewsDir 84*
Advertiser - Edgerton, WI - *AyerDirPub 83*
Advertiser - Sun Prairie, WI - *AyerDirPub 83*
Advertiser - Wisconsin Rapids, WI - *AyerDirPub 83*
Advertiser - Beaverlodge, AB, Canada - *AyerDirPub 83; Ed&PubIntYB 82*
Advertiser - Armstrong, BC, Canada - *Ed&PubIntYB 82*
Advertiser - Grand Falls, NF, Canada - *AyerDirPub 83*
Advertiser - Kentville, NS, Canada - *AyerDirPub 83; Ed&PubIntYB 82*
Advertiser - Frankford, ON, Canada - *AyerDirPub 83; Ed&PubIntYB 82*
Advertiser - Toronto, ON, Canada - *Ed&PubIntYB 82*
Advertiser - Woodbridge, ON, Canada - *Ed&PubIntYB 82*
Advertiser-Advance, The - El Paso, IL - *Ed&PubIntYB 82*
Advertiser & Bastrop County News - Bastrop, TX - *AyerDirPub 83*
Advertiser-Courier - Hermann, MO - *AyerDirPub 83; Ed&PubIntYB 82*
Advertiser Democrat - Norway, ME - *AyerDirPub 83; Ed&PubIntYB 82*
Advertiser-Free Press [of Scottsboro Newspapers] - Scottsboro, AL - *NewsDir 84*
Advertiser-Gleam - Guntersville, AL - *AyerDirPub 83; Ed&PubIntYB 82*
Advertiser Inc. - Marion, WI - *AyerDirPub 83*
Advertiser-Journal [of Advertiser Co.] - Montgomery, AL - *Ed&PubIntYB 82*
Advertiser Photo News - Warwick, NY - *AyerDirPub 83; BaconPubCkNews 84*
Advertiser Post - North Battleford, SK, Canada - *AyerDirPub 83*
Advertiser, The - Branford, CT - *AyerDirPub 83*
Advertiser, The - East Haven, CT - *Ed&PubIntYB 82*
Advertiser, The - Elmwood, IL - *AyerDirPub 83*
Advertiser, The - Buchanan, MI - *AyerDirPub 83*
Advertiser, The - Edmore, MI - *AyerDirPub 83*
Advertiser, The - Elsie, MI - *AyerDirPub 83*
Advertiser, The - Durham, NC - *AyerDirPub 83*
Advertiser, The [of G.T.S. Publications] - Bellfontaine, OH - *NewsDir 84*
Advertiser-Topic - Petrolia, ON, Canada - *Ed&PubIntYB 82*
Advertiser-Tribune - Tiffin, OH - *AyerDirPub 83; Ed&PubIntYB 82*
Advertisers Broadcasting Co. - New York, NY - *Tel&CabFB 84C*
Advertisers Co-Op - Wheaton, MD - *ArtMar 84; StaDirAdAg 2-84*
Advertisers Digest [of Executive Review Publishers] - Chicago, IL - *MagDir 84*
Advertisers Exchange Inc. - Sparta, NJ - *Ed&PubIntYB 82*
Advertisers Research - Minneapolis, MN - *IntDirMarRes 83*
Advertiser's Services Inc. - Fullerton, CA - *StaDirAdAg 2-84*
Advertising Age [of Crain Communications Inc.] - Chicago, IL - *BaconPubCkMag 84; Folio 83; LitMarPl 83, 84; NewsBur 6; WritMar 84*
Advertising Age [of Crain Communications Inc.] - New York, NY - *MagDir 84; MagIndMarPl 82-83*
Advertising Age (Cite Service) - Chicago, IL - *ProGuPRSer 4*
Advertising Age (Electronic Media Edition) - Chicago, IL - *BaconPubCkMag 84*
Advertising Agency Associates - Newton Center, MA - *StaDirAdAg 2-84*
Advertising Agency Inc., The - Chicago, IL - *StaDirAdAg 2-84*
Advertising Agency Partnership Ltd. - London, England - *StaDirAdAg 2-84*
Advertising Alliance Inc., The - Minnetonka, MN - *StaDirAdAg 2-84*
Advertising & Art Council - Birmingham, AL - *AdAge 3-28-84; AvMarPl 83; StaDirAdAg 2-84*
Advertising & Marketing Associates Inc. - Miami, FL - *StaDirAdAg 2-84*
Advertising & Marketing Inc. - Jackson, MS - *StaDirAdAg 2-84*
Advertising & Marketing Intelligence [of New York Times Information Service Inc.] - Parsippany, NJ - *CompReadDB 82; DBBus 82; EISS 83*
Advertising Assistance Inc. - Weston, MA - *StaDirAdAg 2-84*
Advertising Associates - Northbrook, IL - *AdAge 3-28-84; StaDirAdAg 2-84*
Advertising Associates - Tyler, TX - *StaDirAdAg 2-84*
Advertising Associates Inc. - St. Louis, MO - *DirMarMP 83*
Advertising, Boelter & Lincoln - Madison, WI - *StaDirAdAg 2-84*
Advertising Checking Bureau Inc. - New York, NY - *MagIndMarPl 82-83; ProGuPRSer 4*
Advertising Communications Inc. - Davenport, IA - *StaDirAdAg 2-84*
Advertising Communications Times - Philadelphia, PA - *BaconPubCkMag 84; MagDir 84*
Advertising Co. of Offield & Brower, The - Los Gatos, CA - *StaDirAdAg 2-84*
Advertising Co., The - Houston, TX - *StaDirAdAg 2-84*
Advertising Dentist, The - Phoenix, AZ - *BaconPubCkMag 84*
Advertising Design Studios Inc. - Milwaukee, WI - *StaDirAdAg 2-84*
Advertising Development Specialists - Ft. Collins, CO - *StaDirAdAg 2-84*
Advertising Direction Inc. [of Santa Fe Industries] - Chicago, IL - *StaDirAdAg 2-84*
Advertising, Graphics & Marketing Inc. - Ft. Worth, TX - *StaDirAdAg 2-84*
Advertising Impact - Memphis, TN - *AdAge 3-28-84; StaDirAdAg 2-84*
Advertising Inc. - Greenville, NC - *StaDirAdAg 2-84*
Advertising Inc. - Tulsa, OK - *AdAge 3-28-84; StaDirAdAg 2-84*
Advertising Inc. - Charleston, WV - *StaDirAdAg 2-84*
Advertising Management - Brooklyn, NY - *AdAge 3-28-84; MagIndMarPl 82-83; StaDirAdAg 2-84*
Advertising, Marketing, & Sales Promotion Book Club, The - Middle Island, NY - *LitMarPl 83, 84*
Advertising/Marketing Associates Inc. - Sparta, NJ - *StaDirAdAg 2-84*
Advertising Media Services Inc. - New York, NY - *StaDirAdAg 2-84*
Advertising News Review - Long Island City, NY - *MagIndMarPl 82-83*
Advertising Partners/A.P. Designers Inc. - Clifton, NJ - *StaDirAdAg 2-84*
Advertising Personnel Services - New York, NY - *MagIndMarPl 82-83*
Advertising Plus Inc. - Waco, TX - *StaDirAdAg 2-84*
Advertising Plus Inc. - *See* Lambesis & Associates Inc.
Advertising Promotions Inc. - Denver, CO - *StaDirAdAg 2-84*
Advertising Research Foundation - New York, NY - *BoPubDir 4, 5; Tel&CabFB 84C*
Advertising Service Agency Inc. - Charleston, SC - *StaDirAdAg 2-84*
Advertising Services for Recruitment - Newton, MA - *StaDirAdAg 2-84*
Advertising Techniques [of ADA Publishing Co.] - New York, NY - *BaconPubCkMag 84; MagDir 84; MagIndMarPl 82-83; WritMar 84*
Advertising to Women - New York, NY - *AdAge 3-28-84; ArtMar 84; StaDirAdAg 2-84*
Advertising Trade Service Inc. - New York, NY - *StaDirAdAg 2-84*
Advertising Works - Honolulu, HI - *AdAge 3-28-84; StaDirAdAg 2-84*
Advertising World [of Directories International] - New York, NY - *BaconPubCkMag 84; MagDir 84; MagIndMarPl 82-83; WritMar 84*
Advertizer Advocate - Houston, TX - *AyerDirPub 83*
Advertizer-Herald - Bamberg, SC - *AyerDirPub 83; Ed&PubIntYB 82*
Adviser, The [of The Laurel Group Press] - Scottdale, PA - *NewsDir 84*
Advisor - Utica, MI - *AyerDirPub 83*
Advisor - Toronto, ON, Canada - *BaconPubCkMag 84*
Advisor Newspapers - Utica, MI - *BaconPubCkNews 84*
Advisor, The - Middletown, NJ - *Ed&PubIntYB 82; NewsDir 84*

Advisory Research Institute [Div. of William Knobler Co. Inc.] - Manhasset, NY - *IntDirMarRes 83*
Advisory Unit for Computer Based Education [of Hertfordshire County Council] - Hatfield, England - *EISS 7-83 Sup*
Advo-Systems Inc. - Hartford, CT - *HBIndAd&MS 82-83*
Advocacy Press - Santa Barbara, CA - *BoPubDir 5*
Advocate - Greenville, AL - *AyerDirPub 83*
Advocate - Julesburg, CO - *AyerDirPub 83*
Advocate - Hartford, CT - *AyerDirPub 83*
Advocate [of Connecticut Newspapers Inc.] - Stamford, CT - *AyerDirPub 83; BaconPubCkNews 84; Ed&PubIntYB 82; NewsDir 84*
Advocate - Clifton, IL - *AyerDirPub 83*
Advocate - Greenville, IL - *AyerDirPub 83*
Advocate - West Salem, IL - *AyerDirPub 83*
Advocate - Wilmington, IL - *AyerDirPub 83*
Advocate - Rockwell City, IA - *AyerDirPub 83*
Advocate - Andover, KS - *AyerDirPub 83*
Advocate - Columbus, KS - *AyerDirPub 83*
Advocate - Gypsum, KS - *AyerDirPub 83*
Advocate - Marysville, KS - *AyerDirPub 83*
Advocate - Mt. Sterling, KY - *AyerDirPub 83*
Advocate [of Capital City Press] - Baton Rouge, LA - *AyerDirPub 83; Ed&PubIntYB 82; LitMarPl 84*
Advocate - Princetown, MA - *AyerDirPub 83*
Advocate - Sharon, MA - *AyerDirPub 83*
Advocate - Clarkfield, MN - *AyerDirPub 83*
Advocate - Henning, MN - *AyerDirPub 83*
Advocate - Spencer, NE - *AyerDirPub 83*
Advocate - Camillus, NY - *AyerDirPub 83; Ed&PubIntYB 82*
Advocate - Crestline, OH - *AyerDirPub 83*
Advocate - Greenville, OH - *AyerDirPub 83*
Advocate - London, OH - *AyerDirPub 83*
Advocate - Allen, OK - *AyerDirPub 83*
Advocate - Cleveland, TX - *AyerDirPub 83*
Advocate - Van Horn, TX - *AyerDirPub 83*
Advocate - Victoria, TX - *AyerDirPub 83*
Advocate - Parsons, WV - *AyerDirPub 83*
Advocate - Spooner, WI - *AyerDirPub 83*
Advocate - Red Deer, AB, Canada - *AyerDirPub 83; Ed&PubIntYB 82*
Advocate - Vulcan, AB, Canada - *AyerDirPub 83; Ed&PubIntYB 82*
Advocate - Pictou, NS, Canada - *AyerDirPub 83*
Advocate - Erin, ON, Canada - *AyerDirPub 83*
Advocate - Mitchell, ON, Canada - *AyerDirPub 83*
Advocate - Paisley, ON, Canada - *AyerDirPub 83; Ed&PubIntYB 82*
Advocate-Advertiser - Mt. Sterling, KY - *AyerDirPub 83*
Advocate & Journal - Winner, SD - *Ed&PubIntYB 82*
Advocate Democrat, The - Crawfordville, GA - *Ed&PubIntYB 82*
Advocate Hamiltonian - Hamilton, MO - *AyerDirPub 83; Ed&PubIntYB 82*
Advocate-Leader - Kennebec, SD - *AyerDirPub 83; Ed&PubIntYB 82*
Advocate-Messenger - Danville, KY - *AyerDirPub 83; Ed&PubIntYB 82*
Advocate-News - Ft. Bragg, CA - *AyerDirPub 83*
Advocate News - Durant, IA - *Ed&PubIntYB 82*
Advocate News - Wilton, IA - *AyerDirPub 83*
Advocate Publishing - Hartford, CT - *BaconPubCkNews 84*
Advocate Publishing Group - Reynoldsburg, OH - *LitMarPl 83, 84*
Advocate, The - Los Angeles, CA - *LitMarPl 83, 84*
Advocate, The [of Liberation Publications Inc.] - San Mateo, CA - *LitMag&SmPr 83-84; MagDir 84; MagIndMarPl 82-83; WritMar 84*
Advocate, The - Provincetown, MA - *Ed&PubIntYB 82*
Advocate, The [of Thomson Newspapers Inc.] - Newark, OH - *AyerDirPub 83; Ed&PubIntYB 82; NewsDir 84*
Adwar Video - New York, NY - *AvMarPl 83; MicrocomMPl 83, 84*
Adweek [of A/S/M Communications] - New York, NY - *Folio 83; MagDir 84; MagIndMarPl 82-83*
Adweek/Eastern Advertising News [of A/S/M Communications] - New York, NY - *BaconPubCkMag 84*
Adweek/Midwest Advertising News [of A/S/M Communications] - Chicago, IL - *BaconPubCkMag 84*
Adweek/Southeast Advertising News [of A/S/M Communications] - Atlanta, GA - *BaconPubCkMag 84*
Adweek/Southwest Advertising News [of A/S/M Communications] - Dallas, TX - *BaconPubCkMag 84; MagDir 84*
Adweek/Western Advertising News [of A/S/M Communications] - Los Angeles, CA - *BaconPubCkMag 84; WritMar 84*
Adwell Audio-Visual Co. Inc. - New York, NY - *AvMarPl 83*
Adworks Advertising Inc. - Chicago, IL - *StaDirAdAg 2-84*
AEA Advocate - Phoenix, AZ - *MagDir 84*
AEA Data Base [of Association of European Airlines] - Brussels, Belgium - *EISS 7-83 Sup*
AEB Library Services [of Atomic Energy Board] - Pretoria, South Africa - *EISS 83*
AEDS Monitor - Minneapolis, MN - *BaconPubCkMag 84*
Aegean Books [Aff. of Faubour Marigny Bookstore] - New Orleans, LA - *BoPubDir 4, 5*
Aegean Hills Cablevision [of Times Mirror Cable TV] - Aegean Hills, CA - *Tel&CabFB 84C*
Aegis - Bel Air, MD - *AyerDirPub 83; Ed&PubIntYB 82; NewsDir 84*
Aegis Productions - New York, NY - *Tel&CabFB 84C*
Aegis Systems - Saline, MI - *MicrocomMPl 84*
Aegis Systems Corp. - Tigard, OR - *WhoWMicrocom 83*
AEIOU Inc. - Pleasantville, NY - *LitMarPl 83*
AEL [of Microtel Ltd.] - Burnaby, BC, Canada - *VideoDir 82-83*
AEL Industries Inc. - Laurdale, PA - *HomeVid&CabYB 82-83*
AEL Microtel Ltd. - Burnby, BC, Canada - *DataDirSup 7-83*
AEM Computer Services - Phoenix, AZ - *WhoWMicrocom 83*
AEM Computer Services - Scottsdale, AZ - *MicrocomMPl 83*
Aeolian-Harp Press - Burton, MI - *BoPubDir 4, 5*
Aeolus Press Inc. - Baltimore, MD - *LitMag&SmPr 83-84*
Aeolus Productions Inc. - New York, NY - *AvMarPl 83*
Aeon Communications - Seattle, WA - *BoPubDir 4 Sup, 5*
Aeon Concepts - Pittsburgh, PA - *MicrocomMPl 84*
Aerial Applicator - Santa Fe Springs, CA - *BaconPubCkMag 84; MagDir 84*
Aerial Image Transfer Service - New York, NY - *AvMarPl 83*
Aerial Photography Services/APS Inc. - Charlotte, NC - *BoPubDir 4, 5*
AERIC Canadian Database [of The Conference Board of Canada] - Ottawa, ON, Canada - *DataDirOnSer 84*
AERIC National Database [of The Conference Board of Canada] - Ottawa, ON, Canada - *DirOnDB Spring 84*
AERIC Provincial Database [of The Conference Board of Canada] - Ottawa, ON, Canada - *DataDirOnSer 84; DirOnDB Spring 84*
AERIC Steel Products Databank [of The Conference Board of Canada] - Ottawa, ON, Canada - *DataDirOnSer 84*
AERIC Survey of Consumer Buying Intentions [of The Conference Board of Canada] - Ottawa, ON, Canada - *DataDirOnSer 84; DirOnDB Spring 84*
AERIC System [of The Conference Board of Canada] - Ottawa, ON, Canada - *EISS 83*
Aero [of Macro/Comm Corp.] - Los Angeles, CA - *MagDir 84*
Aero [of Macro/Comm Corp.] - San Clemente, CA - *BaconPubCkMag 84; MagIndMarPl 82-83; WritMar 84*
Aero Adventures - Santa Ynez, CA - *BoPubDir 4, 5*
Aero Facts - Hazelwood, MO - *NewsDir 84*
Aero Mechanic [of Machinists District Lodge 751] - Seattle, WA - *NewsDir 84*
Aero-Medical Consultants Inc. - Largo, FL - *BoPubDir 4, 5*
Aero Press Publishers - Fall River, MA - *BoPubDir 4, 5*
Aero Products Research Inc. - Los Angeles, CA - *ArtMar 84; BoPubDir 4, 5*
Aero Publishers Inc. - Fallbrook, CA - *ArtMar 84; DirMarMP 83; LitMarPl 83, 84; WritMar 84*
Aero Record Inc. - New York, NY - *BillIntBG 83-84*
Aero Sun-Times - Billings, MT - *LitMag&SmPr 83-84*
Aero West Magazine - Broomfield, CO - *MagDir 84*
Aerocomp Inc. - Dallas, TX - *MicrocomMPl 84*
Aerodrome Press - Story City, IA - *BoPubDir 4, 5*
Aerofax Inc. - Austin, TX - *BoPubDir 5*
Aerographics - Deltona, FL - *BoPubDir 4, 5*
Aerolog Productions Inc. - Port Washington, NY - *AvMarPl 83*

Aerophile Inc. - San Antonio, TX - *BoPubDir 4, 5*
Aeroshade Inc. - Waukesha, WI - *AvMarPl 83*
Aerosol Age [of Industry Publications Inc.] - Cedar Grove, NJ - *BaconPubCkMag 84; MagDir 84*
Aerospace [of Aerospace Industries Association] - Washington, DC - *BaconPubCkMag 84; MagDir 84*
Aerospace America - New York, NY - *BaconPubCkMag 84*
Aerospace Canada - Toronto, ON, Canada - *BaconPubCkMag 84*
Aerospace Daily Online - Washington, DC - *BaconPubCkMag 84; DirOnDB Spring 84*
Aerospace Database [of American Institute of Aeronautics & Astronautics] - New York, NY - *DataDirOnSer 84*
Aerospace Historian - Manhattan, KS - *MagIndMarPl 82-83*
Aerospace Medical Association - Washington, DC - *BoPubDir 5*
Aerospace Observer - Colorado Springs, CO - *AyerDirPub 83*
Aerospace Research Applications Center [of Indianapolis Center for Advanced Research] - Indianapolis, IN - *EISS 83*
Aerospace Structures Information & Analysis Center [of U.S. Air Force] - Dayton, OH - *EISS 83*
Aerotravel Research - Cranston, RI - *BoPubDir 4, 5*
AES Data - Montreal, PQ, Canada - *DirInfWP 82*
AES Magazine - Pittsburgh, PA - *MagDir 84*
Aesculapius Publishers Inc. - New York, NY - *LitMarPl 83, 84*
Aesthetic Artist Records - Dayton, OH - *BillIntBG 83-84*
Aesthetic Plastic Surgery - New York, NY - *BaconPubCkMag 84*
Aesthetic Realism Foundation - New York, NY - *BoPubDir 4, 5*
Aesthetic, Reconstructive, & Facial Plastic Surgery - Brookline, MA - *MicroMarPl 82-83*
Aeternium Publishing - Nantucket Island, MA - *BoPubDir 4, 5*
Aetna Data Processing Co. - Chicago Heights, IL - *DataDirOnSer 84*
Aetna Life & Casualty - Hartford, CT - *AvMarPl 83*
Aetna Products Co. Inc. - Hicksville, NY - *DirInfWP 82*
Aetna Telecommunications Consultants - Centerville, MA - *TeleSy&SerDir 2-84*
AF Associates - Northvale, NJ - *AvMarPl 83*
AF-Tronics Associates - Hyde Park, UT - *MicrocomMPl 83*
AFB Micro Controls - El Cajon, CA - *MicrocomMPl 83*
AFC Computer Services - New York, NY - *MagIndMarPl 82-83*
AFEE - Paris, France - *DirOnDB Spring 84*
Affaire de Coeur - Fremont, CA - *WritMar 84*
Affarsdok - Stockholm, Sweden - *DirOnDB Spring 84*
Affiliated Broadcasting Inc. - Boston, MA - *BrCabYB 84*
Affiliated Computer Systems - Dallas, TX - *DataDirSup 7-83*
Affiliated Publications - Boston, MA - *AdAge 6-28-84; BrCabYB 84; KnowInd 83*
Affiliated Publications - *See* McCaw Communications Cos. Inc.
Affirmation Books - Whitinsville, MA - *BoPubDir 4, 5; LitMarPl 84*
Affirmative Action Register - St. Louis, MO - *MagIndMarPl 82-83*
Affton Products Co. Inc. - New York, NY - *AvMarPl 83*
Affton South St. Louis County News - Affton, MO - *BaconPubCkNews 84*
AFI Productions Inc. - Miami, FL - *Tel&CabFB 84C*
AFIPS Press - Arlington, VA - *LitMarPl 83, 84*
AFL-CIO Milwaukee Labor Press [of Milwaukee County Labor Council AFL-CIO] - West Allis, WI - *NewsDir 84*
AFL-CIO News - Washington, DC - *NewsDir 84*
AFP-Agora Data Bases [of French Press Agency] - Paris, France - *EISS 83*
AFP Distributors Inc. - New York, NY - *TelAl 83, 84; Tel&CabFB 84C*
AFP Front Projection [Subs. of Lindahl Specialties Inc.] - Elkhart, IN - *AvMarPl 83*
Afrasian Films - New York, NY - *TelAl 83*
Africa Currents [of Montagu Publications] - Huntingdon, England - *LitMag&SmPr 83-84*
Africa Market Research Co. - Nicosia, Cyprus - *IntDirMarRes 83*
Africa News [of NewsNet Inc.] - Bryn Mawr, PA - *DataDirOnSer 84*
Africa News Service - Durham, NC - *BrCabYB 84; DirOnDB Spring 84; EISS 5-84 Sup p.1668; LitMag&SmPr 83-84*
Africa Publications Trust - Huntingdon, England - *LitMag&SmPr 83-84*
Africa Report - New York, NY - *MagDir 84; MagIndMarPl 82-83; WritMar 84*
Africa Research & Publications Project - Trenton, NJ - *LitMag&SmPr 83-84*
Africa Today - Denver, CO - *LitMag&SmPr 83-84; MagIndMarPl 82-83*
Africa Update - New York, NY - *BaconPubCkMag 84*
African-American News & World Report - Baltimore, MD - *Ed&PubIntYB 82*
African Bibliographic Center - Washington, DC - *BoPubDir 4, 5*
African Book Publishing Record, The [of Hans Zell Publishers] - Oxford, England - *LitMag&SmPr 83-84*
African Imprint Library Services - Falmouth, MA - *MicroMarPl 82-83*
African Network of Administrative Information [of African Training & Research Centre in Administration for Development] - Tangier, Morocco - *EISS 7-83 Sup*
African Newspaper Index, The - Langley Park, MD - *LitMag&SmPr 83-84*
African Policy Institute - Brooklyn, NY - *BoPubDir 4*
African Studies [of Witwatersrand University Press] - Johannesburg, South Africa - *LitMag&SmPr 83-84*
African Studies Association/Crossroads Press - Los Angeles, CA - *BoPubDir 4, 5; LitMarPl 84*
Africana Publishing Co. [Div. of Holmes & Meier Publishers Inc.] - New York, NY - *LitMarPl 83, 84*
Africus - Washington, DC - *BaconPubCkMag 84; WritMar 84*
Afro-Am Publishing Co. Inc. - Chicago, IL - *AvMarPl 83; BoPubDir 4, 5*
Afro-American - Washington, DC - *AyerDirPub 83*
Afro-American - Baltimore, MD - *AyerDirPub 83; Ed&PubIntYB 82*
Afro-American Affairs [of Jackson & Edwards Inc.] - Philadelphia, PA - *LitMag&SmPr 83-84*
Afro-American & Washington Tribune - Washington, DC - *Ed&PubIntYB 82*
Afro-American Research Center Inc. - Annapolis, MD - *BoPubDir 5*
Afro-Americans in New York Life & History - Buffalo, NY - *LitMag&SmPr 83-84*
Afro-Hispanic Review - Washington, DC - *LitMag&SmPr 83-84*
Afro-Lecon Inc. (Watson Industries Div.) - Jamestown, NY - *DirInfWP 82*
Afro Weekly - Orangeburg, SC - *Ed&PubIntYB 82*
AFTA: The Alternative Magazine [of AFTA Press Inc.] - New Brunswick, NJ - *ArtMar 84; LitMag&SmPr 83-84; LitMarPl 83, 84; MagIndMarPl 82-83*
After Dark - New York, NY - *ArtMar 84; BaconPubCkMag 84; MagDir 84; MagIndMarPl 82-83; WritMar 84*
After Dark Datalines - Latham, NY - *DirOnDB Spring 84*
After-Image - Los Angeles, CA - *FBInfSer 80*
Afterimage [of Visual Studies Workshop Press] - Rochester, NY - *LitMag&SmPr 83-84*
Afterimage Book Publishers - Urbana, IL - *BoPubDir 4*
Afterimage Book Publishers - El Paso, TX - *BoPubDir 5; LitMag&SmPr 83-84*
Afternoon TV [of Television Publications] - New York, NY - *WritMar 84*
Afterthought Engineering - San Diego, CA - *MicrocomMPl 83, 84; MicrocomSwDir 1*
Afton American - Afton, OK - *BaconPubCkNews 84; Ed&PubIntYB 82*
Afton Cablevision Inc. - Afton, IA - *Tel&CabFB 84C*
Afton Star Enterprise - Afton, IA - *BaconPubCkNews 84; Ed&PubIntYB 82; NewsDir 84*
Afton Star Valley Independent - Afton, WY - *BaconPubCkNews 84*
Afton TV System [of Bainbridge Video Inc.] - Afton, NY - *Tel&CabFB 84C*
AFTRA - New York, NY - *MagIndMarPl 82-83; NewsDir 84*
AFV/Weapons Book Club [Subs. of Sky Books International Inc.] - New York, NY - *LitMarPl 83, 84*
AG Alert - Sacramento, CA - *BaconPubCkMag 84; MagDir 84*
AG-COM - Muscatine, IA - *MicrocomMPl 83*
AG Consultant & Fieldman - Willoughby, OH - *BaconPubCkMag 84; MagDir 84*

Ag-Data Inc. - Walla Walla, WA - *MicrocomMPl 84; WhoWMicrocom 83*
AG Impact - Batavia, NY - *BaconPubCkMag 84; MagDir 84*
AG Marketer - Yakima, WA - *BaconPubCkMag 84; MagDir 84*
Ag-Pilot International Magazine [of Bio-Aeronautic Publishers Inc.] - Milton-Freewater, OR - *BaconPubCkMag 84; WritMar 84*
AG Plus Software - Ida Grove, IA - *MicrocomMPl 84*
AG Review - Putnam, CT - *BaconPubCkMag 84; MagDir 84*
Ag-Tronics Associates - Hyde Park, UT - *MicrocomMPl 84*
Against the Wall - Westfield, NJ - *LitMag&SmPr 83-84*
Agape - Los Angeles, CA - *LitMag&SmPr 83-84*
Agape - Franklin, LA - *BoPubDir 4, 5; LitMag&SmPr 83-84*
Agape - *See* Hope Publishing Co.
Agassiz Advance - Agassiz, BC, Canada - *AyerDirPub 83; Ed&PubIntYB 82*
Agate Mutual Telephone Co. - Agate, CO - *TelDir&BG 83-84*
Agate Press - New York, NY - *BoPubDir 4, 5*
Agathon Press Inc. - New York, NY - *BoPubDir 4 Sup, 5*
Agawam Direct Marketing Inc. - Rowley, MA - *DirMarMP 83*
Agdata - Edmonton, AB, Canada - *DirOnDB Spring 84*
Age-Dispatch - Strathroy, ON, Canada - *AyerDirPub 83; Ed&PubIntYB 82*
Age Press - Gladstone, MB, Canada - *AyerDirPub 83; Ed&PubIntYB 82*
Agedor - Paris, France - *DirOnDB Spring 84*
Ageless Books - Beverly Hills, CA - *BoPubDir 4, 5*
Agence Francaise d'Extraits de Presse - Paris, France - *ProGuPRSer 4*
Agence France-Presse - New York, NY - *Ed&PubIntYB 82*
Agence France-Presse - Paris, France - *InfIndMarPl 83*
Agence S.O.P. Inc. - Montreal, PQ, Canada - *Ed&PubIntYB 82*
Agencia International Camarasa - Madrid, Spain - *ProGuPRSer 4*
Agency Finder Service - New Canaan, CT - *HBIndAd&MS 82-83*
Agency for Instructional Television - Bloomington, IN - *AvMarPl 83; BrCabYB 84; Tel&CabFB 84C*
Agency Inc., The - Wichita, KS - *StaDirAdAg 2-84*
Agency Quoting Systems - Hartland, WI - *MicrocomMPl 83, 84*
Agency Sales Magazine - Irvine, CA - *WritMar 84*
Agency Sales Magazine - Laguna Hills, CA - *BaconPubCkMag 84*
Agency Sales Magazine - Santa Ana, CA - *MagDir 84*
Agency Services Corp. - New York, NY - *Tel&CabFB 84C*
Agency, The - Irvine, CA - *StaDirAdAg 2-84*
Agenda - Westport, CT - *LitMag&SmPr 83-84*
Agenda - London, England - *LitMag&SmPr 83-84*
Agenda, A Journal of Hispanic Issues - Washington, DC - *MagIndMarPl 82-83*
Agenda Editions - London, England - *LitMag&SmPr 83-84*
Agenda, The - Argyle, WI - *AyerDirPub 83*
Agent Computer Services Inc. - Columbia City, IN - *MicrocomMPl 83, 84*
Agga Music Co. Inc. - *See* Ahlert Music Corp., Fred
Aggregate File of the Drug Abuse Epidemiology Data Center - Ft. Worth, TX - *CompReadDB 82*
Agincourt News - Agincourt, ON, Canada - *Ed&PubIntYB 82*
AGLINE [of Doane-Western Inc.] - St. Louis, MO - *DBBus 82; OnBibDB 3*
Aglow [of Women's Aglow Fellowship] - Lynnwood, WA - *WritMar 84*
Aglow Publications Inc. [Subs. of Women's Aglow Fellowship] - Lynnwood, WA - *WritMar 84*
Agneau 2 - London, England - *LitMag&SmPr 83-84*
Agnekolor Systems Corp. - Paterson, NJ - *AvMarPl 83*
Agner, Dwight Edward - Athens, GA - *LitMarPl 83, 84*
AGNET [of University of Nebraska] - Lincoln, NE - *DataDirOnSer 84; DirOnDB Spring 84; EISS 83*
Agnew, Carter, McCarthy Inc. - Boston, MA - *DirPRFirms 83*
Agni Review, The - Cambridge, MA - *LitMag&SmPr 83-84*
Agni Yoga Society - New York, NY - *BoPubDir 4, 5*
Agora/Adoc - Paris, France - *DirOnDB Spring 84*
Agora/Aeco - Paris, France - *DirOnDB Spring 84*
Agora/Agra - Paris, France - *DirOnDB Spring 84*
Agora Associates Inc. - Baltimore, MD - *DirMarMP 83*
Agora Resources Inc. - Lexington, MA - *DirInfWP 82*
Agoura Las Virgenes Independent Agoura Valley News - Agoura, CA - *NewsDir 84*
Agoura Valley Times - *See* Associated Valley Publications
Agra Europe - Tunbridge Wells, England - *EISS 83*
Agra Industries Ltd. - *See* Cablenet Ltd.
Agra Industries Ltd. - *See* CKO Inc.
Agrafiotis Associates Inc. - Manchester, NH - *DirPRFirms 83; StaDirAdAg 2-84*
Agrend Associates Inc. - New York, NY - *MagIndMarPl 82-83*
AGREP - Plateau du Kirchberg, Luxembourg - *DirOnDB Spring 84*
AGREP Secretariat [of Commission of the European Communities] - Plateau du Kirchberg, Luxembourg - *CompReadDB 82*
Agri Educator - Skokie, IL - *MagDir 84*
Agri-Equipment Today - Yakima, WA - *BaconPubCkMag 84*
Agri Finance [of Century Communications Inc.] - Skokie, IL - *ArtMar 84; BaconPubCkMag 84; BoPubDir 4, 5; MagDir 84; MagIndMarPl 82-83*
Agri-Mark Journal - North Andover, MA - *BaconPubCkMag 84; MagDir 84*
Agri Marketing [of Century Communications Inc.] - Skokie, IL - *ArtMar 84; BaconPubCkMag 84; MagDir 84; MagIndMarPl 82-83*
Agri-Markets Data Service [of Capitol Publications Inc.] - Arlington, VA - *DataDirOnSer 84; DirOnDB Spring 84*
Agri News - Rochester, MN - *WritMar 84*
Agri-News - Billings, MT - *NewsDir 84*
Agri-Practice - Santa Barbara, CA - *BaconPubCkMag 84*
Agri-Star [of AgriData Resources Inc.] - Milwaukee, WI - *DataDirOnSer 84; EISS 7-83 Sup*
Agribusiness Fieldman [of Agribusiness Publications] - Fresno, CA - *BaconPubCkMag 84; MagDir 84*
Agribusiness Worldwide - Minneapolis, MN - *BaconPubCkMag 84*
Agrichemical Age [of California Farmer Publishing Co.] - San Francisco, CA - *BaconPubCkMag 84; MagDir 84; MagIndMarPl 82-83*
AGRICOLA [of U.S. Dept. of Agriculture] - Washington, DC - *DirOnDB Spring 84*
AGRICOLA [of U.S. Dept. of Agriculture] - Beltsville, MD - *OnBibDB 3*
AgriComp - Columbia, MO - *BaconPubCkMag 84; MicrocomMPl 84*
Agricultura de las Americas - Overland Park, KS - *BaconPubCkMag 84*
Agricultura de las Americas [of Intertec Publications Corp.] - Shawnee Mission, KS - *MagDir 84*
Agricultural Advertising & Research Div. [of RHP Inc.] - Ithaca, NY - *StaDirAdAg 2-84*
Agricultural Aviation - Washington, DC - *BaconPubCkMag 84*
Agricultural Chemical News - Fresno, CA - *BaconPubCkMag 84*
Agricultural Commodities Data Base [of Market Analysis Branch, Alberta Agriculture] - Edmonton, AB, Canada - *DataDirOnSer 84; EISS 83*
Agricultural Computer Applications - Davis, CA - *MicrocomMPl 83, 84; MicrocomSwDir 1; WhoWMicrocom 83*
Agricultural Computer Software Inc. - Muscatine, IA - *MicrocomMPl 84*
Agricultural Computing [of Doane Publishing] - St. Louis, MO - *MicrocomMPl 84*
Agricultural Data Bases - St. Leonards, Australia - *DirOnDB Spring 84*
Agricultural Economics [of U.S. Dept. of Agriculture] - Washington, DC - *CompReadDB 82*
Agricultural Economics Research Council of Canada - Ottawa, ON, Canada - *BoPubDir 4, 5*
Agricultural Education - Mississippi State, MS - *MagDir 84; MagIndMarPl 82-83*
Agricultural Education - Columbus, OH - *BaconPubCkMag 84*
Agricultural Engineering [of American Society of Agricultural Engineers] - St. Joseph, MI - *BaconPubCkMag 84; MagDir 84*
Agricultural Engineering Abstracts [of National Institute for Agricultural Engineering] - Silsoe, England - *CompReadDB 82*
Agricultural Forecast Database [of Evans Economics Inc.] - Washington, DC - *DataDirOnSer 84*
Agricultural Information & Documentation Section [of Royal Tropical Institute] - Amsterdam, Netherlands - *EISS 83*
Agricultural Information Bank for Asia [of SE Asian Regional Center for Graduate Study & Research in Agriculture] - Laguna, Philippines - *EISS 83*

Agricultural Information System for Agricultural Sciences & Technology [of Food & Agriculture Organization of the U.N.] - Rome, Italy - *CompReadDB 82*
Agricultural Management Systems Inc. - Boise, ID - *WhoWMicrocom 83*
Agricultural Marketing & Trade Database [of Agriculture Canada] - Ottawa, ON, Canada - *EISS 83*
Agricultural Model Database [of Evans Economics Inc.] - Washington, DC - *DataDirOnSer 84*
Agricultural Network Serving Extension & Research [of University of Kentucky] - Lexington, KY - *EISS 83*
Agricultural Online Access [of U.S. Dept. of Agriculture] - Beltsville, MD - *CompReadDB 82; DataDirOnSer 84; DBBus 82; EISS 83*
Agricultural Research Council (Weed Research Organization) - Oxford, England - *CompReadDB 82*
Agricultural Research Information Centre [of Indian Council of Agricultural Research] - New Delhi, India - *EISS 83*
Agricultural Research Projects Data Base [of Commission of the European Communities] - Plateau du Kirchberg, Luxembourg - *DBBus 82; EISS 83*
Agricultural Research Projects in the European Community [of Commission of the European Communities] - Plateau du Kirchberg, Luxembourg - *CompReadDB 82*
Agricultural Research Review [of NewsNet Inc.] - Bryn Mawr, PA - *DataDirOnSer 84*
Agricultural Software Consultants - Kingsville, TX - *MicrocomMPl 83, 84; MicrocomSwDir 1; WhoWMicrocom 83*
Agricultural Weather Information System [of Weather Services International Corp.] - Bedford, MA - *DataDirOnSer 84*
Agriculture [of Data Resources Inc.] - Lexington, MA - *DataDirOnSer 84*
Agriculture Commodities Data Base [of Alberta Agriculture] - Edmonton, AB, Canada - *DBBus 82*
Agriculture Data Bank - Washington, DC - *DirOnDB Spring 84*
Agriculture Data Bank [of Data Resources Inc.] - Lexington, MA - *DBBus 82*
Agriculture Database [of Evans Economics Inc.] - Washington, DC - *DataDirOnSer 84*
Agriculture Forecast [of Chase Econometrics/Interactive Data Corp.] - Waltham, MA - *DataDirOnSer 84; DBBus 82*
Agriculture Teachers Directory - Greensburg, PA - *MagDir 84*
AgriData Network - *DirOnDB Spring 84*
AgriData Resources Inc. [Subs. of Raintree Publishers Inc.] - Milwaukee, WI - *DataDirOnSer 84*
Agriday Computers Ltd. - Salisbury, England - *MicrocomSwDir 1*
Agrinde Publications Ltd. - New York, NY - *LitMarPl 83*
Agrinfo [of Doane-Western Inc.] - St. Louis, MO - *EISS 83*
AGRIS [of Food & Agriculture Organization of the United Nations] - Rome, Italy - *DirOnDB Spring 84; InfIndMarPl 83; OnBibDB 3*
AGRIS Coordinating Centre (Library & Documentation Systems Div.) - Rome, Italy - *CompReadDB 82*
Agristat - Paris, France - *DirOnDB Spring 84*
Agritex [of Saskatchewan Telecommunications] - Regina, SK, Canada - *EISS 5-84 Sup*
Agritrop Data Base [of Group for the Study & Research of Tropical Agronomy] - Paris, France - *EISS 83*
Agriweek - Don Mills, ON, Canada - *BaconPubCkMag 84*
Agroclimatology Data Bank [of Royal Museum of Central Africa] - Tervuren, Belgium - *EISS 83*
Agroforestry Review [of International Tree Crops Institute] - Gravel Switch, KY - *LitMag&SmPr 83-84*
Agrologist - Ottawa, ON, Canada - *BaconPubCkMag 84*
Agronomy Journal [of American Society of Agronomy] - Madison, WI - *BaconPubCkMag 84; MagDir 84*
AGS/American Guidance Service - Circle Pines, MN - *BoPubDir 4, 5*
AGS & R Studios - Chicago, IL - *AvMarPl 83*
AGS Computers Inc. - Mountainside, NJ - *ADAPSOMemDir 83-84*
AGS Management Systems Inc. - Philadelphia, PA - *DataDirSup 7-83*
AGS Software [Subs. of Astro-Graphics Services Inc.] - Orleans, MA - *MicrocomMPl 83, 84; WhoWMicrocom 83*
Agsu Ararat Quarterly - Saddle Brook, NJ - *LitMag&SmPr 83-84*
AGT Computer Products Inc. - Manhattan Beach, CA - *DirInfWP 82*
Aguiar, Walter R. - New York, NY - *LitMarPl 83, 84; MagIndMarPl 82-83*
Agway Cooperator - Syracuse, NY - *MagDir 84; MagIndMarPl 82-83; WritMar 84*
A.H. Computer Software Services - Boise, ID - *WhoWMicrocom 83*
AHA Medical Device Database - Chicago, IL - *DirOnDB Spring 84*
Ahab Music Co. Inc. - Nashville, TN - *BillIntBG 83-84*
AHEA Action [of American Home Economics Association] - Washington, DC - *BaconPubCkMag 84; MagDir 84*
Ahead Designs - Encinitas, CA - *MicrocomMPl 84*
AHF/Competitive Environment Test [Div. of AHF Marketing Research] - New York, NY - *IntDirMarRes 83*
AHF/Fastrack [Div. of AHF Marketing Research] - New York, NY - *IntDirMarRes 83*
AHF/Legal Research [Div. of AHF Marketing Research] - New York, NY - *IntDirMarRes 83*
AHF Marketing Research - New York, NY - *IntDirMarRes 83*
AHF/WATS Telephone Center [Div. of AHF Marketing Research] - New York, NY - *IntDirMarRes 83*
Ahlert-Burke Corp. - *See* Ahlert Music Corp., Fred
Ahlert Music Corp., Fred - Los Angeles, CA - *BillIntBG 83-84*
AHM & A Public Relations [Div. of Arnold Harwell McClain & Associates Inc.] - Dallas, TX - *DirPRFirms 83*
Ahnene Publications - Maxville, ON, Canada - *LitMag&SmPr 83-84*
Ahoskie News-Herald - Ahoskie, NC - *BaconPubCkNews 84*
Ahoy - New York, NY - *BaconPubCkMag 84*
Ahoy - Halifax, NS, Canada - *WritMar 84*
Ahrend Associates Inc. - New York, NY - *ArtMar 84; DirMarMP 83; HBIndAd&MS 82-83; LitMarPl 83, 84; MagIndMarPl 82-83; StaDirAdAg 2-84*
Ahsahta Press [of Boise State University] - Boise, ID - *LitMag&SmPr 83-84; LitMarPl 84; WritMar 84*
AIA Journal - Washington, DC - *MagIndMarPl 82-83*
AIA Productions Inc. - Sherman Oaks, CA - *AvMarPl 83*
AIAA Journal [of American Institute of Aeronautics & Astronautics] - New York, NY - *BaconPubCkMag 84; MagDir 84*
AIC Photo Inc. - Carle Place, NY - *AvMarPl 83*
AIC Photo Inc. (Soligor Div.) - Carle Place, NY - *AvMarPl 83*
A.I.Ch.E. Journal - New York, NY - *BaconPubCkMag 84*
AICS - University Park, NM - *DirInfWP 82*
AID - Boise, ID - *BrCabYB 84*
AID - Oslo, Norway - *DirOnDB Spring 84*
AID - Stockholm, Sweden - *DirOnDB Spring 84*
Aid Data Systems Inc. - Millersville, MD - *MicrocomMPl 84*
Aid Photo - New York, NY - *AvMarPl 83*
Aid-Update Service [of U.S. Agency for International Development] - Beltsville, MD - *EISS 83*
AIDS Agricultural Census [of Computer Sciences of Australia Pty. Ltd.] - St. Leonards, Australia - *DataDirOnSer 84*
AIDS Computer Center - San Francisco, CA - *MicrocomMPl 83*
A.I.D.S. Inc. - San Francisco, CA - *WhoWMicrocom 83*
AIE Studios Inc. - Houston, TX - *AvMarPl 83*
AIGA Publications - Laie, HI - *BoPubDir 5; LitMag&SmPr 83-84*
Aigner - Chicago, IL - *DirInfWP 82*
Aiken, Alex - Glasgow, Scotland - *LitMag&SmPr 83-84*
Aiken Cablevision Inc. [of Evening Post Publishing Co.] - Aiken, SC - *BrCabYB 84; Tel&CabFB 84C*
Aiken Cablevision Inc. - Edgefield, SC - *Tel&CabFB 84C*
Aiken Cablevision Inc. - Saluda, SC - *Tel&CabFB 84C*
Aiken County Rambler - Aiken, SC - *AyerDirPub 83; Ed&PubIntYB 82*
Aiken Standard - Aiken, SC - *BaconPubCkNews 84; Ed&PubIntYB 82; NewsDir 84*
Aikins, Marling & Morris Inc. - San Francisco, CA - *StaDirAdAg 2-84*
Ailes Communications Inc. - New York, NY - *Tel&CabFB 84C*
Aim - Chicago, IL - *ArtMar 84*
AIM - Lincolnshire, IL - *MicrocomMPl 84*
AIM/ARM [of The National Center for Research in Vocational Education] - Columbus, OH - *DBBus 82; DirOnDB Spring 84*
AIM Computer Associates Inc. - Teaneck, NJ - *IntDirMarRes 83*
A.I.M. Computer Systems Inc. - Wickliffe, OH - *MicrocomMPl 83*
AIM for Health - Boston, MA - *AvMarPl 83*

Aim Records Inc. - San Francisco, CA - *BillIntBG 83-84*
AIM Research - El Paso, TX - *IntDirMarRes 83*
A.I.M. Research - Cambridge, England - *MicrocomSwDir 1*
AIMS International Marketing Services Inc. - Springfield, OH - *LitMarPl 84*
AIMS Media - Glendale, CA - *AvMarPl 83*
Aims Plus - Austin, TX - *MicrocomMPl 84; MicrocomSwDir 1*
Ainsworth Cable TV [of Midcontinent Cable Inc.] - Ainsworth, NE - *BrCabYB 84; Tel&CabFB 84C*
Ainsworth Star Journal - Ainsworth, NE - *BaconPubCkNews 84; Ed&PubIntYB 82*
AIPE Journal [of American Institute of Plant Engineers] - Cincinnati, OH - *BaconPubCkMag 84; MagDir 84*
Air & Cosmos - Palos Verdes Peninsula, CA - *MagDir 84*
Air Base News [of South Miami Community Newspapers] - Miami, FL - *NewsDir 84*
Air Cal Magazine - North Miami, FL - *BaconPubCkMag 84*
Air California Magazine - Laguna Beach, CA - *MagDir 84*
Air Capital Cablevision Inc. [of Multimedia Cablevision Inc.] - Wichita, KS - *BrCabYB 84*
Air Cargo Guide [of Official Airline Guides Inc.] - Hinsdale, IL - *MagDir 84*
Air Cargo Magazine [of The Reuben H. Donnelly Corp.] - New York, NY - *MagDir 84; MagIndMarPl 82-83*
Air Cargo News - Jamaica, NY - *MagIndMarPl 82-83*
Air Cargo News - New York, NY - *MagDir 84*
Air Cargo World - Atlanta, GA - *BaconPubCkMag 84*
Air Classics - Canoga Park, CA - *BaconPubCkMag 84*
Air Conditioning, Heating & Refrigeration News [of Business News Publishing Co.] - Troy, MI - *BaconPubCkMag 84; MagDir 84; WritMar 84*
Air Corp. - Reno, NV - *StaDirAdAg 2-84*
Air Diffusion Council - Chicago, IL - *BoPubDir 5*
Air Force Magazine - Washington, DC - *BaconPubCkMag 84; MagDir 84; MagIndMarPl 82-83*
Air Force Times - Washington, DC - *BaconPubCkMag 84; MagDir 84; MagIndMarPl 82-83*
Air Forwarder - New York, NY - *MagDir 84*
A.I.R. Gallery - New York, NY - *BoPubDir 4, 5*
Air Group One - *Folio 83*
Air Line Employee, The - Chicago, IL - *NewsDir 84*
Air Line Pilot [of Air Line Pilots Association] - Washington, DC - *ArtMar 84; BaconPubCkMag 84; MagDir 84; NewsDir 84; WritMar 84*
Air Market News - Columbia, MD - *BaconPubCkMag 84*
Air Photo Supply - Yonkers, NY - *AvMarPl 83*
Air Pixies/Ben Kocivar - New York, NY - *MagIndMarPl 82-83*
Air-Plus Enterprises - Glassboro, NJ - *ArtMar 84; BoPubDir 4, 5*
Air Pollution Technical Information Center [of U.S. Environmental Protection Agency] - Research Triangle Park, NC - *CompReadDB 82; DBBus 82; OnBibDB 3*
Air Power Media Corp. - New York, NY - *StaDirAdAg 2-84*
Air Progress - Canoga Park, CA - *BaconPubCkMag 84; MagIndMarPl 82-83*
Air Progress Ultralights - Canoga Park, CA - *BaconPubCkMag 84*
Air Pulse [of Omaha Sun Newspapers] - Omaha, NE - *AyerDirPub 83; NewsDir 84*
Air Science Co. - Corning, NY - *InfIndMarPl 83*
Air South Radio Inc. - Fulton, MS - *BrCabYB 84*
Air Time International Inc. - New York, NY - *Tel&CabFB 84C*
Air Transport Association of America - Washington, DC - *BoPubDir 5*
Air Transport Data Bank [of Institute of Air Transport] - De Gaulle, France - *EISS 83*
Air Transport Statistical Program [of International Civil Aviation Organization] - Montreal, PQ, Canada - *EISS 83*
Air Transport World [of Penton/IPC] - Washington, DC - *BaconPubCkMag 84; MagDir 84*
Air Transportation Research Information Service [of Transportation Research Board] - Washington, DC - *CompReadDB 82*
Air Travel Bargains - Miami, FL - *MagDir 84*
Air University Review [of United States Air Force] - Montgomery, AL - *MagDir 84; WritMar 84*
Air/Water Pollution Report - Silver Spring, MD - *BaconPubCkMag 84; DirOnDB Spring 84; MagDir 84*
Air/Water Pollution Report [of NewsNet Inc.] - Bryn Mawr, PA - *DataDirOnSer 84*
Airborn - Flint, MI - *BillIntBG 83-84*
Airborne - Laguna Beach, CA - *MagDir 84*
Airborne - Los Angeles, CA - *BaconPubCkMag 84*
AirCapital Cablevision Inc. [of Multimedia Cablevision Inc.] - Wichita, KS - *Tel&CabFB 84C*
Aircon [of RCA Global Communications Inc.] - New York, NY - *TeleSy&SerDir 2-84*
Aircraft Accident Data Base [of I. P. Sharp Associates Ltd.] - Toronto, ON, Canada - *DataDirOnSer 84*
Aircraft Accident/Incident Reporting System [of International Civil Aviation Organization] - Montreal, PQ, Canada - *EISS 83*
Aircraft Charter & Rental Tariff Information Service of North America - Oak Park, IL - *BoPubDir 4, 5*
Aircraft Owners & Pilots Association - Washington, DC - *BoPubDir 5*
Aircraft Technical Publishers - Brisbane, CA - *DataDirOnSer 84*
Aircraft Technical Publishers - San Francisco, CA - *EISS 83; InfIndMarPl 83; MicroMarPl 82-83*
Airdrie & District Echo - Airdrie, AB, Canada - *AyerDirPub 83*
Airfair Interline Magazine - New York, NY - *BaconPubCkMag 84; MagDir 84; MagIndMarPl 82-83; WritMar 84*
Airforce Magazine - Ottawa, ON, Canada - *BaconPubCkMag 84*
Airland Communication Services Ltd. - Strathroy, ON, Canada - *BrCabYB 84*
Airlift Dispatch [of The Charleston Journal] - Charleston, SC - *AyerDirPub 83; NewsDir 84*
Airline & Travel Food Service - Miami Springs, FL - *BaconPubCkMag 84; MagDir 84; MagIndMarPl 82-83*
Airline Executive [of Airline Publishing Group Inc.] - Washington, DC - *MagDir 84*
Airline Executive - Atlanta, GA - *BaconPubCkMag 84*
Airline Handbook Publishing Co. - Cranston, RI - *BoPubDir 5*
Airline Itineraries [of Dittler Brothers Inc.] - Atlanta, GA - *DataDirOnSer 84; DirOnDB Spring 84*
Airline Job Kit - Boise, ID - *BoPubDir 4 Sup, 5*
Airmark Group Inc., The - Richardson, TX - *StaDirAdAg 2-84*
Airmont Publishing Co. - Bridgeport, CT - *BoPubDir 4*
Airplane Press - Richmond, VA - *LitMag&SmPr 83-84*
Airport Press [of J.A.J. Publishing Co.] - Jamaica, NY - *BaconPubCkMag 84; WritMar 84*
Airport Services Management [of Lakewood Publications] - Minneapolis, MN - *BaconPubCkMag 84; MagDir 84; WritMar 84*
Airport Times [of American Syndicate Newspaper Co. Inc.] - Jamaica, NY - *MagDir 84*
Airports International - New York, NY - *BaconPubCkMag 84*
Airsched [of Source Telecomputing Corp.] - McLean, VA - *DataDirOnSer 84*
Airshow Publishers - Annapolis, MD - *BoPubDir 4, 5*
Airwave Communications Co. - Stilwell, OK - *BrCabYB 84; Tel&CabFB 84C*
Airwave Records - Hollywood, CA - *BillIntBG 83-84*
Airway Heights Cable TV [of Western Satellite Inc.] - Airway Heights, WA - *BrCabYB 84; Tel&CabFB 84C*
Airy Advertising Inc. - Albuquerque, NM - *StaDirAdAg 2-84*
AIS Inc. - Shawnee Mission, KS - *MicrocomMPl 83; WhoWMicrocom 83*
AIS Market Research - Fresno, CA - *IntDirMarRes 83*
AIS Microsystems - Washington, DC - *MicrocomMPl 84*
AIS/Net 1000 [of AT & T Information Systems] - Morristown, NJ - *TeleSy&SerDir 2-84*
AIS/Net 1000 [of American Bell Inc.] - Parsippany, NJ - *TeleSy&SerDir 7-83*
AISL Aircraft Accident Database [of Aviation Information Services Ltd.] - Hounslow, England - *CompReadDB 82*
AISL Aircraft Accident Database [of Aviation Information Services Ltd.] - London, England - *DirOnDB Spring 84*
AITI - Oslo, Norway - *DirOnDB Spring 84*
Aitkin Cablevision Inc. [of Marcus Communications Inc.] - Aitkin, MN - *BrCabYB 84; Tel&CabFB 84C*
Aitkin Independent Age - Aitkin, MN - *BaconPubCkNews 84; Ed&PubIntYB 82; NewsDir 84*
Aitkin-Kynett Co. Inc. - Philadelphia, PA - *BrCabYB 84; TelAl 83, 84*

Aitkin-Kynett Co. Inc. - *See* Byoir & Associates Inc., Carl
Aiuppy, Laurance - Livingston, MT - *LitMarPl 84*
A.J. Publishing Co. - Duluth, MN - *BoPubDir 4, 5*
AJAY Enterprises - Falls Church, VA - *BoPubDir 4, 5*
AJL Newsline - New York, NY - *BaconPubCkMag 84*
AJNR-American Journal of Neuroradiology - Baltimore, MD - *BaconPubCkMag 84*
Ajo Copper News - Ajo, AZ - *AyerDirPub 83; BaconPubCkNews 84; Ed&PubIntYB 82*
Ajo TV Service Co. - Ajo, AZ - *BrCabYB 84; Tel&CabFB 84C p.1663*
AKA Public Relations - Los Angeles, CA - *DirPRFirms 83*
AKA Publishing [Aff. of Forrest Printing] - Grand Haven, MI - *BoPubDir 4, 5*
Akai America Ltd. - Compton, CA - *BillIntBG 83-84*
Akers Cable System Inc. - Martin, KY - *BrCabYB 84; Tel&CabFB 84C*
Akers, Mona Jean Coole - Denver, CO - *BoPubDir 4, 5*
Akhbar-i-Gulrang - Toronto, ON, Canada - *Ed&PubIntYB 82*
Akiba Press - Oakland, CA - *BoPubDir 4, 5; LitMag&SmPr 83-84*
Akili Books of America - South Gate, CA - *BoPubDir 4, 5*
Akra Media [Div. of Media Services Inc.] - Birmingham, AL - *MagIndMarPl 82-83*
Akron Beacon Journal - Akron, OH - *BaconPubCkNews 84; Ed&PubIntYB 82; LitMarPl 83, 84; NewsBur 6; NewsDir 84*
Akron-Corfu Pennysaver - Orchard Park, NY - *AyerDirPub 83*
Akron Legal News - Akron, OH - *Ed&PubIntYB 82; NewsDir 84*
Akron-Mentone News - Akron, IN - *AyerDirPub 83; BaconPubCkNews 84; Ed&PubIntYB 82*
Akron News Reporter - Akron, CO - *BaconPubCkNews 84; Ed&PubIntYB 82*
Akron Register Tribune - Akron, IA - *BaconPubCkNews 84; Ed&PubIntYB 82*
Akron Reporter - Akron, OH - *BaconPubCkNews 84*
Akros - Nottingham, England - *LitMag&SmPr 83-84*
Akton Adhesives Inc. - Glendale, NY - *LitMarPl 83, 84*
Akullian Agency Inc., Helen - New York, NY - *LitMarPl 83, 84; MagIndMarPl 82-83*
Akwesasne Notes [Aff. of Mohawk Nation] - Rooseveltown, NY - *BoPubDir 4, 5; LitMag&SmPr 83-84; MagIndMarPl 82-83*
Al Ahlya Advertising - Damascus, Syria - *StaDirAdAg 2-84*
Al-Bo Music Co. - Yonkers, NY - *BillIntBG 83-84*
Al-Islaah - New York, NY - *Ed&PubIntYB 82; NewsDir 84*
Al-Mashiro - Southfield, MI - *Ed&PubIntYB 82*
Al Ra'id Al Arabi - Toronto, ON, Canada - *Ed&PubIntYB 82*
A.L.A. Black Caucus Publications Committee [Aff. of American Library Association] - New Brunswick, NJ - *BoPubDir 5*
A.L.A. Black Caucus Publications Committee [Aff. of American Library Association] - Greenvale, NY - *BoPubDir 4*
Ala Enterprises Inc. - Los Angeles, CA - *BillIntBG 83-84*
ALA Social Responsibilities Round Table - Brooklyn, NY - *LitMag&SmPr 83-84*
ALA/SRRT Newsletter [of ALA Social Responsibilities Round Table] - Brooklyn, NY - *LitMag&SmPr 83-84*
Alabama Builder [of Walker Printing] - Montgomery, AL - *BaconPubCkMag 84; MagDir 84*
Alabama Cattleman - Montgomery, AL - *BaconPubCkMag 84; MagDir 84*
Alabama Conservation - Montgomery, AL - *MagDir 84*
Alabama Contractor [of Association of Plumbing, Heating, Cooling Contractors of Alabama Inc.] - Birmingham, AL - *BaconPubCkMag 84; MagDir 84*
Alabama Data Products Inc. - Birmingham, AL - *DataDirSup 7-83*
Alabama Dept. of Insurance - Montgomery, AL - *BoPubDir 5*
Alabama Development News - Montgomery, AL - *BaconPubCkMag 84*
Alabama Farm Bureau News - Montgomery, AL - *BaconPubCkMag 84; MagDir 84*
Alabama Food Merchants Journal [of Alabama Food Council] - Montgomery, AL - *BaconPubCkMag 84; MagDir 84*
Alabama Forests - Montgomery, AL - *BaconPubCkMag 84; MagDir 84*
Alabama Game & Fish - Marietta, GA - *BaconPubCkMag 84; WritMar 84*
Alabama Journal [of Advertiser Co.] - Montgomery, AL - *AyerDirPub 83; Ed&PubIntYB 82; LitMarPl 83; NewsDir 84*
Alabama Journal-The Advertiser - Montgomery, AL - *LitMarPl 84*
Alabama Labor Council News Letter - Birmingham, AL - *NewsDir 84*
Alabama Messenger - Birmingham, AL - *Ed&PubIntYB 82*
Alabama Monthly - Montgomery, AL - *BaconPubCkMag 84*
Alabama Municipal Journal [of Alabama League of Municipalities] - Montgomery, AL - *BaconPubCkMag 84; MagDir 84*
Alabama NewChannels - Eufaula, AL - *Tel&CabFB 84C*
Alabama NewChannels - Greenville, AL - *Tel&CabFB 84C*
Alabama NewChannels - Wetumpka, AL - *Tel&CabFB 84C*
Alabama News Magazine - Montgomery, AL - *BaconPubCkMag 84; MagDir 84*
Alabama Office of State Planning & Federal Programs - Montgomery, AL - *BoPubDir 5*
Alabama Press Association Clipping Bureau - Tuscaloosa, AL - *ProGuPRSer 4*
Alabama Purchasor - Birmingham, AL - *BaconPubCkMag 84; MagDir 84*
Alabama Resources Information System [of Auburn University] - Auburn, AL - *EISS 83*
Alabama Review - University, AL - *LitMag&SmPr 83-84*
Alabama School Journal - Montgomery, AL - *BaconPubCkMag 84; MagDir 84*
Alabama State Legislative Reference Service - Montgomery, AL - *EISS 83*
Alabama Trucker - Montgomery, AL - *BaconPubCkMag 84; MagDir 84*
Alabama TV Cable Co. - Aliceville, AL - *BrCabYB 84 p.D-297; Tel&CabFB 84C p.1663*
Alabama TV Cable Co. - Carrollton, AL - *BrCabYB 84*
Alabama TV Cable Co. [of Community Tele-Communications Inc.] - Homewood, AL - *BrCabYB 84; Tel&CabFB 84C*
Alabama TV Cable Co. - Kennedy, AL - *BrCabYB 84*
Alabama TV Cable Inc. [of Community Tele-Communications Inc.] - Pleasant Grove, AL - *Tel&CabFB 84C*
Aladdin Software - Danville, IL - *MicrocomMPl 84*
Alamance News - Graham, NC - *AyerDirPub 83; Ed&PubIntYB 82*
Alamance-Orange Enterprise - Mebane, NC - *AyerDirPub 83; Ed&PubIntYB 82*
Alameda County, Bay Area Observer - San Leandro, CA - *AyerDirPub 83*
Alameda Group, The - San Jose, CA - *DirPRFirms 83*
Alameda Publishing Corp. - Oakland, CA - *BaconPubCkNews 84*
Alameda Times Star [of News Observer Inc.] - Alameda, CA - *BaconPubCkNews 84; Ed&PubIntYB 82; NewsDir 84*
Alamo Ad Center Inc. - San Antonio, TX - *ArtMar 84; StaDirAdAg 2-84*
Alamo Computer Co. - San Antonio, TX - *MicrocomMPl 84*
Alamo Crockett Times - Alamo, TN - *BaconPubCkNews 84; NewsDir 84*
Alamo News - Alamo, TX - *BaconPubCkNews 84; Ed&PubIntYB 82*
Alamo Wheeler County Eagle - Alamo, GA - *BaconPubCkNews 84*
Alamogordo Daily News - Alamogordo, NM - *BaconPubCkNews 84; Ed&PubIntYB 82; NewsDir 84*
Alamosa Cable TV [of Tele-Communications Inc.] - Alamosa, CO - *BrCabYB 84; Tel&CabFB 84C*
Alan Advertising Agency Inc. - Charlotte, NC - *StaDirAdAg 2-84*
Alan Enterprises Inc. - Malibu, CA - *TelAl 83, 84; Tel&CabFB 84C*
Alan Literary Agency, Carol J. - Northridge, CA - *LitMarPl 83*
Alana Herbert - Kentland, IN - *LitMag&SmPr 83-84*
Alanet [of American Library Association] - Chicago, IL - *DirOnDB Spring 84; EISS 5-84 Sup*
Alanthus Data Communication Corp. - Rockville, MD - *InfIndMarPl 83*
Alarion Press Inc. - Boulder, CO - *AvMarPl 83*
Alarm Installer & Dealer - Calabasas, CA - *BaconPubCkMag 84*
Alascom Inc. [Subs. of Pacific Telecom Inc.] - Anchorage, AK - *BrCabYB 84; Tel&CabFB 84C*

Alaska [of Alaska Northwest Publishing] - Edmonds, WA - *Folio 83*
Alaska Analysts/Dittman Research Corp. - Anchorage, AK - *IntDirMarRes 83*
Alaska Attitudes & Social Research - Anchorage, AK - *IntDirMarRes 83*
Alaska Beverage Analyst [of Bell Publications] - Denver, CO - *BaconPubCkMag 84; MagDir 84*
Alaska Business & Industry [of Star International Corp.] - Anchorage, AK - *BaconPubCkMag 84; MagDir 84*
Alaska Cablevision Inc. - Kirkland, WA - *BrCabYB 84 p.D-297; Tel&CabFB 84C p.1663*
Alaska Census Data Network [of Alaska State Dept. of Labor] - Juneau, AK - *EISS 5-84 Sup*
Alaska Construction & Oil [of Vernon Publications Inc.] - Seattle, WA - *BaconPubCkMag 84; MagDir 84*
Alaska Empire [of Morris Communications] - Juneau, AK - *NewsDir 84*
Alaska Farm & Garden - Delta Junction, AK - *BaconPubCkMag 84*
Alaska Film Studios - Anchorage, AK - *AvMarPl 83*
Alaska Fisherman's Journal - Seattle, WA - *BaconPubCkMag 84*
Alaska Highway News - Ft. St. John, BC, Canada - *AyerDirPub 83; Ed&PubIntYB 82*
Alaska Knowledge Base [of Alaska State Dept. of Education] - Juneau, AK - *EISS 83*
Alaska Magazine - Anchorage, AK - *BaconPubCkMag 84; MagDir 84; WritMar 84*
Alaska Nature Press - Eagle River, AK - *WritMar 84*
Alaska Northwest Publishing Co. - Anchorage, AK - *LitMarPl 83; WritMar 84*
Alaska Northwest Publishing Co. - Edmonds, WA - *LitMarPl 84*
Alaska Outdoors - Anchorage, AK - *MagDir 84; MagIndMarPl 82-83*
Alaska Outdoors [of Swensen's Publishing] - Fairbanks, AK - *BaconPubCkMag 84; WritMar 84*
Alaska Pacific University Press - Anchorage, AK - *BoPubDir 4, 5*
Alaska Picture Inc. - Juneau, AK - *AvMarPl 83*
Alaska Quarterly Review, The - Anchorage, AK - *LitMag&SmPr 83-84*
Alaska Repertory Theatre - Anchorage, AK - *WritMar 84*
Alaska Television Network - Anchorage, AK - *BrCabYB 84*
Alaska: The Magazine of Life on the Last Frontier - Anchorage, AK - *MagIndMarPl 82-83*
Alaska Trails - Anchorage, AK - *BoPubDir 4, 5*
Alaska Travel Publications Inc. - Anchorage, AK - *BoPubDir 4, 5*
Alaskafest [of Seattle Northwest Publishing Co.] - Seattle, WA - *ArtMar 84; BaconPubCkMag 84; WritMar 84*
Alaskan Cable Network [of E.D. & D. Inc.] - Eielson AFB, AK - *BrCabYB 84*
Alaskan Cable Network - Eielson Air Force Base, AK - *Tel&CabFB 84C*
Alaskan Cable Network - Ft. Wainwright, AK - *BrCabYB 84*
Alaskan Cable Network Inc. - Greely, AL - *BrCabYB 84*
Alaskaphoto [Div. of Aperture PhotoBank Inc.] - Seattle, WA - *LitMarPl 83, 84*
Alba House [Div. of The Society of St. Paul] - Staten Island, NY - *LitMarPl 83, 84; WritMar 84*
Alba Telephone Co. - Alba, MI - *TelDir&BG 83-84*
Albacore Press - Eastsound, WA - *BoPubDir 4, 5*
Albamar Inc. - New York, NY - *DirPRFirms 83*
Alban Bruce Communications Inc. - Baltimore, MD - *AvMarPl 83*
Alban Co. Inc., The George - Campbell, CA - *StaDirAdAg 2-84*
Albanian Orthodox Church in America Inc. [Aff. of Orthodox Church in America] - South Boston, MA - *BoPubDir 4, 5*
Albany Advertising International Inc. - Chatham, NJ - *StaDirAdAg 2-84*
Albany Agenda Herald - Albany, WI - *AyerDirPub 83; BaconPubCkNews 84*
Albany Cable System [of TCI Growth Inc.] - Albany, TX - *BrCabYB 84; Tel&CabFB 84C*
Albany Clinton County News - Albany, KY - *BaconPubCkNews 84; NewsDir 84*
Albany Democrat-Herald [of Capital Cities Communications Inc.] - Albany, OR - *BaconPubCkNews 84; Ed&PubIntYB 82; NewsDir 84*
Albany Herald [of Gray Communications Systems Inc.] - Albany, GA - *BaconPubCkNews 84; NewsDir 84*
Albany Herald - Albany, WI - *BaconPubCkNews 84; Ed&PubIntYB 82*
Albany Jewish World - Albany, NY - *AyerDirPub 83*
Albany Journal - Albany, GA - *BaconPubCkNews 84; Ed&PubIntYB 82; NewsDir 84*
Albany Knickerbocker News - Albany, NY - *BaconPubCkNews 84; LitMarPl 83*
Albany Ledger - Albany, MO - *BaconPubCkNews 84; Ed&PubIntYB 82*
Albany/Macon Times - Albany, GA - *Ed&PubIntYB 82*
Albany Market Research Co. - Albany, NY - *IntDirMarRes 83*
Albany Mutual Telephone Association - Albany, MN - *TelDir&BG 83-84*
Albany News - Albany, TX - *BaconPubCkNews 84; Ed&PubIntYB 82*
Albany Park News [of Chicago Lerner Newspapers] - Chicago, IL - *AyerDirPub 83; NewsDir 84*
Albany Stearns Morrison Enterprise - Albany, MN - *BaconPubCkNews 84*
Albany Times - Albany, GA - *BaconPubCkNews 84*
Albany Times & Thousand Oaks Times - Berkeley, CA - *NewsDir 84*
Albany Times Journal - Albany, CA - *BaconPubCkNews 84*
Albany Times-Union [of The Hearst Corp.] - Albany, NY - *BaconPubCkNews 84; LitMarPl 83; NewsDir 84*
Albatross Book Store, The - San Francisco, CA - *MagIndMarPl 82-83*
Albatross Publishing House - West Vancouver, BC, Canada - *BoPubDir 4, 5*
Albatross Records Inc. - Seattle, WA - *BillIntBG 83-84*
Albemarle Cable TV - Edenton, NC - *BrCabYB 84; Tel&CabFB 84C*
Albemarle Stanly News & Press - Albemarle, NC - *BaconPubCkNews 84; NewsDir 84*
Alberni Cable Television Ltd. - Port Alberni, BC, Canada - *BrCabYB 84*
Alberni District Museum & Historical Society - Port Alberni, BC, Canada - *BoPubDir 4*
Alberni District Museum & Historical Society - Port Alberni, BC, Canada - *BoPubDir 5*
Alberni Valley Times - Port Alberni, BC, Canada - *AyerDirPub 83; BaconPubCkNews 84; Ed&PubIntYB 82*
Albert City Buena Vista County Journal - Albert City, IA - *BaconPubCkNews 84*
Albert Frank-Guenther Law Inc. [Subs. of Foote, Cone & Belding Communications Inc.] - New York, NY - *StaDirAdAg 2-84*
Albert Lea Tribune - Albert Lea, MN - *BaconPubCkNews 84; NewsDir 84*
Albert Literary Agency - Aptos, CA - *LitMarPl 83*
Albert, Mac S. - Riverdale, NY - *LitMarPl 83, 84*
Albert Regd., F. K. - Pointe Claire, PQ, Canada - *BoPubDir 4 Sup, 5*
Alberta Agriculture (Economics Services) - Edmonton, AB, Canada - *BoPubDir 5*
Alberta Agriculture (Market Analysis Branch) - Edmonton, AB, Canada - *DataDirOnSer 84*
Alberta Broadcasting Corp. Ltd. - Ft. McMurray, AB, Canada - *BrCabYB 84; Tel&CabFB 84C*
Alberta Farm Life - Edmonton, AB, Canada - *AyerDirPub 83; BaconPubCkMag 84*
Alberta Gazette Index [of University of Alberta] - Edmonton, AB, Canada - *DataDirOnSer 84*
Alberta History [of Historical Society of Alberta] - Calgary, AB, Canada - *LitMag&SmPr 83-84*
Alberta Inc. - Vancouver, BC, Canada - *ArtMar 84*
Alberta Land Use Planning Data Bank [of Alberta Municipal Affairs] - Edmonton, AB, Canada - *EISS 83*
Alberta Legislative Information [of University of Alberta] - Edmonton, AB, Canada - *DataDirOnSer 84*
Alberta Magazine [of Naylor Communications Ltd.] - Edmonton, AB, Canada - *BaconPubCkMag 84; WritMar 84*

Alberta Oil Sands Index [of Alberta Oil Sands Information Centre] - Edmonton, AB, Canada - *CompReadDB 82; DataDirOnSer 84; DirOnDB Spring 84*
Alberta Oil Sands Information Centre [Subs. of Alberta Research Council] - Edmonton, AB, Canada - *CompReadDB 82; DataDirOnSer 84; EISS 83; InfIndMarPl 83*
Alberta Report - Edmonton, AB, Canada - *BaconPubCkMag 84*
Alberta Research Council - Edmonton, AB, Canada - *BoPubDir 4, 5; FBInfSer 80*
Alberta Wilderness Association - Calgary, AB, Canada - *BoPubDir 4, 5*
Alberton Cable TV - Alberton, MT - *BrCabYB 84; Tel&CabFB 84C*
Albertville Sand Mountain Reporter - Albertville, AL - *BaconPubCkNews 84; NewsDir 84*
Albetros Ltd. - Basingstoke, England - *MicrocomSwDir 1*
Albi Associates Inc., Dom - New York, NY - *AvMarPl 83; WritMar 84*
Albi Productions Inc., Dom - New York, NY - *ArtMar 84*
Albia Monroe County News - *See* Albia Publishing Co.
Albia Publishing Co. - Albia, IA - *BaconPubCkNews 84*
Albia Union-Republican - Albia, IA - *Ed&PubIntYB 82; NewsDir 84*
Albia Union-Republican - *See* Albia Publishing Co.
Albin Industries - Farmington, MI - *DirInfWP 82*
Albin, James R. - Sausalito, CA - *BoPubDir 4, 5*
Albion Advertiser - Albion, NY - *BaconPubCkNews 84; Ed&PubIntYB 82; NewsDir 84*
Albion Albums - Albion, CA - *BoPubDir 4, 5*
Albion Cable TV Ltd. - Bolton, ON, Canada - *BrCabYB 84*
Albion Corp. - San Rafael, CA - *BoPubDir 4, 5*
Albion Evening Recorder - Albion, MI - *BaconPubCkNews 84; Ed&PubIntYB 82*
Albion-Holley Pennysaver - Albion, NY - *AyerDirPub 83*
Albion Journal of Albion - *See* Journal of Albion Publishers
Albion Journal-Register - Albion, IL - *BaconPubCkNews 84*
Albion New Era - Albion, IN - *AyerDirPub 83; BaconPubCkNews 84; Ed&PubIntYB 82*
Albion News - Albion, NE - *BaconPubCkNews 84; Ed&PubIntYB 82; NewsDir 84*
Albion News - Albion, PA - *BaconPubCkNews 84; Ed&PubIntYB 82*
Albion Noble County American - Albion, IN - *BaconPubCkNews 84*
Albion Prairie Post - Albion, IL - *BaconPubCkNews 84*
Albion Telephone Co. Inc. - Albion, ID - *TelDir&BG 83-84*
Albondocani Press - New York, NY - *BoPubDir 4, 5*
Albrecht, Rodelinde - Amherst, MA - *LitMarPl 83, 84*
Albrecht Rodrigues, Veronika - Corvallis, OR - *LitMarPl 83*
Albright & Price - Lafayette, CA - *AdAge 3-28-84; StaDirAdAg 2-84*
Albright & Street Inc. - Brookfield, WI - *StaDirAdAg 2-84*
Albright Knox Art Gallery [Aff. of Buffalo Fine Arts Academy] - Buffalo, NY - *BoPubDir 4 Sup, 5*
Album Globe Distribution Co. Inc. - Hendersonville, TN - *BillIntBG 83-84*
Albuquerque Cable Television Inc. [of Tribune Cable Communications Inc.] - Albuquerque, NM - *BrCabYB 84; Tel&CabFB 84C*
Albuquerque Cable Television Inc. [of Tribune Cable Communications Inc.] - Paradise Hills, NM - *Tel&CabFB 84C*
Albuquerque Health City Sun - Albuquerque, NM - *BaconPubCkNews 84*
Albuquerque Journal - Albuquerque, NM - *BaconPubCkNews 84; Ed&PubIntYB 82; LitMarPl 83, 84; NewsBur 6; NewsDir 84*
Albuquerque News - Albuquerque, NM - *NewsDir 84*
Albuquerque Tribune [of Scripps-Howard Newspapers] - Albuquerque, NM - *BaconPubCkNews 84; Ed&PubIntYB 82; LitMarPl 83; NewsDir 84*
Alburn Bureau, The - Tucson, AZ - *Ed&PubIntYB 82*
Alcalde - Austin, TX - *WritMar 84*
Alcare Communications Inc. - Philadelphia, PA - *Tel&CabFB 84C*
Alcatraz [of Alcatraz Editions] - Santa Cruz, CA - *LitMag&SmPr 83-84*
Alcatraz Editions - Santa Cruz, CA - *BoPubDir 4, 5; LitMag&SmPr 83-84*
Alcazar Productions - Waterbury, VT - *BillIntBG 83-84*
Alcester Union - Alcester, SD - *BaconPubCkNews 84; Ed&PubIntYB 82*
Alchemical Bakery, The - Monroe, UT - *LitMag&SmPr 83-84*
Alchemist/Light Publishing - San Francisco, CA - *BoPubDir 4, 5; LitMag&SmPr 83-84*
Alchemist, The - LaSalle, PQ, Canada - *LitMag&SmPr 83-84*
Alchemy Books - San Francisco, CA - *LitMag&SmPr 83-84; LitMarPl 83, 84*
Alco Associates Inc. - West Hempstead, NY - *ProGuPRSer 4*
Alco Press - New York, NY - *LitMag&SmPr 83-84*
Alcohol Fuels Installations Data Base [of Solar Energy Research Institute] - Golden, CO - *CompReadDB 82*
Alcohol Information Retrieval System [of Rutgers University] - Piscataway, NJ - *CompReadDB 82; DBBus 82*
Alcohol Use/Abuse [of Bibliographic Retrieval Services Inc.] - Lathan, NY - *DataDirOnSer 84*
Alcohol Use/Abuse Information File [of Hazelden Foundation] - Center City, MN - *CompReadDB 82*
Alcohol Week - Washington, DC - *BaconPubCkMag 84*
Alcoholics Anonymous World Services Inc. [Aff. of General Service Board of Alcoholics Anonymous] - New York, NY - *BoPubDir 4, 5*
Alcoholism [of Alcom Inc.] - Seattle, WA - *ArtMar 84; WritMar 84*
Alcoholism-Clinical & Experimental Research - New York, NY - *MagDir 84*
Alcon Engravers Inc. - New York, NY - *LitMarPl 83, 84; MagIndMarPl 82-83*
Alcona County Cable Corp. - Lincoln, MI - *BrCabYB 84*
Alcona County Herald - Lincoln, MI - *Ed&PubIntYB 82*
Alcona County Review - Harrisville, MI - *AyerDirPub 83; Ed&PubIntYB 82*
Alcone Co. Inc. - New York, NY - *AvMarPl 83*
Alcor Systems - Garland, TX - *MicrocomMPl 84*
Alcuin Society - Richmond, BC, Canada - *BoPubDir 4, 5*
Alcyon Corp. - San Diego, CA - *DataDirSup 7-83*
Aldebaran - Bristol, RI - *LitMag&SmPr 83-84*
Aldebaran Review - Berkeley, CA - *BoPubDir 4, 5*
Alden Advance - Alden, MN - *BaconPubCkNews 84; Ed&PubIntYB 82*
Alden Advertiser - Alden, NY - *BaconPubCkNews 84; Ed&PubIntYB 82; NewsDir 84*
Alden Advertising Agency Inc. - New York, NY - *StaDirAdAg 2-84*
Alden Co., The - Commerce, CA - *StaDirAdAg 2-84*
Alden Computer Systems Corp. - Natick, MA - *DataDirSup 7-83*
Alden Equipment Co. (Alden Research Center) - Westborough, MA - *DirInfWP 82*
Alden Films - Brooklyn, NY - *AvMarPl 83; TelAl 83, 84*
Alden, Jay [Aff. of Mook & Blanchard] - La Puerte, CA - *BoPubDir 4, 5*
Alden Press Inc. [Subs. of John Blair & Co.] - Elk Grove Village, IL - *DataDirOnSer 84*
Alden Press Ltd. [Div. of The Alden Printing Group] - Avon, CT - *LitMarPl 83, 84*
Alden Public Relations Inc., J. S. - New York, NY - *DirPRFirms 83*
Alden Taylor & Associates - New York, NY - *DirPRFirms 83*
Alden Television Inc. - Los Angeles, CA - *BrCabYB 84*
Alder Publishing Co. - Rochester, NY - *LitMag&SmPr 83-84*
Aldergrove Star, The - Aldergrove, BC, Canada - *Ed&PubIntYB 82*
Alderson Enterprises - Altoona, PA - *Ed&PubIntYB 82*
Aldi Music Co. - *See* Notable Music Co. Inc.
Aldine Publishing Co. [Div. of Walter de Gruyter Inc.] - Hawthorne, NY - *LitMarPl 83, 84*
Aldous Demian Publishing Ltd. - New York, NY - *BillIntBG 83-84*
Aldredg-Blair Inc. - Dallas, TX - *BoPubDir 5*
Aldrich & Helm Advertising - Billings, MT - *StaDirAdAg 2-84*
Aledo Times Record - Aledo, IL - *BaconPubCkNews 84; NewsDir 84*
Aleff & Associates Inc., Gloria - Waverly, IA - *StaDirAdAg 2-84*
Aleja Music - Redford, MI - *BillIntBG 83-84*
Aleksandrowicz/Uniphoto, Frank - Bay Village, OH - *AvMarPl 83; MagIndMarPl 82-83*
Alemany Press Ltd. - San Francisco, CA - *BoPubDir 5*

Alembic Press - Plainfield, IN - *BoPubDir 4, 5*
Alenik-Rudman Field Services Inc. - Howard Beach, NY - *IntDirMarRes 83*
Aleph - Takoma Park, MD - *BoPubDir 4, 5*
Aleph [of Hebrew University of Jerusalem] - Jerusalem, Israel - *EISS 7-83 Sup*
Aleph Press - San Francisco, CA - *BoPubDir 4 Sup, 5*
Aleph Publishing - Glendale, CA - *BoPubDir 4, 5*
Alert - Chetek, WI - *AyerDirPub 83*
Alert Cable TV Inc. [of Wometco Cable TV Inc.] - Ft. Benning, GA - *BrCabYB 84; Tel&CabFB 84C*
Alert Cable TV of Goldsboro [of Wometco Cable TV Inc.] - Goldsboro, NC - *BrCabYB 84; Tel&CabFB 84C*
Alert Cable TV of North Carolina Inc. [of Wometco Cable TV Inc.] - Carrboro, NC - *BrCabYB 84; Tel&CabFB 84C*
Alert Cable TV of North Carolina Inc. [of Wometco Cable TV Inc.] - Cary, NC - *BrCabYB 84; Tel&CabFB 84C*
Alert Cable TV of North Carolina Inc. [of Wometco Cable TV Inc.] - Cherry Point, NC - *BrCabYB 84; Tel&CabFB 84C*
Alert Cable TV of North Carolina Inc. [of Wometco Cable TV Inc.] - Elizabethtown, NC - *Tel&CabFB 84C*
Alert Cable TV of North Carolina Inc. [of Wometco Cable TV Inc.] - Fairmont, NC - *Tel&CabFB 84C*
Alert Cable TV of North Carolina Inc. [of Wometco Cable TV Inc.] - Farmville, NC - *BrCabYB 84; Tel&CabFB 84C*
Alert Cable TV of North Carolina Inc. [of Wometco Cable TV Inc.] - Garner, NC - *BrCabYB 84; Tel&CabFB 84C*
Alert Cable TV of North Carolina Inc. [of Wometco Cable TV Inc.] - Guilford County, NC - *BrCabYB 84; Tel&CabFB 84C*
Alert Cable TV of North Carolina Inc. [of Wometco Cable TV Inc.] - Pembroke, NC - *Tel&CabFB 84C*
Alert Cable TV of North Carolina Inc. [of Wometco Cable TV Inc.] - Reidsville, NC - *BrCabYB 84*
Alert Cable TV of North Carolina Inc. [of Wometco Cable TV Inc.] - Selma, NC - *BrCabYB 84; Tel&CabFB 84C*
Alert Cable TV of North Carolina Inc. [of Wometco Cable TV Inc.] - Stoneville, NC - *BrCabYB 84; Tel&CabFB 84C*
Alert Cable TV of North Carolina Inc. [of Wometco Cable TV Inc.] - Wake Forest, NC - *BrCabYB 84; Tel&CabFB 84C*
Alert Cable TV of North Carolina Inc. [of Wometco Cable TV Inc.] - Wendell, NC - *BrCabYB 84; Tel&CabFB 84C*
Alert Cable TV of North Carolina Inc. - *See* Wometco Cable TV Inc.
Alert Cable TV of Oklahoma Inc. [of Wometco Cable TV Inc.] - Pryor, OK - *BrCabYB 84; Tel&CabFB 84C*
Alert Cable TV of South Carolina Inc. [of Wometco Cable TV Inc.] - Andrews, SC - *BrCabYB 84; Tel&CabFB 84C*
Alert Cable TV of South Carolina Inc. [of Wometco Cable TV Inc.] - Bishopville, SC - *BrCabYB 84; Tel&CabFB 84C*
Alert Cable TV of South Carolina Inc. [of Wometco Cable TV Inc.] - Georgetown, SC - *BrCabYB 84; Tel&CabFB 84C*
Alert Cable TV of South Carolina Inc. [of Wometco Cable TV Inc.] - Lake City, SC - *Tel&CabFB 84C*
Alert Cable TV of South Carolina Inc. - *See* Wometco Cable TV Inc.
Alert Cable TV of Wilson Inc. [of Wometco Cable TV Inc.] - Wilson, NC - *BrCabYB 84; Tel&CabFB 84C*
Alert Interviewing Service Inc. - Levittown, NY - *IntDirMarRes 83*
Alestle - Edwardsville, MO - *NewsDir 84*
Aletha Jane Music - Nashville, TN - *BillIntBG 83-84*
Aletheia Publishers Inc. [Aff. of Alpha Omega Publications] - Tempe, AZ - *BoPubDir 5*
Aletheia Publishers Inc. - Garland, TX - *BoPubDir 4*
Alexa Press Inc. - East Hampton, NY - *BoPubDir 4, 5*
Alexander & Associates Inc., Elwood R. - Toronto, ON, Canada - *DirPRFirms 83*
Alexander Associates - Los Angeles, CA - *StaDirAdAg 2-84*
Alexander City Cablevision Co. - Alexander City, AL - *BrCabYB 84; Tel&CabFB 84C*
Alexander City Outlook [of Tallapoosa Publishers Inc.] - Alexander City, AL - *AyerDirPub 83; BaconPubCkNews 84; NewsDir 84*
Alexander Co. - New York, NY - *DirPRFirms 83; LitMarPl 83, 84; MagIndMarPl 82-83*
Alexander Enterprises, K. - New York, NY - *IntDirMarRes 83*
Alexander Film Services [Div. of Cadence Industries Corp.] - Colorado Springs, CO - *AvMarPl 83*
Alexander Group Inc., The - Raleigh, NC - *StaDirAdAg 2-84*
Alexander, Linc W. - Vancouver, BC, Canada - *BoPubDir 4, 5*
Alexander Marketing Services Inc. - Grand Rapids, MI - *StaDirAdAg 2-84*
Alexander Research & Communications Inc. - New York, NY - *DataDirOnSer 84; EISS 7-83 Sup*
Alexander/Scot Inc. - Dallas, TX - *StaDirAdAg 2-84*
Alexander Typesetting Inc. - Indianapolis, IN - *LitMarPl 84*
Alexander's Local Cartoon Syndicate - Seneca, SC - *Ed&PubIntYB 82*
Alexandria Alexandrian - Alexandria, IN - *BaconPubCkNews 84*
Alexandria Bay Thousand Island Sun - Alexandria Bay, NY - *BaconPubCkNews 84*
Alexandria Daily Town Talk [of McCormick & Co. Inc.] - Alexandria, LA - *Ed&PubIntYB 82; NewsDir 84*
Alexandria Gazette - Alexandria, VA - *BaconPubCkNews 84; Ed&PubIntYB 82; NewsDir 84*
Alexandria Herald - Alexandria, SD - *BaconPubCkNews 84; Ed&PubIntYB 82*
Alexandria House Books [Div. of Kephart Communications Inc.] - Arlington, VA - *LitMarPl 83, 84*
Alexandria House Inc. - Alexandria, IN - *BillIntBG 83-84*
Alexandria Journal - Fairfax, VA - *AyerDirPub 83*
Alexandria Journal [of Journal Newspapers Inc.] - Springfield, VA - *NewsDir 84*
Alexandria Journal - *See* Journal Newspapers
Alexandria Journal, The - Washington, DC - *Ed&PubIntYB 82*
Alexandria Marketing Services Inc. - New York, NY - *HBIndAd&MS 82-83; IntDirMarRes 83*
Alexandria News Weekly - Alexandria, LA - *AyerDirPub 83; BaconPubCkNews 84; Ed&PubIntYB 82; NewsDir 84*
Alexandria Newspapers Inc. - Alexandria, MN - *BaconPubCkNews 84*
Alexandria Packet, The - Alexandria, VA - *Ed&PubIntYB 82*
Alexandria-Pineville Town Talk - Alexandria, LA - *BaconPubCkNews 84*
Alexandria Times-Tribune - Alexandria, IN - *BaconPubCkNews 84; NewsDir 84*
Alexis Music Inc. - Malibu, CA - *BillIntBG 83-84*
Alexis Press - *See* Acklin Newspaper Group
Aley Associates, Maxwell - New York, NY - *LitMarPl 83, 84*
Alfa Music Group - Los Angeles, CA - *BillIntBG 83-84*
Alfa Records Inc. - Los Angeles, CA - *BillIntBG 83-84*
Alfalfa County News - Carmen, OK - *Ed&PubIntYB 82*
Alfalfa Publishers - Geneva, IL - *BoPubDir 4 Sup, 5*
ALFCO Publications - Corydon, IN - *BoPubDir 4, 5*
Alford Associates - Richmond, VA - *MicrocomMPl 83, 84; WhoWMicrocom 83*
Alfred Cable System - Alfred, NY - *BrCabYB 84; Tel&CabFB 84C*
Alfred Hitchcock's Mystery Magazine [of Davis Publications] - New York, NY - *ArtMar 84; MagIndMarPl 82-83; WritMar 84*
Alfred Publishing Co. Inc. - Sherman Oaks, CA - *BillIntBG 83-84; LitMarPl 83, 84; WritMar 84*
Alfred Sun, The - Alfred, NY - *Ed&PubIntYB 82*
Alfrod & Bertrand - Watertown, MA - *StaDirAdAg 2-84*
Algee Music Corp. - *See* Gallico Music Corp., Al
Algen Press Corp. - College Point, NY - *LitMarPl 83, 84*
Algol Press - New York, NY - *BoPubDir 4, 5; LitMag&SmPr 83-84*
Algoma Cablevision [of Wisconsin Cablevision & Radio Co. Inc.] - Algoma, WI - *Tel&CabFB 84C*
Algoma News Review - Wawa, ON, Canada - *AyerDirPub 83; Ed&PubIntYB 82*
Algoma Record-Herald - Algoma, WI - *AyerDirPub 83; BaconPubCkNews 84*
Algona Cable TV Inc. [of Cable Communications of Iowa] - Algona, IA - *BrCabYB 84*
Algona Kossuth County Advance - Algona, IA - *Ed&PubIntYB 82*
Algona Kossuth County Advance - *See* Algona Publishing Co. Inc.
Algona Publishing Co. Inc. - Algona, IA - *BaconPubCkNews 84*
Algona Upper Des Moines [of Algona Publishing Co. Inc.] - Algona, IA - *Ed&PubIntYB 82; NewsDir 84*
Algona Upper Des Moines - *See* Algona Publishing Co. Inc.

Algonac Courier Journal [of Sommerville Communications Corp.] - Algonac, MI - *NewsDir 84*
Algonac Courier-Journal - *See* Sommerville Communications Corp.
Algonquin Countryside [of Barrington Press Inc.] - Barrington, IL - *NewsDir 84*
Algor Interactive Systems - Pittsburgh, PA - *DataDirOnSer 84*
Algorithmics Inc. - Wellesley, MA - *DirInfWP 82*
Algorix Software - San Francisco, CA - *MicrocomMPl 83*
Alhambra-Grantfork Telephone Co. - Alhambra, IL - *TelDir&BG 83-84*
Alhambra Independent - San Gabriel, CA - *Ed&PubIntYB 82*
Alhambra Independent - *See* Sun Independent Newspapers
Alhambra Post-Advocate - Alhambra, CA - *Ed&PubIntYB 82*
Alhambra Post-Advocate [of Monterey Park Progress Newspapers] - Monterey Park, CA - *NewsDir 84*
Alhambra Post-Advocate - *See* Southern California Publishing Co.
Alhambra Records Inc. - Opa Locka, FL - *BillIntBG 83-84*
Alhart Music Publishing Co. - Lakeside, CA - *BillIntBG 83-84*
ALI-ABA Course Materials Journal - Philadelphia, PA - *MagIndMarPl 82-83*
Ali Baba Press - Gainesville, GA - *LitMag&SmPr 83-84*
Ali-Ben Music - *See* Skinny Zach Music Inc.
Alias Smith & Jones Inc. - Cincinnati, OH - *DirPRFirms 83*
Alice [of Editrice Bibliografica] - Milan, Italy - *CompReadDB 82; DirOnDB Spring 84*
Alice Echo-News - Alice, TX - *BaconPubCkNews 84; NewsDir 84*
Alicejamesbooks [Div. of Alice James Poetry Cooperative Inc.] - Cambridge, MA - *LitMarPl 83, 84*
Alief Advertizer Advocate - Houston, TX - *NewsDir 84*
Alien Group, The - New York, NY - *MicrocomMPl 84*
Alima Music Publishing - Seattle, WA - *BillIntBG 83-84*
Alimansky Planning Group - New York, NY - *LitMarPl 83*
Alimentos Procesados - Chicago, IL - *BaconPubCkMag 84*
Alin Foundation Press - Berkeley, CA - *BoPubDir 4, 5*
Alinari [Div. of Editorial Photocolor Archives Inc.] - New York, NY - *LitMarPl 83, 84*
Alinda Press - Eureka, CA - *BoPubDir 4, 5*
Aliotta & Manhart Publications Inc. - Chicago, IL - *BoPubDir 4 Sup, 5*
Aliquippa News - Aliquippa, PA - *BaconPubCkNews 84*
Aliquippa Steelworker - Aliquippa, PA - *NewsDir 84*
ALIS - Lyngby, Denmark - *DirOnDB Spring 84*
Alised Enterprises - Bethesda, MD - *BoPubDir 4 Sup, 5*
Alive! [of Christian Board of Publication] - St. Louis, MO - *ArtMar 84*
Alive - Guelph, ON, Canada - *LitMag&SmPr 83-84*
Alive - Toronto, ON, Canada - *BaconPubCkMag 84*
Alive Books [Aff. of Canadian Health Reform Products Ltd.] - Vancouver, BC, Canada - *BoPubDir 4, 5*
Alive for Young Teens [of Christian Board of Publication] - St. Louis, MO - *WritMar 84*
Alive Now! - Nashville, TN - *WritMar 84*
Alive Publications Ltd. - New York, NY - *BoPubDir 4, 5*
Aljean Records - Myerstown, PA - *BillIntBG 83-84*
Aljon International - Ft. Lauderdale, FL - *ArtMar 84*
Aljoni Music Co. - Los Angeles, CA - *BillIntBG 83-84*
Alkatraz Corner Music Co. - San Francisco, CA - *BillIntBG 83-84*
Alkazar Associates - Arlington, VA - *MicrocomSwDir 1*
Alkazu Music - El Cerrito, CA - *BillIntBG 83-84*
All About Snowmobiling - Los Angeles, CA - *MagDir 84*
All About Us/Nous Autres Canada Inc. - Coquitlam, BC, Canada - *BoPubDir 5*
All About Us/Nous Autres Canada Inc. - Ottawa, ON, Canada - *BoPubDir 4*
All American Cable Communications Co. [of Tele-Communications Inc.] - Mokena, IL - *BrCabYB 84; Tel&CabFB 84C*
All American Cable Communications Inc. - Peotone, IL - *BrCabYB 84*
All-American Cablevision [of American TV & Communications Corp.] - Columbus, OH - *BrCabYB 84; Tel&CabFB 84C*
All Bright Promotions - Seattle, WA - *LitMarPl 83, 84*
All Business Assistance - Norwalk, CT - *DirInfWP 82*
All-Canada Baptist Publications [Aff. of Baptist Federation of Canada] - Kentville, NS, Canada - *BoPubDir 4 Sup, 5*
All-Canada Radio & Television - Toronto, ON, Canada - *Tel&CabFB 84C*
All Canada Weekly Summaries [of Canada Law Book Ltd.] - Aurora, ON, Canada - *CompReadDB 82; DBBus 82; DirOnDB Spring 84*
All-Canada Weekly Summaries [of QL Systems Ltd.] - Ottawa, ON, Canada - *DataDirOnSer 84*
All-Channel Cable TV of Illinois [of Tele-Communications Inc.] - Chanute AFB, IL - *BrCabYB 84*
All Channel Cable TV of Illinois - Chapman, IL - *BrCabYB 84*
All Communications Corp. - Pittsfield, MA - *BrCabYB 84*
All Languages Graphics Inc. [Div. of Linguistic Systems Inc.] - Cambridge, MA - *LitMarPl 83, 84*
All Media Services - Sherman Oaks, CA - *LitMarPl 83, 84; MagIndMarPl 82-83*
All of Us Inc. - Boulder, CO - *BoPubDir 4, 5*
All-Over Messenger Service Corp. - New York, NY - *MagIndMarPl 82-83*
All Points Cable TV [of All Points Associates Inc.] - Bellevue, WA - *BrCabYB 84*
All-Rite Addressing & Mailing Service Inc. [Div. of Modern Imprinting Co.] - New York, NY - *LitMarPl 83, 84; MagIndMarPl 82-83*
All-Round Typing Service - Massapequa Park, NY - *LitMarPl 83, 84*
All-State Legal Supply Co. - Mountainside, NJ - *DirInfWP 82*
All-Steel Inc. - Aurora, IL - *DirInfWP 82*
All-Union Institute of Scientific & Technical Information - Moscow, USSR - *EISS 83*
All-Vu Cable TV Inc. - Knox County, KY - *BrCabYB 84*
Allamakee Journal & Lansing Mirror - Lansing, IA - *AyerDirPub 83; Ed&PubIntYB 82*
Allan Advertising & Direct Marketing Inc. - Memphis, TN - *DirMarMP 83*
Allan Advertising Inc. - Miami, FL - *StaDirAdAg 2-84*
Allan & Gray Corp. - New York, NY - *LitMarPl 83, 84*
Allan Co., Michael James - Seattle, WA - *DirPRFirms 83*
Allan Publishers Inc. [Aff. of Offenheimer Publishers Inc.] - Pikesville, MD - *LitMarPl 83, 84*
Allan, The Designing Woman Studio, Judy - New York, NY - *LitMarPl 83, 84*
Allanheld & Schram - Montclair, NJ - *BoPubDir 4*
Allanheld, Osmun & Co. [Subs. of Littlefield, Adams & Co.] - Totowa, NJ - *LitMarPl 83*
Allanheld, Osmun & Co. - *See* Rowman & Allanheld
Allanwood Music - *See* Campbell Music Inc., Glen
Allarcom Pay Television - Edmonton, AB, Canada - *BrCabYB 84*
Allard/Lesiege Inc. - Montreal, PQ, Canada - *StaDirAdAg 2-84*
Allbritton Communications - Washington, DC - *AdAge 6-28-84; BrCabYB 84; KnowInd 83; Tel&CabFB 84S*
Allbritton Newspapers - *Ed&PubIntYB 82*
Allbro Music - *See* Elijah Blue Music
Allegan County News & Gazette [of Kaechele Enterprises] - Allegan, MI - *AyerDirPub 83; BaconPubCkNews 84; Ed&PubIntYB 82; NewsDir 84*
Allegan Flashes - Allegan, MI - *AyerDirPub 83*
Allegany Mountain Press - Olean, NY - *BoPubDir 4, 5; LitMag&SmPr 83-84*
Alleghany Highlander - Clifton Forge, VA - *AyerDirPub 83*
Alleghany News, The - Sparta, NC - *Ed&PubIntYB 82*
Allegheny Business Systems Inc. - Delmont, PA - *DirInfWP 82*
Allegheny Cablevision [of The Essex Group] - Frostburg, MD - *BrCabYB 84*
Allegheny Cablevision [of The Essex Group] - Piedmont, WV - *BrCabYB 84*
Allegheny Mountain Network Stations - State College, PA - *BrCabYB 84*
Allegheny Press - California, PA - *BoPubDir 4*
Allegheny Press - Elgin, PA - *BoPubDir 5; WritMar 84*
Allegheny Reporter Shopper - Turtle Creek, PA - *NewsDir 84*
Allegheny Valley Cable Co. Inc. - San Manuel, AZ - *BrCabYB 84*
Allegro Film Productions - Tamarac, FL - *AvMarPl 83; Tel&CabFB 84C; WritMar 84*
Allegro Film Productions Inc. - New York, NY - *ProGuPRSer 4*
Alleluia Press - Allendale, NJ - *BoPubDir 4, 5*
Allen Advertising Inc., Sander - Chicago, IL - *StaDirAdAg 2-84*
Allen Advocate - Allen, OK - *BaconPubCkNews 84; Ed&PubIntYB 82*

Allen American - Allen, TX - *BaconPubCkNews 84; Ed&PubIntYB 82*
Allen & Associates Inc., Milton - Cleveland, OH - *DataDirOnSer 84*
Allen & Dorward - San Francisco, CA - *AdAge 3-28-84; ArtMar 84; DirPRFirms 83; StaDirAdAg 2-84*
Allen & Mattingly - Atlanta, GA - *AdAge 3-28-84; StaDirAdAg 2-84*
Allen & Unwin Inc. [Subs. of George Allen & Unwin Ltd.] - Winchester, MA - *LitMarPl 83, 84; WritMar 84*
Allen & Yanow Literary Agency - Santa Cruz, CA - *LitMarPl 83, 84*
Allen Associates, Frank - San Diego, CA - *CabTVFinDB 83*
Allen Associates Inc., Ben - New York, NY - *HBIndAd&MS 82-83*
Allen Cable TV - Allen, KY - *BrCabYB 84; Tel&CabFB 84C*
Allen, Carl - Beach, ND - *Tel&CabFB 84C p.1663*
Allen Co. Inc., R. C. - Grand Rapids, MI - *DataDirSup 7-83*
Allen County News - Scottsville, KY - *AyerDirPub 83; Ed&PubIntYB 82*
Allen County Star-Times - New Haven, IN - *AyerDirPub 83; Ed&PubIntYB 82*
Allen, Dorsey & Hatfield Inc. - Los Angeles, CA - *StaDirAdAg 2-84*
Allen, Eleanor - Hackensack, NJ - *LitMarPl 83, 84; MagIndMarPl 82-83*
Allen Enterprises - Texas City, TX - *LitMag&SmPr 83-84*
Allen Enterprises Inc., Howard - Cape Canaveral, FL - *BoPubDir 4, 5*
Allen Group Inc. - Provo, UT - *BoPubDir 5*
Allen Inc., Alice - New York, NY - *DirPRFirms 83; LitMarPl 83, 84; MagIndMarPl 82-83*
Allen Inc., John E. - Park Ridge, NJ - *Tel&CabFB 84C*
Allen-Martin Productions Inc. - Louisville, KY - *BillIntBG 83-84*
Allen Paper Co. - Chicago, IL - *DirInfWP 82*
Allen Parker [of The Mellus Newspapers Inc.] - Lincoln Park, MI - *AyerDirPub 83; NewsDir 84*
Allen Parker - *See* Mellus Newspapers Inc.
Allen Parker, The - Allen Park, MI - *Ed&PubIntYB 82*
Allen, Pat - New York, NY - *LitMarPl 83; MagIndMarPl 82-83*
Allen Photo Service Inc. - Arlington, VA - *AvMarPl 83*
Allen Press Inc. - Lawrence, KS - *MagIndMarPl 82-83*
Allen Publishing Co. - Encino, CA - *WritMar 84*
Allen Publishing Co., Nathan - Milford, MI - *BoPubDir 5*
Allen Secretarial Services Inc. - East Detroit, MI - *DirInfWP 82*
Allen-Wayne Communications - New York, NY - *LitMarPl 84*
Allenbach Industries Inc. - Carlsbad, CA - *ADAPSOMemDir 83-84; MicrocomMPl 83*
Allendale County Citizen, The - Allendale, SC - *Ed&PubIntYB 82*
Allendale Telephone Co. - Allendale, MI - *TelDir&BG 83-84*
Allend'or Productions Inc. - Sherman Oaks, CA - *TelAl 83, 84; Tel&CabFB 84C*
Allen's Press Clipping Bureau - San Francisco, CA - *ProGuPRSer 4*
Allen's TV Cable Service Inc. - Morgan City, LA - *BrCabYB 84; Tel&CabFB 84C p.1663*
Allenson-Breckinridge Books [Subs. of Alec R. Allenson Inc.] - Geneva, AL - *BoPubDir 4, 4 Sup, 5; LitMarPl 83, 84*
Allentown Cable TV [of El-Mar Communications Co.] - Allentown, NY - *BrCabYB 84; Tel&CabFB 84C*
Allentown Call-Chronicle - Allentown, PA - *DirOnDB Spring 84; NewsDir 84*
Allentown Messenger-Press - Allentown, NJ - *BaconPubCkNews 84; NewsDir 84*
Allentown Morning Call - Allentown, PA - *BaconPubCkNews 84; LitMarPl 83*
Allentown Morning Call [of VU/TEXT Information Services] - Philadelphia, PA - *DataDirOnSer 84*
Allentown Mountainville Times - *See* Peerless Publications
Allentown Sunday Call-Chronicle - Allentown, PA - *LitMarPl 83*
Aller Reklamebureau A/S - Copenhagen, Denmark - *StaDirAdAg 2-84*
Allerton Associates Advertising - Hot Springs, AR - *ArtMar 84; StaDirAdAg 2-84*
Allerton Press Inc. - New York, NY - *MagIndMarPl 82-83*
Alley Theatre - Houston, TX - *WritMar 84*
Alliance Community TV [of Tele-Communications Inc.] - Alliance, NE - *BrCabYB 84; Tel&CabFB 84C*
Alliance of Information & Referral Systems - Akron, OH - *EISS 83*
Alliance of Resident Theatres - New York, NY - *BoPubDir 4, 5*
Alliance of the Indianapolis Museum of Art - Indianapolis, IN - *BoPubDir 4, 5*
Alliance Pictures Corp. - Cincinnati, OH - *AvMarPl 83*
Alliance Publishers [Aff. of Southern Program Alliance Publishers] - Ft. Lauderdale, FL - *BoPubDir 4, 5*
Alliance Publishing Co. - Minerva, OH - *BaconPubCkNews 84*
Alliance Review - Alliance, OH - *BaconPubCkNews 84; Ed&PubIntYB 82; NewsDir 84*
Alliance Teleconferencing Services [of American Telephone & Telegraph Co.] - Bedminster, NJ - *TeleSy&SerDir 2-84*
Alliance Theatre - Atlanta, GA - *WritMar 84*
Alliance Times-Herald - Alliance, NE - *BaconPubCkNews 84; Ed&PubIntYB 82; NewsDir 84*
Alliance Witness, The - Nyack, NY - *MagIndMarPl 82-83*
Allied Advertising Agency Inc. - Boston, MA - *HBIndAd&MS 82-83; StaDirAdAg 2-84; TelAl 83, 84*
Allied Artists Music Co. Inc. - New York, NY - *BillIntBG 83-84*
Allied Artists Television Corp. - New York, NY - *Tel&CabFB 84C*
Allied Books & Educational Resources - Los Alamos, NM - *LitMarPl 84*
Allied Books & Educational Resources - Santa Fe, NM - *LitMarPl 83*
Allied Business Consultants Inc. - Washington, DC - *BoPubDir 4*
Allied Cable Systems - St. Louis, MO - *Tel&CabFB 84C*
Allied Color Inc. - Guilford, CT - *MagIndMarPl 82-83*
Allied Computer Service - New York, NY - *MicrocomMPl 83, 84*
Allied Computer Services - Basking Ridge, NJ - *DataDirOnSer 84*
Allied Corp. - Morristown, NJ - *Datamation 6-83; ElecNews 7-25-83; Top100Al 83*
Allied Data - Olympia, WA - *ADAPSOMemDir 83-84; DataDirOnSer 84*
Allied Education Council - Galien, MI - *BoPubDir 4, 5*
Allied Enterprises - Chicago, IL - *BoPubDir 5*
Allied Feature Syndicate - Cleveland, OH - *BaconPubCkNews 84; Ed&PubIntYB 82; LitMarPl 84*
Allied Film Laboratory Inc. - Detroit, MI - *AvMarPl 83*
Allied Gardens/Del Cerro Pennysaver - Mission Viejo, CA - *AyerDirPub 83*
Allied Graphic Arts - New York, NY - *DirMarMP 83*
Allied Industrial Worker - Milwaukee, WI - *NewsDir 84*
Allied Lettercraft Co. - New York, NY - *LitMarPl 83, 84; MagIndMarPl 82-83*
Allied News [of Grove City Allied Newspapers Inc.] - Grove City, PA - *AyerDirPub 83; Ed&PubIntYB 82; NewsDir 84*
Allied Paper Inc. [Subs. of SCM Corp.] - Kalamazoo, MI - *LitMarPl 83, 84*
Allied Photo Color Co. - St. Louis, MO - *AvMarPl 83*
Allied Photo Industries [Div. of Kendale Co. Inc.] - Grand Rapids, MI - *AvMarPl 83*
Allied Press International - Salt Lake City, UT - *Ed&PubIntYB 82*
Allied Press International Inc. - Washington, DC - *BrCabYB 84*
Allied Publishers Private Ltd. - Madras, India - *InfoS 83-84*
Allied Publishers Subscription Agency - Madras, India - *InfIndMarPl 83*
Allied Ribbon & Carbon - New York, NY - *DirInfWP 82*
Allied School & Office Products - Albuquerque, NM - *AvMarPl 83*
Allied Telephone Co. of Arkansas Inc. [Aff. of Allied Telephone Co.] - Little Rock, AR - *TelDir&BG 83-84*
Allied Telephone Co. of Kentucky Inc. [Aff. of Allied Telephone Co.] - Shepherdsville, KY - *TelDir&BG 83-84*
Allied Telephone Co. of Missouri Inc. [Aff. of Allied Telephone Co.] - Dixon, MO - *TelDir&BG 83-84*
Allied Telephone Co. of Oklahoma Inc. [Aff. of Allied Telephone Co.] - Burns Flat, OK - *TelDir&BG 83-84*
Allied Utilities Corp. [Aff. of Allied Telephone Co.] - Crossett, AR - *TelDir&BG 83-84*
Alligator Records - Chicago, IL - *BillIntBG 83-84*
Allin - Oxford, England - *LitMag&SmPr 83-84*

Alling & Cory - Long Island City, NY - *LitMarPl 83, 84; MagIndMarPl 82-83*
Allison, Bob - Kirkland, WA - *Tel&CabFB 84C p.1663*
Allison Butler County Tribune-Journal - Allison, IA - *BaconPubCkNews 84*
Allison, Les - Roland, MB, Canada - *BoPubDir 4, 5*
Allison Publishing - Sturgis, SD - *BaconPubCkNews 84*
Allnet [of Combined Network Inc.] - Chicago, IL - *TeleSy&SerDir 7-83*
Allock TV Cable - Vicco, KY - *BrCabYB 84*
Alloy Computer Products [Subs. of Alloy Engineering Co. Inc.] - Natick, MA - *MicrocomMPl 84; WhoWMicrocom 83*
Alloy Data Center [of U.S. National Bureau of Standards] - Washington, DC - *EISS 83*
Alloy Engineering Inc. - Natick, MA - *MicrocomMPl 83, 84*
Allprint Co. Ltd. - Kitchener, ON, Canada - *BoPubDir 4 Sup, 5*
Allscope Services Inc. - New York, NY - *StaDirAdAg 2-84*
Allservice Phototypesetting Co. of Arizona - Phoenix, AZ - *LitMarPl 83, 84*
Allstate Census Use System [of Allstate Insurance Co.] - Menlo Park, CA - *EISS 83*
Allston Brighton Citizen-Item - Allston/Brighton, MA - *Ed&PubIntYB 82*
Allston-Brighton Citizen-Item - Boston, MA - *AyerDirPub 83*
Allston-Brighton Citizen-Item [of Brookline Citizen Group Publications] - Brookline, MA - *NewsDir 84*
Allston-Brighton Citizen-Item - *See* Citizen Group Publications
Allview Cable Service [of Cablecasting Ltd.] - St. Thomas, ON, Canada - *BrCabYB 84*
Ally [of West Coast Print Center] - Berkeley, CA - *LitMag&SmPr 83-84*
Ally & Gargano - New York, NY - *AdAge 3-28-84; Br 1-23-84; BrCabYB 84; StaDirAdAg 2-84*
Ally Press - St. Paul, MN - *BoPubDir 4, 5; LitMag&SmPr 83-84*
Allyn & Bacon Inc. [Subs. of Esquire Inc.] - Newton, MA - *AvMarPl 83; LitMarPl 83, 84; WritMar 84*
Allyn & Bacon Inc. (College Div.) - Newton, MA - *ArtMar 84*
Allyn & Bacon Inc. (Elhi Div.) - Newton, MA - *ArtMar 84*
Allyn & Bacon Inc. (Longwood Div.) - Newton, MA - *ArtMar 84; DirMarMP 83*
Allyn Associates Inc. - Manchester, NH - *StaDirAdAg 2-84*
Allyn-Mason Inc. - Plainview, NY - *LitMarPl 83; MagIndMarPl 82-83*
Alma Desk Co. - High Point, NC - *DirInfWP 82*
Alma Harlan County Journal - Alma, NE - *BaconPubCkNews 84*
Alma Signal-Enterprise - Alma, KS - *BaconPubCkNews 84*
Alma Telephone Co. - Alma, MO - *TelDir&BG 83-84*
Alma Telephone Co. Inc. - Alma, GA - *TelDir&BG 83-84*
Alma Times - Alma, GA - *Ed&PubIntYB 82*
Alma Times-Statesman - Alma, GA - *BaconPubCkNews 84*
Almaden San Jose Sun - San Jose, CA - *Ed&PubIntYB 82*
Almaden Systems Inc. - San Jose, CA - *WhoWMicrocom 83*
Almanac - Charleroi, PA - *AyerDirPub 83*
Almanac Music Inc. - *See* TRO
Almanac-Press/Russian-English Publications - Los Angeles, CA - *BoPubDir 4, 5*
Almar Press - Binghamton, NY - *BoPubDir 4; LitMarPl 83, 84; WritMar 84*
Almaviva Music Ltd. - *See* Live Music Publishing Group
Almena Plaindealer - Almena, KS - *BaconPubCkNews 84; Ed&PubIntYB 82*
Almi Television Productions - New York, NY - *TelAl 84; Tel&CabFB 84C*
Almitra Music Co. Inc. - *See* Kendor Music Inc.
Almo Music Corp. - *See* Rondor Music International Inc.
Almo Publications - Hollywood, CA - *BoPubDir 4, 5*
Almo Service Inc., Carel - Hicksville, NY - *LitMarPl 84*
Almon Associates - San Antonio, TX - *DirPRFirms 83*
Almond Facts - Sacramento, CA - *BaconPubCkMag 84; MagDir 84*
Almond Telephone Co. - Almond, WI - *TelDir&BG 83-84*
Almont Times-Herald & Dryden News - *See* Tri-City Times
Almonte Gazette, The - Almonte, ON, Canada - *Ed&PubIntYB 82*
Almost Friends - Milford, DE - *BillIntBG 83-84*
ALOCO Inc. - East Greenwich, RI - *IntDirMarRes 83*
Aloha [of Davick Publishing Co.] - Honolulu, HI - *BaconPubCkMag 84; MagDir 84; MagIndMarPl 82-83; WritMar 84*
Aloha Breeze - Aloha, OR - *Ed&PubIntYB 82*
Aloha Breeze [of Hillsboro Argus] - Hillsboro, OR - *NewsDir 84*
Alonso & Associates Inc. - Mexico City, Mexico - *DirPRFirms 83*
Aloray Inc. - Huntington, NY - *BoPubDir 4, 5*
Alotagoodmusic Inc. - *See* Buttermilk Sky Music Publishing Corp.
Aloysius Butler & Clark - Bancroft Mills, DE - *StaDirAdAg 2-84*
Aloysius Butler & Clark - Wilmington, DE - *ArtMar 84*
Alpaugh Advertising - Cranford, NJ - *StaDirAdAg 2-84*
Alpena Advertiser [of Gaylord Weeklies Inc.] - Alpena, MI - *AyerDirPub 83; NewsDir 84*
Alpena Cablevision Inc. [of Cable Information Systems Inc.] - Alpena, MI - *BrCabYB 84; Tel&CabFB 84C*
Alpena Journal - Alpena, SD - *Ed&PubIntYB 82*
Alpena Journal - Wessington Springs, SD - *AyerDirPub 83*
Alpena Journal - *See* Wessington Springs Publishers
Alpena News - Alpena, MI - *BaconPubCkNews 84; Ed&PubIntYB 82; NewsDir 84*
Alpern Advertising, Allen - Chicago, IL - *StaDirAdAg 2-84*
Alpert, Burt - San Francisco, CA - *BoPubDir 4, 5*
Alpert Research Inc. - New York, NY - *IntDirMarRes 83*
Alpha - Wolfville, NS, Canada - *WritMar 84*
Alpha Audio/Candyapple Productions [Div. of Alpha Recording Corp.] - Richmond, VA - *AvMarPl 83*
Alpha Bit Communications Inc. - Dearborn, MI - *MicrocomMPl 84*
Alpha Byte Computer Products - Westlake, CA - *MicrocomMPl 84*
Alpha Byte Computer Products - Westside, CA - *MicrocomMPl 83*
Alpha Cine Lab - Seattle, WA - *AvMarPl 83*
Alpha Cine Service Inc. - Cincinnati, OH - *AvMarPl 83*
Alpha Com - Hamburg, West Germany - *MicroMarPl 82-83*
Alpha Communications - Santa Monica, CA - *AvMarPl 83; BoPubDir 5; LitMag&SmPr 83-84*
Alpha Communications - Dayton, OH - *AvMarPl 83*
Alpha Computer Service - Cypress, CA - *MicrocomMPl 84*
Alpha Data Inc. - Chatsworth, CA - *DataDirSup 7-83*
Alpha Data Services - Port Washington, NY - *LitMarPl 83, 84*
Alpha Et Cetera Ltd. - Shelby, NC - *MicrocomMPl 84*
Alpha Film Music - *See* Alpha Music Inc.
Alpha 460 Television Ltd. - Bristol, England - *EISS 7-83 Sup*
Alpha Gamma Arts - Walnut Creek, CA - *BoPubDir 5*
Alpha Inc. - *See* R.S.M. & K. Inc.
Alpha Iota [of Pi Lambda Theta Publications] - Pomona, CA - *BoPubDir 4, 5*
Alpha Merics Corp. - Chatsworth, CA - *DataDirSup 7-83*
Alpha Microsystems - Irvine, CA - *WhoWMicrocom 83*
Alpha Music Inc. - New York, NY - *BillIntBG 83-84*
Alpha Photo Associates - New York, NY - *AvMarPl 83; MagIndMarPl 82-83*
Alpha Press - Gardenville, NY - *BoPubDir 4, 5*
Alpha Products - Woodhaven, NY - *MicrocomMPl 84*
Alpha Publications Inc. - Blue Bell, PA - *LitMarPl 83, 84*
Alpha Pyramis Publishing Co. [Div. of Bibliotheca Press Inc.] - Atlanta, GA - *LitMag&SmPr 83-84*
Alpha Repertory Television Service [of Hearst/ABC Video Services] - New York, NY - *BrCabYB 84; HomeVid&CabYB 82-83*
Alpha Repertory Television Service - *See* Hearst/ABC Video Services
Alpha Research Group Inc. - Bolingbrook, IL - *IntDirMarRes 83*
Alpha-Robinson - Detroit, MI - *BillIntBG 83-84*
Alpha Software Co. - Churchville, PA - *MicrocomMPl 84*
Alpha Software Corp. - Burlington, MA - *MicrocomMPl 84; MicrocomSwDir 1; WritMar 84*
Alpha Systems Resource - Shelbyville, IN - *EISS 5-84 Sup*
Alpha: The Magazine for Campus Greeks - Memphis, TN - *MagDir 84*
Alpha West - Bonita, CA - *LitMarPl 83, 84*
Alphabet Press - Boston, MA - *BoPubDir 4, 5*
Alphabit Communications Inc. - Dearborn, MI - *MicrocomSwDir 1*
Alphabox Press - London, England - *LitMag&SmPr 83-84*
Alphacom Inc. - Campbell, CA - *MicrocomMPl 83, 84*

Alphanetics - Forestville, CA - *MicrocomMPl 83, 84; MicrocomSwDir 1*
Alphapress [Aff. of LEAD Educational Resources Inc.] - Lexington, MA - *BoPubDir 4, 5*
Alpharetta Neighbor - Alpharetta, GA - *Ed&PubIntYB 82*
Alpharetta Neighbor [of Marietta Neighbor Newspapers Inc.] - Marietta, GA - *AyerDirPub 83; NewsDir 84*
Alphatel Corp. - Vienna, VA - *InfoS 83-84; VideoDir 82-83*
Alphatext [Subs. of Ronalds-Federated Ltd.] - Ottawa, ON, Canada - *DataDirOnSer 84; DirInfWP 82; EISS 83*
Alphatext [Subs. of Ronalds-Federated Ltd.] - Richmond Hill, ON, Canada - *DataDirOnSer 84*
Alphatype Corp. [Subs. of Berthold of North America] - Niles, IL - *DirInfWP 82*
Alphaventure - New York, NY - *BoPubDir 4, 5*
Alpine Advertising - Billings, MT - *AdAge 3-28-84; DirMarMP 83; StaDirAdAg 2-84*
Alpine Avalanche [of Far West Texas Publications] - Alpine, TX - *AyerDirPub 83; BaconPubCkNews 84; Ed&PubIntYB 82; NewsDir 84*
Alpine Cablevision Inc. [of Vision Cable Communications Inc.] - Alexandria, LA - *BrCabYB 84; Tel&CabFB 84C*
Alpine Cablevision Inc. [of Marsh Media Inc.] - Banner Elk, NC - *BrCabYB 84; Tel&CabFB 84C*
Alpine Cablevision Inc. [of Marsh Media Inc.] - Elk Park, NC - *BrCabYB 84; Tel&CabFB 84C*
Alpine Cablevision Inc. [of Marsh Media Cable Television] - Taylorsville, NC - *BrCabYB 84*
Alpine Cablevision Inc. [of Marsh Media Inc.] - Roan Mountain, TN - *BrCabYB 84; Tel&CabFB 84C*
Alpine Enterprises - Dearborn, MI - *BoPubDir 4, 5*
Alpine Film Productions - Denver, CO - *AvMarPl 83*
Alpine Fine Arts Collection Ltd. - New York, NY - *LitMarPl 83, 84*
Alpine Guild - Oak Park, IL - *BoPubDir 4, 5*
Alpine Pennysaver - Mission Viejo, CA - *AyerDirPub 83*
Alpine Press - Stoughton, MA - *LitMarPl 83, 84*
Alpine Publications Inc. - Loveland, CO - *ArtMar 84; BoPubDir 4, 5; WritMar 84*
Alpine Sun - Alpine, CA - *AyerDirPub 83; BaconPubCkNews 84*
Alpine TV Cable Co. Inc. - Alpine, TX - *BrCabYB 84; Tel&CabFB 84C*
Alps - Warren, NJ - *MicrocomMPl 84*
Alps Monthly [of Peace & Pieces Press] - San Francisco, CA - *LitMag&SmPr 83-84*
Alrac Music - *See* Watt Works Inc.
Alrhond - *See* Tree Publishing Co. Inc.
A.L.S. Forum & Newsletter, The [of Titania Publications] - Eugene, OR - *LitMag&SmPr 83-84*
Al's Written Music Publishers - Parsons, KS - *BillIntBG 83-84*
Alsask CATV - Alsask, SK, Canada - *BrCabYB 84*
Alsea River Cable Co. - Waldport, OR - *Tel&CabFB 84C*
Alshire International - Burbank, CA - *BillIntBG 83-84*
Alshire Publishing Cos. - Burbank, CA - *BillIntBG 83-84*
Alsip Edition [of Midlothian Southwest Messenger Newspapers] - Midlothian, IL - *NewsDir 84*
Alsip Express - Alsip, IL - *Ed&PubIntYB 82*
Alsip Express - Midlothian, IL - *AyerDirPub 83*
Alsip Messenger - *See* Southwest Messenger Newspapers
Alspa Computer Inc. - Santa Cruz, CA - *WhoWMicrocom 83*
Alstin Advertising - Philadelphia, PA - *AdAge 3-28-84; StaDirAdAg 2-84*
Alta Advertiser - Alta, IA - *Ed&PubIntYB 82*
Alta Advertiser - *See* Pilot-Tribune Printing Co.
Alta Gaia Society - Millerton, NY - *BoPubDir 4, 5*
Alta Loma-Cucamonga Upland Highlander - *See* Highlander Publications Inc.
Alta Napa Press - Calistoga, CA - *BoPubDir 4, 5; LitMag&SmPr 83-84*
Alta Systems Inc. - Austin, TX - *MicrocomMPl 84; MicrocomSwDir 1*
Alta Technology Inc. - Stamford, CT - *DataDirSup 7-83*
Alta Vista Journal - Alta Vista, KS - *Ed&PubIntYB 82*
Altadena Review Inc., The - Altadena, CA - *LitMag&SmPr 83-84*
Altadenan/Pasadenan Chronicle - Altadena, CA - *AyerDirPub 83; BaconPubCkNews 84; NewsDir 84*
Altair Press - Boulder, CO - *BoPubDir 4 Sup, 5*
Altair Productions - San Francisco, CA - *AvMarPl 83*
Altam Music Corp. - *See* Gallico Music Corp., Al
Altamont Advertising Agency Ltd. - New York, NY - *StaDirAdAg 2-84*
Altamont Cable TV - Altamont, KS - *Tel&CabFB 84C*
Altamont Enterprise - Altamont, NY - *NewsDir 84*
Altamont Enterprise & Albany County Post - Altamont, NY - *AyerDirPub 83; BaconPubCkNews 84*
Altamont Enterprise & Albany County Post - Guilderland, NY - *Ed&PubIntYB 82*
Altamont Journal - Altamont, KS - *BaconPubCkNews 84; Ed&PubIntYB 82*
Altamont News - Altamont, IL - *BaconPubCkNews 84; Ed&PubIntYB 82*
Altamont Times - Altamont, MO - *Ed&PubIntYB 82*
Altar Books - Luray, VA - *BoPubDir 5*
Altara Group - North Haven, CT - *BoPubDir 4, 5*
Altavista Journal - Altavista, VA - *AyerDirPub 83; BaconPubCkNews 84; Ed&PubIntYB 82; NewsDir 84*
Altek Corp. - Silver Spring, MD - *DataDirSup 7-83*
Alten, Cohen & Naish Inc. - *See* Morgan, Cohen & Nash
Alter Associates Research Co., M. W. - Stamford, CT - *IntDirMarRes 83*
Altergo Products Inc. - Woburn, MA - *DataDirSup 7-83*
Alternate Energy Publishing - Albuquerque, NM - *BoPubDir 4, 5*
Alternate Media Center [of New York University] - New York, NY - *TeleSy&SerDir 7-83; VideoDir 82-83*
Alternate Source - Lansing, MI - *MicrocomMPl 83, 84; WhoWMicrocom 83*
Alternate World Simulations - Milpitas, CA - *MicrocomMPl 83*
Alternative Energy - Beverly Hills, CA - *BaconPubCkMag 84*
Alternative Energy Retailer - Waterbury, CT - *BaconPubCkMag 84*
Alternative Magazine - New Brunswick, NJ - *MagDir 84*
Alternative Magazine, The [of Alternative Publications Inc.] - Indianapolis, IN - *WritMar 84*
Alternative Media [of Alternative Press Syndicate] - New York, NY - *LitMag&SmPr 83-84; MagIndMarPl 82-83*
Alternative Music Productions Inc. - Los Angeles, CA - *BillIntBG 83-84*
Alternative Press Syndicate - New York, NY - *BoPubDir 4 Sup, 5; Ed&PubIntYB 82; LitMag&SmPr 83-84*
Alternative Press, The - Grindstone City, MI - *LitMag&SmPr 83-84*
Alternative Research - New York, NY - *LitMarPl 83, 84*
Alternative Software Inc. - Cherry Hill, NJ - *MicrocomSwDir 1*
Alternative Sources of Energy - Milaca, MN - *BaconPubCkMag 84; LitMag&SmPr 83-84; MagDir 84; MagIndMarPl 82-83; WritMar 84*
Alternatives: Perspectives in Society and Environment - Peterborough, ON, Canada - *LitMag&SmPr 83-84*
Alternologies - Ft. Collins, CO - *MicrocomMPl 84*
Altertext - Boston, MA - *DirInfWP 82*
Altertext Report, The - Boston, MA - *DirOnDB Spring 84*
Altertext Systems Inc. - Boston, MA - *DirInfWP 82*
Altman & Weil Report to Legal Management [of NewsNet Inc.] - Bryn Mawr, PA - *DataDirOnSer 84*
Altman & Weil Report to Legal Management, The - Ardmore, PA - *DirOnDB Spring 84; WritMar 84*
Altman Communications Research, Herb - Port Washington, NY - *BrCabYB 84; IntDirMarRes 83; Tel&CabFB 84C*
Altman-Hall Associates - Erie, PA - *StaDirAdAg 2-84*
Altman Information Systems - Chicago, IL - *DataDirOnSer 84; EISS 7-83 Sup*
Altman Stoller Weiss Advertising Inc. - New York, NY - *BrCabYB 84*
Alto Herald - Alto, TX - *BaconPubCkNews 84; Ed&PubIntYB 82*
Alton Citizen - Alton, IL - *AyerDirPub 83; BaconPubCkNews 84; Ed&PubIntYB 82; NewsDir 84*
Alton South Missourian-Democrat - Alton, MO - *BaconPubCkNews 84*
Alton Telegraph - Alton, IL - *BaconPubCkNews 84; Ed&PubIntYB 82; NewsDir 84*
Altoona American - *See* American Newspapers
Altoona Herald-Mitchellville Index - Altoona, IA - *AyerDirPub 83; BaconPubCkNews 84; Ed&PubIntYB 82*
Altoona Herald, The - Altoona, IA - *NewsDir 84*

Altoona Labor-Telegram - *See* American Newspapers
Altoona Mirror - Altoona, PA - *BaconPubCkNews 84; Ed&PubIntYB 82; NewsDir 84*
Altos Computer Systems - San Jose, CA - *DataDirSup 7-83; WhoWMicrocom 83*
Altos Computer Systems - Santa Clara, CA - *DirInfWP 82*
Altro TV Cable - Altro, KY - *BrCabYB 84*
Altro TV Inc. - Altro, KY - *Tel&CabFB 84C*
Altschiller Reitzfeld Solin Advertising - New York, NY - *AdAge 3-28-84; ArtMar 84; StaDirAdAg 2-84*
Alturas Modoc County Record - Alturas, CA - *BaconPubCkNews 84; NewsDir 84*
Altus Times - Altus, OK - *BaconPubCkNews 84; Ed&PubIntYB 82; NewsDir 84*
Altwerger & Co. Inc., Nicholas H. - Southfield, MI - *LitMarPl 83, 84*
Aluminum Association Inc. - Washington, DC - *BoPubDir 5*
Aluminum Forecast - Bala Cynwyd, PA - *DirOnDB Spring 84*
Aluminum Forecasts [of Chase Econometrics/Interactive Data Corp.] - Waltham, MA - *DataDirOnSer 84*
Aluminum Light [of Merkle Press] - St. Louis, MO - *NewsDir 84*
Aluminum Mill Forecast [of Chase Econometrics/Interactive Data Corp.] - Waltham, MA - *DataDirOnSer 84*
Aluminum Workers News [of Local 3911 U.S.W.A.] - Chicago, IL - *NewsDir 84*
Alura: Poetry Quarterly - Livonia, MI - *WritMar 84*
Alva Community TV Inc. - Alva, OK - *BrCabYB 84; Tel&CabFB 84C*
Alva Museum Replicas Inc. - Long Island City, NY - *ArtMar 84*
Alva Records - Los Angeles, CA - *BillIntBG 83-84*
Alva Review-Courier - Alva, OK - *BaconPubCkNews 84; NewsDir 84*
Alva Woods County News - Alva, OK - *BaconPubCkNews 84*
Alvarado Bulletin - Alvarado, TX - *BaconPubCkNews 84; Ed&PubIntYB 82*
Alvarado Cable TV Inc. [of Stephen Cable TV Inc.] - Alvarado, MN - *BrCabYB 84*
Alvera Publishing Co. - Tulsa, OK - *BillIntBG 83-84*
Alvin Journal - *See* Fig Leaf Publishing Co.
Alvin Sun [of Alvin Newspapers Inc.] - Alvin, TX - *AyerDirPub 83; BaconPubCkNews 84; Ed&PubIntYB 82; NewsDir 84*
Alvord News - Alvord, TX - *BaconPubCkNews 84; Ed&PubIntYB 82*
Alyson Publications - Boston, MA - *BoPubDir 4, 4 Sup, 5; LitMag&SmPr 83-84; LitMarPl 83, 84; WritMar 84*
Alyssa Records - East Norwich, NY - *BillIntBG 83-84*
AM Books [Aff. of All-Media Services] - Sherman Oaks, CA - *BoPubDir 4, 4 Sup, 5*
AM Cable TV Industries Inc. - Coopersburg, PA - *HomeVid&CabYB 82-83*
AM Cable TV Industries Inc. - Quakertown, PA - *CabTVFinDB 83*
A.M. Electronics - Ann Arbor, MI - *MicrocomMPl 84*
Am-Fem Co. - New York, NY - *BoPubDir 5*
AM International (Bruning Micrographics Div.) - Itasca, IL - *DirInfWP 82*
AM International (ECRM Div.) - Bedford, MA - *DirInfWP 82*
AM International (Multigraphics Div.) - Mt. Prospect, IL - *DirInfWP 82*
AM International Inc. - Chicago, IL - *DataDirSup 7-83*
AM International Inc. (Varityper Div.) - East Hanover, NJ - *DirInfWP 82*
AM Jacquard Systems Inc. - *See* ATV Jacquard Systems Inc.
Am-Pol Eagle [of Buffalo Standard Printing Corp.] - Buffalo, NY - *NewsDir 84*
Am Records of America - Virginia Beach, VA - *BillIntBG 83-84*
Am Rus Literary Agency - New York, NY - *LitMarPl 83, 84*
AMA Book Club [Div. of American Management Associations] - New York, NY - *LitMarPl 83, 84*
AMA Management Digest [Div. of American Management Associations] - New York, NY - *MagIndMarPl 82-83*
AMA Management Library for Growing Cos., The [Div. of American Management Associations] - New York, NY - *LitMarPl 83*
AMA/NET [of American Medical Association] - Chicago, IL - *EISS 7-83 Sup*
AMA/NET Disease Information Base [of American Medical Association] - Chicago, IL - *DataDirOnSer 84; DirOnDB Spring 84*
AMA/NET Drug Information Base [of American Medical Association] - Chicago, IL - *DataDirOnSer 84; DirOnDB Spring 84*
AMA/NET EMPIRES - Amsterdam, Netherlands - *DirOnDB Spring 84*
AMA/NET Medical Procedure & Service Information Base [of American Medical Association] - Chicago, IL - *DataDirOnSer 84*
AMA/NET Medical Procedure Coding & Nomenclature - Chicago, IL - *DirOnDB Spring 84*
AMA/NET Socio-Economic Bibliographic Information Base [of American Medical Association] - Chicago, IL - *DataDirOnSer 84; DirOnDB Spring 84*
Amachrist Music - *See* Funky but Music Inc.
AMACOM Book Div. [of American Management Associations] - New York, NY - *LitMarPl 83, 84*
Amadeo-Brio Music - *See* Funky but Music Inc.
Amadeo Concha Press - Lawrence, KS - *BoPubDir 4 Sup, 5*
Amadeus Music Co. - New York, NY - *BillIntBG 83-84*
Amador Dispatch - Jackson, CA - *AyerDirPub 83; Ed&PubIntYB 82*
Amador Ledger - Jackson, CA - *AyerDirPub 83*
Amador Ledger - Shawinigan, CA - *Ed&PubIntYB 82*
Amador Progress-News - Ione, CA - *AyerDirPub 83; Ed&PubIntYB 82; NewsDir 84*
Amalgamated Publishers Inc. - New York, NY - *LitMarPl 83*
Amalgamated Tulip Corp. [Div. of Saturn Industries Inc.] - Libertyville, IL - *BillIntBG 83-84*
Amana Society Service Co. (Telephone Div.) - Amana, IA - *TelDir&BG 83-84*
Amaray Sales Corp. - Los Altos, CA - *AvMarPl 83; DirInfWP 82; WhoWMicrocom 83*
Amarillo Daily News [of Southwestern Newspapers] - Amarillo, TX - *BaconPubCkNews 84; Ed&PubIntYB 82; LitMarPl 83, 84; NewsDir 84*
Amarillo Globe-News [of Southwestern Newspapers] - Amarillo, TX - *NewsDir 84*
Amarillo Globe Times - Amarillo, TX - *BaconPubCkNews 84; Ed&PubIntYB 82; LitMarPl 83, 84*
Amarillo Sunday News-Globe - Amarillo, TX - *Ed&PubIntYB 82; LitMarPl 83, 84*
Amarta Press - West Franklin, NH - *BoPubDir 4, 5*
Amaryllis Press Inc. - New York, NY - *BoPubDir 5*
Amateur Athletic Union of the United States (AAU Publications Group) - Indianapolis, IN - *BoPubDir 4, 5*
Amateur Boxer, The [of Taylor Publishing Corp.] - Cobalt, CT - *MagDir 84; WritMar 84*
Amaturo Group Inc. - Ft. Lauderdale, FL - *BrCabYB 84*
Amazing [of Dragon Publishing] - Lake Geneva, WI - *WritMar 84*
Amazing Cinema - Baltimore, MD - *BaconPubCkMag 84*
Amazing Records - Ft. Worth, TX - *BillIntBG 83-84*
Amazon - Milwaukee, WI - *LitMag&SmPr 83-84*
Ambar Database [of American Bar Association] - Chicago, IL - *DirOnDB Spring 84; EISS 5-84 Sup*
Ambassador Advertising Associates Inc. - Paramus, NJ - *StaDirAdAg 2-84*
Ambassador Book Service - Hempstead, NY - *LitMarPl 83, 84*
Ambassador Book Service Inc. - Jericho, NY - *LitMarPl 84*
Ambassador Publications - Clearwater, FL - *BoPubDir 4, 5*
Ambassador Report - Pasadena, CA - *LitMag&SmPr 83-84*
Amber Pass Music Inc. - *See* Big Seven Music Corp.
Amber Publishing Corp. - New York, NY - *BoPubDir 4, 5*
Amber Records - Redford, MI - *BillIntBG 83-84*
Amber Ways Music - *See* Americus Music
Amberley Associates - Cincinnati, OH - *CabTVFinDB 83*
Amberley Greeting Card Co. - Cincinnati, OH - *WritMar 84*
Ambiance Analysis - Hunsdale, IL - *WhoWMicrocom 83*
Ambient Sound Records Inc. - Queens, NY - *BillIntBG 83-84*
Ambiente Environmental Concerns - San Antonio, TX - *BoPubDir 4, 5*
Ambiente Music Productions Inc. - Los Angeles, CA - *BillIntBG 83-84*
Ambit - London, England - *LitMag&SmPr 83-84*

Ambler Gazette [of Montgomery Publishing Co.] - Ambler, PA - *Ed&PubIntYB 82; NewsDir 84*
Ambler Gazette - *See* Montgomery Publishing Co.
Amboy Country Times - Amboy, MN - *BaconPubCkNews 84*
Amboy News - Amboy, IL - *BaconPubCkNews 84; Ed&PubIntYB 82*
Ambrose, Carr Deforest & Linton Ltd. - Toronto, ON, Canada - *StaDirAdAg 2-84*
Amburgey, Cullen - Switzer, WV - *Tel&CabFB 84C p.1664*
AMCO International Inc. - Staten Island, NY - *BoPubDir 4, 5*
Amcodyne Inc. - Longmont, CO - *MicrocomMPl 84*
Amcom Inc. - Atlanta, GA - *CabTVFinDB 83*
Amcomp - Sunnyvale, CA - *DirInfWP 82*
AMCOR Computer Corp. - Louisville, KY - *ADAPSOMemDir 83-84*
AMCOR Systems Inc. - Fountain Valley, CA - *MicrocomMPl 84*
Amcorp Ltd. - Huntington Station, NY - *LitMarPl 83, 84*
Amdahl Communications Systems Div. [of Amdahl Corp.] - Marina del Rey, CA - *DataDirSup 7-83; TeleSy&SerDir 7-83*
Amdahl Corp. - Sunnyvale, CA - *DataDirSup 7-83; Datamation 6-83; Top100Al 83*
Amdax Corp. - Bohemia, NY - *DirInfWP 82*
Amdek Corp. - Elk Grove Village, IL - *MicrocomMPl 84; WhoWMicrocom 83*
Amdur, Sidney - Chicago, IL - *BoPubDir 5*
A.M.E. Zion Publishing House [Aff. of African Methodist Episcopal Zion Church] - Charlotte, NC - *BoPubDir 4, 5*
Ameco Publishing Corp. - Williston Park, NY - *BoPubDir 4, 5; LitMarPl 84*
Amelia & Associates Inc., William - Baltimore, MD - *DirPRFirms 83*
Amelia Bulletin Monitor - Amelia Court House, VA - *AyerDirPub 83; Ed&PubIntYB 82*
Amelia Telephone Corp. [Aff. of Telephone & Data Systems Inc./SE] - Amelia, VA - *TelDir&BG 83-84*
Amen & Associates, Robert - Greenwich, CT - *DirPRFirms 83*
Amen Publishing Co. - Arcadia, CA - *BoPubDir 4, 5; LitMag&SmPr 83-84*
Amenia Harlem Valley Times - Amenia, NY - *BaconPubCkNews 84*
Amer-O-Matic Corp. - Birmingham, AL - *DirInfWP 82*
Amerad Advertising Services Inc. - Elgin, IL - *StaDirAdAg 2-84*
Amereon House [Subs. of Amereon Ltd.] - Mattituck, NY - *LitMarPl 84*
Amereon Ltd. - Mattituck, NY - *LitMarPl 83*
America - New York, NY - *BaconPubCkMag 84; MagDir 84; MagIndMarPl 82-83; WritMar 84*
America Herold-Lincoln - Omaha, NE - *Ed&PubIntYB 82*
America: History & Life [of ABC-Clio Inc.] - Santa Barbara, CA - *CompReadDB 82; DataDirOnSer 84; DirOnDB Spring 84; OnBibDB 3*
America Mideast Education & Training Services - Washington, DC - *BoPubDir 4, 5*
America Ukrainian Catholic Daily - Philadelphia, PA - *Ed&PubIntYB 82*
Americable Associates - Homestead, FL - *BrCabYB 84*
Americable Associates - Miami, FL - *Tel&CabFB 84C p.1664*
Americable Inc. - Merrimack, NH - *BrCabYB 84 p.D-297; Tel&CabFB 84C p.1664*
Americable of Greater Miami - Miami, FL - *Tel&CabFB 84C*
Americable U.S.A. Inc. - North Baltimore, OH - *BrCabYB 84*
American - San Bernardino, CA - *Ed&PubIntYB 82*
American [of American-Republican Inc.] - Waterbury, CT - *NewsDir 84*
American - Weiser, ID - *AyerDirPub 83*
American - West Frankfort, IL - *AyerDirPub 83*
American - Brookville, IN - *AyerDirPub 83*
American - Gary, IN - *AyerDirPub 83*
American - Ellsworth, ME - *AyerDirPub 83*
American - Hattiesburg, MS - *AyerDirPub 83; Ed&PubIntYB 82*
American - Mineola, NY - *AyerDirPub 83*
American - Lakota, ND - *AyerDirPub 83*
American - Afton, OK - *AyerDirPub 83*
American - Antlers, OK - *AyerDirPub 83*
American - El Reno, OK - *AyerDirPub 83*
American - Shawnee, OK - *AyerDirPub 83*
American - Stroud, OK - *AyerDirPub 83*
American - Talihina, OK - *AyerDirPub 83*
American - Altoona, PA - *AyerDirPub 83*
American - Brookville, PA - *AyerDirPub 83*
American - Somerset, PA - *AyerDirPub 83*
American - Odessa, TX - *AyerDirPub 83*
American - Stamford, TX - *AyerDirPub 83*
American Academic Association for Peace in the Middle East [Aff. of Transaction Periodical Consortium] - New York, NY - *BoPubDir 4, 5*
American Academy of Allergy & Immunology - Milwaukee, WI - *BoPubDir 5*
American Advertising Co. of Elgin, The - Elgin, IL - *StaDirAdAg 2-84*
American Advertising Services - Philadelphia, PA - *ArtMar 84; StaDirAdAg 2-84*
American Aeronaut - Burbank, CA - *NewsDir 84*
American Agent & Broker - St. Louis, MO - *BaconPubCkMag 84; MagDir 84; MagIndMarPl 82-83*
American Agricultural Economics Documentation Center [of U.S. Dept. of Agriculture] - Washington, DC - *CompReadDB 82; EISS 83*
American Agriculturist & The Rural New Yorker - Ithaca, NY - *BaconPubCkMag 84; MagDir 84; MagIndMarPl 82-83*
American Album & Tape Inc. - New York, NY - *BillIntBG 83-84*
American Alliance for Health, Physical Education, Recreation, & Dance - Reston, VA - *LitMarPl 83, 84*
American Alpine Club, The - New York, NY - *LitMarPl 83, 84*
American Analysis Corp. - Mill Valley, CA - *WhoWMicrocom 83*
American Angus Association - St. Joseph, MO - *BoPubDir 4, 5*
American Animation Inc. - Moorestown, NJ - *AvMarPl 83*
American Annals of the Deaf - Silver Spring, MD - *MagDir 84; MagIndMarPl 82-83*
American Anthropologist - Washington, DC - *MagIndMarPl 82-83*
American Antiquarian Society - Worcester, MA - *BoPubDir 4, 5*
American Antiquity - Washington, DC - *MagIndMarPl 82-83*
American Apparel Manufacturers Association - Arlington, VA - *BoPubDir 4, 5*
American Appraisal Associates Ltd. - Milwaukee, WI - *DataDirOnSer 84*
American-Arab Message - Detroit, MI - *Ed&PubIntYB 82*
American-Arab Message - Highland Park, MI - *NewsDir 84*
American Archivist, The - Chicago, IL - *BaconPubCkMag 84; MagDir 84; MagIndMarPl 82-83*
American Art Journal, The [of Kennedy Galleries Inc.] - New York, NY - *WritMar 84*
American Artist [of Billboard Publishing Inc.] - New York, NY - *ArtMar 84; BaconPubCkMag 84; LitMarPl 83, 84; MagDir 84; MagIndMarPl 82-83*
American Artist Book Club - *See* Watson-Guptill Book Clubs
American Artist Business Letter - New York, NY - *MagIndMarPl 82-83*
American Arts - New York, NY - *ArtMar 84; BaconPubCkMag 84; WritMar 84*
American Arts Pamphlet Series - Exeter, England - *LitMag&SmPr 83-84*
American Assembly [Aff. of Columbia University] - New York, NY - *BoPubDir 4, 5*
American Assembly of Collegiate Schools of Business - St. Louis, MO - *BoPubDir 4, 5*
American Associated of Diabetes Educators - Pitman, NJ - *BoPubDir 5*
American Associates Inc. - Beverly Hills, CA - *StaDirAdAg 2-84*
American Association for Adult & Continuing Education - Washington, DC - *BoPubDir 4 Sup, 5*
American Association for Counseling & Development - Alexandria, VA - *LitMarPl 84*
American Association for Medical Systems & Informatics - Bethesda, MD - *DataDirOnSer 84; EISS 5-84 Sup*
American Association for State & Local History - Nashville, TN - *BoPubDir 4; LitMarPl 83, 84*
American Association for the Advancement of Science - Washington, DC - *BoPubDir 5; MicroMarPl 82-83*
American Association for the Advancement of Science (Pacific Div.) - San Francisco, CA - *BoPubDir 5*
American Association of Avian Pathologists - Kennett Square, PA - *BoPubDir 4, 5*

American Association of Bible Colleges - Fayetteville, AR - *BoPubDir 5*
American Association of Blood Banks - Washington, DC - *BoPubDir 4, 5*
American Association of Cereal Chemists - St. Paul, MN - *BoPubDir 4, 5*
American Association of Colleges of Pharmacy - Bethesda, MD - *BoPubDir 4 Sup, 5*
American Association of Community & Junior Colleges - Washington, DC - *BoPubDir 4*
American Association of Community & Junior Colleges - Alexandria, VA - *BoPubDir 5*
American Association of Cost Engineers - Morgantown, WV - *BoPubDir 4, 5*
American Association of Engineering Societies - New York, NY - *BoPubDir 4, 5*
American Association of Health Data Systems - Cleveland, OH - *EISS 83*
American Association of Law Libraries - Chicago, IL - *BoPubDir 4, 5; EISS 83*
American Association of Nurserymen - Washington, DC - *BoPubDir 5*
American Association of Petroleum Geologists Explorer - Tulsa, OK - *MagDir 84*
American Association of Physics Teachers [Aff. of American Institute of Physics] - Stony Brook, NY - *BoPubDir 5*
American Association of Retired Persons - Washington, DC - *Ed&PubIntYB 82*
American Association of School Administrators - Arlington, VA - *BoPubDir 4, 5*
American Association of University Women - Washington, DC - *BoPubDir 4, 5*
American Association on Mental Deficiency - Washington, DC - *BoPubDir 4 Sup, 5*
American Astrology [of Clancy Publications Inc.] - Tucson, AZ - *ArtMar 84; MagIndMarPl 82-83; WritMar 84*
American Astronautical Society - San Diego, CA - *MicroMarPl 82-83; WritMar 84*
American Atheist [of Gustav Broukal Press] - Austin, TX - *ArtMar 84; MagDir 84; WritMar 84*
American Atheist Press [Aff. of Society of Separationists Inc.] - Austin, TX - *BoPubDir 4, 5; WritMar 84*
American Audio Visual Inc. - New York, NY - *Ed&PubIntYB 82*
American Automated - Deland, FL - *DataDirOnSer 84*
American Automatic Merchandiser [of Harcourt Brace Jovanovich] - Chicago, IL - *MagDir 84*
American Automatic Merchandiser - Middleburg Heights, OH - *BaconPubCkMag 84*
American Avicultural Art & Science Inc. - St. Louis, MO - *WhoWMicrocom 83*
American Baby - New York, NY - *BaconPubCkMag 84; Folio 83; MagDir 84; MagIndMarPl 82-83; WritMar 84*
American Baby Books [of Harlequin Enterprises] - Milwaukee, WI - *LitMarPl 83, 84; WritMar 84*
American Banker [of International Thomson Holdings Inc.] - New York, NY - *BaconPubCkMag 84; BoPubDir 5; DirMarMP 83; DirOnDB Spring 84; Ed&PubIntYB 82; Folio 83; InfoS 83-84; MagDir 84; NewsBur 6; NewsDir 84; WritMar 84*
American Banker [of NewsNet Inc.] - Bryn Mawr, PA - *DataDirOnSer 84*
American Banker Index [of Bell & Howell Co.] - Wooster, OH - *DataDirOnSer 84; DBBus 82*
American Baptist Churches in the USA - Valley Forge, PA - *MagIndMarPl 82-83*
American Baptist Historical Society [Aff. of American Baptist Churches of United States of America] - Rochester, NY - *BoPubDir 4, 5; MicroMarPl 82-83*
American Baptist, The [of American Baptist Churches, USA] - Valley Forge, PA - *ArtMar 84; LitMarPl 83, 84; MagIndMarPl 82-83*
American Bar Association - Chicago, IL - *BoPubDir 5; DataDirOnSer 84; MagIndMarPl 82-83*
American Bar Association (Committee on Continuing Professional Education) - *See* American Law Institute/American Committee on Continuing Professional Education
American Bar Association Journal [of The American Bar Association] - Chicago, IL - *BaconPubCkMag 84; Folio 83; MagDir 84; MagIndMarPl 82-83*
American Bar Association Press - Chicago, IL - *BoPubDir 4*
American Bar Foundation - Chicago, IL - *LitMarPl 83, 84*
American Bed & Breakfast Inc. - St. Albans, VT - *BoPubDir 5*
American Bee Journal - Hamilton, IL - *BaconPubCkMag 84; MagDir 84; MagIndMarPl 82-83; WritMar 84*
American Bell - Morristown, NJ - *InfoS 83-84*
American Bible Society - New York, NY - *LitMarPl 83, 84*
American Bible Society Record - New York, NY - *ArtMar 84; MagDir 84; MagIndMarPl 82-83*
American Biblical Encyclopedia Society - Monsey, NY - *BoPubDir 4, 5*
American Bibliographical Center [of ABC-Clio Inc.] - Santa Barbara, CA - *CompReadDB 82; EISS 83*
American Bicyclist & Motorcyclist - New York, NY - *BaconPubCkMag 84; MagDir 84; WritMar 84*
American Bindery Co. Inc. - Charlotte, NC - *LitMarPl 83, 84*
American Biographical Center - Williamsburg, VA - *BoPubDir 4, 5*
American Biology Teacher - Reston, VA - *MagDir 84*
American Biology Teacher, The - Laramie, WY - *BaconPubCkMag 84*
American Birds [of National Audubon Society] - New York, NY - *ArtMar 84; MagIndMarPl 82-83*
American Boat & Yacht Council Inc. - Amityville, NY - *BoPubDir 4, 5*
American Book Center - Brooklyn, NY - *LitMarPl 83, 84*
American Book Collector [of The Moretus Press Inc.] - New York, NY - *LitMag&SmPr 83-84; LitMarPl 83, 84; MagIndMarPl 82-83; WritMar 84*
American Book Exports - Los Altos, CA - *LitMarPl 83, 84*
American Book Review, The - New York, NY - *LitMag&SmPr 83-84*
American Book-Stratford Press Inc. - Saddle Brook, NJ - *LitMarPl 83*
American Bookdealers Exchange - La Mesa, CA - *DirMarMP 83; LitMag&SmPr 83-84*
American Books International - New York, NY - *LitMarPl 84*
American Bookseller [of Booksellers Publishing Inc.] - New York, NY - *ArtMar 84; BaconPubCkMag 84; LitMarPl 83, 84; MagIndMarPl 82-83; WritMar 84*
American Brahman Breeders Association - Houston, TX - *BoPubDir 5*
American Brewer - Kearny, NJ - *MagDir 84*
American Brittany, The - Ft. Worth, TX - *MagDir 84*
American Broadcasting Cos. - New York, NY - *AdAge 6-28-84; BrCabYB 84; HomeVid&CabYB 82-83; KnowInd 83; LitMarPl 83, 84; TelAl 83, 84; Tel&CabFB 84C, 84S*
American Broadcasting Music Inc. - Los Angeles, CA - *BillIntBG 83-84*
American Building Supplies [of W. R. C. Smith Publishing Co.] - Atlanta, GA - *MagDir 84*
American Building Supplies - New York, NY - *BaconPubCkMag 84; MagIndMarPl 82-83*
American Bureau of Metal Statistics Inc. - New York, NY - *BoPubDir 4, 5*
American Business [of Avant-Garde Media Inc.] - New York, NY - *BaconPubCkMag 84; DirMarMP 83; LitMarPl 83, 84; MagDir 84; MagIndMarPl 82-83*
American Business & Professional Computer Stores - Tampa, FL - *MicrocomMPl 84*
American Business Communication Association - Urbana, IL - *BoPubDir 4, 5*
American Business Consultants - Chambersburg, PA - *MagIndMarPl 82-83*
American Business Consultants Inc. - Sunnyvale, CA - *BoPubDir 4, 5; LitMag&SmPr 83-84; LitMarPl 84*
American Business Network [of U.S. Chamber of Commerce] - Washington, DC - *BrCabYB 84; TeleSy&SerDir 7-83*
American Business Systems - Richmond, VA - *DirInfWP 82*
American Business Systems Inc. - Westford, MA - *MicrocomMPl 83, 84; MicrocomSwDir 1; WhoWMicrocom 83*
American Buyer's Review [of Lott Publishing Co.] - Santa Monica, CA - *BaconPubCkMag 84; MagDir 84*
American Bystander, The - New York, NY - *WritMar 84*

American Cable Network Inc. - Traverse City, MI - *Tel&CabFB 84C*
American Cable Television Inc. [of Times Mirror Cable Television Inc.] - Phoenix, AZ - *BrCabYB 84 p.D-297; Tel&CabFB 84C p.1664*
American Cable Television Inc. - Tempe, AZ - *BrCabYB 84*
American Cable TV [of American Cablesystems Corp.] - Pompano Beach, FL - *BrCabYB 84*
American Cable TV [of American Cablesystems Corp.] - Tamarac, FL - *BrCabYB 84*
American Cable TV Investors [of Daniels & Associates] - Hanford, CA - *BrCabYB 84; Tel&CabFB 84C*
American Cable TV Investors - Denver, CO - *Tel&CabFB 84C p.1664*
American Cable TV Investors - Gainesville, GA - *Tel&CabFB 84C*
American Cable TV Investors - Asheville, NC - *BrCabYB 84; Tel&CabFB 84C*
American Cablesystems Corp. - Beverly, MA - *BrCabYB 84 p.D-297; CabTVFinDB 83*
American Cablesystems Corp. - Boston, MA - *Tel&CabFB 84C p.1664*
American Cablesystems Corp. - Marion, MA - *Tel&CabFB 84C*
American Cablesystems Corp. - Erwin, TN - *Tel&CabFB 84C*
American Cablesystems Corp. - Greeneville, TN - *Tel&CabFB 84C*
American Cablesystems Corp. - Galax, VA - *Tel&CabFB 84C*
American Cablesystems of NY Inc. - Tarrytown, NY - *Tel&CabFB 84C*
American Cablesystems of Tennessee - Hampton, TN - *BrCabYB 84*
American Cablesystems of Tennessee - Washington County, TN - *BrCabYB 84*
American Cablesystems of Tennessee Inc. - Johnson City, TN - *BrCabYB 84; Tel&CabFB 84C*
American Cablesystems of Tennessee Inc. - Mountain City, TN - *BrCabYB 84*
American Cablesystems of Virginia Inc. - Abingdon, VA - *BrCabYB 84*
American Cablesystems of Virginia Inc. - Chilhowie, VA - *BrCabYB 84*
American Cablesystems of Virginia Inc. - Galax, VA - *BrCabYB 84*
American Cablesystems of Virginia Inc. - Honaker, VA - *BrCabYB 84*
American Cablesystems of Virginia Inc. - Independence, VA - *Tel&CabFB 84C*
American Cablesystems of Virginia Inc. - Lebanon, VA - *BrCabYB 84*
American Cablesystems of Virginia Inc. - Saltville, VA - *BrCabYB 84*
American Cablesystems of Virginia Inc. - St. Paul, VA - *BrCabYB 84*
American Cablevision [Aff. of American Television & Communications Corp.] - South Pasadena, CA - *InterCabHB 3*
American Cablevision [of American Television & Communications Corp.] - Terre Haute, IN - *BrCabYB 84; Tel&CabFB 84C*
American Cablevision [of Alda Communications Corp. of Pennsylvania] - Aston, PA - *BrCabYB 84*
American Cablevision Co. [of Group W Cable] - Lewiston, ID - *BrCabYB 84*
American Cablevision Corp. [of Brazoria Cablevision Inc.] - Angleton, TX - *BrCabYB 84*
American Cablevision Corp. - Bellville, TX - *BrCabYB 84*
American Cablevision Corp. - Bryan, TX - *BrCabYB 84*
American Cablevision Corp. [of Southern Cablevision Corp.] - Buffalo, TX - *Tel&CabFB 84C*
American Cablevision Corp. [of Southern Cablevision Corp.] - Cleveland, TX - *Tel&CabFB 84C*
American Cablevision Corp. - Hempstead, TX - *BrCabYB 84; Tel&CabFB 84C*
American Cablevision Corp. [of Southern Cablevision Corp.] - Jasper, TX - *BrCabYB 84; Tel&CabFB 84C*
American Cablevision Corp. [of Southern Cablevision Corp.] - Madisonville, TX - *BrCabYB 84; Tel&CabFB 84C*
American Cablevision Corp. [of Southern Cablevision Corp.] - Woodville, TX - *BrCabYB 84; Tel&CabFB 84C*
American Cablevision Corp. of Angleton [of Southern Cablevision Corp.] - Angleton, TX - *Tel&CabFB 84C*
American Cablevision Corp. of Bellville [of Southern Cablevision Corp.] - Bellville, TX - *Tel&CabFB 84C*
American Cablevision Corp. of Kingsville [of Southern Cablevision Corp.] - Kingsville, TX - *BrCabYB 84; Tel&CabFB 84C*
American Cablevision Corp. of Sealy [of Southern Cablevision Corp.] - Sealy, TX - *Tel&CabFB 84C*
American Cablevision Inc. - Rio Rico, AZ - *BrCabYB 84*
American Cablevision of Asheboro [of American Television & Communications Corp.] - Asheboro, NC - *BrCabYB 84; InterCabHB 3*
American Cablevision of Coronado (San Diego Div.) - Coronado, CA - *Tel&CabFB 84C*
American Cablevision of Cushing [of American Television & Communications Corp.] - Cushing, OK - *BrCabYB 84*
American Cablevision of Indianapolis Inc. - Indianapolis, IN - *BrCabYB 84; Tel&CabFB 84C*
American Cablevision of Kansas City [Aff. of American Television & Communications Corp.] - Kansas City, MO - *BrCabYB 84; InterCabHB 3; Tel&CabFB 84C*
American Cablevision of Littleton [of American Television & Communications Corp.] - Littleton, CO - *BrCabYB 84; InterCabHB 3; Tel&CabFB 84C*
American Cablevision of Monroeville [of American Television & Communications Corp.] - Monroeville, PA - *Tel&CabFB 84C*
American Cablevision of Northglenn [of American Television & Communications Corp.] - Northglenn, CO - *BrCabYB 84; Tel&CabFB 84C*
American Cablevision of Orange [of American Television & Communications Corp.] - Orange, CA - *BrCabYB 84; Tel&CabFB 84C*
American Cablevision of Pennsylvania Inc. [of American Television & Communications Corp.] - Delaware County, PA - *BrCabYB 84*
American Cablevision of Pennsylvania Inc. [of American Television & Communications Corp.] - Wallingford, PA - *Tel&CabFB 84C*
American Cablevision of Rochester [of American Television & Communications Corp.] - Rochester, NY - *BrCabYB 84*
American Cablevision of Rochester Suburbs - Pittsford, NY - *Tel&CabFB 84C*
American Cablevision of San Marino [of American Television & Communications Corp.] - San Marino, CA - *BrCabYB 84; Tel&CabFB 84C*
American Cablevision of South Pasadena - South Pasadena, CA - *BrCabYB 84; Tel&CabFB 84C*
American Cablevision of St. Louis [of American Television & Communications Corp.] - Ferguson, MO - *BrCabYB 84; Tel&CabFB 84C*
American Cablevision of St. Louis [of American Television & Communications Corp.] - St. Louis County, MO - *BrCabYB 84*
American Cablevision of Thornton Inc. [of American Television & Communications Corp.] - Thornton, CO - *BrCabYB 84; Tel&CabFB 84C*
American Cablevision of Webster [of American Television & Communications Corp.] - Webster, NY - *BrCabYB 84; Tel&CabFB 84C*
American Cablevision of West Memphis [Aff. of American Television & Communications Corp.] - West Memphis, AR - *BrCabYB 84; InterCabHB 3; Tel&CabFB 84C*
American Cablevision of Wheat Ridge Inc. [of American Television & Communications Corp.] - Wheat Ridge, CO - *BrCabYB 84; Tel&CabFB 84C*
American Cablevision Services [of GAC Properties Inc.] - Rio Rico, AZ - *Tel&CabFB 84C*
American Cablevision Services [of GAC Properties Inc.] - Barefoot Bay, FL - *Tel&CabFB 84C*
American Cablevision Services [of Cablevision Industries Inc.] - Golden Gate, FL - *BrCabYB 84; Tel&CabFB 84C*
American Cablevision Services [of GAC Properties Inc.] - Poinciana, FL - *BrCabYB 84; Tel&CabFB 84C*
American Cablevision Services Inc. [of Cablevision Industries Inc.] - Cape Coral, FL - *Tel&CabFB 84C*
American Cage-Bird Magazine - Chicago, IL - *BaconPubCkMag 84; MagIndMarPl 82-83*
American Camping Association - Martinsville, IN - *BoPubDir 4, 5*

American Can Co. - Greenwich, CT - *HomeVid&CabYB 82-83*
American-Canadian Publishers Inc. - Portales, NM - *BoPubDir 4, 5; LitMag&SmPr 83-84*
American Canal & Transportation Center - York, PA - *BoPubDir 4, 5*
American Cartographer, The [of American Congress on Surveying] - Falls Church, VA - *BaconPubCkMag 84; MagDir 84*
American Carwash Review [of Lott Publishing Co.] - Santa Monica, CA - *BaconPubCkMag 84; MagDir 84*
American Catholic Philosophical Association - Washington, DC - *BoPubDir 4, 5*
American Catholic Press - Oak Park, IL - *WritMar 84*
American Cemetery - New York, NY - *BaconPubCkMag 84; MagDir 84*
American Ceramic Society - Columbus, OH - *BoPubDir 4, 5*
American Ceramic Society Bulletin - Columbus, OH - *BaconPubCkMag 84; MagDir 84*
American Ceramics - New York, NY - *BaconPubCkMag 84*
American Chemical Machining Co. - Philadelphia, PA - *LitMarPl 83*
American Chemical Society - Washington, DC - *LitMarPl 83, 84; MagIndMarPl 82-83; MicroMarPl 82-83*
American Chemical Society Primary Journal Database - Washington, DC - *DirOnDB Spring 84*
American Chemical Society Primary Journal Database [of Bibliographic Retrieval Services Inc.] - Lathan, NY - *DataDirOnSer 84*
American Chiropractor - Ft. Wayne, IN - *BaconPubCkMag 84*
American Christmas Tree Journal - Milwaukee, WI - *WritMar 84*
American Cinematographer - Hollywood, CA - *BaconPubCkMag 84; MagIndMarPl 82-83; WritMar 84*
American Cinematographer - Los Angeles, CA - *MagDir 84*
American Circle - Chicago, IL - *LitMarPl 83, 84*
American City & County - Pittsfield, MA - *BaconPubCkMag 84; MagDir 84; MagIndMarPl 82-83*
American Classic Screen - Prairie Village, KS - *BaconPubCkMag 84*
American Classic Screen - Shawnee Mission, KS - *ArtMar 84; MagDir 84; MagIndMarPl 82-83*
American Clay Exchange [of Page One Publications] - La Mesa, CA - *WritMar 84*
American Clean Car [of American Trade Magazines Inc.] - Chicago, IL - *BaconPubCkMag 84; MagDir 84; WritMar 84*
American Cleft Palate Association - Pittsburgh, PA - *BoPubDir 5*
American Clinical Products Review - Fairfield, CT - *BaconPubCkMag 84*
American Coin-Op - Chicago, IL - *BaconPubCkMag 84; MagDir 84; WritMar 84*
American Collector - Kermit, TX - *MagDir 84; MagIndMarPl 82-83; WritMar 84*
American Collector - San Marcos, TX - *BaconPubCkMag 84*
American Collector's Journal, The - Kewanee, IL - *MagDir 84*
American College McCahan Foundation - Bryn Mawr, PA - *BoPubDir 4, 5*
American College of Heraldry Inc. - University, AL - *BoPubDir 4, 5*
American College of Nurse-Midwives - Washington, DC - *BoPubDir 4, 5*
American College of Physicians Observer - Philadelphia, PA - *MagDir 84*
American College Testing Program - Iowa City, IA - *BoPubDir 4, 5*
American Colonial Broadcasting Corp. - San Juan, PR - *BrCabYB 84*
American Commercial Enterprises - Westbury, NY - *AvMarPl 83*
American Communication Enterprises - Taylor, MI - *BillIntBG 83-84*
American Communications & Television Inc. - *See* TeleSat Cablevision
American Communications Systems Corp. - *Tel&CabFB 84C*
American Community Cablevision [of American Television & Communications Corp.] - Ithaca, NY - *BrCabYB 84; Tel&CabFB 84C*
American Compass Music - *See* Radmus Publishing Inc.
American Composers Alliance - New York, NY - *BillIntBG 83-84*
American Composers Edition - *See* American Composers Alliance
American CompuSoft - Laguna Hills, CA - *MicrocomMPl 84*
American Computer Development - Bryan, TX - *MicrocomMPl 83*
American Computer Group - Boston, MA - *ADAPSOMemDir 83-84; DataDirSup 7-83; MicrocomMPl 83, 84*
American Computers & Engineers Inc. - Los Angeles, CA - *MicrocomSwDir 1*
American Concrete Institute - Detroit, MI - *BoPubDir 4, 5; MicroMarPl 82-83*
American Conference of Governmental Industrial Hygienists - Cincinnati, OH - *BoPubDir 4, 5*
American Congress on Surveying & Mapping - Falls Church, VA - *BoPubDir 4, 5*
American Conservatory Theatre Magazine - San Francisco, CA - *MagDir 84*
American Consulting Engineers Council - Washington, DC - *BoPubDir 4, 5*
American Correctional Association - College Park, MD - *BoPubDir 4, 5*
American Council for Competitive Telecommunications - Washington, DC - *TeleSy&SerDir 2-84*
American Council for Nationalities Service - New York, NY - *BoPubDir 4, 5*
American Council for the Arts - New York, NY - *BoPubDir 4; LitMarPl 83, 84; WritMar 84*
American Council of Life Insurance/Health Insurance Association of America - Washington, DC - *BoPubDir 5*
American Council of Voluntary Agencies for Foreign Service Inc. (Technical Assistance Information Clearing House) - New York, NY - *BoPubDir 5*
American Council on Education - Washington, DC - *LitMarPl 83, 84*
American Cowboy-Hoof & Horn [of Longhorn Publishing Co.] - Walsenburg, CO - *BaconPubCkMag 84; WritMar 84*
American Cowboy Music Co. - Nashville, TN - *BillIntBG 83-84*
American Cowboy Songs Inc. - Mt. Juliet, TN - *BillIntBG 83-84*
American Craft [of American Craft Council Publishers] - New York, NY - *BaconPubCkMag 84; LitMarPl 83, 84; MagDir 84; MagIndMarPl 82-83; WritMar 84*
American Craft Council - New York, NY - *BoPubDir 4, 5; DirMarMP 83*
American Creative Entertainment Ltd. - Las Vegas, NV - *BillIntBG 83-84*
American Crystallographic Association - New York, NY - *BoPubDir 4, 5*
American Daily Publishing - *Ed&PubIntYB 82*
American Dairy Review - Mt. Morris, IL - *MagDir 84*
American Dance Guild Book Club [Div. of Princeton Book Co.] - Princeton, NJ - *LitMarPl 83*
American Dance Guild Inc. - New York, NY - *LitMag&SmPr 83-84*
American Dance Guild Newsletter - New York, NY - *LitMag&SmPr 83-84*
American Dane Magazine [of Danish Brotherhood in America] - Omaha, NE - *WritMar 84*
American Data Inc. - Citrus Heights, CA - *WhoWMicrocom 83*
American Data Services Inc. - Portland, OR - *DataDirOnSer 84*
American Datacom - Santa Ana, CA - *DataDirSup 7-83*
American Deafness & Rehabilitation Association - Silver Spring, MD - *BoPubDir 4, 5*
American Demographics [of Dow Jones Inc.] - Ithaca, NY - *ArtMar 84; BaconPubCkMag 84; EISS 83; MagDir 84; MagIndMarPl 82-83; WritMar 84*
American Dental Association - Chicago, IL - *BoPubDir 4, 5; MagIndMarPl 82-83*
American Developing Industries - St. Petersburg, FL - *BoPubDir 4, 5*
American Dream - New York, NY - *BillIntBG 83-84*
American Druggist [of The Hearst Corp.] - New York, NY - *BaconPubCkMag 84; MagDir 84; MagIndMarPl 82-83*
American Drycleaner - Chicago, IL - *BaconPubCkMag 84; MagDir 84; WritMar 84*
American Dyestuff Reporter - New York, NY - *BaconPubCkMag 84; MagDir 84*
American Dynamics Corp. - New York, NY - *BoPubDir 4, 5*
American Econo-Clad Books [Div. of American Cos. Inc.] - Topeka, KS - *LitMarPl 84*

American Econo-Clad Services [Div. of The American Cos. Inc.] - Topeka, KS - *BoPubDir 4 Sup, 5; LitMarPl 83, 84*
American Economic Review - Nashville, TN - *MagDir 84*
American Economics Association - Pittsburgh, PA - *CompReadDB 82*
American Education - Washington, DC - *BaconPubCkMag 84; MagDir 84*
American Educational Films Inc. - Nashville, TN - *AvMarPl 83*
American Educational Research Association - Washington, DC - *BoPubDir 4, 5*
American Educational Services Inc. - Lansing, MI - *MagIndMarPl 82-83*
American Educational Television Network - Irvine, CA - *BrCabYB 84*
American Educator - Washington, DC - *BaconPubCkMag 84; MagIndMarPl 82-83*
American Electrodata Inc. - New Brighton, MN - *DirInfWP 82*
American Electronic Supply Inc. [Subs. of Ametron Rents] - Los Angeles, CA - *AvMarPl 83*
American Engineering Model Society - Aiken, SC - *BoPubDir 4, 5*
American Enterprise Institute for Public Policy Research - Washington, DC - *LitMarPl 83, 84*
American Enterprise Publications - Mercer, PA - *BoPubDir 4, 5*
American Enterprise Publishing Inc. - Orlando, FL - *BoPubDir 4, 5*
American Entertainment General - Hollywood, CA - *BillIntBG 83-84*
American Entertainment Industries Inc. - Hollywood, CA - *BillIntBG 83-84*
American Entertainment Marketing - New York, NY - *StaDirAdAg 2-84*
American Entomological Institute - Ann Arbor, MI - *BoPubDir 4, 5*
American Export Marketer - Boca Raton, FL - *BaconPubCkMag 84*
American Express Co. - New York, NY - *AdAge 6-28-84; HomeVid&CabYB 82-83; KnowInd 83; Top100Al 83*
American Express Co. - *See* Warner Amex Cable Communications Inc.
American Fabrics & Fashions - New York, NY - *BaconPubCkMag 84; MagDir 84*
American Falls Cable TV [of King Videocable Co.] - American Falls, ID - *BrCabYB 84*
American Falls Power County Press - American Falls, ID - *BaconPubCkNews 84*
American Family Communiversity Press - Chicago, IL - *BoPubDir 4, 5*
American Family Corp. - Columbus, GA - *Tel&CabFB 84S*
American Family Corp. (Broadcast Div.) - Columbus, GA - *BrCabYB 84*
American Family Physician - Kansas City, MO - *ArtMar 84; BaconPubCkMag 84; MagDir 84; MagIndMarPl 82-83*
American Farm Tribune - Poterville, CA - *BaconPubCkMag 84*
American Features Syndicate - New York, NY - *Ed&PubIntYB 82*
American Federation of Arts - New York, NY - *BoPubDir 4, 5*
American Federation of Astrologers Inc. - Tempe, AZ - *BoPubDir 4, 5*
American Federation of Information Processing Societies Inc. - Arlington, VA - *EISS 83*
American Federation of Musicians - New York, NY - *AvMarPl 83*
American Federation of Television & Radio Artists - New York, NY - *AvMarPl 83*
American Federationist - Washington, DC - *MagIndMarPl 82-83*
American Fern Journal [of American Fern Society Inc.] - Washington, DC - *MagDir 84*
American Field - Chicago, IL - *BaconPubCkMag 84; MagDir 84; MagIndMarPl 82-83; WritMar 84*
American Film [of American Film Institute] - Washington, DC - *BaconPubCkMag 84; LitMarPl 83, 84; MagDir 84; MagIndMarPl 82-83; WritMar 84*
American Film Factory Inc. - Venice, CA - *AvMarPl 83*
American Film Productions - New York, NY - *AvMarPl 83; TelAl 83, 84; Tel&CabFB 84C*
American Firearms Industry - Ft. Lauderdale, FL - *BaconPubCkMag 84; MagDir 84; MagIndMarPl 82-83; WritMar 84*
American First Day Cover Foundation - Elberon, NJ - *BoPubDir 4, 5*
American Flint - Toledo, OH - *NewsDir 84*
American Forestry Association - Washington, DC - *BoPubDir 4, 5*
American Forests [of American Forestry Association] - Washington, DC - *BaconPubCkMag 84; MagDir 84; MagIndMarPl 82-83; WritMar 84*
American Fork Citizen - American Fork, UT - *Ed&PubIntYB 82*
American Fork Citizen - *See* Newtah News Group
American Forum Corp. - Houston, TX - *IntDirMarRes 83*
American Foundation for the Blind Inc. - New York, NY - *BoPubDir 4, 5*
American Foundrymen's Society - Des Plaines, IL - *BoPubDir 4, 5*
American Franklin Corp. (Data Services Div.) - Springfield, IL - *DirInfWP 82*
American Frozen Food Institute [Aff. of National Association of Frozen Food Processors] - McLean, VA - *BoPubDir 5*
American Fruit Grower - Willoughby, OH - *BaconPubCkMag 84; MagDir 84; MagIndMarPl 82-83*
American Funeral Director [of Kates-Boylston Publications Inc.] - New York, NY - *BaconPubCkMag 84; MagDir 84*
American Gage-Bird - Chicago, IL - *MagDir 84*
American Gas Association Monthly - Arlington, VA - *BaconPubCkMag 84; MagDir 84*
American Genealogy Services - Salt Lake City, UT - *BoPubDir 4*
American Geological Institute - Falls Church, VA - *BoPubDir 4, 5; CompReadDB 82; DataDirOnSer 84; InfIndMarPl 83*
American Geophysical Union - Washington, DC - *BoPubDir 4, 5; MagIndMarPl 82-83; MicroMarPl 82-83*
American Glass Review [of Ebel-Doctorow Publications Inc.] - Clifton, NJ - *BaconPubCkMag 84; MagDir 84; WritMar 84*
American Gloxinia & Gesneriad Society - Ayer, MA - *BoPubDir 4*
American Gloxinia & Gesneriad Society - Beverly Farms, MA - *BoPubDir 5*
American Gold News - Ione, CA - *ArtMar 84; BaconPubCkMag 84; MagDir 84; WritMar 84*
American Graphic Services - Plainfield, NJ - *LitMarPl 84*
American Graphic Services - Warren, NJ - *LitMarPl 83*
American Graphics Corp. - Ft. Lauderdale, FL - *LitMarPl 83, 84*
American Graphics Press - Dallas, TX - *MagIndMarPl 82-83*
American Greetings Corp. - Cleveland, OH - *WritMar 84*
American Grocer - Bay Harbor Islands, FL - *BaconPubCkMag 84*
American Grocer [of Grocery Trade Publishing Co.] - Miami, FL - *MagDir 84*
American Group Practice Association - Alexandria, VA - *BoPubDir 5*
American Group Psychotherapy Association Inc. - New York, NY - *BoPubDir 4, 5*
American Guidance Service - Circle Pines, MN - *MicrocomMPl 84*
American Guide Publications Inc. [Aff. of Paul Wallach Enterprises] - Glendale, CA - *BoPubDir 4, 5*
American Guides Inc. - Lighthouse Point, FL - *BoPubDir 4, 5*
American Hairdresser/Salon Owner [of Service Publications Inc.] - New York, NY - *ArtMar 84; BaconPubCkMag 84; MagDir 84; MagIndMarPl 82-83; WritMar 84*
American Hampshire Herdsman - Peoria, IL - *BaconPubCkMag 84; MagDir 84*
American Handgunner - San Diego, CA - *BaconPubCkMag 84; MagDir 84; MagIndMarPl 82-83*
American Harmony Artist - Omaha, NE - *BillIntBG 83-84*
American Health [of American Health Partners] - New York, NY - *BaconPubCkMag 84; Folio 83; WritMar 84*
American Health Care Association Journal - Washington, DC - *BaconPubCkMag 84*
American Health Consultants - Atlanta, GA - *DirMarMP 83*
American Heart Association Inc. - Dallas, TX - *MagIndMarPl 82-83*
American Heart Journal - St. Louis, MO - *BaconPubCkMag 84; MagDir 84; MagIndMarPl 82-83*

American Hereford Journal - Kansas City, MO - *BaconPubCkMag 84; MagDir 84*

American Heritage - New York, NY - *ArtMar 84; LitMarPl 83, 84; MagIndMarPl 82-83; WritMar 84*

American Heritage Cablevision [Aff. of American Television & Communications Corp.] - Council Bluffs, IA - *BrCabYB 84; InterCabHB 3; Tel&CabFB 84C*

American Heritage Library (Picture Collection) - New York, NY - *LitMarPl 83, 84*

American Heritage Publishing Co. Inc. - New York, NY - *DirMarMP 83; LitMarPl 83, 84*

American Hibiscus Society Publications - Pompano Beach, FL - *BoPubDir 4, 5*

American Historical Review - Bloomington, IN - *MagDir 84*

American Historical Review, The - Washington, DC - *MagIndMarPl 82-83*

American Historical Society of Germans from Russia - Lincoln, NE - *BoPubDir 4, 5*

American History Illustrated - Harrisburg, PA - *ArtMar 84; BaconPubCkMag 84; MagDir 84; MagIndMarPl 82-83; WritMar 84*

American Hockey & Arena - Colorado Springs, CO - *BaconPubCkMag 84; MagDir 84; WritMar 84*

American Home Video Library Inc. - New York, NY - *AvMarPl 83*

American Horse Council - Washington, DC - *BoPubDir 5*

American Horticulturist - Alexandria, VA - *BaconPubCkMag 84; MagDir 84*

American Horticulturist - Mt. Vernon, VA - *ArtMar 84; MagIndMarPl 82-83*

American Hospital Association - Chicago, IL - *LitMarPl 83, 84*

American Hotel Association Directory Corp. - New York, NY - *BoPubDir 4, 5*

American Hotel Register Co. - Chicago, IL - *BoPubDir 4, 5*

American Humane Association - Denver, CO - *BoPubDir 5*

American Humane Association - Englewood, CO - *BoPubDir 4*

American Hungarian Review - St. Louis, MO - *BoPubDir 4, 5*

American Hunter [of National Rifle Association] - Washington, DC - *ArtMar 84; BaconPubCkMag 84; MagDir 84; MagIndMarPl 82-83; WritMar 84*

American Import Export Management [of North American Publishing Co.] - Philadelphia, PA - *BaconPubCkMag 84; MagDir 84*

American Indian Art Magazine [of American Indian Art Inc.] - Scottsdale, AZ - *MagIndMarPl 82-83; WritMar 84*

American Indian Basketry - Portland, OR - *LitMag&SmPr 83-84; WritMar 84*

American Indian Culture & Research Journal [of University of California, Los Angeles] - Los Angeles, CA - *LitMag&SmPr 83-84*

American Indian Studies Center [of University of California, Los Angeles] - Los Angeles, CA - *LitMag&SmPr 83-84*

American Industrial Arts Association - Reston, VA - *BoPubDir 4 Sup, 5*

American Industrial Hygiene Association Journal - Akron, OH - *BaconPubCkMag 84; MagDir 84; MagIndMarPl 82-83*

American Industry [of Publications for Industry] - Great Neck, NY - *BaconPubCkMag 84; MagDir 84; MagIndMarPl 82-83*

American Information Services Inc. - Chicago Heights, IL - *ADAPSOMemDir 83-84; DataDirOnSer 84*

American Information Systems Inc. - Wellsboro, PA - *MicrocomMPl 84*

American Ink Maker - New York, NY - *BaconPubCkMag 84; MagDir 84*

American Institute for Economic Research - Great Barrington, MA - *BoPubDir 4, 5*

American Institute for Marxist Studies - New York, NY - *BoPubDir 4, 5*

American Institute for Property & Liability Underwriters - Malvern, PA - *BoPubDir 4, 5*

American Institute for Writing Research Corp. - New York, NY - *BoPubDir 4, 5*

American Institute of Aeronautics & Astronautics - New York, NY - *BoPubDir 4, 5; MagIndMarPl 82-83*

American Institute of Aeronautics & Astronautics (Technical Information Service) - New York, NY - *CompReadDB 82; DataDirOnSer 84; InfIndMarPl 83*

American Institute of Architects - Washington, DC - *BoPubDir 4, 5*

American Institute of Certified Public Accountants - New York, NY - *CompReadDB 82; InfIndMarPl 83; LitMarPl 84*

American Institute of Certified Public Accountants (Information Retrieval Dept.) - New York, NY - *CompReadDB 82*

American Institute of Chemical Engineers - New York, NY - *LitMarPl 83, 84*

American Institute of Cooperation - Washington, DC - *BoPubDir 4, 5*

American Institute of Discussion - Oklahoma City, OK - *BoPubDir 4, 5*

American Institute of Italian Studies - Morristown, NJ - *BoPubDir 4 Sup, 5*

American Institute of Maintenance - Glendale, CA - *BoPubDir 5*

American Institute of Physics - New York, NY - *CompReadDB 82; DataDirOnSer 84; DirMarMP 83; InfIndMarPl 83; LitMarPl 83, 84; MagIndMarPl 82-83; MicroMarPl 82-83*

American Institute of Plant Engineers - Cincinnati, OH - *BoPubDir 5*

American Institute of Real Estate Appraisers - Chicago, IL - *BoPubDir 4, 5*

American Institute of the History of Pharmacy - Madison, WI - *BoPubDir 4, 5*

American Institutes for Research - Palo Alto, CA - *BoPubDir 4, 5*

American Integrity Systems - Santa Ana, CA - *MicrocomMPl 84*

American Intelligent Machines - Prairie View, IL - *WhoWMicrocom 83*

American International - Lutz, FL - *LitMarPl 83, 84*

American International Data Search Inc. - Century City, CA - *EISS 5-84 Sup*

American International Inc. - New York, NY - *MagIndMarPl 82-83*

American International Publishers [Div. of The Institute of Modern Languages Inc.] - Silver Spring, MD - *LitMarPl 83*

American Iris Society - Wichita, KS - *BoPubDir 4, 5*

American Iron & Steel Institute - Washington, DC - *BoPubDir 5*

American Italian Historical Association Inc. - Glen Rock, NJ - *BoPubDir 4*

American Italian Historical Association Inc. - Staten Island, NY - *BoPubDir 5*

American Jewelry Manufacturer - New York, NY - *BaconPubCkMag 84; MagDir 84; WritMar 84*

American Jewish Archives [Aff. of Hebrew Union College] - Cincinnati, OH - *BoPubDir 4, 5*

American Jewish Broadcasting Service Inc. - Bethesda, MD - *BrCabYB 84*

American Jewish Committee, The - New York, NY - *Tel&CabFB 84C*

American Jewish Historical Society - Waltham, MA - *BoPubDir 4, 5*

American Jewish History - Waltham, MA - *MagIndMarPl 82-83*

American Jewish Periodical Center [of Hebrew Union College] - Cincinnati, OH - *LitMarPl 83, 84; MicroMarPl 82-83*

American Journal [of Durgin-Snow Publishing Co. Inc.] - Westbrook, ME - *AyerDirPub 83; Ed&PubIntYB 82; NewsDir 84*

American Journal of Agricultural Economics - Ames, IA - *MagIndMarPl 82-83*

American Journal of Archaeology - Bryn Mawr, PA - *MagIndMarPl 82-83*

American Journal of Art Therapy - Washington, DC - *MagIndMarPl 82-83*

American Journal of Botany - Miami, FL - *MagIndMarPl 82-83*

American Journal of Cardiology, The - New York, NY - *BaconPubCkMag 84; MagDir 84; MagIndMarPl 82-83*

American Journal of Clinical Nutrition - Bethesda, MD - *BaconPubCkMag 84; MagDir 84; MagIndMarPl 82-83*

American Journal of Clinical Pathology - Philadelphia, PA - *BaconPubCkMag 84; MagDir 84; MagIndMarPl 82-83*

American Journal of Diseases of Children - Tucson, AZ - *BaconPubCkMag 84*

American Journal of Diseases of Children - Chicago, IL - *MagDir 84*

American Journal of Education - Chicago, IL - *MagDir 84; MagIndMarPl 82-83*

American Journal of EEG Technology - Hartford, CT - *MagIndMarPl 82-83*
American Journal of Gastroenterology - New York, NY - *BaconPubCkMag 84; MagDir 84*
American Journal of Hospital Pharmacy [of American Society of Hospital Pharmacists] - Bethesda, MD - *BaconPubCkMag 84; MagDir 84*
American Journal of Infection Control - St. Louis, MO - *BaconPubCkMag 84; MagIndMarPl 82-83*
American Journal of International Law - New York, NY - *MagIndMarPl 82-83*
American Journal of Intravenous Therapy & Clinical Nutrition - Georgetown, CT - *MagDir 84*
American Journal of Mathematical & Management Sciences [of American Sciences Press Inc.] - Syracuse, NY - *LitMag&SmPr 83-84*
American Journal of Medical Technology - New York, NY - *BaconPubCkMag 84; MagDir 84*
American Journal of Medicine, The - New York, NY - *BaconPubCkMag 84; MagDir 84; MagIndMarPl 82-83*
American Journal of Nursing - New York, NY - *BaconPubCkMag 84; Folio 83; LitMarPl 83, 84; MagDir 84; MagIndMarPl 82-83; WritMar 84*
American Journal of Obstetrics & Gynecology - St. Louis, MO - *BaconPubCkMag 84; MagDir 84; MagIndMarPl 82-83*
American Journal of Occupational Therapy - Rockville, MD - *BaconPubCkMag 84; MagDir 84*
American Journal of Ophthalmology - Chicago, IL - *BaconPubCkMag 84; MagDir 84; MagIndMarPl 82-83*
American Journal of Optometry & Physiological Optics - Washington, DC - *MagDir 84*
American Journal of Optometry & Physiological Optics - Baltimore, MD - *BaconPubCkMag 84*
American Journal of Orthodontics [of The C. V. Mosby Co.] - St. Louis, MO - *BaconPubCkMag 84; MagDir 84; MagIndMarPl 82-83*
American Journal of Pathology - Philadelphia, PA - *MagDir 84; MagIndMarPl 82-83*
American Journal of Physical Medicine - Baltimore, MD - *BaconPubCkMag 84; MagDir 84*
American Journal of Physics - St. Louis, MO - *BaconPubCkMag 84; MagDir 84*
American Journal of Political Science - Houston, TX - *MagIndMarPl 82-83*
American Journal of Proctology, Gastroenterology, & C. & R. Surgery - Georgetown, CT - *BaconPubCkMag 84; MagDir 84*
American Journal of Psychiatry - Washington, DC - *MagDir 84; MagIndMarPl 82-83*
American Journal of Psychology - Champaign, IL - *MagDir 84*
American Journal of Public Health [of American Public Health Association Inc.] - Washington, DC - *BaconPubCkMag 84; LitMarPl 83, 84; MagDir 84*
American Journal of Roentgenology - Seattle, WA - *BaconPubCkMag 84; MagDir 84*
American Journal of Science - New Haven, CT - *BaconPubCkMag 84; MagDir 84*
American Journal of Sociology - Chicago, IL - *MagIndMarPl 82-83*
American Journal of Sports Medicine, The - Baltimore, MD - *BaconPubCkMag 84*
American Journal of Surgery - New York, NY - *BaconPubCkMag 84; MagDir 84; MagIndMarPl 82-83*
American Journal of the Medical Sciences - Thorofare, NJ - *BaconPubCkMag 84; MagDir 84*
American Journal of Veterinary Research - Roselle, IL - *MagDir 84*
American Journal of Veterinary Research - Schaumburg, IL - *BaconPubCkMag 84*
American Judicature Society - Chicago, IL - *BoPubDir 4, 5*
American Laboratory - Fairfield, CT - *BaconPubCkMag 84; MagDir 84; MagIndMarPl 82-83*
American Laminating Co. - Albany, NY - *LitMarPl 84*
American Land Development Association - Washington, DC - *BoPubDir 5*
American Laser Systems - Goleta, CA - *AvMarPl 83*
American Latvian Association in the United States Inc. - Rockville, MD - *BoPubDir 4 Sup, 5*
American Laundry Digest - Chicago, IL - *BaconPubCkMag 84; MagDir 84; WritMar 84*
American Law Institute - Philadelphia, PA - *LitMarPl 83, 84*
American Law Institute (American Bar Association Committee on Continuing Professional Education) - Philadelphia, PA - *LitMarPl 83, 84*
American Lawn Applicator - Farmington, MI - *BaconPubCkMag 84*
American Lawn Bowlers Guide - Laguna Beach, CA - *BoPubDir 4, 5*
American Lawyer [of AM-Law Publishing Corp.] - New York, NY - *BaconPubCkMag 84; MagDir 84; NewsDir 84*
American Legion Magazine - Indianapolis, IN - *ArtMar 84; BaconPubCkMag 84; LitMarPl 83, 84; MagDir 84; MagIndMarPl 82-83; WritMar 84*
American Legion National Headquarters - Indianapolis, IN - *BoPubDir 4, 5*
American Libraries [of American Library Association] - Chicago, IL - *ArtMar 84; BaconPubCkMag 84; MagDir 84; MagIndMarPl 82-83; WritMar 84*
American Library Association - Chicago, IL - *CompReadDB 82; LitMarPl 83, 84; MagIndMarPl 82-83; MicroMarPl 82-83*
American Library Publishing Co. Inc. - New York, NY - *LitMarPl 83, 84*
American Life Foundation - Watkins Glen, NY - *LitMarPl 83, 84*
American Literary Review Press, The - Boston, MA - *LitMag&SmPr 83-84*
American Literary Review, The - Boston, MA - *LitMag&SmPr 83-84*
American Literature [of Duke University Press] - Durham, NC - *LitMag&SmPr 83-84; LitMarPl 83, 84; MagDir 84; MagIndMarPl 82-83*
American Logger & Lumberman - Hillsdale, NJ - *BaconPubCkMag 84; MagDir 84*
American Lung Association - New York, NY - *AvMarPl 83*
American Machinist [of McGraw-Hill Inc.] - New York, NY - *BaconPubCkMag 84; Folio 83; MagDir 84; MagIndMarPl 82-83*
American Magnetics Corp. - Carson, CA - *DataDirSup 7-83*
American Mailing Lists Corp. - Falls Church, VA - *MagIndMarPl 82-83*
American Malacologists Inc. - Melbourne, FL - *BoPubDir 4, 5*
American Management Associations - New York, NY - *DirInfWP 82; MagIndMarPl 82-83*
American Management Review - New York, NY - *LitMarPl 83*
American Management Systems Inc. - Arlington, VA - *ADAPSOMemDir 83-84; DataDirOnSer 84; DataDirSup 7-83; EISS 5-84 Sup*
American Map & Hagstrom [Subs. of Langenscheidt Publishers Inc.] - Maspeth, NY - *LitMarPl 83, 84*
American Map Co. Inc. [Subs. of Langenscheidt Publishers Inc.] - Maspeth, NY - *AvMarPl 83; LitMarPl 83, 84*
American Maritime Officer [of District 2 MEBA, AMO, AFL-CIO] - Brooklyn, NY - *NewsDir 84*
American Marketing Association - Chicago, IL - *BoPubDir 4, 5*
American Marketing Services Inc. - Newport Beach, CA - *IntDirMarRes 83*
American Mathematical Monthly, The - Washington, DC - *MagDir 84*
American Mathematical Society - Providence, RI - *CompReadDB 82; DataDirOnSer 84; InfIndMarPl 83; LitMarPl 83, 84; MagIndMarPl 82-83*
American Media - Westlake Village, CA - *BoPubDir 4, 5*
American Media Consultants - Los Angeles, CA - *HBIndAd&MS 82-83; StaDirAdAg 2-84*
American Media Inc. - Des Moines, IA - *AvMarPl 83; WritMar 84*
American Media Inc. - Patchogue, NY - *BrCabYB 84*
American Media Services Inc. - Washington, DC - *MagIndMarPl 82-83*
American Media Tours - Kansas City, MO - *LitMarPl 84*
American Medical Association - Chicago, IL - *DataDirOnSer 84; MagIndMarPl 82-83*
American Medical News - Chicago, IL - *ArtMar 84; BaconPubCkMag 84; MagDir 84; NewsBur 6*
American Medical Publishing Association - Santa Barbara, CA - *BoPubDir 4 Sup, 5; LitMag&SmPr 83-84*

American Medical Software [Subs. of Colwell Systems Inc.] - Champaign, IL - *MicrocomMPl 83, 84; WhoWMicrocom 83*
American Medicine News Service - New York, NY - *BrCabYB 84*
American Men & Women of Science [of Jaques Cattell Press] - Tempe, AZ - *CompReadDB 82; DirOnDB Spring 84*
American Men & Women of Science [of R. R. Bowker Co.] - New York, NY - *DataDirOnSer 84; DBBus 82*
American Men & Women of Science Data Base [of R. R. Bowker Co.] - New York, NY - *EISS 83*
American Mercury, The - Torrance, CA - *MagDir 84*
American Metal Market - New York, NY - *BaconPubCkMag 84; BoPubDir 5; Ed&PubIntYB 82*
American Metal Market/Metalworking News [of Fairchild Publications] - New York, NY - *Folio 83*
American Meteorite Laboratory - Denver, CO - *AvMarPl 83; BoPubDir 4, 5*
American Meteorological Society - Boston, MA - *BoPubDir 4, 5; CompReadDB 82; DataDirOnSer 84; InfIndMarPl 83; MagIndMarPl 82-83*
American Micro Dynamics - Newport Beach, CA - *MicrocomMPl 84; WhoWMicrocom 83*
American Micro Media - Red Hook, NY - *MicrocomMPl 84*
American Micro Products Inc. - Richardson, TX - *MicrocomMPl 84*
American Microcomputer Systems & Services - Encino, CA - *WhoWMicrocom 83*
American Mideast Research - San Francisco, CA - *BoPubDir 4, 5*
American Mining Congress Journal - Washington, DC - *BaconPubCkMag 84; MagDir 84*
American Mitac Corp. - Santa Clara, CA - *MicrocomMPl 84*
American Mizrachi Woman, The - New York, NY - *WritMar 84*
American Monument Association - Worthington, OH - *BoPubDir 5*
American Mosquito Control Association Inc. - Fresno, CA - *BoPubDir 5*
American Motor Carrier - Marietta, GA - *BaconPubCkMag 84; MagDir 84*
American Motorcyclist [of American Motorcyclist Association] - Westerville, OH - *ArtMar 84; BaconPubCkMag 84; MagDir 84; MagIndMarPl 82-83; WritMar 84*
American Motorist - Falls Church, VA - *MagDir 84*
American Museum of Natural History - New York, NY - *AvMarPl 83; BoPubDir 4, 5; MagIndMarPl 82-83*
American Museum of Natural History (Micropaleontology Press) - New York, NY - *BoPubDir 4, 5*
American Music Conference - Wilmette, IL - *BoPubDir 4, 5*
American Music Teacher, The - Cincinnati, OH - *BaconPubCkMag 84; MagDir 84*
American Musicians Union Inc. - Dumont, NJ - *AvMarPl 83*
American Musicological Society - *See* Galaxy Music Corp.
American National Enterprises Inc. - Salt Lake City, UT - *AvMarPl 83*
American National Heritage Association - Alexandria, VA - *BoPubDir 4, 5*
American National Metric Council - Bethesda, MD - *BoPubDir 4, 5*
American Network, The [of American Medical Buildings Inc.] - Milwaukee, WI - *CabTVPrDB 83*
American New Church Sunday School Association - Newton, MA - *BoPubDir 4, 5*
American News - Montevideo, MN - *AyerDirPub 83*
American News - Aberdeen, SD - *AyerDirPub 83*
American Newspaper Carrier [of American Newspaper Boy Press] - Winston-Salem, NC - *MagDir 84; WritMar 84*
American Newspaper Publishers Association Foundation - Washington, DC - *BoPubDir 4, 5*
American Newspaper Representatives Inc. [Subs. of National Newspaper Association] - Brooklyn, NY - *LitMarPl 83, 84*
American Newspapers - Altoona, PA - *BaconPubCkNews 84*
American Notes & Queries [of Erasmus Press] - Lexington, KY - *LitMarPl 83, 84*
American Nuclear Society - La Grange Park, IL - *BoPubDir 4, 5; MicroMarPl 82-83*
American Numismatic Association - Colorado Springs, CO - *BoPubDir 4, 5*
American Numismatic Society - New York, NY - *BoPubDir 4, 5*
American Nurse, The - Kansas City, MO - *BaconPubCkMag 84*
American Nurseryman - Chicago, IL - *BaconPubCkMag 84; MagDir 84*
American Nurses' Association - Kansas City, MO - *BoPubDir 4, 5*
American: Official Journal of the Constitutional Rights Foundation - Texas City, TX - *LitMag&SmPr 83-84*
American Oil & Gas Reporter [of Domestic Petroleum Publishing Inc.] - Wichita, KS - *BaconPubCkMag 84; MagDir 84*
American Oil Chemists' Society - Champaign, IL - *BoPubDir 5*
American Opinion - Belmont, MA - *ArtMar 84; BaconPubCkMag 84; MagDir 84; WritMar 84*
American Opinion Corp. - Niles, IL - *IntDirMarRes 83*
American Optometric Associated - St. Louis, MO - *AvMarPl 83*
American Optometric Association News - St. Louis, MO - *MagDir 84*
American Organist - New York, NY - *BaconPubCkMag 84; MagDir 84; MagIndMarPl 82-83*
American Oriental Society - New Haven, CT - *BoPubDir 4, 5*
American Osteopathic Hospital Association - Arlington Heights, IL - *BoPubDir 5*
American Osteopathic Hospital Association - Park Ridge, IL - *BoPubDir 4*
American Overseas Book Co. Inc. - Ridgefield Park, NJ - *LitMarPl 83, 84*
American Pacific Co. - Desert Center, CA - *Tel&CabFB 84C*
American Pacific Co. - Eagle Mountain, CA - *BrCabYB 84*
American Paint & Coatings Journal - St. Louis, MO - *BaconPubCkMag 84; MagDir 84*
American Paint Journal Co. - St. Louis, MO - *BoPubDir 5*
American Painting Contractor - St. Louis, MO - *BaconPubCkMag 84; MagDir 84; WritMar 84*
American Paper Institute - New York, NY - *BoPubDir 5*
American Personnel & Guidance Association - Falls Church, VA - *AvMarPl 83; LitMarPl 83; MagIndMarPl 82-83*
American Petroleum Institute - Washington, DC - *BoPubDir 5; DataDirOnSer 84*
American Petroleum Institute - New York, NY - *CompReadDB 82; InfIndMarPl 83*
American Petroleum Institute (Central Abstracting & Indexing Service) - New York, NY - *CompReadDB 82; DataDirOnSer 84*
American Pharmaceutical Association - Washington, DC - *BoPubDir 4 Sup, 5*
American Pharmacy [of American Pharmaceutical Association] - Washington, DC - *BaconPubCkMag 84; MagDir 84; MagIndMarPl 82-83*
American Philatelic Society - State College, PA - *BoPubDir 4, 5; WritMar 84*
American Philosophical Society - Philadelphia, PA - *LitMarPl 83, 84*
American Photographer - New York, NY - *BaconPubCkMag 84; MagIndMarPl 82-83*
American Photographic Appliance Corp. - Greenfield, MA - *AvMarPl 83*
American Photographic Instrument Co. Inc. - Emerson, NJ - *AvMarPl 83*
American Physiological Society - Bethesda, MD - *MagIndMarPl 82-83*
American Phytopathological Society - St. Paul, MN - *BoPubDir 4, 5*
American Pigeon Journal - Warrenton, MO - *BaconPubCkMag 84; MagDir 84*
American Pine Barrens Publishing Co. - Slingerlands, NY - *BoPubDir 4, 5*
American Pizzi Offset Corp. [Subs. of Amilcare Pizzi-Arti Grafiche] - New York, NY - *LitMarPl 83, 84*
American Planning Corp. - Alexandria, VA - *MicrocomSwDir 1*
American Plate Number Society - Tampa, FL - *BoPubDir 4, 5*
American Play Co. Inc. - New York, NY - *LitMarPl 83, 84*
American Poetry Anthology [of American Poetry Association] - Santa Cruz, CA - *LitMag&SmPr 83-84; WritMar 84*
American Poetry Association - Santa Cruz, CA - *BoPubDir 4 Sup, 5*
American Poetry Press - Claymont, DE - *BoPubDir 4*
American Poetry Press - Upper Darby, PA - *BoPubDir 5; LitMarPl 84*

American Poetry Review [of Temple University] - Philadelphia, PA - *LitMag&SmPr 83-84; LitMarPl 83, 84; MagIndMarPl 82-83*
American Polarizers Inc. - Reading, PA - *Tel&CabFB 84C*
American Political Science Association - Washington, DC - *BoPubDir 4, 5*
American Political Science Review [of American Political Science Association] - Urbana, IL - *LitMarPl 83*
American Portable Computer Inc. - Nashville, TN - *MicrocomMPl 84*
American Postal Worker - Washington, DC - *MagIndMarPl 82-83; NewsDir 84*
American Potato Journal - Old Town, ME - *MagDir 84*
American Potato Journal - Orono, ME - *BaconPubCkMag 84*
American Premiere - Beverly Hills, CA - *ArtMar 84; WritMar 84*
American Press - Lake Charles, LA - *AyerDirPub 83*
American Press - Boston, MA - *BoPubDir 4, 5; LitMarPl 84; WritMar 84*
American Press [Div. of Standard Publishing] - Columbia, MO - *MagIndMarPl 82-83*
American Press Clipping Service Inc. - New York, NY - *ProGuPRSer 4*
American Press Inc. - Gordonsville, VA - *MagIndMarPl 82-83*
American Printer [of Maclean-Hunter Publishing Corp.] - Chicago, IL - *ArtMar 84; BaconPubCkMag 84; LitMarPl 83, 84; MagDir 84; WritMar 84*
American Printer & Lithographer - Chicago, IL - *MagIndMarPl 82-83*
American Printing & Envelope [Div. of Apec Paper Industries Ltd.] - New York, NY - *AvMarPl 83*
American Printing Equipment & Supply Co. [Div. of American Wood Type Manufacturing Co.] - Long Island City, NY - *LitMarPl 83, 84*
American Printing House for the Blind Inc. - Louisville, KY - *LitMarPl 83, 84*
American Professional Color Corp. - Cedar Falls, IA - *AvMarPl 83*
American Professional Equipment Co. - Tampa, FL - *AvMarPl 83*
American Profile [of Donnelley Marketing] - Stamford, CT - *DBBus 82*
American Program Bureau - Chestnut Hill, MA - *LitMarPl 83, 84*
American Prudential Enterprises - Salisbury, NC - *BoPubDir 5*
American Psychiatric Press Inc. [Subs. of American Psychiatric Association] - Washington, DC - *LitMarPl 83, 84*
American Psychological Association - Washington, DC - *BoPubDir 4, 5; CompReadDB 82; MagIndMarPl 82-83*
American Psychologist - Washington, DC - *BaconPubCkMag 84; MagDir 84; MagIndMarPl 82-83*
American Public Health Association - Washington, DC - *BoPubDir 4, 5*
American Public Power Association - Washington, DC - *BoPubDir 5*
American Public Radio - St. Paul, MN - *BrCabYB 84*
American Public Welfare Association - Washington, DC - *BoPubDir 4, 5*
American Public Works Association - Chicago, IL - *BoPubDir 4, 5*
American Publishers Co. [Subs. of Follett Corp.] - Cary, IL - *BoPubDir 4 Sup, 5; LitMarPl 83, 84*
American Publishing Co. - Madison, WI - *BoPubDir 4, 5*
American Quality Books - Spokane, WA - *BoPubDir 4, 5*
American Quarterly - Philadelphia, PA - *MagIndMarPl 82-83*
American R Corp. - North Hollywood, CA - *AvMarPl 83*
American Rabbit Journal - La Vergne, TN - *MagDir 84*
American Radio - Kalamazoo, MI - *BrCabYB 84*
American Radio Relay League Inc. - Newington, CT - *BoPubDir 4, 5*
American Radio Service - Washington, DC - *BrCabYB 84*
American Radio Theatre - Glendale, CA - *WritMar 84*
American Railway Engineering Association - Washington, DC - *BoPubDir 4 Sup, 5*
American Rainbird Music - Nashville, TN - *BillIntBG 83-84*
American Record Collectors' Exchange - New York, NY - *BoPubDir 4, 5*
American Record Guide - Washington, DC - *MagIndMarPl 82-83*
American Religious Town Hall Meeting Inc. - Dallas, TX - *Tel&CabFB 84C*
American Rental Association - Moline, IL - *BoPubDir 5*
American Repertory Theatre - Cambridge, MA - *WritMar 84*
American Reprints Co. - Ironton, MO - *BoPubDir 4*
American Reprints Co. - Bellingham, WA - *BoPubDir 5*
American Republic - Poplar Bluff, MO - *AyerDirPub 83*
American Resource Bureau Inc. - Wheaton, IL - *StaDirAdAg 2-84*
American Revenue Association - Rockford, IA - *BoPubDir 4, 5*
American Review of Respiratory Disease - Baltimore, MD - *MagIndMarPl 82-83*
American Review of Respiratory Disease - New York, NY - *BaconPubCkMag 84; MagDir 84*
American Rifleman - Washington, DC - *BaconPubCkMag 84; MagDir 84; MagIndMarPl 82-83*
American Romanian Academy of Arts & Sciences - Berkeley, CA - *BoPubDir 4*
American Romanian Academy of Arts & Sciences - Davis, CA - *BoPubDir 5*
American Romanian News - Cleveland, OH - *Ed&PublntYB 82*
American Roofer & Building Improvement Contractor [of Shelter Publications Inc.] - Downers Grove, IL - *MagDir 84*
American Rose [of American Rose Society] - Shreveport, LA - *BaconPubCkMag 84; MagDir 84*
American Rose Society - Shreveport, LA - *BoPubDir 4, 5*
American Sales & Marketing Inc. - Port St. Lucie, FL - *IntDirMarRes 83*
American Salesman, The - Burlington, IA - *BaconPubCkMag 84; MagDir 84; WritMar 84*
American Satellite Co. - Rockville, MD - *DataDirSup 7-83; Tel&CabFB 84C; TeleSy&SerDir 2-84*
American Scholar [of The William Byrd Press] - Washington, DC - *LitMag&SmPr 83-84; LitMarPl 83, 84; MagDir 84; MagIndMarPl 82-83; WritMar 84*
American School & University - Philadelphia, PA - *BaconPubCkMag 84; MagDir 84; MagIndMarPl 82-83*
American School Board Journal - Washington, DC - *BaconPubCkMag 84; MagDir 84; MagIndMarPl 82-83; WritMar 84*
American School Health Association - Kent, OH - *BoPubDir 4, 5*
American School of Astrology - West Orange, NJ - *BoPubDir 4, 5*
American School of Classical Studies at Athens [of Institute for Advanced Study] - Princeton, NJ - *LitMarPl 83, 84*
American Science & Engineering Inc. - Cambridge, MA - *BoPubDir 4, 5*
American Sciences Press Inc. - Syracuse, NY - *LitMag&SmPr 83-84*
American Sciences Press Inc. - Columbus, OH - *BoPubDir 4, 5; LitMarPl 84*
American Scientist - New Haven, CT - *BaconPubCkMag 84; LitMarPl 83, 84; MagDir 84; MagIndMarPl 82-83*
American Seating Co. - Grand Rapids, MI - *DirInfWP 82*
American Self Protection Review - Santa Monica, CA - *MagDir 84*
American Service Associates - Norristown, PA - *ADAPSOMemDir 83-84*
American Shipper [of Howard Publications] - Jacksonville, FL - *BaconPubCkMag 84; MagDir 84; MagIndMarPl 82-83*
American Shoemaking - Cambridge, MA - *BaconPubCkMag 84; MagDir 84*
American Shotgunner - Sparks, NV - *MagIndMarPl 82-83*
American Shotgunner, The - Reno, NV - *ArtMar 84; BaconPubCkMag 84; MagDir 84; WritMar 84*
American Showcase Inc. - New York, NY - *LitMarPl 84*
American Small Business Computers - Pryor, OK - *MicrocomMPl 83, 84*
American Soccer Magazine - Venice, CA - *MagDir 84*
American Society for Education & Religion - Springfield, VA - *BoPubDir 5*
American Society for Engineering Education - Washington, DC - *BoPubDir 4, 5*
American Society for Industrial Security - Washington, DC - *BoPubDir 4, 5*
American Society for Industrial Security - Arlington, VA - *MagDir 84*

American Society for Information Science - Washington, DC - *EISS 83*
American Society for Metals - Metals Park, OH - *BoPubDir 4, 5; CompReadDB 82; DataDirOnSer 84; MagIndMarPl 82-83*
American Society for Metals (Metals Information) - Metals Park, OH - *CompReadDB 82*
American Society for Microbiology - Washington, DC - *BoPubDir 4, 5; MagIndMarPl 82-83*
American Society for Public Administration - Washington, DC - *BoPubDir 4 Sup, 5*
American Society for Training & Development - Washington, DC - *LitMarPl 83, 84*
American Society of Agricultural Engineers - St. Joseph, MI - *BoPubDir 4, 5*
American Society of Agronomy - Madison, WI - *BoPubDir 4, 5*
American Society of Appraisers - Washington, DC - *BoPubDir 4, 5*
American Society of Association Executives - Washington, DC - *ProGuPRSer 4*
American Society of Bookplate Collectors & Designers - Alhambra, CA - *BoPubDir 4, 5*
American Society of Civil Engineers - New York, NY - *LitMarPl 83, 84; MagIndMarPl 82-83*
American Society of Clinical Pathologists (Educational Products Div.) - Chicago, IL - *BoPubDir 4, 5*
American Society of Clinical Pathologists Press - Chicago, IL - *AvMarPl 83; LitMarPl 84*
American Society of Composers, Authors, & Publishers - New York, NY - *Tel&CabFB 84C*
American Society of Genealogists - Vienna, VA - *BoPubDir 4, 5*
American Society of Heating, Refrigerating, & Air-Conditioning Engineers - Atlanta, GA - *BoPubDir 4, 5*
American Society of Hospital Pharmacists - Washington, DC - *BoPubDir 5; CompReadDB 82*
American Society of Hospital Pharmacists - Bethesda, MD - *DataDirOnSer 84; InfIndMarPl 83*
American Society of Indexers - New York, NY - *BoPubDir 5*
American Society of International Executives - Philadelphia, PA - *BoPubDir 5*
American Society of Journalists & Authors - New York, NY - *BoPubDir 5*
American Society of Mechanical Engineers - New York, NY - *LitMarPl 83, 84; MagIndMarPl 82-83*
American Society of Photogrammetry - Falls Church, VA - *BoPubDir 4 Sup, 5*
American Society of Real Estate Counselors [Aff. of National Association of Realtors] - Chicago, IL - *BoPubDir 4, 5*
American Society of Safety Engineers - Park Ridge, IL - *BoPubDir 4 Sup, 5*
American Sociological Association - Washington, DC - *BoPubDir 4, 5; MagIndMarPl 82-83*
American Sociological Review - Washington, DC - *MagDir 84*
American Sociological Review - Bloomington, IN - *MagIndMarPl 82-83*
American Software Corp. - Mill Valley, CA - *MicrocomMPl 83, 84; MicrocomSwDir 1; WhoWMicrocom 83*
American Software Design & Distribution Co. - Cottage Grove, MN - *MicrocomMPl 84*
American Software Publishing Co. - Washington, DC - *EISS 5-84 Sup*
American Solar Energy Society [of International Solar Energy Society] - New York, NY - *LitMarPl 83, 84; WritMar 84*
American Sound Corp. - Warren, MI - *AvMarPl 83*
American Sound Records [Subs. of Cliff Ayers Enterprises Inc.] - Nashville, TN - *AvMarPl 83*
American Spectator, The - Bloomington, IN - *DirMarMP 83; LitMarPl 83, 84; MagIndMarPl 82-83*
American Speech-Language-Hearing Association - Rockville, MD - *BoPubDir 5*
American Sports Sales Inc. - Orangeburg, NY - *BoPubDir 4*
American Square Computers - Jamestown, NC - *MicrocomMPl 83, 84*
American Squaredance [of Burdick Enterprises] - Huron, OH - *ArtMar 84; MagDir 84; WritMar 84*
American Srbobran [of Serb National Federation] - Pittsburgh, PA - *Ed&PubIntYB 82; NewsDir 84*
American Stage Festival - Milford, NH - *WritMar 84*
American-Statesman - Austin, TX - *AyerDirPub 83*
American Statistician [of American Statistical Association] - Washington, DC - *BaconPubCkMag 84; MagDir 84*
American Statistics Index [of Congressional Information Service Inc.] - Washington, DC - *CompReadDB 82; OnBibDB 3*
American Statistics Index [of Congressional Information Service Inc.] - Bethesda, MD - *DataDirOnSer 84*
American Stencil Manufacturing Co. - Mt. Prospect, IL - *DirInfWP 82*
American Stock Photos - Hollywood, CA - *AvMarPl 83; MagIndMarPl 82-83*
American-Stratford Graphic Services Inc. [Div. of American Book-Stratford Press Inc.] - Brattleboro, VT - *LitMarPl 83, 84; MagIndMarPl 82-83*
American Studies Press Inc. - Tampa, FL - *BoPubDir 4, 5; LitMag&SmPr 83-84*
American Sunbeam, The - Springdale, AR - *Ed&PubIntYB 82*
American Surgeon - Philadelphia, PA - *BaconPubCkMag 84; MagDir 84*
American Surveys International - Washington, DC - *DirPRFirms 83*
American Survival Center - New Haven, CT - *BoPubDir 4, 5*
American Syndicate Inc. [Subs. of Media Ventures Inc.] - Cincinnati, OH - *LitMarPl 84*
American Syndicate Inc. - Dayton, OH - *Ed&PubIntYB 82*
American Systems Corp. - Pittsburgh, PA - *MicrocomMPl 84*
American Tape Corp. - Ridgefield, NJ - *BillIntBG 83-84*
American Taste - New York, NY - *MagIndMarPl 82-83*
American Teacher [of American Federation of Teachers] - Washington, DC - *BaconPubCkMag 84; MagDir 84; MagIndMarPl 82-83; NewsDir 84*
American Technical Publishers Inc. - Alsip, IL - *LitMarPl 83, 84*
American Telecom - Anaheim, CA - *DataDirSup 7-83; DirInfWP 82*
American Teleconference Corp. - Atlanta, GA - *TeleSy&SerDir 7-83*
American Teledata Corp. - Denver, CO - *WhoWMicrocom 83*
American Telephone & Telegraph Co. - New York, NY - *DataDirSup 7-83; HomeVid&CabYB 82-83; KnowInd 83; TelDir&BG 83-84; TeleSy&SerDir 2-84*
American Television & Communications Corp. [of Time Inc.] - Englewood, CO - *BrCabYB 84 p.D-297; CabTVFinDB 83; HomeVid&CabYB 82-83; LitMarPl 84; TelAl 83, 84; Tel&CabFB 84C p.1664*
American Television & Communications Corp. - Central Florida Div., FL - *BrCabYB 84*
American Television & Communications Corp. [Subs. of Time Inc.] - New York, NY - *HomeVid&CabYB 82-83*
American Television of Midwest City Inc. - Midwest City, OK - *BrCabYB 84*
American Television Syndication Inc. - Los Angeles, CA - *TelAl 84*
American Television Syndication Inc. - New York, NY - *Tel&CabFB 84C*
American Terminal Leasing Corp. - Boston, MA - *DataDirSup 7-83*
American Textile Machinery Association - Washington, DC - *BoPubDir 4*
American Textile Machinery Association - Falls Church, VA - *BoPubDir 5*
American Textile Manufacturers Institute - Washington, DC - *BoPubDir 5*
American, The - Blackduck, MN - *AyerDirPub 83; Ed&PubIntYB 82*
American Theatre Arts - Hollywood, CA - *WritMar 84*
American Theatre Association - Washington, DC - *BoPubDir 4, 5*
American Themes & Tapes Inc. - New York, NY - *BillIntBG 83-84*
American Theological Library Association - Chicago, IL - *CompReadDB 82; EISS 83*
American Theological Library Association - Princeton, NJ - *LitMarPl 83*
American Theological Library Association (Board of Microtext) - Princeton, NJ - *LitMarPl 84; MicroMarPl 82-83*
American Tool, Die, & Stamping News - Farmington, MI - *BaconPubCkMag 84; MagDir 84*

American Topical Association Inc. - Milwaukee, WI - *BoPubDir 4, 5*
American Towman - Metuchen, NJ - *BaconPubCkMag 84*
American Transcommunications Inc. - Greenwich, CT - *CabTVFinDB 83; Tel&CabFB 84C*
American Transportation Builder - Washington, DC - *BaconPubCkMag 84; MagDir 84*
American Tree Farmer, The - Washington, DC - *BaconPubCkMag 84*
American Trend Publishing Co. - Boulder, CO - *BoPubDir 5*
American Trucker [of American Trucker Marketing] - San Bernardino, CA - *BaconPubCkMag 84; WritMar 84*
American Trucking Association Inc. - Washington, DC - *BoPubDir 5*
American Turf Monthly - New York, NY - *MagDir 84*
American Type Founders [Div. of ATF-Davidson Co.] - Elizabeth, NJ - *LitMarPl 83, 84*
American Universal Artforms Corp. - Austin, TX - *BoPubDir 4, 5*
American Universities Field Staff Inc. - Hanover, NH - *BoPubDir 4*
American Used Computer Co. - Boston, MA - *DataDirSup 7-83*
American Used Software Co. - Boston, MA - *MicrocomMPl 83*
American Uutiset - New York Mills, MN - *Ed&PubIntYB 82*
American/Valley Cablevision [of American Television & Communications Corp.] - North Versailles, PA - *BrCabYB 84*
American Vegan Society - Malaga, NJ - *BoPubDir 4, 5*
American Vegetable Grower - Willoughby, OH - *BaconPubCkMag 84; MagDir 84*
American Vegetarian-Hygienist & American Better Health - Duncannon, PA - *MagDir 84*
American Veterinary Publications Inc. - Santa Barbara, CA - *BoPubDir 4, 5*
American Video Channels Inc. - New York, NY - *AvMarPl 83*
American Video Corp. [of American Cablesystems Corp.] - Pompano Beach, FL - *Tel&CabFB 84C*
American Video Corp. - *See* American Cablesystems Corp.
American Video Laboratory [Subs. of American Motion Picture Co.] - Seattle, WA - *AvMarPl 83*
American Video Productions Inc. - New York, NY - *Tel&CabFB 84C*
American Video Tape/Electric Video Inc. - Ridgefield, NJ - *BillIntBG 83-84*
American Video Teleconferencing Corp. - Oceanside, NJ - *TeleSy&SerDir 2-84*
American Videotex Services - New York, NY - *EISS 5-84 Sup; VideoDir 82-83*
American Vocational Association - Arlington, VA - *BoPubDir 4, 5*
American Voice, The - Bedford, VA - *MagDir 84*
American Water Works Association - Denver, CO - *BoPubDir 4, 5; DataDirOnSer 84; MagDir 84*
American Way - Dallas, TX - *BaconPubCkMag 84; MagIndMarPl 82-83*
American Way - Euless, TX - *MagDir 84*
American Way [of American Airlines] - Ft. Worth, TX - *Folio 83; WritMar 84*
American Way Features Inc. - Jupiter, FL - *Ed&PubIntYB 82; LitMarPl 83, 84; MagIndMarPl 82-83*
American Way Features, The - Pigeon Forge, TN - *AyerDirPub 83*
American West - Tucson, AZ - *BaconPubCkMag 84; DirMarMP 83; LitMarPl 83, 84; MagIndMarPl 82-83; WritMar 84*
American West Associates Inc. - Fairfax, CA - *StaDirAdAg 2-84*
American Wheelman - Baltimore, MD - *ArtMar 84; BaconPubCkMag 84*
American Wine Society - Rochester, NY - *BoPubDir 4, 5*
American Wood Preservers Institute (AWPI Publications) - McLean, VA - *BoPubDir 5*
American World-Wide Sounds & Music Inc. - Fairview, NJ - *BillIntBG 83-84*
American Youth Hostels Inc. - Washington, DC - *BoPubDir 4, 5*
American Zionist, The [of Zionist Organization of America] - New York, NY - *LitMarPl 83, 84; MagDir 84; MagIndMarPl 82-83*
Americana [of Americana Magazine Inc.] - New York, NY - *BaconPubCkMag 84; Folio 83; LitMarPl 83, 84; MagIndMarPl 82-83; WritMar 84*
Americana Advertising [Div. of Americana Concessions Inc.] - Atlanta, GA - *StaDirAdAg 2-84*
Americana & Collectibles Press [Aff. of Hake's Americana] - York, PA - *BoPubDir 4, 5*
Americana Book Club - Watkins Glen, NY - *LitMarPl 83, 84*
Americana Books - Pinellas Park, FL - *BoPubDir 4, 5*
Americana Paper & Frame Co. - Portland, OR - *MagIndMarPl 82-83*
Americana Review - Scotia, NY - *BoPubDir 4, 5*
Americana Unltd. - Tucson, AZ - *MicroMarPl 82-83*
Americangroove Records - Davenport, IA - *BillIntBG 83-84*
AmericanProfile [of Donnelley Marketing Information Services] - Stamford, CT - *DataDirOnSer 84; DirOnDB Spring 84*
Americans for Energy Independence - Washington, DC - *BoPubDir 4, 5*
Americans United for Separation of Church & State - Silver Spring, MD - *BoPubDir 4, 5*
Americas [of Organization of American States] - Washington, DC - *ArtMar 84; MagIndMarPl 82-83; WritMar 84*
America's Textiles - Atlanta, GA - *BaconPubCkMag 84; MagDir 84*
America's Textiles Knitter/Apparel - Greenville, SC - *MagDir 84*
Americatone International USA - Las Vegas, NV - *BillIntBG 83-84*
Americus City CATV - Americus, KS - *BrCabYB 84*
Americus Music - Hendersonville, TN - *BillIntBG 83-84*
Americus Times-Recorder - Americus, GA - *BaconPubCkNews 84; Ed&PubIntYB 82; NewsDir 84*
Amerika Woche - Millbrae, CA - *NewsDir 84*
Amerikai-Kanadai Magyar Elet - Chicago, IL - *Ed&PubIntYB 82*
Amerikai Magyar Nepszava - Cleveland, OH - *Ed&PubIntYB 82*
Amerikai Magyar Szo - New York, NY - *Ed&PubIntYB 82*
Amerikanski Slovenec - Cleveland, OH - *Ed&PubIntYB 82*
Amerikanski Srbobran - Pittsburgh, PA - *Ed&PubIntYB 82*
Amerikas Latvietis - Roxbury, MA - *Ed&PubIntYB 82*
Ameripro - Tarzania, CA - *DirInfWP 82*
Ameriska Domovina - Cleveland, OH - *Ed&PubIntYB 82; NewsDir 84*
Ameristar Music Publishing Co. - *See* Four Star International Inc.
Ameritex Communications Inc. - Ennis, TX - *BrCabYB 84; Tel&CabFB 84C p.1664*
Amerosa Music Inc. - *See* President Music Corp.
Amery Free Press [of Sondreal Enterprises Inc.] - Amery, WI - *BaconPubCkNews 84; Ed&PubIntYB 82; NewsDir 84*
Amery Telephone Co. - Amery, WI - *TelDir&BG 83-84*
Ames & Zak Ltd., Lee - Commack, NY - *LitMarPl 83, 84; MagIndMarPl 82-83*
Ames Daily Tribune - Ames, IA - *Ed&PubIntYB 82; NewsDir 84*
Ames Griffin Records - New York, NY - *BillIntBG 83-84*
Ames Laboratory [of Iowa State University] - Ames, IA - *CompReadDB 82*
Ames Publishing - Chicago, IL - *BillIntBG 83-84*
Ames Tribune - Ames, IA - *BaconPubCkNews 84*
Amesbury Cablevision [of New England Cablevision] - Amesbury, MA - *BrCabYB 84*
Amesbury News - Amesbury, MA - *Ed&PubIntYB 82*
Amesbury News - Ipswich, MA - *AyerDirPub 83; NewsDir 84*
Amesbury News - *See* North Shore Weeklies Inc.
Amestoy Music - Los Angeles, CA - *BillIntBG 83-84*
AMF Geo Space Corp. - Houston, TX - *DataDirSup 7-83*
Amfax Inc. - South Weymouth, MA - *Ed&PubIntYB 82*
Amfon 2 Computer Systems - Los Angeles, CA - *MicrocomMPl 84*
AMG Publishers - Chattanooga, TN - *BoPubDir 4, 5*
Amherst Associates Inc. - Chicago, IL - *DataDirOnSer 84; DataDirSup 7-83*
Amherst Bee - Amherst, NY - *Ed&PubIntYB 82*
Amherst Bee [of Bee Publications Inc.] - Williamsville, NY - *AyerDirPub 83; NewsDir 84*
Amherst Bee - *See* Bee Publications Inc.
Amherst Bulletin - Northampton, MA - *AyerDirPub 83*
Amherst Citizen - Amherst, NS, Canada - *Ed&PubIntYB 82*
Amherst County Cablevision Inc. - Madison Heights, VA - *BrCabYB 84; Tel&CabFB 84C*
Amherst Daily News - Amherst, NS, Canada - *BaconPubCkNews 84; Ed&PubIntYB 82*

Amherst-Nelson Publishing Co. - Amherst, VA - *BaconPubCkNews 84*
Amherst New Era Progress - Amherst, VA - *Ed&PubIntYB 82*
Amherst New Era Progress - *See* Amherst-Nelson Publishing Co.
Amherst News Times - Amherst, OH - *BaconPubCkNews 84*
Amherst News-Times, The - Amherst, ND - *Ed&PubIntYB 82*
Amherst Press - Amherst, TX - *Ed&PubIntYB 82*
Amherst Press [Aff. of Palmer Publications Inc.] - Amherst, WI - *BoPubDir 4, 5*
Amherst Press - *See* Sudan Beacon-News Publishers
Amherst Record - Amherst, MA - *BaconPubCkNews 84*
Amherst Records - Buffalo, NY - *BillIntBG 83-84*
Amherst Student, The - Amherst, MA - *NewsDir 84*
Amherst Telephone Co. - Amherst, WI - *TelDir&BG 83-84*
Amherst Valley Advocate - Amherst, MA - *NewsDir 84*
Amherst Valley Advocate - Hatfield, MA - *Ed&PubIntYB 82*
Amherstburg Echo, The - Amherstburg, ON, Canada - *Ed&PubIntYB 82*
AMI - New York, NY - *DirOnDB Spring 84*
AMI Mailing Service Inc. - Jericho, NY - *LitMarPl 83, 84; MagIndMarPl 82-83*
AMI News Bureau - San Francisco, CA - *BrCabYB 84*
AMI Press [Aff. of The Blue Army of Our Lady of Fatima] - Washington, NJ - *BoPubDir 4, 5*
AMI Records - Hendersonville, TN - *BillIntBG 83-84*
Amicus Journal, The - New York, NY - *LitMag&SmPr 83-84*
Amidon & Associates Inc., Paul S. - St. Paul, MN - *AvMarPl 83; DirPRFirms 83*
Amigo Music Publishing Co. - Philadelphia, PA - *BillIntBG 83-84*
Amigo Press - Laguna Beach, CA - *BoPubDir 4, 5; LitMag&SmPr 83-84*
Amigos Bibliographic Council - Dallas, TX - *EISS 83; InfIndMarPl 83*
Amilon Corp. - Woodside, NY - *AvMarPl 83*
Amira Research Interviewing Service - Melville, NY - *IntDirMarRes 83*
Amiron Music - Chatsworth, CA - *BillIntBG 83-84*
Amistad Brands Inc. - Washington, DC - *LitMag&SmPr 83-84*
Amistad Press - Austin, TX - *BoPubDir 4 Sup, 5*
Amistad Research Center - New Orleans, LA - *MicroMarPl 82-83*
Amit Women - New York, NY - *Tel&CabFB 84C*
Amite New Digest - Amite, LA - *BaconPubCkNews 84*
Amite Tangi News [of Hammond Murray-Huber Publishing Inc.] - Hammond, LA - *NewsDir 84*
Amite Tangi-Talk - Amite, LA - *BaconPubCkNews 84; Ed&PubIntYB 82*
Amity Publications - Cottage Grove, OR - *LitMag&SmPr 83-84*
Amityville Record - Amityville, NY - *BaconPubCkNews 84; Ed&PubIntYB 82; NewsDir 84*
AMJ Publishing Co. Industries - Camarillo, CA - *BoPubDir 4, 5*
Amlyn Corp. - San Jose, CA - *MicrocomMPl 84*
AMM Magazine - New York, NY - *BaconPubCkMag 84*
Ammirati & Puris - New York, NY - *AdAge 3-28-84; BrCabYB 84; HBIndAd&MS 82-83; StaDirAdAg 2-84*
AMMS Co. - Lincolnwood, IL - *EISS 83*
Amnesty International - New York, NY - *BoPubDir 4, 5*
AMNET Inc. - Watertown, MA - *DataDirSup 7-83*
Amnion Stoneware - San Francisco, CA - *MicrocomSwDir 1*
Amoroso Inc., Michael - New York, NY - *HBIndAd&MS 82-83; IntDirMarRes 83*
Amory Advertiser [of Mid South Management] - Amory, MS - *AyerDirPub 83; BaconPubCkNews 84; Ed&PubIntYB 82; NewsDir 84*
Amory Cable TV [of Heritage Communications Inc.] - Amory, MS - *Tel&CabFB 84C*
Amos Press Inc. - Sidney, OH - *DirMarMP 83; MagIndMarPl 82-83*
Amos-Townsend & Associates - Summersville, WV - *StaDirAdAg 2-84*
Amoskeag Press Inc. - Hooksett, NH - *BoPubDir 4, 5*
AMP Inc. - Harrisburg, PA - *ElecNews 7-25-83*
Amperex Electronic Corp. [Subs. of North American Philips Corp.] - Hicksville, NY - *MicrocomMPl 83; WhoWMicrocom 83*
Amperex Electronic Corp. - Slatersville, RI - *AvMarPl 83*
Ampero Software Products - Lakewood, CA - *WhoWMicrocom 83*
Ampersand - Hollywood, CA - *MagIndMarPl 82-83*
Ampersand Communications - Coral Gables, FL - *Ed&PubIntYB 82*
Ampersand Corp. - York, PA - *MicrocomMPl 84; MicrocomSwDir 1*
Ampersand Press - Bristol, RI - *LitMag&SmPr 83-84*
Ampersand Press/Stardancer - Brooklyn, NY - *BoPubDir 5*
Ampersand Publishing Services Inc. - Caledon, ON, Canada - *BoPubDir 4, 5*
Ampex Business Products [Div. of Ampex Corp.] - Dallas, TX - *DirInfWP 82*
Ampex Corp. - El Segundo, CA - *MicrocomMPl 84*
Ampex Corp. - Redwood City, CA - *Top100Al 83*
Ampex Corp. (Memory Products Div.) - El Segundo, CA - *DataDirSup 7-83*
Ampex Letter Service Inc. - New York, NY - *LitMarPl 83, 84; MagIndMarPl 82-83*
Amphibian Publications - Athens, GA - *BoPubDir 5*
Amphoto [of Watson-Guptill Publications] - New York, NY - *LitMarPl 83, 84; WritMar 84*
Amplica Inc. - Newbury Park, CA - *HomeVid&CabYB 82-83*
Amplifier - Indianapolis, IN - *NewsDir 84*
Amplix Services Ltd. - Sevenoaks, England - *MicrocomSwDir 1*
AMPM Inc. - Midland, MI - *StaDirAdAg 2-84*
Amport & Associates Inc. - Chagrin Falls, OH - *DirInfWP 82*
Ampro Productions Inc. - New York, NY - *BillIntBG 83-84*
Ampstek Inc. - Richardson, TX - *MicrocomMPl 84*
A.M.R. Publishing Co. - Seattle, WA - *BoPubDir 4 Sup, 5*
Amron Cable TV - Pleasanton, KS - *BrCabYB 84; Tel&CabFB 84C*
Amron Information Services - Union, NJ - *EISS 83*
AMS Advertising - New York, NY - *AdAge 3-28-84; StaDirAdAg 2-84*
AMS Film Service [Div. of AMS Press Inc.] - New York, NY - *MicroMarPl 82-83*
AMS Inc. - Boise, ID - *MicrocomMPl 84*
AMS Press Inc. - New York, NY - *LitMarPl 83, 84; MagIndMarPl 82-83*
Amsat - Stamford, CT - *Tel&CabFB 84C*
Amsco School Publications Inc. - New York, NY - *BoPubDir 4 Sup, 5; LitMarPl 83, 84*
Amsterdam Advertising - Reading, MA - *AdAge 3-28-84; StaDirAdAg 2-84*
Amsterdam, Marcia - New York, NY - *LitMarPl 83, 84*
Amsterdam News - New York, NY - *AyerDirPub 83*
AMT/OSS Inc. - Lewiston, ME - *LitMarPl 83, 84*
Amtek Systems - Richardson, TX - *MicrocomMPl 84*
Amtel Communications Inc. - Madison, WI - *DataDirSup 7-83*
Amtrak Express [of East-West Network Inc.] - Los Angeles, CA - *ArtMar 84; MagIndMarPl 82-83*
Amtrak Express [of East/West Network Inc.] - New York, NY - *BaconPubCkMag 84; MagDir 84; WritMar 84*
Amtron Corp. - Aptos, CA - *AvMarPl 83*
Amulefi Publishing Co. - Buffalo, NY - *BoPubDir 4 Sup, 5*
Amulet Enterprises Inc. - Garfield Heights, OH - *MicrocomMPl 84*
Amusement Business [of The Billboard Publishing Co.] - Nashville, TN - *BaconPubCkMag 84; BoPubDir 5; MagDir 84; MagIndMarPl 82-83; NewsBur 6; WritMar 84*
Amusement Features Syndicate - New York, NY - *Ed&PubIntYB 82; LitMarPl 84*
Amvid Communication Services Inc. - Manhattan Beach, CA - *AvMarPl 83*
AmVideo Cable Corp. [of Prime Cable Corp.] - Hoboken, NJ - *Tel&CabFB 84C*
AMX Corp. - Dallas, TX - *AvMarPl 83*
AN Consultants [Div. of Eleanor Sherman Associates] - New York, NY - *MagIndMarPl 82-83*
An Gael [of The Irish Arts Center] - New York, NY - *WritMar 84*
A.N. Inc. - Whitefish, MT - *BoPubDir 4, 5*
Ana-Doug Publishing - Fullerton, CA - *LitMag&SmPr 83-84*
ANA Newsletters - New York, NY - *MagIndMarPl 82-83*
Anacom General Corp. - Fullerton, CA - *DataDirSup 7-83; MicrocomMPl 83*
Anacomp Inc. - Carmel, IN - *ADAPSOMemDir 83-84; DataDirSup 7-83*

Anacomp Inc. - Indianapolis, IN - *DataDirOnSer 84; Datamation 6-83; Top100Al 83*
Anacomp Inc. - North Brunswick, NJ - *VideoDir 82-83*
Anacomp Microprinting [Div. of Anacomp Inc.] - Des Plaines, IL - *LitMarPl 83, 84*
Anaconda Cable Television [of Tele-Communications Inc.] - Anaconda, MT - *BrCabYB 84; Tel&CabFB 84C*
Anaconda-Ericsson - Garden Grove, CA - *DataDirSup 7-83; Datamation 6-83*
Anaconda-Ericsson Inc. (Telecommunications Div.) - Garden Grove, CA - *DirInfWP 82*
Anaconda Leader, The - Anaconda, MT - *Ed&PubIntYB 82; NewsDir 84*
Anacortes American - Anacortes, WA - *AyerDirPub 83; BaconPubCkNews 84; Ed&PubIntYB 82; NewsDir 84*
Anadarko Daily News - Anadarko, OK - *BaconPubCkNews 84; Ed&PubIntYB 82; NewsDir 84*
Anadex Inc. - Chatsworth, CA - *DataDirSup 7-83; DirInfWP 82; MicrocomMPl 84; WhoWMicrocom 83*
Anagraphics Inc. - New York, NY - *AvMarPl 83*
Anaheim Bulletin - Anaheim, CA - *AyerDirPub 83; BaconPubCkNews 84; Ed&PubIntYB 82; NewsDir 84*
Anaheim Hills News-Times - *See* Placentia News-Times Publishers
Anaheim Independent - Anaheim, CA - *Ed&PubIntYB 82*
Anaheim Independent [of Garden Grove West Orange Publishing Corp.] - Garden Grove, CA - *AyerDirPub 83; NewsDir 84*
Anaheim Independent - *See* West Orange Publishing Co.
Anaheim MDS Co. - Pasadena, CA - *Tel&CabFB 84C*
Anaheim Publishing Co. - Brea, CA - *BoPubDir 5*
Anaheim Publishing Co. - Fullerton, CA - *BoPubDir 4*
Anahuac - Hollywood, CA - *BillIntBG 83-84*
Anahuac Chambers County Progress - Anahuac, TX - *BaconPubCkNews 84*
Anahuac Progress - Anahuac, TX - *Ed&PubIntYB 82*
Anais - Brisbane, CA - *DirOnDB Spring 84*
Analog & Digital Peripherals Inc. - Troy, OH - *WhoWMicrocom 83*
A.N.A.L.O.G. Computing - Cherry Valley, MA - *MicrocomMPl 83, 84*
A.N.A.L.O.G. Computing - Worcester, MA - *BaconPubCkMag 84; WritMar 84*
Analog Devices Inc. - Norwood, MA - *BoPubDir 4, 5*
Analog Private Line Service [of American Telephone & Telegraph Co.] - Bedminster, NJ - *TeleSy&SerDir 2-84*
Analog Productions - San Francisco, CA - *BoPubDir 4, 5*
Analog Science Fiction/Science Fact - New York, NY - *MagDir 84; MagIndMarPl 82-83*
Analog Software - Worcester, MA - *MicrocomMPl 83*
Analog Technology Corp. - Irwindale, CA - *MicrocomMPl 84*
Analysis of Natural Gases Data Base [of U.S. Bureau of Mines] - Amarillo, TX - *EISS 83*
Analysis Press [Aff. of Merrill Analysis Inc.] - Chappaqua, NY - *BoPubDir 4, 5*
Analysis/Research Ltd. - San Diego, CA - *IntDirMarRes 83*
Analyste-Conseil Systeme Informatique Ltee. - Ste-Foy, PQ, Canada - *DataDirOnSer 84*
Analytic Associates - Rolling Hill Estates, CA - *MicrocomMPl 84; WhoWMicrocom 83*
Analytic Consultants International - Stamford, CT - *IntDirMarRes 83*
Analytic Decisions Corp. - Yonkers, NY - *EISS 7-83 Sup*
Analytic Insights Inc. - New York, NY - *IntDirMarRes 83*
Analytic Investment Management Inc. - Irvine, CA - *BoPubDir 4, 5*
Analytic Press, The - Hillsdale, NJ - *LitMarPl 84*
Analytical Biochemistry - New York, NY - *MagDir 84*
Analytical Chemistry [of American Chemical Society] - Washington, DC - *BaconPubCkMag 84; MagDir 84*
Analytical Computer Service Inc. - Chicago, IL - *IntDirMarRes 83*
Analytical Index to Quebec Periodical Articles [of Bibliotheque Nationale du Quebec] - Montreal, PQ, Canada - *DataDirOnSer 84; EISS 83*
Analytical Processes Corp. - Montrose, CO - *MicrocomMPl 84; MicrocomSwDir 1*
Analytical Research Service Inc. - Deerfield, IL - *MagIndMarPl 82-83*
Analytical Service Associates - Lynn, MA - *MicrocomMPl 84*
Analytical Studies Inc. - New Orleans, LA - *IntDirMarRes 83*
Anamaze Records - Brooklyn, NY - *BillIntBG 83-84*
Anamoose Cable TV [of NoDaKable Inc.] - Anamoose, ND - *BrCabYB 84*
Anamosa Journal Eureka [of Anamosa Newspapers Inc.] - Anamosa, IA - *AyerDirPub 83; BaconPubCkNews 84; Ed&PubIntYB 82; NewsDir 84*
Ananda Marga Publications [Aff. of Ananda Marga Pracharaka Samgha] - Denver, CO - *BoPubDir 4, 5*
Ananda Publications - Nevada City, CA - *BoPubDir 4, 5; LitMarPl 84*
Ananga Ranga Music - *See* Budd Music Corp.
Ananian, Joyce L. - Newton, MA - *LitMarPl 83, 84*
Anapress - Melbourne, Australia - *LitMag&SmPr 83-84*
Anarchist Review [of Cienfuegos Press] - Orkney, Scotland - *LitMag&SmPr 83-84*
Anatom Music - *See* Montana Music, Vincent Jr.
Anatron Inc. - Saline, MI - *MicrocomMPl 84*
Anawan Computer Services - Rehoboth, MA - *MicrocomMPl 84; MicrocomSwDir 1*
Ancaster News Journal - Ancaster, ON, Canada - *AyerDirPub 83*
Ancestral Historian Society [Aff. of J. Stewart & Co.] - Evans, GA - *BoPubDir 4, 5*
Ancestral Routes - Salt Lake City, UT - *BoPubDir 4 Sup, 5*
Anchor - Northwood, IA - *AyerDirPub 83*
Anchor - Providence, RI - *AyerDirPub 83*
Anchor Bay Beacon - New Baltimore, MI - *AyerDirPub 83; Ed&PubIntYB 82; NewsDir 84*
Anchor Pad International Inc. - Marina del Rey, CA - *WhoWMicrocom 83*
Anchor Systems [Aff. of Audio/Visual West Inc.] - San Diego, CA - *AvMarPl 83*
Anchor Systems - Bellevue, WA - *MicrocomMPl 83, 84*
Anchorage Alaska Spotlight - Anchorage, AK - *BaconPubCkNews 84*
Anchorage Daily News [of Northern Publishing Co.] - Anchorage, AK - *BaconPubCkNews 84; Ed&PubIntYB 82; LitMarPl 83, 84; NewsBur 6; NewsDir 84*
Anchorage Great Lander Shopping News - Anchorage, AK - *NewsDir 84*
Anchorage Press Inc. - New Orleans, LA - *BoPubDir 4, 5; LitMag&SmPr 83-84; LitMarPl 84*
Anchorage Telephone Utility - Anchorage, AK - *TelDir&BG 83-84*
Anchorage Times - Anchorage, AK - *BaconPubCkNews 84; Ed&PubIntYB 82; LitMarPl 84; NewsDir 84*
Ancient City Press - Santa Fe, NM - *BoPubDir 4; LitMag&SmPr 83-84; LitMarPl 83, 84*
Anco/Boston - Boston, MA - *AvMarPl 83; LitMarPl 83, 84; MagIndMarPl 82-83; WritMar 84*
Anco TV Cable Co. - Butler, AL - *BrCabYB 84; Tel&CabFB 84C*
Ancona Inc., George - Stony Point, NY - *LitMarPl 83, 84; MagIndMarPl 82-83*
Ancora Publishing - Tempe, AZ - *BillIntBG 83-84*
And All Inc. - Houston, TX - *MicrocomSwDir 1*
And Books - South Bend, IN - *BoPubDir 4; LitMag&SmPr 83-84; LitMarPl 83, 84; WritMar 84*
And/Or Press - Berkeley, CA - *LitMag&SmPr 83-84; LitMarPl 83, 84; WritMar 84*
& Press - Colchester, England - *LitMag&SmPr 83-84*
& Press/Stardancer - Brooklyn, NY - *BoPubDir 4*
And Sew On - Martinsville, NJ - *Ed&PubIntYB 82*
Andacht, Sandra - Little Neck, NY - *BoPubDir 5*
Andalusia Star News - Andalusia, AL - *BaconPubCkNews 84; Ed&PubIntYB 82; NewsDir 84*
Andell Packaging Corp. - Long Island City, NY - *LitMarPl 83, 84*
Andent Inc. - Waukegan, IL - *MicrocomMPl 83, 84; WhoWMicrocom 83*
Ander Publications - La Grange, GA - *BoPubDir 4, 5*
Anders Advertising Inc. - New York, NY - *StaDirAdAg 2-84*
Anders, Paul - Williamstown, MA - *LitMarPl 83, 84*
Andersen & Co., Arthur - Chicago, IL - *DirInfWP 82*
Andersen, Paul - Laguna Hills, CA - *BoPubDir 4, 5*
Anderson Advertising, G. - Hampton, NH - *StaDirAdAg 2-84*
Anderson Advertising Inc. - San Antonio, TX - *StaDirAdAg 2-84*
Anderson & Associates, H. T. - Miami, FL - *Ed&PubIntYB 82*

Anderson & Associates Inc., A. H. - Atlanta, GA - *StaDirAdAg 2-84*
Anderson & Associates Inc., Norman R. - San Antonio, TX - *AdAge 3-28-84; StaDirAdAg 2-84*
Anderson & Berdie Associates Inc. - St. Paul, MN - *IntDirMarRes 83*
Anderson & Co., Gavin - New York, NY - *DirPRFirms 83*
Anderson & Seeds Inc., David - Clinton, NY - *TelAl 83, 84*
Anderson Associates Inc., James - Daytona Beach, FL - *StaDirAdAg 2-84*
Anderson Associates Inc., Mark - Arlington Heights, IL - *DirMarMP 83; StaDirAdAg 2-84*
Anderson Baker Co. - Tulsa, OK - *StaDirAdAg 2-84*
Anderson-Bell - Canon City, CO - *MicrocomMPl 84*
Anderson-Bell - Littleton, CO - *MicrocomSwDir 1*
Anderson, Bob & Jean - Palmer Lake, CO - *BoPubDir 4, 5*
Anderson Bulletin - Anderson, IN - *NewsDir 84*
Anderson Cable Co. - Damascus, VA - *BrCabYB 84; Tel&CabFB 84C*
Anderson Cablevision Associates [of Booth American Co.] - Anderson, SC - *BrCabYB 84; Tel&CabFB 84C*
Anderson Co., H. S. - Searles Valley, CA - *BrCabYB 84; Tel&CabFB 84C*
Anderson Co., Olson - Bay City, MI - *AvMarPl 83*
Anderson Countian - Garnett, KS - *AyerDirPub 83; Ed&PubIntYB 82*
Anderson Daily Bulletin - Anderson, IN - *BaconPubCkNews 84; Ed&PubIntYB 82*
Anderson, Davis & Seeds Inc. - Clinton, NY - *StaDirAdAg 2-84*
Anderson Direct Response - Doylestown, PA - *AdAge 3-28-84; StaDirAdAg 2-84*
Anderson, Doug - New York, NY - *LitMarPl 83, 84*
Anderson, Dunston, Helene Inc. - Edison, NY - *StaDirAdAg 2-84*
Anderson Enterprises, Lee - St. Clair, MO - *BillIntBG 83-84*
Anderson Films, Ken - Winona Lake, IN - *ArtMar 84*
Anderson Graphic - Anderson, MO - *BaconPubCkNews 84*
Anderson Herald - Anderson, IN - *BaconPubCkNews 84; Ed&PubIntYB 82; NewsDir 84*
Anderson House - Hinsdale, NY - *BoPubDir 4, 5*
Anderson Independent-Mail [of Harte-Hanks Communications] - Anderson, SC - *AyerDirPub 83; BaconPubCkNews 84; NewsDir 84*
Anderson Jacobson Inc. - San Jose, CA - *DataDirSup 7-83; InfIndMarPl 83*
Anderson Jacobson Inc. - San Juan, CA - *DirInfWP 82*
Anderson, Jim - Brooklyn, NY - *AvMarPl 83; LitMarPl 84*
Anderson, Julian G. - Naples, FL - *BoPubDir 4, 5*
Anderson, Kenneth D. - *See* Combined Cable Corp.
Anderson, Lembke, Welinder Advertising Inc. [Subs. of Anderson & Lembke AB] - Stamford, CT - *DirMarMP 83*
Anderson-Madison Advertising Inc. - Minneapolis, MN - *StaDirAdAg 2-84*
Anderson Marketing Research - Minneapolis, MN - *IntDirMarRes 83*
Anderson, Merrill Co. Inc., The - *See* Merrill Anderson Co. Inc., The
Anderson/Miller Communications - San Francisco, CA - *StaDirAdAg 2-84*
Anderson Music Co. Inc., John - *See* Gallico Music Corp., Al
Anderson Productions, Paul L. - Ft. Collins, CO - *AvMarPl 83*
Anderson Public Relations, David - New York, NY - *DirPRFirms 83*
Anderson Publishing Co. - Cincinnati, OH - *LitMarPl 83, 84; WritMar 84*
Anderson Report - Simi Valley, CA - *BaconPubCkMag 84*
Anderson Stations - Denver, CO - *BrCabYB 84*
Anderson Valley Advertiser - Boonville, CA - *AyerDirPub 83; Ed&PubIntYB 82*
Anderson Valley Post - Anderson, CA - *BaconPubCkNews 84*
Anderson, Wilbur L. - Big Lake, TX - *Tel&CabFB 84C*
Anderson, Will - New York, NY - *BoPubDir 4, 5*
Anderson World Books Inc. [Aff. of Runner's World Magazine Co.] - Mountain View, CA - *LitMarPl 83, 84*
Andes Advertising Agency Inc. - Lancaster, PA - *StaDirAdAg 2-84*
Andes Community TV Inc. - Andes, NY - *BrCabYB 84*
Andgold Music Publishing - *See* Counterpop Music Group
Andor Publishing Inc. - East Rutherford, NJ - *BoPubDir 4, 5*
Andover Advocate - *See* Times Publishing Co.
Andover Advocate, The - Andover, KS - *Ed&PubIntYB 82*
Andover Journal - Andover, KS - *BaconPubCkNews 84; Ed&PubIntYB 82*
Andover News - Andover, NY - *BaconPubCkNews 84; Ed&PubIntYB 82*
Andover Pymatuning Area News - Andover, OH - *BaconPubCkNews 84*
Andover Townsman - Andover, MA - *AyerDirPub 83; BaconPubCkNews 84; Ed&PubIntYB 82; NewsDir 84*
Andrade Publishing Co. - Stafford, TX - *BillIntBG 83-84*
Andrea & Associates - New York, NY - *DirPRFirms 83*
Andrea Music Co. - Philadelphia, PA - *BillIntBG 83-84*
Andren, Carol - New York, NY - *LitMarPl 83, 84; MagIndMarPl 82-83*
Andreozzi Inc., Gennaro - New York, NY - *AvMarPl 83*
Andre's & Co. - Jersey City, NJ - *BoPubDir 4, 5*
Andrew Associates Inc., Gordon G. - New York, NY - *DirPRFirms 83*
Andrew Corp. - Orlando Park, IL - *HomeVid&CabYB 82-83*
Andrew Mountain Press - Hartford, CT - *BoPubDir 4, 5; LitMag&SmPr 83-84*
Andrew Telephone Co. Inc. - Andrew, IN - *TelDir&BG 83-84*
Andrews Agency Inc., The - Tiburon, CA - *StaDirAdAg 2-84*
Andrews & McMeel Inc. [Subs. of Universal Press Syndicate] - Fairway, KS - *LitMarPl 83, 84; WritMar 84*
Andrews & Thomas Inc. - Chicago, IL - *StaDirAdAg 2-84*
Andrews Associates, Gene - Battle Creek, MI - *AvMarPl 83*
Andrews County News - Andrews, TX - *AyerDirPub 83; BaconPubCkNews 84; Ed&PubIntYB 82; NewsDir 84*
Andrews, Elaine - New York, NY - *LitMarPl 83, 84; MagIndMarPl 82-83*
Andrews Journal - Andrews, NC - *BaconPubCkNews 84; Ed&PubIntYB 82*
Andrews Market Cycle Investing - Cupertino, CA - *MagIndMarPl 82-83*
Andrews Marketing Communications Co., Ray - Northfield, IL - *StaDirAdAg 2-84*
Andrews/Mautner - Milwaukee, WI - *AdAge 3-28-84; StaDirAdAg 2-84*
Andrews/Nelson/Whitehead [Div. of Boise Cascade] - Long Island City, NY - *DirInfWP 82; LitMarPl 83, 84; MagIndMarPl 82-83*
Andrews Records, Bob - Redondo Beach, CA - *BillIntBG 83-84*
Andrews Workshops in Creativity - New York, NY - *IntDirMarRes 83*
Androgyne Books - San Francisco, CA - *BoPubDir 4, 5; LitMag&SmPr 83-84*
Andromeda Associates - Washington, DC - *LitMarPl 84*
Andromeda Computer Systems - Greensboro, NC - *MicrocomMPl 84*
Andromeda Productions - Elmira, NY - *AvMarPl 83*
Andronicus Publishing Co. [Div. of Haldi Associates Inc.] - New York, NY - *LitMarPl 83, 84; MicroMarPl 82-83*
Andrus Gerontological Information Center [of University of Southern California] - Los Angeles, CA - *EISS 83*
Andujar Communication Technologies Inc. - La Jolla, CA - *LitMarPl 83, 84*
Andustin Music - Woodstock, NY - *BillIntBG 83-84*
Andy Warhol's Interview - New York, NY - *MagDir 84*
Andysongs - *See* Marvel Music, Andy
Anemone Press - Washington, DC - *BoPubDir 4, 5; LitMag&SmPr 83-84*
Anesthesia & Analgesia - Cleveland, OH - *BaconPubCkMag 84; MagDir 84*
Anesthesia Progress [of American Dental Society of Anesthesiology] - Bronx, NY - *BaconPubCkMag 84; MagDir 84*
Anesthesiology - Philadelphia, PA - *BaconPubCkMag 84; MagDir 84; MagIndMarPl 82-83*
Anesthesiology News - Georgetown, CT - *BaconPubCkMag 84*
Anesthesiology Review - New York, NY - *BaconPubCkMag 84; MagDir 84*
Aneta Star - Aneta, ND - *Ed&PubIntYB 82*
Aneta Star - *See* Ness Press Inc.
Aneuploidy [of US Dept. of Energy] - Oak Ridge, TN - *DataDirOnSer 84; DirOnDB Spring 84*

Ang Associates Pte. Ltd., T. H. - Singapore, Singapore - *IntDirMarRes 83*
Angel City Books - Hollywood, CA - *BoPubDir 4 Sup, 5*
Angel Music, Johnny - Riverdale, NY - *BillIntBG 83-84*
Angel Press - Monterey, CA - *BoPubDir 4, 5; WritMar 84*
Angelaco Records Inc. - Elkhart, IN - *BillIntBG 83-84*
Angeles Mesa News - Los Angeles, CA - *AyerDirPub 83*
Angeles Mesa Wave [of Los Angeles Central News-Wave Publications] - Los Angeles, CA - *NewsDir 84*
Angell & Associates Inc., B. - Chicago, IL - *IntDirMarRes 83*
Angell & Co. Inc. - New York, NY - *IntDirMarRes 83*
Angelo Advertising - Oklahoma City, OK - *StaDirAdAg 2-84*
Angels Camp Calaveras Californian - *See* Calaveras Publishing Co.
Angel's Gate Press - Playa del Rey, CA - *BoPubDir 4, 5*
Angel's Secretarial & Billing Services - Costa Mesa, CA - *LitMarPl 83, 84*
Angelstone Press - Birmingham, AL - *LitMag&SmPr 83-84*
Angenieux Corp. of America - Hudson, NH - *AvMarPl 83*
Angers Publishing Corp. - Lafayette, LA - *BoPubDir 5*
Angier Independent - Angier, NC - *BaconPubCkNews 84*
Angiology - Great Neck, NY - *BaconPubCkMag 84; MagDir 84*
Angle Publishing, Johnny - Jackson, MS - *BillIntBG 83-84*
Angle Steel [Div. of Kewannee Scientific Equipment] - Plainwell, MI - *DirInfWP 82*
Angler - Oakland, CA - *BaconPubCkMag 84; MagDir 84; WritMar 84*
Angler & Hunter - Peterborough, ON, Canada - *BaconPubCkMag 84*
Angler's & Shooter's Press - Goshen, CT - *BoPubDir 4 Sup, 5*
Angler's News - Keyport, NJ - *BaconPubCkMag 84*
Angleton Times - Angleton, TX - *BaconPubCkNews 84; Ed&PubIntYB 82; NewsDir 84*
Anglican Digest - Eureka Springs, AR - *LitMarPl 83; MagIndMarPl 82-83*
Anglo-Brazilian Information Service - Sao Paulo, Brazil - *EISS 7-83 Sup*
Anglo-Welsh Review, The [of Five Arches Press] - Cardiff, Wales - *LitMag&SmPr 83-84*
Angola Evans Journal - Angola, NY - *BaconPubCkNews 84*
Angola Herald - Angola, IN - *Ed&PubIntYB 82*
Angola Herald-Republican [of Home News Enterprises] - Columbus, IN - *NewsDir 84*
Angola Steuben County Herald-Republican - Angola, IN - *BaconPubCkNews 84*
Angriff Press - Hollywood, CA - *BoPubDir 4, 5*
Angst World Library - Selma, OR - *BoPubDir 4, 5; LitMag&SmPr 83-84*
Angstrom Unit Inc., The - New York, NY - *AvMarPl 83*
Angus Journal - St. Joseph, MO - *BaconPubCkMag 84; MagDir 84*
Angus TV Cable Co. - Colliers, WV - *BrCabYB 84; Tel&CabFB 84C*
Anhinga Press - Tallahassee, FL - *BoPubDir 4, 5*
Anhinga Press (Apalachee Poetry Center) - Tallahassee, FL - *BoPubDir 4, 5*
Anian Press - Vancouver, BC, Canada - *BoPubDir 4 Sup, 5*
Anidata - Blackwood, NJ - *MicrocomMPl 84; MicrocomSwDir 1*
Aniforms [Div. of Comart Associates Inc.] - New York, NY - *AvMarPl 83; Tel&CabFB 84C*
Anima Books [Aff. of Conococheague Associates Inc.] - Chambersburg, PA - *BoPubDir 4, 5; LitMag&SmPr 83-84*
Anima Publications - Chambersburg, PA - *LitMag&SmPr 83-84*
Animal Behaviour Abstracts [of Information Retrieval Ltd.] - London, England - *CompReadDB 82*
Animal Breeding Abstracts [of Commonwealth Bureau of Animal Breeding & Genetics] - Edinburgh, Scotland - *CompReadDB 82*
Animal Disease Occurrence - Slough, England - *DirOnDB Spring 84*
Animal Health Technician, The - Princeton Junction, NJ - *BaconPubCkMag 84*
Animal Kingdom - Bronx, NY - *BaconPubCkMag 84; MagIndMarPl 82-83; WritMar 84*
Animal Nutrition & Health [of California Farmer] - San Francisco, CA - *MagDir 84; MagIndMarPl 82-83*
Animal Nutrition & Health - Mt. Morris, IL - *BaconPubCkMag 84*
Animal Owners Motivation Programs - Frankfort, IL - *BoPubDir 4, 5*
Animal Review [of Stonehedge Co.] - Pocasset, MA - *WritMar 84*
Animal Welfare Institute - Washington, DC - *BoPubDir 4, 5*
Animals - Boston, MA - *WritMar 84*
Animals - Framingham, MA - *MagIndMarPl 82-83*
Animals - Framingham Center, MA - *ArtMar 84*
Animals Animals Enterprises - New York, NY - *LitMarPl 83, 84; MagIndMarPl 82-83*
Animated Display Creators Inc. - Miami, FL - *AvMarPl 83*
Animated Electronics Films Inc. - Annapolis, MD - *AvMarPl 83*
Animated Productions Inc. - New York, NY - *AvMarPl 83; TelAl 83, 84; Tel&CabFB 84C*
Animation Arts Associates Inc. - Philadelphia, PA - *ArtMar 84; AvMarPl 83; WritMar 84*
Animation Filmakers Corp. - Hollywood, CA - *ArtMar 84*
Animation Graphics - Reston, VA - *MicrocomMPl 84*
Animation People, The - London, England - *Tel&CabFB 84C*
Animator, The - Portland, OR - *MagIndMarPl 82-83*
Animcalc - Portland, OR - *MicrocomMPl 84*
ANiME - Ibaraki-Ken, Japan - *DirOnDB Spring 84*
Anita Tribune - Anita, IA - *BaconPubCkNews 84; Ed&PubIntYB 82*
Anitek Software Products - Melbourne, FL - *MicrocomMPl 4*
Anitya Publishing - Miami, FL - *BillIntBG 83-84*
Anixter Bros. Inc. [of Anixter Communications] - Skokie, IL - *CabTVFinDB 83; HomeVid&CabYB 82-83*
Anixter Pruzan - Wharton, NJ - *HomeVid&CabYB 82-83*
Anjou - Toronto, ON, Canada - *LitMag&SmPr 83-84*
Ankeny Press-Citizen - Ankeny, IA - *BaconPubCkNews 84; Ed&PubIntYB 82*
Ankeny Press Citizen [of West Des Moines Express Inc.] - West Des Moines, IA - *NewsDir 84*
Ankhco - Palm Beach Gardens, FL - *BoPubDir 4 Sup, 5*
Anlon Music Co. - *See* Pavanne Music Co.
Anma Libri - Saratoga, CA - *BoPubDir 4, 5*
Ann Arbor Cablevision - Ann Arbor, MI - *BrCabYB 84; Tel&CabFB 84C*
Ann Arbor Cablevision Inc. - Ypsilanti, MI - *BrCabYB 84*
Ann Arbor News [of Booth Newspapers Inc.] - Ann Arbor, MI - *BaconPubCkNews 84; Ed&PubIntYB 82; NewsDir 84*
Ann Arbor Observer - Ann Arbor, MI - *WritMar 84*
Ann Arbor Publishers Inc. - Naples, FL - *BoPubDir 4, 5*
Ann Arbor Science Publishers [Div. of Butterworth Publishers] - Woburn, MA - *LitMarPl 84*
Ann Arbor Science Publishers [Div. of Butterworth Publishers] - Ann Arbor, MI - *LitMarPl 83*
Ann Arbor Software Associates - Ann Arbor, MI - *MicrocomMPl 84; MicrocomSwDir 1*
Ann Arbor Terminals Inc. - Ann Arbor, MI - *DataDirSup 7-83; InfIndMarPl 83; MicrocomMPl 84; WhoWMicrocom 83*
Anna Gazette-Democrat - Anna, IL - *BaconPubCkNews 84; NewsDir 84*
Anna-Jonesboro Cable TV [of Flora Cable TV Co.] - Anna, IL - *BrCabYB 84; Tel&CabFB 84C*
Anna Maria Islander - Anna Maria, FL - *BaconPubCkNews 84*
Anna Maria Islander/Longboat Islander [of The New York Times Co.] - Anna Maria, FL - *NewsDir 84*
Anna Publishing Inc. - Ocoee, FL - *LitMarPl 84; WritMar 84*
Anna Publishing Inc. - Winter Park, FL - *LitMarPl 83*
Annabelle Music - *See* Loring Music Co.
Annals of Allergy - Bloomington, MN - *BaconPubCkMag 84*
Annals of Allergy - Minneapolis, MN - *MagDir 84*
Annals of Emergency Medicine - Dallas, TX - *BaconPubCkMag 84; MagDir 84; MagIndMarPl 82-83*
Annals of Internal Medicine - Philadelphia, PA - *BaconPubCkMag 84; MagDir 84; MagIndMarPl 82-83*
Annals of Mathematics - Princeton, NJ - *MagIndMarPl 82-83*
Annals of Neurology - Boston, MA - *BaconPubCkMag 84*
Annals of Plastic Surgery - Boston, MA - *MagDir 84*
Annals of St. Anne de Beaupre, The - St. Anne, PQ, Canada - *WritMar 84*
Annals of Surgery - Philadelphia, PA - *BaconPubCkMag 84; MagDir 84; MagIndMarPl 82-83*
Annals of the American Academy of Political & Social Science - Philadelphia, PA - *MagDir 84; MagIndMarPl 82-83*

Annals of the Association of American Geographers - Washington, DC - *MagDir 84*
Annals of the Entomological Society of America - College Park, MD - *MagDir 84*
Annals of Thoracic Surgery - Boston, MA - *BaconPubCkMag 84*
Annan, Deborah - Seattle, WA - *LitMarPl 84; MagIndMarPl 82-83*
Annandale Advocate - Annandale, MN - *BaconPubCkNews 84; Ed&PubIntYB 82*
Annapolis Capital - Annapolis, MD - *BaconPubCkNews 84; NewsDir 84*
Annapolis CATV Inc. [of Prime Cable Corp.] - Annapolis, MD - *BrCabYB 84; Tel&CabFB 84C*
Annapolis Valley Radio Ltd. - Kentville, NS, Canada - *BrCabYB 84*
Anne Arundel Times [of Banner Corp.] - Annapolis, MD - *Ed&PubIntYB 82; NewsDir 84*
Anne Arundel Times/Severna Park Village Voice - Annapolis, MD - *AyerDirPub 83*
Annex Computer Report - Phoenix, AZ - *DirOnDB Spring 84*
Annex Computer Report [of NewsNet Inc.] - Bryn Mawr, PA - *DataDirOnSer 84*
Annextra Music - Nashville, TN - *BillIntBG 83-84*
Annick Press Ltd. - Willowdale, ON, Canada - *LitMarPl 83, 84*
Annis Co., R. B. - Indianapolis, IN - *AvMarPl 83*
Anniston NewChannels [of New Channels Corp.] - Anniston, AL - *BrCabYB 84; Tel&CabFB 84C*
Anniston Star [of Consolidated Publishing Co.] - Anniston, AL - *BaconPubCkNews 84; BrCabYB 84; Ed&PubIntYB 82; NewsDir 84*
Announcer - Luverne, MN - *AyerDirPub 83*
Annual Buyers Guide [of International Mobile Air Conditioning Association Inc.] - Dallas, TX - *MagDir 84*
Annual Reports Abstracts [of Predicasts Inc.] - Cleveland, OH - *EISS 7-83 Sup*
Annual Reviews Inc. - Palo Alto, CA - *BoPubDir 4, 5; LitMarPl 84*
Annual Survey of Manufactures [of Chase Econometrics/ Interactive Data Corp.] - Waltham, MA - *DataDirOnSer 84*
Annual Survey of Manufactures - Bala Cynwyd, PA - *DirOnDB Spring 84*
Annuit Coeptis Music Records Tapes Ltd. - Croydon, PA - *BillIntBG 83-84*
Anode Music Publishing - Houston, TX - *BillIntBG 83-84*
Anoka County Union - Anoka, MN - *Ed&PubIntYB 82*
Anoka County Union - Minneapolis, MN - *NewsDir 84*
Anoka County Union - *See* Anoka County Union & Shopper Inc.
Anoka County Union & Shopper Inc. - Anoka, MN - *BaconPubCkNews 84*
Anokye, Akua-Adiki - New York, NY - *BoPubDir 4, 5*
Anolog Science Fiction/Science Fact - New York, NY - *WritMar 84*
Anonym Press - Occidental, CA - *BoPubDir 4, 5*
Anonymous Owl Press - Albuquerque, NM - *LitMag&SmPr 83-84*
Another Direction [Div. of Billy Williams Enterprises Inc.] - New York, NY - *AvMarPl 83*
Another Season [of Willowwood Publishing] - Cologne, MN - *LitMag&SmPr 83-84; WritMar 84*
ANR Advertising Agency Inc. - West Caldwell, NJ - *StaDirAdAg 2-84*
Ansa-Letter [Div. of Latham Process Corp.] - New York, NY - *MagIndMarPl 82-83*
Ansel Productions Inc. - New York, NY - *Tel&CabFB 84C*
Ansley Herald - Broken Bow, NE - *BaconPubCkNews 84*
Ansley Herald, The - Ansley, NE - *Ed&PubIntYB 82*
Anson-Cartwright Editions - Toronto, ON, Canada - *BoPubDir 4, 5*
Anson Record & Messenger & Intelligencer - Wadesboro, NC - *AyerDirPub 83; Ed&PubIntYB 82; NewsDir 84*
Anson Record, The - Wadesboro, NC - *Ed&PubIntYB 82*
Anson Western Observer - Anson, TX - *BaconPubCkNews 84*
Ansonia Evening Sentinel [of Thomson Newspapers Inc.] - Ansonia, CT - *BaconPubCkNews 84; NewsDir 84*
Ansonia Records Inc. - New York, NY - *BillIntBG 83-84*
Anspach Grossman Portugal Inc. - New York, NY - *HBIndAd&MS 82-83*
Anstat Inc. - New York, NY - *ADAPSOMemDir 83-84; DataDirOnSer 84*
Ansuda Publications - Harris, IA - *BoPubDir 4, 5; LitMag&SmPr 83-84*
Answer Group Inc. - Cincinnati, OH - *IntDirMarRes 83*
Answer in Computers, The - San Diego, CA - *MicrocomMPl 84; WhoWMicrocom 83*
Answer Line - Sudbury, MA - *WritMar 84*
Answer Man Newsletter, The - San Francisco, CA - *LitMag&SmPr 83-84*
Answer Software Corp. - Cupertino, CA - *MicrocomMPl 84*
Antaeus [of The Ecco Press] - New York, NY - *LitMag&SmPr 83-84; MagDir 84; MagIndMarPl 82-83*
Antal Persknipseldienst - The Hague, Netherlands - *ProGuPRSer 4*
Antares Foundation - San Francisco, CA - *BoPubDir 4, 5*
Antcliff, Keith - Dugway, UT - *Tel&CabFB 84C p.1664*
Antebi & Co. - Brooklyn, NY - *StaDirAdAg 2-84*
Antech Inc. - Roswell, GA - *MicrocomMPl 84; MicrocomSwDir 1; WhoWMicrocom 83*
Antelope Island Press - St. George, UT - *BoPubDir 4 Sup, 5*
Antelope Valley Cablevision [of Tribune Cable Communications] - California City, CA - *BrCabYB 84*
Antelope Valley Cablevision [of Tribune Cable Communications] - Edwards AFB, CA - *BrCabYB 84*
Antelope Valley Cablevision [of Tribune Cable Communications] - Palmdale, CA - *BrCabYB 84*
Antelope Valley Cablevision [of Tribune Cable Communications] - Quartz Hill, CA - *BrCabYB 84*
Antelope Valley Ledger-Gazette - Lancaster, CA - *AyerDirPub 83; Ed&PubIntYB 82*
Antelope Valley Press - Antelope Valley, CA - *Ed&PubIntYB 82*
Antelope Valley Press - Palmdale, CA - *AyerDirPub 83*
Antenna - San Diego, CA - *LitMag&SmPr 83-84*
Antenna Electronics Co. - Ft. Worth, TX - *MicrocomMPl 84*
Antenne TV de St. Zacharie - St. Zacharie, PQ, Canada - *BrCabYB 84*
Anteresgeo Music - *See* Jamie Music Publishing Co.
Antex Data Systems - Mountain View, CA - *MicrocomMPl 84*
Anthoensen Press - Portland, ME - *LitMarPl 83, 84*
Anthon-Herald - Anthon, IA - *BaconPubCkNews 84; Ed&PubIntYB 82*
Anthony, Dorothy Malone - Ft. Scott, KS - *BoPubDir 5*
Anthony Enterprises, Ray - Los Angeles, CA - *Tel&CabFB 84C*
Anthony Inc., C. & R. - New York, NY - *BoPubDir 4, 5*
Anthony Music Inc., Chuck - Altamonte Springs, FL - *BillIntBG 83-84*
Anthony Press - Alhambra, CA - *BoPubDir 4, 5*
Anthony Public Relations, Carolyn - Brooklyn, NY - *LitMarPl 84*
Anthony Publishing Co. - Stow, MA - *BoPubDir 4, 5*
Anthony Republican & Bulletin - Anthony, KS - *BaconPubCkNews 84; Ed&PubIntYB 82*
Anthony, Travis D. - Rush Springs, OK - *BoPubDir 4, 5*
Anthony Wayne Herald [of Toledo Herald Newspapers] - Toledo, OH - *AyerDirPub 83; NewsDir 84*
Anthony Wayne Standard - Waterville, OH - *Ed&PubIntYB 82*
Anthony's Mobile Home Park Ltd. - Dorchester, ON, Canada - *BrCabYB 84*
Anthro-Digital Inc. - Pittsfield, MA - *MicrocomMPl 84*
Anthro-Photo File - Cambridge, MA - *LitMarPl 83, 84; MagIndMarPl 82-83*
Anthropology Resource Center Inc. - Boston, MA - *BoPubDir 4, 5*
Anthroposophic Press Inc. - Spring Valley, NY - *LitMarPl 83, 84*
Anti-Apartheid Movement - London, England - *LitMag&SmPr 83-84*
Anti-Apartheid News - London, England - *LitMag&SmPr 83-84*
Anti-Defamation League [Aff. of B'nai B'rith] - New York, NY - *BoPubDir 4, 5*
Anti-Ocean Press - Ferndale, MI - *BoPubDir 4, 5*
Anti-Ocean Press - Southfield, MI - *LitMag&SmPr 83-84*
Antic Magazine - San Francisco, CA - *MicrocomMPl 84; WritMar 84*
Antietam Cable TV [of Schurz Communications Inc.] - Hagerstown, MD - *BrCabYB 84; Tel&CabFB 84C*

Antietam Press - Boonsboro, MD - *LitMag&SmPr 83-84; LitMarPl 83, 84*
Antigo Area Shoppers Guide - Antigo, WI - *AyerDirPub 83*
Antigo Cablevision [of Wisconsin Cablevision & Radio Co. Inc.] - Antigo, WI - *BrCabYB 84; Tel&CabFB 84C*
Antigo Daily Journal [of Berner Bros. Publishing Co. Inc.] - Antigo, WI - *Ed&PubIntYB 82; NewsDir 84*
Antigo Journal - Antigo, WI - *BaconPubCkNews 84*
Antigonish Cablevision Ltd. - Antigonish, NS, Canada - *BrCabYB 84*
Antigonish Review, The [of St. Francis Xavier University] - Antigonish, NS, Canada - *LitMag&SmPr 83-84; WritMar 84*
Antioch Bi-State Reporter [of Lakeland Publishers Inc.] - Grayslake, IL - *NewsDir 84*
Antioch Daily Ledger - Antioch, CA - *NewsDir 84*
Antioch News - Antioch, IL - *AyerDirPub 83; Ed&PubIntYB 82*
Antioch News [of Lakeland Publishers Inc.] - Grayslake, IL - *NewsDir 84*
Antioch News - *See* Lakeland Publishers Inc.
Antioch Publication - Kansas City, MO - *AyerDirPub 83*
Antioch Publishing Co. - Yellow Springs, OH - *ArtMar 84; BoPubDir 4 Sup, 5*
Antioch Reporter - Antioch, IL - *AyerDirPub 83; Ed&PubIntYB 82*
Antioch Reporter [of Lakeland Publishers Inc.] - Grayslake, IL - *NewsDir 84*
Antioch Reporter - *See* Lakeland Publishers Inc.
Antioch Review - Yellow Springs, OH - *LitMag&SmPr 83-84; LitMarPl 83, 84; MagIndMarPl 82-83; WritMar 84*
Antiope [of Teledifusion de France] - Paris, France - *InfIndMarPl 83*
Antiope & Telematics Corp. - New York, NY - *VideoDir 82-83*
Antiope Teletext System - Montrouge, France - *EISS 83*
Antiquarian & Landmarks Society Inc., The - Hartford, CT - *MicroMarPl 82-83*
Antiquarian, The - Huntington, NY - *ArtMar 84; WritMar 84*
Antiquarian Traders Services - Los Angeles, CA - *StaDirAdAg 2-84*
Antiquarium - Bethany, CT - *BoPubDir 4, 5*
Antique Automobile - Hershey, PA - *MagDir 84; MagIndMarPl 82-83*
Antique Clocks Publishing - Concord, CA - *BoPubDir 4, 5*
Antique Market Tabloid - Silver Spring, MD - *WritMar 84*
Antique Monthly [of Boone Inc.] - Tuscaloosa, AL - *BaconPubCkMag 84; Ed&PubIntYB 82; MagDir 84; WritMar 84*
Antique Motor News - Long Beach, CA - *BaconPubCkMag 84; MagDir 84; MagIndMarPl 82-83*
Antique Phonograph Monthly - Brooklyn, NY - *LitMag&SmPr 83-84*
Antique Records - Pittsburg, KS - *BillIntBG 83-84*
Antique Trader Weekly, The - Dubuque, IA - *BaconPubCkMag 84; MagDir 84; MagIndMarPl 82-83; WritMar 84*
Antiques - New York, NY - *BaconPubCkMag 84; LitMarPl 83, 84*
Antiques & Art - Vancouver, BC, Canada - *BaconPubCkMag 84*
Antiques & Collectibles - Glen Head, NY - *BaconPubCkMag 84*
Antiques Dealer [of Ebel-Doctorow Publications Inc.] - Clifton, NJ - *ArtMar 84; BaconPubCkMag 84; MagDir 84; MagIndMarPl 82-83; WritMar 84*
Antiquity Reprints - Rockville Centre, NY - *BoPubDir 4, 5*
Antisia Music Inc. - New York, NY - *BillIntBG 83-84*
Antitrust & Trade Regulation Report - Washington, DC - *MagIndMarPl 82-83*
Antler & Baldwin Design Group Inc. - New York, NY - *LitMarPl 83, 84*
Antlers American - Antlers, OK - *BaconPubCkNews 84; Ed&PubIntYB 82*
Anton Star - Anton, TX - *Ed&PubIntYB 82*
Antrim County News - Bellaire, MI - *Ed&PubIntYB 82*
Antwerp Bee-Argus - Antwerp, OH - *AyerDirPub 83; BaconPubCkNews 84; Ed&PubIntYB 82*
Anvil Cases Inc. - Rosemead, CA - *AvMarPl 83*
Anvil Herald - Hondo, TX - *AyerDirPub 83*
Anvil Press - Millville, MN - *BoPubDir 4, 5; LitMag&SmPr 83-84*
Anvil Press Poetry - London, England - *LitMag&SmPr 83-84*
Any Photo Type - New York, NY - *LitMarPl 83, 84*
AOA News (Communications Div.) - St. Louis, MO - *MagIndMarPl 82-83*
AOCPM Advertising - Richmond, VA - *StaDirAdAg 2-84*
AOM Corp. - Birmingham, AL - *DataDirSup 7-83*
AOPA Pilot [of Aircraft Owners & Pilots Association] - Bethesda, MD - *Folio 83; MagIndMarPl 82-83*
AOPA Pilot - Frederick, MD - *BaconPubCkMag 84; MagDir 84; WritMar 84*
AORN Journal - Denver, CO - *BaconPubCkMag 84*
A.P. Consultants Inc. - *See* Advertising Partners/A.P. Designers Inc.
AP Network - Washington, DC - *BrCabYB 84*
AP Newscable - Washington, DC - *Tel&CabFB 84C*
AP Newscable [Div. of The Associated Press] - New York, NY - *BrCabYB 84; CabTVPrDB 83; Tel&CabFB 84C*
AP Newsfeatures [Div. of Associated Press] - New York, NY - *BaconPubCkNews 84; LitMarPl 83, 84; MagIndMarPl 82-83*
AP Stock [of Source Telecomputing Corp.] - McLean, VA - *DataDirOnSer 84*
AP Videotex [of Dialcom Inc.] - Silver Spring, MD - *DataDirOnSer 84*
AP Videotex Service [of Source Telecomputing Corp.] - McLean, VA - *DataDirOnSer 84*
APA Monitor [of American Psychological Association] - Washington, DC - *ArtMar 84; WritMar 84*
A.P.A. Studios Inc. - New York, NY - *TelAl 83, 84*
Apace [of International Airline Passengers Association Inc.] - Dallas, TX - *MagDir 84*
Apache Cablevision - San Carlos, AZ - *Tel&CabFB 84C*
Apache Junction Independent - Apache Junction, AZ - *BaconPubCkNews 84*
Apache News - Apache, OK - *AyerDirPub 83; BaconPubCkNews 84; Ed&PubIntYB 82*
Apache Sentinel - Apache Junction, AZ - *AyerDirPub 83; Ed&PubIntYB 82*
Apalachee Quarterly - Tallahassee, FL - *LitMag&SmPr 83-84; WritMar 84*
Apalachicola Carrabelle Times - Apalachicola, FL - *BaconPubCkNews 84; Ed&PubIntYB 82*
Apartment Owner/Builder [of Apartment News Publications Inc.] - Long Beach, CA - *BaconPubCkMag 84; MagDir 84*
APCO Bulletin - New Smyrna Beach, FL - *BaconPubCkMag 84; MagDir 84; MagIndMarPl 82-83*
APD Business Machines - San Diego, CA - *DirInfWP 82*
Apeco Corp. - Des Plains, IL - *DirInfWP 82*
Apertura - Orford, NH - *AvMarPl 83*
Aperture [Div. of Silver Mountain Foundation] - Millerton, NY - *LitMarPl 83, 84; MagIndMarPl 82-83*
Aperture PhotoBank Inc. - Seattle, WA - *LitMarPl 83, 84*
Apex Music Publications - Cupertino, CA - *BillIntBG 83-84*
Apex Western Wake Herald - Apex, NC - *BaconPubCkNews 84*
Apexton Records Manufacturing Corp. - Long Island City, NY - *BillIntBG 83-84*
APF Electronics - New York, NY - *MicrocomMPl 83*
APG News - Havre de Grace, MD - *AyerDirPub 83*
APH Publishers - Shreveport, LA - *BoPubDir 4, 5*
API Magazine - Milton-Freewater, OR - *BaconPubCkMag 84*
API Monthly & Quarterly Drilling Reports - New York, NY - *DirOnDB Spring 84*
Apicultural Abstracts [of International Bee Research Association] - Gerrards Cross, England - *CompReadDB 82; EISS 83*
APILit [of American Petroleum Institute] - New York, NY - *DataDirOnSer 84; DirOnDB Spring 84; OnBibDB 3*
APIPat [of American Petroleum Institute] - New York, NY - *DataDirOnSer 84; DirOnDB Spring 84*
APL Bibliography [of I. P. Sharp Associates Ltd.] - Toronto, ON, Canada - *CompReadDB 82; DataDirOnSer 84; DirOnDB Spring 84*
APL Computers Inc. - Chappaqua, NY - *MicrocomMPl 84*
APL Market News [of Southwater Corp.] - Mt. Carmel, CT - *BaconPubCkMag 84; MicrocomMPl 84*
APL Press - Palo Alto, CA - *BoPubDir 4, 5*
Aplin, Jim - Brooklyn, NY - *MagIndMarPl 82-83*
Aplogica Inc. - New York, NY - *MicrocomMPl 84*
APM Press [Aff. of APM Library of Recorded Sound] - Brooklyn, NY - *BoPubDir 4, 5; LitMag&SmPr 83-84*
Apocalypse Press - Topeka, KS - *BoPubDir 5*

Apocalypse Press - Millville, MN - *BoPubDir 4*
Apocalypse Publishing Co. - Niagara Falls, NY - *BoPubDir 5*
Apogee Communications Group - Boulder, CO - *AvMarPl 83*
Apogee/Lyrical Ways [of Quixsilver Press] - Baltimore, MD - *LitMag&SmPr 83-84*
Apogee Software - Savannah, GA - *MicrocomMPl 84*
Apollo Ad Service - York, PA - *Ed&PubIntYB 82*
Apollo Advertising Agency - Indian Hills, CO - *StaDirAdAg 2-84*
Apollo Advertising Agency - Rochelle, IL - *DirMarMP 83; StaDirAdAg 2-84*
Apollo Audio Visual [Div. of Apollo Space Systems Inc.] - Bellport, NY - *AvMarPl 83*
Apollo Book - Poughkeepsie, NY - *BoPubDir 4, 5*
Apollo Cablevision - Apollo Beach, FL - *Tel&CabFB 84C*
Apollo Cablevision - Hillsborough County, FL - *Tel&CabFB 84C*
Apollo Communications Inc. - Hays, KS - *Tel&CabFB 84C p.1664*
Apollo Computer Inc. - Chelmsford, MA - *DataDirSup 7-83*
Apollo Entertainment Network - New York, NY - *BrCabYB 84*
Apollo News-Record - Apollo, PA - *AyerDirPub 83; BaconPubCkNews 84; Ed&PubIntYB 82*
Apon Publishing Co. - Long Island City, NY - *BillIntBG 83-84*
Apon Record Co. Inc. - Long Island City, NY - *BillIntBG 83-84*
Aponte y Asociados SA, Jesus - Caracas, Venezuela - *IntDirMarRes 83*
Apopka Planter - Apopka, FL - *BaconPubCkNews 84*
Apothecary, The [of Health Care Marketing Services] - Los Altos, CA - *BaconPubCkMag 84; MagDir 84; WritMar 84*
Appalachia Independent - Appalachia, VA - *BaconPubCkNews 84; Ed&PubIntYB 82*
Appalachia Journal - Boston, MA - *MagDir 84*
Appalachian Cablevision of Ohio - McArthur, OH - *BrCabYB 84; Tel&CabFB 84C*
Appalachian Cablevision of Ohio - Oak Hill, OH - *BrCabYB 84*
Appalachian Community Service Network - Washington, DC - *BrCabYB 84; HomeVid&CabYB 82-83*
Appalachian Consortium Press - Boone, NC - *BoPubDir 4, 5; LitMag&SmPr 83-84; LitMarPl 84*
Appalachian Mountain Club Books - Boston, MA - *LitMarPl 83, 84; WritMar 84*
Appalachian News-Express - Pikeville, KY - *AyerDirPub 83; Ed&PubIntYB 82; NewsDir 84*
Appalachian State University (Albion) - Boone, NC - *BoPubDir 4, 5*
Appalachian, The [of Appalachian State University] - Boone, NC - *NewsDir 84*
Appalachian Trailway News - Harpers Ferry, WV - *MagIndMarPl 82-83*
Appalachian Voice, The - Charleston, WV - *NewsDir 84*
Appaloosa News - Moscow, ID - *ArtMar 84; BaconPubCkMag 84; MagDir 84; WritMar 84*
Appalshop Inc. - Whitesburg, KY - *AvMarPl 83; BillIntBG 83-84*
Apparat Inc. - Denver, CO - *MicrocomMPl 83, 84*
Appareils Electroniques Berube Inc. - Ville St. Georges Ouest, BC, Canada - *BrCabYB 84*
Appareils Electroniques Berube Inc. - Prosper, PQ, Canada - *BrCabYB 84*
Appareils Electroniques Berube Inc. - St. Georges, PQ, Canada - *BrCabYB 84; Tel&CabFB 84C*
Apparel Industry Magazine [of Shore Publishing Co.] - Atlanta, GA - *BaconPubCkMag 84; MagDir 84; WritMar 84*
Apparel News Group - Los Angeles, CA - *NewsBur 6*
Apparel News South [of Apparel News Group] - Los Angeles, CA - *BaconPubCkMag 84; WritMar 84*
Apparel World - New York, NY - *ArtMar 84; BaconPubCkMag 84*
Appeal-Democrat - Marysville, CA - *AyerDirPub 83; BaconPubCkNews 84; Ed&PubIntYB 82*
Appeal-Tribune/Mt. Angel News - Silverton, OR - *AyerDirPub 83*
Appel Color Photography - Twin Lakes, WI - *MagIndMarPl 82-83*
Appel, Paul P. - Mt. Vernon, NY - *BoPubDir 4, 5*
Appel Productions Inc., Mike - New York, NY - *BillIntBG 83-84*
Appelgate Advertising Agency Inc. - Muncie, IN - *StaDirAdAg 2-84*
Appetizer, The - Des Moines, IA - *BaconPubCkMag 84; MagDir 84*
Appetizingly Yours - Brandford, CT - *MagDir 84*
Applause - San Diego, CA - *MagDir 84*
Applause Productions Inc. - Port Washington, NY - *AvMarPl 83*
Applause Publications - Diamond Bar, CA - *BoPubDir 4, 5; LitMag&SmPr 83-84*
Applause Records Inc. - Beverly Hills, CA - *BillIntBG 83-84*
Apple Arts Ltd. - Freehold, NJ - *ArtMar 84*
Apple Assembly Line [of S-C Software Corp.] - Dallas, TX - *MicrocomMPl 84*
Apple Bits [of Neo Apple Corp.] - Euclid, OH - *MicrocomMPl 84*
Apple Cable Television Inc. - Dover Plains, NY - *BrCabYB 84*
Apple Computer Inc. - Cupertino, CA - *AvMarPl 83; DataDirSup 7-83; Datamation 6-83; DirInfWP 82; HomeVid&CabYB 82-83; MicrocomMPl 83, 84; MicrocomSwDir 1; Top100Al 83; VideoDir 82-83; WhoWMicrocom 83*
Apple Country Computers - East Wenatchee, WA - *MicrocomMPl 84*
Apple Educators' Newsletter - Ventura, CA - *MicrocomMPl 84*
Apple for the Teacher - Sacramento, CA - *MicrocomMPl 83, 84; WhoWMicrocom 83*
Apple-Gems - San Francisco, CA - *BoPubDir 4, 5*
Apple-Glass Music [Div. of American Music Co.] - Madison, WI - *BillIntBG 83-84*
Apple Orchard [of International Apple Core] - Santa Clara, CA - *BaconPubCkMag 84; MicrocomMPl 84*
Apple Orchard - Vacaville, CA - *WhoWMicrocom 83*
Apple Paget Sound Program Library Exchange - Seattle, WA - *MicrocomMPl 84*
Apple Peel, The [of Birmingham Apple Corp.] - Birmingham, AL - *MicrocomMPl 84*
Apple Pie Press - Berkeley, CA - *BoPubDir 4, 5*
Apple Press - Milwaukie, OR - *BoPubDir 4, 5; WritMar 84*
Apple Press, An - Mendocino, CA - *LitMag&SmPr 83-84*
Apple Publishing Co. [Aff. of Chiron Association Inc.] - New York, NY - *BoPubDir 4, 5*
Apple Pye Records Inc. - Yonkers, NY - *BillIntBG 83-84*
Apple Seeds - Littleton, CO - *BoPubDir 4, 5*
Apple Tree Lane - Atherton, CA - *BoPubDir 4*
Apple Tree Lane - Woodside, CA - *BoPubDir 5; LitMag&SmPr 83-84*
Apple Tree Press - Flint, MI - *BoPubDir 4, 5*
Apple Valley Cable TV [of Booth American Co.] - Apple Valley, CA - *BrCabYB 84; Tel&CabFB 84C*
Apple Valley Cable TV [of Booth American Co.] - Ft. Irwin, CA - *Tel&CabFB 84C*
Apple Valley Cable TV - Brewster, WA - *BrCabYB 84; Tel&CabFB 84C*
Apple Valley Cable TV - Twisp, WA - *Tel&CabFB 84C*
Apple Valley Cable TV - Winthrop, WA - *Tel&CabFB 84C*
Apple Valley/Lakeville Countryside [of Burnsville Current] - Burnsville, MN - *NewsDir 84*
Apple Valley News - Apple Valley, CA - *BaconPubCkNews 84; Ed&PubIntYB 82*
Apple-Wood Books - Cambridge, MA - *LitMag&SmPr 83-84; LitMarPl 83, 84; WritMar 84*
Applebaum Productions Inc., Stan - New York, NY - *AvMarPl 83*
Applebites [Subs. of E. H. Hurwitz & Associates] - Riverdale, NY - *DataDirOnSer 84*
Appleby, Edna - Canmore, AB, Canada - *BoPubDir 4, 5*
Applecart Programs for Education - Juneau, AK - *MicrocomMPl 84*
Applegarth Follies - Ilderton, ON, Canada - *BoPubDir 4, 5*
Appleman Co. Ltd., The - New York, NY - *StaDirAdAg 2-84*
Appleseed Music Inc. - *See* Sanga Music Inc.
Appleton-Century-Crofts [Div. of Prentice-Hall Inc.] - Norwalk, CT - *LitMarPl 83, 84*
Appleton City Journal - Appleton City, MO - *AyerDirPub 83; BaconPubCkNews 84; Ed&PubIntYB 82*
Appleton Papers Inc. [Subs. of Batus Inc.] - Appleton, WI - *LitMarPl 83, 84; MagIndMarPl 82-83*
Appleton Post-Crescent - Appleton, WI - *BaconPubCkNews 84*
Appleton Press - Appleton, MN - *AyerDirPub 83; BaconPubCkNews 84; Ed&PubIntYB 82*
Applezaba Press - Long Beach, CA - *BoPubDir 4, 5; LitMag&SmPr 83-84*

Appliance [of Dana Chase Publications Inc.] - Hinsdale, IL - *MagDir 84*
Appliance - Oak Brook, IL - *BaconPubCkMag 84*
Appliance Manufacturer [of Cahners Publishing Co.] - Des Plaines, IL - *BaconPubCkMag 84; MagDir 84*
Appliance Service News [of Gamit Enterprises Inc.] - Lombard, IL - *ArtMar 84; BaconPubCkMag 84; MagDir 84; MagIndMarPl 82-83; WritMar 84*
Application Engineering - Orange Park, FL - *MicrocomMPl 84*
Application Techniques Inc. - Pepperell, MA - *MicrocomMPl 84*
Applications Software Inc. - Torrance, CA - *ADAPSOMemDir 83-84; DataDirSup 7-83*
Applications Systems Corp. - Boston, MA - *MicrocomSwDir 1*
Applicon - Burlington, MA - *DataDirSup 7-83*
Applied Analytics Inc. - Upper Marlboro, MD - *WhoWMicrocom 83*
Applied & Environmental Microbiology - Washington, DC - *BaconPubCkMag 84; MagDir 84*
Applied Arts Publishers [Aff. of Sowers Printing Co.] - Lebanon, PA - *BoPubDir 4, 5*
Applied Business Computer Co. - Anaheim, CA - *MicrocomMPl 83*
Applied Business Software - Lawndale, CA - *MicrocomMPl 83, 84*
Applied Business Systems - Dunsmuir, CA - *MicrocomMPl 83, 84*
Applied Business Systems Inc. - Louisville, KY - *DataDirOnSer 84*
Applied Business Technologies Corp. - Houston, TX - *WhoWMicrocom 83*
Applied Business Technologies Inc. - Drexel Hill, PA - *ADAPSOMemDir 83-84*
Applied Communications Inc. - Dayton, OH - *ArtMar 84; AvMarPl 83*
Applied Computer Enterprises [Subs. of Lloyd Bush & Associates] - New York, NY - *DataDirOnSer 84; InfIndMarPl 83*
Applied Computer Research - Phoenix, AZ - *BoPubDir 5; EISS 83*
Applied Computer Services Inc. - Palos Heights, IL - *DataDirOnSer 84*
Applied Computer Systems - Sunnyvale, CA - *WhoWMicrocom 83*
Applied Creative Technology Inc. - Arlington, TX - *MicrocomMPl 84*
Applied Data Communications - Tustin, CA - *WhoWMicrocom 83*
Applied Data Inc. - North Haven, CT - *ADAPSOMemDir 83-84; DataDirSup 7-83*
Applied Data Research Inc. - Princeton, NJ - *ADAPSOMemDir 83-84; DataDirSup 7-83*
Applied Data Systems - Tallahassee, FL - *MicrocomMPl 83*
Applied Decision Systems - Lexington, MA - *EISS 83*
Applied Digital Communications - Moorestown, NJ - *DataDirSup 7-83*
Applied Digital Data Systems Inc. - Hauppauge, NY - *DataDirSup 7-83; DirInfWP 82; InfIndMarPl 83; MicrocomMPl 84; WhoWMicrocom 83*
Applied Dynamics International - Ann Arbor, MI - *DataDirSup 7-83; InfIndMarPl 83*
Applied Economic Analysis - Long Beach, CA - *WhoWMicrocom 83*
Applied Educational Systems - Concord, NH - *MicrocomMPl 84; MicrocomSwDir 1*
Applied Educational Systems - Dunbarton, NH - *MicrocomMPl 83*
Applied Engineering - Dallas, TX - *MicrocomMPl 84*
Applied Financial Systems Inc. - San Mateo, CA - *DataDirSup 7-83*
Applied Information & Data Management Systems Section [of Battelle Memorial Institute] - Columbus, OH - *EISS 83*
Applied Information Dynamics Inc. - Walnut Creek, CA - *MicrocomMPl 83*
Applied Information Systems - Chapel Hill, NC - *ADAPSOMemDir 83-84; MicrocomMPl 83, 84; MicrocomSwDir 1*
Applied Logic Inc. - Jamaica, NY - *MicrocomMPl 84*
Applied Management Systems - Whittier, CA - *WhoWMicrocom 83*
Applied Media Group Inc. - Providence, RI - *AvMarPl 83*
Applied Micro Systems - Leavenworth, KS - *MicrocomSwDir 1*
Applied Micro Technology - Tucson, AZ - *WhoWMicrocom 83*
Applied Microcomputer Systems - Silver Lake, NH - *MicrocomMPl 84; MicrocomSwDir 1; WhoWMicrocom 83*
Applied MicroSystems - Roswell, GA - *MicrocomMPl 84; WhoWMicrocom 83*
Applied Optics - Washington, DC - *BaconPubCkMag 84; MagDir 84*
Applied Physics Laboratory [of Chemical Propulsion Information Agency] - Laurel, MD - *CompReadDB 82*
Applied Pressure Techniques - Munster, IN - *BoPubDir 4, 5*
Applied Probability Trust - Sheffield, England - *LitMag&SmPr 83-84*
Applied Professional Software - Austin, TX - *MicrocomMPl 84*
Applied Radiology [of Brentwood Publishing Corp.] - Los Angeles, CA - *ArtMar 84; BaconPubCkMag 84; MagDir 84; MagIndMarPl 82-83*
Applied Research & Consulting - Loveland, CO - *MicrocomMPl 84*
Applied Research Techniques Inc. - Parsippany, NJ - *IntDirMarRes 83*
Applied Skills Press [Subs. of University Associates Inc.] - San Diego, CA - *LitMarPl 84*
Applied Skills Press [Div. of CMA Publishing Co.] - St. Louis, MO - *LitMarPl 83*
Applied Software - Dix Hills, NY - *MicrocomSwDir 1*
Applied Software Technology - Los Gatos, CA - *MicrocomMPl 84; MicrocomSwDir 1; WhoWMicrocom 83*
Applied Software Technology - Westwood, MA - *WhoWMicrocom 83*
Applied Solutions Inc. - Jacksonville, OR - *MicrocomMPl 84*
Applied Spectroscopy - Manhattan, KS - *BaconPubCkMag 84; MagDir 84*
Applied Systems - St. Clair Shores, MI - *DataDirSup 7-83; MicrocomMPl 83*
Applied Therapeutics Inc. - San Francisco, CA - *BoPubDir 4, 5*
Applitek - London, England - *MicrocomSwDir 1*
Appomattox Cablevision Inc. [of Bahakel Communications Ltd.] - Appomattox, VA - *Tel&CabFB 84C*
Appomattox Times-Virginian [of Atlantic Publications Inc.] - Appomattox, VA - *NewsDir 84*
Appomattox Times-Virginian - *See* Atlantic Publications
Appraisal Institute of Canada/Institut Canadien des Evaluateurs - Winnipeg, MB, Canada - *BoPubDir 4, 5*
Appraisal Journal - Chicago, IL - *BaconPubCkMag 84; MagIndMarPl 82-83*
Appraiser, The - Chicago, IL - *BaconPubCkMag 84*
APR Associates Inc. - Memphis, TN - *StaDirAdAg 2-84*
April Dawn Publishing Co. - Falls Church, VA - *BoPubDir 4, 5; LitMag&SmPr 83-84*
April Enterprises Inc. - Santa Monica, CA - *BoPubDir 5*
April Fool Music Publishing [Div. of SOS Productions Ltd.] - New York, NY - *BillIntBG 83-84*
April Hill Publishers - Springfield, VT - *BoPubDir 4, 5*
April Publishing - Los Angeles, CA - *BoPubDir 5*
Apropos Technology - Camarillo, CA - *MicrocomMPl 84; WritMar 84*
APS Advertising Inc. - Burbank, CA - *StaDirAdAg 2-84*
APS Diplomat [of NewsNet Inc.] - Bryn Mawr, PA - *DataDirOnSer 84*
APS Review [of NewsNet Inc.] - Bryn Mawr, PA - *DataDirOnSer 84*
APS Systems Inc. - Carrollton, TX - *MicrocomMPl 84*
A.P.S.A. - Washington, DC - *BoPubDir 4, 5*
APSI-Monarch - New York, NY - *LitMarPl 83*
Apstek Inc. - Dallas, TX - *MicrocomMPl 84*
Apt Books Inc. - New York, NY - *BoPubDir 4, 5*
Apt Data Processing - Chicago, IL - *MicrocomMPl 84*
Aptech Computer Systems Inc. - Pittsburgh, PA - *ADAPSOMemDir 83-84*
Apter & Associates, David - Washington, DC - *DirPRFirms 83*
APTIC [of Dialog Information Services Inc.] - Palo Alto, CA - *DataDirOnSer 84*
APTIC File [of U.S. Environmental Protection Agency] - Research Triangle Park, NC - *DirOnDB Spring 84; EISS 83*
Aptos Film Productions Inc. - Thomasville, GA - *AvMarPl 83*
APWA Reporter [of American Public Works Association] - Chicago, IL - *BaconPubCkMag 84; MagDir 84; MagIndMarPl 82-83*

AQUA [of General Electric Information Services Co.] - Rockville, MD - *DataDirOnSer 84*
Aqua - Rugby, England - *DirOnDB Spring 84*
Aqua Media [Div. of Agua Magnetics Inc.] - Minneapolis, MN - *StaDirAdAg 2-84*
Aqua Music Publishing - *See* Sure Music & Record Co.
Aqua-Sol Enterprises - Ft. Worth, TX - *BoPubDir 4, 5*
Aquaculture [of Dialog Information Services Inc.] - Palo Alto, CA - *DataDirOnSer 84*
Aquaculture - Washington, DC - *DirOnDB Spring 84*
Aquaculture [of National Oceanic & Atmospheric Administration] - Rockville, MD - *CompReadDB 82; OnBibDB 3*
Aquaculture Data Base [of Virginia Institute of Marine Science] - Gloucester Point, VA - *EISS 83*
Aquaculture Magazine - Little Rock, AR - *MagIndMarPl 82-83*
Aquaculture Magazine [of Achill River Corp.] - Asheville, NC - *BaconPubCkMag 84; MagDir 84*
Aquadoc - Brest, France - *DirOnDB Spring 84*
Aqualine [of Dialog Information Services Inc.] - Palo Alto, CA - *DataDirOnSer 84*
Aqualine [of Medmenham Laboratory] - Marlow, England - *CompReadDB 82; DBBus 82; DirOnDB Spring 84; OnBibDB 3*
Aquari Corp. - Midland, MI - *BoPubDir 4, 5*
Aquarian Agent Book Club [of ASI Publishers] - New York, NY - *LitMarPl 83, 84*
Aquarian Book Publishers - Dallas, TX - *BoPubDir 4, 5*
Aquarian Educational Group - Agoura, CA - *BoPubDir 4, 5*
Aquarian Press [Aff. of Bonnie Prudden Inc.] - Stockbridge, MA - *BoPubDir 4, 5*
Aquarian Press Ltd., The - Wellingborough, England - *WritMar 84*
Aquarian Research Foundation - Philadelphia, PA - *BoPubDir 4, 5*
Aquarius - London, England - *LitMag&SmPr 83-84*
Aquarius Enterprises - Wailuku, HI - *BoPubDir 4, 5*
Aquarius Enterprises - Forked River, NJ - *MicrocomMPl 84*
Aquarius Inc. - Indian Rocks Beach, FL - *MicrocomMPl 84*
Aquarius Transfer Ltd. - New York, NY - *AvMarPl 83*
Aquatarius Music Ltd. - Roslyn Heights, NY - *BillIntBG 83-84*
Aquatic Sciences & Fisheries Abstracts [of Food & Agriculture Organization] - Washington, DC - *CompReadDB 82*
Aquatic Sciences & Fisheries Abstracts [of Cambridge Scientific Abstracts] - Bethesda, MD - *DataDirOnSer 84; DBBus 82; DirOnDB Spring 84; OnBibDB 3*
Aquatic Sciences & Fisheries Abstracts [of QL Systems Ltd.] - Ottawa, ON, Canada - *DataDirOnSer 84*
Aquatic Sciences & Fisheries Information System [of Food & Agriculture Organization] - Rome, Italy - *EISS 83*
Aquatic Weed Information & Retrieval Center [of University of Florida] - Gainesville, FL - *EISS 7-83 Sup*
Aquila Publishing - Portree, Scotland - *LitMag&SmPr 83-84*
Aquila Publishing Ltd./Editions Aquila Ltee. - Toronto, ON, Canada - *LitMarPl 84*
Aquila Publishing Ltd./Editions Aquila Ltee. - Montreal, PQ, Canada - *LitMarPl 83*
Aquinas Subscription Agency - St. Paul, MN - *MagIndMarPl 82-83*
AR-VEE Sound Services - New York, NY - *AvMarPl 83*
Arab American Almanac [of The News Circle Publishing Co.] - Glendale, CA - *LitMag&SmPr 83-84*
Arab News of Toronto - Toronto, ON, Canada - *Ed&PubIntYB 82*
Arab Tribune - Arab, AL - *BaconPubCkNews 84; Ed&PubIntYB 82; NewsDir 84*
Arabesque - New York, NY - *WritMar 84*
Arabi St. Bernard Voice - Arabi, LA - *BaconPubCkNews 84; NewsDir 84*
Arabian Horse Express - Coffeyville, KS - *BaconPubCkMag 84*
Arabian Horse Journal - Mt. Airy, MD - *BaconPubCkMag 84*
Arabian Horse, The - Odessa, MO - *MagDir 84*
Arabian Horse World - Palo Alto, CA - *MagDir 84*
Arabic-English Translation Services [Div. of Intercontinental Bureau of Translators & Interpreters Inc.] - New York, NY - *MagIndMarPl 82-83*
Arabic Teaching & Translation - New York, NY - *MagIndMarPl 82-83*
Arachne Publishing - Mountain View, CA - *BoPubDir 4, 5; LitMag&SmPr 83-84*
Arader, W. Graham III - King of Prussia, PA - *BoPubDir 4, 5*
Aramaic Bible Society of Florida Inc. - St. Petersburg, FL - *BoPubDir 4, 5*
Araness Communications Inc. - New York, NY - *AvMarPl 83*
Aransas Pass Progress - Aransas, TX - *Ed&PubIntYB 82*
Aransas Pass Progress - *See* Richards Enterprises Inc.
Arapaho TV Cable Co. - Arapaho, OK - *Tel&CabFB 84C*
Arapaho TV Cable Co. [of Redden Cable TV] - Vici, OK - *BrCabYB 84*
Arapahoe Cable TV Inc. - Arapahoe, NE - *Tel&CabFB 84C*
Arapahoe Independent - Littleton, CO - *Ed&PubIntYB 82*
Arapahoe Independent [of Littleton Independent Printing Co.] - Watkins, CO - *NewsDir 84*
Arapahoe Public Mirror - Arapahoe, NE - *BaconPubCkNews 84; Ed&PubIntYB 82*
Arapahoe Sentinel - *See* Sentinel Newspapers
Arapahoe Telephone Co. - Arapahoe, NE - *TelDir&BG 83-84*
Ararat Press [of The Armenian General Benevolent Union] - Saddle Brook, NJ - *ArtMar 84; LitMarPl 83; WritMar 84*
Arat Music - *See* Music Music Music Inc.
Arau & Goldberg - Philadelphia, PA - *AdAge 3-28-84; LitMarPl 84; StaDirAdAg 2-84*
Arau & Reinhard Direct Marketing - Paoli, PA - *DirMarMP 83; LitMarPl 83*
ARBAT Systems - Hoboken, NJ - *DataDirSup 7-83*
ARBB Custom Color Lab - Bensalem, PA - *AvMarPl 83*
Arbeitsgemeinschaft Hessische Bibliographie Zentralredaktion - Frankfurt, West Germany - *CompReadDB 82*
Arbeitsgemeinschaft Media-Analyse [of Interactive Market Systems Inc.] - New York, NY - *DataDirOnSer 84*
Arbeitsgemeinschaft Media-Analyse - Frankfurt, West Germany - *DirOnDB Spring 84*
Arbetslivets Information och Dokumentation [of Arbetslivscentrum] - Stockholm, Sweden - *CompReadDB 82*
Arbetslivscentrum - Stockholm, Sweden - *CompReadDB 82*
Arbitron Co., The - New York, NY - *EISS 83*
Arbitron Information on Demand [of Arbitron Ratings Co.] - New York, NY - *DataDirOnSer 84*
Arbitron Radio & Arbitron TV - New York, NY - *DirOnDB Spring 84*
Arbitron Radio Information on Demand [of Arbitron Ratings Co.] - New York, NY - *DataDirOnSer 84*
Arbitron Ratings Co. [Subs. of Control Data Corp.] - New York, NY - *AdAge 5-17-84 p.17; BrCabYB 84; DataDirOnSer 84; InterCabHB 3; Tel&CabFB 84C*
Arbitron Television Information on Demand [of Arbitron Ratings Co.] - New York, NY - *DataDirOnSer 84*
Arbogust Co. Inc., The - Chicago, IL - *StaDirAdAg 2-84*
Arbor Age - Encino, CA - *BaconPubCkMag 84*
Arbor House Publishing Co. [Subs. of Hearst Corp.] - New York, NY - *LitMarPl 83, 84; WritMar 84*
Arbor Inc. - Philadelphia, PA - *IntDirMarRes 83*
Arbor Publications - Ann Arbor, MI - *BoPubDir 4, 5; LitMag&SmPr 83-84*
Arbuckle, Cohen & Trewhella Inc. - *See* QUIP-Arbuckle, Cohen & Trewhella Inc.
Arbuckle, Mrs. Daniel A. - Ottawa, ON, Canada - *BoPubDir 4, 5*
Arbus Films - Gallion, AL - *AvMarPl 83*
Arbuta House - Abington, PA - *LitMarPl 84*
Arbutus PBA Inc. - Baltimore, MD - *BoPubDir 4, 5*
Arbutus Publications Ltd. - Vancouver, BC, Canada - *BoPubDir 4, 5*
Arbutus Times - Arbutus, MD - *Ed&PubIntYB 82*
Arbutus Times - Columbia, MD - *AyerDirPub 83*
Arbutus Times [of Ellicott City Stromberg Publishing Inc.] - Ellicot City, MD - *NewsDir 84*
Arbutus Totalsoft Inc. - Bellingham, WA - *MicrocomMPl 84*
ARC - Mendocino, CA - *LitMag&SmPr 83-84*
ARC/AMS [Subs. of Fireman's Fund Insurance Cos.] - Dallas, TX - *DataDirOnSer 84*
ARC Arabic Journal - Montreal, PQ, Canada - *Ed&PubIntYB 82*
ARC Automation Group Inc. [Subs. of Firemans Fund Insurance Co.] - College Station, TX - *WhoWMicrocom 83*

ARC Automation Services Inc. [Subs. of Fireman's Fund Insurance Co.] - Atlanta, GA - *DataDirOnSer 84*
Arc Music Corp. - *See* Goodman Group, The
A.R.C. Publications [Aff. of Aesthetic Research Centre of Canada] - Vancouver, BC, Canada - *BoPubDir 4, 5*
Arc Publications - Todmorden, England - *LitMag&SmPr 83-84*
ARC Videodance - New York, NY - *AvMarPl 83*
Arcade [of Mead Publishing Corp.] - Long Beach, CA - *ArtMar 84; BaconPubCkMag 84; WritMar 84*
Arcade Herald - Arcade, NY - *AyerDirPub 83; BaconPubCkNews 84; Ed&PubIntYB 82*
Arcade Music - *See* Sulzer Music
Arcade Penny Saver - Springville, NY - *AyerDirPub 83*
Arcade Plus - Santa Barbara, CA - *MicrocomMPl 83*
Arcade Record Co./Arzee Record Co. - Philadelphia, PA - *BillIntBG 83-84*
Arcade Tri-County Publications Inc. - Arcade, NY - *NewsDir 84*
Arcadia Bienville Democrat - Arcadia, LA - *BaconPubCkNews 84; NewsDir 84*
Arcadia Books - Liverpool, NY - *BoPubDir 4, 5*
Arcadia Feature Syndicate - Chicago, IL - *Ed&PubIntYB 82; LitMarPl 84*
Arcadia Highlander - *See* Sun Independent Newspapers
Arcadia News-Leader - Arcadia, WI - *BaconPubCkNews 84; Ed&PubIntYB 82*
Arcadia Press - New York, NY - *BoPubDir 4, 5*
Arcadia Telephone Co. [Aff. of Telephone & Data Systems Inc.] - Arcadia, OH - *TelDir&BG 83-84*
Arcadia Telephone Cooperative - Arcadia, IA - *TelDir&BG 83-84*
Arcadia Tribune [of Arcadia Foothill Intercity Newspapers] - Arcadia, CA - *AyerDirPub 83; Ed&PubIntYB 82; NewsDir 84*
Arcadia Tribune - *See* Foothill Inter-City Newspapers
Arcadian - Arcadia, FL - *AyerDirPub 83; BaconPubCkNews 84; Ed&PubIntYB 82*
Arcana Publishing - Wilmot, WI - *BoPubDir 5*
Arcane Order Press - Falls Church, VA - *BoPubDir 4, 5*
Arcanum Early Bird - Arcanum, OH - *BaconPubCkNews 84*
Arcata Graphics Group - Norwalk, CT - *LitMarPl 83, 84*
Arcata Publications Group - Stamford, CT - *MagIndMarPl 82-83*
Arcata Union - Arcata, CA - *BaconPubCkNews 84; NewsDir 84*
Arceneaux, Thelma Hoffmann Tyler - Thibodaux, LA - *BoPubDir 4, 5*
ARCH [of Ontario Education Research Information System] - Toronto, ON, Canada - *CompReadDB 82*
Archaeology [of Archaeological Institute of America] - New York, NY - *DirMarMP 83; MagDir 84; MagIndMarPl 82-83*
Archbold Buckeye - Archbold, OH - *BaconPubCkNews 84; Ed&PubIntYB 82; NewsDir 84*
Archbold Farmland News - Archbold, OH - *BaconPubCkNews 84; Ed&PubIntYB 82; NewsDir 84*
Archdale Cable TV [of American TV & Communications Corp.] - Archdale, NC - *Tel&CabFB 84C*
Archdale-Trinity News - Archdale, NC - *BaconPubCkNews 84*
Archdiocese of Baltimore (Office of Communications) - Baltimore, MD - *Tel&CabFB 84C*
Archer [of Camas Press] - Camas Valley, OR - *LitMag&SmPr 83-84; WritMar 84*
Archer Advertising Inc. - Clearwater, FL - *StaDirAdAg 2-84*
Archer & Associates Inc., Ward - Memphis, TN - *ArtMar 84; DirPRFirms 83; StaDirAdAg 2-84*
Archer City Cable TV [of Star CATV Investment Corp.] - Archer City, TX - *Tel&CabFB 84C*
Archer County News - Archer City, TX - *BaconPubCkNews 84; Ed&PubIntYB 82*
Archer Courier Systems Inc. - New York, NY - *LitMarPl 83, 84; MagIndMarPl 82-83*
Archer East Associates Inc. - New York, NY - *InfIndMarPl 83; LitMarPl 83, 84; MagIndMarPl 82-83*
Archer Editions Press - Lynnville, TN - *BoPubDir 4, 5; WritMar 84*
Archery Development Corp. [Div. of Bear Archery] - Gainesville, FL - *StaDirAdAg 2-84*
Archery Retailer - Minneapolis, MN - *BaconPubCkMag 84; WritMar 84*
Archery Retailer - Milwaukee, WI - *MagDir 84*
Archery World - Minneapolis, MN - *BaconPubCkMag 84; WritMar 84*
Archery World - St. Louis Park, MN - *MagDir 84*
Archery World - Milwaukee, WI - *MagIndMarPl 82-83*
Archey/Cavala & Associates - San Francisco, CA - *AvMarPl 83*
Archibald, Thomas F. - Hillsboro, OH - *Tel&CabFB 84C p.1664*
Archie Comic Publications Inc. - New York, NY - *MagIndMarPl 82-83*
Archie News - Archie, MO - *Ed&PubIntYB 82*
Archinform - Glendale, CA - *BoPubDir 5*
Archinform - Los Angeles, CA - *BoPubDir 4*
Architect & Contractor - Yountville, CA - *MagDir 84*
Architects & Planners Book Service [of Macmillan Book Clubs Inc.] - New York, NY - *LitMarPl 84*
Architects' Book Club [of McGraw-Hill Book Co.] - New York, NY - *LitMarPl 83, 84*
Architectural Aluminum Manufacturers Association - Chicago, IL - *BoPubDir 5*
Architectural Book Publishing Co. Inc. - New York, NY - *WritMar 84*
Architectural Color Slides - Lexington, MA - *AvMarPl 83; MagIndMarPl 82-83*
Architectural Computer Software - Santa Barbara, CA - *MicrocomMPl 84*
Architectural Digest [of Knapp Communications Corp.] - Los Angeles, CA - *BaconPubCkMag 84; Folio 83; MagDir 84; MagIndMarPl 82-83*
Architectural Handbook [of California Council American Institute of Architects] - San Francisco, CA - *MagDir 84*
Architectural Metals [of National Association of Architectural Metal Manufacturers] - Chicago, IL - *MagDir 84; WritMar 84*
Architectural Periodicals Index [of Royal Institute of British Architects] - London, England - *CompReadDB 82; EISS 83*
Architectural Publications Inc. - Keswick, VA - *BoPubDir 5*
Architectural Record [of McGraw-Hill Inc.] - New York, NY - *BaconPubCkMag 84; Folio 83; MagDir 84; MagIndMarPl 82-83*
Architecture [of American Institute of Architects] - Washington, DC - *MagDir 84*
Architecture - New York, NY - *BaconPubCkMag 84*
Architecture & Engineering Performance Information Center [of University of Maryland] - College Park, MD - *EISS 5-84 Sup*
Architecture California - Sacramento, CA - *BaconPubCkMag 84*
Architecture-Concept - Montreal, PQ, Canada - *BaconPubCkMag 84*
Architecture Minnesota [of Minnesota Society, American Institute of Architects] - Minneapolis, MN - *BaconPubCkMag 84; MagDir 84*
Architecture Technology Corp. - Minneapolis, MN - *TeleSy&SerDir 2-84*
Architekton Publishing Co. Inc. - Cranston, RI - *BoPubDir 4, 5*
Archive Film Productions Inc. - New York, NY - *AvMarPl 83*
Archive for New Poetry - San Diego, CA - *LitMag&SmPr 83-84*
Archive of Italian Data of Geology [of National Research Council] - Milan, Italy - *EISS 5-84 Sup*
Archive Press - Issaquah, WA - *BoPubDir 4, 5*
Archives Canada Microfiches (Picture Div.) - Ottawa, ON, Canada - *MicroMarPl 82-83*
Archives Corp. - Worcester, MA - *MicrocomMPl 83*
Archives Inc. - Davenport, IA - *MicrocomMPl 83; WhoWMicrocom 83*
Archives Ink Ltd. - Haworth, NJ - *BoPubDir 4, 5*
Archives of American Art [of Smithsonian Institution] - Washington, DC - *MagIndMarPl 82-83*
Archives of Dermatology - Chicago, IL - *BaconPubCkMag 84; MagDir 84*
Archives of Environmental Health [of Helen Dwight Reid Educational Foundation] - Washington, DC - *BaconPubCkMag 84; MagDir 84; MagIndMarPl 82-83*
Archives of General Psychiatry - Chicago, IL - *BaconPubCkMag 84; MagDir 84*
Archives of Internal Medicine - Chicago, IL - *BaconPubCkMag 84; MagDir 84; MagIndMarPl 82-83*
Archives of Kitley Township - Toledo, ON, Canada - *BoPubDir 4 Sup, 5*
Archives of Neurology - Chicago, IL - *BaconPubCkMag 84; MagDir 84*
Archives of Ophthalmology - Chicago, IL - *BaconPubCkMag 84; MagDir 84*

Archives of Otolaryngology - Chicago, IL - *BaconPubCkMag 84; MagDir 84*
Archives of Pathology & Laboratory Medicine - Chicago, IL - *BaconPubCkMag 84; MagDir 84*
Archives of Physical Medicine & Rehabilitation - Chicago, IL - *BaconPubCkMag 84; MagDir 84; MagIndMarPl 82-83*
Archives of Social History - Stony Brook, NY - *BoPubDir 4 Sup, 5*
Archives of Surgery - Chicago, IL - *BaconPubCkMag 84; MagDir 84*
Archives of the California Institute of Technology - Pasadena, CA - *MagIndMarPl 82-83*
Arcinco Inc. - Passaic, NJ - *StaDirAdAg 2-84*
Arco Advertiser - Arco, ID - *BaconPubCkNews 84; Ed&PubIntYB 82*
Arco Publishing Co. - Provo, UT - *BoPubDir 4, 5*
Arco Publishing Inc. [Subs. of Prentice-Hall Inc.] - New York, NY - *ArtMar 84; LitMarPl 83, 84; WritMar 84*
Arcola Music Inc. - *See* Croma Music Co. Inc.
Arcola Record-Herald - Arcola, IL - *BaconPubCkNews 84*
Arcon - Erie, PA - *WhoWMicrocom 83*
Arcon Coating Mills Inc. - Oceanside, NY - *LitMarPl 83, 84*
ARCsoft Publishers - Woodsboro, MD - *LitMarPl 83, 84; WritMar 84*
Arctic Environmental Information & Data Center [of University of Alaska] - Anchorage, AK - *EISS 83*
Arctic Institute of North America [of University of Calgary] - Calgary, AB, Canada - *CompReadDB 82; DataDirOnSer 84*
Arctic Science & Technology Information System [of Arctic Institute of North America] - Calgary, AB, Canada - *CompReadDB 82; DataDirOnSer 84; DirOnDB Spring 84; EISS 83; InfIndMarPl 83*
Arctinurus Co. - Bellmawr, NJ - *BoPubDir 4, 5*
Arcturns Inc. - Concord, MA - *MicrocomMPl 84*
Ardavan Music - Hollywood, CA - *BillIntBG 83-84*
Arden Press - Denver, CO - *LitMag&SmPr 83-84*
Ardent Enterprises - Edmonton, AB, Canada - *BoPubDir 4, 5*
Ardis Publishers - Ann Arbor, MI - *LitMag&SmPr 83-84; LitMarPl 83, 84*
Ardis Publishing Co. - *See* Trilogy Publishers/Ardis Publishing Co.
Ardis/Russian Literature - Ann Arbor, MI - *LitMarPl 83, 84*
Ardmore Ardmoreite [of Stauffer Communications Inc.] - Ardmore, OK - *BaconPubCkNews 84; NewsDir 84*
Ardmore Data & Broadband Services Inc. - Ardmore, AL - *BrCabYB 84; Tel&CabFB 84C*
Ardmore Data & Broadband Services Inc. [of Ardmore Telephone Co.] - Elkton, TN - *Tel&CabFB 84C*
Ardmore Democrat - Ardmore, OK - *BaconPubCkNews 84; Ed&PubIntYB 82*
Ardmore Main Line Chronicle - Ardmore, PA - *NewsDir 84*
Ardmore Main Line Chronicle - *See* Chester County Communications Ltd.
Ardmore Main Line Times - Ardmore, PA - *NewsDir 84*
Ardmore Main Line Times - *See* Acme Newspapers Inc.
Ardmore Telephone Co. Inc. - Ardmore, TN - *TelDir&BG 83-84*
Ardmoreite - Ardmore, OK - *AyerDirPub 83*
Ardrey Inc. - Edison, NJ - *DirPRFirms 83*
Ardsley Editorial Services, Naiia - New York, NY - *LitMarPl 83; MagIndMarPl 82-83*
A.R.E. Press [Aff. of Association for Research & Enlightenment] - Virginia Beach, VA - *BoPubDir 4, 5*
Area Auto Racing News - Trenton, NJ - *BaconPubCkMag 84; MagDir 84*
Area Business Databank Inc. - Louisville, KY - *EISS 5-84 Sup*
Area Cablevision - Jacksonville, FL - *BrCabYB 84*
Area Computer Services Inc. - Largo, FL - *DataDirOnSer 84*
Area Development [of Halycyon Business Publications Inc.] - Great Neck, NY - *BaconPubCkMag 84; MagDir 84; MagIndMarPl 82-83; WritMar 84*
Area Magazine - Montgomery, AL - *BaconPubCkMag 84; MagDir 84*
Area Market Research Associates - Little Rock, AR - *IntDirMarRes 83*
Area News - Gillespie, IL - *AyerDirPub 83; Ed&PubIntYB 82*
Area Resource File [of U.S. Public Health Service] - Hyattsville, MD - *EISS 83*
Aregon International Inc. - Stamford, CT - *EISS 83; InfoS 83-84; VideoDir 82-83*
Arena Cablevision Corp. [of Chaney Communications Inc.] - Blossom, TX - *BrCabYB 84; Tel&CabFB 84C*
Arena Lettres - Waldwick, NJ - *LitMarPl 83, 84*
Arena Stage - Washington, DC - *WritMar 84*
Arenac County Independent - Standish, MI - *AyerDirPub 83; Ed&PubIntYB 82*
Arenburg Consultants Ltd., Anneliese - Toronto, ON, Canada - *DirInfWP 82*
Arends Inc., Donald L. - Oak Brook, IL - *AdAge 3-28-84; StaDirAdAg 2-84*
Arens & Associates, William F. [Div. of Inter-Marketing Associates Inc.] - La Jolla, CA - *AdAge 3-28-84; StaDirAdAg 2-84*
Arens Applied Electromagnetics Inc. - Gaithersburg, MD - *DataDirSup 7-83*
Ares [of Dragon Publishing] - Lake Geneva, WI - *ArtMar 84*
Ares Publishers Inc. - Chicago, IL - *LitMarPl 83, 84*
Arete Publications Ltd. - Scottsdale, AZ - *BoPubDir 4, 5*
Arete Publishing Co. - Princeton, NJ - *CompReadDB 82*
Arfon Microelectronics Inc. - Lafayette, LA - *MicrocomMPl 84*
Argall & Associates - Beverly Hills, CA - *DirPRFirms 83*
Argee Publishing Co. - Cheviot Hills, CA - *BoPubDir 4*
Argee Publishing Co. - Sherman Oaks, CA - *BoPubDir 5*
Argentine Center for Scientific & Technological Information [of National Council for Scientific & Technical Research] - Buenos Aires, Argentina - *EISS 83*
Argibusiness Fieldman - Fresno, CA - *MagDir 84*
Argo Books Inc. - Norwich, VT - *BoPubDir 4, 5*
Argo Des Plaines Valley News - Argo, IL - *BaconPubCkNews 84*
Argo Publishing Co. - Oxford, England - *LitMag&SmPr 83-84*
Argonaut Information Systems Inc. - Oakland, CA - *DataDirSup 7-83*
Argonaut Newspapers - Hermosa Beach, CA - *BaconPubCkNews 84*
Argonaut, The - Marina del Rey, CA - *AyerDirPub 83; Ed&PubIntYB 82*
Argonaut, The - Austin, TX - *LitMag&SmPr 83-84*
Argos Computers [Subs. of Argos Inc.] - Fresno, CA - *WhoWMicrocom 83*
Argos Products Co. Inc. - Genoa, IL - *AvMarPl 83*
Argraph Corp. - Carlstadt, NJ - *AvMarPl 83*
Argus - Brinkley, AR - *AyerDirPub 83*
Argus - Fremont, CA - *AyerDirPub 83; Ed&PubIntYB 82*
Argus - Long Beach, CA - *AyerDirPub 83*
Argus - Greenfield, IL - *AyerDirPub 83*
Argus - Rock Island, IL - *AyerDirPub 83; Ed&PubIntYB 82*
Argus - Cynthiana, IN - *AyerDirPub 83*
Argus - Galesburg, MI - *AyerDirPub 83; Ed&PubIntYB 82*
Argus - Caledonia, MN - *AyerDirPub 83*
Argus - Janesville, MN - *AyerDirPub 83*
Argus - White Plains, NY - *AyerDirPub 83*
Argus - Stickney, SD - *AyerDirPub 83*
Argus - Flatonia, TX - *AyerDirPub 83*
Argus - Seattle, WA - *AyerDirPub 83; MagDir 84*
Argus/Aloha Breeze - Hillsboro, OR - *AyerDirPub 83*
Argus & Teulon Times - Argus, MB, Canada - *Ed&PubIntYB 82*
Argus Archives - New York, NY - *BoPubDir 4, 5*
Argus-Champion - Newport, NH - *AyerDirPub 83; Ed&PubIntYB 82*
Argus Communications [Div. of DLM Inc.] - Allen, TX - *LitMarPl 83, 84*
Argus-Courier - Petaluma, CA - *AyerDirPub 83; Ed&PubIntYB 82*
Argus Courier Shopping Guide - Petaluma, CA - *AyerDirPub 83*
Argus de la Presse - Paris, France - *ProGuPRSer 4*
Argus-Herald - Sidney, IA - *AyerDirPub 83*
Argus International de la Presse SA - Zurich, Switzerland - *ProGuPRSer 4*
Argus Leader [of Sioux Falls Newspapers Inc.] - Sioux Falls, SD - *AyerDirPub 83; BaconPubCkNews 84; Ed&PubIntYB 82; LitMarPl 84; NewsDir 84*
Argus-Observer - Ontario, OR - *AyerDirPub 83*
Argus-Press - Owosso, MI - *AyerDirPub 83; Ed&PubIntYB 82; NewsDir 84*
Argus Press Inc. - Albany, NY - *MagIndMarPl 82-83*

Argus Presseburo und Verlag - Stuttgart, West Germany - *ProGuPRSer 4*
Argus Publishers Corp. - West Los Angeles, CA - *DirMarMP 83; MagIndMarPl 82-83*
Argus Record Productions [Div. of Record Room] - Glendora, NJ - *BillIntBG 83-84*
Argus Research - New York, NY - *DirOnDB Spring 84*
Argus-Sentinel Inc. - Trotwood, OH - *BaconPubCkNews 84*
Argus South African Newspapers Ltd. - New York, NY - *Ed&PubIntYB 82*
Argyle Agenda - Argyle, WI - *BaconPubCkNews 84; Ed&PubIntYB 82*
Argyle Cable TV [of Stephen Cable TV Inc.] - Stephen, MN - *BrCabYB 84*
Arhoolie Productions Inc. - El Cerrito, CA - *BillIntBG 83-84*
Aria Records - Brooklyn, NY - *BillIntBG 83-84*
Ariadne Press - Rockville, MD - *BoPubDir 4, 5; LitMag&SmPr 83-84*
Arial Advertising Inc. - Forest Hills, NY - *StaDirAdAg 2-84*
Arial Records & Cassettes/ARC Entertainment Group - San Francisco, CA - *BillIntBG 83-84*
Arian Publications - *See* OAS Music Group Inc.
Ariane Data Bank [of National Federations of Buildings & Public Works] - Paris, France - *DirOnDB Spring 84; EISS 83*
Arica Institute Press [Aff. of Africa Institute Inc.] - New York, NY - *BoPubDir 4, 5*
Arid Lands Abstracts [of Arid Lands Information Center] - Tucson, AZ - *CompReadDB 82*
Arid Lands Information Center [of University of Arizona] - Tucson, AZ - *CompReadDB 82; EISS 83*
Ariel Press [Subs. of Light] - Columbus, OH - *LitMag&SmPr 83-84; LitMarPl 83, 84; WritMar 84*
Ariel Publications - Bellevue, WA - *BoPubDir 5*
Ariel Publications - Mercer Island, WA - *BoPubDir 4*
Aries Agency - Dublin, Ireland - *StaDirAdAg 2-84*
Aries Information Systems Inc. - Minneapolis, MN - *DataDirOnSer 84*
Aries Productions - Grand Prairie, TX - *AvMarPl 83*
Aries Publishing - Hayward, CA - *BoPubDir 5*
Aries Sound International Inc. - New York, NY - *AvMarPl 83*
Arigo International Record Co. - *See* Jacobson, Jeffrey E.
Arinco Computer Systems Inc. - Santa Fe, NM - *DataDirSup 7-83; WhoWMicrocom 83*
Arion Press - San Francisco, CA - *BoPubDir 4, 5*
Aris & Phillips Ltd. - Warminster, England - *MicroMarPl 82-83*
Aris Books [Aff. of Harris Publishing Co. Inc.] - Berkeley, CA - *BoPubDir 5; LitMag&SmPr 83-84; LitMarPl 84*
Arista Corp. [Subs. of Hachette Corp.] - Concord, CA - *LitMarPl 83, 84*
Arista Films Inc. - Encino, CA - *AvMarPl 83*
Arista Music Inc. - *See* Arista Music Publishing Group
Arista Music Publishing Group - Beverly Hills, CA - *BillIntBG 83-84*
Arista Records - New York, NY - *BillIntBG 83-84*
Aristadata Inc. - New York, NY - *ADAPSOMemDir 83-84*
Aristo Graphics Corp. - Randolph, NJ - *DataDirSup 7-83*
Aristos Music - Chapel Hill, NC - *BillIntBG 83-84*
Aristotelian Logicians - Phoenix, AZ - *MicrocomMPl 84*
Arithmetic of God - Kings Mountain, NC - *BoPubDir 4 Sup, 5*
Arithmetic Teacher - Reston, VA - *MagDir 84; MagIndMarPl 82-83*
Arizona Beverage Analyst [of Bell Publications] - Denver, CO - *BaconPubCkMag 84; MagDir 84*
Arizona Beverage Guide - Phoenix, AZ - *BaconPubCkMag 84*
Arizona Business Gazette - Phoenix, AZ - *BaconPubCkMag 84; Ed&PubIntYB 82*
Arizona Business/Industry [of Trailbeau Publications Inc.] - Phoenix, AZ - *MagDir 84*
Arizona Cable TV Inc. [of American Cable Television Inc.] - Arizona City, AZ - *BrCabYB 84*
Arizona Cable TV Inc. [of American Cable TV Inc.] - Eloy, AZ - *BrCabYB 84; Tel&CabFB 84C*
Arizona Cable TV Inc. [of American Cable Television Inc.] - Fountain Hills, AZ - *BrCabYB 84*
Arizona Cable TV Inc. [of American Cable TV Inc.] - Heber, AZ - *BrCabYB 84; Tel&CabFB 84C*
Arizona Cable TV Inc. [of American Cable Television Inc.] - Maricopa County, AZ - *BrCabYB 84*
Arizona Cable TV Inc. [of American Cable TV Inc.] - Phoenix, AZ - *Tel&CabFB 84C*
Arizona Cable TV Inc. - Rio Verde, AZ - *BrCabYB 84*
Arizona Cable TV Inc. [of American Cable Television Inc.] - Superior, AZ - *BrCabYB 84; Tel&CabFB 84C*
Arizona Computer Systems Inc. - Jerome, AZ - *WhoWMicrocom 83*
Arizona Computer Systems Inc. - Tuscon, AZ - *MicrocomMPl 83*
Arizona Daily Star [of Pulitzer Publishing Co.] - Tucson, AZ - *BaconPubCkNews 84; Ed&PubIntYB 82; LitMarPl 83, 84*
Arizona Daily Wildcat [of University of Arizona] - Tucson, AZ - *NewsDir 84*
Arizona Dept. of Mineral Resources - Phoenix, AZ - *BoPubDir 5*
Arizona Desert Bighorn Sheep Society Inc. - Phoenix, AZ - *BoPubDir 4, 5*
Arizona Educator Advocate - Phoenix, AZ - *BaconPubCkMag 84*
Arizona Electronics - Phoenix, AZ - *MagIndMarPl 82-83*
Arizona Farm Bureau News - Phoenix, AZ - *MagDir 84*
Arizona Farmer-Ranchman - Phoenix, AZ - *BaconPubCkMag 84; MagDir 84*
Arizona Grocer [of Arizona Grocers Publishing Co.] - Phoenix, AZ - *BaconPubCkMag 84; MagDir 84*
Arizona Highways - Phoenix, AZ - *BaconPubCkMag 84; MagDir 84; MagIndMarPl 82-83; WritMar 84*
Arizona Historical Foundation - Tempe, AZ - *BoPubDir 4, 5*
Arizona Historical Society - Tucson, AZ - *BoPubDir 4, 5*
Arizona Informant - Phoenix, AZ - *AyerDirPub 83*
Arizona Living - Phoenix, AZ - *BaconPubCkMag 84*
Arizona Magazine - Phoenix, AZ - *ArtMar 84; WritMar 84*
Arizona Medicine - Phoenix, AZ - *BaconPubCkMag 84; MagDir 84*
Arizona Mobile Citizen - Phoenix, AZ - *BaconPubCkMag 84; MagDir 84*
Arizona Mobile Publications [of Apache Junction Sentinel] - Apache Junction, AZ - *NewsDir 84*
Arizona Office of Economic Planning & Development - Phoenix, AZ - *BoPubDir 4 Sup, 5*
Arizona Pharmacist [of Arizona Graphics] - Phoenix, AZ - *BaconPubCkMag 84; MagDir 84*
Arizona Photographic Associates Inc. - Phoenix, AZ - *LitMarPl 83; MagIndMarPl 82-83*
Arizona Professional Engineer [of Sunbelt Media Corp.] - Phoenix, AZ - *BaconPubCkMag 84; MagDir 84*
Arizona Purchasor, The - Phoenix, AZ - *MagDir 84*
Arizona Quarterly - Tucson, AZ - *LitMag&SmPr 83-84*
Arizona Range News - Willcox, AZ - *AyerDirPub 83; BaconPubCkNews 84; Ed&PubIntYB 82*
Arizona Republic [of Phoenix Newspapers Inc.] - Phoenix, AZ - *AyerDirPub 83; BaconPubCkNews 84; Ed&PubIntYB 82; LitMarPl 83, 84; NewsBur 6*
Arizona Research - Mesa, AZ - *IntDirMarRes 83*
Arizona Secretary of State - Phoenix, AZ - *BoPubDir 5*
Arizona Silver Belt - Globe, AZ - *AyerDirPub 83; Ed&PubIntYB 82*
Arizona Sports Digest - Phoenix, AZ - *MagDir 84*
Arizona Sports Network - Phoenix, AZ - *CabTVPrDB 83*
Arizona State University (Center for Latin American Studies) - Tempe, AZ - *BoPubDir 4, 5*
Arizona State University Library - Tempe, AZ - *EISS 83*
Arizona Sun - Flagstaff, AZ - *AyerDirPub 83; BaconPubCkNews 84; Ed&PubIntYB 82*
Arizona Territorial - Tucson, AZ - *AyerDirPub 83*
Arizona Territorial, The - Casas Adobes, AZ - *Ed&PubIntYB 82*
Arizona Today's Business - Tucson, AZ - *BaconPubCkMag 84*
Arizonan - Chandler, AZ - *AyerDirPub 83*
Ark - Bristol, VT - *BoPubDir 4 Sup, 5; LitMag&SmPr 83-84*
Ark & Arbor Press - Little Compton, RI - *BoPubDir 5; LitMag&SmPr 83-84*
Ark-City Cable TV Inc. [of Communications Services Inc.] - Arkansas City, KS - *BrCabYB 84; Tel&CabFB 84C*
Ark Data Systems Inc. - Phoenix, AZ - *ADAPSOMemDir 83-84*
Ark Electronic Products Inc. - Melbourne, FL - *DataDirSup 7-83*
Ark of Glenns Music - Los Angeles, CA - *BillIntBG 83-84*
Ark Records - Tigard, OR - *BillIntBG 83-84*

Ark River Review, The - Wichita, KS - *LitMag&SmPr 83-84; WritMar 84*
Ark, The - Belvedere, CA - *Ed&PubIntYB 82*
Ark, The - Tiburon, CA - *AyerDirPub 83; Ed&PubIntYB 82*
Ark Valley News - Valley Center, KS - *AyerDirPub 83; Ed&PubIntYB 82*
Ark-Vision Inc. - Dover, AR - *BrCabYB 84*
Arkadelphia Cable TV [of TCA Cable TV Inc.] - Arkadelphia, AR - *BrCabYB 84; Tel&CabFB 84C*
Arkadelphia Cable TV [of TCA Cable TV Inc.] - Caddo Valley, AR - *Tel&CabFB 84C*
Arkadelphia Siftings Herald - Arkadelphia, AR - *BaconPubCkNews 84; NewsDir 84*
Arkadelphia Southern Standard - Arkadelphia, AR - *BaconPubCkNews 84; NewsDir 84*
Arkansas Ancestors - Hot Springs, AR - *BoPubDir 4 Sup, 5*
Arkansas Banker, The [of Arkansas Bankers Association] - Little Rock, AR - *BaconPubCkMag 84; MagDir 84*
Arkansas Cable Television Inc. [of Times Mirror Cable Television Inc.] - Jacksonville, AR - *BrCabYB 84; Tel&CabFB 84C*
Arkansas Cattle Business - Little Rock, AR - *BaconPubCkMag 84; MagDir 84*
Arkansas City Traveler [of Stauffer Communications Inc.] - Arkansas City, KS - *BaconPubCkNews 84; Ed&PubIntYB 82; NewsDir 84*
Arkansas Democrat [of Little Rock Newspapers Inc.] - Little Rock, AR - *AyerDirPub 83; Ed&PubIntYB 82; LitMarPl 84; NewsBur 6*
Arkansas Educator - Little Rock, AR - *MagDir 84*
Arkansas Engineer, The [of University of Arkansas] - Fayetteville, AR - *MagDir 84*
Arkansas Gazette - Little Rock, AR - *AyerDirPub 83; Ed&PubIntYB 82; LitMarPl 84; NewsBur 6; NewsDir 84*
Arkansas Grocer [of Arkansas Grocer Publishing Co.] - Pine Bluff, AR - *BaconPubCkMag 84; MagDir 84*
Arkansas LP News [of Arkansas LP Gas Association] - Little Rock, AR - *BaconPubCkMag 84; MagDir 84*
Arkansas Poultry Times - Little Rock, AR - *MagDir 84*
Arkansas Press Association - Little Rock, AR - *ProGuPRSer 4*
Arkansas Sportsman [of Game & Fish Publication Inc.] - Marietta, GA - *BaconPubCkMag 84; WritMar 84*
Arkansas Sun - Heber Springs, AR - *Ed&PubIntYB 82*
Arkansas Symphony Orchestra Society Guild - Little Rock, AR - *BoPubDir 4 Sup, 5*
Arkansas Systems Inc. - Little Rock, AR - *DataDirSup 7-83; WhoWMicrocom 83*
Arkansas Telephone Co. Inc. - Clinton, AR - *TelDir&BG 83-84*
Arkansas-Texas Comic Group - Eldorado, AR - *Ed&PubIntYB 82*
Arkansas Times [of Arkansas Writers' Project Inc.] - Little Rock, AR - *BaconPubCkMag 84; WritMar 84*
Arkansas Traveler [of University of Arkansas] - Fayetteville, AR - *NewsDir 84*
Arkansas Valley Cable Inc. [of Central Kansas Cable Inc.] - Burrton, KS - *Tel&CabFB 84C*
Arkansas Valley Cable Inc. [of Central Kansas Cable Inc.] - Centralia, KS - *Tel&CabFB 84C p.1664*
Arkansas Valley Journal - La Junta, CO - *BaconPubCkMag 84; Ed&PubIntYB 82; MagDir 84; NewsDir 84*
Arkansas Valley Times - Alma, AR - *Ed&PubIntYB 82*
Arkansas Weekly Sentinel - Little Rock, AR - *Ed&PubIntYB 82*
Arkay Computer Inc. - Newton Center, MA - *DataDirSup 7-83*
Arkelian Broadcasting Co. - Naples, FL - *BrCabYB 84*
Arkham House Publishers Inc. - Sauk City, WI - *LitMarPl 83, 84*
ArKos Associates - Idaho Springs, CO - *DataDirOnSer 84*
Arks Ltd. - Dublin, Ireland - *StaDirAdAg 2-84*
Arkwright Inc. [Subs. of Oce'Van der Grinten] - Fiskeville, RI - *AvMarPl 83*
Arlen Communications Inc. - Bethesda, MD - *EISS 5-84 Sup; InterCabHB 3; TeleSy&SerDir 2-84; VideoDir 82-83*
Arlington Advocate - Boston, MA - *AyerDirPub 83*
Arlington Advocate - *See* Century Newspapers Inc.
Arlington Advocate, The - Arlington, MA - *Ed&PubIntYB 82*
Arlington Aluminum Co. - Detroit, MI - *AvMarPl 83*
Arlington Broadcast Group - Phoenix, AZ - *BrCabYB 84*
Arlington Broadcast Group - Santa Monica, CA - *Tel&CabFB 84S*
Arlington Cablesystems Corp. [of American Cablesystems Corp.] - Arlington, MA - *BrCabYB 84; Tel&CabFB 84C*
Arlington Catholic Herald - Arlington, VA - *NewsDir 84*
Arlington Citizen - Arlington, NE - *Ed&PubIntYB 82*
Arlington Citizen [of Blair Enterprise Co. Inc.] - Blair, NE - *NewsDir 84*
Arlington Citizen - *See* Enterprise Publishing Co. Inc.
Arlington Citizen-Journal - Arlington, TX - *BaconPubCkNews 84; Ed&PubIntYB 82; NewsDir 84*
Arlington Enterprise - Arlington, MN - *BaconPubCkNews 84; Ed&PubIntYB 82*
Arlington Heights Daily Herald [of Paddock Publications] - Arlington Heights, IL - *NewsDir 84*
Arlington Heights Daily Herald - Chicago, IL - *AyerDirPub 83*
Arlington Heights Herald - *See* Paddock Publications
Arlington Heights Topics - *See* Journal & Topics Newspapers
Arlington Journal - Fairfax, VA - *AyerDirPub 83*
Arlington Journal [of Journal Newspapers Inc.] - Springfield, VA - *NewsDir 84*
Arlington Journal - *See* Journal Newspapers
Arlington Journal, The - Washington, DC - *Ed&PubIntYB 82*
Arlington Movie Studios - Flushing, NY - *TelAl 83, 84*
Arlington News - Arlington, TX - *BaconPubCkNews 84; NewsDir 84*
Arlington News - Farmers Branch, TX - *Ed&PubIntYB 82*
Arlington News [of Icarus Publishers Inc.] - Arlington, VA - *AyerDirPub 83; NewsDir 84*
Arlington Northern Virginia Sun - Arlington, VA - *NewsDir 84*
Arlington Software & Systems - Arlington, MA - *MicrocomMPl 84; MicrocomSwDir 1*
Arlington Sun - Arlington, SD - *BaconPubCkNews 84; Ed&PubIntYB 82*
Arlington TeleCable Inc. [of TeleCable Corp.] - Arlington, TX - *BrCabYB 84; Tel&CabFB 84C*
Arlington TeleCommunications Corp. [Aff. of Tele-Communications Inc.] - Arlington, VA - *BrCabYB 84; InterCabHB 3*
Arlington Telephone Co. [Aff. of HunTel Systems Inc.] - Blair, NE - *TelDir&BG 83-84*
Arlington Times - Arlington, WA - *BaconPubCkNews 84; Ed&PubIntYB 82*
Arlington TV Cooperative Inc. - Arlington, OR - *BrCabYB 84; Tel&CabFB 84C*
Arlington Urbanite - Arlington, TX - *Ed&PubIntYB 82*
Arloco Music Inc. - *See* Sanga Music Inc.
Arlotta Press - Dayton, OH - *BoPubDir 4, 5; LitMag&SmPr 83-84*
Arlyck Films, Ralph - Poughkeepsie, NY - *AvMarPl 83*
Arma Cablevision - Arma, KS - *Tel&CabFB 84C*
Arma Press - North Brandford, CT - *BoPubDir 4, 5*
Armada Times - Armada, MI - *BaconPubCkNews 84; Ed&PubIntYB 82*
Armadale Co. Ltd. - Canada - *Ed&PubIntYB 82*
Armadillo International Software - Austin, TX - *MicrocomMPl 83*
Armadillo Press - Austin, TX - *BoPubDir 4, 5*
Armado & Moth - Boulder, CO - *BoPubDir 4 Sup*
Arman Enterprises Inc. - Woodstock, CT - *BoPubDir 4, 5*
Arman Publishing Inc., M. - Ormond Beach, FL - *BoPubDir 4, 5; WritMar 84*
Armando & Moth - Boulder, CO - *BoPubDir 5*
Armchair Detective, The - New York, NY - *LitMag&SmPr 83-84*
Armchair Sailor Bookstore, The - Newport, RI - *LitMarPl 84*
Armco Communications Inc. - Olivia, MN - *BrCabYB 84; Tel&CabFB 84C p.1664*
Armco Music - *See* Armstrong Associates Inc., Pat
Armed Forces Comptroller - Mt. Vernon, VA - *MagIndMarPl 82-83*
Armed Forces Journal International - Washington, DC - *BaconPubCkMag 84; LitMarPl 83, 84; MagDir 84; WritMar 84*
Armenian Mirror-Spectator - Watertown, MA - *AyerDirPub 83; Ed&PubIntYB 82*
Armenian Reporter - Rego Park, NY - *Ed&PubIntYB 82; NewsDir 84*
Armenian Reporter, The - Flushing, NY - *AyerDirPub 83*
Armenian Review - Boston, MA - *Ed&PubIntYB 82*
Armenian Weekly [of Hairenik Associates] - Boston, MA - *Ed&PubIntYB 82; NewsDir 84*

Armer Research Counsel - Newton Centre, MA - *IntDirMarRes 83*
Armonk North Castle News - Armonk, NY - *BaconPubCkNews 84; NewsDir 84*
Armor America Inc. - Tucson, AZ - *DirInfWP 82*
Armor Magazine - Ft. Knox, KY - *MagDir 84*
Armory Publications - Tacoma, WA - *BoPubDir 4, 5*
Armour Cable TV - Armour, SD - *Tel&CabFB 84C*
Armour Cable TV - Chamberlain, SD - *BrCabYB 84*
Armour Chronicle - Armour, SD - *BaconPubCkNews 84; Ed&PubIntYB 82*
Armour Independent Telephone Co. - Armour, SD - *TelDir&BG 83-84*
Arms Inc. [Subs. of NSA Inc.] - Cherry Hill, NJ - *ADAPSOMemDir 83-84*
Armstrong Advertising, N. - Lubbock, TX - *StaDirAdAg 2-84*
Armstrong Associates Inc., Pat - Orlando, FL - *BillIntBG 83-84*
Armstrong Cable TV Co. - Armstrong, IA - *BrCabYB 84; Tel&CabFB 84C*
Armstrong Communications Inc. [of Armstrong Utilities Inc.] - Austintown Township, OH - *Tel&CabFB 84C*
Armstrong Communications Ltd. - Welland, ON, Canada - *BrCabYB 84*
Armstrong Co. Inc., D. - Houston, TX - *LitMarPl 84*
Armstrong Genealogical Systems - Greenville, TX - *MicrocomMPl 84*
Armstrong Journal - Armstrong, IA - *BaconPubCkNews 84; Ed&PubIntYB 82*
Armstrong Publishing Co. - Los Angeles, CA - *BoPubDir 4, 5*
Armstrong Telephone Co. - Rising Sun, MD - *TelDir&BG 83-84*
Armstrong Telephone Co. [Aff. of Armstrong Utilities Inc.] - Hamlin, WV - *TelDir&BG 83-84*
Armstrong Utilities Inc. - Ashland, OH - *BrCabYB 84; Tel&CabFB 84C p.1664*
Armstrong Utilities Inc. - Boardman, OH - *BrCabYB 84*
Armstrong Utilities Inc. - Butler, OH - *BrCabYB 84 p.D-297*
Armstrong Utilities Inc. - McDonald, OH - *BrCabYB 84; Tel&CabFB 84C*
Armstrong Utilities Inc. - Medina, OH - *Tel&CabFB 84C*
Armstrong Utilities Inc. - Orrville, OH - *BrCabYB 84*
Armstrong Utilities Inc. - Butler, PA - *BrCabYB 84; CabTVFinDB 83; Tel&CabFB 84C*
Armstrong Utilities Inc. - Ellwood City, PA - *BrCabYB 84; Tel&CabFB 84C*
Armstrong Utilities Inc. - Grove City, PA - *BrCabYB 84; Tel&CabFB 84C*
Armstrong Utilities Inc. - Zelienople, PA - *BrCabYB 84*
Armstrong Utilities Inc. - Hamlin, WV - *BrCabYB 84; Tel&CabFB 84C*
Armstrong Utilities Inc. - Kenova, WV - *Tel&CabFB 84C*
Armstrong World Industries Inc. - Lancaster, PA - *DirInfWP 82*
Army [of Association of the US Army] - Arlington, VA - *ArtMar 84; BaconPubCkMag 84; LitMarPl 83, 84; MagDir 84; MagIndMarPl 82-83; WritMar 84*
Army Aviation - Westport, CT - *BaconPubCkMag 84; MagDir 84*
Army/Navy Store & Outdoor Merchandiser - Elizabeth, NJ - *BaconPubCkMag 84; MagDir 84; WritMar 84*
Army Times - Washington, DC - *BaconPubCkMag 84; MagDir 84; MagIndMarPl 82-83*
Army Times Publishing Co. - Washington, DC - *DirMarMP 83; KnowInd 83; MagIndMarPl 82-83; NewsBur 6*
Army Times Syndicate - Washington, DC - *Ed&PubIntYB 82*
Arnan IV Publishers [Aff. of The Quartus Foundation] - Austin, TX - *BoPubDir 5; LitMag&SmPr 83-84*
Arner Publications Inc. - Westmoreland, NY - *BoPubDir 4, 5*
Arnett Ellis County Capital - Arnett, OK - *BaconPubCkNews 84*
Arnold Advertising - Reading, PA - *AdAge 3-28-84; StaDirAdAg 2-84*
Arnold & Associates - San Francisco, CA - *AvMarPl 83*
Arnold & Associates Inc., Noble - Schaumburg, IL - *AdAge 3-28-84; StaDirAdAg 2-84*
Arnold & Associates, Jack - San Diego, CA - *BoPubDir 4, 5*
Arnold & Co. - Chicago, IL - *IntDirMarRes 83*
Arnold & Co. - Boston, MA - *AdAge 3-28-84; ArtMar 84; StaDirAdAg 2-84; TelAl 83, 84*
Arnold & Palmer & Noble Inc. - *See* Byoir & Associates Inc., Carl
Arnold/Conrad Inc. [Div. of Arnold & Co. Inc.] - Boston, MA - *DirPRFirms 83*
Arnold, Edward [Subs. of Edward Arnold Ltd.] - Baltimore, MD - *LitMarPl 84*
Arnold Entertainment Inc., Kay [Div. of The Kay Arnold Group] - Paramus, NJ - *AvMarPl 83*
Arnold Group, Kay - Paramus, NJ - *Tel&CabFB 84C*
Arnold Harwell McClain & Associates - Dallas, TX - *AdAge 3-28-84; ArtMar 84; StaDirAdAg 2-84*
Arnold Inc., Peter - New York, NY - *LitMarPl 83, 84; MagIndMarPl 82-83*
Arnold Jackson & Smyth Advertising, Maxwell - San Francisco, CA - *StaDirAdAg 2-84*
Arnold Rocket - Festus, MO - *AyerDirPub 83*
Arnold Rocket, The - Arnold, MO - *Ed&PubIntYB 82*
Arnold Romedy & Sullivan - Chattanooga, TN - *StaDirAdAg 2-84*
Arnold Sentinel - Arnold, NE - *BaconPubCkNews 84; Ed&PubIntYB 82*
Arnold's Book Bindery Inc. - Reading, PA - *LitMarPl 83, 84*
Arnprior Chronicle, The - Arnprior, ON, Canada - *Ed&PubIntYB 82*
Arnsberger & Comjean - Boston, MA - *LitMarPl 84*
Arnsberger & Comjean - Charleston, MA - *LitMarPl 83*
ARO Publishing Co. - Provo, UT - *BoPubDir 4, 5*
Aronson, Charles N. - Arcade, NY - *BoPubDir 4, 5*
Aronson Inc., Jason - New York, NY - *LitMarPl 83, 84*
Aronson Publishing Co. - Marina del Rey, CA - *BoPubDir 4*
Aronson Publishing Co. - San Mateo, CA - *BoPubDir 5*
Aroostook Republican & News - Caribou, ME - *Ed&PubIntYB 82*
Arowhena Publishing Co. - Downsview, ON, Canada - *BoPubDir 4, 5*
ARP Films Inc. - New York, NY - *Tel&CabFB 84C*
Arpanet Network Information Center [of SRI International] - Menlo Park, CA - *EISS 83*
Arpell/Pinellas Music Publishing [of Rogue Entertainment Co.] - Woodland Hills, CA - *BillIntBG 83-84*
Arrangement Reticule des Informations pour l'Approche des Notions... [of Centre d'Assistance Technique et de Documentation] - Paris, France - *CompReadDB 82*
Arrets de la Cour Federale du Canada [of Federal Dept. of Justice] - Ottawa, ON, Canada - *CompReadDB 82*
Arriaga Publications - Booneville, AR - *BoPubDir 4, 5*
Arriba Records - Los Angeles, CA - *BillIntBG 83-84*
Arriflex Corp. - Blauvelt, NY - *AvMarPl 83*
Arrington Software Service - Boise, ID - *WhoWMicrocom 83*
Arrival - Vancouver, BC, Canada - *BaconPubCkMag 84*
Arrow - Rolfe, IA - *AyerDirPub 83*
Arrow Book Club [of Scholastic Book Services] - New York, NY - *LitMarPl 83, 84*
Arrow Electronics Inc. - Farmingdale, NY - *DataDirSup 7-83*
Arrow Lakes News - Nakusp, BC, Canada - *AyerDirPub 83; Ed&PubIntYB 82*
Arrowhead Cable TV - Shell Lake, WI - *BrCabYB 84; Tel&CabFB 84C*
Arrowhead Communications Corp. [Aff. of Communications Systems Inc.] - Hector, MN - *TelDir&BG 83-84*
Arrowhead Press - Berkeley, CA - *BoPubDir 4, 5; LitMag&SmPr 83-84*
Arrowsmith Star - Parksville, BC, Canada - *Ed&PubIntYB 82*
Arroyo Grande Five Cities Times-Press-Recorder - Arroyo Grande, CA - *BaconPubCkNews 84; NewsDir 84*
ARS - *See* Research Systems Corp.
ARS Ceramica Ltd. - Ann Arbor, MI - *BoPubDir 4, 5*
ARS Electronics - Kenilworth, IL - *BoPubDir 4, 5*
Ars Inc., O. - Cambridge, MA - *BoPubDir 5*
ARS Publishing Co. - Stockton, CA - *BoPubDir 5*
ARS Semeiotica Press - Boulder, CO - *BoPubDir 4, 5*
Arstark & Co. Inc., L. D. - Woodbury, NY - *LitMarPl 83, 84; MagIndMarPl 82-83; StaDirAdAg 2-84*
Art Alliance Press [Aff. of Associated University Presses] - Cranbury, NJ - *BoPubDir 5*
Art Alliance Press [Aff. of Associated University Presses] - East Brunswick, NJ - *BoPubDir 4*
Art & Antiques - New York, NY - *BaconPubCkMag 84; MagDir 84; MagIndMarPl 82-83*
Art & Antiques Book Club [Subs. of Watson-Guptill Book Clubs] - New York, NY - *LitMarPl 84*

Art & Antiques Book Club - *See* Watson-Guptill Book Clubs
Art & Archaeology [of Centre de Documentation Sciences Humaines] - Paris, France - *CompReadDB 82*
Art & Archaeology Newsletter - Flushing, NY - *LitMag&SmPr 83-84*
Art & Artist [of Foundation for the Community of Artists] - New York, NY - *LitMag&SmPr 83-84*
Art & Artists [of Oil Pastel Association] - Upper-Nyack-on-Hudson, NY - *WritMar 84*
Art & Communications - Carlsbad, NM - *BoPubDir 5*
Art & Copy Overload [Div. of John Borden Advertising Agency] - Minneapolis, MN - *DirMarMP 83*
Art & Literary Digest - Tweed, ON, Canada - *WritMar 84*
Art & Reference House - Brownsboro, TX - *BoPubDir 4, 5*
Art & the Law - New York, NY - *MagIndMarPl 82-83*
Art Attack Records Inc. - Tucson, AZ - *BillIntBG 83-84*
Art Audio Publishing Co. - Detroit, MI - *BillIntBG 83-84*
Art Business News [of Myers Publishing Co. Inc.] - Stamford, CT - *BaconPubCkMag 84; MagDir 84; MagIndMarPl 82-83; WritMar 84*
Art City Publishing Co. - Springville, UT - *BaconPubCkNews 84*
Art Com [of Contemporary Arts Press] - San Francisco, CA - *LitMag&SmPr 83-84*
Art Connection Inc. - Los Angeles, CA - *ArtMar 84*
Art Craft Play Co. - Cedar Rapids, IA - *WritMar 84*
Art Direction [of Advertising Art] - New York, NY - *ArtMar 84; BaconPubCkMag 84; LitMarPl 83, 84; MagDir 84; MagIndMarPl 82-83; WritMar 84*
Art Direction Book Co. - New York, NY - *ArtMar 84; LitMarPl 83, 84; WritMar 84*
Art Education - Reston, VA - *BaconPubCkMag 84; MagDir 84; MagIndMarPl 82-83*
Art Education Inc. - Blauvelt, NY - *BoPubDir 4, 5*
Art Gallery [of Hollycroft Press Inc.] - Ivoryton, CT - *BaconPubCkMag 84; MagDir 84*
Art Gallery of Ontario - Toronto, ON, Canada - *BoPubDir 4, 5; LitMarPl 84*
Art Happenings of Houston - Houston, TX - *BaconPubCkMag 84; MagDir 84*
Art History Publishers - Red Wing, MN - *BoPubDir 4, 5*
Art Image Inc. - Los Angeles, CA - *ArtMar 84*
Art in America [of Whitney Communications Corp.] - New York, NY - *BaconPubCkMag 84; LitMarPl 83, 84; MagDir 84; MagIndMarPl 82-83*
Art Institute of Chicago - Chicago, IL - *BoPubDir 4, 5*
Art Institute of Chicago (Publications Dept.) - Chicago, IL - *LitMarPl 84*
Art Letter - New York, NY - *MagIndMarPl 82-83*
Art Material Trade News [of Syndicate Magazines Inc.] - Atlanta, GA - *BaconPubCkMag 84; MagDir 84*
Art Material Trade News - New York, NY - *MagIndMarPl 82-83*
Art Metropole [Aff. of Art Official Inc.] - Toronto, ON, Canada - *BoPubDir 4, 4 Sup, 5*
Art New England - Brighton, MA - *WritMar 84*
Art News Magazine - New York, NY - *DirMarMP 83*
Art Now Gallery Guide - Kenilworth, NJ - *MagDir 84*
Art Now U.S.A. - Kenilworth, NJ - *BaconPubCkMag 84*
Art Official Inc. - Toronto, ON, Canada - *LitMag&SmPr 83-84*
Art Papers - Atlanta, GA - *LitMag&SmPr 83-84*
Art Product News - St. Petersburg, FL - *BaconPubCkMag 84; MagDir 84*
Art Records Manufacturing Co. - Ft. Lauderdale, FL - *BillIntBG 83-84*
Art Resource Inc. - New York, NY - *LitMarPl 84*
Art Show News, The - Littleton, CO - *ArtMar 84*
Art Spectrum [Div. of Mitch Morse Gallery Inc.] - New York, NY - *ArtMar 84*
Art Therapy Publications - Craftsbury Common, VT - *BoPubDir 4, 5*
Art West - Bozeman, MT - *BaconPubCkMag 84; WritMar 84*
Art/World - New York, NY - *BaconPubCkMag 84; MagDir 84*
Arta Publishing Co. - Don Mills, ON, Canada - *BoPubDir 4, 5*
Artabras Inc. [Div. of Abbeville Press Inc.] - New York, NY - *LitMarPl 83, 84*
Artafax Systems Ltd. Inc. - Manchester, NH - *ArtMar 84*
Artal Music Inc. - *See* Catalogue Music Inc.
Artaud's Elbow - Berkeley, CA - *BoPubDir 4, 5*
ArtBibliographies Modern [of ABC-Clio Inc.] - Santa Barbara, CA - *DataDirOnSer 84; DBBus 82; DirOnDB Spring 84*
ArtBibliographies Modern [of Clio Press Ltd.] - Hinksey Hill, England - *OnBibDB 3*
ArtBibliographies Modern [of Clio Press Ltd.] - Oxford, England - *CompReadDB 82*
Arte Publico Press - Houston, TX - *LitMag&SmPr 83-84*
Artech House Inc. [Subs. of Horizon House Inc.] - Dedham, MA - *LitMarPl 83, 84; WritMar 84*
Artel Art & Electronics - Sante Fe, NM - *MicrocomMPl 84*
Artel Communications - Worcester, MA - *DataDirSup 7-83*
Artemis - Roanoke, VA - *LitMag&SmPr 83-84*
Artemis Project Management Information System [of Metier Management Systems Inc.] - Houston, TX - *EISS 83*
Artemis Records Ltd. - Howard Beach, NY - *BillIntBG 83-84*
Artemisia Press - Colorado Springs, CO - *BoPubDir 4, 5; LitMag&SmPr 83-84*
Arteric Designs Ltd. - Old Bethpage, NY - *StaDirAdAg 2-84*
Arters Public Relations, Linda B. - Media, PA - *DirPRFirms 83*
Artes Graficas USA - Farmingdale, NY - *BaconPubCkMag 84; MagDir 84*
Artesia Daily Press [of Valley Newspapers Inc.] - Artesia, NM - *Ed&PubIntYB 82; NewsDir 84*
Artesian Commonwealth - Artesian, SD - *Ed&PubIntYB 82*
Artesian Commonwealth - Woonsocket, SD - *AyerDirPub 83*
Artfolio Inc., The - Atlanta, GA - *ArtMar 84*
Artforms Card Corp. - Highland Park, IL - *WritMar 84*
Artforum - New York, NY - *BaconPubCkMag 84; MagDir 84; MagIndMarPl 82-83*
Artful Dodge Publications - Bloomington, IN - *LitMag&SmPr 83-84*
Artful Reporter, The [of North West Arts] - Manchester, England - *LitMag&SmPr 83-84*
Arthritis & Rheumatism - Atlanta, GA - *BaconPubCkMag 84; MagDir 84; MagIndMarPl 82-83*
Arthritis Information Clearinghouse [of U.S. Public Health Service] - Bethesda, MD - *EISS 83*
Arthritis Information Clearinghouse Database [of National Institute of Arthritis, Diabetes, & Digestive, & Kidney Diseases] - Bethesda, MD - *CompReadDB 82*
Arthur & Associates, Michael - Santa Monica, CA - *HBIndAd&MS 82-83*
Arthur Associates Inc., Budd - Chicago, IL - *DirPRFirms 83*
Arthur Enterprise - Arthur, NE - *BaconPubCkNews 84; Ed&PubIntYB 82*
Arthur Graphic Clarion - Arthur, IL - *BaconPubCkNews 84*
Arthur, M. J. R. - Carson City, NV - *LitMarPl 83, 84; MagIndMarPl 82-83*
Arthur Mutual Telephone Co. - Defiance, OH - *TelDir&BG 83-84*
Arthur Non-Stock Cooperative Telephone Association - Arthur, NE - *TelDir&BG 83-84*
Arthur Owned Publishing - Philadelphia, PA - *BoPubDir 4, 5*
Arthur Publications Inc. - Jacksonville, FL - *BoPubDir 4, 5*
Arthur's International - Honolulu, HI - *Ed&PubIntYB 82*
Artic Computing Ltd. - Hull, England - *MicrocomSwDir 1*
Artichoke Press - Mountain View, CA - *BoPubDir 4, 5*
Articulate Publications Inc. - Los Angeles, CA - *MicrocomMPl 84*
Artifact [of Iceberg Press] - Flint, MI - *LitMag&SmPr 83-84*
Artificial Intelligence - Seattle, WA - *MicrocomSwDir 1*
Artificial Intelligence Inc. - Renton, VA - *MicrocomMPl 84*
Artificial Intelligence Research Group - Los Angeles, CA - *MicrocomMPl 83, 84*
Artikkel-Indeks Tidsskrifter [of Norsk Senter for Informatikk] - Oslo, Norway - *CompReadDB 82*
Artim Advertisement - Hamilton Square, NJ - *AdAge 3-28-84*
Artim Advertising - Trenton, NJ - *StaDirAdAg 2-84*
Artintype Metro Inc. - New York, NY - *LitMarPl 83, 84*
Artisan Crafts - Springfield, MO - *LitMag&SmPr 83-84*
Artisan Research Inc. - Rye, NY - *IntDirMarRes 83*
Artisan Sales - Thousand Oaks, CA - *BoPubDir 4, 5*
Artistry International/Dave Bartruff - San Anselmo, CA - *MagIndMarPl 82-83*
Artists & Alchemists Publications - Sausalito, CA - *BoPubDir 4, 5; LitMag&SmPr 83-84*
Artists & Writers Publications - San Rafael, CA - *WritMar 84*
Artists & Writers Syndicate - Washington, DC - *Ed&PubIntYB 82*

Artists Associates - New York, NY - *LitMarPl 83, 84; MagIndMarPl 82-83*
Artists Foundation Inc. - Boston, MA - *BoPubDir 4, 5*
Artists International [Subs. of Illustrators International Inc.] - New York, NY - *LitMarPl 83, 84; MagIndMarPl 82-83*
Artist's Magazine, The [of F & W Publishing Co.] - Cincinnati, OH - *WritMar 84*
Artist's Market - Cincinnati, OH - *ArtMar 84*
Artists' Publications in Print [of Umbrella Associates] - Glendale, CA - *LitMag&SmPr 83-84*
Artists Revue Records - Nashville, TN - *BillIntBG 83-84*
Artists 7 Austin - Austin, TX - *AvMarPl 83*
Artkino Pictures Inc. - New York, NY - *Tel&CabFB 84C*
Artmagazine - Toronto, ON, Canada - *BaconPubCkMag 84*
Artman's Press - Berkeley, CA - *BoPubDir 4 Sup, 5; LitMag&SmPr 83-84*
ArtNews - New York, NY - *BaconPubCkMag 84; LitMarPl 83, 84; MagDir 84; MagIndMarPl 82-83*
ArtNews Books [Div. of Annellen Publications Inc.] - New York, NY - *LitMarPl 83, 84*
Artpolice - Minneapolis, MN - *LitMag&SmPr 83-84*
Artquest - Weybridge, England - *DirOnDB Spring 84*
Artra Inc. - Arlington, VA - *MicrocomMPl 84*
Artrepreneur Inc. - New York, NY - *BoPubDir 4 Sup, 5*
Arts - New York, NY - *ArtMar 84; CabTVPrDB 83*
Arts & Activities - San Diego, CA - *BaconPubCkMag 84; MagDir 84; MagIndMarPl 82-83*
Arts & Architecture - Los Angeles, CA - *BaconPubCkMag 84; MagDir 84*
Arts & Architecture Press - Santa Monica, CA - *BoPubDir 4, 5*
Arts & Entertainment [of The Houston Post] - Houston, TX - *LitMarPl 84*
Arts & Entertainment Network - New York, NY - *Tel&CabFB 84C*
Arts & Events Magazine - San Francisco, CA - *MagDir 84*
Arts & Humanities Citation Index [of Institute for Scientific Information] - Philadelphia, PA - *CompReadDB 82*
Arts Club Theatre - Vancouver, BC, Canada - *WritMar 84*
Arts Computer Products Inc. - Boston, MA - *WhoWMicrocom 83*
Arts End Books [Aff. of Nostoc Magazine] - Newton, MA - *BoPubDir 4, 5; LitMag&SmPr 83-84*
Arts Magazine [of The Art Digest Co.] - New York, NY - *BaconPubCkMag 84; LitMarPl 83, 84; MagDir 84; MagIndMarPl 82-83; WritMar 84*
Arts Management - New York, NY - *WritMar 84*
Arts of St. Louis, The - St. Louis, MO - *MagDir 84*
Arts Sales Catalog Database [of The Research Libraries Group Inc.] - Stanford, CA - *DataDirOnSer 84*
Artscene - San Francisco, CA - *MagDir 84*
Artsci Inc. - North Hollywood, CA - *MicrocomMPl 83; MicrocomSwDir 1*
Artsci/Softape - North Hollywood, CA - *MicrocomMPl 84*
Artscope Ltd. - New York, NY - *TelAl 83*
Artsongs Publishing - Ft. Lauderdale, FL - *BillIntBG 83-84*
Artviews [of Visual Arts Ontario] - Totonto, ON, Canada - *WritMar 84*
Artweek - Oakland, CA - *BaconPubCkMag 84; MagIndMarPl 82-83*
Artworkers News - New York, NY - *MagIndMarPl 82-83*
Artworx Software Co. - Fairport, NY - *MicrocomMPl 83, 84*
Artz Camera Supply - Aberdeen, SD - *AvMarPl 83*
Artzien [of Kontexts Publications] - Amsterdam, Netherlands - *LitMag&SmPr 83-84*
Arvada East Jefferson Star - *See* Jeffco Publications
Arvada Sentinel [of Community Publications Co.] - Arvada, CO - *NewsDir 84*
Arvada Sentinel - *See* Sentinel Newspapers
Arvak - Rockland, ME - *LitMarPl 84*
Arvida-Clearview Cable Television Corp. - Palm Valley, FL - *BrCabYB 84*
Arvida-Clearview Cable Television Corp. - Ponte Vedra Beach, FL - *BrCabYB 84; Tel&CabFB 84C*
Arvidson Press, J. - Helena, MT - *BoPubDir 4, 5*
Arvig Telephone Co. [Aff. of Bridge Water Telephone Co.] - Pequot Lakes, MN - *TelDir&BG 83-84*
Arvilla Press - Van Buren, AR - *BoPubDir 4, 5*
Arvin Cablevision [of American Television & Communications Co.] - Arvin, CA - *BrCabYB 84*
Arvin Industries Inc. - Columbus, IN - *HomeVid&CabYB 82-83*
Arvin Tiller - Arvin, CA - *BaconPubCkNews 84; Ed&PubIntYB 82*
ARX [of ITT World Communications Inc.] - New York, NY - *TeleSy&SerDir 7-83*
Arztco Pictures Inc. - New York, NY - *AvMarPl 83; TelAl 83, 84; WritMar 84*
As Is/So & So Press - San Francisco, CA - *BoPubDir 4, 5*
ASA Inc. - Southborough, MA - *DataDirOnSer 84*
ASA International Trade Services Inc. - Salem, NH - *DataDirOnSer 84; DataDirSup 7-83*
ASAI Music Corp. - *See* Penny Pincher Music
ASAI Record Corp. - Vansant, VA - *BillIntBG 83-84*
ASAP Photolab Inc. - New York, NY - *AvMarPl 83*
A.S.A.P. Word Processing Inc. - Chicago, IL - *DirInfWP 82*
Asbarez - Los Angeles, CA - *AyerDirPub 83; Ed&PubIntYB 82*
Asbarez Weekly - Glendale, CA - *NewsDir 84*
Asbestos [of D & B Enterprises Inc.] - Lakeville, PA - *BaconPubCkMag 84; MagDir 84*
Asbestos [of Informatheque-PRAUS] - Sherbrooke, PQ, Canada - *DataDirOnSer 84; DirOnDB Spring 84*
Asbestos Information [of QL Systems Ltd.] - Ottawa, ON, Canada - *DataDirOnSer 84*
Asbestos Information [of Universite de Sherbrooke] - Sherbrooke, PQ, Canada - *CompReadDB 82*
Asbestos Worker, The - Washington, DC - *NewsDir 84*
Asbury & James TV Cable Service Corp. - Loudendale, WV - *BrCabYB 84*
Asbury & James TV Cable Service Corp. - Montgomery, WV - *BrCabYB 84 p.D-297*
Asbury Park Press - Asbury Park, NJ - *AyerDirPub 83; BaconPubCkNews 84; Ed&PubIntYB 82; LitMarPl 83, 84; NewsBur 6; NewsDir 84*
Asbury Publishing Co. Inc., Francis - Wilmore, KY - *BoPubDir 4, 5*
ASC Films Inc. [Div. of DAS Productions Inc.] - Malibu, CA - *AvMarPl 83*
ASC Music Co. Inc. - Binghamton, NY - *BillIntBG 83-84*
ASCAP in Action - New York, NY - *WritMar 84*
Ascension Academy - Alexandria, VA - *BoPubDir 4, 5*
Ascension from the Ashes [of AFTA Press] - New Brunswick, NJ - *WritMar 84*
Asch Musical Advertising, Andrew - New York, NY - *AvMarPl 83*
Asch/Seidenbaum Ltd. - New York, NY - *StaDirAdAg 2-84*
Ascham Press, Roger - Toronto, ON, Canada - *BoPubDir 4, 5*
Ascher Music Inc., Emil - New York, NY - *AvMarPl 83*
Ascher Syndicate, Sidney - Mays Landing, NJ - *Ed&PubIntYB 82*
Asciutto, Mary Anne - New York, NY - *LitMarPl 83, 84*
Asdek Publishing - Elmhurst, NY - *Ed&PubIntYB 82*
Aser Publicidad - Bogota, Colombia - *StaDirAdAg 2-84*
Ash Advertising Inc. - Elkhart, IN - *StaDirAdAg 2-84*
Ash Grove Commonwealth - Ash Grove, MO - *BaconPubCkNews 84; Ed&PubIntYB 82*
Ash Inc., Rene L. - New York, NY - *DirPRFirms 83*
Ash-Kar Press - San Francisco, CA - *BoPubDir 4, 5; LitMag&SmPr 83-84*
Ash Lad Press - Canton, NY - *BoPubDir 4, 5; LitMag&SmPr 83-84*
Ash/LeDonne Inc. - New York, NY - *ArtMar 84; StaDirAdAg 2-84*
Ash Publications Inc., David - Orangeburg, NY - *BoPubDir 5*
Ash Valley Music Inc. - Nashville, TN - *BillIntBG 83-84*
ASHA - Rockville, MD - *BaconPubCkMag 84; MagIndMarPl 82-83*
Ashar Enterprises - Fremont, CA - *MicrocomMPl 84*
Ashbrook Publishing - Johnstown, OH - *BaconPubCkNews 84*
Ashburn Associates, Benjamin - Los Angeles, CA - *DirPRFirms 83*
Ashburn Wiregrass Farmer & Stockman - Ashburn, GA - *BaconPubCkNews 84*
Ashby & Associates Inc. - Cleveland, OH - *DirPRFirms 83*
Ashby, Dillon & Meade - Rocky River, OH - *AdAge 3-28-84; StaDirAdAg 2-84*

Ashcroft Cache Creek Journal - Ashcroft, BC, Canada - *AyerDirPub 83*
Ashdown Cablevision Inc. - Ashdown, AR - *BrCabYB 84; Tel&CabFB 84C*
Ashdown Editorial & Design Services, Ellen - Tallahassee, FL - *LitMarPl 83, 84*
Ashdown Little River News - Ashdown, AR - *BaconPubCkNews 84*
Asheboro Courier-Tribune - Asheboro, NC - *BaconPubCkNews 84; NewsDir 84*
Asheboro Randolph Guide - Asheboro, NC - *BaconPubCkNews 84*
Asher Agency - Ft. Wayne, IN - *AdAge 3-28-84*
Asher, Camuso & Gibbs Inc. - Seattle, WA - *StaDirAdAg 2-84*
Asher/Gould Advertising Inc. - Beverly Hills, CA - *StaDirAdAg 2-84*
Asheville Citizen - Asheville, NC - *BaconPubCkNews 84; LitMarPl 83; NewsDir 84*
Asheville Citizen-Times - Asheville, NC - *LitMarPl 83*
Asheville Times - Asheville, NC - *BaconPubCkNews 84; LitMarPl 83; NewsDir 84*
Ashford Press - Clinton, CT - *BoPubDir 5; LitMag&SmPr 83-84*
Ashford Press - Willimantic, CT - *BoPubDir 4*
Ashford Publications [Aff. of Inform-Science Corp.] - Houston, TX - *BoPubDir 4, 5*
Ashira Associates - Los Angeles, CA - *AvMarPl 83*
Ashland Boone County Journal - Ashland, MO - *BaconPubCkNews 84*
Ashland Cable TV - Ashland, KS - *BrCabYB 84*
Ashland Cable TV - Ashland, MT - *BrCabYB 84*
Ashland City Times - Ashland City, TN - *BaconPubCkNews 84; Ed&PubIntYB 82*
Ashland Clark County Clipper - Ashland, KS - *BaconPubCkNews 84*
Ashland County Cable Service Inc. - Loudenville, OH - *Tel&CabFB 84C*
Ashland County Cable Service Inc. [of Lodi Cable Service Co.] - Loudonville, OH - *BrCabYB 84*
Ashland Daily Independent - Ashland, KY - *BaconPubCkNews 84; Ed&PubIntYB 82; NewsDir 84*
Ashland Daily Press - Ashland, WI - *NewsDir 84*
Ashland Daily Tidings - Ashland, OR - *BaconPubCkNews 84*
Ashland Gazette - Ashland, NE - *BaconPubCkNews 84; Ed&PubIntYB 82*
Ashland-Hanover Herald Progress - Ashland, VA - *BaconPubCkNews 84*
Ashland Poetry Press, The - Ashland, OH - *LitMag&SmPr 83-84*
Ashland Progress - Ashland, AL - *BaconPubCkNews 84; Ed&PubIntYB 82*
Ashland Sentinel - Ashland, IL - *BaconPubCkNews 84; Ed&PubIntYB 82*
Ashland Southern Advocate - Ashland, MS - *BaconPubCkNews 84; Ed&PubIntYB 82*
Ashland Times-Gazette - Ashland, OH - *BaconPubCkNews 84; Ed&PubIntYB 82; NewsDir 84*
Ashland Video Co. Inc. - Ashland, PA - *BrCabYB 84*
Ashlar Press [Aff. of Educational Program Development Associates Inc.] - Nashville, TN - *BoPubDir 4, 5*
Ashley, Allen - Pasadena, CA - *WhoWMicrocom 83*
Ashley Books Inc. - Port Washington, NY - *ArtMar 84*
Ashley County Ledger - Hamburg, AR - *AyerDirPub 83; Ed&PubIntYB 82*
Ashley Inc., Aaron - New York, NY - *ArtMar 84*
Ashley News - Ashley, IL - *BaconPubCkNews 84; Ed&PubIntYB 82*
Ashley News Observer, The - Crossett, AR - *AyerDirPub 83; Ed&PubIntYB 82; NewsDir 84*
Ashley Publications Inc. - Carlstadt, NJ - *BillIntBG 83-84*
Ashley Record Co. - Hendersonville, TN - *BillIntBG 83-84*
Ashley Tribune - Ashley, ND - *BaconPubCkNews 84; Ed&PubIntYB 82*
Ashley Video - Hamburg, AR - *BrCabYB 84; Tel&CabFB 84C*
Ashod Press - New York, NY - *BoPubDir 4; LitMag&SmPr 83-84; LitMarPl 83, 84*
ASHRAE Journal [of American Society of Heating, Refrigerating & Air Conditioning Engineers] - Atlanta, GA - *BaconPubCkMag 84; MagIndMarPl 82-83*
ASHRAE Journal [of American Society of Heating, Refrigerating & Air Conditioning Engineers] - Norcross, GA - *MagDir 84*
Ashtabula County Sentinel [of Gazette Printing Co. Inc.] - Jefferson, OH - *NewsDir 84*
Ashtabula Star Beacon - Ashtabula, OH - *BaconPubCkNews 84; NewsDir 84*
Ashton Communications Systems - Vestal, NY - *AvMarPl 83*
Ashton Gazette - Ashton, IL - *BaconPubCkNews 84; Ed&PubIntYB 82*
Ashton Herald - Ashton, ID - *Ed&PubIntYB 82*
Ashton Herald - *See* Standard-Journal Inc.
Ashton-Tate [Subs. of Software Plus] - Culver City, CA - *ADAPSOMemDir 83-84; MicrocomMPl 83, 84; MicrocomSwDir 1; WhoWMicrocom 83*
Ashurst & Kincade Cable TV Co. - Gardnerville, NV - *BrCabYB 84; Tel&CabFB 84C*
Ashworth Book Marketing Inc. - Larchmont, NY - *LitMarPl 83*
ASI - Bethesda, MD - *DirOnDB Spring 84*
ASI - New York, NY - *ArtMar 84*
ASI Data Base [of Aviation Safety Institute] - Worthington, OH - *EISS 5-84 Sup*
ASI Healing Arts Book Club [Div. of ASI Publishing Co.] - New York, NY - *LitMarPl 83, 84*
ASI Market Research [Subs. of IDC Services] - New York, NY - *AdAge 5-17-84 p.32; HBIndAd&MS 82-83; IntDirMarRes 83; MagIndMarPl 82-83*
ASI Publishers - New York, NY - *BoPubDir 4 Sup, 5; LitMag&SmPr 83-84; LitMarPl 83, 84; WritMar 84*
Asia - New York, NY - *BaconPubCkMag 84; MagDir 84; MagIndMarPl 82-83*
Asia Advertising Agency Inc. - Tokyo, Japan - *StaDirAdAg 2-84*
Asia Book Corp. of America - Queens Village, NY - *LitMarPl 83, 84*
Asia Library Services - Auburn, NY - *MicroMarPl 82-83*
Asia Mail, The - Alexandria, VA - *MagDir 84*
Asia-Pacific Broadcasting Union - Kuala Lumpur, Malaysia - *TeleSy&SerDir 2-84*
Asia-Pacific Defense Forum - Camp H. M. Smith, HI - *WritMar 84*
Asia-Pacific Telecommunity - Bangkok, Thailand - *TelDir&BG 83-84*
Asia Publishing House - New York, NY - *BoPubDir 4, 5*
Asia Society Inc. - New York, NY - *BoPubDir 4, 5*
Asia Times - Toronto, ON, Canada - *Ed&PubIntYB 82*
Asian Bookmarket Information Service - Glen Oaks, NY - *LitMarPl 83*
Asian Data Bank [of Data Resource Inc.] - Lexington, MA - *DBBus 82*
Asian Network for Industrial Technology Information & Extension - Singapore, Singapore - *EISS 83*
Asian Profiles [of Interactive Market Systems Inc.] - New York, NY - *DataDirOnSer 84*
Asian Profiles - London, England - *DirOnDB Spring 84*
Asian Studies Center [of Michigan State University] - East Lansing, MI - *LitMag&SmPr 83-84*
Asian Survey [of University of California Press] - Berkeley, CA - *LitMag&SmPr 83-84*
Asiatic Advertising Ltd. - Karachi, Pakistan - *StaDirAdAg 2-84*
Asilomar Music [Div. of RBR Communications Inc.] - New York, NY - *BillIntBG 83-84*
Ask America - Greensboro, NC - *IntDirMarRes 83*
ASK Associates - Woodland Hills, CA - *ADAPSOMemDir 83-84*
Ask Aunt Madge - San Jose, CA - *Ed&PubIntYB 82*
ASK Computer Systems Inc. - Los Altos, CA - *DataDirOnSer 84; DataDirSup 7-83*
ASK Micro Software - Folsom, CA - *MicrocomSwDir 1*
ASK Productions Inc. - Nashville, TN - *AvMarPl 83*
Askey Associates - Keene, NH - *StaDirAdAg 2-84*
Askin Publishers Ltd. - London, England - *LitMag&SmPr 83-84; MicroMarPl 82-83*
Askov American - Askov, MN - *AyerDirPub 83; BaconPubCkNews 84; Ed&PubIntYB 82*
Askwith, Herbert - Larchmont, NY - *LitMarPl 83, 84*
Aslan - Boulder, CO - *BoPubDir 4, 5*
ASLIB - London, England - *EISS 83; InfIndMarPl 83*
ASLIB (Information Services Dept.) - London, England - *InfIndMarPl 83*

ASM News - Washington, DC - *MagDir 84*
ASME Student News - New York, NY - *BaconPubCkMag 84*
Asociacion de Exhibidores Centro Americanos - Coral Gables, FL - *AvMarPl 83*
Asociacion de Literatura Femenina Hispanica - Beaumont, TX - *BoPubDir 4, 5*
Asotin County Sentinel - Clarkston, WA - *AyerDirPub 83*
Asotin County Sentinel - *See* Tribune Newspapers Inc.
Asotin Telephone Co. [Aff. of Telephone & Data Systems Inc.] - Asotin, WA - *TelDir&BG 83-84*
A.S.P. Communications - Toronto, ON, Canada - *BoPubDir 4, 5*
Aspect Composition - Somerville, MA - *LitMarPl 83, 84*
Aspen Flyer - *See* Mountain States Communications Inc.
Aspen Institute Publications - Queenstown, MD - *LitMarPl 84*
Aspen Institute Publications - New York, NY - *LitMarPl 83*
Aspen Institute Publishing Program [Aff. of Aspen Institute for Humanistic Studies] - Palo Alto, CA - *BoPubDir 4*
Aspen Ribbons Inc. - Boulder, CO - *DirInfWP 82; MicrocomMPl 83; WhoWMicrocom 83*
Aspen Software Co. - Tijeras, NM - *MicrocomMPl 83*
Aspen Systems Corp. - Germantown, MD - *DirInfWP 82*
Aspen Systems Corp. [Subs. of Walters Samson U.S. Corp.] - Rockville, MD - *DataDirOnSer 84; DirMarMP 83; InfoS 83-84; LitMarPl 83, 84*
Aspen Times [of Mountain States Communications Inc.] - Aspen, CO - *Ed&PubIntYB 82; NewsDir 84*
Aspen Times - *See* Mountain States Communications Inc.
Aspermont News - Aspermont, TX - *BaconPubCkNews 84*
Asphodel [of Blackbird Press] - Pitman, NJ - *LitMag&SmPr 83-84*
Aspinall, John - Flushing, NY - *MagIndMarPl 82-83*
Aspire - Denver, CO - *WritMar 84*
ASPO - Paris, France - *DirOnDB Spring 84*
Assabet Valley Beacon [of Beacon Minute-Man Corp.] - Acton, MA - *AyerDirPub 83; Ed&PubIntYB 82; NewsDir 84*
Assaria Telephone Exchange Inc. - Assaria, KS - *TelDir&BG 83-84*
ASSASSIN [of Imperial Chemical Industries Ltd.] - Cleveland, England - *EISS 83*
ASSAYS [Div. of Calle & Co.] - Greenwich, CT - *IntDirMarRes 83*
Assemblages - Norwalk, CT - *AvMarPl 83*
Assemblee Nationale (Service de l'Information Parlementaire) - Paris, France - *InfIndMarPl 83*
Assembling Press [Aff. of Participation Projects Foundation] - Brooklyn, NY - *BoPubDir 4, 5; LitMag&SmPr 83-84*
Assembly Engineering [of American Broadcasting Cos. Inc.] - Wheaton, IL - *BaconPubCkMag 84; MagDir 84; MagIndMarPl 82-83; WritMar 84*
Assert Newsletter [of Impact Publishers Inc.] - San Luis Obispo, CA - *LitMag&SmPr 83-84*
Assessor - Waltham, MA - *IntDirMarRes 83*
Assiniboia Times - Assiniboia, SK, Canada - *Ed&PubIntYB 82*
Assistance in Marketing Inc. - Cincinnati, OH - *IntDirMarRes 83*
Assistance in Marketing Inc. - Charleston, WV - *AdAge 3-28-84; StaDirAdAg 2-84*
Associated Advertising Agency - Wichita, KS - *AdAge 3-28-84; StaDirAdAg 2-84*
Associated Advertising of Roanoke Inc. - Roanoke, VA - *StaDirAdAg 2-84*
Associated Audio Services - Port Chester, NY - *AvMarPl 83*
Associated Audio-Visual Corp. - Evanston, IL - *ArtMar 84; AvMarPl 83; WritMar 84*
Associated Bag - Milwaukee, WI - *AvMarPl 83*
Associated Book Publishers Inc. - Scottsdale, AZ - *BoPubDir 4, 5; WritMar 84*
Associated Booksellers - Bridgeport, CT - *LitMarPl 83, 84; WritMar 84*
Associated Broadcast NewsAmerica Inc. - Washington, DC - *BrCabYB 84*
Associated Builders & Contractors Inc. (ABC Publications) - Washington, DC - *BoPubDir 5*
Associated Business Consultants & Marketing Research - *See* American Forum Corp.
Associated Business Systems Inc. - Littleton, CO - *TeleSy&SerDir 2-84*
Associated Church Press - Geneva, IL - *BoPubDir 5*
Associated Communications Corp. - Pittsburgh, PA - *BrCabYB 84*
Associated Computer Services - Portland, OR - *ADAPSOMemDir 83-84*
Associated Consultants - Wheaton, IL - *LitMarPl 83*
Associated Creative Writers - La Mesa, CA - *BoPubDir 4 Sup, 5; LitMag&SmPr 83-84*
Associated Editors - Stamford, CT - *LitMarPl 83*
Associated Editors - New York, NY - *LitMarPl 83, 84; MagIndMarPl 82-83*
Associated Educational Materials Co. - Raleigh, NC - *AvMarPl 83*
Associated Equipment Distributors - Oak Brook, IL - *BoPubDir 5*
Associated Faculty Press Inc. - Port Washington, NY - *LitMarPl 84*
Associated Faculty Press Inc. - Tarrytown, NY - *LitMarPl 83*
Associated Features Inc. - New York, NY - *LitMarPl 83, 84*
Associated General Contractors of America - Washington, DC - *BoPubDir 5*
Associated Information Consultants - Ann Arbor, MI - *EISS 83*
Associated Information Managers - Washington, DC - *EISS 83*
Associated Landscape Contractors of America - McLean, VA - *BoPubDir 5*
Associated Libraries Inc. - Philadelphia, PA - *LitMarPl 83, 84*
Associated Media Service Corp. - Chicago, IL - *StaDirAdAg 2-84*
Associated Music Publishers Inc. - *See* Schirmer Inc., G.
Associated Newspapers Inc. - Wayne, MI - *BaconPubCkNews 84*
Associated Office Services - Boulder, CO - *DirInfWP 82*
Associated Press - Washington, DC - *BrCabYB 84*
Associated Press - New York, NY - *BaconPubCkNews 84; Ed&PubIntYB 82; LitMarPl 83, 84; MagIndMarPl 82-83; NewsBur 6; TelAl 83, 84; Tel&CabFB 84C*
Associated Press - Cleveland, OH - *NewsBur 6*
Associated Press - Columbus, OH - *NewsBur 6*
Associated Publications [Aff. of College of Divine Metaphysics] - Glendora, CA - *BoPubDir 5*
Associated Publishers & Authors Inc. - Lafayette, IN - *LitMarPl 83, 84*
Associated Publishers Inc. [Aff. of Association for the Study of Afro-American Life & History Inc.] - Washington, DC - *BoPubDir 4, 5*
Associated Record Producers Inc. - Hialeah Gardens, FL - *BillIntBG 83-84*
Associated Recording Cos. [Div. of Associated Industries] - Philadelphia, PA - *BillIntBG 83-84*
Associated Recording Studios - New York, NY - *AvMarPl 83*
Associated Release Service Inc. - Chicago, IL - *Ed&PubIntYB 82*
Associated Sales & Bag Co. - Milwaukee, WI - *DataDirSup 7-83*
Associated Southern Publisher's Representatives - Lynnville, TN - *LitMarPl 83, 84*
Associated Systems Inc. - Wichita, KS - *MicrocomSwDir 1*
Associated Technical Services Inc. - Glen Ridge, NJ - *EISS 83*
Associated Technology Co. - Estill Springs, TN - *EISS 83*
Associated Telemanagement Inc. - Boston, MA - *TeleSy&SerDir 7-83*
Associated Texas Newspapers Inc. - Hondo, TX - *BaconPubCkNews 84*
Associated Theatrical Contractors Inc. - Kansas City, MO - *AvMarPl 83*
Associated Valley Publications - Encino, CA - *BaconPubCkNews 84*
Associated Video - Atlanta, GA - *AvMarPl 83*
Associated Warehouses Inc. - New York, NY - *BoPubDir 5*
Associated Writing Programs [of Old Dominion University] - Norfolk, VA - *BoPubDir 4 Sup, 5; LitMag&SmPr 83-84*
Associates & Larranaga - Bloomington, MN - *DirMarMP 83*
Associates & Larranaga Inc. - Minnetonka, MN - *StaDirAdAg 2-84*
Associates for Research in Behavior Inc. - *See* ARBOR Inc.
Associates in Diagnostic Research [Div. of Starch INRA Hooper Inc.] - Mamaroneck, NY - *IntDirMarRes 83*
Associates Inc. - Oklahoma City, OK - *ArtMar 84*
Associates Interviewing Services - Springfield, PA - *IntDirMarRes 83*
Association & Society Manager [of Brentwood Publishing Corp.] - Los Angeles, CA - *ArtMar 84; BaconPubCkMag 84; MagDir 84; MagIndMarPl 82-83*
Association Films Inc. - New York, NY - *ProGuPRSer 4*

Association for Childhood Education International - Washington, DC - *BoPubDir 4, 5*
Association for Computational Linguistics - Menlo Park, CA - *MicroMarPl 82-83*
Association for Computers & the Humanities - New Orleans, LA - *EISS 83*
Association for Computing Machinery - New York, NY - *BoPubDir 4 Sup, 5; EISS 83*
Association for Consumer Research - Ann Arbor, MI - *BoPubDir 4*
Association for Consumer Research - Provo, UT - *BoPubDir 5*
Association for Creative Change Within Religious & Other Social Systems - Syracuse, NY - *BoPubDir 5*
Association for Development of Computer-Based Instructional Systems - Bellingham, WA - *EISS 83*
Association for Educational Communications & Technology - Washington, DC - *BoPubDir 4, 5; InterCabHB 3*
Association for Educational Data Systems - Washington, DC - *EISS 83*
Association for Humanistic Psychology - San Francisco, CA - *BoPubDir 4, 5*
Association for Information & Image Management, The - Silver Spring, MD - *LitMarPl 84*
Association for Jewish Studies - Cambridge, MA - *BoPubDir 4, 5*
Association for Library & Information Science Education - State College, PA - *BoPubDir 5*
Association for Library Information - Pittsburgh, PA - *EISS 7-83 Sup*
Association for Literary & Linguistic Computing - Cambridge, England - *EISS 83*
Association for Northern California Records & Research - Chico, CA - *BoPubDir 4, 5*
Association for Population/Family Planning Libraries & Information Centers - Chapel Hill, NC - *EISS 83*
Association for Public Justice Education Fund - Washington, DC - *BoPubDir 4, 5*
Association for Supervision & Curriculum Development - Alexandria, VA - *BoPubDir 4, 5*
Association for Systems Management - Cleveland, OH - *BoPubDir 4, 5; EISS 83*
Association for the Advancement of Medical Instrumentation - Arlington, VA - *BoPubDir 4, 5*
Association for the Development of Religious Information Systems - Milwaukee, WI - *EISS 83*
Association for the Study of Animated & Comic Art Inc. - New York, NY - *LitMag&SmPr 83-84*
Association for the Study of Family Living - Brooklyn, NY - *BoPubDir 4, 5*
Association for the Understanding of Man Inc. - Austin, TX - *BoPubDir 4, 5*
Association for Union Democracy Inc. - Brooklyn, NY - *BoPubDir 4 Sup, 5*
Association for University Business & Economic Research - Athens, GA - *BoPubDir 5*
Association for World Education - Huntington, NY - *BoPubDir 4, 5*
Association Francaise de Normalisation - Paris, France - *CompReadDB 82; InfIndMarPl 83*
Association Francaise pour l'Etude des Eaux - Paris, France - *InfIndMarPl 83*
Association Management [of American Society of Association Executives] - Washington, DC - *BaconPubCkMag 84; MagDir 84; MagIndMarPl 82-83*
Association of American Colleges (Project on the Status & Education of Women) - Washington, DC - *BoPubDir 5*
Association of American Feed Control Officials Inc. - College Station, TX - *BoPubDir 5*
Association of American Geographers - Washington, DC - *BoPubDir 4, 5*
Association of American Publishers - New York, NY - *BoPubDir 4, 5*
Association of Canadian Pension Management - Toronto, ON, Canada - *BoPubDir 4, 5*
Association of Christian Librarians Inc. - West Seneca, NY - *BoPubDir 4, 5*
Association of College & Research Libraries [Aff. of American Library Association] - Chicago, IL - *BoPubDir 5*
Association of College & University Telecommunications Administrators - Madison, WI - *TeleSy&SerDir 7-83*
Association of Computer Users - Boulder, CO - *BoPubDir 5; EISS 83*
Association of Consulting Chemists & Chemical Engineers Inc. - New York, NY - *BoPubDir 5*
Association of Consulting Engineers of Canada - Ottawa, ON, Canada - *BoPubDir 4 Sup, 5*
Association of Data Communications Users - Bloomington, MN - *TeleSy&SerDir 7-83*
Association of Data Communications Users - New York, NY - *EISS 83*
Association of Database Producers - London, England - *EISS 83*
Association of European Airlines - Brussels, Belgium - *DirOnDB Spring 84*
Association of European Airlines [of I. P. Sharp Associates Ltd.] - Toronto, ON, Canada - *DataDirOnSer 84*
Association of European Airlines Data Base - Brussels, Belgium - *DBBus 82*
Association of European Host Operators Group - Luxembourg, Luxembourg - *EISS 7-83 Sup*
Association of Home Appliance Manufacturers - Chicago, IL - *BoPubDir 4 Sup, 5*
Association of Independent Camps Inc. - New York, NY - *BoPubDir 4, 5*
Association of Independent Commercial Producers - Los Angeles, CA - *AvMarPl 83*
Association of Information & Dissemination Centers - Athens, GA - *EISS 83*
Association of Iron & Steel Engineers - Pittsburgh, PA - *BoPubDir 5*
Association of Korean Christian Scholars in North America Inc. - Princeton Junction, NJ - *BoPubDir 5*
Association of National Advertisers Seminars - New York, NY - *HBIndAd&MS 82-83*
Association of National Non-Profit Artists Centres - Toronto, ON, Canada - *BoPubDir 4, 5*
Association of Official Analytical Chemists - Arlington, VA - *BoPubDir 4, 5*
Association of Professional Genealogists - Salt Lake City, UT - *BoPubDir 5*
Association of Public Data Users - Princeton, NJ - *EISS 83*
Association of Records Managers & Administrators - Prairie Village, KS - *EISS 83*
Association of Research Libraries - Washington, DC - *EISS 83*
Association of School Business Officials of the United States & Canada Research Corp. - Park Ridge, IL - *BoPubDir 4, 5*
Association of Science-Technology Centers - Washington, DC - *BoPubDir 4, 5*
Association of Sexologists - San Francisco, CA - *BoPubDir 4, 5*
Association of Systematics Collections - Lawrence, KS - *BoPubDir 5*
Association of Universities & Colleges of Canada - Ottawa, ON, Canada - *BoPubDir 4, 5*
Association of Viewdata Information Providers Ltd. - London, England - *EISS 83*
Association on American Indian Affairs Inc. - New York, NY - *BoPubDir 4, 5*
Association pour la Conservation et la Reproduction Photographique de la Presse - Paris, France - *MicroMarPl 82-83*
Association pour la Recherche et le Developpement en Informatique Chimique [of Centre Informatique de la Documentation Automatique] - Paris, France - *InfIndMarPl 83*
Association Systems Inc. - Weehawken, NJ - *DataDirOnSer 84*
Association Thermodata - St.-Martin-d'Heres, France - *InfIndMarPl 83*
Association Trends [of Martineau Corp.] - Washington, DC - *MagDir 84*
Association Trends [of Martineau Corp.] - Bethesda, MD - *BaconPubCkMag 84; DirMarMP 83*
Assumption Golden Prairie News - Assumption, IL - *BaconPubCkNews 84; NewsDir 84*
Assumption Pioneer - Napoleonville, LA - *AyerDirPub 83*
Assumption Pioneer, The - Assumption, LA - *Ed&PubIntYB 82*
Assured Systems Development - Cleveland, OH - *ADAPSOMemDir 83-84*

Assyst Computer Services Ltd. - Washington, England - *MicrocomSwDir 1*
AST Research Inc. - Irvine, CA - *MicrocomMPl 83, 84; MicrocomSwDir 1; WhoWMicrocom 83*
ASTA Travel News - New York, NY - *BaconPubCkMag 84; MagDir 84; WritMar 84*
Astara Inc. - Upland, CA - *BoPubDir 4, 5*
Astec Inc. - Needham, MA - *MicrocomMPl 84*
Asten & Associates Inc., Ken - Glendale, CA - *TeleSy&SerDir 2-84*
Astim/Sadtler Infrared Data Program [of Sadtler Research Laboratories Inc.] - Philadelphia, PA - *EISS 83*
ASTIS Online Database [of Arctic Institute of North America] - Calgary, AB, Canada - *DBBus 82*
Astle, David - Toronto, ON, Canada - *BoPubDir 4, 5*
ASTM - Philadelphia, PA - *BoPubDir 4, 5*
ASTM Standardization News - Philadelphia, PA - *BaconPubCkMag 84; MagDir 84*
Aston Electronic Developments Ltd. - Surrey, England - *VideoDir 82-83*
Aston Hall Publications Inc. [Aff. of Nationwide Syndications Inc.] - Rolling Meadows, IL - *BoPubDir 4, 5*
Astor Indexers - New York, NY - *LitMarPl 83, 84; MagIndMarPl 82-83*
Astor Place Magazine & Book Shop - New York, NY - *ProGuPRSer 4*
Astoria Daily Astorian - Astoria, OR - *NewsDir 84*
Astoria South Fulton Argus - Astoria, IL - *AyerDirPub 83; BaconPubCkNews 84*
Astoria Tribune [of Flushing Queens Tribune] - Flushing, NY - *NewsDir 84*
Astra Photo Service - Chicago, IL - *AvMarPl 83*
Astrafilms Inc. - Washington, DC - *Tel&CabFB 84C*
Astral-Image - San Rafael, CA - *MicrocomMPl 84*
Astro Artz - Los Angeles, CA - *BoPubDir 4, 5; LitMag&SmPr 83-84*
Astro Black Books - Sioux Falls, SD - *BoPubDir 4 Sup, 5; LitMag&SmPr 83-84*
Astro Cablevision Corp. [of NewChannels Corp.] - Corapolis, PA - *BrCabYB 84*
Astro-Computing Books - Washington, DC - *BoPubDir 4, 5*
Astro Computing Services - San Diego, CA - *BoPubDir 4; WritMar 84*
Astro-4 Drug Information System [of U.S. Public Health Service] - Rockville, MD - *EISS 83*
Astro-International Syndication - Garden Grove, CA - *Ed&PubIntYB 82; LitMarPl 84*
Astro-Star Enterprises - Rocklin, CA - *MicrocomMPl 83, 84; MicrocomSwDir 1*
Astrocom Corp. - St. Paul, MN - *DataDirSup 7-83*
Astrofilm Service - Hollywood, CA - *AvMarPl 83*
Astronautics & Aeronautics - New York, NY - *MagDir 84; MagIndMarPl 82-83*
Astronette Publishing Co. - Albuquerque, NM - *BillIntBG 83-84*
Astronomical Calendar - Greenville, SC - *BoPubDir 4, 5*
Astronomical Data Center [of U.S. National Aeronautics & Space Administration] - Greenbelt, MD - *EISS 83*
Astronomy - Milwaukee, WI - *BaconPubCkMag 84; MagDir 84; MagIndMarPl 82-83*
Astronomy Book Club [of Macmillan Book Clubs Inc.] - New York, NY - *LitMarPl 83, 84*
Astronomy Quarterly, The [of Pachart Publishing House] - Tucson, AZ - *LitMag&SmPr 83-84*
Astrophysical Journal - Tucson, AZ - *MagDir 84*
Astrosonics Research Institute - Lennox, CA - *BoPubDir 4, 5; LitMag&SmPr 83-84*
ASU Travel Guide - San Francisco, CA - *BaconPubCkMag 84; WritMar 84*
Asura Publications - Austin, TX - *BoPubDir 5*
Asylum Hill Inc. - Hartford, CT - *BoPubDir 4, 5*
Asylum's Press - New York, NY - *BoPubDir 4, 5*
Asyst Design Services - Cortland, NY - *WhoWMicrocom 83*
AT & T - Parsippany, NJ - *VideoDir 82-83*
AT & T Communications [of American Telephone & Telegraph Co.] - Bedminster, NJ - *BrCabYB 84; TeleSy&SerDir 2-84*
AT & T Dial-It 900 Service [of American Telephone & Telegraph Co.] - Bedminster, NJ - *TeleSy&SerDir 2-84*
AT & T 800 Service [of American Telephone & Telegraph Co.] - Bedminster, NJ - *TeleSy&SerDir 2-84*
AT & T-GTE [of American Telephone & Telegraph Co.] - Bedminster, NJ - *Tel&CabFB 84C*
AT & T International [of American Telephone & Telegraph Co.] - Basking Ridge, NJ - *ADAPSOMemDir 83-84; TelDir&BG 83-84; VideoDir 82-83*
AT & T Long Distance Service [of American Telephone & Telegraph Co.] - Bedminster, NJ - *TeleSy&SerDir 2-84*
AT & T Long Lines [of American Telephone & Telegraph Co.] - Bedminster, NJ - *BrCabYB 84*
AT & T WATS [of American Telephone & Telegraph Co.] - Bedminster, NJ - *TeleSy&SerDir 2-84*
At Ease [of Home Missions, Assemblies of God] - Springfield, MO - *WritMar 84*
ATA Advertising Ltd. - London, England - *StaDirAdAg 2-84*
Ata Books - Berkeley, CA - *BoPubDir 4, 5; LitMag&SmPr 83-84*
ATA Univas [of the Univas Network] - Milan, Italy - *StaDirAdAg 2-84*
Atacosa County Cable TV Inc. - Pleasanton, TX - *Tel&CabFB 84C*
Atalla Corp. - San Jose, CA - *DataDirSup 7-83*
Atari Connection [of Atari Inc.] - San Jose, CA - *MicrocomMPl 84*
Atari Inc. - Sunnyvale, CA - *DirInfWP 82; VideoDir 82-83*
Atari Inc. (Home Computer Div.) - Sunnyvale, CA - *WhoWMicrocom 83*
Atascadero News - Atascadero, CA - *BaconPubCkNews 84; Ed&PubIntYB 82; NewsDir 84*
Atascosa County Cable TV Inc. - Pleasanton, TX - *BrCabYB 84*
Atasi Corp. - San Jose, CA - *MicrocomMPl 84; WhoWMicrocom 83*
Atavist, The - Berkeley, CA - *WritMar 84*
ATC Cablevision [of American TV & Communications Corp.] - Urbana, IL - *Tel&CabFB 84C*
ATC Software - Estill Springs, TN - *MicrocomSwDir 1*
Atchison Cablevision Inc. [of Communications Services Inc.] - Atchison, KS - *Tel&CabFB 84C*
Atchison County Mail - Rock Port, MO - *AyerDirPub 83; Ed&PubIntYB 82*
Atchison Globe - Atchison, KS - *BaconPubCkNews 84; Ed&PubIntYB 82; NewsDir 84*
Atchison Sunday Globe - Atchison, KS - *Ed&PubIntYB 82*
Atcom Inc. - New York, NY - *DirMarMP 83; EISS 5-84 Sup*
ATE Information Services [of ATE Management & Service Co. Inc.] - Cincinnati, OH - *EISS 7-83 Sup*
Atec Computer Services Ltd. - Lydney, England - *MicrocomSwDir 1*
Atec Inc. [Subs. of The Eastman Kodak Co.] - Bedford, MA - *LitMarPl 83*
Atelier Parisien d'Urbanisme/Paris Office of Urbanization - Paris, France - *InfIndMarPl 83*
Atelier Saunier - New York, NY - *ArtMar 84*
Atene, Ann - Philadelphia, PA - *LitMarPl 83, 84*
Atex Inc. [Subs. of The Eastman Kodak Co.] - Bedford, MA - *LitMarPl 84*
Atgood Publications Ltd. - Calgary, AB, Canada - *BoPubDir 4 Sup, 5*
Athena Cablevision Corp. - Richmond, CA - *BrCabYB 84*
Athena Cablevision Corp. [of Athena Communications Corp.] - Knox County, TN - *Tel&CabFB 84C*
Athena Cablevision Inc. [of Tele-Communications Inc.] - Knoxville, TN - *BrCabYB 84*
Athena Cablevision of Corpus Christi [of Athena Communications Corp.] - Corpus Christi, TX - *BrCabYB 84; Tel&CabFB 84C*
Athena Communications Corp. - Denver, CO - *Tel&CabFB 84C p.1665*
Athena Communications Corp. - Englewood, CO - *HomeVid&CabYB 82-83*
Athena Communications Corp. - Pineville, KY - *Tel&CabFB 84C*
Athena Communications Corp. - *See* Tele-Communications Inc.
Athena Press - Grand Forks, ND - *BoPubDir 4, 5; LitMag&SmPr 83-84*
Athena Press - Athena, OR - *BaconPubCkNews 84; Ed&PubIntYB 82*
Athena Press Inc. - Vienna, VA - *BoPubDir 4, 5*
Athena Publications - Moravia, NY - *BoPubDir 4, 5*

Athena Software - Newark, DE - *MicrocomMPl 84*
Athenaeum of Philadelphia - Philadelphia, PA - *BoPubDir 4, 5*
Athenaeum Technology Inc. - Braintree, MA - *MicrocomMPl 84*
Atheneum Publishers [Div. of The Scribner Book Co.] - New York, NY - *LitMarPl 83, 84; WritMar 84*
Atheneum Publishers (Juvenile Div.) - New York, NY - *ArtMar 84; WritMar 84*
Athenian House Publishers - Nashville, TN - *BoPubDir 4, 5*
Athenian, The - Athens, GA - *WritMar 84*
Athens - Detroit, MI - *Ed&PubIntYB 82*
Athens Banner-Herald - Athens, GA - *BaconPubCkNews 84; Ed&PubIntYB 82*
Athens Cable TV [of Texas Community Antennas Inc.] - Athens, TX - *BrCabYB 84*
Athens Daily News - Athens, GA - *BaconPubCkNews 84; Ed&PubIntYB 82; NewsDir 84*
Athens Daily Post-Athenian Co. Inc. - Athens, TN - *NewsDir 84*
Athens Daily Review [of Community Information Center Inc.] - Athens, TX - *BaconPubCkNews 84; Ed&PubIntYB 82; NewsDir 84*
Athens Messenger - Athens, OH - *BaconPubCkNews 84; NewsDir 84*
Athens News Courier - Athens, AL - *BaconPubCkNews 84; Ed&PubIntYB 82; NewsDir 84*
Athens Newspapers Inc. - *See* Morris Communications Corp.
Athens Observer, The - Athens, GA - *Ed&PubIntYB 82; NewsDir 84*
Athens Paper Co. - Nashville, TN - *MagIndMarPl 82-83*
Athens Telephone Co. Inc. [Aff. of Century Telephone Enterprises Inc.] - Plain Dealing, LA - *TelDir&BG 83-84*
Athens TV Cable [of TCA Cable TV Group] - Athens, TX - *Tel&CabFB 84C*
Athens TV Cable Co. [of National TV Cable Co.] - Athens, TN - *BrCabYB 84*
Athens TV Cable of Alabama [of MultiVision Northwest Inc.] - Athens, AL - *BrCabYB 84; Tel&CabFB 84C*
Athens Urban Star - Athens, GA - *AyerDirPub 83*
Athens Weekly Review - Athens, TX - *Ed&PubIntYB 82*
Athens Weekly Review - *See* Community Information Center Inc.
Athlete's Outfitter, The - Chicago, IL - *DirOnDB Spring 84*
Athletes Un-Ltd. - Sudbury, MA - *BoPubDir 5*
Athletic Administration - Cleveland, OH - *BaconPubCkMag 84; MagDir 84*
Athletic Institute, The - North Palm Beach, FL - *AvMarPl 83*
Athletic Journal - Evanston, IL - *BaconPubCkMag 84; MagDir 84; MagIndMarPl 82-83*
Athletic Press [Aff. of Golden West Books] - Pasadena, CA - *ArtMar 84; BoPubDir 4, 5; WritMar 84*
Athletic Purchasing & Facilities - Madison, WI - *BaconPubCkMag 84; MagDir 84*
Athletic Training - Greenville, NC - *MagDir 84*
Athletics - Willowdale, ON, Canada - *BaconPubCkMag 84*
Athol Daily News - Athol, MA - *Ed&PubIntYB 82; NewsDir 84*
Athol News - Athol, MA - *BaconPubCkNews 84*
Athon Music Co. - *See* Graham Music Publisher, Roger
ATI Video Enterprises Inc. - New York, NY - *Tel&CabFB 84C*
Atkins & Associates Advertising Inc. - San Antonio, TX - *ArtMar 84; StaDirAdAg 2-84*
Atkins & Reilly Inc. - Boston, MA - *AvMarPl 83*
Atkins Chronicle - Atkins, AR - *BaconPubCkNews 84; Ed&PubIntYB 82*
Atkins Cooperative Telephone Co. - Akkins, IA - *TelDir&BG 83-84*
Atkinson Advertising Associates Inc. - Oklahoma City, OK - *StaDirAdAg 2-84*
Atkinson & Associates Inc. - Chesterfield, MO - *StaDirAdAg 2-84*
Atkinson-Annawan News - Atkinson, IL - *AyerDirPub 83; Ed&PubIntYB 82*
Atkinson Annawan News - *See* News Publishing Co.
Atkinson, Carol Zane - New York, NY - *LitMarPl 83, 84*
Atkinson County Citizen - Pearson, GA - *AyerDirPub 83; Ed&PubIntYB 82*
Atkinson Film-Arts Ltd. - Ottawa, ON, Canada - *AvMarPl 83*
Atkinson Graphic - Atkinson, NE - *AyerDirPub 83; BaconPubCkNews 84; Ed&PubIntYB 82*
Atkinson, Mary D. - College Park, MD - *BoPubDir 4, 5*
Atkinson Programs, Chuck - Benbrook, TX - *MicrocomMPl 84; MicrocomSwDir 1*
Atkinson, R. B. - Duncan, BC, Canada - *Tel&CabFB 84C*
ATLA Religion Database [of ATLA Religion Indexes] - Chicago, IL - *DataDirOnSer 84; DirOnDB Spring 84*
ATLA Religion Database [of Bibliographic Retrieval Services Inc.] - Lathan, NY - *DataDirOnSer 84*
ATLA Religion Indexes [of American Theological Library Association] - Chicago, IL - *DataDirOnSer 84*
Atlanta Audio-Visuals - Atlanta, GA - *ArtMar 84; AvMarPl 83*
Atlanta Buckhead - Atlanta, GA - *Ed&PubIntYB 82*
Atlanta Business Chronicle [of Atlanta Business Chronicle Inc.] - Atlanta, GA - *BaconPubCkMag 84; MagDir 84*
Atlanta Citizens Journal - Atlanta, TX - *BaconPubCkNews 84; NewsDir 84*
Atlanta Constitution [of Cox Enterprises Inc.] - Atlanta, GA - *BaconPubCkNews 84; LitMarPl 83; NewsBur 6; NewsDir 84*
Atlanta Daily World - Atlanta, GA - *BaconPubCkNews 84; Ed&PubIntYB 82; NewsDir 84*
Atlanta Field Services Co. - Atlanta, GA - *IntDirMarRes 83*
Atlanta Information Services - Atlanta, GA - *EISS 83*
Atlanta Inquirer - Atlanta, GA - *BaconPubCkNews 84; Ed&PubIntYB 82; NewsDir 84*
Atlanta Journal [of Atlanta Newspapers] - Atlanta, GA - *BaconPubCkNews 84; LitMarPl 83; NewsBur 6; NewsDir 84*
Atlanta Journal & Constitution - Atlanta, GA - *LitMarPl 83; WritMar 84*
Atlanta Magazine - Atlanta, GA - *BaconPubCkMag 84; MagDir 84; WritMar 84*
Atlanta Montmorency County Tribune - Atlanta, MI - *BaconPubCkNews 84*
Atlanta Newspapers [of Cox Enterprises] - Atlanta, GA - *DirMarMP 83*
Atlanta People's Crusader - Atlanta, GA - *Ed&PubIntYB 82; NewsDir 84*
Atlanta Skier - Atlanta, GA - *BaconPubCkMag 84*
Atlanta Southern Struggle [of Southern Conference Educational Fund] - Atlanta, GA - *NewsDir 84*
Atlanta Times - Atlanta, TX - *BaconPubCkNews 84; Ed&PubIntYB 82*
Atlanta Voice - Atlanta, GA - *BaconPubCkNews 84; Ed&PubIntYB 82; NewsDir 84*
Atlanta Weekly [of Atlanta Newspapers] - Atlanta, GA - *MagIndMarPl 82-83; WritMar 84*
Atlanta's Best Buys - Atlanta, GA - *BoPubDir 5*
Atlanta's Video Music Channel - Atlanta, GA - *CabTVPrDB 83*
Atlantic American Holdings - Tampa, FL - *Tel&CabFB 84C p.1665*
Atlantic Business - Halifax, NS, Canada - *BaconPubCkMag 84*
Atlantic Cable Co. [of Jones Intercable Inc.] - Attalla, AL - *BrCabYB 84*
Atlantic Cablevision Systems Inc. [of Cable Communications of Iowa] - Atlantic, IA - *BrCabYB 84*
Atlantic Cablevision Systems Inc. [of Cable Communications of Iowa] - Audubon, IA - *BrCabYB 84*
Atlantic Camera Repair Corp. - West Islip, NY - *AvMarPl 83*
Atlantic City Computer Corp. - Turnersville, NJ - *WhoWMicrocom 83*
Atlantic City Magazine [of Menus International Inc.] - Atlantic City, NJ - *ArtMar 84; BaconPubCkMag 84; MagDir 84; MagIndMarPl 82-83; WritMar 84*
Atlantic City Press - Atlantic City, NJ - *BaconPubCkNews 84; NewsBur 6; NewsDir 84*
Atlantic City Stage Lighting Inc. - Pleasantville, NJ - *AvMarPl 83*
Atlantic City Stage Lighting Inc. - Philadelphia, PA - *AvMarPl 83*
Atlantic Coast TV Cable Corp. - Atlantic City, NJ - *BrCabYB 84; Tel&CabFB 84C*
Atlantic Communications Group - Framingham, MA - *Tel&CabFB 84C*
Atlantic Community Quarterly, The - Washington, DC - *MagIndMarPl 82-83*
Atlantic Control States Beverage Journal [of Club & Tavern Inc.] - Wheeling, WV - *BaconPubCkMag 84; MagDir 84*
Atlantic Council of the United States - Washington, DC - *BoPubDir 4, 5*

Atlantic County Record - Mays Landing, NJ - *AyerDirPub 83; Ed&PubIntYB 82*
Atlantic Data Services Inc. - Quincy, MA - *ADAPSOMemDir 83-84*
Atlantic Gallery - Washington, DC - *ArtMar 84*
Atlantic Insight - Halifax, NS, Canada - *BaconPubCkMag 84*
Atlantic Institute [Aff. of Atcom Inc.] - New York, NY - *BoPubDir 4 Sup, 5*
Atlantic Institute of Education - Halifax, NS, Canada - *BoPubDir 4, 5*
Atlantic Metrovision Corp. - Woodford, VA - *Tel&CabFB 84C p.1665*
Atlantic Monthly Press - Boston, MA - *LitMarPl 83, 84; WritMar 84*
Atlantic Monthly, The - Boston, MA - *ArtMar 84; WritMar 84*
Atlantic National Advertising Inc. - Richmond, VA - *StaDirAdAg 2-84*
Atlantic News-Telegraph - Atlantic, IA - *BaconPubCkNews 84; Ed&PubIntYB 82; NewsDir 84*
Atlantic Province Reports [of Maritime Law Book Co. Ltd.] - Frederickton, NB, Canada - *CompReadDB 82*
Atlantic Province Reports - Fredrickton, NB, Canada - *DirOnDB Spring 84*
Atlantic Province Reports [of Canadian Law Information Council] - Ottawa, ON, Canada - *DataDirOnSer 84*
Atlantic Provinces Economic Council - Halifax, NS, Canada - *BoPubDir 4, 5*
Atlantic Publications - Accomac, VA - *BaconPubCkNews 84*
Atlantic Recording Corp. - New York, NY - *BillIntBG 83-84*
Atlantic Releasing Corp. - Los Angeles, CA - *AvMarPl 83*
Atlantic Research Corp. - Alexandria, VA - *CabTVFinDB 83; DataDirSup 7-83; DirInfWP 82; FBInfSer 80; InterCabHB 3*
Atlantic Salmon Association - Montreal, PQ, Canada - *BoPubDir 4 Sup, 5*
Atlantic Salmon Journal - Montreal, PQ, Canada - *BaconPubCkMag 84*
Atlantic Satellite Network - Halifax, NS, Canada - *BrCabYB 84*
Atlantic Sun [of Florida Atlantic University] - Boca Raton, FL - *NewsDir 84*
Atlantic Telephone Membership Corp. - Shallote, NC - *TelDir&BG 83-84*
Atlantic Television Inc. - Los Angeles, CA - *TelAl 83, 84; Tel&CabFB 84C*
Atlantic, The [of The Atlantic Monthly Co.] - Boston, MA - *BaconPubCkMag 84; Folio 83; LitMarPl 83, 84; MagDir 84; MagIndMarPl 82-83*
Atlantic Truck Transport Review - Riverview, NB, Canada - *BaconPubCkMag 84*
Atlantis - Halifax, NS, Canada - *LitMag&SmPr 83-84*
Atlantis Editions - Philadelphia, PA - *BoPubDir 4, 5*
Atlantis Entertainment Network [of Lexicom Industries Inc.] - Riverside, NJ - *CabTVPrDB 83; HomeVid&CabYB 82-83; Tel&CabFB 84C*
Atlantis Productions Inc. - Thousand Oaks, CA - *Tel&CabFB 84C*
Atlantis Publishers Inc. - New York, NY - *LitMarPl 83*
Atlantis Publishing Co. - Hollywood, FL - *BoPubDir 4 Sup, 5; LitMarPl 84*
Atlas Cable TV Co. - Afton, OK - *Tel&CabFB 84C*
Atlas Energy Systems - South El Monte, CA - *DataDirSup 7-83; DirInfWP 82*
Atlas Software Sales [Subs. of Atlas Towing Inc.] - St. Louis, MO - *WhoWMicrocom 83*
Atlas Telephone Co. Inc. - Big Cabin, OK - *TelDir&BG 83-84*
Atlis Systems - Gales Ferry, CT - *DirInfWP 82*
Atmore Advance - Atmore, AL - *BaconPubCkNews 84; Ed&PubIntYB 82; NewsDir 84*
ATN Publishing - *See* Rumblin' Songs
ATO Palm, The - Champaign, IL - *MagIndMarPl 82-83*
Atoka Cablevision Co. - Atoka, OK - *BrCabYB 84*
Atoka County Times - Atoka, OK - *BaconPubCkNews 84; Ed&PubIntYB 82; NewsDir 84*
Atoka Indian Citizen - Atoka, OK - *BaconPubCkNews 84; Ed&PubIntYB 82*
Atom Tabloid - Rahway, NJ - *AyerDirPub 83; Ed&PubIntYB 82*
Atomic Collision Cross Section Data [of University of Colorado] - Boulder, CO - *EISS 83*
Atomic Energy Levels Data Center [of U.S. National Bureau of Standards] - Washington, DC - *EISS 83*
Atomic Industrial Forum Inc. - Washington, DC - *BoPubDir 4, 5*
Atomic Spectroscopy - Norwalk, CT - *MagIndMarPl 82-83*
Aton International Inc. - Santa Clara, CA - *MicrocomMPl 84; MicrocomSwDir 1*
Atoz Images - Chicago, IL - *MagIndMarPl 82-83*
ATP Clipping Bureau - New York, NY - *LitMarPl 83, 84; ProGuPRSer 4*
Atra Cablevision Inc. - Inola, OK - *BrCabYB 84*
ATS Typography Service - Scotia, NY - *EISS 7-83 Sup*
Atsuko Computing International - Huntsville, AL - *WhoWMicrocom 83*
Attago Music - Madison, TN - *BillIntBG 83-84*
Attalla Etowah News Journal [of Helderman Enterprises] - Attalla, AL - *BaconPubCkNews 84; NewsDir 84*
Attaway Broadcast Group Inc. - Shreveport, LA - *Tel&CabFB 84C*
Attaway Investments Inc. - Shreveport, LA - *BrCabYB 84*
Attaway Newspaper Group - Conroe, TX - *Ed&PubIntYB 82*
Attco Inc. - Honolulu, HI - *AvMarPl 83*
Attenzione [of Adam Publications Inc.] - New York, NY - *BaconPubCkMag 84; MagIndMarPl 82-83; WritMar 84*
Attic Books Ltd. [Aff. of Alex G. Malloy Inc.] - South Salem, NY - *BoPubDir 4, 5*
Attic Press Inc. - Greenwood, SC - *BoPubDir 4, 5*
Attica Daily Ledger Tribune [of Twin State Publishing Co. Inc.] - Attica, IN - *NewsDir 84*
Attica Friendly Oracle, The - Attica, IN - *Ed&PubIntYB 82*
Attica Hub - Attica, OH - *Ed&PubIntYB 82*
Attica Hub - *See* Seneca Publishing Inc.
Attica Independent - Attica, KS - *BaconPubCkNews 84; Ed&PubIntYB 82*
Attica Ledger-Tribune - Attica, IN - *BaconPubCkNews 84*
Attica News/Wyoming County Times - Attica, NY - *Ed&PubIntYB 82*
Attica News/Wyoming County Times - *See* Sanders Publications
Attica Pennysaver - Orchard Park, NY - *AyerDirPub 83*
Attica Richland Press - Attica, IN - *BaconPubCkNews 84*
Atticus Press - San Diego, CA - *LitMag&SmPr 83-84*
Atticus Review - San Diego, CA - *LitMag&SmPr 83-84*
Attie, David - New York, NY - *MagIndMarPl 82-83*
Attitude Measurement Corp. - Southampton, PA - *IntDirMarRes 83*
Attleboro Sun Chronicle - Attleboro, MA - *BaconPubCkNews 84; NewsDir 84*
Attorney General's Ministry - Victoria, BC, Canada - *CompReadDB 82*
Attorneys' Aid Publications - Kew Gardens, NY - *BoPubDir 4, 5*
Attorneys Computer Report [of Professional Publications Inc.] - Atlanta, GA - *MicrocomMPl 84*
ATV Jacquard Inc. [of AM International Inc.] - Santa Ana, CA - *DataDirSup 7-83; DirInfWP 82; InfIndMarPl 83; WhoWMicrocom 83*
ATV Music Corp. - Hollywood, CA - *BillIntBG 83-84*
ATV News - Long Beach, CA - *BaconPubCkMag 84; MagIndMarPl 82-83*
ATV Research - Dakota City, NE - *WhoWMicrocom 83*
A.T.W. Research Inc. - Beaverton, OR - *IntDirMarRes 83*
Atwater Herald - Atwater, MN - *BaconPubCkNews 84; Ed&PubIntYB 82*
Atwater New Times - *See* Waterford News Publishers
Atwater Signal [of Lesher Newspapers Inc.] - Atwater, CA - *BaconPubCkNews 84; Ed&PubIntYB 82; NewsDir 84*
Atwell's Cable TV - Hyndman, PA - *BrCabYB 84*
Atwood Cable Systems Inc. - Atwood, KS - *Tel&CabFB 84C*
Atwood Citizen-Patriot - Atwood, KS - *BaconPubCkNews 84*
Atwood Herald - Atwood, IL - *BaconPubCkNews 84; Ed&PubIntYB 82*
Atwood Richards Inc. - New York, NY - *HBIndAd&MS 82-83; StaDirAdAg 2-84*
Au Gres Telephone Co. [Aff. of Century Telephone Enterprises Inc.] - Chesaning, MI - *TelDir&BG 83-84*
Au Sable Communications Inc. [of Wometco Cable TV Inc.] - Jay, NY - *Tel&CabFB 84C*
Au Sable Communications Inc. [of Wometco Cable TV Inc.] - Plattsburgh, NY - *BrCabYB 84*

Au Sable Forks Adirondack Record Post - *See* Denton Publications Inc.
AU Software - Colleyville, TX - *MicrocomMPl 84*
Aubrey Thomas Inc. - New York, NY - *MagIndMarPl 82-83*
Auburn Bulletin/Eagle - Auburn, AL - *BaconPubCkNews 84; Ed&PubIntYB 82*
Auburn Cable TV - Auburn, CA - *BrCabYB 84*
Auburn Cablevision [of MetroVision Inc.] - Auburn, NE - *Tel&CabFB 84C*
Auburn Cablevision Inc. - Auburn, NY - *BrCabYB 84; Tel&CabFB 84C*
Auburn Citizen - Auburn, IL - *Ed&PubIntYB 82*
Auburn Citizen [of Howard Publications] - Auburn, NY - *BaconPubCkNews 84; NewsDir 84*
Auburn Citizen - *See* South County Publications
Auburn Daily Globe News - Kent, WA - *Ed&PubIntYB 82*
Auburn Enterprise - Auburn, IA - *Ed&PubIntYB 82*
Auburn Enterprise & Tri-County Special - Auburn, IA - *BaconPubCkNews 84*
Auburn Evening Star [of Kendallville Publishing Co.] - Auburn, IN - *Ed&PubIntYB 82; NewsDir 84*
Auburn House Publishing Co. - Boston, MA - *LitMarPl 83, 84*
Auburn Journal - Auburn, CA - *BaconPubCkNews 84; Ed&PubIntYB 82; NewsDir 84*
Auburn Nemaha County Herald - *See* Auburn Newspapers
Auburn News - Auburn, MA - *AyerDirPub 83; BaconPubCkNews 84*
Auburn Newspapers - Auburn, NE - *BaconPubCkNews 84*
Auburn Press Tribune [of Auburn Newspapers] - Auburn, NE - *Ed&PubIntYB 82; NewsDir 84*
Auburn Press-Tribune - *See* Auburn Newspapers
Auburn Star - Auburn, IN - *BaconPubCkNews 84*
Auburn TeleCable Corp. [of TeleCable Corp.] - Auburn, AL - *BrCabYB 84; Tel&CabFB 84C*
Auburndale Star - Auburndale, FL - *BaconPubCkNews 84; Ed&PubIntYB 82; NewsDir 84*
Auckland Online Users Group [of Herald Information Services] - Auckland, New Zealand - *InfIndMarPl 83*
Aucoin Management Inc. - New York, NY - *BillIntBG 83-84*
Auction Bottom Line, The - New Paris, OH - *WritMar 84*
Auctioneer - Stettler, AB, Canada - *Ed&PubIntYB 82*
Aud Arena Stadium Guide [of The Billboard Publishing Co.] - Nashville, TN - *MagDir 84*
Audecibel - Livonia, MI - *BaconPubCkMag 84; MagDir 84*
Audel & Co., Theodore [Div. of The Bobbs-Merrill Co. Inc.] - Indianapolis, IN - *LitMarPl 83*
Audel & Co., Theodore [Div. of The Bobbs-Merrill Co. Inc.] - New York, NY - *LitMarPl 84*
Audible Images - Cupertino, CA - *BillIntBG 83-84*
Audible Music Publishing Co. - Brooklyn, NY - *BillIntBG 83-84*
Audico Inc. - Elk Grove, IL - *AvMarPl 83*
Audience Research & Development - San Francisco, CA - *BrCabYB 84*
Audience Research & Development - Dallas, TX - *CabTVFinDB 83*
Audigram Songs Inc. [Div. of Audigram Inc.] - Nashville, TN - *BillIntBG 83-84*
Audio [of CBS Publications] - New York, NY - *BaconPubCkMag 84; MagDir 84; MagIndMarPl 82-83; WritMar 84*
Audio Accessories Co. - Batavia, IL - *BillIntBG 83-84*
Audio Alternatives - Midlothian, VA - *BaconPubCkMag 84*
Audio Amateur - Peterborough, NH - *MagIndMarPl 82-83*
Audio Archive [Div. of Films of the Humanities Inc.] - Princeton, NJ - *AvMarPl 83*
Audio Arts Publishing Co. - Los Angeles, CA - *BillIntBG 83-84*
Audio Book Co. - Pasadena, CA - *AvMarPl 83*
Audio Brandon Films Inc. - Mt. Vernon, NY - *ProGuPRSer 4; Tel&CabFB 84C*
Audio Dept. Inc., The - New York, NY - *AvMarPl 83; HBIndAd&MS 82-83*
Audio-Digest Foundation - Glendale, CA - *MagIndMarPl 82-83*
Audio Fidelity Corp. - Richmond, VA - *AvMarPl 83*
Audio-Forum [Div. of Jeffrey Norton Publishers Inc.] - Guilford, CT - *AvMarPl 83*
Audio Graphic Films & Video [Div. of AGF Industries Inc.] - Hollywood, CA - *AvMarPl 83*
Audio Graphic Services - Royal Oak, MI - *AvMarPl 83*
Audio Graphic Systems [Subs. of Jayark Corp.] - Houston, TX - *AvMarPl 83*
Audio Plus Video International Inc. - Northvale, NJ - *AvMarPl 83*
Audio Productions [Div. of Reeves Communications] - New York, NY - *AvMarPl 83; TelAl 83, 84; Tel&CabFB 84C*
Audio Research Inc. - Lisle, IL - *DirMarMP 83*
Audio Services Corp. - New York, NY - *AvMarPl 83*
Audio/Tek Inc. - Campbell, CA - *AvMarPl 83*
Audio Times - New York, NY - *BaconPubCkMag 84; MagDir 84*
Audio Trade News - New York, NY - *MagDir 84*
Audio-Video - Menands, NY - *AvMarPl 83; WritMar 84*
Audio-Video Craft Inc. - Los Angeles, CA - *AvMarPl 83*
Audio-Video News - Falls Church, VA - *BrCabYB 84*
Audio-Video Products Inc. - Burbank, CA - *AvMarPl 83*
Audio-Video Recorders of Arizona Inc. - Phoenix, AZ - *AvMarPl 83*
Audio Vistas Inc. - New York, NY - *AvMarPl 83*
Audio-Visual Associates of New England [Div. of Barbeau Associates Inc.] - Barrinton, RI - *AvMarPl 83*
Audio-Visual Center [Div. of American Audio Visual Corp.] - Palo Alto, CA - *AvMarPl 83*
Audio-Visual Center - Philadelphia, PA - *AvMarPl 83*
Audio-Visual Communications - New York, NY - *BaconPubCkMag 84; MagDir 84; MagIndMarPl 82-83*
Audio-Visual Contractors - Denver, CO - *AvMarPl 83*
Audio-Visual Device Inc. [Div. of Wolsten's Projector House Inc.] - East Orange, NJ - *AvMarPl 83*
Audio-Visual Directions - Torrance, CA - *BaconPubCkMag 84; MagDir 84; WritMar 84*
Audio-Visual Displays - Denver, CO - *AvMarPl 83*
Audio-Visual Dynamics Staging & Rentals [Div. of B.B. Productions] - Newark, NJ - *AvMarPl 83*
Audio-Visual Educational Systems - Houston, TX - *AvMarPl 83*
Audio-Visual Group, The - Philadelphia, PA - *MagIndMarPl 82-83*
Audio-Visual Impact Group - Chicago, IL - *AvMarPl 83*
Audio-Visual Laboratories Inc. - Atlantic Highlands, NJ - *AvMarPl 83*
Audio-Visual Media Inc. - Mansfield, OH - *AvMarPl 83*
Audio-Visual Medical Marketing Inc. - New York, NY - *AvMarPl 83*
Audio-Visual Productions - Brick, NJ - *AvMarPl 83*
Audio-Visual Promotion Aid Inc. - New York, NY - *AvMarPl 83*
Audio-Visual Rentals Inc. - Denver, CO - *AvMarPl 83*
Audio-Visual Rentals Inc. - New York, NY - *AvMarPl 83*
Audio-Visual School Service [Div. of Filmstrip Corp. of America] - New York, NY - *AvMarPl 83*
Audio-Visual Specialists - Ft. Wayne, IN - *AvMarPl 83*
Audio-Visual Systems Inc. - Dayton, OH - *AvMarPl 83*
Audio-Visual Systems Technology - New York, NY - *AvMarPl 83*
Audio-Visual Technology Inc. - Alhambra, CA - *AvMarPl 83*
Audio-Visual Workshop Inc. - New York, NY - *AvMarPl 83*
Audio-Visuals of Tampa Inc. - Tampa, FL - *AvMarPl 83*
Audiocom Inc. - Miami, FL - *CabTVFinDB 83*
Audiocraft Recording Co. - Cincinnati, OH - *AvMarPl 83*
Audiofidelity Enterprises Inc. - Rahway, NJ - *BillIntBG 83-84*
Audiofonics Inc. - Raleigh, NC - *AvMarPl 83*
Audiograph Records & Tapes - Nashville, TN - *BillIntBG 83-84*
Audiophile Records - Decatur, GA - *BillIntBG 83-84*
Audiorama Records Corp. - New York, NY - *BillIntBG 83-84*
Audiotechniques Inc. - Stamford, CT - *AvMarPl 83*
Audiotronics Corp. - North Hollywood, CA - *AvMarPl 83*
Audiovideo International - New York, NY - *BaconPubCkMag 84; MagDir 84*
Audiovisions - Burlington, VT - *BillIntBG 83-84*
Audiovisual Design Studio Inc. - Rocky Hill, CT - *AvMarPl 83*
Audiovisual Inc. - Bismarck, ND - *AvMarPl 83*
Audiovisual Washington Inc. - Fairfax, VA - *AvMarPl 83*
Audiovisuals On-line [of National Library of Medicine] - Bethesda, MD - *CompReadDB 82; DataDirOnSer 84*
Audiscan Inc. - Shreveport, LA - *BrCabYB 84*
Audiscan Products Co. [Subs. of Indal Corp.] - Bellevue, WA - *AvMarPl 83*
Audit Bureau of Circulations - Schaumburg, IL - *MagIndMarPl 82-83*

Auditions by Soundmasters - Chicago, IL - *ArtMar 84*
Auditorium News [of International Association of Auditorium Managers] - Chicago, IL - *BaconPubCkMag 84; MagDir 84*
Audits & Surveys - New York, NY - *AdAge 5-17-84 p.24; IntDirMarRes 83*
Audubon [of National Audubon Society] - New York, NY - *BaconPubCkMag 84; Folio 83; LitMarPl 83, 84; MagDir 84; MagIndMarPl 82-83; WritMar 84*
Audubon Broadcasting Co. - Columbia, SC - *BrCabYB 84*
Audubon News-Advocate - Audubon, IA - *BaconPubCkNews 84; Ed&PubIntYB 82*
Audubon Nishna Valley Tribune - Audubon, IA - *BaconPubCkNews 84*
Audubon Society of Portland Inc. - Portland, OR - *BoPubDir 4, 5*
Auerbach & Co. Inc., Leon - New York, NY - *StaDirAdAg 2-84*
Auerbach Co. Inc., S. Frederic - New York, NY - *LitMarPl 83, 84; StaDirAdAg 2-84*
Auerbach Compar - Pennsauken, NJ - *DBBus 82*
Auerbach Public Relations Inc., George - New York, NY - *DirPRFirms 83*
Auerbach Publishers Inc. [Subs. of Warren, Gorham & Lamont] - Pennsauken, NJ - *ADAPSOMemDir 83-84; DirMarMP 83; EISS 83; LitMarPl 83, 84*
Auerbach, Sylvia - New York, NY - *LitMarPl 83, 84; MagIndMarPl 82-83*
Aufbau - New York, NY - *Ed&PubIntYB 82; LitMag&SmPr 83-84; NewsDir 84*
Augat Inc. - Mansfield, MA - *CabTVFinDB 83; HomeVid&CabYB 82-83*
Augsburg Publishing - Seattle, WA - *AvMarPl 83*
Augsburg Publishing House [Div. of Publishing for the American Lutheran Church] - Minneapolis, MN - *AvMarPl 83; BillIntBG 83-84; DirMarMP 83; LitMarPl 83, 84; MagIndMarPl 82-83; WritMar 84*
Augsburg Reading Club - Minneapolis, MN - *LitMarPl 83, 84*
August House Inc. - Little Rock, AR - *BoPubDir 4; LitMag&SmPr 83-84; LitMarPl 83, 84*
Augusta Advocate - Augusta, AR - *BaconPubCkNews 84*
Augusta Advocate - McCrory, AR - *Ed&PubIntYB 82*
Augusta Area Times - Augusta, WI - *AyerDirPub 83; BaconPubCkNews 84; Ed&PubIntYB 82*
Augusta Cable TV [of Community Tele-Communications Inc.] - Augusta, KS - *Tel&CabFB 84C*
Augusta Cable TV [of Community Tele-Communications Inc.] - Rose Hill, KS - *Tel&CabFB 84C*
Augusta Cable TV Inc. - Mellen, WI - *BrCabYB 84*
Augusta Chronicle [of Southeastern Newspapers Corp.] - Augusta, GA - *BaconPubCkNews 84; LitMarPl 83; NewsDir 84*
Augusta Chronicle & Herald - Augusta, GA - *LitMarPl 83*
Augusta County Courier - Augusta, GA - *BaconPubCkNews 84*
Augusta Daily Gazette - Augusta, KS - *BaconPubCkNews 84; Ed&PubIntYB 82; NewsDir 84*
Augusta Eagle - Augusta, IL - *BaconPubCkNews 84; Ed&PubIntYB 82*
Augusta Herald [of Southeastern Newspapers Corp.] - Augusta, GA - *BaconPubCkNews 84; LitMarPl 83; NewsDir 84*
Augusta News Review - Augusta, GA - *BaconPubCkNews 84*
Augusta Spectator - Augusta, GA - *WritMar 84*
Augusta Telephone Co. [Aff. of Telephone & Data Systems Inc.] - Augusta, MI - *TelDir&BG 83-84*
Augusta Times - Augusta, KY - *BaconPubCkNews 84; Ed&PubIntYB 82*
Augusta Video [of Signet Cablevision Co.] - Fishersville, VA - *BrCabYB 84; Tel&CabFB 84C*
Augusta Video - Stuarts Draft, VA - *BrCabYB 84*
Augusta Video Inc. [of WEHCO Video Inc.] - Augusta, AR - *Tel&CabFB 84C*
Augustana College (Center for Western Studies) - Sioux Falls, SD - *BoPubDir 4, 5*
Augustana College Library - Rock Island, IL - *BoPubDir 4, 5*
Augustana College Press - Sioux Falls, SD - *BoPubDir 4, 5*
Augustana Historical Society - Rock Island, IL - *BoPubDir 4, 5*
Augustin Inc., J. J. - Locust Valley, NY - *LitMarPl 83, 84*
AUI Data Graphics - Washington, DC - *EISS 83*
Aukland Associates - Spokane, WA - *WhoWMicrocom 83*
AUK's - Sacramento, CA - *WhoWMicrocom 83*
Auld Advertising Inc. - Dallas, TX - *StaDirAdAg 2-84*
Auletta & Co. Inc., R. C. - New York, NY - *DirPRFirms 83*
Aulos Music Publishers - Montgomery, NY - *BillIntBG 83-84*
Ault Highland Today - Ault, CO - *NewsDir 84*
Aum Publications [Subs. of Agni Press] - Jamaica, NY - *LitMarPl 83, 84*
Aura Books [Aff. of Aura Enterprises Inc.] - Los Angeles, CA - *BoPubDir 4, 5*
Aura Love Publishing - Casselberry, FL - *BillIntBG 83-84*
Aura Publishing Co. - Brooklyn, NY - *BoPubDir 4, 5*
Aura-Sonic Ltd. - Flushing, NY - *AvMarPl 83*
Auravox Communications - New York, NY - *BillIntBG 83-84*
Aurelia Music - *See* Williams Music Group, Don
Aurelia Sentinel - Aurelia, IA - *BaconPubCkNews 84; Ed&PubIntYB 82*
Aurelio & Friends - Miami, FL - *ArtMar 84*
Aurelius Music - *See* Williams Music Group, Don
Auricle Press - Santa Rosa, CA - *BoPubDir 4*
Auricle Press - Sebastopol, CA - *BoPubDir 5*
Aurico Publishing Co. - Somerville, MA - *BoPubDir 4, 5*
Auriga - Clifton Park, NY - *BoPubDir 4, 5*
Auromere [of Indragni Phototypesetting] - Pomona, CA - *LitMag&SmPr 83-84; LitMarPl 83, 84*
Aurora - Madison, WI - *LitMag&SmPr 83-84*
Aurora - Greenwood, NS, Canada - *AyerDirPub 83*
Aurora Advertiser [of Lawrence County Newspapers Inc.] - Aurora, MO - *BaconPubCkNews 84; NewsDir 84*
Aurora Advocate - Aurora, OH - *AyerDirPub 83; Ed&PubIntYB 82*
Aurora Advocate - *See* Record Publishing Co.
Aurora Arapahoe News Press - *See* Douglas County News Publishing
Aurora Beacon-News, The [of Copley Press Inc.] - Aurora, IL - *NewsDir 84*
Aurora Cable TV Ltd. - Aurora, ON, Canada - *BrCabYB 84*
Aurora County Standard - White Lake, SD - *AyerDirPub 83*
Aurora County Standard & White Lake Wave - White Lake, SD - *Ed&PubIntYB 82*
Aurora General Entertainment - Hollywood, FL - *TelAl 84; Tel&CabFB 84C*
Aurora-Hoyt Lakes Range Facts - Aurora, MN - *BaconPubCkNews 84*
Aurora Journal - Aurora, CO - *NewsDir 84*
Aurora Journal Press - *See* Register Publications Inc.
Aurora News-Register - Aurora, NE - *BaconPubCkNews 84; Ed&PubIntYB 82; NewsDir 84*
Aurora Paperboard [Div. of The Davey Co.] - Aurora, IL - *LitMarPl 83, 84*
Aurora Report [of I. P. Sharp Associates Ltd.] - Toronto, ON, Canada - *DataDirOnSer 84*
Aurora Sentinel - *See* Sentinel Newspapers
Aurora Software - Arlington Heights, IL - *MicrocomMPl 84*
Aurora Sun, The - Aurora, CO - *Ed&PubIntYB 82*
Aurora Sun, The - Wheat Ridge, CO - *NewsDir 84*
Aurora Systems Inc. - Madison, WI - *MicrocomMPl 84*
Aurora, The - Labrador, NF, Canada - *AyerDirPub 83; Ed&PubIntYB 82*
Aurora Village Squire - Castle Rock, CO - *AyerDirPub 83*
Aurum Records [Div. of RBR Communications Inc.] - New York, NY - *BillIntBG 83-84*
Aurvid Productions [Div. of International Treasures] - Philadelphia, PA - *Tel&CabFB 84C*
Ausable Forks Adirondack Record Post [of Elizabethtown Denton Publications Inc.] - Elizabethtown, NY - *NewsDir 84*
AuSable Valley Telephone Co. Inc. - Keeseville, NY - *TelDir&BG 83-84*
Auschwitz Study Foundation Inc. - Huntington Beach, CA - *BoPubDir 4, 5*
Auscom Inc. - Austin, TX - *DataDirSup 7-83*
AUSINET [of ACI Computer Services] - Clayton, Australia - *InfIndMarPl 83*
Auslender Films, Leland - Los Angeles, CA - *AvMarPl 83*
Auspex Music - Studio City, CA - *BillIntBG 83-84*
Auspex Records - Studio City, CA - *BillIntBG 83-84*
Austar Communication Products Inc. - Aurora, CO - *AvMarPl 83*
Austar-Optisonics Inc. [Subs. of Hanimex USA Inc.] - Tucson, AZ - *AvMarPl 83*

Austell Neighbor - Austell, GA - *Ed&PubIntYB 82*
Austell Neighbor [of Marietta Neighbor Newspapers Inc.] - Marietta, GA - *NewsDir 84*
Austerman, Miriam - San Diego, CA - *LitMarPl 84*
Austin [of Austin Chamber of Commerce] - Austin, TX - *WritMar 84*
Austin American-Statesman [of Cox Newspapers] - Austin, TX - *BaconPubCkNews 84; Ed&PubIntYB 82; LitMarPl 83, 84; NewsBur 6; NewsDir 84*
Austin Associates Inc. - Scottsdale, AZ - *StaDirAdAg 2-84*
Austin CableVision [of American TV & Communications Corp.] - Austin, TX - *Tel&CabFB 84C*
Austin Capital City Argus - Austin, TX - *BaconPubCkNews 84*
Austin Chronicle, The - Austin, IN - *Ed&PubIntYB 82*
Austin Citizen [of Austin Publishing Co.] - Austin, TX - *NewsDir 84*
Austin Computer Technologies - Austin, TX - *WhoWMicrocom 83*
Austin-Crothersville News - Austin, IN - *AyerDirPub 83; BaconPubCkNews 84; NewsDir 84*
Austin Group - Austin, TX - *Ed&PubIntYB 82*
Austin Herald [of Thomson Newspapers] - Austin, MN - *BaconPubCkNews 84; Ed&PubIntYB 82; NewsDir 84*
Austin Hill Press Inc. - San Diego, CA - *BoPubDir 4, 5*
Austin Homes & Gardens [of Diversified Productions Inc.] - Austin, TX - *BaconPubCkMag 84; WritMar 84*
Austin Junior Forum Publications - Austin, TX - *BoPubDir 5*
Austin Living [of Baker Publications] - Austin, TX - *BaconPubCkMag 84; MagDir 84; WritMar 84*
Austin Living - Dallas, TX - *MagIndMarPl 82-83*
Austin Management Consulting - Evanston, IL - *IntDirMarRes 83*
Austin Micro Systems Inc. - Austin, TX - *MicrocomMPl 83, 84*
Austin Reese River Reveille - *See* Central Nevada Newspapers Inc.
Austin Subscription Agency - Savannah, GA - *MagIndMarPl 82-83*
Austin Westlake Picayune - Austin, TX - *BaconPubCkNews 84*
Austinite [of Chicago Passage Publications] - Chicago, IL - *AyerDirPub 83; Ed&PubIntYB 82; NewsDir 84*
Austintown Leader - Austintown, OH - *AyerDirPub 83; Ed&PubIntYB 82*
Austintown Leader [of Phoenix Publications Inc.] - Niles, OH - *NewsDir 84*
Austintown Leader - *See* Phoenix Publications Inc.
Australia [of Chase Econometrics/Interactive Data Corp.] - Waltham, MA - *DataDirOnSer 84*
Australia - Bala Cynwyd, PA - *DirOnDB Spring 84*
Australia-Wide Survey of Readership of Magazines [of Interactive Market Systems Inc.] - New York, NY - *DataDirOnSer 84*
Australia-Wide Survey of Readership of Magazines - Melbourne, Australia - *DirOnDB Spring 84*
Australian Bank Bill Rates [of I. P. Sharp Associates Ltd.] - Toronto, ON, Canada - *DataDirOnSer 84*
Australian Bibliographic Network [of National Library of Australia] - Canberra, Australia - *EISS 83*
Australian Bibliographic Network [of National Library of Australia] - Parkes, Australia - *InfIndMarPl 83*
Australian Bibliography of Agriculture - East Melbourne, Australia - *DirOnDB Spring 84*
Australian Broadcasting Commission - New York, NY - *Ed&PubIntYB 82*
Australian Bureau of Statistics - Belconnen, Australia - *EISS 83*
Australian Bureau of Statistics - St. Leonards, Australia - *DirOnDB Spring 84*
Australian Bureau of Statistics Data Base [of I. P. Sharp Associates Ltd.] - Toronto, ON, Canada - *DataDirOnSer 84; DBBus 82*
Australian Business Index - Hawthorn, Australia - *DirOnDB Spring 84; EISS 5-84 Sup; InfIndMarPl 83*
Australian Commodities - Sydney, Australia - *DirOnDB Spring 84*
Australian Commodities [of I. P. Sharp Associates Ltd.] - Toronto, ON, Canada - *DataDirOnSer 84*
Australian Consolidated Press - New York, NY - *Ed&PubIntYB 82; MagIndMarPl 82-83*
Australian Council for Educational Research - Hawthorn, Australia - *CompReadDB 82; InfIndMarPl 83*
Australian Demographic Data Bank [of Australian National University] - Canberra, Australia - *EISS 83*
Australian Earth Sciences Information System [of Australian Mineral Foundation] - Glenside, Australia - *DirOnDB Spring 84; EISS 83*
Australian Economic Statistics [of I. P. Sharp Associates Ltd.] - Toronto, ON, Canada - *DataDirOnSer 84; DirOnDB Spring 84*
Australian Education Index [of Australian Council for Educational Research] - Hawthorn, Australia - *CompReadDB 82; DirOnDB Spring 84; EISS 83*
Australian Export Statistics - Belconnen, Australia - *DirOnDB Spring 84*
Australian Export Statistics [of I. P. Sharp Associates Ltd.] - Toronto, ON, Canada - *DataDirOnSer 84*
Australian Film Commission - Los Angeles, CA - *AvMarPl 83; Tel&CabFB 84C*
Australian Financial Data Base [of I. P. Sharp Associates Ltd.] - Toronto, ON, Canada - *DataDirOnSer 84; DirOnDB Spring 84*
Australian Financial Markets - Sydney, Australia - *DirOnDB Spring 84*
Australian Financial Markets [of I. P. Sharp Associates Ltd.] - Toronto, ON, Canada - *DataDirOnSer 84*
Australian Financial Review Information Service - Sydney, Australia - *DirOnDB Spring 84; EISS 7-83 Sup*
Australian Funds Markets - Sydney, Australia - *DirOnDB Spring 84*
Australian Funds Markets [of I. P. Sharp Associates Ltd.] - Toronto, ON, Canada - *DataDirOnSer 84*
Australian Graduate School of Management [of I. P. Sharp Associates Ltd.] - Toronto, ON, Canada - *DataDirOnSer 84*
Australian Graduate School of Management (Centre for Management Research & Development) - Kensington, Australia - *InfIndMarPl 83*
Australian Graduate School of Management (Corporate Data) - Kensington, Australia - *DirOnDB Spring 84*
Australian Graduate School of Management (Corporate Data) - Toronto, ON, Canada - *DataDirOnSer 84*
Australian Input-Output Database - Belconnen, Australia - *DirOnDB Spring 84*
Australian Input-Output Database [of I. P. Sharp Associates Ltd.] - Toronto, ON, Canada - *DataDirOnSer 84*
Australian Medline Network [of National Library of Australia] - Canberra, Australia - *EISS 5-84 Sup*
Australian Mineral Foundation - Glenside, Australia - *InfIndMarPl 83*
Australian Municipal Information System [of Computer Sciences of Australia Pty. Ltd.] - St. Leonards, Australia - *DataDirOnSer 84; DirOnDB Spring 84*
Australian National Bibliography [of National Library of Australia] - Canberra, Australia - *CompReadDB 82; DirOnDB Spring 84*
Australian National Gallery Library - Canberra, Australia - *EISS 7-83 Sup*
Australian National University Press - New York, NY - *LitMarPl 84*
Australian Newspapers Service - New York, NY - *Ed&PubIntYB 82*
Australian Public Affairs Information Service [of National Library of Australia] - Canberra, Australia - *CompReadDB 82; DirOnDB Spring 84*
Australian Road Index [of Australian Road Research Board] - Nunawading, Australia - *CompReadDB 82; EISS 83*
Australian Road Research Board - Nunawading, Australia - *CompReadDB 82; InfIndMarPl 83*
Australian Road Research Documentation - Nunawading, Australia - *DirOnDB Spring 84*
Australian Science Index [of Commonwealth Scientific & Industrial Research Organisation] - East Melbourne, Australia - *CompReadDB 82; DirOnDB Spring 84*
Australian Scientific & Technological Reports Data Base [of National Library of Australia] - Canberra, Australia - *CompReadDB 82*
Australian Sector Cash Flow - Sydney, Australia - *DirOnDB Spring 84*
Australian Sector Cash Flow [of I. P. Sharp Associates Ltd.] - Toronto, ON, Canada - *DataDirOnSer 84*
Australian Stock Exchange Indices - Sydney, Australia - *DirOnDB Spring 84*

Australian Stock Exchange Indices [of I. P. Sharp Associates Ltd.] - Toronto, ON, Canada - *DataDirOnSer 84*
Australian Transport Literature Information System - Canberra, Australia - *DirOnDB Spring 84*
Australian Video & Communications [of General Magazine Co. Pty. Ltd.] - Glen Iris, Australia - *WritMar 84*
Australian Women's Weekly - Sydney, Australia - *ArtMar 84*
Australiana Publications [Aff. of Dryden Press Australia] - Coral Gables, FL - *BoPubDir 4, 5*
Austrian INIS Center - Seibersdorf, Austria - *InfIndMarPl 83*
Austrian Tymnet/Telenet Node [of Radio Austria AG] - Vienna, Austria - *InfIndMarPl 83*
Autex Systems - Wellesley, MA - *EISS 83; InfoS 83-84*
Authenticated News International - Katonah, NY - *AvMarPl 83; Ed&PubIntYB 82; LitMarPl 83, 84; MagIndMarPl 82-83*
Author Aid Associates - New York, NY - *LitMarPl 83, 84; MagIndMarPl 82-83*
Author! Author! Publishing Co. - New York, NY - *BoPubDir 4, 5*
Author/Publisher Services - Oakhurst, CA - *LitMarPl 83*
Author, The [of Society of Authors] - London, England - *LitMag&SmPr 83-84*
Authors & Anthropologists Services of North America Inc. - Kalispell, MT - *BrCabYB 84*
Authors' Co-Op Publishing Co. - Franklin, TN - *BoPubDir 4, 5; LitMag&SmPr 83-84*
Authors Edition Inc. - Lenox, MA - *BoPubDir 4, 5*
Author's Friend, The - New York, NY - *LitMarPl 83, 84*
Authors Guild Bulletin - New York, NY - *MagIndMarPl 82-83*
Authors Management International - New York, NY - *LitMarPl 83*
Authors Marketing Services Ltd. - Toronto, ON, Canada - *LitMarPl 83, 84*
Author's Roundtable [Div. of Sheridan-Elson Communications Inc.] - New York, NY - *LitMarPl 83, 84*
Auto & Flat Glass Journal [of Grawin Publications Inc.] - Seattle, WA - *BaconPubCkMag 84; MagDir 84*
Auto Book Press - San Marcos, CA - *WritMar 84*
Auto-Cite [of The Lawyers Co-Operative Publishing Co.] - Rochester, NY - *DirOnDB Spring 84; EISS 83; MicrocomMPl 84*
Auto-Cite [of Mead Data Central] - Dayton, OH - *DataDirOnSer 84*
Auto Collision Repair Information System - Hayward, CA - *DirOnDB Spring 84*
Auto-Graphics Inc. - Monterey Park, CA - *LitMarPl 83, 84; MagIndMarPl 82-83*
Auto Laundry News [of Columbia Communications Inc.] - New York, NY - *BaconPubCkMag 84; MagDir 84; WritMar 84*
Auto Merchandising News [of Mortimer Communications Inc.] - Fairfield, CT - *BaconPubCkMag 84; MagDir 84; MagIndMarPl 82-83*
Auto Motor & Sport - Palos Verdes Peninsula, CA - *MagDir 84*
Auto News Syndicate - Daytona Beach, FL - *Ed&PubIntYB 82*
Auto News Syndicate - Flagler Beach, FL - *LitMarPl 84*
Auto Racing Digest - Evanston, IL - *BaconPubCkMag 84; MagIndMarPl 82-83*
Auto Reports - Van Nuys, CA - *MagDir 84*
Auto Screen/Lehigh - Pennsauken, NJ - *LitMarPl 83, 84*
Auto/Sport - Mississauga, ON, Canada - *BaconPubCkMag 84*
Auto Tell Services Inc. - Villanova, PA - *DataDirOnSer 84*
Auto Trim News [of National Association of Auto Trim Shops] - Baldwin, NY - *ArtMar 84; BaconPubCkMag 84; MagDir 84; WritMar 84*
Auto-Trol Technology Corp. - Denver, CO - *DataDirSup 7-83*
Auto Week [of Crain Communications Inc.] - Detroit, MI - *Folio 83*
Autobody & the Reconditioned Car [of Spokesman Publishing] - Cincinnati, OH - *BaconPubCkMag 84; MagDir 84*
Autobuff Magazine [of Carnaby Communications Corp.] - Atlanta, GA - *WritMar 84*
Autocom II Message Switching Service [of Teleglobe Canada] - Montreal, PQ, Canada - *TeleSy&SerDir 7-83*
Autographix - Waltham, MA - *AvMarPl 83*
Autolist-From Resource Systems - San Jose, CA - *MagIndMarPl 82-83*
Autologic Inc. [Subs. of Volt Information Sciences Inc.] - Newbury Park, CA - *DirInfWP 82; LitMarPl 83, 84*
Autolost [Div. of Resource Publications Inc.] - San Jose, CA - *MagIndMarPl 82-83*
Automail [of ADP Autonet] - Ann Arbor, MI - *TeleSy&SerDir 2-84*
Automatech Graphics Corp. [Div. of Rudor Consolidated Industries] - New York, NY - *DataDirOnSer 84; EISS 83; LitMarPl 83, 84; MagIndMarPl 82-83*
Automated Accounting Systems - Vinton, VA - *MicrocomMPl 84; MicrocomSwDir 1*
Automated Analysis - Van Nuys, CA - *MicrocomMPl 84*
Automated Bookkeeping Corp. - New York, NY - *WhoWMicrocom 83*
Automated Cable Corp. - Atlantis, FL - *Tel&CabFB 84C*
Automated Circulation System [of Oberlin College Library] - Oberlin, OH - *EISS 83*
Automated Citation Verification Service [of Lawyer's Co-Operative Publishing Co.] - Rochester, NY - *CompReadDB 82; DBBus 82*
Automated Composition Service Inc. - New York, NY - *LitMarPl 83, 84*
Automated Court Systems Inc. - San Diego, CA - *WhoWMicrocom 83*
Automated Financial Systems Inc. - King of Prussia, PA - *ADAPSOMemDir 83-84; DataDirSup 7-83*
Automated Hospital Information System [of U.S. Veterans Administration Medical Center] - Washington, DC - *EISS 83*
Automated Information Inc. - St. Louis, MO - *DataDirOnSer 84*
Automated Information Resultants Ltd. - Jackson Heights, NY - *DirInfWP 82*
Automated Information Transfer System [of U.S. Dept. of Commerce] - Washington, DC - *InfIndMarPl 83*
Automated Library Information System [of Dataphase Systems Inc.] - Kansas City, MO - *EISS 83*
Automated Library Information System [of Danmarks Tekniske Bibliotek] - Lyngby, Denmark - *CompReadDB 82; EISS 83*
Automated Library Services [of Missouri State Library] - St. Louis, MO - *EISS 83*
Automated Management Services Inc. - Aurora, CO - *MicrocomMPl 83*
Automated Marketing Systems Inc. - Dallas, TX - *EISS 5-84 Sup*
Automated Media Management Systems [Subs. of Research Technology International] - Lincolnwood, IL - *AvMarPl 83*
Automated Medical Systems Inc. - Philadelphia, PA - *DataDirOnSer 84*
Automated Office Resources - Aptos, CA - *DirInfWP 82*
Automated Productions Inc. - *See* Bloom Cos. Inc., The
Automated Quill Inc. - Englewood, CO - *DataDirSup 7-83; MicrocomMPl 83*
Automated Resource Management - Glendora, CA - *MicrocomMPl 84*
Automated Simulations Inc. - Mountain View, CA - *MicrocomMPl 83; WhoWMicrocom 83*
Automated Standards & Regulations Information Online [of French Association for Standardization] - Paris, France - *EISS 83*
Automated Systems Inc. - Dayton, OH - *ADAPSOMemDir 83-84; DataDirOnSer 84*
Automatic Business Centers Inc. - Moorestown, NJ - *ADAPSOMemDir 83-84*
Automatic Data Processing - Clifton, NJ - *ADAPSOMemDir 83-84; DataDirOnSer 84; DataDirSup 7-83; Datamation 6-83; Top100Al 83*
Automatic Data Processing Inc. - Roseland, NJ - *DataDirOnSer 84*
Automatic Devices Co. - Allentown, PA - *AvMarPl 83*
Automatic Fulfillment Services - Dover, NJ - *MagIndMarPl 82-83*
Automatic Funds Transfer Services Inc. - Seattle, WA - *DataDirSup 7-83*
Automatic Machining - Rochester, NY - *ArtMar 84; BaconPubCkMag 84; MagDir 84; MagIndMarPl 82-83; WritMar 84*
Automatic Mail Services Inc. - Long Island City, NY - *MagIndMarPl 82-83*
Automatic Typewritten Letters Corp. - New York, NY - *LitMarPl 83, 84; MagIndMarPl 82-83*

Automation Center of Ottawa - Ottawa, ON, Canada - *DirInfWP 82*
Automation Consultants - Menlo Park, CA - *MicrocomMPl 84; MicrocomSwDir 1; WhoWMicrocom 83*
Automation Consultants International - Encino, CA - *DataDirSup 7-83*
Automation Electronics Corp. - Oakland, CA - *DataDirSup 7-83*
Automation in Housing & Systems Building News [of CMN Associates Inc.] - Carpinteria, CA - *BaconPubCkMag 84; MagDir 84; WritMar 84*
Automation Inc. - Omaha, NE - *DataDirOnSer 84*
Automation Management Inc. - Houston, TX - *MicrocomMPl 84*
Automation Management Services Inc. - Waukesha, WI - *DataDirSup 7-83*
Automation News - New York, NY - *BaconPubCkMag 84*
Automation Techniques - Tulsa, OK - *AvMarPl 83*
Automobile International [of Johnston International Publishing Corp.] - New York, NY - *BaconPubCkMag 84; MagDir 84*
Automobile Quarterly - Princeton, NJ - *ArtMar 84; DirMarMP 83; LitMarPl 83, 84; MagDir 84; MagIndMarPl 82-83; WritMar 84*
Automobile Quarterly Publications - Kutztown, PA - *LitMarPl 83, 84*
Automotive Aftermarket News - Chicago, IL - *BaconPubCkMag 84*
Automotive Age [of Freed-Crown-Lee Publishing Inc.] - Van Nuys, CA - *ArtMar 84; BaconPubCkMag 84; MagDir 84; MagIndMarPl 82-83; NewsBur 6; WritMar 84*
Automotive Body Repair News - Chicago, IL - *BaconPubCkMag 84; MagIndMarPl 82-83*
Automotive Booster of California [of McAnally & Associates Inc.] - La Canada, CA - *BaconPubCkMag 84; MagDir 84; WritMar 84*
Automotive Chain Store [of Babcox Automotive Publications] - Akron, OH - *BaconPubCkMag 84; MagDir 84*
Automotive Competitive Assessment Data Bank - Media, PA - *DirOnDB Spring 84*
Automotive Cooling Journal [of National Automotive Radiator Service Association Inc.] - Kulpsville, PA - *MagDir 84*
Automotive Cooling Journal - Lansdale, PA - *BaconPubCkMag 84*
Automotive Design & Development [of Bobit Publishing Co.] - Redondo Beach, CA - *MagDir 84*
Automotive Design & Development [of Cummins Publishing Co.] - Troy, MI - *NewsDir 84*
Automotive Engineering - Warrendale, PA - *BaconPubCkMag 84*
Automotive Executive [of National Automobile Dealers Service Corp.] - McLean, VA - *BaconPubCkMag 84; MagDir 84*
Automotive Features - Milwaukee, WI - *Ed&PublIntYB 82*
Automotive Fleet [of Bobit Publishing Co.] - Redondo Beach, CA - *BaconPubCkMag 84; MagDir 84; MagIndMarPl 82-83*
Automotive Independent - Bedford, TX - *BaconPubCkMag 84*
Automotive Industries - Chicago, IL - *NewsBur 6*
Automotive Industries - Radnor, PA - *BaconPubCkMag 84; MagIndMarPl 82-83*
Automotive Market Report [of Auto Auction Publishing Inc.] - Pittsburgh, PA - *BaconPubCkMag 84; MagDir 84*
Automotive Marketer - Toronto, ON, Canada - *BaconPubCkMag 84*
Automotive Marketing - Radnor, PA - *BaconPubCkMag 84*
Automotive Messenger - Hazelwood, MO - *BaconPubCkMag 84; MagIndMarPl 82-83*
Automotive Messenger, The [of Hansen Publishing Inc.] - St. Louis, MO - *MagDir 84*
Automotive News [of Crain Communications Inc.] - Detroit, MI - *BaconPubCkMag 84; Folio 83; MagDir 84; MagIndMarPl 82-83; NewsBur 6*
Automotive News Data Bank [of Data Resources Inc.] - Lexington, MA - *DataDirOnSer 84*
Automotive News Data Bank - Detroit, MI - *DirOnDB Spring 84*
Automotive News of the Pacific Northwest - Milwaukie, OR - *BaconPubCkMag 84; MagDir 84*
Automotive Parts Rebuilders Association - McLean, VA - *BoPubDir 5*
Automotive Rebuilder [of Babcox Automotive Publications] - Akron, OH - *BaconPubCkMag 84; MagDir 84; WritMar 84*
Automotive Retailer - Vancouver, BC, Canada - *BaconPubCkMag 84*
Automotive Service Market [of Kaufman-Laverty Publishing Co. Inc.] - Tenafly, NJ - *BaconPubCkMag 84; MagDir 84*
Automotive Volume Distribution - Lincolnwood, IL - *BaconPubCkMag 84; WritMar 84*
Automotive Week [of Automotive Buyer Publishing Co.] - Wayne, NJ - *BaconPubCkMag 84; MagDir 84*
Automovil Internacional [of Johnston International Publishing Corp.] - New York, NY - *BaconPubCkMag 84; MagDir 84*
AutoNet/AutoBase - *DirOnDB Spring 84*
Autopage Book Composition Inc. - Oceanside, NY - *LitMarPl 83, 84; MagIndMarPl 82-83*
Autoscene, The - Westlake Village, CA - *BaconPubCkMag 84*
AutoScript Inc. - Bloomfield, CT - *DataDirOnSer 84; DataDirSup 7-83*
Autosound & Communications - New York, NY - *BaconPubCkMag 84*
Autospec Inc. - Pacific Grove, CA - *WhoWMicrocom 83*
Autotransaction Industry Report [of International Data Corp.] - Waltham, MA - *MagDir 84*
Autotype Word Processing Services Inc. - Denver, CO - *DirInfWP 82*
Autoweek [of Crain Consumer Group Inc.] - Detroit, MI - *BaconPubCkMag 84; MagDir 84; WritMar 84*
Autumn International Records - Garland, TX - *BillIntBG 83-84*
Autumn Press Inc. - Boston, MA - *LitMag&SmPr 83-84*
Auxiliary System for Interactive Statistics [of National Central Bureau of Statistics] - Stockholm, Sweden - *EISS 83*
Auxipress - Brussels, Belgium - *ProGuPRSer 4*
AV Associates - Storrs, CT - *AvMarPl 83*
AV Computer Graphic - Birmingham, MI - *AvMarPl 83*
AV Concepts Corp. - Oakdale, NY - *WritMar 84*
AV-ED Films [Subs. of Color Stock Library Inc.] - Tampa, FL - *AvMarPl 83*
AV Guide - Des Plaines, IL - *BaconPubCkMag 84*
AV Insights Inc. [Div. of Herbert's Camera House Inc.] - Englewood, NJ - *AvMarPl 83*
AV Magic - New York, NY - *AvMarPl 83*
AV Media Craftsman Inc. - New York, NY - *ArtMar 84; AvMarPl 83; WritMar 84*
AV Services - New York, NY - *AvMarPl 83*
AV Systems Inc. - Los Angeles, CA - *MicrocomMPl 84*
Ava Cablevision [of Semo Communications Inc.] - Ava, MO - *Tel&CabFB 84C*
Ava Douglas County Herald - Ava, MO - *BaconPubCkNews 84; NewsDir 84*
AVA Instrumentation Inc. - Ben Lomond, CA - *WhoWMicrocom 83*
AVA Tech Inc. - Sarasota, FL - *AvMarPl 83*
Avalanche-Journal - Lubbock, TX - *AyerDirPub 83*
Avalon Books [of Thomas Bouregy & Co.] - New York, NY - *WritMar 84*
Avalon Cablevision Ltd. - St. John's, NF, Canada - *BrCabYB 84*
Avalon Catalina Islander - Avalon, CA - *BaconPubCkNews 84*
Avalon Communications Inc. - Hewlett, NY - *LitMarPl 83, 84*
Avalon Editions - York, England - *LitMag&SmPr 83-84*
Avalon Hill Microcomputer Games [Subs. of Monarch Avalon Inc.] - Baltimore, MD - *MicrocomMPl 83; WhoWMicrocom 83*
Avant - West Concord, MA - *AvMarPl 83; DataDirSup 7-83*
Avant Books [Aff. of The Word Shop Publications] - San Diego, CA - *BoPubDir 4, 5; LitMag&SmPr 83-84; WritMar 84*
Avant-Garde Computing Inc. - Cherry Hill, NJ - *DataDirOnSer 84*
Avant-Garde Creations - Eugene, OR - *BoPubDir 4; MicrocomMPl 83, 84; WritMar 84*
Avant-Garde Records Inc. - New York, NY - *AvMarPl 83; BillIntBG 83-84*
Avant Inc. - Concord, MA - *DirInfWP 82*
Avante Book Co. - Pasadena, CA - *BoPubDir 4, 5*
Avanti Associates - Mercerville, NJ - *LitMag&SmPr 83-84*
Avanti Communications - Newport, RI - *DataDirSup 7-83; WhoWMicrocom 83*
Avas Corp. - Hackensack, NJ - *AvMarPl 83; MicrocomMPl 84*
Avatar Press - Atlanta, GA - *BoPubDir 4, 5*
Avatar Systems Inc. - Potomac, MD - *EISS 83*
AVC Corp. - Indianapolis, IN - *AvMarPl 83*
Avco Computer Services [of Avco Corp.] - Wilmington, MA - *ADAPSOMemDir 83-84; DataDirOnSer 84; DataDirSup 7-83; EISS 83*

Avco Corp. - Greenwich, CT - *KnowInd 83*
Avcom - Brisbane, CA - *DirOnDB Spring 84*
Avcom Audio-Visual - Washington, DC - *AvMarPl 83*
Avcom Systems Inc. - Cutchogue, NY - *AvMarPl 83*
Avcor - Toronto, ON, Canada - *EISS 5-84 Sup*
Avdec Corp. - Baldwin, NY - *DirInfWP 82*
Ave Maria Press - Notre Dame, IN - *LitMarPl 83, 84; WritMar 84*
Avebury Publishing Co. - *See* Gregg International
AVEDEX Inc. - Wilmette, IL - *AvMarPl 83*
Avekta Productions - New York, NY - *WritMar 84*
Avenue - New York, NY - *BaconPubCkMag 84; WritMar 84*
Avenue M - Chicago, IL - *BaconPubCkMag 84; MagDir 84*
Avenue TV Cable Service Inc. - New Cuyama, CA - *BrCabYB 84*
Avenue TV Cable Service Inc. - Ventura, CA - *BrCabYB 84 p.D-297; Tel&CabFB 84C p.1665*
Avenue Victor Hugo Inc. - Boston, MA - *BoPubDir 4, 5*
Avery Color Studios - Au Train, MI - *BoPubDir 4, 5; LitMarPl 84*
Avery Index to Architectural Periodicals [of The Research Libraries Group Inc.] - Stanford, CA - *DataDirOnSer 84*
Avery Index to Architectural Periodicals [of Columbia University] - New York, NY - *DirOnDB Spring 84; EISS 83*
Avery-Knodel Television - New York, NY - *TelAl 83, 84*
Avery Publishing Group Inc. - Wayne, NJ - *LitMarPl 83, 84*
Avery Telephone Co. [Aff. of Century Telephone Enterprises Inc.] - Hooks, TX - *TelDir&BG 83-84*
Aves Advertising Inc. - Grand Rapids, MI - *StaDirAdAg 2-84*
AVI Producers Workshop - Hollywood, CA - *AvMarPl 83*
AVI Publishing Co. - Westport, CT - *LitMarPl 83, 84; WritMar 84*
AVI Records Inc./Out of Town Records Distributing Corp. - Hollywood, CA - *BillIntBG 83-84*
Avian Publications Inc. - Elizabethtown, KY - *BoPubDir 4, 5*
Aviation - Brookfield, CT - *BaconPubCkMag 84*
Aviation Analysis Inc. - Hinsdale, IL - *MicrocomMPl 84; MicrocomSwDir 1*
Aviation Book Co. - Glendale, CA - *LitMag&SmPr 83-84; LitMarPl 83, 84; WritMar 84*
Aviation Consumer [of Belvoir Publications Inc.] - Riverside, CT - *BaconPubCkMag 84; MagDir 84*
Aviation Convention News - Midland Park, NJ - *BaconPubCkMag 84*
Aviation Daily - Washington, DC - *BaconPubCkMag 84*
Aviation Equipment Maintenance [of The Irving-Cloud Publishing Co.] - Lincolnwood, IL - *BaconPubCkMag 84; WritMar 84*
Aviation Information Services - Hounslow, England - *CompReadDB 82; EISS 83*
Aviation Language School Inc. - Miami, FL - *BoPubDir 5*
Aviation Magazine - Brookfield, CT - *MagIndMarPl 82-83*
Aviation Maintenance Publishers - Basin, WY - *AvMarPl 83; BoPubDir 4, 5*
Aviation Marketing Communications - Wilmington, DE - *DirPRFirms 83*
Aviation Mechanics Bulletin - Arlington, VA - *BaconPubCkMag 84; MagDir 84*
Aviation Mechanics Journal [of Aviation Maintenance Publishers Inc.] - Basin, WY - *BaconPubCkMag 84; MagDir 84; MagIndMarPl 82-83*
Aviation Publications [Aff. of Graphic Communications Center Inc.] - Appleton, WI - *BoPubDir 4, 5*
Aviation Publications Inc. - Gainesville, FL - *BoPubDir 4, 5*
Aviation Publishers Co. Ltd. - Ottawa, ON, Canada - *BoPubDir 4, 5*
Aviation Safety Institute - Worthington, OH - *DataDirOnSer 84; DirOnDB Spring 84*
Aviation Safety Institute Information [of Aviation Safety Institute] - Worthington, OH - *DataDirOnSer 84*
Aviation, Space, & Environmental Medicine - Washington, DC - *MagDir 84*
Aviation Space & Environmental Medicine - San Antonio, TX - *BaconPubCkMag 84*
Aviation Space Magazine - Washington, DC - *MagIndMarPl 82-83*
Aviation Training Systems Ltd. - Saskatoon, SK, Canada - *BoPubDir 4, 5*
Aviation Weather Information System [of Weather Services International Corp.] - Bedford, MA - *DataDirOnSer 84*
Aviation Week & Space Technology [of McGraw-Hill Inc.] - New York, NY - *BaconPubCkMag 84; Folio 83; MagDir 84; MagIndMarPl 82-83; NewsBur 6*
Aviators Guild [of TAB Books Inc.] - Summit, PA - *LitMarPl 84*
Avicultural Book Club [Div. of Avicultural Book Co.] - East Elmhurst, NY - *LitMarPl 84*
Avid Services - Glovertown, NF, Canada - *BoPubDir 5*
Avikon Holdings Ltd. - Edmonton, AB, Canada - *BoPubDir 4 Sup, 5*
Avilla News - *See* Tri-County Publishing Inc.
Avilla News, The - Avilla, IN - *Ed&PubIntYB 82*
Avionics News - Independence, MO - *BaconPubCkMag 84*
Avis & Associates Inc., George - Baltimore, MD - *StaDirAdAg 2-84*
Avis Associates - Bryn Mawr, PA - *HBIndAd&MS 82-83*
AVLine [of U.S. National Library of Medicine] - Bethesda, MD - *DirOnDB Spring 84; EISS 83*
AVMARC [of British Library] - London, England - *CompReadDB 82; DirOnDB Spring 84*
Avnet Inc. - New York, NY - *ElecNews 7-25-83*
Avoca Cablevision Ltd. - Avoca, IA - *Tel&CabFB 84C*
Avoca Journal Herald - Avoca, IA - *BaconPubCkNews 84*
Avoca TV Cable Corp. - Avoca, NY - *BrCabYB 84; Tel&CabFB 84C*
Avocado Grower - Vista, CA - *MagDir 84*
Avocado Grower Magazine - Vista, CA - *WritMar 84*
Avocet Inc. - Menlo Park, CA - *BoPubDir 5*
Avocet Systems Inc. - Dover, DE - *MicrocomMPl 83, 84; WhoWMicrocom 83*
Avocet Two - Millwood, VA - *AvMarPl 83*
Avon Books [Div. of The Hearst Corp.] - New York, NY - *ArtMar 84; DirMarMP 83; LitMarPl 83, 84; WritMar 84*
Avon Clarion - Avon, SD - *BaconPubCkNews 84; Ed&PubIntYB 82*
Avon Danville Gazette - *See* Mid State Newspapers Inc.
Avon Herald News - Avon, NY - *Ed&PubIntYB 82*
Avon Herald News & Rush Henrietta Herald - Geneseo, NY - *AyerDirPub 83*
Avon Herald News/Rush Henrietta Record - *See* Sanders Publications
Avon Lake Press - Avon Lake, OH - *AyerDirPub 83; BaconPubCkNews 84; Ed&PubIntYB 82*
Avon Messenger - *See* Bulletin Publishing Co.
Avon Park Sun - Avon Park, FL - *AyerDirPub 83; BaconPubCkNews 84; Ed&PubIntYB 82; NewsDir 84*
Avon Sentinel - Avon, IL - *Ed&PubIntYB 82*
Avon Sentinel [of Roseville Carlberg Publishing Co.] - Roseville, IL - *AyerDirPub 83; NewsDir 84*
Avon Sentinel - *See* Acklin Newspaper Group
Avondale Press - Willowdale, ON, Canada - *BoPubDir 4, 5; LitMag&SmPr 83-84*
Avon's Research Publications - La Canada, CA - *BoPubDir 4, 5*
Avoyelles Cable TV Inc. [of Scotts Cable Communications Inc.] - Marksville, LA - *BrCabYB 84; Tel&CabFB 84C*
Avoyelles Journal, The - Marksville, LA - *NewsDir 84*
Avoyelles News-Leader - Marksville, LA - *AyerDirPub 83; Ed&PubIntYB 82*
Avoyelles Press - Marksville, LA - *AyerDirPub 83*
AVP Communication - Westborough, MA - *AvMarPl 83*
Avpro Inc. - Kennebunk, ME - *CabTVFinDB 83*
AVPS Corp. - New York, NY - *AvMarPl 83*
Avrea/Pugliese - Dallas, TX - *StaDirAdAg 2-84*
Avrett, Free & Ginsberg - New York, NY - *AdAge 3-28-84; ArtMar 84; StaDirAdAg 2-84*
AVS Distributors - Sykesville, MD - *MicrocomMPl 84*
AVS Intext Ltd. - London, England - *EISS 83*
Avtec Industries Inc. - Teterboro, NJ - *TeleSy&SerDir 2-84*
AVTech - Dayton, OH - *AvMarPl 83*
Avtech Electronics Inc. - Long Island City, NY - *AvMarPl 83*
AVW Productions - Dallas, TX - *ArtMar 84*
Awakener Magazine, The - Hermosa Beach, CA - *LitMag&SmPr 83-84*
Awakener Press, The - Hermosa Beach, CA - *LitMag&SmPr 83-84*
Awakening Productions Inc. - Culver City, CA - *BoPubDir 4, 5*

Awani Press Inc. - Fredericksburg, TX - *BoPubDir 4, 5*
Award Films - Chicago, IL - *TelAl 83, 84; Tel&CabFB 84C*
Award Masters Inc. - Baltimore, MD - *BillIntBG 83-84*
Awareness Techniques - Dover, MA - *BoPubDir 4, 5*
Away - Wellesley, MA - *MagDir 84; WritMar 84*
A.W.M. Co. - Ann Arbor, MI - *BoPubDir 4, 5*
AWP Newsletter - Norfolk, VA - *LitMag&SmPr 83-84*
Axbar Productions - San Antonio, TX - *BillIntBG 83-84*
Axbar Records - San Antonio, TX - *BillIntBG 83-84*
Axe Handle Music - *See* Axbar Productions
Axelband & Brown & Associates Inc. - Cleveland, OH - *StaDirAdAg 2-84*
Axelrod Agency, The - New York, NY - *LitMarPl 84*
Axelrod Associates Inc., Elliot J. - New York, NY - *HBIndAd&MS 82-83*
Axelrod Associates, Norman N. - New York, NY - *AvMarPl 83*
Axelrod Bindery Inc. - Clifton, NY - *MagIndMarPl 82-83*
Axelrod Co., The - Old Bridge, NJ - *StaDirAdAg 2-84*
Axelrod, Jerome - Philadelphia, PA - *LitMarPl 83, 84*
Axess - Paris, France - *DirOnDB Spring 84*
Axiom Corp. - Glendale, CA - *DirInfWP 82; WhoWMicrocom 83*
Axiom Corp. - San Francisco, CA - *MicrocomMPl 84*
Axiom Press - Burlingame, CA - *BoPubDir 4, 5*
Axiom Press Publishers - Burlingame, CA - *LitMag&SmPr 83-84*
Axion - San Jose, CA - *MicrocomMPl 84*
Axios - Fullerton, CA - *ArtMar 84; LitMag&SmPr 83-84*
Axios - Los Angeles, CA - *BoPubDir 4 Sup, 5; WritMar 84*
Axios Newsletter Inc. - Fullerton, CA - *LitMag&SmPr 83-84*
Axis Cablewave - Boulder, CO - *Tel&CabFB 84C*
Axis Inc. - San Diego, CA - *WhoWMicrocom 83*
Axlon Inc. - San Jose, CA - *WhoWMicrocom 83*
Axxa [Div. of Anaconda-Ericsson Inc.] - Woodland Hills, CA - *DirInfWP 82*
AYA Associates Inc. - Paramus, NJ - *DataDirOnSer 84*
Aya Press - Toronto, ON, Canada - *BoPubDir 4, 5; LitMag&SmPr 83-84; LitMarPl 84*
Ayden News Leader - Ayden, NC - *BaconPubCkNews 84; Ed&PubIntYB 82*
Aydin Computer Systems [Subs. of Aydin Corp.] - Ft. Washington, PA - *DataDirSup 7-83; WhoWMicrocom 83*
Aydin Controls [Div. of Aydin Corp.] - Ft. Washington, PA - *DataDirSup 7-83*
Aydin Monitor Systems - Ft. Washington, PA - *DataDirSup 7-83*
Ayer Direct [Div. of N. W. Ayer Inc.] - New York, NY - *DirMarMP 83*
Ayer Ft. Devens Sentry - *See* Public Spirit Publishing Co. Inc.
Ayer Inc., N. W. - Los Angeles, CA - *ArtMar 84*
Ayer Inc., N. W. - New York, NY - *AdAge 3-28-84, 6-25-84; Br 1-23-84; BrCabYB 84; DirPRFirms 83; HomeVid&CabYB 82-83; StaDirAdAg 2-84; TelAl 83, 84*
Ayer Information Center [of N. W. Ayer Inc.] - New York, NY - *EISS 83; ProGuPRSer 4*
Ayer Public Spirit - *See* Public Spirit Publishing Co. Inc.
Ayers/Blake Public Relations - Denver, CO - *DirPRFirms 83*
Ayers Store & TV Cable Inc. - Murray City, OH - *BrCabYB 84; Tel&CabFB 84C*
Ayers, Whitmore & Co. Inc. - New York, NY - *IntDirMarRes 83*
Ayersville Telephone Co. Inc. - Defiance, OH - *TelDir&BG 83-84*
Aylin/Mead & Stewart Advertising Agency Inc. - Houston, TX - *StaDirAdAg 2-84*
Aylmer Heritage Association - Aylmer, PQ, Canada - *BoPubDir 4, 5*
Aylmer Press - Madison, WI - *BoPubDir 4, 5*
Aylmer Reporter Inc. - Aylmer, PQ, Canada - *Ed&PubIntYB 82*
Aylsworth Publishing Co. - Hancock, MI - *BoPubDir 4, 5*
Aylward Enterprises - Wainanae, HI - *MicrocomMPl 84*
Ayorama Editions - Alexandria, ON, Canada - *BoPubDir 4 Sup, 5*
AYR Viewdata Ltd. [of Keycom Electronic Publishing] - Schaumburg, IL - *VideoDir 82-83*
Ayres & Associates Inc. - Lincoln, NE - *DirMarMP 83; StaDirAdAg 2-84*
Ayrshire Digest, The - Brandon, VT - *BaconPubCkMag 84; MagDir 84*
Ayrshire Telephone Co. - Ayrshire, IA - *TelDir&BG 83-84*
Azen & Associates - Ft. Lauderdale, FL - *DirPRFirms 83*
Azinda Publications - Marietta, GA - *BillIntBG 83-84*
Azle News - Azle, TX - *Ed&PubIntYB 82*
Azle News Advertiser [of Azle Tri-County Advertiser Inc.] - Azle, TX - *BaconPubCkNews 84; NewsDir 84*
Azra International Records - Maywood, CA - *BillIntBG 83-84*
Azrex Inc. - Burlington, MA - *DataDirSup 7-83*
Aztec Data Processing Inc. - Forest Hills, NY - *ADAPSOMemDir 83-84*
Aztec Independent-Review - Aztec, NM - *BaconPubCkNews 84*
Azteca Films Inc. - Hollywood, CA - *Tel&CabFB 84C*
Azteca Record Inc. - Burbank, CA - *BillIntBG 83-84*
Aztech Corp. - Washington, DC - *ADAPSOMemDir 83-84; DataDirOnSer 84*
Aztex Corp. - Tucson, AZ - *ArtMar 84; LitMarPl 83, 84; WritMar 84*
Aztlan: International Journal of Chicano Studies Research [of Chicano Studies Research Center Publications] - Los Angeles, CA - *LitMag&SmPr 83-84*
Azurdata Inc. - Redmond, WA - *DataDirSup 7-83; MicrocomMPl 83, 84; MicrocomSwDir 1; WhoWMicrocom 83*
Azure Coast Publishing Co. [Aff. of Werner R. Hashagen & Associates] - La Jolla, CA - *BoPubDir 4 Sup, 5*
Azure Press - Sidney, BC, Canada - *BoPubDir 4, 5*
Azusa Glendora Press [of Highlander Publications] - Azusa, CA - *NewsDir 84*
Azusa Herald - Azusa, CA - *AyerDirPub 83; Ed&PubIntYB 82*
Azusa Herald/Glendora Press - Azusa, CA - *BaconPubCkNews 84; Ed&PubIntYB 82*

B

B & B Direct Inc. - *See* Benton & Bowles Inc.
B & B Publishing - Saugus, CA - *BoPubDir 5*
B & B Publishing Inc. - Everman, TX - *BaconPubCkNews 84*
B & B Research Services Inc. - Cincinnati, OH - *IntDirMarRes 83*
B & B Software - Ann Arbor, MI - *MicrocomMPl 83; MicrocomSwDir 1; WhoWMicrocom 83*
B & B Sound Studios - Burbank, CA - *AvMarPl 83*
B & C Associates Inc. - High Point, NC - *DirPRFirms 83*
B & E International [of Borgen Publishing Co.] - Houston, TX - *NewsDir 84*
B & F Broadcasting Inc. - Milwaukee, WI - *Tel&CabFB 84C*
B & J Photo Inc. - Findlay, OH - *AvMarPl 83*
B & L Information Systems Inc. - Bridgman, MI - *MicrocomSwDir 1*
B & L Sales Inc. - North Hollywood, CA - *AvMarPl 83*
B & M Cable - Lewis County, WA - *Tel&CabFB 84C*
B & R Publishing - Centerville, IN - *BaconPubCkNews 84*
B & R Samizdat Express - West Roxbury, MA - *BoPubDir 4, 5; LitMag&SmPr 83-84*
B & W Press Inc. - Danvers, MA - *MagIndMarPl 82-83*
B-Atlas & Jody Records - Brooklyn, NY - *BillIntBG 83-84*
B Bering Straights [of Gold Dust Publications] - Nome, AK - *Ed&PubIntYB 82*
B-C Cable Inc. - Juneau, AK - *BrCabYB 84*
B/C Enterprises Inc. - Los Angeles, CA - *Tel&CabFB 84C*
B 5 Software - Columbus, OH - *MicrocomMPl 84*
B-G News, The [of Bowling Green State University] - Bowling Green, OH - *NewsDir 84*
B-H Computer Systems Inc. [Subs. of Pace Resources Inc.] - York, PA - *DataDirOnSer 84*
B Major Music - Sherman Oaks, CA - *BillIntBG 83-84*
B$2C Adventures - Annapolis, MD - *BoPubDir 4, 5*
B-W Advertising Agency - Phoenix, AZ - *StaDirAdAg 2-84*
BA Cable TV - Briarwood Village, FL - *BrCabYB 84*
BA Cable TV - Lantana Cascade, FL - *BrCabYB 84*
BA Cable TV - Shadow Lakes, FL - *BrCabYB 84*
Ba-Dake Music Inc. - *See* Schroeder International Ltd., A.
BA-United Service Corp. Inc. - Lake Worth, FL - *Tel&CabFB 84C*
Babbage Institute for the History of Information Processing, Charles [of University of Minnesota] - Minneapolis, MN - *EISS 83*
Babbage Research Centre, Charles - St. Pierre, MB, Canada - *BoPubDir 4, 5*
Babbitt Weekly News - Babbitt, MN - *BaconPubCkNews 84; Ed&PubIntYB 82*
Babcock Agency, The William - Greensboro, NC - *StaDirAdAg 2-84*
Babcock & Wilcox [Subs. of McDermott Inc.] - Lynchburg, VA - *ADAPSOMemDir 83-84; DataDirOnSer 84; DataDirSup 7-83*
Babcock North Music - San Antonio, TX - *BillIntBG 83-84*
Babcox Publications - Akron, OH - *MagIndMarPl 82-83*
Baby Care - New York, NY - *MagDir 84*
Baby Talk - New York, NY - *BaconPubCkMag 84; MagDir 84; MagIndMarPl 82-83; WritMar 84*
Baby Tate Music Corp. - Rosendale, NY - *BillIntBG 83-84*
Babylon Beacon - Babylon, NY - *BaconPubCkNews 84; Ed&PubIntYB 82; NewsDir 84*
Babylon South Bay's Newspaper - Lindenhurst, NY - *NewsDir 84*
Babylon TV Cable Corp. [of Communications Systems Corp.] - Babylon, NY - *Tel&CabFB 84C*
Bac-Data Medical Information Systems Inc. - Totowa, NJ - *EISS 83*
Baca Valley Telephone Co. Inc. - Des Moines, NM - *TelDir&BG 83-84*
Bacal Inc., Griffin - New York, NY - *AdAge 3-28-84*
Bacchus [of CompuServe Inc.] - Columbus, OH - *DataDirOnSer 84*
Bacchus Data Services - Los Angeles, CA - *EISS 5-84 Sup*
Bacchus Data Services Wine Information - Los Angeles, CA - *DirOnDB Spring 84*
Bacchus Press - Seal Beach, CA - *BoPubDir 4, 5; LitMarPl 83*
Bacchus Wine Guide [of Bacchus Data Services] - Los Angeles, CA - *DataDirOnSer 84*
Bach & Co. Inc., Melvin E. - Montclair, NJ - *StaDirAdAg 2-84*
Bach Communications Corp. - Dallas, TX - *Tel&CabFB 84C*
Bach Literary Agency Inc., Julian - New York, NY - *LitMarPl 83, 84*
Bachelis, Faren - Sacramento, CA - *LitMarPl 84*
Bachelis, Faren - San Luis Obispo, CA - *LitMarPl 83; MagIndMarPl 82-83*
Bachert & Associates Inc., R. E. - Lynnwood, WA - *StaDirAdAg 2-84*
Bachner Productions Inc. - New York, NY - *AvMarPl 83; WritMar 84*
Back Bay Music - *See* Mietus Copyright Management
Back Country Trader - Lakeside, CA - *AyerDirPub 83*
Back Door Press [Aff. of Steves Wide World Studios] - Edmonds, WA - *BoPubDir 4 Sup, 5*
Back Fork Books Inc. - Webster Springs, WV - *BoPubDir 5*
Back Home in Kentucky - Bowling Green, KY - *BaconPubCkMag 84*
Back of the Yards Journal - Chicago, IL - *Ed&PubIntYB 82*
Back Pages Books - Columbus, OH - *BoPubDir 4, 5*
Back Row Press - St. Paul, MN - *BoPubDir 4, 5; LitMag&SmPr 83-84*
Back Stage - New York, NY - *BaconPubCkMag 84; MagDir 84; NewsBur 6*
Backcountry Publications Inc. - Woodstock, VT - *LitMarPl 83, 84*
Backeddy Books - Cambridge, ID - *BoPubDir 4, 5*
Backer & Spielvogel - New York, NY - *AdAge 3-28-84; Br 1-23-84; BrCabYB 84; StaDirAdAg 2-84*
Backer Associates Inc., H. H. - Tucson, AZ - *DirPRFirms 83*
Backpacker [of Ziff-Davis] - New York, NY - *BaconPubCkMag 84; MagIndMarPl 82-83; WritMar 84*
Backpacker - Dorset, VT - *MagDir 84*
Backroads - Wilson, WY - *BoPubDir 4, 5; LitMag&SmPr 83-84*

Backstage Records Inc. - Beverly Hills, CA - *BillIntBG 83-84*
Backstreet Editions Inc. - Port Jefferson, NY - *BoPubDir 5; LitMag&SmPr 83-84*
Backstretch, The - Detroit, MI - *BaconPubCkMag 84; MagDir 84; WritMar 84*
Backus Data Systems Inc. - San Jose, CA - *DataDirSup 7-83; MicrocomMPl 84; WhoWMicrocom 83*
Backus/SCF Advertising Inc. - Miami, FL - *StaDirAdAg 2-84*
Backwoods Publications - Kettering, OH - *BoPubDir 5*
Bacon, Josephine - Garden Grove, CA - *LitMarPl 84*
Bacon Memorial Library, Asa S. [of American Hospital Association] - Chicago, IL - *EISS 83*
Bacon Printing Co., The - Derby, CT - *MagIndMarPl 82-83*
Bacon Street Press - Newton, MA - *BoPubDir 5*
Bacon Studios, Paul - New York, NY - *LitMarPl 84*
Bacon's Cable TV - Wibaux, MT - *Tel&CabFB 84C*
Bacon's Clipping Bureau - Chicago, IL - *LitMarPl 83, 84; ProGuPRSer 4*
Bacon's Information International Inc. - Chicago, IL - *ProGuPRSer 4*
Bactrianus Enterprises - Asker, Norway - *LitMag&SmPr 83-84*
Bad Axe Huron Daily Tribune [of Lindsay-Schaub Michigan Inc.] - Bad Axe, MI - *NewsDir 84*
Bad Henry Review, The [of 44 Press Inc.] - Brooklyn, NY - *LitMag&SmPr 83-84*
Bader Rutter & Associates - Brookfield, WI - *AdAge 3-28-84; StaDirAdAg 2-84*
Bader Rutter & Associates (Public Relations Group) - Brookfield, WI - *DirPRFirms 83*
Badger Books - San Francisco, CA - *BoPubDir 4, 5*
Badger CATV [of Marcus Communications Inc.] - Bloomer, WI - *BrCabYB 84*
Badger CATV [of Marcus Communications Inc.] - Tomah, WI - *BrCabYB 84*
Badger Enterprise - Badger, MN - *BaconPubCkNews 84; Ed&PubIntYB 82*
Badger Farm Bureau News - Madison, WI - *BaconPubCkMag 84; MagDir 84*
Badger Infosearch - Milwaukee, WI - *FBInfSer 80*
Badger Mountain Cable TV - Umatilla, OR - *BrCabYB 84*
Badger Mountain Cable TV - Benton City, WA - *BrCabYB 84*
Badger Mountain Cable TV - Richland, WA - *Tel&CabFB 84C p.1665*
Badger Mountain Cable TV - West Richland, WA - *BrCabYB 84*
Badger Press - Cross Plains, WI - *BoPubDir 4, 5*
Badger Printing Corp. [Div. of Graphic Communications Center Inc.] - Appleton, WI - *MagIndMarPl 82-83*
Badger State Telephone Co. [Aff. of Telephone & Data Systems Inc.] - Neillsville, WI - *TelDir&BG 83-84*
Badiyan Productions, Fred - Minneapolis, MN - *AvMarPl 83*
Badlands Natural History Association - Interior, SD - *BoPubDir 4, 5*
Baer Inc., Daniel H. - Sherman Oaks, CA - *DirPRFirms 83*
Baerenreiter - *See* European American Music Corp.
Bafetti Communications - San Diego, CA - *DirPRFirms 83*
Bagdad Copper Country Journal - Bagdad, AZ - *BaconPubCkNews 84*
Bagley Farmers Independent - Bagley, MN - *BaconPubCkNews 84*
Bagley Gazette - Bagley, IA - *BaconPubCkNews 84; Ed&PubIntYB 82*
Bagley Public Utilities Commission - Bagley, MN - *BrCabYB 84; Tel&CabFB 84C*
Bagley, Toni - Lakeland, FL - *BoPubDir 4, 5*
Baha'i Publishing Trust - Wilmette, IL - *LitMarPl 83, 84*
Bahakel Communications, Cy N. - Charlotte, NC - *BrCabYB 84; Tel&CabFB 84C p.1665, 84S*
Bahamas International Publishing Co. Ltd. - Nassau, Bahamas - *WritMar 84*
Bahm, Archie J. - Albuquerque, NM - *BoPubDir 4, 5*
Bahn & Co., Marty - North Miami, FL - *AvMarPl 83*
Bahrain Telecommunications Co. - Manama, Bahrain - *TeleSy&SerDir 2-84*
Baier Publishing Co. - Cissna Park, IL - *BaconPubCkNews 84*
Baikar - Watertown, MA - *AyerDirPub 83; Ed&PubIntYB 82*
Baikie, Kenneth - Scottsdale, AZ - *BoPubDir 4, 5*
Bailey & Associates, Gordon - Stone Mountain, GA - *AdAge 3-28-84; StaDirAdAg 2-84*
Bailey & Lucas - Phoenix, AZ - *DirPRFirms 83*
Bailey Associates Inc., Kenneth D. - Tulsa, OK - *IntDirMarRes 83*
Bailey County Journal - Muleshoe, TX - *Ed&PubIntYB 82*
Bailey Films Inc., Doug - Rockville, MD - *AvMarPl 83*
Bailey Lewis & Associates - Lincoln, NE - *AdAge 3-28-84; StaDirAdAg 2-84*
Bailey Printing & Publishing Inc. - Coal City, IL - *BaconPubCkNews 84*
Bailey Productions, Lem [Subs. of Color Stock Library Inc.] - Tampa, FL - *AvMarPl 83*
Bailey, Richard E. [of Lykens TV Co.] - Lykens, PA - *BrCabYB 84 p.D-297; Tel&CabFB 84C p.1665*
Bailey, William - Santa Barbara, CA - *BoPubDir 4, 5*
Baily County Journal - Muleshoe, TX - *AyerDirPub 83*
Bain Associates, Elizabeth - Cos Cob, CT - *CabTVFinDB 83*
Bainbridge Entertainment Co. Inc. - Los Angeles, CA - *BillIntBG 83-84*
Bainbridge Inc. - Edwardsville, IL - *BoPubDir 4 Sup, 5*
Bainbridge Island Review - Bainbridge Island, WA - *BaconPubCkNews 84*
Bainbridge Post-Searchlight - Bainbridge, GA - *AyerDirPub 83; BaconPubCkNews 84; NewsDir 84*
Bainbridge Review - Bainbridge Island, WA - *Ed&PubIntYB 82; NewsDir 84*
Bainbridge Review - Winslow, WA - *AyerDirPub 83*
Bainbridge TV Cable - Bainbridge Island, WA - *BrCabYB 84; Tel&CabFB 84C*
Bainbridge Video Inc. - Afton, NY - *BrCabYB 84*
Bainbridge Video Inc. - Bainbridge, NY - *Tel&CabFB 84C p.1665*
Bair, Lowell - Woodstock, NY - *LitMarPl 83, 84; MagIndMarPl 82-83*
Baird Callahan County Star - Baird, TX - *BaconPubCkNews 84*
Baisch, Blake & Panella Inc. - Cleveland, OH - *StaDirAdAg 2-84*
Baja Books - Woodland Hills, CA - *BoPubDir 4, 5*
Baja Enterprises - Costa Mesa, CA - *LitMag&SmPr 83-84*
Baja Trail Publications Inc. - Huntington Beach, CA - *BoPubDir 4 Sup, 5; LitMag&SmPr 83-84*
Bajus-Jones Film Corp. - Minneapolis, MN - *Tel&CabFB 84C*
BAKCO Data Inc. - Arlington Heights, IL - *DataDirSup 7-83*
Baker, Abbs, Cunningham & Klepinger - Birmingham, MI - *AdAge 3-28-84; BrCabYB 84; StaDirAdAg 2-84*
Baker Advertising, Erle - Chicago, IL - *StaDirAdAg 2-84*
Baker Advertising Inc. - Hatboro, PA - *StaDirAdAg 2-84*
Baker Advertising Inc., R. J. - Troy, MI - *AdAge 3-28-84; StaDirAdAg 2-84*
Baker & Associates Advertising Inc. - Springfield, MO - *StaDirAdAg 2-84*
Baker & Associates Inc., Erwin H. - East Orange, NJ - *MagIndMarPl 82-83*
Baker & Associates Inc., Lee - Milwaukee, WI - *DirPRFirms 83*
Baker & Taylor Co., The [Div. of W. R. Grace & Co.] - Somerville, NJ - *LitMarPl 83, 84*
Baker & Taylor Co., The [Div. of W. R. Grace & Co.] - New York, NY - *LitMarPl 83, 84*
Baker, Bob - Carmichael, CA - *MicrocomMPl 83*
Baker Book House - Grand Rapids, MI - *LitMarPl 83, 84; WritMar 84*
Baker Cable TV - Baker, MT - *BrCabYB 84; Tel&CabFB 84C*
Baker Campbell & Farley - Virginia Beach, VA - *StaDirAdAg 2-84*
Baker Co., Walter H. - Boston, MA - *LitMag&SmPr 83-84*
Baker County Cablevision - Macclenny, FL - *BrCabYB 84*
Baker County Press, The - MacClenny, FL - *AyerDirPub 83; Ed&PubIntYB 82; NewsDir 84*
Baker Enterprises - Atco, NJ - *WhoWMicrocom 83*
Baker Fallon County Times - Baker, MT - *BaconPubCkNews 84*
Baker Films, Fred - New York, NY - *AvMarPl 83*
Baker, Frasier & Tucker Inc. - Buffalo, NY - *StaDirAdAg 2-84*
Baker, Janet H. - Media, PA - *LitMarPl 83, 84; MagIndMarPl 82-83*
Baker Lovick Ltd. - Toronto, ON, Canada - *StaDirAdAg 2-84*
Baker Observer - *See* Louisiana Suburban Press
Baker Observer, The - Baker, LA - *Ed&PubIntYB 82; NewsDir 84*
Baker Productions, Bob - Los Angeles, CA - *AvMarPl 83*
Baker Productions Inc. - Philadelphia, PA - *ArtMar 84*

Baker Publications Inc. - Dallas, TX - *MagIndMarPl 82-83*
Baker Record-Courier - Baker, OR - *BaconPubCkNews 84; Ed&PubIntYB 82; NewsDir 84*
Baker Stations, Vernon H. - Blacksburg, VA - *BrCabYB 84*
Baker Street Productions Ltd. - North Mankato, MN - *LitMarPl 83, 84*
Bakers Digest [of Siebel Publishing Co.] - Chicago, IL - *MagDir 84*
Bakers Digest - Kansas City, MO - *BaconPubCkMag 84*
Bakers Journal - Port Credit, ON, Canada - *BaconPubCkMag 84*
Baker's Mule - *See* Kicking Mule Publishing Inc.
Baker's Play Publishing Co. - Boston, MA - *WritMar 84*
Bakersfield Cable TV Inc. [of Cox Cable Communications Inc.] - Bakersfield, CA - *Tel&CabFB 84C*
Bakersfield Californian - Bakersfield, CA - *BaconPubCkNews 84; Ed&PubIntYB 82; NewsDir 84; VideoDir 82-83*
Bakersfield Lifestyle - Bakersfield, CA - *WritMar 84*
Bakersfield News Observer - Bakersfield, CA - *Ed&PubIntYB 82*
Bakery Production & Marketing [of Gorman Publishing] - Chicago, IL - *BaconPubCkMag 84; MagDir 84; MagIndMarPl 82-83*
Baki Arab Advertising Inc. - New York, NY - *ArtMar 84; DirMarMP 83; StaDirAdAg 2-84*
Baking Industry [of Putman Publishing Co.] - Chicago, IL - *BaconPubCkMag 84; MagDir 84; MagIndMarPl 82-83*
Baking Today [of Maclaren Publishers Ltd.] - Croydon, England - *WritMar 84*
Bakke, Mary Sterling - Lyme, CT - *BoPubDir 4 Sup, 5*
Bakke Press - Durham, NC - *BoPubDir 5*
Bakke Press - Hillsborough, NC - *BoPubDir 4*
Bal & Bal Music Publishing Co. - La Canada, CA - *BillIntBG 83-84*
Bal Corp., William - Elizabeth, NJ - *LitMarPl 83, 84*
Bala Books - New York, NY - *BoPubDir 5*
Bala Productions - Lynbrook, NY - *BoPubDir 4*
BALA Publications [Aff. of Bay Area Lawyers for the Arts] - San Francisco, CA - *BoPubDir 4, 5*
Balaban, H. & E. - Chicago, IL - *Tel&CabFB 84S*
Balaban Stations - Chicago, IL - *BrCabYB 84*
Balamp Publishing - Detroit, MI - *BoPubDir 4, 5*
Balance Beam Press Inc. - Dayton, MN - *LitMag&SmPr 83-84*
Balance of Payments [of International Monetary Fund] - Washington, DC - *DataDirOnSer 84; DirOnDB Spring 84*
Balance Sheet Computer Service, The - Bakersfield, CA - *WhoWMicrocom 83*
Balassanian, Sonia - New York, NY - *BoPubDir 5*
Balaton Russell Press-Tribune-Record - Balaton, MN - *AyerDirPub 83; BaconPubCkNews 84*
Balboa Publishing - San Francisco, CA - *BoPubDir 4, 5*
Balboa Record Co. - Sepulveda, CA - *BillIntBG 83-84*
Balch Springs News - Seagoville, TX - *BaconPubCkNews 84*
Balch Springs Sentinel - Balch Springs, TX - *Ed&PubIntYB 82*
Balcom Books - Ketchikan, AK - *BoPubDir 4, 5*
Balcones Computer Corp. - Austin, TX - *MicrocomMPl 84*
Balcourt Representatives, Ed - New York, NY - *MagIndMarPl 82-83*
Bald Eagle Press [Aff. of Penn State Press] - University Park, PA - *BoPubDir 4, 5*
Bald Knob Banner - Bald Knob, AR - *BaconPubCkNews 84; Ed&PubIntYB 82*
Bald Knob Cable TV [of TCA Cable TV Inc.] - Bald Knob, AR - *BrCabYB 84; Tel&CabFB 84C*
Baldridge, Edwin T. - Coushatta, LA - *BrCabYB 84*
Baldridge, Edwin T. - Many, LA - *Tel&CabFB 84C p.1665*
Baldrige Enterprises Inc., Letitia - New York, NY - *DirPRFirms 83*
Baldur Gazette, The - Baldur, MB, Canada - *Ed&PubIntYB 82*
Baldwin & Partners Ltd., Angus - Toronto, ON, Canada - *StaDirAdAg 2-84*
Baldwin Bulletin - Baldwin, WI - *BaconPubCkNews 84; Ed&PubIntYB 82*
Baldwin Citizen-Beacon - Baldwin, NY - *BaconPubCkNews 84*
Baldwin Citizen, The - Baldwin, NY - *Ed&PubIntYB 82; NewsDir 84*
Baldwin Clearview Cable TV [of Florida Clearview Inc.] - Baldwin, FL - *BrCabYB 84; Tel&CabFB 84C*
Baldwin Courier - Uniondale, NY - *NewsDir 84*
Baldwin Data Service [Subs. of Baldwin United] - Denver, CO - *DataDirOnSer 84*
Baldwin-Gegenheimer [Div. of Baldwin Technology Corp.] - Stamford, CT - *LitMarPl 83, 84*
Baldwin, Grace Loney - Jamaica, NY - *LitMarPl 83, 84*
Baldwin Lake County Star - Baldwin, MI - *BaconPubCkNews 84*
Baldwin, Laura - Hamilton, ON, Canada - *BoPubDir 4 Sup, 5*
Baldwin Literary Services - Baldwin, NY - *LitMarPl 83, 84*
Baldwin Paper Co. [Div. of Unisource Corp.] - New York, NY - *LitMarPl 83, 84; MagIndMarPl 82-83*
Baldwin Park Herald-Press - Baldwin Park, CA - *Ed&PubIntYB 82*
Baldwin Park Highlander - *See* Highlander Publications Inc.
Baldwin Pennysaver - Freeport, NY - *AyerDirPub 83*
Baldwin South Shore Reporter [of Lawrence Bi-County Publishers Inc.] - Lawrence, NY - *NewsDir 84*
Baldwin South Shore Reporter - *See* Richner Publications Inc.
Baldwin, Ted - New York, NY - *TelAl 83, 84*
Baldwin Tele-News - Baldwin, KS - *BaconPubCkNews 84*
Baldwin TeleComm Inc. - Baldwin, WI - *Tel&CabFB 84C*
Baldwin Telephone Exchange - Baldwin, WI - *TelDir&BG 83-84*
Baldwin Times - Bay Minette, AL - *AyerDirPub 83; Ed&PubIntYB 82*
Baldwinsville Messenger [of Baldwinsville Onon-Town Publishing Co. Inc.] - Baldwinsville, NY - *NewsDir 84*
Baldwinsville Messenger - *See* Brown Newspapers Co. Inc.
Baldwinsville Pennysaver - Syracuse, NY - *AyerDirPub 83*
Baldwyn Community Antenna System Inc. [of Heritage Communications Inc.] - Baldwyn, MS - *Tel&CabFB 84C*
Baldwyn News - Baldwyn, MS - *BaconPubCkNews 84; Ed&PubIntYB 82*
Bale Books [Aff. of Bale Publications] - New Orleans, LA - *BoPubDir 4; LitMarPl 83, 84; WritMar 84*
Balfour, Bernice & Leo - Anaheim, CA - *LitMarPl 83, 84*
Balkan Music Co. - Berwyn, IL - *BillIntBG 83-84*
Balkin Agency, The - New York, NY - *LitMarPl 83, 84*
Ball Advertising - West Chicago, IL - *StaDirAdAg 2-84*
Ball & Chain Studios - Cos Cob, CT - *AvMarPl 83*
Ball Communications Inc. - Evansville, IN - *AvMarPl 83*
Ball Computer Products - Boulder, CO - *WhoWMicrocom 83*
Ball Jar Music - *See* Terrace Music Group Inc.
Ball State Daily News [of Ball State University] - Muncie, IN - *NewsDir 84*
Ball State University Forum - Muncie, IN - *LitMag&SmPr 83-84*
Ball-Stick-Bird Publications Inc. - Stony Brook, NY - *LitMarPl 83, 84*
Ballantine Books [Div. of Random House Inc.] - New York, NY - *LitMarPl 83; WritMar 84*
Ballantine/Del Rey/Fawcett Books [Div. of Random House Inc.] - New York, NY - *LitMarPl 84*
Ballard/Advertising Inc., Perry - St. Joseph, MI - *AdAge 3-28-84; DirMarMP 83; StaDirAdAg 2-84*
Ballard Broadcasting Co. - Lampasas, TX - *BrCabYB 84*
Ballard Cannon Inc. - Seattle, WA - *StaDirAdAg 2-84*
Ballard Rural Telephone Cooperative Corp. Inc. - La Center, KY - *TelDir&BG 83-84*
Ballen Booksellers International Inc. - Commack, NY - *LitMarPl 83, 84*
Ballena Press - Los Altos, CA - *BoPubDir 4, 5*
Ballet News [of The Metropolitan Opera Guild Inc.] - New York, NY - *LitMag&SmPr 83-84; MagIndMarPl 82-83; WritMar 84*
Balletmonographs - South San Francisco, CA - *BoPubDir 4, 5*
Balli Books - Toronto, ON, Canada - *LitMarPl 84*
Ballinger Ledger - Ballinger, TX - *BaconPubCkNews 84; Ed&PubIntYB 82*
Ballinger Publishing Co. [Subs. of Harper & Row Publishers Inc.] - Cambridge, MA - *DirMarMP 83; LitMarPl 83, 84; WritMar 84*
Balloon Digest - Santa Barbara, CA - *BoPubDir 4, 5*
Ballot Research Co. - Mamaroneck, NY - *IntDirMarRes 83*
Ballotta Napurano & Co. Inc. - Springfield, NJ - *AdAge 3-28-84; StaDirAdAg 2-84*
Balls & Strikes [of Amateur Softball Association] - Oklahoma City, OK - *ArtMar 84; WritMar 84*
Ballston Journal - Ballston Spa, NY - *AyerDirPub 83; Ed&PubIntYB 82; NewsDir 84*

Ballston Journal - *See* Journal Newspapers
Balmoral Publishing - Oshawa, ON, Canada - *BoPubDir 4 Sup, 5*
Balmorhea Satellite Cablevision - Balmorhea, TX - *Tel&CabFB 84C*
Balmorhea TV Cable Inc. - Alpine, TX - *BrCabYB 84*
Balock, John Jr. - Melstone, MT - *Tel&CabFB 84C p.1665*
Balsam Films Inc., Jerome - New York, NY - *Tel&CabFB 84C*
Balsam Lake Polk County Ledger [of Ledger Publications Inc.] - Balsam Lake, WI - *BaconPubCkNews 84; NewsDir 84*
Baltic Avenue Press - Birmingham, AL - *LitMag&SmPr 83-84*
Baltic Beacon - Baltic, SD - *Ed&PubIntYB 82*
Baltic Beacon [of Dell Rapids Tribune Inc.] - Dell Rapids, SD - *NewsDir 84*
Baltic Beacon - *See* Prairie Publications
Baltic Cooperative Telephone Co. - Baltic, SD - *TelDir&BG 83-84*
Baltimore Afro American - Baltimore, MD - *AyerDirPub 83; BaconPubCkNews 84; NewsDir 84*
Baltimore East Baltimore Guide [of Guide Publications Inc.] - Baltimore, MD - *NewsDir 84*
Baltimore Enterprise - Baltimore, MD - *BaconPubCkNews 84; NewsDir 84*
Baltimore Fairfield Leader - Baltimore, OH - *BaconPubCkNews 84; NewsDir 84*
Baltimore Jewish Times - Baltimore, MD - *NewsDir 84; WritMar 84*
Baltimore Magazine - Baltimore, MD - *BaconPubCkMag 84; MagDir 84; WritMar 84*
Baltimore Museum of Art - Baltimore, MD - *BoPubDir 4, 5*
Baltimore News American [of The Hearst Corp.] - Baltimore, MD - *BaconPubCkNews 84; LitMarPl 83; NewsBur 6; NewsDir 84*
Baltimore NRHS Publications [Aff. of National Railway Historical Society Inc.] - Baltimore, MD - *BoPubDir 4, 5*
Baltimore Purchaser - Baltimore, MD - *MagDir 84*
Baltimore Research Agency Inc. - Baltimore, MD - *IntDirMarRes 83*
Baltimore Sun [of The A. S. Abell Publishing Co.] - Baltimore, MD - *AyerDirPub 83; BaconPubCkNews 84; NewsBur 6; NewsDir 84*
Baltimore Sun, The (Sun Magazine) - Baltimore, MD - *MagIndMarPl 82-83*
Baltimore Sunpapers Stations - *See* Abell Communications Corp.
Baltimore Towson Jeffersonian - Baltimore, MD - *BaconPubCkNews 84*
Baltimore-Warner Paper Co. [Div. of Hammermill Paper Co.] - Baltimore, MD - *LitMarPl 83, 84*
Baltzer Co., Charles - Cincinnati, OH - *StaDirAdAg 2-84*
Balun, Thomas - Centreville, MD - *Tel&CabFB 84C p.1665*
Bam, The California Music Magazine - Oakland, CA - *BaconPubCkMag 84; MagDir 84*
Bamberg Advertizer-Herald - Bamberg, SC - *BaconPubCkNews 84; NewsDir 84*
Bamberger Public Relations, Gabrielle - New York, NY - *DirPRFirms 83*
Bamboo Music - *See* Creative Music Group
BAMCO Group - Staunton, VA - *BrCabYB 84*
Bamundo Qualitative Research, Annette - Brooklyn, NY - *IntDirMarRes 83*
Banana Inc. - Toledo, OH - *MicrocomMPl 84*
Banana Productions - Vancouver, BC, Canada - *BoPubDir 5; LitMag&SmPr 83-84*
Banana Rag [of Banana Productions] - Vancouver, BC, Canada - *LitMag&SmPr 83-84*
Banana Records - Elizabeth, NJ - *BillIntBG 83-84*
Bancall II [of ADP Network Services Inc.] - Ann Arbor, MI - *DataDirOnSer 84*
Bancompare [of ADP Network Services Inc.] - Ann Arbor, MI - *DataDirOnSer 84*
Bancompare [of Cates, Lyons & Co.] - New York, NY - *DBBus 82; DirOnDB Spring 84*
Bancroft & Friends, Carol - Weston, CT - *LitMarPl 83, 84; MagIndMarPl 82-83*
Bancroft Books - Berkeley, CA - *BoPubDir 4, 5*
Bancroft, John C. - Chicago, IL - *BoPubDir 4 Sup, 5*
Bancroft-Parkman Inc. - New York, NY - *CompReadDB 82*
Bancroft Press - San Rafael, CA - *BoPubDir 4 Sup, 5*
Bancroft Register - Bancroft, IA - *AyerDirPub 83; BaconPubCkNews 84; Ed&PubIntYB 82*
Bancroft-Whitney Co. [Aff. of Lawyers Cooperative Publishing Co.] - San Francisco, CA - *BoPubDir 4, 5*
BancShare - Columbus, OH - *DirOnDB Spring 84*
BancTec Inc. - Dallas, TX - *DataDirSup 7-83*
Bandanna Books - Santa Barbara, CA - *BoPubDir 4 Sup; LitMag&SmPr 83-84; LitMarPl 83*
Bandar-Log Music Corp. - New York, NY - *BillIntBG 83-84*
Bandelier Films - Albuquerque, NM - *Tel&CabFB 84C*
Bander & Associates - Sarasota, FL - *IntDirMarRes 83*
Bander Surveys, Mildred - Warwick, RI - *IntDirMarRes 83*
Bandera Bulletin - Bandera, TX - *BaconPubCkNews 84; Ed&PubIntYB 82*
Bandera Enterprises - Studio City, CA - *AvMarPl 83; Tel&CabFB 84C*
Bandon Historical Society Press - Bandon, OR - *BoPubDir 4, 5*
Bandon Western World - Bandon, OR - *BaconPubCkNews 84; Ed&PubIntYB 82*
Bandwagon - Mulvane, KS - *AyerDirPub 83*
Bane Advertising - San Francisco, CA - *StaDirAdAg 2-84*
Banff Community Antenna Ltd. - Banff, AB, Canada - *BrCabYB 84*
Banff Crag & Canyon - Banff, AB, Canada - *Ed&PubIntYB 82*
Bang & Olufsen of America - Mt. Prospect, IL - *BillIntBG 83-84*
Bangladesh National Scientific & Technical Documentation Centre - Dacca, Bangladesh - *EISS 83*
Bangor Advance - Bangor, MI - *BaconPubCkNews 84; Ed&PubIntYB 82; NewsDir 84*
Bangor Daily News [of Bangor Publishing Co.] - Bangor, ME - *BaconPubCkNews 84; Ed&PubIntYB 82; LitMarPl 83, 84; NewsBur 6; NewsDir 84*
Bangs Brown County Gazette - Bangs, TX - *BaconPubCkNews 84*
Banjar Publications Inc. - Minneapolis, MN - *BillIntBG 83-84*
Banjo Newsletter - Greensboro, MD - *MagIndMarPl 82-83*
Bank Administration Institute - Rolling Meadows, IL - *BoPubDir 5; DataDirOnSer 84*
Bank Administration Magazine - Rolling Meadows, IL - *BaconPubCkMag 84*
Bank Analysis Service [of Data Resources Inc.] - Lexington, MA - *DataDirOnSer 84*
Bank Analysis System [of Control Data Corp.] - Greenwich, CT - *DataDirOnSer 84*
Bank Analysis System [of Robinson-Humphrey Co. Inc.] - Atlanta, GA - *DBBus 82*
Bank Branch Data Base - Bala Cynwyd, PA - *DirOnDB Spring 84*
Bank Branch Database [of Chase Econometrics/Interactive Data Corp.] - Waltham, MA - *DataDirOnSer 84*
Bank Director & Stockholder - Orlando, FL - *WritMar 84*
Bank81 - Montreal, PQ, Canada - *DirOnDB Spring 84*
Bank Executives Report - New York, NY - *BaconPubCkMag 84*
Bank for International Settlements [of I. P. Sharp Associates Ltd.] - Toronto, ON, Canada - *DataDirOnSer 84*
Bank for International Settlements - Basel, Switzerland - *DirOnDB Spring 84*
Bank for International Settlements Quarterly [of I. P. Sharp Associates Ltd.] - Toronto, ON, Canada - *DataDirOnSer 84*
Bank Group for Automation in Management - Paris, France - *EISS 83*
Bank Installment Lending Newsletter - New York, NY - *BaconPubCkMag 84*
Bank Marketing [of Bank Marketing Association] - Chicago, IL - *BaconPubCkMag 84; MagDir 84*
Bank Marketing Association - Chicago, IL - *BoPubDir 4, 5*
Bank Marketing Research Inc. - Beverly Hills, CA - *IntDirMarRes 83*
Bank Network News [of Barlo Communications Corp.] - Chicago, IL - *EISS 5-84 Sup; TeleSy&SerDir 2-84*
Bank Network News [of NewsNet Inc.] - Bryn Mawr, PA - *DataDirOnSer 84*
Bank News - Kansas City, MO - *BaconPubCkMag 84; MagDir 84*
Bank Note Reporter [of Krause Publications] - Iola, WI - *WritMar 84*
Bank of America - San Francisco, CA - *ADAPSOMemDir 83-84*

Bank of Canada Weekly Financial Statistics [of I. P. Sharp Associates Ltd.] - Toronto, ON, Canada - *DataDirOnSer 84; DBBus 82; DirOnDB Spring 84*
Bank of England [of ADP Network Services Inc.] - Ann Arbor, MI - *DataDirOnSer 84*
Bank of England - London, England - *DirOnDB Spring 84*
Bank Systems & Equipment [of Gralla Publications] - New York, NY - *BaconPubCkMag 84; MagDir 84; MagIndMarPl 82-83; WritMar 84*
Bank Teller's Report - Cheshire, MA - *BaconPubCkMag 84*
Bankanal System [of Robinson-Humphrey Co. Inc.] - Atlanta, GA - *DirOnDB Spring 84; EISS 83*
Bankdata [of Time Sharing Resources Inc.] - Great Neck, NY - *DataDirOnSer 84*
Banker [of SDC Search Service] - Santa Monica, CA - *DataDirOnSer 84*
Banker [of Bell & Howell Co.] - Wooster, OH - *DirOnDB Spring 84; OnBibDB 3*
Banker & Brisebois Co. - Detroit, MI - *Ed&PubIntYB 82*
Banker & Tradesman [of Warren Publishing Corp.] - Boston, MA - *BaconPubCkMag 84; MagDir 84*
Bankers Box/Records Storage Systems - Itasca, IL - *DirInfWP 82*
Bankers Digest - Dallas, TX - *BaconPubCkMag 84; MagDir 84*
Banker's Information Systems & Services Inc. - Houston, TX - *MicrocomMPl 84*
Bankers Letter of the Law, The - New York, NY - *BaconPubCkMag 84*
Bankers Magazine, The [of Warren, Gorham & Lamont Inc.] - New York, NY - *BaconPubCkMag 84; MagDir 84*
Bankers Monthly - Northbrook, IL - *BaconPubCkMag 84; MagDir 84*
Bankers Press Inc. [Aff. of George Edward Neal Foundation] - Chicago, IL - *BoPubDir 4, 5*
Bankers Publishing Co. - Boston, MA - *LitMarPl 83, 84; WritMar 84*
Bankers Service Co. - Boston, MA - *BoPubDir 4 Sup, 5*
Bankers Trust Co. - New York, NY - *MagIndMarPl 82-83*
Bankers Trust Co. (Corporate Financial Services) - New York, NY - *CabTVFinDB 83*
Banking Law Journal - New York, NY - *BaconPubCkMag 84*
Banking Law Journal, The - Boston, MA - *MagDir 84*
Banking Regulator - Wilmington, DE - *DirOnDB Spring 84*
Banking Regulator [of NewsNet Inc.] - Bryn Mawr, PA - *DataDirOnSer 84*
Banking Systems Inc. - Dallas, TX - *DataDirSup 7-83*
Bankmatic Systems Inc. - Beaverton, OR - *ADAPSOMemDir 83-84*
Bankphone/Telebank [of Payment & Telecommunication Services Corp.] - New York, NY - *TeleSy&SerDir 7-83*
Bankruptcy Law Letter - Boston, MA - *BaconPubCkMag 84*
Banks-Baldwin Law Publishing Co. - Cleveland, OH - *LitMarPl 83, 84*
Banks County News, The - Homer, GA - *Ed&PubIntYB 82*
Bankwire [of Payment & Telecommunication Services Corp.] - New York, NY - *TeleSy&SerDir 7-83*
Banner - San Francisco, CA - *AyerDirPub 83*
Banner - St. Elmo, IL - *AyerDirPub 83*
Banner - Brownstown, IN - *AyerDirPub 83*
Banner - Sebree, KY - *AyerDirPub 83*
Banner [of Evening Post Publishing Co.] - Cambridge, MD - *AyerDirPub 83; Ed&PubIntYB 82; NewsDir 84*
Banner - Brown City, MI - *AyerDirPub 83*
Banner - Hastings, MI - *AyerDirPub 83*
Banner - Belzoni, MS - *AyerDirPub 83*
Banner - Creighton, MO - *AyerDirPub 83*
Banner - Oak Grove, MO - *AyerDirPub 83*
Banner - Warrenton, MO - *AyerDirPub 83*
Banner - Belmont, NC - *AyerDirPub 83*
Banner - Hillsboro, ND - *AyerDirPub 83*
Banner - Duncan, OK - *AyerDirPub 83*
Banner [of Cleveland Newspapers Inc.] - Cleveland, TN - *AyerDirPub 83; Ed&PubIntYB 82; LitMarPl 84*
Banner - McKenzie, TN - *AyerDirPub 83*
Banner - Nashville, TN - *AyerDirPub 83*
Banner - Bennington, VT - *AyerDirPub 83*
Banner - Logan, WV - *AyerDirPub 83*
Banner - Russell, MB, Canada - *AyerDirPub 83*
Banner - Gravenhurst, ON, Canada - *AyerDirPub 83*
Banner - Listowel, ON, Canada - *AyerDirPub 83*
Banner - Orangeville, ON, Canada - *AyerDirPub 83*
Banner & Greif Ltd. - New York, NY - *DirPRFirms 83*
Banner-Argus - Bruning, NE - *Ed&PubIntYB 82*
Banner Associates Inc., Bob - Los Angeles, CA - *TelAl 83, 84; Tel&CabFB 84C*
Banner Cablevision - Brownstown, IN - *Tel&CabFB 84C*
Banner County Outlook, The - Flora, MS - *Ed&PubIntYB 82*
Banner-Democrat - Lake Providence, LA - *AyerDirPub 83; Ed&PubIntYB 82*
Banner-Gazette - Pekin, IN - *AyerDirPub 83*
Banner-Gazette, The - New Albany, IN - *Ed&PubIntYB 82*
Banner-Graphic - Greencastle, IN - *AyerDirPub 83; Ed&PubIntYB 82*
Banner-Herald [of Athens Newspapers Inc.] - Athens, GA - *AyerDirPub 83; NewsDir 84*
Banner-Herald & Daily News [of Athens Newspapers Inc.] - Athens, GA - *AyerDirPub 83; NewsDir 84*
Banner Independent - Booneville, MS - *AyerDirPub 83; Ed&PubIntYB 82*
Banner Journal - Black River Falls, WI - *AyerDirPub 83; Ed&PubIntYB 82*
Banner-Journal, The - Pierz-Royalton, MN - *Ed&PubIntYB 82*
Banner-News - Magnolia, AR - *AyerDirPub 83; Ed&PubIntYB 82*
Banner of Truth - Carlisle, PA - *BoPubDir 4, 5*
Banner Post - Manning, AB, Canada - *Ed&PubIntYB 82*
Banner Press - Chicago, IL - *BoPubDir 4, 5*
Banner-Press - Marble Hill, MO - *AyerDirPub 83*
Banner-Press - David City, NE - *AyerDirPub 83; Ed&PubIntYB 82*
Banner Press - Brenham, TX - *AyerDirPub 83*
Banner Press Inc. - Birmingham, AL - *BoPubDir 4, 5*
Banner-Press, The - Bollinger County, MO - *Ed&PubIntYB 82*
Banner Publishing Co. - Hoosick Falls, NY - *BaconPubCkNews 84*
Banner, The - Gary, IN - *NewsDir 84*
Banner, The - Elkton, VA - *Ed&PubIntYB 82*
Banner, The - Aurora, ON, Canada - *Ed&PubIntYB 82*
Banner, The - Barrie, ON, Canada - *Ed&PubIntYB 82*
Banner-Tribune - Franklin, LA - *AyerDirPub 83*
Banning Co. - Los Angeles, CA - *ArtMar 84; StaDirAdAg 2-84*
Banning Record Gazette - Banning, CA - *BaconPubCkNews 84; NewsDir 84*
Banque [of Questel Inc.] - Washington, DC - *DataDirOnSer 84*
Banque Bibliographique d'Histoire du Quebec et du Canada [of Informatech] - Montreal, PQ, Canada - *DataDirOnSer 84*
Banque de Donnees Locales - Paris, France - *DirOnDB Spring 84*
Banque des Donnees du Sous-Sol Francais - Orleans, France - *DirOnDB Spring 84*
Banque d'Information Industrielle de Pont-a-Mousson [of Centre de Recherches de Pont a Mousson] - Pont-a-Mousson, France - *CompReadDB 82*
Banque d'Information Politique et d'Actualite [of Direction de la Documentation Francaise] - Paris, France - *CompReadDB 82*
Banque d'Urbanisme, de Planification Territoriale et d'Environnement [of Informatech] - Montreal, PQ, Canada - *DataDirOnSer 84*
Banque Gravemitrique Mondiale - Orleans, France - *DirOnDB Spring 84*
Banque Quebecoise d'Information sur l'Environment [of Informatech] - Montreal, PQ, Canada - *DataDirOnSer 84*
Banster Press - Menlo Park, CA - *BoPubDir 4, 5*
Banta Co. [Subs. of George Banta Co. Inc.] - Menasha, WI - *LitMarPl 83, 84; MagIndMarPl 82-83*
Banta Harrisonburg [Subs. of George Banta Co. Inc.] - Harrisonburg, VA - *LitMarPl 83, 84*
Bantam Books Inc. - New York, NY - *ArtMar 84; DirMarMP 83; LitMarPl 83, 84; WritMar 84*
Bantco [of Tele-Communications Inc.] - Brookside, OH - *BrCabYB 84*
Bantey & Associates, Bill - Montreal, PQ, Canada - *DirPRFirms 83*
Banting Publishers - Regina, SK, Canada - *BoPubDir 4, 5*
Banyan Books Inc. - Miami, FL - *LitMarPl 83, 84; WritMar 84*

Banyan International Corp. - Abilene, TX - *DirMarMP 83*
Banyan Tree Books - Berkeley, CA - *BoPubDir 4, 5; LitMag&SmPr 83-84*
Bap$ Software - Houston, TX - *MicrocomMPl 83*
Baptist & Reflector - Brentwood, TN - *MagDir 84*
Baptist Herald - Oakbrook Terrace, IL - *WritMar 84*
Baptist Information Retrieval System [of Southern Baptist Convention Historical Commission] - Nashville, TN - *CompReadDB 82; EISS 83*
Baptist Leader - Valley Forge, PA - *WritMar 84*
Baptist News Service [Aff. of Baptist Missionary Association of America] - Jacksonville, TX - *BoPubDir 5*
Baptist Press - Nashville, TN - *Ed&PubIntYB 82*
Baptist Publishing House [Div. of Southern Baptist Convention] - El Paso, TX - *LitMarPl 84*
Baptist Record, The - Jackson, MS - *MagDir 84*
Baptist Spanish Publishing House [Aff. of Foreign Mission Board of the Southern Baptist Convention] - El Paso, TX - *BoPubDir 4, 5*
Baptist Standard - Dallas, TX - *MagDir 84*
Baptist Union of Western Canada (Christian Studies Div.) - Calgary, AB, Canada - *BoPubDir 4, 5*
BAR - New York, NY - *DirOnDB Spring 84*
Bar-B Broadcasting Inc. - El Campo, TX - *BrCabYB 84*
Bar Code News [of North American Technology] - Peterborough, NH - *BaconPubCkMag 84; MicrocomMPl 84*
Bar Harbor Times - Bar Harbor, ME - *AyerDirPub 83; BaconPubCkNews 84; Ed&PubIntYB 82; NewsDir 84*
Bar None Music - *See* Kenwon Music
Baraboo News-Republic - Baraboo, WI - *BaconPubCkNews 84; NewsDir 84*
Baradat Music - Tulare, CA - *BillIntBG 83-84*
Baraga Telephone Co. - Baraga, MI - *TelDir&BG 83-84*
Baraka Books [Div. of Golden Communications Inc.] - Santa Monica, CA - *LitMarPl 83, 84*
Baranski & Associates Advertising & Public Relations [Div. of Barancorp Holding Co.] - Topeka, KS - *StaDirAdAg 2-84*
Baranski Publishing Corp. - Topeka, KS - *BoPubDir 5*
Baray Music Inc. - Nashville, TN - *BillIntBG 83-84*
Barbara Dolls - Bowie, MD - *BoPubDir 4, 5*
Barbato Features, Joseph - Elmhurst, NY - *LitMarPl 83, 84*
Barbeau Associates Inc. - Barrington, RI - *DirPRFirms 83*
Barber & Drullard Inc. - Buffalo, NY - *TelAl 83, 84*
Barber County Index - Medicine Lodge, KS - *AyerDirPub 83; Ed&PubIntYB 82*
Barber Literary Agency Inc., Virginia - New York, NY - *LitMarPl 83, 84*
Barber, Ray - Brooklyn, NY - *LitMarPl 83, 84; MagIndMarPl 82-83*
Barberton Herald - Barberton, OH - *BaconPubCkNews 84; Ed&PubIntYB 82; NewsDir 84*
Barbetta Miller Inc. - Fairfield, NJ - *StaDirAdAg 2-84*
Barbizon Electric Co. Inc. - New York, NY - *AvMarPl 83*
Barbizon Light of New England Inc. - Woburn, MA - *AvMarPl 83*
Barbo Music - *See* Brunswick Music Publishing Co. Inc.
Barbour Democrat - Philippi, WV - *AyerDirPub 83; Ed&PubIntYB 82*
Barbour, Judy - Bay City, TX - *BoPubDir 5*
Barboursville Cabell County Bulletin - *See* P.C. Publishing Co.
Barbourville Cable TV Inc. [of Tennessee-Kentucky Systems Inc.] - Barbourville, KY - *BrCabYB 84*
Barbourville Mountain Advocate - Barbourville, KY - *BaconPubCkNews 84; Ed&PubIntYB 82; NewsDir 84*
Barbre Productions Inc. [Div. of Combined Communications Corp.] - Denver, CO - *TelAl 83, 84*
Barclay Bridge Supplies Inc. - Port Chester, NY - *BoPubDir 4, 5; MicrocomMPl 83; WhoWMicrocom 83*
Barclay Press [Aff. of Northwest Yearly Meeting of Friends Church] - Newberg, OR - *BoPubDir 4, 5*
Barco, George - *See* Meadville Master Antenna Inc.
Barco, Yolanda - *See* Meadville Master Antenna Inc.
Bard Press [Aff. of New York State Waterways Project] - New York, NY - *BoPubDir 4 Sup, 5*
Bard Software - San Jose, CA - *MicrocomMPl 84*
Barden Cablevision of Inkster Inc. - Inkster, MI - *Tel&CabFB 84C*
Barden Communications Inc. - Inkster, MI - *Tel&CabFB 84C p.1665*
Bardes Products Inc. - Milwaukee, WI - *AvMarPl 83*
Bardic Echoes Brochures - Grand Rapids, MI - *BoPubDir 4, 5*
Barding Publishing, Leroy F. - Ft. Myers, FL - *BoPubDir 4 Sup, 5*
Bardstown Kentucky Standard - Bardstown, KY - *BaconPubCkNews 84*
Bare Feet & Happy People Press, The - Jemez Springs, NM - *LitMag&SmPr 83-84*
Barfield Consulting Inc. - Washington, DC - *DataDirSup 7-83*
Bargain Book - Brownsville, TX - *AyerDirPub 83*
Baric Viewdata [of Baric Computing Services Ltd.] - Feltham, England - *EISS 83*
Barickman Advertising - Denver, CO - *BrCabYB 84*
Barickman Advertising [Div. of Doyle, Dane & Bernbach Advertising Inc.] - Kansas City, MO - *BrCabYB 84; StaDirAdAg 2-84*
Barish Associates Inc., Mort - Princeton, NJ - *AdAge 3-28-84; LitMarPl 83, 84; StaDirAdAg 2-84*
Bark-Back - Glenshaw, PA - *BoPubDir 4, 5*
Barker, Joseph - Phoenix, AZ - *BoPubDir 5*
Barkham Reviews, John - New York, NY - *LitMarPl 83, 84*
Barkin, Herman, Solochek & Paulsen Inc. - Milwaukee, WI - *ArtMar 84; DirPRFirms 83*
Barkley & Evergreen of Kansas City Inc. - Shawnee Mission, KS - *StaDirAdAg 2-84*
Barks Publications Inc. - Chicago, IL - *BoPubDir 4 Sup, 5*
Barksdale Agri-Comm - Memphis, TN - *AvMarPl 83*
Barksdale Foundation - Idyllwild, CA - *BoPubDir 4, 5*
Barkus Co. Inc., Ted - Philadelphia, PA - *AdAge 3-28-84; ArtMar 84; LitMarPl 84; StaDirAdAg 2-84*
Barlenmir House [Aff. of Barry L. S. Mirenburg Communications] - Bronx, NY - *BoPubDir 4 Sup, 5*
Barlenmir House of Graphics [Subs. of Barry L. S. Mirenburg Designers] - New York, NY - *LitMarPl 83, 84*
Barleycorn Books [Aff. of Tom Wiecks & Associates Inc.] - West Linn, OR - *BoPubDir 4, 5*
Barling Cable TV [of Transwestern Video Inc.] - Barling, AR - *BrCabYB 84*
Barlog Software - Kirkwood, MO - *MicrocomMPl 84*
Barlow, George - New York, NY - *HBIndAd&MS 82-83*
Barmaray Corp. - Hoboken, NJ - *LitMarPl 84*
Barmmer Elliott Inc. [Subs. of Hirsch Elliott Inc.] - Westbrook, CT - *DirPRFirms 83*
Barn Hill - Huntingdon Valley, PA - *BoPubDir 4*
Barn Hill - Philadelphia, PA - *BoPubDir 5*
Barn Owl Books - Berkeley, CA - *BoPubDir 4 Sup, 5; LitMag&SmPr 83-84*
Barnaby Records - Los Angeles, CA - *BillIntBG 83-84*
Barnard Enterprises, Slim - Hollywood, CA - *AvMarPl 83; Tel&CabFB 84C*
Barnard, Roberts & Co. Inc. - Baltimore, MD - *LitMarPl 83*
Barnardsville Telephone Co. [Aff. of Telephone & Data Systems/SE] - Barnardsville, NC - *TelDir&BG 83-84*
Barnegat light Press - Barnegat Light, NJ - *BoPubDir 4 Sup, 5*
Barnell Loft Ltd. - Baldwin, NY - *BoPubDir 4, 5*
Barner & Associates Inc. - Tampa, FL - *StaDirAdAg 2-84*
Barnes & Co. Inc. - Scarsdale, NY - *LitMarPl 84*
Barnes & Co. Inc., A. S. [Subs. of Leisure Dynamics Inc.] - San Diego, CA - *LitMarPl 83, 84; WritMar 84*
Barnes & Noble Books [Div. of Harper & Row Publishers Inc.] - New York, NY - *LitMarPl 83, 84; WritMar 84*
Barnes & Noble Books (Imports & Reprints) - Totowa, NJ - *LitMarPl 83, 84*
Barnes Associates Inc. - New York, NY - *DirPRFirms 83*
Barnes, Billy E. - Chapel Hill, NC - *AvMarPl 83; LitMarPl 84*
Barnes, C. Virginia - New York, NY - *BoPubDir 4, 5*
Barnes Chief - *See* Record Publishing Co.
Barnes City Cooperative Telephone Co. Inc. - Barnes City, IA - *TelDir&BG 83-84*
Barnes, Dennis & Associates Inc. - Greensboro, NC - *StaDirAdAg 2-84*
Barnes, Edwin L., Frank S. Jr. & John M. - Rock Hill, SC - *Tel&CabFB 84C p.1665*
Barnes, Kathleen - New York, NY - *LitMarPl 83, 84*
Barnes Newspapers, Ray - *Ed&PubIntYB 82*

Barnes Publishing Inc., John W. Jr. - Scarsdale, NY - *LitMarPl 83*
Barnesboro Star - Barnesboro, PA - *BaconPubCkNews 84; Ed&PubIntYB 82; NewsDir 84*
Barnesville Cable TV Inc. - Barnesville, GA - *BrCabYB 84; Tel&CabFB 84C*
Barnesville Cable TV Inc. - Barnesville, MN - *Tel&CabFB 84C*
Barnesville Enterprise - Barnesville, OH - *BaconPubCkNews 84; Ed&PubIntYB 82; NewsDir 84*
Barnesville Herald Gazette - Barnesville, GA - *BaconPubCkNews 84; Ed&PubIntYB 82*
Barnesville Municipal Telephone Co. - Barnesville, MN - *TelDir&BG 83-84*
Barnesville Record Review - Barnesville, MN - *BaconPubCkNews 84*
Barnett/Raus Advertising Inc. - Long Beach, CA - *StaDirAdAg 2-84*
Barney [of Fred & Barney Press] - Venice, CA - *LitMag&SmPr 83-84*
Barney & Patrick Advertising - Mobile, AL - *AdAge 3-28-84; StaDirAdAg 2-84*
Barney Music - *See* Blanchris Music
Barney Press - Bakersfield, CA - *BoPubDir 4 Sup, 5*
Barnhart & Co. - Denver, CO - *StaDirAdAg 2-84*
Barnhart Dictionary Companion, The - Cold Spring, NY - *LitMag&SmPr 83-84*
Barnhart Inc., Clarence L. - Bronxville, NY - *BoPubDir 4*
Barnhart Inc., Clarence L. - Cold Spring Harbor, NY - *BoPubDir 5*
Barnhouse Co., C. L. - Oskaloosa, IA - *BillIntBG 83-84*
Barnsdall Times - Barnsdall, OK - *AyerDirPub 83; BaconPubCkNews 84; Ed&PubIntYB 82*
Barnstable Books - New York, NY - *BoPubDir 4, 5*
Barnstable Patriot, The - Hyannis, MA - *AyerDirPub 83*
Barnum Communications - New York, NY - *AdAge 3-28-84; StaDirAdAg 2-84*
Barnum Group, The - New York, NY - *StaDirAdAg 2-84*
Barnum/Secunda Associates [Subs. of Barnum Communications] - New York, NY - *DirPRFirms 83*
Barnwell People Sentinel - Barnwell, SC - *BaconPubCkNews 84; NewsDir 84*
Barnwood - Daleville, IN - *LitMag&SmPr 83-84*
Barnwood Music - *See* Merit Music Corp.
Barnwood Press - Daleville, IN - *BoPubDir 4, 5; LitMag&SmPr 83-84*
Barnwood Press Cooperative - Daleville, IN - *ArtMar 84*
Baroid News Bulletin - Houston, TX - *WritMar 84*
Baron Advertising Inc. - Cleveland, OH - *StaDirAdAg 2-84*
Baron Agency Inc., The Leo - New York, NY - *StaDirAdAg 2-84*
Baron & Zaretsky - New York, NY - *AdAge 3-28-84*
Baron/Canning & Co. Inc. - New York, NY - *DirPRFirms 83*
Baron Enterprises Inc. - Los Angeles, CA - *Tel&CabFB 84C*
Baron, Herman - Moylan, PA - *FBInfSer 80; InfIndMarPl 83*
Baron Information Services - Moylan, PA - *EISS 83*
Baron/O'Brien Inc. - New York, NY - *DirPRFirms 83*
Baron Publishing Co. Inc., Richard W. - New York, NY - *LitMarPl 83, 84*
Baron Stage Curtain & Equipment Co. Inc. - Baltimore, MD - *AvMarPl 83*
Barone & Co. - Washington, DC - *BoPubDir 4, 5*
Baron's Microcomputing Reports - New York, NY - *BaconPubCkMag 84*
Barr Films - Pasadena, CA - *ArtMar 84; AvMarPl 83; Tel&CabFB 84C*
Barr Music, James - New York, NY - *AvMarPl 83*
Barre Gazette - Barre, MA - *AyerDirPub 83; BaconPubCkNews 84; Ed&PubIntYB 82*
Barre-Montpelier Times-Argus - Barre, VT - *AyerDirPub 83; NewsDir 84*
Barre Publishing Co. Inc. [Div. of Clarkson N. Potter Inc.] - New York, NY - *LitMarPl 83, 84*
Barren County Progress - Cave City, KY - *AyerDirPub 83; Ed&PubIntYB 82*
Barrett Associates Inc., R. Reece - Baltimore, MD - *ArtMar 84; StaDirAdAg 2-84*
Barrett Book Co. - Stamford, CT - *BoPubDir 4, 5*
Barrett, Gerald W. - New York, NY - *LitMarPl 83, 84*
Barrett's Big Pond TV Cable System - Big Pond, PA - *BrCabYB 84; Tel&CabFB 84C*
Barrhead Anniversary Book Committee [Aff. of Barrhead & District Chamber of Commerce] - Barrhead, AB, Canada - *BoPubDir 4, 5*
Barrie Cable TV/FM [of Trillium Cable Communications Ltd.] - Barrie, ON, Canada - *BrCabYB 84*
Barrington Banner - Barrington, IL - *Ed&PubIntYB 82*
Barrington Banner [of Free Press Inc.] - Cary, IL - *AyerDirPub 83; NewsDir 84*
Barrington Banner - *See* Free Press Inc.
Barrington Countryside Reminder News - *See* Barrington Press Inc.
Barrington Courier-Review [of Barrington Press Inc.] - Barrington, IL - *AyerDirPub 83; Ed&PubIntYB 82; NewsDir 84*
Barrington Courier-Review - *See* Barrington Press Inc.
Barrington Educational Computer Co-Operative - Barrington, IL - *MicrocomMPl 84; MicrocomSwDir 1*
Barrington Hall Press - Greeley, IA - *BoPubDir 5*
Barrington Herald - Barrington, IL - *Ed&PubIntYB 82*
Barrington Herald [of Paddock Publications] - Mundelein, IL - *NewsDir 84*
Barrington Herald - *See* Paddock Publications
Barrington International Corp. - Ann Arbor, MI - *WhoWMicrocom 83*
Barrington Lakes Countryside - *See* Barrington Press Inc.
Barrington Press Inc. - Barrington, IL - *BaconPubCkNews 84*
Barrington Times - Barrington, RI - *Ed&PubIntYB 82*
Barrington Times [of Bristol Phoenix-Times Publishing Co.] - Bristol, RI - *NewsDir 84*
Barrington Times - *See* Phoenix-Times Newspapers
Barrister - Chicago, IL - *BaconPubCkMag 84; WritMar 84*
Barrister Information Systems Corp. - Buffalo, NY - *DirInfWP 82; WhoWMicrocom 83*
BarriTech Ltd. - New York, NY - *MicrocomMPl 84; MicrocomSwDir 1; WhoWMicrocom 83*
Barron! Advertising & Promotion, Mike - Randolph, MA - *StaDirAdAg 2-84*
Barron Cable Co. - Barron, WI - *BrCabYB 84 p.D-297*
Barron Cable Co. Inc. - Chetek, WI - *BrCabYB 84; Tel&CabFB 84C p.1665*
Barron County News Shield [of Bell Press Inc.] - Barron, WI - *AyerDirPub 83; BaconPubCkNews 84; NewsDir 84*
Barron Enterprises - Santa Barbara, CA - *MicrocomMPl 84*
Barron, Hillman & Mellnick - Boston, MA - *AdAge 3-28-84; StaDirAdAg 2-84*
Barron's [of Dow Jones & Co.] - New York, NY - *Folio 83*
Barron's Educational Series Inc. - Woodbury, NY - *LitMarPl 83, 84; WritMar 84*
Barron's National Business & Financial Weekly [of Dow Jones & Co. Inc.] - New York, NY - *BaconPubCkMag 84; LitMarPl 83, 84; MagDir 84; MagIndMarPl 82-83; WritMar 84*
Barron's Weekly - New York, NY - *NewsBur 6*
Barrow Cable TV [of Arctic Slope Regional Corp.] - Barrow, AK - *BrCabYB 84; Tel&CabFB 84C*
Barry Agency, The - Milwaukee, WI - *StaDirAdAg 2-84*
Barry & Associates, Ben - New York, NY - *TelAl 83; Tel&CabFB 84C*
Barry & Associates Inc., Ben - Los Angeles, CA - *TelAl 84*
Barry & Enright Productions - Los Angeles, CA - *TelAl 83, 84*
Barry Cable Management, Jack - Westchester, CA - *BrCabYB 84*
Barry Cable TV, Jack - Los Angeles, CA - *Tel&CabFB 84C p.1665*
Barry Cable TV, Jack - Westchester, CA - *Tel&CabFB 84C*
Barry County Telephone Co. - Delton, MI - *TelDir&BG 83-84*
Barry Pike County News - Barry, IL - *BaconPubCkNews 84*
Barsky & Associates Inc. - Ann Arbor, MI - *StaDirAdAg 2-84*
Barsky Inc., Arnold - Oceanside, NY - *LitMarPl 83, 84*
Barstow Desert Dispatch [of Thomson Newspapers Inc.] - Barstow, CA - *BaconPubCkNews 84; NewsDir 84*
Barstrann Corp. - Dayton, OH - *MicrocomMPl 83, 84*
Bartczak Associates Inc., Gene - North Bellmore, NY - *ArtMar 84; DirPRFirms 83*
Bartel Dental Book Co. Inc. - Brooklyn, NY - *MagIndMarPl 82-83*
Bartel, Lloyd - Lodi, OH - *Tel&CabFB 84C p.1665*
Bartender - Livingston, NJ - *WritMar 84*

Barter Business News [of National Barter Reserve System] - Portland, OR - *NewsDir 84*
Barter Communique [of Full Circle Marketing Corp.] - Sarasota, FL - *ArtMar 84; WritMar 84*
Barter News [of Barter Exchange Credit Corp.] - Portland, OR - *NewsDir 84*
Barter Publishing - Chicago, IL - *BoPubDir 4 Sup, 5; LitMag&SmPr 83-84*
Barter Theatre - Abingdon, VA - *WritMar 84*
Barter Worldwide Inc. - Culver City, CA - *DataDirOnSer 84; EISS 83*
Barth, Diana - New York, NY - *LitMarPl 83, 84; MagIndMarPl 82-83*
Barth, Elizabeth - New York, NY - *LitMarPl 83, 84*
Barth Inc., Frank - New York, NY - *AdAge 3-28-84; DirPRFirms 83; StaDirAdAg 2-84*
Barth, Robert L. - Florence, KY - *LitMag&SmPr 83-84*
Bartholomew Enterprises Inc. - Des Plaines, IL - *AvMarPl 83*
Bartholomew/Uniphoto, Jim - Santa Monica, CA - *AvMarPl 83*
Bartholomew's Cobble - West Hartford, CT - *LitMag&SmPr 83-84*
Bartleby's Software Service Inc. - New York, NY - *MicrocomMPl 84*
Bartlesville Cablevision [of Donrey Media Group Inc.] - Bartlesville, OK - *BrCabYB 84; Tel&CabFB 84C*
Bartlesville Examiner-Enterprise [of Western Publishing Co.] - Bartlesville, OK - *BaconPubCkNews 84; NewsDir 84*
Bartlesville Tri-County News Review - Bartlesville, OK - *BaconPubCkNews 84*
Bartlesville Wednesday American - Bartlesville, OK - *BaconPubCkNews 84*
Bartlett Associates, Scott - New York, NY - *LitMarPl 83, 84*
Bartlett Star - Bartlett, IL - *Ed&PubIntYB 82*
Bartlett Tribune - Bartlett, TX - *Ed&PubIntYB 82*
Bartlett Tribune-Progress - *See* Taylor Newspapers Inc.
Bartlett Wheeler County Independent - *See* Burwell Newspapers
Bartley Music, Jock - *See* Williams Music Group, Don
Barton & Associates Inc., Buzz - Oak Brook, IL - *StaDirAdAg 2-84*
Barton, Duer & Koch Paper Co. - Baltimore, MD - *DirInfWP 82*
Barton Film Co. - Jacksonville, FL - *AvMarPl 83; WritMar 84*
Barton McBride Associates - New York, NY - *DirInfWP 82*
Barton Music Corp. - Los Angeles, CA - *BillIntBG 83-84*
Barton Music Inc., Earl - Springfield, MO - *BillIntBG 83-84*
Barton Press Writers' Co-Operative - Toronto, ON, Canada - *BoPubDir 4 Sup, 5*
Barton TV Cable Co. Inc. - Barton, MD - *BrCabYB 84*
Barton's TV Service - Haysi, VA - *BrCabYB 84*
Bartonville Limestone Independent News - Bartonville, IL - *BaconPubCkNews 84*
Bartonville Limestone Independent News - Peoria, IL - *NewsDir 84*
Bartow Polk County Democrat - Bartow, FL - *BaconPubCkNews 84*
Baruch Retrieval of Automated Information for Negotiations [of City University of New York] - New York, NY - *EISS 83*
Basch Feature Syndicate, Buddy - New York, NY - *Ed&PubIntYB 82*
Basch, Peter - New York, NY - *LitMarPl 83*
Bascom Mutual Telephone Co. - Bascom, OH - *TelDir&BG 83-84*
Bascome Syndicate, The - Shelter Island, NY - *Ed&PubIntYB 82; LitMarPl 84*
Base Brown & Partners Ltd. - Toronto, ON, Canada - *StaDirAdAg 2-84*
Base-Line Systems Corp. - Moorestown, NJ - *EISS 5-84 Sup; InfoS 83-84*
Base Metals Forecast [of Chase Econometrics/Interactive Data Corp.] - Waltham, MA - *DataDirOnSer 84*
Base 2 Inc. - Fullerton, CA - *DirInfWP 82*
Baseball Digest - Evanston, IL - *MagIndMarPl 82-83*
Baseball Facts Co. - Trenton, NJ - *BoPubDir 4 Sup, 5*
Baseball Guidebook - New York, NY - *MagDir 84*
Baseball Music Publishing Co. - *See* Neverland Music Publishing Co.
Basehor Sentinel - Basehor, KS - *BaconPubCkNews 84; Ed&PubIntYB 82*
Basehor Sentinel - Bonner Springs, KS - *AyerDirPub 83*
Basel Information Center for Chemistry - Basel, Switzerland - *EISS 83*
Baseline [of American Telephone & Telegraph Co.] - Bedminster, NJ - *TeleSy&SerDir 2-84*
Basement Workshop Inc. - New York, NY - *LitMag&SmPr 83-84*
BASF Systems Corp. [Subs. of BASF America Corp.] - Bedford, MA - *AvMarPl 83; DataDirSup 7-83; Datamation 6-83; MicrocomMPl 83; WhoWMicrocom 83*
BASF Systems Corp. (Business Products Group) - Bedford, MA - *DirInfWP 82*
Bash Educational Services Inc. - San Leandro, CA - *BoPubDir 4, 5; LitMarPl 84*
Bashaw Star & Alix Promoter, The - Bashaw, AB, Canada - *Ed&PubIntYB 82*
B.A.S.I.C. - Santa Barbara, CA - *Ed&PubIntYB 82*
Basic Books Inc. [Subs. of Harper & Row Publishers Inc.] - New York, NY - *LitMarPl 83, 84; WritMar 84*
Basic Business Control - Grand Rapids, MI - *DirInfWP 82*
Basic Business Solutions Inc. - St. Charles, IL - *MicrocomMPl 83*
Basic-Chess Features - Freeport, NY - *Ed&PubIntYB 82*
Basic Computing - Tacoma, WA - *BaconPubCkMag 84; MicrocomMPl 84*
Basic Education Inc. - Arlington, VA - *AvMarPl 83*
Basic English Revisited - Burlington, WI - *BoPubDir 4, 5*
Basic/Four Corp. [Div. of Management Assistance Inc.] - Tustin, CA - *DirInfWP 82*
Basic Information Systems Inc. - Inglewood, CA - *MicrocomSwDir 1*
Basic Science Press - Palos Verdes Estates, CA - *BoPubDir 4, 5*
Basics & Beyond Inc. - Amawalk, NY - *MicrocomMPl 83, 84; MicrocomSwDir 1; WhoWMicrocom 83*
Basik Computer Inc. - Gaithersburg, MD - *MicrocomMPl 83*
Basil Cable Systems Inc. - New York, NY - *Tel&CabFB 84C p.1665*
Basil Inc. - Oklahoma City, OK - *StaDirAdAg 2-84*
Basile Weekly - Basile, LA - *AyerDirPub 83; BaconPubCkNews 84; Ed&PubIntYB 82*
Basilian Press [Aff. of Basilian Fathers, St. Basil's College] - Toronto, ON, Canada - *BoPubDir 4 Sup, 5*
Basilisk Press - Fredonia, NY - *BoPubDir 4, 5; LitMag&SmPr 83-84*
Basin Publishing Co. - Garden City, NY - *BoPubDir 4, 5*
Basin Republican-Rustler - Basin, WY - *BaconPubCkNews 84*
Basinger Co., The - Evanston, IL - *StaDirAdAg 2-84*
BASIS [of Battelle Memorial Institute] - Columbus, OH - *EISS 83*
Basis Inc. - Scotts Valley, CA - *MicrocomMPl 84*
Basketball Digest - Evanston, IL - *MagIndMarPl 82-83*
Basketball Weekly - Detroit, MI - *MagDir 84; WritMar 84*
Basler & Associates, Victoria - Pasadena, CA - *StaDirAdAg 2-84*
BASS - Palo Alto, CA - *DirOnDB Spring 84*
Bass & Associates, Walter - Cooperstown, NY - *TeleSy&SerDir 7-83*
Bass & Co. Inc. - New York, NY - *DirPRFirms 83; StaDirAdAg 2-84*
Bass Clef Music - Fanwood, NJ - *BillIntBG 83-84*
Bass/Francis Productions - San Francisco, CA - *AvMarPl 83; Tel&CabFB 84C*
Bass/Herb Yager & Associates, Saul - Los Angeles, CA - *AvMarPl 83*
Bassano Times, The - Bassano, AB, Canada - *AyerDirPub 83*
Basser Advertising Inc., Phillip B. - Philadelphia, PA - *StaDirAdAg 2-84*
Basset Co., Russ - Whittier, CA - *DirInfWP 82*
Bassett CableVision [of Rock County Telephone Co.] - Bassett, NE - *Tel&CabFB 84C*
Bassett Rock County Leader - Bassett, NE - *BaconPubCkNews 84*
Bassinnova - New York, NY - *HBIndAd&MS 82-83*
Bassmaster Magazine [of B.A.S.S. Publications] - Montgomery, AL - *Folio 83; MagDir 84; MagIndMarPl 82-83; WritMar 84*
Basso & Associates - Newport Beach, CA - *AdAge 3-28-84; DirPRFirms 83; StaDirAdAg 2-84*
Basso Survey Services Ltd. - Richmond, VA - *IntDirMarRes 83*
Bastrop Advertiser & County News - Bastrop, TX - *BaconPubCkNews 84; Ed&PubIntYB 82*
Bastrop Cable TV [of TCA Cable TV Inc.] - Bastrop, LA - *BrCabYB 84; Tel&CabFB 84C*

Bastrop Cablevision Corp. - Bastrop, TX - *Tel&CabFB 84C*
Bastrop Cablevision Corp. - Bryan, TX - *BrCabYB 84*
Bastrop Clarion - Bastrop, LA - *NewsDir 84*
Bastrop County Times - Smithville, TX - *AyerDirPub 83; Ed&PubIntYB 82*
Bastrop Daily Enterprise - Bastrop, LA - *Ed&PubIntYB 82; NewsDir 84*
Bastrop Enterprise - Bastrop, LA - *BaconPubCkNews 84*
Basys-Business & Administration Systems Ltd. - Borehamwood, England - *MicrocomSwDir 1*
Bat Music - *See* Moody Music, Doug
Batavia Beacon - Batavia, IA - *Ed&PubIntYB 82*
Batavia Beacon - Eldon, IA - *AyerDirPub 83*
Batavia Beacon/Eldon Forum - *See* Quad County Newspapers
Batavia Chronicle - Batavia, IL - *AyerDirPub 83; Ed&PubIntYB 82*
Batavia Chronicle - *See* Chronicle Publishing Co.
Batavia Clermont Courier [of Queen City Suburban Press] - Cincinnati, OH - *NewsDir 84*
Batavia Clermont Sun - Batavia, OH - *BaconPubCkNews 84*
Batavia Daily News [of Batavia Newspapers Corp.] - Batavia, NY - *NewsDir 84*
Batavia News - Batavia, NY - *BaconPubCkNews 84*
Batchelor, Ted - New York, NY - *LitMarPl 83*
Batelle's Columbus Laboratories - Columbus, OH - *DataDirSup 7-83*
Bates Advertising Inc., David Dean - Laguna Beach, CA - *StaDirAdAg 2-84*
Bates Advertising, Ted - New York, NY - *Br 1-23-84; StaDirAdAg 2-84; TelAl 83, 84*
Bates & Associates Inc., Don - New York, NY - *DirPRFirms 83*
Bates & Associates Inc., Keith - Chicago, IL - *AdAge 3-28-84; DirMarMP 83; StaDirAdAg 2-84*
Bates & Co. Inc., Ted - New York, NY - *BrCabYB 84; HomeVid&CabYB 82-83*
Bates & Fawcett - Darien, CT - *AdAge 3-28-84; StaDirAdAg 2-84*
Bates Communications Corp. - New Matamoras, OH - *BrCabYB 84*
Bates Communications Corp. - New Martinsville, WV - *Tel&CabFB 84C p.1666*
Bates County News Headliner - Butler, MO - *AyerDirPub 83; Ed&PubIntYB 82*
Bates, Edward L. - Houston, TX - *WhoWMicrocom 83*
Bates, Marvin L. Sr. - *See* Bates Communications Corp.
Bates Worldwide Inc., Ted - New York, NY - *AdAge 3-28-84, 6-25-84; StaDirAdAg 2-84*
Batesburg Twin-City News - Batesburg, SC - *BaconPubCkNews 84; NewsDir 84*
Batesville Cable TV [of TCA Cable TV Inc.] - Batesville, AR - *BrCabYB 84; Tel&CabFB 84C*
Batesville Cablevision [of Cardinal Communications Inc.] - Batesville, IN - *BrCabYB 84; Tel&CabFB 84C*
Batesville Guard - Batesville, AR - *BaconPubCkNews 84; Ed&PubIntYB 82; NewsDir 84*
Batesville Herald Tribune - Batesville, IN - *BaconPubCkNews 84; NewsDir 84*
Batesville Panolian - Batesville, MS - *BaconPubCkNews 84; NewsDir 84*
Batesville Record - Batesville, AR - *Ed&PubIntYB 82*
Bath & Domestics [of Dogan Publications] - Delray Beach, FL - *BaconPubCkMag 84; MagDir 84*
Bath & Kitchen Marketer - Don Mills, ON, Canada - *BaconPubCkMag 84*
Bath CATV Inc. - Hot Springs, VA - *BrCabYB 84; Tel&CabFB 84C*
Bath County News Outlook - Owingsville, KY - *AyerDirPub 83; Ed&PubIntYB 82*
Bath Home News - Bath, PA - *BaconPubCkNews 84*
Bath Pennysaver - Bath, NY - *AyerDirPub 83*
Bath Steuben Courier-Advocate - Bath, NY - *BaconPubCkNews 84*
Bath Street Press - Ann Arbor, MI - *BoPubDir 4, 5*
Bath Television & Service Corp. - Bath, NY - *BrCabYB 84; Tel&CabFB 84C*
Bath University Library - Bath, England - *CompReadDB 82*
Bathco Cable TV Co. - Salt Lick, KY - *BrCabYB 84*
Batiment - Toronto, ON, Canada - *BaconPubCkMag 84*
Batish Recording Enterprises - Santa Cruz, CA - *BillIntBG 83-84*
Batjac Productions Inc. - Beverly Hills, CA - *Tel&CabFB 84C*
Batkivschyna - Toronto, ON, Canada - *Ed&PubIntYB 82*
Baton Rouge Advocate [of Capital City Press] - Baton Rouge, LA - *LitMarPl 83; NewsDir 84*
Baton Rouge Alexandria Community Leader - Baton Rouge, LA - *NewsDir 84*
Baton Rouge Catholic Commentator [of Diocese of Baton Rouge] - Baton Rouge, LA - *NewsDir 84*
Baton Rouge Community Leader - Baton Rouge, LA - *BaconPubCkNews 84; NewsDir 84*
Baton Rouge Lake Charles Community Leader - Baton Rouge, LA - *NewsDir 84*
Baton Rouge Morning Advocate - Baton Rouge, LA - *BaconPubCkNews 84*
Baton Rouge State Times [of Capital City Press] - Baton Rouge, LA - *BaconPubCkNews 84; LitMarPl 83; NewsDir 84*
Bator & Associates, Robert - Chicopee, MA - *ArtMar 84*
Batsch Co. Inc. - Camp Hill, PA - *LitMarPl 83, 84; MagIndMarPl 82-83*
Batsch Spectracomp - Camp Hill, PA - *DataDirOnSer 84*
Batsford, B. T. - North Pomfret, VT - *LitMarPl 83, 84*
Battalion, The [of Texas A & M Student Publications] - Brazos, TX - *NewsDir 84*
Battelle Columbus Laboratories [Subs. of Battelle Memorial Institute] - Columbus, OH - *DataDirOnSer 84*
Battelle Computer & Information Systems - Vienna, VA - *InfoS 83-84*
Battelle Memorial Institute - Columbus, OH - *DataDirSup 7-83*
Battelle Press - Columbus, OH - *BoPubDir 4, 5*
Batten, Barton, Durstine & Osborn Inc. - Minneapolis, MN - *ArtMar 84*
Batten, Barton, Durstine & Osborn Inc. - New York, NY - *BrCabYB 84*
Batten, Batten, Hudson & Swab Inc. (Creative Media Div.) - Des Moines, IA - *AvMarPl 83*
Batten, Karin - New York, NY - *LitMarPl 83, 84; MagIndMarPl 82-83*
Battenberg, Fillhardt & Wright - San Jose, CA - *AdAge 3-28-84; StaDirAdAg 2-84*
Battenkill NewChannels - Cambridge, NY - *BrCabYB 84*
Battenkill NewChannels - Greenwich, NY - *Tel&CabFB 84C*
Batteries Today - Dana Point, CA - *BaconPubCkMag 84*
Battery Forecast [of Chase Econometrics/Interactive Data Corp.] - Waltham, MA - *DataDirOnSer 84*
Battery Lane Publications - Gaithersburg, MD - *DataDirOnSer 84*
Battery Man, The [of Independent Battery Manufacturers Association Inc.] - Largo, FL - *BaconPubCkMag 84; MagDir 84; WritMar 84*
Battery Press Inc. - Nashville, TN - *BoPubDir 4, 5; LitMag&SmPr 83-84; LitMarPl 84*
Battin, Loris - Rego Park, NY - *LitMarPl 83, 84; MagIndMarPl 82-83*
Battle Creek Enquirer [of Federated Publications Inc.] - Battle Creek, MI - *BaconPubCkNews 84; LitMarPl 84; NewsDir 84*
Battle Creek Enquirer & News - Battle Creek, MI - *LitMarPl 83; NewsBur 6*
Battle Creek Enterprise - Battle Creek, NE - *BaconPubCkNews 84; Ed&PubIntYB 82*
Battle Creek Times - Battle Creek, IA - *BaconPubCkNews 84; Ed&PubIntYB 82*
Battle Ground Reflector - Battle Ground, WA - *BaconPubCkNews 84; NewsDir 84*
Battle Lake Cable TV - Battle Lake, MN - *BrCabYB 84*
Battle Lake Review - Battle Lake, MN - *BaconPubCkNews 84; Ed&PubIntYB 82*
Battle Mountain Cable TV [of Tele-Communications Inc.] - Battle Mountain, NV - *Tel&CabFB 84C*
Battle Publications, Dennis M. - Elyria, OH - *BoPubDir 4, 5*
Battlefield Cable TV - Chickamauga, GA - *BrCabYB 84*
Battlefield Cable TV - Rossville, GA - *Tel&CabFB 84C*
Battleford Telegraph - Battleford, SK, Canada - *AyerDirPub 83; Ed&PubIntYB 82*
Battleford's Advertiser-Post, The - North Battleford, SK, Canada - *Ed&PubIntYB 82*
Battleford's Community Cablevision Co-Op - North Battleford, SK, Canada - *BrCabYB 84*

Battles & Gary L. Hayes/Starlight, Elmer E. - Dudley, MO - *Tel&CabFB 84C*
Battles, Howard K. - Branford, CT - *LitMarPl 83, 84*
Batutis, Edward J. - Cary, NC - *DataDirOnSer 84*
Batz Hodgson Neuwoehner - St. Louis, MO - *AdAge 3-28-84; StaDirAdAg 2-84*
Bauce, Bill - Oakridge, OR - *Tel&CabFB 84C p.1666*
Bauch Design, Jon - New York, NY - *LitMarPl 83, 84; MagIndMarPl 82-83*
Baudette Region - Baudette, MN - *BaconPubCkNews 84; Ed&PubIntYB 82*
Bauer & Co. Inc., Richard - New York, NY - *LitMarPl 83, 84*
Bauer Audio Video Inc. - Dallas, TX - *AvMarPl 83*
Bauerlein Inc. - New Orleans, LA - *AdAge 3-28-84; DirPRFirms 83; StaDirAdAg 2-84; TelAl 83, 84*
Baufo - Stuttgart, West Germany - *DirOnDB Spring 84*
Bauforschungsprojekte [of Informationsverbundzentrum RAUM und BAU der Fraunhofer-Gesselschaft] - Stuttgart, West Germany - *CompReadDB 82*
Baughman Syndicate - Cleveland, OH - *Ed&PubIntYB 82*
Baughman, William C. - Cleveland, OH - *LitMarPl 83, 84*
Bauhan, William L. - Dublin, NH - *LitMag&SmPr 83-84; LitMarPl 83, 84*
Baum Family, Theodore - *See* Helicon Corp.
Baum, Theodore - *See* Helicon Corp.
Bauman Associates, Frances - Marlboro, NJ - *IntDirMarRes 83*
Bauman Bible Telecasts - Arlington, VA - *AvMarPl 83; Tel&CabFB 84C*
Bausch & Lomb - Austin, TX - *MicrocomMPl 83, 84*
Bavarian Agricultural Information System [of Bavarian Ministry for Food, Agriculture, & Forestry] - Munich, West Germany - *EISS 83*
Bawden Printing Inc. - Eldridge, IA - *BoPubDir 4 Sup, 5*
Baxley News-Banner - Baxley, GA - *BaconPubCkNews 84; Ed&PubIntYB 82; NewsDir 84*
Baxter Advertising Inc., Wm. L. - Minneapolis, MN - *AdAge 3-28-84; StaDirAdAg 2-84*
Baxter & Korge Inc. - Houston, TX - *DirMarMP 83*
Baxter Brothers Inc. - Greenwich, CT - *DirMarMP 83*
Baxter Bulletin - Mountain Home, AR - *AyerDirPub 83; Ed&PubIntYB 82*
Baxter, Gurian & Mazzei - Beverly Hills, CA - *AdAge 3-28-84; StaDirAdAg 2-84*
Baxter Publishing Co. - Toronto, ON, Canada - *LitMarPl 83*
Baxter Research Interviewing - Villa Park, IL - *IntDirMarRes 83*
Baxter/Seivert Associates Inc. - Dallas, TX - *StaDirAdAg 2-84*
Baxter Springs Cablevision - Baxter Springs, KS - *Tel&CabFB 84C*
Baxter Springs Citizen - Baxter Springs, KS - *BaconPubCkNews 84; Ed&PubIntYB 82; NewsDir 84*
Bay & Delta Yachtsman [of Recreation Publications] - Alameda, CA - *ArtMar 84; BaconPubCkMag 84; WritMar 84*
Bay Area Arts Services [Aff. of Intersection Arts Center] - San Francisco, CA - *BoPubDir 4, 5*
Bay Area Cable Interconnect - San Jose, CA - *CabTVPrDB 83*
Bay Area Mobile Tape - San Carlos, CA - *Tel&CabFB 84C*
Bay Area Reference Center [of San Francisco Public Library] - San Francisco, CA - *EISS 83*
Bay Area Religious Channel - Menlo Park, CA - *CabTVPrDB 83*
Bay Area Spatial Information System [of Geogroup Corp.] - Berkeley, CA - *EISS 83*
Bay Area Writers Newsletter [of Life Style Publications] - Stanford, CA - *LitMag&SmPr 83-84*
Bay Books Ltd. - Oakland, CA - *BoPubDir 4, 5*
Bay Cable TV Associates - Marion, MA - *BrCabYB 84*
Bay Cablevision [of Athena Cablevision Corp.] - Travis Air Force Base, CA - *BrCabYB 84*
Bay Cablevision Inc. [of Athena Communications Corp.] - Hercules, CA - *Tel&CabFB 84C*
Bay Cablevision Inc. [of Athena Communications Corp.] - Richmond, CA - *Tel&CabFB 84C*
Bay Cablevision Ltd. - Nanoose Bay, BC, Canada - *BrCabYB 84*
Bay City Democrat - Bay City, MI - *BaconPubCkNews 84*
Bay City Democrat & Bay County Press - Bay City, MI - *Ed&PubIntYB 82*
Bay City Public Relations Inc. - San Francisco, CA - *DirPRFirms 83*
Bay City Times [of Booth Newspapers Inc.] - Bay City, MI - *BaconPubCkNews 84; Ed&PubIntYB 82; LitMarPl 83, 84; NewsDir 84*
Bay City Valley Farmer - Bay City, MI - *BaconPubCkNews 84; NewsDir 84*
Bay County Legal News & Democrat - Bay City, MI - *AyerDirPub 83*
Bay Film Associates - San Francisco, CA - *BrCabYB 84*
Bay Indies Mobile Park Properties Inc. - Bay Indies Mobile Park, FL - *BrCabYB 84*
Bay Minette Baldwin Times - Bay Minette, AL - *BaconPubCkNews 84; NewsDir 84*
Bay News [of Courier-Life Inc.] - Brooklyn, NY - *AyerDirPub 83; Ed&PubIntYB 82; NewsDir 84*
Bay News - *See* Courier-Life Inc.
Bay Photo Lab - Soquel, CA - *AvMarPl 83*
Bay Port Press - National City, CA - *LitMarPl 83, 84*
Bay Press - Port Townsend, WA - *BoPubDir 5; LitMag&SmPr 83-84*
Bay Printing Inc. - Baltimore, MD - *MagIndMarPl 82-83*
Bay Publications, Mel - Pacific, MO - *BillIntBG 83-84*
Bay Records - Alameda, CA - *BillIntBG 83-84*
Bay Reporter - Yukon, OK - *AyerDirPub 83*
Bay Reporter, The - Coos Bay, OR - *Ed&PubIntYB 82*
Bay Review, The - Berkeley, CA - *LitMag&SmPr 83-84*
Bay Shore Cable TV Associates - Weymouth, MA - *Tel&CabFB 84C*
Bay Shore Islip Town Bulletin - Bay Shore, NY - *NewsDir 84*
Bay Shore Sun - La Porte, TX - *Ed&PubIntYB 82*
Bay Springs Jasper County News - *See* Buckley Newspapers Inc.
Bay Springs Jasper County News, The - Bay Springs, MS - *NewsDir 84*
Bay Springs Telephone Co. [Aff. of National Telephone of Alabama] - Bay Springs, MS - *TelDir&BG 83-84*
Bay St. George Cablevision - Stephenville, NF, Canada - *BrCabYB 84*
Bay St. Louis Sea Coast Echo [of Bay St. Louis Newspapers Inc.] - Bay St. Louis, MS - *BaconPubCkNews 84; NewsDir 84*
Bay State Banner - Boston, MA - *AyerDirPub 83; BaconPubCkNews 84; Ed&PubIntYB 82; NewsDir 84*
Bay State Business World [of 128 Publishing Co. Inc.] - Norwood, MA - *BaconPubCkMag 84; MagDir 84*
Bay Technical Associates Inc. - Bay St. Louis, MS - *MicrocomMPl 84*
Bay Times [of Chesapeake Publishing Corp.] - Chester, MD - *NewsDir 84*
Bay Times - Easton, MD - *AyerDirPub 83*
Bay Times - Lorain, OH - *NewsDir 84*
Bay Viewer - South Milwaukee, WI - *AyerDirPub 83; NewsDir 84*
Bay Viewer - *See* Quality Newspapers/Suburban Publications
Bay Village Bay Times - *See* Gottschalk Publishing Co., E. J.
Bay Window, The - Newport Beach, CA - *BaconPubCkMag 84*
Bayard News - Bayard, IA - *BaconPubCkNews 84; Ed&PubIntYB 82*
Bayard Publications Inc. - Stamford, CT - *BoPubDir 4, 5*
Bayard Transcript - Bayard, NE - *AyerDirPub 83; BaconPubCkNews 84; Ed&PubIntYB 82*
Bayer AG - Leverkusen, West Germany - *CompReadDB 82; InfIndMarPl 83*
Bayer, Constance Pole - Toronto, ON, Canada - *BoPubDir 4, 5*
Bayer Publications - Neenah, WI - *BoPubDir 4, 5*
Bayfield Cable TV Co. - Bayfield, WI - *BrCabYB 84; Tel&CabFB 84C*
Bayfield County Press - Bayfield, WI - *BaconPubCkNews 84*
Bayfield County Press, The - Bayfield County, WI - *Ed&PubIntYB 82*
Bayland Telephone Inc. - Abrams, WI - *TelDir&BG 83-84*
Bayles, Dal - Milwaukee, WI - *MagIndMarPl 82-83*
Bayless Enterprises Inc. - Seattle, WA - *BoPubDir 4 Sup, 5*
Bayless-Kerr & Palm Inc. - Cleveland, OH - *ArtMar 84; BrCabYB 84*
Baylinson, Adele - New York, NY - *LitMarPl 83, 84*
Baylor County Banner - Seymour, TX - *AyerDirPub 83; Ed&PubIntYB 82; NewsDir 84*
Baylor Lariat, The [of Baylor University] - Waco, TX - *NewsDir 84*

Baylor University (Armstrong Browning Library) - Waco, TX - *BoPubDir 4, 5*
Baylor University Press - Waco, TX - *BoPubDir 4, 5; LitMarPl 84*
Bayonet, The - Columbus, GA - *AyerDirPub 83*
Bayonne Facts - Bayonne, NJ - *Ed&PubIntYB 82; NewsDir 84*
Bayonne Facts - *See* West New Yorker Inc.
Bayou Cable TV - Plaquemine, LA - *Tel&CabFB 84C p.1666*
Bayou Cablevision - Mobile County, AL - *Tel&CabFB 84C*
Bayou Cablevision Corp. - Mobile, AL - *BrCabYB 84*
Bayou La Batre Mobile County News - Bayou La Batre, AL - *BaconPubCkNews 84*
Bayou Times - Valparaiso, FL - *Ed&PubIntYB 82*
Bayshore Associates - Weymouth, MA - *BrCabYB 84*
Bayshore Books - Nokomis, FL - *BoPubDir 4, 5; LitMag&SmPr 83-84*
Bayshore CATV Inc. - Exmore, VA - *BrCabYB 84*
Bayshore CATV Inc. - Onancock, VA - *BrCabYB 84; Tel&CabFB 84C*
Bayshore Independent, The - Hazlet/Matawan, NJ - *Ed&PubIntYB 82*
Bayshore Independent, The [of Monmouth Communications Corp.] - Keyport, NJ - *NewsDir 84*
Bayshore Islip Bulletin - Bayshore, NY - *BaconPubCkNews 84*
Bayshore Sun, The - La Porte, TX - *AyerDirPub 83*
Bayside Advertiser - Great Neck, NY - *AyerDirPub 83*
Bayside Little Neck Glen Oaks Ledger - Bayside, NY - *BaconPubCkNews 84*
Bayside-Oakland Gardens Pennysaver - Jericho, NY - *AyerDirPub 83*
Bayside Pennysaver - Jericho, NY - *AyerDirPub 83*
Bayside Times - Bayside, NY - *BaconPubCkNews 84; Ed&PubIntYB 82*
Bayside Times - Flushing, NY - *AyerDirPub 83; NewsDir 84*
Bayside Tribune [of Flushing Queens Tribune] - Flushing, NY - *NewsDir 84*
Baytown Sun - Baytown, TX - *AyerDirPub 83; BaconPubCkNews 84; Ed&PubIntYB 82; NewsDir 84*
Baywood Publishing Co. Inc. - Farmingdale, NY - *LitMarPl 83, 84; MagIndMarPl 82-83*
Baze Music, Aleph - Sun Valley, CA - *BillIntBG 83-84*
Bazine Cable Co. - Bazine, KS - *Tel&CabFB 84C*
BB & W Advertising - Boise, ID - *ArtMar 84; StaDirAdAg 2-84*
BB Books - Blackburn, England - *LitMag&SmPr 83-84*
BBC - London, England - *TelAl 83*
BBC Ceefax - London, England - *InfIndMarPl 83*
BBC Data [of British Broadcasting Corp.] - London, England - *EISS 83*
BBC Data Enquiry Service - London, England - *InfIndMarPl 83*
BBC Television Enterprises - London, England - *TelAl 84*
BBDM Inc. - Chicago, IL - *AdAge 3-28-84; HBIndAd&MS 82-83; StaDirAdAg 2-84*
BBDO - New York, NY - *Br 1-23-84*
BBDO Chicago Inc. - Chicago, IL - *TelAl 83, 84*
BBDO Direct - New York, NY - *StaDirAdAg 2-84*
BBDO International - New York, NY - *AdAge 3-28-84, 6-25-84; HomeVid&CabYB 82-83; StaDirAdAg 2-84*
BBDO/West - Los Angeles, CA - *ArtMar 84*
BBG & W Advertising & Public Relations Inc. - Kalamazoo, MI - *StaDirAdAg 2-84*
BBI [of Metromedia Inc.] - Boston, MA - *TelAl 83, 84*
BBM Bureau of Measurement - Don Mills, ON, Canada - *BrCabYB 84; DataDirOnSer 84; DirOnDB Spring 84; EISS 83; Tel&CabFB 84C*
BBN Computer Corp. - Cambridge, MA - *DataDirSup 7-83*
BBN Information Management Corp. - Cambridge, MA - *DirInfWP 82*
BBPP Press Books - Missoula, MT - *LitMag&SmPr 83-84*
BBW: Big Beautiful Woman: Fashions for the Large-Size Woman - Woodland Hills, CA - *MagIndMarPl 82-83*
BBW Inc. - San Francisco, CA - *IntDirMarRes 83*
BBW Records - Livingston, NJ - *BillIntBG 83-84*
BC & T News - Washington, DC - *NewsDir 84*
B.C. Business - Vancouver, BC, Canada - *ArtMar 84; BaconPubCkMag 84*
B.C. Cable Co. - Juneau, AK - *Tel&CabFB 84C*
B.C. Cablevision Inc. - Macclenny, FL - *Tel&CabFB 84C*
BC Computer Co. - Summerville, MO - *MicrocomMPl 83*
BC Discovery - Victoria, BC, Canada - *BaconPubCkMag 84*
BC Enterprises of Memphis Inc. - Memphis, TN - *BillIntBG 83-84*
B.C. Hotelman - North Vancouver, BC, Canada - *BaconPubCkMag 84*
B.C. Lumberman Magazine - Vancouver, BC, Canada - *WritMar 84*
B.C. Outdoors - Vancouver, BC, Canada - *BaconPubCkMag 84*
B.C. Professional Engineer, The - Vancouver, BC, Canada - *BaconPubCkMag 84*
BC Records - Brooklyn, NY - *BillIntBG 83-84*
BC Systems Inc. - Lagrange Park, IL - *MicrocomMPl 84*
B.C. Teacher - Vancouver, BC, Canada - *BaconPubCkMag 84*
BCD Associates Inc. - Oklahoma City, OK - *MicrocomMPl 83, 84; WhoWMicrocom 83*
BCD Library & Automation Consultants - Regina, SK, Canada - *EISS 83*
BCI Casting Inc. - New York, NY - *HBIndAd&MS 82-83*
BCI Inc. - McLean, VA - *VideoDir 82-83*
BCI-TV - Boise, ID - *BrCabYB 84*
BCM Publications [Aff. of BCM International Inc.] - Upper Darby, PA - *BoPubDir 4, 5*
BCP Advertising Ltd. - Montreal, PQ, Canada - *StaDirAdAg 2-84*
BCS Network Services Div. [of Boeing Computer Services Co.] - Vienna, VA - *TeleSy&SerDir 7-83*
B.D. Co., The - Erie, PA - *AvMarPl 83*
BD Software - Brighton, MA - *MicrocomMPl 84; WhoWMicrocom 83*
BDA/BBDO - Atlanta, GA - *AdAge 3-28-84; BrCabYB 84*
BDI - Oslo, Norway - *DirOnDB Spring 84*
BDK Advertising Inc. - St. Petersburg, FL - *StaDirAdAg 2-84*
BDM - Paris, France - *DirOnDB Spring 84*
BDP Systems Inc. [Subs. of Burlington Data Processing Inc.] - Burlington, VT - *WhoWMicrocom 83*
BDR Learning Products Inc. [Aff. of Berkeley Development Resources Inc.] - Londontowne, MD - *BoPubDir 5*
BDR Learning Products Inc. [Aff. of Berkeley Development Resources Inc.] - Morris Plains, NJ - *BoPubDir 4*
BDS Computer Corp. - Menlo Park, CA - *DirInfWP 82*
BDS Corp. - Menlo Park, CA - *DataDirSup 7-83*
Be All Books - Sonoma, CA - *BoPubDir 4, 5*
Be Better Families [of Be Center Inc.] - Fairview, NC - *WritMar 84*
Be Free To Live - Dallas, TX - *LitMag&SmPr 83-84*
Beach Golden Valley News - *See* Golden Valley News Publishers
Beach Haven Times - Long Beach Island, NJ - *Ed&PubIntYB 82*
Beach Haven Times [of Manahawkin Times-Beacon Co.] - Manahawkin, NJ - *AyerDirPub 83; NewsDir 84*
Beach Journal - Great Neck, NY - *AyerDirPub 83*
Beach Music Inc., Howard - *See* Sanga Music Inc.
Beach, Ross - Hays, KS - *BrCabYB 84 p.D-297; Tel&CabFB 84C p.1666*
Beach-Schmidt Group - Hays, KS - *BrCabYB 84*
Beacham, Roger - Austin, TX - *BoPubDir 4, 5*
Beachcomber - Beach Haven, NJ - *AyerDirPub 83; NewsDir 84*
Beachcomber Music - *See* Dawn Productions Ltd.
Beaches Leader, The - Jacksonville Beach, FL - *Ed&PubIntYB 82*
Beaches Tribune - Toronto/Beaches, ON, Canada - *Ed&PubIntYB 82*
Beachwood Sun Messenger - Beachwood, OH - *BaconPubCkNews 84*
Beacon - Mobile, AL - *Ed&PubIntYB 82*
Beacon - Mendocino, CA - *AyerDirPub 83*
Beacon - Spirit Lake, IA - *AyerDirPub 83*
Beacon - Cannon Falls, MN - *AyerDirPub 83*
Beacon - Melrose, MN - *AyerDirPub 83*
Beacon - Macon, MS - *AyerDirPub 83*
Beacon - Branson, MO - *AyerDirPub 83*
Beacon - Trenton, NJ - *NewsDir 84*
Beacon - Grants, NM - *AyerDirPub 83*
Beacon - Babylon, NY - *AyerDirPub 83*
Beacon - Hempstead, NY - *AyerDirPub 83; Ed&PubIntYB 82*
Beacon - Cordell, OK - *AyerDirPub 83*
Beacon - Warwick, RI - *AyerDirPub 83*
Beacon - Crowley, TX - *AyerDirPub 83*
Beacon - Palacios, TX - *AyerDirPub 83*

Beacon - Oconto, WI - *AyerDirPub 83*
Beacon Advertising Inc. - New York, NY - *StaDirAdAg 2-84*
Beacon & Alabama Citizen - Mobile, AL - *AyerDirPub 83*
Beacon & Lambertville Record, The - Lambertville, NJ - *Ed&PubIntYB 82*
Beacon & Leader - Branson, MO - *AyerDirPub 83*
Beacon & Wayland News - Winfield, IA - *AyerDirPub 83*
Beacon Broadcasting Inc. - Columbus, GA - *BrCabYB 84*
Beacon Chemical Co. Inc. - Mt. Vernon, NY - *LitMarPl 83, 84*
Beacon Distributing - Whitby, ON, Canada - *BoPubDir 4 Sup, 5*
Beacon Films - Norwood, MA - *AvMarPl 83*
Beacon Free Press [of Wappingers Falls Shopper Inc.] - Beacon, NY - *Ed&PubIntYB 82; NewsDir 84*
Beacon Herald - Stratford, ON, Canada - *AyerDirPub 83; BaconPubCkNews 84; Ed&PubIntYB 82*
Beacon Hill Music - *See* Lillenas Music Inc.
Beacon Hill News - Seattle, WA - *AyerDirPub 83*
Beacon Hill Press of Kansas City [Subs. of Nazarene Publishing House] - Kansas City, MO - *LitMarPl 84*
Beacon House Inc. [Aff. of American Society of Group Psychotherapy & Psychodrama] - Beacon, NY - *BoPubDir 4, 5*
Beacon Journal - Akron, OH - *AyerDirPub 83*
Beacon Light [of Mahopac Putnam County Press] - Mahopac, NY - *AyerDirPub 83; NewsDir 84*
Beacon Light - *See* Gateway Papers
Beacon News - Jupiter, FL - *Ed&PubIntYB 82*
Beacon News - Aurora, IL - *AyerDirPub 83; BaconPubCkNews 84; Ed&PubIntYB 82*
Beacon-News - Marengo, IL - *AyerDirPub 83; Ed&PubIntYB 82*
Beacon-News - Paris, IL - *AyerDirPub 83*
Beacon-News - Sudan, TX - *AyerDirPub 83*
Beacon News, The - New Hope, PA - *AyerDirPub 83*
Beacon-Observer - Overton, NE - *AyerDirPub 83; Ed&PubIntYB 82*
Beacon Press - Boston, MA - *LitMarPl 83, 84; WritMar 84*
Beacon Press Inc. - Richmond, VA - *MagIndMarPl 82-83*
Beacon-Record [of Delaware Valley Publishing Co. Inc.] - Lambertville, NJ - *AyerDirPub 83; NewsDir 84*
Beacon Sun Newspapers - Bolingbrook, IL - *BaconPubCkNews 84*
Beacon, The - Riverside, CA - *AyerDirPub 83; NewsDir 84*
Beacon, The - Windsor, CO - *AyerDirPub 83*
Beacon, The - Manahawkin, NJ - *AyerDirPub 83; Ed&PubIntYB 82; NewsDir 84*
Beacon, The - Merrick, NY - *Ed&PubIntYB 82*
Beacon, The - Uniondale, NY - *Ed&PubIntYB 82*
Beacon, The - Parry Sound, ON, Canada - *AyerDirPub 83*
Beacon Times - Port Elgin, ON, Canada - *AyerDirPub 83; Ed&PubIntYB 82*
Beagle Publishing Co. - Biglerville, PA - *BillIntBG 83-84*
Beallsville Telephone Co. - Beallsville, PA - *TelDir&BG 83-84*
Beals Advertising Agency Inc. - Oklahoma City, OK - *StaDirAdAg 2-84*
Beam Broadcasters Ltd. - Chicago, IL - *Tel&CabFB 84S*
Beam Communications Corp. - Key Biscayne, FL - *BrCabYB 84*
Beam, The [of Air Couriers International Inc.] - Phoenix, AZ - *TeleSy&SerDir 2-84*
Beaman Porter Inc. - Harrison, NY - *MicrocomMPl 83, 84; MicrocomSwDir 1; WhoWMicrocom 83*
Bean Advertising Agency - Indianapolis, IN - *TelAl 83, 84*
Bean & Son Inc., W. R. - Atlanta, GA - *LitMarPl 83, 84; MagIndMarPl 82-83*
Bean Commission Journal, The - Lansing, MI - *BaconPubCkMag 84*
Bean Publishing Ltd., Carolyn - San Francisco, CA - *WritMar 84*
Bean, Tom - Flagstaff, AZ - *LitMarPl 84*
Beanblossom Publishers - Bloomington, IN - *BoPubDir 4, 5*
Beanie Books - St. Louis, MO - *BoPubDir 4, 5*
Beantown Music Ltd. - Boston, MA - *BillIntBG 83-84*
Bear Advertising - Hollywood, CA - *ArtMar 84; StaDirAdAg 2-84*
Bear & Co. - Santa Fe, NM - *LitMarPl 83, 84*
Bear Claw Press - Ann Arbor, MI - *BoPubDir 4*
Bear Claw Press - Flint, MI - *BoPubDir 5*
Bear Claw Press - Hanover, NH - *LitMag&SmPr 83-84*
Bear Computer - Bloomington, IL - *MicrocomMPl 84*
Bear Hug Books - Berkeley, CA - *BoPubDir 4, 5*
Bear Lake Manistee County Pioneer Press - Bear Lake, MI - *BaconPubCkNews 84*
Bear Publications - Cambridge, NY - *BoPubDir 4, 5*
Bear River Cable - Randolph, WY - *Tel&CabFB 84C*
Bear Tracks - *See* Hot Bear Enterprises
Bear Tribe - Spokane, WA - *LitMag&SmPr 83-84*
Bear Tribe Medicine Society - Spokane, WA - *BoPubDir 4, 5*
Bear Wallow Publishing Co. - Union, OR - *BoPubDir 4, 5*
Beardsley Advertising, Charles F. - Narberth, PA - *StaDirAdAg 2-84*
Beardsley, James W. - Acton, MA - *LitMarPl 83, 84*
Beardstown Gazette - Beardstown, IL - *BaconPubCkNews 84*
Beardstown Illinoian Star [of Beardstown Newspapers Inc.] - Beardstown, IL - *BaconPubCkNews 84; NewsDir 84*
Bearly Ltd. - Buffalo, NY - *BoPubDir 5*
Bearsville Records Inc. - Bearsville, NY - *BillIntBG 83-84*
Beasley Broadcast Group - Goldsboro, NC - *BrCabYB 84*
Beasley Cablevision of Eastern Carolina - Surf City, NC - *BrCabYB 84*
Beasley Cablevision of Eastern North Carolina Inc. - Goldsboro, NC - *Tel&CabFB 84C p.1666*
Beasley Cablevision of Eastern North Carolina Inc. - Warsaw, NC - *Tel&CabFB 84C*
Beatlefan [of The Goody Press] - Decatur, GA - *WritMar 84*
Beatniks from Space [of The Neither/Nor Press] - Ann Arbor, MI - *LitMag&SmPr 83-84; WritMar 84*
Beatrice Cable TV [of Rogers UA Cablesystems Inc.] - Marysville, KS - *BrCabYB 84*
Beatrice Cable TV [of Rogers UA Cablesystems Inc.] - Beatrice, NE - *BrCabYB 84; Tel&CabFB 84C*
Beatrice Daily Sun [of Stauffer Communications Inc.] - Beatrice, NE - *Ed&PubIntYB 82; NewsDir 84*
Beatrice Sun - Beatrice, NE - *BaconPubCkNews 84*
Beatty & Church Co. - Toronto, ON, Canada - *BoPubDir 4 Sup, 5*
Beatty Books - Boise, ID - *BoPubDir 4, 5*
Beattyville Enterprise - Beattyville, KY - *AyerDirPub 83*
Beattyville Enterprise - Jackson, KY - *Ed&PubIntYB 82*
Beattyville Enterprise - *See* Intermountain Publishing Co.
Beau-Di Music Inc. - *See* Beau-Jim Music Inc.
Beau Fleuve Series [of Intrepid Press] - Buffalo, NY - *LitMag&SmPr 83-84*
Beau-Jim Music Inc. - Hermitage, TN - *BillIntBG 83-84*
Beau-Jim Records Inc. - Hermitage, TN - *BillIntBG 83-84*
Beau Lac Publishers - Chuluota, FL - *BoPubDir 4, 5; WritMar 84*
Beau Rivage Press - New York, NY - *BoPubDir 4, 5*
Beauce Distribution TV Inc. - Beauceville Est., PQ, Canada - *BrCabYB 84*
Beauce Nouvelle - St. Georges-de-Beauce, PQ, Canada - *Ed&PubIntYB 82*
Beauce Video Ltee. - Beauce, PQ, Canada - *BrCabYB 84*
Beauchemin, Jean - *See* Video St. Laurent Inc.
Beaudoin Syndicate - Tallahassee, FL - *Ed&PubIntYB 82*
Beaufort Book Co. - Beaufort, SC - *BoPubDir 4, 5*
Beaufort Books Inc. - New York, NY - *LitMarPl 83, 84; WritMar 84*
Beaufort Cable TV Inc. [of Tar River Communications Inc.] - Washington, NC - *BrCabYB 84; Tel&CabFB 84C*
Beaufort Gazette - Beaufort, SC - *BaconPubCkNews 84; Ed&PubIntYB 82; NewsDir 84*
Beaumont-Bennett Inc. - New York, NY - *HBIndAd&MS 82-83; LitMarPl 83, 84; StaDirAdAg 2-84*
Beaumont Enterprise [of The Enterprise Co.] - Beaumont, TX - *BaconPubCkNews 84; Ed&PubIntYB 82; LitMarPl 83, 84; NewsDir 84*
Beaumont Enterprise-Journal - Beaumont, TX - *Ed&PubIntYB 82; LitMarPl 83*
Beaumont, Heller & Sperling - Reading, PA - *AdAge 3-28-84; StaDirAdAg 2-84*
Beaumont Journal - Beaumont, TX - *BaconPubCkNews 84; Ed&PubIntYB 82; LitMarPl 83*
Beaumont MDS Co. - New York, NY - *Tel&CabFB 84C*
Beaumont Organization Ltd., The - New York, NY - *IntDirMarRes 83*
Beauregard, Landry, Nantel, Jasmin et Associes Inc. - Montreal, PQ, Canada - *DirPRFirms 83*
Beauregard News - De Ridder, LA - *AyerDirPub 83*

Beautiful America Publishing Co. - Beaverton, OR - *LitMarPl 83, 84*
Beautiful Day Books - College Park, MD - *BoPubDir 4, 5*
Beautiful Day Music - Brookville, NY - *BillIntBG 83-84*
Beauty & Barber Dealer's World - New York, NY - *MagDir 84*
Beauty Culture Digest, The [of Beauty Bureau Co.] - Dallas, TX - *MagDir 84*
Beauty Digest - New York, NY - *MagIndMarPl 82-83*
Beauty Fashion - New York, NY - *BaconPubCkMag 84; MagDir 84; MagIndMarPl 82-83*
Beauty Handbook - New York, NY - *MagDir 84*
Beauty School World - New York, NY - *MagDir 84*
Beauty Trade Magazine - New York, NY - *MagDir 84*
Beaver - Napanee, ON, Canada - *Ed&PubIntYB 82*
Beaver - Oakville, ON, Canada - *AyerDirPub 83*
Beaver Cable TV System - Beaver, OK - *BrCabYB 84; Tel&CabFB 84C*
Beaver City Times-Tribune - Beaver City, NE - *BaconPubCkNews 84*
Beaver County News - Milford, UT - *AyerDirPub 83; Ed&PubIntYB 82*
Beaver County Times - Beaver, PA - *AyerDirPub 83; BaconPubCkNews 84; Ed&PubIntYB 82; NewsDir 84*
Beaver Creek Telephone Co. - Beaver Creek, OR - *TelDir&BG 83-84*
Beaver Dam Daily Citizen - Beaver Dam, WI - *NewsDir 84*
Beaver Dam Ohio County Messenger - Beaver Dam, KY - *BaconPubCkNews 84; NewsDir 84*
Beaver Herald-Democrat - Beaver, OK - *BaconPubCkNews 84; Ed&PubIntYB 82*
Beaver Kosmos - Vancouver, BC, Canada - *BoPubDir 4, 5*
Beaver Lake Cable TV Co. Inc. - Beaver Lake, OK - *Tel&CabFB 84C*
Beaver Lake Cable TV Inc. - Beaver Shores, AR - *Tel&CabFB 84C*
Beaver Lodge Press - Vancouver, BC, Canada - *LitMag&SmPr 83-84*
Beaver Music Publishing Corp. - *See* Webman & Co., H. B.
Beaver Press - Beaver, UT - *BaconPubCkNews 84; Ed&PubIntYB 82*
Beaver Springs Mutual TV Association - Beaver Springs, PA - *BrCabYB 84; Tel&CabFB 84C*
Beaver Valley Cable TV - Beaver Valley, NY - *BrCabYB 84*
Beaver Valley Cable TV Co. - Raccoon Township, PA - *Tel&CabFB 84C*
Beaverbrook Art Gallery - Fredericton, NB, Canada - *BoPubDir 4 Sup, 5*
Beavercreek Computer Systems - Dayton, OH - *WhoWMicrocom 83*
Beavercreek Daily News - Beavercreek, OH - *BaconPubCkNews 84*
Beavercreek Daily News - Dayton, OH - *AyerDirPub 83; Ed&PubIntYB 82; NewsDir 84*
Beavers - Laporte, MN - *BoPubDir 4, 5*
Beaverton Valley Times - Beaverton, OR - *BaconPubCkNews 84*
Beaverton Valley Times, The [of Guard Publishing Co.] - Portland, OR - *NewsDir 84*
Bebell Inc. (Motion Picture Lab Div.) - New York, NY - *Tel&CabFB 84C*
Bebell Inc. (Slide & Filmstrip Lab Div.) - New York, NY - *Tel&CabFB 84C*
Beber, Silverstein & Partners Advertising Inc. - Miami, FL - *AdAge 3-28-84; StaDirAdAg 2-84*
Bebidas [of All Americas Publishers Service Inc.] - Chicago, IL - *MagDir 84*
Bebidas - Winnetka, IL - *BaconPubCkMag 84*
Bece Cable Inc. - Sumiton, AL - *BrCabYB 84*
Bece Cable Inc. - Tuskegee, AL - *Tel&CabFB 84C p.1666*
Bechtos International Inc., Ramona - New York, NY - *HBIndAd&MS 82-83*
Beck Engraving Co., The - Philadelphia, PA - *LitMarPl 83, 84*
Beck, Ernest W. - Lake Forest, IL - *LitMarPl 83*
Beck Films Inc., Alexander - New York, NY - *TelAl 83, 84; Tel&CabFB 84C*
Beck Inc., Thomas - Sausalito, CA - *ADAPSOMemDir 83-84*
Beck Public Relations, Roger - Sherman Oaks, CA - *DirPRFirms 83*
Beck-Ross Communications Inc. - Rockville Centre, NY - *BrCabYB 84*
Beckenhorst Press Inc. - Columbus, OH - *BillIntBG 83-84*
Becker Advertising Agency Inc., Fred R. - Louisville, KY - *StaDirAdAg 2-84*
Becker & Hayes Inc. - Santa Monica, CA - *EISS 83; InfIndMarPl 83*
Becker, Beverly - Park Ridge, IL - *BoPubDir 4, 5*
Becker Broadcasting - El Paso, TX - *Tel&CabFB 84C*
Becker County Record - Detroit Lakes, MN - *AyerDirPub 83*
Becker Electronics - Chapel Hill, NC - *MicrocomMPl 84*
Becker Inc., Robert A. - New York, NY - *AdAge 3-28-84; StaDirAdAg 2-84*
Becker, Maximilian - New York, NY - *LitMarPl 83, 84*
Becker Research Corp. - Boston, MA - *IntDirMarRes 83*
Becker, W. - *See* Northern Cablevision Ltd.
Beckerman Animation Inc., Howard - New York, NY - *AvMarPl 83*
Beckerman Group Inc., The - Bernardsville, NJ - *StaDirAdAg 2-84*
BECKET - New York, NY - *IntDirMarRes 83*
Becket Records - New York, NY - *BillIntBG 83-84*
Beckett Paper Co., The [Div. of Hammermill Paper Co.] - Hamilton, OH - *LitMarPl 83, 84*
Beckham County Democrat - Erick, OK - *AyerDirPub 83; Ed&PubIntYB 82*
Beckie Publishing Co. - Memphis, TN - *BillIntBG 83-84*
Beckley Post-Herald [of Clay Communications Inc.] - Beckley, WV - *BaconPubCkNews 84; Ed&PubIntYB 82; NewsDir 84*
Beckley Post-Herald Raleigh Register - Beckley, WV - *Ed&PubIntYB 82*
Beckley TeleCable [of TeleCable Corp.] - Beckley, WV - *BrCabYB 84; Tel&CabFB 84C*
Beckman & Associates, Tom - Cincinnati, OH - *BoPubDir 4, 5*
Beckman Associates Advertising Agency Inc. - Albany, NY - *StaDirAdAg 2-84*
Becktold Co. - St. Louis, MO - *LitMarPl 83, 84*
Beckwith, Burnham P. - Palo Alto, CA - *BoPubDir 4 Sup, 5*
Bed & Breakfast West Coast - Carpinteria, CA - *BoPubDir 4 Sup, 5*
Bedacom Co. Inc., The - Santa Clara, CA - *InterCabHB 3*
Bedding [of National Association of Bedding Manufacturers] - Arlington, VA - *BaconPubCkMag 84; MagDir 84*
Bedding Plants Inc. - Okemos, MI - *BoPubDir 5*
Bedell Inc. - Ft. Smith, AR - *AdAge 3-28-84; StaDirAdAg 2-84*
Bedford Books [Aff. of St. Martin's Press Inc.] - Boston, MA - *BoPubDir 4 Sup, 5*
Bedford Bulletin-Democrat - Bedford, VA - *BaconPubCkNews 84; NewsDir 84*
Bedford Cable TV [of Buford Television Inc.] - Bedford, IN - *BrCabYB 84*
Bedford Cablevision Co. [of DoKel Communications Corp.] - Bedford, VA - *BrCabYB 84; Tel&CabFB 84C*
Bedford Cablevision Inc. [of Maclean Hunter Cable TV Ltd.] - Bedford Township, MI - *BrCabYB 84; Tel&CabFB 84C*
Bedford Computer Systems Inc. - Bedford, MA - *DirInfWP 82*
Bedford County Press - Everett, PA - *AyerDirPub 83; Ed&PubIntYB 82*
Bedford County Shopper's Guide - Everett, PA - *AyerDirPub 83*
Bedford Daily Gazette - Bedford, PA - *Ed&PubIntYB 82*
Bedford Gazette - Bedford, PA - *BaconPubCkNews 84; NewsDir 84*
Bedford Group Inc., The - Bedford, NY - *DirMarMP 83*
Bedford Heights Cleveland Metro - Bedford Heights, OH - *BaconPubCkNews 84*
Bedford Improved TV Inc. - Bedford, PA - *BrCabYB 84; Tel&CabFB 84C*
Bedford Inquirer - Bedford, PA - *BaconPubCkNews 84; Ed&PubIntYB 82*
Bedford Minute-Man - Acton, MA - *AyerDirPub 83*
Bedford Minute-Man - Bedford, MA - *Ed&PubIntYB 82*
Bedford Minute-Man [of Minute-Man Publications Inc.] - Lexington, MA - *NewsDir 84*
Bedford Minute Man - *See* Minute-Man Publications Inc.
Bedford Sun Banner - Bedford, OH - *Ed&PubIntYB 82*

Bedford Sun Banner - *See* Sun Newspapers
Bedford Times Mail [of Schurz Communications Inc.] - Bedford, IN - *BaconPubCkNews 84; NewsDir 84*
Bedford Times-Press - Bedford, IA - *BaconPubCkNews 84; Ed&PubIntYB 82*
Bedford Times-Register - Bedford, OH - *Ed&PubIntYB 82*
Bedford Times-Register [of Cuyahoga Falls News] - Cuyahoga Falls, OH - *NewsDir 84*
Bedford Times-Register - *See* Record Publishing Co.
Bedford Trimble-Banner Democrat - Bedford, KY - *BaconPubCkNews 84*
Bedfordshire Magazine [of White Crescent Press] - Luton, England - *LitMag&SmPr 83-84*
Bedick, Barbara - Brooklyn, NY - *LitMarPl 84*
Bedous Press - Beaverton, OR - *BoPubDir 4, 5*
Bedpress Books [Aff. of New Bedford Press] - Los Angeles, CA - *BoPubDir 4, 5*
Bedrick Books Inc., Peter - New York, NY - *LitMarPl 84*
Bedrosian & Associates - Alpine, NJ - *HBIndAd&MS 82-83*
Bee - De Queen, AR - *AyerDirPub 83*
Bee - Fresno, CA - *AyerDirPub 83*
Bee - Sacramento, CA - *AyerDirPub 83*
Bee - Soledad, CA - *AyerDirPub 83*
Bee - Sandpoint, ID - *Ed&PubIntYB 82*
Bee - Jefferson, IA - *AyerDirPub 83*
Bee - Ossian, IA - *AyerDirPub 83*
Bee - Ripley, OH - *AyerDirPub 83*
Bee - Silsbee, TX - *AyerDirPub 83*
Bee - Danville, VA - *AyerDirPub 83; Ed&PubIntYB 82; NewsDir 84*
Bee & Herald Publishing Co. - Jefferson, IA - *BaconPubCkNews 84*
Bee Cool Music Co. - *See* Jamie Music Publishing Co.
Bee Hive Jazz Records - Evanston, IL - *BillIntBG 83-84*
Bee Jay Recording Studios - Orlando, FL - *AvMarPl 83; BillIntBG 83-84*
Bee-Journal - Canastota, NY - *AyerDirPub 83*
Bee Line - Beeville, TX - *AyerDirPub 83*
Bee Line Inc. - Houlton, ME - *BrCabYB 84 p.D-297; Tel&CabFB 84C p.1666*
Bee Line Inc. - Millinocket, ME - *BrCabYB 84*
Bee Line Inc. - Skowhegan, ME - *BrCabYB 84; Tel&CabFB 84C*
Bee/Mor Music - Los Angeles, CA - *BillIntBG 83-84*
Bee Music, Clauda - *See* Anode Music Publishing
Bee-Picayune - Beeville, TX - *AyerDirPub 83*
Bee Productions, Tom - Albuquerque, NM - *BillIntBG 83-84*
Bee Publications Inc. - Williamsville, NY - *BaconPubCkNews 84*
Bee-Ray Music - Hollywood, CA - *BillIntBG 83-84*
Bee Specialist, The - Las Cruces, NM - *LitMag&SmPr 83-84*
Bee, The - Hutchinson, KS - *AyerDirPub 83*
Bee, The - Portland, OR - *Ed&PubIntYB 82*
Bee, The - Phillips, WI - *AyerDirPub 83; Ed&PubIntYB 82*
Bee Two - *See* Kaye Publications, Richard
Beebe News - Beebe, AR - *BaconPubCkNews 84; Ed&PubIntYB 82*
Beebug - St. Albans, England - *MicrocomSwDir 1*
Beech Cable Co. - Beech Bottom, WV - *BrCabYB 84; Tel&CabFB 84C*
Beech Creek TV Cable System - Beech Creek, PA - *Tel&CabFB 84C*
Beech Creek TV Cable System - Blanchard, PA - *BrCabYB 84*
Beech Grove Perry Weekly - Beech Grove, IN - *BaconPubCkNews 84; NewsDir 84*
Beech Hill Publishing - Mt. Desert, ME - *BoPubDir 4, 5; LitMarPl 84*
Beech Leaf Press [Aff. of Kalamazoo Nature Center Inc.] - Kalamazoo, MI - *BoPubDir 4, 5*
Beech Tree Communications - Port Washington, NY - *DirPRFirms 83*
Beecher City Journal - Beecher, IL - *Ed&PubIntYB 82*
Beecher Herald - Beecher, IL - *Ed&PubIntYB 82*
Beecher Herald - *See* Russell Publications
Beecher Peck & Lewis - Detroit, MI - *MagIndMarPl 82-83*
Beechmont Music Publishing Corp. - *See* Webman & Co., H. B.
Beechwold/Clintonville News - Beechwold/Clintonville, OH - *Ed&PubIntYB 82*
Beechwold/Clintonville News - *See* Suburban News Publications
Beechwood Music Corp. - Hollywood, CA - *BillIntBG 83-84*
Beechwood Software Inc. - Rochester, NY - *MicrocomMPl 83, 84; MicrocomSwDir 1; WhoWMicrocom 83*
Beef [of The Webb Co.] - St. Paul, MN - *BaconPubCkMag 84; MagDir 84; MagIndMarPl 82-83; WritMar 84*
Beef Digest - Columbia, MO - *BaconPubCkMag 84*
Beef Empire Stations - Norfolk, NE - *BrCabYB 84*
Beef Improvement News - Ames, IA - *MagDir 84*
Beef Progress - Manhattan, KS - *BaconPubCkMag 84; MagIndMarPl 82-83*
Beefweek - Macon, GA - *BaconPubCkMag 84*
Beehive International - Salt Lake City, UT - *DataDirSup 7-83; InfIndMarPl 83*
Beehive Telephone Co. Inc. - Salt Lake City, UT - *TelDir&BG 83-84*
Beekman Hill Press - New York, NY - *LitMag&SmPr 83-84*
Beekman Paper Co. Inc. - New York, NY - *LitMarPl 83, 84*
Beekman Publishers Inc. - Woodstock, NY - *LitMag&SmPr 83-84; LitMarPl 83, 84*
Beel, Marianne - Valentine, NE - *MagIndMarPl 82-83*
Beeler & Davis - Ottumwa, IA - *Tel&CabFB 84C*
Beeline Cable TV - Bayamon, PR - *Tel&CabFB 84C*
Beer - Anaheim, CA - *BaconPubCkMag 84*
Beer Wholesaler [of Dogan Enterprises Inc.] - Delray Beach, FL - *BaconPubCkMag 84; MagDir 84; WritMar 84*
Beethoven Music Co. - *See* Harrison Music Corp.
Beeton-Schomberg Record-Sentinel - Beeton, ON, Canada - *AyerDirPub 83; Ed&PubIntYB 82*
Beeville Bee-Picayune - Beeville, TX - *Ed&PubIntYB 82; NewsDir 84*
Beeville Bee-Picayune - *See* Beeville Publishing Co. Inc.
Beeville Beeline - *See* Beeville Publishing Co. Inc.
Beeville Cable TV Service Inc. [of Communications Services Inc.] - Beeville, TX - *BrCabYB 84; Tel&CabFB 84C*
Beeville Publishing Co. Inc. - Beeville, TX - *BaconPubCkNews 84*
Before Columbus Foundation - Berkeley, CA - *BoPubDir 4 Sup, 5; LitMarPl 83, 84*
Before the Rapture - Chicago, IL - *LitMag&SmPr 83-84*
Beggs Outlook - Beggs, OK - *Ed&PubIntYB 82*
Beggs Telephone Co. - Beggs, OK - *TelDir&BG 83-84*
Beginner Books [Div. of Random House Inc.] - New York, NY - *LitMarPl 83, 84*
Beginning Readers' Program [of Grolier Enterprises Inc.] - Danbury, CT - *LitMarPl 83, 84*
Beginnings: The Magazine for Writers in the Community [of Human Potential Press] - Iowa City, IA - *LitMag&SmPr 83-84*
Behan Broadcasting - Tucson, AZ - *BrCabYB 84*
Behar Advertising, Albert - Westport, CT - *StaDirAdAg 2-84*
Behavior Today - New York, NY - *DirOnDB Spring 84*
Behavior Today [of NewsNet Inc.] - Bryn Mawr, PA - *DataDirOnSer 84*
Behavioral Analysis Inc. - Irvington, NY - *IntDirMarRes 83*
Behavioral & Brain Sciences, The - New York, NY - *MagDir 84*
Behavioral Books Institute [of Prentice-Hall Inc.] - Englewood, NJ - *LitMarPl 83, 84*
Behavioral Controls [Div. of ALPS Inc.] - Milwaukee, WI - *AvMarPl 83*
Behavioral Medicine - New York, NY - *MagDir 84; MagIndMarPl 82-83*
Behavioral Publishing Co. [Aff. of Behavioral Therapy Institute] - Altadena, CA - *BoPubDir 4*
Behavioral Publishing Co. [Aff. of Behavioral Therapy Institute] - Pasadena, CA - *BoPubDir 5*
Behavioral Research Council [Aff. of American Institute for Economic Research] - Great Barrington, MA - *BoPubDir 4, 5*
Behavioral Science Book Service [of Macmillan Book Clubs Inc.] - New York, NY - *LitMarPl 83, 84*
Behavioral Science Research - Coral Gables, FL - *IntDirMarRes 83*
Behavioral Science Research Div. [of Tuskegee Institute] - Tuskegee Institute, AL - *EISS 83*
Behaviorial Neuropsychiatry - New York, NY - *MagDir 84*
Behaviorscan [of Information Resources Inc.] - Chicago, IL - *EISS 83*
Behavioural Engineering - Scotts Valley, CA - *MicrocomSwDir 1*
Behlman Engineering Corp. - Carpinteria, CA - *DirInfWP 82*

Behrends & Co. - High Point, NC - *AdAge 3-28-84; BrCabYB 84; StaDirAdAg 2-84; TelAl 83, 84*
Behrens Co. Inc., The - Miami, FL - *TelAl 83, 84; Tel&CabFB 84C*
Behrman House Inc. - New York, NY - *LitMarPl 83, 84*
Beil, Frederic C. - New York, NY - *BoPubDir 5*
Beilstein Institute for Literature in Organic Chemistry - Frankfurt, East Germany - *EISS 83*
Beinfeld Publishing Inc. - North Hollywood, CA - *BoPubDir 4, 5*
Being Books Inc. - Northridge, CA - *BoPubDir 4, 5*
Being Publications - Grand Rapids, MI - *BoPubDir 4 Sup, 5*
Beinner Associates Inc., Michael D. - New York, NY - *DirPRFirms 83; LitMarPl 83, 84*
Beitzell, Edwin W. - Abell, MD - *BoPubDir 4, 5*
Bejan & Co. Inc. - New York, NY - *DirPRFirms 83*
BEK Telephone Mutual Aid Corp. - Steele, ND - *TelDir&BG 83-84*
Bel-Park Leader [of Leader Papers Inc.] - Chicago, IL - *AyerDirPub 83; NewsDir 84*
Bel Park Leader - *See* Leader Papers Inc.
Belaieff Editors - *See* Peters Corp., C. F.
Belair Aegis - Belair, MD - *BaconPubCkNews 84*
Belair Road Booster - Baltimore, MD - *AyerDirPub 83*
Belcher Advertising Associates Inc. - Springfield, MA - *StaDirAdAg 2-84*
Belchertown Sentinel [of Palmer Pioneer Enterprises Inc.] - Palmer, MA - *NewsDir 84*
Belchertown Sentinel, The - Belchertown, MA - *Ed&PubIntYB 82*
Belden & Frenz & Lehman Inc. - Westlake, OH - *StaDirAdAg 2-84*
Belden Associates - Dallas, TX - *IntDirMarRes 83*
Belden Communications Inc. - New York, NY - *AvMarPl 83*
Belden Electronics [Div. of Cooper Industries] - Geneva, IL - *DataDirSup 7-83*
Belen Cablevision Inc. - Belen, NM - *BrCabYB 84; Tel&CabFB 84C*
Belen News-Bulletin - Belen, NM - *Ed&PubIntYB 82*
Belen Valencia County News-Bulletin - Belen, NM - *NewsDir 84*
Belew Sound & Visual Inc. - Bristol, TN - *AvMarPl 83*
Belfaire Products - Darien, CT - *AdAge 3-28-84; StaDirAdAg 2-84*
Belfast Music - *See* Duce Music
Belfast Progressive Advertising Ltd. - *See* Royds Advertising Group Ltd., The
Belfast Republican Journal [of Norumlega Publishing Co.] - Belfast, ME - *BaconPubCkNews 84; NewsDir 84*
Belgian American Chamber of Commerce in the U.S. Inc. - New York, NY - *BoPubDir 5*
Belgian Archives for the Social Sciences [of Catholic University of Louvain] - Louvain-la-Neuve, Belgium - *EISS 83*
Belgian Information & Dissemination Service [of Ministry of Economic Affairs] - Brussels, Belgium - *EISS 83; InfIndMarPl 83*
Belgian Online User Group [of Association Belge de Documentation/Belgische Vereniging voor Documentatie] - Brussels, Belgium - *InfIndMarPl 83*
Belgrade Observer - Belgrade, MN - *BaconPubCkNews 84*
Belhaven Cable TV [of MultiChannel Communications Inc.] - Belhaven, NC - *Tel&CabFB 84C*
Belier Press Inc. - New York, NY - *BoPubDir 4, 5*
Believers Bookshelf Inc. - Sunbury, PA - *BoPubDir 4 Sup, 5*
Belington TV Cable Co. - Belington, WV - *BrCabYB 84; Tel&CabFB 84C*
Belisle Enterprise - Bruceton Mills, WV - *BrCabYB 84*
Belisle Enterprises - Confluence, PA - *Tel&CabFB 84C p.1666*
Beljan - Dexter, MI - *LitMarPl 83, 84; MagIndMarPl 82-83*
Belkin Productions Inc. - Cleveland, OH - *BillIntBG 83-84*
Belknap Data Solutions Ltd. - Greenwich, CT - *IntDirMarRes 83*
Bell Advertising Inc., Don - Jacksonville, FL - *StaDirAdAg 2-84*
Bell Advertising Service - Pittsburgh, PA - *StaDirAdAg 2-84*
Bell & Howell - Chicago, IL - *DataDirSup 7-83; HomeVid&CabYB 82-83; MicrocomMPl 83*
Bell & Howell - Lincolnwood, IL - *MicrocomMPl 84*
Bell & Howell (Micro Photo Div.) - Wooster, OH - *AvMarPl 83; BoPubDir 4, 5; CompReadDB 82; DataDirOnSer 84; DirInfWP 82; InfIndMarPl 83; LitMarPl 83, 84; MagIndMarPl 82-83; MicroMarPl 82-83*
Bell & Howell/Columbia Pictures Video Services - Northbrook, IL - *AvMarPl 83*
Bell & Stanton - *See* Manning, Selvage & Lee Inc.
Bell Associates Inc., Dave - Hollywood, CA - *Tel&CabFB 84C*
Bell Association for the Deaf Inc., The Alexander Graham - Washington, DC - *LitMarPl 83, 84*
Bell Books - Youngstown, OH - *BoPubDir 4, 5*
Bell Cablevision Inc. [of Tele-Communications Inc.] - Pineville, KY - *BrCabYB 84*
Bell Canada - Hull, PQ, Canada - *VideoDir 82-83*
Bell, D. Rayford - Louisville, KY - *BoPubDir 4 Sup, 5*
Bell Data Systems - West Palm Beach, FL - *MicrocomMPl 84*
Bell Editions Inc. [Aff. of Folio Inc.] - Scottsdale, AZ - *BoPubDir 4, 5*
Bell-Enterprise - Remsen, IA - *AyerDirPub 83*
Bell Enterprises Inc. - Pine Bluff, AR - *BoPubDir 4, 5*
Bell Flower Herald American - *See* Hearst Community Newspapers
Bell Gardens Review - Bell, CA - *AyerDirPub 83; Ed&PubIntYB 82; NewsDir 84*
Bell Gardens Review - *See* Hearst Community Newspapers
Bell Industrial Post - Bell, CA - *AyerDirPub 83*
Bell, James - Ossining, NY - *LitMarPl 83, 84*
Bell, James M. - Boston, MA - *MagIndMarPl 82-83*
Bell, Jewell - Portageville, MO - *Tel&CabFB 84C p.1666*
Bell Laboratories Library Network [of Bell Telephone Laboratories Inc.] - Murray Hill, NJ - *EISS 83*
Bell-Maywood-Cudahy Industrial Post [of Hearst Corp.] - Bell, CA - *NewsDir 84*
Bell Maywood Industrial Post - Bell, CA - *Ed&PubIntYB 82*
Bell Maywood Industrial Post - *See* Hearst Community Newspapers
Bell Music Publishing Co., Mom - Philadelphia, PA - *BillIntBG 83-84*
Bell Music, Rocky - *See* White Cat Music
Bell-Northern Research - Ottawa, ON, Canada - *VideoDir 82-83; WhoWMicrocom 83*
Bell of the Cape - East Dennis, MA - *StaDirAdAg 2-84*
Bell Press Inc., The Ovid - Fulton, MO - *LitMarPl 83, 84; MagIndMarPl 82-83*
Bell Publicom Inc. - Dayton, OH - *ArtMar 84; DirPRFirms 83*
Bell Publishing - East Brunswick, NJ - *BoPubDir 5; LitMag&SmPr 83-84; LitMarPl 84*
Bell, Robert L. - Melrose, MA - *BoPubDir 4, 5*
Bell Springs Publishing Co. - Laytonville, CA - *BoPubDir 4, 5*
Bell, Steve - Dexter, MO - *BrCabYB 84 p.D-297*
Bell, Steve V. - Portageville, MO - *Tel&CabFB 84C p.1666*
Bell Telephone Co. of Pennsylvania, The - Philadelphia, PA - *TelDir&BG 83-84*
Bell Telephone Laboratories Inc. - Murray Hill, NJ - *TelDir&BG 83-84*
Bella Vista Weekly Vista - Bella Vista, AR - *BaconPubCkNews 84*
Bellaire Antenna Systems Inc. - Bellaire, OH - *BrCabYB 84; Tel&CabFB 84C*
Bellaire Antrim County News - Bellaire, MI - *BaconPubCkNews 84*
Bellaire Records - Bellaire, TX - *BillIntBG 83-84*
Bellaire Texan, The - Bellaire, TX - *NewsDir 84*
Bellamy & Halbin - Cleveland, OH - *DirPRFirms 83*
Belle Banner, The - Belle, MO - *AyerDirPub 83; Ed&PubIntYB 82*
Belle Banner, The - *See* Lewis Publishing Co. Inc.
Belle Center Herald-Voice - Belle Center, OH - *BaconPubCkNews 84*
Belle Chasse Plaquemines Parish Gazette - Belle Chasse, LA - *BaconPubCkNews 84*
Belle Fontaine Press - Marquette, MI - *BoPubDir 4, 5*
Belle Fourche Bee - Belle Fourche, SD - *BaconPubCkNews 84; Ed&PubIntYB 82*
Belle Fourche Daily Post [of Northwest Publishers Inc.] - Belle Fourche, SD - *BaconPubCkNews 84; NewsDir 84*
Belle Glade/Pahokee Herald Observer - *See* Hammel Newspapers of Florida Inc.
Belle Mead Hillsborough Beacon - *See* Princeton Packet Inc.
Belle Plaine Herald - Belle Plaine, MN - *BaconPubCkNews 84; Ed&PubIntYB 82*

Belle Plaine News - Belle Plaine, KS - *BaconPubCkNews 84; Ed&PubIntYB 82*
Belle Plaine Newspapers of Benton County [of Marengo Publishing Corp.] - Belle Plaine, IA - *NewsDir 84*
Belle Plaine Union - Belle Plaine, IA - *BaconPubCkNews 84; Ed&PubIntYB 82*
Bellefontaine Examiner [of Hubbard Publishing Co. Inc.] - Bellefontaine, OH - *BaconPubCkNews 84; Ed&PubIntYB 82; NewsDir 84*
Bellefonte Centre Democrat - Bellefonte, PA - *BaconPubCkNews 84; NewsDir 84*
Belleridge Press - Rancho Santa Fe, CA - *BoPubDir 4, 5; LitMag&SmPr 83-84*
Bellerophon Books - Santa Barbara, CA - *LitMag&SmPr 83-84; LitMarPl 83, 84*
Belleview Leader - Ocala, FL - *AyerDirPub 83*
Belleview Leader, The [of Pinellas Park Post] - Pinellas Park, FL - *NewsDir 84*
Belleview Voice of South Marion - Belleview, FL - *NewsDir 84*
Belleville Area CATV System [of Zampelli TV] - Belleville, PA - *Tel&CabFB 84C*
Belleville Area CATV System - Lewistown, PA - *BrCabYB 84*
Belleville CATV Inc. - Belleville, WI - *Tel&CabFB 84C*
Belleville Community Antenna Systems - Belleville, KS - *BrCabYB 84; Tel&CabFB 84C*
Belleville Enterprise - Wayne, MI - *AyerDirPub 83; NewsDir 84*
Belleville Enterprise, The - Belleville, MI - *Ed&PubIntYB 82*
Belleville Enterprise, The - *See* Associated Newspapers Inc.
Belleville Journal - Belleville, IL - *AyerDirPub 83; Ed&PubIntYB 82*
Belleville Journal - *See* Journal Newspapers of Southern Illinois
Belleville Labor News - Belleville, IL - *NewsDir 84*
Belleville Messenger - Belleville, IL - *BaconPubCkNews 84*
Belleville News-Democrat [of Capital Cities] - Belleville, IL - *NewsDir 84*
Belleville Recorder - Belleville, WI - *BaconPubCkNews 84; Ed&PubIntYB 82*
Belleville Telegram - Belleville, NJ - *NewsDir 84*
Belleville Telescope - Belleville, KS - *BaconPubCkNews 84; Ed&PubIntYB 82; NewsDir 84*
Belleville Times-News - Belleville, NJ - *BaconPubCkNews 84; Ed&PubIntYB 82*
Belleville Times-News - Nutley, NJ - *AyerDirPub 83*
Belleville Times-News, The [of Nutley Sunbank Newspapers] - Adelphia, NJ - *NewsDir 84*
Bellevue Cable TV Co. - Bellevue, IA - *Tel&CabFB 84C*
Bellevue Gazette - Bellevue, MI - *BaconPubCkNews 84; Ed&PubIntYB 82*
Bellevue Gazette - Bellevue, OH - *AyerDirPub 83; BaconPubCkNews 84; Ed&PubIntYB 82; NewsDir 84*
Bellevue-Geddes Pennysaver - Syracuse, NY - *AyerDirPub 83*
Bellevue Herald-Leader - Bellevue, IA - *BaconPubCkNews 84*
Bellevue Journal-American - Bellevue, WA - *Ed&PubIntYB 82*
Bellevue Leader [of Omaha Sun Newspapers] - Bellevue, NE - *NewsDir 84*
Bellevue Leader - Omaha, NE - *BaconPubCkNews 84*
Bellevue News - Bellevue, TX - *Ed&PubIntYB 82*
Bellevue Press - Bellevue, NE - *Ed&PubIntYB 82*
Bellevue Press - Binghamton, NY - *BoPubDir 4, 5; LitMag&SmPr 83-84*
Bellevue RFD News - Bellevue, OH - *BaconPubCkNews 84*
Bellevue Suburban Life [of Dardanell Publications Inc.] - Monroeville, PA - *NewsDir 84*
Bellevue Suburban Life - *See* Gateway Press Inc.
Bellevue Times - Bellevue, TX - *Ed&PubIntYB 82*
Bellflower Herald American - Bellflower, CA - *Ed&PubIntYB 82*
Bellflower Herald American - South Gate, CA - *AyerDirPub 83*
Bellflower Herald American Newspapers [of W. J. McGiffin Newspaper Co.] - Bellflower, CA - *NewsDir 84*
Bellflower/Paramount Herald American - Bellflower, CA - *Ed&PubIntYB 82*
Bellflower/Paramount Herald American - *See* Hearst Community Newspapers
Bellido Co., George - New York, NY - *LitMarPl 83, 84; MagIndMarPl 82-83*
Bellinger, Steve - *See* Prairieland Stations
Bellingham Herald [of Federated Publications Inc.] - Bellingham, WA - *BaconPubCkNews 84; Ed&PubIntYB 82; NewsDir 84*
Bellingham Review, The [of Signpost Press Inc.] - Bellingham, WA - *LitMag&SmPr 83-84*
Bellman Publishing Co. - Arlington, MA - *BoPubDir 4, 5*
Bellmore Life [of L & M Publications] - Bellmore, NY - *BaconPubCkNews 84; Ed&PubIntYB 82; NewsDir 84*
Bellmore-Merrick Advertiser - Levittown, NY - *AyerDirPub 83*
Bellmore-Merrick Observer - Bellmore, NY - *AyerDirPub 83*
Bellmore-Merrick Observer - *See* Observer Newspapers
Bellotto, Nicholas F. - New York, NY - *LitMarPl 83, 84*
Bellows Falls-Springfield Windsor Shopper - Bellows Falls, VT - *AyerDirPub 83*
Bells Crockett County Sentinel - *See* Alamo Crockett Times
Bellview Community Cable - Bellview, WV - *Tel&CabFB 84C*
Bellville Star & Tri-Forks Press - Bellville, OH - *BaconPubCkNews 84; Ed&PubIntYB 82*
Bellville Times [of Austin County Publishing Co. Inc.] - Bellville, TX - *BaconPubCkNews 84; NewsDir 84*
Bellville Times, The - Austin, TX - *Ed&PubIntYB 82*
Belmar Camera Shop Inc. - Belmar, NJ - *AvMarPl 83*
Belmark Book Co. - Westbury, NY - *LitMarPl 83, 84*
Belmond Independent - Belmond, IA - *BaconPubCkNews 84; Ed&PubIntYB 82*
Belmont Banner - Belmont, NC - *BaconPubCkNews 84; Ed&PubIntYB 82*
Belmont Central Leader [of Chicago Leader Newspapers-Leader Papers Inc.] - Chicago, IL - *AyerDirPub 83; NewsDir 84*
Belmont Central News - Chicago, IL - *AyerDirPub 83*
Belmont Citizen - Belmont, MA - *AyerDirPub 83; Ed&PubIntYB 82; NewsDir 84*
Belmont Citizen - *See* Century Newspapers Inc.
Belmont Courier-Bulletin - Belmont, CA - *Ed&PubIntYB 82*
Belmont Courier-Bulletin [of Menlo Park Nowels Publishing] - Menlo Park, CA - *NewsDir 84*
Belmont Courier-Bulletin - *See* Regal Publishing Co.
Belmont-Cragin Passage - Chicago, IL - *AyerDirPub 83*
Belmont Herald [of Belmont Offset Printing & Publishing Co. Inc.] - Belmont, MA - *Ed&PubIntYB 82; NewsDir 84*
Belmont Herald - *See* Herald Publishing Co.
Belmont Music Publishers - Los Angeles, CA - *BillIntBG 83-84*
Belmont Records [Div. of John Penny Enterprises Inc.] - Belmont, MA - *BillIntBG 83-84*
Belmont Telephone Co. - Platteville, WI - *TelDir&BG 83-84*
Belmont-Tishomingo Journal - Belmont, MS - *BaconPubCkNews 84; Ed&PubIntYB 82*
Belmont TV Cable Service - Belmont, MS - *BrCabYB 84*
Belo Broadcasting Corp. - Dallas, TX - *BrCabYB 84; Tel&CabFB 84S*
Belo Corp., A. H. - Dallas, TX - *AdAge 6-28-84; Ed&PubIntYB 82; KnowInd 83*
Belo Information Systems [Div. of A. H. Belo Corp.] - Dallas, TX - *VideoDir 82-83*
Belo Information Systems Online Network - Dallas, TX - *EISS 83*
Beloit Cable TV [of American TV & Communications Corp.] - Beloit, WI - *BrCabYB 84; Tel&CabFB 84C*
Beloit Call - Beloit, KS - *BaconPubCkNews 84*
Beloit Call-Gazette - Beloit, KS - *BaconPubCkNews 84*
Beloit Chronicle - Beloit, WI - *BaconPubCkNews 84*
Beloit Daily Call - Beloit, KS - *Ed&PubIntYB 82; NewsDir 84*
Beloit Daily News - Beloit, WI - *BaconPubCkNews 84; Ed&PubIntYB 82; NewsDir 84*
Beloit Poetry Journal - Beloit, WI - *LitMag&SmPr 83-84; LitMarPl 83, 84; WritMar 84*
Beloit Solomon Valley Post - Beloit, KS - *BaconPubCkNews 84*
Belsten Publishing Ltd. - Maple, ON, Canada - *BoPubDir 4, 5*
Belt Publishes, Simon - Bluff, UT - *BoPubDir 4, 5*
Belt Valley Times - Belt, MT - *BaconPubCkNews 84; Ed&PubIntYB 82*
Beltel [of Post & Telecommunications] - Pretoria, South Africa - *VideoDir 82-83*
Belton Journal - Belton, TX - *BaconPubCkNews 84; Ed&PubIntYB 82*
Belton News - Belton, SC - *BaconPubCkNews 84; Ed&PubIntYB 82*

Belton-Raymore Star Herald [of The Belton Banner Inc.] - Belton, MO - *AyerDirPub 83; BaconPubCkNews 84; Ed&PubIntYB 82; NewsDir 84*
Belvedere Citizen - Belvedere, CA - *Ed&PubIntYB 82*
Belvedere Citizen [of Northeast Los Angeles Publishing Co.] - Los Angeles, CA - *AyerDirPub 83; NewsDir 84*
Belvedere Citizen - *See* Northeast Los Angeles Publishing Co.
Belvedere Publishing Co. - New York, NY - *BoPubDir 4, 5*
Belvidere Daily Republican - Belvidere, IL - *BaconPubCkNews 84; Ed&PubIntYB 82*
Belvidere News - Belvidere, NJ - *BaconPubCkNews 84*
Belvidere Republican - Belvidere, IL - *NewsDir 84*
Belview Independent - Belview, MN - *Ed&PubIntYB 82*
Belwin-Mills Publishing Corp. - New York, NY - *BillIntBG 83-84*
Belzoni Banner - Belzoni, MS - *BaconPubCkNews 84; Ed&PubIntYB 82*
Bement Register - Bement, IL - *Ed&PubIntYB 82*
Bemidji Pioneer - Bemidji, MN - *BaconPubCkNews 84; NewsDir 84*
Bemrose Information Services - Derby, England - *InfIndMarPl 83*
Ben Lomand Rural Telephone Cooperative Inc. - McMinnville, TN - *TelDir&BG 83-84*
Ben Lomond Beacon - North Ogden, UT - *Ed&PubIntYB 82*
Ben Lomond Beacon [of Roy Printing Co. Newspapers] - Roy, UT - *NewsDir 84*
Benaul Associates Advertising - New York, NY - *StaDirAdAg 2-84*
Benben Publications [Aff. of Benben Enterprises Inc.] - Mississauga, ON, Canada - *BoPubDir 4, 5; LitMarPl 84*
Benbow, D. R. - Decatur, GA - *BoPubDir 4 Sup, 5*
Benbrook News [of Suburban Newspapers Inc.] - Ft. Worth, TX - *AyerDirPub 83; NewsDir 84*
Benbrook News - *See* Suburban Newspapers Inc.
Bench History Hustlers - Gull Lake, SK, Canada - *BoPubDir 4 Sup, 5*
Bench Press - Oakland, CA - *BoPubDir 4, 5*
Bench Press [Aff. of Nebraska State Penitentiary] - Lincoln, NE - *BoPubDir 4 Sup, 5*
Bencher Inc. - Chicago, IL - *AvMarPl 83*
Benchmark Computing Services - Providence, UT - *MicrocomMPl 83; WhoWMicrocom 83*
Benchmark Films Inc. - Briarcliff Manor, NY - *AvMarPl 83*
Benchmark Software - Pittsburgh, PA - *MicrocomMPl 83*
Benchmark Systems Inc. - Arlington, VA - *DataDirSup 7-83*
Bend Bulletin [of Western Communications Inc.] - Bend, OR - *BaconPubCkNews 84; NewsDir 84*
Bend Community Antenna Co. [of Liberty Communications Inc.] - Bend, OR - *BrCabYB 84; Tel&CabFB 84C*
Bend of the River Magazine - Perrysburg, OH - *ArtMar 84; WritMar 84*
Bender & Co. Inc., Matthew [Subs. of Times Mirror Corp.] - Albany, NY - *DirMarMP 83*
Bender & Co. Inc., Matthew [Subs. of Times Mirror Co.] - New York, NY - *LitMarPl 83, 84*
Bender Industrial Design Inc., May - New York, NY - *HBIndAd&MS 82-83*
Bender Photographic - Bloomington, IL - *AvMarPl 83*
Bender Publishing, R. James - San Jose, CA - *BoPubDir 4, 5*
Bender Reference Library, Matthew - New York, NY - *DirOnDB Spring 84*
Bendick Associates Inc. - Guilford, CT - *AvMarPl 83*
Bendig Music Corp. - *See* Fermata International Melodies Inc.
Benedek, A. Richard - New York, NY - *Tel&CabFB 84S*
Benedetti Music, Quint - Toluca Lake, CA - *BillIntBG 83-84*
Benedictine Sisters of Perpetual Adoration - San Diego, CA - *BoPubDir 4, 5*
Benefic Press [Div. of Coronado Publishers Inc.] - San Diego, CA - *LitMarPl 83*
Beneficial Computer Services [Subs. of Beneficial Standard Corp.] - Los Angeles, CA - *ADAPSOMemDir 83-84; DataDirOnSer 84*
Benefield, Levinger & Associates - Santa Rosa, CA - *AdAge 3-28-84; StaDirAdAg 2-84*
Benefits Canada - Toronto, ON, Canada - *BaconPubCkMag 84; WritMar 84*
Benetics Corp. - Mountain View, CA - *ADAPSOMemDir 83-84*
Benewah Cable Co. Inc. - St. Maries, ID - *BrCabYB 84; Tel&CabFB 84C*
Benfel Music - Berkeley, CA - *BillIntBG 83-84*
Benfey, Theodor - Greensboro, NC - *BoPubDir 4, 5*
Bengal Press Inc. - Grand Rapids, MI - *ArtMar 84; BoPubDir 4, 5*
Bengston Market Research - Minnetonka, MN - *IntDirMarRes 83*
Benham Community TV - Benham, KY - *BrCabYB 84; Tel&CabFB 84C*
Benicia Herald - Benicia, CA - *BaconPubCkNews 84; Ed&PubIntYB 82*
Benin Press Ltd. - Chicago, IL - *BoPubDir 4, 5*
Beninda Books - Canton, OH - *BoPubDir 4, 5; LitMag&SmPr 83-84*
Benito Advertising, Louis - Tampa, FL - *AdAge 3-28-84; StaDirAdAg 2-84*
Benjamin & Associates, Robert S. - Mexico City, Mexico - *DirPRFirms 83*
Benjamin Associates, Herbert S. - Baton Rouge, LA - *ArtMar 84; DirMarMP 83; StaDirAdAg 2-84; TelAl 83, 84*
Benjamin Co. Inc. - Elmsford, NY - *LitMarPl 83, 84; WritMar 84*
Benjamin/Cummings Publishing Co., The [Subs. of Addison-Wesley Publishing Co.] - Menlo Park, CA - *ArtMar 84; LitMarPl 83, 84*
Benjamin, Curtis - Weston, CT - *LitMarPl 83, 84*
Benjamin Electroproducts Inc. - Commack, NY - *AvMarPl 83*
Benjamins North America Inc., John [Aff. of John Benjamins BV] - Philadelphia, PA - *BoPubDir 4, 5; LitMarPl 83, 84*
Benkelman Post - Benkelman, NE - *BaconPubCkNews 84*
Benkelman Post & News-Chronicle - Benkelman, NE - *Ed&PubIntYB 82*
Benkelman Telephone Co. - Benkelman, NE - *Tel&CabFB 84C p.1666; TelDir&BG 83-84*
Benkovich & Associates Ltd. - Rockford, IL - *DirPRFirms 83*
Benld Enterprise - Benld, IL - *BaconPubCkNews 84; Ed&PubIntYB 82*
Benn & MacDonough Inc. - New York, NY - *ArtMar 84; DirPRFirms 83; StaDirAdAg 2-84*
Benn Hall Associates [Div. of Jones, Brakeley & Rockwell Inc.] - New York, NY - *MagIndMarPl 82-83*
Benn, John [Aff. of Ferocious Tiger-Lion Club] - Ottawa, ON, Canada - *BoPubDir 4, 5*
Bennett & Associates, Aleon - Sherman Oaks, CA - *DirPRFirms 83*
Bennett & Associates, Suzanne - New York, NY - *LitMarPl 83, 84*
Bennett Co., Walter F. - Chicago, IL - *TelAl 83, 84*
Bennett Co., Walter F. - Philadelphia, PA - *BrCabYB 84; StaDirAdAg 2-84*
Bennett County Booster - Martin, SD - *Ed&PubIntYB 82*
Bennett Laboratory Inc. - Columbus, OH - *AvMarPl 83*
Bennett Music Co., Phil - New York, NY - *BillIntBG 83-84*
Bennett Publishing Co. - Peoria, IL - *LitMarPl 83, 84; WritMar 84*
Bennett, Robert - Bala Cynwyd, PA - *BoPubDir 4, 5*
Bennett Studios - Bridgeville, DE - *ArtMar 84*
Bennett's Valley News - Weedville, PA - *Ed&PubIntYB 82*
Bennettsville Marlboro Herald-Advocate [of Marlboro Publishing Co. Inc.] - Bennettsville, SC - *BaconPubCkNews 84; NewsDir 84*
Bennettsville McColl Messenger - Bennettsville, SC - *BaconPubCkNews 84*
Bennington Banner - Bennington, VT - *BaconPubCkNews 84; Ed&PubIntYB 82; NewsDir 84*
Bennington Pennysaver Press [of Hadwen Inc.] - Bennington, VT - *NewsDir 84*
Benoit, Edouard - Riviere-a-Pierre, PQ, Canada - *BrCabYB 84*
Bensalem Advisor - Bensalem, PA - *AyerDirPub 83*
Bensalem Advisor - *See* Intercounty Newspaper Group
Bensenville Banner - Bensenville, IL - *Ed&PubIntYB 82*
Bensenville Banner [of Roselle Copley Record Newspapers] - Schaumburg, IL - *NewsDir 84*
Bensenville Chronicle, The - Bensenville, IL - *Ed&PubIntYB 82*
Bensenville-Wood Dale Voice - *See* Voice Newspapers
Benson & Associates Inc., J. C. - Rockford, IL - *DirPRFirms 83; StaDirAdAg 2-84*
Benson & Benson - Omaha, NE - *WhoWMicrocom 83*

Benson & Co. Inc., W. S. - Austin, TX - *BoPubDir 4, 5*
Benson Broadcasting Co. - Benson, NC - *BrCabYB 84*
Benson Co. Inc. - Nashville, TN - *BillIntBG 83-84; BoPubDir 4, 5; DirMarMP 83*
Benson Co., Philip B. - Washington, DC - *EISS 7-83 Sup*
Benson Co., The - Park Ridge, IL - *MagIndMarPl 82-83*
Benson County Farmers Press - Benson County, ND - *Ed&PubIntYB 82*
Benson County Farmers Press - Minnewaukan, ND - *AyerDirPub 83; NewsDir 84*
Benson Inc. - San Jose, CA - *DataDirSup 7-83*
Benson Mailing & Shipping Service - New York, NY - *LitMarPl 83*
Benson Publishing Co. Inc., John T. - *See* Paragon/Benson Publishing Group
Benson Review - Benson, NC - *Ed&PubIntYB 82*
Benson Review - *See* County Press Publishers
Benson San Pedro Valley News-Sun - *See* Arizona Range News Inc.
Benson Sun [of Sun Newspapers] - Omaha, NE - *Ed&PubIntYB 82; NewsDir 84*
Benson Sun & Northwest Omaha Sun - Omaha, NE - *AyerDirPub 83*
Benson Sun & Northwest Omaha Sun - *See* Sun Newspapers
Benson Swift County Monitor - *See* Swift County Monitor & News Inc.
Benson Swift County News - *See* Swift County Monitor & News Inc.
Benson Swift County News & Monitor - Benson, MN - *NewsDir 84*
Bent County Democrat - Las Animas, CO - *Ed&PubIntYB 82*
Bent of Tau Beta Pi, The - Knoxville, TN - *BaconPubCkMag 84; MagDir 84; MagIndMarPl 82-83*
Bent Records Inc. - New York, NY - *BillIntBG 83-84*
Bente Records - New York, NY - *BillIntBG 83-84*
Bentley, Barnes & Lynn - Chicago, IL - *AdAge 3-28-84; HBIndAd&MS 82-83; StaDirAdAg 2-84*
Bentley, Huggins, Smith & Whittington Inc. - Birmingham, AL - *StaDirAdAg 2-84*
Bentley Inc., Robert - Cambridge, MA - *LitMarPl 83, 84*
Bentley, Richard P. - Tupper Lake, NY - *BoPubDir 4, 5*
Bentley, Ruth - New York, NY - *MagIndMarPl 82-83*
Bentleyville Courier - Lewistown, PA - *AyerDirPub 83*
Bentleyville Courier [of Pioneer Newspapers Inc.] - Monongahela, PA - *AyerDirPub 83; NewsDir 84*
Bentleyville Telephone Co. - Bentleyville, PA - *TelDir&BG 83-84*
Benton & Bowles - New York, NY - *AdAge 3-28-84, 6-25-84; Br 1-23-84; BrCabYB 84; HomeVid&CabYB 82-83; StaDirAdAg 2-84; TelAl 83, 84*
Benton Banner, The - Benton, KS - *Ed&PubIntYB 82*
Benton Bossier Banner-Progress - Benton, LA - *BaconPubCkNews 84*
Benton Bulletin - Philomath, OR - *Ed&PubIntYB 82*
Benton Cable TV Co. [of Flora Cable TV Co.] - Benton, KY - *BrCabYB 84; Tel&CabFB 84C*
Benton City-Benton County Times - Clarkston, WA - *AyerDirPub 83*
Benton City Times - *See* Tribune Newspapers Inc.
Benton Cooperative Telephone Co. - Rice, MN - *TelDir&BG 83-84*
Benton County Broadcasting Co. - Camden, TN - *BrCabYB 84*
Benton County Daily Democrat - Bentonville, AR - *AyerDirPub 83; BaconPubCkNews 84; Ed&PubIntYB 82; NewsDir 84*
Benton County Enterprise - Warsaw, MO - *AyerDirPub 83; Ed&PubIntYB 82*
Benton County News - Foley, MN - *AyerDirPub 83; Ed&PubIntYB 82*
Benton County Tribune - Fowler, IN - *Ed&PubIntYB 82*
Benton Courier - Benton, AR - *AyerDirPub 83; BaconPubCkNews 84; Ed&PubIntYB 82*
Benton Daily Courier [of Benton County Publishing Co.] - Benton, AR - *NewsDir 84*
Benton Harbor-St. Joseph Herald Palladium - St. Joseph, MI - *NewsDir 84*
Benton News - Benton, IL - *BaconPubCkNews 84; NewsDir 84*
Benton Polk County News - Benton, TN - *BaconPubCkNews 84*
Benton Review - Fowler, IN - *AyerDirPub 83; Ed&PubIntYB 82*
Benton Review Publishing Co. Inc. - Fowler, IN - *MagIndMarPl 82-83*
Benton Ridge Telephone Co. - Benton Ridge, OH - *TelDir&BG 83-84*
Benton Tribune-Courier - Benton, KY - *BaconPubCkNews 84; Ed&PubIntYB 82; NewsDir 84*
Bentonville Cable TV [of Texas Community Antennas Inc.] - Bentonville, AR - *BrCabYB 84*
Benzene - New York, NY - *LitMag&SmPr 83-84*
Benzene Editions - New York, NY - *LitMag&SmPr 83-84*
Benzer Public Relations, Shirley L. - New York, NY - *DirPRFirms 83*
Benzie County Ad-Visor - Frankfort, MI - *AyerDirPub 83*
Benzie County Record-Patriot - Frankfort, MI - *Ed&PubIntYB 82*
Berandol Music Ltd. - Toronto, ON, Canada - *BoPubDir 4 Sup, 5*
Berdoo Music - Universal City, CA - *BillIntBG 83-84*
Berea Cablevision Co. [of OVC Telecommunications Inc.] - Berea, KY - *BrCabYB 84*
Berea Citizen - Berea, KY - *BaconPubCkNews 84; Ed&PubIntYB 82*
Berea News Sun [of Cleveland Sun Newspapers] - Cleveland, OH - *AyerDirPub 83; NewsDir 84*
Berea Valley View News Sun - *See* Sun Newspapers
Berenson & Isham - Boston, MA - *AdAge 3-28-84; StaDirAdAg 2-84*
Berenter Greenhouse Elgort Inc. - New York, NY - *StaDirAdAg 2-84*
Beres & Associates Inc., Lou - Chicago, IL - *StaDirAdAg 2-84*
Beresford Cablevision - Beresford, SD - *Tel&CabFB 84C*
Beresford Municipal Telephone Co. - Beresford, SD - *TelDir&BG 83-84*
Beresford Republic - Beresford, SD - *BaconPubCkNews 84; Ed&PubIntYB 82*
Berg & Associates - San Diego, CA - *AvMarPl 83; LitMarPl 84*
Berg Public Relations, Stephen - New York, NY - *DirPRFirms 83*
Bergelt Advertising - New York, NY - *AdAge 3-28-84; StaDirAdAg 2-84*
Bergelt Public Relations Inc. - New York, NY - *DirPRFirms 83*
Bergen & Lee Inc. - Los Angeles, CA - *DirPRFirms 83*
Bergen Bulletin - Palisades Park, NJ - *AyerDirPub 83; Ed&PubIntYB 82*
Bergen Citizen - Edgewater, NJ - *AyerDirPub 83; Ed&PubIntYB 82*
Bergen Evening Record Corp. - Hackensack, NJ - *KnowInd 83*
Bergen Expo Systems - Clifton, NJ - *AvMarPl 83; ProGuPRSer 4*
Bergen Free Press - Fairview, NJ - *AyerDirPub 83; Ed&PubIntYB 82*
Bergen Free Press - *See* West New Yorker Inc.
Bergen Free Press & Jersey Pictorial [of Fairview West New Yorker Inc.] - Fairview, NJ - *NewsDir 84*
Bergen Graphics, Lorenzo - New Orleans, LA - *ArtMar 84*
Bergen News - Palisades Park, NJ - *AyerDirPub 83; Ed&PubIntYB 82*
Bergen News-Palisades Edition - Ft. Lee, NJ - *Ed&PubIntYB 82*
Bergen News Publishing Corp. - Palisades Park, NJ - *BaconPubCkNews 84*
Bergen Telephone Co., The - Sharon, WI - *TelDir&BG 83-84*
Bergen Today [of Wayne Today Newspapers] - Wayne, NJ - *NewsDir 84*
Bergenfield Twin Boro News - Bergenfield, NJ - *BaconPubCkNews 84*
Bergenholz & Arnesen - *See* Dancer Fitzgerald Sample Inc.
Berger Advertising Inc., I. H. - New York, NY - *StaDirAdAg 2-84*
Berger & Co. Inc. - Allentown, PA - *StaDirAdAg 2-84*
Berger Associates Inc., Bill - New York, NY - *LitMarPl 83, 84*
Berger, David - Long Island City, NY - *LitMarPl 83; MagIndMarPl 82-83*
Berger, Helen R. - Jersey City, NJ - *LitMarPl 84*
Berger, Helen R. - Union City, NJ - *LitMarPl 83*
Berger, Stone & Partners Inc. - New York, NY - *StaDirAdAg 2-84*
Bergerie, Maurine - New Iberia, LA - *BoPubDir 4, 5*
Bergeron & Frere Ltee., J. - St. Tite, PQ, Canada - *BrCabYB 84*

Bergin & Garvey Publishers Inc. - South Hadley, MA - *LitMarPl 84*
Bergin Publishers Inc., J. F. - South Hadley, MA - *LitMarPl 83*
Bergman & Associates Inc., Lester V. - Cold Spring, NY - *AvMarPl 83; LitMarPl 83, 84*
Bergseth, Leonard - Edmonds, WA - *Tel&CabFB 84C p.1666*
Bergthold, Filhardt & Wright Inc. - San Jose, CA - *ArtMar 84*
Bergwall - Garden City, NY - *MicrocomMPl 84*
Bergwall Productions Inc. - Uniondale, NY - *AvMarPl 83*
Berinsky, Burton - New York, NY - *MagIndMarPl 82-83*
Berk & Co. Inc. - Boston, MA - *StaDirAdAg 2-84*
Berk Personnel Inc., Margo - New York, NY - *InfIndMarPl 83; MagIndMarPl 82-83*
Berk-Tek Inc. - Reading, PA - *DataDirSup 7-83*
Berkel, Boyce N. - Clearwater, FL - *BoPubDir 4 Sup, 5*
Berkeley-Albany American [of Oakland Neighborhood Journal] - Oakland, CA - *NewsDir 84*
Berkeley Cable TV Co. - Moncks Corner, SC - *BrCabYB 84*
Berkeley Cooperative Publishers - *See* Kicking Mule Publishing Inc.
Berkeley Cottage Software - Berkeley, CA - *MicrocomMPl 83*
Berkeley Democrat - Moncks Corner, SC - *AyerDirPub 83; Ed&PubIntYB 82*
Berkeley Enterprises Inc. - Newtonville, MA - *BoPubDir 5*
Berkeley Fiction Review - Berkeley, CA - *LitMag&SmPr 83-84*
Berkeley Gazette [of North Bay Newspapers] - Berkeley, CA - *LitMarPl 84*
Berkeley Gazette [of Ingersoll Publications] - Richmond, CA - *Ed&PubIntYB 82; LitMarPl 83; NewsDir 84*
Berkeley Heights-New Providence Press - Berkeley Heights, NJ - *AyerDirPub 83; Ed&PubIntYB 82*
Berkeley Heights-New Providence Press [of New Providence Passaic Valley Independent Press] - New Providence, NJ - *NewsDir 84*
Berkeley Heights-New Providence Press - *See* Passaic Valley Independent Press
Berkeley Independent & Gazette [of Brown Newspaper Publishing Co. Inc.] - Berkeley, CA - *NewsDir 84*
Berkeley Literary Office - Berkeley, CA - *LitMarPl 83, 84*
Berkeley Metro Reporter - San Francisco, CA - *NewsDir 84*
Berkeley Metro Reporter - *See* Reporter Publishing Co.
Berkeley Monthly, The - Berkeley, CA - *LitMag&SmPr 83-84*
Berkeley Particle Data Center [of University of California] - Berkeley, CA - *EISS 83; InfIndMarPl 83*
Berkeley Poets Cooperative [of Berkeley Poets Workshop & Press] - Berkeley, CA - *LitMag&SmPr 83-84*
Berkeley Poets Workshop & Press - Berkeley, CA - *BoPubDir 4, 5; LitMag&SmPr 83-84*
Berkeley Post - Oakland, CA - *AyerDirPub 83*
Berkeley Post - *See* Alameda Publishing Corp.
Berkeley Press [of Press Publications] - Oakland, CA - *NewsDir 84*
Berkeley Press - *See* Press Publications
Berkeley Scientific Publications [Aff. of Scientific Newsletter Inc.] - Anaheim, CA - *BoPubDir 4, 5; DirMarMP 83*
Berkeley Slavic Specialties - Berkeley, CA - *BoPubDir 4*
Berkeley Slavic Specialties - Oakland, CA - *BoPubDir 5*
Berkeley Solar Group - Berkeley, CA - *DataDirOnSer 84*
Berkeley Springs Morgan Messenger - Berkeley Springs, WV - *BaconPubCkNews 84*
Berkeley Stage Co. - Berkeley, CA - *WritMar 84*
Berkeley Systems Works - Berkeley, CA - *WhoWMicrocom 83*
Berkeley Works - Berkeley, CA - *LitMag&SmPr 83-84*
Berkey K & L Custom Services - New York, NY - *AvMarPl 83*
Berkhemer & Kline Inc. - Los Angeles, CA - *DirPRFirms 83*
Berklee Press Publications - Boston, MA - *BoPubDir 4, 5*
Berkley, Miriam - New York, NY - *LitMarPl 83, 84; MagIndMarPl 82-83*
Berkley Publishing Group [Subs. of The Putnam Publishing Group] - New York, NY - *LitMarPl 83, 84; WritMar 84*
Berkman & Daniels - San Diego, CA - *DirPRFirms 83*
Berkowitz, Isabel - New York, NY - *LitMarPl 83*
Berkowitz/Linsman Group, The - New York, NY - *DirPRFirms 83*
Berks Community Television - Reading, PA - *TeleSy&SerDir 7-83*
Berks County Record - Reading, PA - *Ed&PubIntYB 82*
Berks-Mont Newspapers Inc. - Boyertown, PA - *BaconPubCkNews 84*
Berks Suburban TV Cable [of American TV & Communications Corp.] - Reading, PA - *BrCabYB 84; InterCabHB 3; Tel&CabFB 84C*
Berkshire Cable TV Co. [of Century Communications Corp.] - Great Barrington, MA - *BrCabYB 84*
Berkshire Courier - Great Barrington, MA - *AyerDirPub 83; Ed&PubIntYB 82; NewsDir 84*
Berkshire Eagle - Pittsfield, MA - *AyerDirPub 83; BaconPubCkNews 84; Ed&PubIntYB 82; NewsDir 84*
Berkshire Group - North Adams, MA - *BrCabYB 84*
Berkshire News - Springfield, IL - *MagDir 84*
Berkshire News - Lebanon, IN - *BaconPubCkMag 84*
Berkshire Paper Co. - Great Barrington, MA - *MagIndMarPl 82-83*
Berkshire Telephone Corp. - Kinderhook-Valatie, NY - *TelDir&BG 83-84*
Berkshire Traveller Press - Stockbridge, MA - *LitMarPl 83, 84*
Berland, Ernie - Plentywood, MT - *Tel&CabFB 84C p.1666*
Berlin Cablevision Inc. - Berlin, WI - *Tel&CabFB 84C*
Berlin Eagle, The [of West Hartford Imprint Newspapers] - West Hartford, CT - *NewsDir 84*
Berlin Journal - Berlin, WI - *AyerDirPub 83; Ed&PubIntYB 82; NewsDir 84*
Berlin Journal - *See* Journal Co., The
Berlin Reporter [of Berlin Munro Enterprises Inc.] - Berlin, NH - *BaconPubCkNews 84; Ed&PubIntYB 82; NewsDir 84*
Berlin, Saretta - Jenkintown, PA - *LitMarPl 83; MagIndMarPl 82-83*
Berliner Audio/Music Productions, Ralph - New York, NY - *AvMarPl 83*
Berliner Computer Center - New Hyde Park, NY - *MicrocomMPl 84*
Berliner Research Center Inc. - Danbury, CT - *LitMarPl 83, 84*
Berlinersoft - New Hyde Park, NY - *MicrocomMPl 83*
Berlitz Publications [Subs. of Macmillan Inc.] - New York, NY - *BillIntBG 83-84; LitMarPl 83, 84*
Berlitz Translation Service - New York, NY - *MagIndMarPl 82-83*
Berman Associates Inc. - Sterling, VA - *MicrocomMPl 83, 84*
Berman, Linda - Merrick, NY - *LitMarPl 83, 84*
Berman, Lois - New York, NY - *LitMarPl 83, 84*
Bermingham & Prosser [Div. of The Mead Corp.] - Hillside, IL - *LitMarPl 83, 84; MagIndMarPl 82-83*
Bermond Art Ltd. - Lake Success, NY - *ArtMar 84*
Bermont, Hubert - Washington, DC - *LitMarPl 83, 84*
Bermuda Biological Station (Special Publications Program) - Cambridge, MA - *BoPubDir 4, 5*
Bermuda Sun - Hamilton, Bermuda - *AyerDirPub 83*
Bermudez & Associates - Beverly Hills, CA - *AdAge 3-28-84; StaDirAdAg 2-84*
Bern Doubt Music - *See* Kaye Publications, Richard
Bern Publishers, Karl - Sun City, AZ - *BoPubDir 4, 5; LitMag&SmPr 83-84*
Bernan Associates [Subs. of Kraus Thomson Organization Ltd.] - Lanham, MD - *BoPubDir 4 Sup, 5; LitMarPl 84; MagIndMarPl 82-83*
Bernard & Co. - Arlington Heights, IL - *AdAge 3-28-84; StaDirAdAg 2-84*
Bernard Associates [Subs. of Kraus Thomson Organization Ltd.] - Lanham, MD - *LitMarPl 83*
Bernard, Jean B. - Washington, DC - *LitMarPl 83, 84; MagIndMarPl 82-83*
Bernard Picture Co. Inc. - Stamford, CT - *ArtMar 84*
Bernard Publications, Ros - Teaneck, NJ - *BoPubDir 4 Sup, 5*
Bernard Telephone Co. Inc. [Aff. of Lost Nation-Elwood Telephone Co.] - Bernard, IA - *TelDir&BG 83-84*
Bernardsville News [of Bernardsville Recorder Publishing Co.] - Bernardsville, NJ - *Ed&PubIntYB 82; NewsDir 84*
Bernardsville News - *See* Recorder Publishing Co.
Bernays, Edward L. - Cambridge, MA - *DirPRFirms 83*
Bernays, Hella Freud - Columbus, OH - *LitMarPl 83, 84; MagIndMarPl 82-83*
Berne News - Berne, IN - *AyerDirPub 83*

Berne Tri-Weekly News [of Economy Printing Concern] - Berne, IN - *Ed&PubIntYB 82; NewsDir 84*
Berner Associates, Robert K. - Clifton, NJ - *DirPRFirms 83*
Berner Associates, Robert K. - Paterson, NJ - *DirPRFirms 83*
Berneta Communications Inc. - Amarillo, TX - *StaDirAdAg 2-84*
Bernett Research Services - Somerville, MA - *IntDirMarRes 83*
Bernhard & Co., Arnold - New York, NY - *BoPubDir 5; KnowInd 83; MicroMarPl 82-83*
Bernhart Associates Ltd., Alfred P. - Toronto, ON, Canada - *BoPubDir 4 Sup, 5*
Bernheim, Kurt - New York, NY - *LitMarPl 83, 84*
Berni Corp., Alan - Greenwich, CT - *ArtMar 84; HBIndAd&MS 82-83*
Bernice News Journal - Bernice, LA - *Ed&PubIntYB 82*
Bernie Post-Tribune - Bernie, MO - *BaconPubCkNews 84*
Berns Advertising, Robert J. - Morton Grove, IL - *StaDirAdAg 2-84*
Berns & Associates Inc., Ron - Chicago, IL - *StaDirAdAg 2-84*
Berns Bureau, The - Washington, DC - *BrCabYB 84*
Berns Camera Stores Inc. - Albany, NY - *AvMarPl 83*
Bernsen's International Press Service Ltd. - San Ramon, CA - *LitMarPl 84*
Bernsen's International Press Service Ltd. - New York, NY - *Ed&PubIntYB 82*
Bernstein Agency, Ron - New York, NY - *LitMarPl 84*
Bernstein & Associates Inc., Ronald A. - Chicago, IL - *StaDirAdAg 2-84*
Bernstein Associates Inc., Jack - New York, NY - *DirPRFirms 83*
Bernstein Associates Inc., Ted - New York, NY - *StaDirAdAg 2-84; TelAl 83, 84*
Bernstein, Leibstone & Rosen Inc. - Old Bethpage, NY - *StaDirAdAg 2-84*
Bernstein, Marion - New York, NY - *LitMarPl 83, 84; MagIndMarPl 82-83*
Bernstein, Meredith G. - New York, NY - *LitMarPl 83, 84*
Bernstein Music Publishing Co., M. - Aurora, CO - *BillIntBG 83-84*
Bernstein Public Relations Inc., Jay - Los Angeles, CA - *DirPRFirms 83*
Bernstein Rein Advertising - Kansas City, MO - *AdAge 3-28-84; StaDirAdAg 2-84*
Bernstein Research Inc., Carol - New York, NY - *IntDirMarRes 83*
Berot Book Inc. - Lansing, MI - *BoPubDir 4, 5*
Berrien County Record - Buchanan, MI - *AyerDirPub 83; Ed&PubIntYB 82*
Berrien Press - Nashville, GA - *AyerDirPub 83; Ed&PubIntYB 82*
Berrien Springs Journal-Era - Berrien Springs, MI - *BaconPubCkNews 84*
Berry & Co., L. M. - Dayton, OH - *DirMarMP 83*
Berry & Homer Inc. - Philadelphia, PA - *AvMarPl 83*
Berry Associates Public Relations Inc. - Chatham, NJ - *DirPRFirms 83*
Berry Co., Paul - Dallas, TX - *StaDirAdAg 2-84*
Berry Fine Publishing Co. - Salem, OR - *BoPubDir 4, 5*
Berryville Clarke Courier - Berryville, VA - *BaconPubCkNews 84*
Berryville Star-Progress - Berryville, AR - *BaconPubCkNews 84; NewsDir 84*
Berstein Agency, Ron - New York, NY - *LitMarPl 83*
Bert & I Inc. - Ipswich, MA - *BillIntBG 83-84*
Bertamax Inc. - Seattle, WA - *MicrocomMPl 83, 84; WhoWMicrocom 83*
Bertelsmann Corp., The - New York, NY - *KnowInd 83*
Bertelsmann Publishing Group [Aff. of Verlagsgruppe Bertelsmann] - New York, NY - *LitMarPl 83, 84*
Bertha Herald - Bertha, MN - *BaconPubCkNews 84; Ed&PubIntYB 82*
Berthelot & Associates, John - New Orleans, LA - *BillIntBG 83-84*
Berthold of North America - Paramus, NJ - *DirInfWP 82*
Berthold Tribune - Berthold, ND - *BaconPubCkNews 84; Ed&PubIntYB 82*
Bertie Ledger-Advance [of Parker Bros. Inc.] - Windsor, NC - *AyerDirPub 83; Ed&PubIntYB 82; NewsDir 84*
Bertman Corp. - Vienna, VA - *CabTVFinDB 83; InterCabHB 3; TeleSy&SerDir 7-83*
Bertman Group Inc., The - Vienna, VA - *VideoDir 82-83*
Bertram, Blake & Russell - Chicago, IL - *StaDirAdAg 2-84*
Bertrand Advertising Agency Inc. - Hollywood, CA - *StaDirAdAg 2-84*
Bertrand Herald - Bertrand, NE - *BaconPubCkNews 84; Ed&PubIntYB 82*
Bertrand Languages Inc. - New York, NY - *MagIndMarPl 82-83*
Bertsch & Co. Advertising Inc. - New York, NY - *StaDirAdAg 2-84*
Bertucci Associates Inc., Andrew - Bristol, PA - *StaDirAdAg 2-84*
Berube Electronic Appliances Inc. - *See* Appareils Electroniques Berube Inc.
Berul Associates Ltd. - Rockville, MD - *ADAPSOMemDir 83-84; EISS 83; InfoS 83-84*
Berwick Enterprise - Bloomsburg, PA - *Ed&PubIntYB 82; NewsDir 84*
Berwitz Research & Analysis, Ken - Marlboro, NJ - *IntDirMarRes 83*
Berwyn Life [of Life Printing & Publishing Co.] - Berwyn, IL - *NewsDir 84*
Berwyn Life Sun - *See* Life Printing & Publishing Co.
Berzurk Systems - Berkeley, CA - *MicrocomMPl 84; MicrocomSwDir 1*
Besancourt Publishers - Brockville, ON, Canada - *BoPubDir 4, 5*
Besches' Bread 'n' Butter Productions Inc. - Georgetown, DE - *BoPubDir 4, 5*
Beseler Co. Inc., Charles - Florham Park, NJ - *AvMarPl 83*
Beserkley Records - Berkeley, CA - *BillIntBG 83-84*
Beslow Associates Inc. - Chicago, IL - *MagIndMarPl 82-83*
Bess Press - Honolulu, HI - *BoPubDir 4 Sup, 5; LitMag&SmPr 83-84*
Bessemer Advertiser - Bessemer, AL - *BaconPubCkNews 84; Ed&PubIntYB 82*
Bessemer City Record - Bessemer City, NC - *BaconPubCkNews 84; Ed&PubIntYB 82*
Bessemer News, The - Bessemer, AL - *Ed&PubIntYB 82*
Bessemer Sun [of Birmingham Sun Newspapers South & West] - Birmingham, AL - *NewsDir 84*
Best Book Club Ever [of Grolier Enterprises Inc.] - Danbury, CT - *LitMarPl 84*
Best Books Inc. - Oak Park, IL - *BoPubDir 4, 5*
Best Buys - New York, NY - *BaconPubCkMag 84; WritMar 84*
Best Cassettes [Div. of N. Bellow Co.] - Thornton, IL - *AvMarPl 83*
Best Color Photographic Lab - New York, NY - *AvMarPl 83*
Best Co., A. M. - Oldwick, NJ - *BoPubDir 4, 5; DataDirOnSer 84*
Best Computer Stores Inc. - Hayward, CA - *MicrocomMPl 83*
Best Corporate Insurance, A. M. - *See* Best Property-Casualty: Financial, A. M.
Best Database, A. M. - Oldwick, NJ - *DirOnDB Spring 84*
Best Executive Data Service [of A. M. Best Co.] - Oldwick, NJ - *DBBus 82*
Best Film & Video Corp. - Great Neck, NY - *TelAl 83, 84; WritMar 84*
Best Friends Music - *See* Right Note Music
Best in Books - Roswell, GA - *LitMarPl 83, 84*
Best Insurance Data Base, A. M. - Oldwick, NJ - *DirOnDB Spring 84*
Best Newspapers in Illinois Inc. - Sullivan, IL - *BaconPubCkNews 84*
Best of Bridge Publishing Ltd. - Calgary, AB, Canada - *BoPubDir 4, 5*
Best of Omni Science Fiction [of Omni Publications International Ltd.] - New York, NY - *LitMarPl 84*
Best People Inc., The - New York, NY - *AvMarPl 83; Tel&CabFB 84C*
Best Printing Co. Ltd., T. H. - Don Mills, ON, Canada - *LitMarPl 83, 84*
Best Programs - Alexandria, VA - *MicrocomMPl 84; MicrocomSwDir 1*
Best Property-Casualty: Financial, A. M. - Oldwick, NJ - *DirOnDB Spring 84*
Best Property-Casualty: Marketing, A. M. - Oldwick, NJ - *DirOnDB Spring 84*
Best Property-Casualty: National Quarterly, A. M. - *See* Best Property-Casualty: Marketing, A. M.

Best Publishing - Boston, MA - *BoPubDir 5*
Best View Cablevision Inc. [of Galanis Brothers Trust] - Abbeville, SC - *BrCabYB 84; Tel&CabFB 84C*
Best Western Press - Bakersfield, CA - *BoPubDir 5*
Best Wishes - Toronto, ON, Canada - *ArtMar 84*
Beston Electronics Inc. - Olathe, KS - *AvMarPl 83*
Best's Insurance Database Service [of A. M. Best Co.] - Oldwick, NJ - *DataDirOnSer 84*
Best's Review, Life/Health - Oldwick, NJ - *BaconPubCkMag 84; MagDir 84*
Best's Review, Property/Casualty - Oldwick, NJ - *BaconPubCkMag 84; MagDir 84*
Bestsellers Inc. - Toronto, ON, Canada - *BoPubDir 4, 5; LitMarPl 83*
Bestview Cable Video Inc. - Metaline Falls, WA - *BrCabYB 84; Tel&CabFB 84C*
Bestways - Carson City, NV - *BaconPubCkMag 84; MagIndMarPl 82-83; WritMar 84*
Bet-Ken Productions - San Jose, CA - *BoPubDir 4, 5*
Bet Yoatz Library Services - Chicago, IL - *FBInfSer 80*
Beta Business Systems - San Diego, CA - *DirInfWP 82*
Beta Communications Inc. - Aspermont, TX - *Tel&CabFB 84C*
Beta Computer Services Pty. Ltd. - Cape Town, South Africa - *ADAPSOMemDir 83-84*
Beta Phi Mu - Lexington, KY - *BoPubDir 4, 5*
Beta Principles Inc. - Waban, MA - *MicrocomSwDir 1*
Beta Research Corp. - Syosset, NY - *IntDirMarRes 83*
Betancourt Advertising & Art - San Diego, CA - *Ed&PubIntYB 82; StaDirAdAg 2-84*
Betcher, Peter - Los Angeles, CA - *LitMarPl 83*
Betdolph Music Co. - *See* Notable
Bete Co. Inc., Channing L. - South Deerfield, MA - *AvMarPl 83; DirMarMP 83*
Betelgeuse Books - Weston, ON, Canada - *BoPubDir 4, 5*
Beth-Ann Music Co. - Wilmington, DE - *BillIntBG 83-84*
Beth-Ridge Music Co. - *See* GCS Music Publications
Bethalon American - Alton, IL - *AyerDirPub 83*
Bethalto American - *See* Alton Citizen Inc.
Bethalto American, The - Alton, IL - *Ed&PubIntYB 82*
Bethan Hi-Vu - Carnegie, OK - *BrCabYB 84; Tel&CabFB 84C*
Bethany-Albany CATV - Albany, MO - *BrCabYB 84*
Bethany-Albany CATV - Bethany, MO - *BrCabYB 84*
Bethany Cable TV - Bethany, MO - *Tel&CabFB 84C*
Bethany College Publications - Lindsborg, KS - *BoPubDir 4, 5*
Bethany House Publishers [Div. of Bethany Fellowship Inc.] - Minneapolis, MN - *LitMarPl 83, 84*
Bethany House Publishing - Minneapolis, MN - *WritMar 84*
Bethany Press, The [Div. of Christian Board of Publication] - St. Louis, MO - *LitMarPl 83, 84*
Bethany Republican-Clipper - Bethany, MO - *BaconPubCkNews 84; Ed&PubIntYB 82; NewsDir 84*
Bethany Tribune-Review - Bethany, OK - *BaconPubCkNews 84; NewsDir 84*
Bethel & Mt. Aetna Telephone & Telegraph Co. [Aff. of GTE Corp.] - Erie, PA - *TelDir&BG 83-84*
Bethel Cablevision Inc. - Bethel, AK - *BrCabYB 84; Tel&CabFB 84C*
Bethel Home News - Bethel, CT - *Ed&PubIntYB 82*
Bethel Home News [of Ridgefield Acorn Press Inc.] - Ridgefield, CT - *NewsDir 84*
Bethel Home News - *See* Acorn Press Inc.
Bethel Journal - Bethel, OH - *AyerDirPub 83; BaconPubCkNews 84; Ed&PubIntYB 82*
Bethel Oxford County Citizen - Bethel, ME - *BaconPubCkNews 84; Ed&PubIntYB 82*
Bethel Park TV Cable [of Adelphia Communications Corp.] - Bethel Park, PA - *BrCabYB 84; Tel&CabFB 84C*
Bethel Publishing [Aff. of Missionary Church Inc.] - Elkhart, IN - *BoPubDir 4, 5*
Bethesda-Chevy Chase Advertiser - Bethesda, MD - *AyerDirPub 83*
Bethesda-Chevy Chase Advertiser - *See* Morkap Publishing
Bethlehem Bulletin - *See* Peerless Publications
Bethlehem Globe-Times - Bethlehem, PA - *BaconPubCkNews 84; NewsDir 84*
Bethlehem Records - New York, NY - *BillIntBG 83-84*
Bethlehem Video [of Adams-Russell Co. Inc.] - Bethlehem, NY - *BrCabYB 84; Tel&CabFB 84C*
Bethpage Newsgram - Bethpage, NY - *Ed&PubIntYB 82*
Bethpage Newsgram - *See* Litmore Publications
Bethpage Tribune - Bethpage, NY - *Ed&PubIntYB 82*
Bethune Institute, Norman - Toronto, ON, Canada - *BoPubDir 4, 5; LitMag&SmPr 83-84*
Betmar & Associates - Washington, DC - *StaDirAdAg 2-84*
Betong-Indeks [of Aalborg Portland] - Aalborg, Denmark - *CompReadDB 82*
Betriebsforschungsinstitut - *See* Verein Deutscher Eisenhuttenleute
Betta Book Service Inc., A - Hauppauge, NY - *LitMarPl 83, 84*
Bettendorf News [of Lee Enterprises] - Bettendorf, IA - *BaconPubCkNews 84; Ed&PubIntYB 82; NewsDir 84*
Better Baby Press [Aff. of Institutes for the Achievement of Human Potential] - Philadelphia, PA - *BoPubDir 4, 5*
Better Beef Business - Platte City, MO - *BaconPubCkMag 84; MagDir 84*
Better Broadcasting Inc. - Washington, GA - *BrCabYB 84*
Better Business [of National Minority Business Council Inc.] - New York, NY - *MagDir 84; WritMar 84*
Better Cable TV - Waterville, ME - *BrCabYB 84; Tel&CabFB 84C p.1666*
Better Computer Supplies - Pinellas Park, FL - *DataDirSup 7-83*
Better Crops with Plant Food - Atlanta, GA - *BaconPubCkMag 84*
Better-Half Music Co. - Bedford Hills, NY - *BillIntBG 83-84*
Better Healthkeeping - New York, NY - *MagDir 84*
Better Homes & Gardens [of Meredith Corp.] - Des Moines, IA - *ArtMar 84; BaconPubCkMag 84; Folio 83; LitMarPl 84; MagDir 84; MagIndMarPl 82-83; NewsBur 6; WritMar 84*
Better Homes & Gardens Books [of Meredith Book Publishing Group] - Des Moines, IA - *DirMarMP 83; LitMarPl 83, 84; WritMar 84*
Better Homes & Gardens Building Ideas - Des Moines, IA - *BaconPubCkMag 84; MagDir 84; MagIndMarPl 82-83*
Better Homes & Gardens Christmas Ideas - Des Moines, IA - *BaconPubCkMag 84; MagDir 84*
Better Homes & Gardens/Cook's Underground - Des Moines, IA - *DirOnDB Spring 84*
Better Homes & Gardens/Cook's Underground [of CompuServe Inc.] - Columbus, OH - *DataDirOnSer 84*
Better Homes & Gardens Decorating Ideas - Des Moines, IA - *BaconPubCkMag 84; MagIndMarPl 82-83*
Better Homes & Gardens Family Book Service & Crafts Club [of Meredith Corp.] - Des Moines, IA - *LitMarPl 83, 84*
Better Homes & Gardens Furnishings & Decorating Ideas - Des Moines, IA - *MagDir 84*
Better Homes & Gardens Garden Ideas & Outdoor Ideas - Des Moines, IA - *MagDir 84*
Better Homes & Gardens Holiday Cooking & Entertaining - Des Moines, IA - *MagDir 84*
Better Homes & Gardens Holiday Crafts - Des Moines, IA - *MagDir 84*
Better Homes & Gardens Home Furnishings Ideas - Des Moines, IA - *MagDir 84*
Better Homes & Gardens Houseplants - Des Moines, IA - *MagDir 84*
Better Homes & Gardens Ideas & Outdoor Living - Des Moines, IA - *BaconPubCkMag 84*
Better Homes & Gardens Kitchen & Bath Ideas - Des Moines, IA - *BaconPubCkMag 84; MagDir 84; MagIndMarPl 82-83*
Better Homes & Gardens Kitchen & Family Room Ideas - Des Moines, IA - *MagDir 84*
Better Homes & Gardens Remodeling Ideas - Des Moines, IA - *BaconPubCkMag 84; MagDir 84; MagIndMarPl 82-83*
Better Homes & Gardens Traditional Home - Des Moines, IA - *BaconPubCkMag 84*
Better Homes & Gardens Window & Wall Decorating Ideas - Des Moines, IA - *BaconPubCkMag 84*
Better Investing - Royal Oak, MI - *BaconPubCkMag 84; MagDir 84; MagIndMarPl 82-83*
Better Life for You, A [of The National Research Bureau Inc.] - Burlington, IA - *WritMar 84*
Better Living - Sunnyvale, CA - *MagDir 84*
Better Living - New York, NY - *MagIndMarPl 82-83*
Better Mileage Co. - Tucson, AZ - *BoPubDir 4, 5*

Better Monitoring Service Inc. - New York, NY - *ProGuPRSer 4*
Better Music Type & Better Typesetting - Nashville, TN - *LitMarPl 83, 84; MagIndMarPl 82-83*
Better Nutrition - New York, NY - *BaconPubCkMag 84; MagDir 84; MagIndMarPl 82-83*
Better Roads - Park Ridge, IL - *BaconPubCkMag 84; MagDir 84*
Better Times - Lauderdale-By-The-Sea, FL - *BaconPubCkMag 84*
Better Times - New York, NY - *MagDir 84*
Better Times Weekly - Morgantown, WV - *Ed&PubIntYB 82*
Better TV Inc. [of Adelphia Communications Group] - Hoosick Falls, NY - *Tel&CabFB 84C*
Better TV Inc. of Bennington [of Adelphia Communications Corp.] - Bennington, VT - *BrCabYB 84; Tel&CabFB 84C*
Better TV Inc. of Dutchess County [of Colony Communications Inc.] - Hyde Park, NY - *BrCabYB 84*
Better Vision Cable Co. - Roanoke, AL - *BrCabYB 84; Tel&CabFB 84C*
Betterview Cablevision of Oregon [of Jones Intercable Inc.] - Canyonville, OR - *BrCabYB 84; Tel&CabFB 84C*
Betterview Cablevision of Oregon [of Jones Intercable] - Myrtle Creek, OR - *BrCabYB 84; Tel&CabFB 84C*
Betterview Cablevision of Oregon [of Jones Intercable] - Winston, OR - *BrCabYB 84; Tel&CabFB 84C*
Betterview TV Cable Co. [of Huntingdon TV Cable Co. Inc.] - Saxton, PA - *BrCabYB 84; Tel&CabFB 84C*
Betterway Publications Inc. - White Hall, VA - *BoPubDir 4; LitMarPl 83, 84; WritMar 84*
Bettis & Schwartz Advertising Inc. - El Paso, TX - *StaDirAdAg 2-84*
Bettles Advertising - Buenos Aires, Argentina - *StaDirAdAg 2-84*
Bettmann Archive [Div. of Kraus-Thomson Organization Ltd.] - New York, NY - *AvMarPl 83; LitMarPl 83, 84*
Betts, Glynne Robinson - New York, NY - *LitMarPl 83, 84*
Between the Lines - Toronto, ON, Canada - *BoPubDir 4; LitMag&SmPr 83-84; LitMarPl 83, 84*
Betz Publishing Co. Inc. - Bethesda, MD - *BoPubDir 5*
Betzer Productions Inc. - Chicago, IL - *ArtMar 84; AvMarPl 83; Tel&CabFB 84C*
Beulah Beacon - Beulah, ND - *BaconPubCkNews 84; Ed&PubIntYB 82*
Beulah Cable TV Inc. - Beulah, ND - *BrCabYB 84*
Beulah Records & Publishing Co. - Crossville, IL - *BoPubDir 4, 5*
Beverage Alcohol Market Report - New York, NY - *BaconPubCkMag 84*
Beverage Alcohol Reporter - North York, ON, Canada - *BaconPubCkMag 84*
Beverage Analyst Group, The [of Bevan Inc.] - Denver, CO - *MagDir 84*
Beverage Beacon - Los Angeles, CA - *BaconPubCkMag 84*
Beverage Bulletin [of California Beverage Publications] - Beverly Hills, CA - *BaconPubCkMag 84; MagDir 84*
Beverage Canada - Mississauga, ON, Canada - *BaconPubCkMag 84*
Beverage Industry [of Harcourt Brace Jovanovich] - New York, NY - *MagDir 84; MagIndMarPl 82-83*
Beverage Industry - Cleveland, OH - *BaconPubCkMag 84*
Beverage Industry News [of Industry Publications Inc.] - San Francisco, CA - *MagDir 84*
Beverage Marketing Corp. - Mingo Junction, OH - *BoPubDir 4 Sup, 5; EISS 83*
Beverage Media - New York, NY - *BaconPubCkMag 84; MagDir 84*
Beverage News, Kansas Edition - Wichita, KS - *BaconPubCkMag 84*
Beverage Record, The [of Anderson Publications] - Lake Arrowhead, CA - *BaconPubCkMag 84; MagDir 84*
Beverage Register, The [of Anderson Publications] - Lake Arrowhead, CA - *MagDir 84*
Beverage Retailer Weekly - Wayne, NJ - *BaconPubCkMag 84*
Beverage Retailer Weekly - New York, NY - *MagDir 84*
Beverage World [of Keller International Publishing Corp.] - Great Neck, NY - *ArtMar 84; BaconPubCkMag 84; MagDir 84; MagIndMarPl 82-83*
Beverage World En Espanol - Great Neck, NY - *BaconPubCkMag 84*
Beverage World Periscope - Great Neck, NY - *BaconPubCkMag 84*
Beverages [of All America's Publishers Service] - Chicago, IL - *MagDir 84*
Beverages - Winnetka, IL - *BaconPubCkMag 84*
Beveridge Organization Inc. - Chicago, IL - *DirPRFirms 83*
Beverly, Baron, Drumm & Associates Inc. - Metairie, LA - *StaDirAdAg 2-84*
Beverly Books Inc. - Linden, NJ - *BoPubDir 4 Sup, 5; LitMarPl 83, 84*
Beverly Hills By-Line - Los Angeles, CA - *Ed&PubIntYB 82*
Beverly Hills Courier - Beverly Hills, CA - *BaconPubCkNews 84; Ed&PubIntYB 82; NewsDir 84*
Beverly Hills Independent - Beverly Hills, CA - *Ed&PubIntYB 82*
Beverly Hills Independent [of Santa Monica United Western Newspapers Inc.] - Santa Monica, CA - *AyerDirPub 83; NewsDir 84*
Beverly Hills Independent - *See* Copley Press Inc.
Beverly Hills Music [Div. of Lawrence Herbst Investment Trust Fund] - Beverly Hills, CA - *BillIntBG 83-84*
Beverly Hills Post [of Los Angeles Post Newspaper Group] - Los Angeles, CA - *NewsDir 84*
Beverly Hills Post - *See* Post Newspaper Group
Beverly News [of Southwest Messenger Newspapers] - Midlothian, IL - *AyerDirPub 83; NewsDir 84*
Beverly News - *See* Southwest Messenger Newspapers
Beverly-Peabody Times - Beverly, MA - *BaconPubCkNews 84*
Beverly Review - Chicago, IL - *AyerDirPub 83*
Beverly Times [of Ottoway Newspapers] - Beverly, MA - *Ed&PubIntYB 82; NewsDir 84*
Bev's Carson Cablevision - Carson, WA - *BrCabYB 84; Tel&CabFB 84C*
Bewick Advertising Inc., Douglas - Springfield, MA - *StaDirAdAg 2-84*
Bexar County Cablevision [of Television Access Inc.] - Bexar County, TX - *Tel&CabFB 84C*
Bexley Publishing Co. - Memphis, TN - *BillIntBG 83-84*
Beyda Associates Inc. - Van Nuys, CA - *LitMarPl 83, 84*
Beyda, Barbara M. - Rockville Centre, NY - *LitMarPl 83, 84*
Beyer Dynamic Inc. - Hicksville, NY - *AvMarPl 83*
Beyl & Boyd Inc. - San Francisco, CA - *DirPRFirms 83*
Beyl Public Relations Inc., Ernest - San Francisco, CA - *DirPRFirms 83*
Beyond - Hollywood, CA - *MagIndMarPl 82-83*
Beyond Baroque Foundation Publications - Venice, CA - *LitMag&SmPr 83-84*
Beyond Science Fiction [of Cosmic Circus Productions] - Richmond, CA - *LitMag&SmPr 83-84*
Beyond Words - Minneapolis, MN - *AvMarPl 83*
Bezkorovainy, Anatoly - Lincolnwood, IL - *BoPubDir 4 Sup, 5*
BFLO Magazine - Boston, MA - *MagDir 84*
B.F.O. Inc. - Forest Hills, NY - *Ed&PubIntYB 82*
BFR Stations - *See* Midcontinent Broadcasting Co.
BG Enterprises - Scottsdale, AZ - *MicrocomMPl 83, 84*
BGM Colour Laboratories Ltd. - Toronto, ON, Canada - *AvMarPl 83*
BGO Music Inc. - Doraville, GA - *BillIntBG 83-84*
BGO Records Inc. - Doraville, GA - *BillIntBG 83-84*
BGS Systems Inc. - Waltham, MA - *DataDirSup 7-83*
B.G.W. Associates [Subs. of Broad Street Communications] - Riverside, CT - *CabTVFinDB 83*
BH & G Data Base [of Better Homes & Gardens] - Des Moines, IA - *EISS 7-83 Sup*
Bhaktivedanta Book Trust - Los Angeles, CA - *BoPubDir 4, 5*
Bharati - Toronto, ON, Canada - *Ed&PubIntYB 82*
BHN/Direct Marketing [Div. of Batz-Hodgson-Neuwoehner Inc.] - Kansas City, MO - *DirMarMP 83*
BHN-PR [Div. of Batz-Hodgson-Neuwoehner Inc.] - St. Louis, MO - *DirPRFirms 83*
BHRA Fluid Engineering [of Dialog Information Services Inc.] - Palo Alto, CA - *DataDirOnSer 84*
BHRA Fluid Engineering - Bedford, England - *InfIndMarPl 83*
BHRA Fluid Engineering [of British Hydromechanics Research Association] - Cranfield, England - *CompReadDB 82; DBBus 82; OnBibDB 3*
BHRA Fluid Engineering - Preston, England - *DirOnDB Spring 84*

BI Associates Inc. - Kensington, MD - *EISS 83*
BI/CAS - New York, NY - *DirOnDB Spring 84*
Bi-County Herald - Hudson, MI - *AyerDirPub 83*
Bi-County Messenger, The - Monett, MO - *AyerDirPub 83*
BI/Data [of Business International Corp.] - New York, NY - *CompReadDB 82; DataDirOnSer 84; DBBus 82; DirOnDB Spring 84; EISS 83; InfIndMarPl 83*
BI/Data Forecasts [of Business International Corp.] - New York, NY - *DataDirOnSer 84; DirOnDB Spring 84*
BI Language Services - El Paso, TX - *MagIndMarPl 82-83*
Bi-Science Publications - Webster Groves, MO - *BoPubDir 4, 5*
Bi-State Reporter - Antioch, IL - *AyerDirPub 83*
Bi-Tech Enterprises - Bohemia, NY - *MicrocomMPl 84*
Bibas-Redford Inc. - Port Chester, NY - *AvMarPl 83*
Bibb Cable TV - Centreville, AL - *Tel&CabFB 84C*
Bibb, Mary - Grants Pass, OR - *BoPubDir 5*
Bible Broadcasting Network - Chesapeake, VA - *Tel&CabFB 84C*
Bible Broadcasting Network - Norfolk, VA - *BrCabYB 84*
Bible-In-Life Friends [of David C. Cook Publishing Co.] - Elgin, IL - *WritMar 84*
Bible-In-Life Pix [of David C. Cook Publishing Co.] - Elgin, IL - *WritMar 84*
Bible Light Publications - Bronx, NY - *BoPubDir 4 Sup, 5*
Bible Literature Publications - Lake Almanor Peninsula, CA - *BoPubDir 4, 5*
Bible Research Press - Abilene, TX - *BoPubDir 4*
Bible Research Systems - Austin, TX - *MicrocomMPl 84*
Bible-Speak Enterprises - Mountain View, CA - *BoPubDir 5; LitMag&SmPr 83-84*
Bible Stories Alive - Toronto, ON, Canada - *BoPubDir 4 Sup, 5*
Bible Temple Publications - Portland, OR - *BoPubDir 4, 5; LitMarPl 84*
Biblical Archeologist - Ann Arbor, MI - *MagIndMarPl 82-83*
Biblical Illustrator - Nashville, TN - *WritMar 84*
Biblical Research Press - Abilene, TX - *BoPubDir 5; LitMarPl 84*
Biblicom - Montreal, PQ, Canada - *DirOnDB Spring 84*
Biblio-Data [of German National Library] - Frankfurt, West Germany - *DirOnDB Spring 84; EISS 83*
Biblio Distribution Centre [Div. of Littlefield, Adams & Co.] - Totowa, NJ - *LitMarPl 83, 84*
Biblio Press - Fresh Meadows, NY - *BoPubDir 4, 5; LitMag&SmPr 83-84*
Biblio-Techniques Inc. - Olympia, WA - *EISS 7-83 Sup*
Bibliocentre [of Centennial College] - Scarborough, ON, Canada - *EISS 83*
Bibliocom [of Institut International de la Communication] - Montreal, PQ, Canada - *CompReadDB 82*
Bibliofem [of City of London Polytechnic] - London, England - *EISS 83*
Bibliografia Nazionale Italiana [of Centro per la Documentazione Automatica] - Rome, Italy - *CompReadDB 82*
Bibliographic Access & Control System [of Washington University] - St. Louis, MO - *EISS 83*
Bibliographic Index of Health Education Periodicals [of Indiana University] - Bloomington, IN - *EISS 7-83 Sup*
Bibliographic Information on Southeast Asia [of University of Sydney] - Sydney, Australia - *CompReadDB 82; DirOnDB Spring 84; EISS 83*
Bibliographic Publishing Co. - Milan, Italy - *EISS 7-83 Sup*
Bibliographic Retrieval Services [Div. of Indian Head Inc.] - Latham, NY - *ADAPSOMemDir 83-84; CompReadDB 82; DataDirOnSer 84; EISS 83, 7-83 Sup, 5-84 Sup; InfIndMarPl 83; InfoS 83-84*
Bibliographic Retrieval Services (Education Service Group) - Latham, NY - *CompReadDB 82*
Bibliographic Services Div. [of British Library] - London, England - *EISS 83*
Bibliographical Center for Research [Subs. of Rocky Mountain Region Inc.] - Denver, CO - *DataDirOnSer 84; EISS 83; InfIndMarPl 83*
Bibliographical Society of America - New York, NY - *BoPubDir 4, 5*
Bibliographical Society of Canada/Societe Bibliographique du Canada - Guelph, ON, Canada - *BoPubDir 4*
Bibliographical Society of Canada/Societe Bibliographique du Canada - London, ON, Canada - *BoPubDir 5*
Bibliographie Internationale de la Documentation en Langue Francaise [of Informatech] - Montreal, PQ, Canada - *DataDirOnSer 84*
Bibliographie Internationale de Langue Francaise sur la Communication [of Informatech] - Montreal, PQ, Canada - *DataDirOnSer 84*
Bibliographie Linguistischer Literatur [of Stadt und Universitatbibliothek Frankfurt] - Frankfurt, West Germany - *CompReadDB 82*
Bibliography of Gamma Ray Transitions [of Indian Institute of Technology] - Kanpur, India - *CompReadDB 82*
Bibliography of Linguistic Literature [of Frankfurt City & University Library] - Frankfurt, East Germany - *EISS 7-83 Sup*
Bibliophile Legion Books - Silver Spring, MD - *BoPubDir 4, 5*
Biblios [of Direction de la Documentation Francaise] - Paris, France - *CompReadDB 82*
Biblios Hawaii [of Hawaii State Dept. of Education] - Honolulu, HI - *EISS 83*
Biblioservices - Lexington, MA - *EISS 7-83 Sup*
Biblioteca Nazionale Italiana - Florence, Italy - *InfIndMarPl 83*
Biblioteca Siglo de Oro - Charlottesville, VA - *BoPubDir 4, 5*
Bibliotecas Publicas del Estado en las Capitales de Provincia [of Ministerio de Cultura] - Madrid, Spain - *InfIndMarPl 83*
Bibliotheca Islamica Inc. - Chicago, IL - *BoPubDir 4, 5*
Bibliotheca Press - Atlanta, GA - *LitMag&SmPr 83-84*
Bibliotheca Press Southwest [of Bibliotheca Press Inc.] - Houston, TX - *BoPubDir 4 Sup, 5*
Bibliotheca Press Update - Atlanta, GA - *LitMag&SmPr 83-84*
Bibliotheck, The - Edinburgh, Scotland - *LitMag&SmPr 83-84*
Bibliotheque d'Humanisme et Renaissance - Geneva, Switzerland - *LitMag&SmPr 83-84*
Bibliotheque Nationale du Quebec [of Ministere des Affaires Culturelles du Quebec] - Montreal, PQ, Canada - *DataDirOnSer 84*
Bibliotheque Nationale du Quebec (Service de Microphotographie) - Montreal, PQ, Canada - *MicroMarPl 82-83*
Bibulophile Press - Bantam, CT - *LitMag&SmPr 83-84*
Bicentennial Era Enterprises - Scappoose, OR - *BoPubDir 4, 5; LitMag&SmPr 83-84*
Bicentennial Studies in Sangamon History - Springfield, IL - *BoPubDir 4, 5*
Bicknell Knox County Daily News - Bicknell, IN - *NewsDir 84*
Bicsi - Puunene, HI - *MicrocomMPl 84*
Bicycle Business Journal - Ft. Worth, TX - *BaconPubCkMag 84; WritMar 84*
Bicycle Dealer Showcase - Irvine, CA - *BaconPubCkMag 84; WritMar 84*
Bicycle Dealer Showcase - Santa Ana, CA - *MagDir 84*
Bicycle Forum - Missoula, MT - *BaconPubCkMag 84*
Bicycle Journal - Ft. Worth, TX - *MagDir 84*
Bicycle Music Co. - Los Angeles, CA - *BillIntBG 83-84*
Bicycling [of Rodale Press Inc.] - Emmaus, PA - *BaconPubCkMag 84; Folio 83; MagDir 84; MagIndMarPl 82-83; WritMar 84*
Biddick Co. - Northridge, CA - *Tel&CabFB 84C*
Biddle & Associates Inc. - Sacramento, CA - *EISS 7-83 Sup*
Biddle Newspapers - Huntingdon, PA - *Ed&PubIntYB 82*
Biederman & Associates Inc., R. - Mission, KS - *HBIndAd&MS 82-83*
Bielaruski Holas - Toronto, ON, Canada - *Ed&PubIntYB 82*
Bieler Press - St. Paul, MN - *BoPubDir 4, 5; LitMag&SmPr 83-84*
Bienstock Music, Johnny - New York, NY - *BillIntBG 83-84*
Bienville Democrat - Arcadia, LA - *AyerDirPub 83; Ed&PubIntYB 82*
Bier & Associates, T. M. - Long Island City, NY - *ADAPSOMemDir 83-84*
Biespiel Advertising, Lee S. - St. Joseph, MI - *StaDirAdAg 2-84*
Biffel Creative Press - Lawrenceville, NJ - *BoPubDir 4*
Big Apple Music Associates - *See* Entertainment Co., The
Big B Publications - Ridgewood, NY - *LitMag&SmPr 83-84*
Big Basin Herald - Muldrow, OK - *Ed&PubIntYB 82*
Big Bear Life & The Grizzly - Big Bear Lake, CA - *AyerDirPub 83; BaconPubCkNews 84; Ed&PubIntYB 82; NewsDir 84*
Big Bear Music - Fairview Heights, IL - *BillIntBG 83-84*

Big Bend Broadcasting Corp. - Quincy, FL - *BrCabYB 84*
Big Bend Communications Inc. - Alpine, TX - *Tel&CabFB 84C p.1666*
Big Bend Communications Inc. - Comstock, TX - *BrCabYB 84*
Big Bend Communications Inc. - Lajitas, TX - *BrCabYB 84*
Big Bend Communications Inc. - Sanderson, TX - *BrCabYB 84*
Big Bend Communications Inc. - Shafter, TX - *BrCabYB 84*
Big Bend Natural History Association Inc. - Big Bend National Park, TX - *BoPubDir 4, 5*
Big Bend Sentinel - Marfa, TX - *AyerDirPub 83; Ed&PubIntYB 82*
Big Bend Telephone Co. Inc. - Alpine, TX - *TelDir&BG 83-84*
Big Book Update, The [of Slater Publications Inc.] - Needham Heights, MA - *MagDir 84*
Big Canoe Cable TV System - Big Canoe, GA - *BrCabYB 84*
Big Canoe Corp. - Big Canoe, GA - *Tel&CabFB 84C*
Big Country Voice, The - Hafford, SK, Canada - *Ed&PubIntYB 82*
Big Daddy Records - Yonkers, NY - *BillIntBG 83-84*
Big Dot Publications - Westmoreland City, PA - *BoPubDir 4 Sup, 5*
Big Elk Music - *See* Williams Music Group, Don
Big Falls CATV - Big Falls, MN - *Tel&CabFB 84C*
Big Farmer Entrepreneur - Frankfort, IL - *MagDir 84; MagIndMarPl 82-83*
Big Fights Inc., The - New York, NY - *Tel&CabFB 84C*
Big Five Software - Van Nuys, CA - *MicrocomMPl 83, 84*
Big Heart Music Inc. - Beverly Hills, CA - *BillIntBG 83-84*
Big Horn Televents Inc. - Greybull, WY - *BrCabYB 84; Tel&CabFB 84C*
Big Hurry Music Co. Inc. - Palisades Park, NJ - *BillIntBG 83-84*
Big Idea Advertising Agency, The - Denver, CO - *StaDirAdAg 2-84*
Big Island Computer Systems Inc. - Pahala, HI - *MicrocomSwDir 1*
Big Island Music - Woodland Hills, CA - *BillIntBG 83-84*
Big Kahuna Music - Memphis, TN - *BillIntBG 83-84*
Big L Productions Ltd. Inc. - Garland, TX - *BillIntBG 83-84*
Big Lake Wildcat - Big Lake, TX - *BaconPubCkNews 84; Ed&PubIntYB 82*
Big Mama Rag - Denver, CO - *LitMag&SmPr 83-84*
Big Mike Music - New York, NY - *BillIntBG 83-84*
Big Monkey Records - Jackson, MS - *BillIntBG 83-84*
Big Moose Press - Big Moose, NY - *BoPubDir 4, 5*
Big Muddy Roundup - Bengough, SK, Canada - *Ed&PubIntYB 82*
Big Muddy Roundup - Radville, SK, Canada - *AyerDirPub 83*
Big Music [Div. of Trod Nossel Artists] - Wallingford, CT - *BillIntBG 83-84*
Big Orange Production Co., The - Miami, FL - *AvMarPl 83*
Big Pasture News - Grandfield, OK - *AyerDirPub 83; Ed&PubIntYB 82*
Big Pine Cable TV - Round Valley, CA - *Tel&CabFB 84C*
Big Rapids Pioneer [of Conine Publishing Co. Inc.] - Big Rapids, MI - *BaconPubCkNews 84; NewsDir 84*
Big Red - Brooklyn, NY - *Ed&PubIntYB 82*
Big Red - New York, NY - *AyerDirPub 83*
Big Reel, The - Madison, NC - *ArtMar 84*
Big Reel, The - Summerfield, NC - *MagIndMarPl 82-83*
Big River Association - St. Louis, MO - *LitMag&SmPr 83-84*
Big Run Telephone Co. [Aff. of Citizens Utilities Co.] - New Bethlehem, PA - *TelDir&BG 83-84*
Big Sandy & Hawkins Journal & Tri Area News - Big Sandy, TX - *AyerDirPub 83; BaconPubCkNews 84; Ed&PubIntYB 82*
Big Sandy Cable [of Belisle Enterprises] - Bruceton Mills, PA - *Tel&CabFB 84C*
Big Sandy Mountaineer - Big Sandy, MT - *BaconPubCkNews 84; Ed&PubIntYB 82*
Big Sandy News - Louisa, KY - *AyerDirPub 83; Ed&PubIntYB 82*
Big Sandy Telecom - Simla, CO - *TelDir&BG 83-84*
Big Sandy TV Cable - Van Lear, KY - *BrCabYB 84*
Big Scream - Grandville, MI - *LitMag&SmPr 83-84*
Big Seven Music Corp. - New York, NY - *BillIntBG 83-84*
Big Sky - Bolinas, CA - *BoPubDir 4, 5*
Big Sky Music - *See* Special Rider Music
Big Spring Cable TV Inc. [of TCA Cable TV Group] - Big Spring, TX - *Tel&CabFB 84C*
Big Spring Cable TV Inc. - Tyler, TX - *BrCabYB 84 p.D-297*
Big Spring Herald [of Harte-Hanks Newspapers Inc.] - Big Spring, TX - *BaconPubCkNews 84; Ed&PubIntYB 82; NewsDir 84*
Big State Music Publishing - Duncanville, TX - *BillIntBG 83-84*
Big Stone Gap Post - Big Stone Gap, VA - *BaconPubCkNews 84*
Big Sur Publications - Monterey, CA - *BoPubDir 4, 5*
Big Swan Publishing Co. - Summertown, TN - *BillIntBG 83-84*
Big Swing Publishing - Oklahoma City, OK - *BillIntBG 83-84*
Big Thicket Museum - Saratoga, TX - *BoPubDir 5*
Big Timber Cable TV [of Communications Investment Corp.] - Big Timber, MT - *BrCabYB 84; Tel&CabFB 84C*
Big Timber Pioneer - Big Timber, MT - *BaconPubCkNews 84; Ed&PubIntYB 82*
Big Time Picture Co. Inc. - Pacific Palisades, CA - *AvMarPl 83*
Big Toad Press - Sacramento, CA - *BoPubDir 4 Sup, 5*
Big Trees Software Corp. - Arnold, CA - *MicrocomMPl 84*
Big Valley [of World of Communications Inc.] - Sepulveda, CA - *BaconPubCkMag 84; WritMar 84*
Big Valley Cablevision - Manteca, CA - *BrCabYB 84*
Big Valley Cablevision Inc. [of Continental Cablevision Inc.] - Stockton, CA - *BrCabYB 84; Tel&CabFB 84C*
Big Wedge Music - *See* Dawn Productions Ltd.
Biggers, Patterson & Parke Inc. - Orlando, FL - *StaDirAdAg 2-84*
Biggs, Cliff & Marge - Grand Terrace, CA - *BoPubDir 4, 5*
Biggs/Gilmore Associates Inc., William R. - Kalamazoo, MI - *AdAge 3-28-84; DirPRFirms 83; StaDirAdAg 2-84*
Biggs, Ken - Los Angeles, CA - *MagIndMarPl 82-83*
Biggs News - Biggs, CA - *BaconPubCkNews 84; Ed&PubIntYB 82*
BIIPAM-CTIF [of Centre de Recherches de Pont-a-Mousson] - Pont-a-Mousson, France - *DBBus 82; DirOnDB Spring 84*
Bijou Ridge Music - Wakonda, SD - *BillIntBG 83-84*
Bijou Telephone Cooperative - Byers, CO - *TelDir&BG 83-84*
Bikepress - Franklin Centre, PQ, Canada - *BoPubDir 5*
BikePress U.S.A./BikePress Canada - Mars, PA - *LitMag&SmPr 83-84*
Bikereport [of Bikecentennial Inc.] - Missoula, MT - *ArtMar 84; WritMar 84*
Bike's Marketing Services Group - Westchester, IL - *StaDirAdAg 2-84*
Bilbat Broadcast Group, The - Hornell, NY - *BrCabYB 84*
BILD - Helsinski, Finland - *DirOnDB Spring 84*
Bildor, The [of Builders Association of Southeastern Michigan] - Southfield, MI - *BaconPubCkMag 84; MagDir 84*
Bildschirmtext [of Deutsche Bundespost] - Bonn, West Germany - *VideoDir 82-83*
Bildschirmtext [of Deutsche Bundespost] - Darmstadt, West Germany - *EISS 83; InfIndMarPl 83*
Bildschirmzeitung [of Arbeitsgemeinschaft der Offentlich-Rechtlichen Rundfunkanstalten] - Berlin, West Germany - *VideoDir 82-83*
Bile [of No Tickee/No Washee Enterprises Ltd.] - Chicago, IL - *LitMag&SmPr 83-84*
Bilingual Books Inc. [Subs. of Outdoor Empire Publishing] - Seattle, WA - *LitMarPl 83, 84*
Bilingual Education Abstracts [of Bibliographic Retrieval Services Inc.] - Latham, NY - *DataDirOnSer 84*
Bilingual Education Bibliographic Abstracts [of National Clearinghouse for Bilingual Education] - Arlington, VA - *CompReadDB 82; OnBibDB 3*
Bilingual Education Bibliographic Abstracts - Rosslyn, VA - *DirOnDB Spring 84*
Bilingual Educational Services Inc. - Los Angeles, CA - *LitMarPl 84*
Bilingual Educational Services Inc. - South Pasadena, CA - *ArtMar 84; AvMarPl 83; BoPubDir 4 Sup, 5; LitMarPl 83; WritMar 84*
Bilingual Publications Co. - New York, NY - *BoPubDir 4 Sup, 5; LitMarPl 83, 84*
Bilingual Review Press [of Eastern Michigan University] - Ypsilanti, MI - *BoPubDir 4, 5; LitMag&SmPr 83-84*
Bilingue Publications - Las Cruces, NM - *BoPubDir 4 Sup, 5; LitMag&SmPr 83-84*
Bilko Press [Aff. of Lakewood Graphics Ltd.] - Kenora, ON, Canada - *BoPubDir 4, 5*

Bill Communications - New York, NY - *DirMarMP 83; KnowInd 83; MagIndMarPl 82-83*
Bill-Lee Music - *See* Ren-Maur Music Corp.
Bill of Rights in Action - Los Angeles, CA - *MagIndMarPl 82-83*
Bill Status System [of Legislative Information System] - Springfield, IL - *DataDirOnSer 84*
Billboard - Los Angeles, CA - *NewsBur 6*
Billboard - Cloquet, MN - *AyerDirPub 83*
Billboard [of Billboard Publications Inc.] - New York, NY - *BaconPubCkMag 84; Folio 83; MagDir 84; MagIndMarPl 82-83; WritMar 84*
Billboard Information Network [of Billboard Publications Inc.] - New York, NY - *CompReadDB 82; DataDirOnSer 84; DBBus 82; DirOnDB Spring 84; EISS 83; MicrocomMPl 84*
Billboard Publications Inc. - New York, NY - *CompReadDB 82; DataDirOnSer 84; KnowInd 83; MagIndMarPl 82-83*
Billee Music - *See* Ren-Maur Music Corp.
Billel Creative Press - Lawrenceville, NJ - *BoPubDir 5*
Billerica Minute-Man - Acton, MA - *AyerDirPub 83*
Billerica Minute-Man [of Beacon/Minute-Man Corp.] - Billerica, MA - *Ed&PubIntYB 82; NewsDir 84*
Billerica Minute Man - *See* Minute-Man Publications Inc.
Billerica News, The - Billerica, MA - *Ed&PubIntYB 82*
Billerica News, The - North Billerica, MA - *NewsDir 84*
Billetdoux Music Publishing - Chicago, IL - *BillIntBG 83-84*
Billiards Digest [of National Bowlers Journal Inc.] - Chicago, IL - *WritMar 84*
Billing, Estelle - Scottsdale, AZ - *LitMarPl 83, 84*
Billings Computer Corp. - Grandview, MO - *MicrocomMPl 84*
Billings Computer Corp. [Subs. of Billings Energy Corp.] - Independence, MO - *MicrocomMPl 84; WhoWMicrocom 83*
Billings County Pioneer - Medora, ND - *AyerDirPub 83*
Billings County Pioneer - *See* Golden Valley News Publishers
Billings Gazette [of Lee Enterprises Inc.] - Billings, MT - *BaconPubCkNews 84; Ed&PubIntYB 82; LitMarPl 83, 84; NewsBur 6; NewsDir 84*
Billings Group, The - Concord, MA - *IntDirMarRes 83*
Billings McEachern Inc. - Foster City, CA - *WhoWMicrocom 83*
Billings News - Garber, OK - *BaconPubCkNews 84*
Billings Times - Billings, MT - *BaconPubCkNews 84; Ed&PubIntYB 82*
Billion Books [Subs. of Billion Interplanetary] - Ft. Worth, TX - *DirMarMP 83*
Billyou, Scott - West Hartford, CT - *LitMarPl 83, 84*
Biloxi-North Biloxi Press - Biloxi, MS - *BaconPubCkNews 84*
Biloxi Reporter, The - Biloxi, MS - *Ed&PubIntYB 82*
BIN Merchandiser [of Industry Publications Inc.] - San Francisco, CA - *BaconPubCkMag 84; MagDir 84*
BIN of California - San Francisco, CA - *BaconPubCkMag 84*
Binary Computer Products - Berkley, MI - *MicrocomMPl 84*
Binary Devices - Noblesville, IN - *MicrocomMPl 84*
Binford & Mort - Portland, OR - *LitMarPl 83, 84; WritMar 84*
Bing Advertising Co., Ralph [Aff. of Marketing Associates Corp.] - San Diego, CA - *ArtMar 84; BrCabYB 84; StaDirAdAg 2-84; TelAl 83, 84*
Bing, Bing, Bing Music - *See* Marvel Music, Andy
Bingham County Cable TV [of Vukasovich Broadcasting Inc.] - Blackfoot, ID - *BrCabYB 84; Tel&CabFB 84C*
Binghamton Evening Press - Binghamton, NY - *BaconPubCkNews 84; LitMarPl 83*
Binghamton NewChannels [Aff. of New Channels Corp.] - Binghamton, NY - *Tel&CabFB 84C*
Binghamton NewChannels [Aff. of NewChannels Corp.] - Vestal, NY - *InterCabHB 3*
Binghamton Press, The - Binghamton, NY - *LitMarPl 83*
Binghamton Sun-Bulletin [of Gannett Co. Inc.] - Binghamton, NY - *BaconPubCkNews 84; LitMarPl 83; NewsDir 84*
Binghamton/Vestal NewChannels Corp. [Aff. of NewChannels Corp.] - Binghamton, NY - *BrCabYB 84*
Bingo Bugle Inc. - Gig Harbor, WA - *LitMag&SmPr 83-84*
Bingo Operator Newsmagazine, The - Clayton, MO - *BaconPubCkMag 84*
Binns Graphics, Betty - New York, NY - *LitMarPl 83, 84; MagIndMarPl 82-83*
Binns, Joseph J. - Bethesda, MD - *LitMarPl 83, 84*
Bio Cycle-Journal of Waste Recycling - Emmaus, PA - *BaconPubCkMag 84; MagDir 84*
Bio-Dynamic Literature [Aff. of Bio-Dynamic Farming & Gardening Association Inc.] - Wyoming, RI - *BoPubDir 4, 5*
Bio-Energy Council - Washington, DC - *BoPubDir 4 Sup, 5*
Bio Engineering News - Willits, CA - *BaconPubCkMag 84*
Bio Medi Dent Research Center - Aiea, HI - *BoPubDir 4 Sup, 5*
Bio-Medical Insight - Miami, FL - *BaconPubCkMag 84; MagDir 84*
Bio/Technology - New York, NY - *BaconPubCkMag 84*
Biobehavioral Press/Wendover Press - Houston, TX - *BoPubDir 4*
Biobehavioral Publishers & Distributors Inc. - Houston, TX - *BoPubDir 5; LitMag&SmPr 83-84*
Biocal Software Inc. - Fairfax, CA - *MicrocomMPl 84*
Biochemistry Abstracts Part 1 (Biological Membranes) - London, England - *CompReadDB 82*
Biochemistry Abstracts Part 2 (Nucleic Acids) - London, England - *CompReadDB 82*
Biochemistry Abstracts Part 3 (Amino-Acids, Peptides, & Proteins) - London, England - *CompReadDB 82*
Biocodes [of Biosciences Information Service] - Philadelphia, PA - *CompReadDB 82; DataDirOnSer 84*
Biodeterioration Centre [of University of Aston] - Birmingham, England - *EISS 83*
Biodoc [of Servi-Tech] - Waterloo, Belgium - *DirOnDB Spring 84; EISS 7-83 Sup*
Bioethics Information Retrieval System [of Georgetown University] - Washington, DC - *EISS 83*
Bioethicsline [of National Library of Medicine] - Washington, DC - *CompReadDB 82; DataDirOnSer 84; DBBus 82; DirOnDB Spring 84; OnBibDB 3*
Biofeedback & Advanced Therapy Institute Inc. [Aff. of Biofeedback Institute of San Francisco] - San Francisco, CA - *BoPubDir 5*
Biofeedback Press [Aff. of Biofeedback Institute of San Francisco] - San Francisco, CA - *BoPubDir 4, 5*
Biofeedback Research Institute - Los Angeles, CA - *BoPubDir 4, 5*
Biograph Records Inc. - Chatham, NY - *BillIntBG 83-84*
Biography Master Index [of Dialog Information Services Inc.] - Palo Alto, CA - *DataDirOnSer 84*
Biography Master Index [of Gale Research Co.] - Detroit, MI - *CompReadDB 82; DBBus 82; DirOnDB Spring 84; EISS 83; OnBibDB 3*
Biography Press - Aransas Pass, TX - *BoPubDir 4, 5*
Biohydrant Publications - St. Albans, VT - *BoPubDir 4 Sup, 5*
Biokinesiology Institute - Shady Cove, OR - *BoPubDir 5*
Biokinesiology Institute - Talent, OR - *BoPubDir 4*
Biological Abstracts on Tape [of Biosciences Information Service] - Philadelphia, PA - *CompReadDB 82; DataDirOnSer 84*
Biological Abstracts/RRM [of BioSciences Information Service] - Philadelphia, PA - *MagDir 84*
Biological Information Service [of Julie Moore & Associates] - Riverside, CA - *CompReadDB 82; EISS 83; FBInfSer 80; InfIndMarPl 83*
Biological Photo Service - Moss Beach, CA - *LitMarPl 83, 84*
Biological Records Centre [of Institute of Terrestrial Ecology] - Huntingdon, England - *EISS 83*
Biologische Bundesanstalt fur Land- & Forstwirtschaft - Berlin, West Germany - *InfIndMarPl 83*
Biology Bookist, The - Half Moon Bay, CA - *LitMarPl 83, 84*
Biology Digest [of Plexus Publishing Inc.] - Medford, NJ - *LitMag&SmPr 83-84*
Biomanagement & Research Enterprises - Sault Ste. Marie, ON, Canada - *BoPubDir 4, 5*
Biomass Digest - Ft. Lee, NJ - *BaconPubCkMag 84*
BioMedical Associates - Alexandria, VA - *LitMarPl 84*
Biomedical Communications - New York, NY - *BaconPubCkMag 84; MagDir 84*
Biomedical Computing Technology Information Center [of Vanderbuilt University Medical School] - Nashville, TN - *EISS 83; InfIndMarPl 83*
Biomedical Documentation & Information Center [of University of Valencia] - Valencia, Spain - *EISS 83*
Biomedical Engineering Current Awareness Notification [of Clinical Research Centre] - Harrow, England - *CompReadDB 82*
Biomedical Information Dept. [of State University of Utrecht Library] - Utrecht, Netherlands - *EISS 7-83 Sup*

Biomedical Information Service [of University of Sheffield] - Sheffield, England - *EISS 83*
Biomedical Products - Dover, NJ - *BaconPubCkMag 84; MagDir 84*
Biomedical Publications - Davis, CA - *BoPubDir 4, 5; WritMar 84*
Biomedical Safety & Standards - Brea, CA - *BaconPubCkMag 84*
Biomedical Technology Information Service - Brea, CA - *BaconPubCkMag 84; MagDir 84*
Biomedicina Slovenica [of University of Ljubljana] - Ljubljana, Yugoslavia - *CompReadDB 82*
Biometrics - Washington, DC - *MagDir 84*
Biondo, Joseph R. - Matamoras, PA - *Tel&CabFB 84C p.1666*
Bioscience [of American Institute of Biological Sciences] - Arlington, VA - *BaconPubCkMag 84; MagDir 84; MagIndMarPl 82-83*
Biosciences Information Service - Philadelphia, PA - *CompReadDB 82; DataDirOnSer 84; EISS 83; InfIndMarPl 83; MicroMarPl 82-83*
Bioscope Manufacturing Co. - Tulsa, OK - *AvMarPl 83*
Bioservice Corp. - Chicago, IL - *BoPubDir 4, 5*
BIOSIS (Professional Services Div.) - Philadelphia, PA - *LitMarPl 83*
BIOSIS/CAS Selects [of BioSciences Information Service] - Philadelphia, PA - *MagDir 84*
BIOSIS Previews [of BioSciences Information Service] - Philadelphia, PA - *CompReadDB 82; DataDirOnSer 84; DBBus 82; DirOnDB Spring 84; OnBibDB 3*
BIOSIS Previews Authority Files [of BioSciences Information Service] - Philadelphia, PA - *DataDirOnSer 84*
Biotechniques - Natick, MA - *BaconPubCkMag 84*
Biotechnology [of SDC Search Service] - Santa Monica, CA - *DataDirOnSer 84*
Biotechnology Abstracts [of Derwent Publications Ltd.] - London, England - *DirOnDB Spring 84; EISS 7-83 Sup*
Biotechnology Investment Opportunities - Brattleboro, VT - *DirOnDB Spring 84; WritMar 84*
Biotechnology News - Summit, NJ - *BaconPubCkMag 84*
BIPACS-Bilingual Publications & Computer Services Inc. - Long Beach, NY - *WhoWMicrocom 83*
Bips London - New York, NY - *Ed&PubIntYB 82*
Birch Bluff Music - *See* Wrensong Inc.
Birch Hills Gazette - Kinistino, SK, Canada - *AyerDirPub 83*
Birch Hills Gazette, The - Birch Hills, SK, Canada - *Ed&PubIntYB 82*
Birch Island Music Press - *See* Barnhouse Co., C. L.
Birch Radio Inc. - Coral Springs, FL - *BrCabYB 84*
Birch Records - Wilmette, IL - *BillIntBG 83-84*
Birch Run Banner - Birch Run, MI - *Ed&PubIntYB 82*
Birch Tree Group Ltd. - Princeton, NJ - *BillIntBG 83-84; LitMarPl 83, 84*
Birch Tree Press - Pasadena, CA - *BoPubDir 4, 5*
Birchwood Associates Ltd. - Chappaqua, NY - *LitMarPl 83*
BIRD - Paris, France - *DirOnDB Spring 84*
Bird & Bull Press - Newtown, PA - *BoPubDir 5*
Bird & Bull Press - North Hills, PA - *BoPubDir 4*
Bird & Co. - Old Greenwich, CT - *ADAPSOMemDir 83-84*
Bird & Falborn Inc. - New York, NY - *StaDirAdAg 2-84*
Bird Associates Inc. - Oradell, NJ - *BoPubDir 4, 5*
Bird City Times - Bird City, KS - *BaconPubCkNews 84; Ed&PubIntYB 82*
Bird in the Bush - Iowa City, IA - *BoPubDir 4, 5; LitMag&SmPr 83-84*
Bird Island Union - Bird Island, MN - *BaconPubCkNews 84; Ed&PubIntYB 82*
Bird, Paul C. - St. Augustine, FL - *BoPubDir 4, 5*
Bird Talk Magazine - Angels Camp, CA - *LitMag&SmPr 83-84*
Bird Watcher's Digest [of Pardson Corp.] - Marietta, OH - *ArtMar 84; WritMar 84*
Birding - Austin, TX - *MagIndMarPl 82-83*
Birding Book Society [of North American Book Clubs Inc.] - Dover, NH - *LitMarPl 83, 84*
Birds' Meadow Publishing Co. Inc. - Rogers, AR - *BoPubDir 4, 5*
Birdsboro News of Southern Berks - *See* Berks-Mont Newspapers Inc.
Birdseed Press - Oakland, CA - *BoPubDir 4, 5*
Birdwell Marketing Research, Al E. - Houston, TX - *IntDirMarRes 83*
Birkenmeier, Fraser, Vorderstrasse & Lashly Inc. - St. Louis, MO - *StaDirAdAg 2-84*
Birkhauser Boston Inc. [Aff. of Birkhauser Verlag] - Cambridge, MA - *BoPubDir 4; LitMarPl 83, 84*
Birmingham Advertiser, The - Birmingham, AL - *NewsDir 84*
Birmingham Alabama Messenger - Birmingham, AL - *BaconPubCkNews 84*
Birmingham-Bloomfield Eccentric [of Suburban Communications Corp.] - Livonia, MI - *AyerDirPub 83; NewsDir 84*
Birmingham-Bloomfield Eccentric - *See* Observer & Eccentric Newspapers
Birmingham Cable Communications [of American Television & Communications Corp.] - Birmingham, AL - *BrCabYB 84; Tel&CabFB 84C*
Birmingham MDS Co. - Jackson, MS - *Tel&CabFB 84C*
Birmingham News [of Newhouse Newspapers] - Birmingham, AL - *BaconPubCkNews 84; Ed&PubIntYB 82; LitMarPl 83, 84; NewsBur 6; NewsDir 84*
Birmingham News-Birmingham Post Herald Index [of Birmingham Public & Jefferson County Free-Library] - Birmingham, AL - *EISS 83*
Birmingham One Voice - Birmingham, AL - *NewsDir 84*
Birmingham Post Herald - Birmingham, AL - *BaconPubCkNews 84; NewsBur 6; NewsDir 84*
Birmingham Shades Valley Sun - Birmingham, AL - *BaconPubCkNews 84*
Birmingham Times - Birmingham, AL - *BaconPubCkNews 84; NewsDir 84*
Birmingham World - Birmingham, AL - *NewsDir 84*
Birmy Graphics of America - Miami, FL - *LitMarPl 84*
Birnbaum Co., Bob - Mountainside, NJ - *EISS 83; InfIndMarPl 83; InfoS 83-84; MagIndMarPl 82-83*
Birns & Sawyer Inc. - Los Angeles, CA - *AvMarPl 83*
Birth - Berkeley, CA - *BaconPubCkMag 84*
Birth Day Publishing Co. - San Diego, CA - *BoPubDir 4, 5; LitMag&SmPr 83-84*
Birth Defects Information System [of Center for Birth Defects Information Services] - Boston, MA - *DataDirOnSer 84; DirOnDB Spring 84; EISS 83*
Birthday Game, The - New Haven, CT - *Ed&PubIntYB 82*
Birthday Music Inc. - *See* Music Music Music Inc.
Birthright Music - Los Angeles, CA - *BillIntBG 83-84*
Birthright Records - Los Angeles, CA - *BillIntBG 83-84*
Birthscope - Dayton, OH - *Ed&PubIntYB 82*
Birtle Eye-Witness, The - Birtle, MB, Canada - *Ed&PubIntYB 82*
Bisbee Brewery Gulch Gazette - Bisbee, AZ - *BaconPubCkNews 84*
Bisbee CATV - Bisbee, AZ - *BrCabYB 84; Tel&CabFB 84C*
Bisbee Daily Review - Bisbee, AZ - *NewsDir 84*
Bisbee Daily Review - Sierra Vista, AZ - *Ed&PubIntYB 82*
Bisbee Press Collective - Bisbee, AZ - *BoPubDir 4, 5; LitMag&SmPr 83-84*
Bisch & Partners Inc., Damian - New York, NY - *StaDirAdAg 2-84*
Bisel Co., George T. - Philadelphia, PA - *BoPubDir 4, 5*
Bishop, Bryant & Associates - Washington, DC - *DirPRFirms 83*
Bishop Cable TV - Bishop, TX - *BrCabYB 84*
Bishop Cable TV Ltd. - Big Pine, CA - *Tel&CabFB 84C*
Bishop Cable TV Ltd. - Bishop, CA - *BrCabYB 84*
Bishop Graphics Inc. - Westlake Village, CA - *BoPubDir 4, 5*
Bishop Museum Press [Aff. of Bernice P. Bishop Museum] - Honolulu, HI - *BoPubDir 4, 5*
Bishop Productions, Katy - Los Angeles, CA - *AvMarPl 83*
Bisiar Music Publishing - Arvada, CO - *BillIntBG 83-84*
Bismarck-Mandan Cable TV [of Meyer Broadcasting Co.] - Bismarck, ND - *BrCabYB 84; Tel&CabFB 84C*
Bismarck-Mandan Finder - Mandan, ND - *AyerDirPub 83*
Bismarck Tribune - Bismarck, ND - *BaconPubCkNews 84; Ed&PubIntYB 82; LitMarPl 84; NewsDir 84*
Bismark Corp. - New York, NY - *HBIndAd&MS 82-83*
Bison Products - Van Nuys, CA - *MicrocomMPl 83*
Bison Research Service - Buffalo, MN - *LitMarPl 83; MagIndMarPl 82-83*
Bison State Telephone Co. [Aff. of Continental Telephone Corp.] - Custer, SD - *TelDir&BG 83-84*

Bison Telephone Co. Inc. - Bison, KS - *TelDir&BG 83-84*
Bit-Better Software, A - Laurel, MD - *MicrocomSwDir 1; WritMar 84*
Bit Software Inc. - Milpitas, CA - *MicrocomMPl 84; MicrocomSwDir 1*
Bit 3 Computer Corp. - Minneapolis, MN - *MicrocomMPl 83, 84*
Bitek International Corp. - Long Beach, CA - *DataDirSup 7-83*
Biting Idge Press - Sandusky, OH - *BoPubDir 4 Sup, 5; LitMag&SmPr 83-84*
Bitker, Marjorie M. - Milwaukee, WI - *LitMarPl 83, 84; MagIndMarPl 82-83*
Bitner Public Relations Inc., Gary - Ft. Lauderdale, FL - *DirPRFirms 83*
Bits Press - Cleveland, OH - *LitMag&SmPr 83-84; LitMarPl 84*
Bits'n Bytes Gazette [of Computer Science Press Inc.] - Rockville, MD - *MicrocomMPl 84*
Bitstream Inc. - Loxahatchee, FL - *MicrocomMPl 84*
Bitterroot - Brooklyn, NY - *LitMag&SmPr 83-84; WritMar 84*
Bittinger, Michael - Clarks, NE - *Tel&CabFB 84C p.1666*
Bitton Advertising Agency - Idaho Falls, ID - *StaDirAdAg 2-84*
Bitton & Associates, Daniel - Madison, WI - *DirPRFirms 83*
Biuro Wycinkow Prasowych GLOB - Warsaw, Poland - *ProGuPRSer 4*
Bivens Music - Nashville, TN - *BillIntBG 83-84*
Biviano Inc., Ronald S. - Crete, IL - *BoPubDir 4, 5*
Biwabik Times - Biwabik, MN - *AyerDirPub 83; BaconPubCkNews 84; Ed&PubIntYB 82*
Biworld Publishers [Subs. of BiWorld Industries Inc.] - Orem, UT - *BoPubDir 4, 5; LitMarPl 84; WritMar 84*
Bixby Bulletin - Bixby, OK - *BaconPubCkNews 84; Ed&PubIntYB 82*
Bixby Bulletin [of McWilliams Publications Inc.] - Broken Arrow, OK - *NewsDir 84*
Bixby Cablevision [of Multimedia Cablevision Inc.] - Bixby, OK - *Tel&CabFB 84C*
Bixby Telephone Co. - Bixby, OK - *TelDir&BG 83-84*
Bizcomp Corp. - Menlo Park, CA - *DataDirSup 7-83*
Bizcomp Corp. - Sunnyvale, CA - *MicrocomMPl 84*
Bizdate [of Source Telecomputing Corp.] - McLean, VA - *DataDirOnSer 84*
Biziwerks Inc. - Grants, NM - *MicrocomMPl 84*
Biznet [of U.S. Chamber of Commerce] - Washington, DC - *CabTVPrDB 83*
BJ Press - Brooklyn, NY - *LitMag&SmPr 83-84*
BJR Public Relations - Culver City, CA - *DirPRFirms 83*
Bjus - Brussels, Belgium - *DirOnDB Spring 84*
BJZ Public Relations [Div. of Brooks, Johnson, Zausmer Advertising Inc.] - San Antonio, TX - *DirPRFirms 83*
BK Associates - Wayzata, MN - *EISS 5-84 Sup*
BK Publications Inc. - Tucson, AZ - *BoPubDir 4, 5*
BKLI - Blackfoot, ID - *BrCabYB 84*
BKMK Press [of University of Missouri at Kansas City] - Kansas City, MO - *ArtMar 84; BoPubDir 4, 5; LitMag&SmPr 83-84; LitMarPl 84; WritMar 84*
BKP Television Systems Inc. [of Service Electric Cable TV] - Sunbury, PA - *BrCabYB 84*
B.L. & H. Music Corp. - *See* Webman & Co., H. B.
Black-A-Moors - Philadelphia, PA - *BoPubDir 4, 5*
Black American Literature Forum - Terre Haute, IN - *LitMag&SmPr 83-84*
Black American, The - New York, NY - *Ed&PubIntYB 82; NewsDir 84*
Black & Musen - East Longmeadow, MA - *AdAge 3-28-84; StaDirAdAg 2-84*
Black & White Publishing Co. - Cambridge, MA - *BoPubDir 4, 5*
Black Artists in America - Spring Valley, NY - *BoPubDir 4, 5*
Black Associates, Gordon S. - Rochester, NY - *IntDirMarRes 83*
Black Bart - Canyon, CA - *LitMag&SmPr 83-84*
Black Belt [of Rainbow Publications Inc.] - Burbank, CA - *MagDir 84; WritMar 84*
Black Books Bulletin - Chicago, IL - *MagIndMarPl 82-83*
Black Box Catalog - Pittsburgh, PA - *DataDirSup 7-83*
Black Box Corp. - Pittsburgh, PA - *MicrocomMPl 84*
Black Box Magazine [of Watershed Intermedia] - Washington, DC - *LitMag&SmPr 83-84*
Black Buzzard Press - Bethesda, MD - *BoPubDir 4*
Black Buzzard Press - Arlington, VA - *BoPubDir 5; LitMag&SmPr 83-84*
Black Careers [of Project Magazine Inc.] - Philadelphia, PA - *BaconPubCkMag 84; MagDir 84; MagIndMarPl 82-83*
Black Cat Press [Aff. of The Norman Press-Normandie House] - Skokie, IL - *BoPubDir 4, 5*
Black Chronicle - Oklahoma City, OK - *Ed&PubIntYB 82*
Black Classic Press - Baltimore, MD - *BoPubDir 4, 5*
Black Coffee Music Inc. - *See* Prophecy Publishing Inc.
Black Collegian, The - New Orleans, LA - *ArtMar 84; MagDir 84; MagIndMarPl 82-83; WritMar 84*
Black Data Weekly - New Orleans, LA - *Ed&PubIntYB 82*
Black Diamond - Chicago, IL - *BaconPubCkMag 84; MagDir 84*
Black Diamond Cablevision - Martinsburg, WV - *BrCabYB 84*
Black Diamond Cablevision Corp. - Kingwood, WV - *Tel&CabFB 84C p.1666*
Black Diamond Recording Corp. - Copiague, NY - *BillIntBG 83-84*
Black Dispatch - Oklahoma City, OK - *Ed&PubIntYB 82*
Black Earth Telephone Co. [Aff. of Telephone & Data Systems Inc.] - Black Earth, WI - *TelDir&BG 83-84*
Black Enterprise [of Earl G. Graves Publishing Co. Inc.] - New York, NY - *BaconPubCkMag 84; Folio 83; MagDir 84; MagIndMarPl 82-83; WritMar 84*
Black Entertainment Television - Washington, DC - *BrCabYB 84; CabTVPrDB 83; HomeVid&CabYB 82-83; Tel&CabFB 84C*
Black Family - Chicago, IL - *BaconPubCkMag 84*
Black Fire Records - Washington, DC - *BillIntBG 83-84*
Black Fly Review, The - Fort Kent, ME - *LitMag&SmPr 83-84*
Black Forest News, The - Black Forest, CO - *Ed&PubIntYB 82*
Black Forest News, The - Colorado Springs, CO - *NewsDir 84*
Black Future [of Williams Communications Inc.] - Orangeburg, SC - *ArtMar 84; WritMar 84*
Black, Gilbert J. - Harrison, NY - *MagIndMarPl 82-83*
Black, Gilbert J. - Lewisburg, PA - *LitMarPl 83, 84*
Black Gold Cooperative Library System - Ventura, CA - *EISS 83*
Black Graphics International [Aff. of Associated Black Publishers of Detroit Inc.] - Detroit, MI - *BoPubDir 4, 5*
Black Hawk County Sun - Evansdale, IA - *AyerDirPub 83; Ed&PubIntYB 82*
Black Heritage - Reston, VA - *MagIndMarPl 82-83*
Black Hills Press - Sturgis, SD - *AyerDirPub 83*
Black Hills Weekly - Lead, SD - *Ed&PubIntYB 82*
Black Hole School of Poethnics [Aff. of Earth Campus] - Port Jefferson, NY - *BoPubDir 4, 5*
Black Horse/Civic Press Suburban - Cherry Hill, NJ - *AyerDirPub 83*
Black Horse/Civic Press Suburban, The - Bellmawr, NJ - *Ed&PubIntYB 82*
Black Ice Publishers - Worcester, MA - *BoPubDir 4, 5*
Black Inc., Walter J. - Roslyn, NY - *LitMarPl 83, 84*
Black Ink Typographers - New York, NY - *LitMarPl 83, 84; MagIndMarPl 82-83*
Black Letter Press [Aff. of Don's Book Store] - Grand Rapids, MI - *BoPubDir 4, 5*
Black Magazine Agency - Logansport, IN - *MagIndMarPl 82-83*
Black Maria - Chicago, IL - *LitMag&SmPr 83-84*
Black Market Press [Aff. of SCAMCO International] - Brooklyn, NY - *BoPubDir 4, 5; LitMag&SmPr 83-84*
Black Moss Press - Coatsworth, ON, Canada - *BoPubDir 4, 5*
Black Mountain Books - State College, PA - *BoPubDir 4, 5*
Black Mountain News - Cave Creek, AZ - *AyerDirPub 83; Ed&PubIntYB 82*
Black Mountain News - Black Mountain, NC - *BaconPubCkNews 84; Ed&PubIntYB 82*
Black Music Cable Channel [of Inner City Broadcasting] - New York, NY - *HomeVid&CabYB 82-83*
Black News - Columbia, SC - *Ed&PubIntYB 82*
Black Newspaper Clipping Bureau - New York, NY - *LitMarPl 83, 84*
Black Note Publishing - *See* Funky but Music Inc.
Black Oak Press - Lincoln, NE - *BoPubDir 4, 5; LitMag&SmPr 83-84*
Black Oyster Press - Chicago, IL - *LitMag&SmPr 83-84*
Black Powder Times - Mt. Vernon, WA - *WritMar 84*
Black Press Service Inc. - New York, NY - *BaconPubCkNews 84; Ed&PubIntYB 82*

Black Radio Network Inc. - New York, NY - *BrCabYB 84*
Black Rainbow Publications - Willowdale, ON, Canada - *BoPubDir 4, 5*
Black Resource Guide Inc. - Washington, DC - *BoPubDir 5*
Black River Cablevision - Black River Falls, WI - *Tel&CabFB 84C*
Black River Falls Banner-Journal - Black River Falls, WI - *BaconPubCkNews 84; NewsDir 84*
Black River Tribune, The - Ludlow, VT - *AyerDirPub 83; Ed&PubIntYB 82*
Black Rose Books Ltd. - Montreal, PQ, Canada - *BoPubDir 4; LitMarPl 83, 84*
Black Scholar [of Black World Foundation] - San Francisco, CA - *LitMag&SmPr 83-84; LitMarPl 84; MagDir 84; MagIndMarPl 82-83*
Black Scholar [of Black World Foundation] - Sausalito, CA - *LitMarPl 83*
Black Scholar Press, The - San Francisco, CA - *LitMag&SmPr 83-84*
Black Sheep Records - Marina del Rey, CA - *BillIntBG 83-84*
Black Sparrow Press - Santa Barbara, CA - *LitMag&SmPr 83-84; LitMarPl 83, 84*
Black Stallion Country Publishers - Culver City, CA - *BillIntBG 83-84*
Black Star Publishing Co. - New York, NY - *AvMarPl 83; Ed&PubIntYB 82; LitMarPl 83, 84; MagIndMarPl 82-83*
Black Stars - Chicago, IL - *MagDir 84*
Black Sun Music - *See* Mayflower Music Corp.
Black Swan Books Ltd. - Redding Ridge, CT - *BoPubDir 4, 5; LitMag&SmPr 83-84; LitMarPl 84*
Black Swan Press - Chicago, IL - *LitMag&SmPr 83-84*
Black Swan Press/Surrealist Editions - Chicago, IL - *BoPubDir 4, 5*
Black Tennis - Dallas, TX - *BaconPubCkMag 84*
Black-Turtle Systems - Columbus, OH - *WhoWMicrocom 83*
Black Voice News - Riverside, CA - *AyerDirPub 83; Ed&PubIntYB 82*
Black Warrior Review, The [of The University of Alabama] - University, AL - *ArtMar 84; LitMag&SmPr 83-84; WritMar 84*
Black Willow Poetry - Norristown, PA - *BoPubDir 5; LitMag&SmPr 83-84*
Black Willow Press - Norristown, PA - *LitMag&SmPr 83-84*
Blackberry - Brunswick, ME - *BoPubDir 4, 5*
Blackberry - Albuquerque, NM - *BoPubDir 4, 5*
Blackberry Books - Bolinas, CA - *BoPubDir 4, 5*
Blackbird Press - Pitman, NJ - *LitMag&SmPr 83-84*
Blackbourn Inc. - Eden Prairie, MN - *AvMarPl 83*
Blackburn & Co. Inc. - Washington, DC - *CabTVFinDB 83*
Blackburn, W. E. - Shamrock, TX - *Tel&CabFB 84C p.1666*
Blackduck American - Blackduck, MN - *BaconPubCkNews 84*
Blackduck Cablevision Inc. - Blackduck, MN - *Tel&CabFB 84C*
Blackduck Telephone Co. - Blackduck, MN - *TelDir&BG 83-84*
Blackfish Books - Canada - *BoPubDir 4, 5*
Blackfoot Morning News - Blackfoot, ID - *BaconPubCkNews 84; NewsDir 84*
Blackfoot Telephone Cooperative Inc. - Missoula, MT - *TelDir&BG 83-84*
Blackhawk Films Inc. - Davenport, IA - *AvMarPl 83; BillIntBG 83-84*
Blackheart Music - St. Louis, MO - *BillIntBG 83-84*
Blackhole School of Poethnics, The - Port Jefferson, NY - *LitMag&SmPr 83-84*
Blackjack & Valley Grapevine [of Seven Buffaloes Press] - Big Timber, MT - *LitMag&SmPr 83-84*
Blackjack Forum, R.G.E. - Berkeley, CA - *LitMag&SmPr 83-84*
Blackmore Public Relations Inc. - Arlington, TX - *StaDirAdAg 2-84*
Black's Guide - Red Bank, NJ - *DataDirOnSer 84; EISS 83; InfIndMarPl 83*
Black's Research Service [of Black's Guide Inc.] - Red Bank, NJ - *DataDirOnSer 84*
Blacks Unltd. - Webster City, IA - *ArtMar 84; WritMar 84*
Blacksburg Cable TV [of Booth American Co.] - Blacksburg, VA - *BrCabYB 84; Tel&CabFB 84C*
Blacksburg-Christiansburg News Messenger - Christiansburg, VA - *AyerDirPub 83*
Blacksburg Group Inc., The - Blacksburg, VA - *LitMarPl 83, 84; WritMar 84*
Blacksburg Sun - Blacksburg, VA - *AyerDirPub 83; NewsDir 84*
Blacksburg Times - Blacksburg, SC - *BaconPubCkNews 84*
Blackshear Cable TV Inc. - Blackshear, GA - *BrCabYB 84; Tel&CabFB 84C*
Blackshear Times - Blackshear, GA - *BaconPubCkNews 84; Ed&PubIntYB 82*
Blackside Inc. - Boston, MA - *AvMarPl 83; WritMar 84*
Blackstone/Associates, Milton - La Jolla, CA - *TelAl 83, 84*
Blackstone Courier-Record - Blackstone, VA - *BaconPubCkNews 84; NewsDir 84*
Blackstone Productions - Springfield, OR - *AvMarPl 83*
Blackstone-Shelburne N.Y. Inc. - New York, NY - *Ed&PubIntYB 82*
Blackstone Valley Tribune/Advertiser [of Nanlo Inc.] - Whitinsville, MA - *AyerDirPub 83; Ed&PubIntYB 82; NewsDir 84*
Blackwell Journal-Tribune [of Midway Publishing Co.] - Blackwell, OK - *BaconPubCkNews 84; Ed&PubIntYB 82; NewsDir 84*
Blackwell North America Inc. [Aff. of B. H. Blackwell Ltd.] - Lake Oswego, OR - *LitMarPl 83, 84*
Blackwell North America Inc. - Portland, OR - *CompReadDB 82*
Blackwell North America Master Cataloging File [of Blackwell North America Inc.] - Portland, OR - *CompReadDB 82*
Blackwell Scientific Publications Inc. - Boston, MA - *ArtMar 84; LitMarPl 83, 84*
Blackwell Technical Services [of B. H. Blackwell Ltd.] - Oxford, England - *EISS 83*
Blackwell Times-Record - Blackwell, OK - *BaconPubCkNews 84; Ed&PubIntYB 82*
Blackwell TV Cable [of Donrey Media Group Inc.] - Blackwell, OK - *BrCabYB 84; Tel&CabFB 84C*
Blackwood Associates - Wellesley Hills, MA - *AdAge 3-28-84; StaDirAdAg 2-84*
Blackwood/Martin & Associates Inc. - Fayetteville, AR - *StaDirAdAg 2-84*
Blackwood Music - *See* Ren-Maur Music Corp.
Blackwood Music Inc. - *See* CBS Songs
Blackwood Music, Ron - Memphis, TN - *BillIntBG 83-84*
Blackwood Observer - Blackwood, NJ - *Ed&PubIntYB 82*
Blackwood Observer - *See* Cam-Glo Newspapers Inc.
Blackwood Productions - Memphis, TN - *BillIntBG 83-84*
Blackwood Productions Inc. - New York, NY - *AvMarPl 83*
Blackwood Washington Township News Report - *See* Cam-Glo Newspapers Inc.
Blade - Fairbury, IL - *AyerDirPub 83*
Blade - Toledo, OH - *AdAge 6-28-84; AyerDirPub 83; Ed&PubIntYB 82; LitMarPl 84; NewsBur 6*
Blade-Atlas - Blanchardville, WI - *AyerDirPub 83; Ed&PubIntYB 82*
Blade-Crescent - Sebewaing, MI - *AyerDirPub 83*
Blade Echo - Bowie, MD - *AyerDirPub 83*
Blade-Empire - Concordia, KS - *AyerDirPub 83; Ed&PubIntYB 82*
Blade Magazine, The - Toledo, OH - *ArtMar 84; WritMar 84*
Blade Magazine, The - Chattanooga, TN - *BaconPubCkMag 84; WritMar 84*
Blade/Market Place - Brighton, CO - *AyerDirPub 83*
Blade-Tribune [of South Coast Newspapers Inc.] - Oceanside, CA - *AyerDirPub 83; BaconPubCkNews 84; Ed&PubIntYB 82; LitMarPl 83, 84*
Bladen Journal [of Park Newspapers of Lumberton Inc.] - Elizabethtown, NC - *AyerDirPub 83; NewsDir 84*
Blagrove Publications - Manchester, CT - *BoPubDir 4, 5*
Blaine Group, The - Los Angeles, CA - *DirPRFirms 83; LitMarPl 83, 84; MagIndMarPl 82-83*
Blaine-Spring Lake Park Life - Blaine-Spring Lake Park, MN - *Ed&PubIntYB 82*
Blaine Spring Lake Park Life - Coon Rapids, MN - *AyerDirPub 83*
Blaine-Spring Lake Park Life [of Anoka County Union & Shopper Inc.] - Minneapolis, MN - *NewsDir 84*
Blaine-Spring Lake Park Life - *See* Anoka County Union & Shopper Inc.
Blair Advertising - Rochester, NY - *AdAge 3-28-84; StaDirAdAg 2-84*

Blair & Co., John - New York, NY - *HomeVid&CabYB 82-83; KnowInd 83; Tel&CabFB 84S*
Blair & Co., John (Owned Stations Div.) - New York, NY - *BrCabYB 84*
Blair & Ketchum's Country Journal [of Country Journal Publishing Co.] - Brattleboro, VT - *Folio 83; LitMarPl 83, 84; MagDir 84; MagIndMarPl 82-83*
Blair & Ketchum's Country Journal - Manchester, VT - *BaconPubCkMag 84; WritMar 84*
Blair Associates Inc., K. C. - Lambertville, NJ - *IntDirMarRes 83*
Blair Corp., D. L. - Great Neck, NY - *DirMarMP 83; StaDirAdAg 2-84*
Blair County Shopper's Guide - Altoona, PA - *AyerDirPub 83*
Blair County Shopper's Guide [of Everett Bedford County Press] - Everett, PA - *NewsDir 84*
Blair Enterprise - Blair, OK - *BaconPubCkNews 84; Ed&PubIntYB 82*
Blair Enterprise - *See* Enterprise Publishing Co. Inc.
Blair Enterprise, The - Blair, NE - *Ed&PubIntYB 82*
Blair Inc. - Baileys Crossroads, VA - *AvMarPl 83*
Blair, John F. - Winston-Salem, NC - *LitMarPl 83, 84; WritMar 84*
Blair Pilot-Tribune [of Blair Enterprise Co. Inc.] - Blair, NE - *NewsDir 84*
Blair Pilot-Tribune - *See* Enterprise Publishing Co. Inc.
Blair Press - Hollidaysburg, PA - *Ed&PubIntYB 82*
Blair Press - Blair, WI - *BaconPubCkNews 84; Ed&PubIntYB 82*
Blair Publishing Co. - Fairfield, CA - *BoPubDir 5*
Blair Telephone Co. [Aff. of HunTel Systems Inc.] - Blair, NE - *TelDir&BG 83-84*
Blair Television - New York, NY - *TelAl 83, 84*
Blair Video Enterprises - New York, NY - *TelAl 84*
Blairsat Inc. [Subs. of John Blair & Co.] - New York, NY - *BrCabYB 84*
Blairstown Press [of Cam-Glo Newspapers Inc.] - Blairstown, NJ - *BaconPubCkNews 84; Ed&PubIntYB 82; NewsDir 84*
Blairstown South Benton-Star-Press - Blairstown, IA - *BaconPubCkNews 84*
Blairsville Dispatch - Blairsville, PA - *BaconPubCkNews 84*
Blairsville North Georgia News - Blairsville, GA - *BaconPubCkNews 84; NewsDir 84*
Blake, An Illustrated Quarterly - Albuquerque, NM - *LitMag&SmPr 83-84*
Blake & Associates, George - Sarasota, FL - *AdAge 3-28-84 p.112; StaDirAdAg 2-84*
Blake Music Recording, Eubie - Brooklyn, NY - *BillIntBG 83-84*
Blakely, Alton - Somerset, KY - *Tel&CabFB 84C p.1666*
Blakely, Alton - LaFollette, TN - *BrCabYB 84*
Blakely, Alton - Livingston, TN - *BrCabYB 84*
Blakely Cable Television Inc. - Blakely, GA - *BrCabYB 84; Tel&CabFB 84C*
Blakely Early County News - Blakely, GA - *BaconPubCkNews 84*
Blakeney Design, Edgar & Barbara - New York, NY - *LitMarPl 83, 84*
Blakeslee Advertising, T. W. - Highland Park, IL - *StaDirAdAg 2-84*
Blakeslee-Lane Inc. - Baltimore, MD - *AvMarPl 83*
Blanca Telephone Co., The - Blanca, CO - *TelDir&BG 83-84*
Blanchard & Associates - Minneapolis, MN - *AdAge 3-28-84; StaDirAdAg 2-84*
Blanchard News - Blanchard, OK - *BaconPubCkNews 84; Ed&PubIntYB 82*
Blanchard Telephone Association Inc. - Blanchard, MI - *TelDir&BG 83-84*
Blanchard Training & Development Inc. - Escondido, CA - *BoPubDir 4, 5*
Blanchard-Wayne Cable TV Ltd. - Wayne, OK - *BrCabYB 84*
Blanchardville Blade-Atlas - Blanchardville, WI - *BaconPubCkNews 84*
Blanche Consultants Inc., Ernest E. - Kensington, MD - *EISS 5-84 Sup*
Blanchester Star-Republican - Blanchester, OH - *BaconPubCkNews 84*
Blanchris Music - New York, NY - *BillIntBG 83-84*
Blanco & Sons Inc., G. A. - Great Barrington, MA - *DirInfWP 82*
Blanco Cablevision Corp. - Blanco, TX - *BrCabYB 84; Tel&CabFB 84C*
Blanco County News - Blanco, TX - *AyerDirPub 83; BaconPubCkNews 84; Ed&PubIntYB 82*
Bland Courier - *See* Lewis Publishing Co. Inc.
Bland Courier, The - Bland, MO - *AyerDirPub 83; Ed&PubIntYB 82*
Bland Messenger, The - Bland, VA - *Ed&PubIntYB 82*
Bland Messenger, The - Wytheville, VA - *NewsDir 84*
Bland, Paul - *See* Crater General Communications Inc.
Blandinsville Star Gazette [of Roseville Carlberg Publishing Co.] - Roseville, IL - *NewsDir 84*
Blandinsville Star-Gazette - *See* Acklin Newspaper Group
Blands Audio Visual Service - Savannah, GA - *AvMarPl 83*
Blank & Associates Inc., Larry - Dayton, OH - *StaDirAdAg 2-84*
Blank & Co. Inc., Arthur - Boston, MA - *DataDirSup 7-83*
Blank Associates Inc., Edward - New York, NY - *IntDirMarRes 83*
Blank Communications Inc., Rolf - Chicago, IL - *DirPRFirms 83*
Blank Tape - Brooklyn, NY - *LitMag&SmPr 83-84*
Blankenship Agency, The - Coral Gables, FL - *StaDirAdAg 2-84*
Blanton Software Service - San Antonio, TX - *WhoWMicrocom 83*
Blasdell-Woodlawn Front Page - Blasdell, NY - *Ed&PubIntYB 82*
Blasdell-Woodlawn Front Page [of Lackawanna Front Page Inc.] - Lackawanna, NY - *NewsDir 84*
Blasdell-Woodlawn Front Page - *See* Front Page Inc.
Blasdell-Woodlawn Penny Saver - Hamburg, NY - *AyerDirPub 83*
Blassingame, McCauley & Wood - New York, NY - *LitMarPl 83, 84*
Blast - Santa Barbara, CA - *LitMag&SmPr 83-84*
Blat Research & Development Corp. - Edmonds, WA - *MicrocomMPl 84*
Blatant Image, The - Wolf Creek, OR - *LitMag&SmPr 83-84*
Blate Associates, Samuel R. - Gaithersburg, MD - *AvMarPl 83; LitMarPl 83, 84*
Blattler TV & Cable - Clarington, OH - *BrCabYB 84*
Blau & Partners, Barry - Westport, CT - *AdAge 3-28-84; StaDirAdAg 2-84*
Blau & Partners, Barry - Wilton, CT - *DirMarMP 83*
Blaufox Associates - Milford, CT - *LitMarPl 83; MagIndMarPl 82-83*
Blavat Advertising Inc. - Erdenheim, PA - *StaDirAdAg 2-84*
Blavat Advertising Inc. - Philadelphia, PA - *DirPRFirms 83*
Blazer - Jackson, MI - *AyerDirPub 83; Ed&PubIntYB 82*
BLCMP Library Service Ltd. [of University of Birmingham] - Birmingham, England - *EISS 83; InfIndMarPl 83*
Blechman Enterprises - Canoga Park, CA - *MicrocomMPl 83, 84; MicrocomSwDir 1; WhoWMicrocom 83*
Bledsoe-Helton Cable TV - Helton, KY - *Tel&CabFB 84C*
Bledsoe Telephone Co-Op - Dunlap, TN - *Tel&CabFB 84C*
Bledsoe Telephone Co-Op - Pikeville, TN - *Tel&CabFB 84C; TelDir&BG 83-84*
Bledsonian Banner - Pikeville, TN - *AyerDirPub 83; Ed&PubIntYB 82*
Bleecker Street Associates Inc. - New York, NY - *LitMarPl 83, 84*
Bleecker Street Music - *See* Katch Nazar Music
Bleecker Street Studio, The - New York, NY - *LitMarPl 83, 84*
Blendingwell Music Inc. - Englewood, NJ - *BillIntBG 83-84*
Blessing Cable TV Corp. - Blessing, TX - *Tel&CabFB 84C*
Blewointmentpress - Vancouver, BC, Canada - *BoPubDir 4, 5; LitMag&SmPr 83-84*
Blex - Brussels, Belgium - *DirOnDB Spring 84*
Bley Cale Inc. - Beardstown, IL - *BrCabYB 84*
Blind Alleys [of Seventh Son Press] - Baltimore, MD - *LitMag&SmPr 83-84*
Blind Basement Music - Silver Spring, MD - *BillIntBG 83-84*
Blind Beggar Press - Bronx, NY - *BoPubDir 4 Sup, 5; LitMag&SmPr 83-84*
Blind Pig Records - Ann Arbor, MI - *BillIntBG 83-84*
Blis Press - Brightwaters, NY - *BoPubDir 5*
Bliss Associates Inc., Robert L. - New Canaan, CT - *DirPRFirms 83*
Bliss, Barefoot & Associates Inc. - New York, NY - *DirPRFirms 83*
Bliss Cable - Gardnerville, NV - *Tel&CabFB 84C*

Bliss Co. Inc., Ben B. - New York, NY - *StaDirAdAg 2-84*
Bliss Co., P. H. - Middletown, CT - *MagIndMarPl 82-83*
Bliss Electronics Corp. - Gardnerville, NV - *BrCabYB 84*
Bliss, John S. & Carolyn - Gardnerville, NV - *Tel&CabFB 84C p.1666*
Bliss, John S. & Carolyn - Minden, NV - *Tel&CabFB 84C*
Blissfield Advance - Blissfield, MI - *Ed&PubIntYB 82*
Blissfield Advance/Raisin River Advocate - Blissfield, MI - *BaconPubCkNews 84*
Blitz - Los Angeles, CA - *LitMag&SmPr 83-84*
Blitz Media Direct [Subs. of LK Advertising] - Middle Island, NY - *LitMarPl 83, 84*
Blitzer Inc., Barbara - Rumson, NJ - *LitMarPl 83, 84*
Blizzard, William C. - Beckley, WV - *MagIndMarPl 82-83*
BLL - Frankfurt, West Germany - *DirOnDB Spring 84*
Bloch & Co. - Cleveland, OH - *BoPubDir 4, 5; MicroMarPl 82-83*
Bloch, Barbara J. - White Plains, NY - *LitMarPl 83, 84*
Bloch Brothers Paper Co. Inc. - New York, NY - *LitMarPl 83, 84*
Bloch Publishing Co. Inc. - New York, NY - *LitMarPl 83, 84*
Block Advertising Inc., David H. - Bloomfield, NJ - *ArtMar 84*
Block Advertising Inc., David H. - Montclair, NJ - *StaDirAdAg 2-84*
Block & Co. Inc. - Wheeling, IL - *DirInfWP 82*
Block Associates, Frank - St. Louis, MO - *ArtMar 84; StaDirAdAg 2-84; TelAl 83, 84*
Block Co., H. & R. - Statesville, NC - *WhoWMicrocom 83*
Block, Dick - Hollywood, CA - *CabTVFinDB 83*
Block Island Cable TV - New Shoreham, RI - *Tel&CabFB 84C*
Block Newspapers - Pittsburgh, PA - *Ed&PubIntYB 82*
Block, Robert S. - *See* B & F Broadcasting Inc.
Blockbuster Music Co. - *See* Jamie Music Publishing Co.
Blomquist Agencies Inc., The - Stockholm, Sweden - *StaDirAdAg 2-84*
Blonder-Tongue Laboratories - Old Bridge, NJ - *AvMarPl 83; HomeVid&CabYB 82-83*
Blood-Horse [Aff. of Thoroughbred Owners & Breeders Association] - Lexington, KY - *BaconPubCkMag 84; BoPubDir 4, 5; MagDir 84*
Blood, Journal of American Society of Hematology - New York, NY - *MagDir 84*
Blood-Journal of American Society of Hematology - Seattle, WA - *BaconPubCkMag 84*
Bloodlines - Kalamazoo, MI - *MagDir 84*
Bloodroot - Grand Forks, ND - *BoPubDir 4, 5; LitMag&SmPr 83-84*
Bloodstock Research [of Bloodstock Research Information Services Inc.] - Lexington, KY - *MicrocomMPl 84*
Bloodstock Research Information Services - Lexington, KY - *ADAPSOMemDir 83-84; DataDirOnSer 84; EISS 83; InfIndMarPl 83*
Bloom Advertising Agency Inc. - Dallas, TX - *DirMarMP 83*
Bloom Agency Inc., James M. - Great Neck, NY - *ArtMar 84; StaDirAdAg 2-84*
Bloom & Gelb - New York, NY - *AdAge 3-28-84; DirMarMP 83; MagIndMarPl 82-83; StaDirAdAg 2-84*
Bloom Cos. Inc., The - Dallas, TX - *AdAge 3-28-84; StaDirAdAg 2-84*
Bloom Inc., Bruce J. - New York, NY - *BrCabYB 84; StaDirAdAg 2-84*
Bloom TV Productions, Aaron S. - San Francisco, CA - *Tel&CabFB 84C*
Bloomberg Public Relations Inc., Mimi - New York, NY - *DirPRFirms 83*
Bloomer Advance - Bloomer, WI - *BaconPubCkNews 84; Ed&PubIntYB 82; NewsDir 84*
Bloomer Telephone Co. - Bloomer, WI - *TelDir&BG 83-84*
Bloomfield Cable TV Inc. [of Horizon Communications Corp.] - Bloomfield, IN - *Tel&CabFB 84C*
Bloomfield Cablevision [of Cable Communications of Iowa] - Bloomfield, IA - *BrCabYB 84*
Bloomfield Davis County Republican - Bloomfield, IA - *BaconPubCkNews 84*
Bloomfield Democrat - Bloomfield, IA - *BaconPubCkNews 84; Ed&PubIntYB 82*
Bloomfield Independent Press [of Worrall Papers] - Bloomfield, NJ - *Ed&PubIntYB 82; NewsDir 84*
Bloomfield Independent Press - *See* Worrall Publications
Bloomfield Journal [of Imprint Newspapers] - Windsor, CT - *NewsDir 84*
Bloomfield Monitor - Bloomfield, NE - *BaconPubCkNews 84; Ed&PubIntYB 82*
Bloomfield Music, Mike - *See* Iguana Music Inc.
Bloomfield News - Bloomfield, IN - *AyerDirPub 83; BaconPubCkNews 84; Ed&PubIntYB 82*
Bloomfield Vindicator - Bloomfield, MO - *BaconPubCkNews 84; Ed&PubIntYB 82*
Bloomfield World - Bloomfield, IN - *BaconPubCkNews 84*
Blooming Grove Times - Blooming Grove, TX - *AyerDirPub 83; BaconPubCkNews 84; Ed&PubIntYB 82*
Blooming Prairie Times - Blooming Prairie, MN - *AyerDirPub 83; BaconPubCkNews 84*
Bloomingdale Home Telephone Co. - Bloomingdale, IN - *TelDir&BG 83-84*
Bloomingdale Press - Bloomingdale, IL - *Ed&PubIntYB 82*
Bloomingdale Press [of Elmhurst Press Publications] - Elmhurst, IL - *AyerDirPub 83; NewsDir 84*
Bloomingdale Press - *See* Press Publications
Bloomingdale Star - Bloomingdale, IL - *Ed&PubIntYB 82*
Bloomingdale Telephone Co. - Bloomingdale, MI - *TelDir&BG 83-84*
Bloomingdale Van Buren County Advertiser - Bloomingdale, MI - *BaconPubCkNews 84; NewsDir 84*
Bloomington Broadcasting Corp. - Bloomington, IL - *BrCabYB 84*
Bloomington Cable Co. [of Del-Cal Cable Inc.] - Bloomington, TX - *BrCabYB 84; Tel&CabFB 84C*
Bloomington Daily Pantagraph [of Evergreen Communications Inc.] - Bloomington, IL - *NewsDir 84*
Bloomington Herald Telephone - Bloomington, IN - *BaconPubCkNews 84; NewsDir 84*
Bloomington Penny Saver - Bloomington, IL - *AyerDirPub 83*
Bloomington Sun - Bloomington, MN - *Ed&PubIntYB 82*
Bloomington Sun - Edina, MN - *AyerDirPub 83*
Bloomington Sun - *See* Sun Newspapers
Bloomington Sun & Free Section [of Minnesota Suburban Newspapers Inc.] - Minneapolis, MN - *NewsDir 84*
Bloomsburg Morning Press - Bloomsburg, PA - *NewsDir 84*
Bloomsbury Review - Denver, CO - *ArtMar 84; LitMag&SmPr 83-84; WritMar 84*
Bloomville Gazette - *See* Seneca Publishing Inc.
Bloomville Gazette, The - Bloomville, OH - *Ed&PubIntYB 82*
Bloomville TV Club - Bloomville, NY - *Tel&CabFB 84C*
Bloor/Yonge Word Processing Service Bureau - Toronto, ON, Canada - *DirInfWP 82*
Blore & Don Richman Inc., Chuck - Hollywood, CA - *HBIndAd&MS 82-83*
Blossom Telephone Co. Inc. - Blossom, TX - *TelDir&BG 83-84*
Blossom Valley Press - Mountain View, CA - *BoPubDir 4, 5; LitMag&SmPr 83-84*
Blotnick, Elihu - Berkeley, CA - *AvMarPl 83*
Blotto Industries Inc. - Albany, NY - *BillIntBG 83-84*
Blountstown County Record - Blountstown, FL - *BaconPubCkNews 84*
Blountsville Telephone Co. - Blountsville, AL - *TelDir&BG 83-84*
Blountville Sullivan County News - Blountville, TN - *BaconPubCkNews 84*
Blow [of Grey Whale Press] - Portland, OR - *LitMag&SmPr 83-84*
Blowing Rock Blowing Rocket [of Rivers Printing Co.] - Blowing Rock, NC - *BaconPubCkNews 84; NewsDir 84*
Blowing Rocket - Boone, NC - *AyerDirPub 83*
Blowing Rocket, The - Blowing Rock, NC - *Ed&PubIntYB 82*
BLS Consumer Price Index [of Dialog Information Services Inc.] - Palo Alto, CA - *DataDirOnSer 84*
BLS Consumer Price Index - Washington, DC - *DirOnDB Spring 84*
BLS Employment, Hours, & Earnings [of Dialog Information Services Inc.] - Palo Alto, CA - *DataDirOnSer 84*
BLS Employment, Hours, & Earnings - Washington, DC - *DirOnDB Spring 84*
BLS Labor Force [of Dialog Information Services Inc.] - Palo Alto, CA - *DataDirOnSer 84*
BLS Labor Force - Washington, DC - *DirOnDB Spring 84*

BLS Producer Price Index [of Dialog Information Services Inc.] - Palo Alto, CA - *DataDirOnSer 84*
BLS Producer Price Index - Washington, DC - *DirOnDB Spring 84*
BLT Business Systems Inc. - Euless, TX - *WhoWMicrocom 83*
BLT Records - Ft. Worth, TX - *BillIntBG 83-84*
Blue Anchor - Sacramento, CA - *MagDir 84*
Blue Band Music - *See* Blue Echo Music
Blue Book Addressing & List Service [Subs. of A. F. Lewis & Co. Inc.] - New York, NY - *LitMarPl 83, 84*
Blue Book Music - Bakersfield, CA - *BillIntBG 83-84*
Blue Book of Fur Farming [of Communications Marketing Inc.] - Brookfield, WI - *MagDir 84*
Blue-Book Publishers - White Plains, NY - *BoPubDir 4, 5*
Blue Buildings - Des Moines, IA - *LitMag&SmPr 83-84*
Blue Candle Music - *See* Blue Echo Music
Blue Canyon Music - San Rafael, CA - *BillIntBG 83-84*
Blue Chip Software - Woodland Hills, CA - *MicrocomMPl 84*
Blue Chip Stamps - Los Angeles, CA - *KnowInd 83*
Blue Chip Stock Photography Inc. - New York, NY - *AvMarPl 83; MagIndMarPl 82-83*
Blue Cloud Abbey - Marvin, SD - *BoPubDir 4, 5*
Blue Cloud Quarterly - Marvin, SD - *LitMag&SmPr 83-84; MagIndMarPl 82-83*
Blue Devil Cable TV Inc. [of Bates Communications Corp.] - Avella, PA - *Tel&CabFB 84C*
Blue Devil Cable TV Inc. [of Bates Communications Corp.] - Burgettstown, PA - *BrCabYB 84; Tel&CabFB 84C*
Blue Devil Cable TV Inc. [of Bates Communications Corp.] - Claysville, PA - *Tel&CabFB 84C*
Blue Devil Cable TV Inc. [of Bates Communications Corp.] - Bethany, WV - *Tel&CabFB 84C*
Blue Diamond Co. - Canonsburg, PA - *BillIntBG 83-84*
Blue Diamond Press - Bronx, NY - *BoPubDir 5*
Blue Dove Records - North Hollywood, CA - *BillIntBG 83-84*
Blue Dragon Press [Aff. of Artists Embassy International] - Oakland, CA - *BoPubDir 4 Sup, 5*
Blue Earth Cablevision Inc. [of Marcus Communications Inc.] - Blue Earth, MN - *BrCabYB 84; Tel&CabFB 84C*
Blue Earth Post Ambassador - Blue Earth, MN - *BaconPubCkNews 84*
Blue Earth Valley Telephone Co. - Blue Earth, MN - *TelDir&BG 83-84*
Blue Echo Music - Nashville, TN - *BillIntBG 83-84*
Blue Fox Associates - Milford, CT - *LitMarPl 84*
Blue Gem Records - Los Angeles, CA - *BillIntBG 83-84*
Blue Goose Inc. - Hagerstown, MD - *BoPubDir 4, 5*
Blue Harbor Press - Lomita, CA - *BoPubDir 4, 5*
Blue Haven Foundation - Marble Falls, TX - *BoPubDir 4, 5*
Blue Heron Press - Alliston, ON, Canada - *BoPubDir 4, 5; LitMag&SmPr 83-84*
Blue Hill Leader - Blue Hill, NE - *BaconPubCkNews 84; Ed&PubIntYB 82*
Blue Hill Weekly Packet - Blue Hill, ME - *BaconPubCkNews 84*
Blue Horizon Press - Greenville, TN - *BoPubDir 4, 5*
Blue Horizons Advertising - Richmond, VA - *StaDirAdAg 2-84*
Blue Horse Publications - Augusta, GA - *BoPubDir 4, 5; LitMag&SmPr 83-84*
Blue Island Music - Los Angeles, CA - *BillIntBG 83-84*
Blue Island Records - Los Angeles, CA - *BillIntBG 83-84*
Blue Island Sun Standard - Blue Island, IL - *BaconPubCkNews 84*
Blue Island Sun Standard [of Chicago Daily Southtown Economist Newspapers] - Chicago, IL - *NewsDir 84*
Blue Lagoon Publishers - Studio City, CA - *BoPubDir 4, 5*
Blue Lake Music - *See* Terrace Music Group
Blue Lakes Software - Madison, WI - *MicrocomMPl 83*
Blue Light Film Co. - New York, NY - *AvMarPl 83*
Blue List Div. [of Standard & Poor's Corp.] - New York, NY - *EISS 83*
Blue List Retrieval [of Standard & Poor's Corp.] - New York, NY - *DataDirOnSer 84*
Blue Mace Music - Virginia Beach, VA - *BillIntBG 83-84*
Blue Melody Music - *See* Blue Echo Music
Blue Menu Music Co. - *See* Green Menu Music Co.
Blue Moon Press Inc. - Tucson, AZ - *BoPubDir 4, 5*
Blue Mound Leader - Blue Mound, IL - *BaconPubCkNews 84; Ed&PubIntYB 82*
Blue Mountain Arts Inc. - Boulder, CO - *LitMarPl 83, 84; WritMar 84*
Blue Mountain Cable Co. - Monticello, UT - *Tel&CabFB 84C p.1666*
Blue Mountain Eagle, The - John Day, OR - *AyerDirPub 83; Ed&PubIntYB 82*
Blue Mountain Press - Kalamazoo, MI - *BoPubDir 4, 5*
Blue Mountain Press - South Haven, MI - *LitMag&SmPr 83-84*
Blue Mountain TV Cable Co. - Mt. Vernon, OR - *BrCabYB 84 p.D-297; Tel&CabFB 84C p.1667*
Blue Mouse Studio - Union, MI - *LitMag&SmPr 83-84*
Blue Oak Press - Sattley, CA - *BoPubDir 4, 5; LitMag&SmPr 83-84*
Blue Ox Word Processing - San Francisco, CA - *DirInfWP 82*
Blue Pencil Group - Reston, VA - *LitMarPl 83, 84*
Blue Print - Columbus, MS - *AyerDirPub 83*
Blue Rain Records Inc. - Chicago, IL - *BillIntBG 83-84*
Blue Rapids Times - Blue Rapids, KS - *BaconPubCkNews 84; Ed&PubIntYB 82*
Blue Ridge Broadcasting Co. - Seneca, SC - *BrCabYB 84*
Blue Ridge Cable of Central Pennsylvania Inc. [of Pencor Services Inc.] - Dushore, PA - *BrCabYB 84*
Blue Ridge Cable of New York - Narrowsburg, PA - *BrCabYB 84*
Blue Ridge Cable of New York Inc. [of Pencor Services Inc.] - Barryville, NY - *Tel&CabFB 84C*
Blue Ridge Cable of New York Inc. - Highland, NY - *BrCabYB 84*
Blue Ridge Cable TV Inc. [of Pencor Services Inc.] - Dushore, PA - *Tel&CabFB 84C*
Blue Ridge Cable TV Inc. [of Pencor Services Inc.] - Greentown, PA - *Tel&CabFB 84C*
Blue Ridge Cable TV Inc. [of Pencor Services Inc.] - Hawley, PA - *BrCabYB 84; Tel&CabFB 84C*
Blue Ridge Cable TV Inc. [of Pencor Services Inc.] - Hemlock Farms, PA - *BrCabYB 84*
Blue Ridge Cable TV Inc. [of Pencor Services Inc.] - Hemlock Farms Development, PA - *Tel&CabFB 84C*
Blue Ridge Cable TV Inc. [of Pencor Services Inc.] - Laceyville, PA - *BrCabYB 84; Tel&CabFB 84C*
Blue Ridge Cable TV Inc. [of Pencor Services Inc.] - Lansford, PA - *BrCabYB 84; Tel&CabFB 84C*
Blue Ridge Cable TV Inc. [of Retel TV Cable Co.] - Lemon Township, PA - *BrCabYB 84*
Blue Ridge Cable TV Inc. [of Pencor Services Inc.] - Mehoopany Township, PA - *BrCabYB 84*
Blue Ridge Cable TV Inc. [of Pencor Services Inc.] - Meshoppen, PA - *Tel&CabFB 84C*
Blue Ridge Cable TV Inc. [of Milford Community Television Inc.] - Milford, PA - *BrCabYB 84; Tel&CabFB 84C*
Blue Ridge Cable TV Inc. [of Pencor Services Inc.] - Mt. Pocono, PA - *BrCabYB 84*
Blue Ridge Cable TV Inc. [of Pencor Services Inc.] - Noxen, PA - *BrCabYB 84; Tel&CabFB 84C*
Blue Ridge Cable TV Inc. [of Pencor Services Inc.] - Palmerton, PA - *BrCabYB 84; Tel&CabFB 84C*
Blue Ridge Cable TV Inc. [of Pencor Services Inc.] - Stroudsburg, PA - *BrCabYB 84; Tel&CabFB 84C*
Blue Ridge Cable TV Inc. [of Pencor Services Inc.] - Tunkhannock, PA - *BrCabYB 84; Tel&CabFB 84C*
Blue Ridge Cable TV Inc. [of Pencor Services Inc.] - Walnutport, PA - *Tel&CabFB 84C*
Blue Ridge Cable TV Inc. [of Pencor Services Inc.] - Wyalusing, PA - *Tel&CabFB 84C*
Blue Ridge Cable TV Inc. - *See* Pencor Services Inc.
Blue Ridge CATV Inc. [of Pencor Services Inc.] - Ephrata, PA - *BrCabYB 84; Tel&CabFB 84C*
Blue Ridge Summit Post - Blue Ridge, GA - *AyerDirPub 83; BaconPubCkNews 84; Ed&PubIntYB 82*
Blue Ridge Telephone Co. Inc. - Blue Ridge, GA - *TelDir&BG 83-84*
Blue Ridge TV Cable Inc. - Sophia, WV - *Tel&CabFB 84C p.1667*
Blue River Cablevision Inc. - Edinburgh, IN - *BrCabYB 84; Tel&CabFB 84C*

Blue River Music Inc. - Hollywood, CA - *BillIntBG 83-84*
Blue River Publishing Co. - Sheboygan, WI - *BoPubDir 4, 5*
Blue River Records - Hollywood, CA - *BillIntBG 83-84*
Blue Run TV Cable Co. [of Mikelson Media Inc.] - Dunnellon, FL - *BrCabYB 84; Tel&CabFB 84C*
Blue Sky Marketing Inc. - St. Paul, MN - *BoPubDir 5*
Blue Sky Press Ltd. - Aurora, ON, Canada - *BoPubDir 4 Sup, 5*
Blue Sky Records Inc. - New York, NY - *BillIntBG 83-84*
Blue Star Press - Brooklyn, NY - *BoPubDir 4 Sup, 5*
Blue Umbrella Music Publishing Co. - Brooklyn, NY - *BillIntBG 83-84*
Blue Unicorn - Kensington, CA - *BoPubDir 4 Sup, 5; LitMag&SmPr 83-84; WritMar 84*
Blue Valley Telephone Co. - Home, KS - *TelDir&BG 83-84*
Blue Water Cable Inc. [of Cardiff Cablevision Inc.] - Blue Rapids, KS - *BrCabYB 84*
Blue Water Cable Inc. [of Cardiff Cablevision Inc.] - Onaga, KS - *Tel&CabFB 84C*
Blue Water Systems - Oceanside, CA - *MicrocomMPl 84*
Bluebirds Computer Software - Wyandotte, MI - *MicrocomMPl 84*
Bluebird's Inc. - Wyandotte, MI - *WhoWMicrocom 83*
Bluebonnet Cable - Wells Branch, TX - *BrCabYB 84*
Bluefield Cablesystems Corp. [of American Cablesystems Corp.] - Bluefield, WV - *BrCabYB 84; Tel&CabFB 84C*
Bluefield Cablesystems Corp. - Green Valley, WV - *BrCabYB 84*
Bluefield Cablesystems Corp. [of American Cablesystems Corp.] - Kimball, WV - *BrCabYB 84*
Bluefield Daily Telegraph - Bluefield, WV - *BaconPubCkNews 84; Ed&PubIntYB 82; NewsDir 84*
Bluefish - Southampton, NY - *LitMag&SmPr 83-84*
Blueford Music - *See* Mercantile Music
Bluegrass Broadcasting Co. - Lexington, KY - *BrCabYB 84*
Bluegrass Cablevision Inc. - Marshall County, KY - *Tel&CabFB 84C*
Bluegrass Literary Review, The - Midway, KY - *LitMag&SmPr 83-84*
Bluegrass Unltd. - Broad Run, VA - *ArtMar 84; BaconPubCkMag 84; WritMar 84*
Bluegrass Unltd. - Manassas, VA - *MagDir 84*
Blueline - Blue Mountain Lake, NY - *LitMag&SmPr 83-84*
Bluestem Productions - Wayzata, MN - *BoPubDir 5*
Bluewater TV Cable Ltd. - Clinton, ON, Canada - *BrCabYB 84*
Bluewater TV Cable Ltd. - Terrace Bay, ON, Canada - *Tel&CabFB 84C*
Bluffon Telephone & Appliance Co. Inc. - Bluffton, SC - *TelDir&BG 83-84*
Bluffs Meredosia Budget - Bluffs, IL - *BaconPubCkNews 84*
Bluffs Times - Bluffs, IL - *BaconPubCkNews 84; Ed&PubIntYB 82*
Bluffton Cable TV Co. [of Omega Communications Inc.] - Bluffton, IN - *BrCabYB 84; Tel&CabFB 84C*
Bluffton News - Bluffton, OH - *BaconPubCkNews 84; Ed&PubIntYB 82; NewsDir 84*
Bluffton News-Banner - Bluffton, IN - *BaconPubCkNews 84; NewsDir 84*
Blum Records - Ft. Worth, TX - *BillIntBG 83-84*
Blumberg Photo Sound Co. - Minneapolis, MN - *AvMarPl 83*
Blumberg Photo Sound Co. of Florida Inc. [Subs. of Blumberg Photo Sound Co.] - Ft. Lauderdale, FL - *AvMarPl 83*
Blumberg, Rhoda - New York, NY - *LitMarPl 83, 84*
Blumenfeld & Associates Inc., Jeff - New York, NY - *DirPRFirms 83*
Blumenfeld Direct Marketing & Advertising Inc., Sol - New York, NY - *DirMarMP 83*
Blumenthal Associates, David - New York, NY - *AvMarPl 83*
Blumenthal/Herman Advertising - Blue Bell, PA - *AdAge 3-28-84; StaDirAdAg 2-84*
Blumenthal, Shirley - New York, NY - *LitMarPl 83; MagIndMarPl 82-83*
Blumenthals - Olean, NY - *AvMarPl 83*
Blum's Farmers & Planters Almanac - Winston-Salem, NC - *MagDir 84*
Blustein/Geary Associates - Waltham, MA - *BoPubDir 4, 5*
Blvd. - Kansas City, MO - *BaconPubCkMag 84*
Bly Communications, Bob - New York, NY - *DirPRFirms 83*
Bly Marketing Communications, Bob - New York, NY - *HBIndAd&MS 82-83*
Blythe-Nelson - Dallas, TX - *DirInfWP 82*
Blythe Palo Verde Valley Times - Blythe, CA - *BaconPubCkNews 84; NewsDir 84*
Blythe Spirit - Blytheville, AR - *AyerDirPub 83; BaconPubCkNews 84*
Blytheville Courier News - Blytheville, AR - *BaconPubCkNews 84; NewsDir 84*
Blytheville TV Cable Co. - Blytheville, AR - *BrCabYB 84; Tel&CabFB 84C*
BM/E-Broadcast Management/Engineering - New York, NY - *BaconPubCkMag 84; MagDir 84*
BMA Audio Cassettes [Div. of Guilford Publications] - New York, NY - *AvMarPl 83; DirMarMP 83*
BMA Data Processing Inc. [Subs. of Central Bank & Trust] - Salt Lake City, UT - *DataDirOnSer 84*
BMB Publishing Co. - Boston, MA - *BoPubDir 4, 5*
BMC Computer Corp. [Subs. of Technology Group Inc.] - Carson, CA - *WhoWMicrocom 83*
BMC Software Inc. - Sugar Land, TX - *ADAPSOMemDir 83-84*
BMDP Statistical Software Inc. - Los Angeles, CA - *BoPubDir 4 Sup, 5; DataDirSup 7-83; EISS 83*
BMH Books [Aff. of Fellowship of Grace Brethren Churches] - Winona Lake, IN - *BoPubDir 4, 5*
BMI Educational Services - Dayton, NJ - *LitMarPl 83, 84*
BMP Publications - *See* Business Man's Publications
BMR - San Francisco, CA - *DirMarMP 83*
BMS Data - Riverside, CA - *DataDirSup 7-83*
BMT Inc. - Tuscaloosa, AL - *BoPubDir 4*
BMT Inc. - Ft. Myers, FL - *BoPubDir 5*
BMX Action [of Wizard Publications] - Torrance, CA - *BaconPubCkMag 84; MagDir 84; WritMar 84*
BMX Plus Magazine [of Daisy/Hi-Torque Publishing Co. Inc.] - Mission Hills, CA - *WritMar 84*
BNA Books [Div. of The Bureau of National Affairs Inc.] - Washington, DC - *LitMarPl 83, 84*
BNA Communications Inc. [of The Bureau of National Affairs Inc.] - Rockville, MD - *AvMarPl 83; WritMar 84*
BNA Policy & Practice Series - Washington, DC - *MagIndMarPl 82-83*
BNA Research & Special Information Services - Washington, DC - *InfoS 83-84*
BNA Video Group [Div. of The Bureau of National Affairs Inc.] - Washington, DC - *InfoS 83-84*
B'nai B'rith International Jewish Monthly, The - Washington, DC - *ArtMar 84; MagIndMarPl 82-83*
BNA's Law Reprints - Washington, DC - *MicroMarPl 82-83*
BNF Metals Abstracts [of BNF Metals Technology Centre] - Wantage, England - *OnBibDB 3*
BNF Metals Abstracts - *See* Nonferrous Metals Abstracts
BNF Metals Technology Centre [Subs. of Grove Laboratories] - Wantage, England - *CompReadDB 82; DataDirOnSer 84; InfIndMarPl 83*
BNF Non-Ferrous Metals Abstracts [of BNF Metals Technology Centre] - Wantage, England - *DataDirOnSer 84*
BNR Press - Port Clinton, OH - *BoPubDir 4, 5*
BNRR Needham Ltd. - *See* Needham, Harper & Steers Inc.
Bo-Gal Music - Wheeling, WV - *BillIntBG 83-84*
Bo-Mar Research - Kalamazoo, MI - *IntDirMarRes 83*
Bo-Sherrel Co. - Newark, CA - *DataDirSup 7-83; WhoWMicrocom 83*
Bo-Sherrel Co. Inc. - Fremont, CA - *MicrocomMPl 84*
BOA Editions Ltd. - Brockport, NY - *BoPubDir 4; LitMag&SmPr 83-84; LitMarPl 83, 84*
Boal Productions Inc., Bill - New York, NY - *AvMarPl 83*
Board & Sail Magazine - Sacramento, CA - *MagDir 84*
Board of Certified Safety Professionals - Savoy, IL - *BoPubDir 5*
Board of Jewish Education of New York - New York, NY - *AvMarPl 83; WritMar 84*
Board Report for Graphic Artists - Harrisburg, PA - *MagIndMarPl 82-83*
Boardman Community TV Inc. - Boardman, OR - *BrCabYB 84; Tel&CabFB 84C*
Boardman News - Boardman, OH - *BaconPubCkNews 84*
Boardman News - Youngstown, OH - *AyerDirPub 83; Ed&PubIntYB 82; NewsDir 84*
Boardroom - New York, NY - *DirMarMP 83*

Boardroom Books Inc. [Aff. of Boardroom Reports Inc.] - New York, NY - *BoPubDir 4, 5*
Boardroom Inc. - Playa del Rey, CA - *StaDirAdAg 2-84*
Boardroom Reports - New York, NY - *BaconPubCkMag 84; LitMarPl 83, 84; MagIndMarPl 82-83*
Boardwalk Film & Tape - Hollywood, CA - *Tel&CabFB 84C*
Boardwalker International Magazine - Atlantic City, NJ - *BaconPubCkMag 84*
Boarts International Inc. - New York, NY - *LitMarPl 83, 84; MagIndMarPl 82-83*
Boasberg Co., The - Kansas City, MO - *DirPRFirms 83; StaDirAdAg 2-84*
Bose Massimi Pollitt Ltd. [of the Univas Network] - London, England - *StaDirAdAg 2-84*
Boat & Motor Dealer - Wilmette, IL - *BaconPubCkMag 84; MagDir 84; MagIndMarPl 82-83*
Boat Records - Madison, WI - *BillIntBG 83-84*
Boating - New York, NY - *ArtMar 84; BaconPubCkMag 84; MagDir 84; MagIndMarPl 82-83; WritMar 84*
Boating Accident Reports System [of U.S. Coast Guard] - Washington, DC - *EISS 83*
Boating Business - Parry Sound, ON, Canada - *BaconPubCkMag 84*
Boating Industry - New York, NY - *BaconPubCkMag 84; MagDir 84; MagIndMarPl 82-83; WritMar 84*
Boating Industry Associations - Chicago, IL - *Tel&CabFB 84C*
Boating Product News [of Whitney Communications Inc.] - New York, NY - *BaconPubCkMag 84; MagDir 84; MagIndMarPl 82-83*
Boaz News Leader - Boaz, AL - *Ed&PubIntYB 82; NewsDir 84*
Bob & Ethel Music - Columbia, SC - *BillIntBG 83-84*
Bob Jones University Press - Greenville, SC - *BoPubDir 4, 5; LitMarPl 84*
Bobbi Enterprises - Mt. Iron, MN - *BoPubDir 4, 5*
Bobbin, The - Columbia, SC - *BaconPubCkMag 84; MagDir 84*
Bobbs-Merrill Co. Inc., The [Subs. of Howard W. Sams & Co. Inc.] - Indianapolis, IN - *LitMarPl 83, 84*
Bobbs-Merrill Co. Inc., The - New York, NY - *WritMar 84*
Bobbs-Merrill Educational Productions Co. - Indianapolis, IN - *AvMarPl 83*
Bobby O Music - *See* Lipservices
Bobby's Beat Music - *See* Fischer Music, Bobby
Bobcat Music Inc. - *See* PPX Publishers
Bobit Publishing Co. - Redondo Beach, CA - *MagIndMarPl 82-83*
Bobley Publishing Corp. [Subs. of Illustrated World Encyclopedia Inc.] - Woodbury, NY - *LitMarPl 83, 84*
Bobrow Consulting Group Inc. - New York, NY - *IntDirMarRes 83*
Bob's TV Cable - Birch River, WV - *Tel&CabFB 84C*
Boca Raton [of JES Publishing Corp.] - Boca Raton, FL - *BaconPubCkMag 84; WritMar 84*
Boca Raton Monday Paper - Boca Raton, FL - *BaconPubCkNews 84*
Boca Raton News [of Knight-Ridder Newspapers Inc.] - Boca Raton, FL - *AyerDirPub 83; BaconPubCkNews 84; Ed&PubIntYB 82; NewsDir 84*
Boca Raton Review [of Lawrence Bi-County Publishers Inc.] - Lawrence, NY - *NewsDir 84*
Boccard Advertising Inc. - Denver, CO - *StaDirAdAg 2-84*
Bocephus Music - *See* Merit Music Corp.
Boces Geneseo Migrant Center - Geneseo, NY - *BoPubDir 5*
Bock Music Co., Fred - Tarzana, CA - *BillIntBG 83-84*
Bockel & Associates Inc., David - Decatur, GA - *StaDirAdAg 2-84*
Bodacious Audio - Sausalito, CA - *AvMarPl 83*
Boddie Record Manufacturing & Recording Inc. - Cleveland, OH - *BillIntBG 83-84*
Bodek & Associates Inc., Norman - Stamford, CT - *InfIndMarPl 83*
Bodenhamer, William S. - Miami, FL - *AvMarPl 83*
Bodil - Stockholm, Sweden - *DirOnDB Spring 84*
Bodine & Associates Inc. - Baltimore, MD - *BoPubDir 4, 5*
Bodley Head, The - Salem, NH - *LitMarPl 83, 84*
Bodnar Associates Inc. - Atlanta, GA - *MicrocomMPl 84*
Bodner Advertising Inc., Stan - Miami, FL - *StaDirAdAg 2-84*
Bodo - Stuttgart, West Germany - *DirOnDB Spring 84*
Body & Co. - Portland, ME - *HBIndAd&MS 82-83; StaDirAdAg 2-84*
Body Fashions/Intimate Apparel [of Harcourt Brace Jovanovich Publications Inc.] - New York, NY - *ArtMar 84; BaconPubCkMag 84; MagDir 84; WritMar 84*
Body Forum, The - Atlanta, GA - *MagDir 84*
Body Politic, The [of Pink Triangle Press] - Toronto, ON, Canada - *LitMag&SmPr 83-84*
Body Rock - New York, NY - *BillIntBG 83-84*
Body Shop Business - Akron, OH - *BaconPubCkMag 84*
Bodyshop - Toronto, ON, Canada - *BaconPubCkMag 84*
Boeckh Building Cost System [of E. H. Boeckh Co.] - Milwaukee, WI - *DBBus 82*
Boeckh Co., E. H. [Aff. of American Appraisal Associates] - Milwaukee, WI - *BoPubDir 4, 5; DataDirOnSer 84*
Boeckh Computerized Building Cost Estimating, E. H. - Milwaukee, WI - *DirOnDB Spring 84*
Boehm Communications Services - Burnsville, CA - *StaDirAdAg 2-84*
Boehm Literary Agency, Richard - New York, NY - *LitMarPl 83, 84*
Boehm/Uniphoto, J. Kenneth - Ridgefield, CT - *AvMarPl 83*
Boeing Co., The - Bellevue, WA - *Datamation 6-83*
Boeing Computer Services Co. - Morristown, NJ - *DataDirOnSer 84; EISS 83*
Boeing Computer Services Co. - Vienna, VA - *ADAPSOMemDir 83-84*
Boeing Computer Services Co. [Div. of The Boeing Co.] - Bellevue, WA - *DataDirOnSer 84; DataDirSup 7-83*
Boeing Computer Services Co. [Div. of Boeing Co.] - Seattle, WA - *Top100Al 83*
Boeing Computer Services Co. (Education & Training Div.) - Seattle, WA - *AvMarPl 83*
Boeing Computer Services Ltd. - London, England - *MicrocomSwDir 1*
Boelter & Lincoln Advertising - Milwaukee, WI - *AdAge 3-28-84*
BOENERGI [of Swedish Institute of Building Documentation] - Stockholm, Sweden - *CompReadDB 82*
Boerne Star - Boerne, TX - *BaconPubCkNews 84; Ed&PubIntYB 82*
Boerner Public Relations Inc. - New York, NY - *DirPRFirms 83*
Boeschen & Co., John - Richmond, CA - *MagIndMarPl 82-83*
BOFORSK [of Swedish Institute of Building Documentation] - Stockholm, Sweden - *CompReadDB 82*
Bog Viewer - South Milwaukee, WI - *NewsDir 84*
Bogalusa Daily News & Sunday News - Bogalusa, LA - *NewsDir 84*
Bogart & Co. - New York, NY - *DirPRFirms 83*
Bogart-Brociner Associates - Annapolis, MD - *DataDirOnSer 84; EISS 83; FBInfSer 80; InfIndMarPl 83*
Bogata News - Bogata, TX - *Ed&PubIntYB 82*
Boger, Martin, Fairchild & Co. Inc. - Elkhart, IN - *StaDirAdAg 2-84*
Bogg Magazine - Arlington, VA - *LitMag&SmPr 83-84*
Bogg Publications - Arlington, VA - *BoPubDir 4, 5; LitMag&SmPr 83-84*
Boggle Publications - New York, NY - *BoPubDir 4, 5*
Boggy Depot Music - *See* O.L. Records & Productions Inc.
Bohle Co., The - Los Angeles, CA - *DirPRFirms 83*
Boilermakers-Blacksmiths Reporter [of Affiliated Graphics] - Kansas City, KS - *NewsDir 84*
Boise Ada Cablevision - Ada County, ID - *BrCabYB 84*
Boise Cascade - Portland, OR - *LitMarPl 83, 84; MagIndMarPl 82-83*
Boise Cascade (Specialty Paperboard Div., Lexide Fiber Products) - Beaver Falls, NY - *LitMarPl 83, 84*
Boise Cascade (Specialty Paperboard Div., Pajco Products) - Lowville, NY - *LitMarPl 84*
Boise City News - Boise City, OK - *BaconPubCkNews 84; Ed&PubIntYB 82*
Boise Idaho Register - Boise, ID - *BaconPubCkNews 84; NewsDir 84*
Boise Idaho Statesman - Boise, ID - *BaconPubCkNews 84*
Boise Journal of Commerce - Boise, ID - *NewsDir 84*
Boise State University (Ahsahta Press) - Boise, ID - *BoPubDir 4, 5*

Boitnott Visual Communications Corp. - Richmond, VA - *AvMarPl 83*
Bojan Music Corp. - Nashville, TN - *BillIntBG 83-84*
Bola Publications - Hesperia, CA - *BoPubDir 4 Sup, 5*
Bolchazy-Carducci Publishers - Chicago, IL - *BoPubDir 4 Sup, 5*
Bold Brass Studios & Publications - Vancouver, BC, Canada - *BoPubDir 4, 5*
Bold Strummer Ltd. - Westport, CT - *BoPubDir 4, 5; LitMag&SmPr 83-84*
Bolding Tab Service Inc. - Stamford, CT - *IntDirMarRes 83*
Boldt Publishing Co. - San Rafael, CA - *BoPubDir 4, 5*
Bolen Industries Inc. - Hackensack, NJ - *DirInfWP 82*
Boletin Anglohispano - Hesperia, CA - *LitMag&SmPr 83-84*
Boley Subscription Agency Inc. - Great Neck, NY - *MagIndMarPl 82-83*
Boling Co. - Silver City, NC - *DirInfWP 82*
Bolingbrook Beacon - Lockport, IL - *NewsDir 84*
Bolingbrook Beacon - *See* Beacon Sun Newspapers
Bolingbrook Beacon, The - Bolingbrook, IL - *Ed&PubIntYB 82*
Bolingbrook Metropolitan - Bolingbrook, IL - *Ed&PubIntYB 82*
Bolinger Co., Paul - Ft. Worth, TX - *DirInfWP 82*
Bolivar Bulletin Times [of Delphos Herald Inc.] - Bolivar, TN - *BaconPubCkNews 84; NewsDir 84*
Bolivar Cable Co. Inc. [of Tennessee-Kentucky CATV Co.] - Bolivar, KY - *BrCabYB 84*
Bolivar Commercial - Cleveland, MS - *AyerDirPub 83; BaconPubCkNews 84; Ed&PubIntYB 82*
Bolivar Herald-Free Press - Bolivar, MO - *AyerDirPub 83; BaconPubCkNews 84; NewsDir 84*
Bolivia Records - Brewton, AL - *BillIntBG 83-84*
Bolling Beam [of Rockville Sentinel Newspapers] - Rockville, MD - *NewsDir 84*
Bollinger County Banner-Press - Marble Hill, MO - *BaconPubCkNews 84*
Bollman International Records - Dallas, TX - *BillIntBG 83-84*
Bologna International Inc., William J. - New York, NY - *AdAge 3-28-84; StaDirAdAg 2-84*
Bolster & King - Providence, RI - *AdAge 3-28-84; StaDirAdAg 2-84*
Bolt Advertising Inc. - Roanoke, VA - *StaDirAdAg 2-84*
Bolt Beranek & Newman Inc. - Cambridge, MA - *EISS 83*
Bolton Associates, Ted - Philadelphia, PA - *VideoDir 82-83*
Bolton, D. J. - San Jose, CA - *BoPubDir 4*
Bolton, D. J. - Santa Fe, NM - *BoPubDir 5*
Bolton Enterprise - Bolton, ON, Canada - *Ed&PubIntYB 82*
Bomac Batten Ltd. (Syndicate Dept.) - Toronto, ON, Canada - *Ed&PubIntYB 82*
Bomp Records Inc. - Los Angeles, CA - *BillIntBG 83-84*
Bomstein Agency, The - Washington, DC - *StaDirAdAg 2-84*
Bomze Graphic Design/Photographics, Rich - Southampton, PA - *LitMarPl 83, 84*
Bon Ami Film Distributing Corp. - New York, NY - *Tel&CabFB 84C*
Bon Appetit [of Knapp Communications Corp.] - Los Angeles, CA - *ArtMar 84; BaconPubCkMag 84; MagIndMarPl 82-83; NewsBur 6; WritMar 84*
Bon Appetit [of Knapp Communications Corp.] - New York, NY - *Folio 83*
Bon Mot Publications - Pigeon Forge, TN - *BoPubDir 4*
Bon Mot Publications - Sevierville, TN - *BoPubDir 5*
Bon Vivant - Downsview, ON, Canada - *BaconPubCkMag 84*
Bonanza Inc. - Sparks, NV - *BoPubDir 4, 5*
Bonanza Valley Voice - Brooten, MN - *Ed&PubIntYB 82*
Bonaparte Record-Republican - Bonaparte, IA - *Ed&PubIntYB 82*
Bonaventure Cablevision - Broward County, FL - *Tel&CabFB 84C*
Bond, Alison M. - New York, NY - *LitMarPl 83, 84*
Bond Analysis Spread System [of Remote Computing Corp.] - Palo Alto, CA - *DataDirOnSer 84*
Bond, Beverly [Aff. of Michael Larson/Elizabeth Pomada Literary Agents] - Houston, TX - *LitMarPl 83, 84*
Bond Buyer, The - New York, NY - *BaconPubCkMag 84; DirMarMP 83; NewsBur 6*
Bond, Dorothy - Cottage Grove, OR - *BoPubDir 4 Sup, 5*
Bond 007 Fan Club, James - Bronxville, NY - *BoPubDir 4 Sup, 5*
Bond, James O. - Rockville, MD - *BoPubDir 5*
Bond, John H. Jr. - Baltimore, MD - *Tel&CabFB 84C*
Bond Wheelwright Co. - *See* Cumberland Press Inc./Bond Wheelwright Co.
Bondata [of FRI Information Services Ltd.] - Montreal, PQ, Canada - *DataDirOnSer 84; DirOnDB Spring 84*
Bonded Services [Div. of Novo Communications Inc.] - Ft. Lee, NJ - *Tel&CabFB 84C*
Bonded Services - New York, NY - *ProGuPRSer 4*
Bonder Ltd., Ronne - New York, NY - *StaDirAdAg 2-84*
Bonduel Cable TV - Bonduel, WI - *Tel&CabFB 84C*
Bonduel Telephone Co. [Aff. of Telephone & Data Systems Inc.] - Bonduel, WI - *TelDir&BG 83-84*
Bondweek [of Institutional Investor] - New York, NY - *BaconPubCkMag 84; NewsDir 84*
Bone, Louis - Gatesville, TX - *Tel&CabFB 84C p.1667*
Bonesteel Enterprise - Bonesteel, SD - *BaconPubCkNews 84; Ed&PubIntYB 82*
Bonfield & Associates - San Francisco, CA - *AdAge 3-28-84; StaDirAdAg 2-84*
Bonfiglio, Peggy - Marcella, NJ - *MagIndMarPl 82-83*
Bonham Daily Favorite - Bonham, TX - *NewsDir 84*
Bonham Favorite - Bonham, TX - *BaconPubCkNews 84*
Bonham Herald - Bonham, TX - *Ed&PubIntYB 82*
Bonifay Holmes County Advertiser - Bonifay, FL - *BaconPubCkNews 84; NewsDir 84*
Bonita Banner - Bonita Springs, FL - *AyerDirPub 83; Ed&PubIntYB 82*
Bonita Banner - *See* Sunbelt Publishing Co.
Bonjoel Enterprises - Des Plaines, IL - *MicrocomMPl 83, 84; WhoWMicrocom 83*
Bonnell Palm Coast News Tribune - Bonnell, FL - *BaconPubCkNews 84*
Bonner & Moore Computing Co. [Subs. of Bonner & Moore Associates] - Houston, TX - *ADAPSOMemDir 83-84; DataDirOnSer 84*
Bonner Springs Chieftain - Bonner Springs, KS - *Ed&PubIntYB 82*
Bonner Springs-Edwardsville Chieftain - Bonner Springs, KS - *BaconPubCkNews 84; NewsDir 84*
Bonners Ferry Cablevision [of Rock Associates Inc.] - Bonners Ferry, ID - *Tel&CabFB 84C*
Bonners Ferry Herald - Bonners Ferry, ID - *BaconPubCkNews 84; Ed&PubIntYB 82*
Bonneville Ad Services - Los Angeles, CA - *StaDirAdAg 2-84*
Bonneville International Corp. [Subs. of Deseret Management Corp.] - Salt Lake City, UT - *AdAge 6-28-84; BrCabYB 84; KnowInd 83; LitMarPl 84; Tel&CabFB 84S*
Bonneville Productions - Salt Lake City, UT - *Tel&CabFB 84C*
Bonney Inc. - Chicago, IL - *StaDirAdAg 2-84*
Bonney Lake Cable TV - Bonney Lake, WA - *BrCabYB 84; Tel&CabFB 84C*
Bonnin Electronics Inc. - Santurce, PR - *AvMarPl 83*
Bonnyville Nouvelle - Bonnyville, AB, Canada - *Ed&PubIntYB 82*
Bono Cable TV [of Spectrum Teltronics Inc.] - Bono, AR - *BrCabYB 84*
Bonsib Inc. - Washington, DC - *DirPRFirms 83; StaDirAdAg 2-84*
Bonsib Inc. - Ft. Wayne, IN - *StaDirAdAg 2-84*
Bonsib Marketing Services - Ft. Wayne, IN - *AdAge 3-28-84*
Boo Hoo Bookies [Aff. of The Original Kleptonian Neo-American Church] - Arcata, CA - *BoPubDir 5*
Boo Hoo Bookies [Aff. of The Original Kleptonian Neo-American Church] - Philadelphia, PA - *BoPubDir 4*
Book & Magazine Production - Northbrook, IL - *MagIndMarPl 82-83*
Book & Tackle Shop - Chestnut Hill, PA - *BoPubDir 4, 5*
Book Arts Review [of The Center for Book Arts] - New York, NY - *LitMag&SmPr 83-84; LitMarPl 84; WritMar 84*
Book Automation Inc. - Stamford, CT - *LitMarPl 83, 84*
Book Business Mart [of Premier Wholesale Book News] - Ft. Worth, TX - *LitMag&SmPr 83-84*
Book Carrier Inc., The - Gaithersburg, MD - *LitMarPl 83, 84*
Book Center Inc. - Montreal, PQ, Canada - *LitMarPl 84*
Book Choice Library Services Ltd. - Pleasantville, NY - *LitMarPl 84*
Book Club for Poetry - Francestown, NH - *LitMarPl 83, 84*
Book Club for the Martial Arts Inc. [Subs. of The Karate & Self Defense Book Club Inc.] - Middle Island, NY - *LitMarPl 83, 84*

Book Collecting World - Chicago, IL - *BaconPubCkMag 84; MagDir 84*
Book Collector's Book Shelf [Subs. of The Moretus Press Inc.] - New York, NY - *LitMarPl 83, 84*
Book Co., The - Los Angeles, CA - *MicrocomMPl 83*
Book Consolidation Service Inc. - Carlstadt, NJ - *LitMarPl 83*
Book Covers Inc. - Newark, NJ - *LitMarPl 83, 84*
Book Crafters Inc. - Chelsea, MI - *LitMarPl 83*
Book Creations Inc. - Canaan, NY - *LitMarPl 83, 84*
Book Dealers World [of American Bookdealers Exchange] - La Mesa, CA - *LitMag&SmPr 83-84; WritMar 84*
Book Dept. - Hartford, CT - *BoPubDir 4, 5*
Book Dept. Inc., The - Boston, MA - *LitMarPl 83, 84*
Book Digest - New York, NY - *MagDir 84; MagIndMarPl 82-83*
Book Dynamics Inc. - New York, NY - *LitMarPl 83, 84*
Book Express Plus/OLAS [of Brodart Inc.] - Williamsport, PA - *DataDirOnSer 84; DBBus 82; DirOnDB Spring 84*
Book Fiend - Toronto, ON, Canada - *BoPubDir 4 Sup, 5; LitMarPl 83, 84*
Book Forum [of Hudson River Press] - New York, NY - *LitMag&SmPr 83-84; MagIndMarPl 82-83; WritMar 84*
Book Home, The (Periodical Dept.) - Colorado Springs, CO - *MagIndMarPl 82-83*
Book House Inc., The - Jonesville, MI - *LitMarPl 83, 84*
Book Industry Study Group Inc. - New York, NY - *BoPubDir 4 Sup, 5*
Book Industry Systems Advisory Committee - New York, NY - *EISS 83*
Book Inventory Systems Inc. - Ann Arbor, MI - *BoPubDir 4 Sup, 5*
Book Jobbers Hawaii Inc. - Honolulu, HI - *LitMarPl 83, 84*
Book-Lab [Aff. of Annmaur Corp.] - North Bergen, NJ - *BoPubDir 4 Sup; LitMarPl 83, 84*
Book Launching Publicity Service - New York, NY - *LitMarPl 83*
Book Lover - New York, NY - *LitMarPl 84*
Book-Mart Press Inc. - North Bergen, NJ - *LitMarPl 83, 84; MagIndMarPl 82-83*
Book-Mart, The - Lake Wales, FL - *LitMag&SmPr 83-84; WritMar 84*
Book-of-the-Month Club Inc. [Subs. of Time Inc.] - New York, NY - *LitMarPl 83, 84*
Book-of-the-Month Club/Science - *See* Book-of-the-Month Club Inc.
Book Page - Los Angeles, CA - *BoPubDir 4, 5*
Book Press Inc., The - Brattleboro, VT - *LitMarPl 83, 84*
Book Press Ltd. - Toronto, ON, Canada - *BoPubDir 5*
Book Publishers Inc. - Fresno, CA - *BoPubDir 4, 5*
Book Publishers of Texas - Tyler, TX - *LitMag&SmPr 83-84*
Book Publishers Projects Inc. - New York, NY - *LitMarPl 83, 84*
Book Publishing Co., The - Summertown, TN - *LitMag&SmPr 83-84; LitMarPl 83, 84*
Book Review Index [of Dialog Information Services Inc.] - Palo Alto, CA - *DataDirOnSer 84*
Book Review Index [of Gale Research Co.] - Detroit, MI - *CompReadDB 82; DBBus 82; DirOnDB Spring 84; EISS 83; OnBibDB 3*
Book Review, The [of Los Angeles Times] - Los Angeles, CA - *LitMarPl 83, 84*
Book Room Ltd. - Halifax, NS, Canada - *BoPubDir 4, 5*
Book Sales Inc. - Secaucus, NJ - *LitMarPl 83, 84*
Book Searchers - Forest Grove, OR - *BoPubDir 4, 5*
Book Services International [Div. of Key Book Service Inc.] - Bridgeport, CT - *LitMarPl 83, 84*
Book Society of Canada Ltd. - Agincourt, ON, Canada - *BoPubDir 4 Sup, 5; LitMarPl 83, 84*
Book Studio Inc., The - Croton-on-Hudson, NY - *LitMarPl 83, 84*
Book Talk - Albuquerque, NM - *LitMag&SmPr 83-84*
Book Trading Ltd. - New York, NY - *LitMarPl 83*
Book Trak Library Management System [of Follett Library Book Co.] - Crystal Lake, IL - *EISS 5-84 Sup*
Book World [of The Washington Post] - Washington, DC - *LitMarPl 83, 84*
Book World Promotions Inc. - Newark, NJ - *LitMarPl 83, 84*
Bookazine Co. Inc. - New York, NY - *LitMarPl 83, 84*
Bookbinders Inc. - Jersey City, NY - *LitMarPl 84*
Bookcraft Inc. - Salt Lake City, UT - *BoPubDir 4, 5; WritMar 84*
BookCrafters Inc. - Chelsea, MI - *LitMarPl 84*
Booke & Co. - New York, NY - *DirPRFirms 83*
Booke & Co. (Communications Div.) - Winston-Salem, NC - *AvMarPl 83*
Booker Associates Inc., James E. - New York, NY - *DirPRFirms 83*
Booker News - Booker, TX - *BaconPubCkNews 84; Ed&PubIntYB 82*
Booker Trailer Court - Booker, TX - *BrCabYB 84; Tel&CabFB 84C*
Bookers, The [Subs. of Morton D. Wax & Associates] - New York, NY - *LitMarPl 83, 84*
Bookery - Redding, CA - *BoPubDir 4, 5; LitMag&SmPr 83-84*
Bookfile - Oxford, England - *DirOnDB Spring 84*
Bookfinger - New York, NY - *BoPubDir 4, 5*
Booklegger Press - San Francisco, CA - *BoPubDir 4, 5; LitMag&SmPr 83-84*
Bookline [of Bancroft-Parkman Inc.] - New York, NY - *EISS 83; InfIndMarPl 83*
Bookline Alert: Missing Books & Manuscripts - Washington, CT - *DirOnDB Spring 84*
Bookline Alert: Missing Books & Manuscripts [of Bancroft-Parkman Inc.] - New York, NY - *CompReadDB 82*
Bookline: Utopia - Washington, CT - *DirOnDB Spring 84*
Booklink Distributors [Div. of Padre Productions] - San Luis Obispo, CA - *BoPubDir 4 Sup, 5; LitMarPl 83, 84*
Booklist - Chicago, IL - *BaconPubCkMag 84; MagDir 84; MagIndMarPl 82-83*
Booklook - Kansas City, MO - *Ed&PubIntYB 82*
Booklore Publishers Inc. - Sarasota, FL - *BoPubDir 4, 5*
Bookmaker Publishing - Burnsville, MN - *BoPubDir 4, 5*
Bookmakers Inc., The - Wilkes-Barre, PA - *LitMarPl 84*
Bookmakers Inc. - Westport, CT - *LitMarPl 83, 84*
Bookman Publishing [Aff. of Rookman Dan Inc.] - Baltimore, MD - *BoPubDir 4, 5; LitMarPl 84*
Bookmark Publishing Associates Ltd. - White Plains, NY - *LitMarPl 83, 84*
Bookmarketers of America Ltd. - Wappingers Falls, NY - *LitMarPl 83, 84*
Bookmart - Gardiner, NY - *MagIndMarPl 82-83*
Bookmaster - Narragansett, RI - *LitMarPl 83, 84*
Bookmen Inc. - Minneapolis, MN - *LitMarPl 83, 84*
Bookmill, The - Santa Monica, CA - *LitMarPl 83, 84; MagIndMarPl 82-83*
Bookpeople - Berkeley, CA - *BoPubDir 4 Sup, 5; LitMarPl 83, 84*
Bookplan, The - New York, NY - *LitMarPl 83, 84*
Bookplates in the News - Alhambra, CA - *ArtMar 84*
Books - Waukegan, IL - *BoPubDir 4, 5*
Books Alive Inc. - Montclair, NJ - *LitMarPl 83, 84*
Books Americana Inc. - Florence, AL - *BoPubDir 4, 5; LitMarPl 84*
Books & Production East Inc. - Manchester-by-the-Sea, MA - *LitMarPl 83*
Books for Accountants [of Prentice-Hall Inc.] - Englewood, NJ - *LitMarPl 83, 84*
Books for All Times Inc. - Alexandria, VA - *BoPubDir 4, 5; LitMag&SmPr 83-84*
Books for Business Inc. [Subs. of Athena Publishing Group BV] - Washington, DC - *LitMarPl 83, 84; WritMar 84*
Books for College Libraries [of American Library Association] - Chicago, IL - *CompReadDB 82*
Books from Magazines Inc. - Commack, NY - *LitMarPl 83, 84*
Books in Canada [of Canadian Review of Books Ltd.] - Toronto, ON, Canada - *BaconPubCkMag 84; LitMag&SmPr 83-84*
Books in Focus - New York, NY - *LitMarPl 83, 84*
Books in Print - Middletown, NY - *LitMarPl 84*
Books in Print [of R. R. Bowker Co.] - New York, NY - *CompReadDB 82; DataDirOnSer 84; DBBus 82; DirOnDB Spring 84; OnBibDB 3*
Books in Print Data Base [of R. R. Bowker Co.] - New York, NY - *EISS 83*
Books Inc. - Montgomery, GA - *LitMarPl 84*
Books Information [of Bibliographic Retrieval Services Inc.] - Lathan, NY - *DataDirOnSer 84*

Books Information [of Brodart Inc.] - Williamsport, PA - *CompReadDB 82*
Books Marc-Us - Ojai, CA - *BoPubDir 4, 5*
Books of a Feather - Los Angeles, CA - *BoPubDir 4 Sup, 5; LitMag&SmPr 83-84*
Books of Light - Columbus, OH - *LitMarPl 83, 84*
Books of the Southwest - Tucson, AZ - *LitMag&SmPr 83-84*
Books of Wall Street - Dallas, TX - *BoPubDir 4, 5*
Books on Tape Inc. - Newport Beach, CA - *AvMarPl 83; DirMarMP 83*
Books Unltd. [Aff. of Junior League of Shreveport] - Shreveport, LA - *BoPubDir 4, 5*
BookServ Inc. - Dayton, NJ - *LitMarPl 83*
BookServ Inc. - Somerset, NJ - *LitMarPl 84*
Booksinfo [of Brodart Inc.] - Williamsport, PA - *DataDirOnSer 84; DirOnDB Spring 84; OnBibDB 3*
Bookslinger - St. Paul, MN - *BoPubDir 4 Sup, 5; LitMarPl 83, 84*
Booksmith Inc. - New York, NY - *LitMarPl 83*
Booksmith Promotional Co. - New York, NY - *LitMarPl 84*
Booksource - Los Angeles, CA - *BoPubDir 4 Sup, 5*
Bookstore Journal [of CBA Service Corp. Inc.] - Colorado Springs, CO - *BaconPubCkMag 84; LitMarPl 83, 84; MagDir 84; MagIndMarPl 82-83*
Bookthrift [Aff. of Simon & Schuster] - New York, NY - *BoPubDir 4 Sup, 5; LitMarPl 83*
Bookviews - New York, NY - *MagDir 84*
Bookworks Inc., The - Chicago, IL - *LitMarPl 84*
Bookworld Communications Corp. - Louisville, KY - *BoPubDir 4, 5*
Bookworm Publishing Co. - Russellville, AR - *BoPubDir 5; LitMag&SmPr 83-84*
Bookworm Publishing Co. Inc. [Aff. of North American Bait Farms Inc.] - Ontario, CA - *BoPubDir 4*
Boole & Babbage Inc. - Sunnyvale, CA - *DataDirSup 7-83*
Boom! Graphics Inc. - Los Angeles, CA - *StaDirAdAg 2-84*
Boombah Herald - Lancaster, NY - *LitMag&SmPr 83-84*
Boomerang - Laramie, WY - *AyerDirPub 83*
Boomerang Music Publishing Co. - *See* S & R Music Publishing Inc.
Boon, Clarence A. - Virden, MB, Canada - *BoPubDir 4, 5*
Boone Advertising Inc. - Houston, TX - *StaDirAdAg 2-84*
Boone & Crockett Club - Alexandria, VA - *BoPubDir 4, 5*
Boone Cablevision [of Booth American Co.] - Boone, NC - *BrCabYB 84; Tel&CabFB 84C*
Boone Corp. - Costa Mesa, CA - *MicrocomMPl 84*
Boone County Headlight - Harrison, AR - *Ed&PubIntYB 82*
Boone County Journal - Ashland, MO - *Ed&PubIntYB 82*
Boone County Recorder - Burlington, KY - *AyerDirPub 83; NewsDir 84*
Boone County Recorder, The - Boone County, KY - *Ed&PubIntYB 82*
Boone County Shopper - Belvidere, IL - *AyerDirPub 83*
Boone County Shopping News - Ames, IA - *AyerDirPub 83*
Boone County Shopping News - Boone, IA - *AyerDirPub 83*
Boone, Jerry - Bixby, OK - *Tel&CabFB 84C p.1667*
Boone News-Republican [of Schaub Publishing Inc.] - Boone, IA - *BaconPubCkNews 84; NewsDir 84*
Boone Newspaper Group - Natchez, MS - *Ed&PubIntYB 82*
Boone, Steve - Point Pleasant Beach, NJ - *LitMarPl 83, 84*
Boone Watauga Democrat [of Rivers Printing Co.] - Boone, NC - *BaconPubCkNews 84; NewsDir 84*
Boones Tunes - *See* Kaye Publications, Richard
Booneville Banner-Independent [of The New York Times Co.] - Booneville, MS - *BaconPubCkNews 84; NewsDir 84*
Booneville Democrat - Booneville, AR - *BaconPubCkNews 84; Ed&PubIntYB 82*
Booneville Yadkin Enterprise - Booneville, NC - *BaconPubCkNews 84*
Boonslick Historical Society - Boonville, MO - *BoPubDir 4, 5*
Boonville Anderson Valley Advertiser - Boonville, CA - *BaconPubCkNews 84*
Boonville Cable TV [of Horizon Communications Corp.] - Boonville, IN - *Tel&CabFB 84C*
Boonville Cable TV [of American TV & Communications Corp.] - Boonville, MO - *BrCabYB 84; Tel&CabFB 84C*
Boonville Cooper County Record - Boonville, MO - *BaconPubCkNews 84*
Boonville Daily News - Boonville, MO - *NewsDir 84*
Boonville Daily News & Advertiser - Boonville, MO - *Ed&PubIntYB 82*
Boonville Herald & Adirondack Tourist - Boonville, NY - *Ed&PubIntYB 82; NewsDir 84*
Boonville News & Advertiser - Boonville, MO - *BaconPubCkNews 84*
Boonville Standard - Boonville, IN - *BaconPubCkNews 84; Ed&PubIntYB 82; NewsDir 84*
Boonville Warrick Enquirer - Boonville, IN - *BaconPubCkNews 84; NewsDir 84*
Boorum & Pease/Vernon McMillan - Elizabeth, NJ - *DirInfWP 82*
Boosey & Hawkes Inc. - Farmingdale, NY - *BoPubDir 4, 5*
Boosey & Hawkes Inc. - New York, NY - *BillIntBG 83-84; Tel&CabFB 84C*
Boost Publishing Co. - Staunton, VA - *LitMag&SmPr 83-84*
Booster - Ireton, IA - *AyerDirPub 83*
Booster [of CM Media] - Columbus, OH - *AyerDirPub 83; Ed&PubIntYB 82; NewsDir 84*
Booster - Germantown, OH - *AyerDirPub 83*
Booster - Innisfail, AB, Canada - *AyerDirPub 83*
Booster - Jasper, AB, Canada - *AyerDirPub 83*
Booster & Weld County News - Greeley, CO - *Ed&PubIntYB 82*
Booster News - Farmingdale, NJ - *AyerDirPub 83*
Booster News - Howell, NJ - *Ed&PubIntYB 82; NewsDir 84*
Booster Newspaper Group [of Chicago Lerner Newspapers] - Chicago, IL - *NewsDir 84*
Booster, The [of Chicago Lerner Newspapers] - Chicago, IL - *Ed&PubIntYB 82; NewsDir 84*
Booster's Community News - London, OH - *AyerDirPub 83*
Boot Records Inc. - Nashville, TN - *BillIntBG 83-84*
Boote-Marketing Research & Analysis, Alfred S. - Bedford, NY - *IntDirMarRes 83*
Booth American Co. - Detroit, MI - *BrCabYB 84 p.D-298; Tel&CabFB 84C p.1667*
Booth & Watson Music - Nashville, TN - *BillIntBG 83-84*
Booth Communications - Birmingham, MI - *BrCabYB 84*
Booth Michigan Newspapers [Div. of Newhouse Newspapers] - New York, NY - *LitMarPl 83, 84*
Booth Newspapers - *See* Newhouse Newspapers
Boothbay Register - Boothbay Harbor, ME - *AyerDirPub 83; BaconPubCkNews 84; Ed&PubIntYB 82; NewsDir 84*
Bootheel Video Inc. [of Adams-Russell Co. Inc.] - Caruthersville, MO - *BrCabYB 84; Tel&CabFB 84C*
Bootstrap Toolkit - South Orange, NJ - *MicrocomMPl 83, 84*
Booz-Allen & Hamilton Inc. - Bethesda, MD - *DirInfWP 82*
Booz-Allen & Hamilton Inc. - New York, NY - *InfoS 83-84; InterCabHB 3*
BOP [of Kitchen Sink Press] - Willow Springs, MO - *LitMag&SmPr 83-84*
Bop Talk Music - Massena, NY - *BillIntBG 83-84*
Borchardt Inc., Georges - New York, NY - *LitMarPl 83, 84*
Borden & Associates, John - Brooklyn Park, MN - *StaDirAdAg 2-84*
Borden & Associates, John - Minneapolis, MN - *ArtMar 84*
Borden & Associates, Robert E. - Chicago, IL - *ArtMar 84; DirPRFirms 83*
Borden Cable Television Ltd. [of Trillium Cable Communications Ltd.] - Alliston, ON, Canada - *BrCabYB 84*
Borden Productions - Concord, MA - *TelAl 83, 84; Tel&CabFB 84C*
Borden Star, The - Gail, TX - *Ed&PubIntYB 82*
Bordentown Register-News [of Lorraine Publishing Inc.] - Bordentown, NJ - *NewsDir 84*
Bordentown Register-News - *See* Lorraine Publishing Inc.
Border Area Cable TV Inc. - Baudette, MN - *BrCabYB 84; Tel&CabFB 84C*
Border Community TV Inc. - Rock Island, PQ, Canada - *BrCabYB 84*
Borderland Sciences Research Foundation - Vista, CA - *BoPubDir 4, 5; LitMag&SmPr 83-84*
Borders, Perrin & Norrander - Portland, OR - *AdAge 3-28-84; StaDirAdAg 2-84*

Borea Photography, Raimondo - New York, NY - *LitMarPl 83, 84; MagIndMarPl 82-83*
Boreal [of University of Alberta] - Edmonton, AB, Canada - *DataDirOnSer 84*
Boreal Codes [of University of Alberta] - Edmonton, AB, Canada - *DataDirOnSer 84*
Boreal Institute for Northern Studies - Edmonton, AB, Canada - *CompReadDB 82*
Boreal Institute for Northern Studies Library - Edmonton, AB, Canada - *EISS 83*
Boreal Library Catalogue [of University of Alberta] - Edmonton, AB, Canada - *CompReadDB 82; DataDirOnSer 84; DirOnDB Spring 84*
Boreal Northern Titles [of University of Alberta] - Edmonton, AB, Canada - *CompReadDB 82; DataDirOnSer 84; DirOnDB Spring 84*
Borealis Press Ltd. - Nepean, ON, Canada - *LitMag&SmPr 83-84; WritMar 84*
Borealis Press Ltd. - Ottawa, ON, Canada - *BoPubDir 4; LitMarPl 83, 84*
Borf Books - Brownsville, KY - *BoPubDir 4, 5; LitMag&SmPr 83-84*
Borg-Warner Educational Systems [Div. of Borg-Warner Corp.] - Arlington Heights, IL - *AvMarPl 83; MicrocomMPl 83, 84*
Borgen Broadcasting Co. - Preston, MN - *BrCabYB 84*
Borger News-Herald [of Donrey Media Group] - Borger, TX - *BaconPubCkNews 84; Ed&PubIntYB 82; NewsDir 84*
Borgo Press, The - San Bernardino, CA - *LitMag&SmPr 83-84; LitMarPl 83, 84; WritMar 84*
Borgstedt, Doug & Jean - Paoli, PA - *Ed&PubIntYB 82*
Borio, Clarice - New York, NY - *LitMarPl 83, 84; MagIndMarPl 82-83*
Boris Color Lab Inc. - Boston, MA - *AvMarPl 83*
Borja Studio, The - Chicago, IL - *LitMarPl 83, 84; MagIndMarPl 82-83*
Borland International - Scotts Valley, CA - *MicrocomMPl 84*
Borlaug Publishing Co. - Washburn, ND - *BaconPubCkNews 84*
Borman/Williams Inc. - New York, NY - *DirPRFirms 83*
Borns, Steven - New York, NY - *LitMarPl 83, 84; MagIndMarPl 82-83*
Bornstein School of Memory Training - Los Angeles, CA - *BoPubDir 4, 5*
Boro News - Homestead, PA - *AyerDirPub 83*
Boron Cable TV - Boron, CA - *BrCabYB 84*
Borst Inc., H. Shaw - Mt. Kisco, NY - *LitMarPl 83, 84*
Borthwick Associates - Plymouth, MN - *LitMarPl 83, 84*
Bortin, Jeff - San Francisco, CA - *LitMarPl 83, 84*
Borum, Michael G. - Nashville, TN - *MagIndMarPl 82-83*
BOS National Inc. - Dallas, TX - *MicrocomMPl 84*
Boschert Inc. - Sunnyvale, CA - *DirInfWP 82*
Bosco Associates, Joseph - Oak Prk, IL - *StaDirAdAg 2-84*
Bosco Multimedia, Don [Subs. of Salesian Society Inc.] - New Rochelle, NY - *BoPubDir 4; LitMarPl 84*
Bosco Publications, Don [Div. of Don Bosco Multimedia] - New Rochelle, NY - *LitMag&SmPr 83-84; WritMar 84*
Boscobel Cable Co. - Boscobel, WI - *BrCabYB 84; Tel&CabFB 84C*
Boscobel Dial - Boscobel, WI - *Ed&PubIntYB 82; NewsDir 84*
Boscobel Dial - *See* Boscobel Publishers Inc.
Boscobel Publishers Inc. - Boscobel, WI - *BaconPubCkNews 84*
Bose Corp. - Framingham, MA - *AvMarPl 83*
Boss - New York, NY - *LitMag&SmPr 83-84*
Boss Apple Tunes - Minneapolis, MN - *BillIntBG 83-84*
Boss Books - New York, NY - *LitMag&SmPr 83-84*
Boss Tweed Music - Sun Valley, CA - *BillIntBG 83-84*
Bossier Banner Progress - Benton, LA - *Ed&PubIntYB 82*
Bossier City Cable TV Corp. [of United Cable TV Corp.] - Bossier City, LA - *Tel&CabFB 84C*
Bossier Press [of Bossier Caddo Newspapers Inc.] - Bossier City, LA - *AyerDirPub 83; BaconPubCkNews 84; NewsDir 84*
Bostelman Associates - Tenafly, NJ - *DirPRFirms 83*
Bostick, M. N. - Waco, TX - *Tel&CabFB 84S*
Boston & Maine Railroad Historical Society Inc. - littleton, MA - *BoPubDir 4, 5*
Boston Bulletin - Englishtown, NJ - *MagDir 84*
Boston Business Journal - Boston, MA - *BaconPubCkMag 84*
Boston College (Mathematics Institute) - Chestnut Hill, MA - *BoPubDir 4, 5*
Boston Critic Inc. - Cambridge, MA - *LitMag&SmPr 83-84*
Boston Dorchester Argus-Citizen - *See* Tribune Publishing Co.
Boston Educational Computing Inc. - Boston, MA - *MicrocomMPl 84*
Boston Financial & Equity Corp. - Boston, MA - *DataDirSup 7-83*
Boston Globe - Boston, MA - *BaconPubCkNews 84; Ed&PubIntYB 82; LitMarPl 83, 84; NewsBur 6; NewsDir 84*
Boston Globe Magazine - Boston, MA - *WritMar 84*
Boston Hellenic Chronicle - Boston, MA - *BaconPubCkNews 84; NewsDir 84*
Boston Herald [of News Group Boston Inc.] - Boston, MA - *BaconPubCkNews 84; LitMarPl 84*
Boston Herald American [of Hearst Corp.] - Boston, MA - *Ed&PubIntYB 82; LitMarPl 83; NewsBur 6; NewsDir 84*
Boston International [Div. of General Idea Inc.] - Boston, MA - *BillIntBG 83-84*
Boston Jamaica Plain Citizen - *See* Tribune Publishing Co.
Boston Ledger - Boston, MA - *Ed&PubIntYB 82*
Boston Ledger [of Citizen Group Publications] - Brookline, MA - *AyerDirPub 83; NewsDir 84*
Boston Ledger - *See* Citizen Group Publications
Boston Library Consortium - Boston, MA - *EISS 83*
Boston Literary Agency, The - Manchester, MA - *LitMarPl 83, 84*
Boston Magazine [of Municipal Publications] - Boston, MA - *ArtMar 84; BaconPubCkMag 84; Folio 83; MagDir 84; MagIndMarPl 82-83; WritMar 84*
Boston Marathon, The [of Boston Phoenix Inc.] - Boston, MA - *BaconPubCkMag 84; WritMar 84*
Boston Marine Guide - Boston, MA - *MagDir 84*
Boston Mills Press [Div. of One Man's Way Ltd.] - Erin, ON, Canada - *BoPubDir 4; LitMarPl 83, 84*
Boston Music Co. [Aff. of Hammerstein Music & Theater Co. Inc.] - Boston, MA - *BillIntBG 83-84; BoPubDir 4, 5; DirMarMP 83*
Boston On-Line - Boston, MA - *DirOnDB Spring 84*
Boston Phoenix - Boston, MA - *BaconPubCkNews 84; LitMarPl 83, 84; MagIndMarPl 82-83; NewsDir 84; WritMar 84*
Boston Pilot - Boston, MA - *NewsDir 84*
Boston Post-Gazette - Boston, MA - *NewsDir 84*
Boston Publishing Co. Inc. [Subs. of Time-Life Books] - Boston, MA - *BoPubDir 4 Sup, 5; LitMarPl 84*
Boston Review [of Boston Critic Inc.] - Cambridge, MA - *ArtMar 84; LitMag&SmPr 83-84; MagDir 84; WritMar 84*
Boston Risk Management Corp. - Boston, MA - *BoPubDir 5*
Boston South Boston Tribune - Boston, MA - *BaconPubCkNews 84*
Boston Sunday Globe, The - Boston, MA - *Ed&PubIntYB 82; LitMarPl 84*
Boston Systems Office Inc. - Waltham, MA - *MicrocomMPl 84; MicrocomSwDir 1*
Boston University (African Studies Center) - Boston, MA - *BoPubDir 4, 5*
Boston University (Krasker Memorial Film Library) - Boston, MA - *AvMarPl 83*
Boston University (School of Theology) - Boston, MA - *BoPubDir 4 Sup, 5*
Boston Valley Cable TV Co. - Boston, NY - *Tel&CabFB 84C*
Boston Women's Health Book Collective Inc. - West Somerville, MA - *BoPubDir 4, 5*
Boston Word Works - Van Nuys, CA - *LitMarPl 83, 84*
Boston's Finest Music Publishing - Boston, MA - *BillIntBG 83-84*
Bosustow Productions - Santa Monica, CA - *AvMarPl 83*
Boswell Associates, John - New York, NY - *LitMarPl 83, 84*
Boswell Enterprise - Boswell, IN - *BaconPubCkNews 84; Ed&PubIntYB 82*
Boswell Frantz Associates - New York, NY - *MagIndMarPl 82-83*
Boswell Frantz Associates - *See* Frantz & Co., V. M.
Boswell Times - Boswell, OK - *BaconPubCkNews 84; Ed&PubIntYB 82*
Botanical Type Specimen Register [of Smithsonian Institution] - Washington, DC - *EISS 83*
Botebooks - DeLeon Springs, FL - *BoPubDir 4, 5*

Botek Instruments - Utica, MI - *MicrocomMPl 84*
Both Sides Now [of Free People Press] - Tyler, TX - *LitMag&SmPr 83-84*
Bothell Northshore Citizen - Bothell, WA - *BaconPubCkNews 84; NewsDir 84*
Bothwell Times - Bothwell, ON, Canada - *AyerDirPub 83; Ed&PubIntYB 82*
Botkins-Anna Times - Botkins, OH - *Ed&PubIntYB 82*
Botkins-Anna Times - *See* Daily News Printing Co.
Botna Valley Times - Carson, IA - *Ed&PubIntYB 82*
Botsford, Ketchum Inc. - San Francisco, CA - *ArtMar 84; BrCabYB 84; TelAl 83, 84*
Bott Advertising, Leo P. Jr. - Chicago, IL - *StaDirAdAg 2-84; TelAl 83, 84*
Bott Broadcasting - Independence, MO - *BrCabYB 84*
Bottin Data Bases [of Didot-Bottin] - Paris, France - *EISS 83*
Bottineau Cable TV [of NoDaKable Inc.] - Bottineau, ND - *BrCabYB 84*
Bottineau Courant - Bottineau, ND - *BaconPubCkNews 84; Ed&PubIntYB 82; NewsDir 84*
Botto, Roessner, Horne & Messinger Inc. - New York, NY - *StaDirAdAg 2-84*
Bottom Line Inc., The - Greenville, SC - *StaDirAdAg 2-84*
Bottom Line Media - San Francisco, CA - *StaDirAdAg 2-84*
Bottom Line Personal - New York, NY - *BaconPubCkMag 84*
Bottom Line Press - San Francisco, CA - *BoPubDir 4, 5*
Bottom Line, The - Bruce, MS - *Ed&PubIntYB 82*
Bottomfish Magazine - Cupertino, CA - *LitMag&SmPr 83-84*
Botway Inc., Clifford A. - New York, NY - *HBIndAd&MS 82-83; StaDirAdAg 2-84*
Bouchard, Madame L. - New York, NY - *Ed&PubIntYB 82*
Bouchard, Walton Productions - Kingston, MA - *ArtMar 84; AvMarPl 83; WritMar 84*
Bouche, Len - Santa Fe, NM - *LitMarPl 84*
Boucher Associates - Londonderry, NH - *DirInfWP 82*
Boulder Cable TV [of Community Tele-Communications Inc.] - Boulder, CO - *BrCabYB 84; Tel&CabFB 84C*
Boulder City News [of Henderson Home News] - Boulder City, NV - *AyerDirPub 83; BaconPubCkNews 84; Ed&PubIntYB 82; NewsDir 84*
Boulder Daily Camera [of Knight-Ridder Newspapers Inc.] - Boulder, CO - *BaconPubCkNews 84; NewsDir 84*
Boulder Daily Camera Focus Magazine - Boulder, CO - *WritMar 84*
Boulder Monitor - Boulder, MT - *BaconPubCkNews 84; Ed&PubIntYB 82*
Boulder Town & Country Review - Boulder, CO - *NewsDir 84*
Boulevard Banner - Encino, CA - *AyerDirPub 83*
Boulevard Recording Studios Inc. - Oak Park, IL - *AvMarPl 83*
Boulind, Richard - New York, NY - *LitMarPl 83*
Boultinghouse & Boultinghouse - New York, NY - *LitMarPl 83, 84*
Boultinghouse Inc., Ray - New York, NY - *LitMarPl 83, 84*
Boultinghouse, Marquis - Lexington, KY - *BoPubDir 4 Sup, 5*
Bound Brook Chronicle - Bound Brook, NJ - *Ed&PubIntYB 82*
Bound Brook Chronicle - *See* Somerset Press
Bound to Stay Bound Books Inc. - Jacksonville, IL - *LitMarPl 83, 84*
Bounty Hunter International - Washington, DC - *WritMar 84*
Bouquet-Orchid Enterprises - Shreveport, LA - *BillIntBG 83-84*
Bourbeuse Telephone Co. - Sullivan, MO - *TelDir&BG 83-84*
Bourbon Beacon - Bourbon, MO - *AyerDirPub 83; BaconPubCkNews 84; Ed&PubIntYB 82*
Bourbon News-Mirror - Bourbon, IN - *BaconPubCkNews 84; Ed&PubIntYB 82*
Bourbonnais Herald [of B & B Publishing Co. Inc.] - Bourbonnais, IL - *AyerDirPub 83; BaconPubCkNews 84; NewsDir 84*
Bouregy & Co. Inc., Thomas - New York, NY - *LitMarPl 83, 84; WritMar 84*
Bouressa, Lavonne - Sacramento, CA - *BoPubDir 5*
Bourinot, Mrs. Arthur S. - Ottawa, ON, Canada - *BoPubDir 4, 5*
Bourne Co. - New York, NY - *BillIntBG 83-84*
Bourne Courier - Bourne, MA - *Ed&PubIntYB 82*
Bourne Courier [of MPG Communications Inc.] - Wareham, MA - *AyerDirPub 83; NewsDir 84*
Bourne Courier - *See* MPG Communications Inc.
Bourne, D. W. - Woods Hole, MA - *LitMarPl 84*
Bourne Educational Software - Winchester, England - *MicrocomSwDir 1*
Boutique & Villager - Burlingame, CA - *NewsDir 84*
Boutwell, Ralph - Greenville, AL - *Tel&CabFB 84C p.1667*
Bova Literary Agency, The Barbara - New York, NY - *LitMarPl 83, 84*
Bovey Scenic Range News - Bovey, MN - *BaconPubCkNews 84*
Bovill TV Cable Co. - Bovill, ID - *BrCabYB 84; Tel&CabFB 84C*
Bovina Blade - Bovina, TX - *BaconPubCkNews 84; Ed&PubIntYB 82*
Bovincular Atavists Co. - Santa Barbara, CA - *LitMag&SmPr 83-84*
Bow & Arrow - Capistrano Beach, CA - *ArtMar 84; BaconPubCkMag 84; MagDir 84; MagIndMarPl 82-83; WritMar 84*
Bow & Swing - Palmetto, FL - *MagDir 84*
Bow Hook, The [of Island Publications] - Charleston, SC - *NewsDir 84*
Bow Records - Newton, MA - *BillIntBG 83-84*
Bowab, J. Alex - Mobile, AL - *Tel&CabFB 84C p.1667*
Bowbells Burke County Tribune - Bowbells, ND - *BaconPubCkNews 84*
Bowden Research Services Inc. - Richmond, VA - *IntDirMarRes 83*
Bowden's News Wire Monitor - Ottawa, ON, Canada - *ProGuPRSer 4*
Bowden's Press Clippings - Toronto, ON, Canada - *ProGuPRSer 4*
Bowden's Radio/TV Monitoring - Toronto, ON, Canada - *ProGuPRSer 4*
Bowdle Pioneer - Bowdle, SD - *BaconPubCkNews 84; Ed&PubIntYB 82*
Bowdoin College (Museum of Art) - Brunswick, ME - *BoPubDir 4, 5*
Bowdoin Print Inc. - Everett, MA - *MagIndMarPl 82-83*
Bowdon Bulletin - Bowdon, GA - *BaconPubCkNews 84; Ed&PubIntYB 82*
Bowen & Associates Inc. - San Diego, CA - *StaDirAdAg 2-84*
Bowen Island Historians - Bowen Island, BC, Canada - *BoPubDir 4, 5*
Bowen Reports, F. A. - Janesville, WI - *BoPubDir 4, 5*
Bowen's Publishing - Bedford, MA - *BoPubDir 5*
Bower & Associates, Michael [Div. of Bower Communications Inc.] - Huntington Beach, CA - *StaDirAdAg 2-84*
Bower & Associates, Michael - Los Alamitos, CA - *DirPRFirms 83*
Bower Associates, Earle - New York, NY - *AdAge 3-28-84; StaDirAdAg 2-84*
Bower Dorsey O'Neill - Houston, TX - *StaDirAdAg 2-84*
Bower-Stewart & Associates - Hawthorne, CA - *WhoWMicrocom 83*
Bowers & Morena Galleries - Wolfeboro, NH - *BoPubDir 5*
Bowers & Ruddy Galleries Inc. [Aff. of General Mills Inc.] - Los Angeles, CA - *BoPubDir 4*
Bowers, John Dallas - Radnor, PA - *BoPubDir 4, 5*
Bowery Publishing Co. - Reno, NV - *BoPubDir 4, 5*
Bowes/Hanlon Advertising - Atlanta, GA - *AdAge 3-28-84; HBIndAd&MS 82-83; StaDirAdAg 2-84*
Bowes Publishers Ltd. - Canada - *Ed&PubIntYB 82*
Bowhook, The [of The Charleston Journal] - Charleston, SC - *NewsDir 84*
Bowhunter - Ft. Wayne, IN - *ArtMar 84; BaconPubCkMag 84; MagIndMarPl 82-83; WritMar 84*
Bowie Blade - Bowie, MD - *Ed&PubIntYB 82; NewsDir 84*
Bowie Blade News - Bowie, MD - *AyerDirPub 83; Ed&PubIntYB 82*
Bowie Blade News - *See* Capital Gazette Newspapers
Bowie County News, The - New Boston, TX - *Ed&PubIntYB 82*
Bowie News - Bowie, TX - *BaconPubCkNews 84; Ed&PubIntYB 82; NewsDir 84*
Bowker Co., R. R. [Subs. of Xerox Publishing Group] - New York, NY - *CompReadDB 82; DataDirOnSer 84; DirMarMP 83; EISS 83; InfoS 83-84; LitMarPl 83, 84; MagIndMarPl 82-83; MicroMarPl 82-83; WritMar 84*
Bowker Co., R. R. (Bowker Information Services) - New York, NY - *InfIndMarPl 83*

Bowker Serials Bibliography Database [of R. R. Bowker Co.] - New York, NY - *CompReadDB 82; DataDirOnSer 84*
Bowlers Journal - Chicago, IL - *ArtMar 84; BaconPubCkMag 84; MagDir 84; WritMar 84*
Bowles, Gerald - Hallock, MN - *Tel&CabFB 84C p.1667*
Bowling - Greendale, WI - *BaconPubCkMag 84; MagDir 84; MagIndMarPl 82-83; WritMar 84*
Bowling Cable TV, G. D. - Hyden, KY - *BrCabYB 84; Tel&CabFB 84C*
Bowling Digest - Evanston, IL - *BaconPubCkMag 84*
Bowling Green Cable TV [of GS Communications Inc.] - Bowling Green, VA - *BrCabYB 84; Tel&CabFB 84C*
Bowling Green Caroline Progress - *See* Atlantic Publications
Bowling Green Caroline Progress, The [of Atlantic Publications Inc.] - Bowling Green, VA - *NewsDir 84*
Bowling Green Daily News - Bowling Green, KS - *BaconPubCkNews 84*
Bowling Green Park City Daily News - Bowling Green, KY - *NewsDir 84*
Bowling Green Sentinel-Tribune - Bowling Green, OH - *BaconPubCkNews 84; NewsDir 84*
Bowling Green State University (Cue Project Publications) - Bowling Green, OH - *BoPubDir 4, 5*
Bowling Green State University (Philosophy Documentation Center) - Bowling Green, OH - *BoPubDir 4, 5*
Bowling Green Times - Bowling Green, MO - *BaconPubCkNews 84; Ed&PubIntYB 82; NewsDir 84*
Bowling Green University Popular Press - Bowling Green, OH - *ArtMar 84*
Bowling Highlights News - Liberty, NY - *NewsDir 84*
Bowling-Moorman Publications - Tipp City, OH - *BaconPubCkNews 84*
Bowling Proprietor - Arlington, TX - *BaconPubCkMag 84; MagDir 84*
Bowman Cablevision Inc. [of Tioga Cablevision Inc.] - Bowman, ND - *Tel&CabFB 84C*
Bowman County Pioneer - Bowman, ND - *BaconPubCkNews 84*
Bowman Finder - Bowman, ND - *BaconPubCkNews 84; NewsDir 84*
Bowman/Harris Partnership Ltd. - *See* Royds Advertising Group Ltd., The
Bowman, Pearl - New York, NY - *LitMarPl 84*
Bowman, Phylis - Prince Rupert, BC, Canada - *BoPubDir 4, 5*
Bowman Pioneer - Bowman, ND - *Ed&PubIntYB 82*
Bowman, Terri J. - Imperial, NE - *Tel&CabFB 84C p.1667*
Bowmar/Noble Publishers [Div. of The Economy Co.] - Los Angeles, CA - *AvMarPl 83; LitMarPl 83*
Bowne Information Systems [Subs. of Bowne & Co. Inc.] - New York, NY - *DataDirOnSer 84; DataDirSup 7-83; DirInfWP 82; EISS 83; InfIndMarPl 83; LitMarPl 83, 84; MagIndMarPl 82-83; MicrocomSwDir 1*
Box Elder Journal - Brigham City, UT - *AyerDirPub 83; Ed&PubIntYB 82; NewsDir 84*
Box Elder News - Brigham City, UT - *AyerDirPub 83; Ed&PubIntYB 82; NewsDir 84*
Box Seat - Carlsbad, CA - *Tel&CabFB 84C*
Box 749 [of The Printable Arts Society Inc.] - New York, NY - *LitMag&SmPr 83-84*
Boxboard Containers - Chicago, IL - *BaconPubCkMag 84; MagDir 84; MagIndMarPl 82-83*
Boxer Music - Nashville, TN - *BillIntBG 83-84*
Boxer Review - Beverly Hills, CA - *MagDir 84*
Boxoffice - Hollywood, CA - *BaconPubCkMag 84; WritMar 84*
Boxoffice [of Associated Publications Inc.] - Kansas City, MO - *MagDir 84*
Boxwood Press, The - Pacific Grove, CA - *LitMag&SmPr 83-84; LitMarPl 83, 84*
Boy Scouts of America - Irving, TX - *BoPubDir 4*
Boy Scouts of America (National Office) - Irving, TX - *BoPubDir 5*
Boyar Advertising, Beaver - New York, NY - *LitMarPl 83*
Boyar Inc., Steve - New York, NY - *LitMarPl 84*
Boyars Publishers Inc., Marion - Salem, NH - *LitMarPl 83*
Boyars Publishers Inc., Marion - New York, NY - *LitMag&SmPr 83-84; LitMarPl 84*
Boyce Enterprises - Santa Maria, CA - *DirInfWP 82*
Boyceville Press Reporter - Boyceville, WI - *BaconPubCkNews 84; Ed&PubIntYB 82*
Boyceville Press-Reporter - Colfax, WI - *AyerDirPub 83*
Boyd & Fraser Publishing Co. - San Francisco, CA - *LitMag&SmPr 83-84; LitMarPl 83, 84*
Boyd Printing Co. Inc., The William - Albany, NY - *LitMarPl 83, 84; MagIndMarPl 82-83*
Boyd Records - Oklahoma City, OK - *BillIntBG 83-84*
Boyd's City Dispatch Inc. - Sharon, CT - *LitMarPl 83, 84*
Boyer, Carl III - Newhall, CA - *BoPubDir 4, 5*
Boyer Co., The Herbert - New York, NY - *InterCabHB 3*
Boyer, Dale E. - Mountain View, CA - *MagIndMarPl 82-83*
Boyer, Ralph - Portageville, MO - *Tel&CabFB 84C p.1667*
Boyertown Area Times, The - Boyertown, PA - *AyerDirPub 83; NewsDir 84*
Boyertown Publishing Co. - Boyertown, PA - *MagIndMarPl 82-83*
Boyertown Times - *See* Berks-Mont Newspapers Inc.
Boykin, James H. - Miami, FL - *BoPubDir 4, 5*
Boyle, Helen D. - Guilford, CT - *LitMarPl 84*
Boyle/Lopez Advertising - Los Angeles, CA - *StaDirAdAg 2-84*
Boyne City Charlevoix County Press - Boyne City, MI - *BaconPubCkNews 84*
Boynton Beach News Journal - Boynton Beach, FL - *Ed&PubIntYB 82*
Boynton/Cook Publishers Inc. - Upper Montclair, NJ - *LitMarPl 83, 84*
Boynton, Mrs. Holmes - Vancouver, BC, Canada - *BoPubDir 4 Sup, 5*
Boynton Shoppers Guide - Pompano Beach, FL - *AyerDirPub 83*
Boys Clubs of America - New York, NY - *BoPubDir 4, 5*
Boys' Life [of Boy Scouts of America] - New York, NY - *Folio 83*
Boys' Life - Dallas, TX - *BaconPubCkMag 84*
Boy's Life [of Boy Scouts of America] - Irving, TX - *LitMarPl 83, 84; MagDir 84; MagIndMarPl 82-83; WritMar 84*
Boys Town Center (Communications & Public Service Div.) - Boys Town, NE - *BoPubDir 4 Sup, 5*
Bozell & Jacobs - Los Angeles, CA - *ArtMar 84*
Bozell & Jacobs - New York, NY - *AdAge 3-28-84; Br 1-23-84; BrCabYB 84; StaDirAdAg 2-84*
Bozell & Jacobs - Dallas, TX - *ArtMar 84*
Bozell & Jacobs - Houston, TX - *ArtMar 84*
Bozell & Jacobs Direct Marketing Div. [of Bozell & Jacobs International Inc.] - New York, NY - *DirMarMP 83*
Bozell & Jacobs Inc. (B-R-M International Div.) - Union, NJ - *Ed&PubIntYB 82*
Bozell & Jacobs International - Palo Alto, CA - *ArtMar 84*
Bozell & Jacobs International - New York, NY - *ArtMar 84*
Bozell & Jacobs/Public Relations [Div. of Bozell & Jacobs] - New York, NY - *DirPRFirms 83*
Bozeman Cable TV [of Community Tele-Communications Inc.] - Bozeman, MT - *BrCabYB 84; Tel&CabFB 84C*
Bozeman Chronicle [of Gallatin Publishing Co.] - Bozeman, MT - *BaconPubCkNews 84; NewsDir 84*
Bozeman Daily Chronicle [of Galatin Publishing Co.] - Bozeman, MT - *Ed&PubIntYB 82; LitMarPl 83, 84*
BP & R Advertising Co. - *See* Pesce Advertising
BP Report - White Plains, NY - *BaconPubCkMag 84*
BPCS - Duluth, MN - *MagIndMarPl 82-83*
BPI Systems Inc. - Austin, TX - *MicrocomMPl 84; MicrocomSwDir 1*
BPS Inc. - Cambridge, MA - *MicrocomMPl 84*
B.R. Syndication Inc. - Millbrook, NY - *Tel&CabFB 84C*
BR3 Press - Ann Arbor, MI - *BoPubDir 5*
Braasch, Gary - Portland, OR - *LitMarPl 84*
Brace, Beverly W. - Sunnyvale, CA - *BoPubDir 4, 5*
Brace, Brad - Halifax, NS, Canada - *BoPubDir 4 Sup, 5*
Brace Independent Editorial Services, Edward R. - Towanda, PA - *LitMarPl 83*
Bracebridge Examiner - Bracebridge, ON, Canada - *Ed&PubIntYB 82*
Braceland Brothers Inc. - Philadelphia, PA - *LitMarPl 83, 84*
Bracken Cable Vision Inc. [of Standard Tobacco Co. Inc.] - Augusta, KY - *BrCabYB 84; Tel&CabFB 84C*
Bracken County News - Brooksville, KY - *AyerDirPub 83; Ed&PubIntYB 82*

Bracker Communications - Northfield, IL - *DirPRFirms 83; StaDirAdAg 2-84*
Brackettville TV Cable Co. Inc. [of Television Cable Co. of Brackettville] - Brackettville, TX - *BrCabYB 84*
Brackman Associates, Henrietta - New York, NY - *LitMarPl 83; MagIndMarPl 82-83*
Braco Advertising Agency Inc. - Scarsdale, NY - *StaDirAdAg 2-84*
Bracy & Bracy - Olmsted, OH - *StaDirAdAg 2-84*
Bradbury Press Inc. [Subs. of Macmillan Inc.] - Scarsdale, NY - *LitMarPl 83, 84; WritMar 84*
Braddock Free Press - Braddock, PA - *BaconPubCkNews 84; NewsDir 84*
Braddock Publications Inc. - Washington, DC - *BoPubDir 5*
Braden Books, John - Madoc, ON, Canada - *BoPubDir 5*
Braden Stations - Middletown, OH - *BrCabYB 84*
Bradenton Herald - Bradenton, FL - *BaconPubCkNews 84; Ed&PubIntYB 82; NewsDir 84*
Bradford County Telegraph - Starke, FL - *AyerDirPub 83; Ed&PubIntYB 82*
Bradford Era - Bradford, PA - *BaconPubCkNews 84; Ed&PubIntYB 82; NewsDir 84*
Bradford Information Systems - Spring, TX - *DataDirSup 7-83*
Bradford Journal [of McKean County Press Inc.] - Bradford, PA - *Ed&PubIntYB 82; NewsDir 84*
Bradford Journal - *See* McKean County Press Inc.
Bradford Journal Opinion/Second Opinion - Bradford, VT - *BaconPubCkNews 84*
Bradford-La Riviere Inc. - Saginaw, MI - *AvMarPl 83*
Bradford-La Riviere Inc. - Southfield, MI - *DirPRFirms 83*
Bradford, Leroy - Seattle, WA - *BoPubDir 4, 5*
Bradford, Linda - New York, NY - *LitMarPl 83, 84; MagIndMarPl 82-83*
Bradford National Computer Services [Subs. of Bradford National Corp.] - Teaneck, NJ - *DataDirOnSer 84*
Bradford National Corp. - New York, NY - *ADAPSOMemDir 83-84; Datamation 6-83; Top100Al 83*
Bradford Republican - Bradford, IL - *BaconPubCkNews 84; Ed&PubIntYB 82*
Bradford Video - Starke, FL - *BrCabYB 84; Tel&CabFB 84C*
Bradford Witness, The - Bradford, ON, Canada - *AyerDirPub 83*
Bradford's Directory - Fairfax, VA - *BoPubDir 4, 5*
Bradham-Hamilton Advertising Inc. - Charleston, SC - *ArtMar 84; StaDirAdAg 2-84*
Bradley Associates - Norfolk, VA - *CabTVFinDB 83*
Bradley Co., Milton - East Longmeadow, MA - *AvMarPl 83*
Bradley Co., Milton - Springfield, MA - *LitMarPl 83*
Bradley Co., Milton (Education Div.) - East Longmeadow, MA - *MicrocomSwDir 1*
Bradley CPA Study Aids Inc. - Woodland Hills, CA - *BoPubDir 4, 5*
Bradley David Associates Ltd. - New York, NY - *BoPubDir 4, 5*
Bradley, Dimmock & Hungerford - New York, NY - *AdAge 3-28-84; StaDirAdAg 2-84*
Bradley, Gelman & Associates Inc. - Detroit, MI - *StaDirAdAg 2-84*
Bradley, Glenn P. - Norman, OK - *LitMarPl 83, 84*
Bradley, Graham & Hamby Advertising Agency Inc. - Columbia, SC - *StaDirAdAg 2-84*
Bradley Press [of B & B Publishing Co. Inc.] - Bourbonnais, IL - *AyerDirPub 83; NewsDir 84*
Bradley Publishing - Little Rock, AR - *LitMag&SmPr 83-84*
Bradley TV Cable Service Inc. - Dansville, NY - *BrCabYB 84; Tel&CabFB 84C*
Bradmark Inc. - Kansas City, KS - *StaDirAdAg 2-84*
Bradner Smith & Co. [Div. of Bradner Central Co.] - Chicago, IL - *LitMarPl 83, 84*
Brador Publications Inc. - Livonia, NY - *BaconPubCkNews 84*
Bradson Press - Thousand Oaks, CA - *BoPubDir 4, 5; LitMag&SmPr 83-84; WritMar 84*
Bradt Enterprises - Cambridge, MA - *BoPubDir 4; LitMag&SmPr 83-84; LitMarPl 83, 84*
Bradwell & Associates Inc., David - San Rafael, CA - *EISS 83*
Brady Advertising Inc. - Chattanooga, TN - *DirMarMP 83*
Brady Co., Robert J. [Div. of Prentice-Hall Co.] - Bowie, MD - *ArtMar 84; BoPubDir 4; LitMarPl 83, 84; MicrocomMPl 84; WritMar 84*
Brady Co., The - Menomonee Falls, WI - *AdAge 3-28-84; StaDirAdAg 2-84*
Brady Co., The (Public Relations Dept.) - Menomonee Falls, WI - *DirPRFirms 83*
Brady, Goode & Aiken Advertising Inc. - Chattanooga, TN - *StaDirAdAg 2-84*
Brady Herald - Brady, TX - *Ed&PubIntYB 82*
Brady Herald - *See* Brady Herald Publishers
Brady Herald Publishers - Brady, TX - *BaconPubCkNews 84*
Brady Standard - *See* Brady Herald Publishers
Brady Standard-Herald Publishers - Brady, TX - *NewsDir 84*
Brady Standard, The - Brady, TX - *Ed&PubIntYB 82*
Braegen Corp. - Cupertino, CA - *InfIndMarPl 83*
Braemar Computer Devices Inc. - Burnsville, MN - *WhoWMicrocom 83*
Bragaw Public Relations Services - Palatine, IL - *ArtMar 84; DirPRFirms 83*
Bragdon Publishers, Allen D. - New York, NY - *BoPubDir 4, 5*
Bragg's Furniture & TV Inc. - McConnellsville, OH - *Tel&CabFB 84C*
Bragg's Service - McConnelsville, OH - *BrCabYB 84*
Braham Journal, The - Braham, MN - *Ed&PubIntYB 82*
Brahms Advertising Inc., Jack - Baltimore, MD - *AdAge 3-28-84; StaDirAdAg 2-84*
Braidwood Index - Wilmington, IL - *AyerDirPub 83*
Braidwood Index - *See* G.W. Communications
Braidwood Journal - Braidwood, IL - *Ed&PubIntYB 82*
Braidwood Journal - *See* Bailey Printing & Publishing Inc.
Braille Inc. - Falmouth, MA - *LitMarPl 83, 84*
Braille Institute Press [Subs. of Braille Institute of America Inc.] - Los Angeles, CA - *LitMarPl 83, 84*
Brain Bank Inc. - New York, NY - *MicrocomMPl 84; MicrocomSwDir 1*
Brain-Box: The Computer Tutor - New York, NY - *MicrocomMPl 83*
Brain-Image Power Press - Hollywood, CA - *BoPubDir 5*
Brain Information Service-Brain Research Institute [of University of California, Los Angeles] - Los Angeles, CA - *MagIndMarPl 82-83*
Brain/Mind Bulletin [of Interface Press] - Los Angeles, CA - *LitMag&SmPr 83-84*
Brain Wave Concepts - Conshohocken, PA - *BillIntBG 83-84*
Brainerd Dispatch - Brainerd, MN - *BaconPubCkNews 84; Ed&PubIntYB 82; NewsDir 84*
Brainin, Frederick - Forest Hills, NY - *MagIndMarPl 82-83*
Brainin Translanguage Service, Frederick - Rego Park, NY - *LitMarPl 83, 84*
Brainreserve Inc. - New York, NY - *HBIndAd&MS 82-83; StaDirAdAg 2-84*
BrainStorm Books [Subs. of Brainstorming Systems] - Tustin, CA - *LitMag&SmPr 83-84; LitMarPl 83, 84*
Brainstorm Productions Inc. - New York, NY - *AvMarPl 83*
Braintree Forum & Observer [of Weymouth Publications Inc.] - Braintree, MA - *AyerDirPub 83; BaconPubCkNews 84; Ed&PubIntYB 82; NewsDir 84*
Braintree Music - Los Angeles, CA - *BillIntBG 83-84*
Braintree Star - Braintree, MA - *BaconPubCkNews 84; NewsDir 84*
Braithwaite, Daniel - Toronto, ON, Canada - *BoPubDir 4, 5*
Braithwaite, Rella - West Hill, ON, Canada - *BoPubDir 4, 5*
Brake & Front End [of Babcox Automotive Publications Inc.] - Akron, OH - *BaconPubCkMag 84; MagDir 84; MagIndMarPl 82-83; WritMar 84*
Bram & Associates Inc., Milton - Chicago, IL - *StaDirAdAg 2-84*
Bram Inc. - Seattle, WA - *WritMar 84*
Braman & Associates Inc., Don - *See* Doremus & Co.
Braman Leader - Braman, OK - *Ed&PubIntYB 82*
Bramble Minibooks - Lansing, MI - *BoPubDir 4, 5*
Brammer Cable TV Inc. [of MBS Cable Corp.] - Chester, WV - *Tel&CabFB 84C*
Brammer Cable TV Inc. - Hancock County, WV - *BrCabYB 84*
Brampton Daily Times - Brampton, ON, Canada - *AyerDirPub 83*
Brampton Guardian - Brampton, ON, Canada - *Ed&PubIntYB 82*
Brancaleone Educational Co. - Upper Montclair, NJ - *BoPubDir 4, 5*
Branch International Music - Dallas, TX - *BillIntBG 83-84*
Branch International Records - Dallas, TX - *BillIntBG 83-84*

Branch of Geographic Names [of U.S. Geological Survey] - Reston, VA - *EISS 83*
Branch-Smith Inc. - Ft. Worth, TX - *LitMarPl 83; MagIndMarPl 82-83*
Brand - Hereford, TX - *AyerDirPub 83*
Brand Advertising - Chicago, IL - *AdAge 3-28-84; StaDirAdAg 2-84*
Brand & Gerber & Shick - Cleveland, OH - *AdAge 3-28-84; StaDirAdAg 2-84*
Brand & Son Inc., Paul L. - Falls Church, VA - *AvMarPl 83*
Brand-Edmonds Associates - Salem, VA - *StaDirAdAg 2-84*
Brand Edmonds Packett - Salem, VA - *DirMarMP 83*
Brand, Gruber & Co. - Southfield, MI - *HBIndAd&MS 82-83; IntDirMarRes 83*
Brand Management Report - Syosset, NY - *BaconPubCkMag 84*
Brand Projection Service & Studios - Brisbane, CA - *AvMarPl 83*
Brand Public Relations [Div. of Brand & Gerber & Schick Inc.] - Cleveland, OH - *DirPRFirms 83*
Branden, Elsa - New York, NY - *LitMarPl 83, 84; MagIndMarPl 82-83*
Branden Press Inc. - Boston, MA - *LitMarPl 83, 84*
Brandenburg Meade County Messenger - Brandenburg, KY - *BaconPubCkNews 84; NewsDir 84*
Brandenburg Telephone Co. Inc. - Brandenburg, KY - *TelDir&BG 83-84*
Brandon Broadcasting - Arroyo Grande, CA - *BrCabYB 84*
Brandon Consulting Group Inc. - New York, NY - *WhoWMicrocom 83*
Brandon Films Inc. - Mt. Vernon, NY - *TelAl 83, 84*
Brandon House Inc. - Bronx, NY - *BoPubDir 4, 5*
Brandon News - Brandon, FL - *Ed&PubIntYB 82; NewsDir 84*
Brandon News - *See* Hillsborough Community Pub. Inc.
Brandon Rankin County News - Brandon, MS - *BaconPubCkNews 84*
Brandon/Ray & Associates Inc. - Little Rock, AR - *ArtMar 84; StaDirAdAg 2-84*
Brandon Shopper - Brandon, FL - *AyerDirPub 83*
Brandon Sun, The - Brandon, MB, Canada - *BaconPubCkNews 84; Ed&PubIntYB 82*
Brandon Valley Reporter - Brandon, SD - *Ed&PubIntYB 82*
Brandon Westman Rural - Brandon, MB, Canada - *AyerDirPub 83*
Brandons Inc. - Jacksonville, FL - *AvMarPl 83*
Brandon's Shipper & Forwarder - New York, NY - *BaconPubCkMag 84; MagDir 84*
Brandstead Press - Carlisle, ON, Canada - *BoPubDir 4, 5*
Brandt & Brandt Literary Agents Inc. - New York, NY - *LitMarPl 83, 84*
Brandt Corp., The - New Orleans, LA - *AvMarPl 83*
Brandt Stewart - Minneapolis, MN - *StaDirAdAg 2-84*
Brandwood Music Inc. - Nashville, TN - *BillIntBG 83-84*
Brandy River Music Co. - Durham, NH - *BillIntBG 83-84*
Brandywine [of Media Town Talk Newspapers] - Media, PA - *NewsDir 84*
Brandywine Cablevision - Kennett Square, PA - *Tel&CabFB 84C*
Brandywine Records - Durham, NH - *BillIntBG 83-84*
Branford Co., Charles T. - Newton Centre, MA - *LitMarPl 83, 84; WritMar 84*
Branford News - Branford, FL - *BaconPubCkNews 84; Ed&PubIntYB 82*
Branford Review - Branford, CT - *AyerDirPub 83; BaconPubCkNews 84; Ed&PubIntYB 82; NewsDir 84*
Brangus Journal - San Antonio, TX - *BaconPubCkMag 84*
Branham Newspaper Sales - New York, NY - *LitMarPl 83, 84*
Braniff's Flying Colors - Miami, FL - *MagDir 84; MagIndMarPl 82-83*
Brann Agency Inc., The Helen - New York, NY - *LitMarPl 83, 84*
Brann, Roger - New York, NY - *HBIndAd&MS 82-83*
Bran's Head at the Hunting Raven Press - Frome, England - *LitMag&SmPr 83-84*
Bransby Productions Ltd., John - New York, NY - *ArtMar 84; AvMarPl 83*
Branson Beacon - Branson, MO - *Ed&PubIntYB 82*
Branson Beacon - *See* Tri-Lakes Newspapers Inc.
Branson Beacon & Leader - Branson, MO - *NewsDir 84*
Branson Beacon & Leader - *See* Tri-Lakes Newspapers Inc.
Brant Computer Services Ltd. - Burlington, ON, Canada - *DataDirOnSer 84*
Brant-Lompa Press - Point Richmond, CA - *BoPubDir 4, 5*
Brant News - Brantford, ON, Canada - *AyerDirPub 83; Ed&PubIntYB 82*
Brantex Inc. (Color Software Services Div.) - Greenville, TX - *MicrocomMPl 84*
Brantford Expositor, The - Brantford, ON, Canada - *BaconPubCkNews 84; Ed&PubIntYB 82*
Brantley Enterprise - Nahunta, GA - *AyerDirPub 83; Ed&PubIntYB 82*
Brantley Telephone Co. Inc. - Nahunta, GA - *TelDir&BG 83-84*
Brantley TV Cable Service - Brantley, AL - *BrCabYB 84*
Brantronics - New Canaan, CT - *AvMarPl 83*
Brashe Advertising Inc. - Jericho, NY - *StaDirAdAg 2-84*
Brasilia Records & Tapes Corp. - New York, NY - *BillIntBG 83-84*
Brason-Sargar Publications - Reseda, CA - *BoPubDir 4, 5; LitMag&SmPr 83-84*
Brass Music Ltd. - *See* Brass Press
Brass Press - Nashville, TN - *BillIntBG 83-84; BoPubDir 4, 5*
Brassey's Naval Record [of Brassey's Publishers Ltd.] - Oxford, England - *DirOnDB Spring 84; EISS 5-84 Sup*
Brat Music - *See* Two Fifty Nine Music
Bratstvo - Toronto, ON, Canada - *Ed&PubIntYB 82*
Brattle Publications - Cambridge, MA - *BoPubDir 4, 5; LitMag&SmPr 83-84*
Brattleboro Reformer [of The Eagle Publishing Corp.] - Brattleboro, VT - *BaconPubCkNews 84; Ed&PubIntYB 82; NewsDir 84*
Bratton/Crews/Cumming & Associates Ltd. - Toronto, ON, Canada - *VideoDir 82-83*
Brauer Computer Support - San Diego, CA - *MicrocomMPl 84*
Braun Advertising Inc. - New York, NY - *StaDirAdAg 2-84*
Braun & Braun Educational Enterprises Ltd. - Calgary, AB, Canada - *BoPubDir 4, 5*
Braun & Co. - Los Angeles, CA - *DirPRFirms 83*
Braun-Brumfield Inc. [Subs. of Heritage Communications Inc.] - Ann Arbor, MI - *LitMarPl 83, 84*
Braverman-Mirisch Inc. - Los Angeles, CA - *LitMarPl 83; StaDirAdAg 2-84; TelAl 83, 84*
Braverman Productions Inc. - Santa Monica, CA - *TelAl 83, 84*
Braverman Productions Inc., Robert - Jericho, NY - *AvMarPl 83*
Bravo [of King & Cowen] - Teaneck, NJ - *LitMag&SmPr 83-84*
Bravo! [of Rainbow Programming Services] - Woodbury, NY - *BrCabYB 84; CabTVPrDB 83; HomeVid&CabYB 82-83; Tel&CabFB 84C*
Brawley News [of Associated Desert Newspapers] - Brawley, CA - *BaconPubCkNews 84; NewsDir 84*
Brawley News - El Centro, CA - *AyerDirPub 83; Ed&PubIntYB 82*
Braxton Cablevision Corp. [of TCI Growth Inc.] - Gassaway, WV - *Tel&CabFB 84C*
Braxton Central [of Glenville Gilmer Graphics Inc.] - Glenville, WV - *NewsDir 84*
Braxton Central - Sutton, WV - *Ed&PubIntYB 82*
Braxton Democrat [of Glenville Gilmer Graphics Inc.] - Glenville, WV - *NewsDir 84*
Braxton Democrat [of Sutton Braxton Central] - Sutton, WV - *Ed&PubIntYB 82; NewsDir 84*
Bray Studios Inc. - Westport, CT - *AvMarPl 83; TelAl 84; Tel&CabFB 84C*
Bray Studios Inc. - New York, NY - *TelAl 83*
Brayden Books, John - Madoc, ON, Canada - *BoPubDir 4*
Braymer Bee - Braymer, MO - *BaconPubCkNews 84; Ed&PubIntYB 82*
Brazeal, Bill - Steamboat Springs, CO - *Tel&CabFB 84C p.1667*
Brazell Advertising Agency - Houston, TX - *StaDirAdAg 2-84*
Brazil Times - Brazil, IN - *BaconPubCkNews 84; Ed&PubIntYB 82; NewsDir 84*
Brazilian Institute for Information in Science & Technology [of National Council of Scientific & Technological Development] - Brasilia, Brazil - *EISS 83*
Braziller Inc., George - New York, NY - *ArtMar 84; LitMarPl 83, 84; WritMar 84*
Brazoria Cable TV Systems - Brazoria, TX - *Tel&CabFB 84C*

Brazoria Cablevision Associates [of Community Tele-Communications Inc.] - Clute, TX - *Tel&CabFB 84C*
Brazoria Cablevision Associates - Lake Jackson, TX - *BrCabYB 84*
Brazoria County News - West Columbia, TX - *AyerDirPub 83; Ed&PubIntYB 82*
Brazoria County News Publishers - West Columbia, TX - *BaconPubCkNews 84*
Brazoria Telephone Co. - Brazoria, TX - *TelDir&BG 83-84*
Brazorian News - Lake Jackson, TX - *AyerDirPub 83; Ed&PubIntYB 82*
Brazos Cable TV Co. - West Columbia, TX - *BrCabYB 84; Tel&CabFB 84C*
Brazos Telephone Cooperative Inc. - Olney, TX - *TelDir&BG 83-84*
Brazosport Facts - Clute, TX - *BaconPubCkNews 84; Ed&PubIntYB 82*
Brazosport Facts - Freeport, TX - *AyerDirPub 83*
BRC Associates Inc. - Bethesda, MD - *EISS 83*
Brea-News Times - Brea, CA - *Ed&PubIntYB 82*
Brea News-Times - *See* Placentia News-Times Publishers
Bread [of Nazarene Publishing House] - Kansas City, MO - *ArtMar 84; WritMar 84*
Bread & Butter Press - Denver, CO - *LitMag&SmPr 83-84*
Bread 'n Honey - Ventura, CA - *BillIntBG 83-84*
Break of Dawn Music Inc. - *See* Songs for Real
Breaking Point Inc. - Wharton, NJ - *BoPubDir 4, 5*
Breakthrough Publications - New York, NY - *LitMarPl 83, 84*
Breakwater Books Ltd. - St. Johns, NF, Canada - *BoPubDir 4; LitMarPl 83, 84*
Brean Murray, Foster Securities - New York, NY - *ADAPSOMemDir 83-84*
Breathingspace [of Watershed Intermedia] - Washington, DC - *LitMag&SmPr 83-84*
Breckenridge American - Breckenridge, TX - *AyerDirPub 83; BaconPubCkNews 84; Ed&PubIntYB 82*
Breckenridge Broadcasting Co. - Breckenridge, TX - *BrCabYB 84*
Breckenridge Bulletin - Breckenridge, MO - *Ed&PubIntYB 82*
Breckenridge Cable [of Rock Associates Inc.] - Breckenridge, CO - *Tel&CabFB 84C*
Breckenridge Summit County Journal - Breckenridge, CO - *BaconPubCkNews 84; NewsDir 84*
Breckenridge TV Cable [of Tele-Communications Inc.] - Breckenridge, TX - *BrCabYB 84; Tel&CabFB 84C*
Brecker & Merryman Inc. - New York, NY - *AvMarPl 83*
Breckinridge County Herald-News - Hardinsburg, KY - *Ed&PubIntYB 82; NewsDir 84*
Breda News - Breda, IA - *BaconPubCkNews 84; Ed&PubIntYB 82*
Breda Telephone Corp. - Breda, IA - *TelDir&BG 83-84*
Breeder & Feeder - Toronto, ON, Canada - *BaconPubCkMag 84*
Breese Journal - Breese, IL - *BaconPubCkNews 84; Ed&PubIntYB 82; NewsDir 84*
Breeze - Gretna, NE - *AyerDirPub 83*
Breeze - Wauneta, NE - *AyerDirPub 83*
Breeze Advertiser - Gardena, CA - *Ed&PubIntYB 82*
Breeze Advertiser - Torrance, CA - *AyerDirPub 83*
Breeze-Courier - Taylorville, IL - *AyerDirPub 83*
Breeze Newspapers - Torrance, CA - *BaconPubCkNews 84*
Breeze-QSD - Dallas, TX - *MicrocomMPl 83*
Breeze, The - Cape Coral, FL - *Ed&PubIntYB 82*
Breeze, The [of Inter County Publishing Co.] - Philadelphia, PA - *NewsDir 84*
Breeze, The - Rockledge, PA - *Ed&PubIntYB 82*
Breezeway Publishing Co. - *See* Hat Band Music
Breezewood Telephone Co. - Breezewood, PA - *TelDir&BG 83-84*
Breezy Creeks Press - Aurora, ON, Canada - *BoPubDir 4, 5*
Brehl & Associates Marketing Research Co. Inc. - Great Neck, NY - *IntDirMarRes 83*
Breitenbush Publications - Portland, OR - *BoPubDir 4, 5; LitMag&SmPr 83-84*
Bremen Enquirer - Bremen, IN - *BaconPubCkNews 84; Ed&PubIntYB 82*
Bremen Gateway - Bremen, GA - *Ed&PubIntYB 82*
Bremen Gateway [of Carroll Publishing Co.] - Carrollton, GA - *NewsDir 84*
Bremen Gateway - *See* Harte-Hanks Communications Inc.
Bremer County Independent - Waverly, IA - *AyerDirPub 83; Ed&PubIntYB 82*
Bremer County Independent Publishers - Waverly, IA - *BaconPubCkNews 84*
Bremerton Sun - Bremerton, WA - *BaconPubCkNews 84; Ed&PubIntYB 82; LitMarPl 83, 84; NewsDir 84*
Bremond Press - Bremond, TX - *BaconPubCkNews 84; Ed&PubIntYB 82*
Bren-Tru Press - New York, NY - *BoPubDir 5*
Brenham Banner-Press - Brenham, TX - *BaconPubCkNews 84; Ed&PubIntYB 82; NewsDir 84*
Brennan Advertising, Leo J. - Troy, MI - *StaDirAdAg 2-84*
Brennan & Associates, Anne - New York, NY - *DirMarMP 83*
Brennan & Brennan Public Affairs/Public Relations - New York, NY - *DirPRFirms 83*
Brennan & Co. Inc., E. A. - Garden Grove, CA - *BoPubDir 4, 5*
Brennen & Co. Inc., W. E. - Evanston, IL - *IntDirMarRes 83*
Brenner Advertising, Harry - Chicago, IL - *StaDirAdAg 2-84*
Brentwood Cable Co. Ltd. - Strathmore, AB, Canada - *BrCabYB 84*
Brentwood Journal - Brentwood, TN - *BaconPubCkNews 84*
Brentwood News - Brentwood, CA - *BaconPubCkNews 84; Ed&PubIntYB 82*
Brentwood Post [of Small Newspapers] - Pacific Palisades, CA - *AyerDirPub 83; NewsDir 84*
Brentwood Publishing Corp. - Los Angeles, CA - *MagIndMarPl 82-83*
Brentwood Publishing Group - Brentwood, TN - *BillIntBG 83-84*
Brentwood Records - Brentwood, TN - *BillIntBG 83-84*
Brentwood Westwood Hills Press - *See* Copley Press Inc.
Brentwood Westwood Press [of United Western Newspapers Inc.] - Santa Monica, CA - *AyerDirPub 83; NewsDir 84*
Brentwood-Westwood Press - Westwood, CA - *Ed&PubIntYB 82*
Bressen, Barbara G. - New York, NY - *MagIndMarPl 82-83*
Bressen Communications - New York, NY - *DirPRFirms 83*
Bressoud Inc., Louis - New York, NY - *LitMarPl 83, 84*
Bretford Manufacturing - Schiller Park, IL - *AvMarPl 83; DirInfWP 82; WhoWMicrocom 83*
Breth Inc., R. C. - Green Bay, WI - *TelAl 83, 84*
Brethren Press [Aff. of Church of the Brethren] - Elgin, IL - *BoPubDir 4, 5; LitMarPl 84*
Brethren Publishing Co. [Aff. of The General Conference of the Brethren Church] - Ashland, OH - *BoPubDir 4, 5*
Breton Publishers [Div. of Wadsworth Publishing Co. Inc.] - North Scituate, MA - *LitMarPl 83, 84*
Brett, Fay L. - Naples, FL - *LitMarPl 83, 84*
Bretton Woods [Aff. of Bretton Woods Associates] - Bretton Woods, NH - *TelDir&BG 83-84*
Brevard Transylvania Times - Brevard, NC - *BaconPubCkNews 84; NewsDir 84*
Brevet Press Inc. - Sioux Falls, SD - *BoPubDir 4, 5; WritMar 84*
Brevity Press - Nashville, TN - *LitMag&SmPr 83-84*
Brewer Associates Inc. - Dearborn, MI - *StaDirAdAg 2-84*
Brewer Broadcasting - Windsor, CO - *BrCabYB 84*
Brewer Broadcasting Corp. - Tell City, IN - *BrCabYB 84*
Brewer, F. R. - Richmond Hill, NY - *BoPubDir 4, 5*
Brewer, Jones & Feldman Inc. - Cincinnati, OH - *DirMarMP 83; StaDirAdAg 2-84*
Brewers Association of Canada - Ottawa, ON, Canada - *BoPubDir 4 Sup, 5*
Brewers Bulletin - Crystal Lake, IL - *MagDir 84*
Brewers Bulletin - Woodstock, IL - *BaconPubCkMag 84*
Brewers Digest [of Siebel Publishing Co.] - Chicago, IL - *BaconPubCkMag 84; MagDir 84*
Brewery Gulch Gazette - Bisbee, AZ - *AyerDirPub 83; Ed&PubIntYB 82*
Brewing Industry News, The - Riverdale, IL - *BaconPubCkMag 84*
Brewster Advertising - Cambridge, MA - *AdAge 3-28-84*
Brewster Corp. - Old Saybrook, CT - *DirInfWP 82*
Brewster Quad-City Herald - Brewster, WA - *BaconPubCkNews 84; Ed&PubIntYB 82*
Brewster Radio & TV Service - Newhall, WV - *BrCabYB 84; Tel&CabFB 84C*
Brewster Standard - Brewster, NY - *BaconPubCkNews 84*
Brewster Times - Brewster, NY - *Ed&PubIntYB 82*

Brewster Times [of Putnam County Press] - Mahopac, NY - *AyerDirPub 83; NewsDir 84*
Brewster Times - *See* Gateway Papers
Brewster Tribune - Brewster, MN - *Ed&PubIntYB 82*
Brewton Standard - Brewton, AL - *BaconPubCkNews 84; Ed&PubIntYB 82; NewsDir 84*
Brian Film Productions - New York, NY - *AvMarPl 83*
Brian's House Inc. - West Chester, PA - *BoPubDir 5*
Briar Rose Productions - Enid, OK - *BillIntBG 83-84*
Briarcliff Press - Jericho, NY - *ArtMar 84; WritMar 84*
Briarcliff Publishing Co. - Dayton, OH - *BoPubDir 4, 5*
Briarfields Press, The - Hartwood, VA - *LitMag&SmPr 83-84*
Briarmeade Music Unltd. - Gretna, LA - *BillIntBG 83-84*
Briarpatch Press - Davidson, NC - *BoPubDir 4, 5*
Bricelyn Mutual Telephone Co. - Bricelyn, MN - *TelDir&BG 83-84*
Bricelyn Sentinel - Bricelyn, MN - *Ed&PubIntYB 82*
Brick - Ilderton, ON, Canada - *LitMag&SmPr 83-84*
Brick & Clay Record [of Cahners Publishing Co.] - Des Plaines, IL - *BaconPubCkMag 84; MagDir 84; WritMar 84*
Brick Books - Ilderton, ON, Canada - *BoPubDir 4, 5; LitMag&SmPr 83-84*
Brick House Publishing Co. - Andover, MA - *LitMag&SmPr 83-84; LitMarPl 83, 84; WritMar 84*
Brick Town News - Brick, NJ - *Ed&PubIntYB 82*
Brickman Associates, Arthur - Miami Beach, FL - *Ed&PubIntYB 82*
Brickman, Robin - Providence, RI - *LitMarPl 83, 84*
Brickner, Alice - Bronx, NY - *LitMarPl 83, 84*
Brickyard Ltd., The (Motion Picture Arts Div.) - Salt Lake City, UT - *TelAl 83, 84*
Bridal Apparel News - Los Angeles, CA - *BaconPubCkMag 84*
Bride Broadcasting Inc. - Ambridge, PA - *BrCabYB 84*
Bride Guide Enterprises - Sherman Oaks, CA - *BoPubDir 4 Sup, 5*
Bride's [of Conde Nast Publications] - New York, NY - *BaconPubCkMag 84; Folio 83; LitMarPl 83, 84; MagDir 84; MagIndMarPl 82-83; WritMar 84*
Bridge: Asian American Perspectives - New York, NY - *LitMag&SmPr 83-84*
Bridge Building Music - *See* Brentwood Publishing Group
Bridge City Cablevision Inc. - Bridge City, TX - *BrCabYB 84; Tel&CabFB 84C*
Bridge Co., The Harry P. - Philadelphia, PA - *StaDirAdAg 2-84*
Bridge Computer Co. - Newton, MA - *MicrocomMPl 84*
Bridge Data Co. - St. Louis, MO - *DataDirOnSer 84; EISS 83; InfIndMarPl 83*
Bridge Data Stock & Options Real Time Information System [of Bridge Data Co.] - St. Louis, MO - *DBBus 82*
Bridge Data Stock & Options Real Time Information System - *See* Bridge Information System: Brokerage Service
Bridge Information System [of Bridge Data Co.] - St. Louis, MO - *DataDirOnSer 84*
Bridge Information System: Brokerage Service - St. Louis, MO - *DirOnDB Spring 84*
Bridge Publications Inc. - Los Angeles, CA - *LitMag&SmPr 83-84; LitMarPl 83, 84*
Bridge Publishing Inc. - South Plainfield, NJ - *BoPubDir 5; LitMarPl 84*
Bridge River-Lillooet News - Lillooet, BC, Canada - *AyerDirPub 83; Ed&PubIntYB 82*
Bridge Software - Stockport, England - *MicrocomSwDir 1*
Bridge Water Telephone Co. [Aff. of Arvig Telephone Co.] - Monticello, MN - *TelDir&BG 83-84*
Bridgeberg Books - Kentfield, CA - *BoPubDir 4, 5; LitMag&SmPr 83-84*
Bridgeport-Birch Run Weekly News - *See* Saginaw Valley News Inc.
Bridgeport Cable TV - Bridgeport, NE - *BrCabYB 84*
Bridgeport Cablevision [of Omni Cable TV Corp.] - Reese Township, MI - *Tel&CabFB 84C*
Bridgeport Fairfield Advocate - *See* Advocate Publishing
Bridgeport-Frankenmuth Cablevision - Frankenmuth, MI - *BrCabYB 84*
Bridgeport Future Views - Bridgeport, MI - *Ed&PubIntYB 82*
Bridgeport Index - Bridgeport, TX - *BaconPubCkNews 84; Ed&PubIntYB 82; NewsDir 84*
Bridgeport Leader Times - Bridgeport, IL - *BaconPubCkNews 84*
Bridgeport News - Bridgeport, IL - *Ed&PubIntYB 82*
Bridgeport News - Chicago, IL - *AyerDirPub 83*
Bridgeport News-Blade - Bridgeport, NE - *BaconPubCkNews 84; Ed&PubIntYB 82*
Bridgeport Post - Bridgeport, CT - *BaconPubCkNews 84; Ed&PubIntYB 82; LitMarPl 83, 84; NewsDir 84*
Bridgeport Telegram [of Post Publishing Co.] - Bridgeport, CT - *BaconPubCkNews 84; NewsDir 84*
Bridger Music Publishing Co. - Sikeston, MO - *BillIntBG 83-84*
Bridger Valley Pioneer [of Green River Star] - Green River, WY - *NewsDir 84*
Bridger Valley Pioneer - Lyman, WY - *AyerDirPub 83*
Bridges Press - Denver, CO - *BoPubDir 4, 5*
Bridges to the Sound Publishing Corp. - Tampa, FL - *BoPubDir 4, 5*
Bridgeton Evening News - Bridgeton, NJ - *BaconPubCkNews 84; Ed&PubIntYB 82; NewsDir 84*
Bridgeview-Hills Reporter - *See* Reporter Publications
Bridgeview Independent - Bridgeview, IL - *Ed&PubIntYB 82*
Bridgeview Independent [of Southwest Messenger Newspapers] - Midlothian, IL - *AyerDirPub 83; NewsDir 84*
Bridgeview Independent - *See* Southwest Messenger Newspapers
Bridgeville Area News - Bridgeville, PA - *AyerDirPub 83; BaconPubCkNews 84; Ed&PubIntYB 82*
Bridgewater Independent - Bridgewater, MA - *BaconPubCkNews 84; Ed&PubIntYB 82*
Bridgewater Tribune - Bridgewater, SD - *BaconPubCkNews 84; Ed&PubIntYB 82*
Bridgman Associates Inc. - Annapolis, MD - *DirMarMP 83; StaDirAdAg 2-84*
Bridgman Community Enterprise - Bridgman, MI - *Ed&PubIntYB 82*
Bridgton News - Bridgton, ME - *AyerDirPub 83; BaconPubCkNews 84; Ed&PubIntYB 82; NewsDir 84*
Briedwell, Larry - *See* Tri-Star Cablevision Inc.
Brien Broadcasting Stations - Montgomery, AL - *BrCabYB 84*
Brigade Leader - Wheaton, IL - *ArtMar 84; WritMar 84*
Brigadoon Publications Inc. - Staten Island, NY - *BoPubDir 4, 5*
Brigantine Music - Cherry Hill, NJ - *BillIntBG 83-84*
Briggs Associates, Robert - Mill Valley, CA - *BoPubDir 5*
Brigham Box Elder Journal - Brigham, UT - *BaconPubCkNews 84*
Brigham/Scully Inc. - Los Angeles, CA - *StaDirAdAg 2-84*
Brigham Street House - Salt Lake City, UT - *BoPubDir 4, 5*
Brigham Young University (Religious Studies Center) - Provo, UT - *BoPubDir 5*
Brigham Young University Press - Provo, UT - *LitMarPl 83, 84; WritMar 84*
Brigham Young University Studies - Provo, UT - *MagIndMarPl 82-83*
Bright & Associates - Los Angeles, CA - *HBIndAd&MS 82-83*
Bright Books - Akron, IN - *BoPubDir 4, 5*
Bright Spirit Press - San Rafael, CA - *BoPubDir 4, 5*
Bright Star Communications Ltd. - Upper Saddle River, NJ - *BrCabYB 84*
Brightman Co., The - Waltham, MA - *StaDirAdAg 2-84*
Brightman, Robert - Great Neck, NY - *LitMarPl 83, 84*
Brightmoor Journal - *See* Suburban Newspapers
Brighton Argus - Brighton, MI - *AyerDirPub 83; Ed&PubIntYB 82*
Brighton Argus [of Sliger Home Newspapers] - Northville, MI - *NewsDir 84*
Brighton Argus - *See* Sliger Livingston Publications
Brighton Blade [of Brighton Newspapers Inc.] - Brighton, CO - *Ed&PubIntYB 82; NewsDir 84*
Brighton Blade-Market Place [of Denver Community Publications Co.] - Brighton, CO - *BaconPubCkNews 84; NewsDir 84*
Brighton Park Life - Chicago, IL - *AyerDirPub 83*
Brighton-Pittsford Post [of Pittsford Wolfe Publications Inc.] - Pittsford, NY - *AyerDirPub 83; Ed&PubIntYB 82; NewsDir 84*
Brighton Publications - New Brighton, MN - *BoPubDir 4, 5*
Brighton Publishing Co. - Salt Lake City, UT - *LitMarPl 83, 84*
Brighton Southwestern Journal - Brighton, IL - *Ed&PubIntYB 82*
Brighton Sun, The [of Howell Livingston County Press] - Howell, MI - *NewsDir 84*
Briley Software - Livermore, CA - *MicrocomMPl 83, 84*

Brill Media Co. Inc. - Evansville, IN - *BrCabYB 84*
Brill Productions, Richard [Div. of Amazon Explorers Inc.] - Parlin, NJ - *AvMarPl 83*
Brilliant Enterprises - Santa Barbara, CA - *WritMar 84*
Brillig Systems Inc. - Burke, VA - *MicrocomMPl 83*
Brillig Systems Inc. - Springfield, VA - *MicrocomMPl 84*
Brillion Cablevision [of Wisconsin Cablevision & Radio Co. Inc.] - Brillion, WI - *Tel&CabFB 84C*
Brillon News - Brillon, WI - *BaconPubCkNews 84*
Brimfield Tribune-Gazette - Brimfield, OH - *Ed&PubIntYB 82*
Brimfield Tribune-Gazette - Kent, OH - *NewsDir 84*
Brindamour, Jean-Louis - San Francisco, CA - *LitMarPl 83, 84; MagIndMarPl 82-83*
Brindlee Mountain Telephone Co. - Arab, AL - *TelDir&BG 83-84*
Briner Chase Group - Salt Lake City, UT - *BillIntBG 83-84*
Bring Out Your Dead Records - Sacramento, CA - *BillIntBG 83-84*
Brinkley Argus - Brinkley, AR - *BaconPubCkNews 84; BrCabYB 84; Ed&PubIntYB 82; NewsDir 84*
Brintle, Mary M. - Whitestone, NY - *LitMarPl 83, 84*
Briod Inc., Andre E. - Newark, NJ - *DirPRFirms 83*
Brisbane Bee - South San Francisco, CA - *AyerDirPub 83; NewsDir 84*
Brisbane Bee - *See* San Mateo Times Group Newspapers
Brisbane Bee-Democrat - Brisbane, CA - *Ed&PubIntYB 82*
Brisbane Cable TV Inc. - Brisbane, CA - *BrCabYB 84*
Briscoe County News - Silverton, TX - *Ed&PubIntYB 82*
Brisebois Cable Engineering - Chateauguay, PQ, Canada - *BrCabYB 84*
Brisendine & Associates Inc. - Ft. Worth, TX - *IntDirMarRes 83*
Brisk, Rubin & Steinberg - Evanston, IL - *LitMarPl 83, 84*
Briskin Associates Inc. - Freeport, NY - *StaDirAdAg 2-84*
Bristol Banner - Bristol, IN - *BaconPubCkNews 84; Ed&PubIntYB 82*
Bristol Enterprise - Bristol, NH - *BaconPubCkNews 84*
Bristol Herald-Courier - Bristol, VA - *BaconPubCkNews 84; NewsDir 84*
Bristol Information Systems - Fall River, MA - *DataDirSup 7-83; DirInfWP 82; MicrocomSwDir 1*
Bristol International Corp. - Bristol, CT - *LitMarPl 83, 84; MagIndMarPl 82-83*
Bristol Langford Shaw - Deland, FL - *AvMarPl 83*
Bristol-Myers New York - New York, NY - *WritMar 84*
Bristol Phoenix - Bristol, RI - *Ed&PubIntYB 82; NewsDir 84*
Bristol Phoenix - *See* Phoenix-Times Newspapers
Bristol Press - Bristol, CT - *AyerDirPub 83; BaconPubCkNews 84; Ed&PubIntYB 82; NewsDir 84*
Bristol Software Factory - Bristol, England - *MicrocomSwDir 1*
Bristol Virginia-Tennessean - Bristol, VA - *BaconPubCkNews 84; NewsDir 84*
Bristow News - *See* Bristow News Co.
Bristow News Co. - Bristow, OK - *BaconPubCkNews 84; Ed&PubIntYB 82*
Bristow Record-Citizen - *See* Bristow News Co.
Bristow, Walter S. III - Eugene, OR - *DataDirOnSer 84*
Britannica 3 [of Encyclopaedia Britannica Inc.] - Chicago, IL - *DBBus 82*
Britches [of Kearns Productions Inc.] - San Francisco, CA - *WritMar 84*
British Architectural Library [of Royal Institute of British Architects] - London, England - *CompReadDB 82*
British Book News - London, England - *LitMag&SmPr 83-84*
British Broadcasting Corp. - New York, NY - *TelAl 83, 84*
British Columbia Genealogical Society - Richmond, BC, Canada - *BoPubDir 4, 5*
British Columbia Historical News - Victoria, BC, Canada - *LitMag&SmPr 83-84*
British Columbia Library Network - Vancouver, BC, Canada - *EISS 5-84 Sup*
British Columbia Lumberman - Vancouver, BC, Canada - *BaconPubCkMag 84*
British Columbia Railway Historical Association [Aff. of British Columbia Ministry of Consumer & Corporate Affairs] - Victoria, BC, Canada - *BoPubDir 4 Sup, 5*
British Columbia Superintendent of Brokers, Insurance, & Real Estate [Aff. of British Columbia Ministry of Consumer & Corporate Affairs] - Vancouver, BC, Canada - *BoPubDir 4 Sup, 5*
British Columbia Telephone Co. - Burnaby, BC, Canada - *VideoDir 82-83*
British Columbia Television Broadcasting System Ltd. - Vancouver, BC, Canada - *BrCabYB 84*
British Computer Society - London, England - *EISS 83*
British Council, The - Vienna, Austria - *InfIndMarPl 83*
British Defence Directory [of Brassey's Publishers Ltd.] - Oxford, England - *EISS 5-84 Sup*
British Education Index [of The British Library] - London, England - *DirOnDB Spring 84; OnBibDB 3*
British Heritage [of Historical Times Inc.] - Harrisburg, PA - *LitMarPl 83, 84; MagDir 84; MagIndMarPl 82-83; WritMar 84*
British Humanities Index [of Library Association Publishing Ltd.] - London, England - *EISS 83*
British Hydromechanics Research Association - Cranfield, England - *CompReadDB 82*
British Information Services - New York, NY - *BrCabYB 84; Tel&CabFB 84C*
British Journal of Aesthetics [of Oxford University Press] - Oxford, England - *LitMag&SmPr 83-84*
British Library (Bibliographic Services Div.) - London, England - *CompReadDB 82; InfIndMarPl 83; MicroMarPl 82-83*
British Library (Newspaper Library) - London, England - *MicroMarPl 82-83*
British Library Automated Information Service - London, England - *EISS 83*
British Library Lending - Wetherby, England - *CompReadDB 82*
British Museum Publications - London, England - *MicroMarPl 82-83*
British National Readership Survey [of Interactive Market Systems Inc.] - New York, NY - *DataDirOnSer 84*
British Naturalists' Association, Country-Side - Roughlee, England - *LitMag&SmPr 83-84*
British Non-Ferrous Metals Abstracts [of BNF Metals Technology Centre] - Wantage, England - *CompReadDB 82*
British Railway Modellers of North America - Calgary, AB, Canada - *BoPubDir 4, 5*
British Science Fiction Association Ltd. - Reading, England - *LitMag&SmPr 83-84*
British Telecom International - *See* International Packet Switching Service
British Theatre Institute Newsletter & Report - Essex, England - *LitMag&SmPr 83-84*
British Tourist Authority - Salem, NH - *LitMarPl 83, 84*
British Universities Film Council Ltd. - London, England - *MicroMarPl 82-83*
British Videotex & Teletext - *See* Logica Inc.
Britt News-Tribune [of Britt Town & Country Advertiser] - Britt, IA - *AyerDirPub 83; Ed&PubIntYB 82; NewsDir 84*
Britt News-Tribune - *See* Britt Publishing Co.
Britt Publishing Co. - Britt, IA - *BaconPubCkNews 84*
Britt-Pugh Associates - New York, NY - *BillIntBG 83-84*
Britt Town & County Advertiser - *See* Britt Publishing Co.
Brittains Papers Inc. [Subs. of Tullis Russell & Co. Ltd.] - Stamford, CT - *LitMarPl 83, 84*
Britteu Music - *See* Brown Moon Music
Britton Cable TV - Britton, SD - *BrCabYB 84*
Britton Color Services Inc. - Auburn, NY - *MagIndMarPl 82-83*
Britton Community Cable TV - Britton, SD - *Tel&CabFB 84C*
Britton Journal - Britton, SD - *BaconPubCkNews 84; Ed&PubIntYB 82*
Britton-Lee Inc. - Los Gatos, CA - *DataDirSup 7-83*
BRIX [of Dept. of the Environment] - Watford, England - *EISS 83*
Broad Band Cablevision Inc. - Leland, MS - *Tel&CabFB 84C*
Broad River Press Inc. - Columbia, SC - *BoPubDir 4, 5*
Broad River Publishing Co. - Cowen, WV - *BillIntBG 83-84*
Broad Street Communications Corp. - New Haven, CT - *BrCabYB 84*
Broad Top Bulletin - Saxton, PA - *AyerDirPub 83; Ed&PubIntYB 82*
Broadband Cablevision - Leland, MS - *BrCabYB 84*

Broadband Communications Inc. - New York, NY - *InterCabHB 3*
Broadband Services Inc. - Weatherford, OK - *Tel&CabFB 84C p.1667*
Broadbent, Marv - Beltsville, MD - *MagIndMarPl 82-83*
Broadcast Advertisers Reports [of Interactive Market Systems Inc.] - New York, NY - *BrCabYB 84; DataDirOnSer 84; DBBus 82; EISS 83; Tel&CabFB 84C*
Broadcast Business Consultants - New York, NY - *HBIndAd&MS 82-83*
Broadcast Communications - Overland, KS - *BaconPubCkMag 84*
Broadcast Data Corp. - Pasadena, MD - *Tel&CabFB 84C*
Broadcast Dept. Inc., The - New York, NY - *AvMarPl 83; HBIndAd&MS 82-83*
Broadcast Engineering - Overland Park, KS - *BaconPubCkMag 84; MagIndMarPl 82-83; WritMar 84*
Broadcast Engineering - Shawnee Mission, KS - *MagDir 84*
Broadcast Enterprises National Inc. - Philadelphia, PA - *BrCabYB 84*
Broadcast Information Bureau Inc. - Long Island, NY - *BrCabYB 84*
Broadcast Information Services Inc. - Denver, CO - *ProGuPRSer 4; Tel&CabFB 84C*
Broadcast Management Corp. - Fairfield, OH - *BrCabYB 84*
Broadcast Management/Engineering - New York, NY - *WritMar 84*
Broadcast Marketing Co. - San Francisco, CA - *InterCabHB 3*
Broadcast Music Inc. - New York, NY - *Tel&CabFB 84C*
Broadcast News Ltd. - Toronto, ON, Canada - *BrCabYB 84; Ed&PubIntYB 82; Tel&CabFB 84C*
Broadcast News Service - Boston, MA - *BrCabYB 84*
Broadcast News Service Inc. - New York, NY - *BrCabYB 84*
Broadcast News Services Inc. - Dallas, TX - *ProGuPRSer 4*
Broadcast Pro-File - Hollywood, CA - *BrCabYB 84*
Broadcast Programming & Production - Los Angeles, CA - *MagDir 84*
Broadcast Properties - College Station, TX - *BrCabYB 84*
Broadcast Properties West Inc. - Seattle, WA - *CabTVFinDB 83*
Broadcast Service Bureau Inc. - Washington, DC - *BrCabYB 84*
Broadcast Services Inc. - Spokane, WA - *Tel&CabFB 84C p.1667*
Broadcast Systems Div. [of RCA Corp.] - Camden, NJ - *Tel&CabFB 84C*
Broadcast Technology - Bolton, ON, Canada - *BaconPubCkMag 84; WritMar 84*
Broadcast Time Inc. - Roslyn, NY - *StaDirAdAg 2-84*
Broadcast Week - New York, NY - *BaconPubCkMag 84*
Broadcaster - Nashua, NH - *AyerDirPub 83*
Broadcaster - Toronto, ON, Canada - *BaconPubCkMag 84; WritMar 84*
Broadcasters Audience Research Board [of Interactive Market Systems Inc.] - New York, NY - *DataDirOnSer 84*
Broadcasters Audience Research Board - London, England - *DirOnDB Spring 84*
Broadcasting - Washington, DC - *BaconPubCkMag 84; MagDir 84; MagIndMarPl 82-83; NewsBur 6*
Broadcasting Foundation of America - New York, NY - *AvMarPl 83; TelAl 83, 84*
Broadcasting Publications Inc. - Washington, DC - *BoPubDir 4, 5*
Broadman Films [Subs. of Baptist Sunday School Board] - Nashville, TN - *AvMarPl 83*
Broadman Press - Nashville, TN - *BillIntBG 83-84; LitMarPl 83, 84; WritMar 84*
Broadmoor Advertising Agency Ltd., The - Colorado Springs, CO - *StaDirAdAg 2-84*
Broadsheet - Auckland, New Zealand - *LitMag&SmPr 83-84*
Broadside/Community Journal, The - Berlin, NJ - *AyerDirPub 83*
Broadside/Crummel Press - Highland Park, MI - *BoPubDir 4*
Broadside Press - Highland Park, MI - *BoPubDir 5*
Broadus & Associates Inc., R. F. - Atlanta, GA - *StaDirAdAg 2-84*
Broadus Powder River Examiner - Broadus, MT - *BaconPubCkNews 84*
Broadview Associates - Ft. Lee, NJ - *ADAPSOMemDir 83-84*
Broadview Savings & Loan Co., The - Cleveland, OH - *DataDirSup 7-83*
Broadway Costumes Inc. - Chicago, IL - *AvMarPl 83*
Broadway/Hollywood International Music Publishers - Beverly Hills, CA - *BillIntBG 83-84*
Broadway Software - New York, NY - *MicrocomMPl 84; MicrocomSwDir 1*
Brochure People [Div. of Intermedia Consultants Inc.] - New York, NY - *DirMarMP 83*
Brock Management Library Ltd. - Don Mills, ON, Canada - *BoPubDir 4, 5*
Brock Publishing Co. - Chico, CA - *BoPubDir 4, 5*
Brock Publishing, John - Los Angeles, CA - *BillIntBG 83-84*
Brocke & Sons Inc., George F. - Kendrick, ID - *BrCabYB 84; Tel&CabFB 84C*
Brockman Associates Inc., John - New York, NY - *LitMarPl 83, 84*
Brockmeyer, Vernon - Beach, ND - *Tel&CabFB 84C p.1667*
Brockport Post [of Wolfe Publications Inc.] - Pittsford, NY - *AyerDirPub 83; NewsDir 84*
Brockport Post - *See* Wolfe Publications Inc.
Brockport Post, The - Brockport, NY - *Ed&PubIntYB 82*
Brockport Tri-County Advertiser - Brockport, NY - *NewsDir 84*
Brockton Cablevision Co. Inc. - Brockton, MA - *BrCabYB 84*
Brockton Enterprise, The - Brockton, MA - *NewsDir 84*
Brockville Cable Telecommunications Inc. [of Utilities Management Group] - Brockville, ON, Canada - *BrCabYB 84*
Brockville Recorder & Times - Brockville, ON, Canada - *LitMarPl 83*
Brockway Record - Brockway, PA - *BaconPubCkNews 84; Ed&PubIntYB 82*
Brockway Television Inc. - Brockway, PA - *BrCabYB 84; Tel&CabFB 84C*
Brod Literary Agency, Ruth Hagy - New York, NY - *LitMarPl 83, 84*
Brodart Books - Williamsport, PA - *LitMarPl 84*
Brodart Co. - Williamsport, PA - *BoPubDir 4 Sup, 5; CompReadDB 82; DataDirOnSer 84; LitMarPl 83, 84*
Brodatz, Phil - Coral Gables, FL - *LitMarPl 83, 84; MagIndMarPl 82-83*
Broderbund Software - San Rafael, CA - *MicrocomMPl 83, 84; WhoWMicrocom 83; WritMar 84*
Broderick & Associates - Dallas, TX - *MicrocomMPl 83, 84; MicrocomSwDir 1; WhoWMicrocom 83*
Brodhead Independent-Register - Brodhead, WI - *BaconPubCkNews 84*
Brodsky Advertising Inc., George - Chicago, IL - *StaDirAdAg 2-84*
Brodt Music Co. - Charlotte, NC - *BillIntBG 83-84*
Brody Advertising Ltd., Frederick - Northbrook, IL - *StaDirAdAg 2-84*
Brody & Associates, David L. [Subs. of Sun Group Inc.] - Chicago, IL - *DirMarMP 83; StaDirAdAg 2-84*
Broekel, Ray - Ipswich, MA - *LitMarPl 83, 84*
Broh & Associates Inc., Irwin - Des Plaines, IL - *BoPubDir 5; IntDirMarRes 83*
Broiler Business - Mt. Morris, IL - *MagDir 84*
Broiler Industry - Sea Isle City, NJ - *BaconPubCkMag 84; MagDir 84*
Brokaw Photography, Dennis - Carmel, CA - *LitMarPl 83, 84; MagIndMarPl 82-83*
Broken Arrow Ledger - Broken Arrow, OK - *BaconPubCkNews 84; Ed&PubIntYB 82*
Broken Bow Community TV Cable - Broken Bow, OK - *BrCabYB 84*
Broken Bow Custer County Chief - Broken Bow, NE - *BaconPubCkNews 84; NewsDir 84*
Broken Bow News - Broken Bow, OK - *BaconPubCkNews 84; Ed&PubIntYB 82*
Broken Bow TV Cable Co. Inc. - Broken Bow, OK - *Tel&CabFB 84C*
Broken Streets - Bristol, CT - *LitMag&SmPr 83-84*
Broken Twig Press - Detroit, MI - *BoPubDir 4, 5*
Broken Whisker Studio - Chicago, IL - *BoPubDir 4, 5; LitMag&SmPr 83-84*
Broker Services Inc. - Englewood, CO - *DataDirOnSer 84; DirOnDB Spring 84; EISS 83*
Broker, The - San Francisco, CA - *BaconPubCkMag 84*
Broker World - Kansas City, MO - *BaconPubCkMag 84*
Brokerage Systems Inc. - Chicago, IL - *ADAPSOMemDir 83-84*

Brokering Press - Minneapolis, MN - *BoPubDir 4 Sup, 5*
Brolet Press, The [Div. of Van Valkenburgh, Nooger & Neville Inc.] - New York, NY - *LitMarPl 83, 84*
Brom Microsystems Engineering Inc. - Winona, MN - *MicrocomSwDir 1*
Brombacher Books [Aff. of Independent Printing Co. Inc.] - Richmond, CA - *BoPubDir 4, 5*
Bromelaid Society Inc. - Los Angeles, CA - *BoPubDir 4, 5*
Bromfield Sy. Educational Foundation - Boston, MA - *LitMag&SmPr 83-84*
Bromide Telephone Co. - Fittstown, OK - *TelDir&BG 83-84*
Brondum, Marshall - Milltown, MT - *Tel&CabFB 84C p.1667*
Bronjo Music Publishing - Brooklyn, NY - *BillIntBG 83-84*
Bronson & Co. Inc., Howard - New York, NY - *DirPRFirms 83*
Bronson Inc., Dick - Bangor, ME - *StaDirAdAg 2-84*
Bronson Journal - Bronson, MI - *BaconPubCkNews 84; Ed&PubIntYB 82*
Bronson Levy County Journal - Bronson, FL - *BaconPubCkNews 84*
Bronte Enterprise - Bronte, TX - *Ed&PubIntYB 82*
Bronte Enterprise - *See* Bronte Enterprise Publishers
Bronte Enterprise Publishers - Bronte, TX - *BaconPubCkNews 84*
Bronte Press - Kankakee, IL - *BoPubDir 4, 5*
Bronx Co-Op City Times [of Riverbay Corp.] - Bronx, NY - *NewsDir 84*
Bronx News - Bronx, NY - *NewsDir 84*
Bronx News - New York, NY - *AyerDirPub 83*
Bronx Parkway News, The - Bronx, NY - *NewsDir 84*
Bronx Press-Review - Bronx, NY - *Ed&PubIntYB 82; NewsDir 84*
Bronx Press-Review - New York, NY - *AyerDirPub 83*
Bronx Riverdale Press - Bronx, NY - *BaconPubCkNews 84*
Bronxville Review Press & Reporter [of Westchester Rockland Newspapers] - Mt. Vernon, NY - *BaconPubCkNews 84; NewsDir 84*
Bronze Music Inc. - *See* Sure-Fire Music Co. Inc.
Brook Farm Books - Glassville, NB, Canada - *BoPubDir 5; LitMag&SmPr 83-84*
Brook Reporter - Brook, IN - *BaconPubCkNews 84; Ed&PubIntYB 82*
Brookdale Press - Stamford, CT - *BoPubDir 4, 5*
Brooke Cable Co. - Brooke County, WV - *BrCabYB 84; Tel&CabFB 84C*
Brooke Computer Corp. - New York, NY - *MicrocomMPl 84; WhoWMicrocom 83*
Brooke News - Wellsburg, WV - *AyerDirPub 83; Ed&PubIntYB 82*
Brooker Sales International Inc., Paul - Wichita, KS - *DirMarMP 83*
Brookes Publishing Co., Paul H. - Baltimore, MD - *BoPubDir 4; LitMarPl 83, 84*
Brookfield Citizen [of La Grange Suburban Life/Citizen] - La Grange, IL - *NewsDir 84*
Brookfield Courier - Brookfield, NY - *Ed&PubIntYB 82*
Brookfield Daily News-Bulletin - Brookfield, MO - *NewsDir 84*
Brookfield-Elm Grove Post [of West Allis Suburban Milwaukee Post Newspapers] - Milwaukee, WI - *NewsDir 84*
Brookfield Journal [of Housatonic Valley Publishing Co.] - Brookfield, CT - *Ed&PubIntYB 82; NewsDir 84*
Brookfield Journal - *See* Housatonic Valley Publishing Co.
Brookfield-Masury News - Niles, OH - *AyerDirPub 83*
Brookfield-Masury News - *See* Phoenix Publications Inc.
Brookfield News - Brookfield, WI - *Ed&PubIntYB 82*
Brookfield News - Oak Creek, WI - *AyerDirPub 83*
Brookfield News - *See* Community Newspapers Inc.
Brookfield News-Bulletin - Brookfield, MO - *BaconPubCkNews 84*
Brookfield Suburban Life Citizen - *See* Life Printing & Publishing Co.
Brookfield Sun - La Grange, IL - *AyerDirPub 83*
Brookfield Times [of Lyons Enterprise Publishing Co.] - Lyons, IL - *NewsDir 84*
Brookhaven Buyers Guide - Brookhaven, MS - *AyerDirPub 83*
Brookhaven Cable TV Inc. [of Rogers UA Cablesystems Inc.] - Brookhaven, NY - *BrCabYB 84; Tel&CabFB 84C*
Brookhaven Daily Leader [of Southwest Publishers Inc.] - Brookhaven, MS - *BaconPubCkNews 84; NewsDir 84*
Brookhaven National Laboratory [of Associated Universities Inc.] - Upton, NY - *CompReadDB 82*
Brookhaven Press [Div. of Northern Micrographics] - La Crosse, WI - *LitMarPl 83, 84; MicroMarPl 82-83*
Brookhaven Review - Brookhaven, NY - *AyerDirPub 83*
Brookhaven Review - Brookhaven Township, NY - *Ed&PubIntYB 82*
Brookhaven Review - Ronkonkoma, NY - *NewsDir 84*
Brookhaven Review - *See* Ronkonkoma Review Publishers
Brookings Curry Coastal Pilot - Brookings, OR - *BaconPubCkNews 84*
Brookings Daily Register [of Stauffer Communications Inc.] - Brookings, SD - *Ed&PubIntYB 82; NewsDir 84*
Brookings Institution, The - Washington, DC - *LitMarPl 83, 84*
Brookings Register - Brookings, SD - *BaconPubCkNews 84*
Brookline Chronicle-Citizen - Brookline, MA - *Ed&PubIntYB 82; NewsDir 84*
Brookline Chronicle-Citizen - *See* Citizen Group Publications
Brookline Journal, The - Pittsburgh, PA - *Ed&PubIntYB 82*
Brooklyn Academy of Music - San Francisco, CA - *MagDir 84*
Brooklyn-Belvedere Comet - Los Angeles, CA - *AyerDirPub 83*
Brooklyn Bensonhurst News - Brooklyn, NY - *NewsDir 84*
Brooklyn Bensonhurst News - *See* Home Reporter & Sunset News Inc.
Brooklyn Botanic Garden - Brooklyn, NY - *BoPubDir 4, 5*
Brooklyn Canarsie Courier - Brooklyn, NY - *BaconPubCkNews 84*
Brooklyn Center Post - Brooklyn Center, MN - *Ed&PubIntYB 82*
Brooklyn Center Post [of Post Newspapers] - Minneapolis, MN - *AyerDirPub 83; NewsDir 84*
Brooklyn Center Post - *See* Post Publications Inc.
Brooklyn Challenge - Brooklyn, NY - *BaconPubCkNews 84*
Brooklyn Chronicle - Brooklyn, IA - *BaconPubCkNews 84*
Brooklyn City Sun - Brooklyn, NY - *BaconPubCkNews 84*
Brooklyn College (Institute for Studies in American Music) - Brooklyn, NY - *BoPubDir 4, 5*
Brooklyn Country Records - New York, NY - *BillIntBG 83-84*
Brooklyn Courier [of Courier-Life Inc.] - Brooklyn, NY - *AyerDirPub 83; Ed&PubIntYB 82; NewsDir 84*
Brooklyn Daily Bulletin [of Earle Associates Inc.] - Brooklyn, NY - *AyerDirPub 83; Ed&PubIntYB 82; NewsDir 84*
Brooklyn Exponent - Brooklyn, MI - *BaconPubCkNews 84; Ed&PubIntYB 82; NewsDir 84*
Brooklyn Graphic - Brooklyn, NY - *BaconPubCkNews 84; Ed&PubIntYB 82; NewsDir 84*
Brooklyn Greenpoint Gazette/Advertiser - Brooklyn, NY - *NewsDir 84*
Brooklyn Heights Press - Brooklyn, NY - *AyerDirPub 83; BaconPubCkNews 84; Ed&PubIntYB 82; NewsDir 84*
Brooklyn Home Reporter & Sunset News - Brooklyn, NY - *NewsDir 84*
Brooklyn Journal, The - Brooklyn, NY - *NewsDir 84*
Brooklyn Longshoreman [of Local 1814, ILA] - Brooklyn, NY - *NewsDir 84*
Brooklyn Museum (Publications & Marketing Services Div.) - Brooklyn, NY - *BoPubDir 4, 5*
Brooklyn Mutual Telephone Co. - Brooklyn, IA - *TelDir&BG 83-84*
Brooklyn New York Recorder - Brooklyn, NY - *BaconPubCkNews 84; NewsDir 84*
Brooklyn Paper, The - Brooklyn, IA - *Ed&PubIntYB 82*
Brooklyn Paper, The - Brooklyn, NY - *AyerDirPub 83; Ed&PubIntYB 82*
Brooklyn Park Post - Brooklyn Park, MN - *Ed&PubIntYB 82*
Brooklyn Park Post - Minneapolis, MN - *AyerDirPub 83; NewsDir 84*
Brooklyn Park Post - *See* Post Publications Inc.
Brooklyn Phoenix - Brooklyn, NY - *Ed&PubIntYB 82; NewsDir 84*
Brooklyn Record - Brooklyn, NY - *AyerDirPub 83; BaconPubCkNews 84; NewsDir 84*
Brooklyn Rediscovery [Aff. of The Brooklyn Educational & Cultural Alliance] - Brooklyn, NY - *BoPubDir 4, 5*
Brooklyn Ridgewood Times - Brooklyn, NY - *NewsDir 84*
Brooklyn Ridgewood Times - Queens & Kings Counties, NY - *Ed&PubIntYB 82*
Brooklyn Spectator - Brooklyn, NY - *BaconPubCkNews 84; Ed&PubIntYB 82; NewsDir 84*
Brooklyn Times - Brooklyn, NY - *AyerDirPub 83; BaconPubCkNews 84; Ed&PubIntYB 82; NewsDir 84*

Brookneal Union Star - Brookneal, VA - *BaconPubCkNews 84*
Brooks Advertising Co. - Toronto, ON, Canada - *StaDirAdAg 2-84*
Brooks Advertising Inc. - Palos Heights, IL - *StaDirAdAg 2-84*
Brooks Advertising Inc., Bernard M. - San Antonio, TX - *StaDirAdAg 2-84*
Brooks Associates, Anita Helen - New York, NY - *ArtMar 84; DirPRFirms 83; LitMarPl 83, 84*
Brooks Bros. Publishers - Nashville, TN - *BillIntBG 83-84*
Brooks Bulletin, The - Brooks, AB, Canada - *Ed&PubIntYB 82*
Brooks Cameras Inc. - San Mateo, CA - *AvMarPl 83*
Brooks/Cole Publishing Co. [Div. of Wadsworth Inc.] - Monterey, CA - *LitMarPl 83, 84*
Brooks Community Newspapers - Westport, CT - *BaconPubCkNews 84*
Brooks Community Television Ltd. - Taber, AB, Canada - *BrCabYB 84*
Brooks Co., Stanley J. - Los Angeles, CA - *BoPubDir 4, 5*
Brooks-Hill, Helen - Oakville, ON, Canada - *BoPubDir 4, 5*
Brooks-Pollard Co. - Little Rock, AR - *StaDirAdAg 2-84*
Brooks Publishing Co. - Bakersfield, CA - *LitMarPl 83*
Brooks Publishing Co. - Carmichael, CA - *LitMarPl 84*
Brooks-Sterling Co. - Danville, CA - *BoPubDir 4, 5*
Brookshire Banner - Brookshire, TX - *AyerDirPub 83; BaconPubCkNews 84; Ed&PubIntYB 82*
Brookside Cable Service Inc. - Brookside, AL - *Tel&CabFB 84C*
Brookside Music Corp. - New York, NY - *BillIntBG 83-84*
Brooksville Bracken County News - *See* Poage Publishing Co.
Brooksville Sun Journal [of Park Newspapers Inc.] - Brooksville, FL - *BaconPubCkNews 84; NewsDir 84*
Brookville American [of McMurray Co.] - Brookville, PA - *Ed&PubIntYB 82; NewsDir 84*
Brookville American - *See* McMurray Co.
Brookville American - *See* Whitewater Publications Inc.
Brookville American-Democrat - Brookville, IN - *NewsDir 84*
Brookville American, The - Brookville, IN - *Ed&PubIntYB 82*
Brookville Cable TV [of Connersville Cable TV Inc.] - Brookville, IN - *BrCabYB 84*
Brookville Cablevision [of Cardinal Communications Inc.] - Brookville, IN - *Tel&CabFB 84C*
Brookville Democrat - *See* Whitewater Publishing Inc.
Brookville Democrat, The - Brookville, IN - *Ed&PubIntYB 82*
Brookville Jeffersonian Democrat - *See* McMurray Co.
Brookville Sentinel - *See* Argus-Sentinel Inc.
Brookville Star - Brookville, OH - *BaconPubCkNews 84; Ed&PubIntYB 82*
Brookville Telephone Co. [Aff. of Mid-Continent Telephone Corp.] - Brookville, PA - *TelDir&BG 83-84*
Broom, Brush, & Mop - Arcola, IL - *BaconPubCkMag 84; MagDir 84*
Broomall Industries Inc. - Broomall, PA - *DataDirSup 7-83*
Broome Associates Inc., John R. - Washington, DC - *ADAPSOMemDir 83-84*
Broome Closet - North Hollywood, CA - *BoPubDir 5*
Broome County Historical Society [Aff. of Roberson Center for the Arts & Sciences] - Binghamton, NY - *BoPubDir 4, 5*
Broome County Living - Binghamton, NY - *BaconPubCkMag 84*
Broomfield Enterprise [of Denver Community Publications Co.] - Broomfield, CO - *AyerDirPub 83; NewsDir 84*
Broomstick - San Francisco, CA - *LitMag&SmPr 83-84*
Brophy, Judith - West Hartford, CT - *LitMarPl 83, 84; MagIndMarPl 82-83*
Brose Productions Inc. - North Hollywood, CA - *AvMarPl 83*
Brother Bear Music - *See* DeWhit Music
Brother International Corp. - Piscataway, NJ - *DirInfWP 82*
Brother Publishing Co. - Beverly Hills, CA - *BillIntBG 83-84*
Brotherhood of Life Inc. - Albuquerque, NM - *BoPubDir 4, 5; LitMarPl 84*
Brotherhood of Maintenance of Way Employes - Highland Park, MI - *MagDir 84*
Brotherhood of Maintenance of Way Employes Journal - Detroit, MI - *ArtMar 84; WritMar 84*
Brothers Publishing Ltd. - Sackville, NB, Canada - *BoPubDir 4 Sup, 5*
Brotman & Associates Inc., Charles J. - Washington, DC - *DirPRFirms 83*
Broude Bros. Ltd. - New York, NY - *BillIntBG 83-84*
Broude International Editions Inc. - Williamstown, MA - *BoPubDir 5*
Broude International Editions Inc. - New York, NY - *BoPubDir 4*
Broude International Editors - *See* Broude Bros. Ltd.
Brouillard Communications [of J. Walter Thompson Co.] - New York, NY - *AdAge 3-28-84; DirPRFirms 83; StaDirAdAg 2-84*
Broussard Feeds Inc. - Lafayette, LA - *MicrocomMPl 84*
Broussard, Thomas R. - Lafayette, LA - *MicrocomMPl 83*
Broward Cablevision Inc. [of Buford TV Inc.] - Broward County, FL - *Tel&CabFB 84C*
Broward Cablevision Inc. [of Buford Television Inc.] - Lauderdale Lakes, FL - *BrCabYB 84*
Broward Jewish Journal - Ft. Lauderdale, FL - *Ed&PubIntYB 82*
Broward Life Magazine - Ft. Lauderdale, FL - *MagDir 84*
Broward Neighbors - Tamarac, FL - *AyerDirPub 83*
Broward Review - Ft. Lauderdale, FL - *Ed&PubIntYB 82; NewsDir 84*
Browder, Nathaniel C. - Raleigh, NC - *BoPubDir 4, 5*
Browerville Blade - Browerville, MN - *BaconPubCkNews 84; Ed&PubIntYB 82*
Brown Advertising - Somerset, NJ - *AdAge 3-28-84; StaDirAdAg 2-84*
Brown Advertising Agency Inc., E. H. - Chicago, IL - *StaDirAdAg 2-84*
Brown Advertising, Brian - Toronto, ON, Canada - *StaDirAdAg 2-84*
Brown Advertising, E. H. - Chicago, IL - *AdAge 3-28-84*
Brown Advertising Ltd., Joseph - Huntington, NY - *StaDirAdAg 2-84*
Brown & Associates Inc., Dave - Oak Brook, IL - *DirPRFirms 83*
Brown & Associates Inc., Earle Palmer - Bethesda, MD - *DirPRFirms 83*
Brown & Associates Inc., J. Aaron - Nashville, TN - *BillIntBG 83-84*
Brown & Associates Inc., Norman - Providence, RI - *LitMarPl 83, 84; MagIndMarPl 82-83*
Brown & Brothers Inc., Arthur - New York, NY - *LitMarPl 83*
Brown & Co. Ltd., T. Stewart - Vancouver, BC, Canada - *StaDirAdAg 2-84*
Brown & Koby Inc. - Houston, TX - *StaDirAdAg 2-84*
Brown & Partners, John - Seattle, WA - *AdAge 3-28-84; StaDirAdAg 2-84*
Brown & Sons, Alex. - Baltimore, MD - *ADAPSOMemDir 83-84*
Brown & Wilson Corp. - Carmel, CA - *BaconPubCkNews 84*
Brown, Andrea - New York, NY - *LitMarPl 83, 84*
Brown Associates Inc., Clare - Garwood, NJ - *IntDirMarRes 83*
Brown Associates, Tom - Dallas, TX - *LitMarPl 83, 84*
Brown Book Co. [Aff. of Overstock Book Co. Inc.] - Farmingdale, NY - *BoPubDir 4, 5*
Brown Books, D. - San Francisco, CA - *BoPubDir 4, 5*
Brown Boxenbaum Inc. - New York, NY - *DirPRFirms 83; StaDirAdAg 2-84*
Brown Brillig Productions Inc., Barry - New York, NY - *TelAl 83, 84*
Brown Brothers - Sterling, PA - *MagIndMarPl 82-83*
Brown, C. C. - Airway Heights, WA - *BoPubDir 4, 5*
Brown City Banner - Brown City, MI - *BaconPubCkNews 84; Ed&PubIntYB 82*
Brown Cos., Earle Palmer - Bethesda, MD - *AdAge 3-28-84; StaDirAdAg 2-84*
Brown Co., E. Arthur - Alexandria, MN - *LitMag&SmPr 83-84; MicrocomMPl 84*
Brown Co., William C. - Dubuque, IA - *DirMarMP 83; WritMar 84*
Brown County Broadcasting Co. Inc. - Brownwood, TX - *Tel&CabFB 84C p.1667*
Brown County Democrat - Nashville, IN - *AyerDirPub 83; Ed&PubIntYB 82*
Brown County Gazette - Bangs, TX - *AyerDirPub 83; Ed&PubIntYB 82*
Brown County News - Frederick, SD - *AyerDirPub 83; Ed&PubIntYB 82*
Brown County Press [of The Batavia Buying Guide] - Batavia, OH - *NewsDir 84*

Brown County Press, The - Mt. Orab, OH - *Ed&PubIntYB 82*
Brown County World - Hiawatha, KS - *AyerDirPub 83*
Brown Daily Herald - Providence, RI - *NewsDir 84*
Brown Deer Herald - Brown Deer, WI - *Ed&PubIntYB 82*
Brown Deer Herald - Oak Creek, WI - *AyerDirPub 83*
Brown Deer Herald - *See* Community Newspapers Inc.
Brown Direct [Div. of Earle Palmer Brown Associates Inc.] - Bethesda, MD - *StaDirAdAg 2-84*
Brown, Dorothy E. - Placerville, CA - *BoPubDir 5*
Brown, Dowling & Kitten - *See* BDK Advertising Inc.
Brown Enterprises, Gary - Philomath, OR - *MicrocomMPl 84*
Brown, Frank - Winkler, MB, Canada - *BoPubDir 4, 5*
Brown Group Inc., The - Avalon, NJ - *ADAPSOMemDir 83-84*
Brown Group, Wm. C. - Dubuque, IA - *LitMarPl 83, 84*
Brown, Henry - New York, NY - *Tel&CabFB 84C*
Brown Inc., Ned - Beverly Hills, CA - *LitMarPl 83, 84*
Brown Information Center Inc., Arlin J. - Ft. Belvoir, VA - *BoPubDir 4, 5*
Brown International Communications - Kenal, AK - *BrCabYB 84*
Brown International Communications - Houston, TX - *Tel&CabFB 84C p.1667*
Brown, James E. - Dalton, GA - *Tel&CabFB 84C p.1667*
Brown Keefe Marine/Bowes - Los Angeles, CA - *StaDirAdAg 2-84*
Brown, Koff & Fried Inc. - New York, NY - *IntDirMarRes 83*
Brown, Lewis S. - Kingston, NY - *BoPubDir 5*
Brown Ltd., Curtis - New York, NY - *LitMarPl 83, 84*
Brown Moon Music - Houston, TX - *BillIntBG 83-84*
Brown Mouse Publishing Co. - Houston, TX - *BoPubDir 4, 5; LitMag&SmPr 83-84*
Brown Newspapers Co. Inc. - Baldwinsville, NY - *BaconPubCkNews 84*
Brown-Olmstead Associates, A. - Atlanta, GA - *DirPRFirms 83; StaDirAdAg 2-84*
Brown Printing Central - Franklin, KY - *MagIndMarPl 82-83*
Brown Productions, Richard - New York, NY - *AvMarPl 83*
Brown Public Relations/Public Relations Services Inc., Cassidy - Gloucester, MA - *LitMarPl 84*
Brown Publishers, William C. - Dubuque, IA - *ArtMar 84; MicrocomMPl 84*
Brown Rabbit Press - Houston, TX - *BoPubDir 4, 5; LitMag&SmPr 83-84*
Brown, Reichelt & Co. - Los Angeles, CA - *CabTVFinDB 83*
Brown, Sanders & Associates Inc. - Noblesville, IN - *DataDirSup 7-83*
Brown Swiss Bulletin - Beloit, WI - *BaconPubCkMag 84; MagDir 84*
Brown Thompson Newspapers - Union City, PA - *BaconPubCkNews 84*
Brown University (Copper Beech Press) - Providence, RI - *BoPubDir 4, 5*
Brown University (Hellcoal Press) - Providence, RI - *BoPubDir 4, 5*
Browne Advertising, Burton - Chicago, IL - *StaDirAdAg 2-84*
Browne Book Composition Inc. - Lawrenceville, NJ - *LitMarPl 84*
Browne, Bortz & Coddington - Denver, CO - *CabTVFinDB 83; TeleSy&SerDir 2-84*
Browne, Freda - New York, NY - *LitMarPl 83*
Browne Ltd., Pema - New York, NY - *LitMarPl 83, 84; MagIndMarPl 82-83*
Browne Multimedia Product Development Inc., Jane Jordan - Chicago, IL - *LitMarPl 83, 84*
Browne, Patricia A. - Watertown, MA - *LitMarPl 84*
Browne Time Sharing Inc. - New York, NY - *DirInfWP 82*
Brownell & Staff - Detroit, MI - *DirPRFirms 83*
Brownfield Country Press - Brownfield, TX - *BaconPubCkNews 84*
Brownfield News - Brownfield, TX - *BaconPubCkNews 84; Ed&PubIntYB 82; NewsDir 84*
Browning Glacier Reporter - Browning, MT - *BaconPubCkNews 84*
Browning Publications [Aff. of Mark A. Browning Corp.] - Atlanta, GA - *BoPubDir 4, 5*
Brownrout Productions, Dean - Buffalo, NY - *BillIntBG 83-84*
Brown's Geological Information Service Ltd. - London, England - *EISS 83*
Brown's Guide to Georgia - College Park, GA - *MagIndMarPl 82-83*
Brown's Inc. - Jonesboro, IN - *Tel&CabFB 84C*
Browns TV Cable Service - Cohocton, NY - *BrCabYB 84; Tel&CabFB 84C*
Browns Valley News - Browns Valley, MN - *BaconPubCkNews 84*
Brownsberger, Susan C. - Watertown, MA - *LitMarPl 83, 84; MagIndMarPl 82-83*
Brownsburg Guide - *See* Mid State Newspapers Inc.
Brownstone Books - Madison, IN - *LitMag&SmPr 83-84*
Brownstone Press, The - Toronto, ON, Canada - *LitMarPl 83*
Brownstown Banner - Brownstown, IN - *BaconPubCkNews 84; Ed&PubIntYB 82; NewsDir 84*
Brownstown Cablevision [of V-R Corp.] - Brownstone, IL - *Tel&CabFB 84C*
Brownstown News-Herald - Wyandotte, MI - *AyerDirPub 83*
Brownsville Cable Co. - Brownsville, OR - *BrCabYB 84*
Brownsville Cable TV Co. [of Athena Communications Corp.] - Brownsville, TN - *Tel&CabFB 84C*
Brownsville Edmonson News - Brownsville, KY - *BaconPubCkNews 84*
Brownsville Herald [of Freedom Newspapers] - Brownsville, TX - *BaconPubCkNews 84; Ed&PubIntYB 82; NewsDir 84*
Brownsville States-Graphic [of Family Corp.] - Brownsville, TN - *BaconPubCkNews 84; NewsDir 84*
Brownsville Telegraph - Brownsville, PA - *BaconPubCkNews 84*
Brownsville Times - Brownsville, OR - *BaconPubCkNews 84*
Brownsville Times - Brownsville, TX - *BaconPubCkNews 84; Ed&PubIntYB 82; NewsDir 84*
Brownsville TV Cable Inc. - Brownsville, OR - *Tel&CabFB 84C*
Brownton Bulletin - Brownton, MN - *BaconPubCkNews 84; Ed&PubIntYB 82*
Brownwood Bulletin - Brownwood, TX - *BaconPubCkNews 84; Ed&PubIntYB 82; NewsDir 84*
Brownwood TV Cable Service - Brownwood, TX - *BrCabYB 84; Tel&CabFB 84C p.1667*
Brownwood TV Cable Service Inc. - Cross Plains, TX - *BrCabYB 84*
Brownwood TV Cable Service Inc. [of CATV Systems Inc.] - Electra, TX - *BrCabYB 84*
Brownwood TV Cable Service Inc. - Ft. Worth, TX - *BrCabYB 84 p.D-298*
Brownwood TV Cable Service Inc. - Rising Star, TX - *BrCabYB 84*
Broyles, Allebaugh & Davis - Englewood, CO - *AdAge 3-28-84; ArtMar 84; BrCabYB 84; StaDirAdAg 2-84*
Broyles/Garamella - Hollywood, CA - *StaDirAdAg 2-84*
Brozyna, Edward A. - Bloomsbury, NJ - *LitMarPl 84*
Brozyna, Edward A. - Jamesburg, NJ - *LitMarPl 83; MagIndMarPl 82-83*
BRS/After Dark [of Bibliographic Retrieval Service] - Latham, NY - *EISS 7-83 Sup; MicrocomMPl 84*
BRS Bibliographic Retrieval Services - Latham, NY - *DataDirSup 7-83; MicrocomSwDir 1*
BRS Bulletin - Latham, NY - *DirOnDB Spring 84*
BRS/File - Latham, NY - *DirOnDB Spring 84*
BRS Search Service [of Bibliographic Retrieval Services] - Latham, NY - *MicrocomMPl 84*
B'Ruach Hatorah Publications - Miami Beach, FL - *BoPubDir 4*
B'Ruach Hatorah Publications - Cincinnati, OH - *BoPubDir 5*
Brubaker, E. S. - Lancaster, PA - *BoPubDir 4 Sup, 5*
Bruccoli-Clark Publishers - Bloomfield Hills, MI - *LitMarPl 83*
Bruccoli-Clark Publishers - Columbia, SC - *LitMarPl 84*
Bruce & James Program Publishers Inc. - Dublin, OH - *MicrocomMPl 84; WhoWMicrocom 83*
Bruce Cable TV [of Scott & Krenz TV Systems] - Bruce, WI - *BrCabYB 84; Tel&CabFB 84C*
Bruce Calhoun County Journal - Bruce, MS - *BaconPubCkNews 84; NewsDir 84*
Bruce County Historical Society - Tiverton, ON, Canada - *BoPubDir 4, 5*
Bruce-Green Advertising Ltd. - Bloomington, IL - *StaDirAdAg 2-84*
Bruce, Lennart - Walnut Creek, CA - *LitMarPl 83, 84*
Bruce, Martin M. - Larchmont, NY - *BoPubDir 4*
Bruce Publishers Inc., Waldo [Aff. of Special People's Tours] - Dallas, TX - *BoPubDir 4, 5*

Bruce Publishers, Martin M. - Larchmont, NY - *BoPubDir 5*
Bruce Telephone Co. Inc. - Bruce, MS - *TelDir&BG 83-84*
Bruce Telephone Co. Inc. - Bruce, WI - *TelDir&BG 83-84*
Bruce Trail Association - Hamilton, ON, Canada - *BoPubDir 4, 5*
Bruce TV Cable - Pleasant Valley, NY - *Tel&CabFB 84C*
Bruin Music Corp. - *See* Famous Music Corp.
Brule County News - Kimball, SD - *AyerDirPub 83; Ed&PubIntYB 82*
Brum & Anderson Public Relations Inc. - Minneapolis, MN - *DirPRFirms 83*
Brumac Industries - Huntington Beach, CA - *AvMarPl 83*
Brumfield-Gallagher Inc. - Nashville, TN - *StaDirAdAg 2-84*
Brumley & Sons, Albert E. - Powell, MO - *BillIntBG 83-84*
Brumm, Gordon - Cambridge, MA - *LitMarPl 83, 84*
Brun Press Inc. - Miami, FL - *BoPubDir 4, 5*
Brundidge Banner - Brundidge, AL - *AyerDirPub 83; BaconPubCkNews 84; Ed&PubIntYB 82*
Brune Research - Vernon, NJ - *EISS 5-84 Sup*
Bruner, W. T. - Louisville, KY - *BoPubDir 4, 5*
Brungard, Jan - Haines City, FL - *WritMar 84*
Bruning - Itasca, IL - *DataDirSup 7-83*
Brunner/Mazel Inc. - New York, NY - *LitMarPl 83, 84*
Brunning Advertising & Marketing Ltd. - London, England - *StaDirAdAg 2-84*
Bruno & Ridgway Research Associates Inc. - Princeton, NJ - *IntDirMarRes 83*
Bruno Associates - Garden Grove, CA - *AvMarPl 83*
Bruno Inc., H. A. - Englewood Cliffs, NJ - *DirPRFirms 83*
Brunswich Record Corp. - New York, NY - *BillIntBG 83-84*
Brunswick Beacon - Shallotte, NC - *AyerDirPub 83; Ed&PubIntYB 82; NewsDir 84*
Brunswick Brunswicker - Brunswick, MO - *BaconPubCkNews 84*
Brunswick Cable Communications Associates [of Tele-Communications Inc.] - Brunswick, OH - *Tel&CabFB 84C*
Brunswick Cablevision [of Telecable Communications Corp.] - Baltimore, MD - *BrCabYB 84*
Brunswick, Cecile - New York, NY - *LitMarPl 83, 84*
Brunswick Church World, The - Brunswick, ME - *NewsDir 84*
Brunswick Citizen, The - Brunswick, MD - *Ed&PubIntYB 82*
Brunswick Historical Society - Cropseyville, NY - *BoPubDir 4, 5*
Brunswick Music Publishing Co. - Beverly Hills, CA - *BillIntBG 83-84*
Brunswick News - Brunswick, GA - *BaconPubCkNews 84; Ed&PubIntYB 82*
Brunswick Press - Fredericton, NB, Canada - *LitMarPl 83, 84*
Brunswick Publishing Co. - Lawrenceville, VA - *BoPubDir 4, 5; LitMarPl 84; WritMar 84*
Brunswick Sun Times - Brunswick, OH - *Ed&PubIntYB 82; NewsDir 84*
Brunswick Sun Times - Cleveland, OH - *AyerDirPub 83*
Brunswick Times-Gazette [of Byerly Publications Inc.] - Lawrenceville, VA - *AyerDirPub 83; Ed&PubIntYB 82; NewsDir 84*
Brunswicker, The - Brunswick, MO - *AyerDirPub 83; Ed&PubIntYB 82*
Brush Advertising Agency, Douglas - Berkeley Heights, NY - *StaDirAdAg 2-84*
Brush Associates Ltd., D. J. - Cold Spring, NY - *DirPRFirms 83*
Brush Cable TV [of Community Tele-Communications Inc.] - Brush, CO - *BrCabYB 84; Tel&CabFB 84C*
Brush Country - Brush, CO - *AyerDirPub 83*
Brush Country News-Tribune - Brush, CO - *BaconPubCkNews 84*
Brush, James B. - Punxsutawney, PA - *BrCabYB 84 p.D-298*
Brush, James B. - *See* Adelphia Communications Corp.
Brush News-Tribune, The - Brush, CO - *Ed&PubIntYB 82*
Brushware - Potomac, MD - *BaconPubCkMag 84; MagDir 84*
Bruskin Associates, R. H. - New Brunswick, NJ - *BrCabYB 84; IntDirMarRes 83; Tel&CabFB 84C*
Bruskin International - New Brunswick, NJ - *BrCabYB 84*
Brussels Post, The - Brussels, ON, Canada - *Ed&PubIntYB 82*
Bruster/Archer/Ball Advertising - San Francisco, CA - *StaDirAdAg 2-84*
Brut Music Publishing [Div. of Brut Productions Inc.] - New York, NY - *BillIntBG 83-84*
Bruzaud Associates - Lake Hopatcong, NJ - *MicrocomMPl 84*
Bruzi Enterprises - Toronto, ON, Canada - *BoPubDir 4, 5*
BRX Inc. - Rochester, NY - *IntDirMarRes 83*
Bryan-College Station Eagle - Bryan, TX - *AyerDirPub 83; BaconPubCkNews 84; Ed&PubIntYB 82; NewsDir 84*
Bryan Co., The R. L. - Columbia, SC - *LitMarPl 83, 84*
Bryan County Star - Caddo, OK - *Ed&PubIntYB 82*
Bryan/Donald Inc. - Kansas City, MO - *AdAge 3-28-84; StaDirAdAg 2-84*
Bryan Newspapers - Cullman, AL - *Ed&PubIntYB 82*
Bryan Times - Bryan, OH - *BaconPubCkNews 84; Ed&PubIntYB 82; NewsDir 84*
Bryans Books Inc., James A. - Fairfield, CT - *LitMarPl 84*
Bryans Books Inc., James A. - New York, NY - *LitMarPl 83*
Bryant Advertising & Marketing - Overland Park, KS - *ArtMar 84*
Bryant & Staff, George - Englewood, NJ - *LitMarPl 83, 84*
Bryant Cable TV Service - Big Island, VA - *BrCabYB 84; Tel&CabFB 84C*
Bryant Dakotan - Bryant, SD - *BaconPubCkNews 84*
Bryant Pond Telephone Co. [Aff. of Oxford County Telephone & Telegraph Co.] - Buckfield, ME - *TelDir&BG 83-84*
Bryce, Harvey S. [of Free Lance Photography & Research Services Ltd.] - San Bernardino, CA - *MagIndMarPl 82-83*
Bryles Survey Service Ltd. - Tinley Park, IL - *IntDirMarRes 83*
Bryn Mawr Press Inc. - Bryn Mawr, PA - *BoPubDir 4, 5*
Bryologist [of American Bryological & Lichenological Society Inc.] - Buffalo, NY - *MagDir 84*
Bryson City Smoky Mountain Times - Bryson City, NC - *BaconPubCkNews 84*
BSG Corp. - Minneapolis, MN - *MicrocomMPl 84*
BSI [of Questel Inc.] - Washington, DC - *DataDirOnSer 84*
BSI - Cape Girardeau, MO - *BrCabYB 84*
BSI/Business Science International Inc. - New York, NY - *IntDirMarRes 83*
BSO Records Inc. - Willow Grove, PA - *BillIntBG 83-84*
BSRIA Information Centre [of Building Services Research & Information Association] - Bracknell, England - *EISS 83*
B.T. Enterprises - Centereach, NY - *MicrocomMPl 83*
BTD Directory Management Inc. - Garden Grove, CA - *StaDirAdAg 2-84*
BTE Information Systems [of Bureau of Transport Economics] - Canberra, Australia - *EISS 5-84 Sup*
BTI - Dagenham, England - *LitMag&SmPr 83-84*
BTI Computer Systems - Sunnyvale, CA - *DataDirSup 7-83; DirInfWP 82*
BTJ - Lund, Sweden - *EISS 83*
Bubbl-Tec - Dublin, CA - *DataDirSup 7-83*
Buber Press, Martin - Brooklyn, NY - *BoPubDir 4, 5*
BUC Information Services [of BUC International Corp.] - Ft. Lauderdale, FL - *EISS 83; InfoS 83-84*
BUC International Corp. - Ft. Lauderdale, FL - *BoPubDir 4 Sup, 5; DataDirOnSer 84*
Bucfax [of BUC International Corp.] - Ft. Lauderdale, FL - *DataDirOnSer 84*
Buchan Industries - Clifton Heights, PA - *DirInfWP 82*
Buchan Pictures - Buffalo, NY - *AvMarPl 83*
Buchanan Advertising Agency, Jerry - San Diego, CA - *StaDirAdAg 2-84*
Buchanan Berrien County Record - Buchanan, MI - *BaconPubCkNews 84*
Buchanan County Farmer - Faucett, MO - *AyerDirPub 83*
Buchanan County Farmer - St. Joseph, MO - *Ed&PubIntYB 82*
Buchanan County Reminder - Independence, IA - *AyerDirPub 83*
Buchanan-Haralson County Tribune [of Carroll Publishing Co.] - Carrollton, GA - *NewsDir 84*
Buchanan-Haralson County Tribune - *See* Harte-Hanks Communications Inc.
Buchanan Lake Country Chronicle - Buchanan, MI - *BaconPubCkNews 84*
Buchanan, Vinson & Co. Inc. - San Diego, CA - *StaDirAdAg 2-84*
Buchheit Newspapers - Spartanburg, SC - *Ed&PubIntYB 82*
Buchwald, Ann - Washington, DC - *LitMarPl 83, 84*
Buck Agency, Howard - New York, NY - *LitMarPl 83, 84*
Buck & Berglund Inc. - Burlington, MA - *StaDirAdAg 2-84*
Buck-Harrison/Louis - Burlington, MA - *StaDirAdAg 2-84*
Buck Hill Associates - Johnsburg, NY - *BoPubDir 4, 5; DirMarMP 83*

Buck Hill Falls Co. [of Blue Ridge TV Cable Inc.] - Buck Hill Falls, PA - *BrCabYB 84; Tel&CabFB 84C*
Buck Hill TV Club Inc. - Guilford, VT - *BrCabYB 84; Tel&CabFB 84C*
Buck Inc., Norman W. - Deerfield, IL - *StaDirAdAg 2-84*
Buck Publishing Co. - Birmingham, AL - *BoPubDir 4, 5*
Buckeye - Archbold, OH - *AyerDirPub 83*
Buckeye Advertising - Columbus, OH - *StaDirAdAg 2-84*
Buckeye Cablevision [of Toledo Blade Co.] - Toledo, OH - *BrCabYB 84; CabTVFinDB 83; HomeVid&CabYB 82-83; Tel&CabFB 84C p.1667*
Buckeye Farm News - Columbus, OH - *BaconPubCkMag 84; MagDir 84; MagIndMarPl 82-83; WritMar 84*
Buckeye Music Inc. - *See* Carlson Music Co.
Buckeye Review - Youngstown, OH - *Ed&PubIntYB 82*
Buckeye Telephone & Supply Co. - Columbus, OH - *DataDirSup 7-83*
Buckeye Triune - Columbus, OH - *MagDir 84*
Buckeye Trucker - Indianapolis, IN - *MagDir 84*
Buckeye Valley News - Buckeye, AZ - *AyerDirPub 83; BaconPubCkNews 84; Ed&PubIntYB 82*
Buckhannon Record Delta [of Mountain Statesman Inc.] - Buckhannon, WV - *BaconPubCkNews 84; NewsDir 84*
Buckhead, Atlanta - Atlanta, GA - *MagDir 84*
Buckheim & Rowland - Ann Arbor, MI - *AdAge 3-28-84; StaDirAdAg 2-84*
Buckhorn Music Publishing Co. Inc. - Nashville, TN - *BillIntBG 83-84*
Buckingham Graphics Inc. - Chicago, IL - *LitMarPl 83*
Buckland Telephone Co. - Buckland, OH - *TelDir&BG 83-84*
Buckley Broadcasting Corp. - Greenwich, CT - *BrCabYB 84*
Buckley Dement Direct Mail Advertising - Chicago, IL - *LitMarPl 83, 84*
Buckley Newspapers Inc. - Bay Springs, MS - *BaconPubCkNews 84*
Buckley Publications Inc. - Chicago, IL - *BoPubDir 4, 5; LitMarPl 84*
Bucklin Banner - Bucklin, KS - *BaconPubCkNews 84; Ed&PubIntYB 82*
Bucklin Community TV - Bucklin, KS - *BrCabYB 84; Tel&CabFB 84C*
Bucknell On-Line Circulation System [of Bucknell University Library] - Lewisburg, PA - *EISS 83*
Bucknell Review - Lewisburg, PA - *LitMag&SmPr 83-84*
Bucknell University Press [Subs. of Associated University Presses] - Lewisburg, PA - *LitMarPl 83, 84; WritMar 84*
Bucknellian, The [of Bucknell University] - Lewisburg, PA - *NewsDir 84*
Buckner News Alliance - Seattle, WA - *Ed&PubIntYB 82*
Bucks County Advisor [of Inter County Publishing Co.] - Philadelphia, PA - *NewsDir 84*
Bucks County Cablevision - Warwick, PA - *BrCabYB 84*
Bucks County Courier Times - Levittown, PA - *AyerDirPub 83; BaconPubCkNews 84; Ed&PubIntYB 82*
Bucks County Historical Society - Doylestown, PA - *BoPubDir 4 Sup, 5*
Bucks County Telegraph - Horsham, PA - *AyerDirPub 83*
Bucks County Tribune - Feasterville, PA - *AyerDirPub 83; Ed&PubIntYB 82*
Bucks County Tribune [of Progress Newspapers Inc.] - Langhorne, PA - *NewsDir 84*
Bucks-Mont Courier - Harleysville, PA - *AyerDirPub 83*
Buckskin Press Inc. - Big Timber, MT - *BoPubDir 4 Sup, 5*
Bucksport Free Press - Bucksport, ME - *BaconPubCkNews 84; Ed&PubIntYB 82*
Buckstein & Associates Inc., Murray E. - Don Mills, ON, Canada - *StaDirAdAg 2-84*
Bucktail Broadcasting Corp. - Emporium, PA - *BrCabYB 84; Tel&CabFB 84C*
Buckwheat Street Publishers - New York, NY - *BoPubDir 4, 5*
Bucyrus-Erie Co. - South Milwaukee, WI - *BoPubDir 4, 5*
Bucyrus Telegraph-Forum [of Freedom Newspapers Inc.] - Bucyrus, OH - *BaconPubCkNews 84; NewsDir 84*
Bud Industries - Willoughby, OH - *AvMarPl 83*
Bud Information Systems [Div. of Tessco Inc.] - Timonium, MD - *DirInfWP 82*
Buda Onion Creek Free Press - Buda, TX - *BaconPubCkNews 84*
Budd Films, Billy - New York, NY - *AvMarPl 83*
Budd Music Corp. - Tarzana, CA - *BillIntBG 83-84*
Buddah Music Inc. - New York, NY - *BillIntBG 83-84*
Buddah Records Inc. - New York, NY - *BillIntBG 83-84*
Buddhist Books International [Aff. of Eikyoji Temple] - Beverly Hills, CA - *BoPubDir 4, 5*
Buddhist Study Center [Aff. of Honpa Hongwanji Mission of Hawaii] - Honolulu, HI - *BoPubDir 4 Sup, 5*
Buddhist Text Translation Society - San Francisco, CA - *BoPubDir 4, 5; LitMag&SmPr 83-84*
Buddy Books Paperback Book Club [of Xerox Education Publications] - Middletown, CT - *LitMarPl 83, 84*
Budek Films & Slides - Newport, RI - *ArtMar 84; AvMarPl 83*
Budge Carbon & Ribbons Ltd. - Montreal, PQ, Canada - *DirInfWP 82*
BudgeCo - Piedmont, CA - *MicrocomMPl 83, 84; WhoWMicrocom 83*
Budget - Douglas, WY - *AyerDirPub 83; Ed&PubIntYB 82*
Budget Book Manufacturing Co. - San Diego, CA - *LitMarPl 83*
Budget Computer Systems - San Diego, CA - *MicrocomSwDir 1*
Budget Publishing - Pineville, WV - *MagDir 84*
Budget, The - Sugarcreek, OH - *AyerDirPub 83; Ed&PubIntYB 82*
Budget Video Inc./Hollywood Home Theatre - Los Angeles, CA - *AvMarPl 83; BillIntBG 83-84*
Budgetrack - Washington, DC - *DirOnDB Spring 84*
Budgetrack [of Data Resources Inc.] - Lexington, MA - *DataDirOnSer 84*
Budlong Press Co. - Chicago, IL - *BoPubDir 5*
Budlong Press Co. - Evanston, IL - *BoPubDir 4*
Bud's Cable Service [of Bud's Electric Service Inc.] - Glen Richey, PA - *BrCabYB 84; Tel&CabFB 84C*
Buehrer Associates Inc., Richard - Phoenix, AZ - *LitMarPl 84*
Buehrer Associates Inc., Richard - Mineola, NY - *LitMarPl 83; MagIndMarPl 82-83*
Buena Park News - Buena Park, CA - *Ed&PubIntYB 82*
Buena Park News [of West Orange Publishing Co.] - Garden Grove, CA - *AyerDirPub 83; NewsDir 84*
Buena Park News - *See* West Orange Publishing Co.
Buena Vista Cable TV [of Buena Vista Telecommunications Inc.] - Los Angeles, CA - *BrCabYB 84*
Buena Vista Chaffee County Times - Buena Vista, CO - *BaconPubCkNews 84*
Buena Vista Channel - Los Angeles, CA - *BrCabYB 84*
Buena Vista County Journal - Newell, IA - *Ed&PubIntYB 82*
Buena Vista International Inc. [Subs. of Walt Disney Productions] - Burbank, CA - *TelAl 83, 84*
Buena Vista News & County Press - Buena Vista, VA - *BaconPubCkNews 84*
Buena Vista Patriot-Citizen - Buena Vista, GA - *Ed&PubIntYB 82*
Buena Vista Patriot-Citizen - *See* Tri-County Newspapers Inc.
Buena Vista Telecommunications Inc. - Colton, CA - *Tel&CabFB 84C p.1667*
Buenavision Cable TV - Colton, CA - *BrCabYB 84*
Buenavision Channel - Los Angeles, CA - *CabTVPrDB 83*
Buffalo & Erie County Historical Society - Buffalo, NY - *BoPubDir 4, 5; MicroMarPl 82-83*
Buffalo Bill Music - Hollywood, FL - *BillIntBG 83-84*
Buffalo Books - San Francisco, CA - *BoPubDir 4, 5*
Buffalo Bulletin - Buffalo, WY - *BaconPubCkNews 84; Ed&PubIntYB 82; NewsDir 84*
Buffalo Center Cable TV - Buffalo Center, IA - *BrCabYB 84*
Buffalo Center Tribune - Buffalo Center, IA - *BaconPubCkNews 84; Ed&PubIntYB 82*
Buffalo Challenger - Buffalo, NY - *AyerDirPub 83; BaconPubCkNews 84; Ed&PubIntYB 82; NewsDir 84*
Buffalo County Journal - Alma, WI - *AyerDirPub 83; BaconPubCkNews 84*
Buffalo Courier-Express - Buffalo, NY - *Ed&PubIntYB 82; NewsBur 6; NewsDir 84*
Buffalo Criterion - Buffalo, NY - *BaconPubCkNews 84; Ed&PubIntYB 82; NewsDir 84*
Buffalo Dallas County Courier - Buffalo, MO - *BaconPubCkNews 84*
Buffalo Evening News - Buffalo, NY - *BaconPubCkNews 84; Ed&PubIntYB 82; NewsBur 6*

Buffalo Fine Print News - Buffalo, NY - *BaconPubCkNews 84; Ed&PubIntYB 82; NewsDir 84*
Buffalo Grove Herald - *See* Paddock Publications
Buffalo Grove Topics - *See* Journal & Topics Newspapers
Buffalo Harper County Journal - Buffalo, OK - *BaconPubCkNews 84*
Buffalo Interconnect - West Seneca, NY - *CabTVPrDB 83*
Buffalo Lake News Mirro - Buffalo Lake, MN - *BaconPubCkNews 84*
Buffalo Lake News, The - Buffalo Lake, MN - *Ed&PubIntYB 82*
Buffalo Law Journal - Buffalo, NY - *NewsDir 84*
Buffalo Nation's Center News - Buffalo, SD - *BaconPubCkNews 84*
Buffalo News - Buffalo, NY - *Ed&PubIntYB 82; NewsDir 84*
Buffalo Philharmonic Orchestra Society Inc. (Women's Committee) - Buffalo, NY - *BoPubDir 5*
Buffalo Press - Buffalo, TX - *BaconPubCkNews 84; Ed&PubIntYB 82*
Buffalo Reflex - Buffalo, MO - *AyerDirPub 83; BaconPubCkNews 84; Ed&PubIntYB 82*
Buffalo River Review - Linden, TN - *AyerDirPub 83; Ed&PubIntYB 82*
Buffalo Riverside Review - Buffalo, NY - *BaconPubCkNews 84*
Buffalo Rocket - Buffalo, NY - *AyerDirPub 83*
Buffalo South News [of Front Page Inc.] - Lackawanna, NY - *NewsDir 84*
Buffalo South News - *See* Front Page Inc.
Buffalo Spree - Buffalo, NY - *BaconPubCkMag 84; MagDir 84; MagIndMarPl 82-83; WritMar 84*
Buffalo Televents Inc. - Buffalo, WY - *Tel&CabFB 84C*
Buffalo Tri City Register - *See* Riverton Register Publishing
Buffalo Valley Telephone Co. - Lewisburg, PA - *TelDir&BG 83-84*
Buffalo Volksfreund - Buffalo, NY - *NewsDir 84*
Buffalo Volksfreund - Hamburg, NY - *Ed&PubIntYB 82*
Buffalo West Side Times - Buffalo, NY - *BaconPubCkNews 84; NewsDir 84*
Buffalo Wright County Journal-Press - Buffalo, MN - *BaconPubCkNews 84; NewsDir 84*
Buffington & Associates, Thomas - Washington, DC - *StaDirAdAg 2-84*
Buford Television - Tyler, TX - *BrCabYB 84 p.D-298; Tel&CabFB 84S*
Bug Music - Hollywood, CA - *BillIntBG 83-84*
Bug Tar - San Jose, CA - *LitMag&SmPr 83-84*
Bug Tar Press - San Jose, CA - *LitMag&SmPr 83-84*
Buggs Island Telephone Cooperative - Bracey, VA - *TelDir&BG 83-84*
Bugle - Niles, IL - *AyerDirPub 83; Ed&PubIntYB 82*
Bugle - Langford, SD - *AyerDirPub 83*
Bugle Publications - Niles, IL - *BaconPubCkNews 84*
Bugle, The - Woodstock, NB, Canada - *AyerDirPub 83; Ed&PubIntYB 82*
Bugli Co. Inc., The - New York, NY - *StaDirAdAg 2-84*
Buhl Cable Co. - Richfield, ID - *BrCabYB 84*
Buhl Cable TV - Hazelton, ID - *BrCabYB 84; Tel&CabFB 84C*
Buhl Cable TV Co. - Buhl, ID - *Tel&CabFB 84C*
Buhl Cable TV Co. - Hagerman, ID - *BrCabYB 84; Tel&CabFB 84C*
Buhl Cable TV Co. - Richfield, ID - *Tel&CabFB 84C*
Buhl Cable TV Co. - Shoshone, ID - *BrCabYB 84; Tel&CabFB 84C*
Buhl Cable TV Co. - Buhl, WA - *BrCabYB 84*
Buhl Herald - Buhl, ID - *BaconPubCkNews 84; Ed&PubIntYB 82*
Buhl Industries Inc. - Hawthorne, NJ - *AvMarPl 83*
Buhl Optical - Pittsburgh, PA - *AvMarPl 83*
Buhl Publishing House - Deckerville, MI - *BaconPubCkNews 84*
Buhrman, Peter - Los Angeles, CA - *MagIndMarPl 82-83*
Buiar Associates Inc., Paul - New York, NY - *DirPRFirms 83*
Buie/Geller Music Inc. - *See* BGO Music Inc.
Buildcore Inc. - Willowdale, ON, Canada - *BoPubDir 4, 5*
Builder [of Hanley-Wood Inc.] - Washington, DC - *ArtMar 84; Folio 83; MagDir 84; MagIndMarPl 82-83; WritMar 84*
Builder & Contractor - Washington, DC - *BaconPubCkMag 84; MagDir 84*
Builder Architect-Contractor Engineer [of Info/Media Inc.] - Phoenix, AZ - *BaconPubCkMag 84; MagDir 84*
Builder Developer West [of BDA News Inc.] - Anaheim, CA - *MagDir 84*
Builder Insider [of WBK Publishing Inc.] - Dallas, TX - *BaconPubCkMag 84; MagDir 84; WritMar 84*
Builder, The - Remenburg, NY - *BaconPubCkMag 84*
Builder's & Contractor's Book Service [of Prentice-Hall Inc.] - Englewood, NJ - *LitMarPl 83, 84*
Builders Association News [of Builders Association of Ft. Worth & Tarrant County] - Ft. Worth, TX - *BaconPubCkMag 84; MagDir 84*
Builders of the Adytum Ltd. - Los Angeles, CA - *BoPubDir 4, 5*
Building & Realty Record - Philadelphia, PA - *MagDir 84*
Building Briefs [of Dan Burch Associates] - Louisville, KY - *ArtMar 84*
Building Center - Milan, Italy - *EISS 83*
Building Cost File Inc. - New York, NY - *BoPubDir 5*
Building Design & Construction [of Cahners Publishing Co.] - Des Plaines, IL - *BaconPubCkMag 84; MagDir 84*
Building Failures Forum - Ithaca, NY - *BaconPubCkMag 84*
Building Industry Digest of Hawaii [of Trade Publishing Co.] - Honolulu, HI - *BaconPubCkMag 84; MagDir 84*
Building Information Institute - Helsinki, Finland - *EISS 83*
Building News - Los Angeles, CA - *MagDir 84; MagIndMarPl 82-83*
Building Official & Code Administrator, The - Homewood, IL - *BaconPubCkMag 84; MagDir 84*
Building Operating Management [of Trade Press Publishing Co.] - Milwaukee, WI - *BaconPubCkMag 84; MagDir 84; MagIndMarPl 82-83*
Building Products Digest - Newport Beach, CA - *BaconPubCkMag 84*
Building Profit - Cincinnati, OH - *WritMar 84*
Building Progress [of Stamats Publishing Co.] - Cedar Rapids, IA - *MagDir 84*
Building Services Contractor [of MacNair-Dorland Co.] - New York, NY - *BaconPubCkMag 84; MagDir 84*
Building Standards [of International Conference of Building Officials] - Whittier, CA - *BaconPubCkMag 84; MagDir 84*
Building Stone Magazine - New York, NY - *BaconPubCkMag 84; MagDir 84*
Building Supply & Home Centers - Des Plaines, IL - *BaconPubCkMag 84*
Building Supply News [of Cahners Publishing Co.] - Des Plaines, IL - *Folio 83; MagDir 84*
Building Trades News - Baltimore, MD - *NewsDir 84*
Buildings [of Stamats Publishing Co.] - Cedar Rapids, IA - *BaconPubCkMag 84; MagDir 84*
Buildings Design Journal - Atlanta, GA - *BaconPubCkMag 84*
Buisson, Gilles - Lac aux Sables, PQ, Canada - *BrCabYB 84*
Bukstein, Roy - San Mateo, CA - *ADAPSOMemDir 83-84*
Bulan Cable TV Inc. [of Communications Corp. of America Inc.] - Bulan, KY - *Tel&CabFB 84C*
Bulford, Sally - Columbus, OH - *MagIndMarPl 82-83*
Bulk Shipping & Commodities - *DirOnDB Spring 84*
Bulkley Dunton Linde Lathrop - New York, NY - *LitMarPl 83, 84; MagIndMarPl 82-83*
Bull & Bear - Winter Park, FL - *BaconPubCkMag 84*
Bull, Donald A. - Trumbull, CT - *BoPubDir 4, 5*
Bull Mountain Bugle, The - Stuart, VA - *AyerDirPub 83; Ed&PubIntYB 82*
Bull Publishing Co. - Palo Alto, CA - *LitMag&SmPr 83-84; LitMarPl 83, 84*
Bull Shoals Lake River Times - Bull Shoals, AR - *BaconPubCkNews 84*
Bullard Telegraph - Bullard, TX - *Ed&PubIntYB 82*
Bulldog - San Francisco, CA - *BaconPubCkMag 84*
Bulldog Records Ltd. - New York, NY - *BillIntBG 83-84*
Buller Films Inc. - Henderson, NE - *AvMarPl 83*
Bullet Management - Harvard, MA - *BillIntBG 83-84*
Bulletin - Manteca, CA - *AyerDirPub 83*
Bulletin - Wilton, CT - *AyerDirPub 83*
Bulletin - Bowdon, GA - *AyerDirPub 83*
Bulletin - Chillicothe, IL - *AyerDirPub 83*
Bulletin - Anderson, IN - *AyerDirPub 83*
Bulletin - Denison, IA - *AyerDirPub 83*
Bulletin - New Brighton, MN - *AyerDirPub 83*

Bulletin - Breckenridge, MO - *AyerDirPub 83*
Bulletin - Elwood, NE - *AyerDirPub 83*
Bulletin - Floral Park, NY - *AyerDirPub 83*
Bulletin - Franklin Square, NY - *AyerDirPub 83*
Bulletin - Litchville, ND - *AyerDirPub 83*
Bulletin - Twinsburg, OH - *AyerDirPub 83*
Bulletin - Bixby, OK - *AyerDirPub 83*
Bulletin - Harrisburg, OR - *AyerDirPub 83*
Bulletin - Bethlehem, PA - *AyerDirPub 83*
Bulletin - Dillsburg, PA - *AyerDirPub 83*
Bulletin - Latrobe, PA - *AyerDirPub 83*
Bulletin [of The Providence Journal Co.] - Providence, RI - *AyerDirPub 83; Ed&PubIntYB 82; LitMarPl 84*
Bulletin - Bandera, TX - *AyerDirPub 83*
Bulletin - Brownwood, TX - *AyerDirPub 83*
Bulletin - Wink, TX - *AyerDirPub 83*
Bulletin - Tooele, UT - *AyerDirPub 83*
Bulletin - Martinsville, VA - *AyerDirPub 83; Ed&PubIntYB 82*
Bulletin - Baldwin, WI - *AyerDirPub 83*
Bulletin - Buffalo, WY - *AyerDirPub 83*
Bulletin - Brooks, AB, Canada - *AyerDirPub 83*
Bulletin - Dauphin, MB, Canada - *AyerDirPub 83*
Bulletin - Bridgewater, NS, Canada - *AyerDirPub 83; Ed&PubIntYB 82*
Bulletin - Ft. Frances, ON, Canada - *AyerDirPub 83*
Bulletin - Sioux Lookout, ON, Canada - *AyerDirPub 83*
Bulletin Board - Brick Town, NJ - *BaconPubCkMag 84*
Bulletin-Democrat - Bedford, VA - *AyerDirPub 83; Ed&PubIntYB 82*
Bulletin-Journal - Independence, IA - *AyerDirPub 83; Ed&PubIntYB 82*
Bulletin-Journal - Cape Girardeau, MO - *AyerDirPub 83; Ed&PubIntYB 82*
Bulletin Newspapers - New Brighton, MN - *BaconPubCkNews 84*
Bulletin of Art & History Publications - Social Circle, GA - *BoPubDir 4, 5*
Bulletin of Bibliography - Westport, CT - *MagDir 84*
Bulletin of Hispanic Studies [of Liverpool University Press] - Liverpool, England - *LitMag&SmPr 83-84*
Bulletin of the American Association of Petroleum Geologists [of Geo. Banta Co. Inc.] - Tulsa, OK - *MagDir 84*
Bulletin of the American Mathematical Society - Providence, RI - *MagDir 84*
Bulletin of the American Meteorological Society - Boston, MA - *MagIndMarPl 82-83*
Bulletin of the Atomic Scientists [of Educational Foundation for Nuclear Science] - Chicago, IL - *ArtMar 84; BaconPubCkMag 84; DirMarMP 83; MagDir 84; MagIndMarPl 82-83*
Bulletin of the Board of Celtic Studies [of University of Wales Press] - Cardiff, Wales - *LitMag&SmPr 83-84*
Bulletin of the California Water Pollution Control Association - Lafayette, CA - *BaconPubCkMag 84*
Bulletin of the Center for Children's Books, The [of The University of Chicago Press Journals] - Chicago, IL - *LitMarPl 83, 84*
Bulletin of the Cleveland Museum of Art, The - Cleveland, OH - *MagDir 84; MagIndMarPl 82-83*
Bulletin of the Detroit Institute of Arts (Publications Dept.) - Detroit, MI - *MagIndMarPl 82-83*
Bulletin of the Greater Omaha Medical Society - Omaha, NE - *MagDir 84*
Bulletin of the Hennepin County Medical Society - Minneapolis, MN - *MagDir 84*
Bulletin of the Medical Library Association - Chicago, IL - *MagDir 84; MagIndMarPl 82-83*
Bulletin of the New Jersey Motor Truck Association - East Brunswick, NJ - *BaconPubCkMag 84*
Bulletin of the New York Academy of Medicine - New York, NY - *BaconPubCkMag 84; MagDir 84*
Bulletin of the Pennsylvania School Boards Association - Harrisburg, PA - *MagDir 84*
Bulletin-Press - Sioux Rapids, IA - *AyerDirPub 83*
Bulletin Publishing Co. - Stoughton, MA - *BaconPubCkNews 84*
Bulletin, The - Diamond Bar, CA - *Ed&PubIntYB 82*
Bulletin, The - Ontario, CA - *AyerDirPub 83; Ed&PubIntYB 82*
Bulletin, The - Sarasota, FL - *AyerDirPub 83*
Bulletin, The - Butler, IN - *AyerDirPub 83*
Bulletin, The - New Orleans, LA - *MagDir 84*
Bulletin, The [of Lexington Minute-Man Publications] - Lexington, MA - *NewsDir 84*
Bulletin, The - Bend, OR - *Ed&PubIntYB 82*
Bulletin, The - Alta Loma, TX - *AyerDirPub 83*
Bulletin-Times - Bolivar, TN - *Ed&PubIntYB 82*
Bullfrog Ballades - *See* Folklore Music
Bullfrog Films Inc. - Oley, PA - *ArtMar 84; AvMarPl 83*
Bullhead City Mohave Valley News - Bullhead City, AZ - *BaconPubCkNews 84; NewsDir 84*
Bullitt County Communications Inc. - Shepherdsville, KY - *BrCabYB 84*
Bulloch & Haggart Advertising Inc. - Colorado Springs, CO - *AdAge 3-28-84; StaDirAdAg 2-84*
Bulloch Telephone Cooperative Inc. - Statesboro, GA - *TelDir&BG 83-84*
Bullseye - North Las Vegas, NV - *AyerDirPub 83*
Bullwhip Publishing Co. - *See* Father-Thunder Publishing Co.
Bulwer Lytton Chronicle, The [of High Orchard Press] - Dagenham, England - *LitMag&SmPr 83-84*
Bumblebee Software - Chicago, IL - *MicrocomMPl 84*
Bun Dance Entertainment Co., A - Los Angeles, CA - *BillIntBG 83-84*
Buna East Texas News - Buna, TX - *BaconPubCkNews 84*
Bunchez & Associates Inc., Gert - St. Louis, MO - *WritMar 84*
Bundesanstalt fur Materialprufung - Berlin, West Germany - *InfIndMarPl 83*
Bundesanstalt fur Strassenwesen - Cologne, West Germany - *InfIndMarPl 83*
Bundesforschungsanstalt fur Fischerei, Information & Documentation [of Bundesministerium fur Ernahrung, Landwirtschaft, & Forsten] - Hamburg, West Germany - *InfIndMarPl 83*
Bundesinstitut fur Sportwissenschaft - Cologne, West Germany - *InfIndMarPl 83*
Bundesministerium der Justiz - Bonn, West Germany - *InfIndMarPl 83*
Bundesstelle fur Aussenhandelsinformation - Cologne, West Germany - *InfIndMarPl 83*
Bundestag (Abeilung Wissenschaftliche Dokumentation) - *See* Deutscher Bundestag (Abteilung Wissenschaftliche Dokumentation)
Bundestag (Abteilung Wissenschaftliche Dokumentation) - Bonn, West Germany - *CompReadDB 82*
Bundestelle fur Aussenhandelsinformation - Cologne, West Germany - *CompReadDB 82*
Bunker Hill Gazette-News - Bunker Hill, IL - *BaconPubCkNews 84*
Bunker Ramo Corp. - Oak Brook, IL - *DirInfWP 82*
Bunker Ramo Information Systems [Subs. of Allied Information Systems] - Trumbull, CT - *DataDirOnSer 84; DataDirSup 7-83; InfIndMarPl 83*
Bunkie Cablevision Inc. [of Communications Services Inc.] - Bunkie, LA - *BrCabYB 84; Tel&CabFB 84C*
Bunkie Record - Bunkie, LA - *BaconPubCkNews 84; Ed&PubIntYB 82*
Bunnell Flagler Palm Coast News Tribune - Bunnell, FL - *BaconPubCkNews 84*
Bunny & the Crocodile Press - Ft. Washington, MD - *BoPubDir 4, 5*
Buntin Advertising Inc. - Nashville, TN - *ArtMar 84; StaDirAdAg 2-84*
Bunting & Gable Inc. - Lancaster, PA - *StaDirAdAg 2-84*
Bunting & Lyon Inc. - Wallingford, CT - *BoPubDir 4, 5*
Bunyan Network, Paul - Traverse City, MI - *BrCabYB 84*
Bunyan Rural Telephone Cooperative, Paul - Bemidji, MN - *TelDir&BG 83-84*
Buranelli, Nan - Lawrenceville, NJ - *LitMarPl 83, 84; MagIndMarPl 82-83*
Buranelli, Nan & Vincent - Lawrenceville, NJ - *LitMarPl 83, 84; MagIndMarPl 82-83*
Burbach Broadcasting Co. - Erie, PA - *BrCabYB 84*
Burbank Argus - *See* Tribune Newspapers Inc.
Burbank Daily Review [of Ingersoll Publications] - Burbank, CA - *BaconPubCkNews 84; NewsDir 84*
Burbank Daily Review - Glendale, CA - *Ed&PubIntYB 82*

Burbank Scene [of Tujunga American Publishing Co.] - Tujunga, CA - *AyerDirPub 83; NewsDir 84*
Burbank Scene, The - Burbank, CA - *Ed&PublntYB 82*
Burbank-Stickney Independent [of Southwest Messenger Newspapers] - Midlothian, IL - *AyerDirPub 83; NewsDir 84*
Burbank-Stickney Independent - *See* Southwest Messenger Newspapers
Burbank-Western Walla Walla County Argus - Clarkston, WA - *AyerDirPub 83*
Burch & Worthley Inc. - Burlington, VT - *StaDirAdAg 2-84*
Burch Myers Cuttie - Chicago, IL - *AdAge 3-28-84; HBIndAd&MS 82-83; StaDirAdAg 2-84*
Burcon Inc. - Houston, TX - *MicrocomMPl 83, 84*
Burden Cowley County Reporter - Burden, KS - *BaconPubCkNews 84*
Burden Songs - *See* Hannan-Phillips Music
Burdett Community Development Corp. - Burdett, KS - *BrCabYB 84; Tel&CabFB 84C*
Burdette Advertising - Ft. Myers, FL - *AdAge 3-28-84; StaDirAdAg 2-84*
Burdette Music Co. - Seattle, WA - *BillIntBG 83-84*
Burdick Inc., R. E. - Fair Lawn, NJ - *BoPubDir 4, 5*
Bureau County Cablevision - Chicago, IL - *BrCabYB 84*
Bureau County Cablevision - Ladd, IL - *Tel&CabFB 84C p.1668*
Bureau County Record - Princeton, IL - *Ed&PublntYB 82*
Bureau County Republican - Princeton, IL - *AyerDirPub 83; Ed&PublntYB 82; NewsDir 84*
Bureau de Recherche pour l'Innovation & la Convergence - *See* Transinove International
Bureau de Recherches Geologiques et Minieres - Orleans, France - *CompReadDB 82; InfIndMarPl 83*
Bureau d'Information BIAM - Paris, France - *InfIndMarPl 83*
Bureau d'Informations & de Previsions Economiques - Neuilly-sur-Seine, France - *InfIndMarPl 83*
Bureau Marcel van Dijk SA - Brussels, Belgium - *EISS 83; InfIndMarPl 83*
Bureau Marcel van Dijk SARL - Paris, France - *InfIndMarPl 83*
Bureau National des Donnees Oceaniques [of Centre Oceanologique de Bretagne] - Brest, France - *InfIndMarPl 83*
Bureau of Broadcast Measurement [of Interactive Market Systems Inc.] - New York, NY - *DataDirOnSer 84*
Bureau of Business & Economic Research [of University of New Mexico] - Albuquerque, NM - *EISS 83; FBInfSer 80; InfIndMarPl 83*
Bureau of Business & Public Research [of University of Northern Colorado] - Greeley, CO - *EISS 83*
Bureau of Economic Analysis [of U.S. Dept. of Commerce] - Washington, DC - *EISS 83*
Bureau of Economic & Behavioral Research [Aff. of American Dental Association] - Chicago, IL - *BoPubDir 4, 5*
Bureau of Economic & Business Research [of University of Florida] - Gainesville, FL - *EISS 7-83 Sup*
Bureau of Economic & Business Research [of University of Utah] - Salt Lake City, UT - *EISS 83*
Bureau of Health & Hospital Careers Counseling - Scarsdale, NY - *BoPubDir 4, 5*
Bureau of International Affairs - Pasadena, CA - *BoPubDir 4 Sup, 5*
Bureau of Justice Statistics [Aff. of U.S. Dept. of Justice] - Washington, DC - *BoPubDir 4, 5*
Bureau of Labor Statistics [of U.S. Dept. of Labor] - Washington, DC - *EISS 83*
Bureau of Law & Business Inc. - Stamford, CT - *LitMarPl 84*
Bureau of Municipal Research - Toronto, ON, Canada - *BoPubDir 4 Sup, 5*
Bureau of National Affairs Inc. - Washington, DC - *CompReadDB 82; DataDirOnSer 84; DirMarMP 83; InfoS 83-84; KnowInd 83*
Bureau of Public Secrets - Berkeley, CA - *BoPubDir 4, 5*
Bureau of Statistics [of International Labour Office] - Geneva, Switzerland - *EISS 83*
Bureau of Statistics, Research & Planning [of Pennsylvania State Dept. of Commerce] - Harrisburg, PA - *EISS 7-83 Sup*
Bureau of Transport Economics [of Dept. of Transport & Construction] - Canberra, Australia - *InfIndMarPl 83*
Bureau of Wholesale Sales Representatives - Atlanta, GA - *MagDir 84*
Bureau of Wholesale Sales Representatives News - Atlanta, GA - *BaconPubCkMag 84*
Bureau Valley Chief - Tiskilwa, IL - *Ed&PublntYB 82*
Bureaufax [of Eastern Telecommunications Philippines Inc.] - Manila, Philippines - *TeleSy&SerDir 7-83*
Burelle's Press Clipping Service - Livingston, NJ - *LitMarPl 83*
Buresch, Joe E. - Sarasota, FL - *Ed&PublntYB 82*
Burgaw Pender Chronicle - Burgaw, NC - *BaconPubCkNews 84*
Burgaw Pender Post - Burgaw, NC - *BaconPubCkNews 84*
Burger Associates Ltd., Knox - New York, NY - *LitMarPl 83, 84*
Burger, Felix & Wood Inc. - San Francisco, CA - *StaDirAdAg 2-84*
Burger, Joanne - Lake Jackson, TX - *BoPubDir 4, 5*
Burgess Advertising Agency, Don L. - San Francisco, CA - *StaDirAdAg 2-84*
Burgess Inc., Jack K. - Ft. Lee, NJ - *LitMarPl 83, 84*
Burgess Publishing Co. - Minneapolis, MN - *DirMarMP 83; LitMarPl 83, 84*
Burgettstown Enterprise - Burgettstown, PA - *BaconPubCkNews 84; Ed&PublntYB 82*
Burgi International Inc. - New York, NY - *IntDirMarRes 83*
Burgoyne Inc. - Cincinnati, OH - *IntDirMarRes 83*
Burgundy Press - Southampton, PA - *BoPubDir 4, 5*
Burien Highline Times - Seattle, WA - *NewsDir 84*
Burien Highline Times - *See* Robinson Communications Co.
Burin Post, The - Marystown, NF, Canada - *Ed&PublntYB 82*
Burkburnett Informer Star - Burkburnett, TX - *BaconPubCkNews 84*
Burke Advertising Inc., R. J. - Dallas, TX - *StaDirAdAg 2-84*
Burke Broadcasting Co. - Longview, TX - *BrCabYB 84*
Burke County Tribune - Bowbells, ND - *AyerDirPub 83; Ed&PublntYB 82*
Burke Dowling Adams Inc. - Atlanta, GA - *BrCabYB 84*
Burke Employment Agency Inc., Theresa M. - New York, NY - *InfIndMarPl 83; LitMarPl 83, 84*
Burke Gazette - Burke, SD - *BaconPubCkNews 84; Ed&PublntYB 82*
Burke Herald [of Springfield Independent] - Springfield, VA - *AyerDirPub 83; NewsDir 84*
Burke Inc., Thomas E. - Jacksonville, FL - *DirPRFirms 83*
Burke International Research Inc. of New York - New York, NY - *IntDirMarRes 83*
Burke Marketing Research - Cincinnati, OH - *HBIndAd&MS 82-83; IntDirMarRes 83*
Burke Marketing Services - Cincinnati, OH - *AdAge 5-17-84 p.24*
Burke Publishing Ltd. - Ajax, ON, Canada - *BoPubDir 4, 5*
Burke, Shirley - New York, NY - *LitMarPl 83, 84*
Burke TV System - Burke, ID - *Tel&CabFB 84C*
Burke Word Processing Centre Inc., Heather - Toronto, ON, Canada - *DirInfWP 82*
Burke's Audio-Visual Center Inc. - South Bend, IN - *AvMarPl 83*
Burke's Book Store Inc. - Memphis, TN - *BoPubDir 4 Sup, 5*
Burkes Garden Telephone Co. - Burkes Garden, VA - *TelDir&BG 83-84*
Burkesville Cumberland County News - Burkesville, KY - *BaconPubCkNews 84*
Burkett School Supply Co. [Div. of Burkett Inc.] - Huntsville, AL - *AvMarPl 83*
Burkhaven Press - Contoocook, NH - *BoPubDir 4, 5*
Burlen & Son Inc., Robert - Hingham, MA - *LitMarPl 83, 84*
Burleson County Citizen Tribune - Caldwell, TX - *AyerDirPub 83; Ed&PublntYB 82*
Burleson County Publishing Co. Inc. - Caldwell, TX - *BaconPubCkNews 84*
Burleson Dispatcher - Burleson, TX - *BaconPubCkNews 84; Ed&PublntYB 82*
Burleson Star - Burleson, TX - *BaconPubCkNews 84; Ed&PublntYB 82; NewsDir 84*
Burley Ltd., J. H. - Toronto, ON, Canada - *StaDirAdAg 2-84*
Burley South Idaho Press [of South Idaho Newspapers Inc.] - Burley, ID - *NewsDir 84*
Burlingame Boutique & Villager - Burlingame, CA - *BaconPubCkNews 84*
Burlingame Enterprise-Chronicle - Burlingame, KS - *Ed&PublntYB 82*
Burlingame/Grossman Inc. - Chicago, IL - *StaDirAdAg 2-84; TelAl 83, 84*

Burlingame Leader - Millbrae, CA - *AyerDirPub 83; NewsDir 84*
Burlingame Osage County Chronicle - Burlingame, KS - *BaconPubCkNews 84*
Burlingame Recorder-Progress - *See* San Mateo Times Group Newspapers
Burlington Boone County Recorder - *See* Recorder Newspapers
Burlington, Brighton & Wheatland Telephone Co. [Aff. of Telephone & Data Systems Inc.] - Burlington, WI - *TelDir&BG 83-84*
Burlington Cable TV - Burlington, ND - *BrCabYB 84*
Burlington Cablenet - Burlington, ON, Canada - *BrCabYB 84*
Burlington CATV [of Heritage Communications Inc.] - Burlington, IA - *BrCabYB 84*
Burlington City-County Newspaper - Burlington, NC - *BaconPubCkNews 84*
Burlington Coffey County Today - Burlington, KS - *BaconPubCkNews 84*
Burlington County College - Pemberton, NJ - *InterCabHB 3*
Burlington County Herald - Mt. Holly, NJ - *AyerDirPub 83*
Burlington County News Weekly - Riverton, NJ - *AyerDirPub 83; NewsDir 84*
Burlington County Times [of Calkins Newspapers Inc.] - Willingboro, NJ - *AyerDirPub 83; BaconPubCkNews 84; Ed&PubIntYB 82; NewsDir 84*
Burlington County Times-Advertiser - Pemberton, NJ - *AyerDirPub 83*
Burlington Daily Times-News - Burlington, NC - *NewsDir 84*
Burlington Free Press [of Gannett Co. Inc.] - Burlington, VT - *AyerDirPub 83; BaconPubCkNews 84; Ed&PubIntYB 82; LitMarPl 83, 84; NewsBur 6; NewsDir 84*
Burlington Gazette - Burlington, ON, Canada - *AyerDirPub 83; Ed&PubIntYB 82*
Burlington Hawk Eye - Burlington, IA - *NewsDir 84*
Burlington Look, The [of Burlington Industries] - Greensboro, NC - *ArtMar 84*
Burlington Music Corp. - New York, NY - *BillIntBG 83-84*
Burlington News - Burlington, MA - *AyerDirPub 83; BaconPubCkNews 84; NewsDir 84*
Burlington Record - Burlington, CO - *BaconPubCkNews 84; Ed&PubIntYB 82*
Burlington Social Planning Council - Burlington, ON, Canada - *BoPubDir 4, 5*
Burlington Standard Press - Burlington, WI - *Ed&PubIntYB 82; NewsDir 84*
Burlington Standard Press - *See* Zimmermann & Sons Inc.
Burlington Times-News - Burlington, NC - *BaconPubCkNews 84*
Burlington Times-Union - Acton, MA - *AyerDirPub 83*
Burlington Times-Union [of Minute-Man Publications Inc.] - Burlington, MA - *Ed&PubIntYB 82; NewsDir 84*
Burlington Times-Union - *See* Minute-Man Publications Inc.
Burlington TV Cable System [of Dorate Interstate Inc.] - Burlington, CO - *BrCabYB 84; Tel&CabFB 84C*
Burmar Technical Corp. - Carle Place, NY - *LitMarPl 83, 84*
Burn Books - San Rafael, CA - *BoPubDir 5*
Burnaby Historical Society - Burnaby, BC, Canada - *BoPubDir 4 Sup, 5*
Burnaby Today - Burnaby, BC, Canada - *Ed&PubIntYB 82*
Burnap Inc., David K. - Dayton, OH - *StaDirAdAg 2-84*
Burnet Bulletin - Burnet, TX - *BaconPubCkNews 84; Ed&PubIntYB 82*
Burnet County Bulletin - Burnet, TX - *AyerDirPub 83; NewsDir 84*
Burnett Advertising Inc., John G. - Dallas, TX - *StaDirAdAg 2-84*
Burnett Co. Inc., Leo - Chicago, IL - *AdAge 3-28-84, 6-25-84; Br 1-23-84; BrCabYB 84; HomeVid&CabYB 82-83; StaDirAdAg 2-84; TelAl 83, 84*
Burnett Consultants Inc., Ed - New York, NY - *EISS 83; IntDirMarRes 83; LitMarPl 83, 84; MagIndMarPl 82-83*
Burnett County Sentinel - Grantsburg, WI - *AyerDirPub 83; Ed&PubIntYB 82*
Burney Falls Cablevision Inc. [of CDA Cable Inc.] - Burney, CA - *BrCabYB 84; Tel&CabFB 84C*
Burney Intermountain News - Burney, CA - *BaconPubCkNews 84; NewsDir 84*
Burning Bush Publications - Kemblesville, PA - *BoPubDir 4*
Burning Bush Publications - Norristown, PA - *LitMag&SmPr 83-84*
Burning Deck Press [Aff. of Anyart] - Providence, RI - *BoPubDir 4, 5; LitMag&SmPr 83-84*
Burning Spear Publications - Oakland, CA - *LitMag&SmPr 83-84*
Burning Spear, The - Oakland, CA - *LitMag&SmPr 83-84*
Burns Associates, Charles - Southampton, PA - *WhoWMicrocom 83*
Burns Group Inc. - Minneapolis, MN - *StaDirAdAg 2-84*
Burns/Hines TV Inc. - Burns, OR - *BrCabYB 84; Tel&CabFB 84C*
Burns, J. B. - La Crescenta, CA - *BoPubDir 4, 5*
Burns Media Productions, J. H. - Amherst, NY - *AvMarPl 83*
Burns Times-Herald - Burns, OR - *BaconPubCkNews 84; Ed&PubIntYB 82*
Burnside CATV Corp. - Pulaski County, KY - *BrCabYB 84*
Burnsville Current, The - Burnsville, MN - *Ed&PubIntYB 82*
Burnsville Sun - Burnsville, MN - *Ed&PubIntYB 82*
Burnsville Sun - Edina, MN - *AyerDirPub 83*
Burnsville Yancey Journal - Burnsville, NC - *BaconPubCkNews 84; NewsDir 84*
Burnup & Sims Inc. - Ft. Lauderdale, FL - *HomeVid&CabYB 82-83*
Burnup & Sims Inc. - Plantation, FL - *CabTVFinDB 83*
Buros Institute of Mental Measurements [of University of Nebraska] - Lincoln, NE - *DataDirOnSer 84*
Burr & Co., Ronald E. - Bloomington, IN - *LitMarPl 83, 84; MagIndMarPl 82-83; StaDirAdAg 2-84*
Burr-Brown Industrial Systems Products - Tucson, AZ - *WhoWMicrocom 83*
Burr Publications Ltd. [Aff. of The Aaron Burr Association] - Hightstown, NJ - *BoPubDir 4, 5*
Burr Ridge Doings - Burr Ridge, IL - *AyerDirPub 83; Ed&PubIntYB 82*
Burr Ridge Doings - *See* Doings Newspapers, The
Burr Ridge Suburban Life Graphic - *See* Life Printing & Publishing Co.
Burrell Advertising - Chicago, IL - *AdAge 3-28-84; StaDirAdAg 2-84*
Burrell, Fred - New York, NY - *LitMarPl 83, 84*
Burrelle's Press Clipping Service - Livingston, NJ - *LitMarPl 84; ProGuPRSer 4*
Burrent Current - Burnsville, MN - *AyerDirPub 83*
Burrill-Ellsworth Associates Inc. - Tenafly, NJ - *BoPubDir 4 Sup, 5*
Burro, Erik L. (Marketing & Communications Group) - Willingboro, NJ - *ArtMar 84*
Burroughs Clearing House [of Burroughs Corp.] - Detroit, MI - *MagDir 84*
Burroughs Corp. - Danbury, CT - *DirInfWP 82*
Burroughs Corp. - Detroit, MI - *ADAPSOMemDir 83-84; DataDirSup 7-83; Datamation 6-83; ElecNews 7-25-83; Top100Al 83; WhoWMicrocom 83*
Burroughs Corp. (Terminal Systems Group) - Detroit, MI - *InfIndMarPl 83*
Burroughs Imaging Systems Div. [of Burroughs Corp.] - Danbury, CT - *DataDirSup 7-83*
Burroughs, M. C. - Lewiston, ID - *BoPubDir 4, 5*
Burroughs Micro World - Austin, TX - *BaconPubCkMag 84*
Burroughs New York City Data Center - New York, NY - *DataDirOnSer 84*
Burroughs Processing Services - New York, NY - *DataDirOnSer 84*
Burroughs World - Austin, TX - *BaconPubCkMag 84*
Burrows Institute Inc., Alvina Treut - Manhasset, NY - *MicroMarPl 82-83*
Burrows Systems - Queens Village, NY - *MicroMarPl 82-83*
Burrows Systems (Microfiche Publications) - Queens Village, NY - *MagIndMarPl 82-83*
Burrton Graphic - Burrton, KS - *BaconPubCkNews 84; Ed&PubIntYB 82*
Burrton Graphic - Halstead, KS - *AyerDirPub 83*
Burrud Productions, Bill - Los Angeles, CA - *Tel&CabFB 84C*
Burson-Marsteller [Subs. of Young & Rubicam Inc.] - New York, NY - *DirPRFirms 83*
Burst/Gosa Productions Inc. - Atlanta, GA - *AvMarPl 83*

Burt County Plaindealer - Tekamah, NE - *AyerDirPub 83; Ed&PubIntYB 82*
Burt Telephone Co., The - Burt, IA - *TelDir&BG 83-84*
Burtoff Syndicated Features, Barbara - Washington, DC - *Ed&PubIntYB 82*
Burton Advertising - Detroit, MI - *AdAge 3-28-84; ArtMar 84; StaDirAdAg 2-84*
Burton & Associates Inc., Jon R. - Bensenville, IL - *StaDirAdAg 2-84*
Burton Antenna Co. Inc. - Melvin, KY - *BrCabYB 84*
Burton-Campbell - Atlanta, GA - *AdAge 3-28-84; StaDirAdAg 2-84*
Burton Computer Corp. - Columbia, SC - *WhoWMicrocom 83*
Burton Gallery - Nevada City, CA - *BoPubDir 4*
Burton Gallery [Aff. of Turn the Page Press] - Roseville, CA - *BoPubDir 5*
Burton-Miles Advertising Inc. - New York, NY - *StaDirAdAg 2-84*
Burwell Cable TV [of Mid State Community TV Ltd.] - Burwell, NE - *BrCabYB 84*
Burwell Cable TV Inc. - Imperial, NE - *BrCabYB 84 p.D-298*
Burwell Newspapers - Burwell, NE - *BaconPubCkNews 84*
Burwell Tribune - Burwell, NE - *Ed&PubIntYB 82*
Burwell Tribune - *See* Burwell Newspapers
Burwood Journal [of Survival News Service] - Los Angeles, CA - *LitMag&SmPr 83-84*
Buryn Publications, Ed - San Francisco, CA - *BoPubDir 4 Sup, 5*
Bus & Truck Transport - Toronto, ON, Canada - *BaconPubCkMag 84*
Bus Ride - Spokane, WA - *BaconPubCkMag 84; MagDir 84; WritMar 84*
Bus Tours - Delavan, WI - *BaconPubCkMag 84; WritMar 84*
Bus World - Woodland Hills, CA - *WritMar 84*
Busch Advertising, Addison - Buffalo, NY - *StaDirAdAg 2-84*
Busch & Associates - San Diego, CA - *StaDirAdAg 2-84*
Busch & Associates - Troy, MI - *HBIndAd&MS 82-83*
Busche Photography, Bill - Ventura, CA - *LitMarPl 83*
Buschman & Associates, David R. - Cleveland, OH - *DirPRFirms 83; StaDirAdAg 2-84*
Buscom Systems Inc. - Santa Clara, CA - *DataDirSup 7-83*
Buser & Associates, Joe - Bryan, TX - *StaDirAdAg 2-84*
Bush & Associates, Lloyd - New York, NY - *ADAPSOMemDir 83-84; EISS 83; InfIndMarPl 83*
Bushnell Communications Ltd. - Ottawa, ON, Canada - *BrCabYB 84; Tel&CabFB 84C*
Bushnell McDonough-Democrat - Bushnell, IL - *BaconPubCkNews 84*
Bushnell Ribbon Corp. - Santa Fe Springs, CA - *DirInfWP 82*
Bushnell Sumter County Times [of Landmark Community Newspapers] - Bushnell, FL - *NewsDir 84*
Bushnell Sumter County Times - *See* Citrus Publishing Inc.
Busi-Math Corp. - Ripon, WI - *MicrocomMPl 84*
Business - Heidelberg, West Germany - *DirOnDB Spring 84*
Business Advertising Specialists Inc. - Austin, TX - *StaDirAdAg 2-84*
Business America [of U.S. Dept. of Commerce] - Washington, DC - *BaconPubCkMag 84; MagDir 84*
Business & Acquisition Newsletter - Houston, TX - *BaconPubCkMag 84*
Business & Commercial Aviation [of Ziff-Davis Publishing Co.] - White Plains, NY - *ArtMar 84; BaconPubCkMag 84; Folio 83; MagDir 84*
Business & Health - Washington, DC - *BaconPubCkMag 84*
Business & Industrial Music Services Inc. - El Paso, TX - *Tel&CabFB 84C*
Business & Industry [of Business Magazines Inc.] - Des Moines, IA - *BaconPubCkMag 84; MagDir 84*
Business & Professional Books Inc. - San Jose, CA - *BoPubDir 5*
Business & Professional List Inc. - New York, NY - *MagIndMarPl 82-83*
Business & Professional Software - Cambridge, MA - *MicrocomMPl 83; MicrocomSwDir 1; WhoWMicrocom 83*
Business & Professional Women's Foundation - Washington, DC - *BoPubDir 4 Sup, 5*
Business & Public Administration Reseach Center [of University of Missouri, Columbia] - Columbia, MO - *EISS 83*
Business & Society Review - New York, NY - *BaconPubCkMag 84; MagDir 84*
Business Application Software [Subs. of ELP Development Co. Inc.] - Los Gatos, CA - *MicrocomMPl 84; MicrocomSwDir 1; WhoWMicrocom 83*
Business Application Systems Inc. - Raleigh, NC - *DirInfWP 82*
Business Applications Group - San Diego, CA - *ADAPSOMemDir 83-84; DataDirOnSer 84*
Business Applications Systems Inc. - Oaklanden, IN - *MicrocomMPl 84*
Business Atlanta - Atlanta, GA - *BaconPubCkMag 84*
Business Books Ltd. [Aff. of Renouf/USA Inc.] - Brookfield, VT - *BoPubDir 4 Sup, 5*
Business Communications Co. Inc. - Stamford, CT - *BoPubDir 4, 5*
Business Communications Review - Hinsdale, IL - *BaconPubCkMag 84*
Business Computer [of NewsNet Inc.] - Bryn Mawr, PA - *DataDirOnSer 84*
Business Computer Center - Haverhill, MA - *MicrocomMPl 84*
Business Computer Consultant - Birmingham, MI - *MicrocomMPl 84*
Business Computer Network - San Antonio, TX - *MicrocomMPl 84*
Business Computer Network [of AMP Inc.] - Basin, WY - *TeleSy&SerDir 7-83*
Business Computer Network [of AMP Inc.] - Riverton, WY - *EISS 5-84 Sup; TeleSy&SerDir 2-84*
Business Computer Services Co. - Overland Park, KS - *MicrocomMPl 83; WhoWMicrocom 83*
Business Computer Solutions - Kansas City, MS - *MicrocomMPl 84*
Business Computer Systems [of Cahners Publishing Co.] - Boston, MA - *BaconPubCkMag 84; MicrocomMPl 84*
Business Computer Systems - Bethany, OK - *MicrocomMPl 84; MicrocomSwDir 1*
Business Computer Systems Corp. - Sinking Spring, PA - *DataDirSup 7-83*
Business Computer, The - Madison, WI - *DirOnDB Spring 84*
Business Computers Systems PLC - Borehamwood, England - *InfIndMarPl 83*
Business Computing Consultants - Birmingham, MI - *MicrocomMPl 83*
Business Conditions Digest [of U.S. Dept. of Commerce] - Washington, DC - *DBBus 82; DirOnDB Spring 84*
Business Conditions Digest [of ADP Network Services Inc.] - Ann Arbor, MI - *DataDirOnSer 84*
Business Controls Corp. - Elmwood Park, NJ - *DataDirSup 7-83*
Business Credit Services [of TRW Inc.] - Orange, CA - *DBBus 82; DirOnDB Spring 84; EISS 83*
Business Data Control Systems - Reynoldsburg, OH - *MicrocomSwDir 1; WhoWMicrocom 83*
Business Data Systems - Old Greenwich, CT - *DataDirOnSer 84*
Business Database [of Market Data Retrieval] - Westport, CT - *CompReadDB 82*
Business Decisions Inc. - New York, NY - *IntDirMarRes 83*
Business Decisions Ltd. - London, England - *IntDirMarRes 83*
Business Design Services - Bellevue, WA - *MicrocomMPl 84; WhoWMicrocom 83*
Business Digest - Cynwyd, PA - *BaconPubCkMag 84*
Business Div., The - Longwood, FL - *WritMar 84*
Business Economics - Hackensack, NJ - *MagIndMarPl 82-83*
Business Education Films - Brooklyn, NY - *AvMarPl 83; ProGuPRSer 4*
Business Education Forum - Reston, VA - *BaconPubCkMag 84; MagDir 84*
Business Education World - New York, NY - *BaconPubCkMag 84; MagDir 84*
Business Efficiency Aids Inc. - Skokie, IL - *DirInfWP 82*
Business Efficiency Aids Inc. (Magne-Dex Div.) - Skokie, IL - *DirInfWP 82*
Business Environment Risk Information - New York, NY - *EISS 7-83 Sup*
Business Equipment & Systems Association - Garden Grove, CA - *DirInfWP 82*
Business Facilities - Red Bank, NJ - *BaconPubCkMag 84; MagDir 84; WritMar 84*
Business Farmer - Scottsbluff, NE - *BaconPubCkMag 84; MagDir 84*

Business-Farmer, The - Rural Scottsbluff, NE - *Ed&PubIntYB 82*
Business Forms & Systems - Philadelphia, PA - *BaconPubCkMag 84; MagDir 84*
Business Graphics Corp. - Dallas, TX - *AvMarPl 83*
Business Horizons [of Indiana University Graduate School of Business] - Bloomington, IN - *BaconPubCkMag 84; MagDir 84; MagIndMarPl 82-83*
Business Ideas - Clifton, NJ - *BaconPubCkMag 84; MagDir 84*
Business Index [of Information Access Corp.] - Menlo Park, CA - *EISS 83*
Business Information Analysis Corp. - Haverford, PA - *IntDirMarRes 83*
Business Information Associates Inc. - Glen Echo, MD - *MicrocomSwDir 1*
Business Information Display Inc. (World Energy Industry Information Services) - San Diego, CA - *DataDirOnSer 84*
Business Information International - Copenhagen, Denmark - *EISS 83; InfIndMarPl 83; InfoS 83-84*
Business Information Service [of Financial Times Business Information Ltd.] - London, England - *EISS 83*
Business Information Services [of Control Data Corp.] - Greenwich, CT - *EISS 5-84 Sup*
Business Information Systems Inc. - Chicago, IL - *DataDirOnSer 84*
Business Information Systems Inc. - Ft. Wayne, IN - *ADAPSOMemDir 83-84*
Business Information Systems Inc. - Stafford, TX - *WhoWMicrocom 83*
Business Information Technology - Conroe, TX - *WhoWMicrocom 83*
Business Information Wire - Toronto, ON, Canada - *DirOnDB Spring 84*
Business Insurance - Chicago, IL - *ArtMar 84; BaconPubCkMag 84; MagDir 84; NewsBur 6; WritMar 84*
Business Insurance [of Crain Communications Inc.] - New York, NY - *Folio 83*
Business Intelligence Program [of SRI International] - Menlo Park, CA - *EISS 83*
Business Intelligence Services Inc. - New York, NY - *ADAPSOMemDir 83-84; DataDirSup 7-83*
Business International - New York, NY - *BaconPubCkMag 84; BoPubDir 5; CompReadDB 82; DataDirOnSer 84; EISS 83; InfoS 83-84; MagDir 84*
Business International Corp. - *See* BI/Data
Business International Country Assessment Service [of Business International Corp.] - New York, NY - *DataDirOnSer 84*
Business International Economic Forecast [of I. P. Sharp Associates Ltd.] - Toronto, ON, Canada - *DataDirOnSer 84*
Business International Historical Data [of I. P. Sharp Associates Ltd.] - Toronto, ON, Canada - *DataDirOnSer 84*
Business Journal, The - San Jose, CA - *BaconPubCkMag 84*
Business Journals Inc. - Norwalk, CT - *BoPubDir 4 Sup, 5*
Business Life - Mississauga, ON, Canada - *BaconPubCkMag 84; WritMar 84*
Business Logic - Kentwood, MI - *MicrocomMPl 84*
Business Machine Dealer Data Base [of National Office Machine Dealers Association] - Wood Dale, IL - *EISS 7-83 Sup*
Business Management Research - San Francisco, CA - *LitMarPl 83, 84*
Business Management Sciences Inc. - Rego Park, NY - *BoPubDir 4*
Business Management Services Inc. - Stevens Point, WI - *StaDirAdAg 2-84*
Business Management Systems Inc. - Fairfax, VA - *MicrocomSwDir 1*
Business Man's Publications - Garland, TX - *BoPubDir 4, 5*
Business Marketing [of Crain Communications Inc.] - Chicago, IL - *MagDir 84; WritMar 84*
Business Marketing - New York, NY - *BaconPubCkMag 84*
Business Marketing Services - Bronxville, NY - *IntDirMarRes 83*
Business Master Inc. - Carlsbad, CA - *WhoWMicrocom 83*
Business Micro Products - Glenwood Springs, CO - *MicrocomMPl 84*
Business News - San Diego, CA - *BaconPubCkMag 84; WritMar 84*
Business News - San Francisco, CA - *BoPubDir 5*
Business News - Winfield, IL - *BaconPubCkMag 84*
Business News Publishing Co. - Troy, MI - *BoPubDir 4, 5*
Business: North Carolina - Charlotte, NC - *BaconPubCkMag 84*
Business Opportunities Australia [of NewsNet Inc.] - Bryn Mawr, PA - *DataDirOnSer 84*
Business Opportunities Digest - Dalton, GA - *MagIndMarPl 82-83*
Business Organization Inc. - *See* Byoir & Associates Inc., Carl
Business Owner, The - Hicksville, NY - *BaconPubCkMag 84*
Business Planning International - La Costa, CA - *WhoWMicrocom 83*
Business Planning Systems - Dover, DE - *MicrocomMPl 83; MicrocomSwDir 1; WhoWMicrocom 83*
Business Problem Solvers - Kansas City, MO - *MicrocomMPl 83; WhoWMicrocom 83*
Business/Professional Advertising Association - New York, NY - *BoPubDir 5*
Business/Professional Software Database - *DirOnDB Spring 84*
Business/Professional Software Database [of Dialog Information Services Inc.] - Palo Alto, CA - *DataDirOnSer 84*
Business/Professional Software Database [of Data Courier Inc.] - Louisville, KY - *EISS 5-84 Sup*
Business Promotions Inc. - Portland, OR - *DirMarMP 83*
Business Psychology International - Washington, DC - *BoPubDir 4*
Business Psychology International - Boston, MA - *BoPubDir 5*
Business Publications Inc. [Subs. of Richard D. Irwin Inc.] - Plano, TX - *LitMarPl 83, 84*
Business Publishers Inc. - Silver Spring, MD - *BoPubDir 4, 5; DirMarMP 83*
Business Quarterly - London, ON, Canada - *BaconPubCkMag 84*
Business Radio Action - Carmichael, CA - *BaconPubCkMag 84*
Business Research Bureau [of University of South Dakota] - Vermillion, SD - *EISS 83*
Business Research Publications Inc. - New York, NY - *BoPubDir 4, 5*
Business Research Publications Inc. - Plainview, NY - *DirMarMP 83*
Business Research Services - Houston, TX - *EISS 7-83 Sup*
Business Research Services Inc. - Cleveland, OH - *IntDirMarRes 83*
Business Review [of New York Business Publications Inc.] - Mattydale, NY - *MagDir 84*
Business Review - Regina, SK, Canada - *BaconPubCkMag 84*
Business Review Weekly - Sydney, Australia - *DirOnDB Spring 84*
Business Sale Institute - San Jose, CA - *BoPubDir 4, 5*
Business Screen Magazine - New York, NY - *MagIndMarPl 82-83*
Business Software - Portland, OR - *BaconPubCkMag 84; MicrocomMPl 84; WritMar 84*
Business Solutions Inc. - Kings Park, NY - *MicrocomMPl 84; WhoWMicrocom 83*
Business Systems Inc. - Westchester, IL - *DataDirOnSer 84*
Business Systems Product Update [of Prime Star Research Inc.] - Roselle, IL - *MicrocomMPl 84*
Business Systems Update [of Prime Star Research Inc.] - Roselle, IL - *MicrocomMPl 84*
Business Television Services Inc. - Greenwich, CT - *AvMarPl 83*
Business: The Magazine of Managerial Thought & Action - Atlanta, GA - *MagIndMarPl 82-83*
Business Times, The [of The Connecticut Business Times Inc.] - East Hartford, CT - *MagDir 84; WritMar 84*
Business to Business - Tallahassee, FL - *WritMar 84*
Business Today - Princeton, NJ - *ArtMar 84; MagDir 84*
Business Traveler's Report - New York, NY - *BaconPubCkMag 84*
Business Trend Analysts - Commack, NY - *BoPubDir 4, 5; EISS 7-83 Sup; IntDirMarRes 83*
Business Week [of McGraw-Hill Inc.] - New York, NY - *ArtMar 84; BaconPubCkMag 84; Folio 83; LitMarPl 83, 84; MagDir 84; MagIndMarPl 82-83; NewsBur 6; WritMar 84*
Business Week - Cleveland, OH - *NewsBur 6*
Business Wire - San Francisco, CA - *Ed&PubIntYB 82; NewsDir 84; ProGuPRSer 4*
Business Worcester - Worcester, MA - *BaconPubCkMag 84*
Businessoft International Corp. - Monsey, NY - *MicrocomMPl 84*

Buss: The Independent Newsletter of Health Co. [of Sextant Publishing Co.] - Washington, DC - *MicrocomMPl 84*
Busse & Cummins - San Francisco, CA - *AdAge 3-28-84; StaDirAdAg 2-84*
Busse Associates Inc., A. R. - Houston, TX - *DirPRFirms 83*
Bustleton-Somerton News - *See* News Gleaner Publications
Busy Shopper - Ft. Oglethorpe, GA - *AyerDirPub 83*
Butane-Propane News - Arcadia, CA - *BaconPubCkMag 84; MagDir 84; MagIndMarPl 82-83*
Butcher & Associates Inc., Robert K. - Shreveport, LA - *AdAge 3-28-84; DirPRFirms 83; StaDirAdAg 2-84*
Butcher Block Music - *See* Hello Love Music
Butcher, Faherty & Associates - Belmont, CA - *LitMarPl 83, 84*
Butcher, Paul - Auxier, KY - *BrCabYB 84*
Butcher Productions, Alden - Hollywood, CA - *AvMarPl 83; WritMar 84*
Butchko, Michele - New York, NY - *LitMarPl 83, 84*
Butec Management Corp. (Dynalogic Div.) - Ottawa, ON, Canada - *DataDirSup 7-83*
Buten Museum of Wedgwood - Merion, PA - *BoPubDir 4, 5*
Buteo Books - Vermillion, SD - *BoPubDir 4, 5*
Butera Associates Inc., Sal - *See* SBA Advertising
Buti-Roberts Advertising Inc. - Chicago, IL - *StaDirAdAg 2-84*
Buti-Roberts Public Relations Inc. [Aff. of Buti-Roberts Advertising Inc.] - Chicago, IL - *DirPRFirms 83*
Butler & Associates, Kenneth B. - Mendota, IL - *StaDirAdAg 2-84*
Butler Associates, Thomas - Cambridge, MA - *LitMarPl 83, 84*
Butler Bates County News Headliner - Butler, MO - *BaconPubCkNews 84; NewsDir 84*
Butler-Bremer Telephone Co. - Plainfield, IA - *TelDir&BG 83-84*
Butler Bulletin - Butler, IN - *BaconPubCkNews 84; Ed&PubIntYB 82*
Butler Cablevision Inc. - Butler, MO - *BrCabYB 84; Tel&CabFB 84C*
Butler Choctaw Advocate - Butler, AL - *BaconPubCkNews 84; NewsDir 84*
Butler County News - Georgiana, AL - *AyerDirPub 83; Ed&PubIntYB 82*
Butler County News [of Gannett Co. Inc.] - Zelienople, PA - *AyerDirPub 83; Ed&PubIntYB 82; NewsDir 84*
Butler County Publishing - Dexter, MO - *BaconPubCkNews 84*
Butler County Tribune Journal - Allison, IA - *AyerDirPub 83; Ed&PubIntYB 82*
Butler Cox & Partners Ltd. - London, England - *InfIndMarPl 83*
Butler, Doug - Maryville, MO - *BoPubDir 4, 5*
Butler Eagle - Butler, PA - *BaconPubCkNews 84; Ed&PubIntYB 82; NewsDir 84*
Butler Graphic Design - Mendota, IL - *BoPubDir 4, 5*
Butler Learning Systems - Dayton, OH - *AvMarPl 83*
Butler Literary Associates, Ed - Scottsdale, AZ - *LitMarPl 83*
Butler Paper Co. [Div. of Great Northern Nekoosa] - City of Industry, CA - *LitMarPl 83, 84*
Butler Paper Co. - Port Edwards, WI - *DirInfWP 82*
Butler Service Group - West Palm Beach, FL - *DirInfWP 82*
Butler Suburban Trends & Times Bulletin - Butler, NJ - *BaconPubCkNews 84*
Butler Taylor County News - Butler, GA - *BaconPubCkNews 84*
Butler Telephone Co. Inc. [Aff. of Telephone Electronics Corp.] - Butler, AL - *TelDir&BG 83-84*
Butler-Weed International Corp. - Garden City, NY - *BillIntBG 83-84*
Butner Advertising Inc., Lawrence - New York, NY - *AdAge 3-28-84; BrCabYB 84; StaDirAdAg 2-84*
Butner-Creedmoor News - Creedmoor, NC - *AyerDirPub 83*
Butt Press - Arlington, MA - *BoPubDir 4, 5*
Butte Cable TV [of Community Tele-Communications Inc.] - Butte, MT - *BrCabYB 84; Tel&CabFB 84C*
Butte Gazette - Butte, NE - *BaconPubCkNews 84; Ed&PubIntYB 82*
Butte Montana Standard [of Lee Enterprises Inc.] - Butte, MT - *NewsDir 84*
Butte Valley-Keno Star - Dorris, CA - *Ed&PubIntYB 82*
Butte Valley Star - Dorris, CA - *AyerDirPub 83*
Butten & Bock Inc. - Melbourne, FL - *CabTVFinDB 83*
Butter-Fat - Vancouver, BC, Canada - *ArtMar 84; BaconPubCkMag 84; WritMar 84*
Butterfield Express & Valley Times - Sunnymead, CA - *AyerDirPub 83; Ed&PubIntYB 82*
Butterfly Books Ltd. - Maple Creek, SK, Canada - *BoPubDir 4, 5*
Butterfly Press - Houston, TX - *BoPubDir 4, 5*
Buttermilk Sky Music Publishing Corp. - New York, NY - *BillIntBG 83-84*
Butterworth & Co. Ltd. - Scarborough, ON, Canada - *LitMarPl 83, 84*
Butterworth Publishers [Subs. of Butterworth Ltd.] - Woburn, MA - *LitMarPl 83, 84*
Butterworth Telepublishing Ltd. - London, England - *EISS 83; InfIndMarPl 83*
Butterworths Pty. Ltd. - Sydney, Australia - *MicroMarPl 82-83*
Button Publishing - San Francisco, CA - *BoPubDir 4, 5*
Buttonwillow Times - Buttonwillow, CA - *Ed&PubIntYB 82*
Buttonwillow Times - Shafter, CA - *AyerDirPub 83; BaconPubCkNews 84*
Butwin & Associates - Minneapolis, MN - *AdAge 3-28-84*
Butwin & Associates Advertising Inc. - St. Louis Park, MN - *StaDirAdAg 2-84*
Buxton Advertising Agency - Pasadena, CA - *StaDirAdAg 2-84*
Buxton-Publicity & Promotion, Leslie - New York, NY - *HBIndAd&MS 82-83*
Buy Line [of Data Communications Corp.] - Memphis, TN - *DataDirOnSer 84*
Buy Line, The - Greenville, MI - *AyerDirPub 83*
Buy-Phone - Los Angeles, CA - *DataDirOnSer 84; DirOnDB Spring 84; EISS 5-84 Sup*
Buyer Inc., Alfred S. - Needham Heights, MA - *StaDirAdAg 2-84*
Buyers Guide - Rockford, IL - *AyerDirPub 83*
Buyer's Guide - Gladwin, MI - *AyerDirPub 83*
Buyers Guide - Neenah, WI - *AyerDirPub 83*
Buyers Guide Shopper News - Lewistown, IL - *AyerDirPub 83*
Buying for the Farm - Pewaukee, WI - *BaconPubCkMag 84; MagDir 84*
Buzzard Inc. - Cambridge, MA - *StaDirAdAg 2-84*
Buzzco Productions Inc. - New York, NY - *Tel&CabFB 84C*
Buzzherb Music - *See* Tutt Music, Scott
BVR - Stockholm, Sweden - *DirOnDB Spring 84*
BWA Advertising Inc. - Kansas City, MO - *StaDirAdAg 2-84*
BWB Advertising - Hewitt, TX - *StaDirAdAg 2-84*
BWI Communications Corp. - Washington, DC - *BillIntBG 83-84*
BWJ Technology - Arlington, TX - *MicrocomMPl 83, 84*
B.W.M.T. Inc. - San Francisco, CA - *WritMar 84*
BWP Associates - West Redding, CT - *DirPRFirms 83*
By By Productions - Glendora, CA - *BoPubDir 4, 5*
By Gene Publishing - *See* Beckie Publishing Co.
By Hand & Foot Ltd. - Brattleboro, VT - *LitMag&SmPr 83-84; LitMarPl 83*
By-Lines - Ft. Smith, AR - *ArtMar 84*
BY/Media Inc. - New York, NY - *Tel&CabFB 84C*
BY/Media Inc. - *See* Byoir & Associates Inc., Carl
By-R-Records - Anchorville, MI - *BillIntBG 83-84*
Byad Inc. - Barrington, IL - *MicrocomMPl 84*
Bye CATV Inc. - Crosby, MN - *BrCabYB 84; Tel&CabFB 84C*
Byemoor History Committee - Byemoor, AB, Canada - *BoPubDir 4, 5*
Byer & Bowman Advertising Agency Inc. - Columbus, OH - *BrCabYB 84; DirPRFirms 83; StaDirAdAg 2-84*
Byers Associates - Weston, ON, Canada - *BoPubDir 4, 5*
Byers Communications Corp. - Atlanta, GA - *InterCabHB 3*
Byers-Petrolia Telephone Co. - Byers, TX - *TelDir&BG 83-84*
Byers Photo Equipment Co. - Portland, OR - *AvMarPl 83*
Byesville Cable Co. - Byesville, OH - *BrCabYB 84; Tel&CabFB 84C*
BYGGDOK [of Swedish Institute of Building Documentation] - Stockholm, Sweden - *CompReadDB 82*
Bygosh Music Corp. - Brookfield, VT - *BillIntBG 83-84*
Byk Advertising Inc., Jon - Los Angeles, CA - *StaDirAdAg 2-84*
Byline - Oklahoma City, OK - *LitMag&SmPr 83-84*
BYLS Press [Aff. of Bet Yoatz Library Services] - Chicago, IL - *BoPubDir 4, 5; LitMag&SmPr 83-84; WritMar 84*
Byoir & Associates Inc., Carl [Subs. of Foote, Cone & Belding Communications Inc.] - New York, NY - *DirPRFirms 83*

Byoir & Associates Inc., Carl - *See* Foote, Cone & Belding Communications Inc.
Byoir/Singapore Pty. Ltd. - *See* Byoir & Associates Inc., Carl
Byram Hilltop Press - Andover, NJ - *BoPubDir 4, 5*
Byrd [of The William Byrd Press Inc.] - Richmond, VA - *LitMarPl 84*
Byrd Inc., Clarence - Stittsville, ON, Canada - *BoPubDir 4 Sup, 5*
Byrd Newspapers - Harrisonburg, VA - *Ed&PubIntYB 82*
Byrd PrePress [Div. of The William Byrd Press Inc.] - Springfield, VA - *LitMarPl 83, 84; MagIndMarPl 82-83*
Byrd Press Inc., The William - Washington, DC - *LitMag&SmPr 83-84*
Byrd Press Inc., The William - Richmond, VA - *LitMarPl 83; MagIndMarPl 82-83*
Byrde, Richard & Pound Inc. - New York, NY - *StaDirAdAg 2-84; TelAl 83, 84*
Byrdstown Cable Service - Byrdstown, TN - *Tel&CabFB 84C*
Byrdstown Pickett County Press - Byrdstown, TN - *BaconPubCkNews 84*
Byrne Advertising Inc. - Slidell, LA - *StaDirAdAg 2-84*
Byrne, Charles R. - New York, NY - *LitMarPl 83, 84*
Byrnes & Co., L. W. - Northfield, IL - *StaDirAdAg 2-84*
Byrnes Co., The - Riverside, CA - *StaDirAdAg 2-84*
Byron Motion Pictures Inc. - Washington, DC - *AvMarPl 83; TelAl 83, 84; Tel&CabFB 84C*
Byron Northern Ogle Tempo - *See* North Central Associated Publishers
Byron Press - Nottingham, England - *LitMag&SmPr 83-84*
Byron Review - Byron, MN - *BaconPubCkNews 84; Ed&PubIntYB 82*
Byte [of McGraw Hill] - Peterborough, NH - *BaconPubCkMag 84; Folio 83; MagIndMarPl 82-83; MicrocomMPl 84; WritMar 84*
Byte Book Club [of McGraw-Hill Book Co.] - New York, NY - *LitMarPl 84*
Byte Industries Inc. [Subs. of Logical Machines Corp.] - Hayward, CA - *DirInfWP 82; MicrocomMPl 83, 84; WhoWMicrocom 83*
Byte Publications [Subs. of McGraw-Hill] - Peterborough, NH - *WhoWMicrocom 83*
Bytek - Berkeley, CA - *WhoWMicrocom 83*
Bytek Computer Systems Corp. - Boca Raton, FL - *MicrocomMPl 84*
Bytel Corp. - Berkeley, CA - *MicrocomMPl 84; MicrocomSwDir 1*
Bytewriter - Ithaca, NY - *MicrocomMPl 83, 84*
Bytronix Corp. - Fullerton, CA - *WhoWMicrocom 83*
BYU Today [of Brigham Young University] - Provo, UT - *WritMar 84*
Byzantine Press [Aff. of Marc Wilkinson Printer Inc.] - Las Vegas, NV - *BoPubDir 4, 5*

C

C-A Cablevision [of Community Tele-Communications Inc.] - Artesia, NM - *BrCabYB 84; Tel&CabFB 84C*
C-A Cablevision [of Community Tele-Communications Inc.] - Carlsbad, NM - *BrCabYB 84; Tel&CabFB 84C*
C & B Associates - Boston, MA - *StaDirAdAg 2-84*
C & B TV Cable Co. - Panther, WV - *BrCabYB 84*
C & C Associates [Div. of Couristan Inc.] - New York, NY - *StaDirAdAg 2-84*
C & C Computer Concepts Inc. - Braintree, MA - *MicrocomMPl 84*
C & C Software - Goleta, CA - *MicrocomMPl 84*
C & C Systems & Software - El Cajon, CA - *WhoWMicrocom 83*
C & D Cable Co. - Chama, NM - *BrCabYB 84; Tel&CabFB 84C*
C & E Cable Service - Hardy, KY - *BrCabYB 84*
C & F Communications Inc. - North Providence, RI - *BrCabYB 84*
C & G Publishing Co. - Los Altos, CA - *BoPubDir 4, 5*
C & H Services Inc. - Robert Lee, TX - *Tel&CabFB 84C*
C & H Video - Hershey, PA - *MicrocomMPl 83*
C & L Communications [of CL Co. Inc.] - Falls Church, VA - *DirMarMP 83*
C & M Publications - Austin, TX - *BoPubDir 4, 5*
C & R Cable Systems [of Tele-Communications Inc.] - Shadyside, OH - *BrCabYB 84; Tel&CabFB 84C*
C & R Co. Inc. - Bertha, MN - *Tel&CabFB 84C*
C & R Publications - Kitchener, ON, Canada - *BoPubDir 4 Sup, 5*
C & S [of N.B. Enterprises Inc.] - New York, NY - *BaconPubCkMag 84; MagDir 84; WritMar 84*
C & S Distributors - Camp Hill, PA - *DataDirSup 7-83*
C & S Electronics Mart Ltd. - Milan, MI - *WhoWMicrocom 83*
C & W Network Services [of Cable & Wireless North America Inc.] - Dallas, TX - *TeleSy&SerDir 2-84*
C Books [Aff. of Cartographic Enterprises] - Del Mar, CA - *BoPubDir 5*
C-Channel [of Price Waterhouse Ltd.] - Toronto, ON, Canada - *BrCabYB 84*
C-COR Electronics Inc. - State College, PA - *CabTVFinDB 83; HomeVid&CabYB 82-83*
C-E Crest Engineering - Houston, TX - *TeleSy&SerDir 2-84*
C-E Elgin Electronics - Erie, PA - *DataDirSup 7-83*
C-E Power Systems [Aff. of Combustion Engineering Inc.] - Windsor, CT - *BoPubDir 4 Sup, 5*
C81 Data Bases - St. Leonards, Australia - *DirOnDB Spring 84*
C/F Communications - Ft. Lauderdale, FL - *DirPRFirms 83*
C/J Research Inc. - Palatine, IL - *IntDirMarRes 83*
C-K Video Inc. - Catlettsburg, KY - *BrCabYB 84*
C-K Video Inc. - Kenova, WV - *BrCabYB 84; Tel&CabFB 84C p.1672*
C-Line - Plano, TX - *DirOnDB Spring 84*
C-M-L Telephone Cooperative Association - Meriden, IA - *TelDir&BG 83-84*
C/M News [of National Concrete Masonry Association] - Herndon, VA - *BaconPubCkMag 84; MagDir 84*
C-P Films Inc. - Omaha, NE - *AvMarPl 83*
C-Port [of Interactive Data Services Inc.] - New York, NY - *DataDirOnSer 84*
C-R Telephone Co. - Ransom, IL - *TelDir&BG 83-84*
C/R TV Cable [of Frederick Cablevision Inc.] - Charles Town, WV - *BrCabYB 84; Tel&CabFB 84C*
C-S Computer Systems Inc. - Manville, NJ - *ADAPSOMemDir 83-84*
C71 Data Bases - St. Leonards, Australia - *DirOnDB Spring 84*
C76 Data Bases - St. Leonards, Australia - *DirOnDB Spring 84*
C-SPAN [of National Cable Satellite Co.] - Washington, DC - *BrCabYB 84; CabTVPrDB 83; HomeVid&CabYB 82-83*
C-Store Business - Stamford, CT - *ArtMar 84; BaconPubCkMag 84*
C-Systems - Fullerton, CA - *MicrocomMPl 84; MicrocomSwDir 1*
C-Tek Software - New York, NY - *DataDirOnSer 84*
C13 Nuclear Magnetic Resonance Spectra - Ludwigshafen, West Germany - *DirOnDB Spring 84*
CA Biblio File [of Chemical Abstracts Service] - Columbus, OH - *CompReadDB 82*
CA Chemical Name Dictionary [of Dialog Information Services Inc.] - Palo Alto, CA - *DataDirOnSer 84*
CA Index Guide [of Chemical Abstracts Service] - Columbus, OH - *CompReadDB 82; DataDirOnSer 84*
CA Magazine - Palo Alto, CA - *MagDir 84*
CA Magazine - Toronto, ON, Canada - *BaconPubCkMag 84; WritMar 84*
CA Search [of Chemical Abstracts Service] - Columbus, OH - *CompReadDB 82; DataDirOnSer 84; DBBus 82; DirOnDB Spring 84; OnBibDB 3*
Ca-Song Music - New York, NY - *BillIntBG 83-84*
Ca-Song Records - New York, NY - *BillIntBG 83-84*
CAA Magazine - Chicago, IL - *MagDir 84*
CAB Abstracts [of Dialog Information Services Inc.] - Palo Alto, CA - *DataDirOnSer 84*
CAB Abstracts [of Commonwealth Agricultural Bureaux] - Farnham Royal, England - *OnBibDB 3*
CAB Abstracts [of Commonwealth Agricultural Bureaux] - Slough, England - *DirOnDB Spring 84; EISS 83*
Cabala Press - Chicago, IL - *BoPubDir 4, 5; LitMag&SmPr 83-84*
Caballero & Associates, Jorge - Chicago, IL - *StaDirAdAg 2-84*
Caballero Press - Las Vegas, NV - *BoPubDir 4, 5*
Cabat-Gill Advertising Agency - Tucson, AZ - *StaDirAdAg 2-84*
Cabbage Cases - Columbus, OH - *AvMarPl 83*
Cabbage Patch Circle [Aff. of Cabbage Patch Settlement House] - Louisville, KY - *BoPubDir 4, 5*
Cabbagehead Press, The - Tempe, AZ - *LitMag&SmPr 83-84*
Cabell Bulletin [of Culloden P.C. Publishing Co.] - Culloden, WV - *AyerDirPub 83; NewsDir 84*
Cabell Eanes Inc. - Richmond, VA - *StaDirAdAg 2-84*
Cabell Record - Milton, WV - *AyerDirPub 83; Ed&PubIntYB 82; NewsDir 84*
Cabell Travel Publications - North Hollywood, CA - *BoPubDir 5*
Cabinet Creations by Computer Inc. - Tampa, FL - *WhoWMicrocom 83*

Cable Advertising Network - Olympia, WA - *HomeVid&CabYB 82-83*
Cable Age - New York, NY - *BaconPubCkMag 84*
Cable America - Atlanta, GA - *Tel&CabFB 84C p.1668*
Cable & Communications Corp. [of Mid-Rivers Telephone Co-Op Inc.] - Jordan, MT - *Tel&CabFB 84C*
Cable & Communications Corp. [of Mid-Rivers Telephone Co-op Inc.] - Richey, MT - *Tel&CabFB 84C*
Cable & Communications Corp. [of Mid-Rivers Telephone Co-Op Inc.] - Savage, MT - *Tel&CabFB 84C*
Cable & Wireless PLC - London, England - *TeleSy&SerDir 2-84*
Cable Antenna Systems - Vandenberg, CA - *Tel&CabFB 84C*
Cable Associates Inc. - Lancaster, PA - *BrCabYB 84; Tel&CabFB 84C*
Cable Atlanta Inc. - Atlanta, GA - *BrCabYB 84*
Cable Brazil Inc. [of Omega Communications Inc.] - Brazil, IN - *BrCabYB 84; Tel&CabFB 84C*
Cable Business - Washington, DC - *BaconPubCkMag 84*
Cable Cash Call - Baltimore, MD - *Tel&CabFB 84C*
Cable Communications Co. [of Times Mirror Co.] - Long Beach, CA - *BrCabYB 84*
Cable Communications Consultants - Falls Church, VA - *CabTVFinDB 83; InterCabHB 3*
Cable Communications Corp. of Delaware - Ft. Lauderdale, FL - *Tel&CabFB 84C p.1668*
Cable Communications Equities Inc. - Raymond, CO - *BrCabYB 84*
Cable Communications Equities Inc. [of Community Tele-Communications Inc.] - Ortonville, MN - *Tel&CabFB 84C*
Cable Communications Equities Inc. [of Tele-Communications Inc.] - Raymond, WA - *Tel&CabFB 84C*
Cable Communications Inc. - Albertville, AL - *Tel&CabFB 84C p.1668*
Cable Communications Inc. - North Augusta, SC - *BrCabYB 84 p.D-298; Tel&CabFB 84C p.1668*
Cable Communications Magazine - Kitchener, ON, Canada - *BaconPubCkMag 84; WritMar 84*
Cable Communications of Iowa Inc. - Algona, IA - *BrCabYB 84 p.D-298*
Cable Communications Systems Inc. - Hector, MN - *Tel&CabFB 84C p.1668*
Cable Communications Systems Inc. - *See* North American Cable Systems
Cable Dallas Inc. - Dallas, TX - *Tel&CabFB 84C*
Cable DeKalb Inc. - Decatur, GA - *BrCabYB 84*
Cable East Point/College Park [of Cable America Inc.] - East Point, GA - *BrCabYB 84*
Cable Electronics Inc. [of United Cable Television Corp.] - Anson, TX - *BrCabYB 84; Tel&CabFB 84C*
Cable Electronics Inc. [of United Cable Television Corp.] - Hamlin, TX - *BrCabYB 84*
Cable Electronics Inc. [of United Cable Television Corp.] - Rotan, TX - *BrCabYB 84*
Cable Films/Video - Kansas City, MO - *BillIntBG 83-84; Tel&CabFB 84C*
Cable Finer Living [of Viacom International Inc.] - Redding, CA - *BrCabYB 84*
Cable Fund IX-B Georgia [of Jones Intercable Inc.] - Lowndes County, GA - *BrCabYB 84*
Cable Group A - Greenville, MI - *Tel&CabFB 84C*
Cable Group Management Inc. - Grand Haven, MI - *Tel&CabFB 84C p.1668*
Cable Health Network - New York, NY - *BrCabYB 84; CabTVPrDB 83; HomeVid&CabYB 82-83*
Cable Health Network - *See* Lifetime
Cable Hour TV Magazine - Ft. Wayne, IN - *BaconPubCkMag 84*
Cable Houston Inc. - Houston, TX - *BrCabYB 84; Tel&CabFB 84C*
Cable Information Systems Inc. - New York, NY - *Tel&CabFB 84C p.1668*
Cable Information Systems Inc. - *See* Tele-Communications Inc.
Cable Investments Inc. - Englewood, CO - *CabTVFinDB 83*
Cable Investments Inc. [of Tele-Communications Inc.] - Gettysburg, PA - *Tel&CabFB 84C*
Cable Investments Inc. [of Tele-Communications Inc.] - Red Lion, PA - *Tel&CabFB 84C*
Cable Management Associates Inc. - Hershey, PA - *Tel&CabFB 84C p.1668*
Cable Management Group of Anna - Jackson Center, OH - *Tel&CabFB 84C*
Cable Marketing - New York, NY - *ArtMar 84; BaconPubCkMag 84; WritMar 84*
Cable Marketing Management - Columbus, OH - *CabTVFinDB 83; Tel&CabFB 84C*
Cable Max Corp. - Chatom, AL - *BrCabYB 84*
Cable Net Ltd. - Estevan, SK, Canada - *BrCabYB 84*
Cable Net Ltd. - Weyburn, SK, Canada - *BrCabYB 84*
Cable Networks Inc. - New York, NY - *HomeVid&CabYB 82-83*
Cable New Castle [of Colorado Cable Co.] - New Castle, CO - *Tel&CabFB 84C*
Cable News - Bethesda, MD - *BaconPubCkMag 84*
Cable News [of NewsNet Inc.] - Bryn Mawr, PA - *DataDirOnSer 84*
Cable News Network [of Turner Broadcasting System Inc.] - Atlanta, GA - *BrCabYB 84; CabTVPrDB 83; HomeVid&CabYB 82-83; TelAl 83; Tel&CabFB 84C*
Cable News Network Headline News - Atlanta, GA - *BrCabYB 84*
Cable News Network Headline News - *See* Cable News Network
Cable News Network 2 [of Turner Broadcasting System Inc.] - Atlanta, GA - *HomeVid&CabYB 82-83*
Cable Newspaper Corp. - Epping, NH - *BrCabYB 84*
Cable Oakland - Oakland, CA - *Tel&CabFB 84C*
Cable of Mattawan [of Omega Communications Inc.] - Mattawan, MI - *BrCabYB 84*
Cable Paonia [of Colorado Cable Co.] - Paonia, CO - *Tel&CabFB 84C*
Cable Products/News Video Product News - Palm Springs, CA - *BaconPubCkMag 84; MagDir 84*
Cable Program Services - Reston, VA - *Tel&CabFB 84C*
Cable Satellite Public Affairs Network - Washington, DC - *BrCabYB 84; Tel&CabFB 84C*
Cable-Scope - Greensburg, PA - *Tel&CabFB 84C p.1668*
Cable Service Co. Inc. [of American Cablesystems Corp.] - Kimball, WV - *Tel&CabFB 84C*
Cable Service Ltd. - Moncton, NB, Canada - *BrCabYB 84*
Cable Services Co. Inc. - Williamsport, PA - *HomeVid&CabYB 82-83*
Cable Services Inc. - Jamestown, ND - *BrCabYB 84 p.D-298; Tel&CabFB 84C p.1668*
Cable Services-Oakes - Oakes, ND - *BrCabYB 84*
Cable Services of Lisbon - Lisbon, ND - *BrCabYB 84; Tel&CabFB 84C*
Cable Services of Valley City - Valley City, ND - *BrCabYB 84*
Cable South Inc. [of Oconee Cablevision Inc.] - Jamesville, NC - *Tel&CabFB 84C*
Cable Sparta - Sparta, WI - *BrCabYB 84; Tel&CabFB 84C*
Cable Specialties Ltd. - Atlanta, GA - *Tel&CabFB 84C p.1668*
Cable System Inc. [of Buckeye Cablevision Inc.] - Monroe, MI - *Tel&CabFB 84C*
Cable Systems [of Storer Cable Communications Inc.] - Addison, TX - *BrCabYB 84*
Cable Systems Inc. - Las Animas, CO - *BrCabYB 84; Tel&CabFB 84C p.1668*
Cable Systems Inc. - Liberal, CO - *BrCabYB 84*
Cable Systems Inc. - Ellinwood, KS - *BrCabYB 84; Tel&CabFB 84C*
Cable Systems Inc. - Greensburg, KS - *BrCabYB 84; Tel&CabFB 84C*
Cable Systems Inc. - Lakin, KS - *BrCabYB 84; Tel&CabFB 84C*
Cable Systems Inc. - Liberal, KS - *Tel&CabFB 84C*
Cable Systems Inc. - Meade, KS - *BrCabYB 84; Tel&CabFB 84C*
Cable Systems Inc. - Scott City, KS - *BrCabYB 84; Tel&CabFB 84C*
Cable Systems Inc. - Stafford, KS - *BrCabYB 84*
Cable Systems Inc. - Syracuse, KS - *BrCabYB 84; Tel&CabFB 84C*
Cable Systems Inc. - Anderson, MO - *Tel&CabFB 84C*
Cable Systems of Alabama Inc. [of American TV & Communications Corp.] - Bessemer, AL - *Tel&CabFB 84C*
Cable Systems of Hoxie Inc. - Hoxie, KS - *BrCabYB 84*
Cable Tech - Denver, CO - *MagDir 84*

Cable Television Business - Englewood, CO - *BaconPubCkMag 84; InterCabHB 3; MagDir 84; WritMar 84*
Cable Television Inc. - Dale City, VA - *BrCabYB 84*
Cable Television Information Center - Arlington, VA - *BoPubDir 5; InterCabHB 3*
Cable Television Network of New Jersey - Trenton, NJ - *CabTVPrDB 83; Tel&CabFB 84C*
Cable Television of San Lorenzo Inc. - San Lorenzo, CA - *BrCabYB 84*
Cable Television of Tchula [of Action Communications Co.] - Tchula, MS - *BrCabYB 84*
Cable Television of the Kennebunks - Kennebunk, ME - *BrCabYB 84*
Cable Television Systems of Arkansas [of Satellite Cable TV Corp.] - Cabot, AR - *BrCabYB 84*
Cable TV [Div. of Yazoo Answer Call Inc.] - Rolling Fork, MS - *BrCabYB 84*
Cable TV - Cheyenne, WY - *BrCabYB 84*
Cable TV Co. [of Vision Cable Communications Inc.] - Wilmington, NC - *Tel&CabFB 84C*
Cable TV Co. - Benton, PA - *BrCabYB 84; Tel&CabFB 84C*
Cable TV Co. - Berwick, PA - *BrCabYB 84; Tel&CabFB 84C*
Cable TV Co. - Nuremberg, PA - *BrCabYB 84; Tel&CabFB 84C*
Cable TV Co. Inc., The - Troy, OH - *Tel&CabFB 84C p.1668*
Cable TV Co. Ltd. [of Southmedia Co.] - Chamblee, GA - *Tel&CabFB 84C*
Cable TV Co. of Central New York - Camden, NY - *BrCabYB 84*
Cable TV Co. of Central New York - Pulaski, NY - *BrCabYB 84*
Cable TV Co. of Central New York - Sandy Creek, NY - *Tel&CabFB 84C p.1668*
Cable TV Co. of Greater San Juan Inc. [of Harris Cable Corp.] - Hato Rey, PR - *BrCabYB 84*
Cable TV Co. of Greater San Juan Inc. - San Juan, PR - *Tel&CabFB 84C*
Cable TV Co. of York [of Susquehanna Broadcasting Co.] - York, PA - *BrCabYB 84; Tel&CabFB 84C*
Cable TV Corp. [of Northland Communications Corp.] - Reedsport, OR - *BrCabYB 84*
Cable TV Fund VIII-A [of Jones Intercable Inc.] - Sebastian, FL - *BrCabYB 84*
Cable TV Fund VIII-A [of Jones Intercable Inc.] - Henry County, GA - *BrCabYB 84; Tel&CabFB 84C*
Cable TV Fund VIII-A [of Jones Intercable Inc.] - Douglas, WY - *BrCabYB 84; Tel&CabFB 84C*
Cable TV Fund VIII-A [of Jones Intercable Inc.] - Glenrock, WY - *Tel&CabFB 84C*
Cable TV Fund VIII-A-Florida [of Jones Intercable Inc.] - Palm Bay, FL - *BrCabYB 84*
Cable TV Fund VIII-B [of Jones Intercable Inc.] - Sedalia, MO - *BrCabYB 84; Tel&CabFB 84C*
Cable TV Fund VIII-B [of Jones Intercable Inc.] - Carolina Beach, NC - *BrCabYB 84*
Cable TV Fund VIII-B [of Jones Intercable Inc.] - St. George, UT - *Tel&CabFB 84C*
Cable TV Fund VIII-C [of Jones Intercable Inc.] - Hillsboro, IL - *BrCabYB 84; Tel&CabFB 84C*
Cable TV Fund VIII-C [of Jones Intercable Inc.] - Nokomis, IL - *BrCabYB 84; Tel&CabFB 84C*
Cable TV Fund VIII-C [of Jones Intercable Inc.] - Pana, IL - *Tel&CabFB 84C*
Cable TV Fund VIII-C [of Jones Intercable Inc.] - Donaldsonville, LA - *Tel&CabFB 84C*
Cable TV Fund IX-A [of Jones Intercable Inc.] - Litchfield, IL - *BrCabYB 84; Tel&CabFB 84C*
Cable TV Fund IX-A [of Jones Intercable Inc.] - Taylorville, IL - *BrCabYB 84; Tel&CabFB 84C*
Cable TV Fund IX-A [of Jones Intercable Inc.] - Wilkesboro, NC - *BrCabYB 84*
Cable TV Fund IX-A Panama City Beach [of Jones Intercable Inc.] - Panama City Beach, FL - *BrCabYB 84*
Cable TV Fund IX-B [of Jones Intercable] - Benton, AR - *BrCabYB 84*
Cable TV Fund IX-B [of Jones Intercable Inc.] - Griffin, GA - *BrCabYB 84; Tel&CabFB 84C*
Cable TV Fund IX-B [of Jones Intercable Inc.] - Lowndes County, GA - *Tel&CabFB 84C*
Cable TV Fund IX-B [of Jones Intercable Inc.] - Moody Air Force Base, GA - *BrCabYB 84*
Cable TV Fund IX-B [of Jones Intercable Inc.] - Onalaska, WI - *BrCabYB 84*
Cable TV Fund IX-C [of Jones Intercable Inc.] - Lutcher, LA - *BrCabYB 84*
Cable TV Fund IX-C [of Jones Intercable Inc.] - Minden, LA - *BrCabYB 84*
Cable TV Fund IX-C [of Jones Intercable Inc.] - Gaston County, NC - *BrCabYB 84; Tel&CabFB 84C*
Cable TV Fund IX-C [of Jones Intercable Inc.] - Kings Mountain, NC - *BrCabYB 84*
Cable TV Fund IX-C [of Jones Intercable Inc.] - Shawnee, OK - *BrCabYB 84*
Cable TV Fund IX-C [of Jones Intercable Inc.] - Atlanta, TX - *BrCabYB 84; Tel&CabFB 84C*
Cable TV Fund IX-C [of Jones Intercable Inc.] - Hallsville, TX - *BrCabYB 84; Tel&CabFB 84C*
Cable TV Fund IX-C [of Jones Intercable Inc.] - Jefferson, TX - *BrCabYB 84*
Cable TV Fund IX-C [of Jones Intercable Inc.] - Marshall, TX - *BrCabYB 84; Tel&CabFB 84C*
Cable TV Fund VII-A [of Jones Intercable Inc.] - North Myrtle Beach, SC - *BrCabYB 84*
Cable TV Fund VII-A [of Jones Intercable Inc.] - Lusk, WY - *BrCabYB 84; Tel&CabFB 84C*
Cable TV Fund VII-A [of Jones Intercable Inc.] - Torrington, WY - *Tel&CabFB 84C*
Cable TV Fund VII-A [of Jones Intercable Inc.] - Wheatland, WY - *Tel&CabFB 84C*
Cable TV Fund VII-ABC-Florida [of Jones Intercable Inc.] - Palm Beach County, FL - *BrCabYB 84*
Cable TV Fund VII-ABC-Florida [of Jones Intercable Inc.] - St. Augustine, FL - *BrCabYB 84*
Cable TV Fund VII-B [of Jones Intercable Inc.] - Amite, LA - *BrCabYB 84*
Cable TV Fund VI [of Jones Intercable Inc.] - Benton, IL - *BrCabYB 84*
Cable TV Fund VI [of Jones Intercable Inc.] - DeQuoin, IL - *BrCabYB 84*
Cable TV Fund VI [of Jones Intercable Inc.] - Du Quoin, IL - *Tel&CabFB 84C*
Cable TV Fund VI [of Jones Intercable Inc.] - Olney, IL - *BrCabYB 84; Tel&CabFB 84C*
Cable TV Fund VI [of Jones Intercable Inc.] - Pinckneyville, IL - *BrCabYB 84; Tel&CabFB 84C*
Cable TV Fund VI [of Jones Intercable Inc.] - Hope, IN - *BrCabYB 84*
Cable TV Fund VI [of Jones Intercable Inc.] - Shelbyville, IN - *BrCabYB 84*
Cable TV Fund VI [of Jones Intercable Inc.] - Fairmont, NC - *BrCabYB 84*
Cable TV Fund VI [of Jones Intercable Inc.] - Pembroke, NC - *BrCabYB 84*
Cable TV Fund 10-A [of Jones Intercable Inc.] - Castro Valley, CA - *BrCabYB 84; Tel&CabFB 84C*
Cable TV Fund 10-A [of Jones Intercable Inc.] - Oxnard, CA - *BrCabYB 84; Tel&CabFB 84C*
Cable TV Fund 10-B [of Jones Intercable] - Mehl, AZ - *BrCabYB 84*
Cable TV Fund 10-B [of Jones Intercable Inc.] - Pima County, AZ - *Tel&CabFB 84C*
Cable TV Fund 10-B [of Jones Intercable] - Pima County (North), AZ - *BrCabYB 84*
Cable TV Fund 10-B [of Jones Intercable] - Pima County(South), AZ - *BrCabYB 84*
Cable TV Fund 10-C [Jones Intercable Inc.] - Azusa, CA - *BrCabYB 84; Tel&CabFB 84C*
Cable TV Fund 10-C [of Jones Intercable Inc.] - Glenville, NY - *Tel&CabFB 84C*
Cable TV Fund 10-C [of Jones Intercable Inc.] - Saratoga Springs, NY - *Tel&CabFB 84C*
Cable TV Fund II-A [of Jones Intercable Inc.] - Anne Arundel County, MD - *Tel&CabFB 84C*
Cable TV in Fairmont - Fairmont, MN - *BrCabYB 84*
Cable TV Inc. - Dugger, IN - *BrCabYB 84*
Cable TV Inc. - Chokio, MN - *BrCabYB 84*

Cable TV Inc. - Hancock, MN - *BrCabYB 84*
Cable TV Inc. - Morris, MN - *BrCabYB 84; Tel&CabFB 84C*
Cable TV Inc. - Starbuck, MN - *BrCabYB 84*
Cable TV Inc. - Underwood, ND - *BrCabYB 84*
Cable TV Inc. - Weatherley, PA - *BrCabYB 84*
Cable TV Inc. - Weatherly, PA - *Tel&CabFB 84C*
Cable TV Industries - Los Angeles, CA - *CabTVFinDB 83; HomeVid&CabYB 82-83*
Cable TV Ltd. - Amherst, NS, Canada - *BrCabYB 84*
Cable TV Ltd. [of CFCF Inc.] - Montreal, PQ, Canada - *BrCabYB 84*
Cable TV-Matador - Matador, TX - *BrCabYB 84*
Cable TV of Acadiana [of Wometco Cable TV] - Eunice, LA - *BrCabYB 84; Tel&CabFB 84C*
Cable TV of Adelanto [of Communications Systems Inc.] - Adelanto, CA - *BrCabYB 84*
Cable TV of Antlers - Antlers, OK - *BrCabYB 84; Tel&CabFB 84C*
Cable TV of Bancroft - Bancroft, IA - *BrCabYB 84; Tel&CabFB 84C*
Cable TV of Belzoni Inc. - Belzoni, MS - *BrCabYB 84; Tel&CabFB 84C*
Cable TV of Blair - Blair, OK - *Tel&CabFB 84C*
Cable TV of Blair - Granite, OK - *BrCabYB 84*
Cable TV of Buhl Inc. - Castleford, ID - *Tel&CabFB 84C*
Cable TV of Bunnell [of Southland Communications Inc.] - Bunnell, FL - *BrCabYB 84*
Cable TV of Camrose/Wetaskiwin Ltd. - Camrose, AB, Canada - *BrCabYB 84*
Cable TV of Clarendon - Clarendon, TX - *BrCabYB 84; Tel&CabFB 84C*
Cable TV of Clifton, Mart, & West Texas [of Tele-Communications Inc.] - Mart, TX - *BrCabYB 84*
Cable TV of College City - College City, AR - *Tel&CabFB 84C*
Cable TV of Constantine [of Omega Communications Inc.] - Constantine, MI - *Tel&CabFB 84C*
Cable TV of Constantine & White Pigeon [of Omega Communications Inc.] - Constantine, MI - *BrCabYB 84*
Cable TV of Coral Springs [of Schurz Communications Inc.] - Coral Springs, FL - *BrCabYB 84; Tel&CabFB 84C*
Cable TV of Cuero [of LBJ Co.] - Cuero, TX - *BrCabYB 84*
Cable TV of Dickinson [of Scott Cable Communications Inc.] - Dickinson, ND - *BrCabYB 84; Tel&CabFB 84C*
Cable TV of Dorchester - Dorchester County, PA - *BrCabYB 84*
Cable TV of Durango Inc. [of Community Tele-Communications Inc.] - Durango, CO - *BrCabYB 84; Tel&CabFB 84C*
Cable TV of Eagle Pass [of Karnack Corp.] - Eagle Pass, TX - *BrCabYB 84; Tel&CabFB 84C*
Cable TV of East Providence [of Susquehanna Broadcasting Co.] - East Providence, RI - *BrCabYB 84; Tel&CabFB 84C*
Cable TV of Fairmont [of Medelco Inc.] - Fairmont, MN - *Tel&CabFB 84C*
Cable TV of Fordyce [of Communications Systems Inc.] - Fordyce, AR - *BrCabYB 84; Tel&CabFB 84C*
Cable TV of Ft. Gibson - Ft. Gibson, OK - *BrCabYB 84*
Cable TV of Georgia Inc. - Dahlonega, GA - *Tel&CabFB 84C p.1668*
Cable TV of Goodwell - Goodwell, OK - *Tel&CabFB 84C*
Cable TV of Haileyville-Hartshorne - Haileyville, OK - *Tel&CabFB 84C*
Cable TV of Harlo - Harlowton, MT - *BrCabYB 84; Tel&CabFB 84C*
Cable TV of Harris County [of Communications Systems Inc.] - Harris County, TX - *BrCabYB 84*
Cable TV of Hartshorne - Hartshorne, OK - *BrCabYB 84*
Cable TV of Hartsville - Hartsville, SC - *BrCabYB 84; Tel&CabFB 84C*
Cable TV of Hayward Inc. - Hayward, WI - *Tel&CabFB 84C*
Cable TV of Hernando [of Interchange Cable] - Hernando, MS - *BrCabYB 84; Tel&CabFB 84C*
Cable TV of Hesperia [of Communications Systems Inc.] - Hesperia, CA - *BrCabYB 84; Tel&CabFB 84C*
Cable TV of Hillsboro Inc. [of Communications Systems Inc.] - Hillsboro, TX - *BrCabYB 84; Tel&CabFB 84C*
Cable TV of Jena [of Communications Systems Inc.] - Jena, LA - *BrCabYB 84; Tel&CabFB 84C*
Cable TV of Kalamazoo - Kalamazoo, MI - *BrCabYB 84*
Cable TV of Keystone Heights [of Communicable Inc.] - Keystone Heights, FL - *BrCabYB 84; Tel&CabFB 84C*
Cable TV of La Salle [of Communications Systems Inc.] - Olla, LA - *BrCabYB 84*
Cable TV of La Salle [of Scott Cable Communications Inc.] - Urania, LA - *Tel&CabFB 84C*
Cable TV of Lake Tahoe [of Communications Systems Inc.] - Meyers, CA - *BrCabYB 84*
Cable TV of Lake Tahoe [of Communications Systems Inc.] - South Lake Tahoe, CA - *BrCabYB 84*
Cable TV of Lebanon [of Scott Cable Communications Inc.] - Lebanon, MO - *Tel&CabFB 84C*
Cable TV of Louisiana Inc. - Columbia, LA - *BrCabYB 84*
Cable TV of Loxley - Loxley, AL - *Tel&CabFB 84C*
Cable TV of Lucedale [of Interchange Cable System] - Lucedale, MS - *BrCabYB 84; Tel&CabFB 84C*
Cable TV of Madison [of Satellite Cable TV Corp.] - Madison, AL - *BrCabYB 84; Tel&CabFB 84C*
Cable TV of Matador - Matador, TX - *Tel&CabFB 84C*
Cable TV of Meyers [of Communications Systems Inc.] - Meyers, CA - *Tel&CabFB 84C*
Cable TV of Minot Inc. [of Community Tele-Communications Inc.] - Minot, ND - *BrCabYB 84; Tel&CabFB 84C*
Cable TV of Monroe Inc. - Ouachita Parish, LA - *BrCabYB 84*
Cable TV of Oklahoma [of Scott Cable Communications Inc.] - Eufaula, OK - *Tel&CabFB 84C*
Cable TV of Olathe [of Landmark Cablevision Associates] - Olathe, KS - *Tel&CabFB 84C*
Cable TV of Oswego [of Jerico Cable TV Inc.] - Oswego, KS - *Tel&CabFB 84C*
Cable TV of Palatka [of Communicable Inc.] - Palatka, FL - *BrCabYB 84; Tel&CabFB 84C*
Cable TV of Paola Inc. - La Cygne, KS - *BrCabYB 84*
Cable TV of Paola Inc. - Paola, KS - *BrCabYB 84 p.D-298; Tel&CabFB 84C p.1668*
Cable TV of Paola Inc. - Spring Hill, KS - *BrCabYB 84*
Cable TV of Pearsall [of Karnack Corp.] - Pearsall, TX - *BrCabYB 84*
Cable TV of Pelahatchie - Pelahatchie, MS - *BrCabYB 84*
Cable TV of Pleasure Island - Gulf Shores, AL - *BrCabYB 84; Tel&CabFB 84C*
Cable TV of Pointe Coupee Inc. [of Wometco Cable TV Inc.] - New Roads, LA - *Tel&CabFB 84C*
Cable TV of Pointe Coupee Inc. [of Wometco Cable TV Inc.] - Pointe Coupee Parish, LA - *BrCabYB 84*
Cable TV of Puget Sound [of Tribune Publishing Co.] - Pierce County, WA - *Tel&CabFB 84C*
Cable TV of Quitman Inc. [of Tele-Media Corp.] - Quitman, GA - *BrCabYB 84*
Cable TV of Rio Vista [of Tele-Communications Inc.] - Rio Vista, CA - *BrCabYB 84; Tel&CabFB 84C*
Cable TV of Rushville [of Cardinal Communications Inc.] - Rushville, IN - *Tel&CabFB 84C*
Cable TV of Stanton Inc. - Stanton, NE - *Tel&CabFB 84C*
Cable TV of Talihina - Talihina, OK - *BrCabYB 84; Tel&CabFB 84C*
Cable TV of Tallapoosa Inc. - Tallapoosa, GA - *Tel&CabFB 84C*
Cable TV of Tchula Inc. [of Action Communications Co. Inc.] - Tchula, MS - *Tel&CabFB 84C*
Cable TV of the Kennebunks - Kennebunk, ME - *Tel&CabFB 84C*
Cable TV of Tri-States - Sandyston, PA - *BrCabYB 84*
Cable TV of Tri-States Inc. - Branchville, NJ - *Tel&CabFB 84C*
Cable TV of Virginia [of Communications Systems Inc.] - Radford, VA - *BrCabYB 84; Tel&CabFB 84C*
Cable TV of West Odessa Inc. - Ector County, TX - *Tel&CabFB 84C*
Cable TV of Wilburton - Wilburton, OK - *BrCabYB 84; Tel&CabFB 84C*
Cable TV of Winnsboro [of Scott Cable Communications Inc.] - Winnsboro, LA - *BrCabYB 84; Tel&CabFB 84C*
Cable TV Puget Sound [of Tribune Publishing Co.] - Ft. Lewis, WA - *Tel&CabFB 84C*
Cable TV Puget Sound [of Tribune Publishing Co.] - Gig Harbor Peninsula, WA - *Tel&CabFB 84C*
Cable TV Puget Sound [of Tribune Publishing Co.] - King County, WA - *Tel&CabFB 84C*

Cable TV Puget Sound [of Tribune Cable Communications Inc.] - Pierce County, WA - *BrCabYB 84*
Cable TV Puget Sound [of Tribune Publishing Co.] - Thurston County, WA - *Tel&CabFB 84C*
Cable TV Ste. Veronique Engr. - Ste. Veronique, PQ, Canada - *BrCabYB 84*
Cable TV Systems Inc. [of Communications Services Inc.] - Hutchinson, KS - *BrCabYB 84; Tel&CabFB 84C*
Cable TV Systems Inc. [of Prime Cable Corp.] - Union City, NJ - *Tel&CabFB 84C*
Cable TV Systems Inc. - Chittenango, NY - *BrCabYB 84; Tel&CabFB 84C*
Cable TV Systems of Arkansas [of Satellite Cable TV Corp.] - Cabot, AR - *Tel&CabFB 84C*
Cable TV Technology - Carmel, CA - *BaconPubCkMag 84*
Cable Video Communications Inc. - Bradenton Beach, FL - *BrCabYB 84*
Cable Video Inc. - Dane, WI - *Tel&CabFB 84C*
Cable View of Albert Lea Inc. [of Tele-Communications Inc.] - Albert Lea, MN - *BrCabYB 84*
Cable-Vision - Edna, TX - *BrCabYB 84; Tel&CabFB 84C*
Cable-Vision - Ganado, TX - *Tel&CabFB 84C*
Cable Vision Inc. [of Adams-Russell Co. Inc.] - Lewiston, ME - *Tel&CabFB 84C*
Cable Vision Inc. [of Omega Communications Inc.] - Alma, MI - *Tel&CabFB 84C*
Cable Vision Inc. [of Omega Communications Inc.] - Hart, MI - *BrCabYB 84*
Cable Vision Inc. [of Omega Communications Inc.] - Ludington, MI - *Tel&CabFB 84C*
Cable Vision Inc. [of Omega Communications Inc.] - Mt. Pleasant, MI - *BrCabYB 84; Tel&CabFB 84C*
Cable Vision Inc. - Scottville, MI - *BrCabYB 84*
Cable Vision Inc. [of Omega Communications Inc.] - Shelby, MI - *BrCabYB 84*
Cable Vision Inc. - Shepherd, MI - *BrCabYB 84*
Cable Vision Inc. - Gatesville, TX - *BrCabYB 84*
Cable Vision Industries - Liberty, NY - *LitMarPl 84*
Cable Vision Industries Inc. - *See* Gerry, Alan
Cable-Vision Ltd. - Granado, TX - *BrCabYB 84*
Cable Vision of Edna - Lolita, TX - *BrCabYB 84*
Cable-Vision of New Jersey - Ridgewood, NJ - *BrCabYB 84*
Cable-Vision Services - Haviland, KS - *BrCabYB 84; Tel&CabFB 84C*
Cable-Vista Inc. - Elizabethtown, KY - *BrCabYB 84*
Cable Vue TV Inc. - Baxley, GA - *BrCabYB 84; Tel&CabFB 84C*
Cable West Corp. [of Satellite Communications Cable TV] - Eaton, CO - *Tel&CabFB 84C*
Cable West Corp. [of American Television & Communications Corp.] - Woodmore, CO - *BrCabYB 84*
Cable West Corp. - Kemmerer, WY - *Tel&CabFB 84C*
Cable West Corp. - Pinedale, WY - *Tel&CabFB 84C p.1669*
Cable West TV Ltd. - Red Deer, AB, Canada - *BrCabYB 84*
Cable West TV Ltd. - Castlegar, BC, Canada - *BrCabYB 84*
Cable West TV Ltd. - Nanaimo, BC, Canada - *BrCabYB 84*
Cable West TV Ltd. - Nelson, BC, Canada - *BrCabYB 84*
Cable West TV Ltd. [of Capital Cable TV Ltd.] - North Vancouver, BC, Canada - *BrCabYB 84*
Cable World Inc. - Charleston, MO - *BrCabYB 84*
Cable World of Chaffee Inc. - Chaffee, MO - *Tel&CabFB 84C*
Cable World of Franklin County Inc. - Washington, MO - *BrCabYB 84*
Cable World of Perryville - Perryville, MO - *BrCabYB 84; Tel&CabFB 84C*
Cable World of Sikeston Inc. - Scott City, KS - *BrCabYB 84*
Cable World of Sikeston Inc. - New Madrid, MO - *BrCabYB 84*
Cable World of Sikeston Inc. - Sikeston, MO - *BrCabYB 84; Tel&CabFB 84C*
Cableage - New York, NY - *InterCabHB 3*
CableBus Systems Corp. - Beaverton, OR - *DataDirSup 7-83; HomeVid&CabYB 82-83*
Cablecasting Ltd. - Toronto, ON, Canada - *BrCabYB 84; Tel&CabFB 84C*
Cablecom/Clifton-Morenci [of Capital Cities Communications Inc.] - Clifton, AZ - *Tel&CabFB 84C*
Cablecom Corp. - Chicago, IL - *Tel&CabFB 84C*
Cablecom-General Inc. - Englewood, CO - *LitMarPl 84; TelAl 83*
Cablecom-General Inc. - *See* Capital Cities Cable Inc.
Cablecom-General Inc. - *See* Capital Cities Communications Inc.
Cablecom-General of Modesto Inc. [of Capital Cities Communications Inc.] - Modesto, CA - *Tel&CabFB 84C*
Cablecom of Abilene [of Capital Cities Communications Inc.] - Abilene, KS - *BrCabYB 84; Tel&CabFB 84C*
Cablecom of Altus [of Capital Cities Communications Inc.] - Altus, OK - *BrCabYB 84; Tel&CabFB 84C*
Cablecom of Ardmore [of Capital Cities Communications Inc.] - Ardmore, OK - *BrCabYB 84; Tel&CabFB 84C*
Cablecom of Beloir [of Wheat State Telecable Inc.] - Douglass, KS - *BrCabYB 84*
Cablecom of Beloit [of Capital Cities Communications Inc.] - Beloit, KS - *BrCabYB 84; Tel&CabFB 84C*
Cablecom of Bonham [of Capital Cities Communications Inc.] - Bonham, TX - *BrCabYB 84; Tel&CabFB 84C*
Cablecom of Brookfield [of Capital Cities Communications Inc.] - Brookfield, MO - *BrCabYB 84; Tel&CabFB 84C*
Cablecom of Childress [of Capital Cities Communications Inc.] - Childress, TX - *BrCabYB 84; Tel&CabFB 84C*
Cablecom of Clarksdale [of Capital Cities Cable Inc.] - Clarksdale, MS - *BrCabYB 84*
Cablecom of Clarksdale/Lyon [of Capital Cities Communications Inc.] - Clarksdale, MS - *Tel&CabFB 84C*
Cablecom of Clay Center [of Capital Cities Communications Inc.] - Clay Center, KS - *BrCabYB 84; Tel&CabFB 84C*
Cablecom of Cobre Valley [of Capital Cities Communications Inc.] - Globe/Miami, AZ - *Tel&CabFB 84C*
Cablecom of Cobre Valley [of Capital Cities Cable Inc.] - Miami, AZ - *BrCabYB 84*
Cablecom of Concordia [of Capital Cities Communications Inc.] - Concordia, KS - *BrCabYB 84; Tel&CabFB 84C*
Cablecom of Cottonwood [of Capital Cities Communications Inc.] - Cottonwood, AZ - *BrCabYB 84; Tel&CabFB 84C*
Cablecom of Denison [of Capital Cities Communications Inc.] - Denison, TX - *Tel&CabFB 84C*
Cablecom of Dyersburg Inc. [of Capital Cities Communications Inc.] - Dyersburg, TN - *BrCabYB 84; Tel&CabFB 84C*
Cablecom of Fargo [of Capital Cities Communications Inc.] - Fargo, ND - *BrCabYB 84; Tel&CabFB 84C*
Cablecom of Gila Valley [of Capital Cities Cable Inc.] - Safford, AZ - *BrCabYB 84; Tel&CabFB 84C*
Cablecom of Gulfport [of Capital Cities Communications Inc.] - Gulfport, MS - *BrCabYB 84; Tel&CabFB 84C*
Cablecom of Hobart [of Capital Cities Communications Inc.] - Hobart, OK - *BrCabYB 84; Tel&CabFB 84C*
Cablecom of Holbrook [of Capital Cities Communications Inc.] - Holbrook, AZ - *BrCabYB 84; Tel&CabFB 84C*
Cablecom of Idabel [of Capital Cities Communications Inc.] - Idabel, OK - *Tel&CabFB 84C*
Cablecom of Joplin-Webb City [of Capital Cities Communications Inc.] - Joplin, MO - *BrCabYB 84; Tel&CabFB 84C*
Cablecom of Kirksville [of Capital Cities Communications Inc.] - Kirksville, MO - *BrCabYB 84; Tel&CabFB 84C*
Cablecom of Lampasas [of Capital Cities Communications Inc.] - Lampasas, TX - *BrCabYB 84; Tel&CabFB 84C*
Cablecom of Lufkin [of Capital Cities Communications Inc.] - Lufkin, TX - *BrCabYB 84; Tel&CabFB 84C*
Cablecom of Mangum [of Capital Cities Communications Inc.] - Mangum, OK - *BrCabYB 84; Tel&CabFB 84C*
Cablecom of Memphis [of Capital Cities Communications Inc.] - Memphis, TX - *BrCabYB 84; Tel&CabFB 84C*
Cablecom of Miami [of Capital Cities Communications Inc.] - Miami, OK - *BrCabYB 84; Tel&CabFB 84C*
Cablecom of Modesto Inc. [of Capital Cities Cable Inc.] - Modesto, CA - *BrCabYB 84*
Cablecom of Norfolk [of Capital Cities Communications Inc.] - Norfolk, NE - *BrCabYB 84; Tel&CabFB 84C*
Cablecom of Nowata Inc. [of Capital Cities Communications Inc.] - Nowata, OK - *Tel&CabFB 84C*
Cablecom of Page [of Capital Cities Communications Inc.] - Page, AZ - *BrCabYB 84; Tel&CabFB 84C*
Cablecom of Ponca City [of Capital Cities Communications Inc.] - Ponca City, OK - *BrCabYB 84; Tel&CabFB 84C*
Cablecom of Port Lavaca [of Capital Cities Communications Inc.] - Port Lavaca, TX - *BrCabYB 84; Tel&CabFB 84C*

Cablecom of Roswell [of Capital Cities Communications Inc.] - Roswell, NM - *BrCabYB 84; Tel&CabFB 84C*
Cablecom of Sherman [of Capital Cities Communications Inc.] - Sherman, TX - *BrCabYB 84; Tel&CabFB 84C*
Cablecom of Vinita [of Capital Cities Communications Inc.] - Vinita, OK - *Tel&CabFB 84C*
Cablecom of Wellington [of Capital Cities Communications Inc.] - Wellington, TX - *BrCabYB 84; Tel&CabFB 84C*
Cablecom of White Mountains [of Capital Cities Communications Inc.] - Show Low, AZ - *BrCabYB 84; Tel&CabFB 84C*
Cablecom of Winslow [of Capital Cities Communications Inc.] - Winslow, AZ - *BrCabYB 84; Tel&CabFB 84C*
Cablecom Walton Corp. [of Simmons Communications Inc.] - Walton, NY - *BrCabYB 84*
Cablefacts - Lexington, KY - *CabTVFinDB 83*
Cablegram Service [of MCI International Inc.] - Rye Brook, NY - *TeleSy&SerDir 2-84*
Cablemaster Corp. - Hunter, NY - *BrCabYB 84; Tel&CabFB 84C*
Cablenet Inc. - Mt. Prospect, IL - *BrCabYB 84; Tel&CabFB 84C*
Cablenet Ltd. - Downsview, ON, Canada - *Tel&CabFB 84C*
Cablenet Ltd. [of Cybermedix Ltd.] - Willowdale, ON, Canada - *BrCabYB 84*
CableNews - Bethesda, MD - *DirOnDB Spring 84*
CableNews [of NewsNet Inc.] - Bryn Mawr, PA - *DataDirOnSer 84*
Cablentertainment - Prestonsburg, KY - *BrCabYB 84; Tel&CabFB 84C*
Cablentertainment - Kitzmiller, MD - *BrCabYB 84*
Cablentertainment - Oakland, MD - *BrCabYB 84; Tel&CabFB 84C*
Cablentertainment [of Group W Cable Inc.] - Vineland, NJ - *Tel&CabFB 84C*
Cablentertainment - New York, NY - *CabTVFinDB 83*
Cablentertainment - Richwood, WV - *BrCabYB 84*
Cablentertainment Inc. - Bridgeton, NJ - *Tel&CabFB 84C*
Cablentertainment Inc. - Iselin, NJ - *BrCabYB 84 p.D-298; Tel&CabFB 84C p.1668*
Cablentertainment Inc. - Ocean City, NJ - *Tel&CabFB 84C*
Cablentertainment Inc. - Ventnor City, NJ - *Tel&CabFB 84C*
Cablentertainment Inc. - Rochester, PA - *Tel&CabFB 84C*
Cablentertainment Inc. - Marion, VA - *BrCabYB 84*
Cablentertainment Inc. - Buckhannon, WV - *Tel&CabFB 84C*
Cablentertainment Inc. - Madison, WV - *Tel&CabFB 84C*
Cablentertainment Inc. - Milton, WV - *Tel&CabFB 84C*
Cablentertainment Inc. - Morgantown, WV - *BrCabYB 84; Tel&CabFB 84C*
Cablentertainment Inc. - Mt. Hope, WV - *Tel&CabFB 84C*
Cablentertainment Inc. - Peterstown, WV - *Tel&CabFB 84C*
Cablentertainment Inc. - Point Pleasant, WV - *Tel&CabFB 84C*
Cablentertainment Inc. - Rowlesburg, WV - *BrCabYB 84*
Cablentertainment Inc. - White Sulphur Springs, WV - *Tel&CabFB 84C*
Cablentertainment of New Castle - New Castle, PA - *BrCabYB 84; Tel&CabFB 84C*
Cablentertainment of Ohio Inc. - Dresden, OH - *BrCabYB 84; Tel&CabFB 84C*
Cablentertainment of Ohio Inc. - New Concord, OH - *BrCabYB 84*
Cablentertainment of Ohio Inc. - Zanesville, OH - *BrCabYB 84; Tel&CabFB 84C*
Cablentertainment of Rochester - Rochester, PA - *BrCabYB 84*
Cablentertainment of Virginia Inc. - Pulaski, VA - *BrCabYB 84; Tel&CabFB 84C*
Cablentertainment of West Virginia - Marion, VA - *Tel&CabFB 84C*
Cablentertainment of West Virginia - Rich Creek, VA - *BrCabYB 84*
Cablentertainment of West Virginia - Alderson, WV - *BrCabYB 84*
Cablentertainment of West Virginia - Beverly, WV - *BrCabYB 84*
Cablentertainment of West Virginia - Cairo, WV - *BrCabYB 84*
Cablentertainment of West Virginia - Farmington, WV - *BrCabYB 84*
Cablentertainment of West Virginia - Madison, WV - *BrCabYB 84*
Cablentertainment of West Virginia - Milton, WV - *BrCabYB 84*
Cablentertainment of West Virginia - Mt. Hope, WV - *BrCabYB 84*
Cablentertainment of West Virginia - Pennsboro, WV - *BrCabYB 84*
Cablentertainment of West Virginia - Pine Grove, WV - *BrCabYB 84*
Cablentertainment of West Virginia - Point Pleasant, WV - *BrCabYB 84*
Cablentertainment of West Virginia - Ravenswood, WV - *BrCabYB 84*
Cablentertainment of West Virginia - Richwood, WV - *Tel&CabFB 84C*
Cablentertainment of West Virginia - Ripley, WV - *BrCabYB 84*
Cablentertainment of West Virginia - Salem, WV - *BrCabYB 84*
Cablentertainment of West Virginia - Shinnston, WV - *BrCabYB 84*
Cablentertainment of West Virginia - White Sulphur Springs, WV - *BrCabYB 84*
CableProfile - Media, PA - *DirOnDB Spring 84*
Cablescope [Aff. of Cowles Media Inc.] - Buffalo, NY - *BrCabYB 84; InterCabHB 3; Tel&CabFB 84C*
Cableshare Inc. - London, ON, Canada - *DataDirOnSer 84; DataDirSup 7-83; VideoDir 82-83*
Cableshop, The [of Adams-Russell] - Waltham, MA - *CabTVPrDB 83*
Cablestrie Inc. - Drummondville, PQ, Canada - *BrCabYB 84*
Cablestrie Inc. - Windsor, PQ, Canada - *Tel&CabFB 84C*
CableSystem, The [of Toledo Blade Co.] - Toledo, OH - *BrCabYB 84*
Cablesystems Alberta Ltd. [of Rogers Cablesystems Inc.] - Calgary, AB, Canada - *BrCabYB 84*
Cablesystems of Alabama Inc. - Bessemer, AL - *BrCabYB 84*
Cablesystems Pacific [of Rogers Cablesystems Inc.] - Multnomah County, OR - *BrCabYB 84*
Cablesystems Pacific [of Rogers UA Cablesystems Inc.] - Portland, OR - *BrCabYB 84; InterCabHB 3; Tel&CabFB 84C*
Cabletelevision Advertising Bureau - New York, NY - *InterCabHB 3*
CableText [of Southern Satellite Systems Inc.] - Douglasville, GA - *BrCabYB 84; Tel&CabFB 84C*
CableText [Div. of Southern Satellite Systems Inc.] - Tulsa, OK - *AvMarPl 83; BrCabYB 84*
Cabletronics Inc. - Geneseo, IL - *BrCabYB 84; Tel&CabFB 84C*
Cableview Inc. - Minneapolis, KS - *Tel&CabFB 84C p.1668*
Cableview Inc. - McKenzie, OR - *Tel&CabFB 84C*
Cableview of Albert Lea Inc. - Albert Lea, MN - *Tel&CabFB 84C*
Cablevision [of Titsch Communications Inc.] - Denver, CO - *BaconPubCkMag 84; Folio 83; MagDir 84*
Cablevision [of Scripps-Howard Cable Services Co.] - Leesburg, FL - *BrCabYB 84*
Cablevision - Atlanta, GA - *BrCabYB 84*
Cablevision [Aff. of American Television & Communications Corp.] - Urbana, IL - *InterCabHB 3*
Cablevision [of St. Joseph Cable Communications Inc.] - Wathena, KS - *BrCabYB 84*
Cablevision [of Cablevision Systems Development Corp.] - Woodbury, NY - *HomeVid&CabYB 82-83*
Cablevision - Aloha, WA - *BrCabYB 84*
Cablevision - Newport, WA - *BrCabYB 84*
Cablevision Associates IV - Eldoza, IA - *BrCabYB 84*
Cablevision Cap de la Madeleine [of Cablevision Nationale Ltee.] - Cap de la Madeleine, PQ, Canada - *BrCabYB 84*
Cablevision Communications of New Jersey [of Group W Cable Corp.] - West Milford, NJ - *BrCabYB 84*
Cablevision Co. Inc. - Alabaster, AL - *BrCabYB 84*
Cablevision Co. Inc. - Forestdale, AL - *BrCabYB 84*
Cablevision Co. Inc. - Gardendale, AL - *BrCabYB 84; Tel&CabFB 84C p.1669*
Cablevision Co. Inc. - Trussville, AL - *BrCabYB 84*
Cablevision Co., The [of The Cable TV Co. Inc.] - Fairfield Glade, TN - *Tel&CabFB 84C*
Cablevision Contra Costa [of Televents Inc.] - Moraga, CA - *BrCabYB 84; Tel&CabFB 84C*
Cablevision du Nord de Quebec Inc. - Val d'Or, PQ, Canada - *BrCabYB 84; Tel&CabFB 84C*

Cablevision Enterprises of Tennessee Inc. - Charlotte, TN - *Tel&CabFB 84C p.1669*
Cablevision Inc. - Waianae, HI - *BrCabYB 84; Tel&CabFB 84C*
Cablevision Inc. [of Omega Communications Inc.] - St. Johns, MI - *Tel&CabFB 84C*
Cablevision Inc. of Russellville - Russellville, KY - *BrCabYB 84; Tel&CabFB 84C*
Cablevision Industries Inc. - Daytona, FL - *Tel&CabFB 84C*
Cablevision Industries Inc. - Lakeland, FL - *Tel&CabFB 84C*
Cablevision Industries Inc. - Liberty, NY - *CabTVFinDB 83; Tel&CabFB 84C p.1669*
Cablevision Industries Inc. - Macedon, NY - *BrCabYB 84*
Cablevision Industries Inc. - Palenville, NY - *BrCabYB 84*
Cablevision Ltd. [of Sunflower Telephone Co. Inc.] - Leoti, KS - *BrCabYB 84 p.D-298; Tel&CabFB 84C*
Cablevision Ltd. [of Sunflower Telephone Co. Inc.] - Sharon Springs, KS - *BrCabYB 84; Tel&CabFB 84C*
Cablevision Ltd. [of Sunflower Telephone Co. Inc.] - Tribune, KS - *BrCabYB 84; Tel&CabFB 84C*
Cablevision Ltd. [of Ottawa Cablevision Ltd.] - Arnprior, ON, Canada - *BrCabYB 84*
Cablevision Management Corp. - Sayre, PA - *Tel&CabFB 84C*
Cablevision Medicine Hat Ltd. - Medicine Hat, AB, Canada - *BrCabYB 84*
Cablevision National Ltd. - Montreal, PQ, Canada - *Tel&CabFB 84C*
Cablevision Nationale Ltee. [of Videotron 1979 Ltee.] - Montreal, PQ, Canada - *BrCabYB 84*
Cablevision Nationale Ltee. - Sherbrooke, PQ, Canada - *BrCabYB 84*
Cablevision Nationale Ltee. - Vanier, PQ, Canada - *BrCabYB 84*
Cablevision of Alamance County [of American TV & Communications Corp.] - Burlington, NC - *BrCabYB 84; Tel&CabFB 84C*
Cablevision of Arkansas City - Arkansas City, AR - *BrCabYB 84*
Cablevision of Asheboro [of American TV & Communications Corp.] - Asheboro, NC - *Tel&CabFB 84C*
Cablevision of Augusta [of Signet Communications Inc.] - Augusta, GA - *BrCabYB 84; Tel&CabFB 84C*
Cablevision of Austin - Austin, MN - *BrCabYB 84; Tel&CabFB 84C*
Cablevision of Baton Rouge - Baton Rouge, LA - *Tel&CabFB 84C*
Cablevision of Bayonne - Bayonne, NJ - *BrCabYB 84; Tel&CabFB 84C*
Cablevision of Benton Inc. [of Century Telephone Enterprises Inc.] - Benton, LA - *Tel&CabFB 84C*
Cablevision of Bethany [of Multimedia Cablevision Inc.] - Bethany, OK - *Tel&CabFB 84C*
Cablevision of Bixby [of Multimedia Cablevision Inc.] - Bixby, OK - *BrCabYB 84*
Cablevision of Blowing Rock Inc. [of Fletcher Smith & Associates] - Blowing Rock, NC - *Tel&CabFB 84C*
Cablevision of Breckenridge - Breckenridge, CO - *BrCabYB 84*
Cablevision of Calumet County Inc. - Brillion, WI - *BrCabYB 84*
Cablevision of Calumet County Inc. - New Holstein, WI - *BrCabYB 84*
Cablevision of Canon City [of American TV & Communications Corp.] - Canon City, CO - *BrCabYB 84; Tel&CabFB 84C*
Cablevision of Canton - Canton, MA - *BrCabYB 84*
Cablevision of Canyon Inc. [of Cardiff Cablevision Inc.] - Canyon, TX - *BrCabYB 84; Tel&CabFB 84C*
Cablevision of Chanute [Aff. of American Television & Communications Corp.] - Chanute, KS - *InterCabHB 3*
Cablevision of Charlotte [of American TV & Communications Corp.] - Charlotte, NC - *BrCabYB 84; Tel&CabFB 84C*
Cablevision of Chicago [of Cablevision Systems Development Co.] - Oak Park, IL - *BrCabYB 84; Tel&CabFB 84C*
Cablevision of Connecticut [of Scripps-Howard Cable Services Co.] - Bridgeport, CT - *Tel&CabFB 84C*
Cablevision of Connecticut [of Cablevision Systems Development Co.] - Fairfield County, CT - *BrCabYB 84; Tel&CabFB 84C*
Cablevision of Corry [of Cablevision Industries Inc.] - Corry, PA - *Tel&CabFB 84C*
Cablevision of Del City [of Multimedia Cablevision Inc.] - Del City, OK - *Tel&CabFB 84C*
Cablevision of Duncan [of Community Tele-Communications Inc.] - Duncan, OK - *BrCabYB 84; Tel&CabFB 84C*
Cablevision of Dunn County [of Wisconsin Cablevision & Radio Co. Inc.] - Menomonie, WI - *BrCabYB 84; Tel&CabFB 84C*
Cablevision of Effingham County - Springfield, GA - *Tel&CabFB 84C*
Cablevision of Effingham Inc. - Springfield, GA - *BrCabYB 84*
Cablevision of Emmett Inc. [of Harmon & Co. Inc.] - Emmett, ID - *Tel&CabFB 84C*
Cablevision of Emporia [of American TV & Communications Corp.] - Emporia, KS - *BrCabYB 84; Tel&CabFB 84C*
Cablevision of Estes [of Liberty Communications Co. Inc.] - Estes Park, CO - *BrCabYB 84*
Cablevision of Eudora [of Community Communications Co.] - Eudora, AR - *BrCabYB 84; Tel&CabFB 84C*
Cablevision of Fairhaven/Acushnet Inc. - Fairhaven, MA - *Tel&CabFB 84C*
Cablevision of Fayetteville [of American TV & Communications Corp.] - Fayetteville, NC - *Tel&CabFB 84C*
Cablevision of Floresville Inc. [of Communications Systems Inc.] - Floresville, TX - *BrCabYB 84*
Cablevision of Fond du Lac County Inc. [of Wisconsin Cablevision & Radio Co. Inc.] - Campbellsport, WI - *Tel&CabFB 84C*
Cablevision of Fond du Lac County Inc. [of Wisconsin Cablevision & Radio Co. Inc.] - Fond du Lac, WI - *Tel&CabFB 84C*
Cablevision of Fond du Lac County Inc. [of Wisconsin Cablevision & Radio Co. Inc.] - Lomira, WI - *Tel&CabFB 84C*
Cablevision of Fond du Lac County Inc. [of Wisconsin Cablevision & Radio Co. Inc.] - Oakfield, WI - *Tel&CabFB 84C*
Cablevision of Fond du Lac County Inc. [of Wisconsin Cablevision & Radio Co. Inc.] - Rosendale, WI - *Tel&CabFB 84C*
Cablevision of Fredericksburg Inc. [of Media General Inc.] - Fredericksburg, VA - *BrCabYB 84; Tel&CabFB 84C*
Cablevision of Gastonia [of American TV & Communications Corp.] - Gastonia, NC - *BrCabYB 84; Tel&CabFB 84C*
Cablevision of Geauga County - Chardon, OH - *BrCabYB 84*
Cablevision of Gonzales Inc. [of Communications Services Inc.] - Gonzales, LA - *BrCabYB 84; Tel&CabFB 84C*
Cablevision of Grand Prairie Inc. - England, AR - *BrCabYB 84; Tel&CabFB 84C*
Cablevision of Grand Prairie Inc. - Lonoke, AR - *Tel&CabFB 84C*
Cablevision of Grand Prairie Inc. - Stuttgart, AR - *BrCabYB 84; Tel&CabFB 84C*
Cablevision of Greater Johnstown [of American TV & Communications Corp.] - Johnstown, PA - *Tel&CabFB 84C*
Cablevision of Greensboro [of American TV & Communications Corp.] - Greensboro, NC - *BrCabYB 84; InterCabHB 3; Tel&CabFB 84C*
Cablevision of Greenville - Greenville, IL - *BrCabYB 84; Tel&CabFB 84C*
Cablevision of Guthrie [of Multimedia Cablevision Inc.] - Guthrie, OK - *Tel&CabFB 84C*
Cablevision of Guymon [of Don Rey Comm] - Guymon, OK - *BrCabYB 84*
Cablevision of High Point-Jamestown [of American TV & Communications Corp.] - High Point, NC - *BrCabYB 84; Tel&CabFB 84C*
Cablevision of Independence [of American TV & Communications Corp.] - Independence, KS - *BrCabYB 84; Tel&CabFB 84C*
Cablevision of Inglewood [of TCI-Taft Cablevision Associates] - Inglewood, CA - *Tel&CabFB 84C*
Cablevision of Jackson County - Jackson, OH - *BrCabYB 84; Tel&CabFB 84C*
Cablevision of Jefferson County Inc. - Arnold, MO - *BrCabYB 84*
Cablevision of Jefferson County Inc. - Hillsboro, MO - *Tel&CabFB 84C*
Cablevision of Kewaunee County Inc. [of Wisconsin Cablevision & Radio Co. Inc.] - Kewaunee, WI - *Tel&CabFB 84C*
Cablevision of Knox City - Knox City, TX - *BrCabYB 84; Tel&CabFB 84C*
Cablevision of Knox County - Rockland, ME - *Tel&CabFB 84C*

Cablevision of Lake Travis [of Lakeway Co.] - Lakeway, TX - *BrCabYB 84; Tel&CabFB 84C*
Cablevision of Leander [of McDaniel & Hillard] - Leander, TX - *Tel&CabFB 84C*
Cablevision of Lincoln County Inc. [of Omega Communications Inc.] - Lincoln County, NM - *BrCabYB 84*
Cablevision of Lincoln County Inc. [of Rifkin & Associates] - Ruidoso, NM - *Tel&CabFB 84C*
Cablevision of Lindsay [of Multimedia Cablevision Inc.] - Lindsay, OK - *Tel&CabFB 84C*
Cablevision of Long Island - Woodbury, NY - *TelAl 83*
Cablevision of Lumberton [of American TV & Communications Corp.] - Lumberton, NC - *BrCabYB 84; Tel&CabFB 84C*
Cablevision of Manassas Park Inc. - Manassas Park, VA - *Tel&CabFB 84C*
Cablevision of Marlow Inc. [of Tele-Communications Inc.] - Marlow, OK - *BrCabYB 84; Tel&CabFB 84C*
Cablevision of McCall [of Harmon & Co. Inc.] - McCall, ID - *BrCabYB 84; Tel&CabFB 84C*
Cablevision of Medford [of Wisconsin Cablevision & Radio Co. Inc.] - Medford, WI - *BrCabYB 84; Tel&CabFB 84C*
Cablevision of Missouri [of Cardiff Cablevision Inc.] - California, MO - *BrCabYB 84; Tel&CabFB 84C*
Cablevision of Missouri [of Cardiff Cablevision Inc.] - Eldon, MO - *BrCabYB 84; Tel&CabFB 84C*
Cablevision of Missouri - Kansas City, MO - *Tel&CabFB 84C p.1669*
Cablevision of Missouri [of Cardiff Cablevision Inc.] - Tipton, MO - *Tel&CabFB 84C*
Cablevision of Missouri Inc. [of Cardiff Cablevision Inc.] - Dixon, MO - *BrCabYB 84*
Cablevision of Moore [of Multimedia Cablevision Inc.] - Moore, OK - *Tel&CabFB 84C*
Cablevision of Mt. Airy [of Tele-Communications Inc.] - Mt. Airy, NC - *BrCabYB 84*
Cablevision of Muskogee [of Tele-Communications Inc.] - Muskogee, OK - *BrCabYB 84; Tel&CabFB 84C*
Cablevision of Mustang [of Multimedia Cablevision Inc.] - Mustang, OK - *Tel&CabFB 84C*
Cablevision of Needles - Needles, CA - *Tel&CabFB 84C*
Cablevision of Neodesha [of American TV & Communications Corp.] - Neodesha, KS - *BrCabYB 84; Tel&CabFB 84C*
Cablevision of New Jersey - Bergenfield, NJ - *BrCabYB 84*
Cablevision of Nichols Hills [of Multimedia Cablevision Inc.] - Nichols Hills, OK - *Tel&CabFB 84C*
Cablevision of Parsons [of American TV & Communications Corp.] - Parsons, KS - *BrCabYB 84; Tel&CabFB 84C*
Cablevision of Pennsylvania Inc. - Norristown, PA - *BrCabYB 84; Tel&CabFB 84C*
Cablevision of Peotone [of Tele-Communications Inc.] - Peotone, IL - *Tel&CabFB 84C*
Cablevision of Perry [of Multimedia Cablevision Inc.] - Perry, OK - *BrCabYB 84; Tel&CabFB 84C*
Cablevision of Pflugerville [of McDaniel & Hillard] - Pflugerville, TX - *BrCabYB 84; Tel&CabFB 84C*
Cablevision of Plattsmouth [of Harmon & Co. Inc.] - Plattsmouth, NE - *BrCabYB 84; Tel&CabFB 84C*
Cablevision of Raleigh [of American TV & Communications Corp.] - Raleigh, NC - *BrCabYB 84; Tel&CabFB 84C*
Cablevision of Raleigh/Durham [Aff. of American Television & Communications Corp.] - Raleigh, NC - *InterCabHB 3*
Cablevision of Shreveport [of American TV & Communications Corp.] - Shreveport, LA - *BrCabYB 84; Tel&CabFB 84C*
Cablevision of Soperton Inc. - Soperton, GA - *BrCabYB 84; Tel&CabFB 84C*
Cablevision of Sulphur-Davis [of Harmon & Co. Inc.] - Sulphur, OK - *Tel&CabFB 84C*
Cablevision of Tecumseh [of Teltran Inc.] - Tecumseh, OK - *BrCabYB 84; Tel&CabFB 84C*
Cablevision of the Fox Cities [of American TV & Communications Corp.] - Appleton, WI - *BrCabYB 84; Tel&CabFB 84C*
Cablevision of the Islands [of Palmer Communications Inc.] - Pine Island, FL - *Tel&CabFB 84C*
Cablevision of the Islands [of Palmer Communications Inc.] - Sanibel, FL - *Tel&CabFB 84C*
Cablevision of Topeka [of Horizon Communications Corp.] - Topeka, KS - *Tel&CabFB 84C*
Cablevision of Wadesboro Inc. - Wadesboro, NC - *BrCabYB 84; Tel&CabFB 84C*
Cablevision of Weiser [of Harmon & Co.] - Weiser, ID - *BrCabYB 84; Tel&CabFB 84C*
Cablevision of Westchester [of Cablevision Systems Development Co.] - Yonkers, NY - *BrCabYB 84*
Cablevision of Westville - Westville, OK - *BrCabYB 84*
Cablevision of Winnebago County [of Wisconsin Cablevision & Radio Co. Inc.] - Omro, WI - *BrCabYB 84; Tel&CabFB 84C*
Cablevision Service Co. - Newmarket, NH - *BrCabYB 84*
Cablevision Service Co. Inc. - Bristol, NH - *BrCabYB 84*
Cablevision Service Co. Inc. - Exeter, NH - *Tel&CabFB 84C p.1669*
Cablevision Service Co. Inc. - Hillsboro, NH - *BrCabYB 84*
Cablevision Services Inc. - Cheyenne, WY - *BrCabYB 84; Tel&CabFB 84C*
Cablevision Systems Boston Corp. - Boston, MA - *BrCabYB 84; Tel&CabFB 84C*
Cablevision Systems Development - Woodbury, NY - *BrCabYB 84 p.D-298; CabTVFinDB 83; HomeVid&CabYB 82-83; KnowInd 83; LitMarPl 84; TelAl 84; Tel&CabFB 84C p.1669*
Cablevision Systems Development Co. - Jericho, NY - *TelAl 83*
Cablevision Systems Inc. - Seminole, OK - *BrCabYB 84; Tel&CabFB 84C p.1669*
Cablevision Systems Inc. - Wewoka, OK - *BrCabYB 84; Tel&CabFB 84C*
Cablevision Systems Long Island [of Cablevision Systems Development Co.] - Oyster Bay, NY - *BrCabYB 84*
Cablevision Systems Westchester Corp. - Yonkers, NY - *Tel&CabFB 84C*
Cablevision Victoriaville Ltee. - Victoriaville, PQ, Canada - *BrCabYB 84*
Cablevision Warwick Inc. - Warwick, PQ, Canada - *BrCabYB 84*
Cablevue Ltd. - Belleville, ON, Canada - *BrCabYB 84*
Cablodistribution Cote du Sud Inc. - La Pocatiere, PQ, Canada - *BrCabYB 84*
Cablodistribution Forestville Inc. - Forestville, PQ, Canada - *BrCabYB 84*
Cablodistribution Le Rocher Inc. - Grand'Mere, PQ, Canada - *BrCabYB 84*
Cablotem Inc. - Ville-Marie, PQ, Canada - *BrCabYB 84*
Cablovision Alma Inc. - Alma, PQ, Canada - *BrCabYB 84*
Cablovision Baie-Comeau Inc. - Baie-Comeau, PQ, Canada - *BrCabYB 84*
Cablovision Baie St.-Paul Inc. - Baie St.-Paul, PQ, Canada - *BrCabYB 84*
Cablovision Bas St.-Laurent Ltd. - Rimouski, PQ, Canada - *BrCabYB 84*
Cablovision Haut Richelieu Ltee. [of Telecable Videotron Ltee.] - St. Jean, PQ, Canada - *BrCabYB 84*
Cablovision Inc. - Asbestos, PQ, Canada - *BrCabYB 84*
Cablovision Inc. - *See* Cablestrie Inc.
Cabool Enterprise - Cabool, MO - *BaconPubCkNews 84; Ed&PubIntYB 82*
Caboose Press - Oakland, CA - *BoPubDir 5*
Cabot Advertising - Boston, MA - *StaDirAdAg 2-84*
Cabot & Co., Harold - Boston, MA - *AdAge 3-28-84; DirMarMP 83; TelAl 83, 84*
Cabot Star-Herald - Cabot, AR - *BaconPubCkNews 84; Ed&PubIntYB 82*
Cabrillo Historical Association - San Diego, CA - *BoPubDir 4 Sup, 5*
Cabrillo Times & Green Sheet - Watsonville, CA - *AyerDirPub 83*
Cabriolet Music - Shreveport, LA - *BillIntBG 83-84*
Cabscott Broadcast Productions Inc. - Lindenwold, NJ - *AvMarPl 83; StaDirAdAg 2-84*
CAC Magazine - Cleveland, OH - *BaconPubCkMag 84*
Caceres, Luis R. Jr. - Miami, FL - *LitMarPl 83, 84; MagIndMarPl 82-83*
Cache Citizen - Preston, ID - *AyerDirPub 83*
Cache Creek Pioneer - Cache Creek, BC, Canada - *AyerDirPub 83*
Cache Review [of Cache Press] - Tucson, AZ - *LitMag&SmPr 83-84; WritMar 84*
Cache Valley Newsletter - Preston, ID - *LitMag&SmPr 83-84*

C.A.C.I. - New York, NY - *IntDirMarRes 83*
CACI Inc.-Federal - Arlington, VA - *DataDirOnSer 84; DataDirSup 7-83; InfIndMarPl 83*
Caci Inc.-International - Fleet, England - *MicrocomSwDir 1*
Cacom Teleservices Inc. - Cottonwood Falls, KS - *BrCabYB 84*
Cacom Teleservices Inc. - Sedan, KS - *BrCabYB 84*
Cacom Teleservices Inc. - Strong City, KS - *BrCabYB 84*
Cactus Clyde Productions - Baton Rouge, LA - *LitMarPl 83, 84; MagIndMarPl 82-83*
Cactus Software - Tempe, AZ - *MicrocomSwDir 1*
Cactus Technology Inc. - Phoenix, AZ - *MicrocomMPl 84*
Cactusplot Co., The - Tempe, AZ - *MicrocomMPl 84*
CAD/CAM Technology [of Computer & Automated Systems Association of SME] - Dearborn, MI - *BaconPubCkMag 84; MicrocomMPl 84*
CAD Systems Update [of The Engineering Software Exchange] - Yonkers, NY - *MicrocomMPl 84*
CADAPSO - Ottawa, ON, Canada - *ADAPSOMemDir 83-84*
Cadcom [Subs. of ManTech International Corp.] - Annapolis, MD - *DataDirOnSer 84; WhoWMicrocom 83*
Caddo-Cable Communications Inc. - Daingerfield, TX - *BrCabYB 84; Tel&CabFB 84C*
Caddo-Cable Communications Inc. - Lone Star, TX - *BrCabYB 84*
Caddo-Cable Communications Inc. - Naples, TX - *BrCabYB 84*
Caddo-Cable Communications Inc. - Omaha, TX - *BrCabYB 84*
Caddo Citizen - Vivian, LA - *AyerDirPub 83*
Caddo Mills Mirror - Caddo Mills, TX - *Ed&PubIntYB 82*
Caddoan Telephone Co. [Aff. of Century Telephone Enterprises Inc.] - Plain Dealing, LA - *TelDir&BG 83-84*
Caddylak Systems - Westbury, NY - *DirInfWP 82*
Cade, Lisl - New York, NY - *LitMarPl 83, 84*
Cadence - Silver Spring, MD - *DirOnDB Spring 84*
Cadence - Redwood, NY - *LitMag&SmPr 83-84; WritMar 84*
Cadence Industries Corp. - West Caldwell, NJ - *KnowInd 83*
Cadence Jazz Records - Redwood, NY - *BillIntBG 83-84*
Cadenza Press [Aff. of Econotype Co.] - Columbia Heights, MN - *BoPubDir 4, 5*
Cadet Polka Records - Burnett, WI - *BillIntBG 83-84*
Cadet Records Inc. - Los Angeles, CA - *BillIntBG 83-84*
Cadillac Buyer's Guide - Cadillac, MI - *AyerDirPub 83*
Cadillac Cable TV [of Centel Cable Television Co.] - Cadillac, MI - *BrCabYB 84*
Cadillac News - Cadillac, MI - *BaconPubCkNews 84; Ed&PubIntYB 82; NewsDir 84*
Cadiz Cable TV - Cadiz, KY - *BrCabYB 84*
Cadiz Harrison News Herald - Cadiz, OH - *BaconPubCkNews 84; NewsDir 84*
Cadiz Record, The - Cadiz, KY - *AyerDirPub 83; Ed&PubIntYB 82*
Cadiz Record, The [of Russellville Logan Ink Inc.] - Russellville, KY - *NewsDir 84*
Cadiz Record, The - *See* Smith Communications Inc., Al
Cadmus [of East Brunswick Public Library] - East Brunswick, NJ - *EISS 83*
Cadmus Editions - Belvedere, CA - *LitMarPl 84*
Cadmus Editions - Santa Barbara, CA - *BoPubDir 4*
Cadmus Editions - Tiburon, CA - *BoPubDir 5; LitMag&SmPr 83-84*
CADO/Royal System Inc. - South Plainfield, NJ - *DirInfWP 82*
CADO Systems Corp. - Torrance, CA - *DataDirSup 7-83; DirInfWP 82; InfIndMarPl 83; WhoWMicrocom 83*
Cadott Sentinel - Cadott, WI - *BaconPubCkNews 84; Ed&PubIntYB 82*
Caduceus Systems Inc. - Plano, TX - *MicrocomMPl 84*
Cadwell Davis Partners - New York, NY - *AdAge 3-28-84; StaDirAdAg 2-84*
CAE Inc. - Hamburg, MI - *AvMarPl 83*
Caedmon/Arabesque - New York, NY - *BillIntBG 83-84*
Caelus Associates - Spokane, WA - *ADAPSOMemDir 83-84*
Caelus Memories Inc. - San Jose, CA - *DataDirSup 7-83; WhoWMicrocom 83*
Caere Corp. - Los Gatos, CA - *DataDirSup 7-83; DirInfWP 82*
Caesar Music Corp., Irving - New York, NY - *BoPubDir 4, 5*
Cafe Solo - Atascadero, CA - *LitMag&SmPr 83-84*
Cahn & Associates Inc., Stanley L. - Baltimore, MD - *LitMarPl 83, 84; MagIndMarPl 82-83*
Cahn, Herbert R. - New York, NY - *LitMarPl 83; MagIndMarPl 82-83*
Cahners Direct Marketing Service [of Cahners Publishing Co.] - Des Plaines, IL - *EISS 5-84 Sup*
Cahners Publishing Co. - Chicago, IL - *MagIndMarPl 82-83*
Cahners Publishing Co. [Subs. of Reed Holdings Inc.] - Des Plaines, IL - *DirMarMP 83*
Cahners Publishing Co. - Boston, MA - *AdAge 6-28-84; NewsBur 6*
Cahners Publishing Co. (Publishing Services Div.) - Denver, CO - *MagIndMarPl 82-83*
Cahokia-Dupo Herald - Cahokia, IL - *AyerDirPub 83; BaconPubCkNews 84; Ed&PubIntYB 82*
Cahokia-Dupo Herald [of Capitol Cities Media Inc.] - East St. Louis, IL - *NewsDir 84*
Cahokia Journal - Cakokia (IL), MO - *Ed&PubIntYB 82*
Cahokia Journal - *See* Journal Newspapers of Southern Illinois
Cail Systems Ltd. - Toronto, ON, Canada - *WhoWMicrocom 83*
Cain Inc., William - Portland, OR - *ArtMar 84; StaDirAdAg 2-84*
Cain, Mike - Richmond, OH - *BoPubDir 4, 5*
Cain Publishing, Katherine - Los Gatos, CA - *BoPubDir 4, 5*
Caine, Farber & Gordon Inc. - Pasadena, CA - *ADAPSOMemDir 83-84*
Cairn Terrier Club of America - Port Allegany, PA - *BoPubDir 4, 5*
Cairo Cablevision - Cairo, IL - *BrCabYB 84*
Cairo Evening Citizen - Cairo, IL - *BaconPubCkNews 84; Ed&PubIntYB 82; NewsDir 84*
Cairo Messenger - Cairo, GA - *BaconPubCkNews 84; Ed&PubIntYB 82; NewsDir 84*
Cairo Record - Cairo, NE - *BaconPubCkNews 84; Ed&PubIntYB 82*
Caislan Press - San Jose, CA - *BoPubDir 4, 5; LitMag&SmPr 83-84*
Caitlin Press - Vancouver, BC, Canada - *BoPubDir 4, 5*
Cal-Ad Co. - Burbank, CA - *ArtMar 84*
Cal Data Systems & Software - Santa Cruz, CA - *MicrocomMPl 83, 84*
Cal Media - La Mirada, CA - *BoPubDir 4 Sup, 5*
Cal-Nor Cableview Inc. - Alturas, CA - *Tel&CabFB 84C*
Cal-Nor Cableview Inc. - Yreka, CA - *Tel&CabFB 84C p.1669*
Cal-Nor Cableview Inc. - *See* Miley, Edward
Cal OSHA Reporter - San Pablo, CA - *BaconPubCkMag 84*
Cal Performances - San Francisco, CA - *MagDir 84*
Cal-Tel Systems Inc. - Santa Ana, CA - *DataDirSup 7-83*
Cal Underwriter - Oakland, CA - *BaconPubCkMag 84*
Cal Vista Video - Van Nuys, CA - *AvMarPl 83*
Calabasas Communications Co. - Calabasas Park, CA - *BrCabYB 84; Tel&CabFB 84C*
Calabasas Las Virgenes News Enterprise [of Hearst Community Newspapers Inc.] - Calabasas, CA - *BaconPubCkNews 84; NewsDir 84*
Calabasas Times - Encino, CA - *AyerDirPub 83*
Calabasas Times - *See* Associated Valley Publications
Calais Advertiser - Calais, ME - *BaconPubCkNews 84; Ed&PubIntYB 82; NewsDir 84*
Calamus Books - New York, NY - *BoPubDir 4, 5; LitMag&SmPr 83-84*
Calao Publishers - Midvale, UT - *BoPubDir 5*
Calapooia Publications - Brownsville, OR - *LitMag&SmPr 83-84*
Calapooya Books - Eugene, OR - *BoPubDir 4, 5*
Calaveras Californian - Angels Camp, CA - *Ed&PubIntYB 82*
Calaveras Prospect Weekly-Citizen & Chronicle - San Andreas, CA - *Ed&PubIntYB 82*
Calaveras Publishing Co. - Angels Camp, CA - *BaconPubCkNews 84*
Calaveras Telephone Co. - Copperopolis, CA - *TelDir&BG 83-84*
Calcasieu Cablevision Inc. [of Communications Services Inc.] - Lake Charles, LA - *BrCabYB 84; Tel&CabFB 84C*
Calcified Tissue Abstracts [of Information Retrieval Ltd.] - London, England - *CompReadDB 82*
Calcon Press - Bruce, MS - *BoPubDir 4, 5*
Calcugram Co., The - Walnut Creek, CA - *MicrocomSwDir 1*
Calculon Corp. - Philadelphia, PA - *EISS 83*
Calderon Press Inc. - New York, NY - *LitMarPl 83, 84*
Caldwell/Bartlett/Wood Inc. - Memphis, TN - *ArtMar 84*

Caldwell Burleson County Citizen-Tribune - Caldwell, TX - *NewsDir 84*
Caldwell Burleson County Citizen-Tribune - *See* Burleson County Publishing Co. Inc.
Caldwell Cablevision - Lenoir, NC - *Tel&CabFB 84C*
Caldwell Cablevision - Caldwell, TX - *BrCabYB 84; Tel&CabFB 84C*
Caldwell, Chris - East Smithfield, PA - *Tel&CabFB 84C p.1669*
Caldwell County Times - Princeton, KY - *AyerDirPub 83; Ed&PubIntYB 82*
Caldwell Industries [Div. of Argus Press] - Luling, TX - *LitMarPl 83, 84*
Caldwell Journal & Noble County Leader - Caldwell, OH - *BaconPubCkNews 84; Ed&PubIntYB 82; NewsDir 84*
Caldwell Messenger - Caldwell, KS - *BaconPubCkNews 84; Ed&PubIntYB 82*
Caldwell Progress - Caldwell, NJ - *BaconPubCkNews 84*
Caldwell/Reingold Group - New York, NY - *AdAge 3-28-84; StaDirAdAg 2-84*
Caldwell-Van Riper Inc. - Ft. Wayne, IN - *TelAl 83, 84*
Caldwell-Van Riper Inc. - Indianapolis, IN - *ArtMar 84; DirPRFirms 83; StaDirAdAg 2-84*
Caldwell Watchman-Progress, The - Columbia, LA - *Ed&PubIntYB 82*
Caleden Citizen - Caledon, ON, Canada - *Ed&PubIntYB 82*
Caleden Citizen - Orangeville, ON, Canada - *AyerDirPub 83*
Caledon Advertising Ltd. - Toronto, ON, Canada - *StaDirAdAg 2-84*
Caledonia Advertiser - Caledonia, NY - *BaconPubCkNews 84; Ed&PubIntYB 82*
Caledonia Argus - Caledonia, MN - *BaconPubCkNews 84; Ed&PubIntYB 82*
Caledonia Courier - Ft. St. James, BC, Canada - *AyerDirPub 83; Ed&PubIntYB 82*
Caledonia Courier Press - Caledonia, MO - *Ed&PubIntYB 82*
Caledonia Press - Racine, WI - *LitMarPl 83, 84*
Caledonian-Record - St. Johnsbury, VT - *AyerDirPub 83; Ed&PubIntYB 82*
Calendar Data Base [of Solar Energy Research Institute] - Golden, CO - *CompReadDB 82*
Calet, Hirsch & Spector - New York, NY - *AdAge 3-28-84; BrCabYB 84; StaDirAdAg 2-84*
Calexico Chronicle - Calexico, CA - *BaconPubCkNews 84; Ed&PubIntYB 82*
Calf News - Tarzana, CA - *MagDir 84*
Calgary Cable TV/FM [of Cablecasting Ltd.] - Calgary, AB, Canada - *BrCabYB 84*
Calgary Herald [of Southam Inc.] - Calgary, AB, Canada - *BaconPubCkNews 84; Ed&PubIntYB 82; LitMarPl 83, 84*
Calgary Magazine - Calgary, AB, Canada - *BaconPubCkMag 84*
Calgary Mirror-North - Calgary, AB, Canada - *AyerDirPub 83*
Calgary Southside Mirror - Calgary, AB, Canada - *AyerDirPub 83*
Calgary Sun - Calgary, AB, Canada - *AyerDirPub 83; BaconPubCkNews 84; Ed&PubIntYB 82*
Calgary Sun's North Side Mirror - Calgary, AB, Canada - *Ed&PubIntYB 82*
Calgary Sun's South Side Mirror - Calgary, AB, Canada - *Ed&PubIntYB 82*
Calhoun Antenna Service [of Telephone & Data Systems Inc.] - Calhoun City, MS - *BrCabYB 84; Tel&CabFB 84C*
Calhoun Chronicle [of Calhoun County Publishing Inc.] - Grantsville, WV - *AyerDirPub 83; Ed&PubIntYB 82; NewsDir 84*
Calhoun City Monitor-Herald - Calhoun City, MS - *BaconPubCkNews 84*
Calhoun City Telephone Co. Inc. [Aff. of Telephone & Data Systems/SE] - Calhoun City, MS - *TelDir&BG 83-84*
Calhoun County Journal - Bruce, MS - *AyerDirPub 83; Ed&PubIntYB 82*
Calhoun County Reminder - Rockwell City, IA - *AyerDirPub 83*
Calhoun Courier - Edison, GA - *AyerDirPub 83*
Calhoun Courier - Edison & Arlington, GA - *Ed&PubIntYB 82*
Calhoun Falls News - Abbeville, SC - *BaconPubCkNews 84*
Calhoun Falls News - Calhoun Falls, SC - *Ed&PubIntYB 82*
Calhoun Herald - Hardin, IL - *AyerDirPub 83*
Calhoun Herald, The - Alton, IL - *Ed&PubIntYB 82*
Calhoun McLean County News - Calhoun, KY - *BaconPubCkNews 84*
Calhoun News - Hardin, IL - *AyerDirPub 83; Ed&PubIntYB 82*
Calhoun Times - Calhoun, GA - *BaconPubCkNews 84; NewsDir 84*
Calhoun Times - St. Matthews, SC - *Ed&PubIntYB 82*
Calhoun Times & Gordon County News - Calhoun, GA - *AyerDirPub 83; Ed&PubIntYB 82*
Calibre Press Inc. - Northbrook, IL - *BoPubDir 4, 5*
Calico Mouse - Fillmore, CA - *BoPubDir 5*
Calico Rock Cable Co. - Calico Rock, AR - *BrCabYB 84*
Calico Rock Progress - Calico Rock, AR - *BaconPubCkNews 84*
Caliente Lincoln County Record - Caliente, NV - *BaconPubCkNews 84*
Califone International Inc. [Div. of Interac Corp.] - Los Angeles, CA - *AvMarPl 83*
California Advocate - Fresno, CA - *Ed&PubIntYB 82*
California AFL-CIO News [of California Labor Federation AFL-CIO] - San Francisco, CA - *NewsDir 84*
California Aggie, The [of University of California] - Davis, CA - *NewsDir 84*
California Agriculture - Berkeley, CA - *BaconPubCkMag 84*
California & Western States Grape Grower - Fresno, CA - *BaconPubCkMag 84; MagDir 84*
California Apparel News [of Womens Apparel Trade Newspaper] - Los Angeles, CA - *BaconPubCkMag 84; MagDir 84*
California Arizona Cotton - Fresno, CA - *BaconPubCkMag 84; MagDir 84*
California Arizona Farm Press - Clarksdale, MS - *AyerDirPub 83; BaconPubCkMag 84*
California Avionics Laboratories Inc. - Palo Alto, CA - *AvMarPl 83*
California Books - Irvine, CA - *BoPubDir 4 Sup, 5*
California Books - Stanford, CA - *BoPubDir 4, 5*
California Builder [of Fellom Publishing Co.] - San Francisco, CA - *BaconPubCkMag 84; MagDir 84*
California Builder & Engineer - Palo Alto, CA - *ArtMar 84; BaconPubCkMag 84; MagDir 84; WritMar 84*
California Business - Los Angeles, CA - *BaconPubCkMag 84; MagDir 84; MagIndMarPl 82-83; WritMar 84*
California Business Computer Corp. - Campbell, CA - *MicrocomMPl 83*
California Cablesystems - Garden Grove, CA - *BrCabYB 84*
California Cablesystems [of Rogers Cablesystems Inc.] - La Mirada, CA - *InterCabHB 3; Tel&CabFB 84C*
California Cablesystems Inc. [of Rogers Cablesystems Inc.] - Downey, CA - *BrCabYB 84; Tel&CabFB 84C*
California Cablevision Ltd. - Rancho San Diego, CA - *BrCabYB 84*
California Cattleman - Sacramento, CA - *BaconPubCkMag 84; MagDir 84*
California Citrograph - Los Angeles, CA - *MagDir 84*
California City Enterprise - California City, CA - *BaconPubCkNews 84*
California Communications - Los Angeles, CA - *AvMarPl 83; WritMar 84*
California Communications Network - *See* Colclouth/California Communications Network, William H.
California Computer Products [Subs. of Sanders Associates Inc.] - Anaheim, CA - *WhoWMicrocom 83*
California Computer Products (Digitizer Products Div.) - Scottsdale, AZ - *DataDirSup 7-83*
California Computer Systems Inc. - Sunnyvale, CA - *WhoWMicrocom 83*
California Country Records - Concord, CA - *BillIntBG 83-84*
California Courier - Fresno, CA - *AyerDirPub 83; NewsDir 84*
California Data Corp. - Newbury Park, CA - *MicrocomMPl 83, 84*
California Databank [of Security Pacific National Bank] - Los Angeles, CA - *DataDirOnSer 84; DBBus 82; DirOnDB Spring 84*
California Democrat - California, MO - *BaconPubCkNews 84; Ed&PubIntYB 82; NewsDir 84*
California Dept. of Finance (Population Research Unit) - Sacramento, CA - *BoPubDir 5*

California Digital Engineering - Hollywood, CA - *WhoWMicrocom 83*
California Engineer [of University of California] - Berkeley, CA - *BaconPubCkMag 84; MagDir 84*
California Farm Network - Sacramento, CA - *BrCabYB 84*
California Farmer - San Francisco, CA - *BaconPubCkMag 84; MagDir 84*
California F.P. - San Francisco, CA - *BaconPubCkMag 84; MagDir 84*
California Freie Presse - Millbrae, CA - *Ed&PubIntYB 82*
California Fruit Grower - Sacramento, CA - *BaconPubCkMag 84*
California Geology - Sacramento, CA - *MagIndMarPl 82-83*
California Governor's Office of Appropriate Technology - Sacramento, CA - *BoPubDir 4, 5*
California Grange News - Sacramento, CA - *BaconPubCkMag 84; MagDir 84*
California Health Publications - Carlsbad, CA - *BoPubDir 4, 5*
California Highway Patrolman [of California Association of Highway Patrolmen] - Sacramento, CA - *MagDir 84; WritMar 84*
California Historical Society - Los Angeles, CA - *LitMarPl 83*
California Historical Society - San Francisco, CA - *BoPubDir 4, 5; LitMarPl 84*
California History - San Diego, CA - *MagIndMarPl 82-83*
California Homes Magazine - Laguna Beach, CA - *BaconPubCkMag 84*
California Horse Review [of Related Industries Corp.] - North Highlands, CA - *WritMar 84*
California Institute of International Studies - Stanford, CA - *BoPubDir 4, 5; DataDirOnSer 84*
California Institute of Public Affairs [Aff. of The Claremont Colleges] - Claremont, CA - *LitMarPl 83, 84; WritMar 84*
California Institute of Technology (Munger Africana Library) - Pasadena, CA - *BoPubDir 4, 5*
California Instruments [Div. of Norlin Industries] - San Diego, CA - *DirInfWP 82*
California Insurance - San Francisco, CA - *MagDir 84*
California International Record & Video Inc. - Newport Beach, CA - *BillIntBG 83-84*
California Journal - Sacramento, CA - *MagIndMarPl 82-83; WritMar 84*
California Journal Press [Aff. of The California Center] - Sacramento, CA - *BoPubDir 4, 5*
California Lawyer - San Francisco, CA - *BaconPubCkMag 84; WritMar 84*
California Lawyers' Press Inc. - Los Angeles, CA - *BoPubDir 4 Sup, 5*
California Library Authority for Systems & Services - San Jose, CA - *CompReadDB 82; DataDirOnSer 84; EISS 83; InfIndMarPl 83; MicroMarPl 82-83*
California Living [of San Francisco Sunday Examiner & Chronicle] - San Francisco, CA - *LitMarPl 83, 84; MagIndMarPl 82-83*
California Magazine - Beverly Hills, CA - *Folio 83; MagDir 84*
California Magazine [of Mediatex Communications Corp.] - Los Angeles, CA - *BaconPubCkMag 84; LitMarPl 83, 84; MagIndMarPl 82-83; WritMar 84*
California Management Review - Berkeley, CA - *MagIndMarPl 82-83*
California Men's Stylist - Los Angeles, CA - *BaconPubCkMag 84; MagDir 84*
California Micro Computer - Fountain Valley, CA - *MicrocomMPl 84*
California Mining Journal - Aptos, CA - *BaconPubCkMag 84; MagDir 84*
California Nurse - San Francisco, CA - *BaconPubCkMag 84; MagDir 84*
California Optometry [of California Optometric Association] - Sacramento, CA - *ArtMar 84; BaconPubCkMag 84; MagDir 84*
California-Oregon Broadcasting Investments - Medford, OR - *BrCabYB 84 p.D-298; Tel&CabFB 84C p.1669, 84S*
California-Oregon Telephone Co. [Aff. of United Telecommunications Inc.] - Hood River, OR - *TelDir&BG 83-84*
California Pacific Computer Co. - Davis, CA - *MicrocomMPl 84; MicrocomSwDir 1*
California Parks & Recreation - Sacramento, CA - *BaconPubCkMag 84*
California Pharmacist [of California Pharmacists Association] - Sacramento, CA - *BaconPubCkMag 84; MagDir 84*
California Publisher - Sacramento, CA - *BaconPubCkMag 84; MagDir 84; WritMar 84*
California Quarterly [of University of California] - Davis, CA - *ArtMar 84; LitMag&SmPr 83-84; WritMar 84*
California Real Estate [of California Association of Realtors] - Los Angeles, CA - *BaconPubCkMag 84; MagDir 84; MagIndMarPl 82-83*
California Real Estate Publications - Covina, CA - *BoPubDir 4, 5*
California Senior Citizen [of McAnally & Associates Inc.] - La Canada, CA - *BaconPubCkMag 84; MagDir 84; NewsDir 84*
California Service Agency - Sacramento, CA - *BoPubDir 4, 5*
California Sheepman's Quarterly - Sacramento, CA - *BaconPubCkMag 84; MagDir 84*
California Spanish Language Data Base - Berkeley, CA - *LitMag&SmPr 83-84*
California Spanish Language Data Base [of California State Library] - Oakland, CA - *EISS 7-83 Sup*
California Staats-Zeitung - Los Angeles, CA - *Ed&PubIntYB 82; NewsDir 84*
California Stainless Manufacturing Inc. - Camarillo, CA - *AvMarPl 83*
California State Census Data Center [of California State Dept. of Finance] - Sacramento, CA - *EISS 7-83 Sup*
California State Employee [of California State Employees' Association] - Sacramento, CA - *ArtMar 84; MagDir 84*
California State Library - Sacramento, CA - *EISS 83*
California State Poetry Society Quarterly - Riverside, CA - *WritMar 84*
California State University (Fullerton Oral History Program) - Fullerton, CA - *BoPubDir 4, 5*
California State University (Long Beach Art Museum & Galleries) - Long Beach, CA - *BoPubDir 4, 5*
California State University (Northridge Santa Susana Press) - Northridge, CA - *BoPubDir 4, 5*
California Street - Berkeley, CA - *BoPubDir 4, 5*
California Survey Research - Sherman Oaks, CA - *EISS 5-84 Sup; IntDirMarRes 83*
California Surveyor, The - Santa Rosa, CA - *BaconPubCkMag 84*
California Tomato Grower, The - Stockton, CA - *BaconPubCkMag 84*
California Tomorrow - San Francisco, CA - *LitMag&SmPr 83-84*
California Travel Report - Van Nuys, CA - *BaconPubCkMag 84*
California Union List of Periodicals [of California Library Authority for Systems & Services] - San Jose, CA - *CompReadDB 82; DataDirOnSer 84; DBBus 82*
California Veckoblad - Los Angeles, CA - *AyerDirPub 83; Ed&PubIntYB 82*
California Veterinarian - Moraga, CA - *BaconPubCkMag 84; MagDir 84*
California Voice - Oakland, CA - *AyerDirPub 83*
California Weekly Explorer Inc. - Costa Mesa, CA - *BoPubDir 4, 5*
California Wood Plans - San Luis Obispo, CA - *BoPubDir 4, 5*
Californiai Magyarsag - Los Angeles, CA - *Ed&PubIntYB 82; NewsDir 84*
Californian - Bakersfield, CA - *AyerDirPub 83*
Californian - Salinas, CA - *AyerDirPub 83*
Californian, The - El Cajon, CA - *BaconPubCkNews 84*
Californian, The - Fallbrook, CA - *AyerDirPub 83*
Californian, The [of Marmack Publishing Inc.] - Temecula, CA - *NewsDir 84*
California's Blue-Rose - Jefferson, WI - *BillIntBG 83-84*
Calims/Uniterm [of IFI/Plenum Data Co.] - Alexandria, VA - *DataDirOnSer 84*
Caliornia Courier, The - Fresno, CA - *Ed&PubIntYB 82*
Calipatria Herald - Calipatria, CA - *BaconPubCkNews 84; Ed&PubIntYB 82*
Caliri, Frank - *See* Gavilan Communications
Calistoga Calistogan - Calistoga, CA - *BaconPubCkNews 84*
Calistoga News, The - Calistoga, CA - *AyerDirPub 83*
Calistoga Weekly Calistogan, The - Calistoga, CA - *NewsDir 84*
Calkins Newspapers - Levittown, PA - *Ed&PubIntYB 82; KnowInd 83*
Call - Du Quoin, IL - *Ed&PubIntYB 82*
Call - Beloit, KS - *AyerDirPub 83*

Call - Kansas City, MO - *AyerDirPub 83; Ed&PubIntYB 82*
Call - Piqua, OH - *AyerDirPub 83*
Call - Freedom, OK - *AyerDirPub 83*
Call - Allentown, PA - *AyerDirPub 83*
Call - Woonsocket, RI - *AyerDirPub 83*
Call - Lead, SD - *AyerDirPub 83*
Call & Post - Cleveland, OH - *AyerDirPub 83; Ed&PubIntYB 82; NewsDir 84*
Call-Apple - Kent, WA - *DirOnDB Spring 84*
Call-Chronicle - Allentown, PA - *AyerDirPub 83; NewsBur 6*
Call Computer - Mountain View, CA - *DataDirOnSer 84; EISS 83; WhoWMicrocom 83*
Call-Gazette - Beloit, KS - *AyerDirPub 83*
Call-Leader, The - Elwood, IN - *BaconPubCkNews 84; Ed&PubIntYB 82*
Call Manager Inc. - Mountain View, CA - *MicrocomSwDir 1*
Call-News Dispatch - Chatom, AL - *AyerDirPub 83; Ed&PubIntYB 82*
Call/Pioneer Times - Lead, SD - *Ed&PubIntYB 82*
Call/Sinking Fund Data Base - Bala Cynwyd, PA - *DirOnDB Spring 84*
Call, The - Schuylkill Haven, PA - *AyerDirPub 83; Ed&PubIntYB 82*
Callaghan, Jane - New York, NY - *BoPubDir 4, 5*
Callahan & Day Inc. - Ligonier, PA - *StaDirAdAg 2-84*
Callahan Clearview Cable TV [of Florida Clearview Inc.] - Callahan, FL - *BrCabYB 84; Tel&CabFB 84C*
Callahan County Star - Baird, TX - *Ed&PubIntYB 82*
Callahan Nassau County Record - Callahan, FL - *BaconPubCkNews 84*
Callahan Research Inc. - New York, NY - *IntDirMarRes 83*
Callahan's Guides Inc. - Essex Junction, VT - *BoPubDir 4 Sup, 5*
Callais Cablevision Inc. - Golden Meadow, LA - *BrCabYB 84; Tel&CabFB 84C*
Callaloo - Lexington, KY - *LitMag&SmPr 83-84*
Callan Data Systems Inc. - Westlake Village, CA - *WhoWMicrocom 83*
Callarman House - Port Hueneme, CA - *BoPubDir 4 Sup, 5*
Callaway Courier - Callaway, NE - *BaconPubCkNews 84; Ed&PubIntYB 82*
Callaway Editions - New York, NY - *BoPubDir 4, 5; LitMarPl 84*
Callaway Music - *See* Mustard Tree Music
Callaway Review - Fulton, MO - *AyerDirPub 83*
Callaway Telephone Co. - Callaway, MN - *TelDir&BG 83-84*
Calldata Systems Inc. - Woodbury, NY - *EISS 83*
Calle & Co. - Greenwich, CT - *IntDirMarRes 83*
Callender/Carney Advertising Inc. - Breezy Point, MN - *StaDirAdAg 2-84*
Caller - Corpus Christi, TX - *AyerDirPub 83*
Caller-Times - Corpus Christi, TX - *AyerDirPub 83*
Callicoon Sullivan County Democrat - Callicoon, NY - *BaconPubCkNews 84*
Callie-Pearl Features - Kansas City, KS - *Ed&PubIntYB 82*
Calligranews [of Calligrafree Co.] - Brookville, OH - *WritMar 84*
Calliope - Glen Rock, NJ - *AvMarPl 83*
Calliope [of Ampersand Press] - Bristol, RI - *LitMag&SmPr 83-84*
Calliope Press - North Hollywood, CA - *BoPubDir 4, 5*
Calliope Press [Aff. of The Pawn Review Inc.] - Glenview, IL - *BoPubDir 4, 5; LitMag&SmPr 83-84*
Calliope Press - Toronto, ON, Canada - *BoPubDir 4, 5*
Calliope Productions - Minneapolis, MN - *AvMarPl 83*
Calliopes Corner - Anchorage, AK - *LitMag&SmPr 83-84*
Calli's Tales - Palmetto, FL - *LitMag&SmPr 83-84*
Callon-Love Music - San Pedro, CA - *BillIntBG 83-84*
Calma Co. - Santa Clara, CA - *DataDirSup 7-83*
Calmar Communications Inc. - Chicago, IL - *DirPRFirms 83*
Caloosa Belle - La Belle, FL - *AyerDirPub 83; Ed&PubIntYB 82*
Calsoft - Agoura, CA - *MicrocomMPl 83*
Caltec Cablevision [of Calvert Telecommunications Inc.] - Baltimore County, MD - *BrCabYB 84*
Caltec Marketing Co. - San Diego, CA - *MicrocomSwDir 1*
CalToday - San Jose, CA - *ArtMar 84; WritMar 84*
Calumet - Chicago, IL - *AyerDirPub 83*
Calumet City-Burnham Pointer Economist [of Chicago Daily Southtown Economist Newspapers] - Chicago, IL - *NewsDir 84*
Calumet City-Burnham Pointer Economist - South Holland, IL - *AyerDirPub 83*
Calumet City/Burnham Pointer-Economist - *See* Pointer-Economist Newspapers
Calumet City Pointer Economist - Calumet City, IL - *Ed&PubIntYB 82*
Calumet Copper Island Sentinel - Calumet, MI - *BaconPubCkNews 84*
Calumet County Shopper - Chilton, WI - *AyerDirPub 83*
Calumet Day, The [of Trinity Holding Corp.] - Lansing, IL - *AyerDirPub 83; NewsDir 84*
Calumet Day, The - Whiting, IL - *Ed&PubIntYB 82*
Calumet Globe, The - East Chicago, IN - *AyerDirPub 83; Ed&PubIntYB 82*
Calumet Press - Highland, IN - *AyerDirPub 83; NewsDir 84*
CALURA [of Canada Systems Group Ltd.] - Mississauga, ON, Canada - *DataDirOnSer 84*
Calvary Inc. - Pittsburgh, PA - *BrCabYB 84*
Calvary Records Inc. - Nashville, TN - *BillIntBG 83-84*
Calvert City Cable TV [of Flora Cable TV Co.] - Calvert City, KY - *BrCabYB 84; Tel&CabFB 84C*
Calvert County Recorder - Prince Frederick, MD - *AyerDirPub 83; Ed&PubIntYB 82*
Calvert Independent - Prince Frederick, MD - *AyerDirPub 83; Ed&PubIntYB 82*
Calvert Journal Gazette - Prince Frederick, MD - *Ed&PubIntYB 82*
Calvert Telecommunications - Timonium, MD - *CabTVFinDB 83*
Calvideo Cable TV - Alpine, CA - *Tel&CabFB 84C*
Calvideo Cable TV - Pine Valley, CA - *Tel&CabFB 84C*
Calvideo Inc. - Alpine, CA - *BrCabYB 84*
Calvin Chronicle - Calvin, OK - *AyerDirPub 83; Ed&PubIntYB 82*
Calvin Chronicle - *See* Hughes County Publishing Co.
Calvin Cinequip - Kansas City, MO - *AvMarPl 83*
Calvinist Contact - St. Catharines, ON, Canada - *Ed&PubIntYB 82*
Calwood Publishing Co. - Monsey, NY - *BoPubDir 4, 5*
Calyx: A Journal of Art & Literature by Women - Corvallis, OR - *LitMag&SmPr 83-84*
Calyx Inc. - Corvallis, OR - *WritMar 84*
Calzone Case Co. [Div. of Calzone Ltd.] - Bridgeport, CT - *AvMarPl 83*
C.A.M. Co. - Hortonville, WI - *BoPubDir 5*
Cam-Glo Newspapers Inc. - Blackwood, NJ - *BaconPubCkNews 84*
CAM-I News Alert - Arlington, TX - *BaconPubCkMag 84*
Cam-Tel Co. [of WEHCO Video Inc.] - Camden, AR - *BrCabYB 84; Tel&CabFB 84C*
Cam-Tri Productions - Eugene, OR - *BoPubDir 4 Sup, 5*
Camarillo Cable TV [of Storer Cable Communications Inc.] - Camarillo, CA - *BrCabYB 84; Tel&CabFB 84C*
Camarillo Daily News - Camarillo, CA - *BaconPubCkNews 84; Ed&PubIntYB 82; NewsDir 84*
Camaro Publishing Co. - Los Angeles, CA - *LitMarPl 83, 84; WritMar 84*
Camas Post-Record - Camas, WA - *NewsDir 84*
Camas Post Record - *See* Post Publications Inc.
Camas-Washougal Post Record - Camas, WA - *AyerDirPub 83; NewsDir 84*
Camas-Washougal Post Record & Shopper's Guide - Vancouver, WA - *Ed&PubIntYB 82*
CAMAX Systems Inc. - Minneapolis, MN - *DataDirSup 7-83*
Cambar Business Systems Inc. - Charleston, SC - *ADAPSOMemDir 83-84*
Cambex Corp. - Waltham, MA - *DataDirSup 7-83*
Camblos-Winger - Asheville, NC - *BoPubDir 4, 5*
Cambria Cambrian - Cambria, CA - *BaconPubCkNews 84*
Cambria Heights Pennysaver - Rockville Centre, NY - *AyerDirPub 83*
Cambria TV Distribution Co. [of Tele-Media Corp.] - Carrolltown, PA - *BrCabYB 84*
Cambria TV Distribution Co. [of National Cable Co. of Cambria County] - Loretto, PA - *BrCabYB 84*
Cambrian News - San Jose, CA - *AyerDirPub 83*

Cambrian, The - Cambria, CA - *AyerDirPub 83; Ed&PubIntYB 82*
Cambrian Weekly News - San Jose, CA - *Ed&PubIntYB 82*
Cambric Press - Huron, OH - *BoPubDir 4, 5*
Cambridge Advertising Inc. - New York, NY - *StaDirAdAg 2-84*
Cambridge Banner - Cambridge, MD - *BaconPubCkNews 84*
Cambridge Book Co. [Subs. of Esquire Inc.] - New York, NY - *LitMarPl 83, 84; WritMar 84*
Cambridge Cable TV - Cambridge, NE - *Tel&CabFB 84C*
Cambridge Chronicle - Cambridge, IL - *BaconPubCkNews 84; Ed&PubIntYB 82*
Cambridge Chronicle - Cambridge, MA - *Ed&PubIntYB 82*
Cambridge Chronicle [of Cambridge Sun Publishing Co.] - West Somerville, MA - *NewsDir 84*
Cambridge Chronicle - *See* Dole Publishing Co. Inc.
Cambridge City National Road Traveler - Cambridge City, IN - *BaconPubCkNews 84*
Cambridge Clarion - Cambridge, NE - *BaconPubCkNews 84; Ed&PubIntYB 82*
Cambridge Computer Associates Inc. - Cambridge, MA - *DataDirSup 7-83*
Cambridge Crystallographic [of Canada Institute for Scientific & Technical Information] - Ottawa, ON, Canada - *DataDirOnSer 84*
Cambridge Crystallographic Data Centre - Cambridge, England - *CompReadDB 82*
Cambridge Daily Jeffersonian - Cambridge, OH - *NewsDir 84*
Cambridge Development Laboratory - Waltham, MA - *MicrocomMPl 84*
Cambridge Development Laboratory - Watertown, MA - *MicrocomMPl 83; WhoWMicrocom 83*
Cambridge Documentary Films Inc. - Cambridge, MA - *AvMarPl 83*
Cambridge Dorchester News [of Easton Publishing Co.] - Cambridge, MD - *NewsDir 84*
Cambridge Group, The - Chicago, IL - *HBIndAd&MS 82-83*
Cambridge News - Cambridge, WI - *BaconPubCkNews 84; Ed&PubIntYB 82*
Cambridge Opinion Studies Inc. - Holmdel, NJ - *IntDirMarRes 83*
Cambridge Records Inc. - Framingham, MA - *BillIntBG 83-84*
Cambridge Reporter, The - Cambridge, ON, Canada - *BaconPubCkNews 84*
Cambridge Research Group Ltd. - Charleston, WV - *BrCabYB 84*
Cambridge Research Institute - Cambridge, MA - *ADAPSOMemDir 83-84; InfoS 83-84*
Cambridge Scientific Abstracts - Washington, DC - *CompReadDB 82; InfIndMarPl 83*
Cambridge Scientific Abstracts - Bethesda, MD - *CompReadDB 82; DataDirOnSer 84; InfoS 83-84*
Cambridge Star - Cambridge, MN - *BaconPubCkNews 84; Ed&PubIntYB 82*
Cambridge Systems Group - Los Altos Hills, CA - *ADAPSOMemDir 83-84; DataDirSup 7-83*
Cambridge Telephone Co. - Geneseo, IL - *TelDir&BG 83-84*
Cambridge Telephone Co. - Cambridge, NE - *TelDir&BG 83-84*
Cambridge Telephone Co. Inc. - Cambridge, ID - *TelDir&BG 83-84*
Cambridge Times - Cambridge, ON, Canada - *AyerDirPub 83; Ed&PubIntYB 82*
Cambridge University Press - New York, NY - *LitMarPl 83, 84; MagIndMarPl 82-83; WritMar 84*
Cambridge Upper County News Reporter - Cambridge, ID - *BaconPubCkNews 84*
Cambridge Washington County Post - *See* Banner Publishing Co.
Camden Advance-Journal - Camden, NY - *Ed&PubIntYB 82*
Camden Catholic Star Herald - Camden, NJ - *NewsDir 84*
Camden Chronicle - Camden, TN - *BaconPubCkNews 84; Ed&PubIntYB 82; NewsDir 84*
Camden County Record - Camden, NJ - *Ed&PubIntYB 82*
Camden County Record - Gloucester City, NJ - *AyerDirPub 83; NewsDir 84*
Camden County Record - *See* Gloucester City News Publishers
Camden County Tribune - St. Mary's, GA - *AyerDirPub 83; Ed&PubIntYB 82*
Camden Courier-Post - Camden, NJ - *BaconPubCkNews 84*
Camden Farmers' Advance - Camden, MI - *BaconPubCkNews 84*
Camden Herald [of Coast Papers Inc.] - Camden, ME - *AyerDirPub 83; BaconPubCkNews 84; Ed&PubIntYB 82; NewsDir 84*
Camden House - Columbia, SC - *BoPubDir 4; LitMarPl 83, 84*
Camden News - Camden, AR - *BaconPubCkNews 84; Ed&PubIntYB 82; NewsDir 84*
Camden News - Camden, NJ - *Ed&PubIntYB 82; NewsDir 84*
Camden Preble County News - *See* Oxford Press Inc.
Camden Telephone & Telegraph Co. Inc. - St. Marys, GA - *TelDir&BG 83-84*
Camden Telephone Co. [Aff. of C.C. & S. Systems Inc.] - Camden, MI - *TelDir&BG 83-84*
Camden Telephone Co. Inc. - Camden, IN - *TelDir&BG 83-84*
Camden TV Cable Co. - Camden, TN - *BrCabYB 84; Tel&CabFB 84C*
Camden Wilcox Progress Era - Camden, AL - *BaconPubCkNews 84*
Camdenton Reveille - Camdenton, MO - *Ed&PubIntYB 82*
Camdenton Reveille - *See* Hub City Publishing Co. Inc.
Camelback Cablevision [of Storer Cable Communications] - Buckeye, AZ - *BrCabYB 84*
Camelback Cablevision - Glendale, AZ - *BrCabYB 84; Tel&CabFB 84C*
Camelback Cablevision [of Storer Cable Communications Inc.] - Peoria, AZ - *BrCabYB 84*
Camelback Cablevision Inc. - Phoenix, AZ - *Tel&CabFB 84C p.1669*
Camellia City Telecasters Inc. - Sacramento, CA - *Tel&CabFB 84S*
Camelot Books [Div. of Hearst Corp.] - New York, NY - *WritMar 84*
Camelot Communications Inc. - Dallas, TX - *StaDirAdAg 2-84*
Camelot Publishing Co. - Ormond Beach, FL - *ArtMar 84; LitMarPl 83, 84*
Camelot Publishing Co. - Fridley, MN - *BoPubDir 5*
Cameo Electronics Inc. - Anaheim, CA - *MicrocomMPl 84*
Camera - Boulder, CO - *AyerDirPub 83*
Camera Arts [of Ziff-Davis Publishing Co.] - New York, NY - *WritMar 84*
Camera Arts Book Club - *See* Watson-Guptill Book Clubs
Camera Clix [Div. of Globe Photos Inc.] - New York, NY - *AvMarPl 83; Ed&PubIntYB 82; LitMarPl 83, 84; MagIndMarPl 82-83*
Camera dei Deputati [of Centro per la Documentazione Automatica] - Rome, Italy - *CompReadDB 82; InfIndMarPl 83*
Camera Dollylite Systems - Lodi, CA - *AvMarPl 83*
Camera Hawaii Inc. - Honolulu, HI - *AvMarPl 83*
Camera Obscura: A Journal of Feminism & Film Theory - Los Angeles, CA - *LitMag&SmPr 83-84*
Camera Review - Boulder, CO - *AyerDirPub 83*
Camera 35 - New York, NY - *MagDir 84*
Camerica Music - New York, NY - *BillIntBG 83-84*
Camerique Stock Photos - Blue Bell, PA - *LitMarPl 83, 84; MagIndMarPl 82-83*
Cameron & Co. Inc. - San Francisco, CA - *LitMarPl 83*
Cameron Citizen-Observer - Cameron, MO - *BaconPubCkNews 84; NewsDir 84*
Cameron County Echo - Emporium, PA - *AyerDirPub 83; Ed&PubIntYB 82*
Cameron Herald - Cameron, TX - *BaconPubCkNews 84; Ed&PubIntYB 82; NewsDir 84*
Cameron Organization - Western Springs, IL - *BillIntBG 83-84*
Cameron Parish Pilot - Cameron, LA - *AyerDirPub 83; BaconPubCkNews 84; Ed&PubIntYB 82*
Cameron Printing Press [Div. of Midland-Ross Corp.] - New Brunswick, NJ - *LitMarPl 84*
Cameron Telephone Co. - Sulphur, LA - *Tel&CabFB 84C; TelDir&BG 83-84*
Cameron-Waldron-Hartig [Div. of Midland-Ross Corp.] - New Brunswick, NJ - *LitMarPl 83*
Camilla Enterprise - Camilla, GA - *AyerDirPub 83; BaconPubCkNews 84; Ed&PubIntYB 82; NewsDir 84*
Camillus Advocate - Camillus, NY - *BaconPubCkNews 84*
CAMM Publishing Co. - Miami, FL - *BoPubDir 5*
Cammeron/Star Fox Records - Brentwood, TN - *BillIntBG 83-84*
Camp & Associates Inc., Woodfin - New York, NY - *MagIndMarPl 82-83*

Camp & Co., J. M. - Wheaton, IL - *BrCabYB 84; StaDirAdAg 2-84*
Camp Associates Advertising Ltd. - Toronto, ON, Canada - *StaDirAdAg 2-84*
Camp Cable Television - Wailuku, HI - *BrCabYB 84*
Camp Denali Publishing - McKinley Park, AK - *BoPubDir 4, 5*
Camp Inc. - Wailuku, HI - *Tel&CabFB 84C p.1669*
Camp Lejeune Cablevision [of TeleNational Communications Inc.] - Camp Lejeune, NC - *BrCabYB 84; Tel&CabFB 84C*
Camp Point Journal - Camp Point, IL - *Ed&PubIntYB 82*
Camp Point Journal - *See* Taylor Publishing Co.
Camp Stations - Wheaton, IL - *BrCabYB 84*
Camp Verde Verde View - Camp Verde, AZ - *NewsDir 84*
Campagnani, Aleman & Quelquejeu SA - *See* Burnett Co. Inc., Leo
Campaign [of Lowry Enterprises] - Fallbrook, CA - *WritMar 84*
Campaign Coaches of Long Island [Div. of F.L.A. Inc.] - North Merrick, NY - *TelAl 83, 84*
Campaign Monitor - New York, NY - *IntDirMarRes 83*
Campaigns & Elections - Washington, DC - *WritMar 84*
Campana - New York, NY - *Ed&PubIntYB 82; NewsDir 84*
Campana Art Co. Inc., D. M. - Pampa, TX - *BoPubDir 5*
Campana Art Co. Inc., D. M. - Salem, WI - *BoPubDir 4*
Campbell & Associates Pty. Ltd., Ken - Brisbane, Australia - *StaDirAdAg 2-84*
Campbell & Co. Inc., Alastair - Barrington, IL - *DirMarMP 83*
Campbell Associates, Walter - Cambridge, MA - *EISS 83*
Campbell Citizen - Campbell, MO - *BaconPubCkNews 84; Ed&PubIntYB 82*
Campbell Communications Inc. - Plymouth, MA - *BrCabYB 84; Tel&CabFB 84C p.1669*
Campbell County News [of Applachian Press] - Jacksboro, TN - *NewsDir 84*
Campbell County Recorder - Ft. Thomas, KY - *AyerDirPub 83*
Campbell County Times - Jacksboro, TN - *AyerDirPub 83*
Campbell County Times, The - Jellico, TN - *Ed&PubIntYB 82*
Campbell Enterprises, J. D. - Winnipeg, MB, Canada - *BoPubDir 4 Sup, 5*
Campbell Ewald [Subs. of The Interpublic Group] - Warren, MI - *Br 1-23-84; BrCabYB 84; DirMarMP 83; StaDirAdAg 2-84; TelAl 83, 84*
Campbell-Ewald Co. (Chevrolet Motor Div.) - Warren, MI - *Tel&CabFB 84C*
Campbell-Ewald Ltd. - Toronto, ON, Canada - *ArtMar 84*
Campbell Films Inc./Guidance Information Center - Saxtons River, VT - *AvMarPl 83*
Campbell, Gene - Chelan, WA - *Tel&CabFB 84C p.1669*
Campbell, Henry & Calvin Inc. - Farmington Hills, MI - *StaDirAdAg 2-84*
Campbell, James D. - Grand Forks, ND - *BrCabYB 84 p.D-298; Tel&CabFB 84C p.1669*
Campbell, Lucile M. - Decatur, AL - *BoPubDir 5*
Campbell, Maria B. - New York, NY - *LitMarPl 83, 84*
Campbell-Mithun [of Ted Bates Worldwide] - Minneapolis, MN - *AdAge 3-28-84; Br 1-23-84; BrCabYB 84; DirMarMP 83; StaDirAdAg 2-84; TelAl 83, 84*
Campbell Music Inc., Glen - Los Angeles, CA - *BillIntBG 83-84*
Campbell Press - Campbell, CA - *Ed&PubIntYB 82*
Campbell Press [of Meredith Corp.] - Cupertino, CA - *NewsDir 84*
Campbell Press - Milpitas, CA - *AyerDirPub 83*
Campbell Press - *See* Meredith Newspapers
Campbell River & Area Mirror - Campbell River, BC, Canada - *AyerDirPub 83; Ed&PubIntYB 82*
Campbell River & District Museum & Archives Society - Campbell River, BC, Canada - *BoPubDir 4, 5*
Campbell River Courier, The - Campbell River, BC, Canada - *Ed&PubIntYB 82*
Campbell River TV Association - Campbell River, BC, Canada - *BrCabYB 84*
Campbell River Upper Islander - Campbell River, BC, Canada - *Ed&PubIntYB 82*
Campbell, Sandy - New York, NY - *BoPubDir 4, 5*
Campbell-Sanford Advertising Co. - Chicago, IL - *StaDirAdAg 2-84*
Campbell Scientific Inc. - Logan, UT - *WhoWMicrocom 83*
Campbellford Herald - Campbellford, ON, Canada - *AyerDirPub 83; Ed&PubIntYB 82*
Campbell's Publishing Co. Ltd. - Victoria, BC, Canada - *BoPubDir 4, 5*
Campbellsport News - Campbellsport, WI - *BaconPubCkNews 84; Ed&PubIntYB 82*
Campbellsville Central Kentucky News-Journal [of Landmark Community Newspapers Inc.] - Campbellsville, KY - *BaconPubCkNews 84; NewsDir 84*
Camperways - Blue Bell, PA - *WritMar 84*
Campfire Boys & Girls Children's Museum - Canyon Lake, CA - *BoPubDir 4, 5*
Campground Merchandising - Philadelphia, PA - *MagDir 84*
Camping - Martinsville, IN - *BaconPubCkMag 84; MagDir 84; MagIndMarPl 82-83*
Camping Canada - Montreal, PQ, Canada - *BaconPubCkMag 84*
Camping Industry - Milwaukee, WI - *MagDir 84*
Camping Products Merchandising - Skokie, IL - *MagDir 84*
Campion Language Studies [Aff. of Helix Investments Ltd.] - Toronto, ON, Canada - *BoPubDir 4 Sup, 5*
Campione, Michael J. - Cinnaminson, NJ - *BoPubDir 4, 5*
Campos Qualitative Research, R. Yvonne - Pittsburgh, PA - *IntDirMarRes 83*
Campti-Pleasant Hill Telephone Co. Inc. - Pleasant Hill, LA - *TelDir&BG 83-84*
Campton Wolfe County News - *See* Courier Publishing Co. Inc.
Campus Cablevision [of University of Wisconsin-Platteville] - Platteville, WI - *BrCabYB 84*
Campus Detroiter, The [of University of Detroit] - Detroit, MI - *NewsDir 84*
Campus Film Distributors Corp. - Tuckahoe, NY - *AvMarPl 83*
Campus Life [of Campus Life Publications Inc.] - Carol Stream, IL - *ArtMar 84; BaconPubCkMag 84; MagIndMarPl 82-83; WritMar 84*
Campus Life - Wheaton, IL - *MagDir 84*
Campus Productions Inc., Steve - Tuckahoe, NY - *TelAl 83, 84; Tel&CabFB 84C*
Campus Scope Press - Minneapolis, MN - *BoPubDir 4, 5*
Campus Subscriptions - Port Washington, NY - *MagIndMarPl 82-83*
Campus, The [of Allegheny College] - Meadville, PA - *NewsDir 84*
Campus Times [of Universty of Rochester Students Association] - Rochester, NY - *NewsDir 84*
Campus Voice [of Bloomsburg State College] - Bloomsburg, PA - *NewsDir 84*
Camralab Inc. [Subs. of WPI] - St. Louis, MO - *AvMarPl 83*
Camrass Corp. - Boonton, NJ - *MicrocomMPl 84*
Camrose Booster, The - Camrose, AB, Canada - *AyerDirPub 83; Ed&PubIntYB 82*
Camrose Canadian, The - Camrose, AB, Canada - *Ed&PubIntYB 82*
Camward House - Frederick, MD - *BoPubDir 4, 5*
Can-Am Publishing Co. Ltd. - Calgary, AB, Canada - *BoPubDir 5*
Can Do Books - Napa, CA - *BoPubDir 4, 5; LitMag&SmPr 83-84*
Can-Do Publishing Co. - Toronto, ON, Canada - *BoPubDir 5*
Can-to-Pan Press - Alameda, CA - *BoPubDir 4, 5*
Canaan Associates, Lee - New York, NY - *ArtMar 84; DirPRFirms 83; LitMarPl 83, 84; MagIndMarPl 82-83*
Canaan Echo - Canaan, NY - *BaconPubCkNews 84*
Canada [of Statistics Canada] - Ottawa, ON, Canada - *DataDirOnSer 84*
Canada & Arab World - Toronto, ON, Canada - *Ed&PubIntYB 82*
Canada & the World - Toronto, ON, Canada - *BaconPubCkMag 84*
Canada Bonded Attorney & Legal Directory Ltd. - Toronto, ON, Canada - *BoPubDir 4, 5*
Canada Business Centers Ltd. - Pointe Claire, PQ, Canada - *DirInfWP 82*
Canada Carbon & Ribbon Co. Ltd. - Toronto, ON, Canada - *DirInfWP 82*
Canada Centre for Mineral & Energy Technology [of Dept. of Energy, Mines & Resources] - Ottawa, ON, Canada - *CompReadDB 82; DataDirOnSer 84*
Canada Centre for Remote Sensing - Ottawa, ON, Canada - *DataDirOnSer 84*

Canada Century Home - Port Hope, ON, Canada - *BaconPubCkMag 84*
Canada Commerce - Ottawa, ON, Canada - *BaconPubCkMag 84*
Canada Data Bank - *DirOnDB Spring 84*
Canada Federal Dept. of Justice - Ottawa, ON, Canada - *DataDirOnSer 84*
Canada Geographic Information System [of Environment Canada] - Ottawa, ON, Canada - *EISS 83*
Canada Institute for Scientific & Technical Information [of National Research Council of Canada] - Ottawa, ON, Canada - *CompReadDB 82; DataDirOnSer 84; EISS 83*
Canada Labour Views Co. Ltd. - Toronto, ON, Canada - *BoPubDir 4 Sup, 5*
Canada Law Book Ltd. - Aurora, ON, Canada - *CompReadDB 82; DataDirOnSer 84; EISS 83*
Canada Market Research Ltd. - Toronto, ON, Canada - *IntDirMarRes 83*
Canada Mortgage & Housing Corp. - Toronto, ON, Canada - *BoPubDir 5*
Canada News-Wire Ltd. - Toronto, ON, Canada - *ProGuPRSer 4*
Canada Poultryman - New Westminster, BC, Canada - *ArtMar 84; BaconPubCkMag 84*
Canada-Svensken - Toronto, ON, Canada - *Ed&PubIntYB 82*
Canada Systems Group - Mississauga, ON, Canada - *DataDirOnSer 84*
Canada Systems Group - Ottawa, ON, Canada - *DataDirOnSer 84*
Canada West Foundation - Calgary, AB, Canada - *BoPubDir 4, 5*
Canada West Publications - Summerland, BC, Canada - *BoPubDir 4, 5*
Canada Wide Feature Service Ltd. [Subs. of The Toronto Sun Publishing Corp.] - Toronto, ON, Canada - *BaconPubCkNews 84; Ed&PubIntYB 82; LitMarPl 84*
Canada's Contract Magazine - Concord, ON, Canada - *BaconPubCkMag 84*
Canada's Furniture Magazine - Concord, ON, Canada - *BaconPubCkMag 84*
Canada's Wings Inc. - Stittsville, ON, Canada - *BoPubDir 4, 5; LitMarPl 84*
Canadatum - Toronto, ON, Canada - *FBInfSer 80*
Canadia Theatre Review - Downsview, ON, Canada - *WritMar 84*
Canadian - Camrose, AB, Canada - *AyerDirPub 83*
Canadian - Carleton Place, ON, Canada - *AyerDirPub 83*
Canadian Aeronautics & Space Journal - Ottawa, ON, Canada - *BaconPubCkMag 84*
Canadian Aftermarket, The - Mississauga, ON, Canada - *BaconPubCkMag 84*
Canadian Agricultural Census-1981 [of I. P. Sharp Associates Ltd.] - Toronto, ON, Canada - *DataDirOnSer 84*
Canadian Agriculture [of Chase Econometrics/Interactive Data Corp.] - Waltham, MA - *DataDirOnSer 84*
Canadian Agriculture - Bala Cynwyd, PA - *DirOnDB Spring 84*
Canadian Agriculture Forecast [of Chase Econometrics/Interactive Data Corp.] - Waltham, MA - *DataDirOnSer 84*
Canadian Agriculture Forecast - Bala Cynwyd, PA - *DirOnDB Spring 84*
Canadian Amateur Swimming Association - Ottawa, ON, Canada - *BoPubDir 4, 5*
Canadian Apparel Manufacturer - Montreal, PQ, Canada - *BaconPubCkMag 84*
Canadian Arab World Review - Montreal, PQ, Canada - *Ed&PubIntYB 82*
Canadian Architect, The - Don Mills, ON, Canada - *BaconPubCkMag 84*
Canadian Arctic Resources Committee - Ottawa, ON, Canada - *BoPubDir 4, 5*
Canadian Art Prints Inc. - Vancouver, BC, Canada - *ArtMar 84*
Canadian Artists' Representation Ontario - Toronto, ON, Canada - *BoPubDir 5*
Canadian Association for Adult Education - Toronto, ON, Canada - *BoPubDir 4, 5*
Canadian Association for Children & Adults with Learning Disabilities - Ottawa, ON, Canada - *BoPubDir 4 Sup, 5*
Canadian Association for Health, Physical Education, & Recreation - Vanier, ON, Canada - *BoPubDir 4, 5*
Canadian Association for Information Science - Calgary, AB, Canada - *BoPubDir 4, 5; EISS 83*
Canadian Association for Information Science [of QL Systems Ltd.] - Ottawa, ON, Canada - *DataDirOnSer 84*
Canadian Association for Publishing in Philosophy - Toronto, ON, Canada - *BoPubDir 4, 5*
Canadian Association of Research Libraries - Montreal, PQ, Canada - *BoPubDir 4 Sup, 5*
Canadian Association of Toy Libraries - Toronto, ON, Canada - *BoPubDir 4, 5*
Canadian Author & Bookman - Toronto, ON, Canada - *LitMag&SmPr 83-84; WritMar 84*
Canadian Automotive Trade [of Maclean-Hunter Ltd.] - Toronto, ON, Canada - *BaconPubCkMag 84; WritMar 84*
Canadian Aviation - Toronto, ON, Canada - *BaconPubCkMag 84*
Canadian Aviation Historical Society - Willowdale, ON, Canada - *BoPubDir 4, 5*
Canadian Ayrshire Review - Ottawa, ON, Canada - *BaconPubCkMag 84*
Canadian Banker - Toronto, ON, Canada - *BaconPubCkMag 84; WritMar 84*
Canadian Beverage Review - Port Credit, ON, Canada - *BaconPubCkMag 84*
Canadian Bibliographical Services [of National Library of Canada] - Ottawa, ON, Canada - *EISS 83*
Canadian Boating - Mississauga, ON, Canada - *BaconPubCkMag 84*
Canadian Bondmarket [of I. P. Sharp Associates Ltd.] - Toronto, ON, Canada - *DataDirOnSer 84; DBBus 82*
Canadian Bonds - Toronto, ON, Canada - *DirOnDB Spring 84*
Canadian Book Exchange Centre [of National Library of Canada] - Ottawa, ON, Canada - *EISS 83*
Canadian Broadcasting Corp. - Ottawa, ON, Canada - *BrCabYB 84; Tel&CabFB 84C*
Canadian Building [of Maclean Hunter Ltd.] - Toronto, ON, Canada - *BaconPubCkMag 84; WritMar 84*
Canadian Business - Toronto, ON, Canada - *BaconPubCkMag 84*
Canadian Business & Current Affairs [of Dialog Information Services Inc.] - Palo Alto, CA - *DataDirOnSer 84*
Canadian Business & Current Affairs - Toronto, ON, Canada - *DirOnDB Spring 84*
Canadian Business Index [of QL Systems Ltd.] - Ottawa, ON, Canada - *DataDirOnSer 84*
Canadian Business Index [of Micromedia Ltd.] - Toronto, ON, Canada - *CompReadDB 82*
Canadian Business Periodicals Index [of Micromedia Ltd.] - Toronto, ON, Canada - *DBBus 82*
Canadian Cable Television Association - Ottawa, ON, Canada - *BoPubDir 4, 5*
Canadian Cablevision Inc. [of Scott Cable Communications Inc.] - Canadian, TX - *BrCabYB 84; Tel&CabFB 84C*
Canadian Camping & RV Dealer - Mississauga, ON, Canada - *BaconPubCkMag 84*
Canadian Census-1981 [of I. P. Sharp Associates Ltd.] - Toronto, ON, Canada - *DataDirOnSer 84*
Canadian Century Publishers - Lancaster, ON, Canada - *BoPubDir 4, 5*
Canadian Champion, The - Milton, ON, Canada - *Ed&PubIntYB 82*
Canadian Chartered Banks [of I. P. Sharp Associates] - Toronto, ON, Canada - *DBBus 82*
Canadian Chartered Banks [of FRI Information Services Ltd.] - Monreal, PQ, Canada - *DataDirOnSer 84*
Canadian Chartered Banks Annual [of I. P. Sharp Associates Ltd.] - Toronto, ON, Canada - *DataDirOnSer 84*
Canadian Chartered Banks Monthly [of I. P. Sharp Associates Ltd.] - Toronto, ON, Canada - *DataDirOnSer 84*
Canadian Chartered Banks Quarterly [of I. P. Sharp Associates Ltd.] - Toronto, ON, Canada - *DataDirOnSer 84*
Canadian Chartered Banks Yearly [of I. P. Sharp Associates Ltd.] - Toronto, ON, Canada - *DataDirOnSer 84*
Canadian Chemical Processing - Don Mills, ON, Canada - *BaconPubCkMag 84*
Canadian Children's Literature Press - Guelph, ON, Canada - *BoPubDir 4, 5; LitMag&SmPr 83-84*
Canadian Citizen, The - Montreal, PQ, Canada - *AyerDirPub 83*
Canadian Clay & Ceramics - Willowdale, ON, Canada - *BaconPubCkMag 84*

Canadian Cleaner & Launderer - Montreal, PQ, Canada - *BaconPubCkMag 84*
Canadian Clearinghouse on Ongoing Research in Nursing [of University of Alberta] - Edmonton, AB, Canada - *EISS 83*
Canadian Clinical Laboratory - Toronto, ON, Canada - *BaconPubCkMag 84*
Canadian Clothing Journal - Toronto, ON, Canada - *BaconPubCkMag 84*
Canadian Coin Box - Owen Sound, ON, Canada - *BaconPubCkMag 84*
Canadian Coin News - Mississauga, ON, Canada - *BaconPubCkMag 84*
Canadian Collector - Toronto, ON, Canada - *BaconPubCkMag 84*
Canadian Conference of Catholic Bishops (Publications Service) - Ottawa, ON, Canada - *BoPubDir 4 Sup, 5*
Canadian Conference of the Arts - Ottawa, ON, Canada - *BoPubDir 4 Sup, 5*
Canadian Connection - Toronto, ON, Canada - *WritMar 84*
Canadian Consulting Engineer - Don Mills, ON, Canada - *BaconPubCkMag 84*
Canadian Contractors Equipment - Mississauga, ON, Canada - *BaconPubCkMag 84*
Canadian Controls & Instrumentation - Toronto, ON, Canada - *BaconPubCkMag 84*
Canadian Corporate Names - Mississauga, ON, Canada - *DirOnDB Spring 84*
Canadian Council of Churches - Toronto, ON, Canada - *BoPubDir 4, 5*
Canadian Council on Social Development - Ottawa, ON, Canada - *BoPubDir 4, 5*
Canadian Crafts Council - Ottawa, ON, Canada - *BoPubDir 4, 5*
Canadian Criminal Cases [of Canada Law Book Ltd.] - Aurora, ON, Canada - *CompReadDB 82; DirOnDB Spring 84*
Canadian Criminal Cases [of QL Systems Ltd.] - Ottawa, ON, Canada - *DataDirOnSer 84*
Canadian Database [of Data Resources Inc.] - Lexington, MA - *DataDirOnSer 84*
Canadian Datasystems - Toronto, ON, Canada - *BaconPubCkMag 84; WritMar 84*
Canadian Defence - Toronto, ON, Canada - *BaconPubCkMag 84*
Canadian Dept. of Insurance - Ottawa, ON, Canada - *DBBus 82; DirOnDB Spring 84*
Canadian Dept. of Insurance [of I. P. Sharp Associates Ltd.] - Toronto, ON, Canada - *DataDirOnSer 84*
Canadian Diabetes Association - Toronto, ON, Canada - *BoPubDir 4 Sup, 5*
Canadian Dimension - Winnipeg, MB, Canada - *LitMag&SmPr 83-84*
Canadian Distributor & Retailer - Montreal, PQ, Canada - *BaconPubCkMag 84*
Canadian Do It Yourself [of Centre Public Relations Ltd.] - Scarborough, ON, Canada - *BaconPubCkMag 84; WritMar 84*
Canadian Doctor - Don Mills, ON, Canada - *BaconPubCkMag 84; WritMar 84*
Canadian Driver/Owner - Toronto, ON, Canada - *BaconPubCkMag 84*
Canadian Education Association - Toronto, ON, Canada - *BoPubDir 4, 5*
Canadian Education Index Data Base [of Canadian Education Association] - Toronto, ON, Canada - *EISS 83*
Canadian Electronics Engineering - Toronto, ON, Canada - *BaconPubCkMag 84*
Canadian Emergency Services News - Calgary, AB, Canada - *BaconPubCkMag 84*
Canadian Energy Data Bank - Washington, DC - *DirOnDB Spring 84*
Canadian Energy Data Bank [of Data Resources Inc.] - Lexington, MA - *DataDirOnSer 84*
Canadian Energy Information System [of Conservation & Renewable Energy Branch] - Ottawa, ON, Canada - *EISS 83*
Canadian Energy Research Institute - Calgary, AB, Canada - *BoPubDir 4 Sup, 5*
Canadian Environment [of Environment Canada, Inland Water Directorate] - Ottawa, ON, Canada - *CompReadDB 82; DataDirOnSer 84; DBBus 82; DirOnDB Spring 84*
Canadian Environmental Law Research Foundation - Toronto, ON, Canada - *BoPubDir 4 Sup, 5*
Canadian Exporter - Scarborough, ON, Canada - *BaconPubCkMag 84*
Canadian Facts [Div. of SK/CF Inc.] - Toronto, ON, Canada - *BrCabYB 84; IntDirMarRes 83; Tel&CabFB 84C*
Canadian Family Physician - Willowdale, ON, Canada - *BaconPubCkMag 84*
Canadian Farmer, The - Winnipeg, MB, Canada - *Ed&PubIntYB 82*
Canadian Federal Corporations & Directors [of Canada Systems Group] - Mississauga, ON, Canada - *DataDirOnSer 84; DirOnDB Spring 84*
Canadian Federation of Film Societies (Index Committee) - Toronto, ON, Canada - *BoPubDir 4, 5*
Canadian Federation of University Women (Edmonton Branch) - Edmonton, AB, Canada - *BoPubDir 4, 5*
Canadian Federation of University Women (Maple Ridge) - Maple Ridge, BC, Canada - *BoPubDir 4*
Canadian Federation of University Women (Maple Ridge Branch) - Maple Ridge, BC, Canada - *BoPubDir 5*
Canadian Fertilizer [of Chase Econometrics/Interactive Data Corp.] - Waltham, MA - *DataDirOnSer 84*
Canadian Fertilizer - Bala Cynwyd, PA - *DirOnDB Spring 84*
Canadian Fiction Magazine - Toronto, ON, Canada - *ArtMar 84; LitMag&SmPr 83-84; WritMar 84*
Canadian Figure Skating Association - Ottawa, ON, Canada - *BoPubDir 4, 5*
Canadian Film Digest Yearbook - Toronto, ON, Canada - *BoPubDir 4, 5*
Canadian Financial Database [of FRI Information Services Ltd.] - Montreal, PQ, Canada - *DataDirOnSer 84*
Canadian Firefighter - Toronto, ON, Canada - *BaconPubCkMag 84*
Canadian Fisherman & Ocean Science - Montreal, PQ, Canada - *BaconPubCkMag 84*
Canadian Flight - Ottawa, ON, Canada - *BaconPubCkMag 84*
Canadian Florist, Greenhouse & Nursery - Mississauga, ON, Canada - *BaconPubCkMag 84*
Canadian Footwear Journal - Don Mills, ON, Canada - *BaconPubCkMag 84*
Canadian Forest Industries - Don Mills, ON, Canada - *BaconPubCkMag 84*
Canadian Foundation for Economic Education - Toronto, ON, Canada - *BoPubDir 4, 5*
Canadian Fruitgrower - Delhi, ON, Canada - *BaconPubCkMag 84*
Canadian Funeral Director - Scarboro, ON, Canada - *BaconPubCkMag 84; WritMar 84*
Canadian Funeral News - Calgary, AB, Canada - *BaconPubCkMag 84*
Canadian Geographic - Ottawa, ON, Canada - *BaconPubCkMag 84; WritMar 84*
Canadian Giftware Business - Toronto, ON, Canada - *BaconPubCkMag 84*
Canadian Government Publishing Centre (Supply & Services Canada) - Ottawa, ON, Canada - *LitMarPl 84*
Canadian Grocer - Toronto, ON, Canada - *BaconPubCkMag 84; WritMar 84*
Canadian Hairdresser - Mississauga, ON, Canada - *BaconPubCkMag 84*
Canadian Hereford Digest, The - Calgary, AB, Canada - *BaconPubCkMag 84*
Canadian Heritage Publications - Ottawa, ON, Canada - *BoPubDir 4, 5*
Canadian Historical Association/Societe Historique du Canada - Ottawa, ON, Canada - *BoPubDir 4, 5*
Canadian Horse, The - Markham, ON, Canada - *WritMar 84*
Canadian Hostelling Association (Nova Scotia) - Halifax, NS, Canada - *BoPubDir 4, 5*
Canadian Hotel & Restaurant - Toronto, ON, Canada - *BaconPubCkMag 84*
Canadian Hungarian Authors Association - Lethbridge, AB, Canada - *BoPubDir 4 Sup, 5*
Canadian Hydrological Operational Multipurpose Subprogramme [of Environment Canada, Inland Water Directorate] - Ottawa, ON, Canada - *DataDirOnSer 84; DirOnDB Spring 84*
Canadian India Star - Toronto, ON, Canada - *Ed&PubIntYB 82*
Canadian Industrial Equipment News - Don Mills, ON, Canada - *BaconPubCkMag 84*

Canadian Information Industry Association - Ottawa, ON, Canada - *EISS 83*
Canadian Institute of Chartered Accountants - Toronto, ON, Canada - *BoPubDir 4, 5*
Canadian Institute of Child Health - Ottawa, ON, Canada - *BoPubDir 4 Sup, 5*
Canadian Institute of International Affairs - Toronto, ON, Canada - *LitMarPl 83, 84*
Canadian Institute of Resources Law - Calgary, AB, Canada - *BoPubDir 4 Sup, 5*
Canadian Institute of Steel Construction - Willowdale, ON, Canada - *BoPubDir 4, 5*
Canadian Institute of Strategic Studies - Toronto, ON, Canada - *BoPubDir 5*
Canadian Institute of Travel Counsellors of Ontario - Toronto, ON, Canada - *BoPubDir 5*
Canadian Insurance/Agent & Broker - Toronto, ON, Canada - *BaconPubCkMag 84*
Canadian Intelligence & Security Association - Toronto, ON, Canada - *BoPubDir 4 Sup, 5*
Canadian Interiors - Toronto, ON, Canada - *BaconPubCkMag 84*
Canadian Inventory of Historic Building [of Environment Canada] - Ottawa, ON, Canada - *CompReadDB 82; EISS 83*
Canadian Jeweller - Toronto, ON, Canada - *BaconPubCkMag 84; WritMar 84*
Canadian Jewish Congress (National Archives) - Montreal, PQ, Canada - *BoPubDir 4 Sup, 5*
Canadian Jewish News - Toronto, ON, Canada - *Ed&PubIntYB 82*
Canadian Journal of Chemical Engineering - Ottawa, ON, Canada - *BaconPubCkMag 84*
Canadian Journal of Chemistry - Ottawa, ON, Canada - *BaconPubCkMag 84*
Canadian Journal of Communication - Saskatoon, SK, Canada - *LitMag&SmPr 83-84*
Canadian Journal of Comparative Medicine - Ottawa, ON, Canada - *BaconPubCkMag 84*
Canadian Journal of Medical Technology - Hamilton, ON, Canada - *BaconPubCkMag 84*
Canadian Journal of Optometry - Ottawa, ON, Canada - *BaconPubCkMag 84*
Canadian Journal of Public Health - Ottawa, ON, Canada - *BaconPubCkMag 84*
Canadian Journal of Surgery - Ottawa, ON, Canada - *BaconPubCkMag 84*
Canadian Law Information Council - Ottawa, ON, Canada - *BoPubDir 4, 5; CompReadDB 82; DataDirOnSer 84; EISS 83*
Canadian Lawyer - Toronto, ON, Canada - *BaconPubCkMag 84*
Canadian League of Rights - Vancouver, BC, Canada - *BoPubDir 4, 5*
Canadian Library Association - Ottawa, ON, Canada - *MicroMarPl 82-83*
Canadian library Association (Publishing Dept.) - Ottawa, ON, Canada - *BoPubDir 4, 5; LitMarPl 84*
Canadian Library Journal - Ottawa, ON, Canada - *BaconPubCkMag 84*
Canadian Literature [of University of British Columbia] - Vancouver, BC, Canada - *LitMag&SmPr 83-84; WritMar 84*
Canadian Living - Toronto, ON, Canada - *BaconPubCkMag 84*
Canadian Machine-Readable Cataloging [of National Library of Canada] - Ottawa, ON, Canada - *CompReadDB 82*
Canadian Machinery & Metalworking - Toronto, ON, Canada - *BaconPubCkMag 84; WritMar 84*
Canadian Machinery News [Div. of Hearst Business Media Corp.] - Southfield, MI - *ArtMar 84; DirMarMP 83*
Canadian Macroeconomic Forecast [of Chase Econometrics/ Interactive Data Corp.] - Waltham, MA - *DataDirOnSer 84*
Canadian Macroeconomic Forecast - Bala Cynwyd, PA - *DirOnDB Spring 84*
Canadian Manager - Willowdale, ON, Canada - *BaconPubCkMag 84*
Canadian Manda Group - Vancouver, BC, Canada - *LitMarPl 83, 84*
Canadian Medical & Biological Engineering Society [Aff. of International Federation for Medical & Biological Engineering] - Ottawa, ON, Canada - *BoPubDir 4, 5*
Canadian Medical Association Journal - Ottawa, ON, Canada - *BaconPubCkMag 84*
Canadian Mennonite Bible College (CMBC Publications) - Winnipeg, MB, Canada - *BoPubDir 4, 5*
Canadian Mental Health Association - Toronto, ON, Canada - *BoPubDir 4, 5*
Canadian Microfilming Co. Ltd./Societe Canadienne du Microfilm Inc. - Montreal, PQ, Canada - *MicroMarPl 82-83*
Canadian Micrographic Society - Willowdale, ON, Canada - *EISS 83*
Canadian Middle East Journal - Montreal, PQ, Canada - *Ed&PubIntYB 82*
Canadian Military Historical Society - Rockwood, ON, Canada - *BoPubDir 4 Sup, 5*
Canadian Mineral Occurence Index [of Geological Survey of Canada] - Ottawa, ON, Canada - *EISS 83*
Canadian Mining & Metallurgical Bulletin, The - Montreal, PQ, Canada - *BaconPubCkMag 84*
Canadian Mining Journal - Don Mills, ON, Canada - *BaconPubCkMag 84*
Canadian Motorcycle Business - Toronto, ON, Canada - *BaconPubCkMag 84*
Canadian Motorcycle Rider [of Hodgson Publishing Co.] - Toronto, ON, Canada - *BaconPubCkMag 84; WritMar 84*
Canadian Museums Association/Association des Musees Canadiens - Ottawa, ON, Canada - *BoPubDir 4, 5; WritMar 84*
Canadian Music Trade - Toronto, ON, Canada - *BaconPubCkMag 84*
Canadian Musician - Toronto, ON, Canada - *BaconPubCkMag 84*
Canadian National Committee [of World Energy Conference] - Ottawa, ON, Canada - *BoPubDir 4 Sup, 5*
Canadian Nature Federation [Aff. of Nature Canada] - Ottawa, ON, Canada - *BoPubDir 4, 5*
Canadian News Index [of QL Systems Ltd.] - Ottawa, ON, Canada - *DataDirOnSer 84*
Canadian News Index [of Micromedia Ltd.] - Toronto, ON, Canada - *CompReadDB 82; DBBus 82*
Canadian Newspaper Services International Ltd. - Toronto, ON, Canada - *BoPubDir 4, 5*
Canadian 1981 Agricultural Census [of I. P. Sharp Associates Ltd.] - Toronto, ON, Canada - *DataDirOnSer 84; DirOnDB Spring 84*
Canadian Nuclear Association - Toronto, ON, Canada - *BoPubDir 4, 5*
Canadian Nurse, The - Ottawa, ON, Canada - *BaconPubCkMag 84*
Canadian Occupational Health & Safety News - Don Mills, ON, Canada - *BaconPubCkMag 84*
Canadian Occupational Safety - Delhi, ON, Canada - *BaconPubCkMag 84*
Canadian Office - Port Credit, ON, Canada - *BaconPubCkMag 84*
Canadian Office Products & Stationery - Don Mills, ON, Canada - *BaconPubCkMag 84*
Canadian Online Enquiry System [of Canada Institute for Scientific & Technical Information] - Ottawa, ON, Canada - *EISS 83*
Canadian Operating Statistics - Ottawa, ON, Canada - *DirOnDB Spring 84*
Canadian Operating Statistics [of I. P. Sharp Associates Ltd.] - Toronto, ON, Canada - *DataDirOnSer 84*
Canadian Optician - Whitby, ON, Canada - *BaconPubCkMag 84*
Canadian Packaging - Toronto, ON, Canada - *BaconPubCkMag 84*
Canadian Paperbacks Publishing Ltd. - Ottawa, ON, Canada - *BoPubDir 4, 5*
Canadian Peace Research Institute - Huntsville, ON, Canada - *BoPubDir 5*
Canadian Peace Research Institute - Oakville, ON, Canada - *BoPubDir 4*
Canadian Periodical Index [of Canadian Library Association] - Ottawa, ON, Canada - *EISS 83*
Canadian Petroleum Association - Calgary, AB, Canada - *BaconPubCkMag 84; BoPubDir 4, 5*
Canadian Pharmaceutical Association - Ottawa, ON, Canada - *BoPubDir 4, 5*
Canadian Pharmaceutical Journal - Ottawa, ON, Canada - *BaconPubCkMag 84; WritMar 84*

Canadian Photography - Toronto, ON, Canada - *BaconPubCkMag 84*
Canadian Plains Research Center [of University of Regina] - Regina, SK, Canada - *CompReadDB 82; DataDirOnSer 84*
Canadian Plains Research Inventory [of QL Systems Ltd.] - Ottawa, ON, Canada - *DataDirOnSer 84*
Canadian Plastics - Don Mills, ON, Canada - *BaconPubCkMag 84*
Canadian Pool & Spa Marketing - Toronto, ON, Canada - *BaconPubCkMag 84*
Canadian Portland Cement Association [Aff. of Portland Cement Association] - Ottawa, ON, Canada - *BoPubDir 4, 5*
Canadian Premiums & Incentives [of Maclean Hunter Publishing Co.] - Toronto, ON, Canada - *WritMar 84*
Canadian Press & Broadcast News, The - Toronto, ON, Canada - *Ed&PubIntYB 82*
Canadian Press Clipping Services - Toronto, ON, Canada - *ProGuPRSer 4*
Canadian Press Newstex [of QL Systems Ltd.] - Kingston, ON, Canada - *DBBus 82*
Canadian Printer & Publisher - Toronto, ON, Canada - *BaconPubCkMag 84*
Canadian Process Equipment & Control News - Toronto, ON, Canada - *BaconPubCkMag 84*
Canadian Public Policy-Analyse de Politiques - Vancouver, BC, Canada - *LitMag&SmPr 83-84*
Canadian Pulp & Paper Association - Montreal, PQ, Canada - *BoPubDir 5*
Canadian Real Estate - Don Mills, ON, Canada - *BaconPubCkMag 84*
Canadian Record - Canadian, TX - *BaconPubCkNews 84; Ed&PubIntYB 82*
Canadian Regulatory Reporter [of Canadian Law Information Council] - Ottawa, ON, Canada - *DataDirOnSer 84; DirOnDB Spring 84*
Canadian Research - Toronto, ON, Canada - *BaconPubCkMag 84*
Canadian Research Centre for Anthropology - Ottawa, ON, Canada - *BoPubDir 4, 5*
Canadian Retail Gas Volume - London, ON, Canada - *DirOnDB Spring 84*
Canadian Review of Books Ltd. - Toronto, ON, Canada - *LitMag&SmPr 83-84*
Canadian Satellite Communications Inc. - Toronto, ON, Canada - *BrCabYB 84*
Canadian Schizophrenia Foundation - Regina, SK, Canada - *BoPubDir 4, 5*
Canadian Secretary - Toronto, ON, Canada - *BaconPubCkMag 84*
Canadian Security - Toronto, ON, Canada - *BaconPubCkMag 84*
Canadian Service for the Selective Dissemination of Information - Ottawa, ON, Canada - *EISS 83*
Canadian Shipping & Marine Engineering - Mississauga, ON, Canada - *BaconPubCkMag 84; WritMar 84*
Canadian Slavonic Papers - Toronto, ON, Canada - *LitMag&SmPr 83-84*
Canadian Society of Petroleum Geologists - Calgary, AB, Canada - *BoPubDir 4 Sup, 5*
Canadian Socio-Economic Information Management System [of Statistics Canada] - Ottawa, ON, Canada - *DBBus 82; EISS 83*
Canadian Speakers & Writers' Service Ltd. - Toronto, ON, Canada - *LitMarPl 83, 84*
Canadian Stage & Arts Publications - Toronto, ON, Canada - *BoPubDir 4, 5*
Canadian Statesman - Bowmanville, ON, Canada - *AyerDirPub 83; Ed&PubIntYB 82*
Canadian Stock Options [of I. P. Sharp Associates Ltd.] - Toronto, ON, Canada - *DataDirOnSer 84; DBBus 82; DirOnDB Spring 84*
Canadian Tax Foundation - Toronto, ON, Canada - *BoPubDir 4, 5*
Canadian Telecommunications Group - Toronto, ON, Canada - *DirInfWP 82*
Canadian Teleconference Network Inc. - Toronto, ON, Canada - *TeleSy&SerDir 2-84*
Canadian Textile Journal - Montreal, PQ, Canada - *BaconPubCkMag 84*
Canadian Theatre Review Publications [Aff. of York University] - Downsview, ON, Canada - *BoPubDir 4, 5*
Canadian Tobacco Grower - Delhi, ON, Canada - *BaconPubCkMag 84*
Canadian Toy Testing Council - Ottawa, ON, Canada - *BoPubDir 4, 5*
Canadian Trademarks - *DirOnDB Spring 84*
Canadian Transportation & Distribution Management [of Southam Communications] - Don Mills, ON, Canada - *BaconPubCkMag 84; WritMar 84*
Canadian Transportation Documentation System [of Transport Canada Library & Information Centre] - Ottawa, ON, Canada - *CompReadDB 82; DataDirOnSer 84*
Canadian Travel Courier - Toronto, ON, Canada - *BaconPubCkMag 84*
Canadian Travel Film Library - Chicago, IL - *Tel&CabFB 84C*
Canadian Travel News - Don Mills, ON, Canada - *BaconPubCkMag 84*
Canadian Travel Press - Toronto, ON, Canada - *BaconPubCkMag 84*
Canadian Underwriter - Toronto, ON, Canada - *BaconPubCkMag 84*
Canadian Unitarian Council - Toronto, ON, Canada - *BoPubDir 4, 5*
Canadian Uutiset - Thunder Bay, ON, Canada - *Ed&PubIntYB 82*
Canadian Valley Telephone Co. - Crowder, OK - *TelDir&BG 83-84*
Canadian Vending Magazine - Owen Sound, ON, Canada - *BaconPubCkMag 84*
Canadian Veterinary Journal, The - Ottawa, ON, Canada - *BaconPubCkMag 84*
Canadian Volleyball Association - Ottawa, ON, Canada - *BoPubDir 4, 5*
Canadian Water Well - Exeter, ON, Canada - *BaconPubCkMag 84*
Canadian Welder & Fabricator - Winnipeg, MB, Canada - *BaconPubCkMag 84*
Canadian Whole Earth Research Foundation - Berkeley, CA - *BoPubDir 4, 5*
Canadian Women of Note [of York University] - Downsview, ON, Canada - *CompReadDB 82*
Canadian Women's Educational Press - Toronto, ON, Canada - *LitMarPl 83*
Canadian Word Processing Supply Co. - Toronto, ON, Canada - *DirInfWP 82*
Canadian Workshop [of Nordais Publications] - Scarborough, ON, Canada - *BaconPubCkMag 84; WritMar 84*
Canadian Yachting - Toronto, ON, Canada - *BaconPubCkMag 84*
Canadiana House - Toronto, ON, Canada - *BoPubDir 4, 5*
Canal Fulton Signal [of Buckeye Publishing Co. Inc.] - Canal Fulton, OH - *BaconPubCkNews 84; NewsDir 84*
Canal Publishing Inc. - Indianapolis, IN - *BillIntBG 83-84*
Canal Winchester Times - Canal Winchester, OH - *BaconPubCkNews 84; NewsDir 84*
Canandaigua Broadcasting Co. - Canandaigua, NY - *BrCabYB 84*
Canandaigua Daily Messenger - Canandaigua, NY - *BaconPubCkNews 84; NewsDir 84*
Canandaigua-Victor-Holcomb Shopping News - Canandaigua, NY - *AyerDirPub 83*
Canandaigua Video Corp. - Canandaigua, NY - *BrCabYB 84*
Canap Press - Victoria, BC, Canada - *BoPubDir 5*
Canarsie Courier - Brooklyn, NY - *AyerDirPub 83; NewsDir 84*
Canarsie Courier - Canarsie, NY - *Ed&PubIntYB 82*
Canarsie Digest [of Courier-Life Inc.] - Brooklyn, NY - *AyerDirPub 83; Ed&PubIntYB 82; NewsDir 84*
Canarsie Digest - *See* Courier-Life Inc.
Canary-Yellow Bird Records Co. - Stockton, CA - *BillIntBG 83-84*
Canastota Bee-Journal - Canastota, NY - *BaconPubCkNews 84; Ed&PubIntYB 82*
Canby Herald [of Eagle Newspapers Inc.] - Canby, OR - *BaconPubCkNews 84; Ed&PubIntYB 82; NewsDir 84*
Canby News - Canby, MN - *BaconPubCkNews 84; Ed&PubIntYB 82; NewsDir 84*
Canby Telephone Association - Canby, OR - *TelDir&BG 83-84*
Cancer - Philadelphia, PA - *BaconPubCkMag 84; MagDir 84; MagIndMarPl 82-83*
Cancer Care Inc. - *See* National Cancer Foundation Inc./Cancer Care Inc.

Cancer Control Society-Cancer Book House - Los Angeles, CA - *BoPubDir 4, 5*
Cancer Information Clearinghouse [of U.S. Public Health Service] - Bethesda, MD - *EISS 83*
Cancer Literature [of International Cancer Research Data Bank] - Bethesda, MD - *DataDirOnSer 84*
Cancer Literature Information On-Line [of National Cancer Institute] - Bethesda, MD - *CompReadDB 82*
Cancer Research Projects [of International Cancer Research Data Bank] - Bethesda, MD - *CompReadDB 82; DataDirOnSer 84*
Cancer Therapy Protocols [of International Cancer Research Data Bank] - Bethesda, MD - *DataDirOnSer 84*
Cancerexpress [of International Cancer Research Data Bank] - Bethesda, MD - *DataDirOnSer 84; DirOnDB Spring 84*
Cancerline [of National Library of Medicine] - Bethesda, MD - *OnBibDB 3*
Cancerlit - Bethesda, MD - *DirOnDB Spring 84*
Cancernet [of Questel Inc.] - Washington, DC - *DataDirOnSer 84*
Cancernet [of Institut Gustave-Roussy] - Villejuif, France - *CompReadDB 82; DirOnDB Spring 84; EISS 83; OnBibDB 3*
Cancerproj - Bethesda, MD - *DirOnDB Spring 84*
Candle Corp. - Los Angeles, CA - *DataDirSup 7-83*
Cando Cable TV Inc. - Cando, ND - *BrCabYB 84*
Cando Towner County Record Herald - Cando, ND - *BaconPubCkNews 84*
Candy & Snack Industry [of Magazines for Industry Inc.] - New York, NY - *MagDir 84; MagIndMarPl 82-83*
Candy Industry - New York, NY - *BaconPubCkMag 84*
Candy Industry [of HBJ Publications] - Cleveland, OH - *WritMar 84*
Candy Marketer [of Magazines for Industry Inc.] - New York, NY - *MagDir 84*
Candy Marketer - Cleveland, OH - *BaconPubCkMag 84*
Candy Records - Irving, TX - *BillIntBG 83-84*
Candy Wholesaler [of National Candy Wholesalers Association Inc.] - Washington, DC - *BaconPubCkMag 84; MagDir 84*
Canec Publishing & Supply House [Subs. of The United Church of Canada] - Don Mills, ON, Canada - *LitMarPl 83, 84*
Canexpo Publishers Inc. - Surrey, BC, Canada - *BoPubDir 4, 5*
Caney Cable TV [of Tele-Communications Inc.] - Caney, KS - *BrCabYB 84*
Caney Chronicle - Caney, KS - *BaconPubCkNews 84; Ed&PubIntYB 82*
Caney Research Group - Stamford, CT - *IntDirMarRes 83*
Canfax - Montreal, PQ, Canada - *DirOnDB Spring 84; Ed&PubIntYB 82*
Canho Enterprises - Vernon, BC, Canada - *BoPubDir 4 Sup, 5*
Canine Behavior Institute Library [Aff. of Environmental Research Laboratory] - Agoura, CA - *BoPubDir 5*
Canine Behavior Institute Library - Santa Monica, CA - *BoPubDir 4*
Canine Chronicle [of Routledge Publications Inc.] - Montpelier, IN - *WritMar 84*
Canine Practice - Santa Barbara, CA - *BaconPubCkMag 84; MagDir 84*
Canistota Clipper - Canistota, SD - *BaconPubCkNews 84; Ed&PubIntYB 82*
Canlit - Victoria, BC, Canada - *BoPubDir 4, 5*
Cannell Productions, Stephen J. - Hollywood, CA - *Tel&CabFB 84C*
Cannella Enterprises Inc. - Syracuse, NY - *MicrocomMPl 84*
Cannelton News, The - Cannelton, IN - *NewsDir 84*
Canner & Co., J. S. [Aff. of Plenum Publishing Corp.] - Boston, MA - *BoPubDir 4, 5; LitMarPl 83, 84; MagIndMarPl 82-83; MicroMarPl 82-83*
Canning Publications Inc. - Vista, CA - *BoPubDir 4, 5*
Cannon Advertising Associates Inc. - New York, NY - *StaDirAdAg 2-84*
Cannon Beach Cablevision Co. - Cannon Beach, OR - *Tel&CabFB 84C*
Cannon Beach Television Co. - Cannon Beach, OR - *BrCabYB 84*
Cannon Courier - Woodbury, TN - *Ed&PubIntYB 82*
Cannon Falls Beacon - Cannon Falls, MN - *BaconPubCkNews 84; Ed&PubIntYB 82*
Cannon Features - Canton, NY - *Ed&PubIntYB 82*
Cannon Graphic Inc. - Charleston, WV - *BoPubDir 4, 5*
Cannon, Larry - Menlo Park, CA - *LitMarPl 83*
Cannon, Larry - Palo Alto, CA - *LitMarPl 84*
Cannon Releasing [Div. of The Cannon Group Inc.] - Hollywood, CA - *AvMarPl 83*
Cannon Valley Telephone Co. Inc. - Morristown, MN - *TelDir&BG 83-84*
Cannonade Press - *See* Konocti Books/Cannonade Press
Cannoneer, The - Ft. Sill, OK - *AyerDirPub 83*
Canoe - Ft. Wayne, IN - *MagIndMarPl 82-83*
Canoe [of New England Publications] - Camden, ME - *BaconPubCkMag 84; MagDir 84; WritMar 84*
Canoe [of New England Publications] - Highland Mill, ME - *ArtMar 84*
Canoe Mountain Echo - Valemount, BC, Canada - *AyerDirPub 83; Ed&PubIntYB 82*
Canoga Data Systems - Canoga Park, CA - *DataDirSup 7-83*
Canoga Park Canogan - *See* Associated Valley Publications
Canoga Park Valley View - *See* San Fernando Valley Sun Publishers
Canola Council of Canada - Winnipeg, MB, Canada - *BoPubDir 4, 5*
Canom [of Questel Inc.] - Washington, DC - *DataDirOnSer 84*
Canon & Shea Associates Inc. - New York, NY - *ArtMar 84*
Canon City Daily Record [of Royal Gorge Publishing Co.] - Canon City, CO - *BaconPubCkNews 84; Ed&PubIntYB 82; NewsDir 84*
Canon City Fremont County Sun - Canon City, CO - *BaconPubCkNews 84*
Canon U.S.A. Inc. - Lake Success, NY - *DirInfWP 82; MicrocomMPl 84; WhoWMicrocom 83*
Canonsburg Daily Notes [of Scripps of Pennsylvania] - Canonsburg, PA - *NewsDir 84*
Canopy Creations - Bloomfield, IA - *BoPubDir 4*
Canora Courier - Canora, SK, Canada - *Ed&PubIntYB 82*
Canorient Seniors Group [Aff. of Canorient Christian Association] - Don Mills, ON, Canada - *BoPubDir 4, 5*
Canova Herald - Canova, SD - *BaconPubCkNews 84; Ed&PubIntYB 82*
Canplains [of Canadian Plains Research Center] - Regina, SK, Canada - *CompReadDB 82; DirOnDB Spring 84*
Canplains Research Inventory [of University of Regina] - Regina, SK, Canada - *DataDirOnSer 84*
Canrad-Hanovia - Newark, NJ - *AvMarPl 83*
Canreg - Ottawa, ON, Canada - *DirOnDB Spring 84*
CANSIM [of Statistics Canada] - Ottawa, ON, Canada - *DataDirOnSer 84; DirOnDB Spring 84*
CANSIM Canadian Agriculture [of Chase Econometrics/Interactive Data Corp.] - Waltham, MA - *DataDirOnSer 84*
CANSIM Telichart [of Faxtel Information Systems Ltd.] - Toronto, ON, Canada - *DataDirOnSer 84*
Canstar Communications - Scarborough, ON, Canada - *DataDirSup 7-83*
Can't Stop Music - New York, NY - *BillIntBG 83-84*
Canter Achenbaum Heekin Inc. - New York, NY - *HBIndAd&MS 82-83*
Canter & Associates Inc. - Los Angeles, CA - *BoPubDir 5*
Canterbury Press - Anaheim, CA - *BoPubDir 4, 5*
Canterbury Press - Rome, NY - *LitMarPl 83, 84; MagIndMarPl 82-83*
Cantin & Elliott - New York, NY - *AdAge 3-28-84; StaDirAdAg 2-84*
Canton Automated Systems Inc. [Subs. of Citizens Savings Bank] - Canton, OH - *DataDirOnSer 84*
Canton Cable TV - Canton, GA - *BrCabYB 84; Tel&CabFB 84C*
Canton Cable TV - Canton, SD - *Tel&CabFB 84C*
Canton Cablevision Inc. - Canton, MS - *BrCabYB 84; Tel&CabFB 84C*
Canton Cherokee Tribune - Canton, GA - *BaconPubCkNews 84*
Canton Daily Ledger [of Winsor Newspapers] - Canton, IL - *BaconPubCkNews 84; NewsDir 84*
Canton Eagle [of Wayne Associated Newspapers Inc.] - Wayne, MI - *AyerDirPub 83; NewsDir 84*
Canton Eagle - *See* Associated Newspapers Inc.
Canton Eagle, The - Canton, MI - *Ed&PubIntYB 82*
Canton Enterprise - Canton, NC - *BaconPubCkNews 84; Ed&PubIntYB 82*
Canton Herald - Canton, TX - *BaconPubCkNews 84; Ed&PubIntYB 82*

Canton Independent-Sentinel - Canton, PA - *BaconPubCkNews 84; Ed&PubIntYB 82*
Canton Journal - Canton, MA - *BaconPubCkNews 84; Ed&PubIntYB 82; NewsDir 84*
Canton-La Grange Cablevision [of Semo Communications Inc.] - La Belle, MO - *Tel&CabFB 84C*
Canton-La Grange Cablevision Inc. [of Semo Communications Inc.] - Canton, MO - *BrCabYB 84; Tel&CabFB 84C*
Canton Madison County Herald - Canton, MS - *BaconPubCkNews 84*
Canton Observer - Canton, MI - *Ed&PubIntYB 82*
Canton Observer [of Livonia Suburban Communications Corp.] - Livonia, MI - *AyerDirPub 83; NewsDir 84*
Canton Observer - *See* Observer & Eccentric Newspapers
Canton Pilot - Canton, KS - *BaconPubCkNews 84; Ed&PubIntYB 82*
Canton Press-News Journal - Canton, MO - *BaconPubCkNews 84; Ed&PubIntYB 82; NewsDir 84*
Canton Register - *See* Bulletin Publishing Co.
Canton Repository [of Thomson-Brush-Moore] - Canton, OH - *BaconPubCkNews 84; NewsDir 84*
Canton Sioux Valley News - Canton, SD - *BaconPubCkNews 84*
Canton St. Lawrence Plaindealer - Canton, NY - *BaconPubCkNews 84; NewsDir 84*
Canton Telephone Co. - Canton, PA - *TelDir&BG 83-84*
Canton Times - Canton, OK - *Ed&PubIntYB 82*
Canton, Woodstock The Cherokee Tribune - Canton, GA - *NewsDir 84*
Cantone, Vic - New York, NY - *LitMarPl 83, 84; MagIndMarPl 82-83*
Cantor Advertising Corp. - San Diego, CA - *StaDirAdAg 2-84*
Cantor & Associates - Austin, TX - *StaDirAdAg 2-84*
Cantor, Ruth - New York, NY - *LitMarPl 83, 84*
Cantrell-Colas Inc. - New York, NY - *LitMarPl 83, 84*
Cantrell Publishing Inc. - Little Rock, AR - *ArtMar 84*
Cantwell Inc., Jack - Englewood Cliffs, NJ - *AdAge 3-28-84; HBIndAd&MS 82-83; StaDirAdAg 2-84*
Canty & Associates - Pensacola, FL - *MicrocomMPl 83*
Cantz & Associates, Marvin S. - Encino, CA - *StaDirAdAg 2-84*
CaNUCS - Ottawa, ON, Canada - *DirOnDB Spring 84*
Canute CATV - Canute, OK - *BrCabYB 84*
Canute Community TV - Canute, OK - *Tel&CabFB 84C*
Canyon Cable TV [of United Artists Cablesystems Corp.] - Aspen, CO - *Tel&CabFB 84C*
Canyon Cable TV [of United Artists Cablesystems Corp.] - Basalt, CO - *BrCabYB 84; Tel&CabFB 84C*
Canyon Cable TV [of United Artists Cablesystems Corp.] - Rifle, CO - *BrCabYB 84; Tel&CabFB 84C*
Canyon County Herald - Wilder, ID - *Ed&PubIntYB 82*
Canyon Courier - Evergreen, CO - *AyerDirPub 83; Ed&PubIntYB 82*
Canyon Creek Current - Canyonville, OR - *Ed&PubIntYB 82*
Canyon Crest Records - Alta Loma, CA - *BillIntBG 83-84*
Canyon Crier News, The - North Hollywood, CA - *AyerDirPub 83*
Canyon Lake Times Guardian - Canyon Lake, TX - *BaconPubCkNews 84*
Canyon News - Canyon, TX - *BaconPubCkNews 84; NewsDir 84*
Canyon Records Inc. - Phoenix, AZ - *BillIntBG 83-84*
Canyon TV Service - Cataldo, ID - *BrCabYB 84; Tel&CabFB 84C*
CAO Times - New York, NY - *BoPubDir 4 Sup, 5*
Cap & Gown Press Inc. - Houston, TX - *LitMarPl 83, 84*
Cap Electronics - Tucson, AZ - *WhoWMicrocom 83*
Cap Gemini Sogeti - Vienna, VA - *ADAPSOMemDir 83-84*
Cap Gemini Sogeti - Grenoble, France - *VideoDir 82-83*
CAP Magazine - Costa Mesa, CA - *BaconPubCkMag 84*
Cap Rock Telephone Co. Inc. - Spur, TX - *TelDir&BG 83-84*
C.A.P. Software - York, ME - *MicrocomMPl 84*
Capa - Brussels, Belgium - *DirOnDB Spring 84*
Capac Journal - Capac, MI - *AyerDirPub 83; Ed&PubIntYB 82*
Capac Journal - *See* Tri-City Times
Capac Journal-Tri-City Times - Imlay City, MI - *NewsDir 84*
Capano Music [Div. of Britone Inc.] - Westville, NJ - *BillIntBG 83-84*
Capay Valley Telephone System Inc. - Guinda, CA - *TelDir&BG 83-84*
CAPCON Network Office - Washington, DC - *EISS 83; InfIndMarPl 83*
Cape Breton Cablevision - Sydney, NS, Canada - *BrCabYB 84*
Cape Breton Post - Sydney, NS, Canada - *AyerDirPub 83; BaconPubCkNews 84; Ed&PubIntYB 82*
Cape Cable TV - Orleans, MA - *BrCabYB 84*
Cape Cod Cablevision Corp. [of TCI-Taft Cablevision Associates] - South Yarmouth, MA - *Tel&CabFB 84C*
Cape Cod Life - Osterville, MA - *BaconPubCkMag 84*
Cape Cod News [of Hughes Newspapers Inc.] - Hyannis, MA - *AyerDirPub 83; Ed&PubIntYB 82; NewsDir 84*
Cape Cod Oracle [of Hughes Newspapers Inc.] - Orleans, MA - *AyerDirPub 83; Ed&PubIntYB 82; NewsDir 84*
Cape Cod Times [of Ottaway Newspapers Inc.] - Hyannis, MA - *AyerDirPub 83; BaconPubCkNews 84; Ed&PubIntYB 82; LitMarPl 83, 84; NewsDir 84*
Cape Cod Writers Inc. - Cummaquid, MA - *LitMag&SmPr 83-84*
Cape Codder, The - Orleans, MA - *AyerDirPub 83; Ed&PubIntYB 82; NewsDir 84*
Cape Coral Breeze - Ft. Myers, FL - *AyerDirPub 83*
Cape Coral Evening Breeze - Cape Coral, FL - *BaconPubCkNews 84; NewsDir 84*
Cape Girardeau Bulletin-Journal - Cape Girardeau, MO - *NewsDir 84*
Cape Girardeau Cable TV Inc. - Cape Girardeau, MO - *BrCabYB 84*
Cape Girardeau CATV [of Tele-Communications Inc.] - Cape Girardeau, MO - *Tel&CabFB 84C*
Cape Girardeau Southeast Missourian [of Thomson Newspapers Inc.] - Cape Girardeau, MO - *NewsDir 84*
Cape, Jonathan - Salem, NH - *LitMarPl 83, 84*
Cape May County Herald - Avalon, NJ - *Ed&PubIntYB 82*
Cape May County Herald [of Seawave Corp.] - Cape May, NJ - *AyerDirPub 83; BaconPubCkNews 84; NewsDir 84*
Cape May Star & Wave - Cape May, NJ - *BaconPubCkNews 84; Ed&PubIntYB 82; NewsDir 84*
Cape Rock Music - Cape Girardeau, MO - *BillIntBG 83-84*
Cape Rock, The [of Southeast Missouri State University Press] - Cape Girardeau, MO - *LitMag&SmPr 83-84; WritMar 84*
Capehart Data Services - Kettering, OH - *WhoWMicrocom 83*
Capelin & Landreth Inc. - New York, NY - *DirPRFirms 83*
Capener Co., The - Dalmar, CA - *StaDirAdAg 2-84*
Capetown Records - Cape Girardeau, MO - *BillIntBG 83-84*
Capilano Review, The - North Vancouver, BC, Canada - *LitMag&SmPr 83-84*
Capistrano Valley News - San Juan Capistrano, CA - *AyerDirPub 83*
Capital - Annapolis, MD - *AyerDirPub 83; Ed&PubIntYB 82*
Capital - Columbus, OH - *BaconPubCkMag 84*
Capital - Three Hills, AB, Canada - *AyerDirPub 83*
Capital Advertising Agency Inc. - Lansing, MI - *StaDirAdAg 2-84*
Capital Bird Dog Enterprises - Slingerlands, NY - *BoPubDir 4, 5*
Capital Broadcast News/Newscom Satellite - Washington, DC - *BrCabYB 84*
Capital Cable TV Ltd. - Edmonton, AB, Canada - *BrCabYB 84; CabTVFinDB 83*
Capital Cable Vision - Hoonah, AL - *BrCabYB 84*
Capital Cities Cable [of Capital Cities Communications Inc.] - Bloomfield Hills, MI - *BrCabYB 84 p.D-298; CabTVFinDB 83; HomeVid&CabYB 82-83; TelAl 84*
Capital Cities Cable - Denison, TX - *BrCabYB 84*
Capital Cities Cable Inc. - Clifton, AZ - *BrCabYB 84*
Capital Cities Cable Inc. - Idabel, OK - *BrCabYB 84*
Capital Cities Communications - New York, NY - *AdAge 6-28-84; BrCabYB 84; Ed&PubIntYB 82; HomeVid&CabYB 82-83; KnowInd 83; TelAl 83, 84; Tel&CabFB 84C, 84S*
Capital Cities Communications Inc. - Bloomfield Hills, MI - *Tel&CabFB 84C p.1669*
Capital Cities Television Productions - Philadelphia, PA - *Tel&CabFB 84C*
Capital City Press Inc. - Montpelier, VT - *LitMarPl 83, 84; MagIndMarPl 82-83*
Capital Consortium Network - *See* CAPCON Network Office
Capital Costs Database [of Utility Data Institute] - Washington, DC - *DataDirOnSer 84*
Capital Counselors Inc. - Washington, DC - *DirPRFirms 83*
Capital Distributing Co., The - Derby, CT - *MagIndMarPl 82-83*

Capital District Business Review [of New York Business Publications Inc.] - Albany, NY - *BaconPubCkMag 84; MagDir 84*

Capital District Trader - Scotia, NY - *AyerDirPub 83*

Capital Energy Letter - Washington, DC - *BaconPubCkMag 84*

Capital Flyer [of Rockville Sentinel Newspapers] - Rockville, MD - *NewsDir 84*

Capital Gazette Newspapers - Bowie, MD - *BaconPubCkNews 84*

Capital Information Bureau - Springfield, IL - *BrCabYB 84*

Capital-Journal [of Stauffer Communications Inc.] - Topeka, KS - *AyerDirPub 83; NewsDir 84*

Capital-Journal - Pierre, SD - *AyerDirPub 83*

Capital Market Systems Inc. - Waltham, MA - *InfIndMarPl 83*

Capital News - Jefferson City, MO - *AyerDirPub 83; Ed&PubIntYB 82*

Capital News - Kelowna, BC, Canada - *AyerDirPub 83; Ed&PubIntYB 82*

Capital Planning Information Ltd. - Edinburgh, Scotland - *EISS 83*

Capital Planning Information Ltd. - Tunbridge, Scotland - *FBInfSer 80*

Capital Press - Salem, OR - *AyerDirPub 83; BaconPubCkMag 84; NewsDir 84*

Capital Publishers Inc. - Washington, DC - *BoPubDir 4, 5*

Capital Publishing Corp. - Wellesley Hills, MA - *BoPubDir 4, 5*

Capital Publishing Inc. - Detroit, MI - *BoPubDir 4, 5*

Capital Radio & TV Co. - McMechen, WV - *BrCabYB 84; Tel&CabFB 84C*

Capital Reporter - Jackson, MS - *Ed&PubIntYB 82*

Capital Services Inc. - Washington, DC - *MicroMarPl 82-83*

Capital Star Artist Enterprises Inc. - Rochester, NY - *BillIntBG 83-84*

Capital Systems Group - Kensington, MD - *EISS 83; InfIndMarPl 83; MicrocomMPl 84*

Capital, The - Orange City, IA - *AyerDirPub 83*

Capital Times [of Madison Newspapers Inc.] - Madison, WI - *AyerDirPub 83; Ed&PubIntYB 82; LitMarPl 83, 84*

Capitaland Woman Magazine - Albany, NY - *MagDir 84*

Capitalist Press - Akron, OH - *BoPubDir 4 Sup, 5*

Capitol Audio-Visuals Inc. - Chattanooga, TN - *Tel&CabFB 84C*

Capitol Broadcasting Co. - Jackson, MS - *BrCabYB 84*

Capitol Broadcasting Co. Inc. - Raleigh, NC - *BrCabYB 84*

Capitol Broadcasting Corp. - Mobile, AL - *BrCabYB 84*

Capitol Cable Co. [of American Television & Communications Corp.] - Austin, TX - *BrCabYB 84*

Capitol Cablevision [of American Television & Communications Corp.] - Albany, NY - *BrCabYB 84; Tel&CabFB 84C*

Capitol Cablevision [of American Television & Communications Corp.] - Austin, TX - *HomeVid&CabYB 82-83*

Capitol Cablevision [of American TV & Communications Corp.] - Charleston, WV - *BrCabYB 84; Tel&CabFB 84C*

Capitol Cablevision Inc. [of American TV & Communications Corp.] - Jackson, MS - *BrCabYB 84; Tel&CabFB 84C*

Capitol City Argus - Austin, TX - *Ed&PubIntYB 82*

Capitol Connection News Service - Arlington, VA - *BrCabYB 84*

Capitol Enquiry - Sacramento, CA - *BoPubDir 4, 5*

Capitol Film & Radio Co. Inc. - Richmond, VA - *AvMarPl 83*

Capitol Hill Beacon - Oklahoma City, OK - *AyerDirPub 83; Ed&PubIntYB 82*

Capitol Hill Times - Seattle, WA - *AyerDirPub 83; Ed&PubIntYB 82*

Capitol News Service - Hollywood, CA - *BaconPubCkNews 84*

Capitol News Service - Sacramento, CA - *Ed&PubIntYB 82; NewsBur 6*

Capitol News Service - Augusta, ME - *BrCabYB 84*

Capitol Outlook - Tallahassee, FL - *Ed&PubIntYB 82*

Capitol Production Music [of Capitol Records Inc.] - Hollywood, CA - *AvMarPl 83; Tel&CabFB 84C*

Capitol Publications Inc. - Arlington, VA - *DataDirOnSer 84*

Capitol Records - Hollywood, CA - *BillIntBG 83-84*

Capitol Services Inc. [Subs. of Indian Head Inc.] - Washington, DC - *CompReadDB 82; DataDirOnSer 84; EISS 83; InfIndMarPl 83; InfoS 83-84*

Capitola Cabrillo Times & Green Sheet - Capitola, CA - *BaconPubCkNews 84*

Caplan/Rawley & Associates [Subs. of Sylvia Caplan Productions] - Houston, TX - *AvMarPl 83*

Caplin Music - *See* Biograph Records Inc.

Cap'n Software - San Francisco, CA - *MicrocomMPl 83; WhoWMicrocom 83*

Cappellari, Stephen G. - Boston, MA - *LitMarPl 84*

Capper Inc. - Knoxville, TN - *LitMarPl 83, 84; MagIndMarPl 82-83*

Capper's Weekly [of Stauffer Communications Inc.] - Topeka, KS - *BaconPubCkMag 84; Ed&PubIntYB 82; MagDir 84; MagIndMarPl 82-83; WritMar 84*

Cappiello & Chabrowe Inc. - New York, NY - *StaDirAdAg 2-84*

Capps Broadcast Group - Bend, OR - *BrCabYB 84*

Capra Press - Santa Barbara, CA - *LitMag&SmPr 83-84; LitMarPl 83, 84; WritMar 84*

Capri Music - *See* Alfred Publishing Co. Inc.

Capricorn Books - Tom's River, NJ - *LitMag&SmPr 83-84*

Capricorn Records Inc. - Macon, GA - *BillIntBG 83-84*

Capro Inc. - Garden Grove, CA - *MicrocomMPl 84; WhoWMicrocom 83*

Caprock Cablevision [of Omni Cable TV Corp.] - Crosbyton, TX - *BrCabYB 84*

Caprock Cablevision [of Omni Cable TV Corp.] - Ralls, TX - *BrCabYB 84*

Caprock Developments - Morris Plains, NJ - *AvMarPl 83*

Caprock Press - Lubbock, TX - *BoPubDir 4, 5*

Caprock Telecasting Inc. - Roswell, NM - *BrCabYB 84*

Capron Lighting & Sound Co. Inc. - Needham, MA - *AvMarPl 83*

Capron Publishing Corp. - Wellesley Hills, MA - *BoPubDir 5*

Capstan Records - East Prairie, MO - *BillIntBG 83-84*

CAPTAIN [of Nippon Telegraph & Telephone Public Corp.] - Tokyo, Japan - *EISS 83; InfIndMarPl 83; VideoDir 82-83*

Captain Blue Music Publishing & Records - Hazleton, PA - *BillIntBG 83-84*

Captain Graphics - Boston, MA - *HBIndAd&MS 82-83*

Car & Driver [of Ziff-Davis Publishing Co.] - Ann Arbor, MI - *ArtMar 84; BaconPubCkMag 84; MagDir 84; MagIndMarPl 82-83; WritMar 84*

Car & Driver [of Ziff-Davis Publishing Co.] - New York, NY - *Folio 83*

Car Biz - Troy, MI - *MagDir 84*

Car Care Hot Line - Brooklyn, NY - *Ed&PubIntYB 82*

Car Classics - Chatsworth, CA - *MagDir 84*

Car Collector & Car Classics [of Classic Publishing Inc.] - Atlanta, GA - *BaconPubCkMag 84; MagIndMarPl 82-83; WritMar 84*

Car Craft [of Petersen Publishing Co.] - Los Angeles, CA - *ArtMar 84; BaconPubCkMag 84; Folio 83; MagDir 84; MagIndMarPl 82-83; WritMar 84*

Car Dealer Insider Newsletter - New York, NY - *BaconPubCkMag 84*

Car Exchange [of Krause Publications] - Iola, WI - *ArtMar 84; BaconPubCkMag 84; MagIndMarPl 82-83; WritMar 84*

Car-Lene Research Inc. - Deerfield, IL - *IntDirMarRes 83*

Car Rental & Leasing Insider Newsletter - New York, NY - *BaconPubCkMag 84*

Car Stereo Trade News - New York, NY - *BaconPubCkMag 84*

Cara Publications - *See* Barnhouse Co., C. L.

Carabis, Anne - Latham, NY - *BoPubDir 4, 5*

Caracci, Philip V. - Brooklyn, NY - *LitMarPl 83, 84*

Caragana Records - *See* Coteau Books/Caragana Records

Caratzas, Aristide D. [Div. of Caratzas Publishing Co. Inc.] - New Rochelle, NY - *LitMarPl 84; WritMar 84*

Caratzas Brothers - New Rochelle, NY - *LitMarPl 83*

Caravan Publishing Group [of Thomson Press India] - New York, NY - *LitMarPl 84*

Caravatt Communications Inc. - New York, NY - *Tel&CabFB 84C*

Caravetta Allen Kimbrough [Subs. of BBDO] - Coral Gables, FL - *AdAge 3-28-84*

Caravetta Allen Kimbrough [Subs. of BBDO] - Miami, FL - *StaDirAdAg 2-84*

Caraway Cable TV [of Spectrum Teltronics Inc.] - Caraway, AR - *BrCabYB 84*

Caraway Kemp Communications - Jacksonville, FL - *AdAge 3-28-84; StaDirAdAg 2-84*

CARBEN Surveying Reprints - Rancho Conlova, CA - *BoPubDir 4, 5*

Carberry Marketing Research - Los Angeles, CA - *IntDirMarRes 83*
Carberry, Mary Margaret - Flossmoor, IL - *Ed&PubIntYB 82*
Carberry News Express - Carberry, MB, Canada - *Ed&PubIntYB 82*
Carbide & Tool Journal, The - Bridgeville, PA - *BaconPubCkMag 84; MagDir 84*
Carbon County News - Red Lodge, MT - *AyerDirPub 83; Ed&PubIntYB 82*
Carbon Dioxide Information Center [of U.S. Dept. of Energy] - Oak Ridge, TN - *EISS 7-83 Sup; InfIndMarPl 83*
Carbon-13 Nuclear Magnetic Resonance Spectral Search System [of Computer Sciences Corp.] - Falls Church, VA - *DataDirOnSer 84*
Carbon Village Press - Carbon, AB, Canada - *AyerDirPub 83*
Carbonate Chronicle - Leadville, CO - *AyerDirPub 83; Ed&PubIntYB 82*
Carbondale Cable Television Co. - Carbondale, CO - *BrCabYB 84; Tel&CabFB 84C*
Carbondale Cable TV - Carbondale, KS - *BrCabYB 84*
Carbondale Cablevision [of Cable Information Systems Inc.] - Carbondale, IL - *BrCabYB 84; Tel&CabFB 84C*
Carbondale Miner [of Dallas Pennaprint Inc.] - Dallas, PA - *NewsDir 84*
Carbondale News - Carbondale, PA - *BaconPubCkNews 84; Ed&PubIntYB 82; NewsDir 84*
Carbondale Southern Illinoisan - Carbondale, IL - *BaconPubCkNews 84*
Carbondale Valley Journal - Carbondale, CO - *BaconPubCkNews 84*
Carcanet New Press - Manchester, England - *LitMag&SmPr 83-84*
Carcosa - Chapel Hill, NC - *BoPubDir 4, 5*
Card Caller Service [of American Telephone & Telegraph Co.] - Bedminster, NJ - *TeleSy&SerDir 2-84*
Card Equipment [of GML Corp.] - Lexington, MA - *CompReadDB 82*
Cardamone, Helen M. - Utica, NY - *BoPubDir 5*
Cardco - Witchita, KS - *MicrocomMPl 84*
Carden & Cherry Advertising Agency - Nashville, TN - *StaDirAdAg 2-84*
Cardiff-by-the-Sea Publishing Co. - Cardiff-by-the-Sea, CA - *BoPubDir 5*
Cardiff Cable Ltd. - Cardiff, ON, Canada - *BrCabYB 84*
Cardiff Cablevision Inc. - Denver, CO - *Tel&CabFB 84C p.1670*
Cardiff Cablevision Inc. - Englewood, CO - *BrCabYB 84 p.D-298*
Cardiff Cablevision Inc. - Blue Rapids, KS - *Tel&CabFB 84C*
Cardiff Cablevision Inc. - Onaga, KS - *BrCabYB 84*
Cardiff Communications - Denver, CO - *CabTVFinDB 83; HomeVid&CabYB 82-83*
Cardiff Publishing Co. - Denver, CO - *BoPubDir 5*
Cardiff Publishing Co. - Englewood, CO - *MagIndMarPl 82-83*
Cardin Advertising - Bangor, ME - *StaDirAdAg 2-84*
Cardinal Cablevision [of Continuing Objectives Inc.] - Bolt, WV - *BrCabYB 84*
Cardinal Cablevision [of Continuing Objectives Inc.] - Coal City, WV - *Tel&CabFB 84C*
Cardinal Cablevision [of Continuing Objectives Inc.] - Eccles, WV - *BrCabYB 84; Tel&CabFB 84C*
Cardinal Cablevision [of Continuing Objectives Inc.] - Fairdale, WV - *Tel&CabFB 84C*
Cardinal Cablevision [of Continuing Objectives Inc.] - Lester, WV - *BrCabYB 84; Tel&CabFB 84C*
Cardinal Communications Inc. - Westport, CT - *LitMarPl 84*
Cardinal Communications Inc. - Indianapolis, IN - *Tel&CabFB 84C p.1670*
Cardinal Press - Tulsa, OK - *BoPubDir 4, 5; LitMag&SmPr 83-84*
Cardinal Publishers - Davis, CA - *BoPubDir 4, 5*
Cardinal Systems Corp. - Silver Spring, MD - *AvMarPl 83*
Cardinal Telecable Corp. - Marshall, IL - *BrCabYB 84*
Cardinal Telecable Corp. [of Omega Communications Inc.] - Paris, IL - *BrCabYB 84; Tel&CabFB 84C*
Cardinal Type Service Inc. - New York, NY - *LitMarPl 83, 84*
Cardington Morrow County Independent - Cardington, OH - *BaconPubCkNews 84*
Cardio Music [Div. of Art Attack Records Inc.] - Tucson, AZ - *BillIntBG 83-84*
Cardiology Product News - New York, NY - *BaconPubCkMag 84*
Cardiology Times - New York, NY - *BaconPubCkMag 84*
Cardiovascular Medicine - New York, NY - *MagIndMarPl 82-83*
Cardiovascular Reviews & Reports - New York, NY - *BaconPubCkMag 84*
Cardon, Rose Inc. - Montreal, PQ, Canada - *StaDirAdAg 2-84*
Cardoza School of Blackjack - Santa Cruz, CA - *BoPubDir 5*
Cards Inc. - Elida, OH - *ADAPSOMemDir 83-84; DataDirOnSer 84*
Cardunal Free Press - Carpentersville, IL - *AyerDirPub 83; Ed&PubIntYB 82; NewsDir 84*
Cardunal Free Press - *See* Free Press Inc.
Cardwell House Inc. - Fergus, ON, Canada - *BoPubDir 4, 5*
Care - Reston, VA - *DirOnDB Spring 84*
Care Communications Inc. - Chicago, IL - *BoPubDir 4, 5*
Care Computer Systems - Bellevue, WA - *DataDirOnSer 84*
Career Aids Inc. - Chatsworth, CA - *AvMarPl 83*
Career & Family Publications - Toronto, ON, Canada - *BoPubDir 4, 5*
Career Blazers Agency Inc. [Subs. of Career Blazers Personnel Services] - New York, NY - *LitMarPl 83, 84; MagIndMarPl 82-83*
Career Builders Inc. - New York, NY - *InfIndMarPl 83; LitMarPl 83, 84; MagIndMarPl 82-83*
Career Guidance Foundation (College Catalog Library) - San Diego, CA - *MicroMarPl 82-83*
Career Placement Registry [Subs. of Plenum Publishing Corp.] - Alexandria, VA - *CompReadDB 82; DataDirOnSer 84; EISS 83*
Career Placement Registry/Experienced Personnel [of Dialog Information Services Inc.] - Palo Alto, CA - *DataDirOnSer 84*
Career Placement Registry/Experienced Personnel - Alexandria, VA - *DirOnDB Spring 84*
Career Placement Registry/Student [of Career Placement Registry Inc.] - Alexandria, VA - *DataDirOnSer 84; DirOnDB Spring 84*
Career Publishing Inc. - Orange, CA - *ArtMar 84; LitMag&SmPr 83-84; LitMarPl 83, 84; WritMar 84*
Career Publishing Inc. - Little Falls, NJ - *BoPubDir 4, 5*
Career World [of Curriculum Innovations Inc.] - Highland Park, IL - *MagDir 84; MagIndMarPl 82-83; WritMar 84*
Careerdata [of New Opportunity Press Ltd.] - London, England - *EISS 83*
Careers & Occupational Information Centre [of Manpower Services Commission] - Sheffield, England - *EISS 7-83 Sup*
Careers Music Inc. - *See* Arista Music Publishing Group
Careers Unltd. Inc. - Cincinnati, OH - *MagIndMarPl 82-83*
CareerSystem - West Palm Beach, FL - *DirOnDB Spring 84*
Carefree Script Service - Carefree, AZ - *LitMarPl 83, 84*
Carel-Almo Service Inc. - Hicksville, NY - *LitMarPl 83; MagIndMarPl 82-83*
Carelli, Glynn & Ward - Butler, NJ - *DirPRFirms 83; StaDirAdAg 2-84*
Carey Library, William - Pasadena, CA - *LitMarPl 83, 84*
Carey Progressor-Times, The - Carey, OH - *NewsDir 84*
Carfax Publishing Co. - Oxford, England - *MicroMarPl 82-83*
Cargill, Wilson & Acree Inc. - Atlanta, GA - *BrCabYB 84; StaDirAdAg 2-84*
Cargo Records - Massapequa, NY - *BillIntBG 83-84*
Carib House - Hayward, CA - *BoPubDir 4, 5*
Caribbean Business News - Toronto, ON, Canada - *WritMar 84*
Caribbean Communications Corp. - Charlotte Amalie, VI - *BrCabYB 84*
Caribbean Communications Corp. - St. Thomas, VI - *Tel&CabFB 84C p.1670*
Caribbean Imprint Library Services - West Falmouth, MA - *MicroMarPl 82-83*
Caribbean MDS Co. - San Juan, PR - *Tel&CabFB 84C*
Caribbean Review - Miami, FL - *LitMag&SmPr 83-84*
Cariboo Observer - Quesnel, BC, Canada - *AyerDirPub 83*
Cariboo Radio Network - Quesnel, BC, Canada - *BrCabYB 84*
Caribou Aroostook Republican & News - Caribou, ME - *BaconPubCkNews 84; NewsDir 84*
Caribou County Sun - Soda Springs, ID - *AyerDirPub 83; Ed&PubIntYB 82*
Carillon, The - Steinbach, MB, Canada - *AyerDirPub 83; Ed&PubIntYB 82*
Carl Junction Standard - Carl Junction, MO - *Ed&PubIntYB 82*
Carle, Eric - West Hawley, MA - *LitMarPl 83, 84*
Carleen Gaetana Music - Chicago, IL - *BillIntBG 83-84*

Carleton Corp. - Boston, MA - *WhoWMicrocom 83*
Carleton Messenger - Carleton, MI - *BaconPubCkNews 84; Ed&PubIntYB 82*
Carleton Miscellany - Northfield, MN - *LitMag&SmPr 83-84*
Carleton Place Canadian, The - Carleton Place, ON, Canada - *Ed&PubIntYB 82*
Carleton University (East-West Project) - Ottawa, ON, Canada - *BoPubDir 4, 5*
Carlin Polycomputers Inc., Patrick - Anaheim, CA - *MicrocomMPl 84*
Carline Specifications [of Chase Econometrics/Interactive Data Corp.] - Waltham, MA - *DataDirOnSer 84*
Carline Specifications - Bala Cynwyd, PA - *DirOnDB Spring 84*
Carlinshar & Associates Applied Research - Bolingbrook, IL - *BoPubDir 4, 5*
Carlinsky Features [Div. of Carlinsky & Carlinsky Inc.] - New York, NY - *Ed&PubIntYB 82; LitMarPl 83, 84*
Carlinville Democrat - Carlinville, IL - *BaconPubCkNews 84; Ed&PubIntYB 82; NewsDir 84*
Carlinville Macoupin County Enquirer - Carlinville, IL - *BaconPubCkNews 84; NewsDir 84*
Carlisle Cable TV [of Centel Cable Television Co.] - Carlisle, KY - *BrCabYB 84*
Carlisle Citizen - Carlisle, IA - *BaconPubCkNews 84; Ed&PubIntYB 82*
Carlisle County News - Bardwell, KY - *AyerDirPub 83; BaconPubCkNews 84; Ed&PubIntYB 82*
Carlisle Evening Sentinel [of Howard Publications Inc.] - Carlisle, PA - *NewsDir 84*
Carlisle Graphics - Dubuque, IA - *LitMarPl 84*
Carlisle Independent - Carlisle, AR - *BaconPubCkNews 84; Ed&PubIntYB 82*
Carlisle, L. B. - Burlington, VT - *BoPubDir 4, 5*
Carlisle Mercury - Carlisle, KY - *BaconPubCkNews 84; Ed&PubIntYB 82; NewsDir 84*
Carlisle Publishing Inc. - Hartsdale, NY - *BoPubDir 5*
Carlisle Sentinel - Carlisle, PA - *BaconPubCkNews 84*
Carlmont Enquirer Bulletin - San Carlos, CA - *AyerDirPub 83*
Carlock Chronicle - Carlock, IL - *BaconPubCkNews 84; Ed&PubIntYB 82*
Carlsbad Cablevision [of Daniels & Associates] - Carlsbad, CA - *BrCabYB 84; Tel&CabFB 84C*
Carlsbad Caverns Natural History Association [Aff. of Carlsbad Caverns & Guadalupe Mountains National Parks] - Carlsbad, NM - *BoPubDir 4, 5*
Carlsbad Current-Argus - Carlsbad, NM - *BaconPubCkNews 84; Ed&PubIntYB 82; NewsDir 84*
Carlsbad Journal [of North Coast Publishers Inc.] - Carlsbad, CA - *Ed&PubIntYB 82; NewsDir 84*
Carlsbad Journal - *See* North Coast Publishers Inc.
Carlsbad Pennysaver - Mission Viejo, CA - *AyerDirPub 83*
Carlsbad Publications - Carlsbad, CA - *LitMarPl 83, 84*
Carlson Advertising Co. - Naperville, IL - *StaDirAdAg 2-84*
Carlson & Associates, George - Seattle, WA - *TelAl 83, 84; Tel&CabFB 84C*
Carlson & Co. Inc. - Indianapolis, IN - *StaDirAdAg 2-84*
Carlson Associates Inc., Walter - New York, NY - *DirPRFirms 83*
Carlson Cable TV Inc. - Bovey, MN - *BrCabYB 84; Tel&CabFB 84C*
Carlson Cable TV Inc. - Coleraine, MN - *BrCabYB 84*
Carlson, Diane - Evanston, IL - *LitMarPl 83, 84*
Carlson Graphic Services [Subs. of Seldner & Seldner] - Lincroft, NJ - *LitMarPl 83, 84*
Carlson, Liebowitz & Olshever Inc. - Los Angeles, CA - *StaDirAdAg 2-84*
Carlson Music Co. - Ft. Lauderdale, FL - *BillIntBG 83-84*
Carlson Newspaper Syndicate, Harriett - Wilmette, IL - *Ed&PubIntYB 82*
Carlson, Rockey & Associates Inc. - *See* Rockey Co. Inc., The
Carlson Stations, Ralph J. - Salt Lake City, UT - *BrCabYB 84*
Carlton & Douglas - Cleveland, OH - *DirPRFirms 83*
Carlton Communications Inc. - Richmond, VA - *DirPRFirms 83*
Carlton Inc., Royce - New York, NY - *LitMarPl 83, 84*
Carlton Music Co., Graham - *See* Pie Music Co., S.
Carlwen Industries - Rockville, MD - *AvMarPl 83*
Carlyle Associates - Santa Monica, CA - *BoPubDir 4, 5*
Carlyle Corp., The David Jamison - Los Angeles, CA - *WhoWMicrocom 83*
Carlyle Marketing Corp. - Chicago, IL - *DirMarMP 83*
Carlyle Music Publishing Corp. - *See* Webman & Co., H. B.
Carlyle Union Banner [of Dempsey Publishing Co.] - Carlyle, IL - *BaconPubCkNews 84; NewsDir 84*
Carma Press - St. Paul, MN - *BoPubDir 4, 5*
Carmag [of CARM Publishing Inc.] - Toronto, ON, Canada - *BaconPubCkMag 84; WritMar 84*
Carmel News Journal - Carmel, IN - *BaconPubCkNews 84; NewsDir 84*
Carmel Pine Cone & Outlook - *See* Brown & Wilson Corp.
Carmel Pine Cone, The - Carmel, CA - *Ed&PubIntYB 82*
Carmel Putnam County Courier - Carmel, NY - *BaconPubCkNews 84*
Carmel, Simon J. - Rockville, MD - *BoPubDir 4, 5*
Carmel Tribune [of Pace Publishing Inc.] - Indianapolis, IN - *Ed&PubIntYB 82; NewsDir 84*
Carmel Tribune - *See* Topic Newspapers Inc.
Carmel Valley Outlook [of Carmel Pine Cone] - Carmel, CA - *NewsDir 84*
Carmel Valley Outlook - Carmel Valley, CA - *Ed&PubIntYB 82*
Carmen Alfalfa County News - Carmen, OK - *BaconPubCkNews 84*
Carmi Times - Carmi, IL - *BaconPubCkNews 84; NewsDir 84*
Carmichael & Co. Advertising & Public Relations Inc. - Chapel Hill, NC - *StaDirAdAg 2-84*
Carmichael Citizen [of Sacramento Suburban Newspapers Inc.] - Fair Oaks, CA - *NewsDir 84*
Carmichael Citizen, The - Carmichael, CA - *Ed&PubIntYB 82*
Carmichael-Lynch Advertising Inc. - Minneapolis, MN - *AdAge 3-28-84; StaDirAdAg 2-84*
Carmony, Charles - New York, NY - *LitMarPl 83, 84*
Carn [of Celtic League] - Dublin, Ireland - *LitMag&SmPr 83-84*
Carnation Press - State College, PA - *BoPubDir 4, 5; LitMag&SmPr 83-84*
Carnduff Gazette-Post-News - Carnduff, SK, Canada - *Ed&PubIntYB 82*
Carnegie Associates Inc. - Dallas, TX - *StaDirAdAg 2-84*
Carnegie Endowment for International Peace - Washington, DC - *BoPubDir 4, 5*
Carnegie Foundation for the Advancement of Teaching - Princeton, NJ - *BoPubDir 5*
Carnegie Herald - Carnegie, OK - *BaconPubCkNews 84; Ed&PubIntYB 82*
Carnegie Institute Museum of Art - Pittsburgh, PA - *BoPubDir 5*
Carnegie Institution of Washington - Washington, DC - *BoPubDir 4, 5*
Carnegie-Mellon Magazine [of Carnegie-Mellon University] - Pittsburgh, PA - *WritMar 84*
Carnegie-Mellon University (Hunt Institute for Botanical Documentation) - Pittsburgh, PA - *BoPubDir 4, 5*
Carnegie Press [Aff. of The American Institute for Professional Education] - Madison, NJ - *LitMarPl 83*
Carnegie Signal-Item [of Knepper Press Corp.] - Carnegie, PA - *BaconPubCkNews 84; NewsDir 84*
Carnegie Telephone Co. Inc. - Carnegie, OK - *TelDir&BG 83-84*
Carnes Publication Services Inc. - Beachwood, OH - *LitMarPl 83, 84*
Carneys Point Cablevision [of Salem County Cable] - Carneys Point, NJ - *Tel&CabFB 84C*
Carnival Press Inc. - Minneapolis, MN - *LitMag&SmPr 83-84*
Carnot Press - Lake Oswego, OR - *BoPubDir 4, 5*
Carnuccio, Victor - New York, NY - *LitMarPl 83, 84*
Caro Tuscola County Advertiser - Caro, MI - *BaconPubCkNews 84; NewsDir 84*
Caroe Marketing Inc. - Rye, NY - *StaDirAdAg 2-84*
Carol City-Opa Locka News [of South Miami Community Newspapers] - Miami, FL - *AyerDirPub 83; NewsDir 84*
Carol City-Opa Locka News - *See* Community Newspapers of Florida Inc.
Carol Group Ltd. - New York, NY - *BoPubDir 4, 5*
Carol Nan Music - *See* Coyote Productions Inc.
Carol Stream Examiner - *See* Examiner Newspapers
Carol Stream Examiner, The - Carol Stream, IL - *Ed&PubIntYB 82*

Carol Stream Press - Carol Stream, IL - *Ed&PubIntYB 82*
Carol Stream Press [of Elmhurst Press Publications] - Elmhurst, IL - *AyerDirPub 83; NewsDir 84*
Carol Stream Press - *See* Press Publications
Carolina Academic Press - Durham, NC - *LitMarPl 84*
Carolina Academic Press - Durham, SC - *LitMarPl 83*
Carolina Art Association [Aff. of Gibbes Art Gallery] - Charleston, SC - *BoPubDir 4, 5*
Carolina Beach Coastal Carolinian - Carolina Beach, NC - *BaconPubCkNews 84*
Carolina Beach Island Gazette - Carolina Beach, NC - *BaconPubCkNews 84*
Carolina Biological Supply - Burlington, NC - *ArtMar 84; AvMarPl 83; LitMarPl 83, 84; WritMar 84*
Carolina Cable TV Inc. [of Tele-Media Corp.] - Newberry, SC - *BrCabYB 84*
Carolina Cablevision Properties Inc. - Cheraw, SC - *BrCabYB 84*
Carolina Cablevision Properties Inc. - Latta, SC - *BrCabYB 84*
Carolina Cablevision Properties Inc. - Marion, SC - *BrCabYB 84*
Carolina Cablevision Properties Inc. - *See* Century Communications Corp.
Carolina Christian Broadcasting Inc. - Greenville, SC - *BrCabYB 84*
Carolina Clipping Service - Raleigh, NC - *ProGuPRSer 4*
Carolina Communications [of American TV & Communications Corp.] - Whiteville, NC - *BrCabYB 84; Tel&CabFB 84C*
Carolina Cooperator - Raleigh, NC - *ArtMar 84; BaconPubCkMag 84*
Carolina Country - Raleigh, NC - *ArtMar 84; BaconPubCkMag 84; MagDir 84*
Carolina Edition [of Baltimore Afro-American Newspapers] - Baltimore, MD - *NewsDir 84*
Carolina Food Dealer [of North Carolina Food Dealers Association Inc.] - Charlotte, NC - *BaconPubCkMag 84; MagDir 84*
Carolina Game & Fish [of Game & Fish Publications Inc.] - Marietta, GA - *BaconPubCkMag 84; WritMar 84*
Carolina Indian Voice, The - Pembroke, NC - *AyerDirPub 83*
Carolina Library Services - Chapel Hill, NC - *EISS 83; FBInfSer 80*
Carolina Lifestyle - Columbia, SC - *MagDir 84*
Carolina Lifestyle [of Cygnet Communications] - Norfolk, VA - *WritMar 84*
Carolina LP Gas News [of Bedford Printing Co.] - Raleigh, NC - *BaconPubCkMag 84; MagDir 84*
Carolina Market Research - Greenville, SC - *IntDirMarRes 83*
Carolina Peacemaker - Greensboro, NC - *AyerDirPub 83*
Carolina Population Center [of University of North Carolina] - Chapel Hill, NC - *CompReadDB 82; DataDirOnSer 84; InfIndMarPl 83*
Carolina Population Center (Microfiche Program) - Chapel Hill, NC - *MicroMarPl 82-83*
Carolina Quarterly [of University of North Carolina] - Chapel Hill, NC - *LitMag&SmPr 83-84; WritMar 84*
Carolina Records - Raleigh, NC - *BillIntBG 83-84*
Carolina Telephone & Telegraph Co. [Aff. of United Telecommunications Inc.] - Tarboro, NC - *TelDir&BG 83-84*
Carolina Times - Durham, NC - *AyerDirPub 83; Ed&PubIntYB 82*
Carolina TV Cable Corp. [of Multimedia Cablevision Inc.] - New Bern, NC - *BrCabYB 84*
Carolina Wren Press, The - Chapel Hill, NC - *LitMag&SmPr 83-84*
Caroline House Publishers Inc. [Subs. of Longman Inc.] - Aurora, IL - *BoPubDir 4 Sup, 5; LitMarPl 83, 84*
Caroline Imports [Div. of Virgin Records] - New York, NY - *BillIntBG 83-84*
Caroline Progress - Bowling Green, VA - *AyerDirPub 83*
Caroline Progress, The - Caroline County, VA - *Ed&PubIntYB 82*
Carolinian, The - Raleigh, NC - *AyerDirPub 83; Ed&PubIntYB 82*
Carollo, A. M. Sr. - *See* Sweetwater Cable Television Co.
Carolrhoda Books Inc. - Minneapolis, MN - *LitMarPl 83, 84; WritMar 84*
Caromar Records - Westwood, NJ - *BillIntBG 83-84*
Caron, Roger - St. Benjamin, PQ, Canada - *BrCabYB 84*
Carothers, Merlin R. - Escondido, CA - *BoPubDir 5*
Carousel [of North Coast Publishers Inc.] - Encinitas, CA - *NewsDir 84*
Carousel [of The Writers Center] - Bethesda, MD - *LitMag&SmPr 83-84*
Carousel Books - North Hollywood, CA - *BoPubDir 4, 5*
Carousel Films Inc. - New York, NY - *AvMarPl 83; Tel&CabFB 84C*
Carousel Micro Tools Inc. - El Cerrito, CA - *MicrocomMPl 84*
Carousel Press - Albany, CA - *BoPubDir 4, 5*
Carousel Records Inc. - Los Angeles, CA - *BillIntBG 83-84*
Carousel Records Inc. - Seattle, WA - *BillIntBG 83-84*
Carp Newsletter Quarterly [of Pleasant Valley Press] - Eleva, WI - *LitMag&SmPr 83-84*
Carpatho-Rusyn Research Center Inc. - Fairview, NJ - *BoPubDir 4, 5*
Carpenter & Co., L. E. - Wharton, NJ - *DirInfWP 82*
Carpenter/Offutt Paper Inc. [Div. of The Unisource Corp.] - Carson, CA - *LitMarPl 83, 84*
Carpenter Press - Pomeroy, OH - *BoPubDir 4, 5; LitMag&SmPr 83-84*
Carpenter Reserve Printing Co. - Cleveland, OH - *MagIndMarPl 82-83*
Carpenter, The [of United Brotherhood of Carpenters & Joiners of America] - Washington, DC - *BaconPubCkMag 84; MagDir 84; MagIndMarPl 82-83; NewsDir 84*
Carpenter's Book Development - Chicago, IL - *LitMarPl 83, 84*
Carpentersville Countryside [of Barrington Press Inc.] - Barrington, IL - *NewsDir 84*
Carpet & Rug Industry - Ramsey, NJ - *BaconPubCkMag 84; MagDir 84*
Carpet & Rug Institute Inc. - Dalton, GA - *BoPubDir 4 Sup, 5*
Carpinteria Herald - Carpinteria, CA - *BaconPubCkNews 84; Ed&PubIntYB 82*
Carqueville Co., Walter M. - Elk Grove Village, IL - *LitMarPl 84*
Carr Associates, R. W. - Aurora, CO - *Tel&CabFB 84C p.1670*
Carr Communications Inc. - Manhasset, NY - *BaconPubCkNews 84*
Carr, James F. - New York, NY - *BoPubDir 4, 5*
Carr Liggett - Cleveland, OH - *AdAge 3-28-84; BrCabYB 84; StaDirAdAg 2-84*
Carr Telephone Co. - Carr, MI - *TelDir&BG 83-84*
Carrabasset Electronics Inc. - Norridgewock, ME - *BrCabYB 84*
Carrabelle Franklin County News - *See* News Publishing
Carrafiello-Diehl & Associates - Irvington, NY - *AdAge 3-28-84; StaDirAdAg 2-84*
Carranza Advertising Inc. - Los Angeles, CA - *StaDirAdAg 2-84*
Carrell Associates Inc. - Los Angeles, CA - *DirPRFirms 83*
Carriage Hills Cable TV - Carriage Hills, CA - *Tel&CabFB 84C*
Carrier Pigeon [Subs. of Alyson Publications Inc.] - Boston, MA - *LitMarPl 83, 84; MagIndMarPl 82-83*
Carrier Pigeon - Southampton, PA - *AyerDirPub 83*
Carrington Foster County Independent - Carrington, ND - *BaconPubCkNews 84*
Carrizo Springs Javelin - Carrizo Springs, TX - *BaconPubCkNews 84; Ed&PubIntYB 82*
Carrizozo Lincoln County News - Carrizozo, NM - *BaconPubCkNews 84*
Carrol College Press - Waukesha, WI - *LitMarPl 84*
Carroll & Associates Inc. - Little Rock, AR - *StaDirAdAg 2-84*
Carroll & Graf Publishers Inc. - New York, NY - *BoPubDir 5; LitMarPl 84*
Carroll Associates Inc., James P. - South Bend, IN - *DirPRFirms 83*
Carroll Associates Inc., Tom - Albany, NY - *StaDirAdAg 2-84*
Carroll Cable Co. Inc. - Carroll, IA - *BrCabYB 84*
Carroll College Press - Waukesha, WI - *BoPubDir 4, 5*
Carroll County Comet - Carroll County, IN - *Ed&PubIntYB 82*
Carroll County Comet - Delphi, IN - *NewsDir 84*
Carroll County Comet - Flora, IN - *AyerDirPub 83*
Carroll County Evening Sun - Westminster, MD - *BaconPubCkNews 84; NewsDir 84*
Carroll County Independent - Center Ossipee, NH - *AyerDirPub 83; Ed&PubIntYB 82; NewsDir 84*
Carroll County Mirror-Democrat - Mt. Carroll, IL - *AyerDirPub 83*

Carroll County News - Huntingdon, TN - *AyerDirPub 83; Ed&PubIntYB 82*
Carroll County Review - Thomson, IL - *AyerDirPub 83; Ed&PubIntYB 82; NewsDir 84*
Carroll County Times [of Landmark Community Newspapers Inc.] - Westminster, MD - *AyerDirPub 83; BaconPubCkNews 84; Ed&PubIntYB 82; NewsDir 84*
Carroll County Tribune - Green Forest, AR - *AyerDirPub 83; Ed&PubIntYB 82*
Carroll Daily Times Herald - Carroll, IA - *Ed&PubIntYB 82; NewsDir 84*
Carroll Inc., J. J. - Elgin, IL - *StaDirAdAg 2-84*
Carroll, J. Clark - Westfield, NJ - *MagIndMarPl 82-83*
Carroll News - Hillsville, VA - *AyerDirPub 83; Ed&PubIntYB 82*
Carroll Press, The - Cranston, RI - *LitMarPl 83, 84*
Carroll Society of North America, Lewis - Silver Spring, MD - *BoPubDir 4, 5*
Carroll Telephone Co. Inc. [Aff. of Mid-Continent Telephone Corp.] - Delphi, IN - *TelDir&BG 83-84*
Carroll Times Herald - Carroll, IA - *BaconPubCkNews 84*
Carrollton Chronicle [of Taylor Communications Inc.] - Carrollton, TX - *AyerDirPub 83; NewsDir 84*
Carrollton Conservative - *See* Mid-State Publishing Co. Inc.
Carrollton Democrat - Carrollton, MO - *BaconPubCkNews 84; NewsDir 84*
Carrollton Free Press Standard - Carrollton, OH - *BaconPubCkNews 84; NewsDir 84*
Carrollton Gazette Patriot - Carrollton, IL - *BaconPubCkNews 84*
Carrollton News Democrat [of Landmark Community Newspapers Inc.] - Carrollton, KY - *BaconPubCkNews 84; NewsDir 84*
Carrollton Newspapers Inc. - Carrollton, MO - *Ed&PubIntYB 82*
Carrollton Pickens County Herald - Carrollton, AL - *BaconPubCkNews 84*
Carrollton Press Inc. [Subs. of International Thomson Holdings Inc.] - Arlington, VA - *CompReadDB 82; DataDirOnSer 84; InfIndMarPl 83; InfoS 83-84; LitMarPl 83; MagIndMarPl 82-83*
Carrollton Press, The - *See* Research Publications
Carrollton Times-Chronicle - Carrollton, TX - *BaconPubCkNews 84*
Carrot River Observer - Carrot River, SK, Canada - *AyerDirPub 83*
Carruthers, Deutsch, Garrison & Williams Inc. - Washington, DC - *TeleSy&SerDir 2-84*
Cars [of Arden Communications Inc.] - Mt. Kisco, NY - *BaconPubCkMag 84; WritMar 84*
Cars & Parts - Sidney, OH - *BaconPubCkMag 84; MagIndMarPl 82-83*
Cars Magazine - Amawalk, NY - *MagIndMarPl 82-83*
Carsch, R. E. - San Francisco, CA - *FBInfSer 80; InfIndMarPl 83; LitMarPl 83, 84*
Carson & Shepherd Advertising - Houston, TX - *StaDirAdAg 2-84*
Carson Associates, Anne - Washington, DC - *LitMarPl 83, 84; MagIndMarPl 82-83*
Carson Broadcasting Corp. - Las Vegas, NV - *Tel&CabFB 84S*
Carson Cable Television Co. [of Tele-Communications Inc.] - Carson, CA - *BrCabYB 84; Tel&CabFB 84C*
Carson Cablevision [of TeleNational Communications Inc.] - Ft. Carson, CO - *BrCabYB 84; Tel&CabFB 84C*
Carson City Chronicle - Carson City, NV - *BaconPubCkNews 84; NewsDir 84*
Carson City Gazette - Carson City, MI - *BaconPubCkNews 84; Ed&PubIntYB 82*
Carson City Nevada Appeal [of Donrey Media Group] - Carson City, NV - *BaconPubCkNews 84; NewsDir 84*
Carson City Reminder - Carson City, MI - *AyerDirPub 83*
Carson Courier - Carson, CA - *Ed&PubIntYB 82*
Carson Enterprises, H. Glenn - Deming, NM - *BoPubDir 4, 5*
Carson Press - Carson, ND - *Ed&PubIntYB 82*
Carson Press - *See* Grant County News Publishers
Carson, Ray F. - San Diego, CA - *BoPubDir 4, 5*
Carson Star - *See* Breeze Newspapers
Carson Star-Harbor Mail - Carson, CA - *Ed&PubIntYB 82*
Carson Star-Harbor Mail [of Torrance Press-Herald] - Torrance, CA - *NewsDir 84*
Carson TV Cable [of Community Tele-Communications Inc.] - Carson City, NV - *BrCabYB 84; Tel&CabFB 84C*
Carsonville Journal - *See* Buhl Publishing House
Carsonville-Port Sanilac Journal - Carsonville, MI - *Ed&PubIntYB 82*
Carstens Publications Inc. - Newton, NJ - *BoPubDir 4 Sup, 5; MagIndMarPl 82-83*
Carstens Publications Inc. (Hobby Book Div.) - Newton, NJ - *WritMar 84*
Carswell Co. Ltd. - Agincourt, ON, Canada - *CompReadDB 82*
Carswell Co. Ltd. (Carswell Legal Publications) - Agincourt, ON, Canada - *LitMarPl 83, 84*
Carswell, Keith & Sally - West Vancouver, BC, Canada - *BoPubDir 4 Sup, 5*
Carswell Legal Publications - Agincourt, ON, Canada - *MicroMarPl 82-83*
Carta Abierta - Seguin, TX - *LitMag&SmPr 83-84*
Carter Advertising Inc. - Shreveport, LA - *ArtMar 84; StaDirAdAg 2-84*
Carter & Associates Inc., Robert - Cleveland, OH - *DirPRFirms 83*
Carter & Futter Advertising Inc. - South Bend, IN - *StaDirAdAg 2-84*
Carter Associates - North Egremont, MA - *LitMarPl 83*
Carter, Bill - New York, NY - *MagIndMarPl 82-83*
Carter Cable TV [of Rogers Cablesystems Inc.] - Gainesville, TX - *BrCabYB 84; Tel&CabFB 84C*
Carter Callahan Advertising & PR - San Jose, CA - *AdAge 3-28-84*
Carter, Callahan & Associates - San Francisco, CA - *DirPRFirms 83*
Carter, Callahan & Associates - San Jose, CA - *StaDirAdAg 2-84*
Carter Co. - Cambridge, MA - *DirInfWP 82*
Carter Corporate Communications Inc., David E. - Ashland, KY - *StaDirAdAg 2-84*
Carter County Telephone Co. [Aff. of Century Telephone Enterprises Inc.] - Van Buren, MO - *TelDir&BG 83-84*
Carter Craft Doll House - Hyattsville, MD - *BoPubDir 4 Sup, 5*
Carter-Grant Productions Inc. - Encino, CA - *TelAl 84*
Carter Productions Inc., Paul - Portland, ME - *WritMar 84*
Carter Publishing - Monmouth Junction, NJ - *BoPubDir 4, 5*
Carter Rice Storrs & Bement [Div. of Hammermill Paper Co.] - Boston, MA - *LitMarPl 83, 84*
Carter Secretarial Service Inc. - Ocean City, MD - *LitMarPl 83, 84*
Carter, Virginia B. - St. Louis, MO - *BoPubDir 4, 5*
Carteret County News-Times - Morehead City, NC - *AyerDirPub 83; Ed&PubIntYB 82*
Carterfone Communications Corp. - Dallas, TX - *DataDirSup 7-83*
Cartersville Cable TV - Adairsville, GA - *BrCabYB 84*
Cartersville Cable TV - Cartersville, GA - *BrCabYB 84; Tel&CabFB 84C*
Cartersville Herald Tribune - Cartersville, GA - *BaconPubCkNews 84*
Cartersville Tribune-News - Cartersville, GA - *BaconPubCkNews 84; NewsDir 84*
Carthage Cable TV Co. [of Marsh Media Inc.] - Carthage, TN - *Tel&CabFB 84C*
Carthage Cablevision Inc. - Carthage, MO - *BrCabYB 84; Tel&CabFB 84C*
Carthage Cablevision Inc. - Carthage, TX - *BrCabYB 84; Tel&CabFB 84C*
Carthage Carthaginian - Carthage, MS - *BaconPubCkNews 84*
Carthage College (Southport Press) - Kenosha, WI - *BoPubDir 4, 5*
Carthage Courier - Carthage, TN - *BaconPubCkNews 84; Ed&PubIntYB 82; NewsDir 84*
Carthage Hancock County Journal-Pilot [of The W. J. McGiffin Newspaper Co.] - Carthage, IL - *BaconPubCkNews 84; NewsDir 84*
Carthage-Hartsville Cable TV [of Marsh Cable Television Co. Inc.] - Carthage, TN - *BrCabYB 84*
Carthage NewChannels [of NewChannels Corp.] - Carthage, NY - *BrCabYB 84; Tel&CabFB 84C*
Carthage News - Carthage, SD - *BaconPubCkNews 84; Ed&PubIntYB 82*
Carthage Panola County Post - Carthage, TX - *BaconPubCkNews 84*
Carthage Panola Watchman - Carthage, TX - *BaconPubCkNews 84; NewsDir 84*

Carthage Press [of Thomson Newspapers Inc.] - Carthage, MO - *AyerDirPub 83; BaconPubCkNews 84; Ed&PubIntYB 82; NewsDir 84*
Carthage Republican Tribune - Carthage, NY - *BaconPubCkNews 84; Ed&PubIntYB 82*
Carthage Tribune - Carthage, NY - *AyerDirPub 83*
Carthaginian - Carthage, MS - *AyerDirPub 83; Ed&PubIntYB 82; NewsDir 84*
Carthay Sound Stage - Los Angeles, CA - *TelAl 83, 84*
Carthay Studios Inc. - Los Angeles, CA - *Tel&CabFB 84C*
Cartoon Records - New Rochelle, NY - *BillIntBG 83-84*
Cartoonists & Writers Syndicate - New York, NY - *Ed&PubIntYB 82; LitMarPl 84*
Cartoonmix - New York, NY - *Ed&PubIntYB 82; LitMarPl 84*
Cartoons - Los Angeles, CA - *ArtMar 84*
Cartoons by Johns - Pebble Beach, CA - *LitMarPl 83, 84; MagIndMarPl 82-83*
Cartwheel Publishing - St. Paul, MN - *BoPubDir 4, 5*
Cartwright, Nellie Parodi - Rancho Palos Verdes, CA - *BoPubDir 4, 5*
Caruana, Claudia - Elmont, NY - *LitMarPl 83, 84*
Caruba, Alan [Subs. of The Caruba Organization] - Maplewood, NJ - *LitMarPl 83, 84; MagIndMarPl 82-83*
Caruba Organization, The - Maplewood, NJ - *DirPRFirms 83; Ed&PubIntYB 82; LitMarPl 83, 84; MagIndMarPl 82-83*
Caruthers Adams Co., The - New York, NY - *MagIndMarPl 82-83*
Caruthers/Easton Twin City Times - Caruthers, CA - *Ed&PubIntYB 82*
Caruthers/Easton Twin City Times - Lemoore, CA - *BaconPubCkNews 84*
Caruthersville Democrat-Argus [of Pemiscot Publishing Co.] - Caruthersville, MO - *NewsDir 84*
Caruthersville Democrat-Argus - *See* Pemiscot Publishing Co.
Caruthersville Pemiscot Journal - *See* Pemiscot Publishing Co.
Carvainis Agency, Maria - New York, NY - *LitMarPl 83, 84*
Carver County Herald [of Southwest Suburban Publishing Inc.] - Chaska, MN - *AyerDirPub 83; Ed&PubIntYB 82; NewsDir 84*
Carver County News - Watertown, MN - *AyerDirPub 83; Ed&PubIntYB 82*
Carver Publishing Inc. - Hampton, VA - *BoPubDir 4 Sup, 5*
Carvon Music Inc. - *See* Croma Music Co. Inc.
Carwin Country International - Cleveland, OH - *BillIntBG 83-84*
Carwin Country Records & Tapes - Cleveland, OH - *BillIntBG 83-84*
Cary & Mr. Wilson Music Inc. - *See* Drake Music Group
Cary Grove Clarion [of Free Press Inc.] - Cary, IL - *AyerDirPub 83; NewsDir 84*
Cary Grove Clarion - *See* Free Press Inc.
Cary-Grove Countryside [of Barrington Press Inc.] - Barrington, IL - *NewsDir 84*
Cary News - Cary, NC - *AyerDirPub 83; BaconPubCkNews 84; Ed&PubIntYB 82; NewsDir 84*
CAS Online [of Chemical Abstracts Service] - Columbus, OH - *CompReadDB 82; DataDirOnSer 84; DBBus 82; EISS 83; MicrocomMPl 84*
CAS Online - *See* CA Search & Registry Nomenclature & Structure Service
CAS Source Index [of Chemical Abstracts Service] - Columbus, OH - *DataDirOnSer 84; DBBus 82*
Casa David - *See* Jac Music Co. Inc.
Casa de Oro - *See* Warner Bros. Music
Casa Editorial [Aff. of Casa Hispana de Bellas Artes] - San Francisco, CA - *BoPubDir 4, 5*
Casa Fragoso Inc. - San Juan, PR - *BillIntBG 83-84*
Casa Grande Cablevision Inc. [of American Cable TV Inc.] - Casa Grande, AZ - *BrCabYB 84; Tel&CabFB 84C*
Casa Grande Dispatch [of Casa Grande Valley Newspapers Inc.] - Casa Grande, AZ - *AyerDirPub 83; BaconPubCkNews 84; Ed&PubIntYB 82; NewsDir 84*
Casa Grande Records/Don-Mar Records/Shawmut Records - Woburn, MA - *BillIntBG 83-84*
Casa Grande Valley Newspapers Inc. - Casa Grande, AZ - *BaconPubCkNews 84*
Casa Manana Musicals Inc. - Ft. Worth, TX - *WritMar 84*
Casale Music Inc., Don - Westbury, NY - *BillIntBG 83-84*
Casares & Asociados SA, Hugo - *See* Grey Advertising Inc.
Casat Telecommunications Inc. - Ashland, MS - *Tel&CabFB 84C*
Casavis, James N. - Brooklyn, NY - *BoPubDir 4, 5*
Cascade Antenna Systems - Lyle, OR - *Tel&CabFB 84C*
Cascade Antenna Systems - The Dalles, OR - *BrCabYB 84*
Cascade Cable Systems - Wishram, OR - *BrCabYB 84*
Cascade Cablevision Inc. - Valley Center, CA - *BrCabYB 84*
Cascade Computerware Co. - Everett, WA - *MicrocomMPl 83*
Cascade Courier - Cascade, MT - *BaconPubCkNews 84; Ed&PubIntYB 82*
Cascade Data Inc. - Grand Rapids, MI - *WhoWMicrocom 83*
Cascade Farm Publishing Co. [Aff. of Tau Theta Enterprises Inc.] - Estacada, OR - *BoPubDir 4, 5*
Cascade Mountain Music - Torrance, CA - *BillIntBG 83-84*
Cascade Mountain Records - Torrance, CA - *BillIntBG 83-84*
Cascade Photographics - Olympia, WA - *BoPubDir 4, 5*
Cascade Pioneer Advertiser - Cascade, IA - *BaconPubCkNews 84; Ed&PubIntYB 82*
Cascade Telephone - Cascade, IA - *TelDir&BG 83-84*
Cascade Utilities Inc. - Estacada, OR - *Tel&CabFB 84C; TelDir&BG 83-84*
Cascades East - Bend, OR - *WritMar 84*
Cascino & Purcell Inc. - Atlanta, GA - *StaDirAdAg 2-84*
Casco Cable Television - Brunswick, ME - *BrCabYB 84; Tel&CabFB 84C*
Casco Cable Television of Bath [of Susquehanna Broadcasting Co.] - Bath, ME - *BrCabYB 84; Tel&CabFB 84C*
Casco Telephone Co. - Casco, WI - *TelDir&BG 83-84*
Casco Televideo [of Casco Telephone Co.] - Casco, WI - *Tel&CabFB 84C*
Case Analysis [of Progresiv Publishr] - Chicago, IL - *LitMag&SmPr 83-84*
Case & Associates Inc. - Dallas, TX - *StaDirAdAg 2-84*
Case & Comment - Rochester, NY - *BaconPubCkMag 84; MagDir 84; MagIndMarPl 82-83*
Case & Co. Inc. - New York, NY - *LitMarPl 83, 84*
Case Associates Advertising Ltd. - Toronto, ON, Canada - *StaDirAdAg 2-84*
Case Currents - Washington, DC - *ArtMar 84*
Case, Elisabeth W. - Seattle, WA - *LitMarPl 83*
Case-Hoyt Color Printers - Rochester, NY - *LitMarPl 83*
Case-Hoyt Corp. - Rochester, NY - *LitMarPl 84; MagIndMarPl 82-83*
Case Paper Co. Inc. - Long Island City, NY - *MagIndMarPl 82-83*
Case Western Reserve University (Bellflower Press) - Cleveland, OH - *BoPubDir 4, 5*
Case Western Reserve University (Bits Press) - Cleveland, OH - *BoPubDir 4, 5*
CaseCo Publications - Spartanburg, SC - *LitMag&SmPr 83-84*
Cases Inc. - Gardena, CA - *AvMarPl 83*
Cases Inc. - Seattle, WA - *AvMarPl 83*
Cases Music Group - *See* Goodman Group, The
Casette Gazette, The [of Handshake Editions] - Paris, France - *LitMag&SmPr 83-84*
Casewit, Curtis W. - Denver, CO - *LitMarPl 83, 84; MagIndMarPl 82-83*
Casey County News, The - Liberty, KY - *Ed&PubIntYB 82*
Casey Daily Reporter - Casey, IL - *BaconPubCkNews 84*
Casey Media Inc. - Boston, MA - *StaDirAdAg 2-84*
Casey Mutual Telephone Co. - Casey, IA - *TelDir&BG 83-84*
Casey Newspapers Inc. - King City, CA - *BaconPubCkNews 84*
Cash Associates, Ron - Pittsburgh, PA - *DirPRFirms 83*
Cash Book-Journal - Jackson, MO - *AyerDirPub 83; Ed&PubIntYB 82*
Cash Box - Hollywood, CA - *BaconPubCkMag 84*
Cash Box - New York, NY - *MagDir 84; NewsBur 6*
Cash Crop Farming - Delhi, ON, Canada - *BaconPubCkMag 84*
Cash Manager - Holliston, MA - *BaconPubCkMag 84; MagIndMarPl 82-83*
Ca$h Newsletter - Brookville, FL - *MagIndMarPl 82-83*
Cash Register Sales Inc. - Minneapolis, MN - *DataDirSup 7-83*
Ca$hco - Brooksville, FL - *DirMarMP 83*
Casheab - San Diego, CA - *MicrocomMPl 84*
Cashflow [of Coordinated Capital Resources Inc.] - Glenview, IL - *BaconPubCkMag 84; MagDir 84; WritMar 84*
Cashiers Chronicle - Cashiers, NC - *BaconPubCkNews 84*
Cashmere Record - Cashmere, WA - *Ed&PubIntYB 82*

Cashmere Record/Consumer News - Cashmere, WA - *AyerDirPub 83; BaconPubCkNews 84*
Cashton Record - Cashton, WI - *BaconPubCkNews 84*
Cashwire [of Payment & Telecommunication Services Corp.] - New York, NY - *TeleSy&SerDir 7-83*
Casino - Bala Cynwyd, PA - *DirOnDB Spring 84*
Casino & Sports [of Gamblers Book Club Press] - Las Vegas, NV - *BaconPubCkMag 84; LitMag&SmPr 83-84; WritMar 84*
Casino Chronicle - Cinnaminson, NJ - *BaconPubCkMag 84*
Casino Gaming Seminars [Aff. of Thomas B. Gallagher & Associates] - Solvang, CA - *BoPubDir 5*
Casio Inc. - Fairfield, NJ - *DataDirSup 7-83*
Casket, The - Antigonish, NS, Canada - *Ed&PubIntYB 82*
Cason Productions, Buzz - Nashville, TN - *BillIntBG 83-84*
Casper Journal - Casper, WY - *BaconPubCkNews 84*
Casper MDS Co. - Salt Lake City, UT - *Tel&CabFB 84C*
Casper Midwest Edgerton News - Casper, WY - *BaconPubCkNews 84*
Casper Star-Tribune [of Howard Publications Inc.] - Casper, WY - *BaconPubCkNews 84; NewsBur 6; NewsDir 84*
Caspian Community TV Corp. - Caspian, MI - *BrCabYB 84; Tel&CabFB 84C*
CASRO - Port Jefferson, NY - *IntDirMarRes 83*
Cass Cable TV - Siler City, NC - *BrCabYB 84*
Cass Cable TV Inc. - Beardstown, IL - *Tel&CabFB 84C*
Cass Cable TV Inc. - Havana, IL - *BrCabYB 84*
Cass Cable TV Inc. - Virginia, IL - *BrCabYB 84 p.D-298; Tel&CabFB 84C p.1670*
Cass Cable TV Inc. - Palmyra, MO - *BrCabYB 84*
Cass Cable TV Inc. - Sanford, NC - *BrCabYB 84; Tel&CabFB 84C*
Cass Cablevision Inc. - Tremonton, UT - *BrCabYB 84; Tel&CabFB 84C*
Cass CATV Inc. [of Cass Community Antenna TV Inc.] - Rushville, IL - *BrCabYB 84*
Cass CATV Inc. [of Cass Community Antenna TV Inc.] - Whitehall, MI - *BrCabYB 84*
Cass City Chronicle - Cass City, MI - *BaconPubCkNews 84; Ed&PubIntYB 82; NewsDir 84*
Cass Community Antenna TV Inc. - Pittsfield, IL - *BrCabYB 84*
Cass Community Antenna TV Inc. - Virginia, IL - *BrCabYB 84*
Cass Community Antenna TV Inc. - Troy, NC - *BrCabYB 84*
Cass County Democrat-Missourian - Harrisonville, MO - *AyerDirPub 83; Ed&PubIntYB 82*
Cass County Reporter - Casselton, ND - *Ed&PubIntYB 82*
Cass County Sun - Linden, TX - *Ed&PubIntYB 82*
Cass Lake Times - Cass Lake, MN - *BaconPubCkNews 84; Ed&PubIntYB 82*
Cass Telephone Co. - Virginia, IL - *TelDir&BG 83-84*
Cassadaga Telephone Corp. - Fredonia, NY - *TelDir&BG 83-84*
Cassandra Records - Berkeley, CA - *BillIntBG 83-84*
Cassell Communications Inc. - Port St. Lucie, FL - *BoPubDir 4, 5; LitMag&SmPr 83-84*
Cassell Photographic Products Inc. - Indianapolis, IN - *AvMarPl 83*
Casselton Cass County Reporter - Casselton, ND - *BaconPubCkNews 84; NewsDir 84*
Casserole Music Inc. - *See* Chappell Music Co.
Cassette Book Co. - Pasadena, CA - *WritMar 84*
Cassette Gazette - Washington, DC - *DirOnDB Spring 84*
Cassette Information Services - Glendale, CA - *BoPubDir 4, 5*
CASSI - Columbus, OH - *DirOnDB Spring 84*
Cassidy Brown Public Relations Inc. - Gloucester, MA - *LitMarPl 83; MagIndMarPl 82-83*
Cassil & Associates Inc., Don R. - *See* Watkins/Cassil Associates
Cassizzi, Vic - Asheville, NC - *BoPubDir 4, 5*
Cassopolis Vigilant - Cassopolis, MI - *BaconPubCkNews 84; Ed&PubIntYB 82*
Cassville Democrat - Cassville, MO - *BaconPubCkNews 84; Ed&PubIntYB 82*
Cassville Republican - Cassville, MO - *AyerDirPub 83; BaconPubCkNews 84; Ed&PubIntYB 82*
Castagne Communications - Bedford Hills, NY - *ArtMar 84; DirPRFirms 83; StaDirAdAg 2-84*
Castalia Music - Milwaukee, WI - *BillIntBG 83-84*
Castalia Publishing Co. - Eugene, OR - *BoPubDir 4, 5*
Castalia Records - Milwaukee, WI - *BillIntBG 83-84*
Castell Corp., Faber - Newark, NJ - *LitMarPl 83*
Castelli Graphics Inc. - New York, NY - *BoPubDir 4, 5*
Castenholz & Sons - Pacific Palisades, CA - *BoPubDir 5*
Casting Engineering & Foundry World - Bridgeport, CT - *BaconPubCkMag 84; MagDir 84; MagIndMarPl 82-83*
Castle Books Inc. [Div. of Book Sales Inc.] - Secaucus, NJ - *LitMarPl 83, 84*
Castle Dale Emery County Progress - *See* Sun Advocate Publishers Inc.
Castle Hill Publishing Ltd. - New York, NY - *BillIntBG 83-84*
Castle Music Inc. - Tulsa, OK - *BillIntBG 83-84*
Castle Music Inc. - *See* Spirit & Soul Publishing Co.
Castle Publications - Palo Alto, CA - *BoPubDir 4, 5*
Castle Publishing Co. Ltd. - Stamford, CT - *BoPubDir 4, 5*
Castle Rock Cowlitz County Advocate - Castle Rock, WA - *BaconPubCkNews 84*
Castle Rock Douglas County News - *See* Douglas County News Publishing
Castleberry Telephone Co. - Castleberry, AL - *TelDir&BG 83-84*
Castleton Banner - Indianapolis, IN - *Ed&PubIntYB 82*
Castleton Banner - *See* Topic Newspapers Inc.
Castlewood Hamlin County Republican - Castlewood, SD - *BaconPubCkNews 84*
Castor Advance, The - Castor, AB, Canada - *Ed&PubIntYB 82*
Castor Spanish International - New York, NY - *AdAge 3-28-84; StaDirAdAg 2-84*
Castro County News - Dimmitt, TX - *AyerDirPub 83; Ed&PubIntYB 82*
Castroville News Bulletin - Castroville, TX - *BaconPubCkNews 84*
Casual Living [of Joseph D. Feldman Columbia Communications Inc.] - New York, NY - *BaconPubCkMag 84; MagDir 84*
Casualrama Records - Charlottesville, VA - *BillIntBG 83-84*
Caswell Messenger - Yanceyville, NC - *AyerDirPub 83; Ed&PubIntYB 82*
Cat Anna Press - Madison Heights, MI - *BoPubDir 4, 5*
Cat Fancy [of Fancy Publications Inc.] - San Clemente, CA - *ArtMar 84; BaconPubCkMag 84; MagDir 84; MagIndMarPl 82-83; WritMar 84*
CAT-MAC Corp. - Creston, WA - *BoPubDir 4, 5*
Cat World - Phoenix, AZ - *MagDir 84*
Catahoula News - Jonesville, LA - *AyerDirPub 83*
Catahoula News Booster - Jonesville, LA - *Ed&PubIntYB 82*
Catalina Cablevision Associates [of Tele-Communications Inc.] - Pima County, AZ - *Tel&CabFB 84C*
Catallactics Corp. - Hinsdale, IL - *DataDirSup 7-83*
Catalog Age - New Canaan, CT - *MagDir 84*
Catalog Card Corp. of America - Burnsville, MN - *EISS 83*
Catalog of American Portraits [of Smithsonian Institution] - Washington, DC - *EISS 83*
Catalog of Federal Domestic Assistance [of U.S. Office of Management & Budget] - Washington, DC - *EISS 83*
Catalog of Stellar Radial Velocities [of Marseille Observatory] - Marseille, France - *EISS 83*
Catalog Online [of National Library of Medicine] - Bethesda, MD - *CompReadDB 82; DataDirOnSer 84*
Catalog Showroom Business [of Gralla Publications] - New York, NY - *BaconPubCkMag 84; MagDir 84; MagIndMarPl 82-83*
Catalog Showroom Merchandiser [of CSM Communications Co. Inc.] - Smithtown, NY - *BaconPubCkMag 84; MagDir 84*
Cataloging Distribution Service [of U.S. Library of Congress] - Washington, DC - *EISS 83*
Catalogo Italiano Riviste su Calcolatore Elettronico [of Editrice Bibliografica] - Milan, Italy - *CompReadDB 82*
Catalogue Music Inc. - New York, NY - *BillIntBG 83-84*
Catalpa Publishing Co. - Oklahoma City, OK - *BillIntBG 83-84*
Catalyst - New York, NY - *BoPubDir 4, 5; DataDirOnSer 84; LitMag&SmPr 83-84*
Catalyst [of McKettner Publishing] - Seattle, WA - *LitMag&SmPr 83-84*
Catalyst - Scarborough, ON, Canada - *BoPubDir 4, 5*
Catalyst Communications Inc. - Hollywood, CA - *Tel&CabFB 84C*
Catalyst for Environment/Energy - New York, NY - *BaconPubCkMag 84*
Catalyst for Environmental Quality - New York, NY - *MagDir 84*
Catalyst Group, The - Gwynedd Valley, PA - *LitMarPl 84*
Catalyst Press - Kentfield, CA - *BoPubDir 5*

Catalyst Resources for Women [of Bibliographic Retrieval Services Inc.] - Lathan, NY - *DataDirOnSer 84*
Catalyst Resources for Women - New York, NY - *DataDirOnSer 84; DirOnDB Spring 84; EISS 5-84 Sup*
Catalyst, The [of Philadelphia Section, American Chemical Society] - Philadelphia, PA - *BaconPubCkMag 84; MagDir 84*
Catalysts Unltd. - New York, NY - *LitMarPl 83, 84*
Cataract Press - Chicago, IL - *BoPubDir 4, 5*
Cataract Weekly - Grand Falls, NB, Canada - *AyerDirPub 83; Ed&PubIntYB 82*
Catasauqua Dispatch - Catasauqua, PA - *BaconPubCkNews 84; Ed&PubIntYB 82*
Catawba Services Inc. - Rock Hill, SC - *BrCabYB 84; Tel&CabFB 84C*
Catawba Valley Broadcasting Co. - Hickory, NC - *BrCabYB 84*
Catawba Valley Communications Inc. [of Harris Cable Corp.] - Hickory, NC - *BrCabYB 84; Tel&CabFB 84C*
Catcher Press - Kent, OH - *LitMag&SmPr 83-84*
Catchline - Bend, OR - *WritMar 84*
Catchup Music - Ft. Worth, TX - *BillIntBG 83-84*
CATCO TV Inc. [of Century Telephone Enterprises Inc.] - Hardy, AR - *BrCabYB 84; Tel&CabFB 84C*
Catechist - Dayton, OH - *MagDir 84; MagIndMarPl 82-83; WritMar 84*
CATEL [Div. of United Scientific Corp.] - Santa Clara, CA - *AvMarPl 83; HomeVid&CabYB 82-83*
Caten, Robert M. - Archbold, OH - *Tel&CabFB 84C p.1670*
Catering Industry Employee [of Hotel & Restaurant Employees & Bartenders International] - Washington, DC - *NewsDir 84*
Catero Records - San Carlos, CA - *BillIntBG 83-84*
Caterpillar World [of Caterpillar Tractor Co.] - Peoria, IL - *WritMar 84*
Cates Consulting Analysts Inc. - New York, NY - *EISS 83*
Catfax: Directory of Mail Order Catalogs - New York, NY - *DirOnDB Spring 84*
Cathedral City Pennysaver - Mission Viejo, CA - *AyerDirPub 83*
Cathedral Films - Westlake Village, CA - *Tel&CabFB 84C; WritMar 84*
Cathedral of Knowledge Inc. - Portland, OR - *BoPubDir 4, 5*
Cathedral Voice, The [of St. Willibrord's Press] - Highlandville, MO - *WritMar 84*
Cathlamet TV Cable [of Wright Cablevision] - Cathlamet, WA - *BrCabYB 84*
Cathlamet Wahkiakum County Eagle - Cathlamet, WA - *BaconPubCkNews 84*
Catholic Banner, The [of Catholic Diocese of Charleston] - Columbia, SC - *NewsDir 84*
Catholic Biblical Association of America - Washington, DC - *BoPubDir 4, 5*
Catholic Biblical Quarterly, The - Washington, DC - *MagIndMarPl 82-83*
Catholic Book Club [Div. of The America Press] - New York, NY - *LitMarPl 83, 84*
Catholic Bulletin, The - St. Paul, MN - *NewsDir 84*
Catholic Cemetery, The [of St. Croix Press Inc.] - Des Plaines, IL - *BaconPubCkMag 84; MagDir 84*
Catholic Digest [of College of St. Thomas] - St. Paul, MN - *BaconPubCkMag 84; DirMarMP 83; LitMarPl 83, 84; MagDir 84; MagIndMarPl 82-83; WritMar 84*
Catholic Digest Book Club - New York, NY - *LitMarPl 83, 84*
Catholic Health Association of the United States, The - St. Louis, MO - *LitMarPl 83, 84*
Catholic Heritage Press, The - Santa Fe, NM - *LitMarPl 83*
Catholic Historical Review - Washington, DC - *MagDir 84*
Catholic Hungarians' Sunday [of Franciscan Fathers] - Youngstown, OH - *NewsDir 84*
Catholic Journalist - Rockville Centre, NY - *BaconPubCkMag 84; MagDir 84*
Catholic Library World - Haverford, PA - *BaconPubCkMag 84; LitMarPl 83, 84; MagDir 84*
Catholic Life - Fraser, MI - *WritMar 84*
Catholic Lists Inc. - Mt. Vernon, NY - *LitMarPl 83, 84; MagIndMarPl 82-83*
Catholic Mind - New York, NY - *MagIndMarPl 82-83*
Catholic Near East Magazine [of Catholic Near East Welfare Association] - New York, NY - *WritMar 84*
Catholic Outlook, The [of Diocese of Duluth] - Duluth, MN - *NewsDir 84*
Catholic Press Association - Rockville Centre, NY - *BoPubDir 4, 5*
Catholic Press Directory - Rockville Center, NY - *MagDir 84*
Catholic Review, The - Baltimore, MD - *NewsDir 84*
Catholic Seminary Foundation of Indianapolis Inc. - Indianapolis, IN - *BoPubDir 4, 5*
Catholic Sentinel [of Oregon Catholic Press] - Portland, OR - *NewsDir 84*
Catholic Standard, The [of Carroll Publishing Co.] - Washington, DC - *NewsDir 84*
Catholic Telecommunications Network of America [Subs. of U.S. Catholic Conference] - New York, NY - *AvMarPl 83*
Catholic Television Network [of Bay Area Catholic Dioceses] - Menlo Park, CA - *CabTVPrDB 83*
Catholic Theological Society of America - Bronx, NY - *BoPubDir 5*
Catholic Times, The [of Catholic Diocese of Columbus] - Columbus, OH - *NewsDir 84*
Catholic Truth Society - London, England - *WritMar 84*
Catholic University of America Press - Washington, DC - *LitMarPl 83, 84; MicroMarPl 82-83; WritMar 84*
Catholic Virginian, The - Richmond, VA - *AyerDirPub 83*
Catholic Voice, The - Omaha, NE - *NewsDir 84*
CATJ - Oklahoma City, OK - *BaconPubCkMag 84*
Catline [of U.S. National Library of Medicine] - Bethesda, MD - *DBBus 82; DirOnDB Spring 84; EISS 83; OnBibDB 3*
Cato Citizen - Red Creek, NY - *NewsDir 84*
Cato Citizen - *See* Wayuga Community Newspapers Inc.
Cato Citizen, The - Cato, NY - *Ed&PubIntYB 82*
Cato Institute - Washington, DC - *BoPubDir 4 Sup, 5*
Cato Johnson Inc.-USA [Subs. of Young & Rubicam Inc.] - New York, NY - *StaDirAdAg 2-84*
Cato Johnson/Y & R Inc. - New York, NY - *AdAge 3-28-84*
Cato Yasumura Behaeghel [Subs. of Young & Rubicam Inc.] - New York, NY - *StaDirAdAg 2-84*
Catoctin Cable Communications Inc. [of Storer Cable Communications] - Leesburg, VA - *Tel&CabFB 84C*
Catoctin Enterprise - Thurmont, MD - *AyerDirPub 83; Ed&PubIntYB 82*
Catonsville Times - Catonsville, MD - *Ed&PubIntYB 82*
Catonsville Times - Columbia, MD - *AyerDirPub 83*
Catonsville Times [of Ellicott City Stromberg Publishing Inc.] - Ellicott City, MD - *NewsDir 84*
Catoosa Cablevision Network Inc. - Ringgold, GA - *Tel&CabFB 84C*
Catoosa County News - Ringgold, GA - *Ed&PubIntYB 82*
Catoosa Port of Catoosa Times-Herald - Catoosa, OK - *BaconPubCkNews 84*
Cato's Newsletter on Annual Reports, Sid - Chicago, IL - *DirOnDB Spring 84*
Catpatch Music - *See* Kenwon Music
Cat's Eye - Nashville, TN - *LitMag&SmPr 83-84*
Cats Magazine - Daytona Beach, FL - *MagDir 84*
Cats Magazine - Port Orange, FL - *BaconPubCkMag 84; MagIndMarPl 82-83*
Cats Magazine - Pittsburgh, PA - *WritMar 84*
Cat's Pajamas Press - Oak Park, IL - *BoPubDir 4, 5; LitMag&SmPr 83-84*
Cat's Pajamas, The - Berkeley, CA - *LitMarPl 83, 84*
Cat's Pride - St. Paul, MN - *MagDir 84*
Catskill Art Supply - Woodstock, NY - *BoPubDir 4, 5*
Catskill Greene County News - Catskill, NY - *BaconPubCkNews 84; NewsDir 84*
Catskill Mail - Catskill, NY - *BaconPubCkNews 84; NewsDir 84*
Catskill Mountain News - Margaretville, NY - *AyerDirPub 83; Ed&PubIntYB 82*
Catskill Mountain Publishing Corp. - Margaretville, NY - *BaconPubCkNews 84*
Catskill Mountain Video Inc. - Grand Gorge, NY - *BrCabYB 84*
Catskill Mountain Video Inc. - Hobart, NY - *BrCabYB 84*
Catskill Mountain Video Inc. - Lexington, NY - *BrCabYB 84*
Catskill Mountain Video Inc. - Stamford, NY - *BrCabYB 84 p.D-298; Tel&CabFB 84C p.1670*
CatSS - Toronto, ON, Canada - *DirOnDB Spring 84*

Cattaraugus County Industrial Development Agency - Little Valley, NY - *BoPubDir 5*
Cattell Press, Jaques [Subs. of R. R. Bowker Co.] - Tempe, AZ - *CompReadDB 82; DataDirOnSer 84; InfIndMarPl 83; LitMarPl 83, 84*
Cattell Press, Jaques [Subs. of R. R. Bowker Co.] - New York, NY - *DataDirOnSer 84*
Cattle Business in Mississippi - Jackson, MS - *BaconPubCkMag 84; MagDir 84*
Cattle Guard - Denver, CO - *BaconPubCkMag 84; MagDir 84*
Cattleman, The - Ft. Worth, TX - *ArtMar 84; BaconPubCkMag 84; MagDir 84; MagIndMarPl 82-83*
Cattlemen - Winnipeg, MB, Canada - *BaconPubCkMag 84*
Catton Press, Cliff - Glen Falls, NY - *BoPubDir 5*
CATV Enterprises Inc. - New York, NY - *BrCabYB 84*
CATV Fund IX-C [of Jones Intercable Inc.] - Jefferson, TX - *Tel&CabFB 84C*
CATV Inc. - Logan, KS - *BrCabYB 84*
CATV Inc. - Phillipsburg, KS - *Tel&CabFB 84C*
CATV Inc. - Oxford, NE - *BrCabYB 84*
CATV Inc. - Dimmitt, TX - *BrCabYB 84; Tel&CabFB 84C p.1670*
CATV Inc. - Hart, TX - *BrCabYB 84*
CATV La Plata Co. [of Simmons Communications Inc.] - La Plata, MD - *Tel&CabFB 84C*
CATV Lebreux Electronique Enr. - Grande Valles, PQ, Canada - *BrCabYB 84*
CATV Leonardtown Inc. [of CATV General Corp.] - Leonardtown, MD - *BrCabYB 84*
CATV of Elizabeth [of TKR Cable Co.] - Elizabeth, NJ - *BrCabYB 84; Tel&CabFB 84C*
CATV of Higginsville Inc. [of Comm Management Inc.] - Higginsville, MO - *BrCabYB 84; Tel&CabFB 84C*
CATV of King City-Greenfield Inc. [of Communications Systems Inc.] - King City, CA - *BrCabYB 84; Tel&CabFB 84C*
CATV of Lake Tahoe [of Communications Systems Inc.] - West Lake Tahoe, CA - *Tel&CabFB 84C*
CATV of Ohio Valley Inc. [of Tele-Communications Inc.] - East Liverpool, OH - *BrCabYB 84*
CATV of Ohio Valley Inc. [of Tele-Communications Inc.] - Irondale, OH - *BrCabYB 84*
CATV of Ohio Valley Inc. [of Tele-Communications Inc.] - Chester, WV - *BrCabYB 84*
CATV of Ohio Valley Inc. [of Tele-Communications Inc.] - New Cumberland, WV - *BrCabYB 84*
CATV of Oklahoma [of Communications Systems Inc.] - Eufaula, OK - *BrCabYB 84*
CATV Service Co. [of Storer Cable Communications] - Hackettstown, NJ - *Tel&CabFB 84C*
CATV Service Co. [of Storer Cable Communications] - Lambertville, NJ - *Tel&CabFB 84C*
CATV Service Co. [of Storer Cable Communications] - Washington Township, NJ - *Tel&CabFB 84C*
CATV Systems Inc. - Henrietta, TX - *BrCabYB 84*
CATV Systems Inc. - Lewisville, TX - *BrCabYB 84 p.D-298*
CATV Systems of Colorado - Crested Butte, CO - *BrCabYB 84*
CATV West [of Heritage Communications Inc.] - South El Monte, CA - *Tel&CabFB 84C*
Cauldron, The [of Cleveland State University] - Cleveland, OH - *NewsDir 84*
Cause - Boulder, CO - *BoPubDir 5; EISS 83*
Causey Printing Co., F. M. - Forrest City, AR - *BaconPubCkNews 84*
Cavalcade Pictures Inc. - Los Angeles, CA - *TelAl 83; Tel&CabFB 84C*
Cavalcade Pictures Inc. & Cavalcade Television Programs - Los Angeles, CA - *TelAl 84*
Cavalcade Productions Inc. - Ukiah, CA - *AvMarPl 83*
Cavalcade Television Programs - Los Angeles, CA - *TelAl 83*
Cavalier [of Dugent Publishing Corp.] - Coral Gables, FL - *ArtMar 84; BaconPubCkMag 84; MagIndMarPl 82-83; WritMar 84*
Cavalier Chronicle - Cavalier, ND - *BaconPubCkNews 84; Ed&PubIntYB 82*
Cavalier Computer - Del Mar, CA - *MicrocomMPl 83*
Cavalier County Republican - Langdon, ND - *AyerDirPub 83*
Cavalier Daily, The - Charlottesville, VA - *NewsDir 84*
Cavalier Magazine - Miami, FL - *MagDir 84*
Cavalieri & Kleier Inc. - New York, NY - *StaDirAdAg 2-84*
Cavanagh Associates - Washington, DC - *VideoDir 82-83*
Cave Books [Aff. of Cave Research Foundation] - St. Louis, MO - *BoPubDir 5*
Cave City Barren County Progress - *See* Cave Country Newspapers Inc.
Cave City TV Cable [of TCA Cable TV Inc.] - Cave City, AR - *Tel&CabFB 84C*
Cave Country Newspapers Inc. - Cave City, KY - *BaconPubCkNews 84*
Cave Creek Carefree Black Mountain News - Cave Creek, AZ - *BaconPubCkNews 84*
Cave Junction Illinois Valley News - Cave Junction, OR - *BaconPubCkNews 84*
Caveat Emptor - Orange, NJ - *MagDir 84; MagIndMarPl 82-83*
Caveco - Honolulu, HI - *AvMarPl 83*
Cavendish Corp., Marshall [Subs. of Marshall Cavendish Ltd.] - Freeport, NY - *DirMarMP 83*
Cavesson Music - *See* Merit Music Corp.
Cavior Organization Inc., The - New York, NY - *DirPRFirms 83*
Cavlier, Nina W. - High Bridge, NJ - *LitMarPl 83, 84*
Cavri Systems Inc. - New Haven, CT - *AvMarPl 83; MicrocomMPl 83, 84; WhoWMicrocom 83*
Cawkell Information & Technology Services Ltd. - Uxbridge, England - *EISS 83; TeleSy&SerDir 2-84*
Cawker City Ledger - Cawker City, KS - *Ed&PubIntYB 82*
Cawthon Scientific Group - Dearborn, MI - *MicrocomMPl 83, 84; MicrocomSwDir 1; WhoWMicrocom 83*
Caxton Printers Ltd., The - Caldwell, ID - *LitMarPl 83, 84; WritMar 84*
Caxton Software Ltd. - London, England - *MicrocomSwDir 1; WhoWMicrocom 83*
Cay-Bel Publishing Co. - Brewer, ME - *BoPubDir 4, 5; LitMarPl 84*
Cayman Music Inc. - *See* Sumac Music Inc.
Caytronics Record Corp. - New York, NY - *BillIntBG 83-84*
Cayuga Chief-Chronicle [of Red Creek Wayuga Community Newspapers] - Red Creek, NY - *NewsDir 84*
Cayuga Chief-Chronicle - Weedsport, NY - *Ed&PubIntYB 82*
Cayuga Herald News - Cayuga, IN - *BaconPubCkNews 84*
Cayuscos Books - Monterey, CA - *BoPubDir 4, 5*
Cazenovia Republican - Cazenovia, NY - *BaconPubCkNews 84; Ed&PubIntYB 82; NewsDir 84*
CB City International - Phoenix, AZ - *BoPubDir 5*
CB Magazine - Norman, OK - *MagDir 84*
CBA - Moncton, NB, Canada - *BrCabYB 84*
CBA-FM - Moncton, NB, Canada - *BrCabYB 84*
CBAF - Moncton, NB, Canada - *BrCabYB 84*
CBAF-FM - Moncton, NB, Canada - *BrCabYB 84*
CBAFT - Moncton, NB, Canada - *Tel&CabFB 84S*
C.B.A.S. - Ontario, OH - *MicrocomMPl 83*
CBBK-FM - Kingston, ON, Canada - *BrCabYB 84*
CBBL-FM - London, ON, Canada - *BrCabYB 84*
CBC Advertising Inc. - Sacramento, CA - *StaDirAdAg 2-84*
CBC Enterprises [Subs. of Canadian Broadcasting Corp.] - Toronto, ON, Canada - *LitMarPl 84*
CBC Enterprises (Consumer Products Div.) - Toronto, ON, Canada - *LitMarPl 83*
CBC-Project Iris - Montreal, PQ, Canada - *VideoDir 82-83*
CBCL-FM - London, ON, Canada - *BrCabYB 84*
CBCS-FM - Sudbury, ON, Canada - *BrCabYB 84*
CBCT - Charlottetown, PE, Canada - *Tel&CabFB 84S*
CBCT-FM - Charlottetown, PE, Canada - *BrCabYB 84*
CBD - St. John, NB, Canada - *BrCabYB 84*
CBD-FM - St. John, NB, Canada - *BrCabYB 84*
CBD Online [of United Communications Group] - Silver Spring, MD - *EISS 5-84 Sup*
CBD Plus - Greenwich, CT - *DirOnDB Spring 84*
CBDQ - Wabush, NF, Canada - *BrCabYB 84*
CBE - Windsor, ON, Canada - *BrCabYB 84*
CBEE-FM - Chatham, ON, Canada - *BrCabYB 84*
CBEF - Windsor, ON, Canada - *BrCabYB 84*
CBEG-FM - Sarnia, ON, Canada - *BrCabYB 84*
CBEMA Comment - Washington, DC - *BaconPubCkMag 84*
CBET - Detroit, MI - *TelAl 84*

CBET - Windsor, ON, Canada - *BrCabYB 84; TelAl 83; Tel&CabFB 84S*
CBF - Montreal, PQ, Canada - *BrCabYB 84; NatRadPubDir Summer 83, Spring 84*
CBF-FM - Drummondville, PQ, Canada - *BrCabYB 84*
CBF-FM - Montreal, PQ, Canada - *BrCabYB 84*
CBFL-FM - Maniwaki, PQ, Canada - *BrCabYB 84*
CBFT - Montreal, PQ, Canada - *Tel&CabFB 84S*
CBG - Gander, NF, Canada - *BrCabYB 84*
CBGA - Matane, PQ, Canada - *BrCabYB 84*
CBGAT - Matane, PQ, Canada - *Tel&CabFB 84S*
CBGN - Ste.-Anne-des-Monts, PQ, Canada - *BrCabYB 84*
CBGY - Bonavista Bay, NF, Canada - *BrCabYB 84*
CBH - Halifax, NS, Canada - *BrCabYB 84*
CBH-FM - Halifax, NS, Canada - *BrCabYB 84*
CBH Geografic International Inc. [Aff. of Headstart BEH] - Montreal, PQ, Canada - *BoPubDir 4, 5*
CBH Publishing Inc. [Aff. of Headstart BEH] - Glencoe, IL - *BoPubDir 5*
CBH Publishing Inc. - Northfield, IL - *BoPubDir 4*
CBHM-FM - Richibucto, NB, Canada - *BrCabYB 84*
CBHT - Halifax, NS, Canada - *Tel&CabFB 84S*
CBI - Sydney, NS, Canada - *BrCabYB 84*
CBI - Toronto, ON, Canada - *DirOnDB Spring 84*
CBI-FM - Sydney, NS, Canada - *BrCabYB 84*
CBI Publishing Co. - New York, NY - *LitMarPl 84*
CBI Publishing Co. Inc. [of International Thomson Organisation Ltd.] - Boston, MA - *LitMarPl 83; WritMar 84*
CBIA News [of CBIA Service Corp.] - Hartford, CT - *BaconPubCkMag 84; MagDir 84*
CBIM-FM - Lles-Madeleine, PQ, Canada - *BrCabYB 84*
CBIT - Sydney, NS, Canada - *Tel&CabFB 84S*
CBJ - Chicoutimi, PQ, Canada - *BrCabYB 84*
CBJ-FM - Chicoutimi, PQ, Canada - *BrCabYB 84*
CBJE-FM - Chicoutimi, PQ, Canada - *BrCabYB 84*
CBK - Regina, SK, Canada - *BrCabYB 84*
CBK-FM - Regina, SK, Canada - *BrCabYB 84*
CBKA-FM - La Ronge, SK, Canada - *BrCabYB 84*
CBKF-FM - Regina, SK, Canada - *BrCabYB 84*
CBKS-FM - Saskatoon, SK, Canada - *BrCabYB 84*
CBKST - Saskatoon, SK, Canada - *Tel&CabFB 84S*
CBKT - Regina, SK, Canada - *Tel&CabFB 84S*
CBL - Toronto, ON, Canada - *BrCabYB 84; NatRadPubDir Summer 83, Spring 84*
CBL-FM - Toronto, ON, Canada - *BrCabYB 84; NatRadPubDir Summer 83, Spring 84*
CBLFT - Toronto, ON, Canada - *Tel&CabFB 84S*
CBLT - Toronto, ON, Canada - *Tel&CabFB 84S*
CBM - Montreal, PQ, Canada - *BrCabYB 84; NatRadPubDir Summer 83, Spring 84*
CBM-FM - Montreal, PQ, Canada - *BrCabYB 84; NatRadPubDir Summer 83, Spring 84*
CBMI-FM - Baie-Comenau, PQ, Canada - *BrCabYB 84*
CBMR-FM - Fermont, PQ, Canada - *BrCabYB 84*
CBMT - Montreal, PQ, Canada - *Tel&CabFB 84S*
CBN - St. John's, NF, Canada - *BrCabYB 84*
CBN Cable Network - Virginia Beach, VA - *CabTVPrDB 83; Tel&CabFB 84C*
CBN Continental Broadcasting Network Inc. - Virginia Beach, VA - *BrCabYB 84; Tel&CabFB 84S*
CBN-FM - St. John's, NF, Canada - *BrCabYB 84*
CBNA - St. Anthony, NF, Canada - *BrCabYB 84*
CBNLT - Labrador City, NF, Canada - *Tel&CabFB 84S*
CBNM - Marystown, NF, Canada - *BrCabYB 84*
CBNT - St. John's, NF, Canada - *Tel&CabFB 84S*
CBO - Ottawa, ON, Canada - *BrCabYB 84*
CBO-FM - Ottawa, ON, Canada - *BrCabYB 84*
CBO Management Report [of MLP Enterprises] - Philadelphia, PA - *LitMag&SmPr 83-84*
CBO Records Inc. - Los Angeles, CA - *BillIntBG 83-84*
CBO Records Inc. - Central City, KY - *BillIntBG 83-84*
CBOF - Ottawa, ON, Canada - *BrCabYB 84*
CBOF-FM - Ottawa, ON, Canada - *BrCabYB 84*
CBOFT - Ottawa, ON, Canada - *Tel&CabFB 84S*
CBON-FM - Sudbury, ON, Canada - *BrCabYB 84*
CBOT - Ottawa, ON, Canada - *Tel&CabFB 84S*
CBQ - Thunder Bay, ON, Canada - *BrCabYB 84*
CBQ-FM - Pickle Lake, ON, Canada - *BrCabYB 84*
CBQL-FM - Savant Lake, ON, Canada - *BrCabYB 84*
CBQN-FM - Osnaburgh, ON, Canada - *BrCabYB 84*
CBQR - Rankin Inlet, NT, Canada - *BrCabYB 84*
CBQS-FM - Sioux Narrows, ON, Canada - *BrCabYB 84*
CBQX-FM - Kenora, ON, Canada - *BrCabYB 84*
CBR - Calgary, AB, Canada - *BrCabYB 84*
CBR-FM - Calgary, AB, Canada - *BrCabYB 84*
CBR Publications - Honolulu, HI - *LitMag&SmPr 83-84*
CBRT - Calgary, AB, Canada - *Tel&CabFB 84S*
CBS/Blackhawk Cable Communications Corp. [of CBS Inc.] - Hurst, TX - *Tel&CabFB 84C p.1670*
CBS/Blackhawk Cable Communications Corp. [of CBS Inc.] - Mansfield, TX - *Tel&CabFB 84C*
CBS/Broadcast Group - New York, NY - *BrCabYB 84; VideoDir 82-83*
CBS Broadcast International [Div. of CBS Inc.] - New York, NY - *AvMarPl 83*
CBS Cable [of CBS Inc.] - New York, NY - *HomeVid&CabYB 82-83; TelAl 83*
CBS College Publishing - New York, NY - *LitMarPl 83, 84*
CBS (Discos) International - New York, NY - *BillIntBG 83-84*
CBS Educational & Professional Publishing [Div. of CBS Inc.] - New York, NY - *LitMarPl 83, 84*
CBS/Fox Video - Farmington Hills, MI - *AvMarPl 83*
CBS/Fox Video - New York, NY - *BillIntBG 83-84*
CBS Inc. - New York, NY - *AdAge 6-28-84; BrCabYB 84; HomeVid&CabYB 82-83; KnowInd 83; LitMarPl 83, 84; TelAl 83, 84; Tel&CabFB 84C, 84S*
CBS Inc. - Hurst, TX - *BrCabYB 84*
CBS International Publishing - New York, NY - *LitMarPl 83, 84*
CBS News - New York, NY - *Tel&CabFB 84C*
CBS News - *See* CBS Inc.
CBS Professional Publishing - Philadelphia, PA - *LitMarPl 83, 84*
CBS Publications [of CBS Inc.] - New York, NY - *MagIndMarPl 82-83*
CBS Records - New York, NY - *BillIntBG 83-84*
CBS Records International [Div. of CBS International] - New York, NY - *BillIntBG 83-84*
CBS School Publishing - New York, NY - *LitMarPl 83, 84*
CBS Software - Greenwich, CT - *MicrocomMPl 84*
CBS Songs - New York, NY - *BillIntBG 83-84*
CBS Television Stations National Sales - New York, NY - *TelAl 83, 84*
CBS Venture One [of CBS Inc.] - New York, NY - *EISS 7-83 Sup; InfoS 83-84; VideoDir 82-83*
CBS Video Enterprises - New York, NY - *Tel&CabFB 84C*
CBSI-FM - Sept-Iles, PQ, Canada - *BrCabYB 84*
CBST - Sept-Iles, PQ, Canada - *Tel&CabFB 84S*
CBT - Grand Falls, NF, Canada - *BrCabYB 84*
CBTE-FM - Crawford Bay, BC, Canada - *BrCabYB 84*
CBU - Vancouver, BC, Canada - *BrCabYB 84*
CBU-FM - Vancouver, BC, Canada - *BrCabYB 84*
CBUF-FM - Vancouver, BC, Canada - *BrCabYB 84*
CBUFT - Vancouver, BC, Canada - *Tel&CabFB 84S*
CBUT - Vancouver, BC, Canada - *Tel&CabFB 84S*
CBV - Quebec City, PQ, Canada - *BrCabYB 84*
CBV-FM - Laforge, PQ, Canada - *BrCabYB 84*
CBV-FM - Quebec City, PQ, Canada - *BrCabYB 84*
CBVE-FM - Quebec City, PQ, Canada - *BrCabYB 84*
CBVT - Quebec City, PQ, Canada - *Tel&CabFB 84S*
CBW - Winnipeg, MB, Canada - *BrCabYB 84*
CBW-FM - Winnipeg, MB, Canada - *BrCabYB 84*
CBWFT - Winnipeg, MB, Canada - *Tel&CabFB 84S*
CBWK-FM - Thompson, MB, Canada - *BrCabYB 84*
CBWT - Winnipeg, MB, Canada - *Tel&CabFB 84S*
CBX - Edmonton, AB, Canada - *BrCabYB 84*
CBX-FM - Edmonton, AB, Canada - *BrCabYB 84*
CBXFT - Edmonton, AB, Canada - *Tel&CabFB 84S*
CBXT - Edmonton, AB, Canada - *Tel&CabFB 84S*
CBY - Corner Brook, NF, Canada - *BrCabYB 84*
CBYT - Corner Brook, NF, Canada - *Tel&CabFB 84S*
CBZ - Fredericton, NB, Canada - *BrCabYB 84*
CBZ-FM - Fredericton, NB, Canada - *BrCabYB 84*
CBZF-FM - Fredericton, NB, Canada - *BrCabYB 84*
CC & S Cable TV - Jonesville, VA - *BrCabYB 84; Tel&CabFB 84C*

CC Management Services - New York, NY - *LitMarPl 83, 84*
C.C. Software - Walnut Creek, CA - *MicrocomMPl 84*
CCFX - Chicago, IL - *DirOnDB Spring 84*
CCH Canadian Ltd. [Aff. of Commerce Clearing House Inc.] - Don Mills, ON, Canada - *BoPubDir 4; LitMarPl 83, 84*
CCH State Tax Review - Chicago, IL - *DirOnDB Spring 84*
CCH State Tax Review [of NewsNet Inc.] - Bryn Mawr, PA - *DataDirOnSer 84*
CCH Tax Day - Chicago, IL - *DirOnDB Spring 84*
CCH Tax Day [of NewsNet Inc.] - Bryn Mawr, PA - *DataDirOnSer 84*
C.C.I. Cablevision [of Comark Cable Fund III] - Culver, IN - *Tel&CabFB 84C*
C.C.I. Cablevision [of Comark Cable Fund III] - Hebron, IN - *Tel&CabFB 84C*
C.C.I. Cablevision [of Comark Cable Fund III] - Koontz Lake, IN - *Tel&CabFB 84C*
C.C.I. Cablevision [of Comack Cable Fund III] - Pierceville, IN - *Tel&CabFB 84C*
CCM-Corporate Communications & Marketing Inc. - Tampa, FL - *DirPRFirms 83*
C.C.S. - London, England - *MicrocomSwDir 1*
CCS - Barcelona, Spain - *InfIndMarPl 83*
CCS Computer Business Systems Inc. - Chico, CA - *MicrocomMPl 83*
CCS Inc. - Las Vegas, NV - *MicrocomMPl 83*
C.C.T.E. - Winnipeg, MB, Canada - *BoPubDir 4, 5*
CCX - Conway, AR - *MagIndMarPl 82-83*
CD Market Research - Pompton Plains, NJ - *IntDirMarRes 83*
CDA Cable Inc. - Coeur d'Alene, ID - *BrCabYB 84; Tel&CabFB 84C p.1670*
CDA Online Services [of Computer Directions Advisors Inc.] - Cedar Grove, MD - *DataDirOnSer 84*
CDCC Inc. - Sandusky, OH - *MicrocomSwDir 1*
CDE - Atlanta, GA - *BoPubDir 4, 5*
CDE Associates - Hooksett, NH - *WhoWMicrocom 83*
CDE Records & Tapes/Toll Free Records & Tapes - Atlanta, GA - *BillIntBG 83-84*
CDEX Corp. - Los Altos, CA - *ADAPSOMemDir 83-84; MicrocomMPl 84*
CDF Public Relations Syndicate [Div. of City Desk Features] - Forest Hills, NY - *MagIndMarPl 82-83*
CDI Communications - Chicago, IL - *BrCabYB 84*
CDI Designs Inc. - Bronx, NY - *HBIndAd&MS 82-83*
CDIS - Santa Clara, CA - *DirOnDB Spring 84*
CDNPA Data Base [of Canadian Daily Newspaper Publishers Association] - Toronto, ON, Canada - *EISS 83*
CDS Computing Inc. - Wood Ridge, NJ - *MagIndMarPl 82-83*
CDS Publishing Co. - Jamaica, NY - *BoPubDir 4, 5*
CDS Review [of Chicago Dental Society] - Chicago, IL - *BaconPubCkMag 84; MagDir 84*
CDT - *See* Laymond Publishing Co. Inc.
CE Publications [Aff. of Crossley Communications Ltd.] - Niagara Falls, ON, Canada - *BoPubDir 4, 5*
CE Software - Des Moines, IA - *MicrocomMPl 83*
CE Software [Subs. of Custom Electronics Inc.] - Chicopee, MA - *MicrocomMPl 83, 84; MicrocomSwDir 1; WhoWMicrocom 83*
CEAVCO Audio Visual Co. Inc. - Denver, CO - *AvMarPl 83*
CEBCO Standard Publishing [Div. of Standard Publishing] - Fairfield, NJ - *LitMarPl 83, 84*
Cecil Democrat - Elkton, MD - *Ed&PubIntYB 82*
Cecil Whig - Elkton, MD - *AyerDirPub 83; Ed&PubIntYB 82*
Cecile [of Questel Inc.] - Washington, DC - *DataDirOnSer 84*
Cecile - Paris, France - *DirOnDB Spring 84*
CECO Publishing Co. - *See* Campbell-Ewald Co.
CeCom Corp. - Southfield, MI - *TeleSy&SerDir 2-84*
Cedar County News - Hartington, NE - *AyerDirPub 83; Ed&PubIntYB 82*
Cedar County Republican - Stockton, MO - *Ed&PubIntYB 82*
Cedar County Republican & Stockton Journal - Stockton, MO - *AyerDirPub 83*
Cedar Creek Pilot [of Community Information Center] - Kemp, TX - *AyerDirPub 83; Ed&PubIntYB 82; NewsDir 84*
Cedar Creek Press - DeKalb, IL - *BoPubDir 4, 5*
Cedar Creek Publishers - Ft. Wayne, IN - *BoPubDir 4, 5*
Cedar Falls Record [of Howard Publications] - Cedar Falls, IA - *NewsDir 84*
Cedar Grove Cablevision [of Phoenix Communications Inc.] - Cedar Grove, WV - *BrCabYB 84; Tel&CabFB 84C*
Cedar Grove TV Cable Corp. - Handley, WV - *BrCabYB 84*
Cedar Grove TV Cable Corp. - Mammoth, WV - *BrCabYB 84*
Cedar Grove Villager - Cedar Grove, WI - *BaconPubCkNews 84*
Cedar Hill Chronicle - Cedar Hill, TX - *BaconPubCkNews 84; Ed&PubIntYB 82*
Cedar Hill Chronicle [of Duncanville Suburban] - Duncanville, TX - *NewsDir 84*
Cedar Hill Journal [of DeSoto Journal Publishing Co.] - De Soto, TX - *NewsDir 84*
Cedar Hill Software - Stafford, VA - *MicrocomMPl 83; WhoWMicrocom 83*
Cedar House Enterprises - El Granada, CA - *BoPubDir 4, 5*
Cedar Lake Journal [of Lowell Pilcher Publishing Co.] - Lowell, IN - *AyerDirPub 83; NewsDir 84*
Cedar Park Hill Country News - Cedar Park, TX - *BaconPubCkNews 84*
Cedar Rapids Gazette - Cedar Rapids, IA - *BaconPubCkNews 84; Ed&PubIntYB 82; LitMarPl 83, 84; NewsDir 84*
Cedar Rapids Press - Cedar Rapids, NE - *AyerDirPub 83; BaconPubCkNews 84; Ed&PubIntYB 82*
Cedar Rapids Television Co. - Cedar Rapids, IA - *BrCabYB 84*
Cedar Rock - New Braunfels, TX - *LitMag&SmPr 83-84; WritMar 84*
Cedar Rock Press - New Braunfels, TX - *BoPubDir 4, 5; LitMag&SmPr 83-84*
Cedar Springs Clipper - Cedar Springs, MI - *Ed&PubIntYB 82; NewsDir 84*
Cedar Vale Messenger - Cedar Vale, KS - *Ed&PubIntYB 82*
Cedar Vale Messenger - *See* Star Publications
Cedar Valley Times - Vinton, IA - *AyerDirPub 83; BaconPubCkNews 84; Ed&PubIntYB 82*
Cedarburg News Graphic Pilot - Cedarburg, WI - *BaconPubCkNews 84*
Cedarshouse Press - Bryan, TX - *BoPubDir 4, 5; LitMag&SmPr 83-84; WritMar 84*
Cedartown Standard - Cedartown, GA - *BaconPubCkNews 84; Ed&PubIntYB 82; NewsDir 84*
Cedarville Weekly Wave, The [of Mackinac Island Town Crier] - Mackinac Island, MI - *NewsDir 84*
CedarVision Inc. [of Hartington Telephone Co.] - Hartington, NE - *Tel&CabFB 84C*
Cedarwood - Woodview, ON, Canada - *BoPubDir 4 Sup, 5*
Cedarwood Press - Bloomington, IN - *BoPubDir 4, 5*
Cedarwood Publishing Co. Inc. - Nashville, TN - *BillIntBG 83-84*
CEDIJ - St. Quentin en Yvelines, France - *DirOnDB Spring 84*
CEE [of The Sutton Publishing Co. Inc.] - White Plains, NY - *BaconPubCkMag 84; MagDir 84; MagIndMarPl 82-83*
CEEFAX [of British Broadcasting Corp.] - London, England - *EISS 83; VideoDir 82-83*
Cegmark International Inc. - New York, NY - *IntDirMarRes 83*
Cegos - *See* Cegmark International Inc.
CEHindex - Menlo Park, CA - *DirOnDB Spring 84*
CEI Forecasts - Claremont, CA - *DirOnDB Spring 84*
Ceilidh - Foster City, CA - *LitMag&SmPr 83-84*
CEL Programs - Liverpool, NY - *MicrocomMPl 83, 84*
Celco - Mahwah, NJ - *DataDirSup 7-83*
Celebrate Health Digest [of Bergan Mercy Inc.] - Omaha, NE - *WritMar 84*
Celebrating Women - New York, NY - *BoPubDir 4 Sup, 5*
Celebration - Baltimore, MD - *LitMag&SmPr 83-84*
Celebration Cablevision [of Athena Communications Corp.] - Shelbyville, TN - *BrCabYB 84; Tel&CabFB 84C*
Celebration Press - *See* Bock Music Co., Fred
Celebration Recording Inc. [Subs. of MZH & F Inc.] - New York, NY - *AvMarPl 83*
Celebration Records - Bloomington, MN - *BillIntBG 83-84*
Celebrities Productions - St. Louis, MO - *AvMarPl 83*
Celebrity Press Inc. - Los Angeles, CA - *LitMag&SmPr 83-84*
Celebrity Service Inc. - New York, NY - *BoPubDir 4, 5*
Celedia Music - *See* MizMo Enterprises
Celenza, Tim - Cincinnati, OH - *LitMarPl 83, 84; MagIndMarPl 82-83*
Celeste Courier - Celeste, TX - *Ed&PubIntYB 82*
Celestial Arts [Subs. of Ten Speed Press] - Berkeley, CA - *LitMarPl 84; WritMar 84*

Celestial Arts - Millbrae, CA - *LitMag&SmPr 83-84; LitMarPl 83*
Celestial Democracy - Berkeley, CA - *BoPubDir 4, 5*
Celestial Gifts - Hyattsville, MD - *BoPubDir 4, 5*
Celestial Harmonies [Div. of Mayflower Music Corp.] - Wilton, CT - *BillIntBG 83-84*
Celestial Harmonies - *See* Mayflower Music Corp.
Celestial Otter Press - Mt. Prospect, IL - *BoPubDir 4, 5*
Celestial Press - Boca Raton, FL - *BoPubDir 4, 5*
Celestial Records Releasing Corp. - Las Vegas, NV - *BillIntBG 83-84*
Celex - Plateau du Kirchberg, Luxembourg - *DirOnDB Spring 84*
Celibate Woman, The - Washington, DC - *LitMag&SmPr 83-84; WritMar 84*
Celina Clay Citizen - Celina, TN - *BaconPubCkNews 84*
Celina Clay Statesman - Celina, TN - *BaconPubCkNews 84*
Celina Record - Celina, TX - *BaconPubCkNews 84; Ed&PubIntYB 82*
Celina Standard - Celina, OH - *BaconPubCkNews 84; NewsDir 84*
Cell - Cambridge, MA - *MagIndMarPl 82-83*
Cellar Book Shop - Detroit, MI - *LitMarPl 83, 84*
Cellar Door Cinema - Osterville, MA - *AvMarPl 83*
Cellarway Press - Pittsfield, MA - *LitMag&SmPr 83-84*
Cellular Radio Communications Association - Washington, DC - *TeleSy&SerDir 2-84*
Cellular Radio News - Washington, DC - *DirOnDB Spring 84*
Cellular Radio News [of NewsNet Inc.] - Bryn Mawr, PA - *DataDirOnSer 84*
Cellular Radio News - Fairfax, VA - *BaconPubCkMag 84*
Celo Press - Burnsville, NC - *BoPubDir 4, 5; LitMag&SmPr 83-84*
Celta Music - *See* Shayne Enterprises, Larry
Celtic League - Dublin, Iran - *LitMag&SmPr 83-84*
CEM Co. - Bay City, MI - *BoPubDir 4, 5*
Cembura, Al - Berkeley, CA - *BoPubDir 4, 5*
Cement Overshoes Music - *See* Kentucky Colonel Music
Cemetery Management - Falls Church, VA - *BaconPubCkMag 84*
Cen Private Cable Inc. - Farmington, CT - *Tel&CabFB 84C*
Cen-Tex Cable Co. Inc. - Haskell, TX - *BrCabYB 84*
Cen-Tex Cable Co. Inc. [of Harmon & Co.] - Munday, TX - *BrCabYB 84*
CenArk Inc. [of Twin Lakes TV Corp.] - Fairfield Bay, AR - *BrCabYB 84; Tel&CabFB 84C*
Cencom - Columbia, SC - *InterCabHB 3*
Cencom [of Harbison Development Corp.] - Harbison, SC - *BrCabYB 84; Tel&CabFB 84C*
Cencom Cable Associates Inc. - Shelbyville, KY - *Tel&CabFB 84C p.1670*
Cencom Inc. - Rushford, MN - *Tel&CabFB 84C p.1670; TelDir&BG 83-84*
Cencom Inc. - *See* Valley Video Systems Inc.
Cencom of Eastern Missouri Inc. - Chesterfield, MO - *Tel&CabFB 84C p.1670*
Cencom of Eastern Missouri Inc. - Warrenton, MO - *Tel&CabFB 84C*
Cencom of Kentucky - Eminence, KY - *BrCabYB 84*
Cencom of Kentucky - Shelbyville, KY - *BrCabYB 84; Tel&CabFB 84C*
Cencom of North Carolina - Madison County, NC - *Tel&CabFB 84C*
Cencom of South Carolina [of Cencom Cable Associates Inc.] - Camden, SC - *Tel&CabFB 84C*
Cencom of South Carolina [of Cencom Cable Associates Inc.] - Clinton, SC - *Tel&CabFB 84C*
Cencom of South Carolina [of Cencom Cable Associates Inc.] - Laurens, SC - *Tel&CabFB 84C*
Cencom of South Carolina [of Cencom Cable Associates Inc.] - Simpsonville, SC - *Tel&CabFB 84C*
Cencom of South Carolina [of Cencom Cable Associates Inc.] - Woodruff, SC - *Tel&CabFB 84C*
Cencom of Wisconsin Inc. (Cumberland Telephone Div.) - Cumberland, WI - *TelDir&BG 83-84*
Cencom of Wisconsin Inc. (Milton Telephone Div.) - Milton, WI - *TelDir&BG 83-84*
Cencom of Wisconsin Inc. (Wausaukee Telephone Div.) - Wausaukee, WI - *TelDir&BG 83-84*
Cenex Inc. - Alexandria, VA - *EISS 83*
Cenla Broadcasting Co. - Alexandria, LA - *BrCabYB 84*
Censac - Los Angeles, CA - *DirOnDB Spring 84*
Census of Agriculture [of U.S. Bureau of the Census] - Washington, DC - *EISS 83*
Census of Construction Industries [of U.S. Bureau of the Census] - Washington, DC - *EISS 7-83 Sup*
Census of Governments [of U.S. Bureau of the Census] - Washington, DC - *EISS 83*
Census of Manufactures [of U.S. Bureau of the Census] - Washington, DC - *EISS 7-83 Sup*
Census of Mineral Industries [of U.S. Bureau of the Census] - Washington, DC - *EISS 7-83 Sup*
Census of Retail Trade [of U.S. Bureau of the Census] - Washington, DC - *EISS 5-84 Sup*
Census of Service Industries [of U.S. Bureau of the Census] - Washington, DC - *EISS 7-83 Sup*
Census of Transportation [of U.S. Bureau of the Census] - Washington, DC - *EISS 83*
Census of Wholesale Trade [of U.S. Bureau of the Census] - Washington, DC - *EISS 5-84 Sup*
Census of Women-Owned Businesses [of U.S. Bureau of the Census] - Washington, DC - *EISS 7-83 Sup*
Census Services [of Iowa State University] - Ames, IA - *EISS 83*
CensusPlus [of Donnelley Marketing Information Services] - Stamford, CT - *DataDirOnSer 84; DirOnDB Spring 84*
Centaur - Charleston, IL - *MicrocomMPl 84; WritMar 84*
Centaur - Gaithersburg, MD - *MagIndMarPl 82-83*
Centaur Productions Inc. - Studio City, CA - *BillIntBG 83-84*
Centaur Publications - Alexandria, VA - *BoPubDir 4, 5*
Centaur Records - Rochester, NY - *BillIntBG 83-84*
Centec - Reston, VA - *AvMarPl 83; DataDirSup 7-83*
Centel Cable TV Co. [Aff. of Centel Communications] - Lakeland, FL - *InterCabHB 3*
Centel Cable TV Co. - Chicago, IL - *CabTVFinDB 83*
Centel Cable TV Co. - Des Plaines, IL - *BrCabYB 84 p.D-298*
Centel Cable TV Co. - Elgin, IL - *Tel&CabFB 84C*
Centel Cable TV Co. - Matteson, IL - *Tel&CabFB 84C*
Centel Cable TV Co. - Hanover, IN - *Tel&CabFB 84C*
Centel Cable TV Co. - Algona, IA - *Tel&CabFB 84C*
Centel Cable TV Co. - Audubon, IA - *Tel&CabFB 84C*
Centel Cable TV Co. - Bloomfield, IA - *Tel&CabFB 84C*
Centel Cable TV Co. - Burlington, IA - *Tel&CabFB 84C*
Centel Cable TV Co. - Cherokee, IA - *Tel&CabFB 84C*
Centel Cable TV Co. - Fairfield, IA - *Tel&CabFB 84C*
Centel Cable TV Co. - Glidden, IA - *Tel&CabFB 84C*
Centel Cable TV Co. - Laurens, IA - *Tel&CabFB 84C*
Centel Cable TV Co. - Carlisle, KY - *Tel&CabFB 84C*
Centel Cable TV Co. - Clay County, KY - *Tel&CabFB 84C*
Centel Cable TV Co. - Georgetown, KY - *Tel&CabFB 84C*
Centel Cable TV Co. - Midway, KY - *Tel&CabFB 84C*
Centel Cable TV Co. - Millersburg, KY - *Tel&CabFB 84C*
Centel Cable TV Co. - Olive Hill, KY - *Tel&CabFB 84C*
Centel Cable TV Co. - Richmond, KY - *Tel&CabFB 84C*
Centel Cable TV Co. - Springfield, KY - *Tel&CabFB 84C*
Centel Cable TV Co. - Wilmore, KY - *Tel&CabFB 84C*
Centel Cable TV Co. - Traverse City, MI - *BrCabYB 84*
Centel Cable TV Co. [of Centel Communications Co.] - Harris County, TX - *Tel&CabFB 84C*
Centel Cable TV Co. - *See* Centel Communications Co.
Centel Cable TV Co. of Florida [of Central Communications Co.] - Hernando County, FL - *BrCabYB 84; Tel&CabFB 84C*
Centel Cable TV Co. of Florida [of Centel Communications Co.] - Isla del Sol, FL - *Tel&CabFB 84C*
Centel Cable TV Co. of Florida [of Centel Communications Co.] - Mulberry, FL - *Tel&CabFB 84C*
Centel Cable TV Co. of Florida [of Centel Communications Co.] - Polk County, FL - *BrCabYB 84; Tel&CabFB 84C*
Centel Cable TV Co. of Florida [of Centel Communications Co.] - Sumter County, FL - *Tel&CabFB 84C*
Centel Cable TV Co. of Florida [of Centel Communications Co.] - Winter Haven, FL - *Tel&CabFB 84C*
Centel Cable TV Co. of Illinois [of Centel Communications Co.] - Addison, IL - *BrCabYB 84; Tel&CabFB 84C*
Centel Cable TV Co. of Illinois - Aurora, IL - *BrCabYB 84*
Centel Cable TV Co. of Illinois [of Centel Communications Co.] - Clinton, IL - *BrCabYB 84*
Centel Cable TV Co. of Illinois - Elgin, IL - *BrCabYB 84*

Centel Cable TV Co. of Illinois [of Centel Communications Co.] - Fairbury, IL - *BrCabYB 84; Tel&CabFB 84C*
Centel Cable TV Co. of Illinois [of Centel Communications Co.] - Farmer City, IL - *BrCabYB 84; Tel&CabFB 84C*
Centel Cable TV Co. of Illinois [of Centel Communications Co.] - Gibson City, IL - *BrCabYB 84; Tel&CabFB 84C*
Centel Cable TV Co. of Illinois [of Centel Communications Co.] - Lake Zurich, IL - *BrCabYB 84; Tel&CabFB 84C*
Centel Cable TV Co. of Illinois [of Centel Communications Co.] - Le Roy, IL - *Tel&CabFB 84C*
Centel Cable TV Co. of Illinois [of Centel Communications Co.] - Monticello, IL - *Tel&CabFB 84C*
Centel Cable TV Co. of Illinois - Plano, IL - *BrCabYB 84*
Centel Cable TV Co. of Illinois [of Centel Communications Co.] - Rantoul, IL - *BrCabYB 84; Tel&CabFB 84C*
Centel Cable TV Co. of Illinois [of Centel Communications Co.] - Sandwich, IL - *Tel&CabFB 84C*
Centel Cable TV Co. of Illinois [of Centel Communications Co.] - Vernon Hills, IL - *Tel&CabFB 84C*
Centel Cable TV Co. of Illinois [of Centel Communications Co.] - Warrenville, IL - *Tel&CabFB 84C*
Centel Cable TV Co. of Illinois - Winfield, IL - *BrCabYB 84*
Centel Cable TV Co. of Kentucky [of Centel Communications Co.] - Berea, KY - *Tel&CabFB 84C*
Centel Cable TV Co. of Kentucky [of Centel Communications Co.] - East Bernstadt, KY - *Tel&CabFB 84C*
Centel Cable TV Co. of Kentucky - Madison County, KY - *BrCabYB 84*
Centel Cable TV Co. of Michigan [of Centel Communications Co.] - Cadillac, MI - *Tel&CabFB 84C*
Centel Cable TV Co. of Michigan [of Centel Communications Co.] - Traverse City, MI - *Tel&CabFB 84C*
Centel Cable TV Co. of Michigan-Glen Lake [of Centel Communications Co.] - Empire, MI - *Tel&CabFB 84C*
Centel Cable TV Co. of Ohio [of Centel Communications Co] - Lima, OH - *BrCabYB 84; Tel&CabFB 84C*
Centel Cable TV Co. of Ohio [of Centel Communications Co.] - London, OH - *BrCabYB 84; Tel&CabFB 84C*
Centel Cable TV Co. of Ohio [of Centel Communications Co.] - Marysville, OH - *BrCabYB 84; Tel&CabFB 84C*
Centel Cable TV Co. of Ohio [of Centel Communications Co.] - Richwood, OH - *Tel&CabFB 84C*
Centel Cable TV Co. of Ohio [of Centel Communications Co.] - Troy, OH - *BrCabYB 84; Tel&CabFB 84C*
Centel Cable TV Co. of Ohio [of Centel Communications Co.] - Yellow Springs, OH - *Tel&CabFB 84C*
Centel Cable TV Co. of Texas - Harris County, TX - *BrCabYB 84*
Centel Cable TV Co. of Texas - Houston, TX - *BrCabYB 84*
Centel Communications Co. - Aurora, IL - *Tel&CabFB 84C*
Centel Communications Co. - Des Plaines, IL - *LitMarPl 84*
Centel Communications Co. - Lansing, IL - *Tel&CabFB 84C*
Centel Communications Co. - Oak Brook, IL - *Tel&CabFB 84C p.1670*
Centel Communications Co. - Western Springs, IL - *Tel&CabFB 84C*
Centel Supply Co. - Lincoln, NE - *DataDirSup 7-83*
Centel Videopath - Chicago, IL - *CabTVPrDB 83; TeleSy&SerDir 2-84*
Centennial College Press - Scarborough, ON, Canada - *BoPubDir 4, 5*
Centennial Communications Corp. [of Tele-Communications Inc.] - Hartford City, IN - *BrCabYB 84; Tel&CabFB 84C*
Centennial Computer Products Inc. - Rockville, MD - *DataDirSup 7-83*
Centennial Photo Service - Grantsburg, WI - *BoPubDir 4, 5*
Centennial Review, The - Lansing, MI - *LitMag&SmPr 83-84*
Centennial Software Inc. - Denver, CO - *MicrocomMPl 84*
Center Broadcasting Co. - Center, TX - *Tel&CabFB 84C p.1671*
Center Cable TV Inc. - Center, ND - *BrCabYB 84*
Center Cable TV Inc. [of Center Broadcasting Co.] - Center, TX - *BrCabYB 84; Tel&CabFB 84C*
Center Champion - Center, TX - *BaconPubCkNews 84; NewsDir 84*
Center East Texas Light [of Shelby Newspapers Inc.] - Center, TX - *BaconPubCkNews 84; NewsDir 84*
Center for a Woman's Own Name - Barrington, IL - *BoPubDir 4, 5*
Center for Advanced Professional Education Inc. - Santa Ana, CA - *TeleSy&SerDir 2-84*
Center for African Studies - New York, NY - *BoPubDir 5*
Center for Agricultural Documentation & Information [of Ministry for Food, Agriculture, & Forestry] - Bonn, West Germany - *EISS 83*
Center for Analysis of Public Issues - Princeton, NJ - *BoPubDir 4, 5*
Center for Applications of Psychological Type Inc. - Gainesville, FL - *BoPubDir 4, 5*
Center for Applied Linguistics [of Office of Communication & Publications] - Washington, DC - *LitMarPl 83, 84*
Center for Applied Research in Education Inc. [Aff. of Prentice-Hall Inc.] - West Nyack, NY - *BoPubDir 4 Sup, 5*
Center for Arts Information [Aff. of Clearinghouse for Arts Information Inc.] - New York, NY - *BoPubDir 4, 5*
Center for Bioethics [of Kennedy Institute of Ethics] - Washington, DC - *CompReadDB 82*
Center for Birth Defects (Information Services) - Boston, MA - *DataDirOnSer 84*
Center for Book Arts, The - New York, NY - *LitMag&SmPr 83-84*
Center for Building Technology [of U.S. National Bureau of Standards] - Washington, DC - *EISS 7-83 Sup*
Center for Business & Economic Research [of University of Alabama] - University, AL - *EISS 83*
Center for Business & Economic Research [of University of Tennessee, Knoxville] - Knoxville, TN - *EISS 83*
Center for Chinese Research Materials [of Association of Research Libraries] - Washington, DC - *MicroMarPl 82-83*
Center for Communications Management Inc. - Ramsey, NJ - *EISS 5-84 Sup*
Center for Computer/Law - Los Angeles, CA - *EISS 83*
Center for Concept Development - New York, NY - *IntDirMarRes 83*
Center for Conflict Resolution - Madison, WI - *BoPubDir 5*
Center for Coordination of Research on Social Indicators [of Social Science Research Council] - Washington, DC - *EISS 7-83 Sup*
Center for Economic & Management Research [of University of Oklahoma] - Norman, OK - *EISS 7-83 Sup*
Center for Entrepreneurial Management Inc., The - New York, NY - *DataDirOnSer 84*
Center for Environmental Assessment Services [of U.S. National Oceanic & Atmospheric Administration] - Washington, DC - *EISS 83*
Center for Environmental Information [Aff. of Acid Rain Information Clearinghouse] - Rochester, NY - *BoPubDir 4, 5*
Center for Health & Healing - Los Angeles, CA - *BoPubDir 4, 5*
Center for Hermeneutical Studies in Hellenistic & Modern Culture - Berkeley, CA - *BoPubDir 4, 5*
Center for Historical Social Research - Cologne, West Germany - *EISS 83*
Center for Human Development & Research - Vancouver, BC, Canada - *BoPubDir 4, 5*
Center for Human Environments [of City University of New York] - New York, NY - *CompReadDB 82*
Center for Humanities Inc., The - Mt. Kisco, NY - *AvMarPl 83*
Center for Information & Numerical Data Analysis & Synthesis [of Purdue University] - West Lafayette, IN - *EISS 83*
Center for Information on America - Washington, CT - *BoPubDir 4, 5*
Center for Information Research [of Drexel University] - Philadelphia, PA - *EISS 83*
Center for Interactive Programs [of University of Wisconsin-Extension] - Madison, WI - *TeleSy&SerDir 7-83, 2-84*
Center for International Business Cycle Research [of Rutgers University] - Newark, NJ - *EISS 7-83 Sup*
Center for International Prospective Studies - Paris, France - *EISS 7-83 Sup*
Center for Investigative Reporting [Aff. of Greenpeace] - San Francisco, CA - *BoPubDir 5*
Center for Land Grant Studies - Santa Fe, NM - *BoPubDir 4, 5*

Center for Learning & Telecommunications [of American Association for Higher Education] - Washington, DC - *EISS 7-83 Sup; TeleSy&SerDir 7-83*
Center for Massachusetts Data [of Massachusetts State Executive Office of Communities & Development] - Boston, MA - *EISS 7-83 Sup*
Center for Media Development Inc. - Great Neck, NY - *BoPubDir 4, 5*
Center for Migration Studies - Staten Island, NY - *LitMarPl 84*
Center for Modern Psychoanalytic Studies - New York, NY - *BoPubDir 4, 5*
Center for National Security Studies [Aff. of American Civil Liberties Union] - Washington, DC - *BoPubDir 4, 5*
Center for Non-Broadcasting Television Inc. - New York, NY - *InterCabHB 3*
Center for Nonprofit Organizations Inc. - New York, NY - *LitMarPl 83; WritMar 84*
Center for Nuclear Information [of National Commission for Nuclear Energy] - Rio de Janeiro, RJ, Brazil - *EISS 83*
Center for Nuclear Structure & Reaction Data [of USSR State Committee on the Utilization of Atomic Energy] - Moscow, USSR - *EISS 83*
Center for Population & Family Health [of International Institute for the Study of Human Reproduction] - New York, NY - *InfIndMarPl 83*
Center for Population & Family Health Library [of Columbia University] - New York, NY - *EISS 83*
Center for Population Research & Census [of Portland State University] - Portland, OR - *EISS 83*
Center for Professional Development - Logan, UT - *BoPubDir 5*
Center for Psychological Information & Documentation [of University of Trier] - Trier, West Germany - *EISS 83*
Center for Public Advocacy Research Inc. - New York, NY - *BoPubDir 5*
Center for Research in Finance [of University of New South Wales] - Kensington, Australia - *EISS 7-83 Sup*
Center for Research in Security Prices [of University of Chicago] - Chicago, IL - *EISS 83*
Center for Research Libraries - Chicago, IL - *EISS 83; MicroMarPl 82-83*
Center for Research on Criminal Justice - Oakland, CA - *BoPubDir 4, 5*
Center for Science in the Public Interest - Washington, DC - *BoPubDir 4, 5; LitMag&SmPr 83-84*
Center for Scientific & Humanistic Information [of National Autonomous University of Mexico] - Mexico City, Mexico - *EISS 83*
Center for Scientific & Technical Information & Documentation [of Netherlands Organization for Applied Scientific Research] - Delft, Netherlands - *EISS 83*
Center for Scientific Information in Medicine & Health [of Medical Academy] - Sofia, Bulgaria - *EISS 83*
Center for Scientific, Technical, & Economic Information - Sofia, Bulgaria - *EISS 7-83 Sup*
Center for Self-Sufficiency - Houston, TX - *BoPubDir 4 Sup, 5; LitMag&SmPr 83-84*
Center for Self-Sufficiency Update - Houston, TX - *LitMag&SmPr 83-84*
Center for Social Science Research & Documentation for the Arab Region [of United Nations Educational, Scientific, & Cultural Organization] - Cairo, Egypt - *EISS 83*
Center for Southern Folklore - Memphis, TN - *AvMarPl 83; BoPubDir 4, 5; LitMag&SmPr 83-84*
Center for Southern Folklore Magazine - Memphis, TN - *LitMag&SmPr 83-84*
Center for Strategy Research Inc. - Cambridge, MA - *IntDirMarRes 83*
Center for Study of Multiple Birth - Chicago, IL - *BoPubDir 4 Sup, 5; LitMag&SmPr 83-84*
Center for Survey Research [of University of Massachusetts, Boston] - Boston, MA - *EISS 83*
Center for Technology & Admininstration [of American University] - Washington, DC - *EISS 83*
Center for Telecommunications Information - Laguna Hills, CA - *TeleSy&SerDir 2-84*
Center for Telecommunications Studies [of George Washington University] - Washington, DC - *TeleSy&SerDir 2-84*
Center for Thanatology Research & Education Inc. - Brooklyn, NY - *LitMarPl 83, 84*
Center for the Art of Living - Evanston, IL - *BoPubDir 4, 5; LitMag&SmPr 83-84*
Center for the Scientific Study of Religion - Chicago, IL - *BoPubDir 4, 5*
Center for the Study of Advertising Support - Paris, France - *EISS 83*
Center for the Study of Elephants - Carson, CA - *BoPubDir 5*
Center for the Study of the Presidency - New York, NY - *BoPubDir 4, 5*
Center for the Study on Information Systems in Government - Marseille, France - *EISS 7-83 Sup*
Center for the Utilization of Federal Technology [of U.S. National Technical Information Service] - Springfield, VA - *EISS 5-84 Sup*
Center for Translation Documentation - Paris, France - *EISS 83*
Center for UFO Studies - Lima, OH - *EISS 83*
Center for Urban Policy Research [of Rutgers University] - New Brunswick, NJ - *LitMarPl 83, 84*
Center for Women's Studies & Services - San Diego, CA - *BoPubDir 4, 5*
Center for Word Processing Inc. - New York, NY - *DirInfWP 82*
Center Group Broadcasting Inc. - Tyler, TX - *BrCabYB 84*
Center Junction Independent Telephone Co. - Center Junction, IA - *TelDir&BG 83-84*
Center Line Manufacturing Inc. - Milford Square, PA - *MicrocomMPl 84*
Center Magazine, The - Santa Barbara, CA - *MagIndMarPl 82-83*
Center Moriches Bay Tide - Center Moriches, NY - *NewsDir 84*
Center of Alcohol Studies [of Rutgers University] - Piscataway, NJ - *InfIndMarPl 83*
Center Ossipee Carroll County Independent & Pioneer - Center Ossipee, NH - *BaconPubCkNews 84*
Center Post-Dispatch - Center, CO - *BaconPubCkNews 84; Ed&PubIntYB 82*
Center Press - Berkeley, CA - *BoPubDir 4, 5*
Center Republican - Center, ND - *AyerDirPub 83; Ed&PubIntYB 82*
Center Republican [of Washburn Borlaug Publishing Co.] - Washburn, ND - *NewsDir 84*
Center TV Inc. - Warwood, WV - *Tel&CabFB 84C*
Center Video Center - Chicago, IL - *AvMarPl 83*
Centerburg Gazette - Centerburg, OH - *Ed&PubIntYB 82*
Centerburg Gazette - *See* Ashbrook Publishing
Centereach Mid Island News - *See* Smithtown News Inc.
Centering: A Magazine of Poetry [of Years Press] - Lansing, MI - *LitMag&SmPr 83-84*
Centerline Co. - Phoenix, AZ - *BoPubDir 5*
Centerpoint Music Co. - *See* Rontom Music Co.
Centerpoint Productions Inc. - Los Angeles, CA - *TelAl 84; WritMar 84*
Centerpont Productions Inc. - New York, NY - *Tel&CabFB 84C*
Centerstage Press Inc. - Phoenix, AZ - *WritMar 84*
Centerville-Bellbrook Times - Centerville/Bellbrook, OH - *Ed&PubIntYB 82*
Centerville-Bellbrook Times - Dayton, OH - *AyerDirPub 83*
Centerville-Bellbrook Times [of Kettering Publishing Corp.] - Kettering, OH - *NewsDir 84*
Centerville-Bellbrook Times - *See* Kettering Publishing Corp.
Centerville Cablevision Inc. [of Cable Communications of Iowa] - Centerville, IA - *BrCabYB 84*
Centerville Crusader - *See* B & R Publishing
Centerville Hickman County Times - Centerville, TN - *BaconPubCkNews 84*
Centerville Iowegian [of News Consolidated Inc.] - Centerville, IA - *NewsDir 84*
Centerville Iowegian & Citizen - Centerville, IA - *BaconPubCkNews 84*
Centerville Journal - Centerville, SD - *BaconPubCkNews 84; Ed&PubIntYB 82*
Centerville Leon County News - Centerville, TX - *BaconPubCkNews 84*
Centerville Telecable - Centerville, GA - *BrCabYB 84; Tel&CabFB 84C*
Centerville Telephone Co. - Centerville, PA - *TelDir&BG 83-84*
Centex Cablevision [of Harmon & Co.] - Rule, TX - *BrCabYB 84*

CenTex Cablevision Corp. [of Harmon & Co. Inc.] - Haskell, TX - *Tel&CabFB 84C*
CenTex Cablevision Corp. [of Harmon & Co. Inc.] - Munday, TX - *Tel&CabFB 84C*
CenTex Cablevision Corp. [of Harmon & Co. Inc.] - Stamford, TX - *BrCabYB 84; Tel&CabFB 84C*
Centigram Corp. - Sunnyvale, CA - *DataDirSup 7-83; WhoWMicrocom 83*
Centrac Inc. - Bergenfield, NJ - *IntDirMarRes 83*
Central Abstracting & Indexing Service [of American Petroleum Institute] - New York, NY - *EISS 83*
Central Advertising Agency [Div. of Radio Shack] - Ft. Worth, TX - *StaDirAdAg 2-84*
Central Advertising Agency Inc. - Lima, OH - *StaDirAdAg 2-84*
Central Advertising Service - Chicago, IL - *StaDirAdAg 2-84*
Central Alberta Ad-Viser - Red Deer, AB, Canada - *Ed&PubIntYB 82*
Central All-Channel Cablevision Inc. [of Horizon Communications Corp.] - Alexandria, IN - *Tel&CabFB 84C*
Central All-Channel Cablevision Inc. [of Horizon Communications Corp.] - Elwood, IN - *Tel&CabFB 84C*
Central Archives for Empirical Social Research [of University of Cologne] - Cologne, West Germany - *EISS 83*
Central Area Times - Seattle, WA - *Ed&PubIntYB 82*
Central Arkansas Telephone Cooperative Inc. - Donaldson, AR - *TelDir&BG 83-84*
Central Asian Research Centre Ltd. - London, England - *MicroMarPl 82-83*
Central Audio Visual Inc. - Ft. Lauderdale, FL - *AvMarPl 83*
Central-Bergen News - Palisades Park, NJ - *NewsDir 84*
Central Bergen Reporter - Hackensack, NJ - *AyerDirPub 83*
Central Broadcasting Group, The - Richmond, IN - *BrCabYB 84*
Central Bucks Cable Associates - Doylestown, PA - *BrCabYB 84*
Central Bucks Cable Associates - Upper Meron, PA - *BrCabYB 84*
Central Bureau of Statistics [of Ministry of Finances & Customs] - Oslo, Norway - *EISS 7-83 Sup*
Central Business Services - Media, PA - *DirInfWP 82*
Central Cable Corp. - Central City, NE - *BrCabYB 84*
Central Cable Services Inc. - Clay Center, NE - *BrCabYB 84*
Central Cable Services Inc. - Osceola, NE - *BrCabYB 84*
Central Cable Services Inc. [of Comm Management Inc.] - Shelby, NE - *BrCabYB 84*
Central Cable Services Inc. [of Comm Management Inc.] - Stromsburg, NE - *BrCabYB 84; Tel&CabFB 84C*
Central Cable Services Inc. - Sutton, NE - *BrCabYB 84*
Central Cable Services Inc. - Wymore, NE - *Tel&CabFB 84C p.1671*
Central Cable Systems Ltd. - Grand Falls, NF, Canada - *BrCabYB 84*
Central Cable Television Ltd. - Amherst, NS, Canada - *BrCabYB 84*
Central Cable TV Inc. - Columbus, MT - *BrCabYB 84*
Central Cable TV Ltd. - Amherst, NS, Canada - *Tel&CabFB 84C*
Central CATV - Central, LA - *BrCabYB 84*
Central City-Greenville Broadcasting Co. - Central City, KY - *BrCabYB 84*
Central City Linn News-Letter - Central City, IA - *BaconPubCkNews 84*
Central City Marketing Inc. - Chicago, IL - *HBIndAd&MS 82-83*
Central City Register-Call - Central City, CO - *BaconPubCkNews 84*
Central City Republican Nonpareil - Central City, NE - *BaconPubCkNews 84; Ed&PubIntYB 82; NewsDir 84*
Central City Times-Argus - Central City, KY - *BaconPubCkNews 84; NewsDir 84*
Central Coast Green Sheet - Santa Maria, CA - *AyerDirPub 83; Ed&PubIntYB 82*
Central Coast Sun-Bulletin - Morro Bay, CA - *Ed&PubIntYB 82*
Central Coast Times - San Luis Obispo, CA - *AyerDirPub 83; Ed&PubIntYB 82*
Central Committee for Conscientious Objectors - Philadelphia, PA - *BoPubDir 4, 5*
Central Computer Services Corp. - Syracuse, NY - *WhoWMicrocom 83*
Central Computing Co. - Decatur, IL - *ADAPSOMemDir 83-84*
Central Conference of American Rabbis (CCAR Press) - New York, NY - *BoPubDir 4, 5*
Central County Courier - Debary, FL - *NewsDir 84*
Central County Trade Lines - Eau Claire, MI - *AyerDirPub 83*
Central Data Corp. - Champaign, IL - *MicrocomMPl 83, 84; MicrocomSwDir 1; WhoWMicrocom 83*
Central Delaware County Town Talk [of Media Town Talk Newspapers] - Media, PA - *NewsDir 84*
Central Educational Network - Chicago, IL - *BrCabYB 84; Tel&CabFB 84C*
Central Electric Railfans' Association - Chicago, IL - *BoPubDir 4, 5*
Central Electronic Network for Data Processing & Analysis - Padova, Italy - *EISS 83*
Central Florida Information Research Service Inc. - Lakeland, FL - *EISS 5-84 Sup*
Central Florida Scene [of Central Scene Publications Inc.] - Orlando, FL - *BaconPubCkMag 84; MagDir 84; WritMar 84*
Central Idaho Star-News - McCall, ID - *AyerDirPub 83; Ed&PubIntYB 82*
Central Illinois Cablevision Inc. [of Combined Cable Corp.] - Minonk, IL - *BrCabYB 84*
Central Illinois Cablevision Inc. [of Combined Cable Corp.] - Roanoke, IL - *Tel&CabFB 84C*
Central Indiana Telephone Co. Inc. [Aff. of Century Telephone Enterprises Inc.] - Battle Ground, IN - *TelDir&BG 83-84*
Central Information & Library [of Shell U.K. Administrative Services] - London, England - *EISS 83*
Central Information Exchange [of Community Service Council of Broward County Inc.] - Ft. Lauderdale, FL - *EISS 83*
Central Information Library & Editorial Section [of Commonwealth Scientific & Industrial Research Organization] - East Melbourne, Australia - *EISS 83*
Central Information Service [of University of London] - London, England - *EISS 7-83 Sup, 5-84 Sup*
Central Institute for Information & Documentation - Berlin, West Germany - *EISS 83*
Central Institute for Scientific & Technical Information [of State Committee for Science & Technical Progress] - Sofia, Bulgaria - *InfIndMarPl 83*
Central Interior Cablevision Ltd. - Prince George, BC, Canada - *BrCabYB 84*
Central Islip, Islip News - *See* Smithtown News Inc.
Central Jersey Leader - Freehold, NJ - *AyerDirPub 83*
Central Kansas Cable Inc. - Axtell, KS - *BrCabYB 84*
Central Kansas Cable Inc. - Centralia, KS - *Tel&CabFB 84C p.1671*
Central Kentucky News-Journal - Campbellsville, KY - *AyerDirPub 83; Ed&PubIntYB 82*
Central Lake Torch - Central Lake, MI - *BaconPubCkNews 84*
Central Library & Documentation Branch [of International Labour Office] - Geneva, Switzerland - *EISS 83*
Central Louisiana Telephone Co. Inc. [Aff. of Century Telephone Enterprises Inc.] - Jena, LA - *TelDir&BG 83-84*
Central Maine Interactive Telecommunications System [of Medical Care Development Inc.] - Augusta, ME - *TeleSy&SerDir 7-83*
Central Maine Morning Sentinel - Waterville, ME - *BaconPubCkNews 84; Ed&PubIntYB 82*
Central Marketing Inc. - New York, NY - *IntDirMarRes 83*
Central Medical Library - Helsinki, Finland - *CompReadDB 82*
Central Michigan Life [of Central Michigan University] - Mt. Pleasant, MI - *NewsDir 84*
Central Michigan University (Clarke Historical Library) - Mt. Pleasant, MI - *BoPubDir 4*
Central Michign University (Clarke Historical Library) - Mt. Pleasant, MI - *BoPubDir 5*
Central Military Sun-Press - Kaneohe, HI - *AyerDirPub 83*
Central Minnesota Television Co. - Alexandria, MN - *BrCabYB 84; Tel&CabFB 84S*
Central Missouri Leader - Camdenton, MO - *Ed&PubIntYB 82*
Central Missouri Leader - Osage Beach, MO - *AyerDirPub 83*
Central National Bank - Cleveland, OH - *DataDirSup 7-83*
Central Nebraska Telephone Co. [Aff. of Unitel of Nebraska] - Blair, NE - *TelDir&BG 83-84*
Central Nevada Newspapers Inc. - Tonopah, NV - *BaconPubCkNews 84*

Central New York Business Review - Syracuse, NY - *BaconPubCkMag 84*
Central New York Genealogical Society Inc. - Syracuse, NY - *BoPubDir 4, 5*
Central News - Los Angeles, CA - *AyerDirPub 83*
Central News - Beaver, PA - *Ed&PubIntYB 82*
Central News Agency Inc. - New York, NY - *Ed&PubIntYB 82*
Central News-Wave Publications - Los Angeles, CA - *BaconPubCkNews 84; Ed&PubIntYB 82*
Central Newspapers - Indianapolis, IN - *AdAge 6-28-84; Ed&PubIntYB 82; KnowInd 83*
Central O Kanagan Capital News - Kelowna, BC, Canada - *AyerDirPub 83*
Central Office of Information - London, England - *Tel&CabFB 84C*
Central Okanagan Capital News - Kelowna, BC, Canada - *Ed&PubIntYB 82*
Central Oklahoma Telephone Co. - Davenport, OK - *Tel&CabFB 84C p.1671; TelDir&BG 83-84*
Central Oregonian - Prineville, OR - *AyerDirPub 83*
Central Park - New York, NY - *LitMag&SmPr 83-84*
Central Patents Index [of Derwent Publications Ltd.] - London, England - *CompReadDB 82*
Central Pennsylvania Garment Worker - Harrisburg, PA - *NewsDir 84*
Central Pennsylvania Labor News - Harrisburg, PA - *NewsDir 84*
Central Personnel Data File [of U.S. Office of Personnel Management] - Washington, DC - *EISS 83*
Central Phoenix Sun - Phoenix, AZ - *AyerDirPub 83*
Central Plains Cable TV Inc. - Gregory, SD - *BrCabYB 84*
Central Point Software - Portland, OR - *DataDirSup 7-83; MicrocomMPl 83, 84; MicrocomSwDir 1*
Central Post - Kendall Park, NJ - *AyerDirPub 83; Ed&PubIntYB 82*
Central Press Features of London - New York, NY - *Ed&PubIntYB 82*
Central Project Administration for Current Agric. Research, Netherlands [of Netherlands Organization for Applied Scientific Research] - The Hague, Netherlands - *EISS 83*
Central Publications Co. Inc. - Indianapolis, IN - *LitMarPl 84*
Central Publishing - Ottawa, ON, Canada - *BoPubDir 4 Sup, 5*
Central Publishing Co. Inc. - Indianapolis, IN - *LitMarPl 83*
Central Railway Chronicle - Buffalo, NY - *MagDir 84*
Central Record - Lancaster, KY - *AyerDirPub 83*
Central Record - Medford, NJ - *AyerDirPub 83; Ed&PubIntYB 82*
Central Report Index [of Dow Chemical Co.] - Midland, MI - *EISS 83*
Central Research Services Inc., The - Tokyo, Japan - *IntDirMarRes 83*
Central School Supply Co. - Jackson, MS - *AvMarPl 83*
Central Scot - Eldridge, IA - *TelDir&BG 83-84*
Central Shopper - Lisbon, OH - *AyerDirPub 83*
Central Square Citizen Outlet - *See* Oswego County Weeklies
Central State Telephone Co. [Aff. of Telephone & Data Systems Inc.] - Vesper, WI - *TelDir&BG 83-84*
Central States Archaeological Societies Inc. - St. Louis, MO - *BoPubDir 4, 5*
Central States Products Co. - St. Louis, MO - *LitMarPl 83, 84*
Central Statistical Office [of Chase Econometrics/Interactive Data Corp.] - Waltham, MA - *DataDirOnSer 84*
Central Statistical Office - London, England - *InfIndMarPl 83*
Central Statistical Office - Budapest, Hungary - *EISS 5-84 Sup*
Central Statistics Bureau [of British Columbia Ministry of Industry & Small Business Development] - Victoria, BC, Canada - *EISS 5-84 Sup*
Central Sun Press - Oahu, HI - *Ed&PubIntYB 82*
Central Technical Library [of University of Ljubljana] - Ljubljana, Yugoslavia - *EISS 83*
Central Telelphone Co. of Texas (Central District) - Killeen, TX - *TelDir&BG 83-84*
Central Telephone & Utilities Corp. - Chicago, IL - *HomeVid&CabYB 82-83*
Central Telephone & Utilities Corp. - Lincoln, NE - *TelDir&BG 83-84*
Central Telephone Co. - Ft. Dodge, IA - *TelDir&BG 83-84*
Central Telephone Co. [Aff. of Century Telephone Enterprises Inc.] - Chesaning, MI - *TelDir&BG 83-84*
Central Telephone Co. (Minneapolis Div.) - Burnsville, MN - *TelDir&BG 83-84*
Central Telephone Co. (North Carolina Div.) - Hickory, NC - *TelDir&BG 83-84*
Central Telephone Co. of Illinois [Aff. of Centel Corp.] - Des Plaines, IL - *TelDir&BG 83-84*
Central Telephone Co. of Missouri [Aff. of Centel Corp.] - Jefferson City, IA - *TelDir&BG 83-84*
Central Telephone Co. of Nevada [Aff. of Centel Corp.] - Las Vegas, NV - *TelDir&BG 83-84*
Central Telephone Co. of Ohio [Aff. of Centel Corp.] - Lorain, OH - *TelDir&BG 83-84*
Central Telephone Co. of Texas - Killeen, TX - *TelDir&BG 83-84*
Central Telephone Co. of Texas (Southern District) - Humble, TX - *TelDir&BG 83-84*
Central Telephone Co. of Virginia [Aff. of Centel Corp.] - Charlottesville, VA - *TelDir&BG 83-84*
Central Telephone-Florida [Aff. of Central Telephone & Utilities Corp.] - Tallahassee, FL - *TelDir&BG 83-84*
Central Telephone Interviewing System - Trevose, PA - *IntDirMarRes 83*
Central Texas Cable TV - Hallettsville, TX - *Tel&CabFB 84C*
Central Texas Cable TV - La Grange, TX - *Tel&CabFB 84C*
Central Texas Cable TV - Schulenburg, TX - *Tel&CabFB 84C*
Central Texas Cable TV - Weimar, TX - *Tel&CabFB 84C*
Central Texas Cablevision Inc. [of Combined Cable Corp.] - Granite Shoals, TX - *Tel&CabFB 84C*
Central Texas Telephone Cooperative Inc. - Goldthwaite, TX - *TelDir&BG 83-84*
Central Utah Telephone Inc. - Fairview, UT - *TelDir&BG 83-84*
Central Valley Cablevision Inc. - Hillsboro, ND - *BrCabYB 84*
Central Valley Cablevision Inc. - Mayville, ND - *BrCabYB 84; Tel&CabFB 84C p.1671*
Central Valley Railroad Publications - Wilton, CA - *BoPubDir 4, 5*
Central Video Inc. - Seattle, WA - *AvMarPl 83*
Central Virginian - Louisa, VA - *AyerDirPub 83; Ed&PubIntYB 82; NewsDir 84*
Central Westchester-North White Plains-Elmsford Pennysaver - Yorktown Heights, NY - *AyerDirPub 83*
Central/Western Massachusetts Automated Resource Sharing - Paxton, MD - *EISS 7-83 Sup*
Central Whittier-Hills Highlander - *See* Highlander Publications Inc.
Centralia Cable Systems [of Tele-Communications Inc.] - Centralia, MO - *Tel&CabFB 84C*
Centralia Evening & Sunday Sentinel - Centralia, IL - *NewsDir 84*
Centralia Fireside Guard - Centralia, MO - *BaconPubCkNews 84; Ed&PubIntYB 82*
Centralia Nemaha County Journal Leader - Centralia, KS - *BaconPubCkNews 84*
Centralia Sentinel - Centralia, IL - *BaconPubCkNews 84; Ed&PubIntYB 82*
Centre - Scarborough, ON, Canada - *BaconPubCkMag 84*
Centre Cherokee County Herald - Centre, AL - *BaconPubCkNews 84; NewsDir 84*
Centre Daily Times [of Nittany Printing & Publishing Co.] - State College, PA - *AyerDirPub 83; Ed&PubIntYB 82; NewsDir 84*
Centre d'Assistance Technique et de Documentation [of Federation Nationale du Batiment] - Paris, France - *CompReadDB 82; InfIndMarPl 83*
Centre de Documentation des Industries Utilisatrices de Produits Agricoles [of Association pour la Promotion Industrie-Agriculture] - Massy, France - *CompReadDB 82; InfIndMarPl 83*
Centre de Documentation Internationale - New York, NY - *ProGuPRSer 4*
Centre de Documentation Sciences Humaines [of Centre National de la Recherche Scientifique] - Paris, France - *CompReadDB 82*
Centre de Donnees Stellaires [of Observatoire de Strasbourg] - Strasbourg, France - *InfIndMarPl 83*
Centre de Preparation Documentaire a la Traduction - Paris, France - *MicroMarPl 82-83*
Centre de Recherche Documentaire - Brussels, Belgium - *InfIndMarPl 83*

Centre de Recherches de Pont-a-Mousson (Service de Documentation Industrielle) - Pont-a-Mousson, France - *CompReadDB 82; InfIndMarPl 83*
Centre Democrat - Bellefonte, PA - *AyerDirPub 83; Ed&PubIntYB 82*
Centre d'Enseignement du Management - Paris, France - *InfIndMarPl 83*
Centre d'Etudes & de Recherches de l'Industrie des Liants Hydrauliques [of Centre Technique Industriel] - Paris, France - *InfIndMarPl 83*
Centre d'Etudes des Matieres Plastiques - Paris, France - *CompReadDB 82*
Centre d'Etudes Prospectives & d'Informations Internationales - Paris, France - *InfIndMarPl 83*
Centre d'Information & de Documentation sur le Bruit - Neuilly-sur-Seine, France - *InfIndMarPl 83*
Centre d'Informations Spectroscopiques - Paris, France - *InfIndMarPl 83*
Centre d'Informatique Appliquee au Developpement & l'Agriculture Tropicale [of Musee Royal de l'Afrique Centrale] - Tervuren, Belgium - *InfIndMarPl 83*
Centre d'Informatique Generale de Liege - Alleur, Belgium - *InfIndMarPl 83*
Centre d'Informatique Juridique - St.-Quentin-en-Yvelines, France - *InfIndMarPl 83*
Centre Enterprise - San Francisco, CA - *BoPubDir 4, 5*
Centre Films Inc. - Hollywood, CA - *AvMarPl 83*
Centre for Agicultural Publishing & Documentation [of Ministry of Agriculture & Fisheries] - Wageningen, Netherlands - *EISS 83*
Centre for Catalogue Research [of University of Bath Library] - Bath, England - *EISS 5-84 Sup*
Centre for East Asian Cultural Studies, The - Tokyo, Japan - *MicroMarPl 82-83*
Centre for Information on Standardization & Metrology [of Polish Committee of Standardization, Resources, & Quality] - Warsaw, Poland - *EISS 7-83 Sup*
Centre for Library & Information Management [of Loughborough University of Technology] - Loughborough, England - *EISS 83*
Centre for Library Science & Methodology [of National Szechenyi Library] - Budapest, Hungary - *EISS 83*
Centre for Research on User Studies [of University of Sheffield Library] - Sheffield, England - *EISS 83*
Centre for Scientific & Technical Information [of Council for Scientific & Industrial Research] - Pretoria, South Africa - *EISS 83; InfIndMarPl 83*
Centre for Scientific & Technical Information & Documentation - *See* Nederlandsche Organisatie voor Toegepast-Natuurwetenschappelijk Onderzoek
Centre Francais du Commerce Exterieur - Paris, France - *InfIndMarPl 83*
Centre International d'Enregistrement des Publications en Serie - Paris, France - *CompReadDB 82*
Centre International des Hautes Etudes Agronomiques Mediterraniennes - Montpellier, France - *InfIndMarPl 83*
Centre National de Documentation Scientifique & Technique - Brussels, Belgium - *InfIndMarPl 83*
Centre National de la Recherche Scientifique [of Banque des Connaissances et des Techniques] - Paris, France - *CompReadDB 82*
Centre National de la Recherche Scientifique (Centre de Documentation Sciences Humaines) - Paris, France - *InfIndMarPl 83*
Centre National de la Recherche Scientifique (Centre de Documentation Scientifique & Technique) - Paris, France - *InfIndMarPl 83*
Centre National de l'Information Chimique - Paris, France - *InfIndMarPl 83*
Centre National d'Etudes des Telecommunications [of Service de Documentation Interministerielle] - Issy-les-Moulineaux, France - *CompReadDB 82; InfIndMarPl 83*
Centre National pour l'Exploitation des Oceans [of Bureau National des Donnes Oceaniques] - Brest, France - *CompReadDB 82*
Centre News - Arborg, MB, Canada - *Ed&PubIntYB 82*
Centre of Information Resource & Technology - Singapore, Singapore - *EISS 5-84 Sup*
Centre on Transnational Corps. (Information Analysis Div.) - New York, NY - *InfIndMarPl 83*
Centre Productions Inc. - Boulder, CO - *AvMarPl 83*
Centre Technique des Industries Mecaniques - Senlis, France - *InfIndMarPl 83*
Centre Technique des Industries Mecaniques [of European Space Agency] - Frascati, Italy - *DataDirOnSer 84*
Centre TV Cable Co. [of Horizon Communications Corp.] - Centre, AL - *Tel&CabFB 84C*
Centre TV Inc. - Warwood, WV - *BrCabYB 84*
Centre Video [of Tele-Communications Inc.] - Castle Shannon, PA - *BrCabYB 84*
Centre Video [of Tele-Communications Inc.] - Dormont, PA - *BrCabYB 84*
Centre Video [of Tele-Communications Inc.] - Kane, PA - *BrCabYB 84; Tel&CabFB 84C*
Centre Video [of Tele-Communications Inc.] - Monessen, PA - *BrCabYB 84; Tel&CabFB 84C*
Centre Video [of Tele-Communications Inc.] - Penn Hills Township, PA - *BrCabYB 84*
Centre Video Corp. [of Community Tele-Communications Inc.] - Mingo Junction, OH - *BrCabYB 84; Tel&CabFB 84C p.1671*
Centre Video Corp. [of Tele-Communications Inc.] - Aliquippa, PA - *BrCabYB 84*
Centre Video Corp. - Ambridge, PA - *Tel&CabFB 84C*
Centre Video Corp. [of Tele-Communications Inc.] - Carnegie, PA - *BrCabYB 84; Tel&CabFB 84C*
Centre Video Corp. [of Tele-Communications Inc.] - Clarion, PA - *BrCabYB 84; Tel&CabFB 84C*
Centre Video Corp. [of Tele-Communications Inc.] - McDonald, PA - *BrCabYB 84*
Centre Video Corp. [of Tele-Communications Inc.] - McKees Rocks, PA - *BrCabYB 84; Tel&CabFB 84C*
Centre Video Corp. [of Tele-Communications Inc.] - McKeesport, PA - *BrCabYB 84; Tel&CabFB 84C*
Centre Video Corp. [of Tele-Communications Inc.] - State College, PA - *BrCabYB 84; Tel&CabFB 84C*
Centre Video Corp. [of Tele-Communications Inc.] - Towanda, PA - *BrCabYB 84; Tel&CabFB 84C*
Centre Video Corp. [of Tele-Communications Inc.] - West View, PA - *BrCabYB 84*
Centre Video Corp. - *See* Tele-Communications Inc.
Centre Video Corp. of Ohio Inc. - Mingo Junction, OH - *Tel&CabFB 84C*
Centreville Press [of Central Alabama Publishing Co. Inc.] - Centreville, AL - *BaconPubCkNews 84; Ed&PubIntYB 82; NewsDir 84*
Centreville Queen Anne's Record-Observer - Centreville, MD - *NewsDir 84*
Centreville Record-Observer - Centreville, MD - *BaconPubCkNews 84; Ed&PubIntYB 82*
Centrex Shopper - Copperas Cove, TX - *AyerDirPub 83*
Centro de Comunicacion [of Misioneros Oblatos de Maria Immaculada] - San Antonio, TX - *BoPubDir 4, 5*
Centro de Documentacao Cientifica e Tecnica [of Instituto Nacional de Investigacao Cientifica] - Lisbon, Portugal - *InfIndMarPl 83*
Centro de Documentacion y Informatica Biomedica - Valencia, Spain - *InfIndMarPl 83*
Centro di Riferimento Italiano Diane - Rome, Italy - *InfIndMarPl 83*
Centro Elettronico di Documentazione Giuridica [of Corte Suprema di Cassazione] - Rome, Italy - *InfIndMarPl 83*
Centron Films [Subs. of Coronet Films] - Lawrence, KS - *AvMarPl 83; ProGuPRSer 4*
Centronics Data Computer Corp. - Hudson, NH - *Datamation 6-83; DirInfWP 82; InfIndMarPl 83; MicrocomMPl 83; Top100Al 83; WhoWMicrocom 83*
Centrum voor Landbouwpublikaties & Landbouwdocumentatie - Wageningen, Netherlands - *InfIndMarPl 83*
Centry Virginia Corp. - Bold Camp, VA - *BrCabYB 84*
Centurion Computer Corp. [of EDS Corp.] - Richardson, TX - *WhoWMicrocom 83*
Centurion Industries Inc. - Menlo Park, CA - *AvMarPl 83*
Centurion Press Ltd. - Edmonton, AB, Canada - *BoPubDir 4, 5*
Century Analysis Inc. - Pacheco, CA - *DataDirSup 7-83; MicrocomSwDir 1*

Century Broadcasting Corp. - Chicago, IL - *BrCabYB 84*
Century Cable Management Corp. [of Century Communications Corp.] - Old Lyme, CT - *BrCabYB 84; Tel&CabFB 84C*
Century Cable of Northern California [of Century Communications Corp.] - Albany, CA - *BrCabYB 84*
Century Cable of Northern California [of Century Communications Corp.] - Benicia, CA - *BrCabYB 84; Tel&CabFB 84C*
Century Cable of Northern California [of Century Communications Corp.] - San Pablo, CA - *BrCabYB 84; Tel&CabFB 84C*
Century Cable of Northern California [of Century Communications Corp.] - Ventura, CA - *BrCabYB 84; Tel&CabFB 84C*
Century Cable of Southern California [of Century Communications Corp.] - Brea, CA - *BrCabYB 84; Tel&CabFB 84C*
Century Cable of Southern California [of Century Communications Corp.] - Redondo Beach, CA - *BrCabYB 84; Tel&CabFB 84C*
Century Cable TV - Cullman, AL - *Tel&CabFB 84C*
Century Cable TV - Ft. Payne, AL - *BrCabYB 84*
Century Cable TV - Indianola, MS - *Tel&CabFB 84C*
Century Cable TV [of Century Virginia Corp.] - Clintwood, VA - *BrCabYB 84*
Century Cable TV - Wise County, VA - *BrCabYB 84*
Century Cablenet Inc. [of Century Telephone Enterprises Inc.] - Au Gres, MI - *Tel&CabFB 84C*
Century Cablenet Inc. [of Century Telephone Enterprises Inc.] - Hudsonville, MI - *Tel&CabFB 84C*
Century Carolina Corp. [of Century Communications Corp.] - Cheraw, SC - *Tel&CabFB 84C*
Century Carolina Corp. [of Century Communications Corp.] - Dillon, SC - *Tel&CabFB 84C*
Century Carolina Corp. [of Century Communications Corp.] - Marion, SC - *Tel&CabFB 84C*
Century Carolina Corp. [of Century Communications Corp.] - Mullins, SC - *Tel&CabFB 84C*
Century City Post [of Los Angeles Post Newspaper Group] - Los Angeles, CA - *NewsDir 84*
Century City Post - *See* Post Newspaper Group
Century Color Lab Inc. - East Hartford, CT - *AvMarPl 83*
Century Communications - New Canaan, CT - *BrCabYB 84 p.D-299; CabTVFinDB 83; LitMarPl 84; Tel&CabFB 84C p.1671*
Century Communications Inc. - Skokie, IL - *BoPubDir 4, 5*
Century Computer Corp. - Dallas, TX - *DataDirSup 7-83; WhoWMicrocom 83*
Century Data Systems Inc. [Subs. of Xerox Corp.] - Anaheim, CA - *WhoWMicrocom 83*
Century Enterprises Inc. - Kannapolis, NC - *StaDirAdAg 2-84*
Century Features Inc. - Pittsburgh, PA - *Ed&PubIntYB 82*
Century House Publishing [of American Life Foundation] - Elmira, NY - *LitMarPl 84*
Century House Publishing [of American Life Foundation] - Watkins Glen, NY - *LitMarPl 83*
Century Huntington Co. Inc. [of Century Communications Corp.] - Huntington, WV - *BrCabYB 84; Tel&CabFB 84C*
Century Huntington Inc. [of Century Communications Corp.] - Barboursville, WV - *BrCabYB 84*
Century Media Corp. - New York, NY - *StaDirAdAg 2-84*
Century Micro - Sacramento, CA - *MicrocomMPl 84*
Century Mountain Corp. - Dryden, VA - *BrCabYB 84*
Century Mountain Corp. - Norton, VA - *Tel&CabFB 84C p.1671*
Century Newspapers Inc. - Winchester, MA - *BaconPubCkNews 84*
Century Norwich Corp. [of Century Communications Corp.] - Norwich, CT - *BrCabYB 84; Tel&CabFB 84C*
Century One Press [Aff. of Graphic Services Inc.] - Colorado Springs, CO - *BoPubDir 4, 5*
Century Precision Cine/Optics [Div. of Century Precision Industries] - North Hollywood, CA - *AvMarPl 83*
Century Press - Edmonton, AB, Canada - *BoPubDir 4, 5*
Century Printing Co. Inc. - New York, NY - *LitMarPl 83, 84*
Century Productions Inc. - Sayreville, NJ - *BillIntBG 83-84*
Century Publications Co. - Evanston, IL - *DirMarMP 83*
Century Records Inc. - Pittsburgh, PA - *BillIntBG 83-84*
Century Software Systems [Subs. of Century International Ltd.] - Los Angeles, CA - *MicrocomMPl 83, 84; MicrocomSwDir 1; WhoWMicrocom 83*
Century Telephone Co. Inc. [Aff. of Century Telephone Enterprises Inc.] - Greensbury, LA - *TelDir&BG 83-84*
Century Telephone Enterprises Inc. - Monroe, LA - *Tel&CabFB 84C p.1671; TelDir&BG 83-84*
Century Teleview of Louisiana Inc. - Plain Dealing, LA - *Tel&CabFB 84C*
Century Teleview of Tennessee Inc. [of Century Telephone Enterprises Inc.] - Lafayette, TN - *Tel&CabFB 84C*
Century Teleview of Tennessee Inc. [of Century Telephone Enterprises Inc.] - Red Boiling Springs, TN - *BrCabYB 84; Tel&CabFB 84C*
Century Teleview of Tennessee Inc. [of Century Telephone Enterprises Inc.] - Westmoreland, TN - *Tel&CabFB 84C*
Century Teleview of Tennessee Inc. - Woodbury, TN - *BrCabYB 84*
Century III Electronics International Inc. - Anaheim, CA - *HomeVid&CabYB 82-83*
Century Three Press - Lincoln, NE - *BoPubDir 4, 5*
Century Virginia Corp. [of Century Communications Corp.] - Big Stone Gap, VA - *Tel&CabFB 84C*
Century Virginia Corp. [of Century Communications Corp.] - Norton, VA - *BrCabYB 84; Tel&CabFB 84C*
Ceolfrith Press - Sunderland, England - *LitMag&SmPr 83-84*
CEPA Gallery - Buffalo, NY - *BoPubDir 4, 5*
Ceppos Consultant - New York, NY - *LitMarPl 83, 84*
Ceramic Abstracts [of American Ceramic Society Inc.] - Columbus, OH - *MagDir 84*
Ceramic Arts & Crafts - Livonia, MI - *BaconPubCkMag 84; MagDir 84; MagIndMarPl 82-83*
Ceramic Engineering & Science Proceedings [of American Ceramic Society Inc.] - Columbus, OH - *MagDir 84*
Ceramic Hobbyist - Willowdale, ON, Canada - *BaconPubCkMag 84*
Ceramic Industry [of Cahners Publishing Co.] - Des Plaines, IL - *BaconPubCkMag 84; MagDir 84; WritMar 84*
Ceramic Scope - Los Angeles, CA - *MagDir 84; WritMar 84*
Ceramics - Fresno, CA - *BaconPubCkMag 84*
Ceramics Monthly - Columbus, OH - *BaconPubCkMag 84; MagDir 84; MagIndMarPl 82-83*
Cerberus Book Co. - Ft. Bragg, NC - *BoPubDir 5*
Cerberus Book Co. - Ft. Buchanan, PR - *BoPubDir 4*
Cerberus Group Inc., The - Frenchtown, NJ - *ADAPSOMemDir 83-84; LitMarPl 83, 84*
CERBO Informatique Inc. - Westmount, PQ, Canada - *VideoDir 82-83*
Cereal Chemistry [of American Association of Cereal Chemists] - St. Paul, MN - *BaconPubCkMag 84; MagDir 84*
Cereal Foods World [of American Association of Cereal Chemists] - St. Paul, MN - *BaconPubCkMag 84; MagDir 84*
Cereal Women's Institute - Cereal, AB, Canada - *BoPubDir 4 Sup, 5*
Ceres Courier [of Morris Newspaper Corp.] - Ceres, CA - *BaconPubCkNews 84; Ed&PubIntYB 82; NewsDir 84*
Ceres Press - Woodstock, NY - *BoPubDir 4 Sup, 5; LitMag&SmPr 83-84*
Ceres Software Inc. - Portland, OR - *MicrocomMPl 84*
Cermetek Microelectronics - Sunnyvale, CA - *DataDirSup 7-83; MicrocomMPl 84*
Cerritos/Artesia Community Advocate [of Hearst Corp.] - Artesia, CA - *NewsDir 84*
Cerritos/Artesia Community Advocate - *See* Hearst Community Newspapers
Cerro Gordo News - Cerro Gordo, IL - *BaconPubCkNews 84; Ed&PubIntYB 82*
Certified Surveys Inc. - New York, NY - *IntDirMarRes 83*
Cerulean Press [Subs. of Kent Publications Inc.] - Northridge, CA - *LitMag&SmPr 83-84*
Cervera International Corp. - Hollywood, CA - *StaDirAdAg 2-84*
CESARS - Lansing, MI - *DirOnDB Spring 84*
CESM-TV - Thompson, MB, Canada - *BrCabYB 84*
CESP Presse - Paris, France - *DirOnDB Spring 84*
CETA Learning Systems - Bolton, ON, Canada - *BoPubDir 5*
CETA Learning Systems - Ft. Erie, ON, Canada - *BoPubDir 4*
Cetacean Music - *See* FYDAQ Music

Cetec Gauss [Div. of Cetec Corp.] - Sun Valley, CA - *AvMarPl 83*
Cetec Vega [Div. of Cetec Corp.] - El Monte, CA - *AvMarPl 83*
CETIM - Senilas, France - *DirOnDB Spring 84*
Cetra Music Corp. - Chicago, IL - *BillIntBG 83-84*
Cetta - *See* Jacobson, Jeffrey E.
CFAB - Windsor, NS, Canada - *BrCabYB 84*
CFAC - Calgary, AB, Canada - *BrCabYB 84*
CFAC-TV - Calgary, AB, Canada - *Tel&CabFB 84S*
CFAC-TV - Lethbridge, AB, Canada - *Tel&CabFB 84S*
CFAK - Atikokan, ON, Canada - *BrCabYB 84*
CFAM - Altona, MB, Canada - *BrCabYB 84*
CFAM - Richmond Hill, ON, Canada - *NatRadPubDir Summer 83 p.273, Spring 84 p.275*
CFAN - Newcastle, NB, Canada - *BrCabYB 84*
CFAR - Flin-Flon, MB, Canada - *BrCabYB 84*
CFAX - Victoria, BC, Canada - *BrCabYB 84*
CFB Penhold CATV - Mynarski Park, AB, Canada - *BrCabYB 84*
CFBC - St. John, NB, Canada - *BrCabYB 84*
CFBK - Huntsville, ON, Canada - *BrCabYB 84*
CFBQ - Parry Sound, ON, Canada - *BrCabYB 84*
CFBR - Sudbury, ON, Canada - *BrCabYB 84*
CFBV - Smithers, BC, Canada - *BrCabYB 84*
CFCA-FM - Kitchener, ON, Canada - *BrCabYB 84*
CFCB - Corner Brook, NF, Canada - *BrCabYB 84*
CFCF - Montreal, PQ, Canada - *BrCabYB 84; NatRadPubDir Summer 83, Spring 84*
CFCF-TV - Montreal, PQ, Canada - *Tel&CabFB 84S*
CFCH - North Bay, ON, Canada - *BrCabYB 84*
CFCL - Timmins, ON, Canada - *BrCabYB 84*
CFCL-TV - Timmins, ON, Canada - *Tel&CabFB 84S*
CFCM-TV - Quebec City, PQ, Canada - *Tel&CabFB 84S*
CFCN - Calgary, AB, Canada - *BrCabYB 84*
CFCN-TV [Div. of CFCN Communications Ltd.] - Calgary, AB, Canada - *Tel&CabFB 84C, 84S*
CFCO - Chatham, ON, Canada - *BrCabYB 84*
CFCP - Courtenay, BC, Canada - *BrCabYB 84*
CFCQ-FM - Trois Rivieres, PQ, Canada - *BrCabYB 84*
CFCR-FM - Red Deer, AB, Canada - *BrCabYB 84*
CFCT - Tuktoyaktuk, NT, Canada - *BrCabYB 84*
CFCV-FM - St. Andrews, NF, Canada - *BrCabYB 84*
CFCW - Camrose, AB, Canada - *BrCabYB 84*
CFCY - Charlottetown, PE, Canada - *BrCabYB 84*
CFDA - Victoriaville, PQ, Canada - *BrCabYB 84*
CFDR - Dartmouth, NS, Canada - *BrCabYB 84*
CFED - Chapais, PQ, Canada - *BrCabYB 84*
CFEK - Fernie, BC, Canada - *BrCabYB 84*
CFEM-TV - Rouyn, PQ, Canada - *Tel&CabFB 84S*
CFER-TV - Rimouski, PQ, Canada - *Tel&CabFB 84S*
CFFB - Frobisher Bay, NT, Canada - *BrCabYB 84*
CFFM-FM - Chase, BC, Canada - *BrCabYB 84*
CFFM-FM - Kamloops, BC, Canada - *BrCabYB 84*
CFFM-FM - Pritchard, BC, Canada - *BrCabYB 84*
CFGB - Happy Valley, NF, Canada - *BrCabYB 84*
CFGL-FM - Laval, PQ, Canada - *BrCabYB 84*
CFGM - Richmond Hill, ON, Canada - *BrCabYB 84*
CFGN - Port-aux-Basques, NF, Canada - *BrCabYB 84*
CFGO - Ottawa, ON, Canada - *BrCabYB 84*
CFGP - Grande Prairie, AB, Canada - *BrCabYB 84*
CFGR - Gravelbourg, SK, Canada - *BrCabYB 84*
CFGT - Alma, PQ, Canada - *BrCabYB 84*
CFI - New York, NY - *MicrocomMPl 83*
CFI Computer Solutions - New York, NY - *MicrocomMPl 84*
CFIL-FM - Gillam, MB, Canada - *BrCabYB 84*
CFIQ - Harbour Grace, NF, Canada - *BrCabYB 84*
CFJC - Kamloops, BC, Canada - *BrCabYB 84*
CFJC-TV - Kamloops, BC, Canada - *Tel&CabFB 84S*
CFJR - Brockville, ON, Canada - *BrCabYB 84*
CFKC - Creston, BC, Canada - *BrCabYB 84*
CFLA-TV - Goose Bay, NF, Canada - *Tel&CabFB 84S*
CFLC-FM - Churchill Falls, NF, Canada - *BrCabYB 84*
CFLD - Burns Lake, BC, Canada - *BrCabYB 84*
CFLG-FM - Cornwall, ON, Canada - *BrCabYB 84*
CFLH - Hearst, ON, Canada - *BrCabYB 84*
CFLK - Kapuskasing, ON, Canada - *BrCabYB 84*
CFLM - La Tuque, PQ, Canada - *BrCabYB 84*
CFLN - Goose Bay, NF, Canada - *BrCabYB 84*
CFLP - Rimouski, PQ, Canada - *BrCabYB 84*
CFLS - Levis, PQ, Canada - *BrCabYB 84*
CFLV - Valleyfield, PQ, Canada - *BrCabYB 84*
CFLW - Wabush, NF, Canada - *BrCabYB 84*
CFLY-FM - Kingston, ON, Canada - *BrCabYB 84*
CFMB - Montreal, PQ, Canada - *BrCabYB 84*
CFMB - Westmount, PQ, Canada - *NatRadPubDir Summer 83 p.271, Spring 84 p.273*
CFMC-FM - Saskatoon, SK, Canada - *BrCabYB 84*
CFMF-FM - Fermont, PQ, Canada - *BrCabYB 84*
CFMI-FM - New Westminster, BC, Canada - *BrCabYB 84*
CFMK-FM - Kingston, ON, Canada - *BrCabYB 84*
CFML - Cornwall, ON, Canada - *BrCabYB 84*
CFMO-FM - Ottawa, ON, Canada - *BrCabYB 84*
CFMP-FM - Peterborough, ON, Canada - *BrCabYB 84*
CFMQ-FM - Regina, SK, Canada - *BrCabYB 84*
CFMR - Ft. Simpson, NT, Canada - *BrCabYB 84*
CFMS-FM - Victoria, BC, Canada - *BrCabYB 84*
CFMT-TV - Toronto, ON, Canada - *Tel&CabFB 84S*
CFMU-FM - Hamilton, ON, Canada - *BrCabYB 84*
CFMX-FM - Cobourg, ON, Canada - *BrCabYB 84*
CFNB - Fredericton, NB, Canada - *BrCabYB 84*
CFNI - Port Hardy, BC, Canada - *BrCabYB 84*
CFNL - Ft. Nelson, BC, Canada - *BrCabYB 84*
CFNN-FM - St. Anthony, NF, Canada - *BrCabYB 84*
CFNO-FM - Marathon, ON, Canada - *BrCabYB 84*
CFNS - Saskatoon, SK, Canada - *BrCabYB 84*
CFNW - Port-au-Choix, NF, Canada - *BrCabYB 84*
CFNY-FM - Brampton, ON, Canada - *BrCabYB 84; NatRadPubDir Summer 83 p.272, Spring 84 p.274*
CFOB - Ft. Frances, ON, Canada - *BrCabYB 84*
CFOK - Westlock, AB, Canada - *BrCabYB 84*
CFOR - Orillia, ON, Canada - *BrCabYB 84*
CFOS - Owen Sound, ON, Canada - *BrCabYB 84*
CFOX-FM - Vancouver, BC, Canada - *BrCabYB 84*
CFOZ-FM - Argentia, NF, Canada - *BrCabYB 84*
CFPL - London, ON, Canada - *BrCabYB 84*
CFPL-FM - London, ON, Canada - *BrCabYB 84*
CFPL-TV - London, ON, Canada - *Tel&CabFB 84S*
CFPR - Prince Rupert, BC, Canada - *BrCabYB 84*
CFPS - Port Elgin, ON, Canada - *BrCabYB 84*
CFQC - Saskatoon, SK, Canada - *BrCabYB 84*
CFQC-TV - Saskatoon, SK, Canada - *Tel&CabFB 84S*
CFQM-FM - London, ON, Canada - *BrCabYB 84*
CFQR-FM - Montreal, PQ, Canada - *BrCabYB 84*
CFQX-FM - Selkirk, MB, Canada - *BrCabYB 84*
CFRA - Ottawa, ON, Canada - *BrCabYB 84*
CFRB - Toronto, ON, Canada - *BrCabYB 84; NatRadPubDir Summer 83, Spring 84*
CFRC - Kingston, ON, Canada - *BrCabYB 84*
CFRC-FM - Kingston, ON, Canada - *BrCabYB 84*
CFRD - Richmond, BC, Canada - *BrCabYB 84*
CFRG - Gravelbourg, SK, Canada - *BrCabYB 84*
CFRN - Edmonton, AB, Canada - *BrCabYB 84*
CFRN-TV - Edmonton, AB, Canada - *Tel&CabFB 84S*
CFRO-FM - Vancouver, BC, Canada - *BrCabYB 84; NatRadPubDir Summer 83, Spring 84*
CFRP - Forestville, PQ, Canada - *BrCabYB 84*
CFRU-FM - Guelph, ON, Canada - *BrCabYB 84*
CFRW - Winnipeg, MB, Canada - *BrCabYB 84*
CFRY - Portage la Prairie, MB, Canada - *BrCabYB 84*
CFS Barrington, Sherose Park CATV - Stone Horse, NS, Canada - *BrCabYB 84*
CFS Inc. - West Roxbury, MA - *ADAPSOMemDir 83-84; DataDirSup 7-83*
CFS Mont Apica Cable TV System [of Canadian Forces Station Mont Apica] - Mont Apica, PQ, Canada - *BrCabYB 84*
CFSL - Weyburn, SK, Canada - *BrCabYB 84*
CFSX - Stephenville, NF, Canada - *BrCabYB 84*
CFTI-FM - Timmins, ON, Canada - *BrCabYB 84*
CFTJ - Cambridge, ON, Canada - *BrCabYB 84*
CFTK - Terrace, BC, Canada - *BrCabYB 84*
CFTK-TV - Terrace, BC, Canada - *Tel&CabFB 84S*
CFTM-TV - Montreal, PQ, Canada - *Tel&CabFB 84S*
CFTO-TV - Toronto, ON, Canada - *Tel&CabFB 84S*

CFTR - Toronto, ON, Canada - *BrCabYB 84; NatRadPubDir Summer 83, Spring 84*
CFUN - Vancouver, BC, Canada - *BrCabYB 84*
CFVD - Ville Degelis, PQ, Canada - *BrCabYB 84*
CFVR - Abbotsford, BC, Canada - *BrCabYB 84*
CFWB - Campbell River, BC, Canada - *BrCabYB 84*
CFWH - Whitehorse, YT, Canada - *BrCabYB 84*
CFYK - Yellowknife, NT, Canada - *BrCabYB 84*
CFYN - Sault Ste. Marie, ON, Canada - *BrCabYB 84*
CFYR - Whitecourt, AB, Canada - *BrCabYB 84*
CG & S - Littleton, CO - *MicrocomMPl 84*
CGA Computer Associates - Marlboro, NJ - *ADAPSOMemDir 83-84*
CGA Magazine - Vancouver, BC, Canada - *WritMar 84*
CGRS Microtech Inc. - Langhorne, PA - *MicrocomMPl 83; WhoWMicrocom 83*
CGRS Microtech Inc. - Pendell, PA - *MicrocomMPl 84*
Cha-Cha Records - South Holland, IL - *BillIntBG 83-84*
CHA/Claire Harrison Associates Inc. - San Francisco, CA - *DirPRFirms 83*
CHAB - Moose Jaw, SK, Canada - *BrCabYB 84*
Chabot, Philippe - Lac Edouard, PQ, Canada - *BrCabYB 84*
Chaby Communications - New York, NY - *DirPRFirms 83*
CHAD - Amos, PQ, Canada - *BrCabYB 84*
Chadbourn Columbus County News - Chadbourn, NC - *BaconPubCkNews 84*
Chadonnet, Ann Fox - Chugiak, AK - *BoPubDir 4*
Chadron Cablevision [of Scott Cable Communications Inc.] - Chadron, NE - *BrCabYB 84; Tel&CabFB 84C*
Chadron Record - Chadron, NE - *BaconPubCkNews 84; Ed&PubIntYB 82*
Chadwyck-Healey Inc. - Teaneck, NJ - *BoPubDir 4, 5*
Chadwyck-Healey Ltd. - Cambridge, England - *InfIndMarPl 83; MicroMarPl 82-83*
Chaffee County Times, The - Buena Vista, CO - *Ed&PubIntYB 82*
Chaffee Signal - Chaffee, MO - *BaconPubCkNews 84; Ed&PubIntYB 82*
Chafitz Inc. - Rockville, MD - *WhoWMicrocom 83*
Chagrin Falls Chagrin Valley Times - Chagrin Falls, OH - *BaconPubCkNews 84*
Chagrin Falls Solon Times - Chagrin Falls, OH - *BaconPubCkNews 84*
Chagrin Valley Herald Sun - Chagrin Falls, OH - *Ed&PubIntYB 82*
Chagrin Valley Herald Sun [of Sun Newspapers] - Cleveland, OH - *NewsDir 84*
Chagrin Valley Herald Sun - *See* Sun Newspapers
Chagrin Valley Times - Chagrin Falls, OH - *AyerDirPub 83; Ed&PubIntYB 82; NewsDir 84*
CHAI Survey Service - Charleston, SC - *IntDirMarRes 83*
Chaikin Research Group, Cy - Danbury, CT - *IntDirMarRes 83*
Chaikin, Rhonda - Oakland, CA - *DirInfWP 82*
Chailleann, Clo - Aberfeldy, Scotland - *LitMag&SmPr 83-84*
Chain Drug Review - New York, NY - *BaconPubCkMag 84*
Chain Marketing & Management - New York, NY - *BaconPubCkMag 84*
Chain Merchandiser - Piedmont, CA - *BaconPubCkMag 84; MagDir 84*
Chain Saw Age - Portland, OR - *BaconPubCkMag 84; MagDir 84*
Chain Saw Industry & Power Equipment Dealer - Wadley, GA - *BaconPubCkMag 84*
Chain Saw Industry & Power Equipment Dealer - Shreveport, LA - *MagDir 84; MagIndMarPl 82-83*
Chain Store Age - New York, NY - *ArtMar 84; NewsBur 6*
Chain Store Age/Drug Edition [of Lebhar-Friedman Publications Inc.] - New York, NY - *MagDir 84*
Chain Store Age Executive - New York, NY - *BaconPubCkMag 84; MagDir 84; MagIndMarPl 82-83*
Chain Store Age/General Merchandise Edition - New York, NY - *BaconPubCkMag 84*
Chain Store Age Supermarkets [of Lebhar-Friedman Publications Inc.] - New York, NY - *MagDir 84; MagIndMarPl 82-83*
Chainsigns - New York, NY - *BaconPubCkMag 84*
Chajet Design Group Inc. - New York, NY - *HBIndAd&MS 82-83*
CHAK - Invik, NT, Canada - *BrCabYB 84*
CHAL - St. Pamphile, PQ, Canada - *BrCabYB 84*
Chalco Engineering Corp. - Gardena, CA - *DataDirSup 7-83*
Chalco Publishing Co. - *See* PPX Publishers
Chalet Records/Friederich's Productions - Los Angeles, CA - *BillIntBG 83-84*
Chaleur Evening Stars Inc. [Aff. of New Brunswick Senior Citizens Federation] - Bathurst, NB, Canada - *BoPubDir 4, 5*
Chalfant Press Inc. - Bishop, CA - *BaconPubCkNews 84; BoPubDir 4, 5*
Chalfont Records Inc. - Montgomery, AL - *BillIntBG 83-84*
Chalk, Nissen, Hanft - New York, NY - *AdAge 3-28-84; StaDirAdAg 2-84*
Challenge Books - Woodridge, IL - *BoPubDir 4, 5*
Challenge Press - Dayton, OH - *BoPubDir 4, 5*
Challenge Printing Co. - Wallington, NJ - *LitMarPl 83, 84*
Challenge Publications - Canoga Park, CA - *MagIndMarPl 82-83*
Challenge: The Magazine of Economic Affairs - Armonk, NY - *MagIndMarPl 82-83*
Challis Messenger - Challis, ID - *BaconPubCkNews 84; Ed&PubIntYB 82*
Challove Music - *See* MizMo Enterprises
Chalmac Publishing - *See* PPX Publishers
Chalmers Cookbooks Inc., Irena - New York, NY - *BoPubDir 4; LitMarPl 83, 84*
CHAM - Hamilton, ON, Canada - *BrCabYB 84*
Chamah - Brooklyn, NY - *BoPubDir 4*
Chamah - New York, NY - *BoPubDir 5*
Chamber of Commerce of the U.S. - Washington, DC - *AvMarPl 83*
Chamberlain-Frandolig Inc. - Houston, TX - *StaDirAdAg 2-84*
Chamberlain Interviewing Service - Memphis, TN - *IntDirMarRes 83*
Chamberlain, Mildred Mosher - Warwick, RI - *BoPubDir 4, 5*
Chamberlain Register - Chamberlain, SD - *BaconPubCkNews 84; Ed&PubIntYB 82*
Chambers Cable Communications Inc. - Eugene, OR - *Tel&CabFB 84C p.1671*
Chambers Cable of Edmonds [of Chambers CableComm Inc.] - Edmonds, WA - *Tel&CabFB 84C*
Chambers Cable of Novato [of Chambers CableComm Inc.] - Novato, CA - *Tel&CabFB 84C*
Chambers Cable of Southern California Inc. [of Chambers CableComm Inc.] - San Bernardino, CA - *Tel&CabFB 84C*
Chambers Cable of Southern California Inc. [of Chambers CableComm Inc.] - Sun City, CA - *Tel&CabFB 84C*
Chambers, Lewis R. [Div. of Bethel Agencies] - New York, NY - *LitMarPl 83, 84*
Chambersburg Public Opinion [of Gannett Satellite Information Network Inc.] - Chambersburg, PA - *BaconPubCkNews 84; NewsDir 84*
Chamblee Neighbor [of Marietta Neighbor Newspapers Inc.] - Marietta, GA - *AyerDirPub 83; NewsDir 84*
Chambre de Commerce & d'Industrie de Paris - Paris, France - *InfIndMarPl 83*
Champ Systems Inc. - Sacto, CA - *MicrocomMPl 84*
Champaign Cable Co. Inc. [of Communication Corp. of America Inc.] - Urbana, OH - *Tel&CabFB 84C*
Champaign Computer Co. - Mahomet, IL - *MicrocomMPl 84; MicrocomSwDir 1*
Champaign News Gazette - Champaign, IL - *BaconPubCkNews 84*
Champaign Telephone Co., The - Urbana, OH - *TelDir&BG 83-84*
Champaign-Urbana Communications [of American Television & Communications Corp.] - Champaign, IL - *BrCabYB 84*
Champaign-Urbana Magazine [of Faucett Communications Inc.] - Champaign, IL - *WritMar 84*
Champaign-Urbana News Gazette - Champaign, IL - *Ed&PubIntYB 82; NewsDir 84*
Champion Advertising Agency [Div. of Jerry Hahn & Associates Inc.] - Englewood, NJ - *ArtMar 84; StaDirAdAg 2-84*
Champion Athlete Publishing Co. - Richmond, VA - *BoPubDir 4, 5; WritMar 84*
Champion Inc. - Orlando, FL - *StaDirAdAg 2-84*
Champion Press [Aff. of Tom Hopkins Champions Unltd. Inc.] - Scottsdale, AZ - *BoPubDir 4 Sup, 5*
Champion Publications of Chino Inc. - Chino, CA - *AyerDirPub 83; BaconPubCkNews 84*
Champion, The - Center, TX - *AyerDirPub 83; Ed&PubIntYB 82*

Champion, The - Houston, TX - *WritMar 84*
Champion Video Inc. - Tempe, AZ - *AvMarPl 83*
Champions on Film [Div. of School-Tech Inc.] - Ann Arbor, MI - *AvMarPl 83*
Championship Racefilm Productions - San Pedro, CA - *Tel&CabFB 84C*
Champlain NewChannels [of NewChannels Corp.] - Champlain, NY - *BrCabYB 84*
Champlain NewChannels - Rouses Point, NY - *Tel&CabFB 84C*
Champlain Telephone Co. - Champlain, NY - *TelDir&BG 83-84*
Champlin-Dayton Press - Champlin, MN - *Ed&PubIntYB 82*
Champlin-Dayton Press - Osseo, MN - *AyerDirPub 83*
Champlin-Dayton Press - *See* Larson Publications Inc.
Champoeg Press - Beaverton, OR - *BoPubDir 4, 5*
CHAN-TV - Vancouver, BC, Canada - *Tel&CabFB 84S*
Chancery Publishers - Baltimore, MD - *BoPubDir 4, 5; LitMag&SmPr 83-84*
Chandler & Brownsboro Statesman - Brownsboro, TX - *AyerDirPub 83; BaconPubCkNews 84*
Chandler & Sharp Publishers Inc. - Novato, CA - *LitMag&SmPr 83-84; LitMarPl 83, 84*
Chandler Arizonan [of Cox Arizona Publications] - Chandler, AZ - *BaconPubCkNews 84; Ed&PubIntYB 82; NewsDir 84*
Chandler-Corcoran Inc. - Seattle, WA - *DirPRFirms 83*
Chandler Lincoln County News - Chandler, OK - *BaconPubCkNews 84; NewsDir 84*
Chandler Music Co. Inc. - *See* Loring Music Co.
Chandler Post - Chandler, IN - *Ed&PubIntYB 82; NewsDir 84*
Chandler Tribune - Mesa, AZ - *AyerDirPub 83*
Chandoha Photography, Walter - Annandale, NJ - *LitMarPl 83, 84; MagIndMarPl 82-83*
Chandonnet, Ann Fox - Chugiak, AK - *BoPubDir 5*
Chandos Music - *See* Folklore Music
Chandrabhaga - Orissa Hill, IN - *LitMag&SmPr 83-84*
Chang Laboratories Inc. - Cupertino, CA - *MicrocomMPl 83*
Chang Laboratories Inc. - San Jose, CA - *MicrocomMPl 84*
Change [of Synergetic Press] - Chapel Hill, NC - *LitMag&SmPr 83-84*
Change for Children - San Francisco, CA - *BoPubDir 4, 5*
Change Magazine [of Helen Dwight Reid Educational Foundation] - Washington, DC - *BaconPubCkMag 84; MagDir 84; MagIndMarPl 82-83*
Change Magazine Press [of Council on Learning] - New Rochelle, NY - *LitMarPl 83*
Changing Scene Theater, The - Denver, CO - *WritMar 84*
Changing Times [of The Kiplinger Organization] - Washington, DC - *ArtMar 84; BaconPubCkMag 84; LitMarPl 83, 84; MagDir 84; MagIndMarPl 82-83; WritMar 84*
Changing Times [of The Kiplinger Organization] - New York, NY - *Folio 83*
Channel Black, The - New York, NY - *CabTVPrDB 83*
Channel Data Systems - Santa Barbara, CA - *MicrocomMPl 83, 84; WhoWMicrocom 83*
Channel Films Inc. - New York, NY - *Tel&CabFB 84C*
Channel Master Satellite Systems Inc. - Franklinton, NC - *BrCabYB 84*
Channel Master Satellite Systems Inc. - Knightdale, NC - *BrCabYB 84*
Channel Master Satellite Systems Inc. - Oxford, NC - *Tel&CabFB 84C p.1671*
Channel Music [Div. of Music Associates] - Nashville, TN - *BillIntBG 83-84*
Channel One - Atlanta, GA - *Tel&CabFB 84C*
Channel One - Medford, NJ - *WhoWMicrocom 83*
Channel One Inc. - Waltham, MA - *Tel&CabFB 84C*
Channel One Video Tape Inc. - Miami, FL - *AvMarPl 83*
Channel 6 Inc. - Temple, TX - *BrCabYB 84*
Channel 10 Inc. - Duluth, MN - *BrCabYB 84*
Channel, The [of Mobile Video Services Ltd.] - Washington, DC - *TeleSy&SerDir 7-83*
Channel 2 Broadcasting Co. - Anchorage, AK - *BrCabYB 84*
Channel Two Television Co. - Houston, TX - *BrCabYB 84*
Channel View Inc. - Escondido, CA - *Tel&CabFB 84C*
Channels - Exeter, NH - *MagDir 84; MagIndMarPl 82-83*
Channels of Communications - New York, NY - *BaconPubCkMag 84*
Channeltainment Inc. - Knoxville, TN - *CabTVPrDB 83*
Channelview Sentinel - *See* Houston Community Newspapers
Channick Broadcasting Corp. - Joliet, IL - *BrCabYB 84*
Channing Books - Marion, MA - *BoPubDir 4, 5*
Chanson Editors Co. - *See* Stanyan Music Co.
Chanteyman Press - Woodbridge, NJ - *BoPubDir 4, 5*
Chanticleer Co. Inc. - New York, NY - *LitMarPl 83, 84*
Chanticleer Press Inc. - New York, NY - *LitMarPl 83, 84*
Chantico Publishing Co. - Long Beach, CA - *BoPubDir 4, 5*
Chantry Music Press Inc. - Springfield, OH - *BillIntBG 83-84*
Chantry Press - Midland Park, NJ - *BoPubDir 4 Sup, 5; LitMag&SmPr 83-84*
Chanute This Week - Rantoul, IL - *AyerDirPub 83; Ed&PubIntYB 82*
Chanute Tribune [of Harris Enterprises Inc.] - Chanute, KS - *BaconPubCkNews 84; NewsDir 84*
CHAP - Longlac, ON, Canada - *BrCabYB 84*
Chapel/Bridge Records [Div. of Pacific Press Publishing Association] - Mountain View, CA - *BillIntBG 83-84*
Chapel Hill Newspaper - Chapel Hill, NC - *AyerDirPub 83; BaconPubCkNews 84; Ed&PubIntYB 82; NewsDir 84*
Chapel Hill Weekly Advertiser - Chapel Hill, NC - *AyerDirPub 83*
Chapin West Associates - Encino, CA - *LitMarPl 83*
Chaplaincy - Washington, DC - *MagDir 84*
Chaplin Associates Ltd., Joseph E. - New York, NY - *DirInfWP 82*
Chapman [of Lothlorien] - Edinburgh, Scotland - *LitMag&SmPr 83-84*
Chapman Advertiser - *See* Montgomery Publications Inc.
Chapman Advertiser & Enterprise Journal - Chapman, KS - *AyerDirPub 83; Ed&PubIntYB 82*
Chapman & Hall Ltd. - Andover, England - *MicroMarPl 82-83*
Chapman & Quinn [Subs. of Comhawk Marketing] - New York, NY - *DirMarMP 83; MagIndMarPl 82-83*
Chapman Associates - Atlanta, GA - *CabTVFinDB 83*
Chapman Co., Bruce - Grafton, VT - *Tel&CabFB 84C*
Chapman Corp. - Portland, ME - *LitMarPl 83, 84*
Chapman Direct Marketing Inc. [Subs. of Young & Rubicam Inc.] - New York, NY - *DirMarMP 83*
Chapman Direct Marketing Inc. - *See* Young & Rubicam Inc.
Chapman Inc., James P. - Detroit, MI - *DirPRFirms 83*
Chapman Printing Co. - Huntington, WV - *MagIndMarPl 82-83*
Chapman/Warwick [Aff. of Warwick Advertising] - San Diego, CA - *StaDirAdAg 2-84*
Chappaqua Journal - Armonk, NY - *AyerDirPub 83*
Chappell International-New York - New York, NY - *BillIntBG 83-84*
Chappell Music Co. - New York, NY - *BillIntBG 83-84*
Chappell Register - Chappell, NE - *BaconPubCkNews 84; Ed&PubIntYB 82*
Chapple Films - Chaplin, CT - *AvMarPl 83*
Chapter & Cask [Div. of Collart Enterprises] - Baltimore, MD - *BoPubDir 4; LitMarPl 83*
Chapter & Cask [Div. of Collart Enterprises] - Glyndon, MD - *BoPubDir 5; LitMarPl 84*
Chapter IV - *See* Campbell Music Inc., Glen
Char Barb Music - Swoope, VA - *BillIntBG 83-84*
CHAR-FM - Alert, NT, Canada - *BrCabYB 84*
Char-Liz Music Inc. - New York, NY - *BillIntBG 83-84*
Character Books - San Diego, CA - *LitMag&SmPr 83-84*
Charade Records - Tulare, CA - *BillIntBG 83-84*
Charbuz Music Co. - Philadelphia, PA - *BillIntBG 83-84*
Chardon Geauga Times Leader - Chardon, OH - *NewsDir 84*
Charging for Library Services [of QL Systems Ltd.] - Ottawa, ON, Canada - *DataDirOnSer 84*
Charging for Library Services [of McGill University] - Montreal, PQ, Canada - *CompReadDB 82; DirOnDB Spring 84*
Chariho Times [of Wakefield Narragansett Times] - Wakefield, RI - *NewsDir 84*
Chariho Times, The - Charlestown, RI - *Ed&PubIntYB 82*
Charioteer, The [of Parnassos] - New York, NY - *LitMag&SmPr 83-84*
Charisma [of Plus Communications Inc.] - Winter Park, FL - *WritMar 84*

Charisma Communications Group - Columbus, MS - *BrCabYB 84*
Charisma Press [Aff. of The Province] - Andover, MA - *BoPubDir 4, 5*
Charisma Productions - Deerfield Beach, FL - *AvMarPl 83*
Charisma Publications Inc. - Carmel, IN - *BoPubDir 4*
Charisma Publications Inc. - Indianapolis, IN - *BoPubDir 5*
Charitable Giving [of NewsNet Inc.] - Bryn Mawr, PA - *DataDirOnSer 84*
Charitable Giving Newsletter - Eugene, OR - *DataDirOnSer 84; DirOnDB Spring 84*
Chariton Courier - Keytesville, MO - *AyerDirPub 83; Ed&PubIntYB 82*
Chariton Herald-Patriot [of Chariton Publishing Co.] - Chariton, IA - *Ed&PubIntYB 82; NewsDir 84*
Chariton Herald-Patriot - *See* Chariton Publishing Co.
Chariton Leader - Chariton, IA - *Ed&PubIntYB 82; NewsDir 84*
Chariton Leader - *See* Chariton Publishing Co.
Chariton Publishing Co. - Chariton, IA - *BaconPubCkNews 84*
Chariton Review [of Northeast Missouri State University] - Kirksville, MO - *LitMag&SmPr 83-84; WritMar 84*
Chariton Review Press - Kirksville, MO - *LitMag&SmPr 83-84*
Chariton Valley Telephone Corp. - Bucklin, MO - *TelDir&BG 83-84*
Charlemont TV - Charlemont, MA - *BrCabYB 84; Tel&CabFB 84C*
Charles & Co. Inc. - Southport, CT - *BoPubDir 4, 5*
Charles City Press [of Mid America Publishing Corp.] - Charles City, IA - *AyerDirPub 83; BaconPubCkNews 84; Ed&PubIntYB 82; NewsDir 84*
Charles County Times-Crescent - La Plata, MD - *NewsDir 84*
Charles-Frederick Publishers - St. Paul, MN - *BoPubDir 4, 5*
Charles Mix County News - Geddes, SD - *AyerDirPub 83; Ed&PubIntYB 82*
Charles Press Publishers Inc. - Bowie, MD - *BoPubDir 4, 5*
Charles Publishing, Joseph J. - Hilton, NY - *BoPubDir 5*
Charles Recording Services, Dick - New York, NY - *AvMarPl 83*
Charles River Books Inc. - Charlestown, MA - *LitMarPl 83, 84*
Charles River Data Systems Inc. - Natick, MA - *DataDirSup 7-83; WhoWMicrocom 83*
Charles Street Press - Baltimore, MD - *BoPubDir 4 Sup, 5; LitMag&SmPr 83-84*
Charles Town Spirit Jefferson Advocate - Charles Town, WV - *BaconPubCkNews 84*
Charles TV Cable System - Avis, PA - *BrCabYB 84; Tel&CabFB 84C p.1671*
Charles TV Cable System - Jersey Shore, PA - *BrCabYB 84*
Charles TV Cable System - North Bend, PA - *Tel&CabFB 84C*
Charleston Airlift Dispatch - Charleston, SC - *BaconPubCkNews 84*
Charleston Black Times - Columbia, SC - *AyerDirPub 83*
Charleston Black Times - *See* Juju Publishing Co.
Charleston Cable TV [of Heritage Communications Inc.] - Charleston, MS - *Tel&CabFB 84C*
Charleston Chronicle - Charleston, SC - *BaconPubCkNews 84; Ed&PubIntYB 82; NewsDir 84*
Charleston Coles County Daily Times-Courier - Charleston, IL - *NewsDir 84*
Charleston Courier - Charlestown, IN - *BaconPubCkNews 84*
Charleston Daily Mail [of Clay Communications Inc.] - Charleston, WV - *BaconPubCkNews 84; Ed&PubIntYB 82; LitMarPl 84; NewsDir 84*
Charleston Enterprise-Courier - Charleston, MO - *BaconPubCkNews 84; NewsDir 84*
Charleston Evening Post - Charleston, SC - *BaconPubCkNews 84*
Charleston Express - Charleston, AR - *BaconPubCkNews 84; Ed&PubIntYB 82*
Charleston Gazette - Charleston, WV - *BaconPubCkNews 84; Ed&PubIntYB 82; LitMarPl 84; NewsBur 6; NewsDir 84*
Charleston News & Courier - Charleston, SC - *BaconPubCkNews 84; NewsDir 84*
Charleston Suburban News - *See* Community Press Inc.
Charleston Sun-Sentinel - Charleston, MS - *BaconPubCkNews 84*
Charlestown Cable System [of Telecable Communications Corp.] - Charlestown, MD - *BrCabYB 84*
Charlestown Courier - Charlestown, IN - *Ed&PubIntYB 82; NewsDir 84*
Charlestown Courier - *See* Charleston Courier
Charlestown Leader - Charlestown, IN - *BaconPubCkNews 84; Ed&PubIntYB 82; NewsDir 84*
Charlevoix County Press [of Silbar Communications Inc.] - Boyne City, MI - *AyerDirPub 83; Ed&PubIntYB 82; NewsDir 84*
Charlevoix Courier - Charlevoix, MI - *AyerDirPub 83; BaconPubCkNews 84; Ed&PubIntYB 82; NewsDir 84*
Charlevoix North Woods Call - Charlevoix, MI - *NewsDir 84*
Charlie Books - Petaluma, CA - *BoPubDir 4, 5*
Charlie/Papa Productions - Rockville, MD - *AvMarPl 83*
Charlotte Gazette - Drakes Branch, VA - *AyerDirPub 83; Ed&PubIntYB 82*
Charlotte Magazine - Charlotte, NC - *ArtMar 84; BaconPubCkMag 84; MagDir 84; WritMar 84*
Charlotte Mecklenburg Times - Charlotte, NC - *BaconPubCkNews 84*
Charlotte Message Center Inc. - Ft. Myers, FL - *Tel&CabFB 84C*
Charlotte News [of Knight Publishing Co.] - Charlotte, NC - *BaconPubCkNews 84; Ed&PubIntYB 82; NewsBur 6; NewsDir 84*
Charlotte Observer [of Knight-Ridder Newspapers Inc.] - Charlotte, NC - *ArtMar 84; BaconPubCkNews 84; Ed&PubIntYB 82; LitMarPl 83, 84; NewsBur 6; NewsDir 84*
Charlotte Post - Charlotte, NC - *BaconPubCkNews 84; Ed&PubIntYB 82*
Charlotte Republican Tribune - Charlotte, MI - *AyerDirPub 83; BaconPubCkNews 84; Ed&PubIntYB 82*
Charlotte Shopping Guide - Punta Gorda, FL - *AyerDirPub 83*
Charlotte Star of Zion - Charlotte, NC - *BaconPubCkNews 84*
Charlotte Weekly, The - Charlotte, NC - *AyerDirPub 83*
Charlottesville-Albemarle Tribune - Charlottesville, VA - *BaconPubCkNews 84; Ed&PubIntYB 82; NewsDir 84*
Charlottesville Daily Progress, The - Charlottesville, VA - *Ed&PubIntYB 82*
Charlottesville Observer - Charlottesville, VA - *AyerDirPub 83; Ed&PubIntYB 82*
Charlton County Herald - Folkston, GA - *AyerDirPub 83; Ed&PubIntYB 82*
Charlton, Mabel - Griffin, SK, Canada - *BoPubDir 4 Sup, 5*
Charlton Press [Div. of Charlton International Inc.] - Toronto, ON, Canada - *BoPubDir 4; LitMarPl 83, 84*
Charlton Publications - Derby, CT - *MagIndMarPl 82-83*
Charnas Inc. - Manchester, CT - *StaDirAdAg 2-84*
Charnay, John - Canoga Park, CA - *LitMarPl 83, 84; MagIndMarPl 82-83*
Charnel House - Toronto, ON, Canada - *BoPubDir 4, 5; LitMag&SmPr 83-84*
Charney/Palacios & Co. Inc. - Coral Gables, FL - *StaDirAdAg 2-84*
Charny Co., Dan - Dobbs Ferry, NY - *StaDirAdAg 2-84*
Charriere, Gerard - New York, NY - *LitMarPl 83, 84*
Chart Music Publishing House - *See* Birch Tree Group Ltd.
Charta Records - Nashville, TN - *BillIntBG 83-84*
Chartbound Music Publications Ltd. - *See* GCS Music Publications
Charteng Workshop [of Small-Small Press] - Rumford, ME - *LitMag&SmPr 83-84*
Charter Books [of The Berkley Publishing Group] - New York, NY - *WritMar 84*
Charter Cable TV [of Community Cable Systems Inc.] - Middleville, MI - *Tel&CabFB 84C*
Charter Co., The - Jacksonville, FL - *KnowInd 83*
Charter Control Inc. - Plainsboro, NJ - *WhoWMicrocom 83*
Charter Data Products - Bannockburn, IL - *DirInfWP 82*
Charter Data Services Inc. - Des Moines, IA - *MagIndMarPl 82-83*
Charter Fixture Library [of Maritime Data Network Ltd.] - Stamford, CT - *DataDirOnSer 84*
Charter Oak-San Dimas Highlander - *See* Highlander Publications Inc.
Charter Oak Times - Charter Oak, IA - *Ed&PubIntYB 82*
Charter Oak Ute Newspaper - Charter Oak, IA - *BaconPubCkNews 84*
Charter Publications Inc. - Valley Forge, PA - *BillIntBG 83-84*
Chartered Banks Annual - Toronto, ON, Canada - *DirOnDB Spring 84*
Chartered Banks Monthly Statement of Assets & Liabilities [of I. P. Sharp Associates Ltd.] - Toronto, ON, Canada - *DataDirOnSer 84; DirOnDB Spring 84*

Chartered Banks Quarterly Income Statement [of I. P. Sharp Associates Ltd.] - Toronto, ON, Canada - *DataDirOnSer 84; DirOnDB Spring 84*
Chartex Information Design - Cambridge, MA - *LitMarPl 83, 84*
Charthouse - Canaan, NH - *LitMarPl 84*
Chartiers Valley Times Progress - Homestead, PA - *AyerDirPub 83*
Chartmakers Inc., The - New York, NY - *AvMarPl 83*
Chartmasters - Covington, LA - *BoPubDir 4, 5*
Chartpak [Subs. of Times Mirror Co.] - Leeds, MA - *AvMarPl 83*
Chartpak/Pickett Industries [Subs. of Times Mirror Co.] - Irvine, CA - *LitMarPl 83*
Chartwell Books Inc. [Div. of Book Sales Inc.] - Secaucus, NJ - *LitMarPl 83, 84*
Chartwell Communications Group - Los Angeles, CA - *HomeVid&CabYB 82-83*
CHAS-FM - Sault Ste. Marie, ON, Canada - *BrCabYB 84*
Chase & Co., Laurie - San Francisco, CA - *DirPRFirms 83*
Chase Avenue Press - Winter Park, FL - *LitMag&SmPr 83-84*
Chase City News-Progress - Chase City, VA - *BaconPubCkNews 84*
Chase City News-Progress - Clarksville, VA - *AyerDirPub 83*
Chase County Leader News - Cottonwood Falls, KS - *Ed&PubIntYB 82*
Chase Data Systems - Cincinnati, OH - *MicrocomMPl 83, 84*
Chase Direct Mail Corp. - New York, NY - *MagIndMarPl 82-83*
Chase, Don M. - Sebastopol, CA - *BoPubDir 4, 5*
Chase Econometrics [of Chase Econometrics/Interactive Data Corp.] - Bala Cynwyd, PA - *EISS 83; MicrocomMPl 84*
Chase Econometrics/Interactive Data Corp. [Div. of Chase Manhattan Bank] - Waltham, MA - *ADAPSOMemDir 83-84; DataDirOnSer 84; DataDirSup 7-83; InfIndMarPl 83; InfoS 83-84*
Chase/Ehrenberg & Rosene - Chicago, IL - *AdAge 3-28-84; StaDirAdAg 2-84*
Chase Enterprises Inc. - San Diego, CA - *WhoWMicrocom 83*
Chase Index - *See* Ellsworth Reporter
Chase Index, The - Chase, KS - *Ed&PubIntYB 82*
Chase, Livingston & Co., Cochrane - Irvine, CA - *AdAge 3-28-84; StaDirAdAg 2-84*
Chase Manhattan Bank NA - New York, NY - *VideoDir 82-83*
Chase Manhattan Bank/The Information Center - New York, NY - *FBInfSer 80*
Chase Pickett Inc. - Hillside, IL - *StaDirAdAg 2-84*
Chase Research Inc., D. A. - Atlanta, GA - *IntDirMarRes 83*
Chase/Temkin & Associates Inc. - New York, NY - *StaDirAdAg 2-84*
Chase, The - Lexington, KY - *MagDir 84*
Chase Trade Information Corp. [Subs. of Chase Manhattan Bank NA] - New York, NY - *DirMarMP 83*
Chaska Cable TV [of Zylstra Communications Corp.] - Chaska, MN - *BrCabYB 84*
Chaska Carver County Herald - Chaska, MN - *BaconPubCkNews 84*
Chasqui - Provo, UT - *LitMag&SmPr 83-84*
Chasse Publications - Denver, CO - *BoPubDir 4, 5*
CHAT - Medicine Hat, AB, Canada - *BrCabYB 84*
CHAT-TV - Medicine Hat, AB, Canada - *Tel&CabFB 84S*
Chatawa Music - *See* Malaco Music Co.
Chateau Publishing Inc. - Orlando, FL - *BoPubDir 4, 5*
Chateaugay Record - Chateaugay, NY - *Ed&PubIntYB 82*
Chateaugay Record [of Denton Publications Inc.] - Elizabethtown, NY - *NewsDir 84*
Chateaugay Record - *See* Denton Publications Inc.
Chatelaine - Toronto, ON, Canada - *BaconPubCkMag 84; WritMar 84*
Chatelaine's New Mother - Toronto, ON, Canada - *BaconPubCkMag 84*
Chatfield Cable TV [of Preston Cable TV Inc.] - Chatfield, MN - *BrCabYB 84; Tel&CabFB 84C*
Chatfield Music - Encino, CA - *BillIntBG 83-84*
Chatfield News - Chatfield, MN - *BaconPubCkNews 84; Ed&PubIntYB 82*
Chatfield Paper Corp. [Div. of Mead Corp.] - Cincinnati, OH - *LitMarPl 83, 84*
Chatham & Associates - Atlanta, GA - *DirPRFirms 83*
Chatham Bookseller - Chatham, NJ - *BoPubDir 4, 5*
Chatham Cable TV [of Rogers Cablesystems Inc.] - Chatham, ON, Canada - *BrCabYB 84*
Chatham Clarion - Chatham, IL - *AyerDirPub 83; Ed&PubIntYB 82*
Chatham Clarion - *See* South County Publications
Chatham County Herald, The - Chatham County, NC - *Ed&PubIntYB 82*
Chatham Courier - Chatham, NJ - *BaconPubCkNews 84; Ed&PubIntYB 82; NewsDir 84*
Chatham Courier-Rough Notes - Chatham, NY - *BaconPubCkNews 84; NewsDir 84*
Chatham Courier, The - Chatham, NY - *Ed&PubIntYB 82*
Chatham Daily News, The - Chatham, ON, Canada - *BaconPubCkNews 84*
Chatham House Publishers Inc. - Chatham, NJ - *LitMarPl 83, 84*
Chatham News - Chatham, ON, Canada - *AyerDirPub 83*
Chatham Press - Chatham, NJ - *BaconPubCkNews 84; Ed&PubIntYB 82*
Chatham Press [of The Summit Herald] - Summit, NJ - *NewsDir 84*
Chatham Press, The [Subs. of Devin-Adair Publishers] - Old Greenwich, CT - *WritMar 84*
Chatham Publishing Co. - Burlingame, CA - *BoPubDir 4, 5; LitMag&SmPr 83-84*
Chatham Record, The - Pittsboro, NC - *Ed&PubIntYB 82*
Chatham-Southeast Citizen [of Chicago Weekend] - Chicago, IL - *NewsDir 84*
Chatham Square Press Inc. - New York, NY - *LitMarPl 83, 84*
Chatham Star-Tribune - Chatham, VA - *BaconPubCkNews 84*
Chatham Telephone Co. - Chatham, LA - *TelDir&BG 83-84*
Chatham Telephone Co. - Chatham, MI - *TelDir&BG 83-84*
Chatham Township Independent [of Passaic Valley Independent Press] - New Providence, NJ - *NewsDir 84*
Chatham Township Independent - *See* Passaic Valley Independent Press
Chatom Call-News Dispatch - Chatom, AL - *BaconPubCkNews 84*
Chatsworth Cablevision Co. - Chatsworth, GA - *BrCabYB 84; Tel&CabFB 84C*
Chatsworth Data Corp. - Chatsworth, CA - *DataDirSup 7-83; WhoWMicrocom 83*
Chatsworth Plaindealer - Chatsworth, IL - *AyerDirPub 83; Ed&PubIntYB 82*
Chatsworth Plaindealer - *See* Cornbelt Press Inc.
Chatsworth Studios Ltd. - Toronto, ON, Canada - *BoPubDir 4 Sup, 5*
Chatsworth Times - Encino, CA - *AyerDirPub 83*
Chatsworth Times [of Walls Newspapers Inc.] - Chatsworth, GA - *BaconPubCkNews 84; Ed&PubIntYB 82; NewsDir 84*
Chatsworth Times - *See* Associated Valley Publications
Chattahoochee Cablevision [of McDonald Group] - Newnan, GA - *Tel&CabFB 84C*
Chattahoochee Record Co. - Van Nuys, CA - *BillIntBG 83-84*
Chattahoochee Twin City News - Chattahoochee, FL - *BaconPubCkNews 84*
Chattahoochie Cable Communications Inc. [of Summit Communications Inc.] - Cobb County, GA - *BrCabYB 84*
Chattanooga Cable TV Co. [of Tele-Scripps Cable Co.] - Chattanooga, TN - *Tel&CabFB 84C*
Chattanooga CATV [of Southmedia Co.] - Chattanooga, TN - *BrCabYB 84*
Chattanooga Hamilton County Herald - Chattanooga, TN - *BaconPubCkNews 84*
Chattanooga News-Free Press - Chattanooga, TN - *BaconPubCkNews 84; LitMarPl 83; NewsDir 84*
Chattanooga Times [of Times Printing Co.] - Chattanooga, TN - *BaconPubCkNews 84; Ed&PubIntYB 82; LitMarPl 83, 84; NewsBur 6; NewsDir 84*
Chattaroy Cable Co. - Chattaroy, WV - *BrCabYB 84; Tel&CabFB 84C*
Chatterton Press - Cincinnati, OH - *BoPubDir 4, 5*
Chatto & Windus/The Hogarth Press - Salem, NH - *LitMarPl 83, 84*
CHAU-TV - Carleton, PQ, Canada - *Tel&CabFB 84S*
Chaucer Press Inc., The - Duryea, PA - *LitMarPl 83, 84*
Chautauqua & Erie Telephone Corp. - Westfield, NY - *TelDir&BG 83-84*

Chautauqua Hills Cable Inc. - Dexter, KS - *BrCabYB 84; Tel&CabFB 84C*
Chautauqua Hills Cable Inc. - Shidler, OK - *BrCabYB 84*
Chautauqua News - Mayville, NY - *AyerDirPub 83*
Chautauqua News - Sherman, NY - *Ed&PubIntYB 82*
Chawed Rawzin Press - San Antonio, TX - *BoPubDir 5*
Chawed Rawzin Press - Slaton, TX - *BoPubDir 4*
CHAY-FM - Barrie, ON, Canada - *BrCabYB 84*
Chazy & Westport Telephone Corp. - Westport, NY - *TelDir&BG 83-84*
CHBC-TV - Kelowna, BC, Canada - *Tel&CabFB 84S*
CHCH-TV - Hamilton, ON, Canada - *Tel&CabFB 84S*
Chciuk-Celt, Alexandra - West Hempstead, NY - *LitMarPl 83, 84*
CHCL - Medley, AB, Canada - *BrCabYB 84*
CHCM - Marystown, AB, Canada - *BrCabYB 84*
Cheaha Cablevision Inc. - Albertville, AL - *BrCabYB 84; Tel&CabFB 84C*
Cheaha Cablevision Inc. - Childersburg, AL - *BrCabYB 84*
Cheaha Cablevision Inc. - Southside, AL - *BrCabYB 84*
Cheaha Cablevision Inc. - Talladega, AL - *BrCabYB 84; Tel&CabFB 84C p.1671*
Cheam Publishing Ltd. - Victoria, BC, Canada - *BoPubDir 4, 5*
Cheap Street - New Castle, VA - *BoPubDir 5*
Cheasapeake & Potomac Telephone Cos., The - Washington, DC - *TelDir&BG 83-84*
Cheat Mountain Press - Elkins, WV - *BoPubDir 4 Sup, 5; LitMag&SmPr 83-84*
Cheavoria Music Publishing Co. - Brewton, AL - *BillIntBG 83-84*
Cheboygan Daily Tribune - Cheboygan, MI - *Ed&PubIntYB 82; NewsDir 84*
Cheboygan Observer - Cheboygan, MI - *BaconPubCkNews 84; Ed&PubIntYB 82*
Cheboygan Tribune - Cheboygan, MI - *BaconPubCkNews 84*
CHEC - Edmonton, AB, Canada - *BrCabYB 84*
CHEC - Lethbridge, AB, Canada - *BrCabYB 84*
Check List of Social Science Serials [of Bath University Library] - Bath, England - *CompReadDB 82*
Checkerboard Advertising Co. - St. Louis, MO - *StaDirAdAg 2-84*
Checks-To-Go - La Mesa, CA - *MicrocomMPl 83*
Checotah McIntosh County Democrat - Checotah, OK - *BaconPubCkNews 84*
Cheechako News - Kenai, AK - *AyerDirPub 83; Ed&PubIntYB 82*
Cheektowaga Bee - Cheektowaga, NY - *AyerDirPub 83; Ed&PubIntYB 82*
Cheektowaga Bee [of Bee Publications Inc.] - Williamsville, NY - *NewsDir 84*
Cheektowaga Bee - *See* Bee Publications Inc.
Cheektowaga Journal [of Lackawanna Leader Publishing Co.] - Lackawanna, NY - *NewsDir 84*
Cheektowaga Times - Cheektowaga, NY - *BaconPubCkNews 84; Ed&PubIntYB 82; NewsDir 84*
Cheese Reporter - Madison, WI - *BaconPubCkMag 84; MagDir 84*
Cheesecake - *See* Jacobson, Jeffrey E.
Cheever Publishing - Bloomington, IL - *BoPubDir 4, 5*
CHEF - Granby, PQ, Canada - *BrCabYB 84*
Chef Institutional - Wilton, CT - *BaconPubCkMag 84*
Chef/Institutional - New York, NY - *MagDir 84*
Chef Novati Gourmet Cooking Ltd. - Montreal, PQ, Canada - *BoPubDir 4*
Chef William Lord, Chef's Kitchen - Wakefield, MS - *Ed&PubIntYB 82*
Chek-Chart Service Bulletin, The - San Jose, CA - *WritMar 84*
CHEK-TV - Victoria, BC, Canada - *Tel&CabFB 84S*
Chelan Antenna Inc. - Chelan, WA - *BrCabYB 84; Tel&CabFB 84C*
Chelan Valley Mirror - Chelan, WA - *AyerDirPub 83; BaconPubCkNews 84; Ed&PubIntYB 82*
Chellis, Conwell & Gale Inc. - Portland, ME - *StaDirAdAg 2-84*
Chellman Co., Chuck - Nashville, TN - *BillIntBG 83-84*
Chelmsford Independent - Acton, MA - *AyerDirPub 83*
Chelmsford Newsweekly - Chelmsford, MA - *BaconPubCkNews 84*
Chelmsford-Westford-Tyngsboro Newsweekly - Chelmsford, MA - *AyerDirPub 83; Ed&PubIntYB 82; NewsDir 84*
Cheloniidae Press - Williamsburg, MA - *BoPubDir 4 Sup, 5*
Chelsea - New York, NY - *LitMag&SmPr 83-84; WritMar 84*
Chelsea Clinton News - Chelsea, NY - *Ed&PubIntYB 82*
Chelsea-Clinton News - New York, NY - *AyerDirPub 83*
Chelsea Communications Inc. - Mt. Lebanon, PA - *BrCabYB 84*
Chelsea House Publishers [Div. of Chelsea Educational Communications Inc.] - New York, NY - *LitMarPl 83, 84; WritMar 84*
Chelsea-Lee Books - Los Angeles, CA - *BoPubDir 4, 5*
Chelsea Publishing Co. Inc. - New York, NY - *LitMarPl 83, 84*
Chelsea Record - Chelsea, MA - *BaconPubCkNews 84; NewsDir 84*
Chelsea Reporter - Chelsea, OK - *BaconPubCkNews 84; Ed&PubIntYB 82*
Chelsea Standard - Chelsea, MI - *BaconPubCkNews 84; Ed&PubIntYB 82; NewsDir 84*
Chelsea Theater Center - New York, NY - *WritMar 84*
Cheltenham CATV Co. [of Comcast Corp.] - Cheltenham, PA - *BrCabYB 84*
Chem-Al Inc. - Racine, WI - *WhoWMicrocom 83*
Chem Singly Indexed Substances [of DIALOG Information Services Inc.] - Palo Alto, CA - *DBBus 82*
Chem Systems - Tarrytown, NY - *BoPubDir 5*
Chem Systems International Ltd. - London, England - *EISS 7-83 Sup*
CHEM-TV - Trois Rivieres, PQ, Canada - *Tel&CabFB 84S*
Chemco Physical Properties Data Bank [of Federal Technical University] - Zurich, Switzerland - *EISS 83*
Chemdata Research - Santa Barbara, CA - *EISS 83*
Chemdex [of SDC Search Service] - Santa Monica, CA - *CompReadDB 82; DataDirOnSer 84*
Chemical Abstracts [of SDC Search Service] - Santa Monica, CA - *DataDirOnSer 84*
Chemical Abstracts Service [Div. of American Chemical Society] - Columbus, OH - *CompReadDB 82; DataDirOnSer 84; EISS 83; InfIndMarPl 83; MicroMarPl 82-83*
Chemical Abstracts Service Source Index [of Chemical Abstracts Service] - Columbus, OH - *CompReadDB 82*
Chemical Age Project File [of Morgan-Grampian Process Press Information Service] - London, England - *EISS 7-83 Sup*
Chemical & Engineering News [of American Chemical Society] - Westport, CT - *Folio 83*
Chemical & Engineering News [of American Chemical Society] - Washington, DC - *BaconPubCkMag 84; MagDir 84; MagIndMarPl 82-83; NewsBur 6*
Chemical & Process Engineering Abstracts [of Bayer AG] - Leverkusen, West Germany - *EISS 83*
Chemical Automated Search Terminal [of Computer Corp. of America] - Cambridge, MA - *EISS 83*
Chemical Bank - New York, NY - *VideoDir 82-83*
Chemical-Biological Activities [of Chemical Abstracts Service] - Columbus, OH - *CompReadDB 82*
Chemical Bulletin, The [of Chicago Section, American Chemical Society] - Chicago, IL - *BaconPubCkMag 84; MagDir 84*
Chemical Business - New York, NY - *BaconPubCkMag 84*
Chemical Carcinogenesis Research Information System [of Chemical Information Systems Inc.] - Baltimore, MD - *DataDirOnSer 84*
Chemical Carcinogenesis Research Information System - Bethesda, MD - *DirOnDB Spring 84*
Chemical Data Bank - Washington, DC - *DirOnDB Spring 84*
Chemical Data Banks [of Data Resources Inc.] - Lexington, MA - *DataDirOnSer 84; DBBus 82*
Chemical Data Center Inc. - Columbus, OH - *DataDirOnSer 84; EISS 83; FBInfSer 80; InfIndMarPl 83*
Chemical Data Services [of IPC Industrial Press Ltd.] - Surrey, England - *InfIndMarPl 83*
Chemical Data Services [of IPC Industrial Press Ltd.] - Sutton, England - *EISS 83*
Chemical Dictionary On-line [of National Library of Medicine] - Bethesda, MD - *DataDirOnSer 84*
Chemical Economics Handbook [of SDC Information Services] - Santa Monica, CA - *DataDirOnSer 84*
Chemical Economics Handbook Online [of SRI International] - Menlo Park, CA - *DirOnDB Spring 84; EISS 5-84 Sup*
Chemical Effects Information Center [of Oak Ridge National Laboratory] - Oak Ridge, TN - *CompReadDB 82; EISS 83*
Chemical Engineering [of McGraw-Hill Inc.] - New York, NY - *BaconPubCkMag 84; Folio 83; MagDir 84; MagIndMarPl 82-83*

Chemical Engineering Abstracts [of Pergamon International Information Corp.] - McLean, VA - *DataDirOnSer 84*
Chemical Engineering Abstracts [of The Royal Society of Chemistry Information Services] - Nottingham, England - *DataDirOnSer 84; DirOnDB Spring 84; OnBibDB 3*
Chemical Engineering Progress [of American Institute of Chemical Engineers] - New York, NY - *BaconPubCkMag 84; MagDir 84*
Chemical Engineers' Book Club [of McGraw-Hill Book Co.] - New York, NY - *LitMarPl 83, 84*
Chemical Equipment [of Gordon Publications Inc.] - Dover, NJ - *BaconPubCkMag 84; MagDir 84*
Chemical Equipment [of Gordon Publications Inc.] - Morristown, NJ - *Folio 83*
Chemical Evaluation Search & Retrieval System [of Computer Sciences Corp.] - Falls Church, VA - *DataDirOnSer 84*
Chemical Exposure [of Dialog Information Services Inc.] - Palo Alto, CA - *DataDirOnSer 84*
Chemical Exposure - Oak Ridge, TN - *DirOnDB Spring 84*
Chemical Hazards Response Information System [of U.S. Coast Guard] - Washington, DC - *EISS 83*
Chemical Industry Notes [of Chemical Abstracts Service] - Columbus, OH - *CompReadDB 82; DataDirOnSer 84; DBBus 82; DirOnDB Spring 84*
Chemical Industry Product News [of Putnam Publishing Co.] - Chicago, IL - *BaconPubCkMag 84; MagDir 84; MagIndMarPl 82-83*
Chemical Information & Documentation [of German Chemical Society] - Berlin, West Germany - *EISS 83*
Chemical Information Center [of Indiana University] - Bloomington, IN - *EISS 83; InfIndMarPl 83*
Chemical Information Management Inc. - Cherry Hill, NJ - *EISS 83*
Chemical Information Retrieval System [of U.S. Army] - Washington, DC - *EISS 83*
Chemical Information Systems Inc. [Subs. of Fein-Marquart Associates] - Baltimore, MD - *DataDirOnSer 84*
Chemical Kinetics Data Center [of National Bureau of Standards] - Washington, DC - *EISS 83; InfIndMarPl 83*
Chemical Marketing Reporter [of Schnell Publishing Co.] - New York, NY - *BaconPubCkMag 84; MagDir 84; MagIndMarPl 82-83*
Chemical Processing [of Putnam Publishing Co.] - Chicago, IL - *BaconPubCkMag 84; Folio 83; MagDir 84; MagIndMarPl 82-83*
Chemical Propulsion Abstracts [of Chemical Propulsion Information Agency] - Laurel, MD - *CompReadDB 82*
Chemical Propulsion Information Agency [of Johns Hopkins University] - Laurel, MD - *EISS 83*
Chemical Publishing Co. Inc. - New York, NY - *LitMarPl 83, 84*
Chemical Purchasing [of Myers Publishing Co.] - Stamford, CT - *BaconPubCkMag 84; MagDir 84; MagIndMarPl 82-83*
Chemical Reactions Documentation Service [of SDC Search Service] - Santa Monica, CA - *DataDirOnSer 84*
Chemical Reactions Documentation Service [of Derwent Publications Ltd.] - London, England - *CompReadDB 82; EISS 83; OnBibDB 3*
Chemical Regulations & Guidelines System [of Dialog Information Services Inc.] - Palo Alto, CA - *DataDirOnSer 84*
Chemical Regulations & Guidelines System [of U.S. Environmental Protection Agency] - Washington, DC - *CompReadDB 82*
Chemical Regulations & Guidelines System [of CRC Systems Inc.] - Fairfax, VA - *DirOnDB Spring 84; EISS 83*
Chemical Singly Indexed Substances [of Lockheed Information Systems] - Palo Alto, CA - *CompReadDB 82*
Chemical Society, The - *See* Royal Society of Chemistry, The
Chemical Spotlight - Ridgewood, NJ - *BaconPubCkMag 84*
Chemical Substances Information Network [of U.S. Environmental Protection Agency] - Washington, DC - *EISS 83*
Chemical Thermodynamics Data Center [of U.S. National Bureau of Standards] - Washington, DC - *EISS 83*
Chemical Times & Trends [of Chemical Specialties Manufacturers Association] - Washington, DC - *MagDir 84*
Chemical Times & Trends - Baltimore, MD - *BaconPubCkMag 84; MagIndMarPl 82-83*
Chemical Titles [of Chemical Abstracts Service] - Columbus, OH - *CompReadDB 82; DataDirOnSer 84*
Chemical Week [of McGraw-Hill Inc.] - New York, NY - *BaconPubCkMag 84; Folio 83; MagDir 84; MagIndMarPl 82-83; NewsBur 6*
Chemical Week - Cleveland, OH - *NewsBur 6*
Chemicals Identified in Human Biological Media [of Oak Ridge National Laboratory] - Oak Ridge, TN - *CompReadDB 82*
Chemigraphic Paper Corp. - Rutherford, NJ - *DirInfWP 82*
Chemir Laboratories - Glendale, MO - *DataDirOnSer 84*
Chemist, The [of The American Institute of Chemists Inc.] - Washington, DC - *MagDir 84*
Chemist, The - Bethesda, MD - *BaconPubCkMag 84*
Chemistry in Canada - Ottawa, ON, Canada - *BaconPubCkMag 84*
Chemistry Industry Notes [of American Chemical Society] - Columbus, OH - *OnBibDB 3*
Chemlaw [of The Bureau of National Affairs] - Washington, DC - *CompReadDB 82; DataDirOnSer 84; DBBus 82; EISS 83*
Chemline [of National Library of Medicine] - Bethesda, MD - *CompReadDB 82; EISS 83*
Chemname [of Dialog Information Services Inc.] - Palo Alto, CA - *CompReadDB 82; DataDirOnSer 84*
Chemoreception Abstracts [of Information Retrieval Ltd.] - London, England - *CompReadDB 82*
Chemsafe Data Bank [of Atomic Energy Authority] - Didcot, England - *EISS 83*
Chemsearch [of Dialog Information Services Inc.] - Palo Alto, CA - *CompReadDB 82; DataDirOnSer 84; DBBus 82; DirOnDB Spring 84*
ChemShare Corp. [Subs. of Texas-McCan] - Houston, TX - *DataDirOnSer 84*
Chemsis [of Dialog Information Services Inc.] - Palo Alto, CA - *DataDirOnSer 84; DirOnDB Spring 84*
Chemtech [of American Chemical Society] - Westport, CT - *MagDir 84*
Chemtech [of American Chemical Society] - Summit, NJ - *BaconPubCkMag 84; MagDir 84; MagIndMarPl 82-83*
Chemtran [of Fulton Data Systems] - Atlanta, GA - *DataDirOnSer 84*
Chemtran - Houston, TX - *DirOnDB Spring 84*
Chemung Valley Reporter - Horseheads, NY - *AyerDirPub 83; Ed&PubIntYB 82; NewsDir 84*
Chemzero [of Dialog Information Services Inc.] - Palo Alto, CA - *DataDirOnSer 84; DirOnDB Spring 84*
Chen Information Systems Inc. - Burlingame, CA - *MicrocomSwDir 1; WhoWMicrocom 83*
Chenango American & Whitney Point Reporter - Greene, NY - *AyerDirPub 83; Ed&PubIntYB 82*
Chenango & Unadilla Telephone Corp. [Aff. of Continental Telecom Inc.] - Johnstown, NY - *TelDir&BG 83-84*
Chenault Inc. - New York, NY - *StaDirAdAg 2-84*
Chenery Associates - New York, NY - *LitMarPl 84*
Cheney Cable TV Co. - Cheney, WA - *Tel&CabFB 84C*
Cheney, Donna B. - McCook, NE - *BoPubDir 4, 5*
Cheney Free Press - Cheney, WA - *BaconPubCkNews 84; Ed&PubIntYB 82*
Cheney/Medical Lake TV Cable - Medical Lake, WA - *Tel&CabFB 84C*
Cheney Sentinel - Cheney, KS - *BaconPubCkNews 84; Ed&PubIntYB 82*
Cheng & Tsui Co. Inc. - Boston, MA - *BoPubDir 4, 5; LitMarPl 83, 84*
Chenoa Clipper-Times - Lexington, IL - *Ed&PubIntYB 82*
Chenoa Clipper-Times - *See* Cornbelt Press Inc.
Chenoweth, Ellis, Faulkner & Associates Inc. - Tampa, FL - *StaDirAdAg 2-84*
Chenoweth Films, R. B. - La Habra, CA - *AvMarPl 83*
Chequamegon Telephone Cooperative Inc. - Cable, WI - *TelDir&BG 83-84*
CHER - Sydney, NS, Canada - *BrCabYB 84*
Cheraw Chronicle [of Community Newspapers] - Cheraw, SC - *BaconPubCkNews 84; Ed&PubIntYB 82; NewsDir 84*
Cherbuti Films Inc. - New York, NY - *AvMarPl 83*
Cherenson Group, The - Livingston, NJ - *DirPRFirms 83; StaDirAdAg 2-84*
Cheri [of Cheri Enterprises Inc.] - New York, NY - *Folio 83; WritMar 84*
Cherie Music - Mesquite, TX - *BillIntBG 83-84*

Cherio - New York, NY - *BillIntBG 83-84*
Cherith Publishing Co. - Placentia, CA - *BillIntBG 83-84*
Cherokee County Banner - Rusk, TX - *AyerDirPub 83; Ed&PubIntYB 82*
Cherokee County Chronicle - Tahlequah, OK - *Ed&PubIntYB 82*
Cherokee County Herald - Centre, AL - *AyerDirPub 83; Ed&PubIntYB 82*
Cherokee Daily Times [of Gazette Co.] - Cherokee, IA - *Ed&PubIntYB 82; NewsDir 84*
Cherokee Messenger - *See* Cherokee Publishing Co.
Cherokee Messenger, The - Cherokee, OK - *Ed&PubIntYB 82*
Cherokee Publishing Co. - Covington, GA - *BoPubDir 4, 5*
Cherokee Publishing Co. - Cherokee, OK - *BaconPubCkNews 84*
Cherokee Republican - *See* Cherokee Publishing Co.
Cherokee Republican, The - Cherokee, OK - *Ed&PubIntYB 82*
Cherokee Scout - Murphy, NC - *AyerDirPub 83; Ed&PubIntYB 82*
Cherokee Telephone Co. - Calera, OK - *TelDir&BG 83-84*
Cherokee Times - Cherokee, IA - *BaconPubCkNews 84*
Cherokee Tribune - Canton, GA - *AyerDirPub 83; Ed&PubIntYB 82*
Cherokee TV Cable Co. - Cherokee, AL - *Tel&CabFB 84C*
Cherokee TV Cable System [of Dorate Inc.] - Cherokee, OK - *BrCabYB 84; Tel&CabFB 84C*
Cherokeean, The - Rusk, TX - *Ed&PubIntYB 82*
Cherry Blossom Music Co. - *See* Cherry Lane Music Publishing Co. Inc.
Cherry Creek Inc. - Mankato, MN - *LitMag&SmPr 83-84*
Cherry Diamond, The - St. Louis, MO - *BaconPubCkMag 84*
Cherry Electrical Products - Harpenden, England - *InfIndMarPl 83*
Cherry Hill News - Cherry Hill, NJ - *AyerDirPub 83; NewsDir 84*
Cherry Hill News - *See* Suburban Newspapers
Cherry Hill News Suburban - Cherry Hill, NJ - *Ed&PubIntYB 82*
Cherry Hill Scene, The - Cherry Hill, NJ - *Ed&PubIntYB 82*
Cherry Hill Sterling Suburban - *See* Suburban Newspapers
Cherry/Hufford Advertising & Graphics Inc. - Beloit, WI - *StaDirAdAg 2-84*
Cherry Lane Books [Div. of Cherry Lane Music Co. Inc.] - Port Chester, NY - *LitMarPl 83, 84*
Cherry Lane Music Publishing Co. Inc. - Port Chester, NY - *BillIntBG 83-84*
Cherry Mountain Music - *See* Cherry Lane Music Publishing Co. Inc.
Cherry Publishers - Winnipeg, MB, Canada - *BoPubDir 4, 5*
Cherry Records - Houston, TX - *BillIntBG 83-84*
Cherry River Music Co. - *See* Cherry Lane Music Publishing Co. Inc.
Cherry Valley Editions - Silver Spring, MD - *LitMarPl 83, 84*
Cherrygarth Farms Software Inc. - Auburn, IN - *MicrocomMPl 84*
Cherryvale Cable TV Inc. [of Tele-Communications Inc.] - Cherryvale, KS - *BrCabYB 84*
Cherryvale Citizen - Cherryvale, KS - *BaconPubCkNews 84; Ed&PubIntYB 82*
Cherryville Eagle - Cherryville, NC - *BaconPubCkNews 84*
Chertok & Co. Inc., Harvey - New York, NY - *BrCabYB 84*
Cherubim Publishing Co. - Rockaway, NY - *BoPubDir 4, 5*
Chesaning Montrose Argus - Chesaning, MI - *BaconPubCkNews 84*
Chesaning Saginaw Valley News - Chesaning, MI - *NewsDir 84*
Chesapeake & Potomac Telephone Co. of Maryland, The - Baltimore, MD - *TelDir&BG 83-84*
Chesapeake & Potomac Telephone Co. of Virginia, The - Richmond, VA - *TelDir&BG 83-84*
Chesapeake & Potomac Telephone Co. of West Virginia, The - Carleston, WV - *TelDir&BG 83-84*
Chesapeake Bay Magazine - Annapolis, MD - *BaconPubCkMag 84; MagDir 84; WritMar 84*
Chesapeake CATV Inc. [of Tangier Island TV Corp.] - Tangier Island, VA - *Tel&CabFB 84C*
Chesapeake Information Retrieval Service - Edgewater, MD - *EISS 83*
Chesapeake Post [of Byerly Publications Inc.] - Chesapeake, VA - *AyerDirPub 83; BaconPubCkNews 84; Ed&PubIntYB 82; NewsDir 84*
Chesdel Music Co. - *See* Alshire Publishing Cos.
Chesford Music Publications - *See* Barnhouse Co., C. L.
Cheshire Books - Palo Alto, CA - *BoPubDir 4, 5; LitMag&SmPr 83-84*
Cheshire Cable Corp. - Hinsdale, NH - *BrCabYB 84; Tel&CabFB 84C*
Cheshire Herald - Cheshire, CT - *BaconPubCkNews 84; Ed&PubIntYB 82; NewsDir 84*
Cheshire Music Inc. - *See* TRO
Cheskin Associates-Color Research Institute - Menlo Park, CA - *IntDirMarRes 83*
Chesley Enterprise - Chesley, ON, Canada - *AyerDirPub 83*
Chesley Music Corp. - *See* Denton & Haskins Corp.
Chesley, Paul - Aspen, CO - *LitMarPl 83, 84; MagIndMarPl 82-83*
Chesnee Telephone Co. Inc. - Chesnee, SC - *TelDir&BG 83-84*
Chesopiean Library of Archaeology - Norfolk, VA - *BoPubDir 4, 5*
Chess - Denver, CO - *DirInfWP 82*
Chess Enterprises Inc. - Coraopolis, PA - *LitMag&SmPr 83-84*
Chess Journalist, The [of Chess Journalists of America] - Upper Darby, PA - *LitMag&SmPr 83-84*
Chess Journalists of America - Cincinnati, OH - *LitMag&SmPr 83-84*
Chess Life [of United States Chess Federation] - New Windsor, NY - *ArtMar 84; BaconPubCkMag 84; MagIndMarPl 82-83; WritMar 84*
Chess Nut Books - Montreal, PQ, Canada - *BoPubDir 5*
Chess Nut Books - Westmount, PQ, Canada - *BoPubDir 4*
Chess Records - Englewood, NJ - *BillIntBG 83-84*
Chess Visions Inc. - South Miami, FL - *BoPubDir 4 Sup, 5*
Chesstours - Reno, NV - *Ed&PubIntYB 82*
Chest - Park Ridge, IL - *BaconPubCkMag 84; MagDir 84; MagIndMarPl 82-83*
Chesta e Chida Cookbook - Lafayette, LA - *BoPubDir 5*
Chester Cable TV [of Acton CATV Inc.] - Chester, SC - *BrCabYB 84*
Chester Community TAS - Chester, WV - *Tel&CabFB 84C*
Chester County Broadcasting Co. [of Lenfest Communications Inc.] - Chester County, PA - *Tel&CabFB 84C*
Chester County Broadcasting Co. - Coatesville, PA - *BrCabYB 84*
Chester County Broadcasting Co. [of Lenfest Communications Inc.] - West Chester, PA - *Tel&CabFB 84C*
Chester County Communications Ltd. - Oxford, PA - *BaconPubCkNews 84*
Chester County Independent - Henderson, TN - *Ed&PubIntYB 82*
Chester County Post - Paoli, PA - *Ed&PubIntYB 82*
Chester County Press - Oxford, PA - *AyerDirPub 83; Ed&PubIntYB 82*
Chester, E. B. - Rocky Mt., NC - *Tel&CabFB 84C p.1672*
Chester Herald - Chester, NE - *BaconPubCkNews 84; Ed&PubIntYB 82*
Chester Kent Island Bay Times - Chester, MD - *BaconPubCkNews 84*
Chester Liberty County Times - Chester, MT - *BaconPubCkNews 84*
Chester News & Reporter [of The Springs Co.] - Chester, SC - *BaconPubCkNews 84; NewsDir 84*
Chester Panhandle Press - Chester, WV - *BaconPubCkNews 84*
Chester Progressive - Chester, CA - *Ed&PubIntYB 82*
Chester Progressive - *See* Feather Publishing Co. Inc.
Chester Randolph County Herald Tribune - Chester, IL - *BaconPubCkNews 84; NewsDir 84*
Chester Telephone Co. - Chester, IA - *TelDir&BG 83-84*
Chester Telephone Co. - Chester, SC - *TelDir&BG 83-84*
Chester White Journal - Rochester, IN - *BaconPubCkMag 84; MagDir 84*
Chesterfield Advertiser - Chesterfield, SC - *AyerDirPub 83; Ed&PubIntYB 82*
Chesterfield Cable Communications [of Storer Cable Communications Inc.] - Chesterfield County, VA - *BrCabYB 84*
Chesterfield Cablevision Inc. - Westmoreland, NH - *Tel&CabFB 84C*
Chesterfield Cablevision Inc. [of Storer Cable Communications] - Chesterfield County, VA - *Tel&CabFB 84C*
Chesterfield Gazette - Chesterfield, VA - *AyerDirPub 83*
Chesterfield Journal - Chester, VA - *NewsDir 84*
Chesterfield Music Shops Inc. - New York, NY - *AvMarPl 83*

Chesterton Tribune - Chesterton, IN - *BaconPubCkNews 84; NewsDir 84*
Chestertown Kent County News [of Chesapeake Publishing Corp.] - Chestertown, MD - *BaconPubCkNews 84; NewsDir 84*
Chesterville Record - Chesterville, ON, Canada - *AyerDirPub 83*
Chestler Publishing Co. - Clio, MI - *BillIntBG 83-84*
Chestnut Communications Inc. - Greenwich, CT - *BrCabYB 84*
Chestnut Communications Inc. - New York, NY - *HBIndAd&MS 82-83*
Chestnut Hill Local - Philadelphia, PA - *AyerDirPub 83*
Chestnut House Group Inc. - Chicago, IL - *LitMarPl 83, 84; MagIndMarPl 82-83*
Chestnut Mound Music [Div. of Eddie Crook Co.] - Hendersonville, TN - *BillIntBG 83-84*
CHET - Chetwynd, BC, Canada - *BrCabYB 84*
Chetek Alert - Chetek, WI - *BaconPubCkNews 84; Ed&PubIntYB 82; NewsDir 84*
Chetopa Advance - Chetopa, KS - *BaconPubCkNews 84; Ed&PubIntYB 82*
Chetwynd Haddons - London, England - *StaDirAdAg 2-84*
Cheval Books/Stanyan Books [Aff. of Rod McKuen Enterprises Inc.] - Hollywood, CA - *BoPubDir 4, 5*
Chevalier Publications - Tulare, CA - *BoPubDir 4, 5*
Chevron USA - San Jose, CA - *WritMar 84*
Chewelah Independent - *See* Panorama Publishers
Chewelah Independent, The - Chewelah, WA - *AyerDirPub 83; Ed&PubIntYB 82*
CHEX - Peterborough, ON, Canada - *BrCabYB 84*
CHEX-TV - Peterborough, ON, Canada - *Tel&CabFB 84S*
Cheyenne Music Productions - Pontiac, MI - *BillIntBG 83-84*
Cheyenne Range Ledger - Cheyenne Wells, CO - *BaconPubCkNews 84*
Cheyenne River Sioux Tribe Telephone Authority - Eagle Butte, SD - *TelDir&BG 83-84*
Cheyenne Star - Cheyenne, OK - *BaconPubCkNews 84; Ed&PubIntYB 82*
Cheyenne State Tribune - Cheyenne, WY - *BaconPubCkNews 84*
Cheyenne Wyoming Eagle - Cheyenne, WY - *BaconPubCkNews 84*
CHEZ-FM - Ottawa, ON, Canada - *BrCabYB 84*
CHFA - Edmonton, AB, Canada - *BrCabYB 84*
CHFC - Chruchill, MB, Canada - *BrCabYB 84*
CHFD-TV - Thunder Bay, ON, Canada - *Tel&CabFB 84S*
CHFI-FM - Toronto, ON, Canada - *BrCabYB 84; NatRadPubDir Summer 83, Spring 84*
CHFM-FM - Calgery, AB, Canada - *BrCabYB 84*
CHFX-FM - Halifax, NS, Canada - *BrCabYB 84*
CHGA-FM - Maniwaki, PQ, Canada - *BrCabYB 84*
CHGB - La Pocatiere, PQ, Canada - *BrCabYB 84*
CHGB-FM - La Pocatiere, PQ, Canada - *BrCabYB 84*
CHGG-FM - Limestone, MB, Canada - *BrCabYB 84*
Chi/Cor Information Management Inc. - Chicago, IL - *ADAPSOMemDir 83-84*
Chi Corp. - Beachwood, OH - *DataDirSup 7-83*
Chi-Town Records - Chicago, IL - *BillIntBG 83-84*
Chiaroscuro [of Clearly Obscure Press] - Ithaca, NY - *LitMag&SmPr 83-84*
Chiat/Day - Los Angeles, CA - *AdAge 3-28-84; ArtMar 84; Br 1-23-84; BrCabYB 84; StaDirAdAg 2-84*
Chiat/Day/Livingston Inc. - *See* Livingston & Co.
CHIB - Chibougamau, PQ, Canada - *BrCabYB 84*
Chibardun Telephone Cooperative Inc. - Dallas, WI - *TelDir&BG 83-84*
Chic [of Larry Flynt Publications] - Los Angeles, CA - *ArtMar 84; Folio 83; MagDir 84; MagIndMarPl 82-83; WritMar 84*
Chicago [of WFMT Inc.] - Chicago, IL - *ArtMar 84; BaconPubCkMag 84; Folio 83; LitMarPl 83, 84; MagDir 84; MagIndMarPl 82-83; WritMar 84*
Chicago Advertising Agency - Chicago, IL - *StaDirAdAg 2-84*
Chicago Albany Park News - *See* Myers Publishing Co.
Chicago Apparel News - Los Angeles, CA - *BaconPubCkMag 84*
Chicago Austinite - *See* Passage Publications Inc.
Chicago Back of the Yards Journal - Chicago, IL - *BaconPubCkNews 84; NewsDir 84*
Chicago Belmont Central Leader - *See* Leader Papers Inc.
Chicago Beverly Review - Chicago, IL - *BaconPubCkNews 84*
Chicago Bilalian News - Chicago, IL - *NewsDir 84*
Chicago Board of Trade - Chicago, IL - *BoPubDir 4, 5*
Chicago Board Options Exchange - Chicago, IL - *BoPubDir 5*
Chicago Booster - *See* Lincoln-Belmont Publishing Co.
Chicago Bowler - Westchester, IL - *BaconPubCkMag 84*
Chicago Bridgeport News - Chicago, IL - *BaconPubCkNews 84; NewsDir 84*
Chicago Brighton Park Life - Chicago, IL - *BaconPubCkNews 84*
Chicago Brighton Park-McKinley Park Life - Chicago, IL - *NewsDir 84*
Chicago Catholic, The - Chicago, IL - *BaconPubCkMag 84; NewsDir 84*
Chicago Chatham Citizen - *See* Chicago Citizen
Chicago Citizen - Chicago, IL - *BaconPubCkNews 84*
Chicago-Clear Ridge Reporter [of Chicago Southwest News-Herald] - Chicago, IL - *NewsDir 84*
Chicago Communication Service Inc. - Chicago, IL - *Tel&CabFB 84C*
Chicago Community Reporter - Chicago, IL - *BaconPubCkNews 84*
Chicago County Press - Lindstrom, MN - *Ed&PubIntYB 82*
Chicago Cragin Leader - *See* Leader Papers Inc.
Chicago Creative Directory - Chicago, IL - *BoPubDir 5*
Chicago Daily Calumet [of Midland Communications Inc.] - Chicago, IL - *BaconPubCkNews 84; NewsDir 84*
Chicago Daily Defender [of Robert S. Abbott Publishing Co.] - Chicago, IL - *BaconPubCkNews 84; Ed&PubIntYB 82; NewsDir 84*
Chicago Daily Herald - Arlington Heights, IL - *NewsDir 84*
Chicago Daily Law Bulletin - Chicago, IL - *BaconPubCkMag 84; Ed&PubIntYB 82; NewsDir 84*
Chicago Daily News - *See* Field Newspaper Syndicate
Chicago Daily Southtown Economist - Chicago, IL - *BaconPubCkNews 84*
Chicago Defender - Chicago, IL - *AyerDirPub 83; Ed&PubIntYB 82*
Chicago Downtown/Lake Shore News - Chicago, IL - *BaconPubCkNews 84*
Chicago Edison-Norwood Review - *See* Des Plains Publishing Co.
Chicago El Informador - Chicago, IL - *NewsDir 84*
Chicago Evergreen Gazette - Chicago, IL - *BaconPubCkNews 84; NewsDir 84*
Chicago Fire Fighter - Chicago, IL - *BaconPubCkMag 84; MagDir 84*
Chicago Food Market News - Chicago, IL - *BaconPubCkMag 84*
Chicago Good News Weekly - Chicago, IL - *BaconPubCkNews 84; NewsDir 84*
Chicago Group Inc., The - Chicago, IL - *IntDirMarRes 83*
Chicago Harlem-Foster Times - *See* Lerner Times Newspapers
Chicago Harlem-Irving Leader - *See* Leader Papers Inc.
Chicago Harlem-Irving Times - *See* Lerner Times Newspapers
Chicago Hegewisch News - Chicago, IL - *BaconPubCkNews 84; NewsDir 84*
Chicago Heights Star - Chicago Heights, IL - *AyerDirPub 83; Ed&PubIntYB 82; NewsDir 84*
Chicago Heights Star - *See* Star Publications
Chicago Historical & Architectural Landmarks Commission - Chicago, IL - *BoPubDir 4, 5*
Chicago Historical Society - Chicago, IL - *BoPubDir 4, 5*
Chicago History [of Chicago Historical Society] - Chicago, IL - *MagIndMarPl 82-83; WritMar 84*
Chicago Hyde Park Herald - Chicago, IL - *BaconPubCkNews 84*
Chicago Independent Bulletin - Chicago, IL - *BaconPubCkNews 84; Ed&PubIntYB 82; NewsDir 84*
Chicago Independent Bulletin - South Shore, IL - *Ed&PubIntYB 82*
Chicago Institute of Theology & Culture - Chicago, IL - *BoPubDir 4, 5*
Chicago Jefferson Mayfair Times - *See* Lerner Times Newspapers
Chicago Jefferson Park Leader - *See* Leader Papers Inc.
Chicago Journal - Chicago, IL - *AyerDirPub 83; WritMar 84*
Chicago Journal - *See* Press Newspapers
Chicago La Raza Publications Ltd. - Chicago, IL - *NewsDir 84*
Chicago Lawndale Drum - Chicago, IL - *BaconPubCkNews 84*
Chicago-Lawndale News [of Chicago West Town Publications] - Chicago, IL - *NewsDir 84*
Chicago Lawyer - Chicago, IL - *BaconPubCkMag 84*
Chicago Library System - Chicago, IL - *EISS 83*

Chicago Lincoln-Belmont Booster - *See* Lincoln-Belmont Publishing Co.
Chicago Lincolnwood Life - *See* Myers Publishing Co.
Chicago Logan Square Times - *See* Lerner Times Newspapers
Chicago Market [of Bolger Publications Inc.] - Minneapolis, MN - *BaconPubCkMag 84; MagDir 84*
Chicago Marketing Systems Inc. - Schaumburg, IL - *DirMarMP 83*
Chicago Maroon - Chicago, IL - *NewsDir 84*
Chicago Mayfair Leader - *See* Leader Papers Inc.
Chicago MDS Co. - Pasadena, MD - *Tel&CabFB 84C*
Chicago Medical Book Co. - Niles, IL - *LitMarPl 83, 84*
Chicago Medicine - Chicago, IL - *BaconPubCkMag 84; MagDir 84*
Chicago Metro News - Chicago, IL - *AyerDirPub 83; BaconPubCkNews 84; Ed&PubIntYB 82*
Chicago Mid-West Herald - *See* West Town Publications
Chicago Motor Club Home & Away - Chicago, IL - *BaconPubCkMag 84*
Chicago Music Publishing - Los Angeles, CA - *BillIntBG 83-84*
Chicago Near North News - Chicago, IL - *BaconPubCkNews 84; NewsDir 84*
Chicago Near West Side Herald - *See* West Town Publications
Chicago New Art Association - Chicago, IL - *LitMag&SmPr 83-84*
Chicago New Crusader - Chicago, IL - *BaconPubCkNews 84; NewsDir 84*
Chicago North Center/Irving Park - *See* Lincoln-Belmont Publishing Co.
Chicago North Loop News - Chicago, IL - *BaconPubCkNews 84*
Chicago Northtown News - *See* Myers Publishing Co.
Chicago Northwest Herald - *See* West Town Publications
Chicago Northwest Leader - *See* Leader Papers Inc.
Chicago Northwest Passage - *See* Passage Publications Inc.
Chicago Northwest Side Press - *See* Press Newspapers
Chicago Northwest Sunday Press - *See* Press Newspapers
Chicago Northwest Sunday Times - *See* Lerner Times Newspapers
Chicago Northwest Times - *See* Lerner Times Newspapers
Chicago Observer [of The Woodlawn Organization] - Chicago, IL - *BaconPubCkNews 84; NewsDir 84*
Chicago Online Users Group - Chicago, IL - *InfIndMarPl 83*
Chicago Paper Co. - Des Plaines, IL - *LitMarPl 84*
Chicago Portage Park Leader - *See* Leader Papers Inc.
Chicago Portage Park Passage - *See* Passage Publications Inc.
Chicago Portage Park Times - *See* Lerner Times Newspapers
Chicago Program Group Inc. - Chicago, IL - *Tel&CabFB 84C*
Chicago Psychoanalytic Literature Index [of Institute for Psychoanalysis] - Chicago, IL - *EISS 83*
Chicago Purchasor, The - Chicago, IL - *BaconPubCkMag 84; MagDir 84*
Chicago Racing Form - Chicago, IL - *NewsDir 84*
Chicago Ravenswood-Lincolnite - *See* Myers Publishing Co.
Chicago Ravenswood News - *See* Myers Publishing Co.
Chicago Reader - Chicago, IL - *ArtMar 84; AyerDirPub 83; BaconPubCkNews 84; WritMar 84*
Chicago Reporter [of Chicago Trio Enterprises] - Chicago, IL - *NewsDir 84*
Chicago Review [of University of Chicago] - Chicago, IL - *LitMag&SmPr 83-84; WritMar 84*
Chicago Review Press - Chicago, IL - *LitMarPl 83, 84; WritMar 84*
Chicago Ridge Citizen - Chicago, IL - *BaconPubCkNews 84*
Chicago Ridge Citizen [of Midlothian Southwest Messenger Newspapers] - Midlothian, IL - *AyerDirPub 83; NewsDir 84*
Chicago Ridge Citizen - Ridge, IL - *Ed&PubIntYB 82*
Chicago Ridge Worth-Palos Reporter - Chicago Ridge, IL - *NewsDir 84*
Chicago Rogers Park-Edgewater News - *See* Myers Publishing Co.
Chicago Shoreland News - Chicago, IL - *BaconPubCkNews 84*
Chicago Skyline - *See* Lincoln-Belmont Publishing Co.
Chicago South End Citizen - *See* Chicago Citizen
Chicago Southeast Independent Bulletin - *See* Chicago Independent Bulletin
Chicago Southtown Economist-Central - *See* Southtown Economist Inc.
Chicago Southtown Economist-South - *See* Southtown Economist Inc.
Chicago Southwest Independent Bulletin - *See* Chicago Independent Bulletin
Chicago Southwest News-Herald - *See* Vondrak Publications Inc.
Chicago Sports - Chicago, IL - *BaconPubCkMag 84*
Chicago Studies - Mundelein, IL - *WritMar 84*
Chicago Suburban Leader - *See* Leader Papers Inc.
Chicago Suburban Sun Times - Elk Grove Village, IL - *BaconPubCkNews 84*
Chicago Suburbanite Economist - *See* Southtown Economist Inc.
Chicago Sun Times [of Field Enterprises Inc.] - Chicago, IL - *BaconPubCkNews 84; LitMarPl 83, 84; NewsBur 6; NewsDir 84*
Chicago Sun-Times Show/Book Week - Chicago, IL - *WritMar 84*
Chicago Sunday Booster - *See* Lincoln-Belmont Publishing Co.
Chicago Sunday Life - *See* Myers Publishing Co.
Chicago Sunday Northwest Side Press - Chicago, IL - *NewsDir 84*
Chicago Sunday Star - *See* Myers Publishing Co.
Chicago Systems Software - Chicago, IL - *MicrocomMPl 83*
Chicago Teacher [of Chicago Teachers Union] - Chicago, IL - *NewsDir 84*
Chicago Theological Seminary (Exploration Press) - Chicago, IL - *BoPubDir 4, 5*
Chicago Tribune - Chicago, IL - *BaconPubCkNews 84; Ed&PubIntYB 82; LitMarPl 83, 84; NewsBur 6; NewsDir 84*
Chicago Tribune - *See* Tribune Broadcasting Co.
Chicago Tribune Magazine - Chicago, IL - *MagIndMarPl 82-83*
Chicago Tribune-New York News Syndicate Inc. - New York, NY - *Ed&PubIntYB 82; MagIndMarPl 82-83*
Chicago Tribune Press Service Inc. - New York, NY - *Ed&PubIntYB 82*
Chicago Uptown News - *See* Myers Publishing Co.
Chicago Weekend - *See* Chicago Citizen
Chicago Weekly Reporter - *See* Press Newspapers
Chicago West Belmont Leader - *See* Leader Papers Inc.
Chicago West Side Times [of Chicago West Town Publications] - Chicago, IL - *NewsDir 84*
Chicago West Side Times - *See* West Town Publications
Chicago West Town Herald - *See* West Town Publications
Chicago Westside Journal - Chicago, IL - *BaconPubCkNews 84*
Chicagoland Community Reporter - Chicago, IL - *Ed&PubIntYB 82; NewsDir 84*
Chicagoland Development - Chicago, IL - *BaconPubCkMag 84*
Chicagoland Electronics Engineer - Aurora, IL - *MagDir 84*
Chicagoland's Real Estate Advertiser [of Law Bulletin Publishing Co.] - Chicago, IL - *BaconPubCkMag 84; MagDir 84*
Chicago's Elite - Chicago, IL - *MagDir 84*
Chicago's Northwest Side Press - Chicago, IL - *AyerDirPub 83; Ed&PubIntYB 82; NewsDir 84*
Chicano Studies Research Center Publications [of University of California, Los Angeles] - Los Angeles, CA - *LitMag&SmPr 83-84*
Chichester Telephone - Chichester, NH - *TelDir&BG 83-84*
Chick & Associates, Leo - Los Angeles, CA - *DirMarMP 83*
Chickadee Magazine [of The Young Naturalist Foundation] - Toronto, ON, Canada - *WritMar 84*
Chickamauga Telephone Corp. - Chickamauga, GA - *TelDir&BG 83-84*
Chickasha Cablevision [of Multimedia Cablevision Inc.] - Chickasha, OK - *Tel&CabFB 84C*
Chickasha Daily Express [of Central Publishers Ltd.] - Chickasha, OK - *BaconPubCkNews 84; Ed&PubIntYB 82; NewsDir 84*
Chickasha Star - *See* Star Publishing Co.
Chickasha Star, The - Chickasha, OK - *Ed&PubIntYB 82*
Chickawaw Telephone Co. - Sulphur, OK - *TelDir&BG 83-84*
Chicken Fried Music - *See* Prophecy Publishing Inc.
Chickering/Howell - Los Angeles, CA - *StaDirAdAg 2-84*
Chico Enterprise Record - Chico, CA - *BaconPubCkNews 84; Ed&PubIntYB 82; NewsDir 84*
Chico MDS Communications - Sacramento, CA - *Tel&CabFB 84C*
Chico News & Review [of Chico Community Publishing Inc.] - Chico, CA - *NewsDir 84*
Chico Texan - Chico, TX - *AyerDirPub 83; BaconPubCkNews 84; Ed&PubIntYB 82*
Chicopee Herald - Chicopee, MA - *BaconPubCkNews 84; Ed&PubIntYB 82; NewsDir 84*
Chicorel Music Corp. Inc. - Milwaukee, WI - *BillIntBG 83-84*

Chicot County Newspapers Inc. - Lake Village, AR - *BaconPubCkNews 84*
Chicot Spectator - Lake Village, AR - *AyerDirPub 83; Ed&PubIntYB 82*
Chicot Spectator - *See* Chicot County Newspapers Inc.
Chida Cookbook, Chesta E. - Lafayette, LA - *BoPubDir 4 Sup*
Chief - Apopka, FL - *AyerDirPub 83*
Chief - Perry, IA - *AyerDirPub 83*
Chief - Donaldsonville, LA - *AyerDirPub 83*
Chief - Red Cloud, NE - *AyerDirPub 83*
Chief - Pawnee, OK - *AyerDirPub 83*
Chief - Mukwonago, WI - *AyerDirPub 83*
Chief Cablevision [of Cable Communications of Iowa] - Cherokee, IA - *BrCabYB 84*
Chief-Civil Service Leader, The - New York, NY - *NewsDir 84*
Chief Engineer [of Chief Engineers Association of Chicago] - Orland Park, IL - *BaconPubCkMag 84; MagDir 84*
Chief Executive - New York, NY - *BaconPubCkMag 84; DirMarMP 83; MagDir 84*
Chief Manufacturing Inc. - Burnsville, MN - *AvMarPl 83*
Chief-Union - Upper Sandusky, OH - *AyerDirPub 83*
Chiefland Citizen - Chiefland, FL - *BaconPubCkNews 84; Ed&PubIntYB 82*
Chieftain - Holly, CO - *AyerDirPub 83*
Chieftain - Pueblo, CO - *AyerDirPub 83; Ed&PubIntYB 82*
Chieftain - Bonner Springs, KS - *AyerDirPub 83*
Chieftain - Tecumseh, NE - *AyerDirPub 83*
Chieftain - Olustee, OK - *AyerDirPub 83*
Chieftain Shopper - Bonner Springs, KS - *AyerDirPub 83*
CHIK-FM - Quebec City, PQ, Canada - *BrCabYB 84*
Child Abuse & Neglect [of National Center on Child Abuse & Neglect] - Washington, DC - *CompReadDB 82; DataDirOnSer 84; DBBus 82; DirOnDB Spring 84; OnBibDB 3*
Child Development Abstracts & Bibliography [of Society for Research in Child Development] - University Park, PA - *EISS 83*
Child Evangelism Fellowship Press - Warrenton, MO - *BoPubDir 4, 5; Tel&CabFB 84C*
Child Focus Co. - Manhattan Beach, CA - *BoPubDir 4, 5*
Child Health Association of Sewickley Inc. - Sewickley, PA - *BoPubDir 4, 5*
Child Life [of Benjamin Franklin Library & Medical Society Inc.] - Indianapolis, IN - *ArtMar 84; MagIndMarPl 82-83; WritMar 84*
Child Research Service [Aff. of McCollum/Spielman Inc.] - New York, NY - *IntDirMarRes 83*
Child Ware Corp. - Menlo Park, CA - *MicrocomMPl 84*
Child Welfare - New York, NY - *MagDir 84; MagIndMarPl 82-83*
Child Welfare Information Services Inc. - New York, NY - *EISS 83*
Child Welfare League of America Inc. - New York, NY - *LitMarPl 83, 84*
Childbirth Graphics Ltd. - Rochester, NY - *LitMag&SmPr 83-84*
Childersburg Star - Childersburg, AL - *Ed&PubIntYB 82; NewsDir 84*
Childhood Education [of Association for Childhood Education International] - Washington, DC - *BaconPubCkMag 84; LitMarPl 83, 84; MagDir 84; MagIndMarPl 82-83*
Childlife - Indianapolis, IN - *MagDir 84*
Children First Press - Ann Arbor, MI - *BoPubDir 4, 5*
Children's Art Foundation Inc. - Santa Cruz, CA - *BoPubDir 4, 5*
Children's Book & Music Center - Santa Monica, CA - *AvMarPl 83*
Children's Book Co., The [Subs. of Creative Education Inc.] - Mankato, MN - *LitMarPl 83, 84*
Children's Book Council Inc. - New York, NY - *AvMarPl 83*
Children's Book Press/Imprenta de Libros Infantiles - San Francisco, CA - *LitMag&SmPr 83-84; LitMarPl 83, 84*
Children's Classics on Tape - Springfield, VA - *AvMarPl 83*
Children's Defense Fund - Washington, DC - *BoPubDir 5*
Children's Digest [of Benjamin Franklin Society] - Indianapolis, IN - *ArtMar 84; MagDir 84; MagIndMarPl 82-83; WritMar 84*
Children's Gospel Hour Inc., The - Livingston, TN - *Tel&CabFB 84C*
Children's Health Care - Thorofare, NJ - *MagIndMarPl 82-83*
Children's House/Children's World - Caldwell, NJ - *LitMarPl 83, 84; MagIndMarPl 82-83*
Children's Learning Center Inc. - Indianapolis, IN - *BoPubDir 4, 5*
Childrens' Learning Society - Brooklyn, NY - *BillIntBG 83-84*
Children's Literature - Wendham Center, CT - *WritMar 84*
Children's Museum of Oak Ridge - Oak Ridge, TN - *BoPubDir 5*
Children's Musical Plays - *See* Popular Music Co.
Children's Playmate - Indianapolis, IN - *ArtMar 84; MagIndMarPl 82-83; WritMar 84*
Children's Press [Div. of Regensteiner Publishing Enterprises Inc.] - Chicago, IL - *DirMarMP 83; LitMarPl 83, 84; WritMar 84*
Children's Radio Theatre - Washington, DC - *WritMar 84*
Children's Television Workshop - New York, NY - *DirMarMP 83; TelAl 83, 84*
Children's World - *See* Children's House/Children's World
Childress Index - Childress, TX - *BaconPubCkNews 84; Ed&PubIntYB 82; NewsDir 84*
Childress Radio Group - Sylva, NC - *BrCabYB 84*
Child's World Inc. - Elgin, IL - *ArtMar 84; BoPubDir 4, 5*
Childwrite Inc. - La Crosse, WI - *BoPubDir 5*
Chilhowie Cablesystems [of American Cablesystems Corp.] - Chilhowie, VA - *Tel&CabFB 84C*
Chillicothe Bulletin - Chillicothe, IL - *Ed&PubIntYB 82; NewsDir 84*
Chillicothe Bulletin - *See* Tazewell Publishing Co.
Chillicothe Cable TV [of American TV & Communications Corp.] - Chillicothe, MO - *BrCabYB 84; Tel&CabFB 84C*
Chillicothe Cablevision [of Henry Cablevision] - Chillicothe, IL - *Tel&CabFB 84C*
Chillicothe Cablevision [of McDonald Group Inc.] - Chillicothe, OH - *BrCabYB 84; Tel&CabFB 84C*
Chillicothe Cablevision Inc. - Chillicothe Township, IL - *BrCabYB 84*
Chillicothe Constitution-Tribune - Chillicothe, MO - *BaconPubCkNews 84*
Chillicothe Gazette - Chillicothe, OH - *BaconPubCkNews 84; Ed&PubIntYB 82; NewsDir 84*
Chillicothe Telephone Co., The - Chillicothe, OH - *TelDir&BG 83-84*
Chillicothe Valley News - Chillicothe, TX - *BaconPubCkNews 84*
Chilliwack Cablenet [of Cablenet Ltd.] - Chilliwack, BC, Canada - *BrCabYB 84*
Chilliwack Progress, The - Chilliwack, BC, Canada - *Ed&PubIntYB 82*
Chilmark House - Washington, DC - *BoPubDir 4, 5*
Chilton Book Co. [Subs. of ABC Publishing] - Radnor, PA - *ArtMar 84; LitMarPl 83, 84; MagIndMarPl 82-83; WritMar 84*
Chilton County News - Clanton, AL - *Ed&PubIntYB 82*
Chilton Direct Marketing Co. [Subs. of ABC] - Radnor, PA - *DirMarMP 83*
Chilton Printing Co. - Philadelphia, PA - *MagIndMarPl 82-83*
Chilton Publications - Radnor, PA - *NewsBur 6*
Chilton Research Services [Subs. of American Broadcasting Co.] - Radnor, PA - *AdAge 5-17-84 p.33; IntDirMarRes 83*
Chilton Times Journal [of Vercauteren Publishing] - Chilton, WI - *BaconPubCkNews 84; Ed&PubIntYB 82; NewsDir 84*
Chilton's Energy Newsletter - Radnor, PA - *BaconPubCkMag 84*
CHIM-FM - Kelowna, BC, Canada - *BrCabYB 84*
CHIN - Toronto, ON, Canada - *BrCabYB 84; NatRadPubDir Summer 83, Spring 84*
Chin & Co. Inc., Ted - New York, NY - *AdAge 3-28-84; StaDirAdAg 2-84*
CHIN-FM - Toronto, ON, Canada - *BrCabYB 84; NatRadPubDir Summer 83, Spring 84*
China Book Club & Far East Book Society [Subs. of Eurasia Press Inc.] - New York, NY - *LitMarPl 83, 84*
China Books - San Francisco, CA - *WritMar 84*
China Books & Periodicals Inc. - San Francisco, CA - *BoPubDir 4, 5; LitMarPl 83, 84; MagIndMarPl 82-83*
China Building Information Center - Beijing, China - *EISS 7-83 Sup*
China Business Review [of National Council for US-China Trade] - Washington, DC - *BaconPubCkMag 84; MagDir 84*
China Glass & Tableware [of Ebel-Doctorow Publications Inc.] - Clifton, NJ - *BaconPubCkMag 84; MagDir 84; WritMar 84*

China Grove South Rowan Times - China Grove, NC - *BaconPubCkNews 84*
China Painter - Oklahoma City, OK - *MagIndMarPl 82-83*
China Post - New York, NY - *AyerDirPub 83; Ed&PubIntYB 82; NewsDir 84*
China Quarterly - London, England - *LitMag&SmPr 83-84*
China Telephone Co. - South China, ME - *TelDir&BG 83-84*
China Tribune - New York, NY - *Ed&PubIntYB 82*
Chinese Art Appraisers Association - San Francisco, CA - *BoPubDir 4, 5*
Chinese Canadian Bulletin - Vancouver, BC, Canada - *Ed&PubIntYB 82*
Chinese Culture Service Inc. - Oak Park, IL - *BoPubDir 4, 5*
Chinese Express - Toronto, ON, Canada - *Ed&PubIntYB 82*
Chinese Grocer, The - San Francisco, CA - *DirMarMP 83*
Chinese Literature - Beijing, China - *LitMag&SmPr 83-84*
Chinese Materials Center - San Francisco, CA - *MagIndMarPl 82-83*
Chinese Pacific Weekly - San Francisco, CA - *Ed&PubIntYB 82*
Chinese Times - San Francisco, CA - *AyerDirPub 83; Ed&PubIntYB 82; NewsDir 84*
Chinese Times - Vancouver, BC, Canada - *AyerDirPub 83; Ed&PubIntYB 82*
Chinese Voice, The - Vancouver, BC, Canada - *Ed&PubIntYB 82*
Chinese Wide Angle Weekly - Toronto, ON, Canada - *Ed&PubIntYB 82*
Chinkapin Press Inc. - Eugene, OR - *BoPubDir 4, 5*
Chinmaya Publications [Aff. of Chinmaya Mission] - Piercy, CA - *BoPubDir 4, 5*
Chino Champion - Chino, CA - *Ed&PubIntYB 82*
Chino Champion - *See* Champion Publications of Chino Inc.
Chino South Ontario News - *See* Champion Publications of Chino Inc.
Chino Valley News - Chino, CA - *AyerDirPub 83*
Chino Valley News - *See* Champion Publications of Chino Inc.
Chinook Observer - Long Beach, WA - *AyerDirPub 83; Ed&PubIntYB 82*
Chinook Opinion - Chinook, MT - *BaconPubCkNews 84; Ed&PubIntYB 82*
Chinook Progressive Club TV - Chinook, WA - *BrCabYB 84; Tel&CabFB 84C*
Chintronics Co. - Chelmsford, MA - *MicrocomMPl 84*
CHIP-FM - Ft. Coulonge, PQ, Canada - *BrCabYB 84*
Chipley Washington County News - Chipley, FL - *BaconPubCkNews 84*
Chipper/Shacker [of The Potato Chip/Snack Food Association] - Arlington, VA - *MagDir 84*
Chipper/Snacker - Alexandria, VA - *BaconPubCkMag 84*
Chippewa Communications Inc. - Lac du Flambeau, WI - *Tel&CabFB 84C*
Chippewa County Telephone Co. Inc. - Brimley, MI - *TelDir&BG 83-84*
Chippewa County Telephone Inc. [Aff. of Universal Telephone Inc.] - Hawkins, WI - *TelDir&BG 83-84*
Chippewa Falls Chippewa Herald-Telegram - Chippewa Falls, WI - *NewsDir 84*
Chippewa Herald-Telegram - Chippewa Falls, WI - *Ed&PubIntYB 82*
Chip's Bookshop Inc. - New York, NY - *BoPubDir 4, 5*
CHIQ-FM - Winnipeg, MB, Canada - *BrCabYB 84*
Chirich, Nancy - Sullivan's Island, SC - *BoPubDir 4, 5*
Chiron Corp. Ltd. - Ottawa, ON, Canada - *BoPubDir 5*
Chiron Corp. Ltd. (Publishing Div.) - Ottawa, ON, Canada - *BoPubDir 4*
Chiron Press Inc. - Concord, MA - *BoPubDir 4, 5*
Chisago County Press - Lindstrom, MN - *AyerDirPub 83*
Chisholm Associates Inc., J. - Wakefield, MA - *DirPRFirms 83; StaDirAdAg 2-84*
Chisholm Film Productions Ltd., Jack - Toronto, ON, Canada - *LitMarPl 83, 84*
Chisholm Free Press - *See* Chisholm Free Press Publishers
Chisholm Free Press & Tribune Press - Chisholm, MN - *NewsDir 84*
Chisholm Free Press Publishers - Chisholm, MN - *BaconPubCkNews 84*
Chisholm Tribune-Press - *See* Chisholm Free Press Publishers
Chislovsky/Fuhrman & Partners Ltd. - New York, NY - *StaDirAdAg 2-84*
Chism Communications - Reno, NV - *AvMarPl 83*
Chittenango Bridgeport Times - Chittenango, NY - *AyerDirPub 83; BaconPubCkNews 84; Ed&PubIntYB 82*
Chittick Egan Advertising - Wayne, PA - *DirMarMP 83; HBIndAd&MS 82-83*
CHLC - Hauterive, PQ, Canada - *BrCabYB 84*
CHLG-FM - Brisay, PQ, Canada - *BrCabYB 84*
CHLN - Trois-Rivieres, PQ, Canada - *BrCabYB 84*
CHLO - St. Thomas, ON, Canada - *BrCabYB 84*
CHLQ-FM - Charlottetown, PE, Canada - *BrCabYB 84*
CHLR - Moncton, NB, Canada - *BrCabYB 84*
CHLT - Sherbrooke, PQ, Canada - *BrCabYB 84; NatRadPubDir Summer 83 p.271, Spring 84 p.273*
CHLT-TV - Sherbrooke, PQ, Canada - *Tel&CabFB 84S*
CHLW - St. Paul, AB, Canada - *BrCabYB 84*
CHML - Hamilton, ON, Canada - *BrCabYB 84*
CHMM-FM - Winnipeg, MB, Canada - *BrCabYB 84*
CHMO - Moosonee, ON, Canada - *BrCabYB 84*
CHMP - Flint, MI - *InterCabHB 3*
CHNB-TV - North Bay, ON, Canada - *Tel&CabFB 84S*
CHNC - New Carlisle, PQ, Canada - *BrCabYB 84*
Chnito Productions - Norwich, VT - *BillIntBG 83-84*
CHNL - Clearwater, BC, Canada - *BrCabYB 84*
CHNL - Kamloops, BC, Canada - *BrCabYB 84*
CHNO - Sudbury, ON, Canada - *BrCabYB 84*
CHNR - Simcoe, ON, Canada - *BrCabYB 84*
CHNS - Halifax, NS, Canada - *BrCabYB 84*
CHOC-FM - Jonquiere, PQ, Canada - *BrCabYB 84*
Chocolate News - New York, NY - *BaconPubCkMag 84*
Choctaw Advocate - Butler, AL - *AyerDirPub 83; Ed&PubIntYB 82*
Choctaw County Music - *See* Blackwood Music, Ron
Choctaw/Nicoma Park Free Press - Choctaw, OK - *AyerDirPub 83; Ed&PubIntYB 82*
Choctaw Plaindealer - Ackerman, MS - *AyerDirPub 83; Ed&PubIntYB 82*
Choctaw Telephone Co. - Halltown, MO - *TelDir&BG 83-84*
CHOI-FM - Quebec City, PQ, Canada - *BrCabYB 84*
Choice [of American Library Association] - Middletown, CT - *BaconPubCkMag 84; MagDir 84; MagIndMarPl 82-83*
Choice Magazine Listening - Port Washington, NY - *MagIndMarPl 82-83*
Choice Publications Ltd. - Markham, ON, Canada - *BoPubDir 4, 5*
Choice Records - Sea Cliff, NY - *BillIntBG 83-84*
Choice Retail Systems Inc. - Marietta, GA - *DataDirSup 7-83*
CHOK - Sarnia, ON, Canada - *BrCabYB 84*
Choker Records Inc. - Battle Creek, MI - *BillIntBG 83-84*
Chokio Review - Chokio, MN - *BaconPubCkNews 84; Ed&PubIntYB 82*
CHOM-FM - Montreal, PQ, Canada - *BrCabYB 84*
CHOM-FM - Westmount, PQ, Canada - *NatRadPubDir Summer 83 p.271, Spring 84 p.273*
CHOO - Ajax, ON, Canada - *BrCabYB 84*
Choral Art Publications - *See* Fox Publishing Co. Inc., Sam
Choral Journal, The - Lawton, OK - *MagIndMarPl 82-83*
Choron Inc., Sandra - Teaneck, NJ - *LitMarPl 84*
CHOS-FM - Rattling Brook, NF, Canada - *BrCabYB 84*
Chosen Books [Div. of The Zondervan Corp.] - Lincoln, VA - *LitMarPl 83, 84; WritMar 84*
Choset, Charles - New York, NY - *LitMarPl 83, 84; MagIndMarPl 82-83*
CHOT-TV - Hull, PQ, Canada - *Tel&CabFB 84S*
Chotas, James - New York, NY - *LitMarPl 83, 84; MagIndMarPl 82-83*
Choteau Acantha - Choteau, MT - *BaconPubCkNews 84; Ed&PubIntYB 82*
Choteau Cable TV - Choteau, MT - *Tel&CabFB 84C*
Chou-Chou Press - Shoreham, NY - *BoPubDir 4 Sup, 5*
Chouinard, Guy - St. Pamphile, PQ, Canada - *BrCabYB 84*
Chouteau Review - Kansas City, MO - *LitMag&SmPr 83-84*
Chouteau Telephone Co. - Chouteau, OK - *TelDir&BG 83-84*
CHOW - Welland, ON, Canada - *BrCabYB 84*
Chowan Herald, The - Edenton, NC - *AyerDirPub 83; Ed&PubIntYB 82*

Chowchilla Cable TV [of SanVal Cablevision Inc.] - Chowchilla, CA - *BrCabYB 84; Tel&CabFB 84C*
Chowchilla News - Chowchilla, CA - *BaconPubCkNews 84; Ed&PubIntYB 82*
Chowder Chapbooks - Milton, MA - *LitMag&SmPr 83-84*
Chowder Chapbooks - Wallaston, MA - *BoPubDir 4, 5*
Chowder Review, The [of Chowder Chapbooks] - Milton, MA - *LitMag&SmPr 83-84*
CHOZ-FM - St. John's, NF, Canada - *BrCabYB 84*
CHPQ - Parksville, BC, Canada - *BrCabYB 84*
CHPR - Hawkesbury, ON, Canada - *BrCabYB 84*
CHQB - Powell River, BC, Canada - *BrCabYB 84*
CHQM - Vancouver, BC, Canada - *BrCabYB 84; NatRadPubDir Summer 83, Spring 84*
CHQM-FM - Vancouver, BC, Canada - *BrCabYB 84; NatRadPubDir Summer 83, Spring 84*
CHQR - Calgary, AB, Canada - *BrCabYB 84*
CHQT - Edmonton, AB, Canada - *BrCabYB 84*
CHRB - High River, AB, Canada - *BrCabYB 84*
CHRC - Quebec City, PQ, Canada - *BrCabYB 84*
CHRD - Drummondville, PQ, Canada - *BrCabYB 84*
CHRE-FM - St. Catharines, ON, Canada - *BrCabYB 84*
Chris-Craft Industries - New York, NY - *AdAge 6-28-84; BrCabYB 84; HomeVid&CabYB 82-83; KnowInd 83; Tel&CabFB 84S*
Chris Music Publishing - Manistique, MI - *BillIntBG 83-84*
Chrisman Leader - Chrisman, IL - *BaconPubCkNews 84; Ed&PubIntYB 82*
Chrismol - Poughkeepsie, NY - *BrCabYB 84*
Chrisp's Telephone Co. - Paxton, NE - *TelDir&BG 83-84*
Christ for the Nations - Dallas, TX - *BoPubDir 4, 5*
Christ Video Center, Don - Collingswood, NJ - *AvMarPl 83*
Christendom Publications [Aff. of Christendom Educational Corp.] - Front Royal, VA - *BoPubDir 4 Sup, 5*
Christensen Deman Overseas Ltd. - London, England - *StaDirAdAg 2-84*
Christensen Photography, R. Lans - Litchfield, CT - *MagIndMarPl 82-83*
Christenson, Barclay & Shaw Inc. - Kansas City, MO - *StaDirAdAg 2-84*
Christian Adventurer [of Messenger Publishing House] - Joplin, MO - *WritMar 84*
Christian Artists Corp. - Thousand Oaks, CA - *BillIntBG 83-84*
Christian Association for Psychological Studies - Farmington Hills, MI - *BoPubDir 5*
Christian Board of Publication - St. Louis, MO - *ArtMar 84; MagIndMarPl 82-83*
Christian Book Club of America - Hawthorne, CA - *BoPubDir 4, 5*
Christian Book Distributors - Compton, CA - *BoPubDir 4 Sup, 5*
Christian Books - Goleta, CA - *BoPubDir 4, 5*
Christian Bookseller & Librarian [of Christian Life Missions] - Wheaton, IL - *BaconPubCkMag 84; LitMarPl 83, 84; MagDir 84; MagIndMarPl 82-83; WritMar 84*
Christian Bookshelf, The - Chappaqua, NY - *LitMarPl 83, 84*
Christian Broadcasting Association - Honolulu, HI - *BrCabYB 84*
Christian Broadcasting Network - Virginia Beach, VA - *BrCabYB 84; HomeVid&CabYB 82-83; TelAl 83; WritMar 84*
Christian Broadcasting Network - *See* CBN Continental Network Inc.
Christian Century [of The Christian Century Foundation] - Chicago, IL - *ArtMar 84; BaconPubCkMag 84; LitMarPl 83, 84; MagDir 84; MagIndMarPl 82-83; WritMar 84*
Christian Church/Disciples of Christ - Indianapolis, IN - *AvMarPl 83*
Christian Cinema Inc. - Ambler, PA - *AvMarPl 83*
Christian Classics - Westminster, MD - *LitMarPl 83, 84; WritMar 84*
Christian Herald - Chappaqua, NY - *ArtMar 84; BaconPubCkMag 84; LitMarPl 83, 84; MagDir 84; MagIndMarPl 82-83; WritMar 84*
Christian Herald Association - Chappaqua, NY - *DirMarMP 83*
Christian Herald Family Bookshelf [of Christian Herald Association] - Chappaqua, NY - *LitMarPl 83, 84*
Christian Home & School - Grand Rapids, MI - *MagIndMarPl 82-83*
Christian Home, The - Nashville, TN - *WritMar 84*
Christian Inquirer - Niagara Falls, NY - *MagIndMarPl 82-83*
Christian Institutions Research & Documentation Center - Strasbourg Cedex, France - *EISS 83*
Christian International [Aff. of Christian International University] - Phoenix, AZ - *BoPubDir 4 Sup, 5*
Christian Life Magazine - Wheaton, IL - *BaconPubCkMag 84; MagDir 84; MagIndMarPl 82-83; WritMar 84*
Christian Light Publications Inc. - Harrisonburg, VA - *BoPubDir 4, 5*
Christian Literature Crusade - Elgin, ON, Canada - *BoPubDir 4 Sup, 5*
Christian Living for Senior Highs [of David C. Cook Publishing Co.] - Elgin, IL - *WritMar 84*
Christian Ministry - Chicago, IL - *ArtMar 84; BaconPubCkMag 84; MagDir 84; MagIndMarPl 82-83; WritMar 84*
Christian Press [Aff. of Canadian Conference of Mennonite Brethren Churches] - Winnipeg, MB, Canada - *BoPubDir 4*
Christian Productions Inc. - Madison, TN - *StaDirAdAg 2-84*
Christian Quality Paperback Book Club [Subs. of ABC Publishing Inc.] - Waco, TX - *LitMarPl 83*
Christian Reader - Wheaton, IL - *BaconPubCkMag 84*
Christian Record Braille Foundation - Lincoln, NE - *LitMarPl 83, 84*
Christian Reformed Church (Board of Publications) - Grand Rapids, MI - *BoPubDir 4, 5*
Christian Resource Communications Inc. - Orange, CA - *BoPubDir 4, 5*
Christian Review - Atlanta, GA - *BaconPubCkMag 84*
Christian Schools International - Grand Rapids, MI - *LitMarPl 84*
Christian Schools International - Lincoln, NE - *LitMarPl 83*
Christian Science Monitor - Boston, MA - *AyerDirPub 83; BaconPubCkNews 84; Ed&PubIntYB 82; LitMarPl 83, 84; MagDir 84; NewsBur 6; NewsDir 84; WritMar 84*
Christian Science Monitor (Radio News Service) - Boston, MA - *BrCabYB 84*
Christian Science Monitor News & Photo Service - *See* Register & Tribune Syndicate
Christian Science Publishing Society - Boston, MA - *DirMarMP 83; KnowInd 83; LitMarPl 83, 84*
Christian Single [of Baptist Sunday School Board] - Nashville, TN - *WritMar 84*
Christian Success Publishing House - Irrigon, OR - *BoPubDir 4*
Christian Success Publishing House - Yakima, WA - *BoPubDir 5*
Christian World Inc. - Oklahoma City, OK - *BillIntBG 83-84*
Christian Writer, The - Lakeland, FL - *WritMar 84*
Christianica Center - Chicago, IL - *BoPubDir 4, 5*
Christianity & Crisis - New York, NY - *MagIndMarPl 82-83; WritMar 84*
Christianity Today - Carol Stream, IL - *BaconPubCkMag 84; DirMarMP 83; MagIndMarPl 82-83; WritMar 84*
Christianity Today - Wheaton, IL - *MagDir 84*
Christiansburg Blacksburg News Messenger, The [of Worrell Newspapers Inc.] - Christiansburg, VA - *NewsDir 84*
Christiansen & Associates Inc. - Murfreesboro, TN - *StaDirAdAg 2-84*
Christo Inc., Van - Boston, MA - *StaDirAdAg 2-84*
Christopher Group, The - Short Hills, NJ - *DirPRFirms 83*
Christopher Music - *See* Tessalou Music
Christopher Progress - Christopher, IL - *BaconPubCkNews 84*
Christopher Publishing House - West Hanover, MA - *BoPubDir 4, 5; LitMarPl 84*
Christopher Street - New York, NY - *MagIndMarPl 82-83*
Christopher Systems Corp. - Los Angeles, CA - *MicrocomSwDir 1*
Christopher Thomas Associates - Northport, NY - *AdAge 3-28-84; StaDirAdAg 2-84*
Christopher's Books - Oakland, CA - *BoPubDir 4, 5; LitMag&SmPr 83-84*
Christophers Inc., The - New York, NY - *Tel&CabFB 84C*
Christ's Mission - Hackensack, NJ - *BoPubDir 4, 5*
Christward Ministry - Escondido, CA - *BoPubDir 4, 5*
Chriswald Music Inc. - *See* De Walden Music
CHRL - Roberval, PQ, Canada - *BrCabYB 84*
CHRM - Matane, PQ, Canada - *BrCabYB 84*
CHRO - Pembroke, ON, Canada - *BrCabYB 84*
CHRO-TV - Ottawa, ON, Canada - *Tel&CabFB 84S*

CHRO-TV - Pembroke, ON, Canada - *Tel&CabFB 84S*
Chroma TV Center - Mill Run, PA - *BrCabYB 84*
Chroma TV Center [of Laurel Highlands TV Co.] - Normalville, PA - *BrCabYB 84; Tel&CabFB 84C*
Chromasette Magazine [of Cload Publications Inc.] - Santa Barbara, CA - *MicrocomMPl 84*
Chromatics Inc. - Tucker, GA - *DataDirSup 7-83; WhoWMicrocom 83*
Chromatics Ltd. - Chicago, IL - *AvMarPl 83*
Chrome Forecast - Bala Cynwyd, PA - *DirOnDB Spring 84*
Chrome Yellow Private Press - Crescent City, FL - *BoPubDir 5*
Chrome Yellow Private Press - Gainesville, FL - *BoPubDir 4*
Chronicle - Atkins, AR - *AyerDirPub 83*
Chronicle - Altadena, CA - *Ed&PubIntYB 82*
Chronicle - Calexico, CA - *AyerDirPub 83*
Chronicle - Canoga Park, CA - *AyerDirPub 83*
Chronicle - Livingston, CA - *AyerDirPub 83; Ed&PubIntYB 82*
Chronicle - San Francisco, CA - *AyerDirPub 83; Ed&PubIntYB 82; LitMarPl 84*
Chronicle - Santa Paula, CA - *AyerDirPub 83*
Chronicle - Crested Butte, CO - *AyerDirPub 83; Ed&PubIntYB 82*
Chronicle - Willimantic, CT - *AyerDirPub 83; Ed&PubIntYB 82*
Chronicle - Milford, DE - *AyerDirPub 83; Ed&PubIntYB 82*
Chronicle - Ft. Pierce, FL - *Ed&PubIntYB 82*
Chronicle - Augusta, GA - *AyerDirPub 83; Ed&PubIntYB 82; LitMarPl 84*
Chronicle - Cottonwood, ID - *AyerDirPub 83*
Chronicle - Cambridge, IL - *AyerDirPub 83*
Chronicle - Colchester, IL - *AyerDirPub 83*
Chronicle - De Kalb, IL - *AyerDirPub 83*
Chronicle - Gardner, IL - *AyerDirPub 83*
Chronicle - Scottsburg, IN - *AyerDirPub 83*
Chronicle - Lamoni, IA - *AyerDirPub 83*
Chronicle - Pella, IA - *AyerDirPub 83*
Chronicle - Caney, KS - *AyerDirPub 83*
Chronicle - Colfax, LA - *AyerDirPub 83*
Chronicle - Cambridge, MA - *AyerDirPub 83*
Chronicle - Cass City, MI - *AyerDirPub 83*
Chronicle - Marshall, MI - *AyerDirPub 83*
Chronicle - Muskegon, MI - *AyerDirPub 83*
Chronicle - St. Clair, MO - *AyerDirPub 83*
Chronicle - Bozeman, MT - *AyerDirPub 83*
Chronicle - Carson City, NV - *AyerDirPub 83*
Chronicle - Bound Brook, NJ - *AyerDirPub 83*
Chronicle - Winston-Salem, NC - *AyerDirPub 83; Ed&PubIntYB 82*
Chronicle - Cavalier, ND - *AyerDirPub 83*
Chronicle - La Moure, ND - *AyerDirPub 83*
Chronicle - Uhrichsville, OH - *AyerDirPub 83*
Chronicle - Vandalia, OH - *AyerDirPub 83*
Chronicle - Creswell, OR - *AyerDirPub 83; Ed&PubIntYB 82*
Chronicle - The Dalles, OR - *AyerDirPub 83*
Chronicle - Charleston, SC - *AyerDirPub 83*
Chronicle - Cheraw, SC - *AyerDirPub 83*
Chronicle - Clinton, SC - *AyerDirPub 83*
Chronicle - Honea Path, SC - *AyerDirPub 83*
Chronicle - Armour, SD - *AyerDirPub 83*
Chronicle - Camden, TN - *AyerDirPub 83*
Chronicle - Crossville, TN - *AyerDirPub 83*
Chronicle - Cedar Hill, TX - *AyerDirPub 83*
Chronicle - Houston, TX - *AyerDirPub 83*
Chronicle - Teague, TX - *AyerDirPub 83*
Chronicle - Wills Point, TX - *AyerDirPub 83*
Chronicle - Windsor, VT - *AyerDirPub 83*
Chronicle - Centralia, WA - *AyerDirPub 83*
Chronicle - Elma, WA - *AyerDirPub 83*
Chronicle - Dodgeville, WI - *AyerDirPub 83*
Chronicle - Weyauwega, WI - *AyerDirPub 83*
Chronicle - Lovell, WY - *AyerDirPub 83*
Chronicle - Oliver, BC, Canada - *AyerDirPub 83*
Chronicle - Dunnville, ON, Canada - *AyerDirPub 83*
Chronicle - Durham, ON, Canada - *AyerDirPub 83*
Chronicle - Shellbrook, SK, Canada - *AyerDirPub 83*
Chronicle Ad-Viser - Penn Yan, NY - *AyerDirPub 83*
Chronicle & News Sentinel - Stoughton, MA - *AyerDirPub 83*
Chronicle & Sentinel-Mist, The - St. Helens, OR - *Ed&PubIntYB 82*
Chronicle Books [Div. of Chronicle Publishing Co.] - San Francisco, CA - *ArtMar 84; LitMag&SmPr 83-84; LitMarPl 83, 84; WritMar 84*
Chronicle Broadcasting Co. - San Francisco, CA - *BrCabYB 84; Tel&CabFB 84S*
Chronicle-Citizen - Brookline, MA - *AyerDirPub 83*
Chronicle-Express [of Seneca Media Inc.] - Penn Yan, NY - *AyerDirPub 83; NewsDir 84*
Chronicle Features - San Francisco, CA - *BaconPubCkNews 84; Ed&PubIntYB 82; LitMarPl 83, 84; MagIndMarPl 82-83*
Chronicle Guidance Publications Inc. - Moravia, NY - *LitMarPl 83, 84*
Chronicle Hathaway Publishing Co., The - South Dartmouth, MA - *NewsDir 84*
Chronicle-Headlight-Enquirer - Cullom, IL - *AyerDirPub 83*
Chronicle-Herald - Augusta, GA - *AyerDirPub 83; Ed&PubIntYB 82; LitMarPl 84*
Chronicle-Herald - Macon, MO - *AyerDirPub 83*
Chronicle-Herald, The - Halifax, NS, Canada - *AyerDirPub 83; BaconPubCkNews 84; Ed&PubIntYB 82*
Chronicle-Independent [of Camden Media Co.] - Camden, SC - *AyerDirPub 83; Ed&PubIntYB 82; NewsDir 84*
Chronicle-Journal - Floresville, TX - *AyerDirPub 83*
Chronicle-Journal - Thunder Bay, ON, Canada - *AyerDirPub 83; Ed&PubIntYB 82*
Chronicle-News - Trinidad, CO - *AyerDirPub 83; Ed&PubIntYB 82*
Chronicle of Higher Education - Washington, DC - *ArtMar 84; BaconPubCkMag 84; Folio 83; InfoS 83-84; LitMarPl 83, 84; MagDir 84; MagIndMarPl 82-83*
Chronicle of the Horse - Middleburg, VA - *BaconPubCkMag 84; MagDir 84*
Chronicle Productions - San Francisco, CA - *AvMarPl 83*
Chronicle Publishing Co. - San Francisco, CA - *AdAge 6-28-84; Ed&PubIntYB 82; KnowInd 83*
Chronicle Publishing Co. - St. Charles, IL - *BaconPubCkNews 84*
Chronicle Publishing Co. - *See* Chronicle Broadcasting Co.
Chronicle-Telegram - Elyria, OH - *AyerDirPub 83; Ed&PubIntYB 82*
Chronicle Telegraph - Quebec City, PQ, Canada - *AyerDirPub 83; Ed&PubIntYB 82*
Chronicle, The - Hoopeston, IL - *AyerDirPub 83*
Chronicle, The - Dartmouth, MA - *Ed&PubIntYB 82*
Chronicle, The - South Dartmouth, MA - *AyerDirPub 83*
Chronicle, The - Cranford, NJ - *AyerDirPub 83*
Chronicle, The - Barton, VT - *AyerDirPub 83*
Chronicle, The - Arnprior, ON, Canada - *AyerDirPub 83*
Chronicle-Tribune - Marion, IN - *AyerDirPub 83; Ed&PubIntYB 82*
Chronicler [of Cincinnati AFL-CIO Labor Council] - Cincinnati, OH - *NewsDir 84*
Chrono-Log Corp. - Havertown, PA - *DataDirSup 7-83*
Chronolog Newsletter [of DIALOG Information Services Inc.] - Palo Alto, CA - *DataDirOnSer 84; DBBus 82; DirOnDB Spring 84*
Chronotype - Rice Lake, WI - *AyerDirPub 83*
CHRS - Longueuil, PQ, Canada - *BrCabYB 84*
CHRT - St. Eleuthere, PQ, Canada - *BrCabYB 84*
Chrysalis Music Group - New York, NY - *BillIntBG 83-84*
Chrysalis Publishing Ltd. - Phoenix, AZ - *BoPubDir 4 Sup, 5*
Chrysalis Records - Los Angeles, CA - *BillIntBG 83-84*
Chrysalis Records - New York, NY - *BillIntBG 83-84*
Chrysostom Corp., The - Casper, WY - *BrCabYB 84*
Chrystal Direct Marketing Group Inc., The - Arlington Heights, IL - *DirMarMP 83; StaDirAdAg 2-84*
CHSC - St. Catharines, ON, Canada - *BrCabYB 84*
CHSH-TV - Sherbrooke, PQ, Canada - *Tel&CabFB 84S*
CHSJ - St. John, NB, Canada - *BrCabYB 84*
CHSJ-TV - St. John, NB, Canada - *Tel&CabFB 84S*
CHSK-FM - Saskatoon, SK, Canada - *BrCabYB 84*
CHSM - Steinbach, MB, Canada - *BrCabYB 84*
Chthon Press - Westford, MA - *LitMag&SmPr 83-84*
CHTK - Prince Rupert, BC, Canada - *BrCabYB 84*
CHTM - Thompson, MB, Canada - *BrCabYB 84*
CHTN - Charlottetown, PE, Canada - *BrCabYB 84*
CHUB - Nanaimo, BC, Canada - *BrCabYB 84*
Chubb & Son Inc. - Summit, NJ - *ADAPSOMemDir 83-84*

CHUC - Cobourg, ON, Canada - *BrCabYB 84*
Chud, Harry S. - Ft. Worth, TX - *MicrocomSwDir 1*
Chugiak-Eagle River Star - Eagle River, AK - *AyerDirPub 83*
Chugiak-Eagle River Star, The - Chugiak, AK - *Ed&PubIntYB 82*
Chugwater Telephone Co. - Chugwater, WY - *TelDir&BG 83-84*
Chula Vista North East Pennysaver - Mission Viejo, CA - *AyerDirPub 83*
Chula Vista North West Pennysaver - Mission Viejo, CA - *AyerDirPub 83*
Chula Vista South East Pennysaver - Mission Viejo, CA - *AyerDirPub 83*
Chula Vista South West Pennysaver - Mission Viejo, CA - *AyerDirPub 83*
Chula Vista Star-News - Chula Vista, CA - *Ed&PubIntYB 82*
Chula Vista Star-News - *See* Star-News Publishing Co. Inc.
CHUM - Toronto, ON, Canada - *BrCabYB 84*
CHUM-FM - Toronto, ON, Canada - *BrCabYB 84; NatRadPubDir Summer 83, Spring 84*
Chuo Senko Advertising Co. Ltd. - Tokyo, Japan - *StaDirAdAg 2-84*
CHUR - North Bay, ON, Canada - *BrCabYB 84*
Church Administration - Nashville, TN - *WritMar 84*
Church & Society - *See* Churchnews International
Church & State [of Americans United for Separation of Church & State] - Silver Spring, MD - *WritMar 84*
Church & Synagogue Library Association - Bryn Mawr, PA - *BoPubDir 4, 5*
Church Federation of Greater Indianapolis - Indianapolis, IN - *Tel&CabFB 84C*
Church Growth Book Club [Div. of The William Carey Library] - Pasadena, CA - *LitMarPl 83*
Church Herald, The - Grand Rapids, MI - *BaconPubCkMag 84; MagDir 84; MagIndMarPl 82-83; WritMar 84*
Church History Research & Archives - Gallatin, TN - *BoPubDir 4, 5*
Church League of America - Wheaton, IL - *BoPubDir 4, 5*
Church Management, The Clergy Journal - Austin, TX - *ArtMar 84; BaconPubCkMag 84; MagDir 84; MagIndMarPl 82-83; WritMar 84*
Church Musician, The - Nashville, TN - *WritMar 84*
Church of Jesus Christ of Latter Day Saints (Historical Dept.) - Salt Lake City, UT - *CompReadDB 82; MicroMarPl 82-83*
Church of Light Inc. - Los Angeles, CA - *BoPubDir 4, 5*
Church Point Cable TV Inc. [of Wometco Cable TV Inc.] - Church Point, LA - *BrCabYB 84; Tel&CabFB 84C*
Church Point News - Church Point, LA - *AyerDirPub 83*
Church Programs for Primaries - Springfield, MO - *WritMar 84*
Church Training - Nashville, TN - *WritMar 84*
Church World Service - New York, NY - *Tel&CabFB 84C*
Church World Service/Crop - Elkhart, IN - *Tel&CabFB 84C*
Churchill County Telephone & Telegraph System - Fallon, NV - *TelDir&BG 83-84*
Churchill Films - Los Angeles, CA - *AvMarPl 83*
Churchill/IPR Houston - Houston, TX - *DirPRFirms 83*
Churchill Livingstone Inc. [Subs. of Longman Holdings Inc.] - New York, NY - *LitMarPl 83, 84*
Churchilliana Co. - Sacramento, CA - *BoPubDir 4, 5*
Churchman - St. Petersburg, FL - *ArtMar 84; BaconPubCkMag 84; MagDir 84; MagIndMarPl 82-83*
ChurchNews International - Windsor, CA - *DirOnDB Spring 84*
ChurchNews International [of NewsNet Inc.] - Bryn Mawr, PA - *DataDirOnSer 84*
Churubusco Tri-County Truth - *See* Tri-County Publishing Inc.
Chusid Associates Inc., Leon - New York, NY - *ADAPSOMemDir 83-84*
Chutzpah - Chicago, IL - *BoPubDir 4, 5*
CHVD - Dolbeau, PQ, Canada - *BrCabYB 84*
CHVO - Carbonear, NF, Canada - *BrCabYB 84*
CHWK - Chilliwack, BC, Canada - *BrCabYB 84*
CHWO - Oakville, ON, Canada - *BrCabYB 84*
CHYM [Aff. of Maclean Hunter Ltd.] - Kitchener, ON, Canada - *BoPubDir 4, 5; BrCabYB 84*
CHYQ - Muskgravetown, NF, Canada - *BrCabYB 84*
CHYR - Leamington, ON, Canada - *BrCabYB 84*
Ciani/Musica Inc. - New York, NY - *AvMarPl 83; Tel&CabFB 84C*
Ciano Publishing Co. - Hasbrouck Heights, NJ - *BillIntBG 83-84*
Cibar Inc. - Colorado Springs, CO - *MicrocomSwDir 1*
Cibbarelli & Associates - Huntington Beach, CA - *EISS 83; FBInfSer 80; InfIndMarPl 83*
CIBC-FM - Prince George, BC, Canada - *BrCabYB 84*
CIBDOC [of International Council for Building Research Studies & Documentation] - Stuttgart, West Germany - *EISS 83*
CIBL-FM - Montreal, PQ, Canada - *BrCabYB 84*
Cibley, Phil - New York, NY - *AvMarPl 83*
Cibola Press - Palo Alto, CA - *BoPubDir 4, 5*
CIBQ - Brooks, AB, Canada - *BrCabYB 84*
C.I.C. Cable Inc. - Hardin, MT - *BrCabYB 84*
CIC Cable TV [of Cable Installation & Construction Inc.] - Plains, TX - *BrCabYB 84*
C.I.C. Ltd. - Purley, England - *MicrocomSwDir 1*
CIC Research Inc. - San Diego, CA - *IntDirMarRes 83*
CICA-TV - Toronto, ON, Canada - *Tel&CabFB 84S*
CICC-TV - Yorkton, SK, Canada - *Tel&CabFB 84S*
Cicco Productions Inc. - New York, NY - *BillIntBG 83-84*
Ciccolini Films Inc. - San Francisco, CA - *Tel&CabFB 84C*
Cicero-Berwyn-Stickney Forest View Life - Berwyn, IL - *Ed&PubIntYB 82*
Cicero Life [of Life Printing & Publishing Co.] - Berwyn, IL - *NewsDir 84*
Cicero Life - *See* Life Printing & Publishing Co.
CICI-TV - Sudbury, ON, Canada - *Tel&CabFB 84S*
CIDAT - *See* Centre d'Informatique Appliquee au Developpement & l'Agriculture Tropicale
Cider Mill Press - Stratford, CT - *BoPubDir 4, 5*
Cider Press - Grand Rapids, MI - *BoPubDir 4, 5*
Cie Cablevision de Hawkesbury - Hawkesbury, ON, Canada - *BrCabYB 84*
CIE Systems [Subs. of C. Itoh Electronics] - Irvine, CA - *MicrocomMPl 83; WhoWMicrocom 83*
CIEL-FM - Longqeuil, PQ, Canada - *BrCabYB 84*
Cienfuegos Press - Minneapolis, MN - *BoPubDir 4, 5*
Cienfuegos Press - Orkney, Scotland - *LitMag&SmPr 83-84*
Cifi Publishing Co. - Cincinnati, OH - *BillIntBG 83-84*
CIGB-FM - Trois Rivieres, PQ, Canada - *BrCabYB 84*
CIGL-FM - Belleville, ON, Canada - *BrCabYB 84*
CIGM-FM - Sudbury, ON, Canada - *BrCabYB 84*
CIGO - Port Hawkesbury, NS, Canada - *BrCabYB 84*
CIGV-FM - Penticton, BC, Canada - *BrCabYB 84*
CIHI - Fredericton, NB, Canada - *BrCabYB 84*
CILA-FM - Lethbridge, AB, Canada - *BrCabYB 84*
CILQ-FM - Toronto, ON, Canada - *BrCabYB 84*
CILW - Grande Centre, AB, Canada - *BrCabYB 84*
CIM [of Questel Inc.] - Washington, DC - *DataDirOnSer 84*
CIM Construction Journal - Boston, MA - *MagDir 84*
Cim Tel Cable Inc. - Mannford, OK - *BrCabYB 84 p.D-299; Tel&CabFB 84C p.1672*
Cim Tel Cable Inc. - Pawnee, OK - *BrCabYB 84*
Cimarron Corp. [Subs. of Standun Control Inc.] - Costa Mesa, CA - *MicrocomMPl 84; MicrocomSwDir 1; WhoWMicrocom 83*
Cimarron Jacksonian - Cimarron, KS - *BaconPubCkNews 84; Ed&PubIntYB 82*
Cimarron Review - Stillwater, OK - *LitMag&SmPr 83-84*
Cimarron Telephone Co. - Mannford, OK - *TelDir&BG 83-84*
CIME-FM - Ste. Adele, PQ, Canada - *BrCabYB 84*
CIMF-FM - Hull, PQ, Canada - *BrCabYB 84*
CIMH-FM - Sept-Iles, PQ, Canada - *BrCabYB 84*
CIMO-FM - Magog, PQ, Canada - *BrCabYB 84*
CIMT-TV - Riviere du Loup, PQ, Canada - *Tel&CabFB 84S*
Cin-Pep Music Publishing Co. [Div. of Cameo Inc.] - New York, NY - *BillIntBG 83-84*
Cin Publications - San Francisco, CA - *BoPubDir 4, 5; LitMag&SmPr 83-84*
Cinaco Film & TV Co. Inc. - Los Angeles, CA - *Tel&CabFB 84C*
Cinahl Corp. - Glendale, CA - *BoPubDir 5*
Cinamon Associates Inc. - Brookline, MA - *DirMarMP 83; LitMarPl 83, 84; MagIndMarPl 82-83; StaDirAdAg 2-84*
Cinarco-Elliott Audio Visual & Computer Center - Davenport, IA - *AvMarPl 83*
Cincinnati Bell Inc. - Cincinnati, OH - *TelDir&BG 83-84*
Cincinnati Business Journal - Worthington, OH - *BaconPubCkMag 84*
Cincinnati Call & Post - Cincinnati, OH - *BaconPubCkNews 84*

Cincinnati Catholic Telegraph - Cincinnati, OH - *NewsDir 84*
Cincinnati Chess Federation - Cincinnati, OH - *LitMag&SmPr 83-84*
Cincinnati Clermont Community Journal - Cincinnati, OH - *BaconPubCkNews 84*
Cincinnati Clermont County Review - Cincinnati, OH - *BaconPubCkNews 84*
Cincinnati Clermont Courier - Cincinnati, OH - *BaconPubCkNews 84*
Cincinnati Eastern Hills Journal - Cincinnati, OH - *Ed&PubIntYB 82*
Cincinnati Enquirer [of Gannett Co. Inc.] - Cincinnati, OH - *BaconPubCkNews 84; Ed&PubIntYB 82; LitMarPl 83, 84; NewsBur 6; NewsDir 84*
Cincinnati Enquirer - Columbus, OH - *NewsBur 6*
Cincinnati Enquirer Sunday Magazine - Cincinnati, OH - *ArtMar 84*
Cincinnati Forest Hills Journal - *See* Queen City Suburban Press Inc.
Cincinnati Herald - Cincinnati, OH - *BaconPubCkNews 84; Ed&PubIntYB 82*
Cincinnati Information & Referral Center [of Community Chest & Council of the Cincinnati Area] - Cincinnati, OH - *EISS 83*
Cincinnati Kurier - Cincinnati, OH - *AyerDirPub 83; Ed&PubIntYB 82*
Cincinnati Magazine - Cincinnati, OH - *ArtMar 84; BaconPubCkMag 84; MagDir 84; WritMar 84*
Cincinnati Medicine - Cincinnati, OH - *BaconPubCkMag 84; MagDir 84*
Cincinnati Mt. Washington Press - Cincinnati, OH - *BaconPubCkNews 84*
Cincinnati Music Co. - Cincinnati, OH - *BillIntBG 83-84*
Cincinnati North Echo - Hamilton, OH - *AyerDirPub 83*
Cincinnati Northeast Suburban Life - Cincinnati, OH - *Ed&PubIntYB 82*
Cincinnati Northern Hills Press/Northwest Press - Cincinnati, OH - *Ed&PubIntYB 82*
Cincinnati Norwood Enterprise - Cincinnati, OH - *Ed&PubIntYB 82*
Cincinnati Poetry Review - Cincinnati, OH - *LitMag&SmPr 83-84*
Cincinnati Post [of The E. W. Scripps Co.] - Cincinnati, OH - *BaconPubCkNews 84; Ed&PubIntYB 82; NewsBur 6; NewsDir 84*
Cincinnati Purchasor - Cincinnati, OH - *MagDir 84*
Cincinnati Purchasor - Miamisburg, OH - *BaconPubCkMag 84*
Cincinnati Subscription TV - Cincinnati, OH - *TelAl 83*
Cincinnati Suburban Press - Sharonville, OH - *BaconPubCkNews 84*
Cincinnati Valley Courier - Cincinnati, OH - *BaconPubCkNews 84*
Cincom Systems Inc. - Cincinnati, OH - *ADAPSOMemDir 83-84; DataDirSup 7-83*
Cine Craft Films Inc. - Portland, OR - *AvMarPl 83*
Cine Craft Laboratories [Subs. of Western Cine] - Orlando, FL - *AvMarPl 83*
Cine Design Films - Denver, CO - *AvMarPl 83; WritMar 84*
Cine/Grafic Publications - Hollywood, CA - *BoPubDir 4, 5*
Cine Information - New York, NY - *BoPubDir 4 Sup, 5; EISS 83*
Cine Magnetics Film & Video Laboratories [Div. of Cine Magnetics Inc.] - Mamaroneck, NY - *AvMarPl 83; Tel&CabFB 84C*
Cine-Mark [Div. of Krebs Productions Inc.] - Chicago, IL - *AvMarPl 83*
Cine-Pic Hawaii - Honolulu, HI - *ArtMar 84; AvMarPl 83*
Cine Rent West/Stage A [Subs. of Snazelle Film Tape Inc.] - San Francisco, CA - *AvMarPl 83*
Cine Service Laboratories Inc. - Watertown, MA - *AvMarPl 83*
Cine 60 Inc. - New York, NY - *AvMarPl 83*
Cine-Sonics Sound Transfers - Lincoln Center, MA - *AvMarPl 83*
Cine-Tele Productions - Palm Desert, CA - *Tel&CabFB 84C*
Cineamerica Pay TV Services - Beverly Hills, CA - *TelAl 83*
Cineaste Magazine - New York, NY - *LitMag&SmPr 83-84; MagIndMarPl 82-83; WritMar 84*
Cinecare International - Santa Monica, CA - *AvMarPl 83*
Cinecraft Inc. - Cleveland, OH - *TelAl 83, 84; Tel&CabFB 84C*
Cinefan [of Fandom Unltd. Enterprises] - Sunnyvale, CA - *LitMag&SmPr 83-84*
Cinefantastique - Oak Park, IL - *ArtMar 84*
Cineffects Color Laboratory - New York, NY - *Tel&CabFB 84C*
Cineffects Visuals Inc. - New York, NY - *AvMarPl 83; Tel&CabFB 84C*
Cinefilm Laboratory - Atlanta, GA - *AvMarPl 83*
Cinegraph Slides - Garden Grove, CA - *AvMarPl 83*
Cinema Arts Associates Inc. - New York, NY - *AvMarPl 83*
Cinema Associates - Seattle, WA - *AvMarPl 83*
Cinema Book Society - Hollywood, CA - *LitMarPl 83*
Cinema Canada - Montreal, PQ, Canada - *BaconPubCkMag 84*
Cinema Concept Inc. - Newington, CT - *AvMarPl 83*
Cinema East - Miami, FL - *AvMarPl 83*
Cinema Processors Inc. - Chicago, IL - *AvMarPl 83*
Cinema Products Corp. - Los Angeles, CA - *AvMarPl 83*
Cinema Research Group [Subs. of Kaleidoscope Film Ltd.] - Hollywood, CA - *AvMarPl 83*
Cinema Shares International Television - New York, NY - *TelAl 83, 84; Tel&CabFB 84C*
Cinema Sound Ltd. - New York, NY - *AvMarPl 83*
Cinemagic - New York, NY - *BaconPubCkMag 84*
Cinemakers Inc. - New York, NY - *ArtMar 84; AvMarPl 83; ProGuPRSer 4*
Cineman Movie Reviews - Middleton, NY - *DirOnDB Spring 84*
Cineman Syndicate - Middletown, NY - *DataDirOnSer 84; Ed&PubIntYB 82; LitMarPl 84*
Cinemascore [of Fandom Unltd. Enterprises] - Sunnyvale, CA - *LitMag&SmPr 83-84*
Cinematheque TV Systems - Port Washington, NY - *TelAl 84*
Cinematronics - Ft. Lauderdale, FL - *AvMarPl 83*
Cinemax [of Time Inc.] - New York, NY - *AvMarPl 83; BrCabYB 84; CabTVPrDB 83; HomeVid&CabYB 82-83; TelAl 83; Tel&CabFB 84C*
Cineque Colorfilm Laboratories Inc. - New York, NY - *Tel&CabFB 84C*
Cinetronics - Canoga Park, CA - *AvMarPl 83*
Cinetudes - New York, NY - *WritMar 84*
Cinetudes Film Productions Ltd. - New York, NY - *ArtMar 84; AvMarPl 83; TelAl 83, 84; Tel&CabFB 84C*
Cinevision Corp. - Atlanta, GA - *AvMarPl 83*
Cineworld Corp. - Miami, FL - *TelAl 84*
CING-FM - Burlington, ON, Canada - *BrCabYB 84*
CINL - Princeton, BC, Canada - *BrCabYB 84*
Cinnaminson Journal - *See* Suburban Newspapers
Cinnamon Reggae - *See* Jo-Wee Publishing
Cinopticals Inc. - New York, NY - *Tel&CabFB 84C*
CINQ-FM - Montreal, PQ, Canada - *BrCabYB 84*
CIOI-FM - Prince George, BC, Canada - *BrCabYB 84*
CIOS-FM - Stephenville, NF, Canada - *BrCabYB 84*
CIOZ-FM - Marystown, NF, Canada - *BrCabYB 84*
CIPC - Port-Cartier, PQ, Canada - *BrCabYB 84*
Cipher Data Products Inc. - San Diego, CA - *DataDirSup 7-83; MicrocomMPl 84; Top100Al 83; WhoWMicrocom 83*
Cirascope - Chicago, IL - *MagDir 84*
CIRB - Lac Etchemin, PQ, Canada - *BrCabYB 84*
Circa Library Circulation Systems [of Highsmith Co. Inc.] - Ft. Atkinson, WI - *EISS 5-84 Sup*
Circa Publications Inc. - Pelham, NY - *BoPubDir 4 Sup, 5; LitMarPl 83, 84*
Circe - Milan, Italy - *DirOnDB Spring 84*
Circle [of Circle Forum] - Portland, OR - *LitMag&SmPr 83-84*
Circle Banner - Circle, MT - *AyerDirPub 83; BaconPubCkNews 84*
Circle Banner - Miles City, MT - *Ed&PubIntYB 82*
Circle City Research Inc. - Indianapolis, IN - *IntDirMarRes 83*
Circle Forum - Portland, OR - *LitMag&SmPr 83-84*
Circle K Magazine - Indianapolis, IN - *ArtMar 84; WritMar 84*
Circle Pines Circulating - Circle Pines, MN - *BaconPubCkNews 84*
Circle Pines Quad Community Press - *See* Press Publications
Circle Publications - Madison, WI - *BoPubDir 4 Sup, 5*
Circle Repertory Co. - New York, NY - *WritMar 84*
Circle Software Corp. - Downers Grove, IL - *ADAPSOMemDir 83-84*
Circle, The - Jamaica Plain, MA - *LitMag&SmPr 83-84*
Circle Track - Los Angeles, CA - *BaconPubCkMag 84*
Circleville Cablevision Association [of Nationwide Communications Inc.] - Circleville, OH - *BrCabYB 84*
Circleville Herald - Circleville, OH - *BaconPubCkNews 84; NewsDir 84*

Circleville Mutual Telephone Co. - Circleville, WV - *TelDir&BG 83-84*
Circon Corp. - Santa Barbara, CA - *AvMarPl 83*
Circs - New York, NY - *DirOnDB Spring 84*
Circuit Alert - Los Gatos, CA - *BaconPubCkMag 84*
Circuit Playhouse/Playhouse on the Square - Memphis, TN - *WritMar 84*
Circuits Manufacturing [of Morgan-Grampian Co.] - Boston, MA - *BaconPubCkMag 84; MagDir 84; MagIndMarPl 82-83*
Circulating Pines - Circle Pines, MN - *AyerDirPub 83; Ed&PubIntYB 82*
Circulation - Dallas, TX - *MagDir 84; MagIndMarPl 82-83*
Circulation Fulfillment Services Inc. - Brooklyn, NY - *MagIndMarPl 82-83*
Circulation Library Automated System for Information Control [of Cincinnati Electronics Corp.] - Cincinnati, OH - *EISS 83*
Circulation Research - Dallas, TX - *MagDir 84*
Circulation '79/'80 [of American Newspaper Markets] - Winnetka, IL - *MagDir 84*
Circus [of Circus Enterprises] - New York, NY - *BaconPubCkMag 84; Folio 83; MagDir 84; MagIndMarPl 82-83*
CIRK-FM - Edmonton, AB, Canada - *BrCabYB 84*
CIRPA/ADISQ Foundation, The - Toronto, ON, Canada - *EISS 7-83 Sup*
CIS [of Questel Inc.] - Washington, DC - *DataDirOnSer 84*
CIS Abstracts [of International Occupational Safety & Health Information Centre] - Geneva, Switzerland - *CompReadDB 82; OnBibDB 3*
CIS-Bit - *See* CISDoc
CIS-ILO - *See* CISDoc
CIS/Index [of Congressional Information Service Inc.] - Washington, DC - *DBBus 82; OnBibDB 3*
CIS/Index [of Congressional Information Service Inc.] - Bethesda, MD - *DataDirOnSer 84; DirOnDB Spring 84*
CIS User Support Group [of Computer Sciences Corp.] - Falls Church, VA - *DataDirOnSer 84*
CISCo - Chicago, IL - *DirOnDB Spring 84*
Cisco Computer Systems Co. - Crockett, TX - *MicrocomMPl 84*
Cisco Press - *See* Eastland Country Newspapers
Cisco Press, The - Cisco, TX - *Ed&PubIntYB 82; NewsDir 84*
CISDoc - Geneva, Switzerland - *DirOnDB Spring 84*
CISILO [of International Occupational Safety & Health Information Centre] - Geneva, Switzerland - *DataDirOnSer 84*
CISInetwork - Van Nuys, CA - *DataDirOnSer 84; DataDirSup 7-83; MicrocomMPl 84*
CISL - Richmond, BC, Canada - *BrCabYB 84*
CISN-FM - Edmondton, AB, Canada - *BrCabYB 84*
CISP-FM - Pemberton, BC, Canada - *BrCabYB 84*
Cissi Music Inc. - *See* Sumac Music Inc.
Cissna Park News - Cissna Park, IL - *Ed&PubIntYB 82*
Cissna Park News - *See* Baier Publishing Co.
Cistercian Publications Inc. - Kalamazoo, MI - *LitMarPl 83, 84*
CISTI Current Catalog [of Canada Institute for Scientific & Technical Information] - Ottawa, ON, Canada - *DataDirOnSer 84*
CISV - Winkler-Moden, MB, Canada - *BrCabYB 84*
CISW-FM - Whistler, BC, Canada - *BrCabYB 84*
C.I.T. Financial Corp. [Subs. of RCA Corp.] - Livingston, NJ - *Tel&CabFB 84C*
Citadel Press [Subs. of Lyle Stuart Inc.] - Secaucus, NJ - *LitMarPl 83, 84; WritMar 84*
Citadel, The - Groton, CT - *WhoWMicrocom 83*
Citadel Theatre, The - Edmonton, AB, Canada - *WritMar 84*
Citation - Karnes City, TX - *AyerDirPub 83*
Citation Box & Paper Co. - Chicago, IL - *LitMarPl 83, 84*
Citation Computers Inc. - Houston, TX - *WhoWMicrocom 83*
Citation Group Inc. - Philadelphia, PA - *MicrocomMPl 83*
Citation Systems - Atlanta, GA - *MicrocomMPl 84*
CITE-FM - Montreal, PQ, Canada - *BrCabYB 84*
CITE-FM - Sherbrooke, PQ, Canada - *BrCabYB 84*
Cites Nouvelles - Ste. Genevieve, PQ, Canada - *Ed&PubIntYB 82*
CITF-FM - Quebec City, PQ, Canada - *BrCabYB 84*
CITI-FM - Winnipeg, MB, Canada - *BrCabYB 84*
Citibank - New York, NY - *VideoDir 82-83*
Citibank Economic Database [of Citibank N.A.] - New York, NY - *EISS 83*
Citibank Economics - New York, NY - *InfIndMarPl 83*
Citibank U.S. Economic Forecast - New York, NY - *DirOnDB Spring 84*
Citibase [of Citibank Economics Dept.] - New York, NY - *DataDirOnSer 84; DBBus 82; DirOnDB Spring 84*
Citibase-Weekly [of Citibank] - New York, NY - *DBBus 82; DirOnDB Spring 84*
Citibusiness - Metairie, LA - *BaconPubCkMag 84*
Citicorp Economic Report - New York, NY - *DirOnDB Spring 84*
Citicorp Information Resources - Denver, CO - *DataDirOnSer 84*
Citicorp Information Services - New York, NY - *DataDirOnSer 84*
Citicorp Resources Inc. - Stamford, CT - *DataDirSup 7-83*
Citidata Corp. - Northridge, CA - *DataDirOnSer 84*
Citiforecast [of I. P. Sharp Associates Ltd.] - Toronto, ON, Canada - *DataDirOnSer 84*
Citis Ltd. - Dublin, Ireland - *EISS 83*
Citishare [of Citibank N.A.] - New York, NY - *DataDirOnSer 84; DataDirSup 7-83; EISS 83*
Citishare Information Services [of Citishare Corp.] - New York, NY - *InfoS 83-84; MicrocomMPl 84*
Citiy Music Publishers Co. - Cincinnati, OH - *BillIntBG 83-84*
Citizen - Tucson, AZ - *AyerDirPub 83*
Citizen - De Queen, AR - *AyerDirPub 83*
Citizen - Searcy, AR - *AyerDirPub 83*
Citizen - Elk Grove, CA - *AyerDirPub 83*
Citizen - Florence, CO - *AyerDirPub 83*
Citizen - Glastonbury, CT - *AyerDirPub 83*
Citizen - Milford, CT - *AyerDirPub 83*
Citizen - Winsted, CT - *AyerDirPub 83*
Citizen - Key West, FL - *AyerDirPub 83*
Citizen - Auburn, IL - *AyerDirPub 83*
Citizen - Mahomet, IL - *AyerDirPub 83*
Citizen - Linton, IN - *AyerDirPub 83*
Citizen - Carlisle, IA - *AyerDirPub 83*
Citizen - Iowa Falls, IA - *AyerDirPub 83*
Citizen - Baxter Springs, KS - *AyerDirPub 83*
Citizen - Berea, KY - *AyerDirPub 83*
Citizen - Coushatta, LA - *AyerDirPub 83*
Citizen - Welsh, LA - *AyerDirPub 83*
Citizen - Frostburg, MD - *AyerDirPub 83; Ed&PubIntYB 82*
Citizen - Benton Harbor, MI - *Ed&PubIntYB 82*
Citizen - Washington, MO - *AyerDirPub 83*
Citizen - Arlington, NE - *AyerDirPub 83*
Citizen - Greeley, NE - *AyerDirPub 83*
Citizen - Holdrege, NE - *AyerDirPub 83*
Citizen - Walthill, NE - *AyerDirPub 83*
Citizen - Laconia, NH - *AyerDirPub 83; Ed&PubIntYB 82*
Citizen - Passaic, NJ - *AyerDirPub 83*
Citizen - Auburn, NY - *AyerDirPub 83; Ed&PubIntYB 82*
Citizen - Baldwin, NY - *AyerDirPub 83*
Citizen - Cato, NY - *AyerDirPub 83*
Citizen - Asheville, NC - *AyerDirPub 83; Ed&PubIntYB 82; LitMarPl 84*
Citizen - Red Springs, NC - *AyerDirPub 83*
Citizen - Andover, OH - *AyerDirPub 83*
Citizen - Urbana, OH - *AyerDirPub 83*
Citizen - Cushing, OK - *Ed&PubIntYB 82*
Citizen - Greer, SC - *AyerDirPub 83*
Citizen - Pulaski, TN - *AyerDirPub 83*
Citizen - Frankston, TX - *AyerDirPub 83*
Citizen - Pasadena, TX - *AyerDirPub 83*
Citizen - Waco, TX - *AyerDirPub 83*
Citizen - Webster, TX - *BaconPubCkNews 84*
Citizen - American Fork, UT - *AyerDirPub 83*
Citizen - Woodinville, WA - *AyerDirPub 83*
Citizen - Beaver Dam, WI - *AyerDirPub 83*
Citizen - Prince George, BC, Canada - *AyerDirPub 83; BaconPubCkNews 84; Ed&PubIntYB 82*
Citizen - Thompson, MB, Canada - *Ed&PubIntYB 82*
Citizen - Havelock, ON, Canada - *Ed&PubIntYB 82*
Citizen - Penetanguishene, ON, Canada - *Ed&PubIntYB 82*
Citizen - Kipling, SK, Canada - *AyerDirPub 83; Ed&PubIntYB 82*
Citizen-Advance - Copperhill, TN - *Ed&PubIntYB 82*
Citizen-Advertiser - Paris, KY - *AyerDirPub 83; NewsDir 84*
Citizen & Georgian - Montezuma, GA - *Ed&PubIntYB 82*
Citizen Group Publications - Brookline, MA - *BaconPubCkNews 84; LitMarPl 83*

Citizen Herald - Jesup, IA - *AyerDirPub 83; Ed&PubIntYB 82*
Citizen Herald - Walden, NY - *AyerDirPub 83; Ed&PubIntYB 82*
Citizen-Journal - Columbus, OH - *AyerDirPub 83*
Citizen-Journal - Arlington, TX - *AyerDirPub 83*
Citizen-News - Dalton, GA - *AyerDirPub 83*
Citizen News - Johnston, SC - *AyerDirPub 83*
Citizen News - Zurich, ON, Canada - *Ed&PubIntYB 82*
Citizen Newspapers - Chicago, IL - *Ed&PubIntYB 82*
Citizen of Morris County - Denville, NJ - *AyerDirPub 83; Ed&PubIntYB 82*
Citizen Outlet, The - Central Square, NY - *Ed&PubIntYB 82*
Citizen-Patriot - Atwood, KS - *AyerDirPub 83; Ed&PubIntYB 82*
Citizen Patriot - Jackson, MI - *AyerDirPub 83*
Citizen Printing Co. - Iowa Falls, IA - *BaconPubCkNews 84*
Citizen Publishing Co. Inc. - Preston, ID - *BaconPubCkNews 84*
Citizen Shopper - Squamish, BC, Canada - *Ed&PubIntYB 82*
Citizen Shopper's Guide - Waco, TX - *AyerDirPub 83*
Citizen-Standard [of News Publishing & Printing Co.] - Valley View, PA - *AyerDirPub 83; Ed&PubIntYB 82; NewsDir 84*
Citizen, The - Mansfield, AR - *Ed&PubIntYB 82*
Citizen, The - San Dieguito/Delmar, CA - *Ed&PubIntYB 82*
Citizen, The - Brunswick, MD - *AyerDirPub 83*
Citizen, The - Hamtramck, MI - *Ed&PubIntYB 82*
Citizen, The - Hillside, NJ - *AyerDirPub 83; Ed&PubIntYB 82*
Citizen, The - Amherst, NS, Canada - *AyerDirPub 83; Ed&PubIntYB 82*
Citizen, The [of Southam Inc.] - Ottawa, ON, Canada - *AyerDirPub 83; BaconPubCkNews 84; Ed&PubIntYB 82; LitMarPl 84*
Citizen-Times - Overbrook, KS - *AyerDirPub 83; Ed&PubIntYB 82*
Citizen-Times - Scottsville, KY - *AyerDirPub 83; Ed&PubIntYB 82*
Citizen-Times - Asheville, NC - *AyerDirPub 83; Ed&PubIntYB 82; LitMarPl 84*
Citizen Tribune - Morristown, TN - *AyerDirPub 83; Ed&PubIntYB 82*
Citizen Voice & Times - Irvine, KY - *AyerDirPub 83; Ed&PubIntYB 82*
Citizens Automated Systems [Div. of Citizens Savings Association] - Canton, OH - *DataDirOnSer 84; DataDirSup 7-83*
Citizens Cable Co. [of Times Mirror Cable Television Inc.] - Williamsport, PA - *BrCabYB 84; Tel&CabFB 84C*
Citizens Cable of Allen County Inc. - New Haven, IN - *BrCabYB 84; Tel&CabFB 84C*
Citizens Cable South Inc. - Ossian, IN - *Tel&CabFB 84C*
Citizens Cable TV [of North American Communications Corp.] - Chisholm, MN - *BrCabYB 84; Tel&CabFB 84C*
Citizens CATV Inc. [of Citizens Telephone Co.] - Plains, GA - *Tel&CabFB 84C*
Citizens Committee for New York City - New York, NY - *BoPubDir 4, 5*
Citizens' Committee on Children - Ottawa, ON, Canada - *BoPubDir 4, 5*
Citizens Communication Co. - Drakesville, IA - *Tel&CabFB 84C*
Citizens Emergency Travel Advisory Service [of U.S. Dept. of State] - Washington, DC - *DirOnDB Spring 84; EISS 5-84 Sup*
Citizen's Energy Project - Washington, DC - *BoPubDir 4, 5; LitMag&SmPr 83-84*
Citizens Financial Corp. - Independence, OH - *ADAPSOMemDir 83-84*
Citizens for Privacy in Cable TV - Nashville, TN - *InterCabHB 3*
Citizens in Defense of Civil Liberties - Chicago, IL - *BoPubDir 4 Sup, 5*
Citizens Industrial Financing - Morgantown, WV - *ADAPSOMemDir 83-84*
Citizens Information & Referral Service [of United Way of Dade County] - Miami, FL - *EISS 83*
Citizens Journal - Atlanta, TX - *AyerDirPub 83; Ed&PubIntYB 82*
Citizens Law Library Inc. - Boulder, CO - *BoPubDir 4 Sup, 5*
Citizens Mutual Telephone Co., The - Boomfield, IA - *TelDir&BG 83-84*
Citizens Mutual TV Society - North Bend, PA - *BrCabYB 84*
Citizens Observer, The - Cameron, MO - *Ed&PubIntYB 82*
Citizens Telephone Co. - Brevard, NC - *TelDir&BG 83-84*
Citizens Telephone Co. Inc. - Leslie, GA - *TelDir&BG 83-84*
Citizens Telephone Co. Inc. - Fairmount, IN - *TelDir&BG 83-84*
Citizens Telephone Co. of Hammond, New York Inc. - Hammond, NY - *TelDir&BG 83-84*
Citizens Telephone Co. of Higginsville, Missouri - Higginsville, MO - *TelDir&BG 83-84*
Citizens Telephone Co. of Kecksburg - Mammoth, PA - *TelDir&BG 83-84*
Citizens Telephone Cooperative - Floyd, VA - *TelDir&BG 83-84*
Citizens Telephone Cooperative Inc. - New Auburn, WI - *TelDir&BG 83-84*
Citizens Telephone Corp. - Warren, IN - *TelDir&BG 83-84*
Citizens Utilities Co. - Kingman, AZ - *TelDir&BG 83-84*
Citizens Utilities Co. - Stamford, CT - *TelDir&BG 83-84*
Citizens Utilities Co. of California [Aff. of Citizens Utilities Co.] - Redding, CA - *TelDir&BG 83-84*
Citizens Utilities Co. of Pennsylvania [Aff. of Citizens Utilities Co.] - New Bethlehem, PA - *TelDir&BG 83-84*
Citizens' Voice - Wilkes-Barre, PA - *AyerDirPub 83; Ed&PubIntYB 82*
CITL-TV - Lloydminster, AB, Canada - *Tel&CabFB 84S*
CITR-FM - Vancouver, BC, Canada - *BrCabYB 84*
Citrograph - Los Angeles, CA - *BaconPubCkMag 84*
Citronelle Cable TV Inc. - Citronelle, AL - *Tel&CabFB 84C*
Citrus & Vegetable Magazine - Tampa, FL - *BaconPubCkMag 84; MagDir 84*
Citrus Cablevision Inc. - Lee County, FL - *BrCabYB 84*
Citrus County Chronicle [of Citrus Publishing Inc.] - Inverness, FL - *AyerDirPub 83; Ed&PubIntYB 82; NewsDir 84*
Citrus Heights Bulletin [of Sacramento Suburban Newspapers Inc.] - Fair Oaks, CA - *NewsDir 84*
Citrus Heights Bulletin, The - Citrus Heights, CA - *Ed&PubIntYB 82*
Citrus Industry, The - Bartow, FL - *BaconPubCkMag 84; MagDir 84*
Citrus Publishing Inc. - Inverness, FL - *BaconPubCkNews 84*
CITV-TV - Edmonton, AB, Canada - *Tel&CabFB 84S*
City & Country Home - Toronto, ON, Canada - *BaconPubCkMag 84*
City & Suburban Herald - Pittsburgh, PA - *AyerDirPub 83*
City & Suburban Life - Bellevue, PA - *AyerDirPub 83; Ed&PubIntYB 82*
City & Suburban Life - Pittsburgh, PA - *Ed&PubIntYB 82*
City & Town [of Arkansas Municipal League] - North Little Rock, AR - *BaconPubCkMag 84; MagDir 84*
City & Town of Poughkeepsie - Yorktown Heights, NY - *AyerDirPub 83*
City Animation Co. - Troy, MI - *AvMarPl 83*
City Cable Co. - Greensburg, KY - *BrCabYB 84*
City Cyclist, The - New York, NY - *LitMag&SmPr 83-84*
City Desk Features - Forest Hills, NY - *BaconPubCkNews 84; Ed&PubIntYB 82; MagIndMarPl 82-83*
City Film Productions, City Film Center Inc. - Middle Village, NY - *AvMarPl 83*
City Film Productions, City Film Center Inc. - New York, NY - *TelAl 83*
City Film Productions, City Film Center Inc. - Queens, NY - *TelAl 84*
City Hall Digest - Seabrook, MD - *BaconPubCkMag 84*
City Lights Books - San Francisco, CA - *LitMag&SmPr 83-84; LitMarPl 83, 84*
City Lights Journal [of City Lights Books] - San Francisco, CA - *LitMag&SmPr 83-84*
City Miner - Berkeley, CA - *LitMag&SmPr 83-84*
City Miner Books - Berkeley, CA - *BoPubDir 4, 5*
City News [of Los Angeles Meredith Newspapers] - Los Angeles, CA - *NewsDir 84*
City News - Bronx, NY - *NewsDir 84*
City News Bureau of Chicago - Chicago, IL - *BaconPubCkNews 84; Ed&PubIntYB 82*
City Newspaper - Rochester, NY - *AyerDirPub 83; Ed&PubIntYB 82*
City of Americus Cable TV - Americus, KS - *Tel&CabFB 84C*
City of Big Falls CATV - Big Falls, MN - *BrCabYB 84*
City of Brookings Municipal Telephone Dept. - Brookings, SD - *TelDir&BG 83-84*

City of Calgary Information Service [of Calgary Public Information Dept.] - Calgary, AB, Canada - *EISS 7-83 Sup*
City of Cascade Locks Cable TV - Cascade Locks, OR - *Tel&CabFB 84C*
City of Cawker City - Cawker City, KS - *Tel&CabFB 84C*
City of Covington CATV - Covington, GA - *Tel&CabFB 84C*
City of Crystal Falls - Crystal Falls, MI - *Tel&CabFB 84C*
City of Fosston Cable TV - Fosston, MN - *BrCabYB 84*
City of Marion Cable TV - Marion, KS - *Tel&CabFB 84C*
City of Monroe (Water, Light, & Gas Commission) - Monroe, GA - *Tel&CabFB 84C*
City of Newberry - Newberry, FL - *Tel&CabFB 84C*
City of Norway CATV - Norway, MI - *BrCabYB 84; Tel&CabFB 84C*
City of San Bruno Municipal Cable TV - San Bruno, CA - *Tel&CabFB 84C*
City of Sumas TV Cable System - Sumas, WA - *BrCabYB 84; Tel&CabFB 84C*
City of Taconite Cable TV - Taconite, MN - *Tel&CabFB 84C*
City of Waverly Cable TV - Waverly, KS - *Tel&CabFB 84C*
City of Waverly CATV - Waverly, KS - *BrCabYB 84*
City Park Music - *See* Castalia Music
City Press [of Los Angeles Meredith Newspapers] - Los Angeles, CA - *NewsDir 84*
City Research Associates Ltd. - London, England - *IntDirMarRes 83*
City Slicker Press - Kenosha, WI - *BoPubDir 4, 5*
City Sports Monthly - San Francisco, CA - *WritMar 84*
City Terrace Comet - City Terrace, CA - *Ed&PubIntYB 82*
City Terrace Comet - Los Angeles, CA - *AyerDirPub 83*
City Tribune - Glenwood, WI - *Ed&PubIntYB 82*
CITY-TV - Toronto, ON, Canada - *Tel&CabFB 84S*
City TV Cable Service [of Biltmore-Holiday Corp.] - Lordsburg, NM - *BrCabYB 84; Tel&CabFB 84C*
City TV Inc. - Columbia, KY - *BrCabYB 84; Tel&CabFB 84C*
City Vision Inc. [of Southwest Missouri Cable TV Inc.] - Marionville, MO - *Tel&CabFB 84C*
City Woman - Toronto, ON, Canada - *BaconPubCkMag 84*
CIVA-TV - Noranda, PQ, Canada - *Tel&CabFB 84S*
CIVA-TV - Val d'Or-Amos, PQ, Canada - *Tel&CabFB 84S*
CIVC-TV - Trois Rivieres, PQ, Canada - *Tel&CabFB 84S*
CIVG-TV - Sept-Iles, PQ, Canada - *Tel&CabFB 84S*
CIVH - Vanderhoof, BC, Canada - *BrCabYB 84*
Civic Communication Inc. - Jackson, MS - *BrCabYB 84*
Civic/Data Corp. - Los Angeles, CA - *BoPubDir 4, 5*
Civic Education Association - Tustin, CA - *BoPubDir 5*
Civic Education Service Inc. [Div. of Mafex Associates Inc.] - Johnstown, PA - *AvMarPl 83*
Civic Public Works - Toronto, ON, Canada - *BaconPubCkMag 84*
Civil Aeronautics Board - Washington, DC - *DataDirOnSer 84*
Civil Air Patrol News - Montgomery, AL - *BaconPubCkMag 84; MagDir 84*
Civil & Structural Computing Ltd. - Bradford, England - *MicrocomSwDir 1*
Civil Engineering [of American Society of Civil Engineers] - New York, NY - *ArtMar 84; BaconPubCkMag 84; MagDir 84; MagIndMarPl 82-83; WritMar 84*
Civil Engineers' Book Club [of McGraw-Hill Book Co.] - New York, NY - *LitMarPl 83, 84*
Civil Service Leader [of Leader Publications Inc.] - New York, NY - *MagDir 84*
Civil War Times Illustrated - Harrisburg, PA - *ArtMar 84; MagDir 84; MagIndMarPl 82-83; WritMar 84*
Civitan - Birmingham, AL - *MagDir 84*
Civitas Corp. Ltd. - Montreal, PQ, Canada - *BrCabYB 84*
CIVM-TV - Montreal, PQ, Canada - *Tel&CabFB 84S*
CIVO-TV - Hull, PQ, Canada - *Tel&CabFB 84S*
CIVQ-TV - Quebec City, PQ, Canada - *Tel&CabFB 84S*
CIVR-TV - Rimouski, PQ, Canada - *Tel&CabFB 84S*
CIVS-TV - Sherbrooke, PQ, Canada - *Tel&CabFB 84S*
CIVV-TV - Lac St. Jean, PQ, Canada - *Tel&CabFB 84S*
CIVV-TV - Saguenay, PQ, Canada - *Tel&CabFB 84S*
CIX-TV - Miami, FL - *BrCabYB 84*
CIXX-FM - London, ON, Canada - *BrCabYB 84*
CIYQ - Grand Falls, NF, Canada - *BrCabYB 84*
CIYR - Hinton, AB, Canada - *BrCabYB 84*
CIZL-FM - Regina, SK, Canada - *BrCabYB 84*
CJ Publishing - Chicago, IL - *BillIntBG 83-84*
CJ Record Co. - Chicago, IL - *BillIntBG 83-84*
CJAD - Montreal, PQ, Canada - *BrCabYB 84; NatRadPubDir Summer 83, Spring 84*
CJAF - Cabano, PQ, Canada - *BrCabYB 84*
CJAN - Asbestos, PQ, Canada - *BrCabYB 84*
CJAR - The Pas, MB, Canada - *BrCabYB 84*
CJAT - Trail, BC, Canada - *BrCabYB 84*
CJAT-FM - Trail, BC, Canada - *BrCabYB 84*
CJAV - Port Alberni, BC, Canada - *BrCabYB 84*
CJAX-FM - Edmonton, AB, Canada - *BrCabYB 84*
CJAY-FM - Calgary, AB, Canada - *BrCabYB 84*
CJAZ-FM - Vancouver, BC, Canada - *BrCabYB 84; NatRadPubDir Summer 83, Spring 84*
CJBC - Toronto, ON, Canada - *BrCabYB 84*
CJBC-FM - London, ON, Canada - *BrCabYB 84*
CJBK - London, ON, Canada - *BrCabYB 84*
CJBM - Causapscal, PQ, Canada - *BrCabYB 84*
CJBQ - Belleville, ON, Canada - *BrCabYB 84*
CJBR - Rimouski, PQ, Canada - *BrCabYB 84*
CJBR-FM - Rimouski, PQ, Canada - *BrCabYB 84*
CJBRT - Rimouski, PQ, Canada - *Tel&CabFB 84S*
CJBX-FM - London, ON, Canada - *BrCabYB 84*
CJCA - Edmonton, AB, Canada - *BrCabYB 84*
CJCB - Sydney, NS, Canada - *BrCabYB 84*
CJCB-TV - Sydney, NS, Canada - *Tel&CabFB 84S*
CJCD - Yellowknife, NT, Canada - *BrCabYB 84*
CJCH - Halifax, NS, Canada - *BrCabYB 84*
CJCH-FM - Halifax, NS, Canada - *BrCabYB 84*
CJCH-TV - Halifax, NS, Canada - *Tel&CabFB 84S*
CJCI - Prince George, BC, Canada - *BrCabYB 84*
CJCJ - Woodstock, NB, Canada - *BrCabYB 84*
CJCL - Toronto, ON, Canada - *BrCabYB 84; NatRadPubDir Summer 83, Spring 84*
CJCM-FM - Brandon, MB, Canada - *BrCabYB 84*
CJCS - Stratford, ON, Canada - *BrCabYB 84*
CJCW - Sussex, NB, Canada - *BrCabYB 84*
CJCY - Medicine Hat, AB, Canada - *BrCabYB 84*
CJDC - Dawson Creek, BC, Canada - *BrCabYB 84*
CJDC-TV - Dawson Creek, BC, Canada - *Tel&CabFB 84S*
CJEN-FM - Jenpeg, MB, Canada - *BrCabYB 84*
CJER - St. Jerome, PQ, Canada - *BrCabYB 84*
CJET - Smiths Falls, ON, Canada - *BrCabYB 84*
CJFB-TV - Swift Current, SK, Canada - *Tel&CabFB 84S*
CJFI-FM - Sarnia, ON, Canada - *BrCabYB 84*
CJFM-FM - Montreal, PQ, Canada - *BrCabYB 84; NatRadPubDir Summer 83, Spring 84*
CJFP - Riviere-du-Loup, PQ, Canada - *BrCabYB 84*
CJFX - Antigonish, NS, Canada - *BrCabYB 84*
CJGL-FM - Swift Current, SK, Canada - *BrCabYB 84*
CJGX - Yorkton, SK, Canada - *BrCabYB 84*
CJIB - Vernon, BC, Canada - *BrCabYB 84*
CJIC-TV - Sault Ste. Marie, ON, Canada - *Tel&CabFB 84S*
CJJC - Langley, BC, Canada - *BrCabYB 84*
CJKL - Kirkland Lake, ON, Canada - *BrCabYB 84*
CJLA - Lachute, PQ, Canada - *BrCabYB 84*
CJLB - Thunder Bay, ON, Canada - *BrCabYB 84*
CJLM - Joliette, PQ, Canada - *BrCabYB 84*
CJLS - Yarmouth, NS, Canada - *BrCabYB 84*
CJMC - Ste-Anne-des-Monts, PQ, Canada - *BrCabYB 84*
CJMD - Chibougamau, PQ, Canada - *BrCabYB 84*
CJME - Regina, SK, Canada - *BrCabYB 84*
CJMF-FM - Quebec City, PQ, Canada - *BrCabYB 84*
CJMH - Medicine Hat, AB, Canada - *BrCabYB 84*
CJMR - Mississauga, ON, Canada - *BrCabYB 84*
CJMS - Montreal, PQ, Canada - *BrCabYB 84*
CJMT - Chicoutimi, PQ, Canada - *BrCabYB 84*
CJMX-FM - Sudbury, ON, Canada - *BrCabYB 84*
CJNB - North Battleford, SK, Canada - *BrCabYB 84*
CJNH - Bancroft, ON, Canada - *BrCabYB 84*
CJNL - Merritt, BC, Canada - *BrCabYB 84*
CJNR - Blind River, ON, Canada - *BrCabYB 84*
CJNS - Meadow Lake, SK, Canada - *BrCabYB 84*
CJOB - Winnipeg, MB, Canada - *BrCabYB 84*
CJOC - Lethbridge, AB, Canada - *BrCabYB 84*
CJOH-TV - Ottawa, ON, Canada - *Tel&CabFB 84S*
CJOI - Wetaskiwin, AB, Canada - *BrCabYB 84*

CJOK - Ft. McMurray, AB, Canada - *BrCabYB 84*
CJOM-FM - Windsor, ON, Canada - *BrCabYB 84*
CJON-TV - St. John's, NF, Canada - *Tel&CabFB 84S*
CJOR - Vancouver, BC, Canada - *BrCabYB 84; NatRadPubDir Summer 83, Spring 84*
CJOS-FM - Gander, NF, Canada - *BrCabYB 84*
CJOY - Guelph, ON, Canada - *BrCabYB 84*
CJOZ-FM - Bonavista, NF, Canada - *BrCabYB 84*
CJPM-TV - Chicoutimi, PQ, Canada - *Tel&CabFB 84S*
CJPR - Blairmore, AB, Canada - *BrCabYB 84*
CJQM-FM - Sault Ste. Marie, ON, Canada - *BrCabYB 84*
CJQR-FM - St. Catharines, ON, Canada - *BrCabYB 84*
CJRB - Boissevain, MB, Canada - *BrCabYB 84*
CJRC - Ottawa, ON, Canada - *BrCabYB 84*
CJRE-FM - Riviere au Renard, PQ, Canada - *BrCabYB 84*
CJRG-FM - Gaspe, PQ, Canada - *BrCabYB 84*
CJRL - Kenora, ON, Canada - *BrCabYB 84*
CJRN - Niagara Falls, ON, Canada - *BrCabYB 84*
CJRP - Quebec City, PQ, Canada - *BrCabYB 84*
CJRS - Sherbrooke, ON, Canada - *BrCabYB 84*
CJRT-FM - Toronto, ON, Canada - *BrCabYB 84*
CJRW - Summerside, PE, Canada - *BrCabYB 84*
CJSA - Ste. Agathe des Monts, PQ, Canada - *BrCabYB 84*
CJSB - Ottawa, ON, Canada - *BrCabYB 84*
CJSD-FM - Thunder Bay, ON, Canada - *BrCabYB 84*
CJSL - Estevan, SK, Canada - *BrCabYB 84*
CJSN - Shaunavon, SK, Canada - *BrCabYB 84*
CJSO - Sorel, PQ, Canada - *BrCabYB 84*
CJSS - Cornwall, ON, Canada - *BrCabYB 84*
CJTN - Trenton, ON, Canada - *BrCabYB 84*
CJTR - Trois-Rivieres, PQ, Canada - *BrCabYB 84*
CJTT - New Liskeard, ON, Canada - *BrCabYB 84*
CJUS Data Bank [of Commission of the European Communities] - Kirchberg, Luxembourg - *EISS 83*
CJVA - Carquet, NB, Canada - *BrCabYB 84*
CJVB - Vancouver, BC, Canada - *BrCabYB 84*
CJVI - Victoria, BC, Canada - *BrCabYB 84*
CJVL - Ste-Marie-de-Beauce, PQ, Canada - *BrCabYB 84*
CJVR - Melfort, SK, Canada - *BrCabYB 84*
CJWA - Wawa, ON, Canada - *BrCabYB 84*
CJWN-TV - Corner Brook, NF, Canada - *Tel&CabFB 84S*
CJWW - Saskatoon, SK, Canada - *BrCabYB 84*
CJXX - Grande Prairie, AB, Canada - *BrCabYB 84*
CJYC-FM - St. John, NB, Canada - *BrCabYB 84*
CJYQ - St. John's, NF, Canada - *BrCabYB 84*
CJYR - Edson, AB, Canada - *BrCabYB 84*
CK Enterprises - Spartanburg, SC - *BoPubDir 5*
C.K. Video Inc. - *See* Keyser, James W.
CKAC - Montreal, PQ, Canada - *BrCabYB 84; NatRadPubDir Summer 83, Spring 84*
CKAD - Middleton, NS, Canada - *BrCabYB 84*
CKAL - Vernon, BC, Canada - *BrCabYB 84*
CKAL-FM - Kaslo, BC, Canada - *BrCabYB 84*
CKAL-FM - Nakupso, BC, Canada - *BrCabYB 84*
CKAL-FM - New Denver, BC, Canada - *BrCabYB 84*
CKAN - Newmarket, ON, Canada - *BrCabYB 84*
CKAP - Kapuskasing, ON, Canada - *BrCabYB 84*
CKAR - Oshawa, ON, Canada - *BrCabYB 84; NatRadPubDir Summer 83 p.272, Spring 84 p.274*
CKAT-FM - North Bay, ON, Canada - *BrCabYB 84*
CKAY - Duncan, BC, Canada - *BrCabYB 84*
CKBB - Barrie, ON, Canada - *BrCabYB 84*
CKBC - Bathurst, NB, Canada - *BrCabYB 84*
CKBI - Prince Albert, SK, Canada - *BrCabYB 84*
CKBI-TV - Prince Albert, SK, Canada - *Tel&CabFB 84S*
CKBM - Montmagny, PQ, Canada - *BrCabYB 84*
CKBQ-TV - Star City, SK, Canada - *Tel&CabFB 84S*
CKBS - St. Hyacinthe, PQ, Canada - *BrCabYB 84*
CKBW - Bridgewater, NS, Canada - *BrCabYB 84*
CKBX - Hundred Mile House, BC, Canada - *BrCabYB 84*
CKBY-FM - Ottawa, ON, Canada - *BrCabYB 84*
CKCB - Collingwood, ON, Canada - *BrCabYB 84*
CKCH - Hull, PQ, Canada - *BrCabYB 84*
CKCK - Regina, SK, Canada - *BrCabYB 84*
CKCL - Truro, NS, Canada - *BrCabYB 84*
CKCM - Grand Falls, NF, Canada - *BrCabYB 84*
CKCN - Sept-Iles, PQ, Canada - *BrCabYB 84*
CKCO-TV - Kitchener, ON, Canada - *Tel&CabFB 84S*
CKCQ - Quesnel, BC, Canada - *BrCabYB 84*
CKCR - Revelstoke, BC, Canada - *BrCabYB 84*
CKCU-FM - Ottawa, ON, Canada - *BrCabYB 84*
CKCV - Quebec City, PQ, Canada - *BrCabYB 84*
CKCW - Moncton, NB, Canada - *BrCabYB 84*
CKCW-TV - Moncton, NB, Canada - *Tel&CabFB 84S*
CKCY - Sault Ste. Marie, ON, Canada - *BrCabYB 84*
CKCY-TV - Sault Ste. Marie, ON, Canada - *Tel&CabFB 84S*
CKDA - Victoria, BC, Canada - *BrCabYB 84*
CKDH - Amherst, NS, Canada - *BrCabYB 84*
CKDK - Woodstock, ON, Canada - *BrCabYB 84*
CKDM - Dauphin, MB, Canada - *BrCabYB 84*
CKDQ - Drumheller, ON, Canada - *BrCabYB 84*
CKDR - Dryden, ON, Canada - *BrCabYB 84*
CKDS-FM - Hamilton, ON, Canada - *BrCabYB 84*
CKDY - Digby, NS, Canada - *BrCabYB 84*
CKEC - New Glasgow, NS, Canada - *BrCabYB 84*
CKEG - Nanaimo, BC, Canada - *BrCabYB 84*
CKEK - Cranbrook, BC, Canada - *BrCabYB 84*
CKEN - Kentville, NS, Canada - *BrCabYB 84*
CKER - Edmonton, AB, Canada - *BrCabYB 84*
CKER Radio Ltd. - Edmonton, AB, Canada - *BrCabYB 84*
CKEY - Toronto, ON, Canada - *BrCabYB 84; NatRadPubDir Summer 83, Spring 84*
CKFL - Lac Megantic, PQ, Canada - *BrCabYB 84*
CKFM-FM - Toronto, ON, Canada - *BrCabYB 84; NatRadPubDir Summer 83, Spring 84*
CKGA - Gander, NF, Canada - *BrCabYB 84*
CKGB - Timmins, ON, Canada - *BrCabYB 84*
CKGF - Grand Forks, BC, Canada - *BrCabYB 84*
CKGL-FM - Kitchener, ON, Canada - *BrCabYB 84*
CKGM - Montreal, PQ, Canada - *BrCabYB 84; NatRadPubDir Summer 83, Spring 84*
CKGN-TV - Toronto, ON, Canada - *Tel&CabFB 84S*
CKGO - Hope, BC, Canada - *BrCabYB 84*
CKGO-FM - Boston Bar, BC, Canada - *BrCabYB 84*
CKGR - Golden, BC, Canada - *BrCabYB 84*
CKGY - Red Deer, AB, Canada - *BrCabYB 84*
CKHJ-FM - Fredericton, NB, Canada - *BrCabYB 84*
CKHR-FM - Hay River, NT, Canada - *BrCabYB 84*
CKIK-FM - Calgary, AB, Canada - *BrCabYB 84*
CKIM - Baie Verte, NF, Canada - *BrCabYB 84*
CKIQ - Kelowna, BC, Canada - *BrCabYB 84*
CKIT-FM - Regina, SK, Canada - *BrCabYB 84*
CKIX-FM - St. John's, NF, Canada - *BrCabYB 84*
CKJD - Sarnia, ON, Canada - *BrCabYB 84*
CKJS - Winnipeg, MB, Canada - *BrCabYB 84*
CKJY-FM - Windsor, ON, Canada - *BrCabYB 84*
CKKC - Nelson, BC, Canada - *BrCabYB 84*
CKKR - Rosetown, SK, Canada - *BrCabYB 84*
CKKW - Kitchener, ON, Canada - *BrCabYB 84*
CKLA-FM - Guelph, ON, Canada - *BrCabYB 84*
CKLC - Kingston, ON, Canada - *BrCabYB 84*
CKLD - Thetford Mines, PQ, Canada - *BrCabYB 84*
CKLE-FM - Rimouski, PQ, Canada - *BrCabYB 84*
CKLM - Montreal, PQ, Canada - *BrCabYB 84*
CKLQ - Brandon, MB, Canada - *BrCabYB 84*
CKLR - L'Annonciation, PQ, Canada - *BrCabYB 84*
CKLW - Windsor, ON, Canton Island - *BrCabYB 84*
CKLY - Lindsay, ON, Canada - *BrCabYB 84*
CKMF-FM - Montreal, PQ, Canada - *BrCabYB 84*
CKMI-TV - Quebec City, PQ, Canada - *Tel&CabFB 84S*
CKMK - MacKenzie, BC, Canada - *BrCabYB 84*
CKML - Mont Laurier, PQ, Canada - *BrCabYB 84*
CKMP - Midland, ON, Canada - *BrCabYB 84*
CKMS-FM - Waterloo, ON, Canada - *BrCabYB 84*
CKMV - Grand Falls, NB, Canada - *BrCabYB 84*
CKMW - Brampton, ON, Canada - *BrCabYB 84; NatRadPubDir Summer 83 p.273, Spring 84 p.275*
CKNB - Campbellton, NB, Canada - *BrCabYB 84*
CKNC-TV - Sudbury, ON, Canada - *Tel&CabFB 84S*
CKND-TV - Winnipeg, MB, Canada - *Tel&CabFB 84S*
CKNL - Ft. St. John, BC, Canada - *BrCabYB 84*
CKNR - Elliott Lake, ON, Canada - *BrCabYB 84*
CKNS - Espanola, ON, Canada - *BrCabYB 84*
CKNW - New Westminster, BC, Canada - *BrCabYB 84*

CKNX - Wingham, ON, Canada - *BrCabYB 84*
CKNX-FM - Wingham, ON, Canada - *BrCabYB 84*
CKNX-TV - Wingham, ON, Canada - *Tel&CabFB 84S*
CKNY-TV - North Bay, ON, Canada - *Tel&CabFB 84S*
CKO - Pointe Claire, PQ, Canada - *BrCabYB 84*
CKO-FM - Calgary, AB, Canada - *BrCabYB 84*
CKO-FM - Edmonton, AB, Canada - *BrCabYB 84*
CKO-FM - Vancouver, BC, Canada - *BrCabYB 84*
CKO-FM - London, ON, Canada - *BrCabYB 84*
CKO-FM - Ottawa, ON, Canada - *BrCabYB 84*
CKO-FM - Toronto, ON, Canada - *BrCabYB 84*
CKO Inc. - Toronto, ON, Canada - *BrCabYB 84*
CKOB - Renfrew, ON, Canada - *BrCabYB 84*
CKOC - Hamilton, ON, Canada - *BrCabYB 84*
CKOI-FM - Verdun, PQ, Canada - *BrCabYB 84*
CKOK - Penticton, BC, Canada - *BrCabYB 84*
CKOM - Saskatoon, SK, Canada - *BrCabYB 84*
CKOO - Osoyoos, BC, Canada - *BrCabYB 84*
CKOR-FM - Penticton, BC, Canada - *BrCabYB 84*
CKOS-TV - Yorkton, SK, Canada - *Tel&CabFB 84S*
CKOT - Tillsonburg, ON, Canada - *BrCabYB 84*
CKOT-FM - Tillsonburg, ON, Canada - *BrCabYB 84*
CKOV - Kelowna, BC, Canada - *BrCabYB 84*
CKOY - Ottawa, ON, Canada - *BrCabYB 84*
CKOZ-FM - Corner Brook, NF, Canada - *BrCabYB 84*
CKPC - Brantford, ON, Canada - *BrCabYB 84*
CKPC-FM - Brantford, ON, Canada - *BrCabYB 84*
CKPE-FM - Sydney, NS, Canada - *BrCabYB 84*
CKPG - Prince George, BC, Canada - *BrCabYB 84*
CKPG-TV - Prince George, BC, Canada - *Tel&CabFB 84S*
CKPR - Thunder Bay, ON, Canada - *BrCabYB 84*
CKPR-TV - Thunder Bay, ON, Canada - *Tel&CabFB 84S*
CKPT - Peterborough, ON, Canada - *BrCabYB 84*
CKQM-FM - Peterborough, ON, Canada - *BrCabYB 84*
CKQN-FM - Baker Lake, NT, Canada - *BrCabYB 84*
CKQR - Castlegar, BC, Canada - *BrCabYB 84*
CKQT-FM - Oshawa, ON, Canada - *BrCabYB 84; NatRadPubDir Summer 83 p.273, Spring 84 p.275*
CKRA-FM - Edmonton, AB, Canada - *BrCabYB 84*
CKRB - St. Georges de Peauce, PQ, Canada - *BrCabYB 84*
CKRC - Winnipeg, MB, Canada - *BrCabYB 84*
CKRD - Red Deer, AB, Canada - *BrCabYB 84*
CKRD-TV - Red Deer, AB, Canada - *Tel&CabFB 84S*
CKRE - Red Lake, ON, Canada - *BrCabYB 84*
CKRL-FM - Quebec City, PQ, Canada - *BrCabYB 84*
CKRM - Regina, SK, Canada - *BrCabYB 84*
CKRN - Rouyn, PQ, Canada - *BrCabYB 84*
CKRN-TV - Noranda, PQ, Canada - *Tel&CabFB 84S*
CKRS - Jonquiere, PQ, Canada - *BrCabYB 84*
CKRS-TV - Jonquiere, PQ, Canada - *Tel&CabFB 84S*
CKRT-TV - Riviere du Loup, PQ, Canada - *Tel&CabFB 84S*
CKRV - Drummondville, PQ, Canada - *BrCabYB 84*
CKRW - Whitehorse, YT, Canada - *BrCabYB 84*
CKRY-FM - Calgary, AB, Canada - *BrCabYB 84*
CKSA - Lloydminster, AB, Canada - *BrCabYB 84*
CKSA-TV - Lloydminster, AB, Canada - *Tel&CabFB 84S*
CKSB - St. Boniface, MB, Canada - *BrCabYB 84*
CKSB-FM - Dryden, ON, Canada - *BrCabYB 84*
CKSL - London, ON, Canada - *BrCabYB 84*
CKSL - La Sarre, PQ, Canada - *BrCabYB 84*
CKSM - Shawinigan, PQ, Canada - *BrCabYB 84*
CKSO - Sudbury, ON, Canada - *BrCabYB 84*
CKSP - Summerland, BC, Canada - *BrCabYB 84*
CKSQ - Stettler, AB, Canada - *BrCabYB 84*
CKSS-FM - Red Rocks, NF, Canada - *BrCabYB 84*
CKST - St. Albert, AB, Canada - *BrCabYB 84*
CKSW - Swift Current, SK, Canada - *BrCabYB 84*
CKTA - Taber, AB, Canada - *BrCabYB 84*
CKTB - St. Catharines, ON, Canada - *BrCabYB 84*
CKTK - Kitimat, BC, Canada - *BrCabYB 84*
CKTL - Plessisville, PQ, Canada - *BrCabYB 84*
CKTM-TV - Trois Rivieres, PQ, Canada - *Tel&CabFB 84S*
CKTO-FM - Truro, NS, Canada - *BrCabYB 84*
CKTS - Sherbrooke, PQ, Canada - *BrCabYB 84*
CKTV - Regina, SK, Canada - *Tel&CabFB 84S*
CKUA - Edmonton, AB, Canada - *BrCabYB 84*
CKUA-FM - Drumheller, AB, Canada - *BrCabYB 84*
CKUA-FM - Edmonton, AB, Canada - *BrCabYB 84*
CKUA-FM - Grande Prairie, AB, Canada - *BrCabYB 84*
CKUA-FM - Lethbridge, AB, Canada - *BrCabYB 84*
CKUA-FM - Medicine Hat, AB, Canada - *BrCabYB 84*
CKUA-FM - Peace River, AB, Canada - *BrCabYB 84*
CKUA-FM - Red Deer, AB, Canada - *BrCabYB 84*
CKUE-FM - Smiths Falls, ON, Canada - *BrCabYB 84*
CKUT - Wollaston Lake, SK, Canada - *BrCabYB 84*
CKVD - Val-d'Or, PQ, Canada - *BrCabYB 84*
CKVL - Verdun, PQ, Canada - *BrCabYB 84*
CKVM - Ville-Marie, PQ, Canada - *BrCabYB 84*
CKVO - Clarenville, NF, Canada - *BrCabYB 84*
CKVR-TV - Barrie, ON, Canada - *Tel&CabFB 84S*
CKVU-TV - Vancouver, BC, Canada - *Tel&CabFB 84S*
CKWG-FM - Winnipeg, MB, Canada - *BrCabYB 84*
CKWL - Williams Lake, BC, Canada - *BrCabYB 84*
CKWM-FM - Kentville, NS, Canada - *BrCabYB 84*
CKWR-FM - Kitchener, ON, Canada - *BrCabYB 84*
CKWS - Kingston, ON, Canada - *BrCabYB 84*
CKWS-TV - Kingston, ON, Canada - *Tel&CabFB 84S*
CKWW - Windsor, ON, Canada - *BrCabYB 84*
CKWX - Vancouver, BC, Canada - *BrCabYB 84; NatRadPubDir Summer 83, Spring 84*
CKX-TV - Brandon, MB, Canada - *Tel&CabFB 84S*
CKXL - Calgary, AB, Canada - *BrCabYB 84*
CKXM-FM - Edmonton, AB, Canada - *BrCabYB 84*
CKXR - Salmon Arm, BC, Canada - *BrCabYB 84*
CKY - Winnipeg, MB, Canada - *BrCabYB 84*
CKY-TV - Winnipeg, MB, Canada - *Tel&CabFB 84S*
CKYL - Peace River, AB, Canada - *BrCabYB 84*
CKYQ - Grand Bank, NF, Canada - *BrCabYB 84*
CKYR - Grand Cache, AB, Canada - *BrCabYB 84*
CKYR - Jasper, AB, Canada - *BrCabYB 84*
Clack Sound Studios Inc. - New York, NY - *AvMarPl 83*
Clackamas County News - Estacada, OR - *Ed&PubIntYB 82*
Clackamas County Review, The - Milwaukie, OR - *NewsDir 84*
CLADBIB [of Comision Economica para America Latina] - Santiago, Chile - *CompReadDB 82*
Clafin Tri County News - *See* Dispatch Publishing Co.
Claflin Clarion - Claflin, KS - *Ed&PubIntYB 82*
Claiborne Cable TV - Haynesville, LA - *Tel&CabFB 84C*
Claiborne Progress - Tazewell, TN - *AyerDirPub 83; Ed&PubIntYB 82; NewsDir 84*
Claiborne Telephone Co. Inc. [Aff. of Century Telephone Enterprises Inc.] - New Tazewell, TN - *TelDir&BG 83-84*
Claims/Chem [of IFI/Plenum Data Co.] - Alexandria, VA - *DataDirOnSer 84*
Claims/Chem [of IFI/Plenum Data Co.] - Arlington, VA - *DBBus 82*
Claims/Citation [of IFI/Plenum Data Co.] - Alexandria, VA - *DataDirOnSer 84; DBBus 82*
Claims/Citation [of Search Check Inc.] - Arlington, VA - *DirOnDB Spring 84; EISS 83*
Claims/Class [of IFI/Plenum Data Co.] - Alexandria, VA - *DataDirOnSer 84*
Claims/Class - Arlington, VA - *DirOnDB Spring 84*
Claims/Compound Registry [of Dialog Information Services Inc.] - Palo Alto, CA - *DataDirOnSer 84*
Claims/Compound Registry - Arlington, VA - *DirOnDB Spring 84*
Claims Digest - San Pablo, CA - *BaconPubCkMag 84*
Claims Reporter - San Pablo, CA - *BaconPubCkMag 84*
Claims/Uniterm [of IFI/Plenum Data Co.] - Arlington, VA - *DBBus 82; DirOnDB Spring 84*
Claims/US Patent Abstracts [of IFI/Plenum Data Co.] - Alexandria, VA - *DataDirOnSer 84*
Claims/US Patent Abstracts Weekly [of IFI/Plenum Data Co.] - Alexandria, VA - *DataDirOnSer 84*
Claims/US Patents [of IFI/Plenum Data Co.] - Alexandria, VA - *DataDirOnSer 84*
Claims/US Patents [of IFI/Plenum Data Co.] - Arlington, VA - *DBBus 82; DirOnDB Spring 84*
Claire-Vue Inc. - Plessisville, PQ, Canada - *BrCabYB 84*
Clairemont North Pennysaver - Mission Viejo, CA - *AyerDirPub 83*
Clairmont Camera - Studio City, CA - *AvMarPl 83*
Clairmont Central Pennysaver - Mission Viejo, CA - *AyerDirPub 83*

Clairmont South Pennysaver - Mission Viejo, CA - *AyerDirPub 83*
Clairmonte, Mrs. Glenn - Summit, MO - *MagIndMarPl 82-83*
Clampitt Paper Co. - Houston, TX - *MagIndMarPl 82-83*
Clamshell Press - Santa Rosa, CA - *BoPubDir 4, 5; LitMag&SmPr 83-84*
Clancy, Shulman & Associates Inc. - New York, NY - *IntDirMarRes 83*
Clanton Central Alabama Independent - Clanton, AL - *BaconPubCkNews 84*
Clanton Chilton County News - Clanton, AL - *BaconPubCkNews 84*
Clanton Independent Advertiser - Clanton, AL - *NewsDir 84*
Clapp & Auel Microwave Communications - Sacramento, CA - *Tel&CabFB 84C*
Clappers - Kew Gardens, NY - *BillIntBG 83-84*
Clara City Herald - Clara City, MN - *BaconPubCkNews 84; Ed&PubIntYB 82*
Clara City Telephone - Clara City, MN - *TelDir&BG 83-84*
Clara Music Publishing Corp. - New York, NY - *BillIntBG 83-84*
Clardy's Synergistic Software Inc. - Bellevue, WA - *WhoWMicrocom 83*
Clare County Cleaver - Harrison, MI - *Ed&PubIntYB 82*
Clare Personnel Agency - New York, NY - *MagIndMarPl 82-83*
Clare Sentinel - Clare, MI - *BaconPubCkNews 84; Ed&PubIntYB 82; NewsDir 84*
Claremont Controls Ltd. - Morpeth, England - *MicrocomSwDir 1*
Claremont Courier - Claremont, CA - *Ed&PubIntYB 82; NewsDir 84*
Claremont Courier - *See* Claremont Courier Graphics Corp.
Claremont Courier Graphics Corp. - Claremont, CA - *BaconPubCkNews 84*
Claremont Eagle-Times - Claremont, NH - *BaconPubCkNews 84; LitMarPl 83; NewsDir 84*
Claremont House - San Jose, CA - *BoPubDir 4, 5*
Claremont House Publishing Inc. - *See* OAS Music Group Inc.
Claremont News - Claremont, MN - *BaconPubCkNews 84; Ed&PubIntYB 82*
Claremont Total Library System [of Claremont Colleges] - Claremont, CA - *EISS 5-84 Sup*
Claremore Cable Television - Claremore, OK - *BrCabYB 84; Tel&CabFB 84C*
Claremore Progress - Claremore, OK - *BaconPubCkNews 84; Ed&PubIntYB 82; NewsDir 84*
Claremount Press - New York, NY - *BoPubDir 4, 5*
Clarence Bee - Clarence, NY - *AyerDirPub 83; Ed&PubIntYB 82*
Clarence Bee [of Bee Publications Inc.] - Williamsville, NY - *NewsDir 84*
Clarence Bee - *See* Bee Publications Inc.
Clarence Courier - Clarence, MO - *BaconPubCkNews 84; Ed&PubIntYB 82*
Clarence House Publishers - San Francisco, CA - *BoPubDir 4, 5*
Clarence Telephone Co. Inc. - Clarence, IA - *TelDir&BG 83-84*
Clarenceville Packet, The - Clarenceville, NF, Canada - *Ed&PubIntYB 82*
Clarendon Books - Topsfield, MA - *BoPubDir 4 Sup, 5*
Clarendon Cable Co. [of Real Properties Inc.] - Clarendon, AR - *BrCabYB 84; Tel&CabFB 84C*
Clarendon Cablevision Inc. - Manning, SC - *Tel&CabFB 84C*
Clarendon Cablevision Inc. - Summerton, SC - *BrCabYB 84*
Clarendon Hills Doings - Clarendon Hills, IL - *AyerDirPub 83; Ed&PubIntYB 82*
Clarendon Hills Doings [of The Doings Newspapers] - Hinsdale, IL - *NewsDir 84*
Clarendon Hills Doings - *See* Doings Newspapers, The
Clarendon Hills Suburban Life Graphic - *See* Life Printing & Publishing Co.
Clarendon Monroe County Sun - Clarendon, AR - *BaconPubCkNews 84*
Clarendon Press - Clarendon, TX - *AyerDirPub 83; BaconPubCkNews 84; Ed&PubIntYB 82*
Clarendon Sentinel - Clarendon, AR - *BaconPubCkNews 84*
Clarendon Television Association - Clarendon, PA - *BrCabYB 84; Tel&CabFB 84C*
Claretian Publications - Chicago, IL - *LitMarPl 83, 84*
Claridge Group Ltd., The - New York, NY - *TelAl 83, 84*
Claridge Music [Div. of MPL Communications] - New York, NY - *BillIntBG 83-84*
Clarinda Co., The [Subs. of Nodaway Valley Co.] - Clarinda, IA - *LitMarPl 83, 84*
Clarinda Herald-Journal [of Clarinda Publishing Co. Inc.] - Clarinda, IA - *BaconPubCkNews 84; Ed&PubIntYB 82; NewsDir 84*
Clarion - Dumas, AR - *AyerDirPub 83*
Clarion - Cotati, CA - *AyerDirPub 83*
Clarion - Lakewood, CA - *AyerDirPub 83*
Clarion - Princeton, IN - *AyerDirPub 83*
Clarion - Mt. Hope, KS - *AyerDirPub 83*
Clarion - Rochester, MI - *AyerDirPub 83*
Clarion - Cambridge, NE - *AyerDirPub 83*
Clarion - New Holland, PA - *AyerDirPub 83*
Clarion - Kindersley, SK, Canada - *AyerDirPub 83; Ed&PubIntYB 82*
Clarion Books [of Ticknor & Fields] - New York, NY - *LitMarPl 83, 84; WritMar 84*
Clarion-Ledger [of Mississippi Publishers Corp.] - Jackson, MS - *AyerDirPub 83; Ed&PubIntYB 82; LitMarPl 83, 84*
Clarion Ledger-Jackson Daily News [of Mississippi Publishers Corp.] - Jackson, MS - *AyerDirPub 83; LitMarPl 84*
Clarion News - Clarion, PA - *BaconPubCkNews 84; Ed&PubIntYB 82; NewsDir 84*
Clarion Printing Co. Inc. - Columbia, IL - *BaconPubCkNews 84*
Clarion Productions - *See* Alexandria House Inc.
Clarion, The [of O'Bannon Publishing Co. Inc.] - Corydon, IN - *AyerDirPub 83; NewsDir 84*
Clarion Wright County Monitor - Clarion, IA - *BaconPubCkNews 84; Ed&PubIntYB 82*
Clarissa Independent - Clarissa, MN - *BaconPubCkNews 84; Ed&PubIntYB 82*
Claritas Corp. - Rosslyn, VA - *EISS 83*
Clarity - Berkhamsted, England - *LitMag&SmPr 83-84*
Clarity Books - Winnipeg, MB, Canada - *BoPubDir 4, 5*
Clark Advertising Inc., Walter - Dallas, TX - *StaDirAdAg 2-84*
Clark Advertising, Thomas F. - Summit, NJ - *StaDirAdAg 2-84*
Clark & Associates Inc., E. - Sacramento, CA - *StaDirAdAg 2-84*
Clark & Fritts - New York, NY - *MagIndMarPl 82-83*
Clark Art Institute - Williamstown, MA - *CompReadDB 82*
Clark Boardman Co. Ltd. [Div. of International Thomson Organization Ltd.] - New York, NY - *DirMarMP 83; LitMarPl 83, 84*
Clark, Christina - Studio City, CA - *LitMarPl 84*
Clark Community Cable TV - Clark, SD - *BrCabYB 84*
Clark Co., Arthur H. - Glendale, CA - *LitMag&SmPr 83-84; LitMarPl 83, 84; WritMar 84*
Clark Co., Dick - Burbank, CA - *TelAl 83, 84*
Clark Co. Inc., Charles W. - Brentwood, NY - *AvMarPl 83*
Clark Copy International Corp. - Morton Grove, IL - *DirInfWP 82*
Clark County Cablevision - Jeffersonville, IN - *Tel&CabFB 84C*
Clark County Cablevision Inc. [of Daniels & Associates Inc.] - Clark County, IN - *BrCabYB 84*
Clark County Clipper - Ashland, KS - *AyerDirPub 83; Ed&PubIntYB 82*
Clark County Courier - Clark, SD - *AyerDirPub 83; BaconPubCkNews 84*
Clark County Historical Society - Springfield, OH - *BoPubDir 4, 5*
Clark County Press, The - Neillsville, WI - *AyerDirPub 83; Ed&PubIntYB 82*
Clark, Darwin H. - South Pasadena, CA - *StaDirAdAg 2-84*
Clark Direct Marketing - New York, NY - *AdAge 3-28-84; DirMarMP 83; StaDirAdAg 2-84*
Clark, Edythe S. - Hinsdale, NH - *LitMarPl 83; MagIndMarPl 82-83*
Clark, Edythe S. - Marlborough, NH - *LitMarPl 84*
Clark Enterprises, David J. - New York, NY - *AvMarPl 83*
Clark Executive Recruitment, Toby - New York, NY - *LitMarPl 83, 84; MagIndMarPl 82-83*
Clark-Franklin-Kingston Press Inc. - Westwood, MA - *MagIndMarPl 82-83*
Clark, Howard - Stanfordville, NY - *LitMarPl 83*
Clark Library, Frances - *See* Birch Tree Group Ltd.
Clark Ltd., Alex L. - Toronto, ON, Canada - *AvMarPl 83*
Clark Ltd., T. & T. - Edinburgh, Scotland - *WritMar 84*
Clark, Murphy & Smylie - Brandon, MS - *Tel&CabFB 84C*

Clark Musical Productions - Watseka, IL - *BillIntBG 83-84*
Clark Patriot - Clark, NJ - *AyerDirPub 83*
Clark Patriot [of Tabloid Lithographers Inc.] - Rahway, NJ - *Ed&PubIntYB 82; NewsDir 84*
Clark Patriot - *See* Tabloid Lithographers Inc.
Clark Printing Co. Inc. [A Banta Co.] - North Kansas City, MO - *MagIndMarPl 82-83*
Clark Publishing - Indianapolis, IN - *BillIntBG 83-84*
Clark Publishing Co. - Caldwell, ID - *BoPubDir 4, 5*
Clark, Raymond B. Jr. - St. Michaels, MD - *BoPubDir 4, 5*
Clark Systems - Balesville, IN - *MicrocomMPl 84*
Clark Teleshows Inc., Dick - Burbank, CA - *Tel&CabFB 84C*
Clark University (Center for Technology, Environment, & Development) - Worcester, MA - *BoPubDir 4 Sup, 5*
Clark University Press - Worcester, MA - *BoPubDir 4, 5*
Clarke Advertising, George P. - New York, NY - *AdAge 3-28-84; StaDirAdAg 2-84*
Clarke & Co. - Boston, MA - *DirPRFirms 83*
Clarke & Corcillo - Norwalk, CT - *ArtMar 84; DirMarMP 83; StaDirAdAg 2-84*
Clarke County Democrat, The - Grove Hill, AL - *Ed&PubIntYB 82*
Clarke County Tribune - Quitman, MS - *Ed&PubIntYB 82*
Clarke Courier, The - Berryville, VA - *AyerDirPub 83; Ed&PubIntYB 82*
Clarke Goward Carr & Fitts - Boston, MA - *AdAge 3-28-84; StaDirAdAg 2-84*
Clarke, Irwin & Co. Ltd. - Toronto, ON, Canada - *LitMarPl 83, 84; WritMar 84*
Clarke Literary Agency Inc. - New York, NY - *LitMarPl 83*
Clarkee Music [Div. of Contemporary Artist Enterprises Inc.] - Los Angeles, CA - *BillIntBG 83-84*
Clarkesville Tri-County Advertiser - Clarkesville, GA - *BaconPubCkNews 84*
Clarkfield Advocate - Clarkfield, MN - *BaconPubCkNews 84; Ed&PubIntYB 82*
Clark's Fork Record - Bridger, MT - *Ed&PubIntYB 82*
Clarks Summit Abington Journal - *See* Pennaprint Inc.
Clarks Telephone Co. - Clarks, NE - *TelDir&BG 83-84*
Clarksburg Exponent - Clarksburg, WV - *BaconPubCkNews 84; Ed&PubIntYB 82*
Clarksburg Exponent-Telegram - Clarksburg, WV - *NewsDir 84*
Clarksburg Telegram - Clarksburg, WV - *Ed&PubIntYB 82*
Clarksdale Press Register [of Delta Press Publishing Co. Inc.] - Clarksdale, MS - *BaconPubCkNews 84; NewsDir 84*
Clarkson Colfax County Press - Clarkson, NE - *BaconPubCkNews 84*
Clarkston Herald - Clarkston, WA - *AyerDirPub 83; Ed&PubIntYB 82*
Clarkston Herald - *See* Tribune Newspapers Inc.
Clarkston Neighbor [of Marietta Neighbor Newspapers Inc.] - Marietta, GA - *NewsDir 84*
Clarkston News [of Oxford Leader Inc.] - Clarkston, MI - *BaconPubCkNews 84; Ed&PubIntYB 82; NewsDir 84*
Clarkston Reminder - Clarkston, MI - *BaconPubCkNews 84*
Clarkston Software - Clarkston, MI - *MicrocomMPl 83, 84*
Clarkston Valley American - Clarkston, WA - *BaconPubCkNews 84*
Clarksville Cablevision Co. [of DoKel Communications Corp.] - Clarksville, VA - *BrCabYB 84; Tel&CabFB 84C*
Clarksville Johnson County Graphic - Clarksville, AR - *BaconPubCkNews 84*
Clarksville Leaf Chronicle - Clarksville, TN - *BaconPubCkNews 84*
Clarksville Mecklenburg News, The News-Progress - Chase City, VA - *NewsDir 84*
Clarksville Mutual Telephone Co. - Clarksville, IL - *TelDir&BG 83-84*
Clarksville News-Progress - Clarksville, VA - *BaconPubCkNews 84*
Clarksville Record - Clarksville, MI - *BaconPubCkNews 84; Ed&PubIntYB 82*
Clarksville Star - Clarksville, IA - *BaconPubCkNews 84; Ed&PubIntYB 82*
Clarksville Times - Clarksville, TX - *BaconPubCkNews 84; Ed&PubIntYB 82*
Clarkton Southeastern Times - Clarkton, NC - *BaconPubCkNews 84; Ed&PubIntYB 82*
Clarkwood Corp. [Subs. of Lenz & Riecker Inc.] - Totowa, NJ - *LitMarPl 83, 84*
Clarus Music Ltd. - Yonkers, NY - *AvMarPl 83; BillIntBG 83-84*
Clary Corp. - San Gabriel, CA - *DataDirSup 7-83*
Clary Corp. (Precision Instruments Div.) - San Gabriel, CA - *WhoWMicrocom 83*
CLASS - *See* California Library Authority for Systems & Services
Class Code, Assignee, Index Method Search (Chemistry) - Alexandria, VA - *CompReadDB 82*
Class Code, Assignee, Index, Method Search (Classification) - Alexandria, VA - *CompReadDB 82*
Class Code, Assignee, Index, Method Search (General, Electrical, Mechanical & Chemical) - Alexandria, VA - *CompReadDB 82*
C.L.A.S.S. Magazine [of C.L.A.S.S. Promotions Inc.] - New York, NY - *WritMar 84*
Class 1 Systems - Lansing, IL - *MicrocomSwDir 1*
Class Ontyme-II Communication Network [of Cooperative Library Agency for Systems & Services] - San Jose, CA - *TeleSy&SerDir 2-84*
Classic American Music - Minneapolis, MN - *BillIntBG 83-84*
Classic Audio Visual Inc. - Bloomingdale, IL - *AvMarPl 83*
Classic Car, The - New York, NY - *MagIndMarPl 82-83*
Classic Communications Ltd. - Richmond Hill, ON, Canada - *BrCabYB 84*
Classic Images - Davenport, IA - *LitMag&SmPr 83-84*
Classic Markets Corp. - Norcross, GA - *StaDirAdAg 2-84*
Classic Non-Fiction Library - Woodward, PA - *BoPubDir 4, 5*
Classic Photo Laboratories Inc. - Allentown, PA - *AvMarPl 83*
Classic Publishers - Prospect, KY - *BoPubDir 4, 5*
Classical Calliope - Petersborough, NH - *LitMag&SmPr 83-84*
Classical Folia [Aff. of Institute for Early Christian Iberian Studies] - Worcester, MA - *BoPubDir 4, 5*
Classical Journal - Boulder, CO - *MagDir 84*
Classical Micropublishing Inc. [of Columbia University] - New York, NY - *MicroMarPl 82-83*
Classics Club [Div. of Walter J. Black Inc.] - Roslyn, NY - *LitMarPl 83, 84*
Classics Unltd. Inc. - Caldwell, ID - *BoPubDir 4, 5*
Classified Exchange - Memphis, TN - *BaconPubCkMag 84*
Classified Images Inc. - Toluca Lake, CA - *StaDirAdAg 2-84*
Classified International Advertising Services - Hollywood, FL - *ArtMar 84; Ed&PubIntYB 82*
Classroom Computer Learning - Belmont, CA - *BaconPubCkMag 84*
Classroom Computer News [of Pitman Learning Inc.] - Belmont, CA - *MicrocomMPl 84*
Classroom Consortia Media Inc. - Staten Island, NY - *MicrocomMPl 84*
Classroom World Productions - Raleigh, NC - *ArtMar 84; AvMarPl 83*
Claster Television Productions - Towson, MD - *Tel&CabFB 84C*
Clatskanie Cable TV - Clatskanie, OR - *BrCabYB 84; Tel&CabFB 84C*
Clatskanie Chief - Clatskanie, OR - *BaconPubCkNews 84; Ed&PubIntYB 82*
Clatworthy Colorvues - Santa Cruz, CA - *BoPubDir 4, 5*
Claude & Associates Ltd. - Christchurch, New Zealand - *StaDirAdAg 2-84*
Claude News - Claude, TX - *BaconPubCkNews 84; Ed&PubIntYB 82*
Clausen Associates, Connie - New York, NY - *LitMarPl 83, 84*
Clausen Co., Muriel C. - Oakland, CA - *BoPubDir 4 Sup, 5*
Clavier - Evanston, IL - *ArtMar 84; BaconPubCkMag 84; MagDir 84; WritMar 84*
Claxton Cable Co. [of Tele-Media Corp.] - Claxton, GA - *BrCabYB 84*
Claxton Cablevision Inc. - Claxton, TN - *Tel&CabFB 84C*
Claxton Enterprise - Claxton, GA - *BaconPubCkNews 84; Ed&PubIntYB 82*
Clay Associates Inc., Ev - Coral Gables, FL - *DirPRFirms 83*
Clay Center Dispatch - Clay Center, KS - *BaconPubCkNews 84; Ed&PubIntYB 82; NewsDir 84*
Clay City Cable TV [of Centel Cable Television Co.] - Clay City, KY - *BrCabYB 84*
Clay City County Advocate-Press - Flora, IL - *AyerDirPub 83; NewsDir 84*

Clay City Times [of Hasco Newspapers Inc.] - Clay City, KY - *AyerDirPub 83; BaconPubCkNews 84; Ed&PubIntYB 82; NewsDir 84*
Clay Communications Inc. - Wilmington, NC - *BrCabYB 84*
Clay Communications Inc. - Charleston, WV - *BrCabYB 84; Ed&PubIntYB 82; Tel&CabFB 84S*
Clay County Cable TV Co. Inc. - Louisville, IL - *Tel&CabFB 84C*
Clay County Cablevision Co. Inc. - Louisville, IL - *BrCabYB 84*
Clay County Communications [of Communications Services Inc.] - Kearney, MO - *Tel&CabFB 84C*
Clay County Communications Co. [of Communications Services Inc.] - Gladstone, MO - *BrCabYB 84; Tel&CabFB 84C*
Clay County Courier - Corning, AR - *Ed&PubIntYB 82*
Clay County Crescent - Green Cove Springs, FL - *AyerDirPub 83; Ed&PubIntYB 82*
Clay County Free Press - Clay, WV - *AyerDirPub 83; BaconPubCkNews 84; Ed&PubIntYB 82*
Clay County Leader - Henrietta, TX - *AyerDirPub 83; Ed&PubIntYB 82*
Clay County News - Sutton, NE - *AyerDirPub 83; Ed&PubIntYB 82*
Clay County Republican - Louisville, IL - *Ed&PubIntYB 82*
Clay County Rural Telephone Cooperative Inc. - Cloverdale, IN - *TelDir&BG 83-84*
Clay Dispatch-Tribune [of Townsend Communications Inc.] - Kansas City, MO - *AyerDirPub 83; Ed&PubIntYB 82; NewsDir 84*
Clay Dispatch-Tribune - *See* Townsend Communications Inc.
Clay East/West Shopper News - North Kansas City, MO - *Ed&PubIntYB 82*
Clay Messenger - Clay, WV - *Ed&PubIntYB 82*
Clay Music - *See* Tree International
Clay Pigeon Records [Div. of Clay Pigeon International] - Chicago, IL - *BillIntBG 83-84*
Clay Publicom Inc. - Irvine, CA - *DirPRFirms 83*
Clay Statesman - Celina, TN - *AyerDirPub 83; Ed&PubIntYB 82*
Clay Today - Orange Park, FL - *AyerDirPub 83; Ed&PubIntYB 82*
Clay Video Inc. - Orange Park, FL - *BrCabYB 84; Tel&CabFB 84C*
Clayburn, Barbara B. - Stockton, CA - *BoPubDir 4, 5*
Claymont Communications [Aff. of Coombe Springs Press] - Charles Town, WV - *BoPubDir 4, 4 Sup, 5*
Claysville Weekly Recorder - Claysville, PA - *BaconPubCkNews 84; NewsDir 84*
Clayton Advertising Co., Gene - St. Louis, MO - *StaDirAdAg 2-84*
Clayton & Co. Inc., A. T. - New York, NY - *MagIndMarPl 82-83*
Clayton Associates Inc., Sidney - Chicago, IL - *AdAge 3-28-84; StaDirAdAg 2-84*
Clayton Citizen - Clayton, MO - *Ed&PubIntYB 82*
Clayton Citizen - St. Louis, MO - *Ed&PubIntYB 82; NewsDir 84*
Clayton Citizen, The - Creve Coeur, MO - *AyerDirPub 83*
Clayton County Register [of Griffith Press Inc.] - Elkader, IA - *AyerDirPub 83; Ed&PubIntYB 82; NewsDir 84*
Clayton-Davis & Associates - St. Louis, MO - *AvMarPl 83; BillIntBG 83-84; DirPRFirms 83; StaDirAdAg 2-84*
Clayton Enterprise - Clayton, IL - *Ed&PubIntYB 82*
Clayton Enterprise - *See* Taylor Publishing Co.
Clayton Neighbor - Marietta, GA - *AyerDirPub 83*
Clayton Neighbor, The - Jonesboro, GA - *Ed&PubIntYB 82*
Clayton News - Clayton, NC - *Ed&PubIntYB 82*
Clayton News - *See* County Press Publishers
Clayton News/Daily - Jonesboro, GA - *Ed&PubIntYB 82*
Clayton Publishing House Inc. - St. Louis, MO - *LitMarPl 83, 84*
Clayton Record - Clayton, AL - *BaconPubCkNews 84; Ed&PubIntYB 82*
Clayton Sun - College Park, GA - *AyerDirPub 83*
Clayton Sun [of Decatur News Publishing Co. Inc.] - Decatur, GA - *NewsDir 84*
Clayton Sun - Forest Park/Jonesboro, GA - *Ed&PubIntYB 82*
Clayton Telephone Co. [Aff. of Telephone & Data Systems Inc.] - Clayton, MI - *TelDir&BG 83-84*
Clayton Today - Talihina, OK - *BaconPubCkNews 84*
Clayton Tribune - Clayton, GA - *BaconPubCkNews 84; Ed&PubIntYB 82*
Clayton TV Cable System [of Dorate Interstate Inc.] - Clayton, NM - *BrCabYB 84; Tel&CabFB 84C*
Clayton Union County Leader - Clayton, NM - *BaconPubCkNews 84*
Clayton Watchman Advocate [of St. Louis County Printing & Publishing Co.] - St. Louis, MO - *NewsDir 84*
CLCB Press [Aff. of CLCBI International] - Charlotte, NC - *BoPubDir 4, 5; WritMar 84*
CLCO Inc. - Arlington, VA - *StaDirAdAg 2-84*
Cle Elum Northern Kittitas County Tribune - Cle Elum, WA - *BaconPubCkNews 84*
Clean Cuts Inc. - Baltimore, MD - *BillIntBG 83-84*
Clean Energy Press - Honolulu, HI - *BoPubDir 4, 5; LitMag&SmPr 83-84*
Clean Scene Quarterly - Hallandale, FL - *BaconPubCkMag 84*
Clean Water Report - Silver Spring, MD - *BaconPubCkMag 84*
Cleaning Management [of Harris Communications] - Irvine, CA - *ArtMar 84; BaconPubCkMag 84; MagDir 84*
Clear Beginnings-Women's Writing Workshops - Chesterland, OH - *LitMag&SmPr 83-84*
Clear Cable-Vision Inc. [of BECE Cable Inc.] - Sumiton, AL - *Tel&CabFB 84C*
Clear Cablevision [of Essex Communications Corp.] - Monroeville, AL - *Tel&CabFB 84C*
Clear Cablevision Inc. [of Capital Cities Communications Inc.] - Saline, MI - *BrCabYB 84; Tel&CabFB 84C*
Clear Channel Communications Inc. - San Antonio, TX - *BrCabYB 84*
Clear Channels Cable TV Co. [of Omega Communications] - Freeport, PA - *BrCabYB 84*
Clear Channels Cable TV Co. [of Omega Communications Inc.] - Kittanning, PA - *BrCabYB 84; Tel&CabFB 84C*
Clear Channels Cable TV Co. [of Omega Communications Inc.] - New Bethlehem, PA - *Tel&CabFB 84C*
Clear Creek Courant - Idaho Springs, CO - *AyerDirPub 83; Ed&PubIntYB 82*
Clear Creek Mutual Telephone Co. - Oregon City, OR - *TelDir&BG 83-84*
Clear Crest Cable Television Ltd. - New Liskeard, ON, Canada - *BrCabYB 84*
Clear Lake Cable TV [of North American Communications Corp.] - Clear Lake, SD - *Tel&CabFB 84C*
Clear Lake Citizen - Houston, TX - *NewsDir 84*
Clear Lake Courier - Clear Lake, SD - *BaconPubCkNews 84; Ed&PubIntYB 82*
Clear Lake Independent Telephone Co. - Clear Lake, IA - *TelDir&BG 83-84*
Clear Lake Mirror-Reporter - Clear Lake, IA - *BaconPubCkNews 84; Ed&PubIntYB 82*
Clear Lake Observer American - Clear Lake, CA - *BaconPubCkNews 84; Ed&PubIntYB 82*
Clear Lake Star - Clear Lake, WI - *Ed&PubIntYB 82*
Clear Lake Telephone Co. - Clear Lake, WI - *TelDir&BG 83-84*
Clear Light Inc. - Ft. Lauderdale, FL - *AvMarPl 83; BillIntBG 83-84*
Clear Picture Inc. [of Massillon Cable TV Inc.] - Wooster, OH - *BrCabYB 84; Tel&CabFB 84C*
Clear Ridge Reporter - *See* Vondrak Publications Inc.
Clear Ridge Times [of Lyons Enterprise Publishing Co.] - Lyons, IL - *NewsDir 84*
Clear Television Cable Corp. - Berkeley, NJ - *BrCabYB 84*
Clear Track - Highland, IN - *BaconPubCkMag 84*
Clear TV Cable Corp. - Dover Township, NJ - *BrCabYB 84*
Clear TV Cable Corp. - Toms River, NJ - *Tel&CabFB 84C p.1672*
Clear-View Cable TV Inc. - Chase City, VA - *BrCabYB 84; Tel&CabFB 84C*
Clear-View Cable TV Inc. - Pearlsburg, VA - *BrCabYB 84*
Clear-View Cable TV Inc. - Radford, VA - *Tel&CabFB 84C p.1672*
Clear View Publications - Aurora, IL - *BoPubDir 5*
Clear Vision Cable [of The Essex Group] - Camden, AL - *BrCabYB 84; Tel&CabFB 84C*
Clear Vision Cable [of The Essex Group] - Greensboro, AL - *Tel&CabFB 84C*

Clear Vision Cable [of The Essex Group] - Linden, AL - *BrCabYB 84; Tel&CabFB 84C*
Clear Vision Cable [of The Essex Group] - Livingston, AL - *Tel&CabFB 84C*
Clear Vision Cable [of The Essex Group] - Monroeville, AL - *BrCabYB 84*
Clear Vision Cable [of The Essex Group] - Thomasville, AL - *Tel&CabFB 84C*
Clear Vision Cable [of The Essex Group] - York, AL - *Tel&CabFB 84C*
Clear Vision Cable - Decatur, MS - *BrCabYB 84*
Clear Vision Cable [of The Essex Group] - Houston, MS - *BrCabYB 84*
Clear Vision Cable [of The Essex Group] - Newton, MS - *BrCabYB 84*
Clear Vision Cable [of The Essex Group] - Pontotoc, MS - *BrCabYB 84*
Clear Vision Cable - Union, MS - *BrCabYB 84*
Clear Vision Cable [of The Essex Group] - Water Valley, MS - *BrCabYB 84*
Clear Vision Cable - Lancaster, PA - *NewsDir 84*
Clear Vision Cable [of The Essex Group] - Parsons, TN - *BrCabYB 84*
Clear Vision Cable [of The Essex Group] - Waynesboro, TN - *BrCabYB 84*
Clear Vision Cable of Huntingdon [of The Essex Group] - Bruceton, TN - *Tel&CabFB 84C*
Clear Vision Cable of Huntingdon [of The Essex Group] - Huntingdon, TN - *BrCabYB 84; Tel&CabFB 84C*
Clear Vision Cable of Lewisburg [of The Essex Group] - Lewisburg, TN - *BrCabYB 84; Tel&CabFB 84C*
Clear Vision Cable of Martin [of The Essex Group] - Martin, TN - *BrCabYB 84; Tel&CabFB 84C*
Clear Vision Cable of Martin [of The Essex Group] - Sharon, TN - *BrCabYB 84*
Clear Vision Cable of McKenzie [of The Essex Group] - Atwood, TN - *BrCabYB 84; Tel&CabFB 84C*
Clear Vision Cable of McKenzie [of The Essex Group] - Gleason, TN - *BrCabYB 84; Tel&CabFB 84C*
Clear Vision Cable of McKenzie [of The Essex Group] - McKenzie, TN - *BrCabYB 84; Tel&CabFB 84C*
Clear Vision Cable of McKenzie [of The Essex Group] - Trezevant, TN - *BrCabYB 84*
Clear Vision TV [of Group W Cable] - Lexington, TN - *BrCabYB 84*
Clear Vision TV [of Group W Cable] - Savannah, TN - *BrCabYB 84*
Clear Vision TV [of Group W Cable] - Union City, TN - *BrCabYB 84*
Clear Vision TV of Kosciusko - Kosciusko, MS - *BrCabYB 84; Tel&CabFB 84C*
Clear Vision TV of Milan [of Group W Cable Inc.] - Milan, TN - *BrCabYB 84; Tel&CabFB 84C*
Clear Vision TV of Union City [of Group W Cable Inc.] - Union City, TN - *Tel&CabFB 84C*
Clear-Vu Cable Inc. - Summerville, GA - *BrCabYB 84; Tel&CabFB 84C*
Clear-Vue TV Inc. [of Omni Cable TV Corp.] - Madill, OK - *BrCabYB 84; Tel&CabFB 84C*
Clearfield & Cambria Telephone Co. [Aff. of Mid-Continent Telephone Corp.] - Coalport, PA - *TelDir&BG 83-84*
Clearfield Chronicle - Clearfield, IA - *BaconPubCkNews 84; Ed&PubIntYB 82*
Clearfield Courier - Clearfield, UT - *Ed&PubIntYB 82*
Clearfield Courier [of Roy Printing Co. Newspapers] - Roy, UT - *NewsDir 84*
Clearfield Progress [of Progressive Publishing Co. Inc.] - Clearfield, PA - *NewsDir 84*
Clearing House [of Helen Dwight Reid Educational Foundation] - Washington, DC - *MagIndMarPl 82-83*
Clearing-House for On-Going Research in Cancer Epidemiology [of World Health Organization] - Lyon, France - *EISS 83*
Clearing-House on Conditions of Work [of International Labour Office] - Geneva, Switzerland - *EISS 7-83 Sup*
Clearinghouse for Occupational Safety & Health Information [of U.S. Public Health Service] - Cincinnati, OH - *EISS 83*
Clearinghouse for Occupational Safety & Health Information (Technical Services Div.) - Cincinnati, OH - *CompReadDB 82*
Clearinghouse on Development Communication [of Academy for Educational Development] - Washington, DC - *EISS 5-84 Sup*
Clearinghouse on Health Indexes [of U.S. Public Health Service] - Hyattsville, MD - *EISS 83*
Clearinghouse on the Handicapped [of U.S. Dept. of Education] - Washington, DC - *DataDirOnSer 84; EISS 83*
Clearinghouse Record Corp. - New York, NY - *BillIntBG 83-84*
Clearlake Highlands Clearlake Observer-American - Clearlake Highlands, CA - *NewsDir 84*
Clearly Obscure Press - Ithaca, NY - *LitMag&SmPr 83-84*
Clearsight Cable TV [of Mickelson Media Inc.] - Las Vegas, NM - *BrCabYB 84; Tel&CabFB 84C*
Clearstory - Beltsville, MD - *FBInfSer 80*
Clearview-Auburndale Pennysaver - Jericho, NY - *AyerDirPub 83*
Clearview Cable Co. [of Tele-Communications Inc.] - Gloucester City, NJ - *BrCabYB 84*
Clearview Cable Co. Inc. - Burnsville, NC - *BrCabYB 84*
Clearview Cable Co. Inc. - Spruce Pine, NC - *BrCabYB 84*
Clearview Cable TV [of Group W Cable] - Panama City, FL - *BrCabYB 84*
Clearview Cable TV [of Group W Cable] - Dublin, GA - *BrCabYB 84*
Clearview Cable TV [of Group W Cable] - Milledgeville, GA - *BrCabYB 84*
Clearview Cable TV [of Group W Cable] - Swainsboro, GA - *BrCabYB 84*
Clearview Cable TV [of Group W Cable Inc.] - Valdosta, GA - *BrCabYB 84; Tel&CabFB 84C*
Clearview Cable TV [of Tele-Communications Inc.] - Richmond, IN - *BrCabYB 84; Tel&CabFB 84C*
Clearview Cable TV Corp. [of Communications Services Inc.] - Denham Springs, LA - *Tel&CabFB 84C*
Clearview Cable TV Ltd. - Simcoe, ON, Canada - *BrCabYB 84*
Clearview Cablevision Associates - Surfside Beach, SC - *BrCabYB 84; Tel&CabFB 84C*
Clearview TV Cable - Auburn, WA - *BrCabYB 84*
Clearview TV Cable of Hawaii - Hickam Air Force Base, HI - *BrCabYB 84*
Clearview TV Cable of Hawaii Inc. - Hickman Air Force Base, HI - *Tel&CabFB 84C*
Clearvision [of The Essex Group] - Decatur, MS - *Tel&CabFB 84C*
Clearvision [of The Essex Group] - Houston, MS - *Tel&CabFB 84C*
Clearvision [of The Essex Group] - Louisville, MS - *BrCabYB 84*
Clearvision [of The Essex Group] - Newton, MS - *Tel&CabFB 84C*
Clearvision [of The Essex Group] - Pontotoc, MS - *Tel&CabFB 84C*
Clearvision [of The Essex Group] - Union, MS - *Tel&CabFB 84C*
Clearvision [of The Essex Group] - Water Valley, MS - *Tel&CabFB 84C*
ClearVision Television Inc. [of American Cable Television Inc.] - Nogales, AZ - *BrCabYB 84; Tel&CabFB 84C*
Clearvue Inc. - Chicago, IL - *AvMarPl 83; WritMar 84*
Clearwater Bargain Bill - Largo, FL - *AyerDirPub 83*
Clearwater Cable Vision - Belle Plaine, KS - *BrCabYB 84*
Clearwater Cable Vision - Burden, KS - *BrCabYB 84*
Clearwater Cable Vision - Lee, KS - *BrCabYB 84*
Clearwater Cable Vision - Leon, KS - *BrCabYB 84*
Clearwater Cable Vision Inc. - Belle Plain, KS - *Tel&CabFB 84C*
Clearwater Communications - Headquarters, ID - *BrCabYB 84*
Clearwater Communications - Orofino, ID - *BrCabYB 84; Tel&CabFB 84C*
Clearwater Communications Inc. - Coeur d'Alene, ID - *Tel&CabFB 84C p.1672*
Clearwater Communications Inc. - Grangeville, ID - *BrCabYB 84; Tel&CabFB 84C*
Clearwater Communications Inc. - Weippe, ID - *BrCabYB 84*
Clearwater Journal - La Grande, OR - *LitMag&SmPr 83-84*
Clearwater Navigator - Poughkeepsie, NY - *LitMag&SmPr 83-84*
Clearwater Press - La Grande, OR - *LitMag&SmPr 83-84*
Clearwater Productions - Eugene, OR - *ArtMar 84; WritMar 84*
Clearwater Progress - Kamiah, ID - *AyerDirPub 83; Ed&PubIntYB 82*

Clearwater Publishing Co. Inc. - New York, NY - *LitMarPl 83, 84; MicroMarPl 82-83*
Clearwater Record-Ewing News - Clearwater, NE - *Ed&PublntYB 82*
Clearwater Record-News - Clearwater, NE - *BaconPubCkNews 84*
Clearwater Sun - Clearwater, FL - *BaconPubCkNews 84; Ed&PublntYB 82; NewsDir 84*
Clearwater Times - Belle Plaine, KS - *BaconPubCkNews 84*
Clearwater Times - Clearwater, KS - *Ed&PublntYB 82*
Clearwater Tribune - Orofino, ID - *AyerDirPub 83; Ed&PublntYB 82*
Clearwaters - Bronx, NY - *BaconPubCkMag 84*
Clearwaters - Syracuse, NY - *MagDir 84*
Cleburne County Times - Heber Springs, AR - *AyerDirPub 83; Ed&PublntYB 82; NewsDir 84*
Cleburne Johnson County News - Cleburne, TX - *BaconPubCkNews 84; NewsDir 84*
Cleburne News - Heflin, AL - *AyerDirPub 83; Ed&PublntYB 82*
Cleburne Times-Review [of Donrey Media Group] - Cleburne, TX - *BaconPubCkNews 84; Ed&PublntYB 82; NewsDir 84*
Cleff, Bernie - Philadelphia, PA - *MagIndMarPl 82-83*
Cleis Press - Minneapolis, MN - *BoPubDir 4*
Cleis Press - Pittsburgh, PA - *BoPubDir 5; LitMag&SmPr 83-84*
Cleland, Ward, Smith & Associates Inc. - Winston-Salem, NC - *StaDirAdAg 2-84*
Clement & Ganfield Inc. - New York, NY - *StaDirAdAg 2-84*
Clement Communications - Concordville, PA - *DirMarMP 83*
Clement, David D. [Aff. of Oak Leaf Antiques & Militaria] - Fair Oaks, CA - *BoPubDir 4, 5*
Clement-Petrocik Co., The - New York, NY - *DirPRFirms 83*
Clementine Press - Dubuque, IA - *BoPubDir 5*
Clementon Record Breeze - *See* Cam-Glo Newspapers Inc.
Clements Co., The - Menlo Park, CA - *MicrocomSwDir 1; WhoWMicrocom 83*
Clements, N. R. - *See* Snyder Community Antenna TV Co. Inc.
Clements Research Inc., Mark - New York, NY - *BrCabYB 84; IntDirMarRes 83*
Clements Telephone Co. - Clements, MN - *TelDir&BG 83-84*
Clemmons Courier - Clemmons, NC - *BaconPubCkNews 84; NewsDir 84*
Clemson Messenger - Clemson, SC - *BaconPubCkNews 84; NewsDir 84*
Clermont County Review - Batavia, OH - *Ed&PublntYB 82*
Clermont County Review [of Cincinnati Nichols Printing Co.] - Cincinnati, OH - *AyerDirPub 83; NewsDir 84*
Clermont Courier - Batavia, OH - *AyerDirPub 83; Ed&PublntYB 82*
Clermont Courier - *See* Queen City Suburban Press Inc.
Clermont South Lake Press - Clermont, FL - *BaconPubCkNews 84*
Clermont Sun - Batavia, OH - *AyerDirPub 83; NewsDir 84*
Clermont Sun, The - Clermont County, OH - *Ed&PublntYB 82*
Cleva Computer Ware - Brooklyn, NY - *MicrocomMPl 84*
Cleveland - Cleveland, OH - *ArtMar 84; BaconPubCkMag 84; MagDir 84; MagIndMarPl 82-83*
Cleveland Advocate [of Attaway Investments Inc.] - Cleveland, TX - *BaconPubCkNews 84; Ed&PublntYB 82; NewsDir 84*
Cleveland American - Cleveland, OK - *BaconPubCkNews 84; Ed&PublntYB 82*
Cleveland Area TV Inc. [of Cox Cable Communications Inc.] - Parma, OH - *BrCabYB 84*
Cleveland Athletic Club Magazine - Cleveland, OH - *MagDir 84*
Cleveland Ballet - Cleveland, OH - *BoPubDir 4 Sup, 5*
Cleveland Banner, The - Cleveland, TN - *LitMarPl 83*
Cleveland Bolivar Commercial - Cleveland, MS - *NewsDir 84*
Cleveland Call & Post - Cleveland, OH - *BaconPubCkNews 84*
Cleveland Chess Bulletin - Parma, OH - *LitMag&SmPr 83-84*
Cleveland Citizen, The [of Cleveland Building & Construction Trades Council] - Cleveland, OH - *NewsDir 84*
Cleveland Costume Co. [Div. of Dawson Co.] - Cleveland, OH - *AvMarPl 83*
Cleveland County Herald - Rison, AR - *Ed&PublntYB 82*
Cleveland County Reporter - Lexington/Noble, OK - *Ed&PublntYB 82*
Cleveland County Reporter - Noble, OK - *AyerDirPub 83*
Cleveland County Telephone Co. Inc. - Rison, AR - *TelDir&BG 83-84*
Cleveland Daily Banner - Cleveland, TN - *BaconPubCkNews 84; NewsDir 84*
Cleveland Engineering [of Cleveland Engineering Society] - Cleveland, OH - *MagDir 84*
Cleveland Food Dealer, The [of Cleveland Food Dealers Association Inc.] - Cleveland, OH - *BaconPubCkMag 84; MagDir 84*
Cleveland Garfield Heights Leader - Cleveland, OH - *BaconPubCkNews 84*
Cleveland Integrated Computer System [of Cleveland Public Library] - Cleveland, OH - *EISS 83*
Cleveland/Lyman & Associates - Seattle, WA - *ArtMar 84*
Cleveland/Lyman/Tonkin & Associates - Seattle, WA - *StaDirAdAg 2-84*
Cleveland Metro - Bedford, OH - *Ed&PublntYB 82*
Cleveland Microband Teleservices Inc. - Cleveland, OH - *Tel&CabFB 84C*
Cleveland Museum of Art - Cleveland, OH - *BoPubDir 4, 5*
Cleveland Newspapers - *See* Walls Newspapers
Cleveland On-Line Users [of Diamond Shamrock Corp.] - Painesville, OH - *InfIndMarPl 83*
Cleveland Plain Dealer [of Newhouse Newspapers] - Cleveland, OH - *BaconPubCkNews 84; LitMarPl 83; NewsBur 6; NewsDir 84*
Cleveland Play House, The - Cleveland, OH - *WritMar 84*
Cleveland Point of View - Cleveland, OH - *BaconPubCkNews 84*
Cleveland Press [of The E. W. Scripps Co.] - Cleveland, OH - *Ed&PublntYB 82; NewsBur 6; NewsDir 84*
Cleveland Publishers Inc. - Shelby, NC - *NewsDir 84*
Cleveland South End News - Cleveland, OH - *BaconPubCkNews 84; NewsDir 84*
Cleveland State University (Poetry Center) - Cleveland, OH - *BoPubDir 4, 5; LitMag&SmPr 83-84*
Cleveland Sun Scoop Journal - *See* Post Corp./Sun Newspapers
Cleveland Survey Center - Cleveland, OH - *IntDirMarRes 83*
Cleveland Times - Shelby, NC - *AyerDirPub 83; Ed&PublntYB 82*
Cleveland White County News - Cleveland, GA - *BaconPubCkNews 84*
Clevelander, The - Cleveland, OH - *BaconPubCkMag 84*
Clewiston News - Clewiston, FL - *Ed&PublntYB 82; NewsDir 84*
Clewiston News - *See* Hammel Newspapers of Florida Inc.
Cleworth, Charles W. - Denver, CO - *BoPubDir 4, 5*
Cleworth Publishing Co. Inc. - Cos Cob, CT - *DirMarMP 83; MagIndMarPl 82-83*
Cliche, Maurice - *See* Thetford Video Inc.
Click/Chicago Ltd. - Chicago, IL - *LitMarPl 84*
Clicker City - Haverhill, MA - *LitMarPl 83, 84*
Cliff Catton Press - Glen Falls, NY - *BoPubDir 4*
Clifford/Elliot & Associates - Oakville, ON, Canada - *BoPubDir 4 Sup, 5*
Clifford of Vermont Inc. - Bethel, VT - *DataDirSup 7-83*
Cliffs Notes Inc. - Lincoln, NE - *ArtMar 84; LitMarPl 83, 84; WritMar 84*
Cliffside Park Palisadian - Cliffside Park, NJ - *BaconPubCkNews 84; Ed&PublntYB 82; NewsDir 84*
Clifton-Chebanse Ashkum Advocate - Clifton, IL - *BaconPubCkNews 84*
Clifton Copper Era - Clifton, AZ - *BaconPubCkNews 84*
Clifton Dateline Journal - Clifton, NJ - *BaconPubCkNews 84*
Clifton Forge Daily Review - Clifton Forge, VA - *NewsDir 84*
Clifton Forge-Waynesboro Telephone Co. - Staunton, VA - *TelDir&BG 83-84*
Clifton Independent Prospector - Clifton, NJ - *BaconPubCkNews 84*
Clifton Magazine [of University of Cincinnati] - Cincinnati, OH - *ArtMar 84*
Clifton News Journal, The - Clifton, NJ - *Ed&PublntYB 82*
Clifton News-Tribune - Clifton, KS - *BaconPubCkNews 84; Ed&PublntYB 82*
Clifton Post Eagle - Clifton, NJ - *BaconPubCkNews 84*
Clifton Record - Clifton, TX - *BaconPubCkNews 84; Ed&PublntYB 82*
Clifton Telephone Co. [Aff. of Central Telephone Co. of Texas] - Killeen, TX - *TelDir&BG 83-84*
Climate Assessment Database - Washington, DC - *DirOnDB Spring 84*

Climax Crescent - Climax, MI - *BaconPubCkNews 84; Ed&PubIntYB 82*
Climax Telephone Co. - Climax, MI - *TelDir&BG 83-84*
Clinch County News - Homerville, GA - *AyerDirPub 83; Ed&PubIntYB 82*
Clinch Valley News [of Southwest Virginia Publishers Inc.] - Tazewell, VA - *AyerDirPub 83; Ed&PubIntYB 82; NewsDir 84*
Clinch Valley Times - St. Paul, VA - *AyerDirPub 83; Ed&PubIntYB 82*
Cline-Sigmon Publishers - Hickory, NC - *BoPubDir 4, 5*
Clingstone Press - Jamestown, RI - *BoPubDir 4, 5*
Clinical & Investigative Medicine - Elmsford, NY - *MagDir 84*
Clinical Cardiology - Mahwah, NJ - *BaconPubCkMag 84*
Clinical Chemistry [of American Association for Clinical Chemistry] - Winston-Salem, NC - *BaconPubCkMag 84; MagDir 84; MagIndMarPl 82-83*
Clinical Chemistry Lookout [of Karolinska Institutet] - Stockholm, Sweden - *CompReadDB 82*
Clinical Chemistry News - Washington, DC - *BaconPubCkMag 84*
Clinical Data Design - Milwaukee, WI - *MicrocomMPl 84*
Clinical Lab Letter - Brea, CA - *BaconPubCkMag 84*
Clinical Lab Products - Amherst, NH - *BaconPubCkMag 84; MagDir 84*
Clinical Laboratory International - Del Mar, CA - *BaconPubCkMag 84*
Clinical Nuclear Medicine - Philadelphia, PA - *MagDir 84*
Clinical Obstetrics & Gynecology - Philadelphia, PA - *MagIndMarPl 82-83*
Clinical Orthopaedics & Related Research - Philadelphia, PA - *MagIndMarPl 82-83*
Clinical Pediatrics - Philadelphia, PA - *MagDir 84; MagIndMarPl 82-83*
Clinical Pharmacology & Therapeutics - St. Louis, MO - *MagDir 84; MagIndMarPl 82-83*
Clinical Pharmacy - Bethesda, MD - *BaconPubCkMag 84*
Clinical Preventive Dentistry [of J. B. Lippincott Co.] - Philadelphia, PA - *BaconPubCkMag 84; MagDir 84; MagIndMarPl 82-83*
Clinical Protocols [of National Cancer Institute] - Bethesda, MD - *CompReadDB 82*
Clinical Psychiatry News - Rockville, MD - *BaconPubCkMag 84; MagDir 84; MagIndMarPl 82-83*
Clinical Psychology Publishing Co. - Brandon, VT - *BoPubDir 4, 5; MagIndMarPl 82-83*
Clinical Research - Thorofare, NJ - *BaconPubCkMag 84; MagDir 84; MagIndMarPl 82-83*
Clinical Research Centre (Bioengineering Div.) - Harrow, England - *CompReadDB 82*
Clinical Social Work Journal - New York, NY - *MagIndMarPl 82-83*
Clinical Toxicology of Commercial Products [of Dartmouth Medical School] - Hanover, NH - *EISS 83*
Clinical Toxicology of Commercial Products [of University of Rochester] - Rochester, NY - *DBBus 82*
Clinical Toxicology of Commercial Products [of Computer Sciences Corp.] - Falls Church, VA - *DataDirOnSer 84*
Clinitemp Inc. - Indianapolis, IN - *BoPubDir 4, 5*
Clinprot - Bethesda, MD - *DirOnDB Spring 84*
Clinton Advisor - *See* Advisor Newspapers
Clinton & Graceville Northern Star - Clinton, MN - *BaconPubCkNews 84*
Clinton Cable TV [of North American Communications Corp.] - Clinton, MN - *BrCabYB 84*
Clinton Cable TV Co. Inc. [of Nichols Investment Corp.] - Clinton, IN - *BrCabYB 84; Tel&CabFB 84C*
Clinton Cable TV Inc. [of Tar River Communications Inc.] - Clinton, NC - *BrCabYB 84; Tel&CabFB 84C*
Clinton Cable TV Inc. [of Matrix Enterprises Inc.] - Clinton, TN - *BrCabYB 84*
Clinton Cablevision Service Inc. - Clinton, AR - *BrCabYB 84; Tel&CabFB 84C*
Clinton Cablevision System Inc. - Clinton, MO - *Tel&CabFB 84C*
Clinton Chronicle - Clinton, SC - *BaconPubCkNews 84; Ed&PubIntYB 82; NewsDir 84*
Clinton Clintonian - Clinton, IN - *BaconPubCkNews 84*
Clinton County Cable Corp. [of UltraCom Inc.] - Wilmington, OH - *BrCabYB 84; Tel&CabFB 84C*
Clinton County/County Journal - Belleville, IL - *AyerDirPub 83*
Clinton County Journal - *See* Journal Newspapers of Southern Illinois
Clinton County News - Mascoutah, IL - *NewsDir 84*
Clinton County News - New Baden, IL - *AyerDirPub 83; Ed&PubIntYB 82*
Clinton County News - Albany, KY - *AyerDirPub 83*
Clinton County News - Clinton County, KY - *Ed&PubIntYB 82*
Clinton County News - St. Johns, MI - *AyerDirPub 83; Ed&PubIntYB 82*
Clinton Courier - Clinton, NY - *BaconPubCkNews 84; Ed&PubIntYB 82*
Clinton Courier-News - Clinton, TN - *BaconPubCkNews 84; Ed&PubIntYB 82; NewsDir 84*
Clinton Daily Clintonian [of Clinton Color Crafters Inc.] - Clinton, IN - *NewsDir 84*
Clinton Daily Democrat - Clinton, MO - *NewsDir 84*
Clinton Daily Item [of W. J. Coulter Press Inc.] - Clinton, MA - *Ed&PubIntYB 82; NewsDir 84*
Clinton Daily Journal - Clinton, IL - *BaconPubCkNews 84; Ed&PubIntYB 82; NewsDir 84*
Clinton Daily News - Clinton, OK - *BaconPubCkNews 84; Ed&PubIntYB 82; NewsDir 84*
Clinton Democrat - Clinton, MO - *BaconPubCkNews 84; Ed&PubIntYB 82*
Clinton Eye - Clinton, MO - *BaconPubCkNews 84; Ed&PubIntYB 82*
Clinton-Fraser-Mt. Clemens Advisor - Mt. Clemens, MI - *Ed&PubIntYB 82*
Clinton Herald - Clinton, IA - *BaconPubCkNews 84; Ed&PubIntYB 82; NewsDir 84*
Clinton Item - Clinton, MA - *BaconPubCkNews 84*
Clinton Local - Clinton, MI - *BaconPubCkNews 84; Ed&PubIntYB 82*
Clinton Music Productions - Houston, TX - *AvMarPl 83*
Clinton News - Clinton, MS - *BaconPubCkNews 84; Ed&PubIntYB 82*
Clinton News-Record - Clinton, ON, Canada - *Ed&PubIntYB 82*
Clinton Recorder - Clinton, CT - *BaconPubCkNews 84; Ed&PubIntYB 82; NewsDir 84*
Clinton Sampson Independent - Clinton, NC - *NewsDir 84*
Clinton Topper - Clinton, WI - *BaconPubCkNews 84; Ed&PubIntYB 82*
Clinton Town Talk - Clinton, IA - *BaconPubCkNews 84; NewsDir 84*
Clinton TV Cable Co. Inc. [of Matrix Enterprises Inc.] - Clinton, TN - *Tel&CabFB 84C*
Clinton Van Buren County Democrat - Clinton, AR - *BaconPubCkNews 84; NewsDir 84*
Clinton Watchman - Clinton, LA - *NewsDir 84*
Clinton Watchman - *See* Louisiana Suburban Press
Clintonian - Clinton, IN - *AyerDirPub 83*
Clintonville Shopper's Guide - Clintonville, WI - *AyerDirPub 83*
Clintonville Tribune Gazette [of Clintonville Publishing Co.] - Clintonville, WI - *BaconPubCkNews 84; NewsDir 84*
CLIO Bibliography Series [of American Bibliographical Center] - Santa Barbara, CA - *CompReadDB 82*
Clio Messenger - Clio, MI - *BaconPubCkNews 84; Ed&PubIntYB 82*
Clio Press Ltd. - Oxford, England - *CompReadDB 82*
Clip Bits [of Dynamic Graphics Inc.] - Peoria, IL - *WritMar 84*
Clipper - Elba, AL - *AyerDirPub 83*
Clipper - Los Angeles, CA - *MagDir 84*
Clipper - Stewardson, IL - *AyerDirPub 83*
Clipper - Garrett, IN - *AyerDirPub 83*
Clipper - Duxbury, MA - *AyerDirPub 83*
Clipper - Lexington, NE - *AyerDirPub 83*
Clipper - Shelton, NE - *AyerDirPub 83*
Clipper - Hennessey, OK - *AyerDirPub 83*
Clipper, The - Cunningham, KS - *AyerDirPub 83*
Clipper-Times & Lexington Unit Journal - Chenoa, IL - *AyerDirPub 83*
Clita Music Inc. - *See* Mietus Copyright Management
Cload Magazine - Goleta, CA - *WhoWMicrocom 83*
Cload Magazine - Santa Barbara, CA - *LitMag&SmPr 83-84; MicrocomMPl 83, 84*
Cload Publications Inc. - Santa Barbara, CA - *WritMar 84*

Clock Music - *See* Moody Music, Doug
Clocking Manufacturer's Association of the U.S.A. - New York, NY - *BoPubDir 4 Sup*
Clockus Music Co. - Milford, CA - *BillIntBG 83-84*
Clockwork Software - Colorado Springs, CO - *MicrocomMPl 83*
Clodele Enterprises Inc. - Pine Bluff, AR - *BoPubDir 4, 5*
Clokey Productions Inc. - Covina, CA - *Tel&CabFB 84C*
Clone Publishers [Aff. of Clone Records Inc.] - Rocky Point, NY - *BoPubDir 4, 5*
Clone Records - Akron, OH - *BillIntBG 83-84*
Clone Software - Denver, CO - *MicrocomMPl 84*
Clone Software - Lakewood, CO - *MicrocomMPl 83*
Clonetone Music Co. - New York, NY - *BillIntBG 83-84*
Cloquet Billboard Shopper [of Cloquet Newspapers Inc.] - Cloquet, MN - *NewsDir 84*
Cloquet Cablevision [of North American Communications Corp.] - Cloquet, MN - *Tel&CabFB 84C*
Cloquet Pine Knot [of Cloquet Newspapers Inc.] - Cloquet, MN - *BaconPubCkNews 84; Ed&PubIntYB 82; NewsDir 84*
Closing the Gap [of Random Graphics] - Henderson, MN - *MicrocomMPl 84*
Clothes & Textiles Bibliography [of University of Alberta] - Edmonton, AB, Canada - *DataDirOnSer 84*
Clothing Manufacturers Association of the U.S.A. - New York, NY - *BoPubDir 5*
Cloud Enterprises - Orinda, CA - *BoPubDir 4, 5*
Cloud Hopper Music Inc. - College Park, GA - *BillIntBG 83-84*
Cloudburst Press of America Inc. - Point Roberts, WA - *LitMarPl 83*
Clouse, M. K. - Murdock, KS - *LitMarPl 83*
Clover Herald - Clover, SC - *BaconPubCkNews 84; Ed&PubIntYB 82*
Clover Press - Regina, SK, Canada - *LitMag&SmPr 83-84*
Cloverdale Press Inc. - New York, NY - *LitMarPl 83, 84*
Cloverdale Reveille - Cloverdale, CA - *AyerDirPub 83; Ed&PubIntYB 82; NewsDir 84*
Cloverdale Reveille & Geyserville Press - Cloverdale, CA - *BaconPubCkNews 84*
Cloverfork Inc. [of Matrix Enterprises Inc.] - Evarts, KY - *BrCabYB 84*
Cloverfork Inc. - Crossville, TN - *Tel&CabFB 84C*
Clovernook Printing House for the Blind - Cincinnati, OH - *LitMarPl 83, 84*
Cloverport Cablevision [of Kentuckiana Cablevision Inc.] - Cloverport, KY - *BrCabYB 84; Tel&CabFB 84C*
Clovis Curry County Times - Clovis, NM - *BaconPubCkNews 84*
Clovis Independent Tribune [of El Dorado Newspapers] - Clovis, CA - *BaconPubCkNews 84; Ed&PubIntYB 82; NewsDir 84*
Clovis Laboratory Software - Clovis, CA - *MicrocomMPl 84*
Clovis News-Journal - Clovis, NM - *BaconPubCkNews 84; Ed&PubIntYB 82; NewsDir 84*
CLS & Associates Inc. - Aurora, CO - *AvMarPl 83*
CLU Journal - Bryn Mawr, PA - *MagDir 84*
Club [of Fiona Press Inc.] - Newtown, CT - *BaconPubCkMag 84; Folio 83; MagDir 84*
Club & Food Service - Westbury, NY - *BaconPubCkMag 84; MagDir 84*
Club del Libro [of AIMS International Marketing Services Inc.] - Springfield, OH - *LitMarPl 84*
Club International [of Fiona Press Inc.] - Newtown, CT - *Folio 83*
Club Leabhar - Portree, Scotland - *LitMag&SmPr 83-84*
Club Living - Hartsdale, NY - *MagDir 84*
Club Management [of Commerce Publishing Co.] - St. Louis, MO - *BaconPubCkMag 84; MagDir 84; MagIndMarPl 82-83*
Club Member, The - New York, NY - *BaconPubCkMag 84*
Club TV de Matagami - Matagami, PQ, Canada - *BrCabYB 84*
Clubdate Magazine [of MBC Inc.] - Cleveland, OH - *WritMar 84*
Clubhouse - Berrien Springs, MI - *WritMar 84*
ClusterPlus [of Donnelley Marketing Information Services] - Stamford, CT - *DataDirOnSer 84; DirOnDB Spring 84*
Clute Brazosport Facts [of Review Publishers Inc.] - Clute, TX - *NewsDir 84*
CLW Communications Group Inc. - Chattanooga, TN - *BrCabYB 84*
CLX - Brandon, MB, Canada - *BrCabYB 84*
Clyde & Varius Inc. - Chicago, IL - *StaDirAdAg 2-84*
Clyde Digital Systems Inc. - Provo, UT - *DataDirSup 7-83*
Clyde Enterprise - Clyde, OH - *BaconPubCkNews 84; Ed&PubIntYB 82*
Clyde Journal - Clyde, TX - *BaconPubCkNews 84; Ed&PubIntYB 82*
Clyde Press - Buffalo, NY - *BoPubDir 4, 5; LitMag&SmPr 83-84*
Clyde Republican - Clyde, KS - *BaconPubCkNews 84; Ed&PubIntYB 82*
Clyde Service Corp. - Riverside, IL - *StaDirAdAg 2-84*
Clymer Cable TV Co. - Clymer, PA - *BrCabYB 84*
Clymer Telephone Co. Inc. [Aff. of Mid-Continent Telephone Corp.] - Clymer, NY - *TelDir&BG 83-84*
CM Group Ltd. - London, England - *StaDirAdAg 2-84*
CM Publishing - El Paso, TX - *BoPubDir 4 Sup, 5*
CMA Associates - Yucca Valley, CA - *WhoWMicrocom 83*
CMA Cablevision [of Cable Management Associates Inc.] - Walkersville, MD - *Tel&CabFB 84C*
CMA Cablevision [of Cable Management Associates Inc.] - Alkol, WV - *Tel&CabFB 84C*
CMA Cablevision [of Cable Management Associates Inc.] - Piedmont, WV - *Tel&CabFB 84C*
CMA Cablevision [of Master Telecable Inc.] - Prenter, WV - *BrCabYB 84; Tel&CabFB 84C*
CMA Cablevision Inc. [of Cable Management Associates Inc.] - Boomer, WV - *Tel&CabFB 84C*
CMA Cablevision Inc. [of Cable Management Associates Inc.] - Campbells Creek, WV - *Tel&CabFB 84C*
CMA Cablevision Inc. [of Cable Management Associates Inc.] - Decota, WV - *Tel&CabFB 84C*
CMA Cablevision Inc. [of Cable Management Associates Inc.] - Glen Ferris, WV - *Tel&CabFB 84C*
CMA Cablevision Inc. [of Cable Management Associates Inc.] - Jodie, WV - *Tel&CabFB 84C*
CMA Cablevision Inc. [of Cable Management Associates Inc.] - London, WV - *Tel&CabFB 84C*
CMA Cablevision Inc. [of Cable Management Associates Inc.] - Miami, WV - *Tel&CabFB 84C*
CMA Cablevision Inc. [of Cable Management Associates Inc.] - Racine, WV - *Tel&CabFB 84C*
CMA Cablevision of Chelyan [of Cable Management Associates Inc.] - Chelyan, WV - *Tel&CabFB 84C*
CMA Cablevision of Frostburg [of Cable Management Associates Inc.] - Frostburg, MD - *Tel&CabFB 84C*
CMA Cablevision of Keyser [of Cable Management Associates Inc.] - Keyser, WV - *Tel&CabFB 84C*
CMA Cablevision of Lewisburg [of Cable Management Associates Inc.] - Lewisburg, WV - *Tel&CabFB 84C*
CMA Cablevision of Northfork [of Cable Management Associates Inc.] - Northfork, WV - *Tel&CabFB 84C*
CMA Micro Computer - Yucca Valley, CA - *MicrocomMPl 84; MicrocomSwDir 1*
CMC International [Subs. of Computer Marketing Corp.] - Bellevue, WA - *MicrocomMPl 83, 84; WhoWMicrocom 83*
CMC News Computer & Media Center [of CMC News] - Cannon Falls, MN - *MicrocomMPl 84*
CMEA News - Concord, CA - *BaconPubCkMag 84*
CMG - Winchester, MA - *MagIndMarPl 82-83*
CMG Computer Management Group - Croydon, England - *WhoWMicrocom 83*
CMH Records Inc. - Los Angeles, CA - *BillIntBG 83-84*
CMI Cable Communications Inc. - La Mesa, CA - *Tel&CabFB 84C p.1672*
CMI Corp. - Troy, MI - *ADAPSOMemDir 83-84*
CMI Inc. - Ft. Worth, TX - *HBIndAd&MS 82-83*
CMLS On-Line Data Service [of Computer Multiple Listing Service] - Fairfax, VA - *DataDirOnSer 84; DirOnDB Spring 84*
CMP Data Services Div. [of CMP Publications Inc.] - Manhasset, NY - *DirMarMP 83*
CMR Associates [Div. of LSI Inc.] - Crofton, MD - *BoPubDir 4, 5; LitMarPl 84*
CMS Inc. - Chicago, IL - *WhoWMicrocom 83*
CMS Records Inc. - New York, NY - *BillIntBG 83-84*
CMS Software Systems Inc. - Mesquite, TX - *MicrocomMPl 83, 84; WhoWMicrocom 83*
CMV Software Specialists Inc. - Sioux Falls, SD - *MicrocomMPl 84; MicrocomSwDir 1*
CNEXO - Brest, France - *DirOnDB Spring 84*

CNI - Toronto, ON, Canada - *DirOnDB Spring 84*
CNMR - Delft, Netherlands - *DirOnDB Spring 84*
CNN Headline News [of Turner Broadcasting Systems Inc.] - Atlanta, GA - *CabTVPrDB 83; Tel&CabFB 84C*
CNN Radio [Div. of Turner Broadcasting Systems Inc.] - Atlanta, GA - *LitMarPl 84*
CNRS Centre de Documentation Scientifique et Technique - Paris, France - *InfoS 83-84*
CNRSLAB [of Questel Inc.] - Washington, DC - *DataDirOnSer 84*
CNRSLAB [of Centre National de la Recherche Scientifique] - Paris, France - *CompReadDB 82*
CNRSLAB - *See* Labinfo
CNUCE [of National Research Council] - Pisa, Italy - *EISS 83; InfIndMarPl 83*
Co-Ed [of Scholastic Inc.] - New York, NY - *BaconPubCkMag 84; Folio 83; MagDir 84; MagIndMarPl 82-83*
Co-Evolution Quarterly - Sausalito, CA - *MagIndMarPl 82-83*
Co-Op City News - Bronx, NY - *Ed&PubIntYB 82*
Co-Op City News - New York, NY - *AyerDirPub 83*
Co-Op City Times - Bronx, NY - *Ed&PubIntYB 82*
Co-Op Country News - St. Paul, MN - *BaconPubCkMag 84; MagDir 84*
Co-Op TV Inc. - Wardensville, WV - *BrCabYB 84; Tel&CabFB 84C*
Co-Operative Automation Group - London, England - *EISS 83*
Co-Operative College of Canada - Saskatoon, SK, Canada - *BoPubDir 4, 5*
Co-Operative Housing Federation of Toronto Inc. - Toronto, ON, Canada - *BoPubDir 4, 5*
Co-Ordination Group Inc., The - Chicago, IL - *StaDirAdAg 2-84*
Coach & Athlete - Needham, MA - *MagDir 84; MagIndMarPl 82-83*
Coach House Press - Toronto, ON, Canada - *BoPubDir 4; LitMag&SmPr 83-84; LitMarPl 83, 84*
Coach House Press Inc. - Chicago, IL - *BoPubDir 4, 5; LitMarPl 84*
Coachella Desert Rancher - *See* Desert Associated Newspapers
Coachella Valley Sun - Coachella, CA - *Ed&PubIntYB 82*
Coachella Valley Sun [of Evening News Association] - Indio, CA - *AyerDirPub 83; NewsDir 84*
Coachella Valley Sun - *See* Desert Associated Newspapers
Coachella Valley Television [of Palmer Communications Inc.] - Palm Desert, CA - *BrCabYB 84; Tel&CabFB 84C*
Coaches' Book Club [of Prentice-Hall Inc.] - Englewood, NJ - *LitMarPl 83, 84*
Coaching Review - Ottawa, ON, Canada - *ArtMar 84; WritMar 84*
Coaching Slo'Pitch Softball - Lima, OH - *LitMag&SmPr 83-84*
Coaching Women's Athletics - Madison, CT - *MagDir 84*
COADCO - Kansas City, MO - *StaDirAdAg 2-84*
Coakley Heagerty Cos. Ltd., The - Santa Clara, CA - *AdAge 3-28-84; StaDirAdAg 2-84*
Coal Abstracts [of University of Alberta] - Edmonton, AB, Canada - *DataDirOnSer 84*
Coal Age [of McGraw-Hill Publications Co.] - New York, NY - *BaconPubCkMag 84; EISS 83; MagDir 84; MagIndMarPl 82-83; WritMar 84*
Coal City Courant - *See* Bailey Printing & Publishing Inc.
Coal City Courant, The - Coal City, IL - *Ed&PubIntYB 82*
Coal City Express - Wilmington, IL - *AyerDirPub 83*
Coal City Express - *See* G.W. Communications
Coal Data Bank [of U.S. Dept. of Energy] - Washington, DC - *DBBus 82; DirOnDB Spring 84*
Coal Data Banks [of Data Resources Inc.] - Lexington, MA - *DataDirOnSer 84*
Coal Data Base [of International Energy Agency] - London, England - *CompReadDB 82; DBBus 82; DirOnDB Spring 84; OnBibDB 3*
Coal Dust Music Inc. - *See* Coal Miners Music Inc.
Coal Energy News - St. Clairsville, OH - *MagDir 84*
Coal Industry News - Washington, DC - *MagDir 84; MagIndMarPl 82-83*
Coal Industry News - New York, NY - *WritMar 84*
Coal Miner, The - Vancouver, BC, Canada - *BaconPubCkMag 84*
Coal Miners Music Inc. - Nashville, TN - *BillIntBG 83-84*
Coal Mining & Processing - Chicago, IL - *BaconPubCkMag 84; MagDir 84; MagIndMarPl 82-83*
Coal Model [of Data Resources Inc.] - Lexington, MA - *DataDirOnSer 84*
Coal Operator, The - Beckley, WV - *BaconPubCkMag 84; MagDir 84*
Coal Outlook Marketline [of Pasha Publications] - Arlington, VA - *BaconPubCkMag 84; DataDirOnSer 84*
Coal People - Charleston, WV - *BaconPubCkMag 84*
Coal R & D - Washington, DC - *BaconPubCkMag 84*
Coal Technology Information Centre [of Alberta Research Council] - Edmonton, AB, Canada - *EISS 83*
Coal Valley News - Madison, WV - *AyerDirPub 83; Ed&PubIntYB 82*
Coal Week International - Washington, DC - *BaconPubCkMag 84*
Coale Concepts - Springfield, IL - *DirPRFirms 83*
Coalfield Progress - Norton, VA - *AyerDirPub 83*
Coalgate Cablevision Co. - Coalgate, OK - *BrCabYB 84; Tel&CabFB 84C*
Coalgate Record Register - Coalgate, OK - *BaconPubCkNews 84; Ed&PubIntYB 82*
Coalinga CATV [of McVay Communications Inc.] - Coalinga, CA - *BrCabYB 84; Tel&CabFB 84C*
Coalinga Record - Coalinga, CA - *BaconPubCkNews 84; Ed&PubIntYB 82; NewsDir 84*
Coalink - Kensington, MD - *DirOnDB Spring 84*
Coalition for the Medical Rights of Women - San Francisco, CA - *BoPubDir 4, 5*
Coalition on Women & Religion - Seattle, WA - *BoPubDir 4, 5*
Coalpro - London, England - *DirOnDB Spring 84*
Coalrip - *See* Coalpro
Coalville Summit County Bee - *See* Wave Publishing Co.
Coast - Myrtle Beach, SC - *BaconPubCkMag 84*
Coast Cable Vision Ltd. - Delta, BC, Canada - *Tel&CabFB 84C*
Coast Cablevision Ltd. - Sechelt, BC, Canada - *BrCabYB 84*
Coast Communications Co. Inc. - Ocean Shores, WA - *BrCabYB 84; Tel&CabFB 84C*
Coast Communications Co. Inc. - Pacific Beach, WA - *Tel&CabFB 84C*
Coast Computer Supplies - Novato, CA - *MicrocomMPl 83*
Coast Dispatch Group - Encinitas, CA - *AyerDirPub 83; Ed&PubIntYB 82*
Coast Enterprises - Westlake Village, CA - *DirPRFirms 83*
Coast Guard, The - Shelburne, NS, Canada - *AyerDirPub 83; Ed&PubIntYB 82*
Coast Highway Music - *See* Open End Music
Coast Media News Group - Newport Beach, CA - *BaconPubCkNews 84*
Coast Media Newspapers - Culver City, CA - *BaconPubCkNews 84*
Coast Music - *See* Amestoy Music
Coast News - Dade City, FL - *AyerDirPub 83*
Coast News - Gibsons, BC, Canada - *AyerDirPub 83*
Coast Productions - Hollywood, CA - *AvMarPl 83; TelAl 83, 84; Tel&CabFB 84C*
Coast Special Effects - North Hollywood, CA - *TelAl 83, 84; Tel&CabFB 84C*
Coast Star, The - Manasquan, NJ - *Ed&PubIntYB 82*
Coast Telecourses - Fountain Valley, CA - *AvMarPl 83*
Coast to Coast Advertising - Tampa, FL - *StaDirAdAg 2-84*
Coast to Coast Books - Portland, OR - *BoPubDir 4, 5; LitMag&SmPr 83-84*
Coast to Coast Publishing Group - New York, NY - *BillIntBG 83-84*
Coast to Coast Records Inc. - New York, NY - *BillIntBG 83-84*
Coast TV Cable Inc. - Long Beach, MS - *BrCabYB 84; Tel&CabFB 84C*
Coast Valley Cable Systems Inc. [of Mickelson Media Inc.] - Ft. Coasta, CA - *BrCabYB 84*
Coastal Bend Cablevision [of Capital Cities Communications Inc.] - Aransas Pass, TX - *BrCabYB 84; Tel&CabFB 84C*
Coastal Cable Corp. [of Adams-Russell Co. Inc.] - Bangor, ME - *BrCabYB 84; Tel&CabFB 84C*
Coastal Cable Inc. - Port O'Connor, TX - *BrCabYB 84*
Coastal Cable Services [of Mickelson Media Inc.] - Darien, GA - *Tel&CabFB 84C*

Coastal Cable Services [of Mickelson Media Inc.] - Jekyll Island, GA - *BrCabYB 84; Tel&CabFB 84C*
Coastal Cable TV [of Chinco Properties Inc.] - Chincoteague, VA - *BrCabYB 84; Tel&CabFB 84C*
Coastal Cablevision Corp. - Suwannee, FL - *BrCabYB 84*
Coastal Cablevision Corp. - Hinesville, GA - *BrCabYB 84; Tel&CabFB 84C*
Coastal Computer Systems Inc. - Surfside Beach, SC - *MicrocomMPl 83*
Coastal Courier, The - Hinesville, GA - *AyerDirPub 83; Ed&PubIntYB 82*
Coastal Data Products Inc. - Miami, FL - *DataDirSup 7-83*
Coastal Engineering Information Analysis Center [of U.S. Army] - Ft. Belvoir, VA - *EISS 83*
Coastal Georgia Historical Society - St. Simons Island, GA - *BoPubDir 4, 5*
Coastal Journal - Bath, ME - *AyerDirPub 83*
Coastal Journal - Gloucester, MA - *WritMar 84*
Coastal Magazine - Savannah, GA - *MagDir 84*
Coastal Plains Farmer - Raleigh, NC - *MagDir 84*
Coastal Plains Publishing Co. - Danville, VA - *ArtMar 84*
Coastal Telephone & Electronics Corp. [Aff. of Century Telephone Enterprises Inc.] - Breaux Bridge, LA - *TelDir&BG 83-84*
Coastal Utilities Inc. - Hinesville, GA - *TelDir&BG 83-84*
Coastland Times - Manteo, NC - *AyerDirPub 83*
Coastline Dispatch - San Clemente, CA - *AyerDirPub 83*
Coastside Cable TV Inc. - Ft. Ord, CA - *BrCabYB 84; Tel&CabFB 84C*
Coastside Cable TV Inc. - Half Moon Bay, CA - *BrCabYB 84; Tel&CabFB 84C*
Coastside Cable TV Inc. - Placer County, CA - *Tel&CabFB 84C*
Coastside Cable TV Inc. - Rocklin, CA - *BrCabYB 84; Tel&CabFB 84C*
Coastside Cable TV Inc. - Williams, CA - *Tel&CabFB 84C*
Coastside Cable TV Inc. - *See* Hazen, Dean
Coastside Chronicle - Pacifica, CA - *Ed&PubIntYB 82*
Coastside Chronicle - South San Francisco, CA - *AyerDirPub 83*
Coat of Arms Music - Oak Hill, OH - *BillIntBG 83-84*
Coates Antiques, Pamela - Ardencroft, DE - *BoPubDir 4, 5*
Coatesville Record - Coatesville, PA - *BaconPubCkNews 84*
Coatesville Village News - *See* Chester County Communications Ltd.
Coatings - Oakville, ON, Canada - *BaconPubCkMag 84*
Coatings Technology Journal - Philadelphia, PA - *MagDir 84*
Coaxial Analysts Inc. - Denver, CO - *CabTVFinDB 83; InterCabHB 3*
Coaxial Associates of Florida Ltd. - Sarasota, FL - *Tel&CabFB 84C p.1672*
Coaxial Brokerage Associates Inc. - Denver, CO - *CabTVFinDB 83*
Coaxial Cable Co. [of American TV & Communications Corp.] - Franklin, PA - *BrCabYB 84; Tel&CabFB 84C*
Coaxial Cable TV Corp. [of Times Publishing Co.] - Cambridge Springs, PA - *BrCabYB 84; Tel&CabFB 84C*
Coaxial Communications [of Group W Cable Inc.] - Sarasota, FL - *BrCabYB 84 p.D-299; Tel&CabFB 84C p.1672*
Coaxial Communications - Temple Terrace, FL - *InterCabHB 3*
Coaxial Communications - Columbus, OH - *BrCabYB 84; HomeVid&CabYB 82-83; InterCabHB 3; Tel&CabFB 84C*
Coaxial Development Associates - Washington, DC - *BrCabYB 84 p.D-299*
Coaxial Development Associates - Camden, SC - *BrCabYB 84*
Cobalt Forecast - Bala Cynwyd, PA - *DirOnDB Spring 84*
Cobar Inc. - Anaheim, CA - *DataDirSup 7-83*
Cobb/Dunlop Publisher Services Inc. - New York, NY - *LitMarPl 83, 84; MagIndMarPl 82-83*
Cobbers [Aff. of Martensen Co. Inc.] - Williamsburg, VA - *BoPubDir 4, 5; LitMag&SmPr 83-84*
Cobblesmith - Freeport, ME - *LitMarPl 83, 84; WritMar 84*
Cobblestone - Peterborough, NH - *ArtMar 84; LitMag&SmPr 83-84; MagIndMarPl 82-83; WritMar 84*
Cobblestone Press Ltd. - Vancouver, BC, Canada - *BoPubDir 4, 5*
Cobblestone Publishing Inc. - Peterborough, NH - *LitMag&SmPr 83-84*
Cobbosseeconte Telephone & Telegraph Co. - West Gardiner, ME - *TelDir&BG 83-84*
Cobden Sun, The - Cobden, ON, Canada - *Ed&PubIntYB 82*
Coblentz Society Inc. - Kirkwood, MO - *BoPubDir 4, 5*
Cobleskill Times-Journal - Cobleskill, NY - *NewsDir 84*
Cobleskill Times-Journal - *See* Catskill Mountain Publishing Corp.
Cobourg Daily Star - Cobourg, ON, Canada - *Ed&PubIntYB 82*
Cobra Country Records - Winnetka, CA - *BillIntBG 83-84*
Cobrasoft Inc. - Hawthorne, CA - *MicrocomMPl 84; MicrocomSwDir 1*
Coburg Cable Co. - Coburg, OR - *BrCabYB 84; Tel&CabFB 84C*
Coca-Cola Bottler, The - Atlanta, GA - *MagDir 84*
Cochise Publishing Co. - Athens, TX - *BillIntBG 83-84*
Cochise Record Co. - Athens, TX - *BillIntBG 83-84*
Cochonour, Bob - *See* Tri-Star Cablevision Inc.
Cochonour, Don - *See* Tri-Star Cablevision Inc.
Cochonour, Joe - *See* Tri-Star Cablevision Inc.
Cochran Journal - Cochran, GA - *BaconPubCkNews 84; Ed&PubIntYB 82*
Cochran, Sandford, Jones Advertising Agency Inc. - Memphis, TN - *StaDirAdAg 2-84*
Cochrane, Chase, Livingston & Co. (Public Relations Div.) - Irvine, CA - *DirPRFirms 83*
Cochrane Cooperative Telephone Co. - Cochrane, WI - *TelDir&BG 83-84*
Cochrane Fountain City Recorder - Cochrane, WI - *BaconPubCkNews 84*
Cochrane Recorder - Cochrane, WI - *Ed&PubIntYB 82*
Cochranton Times - Cochranton, PA - *Ed&PubIntYB 82*
Cochrun Inc. - St. Petersburg Beach, FL - *BoPubDir 4, 5*
Cockerham & Associates Inc., John M. - Huntsville, AL - *MicrocomMPl 83, 84*
Cockle & Associates Inc., George R. - Omaha, NE - *BoPubDir 4, 5*
Cockshaw's Construction Labor News & Opinion [of Communications Counselors Inc.] - Newtown Square, PA - *BaconPubCkMag 84; MagDir 84*
CoCo Warehouse - Westland, MI - *MicrocomMPl 84*
Cocoa Central Brevard Shopping News - Melbourne, FL - *AyerDirPub 83*
Cocoa Tribune - Cocoa, FL - *BaconPubCkNews 84*
Cocohut - Houston, TX - *MicrocomMPl 84*
Cocopro - St. Louis, MO - *MicrocomMPl 84*
Coda - Toronto, ON, Canada - *BaconPubCkMag 84; LitMag&SmPr 83-84*
Coda Inc. - Midland Park, NJ - *AvMarPl 83*
Coda: Poets & Writers Newsletter [of Poets & Writers Inc.] - New York, NY - *LitMag&SmPr 83-84; LitMarPl 83, 84; MagIndMarPl 82-83*
Coda Press - Madison, WI - *BoPubDir 4, 5*
Codapro Corp. - Plainview, NY - *WhoWMicrocom 83*
Codata Systems Corp. - Sunnyvale, CA - *WhoWMicrocom 83*
CODE - New York, NY - *DirOnDB Spring 84*
Code Works, The - Santa Barbara, CA - *WhoWMicrocom 83*
Codelco Inc. - Sunnyvale, CA - *MicrocomSwDir 1*
Codex Corp. - Mansfield, MA - *DataDirSup 7-83; WhoWMicrocom 83*
Codex International Records - Cincinnati, OH - *BillIntBG 83-84*
Coding Enterprise - Forest Hills, NY - *IntDirMarRes 83*
Codoc - Guelph, ON, Canada - *DirOnDB Spring 84*
Codoc [of QL Systems Ltd.] - Ottawa, ON, Canada - *DataDirOnSer 84*
Cody Enterprise [of Sage Publishing Co. Inc.] - Cody, WY - *BaconPubCkNews 84; Ed&PubIntYB 82; NewsDir 84*
Cody-Powell Cable TV [of Community Tele-Communications Inc.] - Cody, WY - *BrCabYB 84; Tel&CabFB 84C*
Coe Communications Inc. - Rockville, MD - *AvMarPl 83*
Coe Film Associates Inc. - New York, NY - *Tel&CabFB 84C*
Coeburn Cable Co. - Coeburn, VA - *BrCabYB 84; Tel&CabFB 84C*
Coen Co., The Ray - Santa Monica, CA - *AdAge 3-28-84; StaDirAdAg 2-84*
Coerten SA - *See* Bates Worldwide Inc., Ted
Coeur d'Alene Cablevision Inc. [of CDA Cable Inc.] - Coeur d'Alene, ID - *Tel&CabFB 84C*
Coeur d'Alene Press - Coeur d'Alene, ID - *BaconPubCkNews 84; Ed&PubIntYB 82*
CoEvolution Quarterly [of Whole Earth Catalog] - Sausalito, CA - *LitMag&SmPr 83-84; LitMarPl 83, 84*
Coffee Break - Los Angeles, CA - *NewsDir 84*

Coffee Break Press - Burley, WA - *BoPubDir 4 Sup, 5; LitMag&SmPr 83-84*
Coffee County Progress - Douglas, GA - *Ed&PubIntYB 82*
Coffeeline [of Dialog Information Services Inc.] - Palo Alto, CA - *DataDirOnSer 84*
Coffeeline [of International Coffee Organization] - London, England - *CompReadDB 82; DirOnDB Spring 84; EISS 83; OnBibDB 3*
Coffeeville Courier - Coffeeville, MS - *BaconPubCkNews 84; Ed&PubIntYB 82*
Coffey County Community TV Co. - Gridley, KS - *BrCabYB 84*
Coffey County Reporter - Le Roy, KS - *Ed&PubIntYB 82*
Coffey County Reporter, The - Burlington, KS - *AyerDirPub 83*
Coffey County Today - Burlington, KS - *NewsDir 84*
Coffeyville Cable TV Inc. [of Tele-Communications Inc.] - Coffeyville, KS - *BrCabYB 84; Tel&CabFB 84C*
Coffeyville Journal [of Gannett Co. Inc.] - Coffeyville, KS - *BaconPubCkNews 84; Ed&PubIntYB 82; NewsDir 84*
Coffield's Cable TV Co. - Wishram, WA - *Tel&CabFB 84C*
Coffin-Besser & Summers - *See* Lewis/Coffin/Associates
Coffin, George - Waltham, MA - *BoPubDir 4, 5*
Cogan Books - Fullerton, CA - *LitMarPl 83, 84*
Cogent-Data Technologies - Bellevue, WA - *MicrocomMPl 84*
Cogent Inc. - San Francisco, CA - *StaDirAdAg 2-84*
Coggin Photography Inc., Roy - New York, NY - *MagIndMarPl 82-83*
Coghill Composition Co. - Richmond, VA - *LitMarPl 83, 84*
Cogitan - Palo Alto, CA - *DirInfWP 82*
Cogito Data Systems Inc. - Princeton, NJ - *DataDirOnSer 84*
Cognitec - Del Mar, CA - *MicrocomMPl 84*
Cognitive Products - Bloomington, IN - *WhoWMicrocom 83*
Cognito Productions - Hopkins, MN - *BillIntBG 83-84*
Cognitronics Corp. - Stamford, CT - *DataDirSup 7-83; DirInfWP 82; WhoWMicrocom 83*
Cohan & Paul Inc. - Chicago, IL - *DirMarMP 83; DirPRFirms 83; StaDirAdAg 2-84*
Cohasset Mirror - Cohasset, MA - *Ed&PubIntYB 82*
Cohasset Mirror - Scituate, MA - *AyerDirPub 83*
Cohen & Greenbaum Inc. - Chicago, IL - *StaDirAdAg 2-84*
Cohen & Luckenbacher - Los Angeles, CA - *BillIntBG 83-84*
Cohen & Marino Inc. - New York, NY - *StaDirAdAg 2-84*
Cohen Associates, Georgia M. - San Diego, CA - *LitMarPl 83, 84*
Cohen Inc., Ruth - Menlo Park, CA - *LitMarPl 83, 84*
Cohen Literary Agency Ltd., Hy - New York, NY - *LitMarPl 83, 84*
Cohen Marketing Services Ltd., Aaron - Scarsdale, NY - *IntDirMarRes 83*
Cohen, Mollie L. - New York, NY - *LitMarPl 83, 84*
Cohen Okerlund Smith Advertising & Marketing Inc. - Minneapolis, MN - *StaDirAdAg 2-84*
Cohen Research Inc., Louis - Woodbury, NY - *IntDirMarRes 83*
Cohen, Stephanie - New York, NY - *LitMarPl 84*
Cohen, Sydney Wolfe - New York, NY - *LitMarPl 84*
Coherent Communications Systems Corp. - Hauppauge, NY - *DataDirSup 7-83*
Cohn & Wolfe Inc. - Atlanta, GA - *DirPRFirms 83*
Cohn Music, Bruce - Sonoma, CA - *BillIntBG 83-84*
Cohu Inc. (Electronics Div.) - San Diego, CA - *AvMarPl 83*
COIN [of Bell & Howell Co.] - Wooster, OH - *DataDirOnSer 84*
COIN [of University of Alberta] - Edmonton, AB, Canada - *DataDirOnSer 84*
Coin & Currency Institute Inc. [Aff. of Capitol Coin Co. Inc.] - Ft. Lee, NJ - *BoPubDir 4, 5*
Coin Financial Systems Inc. - Norcross, GA - *DataDirSup 7-83*
Coin Launderer & Cleaner - Glenview, IL - *BaconPubCkMag 84; MagDir 84*
Coin Mart - Encino, CA - *MagDir 84*
Coin Prices - Iola, WI - *MagDir 84; MagIndMarPl 82-83*
Coin Slot, The - Luzerne, PA - *BaconPubCkMag 84*
Coin World - Dayton, OH - *MagDir 84*
Coin World - Sidney, OH - *BaconPubCkMag 84; MagIndMarPl 82-83*
Coinage - Encino, CA - *BaconPubCkMag 84; MagDir 84; MagIndMarPl 82-83*
Coinamatic Age - New York, NY - *BaconPubCkMag 84; MagDir 84*
Coins [of Krause Publications] - Iola, WI - *ArtMar 84; BaconPubCkMag 84; MagDir 84; MagIndMarPl 82-83; WritMar 84*
COINS [of Agriculture Canada] - Ottawa, ON, Canada - *EISS 83*
Coins Records - Tallahassee, FL - *BillIntBG 83-84*
Coinversations - Franklin, MI - *Ed&PubIntYB 82; LitMarPl 84*
Cokato Enterprise - Cokato, MN - *BaconPubCkNews 84; Ed&PubIntYB 82*
Coke County Cablevision - Bronte, TX - *BrCabYB 84*
Coke County Cablevision [of C & H Services Inc.] - Robert Lee, TX - *BrCabYB 84*
Coker Publishing House - Gordonville, TX - *BoPubDir 5*
Coker Publishing House - Houston, TX - *BoPubDir 4; LitMag&SmPr 83-84*
Col-Bob Associates Inc. - New York, NY - *BoPubDir 4 Sup, 5*
COL Ltd. - Hong Kong - *ADAPSOMemDir 83-84*
Colane Cable TV Inc. - Logan County, WV - *Tel&CabFB 84C*
Colane Cable TV Inc. - Omar, WV - *BrCabYB 84*
Colangelo Associates, Ted - White Plains, NY - *StaDirAdAg 2-84*
Colarossi Griswold Inc. [Subs. of Griswold Inc.] - New York, NY - *StaDirAdAg 2-84*
Colasuonno FA Inc. - New York, NY - *IntDirMarRes 83*
Colbert & Associates, Nancy - Toronto, ON, Canada - *LitMarPl 83, 84*
Colbert County Reporter - Tuscumbia, AL - *Ed&PubIntYB 82*
Colbert Television Sales Inc. - Los Angeles, CA - *TelAl 83, 84; Tel&CabFB 84C*
Colborne Chronicle - Colborne, ON, Canada - *Ed&PubIntYB 82*
Colborne Citizen, The - Colborne, ON, Canada - *Ed&PubIntYB 82*
Colburn & Tegg - Hollis, NY - *BoPubDir 4, 5*
Colburn Laboratory Inc., George W. - Chicago, IL - *Tel&CabFB 84C*
Colby Computer [Div. of Colby Research Industries Inc.] - Palo Alto, CA - *MicrocomMPl 84*
Colby Free Press [of Alliance Publishing Co.] - Colby, KS - *BaconPubCkNews 84; Ed&PubIntYB 82; NewsDir 84*
Colchie Associates Inc., Thomas - New York, NY - *LitMarPl 83, 84*
Colclough/California Communications Network, William H. - Santa Rosa, CA - *Tel&CabFB 84C*
Cold [of SDC Search Service] - Santa Monica, CA - *DataDirOnSer 84*
Cold Mountain Press [Aff. of Provision House] - Austin, TX - *BoPubDir 4, 5; LitMag&SmPr 83-84*
Cold Regions Bibliography Project [of Library of Congress] - Washington, DC - *DBBus 82; DirOnDB Spring 84; EISS 83*
Cold Regions Research & Engineering Laboratory [of U.S. Army] - Hanover, NH - *EISS 83*
Cold Regions Science & Technology Bibliography [of Cold Regions Research & Engineering Laboratory] - Hanover, NH - *CompReadDB 82; OnBibDB 3*
Cold Spring Harbor Laboratory - Cold Spring Harbor, NY - *LitMarPl 83, 84*
Cold Spring Putnam County News & Recorder - Cold Spring, NY - *BaconPubCkNews 84*
Cold Spring Record - Cold Spring, MN - *BaconPubCkNews 84; Ed&PubIntYB 82*
Cold Weather Music - *See* Special Rider Music
Coldwater Cablevision Inc. - Coldwater, MI - *BrCabYB 84; Tel&CabFB 84C*
Coldwater Community TV Inc. - Coldwater, KS - *BrCabYB 84; Tel&CabFB 84C*
Coldwater Mercer County Chronicle - Coldwater, OH - *BaconPubCkNews 84; NewsDir 84*
Coldwater Reporter - Coldwater, MI - *BaconPubCkNews 84; Ed&PubIntYB 82; NewsDir 84*
Coldwater Western Star - Coldwater, KS - *BaconPubCkNews 84*
Cole & Weber [Subs. of Ogilvy & Mather International] - Seattle, WA - *AdAge 3-28-84; BrCabYB 84; StaDirAdAg 2-84; TelAl 83, 84*
Cole & Weber Public Relations [Div. of Cole & Weber Inc.] - Seattle, WA - *DirPRFirms 83*
Cole Business Furniture - York, PA - *DirInfWP 82*
Cole Camp Courier - Cole Camp, MO - *BaconPubCkNews 84; Ed&PubIntYB 82*

Cole Communications & Associates - Lansing, IL - *StaDirAdAg 2-84*
Cole Co., Carter L. - Canoga Park, CA - *MicrocomMPl 84*
Cole Co., Carter L. - Woodland Hills, CA - *MicrocomMPl 83*
Cole Co. Inc., Bruce H. - Phoenix, AZ - *StaDirAdAg 2-84*
Cole, E. R. - Cleveland, OH - *LitMarPl 84*
Cole, E. R. - Euclid, OH - *LitMarPl 83; MagIndMarPl 82-83*
Cole/Green/Associates Inc. - Lomita, CA - *IntDirMarRes 83*
Cole Henderson Drake - Atlanta, GA - *AdAge 3-28-84; StaDirAdAg 2-84*
Cole, Irad Dean - Fairfax, VA - *BoPubDir 4, 5*
Cole, Jim - Mill Valley, CA - *BoPubDir 4, 5*
Cole Literary Agency, Joyce K. - Berkeley, CA - *LitMarPl 83, 84*
Cole Publications [Subs. of Metromail Inc.] - Lincoln, NE - *DirMarMP 83*
Cole Publishing Co., M. M. - Chicago, IL - *BillIntBG 83-84*
Cole, Richard D. - Easton, CT - *LitMarPl 83, 84*
Cole Surveys Inc. [Subs. of The Wyatt Co.] - Boston, MA - *DirMarMP 83*
Cole/West, Keith [Subs. of Carnation Co.] - Redwood City, CA - *AvMarPl 83*
Colebrook Cable TV Inc. - Colebrook, NH - *BrCabYB 84; Tel&CabFB 84C*
Colebrook Cable TV Inc. - West Stewartstown, NH - *BrCabYB 84*
Colebrook News & Sentinel - Colebrook, NH - *BaconPubCkNews 84*
Coleco Industries Inc. - Hartford, CT - *HomeVid&CabYB 82-83*
Colee & Co. - West Palm Beach, FL - *StaDirAdAg 2-84*
Coleman Advertising Inc. - Dallas, TX - *Ed&PubIntYB 82*
Coleman & Pellet Inc. - Union, NJ - *DirPRFirms 83*
Coleman County Chronicle - Coleman, TX - *AyerDirPub 83; Ed&PubIntYB 82; NewsDir 84*
Coleman County Chronicle - *See* Coleman County Chronicle Publishers
Coleman County Chronicle Publishers - Coleman, TX - *BaconPubCkNews 84*
Coleman County Telephone Cooperative Inc. - Santa Anna, TX - *TelDir&BG 83-84*
Coleman Democrat-Voice - *See* Coleman County Chronicle Publishers
Coleman Democrat-Voice, The - Coleman, TX - *Ed&PubIntYB 82*
Coleman, Duke - Silver Spring, MD - *BoPubDir 4, 5*
Coleman Enterprises Inc., Earl M. - Crugers, NY - *LitMag&SmPr 83-84*
Coleman, Eugene - Corbin, KY - *Tel&CabFB 84C p.1672*
Coleman Inc., Bruce - New York, NY - *MagIndMarPl 82-83*
Coleman, Mary Garland - Vancouver, BC, Canada - *BoPubDir 4, 5*
Coleman Publication, Ruth - Huntsville, AL - *BoPubDir 4, 5*
Coleman Research - Dallas, TX - *BrCabYB 84*
Coleman, Rita - Willowdale, ON, Canada - *BoPubDir 4, 5*
Coleman Robertson Inc. - New Orleans, LA - *StaDirAdAg 2-84*
Coleman TV Cable Co. - Pike County, KY - *BrCabYB 84*
Coleman TV Cable Co. [of Landmark Cablevision Associates] - Coleman, TX - *Tel&CabFB 84C*
Coleman TV Cable Co. [of Landmark Cablevision Associates] - Concho, TX - *BrCabYB 84*
Colenso Communications Ltd. - *See* BBDO International Inc.
Colenta America Corp. - Paramus, NJ - *AvMarPl 83*
Coleraine Video Inc. - Coleraine, PQ, Canada - *BrCabYB 84*
Coleridge Blade - Coleridge, NE - *BaconPubCkNews 84; Ed&PubIntYB 82*
Coles County Times-Courier - Charleston, IL - *BaconPubCkNews 84; Ed&PubIntYB 82*
Coles Publishing Co. Ltd. [Div. of Coles Book Stores Ltd.] - Rexdale, ON, Canada - *LitMarPl 83, 84; WritMar 84*
Colfax Chronicle - Colfax, LA - *BaconPubCkNews 84; Ed&PubIntYB 82*
Colfax County Press - Clarkson, NE - *AyerDirPub 83; Ed&PubIntYB 82*
Colfax Daily Bulletin - Colfax, WA - *Ed&PubIntYB 82*
Colfax Gazette - Colfax, WA - *BaconPubCkNews 84; Ed&PubIntYB 82; NewsDir 84*
Colfax Jasper County Tribune - Colfax, IA - *BaconPubCkNews 84*
Colfax Messenger - Colfax, WI - *BaconPubCkNews 84; Ed&PubIntYB 82*
Colfax Press - Colfax, IL - *Ed&PubIntYB 82*
Colfax Press - *See* Cornbelt Press Inc.
Colfax Record - Colfax, CA - *BaconPubCkNews 84; Ed&PubIntYB 82*
Colgate Personnel Agency - New York, NY - *LitMarPl 83, 84; MagIndMarPl 82-83*
Colgin Publishing - Manlius, NY - *BoPubDir 4, 5*
Colish Inc., A. - Mt. Vernon, NY - *LitMarPl 83, 84*
Collaboration [of Matagiri] - Mt. Tremper, NY - *LitMag&SmPr 83-84*
Collage Books [Subs. of Whitehall Co.] - Wheeling, IL - *LitMarPl 84*
Collamore Press, The [Div. of D. C. Heath & Co.] - Lexington, MA - *LitMarPl 83, 84*
Collard, Eileen - Burlington, ON, Canada - *BoPubDir 4, 5*
Collart Enterprises - Baltimore, MD - *BoPubDir 4 Sup, 5*
Collateral Group Inc., The - *See* Bloom Cos. Inc., The
Collateral Investment Co. - Birmingham, AL - *DataDirSup 7-83*
Colle & McVoy Advertising Agency - Minneapolis, MN - *AdAge 3-28-84; BrCabYB 84; DirPRFirms 83; StaDirAdAg 2-84*
Colleasius Press - Colorado Springs, CO - *BoPubDir 4, 5*
Collectibles - Don Mills, ON, Canada - *BaconPubCkMag 84*
Collectibles Illustrated [of Yankee Publishing Inc.] - Dublin, NH - *WritMar 84*
Collection Inc. - Memphis, TN - *LitMarPl 83, 84*
Collection Management - New York, NY - *BaconPubCkMag 84*
Collections - Buffalo, NY - *MagDir 84*
Collective Farm - New York, NY - *BoPubDir 5*
Collective for Training & Education - Amsterdam, Netherlands - *EISS 83*
Collective Impressions Ltd. - Towson, MD - *ArtMar 84*
Collector - Claremont, CA - *BoPubDir 5*
Collector - Mentone, CA - *BoPubDir 4*
Collector [of American Collectors Association Inc.] - Minneapolis, MN - *MagDir 84*
Collector Books [Aff. of Schroeder Publishing Co.] - Paducah, KY - *BoPubDir 4, 5; LitMarPl 84; WritMar 84*
Collector Editions Quarterly - New York, NY - *BaconPubCkMag 84; WritMar 84*
Collector Grade Publications - Toronto, ON, Canada - *BoPubDir 4, 5*
Collector Records - Silver Spring, MD - *BillIntBG 83-84*
Collectors Club Inc. - New York, NY - *BoPubDir 4, 5*
Collectors Club Philatelist [of The Moretus Press Inc.] - New York, NY - *LitMag&SmPr 83-84*
Collectors Mart - Wichita, KS - *BaconPubCkMag 84; WritMar 84*
Collectors News - Grundy Center, IA - *BaconPubCkMag 84; MagIndMarPl 82-83; WritMar 84*
College Administration Publications Inc. - Asheville, NC - *BoPubDir 5*
College & Research Libraries - Stanford, CA - *BaconPubCkMag 84; MagDir 84*
College & Research Libraries [of Association of College & Research Libraries] - Chicago, IL - *LitMarPl 83, 84*
College & Research Libraries News [of American Library Association] - Chicago, IL - *BaconPubCkMag 84; MagIndMarPl 82-83*
College & University - Athens, OH - *MagIndMarPl 82-83*
College Bowl Co. Inc. - New York, NY - *Tel&CabFB 84C*
College City Community Cable Inc. - College City, AR - *BrCabYB 84*
College Composition & Communication - Urbana, IL - *BaconPubCkMag 84; MagDir 84; MagIndMarPl 82-83*
College Connections - New York, NY - *DirPRFirms 83*
College Corner News - Liberty, IN - *AyerDirPub 83*
College Corner News - College Corner, OH - *Ed&PubIntYB 82*
College Corner News - Oxford, OH - *AyerDirPub 83*
College Corner News - *See* Oxford Press Inc.
College English [of National Council of Teachers of English] - Urbana, IL - *LitMarPl 83, 84*
College English [of National Council of Teachers of English] - Bloomington, IN - *LitMag&SmPr 83-84*
College Entrance Examination Board - New York, NY - *LitMarPl 83, 84*

College Entrance Examination Board (Communications Div.) - New York, NY - *CompReadDB 82*
College Game, The - New York, NY - *MagDir 84*
College Grove East Pennysaver - Mission Viejo, CA - *AyerDirPub 83*
College Grove West Pennysaver - Mission Viejo, CA - *AyerDirPub 83*
College Heights Herald [of Western Kentucky University] - Bowling Green, KY - *NewsDir 84*
College-Hill Press - San Diego, CA - *LitMarPl 83, 84; WritMar 84*
College Kid's Cookbooks - Ft. Worth, TX - *BoPubDir 4, 5*
College Market 1983, The - New York, NY - *DirOnDB Spring 84*
College Marketing Group Inc. - Winchester, MA - *LitMarPl 83, 84*
College of Cape Breton Press - Sydney, NS, Canada - *BoPubDir 4, 5*
College Placement Council Inc. - Bethlehem, PA - *BoPubDir 4, 5*
College Placer - Clarkston, WA - *AyerDirPub 83*
College Point Tribune [of Flushing Queens Tribune] - Flushing, NY - *NewsDir 84*
College Press Publishing Co. - Jopin, MO - *BoPubDir 4, 5*
College Press Review - Athens, OH - *WritMar 84*
College Press Service - Denver, CO - *BaconPubCkNews 84; DirOnDB Spring 84; Ed&PubIntYB 82; LitMarPl 83, 84; MagIndMarPl 82-83*
College Press Service [of NewsNet Inc.] - Bryn Mawr, PA - *DataDirOnSer 84*
College Selection Service [of Peterson's Guides] - Princeton, NJ - *EISS 83*
College Skills Center [of Speedreading Institute] - Baltimore, MD - *BoPubDir 5*
College Skills Center [of Speedreading Institute] - New York, NY - *BoPubDir 4*
College Store Executive [of Executive Business Media Inc.] - Westbury, NY - *ArtMar 84; BaconPubCkMag 84; LitMarPl 83, 84; MagDir 84; MagIndMarPl 82-83; WritMar 84*
College Store Journal, The - Oberlin, OH - *BaconPubCkMag 84; MagDir 84*
College Student Journal - Chula Vista, CA - *MagDir 84*
College Union - Westbury, NY - *BaconPubCkMag 84; WritMar 84*
Collegeville Independent & Transcript - Collegeville, PA - *BaconPubCkNews 84*
Collegian, The [of The University of Toledo] - Toledo, OH - *NewsDir 84*
Collegiate Career Woman [of Equal Opportunity Publications Inc.] - Greenlawn, NY - *WritMar 84*
Collegiate Microcomputer [of Rose Hulman Institute of Technology] - Terre Haute, IN - *ArtMar 84; BaconPubCkMag 84; MicrocomMPl 84*
Collegiate Publishing Inc. - San Diego, CA - *LitMarPl 83, 84*
Collegiate Woman's Career Magazine - Centerport, NY - *MagDir 84*
Collegium Book Publishers Inc. - Elmsford, NY - *LitMarPl 83*
Collegium Sound Inc. - Jackson Heights, NY - *BillIntBG 83-84*
Collett, Dickenson, Pearce & Partners Ltd. - London, England - *StaDirAdAg 2-84*
Collie Review - Beverly Hills, CA - *MagDir 84*
Collier Agency, Shirley - Los Angeles, CA - *LitMarPl 83*
Collier Associates - New York, NY - *LitMarPl 83, 84*
Collier Graphic Services - New York, NY - *MagIndMarPl 82-83*
Collier Macmillan Canada Inc. [Subs. of Macmillan Publishing Co. Inc.] - Don Mills, ON, Canada - *LitMarPl 83, 84; WritMar 84*
Collier Publications Inc., Robert - Indialantic, FL - *BoPubDir 4, 5*
Collier Shopping Guide - Naples, FL - *AyerDirPub 83*
Collierville Herald - Collierville, TN - *BaconPubCkNews 84; Ed&PubIntYB 82; NewsDir 84*
Collin & Associates - San Rafael, CA - *StaDirAdAg 2-84*
Collingwood Enterprise-Bulletin, The - Collingwood, ON, Canada - *Ed&PubIntYB 82*
Collingwood Times, The - Collingwood, ON, Canada - *Ed&PubIntYB 82*
Collins Advertising Agency, Becky - Honolulu, HI - *DirPRFirms 83*
Collins Associates, Lee R. - Culver City, CA - *LitMarPl 83, 84*
Collins Color Photo Lab - Dallas, TX - *AvMarPl 83*
Collins Consulting Inc., Thom - Pacific Palisades, CA - *EISS 5-84 Sup*
Collins International Trading Corp. - Calabassas, CA - *MicrocomMPl 84*
Collins, James F. & Lela - St. Francis, KS - *Tel&CabFB 84C p.1672*
Collins News-Commercial - Collins, MS - *BaconPubCkNews 84*
Collins, Patrick J. - New Rochelle, NY - *LitMarPl 83*
Collins Sons & Co. Ltd., William - Don Mills, ON, Canada - *LitMarPl 83, 84*
Collinsville Cablevision - Collinsville, OK - *Tel&CabFB 84C*
Collinsville Herald [of Post Corp.] - Collinsville, IL - *BaconPubCkNews 84; Ed&PubIntYB 82; NewsDir 84*
Collinsville Journal - Collinsville, IL - *AyerDirPub 83; Ed&PubIntYB 82*
Collinsville Journal - *See* Journal Newspapers of Southern Illinois
Collinsville News - Collinsville, OK - *AyerDirPub 83; BaconPubCkNews 84; Ed&PubIntYB 82*
Collision [of Kruza Kaleidoscopix Inc.] - Franklin, MA - *BaconPubCkMag 84; MagDir 84; WritMar 84*
Collison, James - Van Nuys, CA - *MagIndMarPl 82-83*
Colloquy - Greenwich, CT - *ArtMar 84*
Colman Argus - Colman, SD - *Ed&PubIntYB 82*
Colman Argus - Dell Rapids, SD - *NewsDir 84*
Colman Argus - *See* Prairie Publications
Colman Publishers - Stockton, CA - *BoPubDir 4, 5*
Colmesneil Telephone Co. - Colmesneil, TX - *TelDir&BG 83-84*
Colo Telephone Co. - Colo, IA - *TelDir&BG 83-84*
Cologne Press - Cologne, NJ - *BoPubDir 4, 5*
Cologne South Jersey Advisor - Cologne, NJ - *NewsDir 84*
Coloma Telephone Co. - Coloma, WI - *TelDir&BG 83-84*
Colombia Information Service - New York, NY - *Ed&PubIntYB 82*
Colon Express - Colon, MI - *BaconPubCkNews 84; Ed&PubIntYB 82*
Colonial Beach Cablevision Co. [of DoKel Communications Corp.] - Colonial Beach, VA - *BrCabYB 84; Tel&CabFB 84C*
Colonial Bindery Inc. - Deer Park, NY - *LitMarPl 84*
Colonial Bird Register [of Cornell University] - Ithaca, NY - *EISS 83*
Colonial Cable TV [of Adelphia Communications Corp.] - Plymouth Meeting, PA - *Tel&CabFB 84C*
Colonial Cable TV [of GSL Electronics Inc.] - Plymouth Township, PA - *BrCabYB 84*
Colonial Cablevision [of Rau Radio Stations] - Anne Arundel County, MD - *BrCabYB 84*
Colonial Cablevision Inc. - Queensbury, NY - *BrCabYB 84*
Colonial Cablevision of Milford - Milford, MA - *BrCabYB 84*
Colonial Cablevision of Revere Inc. - Revere, MA - *BrCabYB 84; Tel&CabFB 84C p.1672*
Colonial Color Corp. - Boston, MA - *AvMarPl 83*
Colonial Data Services Corp. - Hamden, CT - *WhoWMicrocom 83*
Colonial Homes [of Hearst Magazines Div.] - New York, NY - *BaconPubCkMag 84; Folio 83; MagDir 84; MagIndMarPl 82-83*
Colonial Williamsburg Foundation (A-V Distribution) - Williamsburg, VA - *AvMarPl 83*
Colonial Williamsburg Foundation, The - Williamsburg, VA - *LitMarPl 83, 84*
Colonialtown Press - Brewster, NY - *LitMarPl 83*
Colonnade Color - Livonia, MI - *AvMarPl 83*
Colonnades - Elon College, NC - *LitMag&SmPr 83-84*
Colony Cable TV - Colony, KY - *BrCabYB 84*
Colony Cable TV - Laurel County, KY - *BrCabYB 84*
Colony Communications Inc. [of Providence Journal Co.] - Providence, RI - *BrCabYB 84 p.D-299; CabTVFinDB 83; LitMarPl 84; Tel&CabFB 84C p.1672*
Colony/Harbor Cablevision - Wilmington, CA - *BrCabYB 84; Tel&CabFB 84C*
Colony-Microband of Massachusetts Inc. - Providence, RI - *Tel&CabFB 84C*
Colony-Microband of Rhode Island Inc. - Providence, RI - *Tel&CabFB 84C*
Color by Spencer Inc. - Troy, MI - *AvMarPl 83*

Color Cable TV Systems Inc. - Tularosa, NM - *BrCabYB 84*
Color Coded Charting & Filing Systems - Riverside, CA - *BoPubDir 4, 5*
Color Computer [of New England Publications] - Camden, ME - *BaconPubCkMag 84; MicrocomMPl 84; WritMar 84*
Color Computer News [of Remarkable Software] - Muskegon, MI - *MicrocomMPl 84*
Color Country Cable [of Citation Cable Systems] - Hurricane, UT - *Tel&CabFB 84C*
Color Dynamics Inc. - Seattle, WA - *AvMarPl 83*
Color Film Corp. - Santa Monica, CA - *AvMarPl 83*
Color Film Corp. - Landover, MD - *AvMarPl 83*
Color Film Corp. - West Roxbury, MA - *AvMarPl 83*
Color Film Corp. - Mound, MN - *AvMarPl 83*
Color Film Corp. (Video Div.) - Stamford, CT - *AvMarPl 83*
Color Film Service - Upper Darby, PA - *AvMarPl 83*
Color Image Systems - Riverside, CA - *AvMarPl 83*
Color Lab Inc. - Dallas, TX - *AvMarPl 83*
Color Micro Journal [of Computer Publishing Inc.] - Hixson, TN - *BaconPubCkMag 84; MicrocomMPl 84*
Color Photo Service Inc. - Mt. Rainier, MD - *AvMarPl 83*
Color Place, The - Dallas, TX - *AvMarPl 83*
Color Place, The - Houston, TX - *AvMarPl 83*
Color Software Services - Greenville, TX - *MicrocomMPl 83*
Color Stock Library Inc. - Tampa, FL - *AvMarPl 83*
Color Terminals International Inc. - Troy, MI - *DataDirSup 7-83*
Color Video Recording Service Inc. - San Diego, CA - *AvMarPl 83*
Colorado Alliance of Research Libraries - Denver, CO - *EISS 83*
Colorado Alumnus, The [of University of Colorado] - Boulder, CO - *ArtMar 84*
Colorado Associated University Press [of University of Colorado] - Boulder, CO - *ArtMar 84; LitMarPl 83, 84; WritMar 84*
Colorado Beverage Analyst [of Bevan Inc.] - Denver, CO - *BaconPubCkMag 84; MagDir 84*
Colorado Black Lifestyle [of Downing Publishing Inc.] - Denver, CO - *WritMar 84*
Colorado Brand - Boulder, CO - *AvMarPl 83*
Colorado/Business [of Titsch Publishing Inc.] - Denver, CO - *BaconPubCkMag 84; MagDir 84; WritMar 84*
Colorado Business/Economic Data Bank [of University of Colorado] - Boulder, CO - *EISS 83*
Colorado Business Systems Inc. [Subs. of Cabot Business Systems Inc.] - Denver, CO - *WhoWMicrocom 83*
Colorado Cable Co. - Paonia, CO - *Tel&CabFB 84C p.1672*
Colorado Cablevision Inc. - Bennett, CO - *BrCabYB 84*
Colorado Cablevision Inc. - Byers, CO - *BrCabYB 84*
Colorado Cablevision Inc. - Foxridge Farms, CO - *BrCabYB 84*
Colorado Cablevision Inc. - Strasburg, CO - *BrCabYB 84*
Colorado City Record - Colorado City, TX - *BaconPubCkNews 84; Ed&PubIntYB 82*
Colorado College (Press at Colorado College) - Colorado Springs, CO - *BoPubDir 5*
Colorado Color - Colorado Springs, CO - *AvMarPl 83*
Colorado Consulting Group - Denver, CO - *DirInfWP 82*
Colorado Country Life - Denver, CO - *MagDir 84*
Colorado County Citizen - Columbus, TX - *AyerDirPub 83; Ed&PubIntYB 82*
Colorado Daily - Boulder, CO - *NewsDir 84*
Colorado Editor - Denver, CO - *BaconPubCkMag 84; MagDir 84*
Colorado Engineer - Boulder, CO - *BaconPubCkMag 84; MagDir 84*
Colorado Fiber Center Inc. - Boulder, CO - *BoPubDir 4; LitMag&SmPr 83-84*
Colorado Historical Society - Denver, CO - *MicroMarPl 82-83*
Colorado Homes & Lifestyles - Denver, CO - *WritMar 84*
Colorado Intercable Inc. [of Jones Intercable Inc.] - Georgetown, CO - *BrCabYB 84*
Colorado Intercable Inc. [of Jones Intercable Inc.] - Idaho Springs, CO - *BrCabYB 84*
Colorado Intercable Inc. [of Jones Intercable Inc.] - Jefferson County, CO - *BrCabYB 84*
Colorado Labor Advocate - Denver, CO - *NewsDir 84*
Colorado Leader - Denver, CO - *AyerDirPub 83; Ed&PubIntYB 82*
Colorado Library Network [of Colorado State Library] - Denver, CO - *EISS 83*
Colorado Market Research Services Inc. - Denver, CO - *IntDirMarRes 83*
Colorado Medicine - Denver, CO - *BaconPubCkMag 84; MagDir 84*
Colorado Mining Association - Denver, CO - *BoPubDir 4 Sup, 5*
Colorado Municipal League - Denver, CO - *BoPubDir 5*
Colorado Municipalities - Denver, CO - *BaconPubCkMag 84*
Colorado Municipalities [of Colorado Municipal League] - Wheat Ridge, CO - *MagDir 84*
Colorado Natural Heritage Inventory [of Colorado State Dept. of Natural Resources] - Denver, CO - *EISS 7-83 Sup*
Colorado-North Review - Greeley, CO - *LitMag&SmPr 83-84*
Colorado Press Clipping Service - Denver, CO - *ProGuPRSer 4*
Colorado Railroad Museum - Golden, CO - *BoPubDir 4, 5*
Colorado Rancher & Farmer - Denver, CO - *BaconPubCkMag 84; MagDir 84*
Colorado Regional Data Center [Subs. of Citicorp] - Denver, CO - *DataDirOnSer 84*
Colorado River Press - Austin, TX - *BoPubDir 4, 5*
Colorado/Rocky Mountain West Magazine - Denver, CO - *MagDir 84*
Colorado School Journal - Aurora, CO - *BaconPubCkMag 84; MagDir 84*
Colorado School of Mines Press - Golden, CO - *BoPubDir 4, 5*
Colorado School of Mines Press (Publications Dept.) - Golden, CO - *LitMarPl 84*
Colorado Sports Monthly [of Colorado Springs Publishing] - Colorado Springs, CO - *BaconPubCkMag 84; WritMar 84*
Colorado Springs Black Forest News - Colorado Springs, CO - *BaconPubCkNews 84*
Colorado Springs Cablevision Inc. [of American TV & Communications Corp.] - Colorado Springs, CO - *BrCabYB 84; Tel&CabFB 84C*
Colorado Springs Fine Arts Center - Colorado Springs, CO - *BoPubDir 5*
Colorado Springs Gazette Telegraph [of Freedom Newspapers Inc.] - Colorado Springs, CO - *BaconPubCkNews 84; Ed&PubIntYB 82; NewsDir 84*
Colorado Springs Sun - Colorado Springs, CO - *BaconPubCkNews 84; Ed&PubIntYB 82; LitMarPl 83, 84; NewsDir 84*
Colorado State Data Center [of Colorado State Dept. of Local Affairs] - Denver, CO - *EISS 5-84 Sup*
Colorado State Review - Ft. Collins, CO - *LitMag&SmPr 83-84*
Colorado State University (Colorado State Review Press) - Ft. Collins, CO - *BoPubDir 4, 5*
Colorado Statesman - Denver, CO - *AyerDirPub 83; Ed&PubIntYB 82; NewsDir 84*
Colorado Technical Reference Center [of University of Colorado] - Boulder, CO - *DataDirOnSer 84; EISS 83; FBInfSer 80; InfIndMarPl 83*
Colorado Transcript [of Montgomery Publishing Inc.] - Golden, CO - *Ed&PubIntYB 82; NewsDir 84*
Colorado Tribune - Pueblo, CO - *Ed&PubIntYB 82*
Colorado Valley Telephone Cooperative - Lagrange, TX - *TelDir&BG 83-84*
Colorado Video - Boulder, CO - *AvMarPl 83; DataDirSup 7-83; TeleSy&SerDir 7-83*
Colorado Visual Aids - Denver, CO - *AvMarPl 83*
Coloradoan [of Ft. Collins Newspapers Inc.] - Ft. Collins, CO - *AyerDirPub 83; BaconPubCkNews 84; Ed&PubIntYB 82; NewsDir 84*
ColorCorp - Bloomfield Hills, MI - *MicrocomMPl 84; MicrocomSwDir 1*
Colorfax Laboratories - Silver Spring, MD - *AvMarPl 83*
Colorich Color Lab - San Diego, CA - *AvMarPl 83*
Colorlab Ltd. - Providence, RI - *AvMarPl 83*
Colormark Lab [Div. of Markow Photography Inc.] - Phoenix, AZ - *AvMarPl 83*
Colorol Image-Atlanta - Atlanta, GA - *AvMarPl 83*
Colorpix Inc. - New Orleans, LA - *AvMarPl 83*
ColorPlant - Farmington, ME - *MagIndMarPl 82-83*
Colortek - Boston, MA - *AvMarPl 83*

Colortone Aids to Communications - Elmsford, NY - *AvMarPl 83*
Colortone Press - Washington, DC - *LitMarPl 83, 84*
Colortran Inc. - Burbank, CA - *AvMarPl 83*
Colortronics Corp. - Morristown, NJ - *MagIndMarPl 82-83*
Colosseum Records Ltd. - Philadelphia, PA - *BillIntBG 83-84*
Colquitt, Jack N. - San Antonio, TX - *WhoWMicrocom 83*
Colquitt Miller County Liberal - Colquitt, GA - *BaconPubCkNews 84*
Colsky Advertising Inc. - San Francisco, CA - *StaDirAdAg 2-84*
Colt Microfiche Corp. - Red Bank, NJ - *MicroMarPl 82-83*
Colton Courier - Colton, CA - *BaconPubCkNews 84; Ed&PubIntYB 82; NewsDir 84*
Colton, Kay W. - Gould, AR - *FBInfSer 80*
Colton News-Journal - *See* Tribune Newspapers Inc.
Colton Telephone Co. - Colton, OR - *TelDir&BG 83-84*
Coltsfoot Press [Aff. of Spartacus International Ltd.] - New York, NY - *BoPubDir 4, 5*
Columbia [of Knights of Columbus] - New Haven, CT - *ArtMar 84; BaconPubCkMag 84; LitMarPl 83, 84; MagDir 84; MagIndMarPl 82-83; WritMar 84*
Columbia Adair County News - Columbia, KY - *BaconPubCkNews 84*
Columbia Artists Management Inc. - New York, NY - *Tel&CabFB 84C*
Columbia Basin Farmer, The - Othello, WA - *MagDir 84*
Columbia Basin Herald - Moses Lake, WA - *AyerDirPub 83; BaconPubCkNews 84; Ed&PubIntYB 82*
Columbia Basin News - Clarkston, WA - *AyerDirPub 83*
Columbia Black News - Columbia, SC - *AyerDirPub 83; NewsDir 84*
Columbia Black News - *See* Juju Publishing Co.
Columbia Books Inc. - Washington, DC - *BoPubDir 4, 5*
Columbia Cable [of United Artists Cablesystems Corp.] - Kennewick, WA - *Tel&CabFB 84C*
Columbia Cable TV [of Columbia Communications Corp.] - Rosenberg, TX - *BrCabYB 84; Tel&CabFB 84C*
Columbia Cable TV Co. Inc. [of Wometco Cable TV Inc.] - Columbia, SC - *BrCabYB 84; Tel&CabFB 84C*
Columbia Cablevision [of Group W Cable] - Columbia, MO - *BrCabYB 84*
Columbia Caldwell Watchman Progress - Columbia, LA - *BaconPubCkNews 84*
Columbia City Cable TV Inc. - Columbia City, IN - *BrCabYB 84; Tel&CabFB 84C*
Columbia City Post & Commercial-Mail - Columbia City, IN - *BaconPubCkNews 84; NewsDir 84*
Columbia College (Chicago Center for Contemporary Photography) - Chicago, IL - *BoPubDir 4, 5*
Columbia Columbian-Progress/Sunday Mirror - Columbia, MS - *BaconPubCkNews 84*
Columbia Columbian-Progress, The - Columbia, MS - *NewsDir 84*
Columbia Communications Inc. - New York, NY - *MagIndMarPl 82-83*
Columbia Computing Services Inc. - Kent, WA - *DataDirOnSer 84*
Columbia Daily Spectator [of Spectator Publishing Co. Inc.] - New York, NY - *NewsDir 84*
Columbia Daily Tribune - Columbia, MO - *NewsDir 84*
Columbia Data Products Inc. - Columbia, MD - *DataDirSup 7-83; WhoWMicrocom 83*
Columbia Empire Broadcasting Corp. - Yakima, WA - *BrCabYB 84*
Columbia Falls Cable TV [of Group W Cable] - Columbia Falls, MT - *BrCabYB 84*
Columbia Falls Hungry Horse News - Columbia Falls, MT - *BaconPubCkNews 84*
Columbia Features - New York, NY - *BaconPubCkNews 84; Ed&PubIntYB 82; LitMarPl 83, 84; MagIndMarPl 82-83*
Columbia Finishing Mills Ltd. - Cornwall, ON, Canada - *LitMarPl 83, 84*
Columbia Flier [of Patuxent Publishing Corp.] - Columbia, MD - *AyerDirPub 83; Ed&PubIntYB 82; NewsDir 84*
Columbia Flier [of Ellicott City Stromberg Publishing Inc.] - Ellicott City, MD - *NewsDir 84*
Columbia-Great Lakes Corp. - Dayton, OH - *DirInfWP 82*
Columbia Heights St. Anthony Sun - Columbia Heights, MN - *Ed&PubIntYB 82*
Columbia Heights Sun - *See* Sun Newspapers
Columbia Heights Sun & Free Section [of Minnesota Suburban Newspapers Inc.] - Minneapolis, MN - *NewsDir 84*
Columbia Herald - Columbia, TN - *BaconPubCkNews 84*
Columbia Journalism Review [of Columbia University] - New York, NY - *BaconPubCkMag 84; DirMarMP 83; LitMarPl 83, 84; MagDir 84; MagIndMarPl 82-83; WritMar 84*
Columbia Language Services Inc. - Washington, DC - *BoPubDir 4, 5*
Columbia Literary Associates Inc. - Columbia, MD - *LitMarPl 83*
Columbia Literary Associates Inc. - Ellicott City, MD - *LitMarPl 84*
Columbia Microsystems - Columbia, MO - *MicrocomMPl 84*
Columbia Missourian [of Missouri Publishing Association] - Columbia, MO - *BaconPubCkNews 84; Ed&PubIntYB 82; LitMarPl 84; NewsDir 84*
Columbia Monroe County Clarion - Columbia, IL - *NewsDir 84*
Columbia Monroe County Clarion - *See* Clarion Printing Co. Inc.
Columbia News - Martinez, GA - *AyerDirPub 83*
Columbia News - Columbia, PA - *BaconPubCkNews 84; Ed&PubIntYB 82; NewsDir 84*
Columbia Newspapers Inc. - Columbia, SC - *LitMarPl 83*
Columbia Pictures Industries Inc. - New York, NY - *HomeVid&CabYB 82-83; KnowInd 83; Tel&CabFB 84C*
Columbia Pictures International Corp. - New York, NY - *Tel&CabFB 84C*
Columbia Pictures Television [Div. of Columbia Pictures Industries Inc.] - Burbank, CA - *LitMarPl 83; TelAl 83, 84; Tel&CabFB 84C*
Columbia Pictures Television [Div. of Columbia Pictures Industries Inc.] - Sherman Oaks, CA - *TelAl 83, 84*
Columbia Pictures Television Canada [Div. of Columbia Pictures Industries Inc.] - Toronto, ON, Canada - *Tel&CabFB 84C*
Columbia Planograph Co. - Beltsville, MD - *LitMarPl 83, 84*
Columbia Press - Warrenton, OR - *AyerDirPub 83; Ed&PubIntYB 82*
Columbia Publishing Co. Inc. - Frenchtown, NJ - *LitMarPl 83, 84; MagIndMarPl 82-83; WritMar 84*
Columbia Record [of Columbia Newspapers Inc.] - Columbia, SC - *BaconPubCkNews 84; Ed&PubIntYB 82; LitMarPl 84; NewsBur 6; NewsDir 84*
Columbia Ribbon & Carbon Manufacturing Co. Inc. - Union City, NJ - *DirInfWP 82*
Columbia Road Review [of King Publications] - Washington, DC - *LitMag&SmPr 83-84*
Columbia Software - Columbia, MD - *MicrocomMPl 84; MicrocomSwDir 1; WhoWMicrocom 83*
Columbia Software Products - Fairfax, VA - *MicrocomSwDir 1*
Columbia Special Products [Div. of CBS Records] - New York, NY - *AvMarPl 83; BillIntBG 83-84*
Columbia St. Andrews News - Columbia, SC - *BaconPubCkNews 84*
Columbia Star - *See* Clarion Printing Co. Inc.
Columbia Star-Reporter - Columbia, SC - *BaconPubCkNews 84*
Columbia Star, The - Columbia, IL - *Ed&PubIntYB 82*
Columbia State - Columbia, SC - *BaconPubCkNews 84*
Columbia Station Rural-Urban Record - Columbia Station, OH - *BaconPubCkNews 84; NewsDir 84*
Columbia Television Co. [of Rogers UA Cablesystems Inc.] - Kennewick, WA - *BrCabYB 84*
Columbia Television of Hermiston [of Rogers UA Cablesystems Inc.] - Hermiston, OR - *BrCabYB 84*
Columbia Tribune - Columbia, MO - *BaconPubCkNews 84*
Columbia TV of Hermiston [of UA Cablesystems Corp.] - Hermiston, OR - *Tel&CabFB 84C*
Columbia University (Center for International Business Cycle Research) - New York, NY - *DataDirOnSer 84*
Columbia University (Center for the Social Sciences) - New York, NY - *BoPubDir 4 Sup, 5*
Columbia University (Columbia Scholastic Press Association) - New York, NY - *BoPubDir 4, 5*
Columbia University (Council for European Studies) - New York, NY - *BoPubDir 4, 5*
Columbia University (East Asian Institute) - New York, NY - *BoPubDir 4, 5*
Columbia University (Institute on Western Europe) - New York, NY - *BoPubDir 4, 5*

Columbia University (Oral History Research Office) - New York, NY - *BoPubDir 4, 5*
Columbia University (Tutoring & Translation Agency) - New York, NY - *LitMarPl 83, 84; MagIndMarPl 82-83*
Columbia University Music Press - *See* Galaxy
Columbia University Press - New York, NY - *LitMarPl 83, 84; WritMar 84*
Columbian - Vancouver, WA - *AyerDirPub 83; Ed&PubIntYB 82*
Columbian - New Westminster, BC, Canada - *AyerDirPub 83; BaconPubCkNews 84; Ed&PubIntYB 82*
Columbian Advertising Inc. - Chicago, IL - *StaDirAdAg 2-84*
Columbian-Progress - Columbia, MS - *AyerDirPub 83; Ed&PubIntYB 82*
Columbiana Ledger - Columbiana, OH - *Ed&PubIntYB 82*
Columbiana Ledger - Lisbon, OH - *BaconPubCkNews 84*
Columbiana Shelby County Reporter - Columbiana, AL - *BaconPubCkNews 84; NewsDir 84*
Columbine Cablevision [of World Co.] - Ft. Collins, CO - *BrCabYB 84; Tel&CabFB 84C*
Columbine Editions - Toronto, ON, Canada - *BoPubDir 4 Sup, 5; LitMag&SmPr 83-84*
Columbine Independent - Columbine, CO - *Ed&PubIntYB 82*
Columbine Independent - Littleton, CO - *AyerDirPub 83*
Columbine Independent - Watkins, CO - *NewsDir 84*
Columbine Telephone Co. - Hooper, CO - *TelDir&BG 83-84*
Columbus Advocate - Columbus, KS - *BaconPubCkNews 84*
Columbus Blue Print, The - Columbus, MS - *NewsDir 84*
Columbus Booster - Columbus, OH - *BaconPubCkNews 84*
Columbus Business Journal - Worthington, OH - *BaconPubCkMag 84*
Columbus Cable TV [of American TV & Communications Corp.] - Columbus, NE - *BrCabYB 84; Tel&CabFB 84C*
Columbus Cable TV Service [of Communications Services Inc.] - Columbus, TX - *BrCabYB 84; Tel&CabFB 84C*
Columbus Cablevision [of Cox Cable Communications] - Columbus, IN - *BrCabYB 84*
Columbus Cablevision - Columbus, KS - *BrCabYB 84; Tel&CabFB 84C*
Columbus Cablevision Inc. [of Community Tele-Communications Inc.] - Columbus, GA - *BrCabYB 84; Tel&CabFB 84C*
Columbus Call & Post - Columbus, OH - *BaconPubCkNews 84*
Columbus Citizen-Journal [of The E. W. Scripps Co.] - Columbus, OH - *BaconPubCkNews 84; Ed&PubIntYB 82; LitMarPl 83, 84; NewsBur 6; NewsDir 84*
Columbus Citizen Sun - Columbus, MT - *BaconPubCkNews 84*
Columbus Colorado County Citizen - Columbus, TX - *BaconPubCkNews 84*
Columbus Commercial Dispatch - Columbus, MS - *BaconPubCkNews 84; BrCabYB 84; NewsDir 84*
Columbus County News - Chadbourn, NC - *AyerDirPub 83; Ed&PubIntYB 82*
Columbus Daily Advocate - Columbus, KS - *Ed&PubIntYB 82; NewsDir 84*
Columbus Dispatch - Columbus, OH - *BaconPubCkNews 84; Ed&PubIntYB 82; LitMarPl 83, 84; NewsBur 6; NewsDir 84*
Columbus Dispatch Magazine - Columbus, OH - *MagIndMarPl 82-83; WritMar 84*
Columbus Enquirer [of R. W. Page Corp.] - Columbus, GA - *BaconPubCkNews 84; Ed&PubIntYB 82; LitMarPl 83, 84; NewsBur 6; NewsDir 84*
Columbus Free Press - Columbus, OH - *LitMag&SmPr 83-84*
Columbus Ft. Benning Bayonet, The [of R. W. Page Corp.] - Columbus, GA - *NewsDir 84*
Columbus Gazette - Columbus Junction, IA - *AyerDirPub 83; BaconPubCkNews 84; Ed&PubIntYB 82*
Columbus Grove Putnam County Vidette - Columbus Grove, OH - *BaconPubCkNews 84*
Columbus Grove Telephone Co. - Columbus Grove, OH - *TelDir&BG 83-84*
Columbus Herald - Columbus, IN - *BaconPubCkNews 84; Ed&PubIntYB 82*
Columbus Journal-Republican - Columbus, WI - *BaconPubCkNews 84*
Columbus Laboratories Library [of Battelle Memorial Institute] - Columbus, OH - *EISS 83*
Columbus Ledger [of R. W. Page Corp.] - Columbus, GA - *BaconPubCkNews 84; Ed&PubIntYB 82; LitMarPl 83, 84; NewsBur 6; NewsDir 84*
Columbus Ledger-Enquirer, The [of The R. W. Page Corp.] - Columbus, GA - *LitMarPl 83, 84*
Columbus Messenger East, The - Columbus, OH - *Ed&PubIntYB 82*
Columbus Messenger West, The - Columbus, OH - *Ed&PubIntYB 82*
Columbus Modern Light - Columbus, KS - *BaconPubCkNews 84*
Columbus Monthly [of Columbus Monthly Publishing Corp.] - Columbus, OH - *ArtMar 84; BaconPubCkMag 84; MagDir 84; WritMar 84*
Columbus Museum of Arts & Sciences - Columbus, GA - *BillIntBG 83-84*
Columbus Northland News [of Suburban News Publications Inc.] - Columbus, OH - *NewsDir 84*
Columbus Onyx - Columbus, OH - *Ed&PubIntYB 82*
Columbus Republic [of Home News Enterprises] - Columbus, IN - *BaconPubCkNews 84; NewsDir 84*
Columbus, Ronald C. - New York, NY - *LitMarPl 83, 84*
Columbus Silver Wings - Columbus, MS - *BaconPubCkNews 84*
Columbus Telegram [of Freedom Newspapers] - Columbus, NE - *BaconPubCkNews 84; Ed&PubIntYB 82; NewsDir 84*
Columbus Telephone Co. - Columbus, KS - *TelDir&BG 83-84*
Columbus Thermal Belt News Journal - Columbus, NC - *BaconPubCkNews 84*
Columbus Times - Columbus, GA - *AyerDirPub 83; BaconPubCkNews 84; NewsDir 84*
Columbus Tri Village News - *See* Suburban News Publications
Columbus TV Cable Corp. - Columbus, MS - *BrCabYB 84; Tel&CabFB 84C*
Columbus Upper Arlington News [of Suburban News Publications Inc.] - Columbus, OH - *NewsDir 84*
Columbus Upper Arlington News, The - Upper Arlington, OH - *Ed&PubIntYB 82*
Column One Music - Springfield, MO - *BillIntBG 83-84*
Column One Record Co. - Springfield, MO - *BillIntBG 83-84*
Colusa County Farmer - Williams, CA - *AyerDirPub 83; Ed&PubIntYB 82*
Colusa Sun Herald [of Johnson Newspapers Inc.] - Colusa, CA - *BaconPubCkNews 84; Ed&PubIntYB 82; NewsDir 84*
Colville Panoramic Advertisr - *See* Panorama Publishers
Colville Statesman-Examiner - Colville, WA - *BaconPubCkNews 84; Ed&PubIntYB 82; NewsDir 84*
Colville TV Cable Co. [of Tidel Communications Inc.] - Colville, WA - *BrCabYB 84; Tel&CabFB 84C*
Colwell Systems Inc. - Champaign, IL - *MicrocomSwDir 1*
Colwell Systems Ltd. - Brossard, PQ, Canada - *BoPubDir 4 Sup, 5*
Colwood Goldstream Gazette - Victoria, BC, Canada - *Ed&PubIntYB 82*
Com Catalog/Union Com Catalog Project [of Old Dominion University Library] - Norfolk, VA - *EISS 83*
COM Consultants - Diamond Bar, CA - *TeleSy&SerDir 2-84*
Com Data Corp. - Morton Grove, IL - *DataDirSup 7-83; MicrocomMPl 84*
Com Design Inc. - Goleta, CA - *DataDirSup 7-83*
Com/Peripherals Inc. - Great Neck, NY - *WhoWMicrocom 83*
Com-Pro - Charleston, SC - *MicrocomMPl 84*
Com-Pro - *See* Meszaros Associates Inc.
Com-Star Cablevision Inc. - *See* McCubbins, Charles L.
Com/Tech Group, The - St. Petersburg, FL - *AdAge 3-28-84; StaDirAdAg 2-84*
Com/Tech Systems Inc. - New York, NY - *DataDirSup 7-83*
Com-West Inc. - *See* Tele-Communications Inc.
Comanche Chief - Comanche, TX - *BaconPubCkNews 84; Ed&PubIntYB 82; NewsDir 84*
Comanche County Telephone Co. - Deleon, TX - *TelDir&BG 83-84*
Comanche News - Comanche, OK - *BaconPubCkNews 84; Ed&PubIntYB 82*
Comarc Systems - San Francisco, CA - *DataDirSup 7-83*
CoMarco Data Services Inc. - New York, NY - *MagIndMarPl 82-83*
Comark Cable Fund III - West Palm Beach, FL - *Tel&CabFB 84C p.1672*

Comark Corp. - Waltham, MA - *DataDirSup 7-83; WhoWMicrocom 83*
Comark Inc. - West Palm Beach, FL - *Tel&CabFB 84C*
Comart Aniforms [Div. of Comart Associates Inc.] - New York, NY - *StaDirAdAg 2-84*
Combat Handguns [of Harris Publications Outdoor Group] - New York, NY - *WritMar 84*
Combinations, A Journal of Photography - Greenfield Center, NY - *LitMag&SmPr 83-84*
Combine Music Group - Nashville, TN - *BillIntBG 83-84*
Combined Book Exhibit, The [Div. of F. W. Faxon Co. Inc.] - Hawthorne, NY - *MagIndMarPl 82-83*
Combined Cable Corp. - Chicago, IL - *BrCabYB 84 p.D-299; Tel&CabFB 84C p.1673*
Combined Communications Corp. - *See* Gannett Newspapers
Combined Health Information Database [of U.S. Public Health Service] - Bethesda, MD - *EISS 5-84 Sup*
Combined Industry Standards & Military Specifications - Englewood, CO - *DirOnDB Spring 84*
Combined T9/Service Segment [of I. P. Sharp Associates Ltd.] - Toronto, ON, Canada - *DataDirOnSer 84*
Comboni Missions - Cincinnati, OH - *WritMar 84*
Combs/Resneck/Stone & Associates Inc. - Little Rock, AR - *StaDirAdAg 2-84*
Combur Corp. - Palo Verdes Estates, CA - *DataDirSup 7-83*
Combustion - New York, NY - *MagDir 84*
Comcast Cable - St. Clair Shores, MI - *Tel&CabFB 84C*
Comcast Cable Communications - Bala Cynwyd, PA - *BrCabYB 84 p.D-299; CabTVFinDB 83; LitMarPl 84; TelAl 84*
Comcast Cable of Corinth - Corinth, MS - *Tel&CabFB 84C*
Comcast Cable of Paducah Inc. - Paducah, KY - *BrCabYB 84; Tel&CabFB 84C*
Comcast Cable One - Trenton, NJ - *Tel&CabFB 84C*
Comcast Cablevision - Flint, MI - *BrCabYB 84; Tel&CabFB 84C*
Comcast Cablevision Inc. - Willow Grove, PA - *Tel&CabFB 84C*
Comcast Cablevision of Clinton - Clinton Township, MI - *BrCabYB 84*
Comcast Cablevision of Corinth - Corinth, MS - *BrCabYB 84*
Comcast Cablevision of Montgomery County Inc. - Bala Cynwyd, PA - *BrCabYB 84; Tel&CabFB 84C*
Comcast Cablevision of Shelby Inc. - Shelby, MI - *Tel&CabFB 84C*
Comcast Cablevision of Warren [of Comcast Management Corp.] - Warren, MI - *BrCabYB 84*
Comcast Corp. - Warren, MI - *BrCabYB 84*
Comcast Corp. [of International Equity Corp.] - Bala Cynwyd, PA - *HomeVid&CabYB 82-83; KnowInd 83; TelAl 83; Tel&CabFB 84C p.1673*
Comcepts Systems - Notre Dame, IN - *MicrocomSwDir 1*
Comcheq Services Ltd. - Winnipeg, MB, Canada - *DataDirOnSer 84*
Comco Electronics Inc. - Des Plaines, IL - *Tel&CabFB 84C*
COMCOM [Div. of Haddon Craftsmen] - Allentown, PA - *EISS 83; LitMarPl 83, 84; MagIndMarPl 82-83*
Comcorp Data Systems Inc. - New York, NY - *ADAPSOMemDir 83-84*
Comcrash - London, England - *MicrocomSwDir 1*
Comdat - *See* CISCo
Comdesign Inc. - Goleta, CA - *MicrocomMPl 84*
Comdisco Inc. - Rosemont, IL - *Datamation 6-83*
Come-All-Ye [of Legacy Books] - Hatboro, PA - *LitMag&SmPr 83-84*
Comedy Center Inc., The - Wilmington, DE - *Ed&PubIntYB 82*
Comedy Entertainment Network - Minneapolis, MN - *BrCabYB 84; CabTVPrDB 83; Tel&CabFB 84C*
Comer News - Comer, GA - *BaconPubCkNews 84; Ed&PubIntYB 82*
Comet Press, The [Div. of Harwyn Litho Inc.] - New York, NY - *LitMarPl 83, 84*
Comet, The - Aberdeen, SD - *Ed&PubIntYB 82*
Comext [of Informatech] - Montreal, PQ, Canada - *DataDirOnSer 84*
Comext Data Bank [of Commission of the European Communities] - Kirchberg, Luxembourg - *EISS 83*
Comext-Eurostat - Kirchberg, Luxembourg - *DirOnDB Spring 84*
Comfort News - Comfort, TX - *BaconPubCkNews 84; Ed&PubIntYB 82*
Comfort, Randy Lee - Denver, CO - *BoPubDir 4, 5*
Comfrey Times - Comfrey, MN - *AyerDirPub 83; BaconPubCkNews 84; Ed&PubIntYB 82*
Comgraphics [of George Graphics] - San Francisco, CA - *EISS 83*
Comicana Books - Bedford, NY - *BoPubDir 4 Sup, 5*
Comision Economica para America Latina (Central Latinoamericano de Documentacion Economica y Social) - Santiago, Chile - *CompReadDB 82*
Comjean, Marlies - Lincoln, MA - *LitMarPl 83, 84*
Comm Data Computer House - Milford, MI - *MicrocomMPl 83, 84; WritMar 84*
Comm Management Inc. - Topeka, KS - *BrCabYB 84 p.D-299; Tel&CabFB 84C p.1673*
Comm-Pro Associates - Manhattan Beach, CA - *DataDirSup 7-83*
Commack-Kings Park Pennysaver - Huntington, NY - *AyerDirPub 83*
Commack News - Commack, NY - *Ed&PubIntYB 82*
Commack News [of Smithtown News Inc.] - Smithtown, NY - *NewsDir 84*
Commack News - *See* Smithtown News Inc.
Command Broadcast Group - Beacon, NY - *BrCabYB 84*
Command Post - O'Fallon, IL - *AyerDirPub 83*
Command Productions - White Plains, NY - *ArtMar 84; WritMar 84*
Command Products Co. - Evanston, IL - *AvMarPl 83*
Commander Magazine - Tacoma, WA - *MicrocomMPl 84*
Commander Satellite Corp. - Ft. Lauderdale, FL - *Tel&CabFB 84C*
Commander Systems Inc. - Westerville, OH - *DataDirSup 7-83*
Commart Advertising Inc. - Santa Clara, CA - *StaDirAdAg 2-84*
Commcept Publishing Ltd. - Vancouver, BC, Canada - *BoPubDir 4, 5*
Commco Cable Communications Co. - Odem, TX - *BrCabYB 84*
Commco Public Relations Inc. - New York, NY - *DirPRFirms 83*
Commentary - New York, NY - *BaconPubCkMag 84; LitMarPl 83, 84; MagDir 84; MagIndMarPl 82-83; WritMar 84*
Commerce [of Chicago Association of Commerce & Industry] - Chicago, IL - *ArtMar 84; BaconPubCkMag 84; MagDir 84; WritMar 84*
Commerce Advertising Agency Inc. - New York, NY - *StaDirAdAg 2-84*
Commerce Business Daily [of Dialog Information Services Inc.] - Palo Alto, CA - *DataDirOnSer 84*
Commerce Business Daily [of U.S. Dept. of Commerce] - Chicago, IL - *DirOnDB Spring 84; EISS 7-83 Sup*
Commerce City Sentinel [of Community Publications Co.] - Commerce City, CO - *AyerDirPub 83; NewsDir 84*
Commerce City Sentinel - *See* Sentinel Newspapers
Commerce Clearing House Inc. - Atlanta, GA - *MagIndMarPl 82-83*
Commerce Clearing House Inc. - Chicago, IL - *DataDirOnSer 84; Datamation 6-83; DirMarMP 83; KnowInd 83; LitMarPl 83, 84; MicroMarPl 82-83; Top100Al 83*
Commerce Journal [of Harte-Hanks Communications Inc.] - Commerce, TX - *AyerDirPub 83; BaconPubCkNews 84; Ed&PubIntYB 82; NewsDir 84*
Commerce Kings - Lakeland, FL - *DirMarMP 83*
Commerce News - Commerce, GA - *BaconPubCkNews 84; Ed&PubIntYB 82; NewsDir 84*
Commerce Spinal Column Newsweekly - *See* Spinal Column Newsweekly
Commerce-Walled Lake Spinal Column [of Union Lake Spinal Column] - Union Lake, MI - *NewsDir 84*
Commercial - Pine Bluff, AR - *AyerDirPub 83*
Commercial - Dyersville, IA - *AyerDirPub 83*
Commercial Analysts Co. - New York, NY - *IntDirMarRes 83*
Commercial & Financial Chronicle [of National News Service Inc.] - New York, NY - *BaconPubCkMag 84; MagDir 84; NewsBur 6*
Commercial & Home Movie Service Inc. - Allentown, PA - *AvMarPl 83*
Commercial & Legal Services Div. [of Aspen Systems Corp.] - New York, NY - *EISS 83*
Commercial Appeal - Danville, VA - *AyerDirPub 83*

Commercial Appeal, The [of Memphis Publishing Co.] - Memphis, TN - *AyerDirPub 83; Ed&PubIntYB 82; LitMarPl 84; NewsBur 6*
Commercial Bulletin - Boston, MA - *BaconPubCkMag 84; MagDir 84*
Commercial Car Journal - Detroit, MI - *NewsBur 6*
Commercial Car Journal - Radnor, PA - *MagIndMarPl 82-83*
Commercial Carrier Journal - Radnor, PA - *BaconPubCkMag 84*
Commercial Computer Services Inc. - Ft. Worth, TX - *DataDirSup 7-83*
Commercial Dispatch - Columbus, MS - *AyerDirPub 83; Ed&PubIntYB 82*
Commercial Dispatch Publishing - *See* Imes, Birney Jr.
Commercial Electronics Ltd. - Vancouver, BC, Canada - *AvMarPl 83*
Commercial-Express - Vicksburg, MI - *AyerDirPub 83; NewsDir 84*
Commercial Fisheries News - Stonington, ME - *WritMar 84*
Commercial Law Journal - Chicago, IL - *MagDir 84*
Commercial Leader - Lyndhurst, NJ - *AyerDirPub 83*
Commercial Leader-Review - Lyndhurst, NJ - *Ed&PubIntYB 82*
Commercial Lithographers Inc. - Bensenville, IL - *MagIndMarPl 82-83*
Commercial Mail & Columbia City Post, The - Columbia City, IN - *Ed&PubIntYB 82*
Commercial News [of C. A. Page Publishing Corp.] - Lynwood, CA - *BaconPubCkMag 84; MagDir 84*
Commercial-News - Danville, IL - *AyerDirPub 83; Ed&PubIntYB 82*
Commercial News - Saratoga Springs, NY - *AyerDirPub 83*
Commercial Printing Inc. - Des Moines, IA - *MagIndMarPl 82-83*
Commercial Productions Inc. - New York, NY - *AvMarPl 83*
Commercial Radio Institute Inc. - Baltimore, MD - *Tel&CabFB 84S*
Commercial Record [of Record Publishing Co.] - Rocky Hill, CT - *BaconPubCkMag 84; MagDir 84*
Commercial Record - Saugatuck, MI - *AyerDirPub 83; Ed&PubIntYB 82*
Commercial Recorder [of Recorder Publishing Co.] - Ft. Worth, TX - *Ed&PubIntYB 82; NewsDir 84*
Commercial Recorder, The - San Antonio, TX - *Ed&PubIntYB 82*
Commercial Remodeling [of Qualified Remodeler Inc.] - Chicago, IL - *BaconPubCkMag 84; MagDir 84*
Commercial Review - Portland, OR - *BaconPubCkMag 84; MagDir 84*
Commercial Review, The - Portland, IN - *AyerDirPub 83; Ed&PubIntYB 82*
Commercial Software Inc. - New York, NY - *ADAPSOMemDir 83-84*
Commercial Software Systems - Littleton, CO - *MicrocomMPl 84; MicrocomSwDir 1; WhoWMicrocom 83*
Commercial Space Report, The - Sunnyvale, CA - *BaconPubCkMag 84*
Commercial Systems Inc. - Paducah, KY - *ADAPSOMemDir 83-84*
Commercial Systems Laboratories - Auburn, AL - *MicrocomMPl 84*
Commercial West - Eden Prairie, MN - *BaconPubCkMag 84*
Commercial West [of Financial Communications Inc.] - Hopkins, MN - *MagDir 84*
Commex Ltd. - Hartsdale, NY - *DataDirSup 7-83*
Commissariat a l'Energie Atomique [of Departement de Surete Nucleaire] - Fontenay-aux-Roses, France - *InfIndMarPl 83*
Commissie voor Bibliografie & Dokumentatie - Amsterdam, Netherlands - *InfIndMarPl 83*
Commission for the Advancement of Public Interest Organizations - Washington, DC - *BoPubDir 4, 5*
Commission Internationale Mixte - New York, NY - *CompReadDB 82*
Commission of the European Communities - Kirchberg, Luxembourg - *CompReadDB 82; InfIndMarPl 83*
Commission on Professional & Hospital Activities - Ann Arbor, MI - *DirInfWP 82; EISS 83*
Commission on Storage, Automatic Processing, & Retrieval of Geological Data [of International Union of Geological Sciences] - Paris, France - *EISS 83*
Commission on Voluntary Service & Action - New York, NY - *BoPubDir 4, 5*
Committee for Abortion Rights & Against Sterilization Abuse - New York, NY - *BoPubDir 4 Sup, 5*
Committee for Biological Pest Control - Los Angeles, CA - *BoPubDir 4, 5*
Committee for Economic Development - New York, NY - *BoPubDir 4, 5*
Committee for Elimination of Death - San Marcos, CA - *BoPubDir 5*
Committee for Nuclear Responsibility - San Francisco, CA - *BoPubDir 4, 5*
Committee for Single Adoptive Parents - Chevy Chase, MD - *BoPubDir 5*
Committee on Canadian Labour History - St. John's, NF, Canada - *BoPubDir 4, 5*
Committee on Data for Science & Technology [of International Council of Scientific Unions] - Paris, France - *EISS 83; InfIndMarPl 83*
Committee Publishers - Evanston, IL - *BoPubDir 4, 5*
Committee, The - Evanston, IL - *LitMag&SmPr 83-84*
Commline - Wheeling, IL - *BaconPubCkMag 84*
Commodities [of I. P. Sharp Associates Ltd.] - Toronto, ON, Canada - *DataDirOnSer 84*
Commodities - London, England - *DirOnDB Spring 84*
Commodities Data Bank - Washington, DC - *DirOnDB Spring 84*
Commodities Data Information Service [of MJK Associates] - Santa Clara, CA - *EISS 83*
Commodities Futures - Mountain View, CA - *DirOnDB Spring 84*
Commodities/Futures - Memphis, TN - *DirOnDB Spring 84*
Commodities Magazine - Chicago, IL - *MagIndMarPl 82-83*
Commodities Magazine - Cedar Falls, IA - *WritMar 84*
Commodities Market Data Bank [of Commodity Systems Inc.] - Boca Raton, FL - *DataDirOnSer 84*
Commodities Market Data Bank [of Data Resources Inc.] - Lexington, MA - *DataDirOnSer 84; DBBus 82*
Commodities Research Unit Ltd. - London, England - *EISS 83; InfIndMarPl 83*
Commodity Concepts - Phoenix, AZ - *WhoWMicrocom 83*
Commodity Data [of National Computer Network of Chicago] - Chicago, IL - *DataDirOnSer 84*
Commodity Data Information System [of MJK Associates] - Santa Clara, CA - *DBBus 82*
Commodity Futures [of Market Data Systems Inc.] - Memphis, TN - *DataDirOnSer 84*
Commodity Information Services - Chicago, IL - *DataDirOnSer 84; EISS 83; InfIndMarPl 83*
Commodity Journal [of American Association of Commodity Traders] - Concord, NH - *MagIndMarPl 82-83; WritMar 84*
Commodity Microanalysis Inc. - Baltimore, MD - *EISS 83*
Commodity News Services [Subs. of Knight-Ridder Newspapers Inc.] - Leawood, KS - *DataDirOnSer 84; DirOnDB Spring 84; Ed&PubIntYB 82; EISS 83; InfoS 83-84*
Commodity Quotations Inc. - Scarsdale, NY - *Ed&PubIntYB 82*
Commodity Research Bureau Inc. - Jersey City, NJ - *BoPubDir 5*
Commodity Research Bureau Inc. - New York, NY - *BoPubDir 4; EISS 83*
Commodity Systems Inc. - Boca Raton, FL - *DataDirOnSer 84; EISS 83; InfIndMarPl 83*
Commodity Transportation Survey [of ADP Network Services Inc.] - Ann Arbor, MI - *DataDirOnSer 84*
Commodore [of Commodore Business Machines] - West Chester, PA - *BaconPubCkMag 84; MicrocomMPl 84; WritMar 84*
Commodore Business Machines Inc. - Santa Clara, CA - *DirInfWP 82*
Commodore Business Machines Inc. - King of Prussia, PA - *MicrocomMPl 83*
Commodore Business Machines Inc. [Subs. of Commodore International] - Norristown, PA - *WhoWMicrocom 83*
Commodore Business Machines Inc. [Subs. of Commodore International] - West Chester, PA - *MicrocomMPl 84; WhoWMicrocom 83*
Commodore Business Machines Ltd. - Slough, England - *MicrocomSwDir 1*
Commodore Information Network [of Commodore Business Machines] - Wayne, PA - *DirOnDB Spring 84; EISS 7-83 Sup*
Commodore Information Network [of Commodore Business Machines] - West Chester, PA - *TeleSy&SerDir 2-84*

Commodore International Ltd. - Norristown, PA - *Datamation 6-83; HomeVid&CabYB 82-83*
Commodore International Ltd. - West Chester, PA - *DataDirOnSer 84*
Commodore International Ltd. - Nassau, Bahamas - *Top100Al 83*
Commodore Power/Play [of Commodore Computers] - West Chester, PA - *MicrocomMPl 84*
Commodore Record Co. Inc. - New Rochelle, NY - *BillIntBG 83-84*
Common - Chicago, IL - *EISS 83*
Common Carrier Bureau [of U.S. Federal Communications Commission] - Washington, DC - *TeleSy&SerDir 7-83*
Common Carrier Corp. - Hollywood, CA - *Tel&CabFB 84C*
Common Cause Records - Miami, FL - *BillIntBG 83-84*
Common Ground - St. Peters, PA - *LitMag&SmPr 83-84*
Common Knowledge Press [Aff. of Commonweal Inc.] - Bolinas, CA - *BoPubDir 5*
Common Lives/Lesbian Lives - Iowa City, IA - *LitMag&SmPr 83-84*
Common Sense - Miami, FL - *LitMag&SmPr 83-84*
Common Sense Communications Inc. - Saginaw, MI - *StaDirAdAg 2-84*
Common Table - New Haven, CT - *BoPubDir 4, 5*
Commoner - Enderby, BC, Canada - *Ed&PubIntYB 82*
Commoners' Publishing Society Inc. - Ottawa, ON, Canada - *BoPubDir 4; LitMarPl 83, 84; WritMar 84*
Commonground Press - New Paltz, NY - *BoPubDir 4 Sup, 5*
Commonsense Books - Chelmsford, MA - *BoPubDir 4, 5*
Commonweal - New York, NY - *BaconPubCkMag 84; LitMarPl 83, 84; MagDir 84; MagIndMarPl 82-83; WritMar 84*
Commonwealth - San Francisco, CA - *MagDir 84*
Commonwealth - Greenwood, MS - *AyerDirPub 83*
Commonwealth - Ash Grove, MO - *AyerDirPub 83*
Commonwealth - Norfolk, VA - *BaconPubCkMag 84; WritMar 84*
Commonwealth - Virginia Beach, VA - *MagDir 84*
Commonwealth Agricultural Bureaux Abstracts - Slough, England - *CompReadDB 82; DBBus 82; InfIndMarPl 83*
Commonwealth Bank Bond Index - Sydney, Australia - *DirOnDB Spring 84*
Commonwealth Bank Bond Index [of I. P. Sharp Associates Ltd.] - Toronto, ON, Canada - *DataDirOnSer 84*
Commonwealth Bureau of Agricultural Economics - Oxford, England - *CompReadDB 82*
Commonwealth Bureau of Animal Breeding & Genetics - Edinburgh, Scotland - *CompReadDB 82*
Commonwealth Bureau of Animal Health - Weybridge, England - *CompReadDB 82*
Commonwealth Bureau of Animal Health (Central Veterinary Laboratory) - Weybridge, England - *CompReadDB 82*
Commonwealth Bureau of Dairy Science & Technology - Reading, England - *CompReadDB 82*
Commonwealth Bureau of Horticulture & Plantation Crops - Maidstone, England - *CompReadDB 82*
Commonwealth Bureau of Nutrition (Rowett Research Institute) - Aberdeen, Scotland - *CompReadDB 82*
Commonwealth Bureau of Pastures & Field Crops - Maidenhead, England - *CompReadDB 82*
Commonwealth Bureau of Plant Breeding & Genetics - Cambridge, England - *CompReadDB 82*
Commonwealth Bureau of Soils - Harpenden, England - *CompReadDB 82*
Commonwealth Cable Co. - Somerset, KY - *BrCabYB 84*
Commonwealth Cable Systems Inc. - Dallas, PA - *BrCabYB 84*
Commonwealth Cable Systems Inc. - Wilkes-Barre, PA - *Tel&CabFB 84C p.1673*
Commonwealth Cablevision Corp. - Grottoes, VA - *BrCabYB 84*
Commonwealth Cablevision Corp. - Luray, VA - *BrCabYB 84 p.D-299; Tel&CabFB 84C p.1673*
Commonwealth Cablevision of Massachusetts Inc. - Westfield, MA - *BrCabYB 84 p.D-299; Tel&CabFB 84C p.1673*
Commonwealth Communications - Los Angeles, CA - *AvMarPl 83*
Commonwealth Forestry Bureau - Oxford, England - *CompReadDB 82*
Commonwealth Group Inc., The - Stamford, CT - *HBIndAd&MS 82-83*
Commonwealth Institute of Entomology - London, England - *CompReadDB 82*
Commonwealth Institute of Helminthology - St. Albans, England - *CompReadDB 82*
Commonwealth-Journal - Somerset, KY - *AyerDirPub 83; Ed&PubIntYB 82*
Commonwealth Microfilm Library (Marketing Div.) - Willowdale, ON, Canada - *MicroMarPl 82-83*
Commonwealth Mycological Institute - Richmond, England - *CompReadDB 82*
Commonwealth Press - Worcester, MA - *MagIndMarPl 82-83*
Commonwealth-Press - Ripon, WI - *AyerDirPub 83*
Commonwealth Press Inc. - Radford, VA - *BoPubDir 4, 5*
Commonwealth Regional Energy Resources Index [of Commonwealth Scientific & Industrial Research Organisation] - East Melbourne, Australia - *CompReadDB 82*
Commonwealth Regional Renewable Energy Resources Information System - East Melbourne, Australia - *EISS 83*
Commonwealth Scientific & Industrial Research Organisation - East Melbourne, Australia - *CompReadDB 82; InfIndMarPl 83*
Commonwealth Scientific & Industrial Research Organisation Libraries - *See* CSIRO
Commonwealth Systems - Lancaster, PA - *DirInfWP 82*
Commonwealth Telephone Co. [Aff. of Commonwealth Telephone Enterprises Inc.] - Dallas, PA - *TelDir&BG 83-84*
Commonwealth Times [of Virginia Commonwealth University] - Richmond, VA - *NewsDir 84*
Commpute Program [of State University of New York at Stony Brook] - Stony Brook, NY - *EISS 83*
Commsoft - Palo Alto, CA - *MicrocomMPl 83, 84; WhoWMicrocom 83*
Communacad - Wilton, CT - *AvMarPl 83*
Communi-Creations Inc. - Denver, CO - *AvMarPl 83; Tel&CabFB 84C*
Communi-K Inc. - New York, NY - *StaDirAdAg 2-84*
Communica Ltd. - Toronto, ON, Canada - *StaDirAdAg 2-84*
Communicable [of Southland Communications Inc.] - Cocoa Beach, FL - *BrCabYB 84; Tel&CabFB 84C p.1673*
Communicable Inc. - Middletown, IN - *Tel&CabFB 84C*
Communicable of Palmetto [of Cablevision Industries Inc.] - Palmetto, FL - *Tel&CabFB 84C*
Communicable of Texas Inc. - Crane, TX - *BrCabYB 84; Tel&CabFB 84C*
Communicable of Texas Inc. - Kermit, TX - *BrCabYB 84*
CommuniCable of Texas Inc. - Monahans, TX - *BrCabYB 84; Tel&CabFB 84C*
Communicacion Positiva Inc. - San Juan, PR - *DirPRFirms 83*
Communicade - Rochester, NY - *Ed&PubIntYB 82*
Communicate - Beaverlodge, AB, Canada - *WritMar 84*
Communicate America Affiliates Inc. - New York, NY - *DirPRFirms 83*
Communicate with Confidence Inc. - Great Neck, NY - *ProGuPRSer 4*
Communication Advisors Inc. - Southfield, MI - *TeleSy&SerDir 7-83*
Communication Aids International - Los Angeles, CA - *Ed&PubIntYB 82*
Communication & Design Agency Inc. - Latham, NY - *StaDirAdAg 2-84*
Communication Arts [of Coyne & Blanchard Inc.] - Palo Alto, CA - *BaconPubCkMag 84; MagDir 84; MagIndMarPl 82-83*
Communication Arts International - Washington, DC - *MagIndMarPl 82-83*
Communication Channels Inc. - Atlanta, GA - *DirMarMP 83; MagIndMarPl 82-83*
Communication Commission [of National Council of Churches] - New York, NY - *TelAl 83, 84; Tel&CabFB 84C*
Communication Concepts Inc. [Subs. of Retail Computer Services] - Ivyland, PA - *DataDirOnSer 84; MagIndMarPl 82-83*
Communication Controls Inc. - Greenwich, CT - *DataDirSup 7-83*
Communication Corp. Inc. - Washington, DC - *ArtMar 84*
Communication Corp. of America Inc. - Mechanicsburg, OH - *Tel&CabFB 84C*
Communication Corp. of America Inc. - Brentwood, TN - *Tel&CabFB 84C p.1673*
Communication Creativity - Saguache, CO - *LitMag&SmPr 83-84; LitMarPl 83, 84*
Communication Devices Inc. - South Hackensack, NJ - *WhoWMicrocom 83*

Communication Directions Inc. - Newport Beach, CA - *StaDirAdAg 2-84*
Communication Education - Annandale, VA - *MagDir 84*
Communication Illustrated - Bartlesville, OK - *BaconPubCkMag 84*
Communication Northwest Inc. - Seattle, WA - *DirPRFirms 83*
Communication Options - Atlanta, GA - *DirPRFirms 83*
Communication Planners Inc. - Great Neck, NY - *DirPRFirms 83*
Communication Plus - Richardson, TX - *StaDirAdAg 2-84*
Communication Press - San Francisco, CA - *BoPubDir 4, 5; LitMag&SmPr 83-84*
Communication Resources - Haddonfield, NJ - *TeleSy&SerDir 7-83*
Communication Resources - New York, NY - *LitMarPl 83, 84*
Communication Services & Research - Winter Springs, FL - *CabTVFinDB 83*
Communication Skill Builders Inc. - Tucson, AZ - *DirMarMP 83; LitMarPl 83, 84; WritMar 84*
Communication Specialists of America - San Diego, CA - *LitMarPl 84*
Communication Strategies Inc. - Cambridge, MA - *VideoDir 82-83*
Communication Studies - Dallas, TX - *BoPubDir 4, 5*
Communication Systems - Mississauga, ON, Canada - *BaconPubCkMag 84*
Communication Training Consultants Inc. - New York, NY - *TeleSy&SerDir 2-84*
Communication Workshop, The - New York, NY - *HBIndAd&MS 82-83*
Communication World - San Francisco, CA - *MagIndMarPl 82-83*
Communications - Englewood, CO - *BaconPubCkMag 84; MagDir 84*
Communications Advertising Inc. - San Antonio, TX - *StaDirAdAg 2-84*
Communications Analysis Corp. - Framingham, MA - *TeleSy&SerDir 7-83*
Communications & Cablevision Inc. - Monroe, MI - *BrCabYB 84*
Communications & Distributed Resources [of NewsNet Inc.] - Bryn Mawr, PA - *DataDirOnSer 84*
Communications & Distributed Resources Report - Framingham, MA - *BaconPubCkMag 84; DirOnDB Spring 84*
Communications & the Law - Pine Plains, NY - *MagDir 84*
Communications Associates - Miami, FL - *DirPRFirms 83*
Communications Capital Corp. - New York, NY - *CabTVFinDB 83*
Communications Center of Clarksburg - Clarksburg, MD - *TeleSy&SerDir 2-84*
Communications Co. - San Francisco, CA - *BoPubDir 4, 5*
Communications Concepts Inc. - Cape Canaveral, FL - *AvMarPl 83*
Communications Consultants Inc. - Asbury, NJ - *TeleSy&SerDir 7-83*
Communications Corp. Inc. - Washington, DC - *WritMar 84*
Communications Corp. of America - Chicago, IL - *AvMarPl 83*
Communications Corp. of Indiana [Aff. of Telephone & Data Systems Inc.] - Roachdale, IN - *TelDir&BG 83-84*
Communications Counseling Co., The - Pittsburgh, PA - *DirPRFirms 83*
Communications Counselors Network - *See* Local Communications Inc.
Communications Daily - Washington, DC - *BaconPubCkMag 84; DirOnDB Spring 84; MagDir 84*
Communications Daily [of NewsNet Inc.] - Bryn Mawr, PA - *DataDirOnSer 84*
Communications Dept. [of Church of the Nazarene] - Kansas City, MO - *Tel&CabFB 84C*
Communications Electronics - Ann Arbor, MI - *MicrocomMPl 83*
Communications Engineering Digest - Denver, CO - *BaconPubCkMag 84; MagDir 84*
Communications Engineering Magazine - Plainview, NY - *BaconPubCkMag 84*
Communications Equity Associates - Tampa, FL - *CabTVFinDB 83*
Communications Group Inc., The - Toronto, ON, Canada - *DirPRFirms 83*
Communications Group, The - Boca Raton, FL - *DirPRFirms 83*
Communications Group, The - Memphis, TN - *DirPRFirms 83*
Communications Group West - Santa Monica, CA - *AvMarPl 83*
Communications Industry Forum - Pinebrook, NJ - *DirOnDB Spring 84*
Communications Industry Report [of NAVA/ICIA] - Fairfax, VA - *MicrocomMPl 84*
Communications Information [of University of Guelph] - Guelph, ON, Canada - *CompReadDB 82; EISS 83*
Communications Information [of QL Systems Ltd.] - Ottawa, ON, Canada - *DataDirOnSer 84*
Communications International [of Dawson-Butwick Publishers] - Washington, DC - *BaconPubCkMag 84; TeleSy&SerDir 2-84*
Communications Investment Corp. - Salt Lake City, UT - *Tel&CabFB 84C p.1673*
Communications Investment Corp. - *See* Standard Communications Inc.
Communications Management Associates - Stamford, CT - *TeleSy&SerDir 7-83*
Communications Management Systems - Chevy Chase, MD - *ProGuPRSer 4*
Communications/Marketing Co. - New York, NY - *DirMarMP 83; StaDirAdAg 2-84*
Communications Marketing Inc. - El Cajon, CA - *CabTVFinDB 83; IntDirMarRes 83; Tel&CabFB 84C*
Communications Marketing Inc. - La Mesa, CA - *Tel&CabFB 84C*
Communications Marketing Specialists - Chicago, IL - *DirMarMP 83*
Communications Media - Pasadena, MD - *Tel&CabFB 84C*
Communications Media Center [Aff. of New York Law School] - New York, NY - *BoPubDir 5*
Communications Network Service [of Satellite Business Systems] - McLean, VA - *TeleSy&SerDir 7-83*
Communications News [of Harcourt Brace Jovanovich Publications] - Geneva, IL - *BaconPubCkMag 84; Folio 83; MagDir 84; MagIndMarPl 82-83; TeleSy&SerDir 7-83*
Communications of the ACM [of Association for Computing Machinery] - New York, NY - *BaconPubCkMag 84; MagDir 84*
Communications-Pacific Inc. - Honolulu, HI - *DirPRFirms 83*
Communications Planning Corp. - Chicago, IL - *StaDirAdAg 2-84*
Communications Plus - New York, NY - *LitMarPl 83, 84*
Communications Press Inc. - Washington, DC - *LitMarPl 83, 84; WritMar 84*
Communications Properties Inc. - Dubuque, IA - *BrCabYB 84*
Communications Publishing Group Inc. - Boston, MA - *DataDirOnSer 84*
Communications Publishing Group Inc. - Brookline, MA - *DataDirOnSer 84; EISS 5-84 Sup*
Communications Research Corp. - Bellevue, WA - *DataDirSup 7-83*
Communications Research Laboratories - New York, NY - *EISS 83*
Communications Resources L.P. - Greenwich, CT - *Tel&CabFB 84C*
Communications Retailing - New York, NY - *MagDir 84*
Communications Satellite Co. - Washington, DC - *BrCabYB 84; HomeVid&CabYB 82-83; TelDir&BG 83-84; TeleSy&SerDir 7-83*
Communications Services Associates - Flower Mound, TX - *Tel&CabFB 84C*
Communications Services Associates - Highland Village, TX - *Tel&CabFB 84C*
Communications Services Associates - The Colony, TX - *Tel&CabFB 84C*
Communications Services Inc. [Div. of Tandem Productions Inc.] - Junction City, KS - *BrCabYB 84 p.D-299; CabTVFinDB 83; LitMarPl 84; Tel&CabFB 84C p.1673*
Communications Services Inc. - Weston, MO - *BrCabYB 84*
Communications Services Inc. - Allen, TX - *Tel&CabFB 84C*
Communications Services Inc. - McKinney, TX - *Tel&CabFB 84C*
Communications Services Inc. - Wylie, TX - *Tel&CabFB 84C*
Communications-6 Inc. - Montreal, PQ, Canada - *DirPRFirms 83*
Communications Solutions Inc. - Cupertino, CA - *ADAPSOMemDir 83-84*
Communications Studies & Planning International Inc. - New York, NY - *EISS 7-83 Sup; TeleSy&SerDir 7-83*
Communications Supply Inc. - West Chester, PA - *HomeVid&CabYB 82-83*
Communications Systems Corp. - Greenlawn, NY - *Tel&CabFB 84C p.1673*

Communications Systems Inc. - Hector, MN - *TelDir&BG 83-84*
Communications Systems Inc. - Irving, TX - *BrCabYB 84 p.D-299; CabTVFinDB 83*
Communications Systems Inc. - *See* Scott Cable Communications Inc.
Communications Team Inc. - Huntingdon Valley, PA - *StaDirAdAg 2-84*
Communications Technology Management Inc. - McLean, VA - *TeleSy&SerDir 2-84; VideoDir 82-83*
Communications Towers Inc. of Texas - Baton Rouge, LA - *Tel&CabFB 84C*
Communications Unltd. - Charlotte, NC - *TeleSy&SerDir 2-84*
Communications Workshop Inc. - Chicago, IL - *HBIndAd&MS 82-83; IntDirMarRes 83*
Communicator - Los Angeles, CA - *ArtMar 84*
Communicator - Alexandria, VA - *MagIndMarPl 82-83*
Communicators Cable Co. - Senatobia, MS - *Tel&CabFB 84C p.1673*
Communicators Cable Co. - Southaven, MS - *BrCabYB 84; Tel&CabFB 84C*
Communicators Group - Brattleboro, VT - *AdAge 3-28-84; StaDirAdAg 2-84*
Communicators Inc. - Cleveland, OH - *StaDirAdAg 2-84*
Communicators Inc., The - Pomfret Center, CT - *ArtMar 84; AvMarPl 83*
Communicator's Journal - Omaha, NE - *BaconPubCkMag 84; WritMar 84*
Communicators, The - Rockville, MD - *DirPRFirms 83*
Communicom - Culver City, CA - *BrCabYB 84; Tel&CabFB 84C p.1673*
Communicom - La Verne, CA - *BrCabYB 84*
Communicom - Los Angeles, CA - *BrCabYB 84*
Communicom - Tustin, CA - *BrCabYB 84*
Communicraft - Sunland, CA - *DirPRFirms 83*
Communicraft - Chicago, IL - *DirPRFirms 83*
Communicus Inc. - Los Angeles, CA - *IntDirMarRes 83*
Communigraphics - Woodbury, NY - *AdAge 3-28-84; StaDirAdAg 2-84*
Communigraphics Inc. - Baltimore, MD - *StaDirAdAg 2-84*
Communique Inc. - Elm Grove, WI - *StaDirAdAg 2-84*
Communispond Inc. - New York, NY - *ProGuPRSer 4*
Communities [of Communities Publishing Cooperative] - Louisa, VA - *LitMag&SmPr 83-84*
Communities Publishing Cooperative - Louisa, VA - *LitMag&SmPr 83-84*
Communitree Group - San Francisco, CA - *MicrocomMPl 83, 84; WritMar 84*
Community Action on Latin America [Aff. of Madison Campus Ministries] - Madison, WI - *BoPubDir 4 Sup, 5*
Community Advertising - Ft. Worth, TX - *Ed&PubIntYB 82*
Community Advisor - Marshall, MI - *AyerDirPub 83*
Community Advocate - Artesia, CA - *AyerDirPub 83*
Community Aerial Systems [of Community Tele-Communications Inc.] - Mineral Wells, TX - *BrCabYB 84; Tel&CabFB 84C*
Community & Junior College Journal - Washington, DC - *BaconPubCkMag 84; MagDir 84*
Community & Suburban Press Service - Frankfort, KY - *Ed&PubIntYB 82*
Community Animal Control - Tucson, AZ - *MagDir 84; WritMar 84*
Community Antenna Inc. [of Teleservice Corp. of America] - Batesville, AR - *BrCabYB 84*
Community Antenna Inc. [of Teleservice Corp. of America] - Cave City, AR - *BrCabYB 84*
Community Antenna Inc. - Gouverneur, NY - *Tel&CabFB 84C*
Community Antenna Inc. [of Century Communications Corp.] - Laurinburg, NC - *BrCabYB 84; Tel&CabFB 84C*
Community Antenna Service - Elkader, IA - *BrCabYB 84; Tel&CabFB 84C*
Community Antenna Service - Cottageville, WV - *BrCabYB 84*
Community Antenna Systems Inc. - Belleville, KS - *Tel&CabFB 84C*
Community Antenna Systems Inc. - Council Grove, KS - *BrCabYB 84*
Community Antenna Systems Inc. - Manhattan, KS - *BrCabYB 84*
Community Antenna Systems Inc. - Connell, WA - *Tel&CabFB 84C p.1674*
Community Antenna Systems Inc. - Lind, WA - *BrCabYB 84*
Community Antenna Systems Inc. - Tekoa, WA - *BrCabYB 84; Tel&CabFB 84C*
Community Antenna Systems Inc. - Cazenovia, WI - *BrCabYB 84*
Community Antenna Systems Inc. - Elroy, WI - *BrCabYB 84*
Community Antenna Systems Inc. - Hillsboro, WI - *Tel&CabFB 84C*
Community Antenna Systems Inc. - Kendall, WI - *BrCabYB 84*
Community Antenna Systems Ltd. [of Northern Cablevision Ltd.] - St. Paul, AB, Canada - *BrCabYB 84*
Community Antenna Television Association - Fairfax, VA - *InterCabHB 3*
Community Bank President, The - Akron, IA - *BaconPubCkMag 84*
Community Broadcasting Co. - Los Alamos, NM - *BrCabYB 84*
Community Broadcasting Service - Bangor, ME - *BrCabYB 84; Tel&CabFB 84C*
Community Builders Books - Canterbury, NH - *BoPubDir 4, 5*
Community Cable Co. [of Tele-Communications Inc.] - Ortonville, MN - *BrCabYB 84*
Community Cable Co. - Alton, MO - *BrCabYB 84*
Community Cable Co. - Thayer, MO - *BrCabYB 84*
Community Cable Co. - West Plains, MO - *BrCabYB 84; Tel&CabFB 84C p.1674*
Community Cable Co. [of Clemco Inc.] - Boyd, TX - *Tel&CabFB 84C*
Community Cable Co. [of Community Tele-Communications Inc.] - Salem, UT - *Tel&CabFB 84C*
Community Cable Corp. - Hoxie, AR - *Tel&CabFB 84C*
Community Cable Corp. - Walnut Ridge, AR - *BrCabYB 84*
Community Cable Corp. [of Northland Communications Corp.] - Gold Beach, OR - *BrCabYB 84*
Community Cable Corp. [of North Penn Telephone Co.] - East Smithfield, PA - *Tel&CabFB 84C*
Community Cable Corp. [of North Penn Telephone Co.] - Mansfield, PA - *BrCabYB 84; Tel&CabFB 84C*
Community Cable of Utah Inc. [of Tele-Communications Inc.] - Tooele, UT - *BrCabYB 84; Tel&CabFB 84C*
Community Cable of Utah Inc. - Toolele, UT - *BrCabYB 84*
Community Cable Service [of Times Mirror Cable Television Inc.] - Logan, OH - *BrCabYB 84; Tel&CabFB 84C*
Community Cable Systems Inc. - Hastings, MI - *Tel&CabFB 84C p.1674*
Community Cable TV Inc. - Channahon, IL - *BrCabYB 84*
Community Cable TV Inc. - Minooka, IL - *BrCabYB 84*
Community Cable TV Inc. - Sanborn, IA - *Tel&CabFB 84C*
Community Cable TV Inc. [of P.W. Communications Inc.] - Decatur, MI - *BrCabYB 84*
Community Cable TV Inc. - Clark County, NV - *BrCabYB 84*
Community Cable TV Inc. - Las Vegas, NV - *BrCabYB 84; Tel&CabFB 84C*
Community Cable TV Inc. - Delta, OH - *BrCabYB 84; Tel&CabFB 84C*
Community Cable TV Inc. - Swanton, OH - *BrCabYB 84; Tel&CabFB 84C p.1674*
Community Cablesystems Inc. of Texas - Elgin, TX - *Tel&CabFB 84C*
Community Cablesystems Inc. of Texas - Sinton, TX - *Tel&CabFB 84C*
Community Cablevision Co. [of Irvine Co.] - Irvine, CA - *Tel&CabFB 84C*
Community Cablevision Co. [of The Irvine Co.] - Newport Beach, CA - *BrCabYB 84; InterCabHB 3*
Community Cablevision Co. - Collinsville, OK - *BrCabYB 84*
Community Cablevision Co. - Hominy, OK - *BrCabYB 84 p.D-299*
Community Cablevision Corp. [of Southern Cablevision Corp.] - Bryan, TX - *BrCabYB 84; Tel&CabFB 84C*
Community Cablevision Inc. - Belvidere, IL - *BrCabYB 84; Tel&CabFB 84C*
Community Cablevision Inc. - Evanston, IL - *BrCabYB 84; Tel&CabFB 84C p.1674*
Community Cablevision Inc. - Harvard, IL - *BrCabYB 84*
Community Cablevision Inc. [of Topeka Community Cablevision] - Frankfort, KS - *BrCabYB 84; Tel&CabFB 84C*
Community Cablevision Inc. - Fontana, WI - *BrCabYB 84*

Community Cablevision Inc. - Genoa City, WI - *BrCabYB 84; Tel&CabFB 84C*
Community Cablevision Inc. - Sharon, WI - *BrCabYB 84*
Community Cablevision of Framingham - Framingham, MA - *BrCabYB 84; Tel&CabFB 84C*
Community Cablevision of Odessa [of Beta Communications Inc.] - Odessa, TX - *BrCabYB 84; Tel&CabFB 84C*
Community Cablevision Service - Partridge, KY - *Tel&CabFB 84C*
Community Cablevision System Co. - Hattiesburg, MS - *Tel&CabFB 84C*
Community Care Services Inc. - Toronto, ON, Canada - *BoPubDir 4, 5*
Community CATV Corp. [of Manasett Inc.] - Clewiston, FL - *BrCabYB 84 p.D-299; Tel&CabFB 84C*
Community CATV Corp. [of Manasett Corp.] - Colby, KS - *BrCabYB 84; Tel&CabFB 84C*
Community CATV Corp. - Providence, RI - *Tel&CabFB 84C p.1674*
Community Club Awards Inc. - Westport, CT - *Ed&PubIntYB 82*
Community Collaborators - Charlottesville, VA - *BoPubDir 4, 5; LitMag&SmPr 83-84*
Community College Frontiers - Springfield, IL - *MagIndMarPl 82-83*
Community College Press [Aff. of Amos R. Koontz Memorial Foundation Center] - Riverton, VA - *BoPubDir 4, 5*
Community Communications Co. - Monticello, AR - *BrCabYB 84 p.D-299; Tel&CabFB 84C p.1674*
Community Communications Co. [of Tele-Communications Inc.] - Delta, CO - *BrCabYB 84*
Community Computer Corp. - Philadelphia, PA - *DataDirOnSer 84; DataDirSup 7-83*
Community Council of Greater New York - New York, NY - *BoPubDir 4, 5*
Community Crier, The - Plymouth, MI - *AyerDirPub 83; Ed&PubIntYB 82*
Community Development Corp., The - Edgeley, ND - *Tel&CabFB 84C*
Community Development Journal [of Oxford University Press] - Newcastle upon Tyne, England - *LitMag&SmPr 83-84*
Community Development Publications - Silver Spring, MD - *WritMar 84*
Community Environmental Council Inc. - Santa Barbara, CA - *BoPubDir 4, 5*
Community Features - San Francisco, CA - *BaconPubCkNews 84; Ed&PubIntYB 82*
Community Health Information Network [of Mt. Auburn Hospital] - Cambridge, MA - *EISS 83*
Community Herald - New York, NY - *AyerDirPub 83; BaconPubCkNews 84*
Community Herald Newspapers Inc. - Monona, WI - *BaconPubCkNews 84*
Community Herald, The - Manhattan, NY - *Ed&PubIntYB 82*
Community Human Resources Information System [of Federation for Community Planning] - Cleveland, OH - *EISS 83*
Community Information & Referral Services Inc. - Phoenix, AZ - *EISS 83*
Community Information Center Inc. - Athens, TX - *BaconPubCkNews 84*
Community Information Centre of Metropolitan Toronto - Toronto, ON, Canada - *BoPubDir 4, 5; VideoDir 82-83*
Community Information Network [of Telecrafter] - Billings, MT - *CabTVPrDB 83*
Community Information Source [of Dallas Public Library] - Dallas, TX - *EISS 83*
Community Journal [of Queen City Suburban Press] - Cincinnati, OH - *AyerDirPub 83; Ed&PubIntYB 82; NewsDir 84*
Community Journal - Milwaukee, WI - *Ed&PubIntYB 82*
Community Journal, The - Riverhead, NY - *Ed&PubIntYB 82*
Community Leader - Baton Rouge, LA - *Ed&PubIntYB 82*
Community Life - McFarland, WI - *AyerDirPub 83; Ed&PubIntYB 82*
Community Media Corp. - Raymond, WA - *BaconPubCkNews 84*
Community Mirror - Gonzales, LA - *AyerDirPub 83*
Community News - Dora, AL - *AyerDirPub 83*
Community News - Chicago, IL - *AyerDirPub 83; Ed&PubIntYB 82*
Community News - Mt. Clemens, MI - *AyerDirPub 83; BaconPubCkNews 84*
Community News - Cherry Hill, NJ - *AyerDirPub 83*
Community News - Malvern, OH - *AyerDirPub 83*
Community News - Clarksville, TN - *AyerDirPub 83*
Community News - Crosby, TX - *Ed&PubIntYB 82*
Community News - East Houston, TX - *Ed&PubIntYB 82*
Community News - Longview, TX - *AyerDirPub 83*
Community News & Shopper - Clinton, MA - *AyerDirPub 83*
Community News Inc. - Northwood, ND - *BaconPubCkNews 84*
Community News Suburban, The - Pennsauken, NJ - *Ed&PubIntYB 82*
Community News, The - Sumiton, AL - *Ed&PubIntYB 82; NewsDir 84*
Community News, The - Madison, TN - *Ed&PubIntYB 82*
Community News, The - Drayton, ON, Canada - *Ed&PubIntYB 82*
Community Newspapers Inc. - Glen Cove, NY - *BaconPubCkNews 84*
Community Newspapers Inc. - Moravia, NY - *BaconPubCkNews 84*
Community Newspapers Inc. - Wauwatosa, WI - *BaconPubCkNews 84*
Community Newspapers of Florida Inc. - South Miami, FL - *BaconPubCkNews 84*
Community Observer - Bennettsville, SC - *AyerDirPub 83*
Community of TCI of Kansas Inc. [of Community Tele-Communications Inc.] - Leavenworth, KS - *Tel&CabFB 84C*
Community Pacific Broadcasting Corp. - Salinas, CA - *BrCabYB 84*
Community Planning Press - St. John, NB, Canada - *BoPubDir 4, 5*
Community Post - Minster, OH - *AyerDirPub 83; Ed&PubIntYB 82*
Community Press - Cambridge City, IN - *AyerDirPub 83*
Community Press - Charleston, SC - *BaconPubCkNews 84*
Community Press - Carstairs, AB, Canada - *AyerDirPub 83; Ed&PubIntYB 82*
Community Press - Sedgewick, AB, Canada - *AyerDirPub 83*
Community Press Features U.P.A. - Boston, MA - *Ed&PubIntYB 82*
Community Publishing Cooperative [Aff. of Unschool Educational Corp.] - Louisa, VA - *BoPubDir 4, 5*
Community Reporter - Chicago, IL - *AyerDirPub 83*
Community Reporter - Mt. Airy, MD - *AyerDirPub 83; Ed&PubIntYB 82*
Community Research Services [of Illinois State University] - Normal, IL - *EISS 83*
Community Resources Information Service Inc. - Santa Barbara, CA - *EISS 83*
Community Service Broadcasting Inc. - Mt. Vernon, IL - *BrCabYB 84*
Community Service Inc. - Frankfort, KY - *BrCabYB 84; Tel&CabFB 84C*
Community Service Inc. - Yellow Springs, OH - *BoPubDir 4, 5*
Community Service Newsletter - Yellow Springs, OH - *LitMag&SmPr 83-84*
Community Service Telephone Co. - Winthrop, ME - *TelDir&BG 83-84*
Community Service Television - Williston, ND - *BrCabYB 84; Tel&CabFB 84C*
Community System, The - Wilcox, PA - *Tel&CabFB 84C*
Community Systems Inc. [of Eastern Pennsylvania Relay] - Middleburg, PA - *BrCabYB 84; Tel&CabFB 84C*
Community TAS - Chester, WV - *BrCabYB 84*
Community TCI Inc. - La Vista, NE - *Tel&CabFB 84C*
Community TCI of Ohio Inc. [of Tele-Communications Inc.] - Barnesville, OH - *BrCabYB 84; Tel&CabFB 84C*
Community TCI of Ohio Inc. [of Tele-Communications Inc.] - Bethesda, OH - *BrCabYB 84*
Community TCI of Ohio Inc. [of Tele-Communications Inc.] - Cadiz, OH - *BrCabYB 84*
Community TCI of Ohio Inc. [of Community Tele-Communications Inc.] - Chester, OH - *Tel&CabFB 84C*
Community TCI of Ohio Inc. [of Community Tele-Communications Inc.] - East Liverpool, OH - *Tel&CabFB 84C*

Community TCI of Ohio Inc. [of Community Tele-Communications Inc.] - Irondale, OH - *Tel&CabFB 84C*
Community TCI of Ohio Inc. [of Tele-Communications Inc.] - Martins Ferry, OH - *Tel&CabFB 84C*
Community TCI of Ohio Inc. [of Community Tele-Communications Inc.] - Steubenville, OH - *Tel&CabFB 84C*
Community TCI of Ohio Inc. [of Community Tele-Communications Inc.] - Wheeling Township, OH - *Tel&CabFB 84C*
Community TCI of Ohio Inc. [of Community Tele-Communications Inc.] - Moundsville, WV - *BrCabYB 84; Tel&CabFB 84C*
Community TCI of Ohio Inc. [of Tele-Communications Inc.] - New Cumberland, WV - *Tel&CabFB 84C*
Community TCI of Ohio Inc. - *See* Tele-Communications Inc.
Community Tele-Communications Inc. - Denver, CO - *TelAl 83*
Community Tele-Communications Inc. - Lakewood, CO - *BrCabYB 84*
Community Tele-Communications Inc. - Preston, ID - *BrCabYB 84*
Community Tele-Communications Inc. - Centralia, MO - *BrCabYB 84*
Community Tele-Communications Inc. - Jefferson City, MO - *Tel&CabFB 84C*
Community Tele-Communications Inc. - Mountain Grove, MO - *Tel&CabFB 84C*
Community Tele-Communications Inc. - La Vista, NE - *BrCabYB 84*
Community Tele-Communications Inc. - Ogallala, NE - *BrCabYB 84*
Community Tele-Communications Inc. - Holloway, OH - *Tel&CabFB 84C*
Community Tele-Communications Inc. - Gorman, TX - *BrCabYB 84*
Community Tele-Communications Inc. - Culpeper, VA - *Tel&CabFB 84C*
Community Tele-Communications Inc. - Thermopolis, WY - *Tel&CabFB 84C*
Community Tele-Communications Inc. - Worland, WY - *BrCabYB 84*
Community Tele-Communications Inc. - *See* Tele-Communications Inc.
Community Tele-Communications of Ohio Inc. - Holloway, OH - *BrCabYB 84*
Community Tele-Communications of Ohio Inc. - Martins Ferry, OH - *Tel&CabFB 84C*
Community Telecable of Georgia [of McDonald Group] - Manchester, GA - *BrCabYB 84; Tel&CabFB 84C*
Community Telecable of Georgia Inc. [of McDonald Group] - La Grange, GA - *BrCabYB 84; Tel&CabFB 84C*
Community Telecommunications Development - Reading, PA - *InterCabHB 3*
Community Telecommunications Development Foundation - Washington, DC - *TeleSy&SerDir 7-83*
Community Telephone Co. Inc. - Windthorst, TX - *TelDir&BG 83-84*
Community Telephone Co., The - Leipsic, OH - *TelDir&BG 83-84*
Community Times [of Ellicott City Stromberg Publishing Inc.] - Ellicott City, MD - *NewsDir 84*
Community TV [of P & H Electronics] - Beavertown, PA - *Tel&CabFB 84C*
Community TV - Thermopolis, WY - *BrCabYB 84*
Community TV Cable Co. - Marmaduke, AR - *BrCabYB 84; Tel&CabFB 84C*
Community TV Cable Co. - Maynard, AR - *Tel&CabFB 84C*
Community TV Cable Co. - Rector, AR - *BrCabYB 84; Tel&CabFB 84C*
Community TV Cable Co. - Reyno, AR - *BrCabYB 84; Tel&CabFB 84C*
Community TV Cable Co. - Mountain View, MO - *BrCabYB 84*
Community TV Cable Co. - Piedmont, MO - *BrCabYB 84*
Community TV Cable System of Lee County Inc. [of Storer Cable Communications Inc.] - Lehigh Acres, FL - *BrCabYB 84; Tel&CabFB 84C*
Community TV Co. - Ellijay, GA - *BrCabYB 84; Tel&CabFB 84C*
Community TV Corp. - Franklin, NH - *Tel&CabFB 84C*
Community TV Corp. - Laconia, NH - *BrCabYB 84 p.D-299; Tel&CabFB 84C p.1674*
Community TV Inc. - Walkerton Station, KY - *BrCabYB 84*
Community TV Inc. - Havre, MT - *BrCabYB 84*
Community TV Inc. [of Tele-Communications Inc.] - De Leon, TX - *BrCabYB 84; Tel&CabFB 84C*
Community TV Inc. [of Tele-Communications Inc.] - Gorman, TX - *Tel&CabFB 84C*
Community TV Ltd. - Prince Albert, SK, Canada - *BrCabYB 84*
Community TV of Madison [of Midcontinent Cable Systems Co.] - Madison, SD - *BrCabYB 84; Tel&CabFB 84C*
Community TV of Utah Inc. [of Tele-Communications Inc.] - Nephi, UT - *Tel&CabFB 84C*
Community TV of Utah Inc. [of Tele-Communications Inc.] - Ogden, UT - *Tel&CabFB 84C*
Community TV of Utah Inc. [of Tele-Communications Inc.] - Park City, UT - *BrCabYB 84; Tel&CabFB 84C*
Community TV of Utah Inc. [of Tele-Communications Inc.] - Price, UT - *BrCabYB 84; Tel&CabFB 84C*
Community TV of Utah Inc. [of Tele-Communications Inc.] - Provo, UT - *BrCabYB 84; Tel&CabFB 84C*
Community TV of Utah Inc. [of Tele-Communications Inc.] - Salt Lake City, UT - *Tel&CabFB 84C*
Community TV of Utah Inc. [of Tele-Communications Inc.] - Smithfield, UT - *BrCabYB 84; Tel&CabFB 84C*
Community TV of Utah Inc. [of Tele-Communications Inc.] - West Valley City, UT - *Tel&CabFB 84C*
Community TV Service [of Liberty Television Co. Inc.] - Dunnville, KY - *BrCabYB 84*
Community TV System Inc. - Greenwood, MS - *BrCabYB 84; Tel&CabFB 84C*
Commuter Air - Atlanta, GA - *BaconPubCkMag 84*
Commuter On-line Origin-Destination [of I. P. Sharp Associates Ltd.] - Toronto, ON, Canada - *DataDirOnSer 84*
Commuter Origin-Destination - Washington, DC - *DirOnDB Spring 84*
Comnet [of Cantlin Communications Inc.] - Anaheim, CA - *EISS 83*
COMNET - Washington, DC - *DataDirSup 7-83*
Comnet [of Michigan State University] - East Lansing, MI - *TeleSy&SerDir 2-84*
Comnet Ltd. - Mississauga, ON, Canada - *BrCabYB 84; Tel&CabFB 84C*
Como & Associates Inc., Ron - New York, NY - *DirPRFirms 83*
Como Sales Co. Inc. - New York, NY - *LitMarPl 83, 84*
Comox District Free Press - Courtenay, BC, Canada - *AyerDirPub 83; Ed&PubIntYB 82*
Comox Valley Cablenet [of Cablenet Ltd.] - Comox Valley, BC, Canada - *BrCabYB 84*
Comp Info Inc. - New York, NY - *ADAPSOMemDir 83-84*
Comp-Type Business Products - Calgary, AB, Canada - *DirInfWP 82*
Comp-U-Card [of Comp-U-Card of America Inc.] - Stamford, CT - *DataDirOnSer 84*
Comp-U-Card of America Inc. - Stamford, CT - *DataDirOnSer 84; VideoDir 82-83*
Comp-U-Store [of Comp-U-Card International Inc.] - Stamford, CT - *DataDirOnSer 84; DirOnDB Spring 84; TeleSy&SerDir 2-84*
Compac - Chipping Campden, England - *MicrocomSwDir 1*
Compac Systems Inc. - Palatine, IL - *MicrocomMPl 84; MicrocomSwDir 1; WhoWMicrocom 83*
Compact [of National Computer Network of Chicago] - Chicago, IL - *DataDirOnSer 84; DirOnDB Spring 84*
Compact Books Inc. - Hollywood, FL - *LitMarPl 84*
Compact Disc Packaging - Hollywood, CA - *AvMarPl 83*
Compact Publications Inc. - Hollywood, FL - *LitMarPl 83; WritMar 84*
Compact Software International Ltd. - Dorking, England - *MicrocomSwDir 1*
Compact Video Services Inc. - Burbank, CA - *AvMarPl 83*
Compact Video Systems Inc. - Burbank, CA - *HomeVid&CabYB 82-83*
Compagnie Internationale de Services en Informatique - Paris, France - *InfIndMarPl 83*
Compal Inc. - Beverly Hills, CA - *DataDirSup 7-83; MicrocomMPl 84; MicrocomSwDir 1*

Compal Inc. - Encino, CA - *WhoWMicrocom 83*
Compal Inc. - Woodland Hills, CA - *DirInfWP 82*
Compania Telefonica Nacional de Espana (Div. de Informatica) - Madrid, Spain - *InfIndMarPl 83*
Companion of St. Francis & St. Anthony, The [of Conventual Franciscan Friars] - Toronto, ON, Canada - *WritMar 84*
Company Carr, The - Sylvania, OH - *StaDirAdAg 2-84*
Company of Artists Productions Inc. - Hollywood, CA - *TelAl 83, 84*
Company of the Two P(i)eters Inc. - *See* Jamie Music Publishing Co.
Company Technical Document Center [of Hughes Aircraft Co.] - El Segundo, CA - *EISS 83*
Company's Coming Publishing Ltd. - Vermilion, AB, Canada - *BoPubDir 5*
Compaq Computer Corp. - Houston, TX - *WhoWMicrocom 83*
Compass - San Mateo, CA - *DirOnDB Spring 84*
Compass - Louisville, KY - *MicrocomMPl 84*
Compass [of Marine Office of America Corp.] - New York, NY - *WritMar 84*
Compass - Tacoma, WA - *WritMar 84*
Compass [of Compass Poetry & Prose] - Burwood, Australia - *LitMag&SmPr 83-84; WritMar 84*
Compass Films - Newton, NJ - *WritMar 84*
Compass Poetry & Prose - Burwood, Australia - *LitMag&SmPr 83-84*
Compass Rose Editorial Services - Camden, ME - *LitMarPl 83*
Compass, The - Mystic, CT - *AyerDirPub 83; Ed&PubIntYB 82; NewsDir 84*
Compass, The - Marborough, MA - *AyerDirPub 83*
Compass, The - Carbonear, NF, Canada - *Ed&PubIntYB 82*
Compcare Publications [Div. of Comprehensive Care Corp.] - Minneapolis, MN - *ArtMar 84; LitMarPl 83, 84; WritMar 84*
Compco Photographic/Goldberg Brothers - Chicago, IL - *AvMarPl 83*
Compendex [of Engineering Information Inc.] - New York, NY - *DirOnDB Spring 84; OnBibDB 3*
Compendium Inc. - Atlanta, GA - *BillIntBG 83-84*
Compendium of Continuing Education in Dentistry - Lawrenceville, NJ - *BaconPubCkMag 84*
Compensation Review [of American Management Association] - New York, NY - *BaconPubCkMag 84; MagDir 84; MagIndMarPl 82-83*
Competitive Computing Inc. - Watchung, NJ - *MicrocomMPl 84*
Competitive Edge Productions - Albuquerque, NM - *AvMarPl 83; StaDirAdAg 2-84*
Competitive Market Intelligence - Los Angeles, CA - *FBInfSer 80*
Competitivedge [of National Home Furnishings Association] - Chicago, IL - *BaconPubCkMag 84; MagDir 84*
Compilation of Stellar Rotational Velocities Project [of University of Kyoto] - Kyoto, Japan - *EISS 83*
Compiler Systems Inc. - Sierra Madre, CA - *WhoWMicrocom 83*
Compilers Plus Inc. - Pelham Manor, NY - *MagIndMarPl 82-83*
Compinfo Inc. - New York, NY - *MicrocomMPl 84*
Compleat Entertainment Corp. - Nashville, TN - *BillIntBG 83-84*
Compleat Systems - Pittsburgh, PA - *MicrocomMPl 84; WhoWMicrocom 83*
Complete Business Services - Logan, UT - *MicrocomMPl 83, 84; WhoWMicrocom 83*
Complete Business Systems Inc. - Chicago, IL - *WhoWMicrocom 83*
Complete Buyer's Guide to Stereo/Hi-Fi Equipment - Chappaqua, NY - *MagDir 84; MagIndMarPl 82-83*
Complete Channel TV Co. - Madison, WI - *BrCabYB 84; Tel&CabFB 84C p.1674*
Complete Computer Systems - Horsham, PA - *DataDirSup 7-83*
Complete Woman - Chicago, IL - *BaconPubCkMag 84*
Complex Systems Inc. - New York, NY - *DataDirSup 7-83*
Complexible of Brook Park - Brook Park, OH - *Tel&CabFB 84C*
Complexicable - Brook Park, OH - *BrCabYB 84; Tel&CabFB 84C p.1674*
Compliance Alert: Federal Register Digest - Stamford, CT - *DirOnDB Spring 84*
Compliance Alert: Federal Register Digest [of NewsNet Inc.] - Bryn Mawr, PA - *DataDirOnSer 84*
Compmark [of Citishare] - New York, NY - *DataDirOnSer 84; DirOnDB Spring 84*
Compmark Data Services [of Standard & Poor's Corp.] - New York, NY - *EISS 83*
Compo Record Co. - Oklahoma City, OK - *BillIntBG 83-84*
Compolith Graphics - Indianapolis, IN - *MagIndMarPl 82-83*
Composers Music - *See* Contemporary Music
Composers Recordings Inc. - New York, NY - *BillIntBG 83-84*
Composing Room of Michigan Inc., The - Grand Rapids, MI - *LitMarPl 83, 84*
Composing Room of New England - Boston, MA - *LitMarPl 84*
Composition House Ltd. - Sudbury, MA - *LitMarPl 83, 84*
Composition Systems Inc. - Elmsford, NY - *VideoDir 82-83*
Compre Comm Inc. - Champaign, IL - *DataDirSup 7-83*
Comprehensive Automated Learning Resources System [of Elgin Community College] - Elgin, IL - *EISS 83*
Comprehensive Dissertation Index [of University Microfilms International] - Ann Arbor, MI - *CompReadDB 82; DataDirOnSer 84; DBBus 82; EISS 83; OnBibDB 3*
Comprehensive Dissertation Index - *See* Dissertation Abstracts Online
Comprehensive Information Services [of PIRA: Research Association for the Paper & Board, Printing, & Packaging Industries] - Leatherhead, England - *EISS 83*
Comprehensive Information System on Transnational Corps. [of Centre on Transnational Corps.] - New York, NY - *EISS 83*
Comprehensive Software - Redondo Beach, CA - *MicrocomMPl 84*
Comprehensive Tax Systems - Oakland, CA - *WhoWMicrocom 83*
Comprehensive Video Supply Corp. - Northvale, NJ - *AvMarPl 83*
Comprenetics Inc. - Culver City, CA - *WritMar 84*
Comprep Corp. - Orange, CA - *MicrocomMPl 84*
Compress [Div. of Van Nostrand Reinhold] - Wentworth, NH - *LitMarPl 84; MicrocomMPl 83, 84; MicrocomSwDir 1*
Compressed Air [of Ingersoll-Rand Co.] - Washington, NJ - *BaconPubCkMag 84; MagDir 84; MagIndMarPl 82-83; WritMar 84*
Compression Labs Inc. - San Jose, CA - *DataDirSup 7-83; TeleSy&SerDir 2-84*
Comprint Inc. - Mountain View, CA - *MicrocomMPl 84*
Compro Associates - New Paltz, NY - *DataDirSup 7-83; MicrocomMPl 84*
Compro Corp. - Miami, FL - *MicrocomMPl 84; MicrocomSwDir 1*
Compro Productions - Atlanta, GA - *AvMarPl 83; Tel&CabFB 84C*
Compsoft Ltd. - Guildford, England - *MicrocomSwDir 1*
Compstat - Gloulester Point, VA - *MicrocomMPl 83*
Compton Advertising [of Saatchi & Saatchi Compton Worldwide] - New York, NY - *AdAge 3-28-84; Br 1-23-84; BrCabYB 84; HomeVid&CabYB 82-83; TelAl 83, 84*
Compton & Meade TV - Pikeville, KY - *BrCabYB 84*
Compton, Ayres - Temple, TX - *DirPRFirms 83*
Compton Cable TV Ltd. - Uxbridge, ON, Canada - *BrCabYB 84*
Compton Communications Inc. - New York, NY - *StaDirAdAg 2-84*
Compton Co., F. E. [Div. of Encyclopaedia Britannica Inc.] - Chicago, IL - *LitMarPl 83, 84*
Compton Herald American - Compton, CA - *Ed&PubIntYB 82*
Compton Herald American - South Gate, CA - *AyerDirPub 83*
Compton, Joan Callahan - Las Cruces, NM - *LitMarPl 84*
Compton Metropolitan Gazette - *See* Hamm Publications Inc.
Comptype Inc. - Winchester, MA - *LitMarPl 83, 84; MagIndMarPl 82-83*
Compu-Binder Inc. - Folcroft, PA - *DataDirSup 7-83*
Compu-Draw - Rochester, NY - *MicrocomMPl 84*
Compu-Fax - Park Ridge, IL - *BaconPubCkMag 84*
Compu-Law Inc. - Culver City, CA - *MicrocomMPl 84*
Compu-Link Corp. [Subs. of Provencial House Inc.] - Lansing, MI - *ADAPSOMemDir 83-84; DataDirOnSer 84*
Compu-Mark - Mortsel, Belgium - *EISS 83*
Compu-Mark U.S. - Washington, DC - *EISS 5-84 Sup*
Compu-Pix-Rental CPR [Div. of Associated Photographers International] - Canoga Park, CA - *AvMarPl 83*
Compu-Quote - Canoga Park, CA - *MicrocomMPl 83*
Compu-Rite Ribbon Corp. - Tarzana, CA - *DirInfWP 82*
Compu Sense - Wichita, KS - *MicrocomMPl 84*
Compu-Share Inc. - Lubbock, TX - *MicrocomMPl 84*
Compu-Tations - Troy, MI - *MicrocomMPl 83, 84; MicrocomSwDir 1; WhoWMicrocom 83*
Compu-Tome I - Pasadena, CA - *MicrocomMPl 84*

Compu-Trac Inc. - New Orleans, LA - *WhoWMicrocom 83*
Compu-Tutor - Placentia, CA - *WhoWMicrocom 83*
Compu-U-Staff Inc. - Towson, MD - *ADAPSOMemDir 83-84*
Compu-U-Star [of Comp-U-Card of America Inc.] - Stamford, CT - *DBBus 82*
Compubond [of Payne Webber Jackson & Curtis Inc.] - New York, NY - *DataDirOnSer 84; DBBus 82*
Compubyte Inc. - Cape Coral, FL - *MicrocomMPl 84*
CompuCable Corp. - Anaheim, CA - *MicrocomMPl 84*
Compucape Pty. Ltd. - Cape Town, South Africa - *ADAPSOMemDir 83-84*
Compucon - Dallas, TX - *Tel&CabFB 84C; TeleSy&SerDir 2-84*
Compucorp - Los Angeles, CA - *DirInfWP 82; WhoWMicrocom 83*
Compucorp - Santa Monica, CA - *DataDirSup 7-83*
CompuCover - Mary Esther, FL - *MicrocomMPl 83*
Compucraft - Van Nuys, CA - *MicrocomMPl 84*
CompuData Inc. - West Springfield, MA - *ADAPSOMemDir 83-84*
CompuData Inc. - Bala Cynwyd, PA - *WhoWMicrocom 83*
CompuData Inc. - Philadelphia, PA - *DataDirOnSer 84; DataDirSup 7-83; EISS 7-83 Sup; MicrocomMPl 84; MicrocomSwDir 1*
Compudata Systems Inc. - Westport, CT - *DirInfWP 82*
Compudent Management Systems - Heinet, CA - *MicrocomMPl 83*
Compugraphic Corp. - Wilmington, MA - *DirInfWP 82; InfIndMarPl 83; LitMarPl 83, 84*
Compu.Guide - Dedham, MA - *DirOnDB Spring 84*
Compulaw - Washington, DC - *ADAPSOMemDir 83-84*
Compulink Corp. - Longmont, CO - *MicrocomMPl 84; WhoWMicrocom 83*
Compu.Map - Dedham, MA - *DirOnDB Spring 84*
Compumart Corp. - Cambridge, MA - *MicrocomMPl 83*
Compumax Associates Inc. - Menlo Park, CA - *MicrocomMPl 83, 84*
Compumax Associates Inc. - Palo Alto, CA - *WhoWMicrocom 83*
Compupeg Marketing - Waterloo, IA - *MicrocomMPl 84*
Compupixrental [Div. of Associated Photographers International] - Canoga Park, CA - *LitMarPl 83, 84*
Compupower Corp. - Secaucus, NJ - *MagIndMarPl 82-83*
CompuPro [Subs. of Godbout Electronics Inc.] - Oakland, CA - *WhoWMicrocom 83*
CompuScan Inc. - Fairfield, NJ - *DataDirSup 7-83; LitMarPl 83, 84; WhoWMicrocom 83*
CompuScan Inc. - Teterboro, NJ - *DirInfWP 82*
Compusearch Market & Social Research Ltd. - Toronto, ON, Canada - *EISS 83*
Compusense Ltd. - London, England - *MicrocomSwDir 1*
CompuServe [Subs. of H & R Block Inc.] - Columbus, OH - *DataDirOnSer 84; DataDirSup 7-83; DBBus 82; EISS 83; InterCabHB 3; MicrocomMPl 84; VideoDir 82-83*
CompuServe Inc. (Personal Computing Div.) - Columbus, OH - *HomeVid&CabYB 82-83*
CompuServe Information Service [of CompuServe Inc.] - Columbus, OH - *DataDirOnSer 84; EISS 83; TeleSy&SerDir 2-84*
CompuServe Network Services [Div. of CompuServe Inc.] - Columbus, OH - *DataDirOnSer 84; TeleSy&SerDir 7-83*
CompuSource - Cary, NC - *DataDirOnSer 84*
Compusource Corp. - Torrance, CA - *DirInfWP 82*
Compustat [of Standard & Poor's Compustat Services Inc.] - Englewood, CO - *DBBus 82; DirOnDB Spring 84*
Compustat Data Services - Santa Ana, CA - *MicrocomMPl 84*
Compustat Geographic [of ADP Network Services Inc.] - Ann Arbor, MI - *DataDirOnSer 84*
Compustat Services Inc. [of Standard & Poor's Corp.] - Englewood, CO - *EISS 83*
CompuSystems Inc. - Columbia, SC - *MicrocomMPl 83, 84; MicrocomSwDir 1; WhoWMicrocom 83*
Comput-A-Note Inc. - Warrington, PA - *WhoWMicrocom 83*
Comput Distributors - Troy, MI - *MicrocomMPl 84*
Computalker - Santa Monica, CA - *MicrocomMPl 84*
Computalker Consultants - Santa Monica, CA - *MicrocomMPl 83, 84*
Compute! [of Small System Services] - Greensboro, NC - *BaconPubCkMag 84; Folio 83; MicrocomMPl 84; WritMar 84*
Compute-R-Systems Inc. - Plymouth Meeting, PA - *ADAPSOMemDir 83-84*
Computeach Press Inc. - San Jose, CA - *BoPubDir 5*
Computec Systems Corp. - San Juan, Puerto Rico - *WhoWMicrocom 83*
CompuTech - Redondo Beach, CA - *MicrocomSwDir 1*
Computech - Lakewood, NJ - *MicrocomMPl 84*
Computed Systems - St. Clair Shores, MI - *MicrocomMPl 84*
Computek - Canyon Country, CA - *MicrocomMPl 83*
Computek [Subs. of General Automation] - Burlington, MA - *DataDirSup 7-83; MicrocomMPl 83; MicrocomSwDir 1; WhoWMicrocom 83*
Computel Systems Ltd. [Subs. of Royal Trustco Ltd.] - Ottawa, ON, Canada - *DataDirOnSer 84; EISS 83*
Computer [of IEEE Computer Society] - Los Alamitos, CA - *BaconPubCkMag 84; MagDir 84*
Computer Accessories Corp. - Huntington, NY - *DataDirSup 7-83; DirInfWP 82*
Computer Accessories Inc. - San Diego, CA - *MicrocomMPl 84*
Computer Accounting Consultants Inc. - Wellesley, MA - *MicrocomMPl 84*
Computer Accounting Inc. - Tacoma, WA - *DataDirOnSer 84*
Computer-Advanced Ideas - Berkeley, CA - *MicrocomMPl 83, 84; MicrocomSwDir 1*
Computer Advertising News - New York, NY - *BaconPubCkMag 84*
Computer Age - San Francisco, CA - *MicrocomMPl 84*
Computer Age-EDP Weekly - Annandale, VA - *BaconPubCkMag 84*
Computer Age Ltd. [Subs. of Home Computer Centre/SBS Computer Shoppe] - Toronto, ON, Canada - *WhoWMicrocom 83*
Computer Age Software - Silver Spring, MD - *MicrocomMPl 83*
Computer Age World Trade - Annandale, VA - *BaconPubCkMag 84*
Computer Aided Design - San Francisco, CA - *MicrocomSwDir 1; WhoWMicrocom 83*
Computer Aided Design Report - San Diego, CA - *BaconPubCkMag 84*
Computer-Aided Engineering - Cleveland, OH - *BaconPubCkMag 84*
Computer Alternatives - Sterling Heights, MI - *WhoWMicrocom 83*
Computer Analyzed Newspaper Data On-Line [of Newspaper Advertising Bureau Inc.] - New York, NY - *EISS 83*
Computer & Chemistry [of Pergamon Press Inc.] - Elmsford, NY - *MicrocomMPl 84*
Computer & Communications Buyer - New York, NY - *BaconPubCkMag 84*
Computer & Communications Industry Association - Arlington, VA - *EISS 83*
Computer & Control Abstracts [of INSPEC, Institution of Electrical Engineers] - Hitchin, England - *OnBibDB 3*
Computer & Electronics Marketing - Boston, MA - *BaconPubCkMag 84; MicrocomMPl 84*
Computer & Information Science Research Center [of Ohio State University] - Columbus, OH - *EISS 83*
Computer & Information Services [of Corp. for Public Broadcasting] - Washington, DC - *EISS 83*
Computer & Law [of Centre de Documentation Sciences Humaines] - Paris, France - *CompReadDB 82*
Computer & Software News [of Lebhar-Friedman Inc.] - New York, NY - *BaconPubCkMag 84; MicrocomMPl 84*
Computer Applications - Salinas, CA - *MicrocomMPl 84*
Computer Applications Corp. - Memphis, TN - *ADAPSOMemDir 83-84; MicrocomMPl 84; MicrocomSwDir 1*
Computer: Applications Inc. - Miami, FL - *MicrocomSwDir 1*
Computer Applications Unltd. - Rye, NY - *MicrocomMPl 83, 84*
Computer Assistance Inc. - Chambersberg, PA - *DataDirOnSer 84*
Computer-Assisted Instruction Systems - Los Angeles, CA - *WhoWMicrocom 83*
Computer Assisted Instructions Inc. - Grand Rapids, MI - *MicrocomMPl 84*
Computer Assisted Library Instruction Co. Inc. - St. Louis, MO - *MicrocomMPl 84*
Computer Assisted Trading System [of American Meat Exchange Inc.] - Elmhurst, IL - *EISS 5-84 Sup*
Computer Associates Inc. - South Bend, IN - *DataDirOnSer 84; DataDirSup 7-83*

Computer Associates International Inc. - Jericho, NY - *ADAPSOMemDir 83-84; DataDirSup 7-83*
Computer Automation Inc. - Irvine, CA - *InfIndMarPl 83*
Computer Barn - Salinas, CA - *MicrocomMPl 84*
Computer-Based Financial Management System [of Harper & Schuman Inc.] - Cambridge, MA - *EISS 83*
Computer-Based Information Services [of University of Texas, Austin] - Austin, TX - *EISS 83*
Computer-Based Reference Services Committee [of Sterling-Winthrop Research Institute] - Rensselaer, NY - *InfIndMarPl 83*
Computer Book Club, The [of TAB Books Inc.] - Blue Ridge Summit, PA - *LitMarPl 83, 84*
Computer Book Review [of CBR Publications] - Honolulu, HI - *BaconPubCkMag 84; LitMag&SmPr 83-84*
Computer Book Service [Subs. of Chas. Levy Circulation Co.] - Hillside, IL - *LitMarPl 83, 84*
Computer Bugs, The - Boynton Beach, FL - *WhoWMicrocom 83*
Computer Business - Los Angeles, CA - *BaconPubCkMag 84*
Computer Business News - Framingham, MA - *MagIndMarPl 82-83*
Computer/Business Services - Warren, MI - *MicrocomMPl 84*
Computer Cable & Products Inc. - Farmingdale, NY - *DataDirSup 7-83*
Computer Cable TV Inc. - Coconut Creek, FL - *Tel&CabFB 84C*
Computer Caging Corp. - Citrus Heights, CA - *DirMarMP 83*
Computer Cannery - San Jose, CA - *MicrocomMPl 84*
Computer Case Co. - Columbus, OH - *MicrocomMPl 83*
Computer Center [of University of Georgia] - Athens, GA - *EISS 7-83 Sup*
Computer Center - Mission, KS - *MicrocomMPl 83; WhoWMicrocom 83*
Computer Center [of Digibyte Systems Corp.] - New York, NY - *MicrocomMPl 83*
Computer Center Inc. - Baltimore, MD - *ADAPSOMemDir 83-84; DataDirOnSer 84*
Computer Center, The - Waterloo, IA - *WhoWMicrocom 83*
Computer Centre Inc. - Nokomis, FL - *WhoWMicrocom 83*
Computer Color Corp. - New York, NY - *LitMarPl 83; MagIndMarPl 82-83*
Computer Communications Inc. - Torrance, CA - *DataDirSup 7-83; DirInfWP 82*
Computer Communications Networks Group [of University of Waterloo] - Waterloo, ON, Canada - *EISS 83*
Computer Co., The - Richmond, VA - *DataDirOnSer 84; DataDirSup 7-83; EISS 83; InfIndMarPl 83; MicrocomMPl 84*
Computer Co., The (Interactive Database Systems Div.) - Richmond, VA - *DataDirOnSer 84*
Computer Components Inc. - Van Nuys, CA - *WhoWMicrocom 83*
Computer Composition Center [of Hartmann & Heenemann] - Berlin, West Germany - *EISS 83*
Computer Composition Corp. - Madison Heights, MI - *EISS 83; LitMarPl 83, 84; MagIndMarPl 82-83*
Computer Composition Sales - New York, NY - *LitMarPl 83; MagIndMarPl 82-83*
Computer Concepts & Services Inc. - St. Cloud, MN - *ADAPSOMemDir 83-84*
Computer Concepts Inc. - Portland, OR - *DataDirSup 7-83*
Computer Conference Program [of Seybold Publications Inc.] - Media, PA - *TeleSy&SerDir 2-84*
Computer Connection Ltd., The - Englewood, CA - *MicrocomMPl 83*
Computer Connection Ltd., The - Englewood, CO - *MicrocomMPl 84*
Computer Consoles Inc. - Rochester, NY - *DataDirSup 7-83; DirInfWP 82*
Computer Consultants - Dunkirk, NY - *MicrocomMPl 83, 84; MicrocomSwDir 1*
Computer Consultants Ltd. - St. Louis, MO - *DataDirOnSer 84*
Computer Consultants of Iowa Ltd. - Marion, IA - *MicrocomMPl 83*
Computer Consultants of Irvine - Irvine, CA - *DataDirSup 7-83*
Computer Consulting Services - Clearwater, FL - *MicrocomMPl 84; MicrocomSwDir 1*
Computer Consumer [of The Garlic Press] - Rochester, NY - *LitMag&SmPr 83-84*
Computer Control Systems Inc. - Largo, FL - *MicrocomSwDir 1; WhoWMicrocom 83*
Computer Cookbook, The - New York, NY - *DirOnDB Spring 84*
Computer Corp. of America - Cambridge, MA - *DataDirOnSer 84; DataDirSup 7-83*
Computer Cost Estimating Services [of E. H. Boeckh Co.] - Milwaukee, WI - *EISS 83*
Computer Country - Florissant, MO - *WhoWMicrocom 83*
Computer Craft of Austin - Austin, TX - *MicrocomMPl 84*
Computer Creations Inc. - South Bend, IN - *AvMarPl 83*
Computer Crossroads Inc. - Columbia, MD - *WhoWMicrocom 83*
Computer Daily - Annandale, VA - *BaconPubCkMag 84*
Computer Data Access Inc. - Clifton, NJ - *DataDirSup 7-83*
Computer Data & Data Base Source Book, The - Potomac, MD - *DirOnDB Spring 84*
Computer Data Corp. - Los Angeles, CA - *DataDirOnSer 84*
Computer Data Report, The - Potomac, MD - *DirOnDB Spring 84*
Computer Data Services - Amherst, NH - *MicrocomMPl 83, 84*
Computer Data Systems Inc. - Bethesda, MD - *EISS 83*
Computer Database [of Management Contents] - Northbrook, IL - *DataDirOnSer 84; DirOnDB Spring 84; EISS 5-84 Sup*
Computer Dealer [of Gordon Publications Inc.] - Dover, NJ - *BaconPubCkMag 84; MicrocomMPl 84; WritMar 84*
Computer Decisions [of Hayden Publishing Co.] - Rochelle Park, NJ - *ArtMar 84; BaconPubCkMag 84; Folio 83; MagDir 84; MagIndMarPl 82-83; NewsBur 6; WritMar 84*
Computer Depot Inc. - Bloomington, MN - *WhoWMicrocom 83*
Computer Design [of PennWell Publishing Co.] - Littleton, MA - *BaconPubCkMag 84; Folio 83; MagDir 84; MagIndMarPl 82-83; WritMar 84*
Computer Design Labs - Trenton, NJ - *MicrocomMPl 83*
Computer Designed Systems - Minneapolis, MN - *DirInfWP 82*
Computer Detailing - Warminister, PA - *MicrocomMPl 84*
Computer Development Inc. - Beaverton, OR - *DataDirSup 7-83*
Computer Development Specialists of Long Island Inc. - Centereach, NY - *MicrocomMPl 84; MicrocomSwDir 1*
Computer Development Specialists of Long Island Inc. - Melville, NY - *MicrocomMPl 83*
Computer Devices Inc. - Burlington, MA - *DataDirSup 7-83; DirInfWP 82; WhoWMicrocom 83*
Computer Directions Advisors Inc. - Silver Spring, MD - *DataDirOnSer 84*
Computer Directions Group Inc. - New York, NY - *EISS 7-83 Sup*
Computer Discount - West Milford, NJ - *MicrocomMPl 84*
Computer Div. [of Maryland State Dept. of Legislative Reference] - Annapolis, MD - *EISS 83*
Computer Dynamic Systems Inc. - Denver, CO - *DataDirSup 7-83*
Computer Dynamics Inc. - Oakland, CA - *DirInfWP 82*
Computer Dynamics Inc. - Southfield, MI - *ADAPSOMemDir 83-84*
Computer Dynamics Inc. - New York, NY - *DataDirSup 7-83*
Computer Dynamics Inc. - Grier, SC - *MicrocomMPl 84*
Computer Dynamics Inc. - Alexandria, VA - *DataDirOnSer 84*
Computer-Ed - Carmel, NY - *MicrocomMPl 84*
Computer EdiType System - New York, NY - *MicrocomMPl 84*
Computer Education Techniques Inc. - New York, NY - *ADAPSOMemDir 83-84*
Computer/Electronic Service News - Peterborough, NH - *BaconPubCkMag 84*
Computer Electronics [of Ziff-Davis Publishing Co.] - New York, NY - *MicrocomMPl 84*
Computer Engineering Services - Show Low, AZ - *WritMar 84*
Computer Enhancement Corp. - Costa Mesa, CA - *DataDirSup 7-83*
Computer Entrepeneur, The - New York, NY - *MicrocomMPl 84*
Computer Equipment Information Bureau - Boston, MA - *DataDirOnSer 84*
Computer Facilities Management [Subs. of Compumark Inc.] - Newtown Square, PA - *DataDirOnSer 84*
Computer Factory Inc., The - New York, NY - *WhoWMicrocom 83*
Computer Faire Program - Woodside, CA - *MicrocomMPl 84*
Computer Farming Newsletter [of NewsNet Inc.] - Bryn Mawr, PA - *DataDirOnSer 84*

Computer Forum Inc. - Santa Fe Springs, CA - *WhoWMicrocom 83*
Computer Furniture & Accessories Inc. - Gardena, CA - *WhoWMicrocom 83*
Computer Games - New York, NY - *BaconPubCkMag 84*
Computer Gaming World [of Golden Empire Publications Inc.] - Anaheim, CA - *BaconPubCkMag 84; MicrocomMPl 84*
Computer Generated Data [Subs. of Wagener Enterprises] - Virginia Beach, VA - *WhoWMicrocom 83*
Computer Graphics - Minneapolis, MN - *AvMarPl 83*
Computer Graphics - New York, NY - *BaconPubCkMag 84*
Computer Graphics Group Inc. - Atlanta, GA - *MicrocomMPl 84*
Computer Graphics News - Fairfax, VA - *BaconPubCkMag 84*
Computer Graphics Software News, The - Houston, TX - *BaconPubCkMag 84*
Computer Graphics World [of Penwall Publishing Co.] - San Francisco, CA - *BaconPubCkMag 84; MicrocomMPl 84; WritMar 84*
Computer Hardware Inc. - Sacramento, CA - *DataDirSup 7-83; WhoWMicrocom 83*
Computer Headware - San Francisco, CA - *MicrocomMPl 84; MicrocomSwDir 1*
Computer Heroes - East Liverpool, OH - *MicrocomMPl 83, 84*
Computer Horizons Corp. - New York, NY - *ADAPSOMemDir 83-84; DataDirSup 7-83*
Computer House - Mammoth Lakes, CA - *MicrocomMPl 83*
Computer House [Subs. of F.L.C. Inc.] - Jackson, MI - *MicrocomMPl 83; WhoWMicrocom 83*
Computer Identics Corp. - Canton, MA - *WhoWMicrocom 83*
Computer Image Corp. - Denver, CO - *ArtMar 84; AvMarPl 83; Tel&CabFB 84C*
Computer Industry Market Intelligence System - La Jolla, CA - *DirOnDB Spring 84*
Computer Information Index Series [of BP Publications] - Southbury, CT - *EISS 5-84 Sup*
Computer Ink - Seattle, WA - *DataDirSup 7-83*
Computer Innovations - Chicago, IL - *DataDirOnSer 84; DataDirSup 7-83; EISS 5-84 Sup*
Computer Innovations - Lincroft, NJ - *MicrocomMPl 83; WhoWMicrocom 83*
Computer Innovations - Red Bank, NJ - *MicrocomMPl 84; MicrocomSwDir 1*
Computer Insider [of NewsNet Inc.] - Bryn Mawr, PA - *DataDirOnSer 84*
Computer Insider - Madison, WI - *DirOnDB Spring 84*
Computer Installation Data File [of Computer Intelligence Corp.] - La Jolla, CA - *DataDirOnSer 84*
Computer Intelligence Corp. [Subs. of Ziff Davis Publishing Co.] - La Jolla, CA - *ADAPSOMemDir 83-84; DataDirOnSer 84*
Computer Interviewing Corp. of America - Yountville, CA - *IntDirMarRes 83*
Computer Investment Advice Inc. - Coraopolis, PA - *MicrocomMPl 84*
Computer Island - Staten Island, NY - *MicrocomMPl 84*
Computer Kitchen, The - Sunnyvale, CA - *WhoWMicrocom 83*
Computer Knowledge - Worcester, MA - *MicrocomMPl 84*
Computer Language Co. Inc. - New York, NY - *BoPubDir 5*
Computer Languages [of Pergamon Press Inc.] - Elmsford, NY - *MicrocomMPl 84*
Computer Law Advisers - Springfield, VA - *ADAPSOMemDir 83-84*
Computer Law & Tax Report - Woburn, MA - *MagIndMarPl 82-83*
Computer Law Service - Woburn, MA - *MagDir 84*
Computer-Link Corp. - Burlington, MA - *DirInfWP 82*
Computer Magic Inc. - Louisville, KY - *MicrocomMPl 83*
Computer Mail Order - Williamsport, PA - *MicrocomMPl 83*
Computer Mailings Inc. - Los Angeles, CA - *ADAPSOMemDir 83-84*
Computer Management Systems - Santa Rosa, CA - *MicrocomSwDir 1*
Computer Market Observer [of Auerbach Publishers Inc.] - Pennsauken, NJ - *DirOnDB Spring 84; MicrocomMPl 84*
Computer Market Observer [of NewsNet Inc.] - Bryn Mawr, PA - *DataDirOnSer 84*
Computer Marketers Inc. - West Orange, NJ - *MicrocomMPl 84; MicrocomSwDir 1*
Computer Marketing Newsletter - Newport Beach, CA - *BaconPubCkMag 84*
Computer Marketing Services - Cherry Hill, NJ - *MicrocomMPl 84*
Computer Marketing Services - Rochester, NY - *DirMarMP 83; HBIndAd&MS 82-83*
Computer Mart - Troy, MI - *MicrocomMPl 83, 84*
Computer Mart Inc. - Waltham, MA - *MicrocomMPl 84; WhoWMicrocom 83*
Computer Mart Inc. - Clawson, MI - *WhoWMicrocom 83*
Computer Mart of New Jersey - Iselin, NJ - *MicrocomMPl 83*
Computer Mate Inc. - Richardson, TX - *MicrocomMPl 84*
Computer Mathware - Princeton, NJ - *MicrocomMPl 83, 84*
Computer Media Distributors [Div. of Nutshell Systems Inc.] - New York, NY - *MicrocomMPl 84*
Computer Media Products - San Diego, CA - *MicrocomMPl 83*
Computer Memories - Chatsworth, CA - *DataDirSup 7-83; MicrocomMPl 84*
Computer Merchandising [of Eastman Publishing] - Encino, CA - *BaconPubCkMag 84; MicrocomMPl 84; WritMar 84*
Computer Merchant Ltd., The - South Weymouth, MA - *DataDirSup 7-83; MicrocomSwDir 1*
Computer Methods Inc. - Milwaukee, WI - *MicrocomSwDir 1*
Computer Metrics - El Cajon, CA - *MicrocomMPl 83*
Computer Microfilm International Corp. - Arlington, VA - *EISS 83; MicroMarPl 82-83*
Computer Modelling Ltd. - Penn, England - *MicrocomSwDir 1*
Computer Multiple Listing Service - Fairfax, VA - *DataDirOnSer 84*
Computer 'N Things [Subs. of Electronics Technology Inc.] - Austin, TX - *WhoWMicrocom 83*
Computer Network Corp. - Washington, DC - *DataDirOnSer 84; EISS 83; LitMarPl 83, 84; MagIndMarPl 82-83*
Computer News of San Diego [of Singman Publications Inc.] - San Diego, CA - *MicrocomMPl 84*
Computer Operator [of Elexpro Enterprises Inc.] - Aurora, IL - *MagDir 84*
Computer Optics Inc. [Subs. of Four-Phase Systems Inc.] - Bethel, CT - *WhoWMicrocom 83*
Computer Options Inc. - Brockton, MA - *MicrocomSwDir 1*
Computer Palace-Royal Software - Eugene, OR - *MicrocomMPl 84; WritMar 84*
Computer Peripherals & Software - Bethlehem, PA - *MicrocomMPl 84*
Computer Picks - Brunswick, NJ - *Ed&PubIntYB 82*
Computer Pictures [of Back Stage Publications] - New York, NY - *BaconPubCkMag 84; MicrocomMPl 84*
Computer Place Inc., The - Worcester, MA - *WhoWMicrocom 83*
Computer Place, The - Brooklyn Heights, OH - *DataDirSup 7-83*
Computer Place, The [Subs. of Trintronics Ltd.] - Toronto, ON, Canada - *WhoWMicrocom 83*
Computer Possibilities Unltd. - Mountain View, CA - *MicrocomMPl 84*
Computer Power Inc. - Jacksonville, FL - *ADAPSOMemDir 83-84*
Computer Power Inc. - High Bridge, NJ - *WhoWMicrocom 83*
Computer Power Systems - Carson, CA - *WhoWMicrocom 83*
Computer Printers International - Mountain View, CA - *DirInfWP 82; WhoWMicrocom 83*
Computer Pro Corp. - Miami, FL - *MicrocomMPl 84*
Computer Products - Dover, NJ - *BaconPubCkMag 84*
Computer Products - Morristown, NJ - *MagIndMarPl 82-83*
Computer Products [of Gordon Publications Inc.] - Randolph, NJ - *MicrocomMPl 84*
Computer Products International - New Orleans, LA - *MicrocomMPl 83, 84; MicrocomSwDir 1*
Computer Professionals' Book Club [of McGraw-Hill Book Co.] - New York, NY - *LitMarPl 83*
Computer Program Associates - Dallas, TX - *MicrocomMPl 84*
Computer Program Management Inc. - Anderson, IN - *MicrocomMPl 83; WhoWMicrocom 83*
Computer Programs Associates - Dallas, TX - *MicrocomMPl 83*
Computer Projects Inc. - Hoboken, NJ - *DataDirSup 7-83*
Computer Publications Group - Madison, WI - *MicrocomMPl 84*
Computer Publicity News - San Francisco, CA - *BaconPubCkMag 84; MicrocomMPl 84*
Computer Publishing & Advertising Report [of Communications Trends Inc.] - New Rochelle, NY - *MicrocomMPl 84*

Computer Publishing Inc. - Hixson, TX - *MicrocomMPl 84*
Computer Reference Center [of Rutgers University] - Piscataway, NJ - *EISS 83*
Computer Research Co. [Subs. of Comshare Inc.] - Chicago, IL - *DataDirOnSer 84*
Computer Research Corp. - Wheat Ridge, CO - *WhoWMicrocom 83*
Computer Research Inc. - Coraopolis, PA - *ADAPSOMemDir 83-84*
Computer Reserves Inc. - Union, NJ - *IntDirMarRes 83*
Computer Resource Centers - Weston, MA - *MicrocomMPl 84*
Computer Resource Services Inc. - Las Vegas, NV - *DataDirOnSer 84; DataDirSup 7-83*
Computer Resources [Subs. of Herman Miller Inc.] - Grandville, MI - *DataDirOnSer 84*
Computer Resources - Lancaster, PA - *MicrocomMPl 83, 84*
Computer Resources Co. - Allentown, PA - *MicrocomMPl 84*
Computer Resources Inc. - Cleveland, OH - *DataDirSup 7-83; WhoWMicrocom 83*
Computer Resources International Inc. - Monroe, LA - *ADAPSOMemDir 83-84*
Computer Resources Services Inc. [Div. of Data-Corp of Nevada] - Las Vegas, NV - *DataDirOnSer 84*
Computer Retail News [of CMP Publications Inc.] - Manhasset, NY - *BaconPubCkMag 84; MagDir 84*
Computer Retailing [of WRC Smith Publishing] - Atlanta, GA - *BaconPubCkMag 84; MagIndMarPl 82-83; MicrocomMPl 84; WhoWMicrocom 83; WritMar 84*
Computer Retrieval of Information on Scientific Projects [of National Institutes of Health] - Bethesda, MD - *CompReadDB 82*
Computer Ribbon Specialists - Hicksville, NY - *DirInfWP 82*
Computer Science Press Inc. - Rockville, MD - *ArtMar 84; LitMarPl 83, 84; MicroMarPl 82-83; TeleSy&SerDir 2-84; WritMar 84*
Computer Sciences Corp. - El Segundo, CA - *DataDirOnSer 84; DataDirSup 7-83; Datamation 6-83; EISS 83; Top100Al 83*
Computer Sciences Corp. (INFONET Div.) - El Segundo, CA - *ADAPSOMemDir 83-84*
Computer Sciences Div. [of Datatronic Systems Corp.] - Panorama City, CA - *EISS 83*
Computer Sciences of Australia Pty. Ltd. [Subs. of Computer Sciences Corp.] - St. Leonards, Australia - *DataDirOnSer 84*
Computer Search Center [of Illinois Institute of Technology] - Chicago, IL - *EISS 83; FBInfSer 80; InfIndMarPl 83*
Computer Search International Corp. - Baltimore, MD - *DataDirOnSer 84*
Computer Search Service [of British Library] - London, England - *EISS 83*
Computer Secretary Inc. - Tampa, FL - *DirInfWP 82*
Computer Secretary Inc. - Atlanta, GA - *DirInfWP 82*
Computer Service Systems Network - Boston, MA - *WhoWMicrocom 83*
Computer Services - Provo, UT - *MicrocomMPl 84*
Computer Services Corp. - Birmingham, AL - *ADAPSOMemDir 83-84*
Computer Services International [Subs. of Corporate Services Inc.] - Mesa, AZ - *DataDirOnSer 84*
Computer Services International Corp. - Weehawken, NJ - *ADAPSOMemDir 83-84*
Computer Services of Encinitas - Encinitas, CA - *WhoWMicrocom 83*
Computer Services Report - Belmont, MA - *BaconPubCkMag 84*
Computer Shack - Pontiac, MI - *MicrocomMPl 83, 84*
Computer Sharing Services Inc. [Subs. of Rio Grande Industries] - Denver, CO - *ADAPSOMemDir 83-84; DataDirOnSer 84; DataDirSup 7-83; EISS 83*
Computer Shopper [of Patch Publishing Co. Inc.] - Titusville, FL - *DirMarMP 83; MicrocomMPl 84*
Computer Skill Builders - Tucson, AZ - *MicrocomMPl 84; WritMar 84*
Computer Slide Co. Inc., The [Subs. of Benjamin Morse Inc.] - Boston, MA - *AvMarPl 83*
Computer Software Association Inc. - Randolph, MA - *MicrocomMPl 84*
Computer Software/Books R Us - Irvine, CA - *LitMarPl 83, 84; MicrocomMPl 84*
Computer Software Design - Anaheim, CA - *MicrocomMPl 84; MicrocomSwDir 1; WhoWMicrocom 83*
Computer Software for Professionals Inc. - Oakland, CA - *MicrocomMPl 84; WhoWMicrocom 83*
Computer Software Management & Information Center [of University of Georgia] - Athens, GA - *EISS 83*
Computer Solutions - San Antonio, TX - *WhoWMicrocom 83*
Computer Specialties - El Cajon, CA - *MicrocomMPl 83*
Computer Stations Inc. - St. Louis, MO - *MicrocomMPl 83, 84; MicrocomSwDir 1; WhoWMicrocom 83*
Computer Stop - Lawndale, CA - *MicrocomMPl 84*
Computer Stop Corp. - Torrance, CA - *WhoWMicrocom 83*
Computer Store Inc., The - Sudbury, MA - *WhoWMicrocom 83*
Computer Store International - El Cajon, CA - *MicrocomMPl 83*
Computer Store of Gulf Breeze Inc. - Gulf Breeze, FL - *MicrocomMPl 83*
Computer Support Services - Rockville, MD - *ADAPSOMemDir 83-84*
Computer Support Systems Inc. - North Mankato, MN - *WhoWMicrocom 83*
Computer Synthesis - Norcross, GA - *WhoWMicrocom 83*
Computer System Dynamics Inc. - Denver, CO - *WhoWMicrocom 83*
Computer Systems - St. Clair Shores, MI - *WhoWMicrocom 83*
Computer Systems & Programs - Dallas, TX - *MicrocomMPl 83*
Computer Systems Consultants - Conyers, GA - *MicrocomMPl 83, 84*
Computer Systems Design Group - San Diego, CA - *WhoWMicrocom 83*
Computer Systems Dynamics Inc. - Denver, CO - *WhoWMicrocom 83*
Computer Systems Group - Waterloo, ON, Canada - *WhoWMicrocom 83*
Computer Systems Inc. - Baton Rouge, LA - *ADAPSOMemDir 83-84*
Computer Systems Interactive Inc. - New York, NY - *WhoWMicrocom 83*
Computer Systems News [of CMP Publications Inc.] - Manhasset, NY - *BaconPubCkMag 84; Folio 83*
Computer Systems Report for Distribution - Exton, PA - *BaconPubCkMag 84*
Computer Systems Research - Avon, CT - *MicrocomMPl 83, 84; MicrocomSwDir 1*
Computer Talk - Blue Bell, PA - *BaconPubCkMag 84*
Computer Talk Inc. - Morrison, CO - *DataDirSup 7-83*
Computer Task Group - Buffalo, NY - *ADAPSOMemDir 83-84; DataDirOnSer 84; DataDirSup 7-83; MicrocomMPl 84; MicrocomSwDir 1*
Computer Tax Service - Incline Village, NV - *MicrocomMPl 84; MicrocomSwDir 1*
Computer Techniques Corp. - Richmond, VA - *WhoWMicrocom 83*
Computer Technology Group - Chicago, IL - *ADAPSOMemDir 83-84*
Computer Technology Review - Los Angeles, CA - *BaconPubCkMag 84*
Computer Terminal Systems - Hauppauge, NY - *DataDirSup 7-83*
Computer-Time Corp. - Morrison, CO - *DataDirOnSer 84*
Computer Times [of Hayden Publishing Co. Inc.] - Rochelle Park, NJ - *MagDir 84*
Computer Times [of PTN Publishing Co.] - Woodbury, NY - *MagDir 84*
Computer Toolbox Inc. - Waterbury, CT - *MicrocomMPl 84*
Computer Trader Magazine [of Lambert Publishing House] - Birmingham, AL - *MicrocomMPl 84*
Computer Transceiver Systems Inc. - Paramus, NJ - *DataDirSup 7-83; DirInfWP 82; InfIndMarPl 83; MicrocomMPl 84; WhoWMicrocom 83*
Computer Translation Inc. [Subs. of Management Systems Corp.] - Orem, UT - *EISS 83; WhoWMicrocom 83*
Computer Transtation Inc. - Provo, UT - *MicrocomMPl 83*
Computer Tree Inc., The - Endwell, NY - *WhoWMicrocom 83*
Computer Typesetting Services [Subs. of Publishers Services International] - Burbank, CA - *LitMarPl 83, 84*
Computer Typesetting Services - Glendale, CA - *MagIndMarPl 82-83*
Computer Unltd. Inc. - Towson, MD - *WhoWMicrocom 83*

Computer Update [of The Boston Computer Society] - Boston, MA - *BaconPubCkMag 84; MicrocomMPl 84*
Computer Usage Co. - San Francisco, CA - *DataDirOnSer 84; DataDirSup 7-83*
Computer Utilities of Cleveland Inc. - Cleveland, OH - *ADAPSOMemDir 83-84*
Computer Ware - New York, NY - *BaconPubCkMag 84*
Computer Works - Harrisonburg, VA - *MicrocomMPl 83*
Computer Works, The - Culver City, CA - *MicrocomMPl 83*
Computerama Inc. [Subs. of Computer World] - Burbank, CA - *WhoWMicrocom 83*
Computercentrum C. Van de Velden BV - Arnhem, Netherlands - *ADAPSOMemDir 83-84*
Computerdaily [of Computer Age Publications] - Annandale, VA - *EISS 5-84 Sup*
Computerdata - Downsview, ON, Canada - *BaconPubCkMag 84*
Computerised Information from National Criminological Holdings [of Australian Institute of Criminology Library] - Philip, Australia - *EISS 83*
Computeristics Inc. - Hamden, CT - *ADAPSOMemDir 83-84*
Computerized Areal Demographic Information System [of University of New Mexico] - Albuquerque, NM - *EISS 83*
Computerized Bibliographic Services [of University of Wisconsin] - Madison, WI - *DataDirOnSer 84*
Computerized Biology Data & Program Bank [of University of Notre Dame] - Notre Dame, IN - *EISS 83*
Computerized Conferencing & Communications Center [of New Jersey Institute of Technology] - Newark, NJ - *DataDirOnSer 84*
Computerized Data Bank of Women-Owned Business [of National Association of Women Business Owners] - Chicago, IL - *EISS 83*
Computerized Documentation System/Integrated Set of Information Systems [of United Nations Educational, Scientific, & Cultural Organization] - Paris, France - *EISS 83*
Computerized Engineering Index [of Engineering Information Inc.] - New York, NY - *CompReadDB 82; DataDirOnSer 84; DBBus 82*
Computerized Folklore Archive [of University of Detroit] - Detroit, MI - *CompReadDB 82; EISS 83*
Computerized Information Retrieval System of Gas Chromatography Literature [of Preston Publications Inc.] - Niles, IL - *CompReadDB 82*
Computerized Information Unit [of National Institute for Research on Biological Resources] - Veracruz, Mexico - *EISS 83*
Computerized Legislative Information Systems [of Vermont State Legislative Council] - Montpelier, VT - *EISS 83*
Computerized Library Acquisitions System [of Lukac Data Systems] - Hillsboro, OR - *EISS 83*
Computerized Library of Analysed Igneous Rocks [of University of Melbourne] - Parkville, Australia - *EISS 83*
Computerized Library Services [of University of California, Santa Barbara] - Santa Barbara, CA - *EISS 83*
Computerized Library Services [of Northeastern University Libraries] - Boston, MA - *EISS 83*
Computerized Library Services [of University of New Hampshire Library] - Durham, NH - *EISS 83*
Computerized Library Services [of New York State Library] - Albany, NY - *EISS 83*
Computerized Literature Search Service [of Massachusetts Institute of Technology Libraries] - Cambridge, MA - *FBInfSer 80*
Computerized Literature Searching Service [of University of California, San Diego] - La Jolla, CA - *FBInfSer 80*
Computerized London Information Service, A [of Greater London Council] - London, England - *CompReadDB 82*
Computerized Management Decisions - Indianapolis, IN - *ADAPSOMemDir 83-84; DataDirOnSer 84*
Computerized Manufacturing [of Technical Database Corp.] - Conroe, TX - *BaconPubCkMag 84; MicrocomMPl 84*
Computerized Plant Germplasm Inventory System [of U.S. Dept. of Agriculture] - Ft. Collins, CO - *EISS 83*
Computerized Register of Voice Research [of Southern Illinois University] - Carbondale, IL - *CompReadDB 82; EISS 83*
Computerized Resources Information Bank [of U.S. Geological Survey] - Reston, VA - *EISS 83*
Computerized Retrieval Services [of Newfoundland Dept. of Mines & Energy] - St. John's, NF, Canada - *EISS 83*
Computerized Services [of Marshall & Swift Publication Co.] - Los Angeles, CA - *EISS 83*
Computerized System [of U.S. Dept. of Defense] - New York, NY - *EISS 83*
Computerized Text Processing & Retrieval System for City Council Information [of Toronto Dept. of the City Clerk] - Toronto, ON, Canada - *EISS 83*
Computerland Corp. [Subs. of IMS Associates] - San Leandro, CA - *WhoWMicrocom 83*
Computerline Ltd. - Weybridge, England - *MicrocomSwDir 1*
Computerm Corp. - Portland, OR - *DirInfWP 82*
Computerm Corp. - Pittsburgh, PA - *DataDirSup 7-83*
Computermail Associates - Baltimore, MD - *MagIndMarPl 82-83*
Computerpat [of Pergamon International Information Corp.] - McLean, VA - *DataDirOnSer 84; DirOnDB Spring 84*
Computers & Chemical Engineering [of Pergamon Press Inc.] - Elmsford, NY - *MicrocomMPl 84*
Computers & Education [of Pergamon Press Inc.] - Elmsford, NY - *MicrocomMPl 84*
Computers & Electronics [of Ziff-Davis Publishing Co.] - New York, NY - *BaconPubCkMag 84; Folio 83; LitMarPl 83, 84; MagDir 84; WritMar 84*
Computers & Industrial Engineering [of Pergamon Press Inc.] - Elmsford, NY - *MicrocomMPl 84*
Computers & Medicine - Glencoe, IL - *BaconPubCkMag 84*
Computers & Minicomputers [of GML Corp.] - Lexington, MA - *CompReadDB 82*
Computers & People - Newtonville, MA - *BaconPubCkMag 84*
Computers & the Humanities - Flushing, NY - *EISS 83*
Computers Control & Information Theory - Springfield, VA - *BaconPubCkMag 84*
Computers for Design & Construction [of Meta Data Publishing Corp.] - New York, NY - *BaconPubCkMag 84; MagDir 84*
Computers for Marketing Corp. - San Francisco, CA - *DataDirOnSer 84; IntDirMarRes 83*
Computers in Healthcare - Englewood, CO - *BaconPubCkMag 84*
Computers in Mechanical Engineering - New York, NY - *BaconPubCkMag 84*
Computers in Medicine [of Medical Software Co.] - Center Moriches, NY - *MicrocomMPl 84*
Computers in Psychiatry/Psychology - New Haven, CT - *MicrocomMPl 84*
Computers in the Schools - Lubbock, TX - *BaconPubCkMag 84*
Computers in the Telephone Industry - Hazelwood, MO - *BaconPubCkMag 84*
Computers International - Los Angeles, CA - *MicrocomMPl 84*
Computers Plus Inc. - Dubuque, IA - *WhoWMicrocom 83*
Computers, Reading & Language Arts [of Modern Learning Publishers Inc.] - Oakland, CA - *MicrocomMPl 84*
Computer's Voice - Flint, MI - *MicrocomMPl 83, 84*
ComputerTalk for the Pharmacist [of ComputerTalk Associates Inc.] - Blue Bell, PA - *MicrocomMPl 84*
ComputerTalk for the Physician [of ComputerTalk Associates Inc.] - Blue Bell, CA - *MicrocomMPl 84*
ComputerTown News Bulletin [of People's Computer Co.] - Menlo Park, CA - *MicrocomMPl 84*
Computervision Corp. - Bedford, MA - *DataDirSup 7-83; Datamation 6-83; Top100Al 83*
Computerware - Encinitas, CA - *MicrocomMPl 83, 84*
Computerware Inc. - Stillwater, MN - *DataDirSup 7-83*
Computerware Unltd. - Elkhart, IN - *MicrocomSwDir 1*
Computerworks Inc. - Westport, CT - *WhoWMicrocom 83*
Computerworld [of CW Communications Inc.] - Framingham, MA - *ArtMar 84; BaconPubCkMag 84; Folio 83; MagDir 84; MagIndMarPl 82-83; MicrocomMPl 84; NewsBur 6; NewsDir 84; WritMar 84*
Computerworld International Inc. - Golden, CO - *MicrocomMPl 83, 84*
Compute!'s Gazette [of Small System Services] - Greensboro, NC - *BaconPubCkMag 84; MicrocomMPl 84; WritMar 84*
Computex - Webster, TX - *MicrocomMPl 83*
Computhink - Sunnyvale, CA - *WhoWMicrocom 83*
Computing! - San Francisco, CA - *MicrocomMPl 84; MicrocomSwDir 1*
Computing Assistance Program [of Taylor University] - Upland, IN - *EISS 83*

Computing Canada - Willowdale, ON, Canada - *BaconPubCkMag 84; WritMar 84*
Computing Center [of University of Notre Dame] - Notre Dame, IN - *EISS 83*
Computing Information Center [of University of Washington] - Seattle, WA - *EISS 83*
Computing Information Services Inc. - Phoenix, AZ - *LitMarPl 83, 84*
Computing Journal Abstracts [of National Computing Centre Ltd.] - Manchester, England - *CompReadDB 82*
Computing Now! - Toronto, ON, Canada - *BaconPubCkMag 84; WritMar 84*
Computing Publications Inc. - Princeton, NJ - *ADAPSOMemDir 83-84*
Computing Resource Center - Santa Monica, CA - *ADAPSOMemDir 83-84*
Computing Reviews [of Association for Computing Machinery] - New York, NY - *MagDir 84*
Computing Teacher, The [of International Council for Computers of Education] - Eugene, OR - *MicrocomMPl 84*
Computing Trends - Seattle, WA - *BoPubDir 4, 5*
Computofacts - Willowdale, ON, Canada - *BoPubDir 4, 5*
Computoll Group Ltd. - New York, NY - *DirInfWP 82; TeleSy&SerDir 7-83*
Computone Systems Inc. - Atlanta, GA - *ADAPSOMemDir 83-84; DataDirOnSer 84; DataDirSup 7-83*
CompuTool Corp. - Minneapolis, MN - *DataDirSup 7-83*
Computrickx Inc. - Petaluma, CA - *MicrocomSwDir 1*
Computrol Inc. - St. Louis, MO - *DataDirSup 7-83*
Computron Business Solutions Inc. - New York, NY - *MicrocomMPl 84*
Computron Software - New York, NY - *DirInfWP 82*
Computronic Computer Corp. [Subs. of Dominion Energy Group Inc.] - Lawrence, NY - *WhoWMicrocom 83*
Computronics Distributing Inc. - Stratford, CT - *MicrocomMPl 84*
Computx - Oak Ridge, NJ - *MicrocomMPl 84*
Computype Inc. - St. Paul, MN - *LitMarPl 83, 84; MagIndMarPl 82-83*
CompuView Products Inc. - Ann Arbor, MI - *MicrocomMPl 83, 84; WhoWMicrocom 83*
Compuware Corp. - Birmingham, MI - *ADAPSOMemDir 83-84; DataDirSup 7-83*
Compuware Corp. - Southfield, MI - *WhoWMicrocom 83*
Compuware Corp. - Cherry Hill, NJ - *MicrocomMPl 83, 84*
CompuWeigh [Subs. of CompuDyne Corp.] - Cheshire, CT - *WhoWMicrocom 83*
Comreco Music Inc. - New Rochelle, NY - *BillIntBG 83-84*
Comrex International Inc. - Torrance, CA - *MicrocomMPl 84*
Comsat General Corp. - Washington, DC - *BrCabYB 84; Tel&CabFB 84C; TeleSy&SerDir 7-83*
Comsat General Integrated Systems Inc. - Palo Alto, CA - *BrCabYB 84*
Comsat General Telesystems Inc. - Fairfax, VA - *BrCabYB 84*
Comsat Maritime Services [of Comsat World Systems Div.] - Washington, DC - *TeleSy&SerDir 7-83*
Comsat TeleSystems - Fairfax, VA - *DataDirSup 7-83*
Comsat World Systems - Washington, DC - *BrCabYB 84*
Comsearch Inc. - Reston, VA - *Tel&CabFB 84C; TeleSy&SerDir 7-83*
Comsen Inc. - Lemoyne, PA - *MicrocomMPl 84*
Comserv Corp. - Eagan, MN - *ADAPSOMemDir 83-84; DataDirSup 7-83*
Comserv Inc. - Scottsdale, AZ - *CabTVFinDB 83*
Comserv Ltd. [of Schaller Telephone Co.] - Ida Grove, IA - *Tel&CabFB 84C*
Comserv Ltd. [of Schaller Telephone Co.] - Odebolt, IA - *Tel&CabFB 84C*
Comshare Inc. - Atlanta, GA - *MicrocomMPl 84*
Comshare Inc. - Ann Arbor, MI - *ADAPSOMemDir 83-84; DataDirOnSer 84; DataDirSup 7-83; Datamation 6-83; EISS 83; InfIndMarPl 83; Top100Al 83*
Comshare Ltd. - Rexdale, ON, Canada - *DataDirSup 7-83*
Comshare Ltd. - London, England - *MicrocomSwDir 1*
Comshare Target Software - Atlanta, GA - *MicrocomMPl 83; MicrocomSwDir 1*
Comshare-Trust (Service Div.) - Philadelphia, PA - *WhoWMicrocom 83*
ComSoft - Glendale, CA - *MicrocomMPl 83*
ComSoft - West Los Angeles, CA - *MicrocomMPl 84*
Comspec - New York, NY - *DirOnDB Spring 84*
Comstock Bonanza Press - Grass Valley, CA - *LitMag&SmPr 83-84*
Comstock Community Television Inc. - Virginia City, NV - *BrCabYB 84; Tel&CabFB 84C*
Comstock Editions Inc. - Sausalito, CA - *LitMarPl 83, 84*
Comstock News - Comstock, NE - *BaconPubCkNews 84; Ed&PubIntYB 82*
Comstock Records - Shawnee, KS - *BillIntBG 83-84*
Comstow Information Services - Stow, MA - *EISS 7-83 Sup*
Comsul Ltd. - San Francisco, CA - *TeleSy&SerDir 2-84*
Comsumer Electronic Services Div. [of Comp-U-Card of America Inc.] - Stamford, CT - *EISS 83*
Comtact Corp. [Subs. of Klemtner Advertising] - New York, NY - *AvMarPl 83*
Comtal/3M - Altadena, CA - *DataDirSup 7-83*
Comtec Inc. [of Realty Investment Co.] - Hilo, HI - *BrCabYB 84; Tel&CabFB 84C*
Comtec Information Systems Inc. - Cumberland, RI - *DataDirSup 7-83*
Comtech Data Corp. - Scottsdale, AZ - *DataDirSup 7-83*
Comtech Group International Ltd. - Willowdale, ON, Canada - *DataDirOnSer 84; DataDirSup 7-83*
Comtech Systems Inc. - Columbus, OH - *ADAPSOMemDir 83-84*
Comtech Telecommunications Corp. - New York, NY - *HomeVid&CabYB 82-83*
Comtel Inc. - New York, NY - *BrCabYB 84*
Comtrex Systems Corp. - Mt. Laurel, NJ - *DataDirSup 7-83*
Comtronic Systems - Kent, WA - *MicrocomMPl 83, 84*
Comunidade - Toronto, ON, Canada - *Ed&PubIntYB 82*
Comunita Viva - Toronto, ON, Canada - *Ed&PubIntYB 82*
Comvestrix Corp. - New York, NY - *ADAPSOMemDir 83-84*
Comworld International - New York, NY - *Tel&CabFB 84C*
Comworld Productions - Sherman Oaks, CA - *TelAl 84*
Con Brio Music - Nashville, TN - *BillIntBG 83-84*
Con Brio Records Inc. - Nashville, TN - *BillIntBG 83-84*
Concap Computing Systems - Oakland, CA - *DataDirOnSer 84; DataDirSup 7-83*
Concept Development Inc. - Costa Mesa, CA - *DataDirSup 7-83*
Concept Educational Software - Allentown, PA - *MicrocomMPl 84*
Concept 80's - Newtown Square, PA - *AvMarPl 83*
Concept IV Computer Systems Inc. - Albany, NY - *DataDirSup 7-83*
Concept Production Inc. - Madison, WI - *AvMarPl 83*
Concept Publishing - York, NY - *BoPubDir 4, 5*
Concept Systems Inc. - Philadelphia, PA - *DataDirSup 7-83*
Concept Testing Institute, The - New York, NY - *IntDirMarRes 83*
Concept Three - Davison, MI - *StaDirAdAg 2-84*
Concept Visualizers Inc. - Brooklyn, NY - *BoPubDir 4, 5*
Conceptions Southwest - Albuquerque, NM - *LitMag&SmPr 83-84*
Concepts - Ithaca, NY - *BoPubDir 5*
Concepts Systems Inc. - Notre Dame, IN - *MicrocomMPl 84*
Concepts Unltd. Inc. - Acton, MA - *LitMarPl 83, 84*
Conceptual Instruments Co. - Philadelphia, PA - *MicrocomSwDir 1*
Conceptual Resources [Div. of Wallack & Wallack Inc.] - Great Neck, NY - *StaDirAdAg 2-84*
Conceptual Systems Inc. - Burnsville, MN - *MicrocomMPl 83; WhoWMicrocom 83*
Concerning Poetry - Bellingham, WA - *LitMag&SmPr 83-84*
Conch Magazine [Div. of Conch Corp. Co.] - Buffalo, NY - *ArtMar 84; LitMag&SmPr 83-84; LitMarPl 83, 84*
Conch Review of Books [of Conch Magazine Ltd.] - Buffalo, NY - *LitMag&SmPr 83-84*
Conch Typesetting & Graphic Services [Div. of Conch Magazine Ltd.] - Buffalo, NY - *LitMarPl 83, 84; MagIndMarPl 82-83*
Concho Herald - Paint Rock, TX - *AyerDirPub 83; Ed&PubIntYB 82*
Conconully TV Cable Co. - Conconully, WA - *BrCabYB 84; Tel&CabFB 84C*
Concord Books - Seal Beach, CA - *BoPubDir 4 Sup, 5*

Concord Cable Communications - Oxford, MI - *Tel&CabFB 84C p.1674*
Concord Cable Communications Co. Inc. [of Telephone & Data Systems Inc.] - Concord, TN - *BrCabYB 84; Tel&CabFB 84C*
Concord Cablevision Co. Inc. - Concord, MI - *Tel&CabFB 84C*
Concord Computer Products - Anaheim, CA - *MicrocomMPl 83*
Concord Computing Corp. - Bedford, MA - *DataDirOnSer 84; DataDirSup 7-83*
Concord Daily Monitor - Concord, NH - *BaconPubCkNews 84*
Concord Data Systems Inc. - Waltham, MA - *DataDirSup 7-83*
Concord Jazz Inc. - Concord, CA - *BillIntBG 83-84*
Concord Journal [of Oakland Neighborhood Journal] - Oakland, CA - *AyerDirPub 83; NewsDir 84*
Concord Journal - Acton, MA - *AyerDirPub 83*
Concord Journal [of Minute-Man Publications Inc.] - Arlington, MA - *NewsDir 84*
Concord Journal - Concord, MA - *AyerDirPub 83; Ed&PubIntYB 82*
Concord Journal - *See* Minute-Man Publications Inc.
Concord Monitor [of Newspapers of New England Inc.] - Concord, NH - *Ed&PubIntYB 82; NewsDir 84*
Concord News, The - Concord, MI - *Ed&PubIntYB 82*
Concord Patriot - Acton, MA - *Ed&PubIntYB 82*
Concord Patriot, The [of Acton Beacon Publishing Co. Inc.] - Concord, MA - *NewsDir 84*
Concord Spiral Bindery - Los Angeles, CA - *LitMarPl 83, 84; MagIndMarPl 82-83*
Concord Telephone Co. Inc. - Concord, MI - *TelDir&BG 83-84*
Concord Telephone Co., The - Concord, NC - *TelDir&BG 83-84*
Concord Telephone Exchange Inc. [Aff. of TCC Inc.] - Knoxville, TN - *TelDir&BG 83-84*
Concord Transcript [of East Bay Newspapers Inc.] - Concord, CA - *Ed&PubIntYB 82; NewsDir 84*
Concord Tribune - Concord, NC - *BaconPubCkNews 84; Ed&PubIntYB 82; NewsDir 84*
Concord TV Cable - Concord, CA - *BrCabYB 84; Tel&CabFB 84C*
Concordant Publishing Concern Inc. - Canyon Country, CA - *BoPubDir 4, 5*
Concordia Blade-Empire - Concordia, KS - *BaconPubCkNews 84; NewsDir 84*
Concordia Cablevision Inc. [of Communications Services Inc.] - Ferriday, LA - *BrCabYB 84; Tel&CabFB 84C*
Concordia Concordian - Concordia, MO - *BaconPubCkNews 84*
Concordia Kansan - Concordia, KS - *BaconPubCkNews 84; Ed&PubIntYB 82*
Concordia Publishing House - St. Louis, MO - *AvMarPl 83; BillIntBG 83-84; DirMarMP 83; LitMarPl 83, 84; MagIndMarPl 82-83; WritMar 84*
Concordia University (Guidance Information Centre) - Montreal, PQ, Canada - *BoPubDir 4, 5*
Concordian, The - Concordia, MO - *AyerDirPub 83; Ed&PubIntYB 82*
Concours Publishing - Riverside, CA - *BoPubDir 4, 5*
Concrete [of Pit & Quarry Publications Inc.] - Chicago, IL - *BaconPubCkMag 84; MagDir 84; MagIndMarPl 82-83*
Concrete - Leatherhead, England - *WritMar 84*
Concrete Construction - Addison, IL - *BaconPubCkMag 84; MagIndMarPl 82-83; WritMar 84*
Concrete Construction Publications Inc. - Addison, IL - *BoPubDir 5; MagDir 84*
Concrete Herald - Concrete, WA - *BaconPubCkNews 84; Ed&PubIntYB 82*
Concrete Industry Bulletin [of Concrete Industry Board] - New York, NY - *BaconPubCkMag 84; MagDir 84*
Concrete International: Design & Construction [of American Concrete Institute] - Detroit, MI - *BaconPubCkMag 84; MagDir 84; MagIndMarPl 82-83; WritMar 84*
Concrete Products [of Maclean-Hunter Publishing Corp.] - Chicago, IL - *BaconPubCkMag 84; MagDir 84*
Concrete Technology Information Analysis Center [of U.S. Army] - Vicksburg, MS - *EISS 83*
Concrete TV Cable Co. - Concrete, WA - *Tel&CabFB 84C*
Concurrent Corp. - Cincinnati, OH - *MicrocomSwDir 1*
Conde Nast Ltd., The - *Folio 83*
Conde Nast Package of Women, The - *Folio 83*
Conde Nast Publications Inc. - New York, NY - *DirMarMP 83; MagIndMarPl 82-83*
Conde News - Conde, SD - *Ed&PubIntYB 82*
Conditions - Brooklyn, NY - *LitMag&SmPr 83-84*
Condo Management Maintenance Corp. - Clinton, NJ - *BoPubDir 4 Sup, 5*
Condon, Richard W. - Camden, SC - *Tel&CabFB 84C p.1674*
Condon Times-Journal - Condon, OR - *BaconPubCkNews 84*
Condon TV System [of Telephone & Data Systems Inc.] - Condon, OR - *BrCabYB 84; Tel&CabFB 84C*
Condor Cable TV - Marlette, MI - *Tel&CabFB 84C*
Condor Cable TV - Whitmore Lake, MI - *Tel&CabFB 84C p.1674*
Condor Computer Corp. - Ann Arbor, MI - *MicrocomMPl 83, 84; MicrocomSwDir 1; WhoWMicrocom 83*
Condor Corp., The - Birmingham, AL - *DataDirSup 7-83; MicrocomSwDir 1*
Condor Pictures Inc. - Hollywood, CA - *TelAl 83, 84*
Condor Publishing - Ashland, MA - *BoPubDir 4 Sup, 5*
Conduit - Iowa City, IA - *WhoWMicrocom 83*
Conduit - Oakdale, IA - *MicrocomMPl 84*
Condyne (Oceana Group) - Dobbs Ferry, NY - *AvMarPl 83*
Cone-Heiden - Seattle, WA - *DirMarMP 83*
Cone Music Co. - *See* Keene Music Co., Joe
Conejos County Citizen - La Jara, CO - *AyerDirPub 83; Ed&PubIntYB 82*
Conemaugh Cable TV [of Eastern Telecom Corp.] - Conemaugh, PA - *Tel&CabFB 84C*
Conestoga Cablevision Inc. [of TCI Growth Inc.] - Catoosa, OK - *Tel&CabFB 84C*
Conestoga Cablevision Inc. [of TCI Growth Inc.] - Coweta, OK - *Tel&CabFB 84C*
Conestoga Cablevision Inc. [of TCI Growth Inc.] - Owasso, OK - *Tel&CabFB 84C*
Conestoga Telephone & Telegraph Co. of Pennsylvania, The [Aff. of Northern Communications Inc.] - Birdsboro, PA - *TelDir&BG 83-84*
Conex Electro Systems Inc. - Bellingham, WA - *MicrocomMPl 84*
Coney Island Times [of Brooklyn North Brooklyn News] - Brooklyn, NY - *NewsDir 84*
Coney Island Times - Coney Island, NY - *Ed&PubIntYB 82*
Conf - West Germany - *DirOnDB Spring 84*
Confectioner [of Associated Business Publications] - New York, NY - *MagDir 84*
Confectioner, The - Milwaukee, WI - *BaconPubCkMag 84*
Confederate - Mt. Forest, ON, Canada - *AyerDirPub 83; Ed&PubIntYB 82*
Confederate Calendar Works - Austin, TX - *LitMag&SmPr 83-84*
Conference Board - New York, NY - *DataDirOnSer 84; DBBus 82; DirOnDB Spring 84; EISS 83; InfIndMarPl 83; LitMarPl 83, 84*
Conference Board Across the Board - New York, NY - *MagDir 84*
Conference Board Data Base [of The Conference Board] - New York, NY - *DataDirOnSer 84*
Conference Board of Canada, The - Ottawa, ON, Canada - *DataDirOnSer 84*
Conference Management Corp. - Norwalk, CT - *MagIndMarPl 82-83*
Conference on Alternative State & Local Policies - Washington, DC - *BoPubDir 4, 5*
Conference on Data Systems Languages - Washington, DC - *EISS 83*
Conference on Economic Progress - Washington, DC - *BoPubDir 4, 5*
Conference on Inter-American Telecommunications - Washington, DC - *TeleSy&SerDir 2-84*
Conference on Optical Fiber Communication [of Optical Society of America] - Washington, DC - *TeleSy&SerDir 2-84*
Conference Papers Index [of Cambridge Scientific Abstracts] - Washington, DC - *CompReadDB 82*
Conference Papers Index [of Cambridge Scientific Abstracts] - Bethesda, MD - *DataDirOnSer 84; DBBus 82; DirOnDB Spring 84; EISS 83; OnBibDB 3*
Conference Proceedings Index - London, England - *DirOnDB Spring 84*

Conference Proceedings Index [of British Library] - Wetherby, England - *CompReadDB 82; OnBibDB 3*
Conference 600 [of Telecom Canada] - Ottawa, ON, Canada - *TeleSy&SerDir 2-84*
Confersat [of Public Broadcasting Service] - Washington, DC - *TeleSy&SerDir 2-84*
Confertech International Inc. - Arvada, CO - *TeleSy&SerDir 2-84*
Confidential & Information Products [of Bemrose Printing] - Derby, England - *EISS 5-84 Sup*
Confidential Forecaster - Austin, TX - *MagDir 84*
Confidential Forecaster, The - St. Louis, MO - *BaconPubCkMag 84*
Confidential Kick-off [of NewsNet Inc.] - Bryn Mawr, PA - *DataDirOnSer 84*
Confidential Kick-Off - Redmond, WA - *DirOnDB Spring 84*
Confluence Press Inc. - Lewiston, ID - *LitMag&SmPr 83-84; LitMarPl 84*
Confrontation [of Long Island University] - Brooklyn, NY - *LitMag&SmPr 83-84; WritMar 84*
Congdon & Weed Inc. - New York, NY - *LitMarPl 83, 84; WritMar 84*
Congdon Associates Inc., Don - New York, NY - *LitMarPl 84*
Congeros Publications [Aff. of Stump's Printing & Services] - Ontario, CA - *BoPubDir 4, 5*
Conglor Publishing Inc. - Maspeth, NY - *BaconPubCkNews 84*
Congress Graphics Inc. - Detroit, MI - *StaDirAdAg 2-84*
Congress Hill & Associates - Hartville, OH - *StaDirAdAg 2-84*
Congress Monthly [of American Jewish Congress] - New York, NY - *ArtMar 84; LitMarPl 83, 84; MagDir 84; MagIndMarPl 82-83; WritMar 84*
Congressional Digest - Washington, DC - *MagIndMarPl 82-83; MicroMarPl 82-83*
Congressional Digest [of NewsNet Inc.] - Bryn Mawr, PA - *DataDirOnSer 84*
Congressional Information Service - Washington, DC - *CompReadDB 82*
Congressional Information Service [Subs. of Elsevier-NDU-NV] - Bethesda, MD - *DataDirOnSer 84; DirMarMP 83; EISS 83; InfIndMarPl 83; InfoS 83-84; LitMarPl 83, 84; MagIndMarPl 82-83; MicroMarPl 82-83*
Congressional Information Sources Inventories & Directories Data Base [of U.S. General Accounting Office] - Washington, DC - *EISS 83*
Congressional Quarterly [Subs. of St. Petersburg Times Publishing Co.] - Washington, DC - *BrCabYB 84; DirMarMP 83; Ed&PubIntYB 82; EISS 83; InfIndMarPl 83; InfoS 83-84; LitMarPl 83, 84; MicroMarPl 82-83*
Congressional Quarterly Press - Washington, DC - *WritMar 84*
Congressional Quarterly Service - Washington, DC - *Ed&PubIntYB 82*
Congressional Quarterly Weekly Report - Washington, DC - *MagIndMarPl 82-83*
Congressional Record [of Capitol Services Inc.] - Washington, DC - *OnBibDB 3*
Congressional Record Abstracts [of Capitol Services Inc.] - Washington, DC - *CompReadDB 82; DataDirOnSer 84; DBBus 82; DirOnDB Spring 84; EISS 83*
Congressional Record Clippings - Washington, DC - *Ed&PubIntYB 82*
Congressional Staff Directory Ltd. - Mt. Vernon, VA - *BoPubDir 4, 5*
Conifer High Timber Times - Conifer, CO - *BaconPubCkNews 84*
Conifer Publishing Co. - Portland, OR - *LitMag&SmPr 83-84*
Conjunctions - New York, NY - *BoPubDir 4 Sup, 5; LitMag&SmPr 83-84*
Conklin Associates Inc., Bill - Elliott City, MD - *DirInfWP 82*
Conklin Labs & Bebee Inc. - Syracuse, NY - *StaDirAdAg 2-84*
Conland Newspapers - Catskill, NY - *Ed&PubIntYB 82*
Conley Inc., Richard - Palo Alto, CA - *StaDirAdAg 2-84*
Conley TV & Cable Service - Garrett, KY - *Tel&CabFB 84C*
Conn Associates, Frances G. [Div. of National Communications Institute] - Bethesda, MD - *LitMarPl 83, 84*
Conn Information Systems Co. - Bridgeport, CT - *MicrocomMPl 83, 84*
Conneaut Lake Breeze [of Gazette Printing Co. Inc.] - Jefferson, OH - *NewsDir 84*
Conneaut Lake Breeze - Conneaut Lake, PA - *AyerDirPub 83; Ed&PubIntYB 82*
Conneaut Lake Breeze - Linesville, PA - *BaconPubCkNews 84*
Conneaut News-Herald - Ashtabula, OH - *NewsDir 84*
Conneaut News-Herald - Conneaut, OH - *BaconPubCkNews 84*
Conneaut Telephone Co. - Conneaut, OH - *TelDir&BG 83-84*
Conneautville Courier - Conneautville, PA - *BaconPubCkNews 84; Ed&PubIntYB 82*
Connecticut Backgammon Newsletter - Waterbury, CT - *LitMag&SmPr 83-84*
Connecticut Beverage Journal [of Beverage Publications Inc.] - Hamden, CT - *BaconPubCkMag 84; MagDir 84*
Connecticut Business Journal [of Business Journals of America] - Harrison, NY - *BaconPubCkMag 84; MagDir 84; NewsDir 84*
Connecticut Business Review - Hartford, CT - *BaconPubCkMag 84*
Connecticut Cable Interconnect - Seymour, CT - *CabTVPrDB 83*
Connecticut Census Data Center [of Connecticut State Office of Policy & Management] - Hartford, CT - *EISS 83*
Connecticut Construction - Farmington, CT - *BaconPubCkMag 84; MagDir 84*
Connecticut Consulting Group Inc. - Georgetown, CT - *HBIndAd&MS 82-83*
Connecticut Daily Campus - Storrs, CT - *NewsDir 84*
Connecticut Dept. of Economic Development - Hartford, CT - *BoPubDir 5*
Connecticut Fireside Press [Aff. of Connecticut Fireside Magazine] - Hamden, CT - *BoPubDir 4, 5*
Connecticut Historical Society - Hartford, CT - *BoPubDir 4 Sup, 5*
Connecticut Information Systems Co. - Bridgeport, CT - *WhoWMicrocom 83*
Connecticut Italian Bulletin - Hartford, CT - *Ed&PubIntYB 82*
Connecticut Jewish Ledger - Hartford, CT - *AyerDirPub 83*
Connecticut Laminating Co. Inc. - New Haven, CT - *DataDirSup 7-83*
Connecticut Magazine - Fairfield, CT - *ArtMar 84; BaconPubCkMag 84; MagDir 84; MagIndMarPl 82-83; WritMar 84*
Connecticut Micro Computer - Brookfield, CT - *MicrocomMPl 83, 84*
Connecticut Motor Transport News - East Hartford, CT - *BaconPubCkMag 84*
Connecticut Motor Transport News - Hartford, CT - *MagDir 84*
Connecticut Natural Diversity Data Base [of Connecticut State Dept. of Environmental Protection] - Hartford, CT - *EISS 5-84 Sup*
Connecticut Pharmacist - Wethersfield, CT - *BaconPubCkMag 84*
Connecticut Poetry Review, The - New Haven, CT - *LitMag&SmPr 83-84*
Connecticut Printers Inc. - Bloomfield, CT - *LitMarPl 83, 84; MagIndMarPl 82-83*
Connecticut Purchasor - Boston, MA - *BaconPubCkMag 84; MagDir 84*
Connecticut Quarterly - Enfield, CT - *LitMag&SmPr 83-84*
Connecticut Real Estate Journal [of East Coast Publications Inc.] - Accord, MA - *MagDir 84*
Connecticut River Review - Hamden, CT - *LitMag&SmPr 83-84*
Connecticut Travels - New Haven, CT - *BaconPubCkMag 84*
Connecticut Typographers - Stamford, CT - *LitMarPl 83*
Connection Communications Corp. - Newark, NJ - *BrCabYB 84; Tel&CabFB 84C*
Connections - Palm City, FL - *BaconPubCkMag 84*
Connections - Minneapolis, MN - *AvMarPl 83*
Connections Magazine - Putnam Valley, NY - *LitMag&SmPr 83-84; WritMar 84*
Connections Press - Pacific Grove, CA - *BoPubDir 4, 5*
Connections Unltd. Inc. - Wheaton, MD - *BillIntBG 83-84*
Connector for Networked Information Transfer [of Massachusetts Institute of Technology] - Cambridge, MA - *EISS 83*
Connell Franklin County Graphic - Connell, WA - *BaconPubCkNews 84*
Connell, May & Steavenson Ltd. - London, England - *StaDirAdAg 2-84*
Connellsville Daily Courier - Connellsville, PA - *NewsDir 84*
Connelly Editorial Services, Claire - Coventry, CT - *LitMarPl 83, 84; MagIndMarPl 82-83*

Conner Music, Mike - *See* Loring Music Co.
Conner/Sanderson Publishers - Los Gatos, CA - *BoPubDir 4, 5*
Connersville Cable TV Inc. [of Cardinal Communications Inc.] - Connersville, IN - *BrCabYB 84; Tel&CabFB 84C*
Connersville Cable TV Inc. - *See* Cardinal Communications Inc.
Connersville News-Examiner - Connersville, IN - *BaconPubCkNews 84; Ed&PubIntYB 82; NewsDir 84*
Connexcall [of Connex International Inc.] - Danbury, CT - *TeleSy&SerDir 7-83*
Connexions [of People's Translation Service] - Oakland, CA - *LitMag&SmPr 83-84*
Connexions - Cambridge, MA - *DirOnDB Spring 84*
Connexions [of Canadian Information Sharing Service] - Toronto, ON, Canada - *LitMag&SmPr 83-84*
Connoisseur - New York, NY - *BaconPubCkMag 84; MagIndMarPl 82-83*
Connoisseur Society Inc. - New York, NY - *BillIntBG 83-84*
Connoisseurs' Guide to California Wine - San Francisco, CA - *BaconPubCkMag 84*
Connoisseurs Unltd. - St. Paul, MN - *StaDirAdAg 2-84*
Connolly, Dr. Charles - Ames, IA - *BrCabYB 84*
Connor-Sager Associates - North Aurora, IL - *AdAge 3-28-84; StaDirAdAg 2-84*
Connors Antiques & Books for Men, John J. - Toledo, OH - *BoPubDir 5*
Connors Associates Inc. - Boston, MA - *LitMarPl 84*
Connors Inc., Kevin F. - Boston, MA - *LitMarPl 83*
Connors, John J. - Toledo, OH - *BoPubDir 4*
Conowall, Joseph - Archbold, OH - *Tel&CabFB 84C p.1674*
Conposit Development Services Inc. - *See* Gardner Advertising Co. Inc.
Conpub - Ypsilanti, MI - *BoPubDir 4, 5*
Conquest Publications - Lewisville, NC - *BoPubDir 4, 5*
ConQuip - *See* Advant
Conquistador Music - *See* Groovesville Music
Conrac - Covina, CA - *AvMarPl 83; InfIndMarPl 83*
Conrac Corp. - Stamford, CT - *HomeVid&CabYB 82-83*
Conrad Cable TV - Conrad, MT - *Tel&CabFB 84C*
Conrad Direct - Englewood, NJ - *LitMarPl 84*
Conrad Independent Observer - Conrad, MT - *BaconPubCkNews 84*
Conrad Lilly Co. - Newburyport, MA - *BoPubDir 4, 5*
Conrad Music - *See* Goodman Group, The
Conrad Record - Conrad, IA - *BaconPubCkNews 84; Ed&PubIntYB 82*
Conradi, Johnson & Associates Inc. - Clayton, MO - *StaDirAdAg 2-84*
Conradiana - Lubbock, TX - *LitMag&SmPr 83-84*
Conroy, Barbara - Tabernash, CO - *BoPubDir 4, 5; FBInfSer 80*
Conroy-LaPointe/Computer Exchange - Portland, OR - *MicrocomMPl 84*
Conroy, William T. Jr. - New York, NY - *MagIndMarPl 82-83*
Conseil National du Credit - Paris, France - *DirOnDB Spring 84*
Consensus Inc. - New York, NY - *IntDirMarRes 83*
Conservation & Renewable Energy Inquiry & Referral Service [of Dept. of Energy] - Silver Spring, MD - *EISS 83; InfIndMarPl 83*
Conservation Council of Ontario - Toronto, ON, Canada - *BoPubDir 4 Sup, 5*
Conservation Foundation, The - Washington, DC - *LitMarPl 83, 84*
Conservationist, The - Albany, NY - *MagIndMarPl 82-83*
Conservative - Independence, IA - *AyerDirPub 83; Ed&PubIntYB 82*
Conservative - Carrollton, MS - *AyerDirPub 83*
Conservative & Advertiser - Tipton, IA - *AyerDirPub 83*
Conservative Book Club Inc. - Harrison, NY - *LitMarPl 84*
Conservative Digest [of Viguerie Communications] - Falls Church, VA - *ArtMar 84; BaconPubCkMag 84; MagDir 84; MagIndMarPl 82-83; WritMar 84*
Conservative Register [of Proud Eagle Press] - Riverside, CA - *WritMar 84*
Conservative, The - Carrolton, MS - *Ed&PubIntYB 82*
Conservatory of American Literature [Aff. of National Heritage Foundation] - South Thomaston, ME - *BoPubDir 5; LitMag&SmPr 83-84*
Conshohocken Recorder - Conshohocken, PA - *Ed&PubIntYB 82*
Conshohocken Recorder - *See* Intercounty Newspaper Group
Consolidated Advertising Directors Inc. - Los Angeles, CA - *StaDirAdAg 2-84*
Consolidated Amethyst Communications Inc. - Scarborough, ON, Canada - *BoPubDir 4, 5*
Consolidated Cable Corp. [of Bates Communications Corp.] - Clarington, OH - *Tel&CabFB 84C*
Consolidated Cable Corp. [of Bates Communications Corp.] - Newport, OH - *BrCabYB 84; Tel&CabFB 84C*
Consolidated Cable Corp. [of Bates Communications Corp.] - Hannibal, WV - *Tel&CabFB 84C*
Consolidated Cable Corp. [of Bates Communications Corp.] - New Martinsville, WV - *Tel&CabFB 84C*
Consolidated Cable TV Inc. [of Teleservice Corp. of America] - McCrory, AR - *BrCabYB 84*
Consolidated Capital Advertising Inc. - Emeryville, CA - *StaDirAdAg 2-84*
Consolidated Communications Inc. - Harrison, NY - *DataDirSup 7-83*
Consolidated Computer Group - Tacoma, WA - *MicrocomMPl 83, 84*
Consolidated Computer Inc. - Ottawa, ON, Canada - *InfIndMarPl 83*
Consolidated/Drake Press - Philadelphia, PA - *MagIndMarPl 82-83*
Consolidated Film Industries [Div. of Republic Corp.] - Hollywood, CA - *AvMarPl 83; Tel&CabFB 84C*
Consolidated Film Laboratories - *See* Consolidated Film Industries
Consolidated Marketing Services Inc. - New York, NY - *BoPubDir 4, 5; DirMarMP 83*
Consolidated Midwest Cable TV Inc. - Chatham, IL - *BrCabYB 84; Tel&CabFB 84C*
Consolidated Midwest Cable TV Inc. - Pawnee, IL - *BrCabYB 84*
Consolidated Papers Inc. - Chicago, IL - *LitMarPl 83, 84; MagIndMarPl 82-83*
Consolidated Photographic Imports Inc. - West Orange, NJ - *AvMarPl 83*
Consolidated Telephone Co. - Brainerd, MN - *TelDir&BG 83-84*
Consolidated Telephone Co. - Lincoln, NE - *TelDir&BG 83-84*
Consolidated Telephone Cooperative - Dickinson, ND - *TelDir&BG 83-84*
Consolidated TV Cable Service Inc. - Frankfort, KY - *BrCabYB 84; Tel&CabFB 84C*
Consolink Corp. - Longmont, CO - *MicrocomMPl 84*
Consorci d'Informacio & Documentacio de Catalunya - Barcelona, Spain - *InfIndMarPl 83*
Consort Enterprise, The - Consort, AB, Canada - *Ed&PubIntYB 82*
Consortium Communications International Inc. - New York, NY - *TeleSy&SerDir 2-84*
Consortium for Continental Reflection Profiling - Ithaca, NY - *EISS 83*
Consortium House Ltd. - Del Mar, CA - *LitMarPl 83, 84*
Consortium of Rhode Island Academic & Research Libraries - Providence, RI - *EISS 83*
Consorzio Interuniversitario Lombardo per l'Elaborazione Automatica - Milan, Italy - *InfIndMarPl 83*
Constant Communications Co. - Lake Oswego, OR - *BrCabYB 84*
Constantia Books - Greenwich, CT - *BoPubDir 4, 5*
Constantian, The - Pittsburgh, PA - *ArtMar 84*
Constantine Engineering Laboratories Co. - Mahwah, NJ - *AvMarPl 83*
Constech Inc. - Dallas, TX - *DataDirOnSer 84*
Constellate Consultants Ltd. - New Delhi, India - *EISS 83; InfIndMarPl 83*
Constellations [of New Traditions Publications] - Santa Rosa, CA - *LitMag&SmPr 83-84*
Constitution [of Atlanta Newspapers] - Atlanta, GA - *AyerDirPub 83; Ed&PubIntYB 82; LitMarPl 84*
Constitution - Lawton, OK - *AyerDirPub 83; BaconPubCkNews 84*
Constitution-Tribune - Chillicothe, MO - *AyerDirPub 83; Ed&PubIntYB 82; NewsDir 84*
Constitutional Capers - Venice, CA - *BoPubDir 4, 5*
Constitutional Rights Foundation - Texas City, TX - *BoPubDir 4 Sup, 5*
Construccion Pan-Americana [of International Construction Publishing Co.] - Miami, FL - *BaconPubCkMag 84; MagDir 84*

Construction - Arlington, VA - *MagDir 84*
Construction - Falls Church, VA - *BaconPubCkMag 84*
Construction Bargaineer, The - St. Paul, MN - *MagDir 84*
Construction Bulletin - Golden Valley, MN - *BaconPubCkMag 84*
Construction Bulletin [of Chapin Publishing Co.] - Minneapolis, MN - *MagDir 84*
Construction Canada - Toronto, ON, Canada - *BaconPubCkMag 84*
Construction Computer Applications [of NewsNet Inc.] - Bryn Mawr, PA - *DataDirOnSer 84*
Construction Computer Applications Newsletter [of Construction Industry Press] - Silver Spring, MD - *DirOnDB Spring 84; MicrocomMPl 84*
Construction Computer Control Corp. - Milwaukee, WI - *ADAPSOMemDir 83-84; DataDirOnSer 84*
Construction Contracting - Culver City, CA - *BaconPubCkMag 84*
Construction Contracting [of Nolan-Sands Publishing] - Garden Grove, CA - *MagDir 84*
Construction Contracting - Redondo Beach, CA - *MagIndMarPl 82-83*
Construction Data Control Inc. - Norcross, GA - *MicrocomSwDir 1*
Construction Data Control Inc. - Tucker, GA - *MicrocomMPl 83, 84; WhoWMicrocom 83*
Construction Digest - Indianapolis, IN - *BaconPubCkMag 84; MagDir 84; WritMar 84*
Construction Dimensions - Washington, DC - *ArtMar 84; MagDir 84*
Construction Equipment [of Reed Holdings Inc.] - Chicago, IL - *MagIndMarPl 82-83*
Construction Equipment [of Cahners Publishing Co.] - Des Plaines, IL - *BaconPubCkMag 84; Folio 83; MagDir 84*
Construction Equipment Distribution [of Associated Equipment Distributors] - Hinsdale, IL - *MagDir 84*
Construction Equipment Distribution - Oak Brook, IL - *BaconPubCkMag 84*
Construction Equipment Guide [of McKeon Publishing Co.] - Glenside, PA - *BaconPubCkMag 84; MagDir 84*
Construction Equipment Operation & Maintenance [of Construction Publications Inc.] - Cedar Rapids, IA - *ArtMar 84; BaconPubCkMag 84; MagDir 84; WritMar 84*
Construction Estimating Co. - Vallejo, CA - *MicrocomMPl 84*
Construction Industry Press - Silver Spring, MD - *BoPubDir 5; EISS 5-84 Sup*
Construction Labor News Inc. - San Jose, CA - *AyerDirPub 83; NewsDir 84*
Construction News - Little Rock, AR - *BaconPubCkMag 84*
Construction News Publishing Co. [of Construction News Inc.] - Little Rock, AR - *MagDir 84*
Construction Productivity Management - Silver Spring, MD - *DirOnDB Spring 84*
Construction Productivity Management [of NewsNet Inc.] - Bryn Mawr, PA - *DataDirOnSer 84*
Construction Publications - Phoenix, AZ - *BoPubDir 4, 5*
Construction Review [of U.S. Government Printing Office] - Washington, DC - *BaconPubCkMag 84; MagDir 84*
Construction Specifier [of Construction Specifications Institute] - Alexandria, VA - *BaconPubCkMag 84; MagDir 84; WritMar 84*
Construction Supervision & Safety Letter - Waterford, CT - *ArtMar 84; WritMar 84*
Construction Systems Software Inc. - San Antonio, TX - *MicrocomMPl 84*
Construction Times - Stillwater, MN - *BaconPubCkMag 84*
Constructioneer [of Reports Corp.] - Chatham, NJ - *ArtMar 84; BaconPubCkMag 84; MagDir 84; MagIndMarPl 82-83*
Constructive Action Newsletter - Syracuse, NY - *LitMag&SmPr 83-84*
Constructive Computing Co. Inc. - Kansas City, KS - *MicrocomMPl 84*
Constructor [of AGC Information Inc.] - Washington, DC - *BaconPubCkMag 84; MagDir 84; WritMar 84*
Consulate General of the Netherlands (Press & Cultural Section) - New York, NY - *Tel&CabFB 84C*
Consultant - Greenwich, CT - *BaconPubCkMag 84; MagDir 84; MagIndMarPl 82-83*
Consultant Systems Inc. - Santa Barbara, CA - *MicrocomMPl 84; MicrocomSwDir 1*
Consultant, The - Mt. Prospect, IL - *MicrocomSwDir 1*
Consultants Bureau [Subs. of Plenum Publishing Corp.] - New York, NY - *MagIndMarPl 82-83*
Consultants for Information Resource Management Inc. - Bloomingdale, IL - *WhoWMicrocom 83*
Consultants in Public Relations SA - Minnetonka, MN - *DirPRFirms 83*
Consultant's Library [Aff. of Bermont Books Inc.] - Washington, DC - *BoPubDir 4, 5; LitMarPl 84*
Consultants News [Div. of Kennedy & Kennedy Inc.] - Fitzwilliam, NH - *BaconPubCkMag 84; BoPubDir 4, 5; LitMarPl 84*
Consultants on Information Access - Ottawa, ON, Canada - *InfIndMarPl 83*
Consultec Canada Ltd. - Vancouver, BC, Canada - *TeleSy&SerDir 2-84*
Consultech Associates Inc. - Wayne, PA - *ADAPSOMemDir 83-84*
Consultext - Rotsterhaule, Netherlands - *EISS 7-83 Sup; InfIndMarPl 83*
Consulting & Technical Services Div. [of Contel Information Systems Inc.] - Great Neck, NY - *TeleSy&SerDir 7-83*
Consulting Engineer [of Technical Publishing] - Barrington, IL - *BaconPubCkMag 84; MagDir 84*
Consulting Psychologists Press Inc. - Palo Alto, CA - *BoPubDir 4, 5*
Consulting Resources for Management - Peoria, IL - *VideoDir 82-83*
Consumer Affairs Group, The - New York, NY - *HBIndAd&MS 82-83*
Consumer Affairs Letter, The - Washington, DC - *BaconPubCkMag 84*
Consumer Associates - Pittsburgh, PA - *LitMag&SmPr 83-84*
Consumer Automotive Press - San Francisco, CA - *BoPubDir 5*
Consumer Behavior Inc. - New York, NY - *IntDirMarRes 83*
Consumer Communications [Aff. of Creative Enterprises International] - Albuquerque, NM - *BoPubDir 4, 5*
Consumer Credit Project Inc. - Barrington, IL - *BoPubDir 4, 5*
Consumer Data & Research Group Inc. - Des Moines, IA - *DirMarMP 83*
Consumer Data-Tell-A-Market - West Palm Beach, FL - *CabTVFinDB 83*
Consumer Demographics Inc. - Atlanta, GA - *EISS 83*
Consumer Dialogue Center, The - Stamford, CT - *IntDirMarRes 83*
Consumer Economic Service Data [of Data Resources Inc.] - Lexington, MA - *DBBus 82*
Consumer Electronics [Subs. of RCA Corp.] - Indianapolis, IN - *Tel&CabFB 84C*
Consumer Electronics [of CES Publishing Corp.] - New York, NY - *BaconPubCkMag 84; MagIndMarPl 82-83; MicrocomMPl 84*
Consumer Electronics Monthly [of International Thompson Business Press] - New York, NY - *MagDir 84*
Consumer Expenditure Survey [of US Bureau of the Census] - Washington, DC - *DataDirOnSer 84*
Consumer Financial Decisions - Menlo Park, CA - *DirOnDB Spring 84*
Consumer Guide - Cornwall, ON, Canada - *AyerDirPub 83*
Consumer Guide/Publications International Ltd. - Skokie, IL - *LitMarPl 83, 84; MagIndMarPl 82-83*
Consumer/Industrial Research Service - Media, PA - *IntDirMarRes 83*
Consumer Information Agency Inc. - Norcross, GA - *StaDirAdAg 2-84*
Consumer Information Network - Ithaca, NY - *BrCabYB 84*
Consumer Information Publications Inc. - Palm Harbor, FL - *BoPubDir 4 Sup, 5*
Consumer Life - Hicksville, NY - *BaconPubCkMag 84; WritMar 84*
Consumer Mail Panels [of Market Facts Inc.] - New York, NY - *IntDirMarRes 83*
Consumer Network Inc. - Union City, GA - *IntDirMarRes 83*
Consumer News - Cortland, NY - *AyerDirPub 83*
Consumer News Inc. - Washington, DC - *BoPubDir 4, 5; Ed&PubIntYB 82*
Consumer Newsweekly - Bethesda, MD - *BaconPubCkMag 84*

Consumer Opinion Forum [of Market Facts Inc.] - New York, NY - *IntDirMarRes 83*
Consumer Opinion Services Inc. - Seattle, WA - *IntDirMarRes 83*
Consumer Press - Great Falls, MT - *AyerDirPub 83*
Consumer Price Index Database [of Evans Economics Inc.] - Washington, DC - *DataDirOnSer 84*
Consumer Price Index/Producer Price Index [of U.S. Dept. of Labor] - Washington, DC - *DBBus 82*
Consumer Price Indexes [of Wharton Econometric Forecasting Associates] - Philadelphia, PA - *DataDirOnSer 84*
Consumer Prospects [of The Futures Group] - Glastonburg, CT - *DataDirOnSer 84*
Consumer Publishing Co. Inc. - Canton, OH - *DirMarMP 83*
Consumer Pulse Inc. - Englewood, CO - *IntDirMarRes 83*
Consumer Pulse Inc. - *See* SRG International Ltd.
Consumer Reports [of Consumers Union] - Mt. Vernon, NY - *BaconPubCkMag 84; Folio 83; MagDir 84; MagIndMarPl 82-83; WritMar 84*
Consumer Reports Books [of Consumers Union] - Mt. Vernon, NY - *LitMarPl 83, 84; WritMar 84*
Consumer Reports Films - Mt. Vernon, NY - *AvMarPl 83*
Consumer Research of Maine - Portlane, ME - *IntDirMarRes 83*
Consumer Response Corp. - New York, NY - *IntDirMarRes 83; ProGuPRSer 4*
Consumer Response Corp. (Qualitative Div.) - New York, NY - *IntDirMarRes 83*
Consumer Spending Forecast [of Chase Econometrics/Interactive Data Corp.] - Waltham, MA - *DataDirOnSer 84*
Consumer Spending Forecast - Bala Cynwyd, PA - *DirOnDB Spring 84*
Consumer Surveys Co. - Arlington Heights, IL - *IntDirMarRes 83*
Consumer Systems Services Group Inc. [Subs. of Consumer Systems Corp.] - Downers Grove, IL - *DataDirOnSer 84*
Consumer's Advisory Press - Greensboro, NC - *LitMag&SmPr 83-84*
Consumers' Association - London, England - *MicroMarPl 82-83*
Consumers Digest - Chicago, IL - *ArtMar 84; BaconPubCkMag 84; MagIndMarPl 82-83; WritMar 84*
Consumers Marketing Research Inc. - Hackensack, NJ - *MagIndMarPl 82-83*
Consumers' Research Inc. - Washington, NJ - *EISS 83*
Consumers' Research Magazine - Washington, NJ - *BaconPubCkMag 84; MagDir 84; MagIndMarPl 82-83; WritMar 84*
Consumers Union News Digest - Mt. Vernon, NY - *MagIndMarPl 82-83*
Consumers Union of United States Inc. - Mt. Vernon, NY - *KnowInd 83*
Consumertronics Co. - Almogordo, NM - *BoPubDir 4, 5*
ConsumerViews [of Burgoyne Inc.] - Cincinnati, OH - *IntDirMarRes 83*
Contact - Mendocino, CA - *LitMag&SmPr 83-84*
Contact - Perham, MN - *AyerDirPub 83*
Contact Lens Forum - White Plains, NY - *MagDir 84*
Contact Press Images Inc./Contact Camp - New York, NY - *MagIndMarPl 82-83*
Contact/II Publications - New York, NY - *BoPubDir 4, 5; LitMag&SmPr 83-84*
Contact! Visual Communications - Evanston, IL - *AvMarPl 83*
Contact Werbeagentur F.R.C. Hoffmann GmbH - Bremen, West Germany - *StaDirAdAg 2-84*
Contacto-The International Contact Lens Journal - Chicago, IL - *BaconPubCkMag 84; MagDir 84*
Contacts - New York, NY - *BaconPubCkMag 84; MagDir 84; MagIndMarPl 82-83*
Contacts - North Chatham, NY - *ArtMar 84; WritMar 84*
Contacts Influential International Inc. - Portland, OR - *DirMarMP 83*
Container News [of Communication Channels Inc.] - Atlanta, GA - *BaconPubCkMag 84; MagDir 84*
Contel Information Systems - Bethesda, MD - *MicrocomMPl 83*
Contel Information Systems (Software & Systems Div.) - Bethesda, MD - *MicrocomMPl 84*
Contel Information Systems Inc. - Great Neck, NY - *DataDirSup 7-83*
ContelNet [of Contel Information Systems Inc.] - Great Neck, NY - *TeleSy&SerDir 7-83*
Contelvision [of Continental Telephone Services Corp.] - Manassas, VA - *EISS 83*
Contemplative Investments Inc. - Clearwater, FL - *ArtMar 84*
Contempo Communications Inc. - New York, NY - *AvMarPl 83; TelAl 83, 84*
Contempo Vibrato Recordings - New York, NY - *BillIntBG 83-84*
Contemporary Administrator - Nashville, TN - *BaconPubCkMag 84*
Contemporary Advertising Agency Inc. - Spokane, WA - *StaDirAdAg 2-84*
Contemporary Arts Press [Aff. of La Mamelle Inc.] - San Francisco, CA - *BoPubDir 4, 5; LitMag&SmPr 83-84; MicroMarPl 82-83*
Contemporary Books - Chicago, IL - *LitMarPl 83, 84; WritMar 84*
Contemporary Christian Magazine [of CCM Publications Inc.] - Laguna Hills, CA - *ArtMar 84; WritMar 84*
Contemporary Christian Music - Laguna Hills, CA - *BaconPubCkMag 84*
Contemporary Communications Corp. - New Rochelle, NY - *Tel&CabFB 84C*
Contemporary Crafts Inc. - Los Angeles, CA - *BoPubDir 4, 5*
Contemporary Creative Services - *See* Blue River Music Inc.
Contemporary Curriculums - Lockport, IL - *LitMag&SmPr 83-84*
Contemporary Dialysis - Encino, CA - *BaconPubCkMag 84*
Contemporary Drama Service - Downers Grove, IL - *WritMar 84*
Contemporary Educational Services Inc. - North Brunswick, NJ - *LitMarPl 83*
Contemporary Educational Services Inc. - Princeton, NJ - *LitMarPl 84*
Contemporary Lithographers Inc. - Raleigh, NC - *LitMarPl 84*
Contemporary Marketing - Bala Cynwyd, PA - *AdAge 3-28-84; StaDirAdAg 2-84*
Contemporary Marketing Research Inc. (Qualitative Div.) - New York, NY - *IntDirMarRes 83*
Contemporary Marxism [of Synthesis Publications] - San Francisco, CA - *LitMag&SmPr 83-84*
Contemporary Media Broadcasting Group - St. Charles, MO - *BrCabYB 84*
Contemporary Music [Div. of BSO Records] - Hollywood, CA - *BillIntBG 83-84*
Contemporary Novels from Cornerstone Press - Lock Haven, PA - *BoPubDir 4 Sup, 5; LitMag&SmPr 83-84*
Contemporary Ob/Gyn - Oradell, NJ - *BaconPubCkMag 84; MagDir 84; MagIndMarPl 82-83*
Contemporary Optometry - Philadelphia, PA - *BaconPubCkMag 84*
Contemporary Orthopaedics - Redondo Beach, CA - *BaconPubCkMag 84*
Contemporary Perspectives Inc. - New York, NY - *BoPubDir 4, 5*
Contemporary Psychology - Washington, DC - *MagIndMarPl 82-83*
Contemporary Psychology: A Journal of Reviews - Austin, TX - *BaconPubCkMag 84; MagDir 84*
Contemporary Recording Studios Inc. - Broomall, PA - *BillIntBG 83-84*
Contemporary Records Inc. - Los Angeles, CA - *BillIntBG 83-84*
Contemporary Sociology - Storrs, CT - *MagIndMarPl 82-83*
Contemporary Studies Inc. - River Forest, IL - *IntDirMarRes 83*
Contemporary Surgery - Redondo Beach, CA - *BaconPubCkMag 84; MagDir 84; MagIndMarPl 82-83*
Contenova - Vancouver, BC, Canada - *WritMar 84*
Contention Music - Nashville, TN - *BillIntBG 83-84*
Contex Systems - Conrad, CA - *MicrocomMPl 83*
Context Inc. - Narbeth, PA - *InfIndMarPl 83*
Context Management Systems - Torrance, CA - *MicrocomMPl 83, 84; MicrocomSwDir 1; WhoWMicrocom 83*
Context Press [Div. of Consciousness Industries Inc.] - Brooklyn, NY - *LitMarPl 83*
Context Publications - San Francisco, CA - *BoPubDir 4, 5; LitMag&SmPr 83-84*
Conti Advertising Agency Inc. - Montvale, NJ - *AdAge 3-28-84; StaDirAdAg 2-84*
Conti Commodity Services Inc. (Research Computer Center) - Memphis, TN - *DataDirOnSer 84*
Conti-Currency [of Computer Sciences Corp.] - El Segundo, CA - *DataDirOnSer 84*

ContiCurrency - Chicago, IL - *InfIndMarPl 83*
Continental [of East-West Network Inc.] - Los Angeles, CA - *ArtMar 84; BaconPubCkMag 84; MagDir 84; WritMar 84*
Continental Adventures - Bloomfield Hills, MI - *MicrocomMPl 83, 84*
Continental Advertising Associates - Bloomington, MN - *StaDirAdAg 2-84*
Continental Aerographics Inc. - Vancouver, BC, Canada - *BoPubDir 4 Sup, 5*
Continental Aikido Association - Jonesboro, AR - *BoPubDir 5*
Continental Association of Funeral & Memorial Societies Inc. - Washington, DC - *BoPubDir 4, 5*
Continental Book Co. [of Le Cercle du Livre de France Inc.] - Long Island City, NY - *LitMarPl 83*
Continental Broadcasting Network Inc. - Virginia Beach, VA - *BrCabYB 84*
Continental Business Computers Inc. - Santa Cruz, CA - *MicrocomMPl 84*
Continental Cable of York County Inc. [of Continental Cablevision Inc.] - Grafton, VA - *Tel&CabFB 84C*
Continental Cablevision - Jacksonville, FL - *Tel&CabFB 84C*
Continental Cablevision - Saco, ME - *BrCabYB 84*
Continental Cablevision - Beverly, MA - *InterCabHB 3; Tel&CabFB 84C*
Continental Cablevision - Boston, MA - *AdAge 6-28-84; BrCabYB 84 p.D-299; CabTVFinDB 83; DirMarMP 83; HomeVid&CabYB 82-83; KnowInd 83; LitMarPl 84; TelAl 84; Tel&CabFB 84C p.1674*
Continental Cablevision - Brockton, MA - *BrCabYB 84; Tel&CabFB 84C*
Continental Cablevision - Deerfield, MA - *BrCabYB 84*
Continental Cablevision - Reading, MA - *Tel&CabFB 84C*
Continental Cablevision - Saugus, MA - *Tel&CabFB 84C*
Continental Cablevision - Dearborn Heights, MI - *Tel&CabFB 84C*
Continental Cablevision - Southfield, MI - *Tel&CabFB 84C*
Continental Cablevision - Boston, MN - *TelAl 83*
Continental Cablevision - Cheviot, OH - *BrCabYB 84*
Continental Cablevision - Fairborn, OH - *Tel&CabFB 84C*
Continental Cablevision - Xenia, OH - *Tel&CabFB 84C*
Continental Cablevision - Grafton, VA - *BrCabYB 84*
Continental Cablevision of Belleville - Belleville, IL - *BrCabYB 84*
Continental Cablevision of Cook County Inc. - Berkeley, IL - *Tel&CabFB 84C*
Continental Cablevision of Cook County Inc. - Calumet City, IL - *Tel&CabFB 84C*
Continental Cablevision of Cook County Inc. - Chicago Suburbs, IL - *BrCabYB 84*
Continental Cablevision of Cook County Inc. - Forest Park, IL - *Tel&CabFB 84C*
Continental Cablevision of Cook County Inc. - Franklin Park, IL - *Tel&CabFB 84C*
Continental Cablevision of Cook County Inc. - River Grove, IL - *Tel&CabFB 84C*
Continental Cablevision of Cook County Inc. - Riverdale, IL - *Tel&CabFB 84C*
Continental Cablevision of Cook County Inc. - Rosemont, IL - *Tel&CabFB 84C*
Continental Cablevision of Cook County Inc. - Schiller Park, IL - *Tel&CabFB 84C*
Continental Cablevision of Cook County Inc. - Westchester, IL - *Tel&CabFB 84C*
Continental Cablevision of Hazel Park - Hazel Park, MI - *BrCabYB 84; Tel&CabFB 84C*
Continental Cablevision of Illinois Inc. - Carthage, IL - *BrCabYB 84; Tel&CabFB 84C*
Continental Cablevision of Illinois Inc. - Freeport, IL - *BrCabYB 84; Tel&CabFB 84C*
Continental Cablevision of Illinois Inc. - Kewanee, IL - *BrCabYB 84; Tel&CabFB 84C*
Continental Cablevision of Illinois Inc. - Lincoln, IL - *BrCabYB 84; Tel&CabFB 84C*
Continental Cablevision of Illinois Inc. - Morton, IL - *BrCabYB 84; Tel&CabFB 84C*
Continental Cablevision of Illinois Inc. - Pekin, IL - *BrCabYB 84; Tel&CabFB 84C*
Continental Cablevision of Illinois Inc. - Quincy, IL - *BrCabYB 84; Tel&CabFB 84C*
Continental Cablevision of Illinois Inc. - Keokuk, IA - *BrCabYB 84; Tel&CabFB 84C*
Continental Cablevision of James City County - James City County, VA - *BrCabYB 84; Tel&CabFB 84C*
Continental Cablevision of Lansing - Lansing, MI - *BrCabYB 84; Tel&CabFB 84C*
Continental Cablevision of Madison Heights - Madison Heights, MI - *BrCabYB 84; Tel&CabFB 84C*
Continental Cablevision of Massachusetts - Beverly, MA - *BrCabYB 84*
Continental Cablevision of Massachusetts - Newton Center, MA - *BrCabYB 84*
Continental Cablevision of Massachusetts - Reading, MA - *BrCabYB 84*
Continental Cablevision of Massachusetts - Saugus, MA - *BrCabYB 84*
Continental Cablevision of Massachusetts - Watertown, MA - *BrCabYB 84; Tel&CabFB 84C*
Continental Cablevision of Miami Valley Inc. - Kettering, OH - *BrCabYB 84*
Continental Cablevision of Michigan Inc. - Holland, MI - *BrCabYB 84; Tel&CabFB 84C*
Continental Cablevision of Michigan Inc. - Jackson, MI - *BrCabYB 84; Tel&CabFB 84C*
Continental Cablevision of Michigan Inc. - Roseville, MI - *Tel&CabFB 84C*
Continental Cablevision of Morton Grove Inc. - Morton Grove, IL - *BrCabYB 84; Tel&CabFB 84C*
Continental Cablevision of New Hampshire - South Berwick, ME - *BrCabYB 84*
Continental Cablevision of New Hampshire - Lawrence, MA - *BrCabYB 84; Tel&CabFB 84C*
Continental Cablevision of New Hampshire - Dover, NH - *BrCabYB 84; Tel&CabFB 84C*
Continental Cablevision of New Hampshire - Portsmouth, NH - *BrCabYB 84; Tel&CabFB 84C*
Continental Cablevision of New Hampshire Inc. - Berwick, ME - *BrCabYB 84*
Continental Cablevision of New Hampshire Inc. - Eliot, ME - *BrCabYB 84*
Continental Cablevision of New Hampshire Inc. - Kittery, ME - *BrCabYB 84*
Continental Cablevision of New Hampshire Inc. - Saco, ME - *Tel&CabFB 84C*
Continental Cablevision of New Hampshire Inc. - North Andover, MA - *BrCabYB 84*
Continental Cablevision of New Hampshire Inc. - Concord, NH - *BrCabYB 84; Tel&CabFB 84C*
Continental Cablevision of New Hampshire Inc. - New Castle, NH - *BrCabYB 84*
Continental Cablevision of New Hampshire Inc. - Pease Air Force Base, NH - *BrCabYB 84*
Continental Cablevision of New Hampshire Inc. - Pembroke, NH - *BrCabYB 84*
Continental Cablevision of New Hampshire Inc. - Rollinsford, NH - *BrCabYB 84*
Continental Cablevision of New Hampshire Inc. - Rye, NH - *BrCabYB 84*
Continental Cablevision of New Hampshire Inc. - Salem, NH - *BrCabYB 84*
Continental Cablevision of Northampton Inc. - Northampton, MA - *BrCabYB 84*
Continental Cablevision of Northeast Ohio - Bay Village, OH - *Tel&CabFB 84C*
Continental Cablevision of Northeast Ohio - Elyria, OH - *BrCabYB 84; Tel&CabFB 84C*
Continental Cablevision of Northeast Ohio - Mentor, OH - *BrCabYB 84*
Continental Cablevision of Ohio Inc. - Athens, OH - *BrCabYB 84; Tel&CabFB 84C*
Continental Cablevision of Ohio Inc. - Bellevue, OH - *BrCabYB 84; Tel&CabFB 84C*
Continental Cablevision of Ohio Inc. - Cheviot, OH - *Tel&CabFB 84C*
Continental Cablevision of Ohio Inc. - Clyde, OH - *BrCabYB 84*

Continental Cablevision of Ohio Inc. - Englewood, OH - *BrCabYB 84; Tel&CabFB 84C*
Continental Cablevision of Ohio Inc. - Fairborn, OH - *BrCabYB 84*
Continental Cablevision of Ohio Inc. - Findlay, OH - *BrCabYB 84; Tel&CabFB 84C*
Continental Cablevision of Ohio Inc. - Fostoria, OH - *BrCabYB 84; Tel&CabFB 84C*
Continental Cablevision of Ohio Inc. - Galion, OH - *BrCabYB 84; Tel&CabFB 84C*
Continental Cablevision of Ohio Inc. - Huber Heights, OH - *BrCabYB 84; Tel&CabFB 84C*
Continental Cablevision of Ohio Inc. - Kettering, OH - *Tel&CabFB 84C*
Continental Cablevision of Ohio Inc. - Mentor, OH - *Tel&CabFB 84C*
Continental Cablevision of Ohio Inc. - Norwalk, OH - *BrCabYB 84; Tel&CabFB 84C*
Continental Cablevision of Ohio Inc. - Springfield, OH - *BrCabYB 84; Tel&CabFB 84C*
Continental Cablevision of Ohio Inc. - The Plains, OH - *BrCabYB 84*
Continental Cablevision of Ohio Inc. - Tiffin, OH - *BrCabYB 84*
Continental Cablevision of Ohio Inc. - Upper Sandusky, OH - *BrCabYB 84; Tel&CabFB 84C*
Continental Cablevision of Ohio Inc. - Willard, OH - *BrCabYB 84; Tel&CabFB 84C*
Continental Cablevision of Ohio Inc. - Xenia, OH - *BrCabYB 84*
Continental Cablevision of Richmond - Richmond, VA - *BrCabYB 84; Tel&CabFB 84C*
Continental Cablevision of Roseville - Roseville, MI - *BrCabYB 84*
Continental Cablevision of Southfield - Southfield, MI - *BrCabYB 84*
Continental Cablevision of Springfield - Springfield, MA - *BrCabYB 84; Tel&CabFB 84C*
Continental Cablevision of St. Louis County - Belleville, IL - *Tel&CabFB 84C*
Continental Cablevision of St. Louis County - Jennings, MO - *BrCabYB 84; Tel&CabFB 84C*
Continental Cablevision of St. Louis County - Overland, MO - *BrCabYB 84; Tel&CabFB 84C*
Continental Cablevision of Virginia Inc. - Henrico County, VA - *BrCabYB 84; Tel&CabFB 84C*
Continental Cablevision of Winchester Inc. - Winchester, MA - *BrCabYB 84*
Continental Camera Systems - Van Nuys, CA - *AvMarPl 83*
Continental Classified Ad Agency Inc. - Houston, TX - *StaDirAdAg 2-84*
Continental Color - Oakland, CA - *AvMarPl 83*
Continental Communications Inc. - Bridgeport, CT - *StaDirAdAg 2-84*
Continental Corp. - Neptune, NJ - *ADAPSOMemDir 83-84*
Continental Data Processing Inc. - Wilkes-Barre, PA - *ADAPSOMemDir 83-84*
Continental Divide Trail Society - Bethesda, MD - *BoPubDir 4, 5*
Continental Editions - Sioux City, IA - *BoPubDir 4, 5*
Continental Extra - Los Angeles, CA - *MagIndMarPl 82-83*
Continental Feature Inc. - New York, NY - *Ed&PubIntYB 82*
Continental Film Productions Corp. - Chattanooga, TN - *AvMarPl 83; ProGuPRSer 4; Tel&CabFB 84C*
Continental Franchise Review - Denver, CO - *BaconPubCkMag 84*
Continental Heritage Press Inc. - Tulsa, OK - *LitMarPl 83, 84*
Continental Horseman - Weatherford, TX - *BaconPubCkMag 84; WritMar 84*
Continental International Pictures - Greenville, OH - *TelAl 83, 84*
Continental Merchandisers Inc. - St. Paul, MN - *WhoWMicrocom 83*
Continental News-Review - Continental, OH - *BaconPubCkNews 84; Ed&PubIntYB 82*
Continental Publications Ltd. - Carlsbad, CA - *BoPubDir 4, 5*
Continental Publishing Co. - New York, NY - *BoPubDir 4, 5*
Continental Radio - Portsmouth, VA - *BrCabYB 84*
Continental Recordings Inc. - Boston, MA - *BillIntBG 83-84*
Continental Resources Inc. (Softsource Div.) - Bedford, MA - *MicrocomMPl 84*
Continental Software - Los Angeles, CA - *MicrocomMPl 83, 84; MicrocomSwDir 1*
Continental Software Inc. - Culver City, CA - *WhoWMicrocom 83*
Continental Telecom Inc. - Atlanta, GA - *Datamation 6-83; TelDir&BG 83-84; VideoDir 82-83*
Continental Telephone Co. [Aff. of Telephone & Data Systems Inc.] - Continental, OH - *TelDir&BG 83-84*
Continental Telephone Co. of Arkansas [Aff. of Continental Telephone Corp.] - Russellville, AR - *TelDir&BG 83-84*
Continental Telephone Co. of California [Aff. of Continental Telecom Inc.] - Victorville, CA - *TelDir&BG 83-84*
Continental Telephone Co. of Illinois [Aff. of Continental Telephone Corp.] - Sycamore, IL - *TelDir&BG 83-84*
Continental Telephone Co. of Indiana [Aff. of Continental Telephone Corp.] - Seymour, IN - *TelDir&BG 83-84*
Continental Telephone Co. of Iowa [Aff. of Continental Telephone Corp.] - Knoxville, IA - *TelDir&BG 83-84*
Continental Telephone Co. of Kansas Inc. [Aff. of Continental Telephone Corp.] - Gardner, KS - *TelDir&BG 83-84*
Continental Telephone Co. of Kentucky [Aff. of Continental Telephone Corp.] - London, KY - *TelDir&BG 83-84*
Continental Telephone Co. of Maine Inc. [Aff. of Continental Telephone Corp.] - Concord, NH - *TelDir&BG 83-84*
Continental Telephone Co. of Michigan [Aff. of Continental Telephone Corp.] - Pinconning, MI - *TelDir&BG 83-84*
Continental Telephone Co. of Minnesota Inc. [Aff. of Continental Telephone Corp.] - Minneapolis, MN - *TelDir&BG 83-84*
Continental Telephone Co. of Missouri [Aff. of Continental Telephone Corp.] - Wentzville, MO - *TelDir&BG 83-84*
Continental Telephone Co. of Nebraska [Aff. of Continental Telephone Corp.] - Wisner, NE - *TelDir&BG 83-84*
Continental Telephone Co. of New Hampshire [Aff. of Continental Telephone Corp.] - Concord, NH - *TelDir&BG 83-84*
Continental Telephone Co. of New Jersey [Aff. of Continental Telecom Inc.] - Johnstown, NY - *TelDir&BG 83-84*
Continental Telephone Co. of North Carolina [Aff. of Continental Telephone Corp.] - Weaverville, NC - *TelDir&BG 83-84*
Continental Telephone Co. of Northwest [Aff. of Contel Service Corp.] - Bellevue, WA - *TelDir&BG 83-84*
Continental Telephone Co. of Pennsylvania [Aff. of Continental Telephone Corp.] - Hershey, PA - *TelDir&BG 83-84*
Continental Telephone Co. of South Carolina [Aff. of Continental Telephone Corp.] - Simpsonville, SC - *TelDir&BG 83-84*
Continental Telephone Co. of Texas [Aff. of Continental Telephone Corp.] - Dallas, TX - *TelDir&BG 83-84*
Continental Telephone Co. of the South [Aff. of Continental Telecom Inc.] - Pell City, AL - *TelDir&BG 83-84*
Continental Telephone Co. of the West [Aff. of Continental Telecom Inc.] - Phoenix, AZ - *TelDir&BG 83-84*
Continental Telephone Co. of Upstate New York Inc. [Aff. of Continental Telephone Corp.] - Johnstown, NY - *TelDir&BG 83-84*
Continental Telephone Co. of Vermont [Aff. of Continental Telephone Corp.] - Springfield, VT - *TelDir&BG 83-84*
Continental Telephone Co. of Virginia [Aff. of Continental Telecom Inc.] - Mechanicsville, VA - *TelDir&BG 83-84*
Continental Telephone Corp. - Atlanta, GA - *HomeVid&CabYB 82-83*
Continental Times - Toronto, ON, Canada - *Ed&PubIntYB 82*
Continental Translation Service Inc. - New York, NY - *MagIndMarPl 82-83*
Continua - Chicago, IL - *DirOnDB Spring 84*
Continuing Education for the Family Physician - New York, NY - *MagDir 84; MagIndMarPl 82-83*
Continuing Education Systems Inc. - Hinsdale, IL - *BoPubDir 4, 5*
Continuing Legal Education Society of British Columbia - Vancouver, BC, Canada - *BoPubDir 4, 5*
Continuing Library Education Network & Exchange Inc. - Washington, DC - *EISS 83*
Continuing Objectives Inc. - Beckley, WV - *Tel&CabFB 84C p.1675*
Continuing Saga Press - San Francisco, CA - *BoPubDir 4, 5; LitMag&SmPr 83-84*
Continuous Plankton Recorder Survey [of Natural Environment Research Council] - Plymouth, England - *EISS 83*

Continuum Co. Inc., The - Austin, TX - *ADAPSOMemDir 83-84; DataDirOnSer 84; DataDirSup 7-83*
Continuum Publishing Corp., The - New York, NY - *LitMarPl 83, 84; WritMar 84*
Contitronix - Garland, TX - *DirInfWP 82*
Contol Data Corp. - Minneapolis, MN - *ElecNews 7-25-83*
Contra Costa County Rural American [of Oakland Neighborhood Journal] - Oakland, CA - *NewsDir 84*
Contra Costa Independent [of Ingersoll Publications] - Richmond, CA - *Ed&PubIntYB 82; NewsDir 84*
Contra Costa Independent Berkeley Gazette - Richmond, CA - *AyerDirPub 83*
Contra Costa Sun - Lafayette, CA - *AyerDirPub 83; Ed&PubIntYB 82*
Contra Costa Times - Walnut Creek, CA - *AyerDirPub 83; BaconPubCkNews 84; Ed&PubIntYB 82*
Contraband Magazine - Portland, ME - *LitMag&SmPr 83-84*
Contraband Press - Portland, ME - *BoPubDir 4, 5; LitMag&SmPr 83-84*
Contraceptive Technology Update - Atlanta, GA - *BaconPubCkMag 84*
Contract [of Gralla Publications] - New York, NY - *ArtMar 84; BaconPubCkMag 84; MagDir 84; MagIndMarPl 82-83*
Contract Bridge Bulletin, The - Memphis, TN - *MagIndMarPl 82-83*
Contract Carrier Conference [Aff. of American Trucking Associations Inc.] - Washington, DC - *BoPubDir 5*
Contract Interiors - New York, NY - *MagDir 84*
Contract Services Associates - Anaheim, CA - *MicrocomMPl 83, 84; MicrocomSwDir 1; WhoWMicrocom 83*
Contracting Business [of Penton/IPC] - Cleveland, OH - *BaconPubCkMag 84; MagDir 84*
Contracting in the Carolinas [of Virginia Publisher's Wing] - Darlington, SC - *MagDir 84*
Contractor - Barrington, IL - *BaconPubCkMag 84*
Contractor Business Report - New York, NY - *BaconPubCkMag 84*
Contractor Engineer - Phoenix, AZ - *BaconPubCkMag 84*
Contractor Magazine [of Morgan Grampian Publishing Co.] - Pittsfield, MA - *MagDir 84; WritMar 84*
Contractor Management Systems - Reston, VA - *MicrocomMPl 83, 84*
Contractors Guide - Skokie, IL - *BaconPubCkMag 84*
Contrast - Toronto, ON, Canada - *Ed&PubIntYB 82*
Contributors Bulletin [of Freelance Press Services] - Salford, England - *LitMag&SmPr 83-84*
Control-C Software Inc. - Portland, OR - *MicrocomMPl 83, 84; MicrocomSwDir 1*
Control Concepts Corp. - Binghamton, NY - *WhoWMicrocom 83*
Control Concepts Corp. [Subs. of Presearch Inc.] - Manassas, VA - *WhoWMicrocom 83*
Control Craft Inc. - Muskego, WI - *MicrocomMPl 84*
Control Data Corp. - Bloomington, MN - *Datamation 6-83*
Control Data Corp. - Minneapolis, MN - *ADAPSOMemDir 83-84; AvMarPl 83; CompReadDB 82; DataDirOnSer 84; DataDirSup 7-83; DirInfWP 82; InfIndMarPl 83; Top100Al 83; WhoWMicrocom 83*
Control Data Corp. (Business Information Services) - Greenwich, CT - *DataDirOnSer 84; InfIndMarPl 83; WhoWMicrocom 83*
Control Data Corp. (Network Information Services) - Greenwich, CT - *DataDirSup 7-83*
Control Engineering [of Technical Publishing] - Barrington, IL - *BaconPubCkMag 84; Folio 83; MagDir 84; MagIndMarPl 82-83; WritMar 84*
Control Systems - Minneapolis, MN - *MicrocomMPl 84*
Control Transaction Corp. - Fairfield, NJ - *DataDirSup 7-83*
Controlled Fusion Atomic Data Center [of U.S. Dept. of Energy] - Oak Ridge, TN - *EISS 83*
Controlled-Release Database [of Technology Catalysts Inc.] - Arlington, VA - *DataDirOnSer 84*
Contronics - Hudson, NH - *MicrocomMPl 84*
Convenience Store Merchandiser [of Associated Business Publications Inc.] - New York, NY - *BaconPubCkMag 84; MagDir 84*
Convenience Store News [of BMT Publications Inc.] - New York, NY - *BaconPubCkMag 84; MagDir 84; NewsBur 6; WritMar 84*
Convention & Incentive Travel Sales Leads [of Brentwood Publishing Corp.] - Los Angeles, CA - *MagDir 84*
Convention Services: Reporting/Coordinating - Austin, TX - *BoPubDir 4, 5*
Convergence Corp. - Irvine, CA - *AvMarPl 83*
Convergent Technologies - Santa Clara, CA - *DataDirSup 7-83; Datamation 6-83; Top100Al 83; WhoWMicrocom 83*
Conversa-Phone Institute Inc. - Ronkonkoma, NY - *BillIntBG 83-84*
Conversational Voice Terminal Corp. - Gurnee, IL - *DataDirSup 7-83*
Conversion Specialists Inc. [Subs. of Bill King Editorial Services] - New York, NY - *AvMarPl 83*
Converting Magazine - Chicago, IL - *BaconPubCkMag 84*
Convex Industries - Boulder, CO - *BoPubDir 4, 5*
Conway Associates International - New York, NY - *LitMarPl 83, 84; MagIndMarPl 82-83*
Conway Associates, Joseph P. - Upper Brookville, NY - *DirPRFirms 83*
Conway Corp. - Conway, AR - *BrCabYB 84; Tel&CabFB 84C*
Conway County Petit Jean Country Headlight - Morrilton, AR - *AyerDirPub 83; Ed&PubIntYB 82; NewsDir 84*
Conway Field & Herald - Conway, SC - *BaconPubCkNews 84; NewsDir 84*
Conway Log Cabin Democrat - Conway, AR - *NewsDir 84*
Conway/Milliken Corp. - Chicago, IL - *IntDirMarRes 83*
Conway Publications Inc. - Atlanta, GA - *BoPubDir 4, 5*
Conway Springs Star & Argonia Argosy - Conway Springs, KS - *BaconPubCkNews 84; Ed&PubIntYB 82*
Conwed Corp. (Office Interiors Div.) - St. Paul, MN - *DirInfWP 82*
Conyers-Rockdale Cablevision - Conyers, GA - *BrCabYB 84*
Conypol Music Inc. - Willow Grove, PA - *BillIntBG 83-84*
Cooga Mooga Inc. - Los Angeles, CA - *Tel&CabFB 84C*
Cook Advertising Co. - *See* COADCO
Cook Advertising Inc., William - Jacksonville, FL - *AdAge 3-28-84; StaDirAdAg 2-84*
Cook Associates Inc., Elmer P. - Bala Cynwyd, PA - *StaDirAdAg 2-84*
Cook Book Publishers Inc. - Lenexa, KS - *DirMarMP 83*
Cook Cablevision Service - Cyclone, WV - *BrCabYB 84*
Cook, Chester L. - Slidell, LA - *BoPubDir 4, 5*
Cook Communications Services Inc. - Newport Beach, CA - *DirPRFirms 83*
Cook County News-Herald - Grand Marais, MN - *AyerDirPub 83; Ed&PubIntYB 82*
Cook Laboratories Inc. - Norwalk, CT - *BillIntBG 83-84*
Cook Literary Agency Inc., Molly Malone - Provincetown, MA - *LitMarPl 83, 84*
Cook News-Herald - Cook, MN - *BaconPubCkNews 84; Ed&PubIntYB 82*
Cook Public Relations Inc., William [Subs. of William Cook Advertising Inc.] - Jacksonville, FL - *DirPRFirms 83*
Cook Publications, Ray - Poughkeepsie, NY - *BoPubDir 5*
Cook Publishing Co., David C. [of Chariot Books] - Elgin, IL - *ArtMar 84; WritMar 84*
Cook Publishing Co., David C. (Adult General Div.) - Elgin, IL - *WritMar 84*
Cook Publishing Co., David C. (Book Div.) - Elgin, IL - *ArtMar 84; LitMarPl 83, 84*
Cook/Ruef & Associates Inc. - Columbia, SC - *StaDirAdAg 2-84*
Cook/Uniphoto, James - Denver, CO - *AvMarPl 83*
Cookbook Digest [of RPC Publications Corp.] - New York, NY - *LitMarPl 83, 84; MagIndMarPl 82-83*
Cookbooks, USA - Bend, OR - *ArtMar 84*
Cooke Inc., Donald - New York, NY - *TelAl 83, 84*
Cooke Inc., Ralph Kent - Los Angeles, CA - *AdAge 3-28-84; StaDirAdAg 2-84*
Cooke Marketing Research - New York, NY - *IntDirMarRes 83*
Cookery Book Club, The - Port Washington, NY - *LitMarPl 83, 84*
Cookeville Herald-Citizen - Cookeville, TN - *NewsDir 84*
Cookhouse Recording Studios - Minneapolis, MN - *BillIntBG 83-84*

Cookie Press - Des Moines, IA - *BoPubDir 4, 5; LitMag&SmPr 83-84*
Cookin' Records - Harwich Point, MA - *BillIntBG 83-84*
Cooking & Crafts Club - *See* Book-of-the-Month Club Inc.
Cooking for Profit - Fond Du Lac, WI - *BaconPubCkMag 84; MagDir 84; MagIndMarPl 82-83*
Cooks Magazine - Westport, CT - *BaconPubCkMag 84*
Cooley & Shillinglaw Inc. - Houston, TX - *StaDirAdAg 2-84*
Cooley Associates Inc. - Langhorne, PA - *CabTVFinDB 83*
Coolidge & Associates - Austin, TX - *MicrocomMPl 83*
Coolidge Cable TV Co. - Coolidge, TX - *BrCabYB 84; Tel&CabFB 84C*
Coolidge Cablevision Inc. [of Masada Corp.] - Florence, AZ - *Tel&CabFB 84C*
Coolidge Co. Inc., The - New York, NY - *LitMarPl 83, 84*
Coolidge Co., The - *See* Howard Co. Inc., E. T.
Coolidge Examiner - Coolidge, AZ - *AyerDirPub 83; Ed&PubIntYB 82*
Coolidge Examiner - *See* Casa Grande Valley Newspapers Inc.
Coon Creek Telephone Co. - Blairstown, IA - *TelDir&BG 83-84*
Coon Rapids Enterprise - Coon Rapids, IA - *BaconPubCkNews 84; Ed&PubIntYB 82*
Coon Rapids Herald - Coon Rapids, MN - *AyerDirPub 83; Ed&PubIntYB 82*
Coon Rapids Herald [of Anoka County Union & Shopper Inc.] - Minneapolis, MN - *NewsDir 84*
Coon Rapids Herald - *See* Anoka County Union & Shopper Inc.
Coon Rapids Municipal Cable TV System - Coon Rapids, IA - *BrCabYB 84; Tel&CabFB 84C*
Coon Valley Cooperative Telephone Association - Menlo, IA - *TelDir&BG 83-84*
Coon Valley Farmers Telephone Co. Inc. - Coon Valley, WI - *TelDir&BG 83-84*
Coonhound Bloodlines - Kalamazoo, MI - *MagDir 84*
Coons, Corker & Associates Inc. - Spokane, WA - *StaDirAdAg 2-84*
Cooper & Associates, Roger - Auburn, CA - *BrCabYB 84; CabTVFinDB 83; Tel&CabFB 84C*
Cooper & Co. Inc., Cathy - Atlanta, GA - *DirInfWP 82*
Cooper & Cooper - Northfield, IL - *DirMarMP 83*
Cooper, Arthur R. - Tunnelton, WV - *BrCabYB 84*
Cooper Associates Agency Inc., Bill - New York, NY - *LitMarPl 83, 84*
Cooper Associates Inc. - Marlton, NJ - *CabTVFinDB 83*
Cooper, Burch & Howe Inc. - Las Vegas, NV - *StaDirAdAg 2-84*
Cooper-Cameron Inc. - Clifton, NJ - *StaDirAdAg 2-84*
Cooper Clinic, H. K. - Lancaster, PA - *BoPubDir 4, 5*
Cooper Communications Inc. - Encino, CA - *DirPRFirms 83*
Cooper Copy Co. Inc. - East Orange, NJ - *DirInfWP 82*
Cooper County Record - Boonville, MO - *AyerDirPub 83; Ed&PubIntYB 82*
Cooper Data Systems Inc. - New Orleans, LA - *ADAPSOMemDir 83-84; DataDirOnSer 84*
Cooper Leder Inc. - New York, NY - *StaDirAdAg 2-84*
Cooper, Lee - Malibu, CA - *BoPubDir 5*
Cooper Music, Martin - Beverly Hills, CA - *BillIntBG 83-84*
Cooper Productions Inc., William L. - New York, NY - *Tel&CabFB 84C*
Cooper Review - Cooper, TX - *BaconPubCkNews 84; Ed&PubIntYB 82*
Cooper Services - Hastings-on-Hudson, NY - *IntDirMarRes 83*
Cooper Square Advertising Agency [Div. of The Hartz Mountain Corp.] - Harrison, NJ - *StaDirAdAg 2-84*
Cooper, Tony - Steamboat Springs, CO - *Tel&CabFB 84C p.1675*
Cooper VideoCommunications - South Orange, NJ - *AvMarPl 83*
Cooperating Libraries in Consortium - St. Paul, MN - *EISS 83*
Cooperative Builder - Minneapolis, MN - *MagDir 84*
Cooperative College Library Center - Atlanta, GA - *EISS 7-83 Sup*
Cooperative Directory Association - Albuquerque, NM - *BoPubDir 4, 5*
Cooperative Documents Network Project [of University of Guelph] - Guelph, ON, Canada - *CompReadDB 82; EISS 83*
Cooperative Extension Service Telephone Network [of University of Illinois at Champaign-Urbana] - Urbana, IL - *TeleSy&SerDir 7-83*
Cooperative Farmer - Richmond, VA - *BaconPubCkMag 84; MagDir 84; MagIndMarPl 82-83*
Cooperative Information Center for Hospital Management Studies [of University of Michigan] - Ann Arbor, MI - *EISS 83*
Cooperative Information Network - Stanford, CA - *EISS 83*
Cooperative Library Agency for Systems & Services - San Jose, CA - *DataDirOnSer 84; MicrocomMPl 84*
Cooperative Telephone Co. - Victor, IA - *TelDir&BG 83-84*
Cooperative Telephone Exchange - Stanhope, IA - *TelDir&BG 83-84*
Cooperative World - Minneapolis, MN - *BaconPubCkMag 84*
Cooperativo Antigruppo Siciliano [of Sicilian Antigruppo/Cross-Cultural Communications] - Villa Scanimac, Italy - *LitMag&SmPr 83-84*
Coopers & Lybrand (Office Information Systems Group) - Washington, DC - *DirInfWP 82*
Coopersburg Telephone Co. - Coopersburg, PA - *TelDir&BG 83-84*
Coopersmith Literary Agency, Julia - New York, NY - *LitMarPl 83, 84*
Cooperstown Freeman's Journal - Cooperstown, NY - *NewsDir 84*
Cooperstown Griggs County Sentinel-Courier - Cooperstown, ND - *BaconPubCkNews 84*
Cooperstown NewChannels - Cooperstown, NY - *BrCabYB 84*
Cooperstown Sentinel-Courier - Cooperstown, ND - *Ed&PubIntYB 82*
Coordinated Management Systems Inc. - *See* Nielsen Co., A. C.
Coordinated Occupational Information Network [of Bell & Howell Co.] - Maumee, OH - *EISS 83*
Coordinating Information for Texas Educators [of Texas State Education Agency] - Austin, TX - *EISS 83*
Coordination & Information Center [of U.S. Dept. of Energy] - Las Vegas, NV - *EISS 83*
Coordinierte Management Systeme - Frankfurt, West Germany - *InfIndMarPl 83*
Coos Bay Reporter - Coos Bay, OR - *BaconPubCkNews 84*
Coos Bay World [of Southwestern Oregon Publishing Co.] - Coos Bay, OR - *BaconPubCkNews 84; NewsDir 84*
Coos County Democrat - Lancaster, NH - *AyerDirPub 83; Ed&PubIntYB 82; NewsDir 84*
Coosa Cable Co. - Pell City, AL - *BrCabYB 84; Tel&CabFB 84C*
Coosol Inc./Computer Baron - Costa Mesa, CA - *MicrocomMPl 84*
Copan Music - *See* Amiron Music
Cope Associates - Washington, DC - *DirMarMP 83*
Cope Associates - Bethesda, MD - *StaDirAdAg 2-84*
Copeland Co. Inc., The Hal - Dallas, TX - *DirPRFirms 83; LitMarPl 84; StaDirAdAg 2-84*
Copiah County Courier - Hazlehurst, MS - *AyerDirPub 83; Ed&PubIntYB 82; NewsDir 84*
Copley & Associates - Washington, DC - *BoPubDir 4*
Copley Books [Aff. of The Copley Press Inc.] - La Jolla, CA - *BoPubDir 4, 5; LitMag&SmPr 83-84; WritMar 84*
Copley Colony Harbor Cablevision [of Colony Communications Inc.] - San Pedro, CA - *BrCabYB 84*
Copley Communications - Boston, MA - *DirMarMP 83*
Copley News Service [Div. of Copley Press Inc.] - San Diego, CA - *BaconPubCkNews 84; Ed&PubIntYB 82; LitMarPl 84*
Copley Newspaper Group - Schaumburg, IL - *BaconPubCkNews 84*
Copley Newspapers - La Jolla, CA - *AdAge 6-28-84; Ed&PubIntYB 82; KnowInd 83*
Copley Press Inc. - Santa Monica, CA - *BaconPubCkNews 84*
Copley Press Inc., The - San Pedro, CA - *Tel&CabFB 84C p.1675*
Copley Record Newspapers - Schaumburg, IL - *Ed&PubIntYB 82*
Copp Clark Pitman [Subs. of Copp Clark Ltd.] - Toronto, ON, Canada - *LitMarPl 83, 84*
Coppage, A. Maxim - Concord, CA - *BoPubDir 5*
Coppell Cablevision Inc. - Coppell, TX - *BrCabYB 84; Tel&CabFB 84C*
Copper & Brass Forecast - Bala Cynwyd, PA - *DirOnDB Spring 84*
Copper Basin Cablevision Inc. - Kearny, AZ - *Tel&CabFB 84C*

Copper Basin News - Hayden, AZ - *Ed&PubIntYB 82*
Copper Basin News - Kearny, AZ - *AyerDirPub 83*
Copper Beech Press - Providence, RI - *LitMag&SmPr 83-84*
Copper Belt Cablevision Inc. - Kearny, AZ - *BrCabYB 84*
Copper Belt Cablevision Inc. - Winkleman, AZ - *BrCabYB 84*
Copper Belt Cablevision Inc. - *See* Monroe, James E.
Copper Canyon Press - Port Townsend, WA - *BoPubDir 4, 5; LitMag&SmPr 83-84*
Copper Data Center [of Battelle Columbus Laboratories] - Columbus, OH - *DataDirOnSer 84; DirOnDB Spring 84; EISS 83*
Copper Development Association Inc. - New York, NY - *BoPubDir 5*
Copper Development Association Products Handbook [of Battelle Columbus Laboratories] - Columbus, OH - *DataDirOnSer 84*
Copper Era, The [of New Horizon Publishing Co.] - Clifton, AZ - *Ed&PubIntYB 82; NewsDir 84*
Copper Mountain Metropolitan District - Copper Mountain, CO - *BrCabYB 84; Tel&CabFB 84C*
Copper News - Bagdad, AZ - *AyerDirPub 83; Ed&PubIntYB 82*
Copper Orchid Publishing Co. - Jackson, MI - *BoPubDir 5*
Copper Valley Telephone Cooperative Inc. - Valdez, AK - *TelDir&BG 83-84*
Copperas Cove Leader Press [of Taylor Communications Inc.] - Copperas Cove, TX - *AyerDirPub 83; BaconPubCkNews 84; Ed&PubIntYB 82; NewsDir 84*
Copperhill Citizen-Advance - Copperhill, TN - *BaconPubCkNews 84*
Copple House Books - Ossining, NY - *LitMarPl 83*
Copple House Books Inc. - Lakemont, GA - *BoPubDir 4, 5*
Coppola Creative Concepts - San Francisco, CA - *StaDirAdAg 2-84*
Copula - Spokane, WA - *LitMag&SmPr 83-84*
Copy/Chicago - Des Plaines, IL - *BaconPubCkMag 84*
Copy Clearing House - New York, NY - *MagIndMarPl 82-83*
Copy Craft Corp. - Thousand Oaks, CA - *DirInfWP 82*
Copy-Plus Corp. - Milwaukee, WI - *DirInfWP 82*
Copy Pool, The - New York, NY - *HBIndAd&MS 82-83*
Copy Shoppe, The - New York, NY - *HBIndAd&MS 82-83; LitMarPl 83, 84*
Copy-Write Artograph Co. - Brooklyn, NY - *BoPubDir 4, 5*
Copyer Co. Ltd. - Los Angeles, CA - *DirInfWP 82*
Copyright Clearance Center Inc. - Salem, MA - *EISS 83*
Copyright Office Publication & Interactive Cataloging System [of U.S. Library of Congress] - Washington, DC - *EISS 83*
Copyright Service Bureau Ltd. - New York, NY - *BillIntBG 83-84*
Copywriters Council of America [Div. of DMMA Inc.] - Middle Island, NY - *LitMarPl 83, 84*
Coquille Valley Sentinel - Coquille, OR - *AyerDirPub 83; BaconPubCkNews 84; Ed&PubIntYB 82*
Coquitlam Herald - Port Coquitlam, BC, Canada - *AyerDirPub 83; Ed&PubIntYB 82*
Coquitlam/Maple Ridge Today - Coquitlam/Maple Ridge, BC, Canada - *Ed&PubIntYB 82*
Cor-Rell Communications Co. - St. Louis, MO - *AvMarPl 83*
Coraco - Los Angeles, CA - *BoPubDir 4 Sup, 5*
Coral Gables News [of South Miami Community Newspapers] - Miami, FL - *AyerDirPub 83; NewsDir 84*
Coral Gables News - *See* Community Newspapers of Florida Inc.
Coral Gables Printing Service Inc. - Coral Gables, FL - *MagIndMarPl 82-83*
Coral Gables Printing Service Inc. - Miami, FL - *MagIndMarPl 82-83*
Coral Gables Sun Reporter - Coral Gables, FL - *Ed&PubIntYB 82*
Coral Gables Sun Reporter - Miami Beach, FL - *AyerDirPub 83*
Coral Springs Courier - Coral Springs, FL - *Ed&PubIntYB 82*
Coral Springs Courier - Ft. Lauderdale, FL - *AyerDirPub 83*
Coral Springs Forum - Coral Springs, FL - *AyerDirPub 83; BaconPubCkNews 84*
Coralie - Brussels, Belgium - *DirOnDB Spring 84*
Coralville Courier - Coralville, IA - *BaconPubCkNews 84; Ed&PubIntYB 82*
Coralville Courier - Iowa City, IA - *NewsDir 84*
Coraopolis Record - *See* Gateway Press Inc.
Corbell-Hart Video Communications Inc. - Carterville, IL - *Tel&CabFB 84C p.1675*
Corbett Advertising - Rochester, MI - *AdAge 3-28-84*
Corbett Advertising Inc. - Columbus, OH - *ArtMar 84; StaDirAdAg 2-84*
Corbett, B. - Bonita Springs, FL - *BoPubDir 4, 5*
Corbett Inc., Frank J. [Div. of BBDO Health & Medical Communications Inc.] - Chicago, IL - *AdAge 3-28-84; ArtMar 84; StaDirAdAg 2-84*
Corbett, Mildred - Burns, OR - *Tel&CabFB 84C p.1675*
Corbin Publishings - Red Oak, IA - *BoPubDir 4, 5*
Corbin Times-Tribune - Corbin, KY - *BaconPubCkNews 84; NewsDir 84*
Corbus, William - *See* Contemporary Communications Corp.
Corcoran Gallery of Art - Washington, DC - *BoPubDir 4, 5*
Corcoran Journal - Corcoran, CA - *BaconPubCkNews 84; Ed&PubIntYB 82*
Corcoran, Lawrence - Sturgeon Bay, WI - *BoPubDir 4, 5*
CORD - New York, NY - *BoPubDir 4 Sup, 5*
Cord Guns Guide - New York, NY - *MagDir 84*
Cord Hunting - New York, NY - *MagDir 84*
Cord Records - Shreveport, LA - *BillIntBG 83-84*
Cordatum - Bethesda, MD - *EISS 83; InfIndMarPl 83; InfoS 83-84; LitMarPl 83, 84; MagIndMarPl 82-83*
Cordele Dispatch [of Thomson Newspapers Publishing Co. Inc.] - Cordele, GA - *BaconPubCkNews 84; Ed&PubIntYB 82; NewsDir 84*
Cordell Beacon - Cordell, OK - *BaconPubCkNews 84; Ed&PubIntYB 82; NewsDir 84*
Cordell TV Cable System [of Dorate Inc.] - Cordell, OK - *BrCabYB 84; Tel&CabFB 84C*
Cordial Music - *See* Channel Music
Cordova Cablevision [of Alaska Cablevision Inc.] - Cordova, AK - *BrCabYB 84; Tel&CabFB 84C*
Cordova Publishing Co. - *See* Alshire Publishing Cos.
Cordova Telephone Cooperative Inc. - Cordova, AK - *TelDir&BG 83-84*
Cordova Times - Cordova, AK - *AyerDirPub 83; BaconPubCkNews 84; Ed&PubIntYB 82*
Cordovan Corp. - Houston, TX - *BoPubDir 4, 5; MagIndMarPl 82-83*
Cordovan Press [Div. of Cordovan Corp.] - Houston, TX - *WritMar 84*
Cordura Publications Inc. [Subs. of Cordura Corp.] - San Diego, CA - *DataDirOnSer 84; DirMarMP 83; InfoS 83-84*
Core Collection Books Inc. [Aff. of Granger Book Co. Inc.] - Great Neck, NY - *LitMarPl 83, 84*
CORE Publications [Aff. of Congress of Racial Equality] - New York, NY - *BoPubDir 4, 5*
Core Publishing - Kingston, ON, Canada - *BoPubDir 4 Sup, 5*
Corelli-Jacobs Film Music Inc. - New York, NY - *Tel&CabFB 84C*
Corey Products Inc. - New York, NY - *DirInfWP 82*
Corinth Books Inc. - Chevy Chase, MD - *LitMag&SmPr 83-84*
Corinth Daily Corinthian - Corinth, MS - *BaconPubCkNews 84; NewsDir 84*
Corinth House Publishers - Anaheim, CA - *BoPubDir 4, 5*
Corinthian - Corinth, MS - *AyerDirPub 83*
Corinthian Broadcasting [Subs. of Dun & Bradstreet Corp.] - New York, NY - *TelAl 83, 84; Tel&CabFB 84S*
Corinthian Broadcasting - *See* Pembroke Cable
Corinthian Cable Corp. - Hampton, VA - *Tel&CabFB 84C p.1675*
Corinthian Communications Inc. - New York, NY - *StaDirAdAg 2-84*
Corinthian Press, The [Subs. of EDR Corp.] - Shaker Heights, OH - *LitMarPl 83, 84; WritMar 84*
Corita Communications - Los Angeles, CA - *BoPubDir 4, 5*
Corley Printing Co. - St. Louis, MO - *LitMarPl 83, 84*
CORLS Interlibrary Loan & Communication System - Richmond Hill, ON, Canada - *TeleSy&SerDir 2-84*
Corn Belt Telephone Co. - Wall Lake, IA - *TelDir&BG 83-84*
Corn Husker Cablevision [of Tele-Communications Inc.] - Offutt Air Force Base, NE - *Tel&CabFB 84C*
Corn Refiners Association Inc. - Washington, DC - *BoPubDir 5*
Corn Washita County Enterprise - Corn, OK - *BaconPubCkNews 84*
Cornbelt Press Inc. - Fairbury, IL - *BaconPubCkNews 84*

Cornelia Northeast Georgian - Cornelia, GA - *BaconPubCkNews 84; NewsDir 84*
Cornelius Music, Stan - Nashville, TN - *BillIntBG 83-84*
Cornell & Lake Holcombe Courier - Cornell, WI - *AyerDirPub 83; BaconPubCkNews 84; Ed&PubIntYB 82*
Cornell Communications Co. - Lansdowne, PA - *AvMarPl 83*
Cornell Computer Services [of Cornell University] - Ithaca, NY - *DataDirOnSer 84; EISS 83*
Cornell Daily Sun - Ithaca, NY - *NewsDir 84*
Cornell Engineer - Ithaca, NY - *BaconPubCkMag 84*
Cornell Engineer, The - Jacksonville, NY - *MagDir 84*
Cornell Maritime Press Inc. - Centreville, MD - *LitMarPl 83, 84; WritMar 84*
Cornell University (Audio-Visual Resource Center) - Ithaca, NY - *AvMarPl 83*
Cornell University (China-Japan Program) - Ithaca, NY - *BoPubDir 4, 5*
Cornell University (Cornell Modern Indonesia Project) - Ithaca, NY - *BoPubDir 4, 5*
Cornell University (Dept. of Manuscripts) - Ithaca, NY - *MicroMarPl 82-83*
Cornell University (Laboratory of Ornithology) - Ithaca, NY - *AvMarPl 83*
Cornell University (New York State School of Industrial & Labor Relations) - Ithaca, NY - *BoPubDir 4*
Cornell University (School of Hotel Administration) - Ithaca, NY - *BoPubDir 4, 5*
Cornell University (Southeast Asia Program) - Ithaca, NY - *BoPubDir 4, 5*
Cornell University Press - Ithaca, NY - *LitMarPl 83, 84*
Cornell Veterinarian - Jacksonville, NY - *MagDir 84*
Cornell Widow Inc. [Aff. of Cornell Alumni News] - Ithaca, NY - *BoPubDir 4 Sup, 5*
Corner & Gilbert D. Moyle, Sherwood L. - Rapid City, SD - *Tel&CabFB 84S*
Cornerstone - Chicago, IL - *LitMag&SmPr 83-84*
Cornerstone Associates Inc. - Waltham, MA - *AvMarPl 83*
Cornerstone Color [Div. of Conerstone Associates Inc.] - Waltham, MA - *AvMarPl 83*
Cornerstone Library Inc. [Div. of Simon & Schuster] - New York, NY - *LitMarPl 83, 84*
Cornerstone Press - St. Louis, MO - *BoPubDir 4, 5; LitMag&SmPr 83-84*
Cornerstone Press Image Magazine - St. Louis, MO - *ArtMar 84*
Cornerstone Software - San Jose, CA - *MicrocomMPl 83*
Cornfield Literary Agency, Robert - New York, NY - *LitMarPl 83, 84*
Cornfield Review - Marion, OH - *LitMag&SmPr 83-84*
Cornhusker Country - Council Bluffs, IA - *ArtMar 84*
Corning Adams County Free Press - Corning, IA - *BaconPubCkNews 84*
Corning Cable TV Co. Inc. - Corning, AR - *BrCabYB 84*
Corning Clay County Courier - Corning, AR - *BaconPubCkNews 84*
Corning Daily Observer - Corning, CA - *Ed&PubIntYB 82; NewsDir 84*
Corning Free Press - Corning, IA - *Ed&PubIntYB 82*
Corning Leader - Corning, NY - *BaconPubCkNews 84; NewsDir 84*
Corning Museum of Glass - Corning, NY - *BoPubDir 4, 5; MicroMarPl 82-83*
Corning NewChannels [of NewChannels Corp.] - Corning, NY - *BrCabYB 84; Tel&CabFB 84C*
Corning Observer - Corning, CA - *BaconPubCkNews 84*
Corning TV Cable Inc. - Corning, AR - *Tel&CabFB 84C*
Cornish & Brown-Cross Advertising - Philadelphia, PA - *StaDirAdAg 2-84*
Cornsoft Group, The - Indianapolis, IN - *MicrocomMPl 83, 84*
Cornucopia Publications [Aff. of The Living Love Church of Kentucky] - St. Mary, KY - *BoPubDir 4*
Cornucopia Software - Berkeley, CA - *MicrocomMPl 83, 84; MicrocomSwDir 1; WhoWMicrocom 83*
Cornwall Books [Aff. of Consolidated Publishing Corp.] - Cranbury, NJ - *BoPubDir 5*
Cornwall Books [Aff. of Consolidated Publishing Corp.] - East Brunswick, NJ - *BoPubDir 4*
Cornwall CableVision Inc. [of Rogers Cablesystems Inc.] - Cornwall, ON, Canada - *BrCabYB 84*
Cornwall Computer Systems Inc. - Deerfield Beach, FL - *MicrocomMPl 84*
Cornwall Computer Systems Inc. - East Brunswick, NJ - *MicrocomMPl 83*
Cornwall Local - Cornwall, NY - *AyerDirPub 83; BaconPubCkNews 84; Ed&PubIntYB 82*
Cornwall News - Cornwall, ON, Canada - *AyerDirPub 83*
Cornwall Standard-Freeholder - Cornwall, ON, Canada - *LitMarPl 83*
Cornwall Weekly News - Cornwall, ON, Canada - *Ed&PubIntYB 82*
Cornwell Associates, Robert - Paramus, NJ - *LitMarPl 84; MagIndMarPl 82-83*
Corodale Inc. - Boston, MA - *DataDirSup 7-83*
Corona - Bozeman, MT - *LitMag&SmPr 83-84*
Corona Daily Independent - Corona, CA - *BaconPubCkNews 84; Ed&PubIntYB 82; NewsDir 84*
Corona Data Systems - Chatsworth, CA - *MicrocomMPl 83*
Corona Data Systems - Westlake Village, CA - *WhoWMicrocom 83*
Corona-Norco Independent [of Mendouno Publishing Co.] - Corona, CA - *LitMarPl 84*
Corona Publishing Co. - San Antonio, TX - *BoPubDir 4, 5*
Corona Telephone Co. - Corona, NM - *TelDir&BG 83-84*
Coronado Journal - Coronado, CA - *BaconPubCkNews 84; Ed&PubIntYB 82; NewsDir 84*
Coronado Pennysaver - Mission Viejo, CA - *AyerDirPub 83*
Coronado Press Inc. - Lawrence, KS - *BoPubDir 4, 5; LitMarPl 84*
Coronado Publishers Inc. [Subs. of Academic Press Inc.] - San Diego, CA - *LitMarPl 83*
Coronado Record Co. - Oakland, CA - *BillIntBG 83-84*
Coronado Studios - Miami, FL - *AvMarPl 83; WritMar 84*
Coronet [Div. of Esquire Inc.] - Chicago, IL - *AvMarPl 83*
Coronet Films - Chicago, IL - *WritMar 84*
Coronet Industries Inc. [Subs. of RCA Corp.] - Dalton, GA - *Tel&CabFB 84C*
Coronet Instructional Media - Chicago, IL - *ProGuPRSer 4*
COROS - Tucson, AZ - *BoPubDir 4, 5*
Corp - Eggenstein-Leopoldshafen, West Germany - *DirOnDB Spring 84*
Corporate Accounting - Boston, MA - *BaconPubCkMag 84*
Corporate Acquisitions & Dispositions [of NewsNet Inc.] - Bryn Mawr, PA - *DataDirOnSer 84*
Corporate Acquistions & Dispositions of Businesses - Washington, DC - *DirOnDB Spring 84*
Corporate Advertising Agency - Lehigh, FL - *StaDirAdAg 2-84*
Corporate Affiliation [of Computer Intelligence Corp.] - La Jolla, CA - *DataDirOnSer 84*
Corporate Asset Development Inc. - Chappaqua, NY - *ADAPSOMemDir 83-84*
Corporate Business Systems Ltd. - Cheltenham, England - *MicrocomSwDir 1*
Corporate Communications - Detroit, MI - *AvMarPl 83*
Corporate Communications Associates - Glen Ellyn, IL - *DirPRFirms 83*
Corporate Communications Consultants Inc. - New York, NY - *TeleSy&SerDir 2-84*
Corporate Communications Inc. - Englewood, CO - *DirPRFirms 83; StaDirAdAg 2-84*
Corporate Communications Inc. - Seattle, WA - *DirPRFirms 83*
Corporate Communications Report - New York, NY - *BaconPubCkMag 84*
Corporate Consulting Co. - Belmont, MA - *WhoWMicrocom 83*
Corporate Data Exchange Inc. - New York, NY - *BoPubDir 4, 5; EISS 83*
Corporate Data Strategies Inc. - Moorestown, NJ - *ADAPSOMemDir 83-84*
Corporate Design - New York, NY - *BaconPubCkMag 84*
Corporate Earnings Estimator Data Base [of Zacks Investment Research Inc.] - Chicago, IL - *DirOnDB Spring 84; EISS 7-83 Sup*
Corporate Earnings Estimator Data Base [of Dow Jones News/Retrieval Service] - Princeton, NJ - *DataDirOnSer 84*

Corporate Financing Week - New York, NY - *BaconPubCkMag 84*
Corporate Fitness & Recreation - Los Angeles, CA - *ArtMar 84; BaconPubCkMag 84*
Corporate Intelligence Inc. - St. Paul, MN - *CompReadDB 82; DataDirOnSer 84; IntDirMarRes 83*
Corporate Management & Marketing Consultants - Morris Plains, NJ - *ADAPSOMemDir 83-84*
Corporate Management Inc. - Seattle, WA - *ADAPSOMemDir 83-84; DataDirOnSer 84*
Corporate Management Systems - Denver, CO - *EISS 83*
Corporate Media Communications Inc. - Atlanta, GA - *AvMarPl 83*
Corporate Meetings & Incentives - New York, NY - *BaconPubCkMag 84*
Corporate Monthly - Philadelphia, PA - *BaconPubCkMag 84; WritMar 84*
Corporate Public Issues - Stamford, CT - *BaconPubCkMag 84*
Corporate Report-Kansas City - Kansas City, MO - *BaconPubCkMag 84*
Corporate Report-Minnesota [of Dorn Communications Inc.] - Minneapolis, MN - *BaconPubCkMag 84; MagDir 84*
Corporate Security - New York, NY - *BaconPubCkMag 84*
Corporate Services Inc. - Mesa, AZ - *DataDirOnSer 84*
Corporate Shareholder [of NewsNet Inc.] - Bryn Mawr, PA - *DataDirOnSer 84*
Corporate Shareholder Press - New York, NY - *EISS 5-84 Sup*
Corporate Shareholder, The - New York, NY - *DirOnDB Spring 84*
Corporate Technical Library [of Upjohn Co.] - Kalamazoo, MI - *EISS 83*
Corporate Time Sharing Services Inc. - New York, NY - *DataDirOnSer 84; EISS 83*
Corporate Video Services - New York, NY - *AvMarPl 83*
Corporatewatch - New York, NY - *DirOnDB Spring 84*
Corporation for Enterprise Development - Washington, DC - *BoPubDir 4 Sup, 5*
Corporation for Entertainment & Learning Inc., The - New York, NY - *AvMarPl 83; TelAl 84*
Corporation for Public Broadcasting - Washington, DC - *BoPubDir 5; BrCabYB 84; InterCabHB 3*
Corporation House Ltd. - Ottawa, ON, Canada - *DirPRFirms 83*
Corporation Records, Daily News - New York, NY - *Ed&PubIntYB 82*
Corps of Engineers Guide Specifications [of Bowne Information Systems Inc.] - New York, NY - *DataDirOnSer 84*
Corpus Books - Don Mills, ON, Canada - *BoPubDir 4 Sup, 5*
Corpus Christi Caller [of Harte-Hanks Communications Co.] - Corpus Christi, TX - *BaconPubCkNews 84; Ed&PubIntYB 82; LitMarPl 84; NewsDir 84*
Corpus Christi Caller-Times - Corpus Christi, TX - *Ed&PubIntYB 82; LitMarPl 84*
Corpus Christi Magazine - Corpus Christi, TX - *BaconPubCkMag 84*
Corpus Christi Times - Corpus Christi, TX - *BaconPubCkNews 84; Ed&PubIntYB 82; LitMarPl 84*
Corpus Information Services [Div. of Southam Communications Ltd.] - Don Mills, ON, Canada - *LitMarPl 83, 84*
Corradine & Associates, Tom J. - Hollywood, CA - *TelAl 83, 84; Tel&CabFB 84C*
Corrections Magazine - New York, NY - *BaconPubCkMag 84; MagDir 84; MagIndMarPl 82-83*
Corrections Today - College Park, MD - *BaconPubCkMag 84; MagDir 84*
Correctionville News - Correctionville, IA - *BaconPubCkNews 84; Ed&PubIntYB 82*
Correio Portugues - Toronto, ON, Canada - *Ed&PubIntYB 82*
Correlan Publications - Watsonville, CA - *BoPubDir 4, 5*
Correspondent [of Aid Association for Lutherans] - Appleton, WI - *WritMar 84*
Corriere Canadese - Toronto, ON, Canada - *AyerDirPub 83; Ed&PubIntYB 82*
Corriere del Berkshire - Pittsfield, MA - *Ed&PubIntYB 82*
Corriere Illustrato - Toronto, ON, Canada - *Ed&PubIntYB 82*
Corriere Italiano - Montreal, PQ, Canada - *Ed&PubIntYB 82*
Corrigan Times - Corrigan, TX - *Ed&PubIntYB 82*
Corrigan Times - *See* Polk County Publishing
Corrosion - New York, NY - *DirOnDB Spring 84*
Corrosion - Houston, TX - *BaconPubCkMag 84*
Corrosion Control - Oakville, ON, Canada - *BaconPubCkMag 84*
Corry Journal - Corry, PA - *BaconPubCkNews 84; Ed&PubIntYB 82; NewsDir 84*
Corsica Globe - Corsica, SD - *BaconPubCkNews 84; Ed&PubIntYB 82*
Corsicana Cable TV - Corsicana, TX - *BrCabYB 84; Tel&CabFB 84C*
Corsicana Sun [of Harte-Hanks Communications Co.] - Corsicana, TX - *BaconPubCkNews 84; Ed&PubIntYB 82; NewsDir 84*
Corsicana Weekly Light - Corsicana, TX - *Ed&PubIntYB 82*
Corson County News - McIntosh, SD - *Ed&PubIntYB 82*
Cortani/Brown/Rigoli - Mountain View, CA - *StaDirAdAg 2-84*
Corte Madera Twin Cities Times - Corte Madera, CA - *BaconPubCkNews 84; NewsDir 84*
Cortex Systems Ltd. - Montreal, PQ, Canada - *WhoWMicrocom 83*
Cortez Cable [of CATV Investors] - Cortez, CO - *Tel&CabFB 84C*
Cortez Montezuma Valley Journal - Cortez, CO - *Ed&PubIntYB 82; NewsDir 84*
Cortez Montezuma Valley Journal - *See* Cortez Newspapers Inc.
Cortez Newspapers Inc. - Cortez, CO - *BaconPubCkNews 84*
Cortez Sentinel - Cortez, CO - *NewsDir 84*
Cortez Sentinel - *See* Cortez Newspapers Inc.
Cortina Co. Inc., R. D. - Westport, CT - *WritMar 84*
Cortina Learning International Inc. - Westport, CT - *ArtMar 84; LitMarPl 83, 84*
Cortland County Farm & Home News - Syracuse, NY - *MagDir 84*
Cortland Data Systems - Chicago, IL - *MicrocomMPl 84*
Cortland Democrat - Cortland, NY - *BaconPubCkNews 84; Ed&PubIntYB 82; NewsDir 84*
Cortland Home News - Cortland, OH - *Ed&PubIntYB 82*
Cortland Home News [of Niles Phoenix Publications Inc.] - Niles, OH - *AyerDirPub 83; NewsDir 84*
Cortland Home News - *See* Phoenix Publications Inc.
Cortland Standard - Cortland, NY - *BaconPubCkNews 84; Ed&PubIntYB 82; NewsDir 84*
Corvallis Gazette-Times [of Lee Enterprises Inc.] - Corvallis, OR - *BaconPubCkNews 84; Ed&PubIntYB 82; NewsDir 84*
Corvallis Software Inc. - Corvallis, OR - *BoPubDir 5*
Corvallis TV Cable Co. [of Liberty Communications Inc.] - Albany, OR - *BrCabYB 84*
Corvallis TV Cable Co. [of Liberty Communications Inc.] - Corvallis, OR - *BrCabYB 84*
Corvallis TV Cable Co. [of Liberty Communications Inc.] - Philomath, OR - *BrCabYB 84*
Corvette Fever [of Prospect Publishing Co. Inc.] - Ft. Washington, MD - *ArtMar 84; BaconPubCkMag 84; WritMar 84*
Corvette News - Warren, MI - *WritMar 84*
Corvus Information Center [of Corvus International Co.] - Severna Park, MD - *EISS 83*
Corvus Systems Inc. - San Diego, CA - *DirInfWP 82*
Corvus Systems Inc. - San Jose, CA - *DataDirSup 7-83; MicrocomMPl 84; WhoWMicrocom 83*
Corwen Associates - New York, NY - *LitMarPl 83, 84; MagIndMarPl 82-83*
Corwith Herald - Corwith, IA - *BaconPubCkNews 84; Ed&PubIntYB 82*
Cory Sound Co. - San Francisco, CA - *AvMarPl 83; WritMar 84*
Corycian Press - Iowa City, IA - *BoPubDir 4, 5*
Corydon Cablevision Inc. [of Heritage Communications Inc.] - Corydon, IA - *Tel&CabFB 84C*
Corydon Clarion - Corydon, IN - *BaconPubCkNews 84*
Corydon Democrat - Corydon, IN - *BaconPubCkNews 84; Ed&PubIntYB 82; NewsDir 84*
Corydon Harrison County Press - *See* Charleston Courier
Corydon Times-Republican - Corydon, IA - *BaconPubCkNews 84; Ed&PubIntYB 82; NewsDir 84*
Coryell Publishing Co. - *See* Mayflower Music Corp.
COS Information Inc. - Montreal, PQ, Canada - *DirInfWP 82*
Cosar Corp. - Garland, TX - *AvMarPl 83*

Cosay, Werner & Associates Inc. - Beverly Hills, CA - *LitMarPl 83*
Coshocton Tribune - Coshocton, OH - *BaconPubCkNews 84; Ed&PubIntYB 82; NewsDir 84*
Coslett Publishing Co. - Williamsport, PA - *BoPubDir 4, 5*
Cosmep Newsletter - San Francisco, CA - *LitMag&SmPr 83-84*
Cosmep Prison Project Newsletter, The - Greenfield Center, NY - *LitMag&SmPr 83-84*
Cosmetic Insiders Report - New York, NY - *BaconPubCkMag 84*
Cosmetic Technology - Inglewood, CA - *MagIndMarPl 82-83*
Cosmetic, Toiletry, & Fragrance Association - Washington, DC - *BoPubDir 5*
Cosmetic World - New York, NY - *BaconPubCkMag 84*
Cosmetics - Don Mills, ON, Canada - *BaconPubCkMag 84*
Cosmetics & Toiletries [of Allured Publishing Corp.] - Wheaton, IL - *BaconPubCkMag 84; MagDir 84*
Cosmic Circus Productions - Richmond, CA - *LitMag&SmPr 83-84*
Cosmic Communication Co. - Decorah, IA - *BoPubDir 4, 5*
Cosmopolitan [of Hearst Corp.] - New York, NY - *ArtMar 84; BaconPubCkMag 84; Folio 83; LitMarPl 83, 84; MagDir 84; MagIndMarPl 82-83; WritMar 84*
Cosmopolitan Contact [of Pantheon Press] - Fontana, CA - *LitMag&SmPr 83-84; WritMar 84*
Cosmopolitan Electronics Corp. - Ann Arbor, MI - *MicrocomMPl 84*
Cosmopolitan Electronics Corp. - Canton, MI - *MicrocomMPl 83*
Cosmopolitan's Beauty Guide - New York, NY - *BaconPubCkMag 84*
Cosmopolitan's Super Diets & Exercise Guide - New York, NY - *BaconPubCkMag 84*
Cosmopolite Herald - Girard, PA - *AyerDirPub 83; Ed&PubIntYB 82*
Cosmopolite Herald [of Brown-Thompson Newspapers] - Union City, PA - *NewsDir 84*
Cosmopulos, Crowley & Daly - Boston, MA - *AdAge 3-28-84; ArtMar 84; StaDirAdAg 2-84*
Cosmos - New York, NY - *MagIndMarPl 82-83*
Cosmos Broadcasting - Greenville, SC - *BrCabYB 84; Tel&CabFB 84S*
Cosmos Communications - Pleasantville, IA - *Tel&CabFB 84C p.1675*
Cosmos Communications - New York, NY - *DataDirOnSer 84*
Cosmos Computers - Sacramento, CA - *MicrocomMPl 83*
Cosmos Inc. - Morton, WA - *MicrocomSwDir 1*
Cosmos Store [Aff. of Carl Sagan Productions Inc.] - Montrose, CA - *BoPubDir 4, 5*
Cosmos Sun, The - Cosmos, MN - *Ed&PubIntYB 82*
Cosmotic Concerns - Granada Hills, CA - *LitMag&SmPr 83-84*
Cosmotic Concerns [Aff. of Jacef Relations] - Hollywood, CA - *BoPubDir 5*
Cosray Research Institute - Salt Lake City, UT - *BoPubDir 4 Sup, 5*
Cossette Productions, Pierre - Los Angeles, CA - *Tel&CabFB 84C*
Cossou, Charlene - *See* Jerico Cable TV Inc.
Cossou, Jerry L. - *See* Jerico Cable TV Inc.
Cossu, Franco - South Pasadena, CA - *MagIndMarPl 82-83*
Cost & Management - Hamilton, ON, Canada - *BaconPubCkMag 84*
Cost Engineering - Morgantown, WV - *BaconPubCkMag 84; MagDir 84*
Cost Forecasting Data Banks - Washington, DC - *DirOnDB Spring 84*
Cost Forecasting Data Banks [of Data Resources Inc.] - Lexington, MA - *DataDirOnSer 84; DBBus 82*
Cost Information Systems Div. [of McGraw-Hill Information Systems Co.] - New York, NY - *EISS 83*
Cost Programs [of Marshall & Swift Publication Co.] - Los Angeles, CA - *DBBus 82*
Cost-Saving Data Systems Inc. - Davenport, IA - *ADAPSOMemDir 83-84*
Cost Systems Engineers Inc. - Ft. Worth, TX - *BoPubDir 5; DataDirOnSer 84; InfIndMarPl 83*
Costa Mesa - Anaheim, CA - *DirInfWP 82*
Costa Mesa News - Costa Mesa, CA - *AyerDirPub 83*
Costa Mesa News - *See* Coast Media News Group
Costello & Co., Don - Chicago, IL - *AdAge 3-28-84; BrCabYB 84; HBIndAd&MS 82-83; StaDirAdAg 2-84*
Costello, Brennand & Associates - Ft. Myers, FL - *StaDirAdAg 2-84*
Costich & McConnell Inc. - Hauppauge, NY - *StaDirAdAg 2-84*
Costilla County Free Press - San Luis, CO - *Ed&PubIntYB 82*
Cotati Rohnent Park-Cotati Clarion - Cotati, CA - *BaconPubCkNews 84*
Cote, Leo Paul - *See* Tele Cable Enrg.
Coteau Books/Caragana Records - Moose Jaw, SK, Canada - *BoPubDir 4, 5*
Cotec - Saratoga, CA - *MicrocomMPl 84*
Cotillion Music Inc. - New York, NY - *BillIntBG 83-84*
Cottage Books [Aff. of Sam Yette Enterprises] - Silver Spring, MD - *BoPubDir 4 Sup, 5*
Cottage Grove Sentinel [of Capital Cities Communications Inc.] - Cottage Grove, OR - *BaconPubCkNews 84; Ed&PubIntYB 82; NewsDir 84*
Cottage Industries - Cobalt, CT - *BoPubDir 4, 5*
Cottagers' Security & Service Ltd. - Minden, ON, Canada - *BrCabYB 84*
Cotter-Gassville TV Cable Co. [of Pinion Corp.] - Cotter, AR - *BrCabYB 84*
Cotter Media Group, The - San Jose, CA - *CabTVFinDB 83*
Cottman/Mazza Public Relations - Los Angeles, CA - *LitMarPl 84*
Cotton Blossom Music - Bismarck, ND - *BillIntBG 83-84*
Cotton Country Communications Inc. [of Commco Cable] - Hollandale, MS - *BrCabYB 84*
Cotton Digest International - Houston, TX - *BaconPubCkMag 84; MagDir 84*
Cotton Farming - Memphis, TN - *BaconPubCkMag 84; MagDir 84*
Cotton Gin & Oil Mill Press - Dallas, TX - *MagDir 84*
Cotton Gin & Oil Mill Press - Mesquite, TX - *BaconPubCkMag 84*
Cotton Grower - Memphis, TN - *BaconPubCkMag 84; MagDir 84*
Cotton Hill Cablevision Co. - Campbell, MO - *BrCabYB 84*
Cotton Hill Cablevision Inc. - Malden, MO - *BrCabYB 84; Tel&CabFB 84C p.1675*
Cotton International - Willoughby, OH - *MagDir 84*
Cotton International - Memphis, TN - *MagDir 84*
Cotton Lane Press - Augusta, GA - *BoPubDir 4, 5; LitMag&SmPr 83-84*
Cotton Plant Democrat - McCrory, AR - *Ed&PubIntYB 82*
Cottontail Publications - Indianapolis, IN - *LitMag&SmPr 83-84*
Cottontail Publications - Trafalgar, IN - *BoPubDir 4 Sup, 5*
Cottonwood - Lawrence, KS - *LitMag&SmPr 83-84*
Cottonwood Chronicle - Cottonwood, ID - *BaconPubCkNews 84; Ed&PubIntYB 82*
Cottonwood County Citizen - Windom, MN - *AyerDirPub 83; Ed&PubIntYB 82*
Cottonwood County Historical Society - Windom, MN - *BoPubDir 4, 5*
Cottonwood Current - Cottonwood, MN - *Ed&PubIntYB 82*
Cottonwood News - Cottonwood, MN - *BaconPubCkNews 84*
Cottonwood Press - Lawrence, KS - *LitMag&SmPr 83-84*
Cottonwood Verde Independent [of Western Newspaper Inc.] - Cottonwood, AZ - *BaconPubCkNews 84; NewsDir 84*
Cottonwood Verde Valley View - Cottonwood, AZ - *BaconPubCkNews 84*
Cotulla Cable TV Inc. - Cotulla, TX - *BrCabYB 84*
Cotulla Record - Cotulla, TX - *Ed&PubIntYB 82*
Cotulla Record - *See* Frio-Nueces Publications Ltd.
Couch & Co., R. L. - Irvine, CA - *StaDirAdAg 2-84*
Couch Cable TV Service - Brownsfork, KY - *Tel&CabFB 84C*
Coudersport Potter Enterprise - Coudersport, PA - *BaconPubCkNews 84*
Coudersport TV Cable Co. - Coudersport, PA - *BrCabYB 84; Tel&CabFB 84C*
Couer d'Alene Press - Couer d'Alene, ID - *NewsDir 84*
Cougar Books - Sacramento, CA - *LitMag&SmPr 83-84; LitMarPl 83, 84; WritMar 84*
Cougar Mountain Software Inc. - Boise, ID - *MicrocomMPl 84*
Cougar Record Co. - Bakersfield, CA - *BillIntBG 83-84*
Coughlin/Adler Associates Inc. - Miami, FL - *MagIndMarPl 82-83*

Coughlin, Michael E. - St. Paul, MN - *BoPubDir 4, 5; LitMag&SmPr 83-84*
Coulee Cable TV - Elmer City, WA - *BrCabYB 84*
Coulee Cable TV [of Tele-Communications Inc.] - Grand Coulee, WA - *BrCabYB 84; Tel&CabFB 84C*
Coulee Cable TV [of Tele-Communications Inc.] - Nespelem, WA - *Tel&CabFB 84C*
Coulee City News-Standard - Coulee City, WA - *BaconPubCkNews 84*
Council Adams County Leader - Council, ID - *BaconPubCkNews 84*
Council Bluffs Daily Nonpareil [of Thomson Newspapers Ltd.] - Council Bluffs, IA - *NewsDir 84*
Council Bluffs Farmer Labor Press - Council Bluffs, IA - *NewsDir 84*
Council Bluffs Nonpareil - Council Bluffs, IA - *BaconPubCkNews 84; LitMarPl 83*
Council for Advancement & Support of Education - Washington, DC - *BoPubDir 4 Sup, 5*
Council for Career Planning Inc. - New York, NY - *BoPubDir 4, 5*
Council for Exceptional Children - Reston, VA - *CompReadDB 82; DataDirOnSer 84; InfIndMarPl 83; MicroMarPl 82-83*
Council for Indian Education - Billings, MT - *LitMag&SmPr 83-84*
Council for Social & Economic Studies - Washington, DC - *BoPubDir 4, 5*
Council for Yukon Indians - Whitehorse, YT, Canada - *BoPubDir 4, 5*
Council Grove Republican - Council Grove, KS - *BaconPubCkNews 84; NewsDir 84*
Council Grove Telephone Co. - Council Grove, KS - *TelDir&BG 83-84*
Council of American Survey Research Organizations - *See* CASRO
Council of Biology Editors Inc. - Bethesda, MD - *BoPubDir 4, 5*
Council of Fleet Specialists - Shawnee Mission, KS - *BoPubDir 5*
Council of National Library & Information Associations - Haverford, PA - *EISS 83*
Council of New Mexico Academic Libraries - Roswell, NM - *EISS 83*
Council of Ontario Universities - Toronto, ON, Canada - *BoPubDir 4 Sup, 5*
Council of Planning Librarians - Chicago, IL - *LitMarPl 84*
Council of Professional Associations on Federal Statistics - Washington, DC - *EISS 5-84 Sup*
Council of State Governments - Lexington, KY - *BoPubDir 4, 5*
Council of Wisconsin Librarians - Madison, WI - *EISS 83*
Council on Economic Priorities - New York, NY - *BoPubDir 4, 5*
Council on Foreign Relations - New York, NY - *BoPubDir 4, 5*
Council on Homosexuality & Religion Inc. - Winnipeg, MB, Canada - *BoPubDir 4, 5*
Council on Interracial Books for Children - New York, NY - *LitMag&SmPr 83-84*
Council on Library Resources - Washington, DC - *EISS 83*
Council on Municipal Performance - New York, NY - *BoPubDir 4, 5*
Council on Postsecondary Accreditation [Aff. of National Center for Higher Education] - Washington, DC - *BoPubDir 4, 5*
Council on Religion & International Affairs - New York, NY - *BoPubDir 4, 5*
Council on Research in Bibliography Inc. - Flushing, NY - *BoPubDir 4, 5*
Council on Social Work Education - New York, NY - *BoPubDir 4 Sup, 5*
Council on the Study of Religion - Waterloo, ON, Canada - *BoPubDir 5*
Council Rock Music - *See* Creative Music Group
Counsel House Research [Div. of The Frederic C. Decker Co. Inc.] - Brookfield Center, CT - *MagIndMarPl 82-83*
Counseling & Consulting Services Publications - San Jose, CA - *BoPubDir 5*
Counselor, The [of Advertising Specialty Institute] - Langhorne, PA - *BaconPubCkMag 84; MagDir 84; WritMar 84*
Counselor's Information Service - Washington, DC - *MagDir 84*
Count Dracula Fan Club Newsletter-Journal, The [of Dracula Press] - New York, NY - *LitMag&SmPr 83-84*
Counter-Propaganda Press, The - Park Forest, IL - *LitMag&SmPr 83-84*
Counter Spy - Washington, DC - *MagIndMarPl 82-83*
Counterforce [of Dolly Varden Publications] - Rio Rancho, NM - *LitMag&SmPr 83-84*
Counterman - Akron, OH - *BaconPubCkMag 84*
Counterpart Music - Cincinnati, OH - *BillIntBG 83-84*
Counterpoint Software Inc. - Minneapolis, MN - *MicrocomMPl 84*
Counterpop Music Group - Atlanta, GA - *BillIntBG 83-84*
Counterpop Music Publishing - *See* Counterpop Music Group
Counterport Co. - Jamaica, NY - *DirInfWP 82*
Counterspy - Washington, DC - *LitMag&SmPr 83-84*
Counting House Publishing Co. - Thiensville, WI - *BoPubDir 4, 5*
Country - Maryville, MO - *AyerDirPub 83*
Country Almanac - Redwood City, CA - *NewsDir 84*
Country Almanac - Woodside, CA - *AyerDirPub 83; Ed&PubIntYB 82*
Country Almanac - New York, NY - *BaconPubCkMag 84*
Country Bazaar Publishing & Distributing [Aff. of Honey Inc.] - Berryville, AR - *BoPubDir 4, 5*
Country Boy Publishing - *See* Glolite Publishing Co.
Country Cable - San Diego, CA - *BrCabYB 84*
Country Cable Co. - Corning, OH - *BrCabYB 84; Tel&CabFB 84C*
Country Cable Inc. - San Diego Country Estates, CA - *Tel&CabFB 84C*
Country Cable Inc. - Thayer, KS - *Tel&CabFB 84C p.1675*
Country Cable Systems - Palo Cedro, CA - *Tel&CabFB 84C*
Country Cable TV Inc. - Elgin, TX - *BrCabYB 84*
Country Chronicle - Denmark, WI - *BaconPubCkMag 84*
Country Chronicle, The - Green Bay, WI - *MagDir 84*
Country Classics Music Publishing Co. - Oklahoma City, OK - *BillIntBG 83-84*
Country Club Golfer - Irvine, CA - *MagIndMarPl 82-83*
Country Courier, The - Conklin, NY - *Ed&PubIntYB 82*
Country Dance & Song Society of America - New York, NY - *BoPubDir 4, 5*
Country Decorating Ideas - New York, NY - *BaconPubCkMag 84*
Country Estate - Terra Cotta, ON, Canada - *WritMar 84*
Country Estate - Toronto, ON, Canada - *BaconPubCkMag 84*
Country Evaluation Indicator System [of Chase Econometrics/ Interactive Data Corp.] - Waltham, MA - *DataDirOnSer 84*
Country Evaluation Indicator System - *See* GLOBE
Country Evaluation System [of I. P. Sharp Associates Ltd.] - Toronto, ON, Canada - *DataDirOnSer 84*
Country Folks West - Palatine Bridge, NY - *BaconPubCkMag 84*
Country Garden Press - Duluth, MN - *BoPubDir 4 Sup, 5*
Country Gentleman - Indianapolis, IN - *LitMarPl 83; MagDir 84; MagIndMarPl 82-83*
Country Guide - Winnipeg, MB, Canada - *BaconPubCkMag 84*
Country in the City Records - Romulus, MI - *BillIntBG 83-84*
Country International Records - Nashville, TN - *BillIntBG 83-84*
Country Journal - Springfield, IL - *MagDir 84*
Country Leader - *See* Marple Publishing Co. Inc.
Country Life in British Columbia - White Rock, BC, Canada - *BaconPubCkMag 84*
Country Living [of The Hearst Corp.] - New York, NY - *BaconPubCkMag 84; Folio 83; MagIndMarPl 82-83*
Country Living Magazine - Columbus, OH - *MagDir 84*
Country Magazine [of Country Sun Inc.] - Alexandria, VA - *BaconPubCkMag 84; WritMar 84*
Country Moon Publishing Inc. - *See* Crescent Music Group
Country Music - New York, NY - *MagDir 84; MagIndMarPl 82-83*
Country Music Foundation Press - Nashville, TN - *BoPubDir 4, 5*
Country Music TV - Englewood, CO - *Tel&CabFB 84C*
Country Outlook - Oshkosh, WI - *AyerDirPub 83*
Country People - Greendale, WI - *BaconPubCkMag 84*
Country Post, The - Batavia, NY - *Ed&PubIntYB 82*
Country Press - New York, NY - *BoPubDir 4, 5; LitMag&SmPr 83-84*
Country Press - Scottsville, NY - *BoPubDir 4, 5*
Country Press - Brownfield, TX - *AyerDirPub 83; Ed&PubIntYB 82*
Country Press Inc., The - Middleborough, MA - *LitMarPl 83, 84*

Country Reporting System - Toronto, ON, Canada - *DirOnDB Spring 84*
Country Road Music Inc. - Los Angeles, CA - *BillIntBG 83-84*
Country Road Press - Santa Ana, CA - *BoPubDir 4, 5*
Country Showcase America Records - Beltsville, MD - *BillIntBG 83-84*
Country Side [of P. A. Benjamin & Co.] - Northampton, MA - *WritMar 84*
Country-Side - Roughlee, England - *LitMag&SmPr 83-84*
Country Song Roundup - Derby, CT - *BaconPubCkMag 84; MagDir 84; MagIndMarPl 82-83*
Country Star Music - Franklin, PA - *BillIntBG 83-84*
Country Stream Music & Record Co. - St. Louis, MO - *BillIntBG 83-84*
Country Today, The - Eau Claire, WI - *AyerDirPub 83*
Country Women - Albion, CA - *BoPubDir 4, 5*
Countryman-Klang Inc. - Minneapolis, MN - *Tel&CabFB 84C*
Countryman Press Inc., The - Chicago, IL - *LitMarPl 84*
Countryman Press Inc., The - Woodstock, VT - *LitMarPl 83*
Countryman, The - Burford, England - *LitMag&SmPr 83-84*
Countryside - Apple Valley/Lakeville, MN - *Ed&PubIntYB 82*
Countryside - Burnsville, MN - *AyerDirPub 83*
Countryside - Waterloo, WI - *MagDir 84; MagIndMarPl 82-83*
Countryside Books - Milwaukee, WI - *LitMarPl 83, 84*
Countryside Data Inc. - Idaho Falls, ID - *MicrocomMPl 83, 84*
Countryside/Dunedin Bargain Bill - Largo, FL - *AyerDirPub 83*
Countryside Herald [of The Tarpon Springs Herald Newspapers] - Tarpon Springs, FL - *NewsDir 84*
Countryside Publications Ltd. - Waterloo, WI - *DirMarMP 83*
Countryside Reminder News [of Barrington Press Inc.] - Barrington, IL - *AyerDirPub 83; NewsDir 84*
Countryside Reminder News - Buffalo Grove, IL - *Ed&PubIntYB 82*
Countryside Sun - La Grange, IL - *AyerDirPub 83*
Countryside Sun [of Overland Park Sun Newspapers] - Shawnee Mission, KS - *NewsDir 84*
Countrystyle - Franklin Park, IL - *MagDir 84*
Countrywide Tape & Record Distributors Inc. - Jericho, NY - *BillIntBG 83-84*
County Advertiser, The - Gaithersburg, MD - *Ed&PubIntYB 82*
County Agriculture [of Chase Econometrics/Interactive Data Corp.] - Waltham, MA - *DataDirOnSer 84*
County Agriculture - Bala Cynwyd, PA - *DirOnDB Spring 84*
County Argus, The [of The Northville Sliger Home Newspapers] - Northville, MI - *NewsDir 84*
County Booster, The - St. Paris, OH - *AyerDirPub 83*
County Building Permits [of Chase Econometrics/Interactive Data Corp.] - Waltham, MA - *DataDirOnSer 84*
County Building Permits - Bala Cynwyd, PA - *DirOnDB Spring 84*
County Business Patterns [of U.S. Bureau of the Census] - Washington, DC - *EISS 83*
County Business Patterns - *See* County Business Structures
County Business Structures [of Chase Econometrics/Interactive Data Corp.] - Waltham, MA - *DataDirOnSer 84*
County Business Structures - Bala Cynwyd, PA - *DirOnDB Spring 84*
County Cable Corp. - Bixby, OK - *Tel&CabFB 84C p.1675*
County Cable Ltd. - Listowel, ON, Canada - *BrCabYB 84*
County Cablevision - Wabasha, MN - *BrCabYB 84; Tel&CabFB 84C*
County Cablevision Corp. - Pima County, AZ - *Tel&CabFB 84C*
County Cablevision Inc. - Zeigler, IL - *Tel&CabFB 84C p.1675*
County Cablevision Inc. [of Fundy Cablevision Ltd.] - Madawaska, ME - *BrCabYB 84; Tel&CabFB 84C*
County Carrier - Madison, FL - *Ed&PubIntYB 82*
County Chronicle - Kingfisher, OK - *AyerDirPub 83*
County Courier - Conklin, NY - *AyerDirPub 83*
County Courier - Clark, SD - *Ed&PubIntYB 82*
County Courier [of Dallas Tribune Printing Co. Inc.] - Dallas, TX - *AyerDirPub 83; NewsDir 84*
County Courier, The - St. Albans, VT - *Ed&PubIntYB 82*
County Courier, The - Swanton, VT - *AyerDirPub 83*
County Democrat - Shawnee, OK - *AyerDirPub 83; Ed&PubIntYB 82*
County Demographic Database [of Demograpic Research Co. Inc.] - Santa Monica, CA - *DataDirOnSer 84*
County Echo, The - Pequot Lakes, MN - *AyerDirPub 83*
County Employment & Wages [of Chase Econometrics/Interactive Data Corp.] - Waltham, MA - *DataDirOnSer 84*
County Employment & Wages - Bala Cynwyd, PA - *DirOnDB Spring 84*
County Leader [of Marple Publishing Co. Inc.] - Newtown Square, PA - *AyerDirPub 83; NewsDir 84*
County Life [of Radius Magazines Inc.] - Mamaroneck, NY - *BaconPubCkMag 84; MagDir 84; WritMar 84*
County Life Magazine - Reading, PA - *MagDir 84*
County Line Music - *See* Skinny Zach Music Inc.
County Line Observer - Illipolis, IL - *AyerDirPub 83*
County Line Observer - Niantic, IL - *Ed&PubIntYB 82*
County Neighbours, The - Stratford, ON, Canada - *AyerDirPub 83*
County News [of National Association of Counties] - Washington, DC - *NewsDir 84*
County News - Warner, OK - *AyerDirPub 83*
County News-Shield - Barron, WI - *Ed&PubIntYB 82*
County Observer - Reedsville, PA - *NewsDir 84*
County Observer, The - Lewistown, PA - *Ed&PubIntYB 82*
County Personal Income, Population, & Employment [of Chase Econometrics/Interactive Data Corp.] - Waltham, MA - *DataDirOnSer 84*
County Personal Income, Population, & Employment - Bala Cynwyd, PA - *DirOnDB Spring 84*
County Photo Compositing Corp. - Jefferson, MA - *DirInfWP 82; LitMarPl 83, 84*
County Post, The - Millsboro, DE - *AyerDirPub 83; Ed&PubIntYB 82*
County Press - Eads, CO - *Ed&PubIntYB 82*
County Press - Refugio, TX - *Ed&PubIntYB 82*
County Press Publishers - Benson, NC - *BaconPubCkNews 84*
County Progress - Brownwood, TX - *BaconPubCkMag 84*
County Record - Denton, MD - *AyerDirPub 83; Ed&PubIntYB 82*
County Record, The - Blountstown, FL - *Ed&PubIntYB 82*
County Records - Floyd, VA - *BillIntBG 83-84*
County Reporter - Green Lake, WI - *Ed&PubIntYB 82*
County Star - Tolono, IL - *AyerDirPub 83; Ed&PubIntYB 82*
County Tribune - Goodhue, MN - *Ed&PubIntYB 82*
County Weekly - Grenada, MS - *Ed&PubIntYB 82*
County Weekly, The [of Johnson Lamoille County Weekly] - Essex Junction, VT - *AyerDirPub 83; NewsDir 84*
County Wide News - Tecumseh, OK - *AyerDirPub 83*
Countyman Press - Woodstock, VT - *LitMag&SmPr 83-84*
Countywide New-Record - Harriman, TN - *AyerDirPub 83*
Countywide Shopper [of Pinellas Park Post] - Pinellas Park, FL - *NewsDir 84*
Couple to Couple League - Cincinnati, OH - *BoPubDir 4, 5*
Courant - Evergreen, AL - *AyerDirPub 83*
Courant - Coal City, IL - *AyerDirPub 83*
Courant - Bottineau, ND - *AyerDirPub 83*
Courart-Citizen - Howard, KS - *AyerDirPub 83*
Courier - Tuscaloosa, AL - *Ed&PubIntYB 82*
Courier [of Prescott Newspapers Inc.] - Prescott, AZ - *AyerDirPub 83; Ed&PubIntYB 82; NewsDir 84*
Courier - Beverly Hills, CA - *AyerDirPub 83*
Courier - Ceres, CA - *AyerDirPub 83*
Courier - Colton, CA - *AyerDirPub 83*
Courier - Covina, CA - *AyerDirPub 83*
Courier - Cupertino, CA - *AyerDirPub 83*
Courier - Monroe, CT - *AyerDirPub 83*
Courier - Jupiter, FL - *Ed&PubIntYB 82*
Courier - Plant City, FL - *AyerDirPub 83; Ed&PubIntYB 82*
Courier - Macon, GA - *AyerDirPub 83; Ed&PubIntYB 82*
Courier - Thomasville, GA - *NewsDir 84*
Courier - Gibson City, IL - *AyerDirPub 83*
Courier - Jacksonville, IL - *AyerDirPub 83; Ed&PubIntYB 82*
Courier - Lincoln, IL - *AyerDirPub 83*
Courier - Morton, IL - *AyerDirPub 83; Ed&PubIntYB 82*
Courier - Washington, IL - *AyerDirPub 83*
Courier - Evansville, IN - *AyerDirPub 83*
Courier - Madison, IN - *AyerDirPub 83*
Courier - Morocco, IN - *AyerDirPub 83*
Courier - Coralville, IA - *AyerDirPub 83*
Courier - Ottumwa, IA - *AyerDirPub 83*
Courier - Reinbeck, IA - *AyerDirPub 83*
Courier - Sutherland, IA - *AyerDirPub 83*

Courier - Thompson, IA - *AyerDirPub 83*
Courier - Waterloo, IA - *AyerDirPub 83*
Courier - Stafford, KS - *AyerDirPub 83*
Courier - Winfield, KS - *AyerDirPub 83*
Courier - Hickman, KY - *AyerDirPub 83*
Courier - Wareham, MA - *AyerDirPub 83*
Courier - Temperance, MI - *Ed&PubIntYB 82*
Courier - Coffeeville, MS - *AyerDirPub 83*
Courier - Magee, MS - *AyerDirPub 83*
Courier - Clarence, MO - *AyerDirPub 83*
Courier - Cole Camp, MO - *AyerDirPub 83*
Courier - Kearney, MO - *AyerDirPub 83*
Courier - Glasgow, MT - *AyerDirPub 83*
Courier - Callaway, NE - *AyerDirPub 83*
Courier - Gering, NE - *AyerDirPub 83*
Courier - Chatham, NJ - *AyerDirPub 83*
Courier - Clinton, NY - *AyerDirPub 83*
Courier - Deposit, NY - *AyerDirPub 83*
Courier - Valley Stream, NY - *AyerDirPub 83*
Courier - Forest City, NC - *AyerDirPub 83*
Courier - Canfield, OH - *Ed&PubIntYB 82*
Courier - Eldorado, OK - *AyerDirPub 83*
Courier - Grants Pass, OR - *AyerDirPub 83*
Courier - Conneautville, PA - *AyerDirPub 83*
Courier - Connellsville, PA - *AyerDirPub 83*
Courier - Clear Lake, SD - *AyerDirPub 83*
Courier - Freeman, SD - *AyerDirPub 83*
Courier - Sisseton, SD - *AyerDirPub 83*
Courier - Carthage, TN - *AyerDirPub 83*
Courier - Savannah, TN - *AyerDirPub 83*
Courier - Moody, TX - *AyerDirPub 83*
Courier - Munday, TX - *AyerDirPub 83*
Courier - Sanger, TX - *AyerDirPub 83*
Courier - Clearfield, UT - *AyerDirPub 83*
Courier - Milton, WI - *AyerDirPub 83*
Courier - Milwaukee, WI - *AyerDirPub 83*
Courier - Thorp, WI - *AyerDirPub 83*
Courier - Waterloo, WI - *AyerDirPub 83*
Courier - Campbell River, BC, Canada - *AyerDirPub 83*
Courier - Kelowna, BC, Canada - *AyerDirPub 83*
Courier - Digby, NS, Canada - *AyerDirPub 83; Ed&PubIntYB 82*
Courier - Perth, ON, Canada - *AyerDirPub 83*
Courier - Canora, SK, Canada - *AyerDirPub 83*
Courier & Freeman - Potsdam, NY - *AyerDirPub 83*
Courier & Press - Evansville, IN - *AyerDirPub 83*
Courier & State Line News - Winchendon, MA - *AyerDirPub 83*
Courier & Terrebonne Press - Houma, LA - *AyerDirPub 83*
Courier Chronicle, The - Humboldt, TN - *Ed&PubIntYB 82*
Courier Color - Lowell, MA - *MagIndMarPl 82-83*
Courier Communications Group - Milwaukee, WI - *BaconPubCkNews 84*
Courier Crescent - Orrville, OH - *AyerDirPub 83; Ed&PubIntYB 82*
Courier-Democrat [of Arkansas Newspapers Inc.] - Russellville, AR - *AyerDirPub 83; NewsDir 84*
Courier Express - Du Bois, PA - *AyerDirPub 83; Ed&PubIntYB 82; NewsDir 84*
Courier-Gazette - Rockland, ME - *AyerDirPub 83; Ed&PubIntYB 82*
Courier-Gazette - Newark, NY - *AyerDirPub 83; Ed&PubIntYB 82; NewsDir 84*
Courier-Gazette - McKinney, TX - *AyerDirPub 83*
Courier Graphics [Div. of J. P. Stevens] - Louisville, KY - *LitMarPl 83, 84*
Courier-Herald - Dublin, GA - *AyerDirPub 83; Ed&PubIntYB 82*
Courier-Herald - Enumclaw, WA - *AyerDirPub 83*
Courier Highlights - Jupiter, FL - *AyerDirPub 83*
Courier Hub - Stoughton, WI - *AyerDirPub 83*
Courier-Index - Marianna, AR - *AyerDirPub 83; Ed&PubIntYB 82*
Courier-Journal - Crescent City, FL - *Ed&PubIntYB 82*
Courier-Journal - Louisville, KY - *AyerDirPub 83; BaconPubCkNews 84; Ed&PubIntYB 82; NewsBur 6; NewsDir 84*
Courier-Journal - Algonac, MI - *AyerDirPub 83; Ed&PubIntYB 82*
Courier Journal - Festus, MO - *AyerDirPub 83; Ed&PubIntYB 82*
Courier Journal - Palmyra, NY - *AyerDirPub 83; Ed&PubIntYB 82*
Courier Journal - Rochester, NY - *Ed&PubIntYB 82*
Courier-Journal & Louisville Times Co. - Louisville, KY - *AdAge 6-28-84; KnowInd 83; VideoDir 82-83*
Courier-Journal Magazine, The - Louisville, KY - *WritMar 84*
Courier-Laval - Laval, PQ, Canada - *Ed&PubIntYB 82*
Courier-Leader - Paw Paw, MI - *AyerDirPub 83; Ed&PubIntYB 82*
Courier-Life Inc. - Brooklyn, NY - *BaconPubCkNews 84*
Courier News - Blytheville, AR - *AyerDirPub 83; Ed&PubIntYB 82*
Courier-News - Elgin, IL - *AyerDirPub 83; Ed&PubIntYB 82*
Courier News [of St. Louis Suburban Newspapers Inc.] - St. Louis, MO - *AyerDirPub 83; NewsDir 84*
Courier-News - Bridgewater, NJ - *BaconPubCkNews 84; Ed&PubIntYB 82*
Courier-News - Somerville, NJ - *AyerDirPub 83; NewsDir 84*
Courier-News - Clinton, TN - *AyerDirPub 83*
Courier Newspapers Inc. - Olney, MD - *Ed&PubIntYB 82*
Courier-Post - Hannibal, MO - *AyerDirPub 83*
Courier-Post - Camden, NJ - *AyerDirPub 83; NewsBur 6*
Courier-Post [of Southern New Jersey Newspapers Inc.] - Cherry Hill, NJ - *Ed&PubIntYB 82; NewsDir 84*
Courier Press - Prairie du Chien, WI - *AyerDirPub 83; Ed&PubIntYB 82; NewsDir 84*
Courier Press - Wallaceburg, ON, Canada - *AyerDirPub 83; Ed&PubIntYB 82*
Courier Printing Co. Inc. - Murfreesboro, TN - *MagIndMarPl 82-83*
Courier Publishing Co. Inc. - Liberty, KY - *BaconPubCkNews 84*
Courier-Record - Blackstone, VA - *AyerDirPub 83; Ed&PubIntYB 82*
Courier Records - New York, NY - *BillIntBG 83-84*
Courier-Rough Notes - Chatham, NY - *AyerDirPub 83*
Courier-Sentinel, The - Kiester, MN - *AyerDirPub 83; Ed&PubIntYB 82*
Courier-Standard-Enterprise - Canajoharie, NY - *AyerDirPub 83*
Courier-Standard-Enterprise [of Tri-Village Publishers Inc.] - Ft. Plain, NY - *Ed&PubIntYB 82; NewsDir 84*
Courier Systems Inc. - South Kearny, NJ - *LitMarPl 83, 84*
Courier Terminal Systems Inc. - Tempe, AZ - *InfIndMarPl 83*
Courier, The - Stockton, CA - *NewsDir 84*
Courier, The - Damascus, MD - *Ed&PubIntYB 82*
Courier, The - Chesaning, MI - *Ed&PubIntYB 82*
Courier, The - Minden, NE - *Ed&PubIntYB 82*
Courier, The - Middletown, NJ - *AyerDirPub 83; Ed&PubIntYB 82*
Courier, The - Clemmons, NC - *Ed&PubIntYB 82*
Courier, The [of Findlay Publishing Co.] - Findlay, OH - *AyerDirPub 83; Ed&PubIntYB 82; NewsDir 84*
Courier, The - Bentleyville, PA - *Ed&PubIntYB 82*
Courier, The [of Attaway Newspaper Group] - Conroe, TX - *AyerDirPub 83; Ed&PubIntYB 82; NewsDir 84*
Courier-Times - New Castle, IN - *AyerDirPub 83; Ed&PubIntYB 82*
Courier Times - Sutherland, NE - *AyerDirPub 83; Ed&PubIntYB 82*
Courier-Times - Roxboro, NC - *AyerDirPub 83; Ed&PubIntYB 82*
Courier Times [of T. B. Butler Publishing Co. Inc.] - Tyler, TX - *AyerDirPub 83; NewsDir 84*
Courier Times-Telegraph [of T. B. Butler Publishing Co. Inc.] - Tyler, TX - *AyerDirPub 83; NewsDir 84*
Courier Tribune - Seneca, KS - *AyerDirPub 83*
Courier-Tribune - Asheboro, NC - *AyerDirPub 83; Ed&PubIntYB 82*
Courier-Wedge - Durand, WI - *AyerDirPub 83; Ed&PubIntYB 82*
Courier Weekend - St. Stephen, NB, Canada - *AyerDirPub 83*
Courrier-Ahuntsic - Ahuntsic, PQ, Canada - *Ed&PubIntYB 82*
Courrier-Laurentides - St. Jerome, PQ, Canada - *Ed&PubIntYB 82*
Courrier-Sud - Nicolet, PQ, Canada - *Ed&PubIntYB 82*
Courses by Newspapers - La Jolla, CA - *Ed&PubIntYB 82*
Courseware Inc. - San Diego, CA - *BoPubDir 4, 5; MicrocomMPl 84*
Courseware Report Card [of Educational Insight] - Compton, CA - *MicrocomMPl 84*
Court-Butternut Pennysaver - Syracuse, NY - *AyerDirPub 83*
Court Cable Co. [of MacDonald Group Inc.] - Washington Court House, OH - *BrCabYB 84; Tel&CabFB 84C*
Court Cablevision Inc. - Sabina, OH - *BrCabYB 84*

Court Club Sports - Barrington, IL - *BaconPubCkMag 84*
Court Index - Cincinnati, OH - *Ed&PubIntYB 82; NewsDir 84*
Court Scribe - Eugene, OR - *BoPubDir 4 Sup, 5*
Courtland Cable TV - Courtland, KS - *Tel&CabFB 84C*
Courtland Cable TV [of Sleepy Eye CATV Inc.] - Courtland, MN - *BrCabYB 84*
Courtland Journal - Courtland, KS - *BaconPubCkNews 84; Ed&PubIntYB 82*
Courtney/Wilson Advertising - Calabasas, CA - *StaDirAdAg 2-84*
Coushatta Citizen - Coushatta, LA - *BaconPubCkNews 84*
Coushatta Citizen - Red River Parish, LA - *Ed&PubIntYB 82*
Cousins & Associates Inc., Morison S. - New York, NY - *HBIndAd&MS 82-83*
Cousins Music Inc. - Upper Nyack, NY - *BillIntBG 83-84*
Coutts Library Service Inc. - Lewiston, NY - *LitMarPl 83, 84; MagIndMarPl 82-83*
Covalt Advertising Agency Inc. - Miami, FL - *StaDirAdAg 2-84*
Cove, Cooper, Lewis Inc. - New York, NY - *BrCabYB 84; DirPRFirms 83; StaDirAdAg 2-84*
Cove Press - Severna Park, MD - *LitMag&SmPr 83-84*
Cove Press - Prince Rupert, BC, Canada - *BoPubDir 4, 5*
Cove View Press - Arcata, CA - *BoPubDir 4 Sup, 5; LitMag&SmPr 83-84*
Covelo Round Valley News - Covelo, CA - *BaconPubCkNews 84*
Covenant Companion, The - Chicago, IL - *ArtMar 84; WritMar 84*
Covenant Music - *See* Alexandria House Inc.
Covenant Press [Aff. of The Evangelical Covenant Church of America] - Chicago, IL - *BoPubDir 4, 5*
Covenant Recording Inc. - Salt Lake City, UT - *BillIntBG 83-84*
Cover Craft Corp. - Amherst, NH - *WhoWMicrocom 83*
Cover Publishing Co. - Tampa, FL - *BoPubDir 4, 5*
Cover to Cover Inc. - New York, NY - *LitMarPl 83, 84; MagIndMarPl 82-83*
Covey & Koons - Canton, OH - *AdAge 3-28-84; StaDirAdAg 2-84*
Covina Inter-City Express [of Thomson Newspapers Inc.] - West Covina, CA - *NewsDir 84*
Covington Cable TV [of Athena Communications Corp.] - Covington, TN - *Tel&CabFB 84C*
Covington Cable TV Inc. - Covington, IN - *BrCabYB 84; Tel&CabFB 84C*
Covington Co., Ben H. - Columbia, SC - *AvMarPl 83*
Covington Fountain County Star - Covington, IN - *BaconPubCkNews 84*
Covington Kentucky Post [of E. W. Scripps Co.] - Covington, KY - *NewsDir 84*
Covington Leader - Covington, TN - *BaconPubCkNews 84; Ed&PubIntYB 82; NewsDir 84*
Covington Messenger, The - Covington, KY - *NewsDir 84*
Covington Multi-County Star [of Covington News] - Covington, GA - *NewsDir 84*
Covington News - Covington, GA - *BaconPubCkNews 84; Ed&PubIntYB 82*
Covington, Paul [Div. of Pierron Publishing Industries] - Northvale, NJ - *LitMarPl 83, 84*
Covington Record - Covington, OK - *BaconPubCkNews 84; Ed&PubIntYB 82*
Covington St. Tammany Farmer - Covington, LA - *BaconPubCkNews 84; Ed&PubIntYB 82; NewsDir 84*
Covington St. Tammany News-Banner - Covington, LA - *BaconPubCkNews 84; NewsDir 84*
Covington Stillwater Valley Advertiser - Covington, OH - *BaconPubCkNews 84*
Covington Suspension Press - Covington, KY - *BaconPubCkNews 84*
Covington Virginian - Covington, VA - *AyerDirPub 83; BaconPubCkNews 84; Ed&PubIntYB 82; NewsDir 84*
Cow Bay Computing - Manhasset, NY - *MicrocomMPl 84; MicrocomSwDir 1*
Cow Bay Computing - Plandome, NY - *MicrocomMPl 83*
Cow Country - Cheyenne, WY - *BaconPubCkMag 84; MagDir 84*
Cowan Advertising, T. N. - Alvarado, TX - *DirMarMP 83*
Cowan Publishing Corp. - Port Washington, NY - *MagIndMarPl 82-83*
Cowan, R. Don - Tyler, TX - *BrCabYB 84 p.D-299*
Cowan, Robert G. - Los Angeles, CA - *BoPubDir 4, 5*
Coward, McCann & Geoghegan - New York, NY - *WritMar 84*
Coward McCann Inc. - New York, NY - *WritMar 84*
Coward McCann Inc. - *See* Putnam Publishing Group
Cowboy Carl/Neon Records - Park Forest, IL - *BillIntBG 83-84*
Cowboy Junction Publishing Co. - Lecanto, FL - *BillIntBG 83-84*
Cowell, Jack - New York, NY - *HBIndAd&MS 82-83*
Coweta Cable Corp. [of Hurst-Mullinax Group] - Newnan, GA - *BrCabYB 84*
Coweta Times Star - Coweta, OK - *Ed&PubIntYB 82*
Coweta Times-Star [of Wagoner Newspapers Inc.] - Wagoner, OK - *NewsDir 84*
Coweta Times-Star - *See* Wagoner Newspapers Inc.
Cowichan Cablevision Ltd. - Duncan, BC, Canada - *BrCabYB 84*
Cowichan Leader - Duncan, BC, Canada - *AyerDirPub 83; Ed&PubIntYB 82*
Cowichan News - Duncan, BC, Canada - *AyerDirPub 83; Ed&PubIntYB 82*
Cowichan Pictorial - Duncan, BC, Canada - *AyerDirPub 83*
Cowiche Telephone Co. - Cowiche, WA - *TelDir&BG 83-84*
Cowle Enterprises Ltd. - Ames, IA - *BrCabYB 84*
Cowles Broadcasting Inc. - Daytona Beach, FL - *Tel&CabFB 84S*
Cowles Communications Inc. - Daytona Beach, FL - *BrCabYB 84; HomeVid&CabYB 82-83*
Cowles Media Co. - Minneapolis, MN - *AdAge 6-28-84; KnowInd 83*
Cowles Newspapers - Minneapolis, MN - *Ed&PubIntYB 82*
Cowles Publishing Co. - Spokane, WA - *BrCabYB 84; VideoDir 82-83*
Cowley Cablevision Inc. [of Communications Services Inc.] - Winfield, KS - *BrCabYB 84; Tel&CabFB 84C*
Cowley County Reporter - Burden, KS - *AyerDirPub 83; Ed&PubIntYB 82*
Cowley Literary Management, Glenn - New York, NY - *LitMarPl 83*
Cowley Publications [Aff. of Society of St. John the Evangelist] - Cambridge, MA - *BoPubDir 4, 5*
Cowlitz Cableview Co. [of Longview Publishing Co.] - Longview, WA - *BrCabYB 84; Tel&CabFB 84C*
Cowlitz County Advocate - Castle Rock, WA - *Ed&PubIntYB 82*
Cox Advertising Inc. - Atlanta, GA - *StaDirAdAg 2-84*
Cox & Burch Advertising Co., The - Newport Beach, CA - *StaDirAdAg 2-84*
Cox Broadcasting Corp. - Atlanta, GA - *HomeVid&CabYB 82-83*
Cox Cable [of Cox Cable Communications Inc.] - Jefferson Parish, LA - *BrCabYB 84*
Cox Cable Aberdeen [of Cox Cable Communications Corp.] - Aberdeen, WA - *BrCabYB 84; Tel&CabFB 84C*
Cox Cable Astoria - Astoria, OR - *BrCabYB 84*
Cox Cable Bakersfield - Bakersfield, CA - *BrCabYB 84*
Cox Cable Berkshire - North Adams, MA - *BrCabYB 84*
Cox Cable Camas/Washougal [of Rogers UA Cablesystems] - Camas, WA - *BrCabYB 84*
Cox Cable Cedar Rapids Inc. - Cedar Rapids, IA - *BrCabYB 84; Tel&CabFB 84C*
Cox Cable Cleveland Area [of Cox Cable Communications Inc.] - Parma, OH - *Tel&CabFB 84C*
Cox Cable Columbus [of Cox Cable Communications Inc.] - Columbus, IN - *Tel&CabFB 84C*
Cox Cable Communications - Atlanta, GA - *BrCabYB 84 p.D-300; CabTVFinDB 83; HomeVid&CabYB 82-83; LitMarPl 84; TelAl 83, 84; Tel&CabFB 84C p.1675*
Cox Cable Cranston/Johnston Inc. - Cranston, RI - *BrCabYB 84; Tel&CabFB 84C*
Cox Cable Eureka [of Cox Cable Communications Inc.] - Eureka, CA - *BrCabYB 84*
Cox Cable Ft. Wayne - Ft. Wayne, IN - *BrCabYB 84; Tel&CabFB 84C*
Cox Cable Gainesville - Gainesville, FL - *BrCabYB 84*
Cox Cable Greater Hartford Inc. [of Cox Cable Communications Inc.] - Manchester, CT - *Tel&CabFB 84C*
Cox Cable Green Mountain [of Cox Cable Communications Corp.] - Burlington, VT - *BrCabYB 84; Tel&CabFB 84C*
Cox Cable Humboldt Bay [of Trans-Video Corp.] - Arcata, CA - *BrCabYB 84*
Cox Cable Humboldt Bay [of Cox Cable Communications Inc.] - Eureka, CA - *Tel&CabFB 84C*

Cox Cable Iron Range [of Telesystems Corp.] - Marquette, MI - *BrCabYB 84*
Cox Cable Jacksonville Beach Inc. [of Cox Cable Communications Inc.] - Jacksonville Beach, FL - *BrCabYB 84; Tel&CabFB 84C*
Cox Cable Jefferson Parish [of Cox Cable Communications Inc.] - Harahan, LA - *HomeVid&CabYB 82-83*
Cox Cable Lake County [of Cox Cable Communications Inc.] - Libertyville, IL - *BrCabYB 84; Tel&CabFB 84C*
Cox Cable Lewistown - Lewistown, PA - *BrCabYB 84; Tel&CabFB 84C*
Cox Cable Lock Haven [of Cox Cable Communications Inc.] - Lock Haven, PA - *BrCabYB 84; Tel&CabFB 84C*
Cox Cable Long Beach [of Cox Cable Communications Inc.] - Long Beach, WA - *BrCabYB 84*
Cox Cable Lower Columbia [of Cox Cable Communications Inc.] - Long Beach, WA - *Tel&CabFB 84C*
Cox Cable Lubbock [of Cox Cable Communications Inc.] - Lubbock, TX - *BrCabYB 84; Tel&CabFB 84C*
Cox Cable Macon [of Cox Cable Communications Inc.] - Macon, GA - *BrCabYB 84; Tel&CabFB 84C*
Cox Cable Maywood - Maywood, IL - *BrCabYB 84; Tel&CabFB 84C*
Cox Cable Michigan City - Michigan City, IN - *BrCabYB 84; Tel&CabFB 84C*
Cox Cable Montpelier [of Cox Cable Communications Inc.] - Montpelier, VT - *BrCabYB 84; Tel&CabFB 84C*
Cox Cable New Orleans - New Orleans, LA - *Tel&CabFB 84C*
Cox Cable New York - Great Neck, NY - *BrCabYB 84; Tel&CabFB 84C*
Cox Cable Norfolk [of Cox Cable Communications Inc.] - Norfolk, VA - *BrCabYB 84*
Cox Cable Ocala - Ocala, FL - *BrCabYB 84*
Cox Cable Oklahoma City - Oklahoma City, OK - *BrCabYB 84; Tel&CabFB 84C*
Cox Cable Omaha [Aff. of Cox Cable Communications Inc.] - Omaha, NE - *HomeVid&CabYB 82-83; InterCabHB 3; Tel&CabFB 84C*
Cox Cable Orland Park [of Cox Cable Communications Inc.] - Orland Park, IL - *BrCabYB 84; Tel&CabFB 84C*
Cox Cable Owosso - Owosso, MI - *Tel&CabFB 84C*
Cox Cable Park Forest - Park Forest, IL - *BrCabYB 84; Tel&CabFB 84C*
Cox Cable Pensacola [of Cox Cable Communications Inc.] - Pensacola, FL - *BrCabYB 84; Tel&CabFB 84C*
Cox Cable Peru - Peru, IN - *BrCabYB 84; Tel&CabFB 84C*
Cox Cable Porterville [of Cox Cable Communications Inc.] - Porterville, CA - *BrCabYB 84; Tel&CabFB 84C*
Cox Cable Portsmouth Inc. - Portsmouth, VA - *BrCabYB 84; Tel&CabFB 84C*
Cox Cable Quint-Cities - Moline, IL - *BrCabYB 84; Tel&CabFB 84C*
Cox Cable Roanoke - Roanoke, VA - *BrCabYB 84*
Cox Cable Robinson - Robinson, IL - *BrCabYB 84; Tel&CabFB 84C*
Cox Cable Rutland [of Cox Cable Communications Inc.] - Rutland, VT - *BrCabYB 84; Tel&CabFB 84C*
Cox Cable Saginaw - Saginaw, MI - *BrCabYB 84; Tel&CabFB 84C*
Cox Cable San Diego [Aff. of Cox Cable Communications Inc.] - San Diego, CA - *BrCabYB 84; CabTVPrDB 83; HomeVid&CabYB 82-83; InterCabHB 3; Tel&CabFB 84C*
Cox Cable Santa Barbara [of Cox Cable Communications Inc.] - Santa Barbara, CA - *BrCabYB 84; Tel&CabFB 84C*
Cox Cable Seaside [of Cox Cable Communications Inc.] - Seaside, OR - *BrCabYB 84*
Cox Cable Sebring/Avon Park [of Cox Cable Communications Inc.] - Sebring, FL - *BrCabYB 84; Tel&CabFB 84C*
Cox Cable South Carolina - Myrtle Beach, SC - *BrCabYB 84; Tel&CabFB 84C*
Cox Cable Spokane - Spokane, WA - *BrCabYB 84; Tel&CabFB 84C*
Cox Cable The Dalles [of Cox Cable Communications Inc.] - The Dalles, OR - *BrCabYB 84; Tel&CabFB 84C*
Cox Cable Tidewater [of Cox Cable Communications Inc.] - Virginia Beach, VA - *HomeVid&CabYB 82-83*
Cox Cable Tidewater Inc. - Norfolk, VA - *Tel&CabFB 84C*
Cox Cable Tucson - Tucson, AZ - *BrCabYB 84; Tel&CabFB 84C*
Cox Cable TV [of Cox Cable Communications Inc.] - St. Clair Shores, MI - *BrCabYB 84*
Cox Cable Tyrone [of Cox Cable Communications Inc.] - Tyrone, PA - *BrCabYB 84; Tel&CabFB 84C*
Cox Cable University City [of Cox Cable Communications Inc.] - Gainesville, FL - *Tel&CabFB 84C*
Cox Cable Vancouver/Clark County - Vancouver, WA - *BrCabYB 84; Tel&CabFB 84C*
Cox Cable Virginia Beach Inc. [of Cox Cable Communications Inc.] - Virginia Beach, VA - *BrCabYB 84; Tel&CabFB 84C*
Cox Cable Wabash - Wabash, IN - *BrCabYB 84; Tel&CabFB 84C*
Cox Cable Warner Robins [of Cox Cable Communications Inc.] - Warner Robins, GA - *BrCabYB 84; Tel&CabFB 84C*
Cox Cable Yakima [of Cox Cable Communications Inc.] - Yakima, WA - *BrCabYB 84; Tel&CabFB 84C*
Cox Cablevision Corp. [of Cox Cable Communications Inc.] - Ocala, FL - *Tel&CabFB 84C*
Cox Communications - Atlanta, GA - *AdAge 6-28-84; BrCabYB 84; KnowInd 83; TelAl 83, 84; Tel&CabFB 84S*
Cox, Dorothy A. - Farmington Hills, MI - *BoPubDir 4, 5*
Cox Enterprises - Atlanta, GA - *AdAge 6-28-84; Ed&PubIntYB 82; KnowInd 83*
Cox Film Enterprises, William G. - Sun City, AZ - *TelAl 83, 84*
Cox, Harold E. - Forty Ft., PA - *BoPubDir 4, 5*
Cox Inc., James - Houston, TX - *DirPRFirms 83*
Cox, J. Cunningham - Bryn Mawr, PA - *StaDirAdAg 2-84*
Cox, Lloyd Associates Ltd. - New York, NY - *HBIndAd&MS 82-83; IntDirMarRes 83*
Cox, Melvin H. - North Oakland, CA - *BrCabYB 84*
Cox Newspapers - *See* Cox Communications Inc.
Cox Publications - El Cerrito, CA - *BoPubDir 5*
Cox Subscription Agency, W. T. - Goldsboro, NC - *MagIndMarPl 82-83*
Coxe Group, The - Philadelphia, PA - *DirPRFirms 83*
Coy Hunt & Co. [Div. of A. T. Clayton & Co. Inc.] - New York, NY - *LitMarPl 83, 84*
Coyote Books - Berkeley, CA - *BoPubDir 4, 5*
Coyote Flats Historical Society - Canada - *BoPubDir 4, 5*
Coyote Love Press - Portland, ME - *LitMag&SmPr 83-84*
Coyote Productions Inc. - Marina del Rey, CA - *BillIntBG 83-84*
Cozad & Associates Inc., R. P. - Los Angeles, CA - *DirPRFirms 83*
Cozad-Benskin & Associates Inc. - Encino, CA - *StaDirAdAg 2-84*
Cozad Cable TV - Gothenburg, NE - *Tel&CabFB 84C*
Cozad Telephone Co. - Cozad, NE - *TelDir&BG 83-84*
Cozad Tri-City Tribune - Cozad, NE - *BaconPubCkNews 84*
Cozgem Music - Seattle, WA - *BillIntBG 83-84*
Cozgem Records - Seattle, WA - *BillIntBG 83-84*
CP Aids - Kent, OH - *MicrocomMPl 83, 84; MicrocomSwDir 1; WhoWMicrocom 83*
CP/$ - Plano, TX - *MicrocomMPl 84*
CP/M Review - Mercer Island, WA - *BaconPubCkMag 84; MicrocomMPl 84*
CP National - Piscataway, NJ - *DataDirSup 7-83*
CP National Corp. - Concord, CA - *TelDir&BG 83-84*
C.P. Press - Montclair, NJ - *BoPubDir 5*
C.P. Press - Flushing, NY - *BoPubDir 4*
CP Software - Brighton, England - *MicrocomSwDir 1*
CPA Computer Report [of Professional Publications Inc.] - Atlanta, GA - *MicrocomMPl 84*
CPA 83 - Dallas, TX - *BaconPubCkMag 84*
CPA Journal, The [of The New York State Society of CPAs] - New York, NY - *BaconPubCkMag 84; MagDir 84; MagIndMarPl 82-83*
CPA Software & Systems - Colorado Springs, CO - *MicrocomMPl 84*
CPC Associates Inc. - Hollywood, CA - *TelAl 83, 84*
CPC Library Data Base [of University of North Carolina] - Chapel Hill, NC - *EISS 83*
CPC System - St. Paul, MN - *DirOnDB Spring 84*
CPDA News - New York, NY - *BaconPubCkMag 84*
CPF Group Inc. - New York, NY - *AvMarPl 83*
CPI - New York, NY - *ArtMar 84; LitMarPl 83, 84*
CPI Music [Div. of Centaur Productions Inc.] - Studio City, CA - *BillIntBG 83-84*
CPI of Arkansas Inc. [of Times Mirror Cable TV] - North Little Rock, AR - *BrCabYB 84; Tel&CabFB 84C*

CPI/PPI - Washington, DC - *DirOnDB Spring 84*
CPI Publishing Inc. - New York, NY - *LitMarPl 83, 84*
CPI Purchasing - Boston, MA - *BaconPubCkMag 84*
CPL Bibliographies [Aff. of Council of Planning Librarians] - Chicago, IL - *BoPubDir 4, 5*
CPM Inc. - Chicago, IL - *HBIndAd&MS 82-83; StaDirAdAg 2-84*
CPM Systems - New York, NY - *Tel&CabFB 84C*
C.P.S. Cable Vision - Coalport, PA - *BrCabYB 84; Tel&CabFB 84C*
CPT Corp. - Eden Prairie, MN - *Datamation 6-83; Top100Al 83*
CPT Corp. - Minneapolis, MN - *DataDirSup 7-83; DirInfWP 82*
C.P.U. Computer Corp. - Charlestown, MA - *MicrocomMPl 83*
CPU Inc. - Montgomery, AL - *WhoWMicrocom 83*
CQ: The Radio Amateur's Journal - Hicksville, NY - *BaconPubCkMag 84; MagDir 84; MagIndMarPl 82-83; WritMar 84*
CQ Washington Alert Service - Washington, DC - *DirOnDB Spring 84*
CRA Inc. - Los Angeles, CA - *IntDirMarRes 83*
Crab Creek Review - Ephrata, WA - *LitMag&SmPr 83-84*
Crabshaw Music - San Francisco, CA - *BillIntBG 83-84*
Crabtree Publishing - Federal Way, WA - *BoPubDir 4, 5*
Crabtree-Vickers Inc. - Englewood Cliffs, NJ - *LitMarPl 83, 84*
Cracked Lens at Sundown - Detroit, MI - *LitMag&SmPr 83-84*
Craft & Art Market - Greenwood, MS - *BaconPubCkMag 84*
Craft & Needlework Age - Englishtown, NJ - *BaconPubCkMag 84; MagDir 84*
Craft & Needlework Age - New York, NY - *MagIndMarPl 82-83*
Craft International - New York, NY - *BaconPubCkMag 84*
Craft, Jerry - Jacksboro, TX - *Tel&CabFB 84C p.1675*
Craft Patterns Home Workshop Feature - St. Charles, IL - *Ed&PubIntYB 82*
Craft Range - Denver, CO - *WritMar 84*
Craftrends - Norcross, GA - *BaconPubCkMag 84*
Crafts [of PJS Enterprises Inc.] - Peoria, IL - *BaconPubCkMag 84; Folio 83; MagIndMarPl 82-83*
Crafts 'n Things - Park Ridge, IL - *BaconPubCkMag 84; MagDir 84; MagIndMarPl 82-83; WritMar 84*
Crafts Report, The - Seattle, WA - *BaconPubCkMag 84*
Craftsbury Software - Washington, DC - *MicrocomMPl 84*
Craftsman - Chicago, IL - *NewsDir 84*
Craftsman Book Co. - Carlsbad, CA - *ArtMar 84; LitMag&SmPr 83-84; LitMarPl 83, 84; WritMar 84*
Craftsman Press - Seattle, WA - *MagIndMarPl 82-83*
Craftsman Publications Inc./Western Sports Guides - El Paso, TX - *BoPubDir 4, 5*
Craftswoman [of Daedalus Publications Inc.] - Deerfield, IL - *WritMar 84*
Crag & Canyon - Banff, AB, Canada - *AyerDirPub 83*
Cragin Leader [of Chicago Leader Newspapers-Leader Papers Inc.] - Chicago, IL - *AyerDirPub 83; NewsDir 84*
Cragmont Publications - San Francisco, CA - *LitMag&SmPr 83-84; LitMarPl 83, 84*
Craig & Co. - *See* Graham Music Publisher, Roger
Craig Corp. - Compton, CA - *AvMarPl 83; DirInfWP 82*
Craig-Ellis Co. - *See* Graham Music Publisher, Roger
Craig Empire-Courier - Craig, CO - *Ed&PubIntYB 82*
Craig Envelope Corp. - Long Island City, NY - *MagIndMarPl 82-83*
Craig, J. D. - Carmel, CA - *BoPubDir 4, 5*
Craig, Lamm, Hensley & Alderman Advertising - Houston, TX - *AdAge 3-28-84; StaDirAdAg 2-84*
Craig Services - Morristown, TN - *LitMarPl 84*
Craig Snake River Press - *See* Northwest Colorado Press
Craig Telephone Co. - Craig, NE - *TelDir&BG 83-84*
Craigmont TV Cable Service - Craigmont, ID - *Tel&CabFB 84C*
Craigville Telephone Corp. - Craigville, IL - *TelDir&BG 83-84*
Crain Books [Div. of Crain Communications Inc.] - Chicago, IL - *LitMarPl 83, 84; WritMar 84*
Crain Communications - Chicago, IL - *DirMarMP 83; KnowInd 83; MagIndMarPl 82-83*
Crain Communications Computer Services - Chicago, IL - *MagIndMarPl 82-83*
Crain's Chicago Business [of Crain Communications Inc.] - Chicago, IL - *BaconPubCkMag 84; Folio 83; MagDir 84; NewsDir 84*
Crain's Cleveland Business - Cleveland, OH - *BaconPubCkMag 84; WritMar 84*
Crain's Illinois Business [of Crain Communications Inc.] - Chicago, IL - *BaconPubCkMag 84; MagDir 84*
Cram Co. Inc., The George F. - Indianapolis, IN - *AvMarPl 83; LitMarPl 83, 84*
Crambruck Press [Aff. of Cramer Products] - New York, NY - *BoPubDir 4, 5*
Cramer Bookstore - Kansas City, MO - *BoPubDir 4, 5*
Cramer Co., H. G. [Div. of Florida Fabricators Inc.] - Sarasota, FL - *AvMarPl 83*
Cramer Industries Inc. - Kansas City, KS - *DirInfWP 82*
Cramer-Krasselt - Milwaukee, WI - *AdAge 3-28-84; ArtMar 84; BrCabYB 84; StaDirAdAg 2-84; TelAl 83, 84*
Cramer-Krasselt/Direct [Div. of Cramer-Krasselt] - Chicago, IL - *DirMarMP 83*
Crammond Public Relations Inc. - Butler, NJ - *DirPRFirms 83*
Cranberries - Cobalt, CT - *BaconPubCkMag 84; MagDir 84; WritMar 84*
Cranbrook Institute of Science [Aff. of Cranbrook Educational Community] - Bloomfield Hills, MI - *BoPubDir 4, 5*
Cranbrook Publishing Co. - Ann Arbor, MI - *BoPubDir 4, 5*
Cranbrook Television Ltd. - Cranbrook, BC, Canada - *BrCabYB 84*
Cranbury Press - Cranbury, NJ - *Ed&PubIntYB 82*
Cranbury Press - *See* Princeton Packet Inc.
Crandall Associates - Houston, TX - *BoPubDir 4 Sup, 5; LitMarPl 83, 84*
Crandall Associates Inc., Richard - Katonah, NY - *StaDirAdAg 2-84*
Crandall Communications Inc. - New York, NY - *AvMarPl 83*
Crandon Forest Republican - Crandon, WI - *BaconPubCkNews 84*
Crandon Telephone Co. - Crandon, WI - *TelDir&BG 83-84*
Crane Chronicle/Stone County Republican - Crane, MO - *AyerDirPub 83; BaconPubCkNews 84*
Crane Chronicle, The - Crane, MO - *Ed&PubIntYB 82*
Crane Collection of Photographic History, Arnold H. - Chicago, IL - *MagIndMarPl 82-83*
Crane Duplicating Service Inc. - Barnstable, MA - *LitMarPl 83, 84; MagIndMarPl 82-83*
Crane News - Crane, TX - *AyerDirPub 83; BaconPubCkNews 84; Ed&PubIntYB 82*
Crane Publishing Co. [Div. of MLP] - Trenton, NJ - *LitMarPl 83, 84*
Crane, Russak & Co. Inc. - New York, NY - *LitMarPl 83, 84; MagIndMarPl 82-83*
Crane Software Inc. - Huntington Beach, CA - *MicrocomMPl 83*
Cranfill Advertising Agency Inc. - Indianapolis, IN - *StaDirAdAg 2-84*
Cranford Chronicle [of Awbrey Communications in New Jersey Inc.] - Cranford, NJ - *BaconPubCkNews 84; Ed&PubIntYB 82; NewsDir 84*
Cranford/Johnson/Hunt & Associates - Little Rock, AR - *StaDirAdAg 2-84*
Cranston-Csuri Productions Inc. - Columbus, OH - *AvMarPl 83*
Cranston Herald [of Southern R.I. Publications] - Cranston, RI - *BaconPubCkNews 84; Ed&PubIntYB 82; NewsDir 84*
Cranston Herald - Providence, RI - *NewsDir 84*
Cranston Herald - Warwick, RI - *AyerDirPub 83*
Cranston Mirror - Cranston, RI - *ArtMar 84; BaconPubCkNews 84; Ed&PubIntYB 82*
Cranston Mirror - Providence, RI - *NewsDir 84*
Crater General Communications Inc. - Petersburg, VA - *Tel&CabFB 84C p.1675*
Craven Design Studios Inc. - New York, NY - *LitMarPl 83, 84*
Craven Film Corp., Thomas - New York, NY - *AvMarPl 83; TelAl 83, 84; Tel&CabFB 84C*
Craw-Kan Telephone Cooperative Inc. - Girard, KS - *TelDir&BG 83-84*
Crawford AD-Visor - Meadville, PA - *AyerDirPub 83*
Crawford & Associates - Atlanta, GA - *AdAge 3-28-84; StaDirAdAg 2-84*
Crawford Broadcasting Co. - Flourtown, PA - *BrCabYB 84*
Crawford Cable Co. - Alma, NE - *Tel&CabFB 84C*
Crawford Cable Co. - Franklin, NE - *Tel&CabFB 84C*
Crawford Cable Co. - North Platte, NE - *Tel&CabFB 84C p.1675*
Crawford Cable Co. - Red Cloud, NE - *Tel&CabFB 84C*

Crawford Cable Co. - Wills Point, TX - *Tel&CabFB 84C*
Crawford Clipper/Harrison Sun - Crawford, NE - *BaconPubCkNews 84*
Crawford County Avalanche - Grayling, MI - *AyerDirPub 83; Ed&PubIntYB 82*
Crawford County Bulletin - Mulberry, AR - *Ed&PubIntYB 82*
Crawford County Cable Inc. [of Cardiff Cablevision Inc.] - Frontenac, KS - *Tel&CabFB 84C*
Crawford County Cable Inc. [of Cardiff Cablevision Inc.] - Frontenac/Girard, KS - *BrCabYB 84*
Crawford County Democrat - English, IN - *Ed&PubIntYB 82*
Crawford County Democrat-News Messenger - English, IN - *AyerDirPub 83*
Crawford County Independent - Gays Mills, WI - *Ed&PubIntYB 82*
Crawford County Independent & Kickapoo Scout [of Boscobel Publishers Inc.] - Boscobel, WI - *NewsDir 84*
Crawford County Independent & Kickapoo Scout - Gays Mills, WI - *AyerDirPub 83*
Crawford County Independent, The - Boscobel, WI - *Ed&PubIntYB 82*
Crawford Data Systems - Somis, CA - *MicrocomMPl 84; WritMar 84*
Crawford Furniture & TV Inc. - Erick, OK - *BrCabYB 84; Tel&CabFB 84C*
Crawford Memorial Society, The F. Marion - Nashville, TN - *LitMag&SmPr 83-84*
Crawford Mirror [of Missourian Publishing Co. Inc.] - Steelville, MO - *AyerDirPub 83; Ed&PubIntYB 82; NewsDir 84*
Crawford Press - Hutsonville, IL - *AyerDirPub 83; Ed&PubIntYB 82*
Crawfordsville Community Cable Corp. - Crawfordsville, IN - *BrCabYB 84; Tel&CabFB 84C*
Crawfordsville Community Cable Corp. - *See* Cardinal Communications Inc.
Crawfordsville Journal-Review - Crawfordsville, IN - *BaconPubCkNews 84; Ed&PubIntYB 82; NewsDir 84*
Crawfordville Advocate-Democrat - Crawfordville, GA - *BaconPubCkNews 84*
Crawfordville Wakulla News - *See* News Publishing
Crawl Out Your Window - San Diego, CA - *LitMag&SmPr 83-84*
Crawley & Co. Inc. - Boston, MA - *DirPRFirms 83*
Crawley Associates, David - Los Angeles, CA - *StaDirAdAg 2-84*
Crawley Book Machinery Co. - Newport, KY - *LitMarPl 83, 84*
Crawley, Emmett L. - Columbus, OH - *MagIndMarPl 82-83*
Crawley Films - Ottawa, ON, Canada - *AvMarPl 83; Tel&CabFB 84C*
Crawlspace - Belvidere, IL - *LitMag&SmPr 83-84*
Crawshaw, Todd - San Francisco, CA - *LitMarPl 83, 84*
Cray Research Inc. - Minneapolis, MN - *DataDirSup 7-83; Datamation 6-83; Top100Al 83*
Crazy Cajun Music - Houston, TX - *BillIntBG 83-84*
Crazy Lady Productions - *See* Rothstein Music Ltd.
Crazyhorse - Little Rock, AR - *LitMag&SmPr 83-84*
CRB Broadcasting - New York, NY - *BrCabYB 84*
CRB Microtools - Phoenix, AZ - *MicrocomMPl 84*
CRB Research - Commack, NY - *BoPubDir 4, 5*
CRC Information Systems Inc. - New York, NY - *ADAPSOMemDir 83-84; DataDirOnSer 84; IntDirMarRes 83*
CRC Music - *See* MRI Music
CRC Press Inc. - Boca Raton, FL - *DirMarMP 83; LitMarPl 83, 84; MagIndMarPl 82-83*
CRCNET Inc. - New York, NY - *IntDirMarRes 83*
CRCS Publications - Reno, NV - *LitMag&SmPr 83-84; LitMarPl 83, 84*
CRDS - McLean, VA - *DirOnDB Spring 84*
CRE Inc. - Brazil, IN - *AdAge 3-28-84; StaDirAdAg 2-84*
Cream City Review - Milwaukee, WI - *LitMag&SmPr 83-84*
Cream Publishing Group - Los Angeles, CA - *BillIntBG 83-84*
Cream Records Inc. - Los Angeles, CA - *BillIntBG 83-84*
Cream Valley Telephone Co. [Aff. of Universal Telephone Inc.] - Hawkins, WI - *TelDir&BG 83-84*
Creamania - Boston, MA - *LitMag&SmPr 83-84*
Creamer Dickson Basford [Subs. of Creamer Inc.] - New York, NY - *DirPRFirms 83*
Creamer Inc. - Hartford, CT - *ArtMar 84*
Creamer Inc. - New York, NY - *BrCabYB 84; StaDirAdAg 2-84*
Creation/Evolution Journal - Buffalo, NY - *LitMag&SmPr 83-84*
Creation House [Aff. of Christian Life Missions] - Carol Stream, IL - *BoPubDir 4 Sup, 5*
Creation-Life Publishers Inc. - San Diego, CA - *BoPubDir 4, 5; LitMarPl 84*
Creative - New York, NY - *BaconPubCkMag 84; MagDir 84*
Creative AD/Ventures Inc. - New York, NY - *LitMarPl 83, 84; MagIndMarPl 82-83; StaDirAdAg 2-84*
Creative Advertising [Div. of Creative Press Inc.] - Evansville, IN - *StaDirAdAg 2-84*
Creative Advertising Agency - Biddeford, ME - *StaDirAdAg 2-84*
Creative Advertising Agency Inc. - Mt. Vernon, NY - *StaDirAdAg 2-84*
Creative Advertising Co., The - Phoenix, AZ - *AdAge 3-28-84; StaDirAdAg 2-84*
Creative Alliance Inc. - New York, NY - *StaDirAdAg 2-84*
Creative Analysis - New York, NY - *IntDirMarRes 83*
Creative Answers - Houston, TX - *BoPubDir 4, 5*
Creative Artists Agency Inc. - Los Angeles, CA - *LitMarPl 83, 84*
Creative Arts Book Co. - Berkeley, CA - *LitMag&SmPr 83-84; LitMarPl 83, 84; WritMar 84*
Creative Arts Development - Soquel, CA - *LitMag&SmPr 83-84*
Creative Associates Inc. - Dallas, TX - *StaDirAdAg 2-84*
Creative Book Co. [Div. of Marshall/Creative Enterprises] - Van Nuys, CA - *LitMag&SmPr 83-84; LitMarPl 83, 84; WritMar 84*
Creative Books - Carmel, CA - *BoPubDir 4, 5*
Creative Color Service - Salt Lake City, UT - *AvMarPl 83*
Creative Communications - Rochester, NY - *Ed&PubIntYB 82*
Creative Communications - Philadelphia, PA - *DirMarMP 83*
Creative Communications - Port Angeles, WA - *BoPubDir 5*
Creative Communications Associates Inc. - Orange, CA - *StaDirAdAg 2-84*
Creative Communications Center - Delavan, WI - *StaDirAdAg 2-84*
Creative Communications Group - Dallas, TX - *AvMarPl 83*
Creative Composition [Aff. of Polish Heritage Products] - Cherry Hill, NJ - *BoPubDir 4, 5*
Creative Computer Center - Orlando, FL - *MicrocomMPl 84*
Creative Computer Consultants Inc. - Norwalk, CT - *WhoWMicrocom 83*
Creative Computer Services Inc. - Dallas, TX - *DirMarMP 83*
Creative Computing [of AHL Computing Inc.] - Morris Plains, NJ - *BaconPubCkMag 84; Folio 83; LitMag&SmPr 83-84; LitMarPl 83, 84; MagDir 84; MagIndMarPl 82-83; MicrocomMPl 84; WhoWMicrocom 83; WritMar 84*
Creative Computing - Morristown, NJ - *WhoWMicrocom 83*
Creative Computing Press [Aff. of Ziff-Davis Publishing Co.] - Morris Plains, NJ - *BoPubDir 4, 5; LitMag&SmPr 83-84*
Creative Computing Press [Subs. of Ziff-Davis Publishing Co.] - New York, NY - *LitMarPl 84*
Creative Computing Services - Dryden, ME - *EISS 83*
Creative Computing Video & Arcade Games - Morris Plains, NJ - *BaconPubCkMag 84*
Creative Concepts Publishing Corp. - Ojai, CA - *BillIntBG 83-84*
Creative Consortium Ltd. - Arlington Heights, IL - *DirMarMP 83; StaDirAdAg 2-84*
Creative Consumer Research - Houston, TX - *IntDirMarRes 83*
Creative Corps. - Hollywood, CA - *BillIntBG 83-84*
Creative Crafts - Newton, NJ - *MagDir 84; MagIndMarPl 82-83*
Creative Crafts & Miniatures - Newton, NJ - *ArtMar 84; BaconPubCkMag 84; WritMar 84*
Creative Curriculum Inc. - Huntington Beach, CA - *AvMarPl 83; BoPubDir 4 Sup, 5*
Creative Data Inc. - Van Nuys, CA - *IntDirMarRes 83*
Creative Dept. Inc., The - Philadelphia, PA - *HBIndAd&MS 82-83*
Creative Dept. Inc., The - Milwaukee, WI - *HBIndAd&MS 82-83*
Creative Dimensions [Div. of The Creative Group Inc.] - Appleton, WI - *StaDirAdAg 2-84*
Creative Education Foundation Inc. - Buffalo, NY - *BoPubDir 4, 5*
Creative Education Inc. [Aff. of Child's World Inc.] - Mankato, MN - *LitMarPl 83, 84*
Creative Encounters Inc. - *See* Empire City Marketing
Creative Establishment, The - Chicago, IL - *ArtMar 84*

Creative Establishment, The - New York, NY - *ArtMar 84; WritMar 84*
Creative Exchange Inc. - Dayton, OH - *AvMarPl 83*
Creative Eye Press - Phoenix, AZ - *BoPubDir 5*
Creative Eye Press - Modesto, CA - *BoPubDir 4*
Creative Film Society - Reseda, CA - *AvMarPl 83*
Creative Forum, The - New York, NY - *MagIndMarPl 82-83*
Creative Freelancers Inc. - New York, NY - *InfIndMarPl 83; LitMarPl 83, 84*
Creative Group Inc., The - New Haven, CT - *StaDirAdAg 2-84*
Creative Hair Designer [of Business Journals] - Norwalk, CT - *MagDir 84*
Creative Homeowner Press [Aff. of Federal Marketing Corp.] - Passaic, NJ - *BoPubDir 5*
Creative Homeowner Press [Aff. of Federal Marketing Corp.] - Milwaukee, WI - *BoPubDir 4*
Creative House Advertising Inc. - Southfield, MI - *ArtMar 84; StaDirAdAg 2-84*
Creative Infomatics Inc. - Minnetonka, MN - *BoPubDir 4, 5*
Creative Information Systems - Portland, OR - *DataDirOnSer 84*
Creative Learning Inc. - Warren, RI - *AvMarPl 83*
Creative Learning Press Inc. - Mansfield Center, CT - *BoPubDir 4, 5; LitMarPl 84*
Creative List Services Inc. - Farmingdale, NY - *EISS 5-84 Sup*
Creative Living - New York, NY - *MagDir 84*
Creative Mailing Consultants of America Inc. - Capitol Heights, MD - *DirMarMP 83; MagIndMarPl 82-83*
Creative Marketing - Fairfield, NJ - *StaDirAdAg 2-84*
Creative Marketing Associates - Pittsburgh, PA - *DirMarMP 83; StaDirAdAg 2-84*
Creative Marketing Concepts Ltd. - Cranston, RI - *StaDirAdAg 2-84*
Creative Marketing Management - New York, NY - *HBIndAd&MS 82-83*
Creative Media Agency - New York, NY - *StaDirAdAg 2-84*
Creative Media Development - Portland, OR - *AvMarPl 83*
Creative Media Productions [Div. of Ikonographics Inc.] - Louisville, KY - *AvMarPl 83*
Creative Microlibraries Inc. [Div. of Svobodny Development Corp.] - Manhasset, NY - *MicroMarPl 82-83*
Creative Mind Workshop, The - Columbus, OH - *MicrocomMPl 84*
Creative Music Group - Hollywood, CA - *BillIntBG 83-84*
Creative Options Publishing - Edmonds, WA - *BoPubDir 4, 5; LitMag&SmPr 83-84*
Creative Penthouse - New York, NY - *HBIndAd&MS 82-83*
Creative People Inc. - Chicago, IL - *HBIndAd&MS 82-83*
Creative Press Inc. - *See* Creative Advertising
Creative Product News - Lake Forest, IL - *WritMar 84*
Creative Productions - Orange, NJ - *AvMarPl 83; WritMar 84*
Creative Productions - New York, NY - *AvMarPl 83; HBIndAd&MS 82-83*
Creative Products News - Lake Forest, IL - *BaconPubCkMag 84*
Creative Products Source - Ft. Lee, NJ - *HBIndAd&MS 82-83*
Creative Professional Service - Woburn, MA - *DirInfWP 82*
Creative Programming - Pasadena, CA - *ADAPSOMemDir 83-84*
Creative Programming - Weston, CT - *Tel&CabFB 84C*
Creative Programming - Arlington Heights, IL - *LitMarPl 84; MicrocomMPl 84*
Creative Programs Unltd. - Seattle, WA - *MicrocomMPl 84*
Creative Publications [Aff. of Westinghouse Learning Corp.] - Palo Alto, CA - *LitMarPl 83, 84*
Creative Publishing - College Station, TX - *LitMarPl 83, 84; WritMar 84*
Creative Publishing Report - Edmonds, WA - *BaconPubCkMag 84*
Creative Research & Educational Systems for Today - Flushing, NY - *BoPubDir 4, 5*
Creative Research Associates Inc. - Chicago, IL - *IntDirMarRes 83*
Creative Research Group Ltd., The - Toronto, ON, Canada - *IntDirMarRes 83*
Creative Research Services Inc. - New York, NY - *IntDirMarRes 83*
Creative Research Systems - San Francisco, CA - *MicrocomMPl 84; MicrocomSwDir 1*
Creative Resource Group - Buffalo, NY - *StaDirAdAg 2-84*
Creative Resources - Miami, FL - *ArtMar 84*
Creative Resources - Cincinnati, OH - *BoPubDir 5; LitMag&SmPr 83-84*
Creative Roots Inc. - New York, NY - *LitMag&SmPr 83-84*
Creative Sales Promotion Associates Inc. - St. Louis, MO - *StaDirAdAg 2-84*
Creative Selling - Lake Forest, IL - *BaconPubCkMag 84; MagIndMarPl 82-83*
Creative Selling - Carnegie, PA - *AvMarPl 83*
Creative Services - Carmel, CA - *LitMarPl 83, 84; MagIndMarPl 82-83*
Creative Services - Chicago, IL - *StaDirAdAg 2-84*
Creative Services - Merion, PA - *LitMarPl 84*
Creative Socio-Medics Inc. [Subs. of Advanced Computer Techniques Corp.] - New York, NY - *DataDirOnSer 84*
Creative Software Development - West Valley City, UT - *MicrocomMPl 83*
Creative Software Inc. - Madison, WI - *MicrocomMPl 84*
Creative Solutions Inc. - Rockville, MD - *MicrocomMPl 84; MicrocomSwDir 1*
Creative Solutions Inc. - Ann Arbor, MI - *MicrocomSwDir 1*
Creative Sound Recording Studios - Brazil, IN - *BillIntBG 83-84*
Creative Source Music - *See* I've Got the Music Co.
Creative Storytime Press - Minneapolis, MN - *BoPubDir 4, 5*
Creative Strategies International - San Jose, CA - *BoPubDir 5; InfoS 83-84*
Creative Technical Consultants - Cedar Crest, NM - *MicrocomMPl 84*
Creative Technologies Inc. - Annandale, VA - *AvMarPl 83; DataDirSup 7-83*
Creative Touch Ltd. - New Berlin, WI - *StaDirAdAg 2-84*
Creative Venture Films [Subs. of Forney Miller Film Associates] - Spring House, PA - *AvMarPl 83*
Creative Ventures Inc. - West Lafayette, IN - *BoPubDir 5*
Creative Visuals - Minneapolis, MN - *AvMarPl 83*
Creative Visuals [Div. of Gamco Industries Inc.] - Big Spring, TX - *WritMar 84*
Creative with Words Publications - Carmel, CA - *BoPubDir 4 Sup, 5; LitMag&SmPr 83-84*
Creative Woman, The - Park Forest South, IL - *LitMag&SmPr 83-84*
Creative Workshop Inc. - Ft. Lauderdale, FL - *DirPRFirms 83*
Creative World Inc. - Los Angeles, CA - *BillIntBG 83-84*
Creative Years - Gainesville, FL - *WritMar 84*
Creativision - Stamford, CT - *TelAl 83, 84*
Creativity - Toronto, ON, Canada - *BaconPubCkMag 84*
Creatures at Large - Pacifica, CA - *BoPubDir 4, 5*
Credences: Journal of Twentieth Century Poetry & Poetics - Buffalo, NY - *LitMag&SmPr 83-84*
Credit [of American Financial Services Association] - Washington, DC - *BaconPubCkMag 84; MagDir 84*
Credit & Financial Management [of National Association of Credit Management] - New York, NY - *BaconPubCkMag 84; MagDir 84; MagIndMarPl 82-83*
Credit Card Journal - New York, NY - *BaconPubCkMag 84*
Credit Consultant Inc. - Tokyo, Japan - *IntDirMarRes 83*
Credit Data [of TRW Inc.] - Orange, CA - *DBBus 82; DirOnDB Spring 84; EISS 83*
Credit Executive [of NY Credit & Financial Management Association] - New York, NY - *BaconPubCkMag 84; MagDir 84*
Credit Research Foundation Inc. [Aff. of National Association of Credit Management] - Lake Success, NY - *BoPubDir 4, 5*
Credit Union Executive - Madison, WI - *BaconPubCkMag 84*
Credit Union Life - Eau Claire, WI - *MagDir 84*
Credit Union Magazine [of Credit Union National Association] - Madison, WI - *BaconPubCkMag 84; MagDir 84; MagIndMarPl 82-83*
Credit Union National Association - Madison, WI - *BoPubDir 5*
Credit Union News - New York, NY - *BaconPubCkMag 84*
Credit Union Regulator - Wilmington, DE - *DirOnDB Spring 84*
Credit Union Regulator [of NewsNet Inc.] - Bryn Mawr, PA - *DataDirOnSer 84*
Credit Valley Cable TV/FM Ltd. - Scarborough, ON, Canada - *Tel&CabFB 84C*
Credit Valley Cable TV/FM Ltd. - *See* Rogers Cablesystems Inc.

Credit World, The [of International Consumer Credit Association] - St. Louis, MO - *BaconPubCkMag 84; MagDir 84; MagIndMarPl 82-83*
Creditalk - New York, NY - *MagDir 84*
Credithriftalk [of Credithrift Financial] - Evansville, IN - *ArtMar 84; WritMar 84*
Credo Publications - West Stockbridge, MA - *BoPubDir 4, 5*
Credoc/Bjus - *See* Bjus
Credoc/Blex - *See* Blex
Credoc/Coralie - *See* Coralie
Cree Productions Inc. [Aff. of Native Heritage & Cultural Centre] - Edmonton, AB, Canada - *BoPubDir 4 Sup, 5*
Creed Associates Inc. - Boston, MA - *TelAl 83, 84*
Creed Public Relations & Marketing Services, Dudley - San Francisco, CA - *DirPRFirms 83*
Creede Mineral County Miner - Creede, CO - *BaconPubCkNews 84*
Creedmoor Butner-Creedmoor News - Creedmoor, NC - *BaconPubCkNews 84; NewsDir 84*
Creek House - Ojai, CA - *BoPubDir 4, 5*
CreekSide Music Publishing Co. - Tabor City, NC - *BillIntBG 83-84*
Creekwood Press - Birmingham, AL - *BoPubDir 4, 5; LitMag&SmPr 83-84*
Creelman Celebrate Saskatchewan Committee - Creelman, SK, Canada - *BoPubDir 4 Sup, 5*
Creem - Birmingham, MI - *BaconPubCkMag 84; MagDir 84; MagIndMarPl 82-83; WritMar 84*
Creemore Star, The - Creemore, ON, Canada - *Ed&PubIntYB 82*
Crehore, John Davenport - Oakland, CA - *BoPubDir 4, 5*
Creighton Banner - Creighton, MO - *BaconPubCkNews 84; Ed&PubIntYB 82*
Creighton News - Creighton, NE - *BaconPubCkNews 84; Ed&PubIntYB 82*
Creighton, Tom - Jacksboro, TX - *Tel&CabFB 84C p.1676*
Cren Publishing Ltd. - Ottawa, ON, Canada - *LitMag&SmPr 83-84*
Crenshaw News - Crenshaw, CA - *Ed&PubIntYB 82*
Crenshaw News [of Culver City Coast Media Newspapers] - Culver City, CA - *AyerDirPub 83; NewsDir 84*
Crenshaw News - *See* Coast Media Newspapers
Crescendo Publishing - New York, NY - *WritMar 84*
Crescendo Record Co. - Astoria, NY - *BillIntBG 83-84*
Crescent - Saguache, CO - *AyerDirPub 83*
Crescent - Climax, MI - *AyerDirPub 83*
Crescent - Hills, MN - *AyerDirPub 83; Ed&PubIntYB 82*
Crescent City Courier-Journal - Crescent City, FL - *BaconPubCkNews 84*
Crescent City Del Norte Triplicate [of Hadley Newspapers Inc.] - Crescent City, CA - *BaconPubCkNews 84; NewsDir 84*
Crescent International Toronto - Willowdale, ON, Canada - *Ed&PubIntYB 82*
Crescent Lake Clearview Cable TV - Crescent City, FL - *BrCabYB 84*
Crescent Logan County News - Crescent, OK - *BaconPubCkNews 84*
Crescent Music Group - Los Angeles, CA - *BillIntBG 83-84*
Crescent News - Defiance, OH - *AyerDirPub 83; BaconPubCkNews 84; Ed&PubIntYB 82*
Crescent Records - Los Angeles, CA - *BillIntBG 83-84*
Crescenta Valley Cable TV [of SSE Communications] - La Crescenta, CA - *Tel&CabFB 84C*
Cresco Times-Plain Dealer [of T.P.D. Publishing Inc.] - Cresco, IA - *BaconPubCkNews 84; NewsDir 84*
Cresmer, Woodward, O'Mara & Ormsbee Inc. - New York, NY - *Ed&PubIntYB 82; LitMarPl 83, 84*
Cresset Publishers - Philadelphia, PA - *BoPubDir 4, 5*
Cresson-Gallitzin Mainliner - Cresson, PA - *Ed&PubIntYB 82*
Cresson Gallitzin Mainliner - *See* Sedloff Publications Inc.
Crest Antenna Systems Inc. - Arnold, MO - *Tel&CabFB 84C*
Crest Challenge Books - Loma Linda, CA - *BoPubDir 4 Sup, 5*
Crest Communications Inc. [of Tele-Communications Inc.] - Derby, KS - *Tel&CabFB 84C*
Crest Communications Inc. [of Tele-Communications Inc.] - El Dorado, KS - *Tel&CabFB 84C*
Crest Communications Inc. - Rose Hill, KS - *BrCabYB 84*
Crest Electronics - Los Angeles, CA - *AvMarPl 83*
Crest Litho Inc. - Albany, NY - *LitMarPl 83, 84; MagIndMarPl 82-83*
Crest National Videotape & Film Laboratories - Hollywood, CA - *AvMarPl 83*
Crested Butte Cable - Crested Butte, CO - *Tel&CabFB 84C*
Crested Butte Chronicle - Crested Butte, CO - *BaconPubCkNews 84*
Crested Butte Pilot - Crested Butte, CO - *BaconPubCkNews 84; Ed&PubIntYB 82*
Crestline Advocate - Crestline, OH - *BaconPubCkNews 84; Ed&PubIntYB 82*
Crestline Mountain Courier - Crestline, CA - *BaconPubCkNews 84*
Crestline Publishing Co. Inc. - Sarasota, FL - *BoPubDir 4, 5*
Creston Cabled-Video Ltd. - Creston, BC, Canada - *BrCabYB 84*
Creston Cablevision Inc. [of Heritage Communications Inc.] - Creston, IA - *Tel&CabFB 84C*
Creston News-Advertiser - Creston, IA - *BaconPubCkNews 84; Ed&PubIntYB 82; NewsDir 84*
Creston Review, The - Creston, BC, Canada - *Ed&PubIntYB 82*
Creston Valley Advance, The - Creston, BC, Canada - *Ed&PubIntYB 82*
Crestview Cable TV [of California-Oregon Broadcasting Inc.] - Enterprise, OR - *BrCabYB 84; Tel&CabFB 84C*
Crestview Cable TV [of California-Oregon Broadcasting Inc.] - Madras, OR - *BrCabYB 84; Tel&CabFB 84C*
Crestview Cable TV [of California-Oregon Broadcasting Inc.] - Prineville, OR - *BrCabYB 84; Tel&CabFB 84C*
Crestview North Okaloosa Bulletin - Crestview, FL - *BaconPubCkNews 84*
Crestview Okaloosa News-Journal [of Scripps League Newspapers Inc.] - Crestview, FL - *BaconPubCkNews 84; NewsDir 84*
Crestwood House Inc. - Mankato, MN - *LitMarPl 83, 84; WritMar 84*
Crestwood Micro Systems Inc. - West Hurley, NY - *MicrocomMPl 84*
Creswell Chronicle - Creswell, OR - *BaconPubCkNews 84; NewsDir 84*
Creswell, Munsell, Fultz & Zirbel [of Young & Rubicam] - Cedar Rapids, IA - *AdAge 3-28-84; BrCabYB 84; DirPRFirms 83; LitMarPl 83, 84; TelAl 83, 84*
Creswell, Munsell, Fultz & Zirbel Inc. - Des Moines, IA - *TelAl 83*
Crete News - Crete, NE - *BaconPubCkNews 84; Ed&PubIntYB 82; NewsDir 84*
Crete-Park Forest South Star [of Chicago Heights Star Publications] - Chicago Heights, IL - *NewsDir 84*
Crete-Park Forest South Star - Crete, IL - *AyerDirPub 83*
Crete-Park Forest South Star - Park Forest South, IL - *Ed&PubIntYB 82*
Crete-Park Forest South Star - *See* Star Publications
Crete Record - *See* Russell Publications
Creutz & Co., Robert T. - Boston, MA - *LitMarPl 83, 84; MagIndMarPl 82-83*
Creveling, Joanne - New York, NY - *DirPRFirms 83*
Crewe-Burkeville Journal - Crewe, VA - *AyerDirPub 83; BaconPubCkNews 84; Ed&PubIntYB 82; NewsDir 84*
Cricket Letter Inc., The - Ardmore, PA - *Ed&PubIntYB 82*
Cricket Publications - Toledo, OH - *ArtMar 84; WritMar 84*
Cricket: The Magazine for Children [of Open Court Publishing Co.] - La Salle, IL - *DirMarMP 83; LitMarPl 83, 84; MagDir 84; MagIndMarPl 82-83*
Cricket Theatre, The - Minneapolis, MN - *WritMar 84*
Crier - Lake Lillian, MN - *AyerDirPub 83*
Crime & Delinquency - Hackensack, NJ - *MagDir 84; MagIndMarPl 82-83*
Crime & Social Justice Associates Inc. - San Francisco, CA - *BoPubDir 4, 5; LitMag&SmPr 83-84*
Criminal Justice Archive Directory - Ann Arbor, MI - *DirOnDB Spring 84*
Criminal Justice Career Digest - Phoenix, AZ - *WritMar 84*
Criminal Justice Periodical Index [of University Microfilms International] - Ann Arbor, MI - *CompReadDB 82; DirOnDB Spring 84; EISS 83; OnBibDB 3*
Criminal Justice Periodicals Index [of Dialog Information Services Inc.] - Palo Alto, CA - *DataDirOnSer 84*
Criminal Law Bulletin - New York, NY - *BaconPubCkMag 84*
Crimmins & Co., Ed - Fairfield, CT - *HBIndAd&MS 82-83*

Crimmins Public Relations Inc., Thomas - Huntington, NY - *DirPRFirms 83*
Crimson Camera Technical Sales Inc. - Cambridge, MA - *AvMarPl 83*
Crimson Dynasty Record Corp. - Jenkintown, PA - *BillIntBG 83-84*
Crimson Printing Co. - Cambridge, MA - *LitMarPl 83, 84*
Crimson-White [of The University of Alabama] - Stewart, AL - *NewsDir 84*
Cripple Creek Gold Rush - Cripple Creek, CO - *BaconPubCkNews 84*
CRIS/USDA - Beltsville, MD - *DirOnDB Spring 84*
Crises Research Press [Aff. of American Buddhist Movement] - New York, NY - *BoPubDir 5*
Crisfield CATV [of Stewart Spitz & Associates] - Crisfield, MD - *BrCabYB 84; Tel&CabFB 84C*
Crisfield Times - Crisfield, MD - *BaconPubCkNews 84; Ed&PubIntYB 82*
Crisis, The - Brooklyn, NY - *BaconPubCkMag 84*
Crisis, The - New York, NY - *MagDir 84; MagIndMarPl 82-83*
Crisler & Co. Inc., R. C. - Cincinnati, OH - *CabTVFinDB 83*
Crisman, Don R. - Troy, PA - *Tel&CabFB 84C p.1676*
Crisman, Naomi L. - Troy, PA - *Tel&CabFB 84C p.1676*
Crisp & Harrison Agency - Jacksonville, FL - *StaDirAdAg 2-84*
Crisp Area Scene - Cordele, GA - *AyerDirPub 83*
Crispin & Associates, Samuel B. - Coral Gables, FL - *StaDirAdAg 2-84*
Crissey, Harrington E. Jr. - Philadelphia, PA - *BoPubDir 5*
Crista Broadcasting - Seattle, WA - *BrCabYB 84*
Criswell Div. Inc. - San Francisco, CA - *StaDirAdAg 2-84*
CRIT Criterion News/Advertiser, The - Metuchen, NJ - *AyerDirPub 83*
Criterion - Dodge, NE - *AyerDirPub 83*
Criterion - Dallas, TX - *EISS 83*
Criterion Music Corp. - Hollywood, CA - *BillIntBG 83-84; BoPubDir 4, 5*
Criterion Photocraft Co. - New York, NY - *LitMarPl 83, 84*
Criterion, The - Indianapolis, IN - *NewsDir 84*
Critical Care Medical Library - Latham, NY - *DirOnDB Spring 84*
Critical Care Medicine - Baltimore, MD - *BaconPubCkMag 84; MagDir 84*
Critical Care Medicine [of Bibliographic Retrieval Services Inc.] - Latham, NY - *DataDirOnSer 84*
Critical Care Nurse - Bridgewater, NJ - *BaconPubCkMag 84*
Critical Review, The - Canberra, Austria - *LitMag&SmPr 83-84*
Criticality Experiments, 1943-1978-An Annotated Bibliography [of Lawrence Livermore National Laboratory] - Livermore, CA - *CompReadDB 82*
Critique: A Journal of Conspiracy & Metaphysics [of Critique Foundation] - Santa Rosa, CA - *WritMar 84*
Critique Music Publishing Co. Inc. - Reading, MA - *BillIntBG 83-84*
Critique: Studies in Modern Fiction - Atlanta, GA - *LitMag&SmPr 83-84; LitMarPl 83*
Crittenden Bulletin [of NewsNet Inc.] - Bryn Mawr, PA - *DataDirOnSer 84*
Crittenden-North Concepts [Aff. of Healthworks Medical Group Inc.] - South Laguna, CA - *BoPubDir 5*
Crittenden Press - Marion, KY - *AyerDirPub 83; Ed&PubIntYB 82; NewsDir 84*
Crittenden Report [of NewsNet Inc.] - Bryn Mawr, PA - *DataDirOnSer 84*
CRK Advertising - New York, NY - *StaDirAdAg 2-84*
CRM/McGraw-Hill - Del Mar, CA - *Tel&CabFB 84C*
CRM/McGraw-Hill - Solana Beach, CA - *LitMarPl 84*
Crocco Co., W. C. - Glen Rock, NJ - *DirPRFirms 83*
Crocker & Hull Advertising Inc. - New York, NY - *StaDirAdAg 2-84*
Crockett Cable TV Co. Inc. [of Tribune Cable Communications Inc.] - Alamo, TN - *BrCabYB 84; Tel&CabFB 84C*
Crockett County Sentinel - Bells, TN - *AyerDirPub 83; Ed&PubIntYB 82*
Crockett Houston County Courier - Crockett, TX - *Ed&PubIntYB 82; NewsDir 84*
Crockett Houston County Courier - *See* Polk County Publishing
Crockett Telephone Co. - Friendship, TN - *TelDir&BG 83-84*
Crockett Times - Alamo, TN - *AyerDirPub 83; Ed&PubIntYB 82*
Croft Associates, Susan - Los Angeles, CA - *DirPRFirms 83*
Crofton Journal - Crofton, NE - *BaconPubCkNews 84; Ed&PubIntYB 82*
Crofton News-Crier [of Bowie News/Prince Georges County News] - Bowie, MD - *NewsDir 84*
Crofton News Crier - Crofton, MD - *Ed&PubIntYB 82*
Crofton News-Crier - *See* Capital Gazette Newspapers
Crofton Publishing Corp. - Brookline, MA - *BoPubDir 4, 5*
Croissant & Co. - Athens, OH - *BoPubDir 4, 5; LitMag&SmPr 83-84*
Croma Music Co. Inc. - New York, NY - *BillIntBG 83-84*
Cromar's Audio Visual Center - Denver, CO - *AvMarPl 83; Tel&CabFB 84C*
Cromelin, Paul L. - Savannah, GA - *BoPubDir 4, 5*
Cromemco Inc. - Mountain View, CA - *DataDirSup 7-83; DirInfWP 82; MicrocomMPl 83, 84; WhoWMicrocom 83*
Cromemco Local Area Network [of Cromemco Inc.] - Mountain View, CA - *TeleSy&SerDir 7-83*
Cromlech Press - Hamilton, ON, Canada - *BoPubDir 4, 5*
Cromona Letcher County Community Press - Cromona, KY - *BaconPubCkNews 84; NewsDir 84*
Cromwel Press - Santa Margarita, CA - *BoPubDir 4, 5*
Cromwell Music Inc. - *See* TRO
Cromwell-Smith Services - La Jolla, CA - *BoPubDir 4, 5*
Crone Associates, Charles - Raleigh, NC - *StaDirAdAg 2-84*
Cronenwett Associates - Holton, MI - *DirPRFirms 83*
Crones' Own Press - Durham, NC - *LitMag&SmPr 83-84*
Cronin & Associates, Sylvia - Miami, FL - *DirPRFirms 83*
Cronin & Co. Inc. - Glastonbury, CT - *StaDirAdAg 2-84*
Cronin Feature Syndicating Inc. [Div. of Consumer Information Advisor] - Miami, FL - *Ed&PubIntYB 82; LitMarPl 84*
CRONOS [of CISInetwork] - Van Nuys, CA - *DataDirOnSer 84*
CRONOS Data Bank [of Commission of the European Communities] - Kirchberg, Luxembourg - *EISS 83*
CRONOS-Eurostat - Luxembourg - *DirOnDB Spring 84*
Cronquist, Jack - Grand Forks Air Force Base, ND - *Tel&CabFB 84C p.1676*
Crook Advertising Agency Inc. - Dallas, TX - *StaDirAdAg 2-84*
Crook Co., Eddie - Hendersonville, TN - *BillIntBG 83-84*
Crookston Cable TV [of Southern Minnesota Broadcasting Association] - Crookston, MN - *BrCabYB 84; Tel&CabFB 84C*
Crookston Shopper - Crookston, MN - *AyerDirPub 83*
Crookston Times - Crookston, MN - *BaconPubCkNews 84; Ed&PubIntYB 82; NewsDir 84*
Crop Dust - Bealeton, VA - *LitMag&SmPr 83-84*
Crop Dust Press - Bealeton, VA - *LitMag&SmPr 83-84*
Crop Science [of Crop Science Society of America] - Madison, WI - *BaconPubCkMag 84; MagDir 84*
Crops & Soils Magazine [of American Society of Agronomy] - Madison, WI - *BaconPubCkMag 84; MagDir 84*
Crosby Cable Inc. - Indianola, MS - *BrCabYB 84*
Crosby Cablevision Inc. [of Tioga Cablevision Inc.] - Crosby, ND - *Tel&CabFB 84C*
Crosby Divide County Journal - Crosby, ND - *BaconPubCkNews 84*
Crosby, Edward L. III - Indialantic, FL - *LitMarPl 84*
Crosby-Ironton Courier - Crosby, MN - *AyerDirPub 83; BaconPubCkNews 84; Ed&PubIntYB 82*
Crosby Journal [of The Divide County Journal] - Crosby, ND - *NewsDir 84*
Crosby Productions Inc., Bing - Hollywood, CA - *TelAl 83, 84*
Crosby Typographers [Subs. of Capitol-Crosby Typographers Inc.] - New York, NY - *LitMarPl 83, 84*
Crosbyton Review - Crosbyton, TX - *BaconPubCkNews 84; Ed&PubIntYB 82*
Crosley Inc. - Jonesboro, AR - *BoPubDir 4, 5*
Cross Associates Inc., B. - Indianapolis, IN - *ADAPSOMemDir 83-84*
Cross Books - North Providence, RI - *BoPubDir 4, 5*
Cross-Canada Writers' Quarterly [of Columbine Editions] - Toronto, ON, Canada - *LitMag&SmPr 83-84*
Cross City Dixie County Advocate - Cross City, FL - *BaconPubCkNews 84*
Cross Communications Co. - Boulder, CO - *DirInfWP 82*
Cross Country Cable Ltd. - Warren, NJ - *Tel&CabFB 84C p.1676*
Cross Country Cable Ltd. - Chesapeake, VA - *Tel&CabFB 84C*

Cross Country Network Inc. - Chicago, IL - *Tel&CabFB 84C*
Cross Country Press Ltd. - Flushing, NY - *BoPubDir 4, 5; LitMag&SmPr 83-84*
Cross Country Ski - New York, NY - *BaconPubCkMag 84*
Cross County Shopper - Saskatoon, SK, Canada - *AyerDirPub 83*
Cross County Times - Parkin, AR - *AyerDirPub 83; Ed&PubIntYB 82*
Cross-Cultural Communications [Aff. of Coop Antigruppo Siciliano] - Merrick, NY - *BoPubDir 4, 5*
Cross Currents - Dobbs Ferry, NY - *LitMarPl 83, 84; MagIndMarPl 82-83*
Cross-Database Search System [of Bibliographic Retrieval Services Inc.] - Latham, NY - *CompReadDB 82*
Cross Educational Software - Ruston, LA - *MicrocomMPl 84; MicrocomSwDir 1; WhoWMicrocom 83*
Cross, Henry B. Jr. - New Milford, CT - *Tel&CabFB 84C p.1676*
Cross Information Co. - Boulder, CO - *DataDirOnSer 84; EISS 7-83 Sup; MicrocomMPl 84*
Cross Keys Advertising - Doylestown, PA - *AdAge 3-28-84*
Cross Keys Publishing Co. Inc. - *See* Tree International
Cross Plains Review - Cross Plains, TX - *BaconPubCkNews 84; Ed&PubIntYB 82*
Cross, Ruth C. - Woods Hole, MA - *LitMarPl 83, 84*
Cross Siclare/New York Inc. - Staten Island, NY - *LitMarPl 83, 84; MagIndMarPl 82-83*
Cross Telephone Co. of Oklahoma Inc. - Warner, OK - *TelDir&BG 83-84*
Cross Timbers Music - *See* Booth & Watson Music
Crossan Research Consultants Inc. - Van Nuys, CA - *IntDirMarRes 83*
Crossbow [of Fraser Williams Scientific Systems Ltd.] - Poynton, England - *EISS 83*
Crosscountry - Flushing, NY - *LitMag&SmPr 83-84*
Crosscurrents - Westlake Village, CA - *ArtMar 84; WritMar 84*
Crosscurrents [of Greenwich-Meridian] - Saskatoon, SK, Canada - *LitMag&SmPr 83-84*
Crosscut Saw Press - Berkeley, CA - *BoPubDir 4, 5*
Crossett Ashley News Observer - Crossett, AR - *BaconPubCkNews 84*
Crossett Cable TV [of Communications Systems Inc.] - Crossett, AR - *BrCabYB 84; Tel&CabFB 84C*
Crosseyed Bear Music - *See* Harlem Music
Crossfield History Group - Crossfield, AB, Canada - *BoPubDir 4 Sup, 5*
Crossing Press, The - Trumansburg, NY - *ArtMar 84; LitMag&SmPr 83-84; LitMarPl 83, 84; WritMar 84*
Crosslake Telephone Co. - Crosslake, MN - *TelDir&BG 83-84*
Crossley, Dorothy I. - Franconia, NH - *MagIndMarPl 82-83*
Crossley Surveys Inc. - New York, NY - *BrCabYB 84; IntDirMarRes 83; Tel&CabFB 84C*
Crossly Youth-Student Surveys/Consultants - New York, NY - *IntDirMarRes 83*
Crossman Co., M. R. - North Hollywood, CA - *StaDirAdAg 2-84*
Crossover Programming Co. - Santa Monica, CA - *TelAl 83, 84*
Crosspoint Latch Corp. - Union, NJ - *AvMarPl 83*
Crossroad Publishing Co., The [Subs. of W. H. Smith Publishers Inc.] - New York, NY - *LitMarPl 83, 84*
Crossroads - Los Angeles, CA - *BoPubDir 4, 5*
Crossroads - Evanston, IL - *MagIndMarPl 82-83*
Crossroads Press [Div. of African Studies Association] - Los Angeles, CA - *LitMarPl 83, 84*
Crossroads Press - *See* African Studies Association/Crossroads Press
Crossville Cable Television Inc. - Crossville, AL - *BrCabYB 84*
Crossville Cable Television Inc. [of Matrix Enterprises Inc.] - Crossville, TN - *BrCabYB 84*
Crossville Chronicle - Crossville, TN - *BaconPubCkNews 84; Ed&PubIntYB 82; NewsDir 84*
Crossville Cumberland County Times - Crossville, TN - *NewsDir 84*
Crossville Telephone Co. - Crossville, IL - *TelDir&BG 83-84*
Crossway Books [Aff. of Good News Publishers] - Westchester, IL - *BoPubDir 4, 5; LitMarPl 84; WritMar 84*
Crosswicks Cable TV [of Times Mirror Cable Television Inc.] - Brick Town, NJ - *BrCabYB 84*
Crosswicks Industries [of Times Mirror Cable Television Inc.] - Brick Township, NJ - *Tel&CabFB 84C*
Crosswind - Oak Harbor, WA - *AyerDirPub 83*
Croswell Jeffersonian/Advisor - Croswell, MI - *BaconPubCkNews 84*
Croswell Sanilac Jeffersonian/Advisor - Croswell, MI - *NewsDir 84*
Croton Cortlandt News [of Carmel Putnam County Courier] - Carmel, NY - *NewsDir 84*
Croton Cortlandt News - Croton-on-Hudson, NY - *Ed&PubIntYB 82*
Croton Review [of Croton Council on the Arts Inc.] - Croton-on-Hudson, NY - *LitMag&SmPr 83-84; WritMar 84*
Crow Cable TV - Crow Agency, MT - *BrCabYB 84*
Crow Production - Sacramento, CA - *BoPubDir 4, 5*
Crow Production - Long Beach, NY - *BillIntBG 83-84*
Crow Ridge Associates Inc. - New Scotland, NY - *MicrocomMPl 84*
Crow River Cable TV [of Mickelson Media Inc.] - Hutchinson, MN - *BrCabYB 84; Tel&CabFB 84C*
Crow River News - Osseo, MN - *AyerDirPub 83*
Crow River News - St. Michael, MN - *Ed&PubIntYB 82*
Crow Wing County Review - Brainerd, MN - *Ed&PubIntYB 82*
Crowe Advertising Agency, John - Springfield, IL - *ArtMar 84; StaDirAdAg 2-84*
Crowell Foard County News - Crowell, TX - *BaconPubCkNews 84*
Crowell/Lippincott Junior Books - *See* Harper & Row (Junior Books Group)
Crowell McKay Inc. - Irvine, CA - *DirPRFirms 83; StaDirAdAg 2-84*
Crowfoot Press - Ann Arbor, MI - *BoPubDir 4, 5*
Crowhaven - Denver, CO - *ArtMar 84*
Crowley & Associates Inc., John H. - Milwaukee, WI - *StaDirAdAg 2-84*
Crowley Beacon - Crowley, TX - *BaconPubCkNews 84; Ed&PubIntYB 82*
Crowley Cable TV [of TCA Cable TV Inc.] - Crowley, LA - *BrCabYB 84; Tel&CabFB 84C*
Crowley Post-Signal - Crowley, LA - *BaconPubCkNews 84; Ed&PubIntYB 82; NewsDir 84*
Crowley Ridge Chronicle - Forrest City, AR - *Ed&PubIntYB 82*
Crowley the Magazine Man Inc. - Bronx, NY - *MagIndMarPl 82-83*
Crown Bindery Service - Frankford, ON, Canada - *LitMarPl 83, 84*
Crown International Literature & Arts Agency, Bonnie R. - New York, NY - *LitMarPl 83, 84*
Crown International Pay Television Inc. - Beverly Hills, CA - *Tel&CabFB 84C*
Crown Music Press - *See* Brass Press
Crown Paper Board Co. Inc. - Philadelphia, PA - *LitMarPl 83, 84*
Crown Point Lake County Star - Crown Point, IN - *BaconPubCkNews 84*
Crown Point Lake County Star-Register Newspapers - Crown Point, IN - *NewsDir 84*
Crown Point Register - Crown Point, IN - *BaconPubCkNews 84; Ed&PubIntYB 82*
Crown Point Telephone Corp. - Crown Point, NY - *TelDir&BG 83-84*
Crown Publishers Inc. - New York, NY - *AvMarPl 83; KnowInd 83; LitMarPl 83, 84; WritMar 84*
Crown Record Co. Ltd. - Los Angeles, CA - *BillIntBG 83-84*
Crown Syndicate Inc. - Weatherford, TX - *Ed&PubIntYB 82*
Crown Zellerbach Corp. - San Francisco, CA - *LitMarPl 83, 84*
Crownpoint Cable TV - Crownpoint, OK - *BrCabYB 84*
Crownset Clarion, The - Sparwood, BC, Canada - *Ed&PubIntYB 82*
Crownsoft Applications Inc. - Furlong, PA - *MicrocomMPl 84*
Crow's Mark Press, The - Wolcott, VT - *LitMag&SmPr 83-84*
Crow's Weekly Letter - Portland, OR - *BaconPubCkMag 84; MagDir 84*
Crowsnest Cablevision Ltd. - Blairmore, AB, Canada - *BrCabYB 84*
Crowsnest Cablevision Ltd. - Pincher Creek, AB, Canada - *BrCabYB 84*
CRS Consultants Press - Key Biscayne, FL - *LitMag&SmPr 83-84*

CRU Consultants Inc. [Aff. of Commodities Research Unit Ltd.] - New York, NY - *BoPubDir 5; DataDirOnSer 84*
CRU Lead/Zinc/Silver Cost Model [of CRU Consultants Inc.] - New York, NY - *DataDirOnSer 84*
CRU Lead/Zinc/Silver Mine Revenue & Concentrate Supply Model - New York, NY - *DirOnDB Spring 84*
CRU Mine Smelter & Refinery Databank [ADP Network Services Inc.] - Ann Arbor, MI - *DataDirOnSer 84*
CRU Mine Smelter & Refinery Databank - New York, NY - *DirOnDB Spring 84*
Crucible Press [Aff. of John S. Crosbie Ltd.] - Toronto, ON, Canada - *BoPubDir 5*
Crude Oil Analysis Data Bank [of U.S. Dept. of Energy] - Bartlesville, OK - *EISS 7-83 Sup*
Crude Oil Analysis System - Washington, DC - *DirOnDB Spring 84*
Cruise & Tours Everywhere - New York, NY - *MagDir 84*
Cruise Travel [of Century Publishing Co.] - Evanston, IL - *BaconPubCkMag 84; MagIndMarPl 82-83*
Cruising World - Newport, RI - *BaconPubCkMag 84; MagDir 84; MagIndMarPl 82-83; WritMar 84*
Cruising World Publications Inc. - Newport, RI - *DirMarMP 83*
Crumbley & Associates - Atlanta, GA - *AdAge 3-28-84; StaDirAdAg 2-84*
Crume & Associates Inc. - Dallas, TX - *StaDirAdAg 2-84*
Crump Media Syndicate - Coopersville, MI - *Ed&PubIntYB 82*
Crumpark Publishing Co. - Harrison, AK - *BoPubDir 4, 5*
Crunch Bird Studios Inc. - Farmington Hills, MI - *AvMarPl 83*
Crusade Bible Publishers Inc. [Subs. of Dove Bible Publishers Inc.] - Wichita, KS - *LitMarPl 84*
Crusade Bible Publishers Inc. [Subs. of Dove Bible Publishers Inc.] - Mt. Juliet, TN - *LitMarPl 83*
Crusade Publications - El Monte, CA - *BoPubDir 4, 5*
Crusader - San Diego, CA - *NewsDir 84*
Crusader - Gary, IN - *AyerDirPub 83*
Crusader - Grand Rapids, MI - *ArtMar 84; WritMar 84*
Crusader [of Baptist Brotherhood Commission] - Memphis, TN - *ArtMar 84*
Crusader, The - Centerville, IN - *AyerDirPub 83; Ed&PubIntYB 82*
Crutch Music - *See* Widget Publishing
Crutcher, Marian - Chicago, IL - *HBIndAd&MS 82-83*
Crux Publications [Aff. of Gabriel Publishing Co. Inc.] - Albany, NY - *BoPubDir 4, 5*
Cruzada Spanish Publications - Miami, FL - *BoPubDir 4, 5*
Cryobiology - New York, NY - *MagDir 84*
Cryptologia [of Rose-Hulman Institute of Technology] - Terre Haute, IN - *ArtMar 84*
Cryst - Cambridge, England - *DirOnDB Spring 84*
Crystal City Zavala County Sentinel - Crystal City, TX - *BaconPubCkNews 84*
Crystal Clear CATV Inc. - Florence, MS - *BrCabYB 84*
Crystal Clear Records Inc. - San Francisco, CA - *BillIntBG 83-84*
Crystal Color Co. - Pensacola, FL - *MagIndMarPl 82-83*
Crystal Data Center [of U.S. National Bureau of Standards] - Washington, DC - *EISS 83*
Crystal Falls CATV - Crystal Falls, MI - *BrCabYB 84*
Crystal Falls Diamond Drill - Crystal Falls, MI - *BaconPubCkNews 84; NewsDir 84*
Crystal Fluid Filter - Woodside, NY - *AvMarPl 83*
Crystal Lake Countryside [of Barrington Press Inc.] - Barrington, IL - *AyerDirPub 83; NewsDir 84*
Crystal Lake Morning Herald [of Free Press Inc.] - Crystal Lake, IL - *BaconPubCkNews 84; Ed&PubIntYB 82; NewsDir 84*
Crystal Lake News & McHenry County Guide - Crystal Lake, IL - *BaconPubCkNews 84; Ed&PubIntYB 82; NewsDir 84*
Crystal Pictures Inc. - New York, NY - *ArtMar 84; BillIntBG 83-84; TelAl 83, 84; Tel&CabFB 84C*
Crystal Press Ltd. - Crystal Bay, NV - *BoPubDir 4, 5; LitMag&SmPr 83-84*
Crystal Productions - Aspen, CO - *AvMarPl 83*
Crystal Record Co. - Sedro Woolley, WA - *BillIntBG 83-84*
Crystal Research Ltd. - Torquay, England - *MicrocomSwDir 1*
Crystal River Suncoast Sentinel - Crystal River, FL - *NewsDir 84*
Crystal Springs Meteor - Crystal Springs, MS - *BaconPubCkNews 84*
Crystallographic Data Centre [of Cambridge University] - Cambridge, England - *EISS 83; InfIndMarPl 83*
Crystallographic Data Centre (Bibliographic File) - Cambridge, England - *CompReadDB 82*
Crystallographic Data Centre (Chemical Connectivity File) - Cambridge, England - *CompReadDB 82*
Crystallographic Data Centre (Structural Data) - Cambridge, England - *CompReadDB 82*
CS Publications [Aff. of Career Services Inc.] - El Cajon, CA - *BoPubDir 4, 5*
CSA Inc. - Danbury, CT - *StaDirAdAg 2-84*
CSA Micro Systems - Gerrards Cross, England - *MicrocomSwDir 1*
Csaki, Cuppo Luciana - Bronx, NY - *LitMarPl 84*
Csaki, Luciana - Kansas City, MO - *LitMarPl 83; MagIndMarPl 82-83*
Csaky & Associates Advertising Inc. - Richmond, VA - *StaDirAdAg 2-84; TelAl 83, 84*
CSC Business Systems Inc. - Pleasant Hill, CA - *WhoWMicrocom 83*
CSG Ltd. - Don Mills, ON, Canada - *DirInfWP 82*
CSG Press [Aff. of Capital Systems Group Inc.] - Kensington, MD - *BoPubDir 4, 5*
CSI Business Systems [Subs. of Conceptual Systems Inc.] - Burnsville, MN - *WhoWMicrocom 83*
CSI Career Network - Baltimore, MD - *DirOnDB Spring 84*
CSI Futures-Financial-Options Base [of Commodity Systems Inc.] - Boca Raton, FL - *DirOnDB Spring 84; MicrocomMPl 84*
CSI International Corp. - New York, NY - *StaDirAdAg 2-84*
CSI New Product Testing Centers - Danbury, CT - *HBIndAd&MS 82-83; IntDirMarRes 83*
CSI Piemonte - Torino, Italy - *EISS 83*
CSIRO - East Melbourne, Australia - *MicroMarPl 82-83*
CSIRONET [of Commonwealth Scientific & Industrial Research Organization] - East Melbourne, Australia - *InfIndMarPl 83*
CSL Microdata - Blackrod, England - *MicrocomSwDir 1*
CSO - London, England - *DirOnDB Spring 84*
CSO Macro-Economic Data Bank [of Central Statistical Office] - London, England - *EISS 83*
CSP International - New York, NY - *InterCabHB 3; VideoDir 82-83*
CSP International - London, England - *InfIndMarPl 83*
C.S.P. World News [of Edition Stencil] - Ottawa, ON, Canada - *BoPubDir 4, 5; LitMag&SmPr 83-84*
CSR Inc. - Washington, DC - *EISS 5-84 Sup*
CSRA Cablevision [of Cable Communications Inc.] - North Augusta, SC - *BrCabYB 84; Tel&CabFB 84C*
CSRA Cablevision [of Cable Communications Inc.] - Thomson, SC - *BrCabYB 84*
CSRA Cablevision - *See* Cable Communications Inc.
CSS Publications - Iowa Falls, IA - *BoPubDir 5; LitMag&SmPr 83-84*
CSS/Quotes [of National CSS Inc.] - Wilton, CT - *DBBus 82; DirOnDB Spring 84*
CSWH Univas SA [of the Univas Network] - Zurich, Switzerland - *StaDirAdAg 2-84*
CSX Corp. - Richmond, VA - *KnowInd 83*
CT Journal of Computed Tomography - New York, NY - *BaconPubCkMag 84*
CTA/NEA Action - Santa Ana, CA - *MagDir 84; MagIndMarPl 82-83*
CTC Electronics [Div. of Comm Tech Corp.] - Los Angeles, CA - *MicrocomMPl 84*
CTC of the South [Aff. of Continental Telecom Inc.] - Thomaston, GA - *TelDir&BG 83-84*
CTC of the South-Florida [Aff. of Continental Telephone Corp.] - Marianna, FL - *TelDir&BG 83-84*
CTCI Cablevision Inc. - *See* Tele-Communications Inc.
CTCI of Attica & Williamsport [of Tele-Communications Inc.] - Attica, IN - *BrCabYB 84; Tel&CabFB 84C*
CTCP - Washington, DC - *DirOnDB Spring 84*
CTI - Orem, UT - *MicrocomMPl 83*
CTIC Associates - Arlington, VA - *CabTVFinDB 83; InterCabHB 3*
CTIS - *See* Central Telephone Interviewing System
CTL Electronics Inc. - New York, NY - *AvMarPl 83*

C.T.N.E. Videotex [of Compania Telefonica National de Espana] - Madrid, Spain - *VideoDir 82-83*
CTR Computer Records - Baltimore, MD - *BillIntBG 83-84*
CTR/McGraw-Hill - Monterey, CA - *LitMarPl 84*
CTRAC Computer Services - Middleburg Heights, OH - *ADAPSOMemDir 83-84*
CTS Associates - Detroit, MI - *AdAge 3-28-84; StaDirAdAg 2-84*
CTS Services Inc. - Dallas, TX - *DataDirOnSer 84*
CTV Television Network - Toronto, ON, Canada - *BrCabYB 84; Tel&CabFB 84C*
Cuadra Associates - Santa Monica, CA - *BoPubDir 5; EISS 83; InfIndMarPl 83; InfoS 83-84; WhoWMicrocom 83*
Cuba Cable Co. Inc. - Cuba, NY - *BrCabYB 84; Tel&CabFB 84C*
Cuba City Telephone Exchange Co. [Aff. of Central Western Communications Inc.] - Cuba City, WI - *TelDir&BG 83-84*
Cuba City Tri-County Press - Cuba City, WI - *BaconPubCkNews 84; NewsDir 84*
Cuba Free Press - Cuba, MO - *BaconPubCkNews 84; Ed&PubIntYB 82; NewsDir 84*
Cuba Journal, The - Cuba, IL - *Ed&PubIntYB 82*
Cuba Patriot & Free Press - Cuba, NY - *BaconPubCkNews 84; Ed&PubIntYB 82*
Cube Publications Inc. - Port Jefferson, NY - *LitMag&SmPr 83-84*
Cubic Corp. - San Diego, CA - *DirInfWP 82*
CUC Inc. - Kettering, OH - *DataDirSup 7-83*
CUC Insurance Services Inc. - Stamford, CT - *EISS 7-83 Sup*
CUC Ltd. - Scarborough, ON, Canada - *Tel&CabFB 84C*
CUC Ltd. - *See* Northern Cable Services Ltd.
Cucamonga Ranch Times - *See* Ontario Daily Report
Cudahy Reminder-Enterprise - *See* Community Newspapers Inc.
Cudahy-St. Francis Advisor Press - South Milwaukee, WI - *AyerDirPub 83*
Cudahy-St. Francis Advisor Press - *See* Quality Newspapers/ Suburban Publications
Cudahy-St. Francis Free Press - Cudahy, WI - *Ed&PubIntYB 82*
Cudahy-St. Francis Free Press [of South Milwaukee Voice-Journal] - South Milwaukee, WI - *NewsDir 84*
Cudahy-St. Francis Reminder - Oak Creek, WI - *AyerDirPub 83*
Cude & Pickens Publishing - Daytona Beach, FL - *BillIntBG 83-84*
Cue New York - New York, NY - *MagDir 84*
Cue Recordings Studios Inc. - New York, NY - *AvMarPl 83*
Cue Track - Winnipeg, MB, Canada - *BoPubDir 4, 5*
Cuero Record - Cuero, TX - *AyerDirPub 83; BaconPubCkNews 84; Ed&PubIntYB 82; NewsDir 84*
Cuesta Systems Inc. - San Luis Obispo, CA - *MicrocomMPl 84; WhoWMicrocom 83*
Cuff Publications Ltd., Harry - St. John's, NF, Canada - *BoPubDir 4, 5; LitMarPl 84*
Cuffari & Co. Inc. - Montclair, NJ - *StaDirAdAg 2-84*
Cuisinart Cooking Club [Aff. of Cuisinarts Inc.] - Greenwich, CT - *BoPubDir 4, 5*
Cuisine [of CBS Publications Inc.] - New York, NY - *ArtMar 84; BaconPubCkMag 84; Folio 83; LitMarPl 84; MagIndMarPl 82-83; WritMar 84*
Cuisine Tampa Bay [of La Fray Publishing Co.] - St. Petersburg, FL - *LitMag&SmPr 83-84*
Culbertson King Candiles & Ross Advertising Inc. - Brentwood, TN - *StaDirAdAg 2-84*
Culbertson Searchlight - *See* Herald-News Publishers Inc.
Culdan Agency Inc., The - Paramus, NJ - *StaDirAdAg 2-84*
Culdesac Cable TV - Culdesac, ID - *Tel&CabFB 84C*
Culdesac TV Association - Culdesac, ID - *BrCabYB 84; Tel&CabFB 84C*
Culinarian, The - San Francisco, CA - *BaconPubCkMag 84*
Culinary Art Press Inc. - Reading, PA - *BoPubDir 4, 5*
Cullers Advertising Inc., Vince - Chicago, IL - *StaDirAdAg 2-84*
Cullinet Software - Westwood, MA - *DataDirSup 7-83; MicrocomSwDir 1*
Cullman Times - Cullman, AL - *BaconPubCkNews 84; Ed&PubIntYB 82; NewsDir 84*
Cullman Tribune - Cullman, AL - *BaconPubCkNews 84; Ed&PubIntYB 82; NewsDir 84*
Culloden Putnam Post - *See* P.C. Publishing Co.
Cullom Chronicle - *See* Cornbelt Press Inc.
Cullom Chronicle-Headlight-Enquirer - Cullom, IL - *Ed&PubIntYB 82*
Culnane-Fattori Associates Ltd. - Burlington, ON, Canada - *StaDirAdAg 2-84*
CULP - San Jose, CA - *DirOnDB Spring 84*
Culp Productions, James - San Francisco, CA - *AvMarPl 83*
Culpeper News - Charlottesville, VA - *NewsDir 84*
Culpeper News - Culpeper, VA - *AyerDirPub 83; Ed&PubIntYB 82*
Culpeper Star-Exponent [of Newspaper Publishing Corp.] - Culpeper, VA - *BaconPubCkNews 84; NewsDir 84*
Culpepper & Associates Inc. - Atlanta, GA - *ADAPSOMemDir 83-84*
Cultural Integration Fellowship - San Francisco, CA - *BoPubDir 4, 5*
Cultural Studies Institute - San Jose, CA - *BoPubDir 4 Sup, 5*
Culturama Inc. - Willowdale, ON, Canada - *BoPubDir 4, 5*
Cultvideo - Los Angeles, CA - *BillIntBG 83-84*
Culver & Associates - Dedham, MA - *StaDirAdAg 2-84*
Culver Citizen, The - Culver, IN - *Ed&PubIntYB 82*
Culver City Good Life - *See* Independent-Journal Newspapers
Culver City Hawthorne Community News - Culver City, CA - *BaconPubCkNews 84*
Culver City Independent - Culver City, CA - *Ed&PubIntYB 82*
Culver City Independent - *See* Copley Press Inc.
Culver City Independent & Star News [of Santa Monica United Western Newspapers Inc.] - Santa Monica, CA - *AyerDirPub 83; NewsDir 84*
Culver City Journal [of Santa Monica Independent Journal Newspapers] - Santa Monica, CA - *NewsDir 84*
Culver City News - Culver City, CA - *AyerDirPub 83; Ed&PubIntYB 82*
Culver City News - *See* Coast Media Newspapers
Culver City Wave - *See* Central News-Wave Publications
Culver Pictures Inc. - New York, NY - *AvMarPl 83; LitMarPl 83, 84; MagIndMarPl 82-83*
Culverin Corp. - Dayton, OH - *ADAPSOMemDir 83-84*
Cumberland Advocate - Cumberland, WI - *AyerDirPub 83; BaconPubCkNews 84; Ed&PubIntYB 82; NewsDir 84*
Cumberland Cable TV Inc. [of Century Telephone Enterprises Inc.] - Woodbury, TN - *Tel&CabFB 84C*
Cumberland County News - Burkesville, KY - *AyerDirPub 83; Ed&PubIntYB 82; NewsDir 84*
Cumberland County Times - Crossville, TN - *AyerDirPub 83; BaconPubCkNews 84; Ed&PubIntYB 82*
Cumberland Evening Times - Cumberland, MD - *BaconPubCkNews 84*
Cumberland Journal - Camp Hill, PA - *LitMag&SmPr 83-84*
Cumberland Lincoln Observer - Pawtucket, RI - *NewsDir 84*
Cumberland News [of The Times & Alleganian Co.] - Cumberland, MD - *BaconPubCkNews 84; NewsDir 84*
Cumberland Poetry Review - Nashville, TN - *LitMag&SmPr 83-84*
Cumberland Press Inc. - Freeport, ME - *LitMarPl 83, 84; WritMar 84*
Cumberland Telephone Co. - Cumberland, IA - *TelDir&BG 83-84*
Cumberland Tri-City News - Cumberland, KY - *BaconPubCkNews 84; NewsDir 84*
Cumberland TV Inc. - Cumberland, KY - *BrCabYB 84; Tel&CabFB 84C*
Cumberland Valley Cable TV Corp. - Somerset, KY - *Tel&CabFB 84C p.1676*
Cumberland Valley Cable TV Corp. [of G.S. Communications Inc.] - Greencastle, PA - *BrCabYB 84; Tel&CabFB 84C*
Cumberland Valley Cablevision [of Tennessee-Kentucky Cable TV Co.] - Jamestown, KY - *Tel&CabFB 84C*
Cumberland Valley Cablevision [of Tennessee-Kentucky Cable TV Co.] - Monticello, KY - *BrCabYB 84; Tel&CabFB 84C*
Cumberland Valley Cablevision [of Century Telephone Enterprises Inc.] - Mt. Juliet, TN - *Tel&CabFB 84C*
Cumberland Valley Photographic Workshops - Nashville, TN - *LitMarPl 84*
Cumberlands [of Pikeville College Press] - Pikeville, KY - *LitMag&SmPr 83-84*
Cumby Telephone Cooperative Inc. - Cumby, TX - *TelDir&BG 83-84*
Cumming Associates - Seattle, WA - *InfIndMarPl 83*

Cumming Forsyth County News - Cumming, GA - *BaconPubCkNews 84; NewsDir 84*
Cumming Publishers - Stratford, ON, Canada - *BoPubDir 4, 5*
Cummings Advertising Inc. - Rockford, IL - *StaDirAdAg 2-84*
Cummings, Alan - *See* Community Cablevision Inc.
Cummings & Co., Ross - Oklahoma City, OK - *AdAge 3-28-84; DirPRFirms 83; StaDirAdAg 2-84*
Cummings & Hester Advertising Agency Inc. - Houston, TX - *ArtMar 84*
Cummings Printing/Lew A. Cummings Co. Inc. - Manchester, NH - *MagIndMarPl 82-83*
Cummings Productions - Baltimore, MD - *TelAl 83, 84*
Cummington Publishing Inc. - New Rochelle, NY - *BoPubDir 4, 5*
Cummins, MacFail & Nutry Inc. - Somerset, NJ - *StaDirAdAg 2-84*
Cummins, Rachel - Austin, TX - *LitMarPl 83*
Cumulative Book Index - Bronx, NY - *MagDir 84*
Cumulative Index to Nursing & Allied Health Literature [of Glendale Adventist Medical Center] - Glendale, CA - *EISS 5-84 Sup*
Cumulus Press Ltd. - Moscow, ID - *BoPubDir 4, 5*
Cumulus Systems Ltd. - Rickmansworth, England - *EISS 5-84 Sup*
Cundall/Whitehead Advertising Inc. - Sausalito, CA - *ArtMar 84; DirMarMP 83*
Cuneo Co., John F. - Melrose Park, IL - *LitMarPl 83*
Cuneo, Silton, Turner Inc. - Boston, MA - *StaDirAdAg 2-84*
Cunningham, A. Eileen Smith - Carrollton, IL - *BoPubDir 4, 5*
Cunningham & Walsh - Los Angeles, CA - *ArtMar 84*
Cunningham & Walsh - San Francisco, CA - *ArtMar 84*
Cunningham & Walsh - Chicago, IL - *LitMarPl 83, 84; TelAl 83, 84*
Cunningham & Walsh [of Mickelberry Co.] - New York, NY - *AdAge 3-28-84; ArtMar 84; Br 1-23-84; BrCabYB 84; DirPRFirms 83; HomeVid&CabYB 82-83; StaDirAdAg 2-84*
Cunningham Clipper - Cunningham, KS - *BaconPubCkNews 84; Ed&PubIntYB 82*
Cunningham, Dale S. - Haddonfield, NJ - *LitMarPl 83*
Cunningham Publishing Co. - Buffalo, NY - *BoPubDir 5*
Cunningham Root & Craig - Los Angeles, CA - *AdAge 3-28-84; StaDirAdAg 2-84*
Cunningham, Sly & Associates Inc. - Shreveport, LA - *StaDirAdAg 2-84*
Cunningham Telephone Co. Inc. - Glen Elder, IA - *TelDir&BG 83-84*
CUNY Data Service [of the City University of New York] - New York, NY - *IntDirMarRes 83*
Cupertino Courier [of Meredith Corp.] - Cupertino, CA - *Ed&PubIntYB 82; NewsDir 84*
Cupertino Courier - *See* Meredith Newspapers
Cupola Productions - Philadelphia, PA - *LitMag&SmPr 83-84*
Curator - New York, NY - *BaconPubCkMag 84; MagDir 84*
Curators of the University of Missouri, The - Columbia, MO - *BrCabYB 84*
Curb Records - Burbank, CA - *BillIntBG 83-84*
Curbstone Press - Willimantic, CT - *BoPubDir 4; LitMag&SmPr 83-84; LitMarPl 83, 84*
Curbstone Publishing Co. - Austin, TX - *BoPubDir 4, 5; LitMag&SmPr 83-84*
Curcio Inc., Andrew - Boston, MA - *StaDirAdAg 2-84*
Curious Archives - Woodbridge, NJ - *BrCabYB 84*
Curious Naturalist - Lincoln, MA - *MagIndMarPl 82-83*
Curlew Press, The - Harrogate, England - *LitMag&SmPr 83-84*
Curlew Telephone Co. - Glen Ullin, ND - *TelDir&BG 83-84*
Curley & Associates Inc., John - South Yarmouth, MA - *LitMarPl 83, 84*
Curran, Hitomi & Associates - Sacramento, CA - *StaDirAdAg 2-84*
Currency [of I. P. Sharp Associates Ltd.] - Toronto, ON, Canada - *DBBus 82*
Currency Exchange Data Base - Washington, DC - *DBBus 82*
Currency Exchange Data Base - Rockville, MD - *DirOnDB Spring 84*
Currency Exchange Rates [of I. P. Sharp Associates Ltd.] - Toronto, ON, Canada - *DataDirOnSer 84; DirOnDB Spring 84*
Current [of Helen Dwight Reid Educational Foundation] - Washington, DC - *MagIndMarPl 82-83*
Current Affairs [Div. of Key Productions Inc.] - Ridgefield, CT - *AvMarPl 83*
Current Agricultural Research Information System [of Food & Agriculture Organization] - Rome, Italy - *EISS 83*
Current-Argus - Carlsbad, NM - *AyerDirPub 83*
Current Awareness in Biological Sciences - McLean, VA - *DirOnDB Spring 84*
Current Awareness Literature Service [of U.S. Dept. of Agriculture] - Beltsville, MD - *EISS 83*
Current Biography - Bronx, NY - *MagDir 84*
Current Biotechnology Abstracts [of Royal Society of Chemistry] - Nottingham, England - *DirOnDB Spring 84; EISS 5-84 Sup*
Current Concepts Inc. - *See* Rosenthal Inc., Rolf Werner
Current Consumer - Highland Park, IL - *MagIndMarPl 82-83*
Current Digest of the Soviet Press - Columbus, OH - *EISS 83; MicroMarPl 82-83*
Current Economic Indicators Data Bank [of Data Resources Inc.] - Lexington, MA - *DataDirOnSer 84*
Current Events - Middletown, CT - *MagDir 84*
Current Health - Highland Park, IL - *ArtMar 84; BaconPubCkMag 84*
Current Health 1 - Highland Park, IL - *MagIndMarPl 82-83*
Current Health 1 & 2 - Highland Park, IL - *MagDir 84*
Current Health 2 - Highland Park, IL - *MagIndMarPl 82-83*
Current History - Furlong, PA - *MagIndMarPl 82-83*
Current Index to Journals in Education [of Educational Resources Information Center] - Washington, DC - *CompReadDB 82*
Current Index to Journals in Education [of ORI Inc.] - Bethesda, MD - *DataDirOnSer 84*
Current Issues Publications - Berkeley, CA - *BoPubDir 4, 5*
Current Lifestudies - Highland Park, IL - *MagIndMarPl 82-83*
Current Lines - Norristown, PA - *NewsDir 84*
Current Literature on Water [of South African Water Information Centre] - Pretoria, South Africa - *CompReadDB 82*
Current Local - Van Buren, MO - *AyerDirPub 83; Ed&PubIntYB 82*
Current Physics Information [of American Institute of Physics] - New York, NY - *EISS 83*
Current Podiatry - Orlando, FL - *BaconPubCkMag 84*
Current Quotes [of Dow Jones News/Retrieval Service] - Princeton, NJ - *DataDirOnSer 84*
Current Research in Library & Information Science [of Library Association Publishing Ltd.] - London, England - *EISS 5-84 Sup*
Current Research Information System [of Dialog Information Services Inc.] - Palo Alto, CA - *DataDirOnSer 84*
Current Research Information System [of U.S. Dept. of Agriculture] - Beltsville, MD - *CompReadDB 82; DBBus 82; EISS 83*
Current Science - Middletown, CT - *BaconPubCkMag 84; MagDir 84*
Current Surgery - Philadelphia, PA - *MagDir 84*
Current Technology Index [of Pergamon International Information Corp.] - McLean, VA - *DataDirOnSer 84*
Current Technology Index [of Library Association Publishing Ltd.] - London, England - *DirOnDB Spring 84; EISS 83*
Current, The - Buffalo, NY - *AyerDirPub 83*
Current Wave - Eminence, MO - *AyerDirPub 83; Ed&PubIntYB 82*
Current World Leaders [of International Academy at Santa Barbara] - Santa Barbara, CA - *LitMag&SmPr 83-84*
Currents [of National Organization for River Sports] - Colorado Springs, CO - *WritMar 84*
Curriculum Applications - Arlington, MA - *MicrocomMPl 84*
Curriculum Associates Inc. - North Billerica, MA - *DirMarMP 83*
Curriculum Guidelines [of Ontario Education Research Information System] - Toronto, ON, Canada - *CompReadDB 82*
Curriculum Innovations Inc. - Highland Park, IL - *MagIndMarPl 82-83*
Curriculum Product Review - Belmont, CA - *BaconPubCkMag 84; MagDir 84*
Curriculum Product Review - Palo Alto, CA - *MagIndMarPl 82-83*
Curriculum Review - Chicago, IL - *ArtMar 84; MagIndMarPl 82-83; WritMar 84*

Currie & Ives Advertising - Newtown Square, PA - *StaDirAdAg 2-84*
Currie Spain & Associates - Palo Alto, CA - *ADAPSOMemDir 83-84*
Curry Coastal Pilot [of Western Communications Inc.] - Brookings, OR - *Ed&PubIntYB 82; NewsDir 84*
Curry County Reporter - Gold Beach, OR - *AyerDirPub 83; Ed&PubIntYB 82*
Curry County Times - Clovis, NM - *AyerDirPub 83; Ed&PubIntYB 82*
Curson House Inc. - Philadelphia, PA - *BoPubDir 4, 5*
Curtains [of Pressed Curtains] - Kent, ME - *LitMag&SmPr 83-84*
Curtin & London Inc. - Somerville, MA - *LitMarPl 83, 84; WritMar 84*
Curtin Associates [Div. of Creative Gaming Technology Inc.] - New York, NY - *StaDirAdAg 2-84*
Curtis Associates Inc., Richard - New York, NY - *LitMarPl 83, 84*
Curtis Books, Ralph - Hollywood, FL - *BoPubDir 4, 5*
Curtis Cable TV Co. Inc. [of Curtis Telephone Co.] - Curtis, NE - *BrCabYB 84; Tel&CabFB 84C*
Curtis Circulation Co. - West Caldwell, NJ - *MagIndMarPl 82-83*
Curtis, Clark & Rigan - Santa Barbara, CA - *LitMarPl 83, 84*
Curtis Co., Cally - Hollywood, CA - *AvMarPl 83*
Curtis, Heller Advertising - Louisville, KY - *StaDirAdAg 2-84*
Curtis Hi Line Enterprise - Curtis, NE - *BaconPubCkNews 84*
Curtis Manufacturing Co. Inc. - Peterborough, NH - *MicrocomMPl 84*
Curtis Manufacturing Co. Inc. - Winchester, NH - *WhoWMicrocom 83*
Curtis Paper [Div. of James River Corp.] - Newark, DE - *LitMarPl 83*
Curtis Paper - Southampton, PA - *LitMarPl 84*
Curtis Publishing Co., The - Indianapolis, IN - *MagIndMarPl 82-83*
Curtis Telephone Co. - Curtis, NE - *TelDir&BG 83-84*
Curtiss-Wright Corp. - Wood-Ridge, NJ - *ADAPSOMemDir 83-84*
Curulli, Vincent - Brooklyn, NY - *LitMarPl 83, 84; MagIndMarPl 82-83*
Curvd H & Z - Weston, ON, Canada - *BoPubDir 4, 5*
Cushing Citizen - Cushing, OK - *BaconPubCkNews 84; NewsDir 84*
Cushing-Malloy Inc. - Ann Arbor, MI - *LitMarPl 83, 84*
Cushing News - Cushing, TX - *Ed&PubIntYB 82*
Cushman & Associates Inc., Aaron D. - Chicago, IL - *DirPRFirms 83*
Custer, Arthur - New York, NY - *AvMarPl 83*
Custer County Chief - Broken Bow, NE - *AyerDirPub 83; Ed&PubIntYB 82*
Custer County Chronicle - Clinton, OK - *Ed&PubIntYB 82*
Custer County Chronicle - Custer, SD - *AyerDirPub 83; BaconPubCkNews 84; Ed&PubIntYB 82*
Custer, Ellen R. - West Hollywood, FL - *BoPubDir 4, 5*
Custer Telephone Cooperative Inc. - Challis, ID - *TelDir&BG 83-84*
Custom Applicator [of Little Publications Inc.] - Memphis, TN - *BaconPubCkMag 84; MagDir 84; WritMar 84*
Custom Audience Consultants Inc. - Landover, MD - *BrCabYB 84; Tel&CabFB 84C*
Custom Bike - Compton, CA - *MagDir 84*
Custom Bike/Choppers [of Touring Bike Publishing Inc.] - Anaheim, CA - *BaconPubCkMag 84; MagDir 84; MagIndMarPl 82-83; WritMar 84*
Custom Cable of Colorado Inc. - Denver, CO - *Tel&CabFB 84C p.1676*
Custom Cable Systems Inc. [of Custom Cable of Colorado Inc.] - Bayfield, CO - *Tel&CabFB 84C*
Custom Color Communications Inc. - Hackensack, NJ - *LitMarPl 83*
Custom Color Communications Inc. [Div. of Custom Communications Services Inc.] - Northvale, NJ - *LitMarPl 84*
Custom Color Corp. - Kansas City, MO - *AvMarPl 83*
Custom Color of California - Inglewood, CA - *AvMarPl 83*
Custom Co. - Buena Vista, CO - *MicrocomMPl 84*
Custom Composition Co. - York, PA - *MagIndMarPl 82-83*
Custom Computer Services Inc. - Fresno, CA - *ADAPSOMemDir 83-84; DataDirOnSer 84*
Custom Computer Technology - West Sedona, AZ - *MicrocomMPl 84*
Custom Consulting Services - Seattle, WA - *DataDirSup 7-83*
Custom Data - Alamogordo, NM - *MicrocomMPl 83, 84; MicrocomSwDir 1; WhoWMicrocom 83*
Custom Data Services Inc. - Pennsauken, NJ - *ADAPSOMemDir 83-84*
Custom Electronics Inc. - Chicopee, MA - *MicrocomMPl 83; WhoWMicrocom 83*
Custom Films/Video Inc. - Westport, CT - *AvMarPl 83; Tel&CabFB 84C*
Custom House Press [Aff. of Custom Technologies Group] - Zanesville, OH - *BoPubDir 4, 5*
Custom Marketing Inc. - *See* Bates Worldwide Inc., Ted
Custom Micro Systems Ltd. - Edmonton, AB, Canada - *MicrocomSwDir 1*
Custom Process - Berkeley, CA - *AvMarPl 83*
Custom Publishing Co. - Costa Mesa, CA - *BoPubDir 5*
Custom Records - Tyler, TX - *BillIntBG 83-84*
Custom Records/Kent Music - Los Angeles, CA - *BillIntBG 83-84*
Custom Research Center Inc. - Carolina, PR - *IntDirMarRes 83*
Custom Research Inc. - Minneapolis, MN - *AdAge 5-17-84 p.38; IntDirMarRes 83*
Custom Software - Bedford, TX - *MicrocomMPl 84*
Custom Software Engineering Inc. - Cocoa Beach, FL - *MicrocomMPl 84*
Custom Tailored Software Inc. - East Orange, NJ - *WhoWMicrocom 83*
Custom Tailored Software Inc. - Wayne, NJ - *MicrocomMPl 83*
Custom Terminals [Subs. of Computer Horizons Corp.] - Hauppauge, NY - *DirInfWP 82; WhoWMicrocom 83*
Custombook Inc. [Div. of Custom Communications Services Inc.] - Northvale, NJ - *LitMarPl 84*
Custombook Inc. [Div. of Custom Communications Services Inc.] - South Hackensack, NJ - *LitMarPl 83*
Customcraft Studio Inc. - Washington, DC - *AvMarPl 83*
Customer Satisfaction Research Institute - Shawnee Mission, KS - *IntDirMarRes 83*
Customer's Individual Advisory Board - Erie, PA - *MicrocomMPl 84*
Customized Mailing Lists Inc. - Jamaica Estates, NY - *MagIndMarPl 82-83*
Customized Research - Freehold, NJ - *MicrocomMPl 84*
Customs Computing Systems Inc. - Kirtland, OH - *MicrocomMPl 83, 84*
Customtel - Minneapolis, MN - *IntDirMarRes 83*
Customusic Div. [of Rowe International Inc.] - Whippany, NJ - *Tel&CabFB 84C*
Cut Bank Pioneer Press - Cut Bank, MT - *BaconPubCkNews 84; Ed&PubIntYB 82*
Cutbank [of SmokeRoot] - Missoula, MT - *LitMag&SmPr 83-84*
Cuthbert Times & News Record - Cuthbert, GA - *BaconPubCkNews 84; Ed&PubIntYB 82*
Cuthbertson & Co. Ltd., D. C. - *See* Stewart & Associates Ltd./IMAA Inc., Rex
Cutis - New York, NY - *BaconPubCkMag 84; MagDir 84*
Cutler Advertising Co., H. Whitney - Fairfield, NJ - *StaDirAdAg 2-84*
Cutler Music Co., V. & M. - Chatsworth, CA - *BillIntBG 83-84*
Cutsinger, Jan - St. Charles, MO - *FBInfSer 80*
Cutting Data Information Center [of Technical University of Aachen] - Aachen, West Germany - *EISS 83*
Cutting Tool Engineering - Wheaton, IL - *BaconPubCkMag 84; MagDir 84*
Cuvantul Romanesc - Hamilton, ON, Canada - *Ed&PubIntYB 82*
Cuyahoga Falls News-Press - Cuyahoga Falls, OH - *Ed&PubIntYB 82*
Cuyahoga Falls News-Press - *See* Record Publishing Co.
CVM Productions Inc. - New York, NY - *AvMarPl 83*
CVN/Box Seat [of Daniels & Associates] - Carlsbad, CA - *CabTVPrDB 83*
CVP - Los Angeles, CA - *ArtMar 84; BaconPubCkMag 84; MagDir 84; MagIndMarPl 82-83*
C.W. Communications Inc. [Subs. of International Data Group] - Framingham, MA - *DirMarMP 83; MagIndMarPl 82-83*

C.W. Systems Inc. - Richmond, VA - *MicrocomSwDir 1; WhoWMicrocom 83*
CWA News [of Communications Workers of America] - Washington, DC - *NewsDir 84*
CWARE - North Salt Lake, UT - *MicrocomMPl 83*
CWPCA Bulletin - Lafayette, CA - *MagDir 84*
CWS Group Press - Vinton, IA - *BoPubDir 4, 5*
Cyber Engineering Corp. - Huntsville, AL - *MicrocomMPl 84*
Cyber-Tech - Chatsworth, CA - *MicrocomMPl 83*
Cyberan Software [Subs. of Cyberan Corp.] - Houston, TX - *MicrocomMPl 83, 84; WhoWMicrocom 83*
Cyberdata Corp. - Monterey, CA - *DataDirSup 7-83*
Cyberex Inc. - Mentor, OH - *DirInfWP 82*
Cyberia Inc. - Ames, IA - *MicrocomMPl 83, 84; MicrocomSwDir 1; WhoWMicrocom 83*
Cybermedix Ltd. - Toronto, ON, Canada - *Tel&CabFB 84C*
Cybern Film Systems Inc. - Chicago, IL - *AvMarPl 83*
Cybernet Services [of Control Data Corp.] - Minneapolis, MN - *EISS 83*
Cybernetic Corp. - Agana, GU - *ADAPSOMemDir 83-84*
Cybernetic Information Systems - Schenectady, NY - *MicrocomMPl 84*
Cybernetics Inc. - Huntington Beach, CA - *MicrocomMPl 83, 84; WhoWMicrocom 83*
Cybernetics Resource Corp. - Port Washington, NY - *MicrocomMPl 84*
Cybershare Ltd. - Winnipeg, MB, Canada - *DataDirSup 7-83*
CyberSoft - Plano, TX - *WhoWMicrocom 83*
Cybersystems Inc. - Huntsville, AL - *WhoWMicrocom 83*
Cybertec Inc. - La Jolla, CA - *WhoWMicrocom 83*
Cybertek Computer Products Inc. - Culver City, CA - *DataDirOnSer 84; MicrocomSwDir 1*
Cybertel Videotex Service [of Control Data Australia Pty. Ltd.] - Melbourne, Australia - *EISS 5-84 Sup*
Cybertronics International Inc. - Morristown, NJ - *MicrocomMPl 83, 84*
Cyberway - New York, NY - *DirInfWP 82*
Cyberyan Corp. - Houston, TX - *MicrocomMPl 83*
Cybix Intelligent Systems Inc. - Chatsworth, CA - *MicrocomSwDir 1*
Cyborg Corp. - Newton, MA - *MicrocomMPl 84*
Cyborg Systems Inc. - Chicago, IL - *ADAPSOMemDir 83-84*
Cycare System Inc. - Dubuque, IA - *ADAPSOMemDir 83-84; DataDirOnSer 84*
Cycle - Thousand Oaks, CA - *MagDir 84*
Cycle [of Ziff-Davis Publishing Co.] - Westlake Village, CA - *BaconPubCkMag 84; MagIndMarPl 82-83; WritMar 84*
Cycle Canada [of Brave Beaver Pressworks Ltd.] - Toronto, ON, Canada - *BaconPubCkMag 84; WritMar 84*
Cycle Guide - Torrance, CA - *BaconPubCkMag 84; MagDir 84; MagIndMarPl 82-83*
Cycle Illustrated - New York, NY - *MagDir 84*
Cycle News/East - Tucker, GA - *MagDir 84*
Cycle News/West - Long Beach, CA - *ArtMar 84; BaconPubCkMag 84; MagDir 84; MagIndMarPl 82-83; WritMar 84*
Cycle Times - Chicago, IL - *MagDir 84*
Cycle World - Newport Beach, CA - *ArtMar 84; BaconPubCkMag 84; MagDir 84; MagIndMarPl 82-83; WritMar 84*
Cycling USA - Nevada City, CA - *BaconPubCkMag 84*
Cyclone Software - Cupertino, CA - *MicrocomSwDir 1*
Cyclopedia Publishing Co. - Pleasant Valley, NY - *BoPubDir 4, 5*
Cyclops Music - White Plains, NY - *BillIntBG 83-84*
Cyclops Record Inc. - White Plains, NY - *BillIntBG 83-84*
Cycon Communications Inc. - Lombard, IL - *StaDirAdAg 2-84*
Cydex Corp. - North Hollywood, CA - *DataDirOnSer 84*
Cyex Software Corp. - Palatine, IL - *DirInfWP 82*
Cygnus Software - Mesa, AZ - *MicrocomMPl 83, 84*
Cygnus Technologies Corp. - New York, NY - *ADAPSOMemDir 83-84*
Cykx Books [Aff. of Cykx Inc.] - New York, NY - *BoPubDir 4, 5*
Cylix Communications Network - Memphis, TN - *InfIndMarPl 83*
Cyma Corp. - Mesa, AZ - *MicrocomMPl 84; WhoWMicrocom 83*
Cynthia Peripheral Corp. [Subs. of Cii Honeywell Bull] - Palo Alto, CA - *DataDirSup 7-83; WhoWMicrocom 83*
Cynthiana Argus - Cynthiana, IN - *BaconPubCkNews 84; Ed&PubIntYB 82*
Cynthiana CATV Inc. - Cynthiana, KY - *BrCabYB 84; Tel&CabFB 84C*
Cynthiana Democrat - Cynthiana, KY - *BaconPubCkNews 84; Ed&PubIntYB 82; NewsDir 84*
Cynwyn - New York, NY - *MicrocomMPl 84*
Cyometrics Inc. - Bel Air, MD - *BoPubDir 5*
Cypher - San Francisco, CA - *MicrocomMPl 84*
Cypress Gardens Productions - Cypress Gardens, FL - *StaDirAdAg 2-84*
Cypress/La Palma Community Advocate - *See* Hearst Community Newspapers
Cypress Publishing Corp. - Glendale, CA - *AvMarPl 83; DirMarMP 83; LitMarPl 83, 84*
Cypress Review Press - Half Moon Bay, CA - *LitMag&SmPr 83-84*
Cypress Review, The - Half Moon Bay, CA - *LitMag&SmPr 83-84*
Cyr Color Photo Agency - Norwalk, CT - *AvMarPl 83; LitMarPl 83, 84; MagIndMarPl 82-83*
Cyril News - Cyril, OK - *BaconPubCkNews 84; Ed&PubIntYB 82*
Cyrk Inc. - Sarasota, FL - *MicroMarPl 82-83*
Cytrol Inc. - Edina, MN - *ADAPSOMemDir 83-84*
Cyzern Inc. - Fayetteville, AR - *MicrocomMPl 84*
Czas - Winnipeg, MB, Canada - *Ed&PubIntYB 82*
Czechoslovak Daily-Herald/The Denni Hlasatel - Berwyn, IL - *NewsDir 84*
Czuy, Ted - New York, NY - *HBIndAd&MS 82-83*

D

D & A Publishing - Phoenix, AZ - *BoPubDir 4 Sup, 5*
D & B Computing Services Inc. [Div. of The Dun & Bradstreet Corp.] - Wilton, CT - *DataDirOnSer 84*
D & B-Dun's Market Identifiers - Parsippany, NJ - *DirOnDB Spring 84*
D & B-Million Dollar Directory - Parsippany, NJ - *DirOnDB Spring 84*
D & B-Principal International Businesses [of Dialog Information Services Inc.] - Palo Alto, CA - *DataDirOnSer 84*
D & B-Principal International Businesses - New York, NY - *DirOnDB Spring 84*
D & B Reports [of The Dun & Bradstreet Corp.] - New York, NY - *BaconPubCkMag 84; MagIndMarPl 82-83; WritMar 84*
D & B Service Center - Colfax, WA - *Tel&CabFB 84C*
D & D Records Inc. - Hollywood, CA - *BillIntBG 83-84*
D & M Cable - Corsica, SD - *Tel&CabFB 84C*
D & M Software - Tacoma, WA - *MicrocomMPl 83*
D & N Micro Products Inc. - Ft. Wayne, IN - *MicrocomMPl 83*
D & R Productions Inc. - New York, NY - *Tel&CabFB 84C*
D & S Advertising Services - Ft. Lauderdale, FL - *StaDirAdAg 2-84*
D & S Marketing Associates - Pequannock, NJ - *StaDirAdAg 2-84*
D & S Systems Inc. - Memphis, TN - *MicrocomSwDir 1*
D/C Marketing - Springfield, IL - *IntDirMarRes 83*
D4 Film Studios Inc. - Needham Heights, MA - *ArtMar 84; AvMarPl 83; Tel&CabFB 84C*
D Magazine [of Southwest Media Corp.] - Dallas, TX - *BaconPubCkMag 84; Folio 83; MagDir 84; MagIndMarPl 82-83; WritMar 84*
D-Town Records Inc. - West Hollywood, CA - *BillIntBG 83-84*
D2 Enterprises - Shalimar, FL - *MicrocomMPl 84*
D-Zyne Video Products Inc. - Waterford, CT - *MicrocomMPl 84*
Da Capo Press Inc. [Subs. of Plenum Publishing Corp.] - New York, NY - *LitMarPl 83, 84*
Da-Lite Screen Co. Inc. - Warsaw, IN - *AvMarPl 83*
Da Silva & Other Filmmakers, Raul - New York, NY - *ArtMar 84; AvMarPl 83; WritMar 84*
Daan Graphics - Middlesex, NJ - *BoPubDir 5*
DAAS - *See* Drilling Analysis Data On-Line
Daatselaar & Associates Inc., Joseph - Rochester, NY - *StaDirAdAg 2-84*
DABAS [of Central Telecommunications Office] - The Hague, Netherlands - *EISS 83; InfIndMarPl 83*
D'Abo Songs Inc. - *See* Mayflower Music Corp.
D.A.C. Journal - New York, NY - *BaconPubCkMag 84; MagDir 84*
D.A.C. News [of Detroit Athletic Club] - Detroit, MI - *BaconPubCkMag 84; MagDir 84; WritMar 84*
Dacie Music - *See* Callon-Love Music
Dacon Electronics Inc. - Upper Saddle River, NJ - *DataDirSup 7-83*
D.A.D. Films Ltd. - Los Angeles, CA - *Tel&CabFB 84C*
Dada Center Publications - Healdsburg, CA - *BoPubDir 4, 5; LitMag&SmPr 83-84*
Dadant & Sons Inc. - Hamilton, IL - *BoPubDir 4, 5*
Dade Cable TV Inc. [of Storer Cable Communications] - Kendall, FL - *BrCabYB 84; Tel&CabFB 84C*
Dade City Pasco News - Dade City, FL - *BaconPubCkNews 84; NewsDir 84*
Dade County Sentinel - Trenton, GA - *AyerDirPub 83; Ed&PubIntYB 82*
Dadeville Record - Dadeville, AL - *BaconPubCkNews 84; Ed&PubIntYB 82*
DAE Inc. - Dallas, TX - *WhoWMicrocom 83*
Daedalus [of The American Academy of Arts & Sciences] - Cambridge, MA - *LitMag&SmPr 83-84; LitMarPl 83, 84; MagIndMarPl 82-83*
Daedalus Books Inc. - Washington, DC - *LitMarPl 83*
Daedalus Digital Inc. - Lafayette, LA - *MicrocomMPl 84*
DAFSA - Paris, France - *EISS 83*
DAFSA Information Services - *See* Documentation & Analyse Financiere SA
Dagar - New Haven, CT - *MicrocomMPl 83*
Dagar Enterprises Inc. - Woodbridge, CT - *WhoWMicrocom 83*
Dagar, James M. - Pineville, LA - *LitMarPl 83*
Dage-MTI Inc. - Michigan City, IN - *AvMarPl 83*
Dagg Associates, Michael A. - Ottawa, ON, Canada - *EISS 83; FBInfSer 80; InfIndMarPl 83*
D'Agostino, Lena V. - Davenport Center, NY - *BoPubDir 4, 5*
Dahill Music Co. - *See* Spier Inc., Larry
Dahl & Sarto - Oslo, Norway - *StaDirAdAg 2-84*
Dahl Co., A. J. - Minneapolis, MN - *LitMarPl 83, 84*
Dahlonega Nugget - Dahlonega, GA - *AyerDirPub 83; BaconPubCkNews 84; Ed&PubIntYB 82*
Dahms, Vern - Armstrong, IA - *Tel&CabFB 84C p.1676*
Dai Nippon Printing Co. Ltd. [Subs. of DNP America Inc.] - New York, NY - *LitMarPl 83, 84*
Daigle & Associates - Houston, TX - *StaDirAdAg 2-84*
Daiko Advertising Inc. - Osaka, Japan - *StaDirAdAg 2-84*
Dailey & Associates [Subs. of The Interpublic Group of Cos. Inc.] - Los Angeles, CA - *Br 1-23-84; StaDirAdAg 2-84*
Dailey & Associates - San Francisco, CA - *ArtMar 84; DirPRFirms 83*
Dailey Antiguarian Books, William & Victoria - Los Angeles, CA - *BoPubDir 5*
Dailey-Antiquarian Books, William & Victoria - Los Angeles, CA - *BoPubDir 4*
Dailey International Group - Los Angeles, CA - *AdAge 3-28-84*
Dailey Planet Almanac Inc. - Boulder, CO - *BoPubDir 4*
Daily - Decatur, AL - *AyerDirPub 83*
Daily - Millville, NJ - *AyerDirPub 83*
Daily Advance, The - Dover, NJ - *Ed&PubIntYB 82*
Daily Advance, The - Elizabeth City, NC - *Ed&PubIntYB 82*
Daily Advance, The - Lynchburg, VA - *Ed&PubIntYB 82*
Daily Advertiser, The - Lafayette, LA - *Ed&PubIntYB 82*
Daily Advocate [of Thomson Newspapers Inc.] - Greenville, OH - *Ed&PubIntYB 82; NewsDir 84*
Daily American - Somerset, PA - *BaconPubCkNews 84; Ed&PubIntYB 82*

Daily American Republic - Poplar Bluff, MO - *BaconPubCkNews 84; Ed&PubIntYB 82*
Daily American, The - West Frankfort, IL - *Ed&PubIntYB 82*
Daily Ardmoreite, The - Ardmore, OK - *Ed&PubIntYB 82*
Daily Argus Observer - Ontario, OR - *BaconPubCkNews 84; Ed&PubIntYB 82*
Daily Astorian, The - Astoria, OR - *BaconPubCkNews 84; Ed&PubIntYB 82*
Daily Athenaeum [of West Virginia University Board of Regents] - Morgantown, WV - *NewsDir 84*
Daily Aztec [of San Diego State University] - San Diego, CA - *NewsDir 84*
Daily Bond Buyer, The - New York, NY - *Ed&PubIntYB 82; NewsDir 84*
Daily Breeze - Torrance, CA - *AyerDirPub 83; BaconPubCkNews 84; Ed&PubIntYB 82*
Daily Bulletin - Dauphin, MB, Canada - *BaconPubCkNews 84; Ed&PubIntYB 82*
Daily Bulletin - Sioux Lookout, ON, Canada - *BaconPubCkNews 84; Ed&PubIntYB 82*
Daily Bulletin, The - Kimberley, BC, Canada - *BaconPubCkNews 84; Ed&PubIntYB 82*
Daily Bulletin, The - Ft. Frances, ON, Canada - *BaconPubCkNews 84; Ed&PubIntYB 82*
Daily Business Products Inc. - Hauppauge, NY - *WhoWMicrocom 83*
Daily Business Products Inc. - New York, NY - *DirInfWP 82*
Daily Californian [of Independent Berkeley Student Publishing Co. Inc.] - Berkeley, CA - *NewsDir 84*
Daily Californian, The - El Cajon, CA - *AyerDirPub 83; Ed&PubIntYB 82*
Daily Calumet, The - Chicago, IL - *Ed&PubIntYB 82*
Daily Camera - Boulder, CO - *Ed&PubIntYB 82*
Daily Campus, The [of SMU] - Dallas, TX - *NewsDir 84*
Daily Capital Journal - Pierre, SD - *Ed&PubIntYB 82*
Daily Cardinal, The - Madison, WI - *NewsDir 84*
Daily Challenge, The - Brooklyn, NY - *Ed&PubIntYB 82*
Daily Chicago Southtown Economist - Chicago, IL - *AyerDirPub 83*
Daily Chief-Union, The - Upper Sandusky, OH - *Ed&PubIntYB 82*
Daily Chronicle - De Kalb, IL - *Ed&PubIntYB 82*
Daily Chronicle, The - Santa Paula, CA - *Ed&PubIntYB 82*
Daily Chronicle, The [of Lafromboise Newspapers] - Centralia, WA - *BaconPubCkNews 84; Ed&PubIntYB 82; NewsDir 84*
Daily Citizen - Beaver Dam, WI - *BaconPubCkNews 84; Ed&PubIntYB 82*
Daily Citizen-News, The - Dalton, GA - *Ed&PubIntYB 82*
Daily Citizen, The [of Arkansas Newspapers Inc.] - Searcy, AR - *Ed&PubIntYB 82; NewsDir 84*
Daily Citizen, The - Webster, TX - *Ed&PubIntYB 82*
Daily City Record - South San Francisco, CA - *AyerDirPub 83*
Daily Clay County Advocate-Press - Flora, IL - *Ed&PubIntYB 82; NewsDir 84*
Daily Clintonian, The - Clinton, IN - *Ed&PubIntYB 82*
Daily Collegian [of University of Massachusetts] - Amherst, MA - *NewsDir 84*
Daily Collegian Inc., The - University Park, PA - *NewsDir 84*
Daily Collegian, The [of California State University Associated Students] - Fresno, CA - *NewsDir 84*
Daily Comet, The - Thibodaux, LA - *Ed&PubIntYB 82*
Daily Comment - Belmont, CA - *DirOnDB Spring 84*
Daily Commerce [of Daily Journal Co.] - Los Angeles, CA - *BaconPubCkMag 84; Ed&PubIntYB 82; MagDir 84; NewsDir 84*
Daily Commercial News - San Francisco, CA - *BaconPubCkMag 84; Ed&PubIntYB 82; MagDir 84; NewsDir 84*
Daily Commercial News - Toronto, ON, Canada - *Ed&PubIntYB 82*
Daily Commercial News & Construction Record - Toronto, ON, Canada - *BaconPubCkMag 84*
Daily Commercial News & Shipping Guide [of C. A. Page Publishing Corp.] - Lynwood, CA - *BaconPubCkMag 84; MagDir 84*
Daily Commercial Record - Dallas, TX - *Ed&PubIntYB 82; NewsDir 84*
Daily Construction Service [of Withers Publishing Co.] - Los Angeles, CA - *BaconPubCkMag 84; Ed&PubIntYB 82; MagDir 84; NewsDir 84*
Daily Construction Service [of Wade Publishing Co.] - San Francisco, CA - *BaconPubCkMag 84; MagDir 84*
Daily Corinthian, The - Corinth, MS - *Ed&PubIntYB 82*
Daily Cougar, The [of University of Houston] - Houston, TX - *NewsDir 84*
Daily Courier - St. Joseph, MO - *NewsDir 84*
Daily Courier - Forest City, NC - *BaconPubCkNews 84; Ed&PubIntYB 82*
Daily Courier-Democrat - Russellville, AR - *Ed&PubIntYB 82*
Daily Courier-News [of Copley Press Inc.] - Elgin, IL - *NewsDir 84*
Daily Courier, The - Connellsville, PA - *BaconPubCkNews 84; Ed&PubIntYB 82*
Daily Courier, The - Kelowna, BC, Canada - *Ed&PubIntYB 82*
Daily Court Reporter - Dayton, OH - *Ed&PubIntYB 82; NewsDir 84*
Daily Court Review - Houston, TX - *Ed&PubIntYB 82; NewsDir 84*
Daily Defender - Chicago, IL - *AyerDirPub 83*
Daily Democrat - Marlin, TX - *AyerDirPub 83*
Daily Democrat, The [of Ed. E. Leake Publishing Co. Inc.] - Woodland, CA - *BaconPubCkNews 84; Ed&PubIntYB 82; NewsDir 84*
Daily Democrat, The - Ft. Madison, IA - *Ed&PubIntYB 82*
Daily Dispatch, The [of Douglas Dispatch Inc.] - Douglas, AZ - *Ed&PubIntYB 82*
Daily Dispatch, The - Moline, IL - *Ed&PubIntYB 82*
Daily Dunklin Democrat - Kennett, MO - *BaconPubCkNews 84; Ed&PubIntYB 82*
Daily Eastern News, The [of Eastern Illinois University] - Charleston, IL - *NewsDir 84*
Daily Egyptian [of Southern Illinois University] - Carbondale, IL - *NewsDir 84*
Daily Evening Item - Lynn, MA - *Ed&PubIntYB 82; NewsDir 84*
Daily Events - Springfield, MO - *Ed&PubIntYB 82*
Daily Evergreen [of Student Publications Board for WSU Student Body] - Pullman, WA - *NewsDir 84*
Daily Forty-Niner, The [of California State University] - Long Beach, CA - *NewsDir 84*
Daily Forum - Maryville, MO - *AyerDirPub 83; BaconPubCkNews 84; Ed&PubIntYB 82*
Daily Free Press, The [of Back Bay Publishing Co. Inc.] - Boston, MA - *NewsDir 84*
Daily Freeman-Journal, The - Webster City, IA - *Ed&PubIntYB 82*
Daily Freeman, The - Kingston, NY - *Ed&PubIntYB 82*
Daily Ft. Gateway Guide - Waynesville, MO - *Ed&PubIntYB 82*
Daily Gate City - Keokuk, IA - *Ed&PubIntYB 82*
Daily Gazette, The - Sterling, IL - *Ed&PubIntYB 82*
Daily Gazette, The - Xenia, OH - *Ed&PubIntYB 82*
Daily Gleaner, The [of University Press of New Brunswick Ltd.] - Fredericton, NB, Canada - *AyerDirPub 83; BaconPubCkNews 84; Ed&PubIntYB 82; LitMarPl 84*
Daily Globe News - Auburn, WA - *BaconPubCkNews 84*
Daily Globe, The - Shelby, OH - *Ed&PubIntYB 82*
Daily Graphic [of Vopni Press Ltd.] - Portage La Prairie, MB, Canada - *BaconPubCkNews 84; Ed&PubIntYB 82; LitMarPl 83, 84*
Daily Hampshire Gazette [of H. S. Gere & Sons Inc.] - Northampton, MA - *Ed&PubIntYB 82; LitMarPl 84*
Daily Herald - Arlington Heights, IL - *Ed&PubIntYB 82*
Daily Herald - Biloxi, MS - *BaconPubCkNews 84; Ed&PubIntYB 82; NewsBur 6*
Daily Herald - Roanoke Rapids, NC - *Ed&PubIntYB 82*
Daily Herald - Killeen, TX - *Ed&PubIntYB 82*
Daily Herald-Dispatch - Sierra Vista, AZ - *Ed&PubIntYB 82*
Daily Herald News - Punt· Gorda, FL - *BaconPubCkNews 84; Ed&PubIntYB 82*
Daily Herald, The - Monongahela, PA - *Ed&PubIntYB 82*
Daily Herald, The [of Columbia Publishing Co.] - Columbia, TN - *Ed&PubIntYB 82; NewsDir 84*
Daily Herald, The - Provo, UT - *BaconPubCkNews 84; Ed&PubIntYB 82*
Daily Herald, The - Wausau, WI - *Ed&PubIntYB 82*

Daily Herald-Tribune - Grande Prairie, AB, Canada - *Ed&PubIntYB 82*
Daily Highlander - Lake Wales, FL - *Ed&PubIntYB 82*
Daily Home [of Talladega Publishing Co. Inc.] - Talladega, AL - *Ed&PubIntYB 82; NewsDir 84*
Daily Home-Sylacauga News - Talladega, AL - *BaconPubCkNews 84*
Daily Iberian - New Iberia, LA - *BaconPubCkNews 84; Ed&PubIntYB 82*
Daily Illini, The [of Illini Publishing Co.] - Champaign, IL - *NewsDir 84*
Daily Independent - Corona, CA - *LitMarPl 83*
Daily Independent - Ridgecrest, CA - *BaconPubCkNews 84; Ed&PubIntYB 82*
Daily Independent - Kannapolis, NC - *Ed&PubIntYB 82*
Daily Industrial Index Analyzer - Boston, MA - *DirOnDB Spring 84*
Daily Industrial Index Analyzer [of NewsNet Inc.] - Bryn Mawr, PA - *DataDirOnSer 84*
Daily Inquirer - Gonzales, TX - *Ed&PubIntYB 82*
Daily Intelligencer, The - Doylestown, PA - *BaconPubCkNews 84; Ed&PubIntYB 82*
Daily Inter Lake, The - Kalispell, MT - *Ed&PubIntYB 82*
Daily Iowan, The [of Student Publications Inc.] - Coralville, IA - *NewsDir 84*
Daily Iowan, The - Iowa City, IA - *BaconPubCkNews 84*
Daily Item, The - Sunbury, PA - *BaconPubCkNews 84; Ed&PubIntYB 82*
Daily Jefferson County Union - Ft. Atkinson, WI - *BaconPubCkNews 84; Ed&PubIntYB 82*
Daily Jeffersonian, The - Cambridge, OH - *BaconPubCkNews 84; Ed&PubIntYB 82*
Daily Journal [of McGraw-Hill Information Systems C] - Denver, CO - *BaconPubCkMag 84; Ed&PubIntYB 82; MagDir 84; NewsDir 84*
Daily Journal [of Home News Enterprises] - Franklin, IN - *BaconPubCkNews 84; Ed&PubIntYB 82; NewsDir 84*
Daily Journal - Fergus Falls, MN - *Ed&PubIntYB 82*
Daily Journal - Elizabeth, NJ - *BaconPubCkNews 84; Ed&PubIntYB 82*
Daily Journal Flat River, The [of Eastern Missouri Publishing Co.] - Flat River, MO - *NewsDir 84*
Daily Journal of Commerce - New Orleans, LA - *BaconPubCkMag 84; Ed&PubIntYB 82; MagDir 84*
Daily Journal of Commerce - Portland, OR - *BaconPubCkMag 84; Ed&PubIntYB 82; MagDir 84*
Daily Journal of Commerce - Seattle, WA - *BaconPubCkMag 84; MagDir 84*
Daily Journal, The - Wheaton, IL - *Ed&PubIntYB 82*
Daily Journal, The - International Falls, MN - *Ed&PubIntYB 82*
Daily Journal, The - Flat River, MO - *BaconPubCkNews 84; Ed&PubIntYB 82*
Daily Kent Stater [of Kent State University] - Kent, OH - *NewsDir 84*
Daily Lass-o, The - Denton, TX - *NewsDir 84*
Daily Leader - Fulton, KY - *AyerDirPub 83*
Daily Leader - Brookhaven, MS - *Ed&PubIntYB 82*
Daily Leader - Frederick, OK - *Ed&PubIntYB 82*
Daily Leader, The - Pontiac, IL - *Ed&PubIntYB 82*
Daily Leader, The - Lewisville, TX - *Ed&PubIntYB 82*
Daily Ledger - Antioch, CA - *BaconPubCkNews 84; Ed&PubIntYB 82*
Daily Ledger - Canton, IL - *Ed&PubIntYB 82*
Daily Legal News - Baton Rouge, LA - *Ed&PubIntYB 82*
Daily Legal News - Shreveport, LA - *Ed&PubIntYB 82*
Daily Legal News [of Dexter Publishing Co.] - Tulsa, OK - *NewsDir 84*
Daily Legal News Inc. - Youngstown, OH - *Ed&PubIntYB 82; NewsDir 84*
Daily Local News - West Chester, PA - *Ed&PubIntYB 82*
Daily Mail - Olney, IL - *AyerDirPub 83; Ed&PubIntYB 82*
Daily Mail - Catskill, NY - *Ed&PubIntYB 82*
Daily Mail, The - Hagerstown, MD - *Ed&PubIntYB 82*
Daily Market Record - Minneapolis, MN - *BaconPubCkMag 84; Ed&PubIntYB 82; NewsDir 84*
Daily Meditation - San Antonio, TX - *WritMar 84*
Daily Mercury, The - Guelph, ON, Canada - *BaconPubCkNews 84; Ed&PubIntYB 82*
Daily Messenger, The - Canandaigua, NY - *Ed&PubIntYB 82*
Daily Metals Report - Boston, MA - *DirOnDB Spring 84*
Daily Metals Report [of NewsNet Inc.] - Bryn Mawr, PA - *DataDirOnSer 84*
Daily Midway Driller - Taft, CA - *Ed&PubIntYB 82*
Daily Miner & News - Kenora, ON, Canada - *Ed&PubIntYB 82*
Daily Mining Gazette, The - Houghton, MI - *Ed&PubIntYB 82*
Daily Mississippian, The - University, MS - *NewsDir 84*
Daily Morning Peoples' Press - Yazoo City, MS - *Ed&PubIntYB 82*
Daily Mountain Eagle [of Jasper Newspapers Inc.] - Jasper, AL - *Ed&PubIntYB 82*
Daily Nebraskan, The [of University of Nebraska] - Lincoln, NE - *NewsDir 84*
Daily News - Indio, CA - *BaconPubCkNews 84; Ed&PubIntYB 82*
Daily News - Red Bluff, CA - *Ed&PubIntYB 82*
Daily News - Van Nuys, CA - *AyerDirPub 83; BaconPubCkNews 84; Ed&PubIntYB 82; LitMarPl 84; NewsDir 84; WritMar 84*
Daily News - Effingham, IL - *AyerDirPub 83*
Daily News - Bowling Green, KY - *AyerDirPub 83*
Daily News - Bogalusa, LA - *BaconPubCkNews 84; Ed&PubIntYB 82*
Daily News [of Republican Co.] - Springfield, MA - *NewsBur 6; NewsDir 84*
Daily News - Jacksonville, NC - *Ed&PubIntYB 82*
Daily News - Minot, ND - *AyerDirPub 83*
Daily News - Wahpeton, ND - *AyerDirPub 83; Ed&PubIntYB 82*
Daily News - Philadelphia, PA - *AyerDirPub 83*
Daily News - Kingsport, TN - *Ed&PubIntYB 82*
Daily News - Memphis, TN - *Ed&PubIntYB 82; NewsDir 84*
Daily News [of Longview Newspapers Inc.] - Longview, TX - *NewsDir 84*
Daily News - Lewisburg, WV - *Ed&PubIntYB 82*
Daily News - Williamson, WV - *Ed&PubIntYB 82*
Daily News - Chatham, ON, Canada - *Ed&PubIntYB 82*
Daily News Broadcasting Co. - Bowling Green, KY - *BrCabYB 84*
Daily News Journal - Murfreesboro, TN - *Ed&PubIntYB 82*
Daily News Journal - Kent, WA - *BaconPubCkNews 84; Ed&PubIntYB 82*
Daily News of Johnson County, The - Olathe, KS - *Ed&PubIntYB 82*
Daily News Printing Co. - Wapakoneta, OH - *BaconPubCkNews 84*
Daily News Record [of Fairchild Publications] - New York, NY - *BaconPubCkMag 84; Ed&PubIntYB 82; Folio 83*
Daily News-Record - Harrisonburg, VA - *Ed&PubIntYB 82*
Daily News Record - *See* Fairchild Syndication Service
Daily News Sun - Sun City, AZ - *BaconPubCkNews 84; Ed&PubIntYB 82*
Daily News, The - Whittier, CA - *Ed&PubIntYB 82*
Daily News, The [of Harris Enterprises] - Olathe, KS - *NewsDir 84*
Daily News, The - Newburyport, MA - *Ed&PubIntYB 82*
Daily News, The - Greenville, MI - *NewsDir 84*
Daily News, The - Iron Mountain, MI - *BaconPubCkNews 84; Ed&PubIntYB 82; NewsDir 84*
Daily News, The - Richmond, MO - *Ed&PubIntYB 82; NewsDir 84*
Daily News, The - Batavia, NY - *Ed&PubIntYB 82*
Daily News, The - Springfield, OH - *Ed&PubIntYB 82*
Daily News, The [of Janson Publishing Co. Inc.] - Bangor, PA - *BaconPubCkNews 84; NewsDir 84*
Daily News, The - Huntingdon, PA - *Ed&PubIntYB 82*
Daily News, The - Lebanon, PA - *Ed&PubIntYB 82*
Daily News, The - McKeesport, PA - *BaconPubCkNews 84*
Daily News, The - Longview, WA - *Ed&PubIntYB 82*
Daily News, The - Port Angeles, WA - *Ed&PubIntYB 82*
Daily News, The - Nelson, BC, Canada - *BaconPubCkNews 84*
Daily News, The - Prince Rupert, BC, Canada - *BaconPubCkNews 84; Ed&PubIntYB 82*
Daily News, The - St. John's, NF, Canada - *BaconPubCkNews 84; Ed&PubIntYB 82*

Daily News, The - Lower Sackville, NS, Canada - *Ed&PubIntYB 82*
Daily News, The - Truro, NS, Canada - *Ed&PubIntYB 82*
Daily News Tribune - Fullerton, CA - *Ed&PubIntYB 82*
Daily Nonpareil, The - Council Bluffs, IA - *Ed&PubIntYB 82; LitMarPl 84*
Daily Northwest Colorado Press, The - Craig, CO - *BaconPubCkNews 84*
Daily Northwestern [of Students Publishing Co.] - Evanston, IL - *NewsDir 84*
Daily Northwestern - Oshkosh, WI - *BaconPubCkNews 84*
Daily O'Collegian - Stillwater, OK - *NewsDir 84*
Daily Oklahoman, The [of Oklahoma Publishing Co.] - Oklahoma City, OK - *Ed&PubIntYB 82; LitMarPl 83, 84; NewsBur 6*
Daily Olympian - Olympia, WA - *BaconPubCkNews 84; Ed&PubIntYB 82; LitMarPl 83*
Daily Orange Corp. - Syracuse, NY - *NewsDir 84*
Daily Pacific Builder [of McGraw-Hill Inc.] - San Francisco, CA - *BaconPubCkMag 84; Ed&PubIntYB 82; MagDir 84; NewsDir 84*
Daily Packet & Times - Orillia, ON, Canada - *BaconPubCkNews 84; Ed&PubIntYB 82*
Daily Pantagraph, The - Bloomington, IL - *Ed&PubIntYB 82*
Daily Peabody Times, The - Peabody, MA - *Ed&PubIntYB 82*
Daily Pennsylvanian, The [of University of Pennsylvania] - Philadelphia, PA - *NewsDir 84*
Daily Petro Futures - Boston, MA - *DirOnDB Spring 84*
Daily Petro News [of NewsNet Inc.] - Bryn Mawr, PA - *DataDirOnSer 84*
Daily Planet Almanac Inc. - Boulder, CO - *BoPubDir 5*
Daily Planet, The [of Greater Philadelphia Group Inc.] - Philadelphia, PA - *NewsDir 84*
Daily Post-Athenian, The - Athens, TN - *BaconPubCkNews 84*
Daily Press - Paragould, AR - *AyerDirPub 83*
Daily Press - Artesia, NM - *BaconPubCkNews 84*
Daily Press - Utica, NY - *Ed&PubIntYB 82*
Daily Press - Newport News, VA - *BaconPubCkNews 84; BrCabYB 84 p.D-300; Ed&PubIntYB 82; LitMarPl 84; Tel&CabFB 84C p.1676*
Daily Press, The - Paso Robles, CA - *Ed&PubIntYB 82*
Daily Press, The - Escanaba, MI - *BaconPubCkNews 84; Ed&PubIntYB 82*
Daily Press, The - St. Marys, PA - *BaconPubCkNews 84; Ed&PubIntYB 82*
Daily Press, The - Ashland, WI - *BaconPubCkNews 84*
Daily Press, The - Timmins, ON, Canada - *BaconPubCkNews 84; Ed&PubIntYB 82*
Daily Princetonian, The - Princeton, NJ - *NewsDir 84*
Daily Progress, The [of Worrell Newspapers Inc.] - Charlottesville, VA - *BaconPubCkNews 84; NewsDir 84*
Daily Racing Form - Los Angeles, CA - *Ed&PubIntYB 82*
Daily Racing Form - Chicago, IL - *Ed&PubIntYB 82*
Daily Racing Form - Hightstown, NJ - *Ed&PubIntYB 82*
Daily Racing Form - Toronto, ON, Canada - *Ed&PubIntYB 82*
Daily Record - Peoria, IL - *Ed&PubIntYB 82*
Daily Record - Des Moines, IA - *Ed&PubIntYB 82*
Daily Record - Wichita, KS - *AyerDirPub 83*
Daily Record - Baltimore, MD - *Ed&PubIntYB 82; NewsDir 84*
Daily Record - Kansas City, MO - *Ed&PubIntYB 82; NewsDir 84*
Daily Record - Omaha, NE - *Ed&PubIntYB 82; NewsDir 84*
Daily Record - Morristown, NJ - *BaconPubCkNews 84; Ed&PubIntYB 82; NewsDir 84*
Daily Record - Wooster, OH - *BaconPubCkNews 84; Ed&PubIntYB 82*
Daily Record - Ellensburg, WA - *Ed&PubIntYB 82*
Daily Record Chronicle - Kent, WA - *Ed&PubIntYB 82*
Daily Record Chronicle - Renton, WA - *BaconPubCkNews 84*
Daily Record Inc. - Louisville, KS - *Ed&PubIntYB 82*
Daily Record, The - Lawrenceville, IL - *Ed&PubIntYB 82*
Daily Record, The - New Orleans, LA - *NewsDir 84*
Daily Record, The - Rochester, NY - *Ed&PubIntYB 82*
Daily Record, The - Dunn, NC - *AyerDirPub 83; BaconPubCkNews 84; Ed&PubIntYB 82*
Daily Recorder, The [of Sacramento Legal Press Inc.] - Sacramento, CA - *Ed&PubIntYB 82; NewsDir 84*
Daily Reflector, The - Greenville, NC - *BaconPubCkNews 84*
Daily Register, The - Harrisburg, IL - *Ed&PubIntYB 82*
Daily Register, The - Shrewsbury, NJ - *BaconPubCkNews 84; Ed&PubIntYB 82*
Daily Report, The - Ontario, CA - *BaconPubCkNews 84; Ed&PubIntYB 82*
Daily Reporter - Tucson, AZ - *Ed&PubIntYB 82*
Daily Reporter [of Clark County Publishing Co.] - Casey, IL - *Ed&PubIntYB 82; NewsDir 84*
Daily Reporter - Sioux City, IA - *Ed&PubIntYB 82; NewsDir 84*
Daily Reporter - Spencer, IA - *Ed&PubIntYB 82*
Daily Reporter [of Gant Publishing Co.] - Lincoln, NE - *Ed&PubIntYB 82; NewsDir 84*
Daily Reporter [of Reporter Publishing Co.] - Columbus, OH - *Ed&PubIntYB 82; NewsDir 84*
Daily Reporter - Milwaukee, WI - *Ed&PubIntYB 82; NewsDir 84*
Daily Reporter - Cambridge, ON, Canada - *Ed&PubIntYB 82*
Daily Reporter, The - Greenfield, IN - *BaconPubCkNews 84; Ed&PubIntYB 82*
Daily Republic & Green Sheet - Fairfield, CA - *BaconPubCkNews 84*
Daily Republic, The - Fairfield, CA - *Ed&PubIntYB 82*
Daily Republican-Register - Mt. Carmel, IL - *Ed&PubIntYB 82*
Daily Republican, The - Burlington, KS - *Ed&PubIntYB 82*
Daily Reveille, The [of Louisiana State University] - Baton Rouge, LA - *NewsDir 84*
Daily Review - Bisbee, AZ - *AyerDirPub 83*
Daily Review - Towanda, PA - *BaconPubCkNews 84; Ed&PubIntYB 82*
Daily Review - Clifton Forge, VA - *AyerDirPub 83; BaconPubCkNews 84*
Daily Review Atlas - Monmouth, IL - *Ed&PubIntYB 82*
Daily Review, The - Hayward, CA - *Ed&PubIntYB 82; NewsDir 84*
Daily Review, The [of Morgan City Newspapers Inc.] - Morgan City, LA - *Ed&PubIntYB 82; NewsDir 84*
Daily Rocket-Miner - Rock Springs, WY - *Ed&PubIntYB 82*
Daily Sec Advance - Washington, DC - *DirOnDB Spring 84*
Daily Sentinel [of Grand Junction Newspapers Inc.] - Grand Junction, CO - *Ed&PubIntYB 82; LitMarPl 83, 84; NewsDir 84*
Daily Sentinel [of Woodstock Publishing Co.] - Woodstock, IL - *BaconPubCkNews 84; Ed&PubIntYB 82; NewsDir 84*
Daily Sentinel - Rome, NY - *BaconPubCkNews 84; Ed&PubIntYB 82*
Daily Sentinel-Review, The - Woodstock, ON, Canada - *BaconPubCkNews 84; Ed&PubIntYB 82*
Daily Sentinel-Star, The - Grenada, MS - *Ed&PubIntYB 82*
Daily Sentinel, The - Pomeroy, OH - *Ed&PubIntYB 82*
Daily Sentinel, The - Nacogdoches, TX - *Ed&PubIntYB 82*
Daily Sentinel-Tribune, The - Bowling Green, OH - *Ed&PubIntYB 82*
Daily Shipping News - Portland, OR - *Ed&PubIntYB 82; NewsDir 84*
Daily Signal - Downey, CA - *Ed&PubIntYB 82*
Daily Sitka Sentinel - Sitka, AK - *BaconPubCkNews 84; NewsDir 84*
Daily South Suburban Southtown Economist - Chicago, IL - *AyerDirPub 83*
Daily Southeast News & Downey Champion, The - Downey, CA - *Ed&PubIntYB 82*
Daily Southtown Economist - Chicago, IL - *NewsDir 84*
Daily Southwest Suburban Southtown Economist - Chicago, IL - *AyerDirPub 83*
Daily Spectrum - St. George, UT - *BaconPubCkNews 84*
Daily Spectrum/Iron County Record Edition, The [of Spectrum Publishing Co. Inc.] - Cedar City, UT - *NewsDir 84*
Daily Standard - Excelsior Springs, MO - *BaconPubCkNews 84*
Daily Standard - Sikeston, MO - *Ed&PubIntYB 82*
Daily Standard-Observer - Irwin, PA - *Ed&PubIntYB 82*
Daily Standard, The - Celina, OH - *Ed&PubIntYB 82*
Daily Star-Journal, The - Warrensburg, MO - *BaconPubCkNews 84*
Daily Star-Progress - La Habra, CA - *Ed&PubIntYB 82*
Daily Star, The - Hammond, LA - *Ed&PubIntYB 82*
Daily Star, The - Niles, MI - *Ed&PubIntYB 82*
Daily Star, The - Oneonta, NY - *Ed&PubIntYB 82*
Daily Star, The - Sault Ste. Marie, ON, Canada - *BaconPubCkNews 84*

Daily Statesman - Dexter, MO - *AyerDirPub 83; Ed&PubIntYB 82*
Daily Sun Journal, The - Brooksville, FL - *Ed&PubIntYB 82*
Daily Sun-Post - San Clemente, CA - *Ed&PubIntYB 82*
Daily Sun, The - Warner Robins, GA - *Ed&PubIntYB 82*
Daily/Sunday Register, The [of Capital Cities Communications Inc.] - Red Bank, NJ - *NewsDir 84*
Daily Sundial [of California State University, Northridge] - Northridge, CA - *NewsDir 84*
Daily Tar Heel - Chapel Hill, NC - *NewsDir 84*
Daily Targum, The - New Brunswick, NJ - *NewsDir 84*
Daily Tax Advance - Washington, DC - *DirOnDB Spring 84*
Daily Telegram, The - Adrian, MI - *BaconPubCkNews 84; Ed&PubIntYB 82*
Daily Telegraph Printing Co. - Bluefield, WV - *BrCabYB 84; Tel&CabFB 84S*
Daily Territorial, The - Tucson, AZ - *NewsDir 84*
Daily Texan [of Texas Student Publications] - Austin, TX - *NewsDir 84*
Daily Tidings, The - Yukon, OK - *AyerDirPub 83*
Daily Tidings, The [of Capital Cities Communications Inc.] - Ashland, OR - *Ed&PubIntYB 82; NewsDir 84*
Daily Times - Slidell, LA - *Ed&PubIntYB 82*
Daily Times - Gloucester, MA - *Ed&PubIntYB 82*
Daily Times - Erie, PA - *NewsDir 84*
Daily Times & Chronicle - Woburn, MA - *Ed&PubIntYB 82; NewsDir 84*
Daily Times Leader - West Point, MS - *AyerDirPub 83; Ed&PubIntYB 82*
Daily Times-News, The - Burlington, NC - *Ed&PubIntYB 82*
Daily Times-Republic - Watseka, IL - *Ed&PubIntYB 82*
Daily Times, The - Ottawa, IL - *Ed&PubIntYB 82*
Daily Times, The - Salisbury, MD - *Ed&PubIntYB 82*
Daily Times, The - Portsmouth, OH - *Ed&PubIntYB 82; NewsDir 84*
Daily Times, The - Pryor, OK - *Ed&PubIntYB 82*
Daily Times, The [of Maryville-Alcoa Newspapers Inc.] - Maryville, TN - *Ed&PubIntYB 82; LitMarPl 84*
Daily Times, The - Brampton, ON, Canada - *BaconPubCkNews 84; Ed&PubIntYB 82*
Daily Titan - Fullerton, CA - *NewsDir 84*
Daily Townsman - Cranbrook, BC, Canada - *BaconPubCkNews 84; Ed&PubIntYB 82*
Daily Transcript - Colorado Springs, CO - *Ed&PubIntYB 82*
Daily Transcript - Dedham, MA - *Ed&PubIntYB 82; NewsDir 84*
Daily Tribune - Royal Oak, MI - *BaconPubCkNews 84; Ed&PubIntYB 82; NewsDir 84*
Daily Tribune [of Bay City Newspapers Inc.] - Bay City, TX - *BaconPubCkNews 84; Ed&PubIntYB 82; NewsDir 84*
Daily Tribune - Wisconsin Rapids, WI - *Ed&PubIntYB 82*
Daily Tribune News, The - Cartersville, GA - *Ed&PubIntYB 82*
Daily Tribune, The - Roseville, CA - *Ed&PubIntYB 82*
Daily Trojan [of University of Southern California] - Los Angeles, CA - *NewsDir 84*
Daily Union - Shelbyville, IL - *Ed&PubIntYB 82*
Daily Union, The - Junction City, KS - *Ed&PubIntYB 82*
Daily Universe, The [of Brigham Young University] - Provo, UT - *NewsDir 84*
Daily Utah Chronicle, The [of University of Utah, University Union] - Salt Lake City, UT - *NewsDir 84*
Daily Variety [of Variety Inc.] - Hollywood, CA - *BaconPubCkMag 84; Ed&PubIntYB 82; LitMarPl 83, 84*
Daily Variety [of Variety Inc.] - Los Angeles, CA - *MagDir 84; NewsDir 84*
Daily Vidette, The [of Illinois State University] - Normal, IL - *NewsDir 84*
Daily Washington Law Reporter, The - Washington, DC - *Ed&PubIntYB 82; NewsDir 84*
Daily Word - Unity Village, MO - *MagIndMarPl 82-83*
Daily World [of Long View Publishing Co. Inc.] - New York, NY - *AyerDirPub 83; BaconPubCkNews 84; Ed&PubIntYB 82; NewsDir 84*
Daily World, The - Opelousas, LA - *Ed&PubIntYB 82*
Daily World, The - Aberdeen, WA - *BaconPubCkNews 84; Ed&PubIntYB 82*
Dain & DeJoy - Los Angeles, CA - *BillIntBG 83-84*
Daingerfield Steel Country Bee - Daingerfield, TX - *BaconPubCkNews 84*
Dairy & Food Sanitation - Ames, IA - *BaconPubCkMag 84*
Dairy & Ice Cream Field [of Harcourt Brace Jovanovich] - New York, NY - *MagDir 84*
Dairy Field - New York, NY - *MagIndMarPl 82-83*
Dairy Field - Cleveland, OH - *BaconPubCkMag 84*
Dairy Goat Journal - Scottsdale, AZ - *BaconPubCkMag 84; MagDir 84; MagIndMarPl 82-83; WritMar 84*
Dairy Herd Management - Minneapolis, MN - *BaconPubCkMag 84; MagDir 84; MagIndMarPl 82-83*
Dairy Industry Newsletter - McLean, VA - *BaconPubCkMag 84*
Dairy Magazine - Denver, CO - *BaconPubCkMag 84; MagDir 84*
Dairy Record - Chicago, IL - *BaconPubCkMag 84; MagIndMarPl 82-83*
Dairy Research Digest - Rosemont, IL - *BaconPubCkMag 84*
Dairy Science Abstracts [of Commonwealth Bureau of Dairy Science & Technology] - Reading, England - *CompReadDB 82*
Dairy Scope - Napa, CA - *BaconPubCkMag 84; WritMar 84*
Dairy Scope - Penngrove, CA - *MagDir 84*
Dairy World - Millbury, MA - *BaconPubCkMag 84; MagDir 84*
Dairyland Productions Inc. - Milwaukee, WI - *BillIntBG 83-84*
Dairyman, The - Corona, CA - *BaconPubCkMag 84; MagDir 84; WritMar 84*
Dairymen's Digest - Schaumburg, IL - *BaconPubCkMag 84; MagDir 84*
Dairymen's Digest - Arlington, TX - *ArtMar 84; WritMar 84*
Dairynews - Syracuse, NY - *BaconPubCkMag 84; MagDir 84; WritMar 84*
Daisy Publishing Inc. - Seattle, WA - *BoPubDir 4, 5; LitMarPl 84*
Daisy Wheel Ribbon Co. Inc. - Cucamonga, CA - *DirInfWP 82; MicrocomMPl 83, 84; WhoWMicrocom 83*
Daisytek Inc. - Richardson, TX - *DirInfWP 82*
Dakin 5 Corp. - Denver, CO - *MicrocomSwDir 1; WhoWMicrocom 83*
Dakis Concern, The - Orinda, CA - *StaDirAdAg 2-84*
Dakota Broadcasting Co. - Rapid City, SD - *BrCabYB 84*
Dakota Central Rural Telephone Cooperative Association - Carrington, ND - *TelDir&BG 83-84*
Dakota Cooperative Telecommunications Inc. - Irene, SD - *TelDir&BG 83-84*
Dakota County Tribune - Farmington, MN - *AyerDirPub 83; Ed&PubIntYB 82; NewsDir 84*
Dakota Farmer, The - Aberdeen, SD - *MagDir 84*
Dakota Giant Network - Bismarck, ND - *BrCabYB 84*
Dakota Graphics Inc. - Lakewood, CO - *LitMarPl 83, 84; MicroMarPl 82-83*
Dakota Interviewing Service - Minot, ND - *IntDirMarRes 83*
Dakotan - Isabel, SD - *AyerDirPub 83*
Daksel/Seldak Music Corp. - New York, NY - *BillIntBG 83-84*
Dalcon Computer Center - Nashville, TN - *MicrocomMPl 84*
Dale Books - Waterbury, CT - *BoPubDir 4, 5*
Dale Books Inc. - New York, NY - *BoPubDir 4, 5*
Dale City Cable TV [of Prestige Cable TV Inc.] - Dale City, VA - *Tel&CabFB 84C*
Dale Data - Portland, OR - *MicrocomMPl 84*
Dale Industries Inc. - Waynesville, NC - *AvMarPl 83*
Dale Market Research, Tom - New York, NY - *IntDirMarRes 83*
Dale-Muldoon, Nancy - Brookfield Center, CT - *LitMarPl 83*
Dale News - *See* Ferdinand News Publishers
Dale News, The - Ferdinand, IN - *Ed&PubIntYB 82*
Dalee Bookbinding Co. Inc. - Brooklyn, NY - *LitMarPl 83, 84*
Dale's Electronic & Cable Service - Ft. Ridge, WV - *Tel&CabFB 84C*
Dale's Electronic Service - Marshal County, WV - *BrCabYB 84*
Daleville-Ft. Rucker Cable Fund Ltd. - Daleville, AL - *BrCabYB 84*
Daley Agency Inc., Mae - New York, NY - *LitMarPl 84*
Dalgleish Enterprises Ltd., George - Winnipeg, MB, Canada - *BoPubDir 4 Sup, 5*
Dalhart Daily Texan - Dalhart, TX - *BaconPubCkNews 84; Ed&PubIntYB 82; NewsDir 84*
Dalhart TV Cable System [of Dorate Interstate Inc.] - Dalhart, TX - *BrCabYB 84; Tel&CabFB 84C*
Dalhousie Cable TV - Dalhousie, NB, Canada - *BrCabYB 84*
Dalhousie News - Dalhousie, NB, Canada - *Ed&PubIntYB 82*

Dalhousie Review, The - Halifax, NS, Canada - *LitMag&SmPr 83-84*
Dalhousie University (Institute of Public Affairs) - Halifax, NS, Canada - *BoPubDir 4, 5*
Dalhousie University (School of Library Service) - Halifax, NS, Canada - *BoPubDir 4 Sup, 5*
Dali Foundation Inc., Salvador - St. Petersburg, FL - *BoPubDir 4, 5*
Dallas Cablevision [of Cable Management Associates Inc.] - Dallas, WV - *Tel&CabFB 84C*
Dallas Center Northeast Dallas Record - *Ed&PubIntYB 82*
Dallas Center Times - *See* Northeast Dallas County Record
Dallas City Enterprise - Dallas City, IL - *BaconPubCkNews 84; Ed&PubIntYB 82*
Dallas County Courier - Buffalo, MO - *Ed&PubIntYB 82*
Dallas County News - Adel, IA - *AyerDirPub 83; Ed&PubIntYB 82*
Dallas Craftsman, The [of Reilly Printing Inc.] - Dallas, TX - *NewsDir 84*
Dallas/Ft. Worth Business [of Scripps-Howard News] - Dallas, TX - *BaconPubCkMag 84; MagDir 84*
Dallas-Ft. Worth Home & Garden - Dallas, TX - *BaconPubCkMag 84; MagDir 84*
Dallas/Ft. Worth Living [of Baker Publications] - Dallas, TX - *BaconPubCkMag 84; MagDir 84; MagIndMarPl 82-83; WritMar 84*
Dallas Ft. Worth Texas Jewish Post - Ft. Worth, TX - *AyerDirPub 83*
Dallas Historical Society - Dallas, TX - *BoPubDir 4, 5*
Dallas Itemizer-Observer - Dallas, OR - *BaconPubCkNews 84*
Dallas, Leonard & Pease Inc. - Bala Cynwyd, PA - *StaDirAdAg 2-84*
Dallas Life Magazine [of Belo Corp.] - Dallas, TX - *WritMar 84*
Dallas Magazine [of Dallas Chamber of Commerce] - Dallas, TX - *BaconPubCkMag 84; MagDir 84; WritMar 84*
Dallas Morning News [of A. H. Belo Corp.] - Dallas, TX - *AyerDirPub 83; BaconPubCkNews 84; Ed&PubIntYB 82; LitMarPl 83, 84; NewsBur 6; NewsDir 84*
Dallas Museum of Fine Arts - Dallas, TX - *BoPubDir 4, 5*
Dallas New Era - Dallas, GA - *BaconPubCkNews 84; Ed&PubIntYB 82; NewsDir 84*
Dallas North Carrollton News - Dallas, TX - *NewsDir 84*
Dallas Oak Cliff Tribune - *See* Zauber Publishing
Dallas Park Cities News - Dallas, TX - *BaconPubCkNews 84; NewsDir 84*
Dallas Polk County Itemizer-Observer [of Eagle Newspapers Inc.] - Dallas, OR - *NewsDir 84*
Dallas Post [of Pennaprint Inc.] - Dallas, PA - *Ed&PubIntYB 82; NewsDir 84*
Dallas Post - *See* Pennaprint Inc.
Dallas Post Tribune - Dallas, TX - *BaconPubCkNews 84*
Dallas Public Library (Custom Research Services) - Dallas, TX - *FBInfSer 80*
Dallas Star Records - Dallas, TX - *BillIntBG 83-84*
Dallas Suburban Tribune - Dallas, TX - *BaconPubCkNews 84; NewsDir 84*
Dallas Theater Center - Dallas, TX - *WritMar 84*
Dallas Times Herald [of The Times Mirror Co.] - Dallas, TX - *BaconPubCkNews 84; Ed&PubIntYB 82; LitMarPl 83, 84; NewsBur 6; NewsDir 84*
Dallas Weekly [of Davis & Associates] - Dallas, TX - *AyerDirPub 83; BaconPubCkNews 84; Ed&PubIntYB 82; NewsDir 84*
Dallas White Rocker News - Dallas, TX - *BaconPubCkNews 84; NewsDir 84*
Dallastex Music Publishing Co. - Dallas, TX - *BillIntBG 83-84*
Dalles Chronicle, The [of Mid-Columbia Publishing Co.] - The Dalles, OR - *BaconPubCkNews 84; Ed&PubIntYB 82; NewsDir 84*
Dally Advertising - Ft. Worth, TX - *AdAge 3-28-84; StaDirAdAg 2-84*
Dalmar Cablevision Inc. - Del Mar, CA - *BrCabYB 84*
Dalmas & Ricour - Fayetteville, NC - *BoPubDir 4, 5*
Dalton & Associates Inc., Ralph W. - Troy, OH - *StaDirAdAg 2-84*
Dalton Bookseller, B. - Minneapolis, MN - *LitMarPl 83*
Dalton Daily Citizen-News - Dalton, GA - *BaconPubCkNews 84; NewsDir 84*
Dalton Gazette & Kidron News - Dalton, OH - *BaconPubCkNews 84; Ed&PubIntYB 82*
Dalton News-Record - Dalton, MA - *BaconPubCkNews 84; Ed&PubIntYB 82*
Dalton Telephone Co. Inc. - Dalton, NE - *TelDir&BG 83-84*
Dalton's Directory - Haverford, PA - *BoPubDir 4, 5*
Daly Agency Inc., Mae - New York, NY - *LitMarPl 83*
Daly City Record - Daly City, CA - *Ed&PubIntYB 82*
Daly City Record - South San Francisco, CA - *NewsDir 84*
Daly City Record - *See* San Mateo Times Group Newspapers
Dalya Music Co. - *See* Better Half Music Co.
Daman - Huntsville, AL - *MicrocomMPl 83*
Damariscotta Lincoln County News - Damariscotta, ME - *BaconPubCkNews 84*
Damart Advertising Associates Inc. - Minneapolis, MN - *StaDirAdAg 2-84*
Damas Publishing Co. - Hollywood, CA - *BoPubDir 4, 5*
Damascus Courier-Gazette [of Gaithersburg Publishing Co.] - Gaithersburg, SC - *NewsDir 84*
Damascus Road Press - Wescosville, PA - *BoPubDir 4, 5*
Damascus Weekly Courier - Damascus, MD - *BaconPubCkNews 84*
D'Amato, Alex - Bronxville, NY - *LitMarPl 83, 84; MagIndMarPl 82-83*
D'Amato, Janet P. - Bronxville, NY - *LitMarPl 83, 84*
D'Amato Research Inc. - Plainfield, NJ - *IntDirMarRes 83*
Dame & Co. Inc., Nathaniel - Cambridge, MA - *LitMarPl 83*
Dame Inc., Robert F. [Subs. of Olson Research Inc.] - Richmond, VA - *LitMarPl 83, 84; WritMar 84*
Dame Publications Inc. - Houston, TX - *LitMarPl 83, 84*
D'Amico, Paul M. - Livingston Manor, NY - *BoPubDir 5*
Damisch Advertising & Marketing Agency - Northbrook, IL - *StaDirAdAg 2-84*
Damon (Instructional Systems Div.) - Westwood, MA - *AvMarPl 83*
Damron Enterprises Inc., Bob - San Francisco, CA - *BoPubDir 5*
Dan Advertising Agency - Norfolk, VA - *StaDirAdAg 2-84*
Dan Advertising & Public Relations - Norfolk, VA - *ArtMar 84*
Dan River Press - South Thomaston, ME - *LitMag&SmPr 83-84*
Dan River Press [Aff. of Olmsted Publishing Enterprises Corp.] - Stafford, VA - *BoPubDir 4; LitMarPl 83*
Dan the Man Music Publishing Co. - Cleveland, OH - *BillIntBG 83-84*
Dana Point/Capo Beach - Mission Viejo, CA - *AyerDirPub 83*
Dana Productions [Div. of Saparoff Films Inc.] - North Hollywood, CA - *AvMarPl 83*
Dana Publishing Co. - Miami Beach, FL - *BillIntBG 83-84*
Danbury News Times [of Ottaway Newspapers Inc.] - Danbury, CT - *BaconPubCkNews 84; NewsDir 84*
Danbury Press - Suffern, NY - *BoPubDir 4, 5*
Danbury Printing & Litho - Danbury, CT - *MagIndMarPl 82-83*
Danbury Reporter - Danbury, NC - *Ed&PubIntYB 82*
Danbury Reporter - *See* Pepper Publishing Co.
Danbury Reporter-Stokes Record - Danbury, NC - *AyerDirPub 83*
Danbury Review - Danbury, IA - *BaconPubCkNews 84; Ed&PubIntYB 82*
Danca, Vince - Rockford, IL - *BoPubDir 4, 5*
Dance-A-Thon Records - Atlanta, GA - *BillIntBG 83-84*
Dance Art Co. - San Francisco, CA - *AvMarPl 83*
Dance Book Club [of Princeton Book Co.] - Princeton, NJ - *LitMarPl 84*
Dance Book Forum - New York, NY - *MagIndMarPl 82-83*
Dance Films Association Inc. - New York, NY - *BoPubDir 4, 5*
Dance Horizons - Brooklyn, NY - *BoPubDir 4, 5; LitMarPl 84; WritMar 84*
Dance in Canada - Toronto, ON, Canada - *LitMag&SmPr 83-84; WritMar 84*
Dance Magazine - New York, NY - *ArtMar 84; MagDir 84; MagIndMarPl 82-83; WritMar 84*
Dance News - New York, NY - *MagDir 84*
Dance Notation Bureau Inc. - New York, NY - *BoPubDir 4, 5*
Dance Record Distributors Ltd. - Newark, NJ - *AvMarPl 83*
Dance Scope [of American Dance Guild Inc.] - New York, NY - *LitMag&SmPr 83-84*

Dance Teacher Now [of SMW Communications Inc.] - Davis, CA - *MagIndMarPl 82-83; WritMar 84*
Dancer Fitzgerald Sample - New York, NY - *AdAge 3-28-84, 6-25-84; ArtMar 84; Br 1-23-84; BrCabYB 84; HomeVid&CabYB 82-83; StaDirAdAg 2-84*
Dancer-Miller Publishing - San Francisco, CA - *BillIntBG 83-84*
Dancing Crow Press - Larkspur, CA - *LitMag&SmPr 83-84*
Dancy Productions Inc., Nicholas - New York, NY - *WritMar 84*
Dandelion Music Co. - *See* Jamie Music Publishing Co.
Dandelion, The [of Michael J. Coughlin] - St. Paul, MN - *LitMag&SmPr 83-84*
Dando-Schaff Printing & Publishing Co. - Philadelphia, PA - *MagIndMarPl 82-83*
Dandy Dittys - *See* Schroeder International Ltd., A.
Dandy Lion Publications - San Luis Obispo, CA - *BoPubDir 4, 5*
Danel Enterprises - New York, NY - *DirMarMP 83*
Danforth Tribune - Toronto/Danforth, ON, Canada - *Ed&PubIntYB 82*
Dangary Publishing Co. Inc. - Baltimore, MD - *BoPubDir 4, 5*
Dani Records [Div. of Hilton House Inc.] - Cleveland, OH - *BillIntBG 83-84*
Danica - Chicago, IL - *Ed&PubIntYB 82*
Danica-Morning Star - Chicago, IL - *NewsDir 84*
Daniel & Charles Associates Inc. - New York, NY - *BrCabYB 84; HBIndAd&MS 82-83*
Daniel Books of Toronto - Toronto, ON, Canada - *BoPubDir 4, 5*
Daniel, James & Associates Inc. - Tulsa, OK - *StaDirAdAg 2-84*
Danielle Music Co. [Div. of Hilton House Inc.] - Cleveland, OH - *BillIntBG 83-84*
Daniels & Associates - Lake San Marcos, CA - *BrCabYB 84*
Daniels & Associates Inc. - Denver, CO - *BrCabYB 84 p.D-300; CabTVFinDB 83; HomeVid&CabYB 82-83; InterCabHB 3; LitMarPl 84; Tel&CabFB 84C p.1676*
Daniels Associates, Aaron - New York, NY - *LitMarPl 84*
Daniels, Bill - *See* Daniels & Associates Inc.
Daniels Cablevision - *See* Daniels & Associates Inc.
Daniels Cablevision Inc. - Del Mar, CA - *Tel&CabFB 84C*
Daniels Cablevision Inc. - Fallbrook, CA - *Tel&CabFB 84C*
Daniels Cablevision Inc. - Lake San Marcos, CA - *Tel&CabFB 84C*
Daniels County Leader - Scobey, MT - *Ed&PubIntYB 82*
Daniels, Delia - Hancock, NH - *LitMarPl 83*
Daniels, Devra - Glasgow, MT - *Tel&CabFB 84C p.1676*
Daniels, Ernestine R. - New York, NY - *LitMarPl 83, 84*
Daniels, Guy - New York, NY - *LitMarPl 83, 84*
Daniels, Harold L. - *See* Kansas Cablevision Inc.
Daniels, Nancy L. - Lemont, PA - *LitMarPl 83, 84*
Danielson Best Deal - Danielson, CT - *NewsDir 84*
Danielson Windham County Journal-Transcript - Danielson, CT - *BaconPubCkNews 84*
Danielsville Monitor - Danielsville, GA - *BaconPubCkNews 84; Ed&PubIntYB 82*
Danis Research Inc. - Fairfield, NJ - *IntDirMarRes 83*
Danish Committee for Scientific & Technical Information & Documentation - Copenhagen, Denmark - *EISS 83*
Danish Diane Center - Lyngby, Denmark - *EISS 83*
Danish Teledata System [of Denmark Telecommunications Administration] - Copenhagen, Denmark - *EISS 7-83 Sup; TeleSy&SerDir 7-83*
Danish Terminological Data Bank [of Copenhagen School of Economics & Business Administration] - Copenhagen, Denmark - *EISS 83*
Danish Tymnet/Telenet Access - Roedovre, Denmark - *InfIndMarPl 83*
Danmark & Michaels Inc. - Hicksville, NY - *LitMarPl 84*
Danmark & Michaels Inc. - Westbury, NY - *LitMarPl 83; MagIndMarPl 82-83*
Danmarks Tekniske Bibliotek/National Technological Library of Denmark - Lyngby, Denmark - *CompReadDB 82; InfIndMarPl 83*
Dannen, Kent & Donna - Estes Park, CO - *LitMarPl 84*
Danner Press Corp. - Canton, OH - *LitMarPl 83, 84; MagIndMarPl 82-83*
Danoff Music Co. - Washington, DC - *BillIntBG 83-84*
Danske Pioneer - Chicago, IL - *Ed&PubIntYB 82*
Dansville Genesee Country Express [of Greenhow Newspapers Inc.] - Dansville, NY - *BaconPubCkNews 84; NewsDir 84*
Dansville Press II - Dansville, NY - *LitMarPl 83*
Dansville Press II [Div. of Denie Filter] - New York, NY - *LitMarPl 84*
Dante University of America Press - Brookline Village, MA - *DirMarMP 83; LitMarPl 84*
Dante University of America Press Inc. - Weston, MA - *WritMar 84*
Dantek Software Inc. - Batavia, OH - *WhoWMicrocom 83*
Danube Inc. - Kent, OH - *BoPubDir 5*
Danube Telephone Co. - Danube, MN - *TelDir&BG 83-84*
Danubian Press Inc. [Aff. of American Hungarian Literary Guild] - Astor, FL - *BoPubDir 4, 5; LitMarPl 84*
Danvers Herald - Danvers, MA - *Ed&PubIntYB 82*
Danvers Herald - Ipswich, MA - *AyerDirPub 83; NewsDir 84*
Danvers Herald - *See* North Shore Weeklies Inc.
Danville Advocate-Messenger - Danville, KY - *BaconPubCkNews 84; NewsDir 84*
Danville Bee - Danville, VA - *BaconPubCkNews 84*
Danville Cablevision [of The Daily Press Inc.] - Danville, VA - *BrCabYB 84; Tel&CabFB 84C*
Danville Cablevision Co. [of The Daily Press Inc.] - Altavista, VA - *Tel&CabFB 84C*
Danville CATV Service Inc. - Danville, PA - *BrCabYB 84; Tel&CabFB 84C*
Danville Commercial Appeal - Danville, VA - *BaconPubCkNews 84; Ed&PubIntYB 82; NewsDir 84*
Danville Commercial-News [of Northwestern Publishing Co.] - Danville, IL - *BaconPubCkNews 84; NewsDir 84*
Danville Examiner - Danville, KY - *Ed&PubIntYB 82*
Danville Gazette - Danville, IN - *Ed&PubIntYB 82*
Danville-Lancaster Cablevision Inc. [of Communications Systems Inc.] - Danville, KY - *BrCabYB 84; Tel&CabFB 84C*
Danville Mutual Telephone Co. - Danville, IA - *TelDir&BG 83-84*
Danville News [of Progressive Publishing Co. Inc.] - Danville, PA - *AyerDirPub 83; BaconPubCkNews 84; Ed&PubIntYB 82; NewsDir 84*
Danville News & Observer - Danville, VA - *Ed&PubIntYB 82*
Danville Register - Danville, VA - *BaconPubCkNews 84; Ed&PubIntYB 82*
Danville Republican - Danville, IN - *BaconPubCkNews 84*
Danville Times Advertiser - Danville, OH - *Ed&PubIntYB 82*
Danville Times Advertiser - *See* Knox Printing Co.
Danville Valley Pioneer [of Lesher Communications Inc.] - Danville, CA - *BaconPubCkNews 84; NewsDir 84*
Danville Yell County Record - Danville, AR - *BaconPubCkNews 84*
Dany News Service - Syosset, NY - *Ed&PubIntYB 82; LitMarPl 84*
DANYL Corp. - Moorestown, NJ - *DataDirSup 7-83*
Danz Stations, Fredric A. - *See* Sterling Recreation Organization
Danzig, Phillip I. - Montclair, NJ - *MagIndMarPl 82-83*
DAP TV Associates - Los Angeles, CA - *Tel&CabFB 84C*
Daphne Advertising Inc. - New York, NY - *StaDirAdAg 2-84*
Dar Systems International - Miami, FL - *MicrocomMPl 84*
Daratech Inc. - Cambridge, MA - *BoPubDir 4 Sup, 5*
Darbininkas - Brooklyn, NY - *Ed&PubIntYB 82*
Darby Media Group [Subs. of Darby Graphics Inc.] - Chicago, IL - *AvMarPl 83*
Darc Pluridata System [of Association for Research & Development of Chemical Informatics] - Paris, France - *DirOnDB Spring 84; EISS 83*
Darcy Associated Counselors Inc. - Hilton Head, SC - *DirPRFirms 83*
Darcy Communications Inc. - Denver, CO - *DirPRFirms 83*
D'Arcy-MacManus & Masius - Atlanta, GA - *ArtMar 84*
D'Arcy-MacManus & Masius - Bloomfield Hills, MI - *ArtMar 84; DirMarMP 83*
D'Arcy-MacManus & Masius - St. Louis, MO - *ArtMar 84*
D'Arcy-MacManus & Masius - New York, NY - *Br 1-23-84; BrCabYB 84; HomeVid&CabYB 82-83; StaDirAdAg 2-84; TelAl 83, 84*
D'Arcy MacManus Masius - New York, NY - *AdAge 3-28-84, 6-25-84*
Dardanelle Cable TV [of WEHCO Video Inc.] - Dardanelle, AR - *BrCabYB 84; Tel&CabFB 84C*
Dardanelle Post Dispatch - Dardanelle, AR - *BaconPubCkNews 84; Ed&PubIntYB 82*

DARDO [of Italcable] - Rome, Italy - *InflndMarPl 83*
Dare Inc. - Rockford, IL - *BoPubDir 4 Sup*
Darhansoff, Liz - New York, NY - *LitMarPl 83, 84*
Darien Community Association Inc. - Darien, CT - *BoPubDir 4, 5*
Darien Dupage Progress, The - Darien, IL - *Ed&PubIntYB 82*
Darien Metropolitan - Darien, IL - *Ed&PubIntYB 82*
Darien News [of Brooks Community Newspapers Inc.] - Darien, CT - *Ed&PubIntYB 82; NewsDir 84*
Darien News - Darien, GA - *BaconPubCkNews 84; Ed&PubIntYB 82*
Darien News-Review - *See* Brooks Community Newspapers
Darien Review, The - Darien, CT - *Ed&PubIntYB 82; NewsDir 84*
Darien, Russell, Hill & Dahl - San Jose, CA - *AdAge 3-28-84; StaDirAdAg 2-84*
Darien Suburban Life Graphic - *See* Life Printing & Publishing Co.
Darien Telephone Co. Inc. - Darien, GA - *TelDir&BG 83-84*
Daring Press - Canton, OH - *LitMarPl 83, 84*
Darino, Ed - New York, NY - *BoPubDir 4, 5*
Darino Films - New York, NY - *ArtMar 84; AvMarPl 83*
Dark Horse [of Dark Horse Poets Inc.] - Somerville, MA - *LitMag&SmPr 83-84*
Dark Horse Poets Inc. - Somerville, MA - *LitMag&SmPr 83-84*
Dark Star Systems - Greenford, England - *MicrocomSwDir 1*
Darke County Early Bird, The - Arcanum, OH - *NewsDir 84*
Darke County Farmer [of The Daily Advocate] - Greenville, OH - *NewsDir 84*
Darkhorse Bookmakers - Ashby, MA - *LitMag&SmPr 83-84*
Darkroom Photography - San Francisco, CA - *ArtMar 84; BaconPubCkMag 84; MagIndMarPl 82-83*
Darkroom Products Ltd. - Calendonia, IL - *AvMarPl 83*
Darkroom Techniques - Chicago, IL - *MagIndMarPl 82-83*
Darkroom Techniques [of Preston Publications Inc.] - Niles, IL - *BaconPubCkMag 84; WritMar 84*
Darksilver Records Inc. - Amarillo, TX - *BillIntBG 83-84*
Darksongs Music - Ft. Worth, TX - *BillIntBG 83-84*
Darlene's Secretarial Service - Fountain Valley, CA - *LitMarPl 83, 84; MagIndMarPl 82-83*
Darley, Terry - *See* Oconee Cablevision Inc.
Darlington Cablevision [of Quality CATV Inc.] - Darlington, IN - *BrCabYB 84*
Darlington News & Press - Darlington, SC - *BaconPubCkNews 84; NewsDir 84*
Darlington Republican Journal [of Monroe Publishing Co.] - Darlington, WI - *BaconPubCkNews 84; NewsDir 84*
Darome Connection [of Darome Inc.] - Chicago, IL - *TeleSy&SerDir 7-83*
Darome Inc. - Harvard, IL - *DataDirSup 7-83*
Darr Subscription Agency, Dale C. - Centralia, KS - *MagIndMarPl 82-83*
Darrah, William C. - Gettysburg, PA - *BoPubDir 4, 5*
Darrington Cable TV [of Summit Communications Inc.] - Darrington, WA - *BrCabYB 84*
Darrington Illustrated Press - Darrington, WA - *Ed&PubIntYB 82*
Darrington TV Cable Co. - Darrington, WA - *Tel&CabFB 84C*
Dart C.P. Services Ltd. - Scarborough, ON, Canada - *WhoWMicrocom 83*
Dart News - Atlanta, GA - *BaconPubCkMag 84*
Dartmoor Music - *See* Bicycle Music Co., The
Dartmouth Cable TV Ltd. - Dartmouth, NS, Canada - *BrCabYB 84; Tel&CabFB 84C*
Dartmouth Chronicle [of Somerset Spectator Publishing Corp.] - Fall River, MA - *NewsDir 84*
Dartmouth College (Kiewit Computation Center) - Hanover, NH - *DataDirOnSer 84*
Dartmouth College (Office of Instructional Services) - Hanover, NH - *AvMarPl 83*
Dartmouth College Library - Hanover, NH - *MicroMarPl 82-83*
Dartmouth College Time Sharing [of Dartmouth College] - Hanover, NH - *EISS 83*
Dartmouth Free Press - Dartmouth, NS, Canada - *Ed&PubIntYB 82*
Dartmouth Printing Co. - Hanover, NH - *MagIndMarPl 82-83*
Dartmouth, The - Hanover, NH - *NewsDir 84*
Dartmouth-Westport Chronicle - *See* Hathaway Publishing Corp.
Dartnell Corp. - Chicago, IL - *AvMarPl 83; DirMarMP 83; LitMarPl 83, 84; WritMar 84*
Dartnell Sales & Marketing Executive Report - Chicago, IL - *BaconPubCkMag 84*
Dartnell Sales & Marketing Newsletter - Chicago, IL - *BaconPubCkMag 84*
Darva Records [Div. of MBA Productions] - Austin, TX - *BillIntBG 83-84*
Darvill Outdoor Publications - Mt. Vernon, WA - *BoPubDir 4, 5*
Darwin Press Inc., The - Princeton, NJ - *LitMarPl 83, 84*
Darwin Publications - Burbank, CA - *BoPubDir 5; LitMag&SmPr 83-84; WritMar 84*
Darwin Publications - Sherman Oaks, CA - *BoPubDir 4*
Das Motorrad - Palos Verdes Peninsula, CA - *MagDir 84*
Dasein-Jupiter Hammon Publishing Co. [Aff. of Dasein Literary Society] - New York, NY - *BoPubDir 4, 5*
Dash - Wheaton, IL - *ArtMar 84; WritMar 84*
Dash, James Allen - *See* Birch Tree Group Ltd.
Dasilva, Ladis - Mississauga, ON, Canada - *BoPubDir 4, 5*
Dasi's Directory, Davi - Coconut Grove, FL - *BoPubDir 5*
Dassel Dispatch - Dassel, MN - *BaconPubCkNews 84; Ed&PubIntYB 82*
DASTEK Corp. - Los Gatos, CA - *DataDirSup 7-83*
Data Access Corp. - Coral Gables, FL - *MicrocomMPl 84; MicrocomSwDir 1; WhoWMicrocom 83*
Data Access Management Service - Charleston, SC - *MicrocomSwDir 1*
Data Access Systems Inc. - Blackwood, NJ - *DataDirSup 7-83; DirInfWP 82*
Data & Analysis Center for Software - Franklin Springs, NY - *CompReadDB 82*
Data & Analysis Center for Software [of IIT Research Institute] - Griffiss AFB, NY - *EISS 83*
Data & Analytical Services [of National Center for Higher Education Management Systems] - Boulder, CO - *EISS 83*
Data & Program Archive for the Social Sciences [of University of Milan] - Milan, Italy - *EISS 83*
Data & Program Library Service [of University of Wisconsin-Madison] - Madison, WI - *EISS 83*
Data & Research Technology Corp. - Pittsburgh, PA - *WritMar 84*
Data Anilas Ltd. [Subs. of Development Consultants Inc.] - Salina, KS - *MicrocomSwDir 1; WhoWMicrocom 83*
Data Architects Inc. - Waltham, MA - *DataDirSup 7-83*
Data Archives [of University of Northern Iowa] - Cedar Falls, IA - *EISS 83*
Data Archives [of Mississippi State University] - Mississippi State, MS - *EISS 83*
Data Archives [of University of Cincinnati] - Cincinnati, OH - *EISS 83*
Data Archives [of Temple University] - Philadelphia, PA - *EISS 83*
Data-Assette - Oxford, PA - *MicrocomMPl 84*
Data-Assette - London, England - *MicrocomSwDir 1*
Data Automation Services International Inc. - Alachua, FL - *MicrocomMPl 84*
Data Automation Services International Inc. - Gainesville, FL - *WhoWMicrocom 83*
Data Bank Access Service [of Portuguese Radio Marconi Co.] - Lisbon, Portugal - *EISS 7-83 Sup*
Data Bank for Medicaments - Paris, France - *EISS 83*
Data Bank Information Center - Paris, France - *EISS 83*
Data Bank of European Doctoral Theses in Management [of European Institute for Advanced Studies in Management] - Brussels, Belgium - *EISS 83*
Data Bank on Substances Harmful to Water [of Dortmund Institute for Water Research] - Schwerte-Geisecke, West Germany - *EISS 83*
Data Bank Service [of Tokyo Shoko Research Ltd.] - Tokyo, Japan - *EISS 5-84 Sup*
Data Barter [of Source Telecomputing Corp.] - McLean, VA - *DataDirOnSer 84*
Data Base Alert - White Plains, NY - *BaconPubCkMag 84*
Data Base Consultation Service [of National Council of Science & Technology] - Mexico City, Mexico - *EISS 83*
Data Base Decisions - Atlanta, GA - *MicrocomMPl 84*

Data Base Index [of SDC Search Service] - Santa Monica, CA - *DataDirOnSer 84; DBBus 82*
Data Base Monthly - Austin, TX - *BaconPubCkMag 84*
Data Base Newsletter - Newton Lower Falls, MA - *BaconPubCkMag 84*
Data Base Publishing Div. [of Carlton Graphics] - South Bend, IN - *EISS 83*
Data Base Research Corp. - Lakewood, CO - *MicrocomMPl 84*
Data Base User Service [of Knowledge Industry Publications Inc.] - White Plains, NY - *EISS 5-84 Sup*
Data Based Advisor [of Data Based Solutions Inc.] - San Diego, CA - *MicrocomMPl 84*
Data Based Solutions Inc. - San Diego, CA - *MicrocomMPl 84*
Data Basic Inc. - Mt. Pleasant, MI - *MicrocomSwDir 1*
Data Basics Corp. - New York, NY - *ADAPSOMemDir 83-84*
Data-Basics Inc. - Cleveland, OH - *MicrocomMPl 84*
Data Business Visions Inc. - San Diego, CA - *DataDirSup 7-83*
Data Card Corp. - Minneapolis, MN - *DataDirSup 7-83*
Data-Care [of Radio-Suisse Ltd.] - Berne, Switzerland - *TeleSy&SerDir 7-83*
Data Center [Aff. of Investigative Resource Center] - Oakland, CA - *BoPubDir 4, 5*
Data Center [of International Copper Research Association] - New York, NY - *EISS 83*
Data Center on Atomic Transition Probabilities & Atomic Line Shapes & Shifts [of National Bureau of Standards] - Washington, DC - *EISS 83; InfIndMarPl 83*
Data Channels - Bethesda, MD - *BaconPubCkMag 84; DirOnDB Spring 84; MagIndMarPl 82-83*
Data Channels [of NewsNet Inc.] - Bryn Mawr, PA - *DataDirOnSer 84*
Data Clean Corp. - Keyport, NJ - *WhoWMicrocom 83*
Data Collection on Atomic Line Shapes & Shifts [of U.S. National Bureau of Standards] - Washington, DC - *EISS 83*
Data Command - Kankakee, IL - *MicrocomMPl 84*
Data Command Systems Co. - Coral Gables, FL - *MicrocomMPl 83*
Data Communication Service [of Regie des Telegraphes et des Telephones] - Brussels, Belgium - *TeleSy&SerDir 2-84*
Data Communications [of McGraw-Hill Publications Co.] - New York, NY - *BaconPubCkMag 84; Folio 83; MagDir 84; MagIndMarPl 82-83*
Data Communications Brokers Inc. - Champaign, IL - *DataDirSup 7-83*
Data Communications Corp. - Memphis, TN - *DataDirOnSer 84; DataDirSup 7-83; DirInfWP 82; EISS 83*
Data Communications Systems Center - Irving, TX - *ADAPSOMemDir 83-84*
Data Composition Associates Inc. - East Meadow, NY - *MagIndMarPl 82-83*
Data Concepts Inc. - Little Rock, AR - *MicrocomMPl 84*
Data Consultants - Johnstown, PA - *DataDirOnSer 84*
Data Consultants Inc. - Rockville, MD - *DataDirSup 7-83*
Data Consulting Associates - Occidental, CA - *MicrocomMPl 83, 84*
Data Control Branch [of U.S. National Oceanic & Atmospheric Administration] - Rockville, MD - *EISS 83*
Data Control Group Inc. - New Haven, CT - *DataDirSup 7-83*
Data-Control Systems Inc. - Rockville, MD - *DataDirSup 7-83*
Data Coordination Div. [of Detroit City Planning Dept.] - Detroit, MI - *EISS 83*
Data Courier [Subs. of The Courier-Journal & Louisville Times Co.] - Louisville, KY - *CompReadDB 82; DataDirOnSer 84; EISS 83; InfIndMarPl 83; InfoS 83-84; MicroMarPl 82-83*
Data Design Associates Inc. - Sunnyvale, CA - *ADAPSOMemDir 83-84*
Data Design Logic Systems Inc. - Santa Clara, CA - *DataDirSup 7-83*
Data Development Corp. - New York, NY - *AdAge 5-17-84 p.34; HBIndAd&MS 82-83; IntDirMarRes 83*
Data Devices International Inc. - Chatsworth, CA - *DataDirSup 7-83*
Data Directions Inc. - Bloomfield, CT - *DataDirSup 7-83*
Data Disk Systems - Poway, CA - *WhoWMicrocom 83*
Data Display - New York, NY - *MicrocomMPl 84*
Data Documents - Omaha, NE - *DataDirSup 7-83*
Data Domain - Ft. Wayne, IN - *MicrocomSwDir 1*
Data Dynamics Technology [Aff. of Interface Age Magazine Inc.] - Cerritos, CA - *BoPubDir 5*
Data-Easy - Foster City, CA - *MicrocomMPl 84*
Data Ed - Salem, NH - *MicrocomMPl 83*
Data Electronics Inc. - San Diego, CA - *DataDirSup 7-83; WhoWMicrocom 83*
Data Enterprises Inc. - Bellmore, NY - *DirInfWP 82*
Data Entry Management Association - Stamford, CT - *EISS 83*
Data Entry Services Corp. - Dearborn, MI - *ADAPSOMemDir 83-84*
Data Equipment Inc. [Subs. of Pretoria Inc.] - Sunnyvale, CA - *WhoWMicrocom 83*
Data Equipment Supply Corp. - Downey, CA - *MicrocomMPl 83, 84*
Data Executives Ltd. - New York, NY - *ADAPSOMemDir 83-84*
Data Facility [of Rand Corp.] - Santa Monica, CA - *EISS 83*
Data Fund [of International Monetary Fund] - Washington, DC - *EISS 83*
Data General Corp. - Westboro, MA - *DataDirSup 7-83; Datamation 6-83; DirInfWP 82; ElecNews 7-25-83; InfIndMarPl 83; Top100Al 83; WhoWMicrocom 83*
Data Group Inc., The - Philadelphia, PA - *IntDirMarRes 83*
Data Impact Products Inc. [Subs. of Advanced Electronics] - Boston, MA - *MicrocomMPl 84; WhoWMicrocom 83*
DATA Inc. [Aff. of Cordura Publications Inc.] - San Diego, CA - *BoPubDir 4, 5; EISS 83; LitMarPl 84*
Data Inc. - Arlington, VA - *ADAPSOMemDir 83-84*
Data Index Inc. - Dallas, TX - *ADAPSOMemDir 83-84*
Data Information Science Center - Salem, OR - *ADAPSOMemDir 83-84*
Data Information Service [of European Consortium for Political Research] - Bergen, Norway - *EISS 83*
Data Insights - *See* Marketing Investigations Inc.
Data Library [of University of Alberta] - Edmonton, AB, Canada - *DataDirOnSer 84*
Data Library [of University of British Columbia] - Vancouver, BC, Canada - *EISS 83*
Data Line Corp. - Englewood, NJ - *DataDirSup 7-83*
Data Line Service Co. - Covina, CA - *DataDirOnSer 84*
Data Line Systems Inc. - Spokane, WA - *DataDirSup 7-83*
Data-Link [of Radio-Suisse Ltd.] - Berne, Switzerland - *TeleSy&SerDir 7-83*
Data Magnetics Co. - Santa Clara, CA - *WhoWMicrocom 83*
Data-Mail [of Radio-Suisse Ltd.] - Berne, Switzerland - *TeleSy&SerDir 7-83*
Data Man Ltd. - Calgary, AB, Canada - *DataDirSup 7-83*
Data Management [of Data Processing Management Association] - Park Ridge, IL - *BaconPubCkMag 84; MagDir 84; WritMar 84*
Data Management Associates - Warwick, NY - *EISS 5-84 Sup*
Data Management Systems - Encinitas, CA - *MicrocomMPl 84*
Data Mark Corp. - Chicago, IL - *ADAPSOMemDir 83-84*
Data Match Corp. - Doraville, GA - *MicrocomMPl 84; WhoWMicrocom 83*
Data Most - Chatsworth, CA - *MicrocomMPl 83*
Data Nexus - Salt Lake City, UT - *MicrocomMPl 84*
Data Node Inc. - San Jose, CA - *WhoWMicrocom 83*
Data Notes Publishing Co. - Houston, TX - *BoPubDir 4 Sup, 5; LitMag&SmPr 83-84*
Data Operations Inc. - New York, NY - *ADAPSOMemDir 83-84*
Data Packaging Corp. - Cambridge, MA - *WhoWMicrocom 83*
Data Plus - Bloomfield, CT - *MicrocomMPl 84*
Data Printer Corp. - Malden, MA - *DataDirSup 7-83; WhoWMicrocom 83*
Data Probe Inc. - New York, NY - *IntDirMarRes 83*
Data Processing & Accounting Services - San Francisco, CA - *ADAPSOMemDir 83-84*
Data Processing & Communications Security - Madison, WI - *BaconPubCkMag 84*
Data Processing & Information Science Contents [of Bibliographic Retrieval Services] - Latham, NY - *DataDirOnSer 84; EISS 7-83 Sup*
Data Processing Book Service [of Prentice-Hall Inc.] - Englewood, NJ - *LitMarPl 83, 84*
Data Processing Center Inc. - New Orleans, LA - *DataDirOnSer 84*
Data Processing Consultants - Albuquerque, NM - *MicrocomMPl 83*

Data Processing Consultants - Alburquerque, NM - *MicrocomMPl 84*
Data Processing Consultants - Paris, TN - *WhoWMicrocom 83*
Data Processing Consulting - Boulder, CO - *WhoWMicrocom 83*
Data Processing Design - Placentia, CA - *DataDirSup 7-83; DirInfWP 82*
Data Processing Design Inc. - New York, NY - *MicrocomMPl 83*
Data Processing Digest - Davis, CA - *BaconPubCkMag 84*
Data Processing Digest - Los Angeles, CA - *MagIndMarPl 82-83*
Data Processing Div. [of Kentucky State Legislative Research Commission] - Frankfort, KY - *EISS 83*
Data Processing Enterprises - Los Angeles, CA - *DataDirOnSer 84*
Data Processing Management Association - Park Ridge, IL - *EISS 83*
Data Processors Inc. - Casper, WY - *ADAPSOMemDir 83-84*
Data Product News - Toronto, ON, Canada - *BaconPubCkMag 84*
Data Products [of Toronto Stock Exchange] - Toronto, ON, Canada - *EISS 83*
Data Professionals - Dracut, MA - *DataDirSup 7-83*
Data Publishing International - Amsterdam, Netherlands - *EISS 83*
Data/Quick - New York, NY - *IntDirMarRes 83*
Data Recording Products Div. [of 3M Co.] - St. Paul, MN - *WhoWMicrocom 83*
Data Reference System [of Environment Canada, Inland Water Directorate] - Ottawa, ON, Canada - *CompReadDB 82; DataDirOnSer 84; DirOnDB Spring 84*
Data Research Center Inc. - Traverse City, MI - *EISS 83*
Data Resources - Dayton, OH - *WhoWMicrocom 83*
Data Resources Inc. [Subs. of McGraw-Hill Inc.] - Lexington, MA - *DataDirOnSer 84; DataDirSup 7-83; EISS 83; InfIndMarPl 83; InfoS 83-84; MicrocomMPl 84*
Data Retrieval Corp. of America - Milwaukee, WI - *EISS 83*
Data/Rex Inc. - Detroit, MI - *DataDirSup 7-83*
Data SA - Buenos Aires, Argentina - *ADAPSOMemDir 83-84*
Data-Search - Bethesda, MD - *InfIndMarPl 83*
Data-Search - Pittsboro, NC - *DataDirOnSer 84; EISS 83; FBInfSer 80*
Data Security Concepts - Des Peres, MO - *MicrocomMPl 83, 84*
Data Service Center Inc. - Salina, KS - *WhoWMicrocom 83*
Data Service Center of Lincoln - Lincoln, NE - *MicrocomMPl 84*
Data Services Operations [of Informatics Inc.] - Fairfield, NJ - *EISS 83*
Data Set Directory System [of Washington State University] - Pullman, WA - *EISS 83*
Data-Soft of New Hampshire - Merrimack, NH - *MicrocomMPl 84*
Data Specialties Inc. - Northbrook, IL - *DataDirSup 7-83; MicrocomMPl 84*
Data-Star - Berne, Switzerland - *EISS 83*
Data-Star - Geneva, Switzerland - *InfIndMarPl 83*
Data Strategies Inc. - Escondido, CA - *MicrocomMPl 84*
Data Strategies Inc. - San Diego, CA - *MicrocomSwDir 1; WhoWMicrocom 83*
Data Switch Corp. - Norwalk, CT - *DataDirSup 7-83*
Data Systems - Fern Park, FL - *MicrocomMPl 83*
Data Systems - Chicago, IL - *MicrocomMPl 84*
Data Systems [of Tri-County Regional Planning Commission] - Lansing, MI - *EISS 83*
Data Systems [of National Association of Insurance Commissioners] - Brookfield, WI - *EISS 83*
Data Systems Analysts Inc. - Pennsauken, NJ - *DataDirSup 7-83*
Data Systems Design Inc. - San Jose, CA - *DataDirSup 7-83*
Data Systems Management Div. [of U.S. Civil Aeronautics Board] - Washington, DC - *EISS 83*
Data Systems Marketing - Mountain View, CA - *WhoWMicrocom 83*
Data Systems Northwest - Bremerton, WA - *MicrocomMPl 84*
Data Systems of Baton Rouge - Baton Rouge, LA - *MicrocomMPl 83, 84*
Data Systems of Connecticut Inc. - Milford, CT - *WhoWMicrocom 83*
Data Technology Inc. - Woburn, MA - *DataDirSup 7-83; WhoWMicrocom 83*
Data Technology Inc. [Subs. of Computer Applied Systems] - York, PA - *DataDirOnSer 84*
Data Technology Industries - San Leandro, CA - *MicrocomMPl 83, 84; MicrocomSwDir 1; WhoWMicrocom 83*
Data-Tek - Philadelphia, PA - *DataDirOnSer 84*
Data-Tek Inc. - Bethesda, MD - *DataDirSup 7-83*
Data Terminal Systems Inc. - Maynard, MA - *DataDirSup 7-83*
Data Terminals & Communications - Campbell, CA - *DataDirSup 7-83; DirInfWP 82; MicrocomMPl 84; WhoWMicrocom 83*
Data Train Inc. - Grants Pass, OR - *MicrocomMPl 83; WhoWMicrocom 83*
Data Training [of Warren/Weingarten Inc.] - Boston, MA - *BaconPubCkMag 84; MicrocomMPl 84*
Data Transforms Inc. - Denver, CO - *MicrocomMPl 83, 84; MicrocomSwDir 1*
Data Trek - Ft. Wayne, IN - *MicrocomSwDir 1*
Data Trend - Salt Lake City, UT - *MicrocomMPl 84*
Data Type Inc. - Corona, NY - *LitMarPl 83*
Data Unit [of Centre for the Study of Developing Societies] - Delhi, India - *EISS 7-83 Sup*
Data Universal Corp. - Teaneck, NJ - *ADAPSOMemDir 83-84; DataDirSup 7-83*
Data Use & Access Laboratories - Arlington, VA - *EISS 83*
Data User Services Div. [of U.S. Bureau of the Census] - Washington, DC - *EISS 83*
Data Video Systems Inc. [of R & D Communications Inc.] - Eagle Bend, MN - *Tel&CabFB 84C*
DataArkiv i Stockholm AB [of Informationsvarden i Stockholm AB] - Stockholm, Sweden - *EISS 5-84 Sup; InfIndMarPl 83*
Databank Corp. - Ft. Lauderdale, FL - *WhoWMicrocom 83*
Database [of Online Inc.] - Weston, CT - *MicrocomMPl 84*
Database Hong Kong Ltd. [of Printrite Hong Kong Ltd.] - Hong Kong - *EISS 83; InfoS 83-84*
Database Index [of System Development Corp.] - Santa Monica, CA - *CompReadDB 82*
Database on Atomic & Molecular Physics [of Queen's University of Belfast] - Belfast, Ireland - *EISS 83*
Database Services - Los Altos, CA - *BoPubDir 4, 5; EISS 83; InfoS 83-84*
Databike [of Bikelibrary] - Emporia, KS - *EISS 83*
Databnk [of University of Washington] - Seattle, WA - *EISS 83; InfIndMarPl 83*
Databridge [of ITT World Communications Inc.] - New York, NY - *TeleSy&SerDir 7-83*
Datac [of Radio-Suisse Ltd.] - Berne, Switzerland - *InfIndMarPl 83; TeleSy&SerDir 7-83*
DataCable News [of NewsNet Inc.] - Bryn Mawr, PA - *DataDirOnSer 84*
Datacenter [of Southeast Michigan Council of Governments] - Detroit, MI - *EISS 7-83 Sup*
Datacenter [of A. M. Best Co.] - Oldwick, NJ - *EISS 83*
Datacentralen - *See* I/S Datacentralen
Datacom Inc. - Ft. Walton Beach, FL - *DataDirSup 7-83; WhoWMicrocom 83*
Datacom Northwest Inc. - Seattle, WA - *DataDirSup 7-83*
Datacom Reader Service [of Architecture Technology Corp.] - Minneapolis, MN - *MicrocomMPl 84*
Datacom Systems Corp. - New York, NY - *LitMarPl 83, 84*
Datacomm Advisor [of International Data Corp.] - Los Angeles, CA - *MagDir 84*
Datacomm Management Sciences Inc. - East Norwalk, CT - *DataDirSup 7-83*
Datacorp - Beaverton, OR - *EISS 83*
Datacount Inc. - Opelika, AL - *MicrocomMPl 84*
Datacq Corp. - Monterey, CA - *WhoWMicrocom 83*
Datacrown Inc. [Div. of Crowntek Inc.] - Willowdale, ON, Canada - *ADAPSOMemDir 83-84; DataDirOnSer 84; EISS 83*
Datadyne Corp. - King of Prussia, PA - *WhoWMicrocom 83*
Datadyne Corp. - Norristown, PA - *DataDirSup 7-83*
Dataface Inc. - Santa Clara, CA - *MicrocomMPl 84*
DataFamiliae - Columbus, OH - *DirOnDB Spring 84*
Dataflow Systems Inc. - Bethesda, MD - *EISS 83; FBInfSer 80; InfIndMarPl 83; MagIndMarPl 82-83; MicroMarPl 82-83*
Datafrance - Paris, France - *DirOnDB Spring 84*
Datagest International - Milan, Italy - *InfIndMarPl 83; InfoS 83-84*
Datagraf - Rockville, MD - *DirOnDB Spring 84*

Datagram Corp. - East Greenwich, RI - *DataDirSup 7-83*
Datagram Service [of Western Union Telegraph Co.] - Upper Saddle River, NJ - *TeleSy&SerDir 7-83*
Datagraph - Arnold, CA - *MicrocomMPl 83*
Datagraphics - Tempe, AZ - *LitMarPl 83, 84; MagIndMarPl 82-83*
Datagraphix Inc. [Subs. of General Dynamics Corp.] - San Diego, CA - *DataDirSup 7-83; DirInfWP 82; InfIndMarPl 83; WhoWMicrocom 83*
Datair Systems - Chicago, IL - *DataDirSup 7-83*
Datalab Inc. - Haverford, PA - *MicrocomSwDir 1*
Datalex Co. - San Francisco, CA - *MicrocomMPl 83, 84; MicrocomSwDir 1; WhoWMicrocom 83*
Datalib Resources [of University of Alberta] - Edmonton, AB, Canada - *DataDirOnSer 84*
Dataline Inc. - Toronto, ON, Canada - *DataDirOnSer 84; DataDirSup 7-83; EISS 83*
Dataline Securities Database - Toronto, ON, Canada - *DirOnDB Spring 84*
Datalink [of RCA Global Communications Inc.] - New York, NY - *TeleSy&SerDir 2-84*
Datalink [of Telecom Canada] - Ottawa, ON, Canada - *TeleSy&SerDir 7-83, 2-84*
DataLinx - Westwood, MA - *DirOnDB Spring 84*
Datalogic Inc. - Chattanooga, TN - *WhoWMicrocom 83*
Datalogics Inc. - Chicago, IL - *EISS 83*
Datalogics Inc. [Subs. of Interscience Inc.] - Cleveland, OH - *DataDirOnSer 84*
Datam Consultants - Dekalb, IL - *MicrocomMPl 84*
Datamac Computer Systems - Sunnyvale, CA - *MicrocomMPl 84; WhoWMicrocom 83*
Datamap Inc. - Eden Prairie, MN - *EISS 83*
Datamarc - Richardson, TX - *DirInfWP 82*
Datamark Business Systems - St. Paul, MN - *MicrocomSwDir 1*
Datamatics - Fords, NJ - *MicrocomMPl 84*
Datamatics Management Services Inc. - Englewood Cliffs, NJ - *MicrocomMPl 83*
Datamation [of Technical Publishing] - New York, NY - *ArtMar 84; BaconPubCkMag 84; Folio 83; MagDir 84; MagIndMarPl 82-83; MicrocomMPl 84; NewsBur 6; WritMar 84*
DataMax Computer Services Inc. - Ft. Myers, FL - *MicrocomMPl 83*
Datamax Inc. - Elk Grove Village, IL - *AvMarPl 83*
Datamaxx USA Corp. - Tallahassee, FL - *DataDirSup 7-83*
Datamed Research Inc. - Los Angeles, CA - *MicrocomMPl 83, 84*
Datamedia Corp. - Pennsauken, NJ - *DataDirSup 7-83; InfIndMarPl 83*
Datamension Corp. - Northbrook, IL - *MicrocomMPl 84; MicrocomSwDir 1*
Datamics - New York, NY - *MicroMarPl 82-83*
Datamost Inc. - Chatsworth, CA - *MicrocomMPl 84*
Datanetwork [of Honeywell Inc.] - Minneapolis, MN - *EISS 83; InfoS 83-84*
Datanex Inc. - Eugene, OR - *MicrocomMPl 84*
Datapac [of Transcanada Telephone System] - Ottawa, ON, Canada - *TeleSy&SerDir 7-83, 2-84*
Datapac [of Transcanada Telephone System] - Toronto, ON, Canada - *EISS 83*
Datapage Div. [of Western Publishing Co. Inc.] - O'Fallon, MO - *EISS 5-84 Sup*
Datapath [of ADP Network Services Inc.] - Ann Arbor, MI - *MicrocomMPl 84*
Dataplan - Calistoga, CA - *BoPubDir 5*
Dataplan - Rohnert Park, CA - *BoPubDir 4*
Datapoint Corp. - San Antonio, TX - *DataDirSup 7-83; Datamation 6-83; DirInfWP 82; InfIndMarPl 83; Top100Al 83; WhoWMicrocom 83*
Datapoint Support Services - San Diego, CA - *DirInfWP 82*
Datapro/On-Line [of Data Resources Inc.] - Lexington, MA - *DataDirOnSer 84*
Datapro/Online [of McGraw-Hill Information Systems Co.] - Delran, NJ - *DirOnDB Spring 84; EISS 5-84 Sup*
Datapro Research Corp. [of McGraw-Hill Information Systems Co.] - Delran, NJ - *EISS 83*
Dataproducts Corp. - Woodland Hills, CA - *DataDirSup 7-83; Datamation 6-83; DirInfWP 82; MicrocomMPl 84; Top100Al 83; WhoWMicrocom 83*
Dataproducts New England Inc. - Wallingford, CT - *DataDirSup 7-83*
Dataquest Inc. - Cupertino, CA - *EISS 83; InfoS 83-84*
Dataquest International Inc. - Chicago, IL - *EISS 83; FBInfSer 80*
Datar Publishing Co. - St. Louis, MO - *BoPubDir 4, 5*
Dataram Corp. - Cranbury, NJ - *DataDirSup 7-83*
Dataroute [of Telecom Canada] - Ottawa, ON, Canada - *TeleSy&SerDir 7-83, 2-84*
Dataroyal Inc. - Nashua, NH - *DirInfWP 82; MicrocomMPl 84; WhoWMicrocom 83*
Datarule Publishing Co. - New Canaan, CT - *BoPubDir 4, 5*
Datascan America Inc. - Atlanta, GA - *ADAPSOMemDir 83-84*
Datasearch Business Information Ltd. - Bath, England - *EISS 7-83 Sup*
Datasmith - Shawnee Mission, KS - *MicrocomMPl 83, 84; MicrocomSwDir 1; WhoWMicrocom 83*
Datasoft Inc. - Chatsworth, CA - *MicrocomMPl 84*
Datasoft Inc. - Northridge, CA - *MicrocomMPl 83; WhoWMicrocom 83*
Datasouth Computer Corp. - Charlotte, NC - *DataDirSup 7-83; DirInfWP 82; MicrocomMPl 83, 84; WhoWMicrocom 83*
Datasphere Inc. - Cranford, NJ - *DataDirSup 7-83*
Datasphere Sales Ltd. - Mississauga, ON, Canada - *DataDirSup 7-83*
DataStat - Atlanta, GA - *DirOnDB Spring 84*
Datastream Communications Inc. - Santa Clara, CA - *DataDirSup 7-83*
Datastream International - San Diego, CA - *BaconPubCkMag 84*
Datastream International Ltd. - London, England - *DirOnDB Spring 84; EISS 83; InfIndMarPl 83*
Datatab Inc. - Chicago, IL - *ADAPSOMemDir 83-84*
Datatab Inc. - New York, NY - *DataDirOnSer 84; IntDirMarRes 83; LitMarPl 83, 84; MagIndMarPl 82-83*
Datatec Industries - Englewood, NJ - *DataDirSup 7-83*
Datatech Business Machines - Montreal, PQ, Canada - *DirInfWP 82*
Datatech Software Systems Inc. - Aurora, CO - *MicrocomMPl 84*
Datatek Inc. - Clearwater, FL - *MicrocomMPl 84*
Datatel Inc. - Cherry Hill, NJ - *DataDirSup 7-83*
Datatel Inc. - Alexandria, VA - *ADAPSOMemDir 83-84; DataDirOnSer 84*
Datatrack Inc. - Grand Rapids, MI - *IntDirMarRes 83*
Datatrol Inc. - Hudson, MA - *DataDirSup 7-83*
Datatronic Systems Corp. (Computer Sciences Div.) - Panorama City, CA - *DataDirOnSer 84*
Dataview Inc. - Malden, MA - *InfIndMarPl 83*
Dataview Ltd. - Colchester, England - *MicrocomSwDir 1*
DataVision [of Central Administration of Swedish Telecommunications] - Stockholm, Sweden - *VideoDir 82-83*
Datavue Corp. [Subs. of Intelligent Systems Corp.] - Seattle, WA - *MicrocomMPl 84; WhoWMicrocom 83*
Datavue Products - Wabash, IN - *DirInfWP 82*
Dataware Systems - Pontiac, MI - *MicrocomMPl 84*
Dataword [Div. of Orowac Inc.] - Bay Shore, NY - *LitMarPl 84*
Dataworld Inc. - Knoxville, TN - *MicrocomMPl 84*
Date Line International Records - New York, NY - *BillIntBG 83-84*
Date Research - Suffern, NY - *LitMarPl 84*
Datec Inc. - Chapel Hill, NC - *DataDirSup 7-83; MicrocomMPl 84; WhoWMicrocom 83*
Datel [of RCA Global Communications Inc.] - New York, NY - *TeleSy&SerDir 2-84*
Datel [of Radio-Suisse Ltd.] - Berne, Switzerland - *TeleSy&SerDir 7-83*
Datel-Intersil - Mansfield, MA - *DataDirSup 7-83*
Datel Service [of ITT World Communications Inc.] - New York, NY - *TeleSy&SerDir 7-83*
Datel Services [of German Post & Telecommunication Administration] - Darmstadt, West Germany - *EISS 83*
Dateline Clifton - Clifton, NJ - *NewsDir 84*
Dateline Communications - Santa Monica, CA - *DirPRFirms 83*
Dateline Washington - Washington, DC - *Ed&PubIntYB 82*
Datennachweis Informationssystem [of Informationszentrum Sozialwissenschaften] - Bonn, West Germany - *CompReadDB 82*
DATEV - Nuremberg, West Germany - *InfIndMarPl 83*

DATEX Nordic Public Data Network [of General Directorate of Posts & Telegraphs] - Copenhagen, Denmark - *EISS 83*
Dati Eletorali [of Centro per la Documentazione Automatica] - Rome, Italy - *CompReadDB 82*
Datos CA - Caracas, Venezuela - *IntDirMarRes 83*
Datotek Inc. - Dallas, TX - *DataDirSup 7-83*
Datronic Rental Corp. - Chicago, IL - *DataDirSup 7-83*
Datronix - Cherry Hill, NJ - *WhoWMicrocom 83*
Dat's All Music - *See* Kaye Publications, Richard
Datum Inc. - Anaheim, CA - *DataDirSup 7-83*
Datum Institute for ADP-Supported Development Planning - Bonn, West Germany - *EISS 83*
Datum Oy - *See* Taucher Group
Daugherty Audio - Fairfax, VA - *AvMarPl 83*
Daughters of Sarah - Chicago, IL - *WritMar 84*
Daughters of St. Paul - Boston, MA - *AvMarPl 83; LitMarPl 83, 84*
Daughters of the American Revolution Magazine - Washington, DC - *MagIndMarPl 82-83*
Daughtry Newspapers Inc. - Galveston, TX - *Ed&PubIntYB 82*
Dauncey Records - Warren, MI - *BillIntBG 83-84*
Dauphin Parkland Enterprise - Dauphin, MB, Canada - *AyerDirPub 83*
Dauphin Schulykill Area Merchandiser - Lebanon, PA - *AyerDirPub 83*
D'Aurora Press - Mill Valley, CA - *BoPubDir 4, 5*
Daval Music Co. - *See* Alshire Publishing Cos.
Davco Publishers [Div. of United States History Society] - Skokie, IL - *AvMarPl 83*
Davco Records - Smithtown, NY - *BillIntBG 83-84*
Davell Custom Software - Cleveland, TN - *MicrocomSwDir 1*
Davenport Agency - Atlanta, GA - *StaDirAdAg 2-84*
Davenport & Son Co., A. C. - Palatine, IL - *AvMarPl 83*
Davenport Cable TV [of Western Satellite Inc.] - Davenport, WA - *Tel&CabFB 84C*
Davenport Films - Delaplane, VA - *AvMarPl 83*
Davenport Publishers, May - Los Altos Hills, CA - *BoPubDir 4, 5; WritMar 84*
Davenport Quad-City Times - Davenport, IA - *NewsDir 84*
Davenport Studio, Bill - Santa Fe, NM - *MagIndMarPl 82-83*
Davenport Times - Davenport, WA - *BaconPubCkNews 84; Ed&PubIntYB 82*
Daves Cable Co. - Carrollton, MS - *BrCabYB 84*
Daves Cable Co. - Coffeeville, MS - *BrCabYB 84*
Daves Cable Co. - Duck Hill, MS - *BrCabYB 84*
Dave's Cable Systems Inc. - Cave Springs, AR - *BrCabYB 84*
Dave's Cable Systems Inc. - Springdale, AR - *Tel&CabFB 84C*
Dave's Cable Systems Inc. - Watts, OK - *BrCabYB 84*
Daves, Joan - New York, NY - *LitMarPl 83, 84*
Daves, M. E. - Winona, MS - *BrCabYB 84 p.D-300; Tel&CabFB 84C p.1676*
Davey Co., The - Jersey City, NJ - *LitMarPl 83, 84*
David Advertising Inc. - Cleveland, OH - *StaDirAdAg 2-84*
David & Associates, E. - Storrs, CT - *MicrocomMPl 84*
David & Charles Inc. - North Pomfret, VT - *DirMarMP 83; LitMarPl 83, 84*
David & Co., R. I. - Chicago, IL - *StaDirAdAg 2-84*
David City Banner-Press - David City, NE - *BaconPubCkNews 84; NewsDir 84*
David Marketing Services Inc., Tim - New York, NY - *StaDirAdAg 2-84*
David Music - New York, NY - *BillIntBG 83-84*
David Publishers Inc., Jonathan - Middle Village, NY - *LitMarPl 83*
David-Stewart Publishing Co. - Brookton, ME - *BoPubDir 4, 5*
David, Stuart - New York, NY - *LitMarPl 83, 84*
Davida Publications - Grand Junction, CO - *BoPubDir 4, 5*
Davidson Advertising Agency Inc., W. N. - Evanston, IL - *StaDirAdAg 2-84*
Davidson & Associates - Rancho Palos Verdes, CA - *MicrocomMPl 84; MicrocomSwDir 1*
Davidson, Dianne F. - Marietta, GA - *LitMarPl 83*
Davidson, Dianne F. - Grand Prairie, TX - *LitMarPl 84*
Davidson, Dusty - Oakridge, OR - *Tel&CabFB 84C p.1676*
Davidson, Gary M. - Fripp Island, SC - *Tel&CabFB 84C p.1676*
Davidson Inc., Harlan - Arlington Heights, IL - *LitMarPl 83, 84*
Davidson, John W. - Batesburg, SC - *Tel&CabFB 84C p.1676*
Davidson Ltd., Dixie Lee - Omaha, NE - *LitMarPl 83*
Davidson, Mary Frances - Gatlinburg, TN - *BoPubDir 4, 5*
Davidson Mecklenburg Gazette - Davidson, NC - *BaconPubCkNews 84*
Davidson-Peterson Associates Inc. - New York, NY - *IntDirMarRes 83*
Davidson Printing Co. - Duluth, MN - *MagIndMarPl 82-83*
Davidson Software Systems - Lansing, MI - *MicrocomMPl 83, 84; MicrocomSwDir 1*
Davie-Cooper City News - Ft. Lauderdale, FL - *AyerDirPub 83*
Davie County Enterprise Record - Mocksville, NC - *AyerDirPub 83; Ed&PubIntYB 82*
Davies & Rourke Advertising Inc. - Boise, ID - *StaDirAdAg 2-84*
Davies, Nina S. - New Orleans, LA - *BoPubDir 5*
Daviess-Martin County Rural Telephone Corp. - Montgomery, IN - *TelDir&BG 83-84*
Davis Advertising - Philadelphia, PA - *HBIndAd&MS 82-83; StaDirAdAg 2-84*
Davis Advertising, Bruce Henry - Houston, TX - *StaDirAdAg 2-84*
Davis Advertising Inc., Joseph A. - New York, NY - *StaDirAdAg 2-84*
Davis Advertising Inc., Leonard - Worcester, MA - *AdAge 3-28-84; StaDirAdAg 2-84*
Davis & Dorand Inc. - New York, NY - *StaDirAdAg 2-84*
Davis & Matos Inc. - Tulsa, OK - *StaDirAdAg 2-84*
Davis & Phillips Inc. - Norfolk, VA - *StaDirAdAg 2-84*
Davis & Sanford Co. Inc. - New Rochelle, NY - *AvMarPl 83*
Davis Associates, Bert - New York, NY - *LitMarPl 83, 84; MagIndMarPl 82-83*
Davis Associates, Diane - Boston, MA - *DirPRFirms 83*
Davis Audio-Visual Co. - Green Bay, WI - *AvMarPl 83*
Davis Audio-Visual Inc. - Denver, CO - *AvMarPl 83*
Davis Blue Artwork - Culver City, CA - *ArtMar 84*
Davis Cable Cooperative - Davis, CA - *BrCabYB 84*
Davis Cable TV Inc., Jeff [of Wometco Cable TV Inc.] - Jennings, LA - *BrCabYB 84; Tel&CabFB 84C*
Davis Cablevision - Smethport, PA - *BrCabYB 84; Tel&CabFB 84C*
Davis Catalogue, Mac - *See* Tree International
Davis Coding Service Inc., Steve - New York, NY - *IntDirMarRes 83*
Davis-Cohen Associates - New York, NY - *LitMarPl 83, 84*
Davis Color Slides Inc. - New York, NY - *AvMarPl 83*
Davis Communications Consultants - Stevensville, MT - *TeleSy&SerDir 7-83*
Davis Co., F. A. - Philadelphia, PA - *LitMarPl 83, 84*
Davis Co., H. B. - New York, NY - *BoPubDir 4 Sup, 5*
Davis Co. Inc., Grant - Lewisville, TX - *BoPubDir 4, 5*
Davis County Clipper - Bountiful, UT - *Ed&PubIntYB 82; NewsDir 84*
Davis County Republican - Bloomfield, IA - *AyerDirPub 83; Ed&PubIntYB 82*
Davis Delaney Arrow [Div. of TCI] - New York, NY - *LitMarPl 83, 84*
Davis, Elizabeth - Seattle, WA - *Tel&CabFB 84C p.1676*
Davis Enterprise - Davis, CA - *BaconPubCkNews 84; Ed&PubIntYB 82; NewsDir 84*
Davis Enterprises - Maple Shade, NJ - *Tel&CabFB 84C p.1676*
Davis-Erskine Inc. - Hurricane, WV - *BoPubDir 4 Sup, 5*
Davis/Fowler/Weaver Broadcasting - San Jose, CA - *BrCabYB 84*
Davis Harrison Advertising - Chicago, IL - *StaDirAdAg 2-84*
Davis, Howard - *See* Davis Enterprises
Davis, Joe D. - Ft. Smith, AR - *Tel&CabFB 84C p.1676*
Davis, Joe D. - *See* Transwestern Video Inc.
Davis, John - Seattle, WA - *Tel&CabFB 84C p.1677*
Davis, Johnson, Mogul & Colombatto - Los Angeles, CA - *AdAge 3-28-84; StaDirAdAg 2-84; TelAl 83, 84*
Davis, Judy Lyon - Forest Hills, NY - *LitMarPl 84*
Davis, Lane E. - Houston, MO - *Tel&CabFB 84C p.1677*
Davis Market Research Services Inc. - Woodland Hills, CA - *IntDirMarRes 83*
Davis, Mary Ann - Seattle, WA - *Tel&CabFB 84C p.1677*
Davis/Muender/Ostir - Rockford, IL - *AdAge 3-28-84; BrCabYB 84; StaDirAdAg 2-84*
Davis-Newman-Payne - Knoxville, TN - *StaDirAdAg 2-84*

Davis News - Davis, OK - *AyerDirPub 83; BaconPubCkNews 84; Ed&PubIntYB 82*
Davis News Journal - Layton, UT - *Ed&PubIntYB 82*
Davis, Patrick - Seattle, WA - *Tel&CabFB 84C p.1677*
Davis Printing Corp. [Div. of Racanelle/Davis Corp.] - Carlstadt, NJ - *LitMarPl 83, 84*
Davis Public Relations - New York, NY - *DirPRFirms 83*
Davis Public Relations, Alison - Ridgefield Park, NJ - *LitMarPl 84*
Davis Publications Inc. - Worcester, MA - *LitMarPl 83, 84; WritMar 84*
Davis Publications Inc. - New York, NY - *LitMarPl 83, 84; MagIndMarPl 82-83*
Davis Publishing Co. Inc. - Santa Cruz, CA - *BoPubDir 4, 5*
Davis Publishing Co., K. C. - San Diego, CA - *BoPubDir 5*
Davis Publishing, Steve - Dallas, TX - *WritMar 84*
Davis Research, M. J. - New York, NY - *IntDirMarRes 83*
Davis, Roger - *See* Davis Enterprises
Davis Stephenson County Scope - *See* North Central Associated Publishers
Davis, Thomas - Seattle, WA - *Tel&CabFB 84C p.1677*
Davison Cablevision Ltd. - Davison, MI - *Tel&CabFB 84C*
Davison Index - Davison, MI - *BaconPubCkNews 84; Ed&PubIntYB 82; NewsDir 84*
Davison, Marguerite Porter - Swarthmore, PA - *BoPubDir 4, 5*
Davison Publishing Co. - Ridgewood, NJ - *BoPubDir 4, 5*
DAVKA Corp. - Chicago, IL - *MicrocomMPl 84*
Davong Systems Inc. - Sunnyvale, CA - *MicrocomMPl 84; MicrocomSwDir 1; WhoWMicrocom 83*
Davy & Lovett Enterprises Inc. - Capon Bridge, WV - *Tel&CabFB 84C*
Davy TV Cable Co. - Davy, WV - *BrCabYB 84; Tel&CabFB 84C*
Daw Books Inc. [Aff. of The New American Library] - New York, NY - *LitMarPl 83, 84; WritMar 84*
Dawg Music - *See* Iguana Music Inc.
Dawn - Laguna Hills, CA - *BaconPubCkMag 84*
Dawn Heron Press - San Francisco, CA - *BoPubDir 4, 5*
Dawn Horse Press, The - Clearlake Highlands, CA - *LitMag&SmPr 83-84; LitMarPl 83, 84*
Dawn Productions - Manheim, PA - *BillIntBG 83-84*
Dawn Publishing Co. Ltd. [Aff. of Canadian Jewish Herald] - Dollard-des-Ormeaux, PQ, Canada - *BoPubDir 5*
Dawn Treader Music [Div. of Star Song Records] - Pasadena, TX - *BillIntBG 83-84*
Dawn Valley Press [Aff. of Westminster College] - New Wilmington, PA - *BoPubDir 4, 5; LitMag&SmPr 83-84*
Dawnbreaker Music Co. - San Fernando, CA - *BillIntBG 83-84*
Dawnfire Books - Berkeley, CA - *BoPubDir 5*
Dawson Advertising Consultant, Don - Portland, OR - *StaDirAdAg 2-84*
Dawson & Sons Ltd., Wm. - Folkestone, England - *MicroMarPl 82-83*
Dawson Cable TV [of Rapids Cable TV Inc.] - Dawson, MN - *Tel&CabFB 84C*
Dawson County Advertiser & News - Dawsonville, GA - *AyerDirPub 83; Ed&PubIntYB 82*
Dawson County Herald - Lexington, NE - *Ed&PubIntYB 82*
Dawson, Daniels, Sullivan & Dillon Inc. - Nashville, TN - *StaDirAdAg 2-84*
Dawson, Johns & Black - Chicago, IL - *AdAge 3-28-84; StaDirAdAg 2-84*
Dawson News - Dawson, GA - *BaconPubCkNews 84; Ed&PubIntYB 82*
Dawson Productions - San Francisco, CA - *AvMarPl 83*
Dawson, Richard M. - Redlands, CA - *LitMarPl 84*
Dawson Sentinel - Dawson, MN - *BaconPubCkNews 84; Ed&PubIntYB 82*
Dawson Springs Progress - Dawson Springs, KY - *BaconPubCkNews 84; Ed&PubIntYB 82; NewsDir 84*
Dawson Springs TV Cable Co. [of Horizon Communications Corp.] - Dawson Springs, KY - *Tel&CabFB 84C*
Dawsonville Dawson County Advertiser - Dawsonville, GA - *BaconPubCkNews 84*
Dax Action Books - Williamston, MI - *BoPubDir 4, 5*
Day - New London, CT - *AyerDirPub 83; Ed&PubIntYB 82*
Day & Co. Inc., Wesley - Des Moines, IA - *BrCabYB 84; StaDirAdAg 2-84*
Day & Night Video Banking Pilot [of First Interstate Bank of California] - Los Angeles, CA - *TeleSy&SerDir 2-84*
Day Care & Early Education - New York, NY - *MagDir 84; MagIndMarPl 82-83*
Day Care Council of America Inc. - Mt. Rainier, MD - *BoPubDir 4, 5*
Day Communications, Robert - Los Angeles, CA - *StaDirAdAg 2-84*
Day, Nancy R. - Sonoma, CA - *LitMarPl 83*
Day of Discovery - Grand Rapids, MI - *Tel&CabFB 84C*
Day Productions, Gordon M. - New York, NY - *TelAl 83*
Day Tonight/Night Today - Hull, MA - *LitMag&SmPr 83-84; WritMar 84*
Daycom Corp. - Dayton, OH - *Tel&CabFB 84C*
Daylight TV - New York, NY - *MagDir 84*
Dayner/Hall Inc. - Winter Park, FL - *StaDirAdAg 2-84*
Dayspring Publications of California - Whittier, CA - *BoPubDir 4, 5*
Daystar Publishing Co. - Angwin, CA - *BoPubDir 4, 5*
Daystar Publishing Co. - *See* Euro Tec Publishing
Daystar Records - Baltimore, MD - *BillIntBG 83-84*
Daystar Systems Inc. - Dallas, TX - *MicrocomMPl 84*
Daytime [of Hearst/ABC Video Services] - New York, NY - *BrCabYB 84; CabTVPrDB 83; HomeVid&CabYB 82-83*
Daytime - *See* Hearst/ABC Video Services
Daytime - *See* Lifetime
Daytime Stars - New York, NY - *MagDir 84; MagIndMarPl 82-83*
Daytime TV - New York, NY - *MagDir 84; MagIndMarPl 82-83*
Daytimers - Los Angeles, CA - *MagDir 84*
Dayton Chronicle - Dayton, WA - *BaconPubCkNews 84; Ed&PubIntYB 82*
Dayton Daily News [of Dayton Newspapers Inc.] - Dayton, OH - *BaconPubCkNews 84; Ed&PubIntYB 82; LitMarPl 83, 84; NewsBur 6; NewsDir 84*
Dayton-Forester Inc. - Northbridge, CA - *MicrocomMPl 84*
Dayton Herald - Dayton, TN - *Ed&PubIntYB 82*
Dayton Herald-News - Dayton, TN - *BaconPubCkNews 84*
Dayton Huber Heights Courier - Dayton, OH - *NewsDir 84*
Dayton Human Relations Council - Dayton, OH - *BoPubDir 5*
Dayton Jet Stone Newspaper Inc. - Dayton, OH - *NewsDir 84*
Dayton Jewish Chronicle - Dayton, OH - *AyerDirPub 83*
Dayton Journal Herald - Dayton, OH - *BaconPubCkNews 84; NewsDir 84*
Dayton Magazine [of Dayton Area Chamber of Commerce] - Dayton, OH - *BaconPubCkMag 84; MagDir 84; WritMar 84*
Dayton Press - Lorain, OH - *BoPubDir 4, 5*
Dayton Review - Dayton, IA - *BaconPubCkNews 84; Ed&PubIntYB 82*
Dayton Tribune - Dayton, OR - *BaconPubCkNews 84; Ed&PubIntYB 82*
Daytona Beach Evening News [of News-Journal Corp.] - Daytona Beach, FL - *BaconPubCkNews 84; NewsDir 84*
Daytona Beach Journal [of News-Journal Corp.] - Daytona Beach, FL - *NewsDir 84*
Daytona Beach Morning Journal - Daytona Beach, FL - *BaconPubCkNews 84*
Daytona Beach Times - Daytona Beach, FL - *BaconPubCkNews 84*
Daytona MDS Co. - New York, NY - *Tel&CabFB 84C*
Daytona Pennysaver [of Volusia Pennysaver Inc.] - Ormond Beach, FL - *AyerDirPub 83; NewsDir 84*
Daytona Times - Daytona Beach, FL - *AyerDirPub 83*
D'Azure Music Inc. - *See* Music Music Music Inc.
DB/DC Software Association - Manchester, NH - *MicrocomMPl 84*
DB Records - Decatur, GA - *BillIntBG 83-84*
DB Software Co. - Portland, OR - *MicrocomMPl 83; WhoWMicrocom 83*
DB: The Sound Engineering Magazine - Plainview, NY - *MagDir 84*
DB TV Cable Inc. - Oakfield, ME - *BrCabYB 84*
DBA Records - New York, NY - *BillIntBG 83-84*
DBA Secretarial Systems - Midland, MI - *DirInfWP 82*
D.B.C. - Webster, NY - *BoPubDir 5*
DBD Systems Inc. - Alexandria, VA - *EISS 83*

DBG & H Unltd. - Dallas, TX - *AdAge 3-28-84; StaDirAdAg 2-84*
DBI Books Inc. [Subs. of Dun & Bradstreet Technical Publishing Co.] - Northfield, IL - *LitMarPl 83, 84; WritMar 84*
D.B.I.S. - Eastchester, NY - *MicrocomSwDir 1*
DBS News - Bethesda, MD - *DirOnDB Spring 84*
DBS News [of NewsNet Inc.] - Bryn Mawr, PA - *DataDirOnSer 84*
DC Gazette - Washington, DC - *BoPubDir 4, 5*
DC Health - Lexington, MA - *MicrocomMPl 84*
DC-Jura - Copenhagen, Denmark - *DirOnDB Spring 84*
DC Sound Enterprises - Ft. Worth, TX - *BillIntBG 83-84*
DCA Educational Products [Div. of DCA Inc.] - Warrington, PA - *AvMarPl 83*
DCA Film/Video Productions [Div. of DCA Inc.] - Warrington, PA - *AvMarPl 83*
DCA Productions [Div. of Taft Broadcasting] - Bethesda, MD - *AvMarPl 83*
DCAS Records - Placentia, CA - *BillIntBG 83-84*
DCC Financial Systems - Guernsey, England - *MicrocomSwDir 1*
DCCN: Dimensions of Critical Care Nursing - Philadelphia, PA - *MagIndMarPl 82-83*
DCD Co. [Div. of Borg Enterprises] - Minneapolis, MN - *MicrocomMPl 84; MicrocomSwDir 1*
DCNQ - Brush, CO - *BrCabYB 84*
DCR/Datasmith Inc. - Pensacola, FL - *MicrocomMPl 84*
DCT Corp. - Minneapolis, MN - *MicrocomMPl 84*
DDB Group Two Inc. - New York, NY - *BrCabYB 84*
D.D.B. Press Inc. - Tallahassee, FL - *BoPubDir 4, 5*
DDP Systems Inc. - New York, NY - *DirInfWP 82*
D.D.S. Inc. - Severna Park, MD - *WhoWMicrocom 83*
De Baca County News - Ft. Sumner, NM - *AyerDirPub 83; Ed&PubIntYB 82*
De Barv-Deltona Enterprise - Orange City, FL - *AyerDirPub 83*
De Bono School of Thinking, Edward - New York, NY - *BoPubDir 5*
De Boo Ltd., Richard [Aff. of International Thomson Ltd.] - Don Mills, ON, Canada - *BoPubDir 4 Sup, 5*
De Bord & Owen Inc. - Bowling Green, KY - *ArtMar 84*
De Bow & Partners Inc., Jay - New York, NY - *DirPRFirms 83*
De-Cal Cable Inc. - Port Lavaca, TX - *Tel&CabFB 84C p.1677*
De Colores Inc. - Albuquerque, NM - *BoPubDir 4 Sup, 5*
De Colores Journal - Albuquerque, NM - *MagDir 84*
DE/Domestic Engineering - Elmhurst, IL - *BaconPubCkMag 84*
De Elorza Associates, John - Union, NJ - *DirPRFirms 83*
De Filippes Corp., The N. - New York, NY - *Ed&PubIntYB 82*
De Forest Times-Tribune - De Forest, WI - *BaconPubCkNews 84*
De Funiak - Hinsdale, IL - *BoPubDir 4, 5*
De Gamez, Tana - Key West, FL - *LitMarPl 83, 84*
De Gar Music - San Francisco, CA - *BillIntBG 83-84*
De Graff Inc., John - Camden, ME - *WritMar 84*
De Graff Inc., John - Clinton Corners, NY - *LitMarPl 83, 84*
De Gruyter Inc., Walter - Hawthorne, NY - *LitMarPl 83, 84; MicroMarPl 82-83*
De Haen Drug Information Systems, Paul [of Micromedex Inc.] - Englewood, CO - *EISS 83*
De Hollandse Krant - Langley, BC, Canada - *Ed&PubIntYB 82*
De Jesse Inc., Paul A. - Freehold, NJ - *ArtMar 84; StaDirAdAg 2-84*
DE Kalb Cable Co. [of Omega Communications Inc.] - Auburn, IN - *Tel&CabFB 84C*
De Kalb County Advertiser - Garrett, IN - *AyerDirPub 83; NewsDir 84*
De Kalb County Record-Herald - Maysville, MO - *AyerDirPub 83*
De Kalb Kemper County Messenger - De Kalb, MS - *BaconPubCkNews 84*
De Kalb News - De Kalb, TX - *BaconPubCkNews 84; Ed&PubIntYB 82*
De Karsan Publishing Co. [Aff. of W. F. Hay & Co.] - San Diego, CA - *BoPubDir 4, 5*
De Krig Advertising - New York, NY - *StaDirAdAg 2-84*
De la Cuesta-Hispanic Monographs, Juan - Newark, DE - *LitMarPl 83, 84*
De la Haba Associates, Lois - New York, NY - *LitMarPl 83, 84*
De la Hunt Group - Park Rapids, MN - *BrCabYB 84*
De la Ree Publications, Gerry - Saddle River, NJ - *BoPubDir 4, 5; LitMag&SmPr 83-84*
De Land Pennysaver - De Land, FL - *AyerDirPub 83*
De Land Sun News - De Land, FL - *Ed&PubIntYB 82*
De Launiere, Louis-Georges - Chambord, PQ, Canada - *BrCabYB 84*
De Leeuw, Randall [of Lake End Graphics Ltd.] - New York, NY - *LitMarPl 83, 84*
De Leon Free Press - De Leon, TX - *BaconPubCkNews 84; Ed&PubIntYB 82*
De-Lite Records - New York, NY - *BillIntBG 83-84*
De Luca Publicidad SA, Ricardo - Buenos Aires, Argentina - *StaDirAdAg 2-84*
De Martini Associates - Haddon Heights, NJ - *ArtMar 84; StaDirAdAg 2-84*
De Martini Educational Films, Alfred [Div. of De Martini Associates Inc.] - Haddon Heights, NJ - *AvMarPl 83; WritMar 84*
De Nederlandse Courant - Scarborough, ON, Canada - *Ed&PubIntYB 82*
De Oro Books - Los Osmos, CA - *BoPubDir 4, 5*
De Palma & Hogan Inc. - White Plains, NY - *StaDirAdAg 2-84*
De Pauw, The [of Student Publications Board] - Greencastle, IN - *NewsDir 84*
De Pencier Books, Greey - Toronto, ON, Canada - *LitMarPl 83*
De Pere Journal - De Pere, WI - *BaconPubCkNews 84; Ed&PubIntYB 82; NewsDir 84*
De Perri Inc. - Pleasantville, NY - *StaDirAdAg 2-84*
De Queen Bee - De Queen, AR - *BaconPubCkNews 84; Ed&PubIntYB 82*
De Queen Citizen - De Queen, AR - *BaconPubCkNews 84*
De Queen Daily Citizen [of De Queen Bee Co.] - De Queen, AR - *Ed&PubIntYB 82; NewsDir 84*
De Quincy News - De Quincy, LA - *BaconPubCkNews 84; Ed&PubIntYB 82; NewsDir 84*
De Ridder Beauregard News & Enterprise - De Ridder, LA - *BaconPubCkNews 84; Ed&PubIntYB 82; NewsDir 84*
De Ridder Cable TV [of TCA Cable TV Inc.] - De Ridder, LA - *Tel&CabFB 84C*
De Ridder Enterprise - De Ridder, LA - *Ed&PubIntYB 82; NewsDir 84*
De Riemer Associates, Jane - Wilmington, DE - *IntDirMarRes 83*
De Rue Inc. - Dumont, NJ - *WhoWMicrocom 83*
De Ruyter, Carol L. - San Jose, CA - *LitMarPl 83*
De Smet News - De Smet, SD - *BaconPubCkNews 84; Ed&PubIntYB 82*
De Soto Banner - De Soto, TX - *AyerDirPub 83*
De Soto Cable TV - De Soto, IL - *BrCabYB 84*
De Soto Jefferson Republic - *See* Marten Publications Inc.
De Soto Journal - De Soto, TX - *Ed&PubIntYB 82*
De Soto Leader - De Soto, TX - *Ed&PubIntYB 82*
De Soto News - Gardner, KS - *BaconPubCkNews 84*
De Soto News-Advertiser - De Soto, TX - *BaconPubCkNews 84; Ed&PubIntYB 82; NewsDir 84*
De Soto Press [of Marten Publications Inc.] - De Soto, MO - *Ed&PubIntYB 82; NewsDir 84*
De Soto Press - *See* Marten Publications Inc.
De Sutter Cable - Sanborn, MN - *BrCabYB 84*
De Valls Bluff Times - Hazen, AR - *BaconPubCkNews 84*
De Villiers & Co. [of the Univas Network] - Johannesburg, South Africa - *StaDirAdAg 2-84*
De Vore, Nicholas III - Aspen, CO - *LitMarPl 83, 84*
De Vorss & Co. - Marina del Rey, CA - *LitMarPl 83, 84*
De Voto/Weiner Films Inc. - New York, NY - *AvMarPl 83*
De Vries Ltd., Madeline - New York, NY - *DirPRFirms 83*
De Wachter - Grand Rapids, MI - *Ed&PubIntYB 82*
De Walden Music - Hollywood, CA - *BillIntBG 83-84*
De Wan, Michael - New York, NY - *LitMarPl 83, 84*
De Witt Bath Review - De Witt, MI - *AyerDirPub 83*
De Witt County View - Yorktown, TX - *AyerDirPub 83*
De Witt Era-Enterprise - De Witt, AR - *BaconPubCkNews 84; Ed&PubIntYB 82*
De Witt Observer - De Witt, IA - *BaconPubCkNews 84*
De Witt Times-News - De Witt, NE - *BaconPubCkNews 84*
De Wolfe & Fiske Inc. [Subs. of Chadwick-Miller Inc.] - Canton, MA - *LitMarPl 83, 84*

De Wolfe Music Library Inc. - New York, NY - *AvMarPl 83; Tel&CabFB 84C*
De Wys Inc., Leo - New York, NY - *LitMarPl 83, 84*
De Young Cable TV Co. - Le Mars, IA - *Tel&CabFB 84C p.1677*
De Young Press [Aff. of Minnesota Institute of Philosophy] - Hull, IA - *BoPubDir 4, 5*
DEA - Rome, Italy - *DirOnDB Spring 84*
DEA Software - Fremont, CA - *MicrocomMPl 84*
Dead Angel Press - Atlanta, GA - *LitMag&SmPr 83-84*
Dead Mountain Echo - Oakridge, OR - *Ed&PubIntYB 82*
Deadline Data on World Affairs - Bridgeport, CT - *DirOnDB Spring 84*
Deadline Data on World Affairs [of New York Times Information Service Inc.] - Parsippany, NJ - *EISS 83*
Deadspawn - Narberth, PA - *LitMag&SmPr 83-84*
Deadwood Pioneer-Times - Deadwood, SD - *BaconPubCkNews 84*
Deaf American - Silver Spring, MD - *MagDir 84*
Deaf Canadian Magazine, The - Edmonton, AB, Canada - *ArtMar 84; WritMar 84*
Deal & Associates, S. - San Diego, CA - *BoPubDir 4, 5; LitMag&SmPr 83-84*
Dealer Buying Price [of I. P. Sharp Associates Ltd.] - Toronto, ON, Canada - *DataDirOnSer 84*
Dealers Association of Computerized Products - Rockville, MD - *WhoWMicrocom 83*
Dealer's Audio Visual Supply Corp. - East Rutherford, NJ - *AvMarPl 83*
Dealerscope [of Bartex Publishing Group] - Waltham, MA - *BaconPubCkMag 84; MagDir 84; MagIndMarPl 82-83*
Dealerscope (Mid-Atlantic Edition) - Waltham, MA - *MagDir 84*
Dealerscope (10 Area Editions) - Waltham, MA - *MagDir 84*
Deals on Wheels - Newport Beach, CA - *MagDir 84*
Dean Associates, Bill - Whitestone, NY - *LitMarPl 83*
Dean Books Ltd., Bill - New York, NY - *LitMarPl 83, 84*
Dean Publications - Rancho Cordova, CA - *BoPubDir 4, 5*
Dean's Cable Communications Co. - McCracken, KS - *BrCabYB 84*
Deans Cable Vision Inc. - Lamoni, IA - *BrCabYB 84; Tel&CabFB 84C*
Dear Contributor [of DoubleLeo Publications] - New York, NY - *LitMag&SmPr 83-84*
Dear Kids Publishers - Newton, NH - *BoPubDir 4, 5*
Dear Newspapers - Washington, DC - *Ed&PubIntYB 82*
Dear Publication & Radio Inc. - Washington, DC - *Ed&PubIntYB 82*
Dearborn Cablevision [of Fairbanks Cable of Indiana] - Lawrenceburg, IN - *BrCabYB 84; Tel&CabFB 84C*
Dearborn Computer Co. - Park Ridge, IL - *DataDirSup 7-83*
Dearborn County Register - Lawrenceburg, IN - *AyerDirPub 83; Ed&PubIntYB 82*
Dearborn Heights Leader - Dearborn Heights, MI - *AyerDirPub 83; Ed&PubIntYB 82*
Dearborn Heights Leader - *See* Dearborn Press & Guide Newspapers
Dearborn Heights Leader & Dearborn Ledger & Garden - Dearborn Heights, MI - *NewsDir 84*
Dearborn Heights Times-Herald - Dearborn, MI - *NewsDir 84*
Dearborn Heights Times-Herald - *See* Dearborn Publishing Co.
Dearborn Press & Guide - Dearborn, MI - *BaconPubCkNews 84; Ed&PubIntYB 82; NewsDir 84*
Dearborn Publishing Co. - Dearborn, MI - *BaconPubCkNews 84*
Dearborn Times-Herald - *See* Dearborn Publishing Co.
Dearing Associates, L. M. - Studio City, CA - *AvMarPl 83*
Deary Television Co-Op Inc. - Deary, ID - *BrCabYB 84; Tel&CabFB 84C*
Death - New York, NY - *MagDir 84*
Deaton, John G. - Austin, TX - *LitMarPl 84*
DebDave Music Inc. - Nashville, TN - *BillIntBG 83-84*
Debmar Music - *See* Hoffman, Ivan
DeBolt & District Pioneer Museum Society - DeBolt, AB, Canada - *BoPubDir 4, 5*
Debord & Owen Inc. - Bowling Green, KY - *StaDirAdAg 2-84*
DeBow & Co. Ltd., T. J. - New York, NY - *DirMarMP 83*
DeBruyn-Rettig Advertising Inc. - El Paso, TX - *AdAge 3-28-84; StaDirAdAg 2-84*
DEBS Confectionary Marketing Data Base [of Management Science Associates Inc.] - Pittsburgh, PA - *DataDirOnSer 84*
DEBS Confectionery Marketing Data Base - Ann Arbor, MI - *DirOnDB Spring 84*
Debt; New Issues - New York, NY - *DirOnDB Spring 84*
DEC Computing - Garrett, IN - *MicrocomMPl 84; MicrocomSwDir 1*
DEC Graphics Inc. - New York, NY - *LitMarPl 83, 84*
DEC Professional, The [of Professional Press] - Ambler, PA - *BaconPubCkMag 84; MicrocomMPl 84; WritMar 84*
Decade Media Books Inc. - New York, NY - *BoPubDir 4 Sup, 5*
DeCal Cable Inc. - Yorktown, TX - *BrCabYB 84*
Decatur Cable Co. [of Omega Communications Inc.] - Decatur, IN - *BrCabYB 84; Tel&CabFB 84C*
Decatur Daily [of Tennessee Valley Printing Co. Inc.] - Decatur, AL - *BaconPubCkNews 84; Ed&PubIntYB 82; NewsDir 84*
Decatur-DeKalb News/Era [of Decatur News Publishing Co. Inc.] - Decatur, GA - *AyerDirPub 83; Ed&PubIntYB 82; NewsDir 84*
Decatur Dekalb News/Era - *See* Decatur News Publishing Co. Inc.
Decatur Democrat - Decatur, IN - *AyerDirPub 83; BaconPubCkNews 84; Ed&PubIntYB 82; NewsDir 84*
Decatur Genealogical Society - Decatur, IL - *BoPubDir 4, 5*
Decatur Herald & Review - Decatur, IL - *BaconPubCkNews 84; NewsDir 84*
Decatur Meigs County Statesman - Decatur, TN - *BaconPubCkNews 84*
Decatur News Publishing Co. Inc. - Decatur, GA - *BaconPubCkNews 84*
Decatur News Sentinel - Decatur, AR - *BaconPubCkNews 84*
Decatur North Dekalb News/Sun - *See* Decatur News Publishing Co. Inc.
Decatur Republican - Decatur, MI - *BaconPubCkNews 84; Ed&PubIntYB 82*
Decatur South Dekalb News/Sun - *See* Decatur News Publishing Co. Inc.
Decatur TeleCable Corp. - Decatur, AL - *BrCabYB 84; Tel&CabFB 84C*
Decatur Telephone Co. - Decatur, MS - *TelDir&BG 83-84*
Decatur Telephone Co. Inc. - Decatur, AR - *TelDir&BG 83-84*
Decatur-Tucker-Stone Mountain Dekalb Neighbor - Tucker, GA - *Ed&PubIntYB 82*
Decatur Voice - Decatur, IL - *BaconPubCkNews 84; Ed&PubIntYB 82*
Decatur Voice of the Black Community, The - Decatur, IL - *NewsDir 84*
Decatur Wise County Messenger - Decatur, TX - *BaconPubCkNews 84; NewsDir 84*
Decatur Wise Times - Decatur, TX - *BaconPubCkNews 84*
DecComp Inc. - Tustin, CA - *MicrocomMPl 84*
December Magazine [of December Press] - Highland Park, IL - *LitMag&SmPr 83-84*
December Press - Chicago, IL - *BoPubDir 4*
December Press - Highland Park, IL - *BoPubDir 5; LitMag&SmPr 83-84*
Decennial Census Div. [of U.S. Bureau of the Census] - Washington, DC - *EISS 83*
Dechant & Associates, Carol - Chicago, IL - *LitMarPl 83, 84*
Dechema - Frankfurt, West Germany - *DirOnDB Spring 84; InfIndMarPl 83*
Dechema Chemical Engineering Abstracts Data Bank [of German Society for Chemical Equipment] - Frankfurt, West Germany - *CompReadDB 82*
Dechema Chemical Equipment Suppliers Referral Service [of German Society for Chemical Equipment] - Frankfurt, West Germany - *EISS 83*
Dechema Chemical Technology Information Service [of German Society for Chemical Equipment] - Frankfurt, West Germany - *EISS 83*
Dechema Corrosion Consulting Service [of German Society for Chemical Equipment] - Frankfurt, West Germany - *EISS 83*
Dechema Data Service [of German Society for Chemical Equipment] - Frankfurt, West Germany - *EISS 83*
Dechema Thermophysical Properties Data Bank [of German Society for Chemical Equipment] - Frankfurt, West Germany - *CompReadDB 82; DBBus 82*

Dechy Univas [of the Univas Network] - Brussels, Belgium - *StaDirAdAg 2-84*
Decibel Books - Norman, OK - *BoPubDir 4, 5*
Decibel Inc. - Daveluyville, PQ, Canada - *BrCabYB 84*
Decibel Inc. - Nicolet, PQ, Canada - *BrCabYB 84*
Decibel Inc. - St. Leonard D'Aston, PQ, Canada - *BrCabYB 84*
Decision Analyst Inc. - Arlington, TX - *IntDirMarRes 83*
Decision Consultants Inc. - Southfield, MI - *ADAPSOMemDir 83-84*
Decision Data & Services Inc. - Ames, IA - *MicrocomSwDir 1*
Decision Data Computer Corp. - Horsham, PA - *DataDirSup 7-83; Datamation 6-83; DirInfWP 82; InfIndMarPl 83; Top100Al 83*
Decision Development Corp. - Walnut Creek, CA - *MicrocomMPl 83*
Decision Economics Inc. - Cedar Knolls, NJ - *MicrocomMPl 84*
Decision Graphics Inc. - Southboro, MA - *DataDirSup 7-83*
Decision Information Services Ltd. - Palo Alto, CA - *EISS 83; FBInfSer 80; InfIndMarPl 83*
Decision Magazine - Minneapolis, MN - *MagDir 84; WritMar 84*
Decision Making Information - Santa Ana, CA - *EISS 83; IntDirMarRes 83; Tel&CabFB 84C*
Decision Micro Systems - New York, NY - *DirInfWP 82*
Decision Net [of NCR Corp.] - Dayton, OH - *TeleSy&SerDir 7-83*
Decision Research Corp. - Lexington, MA - *IntDirMarRes 83*
Decision Resources - Weston, CT - *MicrocomMPl 83*
Decision Resources - Westport, CT - *MicrocomMPl 84; MicrocomSwDir 1*
Decision Resources Corp. - Washington, DC - *ADAPSOMemDir 83-84*
Decision Science Corp. - Jenkintown, PA - *MagIndMarPl 82-83*
Decision Science Software Inc. - Austin, TX - *MicrocomMPl 84*
Decision Services Corp. of America - Paramus, NJ - *IntDirMarRes 83*
Decision Support & Information Services - San Antonio, TX - *EISS 7-83 Sup*
Decision Support Software - McLean, VA - *MicrocomMPl 83, 84; MicrocomSwDir 1; WhoWMicrocom 83*
Decision Support Systems - Washington, DC - *MicrocomSwDir 1*
Decision Systems Inc. - Minneapolis, MN - *ADAPSOMemDir 83-84*
Decision Technology - East Molesey, England - *MicrocomSwDir 1*
Décisionex Inc. - Westport, CT - *ADAPSOMemDir 83-84*
Decisions & Developments - Wayland, MA - *BaconPubCkMag 84*
Decisions Center Inc. - New York, NY - *AdAge 5-17-84 p.36; IntDirMarRes 83*
Decisions de l'Orateur [of QL Systems Ltd.] - Ottawa, ON, Canada - *CompReadDB 82; DataDirOnSer 84; DirOnDB Spring 84*
Decitek Corp. - Westboro, MA - *DataDirSup 7-83*
Decker Associates, M. F. - Mamaroneck, NY - *MagIndMarPl 82-83*
Decker, Charles - Long Island City, NY - *LitMarPl 83, 84*
Decker Co. Inc., The Frederic C. - Brookfield Center, CT - *MagIndMarPl 82-83*
Decker Guertin & Cheyne - Hartford, CT - *AdAge 3-28-84; StaDirAdAg 2-84*
Decker, M. C. - Nipomo, CA - *MicrocomMPl 83, 84*
Decker Press Inc. - Grand Junction, CO - *BoPubDir 4 Sup, 5; LitMarPl 84*
Deckerville Recorder - *See* Buhl Publishing House
Deckerville Recorder, The - Deckerville, MI - *Ed&PubIntYB 82*
Declarations [of Direction de la Documentation Francaise] - Paris, France - *CompReadDB 82*
Declassified Documents Reference System [of Carrollton Press Inc.] - Arlington, VA - *EISS 83*
Deco Arts Ltd. - Boca Raton, FL - *ArtMar 84*
DeCoo, George - Long Island, NY - *HBIndAd&MS 82-83*
Decor [of Commerce Publications Inc.] - St. Louis, MO - *ArtMar 84; BaconPubCkMag 84; MagDir 84*
Decorah Journal [of Decorah News Co.] - Decorah, IA - *Ed&PubIntYB 82; NewsDir 84*
Decorah Journal - *See* Decorah News Co.
Decorah News Co. - Decorah, IA - *BaconPubCkNews 84*
Decorah Public Opinion [of Decorah News Co.] - Decorah, IA - *Ed&PubIntYB 82; NewsDir 84*
Decorah Public Opinion - *See* Decorah News Co.
Decorating & Craft Ideas [of Southern Living Inc.] - Birmingham, AL - *BaconPubCkMag 84; Folio 83; MagDir 84; MagIndMarPl 82-83*
Decorating Dealer - Don Mills, ON, Canada - *BaconPubCkMag 84*
Decorating Products Dealers Association of New York - Bayside, NY - *BoPubDir 5*
Decorating Quarterlies - New York, NY - *MagDir 84*
Decorating Retailer - St. Louis, MO - *BaconPubCkMag 84; MagDir 84*
Decorative Design Studio Inc. - Smithsburg, MD - *BoPubDir 5*
Decorative Products World - St. Louis, MO - *BaconPubCkMag 84; MagDir 84; WritMar 84*
Decormag - Montreal, PQ, Canada - *BaconPubCkMag 84*
Dectur Corp. - Denver, CO - *BoPubDir 4, 5*
Dedham Daily Transcript - Dedham, MA - *BaconPubCkNews 84*
Dedicated Systems Corp. - Ft. Lauderdale, FL - *MicrocomMPl 84; MicrocomSwDir 1*
Dee-Bee Recording Service - Myrtle Beach, SC - *BillIntBG 83-84*
Dee Communications Inc., Jessica - New York, NY - *DirPRFirms 83*
Dee, Ivan R. - Chicago, IL - *LitMarPl 83*
Dee Publishing Co. - Salem, OR - *BoPubDir 4, 5*
Deeg & Associates, Frederick E. - Marina Del Rey, CA - *MicrocomMPl 83*
Deej Publishing Co. Inc. - Stilwell, KS - *BoPubDir 4 Sup, 5*
Deejoy Musical Works - Los Angeles, CA - *BillIntBG 83-84*
Deemar Co. Ltd. - *See* SRG International Ltd.
Deep Cover Publications - New York, NY - *BoPubDir 4*
Deep Foundations Institute - Springfield, NJ - *BoPubDir 5*
Deep River Mutual Telephone Co. - Deep River, IA - *TelDir&BG 83-84*
Deep River New Era - Deep River, CT - *Ed&PubIntYB 82*
Deep River Press - Long Beach, CA - *BoPubDir 4 Sup, 5*
Deep River Video Ltd. - Deep River, ON, Canada - *BrCabYB 84*
Deep South Records - Nashville, TN - *BillIntBG 83-84*
Deep Water Records - Cleveland, OH - *BillIntBG 83-84*
Deer & Deer Hunting [of The Stump Sitters Inc.] - Appleton, WI - *ArtMar 84; BaconPubCkMag 84; WritMar 84*
Deer Creek Pilot - Rolling Fork, MS - *AyerDirPub 83; Ed&PubIntYB 82*
Deer Lodge Cable TV [of Community Tele-Communications Inc.] - Deer Lodge, MT - *BrCabYB 84; Tel&CabFB 84C*
Deer Lodge Silver State Post - Deer Lodge, MT - *BaconPubCkNews 84*
Deer Park Argus Tribune - Deer Park, WA - *BaconPubCkNews 84*
Deer Park Cable TV Inc. [of Western Satellite Inc.] - Deer Park, WA - *BrCabYB 84; Tel&CabFB 84C*
Deer Park-North Babylon Edition [of Lindenhurst South Bay's Newspapers] - Lindenhurst, NY - *NewsDir 84*
Deer Park Progress - Deer Park, TX - *Ed&PubIntYB 82; NewsDir 84*
Deer Park Progress & Broadcaster - Deer Park, TX - *BaconPubCkNews 84*
Deer Park Tri-County Tribune - Deer Park, WA - *Ed&PubIntYB 82; NewsDir 84*
Deer River Broadcasting Group - New York, NY - *BrCabYB 84*
Deer River Cablevision [of Northern Communications Inc.] - Deer River, MN - *Tel&CabFB 84C*
Deer River Telephone Co. - Deer River, MN - *TelDir&BG 83-84*
Deer River Western Itasca Review - Deer River, MN - *BaconPubCkNews 84*
Deer Trail Tri-County Tribune - Deer Trail, CO - *BaconPubCkNews 84*
Deerfield Beach Lighthouse Point Observer - Deerfield Beach, FL - *Ed&PubIntYB 82*
Deerfield Beach Observer - Deerfield Beach, FL - *BaconPubCkNews 84*
Deerfield Cable Systems Inc. [of Continental Cablevision Inc.] - Bernardston, MA - *BrCabYB 84; Tel&CabFB 84C*
Deerfield Cable Systems Inc. [of Continental Cablevision Inc.] - Conway, MA - *BrCabYB 84*
Deerfield Cable Systems Inc. - Northfield, MA - *BrCabYB 84*
Deerfield Cable Systems Inc. [of Continental Cablevision Inc.] - Sunderland, MA - *BrCabYB 84*

Deerfield Communications Corp. - New York, NY - *StaDirAdAg 2-84*
Deerfield Farmers Telephone Co. - Deerfield, MI - *TelDir&BG 83-84*
Deerfield Independent - Deerfield, WI - *NewsDir 84*
Deerfield Independent - *See* Royle Publishing Co. Inc.
Deerfield Life - Deerfield, IL - *Ed&PubIntYB 82*
Deerfield Life - *See* Lerner Life Newspapers
Deerfield/Lincolnshire Life - Deerfield, IL - *AyerDirPub 83*
Deerfield News-Advertiser - Deerfield, IL - *Ed&PubIntYB 82*
Deerfield News Advertiser - Highland Park, IL - *AyerDirPub 83*
Deerfield News-Advertiser - *See* Singer Printing & Publishing Co.
Deerfield Review - Deerfield, IL - *Ed&PubIntYB 82*
Deerfield Review [of Pioneer Press Inc.] - Wilmette, IL - *AyerDirPub 83; NewsDir 84*
Deerfield Review - *See* Pioneer Press Inc.
Deerfield Telephone Co. Inc. - Deerfield, VA - *TelDir&BG 83-84*
Deering & Holmes Inc. - *See* Holmes Co. Inc., Michael
Deerland Distributors Inc. - Minneapolis, MN - *WhoWMicrocom 83*
Deermouse Press - Cambridge, MA - *BoPubDir 4, 5*
Deerpath Shopper - Deer River, MN - *AyerDirPub 83*
Dees Communications Inc. - Montgomery, AL - *DirMarMP 83*
Defender - Wilmington, DE - *Ed&PubIntYB 82*
Defender - Louisville, KY - *AyerDirPub 83; Ed&PubIntYB 82*
Defender - Houston, TX - *Ed&PubIntYB 82*
Defender Publishing Co. - West Union, OH - *BaconPubCkNews 84*
Defenders - Washington, DC - *BaconPubCkMag 84*
Defense & Foreign Affairs - Washington, DC - *BaconPubCkMag 84; BoPubDir 5*
Defense Audiovisual Information System [of U.S. Dept. of Defense] - Arlington, VA - *EISS 83*
Defense Daily [of Space Publications Inc.] - Washington, DC - *BaconPubCkMag 84; NewsDir 84*
Defense Data Bank - Washington, DC - *DirOnDB Spring 84*
Defense Data Bank [of Data Resources Inc.] - Lexington, MA - *DataDirOnSer 84*
Defense Electronics [of The Argus Press Holdings PLC] - Palo Alto, CA - *BaconPubCkMag 84; MagDir 84*
Defense Energy Information System [of U.S. Dept. of Defense] - Washington, DC - *EISS 83*
Defense Industry Report - Wilton, CT - *DirOnDB Spring 84*
Defense Logistics Studies Information Exchange [of U.S. Army] - Ft. Lee, VA - *EISS 83*
Defense Management Journal - Alexandria, VA - *BaconPubCkMag 84; MagDir 84*
Defense Market Measures System [of Frost & Sullivan Inc.] - New York, NY - *CompReadDB 82; DBBus 82*
Defense Markets & Technology [of Predicasts Inc.] - Cleveland, OH - *DataDirOnSer 84; EISS 5-84 Sup*
Defense Pest Management Information & Analysis Center [of U.S. Dept. of Defense] - Washington, DC - *EISS 83*
Defense R & D Update - Wilton, CT - *DirOnDB Spring 84*
Defense Science 2000 - Campbell, CA - *BaconPubCkMag 84*
Defense Technical Information Center [Subs. of Defense Logistics Agency] - Alexandria, VA - *CompReadDB 82; DataDirOnSer 84; EISS 83*
Defense Transportation Journal [of National Defense Transportation Association] - College Park, MD - *BaconPubCkMag 84; MagDir 84; MagIndMarPl 82-83*
Defense Week - Washington, DC - *BaconPubCkMag 84*
Defensor-Chieftain - Socorro, NM - *AyerDirPub 83*
Defiance Crescent-News - Defiance, OH - *NewsDir 84*
Defiance Telephone Co. - Defiance, IA - *TelDir&BG 83-84*
Definition Press [Aff. of Aesthetic Realism Foundation] - New York, NY - *BoPubDir 4, 5*
Defotel [of Questel Inc.] - Washington, DC - *DataDirOnSer 84*
Defotel - Paris, France - *DirOnDB Spring 84*
Defuniak Springs Herald-Breeze - Defuniak Springs, FL - *BaconPubCkNews 84*
Degener, Drs. Otto & Isa [Aff. of New York Botanical Garden] - Volcano, HI - *BoPubDir 4, 5*
Deglin & Associates, Ted - New York, NY - *DirPRFirms 83*
Degner Electronic CATV - La Valle, WI - *BrCabYB 84*
Degner Electronic CATV - Union Center, WI - *BrCabYB 84*
Degner Electronic CATV - Wonewoc, WI - *BrCabYB 84; Tel&CabFB 84C p.1677*
DeGruccio/Uniphoto, Paul - Phoenix, AZ - *AvMarPl 83*
DeHart Associates Inc. - Washington, DC - *DirPRFirms 83*
DeHoff Publications - Murfreesboro, TN - *BoPubDir 4, 5*
DEI Teleproducts - Escondido, CA - *DataDirSup 7-83*
Deigh Corp., Phileas - Garden City, NY - *BoPubDir 4, 5*
Deinotation-7 Press - Susquehanna, PA - *BoPubDir 4, 5*
Deiro Music Headquarters - *See* McGinnis & Marx Music Publishing
DeJamus Inc. - *See* James Music Inc., Dick
DeKadt Marketing & Research Inc. - Greenwich, CT - *IntDirMarRes 83*
DeKalb Cable TV [of Omega Communications Inc.] - Auburn, IN - *BrCabYB 84*
DeKalb Daily Chronicle [of Northern Illinois Publishing Co.] - DeKalb, IL - *BaconPubCkNews 84; NewsDir 84*
DeKalb Literary Arts Journal, The - Clarkston, GA - *LitMag&SmPr 83-84*
DeKalb News/Sun [of Decatur News Publishing Co. Inc.] - Decatur, GA - *NewsDir 84*
DeKalb News/Sun North - Decatur, GA - *AyerDirPub 83*
DeKalb News/Sun South - Decatur, GA - *AyerDirPub 83*
DeKalb Telephone Co. Inc. - Alexandria, TN - *TelDir&BG 83-84*
Dekker & Nordemann BV - *See* Elsevier Antiquarian Dept.
Dekker & Sons Inc., John H. - Grand Rapids, MI - *LitMarPl 83, 84*
Dekker Inc., Marcel - New York, NY - *LitMarPl 83, 84; MagIndMarPl 82-83*
Dekko Sound Service [Div. of KIM Productions Inc.] - Boston, MA - *AvMarPl 83*
Dekrig Advertising - New York, NY - *AdAge 3-28-84*
Dektas & Eger Inc. - Cincinnati, OH - *StaDirAdAg 2-84*
Del-Chem Bulletin [of American Chemical Society Delaware Section] - Wilmington, DE - *BaconPubCkMag 84; MagDir 84*
Del City Green Sheet - Del City, OK - *AyerDirPub 83*
Del City News - Del City, OK - *BaconPubCkNews 84; Ed&PubIntYB 82*
Del City News - Oklahoma City, OK - *NewsDir 84*
Del Data Computer Services - Dover, DE - *ADAPSOMemDir 83-84*
Del Gaudio Design Group Inc., Joseph - New York, NY - *LitMarPl 83, 84; MagIndMarPl 82-83*
Del Mar Cablevision [of Cable Management Associates Inc.] - Middletown, DE - *Tel&CabFB 84C*
Del Mar Surfcomber [of North Coast Publishers Inc.] - Del Mar, CA - *Ed&PubIntYB 82; NewsDir 84*
Del Mar Surfcomber - *See* North Coast Publishers Inc.
Del Norte Cablevision [of Tidel Communications Inc.] - Crescent City, CA - *BrCabYB 84; Tel&CabFB 84C*
Del Norte Cablevision [of Tidel Communications Inc.] - Gasquet, CA - *Tel&CabFB 84C*
Del Norte Cablevision [of Tidel Communications Inc.] - Hiouchi, CA - *Tel&CabFB 84C*
Del Norte Cablevision [of Tidel Communications Inc.] - Smith River, CA - *Tel&CabFB 84C*
Del Norte Prospector - Del Norte, CO - *BaconPubCkNews 84; Ed&PubIntYB 82*
Del Norte Triplicate - Crescent City, CA - *AyerDirPub 83; Ed&PubIntYB 82*
Del Oeste Press - Chatsworth, CA - *BoPubDir 5; LitMarPl 84*
Del Oeste Press - Tarzana, CA - *BoPubDir 4*
Del Paeske Productions Inc. - Milwaukee, WI - *AvMarPl 83*
Del Ray News Journal - Del Ray, FL - *BaconPubCkNews 84*
Del Rey Communications - Chicago, IL - *AvMarPl 83; BrCabYB 84*
Del Rio News-Herald [of Harte-Hanks Publishing Corp.] - Del Rio, TX - *BaconPubCkNews 84; Ed&PubIntYB 82; NewsDir 84*
Del Rio TV Cable Corp. [of Times Mirror Cable TV] - Del Rio, TX - *Tel&CabFB 84C*
Del Sound Music - *See* Happy Valley Music
Del Valle, Joseph B. - New York, NY - *LitMarPl 83, 84*
Delacorte Press - New York, NY - *LitMarPl 83*
Delafield Press - Suttons Bay, MI - *BoPubDir 4 Sup, 5*
Delair Publishing Co. [Div. of Delair Enterprises Inc.] - New York, NY - *DirMarMP 83; LitMarPl 83, 84; WritMar 84*

Deland Sun News [of General Newspapers Inc.] - Deland, FL - *BaconPubCkNews 84; NewsDir 84*
Delaney Advertising - Fresno, CA - *StaDirAdAg 2-84*
Delano Eagle - Delano, MN - *AyerDirPub 83; BaconPubCkNews 84; Ed&PubIntYB 82*
Delano Record - Delano, CA - *BaconPubCkNews 84; Ed&PubIntYB 82*
Delapeake Publishing Co. - Wilmington, DE - *LitMag&SmPr 83-84*
Delat Farm Press - Clarksdale, MS - *MagDir 84*
Delavan Enterprise - Delavan, WI - *Ed&PubIntYB 82; NewsDir 84*
Delavan Enterprise & Republican - Delavan, WI - *BaconPubCkNews 84*
Delavan Telephone Co. - Delavan, MN - *TelDir&BG 83-84*
Delavan Times - Delavan, IL - *BaconPubCkNews 84; Ed&PubIntYB 82*
Delavan Total TV - Delavan, WI - *Tel&CabFB 84C*
Delaware Beachcomber [of Atlantic Publications Inc.] - Rehoboth Beach, DE - *NewsDir 84*
Delaware Cable TV [of American TV & Communications Corp.] - Delaware, OH - *BrCabYB 84; Tel&CabFB 84C*
Delaware City Trans-Video Corp. - Delaware City, DE - *BrCabYB 84*
Delaware Coast Press [of Atlantic Publications Inc.] - Rehoboth Beach, DE - *AyerDirPub 83; Ed&PubIntYB 82; NewsDir 84*
Delaware County Cable TV Co. [of Times Mirror Cable TV] - Ridley Township, PA - *Tel&CabFB 84C*
Delaware County Cable TV Co. [of Times Mirror Cable TV] - Upper Darby, PA - *BrCabYB 84; Tel&CabFB 84C*
Delaware County Daily Times - Chester, PA - *AyerDirPub 83*
Delaware County Daily Times [of Central States Publishing Inc.] - Clifton Heights, PA - *NewsDir 84*
Delaware County Daily Times - Primos, PA - *BaconPubCkNews 84; Ed&PubIntYB 82*
Delaware County Journal - Jay, OK - *AyerDirPub 83; Ed&PubIntYB 82*
Delaware County Leader - Hopkinton, IA - *AyerDirPub 83; Ed&PubIntYB 82*
Delaware County Times - Delhi, NY - *AyerDirPub 83*
Delaware Gazette - Delaware, OH - *BaconPubCkNews 84; Ed&PubIntYB 82; NewsDir 84*
Delaware Medical Journal - Wilmington, DE - *BaconPubCkMag 84; MagDir 84*
Delaware On-Line Users Group [of University of Delaware] - Newark, DE - *InfIndMarPl 83*
Delaware Orcal Cable Inc. - Calipatria, CA - *BrCabYB 84; Tel&CabFB 84C*
Delaware Orcal Cable Inc. - Reno, NV - *Tel&CabFB 84C p.1677*
Delaware Orcal Cable Inc. - Beaver, UT - *BrCabYB 84*
Delaware Orcal Cable Inc. - Panguitch, UT - *BrCabYB 84*
Delaware Sentinel, The - Dover, DE - *AyerDirPub 83*
Delaware State Data Center [of Delaware State Development Office] - Dover, DE - *EISS 83*
Delaware State News - Dover, DE - *AyerDirPub 83; BaconPubCkNews 84; Ed&PubIntYB 82*
Delaware Telephone Co. Inc. [Aff. of Continental Telecom Inc.] - Johnstown, NY - *TelDir&BG 83-84*
Delaware Today - Wilmington, DE - *ArtMar 84; BaconPubCkMag 84; MagDir 84; WritMar 84*
Delaware Valley Business Magazine - Philadelphia, PA - *MagDir 84*
Delaware Valley News [of Hunterdon County Democrat] - Flemington, NJ - *NewsDir 84*
Delaware Valley News [of Hunterdon County Democrat] - Frenchtown, NJ - *AyerDirPub 83; Ed&PubIntYB 82; NewsDir 84*
Delcambre Telephone Co. Inc. - Delcambre, LA - *TelDir&BG 83-84*
Delco Associates Inc. - Greenwich, CT - *DirInfWP 82*
Delco Mailing & Advertising - Upper Darby, PA - *MagIndMarPl 82-83*
Delecorte Press - New York, NY - *WritMar 84*
DeLeeuw Hill & Associates - Southfield, MI - *StaDirAdAg 2-84*
Delev Music Co. - Philadelphia, PA - *BillIntBG 83-84*
Delfino Marketing Communications Inc. - Hawthorne, NY - *StaDirAdAg 2-84*
Delft Hydraulics Laboratory - Delft, Netherlands - *InfIndMarPl 83*
Delft Hydraulics Laboratory Library (Information & Documentation) - Delft, Netherlands - *CompReadDB 82*
Delft Hydro [of QL Systems Ltd.] - Ottawa, ON, Canada - *DataDirOnSer 84*
Delft Hydro [of Delft Hydraulics Laboratory Library] - Delft, Netherlands - *CompReadDB 82; DirOnDB Spring 84*
Delgado Advertising & Public Relations, Ed - Santa Fe, NM - *StaDirAdAg 2-84*
Delgren Books - Tucson, AZ - *LitMag&SmPr 83-84*
Delhi Delaware County Times - Delhi, NY - *BaconPubCkNews 84*
Delhi Dispatch - Delhi, LA - *BaconPubCkNews 84*
Delhi Dispatch, The - Richland Parish, LA - *Ed&PubIntYB 82*
Delhi Express - *See* Waterford News Publishers
Delhi NewChannels [of New Channels Corp.] - Delhi, NY - *BrCabYB 84*
Delhi News Record - Delhi, ON, Canada - *Ed&PubIntYB 82*
Delhi Press/Price Hill Press - Cincinnati, OH - *AyerDirPub 83; Ed&PubIntYB 82*
Delhi Press/Price Hill Press - *See* Queen City Suburban Press Inc.
Delhi Telephone Co. - Delhi, NY - *TelDir&BG 83-84*
Deli-Dairy Management - Cedarhurst, NY - *BaconPubCkMag 84; MagDir 84*
Deli News [of Delicatessen Council of Southern California] - Los Angeles, CA - *MagDir 84*
Deli News - Mar Vista, CA - *BaconPubCkMag 84*
Delia Associates - Whitehouse, NJ - *DirPRFirms 83*
Delibes Communications Ltd. - New York, NY - *DirPRFirms 83*
Delicate Music - *See* Rondor Music International Inc.
Delilah Communications Ltd. - New York, NY - *LitMarPl 83, 84*
DeLise Productions, Lou - Willow Grove, PA - *BillIntBG 83-84*
Deliver Music Publishing Co. - *See* Will-Du Music Publishing Co.
Delker Electronics Inc. - Smyrna, TN - *MicrocomMPl 84*
Dell City Hudspeth County Herald Review - Dell City, TX - *BaconPubCkNews 84*
Dell Distributing Co. Inc. [Subs. of Dell Publishing Co. Inc.] - New York, NY - *LitMarPl 83*
Dell Manufacturing Co. Inc. - Farmington, CT - *ADAPSOMemDir 83-84*
Dell-Naatz Publication Arts - Manitou Springs, CO - *LitMarPl 83, 84*
Dell Publishing Co. Inc. [Subs. of Doubleday & Co. Inc.] - New York, NY - *LitMarPl 83, 84; WritMar 84*
Dell Puzzle Publications - New York, NY - *WritMar 84*
Dell Rapids Tribune - Dell Rapids, SD - *Ed&PubIntYB 82*
Dell Rapids Tribune - *See* Prairie Publications
Dell Telephone Cooperative Inc. - Dell City, TX - *TelDir&BG 83-84*
Della Femina, Travisano & Partners - New York, NY - *AdAge 3-28-84; Br 1-23-84; BrCabYB 84; StaDirAdAg 2-84*
Dellee - *See* Alexis Music Inc.
Dellen Publishing Co. [Subs. of Dividend Industries] - Santa Clara, CA - *BoPubDir 4, 5; LitMarPl 84*
Dells Events - Wisconsin Dells, WI - *Ed&PubIntYB 82*
Dellwood Music Co. Inc. - Saddle Brook, NJ - *BillIntBG 83-84*
Delmar Co., The [Subs. of Republic Corp.] - Charlotte, NC - *LitMarPl 83, 84*
Delmar Publishers Inc. [Subs. of Thomas Nelson International Ltd.] - Albany, NY - *LitMarPl 83, 84*
Delmar Publishing Inc. - Albany, NY - *WritMar 84*
Delmar Spotlight - Delmar, NY - *BaconPubCkNews 84*
Delmark Records - Chicago, IL - *BillIntBG 83-84*
Delmarva Broadcasting Co. - Wilmington, DE - *BrCabYB 84*
Delmarva Farmer - Easton, MD - *BaconPubCkMag 84*
Delmarva News [of Atlantic Publications Inc.] - Millsboro, DE - *AyerDirPub 83; Ed&PubIntYB 82; NewsDir 84*
Delmont Record - Delmont, SD - *BaconPubCkNews 84; Ed&PubIntYB 82*
Deloitte, Haskins & Sells - Boston, MA - *CabTVFinDB 83; InterCabHB 3*
Deloitte Haskins & Sells (Office Automation Group) - Miami, FL - *DirInfWP 82*
Delong & Associates - Annapolis, MD - *BoPubDir 4, 5*
Deloraine Times & Star, The - Deloraine, MB, Canada - *Ed&PubIntYB 82*

DeLorme Publishing Co. - Freeport, ME - *BoPubDir 4, 5*
Delos Records Inc. - Santa Monica, CA - *BillIntBG 83-84*
Delphi [of General Videotex Corp.] - Cambridge, MA - *DirOnDB Spring 84; EISS 7-83 Sup; MicrocomMPl 84; TeleSy&SerDir 7-83*
Delphi Books [Aff. of Delphi Information Sciences Corp.] - Santa Monica, CA - *BoPubDir 4, 5*
Delphi Data Systems - Minneapolis, MN - *DirInfWP 82*
Delphi Data Systems Inc. - Eden Prairie, MN - *DataDirOnSer 84*
Delphi Research Center - Lincoln, MA - *BoPubDir 5*
Delphic Systems - St. Louis, MO - *WhoWMicrocom 83*
Delphos Herald - Delphos, OH - *BaconPubCkNews 84; Ed&PubIntYB 82; NewsDir 84*
Delphos Republican - Delphos, KS - *BaconPubCkNews 84; Ed&PubIntYB 82*
Delphos Republican - Glasco, KS - *BaconPubCkNews 84*
Delporte Inc., G. Andre - Syracuse, NY - *StaDirAdAg 2-84*
Delray Beach-Boynton Beach News Journal [of Palm Beach Newspapers Inc.] - Delray Beach, FL - *AyerDirPub 83; NewsDir 84*
Delray Beach News Journal - Delray Beach, FL - *Ed&PubIntYB 82*
Delrieu - *See* Galaxy Music Corp.
Delrieu, Duprat & Associes - Paris, France - *StaDirAdAg 2-84*
Delta - New York, NY - *BrCabYB 84*
Delta Advertising Agency - Huntington Beach, CA - *StaDirAdAg 2-84*
Delta Air Lines - Jamaica, NY - *MagIndMarPl 82-83*
Delta Atlas - Delta, OH - *AyerDirPub 83; BaconPubCkNews 84; Ed&PubIntYB 82; NewsDir 84*
Delta Books [Div. of Dell Publishing Co.] - New York, NY - *WritMar 84*
Delta Cable Television Ltd. - Delta, BC, Canada - *BrCabYB 84*
Delta Cable TV Co. [of Community Tele-Communications Inc.] - Delta, CO - *Tel&CabFB 84C*
Delta Cable TV Co. [of GS Communications Inc.] - Frederick, MD - *BrCabYB 84*
Delta Cable TV Co. [of GS Communications Inc.] - Delta, PA - *Tel&CabFB 84C*
Delta Cablevision [of TCA Cable TV Inc.] - Lake Village, AR - *Tel&CabFB 84C*
Delta Cablevision Inc. [of TCA Cable TV Inc.] - Dermott, AR - *Tel&CabFB 84C*
Delta Cablevision Inc. [of TCA Cable TV Inc.] - McGehee, AR - *Tel&CabFB 84C*
Delta Cablevision Inc. - Delhi, LA - *Tel&CabFB 84C*
Delta Cablevision Inc. - Lake Providence, LA - *BrCabYB 84*
Delta Cablevision Inc. - Oak Grove, LA - *Tel&CabFB 84C*
Delta Cablevision Inc. [of TCA Cable TV Inc.] - Tyler, TX - *BrCabYB 84 p.D-300*
Delta Communications Inc. - Columbia, MD - *MagIndMarPl 82-83*
Delta Computers Inc. - Alexandria, LA - *MicrocomSwDir 1; WhoWMicrocom 83*
Delta County Cooperative Telephone Co. - Paonia, CO - *Tel&CabFB 84C p.1677; TelDir&BG 83-84*
Delta County Independent - Delta, CO - *AyerDirPub 83; BaconPubCkNews 84; Ed&PubIntYB 82; NewsDir 84*
Delta County Tel-Comm Inc. [of Delta County Cooperative Telephone Co.] - Cedaredge, CO - *Tel&CabFB 84C*
Delta County Tel-Comm Inc. [of Delta County Cooperative Telephone Co.] - Hotchkiss, CO - *BrCabYB 84; Tel&CabFB 84C*
Delta Data Systems Corp. - Trevose, PA - *DataDirSup 7-83; DirInfWP 82; InfIndMarPl 83*
Delta Data Systems Inc. - Pocatello, ID - *WhoWMicrocom 83*
Delta Democrat-Times - Greenville, MS - *AyerDirPub 83; Ed&PubIntYB 82; LitMarPl 83, 84*
Delta Design & Graphics Ltd. - Newark, England - *MicrocomSwDir 1*
Delta Design Group - Greenville, MS - *MagIndMarPl 82-83*
Delta Farm Press - Clarksdale, MS - *AyerDirPub 83; BaconPubCkMag 84*
Delta Farming Systems Inc. - Grand Junction, CO - *MicrocomMPl 84*
Delta International Records Inc. - Cleveland, OH - *BillIntBG 83-84*
Delta Lithograph Co. - Van Nuys, CA - *LitMarPl 83, 84; MagIndMarPl 82-83*
Delta Market Research Inc. - Horsham, PA - *IntDirMarRes 83*
Delta Microcomputer - Alexandria, LA - *WhoWMicrocom 83*
Delta Millard County Chronicle - Delta, UT - *BaconPubCkNews 84*
Delta Optimist - Delta, BC, Canada - *AyerDirPub 83; Ed&PubIntYB 82*
Delta Pictures Inc. - Shreveport, LA - *AvMarPl 83*
Delta Publications Associates [Aff. of DPA-LTS Enterprises Inc.] - Alburg, VT - *BoPubDir 4*
Delta Records - Nacogdoches, TX - *BillIntBG 83-84*
Delta Reporter - Gladstone, MI - *AyerDirPub 83; Ed&PubIntYB 82*
Delta Research Services Inc. - Coral Gables, FL - *EISS 83*
Delta Scene - Cleveland, MS - *WritMar 84*
Delta Sky [of Halsey Publishing Co.] - North Miami, FL - *BaconPubCkMag 84; Folio 83; MagIndMarPl 82-83; WritMar 84*
Delta Star - Delta, PA - *BaconPubCkNews 84*
Delta Telephone Co. Inc. - Louise, MS - *TelDir&BG 83-84*
Delta Video Cable Inc. - Tiptonville, TN - *BrCabYB 84; Tel&CabFB 84C*
Delta Video Co. [of Midwest Video Corp.] - Greenville, MS - *BrCabYB 84; Tel&CabFB 84C*
Delta Video Inc. - Bernie, MO - *BrCabYB 84*
Delta Video Inc. - Clarkton, MO - *BrCabYB 84; Tel&CabFB 84C*
Delta Video Inc. - Parma, MO - *BrCabYB 84*
Delta Video Inc. - Portageville, MO - *BrCabYB 84*
Delta Video Inc. - Wardell, MO - *BrCabYB 84*
Deltak Microsystems Inc. - Naperville, IL - *MicrocomMPl 84*
Deltakos U.S.A. - New York, NY - *StaDirAdAg 2-84*
Deltax Corp. - Orem, UT - *MicrocomSwDir 1*
Deltec Corp. [Div. of Gould Inc.] - San Diego, CA - *DirInfWP 82*
Deltek Industries - Pittsburgh, PA - *AvMarPl 83; DirInfWP 82*
Deltiologists of America - Ridley Park, PA - *BoPubDir 4, 5*
Deltiology - Ridley Park, PA - *ArtMar 84*
Deltona Cablevision - Deltona, FL - *BrCabYB 84*
Deluxe Co. - Shreveport, LA - *BoPubDir 4 Sup, 5*
Deluxe Laboratories Inc. [Subs. of Twentieth Century-Fox Film Corp.] - Hollywood, CA - *AvMarPl 83; Tel&CabFB 84C*
Delvy Enterprises Inc., Richard - Los Angeles, CA - *BillIntBG 83-84*
Dem Del Word Processing Center Ltd. - Montreal, PQ, Canada - *DirInfWP 82*
Demaine & Associates, Windsor - Alexandria, VA - *StaDirAdAg 2-84*
Demand Research Corp. - Chicago, IL - *IntDirMarRes 83*
Demaree, Kenneth B. - Southbury, CT - *LitMarPl 83, 84*
Demarest Public Relations - Dallas, TX - *DirPRFirms 83*
Demartin-Marona-Cranstoun-Downes - Wilmington, DE - *HBIndAd&MS 82-83; StaDirAdAg 2-84*
Dembner Books [Div. of Red Dembner Enterprises Corp.] - New York, NY - *LitMarPl 83, 84*
Dembner Enterprises Corp., Red - New York, NY - *WritMar 84*
Demby & Associates Inc. - New York, NY - *IntDirMarRes 83*
Demco Inc. - Madison, WI - *AvMarPl 83; LitMarPl 83, 84*
Demerco Industries - Van Nuys, CA - *WhoWMicrocom 83*
Demi-Software - Medfield, MA - *MicrocomMPl 83, 84*
Deming Headlight - Deming, NM - *BaconPubCkNews 84; Ed&PubIntYB 82; NewsDir 84*
Demiris-Rice & Associates Inc. - Salt Lake City, UT - *StaDirAdAg 2-84*
Democo Inc. - Madison, WI - *MagIndMarPl 82-83*
Democraft Printing & Lithographing Co. - Little Rock, AR - *MagIndMarPl 82-83*
Democrat - Lonoke, AR - *AyerDirPub 83*
Democrat - Trumann, AR - *AyerDirPub 83*
Democrat - Woodland, CA - *AyerDirPub 83*
Democrat - Tallahassee, FL - *AyerDirPub 83*
Democrat - Brookville, IN - *AyerDirPub 83*
Democrat - Corydon, IN - *AyerDirPub 83*
Democrat - Mt. Vernon, IN - *AyerDirPub 83*
Democrat - Bloomfield, IA - *AyerDirPub 83*
Democrat - Emmetsburg, IA - *AyerDirPub 83*
Democrat - Ft. Madison, IA - *AyerDirPub 83*
Democrat - Orange City, IA - *AyerDirPub 83; Ed&PubIntYB 82*

Democrat - Waukon, IA - *AyerDirPub 83*
Democrat - Waverly, IA - *AyerDirPub 83*
Democrat - Cynthiana, KY - *AyerDirPub 83*
Democrat - Natchez, MS - *AyerDirPub 83*
Democrat - Bowling Green, MO - *AyerDirPub 83*
Democrat - California, MO - *AyerDirPub 83*
Democrat - Carrollton, MO - *AyerDirPub 83; Ed&PubIntYB 82*
Democrat - Cassville, MO - *AyerDirPub 83*
Democrat - Clinton, MO - *AyerDirPub 83*
Democrat [of Dear Publication & Radio Inc.] - Sedalia, MO - *AyerDirPub 83; Ed&PubIntYB 82; NewsDir 84*
Democrat - Shelbina, MO - *AyerDirPub 83*
Democrat - Cortland, NY - *AyerDirPub 83*
Democrat - Durant, OK - *AyerDirPub 83*
Democrat - Pauls Valley, OK - *AyerDirPub 83*
Democrat - Hearne, TX - *AyerDirPub 83*
Democrat - Marlin, TX - *AyerDirPub 83*
Democrat - Memphis, TX - *AyerDirPub 83*
Democrat - Sherman, TX - *AyerDirPub 83*
Democrat - Glenville, WV - *AyerDirPub 83*
Democrat - Weston, WV - *AyerDirPub 83*
Democrat Advertiser - Sikeston, MO - *Ed&PubIntYB 82*
Democrat & Chronicle [of Gannett Co. Inc.] - Rochester, NY - *AyerDirPub 83; Ed&PubIntYB 82; LitMarPl 84*
Democrat & Leader [of Frisbie Publishing Co. Inc.] - Ft. Meade, FL - *AyerDirPub 83; NewsDir 84*
Democrat & Town & Country - Pulaski, NY - *AyerDirPub 83*
Democrat-Argus - Caruthersville, MO - *AyerDirPub 83; Ed&PubIntYB 82*
Democrat-Chief - Hobart, OK - *AyerDirPub 83; Ed&PubIntYB 82*
Democrat-Herald [of Western Communications Inc.] - Baker, OR - *BaconPubCkNews 84; Ed&PubIntYB 82; NewsDir 84*
Democrat-Herald Publishing Co. - *See* Capital Cities Communications Inc.
Democrat-Journal - Stilwell, OK - *AyerDirPub 83*
Democrat-Leader - Fayette, MO - *AyerDirPub 83; Ed&PubIntYB 82*
Democrat-Leader - Norborne, MO - *AyerDirPub 83; Ed&PubIntYB 82*
Democrat Message, The - Mt. Sterling, IL - *AyerDirPub 83; Ed&PubIntYB 82*
Democrat-Messenger - Waynesburg, PA - *AyerDirPub 83; Ed&PubIntYB 82; NewsDir 84*
Democrat-News - Fredericktown, MO - *AyerDirPub 83; Ed&PubIntYB 82*
Democrat News - Pulaski, NY - *AyerDirPub 83*
Democrat News, The - Jerseyville, IL - *AyerDirPub 83; Ed&PubIntYB 82; NewsDir 84*
Democrat-News, The - Marshall, MO - *AyerDirPub 83; BaconPubCkNews 84; Ed&PubIntYB 82*
Democrat-Radio - Manchester, IA - *AyerDirPub 83*
Democrat-Reporter - Linden, AL - *AyerDirPub 83; Ed&PubIntYB 82*
Democrat-Rocket, The - Festus, MO - *AyerDirPub 83*
Democrat, The - England, AR - *AyerDirPub 83*
Democrat Tribune - Mineral Point, WI - *AyerDirPub 83; Ed&PubIntYB 82*
Democrat Union - Lawrenceburg, TN - *AyerDirPub 83; Ed&PubIntYB 82*
Democrat-Voice - Coleman, TX - *AyerDirPub 83*
Democratic Left - New York, NY - *LitMag&SmPr 83-84*
Demographic Data Base [of University of Umea] - Umea, Sweden - *EISS 5-84 Sup*
Demographic Database [of Demographic Research Co. Inc.] - Santa Monica, CA - *DataDirOnSer 84*
Demographic Research Co. Inc. - Santa Monica, CA - *DataDirOnSer 84; EISS 83*
Demographic Systems Group [of CACI Inc.] - Arlington, VA - *EISS 83*
Demographics Laboratory - Olympia, WA - *EISS 83*
Demolition Age - Northfield, IL - *BaconPubCkMag 84*
Demopolis CATV Co. - Demopolis, AL - *BrCabYB 84; Tel&CabFB 84C*
Demopolis Times [of Boone Publications] - Demopolis, AL - *AyerDirPub 83; BaconPubCkNews 84; Ed&PubIntYB 82; NewsDir 84*
Demopolis White Bluff Chronicle - Demopolis, AL - *BaconPubCkNews 84*
Demos Music Publications - Houston, TX - *BoPubDir 4, 5*
Demotte Kankakee Valley Post-News - Demotte, IN - *BaconPubCkNews 84*
Demou & Associates, Morris - Burnsville, MN - *BoPubDir 4, 5*
Dempsey, Muriel V. - Heward, SK, Canada - *BoPubDir 4, 5*
Dempsey's TV Service - Laurel Creek, WV - *BrCabYB 84; Tel&CabFB 84C*
Den Danske Pioneer - Chicago, IL - *NewsDir 84*
Dendle & Schraibman - Lexington, KY - *BoPubDir 5*
Deneau Publishers & Co. Ltd. - Ottawa, ON, Canada - *BoPubDir 4; LitMarPl 83, 84; WritMar 84*
Denham Springs Home Almanac [of Hammond Murray-Huber Publishing Inc.] - Hammond, LA - *NewsDir 84*
Denham Springs-Livingston Parish News - Denham Springs, LA - *BaconPubCkNews 84; Ed&PubIntYB 82; NewsDir 84*
Denhard & Stewart Inc. - New York, NY - *LitMarPl 83, 84; StaDirAdAg 2-84*
Denim & Lace Music - *See* Cornelius Music, Stan
Denison & Co. Inc., T. S. - Minneapolis, MN - *LitMarPl 83, 84; WritMar 84*
Denison Bulletin - Denison, IA - *Ed&PubIntYB 82*
Denison Bulletin - *See* Denison Newspapers Inc.
Denison Bulletin & Review - Denison, IA - *NewsDir 84*
Denison Herald - Denison, TX - *BaconPubCkNews 84; Ed&PubIntYB 82; NewsDir 84*
Denison Newspapers Inc. - Denison, IA - *BaconPubCkNews 84*
Denison Propaganda SA - *See* Bates Worldwide Inc., Ted
Denison Review - *See* Denison Newspapers Inc.
Denison Review, The - Denison, IA - *Ed&PubIntYB 82*
Denlinger's Publishers Ltd. - Fairfax, VA - *LitMarPl 83, 84; WritMar 84*
Denman, Frank B. - Seattle, WA - *MagIndMarPl 82-83*
Denmark Press - Denmark, WI - *BaconPubCkNews 84; Ed&PubIntYB 82*
Denni Hlasatel - Berwyn, IL - *AyerDirPub 83*
Denni Hlasatel - Cicero, IL - *Ed&PubIntYB 82*
Dennis & Co. Inc. - Stamford, CT - *IntDirMarRes 83*
Dennis Bulletin - *See* Orleans Hughes Newspapers Inc.
Dennis Bulletin, The - Orleans, MA - *NewsDir 84*
Dennis-Landman Publishers - Santa Monica, CA - *BoPubDir 4, 5*
Dennis Productions, Hal - Hollywood, CA - *Tel&CabFB 84C*
Dennison KYBE Corp. [Subs. of Dennison Manufacturing Co.] - Waltham, MA - *DataDirSup 7-83; DirInfWP 82; WhoWMicrocom 83*
Dennison Manufacturing Co. - Framingham, MA - *DataDirSup 7-83; DirInfWP 82*
Dennison Manufacturing Co. (Carter's Ink Div.) - Waltham, MA - *DirInfWP 82*
Dennison Monarch Systems Inc. [Subs. of Dennison Manufacturing Co.] - New Windsor, NY - *DirInfWP 82*
Dennison/National [Subs. of Dennison Manufacturing Co.] - Holyoke, MA - *DirInfWP 82*
Denny, Walls, Ross & Wright Inc. - Portland, OR - *StaDirAdAg 2-84*
Denon - Foster City, CA - *BillIntBG 83-84*
Denon America Inc./Denon Records - West Caldwell, NJ - *BillIntBG 83-84*
Denoyer Geppert Co. - Chicago, IL - *LitMarPl 83, 84*
Densen Enterprises Inc. - Bakersfield, CA - *Tel&CabFB 84C*
Dent & Associates Inc., Gary A. - Ft. Worth, TX - *CabTVFinDB 83*
Dent & Sons Ltd., J. M. - Don Mills, ON, Canada - *LitMarPl 83*
Dent County TV Cable System - Salem, MO - *BrCabYB 84; Tel&CabFB 84C*
Dental Assistant - Chicago, IL - *BaconPubCkMag 84; MagDir 84*
Dental Computer Newsletter [of Andent Inc.] - Waukegan, IL - *MicrocomMPl 84*
Dental Dealer International Product News [of ESCO Publishing Co.] - San Antonio, TX - *MagDir 84*
Dental Economics [of Petroleum Publishing Co.] - Tulsa, OK - *BaconPubCkMag 84; DirMarMP 83; MagDir 84; MagIndMarPl 82-83; WritMar 84*
Dental Floss Magazine [of Toothpaste Press] - West Branch, IA - *LitMag&SmPr 83-84*

Dental Hygiene [of American Dental Hygienists' Association] - Chicago, IL - *ArtMar 84; BaconPubCkMag 84; MagDir 84; MagIndMarPl 82-83*
Dental Industry News [of Harcourt Brace Jovanovich Publications] - New York, NY - *MagDir 84*
Dental Industry Newsletter - Cleveland, OH - *BaconPubCkMag 84*
Dental Info - Tucson, AZ - *BoPubDir 5*
Dental Lab Products [of Irving-Cloud Publishing Co.] - Skokie, IL - *BaconPubCkMag 84; MagDir 84*
Dental Lab World [of Esco Publishing Co.] - San Antonio, TX - *MagDir 84; MagIndMarPl 82-83*
Dental Laboratory News [of Dental Lab Association of the State of New York] - New York, NY - *BaconPubCkMag 84; MagDir 84; MagIndMarPl 82-83*
Dental Laboratory Review [of Harcourt Brace Jovanovich Publications] - New York, NY - *BaconPubCkMag 84; MagDir 84*
Dental Management [of Harcourt Brace Jovanovich Publications] - New York, NY - *MagDir 84; MagIndMarPl 82-83*
Dental Management - Cleveland, OH - *BaconPubCkMag 84; WritMar 84*
Dental Management [of The Harvest Cos.] - Middleburg Heights, OH - *ArtMar 84*
Dental Products Report [of Irving-Cloud Publishing Co.] - Skokie, IL - *BaconPubCkMag 84; DirMarMP 83; MagDir 84; MagIndMarPl 82-83*
Dental Research Data Office [of U.S. Public Health Service] - Bethesda, MD - *EISS 83*
Dental Student [of Stevens Publishing Corp.] - Waco, TX - *BaconPubCkMag 84; MagDir 84*
Dental Survey [of Harcourt Brace Jovanovich Publications] - New York, NY - *MagDir 84*
Dentcom Inc. - Jenkintown, PA - *MicrocomMPl 84*
Dentistry Today - McLean, VA - *BaconPubCkMag 84*
Dentist's Computer, The - Glen Rock, NJ - *MicrocomMPl 84*
Denton Advertising Inc. - Tampa, FL - *StaDirAdAg 2-84*
Denton & Haskins Corp. - New York, NY - *BillIntBG 83-84*
Denton County Enterprise - Denton, TX - *BaconPubCkNews 84*
Denton County Record - Denton, MD - *BaconPubCkNews 84*
Denton Publications Inc. - Elizabethtown, NY - *BaconPubCkNews 84*
Denton Record - Denton, NC - *BaconPubCkNews 84; Ed&PubIntYB 82*
Denton Record-Chronicle - Denton, TX - *BaconPubCkNews 84; Ed&PubIntYB 82; NewsDir 84*
Denton, Thomas Ltd. - London, ON, Canada - *WhoWMicrocom 83*
Dentronix Systems Inc. - Santa Ana, CA - *DataDirSup 7-83; WhoWMicrocom 83*
Dentsu Inc. - Tokyo, Japan - *BrCabYB 84; StaDirAdAg 2-84*
Denver & Ephrata Telephone & Telegraph Co. - Ephrata, PA - *TelDir&BG 83-84*
Denver Art Museum - Denver, CO - *BoPubDir 4, 5*
Denver Business - Denver, CO - *BaconPubCkMag 84*
Denver Center Theatre Co. - Denver, CO - *WritMar 84*
Denver Chamber of Commerce - Denver, CO - *BoPubDir 4 Sup, 5*
Denver City Press - Denver City, TX - *BaconPubCkNews 84; Ed&PubIntYB 82*
Denver Clarion - Denver, CO - *NewsDir 84*
Denver Colorado Leader - Denver, CO - *BaconPubCkNews 84*
Denver Colorado Statesman - Denver, CO - *BaconPubCkNews 84*
Denver Forum - Denver, IA - *BaconPubCkNews 84*
Denver Herald-Dispatch - Denver, CO - *BaconPubCkNews 84; NewsDir 84*
Denver Living [of Baker Publications] - Aurora, CO - *MagDir 84; WritMar 84*
Denver Living - Dallas, TX - *MagIndMarPl 82-83*
Denver Magazine - Denver, CO - *BaconPubCkMag 84; MagDir 84*
Denver Monthly - Denver, CO - *MagDir 84*
Denver Post [of Times Mirror Corp.] - Denver, CO - *BaconPubCkNews 84; Ed&PubIntYB 82; LitMarPl 83, 84; NewsBur 6; NewsDir 84*
Denver Quarterly [of University of Denver] - Denver, CO - *LitMag&SmPr 83-84; WritMar 84*
Denver Rocky Mountain News - Denver, CO - *NewsDir 84*
Denver Software Co. - Aurora, CO - *MicrocomMPl 83; MicrocomSwDir 1; WhoWMicrocom 83*
Denver Weekly News - Denver, CO - *BaconPubCkNews 84; Ed&PubIntYB 82; NewsDir 84*
Denver Westminster Sentinel - Thornton, CO - *BaconPubCkNews 84*
Denville Citizen of Morris County - Denville, NJ - *BaconPubCkNews 84; NewsDir 84*
Department d'IRO [of University of Montreal] - Montreal, PQ, Canada - *VideoDir 82-83*
Department for Informatics & Science Analysis [of Hungarian Academy of Sciences Library] - Budapest, Hungary - *EISS 5-84 Sup*
Department of Indian Affairs & Northern Development (Northern Research Information & Documentation Service) - Ottawa, ON, Canada - *CompReadDB 82*
Department of Information Services [of Council for Exceptional Children] - Reston, VA - *EISS 83*
Department of Printed Books Current Catalogue - London, England - *DirOnDB Spring 84*
Department Store Economist - New York, NY - *BaconPubCkMag 84*
Departures [of HBC Travel Ltd.] - Don Mills, ON, Canada - *WritMar 84*
Dependable Lists Inc. - New York, NY - *LitMarPl 83, 84; MagIndMarPl 82-83*
Depew Advertising, Dorr M. - Charlotte, NC - *StaDirAdAg 2-84*
Depew Herald - Depew, NY - *AyerDirPub 83; Ed&PubIntYB 82*
Depew Herald [of Bee Publications Inc.] - Williamsville, NY - *NewsDir 84*
Depew Herald - *See* Bee Publications Inc.
Depicto Films Corp. - Paramus, NJ - *TelAl 83, 84*
DEPO - Eagle Point, OR - *TV&RadDir 84*
Deport Times - Deport, TX - *Ed&PubIntYB 82*
Deposit Courier - Deposit, NY - *BaconPubCkNews 84; Ed&PubIntYB 82*
Deposit Telephone Co. Inc. - Deposit, NY - *TelDir&BG 83-84*
Deposit Television Inc. - Deposit, NY - *BrCabYB 84; Tel&CabFB 84C*
Depot Press - Nashville, TN - *LitMag&SmPr 83-84*
Deppe & Associates - St. Louis, MO - *AdAge 3-28-84; StaDirAdAg 2-84*
Depth Research Laboratories Inc. - Brooklyn, NY - *IntDirMarRes 83*
Depue Telephone Co. - Depue, IL - *TelDir&BG 83-84*
Der Angriff Publications - Huntington, WV - *BoPubDir 4, 5*
Der Ausschnitt - Berlin, West Germany - *ProGuPRSer 4*
Der Deutsch-Amerikaner [of German American National Congress] - Mt. Prospect, IL - *Ed&PubIntYB 82; NewsDir 84*
Der Nacht Musik - *See* Rumblin' Songs
Der Yid - Brooklyn, NY - *Ed&PubIntYB 82; NewsDir 84*
Derby Cable TV [of Tele-Communications Inc.] - Derby, KS - *BrCabYB 84*
Derby Cablevision Inc. - Kauai Island, HI - *BrCabYB 84; Tel&CabFB 84C*
Deregulations - Tampa, FL - *BaconPubCkMag 84*
DeRidder Cable TV [of Teleservice Corp. of America Inc.] - DeRidder, LA - *BrCabYB 84*
Derivation & Tabulation Associates Inc. [Aff. of Cordura Corp.] - San Diego, CA - *BoPubDir 5*
Derleth Society Newsletter, August - Uncasville, CT - *LitMag&SmPr 83-84*
Dermal Absorption [of Chemical Information Systems Inc.] - Baltimore, MD - *DataDirOnSer 84*
Dermatology - Wilmette, IL - *BaconPubCkMag 84*
Dermatology Times - New York, NY - *BaconPubCkMag 84*
Dermott Times-News - Dermott, AR - *BaconPubCkNews 84*
Dernbach Associates - Miller Place, NY - *DirPRFirms 83*
Deros [of Miriam Press Inc.] - Alexandria, VA - *LitMag&SmPr 83-84; WritMar 84*
Derrick - Drumright, OK - *AyerDirPub 83*
Derrick - Oil City, PA - *AyerDirPub 83; Ed&PubIntYB 82*
Derry-Decatur TV Cable Inc. - Derry, PA - *BrCabYB 84*
Derry-Decatur TV Line Inc. [of Cable Management Associates Inc.] - Lewistown, PA - *Tel&CabFB 84C*
Derry-Decatur TV Line Inc. - Mifflinburg, PA - *BrCabYB 84*

Derry Music Co. - San Francisco, CA - *BillIntBG 83-84*
Derry News [of Derry Publishing Co. Inc.] - Derry, NH - *AyerDirPub 83; BaconPubCkNews 84; Ed&PubIntYB 82; NewsDir 84*
Deru's Fine Art Books [Aff. of Petersen Galleries] - Bellflower, CA - *BoPubDir 4, 5*
Derus Media Service Inc. - Chicago, IL - *Ed&PubIntYB 82; LitMarPl 83, 84; MagIndMarPl 82-83*
DeRuyter, Carol L. - San Jose, CA - *MagIndMarPl 82-83*
Derviation & Tabulation Associates Inc. [Aff. of Cordura Corp.] - San Diego, CA - *BoPubDir 4*
Derwent Inc. - McLean, VA - *InfoS 83-84*
Derwent Publications Ltd. [Subs. of Thomson British Holdings Ltd.] - London, England - *CompReadDB 82; DataDirOnSer 84; InfIndMarPl 83; MicroMarPl 82-83*
Derwent-SDC Search Service - Reading, England - *EISS 83; InfIndMarPl 83*
Des Arc White River Journal - Des Arc, AR - *BaconPubCkNews 84*
Des Moines County News - West Burlington, IA - *AyerDirPub 83; Ed&PubIntYB 82*
Des Moines Daily Business Record [of Allstate Realty Co. Inc.] - Des Moines, IA - *NewsDir 84*
Des Moines Highland Park News [of West Des Moines Express] - Des Moines, IA - *BaconPubCkNews 84; NewsDir 84*
Des Moines Interviewing Service - Des Moines, IA - *IntDirMarRes 83*
Des Moines Lee Town News - Des Moines, IA - *BaconPubCkNews 84*
Des Moines New Iowa Bystander - Des Moines, IA - *BaconPubCkNews 84*
Des Moines News - Des Moines, WA - *Ed&PubIntYB 82*
Des Moines News [of Robinson Communications Co.] - Seattle, WA - *NewsDir 84*
Des Moines News - *See* Robinson Communications Co.
Des Moines Register - Des Moines, IA - *BaconPubCkNews 84; Ed&PubIntYB 82; LitMarPl 83, 84; NewsBur 6; NewsDir 84*
Des Moines Register & Tribune Co. - Des Moines, IA - *AdAge 6-28-84; KnowInd 83; Tel&CabFB 84S*
Des Moines Register & Tribune Co. - *See* Register Broadcast Group
Des Moines Register & Tribune Picture Magazine - Des Moines, IA - *MagIndMarPl 82-83*
Des Moines Sunday Register - Des Moines, IA - *Ed&PubIntYB 82; LitMarPl 84*
Des Moines Tribune - Des Moines, IA - *Ed&PubIntYB 82; NewsBur 6; NewsDir 84*
Des Plaines/East Maine Life [of Chicago Lerner Newspapers] - Chicago, IL - *NewsDir 84*
Des Plaines Family Journal - *See* Journal & Topics Newspapers
Des Plaines Golf Mill Highlander [of Pioneer Press Inc.] - Park Ridge, IL - *NewsDir 84*
Des Plaines Herald [of Paddock Publications] - Arlington Heights, IL - *NewsDir 84*
Des Plaines Herald - *See* Paddock Publications
Des Plaines Highlander - Park Ridge, IL - *Ed&PubIntYB 82*
Des Plaines Highlander - Wilmette, IL - *AyerDirPub 83*
Des Plaines Highlander - *See* Pioneer Press Inc.
Des Plaines Journal - Des Plaines, IL - *Ed&PubIntYB 82; NewsDir 84*
Des Plaines Journal - *See* Journal & Topics Newspapers
Des Plaines Life - *See* Myers Publishing Co.
Des Plaines Northwest Journal - *See* Journal & Topics Newspapers
Des Plaines Park Ridge Bugle - *See* Bugle Publications
Des Plaines Publishing Co. - Des Plaines, IL - *BaconPubCkNews 84; MagIndMarPl 82-83*
Des Plaines Suburban Journal - *See* Journal & Topics Newspapers
Des Plaines Suburban Times [of Des Plaines Publishing Co.] - Des Plaines, IL - *Ed&PubIntYB 82; NewsDir 84*
Des Plaines Times - *See* Des Plaines Publishing Co.
Des Plaines Valley News - Argo, IL - *AyerDirPub 83*
Des Plaines Valley News - Summit, IL - *Ed&PubIntYB 82*
DeSano, Philip R. - Providence, RI - *Tel&CabFB 84C p.1677*
Desarrollo Nacional [of Intercontinental Publications Inc.] - Westport, CT - *BaconPubCkMag 84; MagDir 84*
Desberg & Associates, Richard - Cleveland, OH - *StaDirAdAg 2-84*
Desbrow UK/USA Public Relations, Rosetta - New York, NY - *DirPRFirms 83*
Descant [of Texas Christian University Press] - Ft. Worth, TX - *LitMag&SmPr 83-84*
Descant - Toronto, ON, Canada - *LitMag&SmPr 83-84*
Deseret Book Co. [Aff. of The Church of Jesus Christ of Latter-Day Saints] - Salt Lake City, UT - *BoPubDir 4, 5; LitMarPl 84*
Deseret News - Salt Lake City, UT - *AyerDirPub 83; BaconPubCkNews 84; Ed&PubIntYB 82; LitMarPl 84; NewsBur 6*
Deserio Gallery - Mesa, AZ - *BoPubDir 4 Sup, 5*
Desert Advertiser - Indio, CA - *AyerDirPub 83*
Desert Airman [of Territorial Publishers Inc.] - Tucson, AZ - *AyerDirPub 83; NewsDir 84*
Desert Associated Newspapers - Indio, CA - *BaconPubCkNews 84*
Desert Community Newspapers Inc. - Palm Desert, CA - *AyerDirPub 83; NewsDir 84*
Desert Diamond Co. - Casa Grande, AZ - *BoPubDir 4, 5*
Desert Dispatch - Barstow, CA - *AyerDirPub 83; Ed&PubIntYB 82*
Desert Edge & Desert - Bloomington, CA - *NewsDir 84*
Desert First Works Inc. - Tucson, AZ - *BoPubDir 4, 5*
Desert Guest Pennysaver - Mission Viejo, CA - *AyerDirPub 83*
Desert Hot Springs Cablevision [of Daniels & Associates] - Desert Hot Springs, CA - *BrCabYB 84; Tel&CabFB 84C*
Desert Hot Springs Desert Sentinel, The - Desert Hot Springs, CA - *NewsDir 84*
Desert Magazine - Desert Hot Springs, CA - *MagDir 84*
Desert MDS Co. - Palm Desert, CA - *Tel&CabFB 84C*
Desert Morning Records - Quartz Hill, CA - *BillIntBG 83-84*
Desert News - Mojave, CA - *AyerDirPub 83*
Desert Post - Palm Desert, CA - *Ed&PubIntYB 82*
Desert Press - Bouse, AZ - *BoPubDir 4, 5*
Desert Rancher - Coachella, CA - *MagDir 84*
Desert Sentinel - Desert Hot Springs, CA - *AyerDirPub 83; BaconPubCkNews 84; Ed&PubIntYB 82*
Desert Star - Needles, CA - *AyerDirPub 83*
Desert Sun Publishing Co. - Palm Springs, CA - *LitMarPl 84*
Desert Sun, The - Palm Springs, CA - *AyerDirPub 83; Ed&PubIntYB 82; LitMarPl 83; NewsDir 84*
Desert Trail - Twentynine Palms, CA - *AyerDirPub 83; Ed&PubIntYB 82*
Desert Wings - Boron, CA - *AyerDirPub 83*
Deshler Flag - Deshler, OH - *Ed&PubIntYB 82*
Deshler Rustler - Deshler, NE - *BaconPubCkNews 84; Ed&PubIntYB 82*
DeShon, Robert - Kalamazoo, MI - *Tel&CabFB 84C p.1677*
Design Aid's Inc. - Laguna Niguel, CA - *MicrocomMPl 84*
Design Alliance Inc. - New York, NY - *HBIndAd&MS 82-83*
Design & Market Research Laboratory [Div. of Container Corp. of America] - Carol Stream, IL - *IntDirMarRes 83*
Design Automation Inc. - Lexington, MA - *WhoWMicrocom 83*
Design Conceptions/Elaine Abrams - New York, NY - *LitMarPl 83, 84*
Design Cost & Data - Glendora, CA - *BaconPubCkMag 84; MagDir 84*
Design Data Systems Corp. - Cedar Rapids, IA - *MicrocomMPl 84*
Design Element - Los Angeles, CA - *LitMarPl 83, 84; MagIndMarPl 82-83*
Design Engineering - New York, NY - *MagDir 84; MagIndMarPl 82-83*
Design Engineering - Toronto, ON, Canada - *BaconPubCkMag 84*
Design Enterprises of San Francisco - San Francisco, CA - *BoPubDir 4, 5; LitMag&SmPr 83-84; MicrocomMPl 84; WhoWMicrocom 83*
Design for Arts in Education [of Heldref Publications] - Washington, DC - *BaconPubCkMag 84; WritMar 84*
Design for Arts in Education - Indianapolis, IN - *MagDir 84*
Design for Profit [of Florafax International Inc.] - Tulsa, OK - *MagDir 84; WritMar 84*
Design for Selling Inc. - Brooklyn, NY - *StaDirAdAg 2-84*
Design Graphics World - Atlanta, GA - *BaconPubCkMag 84; MagDir 84*

Design Group, The - Greensboro, NC - *HBIndAd&MS 82-83*
Design House Review - Long Beach, CA - *BaconPubCkMag 84*
Design Image Group - New York, NY - *TeleSy&SerDir 7-83*
Design Institute for Physical Property Data [of American Institute of Chemical Engineers] - New York, NY - *EISS 83*
Design Magazine - Washington, DC - *BaconPubCkMag 84*
Design News [of Reed Holdings Inc.] - Boston, MA - *BaconPubCkMag 84; Folio 83; MagDir 84; MagIndMarPl 82-83*
Design Photographers International Inc. - New York, NY - *AvMarPl 83*
Design Planning Group Inc. - Chicago, IL - *HBIndAd&MS 82-83*
Design Product News - Milliken, ON, Canada - *BaconPubCkMag 84*
Design Professions Technical Specialty Index [of National Society of Professional Engineers] - Washington, DC - *EISS 83*
Design Solution Inc. - Fayetteville, AR - *MicrocomMPl 83*
Design Source, The - New York, NY - *LitMarPl 84*
Design Strategies - Jackson, NJ - *MicrocomMPl 84*
Design Systems Inc. - St. Louis, MO - *EISS 83; MicrocomSwDir 1*
Design Technology - San Diego, CA - *MicrocomMPl 84*
Design Trends Ltd. - Wilton, CT - *MicrocomMPl 84; MicrocomSwDir 1*
Designectics International Inc. - Waterloo, ON, Canada - *BoPubDir 4*
Designer Music - *See* Brentwood Publishing Group
Designer Software - Houston, TX - *MicrocomMPl 83; MicrocomSwDir 1*
Designer, The - New York, NY - *BaconPubCkMag 84; MagDir 84*
Designers & Builders of Information Systems - Eastchester, NY - *MicrocomMPl 84; WhoWMicrocom 83*
Designers Book Club - *See* Watson-Guptill Book Clubs
Designers Inc. - Chattanooga, TN - *StaDirAdAg 2-84*
Designers West - Los Angeles, CA - *BaconPubCkMag 84; MagDir 84*
Designetics International Inc. - Waterloo, ON, Canada - *BoPubDir 5*
Designfax - Cleveland, OH - *MagDir 84*
Designfax - Solon, OH - *BaconPubCkMag 84; MagIndMarPl 82-83*
DesignWare Inc. - San Francisco, CA - *AvMarPl 83; MicrocomMPl 84*
Designworks Inc. - Cambridge, MA - *LitMarPl 83, 84; MagIndMarPl 82-83*
Desktop Computer Software - Santa Clara, CA - *MicrocomMPl 84*
Desktop Computing [of Wayne Green Enterprises] - Peterborough, NH - *BaconPubCkMag 84; MicrocomMPl 84; WritMar 84*
DeskTop Software Corp. - Princeton, NJ - *MicrocomSwDir 1; WhoWMicrocom 83*
Desmar Music Inc. - New York, NY - *BillIntBG 83-84*
Desnet [of Destek Group] - Sunnyvale, CA - *TeleSy&SerDir 7-83*
DeSola, Fiore Inc. - New York, NY - *DirPRFirms 83*
DeSoto Shopping Guide - Arcadia, FL - *AyerDirPub 83*
Desporto - Toronto, ON, Canada - *Ed&PubIntYB 82*
Dessauer Inc., John P. - Vineyard Haven, MA - *LitMarPl 83*
Desserco Publishing - Culver City, CA - *BoPubDir 4, 5*
Dest Corp. - San Jose, CA - *DirInfWP 82*
Destek Group - Mountain View, CA - *DirInfWP 82*
Destek Group, The - Sunnyvale, CA - *DataDirSup 7-83; MicrocomMPl 84; WhoWMicrocom 83*
Destin Log - Destin, FL - *BaconPubCkNews 84*
Destination: Philadelphia - Philadelphia, PA - *BaconPubCkMag 84; MagDir 84*
Destinations - Washington, DC - *BaconPubCkMag 84*
Destiny Entertainment Corp. - Beverly Hills, CA - *BillIntBG 83-84*
Destiny Records - Wilmington, MA - *BillIntBG 83-84*
Destiny Records - Sheffield Lake, OH - *BillIntBG 83-84*
DeSutter Cable TV Inc. - Minneota, MN - *Tel&CabFB 84C p.1677*
Desy Scientific Documentation & Information Service [of German Electron-Synchrotron] - Hamburg, West Germany - *EISS 83*
Detective Book Club [Div. of Walter J. Black Inc.] - Roslyn, NY - *LitMarPl 83, 84*
Detective Cases [of Detective Files Group] - Montreal, PQ, Canada - *WritMar 84*
Detective Dragnet [of Detective Files Group] - Montreal, PQ, Canada - *WritMar 84*
Detective Files [of Detective Files Group] - Montreal, PQ, Canada - *WritMar 84*
Determined Productions Inc. - San Francisco, CA - *BoPubDir 4, 5*
Detherm-SDC - Frankfurt, West Germany - *DirOnDB Spring 84*
Detherm-SDR - Frankfurt, West Germany - *DirOnDB Spring 84*
Detjen Philatelic News Service - St. Augustine, FL - *Ed&PubIntYB 82*
Detroit Art Registration Information System [of Detroit Institute of Arts] - Detroit, MI - *EISS 7-83 Sup*
Detroit Building Tradesman - Detroit, MI - *NewsDir 84*
Detroit Business Journal - Detroit, MI - *BaconPubCkMag 84*
Detroit Courier - Detroit, MI - *Ed&PubIntYB 82*
Detroit/Ecorse Telegram - Detroit, MI - *Ed&PubIntYB 82*
Detroit Engineer [of The Engineering Society of Detroit] - Detroit, MI - *ArtMar 84; BaconPubCkMag 84; MagDir 84; WritMar 84*
Detroit Free Press [of Knight-Ridder Newspapers Inc.] - Detroit, MI - *BaconPubCkNews 84; Ed&PubIntYB 82; LitMarPl 83, 84; NewsBur 6; NewsDir 84*
Detroit Harper Woods Herald - *See* Harper Woods Herald
Detroit Institute of Arts - Detroit, MI - *BoPubDir 4, 5*
Detroit Labor News [of Metropolitan Detroit AFL-CIO] - Detroit, MI - *NewsDir 84*
Detroit Lakes Becker County Record [of Detroit Lakes Publishing Co. Inc.] - Detroit Lakes, MN - *BaconPubCkNews 84; NewsDir 84*
Detroit Lakes Tribune [of Detroit Lakes Publishing Co. Inc.] - Detroit Lakes, MN - *NewsDir 84*
Detroit Lawyer, The - Detroit, MI - *MagDir 84*
Detroit Legal News - Detroit, MI - *NewsDir 84*
Detroit Magazine [of The Detroit Free Press] - Detroit, MI - *MagIndMarPl 82-83; WritMar 84*
Detroit Marketing Services Inc. - Southfield, MI - *IntDirMarRes 83*
Detroit Medical Center Cooperative Services - Detroit, MI - *DirInfWP 82*
Detroit Medical News - Detroit, MI - *BaconPubCkMag 84; MagDir 84*
Detroit Michigan Chronicle - Detroit, MI - *BaconPubCkNews 84*
Detroit New Center News - *See* Monday Morning Newspapers
Detroit News [of Evening News Association] - Detroit, MI - *AyerDirPub 83; BaconPubCkNews 84; Ed&PubIntYB 82; LitMarPl 83, 84; NewsBur 6; NewsDir 84*
Detroit News - Detroit, TX - *BaconPubCkNews 84*
Detroit News Magazine - Detroit, MI - *MagIndMarPl 82-83*
Detroit Record - *See* Lakes Publishing Co. Inc.
Detroit Society for Genealogical Research Inc. - Detroit, MI - *BoPubDir 4, 5*
Detroit Suburban News, The - Detroit, MI - *NewsDir 84*
Detroit Tribune - *See* Lakes Publishing Co. Inc.
Detroiter Business News, The [of Greater Detroit Chamber of Commerce] - Detroit, MI - *NewsDir 84*
Detroiter, The [of Greater Detroit Chamber of Commerce] - Detroit, MI - *BaconPubCkMag 84; MagDir 84*
Detrow & Underwood - Ashland, OH - *AdAge 3-28-84; StaDirAdAg 2-84*
Detselig Enterprises Ltd. - Calgary, AB, Canada - *BoPubDir 4; LitMarPl 83, 84; WritMar 84*
Detwiler's Golden Rule Communications Inc. - New Enterprise, PA - *BrCabYB 84*
Detwiler's Golden Rule Communications Inc. - Woodbury, PA - *Tel&CabFB 84C*
Deuel Telephone Cooperative Association - Clear Lake, SD - *TelDir&BG 83-84*
Deulofeu-Wilson Advertising Inc. - Los Angeles, CA - *StaDirAdAg 2-84*
Deusing Film Productions, Murl - Clermont, FL - *AvMarPl 83*
Deutsch Associates, David - New York, NY - *AdAge 3-28-84; StaDirAdAg 2-84*
Deutsch Design, Laurence - Los Angeles, CA - *AvMarPl 83*
Deutsch Shea & Evans [Subs. of Foote, Cone & Belding Communications Inc.] - New York, NY - *HBIndAd&MS 82-83; StaDirAdAg 2-84*

Deutsche Bibliographie [of Deutsche Bibliothek] - Frankfurt, West Germany - *CompReadDB 82*
Deutsche Bibliothek - Frankfurt, West Germany - *CompReadDB 82; InfIndMarPl 83*
Deutsche Gesellschaft fuer Chemisches Apparatewesen - Frankfurt, West Germany - *CompReadDB 82*
Deutscher Bundestag - Bonn, West Germany - *CompReadDB 82*
Deutscher Bundestag (Abteilung Wissenschaftliche Dokumentation) - Bonn, West Germany - *InfIndMarPl 83*
Deutsches Elektronen-Synchrotron - Hamburg, West Germany - *CompReadDB 82; InfIndMarPl 83*
Deutsches Institut fuer Medizinische Dokumentation & Information - Cologne, West Germany - *InfIndMarPl 83*
Deutsches Institut fuer Normung eV/German Institute for Standardization - Berlin, West Germany - *InfIndMarPl 83*
Deutsches Institut fuer Urbanistik - Berlin, West Germany - *CompReadDB 82; InfIndMarPl 83*
Deutsches Krebsforschungszentrum/German Cancer Research Center [of Institut fuer Dokumentation, Information, und Statistik] - Heidelberg, West Germany - *InfIndMarPl 83*
Deutsches Kunstoff-Institut - Darmstadt, West Germany - *CompReadDB 82; InfIndMarPl 83*
Deutsches Musikgeschichtliches Archiv - Kassel, West Germany - *MicroMarPl 82-83*
Devaney Stock Photos - New York, NY - *LitMarPl 83, 84; MagIndMarPl 82-83*
Develcon Electronics Inc. - Doylestown, PA - *DataDirSup 7-83*
Develop Data Base [of Control Data Corp.] - Minneapolis, MN - *DirOnDB Spring 84; EISS 7-83 Sup*
Developing Countries Primary Source Data Bank [of Data Resources Inc.] - Lexington, MA - *DBBus 82*
Developing Country Courier, The - McLean, VA - *LitMag&SmPr 83-84*
Development Associates - Santa Ana, CA - *MicrocomMPl 84*
Development Counsellors International Ltd. - New York, NY - *DirPRFirms 83; HBIndAd&MS 82-83; StaDirAdAg 2-84*
Development Publications Ltd. - Willowdale, ON, Canada - *BoPubDir 4, 5*
Development Reading Distributors - Cape Coral, FL - *BoPubDir 5*
Development Reading Distributors - Laramie, WY - *BoPubDir 4*
Development Systems Corp. - Chicago, IL - *WritMar 84*
Developmental Arts - Arlington, MA - *LitMag&SmPr 83-84*
Developmental Learning Materials - Allen, TX - *MicrocomMPl 84*
Deven Lithographers Inc. - Brooklyn, NY - *LitMarPl 83, 84; MagIndMarPl 82-83*
Devida Publications - Owings Mills, MD - *BoPubDir 4 Sup, 5; LitMag&SmPr 83-84*
Devils Lake Cable TV [of Midcontinent Cable Systems Co.] - Devils Lake, ND - *BrCabYB 84*
Devils Lake Journal - Devils Lake, ND - *BaconPubCkNews 84; Ed&PubIntYB 82; NewsDir 84*
Devils Lake World, The - Ramsey County, ND - *Ed&PubIntYB 82*
Devil's Millhopper, The [of University of South Carolina] - Columbia, SC - *LitMag&SmPr 83-84; WritMar 84*
Devil's River News - Sonora, TX - *AyerDirPub 83; Ed&PubIntYB 82*
Devin-Adair Publishing Co. [Subs. of The Chatham Press] - Old Greenwich, CT - *LitMarPl 83, 84; WritMar 84*
Devine Medina Valley Times - Devine, TX - *BaconPubCkNews 84*
Devine News - Devine, TX - *AyerDirPub 83; BaconPubCkNews 84; Ed&PubIntYB 82*
Devlin & Associates - Stillwater, OK - *StaDirAdAg 2-84*
Devlin Associates Inc. - King of Prussia, PA - *DataDirSup 7-83*
Devlin Productions Inc. - New York, NY - *AvMarPl 83*
Devney Organization Inc., The - New York, NY - *TelAl 83, 84*
Devoke Co. - Palo Alto, CA - *DirInfWP 82*
Devoke Co. Inc. - Santa Clara, CA - *WhoWMicrocom 83*
Devon Music Inc. - *See* TRO
Devon Press Inc. - Berkeley, CA - *BoPubDir 4, 5*
Devon Publishing Co. Inc. - Washington, DC - *BoPubDir 5*
Devorss & Co. - Marina del Rey, CA - *BoPubDir 4, 5*
DeWan, Michael J. - NEw York, NY - *MagIndMarPl 82-83*
Dewar, L. George - O'Leary, PE, Canada - *BoPubDir 4, 5*
Dewey County Record - Selling, OK - *Ed&PubIntYB 82*
Dewey Herald-Record - Dewey, OK - *BaconPubCkNews 84*
Dewey Herald Report - Dewey, OK - *Ed&PubIntYB 82*
Dewey, Jennifer - Santa Fe, NM - *LitMarPl 84*
Dewhirst Corp. Pty. Ltd., The - Melbourne, Australia - *MicrocomSwDir 1*
DeWhit Music - Van Nuys, CA - *BillIntBG 83-84*
DeWitt/Bath Review, The - DeWitt/Bath, MI - *Ed&PubIntYB 82*
DeWitt Conklin Organizations Inc. - *See* Jones, Brakeley & Rockwell Inc.
Dewitt County View - Yorktown, TX - *Ed&PubIntYB 82*
DeWitt Observer - DeWitt, IA - *Ed&PubIntYB 82; NewsDir 84*
Dewitt Petrochemical Newsletters & Price Forecasts [of I. P. Sharp Associates Ltd.] - Toronto, ON, Canada - *DataDirOnSer 84; DirOnDB Spring 84*
Dewolfe & Fiske Inc. - Canton, MA - *LitMarPl 83*
Dexel Systems Corp. - Falls Church, VA - *ADAPSOMemDir 83-84; WhoWMicrocom 83*
Dexfield Review-Sentinel - Redfield, IA - *AyerDirPub 83; Ed&PubIntYB 82*
Dexter & Westbrook Ltd. [of Barnell Loft Ltd.] - Baldwin, NY - *LitMarPl 83, 84*
Dexter Daily Statesman - Dexter, MO - *BaconPubCkNews 84; NewsDir 84*
Dexter Gazette - Dexter, ME - *BaconPubCkNews 84*
Dexter Leader - Dexter, MI - *BaconPubCkNews 84; Ed&PubIntYB 82*
Dexter, Lincoln A. - Brookfield, MA - *BoPubDir 4, 5*
Dexter Productions Inc., Jerry - Beverly Hills, CA - *Tel&CabFB 84C*
Dexter Program Syndication, Jerry - Beverly Hills, CA - *Tel&CabFB 84C*
Dexter Stoddard County News - Dexter, MO - *BaconPubCkNews 84; NewsDir 84*
Deyell Co., John [Subs. of Consolidated Graphics Ltd.] - Lindsay, ON, Canada - *LitMarPl 83, 84*
DFK Advertising - New York, NY - *AdAge 3-28-84; StaDirAdAg 2-84*
DFM Associates - Irvine, CA - *BoPubDir 4, 5*
D.F.M. Operating [of Cardiff Cablevision Inc.] - Henryetta, OK - *BrCabYB 84*
D.G.A. Electronics Ltd. - Toronto, ON, Canada - *WhoWMicrocom 83*
DGJ Records Inc. - Miami, FL - *BillIntBG 83-84*
DGM Metallurgy Information [Aff. of Deutsche Gesellschaft fuer Metallkunde eV] - New York, NY - *BoPubDir 4, 5*
Dharma Press - Oakland, CA - *LitMarPl 83, 84*
Dharma Publishing - Berkeley, CA - *LitMag&SmPr 83-84; LitMarPl 83, 84; WritMar 84*
Dharma Records [Div. of Saturn Industries] - Libertyville, IL - *BillIntBG 83-84*
DHD Inc. - Falls Church, VA - *MicrocomMPl 84*
DHL Cable TV - Valliant, OK - *BrCabYB 84; Tel&CabFB 84C*
Di/An Controls Inc. - Boston, MA - *DataDirSup 7-83; DirInfWP 82; WhoWMicrocom 83*
Di Franza Williamson Inc. - New York, NY - *HBIndAd&MS 82-83*
Di Leo Photographics - Sacramento, CA - *AvMarPl 83*
Di-Tri Books - Madison, WI - *BoPubDir 4, 5*
Diabetes - New York, NY - *BaconPubCkMag 84; MagDir 84; MagIndMarPl 82-83*
Diabetes Care - New York, NY - *MagDir 84; MagIndMarPl 82-83*
Diabetes Educator, The - Pitman, NJ - *BaconPubCkMag 84*
Diabetes Forecast - New York, NY - *MagIndMarPl 82-83*
Diablo Record Co. - Youngstown, OH - *BillIntBG 83-84*
Diablo Systems Inc. - Fremont, CA - *MicrocomMPl 84*
Diablo Systems Inc. - Hayward, CA - *DataDirSup 7-83; DirInfWP 82*
Diablo Valley News - Oakley, CA - *AyerDirPub 83*
Diablo Western Press - Alamo, CA - *BoPubDir 4, 5*
Diack Newsletter - Benzonia, MI - *DirOnDB Spring 84*
Diagnosis - Oradell, NJ - *BaconPubCkMag 84*
Diagnostic Imaging - San Francisco, CA - *BaconPubCkMag 84; MagDir 84; MagIndMarPl 82-83; WritMar 84*
Diagnostic Medicine - Oradell, NJ - *BaconPubCkMag 84; MagDir 84*
Diagnostic Research Inc. - New York, NY - *IntDirMarRes 83*

Diagnostic Testing Laboratory Inc. - Mentor, OH - *WhoWMicrocom 83*
Diagonal Progress - Diagonal, IA - *BaconPubCkNews 84; Ed&PubIntYB 82*
Diagraph-Bradley Industries Inc. - Herrin, IL - *LitMarPl 83, 84*
Dial - Boscobel, WI - *AyerDirPub 83*
Dial-a-Poem Poets LP's [of Giorno Poetry Systems Records] - New York, NY - *LitMag&SmPr 83-84*
Dial-A-Secretary - New York, NY - *LitMarPl 83, 84*
Dial-A-Writer Referral Service [of American Society of Journalists & Authors Inc.] - New York, NY - *HBIndAd&MS 82-83; LitMarPl 83, 84*
Dial Books for Young Readers [Div. of E. P. Dutton Inc.] - New York, NY - *LitMarPl 83, 84*
Dial/Data [of Remote Computing] - Palo Alto, CA - *DataDirOnSer 84*
Dial-Out - New York, NY - *MicrocomMPl 84*
Dial Press, The - New York, NY - *LitMarPl 83; WritMar 84*
Dial, The - New York, NY - *BaconPubCkMag 84*
Dial-Tyme - Washington, DC - *DataDirOnSer 84*
Dialcom Inc. - Silver Spring, MD - *DataDirOnSer 84; EISS 83*
Dialcom International Inc. - Silver Spring, MD - *InfoS 83-84*
Dialindex [of Dialog Information Services Inc.] - Palo Alto, CA - *CompReadDB 82; DataDirOnSer 84*
Dialing for Dollars - Baltimore, MD - *Tel&CabFB 84C*
Dialog [of Dialog Information Services Inc.] - Palo Alto, CA - *MicrocomMPl 84*
Dialog Information Services Inc. [Subs. of Lockheed Corp.] - Palo Alto, CA - *DataDirOnSer 84; DataDirSup 7-83; EISS 83, 7-83 Sup, 5-84 Sup; InfIndMarPl 83; InfoS 83-84*
Dialog Publications [of Dialog Information Services Inc.] - Palo Alto, CA - *DataDirOnSer 84*
Dialog, The - Wilmington, DE - *Ed&PubIntYB 82*
Dialogue [of Dialogue Publications Inc.] - Berwyn, IL - *WritMar 84*
Dialogue House Library - New York, NY - *BoPubDir 4, 5*
Dialogue Press of Man & World - University Park, PA - *BoPubDir 4, 5*
Dialysis & Transplantation - North Hollywood, CA - *BaconPubCkMag 84; MagDir 84; MagIndMarPl 82-83*
Diamant, Anita [Subs. of The Writers Workshop Inc.] - New York, NY - *LitMarPl 83, 84*
Diamond Advertising Agency Inc. - Stratford, CT - *StaDirAdAg 2-84*
Diamond Agency Inc. - Tokyo, Japan - *StaDirAdAg 2-84*
Diamond Art Studio Ltd. - New York, NY - *LitMarPl 83, 84*
Diamond Artists Ltd. - Los Angeles, CA - *Tel&CabFB 84C*
Diamond Bar Bulletin - *See* Pomona Progress Bulletin
Diamond Bar Highlander - *See* Highlander Publications Inc.
Diamond Bar-Walnut-Rowland Heights Bulletin [of Ontario Bonita Publishing Co.] - Ontario, CA - *NewsDir 84*
Diamond Don Records - Poteau, OK - *BillIntBG 83-84*
Diamond Drill - Crystal Falls, MI - *AyerDirPub 83; Ed&PubIntYB 82*
Diamond Engineering Corp. - Redmond, WA - *DataDirSup 7-83*
Diamond Head Software - Honolulu, HI - *MicrocomMPl 84*
Diamond Heights Publishing Co. Inc. - San Francisco, CA - *BoPubDir 4, 5*
Diamond Lake Area Cable TV Co. [of Omega Communications Inc.] - Dowagiac, MI - *BrCabYB 84; Tel&CabFB 84C*
Diamond Market Research Inc., Ruth - Buffalo, NY - *IntDirMarRes 83*
Diamond, Nina S. - Ft. Lee, NJ - *Ed&PubIntYB 82*
Diamond Publishers [Aff. of Grandin Associates] - Diamond Bar, CA - *BoPubDir 4 Sup, 5*
Diamond Registry Bulletin, The - New York, NY - *WritMar 84*
Diamond Software Supply Inc. - Oakland, CA - *MicrocomMPl 84*
Diamond State Telephone Co., The - Wilmington, DE - *TelDir&BG 83-84*
Diamond System - New York, NY - *DirOnDB Spring 84*
Diamond Systems Inc. - Niles, IL - *MicrocomMPl 84*
Diamond Trail News - Sully, IA - *AyerDirPub 83; Ed&PubIntYB 82*
Diamondback, The [of Maryland Media Inc.] - College Park, MD - *NewsDir 84*
Diana's Almanac [of Diana's Press] - Providence, RI - *LitMag&SmPr 83-84*
Diana's Bimonthly Press - Providence, RI - *BoPubDir 4, 5*
Diana's Press - Providence, RI - *LitMag&SmPr 83-84*
Diane Guide - Abingdon, England - *DirOnDB Spring 84*
Diann Inc. - Scottsburg, IN - *BrCabYB 84*
Dianosis - Oradell, NJ - *MagIndMarPl 82-83*
Diapason, The - Des Plaines, IL - *BaconPubCkMag 84; MagDir 84*
Diario las Americas [of The Americas Publishing Co.] - Miami, FL - *AyerDirPub 83; Ed&PubIntYB 82; NewsDir 84*
Dibie-Dash Productions - Hollywood, CA - *AvMarPl 83*
Diboll Free Press - Diboll, TX - *BaconPubCkNews 84*
Dichter Associates International Ltd., Ernest - Peekskill, NY - *Tel&CabFB 84C*
Dichter Motivations Inc., Ernest - Peekskill, NY - *IntDirMarRes 83*
Dick & Bert - Hollywood, CA - *HBIndAd&MS 82-83*
Dick & Co., J. - Highland Park, IL - *BoPubDir 4, 5; EISS 83*
Dick Broadcasting Co. - Knoxville, TN - *BrCabYB 84*
Dick Co., A. B. [Subs. of General Electric Co.] - Chicago, IL - *AvMarPl 83; DataDirSup 7-83; DirInfWP 82*
Dickens Data Systems Inc. - Norcross, GA - *MicrocomMPl 84*
Dickens Data Systems Inc. - Tucker, GA - *MicrocomMPl 83*
Dickey Co. Inc., Donald G. - Mill Valley, CA - *MagIndMarPl 82-83*
Dickey County Leader - Ellendale, ND - *AyerDirPub 83; Ed&PubIntYB 82*
Dickey Rural Telephone Mutual Aid Corp. - Ellendale, ND - *TelDir&BG 83-84*
Dickeyville Telephone Corp. - Dickeyville, WI - *TelDir&BG 83-84*
Dickholtz, Gladys - Temple City, CA - *LitMarPl 83; MagIndMarPl 82-83*
Dickinson Books, Emily - Brentwood, MD - *BoPubDir 4, 5*
Dickinson Brothers - Grand Rapids, MI - *LitMarPl 83, 84*
Dickinson Communications Ltd. - Scottsdale, AZ - *Tel&CabFB 84C p.1677*
Dickinson Direct Response [Subs. of Dickinson Advertising Inc.] - Quincy, MA - *DirMarMP 83*
Dickinson Multi-Media Services Inc. - New York, NY - *LitMarPl 84*
Dickinson Newspaper Services Inc. - New York, NY - *Ed&PubIntYB 82*
Dickinson Pacific Cablesystems - Huntington Beach, CA - *BrCabYB 84; Tel&CabFB 84C*
Dickinson Pacific Cablesystems - Westminster, CA - *BrCabYB 84*
Dickinson Press - Dickinson, ND - *AyerDirPub 83; BaconPubCkNews 84; Ed&PubIntYB 82; NewsDir 84*
Dickinson Research Inc., Shoi Balaban - San Francisco, CA - *HBIndAd&MS 82-83*
Dickinson Research Inc., Shoi Balaban - Ft. Lauderdale, FL - *IntDirMarRes 83*
Dickinson Suburban Journal - Dickinson, TX - *BaconPubCkNews 84*
Dickinson, Terence - Odessa, ON, Canada - *Ed&PubIntYB 82*
Dickison & Rakaseder - Westport, CT - *AdAge 3-28-84; StaDirAdAg 2-84*
Dickison Rakaseder Mosconi Inc. - Westport, CT - *HBIndAd&MS 82-83*
Dickson/Associates - Washington, DC - *DirPRFirms 83*
Dickson-Bennett International Features Service [Div. of Wonders/Bennett/Dell Publications] - St. Joseph, MO - *Ed&PubIntYB 82; LitMarPl 84*
Dickson County Free Press - Dickson, TN - *Ed&PubIntYB 82*
Dickson County Herald - Dickson, TN - *AyerDirPub 83; Ed&PubIntYB 82*
Dickson Free Press - Dickson, TN - *BaconPubCkNews 84; NewsDir 84*
Dickson Herald - Dickson, TN - *BaconPubCkNews 84; NewsDir 84*
Dickson Publishing Co., John A. [Aff. of Processing & Books Inc.] - Melrose Park, IL - *BoPubDir 4, 5*
Dicom Industries Inc. - Sunnyvale, CA - *DataDirSup 7-83*
Dicomed Corp. - Minneapolis, MN - *AvMarPl 83; DataDirSup 7-83*
Dictaphone Corp. - Rye, NY - *DirInfWP 82*
Dictation Disc Co. - New York, NY - *AvMarPl 83*

Diction Books - St. Paul, MN - *BoPubDir 4 Sup, 5*
Dictionary of American Hymnology [of Hymn Society of America] - Springfield, OH - *EISS 83*
Dicul Publishing - Nashville, IN - *BoPubDir 4 Sup, 5*
Didactic Systems Inc. - Cranford, NJ - *BoPubDir 4, 5*
Didactics Corp. - Mansfield, OH - *AvMarPl 83*
Didday & Branch - Cincinnati, OH - *AdAge 3-28-84; StaDirAdAg 2-84*
Didier & Broderick Inc. - Northbrook, IL - *MagIndMarPl 82-83*
Didier Inc., Marcel - Montreal, PQ, Canada - *LitMarPl 83, 84*
Didik TV Productions - Rego Park, NY - *AvMarPl 83*
Didsbury Booster & Mountain View County News - Didsbury, AB, Canada - *Ed&PubIntYB 82*
Didsbury Pioneer & Mountain View County News - Didsbury, AB, Canada - *AyerDirPub 83*
Die Casting Engineer Bi-Monthly - Detroit, MI - *MagDir 84*
Die Casting Management - Des Plaines, IL - *BaconPubCkMag 84*
Die Gilde Werbeagentur GmbH - Hamburg, West Germany - *StaDirAdAg 2-84*
Die Mennonitische Post - Steinbach, MB, Canada - *Ed&PubIntYB 82*
Die Welt Post und Der Staats-Anzeiger - Omaha, NE - *Ed&PubIntYB 82*
Die Zeit - Toronto, ON, Canada - *Ed&PubIntYB 82*
Diebold Group Inc. - New York, NY - *InfIndMarPl 83*
Diebold Inc. - Canton, OH - *DataDirSup 7-83; Datamation 6-83*
Diederichs & Associates Inc., Janet - Chicago, IL - *DirPRFirms 83*
Diegnan & Associates - Oldwick, NJ - *ArtMar 84*
Diegnan & Associates, Norman - Lebanon, NJ - *DirPRFirms 83*
Diehl, Kathryn - Lima, OH - *BoPubDir 4, 5*
Diehl Placement Bureau Inc., Mary - New York, NY - *InfIndMarPl 83; LitMarPl 83, 84; MagIndMarPl 82-83*
Diemer, Smith Publishing Co. - Napa, CA - *BoPubDir 5*
Diener & Associates Inc. - Research Triangle Park, NC - *IntDirMarRes 83; StaDirAdAg 2-84*
Diener/Hauser/Bates Co. Inc. - Los Angeles, CA - *TelAl 83, 84*
Diener/Hauser/Bates Co. Inc. - Ft. Lauderdale, FL - *TelAl 83*
Diener/Hauser/Bates Co. Inc. [of Ted Bates] - New York, NY - *AdAge 3-28-84; StaDirAdAg 2-84*
Dierkes, William H. - Eureka Springs, AR - *LitMarPl 83, 84*
Dierks TV Cable Co. - Dierks, AR - *BrCabYB 84; Tel&CabFB 84C*
Diesel - Guelph, ON, Canada - *BaconPubCkMag 84*
Diesel & Gas Turbine Progress - Milwaukee, WI - *MagDir 84*
Diesel & Gas Turbine Worldwide - Brookfield, WI - *BaconPubCkMag 84*
Diesel Equipment Superintendent - Norwalk, CT - *BaconPubCkMag 84; MagDir 84*
Diesel Motorist - Ft. Lee, NJ - *BaconPubCkMag 84*
Diesel Progress/Diesel & Gas Turbine Worldwide - Brookfield, WI - *WritMar 84*
Diesel Progress North American - Brookfield, WI - *BaconPubCkMag 84; MagIndMarPl 82-83*
Diet & Nutrition Book Club [of Prentice-Hall Inc.] - Englewood, NJ - *LitMarPl 83, 84*
Dietary Research - Seattle, WA - *BoPubDir 4, 5*
Dieter Kaetel Microsystems - Mercer Island, WA - *MicrocomMPl 83*
Dietz Enterprises Inc., Herb - North Miami, FL - *ArtMar 84*
Dietz Press Inc., The - Richmond, VA - *MagIndMarPl 82-83*
Difficulties, The [of Viscerally Press] - Kent, OH - *LitMag&SmPr 83-84*
Diffusion in Metals & Alloys Data Center [of U.S. National Bureau of Standards] - Washington, DC - *EISS 83; InfIndMarPl 83*
Digby Cable TV [of Dartmouth Cable TV Ltd.] - Dartmouth, NS, Canada - *BrCabYB 84*
Digby Mirror, The - Yarmouth, NS, Canada - *AyerDirPub 83*
Digest - Hallandale, FL - *AyerDirPub 83*
Digest for Home Furnishers [of Minnesota '300'] - Minneapolis, MN - *BaconPubCkMag 84; MagDir 84*
Digest of Chiropractic Economics, The - Livonia, MI - *BaconPubCkMag 84*
Digest of Emergency Medical Care - Van Nuys, CA - *BaconPubCkMag 84*
Digestive Diseases & Sciences - New York, NY - *MagDir 84*
Digestive Diseases & Sciences - Philadelphia, PA - *BaconPubCkMag 84*
Digests of Environmental Impact Statements [of Bibliographic Retrieval Services Inc.] - Lathan, NY - *DataDirOnSer 84*
Digger Magazine [of Underground Contractors Association] - San Jose, CA - *MagDir 84*
Digger, The - Milwaukee, OR - *BaconPubCkMag 84*
Dighton Cable Communications Inc. - Dighton, KS - *BrCabYB 84*
Dighton Herald - Dighton, KS - *BaconPubCkNews 84; Ed&PubIntYB 82*
Digi-Data Corp. - Jessup, MD - *DataDirSup 7-83*
Digiac Corp. - Hauppauge, NY - *MicrocomMPl 83*
Digicom Data Products Inc. - San Jose, CA - *DirInfWP 82*
Digicomp Research Corp. - Ithaca, NY - *MicrocomMPl 83, 84; WhoWMicrocom 83*
Digidat Systems Inc. - Elmsford, NY - *DataDirOnSer 84*
Digilog Business Systems - Montgomeryville, PA - *DataDirSup 7-83; InfIndMarPl 83; MicrocomMPl 83; WhoWMicrocom 83*
Digisoft Computers Inc. - New York, NY - *MicrocomMPl 84*
Digit - San Francisco, CA - *MicrocomMPl 84*
Digitab Computing Inc. - Roslyn Heights, NY - *IntDirMarRes 83*
Digital Associates Corp. - Stamford, CT - *DataDirSup 7-83*
Digital Business Systems - Reading, MA - *MicrocomMPl 83, 84*
Digital Communications Associates Inc. - Norcross, GA - *DataDirSup 7-83; TeleSy&SerDir 7-83; WhoWMicrocom 83*
Digital Constructs - Norrestown, PA - *MicrocomMPl 83*
Digital Design [of Morgan Grampian Publication Co.] - Boston, MA - *BaconPubCkMag 84; MagDir 84; MicrocomMPl 84; WritMar 84*
Digital Development Corp. - San Diego, CA - *DataDirSup 7-83*
Digital Digest - Norcross, GA - *DirOnDB Spring 84*
Digital Equipment Corp. - Maynard, MA - *DataDirSup 7-83; Datamation 6-83; DirInfWP 82; ElecNews 7-25-83; InfIndMarPl 83; MicrocomMPl 83; VideoDir 82-83; WhoWMicrocom 83*
Digital Equipment Corp. - Weston, MA - *Top100Al 83*
Digital Equipment Corp. - *See* Digital Press/Digital Equipment Corp.
Digital Forms Inc. - Chicago, IL - *MicrocomMPl 84*
Digital Graphic Systems - Palo Alto, CA - *DataDirSup 7-83; MicrocomMPl 83; WhoWMicrocom 83*
Digital Learning Systems Inc. - Denville, NJ - *MicrocomMPl 84*
Digital Mapping System [of Topographical Survey] - Ottawa, ON, Canada - *EISS 83*
Digital Marketing Corp. - Walnut Creek, CA - *EISS 5-84 Sup; MicrocomMPl 83, 84; MicrocomSwDir 1; WritMar 84*
Digital Microsystems [Subs. of Extel Group Ltd.] - Oakland, CA - *DataDirSup 7-83; WhoWMicrocom 83*
Digital Paging Systems Inc. - Englewood, NJ - *Tel&CabFB 84C*
Digital Press/Digital Equipment Corp. - Bedford, MA - *LitMarPl 83, 84*
Digital Publications Inc. - Norcross, GA - *EISS 83*
Digital Research - Pacific Grove, CA - *ADAPSOMemDir 83-84; MicrocomMPl 83, 84; MicrocomSwDir 1; WhoWMicrocom 83*
Digital Retailing [of Dealerscope Inc.] - Waltham, MA - *BaconPubCkMag 84; MicrocomMPl 84*
Digital Review - Burlington, MA - *BaconPubCkMag 84*
Digital Software Inc. - North Saint Paul, MN - *MicrocomMPl 84*
Digital Solutions Inc. - Edison, NJ - *DataDirOnSer 84*
Digital Switch Corp. - Richardson, TX - *DataDirSup 7-83*
Digital Systems Corp. - Walkersville, MD - *DataDirSup 7-83; MicrocomSwDir 1*
Digital Systems Inc. - Hackensack, NJ - *MicrocomMPl 83*
Digital Technology Inc. - San Diego, CA - *WhoWMicrocom 83*
Digital Technology International [Subs. of Oldham Associates Inc.] - Provo, UT - *WhoWMicrocom 83*
Digital Video Corp. - New York, NY - *InterCabHB 3; VideoDir 82-83*
Digital Video Systems Corp. [Subs. of Scientific Atlanta Inc.] - Toronto, ON, Canada - *AvMarPl 83*
Digital Visions Inc. - New York, NY - *DataDirSup 7-83*
Digitan Systems Inc. - Brooklyn, NY - *MicrocomSwDir 1; WhoWMicrocom 83*
Digitech - Newton, NJ - *MicrocomMPl 84*
Digitech Industries Inc. - Ridgefield, CT - *DataDirSup 7-83*

Digitex [Div. of Inter-Care Systems Inc.] - Los Angeles, CA - *MicrocomMPl 84*
Digitus Corp. - Baltimore, MD - *WhoWMicrocom 83*
Digitype [Div. of Ecotran Corp.] - Beachwood, OH - *EISS 83; LitMarPl 83, 84*
Diglac Corp. - Hauppauge, NY - *MicrocomMPl 84*
Digney Public Relations, Girard M. - Los Angeles, CA *DirPRFirms 83*
Dignity Inc. - Washington, DC - *BoPubDir 4 Sup, 5*
Diiorio, Wergeles Inc. - New York, NY - *StaDirAdAg 2-84*
Dijkstra Literary Agency, Sandra - Del Mar, CA - *LitMarPl 83, 84*
Dikeman Laminating - Clifton, NJ - *LitMarPl 83, 84*
Dilithium Press - Beaverton, OR - *ArtMar 84; LitMarPl 83, 84; MicrocomMPl 83, 84; WritMar 84*
Diliton Publications Inc. - Mesquite, TX - *BoPubDir 4, 5*
Dill City Cable Co. - Dill City, OK - *BrCabYB 84; Tel&CabFB 84C*
Dill City Cable Co., The - Roosevelt, OK - *BrCabYB 84*
Dill Publishing [Aff. of Dill Enterprises] - Lincoln, NE - *BoPubDir 4, 5*
Dillard Music - *See* Gopam Enterprises Inc.
Dillard Paper Co. - Greensboro, NC - *DirInfWP 82*
Diller Telephone - Diller, NE - *TelDir&BG 83-84*
Dilley Cable TV - Dilley, TX - *BrCabYB 84; Tel&CabFB 84C*
Dilley Herald - Dilley, TX - *Ed&PubIntYB 82*
Dilley Herald - *See* Frio-Nueces Publications Ltd.
Dillon Book Co. Inc. [Subs. of Harold Dillon Inc.] - Boulder, CO - *BoPubDir 4 Sup, 5; LitMarPl 83, 84*
Dillon Cable TV [of Tele-Communications Inc.] - Dillon, MT - *BrCabYB 84; Tel&CabFB 84C*
Dillon Herald - Dillon, SC - *BaconPubCkNews 84; Ed&PubIntYB 82; NewsDir 84*
Dillon/Liederbach Inc. - Winston-Salem, NC - *BoPubDir 4, 5*
Dillon Press Inc. - Minneapolis, MN - *LitMarPl 83, 84; WritMar 84*
Dillon Printing Corp. - New York, NY - *LitMarPl 83, 84*
Dillon, R. K. - New York, NY - *AvMarPl 83*
Dillon Summit County Sentinel - Dillon, CO - *BaconPubCkNews 84; NewsDir 84*
Dillon Tribune-Examiner - Dillon, MT - *BaconPubCkNews 84; Ed&PubIntYB 82*
Dillon-Tyler Publishers - Napa, CA - *BoPubDir 4, 5*
Dillsburg Bulletin - Dillsburg, PA - *BaconPubCkNews 84*
Dillsburg Cable TV Co. [of GS Communications Inc.] - Dillsburg, PA - *BrCabYB 84*
Dillsburg Community News - Dillsburg, PA - *Ed&PubIntYB 82*
Dillsburg Weekly Bulletin, The [of Fry Communications] - Dillsburg, PA - *NewsDir 84*
Dilly International Productions - Cincinnati, OH - *WritMar 84*
Dilson, Jesse - New York, NY - *LitMarPl 83, 84; MagIndMarPl 82-83*
Dilworth, Jacqueline V. - Sarasota, FL - *LitMarPl 83; MagIndMarPl 82-83*
Dimco-Gray - Centerville, OH - *AvMarPl 83*
DIMDINET - Cologne, West Germany - *InfIndMarPl 83*
Dimension - Austin, TX - *LitMag&SmPr 83-84*
Dimension Books Inc. - Denville, NJ - *ArtMar 84; LitMarPl 83, 84; WritMar 84*
Dimension Cable Services [of Times Mirror Cable TV] - Haverhill, MA - *Tel&CabFB 84C*
Dimension Films - Los Angeles, CA - *AvMarPl 83*
Dimension Music - *See* Paragon/Benson Publishing Group
Dimension Records - Nashville, TN - *BillIntBG 83-84*
Dimensional Business Systems Inc. - Boca Raton, FL - *WhoWMicrocom 83*
Dimensional Marketing Inc. - Chicago, IL - *StaDirAdAg 2-84*
Dimensionist Press - Highland, CA - *ArtMar 84; BoPubDir 4, 5*
Dimensions & Directions Ltd. - New York, NY - *LitMarPl 83, 84*
Dimensions in Health Service - Ottawa, ON, Canada - *BaconPubCkMag 84; WritMar 84*
Dime's Group Inc. - Mountain View, CA - *BoPubDir 4, 5*
DIMIS Inc. - Ocean, NJ - *DataDirSup 7-83*
Dimitri Music Co. - Severn, MD - *BillIntBG 83-84*
Dimmitt TV Cable Co. [of CATV Inc.] - Dimmitt, TX - *Tel&CabFB 84C*
Dimon & Associates - Burbank, CA - *StaDirAdAg 2-84*
Dimond Publishing [Aff. of Dimond Printers] - Oakland, CA - *BoPubDir 4, 5*
Dimondstein Book Express [Div. of Brodart Inc.] - Williamsport, PA - *LitMarPl 83, 84*
D.I.N. Newservice - Phoenix, AZ - *WritMar 84*
D.I.N. Publications [Aff. of Do It Now Foundation] - Phoenix, AZ - *BoPubDir 4, 5; LitMag&SmPr 83-84*
Dinah - Cincinnati, OH - *LitMag&SmPr 83-84*
Diner Films Inc., Leo - San Francisco, CA - *AvMarPl 83; Tel&CabFB 84C*
Dines Letter - Belvedere, CA - *BaconPubCkMag 84*
Dini Advertising - San Francisco, CA - *AdAge 3-28-84; StaDirAdAg 2-84*
Dinkel & Associates Inc., R. A. - Lansing, MI - *StaDirAdAg 2-84*
Dinkins Online Newsletters, Lloyd - Memphis, TN - *EISS 5-84 Sup*
Dinoff Associates Inc., Lester - Yonkers, NY - *ArtMar 84; DirPRFirms 83*
Dinosaur Cable Television Inc. - Glen Rose, TX - *BrCabYB 84; Tel&CabFB 84C*
Dinuba Sentinel - Dinuba, CA - *BaconPubCkNews 84; Ed&PubIntYB 82*
Diode Cable Co. [of Diller Telephone Co.] - Diller, NE - *Tel&CabFB 84C*
Dion Family - *See* Transvision Disraeli Inc.
Diotima Books - Glen Carbon, IL - *BoPubDir 4, 5*
Dip Inc. - Boston, MA - *DirInfWP 82*
DiPaul, H. Bert - Warminster, PA - *BoPubDir 4, 5*
Diplomacy World [of Pandemonium Press] - Encinitas, CA - *LitMag&SmPr 83-84*
Diplomat Music - *See* Shayne Enterprises, Larry
Diplomatic Press Inc. - Bloomington, IN - *BoPubDir 4, 5*
Direct [of Direct Magazine Partners] - New York, NY - *BaconPubCkMag 84; DirMarMP 83; WritMar 84*
Direct [of Philips Information Systems & Automation] - Eindhoven, Netherlands - *EISS 83*
Direct Access Data Bank [of The University of Quebec] - Ste-Foy, PQ, Canada - *EISS 83*
Direct Access to Remote Data Bases Overseas [of ItalCable] - Rome, Italy - *EISS 5-84 Sup; TeleSy&SerDir 2-84*
Direct-Aid - Boulder, CO - *MicrocomMPl 84*
Direct Broadcast Programs Inc. - Studio City, CA - *Tel&CabFB 84C*
Direct Broadcast Satellite Corp. - Bethesda, MD - *BrCabYB 84; HomeVid&CabYB 82-83*
Direct Broadcast Satellite Service [of Graphic Scanning Corp.] - Teaneck, NJ - *TeleSy&SerDir 2-84*
Direct Channels Inc. [of Times Mirror Cable Television Inc.] - Defiance, OH - *BrCabYB 84*
Direct Channels Inc. [of Times Mirror Cable Television Inc.] - Wauseon, OH - *BrCabYB 84*
Direct Channels of New Bethlehem [of Omega Communications Inc.] - New Bethlehem, PA - *BrCabYB 84*
Direct Cinema Ltd. Inc. - Los Angeles, CA - *AvMarPl 83*
Direct Connection - Honolulu, HI - *DirOnDB Spring 84*
Direct Connection [of CompuServe Inc.] - Columbus, OH - *DataDirOnSer 84*
Direct Disk Laboratories - Newport, TN - *BillIntBG 83-84*
Direct Inc. - Santa Clara, CA - *DataDirSup 7-83*
Direct Inc. - Sunnyvale, CA - *WhoWMicrocom 83*
Direct Information Access Network for Europe [of Commission of the European Communities] - Kirchberg, Luxembourg - *EISS 83; TeleSy&SerDir 7-83*
Direct Mail Lists Rates & Data [of Standard Rate & Data Service] - Skokie, IL - *MagIndMarPl 82-83*
Direct Mail Promotions Inc. - New York, NY - *LitMarPl 83, 84*
Direct Mail Promotions Inc. (Co-Operative Mailing Div.) - New York, NY - *LitMarPl 83, 84*
Direct Mail Specialist Inc. [Subs. of National American Corp.] - Gautier, MS - *DirMarMP 83*
Direct Marketing [of Hoke Communications Inc.] - Garden City, NY - *BaconPubCkMag 84; MagDir 84; MagIndMarPl 82-83*
Direct Marketing Agency - Stamford, CT - *AdAge 3-28-84; DirMarMP 83; HBIndAd&MS 82-83; StaDirAdAg 2-84*
Direct Marketing Concepts - Framingham, MA - *DirMarMP 83*
Direct Marketing Group - San Jose, CA - *BillIntBG 83-84*

Direct Marketing Group Inc., The - New York, NY - *DirMarMP 83; StaDirAdAg 2-84*
Direct Merchandising Services Inc. - Mt. Prospect, IL - *DataDirOnSer 84*
Direct Promotions Inc. - Irvine, CA - *DirMarMP 83*
Direct Response - Rolling Hills, CA - *DirMarMP 83*
Direct Response Broadcasting Network Inc. - Philadelphia, PA - *BrCabYB 84; DirMarMP 83; StaDirAdAg 2-84*
Direct Response Creative [of McKinney Marketing Group Inc.] - New York, NY - *DirMarMP 83*
Direct Response Group Inc. - Dallas, TX - *StaDirAdAg 2-84*
Direct Response Inc. - Minneapolis, MN - *DirMarMP 83*
Direct Response Marketing Inc. - Omaha, NE - *DirMarMP 83*
Direct Response Services Corp. [Subs. of Wausau Insurance Cos.] - St. Louis, MO - *DirMarMP 83*
Direct Response Services Inc. - Clearwater, FL - *DirMarMP 83*
Direction [of National Furniture Warehousemen's Association] - Chicago, IL - *MagDir 84*
Direction - Alexandria, VA - *BaconPubCkMag 84*
Direction de la Documentation Francaise - Paris, France - *CompReadDB 82*
Direction de la Documentation Francaise - *See* La Documentation Francaise
Direction GA - Pittsburgh, PA - *BillIntBG 83-84*
Direction of Trade [of International Monetary Fund] - Washington, DC - *DataDirOnSer 84*
Direction of Trade Data Bank - Washington, DC - *DirOnDB Spring 84*
Directions for Decisions Inc. - New York, NY - *IntDirMarRes 83*
Directions Inc. - Richardson, TX - *DataDirSup 7-83*
Director, The [of NFDA Publications] - Milwaukee, WI - *MagDir 84*
Directorate for Information & Documentation [of National Commission for Scientific & Technological Research] - Santiago, Chile - *EISS 83*
Directories International - Evanston, IL - *BoPubDir 4, 5*
Directories Publishing Co. Inc. - Ormond Beach, FL - *BoPubDir 4, 5*
Directors Guild of America - New York, NY - *AvMarPl 83*
Directory & Locator Data Base [of Solar Energy Research Institute] - Golden, CO - *CompReadDB 82*
Directory Enterprises - New York, NY - *BoPubDir 5*
Directory Marketing Inc. - Chicago, IL - *StaDirAdAg 2-84*
Directory of Companies [of Pergamon International Information Corp.] - McLean, VA - *DataDirOnSer 84*
Directory of Companies - London, England - *DirOnDB Spring 84*
Directory of Directors Co. Inc. - Southport, CT - *BoPubDir 4, 5*
Directory of Federally Supported Research in Universities [of Canada Institute for Scientific & Technical Information] - Ottawa, ON, Canada - *DataDirOnSer 84*
Directory of Incentive Travel International - Encino, CA - *MagDir 84*
Directory of Northern Art Galleries & Studios - Ashington, England - *LitMag&SmPr 83-84*
Directory of Symbols [of Dow Jones News/Retrieval Service] - Princeton, NJ - *DataDirOnSer 84*
Directory of Washington Creative Services - Washington, DC - *BoPubDir 5*
Directory Service Bureau Ltd. - Deerfield, IL - *StaDirAdAg 2-84*
Directory Specialists Inc. - Danville, IL - *StaDirAdAg 2-84*
DIRLine [of National Library of Medicine] - Bethesda, MD - *DataDirOnSer 84*
Dirt Bike - Encino, CA - *MagIndMarPl 82-83*
Dirt Bike - Mission Hills, CA - *BaconPubCkMag 84*
Dirt Bike - San Fernando, CA - *MagDir 84*
Dirt Rider - Los Angeles, CA - *BaconPubCkMag 84*
Dirva - Cleveland, OH - *Ed&PubIntYB 82; NewsDir 84*
Disabled Programmers Inc. - Campbell, CA - *ADAPSOMemDir 83-84*
Disc - Latham, NY - *DirOnDB Spring 84*
Disc Inc. - Baltimore, MD - *DataDirSup 7-83*
DISC Information System [of Drilling Information Service Co.] - Houston, TX - *TeleSy&SerDir 2-84*
Disc Tech One Inc. - Santa Barbara, CA - *WhoWMicrocom 83*
Disciple, The [of Christian Board of Publication] - St. Louis, MO - *ArtMar 84; MagDir 84; MagIndMarPl 82-83; WritMar 84*
Disciplined Order of Christ - Ashland, OH - *BoPubDir 4, 5*
Disclosure Inc. - Washington, DC - *CompReadDB 82; LitMarPl 83*
Disclosure Inc. - Bethesda, MD - *DataDirOnSer 84; EISS 83; InfIndMarPl 83; InfoS 83-84; MicroMarPl 82-83*
Disclosure Online [of Disclosure Inc.] - Washington, DC - *CompReadDB 82*
Disclosure Record [of Newsfeatures Inc.] - Floral Park, NY - *MagDir 84; ProGuPRSer 4*
Disclosure/Spectrum Ownership Data Base [of Disclosure Inc.] - Bethesda, MD - *DataDirOnSer 84; DirOnDB Spring 84; EISS 5-84 Sup*
Disclosure II [of Disclosure Inc.] - Bethesda, MD - *DataDirOnSer 84; DBBus 82; DirOnDB Spring 84*
Disco-Tech Microcomputer Products [Div. of Morton Technologies] - Santa Rosa, CA - *MicrocomMPl 83, 84; MicrocomSwDir 1; WhoWMicrocom 83*
Discocorp - Kensington, CA - *BillIntBG 83-84*
Discolando Records & Tapes Corp. - Union City, NJ - *BillIntBG 83-84*
Discos Latin International Inc. - Los Angeles, CA - *BillIntBG 83-84*
Discount America Guide - New York, NY - *LitMag&SmPr 83-84*
Discount America Publications - New York, NY - *BoPubDir 5*
Discount Corp. of New York Database - New York, NY - *DirOnDB Spring 84; InfIndMarPl 83*
Discount Corp. of New York Database [of CompuServe Inc.] - Columbus, OH - *DataDirOnSer 84*
Discount Long Distance - New Orleans, LA - *TeleSy&SerDir 2-84*
Discount Merchandiser, The [of Chartcom Inc.] - New York, NY - *BaconPubCkMag 84; MagDir 84; MagIndMarPl 82-83*
Discount Software Group - Culver City, CA - *MicrocomMPl 84*
Discount Software Group - Los Angeles, CA - *MicrocomMPl 83*
Discount Store News - New York, NY - *BaconPubCkMag 84*
Discount Video Tapes Inc. - Burbank, CA - *BillIntBG 83-84*
Discover [of Time Inc.] - New York, NY - *BaconPubCkMag 84; Folio 83; LitMarPl 84; MagIndMarPl 82-83*
Discover Hawaii - Honolulu, HI - *BaconPubCkMag 84*
Discover-San Jose to San Mateo - Palo Alto, CA - *BaconPubCkMag 84*
Discover Syndication - New York, NY - *MagIndMarPl 82-83*
Disco'ver the WATS Room - Englewood Cliffs, NJ - *IntDirMarRes 83*
Discoveries - Kansas City, MO - *ArtMar 84; WritMar 84*
Discoveries Publishing Co. [Aff. of Discoveries Inc.] - Glastonbury, CT - *BoPubDir 4, 5*
Discovering Books Paperback Book Club [of Xerox Education Publications] - Middletown, CT - *LitMarPl 83, 84*
Discovery - Chicago, IL - *MagIndMarPl 82-83*
Discovery - Northbrook, IL - *MagDir 84; WritMar 84*
Discovery Cable TV - Discovery, MD - *BrCabYB 84*
Discovery Games - St. Paul, MN - *MicrocomMPl 83, 84*
Discovery Productions - New York, NY - *ArtMar 84; Tel&CabFB 84C*
Discovery Software International - Colorado Springs, CO - *MicrocomSwDir 1*
Disctron Inc. - Milpitas, CA - *MicrocomMPl 84*
Diseases of the Colon & Rectum - Philadelphia, PA - *MagDir 84*
Disk Depot - Colorado Springs, CO - *MicrocomSwDir 1*
Disk Memory Technology Inc. - Lake Oswego, OR - *MicrocomMPl 84*
Disk Memory Technology Inc. - Portland, OR - *WhoWMicrocom 83*
Diskazine/Apple II [of Diskazine Publications] - Columbus, IN - *MicrocomMPl 84*
DiskCount Data - Plano, TX - *MicrocomMPl 84*
Disking International - Liphook, England - *MicrocomSwDir 1*
Dismantlers Digest [of Automotive Dismantlers & Recyclers Association] - Washington, DC - *BaconPubCkMag 84; MagDir 84*
Disney Channel, The [of Walt Disney Productions] - Burbank, CA - *CabTVPrDB 83; Tel&CabFB 84C*
Disney Channel, The [of Walt Disney Productions] - New York, NY - *BrCabYB 84; HomeVid&CabYB 82-83*
Disney Educational Media Co., Walt [Div. of Walt Disney Telecommunications] - Burbank, CA - *AvMarPl 83*
Disney Music Co., Walt - Burbank, CA - *BillIntBG 83-84*

Disney Productions, Walt - Burbank, CA - *HomeVid&CabYB 82-83; KnowInd 83; LitMarPl 83; MicrocomMPl 84; TelAl 83, 84; Tel&CabFB 84C; WritMar 84*
Disney Telecommunications & Non-Theatrical Co. [Subs. of Walt Disney Productions] - Burbank, CA - *Tel&CabFB 84C*
Disney Training & Development Programs, Walt - Burbank, CA - *AvMarPl 83*
Disneyland/Vista Records - Burbank, CA - *BillIntBG 83-84*
Disney's Wonderful World of Reading [of Grolier Enterprises Inc.] - Danbury, CT - *LitMarPl 83, 84*
Dispatch - Douglas, AZ - *AyerDirPub 83*
Dispatch [of El Dorado Newspapers Inc.] - Gilroy, CA - *AyerDirPub 83; Ed&PubIntYB 82; NewsDir 84*
Dispatch - Cordele, GA - *AyerDirPub 83*
Dispatch - Moline, IL - *AyerDirPub 83*
Dispatch - Ringsted, IA - *AyerDirPub 83*
Dispatch - Clay Center, KS - *AyerDirPub 83*
Dispatch - Delhi, LA - *AyerDirPub 83*
Dispatch - Brainerd, MN - *AyerDirPub 83*
Dispatch - Dassel, MN - *AyerDirPub 83*
Dispatch [of Northwest Publications Inc.] - St. Paul, MN - *AyerDirPub 83; NewsDir 84*
Dispatch - New Providence, NJ - *AyerDirPub 83; Ed&PubIntYB 82*
Dispatch - Oneida, NY - *AyerDirPub 83*
Dispatch - Henderson, NC - *AyerDirPub 83*
Dispatch - Lexington, NC - *AyerDirPub 83; BaconPubCkNews 84; Ed&PubIntYB 82*
Dispatch - Columbus, OH - *AyerDirPub 83*
Dispatch - Catasauqua, PA - *AyerDirPub 83*
Dispatch - Pittston, PA - *AyerDirPub 83*
Dispatch - Portage, PA - *AyerDirPub 83*
Dispatch - York, PA - *AyerDirPub 83*
Dispatch - Cookeville, TN - *AyerDirPub 83; BaconPubCkNews 84; Ed&PubIntYB 82*
Dispatch - Lampasas, TX - *AyerDirPub 83*
Dispatch - Post, TX - *AyerDirPub 83*
Dispatch - Eatonville, WA - *AyerDirPub 83*
Dispatch Graphics Inc. - New York, NY - *LitMarPl 83, 84; MagIndMarPl 82-83*
Dispatch-News - Lexington, SC - *AyerDirPub 83; Ed&PubIntYB 82; NewsDir 84*
Dispatch News Service - Union City, NJ - *LitMarPl 84*
Dispatch News Service - New York, NY - *Ed&PubIntYB 82*
Dispatch Printing Co. - Columbus, OH - *AdAge 6-28-84; BrCabYB 84*
Dispatch Printing Co. - *See* VideOhio Inc.
Dispatch Publishing Co. - Hoisington, KS - *BaconPubCkNews 84*
Dispatch, The [of The Summit Herald] - Summit, NJ - *NewsDir 84*
Dispatch, The - Union City, NJ - *AyerDirPub 83; Ed&PubIntYB 82; NewsBur 6*
Dispatch, The - Blairsville, PA - *Ed&PubIntYB 82*
Dispatch-Times - Mendon, IL - *Ed&PubIntYB 82*
Dispatch-Tribune [of Townsend Communications Inc.] - Kansas City, MO - *NewsDir 84*
Dispensing Optician, The - Washington, DC - *BaconPubCkMag 84; MagDir 84*
Display Data Corp. - Hunt Valley, MD - *DataDirSup 7-83*
Display Dimensions - San Francisco, CA - *MagIndMarPl 82-83*
Display Media Inc. [Div. of Gamco Industries Inc.] - Chicago, IL - *AvMarPl 83*
Display Productions Inc. - Dallas, TX - *AvMarPl 83*
Display Terminals [of GML Corp.] - Lexington, MA - *CompReadDB 82*
Displays for Schools Inc. - Gainesville, FL - *BoPubDir 4, 5*
Disques Dual - Portland, ME - *BillIntBG 83-84*
Dissertation Abstracts International [of Bibliographic Retrieval Services Inc.] - Latham, NY - *DataDirOnSer 84*
Dissertation Abstracts Online - Ann Arbor, MI - *DirOnDB Spring 84*
Distant Thunder Press - Milwaukee, WI - *BoPubDir 4, 5; LitMag&SmPr 83-84*
Disti-Pure International - Minneapolis, MN - *BoPubDir 4, 5*
Distinguished Home Plans & Products - Mineola, NY - *BaconPubCkMag 84; MagDir 84*
Distribuco/Foodservice Computer Systems Inc. - Santa Ana, CA - *DataDirSup 7-83*
Distributed Computer Systems - Waltham, MA - *WhoWMicrocom 83*
Distributed Computing Systems - Lombard, IL - *MicrocomMPl 84; MicrocomSwDir 1*
Distributed Logic Corp. - Garden Grove, CA - *MicrocomMPl 84*
Distributed Planning Systems Corp. - Woodland Hills, CA - *MicrocomMPl 84*
Distribution - Radnor, PA - *BaconPubCkMag 84; MagIndMarPl 82-83*
Distribution Information Databases [of Distribution Sciences Inc.] - Chicago, IL - *DataDirOnSer 84*
Distribution Management Systems Inc. - Lexington, MA - *ADAPSOMemDir 83-84*
Distribution Register of Organic Pollutants in Water [of U.S. Environmental Protection Agency] - Washington, DC - *CompReadDB 82*
Distribution Register of Organic Pollutants in Water [of Computer Sciences Corp.] - Falls Church, VA - *DataDirOnSer 84*
Distribution Sciences Inc. - Chicago, IL - *ADAPSOMemDir 83-84; DataDirOnSer 84; WhoWMicrocom 83*
Distribution Systems Inc. - Bristol, PA - *LitMarPl 83, 84; MagIndMarPl 82-83*
Distributors - South Bend, IN - *BoPubDir 4 Sup, 5; LitMarPl 83, 84*
Distributor's Link, The - Emerson, NJ - *BaconPubCkMag 84*
Distributors Magazine [of Gro-Com Group] - Barrington, RI - *MagDir 84*
District Heating [of International District Heating Association] - Washington, DC - *BaconPubCkMag 84; MagDir 84*
District Journal - Delburne, AB, Canada - *Ed&PubIntYB 82*
District 69 Cablevision Inc. - Parksville, BC, Canada - *BrCabYB 84*
District Union 427 Voice - Cleveland, OH - *NewsDir 84*
Dittberner Associates Inc. - Bethesda, MD - *TeleSy&SerDir 2-84*
Dittler Brothers Inc. - Atlanta, GA - *DataDirOnSer 84*
Ditto - Whittensville, MA - *DirInfWP 82*
Ditzel Productions, William - Dayton, OH - *AvMarPl 83*
Diver [of Seagraphic Publications Ltd.] - Vancouver, BC, Canada - *ArtMar 84; WritMar 84*
Diver, The [of Taylor Publishing Corp.] - Cobalt, CT - *WritMar 84*
Divernon News - Divernon, IL - *AyerDirPub 83; Ed&PubIntYB 82*
Divernon News - *See* South County Publications
Diversified Business Communications Ltd. - Mississauga, ON, Canada - *DirInfWP 82*
Diversified Cable Services - Hudson, MI - *Tel&CabFB 84C*
Diversified Communications - Bangor, ME - *Tel&CabFB 84S*
Diversified Communications Inc. - Findlay, OH - *DirPRFirms 83*
Diversified Communications Inc. - *See* New England Cablevision Inc.
Diversified Data Systems Inc. - Tucson, AZ - *DataDirSup 7-83*
Diversified Enterprises Inc. - Alpena, MI - *BoPubDir 5*
Diversified Enterprises Inc. - Posen, MI - *BoPubDir 4*
Diversified Finders, The - Long Beach, CA - *FBInfSer 80*
Diversified Mailing Service - Waldorf, MD - *MagIndMarPl 82-83*
Diversified Sales & Marketing Research Consultants Inc. - Brooklyn, NY - *IntDirMarRes 83*
Diversified Software Research - Rockford, IL - *MicrocomMPl 84*
Diversion - New York, NY - *BaconPubCkMag 84; MagDir 84; MagIndMarPl 82-83*
Diversity Productions - Beaverton, OR - *AvMarPl 83*
Divide County Journal - Crosby, ND - *AyerDirPub 83*
Divine Science Press [Aff. of Divine Science Federation International] - Denver, CO - *BoPubDir 4, 5*
Division - Honolulu, HI - *BrCabYB 84*
Division Executive Alerting & Communication Network [of Dept. of the Interior] - Reston, VA - *TeleSy&SerDir 2-84*
Divisions - Cleveland Heights, OH - *LitMag&SmPr 83-84*
Divry Inc., D. C. - New York, NY - *BoPubDir 4, 5*
Dix & Eaton - Cleveland, OH - *AdAge 3-28-84; DirPRFirms 83; StaDirAdAg 2-84*
Dix Newspapers - Wooster, OH - *Ed&PubIntYB 82*
Dix Stations - Wooster, OH - *BrCabYB 84*

Dix Type Inc. - Syracuse, NY - *LitMarPl 83, 84*
Dixie - New Orleans, LA - *MagIndMarPl 82-83*
Dixie Business - Atlanta, GA - *MagDir 84*
Dixie Cable TV - Alma, GA - *BrCabYB 84; Tel&CabFB 84C*
Dixie Contractor - Decatur, GA - *BaconPubCkMag 84; MagDir 84; WritMar 84*
Dixie County Advocate - Cross City, FL - *AyerDirPub 83; Ed&PubIntYB 82*
Dixie Data Processing Supplies Inc. - Birmingham, AL - *DataDirSup 7-83*
Dixie Data Services - Columbus, GA - *MicrocomMPl 83, 84*
Dixie Gun Works - Union City, TN - *AvMarPl 83*
Dixie News - Florence, KY - *AyerDirPub 83; NewsDir 84*
Dixie Purchasor - Carrollton, GA - *MagDir 84*
Dixon Cable TV Inc. [of Tele-Communications Inc.] - Dixon, IL - *BrCabYB 84; Tel&CabFB 84C*
Dixon Evening Telegraph [of B. F. Shaw Printing Co.] - Dixon, IL - *Ed&PubIntYB 82; NewsDir 84*
Dixon Group Advertising & Public Relations Inc., The - Norfolk, VA - *StaDirAdAg 2-84*
Dixon Inc., Christopher - New York, NY - *AvMarPl 83*
Dixon Pilot - Dixon, MO - *BaconPubCkNews 84; Ed&PubIntYB 82; NewsDir 84*
Dixon Telegraph - Dixon, IL - *BaconPubCkNews 84*
Dixon Telephone Co. - Dixon, IA - *TelDir&BG 83-84*
Dixon Tribune - Dixon, CA - *BaconPubCkNews 84; Ed&PubIntYB 82*
Dixville Telephone Co. - Dixville, NH - *TelDir&BG 83-84*
DJ 'Al' Systems Ltd. - Los Angeles, CA - *MicrocomMPl 83; MicrocomSwDir 1*
DJ Cable TV Inc. [of Service Electric Cable TV] - Nazareth, PA - *BrCabYB 84*
DJ Cable TV Inc. [of Service Electric Cable TV] - Northampton, PA - *BrCabYB 84*
DJC & Associates - Sacramento, CA - *ArtMar 84*
DJEM - Edmundston, NB, Canada - *BrCabYB 84*
DJM - New York, NY - *AvMarPl 83*
DJM Enzyme Report - Willits, CA - *BaconPubCkMag 84*
DJM Records - Nashville, TN - *BillIntBG 83-84*
DJR Associates Inc. - Tarrytown, NY - *MicrocomMPl 84*
DK & A - Washington, DC - *MagIndMarPl 82-83*
D.K. Associates - Dallas, TX - *DirInfWP 82*
DK Halcyon Group Inc. [Aff. of Thom Doran & Partners Inc.] - Dayton, OH - *BoPubDir 4, 5*
D.K. Research - Las Vegas, NV - *BoPubDir 4*
DKA Advertising - Washington, DC - *DirMarMP 83; LitMarPl 83, 84; StaDirAdAg 2-84*
DKF - Bietigheim-Bissingen, West Germany - *DirOnDB Spring 84*
DKI - Darmstadt, West Germany - *DirOnDB Spring 84*
DKI Literaturdatenbank Kuntstoffe Kautschuk Fasern [of Deutsches Kunstoff-Institut] - Darmstadt, West Germany - *CompReadDB 82*
DLM Inc. - Chicago, IL - *DataDirOnSer 84*
DLM Inc. - Allen, TX - *MicrocomMPl 83*
DM Music - *See* Moody Music, Doug
DM News [of Mill Hollow Publications] - New York, NY - *BaconPubCkMag 84; DirMarMP 83; WritMar 84*
DM Studio - Bowie, MD - *MicrocomMPl 84*
DMA Corp. - Goleta, CA - *MicrocomMPl 83*
DMA Productions - New York, NY - *AvMarPl 83*
DMA Systems Corp. - Goleta, CA - *MicrocomMPl 84; WhoWMicrocom 83*
DMC Systems Inc. - Santa Clara, CA - *DataDirSup 7-83*
DMN Cable Investors - Alma, AR - *Tel&CabFB 84C p.1677*
DMR Associates Inc. - Boston, MA - *DirInfWP 82*
D.M.R. Publications Inc. - Milwaukee, WI - *BoPubDir 4, 5*
DMS [of Hydrocomp Inc.] - Mountain View, CA - *DataDirOnSer 84; DirOnDB Spring 84*
DMS Contract Awards [of Data Resources Inc.] - Lexington, MA - *DataDirOnSer 84*
DMS Inc. - Greenwich, CT - *BoPubDir 5; EISS 83*
DMS Market Intelligence Reports On-Line [of Data Resources Inc.] - Lexington, MA - *DataDirOnSer 84*
DMS/Online - Greenwich, CT - *DirOnDB Spring 84*
DMV/DRS Creative Services - Jersey City, NJ - *LitMarPl 84*
DMW Group Inc. - Ann Arbor, MI - *DataDirOnSer 84; DataDirSup 7-83; EISS 83; TeleSy&SerDir 7-83*
DNR Press - La Mesa, CA - *BoPubDir 4, 5*
Do-Bran-Cin Cablevision Inc. - East Brady, PA - *Tel&CabFB 84C p.1677*
DO Industries Inc. - East Rochester, NY - *AvMarPl 83*
Do-It-Yourself Legal Publishers - New York, NY - *BoPubDir 4, 5; LitMag&SmPr 83-84*
D.O., The - Chicago, IL - *BaconPubCkMag 84; MagDir 84*
Doane Agricultural Service Inc. - St. Louis, MO - *BoPubDir 4, 5; CompReadDB 82*
Doane Farm Media Measurement Study - St. Louis, MO - *DirOnDB Spring 84*
Doane Information Center Indexing System [of Doane Agricultural Service Inc.] - St. Louis, MO - *CompReadDB 82*
Doane-Western Inc. - St. Louis, MO - *WritMar 84*
Doane's Agricultural Report - St. Louis, MO - *BaconPubCkMag 84*
Dobbins, M. F. - Glenside, PA - *BoPubDir 5*
Dobbs-Maynard Co. - Jackson, MS - *StaDirAdAg 2-84*
Dobbs Public Relations - New York, NY - *DirPRFirms 83*
Dobert Productions Inc., Stefan - Bethesda, MD - *ArtMar 84; AvMarPl 83*
Dobi Publishing - Olean, NY - *BoPubDir 4 Sup, 5*
Dobie Co., The [Subs. of Eazyway Inc.] - North Royalton, OH - *DirMarMP 83*
Dobra Kniha/Friends of Good Books - Cambridge, ON, Canada - *BoPubDir 4, 5*
Dobson Telephone Co. Inc. - Cheyenne, OK - *TelDir&BG 83-84*
Doc Dick Enterprises - Mt. Vernon, NY - *BillIntBG 83-84*
Doc Ron Productions Inc. - Boynton Beach, FL - *BillIntBG 83-84*
Docent Corp. - South Salem, NY - *AvMarPl 83; BoPubDir 4, 5; LitMarPl 84*
DockxDesign - Boston, MA - *LitMarPl 83, 84; MagIndMarPl 82-83*
Dococean [of Centre National pour l'Exploitation de Oceans] - Brest, France - *CompReadDB 82; DirOnDB Spring 84*
Doctor Jazz Press - Tuscaloosa, AL - *LitMag&SmPr 83-84*
Doctor's Life, The - New York, NY - *MagDir 84*
DOCU/Master [of TSI International] - Norwalk, CT - *EISS 83*
Doculam [Div. of Bryce Corp.] - Memphis, TN - *AvMarPl 83*
Documan Software - Kalamazoo, MI - *MicrocomMPl 83, 84*
Documat Office Technology - London, ON, Canada - *DirInfWP 82*
Document Associates Inc. - New York, NY - *AvMarPl 83*
Document Engineering Co. Inc. - Van Nuys, CA - *EISS 5-84 Sup*
Document Handling & Information Services Facility [of U.S. General Accounting Office] - Gaithersburg, MD - *EISS 83*
Document Ordres et Reglements Statutaires [of Federal Dept. of Justice] - Ottawa, ON, Canada - *CompReadDB 82*
Documentaries for Learning [Div. of Harvard Medical School] - Boston, MA - *AvMarPl 83*
Documentary Educational Resources Inc. - Watertown, MA - *AvMarPl 83*
Documentary Films Inc. - New York, NY - *TelAl 83, 84*
Documentary Publications - Salisbury, NC - *BoPubDir 4, 5*
Documentary Recordings - Los Angeles, CA - *BillIntBG 83-84*
Documentary Research Center - Brussels, Belgium - *EISS 83*
Documentary Service [of International Institute of Refrigeration] - Paris, France - *EISS 5-84 Sup*
Documentation & Health Information Office [of Pan American Health Organization] - Washington, DC - *EISS 83*
Documentation & Information Div. [of Central American Research Institute for Industry] - Guatemala, Guatemala - *EISS 83*
Documentation & Information System for Parliamentary Materials [of German Federal Diet] - Bonn, West Germany - *EISS 83*
Documentation & Information System on Developmental Biology [of Hubrecht Laboratory] - Utrecht, Netherlands - *EISS 83*
Documentation & Information Unit [of United Nations Educational, Scientific, & Cultural Organization] - Geneva, Switzerland - *EISS 83*
Documentation Associates - Santa Monica, CA - *FBInfSer 80*
Documentation Bureau [of International Railway Union] - Paris, France - *EISS 83*
Documentation Center [of Atomic Energy Commission] - Gif-sur-Yvette, France - *EISS 83*
Documentation Center [of Institute of Research on Fruits & Citrus-Fruits] - Paris, France - *EISS 83*

Documentation Center [of French Petroleum Institute] - Rueil-Malmaison, France - *EISS 83*
Documentation Center [of Food & Agriculture Organization] - Rome, Italy - *EISS 83*
Documentation Center [of German Foundation for International Development] - Bonn, West Germany - *EISS 83*
Documentation Center for Human Sciences [of National Center for Scientific Research] - Paris, France - *EISS 83*
Documentation Center for Mechanics [of Technical Center for Mechanical Industries] - Senlis, France - *EISS 83*
Documentation Center for Plant Pathology & Plant Protection [of Federal Biological Research Center for Agriculture & Forestry] - Berlin, West Germany - *EISS 83*
Documentation Center on Animal Production [of University of Hohenheim] - Stuttgart, West Germany - *EISS 83*
Documentation Centre [of International Livestock Centre for Africa] - Addis Ababa, Ethiopia - *EISS 7-83 Sup*
Documentation Centre [of National Institute of Health & Family Welfare] - New Delhi, India - *EISS 5-84 Sup*
Documentation Dept. [of Bureau of Geological & Mining Research] - Orleans, France - *EISS 83*
Documentation Dept. [of Institute of Nutrition] - Giessen, West Germany - *EISS 83*
Documentation et Analyse Financiere SA - Paris, France - *InfIndMarPl 83*
Documentation Section [of Swedish University of Agricultural Sciences] - Uppsala, Sweden - *EISS 83*
Documentation Section [of Volkswagenwerk AG] - Wolfsburg, West Germany - *EISS 83*
Documentation Service [of Merlin Gerin Co.] - Grenoble, France - *EISS 83*
Documentation Service [of Center for Industrial Creation] - Paris, France - *EISS 5-84 Sup*
Documentation Service [of Swiss Academy of Medical Sciences] - Berne, Switzerland - *EISS 83*
Documents for New Poetry [of Archive for New Poetry] - San Diego, CA - *LitMag&SmPr 83-84*
Documents in Calgary Libraries [of University of Alberta] - Edmonton, AB, Canada - *DataDirOnSer 84*
Documents, Ordres et Reglements Statutaires [of QL Systems Ltd.] - Ottawa, ON, Canada - *DataDirOnSer 84; DirOnDB Spring 84*
Docutel/Olivetti Corp. - Tarrytown, NY - *WhoWMicrocom 83*
Docuvid Electronic News Services - New York, NY - *BrCabYB 84; Tel&CabFB 84C*
DoD Nuclear Information & Analysis Center [of Kaman Tempo] - Santa Barbara, CA - *EISS 83*
Dodd, Mead & Co. [Subs. of Thomas Nelson Inc.] - New York, NY - *LitMarPl 83, 84; WritMar 84*
Dodds Music Inc., Malcolm - New York, NY - *HBIndAd&MS 82-83*
Doderipa Records - Newington, CT - *BillIntBG 83-84*
Dodge Center Star-Record - Dodge Center, MN - *BaconPubCkNews 84; Ed&PubIntYB 82*
Dodge City Broadcasting Co. - Dodge City, KS - *BrCabYB 84*
Dodge City Cable TV [of Community Tele-Communications Inc.] - Dodge City, KS - *BrCabYB 84; Tel&CabFB 84C*
Dodge City Globe - Dodge City, KS - *BaconPubCkNews 84; Ed&PubIntYB 82; NewsDir 84*
Dodge City Southwest Kansas Register - Dodge City, KS - *NewsDir 84*
Dodge Construction Analysis System [of McGraw-Hill Information Systems Co.] - New York, NY - *DBBus 82*
Dodge Construction News - Los Angeles, CA - *Ed&PubIntYB 82*
Dodge Construction News [of McGraw-Hill Information Systems Co.] - Monterey Park, CA - *NewsDir 84*
Dodge Construction News [of McGraw-Hill Information Systems Co.] - Chicago, IL - *BaconPubCkMag 84; Ed&PubIntYB 82; NewsDir 84*
Dodge Construction News Green Sheet [of McGraw-Hill Inc.] - Monterey Park, CA - *MagDir 84*
Dodge Construction Potentials Data Bank [of Data Resources Inc.] - Lexington, MA - *DataDirOnSer 84*
Dodge Construction Potentials Data Bank - New York, NY - *DirOnDB Spring 84*
Dodge County Independent - Kasson, MN - *AyerDirPub 83; Ed&PubIntYB 82*
Dodge County Independent-News [of Royle Publishing Inc.] - Juneau, WI - *AyerDirPub 83; Ed&PubIntYB 82; NewsDir 84*
Dodge County Telephone Co. [Aff. of Telephone & Data Systems Inc.] - Reeseville, WI - *TelDir&BG 83-84*
Dodge Criterion - Dodge, NE - *BaconPubCkNews 84; Ed&PubIntYB 82*
Dodge Div. [of McGraw-Hill Informations Systems Co.] - New York, NY - *EISS 83*
Dodge High Plains Journal - Dodge City, KS - *BaconPubCkNews 84*
Dodgeville-Chronicle - Dodgeville, WI - *BaconPubCkNews 84; Ed&PubIntYB 82; NewsDir 84*
Dodo Graphics Inc. - Plattsburgh, NY - *ArtMar 84*
Dodson, Craddock & Born Advertising Inc. - Pensacola, FL - *AdAge 3-28-84; StaDirAdAg 2-84*
Doe-Anderson Advertising Agency Inc. - Louisville, KY - *AdAge 3-28-84; ArtMar 84; BrCabYB 84; StaDirAdAg 2-84*
DOE Energy Data Base [of U.S. Dept. of Energy] - Oak Ridge, TN - *CompReadDB 82; DBBus 82; DirOnDB Spring 84*
DOE/ERS Bibliography for Flywheel Energy Systems [of Lawrence Livermore National Laboratory] - Livermore, CA - *CompReadDB 82*
DOE/ERS Bibliography for Molten Salts-Eutectic Data [of Lawrence Livermore National Laboratory] - Livermore, CA - *CompReadDB 82*
DOE/ERS Technology Information System [of Lawrence Livermore National Laboratory] - Livermore, CA - *CompReadDB 82*
Doe-LP Productions & Co., John - New York, NY - *BillIntBG 83-84*
DOE/RECON [of U.S. Dept. of Energy] - Oak Ridge, TN - *EISS 83*
DOE Technical Information Center [of U.S. Dept of Energy] - Oak Ridge, TN - *InfIndMarPl 83*
Dog Ear Press - Hulls Cove, ME - *BoPubDir 4*
Dog Ear Press - South Harpswell, ME - *BoPubDir 5; LitMag&SmPr 83-84*
Dog Ear Rag [of The Dog Ear Press] - South Harpswell, ME - *LitMag&SmPr 83-84*
Dog Fancy [of Fancy Publications Inc.] - San Clemente, CA - *ArtMar 84; BaconPubCkMag 84; MagDir 84; MagIndMarPl 82-83; WritMar 84*
Dog Hair Press - Iowa City, IA - *LitMag&SmPr 83-84*
Dog River Review [of Trout Creek Press] - Parkdale, OR - *LitMag&SmPr 83-84*
Dog World - Chicago, IL - *BaconPubCkMag 84; MagDir 84; MagIndMarPl 82-83*
DOGE - *See* FRANCIS: DOGE
Doggeral Press - Santa Barbara, CA - *BoPubDir 4, 5; LitMag&SmPr 83-84*
Doheny Music - Los Angeles, CA - *BillIntBG 83-84*
Doherty & Co., John - Ottawa, ON, Canada - *StaDirAdAg 2-84*
Doherty, Helen - Winnipeg, MB, Canada - *BoPubDir 4, 5*
Doings Newspapers, The - Hinsdale, IL - *BaconPubCkNews 84*
D.O.K. Publishers Inc. - Buffalo, NY - *BoPubDir 4, 5; LitMarPl 84*
DOKDI [of Schweizerische Akademie der Medizinischen Wissenschaften] - Berne, Switzerland - *InfIndMarPl 83*
Dokel Communications Corp. - Rocky Mt., VA - *Tel&CabFB 84C p.1677*
DoKel Communications Corp. - *See* Welbac Cable TV Corp.
Dokumentation Krankenhauswesen [of Institut fur Krankenhausbau] - Berlin, West Germany - *InfIndMarPl 83*
Dokumentation Maschinenbau File [of Fachinformationszentrum Technik eV] - Frankfurt, West Germany - *CompReadDB 82*
Dokumentations-und Informationssystem fuer Parlamentsmaterial [of Deutscher Bundestag] - Bonn, West Germany - *CompReadDB 82*
Dokumentationsstelle der Universitat Hohenheim - Stuttgart, West Germany - *InfIndMarPl 83*
Dolan, Charles F. - *See* Cablevision Systems Development Co.
Dolbeau TV Service Inc. - Dolbeau, PQ, Canada - *BrCabYB 84*
DOLDIS - Stockholm, Sweden - *DirOnDB Spring 84*
Dole Publishing Co. Inc. - Somerville, MA - *BaconPubCkNews 84*
Dolezal, Robert J. - Los Angeles, CA - *LitMarPl 83, 84*
Dolger Agency, The Jonathan - New York, NY - *LitMarPl 83, 84*

Doll Collectors of America Inc. - Westford, MA - *BoPubDir 4, 5*
Doll Reader [Subs. of Hobby House Press Inc.] - Cumberland, MD - *WritMar 84*
Doll Talk - Independence, MO - *MagDir 84*
Doll World - Brooksville, FL - *ArtMar 84*
Dollar Records/National Foundation Records, Johnny - Nashville, TN - *BillIntBG 83-84*
Dollar Saver - Fremont, CA - *AyerDirPub 83*
Dollars & Sense [of National Taxpayers Union] - Washington, DC - *ArtMar 84; WritMar 84*
Dollars & Sense - Chicago, IL - *BaconPubCkMag 84*
Dollars & Sense [of Economic Affairs Bureau Inc.] - Somerville, MA - *MagDir 84*
Dollars Per Day Survey - Walnut Creek, CA - *BoPubDir 4 Sup, 5*
Dollarsaver - Hemet, CA - *AyerDirPub 83*
Dolls [of Acquire Publishing Co. Inc.] - New York, NY - *BaconPubCkMag 84; WritMar 84*
Dolly Bee Music - Palm Springs, CA - *BillIntBG 83-84*
Dolnick & Associates, Norman - Chicago, IL - *DirPRFirms 83*
Dolores Star - Dolores, CO - *AyerDirPub 83; BaconPubCkNews 84; Ed&PubIntYB 82*
Dolphin Aquatics - Stamford, CT - *BoPubDir 4*
Dolphin Aquatics - Ft. Dix, NJ - *BoPubDir 5*
Dolphin Book Club - *See* Book-of-the-Month Club Inc.
Dolphin Digest - Miami, FL - *Ed&PubIntYB 82*
Dolphin Editions - Cambridge, MA - *BoPubDir 4, 5*
Dolphin Multi-Media - Palo Alto, CA - *AvMarPl 83*
Dolphin Productions - New York, NY - *ArtMar 84; AvMarPl 83; Tel&CabFB 84C*
Dolphin Records - Durham, NC - *BillIntBG 83-84*
Dolton Pointer [of Chicago Daily Southtown Economist Newspapers] - Chicago, IL - *NewsDir 84*
Dolton Pointer - Dolton, IL - *Ed&PubIntYB 82*
Dolton Pointer - South Holland, IL - *AyerDirPub 83*
Dolton Pointer-Economist - *See* Pointer-Economist Newspapers
DOMA Dokumentation Maschinenbau im FIZ Technik eV - Frankfurt, West Germany - *DirOnDB Spring 84; InfIndMarPl 83*
Doma Press [Aff. of Spiritual Pathways Institute] - Downers Grove, IL - *BoPubDir 4 Sup, 5*
Domain Communications - Wheaton, IL - *BrCabYB 84; StaDirAdAg 2-84*
Dombrower Co. Inc., The Ralph L. - Richmond, VA - *BrCabYB 84*
Dome Consumer News & Design - Evanston, IL - *BaconPubCkMag 84*
D.O.M.E. Services - Colorado Springs, CO - *BoPubDir 4, 5*
Domestic [of National Council for Research & Development] - Tel-Aviv, Israel - *EISS 83*
Domestic Engineering [of Construction Industry Press] - Elmhurst, IL - *ArtMar 84; MagDir 84; WritMar 84*
Domestic, Foreign National, International Standards [of Information Handling Services] - Englewood, CO - *DataDirOnSer 84*
Domesticom/Domestidyne - New Orleans, LA - *Tel&CabFB 84C*
Domina Books - *See* Double M Press/Domina Books
Dominie Press Ltd. - Agincourt, ON, Canada - *LitMarPl 83, 84*
Dominion Directory Co. Ltd. - Burnaby, BC, Canada - *VideoDir 82-83*
Dominion Law Reports [of Canada Law Book Ltd.] - Aurora, ON, Canada - *CompReadDB 82; DirOnDB Spring 84*
Dominion Law Reports [of QL Systems Ltd.] - Ottawa, ON, Canada - *DataDirOnSer 84*
Dominion-Post - Morgantown, WV - *AyerDirPub 83; BaconPubCkNews 84; Ed&PubIntYB 82*
Dominion Press [Aff. of The Invisible Ministry] - San Marcos, CA - *BoPubDir 4, 5; LitMag&SmPr 83-84*
Dominion Research Corp. - Baltimore, MD - *IntDirMarRes 83*
Domino Records - Yonkers, NY - *BillIntBG 83-84*
Domino Records - Garland, TX - *BillIntBG 83-84*
Domjan Studio - Tuxedo Park, NY - *BoPubDir 4, 5*
Domke, J. G. - Lansdowne, PA - *AvMarPl 83*
Domore Office Furniture - Elkhart, IN - *DirInfWP 82*
Domus Books Inc. [of Quality Books Inc.] - Northbrook, IL - *LitMarPl 83*
Don Bosco Publications - New Rochelle, NY - *LitMarPl 83*
Donadio & Associates Inc., Candida - New York, NY - *LitMarPl 83, 84*
Donaghey Publications, John - Garland, TX - *BoPubDir 4, 5*
Donahoe, Edward D. - Louisville, KY - *BoPubDir 4 Sup, 5*
Donahue & Associates Advertising Inc. - New York, NY - *StaDirAdAg 2-84*
Donahue Inc. - Glastonbury, CT - *DirPRFirms 83; StaDirAdAg 2-84*
Donald Art Co. Inc. - Port Chester, NY - *ArtMar 84*
Donaldson Display Co. Inc. - South Hackensack, NJ - *StaDirAdAg 2-84*
Donaldsonville Cable TV Fund VIII-C [of Jones Intercable Inc.] - Donaldsonville, LA - *BrCabYB 84*
Donaldsonville Chief [of Donaldsonville Newspapers Inc.] - Donaldsonville, LA - *BaconPubCkNews 84; NewsDir 84*
Donalsonville News - Donalsonville, GA - *BaconPubCkNews 84; Ed&PubIntYB 82*
Donars Productions - Loveland, CO - *AvMarPl 83*
Donato Music Publishing Co. - New York, NY - *BoPubDir 4, 5*
Donde - Miami Beach, FL - *BaconPubCkMag 84*
Donelson News Diary - Nashville, TN - *AyerDirPub 83*
Doner & Co., W. B. - Baltimore, MD - *AdAge 3-28-84; TelAl 84*
Doner & Co., W. B. - Southfield, MI - *ArtMar 84; Br 1-23-84; BrCabYB 84; StaDirAdAg 2-84; TelAl 83*
Doner & Co., W. B. - Houston, TX - *ArtMar 84*
Dongola Tri-County Record - Dongola, IL - *BaconPubCkNews 84*
Donino Pace Inc. - New York, NY - *StaDirAdAg 2-84*
Doniphan County Cable TV Inc. [of Semo Communications Inc.] - Troy, KS - *BrCabYB 84; Tel&CabFB 84C*
Doniphan Herald - Doniphan, NE - *BaconPubCkNews 84; Ed&PubIntYB 82*
Doniphan Ozark Graphic Weekly - Doniphan, MO - *BaconPubCkNews 84*
Doniphan Prospect-News - Doniphan, MO - *BaconPubCkNews 84; NewsDir 84*
Donley Communications Corp. - New York, NY - *DirPRFirms 83*
Donmark Graphics Inc. - La Canada, CA - *DirInfWP 82*
Donn Advertising Associates - Erie, PA - *StaDirAdAg 2-84*
Donn Corp. - Westlake, OH - *DataDirSup 7-83*
Donna Events News - Donna, TX - *BaconPubCkNews 84*
Donna-Marie Music Publishing - Atlantic City, NJ - *BillIntBG 83-84*
Donna Music Publishing Co. - Woburn, MA - *BillIntBG 83-84*
Donnar Publications - Woodland Hills, CA - *BoPubDir 5*
Donnelley & Sons Co., R. R. - Chicago, IL - *LitMarPl 83, 84; MagIndMarPl 82-83*
Donnelley & Sons Co., R. R. - New York, NY - *MagIndMarPl 82-83*
Donnelley & Sons Co., R. R. (Electronic Graphics Sales Div.) - Oak Brook, IL - *LitMarPl 83, 84; MagIndMarPl 82-83*
Donnelley Cartographic Services [Subs. of R. R. Donnelley & Sons Co.] - Lancaster, PA - *LitMarPl 83, 84*
Donnelley Marketing Information Services [Subs. of The Dun & Bradstreet Corp.] - Stamford, CT - *CabTVFinDB 83; DataDirOnSer 84*
Donnellson Star - Donnellson, IA - *Ed&PubIntYB 82*
Donnellson Star/West Point Bee - Donnellson, IA - *BaconPubCkNews 84*
Donnelly Advertising Co. - St. Louis, MO - *StaDirAdAg 2-84*
Donnelly & Sons Publishing Co. - Colorado Springs, CO - *BoPubDir 4, 5*
Donning Co., The - Norfolk, VA - *ArtMar 84; LitMag&SmPr 83-84; LitMarPl 83, 84; WritMar 84*
Donoghue Organization [Aff. of Cash Management Institute] - Holliston, MA - *BoPubDir 4 Sup, 5*
Donoghue's Money Fund Report [of The Donoghue Organization] - Holliston, MA - *MagIndMarPl 82-83; WritMar 84*
Donohue Associates Inc., Jody - New York, NY - *ArtMar 84; DirPRFirms 83*
Donohue Co., Stephen T. - New York, NY - *DirPRFirms 83*
Donovan Data Systems Inc. - New York, NY - *ADAPSOMemDir 83-84; HBIndAd&MS 82-83*
Donovan Inc., Elizabeth - New York, NY - *IntDirMarRes 83*
Donrey Cablevision - Rogers, AR - *BrCabYB 84*
Donrey Cablevision - Vallejo, CA - *Tel&CabFB 84C*

Donrey Media Group - Ft. Smith, AR - *AdAge 6-28-84; BrCabYB 84 p.D-300; NewsBur 6; Tel&CabFB 84C p.1677*
Donrey Media Group - Las Vegas, NV - *Ed&PubIntYB 82; KnowInd 83*
Don's Office Products Inc. - Ketchikan, AK - *WhoWMicrocom 83*
Don't Ask Software - Los Angeles, CA - *MicrocomMPl 83, 84*
Doodly-Squat Press - Los Angeles, CA - *LitMag&SmPr 83-84*
Doodly-Squat Press - Albuquerque, NM - *BoPubDir 4, 5*
Doolco Inc. - Dallas, TX - *BoPubDir 4, 5*
Dooley, Boyce - Summerville, GA - *Tel&CabFB 84C p.1677*
Dooms Publishing Co. - Waynesboro, VA - *BillIntBG 83-84*
Doon Press - Doon, IA - *BaconPubCkNews 84; Ed&PubIntYB 82; NewsDir 84*
Door County Advocate - Sturgeon Bay, WI - *AyerDirPub 83; Ed&PubIntYB 82*
Door Reminder - Ellison Bay, WI - *AyerDirPub 83*
Doors & Hardware [of Door & Hardware Institute] - McLean, VA - *BaconPubCkMag 84; MagDir 84*
Doorway Publications - Brockville, ON, Canada - *BoPubDir 4 Sup, 5*
Doorways to the Mind [of Aries Productions Inc.] - Creve Coeur, MO - *WritMar 84*
Dooryard Press - Story, WY - *BoPubDir 4, 5; LitMag&SmPr 83-84*
Dora-Clayton Agency Inc. - Atlanta, GA - *TelAl 83, 84*
Dorate Inc. - Sayre, OK - *BrCabYB 84 p.D-300; Tel&CabFB 84C p.1677*
Doraville Neighbor [of Marietta Neighbor Newspapers Inc.] - Marietta, GA - *NewsDir 84*
Dorchester Argus-Citizen - Boston, MA - *AyerDirPub 83*
Dorchester Argus-Citizen - Dorchester, MA - *Ed&PubIntYB 82*
Dorchester Cablevision Inc. [of Wometco Cable TV Inc.] - Summerville, SC - *Tel&CabFB 84C*
Dorchester Eagle-Record - St. George, SC - *AyerDirPub 83*
Dorchester Publishing Co. Inc. - New York, NY - *LitMarPl 84*
Dorchester Suburban Record - Dorchester Center, MA - *NewsDir 84*
Dore Records Ltd. - Hollywood, CA - *BillIntBG 83-84*
Doremus & Co. [Subs. of BBDO International Inc.] - New York, NY - *AdAge 3-28-84; BrCabYB 84; DirPRFirms 83; StaDirAdAg 2-84; TelAl 83, 84*
Doremus Direct [Subs. of BBDO International Inc.] - New York, NY - *DirMarMP 83*
Doremus Inc., John - Chicago, IL - *AvMarPl 83*
Doremus/West - San Francisco, CA - *ArtMar 84*
Dorf/MJH - New York, NY - *DirPRFirms 83; LitMarPl 83, 84*
Dorff, Ralph L. - Mission Viejo, CA - *LitMarPl 83*
Doric Computer Systems - Watford, England - *MicrocomSwDir 1*
DORIS [of CACI Inc.] - Arlington, VA - *DataDirOnSer 84*
Dorison House Publishers Inc. - Boston, MA - *LitMag&SmPr 83-84; LitMarPl 83, 84*
Dorje Ling Publishers - Lagunitas, CA - *BoPubDir 5*
Dorje Ling Publishers - San Rafael, CA - *BoPubDir 4*
Dorland & Sweeney - Philadelphia, PA - *AdAge 3-28-84; StaDirAdAg 2-84*
Dorland Publishing Co., Wayne E. - Mendham, NJ - *BoPubDir 4, 5*
Dormac Inc. - Beaverton, OR - *BoPubDir 4, 5; LitMarPl 84*
Dormant Brain Research & Development Laboratory - Black Hawk, CO - *BoPubDir 4, 5; LitMag&SmPr 83-84*
Dormont News - Homestead, PA - *AyerDirPub 83*
Dorn Books [Aff. of Dorn Communications Inc.] - Minneapolis, MN - *BoPubDir 4 Sup, 5*
Dorn Computer Consultants Inc. - New York, NY - *EISS 83*
Dorn Public Relations [Div. of Dorn Communications Inc.] - Bloomington, MN - *DirPRFirms 83*
Dorn Records - Chatsworth, CA - *BillIntBG 83-84*
Dornan Inc., W. J. - Collingdale, PA - *LitMarPl 83, 84*
Doro International Corp. - South San Francisco, CA - *DirInfWP 82*
Doron, Marcia Nita - Teaneck, NJ - *LitMarPl 84*
Doros Animation Inc. - New York, NY - *AvMarPl 83*
Dorr Public Relations - Toluca Lake, CA - *DirPRFirms 83*
Dorr Research Corp. - Boston, MA - *IntDirMarRes 83*
Dorris Butte Valley Star - Dorris, CA - *BaconPubCkNews 84*
Dorris Telephone Co. - Dorris, CA - *TelDir&BG 83-84*
Dorritie & Lyons - New York, NY - *AdAge 3-28-84; StaDirAdAg 2-84*
Dorrity Advertising Inc. - Memphis, TN - *StaDirAdAg 2-84*
Dorsett Educational Systems Inc. - Norman, OK - *AvMarPl 83; MicrocomMPl 83, 84*
Dorsey Advertising/Public Relations Agency - Mesquite, TX - *StaDirAdAg 2-84*
Dorsey Agency - Dallas, TX - *ArtMar 84*
Dorsey Press, The [Div. of Richard D. Irwin Inc.] - Homewood, IL - *LitMarPl 83*
Dorsey Press, The - New York, NY - *LitMarPl 84*
Dorsey, Shirlene C. - Newport Beach, CA - *LitMarPl 84*
Dort & Co., Dallas C. - Flint, MI - *ArtMar 84; StaDirAdAg 2-84*
Dortmund/Leuven Library System [of International Business Machines Corp.] - Bethesda, MD - *EISS 83*
Dortmund VLE Data Bank [of University of Dortmund] - Dortmund, West Germany - *DirOnDB Spring 84; EISS 83*
Dortmund VLE Database [of ChemShare Corp.] - Houston, TX - *DataDirOnSer 84*
Dorton TV Cable Line - Dorton, KY - *BrCabYB 84; Tel&CabFB 84C*
Dos Palos Star - Dos Palos, CA - *BaconPubCkNews 84; Ed&PubIntYB 82*
Dos Tejedoras/Fiber Arts Publications - St. Paul, MN - *BoPubDir 4, 5; LitMag&SmPr 83-84*
Dosimetry of Special & General Employees [of Creative Information Systems] - Portland, OR - *DataDirOnSer 84*
Dossier, The [of SUNY] - Oneonta, NY - *WritMar 84*
Dot Pasteup Supply Co. - Omaha, NE - *BoPubDir 4, 5*
Dothan Eagle - Dothan, AL - *BaconPubCkNews 84; Ed&PubIntYB 82; NewsDir 84*
Dothard Associates, R. L. - Brattleboro, VT - *BoPubDir 4 Sup, 5*
Dots Publications - Ventura, CA - *BoPubDir 4, 5*
Dotson & Wilson Consulting - Lexington, KY - *WhoWMicrocom 83*
Dottrina Giuridica [of Instituto per la Documentazione Giuridica] - Florence, Italy - *CompReadDB 82*
Doty, Phillips & Laing - Battle Creek, MI - *AdAge 3-28-84; StaDirAdAg 2-84*
Double Arrow Record Co. Inc. - Long Island City, NY - *BillIntBG 83-84*
Double-D Advertising - San Francisco, CA - *StaDirAdAg 2-84*
Double D Associates - Menomonee Falls, WI - *AvMarPl 83*
Double-Gold Software - Saratoga, CA - *MicrocomMPl 83*
Double Harness [of Avalon Editions] - York, England - *LitMag&SmPr 83-84*
Double Helix Press - Los Angeles, CA - *BoPubDir 4, 5*
Double M Industries - Austin, TX - *AvMarPl 83*
Double M Press - Sepulveda, CA - *BoPubDir 4, 5; LitMag&SmPr 83-84*
Double Sharp Music - *See* Groovesville Music
Double Star Catalogs [of U.S. Navy] - Washington, DC - *EISS 83*
Doubleday & Co. Inc. - New York, NY - *ArtMar 84; KnowInd 83; LitMarPl 83, 84; WritMar 84*
Doubleday Book Clubs - Garden City, NY - *LitMarPl 83*
Doubleday Book Clubs [Subs. of Doubleday & Co. Inc.] - New York, NY - *LitMarPl 84*
Doubleday Broadcasting Co. - New York, NY - *BrCabYB 84*
Doubleday Canada Ltd. [Subs. of Doubleday Inc. USA] - Toronto, ON, Canada - *LitMarPl 83, 84; WritMar 84*
Doubleday Syndicate - New York, NY - *Ed&PubIntYB 82*
Doubleo Publications - New York, NY - *BoPubDir 4, 5; LitMag&SmPr 83-84*
Doubletree Music - *See* Merit Music Corp.
Doughty & Associates Inc., Ron - Monroe, LA - *StaDirAdAg 2-84*
Douglas & McIntyre Ltd. - Vancouver, BC, Canada - *LitMarPl 83, 84*
Douglas Budget - Douglas, WY - *BaconPubCkNews 84*
Douglas Coffee County Progress - Douglas, GA - *BaconPubCkNews 84; NewsDir 84*
Douglas Communications of Glens Falls Inc. [of Tribune Cable Communications Inc.] - Glens Falls, NY - *BrCabYB 84*
Douglas Communications of Louisiana Inc. [of Tribune Cable Communications Inc.] - Slidell, LA - *BrCabYB 84*

Douglas Communications of New York Inc. [of Tribune Cable Communications Inc.] - Oneida, NY - *BrCabYB 84*
Douglas Communications of West Tennessee Inc. [of Tribune Cable Communications Inc.] - Jackson, TN - *Tel&CabFB 84C*
Douglas Communications of West Tennessee Inc. [of Tribune Cable Communications Inc.] - Selmer, TN - *Tel&CabFB 84C*
Douglas County Bulletin - Sutherlin, OR - *AyerDirPub 83*
Douglas County Cablevision - Castle Rock, CO - *Tel&CabFB 84C*
Douglas County Cablevision - Denver, CO - *Tel&CabFB 84C p.1678*
Douglas County Cablevision - Sedalia, CO - *BrCabYB 84*
Douglas County Cablevision [of MetroVision Inc.] - Douglas County, NE - *Tel&CabFB 84C*
Douglas County Gazette - Waterloo, NE - *AyerDirPub 83; Ed&PubIntYB 82*
Douglas County Herald - Ava, MO - *AyerDirPub 83; Ed&PubIntYB 82*
Douglas County News - Castle Rock, CO - *Ed&PubIntYB 82*
Douglas County News-Press - Castle Rock, CO - *AyerDirPub 83; BaconPubCkNews 84*
Douglas County Sentinel - Douglasville, GA - *AyerDirPub 83; Ed&PubIntYB 82*
Douglas Dispatch - Douglas, AZ - *BaconPubCkNews 84; NewsDir 84*
Douglas Enterprise - Douglas, GA - *BaconPubCkNews 84; Ed&PubIntYB 82; NewsDir 084*
Douglas Film Industries - Chicago, IL - *AvMarPl 83; Tel&CabFB 84C*
Douglas Neighbor - Marietta, GA - *AyerDirPub 83*
Douglas Neighbor, The - Douglasville, GA - *Ed&PubIntYB 82*
Douglas Televiewers Inc. - Douglas, GA - *BrCabYB 84; Tel&CabFB 84C*
Douglas TV Co. Inc. [of Jim R. Smith & Co. Inc.] - Douglas, AZ - *Tel&CabFB 84C*
Douglas TV Co. Inc. [of Jim R. Smith & Co. Inc.] - Payson, AZ - *Tel&CabFB 84C*
Douglas TV Co. Inc. [of Jim R. Smith & Co. Inc.] - Williams, AZ - *Tel&CabFB 84C*
Douglass Tribune - Douglass, KS - *Ed&PubIntYB 82*
Douglaston-Little Neck Pennysaver - Great Neck, NY - *AyerDirPub 83*
Douglaston-Little Neck Shopping News - Jericho, NY - *AyerDirPub 83*
Douglasville Douglas County Sentinel - Douglasville, GA - *BaconPubCkNews 84; NewsDir 84*
Dousman Index [of Lake Country Reporter Publishers] - Hartland, WI - *NewsDir 84*
Dousman Index - *See* Lake Country Reporter Publishers
Doussard & Associates Inc., Ron - Cary, IL - *LitMarPl 83, 84*
Douthett Enterprises - Wichita, KS - *MicrocomMPl 83, 84*
Dovale Advertising Inc., R. J. - Curacao, Netherlands Antilles - *StaDirAdAg 2-84*
Dove Creek Press - Dove Creek, CO - *AyerDirPub 83; BaconPubCkNews 84; Ed&PubIntYB 82*
Dove Films - Hollywood, CA - *AvMarPl 83*
Dove Films - New York, NY - *AvMarPl 83*
Dovelin Printing Co. - New York, NY - *LitMarPl 83, 84*
Dover Daily Advance - Dover, NJ - *BaconPubCkNews 84; NewsDir 84*
Dover Delaware State News [of Independent Newspapers Inc.] - Dover, DE - *NewsDir 84*
Dover Foster's Daily Democrat [of George J. Foster & Co. Inc.] - Dover, NH - *NewsDir 84*
Dover-Foxcroft Piscataquis Observer - Dover-Foxcroft, ME - *BaconPubCkNews 84; NewsDir 84*
Dover Free Press - *See* Rochester Courier Publishers
Dover Publications Inc. - Mineola, NY - *LitMarPl 84*
Dover Publications Inc. - New York, NY - *DirMarMP 83; LitMarPl 83*
Dover-Sherborn Suburban Press - Dover, MA - *Ed&PubIntYB 82*
Dover-Sherborn Suburban Press [of Suburban World Inc.] - Needham, MA - *AyerDirPub 83; NewsDir 84*
Dover-Sherborn Suburban Press - *See* Suburban World Inc.
Dover Somersworth Free Press - Rochester, NH - *AyerDirPub 83*
Dover Stewart Houston Times - Dover, TN - *BaconPubCkNews 84*
Dow, Clarence B. Jr. - Caribou, ME - *Tel&CabFB 84C p.1678*
Dow Co., James L. Chicago, IL - *StaDirAdAg 2-84*
Dow Jones & Co. Inc. - Princeton, NJ - *BrCabYB 84; HomeVid&CabYB 82-83; InfoS 83-84; InterCabHB 3; Tel&CabFB 84C p.1678*
Dow Jones & Co. Inc. - New York, NY - *AdAge 6-28-84; CompReadDB 82; DirMarMP 83; Ed&PubIntYB 82; HomeVid&CabYB 82-83; KnowInd 83*
Dow Jones Cable News [of Dow Jones & Co.] - Princeton, NJ - *AvMarPl 83; BrCabYB 84; CabTVPrDB 83; Tel&CabFB 84C*
Dow Jones Information Services - Princeton, NJ - *VideoDir 82-83*
Dow Jones International Marketing Services - New York, NY - *Ed&PubIntYB 82*
Dow Jones-Irwin [Subs. of Richard D. Irwin Inc.] - Homewood, IL - *LitMarPl 83, 84; WritMar 84*
Dow Jones News/Retrieval Service [of Dow Jones & Co. Inc.] - Princeton, NJ - *CompReadDB 82; DataDirOnSer 84; DBBus 82; DirOnDB Spring 84; EISS 83; MicrocomMPl 84; OnBibDB 3*
Dow Jones News Services - New York, NY - *BaconPubCkNews 84; Ed&PubIntYB 82; Tel&CabFB 84C*
Dow Jones Quotes - Princeton, NJ - *DirOnDB Spring 84*
Dow Jones Weekly Economic Update [of Dow Jones News/Retrieval Service] - Princeton, NJ - *DataDirOnSer 84*
Dow-Sat of Iowa Inc. [of Dowden Communications Inc.] - Brooklyn, IA - *Tel&CabFB 84C*
Dow-Sat of Iowa Inc. [of Dowden Communications Inc.] - Clarksville, IA - *Tel&CabFB 84C*
Dow-Sat of Iowa Inc. [of Dowden Communications Inc.] - Fredericksburg, IA - *Tel&CabFB 84C*
Dow-Sat of Iowa Inc. [of Dowden Communications Inc.] - North English, IA - *Tel&CabFB 84C*
Dow-Sat of Minnesota Inc. [of Dowden Communications Inc.] - Gaylord, MN - *Tel&CabFB 84C*
Dowagiac News [of Daughtry Newspaper Inc.] - Dowagiac, MI - *BaconPubCkNews 84; Ed&PubIntYB 82; NewsDir 84*
Dowbenko & Associates, Uri - San Francisco, CA - *DirMarMP 83*
Dowcom Inc. - Medway, ME - *BrCabYB 84*
Dowd & Associates, Merle E. - Mercer Island, WA - *Ed&PubIntYB 82; LitMarPl 83, 84*
Dowden & Co. - Drexel Hill, PA - *StaDirAdAg 2-84*
Dowden Communications Inc. - Atlanta, GA - *Tel&CabFB 84C p.1678*
Dowden Communications Inc. - Mound, MN - *Tel&CabFB 84C*
Dowler, Warren L. - Sierra Madre, CA - *BoPubDir 4, 5*
Dowling Manuscript Services, Barbara A. - Malibu, CA - *MagIndMarPl 82-83*
Down Beat - Chicago, IL - *BaconPubCkMag 84; MagDir 84; MagIndMarPl 82-83*
Down East - Camden, ME - *ArtMar 84; BaconPubCkMag 84; MagDir 84; MagIndMarPl 82-83; WritMar 84*
Down East Books [Subs. of Down East Enterprise Inc.] - Camden, ME - *BoPubDir 4; LitMarPl 83, 84; WritMar 84*
Down River News-Herald - Woodhaven, MI - *Ed&PubIntYB 82*
Down There Press - Burlingame, CA - *BoPubDir 4, 5; LitMag&SmPr 83-84*
Down to Earth Gardening Features - Needham, MA - *Ed&PubIntYB 82*
Downeast Digital - Solon, ME - *MicrocomMPl 83, 84; MicrocomSwDir 1; WhoWMicrocom 83*
Downers Grove Hi-Liter - Downers Grove, IL - *BaconPubCkNews 84*
Downers Grove Reporter - Downers Grove, IL - *Ed&PubIntYB 82; NewsDir 84*
Downers Grove Reporter - *See* Reporter Progress Newspapers
Downers Grove Suburban Life Graphic - *See* Life Printing & Publishing Co.
Downey, Charles - Omaha, NE - *InfIndMarPl 83*
Downey Herald American - Downey, CA - *Ed&PubIntYB 82*
Downey Herald American - South Gate, CA - *AyerDirPub 83*
Downey Herald American - *See* Hearst Community Newspapers
Downey, Marion H. & William S. - Whiting, NJ - *LitMarPl 83, 84*
Downey Place Publishing House Inc. - El Cerrito, CA - *LitMag&SmPr 83-84*
Downey Southeast News - South Gate, CA - *BaconPubCkNews 84*

Downey Southeast News & Champion [of Downey Newspapers Inc.] - Downey, CA - *NewsDir 84*
Downieville Mountain Messenger - Downieville, CA - *BaconPubCkNews 84; NewsDir 84*
Downing Industrial Advertising Inc. - Pittsburgh, PA - *StaDirAdAg 2-84*
Downs & Roosevelt Inc. - Washington, DC - *DirPRFirms 83*
Downs Broadcasting - Kannapolis, NC - *BrCabYB 84*
Downs Cable Inc. - Downs, KS - *BrCabYB 84; Tel&CabFB 84C*
Downs Group Inc., The - Charlotte, NC - *StaDirAdAg 2-84*
Downs News - Downs, KS - *BaconPubCkNews 84*
Downs News & Times, The - Downs, KS - *Ed&PubIntYB 82*
Downsview Reporter - Toronto, ON, Canada - *Ed&PubIntYB 82*
Downsville Community Antenna System Inc. - Downsville, NY - *BrCabYB 84; Tel&CabFB 84C*
Downtown Community Television Center - New York, NY - *AvMarPl 83*
Downtown Herald [of New York Herald] - New York, NY - *AyerDirPub 83; NewsDir 84*
Downtown Herald, The - Manhattan, NY - *Ed&PubIntYB 82*
Downtown Idea Exchange - New York, NY - *BaconPubCkMag 84*
Downtown Music Co. - *See* Entertainment Co. Music Group, The
Downtown Poets Co-Op - Brooklyn, NY - *BoPubDir 4, 5; LitMag&SmPr 83-84*
Downtown Research & Development Center - New York, NY - *BoPubDir 4, 5*
Downtown Review, The - New York, NY - *LitMag&SmPr 83-84*
Downtowner [of R.F.D. Publications Inc.] - Portland, OR - *ArtMar 84; WritMar 84*
Dows Advocate - Dows, IA - *BaconPubCkNews 84*
Doyle Advertising Inc., Jack M. - Louisville, KY - *StaDirAdAg 2-84*
Doyle & Co. Inc., William S. - *See* Henderson Friedlich Graf & Doyle Inc.
Doyle & McKenna & Associates Inc. - Reno, NV - *StaDirAdAg 2-84*
Doyle Associates Inc., Richard L. - New York, NY - *DirPRFirms 83; HBIndAd&MS 82-83; StaDirAdAg 2-84*
Doyle Dane Bernbach International Inc. - New York, NY - *AdAge 3-28-84, 6-25-84; Br 1-23-84; BrCabYB 84; HomeVid&CabYB 82-83; StaDirAdAg 2-84; TelAl 83, 84*
Doyle Dane Bernbach Ltd. - Toronto, ON, Canada - *ArtMar 84*
Doyle, Howard A. - East Dennis, MA - *LitMarPl 83, 84*
Doyle, Louis - New York, NY - *LitMarPl 83, 84; MagIndMarPl 82-83*
Doyle/The Consumer Network Inc., Mona - Philadelphia, PA - *HBIndAd&MS 82-83*
Doyle-Van Fossen Inc. - Laguna Hills, CA - *StaDirAdAg 2-84*
Doylen Records - Memphis, TN - *BillIntBG 83-84*
Doylestown Bucks County Telegraph - *See* Progress Newspapers Inc.
Doylestown Daily Intelligencer [of Calkins Newspapers Inc.] - Doylestown, PA - *NewsDir 84*
Doylestown Telephone Co., The - Doyestown, OH - *TelDir&BG 83-84*
DP & W Inc. - Boston, MA - *DataDirOnSer 84*
DP Communications Corp. - Great Neck, NY - *WhoWMicrocom 83*
DP Enterprises - Phoenix, AZ - *BoPubDir 4, 5*
DPA-LTA Enterprises Inc. - Alburg, VT - *BoPubDir 4 Sup, 5*
DPC - Albuquerque, NM - *MicrocomMPl 83*
DPF Computer Leasing Corp. - Hartsdale, NY - *DataDirSup 7-83*
DPG Publishing Co. Ltd. [Aff. of Dumont Press Graphix] - Kitchener, ON, Canada - *BoPubDir 4, 5*
DPS Information Centre [of Data Processing Services Co.] - Cairo, Egypt - *EISS 7-83 Sup*
Dr. Dobb's Journal [Subs. of People's Computer Co.] - Menlo Park, CA - *BaconPubCkMag 84; LitMag&SmPr 83-84; MagIndMarPl 82-83; MicrocomMPl 84; WhoWMicrocom 83*
DR Group Inc., The - Boston, MA - *ArtMar 84; StaDirAdAg 2-84*
DR Group Inc., The - New York, NY - *AdAge 3-28-84; DirMarMP 83; HBIndAd&MS 82-83*
DR Music - *See* Alexis Music Inc.
Dr. Software - Santa Barbara, CA - *MicrocomMPl 83*
Dracula Press [Aff. of The Count Dracula Fan Club] - New York, NY - *BoPubDir 4, 5; LitMag&SmPr 83-84*
Draft Action - Washington, DC - *LitMag&SmPr 83-84*
Drag Racing News & Views - Seattle, WA - *BaconPubCkMag 84*
Drag World - Leawood, KS - *BaconPubCkMag 84*
Dragon Co. - Houston, TX - *BoPubDir 5*
Dragon Enterprises - Genoa, NV - *BoPubDir 4, 5*
Dragon Gate Inc. - Port Townsend, WA - *BoPubDir 4, 5; LitMag&SmPr 83-84*
Dragon International Inc. - Haledon, NJ - *BillIntBG 83-84*
Dragon Magazine [of TSR Hobbies Inc.] - Lake Geneva, WI - *ArtMar 84; WritMar 84*
Dragon Records - Bronx, NY - *BillIntBG 83-84*
Dragonfighter Press - Houston, TX - *BoPubDir 4 Sup, 5*
Dragonfly [Aff. of Western World Haiku Society] - Portland, OR - *BoPubDir 4, 5; LitMag&SmPr 83-84*
Dragonfly Press - Toledo, OH - *BoPubDir 4, 5*
Dragonfly Software - Colesville, MD - *MicrocomMPl 84*
Dragon's Lair Inc., The - Dayton, OH - *MagIndMarPl 82-83*
Dragon's Teeth Press - Georgetown, CA - *BoPubDir 4, 5; LitMag&SmPr 83-84; LitMarPl 84; WritMar 84*
Dragonsbreath Press - Sister Bay, WI - *BoPubDir 4, 5; LitMag&SmPr 83-84; WritMar 84*
Dragonwyck Publishing Inc. - Contoocook, NH - *BoPubDir 4, 5*
Drain Cable & Appliance Inc. - Drain, OR - *BrCabYB 84; Tel&CabFB 84C*
Drain Enterprise - Drain, OR - *BaconPubCkNews 84; Ed&PubIntYB 82*
Drake Advertising Ltd. - Toronto, ON, Canada - *StaDirAdAg 2-84*
Drake & Associates, Tom - Portland, OR - *StaDirAdAg 2-84*
Drake Associates Inc., Kenneth - Detroit, MI - *DirPRFirms 83*
Drake Cable TV [of NoDaKable Inc.] - Bottineau, ND - *BrCabYB 84*
Drake Cable TV [of NoDaKable Inc.] - Drake, ND - *Tel&CabFB 84C*
Drake, Earl - Kalamazoo, MI - *Tel&CabFB 84C p.1678*
Drake Music Group/First Generation Records - Nashville, TN - *BillIntBG 83-84*
Drake Times-Delphic [of Drake University] - Des Moines, IA - *NewsDir 84*
Drakes Branch Charlotte Gazette - Drakes Branch, VA - *NewsDir 84*
Drama Book Publishers - New York, NY - *ArtMar 84; LitMarPl 83, 84; WritMar 84*
Drama Review, The [of The MIT Press] - Cambridge, MA - *LitMarPl 83, 84*
Drama Review, The [of New York University] - New York, NY - *LitMag&SmPr 83-84; MagDir 84; MagIndMarPl 82-83; WritMar 84*
Dramatic Publishing Co., The - Chicago, IL - *LitMarPl 83, 84; WritMar 84*
Dramatics [of International Thespian Society] - Cincinnati, OH - *BaconPubCkMag 84; MagIndMarPl 82-83; WritMar 84*
Dramatika - Tarpon Springs, FL - *BoPubDir 4, 5; LitMag&SmPr 83-84; WritMar 84*
Dramatists Play Service Inc. - New York, NY - *LitMarPl 83, 84*
DRAMCO Sales Inc. - New York, NY - *DirInfWP 82*
Dranetz Engineering Lab Inc. - South Plainfield, NJ - *DirInfWP 82*
Draper Daniels Media Services Inc. - Chicago, IL - *BrCabYB 84; StaDirAdAg 2-84*
Draper Screen Co. - Spiceland, IN - *AvMarPl 83*
Draperies & Window Coverings - North Palm Beach, FL - *BaconPubCkMag 84*
Drate/Drate Design, Spencer - New York, NY - *LitMarPl 83, 84; MagIndMarPl 82-83*
Draugas - Chicago, IL - *Ed&PubIntYB 82*
Draw Music Co. - Waterford, PA - *BillIntBG 83-84*
Drawing Board Greeting Cards Inc. - Dallas, TX - *WritMar 84*
Drawing-Room Graphic Services Ltd. - North Vancouver, BC, Canada - *BoPubDir 4, 5*
Drayeniv Music Publishing Co. - Edgartown, MA - *BillIntBG 83-84*
Drayton Cable TV Inc. - Drayton, ND - *BrCabYB 84*
Drayton Express - Drayton, ND - *Ed&PubIntYB 82*
Drayton Express - *See* Ness Press Inc.
Dreadnaught - Toronto, ON, Canada - *BoPubDir 4, 5; LitMarPl 84; WritMar 84*

Dream Dealers Music - *See* Fricon Entertainment Co. Inc., The
Dream Garden Press - Salt Lake City, UT - *BoPubDir 4 Sup, 5; LitMag&SmPr 83-84; LitMarPl 84; WritMar 84*
Dream International Quarterly - Escondido, CA - *WritMar 84*
Dream Place Publications - Stanford, CA - *BoPubDir 4, 5; LitMag&SmPr 83-84*
Dreams - New York, NY - *LitMag&SmPr 83-84*
Dreams Unltd. - Middleton, WI - *BoPubDir 4, 5*
Dreamstreet Records - Hohokus, NJ - *BillIntBG 83-84*
Dreamworks - New York, NY - *MagIndMarPl 82-83*
Dreena Music - *See* Asilomar Music
Dreenan Press Ltd. - Croton-on-Hudson, NY - *LitMarPl 83*
Dreher Leather Manufacturing Corp. - Newark, NJ - *LitMarPl 83, 84*
Drelwood Publications [Aff. of West-hill Management & Development Inc.] - Portland, OR - *BoPubDir 4 Sup, 5*
Drennan CHR New York Regional Data Base - New York, NY - *DirOnDB Spring 84*
Drennan Communications - White Plains, NY - *LitMarPl 83, 84; MagIndMarPl 82-83*
Drenser, Morris & Tortorello Research Inc. - New York, NY - *IntDirMarRes 83*
Drenthe Telephone Co. - Zeeland, MI - *TelDir&BG 83-84*
Dresden Enterprise - Dresden, TN - *BaconPubCkNews 84; NewsDir 84*
Dresden Enterprise & Sharon Tribune - Dresden, TN - *Ed&PubIntYB 82*
Dresden Post-Transcript - Dresden, OH - *BaconPubCkNews 84; Ed&PubIntYB 82*
Dress for Success - New York, NY - *ProGuPRSer 4*
Dressage & CT - Cleveland, OH - *MagIndMarPl 82-83*
Dresselhaus Computer Products - Glendora, CA - *MicrocomMPl 84*
Dresselhaus Computer Products - Woodland Hills, CA - *MicrocomMPl 83*
Dresser Dispatch - Prescott, WI - *AyerDirPub 83*
Dresser Dispatch - *See* Weekly Newspapers Inc.
Drew Associates Inc. - New York, NY - *Tel&CabFB 84C*
Drew Mark Music Inc. - Metairie, LA - *BillIntBG 83-84*
Drew Sunflower County News - Drew, MS - *BaconPubCkNews 84*
Drewry Group, R. H. - Lawton, OK - *BrCabYB 84; Tel&CabFB 84S*
Drexel Burnham Lambert Inc. - New York, NY - *ADAPSOMemDir 83-84*
Drexel Hill Leader [of Marple Publishing Co. Inc.] - Newtown Square, PA - *NewsDir 84*
Drexel Hill Leader - *See* Marple Publishing Co. Inc.
Drexel Star - Drexel, MO - *BaconPubCkNews 84; Ed&PubIntYB 82*
Drexel Technical Journal [of Drexel University] - Philadelphia, PA - *BaconPubCkMag 84; MagDir 84*
Drexler Interviewing Service, Evelyn - Huntsville, AL - *IntDirMarRes 83*
Drey Co. Inc., Alan - New York, NY - *LitMarPl 83, 84*
Dreyer, Peter H. - Boston-Westwood, MA - *MagIndMarPl 82-83*
DRG Music Inc. - New York, NY - *BillIntBG 83-84*
DRG Records Inc. - New York, NY - *BillIntBG 83-84*
DRI Bank Analysis Service - Washington, DC - *DirOnDB Spring 84*
DRI Capsule [of Data Resources Inc.] - Lexington, MA - *DBBus 82*
DRI Current Economic Indicators Data Bank - Washington, DC - *DirOnDB Spring 84*
DRI Financial & Credit Statistics Data Bank - Washington, DC - *DirOnDB Spring 84*
DRI Financial & Credit Statistics Data Bank [of Data Resources Inc.] - Lexington, MA - *DBBus 82*
DRI Industry Financial Service Data Bank - Washington, DC - *DirOnDB Spring 84*
DRI Industry Financial Service Data Bank [of Data Resources Inc.] - Lexington, MA - *DataDirOnSer 84; DBBus 82*
DRI-SEC [of Data Resources Inc.] - Lexington, MA - *DBBus 82*
DRI Securities Data Bank - Washington, DC - *DirOnDB Spring 84*
Driftwood Records - Nashville, TN - *BillIntBG 83-84*
Driggs Teton Valley News - Driggs, ID - *BaconPubCkNews 84*
Drill Bit [of Hart Publications Inc.] - Midland, TX - *BaconPubCkMag 84; MagDir 84*
Drilling Activity Analysis Systems [of Petroleum Information Corp.] - Denver, CO - *DataDirOnSer 84; DBBus 82*
Drilling Analysis Data On-Line - Littleton, CO - *DirOnDB Spring 84*
Drilling Contractor [of International Association of Drilling Contractors] - Houston, TX - *BaconPubCkMag 84; MagDir 84*
Drilling Information Services [of Adams & Rountree Technology Inc.] - Lafayette, LA - *DirOnDB Spring 84; EISS 5-84 Sup*
Drilling Magazine - Dallas, TX - *BaconPubCkMag 84*
Drilling Wellsite Publication [of Associated Publishers Inc.] - Dallas, TX - *MagDir 84*
Drillsite - Calgary, AB, Canada - *BaconPubCkMag 84*
Drip/Trickle Irrigation - Fresno, CA - *BaconPubCkMag 84*
Driscoll & Associates Inc., Mike - Columbus, OH - *StaDirAdAg 2-84*
Drive-In Music Co. Inc. - Hollywood, CA - *BillIntBG 83-84*
Drivel Press - Santa Cruz, CA - *BoPubDir 4, 5*
Driven Music - Portland, ME - *BillIntBG 83-84*
Driving - Florham Park, NJ - *BaconPubCkMag 84; MagDir 84*
Driving Music - *See* Creative Corps.
DRK Inc. - Boston, MA - *StaDirAdAg 2-84*
DRK Photo - Hartford, WI - *LitMarPl 84*
Drohlich Associates Inc., Robert - St. Louis, MO - *DirPRFirms 83*
Drolet, J. Gilles - Bernierville, PQ, Canada - *BrCabYB 84*
Droopytunes - *See* Marvel Music, Andy
Drop Shipping News - New York, NY - *DirMarMP 83*
Drop Top Music - Chicago, IL - *BillIntBG 83-84*
Drossman Lehmann Marino & Reveley Inc. - New York, NY - *StaDirAdAg 2-84*
Drovers Journal [of Vance Publishing Corp.] - Shawnee Mission, KS - *BaconPubCkMag 84; MagIndMarPl 82-83; NewsDir 84*
Drovers Journal, The - Kansas City, KS - *MagDir 84*
DRS [of Advanced Data Management] - Kingston, NJ - *EISS 83*
DRTV Cable - Stockport, OH - *Tel&CabFB 84C*
DRTV Service - Stockport, OH - *BrCabYB 84*
Druck, Kitty L. - Somerset, NJ - *LitMarPl 83, 84*
Druck Productions, Mark - New York, NY - *HBIndAd&MS 82-83; WritMar 84*
Drucker/Vincent Inc. - San Francisco, CA - *ArtMar 84*
Drug Abuse Council - Washington, DC - *BoPubDir 4, 5*
Drug Abuse Epidemiology Data Center [of Texas Christian University] - Ft. Worth, TX - *CompReadDB 82; EISS 83*
Drug Abuse Reform Enterprises - Rockford, IL - *LitMarPl 83*
Drug Abuse Warning Network [of U.S. Drug Enforcement Administration] - Washington, DC - *EISS 83*
Drug & Cosmetic Industry [of Harcourt Brace Jovanovich Inc.] - New York, NY - *BaconPubCkMag 84; MagDir 84; MagIndMarPl 82-83*
Drug & Poison Information Centre [of University of British Columbia] - Vancouver, BC, Canada - *EISS 83*
Drug Facts & Comparisons [of Harfax Database Publishing] - Cambridge, MA - *DataDirOnSer 84*
Drug Info [of Drug Information Services] - Minneapolis, MN - *CompReadDB 82; DataDirOnSer 84*
Drug Information & Alcohol Use-Abuse [of The Drug Information Services] - Minneapolis, MN - *DBBus 82; DirOnDB Spring 84; OnBibDB 3*
Drug Information Association - Maple Glen, PA - *EISS 83*
Drug Information Fulltext [of American Society of Hospital Pharmacists] - Bethesda, MD - *DirOnDB Spring 84; EISS 5-84 Sup*
Drug Information On-Line [of Excerpta Medica BV] - Amsterdam, Netherlands - *CompReadDB 82*
Drug Information Service [of Memorial Hospital of Long Beach] - Long Beach, CA - *EISS 83*
Drug Information Services [of University of Minnesota] - Minneapolis, MN - *CompReadDB 82; DataDirOnSer 84; EISS 83; InfIndMarPl 83*
Drug Intelligence & Clinical Pharmacy - Cincinnati, OH - *MagDir 84*
Drug Intelligence Publications Inc. - Washington, DC - *BoPubDir 4, 5*

Drug Merchandising - Toronto, ON, Canada - *BaconPubCkMag 84*
Drug Products Information File [of American Society of Hospital Pharmacists] - Washington, DC - *EISS 83*
Drug Store Market Guide - Mohegan Lake, NY - *BoPubDir 4 Sup, 5*
Drug Store News - New York, NY - *BaconPubCkMag 84*
Drug Survival News [of D.I.N. Publications] - Phoenix, AZ - *LitMag&SmPr 83-84*
Drug Therapy [of Biomedical Information Corp.] - New York, NY - *BaconPubCkMag 84; MagDir 84*
Drug Therapy (Hospital Edition) - New York, NY - *MagDir 84; MagIndMarPl 82-83*
Drug Therapy (Office Edition) - New York, NY - *MagIndMarPl 82-83*
Drug Topics [of Litton Publications Inc.] - Oradell, NJ - *BaconPubCkMag 84; MagDir 84; MagIndMarPl 82-83; WritMar 84*
Drugdex [of Micromedex Inc.] - Englewood, CO - *EISS 83*
Drugdoc [of Excerpta Medica BV] - Amsterdam, Netherlands - *CompReadDB 82*
Drugs & Drug Abuse Education - Washington, DC - *MagDir 84*
Druid Books - Ephraim, WI - *BoPubDir 4, 5; LitMag&SmPr 83-84*
Druid Heights Books - Mill Valley, CA - *BoPubDir 4, 5; LitMag&SmPr 83-84*
Druid Press - Birmingham, AL - *LitMag&SmPr 83-84*
Drukker Communications Inc. - Passaic, NJ - *Ed&PubIntYB 82*
Drum Corps World - Madison, WI - *BaconPubCkMag 84*
Drum Records Inc. - Fargo, ND - *BillIntBG 83-84*
Drumheller Mail Ltd. - Drumheller, AB, Canada - *Ed&PubIntYB 82*
Drummer News - Vandalia, OH - *AyerDirPub 83*
Drummond Advertising - Los Gatos, CA - *AdAge 3-28-84; StaDirAdAg 2-84*
Drummond Island Telephone Co. - Carney, MI - *TelDir&BG 83-84*
Drumright Derrick - Drumright, OK - *BaconPubCkNews 84; Ed&PubIntYB 82*
Drumright Journal - Drumright, OK - *Ed&PubIntYB 82*
Drunken Poet Press - Indianapolis, IN - *BoPubDir 4, 5*
Drury, John - Wheeling, WV - *LitMarPl 83, 84*
Dryad Press - San Francisco, CA - *BoPubDir 4, 5; LitMag&SmPr 83-84*
Dryad Press - Takoma Park, MD - *LitMarPl 83, 84; WritMar 84*
Drycleaners News - Waterbury, CT - *BaconPubCkMag 84; MagDir 84*
Dryden Community TV Ltd. - Dryden, ON, Canada - *BrCabYB 84*
Dryden Observer - Dryden, ON, Canada - *Ed&PubIntYB 82*
Dryden Press - *See* CBS Educational & Professional Publishing
Dryden Tompkins Rural News - Dryden, NY - *Ed&PubIntYB 82*
Drytac Corp. - Madison, CT - *AvMarPl 83*
DSA Data Systems Inc. - Brewster, NY - *DataDirSup 7-83*
DSA/Phototech Inc. - Los Angeles, CA - *AvMarPl 83*
D'San Corp. - Flushing, NY - *AvMarPl 83*
DSG Inc. - Philadelphia, PA - *DirInfWP 82*
DSI/Cyzern - Fayettesville, AR - *MicrocomMPl 84*
DSI/Med-Comm Inc. - Lenexa, KS - *MicrocomMPl 84*
DSIR Central Library [of Dept. of Scientific & Industrial Research] - Wellington, New Zealand - *EISS 83*
DSL Computer Products Inc. - Dearborn, MI - *MicrocomMPl 84*
DSM Producers - New York, NY - *AvMarPl 83*
DTI Data Trek - Encinitas, CA - *EISS 7-83 Sup*
DTI Records - San Rafael, CA - *BillIntBG 83-84*
DTSS Inc. [Subs. of Metropolitan Life Insurance Co.] - Hanover, NH - *ADAPSOMemDir 83-84; DataDirOnSer 84; EISS 83; InfoS 83-84*
Du Art Film Laboratories Inc. - New York, NY - *AvMarPl 83*
Du Art Video - Newton, MA - *AvMarPl 83*
Du Art Video [Div. of Du Art Film Laboratories Inc.] - New York, NY - *AvMarPl 83; Tel&CabFB 84C*
Du Bois Area Cable TV Co. [of Vision Cable Communications Inc.] - Du Bois, PA - *BrCabYB 84; Tel&CabFB 84C*
Du Bois Courier-Express - Du Bois, PA - *BaconPubCkNews 84; BrCabYB 84*
Du-My Syndicate - Lancaster, CA - *Ed&PubIntYB 82*
Du Page Doings [of The Doings Newspapers] - Hinsdale, IL - *AyerDirPub 83; NewsDir 84*
Du Page Doings - *See* Doings Newspapers, The
Du Page Progress - Downers Grove, IL - *AyerDirPub 83; NewsDir 84*
Du Page Voice - *See* Voice Newspapers
Du Pont Co. - Wilmington, DE - *HomeVid&CabYB 82-83*
Du Pont Co. (Tyvek Marketing) - Wilmington, DE - *LitMarPl 83, 84*
Du Pre Syndicate - Pine Plains, NY - *Ed&PubIntYB 82*
Du Pree Associates, C. B. - Syracuse, NY - *IntDirMarRes 83*
Du Quaine Lectern Manufacturing Corp. - Kewaunee, WI - *AvMarPl 83*
Du Quoin Call - Du Quoin, IL - *BaconPubCkNews 84*
Du Vall Press Financial Publications - Williamston, MI - *BoPubDir 4, 5*
Dual Systems Corp. - Berkeley, CA - *MicrocomMPl 84; WhoWMicrocom 83*
Duane Music Inc. - Sunnyvale, CA - *BillIntBG 83-84*
Duane TV Relay Inc. - Bulan, KY - *BrCabYB 84*
Duarte Co. - Lewiston, ME - *LitMarPl 83, 84*
Duarte The Duartean - *See* Foothill Inter-City Newspapers
Duartean [of Foothill Inter City Newspapers] - Arcadia, CA - *AyerDirPub 83; NewsDir 84*
Duartean, The - Duarte, CA - *Ed&PubIntYB 82*
Dubbert, Lisa Vey - Baltimore, MD - *LitMarPl 84*
Duber/Grau Inc. - Marina del Rey, CA - *StaDirAdAg 2-84*
Dubie-Do Productions Inc. - Englewood Cliffs, NJ - *Tel&CabFB 84C*
Dubie-Do Productions Inc. - New York, NY - *TelAl 83, 84*
Dubin Bunde Associates - Los Angeles, CA - *BrCabYB 84; StaDirAdAg 2-84*
Dubin, Sidney - Great Neck, NY - *BoPubDir 4 Sup, 5*
Dubitsky Community Relations, Karen - Miami, FL - *DirPRFirms 83*
Dublin & Associates Inc. - San Antonio, TX - *DirPRFirms 83*
Dublin Courier-Herald - Dublin, GA - *BaconPubCkNews 84; NewsDir 84*
Dublin Forum - Dublin, OH - *BaconPubCkNews 84; Ed&PubIntYB 82*
Dublin Press [Aff. of Alden Games] - Sunnyvale, CA - *BoPubDir 4, 5*
Dublin Progress - Dublin, TX - *AyerDirPub 83; BaconPubCkNews 84; Ed&PubIntYB 82*
Dublin Suburbia News - *See* Suburban News Publications
Dubois Cable TV - Dubois, WY - *BrCabYB 84; Tel&CabFB 84C p.1678*
Dubois Cablevision [of Tele-Communications Inc.] - Princeton, IN - *BrCabYB 84*
Dubois CableVision Inc. [of Horizon Communications Corp.] - Jasper, IN - *BrCabYB 84; Tel&CabFB 84C*
Dubois County Historical Society - Jasper, IN - *BoPubDir 4, 5*
Dubois/Ruddy - Birmingham, MI - *AvMarPl 83*
Dubois Telephone Exchange Inc. - Dubois, WY - *TelDir&BG 83-84*
Duboy Advertising Inc., Jess - Richmond, VA - *BrCabYB 84*
Dubuque Leader, The - Dubuque, IA - *NewsDir 84*
Dubuque Telegraph Herald - Dubuque, IA - *NewsDir 84*
Duca-Post - Willowdale, ON, Canada - *Ed&PubIntYB 82*
Duce Music - Los Angeles, CA - *BillIntBG 83-84*
Duchess Music Corp. - *See* MCA Music
Duck Book Digest, The - Cocoa, FL - *LitMag&SmPr 83-84*
Duck Down Press - Fallon, NV - *BoPubDir 4, 5; LitMag&SmPr 83-84; WritMar 84*
Duck Press - New York, NY - *BoPubDir 4, 5*
Duck Soup - Irving, TX - *LitMag&SmPr 83-84*
Duckburg Times, The - Selah, WA - *LitMag&SmPr 83-84*
Ducker Research Co. Inc. - Birmingham, MI - *IntDirMarRes 83*
Ducks Unltd. - Chicago, IL - *MagIndMarPl 82-83*
Ducks Unltd. - Lake Zurich, IL - *MagDir 84*
Duckworth Associates Ltd. - Scarborough, ON, Canada - *DirPRFirms 83*
Ducor Telephone Co. - Ducor, CA - *TelDir&BG 83-84*
Dudden, Adrianne Onderdonk - Bryn Mawr, PA - *LitMarPl 83, 84*
Dude Rancher Magazine [of Dude Ranchers' Association] - Englewood, CO - *MagDir 84*

Dude Ranchers' Association [Aff. of Dude Rancher Magazine] - LaPorte, CO - *BoPubDir 5*
Dudley-Anderson-Yutzy Public Relations Inc. - New York, NY - *DirPRFirms 83*
Dudreck DePaul Ficco & Morgan - Pittsburgh, PA - *AdAge 3-28-84; DirPRFirms 83; StaDirAdAg 2-84*
Duende Press - Oakland, CA - *BoPubDir 4, 5*
Duende Press - Placitas, NM - *LitMag&SmPr 83-84*
Duewel & Associates - Palatine, IL - *ADAPSOMemDir 83-84*
Duff Agency Inc., Charles - Scottsdale, AZ - *StaDirAdAg 2-84*
Duffy & Bentley Consulting Group - Toronto, ON, Canada - *DirInfWP 82*
Duffy & Shanley Inc. - Providence, RI - *DirPRFirms 83; StaDirAdAg 2-84*
Duffy, Bringgold, Knutson & Oberprillers Inc. - Minneapolis, MN - *AdAge 3-28-84; StaDirAdAg 2-84*
Dufour Editions Inc. - Chester Springs, PA - *BoPubDir 4; LitMarPl 83, 84; WritMar 84*
Dufresne, Edouard - Amos, PQ, Canada - *BrCabYB 84*
Dufur TV Corp. - Dufur, OR - *BrCabYB 84; Tel&CabFB 84C*
Dugald Women's Institute - Dugald, MB, Canada - *BoPubDir 4, 5*
Dugan-Farley Communications Associates - Montvale, NJ - *AdAge 3-28-84; StaDirAdAg 2-84*
Duggans, Doyle - Tallahassee, FL - *Tel&CabFB 84C p.1678*
Dugger Cable TV Inc. - Dugger, IN - *Tel&CabFB 84C*
Dugger Color Graphics, Jon - New Castle, PA - *MagIndMarPl 82-83*
Dugway Cable TV Corp. - Dugway, UT - *Tel&CabFB 84C*
Duhamel Broadcasting Enterprises - Rapid City, SD - *BrCabYB 84*
Duir Press - San Francisco, CA - *BoPubDir 4, 5; LitMag&SmPr 83-84*
Dukane Corp. - St. Charles, IL - *AvMarPl 83*
Duke Chronicle [of Duke University Publications Board] - Durham, NC - *NewsDir 84*
Duke Times - Duke, OK - *Ed&PubIntYB 82*
Duke University (Center for International Studies) - Durham, NC - *BoPubDir 4, 5*
Duke University (Center for the Study of Aging & Human Development) - Durham, NC - *BoPubDir 4 Sup, 5*
Duke University (Translation Service) - Durham, NC - *MagIndMarPl 82-83*
Duke University Press - Durham, NC - *LitMag&SmPr 83-84; LitMarPl 83, 84; MagIndMarPl 82-83*
Duke Unltd. Inc. - Kenner, LA - *ArtMar 84; StaDirAdAg 2-84*
Dukengineer [of Engineering Publishing Advisory Council] - Durham, NC - *BaconPubCkMag 84; MagDir 84*
Dulaney Advertising - Louisville, KY - *AdAge 3-28-84; StaDirAdAg 2-84*
Duley Press Inc. - Mishawaka, IN - *MagIndMarPl 82-83*
Duluth Budgeteer-Scenic City News [of Minnesota Newspaper Association] - Duluth, MN - *AyerDirPub 83; BaconPubCkNews 84; Ed&PubIntYB 82; NewsDir 84*
Duluth Herald - Duluth, MN - *Ed&PubIntYB 82; LitMarPl 83*
Duluth News-Tribune - Duluth, MN - *Ed&PubIntYB 82; LitMarPl 83*
Duluth News Tribune & Herald - Duluth, MN - *BaconPubCkNews 84*
DUM, The Newsmagazine of Veterinary Medicine - McLean, VA - *BaconPubCkMag 84*
Dumas Cable TV [of TCA Cable TV Inc.] - Mitchellville, AR - *Tel&CabFB 84C*
Dumas Clarion - Dumas, AR - *BaconPubCkNews 84; Ed&PubIntYB 82; NewsDir 84*
Dumas Moore County News Press - Dumas, TX - *BaconPubCkNews 84; NewsDir 84*
Dumas, Tedd W. - Nucla, CO - *Tel&CabFB 84C p.1678*
Dumont Cablevision - Dumont, IA - *Tel&CabFB 84C*
Dumont Instrumentation Inc. - Commack, NY - *AvMarPl 83*
Dumont Telephone Co. - Dumont, IA - *TelDir&BG 83-84*
Dumoulin, Rejean - Nicolet, PQ, Canada - *BrCabYB 84*
Dun & Bradstreet Canada Ltd. - Toronto, ON, Canada - *BoPubDir 4 Sup, 5*
Dun & Bradstreet Corp. - New York, NY - *AdAge 6-28-84; BoPubDir 5; Datamation 6-83; HomeVid&CabYB 82-83; InfoS 83-84; KnowInd 83; Top100Al 83*
Dun & Bradstreet Corp. - *See* Corinthian Broadcasting Corp.
Dun & Bradstreet Credit Services [Div. of Dun & Bradstreet Corp.] - New York, NY - *DirMarMP 83; InfoS 83-84*
Dun & Bradstreet Operations - New York, NY - *InfoS 83-84*
Duna Studios - Minneapolis, MN - *BoPubDir 5*
Dunaway, William R. - Aspen, CO - *BrCabYB 84*
Dunbar Furniture - Berne, IL - *DirInfWP 82*
Dunbarton Telephone Co. - Dunbarton, NH - *TelDir&BG 83-84*
Duncan Audio Visual Inc. - Rochester, NY - *AvMarPl 83*
Duncan Banner [of Wimberly Investments Inc.] - Duncan, OK - *BaconPubCkNews 84; Ed&PubIntYB 82; NewsDir 84*
Duncan Cable TV Service - Wilmington, VT - *BrCabYB 84; Tel&CabFB 84C*
Duncan, E. - North Hollywood, CA - *LitMarPl 83, 84*
Duncan Eagle - Duncan, OK - *BaconPubCkNews 84*
Duncan, George - Cambridge, MA - *LitMarPl 83, 84; MagIndMarPl 82-83*
Duncan Inc., Victor - Chicago, IL - *AvMarPl 83*
Duncan Inc., Victor - Madison Heights, MI - *AvMarPl 83*
Duncan Inc., Victor - Irving, TX - *AvMarPl 83*
Duncan Media Enterprises Inc. - Kalamazoo, MI - *BrCabYB 84*
Duncannon Area Cable Co. - Duncannon, PA - *BrCabYB 84*
Duncannon Record - Duncannon, PA - *BaconPubCkNews 84; Ed&PubIntYB 82*
Duncanville Cable TV [of Sammons Communications Inc.] - Duncanville, TX - *BrCabYB 84; InterCabHB 3; Tel&CabFB 84C*
Duncanville County Courier - *See* Zauber Publishing
Duncanville Journal [of DeSoto Journal Publishing Co.] - De Soto, TX - *NewsDir 84*
Duncanville Suburban - Duncanville, TX - *AyerDirPub 83; BaconPubCkNews 84; Ed&PubIntYB 82; NewsDir 84*
Dunconor Books - Lake City, CO - *BoPubDir 4, 5*
Dundalk Eagle [of Kimbel Publications Inc.] - Baltimore, MD - *NewsDir 84*
Dundalk Eagle - Dundalk, MD - *AyerDirPub 83; BaconPubCkNews 84; Ed&PubIntYB 82*
Dundas Ancaster Recorder - Dundas, ON, Canada - *AyerDirPub 83*
Dundas Star-Journal - Dundas, ON, Canada - *AyerDirPub 83; Ed&PubIntYB 82*
Dundee Countryside - Barrington, IL - *NewsDir 84*
Dundee Observer - Dundee, NY - *BaconPubCkNews 84; Ed&PubIntYB 82*
Dundee Publishing - Dundee, NY - *LitMag&SmPr 83-84*
Dundee Reporter - Dundee, MI - *Ed&PubIntYB 82*
Dundee Reporter - *See* Reporter Publishing Co.
Dundee Sun - Dundee, NE - *Ed&PubIntYB 82*
Dundee Sun [of Omaha Sun Newspapers] - Omaha, NE - *NewsDir 84*
Dundurn Press Ltd. - Toronto, ON, Canada - *BoPubDir 4; LitMag&SmPr 83-84; LitMarPl 83, 84*
Dune Buggies & Hot VWS [of Wright Publishing Co. Inc.] - Costa Mesa, CA - *BaconPubCkMag 84; MagDir 84; WritMar 84*
Dunedin/Countryside Herald - Dunedin, FL - *AyerDirPub 83*
Dunedin Herald [of The Tarpon Springs Herald Newspapers] - Tarpon Springs, FL - *NewsDir 84*
Dunedin Herald - *See* Pinellas Publishers Inc.
Dunedin Times - Dunedin, FL - *AyerDirPub 83*
Dunes Cable TV - Hauser, OR - *Tel&CabFB 84C*
Dunes Cable TV - North Bend, OR - *BrCabYB 84*
Dunes Enterprises - Beverly Shores, IN - *BoPubDir 4, 5*
Dunham & Marcus Inc. - New York, NY - *HBIndAd&MS 82-83*
Dunhill International List Co. Inc. - Ft. Lauderdale, FL - *LitMarPl 83, 84; MagIndMarPl 82-83*
Dunhill Mailing Lists Inc., Hugo - New York, NY - *EISS 83; MagIndMarPl 82-83*
DUNIS - New York, NY - *DirOnDB Spring 84*
Dunkel Sports Research Service - Ormond Beach, FL - *Ed&PubIntYB 82*
Dunkelberger Advertising Inc., Dennis - Dayton, OH - *StaDirAdAg 2-84*
Dunkerton Sun - Evansdale, IA - *AyerDirPub 83*
Dunkerton Telephone Cooperative - Dunkerton, IA - *TelDir&BG 83-84*
Dunkin County Press - Senath, MO - *Ed&PubIntYB 82*

Dunkirk & Fredonia Telephone Co. - Fredonia, NY - *TelDir&BG 83-84*
Dunkirk Grape Belt - Dunkirk, NY - *BaconPubCkNews 84*
Dunkirk News & Sun - Dunkirk, IN - *BaconPubCkNews 84; Ed&PubIntYB 82*
Dunklin County Press - Senath, MO - *AyerDirPub 83*
Dunklin Democrat - Kennett, MO - *AyerDirPub 83*
Dunlap Reporter - Dunlap, IA - *BaconPubCkNews 84; Ed&PubIntYB 82*
Dunlap Society - Essex, NY - *BoPubDir 4, 5*
Dunlap Society (Visual Documentation Program) - Essex, NY - *MicroMarPl 82-83*
Dunlap Tribune - Dunlap, TN - *BaconPubCkNews 84; Ed&PubIntYB 82*
Dunn Advertising Inc., Mal - Croton Falls, NY - *HBIndAd&MS 82-83*
Dunn & Co. Inc. - South Lancaster, MA - *LitMarPl 83, 84*
Dunn & David Inc. - New York, NY - *IntDirMarRes 83*
Dunn & Hargitt Commodity Service - Lafayette, IN - *EISS 7-83 Sup*
Dunn Broadcasting Co. - El Paso, TX - *BrCabYB 84*
Dunn, Clairice & James E. - La Crosse, WI - *Tel&CabFB 84C p.1678*
Dunn County News - Menomonie, WI - *AyerDirPub 83; Ed&PubIntYB 82*
Dunn County Reminder - Menomonie, WI - *AyerDirPub 83*
Dunn Daily Record - Dunn, NC - *NewsDir 84*
Dunn Dispatch - Dunn, NC - *NewsDir 84*
Dunn Studios Inc., Cal - Chicago, IL - *AvMarPl 83; TelAl 83, 84; Tel&CabFB 84C*
Dunnan & Jeffrey Inc. - Union, NJ - *StaDirAdAg 2-84*
Dunnell Telephone Co. Inc. - Dunnell, MN - *TelDir&BG 83-84*
Dunnville Chronicle - Dunnville, ON, Canada - *Ed&PubIntYB 82*
Dun's Business Month [of Dun & Bradstreet Corp.] - New York, NY - *BaconPubCkMag 84; Folio 83; MagDir 84; MagIndMarPl 82-83; WritMar 84*
Dun's Financial Profiles [of Dun & Bradstreet Corp.] - New York, NY - *DBBus 82*
Dun's Market Identifiers 10+ [of Dun's Marketing ServicesiParsippany, NJ -*DataDirOnSer 84*
Dun's Marketing Services - Hamden, CT - *MicroMarPl 82-83*
Dun's Marketing Services [of Dun & Bradstreet Corp.] - Parsippany, NJ - *BoPubDir 5; DataDirOnSer 84; EISS 83; InfoS 83-84*
Dun's Quest [of Dun & Bradstreet Corp.] - Parsippany, NJ - *DirOnDB Spring 84; EISS 7-83 Sup*
Dun's Review - New York, NY - *NewsBur 6*
Dunseith Cable TV Inc. - Dunseith, ND - *BrCabYB 84*
Dunshee & Co. - Denver, CO - *AdAge 3-28-84; StaDirAdAg 2-84*
Dunsky Advertising Ltd. - Westmount, PQ, Canada - *StaDirAdAg 2-84*
Dunsmuir News - *See* Southern Siskiyou Newspapers Inc.
Dunsmuir News, The - Dunsmuir, CA - *Ed&PubIntYB 82*
Dunsprint [of Dun & Bradstreet Inc.] - New York, NY - *DBBus 82; DirOnDB Spring 84*
Dunwoodie Communications Inc. - New York, NY - *DirPRFirms 83*
Dunwoody-Chamblee-Doraville DeKalb Neighbor - Chamblee, GA - *Ed&PubIntYB 82*
Dunwoody Neighbor - Dunwoody, GA - *Ed&PubIntYB 82*
Dunwoody Neighbor [of Marietta Neighbor Newspapers Inc.] - Marietta, GA - *NewsDir 84*
Duo County Telephone - Jamestown, KY - *TelDir&BG 83-84*
Duosoft Corp. - Savoy, IL - *MicrocomMPl 83, 84; MicrocomSwDir 1; WhoWMicrocom 83*
Dupage Metal Products - Lombard, IL - *AvMarPl 83*
Duplex Music - *See* Live Music Publishing Group
Duplex Records Inc. - New York, NY - *BillIntBG 83-84*
Dupo Journal - *See* Journal Newspapers of Southern Illinois
Dupree West River Progress - Dupree, SD - *BaconPubCkNews 84*
Dupuy Publishing Inc. - Studio City, CA - *BillIntBG 83-84*
Dupuy Records - Studio City, CA - *BillIntBG 83-84*
Duquesne Systems Inc. - Pittsburgh, PA - *ADAPSOMemDir 83-84; DataDirSup 7-83*
Duquesne University Press - Pittsburgh, PA - *LitMarPl 83, 84; WritMar 84*
DuQuoin Evening Call [of Call Publishing Co.] - DuQuoin, IL - *NewsDir 84*
Dura Line - Flat Rock, NC - *DirInfWP 82*
Duracom Corp. - Pennsauken, NJ - *DataDirSup 7-83*
Durafilm Co., The - Hollywood, CA - *AvMarPl 83; Tel&CabFB 84C*
Durak - Rock Stream, NY - *LitMag&SmPr 83-84*
Durand Cable Co. Inc. - Durand, WI - *BrCabYB 84; Tel&CabFB 84C*
Durand Cable Co. Inc. - Mondovi, WI - *Tel&CabFB 84C*
Durand Courier Wedge - Durand, WI - *BaconPubCkNews 84; NewsDir 84*
Durand Express - Durand, MI - *AyerDirPub 83; BaconPubCkNews 84; Ed&PubIntYB 82; NewsDir 84*
Durand Gazette [of Durand North Central Associated Publishers] - Durand, IL - *AyerDirPub 83; Ed&PubIntYB 82; NewsDir 84*
Durand Gazette - *See* North Central Associated Publishers
Durango-Cortez Herald - Durango, CO - *Ed&PubIntYB 82; NewsDir 84*
Durango Herald - Durango, CO - *BaconPubCkNews 84; Ed&PubIntYB 82; NewsDir 84*
Durango Systems Inc. - Cupertino, CA - *DirInfWP 82*
Durango Systems Inc. - San Jose, CA - *DataDirSup 7-83; MicrocomMPl 83, 84; WhoWMicrocom 83*
Durant Bryan County Star - Durant, OK - *BaconPubCkNews 84*
Durant Cablevision - Durant, OK - *BrCabYB 84; Tel&CabFB 84C*
Durant Democrat [of Donrey Inc.] - Durant, OK - *BaconPubCkNews 84; Ed&PubIntYB 82; NewsDir 84*
Durant News - Lexington, MS - *BaconPubCkNews 84*
Durant News & Bryan County Democrat - Durant, OK - *BaconPubCkNews 84; Ed&PubIntYB 82*
Durant News, The - Durant, MS - *Ed&PubIntYB 82*
Durant Plaindealer - Durant, MS - *Ed&PubIntYB 82*
Durant Publishing Co. - Alexandria, VA - *BoPubDir 4 Sup, 5*
Durasell Corp. - New York, NY - *AvMarPl 83; Tel&CabFB 84C; WritMar 84*
Durfee & Solow Advertising Inc. - New York, NY - *StaDirAdAg 2-84*
Durfee Creative Services Inc., Jim - New York, NY - *HBIndAd&MS 82-83*
Durfee's TV Cable Co. - Parkersburg, WV - *BrCabYB 84*
Durham Cablevision [of American TV & Communications Corp.] - Durham, NC - *BrCabYB 84; Tel&CabFB 84C*
Durham Carolina Times - Durham, NC - *BaconPubCkNews 84*
Durham Chronicle, The - Durham, ON, Canada - *Ed&PubIntYB 82*
Durham Morning Herald - Durham, NC - *BaconPubCkNews 84; Ed&PubIntYB 82; LitMarPl 83, 84; NewsDir 84*
Durham North Carolina Anvil - Durham, NC - *BaconPubCkNews 84*
Durham Radio Corp. - Durham, NC - *BrCabYB 84*
Durham Sun [of Durham Herald Co. Inc.] - Durham, NC - *BaconPubCkNews 84; Ed&PubIntYB 82; LitMarPl 83, 84; NewsDir 84*
Durham University Journal, The - New Elvet, England - *LitMag&SmPr 83-84*
Durkee, Mary E. - New York, NY - *LitMarPl 83, 84; MagIndMarPl 82-83*
Duroc News - Peoria, IL - *BaconPubCkMag 84; MagDir 84*
Durocher & Co. Inc. - Detroit, MI - *DirPRFirms 83*
Duroid Products Inc. - New York, NY - *LitMarPl 83, 84*
Durrant's Press Cutting Ltd. - London, England - *ProGuPRSer 4*
Durrell Publications Inc. - Kennebunkport, ME - *BoPubDir 4, 5*
Durst North America Inc. - Tempe, AZ - *AvMarPl 83*
Durst Publications - Long Island City, NY - *WritMar 84*
Durst, Sanford J. - Long Island City, NY - *BoPubDir 5; LitMarPl 84*
Durst, Sanford J. - New York, NY - *BoPubDir 4*
Dusenbury & Alban Inc. - Durham, NC - *StaDirAdAg 2-84*
Dushkin Publishing Group Inc. - Guilford, CT - *LitMarPl 83, 84*
Dushore Sullivan Review - Dushore, PA - *BaconPubCkNews 84*
Dusk & Dawn Records - Adelphi, MD - *BillIntBG 83-84*
Dussault, Paul - Enosburg Falls, VT - *Tel&CabFB 84C p.1678*
Dustbooks - Paradise, CA - *LitMag&SmPr 83-84; LitMarPl 83, 84; WritMar 84*
Dusty Roads Music Corp. - *See* Gallico Music Corp., Al

Dutch State Mines - Geleen, Netherlands - *InfIndMarPl 83*
Dutch Tymnet/Telenet Node - *See* Dabas
Dutton Advance Ltd. - Dutton, ON, Canada - *Ed&PubIntYB 82*
Dutton, E. P. [Subs. of JSD Corp.] - New York, NY - *LitMarPl 83, 84; WritMar 84*
Duty Free International - Miami Springs, FL - *BaconPubCkMag 84*
Duvall Cable TV - Duvall, WA - *BrCabYB 84*
Duvall Radio Sales & Service - Wheeling, WV - *BrCabYB 84*
Duverus Publishing Corp. - Springdale, AR - *BoPubDir 4, 5*
Duxbury Clipper - Duxbury, MA - *Ed&PubIntYB 82*
Duxbury Shoppinguide - Plymouth, MA - *AyerDirPub 83*
Duxbury Systems Inc. - Acton, MA - *MicrocomSwDir 1; WhoWMicrocom 83*
DVJB - Copenhagen, Denmark - *DirOnDB Spring 84*
DVM - New York, NY - *MagDir 84*
Dvorak's Software Review - Albany, CA - *WhoWMicrocom 83*
Dvorkovitz & Associates, Dr. - Ormond Beach, FL - *CompReadDB 82; DataDirOnSer 84; EISS 83*
Dwapara Herald Publishing Inc. - Marble Hill, MO - *BoPubDir 4, 5*
Dwarf Music - *See* Special Rider Music
Dweck & Co., Michael - New York, NY - *StaDirAdAg 2-84*
Dwelley, Citrin & Associates - Poughkeepsie, NY - *StaDirAdAg 2-84*
Dwight Advertising Inc., Hugh - Beaverton, OR - *StaDirAdAg 2-84*
Dwight Star & Herald - Dwight, IL - *BaconPubCkNews 84; Ed&PubIntYB 82*
Dwight's Energydata - Richardson, TX - *DataDirOnSer 84; DBBus 82; EISS 83; InfIndMarPl 83*
Dwight's Energydata Inc. (Oil & Gas Production History) - Richardson, TX - *DirOnDB Spring 84*
Dwight's On-Line System [of Dwight's Energydata Inc.] - Richardson, TX - *DataDirOnSer 84*
Dwight's Seismic Data Brokerage [of Dwight's Energydata Inc.] - Richardson, TX - *DirOnDB Spring 84*
DWJ Associates Inc. - New York, NY - *DirPRFirms 83*
Dwo Quong Fok Lok Sow - New York, NY - *MicrocomMPl 83*
D.W.S. Inc. - Champaign, IL - *BrCabYB 84*
DWU Journal - Englewood, NJ - *NewsDir 84*
Dxtr's, The - Hollywood, CA - *Tel&CabFB 84C*
Dy-Cor Inc. - New York, NY - *BillIntBG 83-84*
Dy-4 Systems Inc. - Ottawa, ON, Canada - *WhoWMicrocom 83*
Dyatron Corp. - Birmingham, AL - *ADAPSOMemDir 83-84; WhoWMicrocom 83*
Dyatron Corp. (General Systems Div.) - Huntsville, AL - *DataDirSup 7-83*
Dye, Van Mol, Lawrence & Erickson - Nashville, TN - *DirPRFirms 83*
Dyer, Audrey - Huntington Beach, CA - *LitMarPl 83, 84*
Dyer-Bennet Records - New York, NY - *BillIntBG 83-84*
Dyer County Tennessean - Newbern, TN - *Ed&PubIntYB 82; NewsDir 84*
Dyer/Kahn - Los Angeles, CA - *StaDirAdAg 2-84*
Dyer/Lynwood/Sauk Village Town & Country - Hammond, IN - *AyerDirPub 83*
Dyer Tri-City Reporter - Dyer, TN - *BaconPubCkNews 84; NewsDir 84*
Dyer, Wells & Associates Inc. - Atlanta, GA - *ADAPSOMemDir 83-84*
Dyersburg State Gazette - Dyersburg, TN - *BaconPubCkNews 84*
Dyersville Commercial - Dyersville, IA - *BaconPubCkNews 84; Ed&PubIntYB 82; NewsDir 84*
Dykeman Associates Inc. - Dallas, TX - *ArtMar 84; AvMarPl 83; DirPRFirms 83*
Dykstra Consultants - Newport Beach, CA - *WhoWMicrocom 83*
Dylakor - Granada Hills, CA - *ADAPSOMemDir 83-84; DataDirSup 7-83*
Dymarc Industries Inc. - Baltimore, MD - *WhoWMicrocom 83*
Dymax - Menlo Park, CA - *BoPubDir 4, 5; MicrocomMPl 84*
Dymax Systems Inc. - Red Bank, NJ - *WhoWMicrocom 83*
Dynabyte - Menlo Park, CA - *DirInfWP 82*
Dynabyte Inc. - Milpitas, CA - *WhoWMicrocom 83*
Dynacom Communications - Montreal, PQ, Canada - *ArtMar 84*
Dynacomp Inc. - Rochester, NY - *MicrocomMPl 84; WhoWMicrocom 83*
Dynair Electronics Inc. - San Diego, CA - *AvMarPl 83*
Dynalogic Info-Tech Corp. Ltd. - Ottawa, ON, Canada - *WhoWMicrocom 83*
Dynamic Business [of Smaller Manufacturers Council] - Pittsburgh, PA - *BaconPubCkMag 84; MagDir 84*
Dynamic Cablevision [Aff. of Colony Communications Inc.] - Hialeah, FL - *BrCabYB 84; InterCabHB 3; Tel&CabFB 84C*
Dynamic Cablevision [of Adelphia Communications Corp.] - West Mifflin, PA - *InterCabHB 3; Tel&CabFB 84C*
Dynamic Cablevision Inc. - Homestead, PA - *BrCabYB 84*
Dynamic Graphics Inc. - Peoria, IL - *Ed&PubIntYB 82*
Dynamic Information Publishing - McLean, VA - *BoPubDir 4 Sup, 5; LitMag&SmPr 83-84*
Dynamic Microprocessor Associates - New York, NY - *MicrocomMPl 83, 84; WhoWMicrocom 83*
Dynamic Operating Systems - Newport Beach, CA - *MicrocomMPl 83*
Dynamic Services - Menlo Park, CA - *EISS 7-83 Sup*
Dynamic Solutions Corp. - Pasadena, CA - *MicrocomMPl 84*
Dynamic Sound - Exeter, NH - *Tel&CabFB 84C*
Dynamic Years [of American Association of Retired Persons] - Long Beach, CA - *ArtMar 84; BaconPubCkMag 84; MagDir 84; MagIndMarPl 82-83; WritMar 84*
Dynamo Publishing Co. - Oakland, CA - *BillIntBG 83-84*
Dynasoft Systems Ltd. - Windsor Junction, NS, Canada - *WhoWMicrocom 83*
Dynasty Records & Video Tapes - Los Angeles, CA - *BillIntBG 83-84*
Dynatech Data Systems - Springfield, VA - *DataDirSup 7-83*
Dynatech Microsoftware Ltd. - Guernsey, England - *MicrocomSwDir 1*
Dynatech Packet Technology Inc. [Subs. of Dynatech Corp.] - Springfield, VA - *WhoWMicrocom 83*
Dynatek Information Systems Inc. - New York, NY - *MicrocomSwDir 1*
Dynatron Computer Systems Inc. - New York, NY - *MagIndMarPl 82-83*
Dynax Inc. - Bell, CA - *MicrocomMPl 84*
Dyncomp Inc. - Rochester, NY - *WritMar 84*
Dysan Corp. - Santa Clara, CA - *Datamation 6-83; Top100Al 83; WhoWMicrocom 83*
Dysart Reporter - Dysart, IA - *AyerDirPub 83; BaconPubCkNews 84; Ed&PubIntYB 82*
DYX Corp. - Dallas, TX - *ADAPSOMemDir 83-84*
Dziennik Polski [of Polish Daily News Inc.] - Detroit, MI - *Ed&PubIntYB 82; NewsDir 84*
Dziennik Zwiazkowy - Chicago, IL - *AyerDirPub 83; Ed&PubIntYB 82*

E

E-A International Inc. - *See* JWT Group Inc.
E & A Design - Liverpool, NY - *ArtMar 84; AvMarPl 83*
E & C Books - Massapequa Park, NY - *BoPubDir 4 Sup, 5*
E & E Cable Service Inc. - Colfax, WV - *BrCabYB 84*
E & E Cable Service Inc. - Fairmont, WV - *Tel&CabFB 84C p.1678*
E & E Cable Service Inc. - Pleasant Valley, WV - *BrCabYB 84*
E & E Cable Service Inc. - Rivesville, WV - *BrCabYB 84*
E & E Cable Service Inc. - Whitehall, WV - *BrCabYB 84; Tel&CabFB 84C*
E & E Enterprises - Longwood, FL - *BoPubDir 4, 5*
E & E Publishing Co. - Souderton, PA - *BoPubDir 4, 5*
E & G Publications - Callaway, NE - *BoPubDir 4, 5*
E & H Software - Baton Rouge, LA - *MicrocomMPl 84*
E & ITV - Danbury, CT - *MagDir 84; MagIndMarPl 82-83*
E & M Advertising Inc. - New York, NY - *StaDirAdAg 2-84*
E & MJ Census of Mining [of McGraw-Hill Publications Co.] - New York, NY - *EISS 83*
E & MJ Mining Activity Digest - New York, NY - *BaconPubCkMag 84*
E & O Systems Ltd. - Santa Clara, CA - *AvMarPl 83*
E-B Advertising Display Inc. - Massillon, OH - *StaDirAdAg 2-84*
E-Com News [of NewsNet Inc.] - Bryn Mawr, PA - *DataDirOnSer 84*
E-Com News - Virginia Beach, VA - *DirOnDB Spring 84*
E-Heart Press - Dallas, TX - *BoPubDir 4 Sup, 5*
E-O Data Corp. - Pennsauken, NJ - *DataDirSup 7-83*
E-Six Lab of Atlanta - Atlanta, GA - *AvMarPl 83*
E-Systems Inc. - Dallas, TX - *ElecNews 7-25-83*
E-Systems Inc. (Garland Div.) - Garland, TX - *DirInfWP 82*
E-Town Ltd. - Hodgenville, KY - *BrCabYB 84*
E/Z Cad Inc. - San Jose, CA - *MicrocomMPl 84*
E-Z Computer Systems - Monsey, NY - *MicrocomMPl 83*
E-Z Interviewing - Elmwood, CT - *IntDirMarRes 83*
E-Z Key - Quincy, MA - *MicrocomMPl 84*
E-Z Learning Methods - Pomona, CA - *BoPubDir 4, 5*
E-Z Software - Mill Valley, CA - *MicrocomMPl 83*
E-Z Software - Novato, CA - *WhoWMicrocom 83*
E-Z Tax Computer Systems Inc. - Spring Valley, NY - *MicrocomMPl 84*
E-Z Vision Inc. - Rusk, TX - *BrCabYB 84; Tel&CabFB 84C*
EAB - Berkeley, CA - *AvMarPl 83*
EABC - Lemon Grove, CA - *MicrocomMPl 84*
Eabs - Ispra, Italy - *DirOnDB Spring 84*
EAD-Equipment Advertiser Digest - Tyler, TX - *BaconPubCkMag 84*
Eads Kiowa County Press - Eads, CO - *BaconPubCkNews 84*
Eads Street Press - Crete, IL - *BoPubDir 4, 5*
Eads, Valerie - New York, NY - *LitMarPl 83, 84; MagIndMarPl 82-83*
Eagan Chronicle - Burnsville, MN - *AyerDirPub 83*
Eagan Chronicle - Eagan, MN - *Ed&PubIntYB 82*
Eagen, Hickman & Associates Inc. - Indianapolis, IN - *StaDirAdAg 2-84*
Eager Consulting Inc. - Houston, TX - *DirPRFirms 83*
Eagle - Dothan, AL - *AyerDirPub 83*
Eagle - Marco Island, FL - *AyerDirPub 83*
Eagle - Augusta, IL - *AyerDirPub 83*
Eagle - Keota, IA - *AyerDirPub 83*
Eagle - Grygla, MN - *AyerDirPub 83*
Eagle - Oxford, MS - *AyerDirPub 83*
Eagle - Ekalaka, MT - *AyerDirPub 83*
Eagle - North Bend, NE - *AyerDirPub 83; Ed&PubIntYB 82*
Eagle - Hubbard, OH - *AyerDirPub 83*
Eagle - Enid, OK - *AyerDirPub 83; Ed&PubIntYB 82*
Eagle - Ringling, OK - *AyerDirPub 83*
Eagle - Butler, PA - *AyerDirPub 83*
Eagle - Reading, PA - *AyerDirPub 83*
Eagle - Junction, TX - *AyerDirPub 83*
Eagle - Moulton, TX - *AyerDirPub 83*
Eagle - Murray, UT - *AyerDirPub 83*
Eagle - Rosetown, SK, Canada - *AyerDirPub 83*
Eagle Advertising Corp. - New Rochelle, NY - *AdAge 3-28-84 p.112; StaDirAdAg 2-84*
Eagle & Swan - New York, NY - *MagIndMarPl 82-83*
Eagle-Beacon - Wichita, KS - *AyerDirPub 83*
Eagle Bend News - Bertha, MN - *BaconPubCkNews 84*
Eagle Bend News, The - Eagle Bend, MN - *Ed&PubIntYB 82*
Eagle Bulletin - Fayetteville, NY - *Ed&PubIntYB 82*
Eagle Bulletin & De Witt News-Times - Fayetteville, NY - *AyerDirPub 83*
Eagle Business Systems - El Toro, CA - *MicrocomMPl 84*
Eagle Butte News - Eagle Butte, SD - *BaconPubCkNews 84; Ed&PubIntYB 82*
Eagle Cable Corp. - Princeton, MO - *Tel&CabFB 84C p.1678*
Eagle Chanter Music Inc. - Shiprock, NM - *BillIntBG 83-84*
Eagle Communications - Los Angeles, CA - *BrCabYB 84*
Eagle Communications - Clayton, MO - *CabTVFinDB 83*
Eagle Computer [Subs. of AVL Inc.] - Los Gatos, CA - *WhoWMicrocom 83*
Eagle Editions [Div. of TPC Ltd.] - Vancouver, BC, Canada - *LitMarPl 83, 84*
Eagle Enterprises - San Francisco, CA - *MicrocomMPl 84; MicrocomSwDir 1; WhoWMicrocom 83*
Eagle Eye [of Student Publications, Lock Haven State College] - Lock Haven, PA - *NewsDir 84*
Eagle-Gazette - Lancaster, OH - *AyerDirPub 83*
Eagle Grove Eagle - Eagle Grove, IA - *AyerDirPub 83; BaconPubCkNews 84; Ed&PubIntYB 82; NewsDir 84*
Eagle International Records - Nashville, TN - *BillIntBG 83-84*
Eagle Lake Cable TV [of Communications Services Inc.] - Eagle Lake, TX - *BrCabYB 84; Tel&CabFB 84C*
Eagle Lake Headlight - Eagle Lake, TX - *BaconPubCkNews 84; Ed&PubIntYB 82; NewsDir 84*
Eagle Magazine - Milwaukee, WI - *BaconPubCkMag 84; MagDir 84*
Eagle Marketing Corp. - Provo, UT - *BoPubDir 4 Sup, 5*
Eagle News [of Eagle Computer Inc.] - Los Gatos, CA - *MicrocomMPl 84*
Eagle North Cable TV - Oakhurst, CA - *BrCabYB 84*

Eagle Pass News Guide - Eagle Pass, TX - *BaconPubCkNews 84; Ed&PubIntYB 82; NewsDir 84*
Eagle Photographics Inc. - Tampa, FL - *AvMarPl 83*
Eagle Record - St. George, SC - *Ed&PubIntYB 82*
Eagle Record Co. - Burbank, CA - *BillIntBG 83-84*
Eagle Recordings Inc. - Nashville, TN - *BillIntBG 83-84*
Eagle River Chugiak Star - Eagle River, AK - *BaconPubCkNews 84*
Eagle River Vilas County News-Review - Eagle River, WI - *BaconPubCkNews 84*
Eagle Rock Sentinel [of Northeast Los Angeles Publishing Co.] - Los Angeles, CA - *AyerDirPub 83; Ed&PubIntYB 82; NewsDir 84*
Eagle Rock Sentinel - *See* Northeast Los Angeles Publishing Co.
Eagle Software Publishing Inc. - Wayne, PA - *MicrocomMPl 84; WhoWMicrocom 83*
Eagle Standard - Fallon, NV - *AyerDirPub 83; NewsDir 84*
Eagle-Star - Marinette, WI - *AyerDirPub 83; Ed&PubIntYB 82*
Eagle Telecommunications Inc. [Aff. of GVNW/National] - Eagle, CO - *TelDir&BG 83-84*
Eagle Telephone System - Richland, OR - *TelDir&BG 83-84*
Eagle Television Club - Lumberport, WV - *BrCabYB 84*
Eagle, The [of The Auburn Bulletin] - Auburn, AL - *NewsDir 84*
Eagle, The [of Human Kinetics Pub. Inc.] - Champaign, IL - *LitMag&SmPr 83-84*
Eagle, The - Cherryville, NC - *Ed&PubIntYB 82*
Eagle-Times [of Eagle Publications Inc.] - Claremont, NH - *AyerDirPub 83; Ed&PubIntYB 82; LitMarPl 84*
Eagle-Tribune - Lawrence, MA - *AyerDirPub 83*
Eagle II - Butler, PA - *AyerDirPub 83*
Eagle Valley Enterprise - Eagle, CO - *AyerDirPub 83; BaconPubCkNews 84; Ed&PubIntYB 82*
Eagle Valley Telephone Co. [Aff. of Communications Systems Inc.] - Clarissa, MN - *TelDir&BG 83-84*
Eagles, Douglas Eaton - Sarnia, ON, Canada - *BoPubDir 4 Sup*
EAK Advertising - Bensalem, PA - *StaDirAdAg 2-84*
Eakin Publications Inc. - Austin, TX - *WritMar 84*
Eakin Publications Inc. - Burnet, TX - *BoPubDir 4, 5*
EAL Enterprises Inc. - Cleveland, OH - *LitMarPl 83, 84*
EAP Co. - Keller, TX - *MicrocomMPl 84*
E.A.R. for Children [of Sound Advice Enterprises] - Roslyn Heights, NY - *LitMag&SmPr 83-84*
Ear Magazine East - New York, NY - *LitMag&SmPr 83-84*
Ear, Nose & Throat Journal - Glen Rock, NJ - *BaconPubCkMag 84*
Ear, Nose & Throat Journal - Williston Park, NY - *MagDir 84; MagIndMarPl 82-83*
Eardley Publications - Rochelle Park, NJ - *BoPubDir 4, 5*
Earl Music Co. - *See* Neverland Music Publishing Co.
Earl Software, George - San Antonio, TX - *MicrocomMPl 83, 84; MicrocomSwDir 1*
Earle Advertising Inc., Lester - Chicago, IL - *StaDirAdAg 2-84*
Earlham Echo - Earlham, IA - *AyerDirPub 83; BaconPubCkNews 84; Ed&PubIntYB 82*
Earling Mutual Telephone Co. - Earling, IA - *TelDir&BG 83-84*
Earlville Leader - Earlville, IL - *BaconPubCkNews 84; Ed&PubIntYB 82*
Early American Industries Association Inc. - Becket, MA - *BoPubDir 4*
Early American Industries Association Inc. - Albany, NY - *BoPubDir 5*
Early American Life [of Historical Times Inc.] - Harrisburg, PA - *BaconPubCkMag 84; Folio 83; MagDir 84; MagIndMarPl 82-83; WritMar 84*
Early & Associates, Jim - Knoxville, TN - *StaDirAdAg 2-84*
Early Bird Music - Tustin, CA - *BillIntBG 83-84*
Early Bird Satellite Services Inc. - Chantilly, VA - *Tel&CabFB 84C*
Early Bird, The - Arcanum, OH - *AyerDirPub 83; Ed&PubIntYB 82*
Early County News - Blakely, GA - *AyerDirPub 83; Ed&PubIntYB 82*
Early Educators Press - Lake Alfred, FL - *BoPubDir 4, 5*
Early Learning Book Club [of Macmillan Book Clubs Inc.] - New York, NY - *LitMarPl 83, 84*
Early News - Early, IA - *BaconPubCkNews 84; Ed&PubIntYB 82*
Early Stages Press - San Francisco, CA - *LitMarPl 83, 84*
Early Stages Press (Contemporary Literature Series) - San Francisco, CA - *LitMag&SmPr 83-84*
Early Years - Darien, CT - *BaconPubCkMag 84; MagDir 84; MagIndMarPl 82-83*
Earlyopt [of Control Data Corp.] - Greenwich, CT - *DataDirOnSer 84*
Earlyopt - Chicago, IL - *DirOnDB Spring 84*
Earmark Inc. - Hampden, CT - *AvMarPl 83*
Earnshaw's Review - New York, NY - *ArtMar 84; BaconPubCkMag 84; MagDir 84*
Earth [of Western Industrial Advertisers] - Los Angeles, CA - *BaconPubCkMag 84; MagDir 84*
Earth - Edgerton, OH - *AyerDirPub 83*
Earth Art Inc. - Kalamazoo, MI - *BoPubDir 4, 5*
Earth Basics Press - Palo Alto, CA - *BoPubDir 4 Sup, 5*
Earth Books - Santa Monica, CA - *BoPubDir 4, 5*
Earth News-Sun - Earth, TX - *BaconPubCkNews 84*
Earth Records Co. - Troy, AL - *BillIntBG 83-84*
Earth Rites Press - Brooklyn, NY - *BoPubDir 4 Sup, 5*
Earth Scenes - New York, NY - *LitMarPl 83, 84; MagIndMarPl 82-83*
Earth Science Associates - Humble, TX - *MicrocomSwDir 1*
Earth Science Publishing Co. - Colorado Springs, CO - *BoPubDir 4, 5*
Earth Sciences Information System [of Netherlands Soil Survey Institute] - Wageningen, Netherlands - *EISS 83*
Earth Shelter Living - Stillwater, MN - *BaconPubCkMag 84*
Earth-Song Press - Sacramento, CA - *LitMag&SmPr 83-84*
Earth View Inc. - Ashford, WA - *BoPubDir 4, 5*
Earthbound Publishing Co. - Dallas, TX - *BillIntBG 83-84*
Earthcare - Wynyard, SK, Canada - *BoPubDir 4 Sup, 5*
Earthenware Computer Services - Eugene, OR - *MicrocomMPl 83*
Earthquake Engineering Research Center [of National Information Service for Earthquake Engineering] - Richmond, CA - *InfIndMarPl 83*
Earthrise Entertainment Inc. - New York, NY - *Tel&CabFB 84C*
Earth's Daughters - Buffalo, NY - *WritMar 84*
Earth's Daughters - Central Park Station, NY - *LitMag&SmPr 83-84*
Earthtone [of Publication Development Inc.] - Portland, OR - *WritMar 84*
Earthtone Recording Co. Inc. - Westerville, OH - *BillIntBG 83-84*
Earthware Computer Services - Eugene, OR - *MicrocomMPl 84; WhoWMicrocom 83*
Earthwise: A Journal of Poetry - Miami, FL - *ArtMar 84; LitMag&SmPr 83-84; WritMar 84*
Earthwise Literary Calendar - Miami, FL - *LitMag&SmPr 83-84*
Earthwise Newsletter - Miami, FL - *LitMag&SmPr 83-84*
Earthwise Publications - Miami, FL - *BoPubDir 4, 5; LitMag&SmPr 83-84*
Earthwork Books - San Francisco, CA - *BoPubDir 4*
Earthwork Books - Minneapolis, MN - *BoPubDir 5*
Earwax Records - Detroit, MI - *BillIntBG 83-84*
Easi Bild Directions Simplified Inc. - Briarcliff Manor, NY - *LitMarPl 83, 84*
Easley Progress - Easley, SC - *BaconPubCkNews 84; Ed&PubIntYB 82; NewsDir 84*
Eason Publications Inc. - Atlanta, GA - *BoPubDir 4, 5*
East African Publishing House - Nairobi, Kenya - *LitMag&SmPr 83-84*
East Allegheny Records Group, The - Newport News, VA - *BillIntBG 83-84*
East Allen Courier - Grabill, IN - *AyerDirPub 83*
East Arkansas Cablevision Inc. [of United Artists Cablesystems Corp.] - Cherry Valley, AR - *BrCabYB 84; Tel&CabFB 84C*
East Arkansas Cablevision Inc. [of United Artists Cablesystems Corp.] - Earle, AR - *Tel&CabFB 84C*
East Arkansas Cablevision Inc. [of United Artists Cablesystems Corp.] - Jonesboro, AR - *BrCabYB 84; Tel&CabFB 84C*
East Arkansas Cablevision Inc. [of United Artists Cablesystems Corp.] - Marked Tree, AR - *BrCabYB 84; Tel&CabFB 84C*
East Arkansas Cablevision Inc. [of United Artists Cablesystems Corp.] - Osceola, AR - *Tel&CabFB 84C*
East Arkansas Video [of WEHCO Video Inc.] - Brinkley, AR - *BrCabYB 84; Tel&CabFB 84C*
East Arkansas Video [of WEHCO Video Inc.] - Forrest City, AR - *BrCabYB 84; Tel&CabFB 84C*

East Arkansas Video [of WEHCO Video Inc.] - Marianna, AR - *BrCabYB 84*
East Arkansas Video [of WEHCO Video Inc.] - Wynne, AR - *BrCabYB 84; Tel&CabFB 84C*
East Ascension Telephone Co. Inc. - Gonzales, LA - *TelDir&BG 83-84*
East Aurora Advertiser - East Aurora, NY - *BaconPubCkNews 84; Ed&PubIntYB 82; NewsDir 84*
East Aurora Pennysaver - Orchard Park, NY - *AyerDirPub 83*
East Baltimore Guide - Baltimore, MD - *AyerDirPub 83*
East Bank Cable TV Inc. [of Cox Cable Communications Inc.] - Kenner, LA - *BrCabYB 84*
East Bank Guide [of Gretna Guide Newspaper Corp.] - Gretna, LA - *NewsDir 84*
East Bay Labor Journal - Oakland, CA - *NewsDir 84*
East Bay Today - Oakland, CA - *LitMarPl 83*
East Berlin Cablevision Corp. [of Telecable Communications Corp.] - East Berlin, PA - *BrCabYB 84*
East Bernard Tribune - East Bernard, TX - *Ed&PubIntYB 82*
East Bernstadt TV Cable Co. [of Centel Cablevision Co. of Kentucky] - East Bernstadt, KY - *BrCabYB 84*
East Boston Times - East Boston, MA - *BaconPubCkNews 84*
East Branch Citizen - Downingtown, PA - *AyerDirPub 83; Ed&PubIntYB 82*
East Branch TV Line Inc. - Hancock, NY - *BrCabYB 84; Tel&CabFB 84C*
East Bridgewater Star - East Bridgewater, MA - *Ed&PubIntYB 82*
East Bridgewater Star - *See* Bridgewater Independent
East Broward Tribune - Ft. Lauderdale, FL - *AyerDirPub 83; Ed&PubIntYB 82*
East Brunswick Sentinel - *See* Sentinel Newspapers
East Brunswick Suburban - *See* Sentinel Newspapers
East Buchanan Telephone Cooperative - Winthrop, IA - *TelDir&BG 83-84*
East Canton Press-News, The - East Canton, OH - *BaconPubCkNews 84; NewsDir 84*
East Carolina University (Poetry Forum Press) - Greenville, NC - *BoPubDir 4, 5*
East Carolinian, The [of East Carolina University] - Greenville, NC - *NewsDir 84*
East Carroll Delta News - Lake Providence, LA - *AyerDirPub 83; Ed&PubIntYB 82*
East Central Florida [of Community Communications Inc.] - Orlando, FL - *WritMar 84*
East Central Minnesota Post/Review [of Forest Lake Times] - Forest Lake, MN - *NewsDir 84*
East Central Minnesota Post Review - Rush City, MN - *Ed&PubIntYB 82*
East Chicago Calumet-Globe - East Chicago, IN - *NewsDir 84*
East Coast Sheet Metal Fabrications Co. - Peekskill, NY - *MicrocomMPl 83, 84; MicrocomSwDir 1*
East Cobb Neighbor - East Cobb, GA - *Ed&PubIntYB 82*
East Cobb Neighbor - Marietta, GA - *AyerDirPub 83*
East Conemaugh Cable TV [of Eastern Telecom Corp.] - East Conemaugh, PA - *Tel&CabFB 84C*
East County Buyer's Guide - El Cajon, CA - *AyerDirPub 83*
East County News - Orchards, WA - *Ed&PubIntYB 82*
East County News - Vancouver, WA - *Ed&PubIntYB 82*
East Dennis Publishing Co. [Aff. of Howard A. Doyle Publishing Co.] - East Dennis, MA - *BoPubDir 4, 5*
East Dubuque Register - East Dubuque, IL - *BaconPubCkNews 84; Ed&PubIntYB 82*
East Dummerston Cable Television Inc. - West Dummerston, VT - *BrCabYB 84*
East Eagle Press - Huron, SD - *BoPubDir 4, 5; LitMag&SmPr 83-84*
East Elgin Cable TV Ltd. - Aylmer, ON, Canada - *BrCabYB 84*
East End Express - Toronto, ON, Canada - *Ed&PubIntYB 82*
East End News - Toronto, ON, Canada - *Ed&PubIntYB 82*
East European Monographs - Boulder, CO - *BoPubDir 4, 5*
East European Quarterly - Boulder, CO - *LitMag&SmPr 83-84*
East Fishkill Record - East Fishkill, NY - *Ed&PubIntYB 82*
East Fishkill Record [of Mahopac Putnam County Press] - Mahopac, NY - *AyerDirPub 83; NewsDir 84*
East Fishkill Record - *See* Gateway Papers
East Grand Forks Exponent - East Grand Forks, MN - *BaconPubCkNews 84*
East Grand Forks Record - East Grand Forks, MN - *BaconPubCkNews 84*
East Greenbush Area News - East Greenbush, NY - *BaconPubCkNews 84; NewsDir 84*
East Greenwich Rhode Island Pendulum - East Greenwich, RI - *BaconPubCkNews 84; NewsDir 84*
East Gwillimbury Communicator, The - Mt. Albert, ON, Canada - *Ed&PubIntYB 82*
East Hampton Star - East Hampton, NY - *BaconPubCkNews 84; Ed&PubIntYB 82; NewsDir 84*
East Hanover Cablevision Inc. - East Hanover, PA - *Tel&CabFB 84C*
East Hartford Gazette - East Hartford, CT - *BaconPubCkNews 84; Ed&PubIntYB 82*
East Kildonan Examiner, The - Winnipeg, MB, Canada - *Ed&PubIntYB 82*
East Kildonan Herald - Winnipeg, MB, Canada - *Ed&PubIntYB 82*
East Lansing Towne Courier - *See* Towne Courier Inc.
East Lauderdale News - Rogersville, AL - *Ed&PubIntYB 82*
East Liverpool Review [of Thomson Newspapers] - East Liverpool, OH - *BaconPubCkNews 84; NewsDir 84*
East Los Angeles Brooklyn Belvedere Comet - East Los Angeles, CA - *Ed&PubIntYB 82*
East Los Angeles Brooklyn-Belvedere Comet - *See* Eastern Group Publications Inc.
East Los Angeles Commerce Tribune - Montebello, CA - *AyerDirPub 83*
East Los Angeles Gazette [of Southern California Publishing Co.] - Montebello, CA - *AyerDirPub 83; NewsDir 84*
East Los Angeles Gazette - *See* Southern California Publishing Co.
East Los Angeles Tribune - Los Angeles, CA - *Ed&PubIntYB 82*
East Los Angeles Tribune [of Southern California Publishing Co.] - Montebello, CA - *NewsDir 84*
East Los Angeles Tribune - *See* Southern California Publishing Co.
East Lycoming Shopper - Hughesville, PA - *AyerDirPub 83*
East Meadow Beacon [of Nassau County Publications] - Hempstead, NY - *NewsDir 84*
East Meadow Beacon - *See* Nassau County Publications
East Meadow Courier - Uniondale, NY - *NewsDir 84*
East Meadow Meadowbrook Times [of Lawrence Bi-County Publishers Inc.] - Lawrence, NY - *NewsDir 84*
East Meadow Meadowbrook Times - *See* Richner Publications Inc.
East Meadow Pennysaver - Levittown, NY - *AyerDirPub 83*
East Memphis Music - *See* Rondor Music International Inc.
East Memphis Shoppers News - Memphis, TN - *AyerDirPub 83*
East Minneapolis & East Suburban Shopping Guide - Minneapolis, MN - *AyerDirPub 83*
East Montco Cable TV [of Relate Inc.] - New Caney, TX - *Tel&CabFB 84C*
East Montco Cable TV - Porter Heights, TX - *Tel&CabFB 84C*
East Orange Record [of Worrall Publications] - East Orange, NJ - *AyerDirPub 83; Ed&PubIntYB 82; NewsDir 84*
East Orange Record - *See* Worrall Publications
East Oregonian - Pendleton, OR - *AyerDirPub 83; BaconPubCkNews 84; Ed&PubIntYB 82*
East Ottertail Telephone Co. - Perham, MN - *Tel&CabFB 84C p.1678; TelDir&BG 83-84*
East Palestine Leader [of The Buckeye Publishing Co.] - East Palestine, OH - *BaconPubCkNews 84; NewsDir 84*
East Palo Alto San Mateo County Advocate - *See* Regal Publishing Co.
East Penn Valley Merchandiser - Hamburg, PA - *AyerDirPub 83*
East Peoria Courier - East Peoria, IL - *Ed&PubIntYB 82*
East Peoria Courier [of Tazewell Publishing Co.] - Morton, IL - *AyerDirPub 83; NewsDir 84*
East Peoria Courier - *See* Tazewell Publishing Co.
East Pepperell Times Free Press - East Pepperell, MA - *BaconPubCkNews 84*
East Point Southside & Fayette Sun - *See* Decatur News Publishing Co. Inc.

East Prairie Eagle - East Prairie, MO - *AyerDirPub 83; BaconPubCkNews 84; Ed&PubIntYB 82*
East Prospect Cable [of American Tele-Systems Corp.] - East Prospect, PA - *BrCabYB 84*
East Providence Post - East Providence, RI - *AyerDirPub 83; BaconPubCkNews 84; Ed&PubIntYB 82*
East River Anthology - Montclair, NJ - *BoPubDir 4, 5; LitMag&SmPr 83-84*
East Rochester Post Herald - East Rochester, NY - *AyerDirPub 83; Ed&PubIntYB 82*
East Rochester Post-Herald [of Wolfe Publications Inc.] - Pittsford, NY - *NewsDir 84*
East Rochester Post Herald - *See* Wolfe Publications Inc.
East Rockaway Lynbrook Observer - East Rockaway, NY - *AyerDirPub 83; BaconPubCkNews 84; Ed&PubIntYB 82; NewsDir 84*
East Rutherford-Carlstadt Free Press - *See* Leader Newspapers Inc.
East San Jose Sun [of Meredith Newspapers] - Cupertino, CA - *NewsDir 84*
East San Jose Sun - Milpitas, CA - *AyerDirPub 83*
East San Jose Sun - San Jose, CA - *Ed&PubIntYB 82*
East San Jose Sun - *See* Meredith Newspapers
East Selah Cable Television Associates - East Selah, WA - *BrCabYB 84; Tel&CabFB 84C*
East Side Express - New York, NY - *AyerDirPub 83; Ed&PubIntYB 82*
East Side Herald [of New York Herald] - New York, NY - *AyerDirPub 83; NewsDir 84*
East Side Herald - *See* Community Herald
East Side Herald, The - Indianapolis, IN - *AyerDirPub 83*
East Side Herald, The - Manhattan, NY - *Ed&PubIntYB 82*
East St. Louis Monitor - East St. Louis, IL - *BaconPubCkNews 84*
East St. Louis News - *See* Journal Newspapers of Southern Illinois
East Suburban Cablevision [of Daniels & Associates Inc.] - Houston, TX - *BrCabYB 84*
East Tawas Iosco County News - East Tawas, MI - *NewsDir 84*
East Tawas Iosco County News Herald - East Tawas, MI - *BaconPubCkNews 84*
East Texas Cable TV Inc. - Kirbyville, TX - *BrCabYB 84*
East Texas Cable TV Inc. - Newton, TX - *BrCabYB 84*
East Texas-ERIC Search System [of East Texas State University Library] - Commerce, TX - *EISS 83*
East Texas Light - Center, TX - *AyerDirPub 83; Ed&PubIntYB 82*
East Texas Light Shopper - Center, TX - *AyerDirPub 83*
East Texas News - Buna, TX - *AyerDirPub 83*
East Texas Television Network - *See* KLMB-TV Inc.
East Timor Human Rights Committee - Syracuse, NY - *LitMag&SmPr 83-84*
East Timor Update [of East Timor Human Rights Committee] - Syracuse, NY - *LitMag&SmPr 83-84*
East Toronto Weekly - Toronto, ON, Canada - *Ed&PubIntYB 82*
East Troy News - East Troy, WI - *BaconPubCkNews 84; Ed&PubIntYB 82*
East Volusia Shopper - Daytona Beach, FL - *AyerDirPub 83*
East Washingtonian - Pomeroy, WA - *AyerDirPub 83; Ed&PubIntYB 82*
East/West Chinese American Journal [of East/West Publishing Co. Inc.] - San Francisco, CA - *AyerDirPub 83; NewsDir 84*
East-West Communication Institute - Honolulu, HI - *BoPubDir 4, 5*
East-West Cultural Center Inc. - Los Angeles, CA - *BoPubDir 4, 5*
East-West Export Books [of University of Hawaii Press] - Honolulu, HI - *LitMarPl 83, 84*
East-West Features Service - Washington, DC - *LitMarPl 83*
East-West Journal - Brookline, MA - *BaconPubCkMag 84; MagDir 84; MagIndMarPl 82-83; WritMar 84*
East-West Marketing Corp. - New York, NY - *StaDirAdAg 2-84*
East-West Music Inc. - *See* Goodman Group, The
East/West Network - Los Angeles, CA - *Folio 83; MagIndMarPl 82-83; NewsBur 6*
East/West Network Inc. - New York, NY - *WritMar 84*
East-West Players - Los Angeles, CA - *WritMar 84*
East-West Population Institute [of East-West Center] - Honolulu, HI - *EISS 83*
East-West Press - Minneapolis, MN - *BoPubDir 4 Sup, 5*
East Whittier-La Mirada Highlander - *See* Highlander Publications Inc.
East Whittier Review - Whittier, CA - *AyerDirPub 83*
East Windsor Historical Society Inc. - Warehouse Point, CT - *BoPubDir 4, 5*
East Woods Press, The - Charlotte, NC - *LitMag&SmPr 83-84; LitMarPl 83, 84; WritMar 84*
East Yolo Record [of Sacramento Suburban Newspapers Inc.] - Fair Oaks, CA - *NewsDir 84*
East Yolo Record, The - Sacramento, CA - *Ed&PubIntYB 82*
Eastbay Today [of Oakland Tribune Inc.] - Oakland, CA - *AyerDirPub 83; Ed&PubIntYB 82; LitMarPl 84*
Eastbench Software Products - Logan, UT - *MicrocomMPl 84*
Eastchester Record - Tuckahoe, NY - *Ed&PubIntYB 82*
Eastchester Record - Yonkers, NY - *AyerDirPub 83*
Eastel [of Eastern Counties Newspapers] - Norwich, England - *EISS 83*
Eastend Enterprise - Eastend, SK, Canada - *Ed&PubIntYB 82*
Easter Publishing - Mobile, AL - *BoPubDir 4, 5*
Easter Seal Society of Alaska [Aff. of National Easter Seal Society] - Anchorage, AK - *BoPubDir 4, 5*
Eastern Aftermarket Journal - Cedarhurst, NY - *BaconPubCkMag 84*
Eastern Air Lines Inc. - Miami, FL - *DataDirSup 7-83*
Eastern Arizona Courier - Safford, AZ - *AyerDirPub 83; Ed&PubIntYB 82; NewsDir 84*
Eastern Automotive Journal - Cedarhurst, NY - *MagDir 84*
Eastern Basketball - West Hempstead, NY - *BaconPubCkMag 84; WritMar 84*
Eastern Book Co. - Portland, ME - *LitMarPl 83, 84*
Eastern Broadcasting Corp. - Washington, DC - *BrCabYB 84*
Eastern Cablevision Ltd. - Truro, NS, Canada - *BrCabYB 84*
Eastern Catholic Life [of Byzantine Catholic Diocese of Passaic] - Passaic, NJ - *NewsDir 84*
Eastern Coal Corp. - Stone, KY - *Tel&CabFB 84C*
Eastern Colorado Cablevision [of Metro Cable Corp.] - Eads, CO - *Tel&CabFB 84C*
Eastern Colorado News - Strasburg, CO - *Ed&PubIntYB 82*
Eastern Colorado Plainsman - Hugo, CO - *AyerDirPub 83; Ed&PubIntYB 82*
Eastern Connecticut Cable Television Inc. - New London, CT - *BrCabYB 84; Tel&CabFB 84C*
Eastern Connecticut State College (Center for Connecticut Studies) - Willimantic, CT - *BoPubDir 4, 5*
Eastern Connecticut State College Foundation Inc. - Willimantic, CT - *BoPubDir 4, 5*
Eastern Echo [of Eastern Michigan University] - Ypsilanti, MI - *NewsDir 84*
Eastern Educational Television Network - Boston, MA - *BrCabYB 84; Tel&CabFB 84C*
Eastern Environmental Radiation Facility [of U.S. Environmental Protection Agency] - Montgomery, AL - *EISS 83*
Eastern Financial Times - Spring Lake, NJ - *BaconPubCkMag 84*
Eastern Grape Grower & Winery News - Watkins Glen, NY - *BaconPubCkMag 84*
Eastern Graphic, The - Montague, PE, Canada - *AyerDirPub 83; Ed&PubIntYB 82*
Eastern Group Publications Inc. - Los Angeles, CA - *BaconPubCkNews 84*
Eastern Hills Journal [of Cincinnati Suburban Newspapers Inc.] - Cincinnati, OH - *AyerDirPub 83; NewsDir 84*
Eastern Hills Journal - *See* Queen City Suburban Press Inc.
Eastern House Software - Winston-Salem, NC - *WhoWMicrocom 83*
Eastern Illinois Cablevision [of Combined Cable Corp.] - Mahomet, IL - *BrCabYB 84; Tel&CabFB 84C*
Eastern Illinois Telephone Corp. [Aff. of Mid-Continent Telephone Corp.] - Rantoul, IL - *TelDir&BG 83-84*
Eastern Iowa Cablevision - Monticello, IA - *Tel&CabFB 84C p.1678*
Eastern Itascan - Nashwauk, MN - *Ed&PubIntYB 82*
Eastern Keyboard Music Co. Ltd. - Brooklyn, NY - *BillIntBG 83-84*

Eastern Lithographing Co. Inc. - Philadelphia, PA - *LitMarPl 83, 84*
Eastern Management Group - Morris Plains, NJ - *TeleSy&SerDir 2-84*
Eastern Microwave Inc. - Syracuse, NY - *BrCabYB 84; Tel&CabFB 84C*
Eastern Missouri CATV Co. [of Cencom of Eastern Missouri Inc.] - Troy, MO - *Tel&CabFB 84C*
Eastern Missouri Telephone Co. - Bowling Green, MO - *TelDir&BG 83-84*
Eastern Nebraska Telephone Co. [Aff. of HunTel Systems Inc.] - Blair, NE - *TelDir&BG 83-84*
Eastern New Mexico University (Film Library) - Portales, NM - *AvMarPl 83*
Eastern News Distributors Inc. - New York, NY - *MagIndMarPl 82-83*
Eastern Oklahoma Catholic [of Diocese of Tulsa] - Tulsa, OK - *NewsDir 84*
Eastern Oklahoma County Green Sheet - Midwest City, OK - *AyerDirPub 83*
Eastern Oregon Telephone Co. - Pilot Rock, OR - *TelDir&BG 83-84*
Eastern Orthodox Books - Willits, CA - *BoPubDir 4, 5*
Eastern Orthodox Church Books [Aff. of Albanian Orthodox Archdiocese in America Inc.] - South Boston, MA - *BoPubDir 4, 5*
Eastern Outdoors - East Lyme, CT - *MagDir 84*
Eastern Pennsylvania Cablevision Inc. [of Lamco Communications Inc.] - Boyertown, PA - *BrCabYB 84*
Eastern Pennsylvania Relay Stations Inc. - Freeburg, PA - *BrCabYB 84*
Eastern Pennsylvania Relay Stations Inc. - Shamokin, PA - *BrCabYB 84; Tel&CabFB 84C p.1678*
Eastern Photo Service - New York, NY - *LitMarPl 83, 84; MagIndMarPl 82-83*
Eastern Press - Bloomington, IN - *BoPubDir 4, 5*
Eastern Press Inc. - New Haven, CT - *LitMarPl 83, 84; MagIndMarPl 82-83*
Eastern Press Inc. (National Fulfillment Div.) - New Haven, CT - *LitMarPl 84*
Eastern Public Radio - Boston, MA - *BrCabYB 84*
Eastern Review - Los Angeles, CA - *MagIndMarPl 82-83*
Eastern Review [of East/West Network Inc.] - New York, NY - *BaconPubCkMag 84; Folio 83; MagDir 84*
Eastern Shore CATV [of United Cable TV Corp.] - Ocean City, MD - *Tel&CabFB 84C*
Eastern Shore Courier - Fairhope, AL - *Ed&PubIntYB 82*
Eastern Shore News, The - Accomac, VA - *AyerDirPub 83*
Eastern Shore News, The - Accomack, VA - *Ed&PubIntYB 82*
Eastern Shore Times [of Atlantic Publications Inc.] - Ocean City, MD - *AyerDirPub 83; Ed&PubIntYB 82; NewsDir 84*
Eastern Slope Rural Telephone Association Inc. - Hugo, CO - *TelDir&BG 83-84*
Eastern Software Distributors - Baltimore, MD - *MicrocomMPl 84*
Eastern Sound Recording Studios - Methuen, MA - *AvMarPl 83*
Eastern Specialities Co. Inc. - Northfield, IL - *DirInfWP 82*
Eastern Telecom Corp. - Monroeville, PA - *BrCabYB 84 p.D-300; Tel&CabFB 84C p.1678*
Eastern Telecommunications Philippines Inc. - Manila, Philippines - *TeleSy&SerDir 7-83*
Eastern Typesetting Co. - South Windsor, CT - *LitMarPl 83, 84*
Eastern Typographics Inc. - Cranford, NJ - *MagIndMarPl 82-83*
Eastern/Western Ontario Farmer - London, ON, Canada - *WritMar 84*
Eastex Shopper - Cleveland, TX - *AyerDirPub 83*
Eastex Telephone Cooperative - Henderson, TX - *TelDir&BG 83-84*
Eastfoto Agency - New York, NY - *LitMarPl 83, 84*
Eastgulf TV Association - Eastgulf, WV - *BrCabYB 84; Tel&CabFB 84C*
Eastham Editions - Prospect, NY - *BoPubDir 4, 5*
Eastin Phelan Corp. - Davenport, IA - *AvMarPl 83*
Eastland Country Newspapers - Eastland, TX - *BaconPubCkNews 84*
Eastland Telegram - Eastland, TX - *Ed&PubIntYB 82*
Eastland Telegram - *See* Eastland Country Newspapers
Eastman Advertising Agency Inc. - Van Nuys, CA - *StaDirAdAg 2-84*
Eastman CableRep - New York, NY - *HomeVid&CabYB 82-83*
Eastman Co., A. Eric - West Bountiful, UT - *MicrocomSwDir 1*
Eastman Inc., Robert - Ithaca, NY - *BoPubDir 4, 5*
Eastman Kodak Co. - Rochester, NY - *DataDirSup 7-83; HomeVid&CabYB 82-83; LitMarPl 83, 84; TelAl 83, 84*
Eastman Kodak Co. (Business Systems Markets Div.) - Rochester, NY - *DirInfWP 82*
Eastman Times Journal Spotlight [of Investments & Counseling Services Inc.] - Eastman, GA - *BaconPubCkNews 84; NewsDir 84*
Easton Bulletin - *See* Bulletin Publishing Co.
Easton Courier - *See* Trumbull Times Publishers
Easton Express - Easton, PA - *BaconPubCkNews 84; BrCabYB 84; NewsDir 84*
Easton Star Democrat - Easton, MD - *BaconPubCkNews 84; NewsDir 84*
Easton Telephone Co. - Easton, MN - *TelDir&BG 83-84*
Eastport Quoddy Tides - Eastport, ME - *BaconPubCkNews 84*
Eastside Journal [of Northeast Los Angeles Publishing Co.] - Los Angeles, CA - *AyerDirPub 83; NewsDir 84*
Eastside Monthly - Providence, RI - *NewsDir 84*
Eastside News - Ft. Worth, TX - *AyerDirPub 83; Ed&PubIntYB 82*
Eastside Suburban Newspapers - Indianapolis, IN - *BaconPubCkNews 84*
Eastside Sun - Los Angeles, CA - *AyerDirPub 83; Ed&PubIntYB 82*
Eastview Editions Inc. - Westfield, NJ - *BoPubDir 4, 5; WritMar 84*
Eastwood Pennysaver - Syracuse, NY - *AyerDirPub 83*
Eastwood Printing Co. - Denver, CO - *MagIndMarPl 82-83*
Eastwood Sound - *See* Sulzer Music
Easy Chair Records - Lubbock, TX - *BillIntBG 83-84*
Easy Data Integrated Library System [of Easy Data Systems Ltd.] - North Vancouver, BC, Canada - *EISS 83*
Easy Home Computer [of Pumpkin Press Inc.] - New York, NY - *BaconPubCkMag 84; MicrocomMPl 84*
Easy Listening Music Corp. - *See* Gallico Music Corp., Al
Easy Living [of The Webb Co.] - St. Paul, MN - *MagDir 84; MagIndMarPl 82-83; WritMar 84*
Easy Living - Surrey, BC, Canada - *ArtMar 84*
Easy Reader - Hermosa Beach, CA - *NewsDir 84*
Easy Reader - South Bay, CA - *Ed&PubIntYB 82*
Easy To Do Decorating - New York, NY - *MagDir 84*
Easylink [of Western Union Electronic Mail Inc.] - McLean, VA - *TeleSy&SerDir 2-84*
Easyriders - Malibu, CA - *BaconPubCkMag 84; MagDir 84; MagIndMarPl 82-83; WritMar 84*
Eat Records [Div. of The Phone Co. Inc.] - Salem, MA - *BillIntBG 83-84*
Eat Your Heart Out Publishing Co. - Calgary, AB, Canada - *BoPubDir 5*
Eaton Corp. - Cleveland, OH - *ElecNews 7-25-83*
Eaton Eagles, Douglas - Sarnia, ON, Canada - *BoPubDir 5*
Eaton Music Inc., Roy - Roosevelt Island, NY - *AvMarPl 83*
Eaton North Weld Herald - Eaton, CO - *BaconPubCkNews 84; Ed&PubIntYB 82*
Eaton Printer Products [Subs. of Eaton Corp.] - Watertown, WI - *WhoWMicrocom 83*
Eaton Printer Products - Riverton, WY - *DataDirSup 7-83*
Eaton Rapids Cable TV Inc. [of MetroVision Inc.] - Eaton Rapids, MI - *Tel&CabFB 84C*
Eaton Rapids Journal - Eaton Rapids, MI - *NewsDir 84*
Eaton Register-Herald - Eaton, OH - *BaconPubCkNews 84*
Eatonton Cable TV [of VCA-TeleCable Inc.] - Eatonton, GA - *Tel&CabFB 84C*
Eatonton Messenger - Eatonton, GA - *BaconPubCkNews 84; Ed&PubIntYB 82*
Eatonville Cable TV [of Vallejo Enterprises Inc.] - Eatonville, WA - *BrCabYB 84; Tel&CabFB 84C*
Eatonville Dispatch - Eatonville, WA - *Ed&PubIntYB 82*
Eatonville Dispatch/Plains News - Eatonville, WA - *BaconPubCkNews 84*

Eatough Associates Advertising - Kansas City, MO - *ArtMar 84*
Eau Claire Country Today - Eau Claire, WI - *BaconPubCkNews 84*
Eau Claire Leader-Telegram - Eau Claire, WI - *BaconPubCkNews 84*
Ebberts & Co., Dan - Anaheim Hills, CA - *StaDirAdAg 2-84*
Ebbets Field Productions - New Rochelle, NY - *AvMarPl 83; Tel&CabFB 84C*
Ebel-Doctorow Publications Inc. - Clifton, NJ - *MagIndMarPl 82-83*
Ebensburg Mountaineer-Herald - Ebensburg, PA - *BaconPubCkNews 84*
Ebensburg News Leader - *See* Sedloff Publications Inc.
Eberhard Engineering - Smithtown, NY - *MicrocomMPl 84*
Eberly Press - East Lansing, MI - *BoPubDir 4, 5*
Ebersold Inc., Fred - Oakbrook Terrace, IL - *StaDirAdAg 2-84*
Ebey, Utley, Van Bronkhorst - Mountain View, CA - *StaDirAdAg 2-84*
EBG Library Consultants - Los Altos, CA - *EISS 7-83 Sup*
EBHA Press [Aff. of Economic & Business History Associates] - Lincoln, NE - *BoPubDir 4, 5*
EBIB [of SDC Search Service] - Santa Monica, CA - *DataDirOnSer 84*
EBIB - Houston, TX - *DirOnDB Spring 84*
Ebony [of Johnson Publishing Co.] - Chicago, IL - *BaconPubCkMag 84; Folio 83; LitMarPl 83, 84; MagDir 84; MagIndMarPl 82-83; WritMar 84*
Ebony Jr! [of Johnson Publishing Co.] - Chicago, IL - *ArtMar 84; LitMarPl 83, 84; MagIndMarPl 82-83; WritMar 84*
EBPR Research Reports - Chicago, IL - *BaconPubCkMag 84*
EBS Inc. - Lynbrook, NY - *LitMarPl 83, 84*
EBS Inc. (Bindery Div.) - Lynbrook, NY - *LitMarPl 83, 84*
EBS Inc. (Subscription Div.) - Lynbrook, NY - *MagIndMarPl 82-83*
EBSCO Industries Inc. - Birmingham, AL - *BoPubDir 4, 5*
EBSCO Subscription Services [Subs. of EBSCO Industries Inc.] - Birmingham, AL - *DataDirOnSer 84; EISS 83; MagIndMarPl 82-83*
EBSCONET [of EBSCO Subscription Services] - Birmingham, AL - *DataDirOnSer 84; DirOnDB Spring 84*
EBW Promotions - New York, NY - *StaDirAdAg 2-84*
Eby & Everson Inc. - *See* Colle & McVoy Advertising Agency Inc.
Eby, Hyatt - Birmingham, MI - *StaDirAdAg 2-84*
EC & M [of McGraw-Hill Inc.] - New York, NY - *Folio 83*
ECA Associates - Chesapeake, VA - *BoPubDir 4, 5; LitMag&SmPr 83-84*
Eccentric, The - Birmingham, MI - *Ed&PubIntYB 82*
Eccentric, The (Troy Edition) - Troy, MI - *Ed&PubIntYB 82*
Eccles Health Sciences Library, Spencer S. [of University of Utah] - Salt Lake City, UT - *CompReadDB 82; DataDirOnSer 84; InfIndMarPl 83*
Ecco Press, The - New York, NY - *LitMag&SmPr 83-84; LitMarPl 83, 84; WritMar 84*
ECD Corp. - *See* GWP Corp.
ECDIN - Luxembourg - *DirOnDB Spring 84*
Echo - Prophetstown, IL - *AyerDirPub 83*
Echo - Elgin, IA - *AyerDirPub 83*
Echo - Ely, MN - *Ed&PubIntYB 82*
Echo - Erskine, MN - *AyerDirPub 83*
Echo - Ligonier, PA - *AyerDirPub 83*
Echo - Mt. Jewett, PA - *AyerDirPub 83*
Echo - Providence, RI - *AyerDirPub 83; Ed&PubIntYB 82; NewsDir 84*
Echo - Eden, TX - *AyerDirPub 83*
Echo - Leavenworth, WA - *AyerDirPub 83*
Echo - Moundsville, WV - *AyerDirPub 83*
Echo - Athabasca, AB, Canada - *AyerDirPub 83; Ed&PubIntYB 82*
Echo - High Level, AB, Canada - *Ed&PubIntYB 82*
Echo - Pincher Creek, AB, Canada - *Ed&PubIntYB 82*
Echo - Hamiota, MB, Canada - *AyerDirPub 83*
Echo - Amherstburg, ON, Canada - *AyerDirPub 83*
Echo - Wiarton, ON, Canada - *AyerDirPub 83*
Echo Communications Corp. - Mountain View, CA - *WhoWMicrocom 83*
Echo Enterprise - Echo, MN - *Ed&PubIntYB 82*
Echo Film Productions Inc. - Boise, ID - *WritMar 84*
Echo-News - Alice, TX - *Ed&PubIntYB 82*
Echo-Pilot - Greencastle, PA - *AyerDirPub 83; Ed&PubIntYB 82*
Echo Publishers West - West Menlo Park, CA - *BoPubDir 4, 5*
Echo-Sentinel - Star City, SK, Canada - *AyerDirPub 83; Ed&PubIntYB 82*
Echo Stage Co. Ltd. - New York, NY - *BoPubDir 5*
Echo, The - Northern Columbia, NY - *Ed&PubIntYB 82*
Echo, The - Oyen, AB, Canada - *AyerDirPub 83*
Echo, The - Chetwynd, BC, Canada - *Ed&PubIntYB 82*
Echo, The - Manitouwadge, ON, Canada - *Ed&PubIntYB 82*
Echoes-Sentinel - Stirling, NJ - *AyerDirPub 83*
Echolab Inc. - Burlington, MA - *AvMarPl 83*
Echoland Shopper - Pequot Lakes, MN - *AyerDirPub 83*
Ecker Consumer Recruiting Inc. - Daly City, CA - *IntDirMarRes 83*
Eckerd Corp., Jack - Clearwater, FL - *HomeVid&CabYB 82-83*
Eckhardt Associates, Fred - Portland, OR - *BoPubDir 4, 5*
Eckhouse Advertising Inc. - New York, NY - *StaDirAdAg 2-84*
Eckles Telphone Co. - New Prague, MN - *TelDir&BG 83-84*
Eckmillion Corp., The - New York, NY - *LitMarPl 83*
Eckstein Social Science Applications, Blanka - New York, NY - *IntDirMarRes 83*
Eckville & District Historical Society - Eckville, AB, Canada - *BoPubDir 4 Sup, 5*
Eclectic Systems Corp. - Addison, TX - *MicrocomMPl 83*
Eclectic Systems Corp. - Dallas, TX - *MicrocomMPl 84*
ECM Newsletters Inc. - Houston, TX - *WritMar 84*
ECO Advertising Agency Ltd. - Stockholm, Sweden - *StaDirAdAg 2-84*
ECO Cos., The - San Marcos, CA - *DataDirSup 7-83*
Ecodoc - *See* FRANCIS: Ecodoc
Ecole Polytechnique Federale de Lausanne (Bibliotheque Centrale) - Lausanne, Switzerland - *InfIndMarPl 83*
Ecological Book Club, The [Subs. of Devin Adair Publishing Co.] - Old Greenwich, CT - *LitMarPl 83, 84*
Ecological Fibers Inc. - South Lancaster, MA - *LitMarPl 83, 84*
Ecology - Ithaca, NY - *MagIndMarPl 82-83*
Ecology Abstracts [of Information Retrieval Ltd.] - London, England - *CompReadDB 82*
Ecology U.S.A. - Silver Spring, MD - *BaconPubCkMag 84*
Ecom Associates Inc. - Milwaukee, WI - *MicrocomMPl 84*
Ecom Consultants Inc. - New York, NY - *DirPRFirms 83*
ECOM Systems Inc. - Memphis, TN - *DataDirSup 7-83*
Ecom Univas [of Univas Network] - Neuilly sur Seine, France - *StaDirAdAg 2-84*
Ecomp - Eggenstein-Leopoldshafen, West Germany - *DirOnDB Spring 84*
Econ-O-Gram [of Air Couriers International Inc.] - Phoenix, AZ - *TeleSy&SerDir 2-84*
Econintel Monitor [of ADP Network Services Inc.] - Ann Arbor, MI - *DataDirOnSer 84*
Econintel Monitor [of Econintel Information Services Ltd.] - London, England - *DirOnDB Spring 84; EISS 83*
Econo Data Inc. - Cincinnati, OH - *ADAPSOMemDir 83-84; DataDirOnSer 84*
Econographics of Knoxville Inc. - Knoxville, TN - *EISS 5-84 Sup*
Econometric Data Bank - Parkville, Australia - *DirOnDB Spring 84*
Econometric Data Bank [of Computer Sciences of Australia Pty. Ltd.] - St. Leonards, Australia - *DataDirOnSer 84*
Economic Analysis & Projections Dept. [of The World Bank] - Washington, DC - *EISS 83*
Economic Analysis Div. [of U.S. Federal Emergency Management] - Washington, DC - *EISS 83*
Economic & Business Research Div. [of University of Arizona] - Tucson, AZ - *EISS 83*
Economic Computer Sales Inc. - Memphis, TN - *DataDirSup 7-83*
Economic Facts [of The National Research Bureau Inc.] - Burlington, IA - *WritMar 84*
Economic Geology - New Haven, CT - *MagDir 84*
Economic Growth Center [of Yale University] - New Haven, CT - *EISS 83*
Economic Information Service [of Ministry of Economic Affairs] - The Hague, Netherlands - *CompReadDB 82; EISS 83; InfIndMarPl 83*

Economic Information Systems [Aff. of Control Data Corp.] - New York, NY - *BoPubDir 4, 5; CompReadDB 82; DataDirOnSer 84; EISS 83; InfIndMarPl 83; InfoS 83-84*
Economic Literature Index [of Dialog Information Services Inc.] - Palo Alto, CA - *DataDirOnSer 84*
Economic Literature Index [of Journal of Economic Literature] - Pittsburgh, PA - *DirOnDB Spring 84; EISS 7-83 Sup*
Economic News Agency - Princeton, NJ - *Ed&PubIntYB 82*
Economic Research Service [of U.S. Dept. of Agriculture] - Washington, DC - *EISS 83*
Economic Salon Ltd. - New York, NY - *BoPubDir 5*
Economic Sciences Corp. - Berkeley, CA - *ADAPSOMemDir 83-84; EISS 83*
Economic Time Series [of Computer Sciences of Australia Pty. Ltd.] - St. Leonards, Australia - *DataDirOnSer 84*
Economic Week - New York, NY - *BaconPubCkMag 84*
Economic World - New York, NY - *BaconPubCkMag 84*
Economics Abstracts International [of Dialog Information Services Inc.] - Palo Alto, CA - *DataDirOnSer 84*
Economics Abstracts International [of Learned Information Ltd.] - Oxford, England - *DBBus 82*
Economics Abstracts International [of Ministry of Economic Affairs] - The Hague, Netherlands - *CompReadDB 82; DirOnDB Spring 84; OnBibDB 3*
Economics & Technology Inc. - Boston, MA - *DirMarMP 83*
Economics Press Inc. - Fairfield, NJ - *BoPubDir 4 Sup, 5*
Economist - New Hampton, IA - *AyerDirPub 83*
Economist & Sun - Markham, ON, Canada - *AyerDirPub 83*
Economist Newspaper Group Inc., The - New York, NY - *DirMarMP 83*
Economist Southtown Shopper [of Chicago Daily Southtown Economist Newspapers] - Chicago, IL - *NewsDir 84*
Economist Statistics Database [of James R. LymBurner & Sons Ltd.] - Toronto, ON, Canada - *DataDirOnSer 84*
Economist Suburban Shopper [of Chicago Daily Southtown Economist Newspapers] - Chicago, IL - *NewsDir 84*
Economist's Statistics [of James R. Lymburner & Sons Ltd.] - Toronto, ON, Canada - *DBBus 82; DirOnDB Spring 84; EISS 83*
Economy Co., The - Oklahoma City, OK - *ArtMar 84; KnowInd 83; LitMarPl 83, 84*
Econoscan Inc. - New York, NY - *MagIndMarPl 82-83*
Econoscope - Warren, NJ - *DirOnDB Spring 84*
Econotec Inc. - Verdun, PQ, Canada - *TeleSy&SerDir 2-84*
Ecorse Advertiser, The - Ecorse, MI - *Ed&PubIntYB 82*
Ecorse Enterprise [of Mellus Newspapers Inc.] - Lincoln Park, MI - *AyerDirPub 83; NewsDir 84*
Ecorse Enterprise - *See* Mellus Newspapers Inc.
Ecorse Enterprise, The - Ecorse, MI - *Ed&PubIntYB 82*
Ecorse River Rouge Herald - Ecorse, MI - *BaconPubCkNews 84*
Ecorse Telegram - Ecorse, MI - *BaconPubCkNews 84; NewsDir 84*
Ecosoft - Indianapolis, IN - *MicrocomMPl 83, 84; MicrocomSwDir 1; WhoWMicrocom 83*
Ecothek - Paris, France - *DirOnDB Spring 84*
Ecotran Corp. - Beachwood, OH - *DataDirOnSer 84; DataDirSup 7-83*
Ecouri Romanesti - Toronto, ON, Canada - *Ed&PubIntYB 82*
Ecphorizer, The - Sunnyvale, CA - *LitMag&SmPr 83-84*
ECRI - Plymouth Meeting, PA - *BoPubDir 5*
Ecrits des Forges Inc. - Trois-Rivieres, PQ, Canada - *BoPubDir 4 Sup, 5*
ECS Microsystems Inc. - San Jose, CA - *WhoWMicrocom 83*
ECTJ/Educational Communication & Technology - Washington, DC - *MagDir 84*
Ecumedia News Service - New York, NY - *BrCabYB 84; Tel&CabFB 84C*
Ecumenical Press - Philadelphia, PA - *BoPubDir 4, 5*
Ecumenical Program for Inter-American Communication & Action [Aff. of National Council of Churches] - Washington, DC - *BoPubDir 4, 5*
Ecusta Paper & Film Group [Subs. of Olin Corp.] - Pisgah Forest, NC - *LitMarPl 83, 84*
ECW Press - Downsview, ON, Canada - *BoPubDir 4; LitMarPl 83, 84*
E.D. & D. Inc. - Haines, AK - *Tel&CabFB 84C p.1678*
'Ed-It - Oakland, CA - *LitMarPl 83, 84*
Ed-Line - Arlington, VA - *DirOnDB Spring 84*
ED-NET [of National School Public Relations Association] - Arlington, VA - *DataDirOnSer 84*
Ed-Net - *See* Ed-Line
Ed-Sci Development - Modesto, CA - *MicrocomMPl 84*
Ed-Sci Development - San Francisco, CA - *MicrocomMPl 83*
Ed-Tech Service - Chatham, NJ - *AvMarPl 83*
Ed-U Press Inc. - Fayetteville, NY - *BoPubDir 4 Sup, 5; LitMag&SmPr 83-84*
Ed-Venture Films - Los Angeles, CA - *Tel&CabFB 84C*
EDAPS - Arlington, VA - *DirOnDB Spring 84*
EDC Publishing [Aff. of Educational Development Corp.] - Tulsa, OK - *ArtMar 84; BoPubDir 4, 5; LitMarPl 84*
Eddy, Frances - Bethesda, MD - *LitMarPl 83; MagIndMarPl 82-83*
Eddy, James E. - *See* E & E Cable Service Inc.
Eddy-Rucker-Nickels Co., The - Cambridge, MA - *AdAge 3-28-84; StaDirAdAg 2-84*
Eddy TV System Inc., James E. - Pleasant Valley, WV - *Tel&CabFB 84C*
Eddyville Herald Ledger - Eddyville, KY - *BaconPubCkNews 84*
Eddyville Tribune - Eddyville, IA - *Ed&PubIntYB 82*
Eddyville Tribune - *See* Quad County Newspapers
Edelman Inc., Daniel J. - Washington, DC - *ArtMar 84*
Edelman Inc., Daniel J. - Chicago, IL - *ArtMar 84; DirPRFirms 83*
Edelman/Uniphoto, Harry - Pittsburgh, PA - *AvMarPl 83*
Edelmann Scott Inc. - Richmond, VA - *DirPRFirms 83; StaDirAdAg 2-84*
Edelstein Associates, Irvin L. - Santa Monica, CA - *StaDirAdAg 2-84*
Edelstein-Okerwall Advertising Agency - Evanston, IL - *StaDirAdAg 2-84; TelAl 83, 84*
Eden Daily News [of Leaksville Publishing Co. Inc.] - Eden, NC - *AyerDirPub 83; BaconPubCkNews 84; Ed&PubIntYB 82; NewsDir 84*
Eden Echo - Eden, TX - *BaconPubCkNews 84; Ed&PubIntYB 82*
Eden Medical Research Inc. - St. Albans, VT - *BoPubDir 4, 5*
Eden Music Corp./Iza Music Corp. - Englewood, NJ - *BillIntBG 83-84*
Eden Personnel Inc./Eden Data Processing - New York, NY - *MagIndMarPl 82-83*
Eden Prairie News - Eden Prairie, MN - *AyerDirPub 83; BaconPubCkNews 84; Ed&PubIntYB 82*
Eden Press Inc. - Montreal, PQ, Canada - *LitMarPl 83, 84*
Eden Records - Allen Park, MI - *BillIntBG 83-84*
Eden Valley Journal - Eden Valley, MN - *BaconPubCkNews 84; Ed&PubIntYB 82*
Eden Valley Press Inc. - Loveland, CO - *BoPubDir 4, 5*
Eden Valley Telephone Co. - Farson, WY - *TelDir&BG 83-84*
Eden's Work [Aff. of Union Center] - Franklin, ME - *BoPubDir 4, 5*
Edenton Chowan Herald - Edenton, NC - *BaconPubCkNews 84*
EDF-DOC [of Questel Inc.] - Washington, DC - *DataDirOnSer 84*
EDF-DOC [of Electricite de France] - Clamart, France - *CompReadDB 82; DirOnDB Spring 84; EISS 83; OnBibDB 3*
Edgar-Athens Record Review - *See* TP Printing Co.
Edgar, Betsy Jordan - Hillsboro, WV - *BoPubDir 4, 5*
Edgar Music Co., Don - Ft. Worth, TX - *BillIntBG 83-84*
Edgartown Vineyard Gazette - Edgartown, MA - *BaconPubCkNews 84*
Edge of an Era - Bala Cynwyd, PA - *BoPubDir 4, 5*
Edgebrook-Sauganash Passage - Chicago, IL - *AyerDirPub 83*
Edgecombe Marketing Inc. - Tarboro, NC - *ArtMar 84; StaDirAdAg 2-84*
Edgefield Advertiser - Edgefield, SC - *BaconPubCkNews 84; Ed&PubIntYB 82*
Edgefield County Press - Edgefield, SC - *AyerDirPub 83*
Edgefield-Johnston Cablevision [of Evening Post Publishing Co.] - Edgefield, SC - *BrCabYB 84*
Edgeley Mail - Edgeley, ND - *BaconPubCkNews 84; Ed&PubIntYB 82*
Edgemont Herald-Tribune - Edgemont, SD - *BaconPubCkNews 84; Ed&PubIntYB 82*
Edgepress - Point Reyes, CA - *BoPubDir 4, 5*
Edgerton Earth - Edgerton, OH - *BaconPubCkNews 84; Ed&PubIntYB 82*

Edgerton Enterprise - Edgerton, MN - *BaconPubCkNews 84; Ed&PubIntYB 82*
Edgerton Platte County Citizen - Edgerton, MO - *BaconPubCkNews 84*
Edgerton Reporter - Edgerton, WI - *BaconPubCkNews 84; Ed&PubIntYB 82; NewsDir 84*
Edges [of American Blade Inc.] - Chattanooga, TN - *WritMar 84*
Edgewater Bergen Citizen - Edgewater, NJ - *BaconPubCkNews 84*
Edgewater Book Co. Inc. - Lakewood, OH - *BoPubDir 4, 5*
Edgewater Cable TV - Edgewater, CO - *Tel&CabFB 84C*
Edgewood Computer Associates Inc. - New York, NY - *TeleSy&SerDir 7-83*
Edgewood Enterprise - Edgewood, TX - *Ed&PubIntYB 82*
Edgewood Enterprise - *See* Howard Publishing Co. Inc.
Edgewood Kenton County Recorder - *See* Recorder Newspapers
Edgewood Press - Clare, MI - *BoPubDir 4, 5*
Edgewood Reminder - Edgewood, IA - *BaconPubCkNews 84; Ed&PubIntYB 82*
Edi Compo - Longueuil, PQ, Canada - *BoPubDir 4, 5*
Edible Records - Urbana, IL - *BillIntBG 83-84*
Ediciones del Norte - Hanover, NH - *LitMag&SmPr 83-84*
Ediciones Hispamerica - Gaithersburg, MD - *BoPubDir 4, 5*
Ediciones Huracan Inc. - Rio Piedras, PR - *BoPubDir 4, 5; LitMarPl 84*
Ediciones NAPA - Asuncion, Paraguay - *LitMag&SmPr 83-84*
Ediciones Universal - Miami, FL - *BoPubDir 4, 5; LitMarPl 84*
Edimedia Inc. - Quebec City, PQ, Canada - *EISS 5-84 Sup*
Edina Sentinel - Edina, MO - *BaconPubCkNews 84; Ed&PubIntYB 82*
Edina Sun - Edina, MN - *AyerDirPub 83; Ed&PubIntYB 82*
Edina Sun - *See* Sun Newspapers
Edinboro Independent & Enterprise News - *See* Brown Thompson Newspapers
Edinburg Herald-Star - Edinburg, IL - *BaconPubCkNews 84*
Edinburg Review [of Hidalgo Publishing Co. Inc.] - Edinburg, TX - *BaconPubCkNews 84; Ed&PubIntYB 82; NewsDir 84*
Edinburgh University Press - Edinburgh, Scotland - *MicroMarPl 82-83*
EDIP - Paris, France - *StaDirAdAg 2-84*
Ediquip [Subs. of J & R Film Co. Inc.] - Hollywood, CA - *AvMarPl 83*
Edison Electric Institute - Washington, DC - *CompReadDB 82*
Edison Lithographing & Printing Corp. - New York, NY - *LitMarPl 83, 84*
Edison-Norwood Park Review - Des Plaines, IL - *AyerDirPub 83*
Edison Technical Services - Bethesda, MD - *BoPubDir 5*
Edit Inc. - Chicago, IL - *LitMarPl 83*
Editcetera - Berkeley, CA - *LitMarPl 83, 84; MagIndMarPl 82-83*
Editec - Cali, Colombia - *EISS 5-84 Sup*
Editec Inc. - Chicago, IL - *FBInfSer 80*
Editel [Div. of Columbia Pictures Industries Inc.] - Chicago, IL - *Tel&CabFB 84C*
Editel Washington - Washington, DC - *TeleSy&SerDir 7-83*
Editing & Publishing Services - Cushing, ME - *LitMarPl 83*
Editing by the Book - New York, NY - *LitMarPl 83*
Editing, Design, & Production Inc. [Subs. of Nodaway Valley Co.] - Philadelphia, PA - *LitMarPl 84*
Editing Unltd. - New Rochelle, NY - *LitMarPl 83, 84; MagIndMarPl 82-83*
Edition am Mehringdamm [Aff. of Edition & Galerie am Mehringdamm] - Rensselaer Falls, NY - *BoPubDir 4 Sup, 5; LitMag&SmPr 83-84*
Edition Speciale - St. Bruno, PQ, Canada - *Ed&PubIntYB 82*
Edition Stencil - Ottawa, ON, Canada - *LitMag&SmPr 83-84*
Editions Cooperatives Albert St.-Martin - Montreal, PQ, Canada - *BoPubDir 5*
Editions Cosmos Enr. - Sherbrooke, PQ, Canada - *BoPubDir 4, 5*
Editions d'Acadie - Moncton, NB, Canada - *BoPubDir 4 Sup, 5*
Editions de la Reunion des Musees Nationaux - Paris, France - *MicroMarPl 82-83*
Editions de l'Avant-Scene - Paris, France - *MicroMarPl 82-83*
Editions de l'Hexagone Enr. - Montreal, PQ, Canada - *BoPubDir 4; LitMarPl 83, 84*
Editions des Deux Mondes - Newark, DE - *BoPubDir 4 Sup, 5*
Editions des Plaines - St.-Boniface, MB, Canada - *BoPubDir 4 Sup, 5*
Editions du Franc-Canada - Montreal, PQ, Canada - *BoPubDir 4, 5*
Editions du Noroit - St.-Lambert, PQ, Canada - *BoPubDir 4, 5; LitMarPl 84*
Editions du Pelican - Quebec, PQ, Canada - *LitMarPl 83, 84*
Editions du Remue-Menage - Montreal, PQ, Canada - *BoPubDir 4, 5*
Editions du Renouveau Pedagogique Inc. - Montreal, PQ, Canada - *LitMarPl 83, 84*
Editions du Trecarre [Aff. of Gage Publishing Ltd.] - St.-Laurent, PQ, Canada - *BoPubDir 5*
Editions Ecole Active - Montreal, PQ, Canada - *LitMarPl 83*
Editions Etincelle [Subs. of SCE Inc.] - Montreal, PQ, Canada - *LitMarPl 83, 84*
Editions Fides - Montreal, PQ, Canada - *LitMarPl 83, 84*
Editions FM - Ville de Laval, PQ, Canada - *LitMarPl 83, 84*
Editions Heritage - St.-Lambert, PQ, Canada - *LitMarPl 83, 84*
Editions Hurtubise HMH Ltee. - Ville Lasalle, PQ, Canada - *LitMarPl 83, 84*
Editions la Liberte Inc. - Ste.-Foy, PQ, Canada - *BoPubDir 4 Sup, 5*
Editions Lemeac Inc. - Montreal, PQ, Canada - *LitMarPl 83, 84*
Editions Marcel Broquet - La Prairie, PQ, Canada - *BoPubDir 4, 5; LitMarPl 84*
Editions Marie-France Ltee. - Montreal, PQ, Canada - *BoPubDir 4, 5; LitMarPl 84*
Editions Nouvelle Optique Inc. - Montreal, PQ, Canada - *BoPubDir 4, 5; LitMarPl 84*
Editions Numismatique et Change - Bar-le-Duc, France - *MicroMarPl 82-83*
Editions of My Country - Montreal, PQ, Canada - *BoPubDir 4, 5*
Editions Publisol - New York, NY - *BoPubDir 4, 5*
Editions Sciences et Culture Inc. - Montreal, PQ, Canada - *BoPubDir 4, 5*
Editions Trait d'Union Publications - Burlington, ON, Canada - *BoPubDir 4, 5*
Editions Vilo Inc. - New York, NY - *LitMarPl 84*
Editiorial Asol Inc. [Aff. of Instituto Nacional de Bellas Letras] - Rio Piedras, PR - *BoPubDir 5*
Editmasters/Mizelle - Washington, DC - *LitMarPl 83, 84*
Editor & Publisher - New York, NY - *ArtMar 84; BaconPubCkMag 84; BoPubDir 4, 5; MagDir 84; MagIndMarPl 82-83; NewsBur 6; WritMar 84*
Editorial & Graphic Services - Martinsville, NJ - *LitMarPl 83, 84; MagIndMarPl 82-83*
Editorial Betania [Aff. of Bethany Fellowship Inc.] - Minneapolis, MN - *BoPubDir 5*
Editorial Caribe - Miami, FL - *BoPubDir 4, 5; LitMarPl 84*
Editorial Consultant Service - West Hempstead, NY - *Ed&PubIntYB 82*
Editorial Consultants Inc. - San Francisco, CA - *BoPubDir 4, 5; LitMarPl 83, 84*
Editorial Consultants Inc. - Wayland, MA - *LitMarPl 83; MagIndMarPl 82-83*
Editorial Consultants Inc. - Seattle, WA - *LitMarPl 83, 84; MagIndMarPl 82-83*
Editorial Dynamics - Forest Hills, NY - *LitMarPl 83, 84*
Editorial Excelsior Corp. - San Jose, CA - *LitMarPl 83, 84; MagIndMarPl 82-83*
Editorial Experts Inc. [Div. of Editorial Experts Inc.] - Alexandria, VA - *BoPubDir 4, 5; LitMarPl 83, 84; MagIndMarPl 82-83*
Editorial Eye, The - Alexandria, VA - *BaconPubCkMag 84; MagIndMarPl 82-83*
Editorial Guild Inc., The - Katonah, NY - *LitMarPl 84*
Editorial Indoamerica - Kansas City, MO - *BoPubDir 4, 5*
Editorial Justa Publications Inc. - Berkeley, CA - *BoPubDir 4, 5; LitMag&SmPr 83-84*
Editorial Options Inc. - New York, NY - *LitMarPl 83, 84*
Editorial Photocolor Archives - New York, NY - *AvMarPl 83; LitMarPl 83; MagIndMarPl 82-83*
Editorial Photocolor Consultants [Div. of Editorial Photocolor Archives Inc.] - New York, NY - *LitMarPl 83*
Editorial Pocho-Che - San Francisco, CA - *BoPubDir 4, 5*
Editorial Research Reports - Washington, DC - *Ed&PubIntYB 82*

Editorial Research Service - Kansas City, MO - *BoPubDir 4, 5; LitMag&SmPr 83-84*
Editorial Services - Bull Shoals, AR - *LitMarPl 83, 84*
Editorial Services Co. - Rockaway, NJ - *BoPubDir 5*
Editorial Services Co. - New York, NY - *BoPubDir 4; LitMag&SmPr 83-84*
Editors Bureau Ltd., The - Westport, CT - *LitMarPl 83, 84*
Editor's Copy Syndicate - Orangeburg, SC - *Ed&PubIntYB 82; LitMarPl 84*
Editor's Forum - Atlanta, GA - *BaconPubCkMag 84; MagDir 84*
Editor's Newsletter - New York, NY - *MagIndMarPl 82-83*
Editors Only - New Britain, CT - *DirOnDB Spring 84*
Editors Press Inc. [Subs. of Kiplinger Washington Editors] - Hyattsville, MD - *LitMarPl 83, 84; MagIndMarPl 82-83*
Editors Press Service Inc. - New York, NY - *BoPubDir 4, 5; Ed&PubIntYB 82*
Editran/Eileen Weppner - Boulder, CO - *LitMarPl 83, 84*
Editrice Bibliografica - Milan, Italy - *CompReadDB 82*
Edits Publishers - San Diego, CA - *BoPubDir 4, 5; WritMar 84*
EDM & Associates Inc. - Washington, DC - *Tel&CabFB 84C; TeleSy&SerDir 2-84*
EDM Digest - Farmington, MI - *BaconPubCkMag 84*
Edman Co., The - Putnam, CT - *Ed&PubIntYB 82*
Edmond Cablevision [of Multimedia Cablevision Inc.] - Edmond, OK - *Tel&CabFB 84C*
Edmond Evening Sun - Edmond, OK - *BaconPubCkNews 84; Ed&PubIntYB 82; NewsDir 84*
Edmond-Montgomery Ltd. - Toronto, ON, Canada - *BoPubDir 5*
Edmond Publishing Co. - Branchport, NY - *BoPubDir 4, 5*
Edmonds Tribune-Review - Edmonds, WA - *Ed&PubIntYB 82; NewsDir 84*
Edmondson/Evans Communications Inc. - New York, NY - *StaDirAdAg 2-84*
Edmonson News - Brownsville, KY - *AyerDirPub 83; Ed&PubIntYB 82*
Edmonton Art Gallery - Edmonton, AB, Canada - *BoPubDir 4 Sup, 5*
Edmonton Commerce & Industry - Edmonton, AB, Canada - *BaconPubCkMag 84*
Edmonton Herald News - Edmonton, KY - *BaconPubCkNews 84; Ed&PubIntYB 82*
Edmonton Journal - Edmonton, AB, Canada - *BaconPubCkNews 84; LitMarPl 83*
Edmonton Magazine - Edmonton, AB, Canada - *BaconPubCkMag 84*
Edmonton Page - Edmonton, AB, Canada - *Ed&PubIntYB 82*
Edmonton Sun, The - Edmonton, AB, Canada - *Ed&PubIntYB 82*
Edmore Cable TV [of Midcontinent Cable Inc.] - Edmore, ND - *BrCabYB 84; Tel&CabFB 84C*
Edmore Herald - Edmore, ND - *Ed&PubIntYB 82*
Edmore Herald - *See* Ness Press Inc.
Edmore Times, The - Edmore, MI - *Ed&PubIntYB 82*
EDN [of Reed Holdings Inc.] - Boston, MA - *BaconPubCkMag 84; Folio 83; MagDir 84; MagIndMarPl 82-83*
Edna Herald - Edna, TX - *BaconPubCkNews 84; Ed&PubIntYB 82; NewsDir 84*
Edna Sun - Edna, KS - *BaconPubCkNews 84*
Ednalite Corp., The - Peekskill, NY - *AvMarPl 83*
Edon Commercial, The - Edon, OH - *AyerDirPub 83; Ed&PubIntYB 82*
EDP Analyzer - Vista, CA - *BaconPubCkMag 84; MagIndMarPl 82-83*
EDP Industry Report [of International Data Corp.] - Framingham, MA - *BaconPubCkMag 84; MagDir 84; MagIndMarPl 82-83*
EDP Performance Review - Phoenix, AZ - *BaconPubCkMag 84*
EDP Services Co. Inc. - Inglewood, CA - *DataDirOnSer 84*
EDP-Software - Waltham, MA - *MicrocomMPl 84*
EDP Supply Cos. - Salem, NH - *DataDirSup 7-83*
EDP Weekly [of EDP News Services Inc.] - Annandale, VA - *MagDir 84*
EDR/Media - Shaker Heights, OH - *TeleSy&SerDir 2-84*
Edric Imports Inc. - Columbia, MD - *AvMarPl 83*
EDS Time-Sharing Systems Inc. [Subs. of Computer Services Inc.] - Milwaukee, WI - *DataDirOnSer 84*
Edson, Bernard - Huntington Station, NY - *LitMarPl 83, 84*
Edson Leader - Edson, AB, Canada - *Ed&PubIntYB 82*
Edstan Studio Inc. - New York, NY - *Tel&CabFB 84C*
EDT - Las Vegas, NV - *MicrocomMPl 83*
Edu Calc Publications [Div. of Educational Calculator Devices Inc.] - Laguna Beach, CA - *DirMarMP 83*
Edu-Comp Inc. - Renton, WA - *MicrocomMPl 83*
Edu Media - Kitchener, ON, Canada - *LitMarPl 83*
Edu-Soft Stekettee Educational Software - Philadelphia, PA - *MicrocomMPl 83*
Edu-Tech Corp., The - Fairfield, CT - *LitMarPl 83, 84*
Edu-Ware Services - Agoura, CA - *MicrocomMPl 83, 84; MicrocomSwDir 1; WhoWMicrocom 83*
Educalc Publications [Aff. of Educational Calculator Devices Inc.] - Laguna Beach, CA - *BoPubDir 4, 5*
Educaltor Inc. - Hudson, MA - *MicrocomMPl 84*
Educat Publishers Inc. - Berkeley, CA - *DirMarMP 83*
Education - Chula Vista, CA - *MagDir 84; MagIndMarPl 82-83*
Education Advisory Bureau - North Hollywood, CA - *MagIndMarPl 82-83*
Education & Training Consultants Co. - Sedona, AZ - *BoPubDir 4, 5*
Education & Training of the Mentally Retarded - Marcus Hook, PA - *MagDir 84*
Education Associates - Athens, GA - *BoPubDir 4, 5; WritMar 84*
Education Associates Inc. - Frankfort, KY - *BoPubDir 4 Sup, 5*
Education Daily Online - Arlington, VA - *DirOnDB Spring 84*
Education Data Base [of Ohio State University Libraries] - Columbus, OH - *CompReadDB 82*
Education Development Center - Newton, MA - *AvMarPl 83*
Education Digest [of Prakken Publications Inc.] - Ann Arbor, MI - *BaconPubCkMag 84; LitMarPl 83, 84; MagDir 84; MagIndMarPl 82-83*
Education Exploration Center Inc. - Minneapolis, MN - *BoPubDir 4*
Education Exploration Center Inc. - Kansas City, MO - *BoPubDir 5*
Education Film Locator [of Consortium of University Film Centers] - Kent, OH - *EISS 83*
Education for Management Inc. [Subs. of Robert A. Farmer Group Inc.] - Watertown, MA - *LitMarPl 83, 84*
Education Funding Research Council - Arlington, VA - *InfIndMarPl 83*
Education Guide Inc. - Randolph, MA - *BoPubDir 4, 5*
Education Industries - Middleton, WI - *BoPubDir 4 Sup, 5*
Education Information Center [of Georgia State Dept. of Education] - Atlanta, GA - *EISS 83*
Education Information Network in the European Community [of Commission of the European Communities] - Brussels, Belgium - *EISS 83*
Education Information Services [of Rhode Island State Dept. of Education] - Providence, RI - *EISS 83*
Education Mailings Clearing House [Div. of Roxbury Press Inc.] - Sweet Springs, MO - *LitMarPl 83, 84*
Education People Inc., The - Chappaqua, NY - *LitMarPl 83, 84*
Education Reports - Washington, DC - *Ed&PubIntYB 82*
Education Research [of Ontario Education Research Information System] - Toronto, ON, Canada - *CompReadDB 82*
Education Research Associates - Amherst, MA - *BoPubDir 4, 5*
Education Service Group [of Bibliographic Retrieval Services] - Latham, NY - *EISS 83*
Education Systems Inc. - Gales Ferry, CT - *LitMarPl 83, 84; MagIndMarPl 82-83*
Education Systems Publisher - Los Angeles, CA - *BoPubDir 5*
Education Tomorrow - Washington, DC - *MagIndMarPl 82-83*
Education Turnkey Systems - Falls Church, VA - *MicrocomMPl 83*
Education USA Newsline & Information Network [of National School Public Relations Association] - Arlington, VA - *DataDirOnSer 84; EISS 7-83 Sup*
Education Week - Washington, DC - *BaconPubCkMag 84*
Educational Activities Inc. - Baldwin, NY - *MicrocomMPl 83, 84; MicrocomSwDir 1*
Educational Activities Inc. - Freeport, NY - *AvMarPl 83; WhoWMicrocom 83*
Educational Affairs Publishers - Columbia, MO - *BoPubDir 4, 5*
Educational & Industrial Television - Danbury, CT - *BaconPubCkMag 84*

Educational Audio Visual Inc. - Pleasantville, NY - *AvMarPl 83; MicrocomMPl 84*
Educational Book Publishers - Guthrie, OK - *BoPubDir 4 Sup, 5*
Educational Broadcasting Corp. - New York, NY - *BrCabYB 84*
Educational Challenges Inc. - Alexandria, VA - *LitMarPl 83, 84*
Educational Communication & Technology Journal - Washington, DC - *BaconPubCkMag 84*
Educational Communications Inc. - Lake Forest, IL - *BoPubDir 5; DirMarMP 83*
Educational Communications Inc. - Northbrook, IL - *BoPubDir 4*
Educational Communications Inc. - King of Prussia, PA - *AvMarPl 83*
Educational Computer Magazine [of EdComp Inc.] - Cupertino, CA - *BaconPubCkMag 84; MicrocomMPl 84*
Educational Computing - Oakton, VA - *MicrocomMPl 84*
Educational Computing Systems - Oak Ridge, TN - *MicrocomMPl 83, 84; WhoWMicrocom 83*
Educational Conference Center [of Luzerne County Community College] - Nanticoke, PA - *TeleSy&SerDir 2-84*
Educational Courseware - Westport, CT - *MicrocomMPl 83, 84; MicrocomSwDir 1; WhoWMicrocom 83*
Educational Database [of Market Data Retrieval] - Westport, CT - *CompReadDB 82*
Educational Dealer - Belmont, CA - *BaconPubCkMag 84*
Educational Dealer - Palo Alto, CA - *MagDir 84; MagIndMarPl 82-83*
Educational Design Inc. - New York, NY - *AvMarPl 83*
Educational Design Services - Wantagh, NY - *LitMarPl 83, 84*
Educational Development Corp. - Tulsa, OK - *ArtMar 84; AvMarPl 83; WritMar 84*
Educational Digest - Toronto, ON, Canada - *BaconPubCkMag 84*
Educational Dimensions Corp. - Stamford, CT - *ArtMar 84; AvMarPl 83*
Educational Direction Inc. - Westport, CT - *AvMarPl 83*
Educational Directions for Dental Auxiliaries [of American Dental Hygienists' Association] - Chicago, IL - *MagDir 84*
Educational Directories Inc. - Mt. Prospect, IL - *BoPubDir 4, 5*
Educational Directory [of American University Press Services Inc.] - New York, NY - *EISS 83; LitMarPl 83, 84*
Educational Dynamics Corp. - King of Prussia, PA - *AvMarPl 83*
Educational Electronics Corp. - Ingelwood, CA - *AvMarPl 83*
Educational Enrichment Materials [Subs. of The New York Times] - Bedford Hills, NY - *AvMarPl 83*
Educational Facilities Laboratories [Aff. of Academy for Educational Development] - New York, NY - *BoPubDir 4 Sup, 5*
Educational Film Center - Annandale, VA - *WritMar 84*
Educational Film Library Association Inc. - New York, NY - *BoPubDir 4, 5*
Educational Filmstrips - Huntsville, TX - *AvMarPl 83*
Educational Foundation for Nuclear Science Inc. - Chicago, IL - *BoPubDir 4, 5; DirMarMP 83*
Educational Images Ltd. - Lyons Falls, NY - *AvMarPl 83; WritMar 84*
Educational Information Services Inc. - Washington, DC - *MicroMarPl 82-83*
Educational Insights - Compton, CA - *AvMarPl 83; LitMarPl 83, 84; WritMar 84*
Educational Leadership - Alexandria, VA - *MagDir 84*
Educational Lists Co. Inc. - Jericho, NY - *LitMarPl 83, 84*
Educational Marketer - White Plains, NY - *BaconPubCkMag 84; MagIndMarPl 82-83*
Educational Materials & Equipment Co. [Div. of EME Corp.] - Pelham, NY - *AvMarPl 83; MicrocomMPl 84*
Educational Materials Distributors - Detroit, MI - *LitMarPl 83, 84*
Educational Media Associates of America Inc. - Berkeley, CA - *BillIntBG 83-84*
Educational Media Corp. - Minneapolis, MN - *BoPubDir 4, 5; LitMarPl 84*
Educational Media International Inc. [Subs. of Educational Media International] - Haymarket, VA - *AvMarPl 83*
Educational Methods [Div. of Development Systems Corp.] - Chicago, IL - *LitMarPl 83, 84*
Educational Micro Systems Inc. - Chester, NJ - *MicrocomMPl 83, 84*
Educational Press Association of America - Glassboro, NJ - *BoPubDir 4, 5*
Educational Programmers Inc. - Roseburg, OR - *BoPubDir 4, 5*
Educational Programming Systems - St. Louis, MO - *WhoWMicrocom 83*
Educational Programs - West Lafayette, IN - *MicrocomMPl 83*
Educational Progress Corp. - Tulsa, OK - *BoPubDir 4, 5*
Educational Projections Corp. - Jacksonville Beach, FL - *AvMarPl 83; BoPubDir 4 Sup, 5*
Educational Publishers Center - Bronxville, NY - *LitMarPl 83*
Educational Publishing Services - Lakewood, OH - *MagIndMarPl 82-83*
Educational Reading Aids Corp. - Carlstadt, NJ - *BoPubDir 4, 5*
Educational Reading Service Inc. - Mahwah, NJ - *LitMarPl 83, 84*
Educational Reading Service Inc. (Audio Visual Div.) - Mahwah, NJ - *AvMarPl 83*
Educational Record - Washington, DC - *BaconPubCkMag 84; MagIndMarPl 82-83*
Educational Research Corp. - Cambridge, MA - *BoPubDir 4, 5*
Educational Research Forum - DeKalb, IL - *DirOnDB Spring 84*
Educational Research Institute - Laguna Hills, CA - *BoPubDir 4, 5*
Educational Research Institute of British Columbia - Vancouver, BC, Canada - *BoPubDir 4, 5*
Educational Research Library [of U.S. National Institute of Education] - Washington, DC - *EISS 83*
Educational Researcher - Washington, DC - *MagDir 84*
Educational Resources Information Center [of National Institute of Education] - Washington, DC - *CompReadDB 82; EISS 83; InfIndMarPl 83*
Educational Resources Information Center [of U.S. Dept. of Education] - Bethesda, MD - *DBBus 82*
Educational Resources Information Center [of The National Center for Research in Vocational Education] - Columbus, OH - *DataDirOnSer 84*
Educational Resources Information Center - *See* ERIC
Educational Sciences [of Centre de Documentation Sciences Humaines] - Paris, France - *CompReadDB 82*
Educational Service Inc. - Stevensville, MI - *BoPubDir 4, 5; LitMarPl 84*
Educational Services - Washington, DC - *AvMarPl 83; BoPubDir 4, 5*
Educational Services Management Corp. - Research Triangle Park, NC - *WhoWMicrocom 83*
Educational Shipping Co. Inc. - New York, NY - *LitMarPl 83, 84*
Educational Software & Design - Flagstaff, AZ - *MicrocomMPl 83*
Educational Software Inc. - Soquel, CA - *MicrocomMPl 84; WritMar 84*
Educational Solutions Inc. - New York, NY - *BoPubDir 4, 5*
Educational Systems Engineering Corp. - Hialeah, FL - *AvMarPl 83*
Educational Teaching Aids - Chicago, IL - *MicrocomMPl 84*
Educational Technology [of Educational Tech Publications Inc.] - Englewood Cliffs, NJ - *BaconPubCkMag 84; LitMarPl 83, 84; MagDir 84; MagIndMarPl 82-83; MicrocomMPl 84*
Educational Teleconference System [of University of Missouri] - Columbia, MO - *TeleSy&SerDir 7-83*
Educational Telephone Network [of University of North Dakota] - Grand Forks, ND - *TeleSy&SerDir 7-83*
Educational Testing Service - Princeton, NJ - *WhoWMicrocom 83*
Educational Testing Service [of Bibliographic Retrieval Services Inc.] - Latham, NY - *DataDirOnSer 84*
Educational Testing Service (Test Collection Database) - Princeton, NJ - *DirOnDB Spring 84; MicroMarPl 82-83*
Educational Turnkey Systems - Falls Church, VA - *MicrocomMPl 84*
Educational TV Services [of Oklahoma State University] - Stillwater, OK - *TeleSy&SerDir 2-84*
Educator Publications [Aff. of The National Educator] - Fullerton, CA - *BoPubDir 4, 5*
Educators' Advocate - Pierre, SD - *BaconPubCkMag 84; MagDir 84*
Educator's Book Club [of Prentice-Hall Inc.] - Englewood, NJ - *LitMarPl 83, 84*

Educators Progress Service Inc. - Randolph, WI - *DirMarMP 83; LitMarPl 83, 84*
Educators Publishing Service Inc. - Cambridge, MA - *LitMarPl 83, 84*
Educom [of The Interuniversity Communications Council Inc.] - Princeton, NJ - *BoPubDir 4, 5; EISS 83*
Educomics - San Francisco, CA - *BoPubDir 4, 5*
Educomp - Vinita, OK - *MicrocomMPl 84*
Educons/Linguicons - Scarsdale, NY - *LitMarPl 83, 84*
Educulture Inc. - Duburque, IA - *MicrocomMPl 84*
Edunet [Subs. of Educom] - Princeton, NJ - *DataDirOnSer 84; TeleSy&SerDir 7-83*
Edupro - Palo Alto, CA - *EISS 5-84 Sup*
EduSoft - Berkeley, CA - *MicrocomMPl 84*
EduTech - Newton Centre, MA - *MicrocomMPl 84*
Edutek Corp. - Palo Alto, CA - *MicrocomMPl 83; WhoWMicrocom 83*
Edwal Scientific Products [Div. of Falcon Safety Products Inc.] - Blue Island, IL - *AvMarPl 83*
Edward Associates - Morton Grove, IL - *MagIndMarPl 82-83*
Edward Press - Rochester, NY - *BoPubDir 4, 5*
Edwardian Studies Association - Dagenham, England - *LitMag&SmPr 83-84*
Edwards Abstract from Records [of The Recorder Printing & Publishing Co.] - San Francisco, CA - *Ed&PubIntYB 82; NewsDir 84*
Edwards Advertising Inc. - High Point, NC - *StaDirAdAg 2-84*
Edwards Air Force Base Desert Wings - California City, CA - *NewsDir 84*
Edwards & Broughton Co. - Raleigh, NC - *MagIndMarPl 82-83*
Edwards & Co. - Bedford, NH - *StaDirAdAg 2-84*
Edwards Brothers Inc. - Ann Arbor, MI - *LitMarPl 83, 84; MagIndMarPl 82-83*
Edwards Brothers Inc., Carolina - Raleigh, NC - *MagIndMarPl 82-83*
Edwards Cable TV - Louisa, KY - *BrCabYB 84*
Edwards Commo-Net Inc. (Marketing Group Div.) - Brookfield, WI - *DirMarMP 83*
Edwards Corp., E. D. - Freeport, NY - *StaDirAdAg 2-84*
Edwards County Independent Times - West Salem, IL - *Ed&PubIntYB 82*
Edwards, Don - Elgin, IL - *BoPubDir 4 Sup, 5*
Edwards, Elmer Eugene [Aff. of Aquarian Astro-Center] - Miami, FL - *BoPubDir 4, 5*
Edwards, Ernest P. - Sweet Briar, VA - *BoPubDir 4, 5*
Edwards, G. F. - Lawton, OK - *BoPubDir 4, 5*
Edwards Inc., J. W. [Aff. of Edwards Brothers Inc.] - Ann Arbor, MI - *BoPubDir 4, 5*
Edwards, J. M. B. - Berkeley, CA - *LitMarPl 83, 84*
Edwards Productions, Ralph - Hollywood, CA - *TelAl 83, 84*
Edwards Productions, Ralph - Los Angeles, CA - *Tel&CabFB 84C*
Edwards Telephone Co. [Aff. of Telephone & Data Systems Inc.] - Edwards, NY - *TelDir&BG 83-84*
Edwardsburg Argus - Cassopolis, MI - *BaconPubCkNews 84*
Edwardsburg Argus - Edwardsburg, MI - *AyerDirPub 83; Ed&PubIntYB 82*
Edwardsville Cable TV [of Union Gas System Inc.] - Edwardsville, KS - *BrCabYB 84; Tel&CabFB 84C*
Edwardsville Intelligencer [of Hearst Corp.] - Edwardsville, IL - *BaconPubCkNews 84; Ed&PubIntYB 82; NewsDir 84*
Edwardsville Journal - Edwardsville, IL - *Ed&PubIntYB 82; NewsDir 84*
Edwardsville Journal - *See* Journal Newspapers of Southern Illinois
EE-Electrical/Electronic Product News - White Plains, NY - *BaconPubCkMag 84*
EECO Inc. - Santa Ana, CA - *DataDirSup 7-83*
EEG Enterprises Inc. - Farmingdale, NY - *AvMarPl 83*
EEI Capsule [of Evans Economics Inc.] - Washington, DC - *DataDirOnSer 84*
EEI Capsule - *See* Evans Economics Inc. (EEICap Database)
Eel Pie Publishing [Aff. of Kampmann & Co.] - New York, NY - *BoPubDir 4 Sup, 5*
Eerdmans Printing Co. - Grand Rapids, MI - *LitMarPl 83, 84*
Eerdmans Publishing Co., William B. - Grand Rapids, MI - *LitMarPl 83, 84; WritMar 84*
Eerie Country - Buffalo, NY - *ArtMar 84; WritMar 84*
EE's Electronics Distributor [of Sutton Publishing Co. Inc.] - White Plains, NY - *BaconPubCkMag 84; MagDir 84; WritMar 84*
Effective Communication Arts - New York, NY - *AvMarPl 83; WritMar 84*
Effective Learning Inc. - Mt. Vernon, NY - *ArtMar 84; LitMarPl 83, 84; MagIndMarPl 82-83; WritMar 84*
Effective Speech Writer's Newsletter - Richmond, VA - *MagIndMarPl 82-83*
Efficient Management Systems Inc. - Concord, CA - *MicrocomMPl 84*
Efficient Management Systems Inc. - Oakland, CA - *MicrocomMPl 83; WhoWMicrocom 83*
Effingham Daily News - Effingham, IL - *BaconPubCkNews 84; Ed&PubIntYB 82; NewsDir 84*
EFM Films [Div. of Education for Management Inc.] - Watertown, MA - *AvMarPl 83*
EFM Systems Inc. - Westport, CT - *DataDirSup 7-83*
EFP Inc. - Jonesboro, AK - *DirInfWP 82*
Efrydiau Athronyddol [of University of Wales Press] - Cardiff, Wales - *LitMag&SmPr 83-84*
EFT Report - Bethesda, MD - *BaconPubCkMag 84; DirOnDB Spring 84*
EFTS-Industry Report - Annandale, VA - *BaconPubCkMag 84*
Egan Advertising - Wayne, PA - *StaDirAdAg 2-84*
Eganville Leader - Eganville, ON, Canada - *AyerDirPub 83; Ed&PubIntYB 82*
Egap Music Inc. - *See* Lear Music Inc.
EGC Associates Inc. - San Antonio, TX - *IntDirMarRes 83*
Egeberg & Vinding - *See* K & E Holdings Inc.
EGG Dallas Broadcasting Inc. - Ft. Worth, TX - *BrCabYB 84*
Egg Harbor News - Egg Harbor City, NJ - *BaconPubCkNews 84; NewsDir 84*
Eggert & Co., R. W. - Dusseldorf, West Germany - *StaDirAdAg 2-84*
Eggplant Press - Denver, CO - *BoPubDir 4, 5*
Eggplant Press - New York, NY - *LitMag&SmPr 83-84*
Eggs Press - Minneapolis, MN - *BoPubDir 4, 5*
E.G.L. Enterprises Inc. - Los Angeles, CA - *BoPubDir 4, 5*
EGM Enterprises - Berkeley Heights, NJ - *BoPubDir 4, 5*
Ego Books - Lincoln, NE - *BoPubDir 4, 5*
Egyptian Marketing Services Bureau - Cairo, Egypt - *IntDirMarRes 83*
Egyptian Telephone Cooperative Association - Steeleville, IL - *TelDir&BG 83-84*
Ehn Graphics Inc. - New York, NY - *LitMarPl 83, 84*
Ehrhart-Babic Associates Inc. - Englewood Cliffs, NJ - *AdAge 5-17-84 p.34; IntDirMarRes 83*
Ehrig & Associates - Seattle, WA - *AdAge 3-28-84; ArtMar 84; StaDirAdAg 2-84*
Ehrlich & Associates, Paul R. - San Francisco, CA - *DirPRFirms 83*
Ehrlich Co. Inc., Harry - New York, NY - *LitMarPl 83, 84*
Ehrlich-Manes & Associates - Washington, DC - *DirPRFirms 83; StaDirAdAg 2-84*
Ehrlich-Manes & Associates - Bethesda, MD - *AdAge 3-28-84; BrCabYB 84*
EHUD International Language Foundation - Walnut Creek, CA - *BoPubDir 5*
E.I. Advertising Agency Corp. - San Francisco, CA - *StaDirAdAg 2-84*
EI Engineering Meetings [of Engineering Information Inc.] - New York, NY - *DataDirOnSer 84; DirOnDB Spring 84*
EIC-Environment Information Center Inc. - New York, NY - *InfIndMarPl 83*
EIC/Intelligence - New York, NY - *BoPubDir 5; InfoS 83-84*
Eichenberg, Fritz - Peace Dale, RI - *LitMarPl 83, 84*
Eichner Systems Inc. - Itasca, IL - *DirInfWP 82; WhoWMicrocom 83*
Eicoff & Co., A. [Div. of Ogilvy & Mather] - Chicago, IL - *Br 1-23-84; BrCabYB 84; StaDirAdAg 2-84*
Eicoff & Co., A. [Div. of Ogilvy & Mather] - New York, NY - *DirMarMP 83*
Eiconics Inc. - Taos, NM - *MicrocomMPl 84; MicrocomSwDir 1; WhoWMicrocom 83*

Eidel Marketing Communications - Briarcliff Manor, NY - *AdAge 3-28-84; StaDirAdAg 2-84*
Eidolon Press - Westport, CT - *LitMarPl 83, 84*
Eidos Systems Corp. [Subs. of Tascon Corp.] - Nashville, TN - *MicrocomSwDir 1; WhoWMicrocom 83*
Eigen Systems - Austin, TX - *MicrocomMPl 84*
Eigen Video - Nevada City, CA - *AvMarPl 83*
8 Ball News [of Bayside Publishing] - Everett, WA - *WritMar 84*
888 Leader - New York, NY - *NewsDir 84*
800 Software - Berkeley, CA - *MicrocomMPl 84*
Eight Miles High Products - Ossett, England - *LitMag&SmPr 83-84*
1802/Z-80 Programs - Latrobe, PA - *MicrocomMPl 83*
18 Almanac - Knoxville, TN - *WritMar 84*
Eighteenth Century Short Title Catalog [of The Research Libraries Group Inc.] - Stanford, CA - *DataDirOnSer 84*
Eighteenth Century Short Title Catalogue [of The British Library] - London, England - *DirOnDB Spring 84; EISS 7-83 Sup; OnBibDB 3*
Eighth of August Publishing Co., The - Oak Park, IL - *MagIndMarPl 82-83*
88 Latviesu Tautas Dejasun Apdares - Don Mills, ON, Canada - *BoPubDir 4, 5*
80 Micro [of Wayne Green Enterprises] - Peterborough, NH - *BaconPubCkMag 84; Folio 83; MicrocomMPl 84; WritMar 84*
80 Northwest Publishing Inc. - Tacoma, WA - *MicrocomMPl 83*
80-User Digest - Lansing, MI - *MicrocomMPl 84*
Eiki International Inc. [Subs. of Eiki Industrial Co. Ltd.] - Laguna Niguel, CA - *AvMarPl 83*
EIM/Europanel - Geneva, Switzerland - *IntDirMarRes 83*
EIMET [of SDC Search Service] - Santa Monica, CA - *DataDirOnSer 84*
Eimicke Associates Inc., V. W. - Yonkers, NY - *DirMarMP 83*
Einhorn & Lewis Inc. - Daytona Beach, FL - *DirPRFirms 83*
Einson Freeman Inc. - Paramus, NJ - *DirMarMP 83; StaDirAdAg 2-84*
Einstein Music - Jamaica, NY - *BillIntBG 83-84*
Eintracht - Skokie, IL - *Ed&PubIntYB 82; NewsDir 84*
Eire-Ireland - St. Paul, MN - *MagIndMarPl 82-83*
EIS Currency Conversion System [of Boeing Computer Services Co.] - Morristown, NJ - *DataDirOnSer 84*
EIS Database of Economic Activity [of Economic Information Systems Inc.] - New York, NY - *CompReadDB 82*
EIS Digests of Environmental Impact Statements [of Information Resources Press] - Arlington, VA - *CompReadDB 82; DBBus 82; EISS 83*
EIS Economic Data - Vienna, VA - *DirOnDB Spring 84*
EIS Establishment Database [of Economic Information Systems Inc.] - New York, NY - *DataDirOnSer 84*
EIS Industrial Plants [of Economic Information Systems Inc.] - New York, NY - *DBBus 82; DirOnDB Spring 84*
EIS Non-Manufacturing Establishments [of Economic Information Systems Inc.] - New York, NY - *DBBus 82*
EIS Non-Manufacturing Establishments - *See* EIS Industrial Plants
EIS Plant Database [of Economic Information Systems Inc.] - New York, NY - *DataDirOnSer 84*
Eisaman, Johns & Laws Advertising Inc. - Los Angeles, CA - *AdAge 3-28-84; BrCabYB 84; StaDirAdAg 2-84*
Eisen Advertising Agency Inc., Henry - New York, NY - *StaDirAdAg 2-84*
Eisen Co. Inc., Alan G. - Old Bethpage, NY - *ArtMar 84; DirPRFirms 83*
Eisen Kramer Associates - Clayton, MO - *DirPRFirms 83*
Eisenbach-Greene Inc. - Los Angeles, CA - *LitMarPl 83, 84*
Eisenberg Educational Enterprises Inc. [Aff. of Tour Tapes of Baltimore] - Baltimore, MD - *BoPubDir 4, 5*
Eisenbrauns - Warsaw, IN - *BoPubDir 4, 5*
Eisenman & Enock - New York, NY - *StaDirAdAg 2-84*
Eisenman-Todd Inc. - Teaneck, NJ - *LitMarPl 83, 84*
Eisner & Associates - Baltimore, MD - *AdAge 3-28-84; ArtMar 84; StaDirAdAg 2-84; TelAl 83, 84*
Eisner & Associates Inc., William - Hales Corners, WI - *AdAge 3-28-84; StaDirAdAg 2-84*
EJ Records - Chicago, IL - *BillIntBG 83-84*
EJAG News Magazine, The [of EJAG Publications] - Carlisle, MA - *WritMar 84*
Ekalaka Eagle - Ekalaka, MT - *BaconPubCkNews 84; Ed&PubIntYB 82*
EKM Nepenthe - Carlton, OR - *LitMarPl 83, 84*
EKS Publishing Co. - Oakland, CA - *BoPubDir 5*
Eksport-Indeks [of Norges Eksportrad] - Oslo, Norway - *CompReadDB 82*
El Arte Tipografico - Philadelphia, PA - *MagDir 84*
El Cajon Daily California, The [of The Californian Publishing Co.] - El Cajon, CA - *NewsDir 84*
El Cajon East Pennysaver - Mission Viejo, CA - *AyerDirPub 83*
El Cajon/Lakeside/Santee Life-News [of Chula Vista Star-News] - Chula Vista, CA - *NewsDir 84*
El Cajon North Pennysaver - Mission Viejo, CA - *AyerDirPub 83*
El Cajon South Pennysaver - Mission Viejo, CA - *AyerDirPub 83*
El Camino Publishers - Santa Barbara, CA - *LitMag&SmPr 83-84*
El Camino Real [of Solana Beach San Dieguito Citizen] - Solana Beach, CA - *NewsDir 84*
El Campo Citizen - El Campo, TX - *Ed&PubIntYB 82*
El Campo Leader News [of El Campo Newspapers Inc.] - El Campo, TX - *AyerDirPub 83; BaconPubCkNews 84; Ed&PubIntYB 82; NewsDir 84*
El Centro Imperial Valley Press [of Associated Desert Newspapers Inc.] - El Centro, CA - *NewsDir 84*
El Centro Imperial Valley Weekly - El Centro, CA - *BaconPubCkNews 84*
El Cerrito Video Systems Inc. [of Televents Inc.] - El Cerrito, CA - *BrCabYB 84*
El Chicano - Colton, CA - *AyerDirPub 83*
El Chicano Music - Chatsworth, CA - *BillIntBG 83-84*
El Continental - El Paso, TX - *AyerDirPub 83; Ed&PubIntYB 82; NewsDir 84*
El Diario-La Prensa - New York, NY - *AyerDirPub 83; Ed&PubIntYB 82*
El Dorado Butler County News - El Dorado, KS - *NewsDir 84*
El Dorado Cablevision [of American TV & Communications Corp.] - El Dorado, AR - *BrCabYB 84; Tel&CabFB 84C*
El Dorado Gazette - Georgetown, CA - *AyerDirPub 83*
El Dorado News-Times [of News-Times Publishing Co.] - El Dorado, AR - *BaconPubCkNews 84; Ed&PubIntYB 82; NewsDir 84*
El Dorado Service League - El Dorado, AR - *BoPubDir 4, 5*
El Dorado Springs Sun - El Dorado Springs, MO - *AyerDirPub 83; Ed&PubIntYB 82*
El Dorado Times - El Dorado, KS - *BaconPubCkNews 84; Ed&PubIntYB 82; NewsDir 84*
El Embotellador [of Keller International Publishing Corp.] - Great Neck, NY - *MagDir 84*
El Exportador - New York, NY - *BaconPubCkMag 84*
El-Hajj Malik Shabazz Press - Washington, DC - *BoPubDir 4, 5*
El Herald - Miami, FL - *DirOnDB Spring 84*
El Hispano - Sacramento, CA - *Ed&PubIntYB 82; NewsDir 84*
El Hispano - Albuquerque, NM - *Ed&PubIntYB 82; NewsDir 84*
EL Hospital - Los Angeles, CA - *ArtMar 84; BaconPubCkMag 84*
EL Hospital - Miami, FL - *MagDir 84*
El Informador - Chicago, IL - *Ed&PubIntYB 82; NewsDir 84*
El Manana - Chicago, IL - *AyerDirPub 83; Ed&PubIntYB 82; NewsDir 84*
El-Mar Communications - Bolivar, NY - *BrCabYB 84; Tel&CabFB 84C*
El Monte Highlander - *See* Sun Independent Newspapers
El Monte Mid Valley News - El Monte, CA - *NewsDir 84*
El Moro Publications - Morro Bay, CA - *BoPubDir 4, 5*
El Mundo [of Oakland Alameda Publishing Corp.] - Oakland, CA - *Ed&PubIntYB 82; NewsDir 84*
El Mundo - San Juan, PR - *AyerDirPub 83*
El Nuevo Dia - San Juan, PR - *AyerDirPub 83*
El Palacio [of Museum of New Mexico Press] - Santa Fe, NM - *ArtMar 84; LitMag&SmPr 83-84; MagDir 84; MagIndMarPl 82-83; WritMar 84*
El Paso County Telephone Co. - Colorado Springs, CO - *TelDir&BG 83-84*
El Paso Field Research Service - El Paso, TX - *IntDirMarRes 83*
El Paso Herald-Post - El Paso, TX - *BaconPubCkNews 84; Ed&PubIntYB 82; LitMarPl 84; NewsDir 84*
El Paso Magazine - El Paso, TX - *BaconPubCkMag 84*

El Paso Public Library Association - El Paso, TX - *BoPubDir 4, 5*
El Paso Record - *See* Cornbelt Press Inc.
El Paso Telephone Co. Inc. - El Paso, IL - *TelDir&BG 83-84*
El Paso Times [of Gannett Co. Inc.] - El Paso, TX - *BaconPubCkNews 84; Ed&PubIntYB 82; LitMarPl 83, 84; NewsBur 6; NewsDir 84*
El Paso Today Magazine [of El Paso Chamber of Commerce] - El Paso, TX - *WritMar 84*
El Popular - Toronto, ON, Canada - *Ed&PubIntYB 82*
El Portal Community TV System - El Portal, CA - *BrCabYB 84; Tel&CabFB 84C*
El Renacimiento Inc. - Lansing, MI - *BoPubDir 4, 5*
El Reno American - El Reno, OK - *BaconPubCkNews 84; Ed&PubIntYB 82*
El Reno Cablevision [of Multimedia Cablevision Inc.] - El Reno, OK - *BrCabYB 84; Tel&CabFB 84C*
El Reno Tribune - El Reno, OK - *BaconPubCkNews 84; Ed&PubIntYB 82; NewsDir 84*
El Reportero - San Juan, PR - *AyerDirPub 83*
El Segundo Beacon - *See* Breeze Newspapers
El Segundo Herald - El Segundo, CA - *Ed&PubIntYB 82*
El Segundo Herald [of Hermosa Beach Cities Newspapers] - Hermosa Beach, CA - *NewsDir 84*
El Segundo Herald - *See* Argonaut Newspapers
El Sereno Star [of Northeast Los Angeles Publishing Co.] - Los Angeles, CA - *AyerDirPub 83; Ed&PubIntYB 82; NewsDir 84*
El Sereno Star - *See* Northeast Los Angeles Publishing Co.
El Sol de Texas - Dallas, TX - *AyerDirPub 83; Ed&PubIntYB 82*
El Sol de Texas - Farmers Branch, TX - *NewsDir 84*
El Sugundo-Hawthorne Beacon [of Torrance Press-Herald] - Torrance, CA - *NewsDir 84*
El Teatro Campesino Inc. [Aff. of El Centro Campesino Cultural Inc.] - San Juan Bautista, CA - *BoPubDir 4, 5*
El Toro/Lake Forest Hills Pennysaver - Mission Viejo, CA - *AyerDirPub 83*
El Vocero de Puerto Rico - San Juan, PR - *AyerDirPub 83*
Elan Image - Montreal, PQ, Canada - *BaconPubCkMag 84*
Elancee - Chicago, IL - *BaconPubCkMag 84*
Elar Publishing Co. Inc. - Plainview, NY - *BoPubDir 4, 5*
Elasac Music - *See* Casale Music Inc., Don
Elastomerics - Atlanta, GA - *BaconPubCkMag 84; MagDir 84; MagIndMarPl 82-83*
Elba Clipper, The - Elba, AL - *Ed&PubIntYB 82*
Elberfeld Telephone Co. Inc. [Aff. of Century Telephone Enterprises Inc.] - Elberfeld, IN - *TelDir&BG 83-84*
Elbert Advertising Agency Inc. - Norwood, MA - *AdAge 3-28-84; StaDirAdAg 2-84*
Elbert County Country Squire, The - Elizabeth, CO - *Ed&PubIntYB 82*
Elbert County News - Castle Rock, CO - *AyerDirPub 83*
Elbert County News - Kiowa, CO - *Ed&PubIntYB 82*
Elberton Star [of North American Publications] - Elberton, GA - *BaconPubCkNews 84; Ed&PubIntYB 82; NewsDir 84*
Elberton Star Beacon, The - Elberton, GA - *AyerDirPub 83*
Elbit Computers Ltd. (Advanced Technology Center) - Haifa, Israel - *InfIndMarPl 83*
Elbit USA Inc. - New York, NY - *DataDirSup 7-83*
Elbow Lake Cable TV - Elbow Lake, MN - *BrCabYB 84; Tel&CabFB 84C*
Elbow Lake Grant County Herald - Elbow Lake, MN - *BaconPubCkNews 84*
Elburn Herald - Elburn, IL - *BaconPubCkNews 84; Ed&PubIntYB 82*
Elburn MDS Co. - Pasadena, MD - *Tel&CabFB 84C*
Elco Systems - Santa Ana, CA - *MicrocomMPl 84; WhoWMicrocom 83*
Elcock Communications - Hurley, SD - *Tel&CabFB 84C*
Elcock Communications - Viborg, SD - *Tel&CabFB 84C*
Elcock, Daryl - Hurley, SD - *Tel&CabFB 84C p.1678*
ELCOM Data Base [of Cambridge Scientific Abstracts] - Bethesda, MD - *EISS 83; OnBibDB 3*
Elcom Data Base [of Cambridge Scientific Abstracts] - Riverdale, MD - *DBBus 82*
Elcom Industries Inc. - St. Louis, MO - *DataDirSup 7-83*
Elcomp-Hofacker - Pomona, CA - *MicrocomSwDir 1*
Elden Enterprises Inc. - Charleston, WV - *AvMarPl 83*
Elder Agency, Joseph - New York, NY - *LitMarPl 83, 84*
Elder Enterprises Inc., Hazel - La Mesa, CA - *IntDirMarRes 83*
Elder, Jim - Jackson Hole, WY - *MagIndMarPl 82-83*
Elder's Book Store - Nashville, TN - *BoPubDir 4, 5*
Eldon Advertiser - Eldon, MO - *BaconPubCkNews 84; Ed&PubIntYB 82*
Eldon Forum - Eldon, IA - *Ed&PubIntYB 82*
Eldora Hardin County Index - Eldora, IA - *BaconPubCkNews 84*
Eldora Herald-Leader - Eldora, IA - *NewsDir 84*
Eldora Herald-Ledger - Eldora, IA - *BaconPubCkNews 84; Ed&PubIntYB 82*
Eldorado Courier - Eldorado, OK - *BaconPubCkNews 84; Ed&PubIntYB 82*
Eldorado Journal [of Carmi Publishing Co.] - Eldorado, IL - *BaconPubCkNews 84; Ed&PubIntYB 82; NewsDir 84*
Eldorado Schleicher County Leader - Eldorado, TX - *BaconPubCkNews 84*
Eldorado Springs Sun - Eldorado Springs, MO - *BaconPubCkNews 84*
Eldridge North Scott Press - Eldridge, IA - *BaconPubCkNews 84; NewsDir 84*
Eldridge Publishing Co. - Franklin, OH - *BoPubDir 4, 5; WritMar 84*
Eldritch Tales [of Yith Press] - Lawrence, KS - *LitMag&SmPr 83-84*
Elecnuc Databank [of Atomic Energy Commission] - Paris, France - *DirOnDB Spring 84; EISS 83*
Electra [of Taft Broadcasting Co.] - Cincinnati, OH - *EISS 7-83 Sup*
Electra Star News - Electra, TX - *BaconPubCkNews 84; Ed&PubIntYB 82*
Electra Telephone Co. - Electra, TX - *TelDir&BG 83-84*
Electranews [of Local Union 1969-IBEW] - Redwood City, CA - *NewsDir 84*
Electri-Onics [of Lake Publishing Corp.] - Libertyville, IL - *BaconPubCkMag 84; MagDir 84*
Electric Abacus, The - Regina, SK, Canada - *MicrocomSwDir 1; WhoWMicrocom 83*
Electric Comfort Conditioning News [of Electrical Information Publications Inc.] - Madison, WI - *BaconPubCkMag 84; MagDir 84*
Electric Co. - New York, NY - *ArtMar 84; MagIndMarPl 82-83*
Electric Consumer - Indianapolis, IN - *BaconPubCkMag 84; MagDir 84*
Electric Light & Power - Barrington, IL - *BaconPubCkMag 84; MagDir 84; MagIndMarPl 82-83; WritMar 84*
Electric Planet Music Publishing - New York, NY - *BillIntBG 83-84*
Electric Planet Productions Inc. - New York, NY - *BillIntBG 83-84*
Electric Power Database [of Electric Power Research Institute] - Palo Alto, CA - *DataDirOnSer 84; DirOnDB Spring 84; EISS 83*
Electric Power Industry Abstracts [of Utility Data Institute] - Washington, DC - *CompReadDB 82; DataDirOnSer 84; DBBus 82; DirOnDB Spring 84; OnBibDB 3*
Electric Power Research Institute - Palo Alto, CA - *DataDirOnSer 84*
Electric Power Research Institute (Research & Development Information System) - Palo Alto, CA - *CompReadDB 82*
Electric Rain Productions Inc. - Cincinnati, OH - *AvMarPl 83*
Electric Utilities - Oak Ridge, TN - *DirOnDB Spring 84*
Electric Utilities [of I. P. Sharp Associates Ltd.] - Toronto, ON, Canada - *DataDirOnSer 84*
Electric Utility Fleet Management - Durham, NH - *BaconPubCkMag 84*
Electric Utility Instrumentation - Durham, NH - *BaconPubCkMag 84*
Electric Utility Week - New York, NY - *MagDir 84*
Electric Vehicle Council [Aff. of Edison Electric Institute] - Washington, DC - *BoPubDir 4 Sup, 5*
Electric Vehicle Council Newsletter - Washington, DC - *BaconPubCkMag 84*
Electric Vehicle Progress [of Alexander Research & Communications Inc.] - New York, NY - *DataDirOnSer 84; DirOnDB Spring 84*

Electric Video Inc. - *See* American Video Tape/Electric Video Inc.
Electric Wastebasket Corp. - New York, NY - *DirInfWP 82*
Electric Weenie, The - Honolulu, HI - *WritMar 84*
Electrical & Electronic Engineering Book Club [of Macmillan Book Clubs Inc.] - New York, NY - *LitMarPl 83, 84*
Electrical & Electronics Abstracts [of INSPEC, Institution of Electrical Engineers] - Hitchin, England - *OnBibDB 3*
Electrical Apparatus [of Barks Publications Inc.] - Chicago, IL - *ArtMar 84; BaconPubCkMag 84; MagDir 84*
Electrical Business - Evanston, IL - *MagIndMarPl 82-83*
Electrical Business [of Rickard Publishing Co.] - Glenview, IL - *MagDir 84*
Electrical Business - Toronto, ON, Canada - *WritMar 84*
Electrical Construction & Maintenance [of McGraw-Hill Publishing Co.] - New York, NY - *BaconPubCkMag 84; MagDir 84; MagIndMarPl 82-83*
Electrical Consultant [of Cleworth Publishing Co. Inc.] - Cos Cob, CT - *BaconPubCkMag 84; MagDir 84; MagIndMarPl 82-83*
Electrical Contractor [of National Electrical Contractors Association Inc.] - Washington, DC - *MagDir 84*
Electrical Contractor - Bethesda, MD - *BaconPubCkMag 84; MagIndMarPl 82-83; WritMar 84*
Electrical Distributor [of National Association of Electrical Distributors] - Stamford, CT - *BaconPubCkMag 84; MagDir 84*
Electrical Energy Management [of Cleworth Publishing Co. Inc.] - Cos Cob, CT - *MagDir 84*
Electrical Engineering Documentation Center [of Technical Information Center] - Frankfurt, West Germany - *EISS 83*
Electrical Equipment [of Sutton Publishing Co. Inc.] - White Plains, NY - *MagDir 84*
Electrical Equipment News - Don Mills, ON, Canada - *BaconPubCkMag 84*
Electrical Marketing - New York, NY - *BaconPubCkMag 84*
Electrical Research Associate - Leatherhead, England - *InfIndMarPl 83*
Electrical South [of Rickard Publishing Co.] - Glenview, IL - *MagDir 84*
Electrical Union World - Fresh Meadows, NY - *NewsDir 84*
Electrical Utility Information - Washington, DC - *DirOnDB Spring 84*
Electrical Utility Week - New York, NY - *BaconPubCkMag 84*
Electrical Wholesaling [of McGraw-Hill Inc.] - New York, NY - *BaconPubCkMag 84; MagDir 84; MagIndMarPl 82-83*
Electrical World [of McGraw-Hill Inc.] - New York, NY - *ArtMar 84; BaconPubCkMag 84; MagDir 84; MagIndMarPl 82-83; NewsBur 6*
Electricite de France [of Direction des Etudes & Recherches] - Clamart, France - *CompReadDB 82; InfIndMarPl 83*
Electricity Canada - Toronto, ON, Canada - *BaconPubCkMag 84; WritMar 84*
Electricity, The Drummer & Univercity [of National News Bureau] - Philadelphia, PA - *WritMar 84*
Electriduct Inc. - Casper, WY - *AvMarPl 83*
Electro Ad Agency Inc. [Div. of Avnet Inc.] - Culver City, CA - *StaDirAdAg 2-84*
Electro Buyers' Guide - Sunnyvale, CA - *BoPubDir 4, 5*
Electro-Chemical Products Corp. - Montclair, NJ - *AvMarPl 83*
Electro-Data Inc. [Subs. of Lizzadro Enterprises] - Hammond, IN - *DataDirOnSer 84*
Electro/General Corp. - Minnetonka, MN - *DataDirSup 7-83*
Electro Nova Productions - New York, NY - *AvMarPl 83*
Electro-Optical Systems Design - Chicago, IL - *MagIndMarPl 82-83*
Electro-Optics [of Cahners Publishing Co.] - Des Plaines, IL - *BaconPubCkMag 84; MagDir 84; WritMar 84*
Electro Rent Corp. - Burbank, CA - *WhoWMicrocom 83*
Electro-Services - North Mankato, MN - *WhoWMicrocom 83*
Electro Standards Laboratory Inc. - Cranston, RI - *DataDirSup 7-83*
Electro-Vision Inc. - La Tuque, PQ, Canada - *BrCabYB 84*
Electro-Voice Inc. [Div. of Gulton Industries] - Buchanan, MI - *AvMarPl 83*
Electrochemical Society Inc. - Pennington, NJ - *BoPubDir 4, 5*
Electrocon International Inc. - Ann Arbor, MI - *MicrocomMPl 84*
Electrodata Inc. - Bedford Heights, OH - *DataDirSup 7-83*
Electrohome Electronics Ltd. - Kitchener, ON, Canada - *AvMarPl 83; DataDirSup 7-83; VideoDir 82-83*
Electromechanical Bench Reference [of Barks Publications Inc.] - Chicago, IL - *ArtMar 84*
Electron, The - Willoughby, OH - *BaconPubCkMag 84*
Electronet Information Systems [Subs. of Policy Studies Corp.] - Springfield, VA - *DataDirOnSer 84; DirOnDB Spring 84; TeleSy&SerDir 2-84*
Electronet/1 [of Policy Studies Corp.] - Springfield, VA - *EISS 7-83 Sup*
ElectroNews - Leesburg, VA - *DataDirOnSer 84; DirOnDB Spring 84; EISS 5-84 Sup*
Electronic Banking - Atlanta, GA - *EISS 7-83 Sup; VideoDir 82-83*
Electronic Banking - Knoxville, TN - *DirOnDB Spring 84*
Electronic Banking [of Bank of Thessalia] - Athens, Greece - *VideoDir 82-83*
Electronic Business [of Cahners Publishing Co.] - Boston, MA - *BaconPubCkMag 84; MagDir 84*
Electronic Buyers Gazette [of Elexpro Enterprises Inc.] - Aurora, IL - *MagDir 84*
Electronic Buyers' Handbook & Directory [of CMP Publications] - Manhasset, NY - *MagDir 84*
Electronic Buyers' News [of CMP Publications] - Manhasset, NY - *BaconPubCkMag 84; Folio 83; MagDir 84; WritMar 84*
Electronic Component News - Radnor, PA - *BaconPubCkMag 84; MagIndMarPl 82-83*
Electronic Components Databank [of European Space Agency] - Rome, Italy - *CompReadDB 82*
Electronic Components Price Forecast - San Mateo, CA - *DirOnDB Spring 84*
Electronic Computer Originated Mail [of U.S. Postal Service] - Washington, DC - *TeleSy&SerDir 7-83*
Electronic Courseware Systems Inc. - Champaign, IL - *BoPubDir 5; MicrocomMPl 84; MicrocomSwDir 1*
Electronic Data Processing Corp. - Riverton, NJ - *DataDirOnSer 84; MagIndMarPl 82-83*
Electronic Data Systems - Rockville, MD - *DataDirSup 7-83*
Electronic Data Systems - Dallas, TX - *ADAPSOMemDir 83-84; DataDirOnSer 84; DataDirSup 7-83; Datamation 6-83; Top100Al 83*
Electronic Design [of Hayden Publishing Co. Inc.] - Rochelle Park, NJ - *BaconPubCkMag 84; Folio 83; MagDir 84; MagIndMarPl 82-83*
Electronic Designers - Hauppauge, NY - *AvMarPl 83*
Electronic Distributing [of Electronic Periodicals Inc.] - Cleveland, OH - *MagDir 84*
Electronic Editions [of the Spokesman-Review & Spokane Chronicle] - Spokane, WA - *DirOnDB Spring 84*
Electronic Education - Tallahassee, FL - *BaconPubCkMag 84*
Electronic Engineering Times [of CMP Publications] - Manhasset, NY - *BaconPubCkMag 84; Folio 83; MagDir 84; MagIndMarPl 82-83*
Electronic Field Productions - Arlington Heights, IL - *AvMarPl 83*
Electronic Fun with Computers & Games - New York, NY - *BaconPubCkMag 84*
Electronic Funds Transfer Association - Washington, DC - *InterCabHB 3; TeleSy&SerDir 7-83*
Electronic Games - New York, NY - *BaconPubCkMag 84*
Electronic Gourmet [of Home Management Systems Inc.] - Winnipeg, MB, Canada - *DataDirOnSer 84*
Electronic Imaging - Boston, MA - *BaconPubCkMag 84*
Electronic Industries Association - Washington, DC - *InterCabHB 3*
Electronic Industry Week - New York, NY - *MagIndMarPl 82-83*
Electronic Information Exchange System [of New Jersey Institute of Technology] - Newark, NJ - *EISS 83*
Electronic Information Systems Inc. - Athens, GA - *MicrocomMPl 83, 84*
Electronic Keyboarding Inc. - Maryland Heights, MO - *EISS 83; LitMarPl 83, 84; MagIndMarPl 82-83*
Electronic Keyboarding Inc. - St. Louis, MO - *LitMarPl 84*
Electronic Learning [of Scholastic Inc.] - New York, NY - *BaconPubCkMag 84; MicrocomMPl 84*
Electronic Legislative Search System [of Commerce Clearing House Inc.] - Chicago, IL - *DataDirOnSer 84*

Electronic Mail & Message Systems [of International Resource Development Inc.] - Norwalk, CT - *MagIndMarPl 82-83; MicrocomMPl 84*
Electronic Materials Information Service [of Institution of Electrical Engineers] - Hitchin, England - *CompReadDB 82; DataDirOnSer 84; DBBus 82; EISS 83*
Electronic Media Associates - New York, NY - *LitMarPl 84*
Electronic Media Committee - Washington, DC - *EISS 83*
Electronic Media Rating Council Inc. - New York, NY - *Tel&CabFB 84C*
Electronic News [of Fairchild Publications] - New York, NY - *BaconPubCkMag 84; Folio 83; MagDir 84; MagIndMarPl 82-83*
Electronic Packaging & Production - Chicago, IL - *MagIndMarPl 82-83*
Electronic Packaging & Production [of Cahners Publishing Co.] - Des Plaines, IL - *BaconPubCkMag 84; MagDir 84; WritMar 84*
Electronic Post [of British Post Office] - London, England - *TeleSy&SerDir 2-84*
Electronic Processors Ltd. [Subs. of Iron & Steel Credit Union] - Birmingham, AL - *ADAPSOMemDir 83-84; DataDirOnSer 84*
Electronic Products [of Hearst Business Communications] - Garden City, NY - *BaconPubCkMag 84; Folio 83; MagDir 84; MagIndMarPl 82-83*
Electronic Program Guide [of United Video Inc.] - Tulsa, OK - *BrCabYB 84; CabTVPrDB 83*
Electronic Properties Information Center [of Thermophysical & Electronic Properties Information Analysis Center] - West Lafayette, IN - *CompReadDB 82*
Electronic Protection Devices - Waltham, MA - *MicrocomMPl 84*
Electronic Publishers Trade Association - Paris, France - *EISS 7-83 Sup*
Electronic Publishing Abstracts [of Pergamon International Information Corp.] - McLean, VA - *DataDirOnSer 84*
Electronic Publishing & Bookselling [of The Oryx Press] - Phoenix, AZ - *MicrocomMPl 84*
Electronic Publishing Div. [of John Wiley & Sons Inc.] - New York, NY - *EISS 83, 7-83 Sup*
Electronic Publishing Service [of The Washington Post] - Washington, DC - *EISS 7-83 Sup*
Electronic Publishing Systems Inc. - Silver Spring, MD - *VideoDir 82-83*
Electronic Rig Stats [of PennWell Publishing Co.] - Tulsa, OK - *DataDirOnSer 84; DirOnDB Spring 84*
Electronic Rig Stats [of Pennwell Publishing Co.] - Houston, TX - *EISS 7-83 Sup*
Electronic Services - Chesterland, OH - *WhoWMicrocom 83*
Electronic Servicing & Technology [of Intertec Publishing Corp.] - Overland Park, KS - *BaconPubCkMag 84; MagIndMarPl 82-83; WritMar 84*
Electronic Servicing & Technology - Shawnee Mission, KS - *MagDir 84*
Electronic Solutions Inc. - Watertown, CT - *MicrocomMPl 84*
Electronic Specialists Inc. - Natick, MA - *MicrocomMPl 83, 84; WhoWMicrocom 83*
Electronic Systems Business News - Los Angeles, CA - *BaconPubCkMag 84*
Electronic Systems Furniture Co. - Carson, CA - *WhoWMicrocom 83*
Electronic Systems Products - Titusville, FL - *AvMarPl 83*
Electronic Tabulating Corp. - Newburgh, NY - *DataDirOnSer 84*
Electronic Technician/Dealer - Duluth, MN - *MagDir 84; MagIndMarPl 82-83*
Electronic Telephone Directory [of French PTT] - Paris, France - *VideoDir 82-83*
Electronic Warfare Digest - Annandale, VA - *BaconPubCkMag 84*
Electronic Washington Post Newsletter [of The Washington Post] - Washington, DC - *DataDirOnSer 84; DirOnDB Spring 84*
Electronic Yellow Pages [of Market Data Retrieval Inc.] - Westport, CT - *DataDirOnSer 84*
Electronic Yellow Pages-Construction Directory - Westport, CT - *DirOnDB Spring 84*
Electronic Yellow Pages-Financial Services Directory - Palo Alto, CA - *DirOnDB Spring 84*
Electronic Yellow Pages-Index [of Dialog Information Services Inc.] - Palo Alto, CA - *DataDirOnSer 84; DirOnDB Spring 84*
Electronic Yellow Pages-Manufacturers Directory - Westport, CT - *DirOnDB Spring 84*
Electronic Yellow Pages-Professionals Directory - Westport, CT - *DirOnDB Spring 84*
Electronic Yellow Pages-Retailers Directory - Westport, CT - *DirOnDB Spring 84*
Electronic Yellow Pages-Services Directory - Westport, CT - *DirOnDB Spring 84*
Electronic Yellow Pages-Wholesalers Directory - Westport, CT - *DirOnDB Spring 84*
Electronics [of McGraw-Hill Publications Co.] - New York, NY - *ArtMar 84; BaconPubCkMag 84; Folio 83; MagDir 84; MagIndMarPl 82-83; NewsBur 6*
Electronics & Communications - Don Mills, ON, Canada - *BaconPubCkMag 84; WritMar 84*
Electronics & Computers [of Cambridge Scientific Abstracts] - Bethesda, MD - *CompReadDB 82; DataDirOnSer 84*
Electronics & Control Engineers' Book Club [of McGraw-Hill Book Co.] - New York, NY - *LitMarPl 83, 84*
Electronics Book Club [of TAB Books Inc.] - Blue Ridge Summit, PA - *LitMarPl 83, 84*
Electronics Book Service [of Prentice-Hall Inc.] - Englewood, NJ - *LitMarPl 83, 84*
Electronics for Kids - New York, NY - *BaconPubCkMag 84*
Electronics Hobbyist - New York, NY - *MagDir 84*
Electronics Insight - Cambridge, MA - *BaconPubCkMag 84*
Electronics of America - Daytona Beach, FL - *MagDir 84*
Electronics of America - Holly Hill, FL - *BaconPubCkMag 84*
Electronics Product News - Toronto, ON, Canada - *BaconPubCkMag 84*
Electronics Products & Technology - Mississauga, ON, Canada - *BaconPubCkMag 84*
Electronics Retailing - New York, NY - *BaconPubCkMag 84; MagIndMarPl 82-83*
Electronics Test [of Morgan-Grampian Publishing Co.] - Boston, MA - *BaconPubCkMag 84; MagDir 84; MagIndMarPl 82-83*
Electronics Today International - Toronto, ON, Canada - *BaconPubCkMag 84; WritMar 84*
Electronics West - Phoenix, AZ - *BaconPubCkMag 84; WritMar 84*
Electrophysics Corp. - Nutley, NJ - *AvMarPl 83*
Electrosonic Systems Inc. - Minneapolis, MN - *AvMarPl 83*
Electrosound Systems Inc. - Holbrook, NY - *DirInfWP 82*
Electrovision Productions - Belvedere, CA - *AvMarPl 83*
Electrum [of Medina Press] - Santa Ana, CA - *LitMag&SmPr 83-84*
Elek Associates/Catalyst, Peter - New York, NY - *LitMarPl 84*
Elek International Rights Agent - New York, NY - *LitMarPl 83, 84*
Elek-Tek Inc. - Chicago, IL - *MicrocomMPl 83*
Elektor - Downey, CA - *MagDir 84*
Elektra/Asylum Music Inc. - Nashville, TN - *BillIntBG 83-84*
Elektra/Asylum/Nonesuch Records - New York, NY - *BillIntBG 83-84*
Elektrokonsult AS - Drammen, Norway - *MicrocomSwDir 1*
Elementary School Journal [of University of Chicago Press] - Chicago, IL - *MagDir 84; MagIndMarPl 82-83*
Elephant Records - Waterbury, VT - *BillIntBG 83-84*
Eleutherian Mills/Hagley Foundation - Wilmington, DE - *BoPubDir 4, 5*
Elevation Enterprises Inc. - Boston, MA - *BillIntBG 83-84*
Elevation Publishing - Boston, MA - *BillIntBG 83-84*
Elevator Constructor, The - Columbia, MD - *NewsDir 84*
Elevator World - Mobile, AL - *BaconPubCkMag 84; MagDir 84*
1199 News [of NUHHC AFL-CIO] - New York, NY - *NewsDir 84*
Elgar Corp. - San Diego, CA - *DirInfWP 82*
Elgee Co. - Spokane, WA - *AdAge 3-28-84; StaDirAdAg 2-84*
Elgen Publishing Co. - Colorado Springs, CO - *BoPubDir 4, 5*
Elgin Courier - Elgin, TX - *Ed&PubIntYB 82*
Elgin Courier - *See* Taylor Newspapers Inc.
Elgin Daily Courier News - Elgin, IL - *BaconPubCkNews 84*
Elgin Echo - Elgin, IA - *BaconPubCkNews 84; Ed&PubIntYB 82*
Elgin Grant County News - *See* Grant County News Publishers
Elgin Herald [of Free Press Inc.] - Carpentersville, IL - *AyerDirPub 83; NewsDir 84*
Elgin Herald - Elgin, IL - *Ed&PubIntYB 82; NewsDir 84*

Elgin Herald - *See* Free Press Inc.
Elgin Review - Elgin, NE - *BaconPubCkNews 84; Ed&PubIntYB 82*
Elgin Syferd - Seattle, WA - *StaDirAdAg 2-84*
Elgin TV Association - Elgin, OR - *BrCabYB 84; Tel&CabFB 84C*
ELIAS - Ottawa, ON, Canada - *DirOnDB Spring 84*
Eliasberg, Jay - New York, NY - *BrCabYB 84*
Elich & Associates, George - Sacramento, CA - *LitMarPl 83, 84; MagIndMarPl 82-83*
Eliezer Associates Inc., J. S. - New York, NY - *MagIndMarPl 82-83*
Elijah Blue Music - Atlanta, GA - *BillIntBG 83-84*
Elins Public Relations, Roberta - New York, NY - *DirPRFirms 83*
Elite - Scottsdale, AZ - *BaconPubCkMag 84*
Elite Communication Systems - Los Angeles, CA - *DataDirOnSer 84*
Elite Entertainment Enterprises - Chicago, IL - *BillIntBG 83-84*
Elite Office Services - Nutley, NJ - *LitMarPl 83, 84*
Elite Software - Pittsburgh, PA - *MicrocomMPl 84*
Elite Software Co. - Heston, England - *MicrocomSwDir 1*
Elite Software Development Inc. - College Station, TX - *MicrocomMPl 84; MicrocomSwDir 1*
Elizabeth City Daily Advance - Elizabeth City, NC - *BaconPubCkNews 84; NewsDir 84*
Elizabeth City Video Inc. [of UltraCom Inc.] - Elizabeth City, NC - *BrCabYB 84; Tel&CabFB 84C*
Elizabeth Islands Telephone Co. - Naushon Island, MA - *TelDir&BG 83-84*
Elizabeth Journal [of Hagadone Newspapers Inc.] - Elizabeth, NJ - *NewsDir 84*
Elizabeth News - Elizabeth, IL - *BaconPubCkNews 84; Ed&PubIntYB 82*
Elizabeth Press [Aff. of Liz Pub Ltd.] - New Rochelle, NY - *BoPubDir 4, 5*
Elizabeth Telephone Co. - Elizabeth, LA - *TelDir&BG 83-84*
Elizabeth Wirt County Journal - Elizabeth, WV - *BaconPubCkNews 84*
Elizabethton Star - Elizabethton, TN - *BaconPubCkNews 84; Ed&PubIntYB 82; NewsDir 84*
Elizabethtown Bladen Journal - Elizabethtown, NC - *BaconPubCkNews 84*
Elizabethtown Chronicle - Elizabethtown, PA - *AyerDirPub 83; BaconPubCkNews 84; Ed&PubIntYB 82; NewsDir 84*
Elizabethtown Ft. Knox Inside the Turret - Elizabethtown, KY - *BaconPubCkNews 84; NewsDir 84*
Elizabethtown Hardin County Independent - Elizabethtown, IL - *BaconPubCkNews 84; NewsDir 84*
Elizabethtown News-Enterprise [of Landmark Communications Inc.] - Elizabethtown, KY - *BaconPubCkNews 84; NewsDir 84*
Elizabethtown Valley News [of Elizabethtown Denton Publications Inc.] - Elizabethtown, NY - *Ed&PubIntYB 82; NewsDir 84*
Elizabethtown Valley News - *See* Denton Publications Inc.
ELJ - St. Louis, MO - *BillIntBG 83-84*
Elk City News - Elk City, OK - *BaconPubCkNews 84; Ed&PubIntYB 82; NewsDir 84*
Elk Grove Chronicle - Hanover Park, IL - *Ed&PubIntYB 82*
Elk Grove Citizen [of Herburger Publications] - Elk Grove, CA - *BaconPubCkNews 84; Ed&PubIntYB 82; NewsDir 84*
Elk Grove Herald - *See* Paddock Publications
Elk Grove Village Daily Herald [of Paddock Publications] - Arlington Heights, IL - *NewsDir 84*
Elk Grove Village Suburban Voice - *See* Voice Newspapers
Elk Horn Kimballton Review - Elk Horn, IA - *AyerDirPub 83; BaconPubCkNews 84*
Elk Island Triangle - Andrew, AB, Canada - *AyerDirPub 83*
Elk Point Cable TV Inc. [of TeleNational Communications Inc.] - Elk Point, SD - *BrCabYB 84; Tel&CabFB 84C*
Elk Point Leader-Courier - Elk Point, SD - *BaconPubCkNews 84*
Elk Rapids Progress - Elk Rapids, MI - *Ed&PubIntYB 82*
Elk Rapids Town Meeting - Elk Rapids, MI - *BaconPubCkNews 84*
Elk River Star News - Elk River, MN - *AyerDirPub 83; BaconPubCkNews 84*
Elk River TV Inc. - Elk River, ID - *BrCabYB 84; Tel&CabFB 84C*
Elk Valley Times & Observer - Fayetteville, TN - *Ed&PubIntYB 82*
Elk Valley Times, Observer & News [of Lakeway Publishers Inc.] - Fayetteville, TN - *NewsDir 84*
Elkader Clayton County Register - Elkader, IA - *BaconPubCkNews 84*
Elkan Music Inc., Henri - Philadelphia, PA - *BillIntBG 83-84*
Elkhart Telephone Co. Inc. - Elkhart, KS - *TelDir&BG 83-84*
Elkhart Tri-State News - Elkhart, KS - *BaconPubCkNews 84; Ed&PubIntYB 82*
Elkhart Truth - Elkhart, IN - *BaconPubCkNews 84; Ed&PubIntYB 82; NewsDir 84*
Elkhart TV Cable Co. - Elkhart, KS - *BrCabYB 84; Tel&CabFB 84C*
Elkhorn City Cable System Inc. - Elkhorn City, KY - *BrCabYB 84; Tel&CabFB 84C*
Elkhorn Independent - Elkhorn, WI - *BaconPubCkNews 84; Ed&PubIntYB 82; NewsDir 84*
Elkhorn Valley Post - *See* Enterprise Publishing Co. Inc.
Elkin Associates - Nutley, NJ - *LitMarPl 83, 84; MagIndMarPl 82-83*
Elkin-Jonesville Tribune, The [of Mid-South Management Co. Inc.] - Elkin, NC - *NewsDir 84*
Elkin, Sandra A. - New York, NY - *LitMarPl 83*
Elkin Tribune - Elkin, NC - *BaconPubCkNews 84*
Elkins Inter-Mountain [of Ogden Newspapers Inc.] - Elkins, WV - *BaconPubCkNews 84; NewsDir 84*
Elkins Randolph Enterprise-Review - Elkins, WV - *BaconPubCkNews 84*
Elkland Electric Co. - Elkland, PA - *BrCabYB 84 p.D-300; Tel&CabFB 84C p.1678*
Elkland Journal - Elkland, PA - *AyerDirPub 83; BaconPubCkNews 84; Ed&PubIntYB 82*
Elkman Advertising - Bala Cynwyd, PA - *AdAge 3-28-84; BrCabYB 84; StaDirAdAg 2-84*
Elkman Advertising (Public Relations Dept.) - Bala Cynwyd, PA - *DirPRFirms 83*
Elko Daily Free Press - Elko, NV - *BaconPubCkNews 84; Ed&PubIntYB 82; NewsDir 84*
Elko Independent - Elko, NV - *BaconPubCkNews 84; Ed&PubIntYB 82*
Elks Magazine, The - Chicago, IL - *ArtMar 84; BaconPubCkMag 84; DirMarMP 83; MagDir 84; MagIndMarPl 82-83; WritMar 84*
Elkton Cecil Democrat, The - Elkton, MD - *NewsDir 84*
Elkton Cecil Whig [of Chesapeake Publishing Corp.] - Elkton, MD - *BaconPubCkNews 84; NewsDir 84*
Elkton Record - Elkton, SD - *Ed&PubIntYB 82*
Elkton Record - *See* Lundgren Publishing Co.
Elkton Todd County Standard - Elkton, KY - *BaconPubCkNews 84*
Elkton Valley Banner - Elkton, VA - *BaconPubCkNews 84*
Elkville Journal - Elkville, IL - *Ed&PubIntYB 82*
Ell Ell Diversified Inc. - Santa Rosa, CA - *BoPubDir 4, 5*
Ellebie Music Publishing Co. - Sharon, PA - *BillIntBG 83-84*
Ellendale Cable TV Inc. - Ellendale, MN - *BrCabYB 84*
Ellendale Dickey County Leader - Ellendale, ND - *BaconPubCkNews 84*
Ellendale Eagle - Ellendale, MN - *BaconPubCkNews 84; Ed&PubIntYB 82*
Ellensburg Record - Ellensburg, WA - *BaconPubCkNews 84; NewsDir 84*
Ellensburg Telephone Co. - Ellensburg, WA - *TelDir&BG 83-84*
Ellentuck & Springer Inc. - Princeton, NJ - *DirMarMP 83*
Ellenville CATV Associates [of Simmons Communications] - Ellenville, NY - *BrCabYB 84; Tel&CabFB 84C*
Ellenville CATV Associates [of Simmons Communications Inc.] - Woodridge, NY - *Tel&CabFB 84C*
Ellenville Journal - Ellenville, NY - *Ed&PubIntYB 82; NewsDir 84*
Ellenville Press [of Ellenville Rondout Valley Publishing Co. Inc.] - Ellenville, NY - *BaconPubCkNews 84; Ed&PubIntYB 82; NewsDir 84*
Ellerbe Telephone Co. - Ellerbe, NC - *TelDir&BG 83-84*
Ellery Queen's Mystery Magazine [of Davis Publications Inc.] - New York, NY - *ArtMar 84; LitMarPl 83, 84; MagIndMarPl 82-83; WritMar 84*

Ellettsville Journal - Ellettsville, IN - *BaconPubCkNews 84*
Elliam Associates - Woodland Hills, CA - *MicrocomMPl 83, 84*
Ellicott City Howard County News - Ellicott City, MD - *BaconPubCkNews 84*
Ellijay Telephone Co. - Ellijay, GA - *TelDir&BG 83-84*
Ellijay Times-Courier - Ellijay, GA - *BaconPubCkNews 84; Ed&PubIntYB 82; NewsDir 84*
Ellingson, Reuben - *See* Nodakable Inc.
Ellingsworth Press Ltd. - Waterbury, CT - *BoPubDir 4, 5*
Ellington Reynolds County Courier - Ellington, MO - *BaconPubCkNews 84*
Ellington Surveys Associates Inc. - Boston, MA - *IntDirMarRes 83*
Ellington Telephone Co. - Ellington, MO - *TelDir&BG 83-84*
Ellinwood Leader - Ellinwood, KS - *AyerDirPub 83; BaconPubCkNews 84; Ed&PubIntYB 82*
Elliot Lake Uranium Mine [of Denison Mines Ltd.] - Elliot Lake, ON, Canada - *BrCabYB 84*
Elliot's Books - Northford, CT - *BoPubDir 4 Sup, 5*
Elliott & Trantow Advertising Inc. - Los Angeles, CA - *StaDirAdAg 2-84*
Elliott County News - Sandy Hook, KY - *AyerDirPub 83; Ed&PubIntYB 82*
Elliott Film Co. Inc. - Minneapolis, MN - *AvMarPl 83*
Elliott Productions, Don - Weston, CT - *Tel&CabFB 84C*
Elliott Productions, Tom (Publishing Div.) - Boston, MA - *BoPubDir 5*
Elliott Research Corp. Ltd. - Toronto, ON, Canada - *Tel&CabFB 84C*
Elliott Research Inc., Ruth - Dayton, OH - *IntDirMarRes 83*
Ellipse - Sherbrooke, PQ, Canada - *LitMag&SmPr 83-84*
Ellipse Broadcast Assignments - Washington, DC - *BrCabYB 84*
Ellipsis Music Corp. - *See* Jamie Music Publishing Co.
Ellis Advertising Co. - Buffalo, NY - *StaDirAdAg 2-84*
Ellis & Co. - *See* Graham Music Publisher, Roger
Ellis Associates - New York, NY - *DirPRFirms 83*
Ellis Cable TV Co. [of KAYS Inc.] - Ellis, KS - *BrCabYB 84; Tel&CabFB 84C*
Ellis, Carol Ann - Columbus, OH - *MagIndMarPl 82-83*
Ellis Computing - San Francisco, CA - *MicrocomMPl 84; WhoWMicrocom 83*
Ellis County Capital - Arnett, OK - *Ed&PubIntYB 82*
Ellis County Star - Hays, KS - *AyerDirPub 83; Ed&PubIntYB 82*
Ellis Enterprises Ltd., Ralph C. - Toronto, ON, Canada - *Tel&CabFB 84C*
Ellis, Joyce W. - Columbus, OH - *LitMarPl 83, 84*
Ellis Press - Peoria, IL - *BoPubDir 4, 5; LitMag&SmPr 83-84*
Ellis Review - Ellis, KS - *BaconPubCkNews 84; Ed&PubIntYB 82*
Ellis Singer Group - Buffalo, NY - *AdAge 3-28-84; StaDirAdAg 2-84*
Ellison Enterprises - Miami Beach, FL - *BoPubDir 4, 5*
Ellison Inc., Michael R. - Phoenix, AZ - *StaDirAdAg 2-84*
Ellison Qualitative Research Inc., Abby - New York, NY - *IntDirMarRes 83*
Ellisville Jones County Progress-Item - Ellisville, MS - *BaconPubCkNews 84*
Ells, Margaret Adelia - Canning, NS, Canada - *BoPubDir 4, 5*
Ellsworth American - Ellsworth, ME - *BaconPubCkNews 84; Ed&PubIntYB 82; NewsDir 84*
Ellsworth Cable Inc. - Ellsworth, KS - *BrCabYB 84; Tel&CabFB 84C*
Ellsworth Cooperative Telephone Association - Ellsworth, IA - *TelDir&BG 83-84*
Ellsworth Pierce County Herald - Ellsworth, WI - *BaconPubCkNews 84*
Ellsworth Record - Ellsworth, WI - *Ed&PubIntYB 82*
Ellsworth Reporter - Ellsworth, KS - *BaconPubCkNews 84; Ed&PubIntYB 82*
Ellwood City Ledger [of Citizens Publishing & Printing Co.] - Ellwood City, PA - *BaconPubCkNews 84; Ed&PubIntYB 82; NewsDir 84*
Elm Grove Elm Leaves - *See* Community Newspapers Inc.
Elm Grove Leaves - Oak Creek, WI - *AyerDirPub 83*
Elm Hollow Syndicate Inc. - Livingston Manor, NY - *Ed&PubIntYB 82; LitMarPl 84*
Elm Leaves - Elmwood Park, IL - *Ed&PubIntYB 82*
Elm Leaves [of Wilmette Pioneer Press Inc.] - Oak Park, IL - *NewsDir 84*
Elm Leaves - Elm Grove, WI - *Ed&PubIntYB 82*
Elm Publishing Co. - Westminster, CA - *BillIntBG 83-84*
Elm Records [Div. of Edd L. McNeely Productions] - Westminster, CA - *BillIntBG 83-84*
Elm Tree Books - North Pomfret, VT - *LitMarPl 83, 84*
Elm Tree Press - Viola, WI - *BoPubDir 4, 5*
Elma Chronicle - Elma, WA - *Ed&PubIntYB 82*
Elma Chronicle - *See* Community Media Corp.
Elma Reminder - Elma, IA - *BaconPubCkNews 84; Ed&PubIntYB 82*
Elma Review - Buffalo, NY - *AyerDirPub 83*
Elman, Barbara - Burbank, CA - *LitMarPl 84*
Elmer, Irene - Berkeley, CA - *LitMarPl 83, 84*
Elmer Times - Elmer, NJ - *AyerDirPub 83; BaconPubCkNews 84; Ed&PubIntYB 82*
Elmer, William B. - Andover, MA - *BoPubDir 4, 5*
Elmhurst Press - Elmhurst, IL - *AyerDirPub 83; Ed&PubIntYB 82; NewsDir 84*
Elmhurst Press - *See* Press Publications
Elmira Star-Gazette - Elmira, NY - *BaconPubCkNews 84; Ed&PubIntYB 82; NewsDir 84*
Elmira Video [of Group W Cable] - Elmira, NY - *BrCabYB 84*
Elmo Agency Inc., Ann - New York, NY - *LitMarPl 83, 84*
Elmont Elmonitor [of Nassau Illustrated News] - Elmont, NY - *AyerDirPub 83; BaconPubCkNews 84; Ed&PubIntYB 82; NewsDir 84*
Elmont Herald - Elmont, NY - *AyerDirPub 83*
Elmont Pennysaver - Rockville Centre, NY - *AyerDirPub 83*
Elmore-Coosa Telephone Co. Inc. [Aff. of Mid-Continent Telephone Corp.] - Eclectic, AL - *TelDir&BG 83-84*
Elms Productions Inc., Charles - Bountiful, UT - *StaDirAdAg 2-84*
Elmsford Record of Greenburgh, The - Elmsford, NY - *NewsDir 84*
Elmvale Lance - Elmvale, ON, Canada - *AyerDirPub 83*
Elmwood Argus - Elmwood, WI - *BaconPubCkNews 84; Ed&PubIntYB 82*
Elmwood Gazette - Elmwood, IL - *Ed&PubIntYB 82*
Elmwood Park Elm Leaves - Wilmette, IL - *AyerDirPub 83*
Elmwood Park Elm Leaves - *See* Pioneer Press Inc.
Elmwood Park-Galewood-Montclare Passage - Chicago, IL - *AyerDirPub 83*
Elmwood Park Post - Chicago, IL - *NewsDir 84*
Elmwood Park Post - Elmwood Park, IL - *AyerDirPub 83*
Elmwood Park Post - *See* Meese' Newspaper Group
Elmwood Park Times - Chicago, IL - *AyerDirPub 83*
Elmwood Park Times - Elmwood Park, IL - *Ed&PubIntYB 82*
Elmwood Park Times - *See* Lerner Times Newspapers
Elnora Telephone Co. [Aff. of Telephone & Data Systems Inc.] - Elnora, IN - *TelDir&BG 83-84*
Elographics Inc. - Oak Ridge, TN - *DataDirSup 7-83; WhoWMicrocom 83*
Eloy Enterprise - Eloy, AZ - *AyerDirPub 83*
Eloy Enterprise - *See* Casa Grande Valley Newspapers Inc.
Elpenor Books - Chicago, IL - *BoPubDir 4, 5; LitMag&SmPr 83-84*
ELRA Group - San Francisco, CA - *BrCabYB 84*
Elra Group - East Lansing, MI - *CabTVFinDB 83; InterCabHB 3*
Elrick & Lavidge Inc. [Subs. of Equifax Inc.] - Chicago, IL - *AdAge 5-17-84 p.32; IntDirMarRes 83*
Elrita Music - *See* Delvy Enterprises Inc., Richard
Elrod Marketing Research Inc. - Atlanta, GA - *IntDirMarRes 83*
Elroy Tribune-Keystone - Elroy, WI - *BaconPubCkNews 84*
ELS Publications [Div. of Washington Educational Research Associates Inc.] - Culver City, CA - *AvMarPl 83; BoPubDir 4, 5*
Elsberry Democrat - Elsberry, MO - *BaconPubCkNews 84; Ed&PubIntYB 82*
Elsevier Antiquarian Dept. - Amsterdam, Netherlands - *MicroMarPl 82-83*
Elsevier-IRCS Ltd. [Subs. of Elsevier-NDU] - Lancaster, England - *DataDirOnSer 84*
Elsevier-NDU nv - Arlington, VA - *KnowInd 83*
Elsevier North-Holland Inc. - New York, NY - *EISS 83*

Elsevier Science Publishing Co. Inc. [Subs. of Elsevier NDU NV] - New York, NY - *LitMarPl 83, 84; MagIndMarPl 82-83*
Elsevier Sequoia SA - Lausanne, Switzerland - *MicroMarPl 82-83*
Elsie Mutual Telephone Co. - Elsie, NE - *TelDir&BG 83-84*
Elsinore Valley Pennysaver - Mission Viejo, CA - *AyerDirPub 83*
ELSS - Chicago, IL - *DirOnDB Spring 84*
Elta Information Service - Washington, DC - *Ed&PubIntYB 82*
Eltech Associates - Los Angeles, CA - *MicrocomMPl 83, 84*
Elvendon Press, The - Reading, England - *LitMag&SmPr 83-84*
Elverston, Catherine C. - Gainesville, FL - *LitMarPl 83, 84; MagIndMarPl 82-83*
Elvis Music Inc. - New York, NY - *BillIntBG 83-84*
Elwell & Donald Smith, Ruth - New York, NY - *LitMarPl 83, 84*
Elwood Bulletin - Elwood, NE - *BaconPubCkNews 84; Ed&PubIntYB 82*
Elwood Call-Leader - Mineola, NY - *NewsDir 84*
Ely Daily Times [of Donrey Media Group] - Ely, NV - *BaconPubCkNews 84; Ed&PubIntYB 82; NewsDir 84*
Ely Echo - Ely, MN - *AyerDirPub 83; BaconPubCkNews 84; NewsDir 84*
Ely Miner - Ely, MN - *BaconPubCkNews 84; Ed&PubIntYB 82*
Elyria Chronicle-Telegram [of Lorain County Printing & Publishing] - Elyria, OH - *BaconPubCkNews 84; NewsDir 84*
Elyria-Lorain Broadcasting Co. - Elyria, OH - *BrCabYB 84*
Elyria Telephone Co. [Aff. of Mid-Continent Telephone Corp.] - Elyria, OH - *TelDir&BG 83-84*
Elysian Enterprise - Elysian, MN - *BaconPubCkNews 84; Ed&PubIntYB 82*
Elysian Fields Publishing [Aff. of Osiris Corp.] - Rockford, IL - *BoPubDir 4, 5*
Emanation Press - Canada - *BoPubDir 4, 5*
EMBase - Amsterdam, Netherlands - *DirOnDB Spring 84*
Embassy Communications - Los Angeles, CA - *TelAl 84*
Embassy Computer Products - Little Neck, NY - *MicrocomMPl 84*
Embassy Home Entertainment - Los Angeles, CA - *BillIntBG 83-84*
Embassy Institute, The - Wilmington, DE - *WhoWMicrocom 83*
Embassy Pictures - Los Angeles, CA - *LitMarPl 83; Tel&CabFB 84C*
Embassy Telecommunications - Los Angeles, CA - *TelAl 83, 84; Tel&CabFB 84C*
Embassy Television - Universal City, CA - *TelAl 83, 84; Tel&CabFB 84C*
Embee Press - Kingston, NY - *BoPubDir 4, 5*
Embers Press - Santa Cruz, CA - *LitMag&SmPr 83-84*
Embry Newspapers Inc. - Beaver Dam, KY - *BoPubDir 4, 5*
Embryonics - Elizaville, NY - *HBIndAd&MS 82-83*
Embryonics New Product Workshop Inc. - Elizaville, NY - *IntDirMarRes 83*
EMC Corp. - St. Paul, MN - *ArtMar 84; AvMarPl 83; LitMarPl 83, 84*
EMC Technology - Gainesville, VA - *BaconPubCkMag 84*
EMCancer - Amsterdam, Netherlands - *DirOnDB Spring 84*
EMCO CATV Inc. - Manchester, VT - *BrCabYB 84 p.D-300; Tel&CabFB 84C p.1678*
Emcom Corp. - Richardson, TX - *DataDirSup 7-83*
Emde Products - Santee, CA - *AvMarPl 83*
EmDrugs - Amsterdam, Netherlands - *DirOnDB Spring 84*
Emerald Graphic Systems - Syracuse, NY - *LitMarPl 84*
Emerald International Records Inc. - Philadelphia, PA - *BillIntBG 83-84*
Emerald Software - Lindenhurst, NY - *MicrocomMPl 84*
Emergency - Carlsbad, CA - *BaconPubCkMag 84; MagDir 84; MagIndMarPl 82-83; WritMar 84*
Emergency Alert Receiver Inc. - New York, NY - *AvMarPl 83*
Emergency Dept. News - New York, NY - *BaconPubCkMag 84*
Emergency Librarian - Vancouver, BC, Canada - *LitMag&SmPr 83-84; WritMar 84*
Emergency Medical Services - North Hollywood, CA - *BaconPubCkMag 84; MagDir 84; MagIndMarPl 82-83*
Emergency Medicine - New York, NY - *BaconPubCkMag 84; MagDir 84; MagIndMarPl 82-83*
Emergency Music Inc. - New York, NY - *BillIntBG 83-84*
Emergency Preparedness News - Silver Spring, MD - *BaconPubCkMag 84*
Emergency Programs Information Center [of U.S. Dept. of Agriculture] - Hyattsville, MD - *EISS 83*
Emergency Records & Filmworks Inc. - New York, NY - *BillIntBG 83-84*
Emergindex [of Micromedex Inc.] - Englewood, CO - *EISS 83*
Emerging Technology Consultants Inc. - Boulder, CO - *MicrocomMPl 84*
Emeritus Corp. - Fresno, CA - *MicrocomMPl 83*
Emeritus Inc. - Cherry Hill, NJ - *BoPubDir 5*
Emerson & Associates - Santa Ana, CA - *StaDirAdAg 2-84*
Emerson Books Inc. - Verplanck, NY - *LitMarPl 83, 84*
Emerson Industrial Controls - Santa Ana, CA - *DirInfWP 82*
Emerson Lane Fortuna - Boston, MA - *AdAge 3-28-84; StaDirAdAg 2-84*
Emerson Marketing Agency - New York, NY - *AdAge 3-28-84; DirMarMP 83; StaDirAdAg 2-84*
Emerson/Nichols/Bailey - Irving, TX - *StaDirAdAg 2-84*
Emerson Tri-County Press - Emerson, NE - *BaconPubCkNews 84*
Emerson, Wajdowicz Studios Inc. - New York, NY - *LitMarPl 83, 84*
Emery Advertising - Hunt Valley, MD - *AdAge 3-28-84; StaDirAdAg 2-84*
Emery Advertising - El Paso, TX - *AdAge 3-28-84 p.112; StaDirAdAg 2-84*
Emery & Associates Inc. - West Hartford, CT - *StaDirAdAg 2-84*
Emery County Farmers Union Telephone Association - Orangeville, UT - *TelDir&BG 83-84*
Emery County Progress - Castle Dale, UT - *AyerDirPub 83; Ed&PubIntYB 82*
Emery Enterprise - Emery, SD - *BaconPubCkNews 84; Ed&PubIntYB 82*
Emery-Pratt Co. - Owosso, MI - *LitMarPl 83, 84*
Emery Worldwide - Wilton, CT - *MagIndMarPl 82-83*
EmForensic - Amsterdam, Netherlands - *DirOnDB Spring 84*
EMH Music - Nashville, TN - *BillIntBG 83-84*
EMHealth - Amsterdam, Netherlands - *DirOnDB Spring 84*
EMI America/Liberty Records [Div. of Capitol Records Inc.] - Los Angeles, CA - *BillIntBG 83-84*
EMI Electronic Flight Services [of Engineering Management Information Corp.] - University City, MO - *EISS 5-84 Sup*
EMI Flight Planning [of Engineering Management Information Corp.] - University City, MO - *DataDirOnSer 84; DirOnDB Spring 84*
EMI Music Worldwide - Hollywood, CA - *BillIntBG 83-84*
Emidata Systems - Garrison, MD - *DirInfWP 82*
Emigrante - Montreal, PQ, Canada - *Ed&PubIntYB 82*
Emily Cooperative Telephone Co. - Emily, MN - *Tel&CabFB 84C; TelDir&BG 83-84*
Eminence Current Wave - Eminence, MO - *BaconPubCkNews 84*
Emington Joker - Emington, IL - *AyerDirPub 83; Ed&PubIntYB 82*
EMIS - New York, NY - *DirOnDB Spring 84*
EMIS - Hitchin, England - *DirOnDB Spring 84*
Emison, Gloria J. - Cincinnati, OH - *LitMarPl 83*
Emissary Publications - South Pasadena, CA - *BoPubDir 5*
Emit Music - *See* Moody Music, Doug
EmKay Records - Tujunga, CA - *BillIntBG 83-84*
Emko Music Corp. [Div. of Emko Talent Associates Corp.] - Monsey, NY - *BillIntBG 83-84*
Emmans, John Stratton - Geraldton, ON, Canada - *Tel&CabFB 84C*
Emmanuel - New York, NY - *WritMar 84*
Emmaus Free Press - Emmaus, PA - *BaconPubCkNews 84*
Emmaus Times - *See* Peerless Publications
Emmerich Enterprises Inc. - Greenwood, MS - *Ed&PubIntYB 82*
Emmerich Enterprises Inc. - McComb, MS - *LitMarPl 84*
Emmerling Inc., John - New York, NY - *AdAge 3-28-84; HBIndAd&MS 82-83; StaDirAdAg 2-84*
Emmet County Ad-Vertiser - Petoskey, MI - *AyerDirPub 83*
Emmetsburg Cable TV - Emmetsburg, IA - *BrCabYB 84; Tel&CabFB 84C*
Emmetsburg Democrat - Emmetsburg, IA - *Ed&PubIntYB 82*
Emmetsburg Democrat - *See* Emmetsburg Publishing Co.
Emmetsburg Publishing Co. - Emmetsburg, IA - *BaconPubCkNews 84*
Emmetsburg Reporter - *See* Emmetsburg Publishing Co.

Emmetsburg Reporter & Democrat - Emmetsburg, IA - *NewsDir 84*
Emmett Messenger Index - Emmett, ID - *BaconPubCkNews 84; NewsDir 84*
Emmett Microform Ltd. - Haslemere, England - *MicroMarPl 82-83*
Emmett Publishing Co. - Minneapolis, MN - *BoPubDir 4, 5*
Emmis Broadcasting Corp. - Indianapolis, IN - *BrCabYB 84*
Emmons County Record - Linton, ND - *AyerDirPub 83; Ed&PubIntYB 82*
Emmons, Dick - Ann Arbor, MI - *Ed&PubIntYB 82*
Emmons Leader-Press - Emmons, MN - *BaconPubCkNews 84*
Emmons Leader, The - Emmons, MN - *Ed&PubIntYB 82*
EMMS-Electronic Mail & Message Systems - Norwalk, CT - *BaconPubCkMag 84*
Emmy - North Hollywood, CA - *BaconPubCkMag 84; WritMar 84*
Emond-Montgomery Ltd. - Toronto, ON, Canada - *BoPubDir 4*
Emory Rains County Leader - Emory, TX - *BaconPubCkNews 84*
Emory University (Center for Research in Social Change) - Atlanta, GA - *BoPubDir 4*
Emory University (Fred Roberts Crawford Witness to the Holocaust Project) - Atlanta, GA - *BoPubDir 5*
Emotions Anonymous - St. Paul, MN - *BoPubDir 5*
EMP Co. - *See* Entertainment Co. Music Group, The
Empac Inc. - Rutherford, NJ - *MicrocomMPl 84*
Emperor Music Inc. - *See* Webman & Co., H. B.
Empire [of Unique Graphics] - Oakland, CA - *LitMag&SmPr 83-84; WritMar 84*
Empire - Syracuse, NY - *MagIndMarPl 82-83*
Empire Advance - Virden, MB, Canada - *AyerDirPub 83; Ed&PubIntYB 82*
Empire Books - New York, NY - *LitMarPl 83, 84*
Empire City Marketing - New York, NY - *DirPRFirms 83*
Empire Films Inc. - New York, NY - *Tel&CabFB 84C*
Empire Messenger Service Inc. - New York, NY - *MagIndMarPl 82-83*
Empire Niagara Purchaser - Buffalo, NY - *BaconPubCkMag 84; MagDir 84*
Empire Press - Waterville, WA - *AyerDirPub 83*
Empire Software [Div. of Melsey Corp.] - Carle Place, NY - *MicrocomMPl 84*
Empire Stages of New York - Long Island City, NY - *AvMarPl 83*
Empire State Press Clipping Service - Scarsdale, NY - *ProGuPRSer 4*
Empire State Railway Museum Inc. - Middletown, NY - *BoPubDir 4, 5*
Empire State Report Monthly [of State Magazine Inc.] - New York, NY - *MagDir 84*
Empire State Weeklies - Webster, NY - *BaconPubCkNews 84*
Empire Telephone Co. [Aff. of Mid-Continent Telephone Corp.] - Comer, GA - *TelDir&BG 83-84*
Empire Telephone Corp. - Prattsburg, NY - *TelDir&BG 83-84*
Empire Tribune - Stephenville, TX - *AyerDirPub 83*
Empirical Research Group Inc. - Milton, WA - *MicrocomMPl 83*
Emploi et Formation - *See* FRANCIS: Emploi et Formation
Employee Benefit Plan Review - Chicago, IL - *BaconPubCkMag 84; MagDir 84*
Employee Relations & Human Resources Bulletin - Waterford, CT - *WritMar 84*
Employee Retirement Plans - Washington, DC - *DirOnDB Spring 84*
Employee Retirement Plans [of NewsNet Inc.] - Bryn Mawr, PA - *DataDirOnSer 84*
Employee Services Management - Chicago, IL - *BaconPubCkMag 84; MagDir 84*
Employment & Professional Training [of Centre de Documentation Sciences Humaines] - Paris, France - *CompReadDB 82*
Employment Information Services - Chico, CA - *BoPubDir 4, 5*
Emporia Gazette [of White Corp. Inc.] - Emporia, KS - *BaconPubCkNews 84; Ed&PubIntYB 82; LitMarPl 83, 84; NewsDir 84*
Emporia Independent Messenger - Emporia, VA - *BaconPubCkNews 84; NewsDir 84*
Emporia Southside Sun [of Byerly Publications Inc.] - Emporia, VA - *BaconPubCkNews 84; NewsDir 84*
Emporium Cameron County Echo - Emporium, PA - *BaconPubCkNews 84; NewsDir 84*
Empress Chinchilla Breeder [of Empress Chinchilla Breeders Co-Op Inc.] - Morrison, CO - *BaconPubCkMag 84; MagDir 84*
Empress Publications - Victoria, BC, Canada - *BoPubDir 4, 5*
Empty Space, The - Seattle, WA - *WritMar 84*
EMR Publications - Bryan, TX - *BoPubDir 4, 5*
Emrose Art Corp. of Florida - Ft. Lauderdale, FL - *ArtMar 84*
EMS Inc. - Tyler, TX - *StaDirAdAg 2-84*
EMTox - Amsterdam, Netherlands - *DirOnDB Spring 84*
Emtrol Systems Inc. - Lancaster, PA - *MicrocomMPl 84*
Emulex Corp. - Costa Mesa, CA - *MicrocomMPl 84*
EMX Telecom - Rockville, MD - *TeleSy&SerDir 2-84*
En Avant Music Co. Inc. - Memphis, TN - *BillIntBG 83-84*
En Passant/Poetry - Wilmington, DE - *BoPubDir 4 Sup, 5; LitMag&SmPr 83-84*
Ena Music Inc. - *See* Live Music Publishing Group
Enabling Systems Inc. - Honolulu, HI - *BoPubDir 4, 5*
Enchantment - Santa Fe, NM - *BaconPubCkMag 84; MagDir 84*
Enchantment Music Co. - Las Cruces, NM - *BillIntBG 83-84*
Encinian - Encino, CA - *AyerDirPub 83; Ed&PubIntYB 82*
Encinitas/Cardiff Pennysaver - Mission Viejo, CA - *AyerDirPub 83*
Encinitas Coast Dispatch [of North Coast Publishers Inc.] - Encinitas, CA - *NewsDir 84*
Encinitas Coast Dispatch - *See* North Coast Publishers Inc.
Encino Encinian - *See* Associated Valley Publications
Encino Press - Austin, TX - *BoPubDir 4, 5*
Enclosed Mall Research of New York Inc. - White Plains, NY - *IntDirMarRes 83*
Encore - Albuquerque, NM - *ArtMar 84; WritMar 84*
Encore - New York, NY - *MagIndMarPl 82-83*
Encore American & Worldwide News - New York, NY - *BaconPubCkMag 84*
Encore Records - Santa Monica, CA - *BillIntBG 83-84*
Encore Studio - New York, NY - *AvMarPl 83*
Encore Theatre - Montreal, PQ, Canada - *WritMar 84*
Encore Visual Education Inc. - Burbank, CA - *AvMarPl 83*
Encounter - London, England - *WritMar 84*
Encyclopaedia Britannica - Chicago, IL - *DirMarMP 83; DirOnDB Spring 84; KnowInd 83; LitMarPl 83, 84*
Encyclopaedia Britannica [of Mead Data Central] - New York, NY - *DataDirOnSer 84*
Encyclopaedia Britannica Data Base - Chicago, IL - *EISS 7-83 Sup*
Encyclopaedia Britannica Educational Corp. [Div. of Encyclopaedia Britannica Inc.] - Chicago, IL - *ArtMar 84; LitMarPl 83, 84; MicrocomMPl 83, 84; MicrocomSwDir 1; Tel&CabFB 84C*
Encyclopaedia Britannica International [Div. of Encyclopaedia Britannica Inc.] - Chicago, IL - *LitMarPl 83, 84*
Encyclopedia [of Dow Jones News/Retrieval Service] - Princeton, NJ - *DataDirOnSer 84*
Encyclopedia of Associations [of Dialog Information Services Inc.] - Palo Alto, CA - *DataDirOnSer 84*
Encyclopedia of Associations [of Gale Research Co.] - Detroit, MI - *CompReadDB 82; DBBus 82; DirOnDB Spring 84; EISS 83*
End of File Inc. - Atlanta, GA - *MicrocomMPl 83*
Endata Inc. - Nashville, TN - *ADAPSOMemDir 83-84; DataDirOnSer 84; DataDirSup 7-83*
Endeavour - Elmsford, NY - *MagDir 84*
Ender, James W. - Wabasha, MN - *Tel&CabFB 84C p.1679*
Enderby Commoner - Enderby, BC, Canada - *AyerDirPub 83*
Enderlin Independent - Enderlin, ND - *BaconPubCkNews 84; Ed&PubIntYB 82*
Endicott Software - Huntsville, AL - *MicrocomMPl 84*
Endicott Tempo of the Town - *See* Southern Tier Publications Inc.
Endless Vacation [of Endless Vacation International] - Indianapolis, IN - *BaconPubCkMag 84; WritMar 84*
Endoc - Luxembourg - *DirOnDB Spring 84*
Endocrinology - Baltimore, MD - *BaconPubCkMag 84; MagDir 84*
Endurance - Santa Barbara, CA - *BoPubDir 4, 5*
Endurance Press - Detroit, MI - *BoPubDir 4, 5*
Enec - Eggenstein-Leopoldshafen, West Germany - *DirOnDB Spring 84*

Enerdata [of ADP Network Services Inc.] - Ann Arbor, MI - *DataDirOnSer 84*
Enerdata - Rome, Italy - *DirOnDB Spring 84*
Energi Data Base - Gif sur Yvette, France - *DirOnDB Spring 84*
Energies, Trends, Cycles - Atlanta, GA - *DirOnDB Spring 84*
Energies, Trends, Cycles [of NewsNet Inc.] - Bryn Mawr, PA - *DataDirOnSer 84*
Energon Co. - Laramie, WY - *BoPubDir 4, 5*
Energy - Stamford, CT - *BaconPubCkMag 84*
Energy [of Chase Econometrics/Interactive Data Corp.] - Waltham, MA - *DataDirOnSer 84; DBBus 82*
Energy - Mt. Kisco, NY - *DirOnDB Spring 84*
Energy - Bala Cynwyd, PA - *DirOnDB Spring 84*
Energy [of QL Systems Ltd.] - Ottawa, ON, Canada - *DataDirOnSer 84; DirOnDB Spring 84*
Energy Analects - Don Mills, ON, Canada - *BaconPubCkMag 84*
Energy & Agriculture Data Base [of Texas A & M University Libraries] - College Station, TX - *EISS 83*
Energy & Economic Data Bank [of International Atomic Energy Agency] - Vienna, Austria - *EISS 83*
Energy & Housing Report - Washington, DC - *BaconPubCkMag 84*
Energy & Mineral Resources [of NewsNet Inc.] - Bryn Mawr, PA - *DataDirOnSer 84*
Energy & Minerals Resources - Silver Spring, MD - *BaconPubCkMag 84; DirOnDB Spring 84*
Energy Bibliography & Index [of Center for Energy & Mineral Resources] - College Station, TX - *OnBibDB 3*
Energy Bibliography & Index [of Gulf Publishing Co.] - Houston, TX - *CompReadDB 82; DBBus 82; EISS 83*
Energy Calendar of Events [of QL Systems Ltd.] - Ottawa, ON, Canada - *CompReadDB 82; DataDirOnSer 84; DBBus 82*
Energy Communications Press Inc. - Manchester, NH - *BoPubDir 4 Sup, 5*
Energy Conservation Digest - Washington, DC - *BaconPubCkMag 84*
Energy Daily, The - Washington, DC - *BaconPubCkMag 84; DirMarMP 83*
Energy Data & Projections System [of Resource & Technology Management Corp.] - Arlington, VA - *EISS 7-83 Sup*
Energy Data Bank [of Data Resources Inc.] - Lexington, MA - *DataDirOnSer 84; DBBus 82*
Energy Data Base [of US Dept. of Energy] - Oak Ridge, TN - *DataDirOnSer 84; OnBibDB 3*
Energy Data Reports - Washington, DC - *DirOnDB Spring 84*
Energy Data Systems Inc. - Wayne, PA - *WhoWMicrocom 83*
Energy Detente International Price/Tax Series - North Hollywood, CA - *DirOnDB Spring 84*
Energy Developments [of Technischer Verlag Resch KG] - Palos Verdes Peninsula, CA - *MagDir 84*
Energy Digest - Washington, DC - *BaconPubCkMag 84; MagDir 84*
Energy Economics [of Centre de Documentation Sciences Humaines] - Paris, France - *CompReadDB 82*
Energy Engineering [of Fairmont Press] - Brooklyn, NY - *BaconPubCkMag 84; MagDir 84; MagIndMarPl 82-83*
Energy Enterprises [of General Electric Information Services Co.] - Denver, CO - *DataDirOnSer 84*
Energy Equipment - Edmonton, AB, Canada - *BaconPubCkMag 84*
Energy Extension Service Clearinghouse [of Michigan State Dept. of Commerce] - Lansing, MI - *EISS 83*
Energy Forum - Toronto, ON, Canada - *BaconPubCkMag 84*
Energy Information Administration [Aff. of U.S. Dept. of Energy] - Washington, DC - *BoPubDir 4 Sup, 5; EISS 83*
Energy Information Database [of International Research & Evaluation] - Eagan, MN - *CompReadDB 82; DataDirOnSer 84; DirOnDB Spring 84*
Energy Information Resources Inventory - Oak Ridge, TN - *DirOnDB Spring 84*
Energy Information Section [of United Nations Educational, Scientific, & Cultural Organization] - Paris, France - *EISS 83*
Energy Information System [of Environment Information Center Inc.] - New York, NY - *EISS 83*
Energy Library [of U.S. Dept. of Energy] - Washington, DC - *EISS 83*
Energy Management Canada - Markham, ON, Canada - *BaconPubCkMag 84*
Energy Management Report [of Energy Publications] - Dallas, TX - *MagDir 84; WritMar 84*
Energy Management Technology [of Walker-Davis Publications Inc.] - Willow Grove, PA - *BaconPubCkMag 84; MagDir 84*
Energy, Mines, & Resources Canada - Ottawa, ON, Canada - *CompReadDB 82*
Energy News [Div. of Harcourt Brace Jovanovich] - Dallas, TX - *BaconPubCkMag 84; WritMar 84*
Energy Notebook - New York, NY - *Ed&PubIntYB 82*
Energy People, The [of PSE & G] - Newark, NJ - *WritMar 84*
Energy Processing/Canada - Calgary, AB, Canada - *BaconPubCkMag 84*
Energy Programs [of QL Systems Ltd.] - Ottawa, ON, Canada - *CompReadDB 82; DataDirOnSer 84; DBBus 82; DirOnDB Spring 84*
Energy Projects [of Energy, Mines, & Resources Canada] - Ottawa, ON, Canada - *CompReadDB 82; DBBus 82*
Energy Publishing Co. - Winter Haven, FL - *BoPubDir 4, 5*
Energy Records - New York, NY - *BillIntBG 83-84*
Energy Research Digest - Washington, DC - *BaconPubCkMag 84*
Energy Research Reports - Framingham, MA - *BaconPubCkMag 84*
Energy Review [of International Academy at Santa Barbara] - Santa Barbara, CA - *LitMag&SmPr 83-84*
Energy Self-Sufficiency - Siloam Springs, AR - *BoPubDir 5*
Energy Sense - Highland Park, IL - *BaconPubCkMag 84*
Energy Studies & Information Center [of French Institute for Energy] - Paris, France - *EISS 83*
Energy Systems Product News - New York, NY - *BaconPubCkMag 84*
Energy Today - Washington, DC - *BaconPubCkMag 84*
Energy User News [of Fairchild Publications] - New York, NY - *BaconPubCkMag 84; MagDir 84; MagIndMarPl 82-83*
Energy Weather Information System [of Weather Services International Corp.] - Bedford, MA - *DataDirOnSer 84*
Energy Week [Div. of Harcourt Brace Jovanovich] - Dallas, TX - *WritMar 84*
Energyline [of Environment Information Center Inc.] - New York, NY - *DataDirOnSer 84; DBBus 82; DirOnDB Spring 84; OnBibDB 3*
Energynet [of Environment Information Center Inc.] - New York, NY - *CompReadDB 82; DataDirOnSer 84; DBBus 82; DirOnDB Spring 84*
Energytapes [of Environment Information Center Inc.] - New York, NY - *CompReadDB 82*
Energyworks Inc. - Watertown, MA - *MicrocomMPl 84*
Enertec Inc. - Lansdale, PA - *MicrocomMPl 83, 84; MicrocomSwDir 1; WhoWMicrocom 83*
Enertech Information Systems - Midland, TX - *MicrocomMPl 84*
Enertronics Research Inc. - St. Louis, MO - *MicrocomMPl 84*
Enfield Cable TV - Enfield, NC - *BrCabYB 84*
Enfield Halifax County This Week - Enfield, NC - *NewsDir 84*
Enfield Northern Connecticut Bazaar [of Enfield Hartford Publications Inc.] - Enfield, CT - *NewsDir 84*
Enfield Northern Connecticut Bazaar - *See* Hartford Publications Inc.
Enfield Press [of Hartford Publications Inc.] - Enfield, CT - *Ed&PubIntYB 82; NewsDir 84*
Enfield Press - *See* Hartford Publications Inc.
Enforcement Journal - Louisville, KY - *BaconPubCkMag 84*
Engage/Social Action - Washington, DC - *WritMar 84*
Engdahl Co., The - Elmhurst, IL - *LitMarPl 83*
Engel Advertising Inc. - Rolling Meadows, IL - *DirMarMP 83; StaDirAdAg 2-84*
Engel & Tirak - Erie, PA - *StaDirAdAg 2-84*
Engel, Henry W. - New York, NY - *LitMarPl 83, 84*
Engelmeier, Philip A. - San Francisco, CA - *BoPubDir 4, 5*
Engendra Press Ltd. - Montreal, PQ, Canada - *BoPubDir 4, 5*
Engergi [of Questel Inc.] - Washington, DC - *DataDirOnSer 84*
Engh, Jeri - Osceola, WI - *LitMarPl 84*
Engh, Jeri - Star Prairie, WI - *LitMarPl 83*
Engh, Rohn - Star Prairie, WI - *LitMarPl 83, 84*
Engineer of California, The - Alhambra, CA - *BaconPubCkMag 84*

Engineer of California, The [of Schilling Graphics] - Alhamburg, CA - *MagDir 84*
Engineered Products Computer Systems Inc. - Greenville, SC - *ADAPSOMemDir 83-84*
Engineering Analysis Software - Ft. Worth, TX - *WhoWMicrocom 83*
Engineering Analysis Software Consultants - Hightstown, NJ - *MicrocomMPl 83*
Engineering & Contract Record - Don Mills, ON, Canada - *BaconPubCkMag 84*
Engineering & Contract Record [of Southam Communications] - Toronto, ON, Canada - *WritMar 84*
Engineering & Mining Journal - New York, NY - *BaconPubCkMag 84; MagDir 84; MagIndMarPl 82-83*
Engineering & Science [of California Institute of Technology & Alumni Association] - Pasadena, CA - *BaconPubCkMag 84; MagDir 84; MagIndMarPl 82-83*
Engineering & Science Review - Cleveland, OH - *BaconPubCkMag 84*
Engineering Contacts - Minneapolis, MN - *BaconPubCkMag 84*
Engineering Digest - Toronto, ON, Canada - *BaconPubCkMag 84*
Engineering Dimensions - Toronto, ON, Canada - *BaconPubCkMag 84*
Engineering Education - Washington, DC - *BaconPubCkMag 84; MagDir 84*
Engineering Foundation - New York, NY - *BoPubDir 4, 5*
Engineering Index Inc. - *See* Engineering Information Inc.
Engineering Information Inc. - New York, NY - *BoPubDir 4, 5; CompReadDB 82; DataDirOnSer 84; EISS 83; InfIndMarPl 83; MicroMarPl 82-83*
Engineering Journal - Montreal, PQ, Canada - *BaconPubCkMag 84*
Engineering Management Information Corp. - University City, MO - *DataDirOnSer 84*
Engineering News-Record [of McGraw-Hill Inc.] - New York, NY - *BaconPubCkMag 84; Folio 83; MagDir 84; MagIndMarPl 82-83*
Engineering Physics Information Centers [of Oak Ridge National Laboratory] - Oak Ridge, TN - *InfIndMarPl 83*
Engineering Press Inc. - San Jose, CA - *BoPubDir 4, 5*
Engineering Sciences Data Unit Ltd. - London, England - *EISS 83*
Engineering Societies Library - New York, NY - *FBInfSer 80*
Engineering Software Exchange - New York, NY - *BaconPubCkMag 84*
Engineering Software Exchange - Yonkers, NY - *MicrocomMPl 84*
Engineering Solutions - Berkeley, CA - *WhoWMicrocom 83*
Engineering Times [of National Society of Professional Engineers] - Washington, DC - *BaconPubCkMag 84; MagDir 84*
Engineering Times, The - Don Mills, ON, Canada - *BaconPubCkMag 84*
Engineerogram, The - Sacramento, CA - *BaconPubCkMag 84*
Engineers' Book Society [of McGraw-Hill Book Co.] - New York, NY - *LitMarPl 83, 84*
Engineer's Digest [of Walker-Davis Publications Inc.] - Willow Grove, PA - *BaconPubCkMag 84; MagDir 84; MagIndMarPl 82-83*
Engineers News [of OELU No. 3] - San Francisco, CA - *NewsDir 84*
Engineers News Report - Phoenix, AZ - *NewsDir 84*
England & Partners Ltd., D. M. - Twyford, England - *InfIndMarPl 83*
England Democrat - England, AR - *BaconPubCkNews 84; Ed&PubIntYB 82*
England Strohl/De Nigris Inc. - New York, NY - *DirPRFirms 83*
Engle Advertising Inc. - Los Angeles, CA - *StaDirAdAg 2-84*
Engle Productions, Morey - Denver, CO - *AvMarPl 83*
Engleman Co., The - Dallas, TX - *DirPRFirms 83*
Englewood Argus - Trotwood, OH - *AyerDirPub 83*
Englewood Argus - *See* Argus-Sentinel Inc.
Englewood Herald - Englewood, FL - *BaconPubCkNews 84; Ed&PubIntYB 82; NewsDir 84*
Englewood Independent - Englewood, OH - *Ed&PubIntYB 82*
Englewood Independent - *See* Bowling-Moorman Publications
Englewood North Jersey Suburbanite, The - Englewood, NJ - *NewsDir 84*
Englewood Press Journal - Englewood, NJ - *BaconPubCkNews 84*
Englewood Sentinel - *See* Sentinel Newspapers
Englewood Sun Coast Times [of Venice Sun Coast Gondolier Inc.] - Venice, FL - *NewsDir 84*
Englewood Sun Coast Times - *See* Sun Coast Media Group Inc.
Englewood Telephone Co. - Englewood, TN - *TelDir&BG 83-84*
English & Associates Inc., Joel - Phoenix, AZ - *StaDirAdAg 2-84*
English Channel, The [of Edward E. Finch & Co.] - New York, NY - *HomeVid&CabYB 82-83*
English Cocker Spaniel Club of America Inc. - Sunderland, MA - *BoPubDir 4, 5*
English Crawford County Democrat & News-Messenger - English, IN - *BaconPubCkNews 84; NewsDir 84*
English, James - Long Beach, MS - *Tel&CabFB 84C p.1679*
English Journal - Tempe, AZ - *BaconPubCkMag 84; MagIndMarPl 82-83*
English Journal [of National Council of Teachers of English] - Urbana, IL - *LitMarPl 83, 84*
English Language Literature Association - Townsville, Australia - *LitMag&SmPr 83-84*
English Studies in Africa-A Journal of the Humanities [of Witwatersrand University Press] - Johannesburg, South Africa - *LitMag&SmPr 83-84*
Engstrom Enterprises - Austin, TX - *AvMarPl 83*
Enhanced Oil & Gas Recovery - Tulsa, OK - *DirOnDB Spring 84*
Enhanceware - Durango, CO - *MicrocomMPl 83, 84*
Enid Cable TV [of Community Tele-Communications Inc.] - Enid, OK - *BrCabYB 84; Tel&CabFB 84C*
Enid Eagle - Enid, OK - *BaconPubCkNews 84; NewsDir 84*
Enid Morning News - Enid, OK - *BaconPubCkNews 84; NewsDir 84*
Enigma Records - Torrance, CA - *BillIntBG 83-84*
Enlightment Press - Massapequa, NY - *BoPubDir 4, 5*
Enlon Associates - Cupertino, CA - *TeleSy&SerDir 2-84*
Enmark Corp. (Publishing Div.) - Westbury, NY - *BoPubDir 5*
E.N.M.R. Telephone Cooperative - Clovis, NM - *TelDir&BG 83-84*
Ennis Creative Research Services, Fay - New York, NY - *IntDirMarRes 83*
Ennis Local - Ennis, TX - *Ed&PubIntYB 82*
Ennis Local - *See* United Publishing Co. Inc.
Ennis News [of United Publishing Co.] - Ennis, TX - *BaconPubCkNews 84; Ed&PubIntYB 82; NewsDir 84*
Ennis Weekly Press - Ennis, TX - *Ed&PubIntYB 82*
Enon Valley Telephone Co. [Aff. of Mid-Continent Telephone Corp.] - Enon Valley, PA - *TelDir&BG 83-84*
Enosburg Franklin County Courier - Enosburg, VT - *BaconPubCkNews 84*
Enosburg Standard - Enosburg, VT - *Ed&PubIntYB 82*
Enquirer - Columbus, GA - *AyerDirPub 83*
Enquirer - Bremen, IN - *AyerDirPub 83*
Enquirer - Cincinnati, OH - *AyerDirPub 83; MagIndMarPl 82-83*
Enquirer & News - Battle Creek, MI - *AyerDirPub 83; Ed&PubIntYB 82*
Enquirer-Gazette - Upper Marlboro, MD - *AyerDirPub 83; Ed&PubIntYB 82*
Enquirer-Journal [of Clay Communications Inc.] - Monroe, NC - *AyerDirPub 83; BaconPubCkNews 84; Ed&PubIntYB 82; NewsDir 84*
Enquiry Press [Aff. of Enquiry Associates] - New York, NY - *BoPubDir 5*
Enrep - Luxembourg - *DirOnDB Spring 84*
Enrich/Ohaus - San Jose, CA - *AvMarPl 83; BoPubDir 4, 5*
Enright & Wessel Advertising Inc. - St. Joseph, MO - *StaDirAdAg 2-84*
Enroute - Metuchen, NJ - *BaconPubCkMag 84*
Enroute - Weston, ON, Canada - *BaconPubCkMag 84*
ENSDF-Medlist - Eggenstein-Leopoldshafen, West Germany - *DirOnDB Spring 84*
ENSDF-NSR - Upton, NY - *DirOnDB Spring 84*
Ensign - Fowler, CA - *AyerDirPub 83*
Ensign - Cornwallis, NS, Canada - *Ed&PubIntYB 82*
Ensign Music Corp. - *See* Famous Music Corp.
Ensign Software - Boise, ID - *MicrocomMPl 84; MicrocomSwDir 1*
Ensign, The - San Mateo, CA - *MagIndMarPl 82-83*
Ensign, The - Raleigh, NC - *BaconPubCkMag 84; MagDir 84*
Enslow Publishers - Hillside, NJ - *LitMarPl 83, 84; WritMar 84*
Ensminger Publishing Co./Pegus Press - Clovis, CA - *BoPubDir 5*

Ensslin & Hall - Tampa, FL - *AdAge 3-28-84; StaDirAdAg 2-84*
Enstar Communications Corp. - Walnut Cove, NC - *Tel&CabFB 84C p.1679*
ENSYS Inc. - Houston, TX - *EISS 5-84 Sup*
EntCo Music - *See* Entertainment Co. Music Group, The
Entelek - Portsmouth, NH - *ArtMar 84; AvMarPl 83; LitMarPl 83, 84; MicrocomMPl 83, 84; WritMar 84*
Enter [of Children's Television Workshop] - New York, NY - *MicrocomMPl 84*
Enter Computer Inc. - San Diego, CA - *MicrocomMPl 84*
Enter-Tel Inc. - Beachwood, OH - *AvMarPl 83; TelAl 84*
Enterprise - Prairie Grove, AR - *AyerDirPub 83*
Enterprise - Boron, CA - *AyerDirPub 83*
Enterprise - California City, CA - *Ed&PubIntYB 82; NewsDir 84*
Enterprise - Davis, CA - *AyerDirPub 83*
Enterprise [of Fallbrook Marmack Publishing] - Fallbrook, CA - *AyerDirPub 83; Ed&PubIntYB 82; NewsDir 84*
Enterprise - Ferndale, CA - *AyerDirPub 83*
Enterprise - Los Banos, CA - *AyerDirPub 83*
Enterprise - Pixley, CA - *AyerDirPub 83*
Enterprise - Selma, CA - *AyerDirPub 83*
Enterprise - Douglas, GA - *AyerDirPub 83*
Enterprise - Clayton, IL - *AyerDirPub 83*
Enterprise - Dallas City, IL - *AyerDirPub 83*
Enterprise - Plainfield, IL - *AyerDirPub 83; Ed&PubIntYB 82*
Enterprise - Boswell, IN - *AyerDirPub 83*
Enterprise - Auburn, IA - *AyerDirPub 83*
Enterprise - Coon Rapids, IA - *AyerDirPub 83*
Enterprise - State Center, IA - *AyerDirPub 83*
Enterprise - Macksville, KS - *AyerDirPub 83*
Enterprise - Harlan, KY - *AyerDirPub 83*
Enterprise - Manchester, KY - *AyerDirPub 83*
Enterprise - Bastrop, LA - *AyerDirPub 83*
Enterprise - Franklinton, LA - *AyerDirPub 83; Ed&PubIntYB 82*
Enterprise - Jeanerette, LA - *AyerDirPub 83*
Enterprise - Mansfield, LA - *AyerDirPub 83*
Enterprise - Ponchatoula, LA - *AyerDirPub 83*
Enterprise - Baltimore, MD - *AyerDirPub 83*
Enterprise [of Chesapeake Publishing Co.] - Lexington Park, MD - *AyerDirPub 83; Ed&PubIntYB 82; NewsDir 84*
Enterprise - Brockton, MA - *BaconPubCkNews 84; Ed&PubIntYB 82*
Enterprise - Falmouth, MA - *AyerDirPub 83*
Enterprise - Marlborough, MA - *AyerDirPub 83; NewsDir 84*
Enterprise - Lakeview, MI - *AyerDirPub 83*
Enterprise - Arlington, MN - *AyerDirPub 83*
Enterprise - Cokato, MN - *AyerDirPub 83*
Enterprise - Edgerton, MN - *AyerDirPub 83*
Enterprise - Elysian, MN - *AyerDirPub 83*
Enterprise - Glencoe, MN - *AyerDirPub 83*
Enterprise - West Concord, MN - *AyerDirPub 83*
Enterprise - Cabool, MO - *AyerDirPub 83*
Enterprise - Nixa, MO - *AyerDirPub 83*
Enterprise - Steele, MO - *AyerDirPub 83*
Enterprise - Livingston, MT - *AyerDirPub 83; Ed&PubIntYB 82*
Enterprise - Arthur, NE - *AyerDirPub 83*
Enterprise - Blair, NE - *AyerDirPub 83*
Enterprise - Spalding, NE - *AyerDirPub 83*
Enterprise - Stapleton, NE - *AyerDirPub 83*
Enterprise - Bristol, NH - *AyerDirPub 83; Ed&PubIntYB 82*
Enterprise - Blackwood, NJ - *AyerDirPub 83*
Enterprise - Lancaster, NY - *AyerDirPub 83*
Enterprise - High Point, NC - *AyerDirPub 83*
Enterprise - Wallace, NC - *AyerDirPub 83*
Enterprise - Clyde, OH - *AyerDirPub 83*
Enterprise - Swanton, OH - *AyerDirPub 83*
Enterprise - Wellington, OH - *AyerDirPub 83*
Enterprise - Drain, OR - *AyerDirPub 83*
Enterprise - Mill City, OR - *AyerDirPub 83*
Enterprise - Berwick, PA - *AyerDirPub 83*
Enterprise - Burgettstown, PA - *AyerDirPub 83*
Enterprise - Mullins, SC - *AyerDirPub 83*
Enterprise - Emery, SD - *AyerDirPub 83*
Enterprise - Platte, SD - *AyerDirPub 83*
Enterprise - Viborg, SD - *AyerDirPub 83*
Enterprise - Wilmot, SD - *AyerDirPub 83*
Enterprise - Dresden, TN - *AyerDirPub 83*
Enterprise - Beaumont, TX - *AyerDirPub 83*
Enterprise - Bronte, TX - *AyerDirPub 83*
Enterprise - Edgewood, TX - *AyerDirPub 83*
Enterprise - Frost, TX - *AyerDirPub 83*
Enterprise - Howe, TX - *AyerDirPub 83*
Enterprise - Mercedes, TX - *AyerDirPub 83*
Enterprise - Muenster, TX - *AyerDirPub 83*
Enterprise - New Ulm, TX - *AyerDirPub 83*
Enterprise - Olney, TX - *AyerDirPub 83*
Enterprise - Winters, TX - *AyerDirPub 83*
Enterprise - Ephraim, UT - *AyerDirPub 83*
Enterprise - South Hill, VA - *AyerDirPub 83; Ed&PubIntYB 82*
Enterprise - Kahlotus, WA - *Ed&PubIntYB 82*
Enterprise - Lynnwood, WA - *AyerDirPub 83*
Enterprise - White Salmon, WA - *AyerDirPub 83*
Enterprise - Glidden, WI - *AyerDirPub 83*
Enterprise - Kewaunee, WI - *AyerDirPub 83*
Enterprise - Lodi, WI - *AyerDirPub 83*
Enterprise - Oconomowoc, WI - *AyerDirPub 83*
Enterprise - Cody, WY - *AyerDirPub 83*
Enterprise - Alliance, AB, Canada - *Ed&PubIntYB 82*
Enterprise - Consort, AB, Canada - *AyerDirPub 83*
Enterprise - Chesley, ON, Canada - *Ed&PubIntYB 82*
Enterprise - Yorkton, SK, Canada - *AyerDirPub 83*
Enterprise & Times - Brockton, MA - *AyerDirPub 83*
Enterprise & Vermonter - Vergennes, VT - *AyerDirPub 83; Ed&PubIntYB 82*
Enterprise-Bulletin - Perham, MN - *AyerDirPub 83*
Enterprise-Bulletin - Collingwood, ON, Canada - *AyerDirPub 83*
Enterprise Cable Television Inc. - Enterprise, AL - *BrCabYB 84; Tel&CabFB 84C*
Enterprise-Chronicle - Burlingame, KS - *AyerDirPub 83*
Enterprise Computer Systems - Jacksonville, FL - *MicrocomMPl 83, 84; MicrocomSwDir 1; WhoWMicrocom 83*
Enterprise-Courier - Charleston, MO - *AyerDirPub 83; Ed&PubIntYB 82*
Enterprise-Courier - Oregon City, OR - *AyerDirPub 83; Ed&PubIntYB 82*
Enterprise Group Inc. - Slidell, LA - *Ed&PubIntYB 82*
Enterprise Inc. - San Francisco, CA - *StaDirAdAg 2-84*
Enterprise-Journal - South San Francisco, CA - *AyerDirPub 83*
Enterprise Journal - Enterprise, KS - *Ed&PubIntYB 82*
Enterprise-Journal - McComb, MS - *AyerDirPub 83; Ed&PubIntYB 82; LitMarPl 83*
Enterprise Journal Newspaper Syndicate - Danville, IL - *Ed&PubIntYB 82*
Enterprise Leasing Co. - Medfield, MA - *WhoWMicrocom 83*
Enterprise Ledger - Enterprise, AL - *BaconPubCkNews 84; Ed&PubIntYB 82; NewsDir 84*
Enterprise Network - Billings, MT - *BrCabYB 84*
Enterprise-News - Wittenberg, WI - *AyerDirPub 83; Ed&PubIntYB 82*
Enterprise-News - Arthur, ON, Canada - *AyerDirPub 83*
Enterprise of Southern Idaho - Gooding, ID - *AyerDirPub 83; Ed&PubIntYB 82*
Enterprise Press - Bath, MI - *BoPubDir 4, 5*
Enterprise Publishing Co. - Brockton, MA - *BrCabYB 84*
Enterprise Publishing Co. Inc. [Aff. of Enterprise Ventures Inc.] - Wilmington, DE - *BoPubDir 4, 5; DirMarMP 83; LitMarPl 83, 84; WritMar 84*
Enterprise Publishing Co. Inc. - Blair, NE - *BaconPubCkNews 84*
Enterprise-Record - Chico, CA - *AyerDirPub 83*
Enterprise-Record - Mishawaka, IN - *Ed&PubIntYB 82*
Enterprise-Recorder - Madison, FL - *AyerDirPub 83*
Enterprise-Republican - Delavan, WI - *AyerDirPub 83*
Enterprise-Review - Greenwich, OH - *AyerDirPub 83*
Enterprise Sun & News - Simi Valley, CA - *BaconPubCkNews 84; Ed&PubIntYB 82*
Enterprise Telephone Co. [Aff. of Enterprise Marketing Services Inc.] - New Holland, PA - *TelDir&BG 83-84*
Enterprise, The - Los Angeles, CA - *Ed&PubIntYB 82*
Enterprise, The - Orange City, FL - *Ed&PubIntYB 82*
Enterprise, The - Tangipahoa Parish, LA - *Ed&PubIntYB 82*
Enterprise, The - Vacherie, LA - *Ed&PubIntYB 82*
Enterprise, The - Hastings, NY - *Ed&PubIntYB 82*

Enterprise, The [of Raleigh News & Observer] - Canton, NC - *AyerDirPub 83; NewsDir 84*
Enterprise, The - Rutherford, NC - *Ed&PubIntYB 82*
Enterprise, The - Williamston, NC - *AyerDirPub 83; Ed&PubIntYB 82*
Enterprise, The - Stuart, VA - *AyerDirPub 83; Ed&PubIntYB 82; NewsDir 84*
Enterprise, The - Owen, WI - *Ed&PubIntYB 82*
Enterprise, The - Coquitiam, BC, Canada - *Ed&PubIntYB 82*
Enterprise, The - Iroquois Falls, ON, Canada - *Ed&PubIntYB 82*
Enterprise-Tocsin - Indianola, MS - *AyerDirPub 83; Ed&PubIntYB 82*
Enterprise Wallowa County Chieftain - Enterprise, OR - *BaconPubCkNews 84*
Enterpriser Magazine - Ottawa, ON, Canada - *BaconPubCkMag 84*
Enterprises Culturelles Enr. - La Prairie, PQ, Canada - *BoPubDir 5; LitMarPl 84*
Enterprises Productions Inc. - Malibu, CA - *Tel&CabFB 84C*
Enterprises Unltd. - New York, NY - *AvMarPl 83*
Entertainer, The - Quincy, FL - *AyerDirPub 83*
Entertainment & Sports Programming Network [of Getty Oil] - Bristol, CT - *AvMarPl 83; BrCabYB 84; HomeVid&CabYB 82-83; TelAl 83*
Entertainment & Sports Programming Network - New York, NY - *CabTVPrDB 83; Tel&CabFB 84C*
Entertainment Channel, The - New York, NY - *HomeVid&CabYB 82-83*
Entertainment Communications Inc. - Bala-Cynwyd, PA - *BrCabYB 84*
Entertainment Co. Music Group, The - New York, NY - *BillIntBG 83-84*
Entertainment Coordinators Inc. - New York, NY - *AvMarPl 83*
Entertainment Factory - Cave Creek, AZ - *BoPubDir 4, 5*
Entertainment Group Ltd., The - Roslyn Heights, NY - *AvMarPl 83*
Entertainment Industry Weekly/Entertainment Digest - Beverly Hills, CA - *WritMar 84*
Entertainment Marketing - Houston, TX - *MicrocomMPl 84*
Entertainment New York - New York, NY - *BaconPubCkMag 84*
Entertainment News - Miami, FL - *MagDir 84*
Entertainment Research Inc. - New York, NY - *IntDirMarRes 83*
Entertainment Systems Inc. - St. Petersburg, FL - *TelAl 83*
Entertainment Systems International - Manhattan Beach, CA - *BillIntBG 83-84*
Entertainment Ventures Inc. - Prescott, AZ - *BillIntBG 83-84*
Entheos [Aff. of Entheos Mountain Agriculture Institute] - Bainbridge Island, WA - *BoPubDir 4, 5*
Entity Publishing Co. - Rowland Heights, CA - *BoPubDir 4, 5*
Entomological Reprint Specialists - Los Angeles, CA - *BoPubDir 4, 5*
Entomological Society of America - College Park, MD - *BoPubDir 4, 5*
Entomology Abstracts [of Information Retrieval Ltd.] - London, England - *CompReadDB 82*
Entree - New York, NY - *BaconPubCkMag 84; MagIndMarPl 82-83; WritMar 84*
Entrepreneur Magazine - Los Angeles, CA - *ArtMar 84; BaconPubCkMag 84; MagIndMarPl 82-83; WritMar 84*
Entrepreneurial Manager [of NewsNet Inc.] - Bryn Mawr, PA - *DataDirOnSer 84*
Entrepreneurial Manager's Newsletter [of Center for Entrepreneurial Management Inc.] - New York, NY - *BaconPubCkMag 84; DirOnDB Spring 84; EISS 7-83 Sup*
Entreprises Culturelles Enr. - La Prairie, PQ, Canada - *BoPubDir 4*
Entropy Ltd. - Lincoln, MA - *BoPubDir 4, 5*
Entropy Negative [of Les Recherches Daniel Say Cie.] - Vancouver, BC, Canada - *LitMag&SmPr 83-84*
Entry Publishing Co. Inc. - New York, NY - *BoPubDir 5*
Entwhistle Books - Glen Ellen, CA - *BoPubDir 4, 5; LitMag&SmPr 83-84*
Entwood Publishing - Wausau, WI - *BoPubDir 4, 5*
Enumclaw Courier Herald & Buckley News Banner - Enumclaw, WA - *BaconPubCkNews 84*
Enumclaw Courier-Herald - Enumclaw, WA - *Ed&PubIntYB 82; NewsDir 84*
Envirodoq - Ottawa, ON, Canada - *DirOnDB Spring 84*
Envirodoq [of Quebec Ministry of the Environment] - Ste. Foy, PQ, Canada - *DBBus 82; EISS 83*
Enviroline [of Environment Information Center Inc.] - New York, NY - *DataDirOnSer 84; DBBus 82; DirOnDB Spring 84; OnBibDB 3*
Environment [of Helen Dwight Reid Educational Foundation] - Washington, DC - *ArtMar 84; BaconPubCkMag 84; MagDir 84; MagIndMarPl 82-83; WritMar 84*
Environment [of WATDOC, Environment Canada] - Ottawa, ON, Canada - *CompReadDB 82*
Environment Canada - Ottawa, ON, Canada - *CompReadDB 82*
Environment Canada (Departmental Library) - Ottawa, ON, Canada - *DataDirOnSer 84*
Environment Information Center Inc. - New York, NY - *CompReadDB 82; DataDirOnSer 84; EISS 83; FBInfSer 80; MicroMarPl 82-83*
Environment Information System [of Environment Information Center Inc.] - New York, NY - *EISS 83*
Environment Libraries Automated System [of Library Services Branch] - Ottawa, ON, Canada - *EISS 83*
Environment Report - Washington, DC - *BaconPubCkMag 84*
Environmental Action Foundation - Washington, DC - *BoPubDir 4, 5; MagIndMarPl 82-83; WritMar 84*
Environmental Assessment Data Systems [of U.S. Environmental Protection Agency] - Research Triangle Park, NC - *EISS 83*
Environmental Audit Letter - New York, NY - *BaconPubCkMag 84*
Environmental Bibliography [of Environmental Studies Institute] - Santa Barbara, CA - *CompReadDB 82; DataDirOnSer 84; DirOnDB Spring 84; OnBibDB 3*
Environmental Chemicals Data & Information Network [of Commission of the European Communities] - Ispra, Italy - *EISS 83*
Environmental Communications - Venice, CA - *BoPubDir 4, 5*
Environmental Control News for Southern Industry - Memphis, TN - *BaconPubCkMag 84*
Environmental Data & Ecological Parameters Data Base [of International Society of Ecological Modelling] - Vaerloese, Denmark - *EISS 83*
Environmental Data & Information Service [of U.S. National Oceanic & Atmospheric Administration] - Washington, DC - *EISS 83*
Environmental Data Network for Project Skywater [of U.S. Bureau of Reclamation] - Denver, CO - *EISS 83*
Environmental Design & Research Center - Foster City, CA - *LitMarPl 83, 84; WritMar 84*
Environmental Design Press [Aff. of Educational & Research Management Inc.] - Reston, VA - *BoPubDir 4, 5*
Environmental Design Research Association - Washington, DC - *BoPubDir 4, 5*
Environmental Educators Inc. - Washington, DC - *DirMarMP 83*
Environmental Entomology [of Entomological Society of America] - College Park, MD - *MagDir 84*
Environmental Fate Data Bases [of Syracuse Research Corp.] - Syracuse, NY - *DataDirOnSer 84; DirOnDB Spring 84; EISS 7-83 Sup*
Environmental Forum - Willimantic, CT - *DirOnDB Spring 84*
Environmental Health News [of Occupational Health Services Inc.] - New York, NY - *DataDirOnSer 84; DirOnDB Spring 84*
Environmental Information & Documentation Centers Data Base [of Commission of the European Communities] - Kirchberg, Luxembourg - *EISS 83*
Environmental Information & Documentation System [of Federal Environmental Agency] - Berlin, West Germany - *EISS 83*
Environmental Information Div. [of Environment Agency] - Ibaraki, Japan - *EISS 83*
Environmental Libraries Automated System [of Canada Institute for Scientific & Technical Information] - Ottawa, ON, Canada - *DataDirOnSer 84*
Environmental Mutagen Information Center [of Oak Ridge National Laboratory] - Oak Ridge, TN - *CompReadDB 82; EISS 83; InfIndMarPl 83*
Environmental Mutagens - Oak Ridge, TN - *DirOnDB Spring 84*
Environmental Periodicals Bibliography [of International Academy at Santa Barbara] - Santa Barbara, CA - *DBBus 82; EISS 83; LitMag&SmPr 83-84*

Environmental Press - Buffalo, NY - *BoPubDir 4*
Environmental Press - Austin, TX - *BoPubDir 5*
Environmental Psychology [of Center for Human Environments] - New York, NY - *CompReadDB 82*
Environmental Publications Associates Ltd. - Melville, NY - *BoPubDir 4, 5*
Environmental Research & Technology Inc. - Concord, MA - *BrCabYB 84; EISS 83*
Environmental Research in the Netherlands [of Netherlands Organization for Applied Scientific Research] - Delft, Netherlands - *CompReadDB 82; DirOnDB Spring 84; EISS 83*
Environmental Research Projects Data Base [of Commission of the European Communities] - Kirchberg, Luxembourg - *EISS 83*
Environmental Science & Technology - Washington, DC - *BaconPubCkMag 84; MagDir 84*
Environmental Science Information Center [of U.S. National Oceanic & Atmospheric Administration] - Rockville, MD - *EISS 83; InfIndMarPl 83*
Environmental Studies Institute - Santa Barbara, CA - *InfIndMarPl 83*
Environmental Technical Applications Center [of U.S. Air Force] - Belleville, IL - *EISS 83*
Environmental Technical Information System [of U.S. Army] - Champaign, IL - *EISS 83*
Environmental Teratology Information Center [of U.S. Dept. of Energy] - Oak Ridge, TN - *CompReadDB 82; DirOnDB Spring 84; EISS 83; InfIndMarPl 83*
Environnement [of Environment Canada, Inland Water Directorate] - Ottawa, ON, Canada - *DataDirOnSer 84; DirOnDB Spring 84*
Envirotapes [of Environment Information Center Inc.] - New York, NY - *CompReadDB 82*
Envision - San Jose, CA - *ADAPSOMemDir 83-84*
Envision Corp. - Boston, MA - *AvMarPl 83*
Envo Publishing Co. Inc. - Lehigh Valley, PA - *BoPubDir 4, 5*
Envoy 100 [of Telecom Canada] - Ottawa, ON, Canada - *TeleSy&SerDir 7-83, 2-84*
Envoypost [of Telecom Canada] - Ottawa, ON, Canada - *TeleSy&SerDir 2-84*
Enwood Personnel Agency - New York, NY - *LitMarPl 83*
E.O. Corp., The - Shelby, NC - *TelAl 83, 84*
EO Press [Aff. of The American Institute for Patristic-Byzantine Studies Inc.] - Kingston, NY - *BoPubDir 5*
EOS Transactions - Washington, DC - *BaconPubCkMag 84; MagDir 84*
EP Microform Ltd. - *See* Microform Ltd.
EPA - Leatherhead, England - *DirOnDB Spring 84*
EPA Clearinghouse Technical Reports Database - Washington, DC - *DirOnDB Spring 84*
EPA Instructional Resources Center [Subs. of SMEAC Information Reference Center] - Columbus, OH - *DataDirOnSer 84*
EPB-Electronic Publishing & Bookselling - Phoenix, AZ - *BaconPubCkMag 84*
EPCA Trade Statistics Database - Brussels, Belgium - *DirOnDB Spring 84*
EPD Color Services Inc. - Hempstead, NY - *AvMarPl 83*
Ephemera & Books - San Diego, CA - *BoPubDir 4, 5*
Ephraim Enterprise - Ephraim, UT - *BaconPubCkNews 84; Ed&PubIntYB 82*
Ephrata Grant County Journal - Ephrata, WA - *BaconPubCkNews 84; NewsDir 84*
Ephrata Review - Ephrata, PA - *BaconPubCkNews 84; Ed&PubIntYB 82; NewsDir 84*
EPIC - San Diego, CA - *DirOnDB Spring 84*
Epic - Evanston, IL - *LitMag&SmPr 83-84*
EPIC - Liege, Belgium - *DirOnDB Spring 84*
Epic Computer Corp. - San Diego, CA - *WhoWMicrocom 83*
Epic Computer Products Inc. - Fountain Valley, CA - *DataDirSup 7-83; MicrocomMPl 83, 84*
Epic Publications Inc. - Orchard Lake, MI - *BoPubDir 4, 5*
EPICOM Inc. - Altamonte Springs, FL - *DataDirSup 7-83*
Epicurean Traveler Press - San Francisco, CA - *BoPubDir 5*
Epidemiology Information System - Oak Ridge, TN - *DirOnDB Spring 84*
EPIE Institute - Stony Brook, NY - *LitMarPl 83*
Epigram Music - Ann Arbor, MI - *AvMarPl 83*
Epilepsy Foundation of America - Landover, MD - *BoPubDir 4 Sup, 5*
Epilepsy Ontario [Aff. of Epilepsy Canada] - Toronto, ON, Canada - *BoPubDir 4 Sup, 5*
Epilepsyline [of U.S. National Institutes of Health] - Bethesda, MD - *CompReadDB 82; DBBus 82; DirOnDB Spring 84; EISS 83*
Epilepsyline [of Bibliographic Retrieval Services Inc.] - Latham, NY - *DataDirOnSer 84*
Epimetheus Press Inc. - New York, NY - *BoPubDir 4; LitMarPl 83, 84*
Epiphany Journal [of Epiphany Press] - San Francisco, CA - *WritMar 84*
Epiphany Records Inc. - San Francisco, CA - *BillIntBG 83-84*
Episcopal Book Club [Div. of Society for Preserving & Encouraging the Arts & Knowledge of the Church] - Eureka Springs, AR - *LitMarPl 83, 84*
Episcopal Churchwomen of Christ [of Episcopal Church] - New Bern, NC - *BoPubDir 4, 5*
Episcopal Radio-TV Foundation Inc., The - Atlanta, GA - *Tel&CabFB 84C; WritMar 84*
Episcopalian, The - Philadelphia, PA - *BaconPubCkMag 84; MagDir 84; MagIndMarPl 82-83; WritMar 84*
Epley Associates Inc. - Charlotte, NC - *DirPRFirms 83*
Epling TV Cable Service - Williamson, WV - *BrCabYB 84; Tel&CabFB 84C*
EPM Publications Inc. - McLean, VA - *LitMarPl 83, 84*
EPO Data Banks [of European Patent Office] - Rijswijk, ZH, Netherlands - *EISS 83*
EPO European Published Patent Applications & Patents [of European Patent Office] - Rijswijk, Netherlands - *CompReadDB 82*
Epoca Pulicidad Ltda. - Bogata, Colombia - *StaDirAdAg 2-84*
Epoch - Ithaca, NY - *LitMag&SmPr 83-84*
Epoch Universal Publications - Phoenix, AZ - *BillIntBG 83-84; BoPubDir 4, 5*
Epperson Stations, Stuart - Winston-Salem, NC - *BrCabYB 84*
Eppinger Furniture Inc. - Stamford, CT - *DirInfWP 82*
Eppley, Rudy H. - Millersburg, OH - *Tel&CabFB 84C p.1679*
Eppley, Rudy H. - *See* Millersburg Community TV Systems Inc.
Eppy, Pearl - New York, NY - *LitMarPl 83, 84; MagIndMarPl 82-83*
EPRI Database for Environmentally Assisted Cracking - Columbus, OH - *DirOnDB Spring 84*
EPRI Journal - Palo Alto, CA - *BaconPubCkMag 84*
EPS Consultants Ltd. - London, England - *MicrocomSwDir 1*
EPS, Entertainment Programming Services Ltd. - Toronto, ON, Canada - *Tel&CabFB 84C*
EPS Inc. - Windham, NH - *MicrocomMPl 84*
EPS Inc. [Subs. of EPS Consultants Ltd.] - Houston, TX - *WhoWMicrocom 83*
Epsilon - Burlington, MA - *AdAge 3-28-84; ADAPSOMemDir 83-84; DataDirOnSer 84; StaDirAdAg 2-84*
Epson America Inc. [Subs. of Epson Corp.] - Torrance, CA - *DataDirSup 7-83; MicrocomMPl 83, 84; WhoWMicrocom 83*
Epstein & Associates Inc., Edward - Syosset, NY - *IntDirMarRes 83*
Epstein Communications Inc. - Albuquerque, NM - *StaDirAdAg 2-84*
Epstein Inc., Herbert - New York, NY - *IntDirMarRes 83*
Epstein Ltd., Susan Baerg - Costa Mesa, CA - *EISS 5-84 Sup*
Epstein Public Relations Inc. - New York, NY - *DirPRFirms 83*
Epstein, Raboy Advertising Inc. - New York, NY - *StaDirAdAg 2-84*
Epstein, Vivian Sheldon - Denver, CO - *BoPubDir 4, 5*
EPW & Associates - Toronto, ON, Canada - *DirInfWP 82*
Epyx Inc. - Sunnyvale, CA - *MicrocomMPl 84*
Equa Music - Fremont, CA - *BillIntBG 83-84*
Equa Records - Fremont, CA - *BillIntBG 83-84*
Equal Opportunity - Centerport, NY - *MagDir 84*
Equal Opportunity [of Equal Opportunity Publications Inc.] - Greenlawn, NY - *WritMar 84*
Equal Time Press - New York, NY - *BoPubDir 4, 5*
Equality Telephone Co. - Equality, IL - *TelDir&BG 83-84*
Equatorial Communications Co. - Mountain View, CA - *TeleSy&SerDir 7-83*

Equifax In-House Advertising Agency [Subs. of Equifax Inc.] - Atlanta, GA - *DirMarMP 83*
Equifax Inc. - Atlanta, GA - *ADAPSOMemDir 83-84; EISS 5-84 Sup; KnowInd 83*
Equine Practice - Santa Barbara, CA - *BaconPubCkMag 84*
Equinox - Camden, ON, Canada - *BaconPubCkMag 84; WritMar 84*
Equinox, The [of Society Ordo Templi Orientis International] - Nashville, TN - *LitMag&SmPr 83-84*
Equipment Advertiser Digest - Minneapolis, MN - *MagIndMarPl 82-83*
Equipment Advertiser Digest - Tyler, TX - *WritMar 84*
Equipment Guide-Book Co. - Palo Alto, CA - *BoPubDir 4, 5*
Equipment Guide News - Palo Alto, CA - *MagIndMarPl 82-83*
Equipment Guide News [of Data Quest Inc.] - San Jose, CA - *BaconPubCkMag 84; MagDir 84*
Equipment Journal - Mississauga, ON, Canada - *BaconPubCkMag 84*
Equipment Maintenance - Westmount, PQ, Canada - *BaconPubCkMag 84*
Equipment Management [of The Irving-Cloud Publishing Co.] - Chicago, IL - *MagDir 84*
Equipment Management - Lincolnwood, IL - *BaconPubCkMag 84; WritMar 84*
Equities/Options-Futures/Options-Network [of Monchik-Weber Corp.] - New York, NY - *DataDirOnSer 84*
Equity; New Issues - New York, NY - *DirOnDB Spring 84*
Equity News [of Actors' Equity Association] - New York, NY - *NewsDir 84*
Equity Publishing Co. - Santa Ana, CA - *BoPubDir 4, 5*
Equity Publishing Corp. - Orford, NH - *BoPubDir 4, 5*
Equity Recording Co. - Atlanta, GA - *BillIntBG 83-84*
Equity, The - Pontiac County, PQ, Canada - *Ed&PubIntYB 82*
Equity, The - Shawville, PQ, Canada - *AyerDirPub 83*
Equus - Gaithersburg, MD - *BaconPubCkMag 84; MagIndMarPl 82-83*
ER586 - Washington, DC - *DirOnDB Spring 84*
ER586 [of I. P. Sharp Associates Ltd.] - Toronto, ON, Canada - *DataDirOnSer 84*
ER586/T9 - Washington, DC - *DirOnDB Spring 84*
Era - Bradford, PA - *AyerDirPub 83*
Era - Lanark, ON, Canada - *Ed&PubIntYB 82*
Era - Newmarket, ON, Canada - *AyerDirPub 83*
Era-Enterprise - De Witt, AR - *AyerDirPub 83*
Era Industries Inc. - Culver City, CA - *BoPubDir 4, 5*
Era-Leader, The - Franklinton, LA - *Ed&PubIntYB 82*
Era Research - San Francisco, CA - *Tel&CabFB 84C*
ERA Technology Ltd. - Leatherhead, England - *InfIndMarPl 83*
Era, The - Windber, PA - *Ed&PubIntYB 82*
Erasmus Press - Lexington, KY - *MicroMarPl 82-83*
ERC Reviews - Dayton, OH - *LitMarPl 84*
Ercona Corp. - Bohemia, NY - *AvMarPl 83*
ERDA Div. of Biological & Environmental Research - Washington, DC - *CompReadDB 82*
Erdmann & Partner Werbeagentur GmbH - Dusseldorf, West Germany - *StaDirAdAg 2-84*
Erdos & Morgan Inc. - New York, NY - *IntDirMarRes 83*
Erewon Press - Berkeley, CA - *BoPubDir 4, 5*
Ergo Productions - London, ON, Canada - *BoPubDir 4, 5*
Ergo Soft - San Diego, CA - *MicrocomMPl 84*
Ergodata [of Rene Descartes University] - Paris, France - *DirOnDB Spring 84; EISS 83*
Ergonomics Information Analysis Centre [of University of Birmingham] - Birmingham, England - *EISS 83*
Ergonomics Newsletter - Santa Monica, CA - *BaconPubCkMag 84*
Ergosyst Associates Inc. - Lawrence, KS - *InfoS 83-84*
Ergotron Inc. - Minneapolis, MN - *MicrocomMPl 84*
ERIC [of the National Institute of Education] - Washington, DC - *MicroMarPl 82-83; OnBibDB 3*
ERIC - Bethesda, MD - *DirOnDB Spring 84*
ERIC Center [of University of North Dakota Library] - Grand Forks, ND - *EISS 83*
ERIC ChESS - Boulder, CO - *InfIndMarPl 83*
ERIC Clearinghouse for Junior Colleges [of U.S. National Institute of Education] - Los Angeles, CA - *EISS 83; InfIndMarPl 83*
ERIC Clearinghouse for Science, Mathematics, & Environmental Education [of U.S. National Institute of Education] - Columbus, OH - *EISS 83; InfIndMarPl 83*
ERIC Clearinghouse for Social Studies/Social Science Education [of U.S. National Institute of Education] - Boulder, CO - *EISS 83*
ERIC Clearinghouse on Adult, Career, & Vocational Education [of U.S. National Institute of Education] - Columbus, OH - *EISS 83; InfIndMarPl 83*
ERIC Clearinghouse on Counseling & Personnel Services [of U.S. National Institute of Education] - Ann Arbor, MI - *DataDirOnSer 84; EISS 83; InfIndMarPl 83; LitMarPl 83, 84; MagIndMarPl 82-83*
ERIC Clearinghouse on Educational Management [of U.S. National Institute of Education] - Eugene, OR - *EISS 83; InfIndMarPl 83*
ERIC Clearinghouse on Elementary & Early Childhood Education [of U.S. National Institute of Education] - Champaign, IL - *EISS 83*
ERIC Clearinghouse on Elementary & Early Childhood Education - Urbana, IL - *InfIndMarPl 83*
ERIC Clearinghouse on Handicapped & Gifted Children [of U.S. National Institute of Education] - Reston, VA - *EISS 83; InfIndMarPl 83*
ERIC Clearinghouse on Higher Education [of U.S. National Institute of Education] - Washington, DC - *EISS 83; InfIndMarPl 83*
ERIC Clearinghouse on Information Resources [of U.S. National Institute of Education] - Syracuse, NY - *EISS 83; InfIndMarPl 83*
ERIC Clearinghouse on Languages & Linguistics [of U.S. National Institute of Education] - Washington, DC - *EISS 83; InfIndMarPl 83*
ERIC Clearinghouse on Reading & Communication Skills [of U.S. National Institute of Education] - Urbana, IL - *EISS 83; InfIndMarPl 83*
ERIC Clearinghouse on Rural Education & Small Schools [of U.S. National Institute of Education] - Las Cruces, NM - *EISS 83; InfIndMarPl 83*
ERIC Clearinghouse on Teacher Education [Aff. of American Association of Colleges for Teacher Education] - Washington, DC - *BoPubDir 5; EISS 83; InfIndMarPl 83*
ERIC Clearinghouse on Tests, Measurement, & Evaluation [of U.S. National Institute of Education] - Princeton, NJ - *EISS 83; InfIndMarPl 83*
ERIC Clearinghouse on Urban Education [of U.S. National Institute of Education] - New York, NY - *EISS 83; InfIndMarPl 83*
ERIC Processing & Reference Facility [Aff. of ORI Inc.] - Bethesda, MD - *BoPubDir 5; EISS 83*
Eric Records [Div. of American Record Sales Inc.] - Westville, NJ - *BillIntBG 83-84*
ERIC Reproduction Service [of U.S. National Institute of Education] - Arlington, VA - *EISS 83*
Erichristian - *See* Smithsongs
Erick Beckham County Democrat - Erick, OK - *BaconPubCkNews 84*
Ericksen Advertising & Design - New York, NY - *AdAge 3-28-84; StaDirAdAg 2-84*
Ericksen Associates - Dennison, MN - *MicrocomMPl 84*
Ericson & Associates Advertising Inc., Eric - Nashville, TN - *AdAge 3-28-84; StaDirAdAg 2-84*
Ericsson Programatic Inc. - Rutherford, NJ - *DataDirSup 7-83; VideoDir 82-83*
Ericsson Telephone Co., L. M. - Stockholm, Sweden - *ElecNews 7-25-83*
Erie & Chautauqua Magazine - Erie, PA - *BaconPubCkMag 84; WritMar 84*
Erie Computer Co. - Erie, PA - *WhoWMicrocom 83*
Erie County Cablevision Inc. [of Toledo Blade Co.] - Sandusky, OH - *BrCabYB 84; Tel&CabFB 84C*
Erie County Farm News - East Aurora, NY - *BaconPubCkMag 84; MagDir 84*
Erie County Reporter - Huron, OH - *AyerDirPub 83; BaconPubCkNews 84*
Erie Daily Times - Erie, PA - *BaconPubCkNews 84; Ed&PubIntYB 82; LitMarPl 84; NewsBur 6*

Erie Morning News [of Times Publishing Co.] - Erie, PA - *BaconPubCkNews 84; LitMarPl 83; NewsBur 6; NewsDir 84*
Erie Motorist, The - Erie, PA - *BaconPubCkMag 84; MagDir 84*
Erie Record - Erie, KS - *BaconPubCkNews 84; Ed&PubIntYB 82*
Erie Review - Erie, IL - *BaconPubCkNews 84*
Erie Street Press - Oak Park, IL - *BoPubDir 4, 5; LitMag&SmPr 83-84*
Erie Telecommunications Inc. [of American Television & Communications Corp.] - Erie, PA - *BrCabYB 84; Tel&CabFB 84C*
Erie Times Daily, The - Erie, PA - *LitMarPl 83*
Erikson/Art Services, Mel - Ronkonkoma, NY - *LitMarPl 83, 84; MagIndMarPl 82-83*
Eriksson, Paul S. - Forest Dale, VT - *LitMarPl 84*
Eriksson, Paul S. - Middlebury, VT - *LitMarPl 83; WritMar 84*
Erin Advocate, The - Erin, ON, Canada - *Ed&PubIntYB 82*
Erin Computer Distributing Corp. - Farmingdale, NY - *WhoWMicrocom 83*
Erin Hills Publishers - San Luis Obispo, CA - *LitMag&SmPr 83-84*
Erini Productions - San Diego, CA - *BillIntBG 83-84*
Erisa Benefit Funds Inc. [Aff. of Prentice-Hall Inc.] - Washington, DC - *BoPubDir 4 Sup, 5*
Erisco Inc. [Subs. of Thomas National Group] - New York, NY - *DataDirOnSer 84*
Erish Communications Management - New York, NY - *DirPRFirms 83*
Erlbaum Associates Inc., Lawrence - Hillsdale, NJ - *LitMarPl 83, 84*
Ernco Sales Inc. - Colorado Springs, CO - *AvMarPl 83*
Ernkel Music Co. [Div. of Ernest Kelley Inc.] - Detroit, MI - *BillIntBG 83-84*
Eroica System for Basic Properties of Organic Compounds [of University of Tokyo] - Tokyo, Japan - *EISS 83*
Eros [of Eros Publications Inc.] - Derby, CT - *Folio 83*
Eros [of IFC Entertainment Ltd.] - New York, NY - *BrCabYB 84; CabTVPrDB 83; HomeVid&CabYB 82-83*
EROS Data Center [of U.S. Geological Survey] - Sioux Falls, SD - *EISS 83*
Eros Publishing Co. Inc. - Reseda, CA - *WritMar 84*
Erotic Art Book Society, The [Subs. of Avant-Garde Media Inc.] - New York, NY - *LitMarPl 83, 84*
Erotic Fiction Quarterly [of EFQ Publications] - San Francisco, CA - *WritMar 84*
ERS Advertising Inc. - Princeton, NJ - *StaDirAdAg 2-84*
Erskine Echo - Erskine, MN - *BaconPubCkNews 84; Ed&PubIntYB 82*
Erskine-Shapiro Theatre Technology Inc. - New York, NY - *AvMarPl 83*
Erva-Latvala Oy - Helsinki, Finland - *StaDirAdAg 2-84*
Erville, Herta - New York, NY - *LitMarPl 83, 84*
Erwin Record - Erwin, TN - *BaconPubCkNews 84; Ed&PubIntYB 82; NewsDir 84*
ESA-Quest [of European Space Agency] - Rome, Italy - *EISS 5-84 Sup*
ESANET [of European Space Agency] - Rome, Italy - *InfIndMarPl 83*
Escalon Times - Escalon, CA - *BaconPubCkNews 84; Ed&PubIntYB 82*
Escambia County Beacon - Pensacola, FL - *Ed&PubIntYB 82*
Escambia Sun-Press, The - Pensacola, FL - *Ed&PubIntYB 82*
Escanaba Daily Press - Escanaba, MI - *NewsDir 84*
ESCAP Bibliographic Information System [of Economic & Social Commission for Asia & The Pacific] - Bangkok, Thailand - *EISS 83*
Escapade - New York, NY - *MagIndMarPl 82-83*
Escapade [of Rainbow Programming Services] - Woodbury, NY - *HomeVid&CabYB 82-83*
Escape Computer Software Inc. - Roswell, GA - *MicrocomMPl 83; MicrocomSwDir 1; WhoWMicrocom 83*
Escape Magazine - St. Cloud, MN - *BaconPubCkMag 84*
Escape Records - Baltimore, MD - *BillIntBG 83-84*
Esccomate [Subs. of Environmental Systems Construction Co.] - Omaha, NE - *MicrocomSwDir 1; WhoWMicrocom 83*
ESCOA Co., The - Lexington, KY - *AvMarPl 83*
Escobosa, Paul - San Francisco, CA - *ADAPSOMemDir 83-84*
Escondido Cablevision [of Times Mirror Co.] - Escondido, CA - *BrCabYB 84*
Escondido North Pennysaver - Mission Viejo, CA - *AyerDirPub 83*
Escondido South Pennysaver - Mission Viejo, CA - *AyerDirPub 83*
Escondido Times Advocate [of The Tribune Co.] - Escondido, CA - *BaconPubCkNews 84; NewsDir 84*
Escondido Weekly Free Press - Escondido, CA - *NewsDir 84*
Escondido West Pennysaver - Mission Viejo, CA - *AyerDirPub 83*
Escortguide - Santa Fe, NM - *BoPubDir 4 Sup, 5*
Escrow Music - St. Louis, MO - *BillIntBG 83-84*
ESDIS - Orlando, FL - *DirOnDB Spring 84*
ESDU International Ltd. - London, England - *MicrocomSwDir 1*
ESE - El Segundo, CA - *AvMarPl 83*
ESE California - La Habra, CA - *BoPubDir 4, 5; DirMarMP 83*
ESE Ltd. - Rexdale, ON, Canada - *DataDirSup 7-83*
ESHAC Inc. - Milwaukee, WI - *BoPubDir 4, 5*
Eshenfelder, Alma - New London, CT - *DirPRFirms 83*
ESI Entertainment Systems International - Bogota, NJ - *AvMarPl 83*
ESIC CATV Ltd. - Roxbury, NY - *BrCabYB 84*
Esker Productions - Washington, DC - *LitMag&SmPr 83-84*
Eskofot America Inc. - San Carlos, CA - *DirInfWP 82*
Eskridge Independent - Eskridge, KS - *BaconPubCkNews 84; Ed&PubIntYB 82*
Esmark Inc. - Mishawaka, IN - *MicrocomMPl 84*
Esner, David R. - Brooklyn, NY - *LitMarPl 84*
Esoteric Publications - Phoenix, AZ - *BoPubDir 4, 5*
ESP Computer Resources Inc. - Hollis, NH - *MicrocomSwDir 1; WhoWMicrocom 83*
ESP-Disk Ltd. - New York, NY - *BillIntBG 83-84*
ESP Management Inc. - New York, NY - *BillIntBG 83-84*
ESPA - Elmsford, NY - *BaconPubCkMag 84*
Espanola Rio Grande Sun - Espanola, NM - *BaconPubCkNews 84; NewsDir 84*
Esparza, Moctesuma - *See* Buena Vision Telecommunications Corp.
Esperanto League for North America Inc. - El Cerrito, CA - *BoPubDir 4, 5*
Esperanto Press - Bailieboro, ON, Canada - *BoPubDir 4, 5*
Esperanto Services - Ottawa, ON, Canada - *BoPubDir 5*
Espial Productions - Toronto, ON, Canada - *EISS 83*
Esplanade Enterprises - Falls Church, VA - *MicrocomMPl 83*
ESPN - Bristol, CT - *BrCabYB 84*
Espree Records - Los Angeles, CA - *BillIntBG 83-84*
Espress Inc. [Aff. of National Spiritual Science Center] - Washington, DC - *ArtMar 84; BoPubDir 4, 5; LitMag&SmPr 83-84*
Esprit Systems Inc. (Hazeltine Terminals Div.) - Commack, NY - *DataDirSup 7-83*
Espy Music Group - Studio City, CA - *BillIntBG 83-84*
Esquire [of 13-30 Corp.] - New York, NY - *ArtMar 84; BaconPubCkMag 84; Folio 83; KnowInd 83; LitMarPl 83, 84; MagDir 84; MagIndMarPl 82-83; WritMar 84*
Esquire Publishing Corp. - New York, NY - *DirMarMP 83*
Ess-Jay Ltd. Inc. - Montgomery, AL - *DirMarMP 83*
Essai Seay Publications - Centreville, IL - *BoPubDir 4 Sup, 5*
Essco - Akron, OH - *WritMar 84*
Esselte Documentation System [of Esselte Group of Booksellers] - Stockholm, Sweden - *EISS 83*
Esselte Pendaflex Corp. - Garden City, NY - *DataDirSup 7-83; DirInfWP 82*
Essence [of Essence Communications Inc.] - New York, NY - *BaconPubCkMag 84; Folio 83; LitMarPl 83, 84; MagDir 84; MagIndMarPl 82-83; NewsBur 6; WritMar 84*
Essence Communications - New York, NY - *DirMarMP 83*
Essence Publications [Aff. of Fred Streit Associates] - Highland Park, NJ - *BoPubDir 4, 5*
Esser Cable TV Inc. - Highland, WI - *Tel&CabFB 84C*
Essertier Software Inc. - Hermosa Beach, CA - *MicrocomMPl 84*
Essex Cable TV - Brewton, AL - *Tel&CabFB 84C*
Essex Cable TV - Evergreen, AL - *BrCabYB 84*
Essex Cable TV [of The Essex Group] - Jackson, AL - *BrCabYB 84*
Essex Cable TV [of The Essex Group] - Livingston, AL - *BrCabYB 84*

Essex Cable TV - Satsuma, AL - *Tel&CabFB 84C*
Essex Cable TV [of The Essex Group] - Gulf Breeze, FL - *BrCabYB 84; Tel&CabFB 84C*
Essex Cable TV [of The Essex Group] - Havana, FL - *Tel&CabFB 84C*
Essex Cable TV - Louisville, MS - *Tel&CabFB 84C*
Essex Cable TV [of The Essex Group] - Hendersonville, NC - *BrCabYB 84; Tel&CabFB 84C*
Essex Cable TV [of The Essex Group] - Sparta, NC - *BrCabYB 84*
Essex Cable TV [of The Essex Group] - West Jefferson, NC - *BrCabYB 84; Tel&CabFB 84C*
Essex Cable TV [of The Essex Group] - Bruceton, TN - *BrCabYB 84*
Essex Cable TV [of The Essex Group] - McKenzie, TN - *Tel&CabFB 84C*
Essex Cable TV [of Rogers Cablesystems Inc.] - Leamington, ON, Canada - *BrCabYB 84*
Essex County Republican - Elizabethtown, NY - *AyerDirPub 83*
Essex County Republican - Keeseville, NY - *Ed&PubIntYB 82*
Essex Engineering Co. - Essex, CT - *DataDirSup 7-83*
Essex Group, The - Jackson, AL - *Tel&CabFB 84C*
Essex Group, The - Greenwich, CT - *BrCabYB 84 p.D-300; Tel&CabFB 84C p.1679*
Essex Group, The - Havana, FL - *BrCabYB 84*
Essex Independent - Essex, IA - *BaconPubCkNews 84; Ed&PubIntYB 82*
Essex Institute - Salem, MA - *BoPubDir 4, 5; MagIndMarPl 82-83*
Essex Journal - *See* Worrall Publications
Essex Junction Suburban List - Essex Junction, VT - *NewsDir 84*
Essex Music Inc. - *See* TRO
Essex Music International Inc. - *See* TRO
Essex Nineteen Eighty-Two Operating - Carrabelle, FL - *BrCabYB 84*
Essig, J. - Webster City, IA - *MicrocomSwDir 1*
Essor [of Questel Inc.] - Washington, DC - *DataDirOnSer 84*
Essor - Trappes, France - *DirOnDB Spring 84*
Estacada Clackamas County News - Estacada, OR - *BaconPubCkNews 84*
Estacado Books - Lubbock, TX - *BoPubDir 4, 5*
Estancia Torrance County Citizen - Estancia, NM - *BaconPubCkNews 84*
Estate Book Sales - Washington, DC - *BoPubDir 4, 5*
Estelline Journal - Estelline, SD - *BaconPubCkNews 84; Ed&PubIntYB 82*
Estes Inc., R. Z. - Houston, TX - *DirPRFirms 83*
Estes Park Trail Gazette - Estes Park, CO - *BaconPubCkNews 84; Ed&PubIntYB 82; NewsDir 84*
Estes Park TV Co. - Estes Park, CO - *Tel&CabFB 84C*
Estey-Hoover Inc. - Newport Beach, CA - *AdAge 3-28-84; ArtMar 84; StaDirAdAg 2-84*
Estherville News [of Mid America Publishing Inc.] - Estherville, IA - *BaconPubCkNews 84; NewsDir 84*
Estill Springs CATV Inc. [of US Cable Corp.] - Estill Springs, TN - *Tel&CabFB 84C*
Estimator; Newscost, The - Toronto, ON, Canada - *DirOnDB Spring 84*
Estimators Handbook - Warren, MI - *BoPubDir 4, 5*
Eston CATV Co-Operative - Eston, SK, Canada - *BrCabYB 84*
Eston Press, The - Eston, SK, Canada - *Ed&PubIntYB 82*
Estrada Publications, Billie - Victoria, BC, Canada - *BoPubDir 4, 5*
Esty Co. Inc., William [Subs. of Ted Bates & Co.] - New York, NY - *AdAge 3-28-84; Br 1-23-84; BrCabYB 84; StaDirAdAg 2-84*
Et cetera - New York, NY - *MagIndMarPl 82-83*
E.T. Software Services - Carpinteria, CA - *MicrocomMPl 83*
Etablering [of Market Intelligence A/S] - Hovik, Norway - *CompReadDB 82*
ETC Associates - Oneida, NY - *BoPubDir 4 Sup, 5; LitMarPl 83, 84*
ETC-Educational Technology & Communication [of Far West Laboratory for Educational Research & Development] - San Francisco, CA - *BaconPubCkMag 84; MicrocomMPl 84*
ETC Publications - Palm Springs, CA - *LitMag&SmPr 83-84; LitMarPl 83, 84; WritMar 84*
ETC Services - New York, NY - *IntDirMarRes 83*
Eternal Enterprises - Sacramento, CA - *BoPubDir 4, 5*
Eternal Word Television Network [of The Catholic Cable Network] - Birmingham, AL - *AvMarPl 83; BrCabYB 84; CabTVPrDB 83; HomeVid&CabYB 82-83; Tel&CabFB 84C; WritMar 84*
Eternity - Philadelphia, PA - *BaconPubCkMag 84; MagDir 84; MagIndMarPl 82-83*
Etex Telephone Cooperative Inc. - Gilmer, TX - *TelDir&BG 83-84*
Ether Card Inc. - Malibu, CA - *MicrocomMPl 84*
Etherseries [of 3COM Corp.] - Mountain View, CA - *TeleSy&SerDir 2-84*
Ethics & Public Policy Center Inc. - Washington, DC - *BoPubDir 4, 5*
Ethics Resource Center Inc. - Washington, DC - *BoPubDir 4, 5*
Ethnic Folk Arts Center Inc. - New York, NY - *BillIntBG 83-84*
Ethnic Press International-News Service - Bethesda, MD - *BrCabYB 84*
Ethnodisc Journal of Recorded Sound, The [of Pachart Publishing House] - Tucson, AZ - *LitMag&SmPr 83-84*
Ethnology [of Centre de Documentation Sciences Humaines] - Paris, France - *CompReadDB 82*
Ethnomusicology Publications Group - Bloomington, IN - *BoPubDir 4, 5*
Ethol Chemicals Inc. - Chicago, IL - *AvMarPl 83*
Ethos Public Relations & Advertising Inc. - Ithaca, NY - *DirPRFirms 83; StaDirAdAg 2-84*
Ethridge Books, Blaine - Detroit, MI - *LitMarPl 83, 84*
Etobicoke Advertiser Guardian - Etobicoke, ON, Canada - *AyerDirPub 83; Ed&PubIntYB 82*
Etobicoke Gazette - Etobicoke, ON, Canada - *Ed&PubIntYB 82*
Etowah Advertiser, The - Attalla, AL - *AyerDirPub 83*
Etowah Enterprise - Etowah, TN - *BaconPubCkNews 84; Ed&PubIntYB 82*
Etowah News-Journal - Attalla, AL - *Ed&PubIntYB 82*
Etowah Records - Attalla, AL - *BillIntBG 83-84*
Etowah TV Cable Co. [of National TV Cable Co.] - Etowah, TN - *BrCabYB 84*
Etreby Computer Co. Inc. - Rowland Heights, CA - *MicrocomMPl 84; MicrocomSwDir 1*
ETS Center - Willoughby, OH - *MicrocomMPl 84*
ETS Record Co. - Honolulu, HI - *BillIntBG 83-84*
ETS Test Collection [of Educational Testing Service] - Princeton, NJ - *EISS 5-84 Sup*
ETS Test Collection Database - *See* Educational Testing Service Test Collection Database
Ettenberg, Eugene M. - Southbury, CT - *LitMarPl 83, 84; MagIndMarPl 82-83*
Ettinger Advertising Associates Inc. - New York, NY - *StaDirAdAg 2-84*
Ettinger, Andrew - Los Angeles, CA - *LitMarPl 84*
Ettlinger Associates, John A. - Hollywood, CA - *Tel&CabFB 84C*
Etude Ipsos II Cadres-Informatique - Paris, France - *DirOnDB Spring 84*
ETV Newsletter - Danbury, CT - *BaconPubCkMag 84*
Euclid Computer Inc. - Torrance, CA - *WhoWMicrocom 83*
Euclid Lake County Leader Journal - *See* Post Corp./Sun Newspapers
Euclid Publishing Co. [Aff. of Bond & Bacon Associates] - New York, NY - *BoPubDir 4, 5*
Euclid Sun Journal - Cleveland, OH - *AyerDirPub 83*
Euclid Sun Journal - Euclid, OH - *Ed&PubIntYB 82*
Euclid Sun Journal - *See* Post Corp./Sun Newspapers
Eudised - Strasbourg, France - *DirOnDB Spring 84*
Eudora Enterprise - Eudora, AR - *Ed&PubIntYB 82*
Eudora Enterprise - Lake Village, AR - *AyerDirPub 83*
Eudora Enterprise - *See* Chicot County Newspapers Inc.
EUE/Screen Gems [Div. of Columbia Pictures Industries Inc.] - Burbank, CA - *AvMarPl 83*
EUE/Screen Gems - Chicago, IL - *AvMarPl 83*
EUE/Screen Gems - New York, NY - *AvMarPl 83; Tel&CabFB 84C*
Eufaula Indian Journal - Eufaula, OK - *BaconPubCkNews 84; Ed&PubIntYB 82*
Eufaula Lake Eufaula World - Eufaula, OK - *BaconPubCkNews 84*

Eufaula Tribune - Eufaula, AL - *BaconPubCkNews 84; Ed&PubIntYB 82; NewsDir 84*
Eugene O'Neill Newsletter, The - Boston, MA - *LitMag&SmPr 83-84*
Eugene Register Guard [of Guard Publishing Co.] - Eugene, OR - *BaconPubCkNews 84; Ed&PubIntYB 82; LitMarPl 83, 84; NewsBur 6; NewsDir 84*
Eugene Television - Eugene, OR - *BrCabYB 84; Tel&CabFB 84S*
Eulenburg Miniature Scores - *See* European American Music Corp.
Eunice News - Eunice, LA - *BaconPubCkNews 84; Ed&PubIntYB 82; NewsDir 84*
Eunice Press - Eunice, NM - *Ed&PubIntYB 82*
Euphoria Records - Revere, MA - *BillIntBG 83-84*
Eupora Webster Progress-Times - Eupora, MS - *BaconPubCkNews 84; NewsDir 84*
Eurabank [of European American Bank & Trust Co.] - New York, NY - *DataDirOnSer 84; DBBus 82; DirOnDB Spring 84*
Eurail Guide Annual - Malibu, CA - *BoPubDir 4, 5*
Euramerica Press - Pittston, PA - *BoPubDir 4, 5*
Euramfore - New York, NY - *DirOnDB Spring 84*
Eurarate [of Control Data Corp.] - Greenwich, CT - *DataDirOnSer 84*
Eurasia Language Service Ltd. - New York, NY - *MagIndMarPl 82-83*
Eurasia Press Inc. - New York, NY - *LitMarPl 83, 84*
Eurastar [of European American Bank] - New York, NY - *EISS 83*
Eureka [of University of Illinois] - Urbana, IL - *EISS 83*
Eureka Cable Inc. - Eureka, IL - *BrCabYB 84*
Eureka Herald - Eureka, KS - *BaconPubCkNews 84; Ed&PubIntYB 82; NewsDir 84*
Eureka MDS Communications - Pasadena, MD - *Tel&CabFB 84C*
Eureka Northwest-Blade - Eureka, SD - *BaconPubCkNews 84*
Eureka Press Inc. - Gloucester, MA - *ArtMar 84; BoPubDir 5*
Eureka Publications - Mantua, NJ - *BoPubDir 5*
Eureka Reporter - Eureka, UT - *Ed&PubIntYB 82*
Eureka Reporter - *See* Art City Publishing Co.
Eureka Review [of Orion Press] - Weston, CT - *LitMag&SmPr 83-84*
Eureka Sentinel - Eureka, NV - *Ed&PubIntYB 82*
Eureka Sentinel - *See* Central Nevada Newspapers Inc.
Eureka Springs Times-Echo - Eureka Springs, AR - *BaconPubCkNews 84; Ed&PubIntYB 82*
Eureka Springs Times-Echo & Flashlight - Eureka Springs, AR - *AyerDirPub 83*
Eureka Times Standard [of Humboldt Newspaper Inc.] - Eureka, CA - *NewsDir 84*
Eureka Tobacco Valley News - Eureka, MT - *BaconPubCkNews 84*
Eureka Woodford County Journal - Eureka, IL - *BaconPubCkNews 84*
EURIS [of Departement Serveur de Honeywell Bull SA] - Brussels, Belgium - *InfIndMarPl 83*
Euro Abstracts [of Commission of the European Communities] - Luxembourg, Luxembourg - *CompReadDB 82; EISS 83; OnBibDB 3*
Euro-Argus - Brussels, Belgium - *ProGuPRSer 4*
Euro-Center Communications Inc. - New York, NY - *HBIndAd&MS 82-83*
Euro Tec Publishing - Incline Village, NV - *BillIntBG 83-84*
Euro Tec Records Inc. - Incline Village, NV - *BillIntBG 83-84*
Eurobooks Inc./The Continental Book Co. - Long Island City, NY - *LitMarPl 83, 84*
Eurocharts [of Rudolph Wolff & Co. Ltd.] - London, England - *EISS 83; InfIndMarPl 83*
Eurocharts Commodities [of Eurocharts] - London, England - *DBBus 82*
Eurocom Group - Neuilly sur Seine, France - *StaDirAdAg 2-84*
Eurocom Group - Paris, France - *AdAge 6-25-84*
Eurodata Foundation - London, England - *EISS 83; TeleSy&SerDir 7-83*
Eurodata Syndicated Loan Database - Bala Cynwyd, PA - *DirOnDB Spring 84*
Eurodicautom [of Commission of the European Communities] - Kirchberg, Luxembourg - *CompReadDB 82; DirOnDB Spring 84; EISS 83*
Eurofile - Delft, Netherlands - *DirOnDB Spring 84*
Eurofile [of European Association of Information Services] - The Hague, Netherlands - *DBBus 82*
Eurolex [of European Law Centre Ltd.] - London, England - *CompReadDB 82; DirOnDB Spring 84; EISS 83*
EURONET [of Commission of European Communities] - Kirchberg, Luxembourg - *InfIndMarPl 83*
EURONET-DIANE Launch Team (Enquiry Service) - Luxembourg, Luxembourg - *InfIndMarPl 83*
Europa Records & Tapes Inc. - New York, NY - *BillIntBG 83-84*
Europe: Magazine of the European Community - Washington, DC - *ArtMar 84; BaconPubCkMag 84; MagIndMarPl 82-83; WritMar 84*
European Aluminium Association - Dusseldorf, West Germany - *InfIndMarPl 83*
European American Bank-Eurastar - New York, NY - *DataDirOnSer 84*
European American Music Distributors Corp. [Aff. of Schott Publications & Universal Edition] - Totowa, NJ - *BillIntBG 83-84; BoPubDir 4, 5*
European Art Color - New York, NY - *AvMarPl 83; MagIndMarPl 82-83; Tel&CabFB 84C*
European Association of Information Services - Newport Pagnell, England - *EISS 83*
European Business Associates On-Line - Bertrange, Luxembourg - *EISS 7-83 Sup*
European Business School Librarians Group - Helsinki, Finland - *CompReadDB 82*
European Businessmen Readership Study [of Interactive Market Systems Inc.] - New York, NY - *DataDirOnSer 84*
European Businessmen Readership Study - Wembly, England - *DirOnDB Spring 84*
European Center for Information in Real Time [of General Services & Management Co.] - Paris, France - *EISS 83*
European Commission Host Organization [of Commission of the European Communities] - Luxembourg, Luxembourg - *EISS 83; InfIndMarPl 83*
European Community Investigation Services - London, England - *FBInfSer 80*
European Community Law [of Honeywell Bull] - Brussels, Belgium - *EISS 83*
European Conference of Ministers of Transport [of Organisation for Economic Co-Operation & Development] - Paris, France - *CompReadDB 82; InfIndMarPl 83*
European Coordination Centre for Research & Documentation in Social Sciences - Vienna, Austria - *EISS 83*
European Documentation & Information System for Education [of Council of Europe] - Strasbourg, France - *EISS 83*
European Documentation Centre [of University of Dundee] - Dundee, Scotland - *EISS 7-83 Sup*
European Economic Indicators [of ADP Network Services Inc.] - Ann Arbor, MI - *DataDirOnSer 84; DirOnDB Spring 84*
European Forecast [of Chase Econometrics/Interactive Data Corp.] - Waltham, MA - *DataDirOnSer 84*
European Forecast - Bala Cynwyd, PA - *DirOnDB Spring 84*
European Information Providers Association - London, England - *EISS 83*
European Journal of Cancer - Elmsford, NY - *MagDir 84*
European Judaism - London, England - *LitMag&SmPr 83-84*
European Law Centre Ltd. - London, England - *CompReadDB 82; InfIndMarPl 83*
European Market Research Bureau Ltd. - London, England - *IntDirMarRes 83*
European Media Representatives Inc. - Long Island City, NY - *Ed&PubIntYB 82*
European National Source Data Banks - London, England - *DirOnDB Spring 84*
European National Source Database [of Data Resources Inc.] - Lexington, MA - *DataDirOnSer 84; DBBus 82*
European Patent Office - Rijswijk, Netherlands - *CompReadDB 82; InfIndMarPl 83*
European Patent Register [of European Patent Office] - Rijswijk, Netherlands - *DBBus 82*
European Patents Register; INPI-2 - Munich, West Germany - *DirOnDB Spring 84*
European Petrochemical Association Trade Statistics Database [of Unilever Computer Services Ltd.] - Watford, England - *EISS 83*

European Petrochemical Industry Computerized System [of Perpinelli Tecnon] - Milan, Italy - *EISS 83*
European Primary Aluminium Association - *See* European Aluminium Association
European Publishers Reps Inc. - Long Island City, NY - *MagIndMarPl 82-83*
European Satellite & Space News - Fleet, England - *TeleSy&SerDir 2-84*
European Space Agency - Rome, Italy - *CompReadDB 82*
European Space Agency (Information Retrieval Service) - Frascati, Italy - *DataDirOnSer 84*
European Space Agency (Information Retrieval Service) - Rome, Italy - *InfIndMarPl 83*
European Telecommunications - Morristown, NJ - *BaconPubCkMag 84*
European Telecommunications Satellite Organization - Paris, France - *TeleSy&SerDir 2-84*
European Television Inc. - New York, NY - *Tel&CabFB 84C*
Europro Inc. - Petaluma, CA - *MicrocomMPl 84; MicrocomSwDir 1*
Europrospects-European Economic Indicators [of ADP Network Services Inc.] - Ann Arbor, MI - *DBBus 82*
EUROSTAT - Luxembourg, Luxembourg - *InfIndMarPl 83*
EUSIREF [of Commission of the European Communities] - Kirchberg, Luxembourg - *InfIndMarPl 83*
Eustace News [of Malakoff Territory Times Publishing Co.] - Malakoff, TX - *NewsDir 84*
Eustis Lake Region News - Eustis, FL - *BaconPubCkNews 84; Ed&PubIntYB 82; NewsDir 84*
Eustis News - Eustis, NE - *BaconPubCkNews 84; Ed&PubIntYB 82*
Eustis Telephone Exchange Inc. - Brady, NE - *TelDir&BG 83-84*
Eutaw Green County Democrat - Eutaw, AL - *BaconPubCkNews 84*
Evaluated Nuclear Structure Data [of Lawrence Berkeley Laboratory] - Berkeley, CA - *CompReadDB 82*
Evaluation & Planning Systems Inc. [Subs. of EPS Consultants Ltd.] - Windham, NH - *DataDirOnSer 84*
Evaluation & Research Associates Inc. - Akron, OH - *BoPubDir 4, 5*
Evaluation, Dissemination & Assessment Center for Bilingual Education [Aff. of Education Service Center Region XIII] - Austin, TX - *BoPubDir 4 Sup, 5*
Evaluation Documentation Center [of U.S. Dept. of Health & Human Services] - Washington, DC - *EISS 5-84 Sup*
Evaluation Engineering - Nokomis, FL - *BaconPubCkMag 84*
Evaluation Engineering - Highland Park, IL - *MagDir 84*
Evaluative Criteria Inc. - Stamford, CT - *IntDirMarRes 83*
Evanel Associates - Northfield, OH - *BoPubDir 4, 5*
Evangel [of Free Methodist Headquarters] - Winona Lake, IN - *ArtMar 84; WritMar 84*
Evangel of Canada - Brantford, ON, Canada - *BoPubDir 4 Sup, 5*
Evangelical Beacon, The - Minneapolis, MN - *WritMar 84*
Evangelical Book Club [Div. of Mott Media Inc.] - Milford, MI - *LitMarPl 83, 84*
Evangelical Sisterhood of Mary - Phoenix, AZ - *BoPubDir 4, 5*
Evangelical Teacher Training Association - Wheaton, IL - *BoPubDir 4, 5*
Evangeline Cable Television Inc. - Mamou, LA - *BrCabYB 84*
Evangeline Cable Television Inc. - Ville Platte, LA - *BrCabYB 84*
Evangeline Telephone Co. [Aff. of Century Telephone Enterprises Inc.] - Breaux Bridge, LA - *TelDir&BG 83-84*
Evangelist Association - Chicago, IL - *BoPubDir 4, 5*
Evangelizing Today's Child [of Child Evangelism Fellowship Inc.] - Warrenton, MO - *WritMar 84*
Evanier, David - New York, NY - *LitMarPl 83, 84; MagIndMarPl 82-83*
Evans Advertising Agency Inc. - Mississauga, ON, Canada - *StaDirAdAg 2-84*
Evans & Bartholomew Inc. - Denver, CO - *ArtMar 84*
Evans & Ciccarone Inc. - Miami, FL - *HBIndAd&MS 82-83; StaDirAdAg 2-84*
Evans & Co. Inc., M. - New York, NY - *LitMarPl 83, 84; WritMar 84*
Evans & Motta Inc. - Phoenix, AZ - *ArtMar 84*
Evans & Sutherland Computer Corp. - Salt Lake City, UT - *DataDirSup 7-83; WhoWMicrocom 83*
Evans Communications - Salt Lake City, UT - *AdAge 3-28-84; StaDirAdAg 2-84*
Evans Economics Agriculture Data Base [of Evans Economics Inc.] - Washington, DC - *DBBus 82; DirOnDB Spring 84*
Evans Economics Consumer Price Index Data Base [of Evans Economics Inc.] - Washington, DC - *DBBus 82*
Evans Economics EEICap Data Base [of Evans Economics Inc.] - Washington, DC - *DirOnDB Spring 84*
Evans Economics Financial Data Base [of Evans Economics Inc.] - Washington, DC - *DBBus 82; DirOnDB Spring 84*
Evans Economics Flow of Funds Data Base [of Evans Economics Inc.] - Washington, DC - *DBBus 82*
Evans Economics Forecast Data Base [of Evans Economics Inc.] - Washington, DC - *DBBus 82; DirOnDB Spring 84*
Evans Economics IMF International Financial Statistics [of Evans Economics Inc.] - Washington, DC - *DBBus 82*
Evans Economics Inc. - Washington, DC - *DataDirOnSer 84; EISS 83; InfIndMarPl 83*
Evans Economics Industry Price Index Data Base [of Evans Economics Inc.] - Washington, DC - *DBBus 82; DirOnDB Spring 84*
Evans Economics International Data Base [of Evans Economics Inc.] - Washington, DC - *DBBus 82; DirOnDB Spring 84*
Evans Economics Metals Data Base [of Evans Economics Inc.] - Washington, DC - *DBBus 82; DirOnDB Spring 84*
Evans Economics Producer Price Data Base [of Evans Economics Inc.] - Washington, DC - *DBBus 82*
Evans Economics Regional Data Base [of Evans Economics Inc.] - Washington, DC - *DirOnDB Spring 84*
Evans Economics Regional Forecasting Service Data Base [of Evans Economics Inc.] - Washington, DC - *DBBus 82*
Evans Economics Regional Housing Service Data Base [of Evans Economics Inc.] - Washington, DC - *DBBus 82*
Evans Economics USA Data Base [of Evans Economics Inc.] - Washington, DC - *DBBus 82; DirOnDB Spring 84*
Evans Electronic News Service - Washington, DC - *DirOnDB Spring 84*
Evans Genealogical Services, Norma Pontiff - Beaumont, TX - *BoPubDir 4, 5*
Evans, H. J. - *See* Ohio Video Service Inc.
Evans Inc., David W. - San Francisco, CA - *ArtMar 84; DirPRFirms 83*
Evans Inc., David W. - Atlanta, GA - *ArtMar 84*
Evans Inc., David W. - Salt Lake City, UT - *BrCabYB 84*
Evans, John Edward - Memphis, TN - *InfIndMarPl 83*
Evans Journal - Angola, NY - *AyerDirPub 83; Ed&PubIntYB 82*
Evans Marketing Group Inc., The Joan - New York, NY - *IntDirMarRes 83*
Evans-Parsons Co. - San Francisco, CA - *MagIndMarPl 82-83*
Evans Press Inc. - Ft. Worth, TX - *MagIndMarPl 82-83*
Evans Publications - Perkins, OK - *BoPubDir 4 Sup, 5; LitMag&SmPr 83-84*
Evans Records Group, Frank - Newport News, VA - *BillIntBG 83-84*
Evans Research Corp. - Etobicoke, ON, Canada - *BoPubDir 5*
Evans, Robert L. - Minneapolis, MN - *BoPubDir 4, 5*
Evans, Sam - Kirkland, WA - *Tel&CabFB 84C p.1679*
Evans Telephone Co. [Aff. of Livingston Telephone Co.] - Patterson, CA - *TelDir&BG 83-84*
Evans/Weinberg Advertising - Los Angeles, CA - *ArtMar 84*
Evansdale Blackhawk County Sun - Evansdale, IA - *BaconPubCkNews 84*
Evanston Advantage - Evanston, IL - *Ed&PubIntYB 82*
Evanston Advertising - Evanston, IL - *StaDirAdAg 2-84*
Evanston North Shore Examiner - Evanston, IL - *BaconPubCkNews 84*
Evanston Review - Evanston, IL - *Ed&PubIntYB 82*
Evanston Review [of Pioneer Press Inc.] - Wilmette, IL - *AyerDirPub 83; NewsDir 84*
Evanston Review - *See* Pioneer Press Inc.
Evanston Uinta County Herald - Evanston, WY - *BaconPubCkNews 84; NewsDir 84*
Evansville Cable Television Inc. - Evansville, IN - *BrCabYB 84; Tel&CabFB 84C*
Evansville Courier - Evansville, IN - *BaconPubCkNews 84; Ed&PubIntYB 82; LitMarPl 83; NewsDir 84*
Evansville Courier & Press - Evansville, IN - *LitMarPl 83*

Evansville Data Processing - Evansville, IN - *DataDirOnSer 84; DataDirSup 7-83; MicrocomMPl 83, 84*
Evansville Leader [of Leader Publishing Corp.] - Evansville, WI - *NewsDir 84*
Evansville Post - Evansville, WI - *Ed&PubIntYB 82*
Evansville Press - Evansville, IN - *BaconPubCkNews 84; Ed&PubIntYB 82; LitMarPl 83, 84; NewsDir 84*
Evansville Review - Evansville, WI - *BaconPubCkNews 84; Ed&PubIntYB 82*
Evant TV Cable - Evant, TX - *BrCabYB 84; Tel&CabFB 84C*
Evanton Music - Inglewood, CA - *BillIntBG 83-84*
Evart Review - Evart, MI - *BaconPubCkNews 84; Ed&PubIntYB 82*
Even Time Inc. - New York, NY - *AvMarPl 83*
Evening Bulletin - Providence, RI - *LitMarPl 83*
Evening Capital - Annapolis, MD - *NewsBur 6*
Evening Chronicle - Uhrichsville, OH - *BaconPubCkNews 84; Ed&PubIntYB 82*
Evening Express [of Guy Gannett Publishing Co.] - Portland, ME - *Ed&PubIntYB 82; LitMarPl 83, 84; NewsBur 6; NewsDir 84*
Evening Free Lance - Hollister, CA - *Ed&PubIntYB 82*
Evening Gazette, The [of Worcester Telegram & Gazette Inc.] - Worchester, ME - *NewsDir 84*
Evening Gazette, The - Worcester, MA - *Ed&PubIntYB 82; LitMarPl 83, 84; NewsBur 6*
Evening Herald - Sanford, FL - *Ed&PubIntYB 82*
Evening Herald - Rock Hill, SC - *Ed&PubIntYB 82*
Evening Independent [of Times Publishing Co.] - St. Petersburg, FL - *Ed&PubIntYB 82; LitMarPl 84*
Evening Independent, The - Massillon, OH - *Ed&PubIntYB 82*
Evening Journal [of The News Journal Co.] - Wilmington, DE - *BaconPubCkNews 84; Ed&PubIntYB 82; NewsDir 84*
Evening Journal [of Lewiston Daily Sun Inc.] - Lewiston, ME - *NewsDir 84*
Evening Journal, The [of Ogden Newspapers Inc.] - Martinsburg, WV - *Ed&PubIntYB 82; NewsDir 84*
Evening Leader, The - St. Marys, OH - *Ed&PubIntYB 82*
Evening News [of Newhouse Newspapers] - Harrisburg, PA - *BaconPubCkNews 84; Ed&PubIntYB 82; LitMarPl 84; NewsBur 6; NewsDir 84*
Evening News Association - Detroit, MI - *AdAge 6-28-84; BrCabYB 84; Ed&PubIntYB 82; KnowInd 83; Tel&CabFB 84S*
Evening News, The - Jeffersonville, IN - *Ed&PubIntYB 82*
Evening News, The - Sault Ste. Marie, MI - *BaconPubCkNews 84; Ed&PubIntYB 82*
Evening News, The - New Glasgow, NS, Canada - *BaconPubCkNews 84; Ed&PubIntYB 82*
Evening Observer [of Dunkirk Printing Co.] - Dunkirk, NY - *BaconPubCkNews 84; Ed&PubIntYB 82; NewsDir 84*
Evening Outlook - Santa Monica, CA - *Ed&PubIntYB 82*
Evening Patriot, The - Charlottetown, PE, Canada - *BaconPubCkNews 84; Ed&PubIntYB 82*
Evening Phoenix, The - Phoenixville, PA - *AyerDirPub 83; Ed&PubIntYB 82*
Evening Post Publishing Co. - Charleston, SC - *BrCabYB 84; Ed&PubIntYB 82; Tel&CabFB 84S*
Evening Post, The - Charleston, SC - *Ed&PubIntYB 82; LitMarPl 83, 84; NewsDir 84*
Evening Press-Enterprise, The - Riverside, CA - *AyerDirPub 83; NewsDir 84*
Evening Press, The [of Gannett Co. Inc.] - Binghamton, NY - *Ed&PubIntYB 82; LitMarPl 84; NewsDir 84*
Evening Review, The - East Liverpool, OH - *Ed&PubIntYB 82*
Evening Sentinel, The - Carlisle, PA - *Ed&PubIntYB 82*
Evening Star, The - Peekskill, NY - *Ed&PubIntYB 82*
Evening Sun, The [of A. S. Abell Co.] - Baltimore, MD - *Ed&PubIntYB 82; LitMarPl 83, 84*
Evening Sun, The - Norwich, NY - *Ed&PubIntYB 82*
Evening Sun, The - Hanover, PA - *Ed&PubIntYB 82*
Evening Telegram - Herkimer, NY - *BaconPubCkNews 84*
Evening Telegram, The [of Rocky Mt. Publishing Co.] - Rocky Mt., NC - *Ed&PubIntYB 82; LitMarPl 84*
Evening Telegram, The - Superior, WI - *Ed&PubIntYB 82*
Evening Telegram, The - St. John's, NF, Canada - *BaconPubCkNews 84; Ed&PubIntYB 82*
Evening Times [of Crittenden Publishing Co.] - West Memphis, AR - *BaconPubCkNews 84; Ed&PubIntYB 82*
Evening Times - West Palm Beach, FL - *Ed&PubIntYB 82*
Evening Times - Cumberland, MD - *NewsDir 84*
Evening Times - Sayre, PA - *BaconPubCkNews 84; Ed&PubIntYB 82; NewsDir 84*
Evening Times-Globe, The - St. John, NB, Canada - *BaconPubCkNews 84*
Evening Times, The - Little Falls, NY - *BaconPubCkNews 84; Ed&PubIntYB 82*
Evening Times, The [of New England Newspapers Inc.] - Pawtucket, RI - *BaconPubCkNews 84; Ed&PubIntYB 82; NewsDir 84*
Evening Tribune, The - San Diego, CA - *NewsBur 6*
Evening Tribune, The - Welland, ON, Canada - *BaconPubCkNews 84; Ed&PubIntYB 82; LitMarPl 83, 84*
Evening World, The [of The Miles Co.] - Bloomfield, IN - *AyerDirPub 83; Ed&PubIntYB 82; NewsDir 84*
Event [of Kwantlen College] - Surrey, BC, Canada - *ArtMar 84; LitMag&SmPr 83-84; WritMar 84*
Event Concepts Inc. - Hermosa Beach, CA - *DirPRFirms 83*
Eventide Clockworks - New York, NY - *AvMarPl 83*
Eventide Inc. - New York, NY - *MicrocomSwDir 1; WhoWMicrocom 83*
Ever Ready Label Corp. - Belleville, NJ - *LitMarPl 83, 84*
Ever Ready Packaging & Assembly Corp. [Subs. of Reliance Folding Carton Corp.] - Bloomfield, NJ - *LitMarPl 83, 84*
Everclear Music - *See* Orb Music Co.
Eveready Superior Products [Aff. of Stanislaus Imports Inc.] - San Francisco, CA - *BoPubDir 4, 5*
Everest Advertising Private Ltd. - Bombay, India - *StaDirAdAg 2-84*
Everest House - New York, NY - *LitMarPl 83*
Everest House - *See* Dodd, Mead & Co.
Everest Record Group - Century City, CA - *BillIntBG 83-84*
Everest World, The - Hiawatha, KS - *Ed&PubIntYB 82*
Everett Bedford County Press - Everett, PA - *BaconPubCkNews 84*
Everett Bedford County Shopper's Guide - Everett, PA - *NewsDir 84*
Everett, Brandt & Bernauer - Independence, MO - *AdAge 3-28-84; DirPRFirms 83; StaDirAdAg 2-84*
Everett/Edwards Inc. - Deland, FL - *AvMarPl 83*
Everett Leader Herald & News - Everett, MA - *BaconPubCkNews 84*
Everett Leader Herald & News Gazette - Everett, MA - *Ed&PubIntYB 82; NewsDir 84*
Everett News Tribune - Everett, WA - *BaconPubCkNews 84*
Everett TV Corp. - Everett, PA - *BrCabYB 84*
Everglades Echo - Everglades, FL - *BaconPubCkNews 84*
Everglades Publishing Co. - Everglades, FL - *BoPubDir 4, 5*
Evergreen Canyon Courier - Evergreen, CO - *BaconPubCkNews 84; NewsDir 84*
Evergreen Country Shopper - Ashland, WI - *AyerDirPub 83*
Evergreen Courant - Evergreen, AL - *BaconPubCkNews 84; Ed&PubIntYB 82; NewsDir 84*
Evergreen Film Service - Eugene, OR - *AvMarPl 83*
Evergreen Intercable Inc. [of Jones Intercable Inc.] - Evergreen, CO - *BrCabYB 84; Tel&CabFB 84C*
Evergreen Media Inc. - Edmonds, WA - *StaDirAdAg 2-84*
Evergreen Paddleways - Two Rivers, WI - *BoPubDir 4 Sup, 5*
Evergreen Park Courier - Evergreen, IL - *Ed&PubIntYB 82*
Evergreen Park Courier [of Southwest Messenger Newspapers] - Midlothian, IL - *AyerDirPub 83; NewsDir 84*
Evergreen Park Courier - *See* Southwest Messenger Newspapers
Evergreen Post - Camas, WA - *AyerDirPub 83; Ed&PubIntYB 82*
Evergreen Press - Pleasant Hill, CA - *BoPubDir 4, 5*
Evergreen Press - Walnut Creek, CA - *LitMarPl 84*
Evergreen Press Ltd. - Vancouver, BC, Canada - *LitMarPl 83, 84*
Everly Communications - Everly, IA - *Tel&CabFB 84C*
Everly Royal News - Everly, IA - *BaconPubCkNews 84*
Everman Kennedale News - *See* B & B Publishing Inc.
Everman Times - Everman, TX - *Ed&PubIntYB 82*
Everman Times - *See* B & B Publishing Inc.
Eversaul, George A. [Aff. of Health Research] - Las Vegas, NV - *BoPubDir 4, 5*

Everson, William A. - Sturgeon Bay, WI - *Tel&CabFB 84C*
Everton Publishers Inc. - Logan, UT - *BoPubDir 4, 5*
Everybody - Omaha, NE - *BaconPubCkMag 84; MagDir 84*
Everybody's Bookshop - Los Angeles, CA - *MagIndMarPl 82-83; ProGuPRSer 4*
Everybody's Money - Madison, WI - *MagIndMarPl 82-83*
Everyday Publications Inc. - Scarborough, ON, Canada - *BoPubDir 4, 5; LitMarPl 84*
Eveshaw News Suburban - *See* Suburban Newspapers
EVG Inc. - Freeport, NY - *AvMarPl 83*
EVM Analysts Inc. - Los Angeles, CA - *DirMarMP 83*
Evolutionary Press - San Francisco, CA - *LitMarPl 83, 84*
Evolutionary Press - Santa Barbara, CA - *LitMag&SmPr 83-84*
Evomada - Toronto, ON, Canada - *Ed&PubIntYB 82*
Evotek - Fremont, CA - *MicrocomMPl 84; WhoWMicrocom 83*
Ewanchuk, Michael - Winnipeg, MB, Canada - *BoPubDir 4, 5*
Ewing & Sons, Jasper - New Orleans, LA - *AvMarPl 83*
Ewing & Sons, Jasper - Jackson, MS - *AvMarPl 83*
Ex-Cell-O Corp. - Irvine, CA - *MicrocomMPl 84*
Ex-Cen Cablevision Ltd. - Exeter, ON, Canada - *BrCabYB 84*
Ex Libris Publications - Sewanee, TN - *BoPubDir 4, 5*
Exact Data System - Bloomington, MN - *DataDirOnSer 84*
Exakta Camera - Bohemia, NY - *AvMarPl 83*
Examiner - San Francisco, CA - *Ed&PubIntYB 82; LitMarPl 84*
Examiner - Elizabethtown, KY - *AyerDirPub 83*
Examiner - Aberdeen, MS - *AyerDirPub 83*
Examiner - Independence, MO - *AyerDirPub 83; Ed&PubIntYB 82; LitMarPl 83, 84*
Examiner - Bellefontaine, OH - *AyerDirPub 83*
Examiner - Eckville, AB, Canada - *AyerDirPub 83; Ed&PubIntYB 82*
Examiner - Edmonton, AB, Canada - *AyerDirPub 83*
Examiner - Barrie, ON, Canada - *AyerDirPub 83; BaconPubCkNews 84; Ed&PubIntYB 82*
Examiner - Peterborough, ON, Canada - *AyerDirPub 83*
Examiner - Westmount, PQ, Canada - *AyerDirPub 83*
Examiner & Chronicle - San Francisco, CA - *AyerDirPub 83; Ed&PubIntYB 82; LitMarPl 84*
Examiner-Enterprise - Bartlesville, OK - *AyerDirPub 83; Ed&PubIntYB 82*
Examiner Newspapers - Winfield, IL - *BaconPubCkNews 84*
Examiner Review - Navasota, TX - *AyerDirPub 83*
Examiner, The - Winfield, IL - *AyerDirPub 83; Ed&PubIntYB 82*
Examiner, The - Muskegon, MI - *NewsDir 84*
Exanimo Press - Segundo, CO - *BoPubDir 4, 5; WritMar 84*
Exbond [of Extel Statistical Services Ltd.] - London, England - *DirOnDB Spring 84; EISS 83*
Excalibur Enterprises - Winston-Salem, NC - *DirMarMP 83*
Excalibur Technologies Corp. - Albuquerque, NM - *MicrocomMPl 84; MicrocomSwDir 1*
Excavating Contractor [of Cummins Publishing Co.] - Troy, MI - *BaconPubCkMag 84; MagDir 84; MagIndMarPl 82-83; NewsDir 84; WritMar 84*
Excel Inc. - Oak Brook, IL - *BoPubDir 5*
Excel Telemedia International Corp. - New York, NY - *Tel&CabFB 84C*
Excellorec Music Co. Inc. - Hollywood, CA - *BillIntBG 83-84*
Excelsior Springs Daily Standard - Excelsior Springs, MO - *NewsDir 84*
Exceptional Child Education Resources [of The Council for Exceptional Children] - Reston, VA - *CompReadDB 82; DataDirOnSer 84; DirOnDB Spring 84; MagDir 84; OnBibDB 3*
Exceptional Children - Reston, VA - *MagDir 84; MagIndMarPl 82-83*
Exceptional Parent Press [Aff. of Psy-Ed Corp.] - Boston, MA - *BoPubDir 4, 5*
Exceptional Parent, The - Boston, MA - *BaconPubCkMag 84; MagDir 84; MagIndMarPl 82-83*
Exceptional Press - San Juan Capistrano, CA - *BoPubDir 4, 5*
Excerpta Medica [Subs. of Elsevier-NDU NV] - Princeton, NJ - *DataDirOnSer 84; InfoS 83-84; OnBibDB 3*
Excerpta Medica [of Excerpta Medica Foundation] - Amsterdam, Netherlands - *CompReadDB 82; DBBus 82; EISS 83; InfIndMarPl 83; MicroMarPl 82-83*
Excerpta Medica - *See* EMBase
Excerpta Medica Database [of Excerpta Medica] - Princeton, NJ - *DataDirOnSer 84*
Exchange - Chicago, IL - *BaconPubCkMag 84*
Exchange - Laurinburg, NC - *AyerDirPub 83*
Exchange: A Journal of Opinion for the Performing Arts - Mankato, MN - *LitMag&SmPr 83-84*
Exchange & Commissary News - Westbury, NY - *BaconPubCkMag 84; MagDir 84*
Exchange Network - Palm Beach Gardens, FL - *DataDirOnSer 84; EISS 5-84 Sup*
Exchange, The - Elizabethton, TN - *AyerDirPub 83*
Exchangite, The - Toledo, OH - *BaconPubCkMag 84; MagDir 84*
Excise Tax Rulings [of Revenue Canada] - Ottawa, ON, Canada - *CompReadDB 82*
Exclamation Point! - Billings, MT - *StaDirAdAg 2-84*
Exclusive News Photos - Santa Monica, CA - *Ed&PubIntYB 82*
Exclusive Press Syndicate - New York, NY - *BaconPubCkNews 84*
Exclusively Yours, Wisconsin - Milwaukee, WI - *BaconPubCkMag 84; MagDir 84*
Exec Software - Lexington, MA - *MicrocomMPl 84*
Exec-U-Mail Inc. - New York, NY - *LitMarPl 83, 84; MagIndMarPl 82-83*
Exec-U-Speak - New York, NY - *ProGuPRSer 4*
Execmail [of Executive Software Inc.] - Los Angeles, CA - *TeleSy&SerDir 2-84*
Execom Corp. - Racine, WI - *MicrocomMPl 83*
Execu-Flow Systems Inc. - Union, NJ - *WhoWMicrocom 83*
Execu-Time - Lake Forest, IL - *BaconPubCkMag 84*
Execucom Systems Corp. - Austin, TX - *ADAPSOMemDir 83-84*
Execunet Commercial Service [of MCI Telecommunications Corp.] - Washington, DC - *TeleSy&SerDir 2-84*
Executaries Four Inc. - Pittsburgh, PA - *DirInfWP 82*
Executec Corp. - Dallas, TX - *ADAPSOMemDir 83-84*
Executime - Lake Forest, IL - *MagIndMarPl 82-83*
Executive [of Airmedia] - Weston, ON, Canada - *BaconPubCkMag 84; WritMar 84*
Executive Administrator, The - Akron, IA - *BaconPubCkMag 84*
Executive Advertising - Canton, OH - *StaDirAdAg 2-84*
Executive Air Fleet Books - Center Moriches, NY - *BoPubDir 4, 5*
Executive Communications Inc. - New York, NY - *BoPubDir 4, 5*
Executive Computer Results Inc. - McLean, VA - *MicrocomSwDir 1*
Executive Data Systems - Atlanta, GA - *MicrocomMPl 84; MicrocomSwDir 1*
Executive Data Systems - Roselle Park, NJ - *MicrocomMPl 83*
Executive Education Press - New York, NY - *ArtMar 84; BoPubDir 5*
Executive Educator - Washington, DC - *BaconPubCkMag 84; MagIndMarPl 82-83*
Executive Enterprises - La Jolla, CA - *BoPubDir 4, 5*
Executive Enterprises Publications Co. Inc. - New York, NY - *LitMarPl 83, 84*
Executive Female, The - New York, NY - *WritMar 84*
Executive Fitness Newsletter - Emmaus, PA - *BaconPubCkMag 84*
Executive Golfer - Irvine, CA - *BaconPubCkMag 84; MagDir 84*
Executive Handbooks - New York, NY - *BoPubDir 4, 5*
Executive Housekeeper [of Bowe Communications Inc.] - Glenview, IL - *MagDir 84*
Executive Housekeeping Today - Columbus, OH - *BaconPubCkMag 84*
Executive Information Service Economic Data [of Boeing Computer Services Co.] - Morristown, NJ - *DataDirOnSer 84*
Executive Jeweler - Des Plaines, IL - *BaconPubCkMag 84*
Executive Magazine - San Francisco, CA - *MagDir 84*
Executive Marketing Service Inc. - Houston, TX - *DirMarMP 83*
Executive Micrographic Systems - Arlington, VA - *WhoWMicrocom 83*
Executive Newsweek - New York, NY - *MagDir 84*
Executive of Los Angeles, The - Los Angeles, CA - *BaconPubCkMag 84*
Executive of Los Angeles, The [of Executive Publications Inc.] - Newport Beach, CA - *MagDir 84*
Executive of Orange County, The [of Executive Publications Inc.] - Newport Beach, CA - *BaconPubCkMag 84; MagDir 84*
Executive of San Francisco Bay Area, The - San Francisco, CA - *BaconPubCkMag 84*

Executive Productivity - Boca Raton, FL - *DirOnDB Spring 84*
Executive Productivity [of NewsNet Inc.] - Bryn Mawr, PA - *DataDirOnSer 84*
Executive Program, The [of Macmillan Book Clubs Inc.] - New York, NY - *LitMarPl 83, 84*
Executive Report [of Riverview Publications] - Pittsburgh, PA - *WritMar 84*
Executive Review - Chicago, IL - *BaconPubCkMag 84; MagDir 84; WritMar 84*
Executive Review Publishers - Chicago, IL - *ArtMar 84*
Executive Salary Research Co. - Lima, OH - *BoPubDir 4, 5*
Executive Sport Publications Ltd. - Edmonton, AB, Canada - *BoPubDir 4, 5*
Executive Wardrobe Engineering - Mamaroneck, NY - *ProGuPRSer 4*
Executive Word Processing Inc. - New York, NY - *DirInfWP 82*
Executive Word Processing Service - Tampa, FL - *DirInfWP 82*
Execuware - Charlotte, NC - *MicrocomMPl 84*
Exelrod Press - Pleasant Hill, CA - *BoPubDir 4, 5*
Exeter Abstract Reference System, The [of Exeter University Teaching Services] - Exeter, England - *EISS 83*
Exeter Beachcomber - *See* Exeter News-Letter Co.
Exeter Fillmore County News - Exeter, NE - *BaconPubCkNews 84*
Exeter News-Letter Co. [of Rockingham County Newspapers] - Exeter, NH - *BaconPubCkNews 84; Ed&PubIntYB 82; NewsDir 84*
Exeter News Letter Kingstonian - *See* Exeter News-Letter Co.
Exeter Sun - *See* Mineral King Publishing
Exeter Sun, The - Exeter, CA - *Ed&PubIntYB 82*
Exhaust News - Burleson, TX - *BaconPubCkMag 84*
Exhibit Builders Inc. - Deland, FL - *AvMarPl 83*
Exhibit Corp. - Long Island City, NY - *MagIndMarPl 82-83*
Exhibit Reporter, The [of Dekotek Inc.] - New York, NY - *MicrocomMPl 84*
Exhorters Inc. - Vienna, VA - *BoPubDir 5*
Exide Electronics Corp. - Raleigh, NC - *DataDirSup 7-83*
Exide Electronics Corp. - Philadelphia, PA - *DirInfWP 82*
Exidy Inc. (Data Products Div.) - Sunnyvale, CA - *DirInfWP 82*
Exile [of Exile Editions Ltd.] - Downsview, ON, Canada - *LitMag&SmPr 83-84*
Exile Editions Ltd. - Toronto, ON, Canada - *LitMag&SmPr 83-84*
Exira Audubon County Journal - Exira, IA - *BaconPubCkNews 84*
Exira Journal - Exira, IA - *Ed&PubIntYB 82*
EXIS 1 [of Expert Information Systems Ltd.] - London, England - *EISS 5-84 Sup*
Existential Books - Minneapolis, MN - *BoPubDir 4, 5*
Exit [of Rochester Routes/Creative Arts Projects] - Rochester, NY - *LitMag&SmPr 83-84*
Expanded Media Editions - Bonn, West Germany - *LitMag&SmPr 83-84*
Expanding Images - Mission Viejo, CA - *AvMarPl 83*
Expecting [of Parents Magazine Enterprises] - New York, NY - *ArtMar 84; MagDir 84; MagIndMarPl 82-83; WritMar 84*
Expedition - Philadelphia, PA - *MagIndMarPl 82-83*
Expedition Press - Kalamazoo, MI - *LitMag&SmPr 83-84*
Experience Inc. - Minneapolis, MN - *IntDirMarRes 83*
Experienced Librarians & Information Personnel in Developing... [of Korea Advanced Institute of Science & Technology] - Seoul, South Korea - *EISS 7-83 Sup*
Experimental Mechanics - Brookfield Center, CT - *BaconPubCkMag 84; MagDir 84*
Experimental Techniques - Brookfield Center, CT - *BaconPubCkMag 84*
Expert Systems Inc. - Redmond, WA - *WhoWMicrocom 83*
Expert Typing Service - New York, NY - *LitMarPl 83, 84*
Expertel - New York, NY - *DirInfWP 82*
Expertype Inc. - New York, NY - *LitMarPl 83, 84*
Explorations Institute - Berkeley, CA - *BoPubDir 4, 5*
Explorations Press - Greenfield, MA - *LitMag&SmPr 83-84*
Explore - Calgary, AB, Canada - *BaconPubCkMag 84*
Explorer Books - Birmingham, AL - *BoPubDir 4 Sup, 5*
Exploring [of Boy Scouts of America] - Irving, TX - *BaconPubCkMag 84; MagDir 84; WritMar 84*
Expo Communications - Wilmington, NC - *AvMarPl 83*
Expo/Extra - Wauseon, OH - *AyerDirPub 83*
Expogroup Inc. - New York, NY - *StaDirAdAg 2-84*
Exponent - Reedley, CA - *AyerDirPub 83*
Exponent - Hagerstown, IN - *AyerDirPub 83*
Exponent - Brooklyn, MI - *AyerDirPub 83*
Exponent - Clarksburg, WV - *AyerDirPub 83*
Exponent - Grandview, MB, Canada - *AyerDirPub 83*
Exponent Data Systems Inc. - New York, NY - *WhoWMicrocom 83*
Exponent Ltd. - Walnut, CA - *BoPubDir 4 Sup, 5*
Exponent Telegram - Clarksburg, WV - *AyerDirPub 83*
Exponent, The [of Iowa Engineering Society] - West Des Moines, IA - *BaconPubCkMag 84; MagDir 84*
Export - New York, NY - *BaconPubCkMag 84*
Export & Exportador [of Johnston International Publishing Corp.] - New York, NY - *MagDir 84*
Export Graficas USA - Farmingdale, NY - *BaconPubCkMag 84; MagDir 84*
Export Software International Ltd. - Edinburgh, Scotland - *MicrocomSwDir 1*
Exporter [of NewsNet Inc.] - Bryn Mawr, PA - *DataDirOnSer 84*
Exporter, The - New York, NY - *DirOnDB Spring 84*
Exporters' Encyclopedia World Marketing Guide [of Dun & Bradstreet International] - New York, NY - *MagDir 84*
Exposition Press Inc. - Smithtown, NY - *LitMarPl 83, 84; MagIndMarPl 82-83*
Expositor - Sparta, TN - *AyerDirPub 83*
Expositor - Brantford, ON, Canada - *AyerDirPub 83*
Expositor, The - Fulton County, OH - *Ed&PubIntYB 82*
Exposure - Lake Bluff, IL - *MagDir 84*
Exposure Booths Inc. - Bensenville, IL - *AvMarPl 83*
Expotek - Phoenix, AZ - *MicrocomMPl 84*
Express - Richmond, CA - *BoPubDir 4, 5*
Express - Winters, CA - *AyerDirPub 83*
Express - Thomaston, CT - *AyerDirPub 83; Ed&PubIntYB 82*
Express - Kinmundy, IL - *AyerDirPub 83*
Express - Knoxville, IA - *AyerDirPub 83*
Express - Monticello, IA - *AyerDirPub 83*
Express - Portland, ME - *AyerDirPub 83*
Express [of Management Decision Systems Inc.] - Waltham, MA - *EISS 83*
Express - Superior, NE - *AyerDirPub 83*
Express - Watkins Glen, NY - *AyerDirPub 83*
Express - Chickasha, OK - *AyerDirPub 83*
Express - Lebanon, OR - *AyerDirPub 83*
Express [of Easton Publishing Co.] - Easton, PA - *AyerDirPub 83; Ed&PubIntYB 82; LitMarPl 83, 84*
Express - Lock Haven, PA - *AyerDirPub 83; BaconPubCkNews 84; Ed&PubIntYB 82*
Express - Pleasanton, TX - *AyerDirPub 83*
Express - San Antonio, TX - *AyerDirPub 83*
Express - Vernal, UT - *AyerDirPub 83*
Express - Aylmer, ON, Canada - *AyerDirPub 83; Ed&PubIntYB 82*
Express - Meaford, ON, Canada - *AyerDirPub 83; Ed&PubIntYB 82*
Express - Broadview, SK, Canada - *Ed&PubIntYB 82*
Express & News - Kirksville, MO - *AyerDirPub 83*
Express & News - San Antonio, TX - *AyerDirPub 83; NewsDir 84*
Expressall - Brookline, MA - *BoPubDir 4, 5*
Expression Co. - Londonderry, NH - *BoPubDir 4, 5*
Expressnet Domestic Private Line Service [of RCA Global Communications Inc.] - New York, NY - *TeleSy&SerDir 2-84*
Exshare [of Extel Computing Ltd.] - London, England - *DBBus 82; DirOnDB Spring 84; EISS 83*
Exstat [of ADP Network Services Inc.] - Ann Arbor, MI - *DataDirOnSer 84*
Exstat [of Extel Statistical Services Ltd.] - London, England - *DBBus 82; DirOnDB Spring 84; EISS 83*
Extel Corp. - Northbrook, IL - *DirInfWP 82*
Extel International Bonds Database [of Chase Econometrics/Interactive Data Corp.] - Waltham, MA - *DataDirOnSer 84*
Extel Statistical Services Ltd. [of Extel Group] - London, England - *InfIndMarPl 83*
Extension Network - Alton, NY - *MagDir 84*
Extension Network - Canandaigua, NY - *BaconPubCkMag 84; MagDir 84*
Extension Review - Washington, DC - *MagDir 84*

Extension Telephone Association - White Clay, NE - *TelDir&BG 83-84*
Extension Today - Brazos, TX - *MagDir 84*
External Debt Data Bank - Washington, DC - *DirOnDB Spring 84*
External Debt Data Base [of Data Resources Inc.] - Lexington, MA - *DataDirOnSer 84*
Extra - Medford, OR - *AyerDirPub 83*
Extragalactic Astronomy Group [of University of Texas, Austin] - Austin, TX - *EISS 83*
Extraprize, The [of Fallbrook Marmack Publishing] - Fallbrook, CA - *AyerDirPub 83; NewsDir 84*
Exxec Inc. - San Francisco, CA - *MicrocomMPl 84*
Exxo Systems Corp. - San Mateo, CA - *MicrocomMPl 84*
Exxon Corp. - New York, NY - *Datamation 6-83*
Exxon Office Systems - Stamford, CT - *DirInfWP 82*
Eye - Clinton, MO - *AyerDirPub 83*
Eye Talk - White Plains, NY - *BaconPubCkMag 84*
Eye View Films Inc. - New York, NY - *AvMarPl 83*
Eye-Witness - Birtle, MB, Canada - *AyerDirPub 83*
Eyeball Music - Chicago, IL - *BillIntBG 83-84*
Eyecontact - New York, NY - *LitMarPl 83*
Eyescan - London, England - *IntDirMarRes 83*
E.Y.R. Programs Inc. - New York, NY - *Tel&CabFB 84C*
Eyring Research Institute Inc. - Provo, UT - *MicrocomMPl 83, 84*
EZ Communications Inc. - Fairfax, VA - *BrCabYB 84*
EZ Cookin' Book Co. - Fountain Valley, CA - *BoPubDir 5*

F

F & F Cable Corp. - Lockney, TX - *Tel&CabFB 84C*
F & L Associates - Long Beach, CA - *BoPubDir 5*
F. & M. Telephone Co. - Farber, MO - *TelDir&BG 83-84*
F & S Ltd. Inc. - Daytona Beach, FL - *LitMarPl 83, 84*
F & S Political Risk Letter - New York, NY - *DirOnDB Spring 84*
F & S Political Risk Letter [of NewsNet Inc.] - Bryn Mawr, PA - *DataDirOnSer 84*
F & S Press [Div. of Frost & Sullivan Inc.] - New York, NY - *LitMarPl 83, 84*
F & SF Book Co. Inc. - Staten Island, NY - *LitMarPl 83, 84*
F & W Publishing Co. - Cincinnati, OH - *DirMarMP 83*
F-V Sound Ltd. - New York, NY - *AvMarPl 83*
F.A. Components - Elmhurst, NY - *MicrocomMPl 84*
FAA General Aviation News [of FAA/DOT] - Washington, DC - *BaconPubCkMag 84; MagDir 84*
Fabbri Representative Offices Inc. [Subs. of Gruppo Editoriale Fabbri] - New York, NY - *LitMarPl 83, 84*
Fabens Valley Independent - Fabens, TX - *BaconPubCkNews 84*
Faber & Co. - Greensboro, NC - *IntDirMarRes 83*
Faber & Faber Inc. [Div. of Faber & Faber Publishers Ltd.] - Winchester, MA - *LitMarPl 83, 84*
Faber Inc., Eberhard - Wilkes-Barre, PA - *AvMarPl 83*
Faber Media Inc., Neil - New York, NY - *StaDirAdAg 2-84*
Faber Shervey Advertising - Minneapolis, MN - *AdAge 3-28-84; DirPRFirms 83; StaDirAdAg 2-84*
Fablewaves Press - Van Nuys, CA - *BoPubDir 4, 5; LitMag&SmPr 83-84*
Fabmath - Warrington, PA - *BoPubDir 4, 5*
Fabricator, The - Rockford, IL - *BaconPubCkMag 84; MagDir 84; MagIndMarPl 82-83*
Fabricnews - New York, NY - *BaconPubCkMag 84; MagDir 84*
Fabrimetal [of Center for Scientific & Technical Research for the Metal Manufacturing Industry] - Brussels, Belgium - *EISS 83; InfIndMarPl 83*
Fabtronics - Brockport, NY - *MicrocomMPl 84*
Fabulous Forgeries Ltd. - New York, NY - *ArtMar 84*
Face to Face - Nashville, TN - *MagDir 84; WritMar 84*
Facemate Corp. - Chicopee, MA - *LitMarPl 83, 84*
Facet Communications - Cincinnati, OH - *TeleSy&SerDir 2-84; WritMar 84*
Facets - Chicago, IL - *MagDir 84; MagIndMarPl 82-83; WritMar 84*
Fachinformationszentrum Chemie GmbH - Berlin, West Germany - *InfIndMarPl 83*
Fachinformationszentrum Energie, Physik, Mathematik GmbH, Karlsruhe - Leopoldshafen, West Germany - *InfIndMarPl 83*
Fachinformationszentrum Energie, Physik, Mathematik GmbH, Karlsruhe (Kernforschungszentrum) - Leopoldshaften, West Germany - *CompReadDB 82*
Fachinformationszentrum Technik eV - Frankfurt, West Germany - *InfIndMarPl 83*
Fachinformationszentrum Technik eV (Dokumentation Maschinenbau) - Frankfurt, West Germany - *CompReadDB 82*
Fachinformationszentrum Technik eV (Zentralstelle Dokumentation Elektrotechnik) - Frankfurt, West Germany - *CompReadDB 82*
Facilitation House - Ottawa, IL - *BoPubDir 4, 5*
Facilities & Services Corp. - Los Angeles, CA - *DataDirOnSer 84*
Facilities Design & Management - New York, NY - *BaconPubCkMag 84; MagDir 84; MagIndMarPl 82-83*
Facility for the Analysis of Chemical Thermodynamics [of McGill University] - Montreal, PQ, Canada - *EISS 83*
Facing South - Durham, NC - *Ed&PubIntYB 82*
Facit-Addo Inc. - Greenwich, CT - *DirInfWP 82; WhoWMicrocom 83*
Facit-Addo Inc. (Data Products Div.) - Greenwich, CT - *DirInfWP 82*
Facit Inc. - Nashua, NH - *DataDirSup 7-83; MicrocomMPl 84*
Fackelman Newspapers - Panama City, FL - *Ed&PubIntYB 82*
Facs Inc. - Washington, DC - *EISS 7-83 Sup; FBInfSer 80; InfIndMarPl 83*
Fact - New York, NY - *BaconPubCkMag 84; WritMar 84*
Fact - Montreal, PQ, Canada - *DirOnDB Spring 84*
Fact, Figures & Film - Syosset, NY - *BaconPubCkMag 84*
Fact Finders - Ridgewood, NJ - *FBInfSer 80*
Factfinders Service [of Control Data Corp.] - Minneapolis, MN - *InfIndMarPl 83*
Factline Inc. - New York, NY - *IntDirMarRes 83*
Factmatcher [of Mini-Computer Systems Inc.] - Elmsford, NY - *EISS 83*
Factor Associates Inc., Mallory - New York, NY - *ArtMar 84; DirPRFirms 83*
Facts - Redlands, CA - *AyerDirPub 83*
Facts - Falfurrias, TX - *AyerDirPub 83*
Facts Center - New York, NY - *IntDirMarRes 83*
Facts Consolidated - Los Angeles, CA - *Tel&CabFB 84C*
Facts for a Fee [of Cleveland Public Library] - Cleveland, OH - *EISS 83; FBInfSer 80; InfIndMarPl 83*
Facts Management Systems - Coral Gables, FL - *MicrocomMPl 84*
Facts 'n Figures - Panorama City, CA - *IntDirMarRes 83*
Facts News - Seattle, WA - *Ed&PubIntYB 82*
Facts of Bayonne - Bayonne, NJ - *AyerDirPub 83*
Facts on File [Subs. of Commerce Clearing House Inc.] - New York, NY - *DirMarMP 83; DirOnDB Spring 84; EISS 5-84 Sup; LitMarPl 83, 84; MicroMarPl 82-83; ProGuPRSer 4; WritMar 84*
Facts Shoppers' Guide - Redlands, CA - *AyerDirPub 83*
Faculty Press Inc. - Brooklyn, NY - *LitMarPl 83, 84; MagIndMarPl 82-83*
Fade In Publishers - Bozeman, MT - *BoPubDir 4, 5*
Fadell Advertising Agency, Mike - Minneapolis, MN - *StaDirAdAg 2-84; TelAl 83, 84*
Fag Rag Books - Boston, MA - *BoPubDir 4, 5; LitMag&SmPr 83-84*
Fahlgren & Ferriss Inc. - Cincinnati, OH - *BrCabYB 84; TelAl 83, 84*

Fahlgren & Ferriss Inc. - Toledo, OH - *ArtMar 84*
Fahlgren & Ferriss Inc. - Parkersburg, WV - *AdAge 3-28-84; DirPRFirms 83; StaDirAdAg 2-84*
Fain Advertising, Michael - New York, NY - *ArtMar 84; StaDirAdAg 2-84*
Fainshaw Press [Aff. of B. R. Smith & Associates Inc.] - Westmoreland, NH - *BoPubDir 4 Sup, 5*
Fair Copy: Consultation in Writing - San Francisco, CA - *LitMarPl 83*
Fair Haven Register - Fair Haven, NY - *Ed&PubIntYB 82*
Fair Haven Register - Red Creek, NY - *NewsDir 84*
Fair Haven Register - *See* Wayuga Community Newspapers Inc.
Fair International - New York, NY - *BaconPubCkMag 84*
Fair Lawn-Elmwood Park-Saddle Brook Shopper - Fair Lawn, NJ - *AyerDirPub 83*
Fair Lawn News-Beacon - Fair Lawn, NJ - *BaconPubCkNews 84; NewsDir 84*
Fair Lawn Shopper - Fair Lawn, NJ - *Ed&PubIntYB 82*
Fair Water-Brandon-Alto Telephone Co. - Brandon, WI - *TelDir&BG 83-84*
Fairbank Associates - Floral Park, NY - *MagIndMarPl 82-83*
Fairbank Sun - Evansdale, IA - *AyerDirPub 83*
Fairbanks Broadcasting Co. - West Palm Beach, FL - *BrCabYB 84*
Fairbanks Broadcasting Co. - Indianapolis, IN - *Tel&CabFB 84C p.1679*
Fairbanks Cable of Florida Inc. [of Fairbanks Broadcasting Co.] - Delray Beach, FL - *BrCabYB 84*
Fairbanks Daily News Miner - Fairbanks, AK - *BaconPubCkNews 84; Ed&PubIntYB 82; NewsDir 84*
Fairbanks Productions, Jerry - Hollywood, CA - *TelAl 83, 84; Tel&CabFB 84C*
Fairborn Daily Herald [of Miami Valley Publishing Co.] - Fairborn, OH - *BaconPubCkNews 84; Ed&PubIntYB 82; NewsDir 84*
Fairbury Blade - Fairbury, IL - *Ed&PubIntYB 82*
Fairbury Blade - *See* Cornbelt Press Inc.
Fairbury Cablevision [of MetroVision Inc.] - Fairbury, NE - *Tel&CabFB 84C*
Fairbury Journal-News - Fairbury, NE - *BaconPubCkNews 84; Ed&PubIntYB 82; NewsDir 84*
Fairchild Books & Visuals [Div. of Fairchild Publications] - New York, NY - *AvMarPl 83; LitMarPl 83, 84*
Fairchild Books & Visuals (Book Div.) - New York, NY - *WritMar 84*
Fairchild Broadcast News - New York, NY - *BrCabYB 84*
Fairchild Music Publishing Corp. - Buena Park, CA - *BillIntBG 83-84*
Fairchild News Service - Cleveland, OH - *NewsBur 6*
Fairchild Publications [Div. of Capital Cities Media Inc.] - New York, NY - *DirMarMP 83; MagIndMarPl 82-83; NewsBur 6*
Fairchild Publications Inc. - *See* Capital Cities Communications Inc.
Fairchild Publications on Microfilm - New York, NY - *MicroMarPl 82-83*
Fairchild Syndicate - New York, NY - *BaconPubCkNews 84; Ed&PubIntYB 82*
FAIReC [of Questel Inc.] - Washington, DC - *DataDirOnSer 84*
FAIReC - Paris, France - *DirOnDB Spring 84*
Fairfax Advertising - New York, NY - *AdAge 3-28-84*
Fairfax Chief - Fairfax, OK - *BaconPubCkNews 84; Ed&PubIntYB 82*
Fairfax Forum - Fairfax, MO - *BaconPubCkNews 84; Ed&PubIntYB 82*
Fairfax Inc. [Subs. of Compton Advertising Inc.] - New York, NY - *BrCabYB 84; StaDirAdAg 2-84; TelAl 83, 84*
Fairfax Journal - Fairfax, VA - *AyerDirPub 83*
Fairfax Journal [of Journal Newspapers] - Springfield, VA - *NewsDir 84*
Fairfax Journal - *See* Journal Newspapers
Fairfax Journal, The - Washington, DC - *Ed&PubIntYB 82*
Fairfax Standard - Fairfax, MN - *BaconPubCkNews 84; Ed&PubIntYB 82*
Fairfield Advocate - Bridgeport, CT - *AyerDirPub 83*
Fairfield Book Co. Inc. - Brookfield Center, CT - *BoPubDir 4 Sup, 5*
Fairfield Broadcasting Co. - Kalamazoo, MI - *BrCabYB 84*
Fairfield Cable TV [of J. M. Schultz Investment Co.] - Fairfield, IL - *BrCabYB 84; Tel&CabFB 84C*
Fairfield Cable TV [of Cable Communications of Iowa] - Fairfield, IA - *BrCabYB 84*
Fairfield Cable TV - Fairfield, MT - *BrCabYB 84*
Fairfield Cablevision [of Nationwide Communications Inc.] - Baltimore, OH - *Tel&CabFB 84C*
Fairfield Cablevision [of Nationwide Communications Inc.] - Circleville, OH - *Tel&CabFB 84C*
Fairfield Cablevision [of Nationwide Communications Inc.] - Lancaster, OH - *BrCabYB 84; Tel&CabFB 84C*
Fairfield Cablevision [of Nationwide Communications Inc.] - Pataskala, OH - *BrCabYB 84; Tel&CabFB 84C*
Fairfield Citizen - *See* Brooks Community Newspapers
Fairfield Citizen-News - Westport, CT - *Ed&PubIntYB 82*
Fairfield Citizen News & Weekly Trader [of Westport News] - Westport, CT - *NewsDir 84*
Fairfield Communications - Green Valley, AZ - *BrCabYB 84; InterCabHB 3; Tel&CabFB 84C*
Fairfield County Advocate [of New Mass Media Inc.] - Bridgeport, CT - *NewsDir 84*
Fairfield County Press - Yonkers, NY - *AyerDirPub 83*
Fairfield Daily Republic [of Fairfield Publishing Co.] - Fairfield, CA - *NewsDir 84*
Fairfield Echo - Fairfield, OH - *BaconPubCkNews 84; Ed&PubIntYB 82*
Fairfield Echo [of Harte-Hanks Communications] - Hamilton, OH - *AyerDirPub 83; NewsDir 84*
Fairfield, Francoise - Westland, MI - *LitMarPl 83, 84*
Fairfield Graphics [Div. of Arcata Graphics Co.] - Fairfield, PA - *LitMarPl 84*
Fairfield-Hamilton Sun - *See* Queen City Suburban Press Inc.
Fairfield Herald - Caldwell, NJ - *NewsDir 84*
Fairfield Herald - *See* Lincoln Park Herald Inc.
Fairfield House - Baltimore, MD - *BoPubDir 4, 5*
Fairfield Leader - Baltimore, OH - *Ed&PubIntYB 82*
Fairfield Ledger - Fairfield, IA - *BaconPubCkNews 84; Ed&PubIntYB 82; NewsDir 84*
Fairfield Recorder - Fairfield, TX - *BaconPubCkNews 84; Ed&PubIntYB 82*
Fairfield Sun - Fairfield, OH - *Ed&PubIntYB 82*
Fairfield Times - Fairfield, MT - *BaconPubCkNews 84; Ed&PubIntYB 82*
Fairfield Travis AFB Tailwind - Fairfield, CA - *NewsDir 84*
Fairfield Wayne County Press - Fairfield, IL - *BaconPubCkNews 84; NewsDir 84*
Fairhope Eastern Shore Courier - Fairhope, AL - *BaconPubCkNews 84; NewsDir 84*
Fairisher Press, The - Rapid City, SD - *LitMag&SmPr 83-84*
Fairleigh Dickinson University Press - Madison, NJ - *LitMarPl 83, 84*
Fairless Union News - Fairless Heights, PA - *NewsDir 84*
Fairmont Photo Press - Fairmont, MN - *BaconPubCkNews 84; NewsDir 84*
Fairmont Press Inc. - Atlanta, GA - *LitMarPl 83, 84; WritMar 84*
Fairmont Records - Santa Monica, CA - *BillIntBG 83-84*
Fairmont Sentinel - Fairmont, MN - *BaconPubCkNews 84; NewsDir 84*
Fairmont Times Messenger - Fairmont, NC - *BaconPubCkNews 84*
Fairmont Times-West Virginian - Fairmont, WV - *BaconPubCkNews 84*
Fairmount Advertising - Ft. Washington, PA - *StaDirAdAg 2-84*
Fairmount Cable TV Inc. - Fairmount, GA - *Tel&CabFB 84C*
Fairmount News - Fairmount, ND - *AyerDirPub 83; Ed&PubIntYB 82*
Fairmount News - *See* Richland Publishing Co.
Fairmount News-Sun - Fairmount, IN - *BaconPubCkNews 84*
Fairmount News, The - Fairmount, IN - *Ed&PubIntYB 82*
Fairmount Telephone Co. Inc. - Fairmount, GA - *TelDir&BG 83-84*
Fairplay International Research Services [of Fairplay Publications Ltd.] - London, England - *EISS 7-83 Sup*
Fairplay Park County Republican & Flume - Fairplay, CO - *BaconPubCkNews 84*
Fairport Community TV [of American Cable Co.] - Fairport, NY - *BrCabYB 84*

Fairport Herald Mail - *See* Empire State Weeklies
Fairport/Penfield Shopping News - Fairport, NY - *AyerDirPub 83*
Fairport Perinton Herald Mail - Fairport, NY - *AyerDirPub 83*
Fairport Perinton Herald Mail [of Empire State Weeklies] - Webster, NY - *NewsDir 84*
Fairpress [of The Gannett Co.] - Norwalk, CT - *AyerDirPub 83; Ed&PubIntYB 82; NewsDir 84*
Fairview Audio-Visual Co. - Tulsa, OK - *AvMarPl 83*
Fairview Community Hospitals (MIS Div.) - Minneapolis, MN - *ADAPSOMemDir 83-84*
Fairview Enterprise - Fairview, KS - *BaconPubCkNews 84; Ed&PubIntYB 82*
Fairview Heights Journal - Fairview Heights, IL - *Ed&PubIntYB 82*
Fairview Heights Journal - *See* Journal Newspapers of Southern Illinois
Fairview Heights/O'Fallon Journal - Fairview Heights, IL - *AyerDirPub 83*
Fairview Heights/O'Fallon Journal - O'Fallon, IL - *Ed&PubIntYB 82*
Fairview Heights Tribune [of Yelvington Publications] - East St. Louis, IL - *NewsDir 84*
Fairview News - Fairview, MT - *AyerDirPub 83; BaconPubCkNews 84; Ed&PubIntYB 82*
Fairview News - Fairview, NJ - *NewsDir 84*
Fairview Post - Fairview, AB, Canada - *Ed&PubIntYB 82*
Fairview Republican - Fairview, OK - *BaconPubCkNews 84; Ed&PubIntYB 82*
Fairview TV Cable System [of Dorate Inc.] - Fairview, OK - *BrCabYB 84; Tel&CabFB 84C*
Fairview Video - Jeffersonville, PA - *AvMarPl 83*
Fairway Sun [of Overland Park Sun Newspapers] - Shawnee Mission, KS - *NewsDir 84*
Fairway Sun - *See* Sun Publications
Fairystone Publishing Co. - Rocky Mt., VA - *BillIntBG 83-84*
Faith & Form [of Interfaith Forum on Religion, Art, & Architecture] - Washington, DC - *BaconPubCkMag 84; MagDir 84*
Faith & Inspiration [of Seraphim Publishing Group Inc.] - Scarsdale, NY - *MagIndMarPl 82-83; WritMar 84*
Faith & Life Press [Aff. of General Conference Mennonite Church] - Newton, KS - *BoPubDir 4, 5*
Faith/at/Work - Columbia, MD - *MagDir 84*
Faith Center Inc. [of Faith Center Global Ministries Inc.] - Glendale, CA - *BrCabYB 84*
Faith for Today - Newbury Park, CA - *Tel&CabFB 84C*
Faith Independent - Faith, SD - *BaconPubCkNews 84; Ed&PubIntYB 82*
Faith Music Inc. - *See* Lillenas Publishing Co.
Faith Publications - Lubbock, TX - *BoPubDir 4, 5*
Faith Publishing House Inc. - Guthrie, OK - *BoPubDir 4, 5*
Falco Data Products - Sunnyvale, CA - *DataDirSup 7-83*
Falcon Ad Agency Inc. - Tokyo, Japan - *StaDirAdAg 2-84*
Falcon Cable Corp. [of Falcon Communications Inc.] - Atascadero, CA - *BrCabYB 84; Tel&CabFB 84C*
Falcon Cable TV [of Falcon Communications Inc.] - Alhambra, CA - *Tel&CabFB 84C*
Falcon Cable TV - Altadena, CA - *BrCabYB 84*
Falcon Cable TV [of Falcon Communications] - Montebello, CA - *BrCabYB 84*
Falcon Cable TV [of Falcon Communications] - Monterey Park, CA - *BrCabYB 84*
Falcon Cable TV [of Falcon Communications Inc.] - Norwalk, CA - *Tel&CabFB 84C*
Falcon Cable TV of Northern California [of Falcon Communications] - Gilroy, CA - *BrCabYB 84*
Falcon Cable TV of Northern California [of Falcon Communications Inc.] - Gonzales, CA - *BrCabYB 84; Tel&CabFB 84C*
Falcon Cable TV of Northern California [of Falcon Communications Inc.] - Hollister, CA - *BrCabYB 84; Tel&CabFB 84C*
Falcon Cable TV of Northern California - Live Oak, CA - *BrCabYB 84*
Falcon Cable TV of Northern California [of Falcon Communications Inc.] - Morgan Hill, CA - *BrCabYB 84; Tel&CabFB 84C*
Falcon Cable TV of Northern California [of Falcon Communications] - Soledad, CA - *BrCabYB 84; Tel&CabFB 84C*
Falcon Cable TV of Southern California [of Falcon Communications Inc.] - Altadena, CA - *Tel&CabFB 84C*
Falcon Cable TV of Southern California [of Falcon Communications Inc.] - La Canada, CA - *Tel&CabFB 84C*
Falcon Cable TV of Southern California [of Falcon Communications Inc.] - Pasadena, CA - *BrCabYB 84*
Falcon Cable TV of Southern California [of Falcon Communications Inc.] - South Pasadena, CA - *Tel&CabFB 84C*
Falcon Cable TV of Tulare County [of Falcon Communications Inc.] - Three Rivers, CA - *Tel&CabFB 84C*
Falcon Cable TV of Tulare County [of Falcon Communications Inc.] - Tulare County, CA - *Tel&CabFB 84C*
Falcon Cable TV of Tulare County [of Falcon Communications] - Woodlake, CA - *BrCabYB 84*
Falcon Communications Inc. - Los Angeles, CA - *BrCabYB 84 p.D-300; Tel&CabFB 84C p.1679*
Falcon Communications of Northern California - Oak Hills, CA - *BrCabYB 84*
Falcon Flyer, The - Colorado Springs, CO - *AyerDirPub 83*
Falcon Hill Press - Sparks, NV - *LitMag&SmPr 83-84*
Falcon Press Publishing Co. Inc. - Helena, MT - *LitMarPl 83, 84; WritMar 84*
Falcon Publishing - Ben Lomond, CA - *BoPubDir 4, 5*
Falcon Publishing [Aff. of Gambit Books] - Venice, CA - *BoPubDir 4, 5*
Falcon Safety Products Inc. - Mountainside, NJ - *AvMarPl 83*
Falcon Word Processing Ltd. - Winnipeg, MB, Canada - *DirInfWP 82*
Falconer Associates, Arthur - Englewood Cliffs, NJ - *AdAge 3-28-84; StaDirAdAg 2-84*
Falconer Records - Inglewood, CA - *BillIntBG 83-84*
Falfurrias Facts - Falfurrias, TX - *BaconPubCkNews 84; Ed&PubIntYB 82*
Fali - Brussels, Belgium - *DirOnDB Spring 84*
Falk Associates Inc., Max - New York, NY - *StaDirAdAg 2-84*
Falk Associates, Richard R. [Subs. of Public Relations Services] - New York, NY - *ArtMar 84; DirPRFirms 83; LitMarPl 83, 84*
Falkynor Books - Davie, FL - *BoPubDir 4, 5; WritMar 84*
Fall Creek Cable TV Co. - Fall Creek, WI - *BrCabYB 84; Tel&CabFB 84C*
Fall Enterprises Inc. - Santee, CA - *StaDirAdAg 2-84*
Fall River Anchor, The - Fall River, MA - *NewsDir 84*
Fall River Area Chamber of Commerce - Fall River, MA - *BoPubDir 5*
Fall River Herald-News - Fall River, MA - *BaconPubCkNews 84; LitMarPl 83*
Fall River Music Inc. - *See* Sanga Music Inc.
Fallbrook Enterprise - Fallbrook, CA - *BaconPubCkNews 84*
Fallbrook Pennysaver - Mission Viejo, CA - *AyerDirPub 83*
Falleder Group Inc., The - New York, NY - *MagIndMarPl 82-83*
Fallen Angel Press - Highland Park, MI - *BoPubDir 4, 5; LitMag&SmPr 83-84*
Faller, Klenk & Quinlan - Buffalo, NY - *AdAge 3-28-84; StaDirAdAg 2-84*
Faller, Klenk & Quinlan - Getzville, NY - *DirPRFirms 83*
Fallon Eagle-Standard - Fallon, NV - *BaconPubCkNews 84*
Fallon Lahontan Valley News - Fallon, NV - *BaconPubCkNews 84; NewsDir 84*
Fallon McElligot Rice - Minneapolis, MN - *StaDirAdAg 2-84*
Fallout Records Centralization - Las Vegas, NV - *DirOnDB Spring 84*
Fallriver Herald News [of Northeast Publishing Inc.] - Fallriver, MA - *NewsDir 84*
Falls Advertiser-News [of Menomonee Falls Publishing Co.] - Menomonee Falls, WI - *NewsDir 84*
Falls Cablevision Inc. [of Marcus Communications Inc.] - International Falls, MN - *BrCabYB 84; Tel&CabFB 84C*
Falls Church News-Advertiser - Falls Church, VA - *Ed&PubIntYB 82*
Falls City Cable TV [of American TV & Communications Corp.] - Falls City, NE - *BrCabYB 84; Tel&CabFB 84C*
Falls City Journal - Falls City, NE - *BaconPubCkNews 84; NewsDir 84*
Falls City Microform - Lexington, KY - *MicroMarPl 82-83*

Falls of the Tar Publications - Rocky Mt., NC - *BoPubDir 4, 5; LitMag&SmPr 83-84*
Falls Record News, The - Smiths Falls, ON, Canada - *Ed&PubIntYB 82*
Falls Weekly Business Journal, The - Spokane, WA - *AyerDirPub 83*
Falmouth Enterprise - Falmouth, MA - *BaconPubCkNews 84; Ed&PubIntYB 82; NewsDir 84*
Falmouth Outlook - Falmouth, KY - *BaconPubCkNews 84; Ed&PubIntYB 82; NewsDir 84*
Falon County Times - Baker, MT - *Ed&PubIntYB 82*
Falt Stations, J. B. Jr. - Huntsville, AL - *BrCabYB 84*
Falter International, Michael - London, England - *MicrocomSwDir 1*
Falvey & Associates, John F. - New York, NY - *DirPRFirms 83*
FAM Book Service - New York, NY - *LitMarPl 83; MagIndMarPl 82-83*
FAM Translation Service - New York, NY - *LitMarPl 83, 84; MagIndMarPl 82-83*
Fama World Circles Inc. - Los Angeles, CA - *BillIntBG 83-84*
Fame Publishing Co. Inc. - Muscle Shoals, AL - *BillIntBG 83-84*
Famiglia Italiana - Weston, ON, Canada - *Ed&PubIntYB 82*
Families - Pleasantville, NY - *MagIndMarPl 82-83*
Families Under Stress - Washington, DC - *Ed&PubIntYB 82*
Family - New York, NY - *BaconPubCkMag 84; MagDir 84*
Family Affair Music - *See* Respect Music Co.
Family Album, A.B.A.A. - Glen Rock, PA - *BoPubDir 4, 5; WritMar 84*
Family & Health Improvement Society - Cambridge, OH - *BoPubDir 4 Sup, 5*
Family Bookshelf - Chappaqua, NY - *LitMarPl 84*
Family Care Workers of Ontario - Ottawa, ON, Canada - *BoPubDir 5*
Family Circle [of The New York Times Co.] - New York, NY - *ArtMar 84; BaconPubCkMag 84; Folio 83; LitMarPl 83, 84; MagDir 84; MagIndMarPl 82-83; WritMar 84*
Family Circle Great Ideas - New York, NY - *MagDir 84; WritMar 84*
Family Computing [of Scholastic Inc.] - New York, NY - *BaconPubCkMag 84; MagDir 84; MicrocomMPl 84*
Family Festivals [of Resource Publications Inc.] - Saratoga, CA - *LitMag&SmPr 83-84*
Family Festivals - Laurel Springs, NJ - *MagIndMarPl 82-83*
Family Films - Panorama City, CA - *TelAl 83, 84; Tel&CabFB 84C*
Family Food Garden, The - Boston, MA - *ArtMar 84; BaconPubCkMag 84; MagDir 84*
Family Friends Publications - Mason City, IA - *BoPubDir 5*
Family Handyman [of Webb Co.] - St. Paul, MN - *BaconPubCkMag 84; DirMarMP 83; Folio 83; MagDir 84; MagIndMarPl 82-83; WritMar 84*
Family Health Magazine - New York, NY - *MagDir 84*
Family Health Media - Aberdeen, SD - *BoPubDir 4, 5*
Family Home Entertainment - Canoga Park, CA - *BillIntBG 83-84*
Family Journal [of Des Plaines Journal-News Publications] - Des Plaines, IL - *NewsDir 84*
Family Journal - Columbia, MO - *BaconPubCkMag 84; WritMar 84*
Family Learning - Belmont, CA - *BaconPubCkMag 84*
Family Life Broadcasting System - Tucson, AZ - *BrCabYB 84*
Family Life Today Magazine - Ventura, CA - *WritMar 84*
Family Motor Coaching - Cincinnati, OH - *ArtMar 84; BaconPubCkMag 84; MagDir 84; WritMar 84*
Family Pastimes - Perth, ON, Canada - *BoPubDir 4, 5*
Family Pet - Tampa, FL - *ArtMar 84; WritMar 84*
Family Physician, The - Oak Brook, IL - *BaconPubCkMag 84*
Family Planning Perspectives - New York, NY - *BaconPubCkMag 84; MagDir 84; MagIndMarPl 82-83*
Family Practice News - Rockville, MD - *BaconPubCkMag 84; MagDir 84; MagIndMarPl 82-83*
Family Practice Recertification - New York, NY - *BaconPubCkMag 84*
Family Process - New York, NY - *MagIndMarPl 82-83*
Family Productions Co. - *See* Mietus Copyright Management
Family Publications - Maitland, FL - *BoPubDir 4, 5*
Family Publishing Co. - Bodega Bay, CA - *BoPubDir 4, 5*
Family Relations: Journal of Applied Family & Child Studies - Blacksburg, VA - *MagIndMarPl 82-83*
Family Resource & Referral Center [of National Council on Family Relations] - Minneapolis, MN - *CompReadDB 82; DataDirOnSer 84; EISS 83*
Family Resources & Referral Center [of Bibliographic Retrieval Services Inc.] - Latham, NY - *DataDirOnSer 84*
Family Resources Database [of National Council on Family Relations] - Minneapolis, MN - *CompReadDB 82; DirOnDB Spring 84; OnBibDB 3*
Family Safety - Chicago, IL - *BaconPubCkMag 84*
Family Service Association of America - New York, NY - *LitMarPl 83, 84*
Family Shopper, The - Walpole, MA - *Ed&PubIntYB 82*
Family Stations Inc. - Oakland, CA - *BrCabYB 84*
Family Theater - Hollywood, CA - *Tel&CabFB 84C*
Family Therapy [of Libra Publishers Inc.] - Roslyn Heights, NY - *LitMag&SmPr 83-84*
Family Therapy News - Upland, CA - *MagIndMarPl 82-83*
Family Weekly [of CBS Publications] - New York, NY - *Folio 83; LitMarPl 83, 84; MagIndMarPl 82-83; NewsBur 6; WritMar 84*
Famous Door Publishing Co. - Milwaukee, WI - *BillIntBG 83-84*
Famous Door Records - Flushing, NY - *BillIntBG 83-84*
Famous Music Corp. [Div. of Gulf & Western Industries Inc.] - New York, NY - *BillIntBG 83-84*
Famous Telephone Supply Co. - Akron, OH - *DataDirSup 7-83*
Fancher, Raymond I. - Winston-Salem, NC - *BoPubDir 4, 5*
Fandango Productions Inc. - New York, NY - *AvMarPl 83*
Fandom Unltd. Enterprises - Sunnyvale, CA - *LitMag&SmPr 83-84*
Fanfare - Tenafly, NJ - *BaconPubCkMag 84*
Fanfare Books Inc. - Stratford, ON, Canada - *BoPubDir 4, 5*
Fanfare Records - Des Moines, IA - *BillIntBG 83-84*
Fannettsburg Cable TV Co. - Fannettsburg, PA - *Tel&CabFB 84C*
Fannin County Special - Bonham, TX - *AyerDirPub 83*
Fanning Personnel Agency Inc. [Subs. of Fanning Enterprises Inc.] - New York, NY - *LitMarPl 83, 84*
Fanning Wholesale Inc. - Idaho Falls, ID - *Tel&CabFB 84C*
Fanon-Courier Corp. - Mission Hills, CA - *AvMarPl 83*
Fantaco Enterprises Inc. - Albany, NY - *BoPubDir 4, 5*
Fantastic Animation Machine, The - New York, NY - *AvMarPl 83*
Fantastic Films - Evanston, IL - *WritMar 84*
Fantasy & Science Fiction [of Mercury Press Inc.] - Cornwall, CT - *LitMarPl 83, 84*
Fantasy Book - Pasadena, CA - *ArtMar 84; WritMar 84*
Fantasy Newsletter - Boca Raton, FL - *LitMag&SmPr 83-84*
Fantasy/Prestige/Milestone/Stax - Berkeley, CA - *BillIntBG 83-84*
Fantasy Publishing Co. Inc. - Alhambra, CA - *BoPubDir 4, 5*
Fantome Press - Warren, OH - *BoPubDir 4, 5*
Fantus Co. - Milburn, NJ - *EISS 83*
Fanzine Directory - Ames, IA - *LitMag&SmPr 83-84*
FAPRS - Washington, DC - *DirOnDB Spring 84*
FAPRS2 [of Control Data Corp.] - Greenwich, CT - *DataDirOnSer 84*
Far Above Music - Canoga Park, CA - *BillIntBG 83-84*
Far East [of Chase Econometrics/Interactive Data Corp.] - Waltham, MA - *DataDirOnSer 84*
Far East - Bala Cynwyd, PA - *DirOnDB Spring 84*
Far East Forecast [of Chase Econometrics/Interactive Data Corp.] - Waltham, MA - *DataDirOnSer 84*
Far East Forecast - Bala Cynwyd, PA - *DirOnDB Spring 84*
Far East Records/Fusion Records - Miami, FL - *BillIntBG 83-84*
Far Eastern Research & Publications Center - Washington, DC - *BoPubDir 4, 5*
Far Northeast Citizen Sentinel - Philadelphia, PA - *AyerDirPub 83; Ed&PubIntYB 82*
Far Out West Publications - South Pasadena, CA - *LitMag&SmPr 83-84*
Far Rockaway Pennysaver - Rockville Centre, NY - *AyerDirPub 83*
Far West - Costa Mesa, CA - *MagDir 84*
Far West Editions - San Francisco, CA - *BoPubDir 4, 5*
Far-West Publishing Co. - La Mesa, CA - *BoPubDir 4, 5*
Far West Research Inc. - San Francisco, CA - *IntDirMarRes 83*
Far West Ski News - Los Angeles, CA - *MagDir 84*

Far Western Philosophy of Education Society - Tempe, AZ - *BoPubDir 4, 5*
Faraday National Corp. - Herndon, VA - *DataDirSup 7-83*
Farallones Institute - Occidental, CA - *BoPubDir 4, 5*
Faran Media Services Inc. - New York, NY - *StaDirAdAg 2-84*
Fargo Forum - Fargo, ND - *LitMarPl 83; NewsBur 6*
Fargo-Moorhead Forum - Fargo, ND - *NewsDir 84*
Faribault Cable TV - Faribault, MN - *BrCabYB 84; Tel&CabFB 84C*
Faribault News - Faribault, MN - *BaconPubCkNews 84; Ed&PubIntYB 82; NewsDir 84*
Faries & Associates, David A. - Los Gatos, CA - *Ed&PubIntYB 82*
Farina News - Farina, IL - *BaconPubCkNews 84; Ed&PubIntYB 82*
Farkas Films Inc. - New York, NY - *Tel&CabFB 84C*
Farley & Associates Inc., Lowell - Ft. Lauderdale, FL - *DirPRFirms 83*
Farley's TV Cable Service Inc. - Mullens, WV - *BrCabYB 84; Tel&CabFB 84C*
Farm Analysis Package [of Food & Agriculture Organization] - Rome, Italy - *EISS 83*
Farm & Country - Toronto, ON, Canada - *BaconPubCkMag 84*
Farm & Dairy - Salem, OH - *BaconPubCkMag 84; MagDir 84*
Farm & Forest - Woodstock, NB, Canada - *WritMar 84*
Farm & Garden, The - Watertown, NY - *MagDir 84*
Farm & Home News - Nappanee, IN - *AyerDirPub 83*
Farm & Home News - Binghamton, NY - *BaconPubCkMag 84*
Farm & Industrial Equipment Institute - Chicago, IL - *DataDirOnSer 84; DBBus 82*
Farm & Industrial Equipment Institute Data Banks - Chicago, IL - *DataDirOnSer 84*
Farm & Power Equipment [of National Farm & Power Services Inc.] - St. Louis, MO - *BaconPubCkMag 84; MagDir 84*
Farm & Ranch Living - Greendale, WI - *BaconPubCkMag 84*
Farm & Ranch Living - Milwaukee, WI - *MagIndMarPl 82-83*
Farm & Ranch Vacations Inc. - *See* Adventure Guides Inc./Farm & Ranch Vacations Inc.
Farm Audience Readership Measurement Service - Mamaroneck, NY - *DirOnDB Spring 84*
Farm Audience Readership Measurement Service [of Interactive Market Systems] - New York, NY - *DataDirOnSer 84*
Farm Bank - Ottawa, ON, Canada - *DirOnDB Spring 84*
Farm Building News [of American Farm Building Service Inc.] - Waukesha, WI - *BaconPubCkMag 84; MagDir 84*
Farm Bureau Acres [of American Farm Bureau Federation] - Park Ridge, IL - *EISS 5-84 Sup*
Farm Bureau Agri-News - Manhattan, KS - *BaconPubCkMag 84; MagDir 84*
Farm Bureau Press - Little Rock, AR - *BaconPubCkMag 84; MagDir 84*
Farm Chemicals [of Meister Publishing Co.] - Willoughby, OH - *BaconPubCkMag 84; MagDir 84*
Farm Computer News [of Successful Farming] - Des Moines, IA - *BaconPubCkMag 84; MicrocomMPl 84*
Farm Equipment [of Johnson Hill Press Inc.] - Ft. Atkinson, WI - *BaconPubCkMag 84; MagDir 84; MagIndMarPl 82-83*
Farm Equipment Quarterly - Exeter, ON, Canada - *BaconPubCkMag 84*
Farm Equipment Wholesalers Association - Iowa City, IA - *BoPubDir 5*
Farm Focus - Yarmouth, NS, Canada - *WritMar 84*
Farm Futures - Milwaukee, WI - *BaconPubCkMag 84*
Farm Impact - Mascoutah, IL - *BaconPubCkMag 84; NewsDir 84*
Farm Industry News - St. Paul, MN - *BaconPubCkMag 84; WritMar 84*
Farm Industry News/Midwest - St. Paul, MN - *MagDir 84*
Farm Industry News/South - St. Paul, MN - *MagIndMarPl 82-83*
Farm Industry News/Sunbelt - St. Paul, MN - *MagDir 84*
Farm Journal - Philadelphia, PA - *BaconPubCkMag 84; DirMarMP 83; KnowInd 83; LitMarPl 84; MagDir 84; MagIndMarPl 82-83; WritMar 84*
Farm Journal Books - Philadelphia, PA - *LitMarPl 83, 84; WritMar 84*
Farm Journal Family Bookshelf [Subs. of Farm Journal Magazine] - Chappaqua, NY - *LitMarPl 83, 84*
Farm Light & Power - Regina, SK, Canada - *BaconPubCkMag 84*
Farm Management Systems of MS Inc. - McLomb, MS - *MicrocomMPl 84*
Farm Market Infodata Service [of Public Broadcasting Service] - Washington, DC - *EISS 5-84 Sup*
Farm Money Management - Minneapolis, MN - *BaconPubCkMag 84; WritMar 84*
Farm News - Marion, IN - *BaconPubCkMag 84; MagDir 84*
Farm Radio News - Leawood, KS - *BrCabYB 84*
Farm Show - Lakeville, MN - *BaconPubCkMag 84; MagDir 84*
Farm Software Development [of NewsNet Inc.] - Bryn Mawr, PA - *DataDirOnSer 84*
Farm Store Merchandising [of ABC Publishing] - Minneapolis, MN - *BaconPubCkMag 84; MagDir 84*
Farm Supplier [of Watt Publishing Co.] - Mt. Morris, IL - *BaconPubCkMag 84; MagDir 84; WritMar 84*
Farm-To-Market Truckers' News - Sioux City, IA - *WritMar 84*
Farm Weekly - Sioux City, IA - *MagDir 84; MagIndMarPl 82-83*
Farm Wife News - Greendale, WI - *BaconPubCkMag 84; MagIndMarPl 82-83*
Farm Wife News - Milwaukee, WI - *WritMar 84*
Farmer & Associates - Sacramento, CA - *MicrocomMPl 84*
Farmer & Miner - Frederick, CO - *AyerDirPub 83*
Farmer & Thomas Music - Washington, DC - *BillIntBG 83-84*
Farmer City Journal - Farmer City, IL - *AyerDirPub 83; Ed&PubIntYB 82*
Farmer-Labor Press, The - Council Bluffs, IA - *NewsDir 84*
Farmer-Minnesota & Dakota - St. Paul, MN - *BaconPubCkMag 84*
Farmer Residence Designer Inc., W. D. - Atlanta, GA - *BoPubDir 4, 5*
Farmer-Stockman of the Midwest [of Nebraska Farmer Stockman Inc.] - Belleville, KS - *BaconPubCkMag 84; Ed&PubIntYB 82; NewsDir 84*
Farmer-Stockman, The - Oklahoma City, OK - *BaconPubCkMag 84; MagIndMarPl 82-83*
Farmer-Stockman, The - Dallas, TX - *MagDir 84*
Farmer, The - St. Paul, MN - *MagDir 84; MagIndMarPl 82-83*
Farmers' Advance News, The [of Suburban Communications Inc.] - Camden, MI - *Ed&PubIntYB 82; NewsDir 84*
Farmers & Business Mens Telephone Co. - Wheatland, IA - *TelDir&BG 83-84*
Farmers & Merchants Mutual Telephone Co. - Wayland, IA - *TelDir&BG 83-84*
Farmers Branch Times [of Taylor Communications Inc.] - Carrollton, TX - *NewsDir 84*
Farmer's Branch Times - Farmer's Branch, TX - *AyerDirPub 83; Ed&PubIntYB 82*
Farmers Cooperative Telephone Co. - Dysart, IA - *TelDir&BG 83-84*
Farmer's Digest - Brookfield, WI - *BaconPubCkMag 84; BoPubDir 4, 5; MagDir 84; MagIndMarPl 82-83*
Farmer's Exchange - New Paris, IN - *AyerDirPub 83; BaconPubCkMag 84; MagDir 84*
Farmers Independent - Bagley, MN - *AyerDirPub 83; Ed&PubIntYB 82*
Farmers Independent Telephone Co. - Grantsburg, WI - *TelDir&BG 83-84*
Farmer's Insight - Peterborough, ON, Canada - *BaconPubCkMag 84*
Farmer's Market - Galesburg, IL - *LitMag&SmPr 83-84*
Farmers Mutual Cooperative Telephone Co. - Harlan, IA - *TelDir&BG 83-84*
Farmers Mutual Cooperative Telephone Co. Inc. - Moulton, IA - *TelDir&BG 83-84*
Farmers Mutual Telephone Co. - Pleasant View, CO - *TelDir&BG 83-84*
Farmers Mutual Telephone Co. - Fruitland, ID - *TelDir&BG 83-84*
Farmers Mutual Telephone Co. - Jesup, IA - *TelDir&BG 83-84*
Farmers Mutual Telephone Co. - Nora Springs, IA - *TelDir&BG 83-84*
Farmers Mutual Telephone Co. - Shellsburg, IA - *TelDir&BG 83-84*
Farmers Mutual Telephone Co. - Stanton, IA - *Tel&CabFB 84C; TelDir&BG 83-84*

Farmers Mutual Telephone Co. - Elsie, MI - *TelDir&BG 83-84*
Farmers Mutual Telephone Co. - Bellingham, MN - *TelDir&BG 83-84*
Farmers Mutual Telephone Co. - Okolona, OH - *TelDir&BG 83-84*
Farmer's Report - Rochelle, IL - *BaconPubCkMag 84*
Farmers Telephone Co-Operative Inc. - Rainsville, AL - *TelDir&BG 83-84*
Farmers Telephone Co. - Batavia, IA - *TelDir&BG 83-84*
Farmers Telephone Co. - Essex, IA - *TelDir&BG 83-84*
Farmers Telephone Co. - Nora Springs, IA - *TelDir&BG 83-84*
Farmers Telephone Co. - Lancaster, WI - *TelDir&BG 83-84*
Farmers Telephone Cooperative Inc. - Kingstree, SC - *TelDir&BG 83-84*
Farmers Weekly Review - Joliet, IL - *AyerDirPub 83; Ed&PubIntYB 82*
Farmersburg News - Farmersburg, IN - *BaconPubCkNews 84*
Farmersville Herald - *See* Mineral King Publishing
Farmersville Panhandle Press - Farmersville, IL - *BaconPubCkNews 84*
Farmersville Princeton Herald - *See* Farmersville Times Inc.
Farmersville Times - Farmersville, TX - *BaconPubCkNews 84; Ed&PubIntYB 82*
Farmerville Cable TV - Farmerville, LA - *BrCabYB 84*
Farmerville Gazette - Farmerville, LA - *BaconPubCkNews 84; Ed&PubIntYB 82*
Farmfutures [of Agridata Resources Inc.] - Milwaukee, WI - *ArtMar 84; MagDir 84; MagIndMarPl 82-83*
Farming Uncle - Liberty, NY - *LitMag&SmPr 83-84*
Farmingdale-Bethpage Pennysaver - Plainview, NY - *AyerDirPub 83*
Farmingdale Observer - Farmingdale, NY - *AyerDirPub 83; Ed&PubIntYB 82*
Farmingdale Observer [of Levittown Observer/Tribune Community Newspapers] - Massapequa Park, NY - *NewsDir 84*
Farmingdale Observer - *See* Hiber Publishing Inc.
Farmingdale Post - Farmingdale, NY - *Ed&PubIntYB 82; NewsDir 84*
Farmington Bugle - Elmwood, IL - *AyerDirPub 83*
Farmington Bugle - Farmington, IL - *Ed&PubIntYB 82*
Farmington Bugle [of Roseville Carlberg Publishing Co.] - Roseville, IL - *NewsDir 84*
Farmington Cablevision Co. - Farmington, MO - *BrCabYB 84; Tel&CabFB 84C*
Farmington Cookbook Committee [Aff. of Farmington Historic Home] - Louisville, KY - *BoPubDir 4, 5*
Farmington County Advertiser [of Farmington News Printing Co. Inc.] - Farmington, MO - *Ed&PubIntYB 82; NewsDir 84*
Farmington Daily - Farmington, NM - *AyerDirPub 83*
Farmington Dakota County Tribune - Farmington, MN - *BaconPubCkNews 84*
Farmington Evening Press [of Smith Newspapers Inc.] - Farmington, MO - *NewsDir 84*
Farmington Forum - *See* Suburban Newspapers
Farmington Franklin Journal & Chronicle - Farmington, ME - *BaconPubCkNews 84; NewsDir 84*
Farmington News - Farmington, MO - *Ed&PubIntYB 82; NewsDir 84*
Farmington Observer - Farmington, MI - *Ed&PubIntYB 82*
Farmington Observer [of Livonia Suburban Communications Corp.] - Livonia, MI - *AyerDirPub 83; NewsDir 84*
Farmington Observer - *See* Observer & Eccentric Newspapers
Farmington Press-Advertiser - Farmington, MO - *BaconPubCkNews 84*
Farmington Times [of New Mexico Newspapers Inc.] - Farmington, NM - *BaconPubCkNews 84; Ed&PubIntYB 82; NewsDir 84*
Farmington Valley Herald - Simsbury, CT - *AyerDirPub 83; Ed&PubIntYB 82*
Farmington Van Buren County Leader - Farmington, IA - *BaconPubCkNews 84*
Farmland News - Kansas City, MO - *BaconPubCkMag 84; MagDir 84; MagIndMarPl 82-83*
Farmland News - Archbold, OH - *AyerDirPub 83*
Farmodex Drug Data Bank [of Farmodex Foundation] - Nijmegen, Netherlands - *EISS 83*
Farmodex Foundation - Nijmegen, Netherlands - *InfIndMarPl 83*
Farmstead Magazine - Freedom, ME - *ArtMar 84; BaconPubCkMag 84; MagIndMarPl 82-83; WritMar 84*
Farmstead Press, The - Freedom, ME - *DirMarMP 83*
Farmville Cable TV [of DoKel Communications Corp.] - Farmville, VA - *BrCabYB 84*
Farmville Cablevision Corp. [of DoKel Communications Corp.] - Farmville, VA - *Tel&CabFB 84C*
Farmville Enterprise - Farmville, NC - *BaconPubCkNews 84; Ed&PubIntYB 82*
Farmville Herald - Farmville, VA - *BaconPubCkNews 84; Ed&PubIntYB 82; NewsDir 84*
Farmweek [of Knightstown Mayhill Publications Inc.] - Knightstown, IN - *AyerDirPub 83; BaconPubCkMag 84; Ed&PubIntYB 82; MagDir 84; NewsDir 84*
Farnham Co. Inc., Frank C. - Philadelphia, PA - *MagIndMarPl 82-83*
Farnsworth Computer Center - Aurora, IL - *WhoWMicrocom 83*
Farnsworth Publishing Co. Inc. - Rockville Centre, NY - *LitMarPl 83, 84; WritMar 84*
Faro Music Publishing - Los Angeles, CA - *BillIntBG 83-84*
Farquharson Ltd., John - New York, NY - *LitMarPl 83, 84*
Farr-Away Music - Madison, TN - *BillIntBG 83-84*
Farr Records - Somerville, NJ - *BillIntBG 83-84*
Farragher Marketing Services [Div. of Airte Ltd. Inc.] - Canfield, OH - *ArtMar 84; DirPRFirms 83; StaDirAdAg 2-84*
Farrar Books - Garden City, NY - *BoPubDir 4, 5*
Farrar, Straus & Giroux Inc. - New York, NY - *LitMarPl 83, 84; WritMar 84*
Farrell International Music Publishing Co., Bobby - St. Petersburg, FL - *BillIntBG 83-84*
Farris Advertising & Marketing Inc. - Kansas City, MO - *StaDirAdAg 2-84*
Farrow, Harold R. - Oakland, CA - *Tel&CabFB 84C p.1679*
Farview Records - Madison, TN - *BillIntBG 83-84*
Farwell, Brice - Morgan Hill, CA - *BoPubDir 4, 5*
Farwell State Line Tribune - Farwell, TX - *BaconPubCkNews 84*
FASB Inflation Databank - New York, NY - *DirOnDB Spring 84*
Fasfax Corp. - Nashua, NH - *DataDirSup 7-83*
Fashion Accessories [of Business Journals Inc.] - Norwalk, CT - *BaconPubCkMag 84; MagDir 84*
Fashion Accessories - New York, NY - *BaconPubCkMag 84; MagDir 84*
Fashion Imprints Associates - Chicago, IL - *BoPubDir 4, 5*
Fashion International - New York, NY - *BaconPubCkMag 84*
Fashion 'n' Figure - Bath, OH - *Ed&PubIntYB 82*
Fashion Newsletter, The - New York, NY - *BaconPubCkMag 84*
Fashion Retailer - Chestnut Hill, MA - *BaconPubCkMag 84*
Fashion Showcase Retailer - Dallas, TX - *BaconPubCkMag 84*
Fasone-Garrett Advertising - Kansas City, MO - *AdAge 3-28-84; StaDirAdAg 2-84*
Fast Agricultural Communications Terminal System [of Purdue University] - West Lafayette, IN - *EISS 83; TeleSy&SerDir 2-84*
Fast Facts [Subs. of Commercial Analysts Co.] - New York, NY - *IntDirMarRes 83*
Fast Permit Reports [of Petroleum Information Corp.] - Littleton, CO - *DBBus 82*
Fast Service - New York, NY - *MagDir 84*
Fast-Track Infoscanners - Mt. Horeb, WI - *EISS 7-83 Sup*
Fastener Business - Ridgefield, CT - *BaconPubCkMag 84*
Fastener Industry News - Ridgefield, CT - *BaconPubCkMag 84*
Fastener Technology - Solon, OH - *BaconPubCkMag 84; MagIndMarPl 82-83*
Fastock II [of ADP Network Services Inc.] - Ann Arbor, MI - *DataDirOnSer 84; DBBus 82; DirOnDB Spring 84*
Fat Tuesday - Los Angeles, CA - *LitMag&SmPr 83-84*
Fate [of Clark Publishing Co.] - Highland Park, IL - *MagDir 84; MagIndMarPl 82-83; WritMar 84*
Fate Records Inc. - Chicago, IL - *BillIntBG 83-84*
Father Music Group - Hollywood, CA - *BillIntBG 83-84*
Father-Thunder Publishing Co. - Northridge, CA - *BillIntBG 83-84*
Fathom Enterprises Inc. - Rancho Palos Verdes, CA - *BoPubDir 4, 5*
Fathom Press - Markesan, WI - *BoPubDir 4, 5*
Fathom Publishing Co. - Cordova, AK - *ArtMar 84; BoPubDir 4, 5*

Faucett Buchanan County Farmer - Faucett, MO - *BaconPubCkNews 84*
Fauer Inc., Jon - New York, NY - *AvMarPl 83*
Faulk & Associates Software - Fullerton, CA - *WhoWMicrocom 83*
Faulk County Record - Faulkton, SD - *Ed&PubIntYB 82*
Faulkner & Associates Inc. - Little Rock, AR - *StaDirAdAg 2-84*
Faulkner Associates Ltd., Mervin G. - Hillsdale, ON, Canada - *MicrocomSwDir 1; WhoWMicrocom 83*
Faulkner Radio Inc. - Bay Minette, AL - *BrCabYB 84*
Faulkton Faulk County Record - Faulkton, SD - *BaconPubCkNews 84*
Fault Press - Union City, CA - *BoPubDir 4, 5*
Fauntleroy Associates, Jack - Silver Spring, MD - *DirMarMP 83*
Fauquier Democrat - Warrenton, VA - *AyerDirPub 83; Ed&PubIntYB 82; NewsDir 84*
Favor Music - *See* Sleepy Deacon Ltd.
Favorite - Franklin, KY - *AyerDirPub 83*
Favorite - Bonham, TX - *AyerDirPub 83; Ed&PubIntYB 82*
Favorite - Hilbert, WI - *AyerDirPub 83*
Fawcett Books - *See* Random House Inc.
Fawcett Library [of City of London Polytechnic] - London, England - *MicroMarPl 82-83*
Fawcett Marketing Services - Greenwich, CT - *MagIndMarPl 82-83*
Fawcett McDermott Cavanagh - Honolulu, HI - *DirPRFirms 83; StaDirAdAg 2-84*
Fax Collector's Editions Inc. - Mercer Island, WA - *BoPubDir 4, 5*
Faxon Communications Corp. - Purchase, NY - *DirInfWP 82*
Faxon Co. Inc., F. W. - Westwood, MA - *DataDirOnSer 84; EISS 83; InfIndMarPl 83; LitMarPl 83, 84; MagIndMarPl 82-83*
Faxpak [of ITT World Communications Inc.] - New York, NY - *TeleSy&SerDir 7-83*
Faxtel Information Systems Ltd. - Toronto, ON, Canada - *DataDirOnSer 84*
Fay, Loren V. - Moravia, NY - *FBInfSer 80*
Faye Productions, Doris - New York, NY - *TelAl 83, 84*
Fayette Advertiser - *See* Fayette Advertiser-Democrat-Leader
Fayette Advertiser-Democrat-Leader - Fayette, MO - *BaconPubCkNews 84*
Fayette Advertiser, The - Fayette, MO - *Ed&PubIntYB 82*
Fayette Cablevision - Uniontown, PA - *BrCabYB 84; Tel&CabFB 84C*
Fayette Cablevision - *See* Helicon Corp.
Fayette Cablevision Inc. - Peachtree City, GA - *BrCabYB 84*
Fayette Cablevision Inc. - Brunswick, MO - *BrCabYB 84*
Fayette Cablevision Inc. - Fayette, MO - *BrCabYB 84*
Fayette Cablevision Inc. - Glasgow, MO - *BrCabYB 84*
Fayette Cablevision Inc. - Lexington, MO - *BrCabYB 84*
Fayette Chronicle - Fayette, MS - *BaconPubCkNews 84; Ed&PubIntYB 82*
Fayette County Broadcaster - Fayette, AL - *Ed&PubIntYB 82; NewsDir 84*
Fayette County Entertainment Services Inc. - Somerville, TN - *Tel&CabFB 84C*
Fayette County News - Fayetteville, GA - *Ed&PubIntYB 82; NewsDir 84*
Fayette County Record - La Grange, TX - *AyerDirPub 83; Ed&PubIntYB 82*
Fayette County Union - West Union, IA - *AyerDirPub 83; Ed&PubIntYB 82*
Fayette Democrat-Leader - *See* Fayette Advertiser-Democrat-Leader
Fayette Falcon - Somerville, TN - *AyerDirPub 83; Ed&PubIntYB 82*
Fayette Leader - Fayette, IA - *BaconPubCkNews 84; Ed&PubIntYB 82*
Fayette Neighbor - Fayetteville, GA - *Ed&PubIntYB 82*
Fayette Neighbor - Marietta, GA - *AyerDirPub 83*
Fayette Review - Fayette, OH - *BaconPubCkNews 84; Ed&PubIntYB 82*
Fayette-Southside Sun - Fayetteville, GA - *Ed&PubIntYB 82*
Fayette Times-Record - Fayette, AL - *BaconPubCkNews 84*
Fayette Tribune - Oak Hill, WV - *AyerDirPub 83; Ed&PubIntYB 82*
Fayetteville Cablevision [of American Television & Communications Corp.] - Fayetteville, NC - *BrCabYB 84*
Fayetteville Community TV [of Rogers UA Cablesystems] - Fayetteville, TN - *BrCabYB 84; Tel&CabFB 84C*
Fayetteville Eagle Bulletin - Fayetteville, NY - *BaconPubCkNews 84*
Fayetteville Eagle-Bulletin & DeWitt News-Times - Fayetteville, NY - *NewsDir 84*
Fayetteville Elk Valley Times - Fayetteville, TN - *BaconPubCkNews 84*
Fayetteville Fayette County News - Fayetteville, GA - *BaconPubCkNews 84*
Fayetteville Northwest Arkansas Times [of Thomson Newspapers Inc.] - Fayetteville, AR - *NewsDir 84*
Fayetteville Observer - Fayetteville, NC - *ArtMar 84; BaconPubCkNews 84; Ed&PubIntYB 82; LitMarPl 83; NewsDir 84*
Fayetteville Observer & Times [of Fayetteville Publishing Co.] - Fayetteville, NC - *Ed&PubIntYB 82; LitMarPl 83, 84*
Fayetteville Telephone Co., The [Aff. of Telephone & Data Systems Inc.] - Fayetteville, OH - *TelDir&BG 83-84*
Fayetteville Times [of Fayetteville Publishing Co.] - Fayetteville, NC - *BaconPubCkNews 84; Ed&PubIntYB 82; LitMarPl 83, 84; NewsDir 84*
Fayetteville Times & Observer - Fayetteville, NC - *NewsDir 84*
Fayettteville Observer [of Fayetteville Publishing Co.] - Fayetteville, NC - *LitMarPl 84*
Fazzary, James - Watkins Glen, NY - *Tel&CabFB 84C p.1679*
FBN Software - Pebble Beach, CA - *WhoWMicrocom 83*
FCA Books for the Arts [Aff. of Foundation for the Community of Artists] - New York, NY - *BoPubDir 4, 5*
FCA Laboratory Ltd. - Tokyo, Japan - *InfoS 83-84*
FCB International Inc. - *BrCabYB 84*
F.C.C. Week [of Dawson-Butwick Publishers] - Washington, DC - *TeleSy&SerDir 2-84*
FCI-Invest/Net - North Miami, FL - *DataDirOnSer 84*
FCO Univas [of the Univas Network] - London, England - *StaDirAdAg 2-84*
FCT Inc. - Hawthorne, CA - *WhoWMicrocom 83*
FCX Carolina Cooperator - Raleigh, NC - *MagDir 84*
FDA Consumer - Rockville, MD - *BaconPubCkMag 84; MagDir 84; WritMar 84*
FDA Document Data Base [of FOI Services Inc.] - Rockville, MD - *CompReadDB 82*
FDA Drug Bulletin - Rockville, MD - *BaconPubCkMag 84*
FDC Publishing Co. - Stewartsville, NJ - *LitMarPl 83, 84*
FDIC - Washington, DC - *DirOnDB Spring 84*
FDIC Report of Condition & Income System [of U.S. Federal Deposit Insurance Corp.] - Washington, DC - *DBBus 82; EISS 83*
FDR Online Inc. [Subs. of Federal Document Retrieval] - Washington, DC - *DataDirOnSer 84*
FDW Arts - Littleton, CO - *BoPubDir 5*
Fearless Taster [of NewsNet Inc.] - Bryn Mawr, PA - *DataDirOnSer 84*
Fearless Taster, The - Windsor, ON, Canada - *DirOnDB Spring 84*
Fearon/Pitman Publishing Co. Inc. - Belmont, CA - *ArtMar 84*
Fearon Reference Systems [Div. of Pitman Learning Inc.] - Belmont, CA - *EISS 83; MicroMarPl 82-83*
Feasterville Bucks County Tribune - *See* Progress Newspapers Inc.
Feasterville Spirit - Feasterville, PA - *Ed&PubIntYB 82*
Feasterville Spirit [of Montgomery Publishing Co.] - Hatboro, PA - *NewsDir 84*
Feasterville Spirit - Lower Southampton, PA - *Ed&PubIntYB 82*
Feasterville Spirit - Warminster, PA - *AyerDirPub 83*
Feasterville Spirit - *See* Montgomery Publishing Co.
Feather Fancier - Forest, ON, Canada - *BaconPubCkMag 84*
Feather Printers Inc., William - Cleveland, OH - *LitMarPl 83*
Feather Printers Inc., William - Oberlin, OH - *LitMarPl 84*
Feather Publishing Co. Inc. - Quincy, CA - *BaconPubCkNews 84*
Feather River Bulletin - Quincy, CA - *Ed&PubIntYB 82*
Feather River Systems Corp. - Auburn, CA - *Tel&CabFB 84C p.1679*
Feather River TV Cable Systems - Quincy, CA - *BrCabYB 84*
Feather River TV Cable Systems Inc. [of Feather River Systems Corp.] - Portola, CA - *Tel&CabFB 84C*

Feathered Violin [of Quorum Editions] - Cranbury, NJ - *WritMar 84*
Feature - New York, NY - *MagDir 84*
Feature Associates - Novato, CA - *LitMarPl 84*
Feature Associates - San Rafael, CA - *Ed&PubIntYB 82*
Feature News Service - St. Louis, MO - *BaconPubCkNews 84; Ed&PubIntYB 82; LitMarPl 83, 84; MagIndMarPl 82-83*
Features International of London - New York, NY - *Ed&PubIntYB 82*
Feckless - Los Angeles, CA - *BillIntBG 83-84*
Fedder Group Inc., The - Baltimore, MD - *MicrocomSwDir 1*
Fedderson Productions, Don - Studio City, CA - *TelAl 83, 84; Tel&CabFB 84C*
Feder Books, T. H. [Aff. of Editorial Photocolor Archives] - New York, NY - *BoPubDir 4, 5*
Feder, Rosalie Brody - New York, NY - *LitMarPl 84*
Federal Assistance Award Data System [of U.S. Bureau of the Census] - Washington, DC - *EISS 83*
Federal Assistance Programs Retrieval System [of U.S. Office of Management & Budget] - Washington, DC - *CompReadDB 82; DBBus 82*
Federal Aviation Administration Master Specifications [of Bowne Information Systems Inc.] - New York, NY - *DataDirOnSer 84*
Federal Aviation Exams Co. - Solvang, CA - *BoPubDir 4, 5*
Federal Business Machine - Rockville, MD - *DataDirSup 7-83*
Federal Communications Bar Association - Washington, DC - *TeleSy&SerDir 7-83*
Federal Court of Canada Reports [of QL Systems Ltd.] - Ottawa, ON, Canada - *DataDirOnSer 84; DirOnDB Spring 84*
Federal Credit Union, The - Rosslyn, VA - *ArtMar 84*
Federal Dept. of Justice - Ottawa, ON, Canada - *CompReadDB 82*
Federal Deposit Insurance Corp. - Washington, DC - *BoPubDir 5*
Federal Document Retrievals Inc. - Washington, DC - *EISS 83*
Federal Election Commission - Washington, DC - *BoPubDir 5*
Federal Employees' News Digest Inc. - Merrifield, VA - *BoPubDir 4, 5*
Federal Employment Decision Search [of Labor Relations Press] - Ft. Washington, PA - *CompReadDB 82*
Federal Energy Data Index [of National Energy Information Center] - Washington, DC - *CompReadDB 82; DataDirOnSer 84; DBBus 82*
Federal Energy Data System - Washington, DC - *DirOnDB Spring 84*
Federal Express - Memphis, TN - *MagIndMarPl 82-83*
Federal Government Research in Progress [of The National Technical Information Service] - Springfield, VA - *DataDirOnSer 84*
Federal Index [of Capitol Services Inc.] - Washington, DC - *CompReadDB 82; DataDirOnSer 84; DBBus 82; DirOnDB Spring 84; EISS 83; OnBibDB 3*
Federal Information Center Program [of U.S. General Services Administration] - Washington, DC - *EISS 83*
Federal Information Processing Standards [of U.S. National Bureau of Standards] - Washington, DC - *EISS 83*
Federal Information Service Inc. - Washington, DC - *EISS 83*
Federal Labor Relations Reporter Database [of Labor Relations Press] - Ft. Washington, PA - *CompReadDB 82*
Federal Legal Information Through Electronics [of U.S. Air Force] - Denver, CO - *EISS 83*
Federal Legal Publications Inc. - New York, NY - *MagIndMarPl 82-83*
Federal Library & Information Network [of U.S. Library of Congress] - Washington, DC - *EISS 83*
Federal Library Committee [of U.S. Library of Congress] - Washington, DC - *EISS 83*
Federal Marking Products Corp. - Norwood, MA - *LitMarPl 83, 84*
Federal Merit Systems Reporter Database [of Labor Relations Press] - Ft. Washington, PA - *CompReadDB 82*
Federal Notes - Saratoga, CA - *LitMag&SmPr 83-84*
Federal Register Abstracts [of Capitol Services Inc.] - Washington, DC - *CompReadDB 82; DataDirOnSer 84; DBBus 82; DirOnDB Spring 84; EISS 83; OnBibDB 3*
Federal Register Notices [of Computer Sciences Corp.] - Falls Church, VA - *DataDirOnSer 84*
Federal Research in Progress - Washington, DC - *DirOnDB Spring 84*
Federal Research in Progress [of U.S. National Technical Information Service] - Springfield, VA - *DirOnDB Spring 84; EISS 5-84 Sup*
Federal Research Report - Silver Spring, MD - *DirOnDB Spring 84*
Federal Research Report [of NewsNet Inc.] - Bryn Mawr, PA - *DataDirOnSer 84*
Federal Reserve Bank of Atlanta - Atlanta, GA - *BoPubDir 5*
Federal Reserve Bank of Kansas City - Kansas City, MO - *BoPubDir 4 Sup, 5*
Federal Reserve Bank of Minneapolis - Minneapolis, MN - *BoPubDir 5*
Federal Reserve Bank of New York - New York, NY - *BoPubDir 5*
Federal Reserve Bank of Philadelphia - Philadelphia, PA - *BoPubDir 5*
Federal Reserve Bank of Richmond - Richmond, VA - *BoPubDir 5*
Federal Reserve Board Weekly - New York, NY - *DirOnDB Spring 84*
Federal Reserve Board Weekly [of I. P. Sharp Associates Ltd.] - Toronto, ON, Caada - *DataDirOnSer 84*
Federal Reserve System Board of Governors - Washington, DC - *BoPubDir 5*
Federal Reserve Week - Silver Spring, MD - *DirOnDB Spring 84*
Federal Reserve Week [of NewsNet Inc.] - Bryn Mawr, PA - *DataDirOnSer 84*
Federal Reserve Y9 Bank Holding Co. Database - New York, NY - *DirOnDB Spring 84*
Federal Software Exchange Center [of U.S. General Services Administration] - Falls Church, VA - *EISS 83*
Federal-State Reports [Subs. of The Martin Haley Cos.] - Falls Church, VA - *CompReadDB 82*
Federal-State Reports (Legislative Tracking System) - Falls Church, VA - *CompReadDB 82*
Federal Systems of Canada - Ottawa, ON, Canada - *MicrocomSwDir 1*
Federal Times [of Army Times Publishing Co.] - Washington, DC - *BaconPubCkMag 84; MagDir 84; MagIndMarPl 82-83*
Federal Way News [of Robinson Newspapers] - Auburn, WA - *NewsDir 84*
Federal Way News - Federal Way, WA - *AyerDirPub 83; Ed&PubIntYB 82*
Federal Way News - *See* Robinson Communications Co.
Federalsburg Times - Federalsburg, MD - *BaconPubCkNews 84; Ed&PubIntYB 82*
Federated Lithographers-Printers Inc. - Providence, RI - *LitMarPl 83, 84*
Federated Media - Elkhart, IN - *BrCabYB 84*
Federated Telephone Cooperative - Chokio, MN - *TelDir&BG 83-84*
Federation for American Immigration Reform - Washington, DC - *BoPubDir 4, 5*
Federation News [of Chicago Federation of Labor & Industrial Union] - Chicago, IL - *NewsDir 84*
Federation News, The [of Los Angeles County Federation of Labor] - Los Angeles, CA - *NewsDir 84*
Federation of American Hospitals Review - Little Rock, AR - *BaconPubCkMag 84; BoPubDir 5; MagDir 84*
Federation of American Societies for Experimental Biology - Bethesda, MD - *BoPubDir 4, 5*
Federation of Canadian Archers - Vanier, ON, Canada - *BoPubDir 4, 5*
Federation Proceedings - Bethesda, MD - *MagDir 84; MagIndMarPl 82-83*
FEDEX - Washington, DC - *DirOnDB Spring 84*
FEDLINK [of Library of Congress] - Washington, DC - *InfIndMarPl 83*
Fedora - Siletz, OR - *LitMag&SmPr 83-84*
Fedwatch - Belmont, CA - *DirOnDB Spring 84*
FEDWIR [of Money Market Services Inc.] - Belmont, CA - *DataDirOnSer 84; DBBus 82*
Fee Bee Music Co. - Pittsburgh, PA - *BillIntBG 83-84*
Fee Bee Record Co. - Pittsburgh, PA - *BillIntBG 83-84*
Fee, Florence A. - Markdale, ON, Canada - *BoPubDir 4, 5*

Feed & Farm Supply Dealer - Winnipeg, MB, Canada - *BaconPubCkMag 84*
Feed & Grain Times [of Johnson Hill Press Inc.] - Ft. Atkinson, WI - *BaconPubCkMag 84; MagDir 84; MagIndMarPl 82-83*
Feed/Back [of California Journalism Foundation Inc.] - San Francisco, CA - *NewsDir 84; WritMar 84*
Feed International - Mt. Morris, IL - *BaconPubCkMag 84*
Feed Management [of Watt Publishing Co.] - Mt. Morris, IL - *BaconPubCkMag 84; MagDir 84*
Feedlot Management - Minneapolis, MN - *BaconPubCkMag 84; MagDir 84*
Feedstuffs [of The Miller Publishing Co.] - Minneapolis, MN - *BaconPubCkMag 84; MagDir 84; MagIndMarPl 82-83*
Feeley Enterprises - Chicago, IL - *DirPRFirms 83*
Feeley Inc., Patricia Falk - Rowayton, CT - *LitMarPl 83, 84*
Feelgreat Publishing Co. [Aff. of The Laugh Factory] - Teaneck, NJ - *BoPubDir 4, 5*
FEES Data Base [of McGill University] - Montreal, PQ, Canada - *DataDirOnSer 84; EISS 83*
Feffer & Simons Inc. [Subs. of Doubleday & Co. Inc.] - New York, NY - *LitMarPl 83, 84; MagIndMarPl 82-83*
Feheley Publishers, M. F. - Toronto, ON, Canada - *BoPubDir 4, 5*
Feher, E. M. - Toronto, ON, Canada - *BoPubDir 4, 5*
Fehl, Fred - New York, NY - *MagIndMarPl 82-83*
Fehlman Advertising & Marketing - Canton, OH - *StaDirAdAg 2-84*
Fehmers Productions Inc., Frank - New York, NY - *BoPubDir 4, 5*
Feil Productions, Edward - Cleveland, OH - *AvMarPl 83*
Fein, Jess - Boston, MA - *BoPubDir 4, 5*
Fein-Marquart Associates - Baltimore, MD - *EISS 83*
Feinberg, Karen - Cincinnati, OH - *LitMarPl 84*
Feiner & Co. Inc., Richard - New York, NY - *Tel&CabFB 84C*
Feinsilver, Lillian Mermin - Easton, PA - *LitMarPl 83, 84; MagIndMarPl 82-83*
Feinsot, Bernice B. - New York, NY - *BoPubDir 4, 5*
Feist Associates, Betsy - New York, NY - *LitMarPl 83*
Feist Resources, Betsy - New York, NY - *LitMarPl 84*
Feith Systems & Software - Bala Cynwyd, PA - *MicrocomMPl 84; MicrocomSwDir 1*
Feith Systems & Software - Elkins Park, PA - *MicrocomMPl 83*
Feith Systems & Software - Wyncote, PA - *WhoWMicrocom 83*
Fejer, Paul Haralyi - Mt. Clemens, MI - *BoPubDir 5*
FEL Publications Ltd. - Los Angeles, CA - *AvMarPl 83; BillIntBG 83-84*
Feld, Joseph - New Rochelle, NY - *LitMarPl 83, 84; MagIndMarPl 82-83*
Felderman/Sharp Communications Inc. - Cleveland, OH - *DirPRFirms 83*
Feldheim Inc., Philipp - New York, NY - *LitMarPl 83, 84*
Feldman Advertising Inc., George - New York, NY - *LitMarPl 83, 84; MagIndMarPl 82-83*
Feldman & Associates, Elane - Brooklyn Heights, NY - *LitMarPl 83, 84; MagIndMarPl 82-83*
Feldman & Co., G. M. - Chicago, IL - *AdAge 3-28-84; StaDirAdAg 2-84*
Feldman & Co., R. S. - Chicago, IL - *AdAge 3-28-84; DirMarMP 83; StaDirAdAg 2-84*
Feldman Interviewing Service Inc., Arline - Providence, RI - *IntDirMarRes 83*
Feldman, Mildred L. B. - Baton Rouge, LA - *BoPubDir 4, 5*
Feldspar - Stanford, CA - *LitMag&SmPr 83-84*
Feldstein Editorial Services, Janice J. - Chicago, IL - *LitMarPl 83, 84*
Felicity Music Inc. - Austin, TX - *BillIntBG 83-84*
Felicity Records Inc. - Austin, TX - *BillIntBG 83-84*
Feline Practice - Santa Barbara, CA - *BaconPubCkMag 84; MagDir 84*
Felix Associates, Frank - Englewood Cliffs, NJ - *DataDirSup 7-83*
Fell Publishers Inc., Frederick - New York, NY - *LitMarPl 83, 84; WritMar 84*
Fellers, Lacy & Gaddis - Austin, TX - *StaDirAdAg 2-84*
Fellman Productions - Malden, MA - *AvMarPl 83*
Fellowship of Reconciliation (Fellowship Publications) - Nyack, NY - *BoPubDir 4, 5; MagIndMarPl 82-83*
Fels & Firn Press - Kentfield, CA - *BoPubDir 4, 5; LitMag&SmPr 83-84*
Felsen, Jerry - Jamaica, NY - *LitMarPl 83, 84*
Felsway Advertising - Totowa, NJ - *StaDirAdAg 2-84*
Felton Telephone Exchange - Felton, MN - *TelDir&BG 83-84*
Feltus, Peter R. - Oakland, CA - *BoPubDir 4, 5*
Fema Music Publications - Naperville, IL - *BillIntBG 83-84*
Female Patient - New York, NY - *BaconPubCkMag 84; MagIndMarPl 82-83*
Feminary - Chapel Hill, NC - *LitMag&SmPr 83-84*
Feminist Bulletin - San Diego, CA - *LitMag&SmPr 83-84*
Feminist Press Inc., The - Old Westbury, NY - *DirMarMP 83; LitMag&SmPr 83-84; LitMarPl 83, 84; WritMar 84*
Feminist Publishing Alliance Inc. - Oakland, CA - *LitMag&SmPr 83-84*
Feminist Review - London, England - *LitMag&SmPr 83-84*
Feminist Studies - College Park, MD - *LitMag&SmPr 83-84*
Feminist Writers' Guild - Berkeley, CA - *BoPubDir 5*
Feminist Writers Guild (National Newsletter) - Berkeley, CA - *LitMag&SmPr 83-84*
Femme-Lines [of Earl Barron Publications] - New York, NY - *BaconPubCkMag 84; MagDir 84*
Fence Industry [of The Argus Press Holdings Co. Inc.] - Atlanta, GA - *BaconPubCkMag 84; MagDir 84; MagIndMarPl 82-83; WritMar 84*
Fenco Micrographic Systems - Burlington, NJ - *DirInfWP 82*
Fender & Latham Inc. - Greenwood, SC - *Tel&CabFB 84C p.1679*
Fenelon Falls Gazette - Fenelon Falls, ON, Canada - *Ed&PubIntYB 82*
Fenichel Co., Norman - Bloomfield, CT - *DirPRFirms 83*
Fenix Timesharing Service [Subs. of Fargo Electronic Services Inc.] - Eden Prairie, MN - *DataDirOnSer 84; EISS 7-83 Sup*
Fennell Subscription Service, Reginald F. - Jackson, MI - *MagIndMarPl 82-83*
Fennimore Telephone Co. [Aff. of Telephone & Data Systems Inc.] - Fennimore, WI - *TelDir&BG 83-84*
Fennimore Times - Fennimore, WI - *BaconPubCkNews 84; Ed&PubIntYB 82*
Fennville Herald - Fennville, MI - *BaconPubCkNews 84; Ed&PubIntYB 82*
Fensholt Inc. - Chicago, IL - *AdAge 3-28-84; StaDirAdAg 2-84*
Fenster Associates Inc., Milton - New York, NY - *DirPRFirms 83*
Fenton Associates, H. T. - Somerville, NJ - *AdAge 3-28-84; StaDirAdAg 2-84*
Fenton Cablevision [of Comcast Cablevision Corp.] - Fenton, MI - *BrCabYB 84; Tel&CabFB 84C*
Fenton Cooperative Telephone Co. - Fenton, IA - *TelDir&BG 83-84*
Fenton Independent - Fenton, MI - *BaconPubCkNews 84; NewsDir 84*
Fenton Journal - Fenton, MO - *Ed&PubIntYB 82*
Fenton Journal - St. Louis, MO - *AyerDirPub 83; NewsDir 84*
Fenton Journal - *See* St. Louis Suburban Newspapers Inc.
Fenton, Lu - New York, NY - *LitMarPl 83, 84*
Fenton Swanger Consumer Research Inc. - Dallas, TX - *IntDirMarRes 83*
Fenton Tri-County News - Fenton, MI - *BaconPubCkNews 84*
Fentress County Leader-Times - Jamestown, TN - *Ed&PubIntYB 82*
Fenvessy & Schwab Inc. - New York, NY - *LitMarPl 84*
Fenvessy Associates Inc. - New York, NY - *LitMarPl 83; MagIndMarPl 82-83*
Fenwick Productions - West Hartford, CT - *AvMarPl 83*
Ferber Co. Management Consulting Inc. - New York, NY - *IntDirMarRes 83*
Ferber Janklow Chimbel Bender - New York, NY - *AdAge 3-28-84; StaDirAdAg 2-84*
Fercom Group Inc., The - Larchmont, NY - *DirPRFirms 83; StaDirAdAg 2-84*
Ferdinand News - *See* Ferdinand News Publishers
Ferdinand News Publishers - Ferdinand, IN - *BaconPubCkNews 84*
Ferdinand News, The - Ferdinand, IN - *Ed&PubIntYB 82*
Fergeson Productions, F. - Marina, CA - *BoPubDir 5*
Fergus-Elora Cable TV Ltd. - Fergus, ON, Canada - *BrCabYB 84*

Fergus-Elora News Express - Fergus, ON, Canada - *AyerDirPub 83; Ed&PubIntYB 82*
Fergus Falls Journal - Fergus Falls, MN - *BaconPubCkNews 84; NewsDir 84*
Ferguson Advertising Inc. - Ft. Wayne, IN - *StaDirAdAg 2-84*
Ferguson Advertising Inc. - Jenkintown, PA - *StaDirAdAg 2-84*
Ferguson & Associates Advertising - Rexburg, ID - *StaDirAdAg 2-84*
Ferguson Associates Inc., Thomas G. - Parsippany, NJ - *AdAge 3-28-84; StaDirAdAg 2-84*
Ferguson Communications - Hillsdale, MI - *LitMarPl 83, 84; MagIndMarPl 82-83*
Ferguson, Goldberg & Associates Inc. - Philadelphia, PA - *DirMarMP 83*
Ferguson Inc., Gary - St. Louis, MO - *DirPRFirms 83*
Ferguson-Minihane Advertising - Wayne, NJ - *StaDirAdAg 2-84*
Ferguson Music USA Inc., Maynard - Ojai, CA - *BillIntBG 83-84*
Ferguson Productions, F. - Berkeley, CA - *BoPubDir 4*
Ferguson Publishing Co., J. G. [Subs. of Doubleday & Co. Inc.] - Chicago, IL - *DirMarMP 83; LitMarPl 83, 84*
Fermata International Melodies Inc. - Hollywood, CA - *BillIntBG 83-84*
Fern-Allan Advertising Agency - Granada Hills, CA - *StaDirAdAg 2-84*
Fern Creek Neighbor, The - Fern Creek, KY - *Ed&PubIntYB 82*
Fern/Hanaway - Providence, RI - *AdAge 3-28-84; StaDirAdAg 2-84*
Fern, Irwin A. - Baltimore, MD - *Tel&CabFB 84C p.1679*
Fernandina Beach News Leader - Fernandina Beach, FL - *BaconPubCkNews 84; NewsDir 84*
Fernandina Cable TV Co. - Fernandina Beach, FL - *BrCabYB 84; Tel&CabFB 84C*
Ferndale Enterprise - Ferndale, CA - *BaconPubCkNews 84; Ed&PubIntYB 82*
Ferndale Westside Record-Journal - Ferndale, WA - *BaconPubCkNews 84*
Ferndock Music [Div. of Wormwood Projects] - Boulder, CO - *BillIntBG 83-84*
Fernley Leader/Courier-Times - Yerington, NV - *AyerDirPub 83*
Fernseh Inc. - Salt Lake City, UT - *AvMarPl 83*
Fernware Inc. - Houston, TX - *WhoWMicrocom 83*
Feron O'Leary Kaprielian Inc. - New York, NY - *StaDirAdAg 2-84*
Ferox Microsystems - Arlington, VA - *ADAPSOMemDir 83-84; DataDirSup 7-83; MicrocomMPl 84; MicrocomSwDir 1; WhoWMicrocom 83; WritMar 84*
Ferrari Inc. - New York, NY - *StaDirAdAg 2-84*
Ferrari Publications - Phoenix, AZ - *BoPubDir 4, 5*
Ferrario & Goodman Advertising - St. Louis, MO - *StaDirAdAg 2-84*
Ferri & Associates, Roger C. - New York, NY - *BoPubDir 4 Sup, 5*
Ferriday Concordia Sentinel - Ferriday, LA - *BaconPubCkNews 84; NewsDir 84*
Ferris Associates - Indianapolis, IN - *MicrocomMPl 84*
Ferris Wheel - Ferris, TX - *BaconPubCkNews 84; Ed&PubIntYB 82*
Ferroalloys & Strategic Metals Forecast [of Chase Econometrics/Interactive Data Corp.] - Waltham, MA - *DataDirOnSer 84*
Ferry Boat Music - Burton, WA - *BillIntBG 83-84*
Fertig Inc., Howard - New York, NY - *LitMarPl 83, 84*
Fertile Journal - Fertile, MN - *BaconPubCkNews 84; Ed&PubIntYB 82*
Fertility & Sterility - Birmingham, AL - *MagDir 84*
Fertility & Sterility - Rochester, MN - *BaconPubCkMag 84; MagIndMarPl 82-83*
Fertilizer Forecast [of Chase Econometrics/Interactive Data Corp.] - Waltham, MA - *DataDirOnSer 84; DBBus 82*
Fertilizer Progress [of The Fertilizer Institute] - Washington, DC - *BaconPubCkMag 84; MagDir 84; WritMar 84*
Fessel, Siegfriedt & Moeller Advertising - Louisville, KY - *AdAge 3-28-84; ArtMar 84; StaDirAdAg 2-84*
Fessenden Cable TV [of NoDaKable Inc.] - Fassenden, ND - *BrCabYB 84*
Fessenden Wells County Free Press - Fessenden, ND - *BaconPubCkNews 84*
Festival Music Party Ltd. - New York, NY - *BillIntBG 83-84*
Festival Publications - Glendale, CA - *LitMag&SmPr 83-84; LitMarPl 83, 84*
Festive Music - Newport News, VA - *BillIntBG 83-84*
Festus-Crystal City News-Democrat [of Jefferson County Newspapers Inc.] - Festus, MO - *NewsDir 84*
Festus Democrat-Rocket, The - Festus, MO - *Ed&PubIntYB 82*
Fetiche Editions - Chiuduno, Italy - *LitMag&SmPr 83-84*
Fetiche Journal - Chiuduno, Italy - *LitMag&SmPr 83-84*
Fetske Associates Inc., Ruth B. - Cobalt, CT - *StaDirAdAg 2-84*
Fetterly & Associates, Fred A. - West Palm Beach, FL - *DirPRFirms 83; StaDirAdAg 2-84*
Fettig & Associates, Art - Battle Creek, MI - *BoPubDir 4*
Fetzer Broadcasting Co. - Kalamazoo, MI - *BrCabYB 84 p.D-300*
Fetzer CableVision [of Fetzer Broadcasting Co.] - Kalamazoo, MI - *BrCabYB 84; Tel&CabFB 84C*
Fetzer Stations, John E. - Kalamazoo, MI - *BrCabYB 84*
Fetzer Television Corp. - Kalamazoo, MI - *Tel&CabFB 84S*
Feulner, Floyd H. - Sylmar, CA - *BoPubDir 4, 5*
Fey Publishing Co. - Wisconsin Rapids, WI - *MagIndMarPl 82-83*
FFL News - Ft. Lauderdale, FL - *MagDir 84*
FFO Communications Inc. - Bronx, NY - *BillIntBG 83-84*
Fforbez Publications - Vancouver, BC, Canada - *BoPubDir 4, 5; LitMarPl 84*
F.I. Communications - Stanford, CA - *BoPubDir 4, 5*
FI Electronics - Santa Rosa, CA - *WhoWMicrocom 83*
Fibar Designs - Menlo Park, CA - *BoPubDir 4, 5; LitMag&SmPr 83-84*
Fiber/Laser News - Bethesda, MD - *BaconPubCkMag 84; DirOnDB Spring 84*
Fiber/Laser News [of NewsNet Inc.] - Bryn Mawr, PA - *DataDirOnSer 84*
Fiber Optics & Communications Newsletter - Brookline, MA - *WritMar 84*
Fiber Optics & Communications Weekly News - Boston, MA - *DirOnDB Spring 84*
Fiber Optics & Communications Weekly News [of NewsNet Inc.] - Bryn Mawr, PA - *DataDirOnSer 84*
Fiber Producer [of W. R. C. Smith Publishing Co.] - Atlanta, GA - *BaconPubCkMag 84; MagDir 84; MagIndMarPl 82-83*
Fiber World - Greenville, SC - *BaconPubCkMag 84*
Fiberarts - Asheville, NC - *BaconPubCkMag 84; WritMar 84*
Fiberbilt Computer Cases - New York, NY - *AvMarPl 83; WhoWMicrocom 83*
Fibonacci Corp. - Goldens Bridge, NY - *BoPubDir 4, 5*
Fibre Market News - New York, NY - *BaconPubCkMag 84; Ed&PubIntYB 82; MagDir 84*
Fibronics International Inc. - Hyannis, MA - *DataDirSup 7-83*
Ficalora Film & Tape Productions, Toni - New York, NY - *ArtMar 84; Tel&CabFB 84C*
Fichman, Pearl - Fresh Meadows, NY - *LitMarPl 83, 84; MagIndMarPl 82-83*
Ficomp Inc. - Fairfax, VA - *TeleSy&SerDir 7-83*
Fiction Collective [of Brooklyn College] - Brooklyn, NY - *BoPubDir 5; LitMag&SmPr 83-84; LitMarPl 83, 84*
Fiction Collective - New York, NY - *BoPubDir 4; LitMag&SmPr 83-84*
Fiction International [of St. Lawrence University] - Canton, NY - *LitMag&SmPr 83-84; LitMarPl 83, 84; WritMar 84*
Fiction, Literature & The Arts Review - Brookline, MA - *LitMag&SmPr 83-84*
Fiction Music Inc. - *See* Fourth Floor Music Inc.
Fiction Network - San Francisco, CA - *LitMag&SmPr 83-84; LitMarPl 84*
Fiddistics Music - *See* Windham Hill Music
Fiddleback Music Publishing Co. Inc. - *See* Valando Publishing Group Inc., Tommy
Fiddlehead Poetry Books - Fredericton, NB, Canada - *BoPubDir 4, 5*
Fiddlehead, The [of University of New Brunswick] - Fredericton, NB, Canada - *LitMag&SmPr 83-84; WritMar 84*
Fideler Co., The - Grand Rapids, MI - *LitMarPl 83, 84*
Fidelity Sound Recordings - Redwood City, CA - *BillIntBG 83-84*
Fidelity Telephone Co. - Sullivan, MO - *TelDir&BG 83-84*
Fidell, H. Bradley - Delray Beach, FL - *LitMarPl 83, 84*
Fiderer Associates Inc., Martin - Englewood Cliffs, NJ - *AdAge 3-28-84; StaDirAdAg 2-84*

Fides/Claretian [Div. of Claretian Publications] - Chicago, IL - *LitMarPl 83*
Fiedler/Berlin Productions Inc. - Studio City, CA - *Tel&CabFB 84C*
Field - Oberlin, OH - *LitMag&SmPr 83-84*
Field Advertising, William Hill - Westport, CT - *StaDirAdAg 2-84*
Field & Harvest, The - Conway, SC - *Ed&PubIntYB 82*
Field & Herald - Conway, SC - *AyerDirPub 83*
Field & Stream [of CBS Publications] - New York, NY - *BaconPubCkMag 84; Folio 83; LitMarPl 84; MagDir 84; MagIndMarPl 82-83; NewsBur 6; Tel&CabFB 84C; WritMar 84*
Field Cablevision [of Field Communications Corp.] - Norton Air Force Base, CA - *BrCabYB 84*
Field Cablevision [of Field Enterprises] - Redlands, CA - *BrCabYB 84*
Field Cablevision of Redlands-Yucaipa Inc. [of Field Communications Corp.] - Redlands, CA - *Tel&CabFB 84C*
Field Cablevision of Riverside County [of Field Communications Corp.] - Sunnymead, CA - *BrCabYB 84; Tel&CabFB 84C*
Field Communications Corp. - San Francisco, CA - *BrCabYB 84 p.D-300; Tel&CabFB 84C p.1679*
Field Crop Abstracts [of Commonwealth Bureau of Pastures & Field Crops] - Maidenhead, England - *CompReadDB 82*
Field Enterprises Inc. - Chicago, IL - *KnowInd 83*
Field House Inc., The - Overland Park, KS - *IntDirMarRes 83*
Field Management Associates - El Cerrito, CA - *IntDirMarRes 83*
Field Management Sacramento - Carmichael, CA - *IntDirMarRes 83*
Field Museum of Natural History - Chicago, IL - *BoPubDir 4, 5*
Field News Service - Chicago, IL - *Ed&PubIntYB 82*
Field Newspaper Syndicate [Subs. of Field Enterprises] - Irvine, CA - *BaconPubCkNews 84; Ed&PubIntYB 82; LitMarPl 83, 84; MagIndMarPl 82-83; NewsBur 6*
Field Research Corp. - San Francisco, CA - *IntDirMarRes 83*
Fields Associates, Jerry - New York, NY - *MagIndMarPl 82-83*
Fieldston Press - New York, NY - *BoPubDir 4, 5*
Fiesta - Paris, France - *DirOnDB Spring 84*
Fiesta City Publishers - Santa Barbara, CA - *BoPubDir 4, 5; WritMar 84*
Fiesta Publishing Corp. - Miami, FL - *LitMarPl 83, 84*
Fiesta Record Co. Inc. - Rockville Centre, NY - *BillIntBG 83-84*
Fiesta! Times - Chula Vista, CA - *WritMar 84*
Fifteen Dance Laboratorium - Toronto, ON, Canada - *BoPubDir 4 Sup, 5*
1557 Labor Journal USWA - Clairton, PA - *NewsDir 84*
1590 Broadcaster - Nashua, NH - *Ed&PubIntYB 82*
Fifteen Years Music - *See* Tompalland Music
Fifth Avenue Shopper [of H & J Price Co.] - Maplewood, NJ - *DataDirOnSer 84; DirOnDB Spring 84*
Fifth Wheel, The - Indianapolis, IN - *BaconPubCkMag 84*
Fifth Wheel, The - Maywood, IN - *MagDir 84*
59/Hobby Radio - Port Washington, NY - *MagDir 84*
50 Plus [of Whitney Communications Corp.] - New York, NY - *BaconPubCkMag 84; Folio 83; MagDir 84; MagIndMarPl 82-83; WritMar 84*
50 States Records [Div. of Accusound Music] - Hendersonville, TN - *BillIntBG 83-84*
Fifty Upward Network [of Network Publications] - Cleveland, OH - *WritMar 84*
Fig Leaf Publishing Co. - Friendswood, TX - *BaconPubCkNews 84*
F.I.G. Ltd. - Northbrook, IL - *BoPubDir 4, 5*
Figgie Systems Management Group - Willoughby, OH - *MicrocomMPl 84*
Fighting Stars [of Rainbow Publications Inc.] - Burbank, CA - *WritMar 84*
Fighting Woman News - New York, NY - *ArtMar 84; LitMag&SmPr 83-84; MagIndMarPl 82-83*
Figlia Publishing Inc. - Carlstadt, NJ - *BillIntBG 83-84*
Figliola & Partners Inc. - New York, NY - *StaDirAdAg 2-84*
Figures - Berkeley, CA - *BoPubDir 4; LitMag&SmPr 83-84*
Figures - Great Barrington, MA - *BoPubDir 5*
Fil-Am-Bel Publications Inc. - Chicago, IL - *WritMar 84*
File Mag [of Art Official Inc.] - Toronto, ON, Canada - *LitMag&SmPr 83-84*
Filer Mutual Telephone Co. - Filer, ID - *TelDir&BG 83-84*
Filion Cable-Vision Inc. - Mont Tremblant, PQ, Canada - *BrCabYB 84*
Filion Cable-Vision Inc. - St. Jovite, PQ, Canada - *BrCabYB 84*
Fillers for Publications - Los Angeles, CA - *MagIndMarPl 82-83*
Fillman Advertising - Champaign, IL - *AdAge 3-28-84; ArtMar 84; StaDirAdAg 2-84*
Fillmore County News - Exeter, NE - *Ed&PubIntYB 82*
Fillmore Herald - Fillmore, CA - *BaconPubCkNews 84; Ed&PubIntYB 82*
Fillmore Millard County Progress - Fillmore, UT - *BaconPubCkNews 84*
Fillmore North Allegany Observer/Bel Blaze - Fillmore, NY - *Ed&PubIntYB 82*
Fillmore North Allegeny Observer/Bel Blaze - *See* Sanders Publications
Film - London, England - *LitMag&SmPr 83-84*
Film America Inc. - Atlanta, GA - *AvMarPl 83*
Film & Television Documentation Center [of State University of New York at Albany] - Albany, NY - *EISS 5-84 Sup*
Film & Video News - La Salle, IL - *BaconPubCkMag 84*
Film & Video Service Inc. - Wheaton, IL - *AvMarPl 83*
Film Center, The - Hyattsville, MD - *AvMarPl 83*
Film Classic Exchange - Los Angeles, CA - *AvMarPl 83*
Film Comment [of Film Society of Lincoln Center] - New York, NY - *BaconPubCkMag 84; LitMarPl 84; MagDir 84; MagIndMarPl 82-83; WritMar 84*
Film Communicators - North Hollywood, CA - *AvMarPl 83*
Film Co., The - New York, NY - *TelAl 83, 84*
Film Core - Hollywood, CA - *Tel&CabFB 84C*
Film Counselors Inc. - New York, NY - *ProGuPRSer 4*
Film Craft Laboratories Inc. - Detroit, MI - *AvMarPl 83*
Film Culture [Aff. of Film Culture Non-Profit Inc.] - New York, NY - *BoPubDir 4, 5; LitMag&SmPr 83-84; MagIndMarPl 82-83*
Film Culture Non-Profit Inc. - New York, NY - *LitMag&SmPr 83-84*
Film Effects of Hollywood - Hollywood, CA - *Tel&CabFB 84C*
Film Group Inc., The - Cambridge, MA - *AvMarPl 83*
Film House Inc., The - Cincinnati, OH - *ArtMar 84*
Film Instruction Co. of America - Milwaukee, WI - *BoPubDir 4, 5*
Film/Jamel Productions Inc. - Beverly Hills, CA - *TelAl 84*
Film/Jamel Productions Inc. - New York, NY - *TelAl 83*
Film Journal [of Pubsun Corp.] - New York, NY - *BaconPubCkMag 84; MagDir 84*
Film Library Quarterly - New York, NY - *LitMag&SmPr 83-84*
Film-Makers' Cooperative - New York, NY - *AvMarPl 83*
Film Makers of Philadelphia Inc. - Philadelphia, PA - *AvMarPl 83*
Film News - La Salle, IL - *MagDir 84*
Film Opticals Inc. - New York, NY - *Tel&CabFB 84C*
Film Presentation Co. Inc. - Iselin, NJ - *AvMarPl 83*
Film Quarterly [of University of California Press] - Berkeley, CA - *BaconPubCkMag 84; LitMag&SmPr 83-84; MagIndMarPl 82-83; WritMar 84*
Film Search Inc. - New York, NY - *AvMarPl 83*
Film Service Corp. - Salt Lake City, UT - *Tel&CabFB 84C*
Film Services Lab Inc. - Boston, MA - *AvMarPl 83*
Film Society of Lincoln Center, The [of Film Comment] - New York, NY - *LitMarPl 83*
Film Systems Inc. - Burbank, CA - *AvMarPl 83*
Filmack Studios - Chicago, IL - *AvMarPl 83; TelAl 83, 84*
Filmack Studios (Television & Industrial Div.) - Chicago, IL - *Tel&CabFB 84C*
FilMagic Products Inc. - Atlanta, GA - *AvMarPl 83*
Filmakers Library Inc. - New York, NY - *AvMarPl 83*
Filmarts - Boston, MA - *AvMarPl 83*
Filmation Associates - Reseda, CA - *AvMarPl 83; Tel&CabFB 84C*
Filmcraft Audio-Visuals [Subs. of Art-Tints Distributors Inc.] - Indianapolis, IN - *AvMarPl 83*
Filmcreations Inc. - West Jordan, UT - *WritMar 84*
Filmfair Communications [Div. of Filmfair Inc.] - Studio City, CA - *AvMarPl 83; Tel&CabFB 84C*
Filmfair Inc. - New York, NY - *Tel&CabFB 84C*
FilmLab Service Inc. - Cleveland, OH - *AvMarPl 83*
Filmlife Inc. - Moonachie, NJ - *AvMarPl 83; Tel&CabFB 84C*

Filmmakers Film & Video Monthly - Ward Hill, MA - *MagIndMarPl 82-83*
Films Around the World Inc. - New York, NY - *Tel&CabFB 84C*
Films Five Inc. - Great Neck, NY - *ArtMar 84; TelAl 83, 84; Tel&CabFB 84C*
Films for Christ Association - Elmwood, IL - *ArtMar 84; WritMar 84*
Films for Educators Inc. - Forest Hills, NY - *AvMarPl 83*
Films for the Humanities Inc. - Princeton, NJ - *AvMarPl 83; WritMar 84*
Films in Review - New York, NY - *BaconPubCkMag 84; MagDir 84; MagIndMarPl 82-83*
Films Inc. [Div. of Public Media Inc.] - Wilmette, IL - *AvMarPl 83; Tel&CabFB 84C*
Films of Distinction - Los Angeles, CA - *AvMarPl 83*
Films of India - Los Angeles, CA - *AvMarPl 83; Tel&CabFB 84C*
Films of the Nations - Brooklyn, NY - *AvMarPl 83; ProGuPRSer 4; TelAl 83, 84; Tel&CabFB 84C*
Filmstrip & Slide Laboratory Inc. - New York, NY - *AvMarPl 83*
Filmtech Inc. - Westfield, MA - *AvMarPl 83*
Filmtel Inc. - Culver City, CA - *TelAl 84*
Filmtreat International Corp. - New York, NY - *Tel&CabFB 84C*
Filmways Inc. - Los Angeles, CA - *HomeVid&CabYB 82-83; KnowInd 83*
Filsinger & Co. Ltd. - New York, NY - *BoPubDir 4, 5*
Filson Club - Louisville, KY - *BoPubDir 4, 5*
Filson, Theodore W. - Rensselaer, IN - *BrCabYB 84 p.D-300; Tel&CabFB 84C p.1679*
Filter Press - Palmer Lake, CO - *LitMarPl 83, 84; WritMar 84*
Filter Press [of Kimbrough Associates Inc.] - Atlanta, GA - *BaconPubCkMag 84; MagDir 84*
FIM Corp. - New York, NY - *LitMarPl 83, 84*
Final Analysis Inc. - New York, NY - *IntDirMarRes 83*
Final Analysis Inc. (Qualitative Div.) - New York, NY - *IntDirMarRes 83*
Final Systems Inc. - Cupertino, CA - *DataDirOnSer 84*
Finance [of IFB Communications] - New York, NY - *MagDir 84*
Finance & Commerce [of Credit Publishing Co.] - Minneapolis, MN - *Ed&PubIntYB 82; NewsDir 84*
Finance & Development - Washington, DC - *MagIndMarPl 82-83*
Financial [of Chase Econometrics/Interactive Data Corp.] - Waltham, MA - *DBBus 82*
Financial - Bala Cynwyd, PA - *DirOnDB Spring 84*
Financial Analysts Federation, The - Broadway, NY - *ProGuPRSer 4*
Financial Analysts Journal [of Financial Analysts Federation] - New York, NY - *BaconPubCkMag 84; MagDir 84*
Financial & Credit Statistics [of Data Resources Inc.] - Lexington, MA - *DataDirOnSer 84*
Financial Associates - Deerfield, IL - *BoPubDir 4, 5*
Financial Computer Systems - Atlanta, GA - *WhoWMicrocom 83*
Financial Computing - Cos Cob, CT - *BaconPubCkMag 84*
Financial Data Bank [of Warner Computer Systems Inc.] - New York, NY - *EISS 83*
Financial Data Products Inc. - Minneapolis, MN - *ADAPSOMemDir 83-84*
Financial Data Services - Bakersfield, CA - *WhoWMicrocom 83*
Financial Database [of Evans Economics Inc.] - Washington, DC - *DataDirOnSer 84*
Financial Executive - Morristown, NJ - *BaconPubCkMag 84*
Financial Executive [of Financial Executives Institute] - New York, NY - *MagDir 84*
Financial Executives Research Foundation [Aff. of Financial Executives Institute] - Morristown, NJ - *BoPubDir 5*
Financial Executives Research Foundation [Aff. of Financial Executives Institute] - New York, NY - *BoPubDir 4*
Financial Forecast [of Chase Econometrics/Interactive Data Corp.] - Waltham, MA - *DataDirOnSer 84; DBBus 82*
Financial Forecast - Bala Cynwyd, PA - *DirOnDB Spring 84*
Financial Freedom Publishers [Aff. of Financial Freedom Consultants] - Clare, MI - *BoPubDir 5*
Financial Freedom Report - Salt Lake City, UT - *WritMar 84*
Financial Information Network [of GTE Telenet] - Vienna, VA - *DataDirOnSer 84*
Financial Information Services [of Quotron Systems Inc.] - Los Angeles, CA - *DataDirOnSer 84*
Financial Institution Data Base [of Control Data Corp.] - Greenwich, CT - *DataDirOnSer 84*
Financial Institution Data Base [of Cates Consulting Analysts Inc.] - New York, NY - *DBBus 82; DirOnDB Spring 84*
Financial Interstate Service Corp. - Knoxville, TN - *DataDirOnSer 84; VideoDir 82-83*
Financial Listing Service - Sausalito, CA - *DirOnDB Spring 84*
Financial Magic Inc. - Irvine, CA - *MicrocomMPl 84*
Financial Management Advisor - Boca Raton, FL - *DirOnDB Spring 84*
Financial Management Advisor [of NewsNet Inc.] - Bryn Mawr, PA - *DataDirOnSer 84*
Financial Management Systems [Subs. of Equifax/Credit Bureau Inc.] - Atlanta, GA - *DataDirOnSer 84*
Financial Marketing Concepts Inc. - Tallahassee, FL - *StaDirAdAg 2-84*
Financial Marketing Group - New York, NY - *StaDirAdAg 2-84*
Financial News - Jacksonville, FL - *Ed&PubIntYB 82*
Financial News & Daily Record, The [of Financial News Corp.] - Jacksonville, FL - *NewsDir 84*
Financial News Network - Santa Monica, CA - *BrCabYB 84; CabTVPrDB 83; Tel&CabFB 84C*
Financial Planner, The [of International Association for Financial Planning] - Atlanta, GA - *BaconPubCkMag 84; MagDir 84; MagIndMarPl 82-83*
Financial Planning Practitioner - Portsmouth, NH - *BaconPubCkMag 84*
Financial Post [of Maclean Hunter Ltd.] - Toronto, ON, Canada - *BaconPubCkMag 84; CompReadDB 82; WritMar 84*
Financial Post Canadian Corporate Database [of Financial Post Investment Databank] - Toronto, ON, Canada - *DataDirOnSer 84; DirOnDB Spring 84*
Financial Post Canadian Corps. [of I. P. Sharp Associates Ltd.] - Toronto, ON, Canada - *DataDirOnSer 84*
Financial Post Corp. Service - Toronto, ON, Canada - *BoPubDir 5*
Financial Post Investment Databank [of Maclean-Hunter Ltd.] - Toronto, ON, Canada - *DataDirOnSer 84; DBBus 82; EISS 83; InfIndMarPl 83*
Financial Post Securities [of I. P. Sharp Associates Ltd.] - Toronto, ON, Canada - *DataDirOnSer 84; DirOnDB Spring 84*
Financial Post Securities Database [of Financial Post Investment Databank] - Toronto, ON, Canada - *DataDirOnSer 84*
Financial Post Survey of Predecessor & Defunct Cos. [of Financial Post Investment Databank] - Toronto, ON, Canada - *DataDirOnSer 84*
Financial Press Inc. - Coral Gables, FL - *BoPubDir 4, 5*
Financial Publishers - Westminster, CA - *BoPubDir 4, 5*
Financial Publishing Co. - Boston, MA - *DirMarMP 83; LitMarPl 83, 84*
Financial Quarterly, The - West Palm Beach, FL - *MagDir 84*
Financial Relations Board Inc., The - Chicago, IL - *DirPRFirms 83*
Financial Review Information Service [of SVP Australia] - Sydney, Australia - *EISS 83*
Financial Securities Data [of National Computer Network of Chicago] - Chicago, IL - *DataDirOnSer 84*
Financial Services Inc. - Glen Rock, NJ - *DataDirOnSer 84*
Financial Shares Corp. - Chicago, IL - *DirPRFirms 83*
Financial Software of America Inc. - Winter Park, FL - *DataDirSup 7-83*
Financial Statistics Div. [of Bank of England] - London, England - *EISS 7-83 Sup*
Financial Systems Technology Inc. - Miami, FL - *WhoWMicrocom 83*
Financial Technology Inc. - Chicago, IL - *DataDirSup 7-83; MicrocomSwDir 1*
Financial Times Actuaries Share Indices [of I. P. Sharp Associates Ltd.] - Toronto, ON, Canada - *DataDirOnSer 84*
Financial Times Actuaries Share Indices - London, England - *DirOnDB Spring 84*
Financial Times Business Information Ltd. - London, England - *FBInfSer 80; InfIndMarPl 83*
Financial Times Currency & Share Index Databank - London, England - *DirOnDB Spring 84*
Financial Times Index - Stockholm, Sweden - *DirOnDB Spring 84*

Financial Times Ltd., The - London, England - *Ed&PubIntYB 82; MicroMarPl 82-83*
Financial Times of Canada - Toronto, ON, Canada - *BaconPubCkMag 84*
Financial Times of London [of Bibliographic Retrieval Services Inc.] - Latham, NY - *DataDirOnSer 84*
Financial Times Share Information [of I. P. Sharp Associates Ltd.] - Toronto, ON, Canada - *DataDirOnSer 84*
Financial Times Share Information - London, England - *DirOnDB Spring 84*
Financial Trend [of Equity Media Inc.] - Dallas, TX - *BaconPubCkMag 84; MagDir 84*
Financial Vision [of Hong Kong Telephone Co. Ltd.] - Hong Kong - *VideoDir 82-83*
Financial World [of Financial World Partners] - New York, NY - *BaconPubCkMag 84; Folio 83; MagDir 84; MagIndMarPl 82-83; NewsBur 6*
Financier [of FinEdit Ltd.] - New York, NY - *BaconPubCkMag 84; MagDir 84; MagIndMarPl 82-83*
Finar Research Inc. - Denver, CO - *DataDirSup 7-83*
Finar Systems Ltd. - Denver, CO - *MicrocomMPl 83*
Fincastle-Botetourt News & Herald - *See* Herald Publishing Corp.
Fincastle Herald, The - Fincastle, VA - *Ed&PubIntYB 82*
Finch Communications Inc. - Pavo, GA - *BrCabYB 84; Tel&CabFB 84C*
Finch, James M. Jr. - *See* Standard Tobacco Inc.
Finch, Pruyn & Co. Inc. - Glens Falls, NY - *LitMarPl 83, 84; MagIndMarPl 82-83*
Finch Recording Co. - Cincinnati, OH - *BillIntBG 83-84*
FinCom Inc. - Los Angeles, CA - *MicrocomMPl 84*
Find/SVP [of Information Clearing House Inc.] - New York, NY - *BoPubDir 5; DataDirOnSer 84; EISS 83; FBInfSer 80; HBIndAd&MS 82-83; InfIndMarPl 83; InfoS 83-84; IntDirMarRes 83; LitMarPl 83; ProGuPRSer 4*
Find/SVP Reports & Studies Index [of Dialog Information Services Inc.] - Palo Alto, CA - *DataDirOnSer 84*
Find/SVP Reports & Studies Index - New York, NY - *CompReadDB 82; DirOnDB Spring 84*
Findata Data Bank [of Stockholm School of Education] - Stockholm, Sweden - *EISS 83*
Finder, The - Bowman, ND - *AyerDirPub 83; Ed&PubIntYB 82*
Findex - Torrance, CA - *WhoWMicrocom 83*
Findhorn Press, The - Morayshire, Scotland - *LitMag&SmPr 83-84*
Findhorn Publications [Aff. of The Findhorn Foundation] - Forest City, OR - *BoPubDir 4*
Findhorn Publications [Aff. of The Findhorn Foundation] - Clinton, WA - *BoPubDir 5*
Findlay Courier, The - Findlay, OH - *BaconPubCkNews 84*
Findlay Enterprise - Findlay, IL - *Ed&PubIntYB 82*
Findlay Enterprise - Sullivan, IL - *AyerDirPub 83*
Findlay Enterprise - *See* Best Newspapers in Illinois Inc.
Findlay Publishing Co., The - Findlay, OH - *BrCabYB 84*
Fine & Associates, Arnold - Washington, DC - *DirPRFirms 83*
Fine Art Resources Inc. - Chicago, IL - *ArtMar 84*
Fine Arts Films Inc. - Studio City, CA - *Tel&CabFB 84C*
Fine Arts Museums of San Francisco - San Francisco, CA - *BoPubDir 4, 5*
Fine Arts Press - Kingsport, TN - *BoPubDir 4, 5; LitMag&SmPr 83-84*
Fine Arts Society - Mishawaka, IN - *BoPubDir 4, 5; LitMag&SmPr 83-84*
Fine Chemicals Directory [of Pergamon International Information Corp.] - McLean, VA - *DataDirOnSer 84*
Fine Chemicals Directory [of Fraser Williams Scientific Systems Ltd.] - Poynton, England - *DirOnDB Spring 84; EISS 83*
Fine Dining [of Connell Publications Inc.] - Miami, FL - *BaconPubCkMag 84; WritMar 84*
Fine Homebuilding [of The Taunton Press Inc.] - Newtown, CT - *BaconPubCkMag 84; MagDir 84; MagIndMarPl 82-83; WritMar 84*
Fine Line Productions - Grand Central Station, NY - *ArtMar 84*
Fine, Peter M. - New York, NY - *MagIndMarPl 82-83*
Fine Print: A Review for the Arts of the Book [of Fine Print Publishing Co.] - San Francisco, CA - *LitMag&SmPr 83-84; LitMarPl 83, 84; WritMar 84*
Fine Print News - Buffalo, NY - *AyerDirPub 83*
Fine Research Inc., George - Hartsdale, NY - *IntDirMarRes 83*
Fine, Travis & Associates Inc. - New York, NY - *IntDirMarRes 83*
Fine Woodworking - Newtown, CT - *BaconPubCkMag 84; MagDir 84; MagIndMarPl 82-83*
Finec - Belmont, CA - *DirOnDB Spring 84*
Finegold Direct Marketing - New York, NY - *LitMarPl 83, 84*
Fineline Co. - New York, NY - *BoPubDir 4, 5*
Finell Musicservices Inc., Judith - New York, NY - *FBInfSer 80*
Finelli Associates, Raymond - Providence, RI - *StaDirAdAg 2-84*
Finescale Modeler [of Kalmbach Publishing Co.] - Milwaukee, WI - *BaconPubCkMag 84; WritMar 84*
Finesse Records - New York, NY - *BillIntBG 83-84*
Finger Lakes Cablevision [of Cablevision Industries Inc.] - Canandaigua, NY - *Tel&CabFB 84C*
Finger Lakes Cablevision [of Cablevision Industries Inc.] - Cayuga, NY - *Tel&CabFB 84C*
Finger Lakes Cablevision [of Cablevision Industries Inc.] - Macedon, NY - *Tel&CabFB 84C*
Finger Lakes Cablevision [of Cablevision Industries Inc.] - Newark, NY - *Tel&CabFB 84C*
Finger Lakes Times - Geneva, NY - *AyerDirPub 83; BaconPubCkNews 84; Ed&PubIntYB 82*
Fingerjig Music - *See* Castalia Music
Fingerote & Grauer/Grauer & Fingerote - Monterey, CA - *StaDirAdAg 2-84*
Fingraph Corp. - Springfield, IL - *DataDirSup 7-83*
Finishers' Management - Glenview, IL - *BaconPubCkMag 84; MagDir 84*
Fink Co., William A. - Gainesville, FL - *MicrocomMPl 84*
Fink Co., William A. - Pompano Beach, FL - *MicrocomMPl 83*
Fink, Joyce - Chehalis, WA - *Ed&PubIntYB 82*
Fink-Pinewood Records - Chesapeake, VA - *BillIntBG 83-84*
Fink, Russell A. - Lorton, VA - *ArtMar 84*
Finke, Blythe Foote - Palisades, NY - *LitMarPl 83; MagIndMarPl 82-83*
Finkel & Associates Inc., M. - Atlanta, GA - *StaDirAdAg 2-84*
Finkelstein & Associates, Arthur J. - Mt. Kisco, NY - *IntDirMarRes 83*
Finland Central Medical Library - Helsinki, Finland - *InfIndMarPl 83*
Finlayson Advertising - Tyler, TX - *StaDirAdAg 2-84*
Finley Broadcasting Co. - Santa Rosa, CA - *BrCabYB 84*
Finley Photographics Inc. - New York, NY - *LitMarPl 83*
Finley Press - Finley, ND - *Ed&PubIntYB 82*
Finley Steele County Press - Finley, ND - *BaconPubCkNews 84*
Finn & Associates Inc., William F. - Tyler, TX - *StaDirAdAg 2-84*
Finn Hill Arts - Silverton, CO - *BoPubDir 4, 5*
Finn Typographic Service Inc. - Stamford, CT - *LitMarPl 83*
Finne, Wladislaw - Yarmouth, ME - *LitMarPl 83, 84*
Finnegan & Agee - Richmond, VA - *AdAge 3-28-84; StaDirAdAg 2-84*
Finnegan Associates, Robert - Wellesley, MA - *IntDirMarRes 83*
Finney Co. - Minneapolis, MN - *BoPubDir 4, 5*
Finnish Council for Scientific Information & Research Libraries - Helsinski, Finland - *EISS 83*
Finnish Online User Group [of Finnish Society for Information Services] - Espoo, Finland - *InfIndMarPl 83*
Finnish Periodicals Index in Economics & Business [of Helsinki School of Economics Library] - Helsinki, Finland - *CompReadDB 82*
Finnish Tymnet/Telenet Access [of General Directorate of Posts & Telecommunications] - Helsinki, Finland - *InfIndMarPl 83*
Finp - Helsinki, Finland - *DirOnDB Spring 84*
Fins & Feathers - Minneapolis, MN - *BaconPubCkMag 84; MagDir 84; MagIndMarPl 82-83*
Finsbury Data Services - London, England - *CompReadDB 82; DataDirOnSer 84; InfIndMarPl 83*
Fintel Co. Newsbase [of Fintel Ltd.] - London, England - *DBBus 82*
Fintel Ltd. [of The Financial Times] - London, England - *CompReadDB 82; InfIndMarPl 83; OnBibDB 3*
Fintex All-Day Exchange Monitor [of NewsNet Inc.] - Bryn Mawr, PA - *DataDirOnSer 84*
Fintex All-Day Foreign Exchange Monitor - New York, NY - *DirOnDB Spring 84*

Fintex International Economic Summaries - New York, NY - *DirOnDB Spring 84*
Fintzenberg Publishers - Long Beach, NY - *BoPubDir 4, 5*
Fiocco Productions - Scottsdale, AZ - *AvMarPl 83*
Fiore Films - Jersey City, NJ - *AvMarPl 83; Tel&CabFB 84C*
Fiore, Quentin - Hopewell, NJ - *LitMarPl 83, 84; MagIndMarPl 82-83*
Fiorentino Associates Inc., Imero - New York, NY - *AvMarPl 83; TeleSy&SerDir 2-84*
Fiorini, Louis M. - Chico, CA - *AvMarPl 83*
Fire Analysis Div. [of National Fire Protection Association] - Quincy, MA - *EISS 83*
Fire Chief [of H. Marvin Ginn Corp.] - Chicago, IL - *BaconPubCkMag 84; MagDir 84*
Fire Engineering [of Technical Publishing Co.] - New York, NY - *BaconPubCkMag 84; MagDir 84; WritMar 84*
Fire Engineering Books [of Technical Publishing Co.] - New York, NY - *BoPubDir 4, 5*
Fire Island News - Ocean Beach, NY - *AyerDirPub 83*
Fire Journal - Quincy, MA - *BaconPubCkMag 84; MagIndMarPl 82-83*
Fire News - Quincy, MA - *BaconPubCkMag 84*
Fire Prevention through Films Inc. - Newton Highlands, MA - *AvMarPl 83*
Fire Protection Topics Inc. - Norwell, MA - *LitMarPl 83, 84*
Fire Research Information Services [of U.S. National Bureau of Standards] - Washington, DC - *EISS 83*
Fire Science Abstracts [of Dept. of the Environment] - Borehamwood, England - *EISS 5-84 Sup*
Fire Service Today - Quincy, MA - *BaconPubCkMag 84; MagIndMarPl 82-83*
Fire Technology - Quincy, MA - *BaconPubCkMag 84*
Firebase System [of U.S. Forest Service] - Boise, ID - *EISS 83*
Firebaugh-Mendota Journal & Times - Firebaugh, CA - *AyerDirPub 83; Ed&PubIntYB 82*
Firebird Press, The - Kingswood, Australia - *LitMag&SmPr 83-84*
Fired-Up Music - *See* Mietus Copyright Management
Firedrum Music Publishers - Albuquerque, NM - *BillIntBG 83-84*
Firefighting in Canada - Delhi, ON, Canada - *BaconPubCkMag 84*
Firefly Books Ltd. - Scarborough, ON, Canada - *BoPubDir 4, 5*
Firefly Press - Cambridge, MA - *BoPubDir 4, 5; LitMag&SmPr 83-84*
Fireflyer Computing - Provo, UT - *MicrocomMPl 83*
Firehouse Color Lab, The - Indianapolis, IN - *AvMarPl 83*
Firehouse Magazine - New York, NY - *BaconPubCkMag 84; MagDir 84; MagIndMarPl 82-83*
Firelight Publishing - Hollywood, CA - *BillIntBG 83-84*
Fireline [of Infotech Publications] - San Francisco, CA - *MagDir 84*
FireNet - Menominee, MI - *DirOnDB Spring 84*
Fireside Books [Div. of Warren H. Green Inc.] - St. Louis, MO - *LitMarPl 83, 84*
Fireside Books [Subs. of Simon & Schuster] - New York, NY - *LitMarPl 83, 84*
Fireside Computing Inc. - Elkridge, MD - *MicrocomMPl 84; MicrocomSwDir 1*
Fireside Guard - Centralia, MO - *AyerDirPub 83*
Fireside Theatre - New York, NY - *LitMarPl 83*
Fireside Theatre - *See* Doubleday Book Clubs
Firestein Books - El Paso, TX - *BoPubDir 4, 5*
Firestone & Associates - New York, NY - *AdAge 3-28-84; DirPRFirms 83; StaDirAdAg 2-84*
Firestone & Associates Inc., John - Canal Winchester, OH - *MagIndMarPl 82-83*
Firestone News Press - Los Angeles, CA - *Ed&PubIntYB 82*
Firestone Park News/Southeast News Press - Los Angeles, CA - *AyerDirPub 83*
Firestone Press, W. D. - Springfield, MO - *BoPubDir 4, 5*
Firestone Program Syndication Co. - Hewlett, NY - *TelAl 83, 84; Tel&CabFB 84C*
Fireweed: A Feminist Quarterly - Toronto, ON, Canada - *LitMag&SmPr 83-84*
Fireweed Press - Sooke, BC, Canada - *BoPubDir 4, 5*
Firey, Walter - Austin, TX - *BoPubDir 4, 5*
Firm Facts Interviewing Service - Stratford, CT - *IntDirMarRes 83*
Firm Foundation Publishing House - Austin, TX - *BoPubDir 4, 5*
First Amendment Press - Stanford, CA - *BoPubDir 4, 5*
First American Bank - Boston, MA - *BoPubDir 4, 5*
First American Records Inc. - Seattle, WA - *BillIntBG 83-84*
First Analysis Corp. System - Chicago, IL - *DataDirOnSer 84; DirOnDB Spring 84*
First Arkansas Cablevision Corp. - Smackover, AR - *BrCabYB 84*
First Artists Music Co. - Beverly Hills, CA - *BillIntBG 83-84*
First Bank System - Minneapolis, MN - *VideoDir 82-83*
First Call for Help [of United Way of Minneapolis] - Minneapolis, MN - *EISS 83*
First Capitol Cablevision [of Group W Cable] - St. Charles, MO - *BrCabYB 84*
First Carolina Communications Inc. - Rocky Mt., NC - *Tel&CabFB 84C p.1679*
First Choice - Santa Barbara, CA - *BoPubDir 4 Sup, 5*
First Choice Cablevision - San Diego, CA - *Tel&CabFB 84C*
First Church of Christ Scientist - Boston, MA - *BoPubDir 4 Sup, 5*
First Class - Palm Springs, CA - *MagDir 84*
First Class - Coral Gables, FL - *BaconPubCkMag 84*
First Commonwealth Communications Inc. - Gloucester, VA - *BrCabYB 84 p.D-300; Tel&CabFB 84C p.1680*
First Communications Inc. - Atlanta, GA - *TeleSy&SerDir 2-84*
First Computer Services - Chicago, IL - *ADAPSOMemDir 83-84*
First Copy - San Jose, CA - *BaconPubCkMag 84*
First Days - Cranford, NJ - *MagDir 84; MagIndMarPl 82-83*
First Dynasty Records Inc. - St. Petersburg, FL - *BillIntBG 83-84*
First East Coast Theatre & Publishing Co. Inc. - New York, NY - *BoPubDir 4, 5; LitMag&SmPr 83-84*
First Generation Programming - New York, NY - *Tel&CabFB 84C*
First Hand [of Firsthand Ltd.] - Teaneck, NJ - *WritMar 84*
First Illinois Cable TV [of Times Mirror Cable Television Inc.] - Springfield, IL - *BrCabYB 84*
First Impressions - Studio City, CA - *ArtMar 84*
First Impressions - Madison, WI - *BoPubDir 4, 5*
First Indiana Cablevision Corp. [of Omni Cable TV Corp.] - Jasonville, IN - *BrCabYB 84; Tel&CabFB 84C*
First Indiana Cablevision Corp. [of Omni Cable TV Corp.] - Oakland City, IN - *Tel&CabFB 84C*
First Indiana Cablevision Corp. - Owensville, IN - *BrCabYB 84*
First Interstate Bank of Arizona Banker - Phoenix, AZ - *ArtMar 84*
First Interstate Bank of California - Los Angeles, CA - *VideoDir 82-83*
First Lady Songs Inc. - Nashville, TN - *BillIntBG 83-84*
First Louisiana Cablevision - Bernice, LA - *BrCabYB 84*
First Marketing Group Inc. - Houston, TX - *StaDirAdAg 2-84*
First Media Corp. - Washington, DC - *BrCabYB 84*
First Michigan Cablevision [of Welbac Cable TV Corp.] - Caro, MI - *Tel&CabFB 84C*
First Michigan Cablevision [of Omni Cable TV Corp.] - Cass City, MI - *BrCabYB 84; Tel&CabFB 84C*
First Michigan Cablevision - Reese, MI - *BrCabYB 84*
First Michigan Cablevision - Vassar, MI - *BrCabYB 84*
First Mountain Foundation [Aff. of Institute for the Advancement of Philosophy for Children] - Montclair, NJ - *BoPubDir 4, 5*
First Person - Palisades, NY - *BoPubDir 4, 5; LitMag&SmPr 83-84*
First Pic Cable TV - Bullitt County, KY - *Tel&CabFB 84C*
First Rural Cable Inc. - Decatur, IL - *Tel&CabFB 84C p.1680*
First Software - Andover, MA - *MicrocomMPl 84*
First Star Software Inc. - New York, NY - *MicrocomMPl 84*
First State Gasoline Dealer News [of Delaware Gasoline Dealers Association] - Wilmington, DE - *MagDir 84*
First TV Corp. - Bremen, IN - *Tel&CabFB 84C*
First Virginia Cablevision - Amherst, VA - *BrCabYB 84*
First West Virginia Cablevision Corp. [of Omni Cable TV Corp.] - Moorefield, WV - *BrCabYB 84; Tel&CabFB 84C*
Firstcable Communications Inc. - Oregon, IL - *BrCabYB 84 p.D-300; Tel&CabFB 84C p.1679*
Firsthand Press - Juneau, AK - *BoPubDir 4 Sup, 5*
Firstline Records - Los Angeles, CA - *BillIntBG 83-84*
Firstworld Travel - Coronado Island, CA - *DataDirOnSer 84*

Firstworld Travel Service - Encino, CA - *DirOnDB Spring 84*
Fischbach, Henry - Hastings-on-Hudson, NY - *MagIndMarPl 82-83*
Fischbach, McCoach & Associates - New York, NY - *IntDirMarRes 83*
Fischbein Advertising Inc. - Minneapolis, MN - *StaDirAdAg 2-84*
Fischer & Associates Inc., Norman - Austin, TX - *CabTVFinDB 83*
Fischer & Lucus Inc. - Nashville, TN - *BillIntBG 83-84*
Fischer Associates Inc., James - Columbus, OH - *CabTVFinDB 83*
Fischer Inc., Carl - New York, NY - *BillIntBG 83-84; BoPubDir 4, 5*
Fischer Kraker Le Fever Inc. - New York, NY - *HBIndAd&MS 82-83*
Fischer Music, Bobby - Nashville, TN - *BillIntBG 83-84*
Fish & Wildlife Reference Service [of Denver Public Library] - Denver, CO - *CompReadDB 82; EISS 83*
Fish Boat, The - Covington, LA - *BaconPubCkMag 84*
Fish Boat, The [of H. L. Peace Publications] - Mandeville, LA - *MagDir 84*
Fish-Head Records - Bay City, MI - *BillIntBG 83-84*
Fish, Kevin R. - San Jose, CA - *LitMarPl 84*
Fishbein Ltd., Frieda - New York, NY - *LitMarPl 83, 84*
Fishburn Productions, Alan M. - Chicago, IL - *AvMarPl 83*
Fisher Advertising - Chicago, IL - *StaDirAdAg 2-84*
Fisher & Gottsman - New York, NY - *EISS 5-84 Sup*
Fisher & Zivi Inc. - Chicago, IL - *DirMarMP 83*
Fisher, B. & K. - Colfax, CA - *BoPubDir 4, 5*
Fisher Brady & LaBrue Advertising Inc. - Seattle, WA - *StaDirAdAg 2-84*
Fisher Broadcasting Inc. - Seattle, WA - *BrCabYB 84; Tel&CabFB 84S*
Fisher Composition Inc. - New York, NY - *LitMarPl 83, 84*
Fisher Corp. - Chatsworth, CA - *BillIntBG 83-84*
Fisher, Diana Duncan - Rockport, MA - *LitMarPl 83*
Fisher/Feld - New York, NY - *AdAge 3-28-84; StaDirAdAg 2-84*
Fisher Group, The - New York, NY - *DirPRFirms 83*
Fisher Institute - Dallas, TX - *BoPubDir 4 Sup, 5; LitMag&SmPr 83-84*
Fisher Music Corp. - New York, NY - *BillIntBG 83-84*
Fisher Organization Inc., The - New York, NY - *IntDirMarRes 83*
Fisher, Ray - Miami, FL - *MagIndMarPl 82-83*
Fisher Reporter - Fisher, IL - *BaconPubCkNews 84; Ed&PubIntYB 82*
Fisher Scientific Co. (Educational Materials Div.) - Chicago, IL - *MicrocomMPl 84*
Fisher-Stevens Inc. - Clifton, NJ - *BoPubDir 5*
Fisherman Group, The - Sag Harbor, NY - *MagDir 84*
Fisherman's Advocate - Port Union, NF, Canada - *Ed&PubIntYB 82*
Fishermen's News - Seattle, WA - *BaconPubCkMag 84; MagDir 84; MagIndMarPl 82-83*
Fisher's Island Telephone Corp., The - Fisher's Island, NY - *TelDir&BG 83-84*
Fishers Sun-Herald - Indianapolis, IN - *Ed&PubIntYB 82*
Fishers Sun Herald - *See* Topic Newspapers Inc.
Fishing & Hunting News [of Outdoor Empire Publishing Co. Inc.] - Seattle, WA - *BaconPubCkMag 84; MagDir 84; MagIndMarPl 82-83; WritMar 84*
Fishing Facts - Menomonee Falls, WI - *BaconPubCkMag 84; MagDir 84; MagIndMarPl 82-83*
Fishing Gazette - Rockland, ME - *BaconPubCkMag 84*
Fishing Gazette - New York, NY - *MagDir 84; WritMar 84*
Fishing in Maryland/Fishing in New Jersey - Phoenix, MD - *MagDir 84*
Fishing Tackle Retailer - Montgomery, AL - *BaconPubCkMag 84; MagIndMarPl 82-83; WritMar 84*
Fishing Tackle Trade News - Wilmette, IL - *BaconPubCkMag 84; MagDir 84*
Fishing World - Floral Park, NY - *BaconPubCkMag 84; MagDir 84; MagIndMarPl 82-83; WritMar 84*
Fishing World - New York, NY - *ArtMar 84*
Fishkill Standard - Fishkill, NY - *Ed&PubIntYB 82*
Fishkill Standard [of Mahopac Putnam County Press] - Mahopac, NY - *AyerDirPub 83; NewsDir 84*
Fishkill Standard - *See* Gateway Papers
Fishman Agency, Shirley - Cleveland, OH - *DirPRFirms 83*
Fishrapper - Wheeler, OR - *Ed&PubIntYB 82*
Fishtraks Communications Group Inc. - Portsmouth, NH - *BillIntBG 83-84*
Fisk Media Services - San Diego, CA - *AvMarPl 83*
Fiske Enterprises - Westlake Village, CA - *BoPubDir 4, 5*
Fist & Rose Publishers Inc. - Afula, IL - *LitMag&SmPr 83-84*
Fit - Mountain View, CA - *BaconPubCkMag 84*
Fitch Music Co., Charlie - Luling, TX - *BillIntBG 83-84*
Fitchburg Cable Communications Group - Fitchburg, WI - *BrCabYB 84; Tel&CabFB 84C*
Fitchburg-Leominster Sentinel & Enterprise [of Thomson Newspapers Inc.] - Fitchburg, MA - *AyerDirPub 83; Ed&PubIntYB 82; NewsDir 84*
Fitchburg Montachusett Review - Fitchburg, MA - *BaconPubCkNews 84*
Fitchburg Paper Co. [Div. of Litton Industries] - Fitchburg, MA - *LitMarPl 83, 84*
Fitchburg Sentinel & Enterprise - Fitchburg, MA - *BaconPubCkNews 84*
Fitchburg Star - Fitchburg, WI - *Ed&PubIntYB 82*
Fitchburg Star - Verona, WI - *AyerDirPub 83*
Fite-Davis & Associates - Oklahoma City, OK - *IntDirMarRes 83*
Fitek [of DAFSA-SNEI SA] - Paris, France - *EISS 83*
Fitness Alternatives Press - Evergreen, CO - *BoPubDir 4 Sup, 5*
Fitness First - Hanover, NH - *BoPubDir 4, 5*
Fitness Industry - North Miami, FL - *BaconPubCkMag 84; WritMar 84*
Fitness Products Ltd. - Washington, DC - *BoPubDir 4, 5*
Fitzgerald Advertising - New Orleans, LA - *AdAge 3-28-84; BrCabYB 84; DirPRFirms 83; StaDirAdAg 2-84*
Fitzgerald Gardner Advertising - New York, NY - *DirPRFirms 83; StaDirAdAg 2-84*
Fitzgerald Herald-Leader - Fitzgerald, GA - *BaconPubCkNews 84*
Fitzgerald, Jerry - Redwood City, CA - *BoPubDir 4, 5*
Fitzgerald Toole & Alden Inc. - Providence, RI - *StaDirAdAg 2-84*
Fitzhenry & Whiteside Ltd. - Don Mills, ON, Canada - *BoPubDir 4 Sup, 5; LitMarPl 83*
Fitzhenry & Whiteside Ltd. - Markham, ON, Canada - *LitMarPl 84*
Fitzpatrick Associates, Don - San Francisco, CA - *BrCabYB 84*
Fitzpatrick Cable TV - Whitesville, NY - *Tel&CabFB 84C*
Fitzpatrick Community TV System - Whitesville, NY - *BrCabYB 84*
Fitzsimons Advertising - Cleveland, OH - *AdAge 3-28-84; StaDirAdAg 2-84*
Fitzsimons Co. Inc., H. T. - Chicago, IL - *BillIntBG 83-84; BoPubDir 4, 5*
Fitzwilliam Enterprises - Guelph, ON, Canada - *BoPubDir 4, 5*
Five Arches Press - Cardiff, Wales - *LitMag&SmPr 83-84*
Five Area Telephone Cooperative Inc. - Muleshoe, TX - *TelDir&BG 83-84*
Five Arms Corp. [Aff. of Weber Systems Inc.] - Chesterland, OH - *BoPubDir 4, 5*
Five Associated University Libraries - Syracuse, NY - *EISS 83; InfIndMarPl 83*
Five Cities Times-Press-Recorder - Arroyo Grande, CA - *AyerDirPub 83; Ed&PubIntYB 82*
Five-P Photographic Processing Inc. - Houston, TX - *AvMarPl 83*
Five Star News - Manchester, PA - *AyerDirPub 83*
Five Starr Productions - Wichita Falls, TX - *BoPubDir 4 Sup, 5; LitMag&SmPr 83-84*
Five Towns Pennysaver - Rockville Centre, NY - *AyerDirPub 83*
Five Village Weekly - Irricana, AB, Canada - *Ed&PubIntYB 82*
Fixx Inc., Alice Kasman - New York, NY - *DirPRFirms 83*
Fjord Press - Corte Madera, CA - *LitMag&SmPr 83-84; LitMarPl 83, 84; WritMar 84*
FLA Groupe la Creatique - Paris, France - *EISS 7-83 Sup; InfIndMarPl 83*
Flack Studio, The - Watertown, MA - *LitMarPl 83, 84*
FLACS [of Florida Section, American Chemical Society] - Boynton Beach, FL - *MagDir 84*
FLACS [of Florida Section, American Chemical Society] - Winter Haven, FL - *BaconPubCkMag 84*
Flag Research Center - Winchester, MA - *BoPubDir 4, 5*

Flager Cable Co. Inc. [of Southland Communications Inc.] - Flager Beach, FL - *BrCabYB 84*
Flagg Films Inc. - Studio City, CA - *AvMarPl 83; Tel&CabFB 84C*
Flagler & Nelson Inc. - Hamburg, NY - *StaDirAdAg 2-84*
Flagler Cable Co. [of Southland Communications Inc.] - Bunnell, FL - *Tel&CabFB 84C*
Flagler News - Flagler, CO - *BaconPubCkNews 84; Ed&PubIntYB 82*
Flagler/Palm Coast News-Tribune - Bunnell, FL - *AyerDirPub 83*
Flagler Tribune, The - Bunnell, FL - *Ed&PubIntYB 82*
Flagstaff Arizona Daily Sun - Flagstaff, AZ - *NewsDir 84*
Flaherty, Joyce A. - St. Louis, MO - *LitMarPl 83, 84*
Flair Communications Agency - Chicago, IL - *HBIndAd&MS 82-83; StaDirAdAg 2-84*
Flair Group Ltd., The - Bala Cynwyd, PA - *StaDirAdAg 2-84*
Flamborough Review - Waterdown, ON, Canada - *AyerDirPub 83; Ed&PubIntYB 82*
Flamm Advertising Inc. - New York, NY - *LitMarPl 83, 84; MagIndMarPl 82-83; StaDirAdAg 2-84*
Flamm/Northam Authors & Publishers Services Inc. - New York, NY - *LitMarPl 83*
Flammer Inc., Harold - *See* Shawnee Press Inc.
Flanagan Advertising Agency, J. R. - New York, NY - *StaDirAdAg 2-84*
Flanagan Home Times - Flanagan, IL - *BaconPubCkNews 84; Ed&PubIntYB 82*
Flandreau Moody County Enterprise - Flandreau, SD - *BaconPubCkNews 84*
Flantzman, Maury - Studio City, CA - *HBIndAd&MS 82-83*
Flare - Toronto, ON, Canada - *BaconPubCkMag 84; WritMar 84*
Flare Books [Div. of Hearst Corp.] - New York, NY - *WritMar 84*
Flashes Shoppers Guide - Eaton Rapids, MI - *AyerDirPub 83*
Flashes Shopping Guide - Stuart, FL - *AyerDirPub 83*
Flat River Cable Services Inc. - Greenville, MI - *BrCabYB 84*
Flat River Lead Belt News - Flat River, MO - *BaconPubCkNews 84; NewsDir 84*
Flat Rock Guardian - Flat Rock, MI - *BaconPubCkNews 84; NewsDir 84*
Flat Rock Mutual Telephone Co. - Flat Rock, IL - *TelDir&BG 83-84*
Flat Rock News-Herald - Wyandotte, MI - *AyerDirPub 83*
Flat Town Music - Ville Platte, LA - *BillIntBG 83-84*
Flatbush Life [of Courier-Life Inc.] - Brooklyn, NY - *AyerDirPub 83; Ed&PubIntYB 82; NewsDir 84*
Flatbush Life - *See* Courier-Life Inc.
Flathead Courier - Polson, MT - *AyerDirPub 83; Ed&PubIntYB 82*
Flatiron Book Distributors Inc. - New York, NY - *BoPubDir 4 Sup, 5; LitMarPl 83, 84*
Flatonia Argus - Flatonia, TX - *BaconPubCkNews 84; Ed&PubIntYB 82*
Flax Advertising - New York, NY - *ArtMar 84; StaDirAdAg 2-84*
Flax Inc., Sam - New York, NY - *LitMarPl 83*
Fleet Information - Providence, RI - *DataDirSup 7-83*
Fleet Maintenance & Specifying - Chicago, IL - *MagDir 84*
Fleet Maintenance & Specifying - Lincolnwood, IL - *BaconPubCkMag 84*
Fleet Owner - New York, NY - *BaconPubCkMag 84; MagDir 84; MagIndMarPl 82-83*
Fleet Press Corp. - New York, NY - *LitMarPl 83, 84; WritMar 84*
Fleet Publishers [Div. of International Thomson Ltd.] - Scarborough, ON, Canada - *LitMarPl 83*
Fleet Service/Media - Ft. Wayne, IN - *StaDirAdAg 2-84*
Fleetwood Graphics [Subs. of Fleetwood Art Studio Inc.] - Madison, WI - *LitMarPl 83, 84*
Fleetwood Inc. - Zeeland, MI - *AvMarPl 83*
Fleetwood Mac Music - Beverly Hills, CA - *BillIntBG 83-84*
Fleetwood Multi-Video Corp. - Fleetwood, PA - *BrCabYB 84*
Fleishman Chatham & Dirico Inc. - Atlanta, GA - *DirPRFirms 83*
Fleishman-Hillard Inc. - St. Louis, MO - *DirPRFirms 83*
Fleming Agency, Peter - Los Angeles, CA - *LitMarPl 83, 84*
Fleming Cable Vision Inc. [of Standard Tobacco Co. Inc.] - Flemingsburg, KY - *BrCabYB 84; Tel&CabFB 84C*
Fleming Gazette - Flemingsburg, KY - *Ed&PubIntYB 82*
Fleming Press - Dundas, ON, Canada - *BoPubDir 4, 5*
Flemingsburg Gazette - Flemingsburg, KY - *AyerDirPub 83; BaconPubCkNews 84*
Flemingsburg Times-Democrat - Flemingsburg, KY - *BaconPubCkNews 84; Ed&PubIntYB 82*
Fles Literary Agency, Barthold - New York, NY - *LitMarPl 83, 84*
Fletcher Herald - Fletcher, OK - *BaconPubCkNews 84; Ed&PubIntYB 82*
Fletcher Hills/El Cajon West Pennysaver - Mission Viejo, CA - *AyerDirPub 83*
Fletcher/Mayo Associates - Atlanta, GA - *ArtMar 84*
Fletcher/Mayo Associates [Subs. of Doyle Dane Bernbach International Inc.] - St. Joseph, MO - *AdAge 3-28-84; ArtMar 84; DirMarMP 83; StaDirAdAg 2-84*
Fletcher-Walker-Gessell Inc. - Midland Park, NJ - *StaDirAdAg 2-84*
Fleurette Records - Claymont, DE - *BillIntBG 83-84*
Flex - Woodland Hills, CA - *BaconPubCkMag 84*
FLEX Inc. - New York, NY - *AvMarPl 83; DirMarMP 83; LitMarPl 83, 84; MagIndMarPl 82-83*
Flex Stream [of American Satellite Co.] - Rockville, MD - *TeleSy&SerDir 2-84*
Flex-Y-Plan Industries Inc. - Erie, PA - *DirInfWP 82*
Flexible Automation - Ho-Ho-Kus, NJ - *MicrocomMPl 84*
Flexible Diskettes [of GML Corp.] - Lexington, MA - *CompReadDB 82*
Flexiduct - Lincoln, NE - *MicrocomMPl 84*
Flexographic Technical Journal - Huntington Station, NY - *BaconPubCkMag 84*
Flick, Cathy - Richmond, IN - *LitMarPl 83, 84*
Flight Line Times [of Data Publications Inc.] - Brookfield, CT - *MagDir 84*
Flight Operations Magazine [of Mucro Communications] - Norcross, GA - *MagDir 84*
Flight Reports [of Peter Katz Productions Inc.] - Yonkers, NY - *WritMar 84*
Flin-Flon Country - Mullen, NE - *BillIntBG 83-84*
Flin-Flon Music - Mullen, NE - *BillIntBG 83-84*
Fling Poetry - Eltham, VI, Australia - *LitMag&SmPr 83-84*
Flinn Communications Corp. - Rockland, ME - *BrCabYB 84*
Flinn Communications of Ohio Inc. - Aberdeen, OH - *BrCabYB 84*
Flinn Communications of Ohio Inc. - Georgetown, OH - *BrCabYB 84*
Flinn Communications of Ohio Inc. - Higginsport, OH - *BrCabYB 84*
Flinn Communications of Ohio Inc. - Manchester, OH - *BrCabYB 84*
Flinn Communications of Ohio Inc. - Ripley, OH - *BrCabYB 84*
Flinn, Lawrence Jr. - Greenwich, CT - *BrCabYB 84 p.D-300*
Flinn, Lawrence Jr. - *See* United Video Cablevision Inc.
Flinn Typographic Service Inc. - Stamford, CT - *LitMarPl 84*
Flint Advertising Agency - Fargo, ND - *AdAge 3-28-84; StaDirAdAg 2-84*
Flint Journal [of Booth Newspapers Inc.] - Flint, MI - *BaconPubCkNews 84; Ed&PubIntYB 82; LitMarPl 83, 84; NewsBur 6; NewsDir 84*
Flint Spokesman, The - Flint, MI - *NewsDir 84*
Flint Suburban News - Flint, MI - *BaconPubCkNews 84*
Flippin TV Cable Inc. - Flippin, AR - *BrCabYB 84; Tel&CabFB 84C*
FlipTrack Learning Systems [Div. of Mosaic Media Inc.] - Glen Ellyn, IL - *AvMarPl 83; MicrocomSwDir 1; WritMar 84*
Flitebrief - Bedford, MA - *DirOnDB Spring 84*
FLM Joint Board Tempo [of Union-FLM Joint Board] - New York, NY - *NewsDir 84*
Floating Island Publications - Point Reyes Station, CA - *BoPubDir 4, 5; LitMag&SmPr 83-84*
Floating Point Systems - Portland, OR - *DataDirSup 7-83; Datamation 6-83; Top100Al 83*
Floating Tones - *See* Prophecy Publishing Inc.
Flomation Tri City Ledger - Flomation, AL - *BaconPubCkNews 84*
Flood & Associates Inc., Jim - Paradise, CA - *DirPRFirms 83*

Floodwood Forum - Floodwood, MN - *BaconPubCkNews 84*
Floor Covering News - Toronto, ON, Canada - *BaconPubCkMag 84*
Floor Covering Weekly [of The Hearst Corp.] - New York, NY - *BaconPubCkMag 84; MagDir 84*
Flooring [of Harcourt Brace & Jovanovich Publications] - New York, NY - *BaconPubCkMag 84; MagDir 84; MagIndMarPl 82-83*
Flora & Fauna Publications Inc. - Gainesville, FL - *BoPubDir 5; LitMarPl 84*
Flora & Fauna Publications Inc. - Kinderhook, NY - *BoPubDir 4*
Flora Associates Inc., Sam - Weston, CT - *StaDirAdAg 2-84*
Flora Cable TV - Flora, IL - *BrCabYB 84 p.D-301; Tel&CabFB 84C p.1680*
Flora Cable TV Inc. - Flora, IN - *Tel&CabFB 84C*
Flora Carroll County Comet - Flora, IN - *BaconPubCkNews 84*
Flora Daily Clay County Advocate Press - Flora, IL - *BaconPubCkNews 84*
Floral Mass Marketing - Chicago, IL - *MagDir 84*
Floral Park-Bellerose Pennysaver/North & South - Jericho, NY - *AyerDirPub 83*
Floral Park Bulletin - Floral Park, NY - *Ed&PubIntYB 82; NewsDir 84*
Floral Park Bulletin - *See* Nassau Border Papers Inc.
Floral Park Dispatch - Floral Park, NY - *AyerDirPub 83; BaconPubCkNews 84; Ed&PubIntYB 82*
Floral Park Gateway - Floral Park, NY - *BaconPubCkNews 84; NewsDir 84*
Floral Park-Glen Oaks Ad World - Great Neck, NY - *AyerDirPub 83*
Florala News - Florala, AL - *BaconPubCkNews 84; Ed&PubIntYB 82*
Florala Telephone Co. Inc., The - Florala, AL - *TelDir&BG 83-84*
Floram Park Eagle - Madison, NJ - *AyerDirPub 83*
Florascope - Glen Ellyn, IL - *BaconPubCkMag 84*
Flordia TV Cable [of American TV & Communications Corp.] - Ormond Beach, FL - *Tel&CabFB 84C*
Florence Black Sun - Columbia, SC - *AyerDirPub 83*
Florence Black Sun - *See* Juju Publishing Co.
Florence Cable Co. - Florence, MI - *Tel&CabFB 84C*
Florence Cable Co. - Iron Mountain, MI - *BrCabYB 84*
Florence Cable TV - Dunes City, OR - *BrCabYB 84*
Florence Cable TV - Florence, OR - *BrCabYB 84*
Florence Citizen - Florence, CO - *BaconPubCkNews 84; Ed&PubIntYB 82*
Florence Courier-Journal - Florence, AL - *BaconPubCkNews 84*
Florence Dixie News - Florence, KY - *BaconPubCkNews 84*
Florence Herald - Florence, AL - *Ed&PubIntYB 82*
Florence Herald-Picture - Florence, AL - *AyerDirPub 83*
Florence Mining News [of Florence Tri-County Independent] - Florence, WI - *NewsDir 84*
Florence Mining News - *See* Florence Mining News Publishers
Florence Mining News Publishers - Florence, WI - *BaconPubCkNews 84*
Florence Morning News [of Thomson Newspapers Inc.] - Florence, SC - *BaconPubCkNews 84; Ed&PubIntYB 82; NewsDir 84*
Florence Reminder & Blade Tribune - Florence, AZ - *AyerDirPub 83*
Florence Reminer & Blade Tribune - *See* Casa Grande Valley Newspapers Inc.
Florence Shoals News-Leader - Florence, AL - *BaconPubCkNews 84*
Florence Siuslaw News - Florence, OR - *BaconPubCkNews 84; NewsDir 84*
Florence Telephone Co. [Aff. of Mid-Continent Telephone Corp.] - Florence, MS - *TelDir&BG 83-84*
Florence Times [of Tri-Cities Newspapers Inc.] - Florence, AL - *BaconPubCkNews 84; NewsDir 84*
Florence Times-Tri Cities Daily [of Tri-Cities Newspapers Inc.] - Florence, AL - *Ed&PubIntYB 82*
Florence Tri-County Independent - Florence, WI - *BaconPubCkNews 84*
Florentine Music - *See* Dawn Productions Ltd.
Florentine Press - Jacksonville, FL - *BoPubDir 5*
Floresville & Poth Cablevision [of Communications Systems Inc.] - Floresville, TX - *Tel&CabFB 84C*
Floresville Chronicle-Journal - Floresville, TX - *BaconPubCkNews 84; Ed&PubIntYB 82; NewsDir 84*
Florham Park Community News - Florham Park, NJ - *Ed&PubIntYB 82*
Florham Park Press Inc. - Florham Park, NJ - *BoPubDir 4, 5*
Florida Banker [of Florida Bankers Association] - Orlando, FL - *ArtMar 84; BaconPubCkMag 84; MagDir 84; WritMar 84*
Florida Bar Journal, The - Tallahassee, FL - *BaconPubCkMag 84; MagDir 84*
Florida Builder [of Peninsula Publishing Co.] - Tampa, FL - *BaconPubCkMag 84; MagDir 84*
Florida Cable TV Network Inc. - Orlando, FL - *Tel&CabFB 84C p.1680*
Florida Cablevision Corp. [of Rogers UA Cablesystems Inc.] - Ft. Pierce, FL - *BrCabYB 84; Tel&CabFB 84C*
Florida Cablevision Corp. [of Rogers UA Cablesystems Inc.] - Vero Beach, FL - *BrCabYB 84; Tel&CabFB 84C*
Florida Catholic, The - Tampa, FL - *NewsDir 84*
Florida Cattleman & Livestock Journal - Kissimmee, FL - *BaconPubCkMag 84; MagDir 84*
Florida Chamber of Commerce - Tallahassee, FL - *BoPubDir 5*
Florida Clearview Inc. - Crescent City, FL - *Tel&CabFB 84C*
Florida Clearview Inc. - Jacksonville, FL - *Tel&CabFB 84C p.1680*
Florida Clearview Inc. - Lake Butler, FL - *Tel&CabFB 84C*
Florida Clearview Inc. - Mayport Naval Air Station, FL - *BrCabYB 84*
Florida Clipping Service - Tampa, FL - *ProGuPRSer 4*
Florida Computer Graphics - Lake Mary, FL - *DataDirSup 7-83; MicrocomMPl 84; WhoWMicrocom 83*
Florida Computer Inc. - North Miami, FL - *DataDirOnSer 84; EISS 7-83 Sup*
Florida Construction Industry [of Technical Communications] - Orlando, FL - *BaconPubCkMag 84; MagDir 84*
Florida Contractor - Tallahassee, FL - *BaconPubCkMag 84; MagDir 84*
Florida Courier - Miami, FL - *Ed&PubIntYB 82*
Florida Data Corp. - Melbourne, FL - *DataDirSup 7-83; DirInfWP 82; MicrocomMPl 84*
Florida Designers Quarterly - Miami, FL - *BaconPubCkMag 84*
Florida Educators' Information Service [of Florida State University] - Tallahassee, FL - *EISS 83*
Florida Explorer - Tampa, FL - *BaconPubCkMag 84; MagDir 84*
Florida Fireman [of Florida State Firemen's Association Inc.] - Avon Park, FL - *BaconPubCkMag 84; MagDir 84*
Florida Flambeau Foundation Inc. - Tallahassee, FL - *NewsDir 84*
Florida Folklife Program [of Florida Dept. of State] - White Springs, FL - *BillIntBG 83-84*
Florida Food & Grocery News - Indian Rocks Beach, FL - *BaconPubCkMag 84; MagDir 84*
Florida Food Dealer [of Retail Grocers Association of Florida Inc.] - Ocala, FL - *BaconPubCkMag 84; MagDir 84; WritMar 84*
Florida Forum [of FRSA Services Corp.] - Winter Park, FL - *BaconPubCkMag 84; MagDir 84; WritMar 84*
Florida Funeral Director - Tallahassee, FL - *BaconPubCkMag 84*
Florida Future Farmer Magazine - Tallahassee, FL - *MagDir 84*
Florida Golfweek - Winter Haven, FL - *BaconPubCkMag 84*
Florida Grocer [of Trade Publishers] - Miami, FL - *BaconPubCkMag 84; MagDir 84*
Florida Grower & Rancher - Orlando, FL - *BaconPubCkMag 84; MagDir 84; WritMar 84*
Florida Gulf Coast Living [of Baker Publications Inc.] - Tampa, FL - *BaconPubCkMag 84; WritMar 84*
Florida Gulf Coast Living - Dallas, TX - *MagIndMarPl 82-83*
Florida Homefurnishings - New York, NY - *BaconPubCkMag 84*
Florida Hotel & Motel News [of Accomodations Inc.] - Tallahassee, FL - *BaconPubCkMag 84; MagDir 84; WritMar 84*
Florida-It Offers You More - Miami, FL - *LitMag&SmPr 83-84*
Florida Keys Keynoter - Florida Keys, FL - *Ed&PubIntYB 82*
Florida Keys Keynoter - Marathon, FL - *AyerDirPub 83*
Florida Keys Magazine [of FKM Publishing Co. Inc.] - Marathon, FL - *WritMar 84*
Florida Library Information Network [of Florida State Library] - Tallahassee, FL - *EISS 83*

Florida MDS Inc. - Gainesville, FL - *Tel&CabFB 84C*
Florida Monthly - Miami, FL - *MagDir 84*
Florida Municipal Record [of Florida League of Cities] - Tallahassee, FL - *BaconPubCkMag 84; MagDir 84*
Florida Music Director - Tampa, FL - *MagDir 84*
Florida Nursing News - Ft. Lauderdale, FL - *BaconPubCkMag 84*
Florida Online Users Groups [of Gould Inc.] - Ft. Lauderdale, FL - *InfIndMarPl 83*
Florida Photo News - West Palm Beach, FL - *Ed&PubIntYB 82*
Florida Production Center - Jacksonville, FL - *AvMarPl 83; WritMar 84*
Florida Publishing Co. - Jacksonville, FL - *Ed&PubIntYB 82*
Florida Purchaser - Jacksonville, FL - *BaconPubCkMag 84; MagDir 84*
Florida Racquet Journal - Jacksonville, FL - *BaconPubCkMag 84; WritMar 84*
Florida Realtor [of Florida Association of Realtors] - Orlando, FL - *MagDir 84*
Florida Restaurant, Hotel, & Motel Journal, The - Pensacola, FL - *MagDir 84*
Florida Restaurateur - North Miami, FL - *BaconPubCkMag 84*
Florida Schools - Tallahassee, FL - *MagDir 84*
Florida Sentinel-Bulletin - Tampa, FL - *AyerDirPub 83*
Florida Shipper - Miami, FL - *BaconPubCkMag 84*
Florida Singles Magazine & Date Book - Palm Beach, FL - *WritMar 84*
Florida Software Services Inc. - Orlando, FL - *DataDirSup 7-83*
Florida Spicifier, The - Orlando, FL - *BaconPubCkMag 84*
Florida Sportsman - Miami, FL - *BaconPubCkMag 84; MagDir 84; MagIndMarPl 82-83*
Florida Star-News - Jacksonville, FL - *Ed&PubIntYB 82*
Florida State University (Friends of the Florida State University Library) - Tallahassee, FL - *BoPubDir 4, 5*
Florida State University (State Library) - Tallahassee, FL - *AvMarPl 83*
Florida Sun Review - Orlando, FL - *AyerDirPub 83; Ed&PubIntYB 82*
Florida Times Union - Jacksonville, FL - *AyerDirPub 83; BaconPubCkNews 84; Ed&PubIntYB 82; LitMarPl 83, 84; NewsBur 6*
Florida Trend - St. Petersburg, FL - *BaconPubCkMag 84; MagDir 84*
Florida Truck News - Tallahassee, FL - *BaconPubCkMag 84; MagDir 84*
Florida TV Cable [of American TV & Communications Corp.] - Melbourne, FL - *Tel&CabFB 84C*
Florida Video [of Group W Cable Inc.] - Perry, FL - *BrCabYB 84; Tel&CabFB 84C*
Floridagriculture - Gainesville, FL - *BaconPubCkMag 84; MagDir 84*
Florissant Buywizer, The [of Florissant Valley Publishing Co.] - Florissant, MO - *NewsDir 84*
Florissant Valley Reporter - Florissant, MO - *BaconPubCkNews 84; Ed&PubIntYB 82; NewsDir 84*
Florist [of Florist's Transworld Delivery] - Southfield, MI - *ArtMar 84; BaconPubCkMag 84; MagDir 84; WritMar 84*
Florists' Review - Chicago, IL - *BaconPubCkMag 84; MagDir 84*
Flotation Sleep Industry - Santa Ana, CA - *BaconPubCkMag 84*
Flournoy & Gibbs Inc. - Toledo, OH - *DirPRFirms 83; StaDirAdAg 2-84*
Flow of Funds [of Evans Economics Inc.] - Washington, DC - *DataDirOnSer 84; DirOnDB Spring 84*
Flow of Funds Accounts [of U.S. Federal Reserve Board] - Washington, DC - *DBBus 82*
Flower & Garden Magazine [of Modern Handcraft Inc.] - Kansas City, MO - *ArtMar 84; BaconPubCkMag 84; Folio 83; MagDir 84; MagIndMarPl 82-83; WritMar 84*
Flower City Printing - Rochester, NY - *MagIndMarPl 82-83*
Flower Films - El Cerrito, CA - *AvMarPl 83*
Flower Mound Community Cable Inc. [of CATV Systems Inc.] - Flower Mound, TX - *BrCabYB 84*
Flower News [of Central Flower News Inc.] - Chicago, IL - *BaconPubCkMag 84; MagDir 84; WritMar 84*
Flower Press [Aff. of Flowerfield Enterprises] - Kalamazoo, MI - *BoPubDir 4, 5; LitMag&SmPr 83-84*
Flowers & - Los Angeles, CA - *BaconPubCkMag 84; WritMar 84*
Flowers & [of Teleflora Inc.] - Redondo Beach, CA - *MagDir 84; MagIndMarPl 82-83*
Flowers Recording Studio - Swoope, VA - *BillIntBG 83-84*
Floyd County Cablevision Inc. - Charles City, IA - *Tel&CabFB 84C*
Floyd County Hesperian - Floydada, TX - *AyerDirPub 83; NewsDir 84*
Floyd County Times - Prestonsburg, KY - *AyerDirPub 83; Ed&PubIntYB 82*
Floyd Press - Floyd, VA - *BaconPubCkNews 84; Ed&PubIntYB 82; NewsDir 84*
Floydada Cable TV [of TCA Cable TV Group] - Floydada, TX - *BrCabYB 84; Tel&CabFB 84C*
Floydada Floyd County Hesperian - Floydada, TX - *BaconPubCkNews 84*
Floydada Hesperian - Floydada, TX - *Ed&PubIntYB 82*
Fluchere, Henri - Irvington, NY - *LitMarPl 83, 84; MagIndMarPl 82-83*
Flue Cured Tobacco Farmer - Raleigh, NC - *BaconPubCkMag 84; MagDir 84*
Flug Revue & Flugwelt International [of Vereinigte Motor-Verlage GmbH & Co.] - Palos Verdes Peninsula, CA - *BaconPubCkMag 84; MagDir 84*
Fluid & Lubricant Ideas - Walnut Creek, CA - *BaconPubCkMag 84*
Fluid Mixtures Data Center [of U.S. National Bureau of Standards] - Boulder, CO - *EISS 7-83 Sup*
Fluker & Associates Advertising Agency - Macon, GA - *ArtMar 84; StaDirAdAg 2-84*
Flushing East Advertiser - Great Neck, NY - *AyerDirPub 83*
Flushing New York Voice - Flushing, NY - *BaconPubCkNews 84; NewsDir 84*
Flushing Observer - Flushing, MI - *BaconPubCkNews 84; Ed&PubIntYB 82; NewsDir 84*
Flushing Pennysaver - Jericho, NY - *AyerDirPub 83*
Flushing Tribune - Flushing, NY - *Ed&PubIntYB 82; NewsDir 84*
Fly Fisherman [of Historical Times Inc.] - Harrisburg, PA - *ArtMar 84; BaconPubCkMag 84; WritMar 84*
Fly Fisherman - Dorset, VT - *MagDir 84; MagIndMarPl 82-83*
Fly Tyer - North Conway, NH - *BaconPubCkMag 84; BoPubDir 5*
Flyer News, The [of University of Dayton] - Dayton, OH - *NewsDir 84*
Flyfisher, The - Idaho Falls, ID - *ArtMar 84; WritMar 84*
Flying [of Ziff-Davis Publishing Co.] - New York, NY - *BaconPubCkMag 84; Folio 83; MagDir 84; MagIndMarPl 82-83; WritMar 84*
Flying A Ltd. - Ithaca, NY - *BillIntBG 83-84*
Flying A Pictures Inc. - Hollywood, CA - *Tel&CabFB 84C*
Flying A, The [of Aeroquip Corp.] - Jackson, MI - *WritMar 84*
Flying Buttress Publications - Endicott, NY - *BoPubDir 4, 5; LitMag&SmPr 83-84*
Flying Buyers' Guide [of Ziff-Davis Publishing Co.] - New York, NY - *MagDir 84*
Flying Camera Inc. - New York, NY - *AvMarPl 83; Ed&PubIntYB 82*
Flying Colors - Miami, FL - *MagDir 84*
Flying Diamond Books - Hettinger, ND - *BoPubDir 4, 5*
Flying Eye Graphics - New York, NY - *AvMarPl 83*
Flying Fish Music - Chicago, IL - *BillIntBG 83-84*
Flying Fish Records Inc. - Chicago, IL - *BillIntBG 83-84*
Flying Lady Music - *See* North Ranch Music
Flying Models - Newton, NJ - *BaconPubCkMag 84; MagDir 84*
Flying Tigers - Los Angeles, CA - *MagIndMarPl 82-83*
Flying Your Way - Boston, MA - *MagDir 84*
Flynt Distributing Co. Inc. - Los Angeles, CA - *MagIndMarPl 82-83*
FM Atlas Publishing Co. - Adolph, MN - *BoPubDir 4, 5*
FM4 Gila River Corp. - Chandler, AZ - *ADAPSOMemDir 83-84*
FMG Corp. - Ft. Worth, TX - *MicrocomMPl 83, 84; WhoWMicrocom 83*
FMJ Inc. - Torrance, CA - *MicrocomMPl 84*
FMQ [of Bibliotheque Nationale du Quebec] - Montreal, PQ, Canada - *DataDirOnSer 84; EISS 83*
FNI Communications Co. - Beverly Hills, CA - *Tel&CabFB 84C p.1680*

FNI Communications Co. - Columbia, TN - *BrCabYB 84; Tel&CabFB 84C*
FNI Communications Co. [of National Telecommunications Corp.] - Cookeville, TN - *BrCabYB 84; Tel&CabFB 84C*
FNI Communications Co. [of National Telecommunications Corp.] - Paris, TN - *BrCabYB 84; Tel&CabFB 84C*
FNI Communications Co. [of Rifkin & Associates] - Tullahoma, TN - *BrCabYB 84; Tel&CabFB 84C*
FNI Communications Co. - *See* National Telecommunications Corp.
FOA Index Group [of Research Institute of National Defense] - Stockholm, Sweden - *EISS 83*
Foard County News - Crowell, TX - *AyerDirPub 83*
Foard County News & Crowell Index, The - Crowell, TX - *Ed&PubIntYB 82*
Focal Point Music - Warner Robins, GA - *BillIntBG 83-84*
Focal Press [Div. of Butterworth Publishers] - Woburn, MA - *LitMarPl 83, 84; WritMar 84*
Focus [of Rockville Sentinel Newspapers] - Rockville, MD - *NewsDir 84*
Focus - Albuquerque, NM - *AyerDirPub 83*
Focus - New York, NY - *WritMar 84*
Focus [of Ohio AFL-CIO] - Columbus, OH - *NewsDir 84*
Focus - Philadelphia, PA - *BaconPubCkMag 84*
Focus [of Hartland Lake Country Reporter] - Hartland, WI - *NewsDir 84*
Focus [of Ontario Library Association] - Toronto, ON, Canada - *LitMag&SmPr 83-84*
Focus [of British Science Fiction Association Ltd.] - Reading, England - *LitMag&SmPr 83-84*
Focus: A Journal for Lesbians [of Daughters of Bilitis] - Cambridge, MA - *LitMag&SmPr 83-84; WritMar 84*
Focus Broadcast Satellite Corp. - Nashville, TN - *BrCabYB 84*
Focus Cable of Oakland Inc. - Oakland, CA - *BrCabYB 84*
Focus International - New York, NY - *AvMarPl 83*
Focus Magazine [of KQED Inc.] - San Francisco, CA - *ArtMar 84*
Focus Market Research Inc. - Bloomington, MN - *IntDirMarRes 83*
Focus/Metro Philadelphia Business Newsweekly [of Business News Inc.] - Philadelphia, PA - *MagDir 84*
Focus/Midwest - St. Louis, MO - *LitMag&SmPr 83-84; MagDir 84; MagIndMarPl 82-83; WritMar 84*
Focus/Midwest Publishing Co. Inc. - St. Louis, MO - *LitMag&SmPr 83-84*
Focus New York - New York, NY - *ArtMar 84; BaconPubCkMag 84*
Focus on Critical Care - St. Louis, MO - *BaconPubCkMag 84*
Focus on Dallas - Dallas, TX - *IntDirMarRes 83*
Focus on Groups - Huntington, NY - *IntDirMarRes 83*
Focus on Information Ltd. - London, England - *FBInfSer 80*
Focus on the Baking Industry - Port Credit, ON, Canada - *BaconPubCkMag 84*
Focus One - Beverly Hills, CA - *IntDirMarRes 83*
Focus Publishing Co. - Farmington Hills, MI - *BoPubDir 5*
Focus Research of Georgia Inc. - Atlanta, GA - *BrCabYB 84*
Focus Research Systems Inc. - West Hartford, CT - *ADAPSOMemDir 83-84*
Focus Room & Field Service of N.Y. Inc., The - Hartsdale, NY - *IntDirMarRes 83*
Focus/Typographers - St. Louis, MO - *MagIndMarPl 82-83*
Focuscope Unltd. - Oak Park, IL - *IntDirMarRes 83*
Fodor's Modern Guides Inc. [Subs. of Morgan-Grampian Inc.] - New York, NY - *LitMarPl 83*
Fodor's Travel Guides [Subs. of Morgan-Grampian Inc.] - New York, NY - *LitMarPl 84; WritMar 84*
Foerster-Forlini Associates Inc. - New York, NY - *LitMarPl 83*
Foerster-Forlini Market Research - New York, NY - *LitMarPl 83*
Fogarty & Klein - Houston, TX - *AdAge 3-28-84; StaDirAdAg 2-84*
Fogel, Stephanie - Brooklyn, NY - *LitMarPl 83; MagIndMarPl 82-83*
Fogerty's Market Research - San Diego, CA - *IntDirMarRes 83*
Fogg Software, Mark - Lafayette, CA - *MicrocomMPl 84*
Fogle Computing Corp. - Spartanburg, SC - *MicrocomMPl 84; MicrocomSwDir 1; WhoWMicrocom 83*
FOI: Newsline - Rockville, MD - *DirOnDB Spring 84*
FOI Services Inc. - Rockville, MD - *CompReadDB 82; EISS 83; InfIndMarPl 83*
Folcroft Library Editions/Norwood Editions - Darby, PA - *LitMarPl 83, 84; WritMar 84*
Folder Editions - Forest Hills, NY - *BoPubDir 4, 5; LitMag&SmPr 83-84*
Foley Advertising Inc. - Oak Brook, IL - *ArtMar 84; StaDirAdAg 2-84*
Foley Agency, The - New York, NY - *LitMarPl 83, 84*
Foley Benton County News - Foley, MN - *BaconPubCkNews 84*
Foley Onlooker - Foley, AL - *BaconPubCkNews 84; Ed&PubIntYB 82*
Foley Public Relations & Promotion - King of Prussia, PA - *DirPRFirms 83*
Folio - London, England - *LitMag&SmPr 83-84*
Folio Advertising Ltd. - Toronto, ON, Canada - *StaDirAdAg 2-84*
Folio Publishing Corp. - New Canaan, CT - *LitMarPl 83, 84*
Folio: The Magazine for Magazine Management - New Canaan, CT - *BaconPubCkMag 84; LitMarPl 83, 84; MagDir 84; MagIndMarPl 82-83; WritMar 84*
Folk Art Studios - El Toro, CA - *BoPubDir 4, 5*
Folk Arts Productions - Huntington, NY - *BillIntBG 83-84*
Folk-Legacy Records Inc. - Sharon, CT - *BillIntBG 83-84; BoPubDir 4, 5*
Folkestone Press - St. Louis, MO - *BoPubDir 4, 5*
Folklore Music - Santa Monica, CA - *BillIntBG 83-84*
Folkraft Publishing Co. Inc. - Newark, NJ - *BillIntBG 83-84*
Folks Upstairs Press, The - Toronto, ON, Canada - *LitMag&SmPr 83-84*
Folksay Press - St. Clairsville, OH - *BoPubDir 4, 5*
Folkston Charlton County Herald - Folkston, GA - *BaconPubCkNews 84*
Folkston Clearview Cable TV [of Group W Cable Inc.] - Folkston, GA - *BrCabYB 84; Tel&CabFB 84C*
Folkways Music Publishers Inc. - *See* TRO
Folkways Records & Service Corp. - New York, NY - *AvMarPl 83; BillIntBG 83-84*
Follansbee Review - Follansbee, WV - *Ed&PubIntYB 82*
Follansbee Review - Wellsburg, WV - *BaconPubCkNews 84*
Follett Library Book Co. [Div. of Follett Corp.] - Crystal Lake, IL - *AvMarPl 83; BoPubDir 4 Sup, 5; LitMarPl 83, 84; MicrocomMPl 84*
Follett Library Book Co. (Micro Computer Div.) - Crystal Lake, IL - *AvMarPl 83*
Follett Lipscomb County Limelight - Follett, TX - *BaconPubCkNews 84*
Follett Publishing Co. [Div. of Follett Corp.] - Chicago, IL - *LitMarPl 83, 84*
Follow Focus - Toluca Lake, CA - *BaconPubCkMag 84*
Followup File - Lancaster, PA - *MagIndMarPl 82-83*
Folsom Ridley Press - *See* Press Publishing Co.
Folsom Shopper - Folsom, CA - *AyerDirPub 83*
Folsom Telegraph - Folson, CA - *Ed&PubIntYB 82*
Folsom Telegraph/Orangevale News [of Foothill Communications Corp.] - Folsom, CA - *NewsDir 84*
Foltz-Wessinger Inc. - Lancaster, PA - *BrCabYB 84; StaDirAdAg 2-84*
Fond du Lac Reporter [of Thomson Newspapers Inc.] - Fond du Lac, WI - *BaconPubCkNews 84; Ed&PubIntYB 82; NewsDir 84*
Fonda Mohawk Valley Democrat - Fonda, NY - *BaconPubCkNews 84*
Fonda Times - Fonda, IA - *BaconPubCkNews 84; Ed&PubIntYB 82*
Fonds Quetelet Library Data Base [of Ministry of Economic Affairs] - Brussels, Belgium - *CompReadDB 82; EISS 83; InfIndMarPl 83*
Fones & Mann - New York, NY - *AdAge 3-28-84; StaDirAdAg 2-84*
Fones Inc., John Scott - New York, NY - *DirPRFirms 83*
Fong Advertising Inc., Ken - Stockton, CA - *StaDirAdAg 2-84*
Font & Vaamond Associates Inc. - New York, NY - *StaDirAdAg 2-84*
Fontana Herald-News - Fontana, CA - *BaconPubCkNews 84; NewsDir 84*
Fontana, John M. - Huntington, NY - *BoPubDir 4, 5*
Fontanelle Observer - Fontanelle, IA - *BaconPubCkNews 84; Ed&PubIntYB 82*

Fontayne Group, The - Marina del Rey, CA - *DirPRFirms 83*
Fonthill Herald - Fonthill, ON, Canada - *AyerDirPub 83*
Food, Agriculture, & Nutrition Inventory [of U.S. Dept. of Agriculture] - Washington, DC - *EISS 83*
Food & Agriculture Organization - Washington, DC - *CompReadDB 82*
Food & Beverage Marketing - New York, NY - *BaconPubCkMag 84; MagIndMarPl 82-83*
Food & Drink Inc. - New York, NY - *HBIndAd&MS 82-83*
Food & Drug Packaging - New York, NY - *MagDir 84; MagIndMarPl 82-83*
Food & Drug Packaging - Cleveland, OH - *BaconPubCkMag 84*
Food & Fiber Letter - McLean, VA - *BaconPubCkMag 84*
Food & Nutrition Information Center [of U.S. Dept. of Agriculture] - Beltsville, MD - *EISS 83; InfIndMarPl 83*
Food & Nutrition Press Inc. - Westport, CT - *LitMarPl 83, 84*
Food & Wine [of American Express Publishing Corp.] - New York, NY - *ArtMar 84; BaconPubCkMag 84; Folio 83; WritMar 84*
Food Chemical News - Washington, DC - *BaconPubCkMag 84*
Food Development - New York, NY - *MagIndMarPl 82-83*
Food Distributor Systems Inc. - Stratford, CT - *DataDirSup 7-83*
Food Distributors Magazine - Barrington, RI - *BaconPubCkMag 84*
Food Distributors News [of National Food Distributors Association] - Chicago, IL - *MagDir 84*
Food, Drug, & Cosmetic Manufacturing [of Putnam Publishing Co.] - Chicago, IL - *MagDir 84*
Food Engineering - Chicago, IL - *NewsBur 6*
Food Engineering - Radnor, PA - *BaconPubCkMag 84; MagIndMarPl 82-83*
Food First Books [Div. of Institute for Food & Development Policy] - San Francisco, CA - *LitMarPl 83, 84*
Food for Thought Publications - Amherst, MA - *LitMag&SmPr 83-84*
Food Group, The - New York, NY - *StaDirAdAg 2-84*
Food Herald [of North Central Texas Food Industry Association] - Dallas, TX - *BaconPubCkMag 84; MagDir 84*
Food in Canada - Toronto, ON, Canada - *BaconPubCkMag 84*
Food Industry Newsletter, The - New York, NY - *BaconPubCkMag 84*
Food Industry Skirmisher, The - Baltimore, MD - *MagDir 84*
Food Management - New York, NY - *BaconPubCkMag 84; MagDir 84*
Food Marketing Communicator - New York, NY - *BaconPubCkMag 84*
Food Merchants Advocate [of NY State Food Merchants Association] - Tarrytown, NY - *BaconPubCkMag 84; MagDir 84*
Food Monitor - New York, NY - *MagIndMarPl 82-83*
Food People - Atlanta, GA - *BaconPubCkMag 84*
Food Plant Ideas - Minneapolis, MN - *BaconPubCkMag 84; MagIndMarPl 82-83*
Food Plant Industry [of Machalek Publishing Co.] - Minneapolis, MN - *MagDir 84*
Food Processing [of Putnam Publishing Co.] - Chicago, IL - *ArtMar 84; BaconPubCkMag 84; MagDir 84; MagIndMarPl 82-83*
Food Processors Institute [Aff. of The National Food Processors Association] - Washington, DC - *BoPubDir 4, 5*
Food Product Development [of Magazines for Industry] - Chicago, IL - *MagDir 84*
Food Production Management [of The Canning Trade Inc.] - Baltimore, MD - *BaconPubCkMag 84; MagDir 84; MagIndMarPl 82-83*
Food Promotions [of Munroe Publications Inc.] - Indian Rocks Beach, FL - *BaconPubCkMag 84; MagDir 84*
Food Research & Action Center Inc. - Washington, DC - *BoPubDir 4, 5*
Food Science & Technology Abstracts [of Dialog Information Services Inc.] - Palo Alto, CA - *DataDirOnSer 84*
Food Science & Technology Abstracts [of International Food Information Service] - Reading, England - *CompReadDB 82; DBBus 82; OnBibDB 3*
Food-Scope - St. Paul, MN - *MagDir 84*
Food Service Marketing - Madison, WI - *MagIndMarPl 82-83*
Food Service Product Alert - Naples, NY - *BaconPubCkMag 84*
Food Technology [of Institute of Food Technologists] - Chicago, IL - *BaconPubCkMag 84; MagDir 84*
Food Trade News [of Best-Met Publishing Co. Inc.] - Ardmore, PA - *BaconPubCkMag 84; MagDir 84; MagIndMarPl 82-83*
Food Transport Week - Arlington, VA - *AyerDirPub 83*
Food World [of Best-Met Publishing Co. Inc.] - Columbia, MD - *BaconPubCkMag 84; MagDir 84*
Foods Adlibra [of Komp Information Services] - Louisville, KY - *CompReadDB 82; DataDirOnSer 84; DBBus 82; DirOnDB Spring 84; EISS 83; OnBibDB 3*
Foodservice & Hospitality - Toronto, ON, Canada - *BaconPubCkMag 84*
Foodservice Distribution Sales - Chicago, IL - *MagDir 84*
Foodservice Equipment Specialist - Chicago, IL - *MagDir 84; MagIndMarPl 82-83*
Foodservice Equipment Specialist - Des Plaines, IL - *BaconPubCkMag 84*
Foodservice Marketing - Madison, WI - *WritMar 84*
Foodservice Product News - New York, NY - *BaconPubCkMag 84; MagDir 84; MagIndMarPl 82-83*
Foodservice Research Center - New York, NY - *IntDirMarRes 83*
Foodsman [of Virginia Food Dealers Association] - Richmond, VA - *BaconPubCkMag 84; MagDir 84*
Fool Court Press - Charlotte, NC - *BoPubDir 5*
Foolproof Press - Berkeley, CA - *LitMag&SmPr 83-84*
Fools Prayer Music Inc. - *See* Big Seven Music Corp.
Football Digest - Evanston, IL - *MagIndMarPl 82-83*
Football News - Detroit, MI - *MagDir 84; MagIndMarPl 82-83; WritMar 84*
Football Publications - Perry, NY - *BoPubDir 4, 5*
Foote & Davies/Mid-America [Subs. of Foote & Davies Inc.] - Lincoln, NE - *LitMarPl 83; MagIndMarPl 82-83*
Foote & Davies/San Francisco [Subs. of J. P. Stevens] - Brisbane, CA - *LitMarPl 83, 84*
Foote, Cone & Belding - Chicago, IL - *AdAge 3-28-84, 6-25-84; Br 1-23-84; BrCabYB 84; StaDirAdAg 2-84*
Foote, Cone & Belding - New York, NY - *DirMarMP 83; HomeVid&CabYB 82-83; TelAl 83, 84*
Foote, Cone & Belding - *See* Byoir & Associates Inc., Carl
Foote, Cone & Belding (Direct Marketing Div.) - Chicago, IL - *DirMarMP 83*
Foote, Cone & Belding/Honig - Los Angeles, CA - *ArtMar 84*
Foote, Cone & Belding/Honig - San Francisco, CA - *ArtMar 84*
Foote Photography, James - Old Greenwich, CT - *AvMarPl 83*
Foothill Inter-City Newspapers - Arcadia, CA - *BaconPubCkNews 84*
Foothill Record - Colfax, CA - *AyerDirPub 83*
Foothills Communications - Larimer County, CO - *Tel&CabFB 84C*
Foothills North - Tucson, AZ - *AyerDirPub 83*
Foothills Press - Pittsfield, MA - *BoPubDir 4, 5*
Foothills Rural Telephone Cooperative Corp. Inc. - Staffordsville, KY - *TelDir&BG 83-84*
Footloose Press - Hayward, CA - *BoPubDir 4 Sup, 5*
Footnotes - Philadelphia, PA - *LitMag&SmPr 83-84*
Footsteps Press - Hobbs, NM - *BoPubDir 4 Sup, 5*
Footville Telephone Co. [Aff. of North-West Telecommunications Inc.] - Footville, WI - *TelDir&BG 83-84*
Footwear Focus [of National Shoe Retailers Association] - New York, NY - *ArtMar 84; BaconPubCkMag 84; WritMar 84*
Footwear Industries of America - Philadelphia, PA - *BoPubDir 4 Sup, 5*
Footwear News [of Capital Cities Media Inc.] - New York, NY - *BaconPubCkMag 84; MagDir 84; MagIndMarPl 82-83*
Footwork Magazine - Paterson, NJ - *LitMag&SmPr 83-84*
For-A Corp. - West Newton, MA - *AvMarPl 83*
For Parents - Eden, NY - *LitMag&SmPr 83-84*
For Seniors Only - New City, NY - *MagDir 84*
For Your Information - New York, NY - *LitMarPl 83*
Foray Associates [Div. of IMC Magnetics Corp.] - Jericho, NY - *ArtMar 84; StaDirAdAg 2-84*
Forbes - New York, NY - *AdAge 6-28-84; BaconPubCkMag 84; Folio 83; KnowInd 83; LitMarPl 83, 84; MagDir 84; MagIndMarPl 82-83; NewsBur 6; WritMar 84*
Forbes & Associates Inc., Paul S. - Fairfax, VA - *DirPRFirms 83*
Forbes & Catoggio Advertising Inc. - New York, NY - *StaDirAdAg 2-84*

Forbes & Weatherall - Minneapolis, MN - *HBIndAd&MS 82-83*

Forbes Communications Corp. - Phoenix, AZ - *DirMarMP 83*

Forbes Directory [of Dow Jones News/Retrieval Service] - Princeton, NJ - *DataDirOnSer 84*

Forbes Directory - New York, NY - *DirOnDB Spring 84*

Forbes, George F. [Aff. of Facts Inc.] - Sepulveda, CA - *BoPubDir 4, 5*

Force, Charles Radley - Jackson, MS - *LitMarPl 83, 84; MagIndMarPl 82-83*

Force Feed Music Publishing Co. - *See* Neverland Music Publishing Co.

Force Publishing Co. - Salinas, CA - *BoPubDir 5*

Force Video - Los Angeles, CA - *BillIntBG 83-84*

Ford Advertising Inc., James A. - Stamford, CT - *StaDirAdAg 2-84*

Ford Aerospace Satellite Services Corp. - Washington, DC - *Tel&CabFB 84C*

Ford Almanac - Woodstock, IL - *BaconPubCkMag 84; MagDir 84*

Ford & Associates Inc., Milton Q. - Memphis, TN - *CabTVFinDB 83*

Ford Associates - Auburn, IN - *BoPubDir 4, 5*

Ford Co. Inc., Harvey A. - Brockton, MA - *StaDirAdAg 2-84*

Ford County Press - Melvin, IL - *Ed&PubIntYB 82*

Ford Foundation - New York, NY - *BoPubDir 5*

Ford, H. C. Jr. - Granite, OK - *Tel&CabFB 84C p.1680*

Ford Inc., Stuart - Richmond, VA - *StaDirAdAg 2-84*

Ford Investment Review - San Diego, CA - *DirOnDB Spring 84*

Ford Investment Review [of NewsNet Inc.] - Bryn Mawr, PA - *DataDirOnSer 84*

Ford Investor Services - San Diego, CA - *EISS 7-83 Sup*

Ford, Jerry - *See* Midway Cable Corp.

Ford Motor Co. - Dearborn, MI - *ElecNews 7-25-83*

Ford Research Services Inc. - Rochester, NY - *IntDirMarRes 83*

Ford Soccer School, Jim - Waterloo, ON, Canada - *BoPubDir 4 Sup, 5*

Ford Times [of Ford Motor Co.] - Dearborn, MI - *ArtMar 84; MagIndMarPl 82-83; WritMar 84*

Forde Motion Picture Laboratories - Seattle, WA - *AvMarPl 83*

Fordel Films Inc. - Fairfax, CA - *AvMarPl 83*

Fordel Films Inc. - San Diego, CA - *TelAl 83, 84*

Fordham Equipment & Publishing Co. - Bronx, NY - *ArtMar 84; AvMarPl 83; BoPubDir 4, 5*

Fordham University Press - Bronx, NY - *LitMarPl 83, 84; WritMar 84*

Ford's Travel Guides - Woodland Hills, CA - *BoPubDir 4, 5*

Fordville Tri-County Sun - Fordville, ND - *Ed&PubIntYB 82*

Fordville Tri-County Sun - *See* Ness Press Inc.

Fordyce News-Advocate - Fordyce, AR - *BaconPubCkNews 84; Ed&PubIntYB 82*

Fore [of Southern California Golf Association] - North Hollywood, CA - *ArtMar 84; BaconPubCkMag 84; MagDir 84*

Forecast! - Washington, DC - *BaconPubCkMag 84; MagDir 84*

Forecast Associates Inc. - Danbury, CT - *BoPubDir 4 Sup, 5*

Forecast for Home Economics - New York, NY - *ArtMar 84; BaconPubCkMag 84; MagDir 84; MagIndMarPl 82-83; WritMar 84*

Forecast Inc. - Manchester Center, VT - *StaDirAdAg 2-84*

Forecaster Publishing Co. Inc. - Tarzana, CA - *BoPubDir 4, 5; DirMarMP 83*

Forecasting & Support Div. [of Washington State Office of Financial Management] - Olympia, WA - *EISS 83*

Forecasting International Ltd. - Arlington, VA - *EISS 83*

Forefront - Namaica, NY - *NewsDir 84*

Foreign Affairs [of Council on Foreign Affairs] - New York, NY - *LitMarPl 83, 84; MagDir 84; MagIndMarPl 82-83; WritMar 84*

Foreign Agricultural Service [of U.S. Dept. of Agriculture] - Washington, DC - *EISS 83*

Foreign Artists Poets & Authors Review [of Le Beacon Presse] - Seattle, WA - *LitMag&SmPr 83-84*

Foreign Exchange Database [of ADP Network Services Inc.] - Ann Arbor, MI - *DataDirOnSer 84*

Foreign Exchange Database - Bala Cynwyd, PA - *DirOnDB Spring 84*

Foreign Exchange Rate Forecast [of Chase Econometrics/ Interactive Data Corp.] - Waltham, MA - *DataDirOnSer 84; DBBus 82*

Foreign Exchange Rate Service [of Conticurrency] - Chicago, IL - *EISS 83*

Foreign Language Studios - Lathrup Village, MI - *MagIndMarPl 82-83*

Foreign Policy - Washington, DC - *MagIndMarPl 82-83*

Foreign Policy Association - New York, NY - *BoPubDir 4, 5*

Foreign Policy Research Institute - Philadelphia, PA - *BoPubDir 4, 5*

Foreign Projects Newsletter [of Richards, Lawrence & Co.] - Santa Monica, CA - *BaconPubCkMag 84; MagDir 84*

Foreign Publications Inc. - Glendale, NY - *LitMarPl 83*

Foreign Resources Associates - Ft. Collins, CO - *MagIndMarPl 82-83*

Foreign Service Journal [of American Foreign Service Association] - Washington, DC - *MagDir 84; MagIndMarPl 82-83; WritMar 84*

Foreign Services Research Institute & Wheat Forders - Washington, DC - *ArtMar 84; BoPubDir 5*

Foreign Trade Div. [of U.S. Bureau of the Census] - Washington, DC - *EISS 83*

Foreign Traders Index [of Dialog Information Services Inc.] - Palo Alto, CA - *DataDirOnSer 84*

Foreign Traders Index [of U.S. Dept. of Commerce] - Washington, DC - *CompReadDB 82; DBBus 82; DirOnDB Spring 84; EISS 83*

Foreman Public Relations, Bill - Memphis, TN - *DirPRFirms 83*

Foreman Publishing Co., Gloria - Oklahoma City, OK - *BoPubDir 4, 5*

Foreman's Letter, The - Waterford, CT - *ArtMar 84; WritMar 84*

Forensic Services Directory - Lawrenceville, NJ - *DirOnDB Spring 84*

Forer & Co. Inc., D. - New York, NY - *WritMar 84*

Foresight Magazine - Birmingham, England - *LitMag&SmPr 83-84*

Forest [of Forest Products Research Society] - Madison, WI - *DataDirOnSer 84; DirOnDB Spring 84*

Forest Advertising Corp. - Brockton, MA - *StaDirAdAg 2-84*

Forest Atwood Paper Co. - Elk Grove Village, IL - *MagIndMarPl 82-83*

Forest-Blade - Swainsboro, GA - *AyerDirPub 83; Ed&PubIntYB 82*

Forest Bugle Leader, The [of Pinellas Park Post] - Pinellas Park, FL - *NewsDir 84*

Forest City News - Forest City, PA - *BaconPubCkNews 84; Ed&PubIntYB 82*

Forest City Summit [of Summit Printing Co. Inc.] - Forest City, IA - *AyerDirPub 83; BaconPubCkNews 84; Ed&PubIntYB 82; NewsDir 84*

Forest City TV Cable Corp. - Forest City, PA - *BrCabYB 84; Tel&CabFB 84C*

Forest Dale Cable Co. - Forest Dale, VT - *Tel&CabFB 84C*

Forest Farmer - Atlanta, GA - *BaconPubCkMag 84; MagDir 84*

Forest Grove-Cornelius News Times - *See* Times Publishing Co.

Forest Grove Washington County News-Times - Forest Grove, OR - *NewsDir 84*

Forest Hills-Central Pennysaver - Rockville Centre, NY - *AyerDirPub 83*

Forest Hills Journal [of Queen City Suburban Press] - Cincinnati, OH - *AyerDirPub 83; NewsDir 84*

Forest Hills Journal - Forest Hills, OH - *Ed&PubIntYB 82*

Forest Hills-Kew Gardens Pennysaver - Rockville Centre, NY - *AyerDirPub 83*

Forest Hills News - *See* B & B Publishing Inc.

Forest Hills-Rego Park Pennysaver - Rockville Centre, NY - *AyerDirPub 83*

Forest Hills Tribune [of Flushing Queens Tribune] - Flushing, NY - *Ed&PubIntYB 82; NewsDir 84*

Forest Industries - San Francisco, CA - *BaconPubCkMag 84; MagDir 84; MagIndMarPl 82-83*

Forest Information Retrieval System [of Forest Products Research Society] - Madison, WI - *EISS 7-83 Sup*

Forest Inventory Data Processing System [of Food & Agriculture Organization] - Rome, Italy - *EISS 83*

Forest Lake Times - *See* Sell Publishing Co.

Forest Lake Times, The - Forest Lake, MN - *Ed&PubIntYB 82*

Forest Leaves - Forest Park, IL - *Ed&PubIntYB 82*

Forest Leaves - River Forest, IL - *Ed&PubIntYB 82*

Forest Leaves [of Wilmette Pioneer Press Inc.] - Wilmette, IL - *NewsDir 84*
Forest Library of Edentata [Aff. of Poet Papers] - Redway, CA - *BoPubDir 4 Sup, 5*
Forest of Peace Books Inc. - Easton, KS - *BoPubDir 4 Sup, 5*
Forest Park Forest Leaves - Wilmette, IL - *AyerDirPub 83*
Forest Park Review - Forest Park, IL - *BaconPubCkNews 84; Ed&PubIntYB 82*
Forest Press [Aff. of Lake Placid Education Foundation] - Albany, NY - *BoPubDir 4, 5*
Forest Press - Tionesta, PA - *AyerDirPub 83; Ed&PubIntYB 82; NewsDir 84*
Forest Products: Abstract Information Digest Service [of Forest Products Research Society] - Madison, WI - *DBBus 82; OnBibDB 3*
Forest Products Abstracts [of Commonwealth Forestry Bureau] - Oxford, England - *CompReadDB 82*
Forest Products Data Bank [of Data Resources Inc.] - Lexington, MA - *DataDirOnSer 84*
Forest Products Journal - Madison, WI - *BaconPubCkMag 84; MagDir 84*
Forest Products Research Society - Madison, WI - *BoPubDir 4, 5; DataDirOnSer 84*
Forest Products Service Data Banks - Washington, DC - *DirOnDB Spring 84*
Forest Republican - Crandon, WI - *AyerDirPub 83; Ed&PubIntYB 82*
Forest Scott County Times - Forest, MS - *BaconPubCkNews 84; NewsDir 84*
Forest-Soil Data System [of U.S. Dept. of Agriculture] - Washington, DC - *EISS 7-83 Sup*
Forest Standard - Forest, ON, Canada - *Ed&PubIntYB 82*
Forester - Huntsville, ON, Canada - *AyerDirPub 83; Ed&PubIntYB 82*
Foresthill Telephone Co. Inc. - Foresthill, CA - *TelDir&BG 83-84*
Forestry Abstracts [of Commonwealth Forestry Bureau] - Oxford, England - *CompReadDB 82*
Forestry Data Banks [of Data Resources Inc.] - Lexington, MA - *DBBus 82*
Forestry Marketing Bulletin - Columbus, OH - *BaconPubCkMag 84*
Forests & People [of Louisiana Forestry Association] - Alexandria, LA - *BaconPubCkMag 84; MagDir 84; WritMar 84*
Forestville Telephone Co. Inc. [Aff. of Universal Telephone Inc.] - Forestville, WI - *TelDir&BG 83-84*
Foret et Papier - Montreal, PQ, Canada - *ArtMar 84; WritMar 84*
Foreword Books - South Portland, ME - *BoPubDir 4 Sup, 5*
Foreworks Publishing - North Hollywood, CA - *BoPubDir 4 Sup, 5*
Forge Press Inc. - New York, NY - *BoPubDir 4, 5*
Forge Publications, The - *See* Red Flag Publishing/The Forge Publications
FORIS - Bonn, West Germany - *DirOnDB Spring 84*
Foris Publications/USA - Cinnaminson, NJ - *BoPubDir 4, 5; LitMag&SmPr 83-84*
Forkner Publishing Corp. - Ridgewood, NY - *BoPubDir 4*
Forkner Publishing Corp. - Agincourt, ON, Canada - *BoPubDir 5*
Forks Forum & Peninsula Herald - Forks, WA - *AyerDirPub 83; BaconPubCkNews 84; Ed&PubIntYB 82*
Forks TeleCable Inc. - Forks, WA - *BrCabYB 84; Tel&CabFB 84C*
Form - Alexandria, VA - *BaconPubCkMag 84*
Form 41 - Washington, DC - *DirOnDB Spring 84*
Form 41 [of I. P. Sharp Associates Ltd.] - Toronto, ON, Canada - *DataDirOnSer 84*
Formaad, Dr. William - Brooklyn, NY - *ProGuPRSer 4*
Formac Publishing Co. Ltd. - Antigonish, NS, Canada - *BoPubDir 4; LitMarPl 83*
Formac Publishing Co. Ltd. - Halifax, NS, Canada - *BoPubDir 5; LitMarPl 84*
Forman/Photo Research & Photo Editing, Alan - New York, NY - *LitMarPl 83, 84*
Forman Productions Inc. - New York, NY - *Tel&CabFB 84C*
Forman Publishing - Los Angeles, CA - *LitMarPl 83, 84; WritMar 84*
Formaster Corp. - San Jose, CA - *WhoWMicrocom 83*
Format - Montreal, PQ, Canada - *EISS 7-83 Sup*
Format: Art & the World [of Seven Oaks Press] - St. Charles, IL - *ArtMar 84; LitMag&SmPr 83-84; WritMar 84*
Format Productions - Tarzana, CA - *TelAl 83, 84; Tel&CabFB 84C*
Format 2 [Div. of The Darkroom Inc.] - Pittsburgh, PA - *AvMarPl 83; WritMar 84*
Formation Inc. - Mt. Laurel, NJ - *DataDirSup 7-83*
Formats Unltd. Inc. - Floral Park, NY - *DirInfWP 82*
Formby Stations, The - Hereford, TX - *BrCabYB 84*
Forms: The Review of Anthropos Theophoros - San Francisco, CA - *ArtMar 84; WritMar 84*
Formula Music Inc. - *See* Muscle Shoals Sound Publishing Co. Inc.
Forney Messenger - Forney, TX - *BaconPubCkNews 84; Ed&PubIntYB 82*
Forox Corp. - Stamford, CT - *AvMarPl 83*
Forrest City Crowley Ridge Chronical - *See* Causey Printing Co., F. M.
Forrest City Times Herald - Forrest City, AR - *BaconPubCkNews 84; NewsDir 84*
Forrest, Mark Associates - Vineland, NJ - *StaDirAdAg 2-84*
Forrest News - *See* Cornbelt Press Inc.
Forrest Publications Inc. - Morristown, NJ - *BoPubDir 4, 5*
Forrestal & Associates Inc. - St. Louis, MO - *DirPRFirms 83*
Forreston Journal - Forreston, IL - *BaconPubCkNews 84; Ed&PubIntYB 82*
FORS - Stuttgart, West Germany - *DirOnDB Spring 84*
Forschungsdokumentation zur Arbeitsmarkt-und-Berufsforschung [of Institut fur Arbeitsmarkt und Berufsforschung] - Nuremberg, West Germany - *CompReadDB 82*
Forschungsprojekte Raumordnung, Stadtebau, Wohnungswesen [of Informationsverbundzentrum RAUM und BAU der Fraunhofer-Gesellschaft] - Stuttgart, West Germany - *CompReadDB 82*
Forse Manufacturing Co. - St. Louis, MO - *AvMarPl 83*
Forssberg Inc., Hank - Hackensack, NJ - *StaDirAdAg 2-84*
Forstenzer Inc., Peter - New York, NY - *AdAge 3-28-84; StaDirAdAg 2-84*
Forster & Associates Inc., Reginald Bishop - Sacramento, CA - *BoPubDir 5*
Forster & Associates Inc., Reginald Bishop - Minneapolis, MN - *BoPubDir 4*
Forsyth Cable TV Co. - Forsyth, MT - *BrCabYB 84; Tel&CabFB 84C*
Forsyth Cablevision - Forsyth, GA - *BrCabYB 84; Tel&CabFB 84C*
Forsyth County News - Cumming, GA - *Ed&PubIntYB 82*
Forsyth Independent/Ashland Story - Forsyth, MT - *BaconPubCkNews 84*
Forsyth Taney County Republican - *See* Tri-Lakes Newspapers Inc.
Forsythe Computers Inc. [Subs. of Gramex Corp.] - Clayton, MO - *WhoWMicrocom 83*
Forte Associates, Betsy - Washington, DC - *DirPRFirms 83*
Fortel Inc. - Norcross, GA - *AvMarPl 83*
Forth Dimension, The - Middletown, PA - *MicrocomMPl 84*
Forth Inc. - Hermosa Beach, CA - *MicrocomMPl 83, 84; MicrocomSwDir 1; WhoWMicrocom 83*
Forthpower [Subs. of Main Services Inc.] - San Rafael, CA - *WhoWMicrocom 83*
Fortier, Jean-Guy - Courcelles, PQ, Canada - *BrCabYB 84*
Fortier, Jean-Guy - Frontenac, PQ, Canada - *BrCabYB 84*
Fortin, Paul L. - Hanson, MA - *LitMarPl 83, 84; MagIndMarPl 82-83*
Fortis Fortis Advertising - Chicago, IL - *AdAge 3-28-84; StaDirAdAg 2-84*
Fortress Press - Philadelphia, PA - *BillIntBG 83-84; LitMarPl 83, 84; WritMar 84*
Fortuna Advance & Humboldt Beacon - Fortuna, CA - *NewsDir 84*
Fortuna Book Sales - Brooksville, FL - *BoPubDir 4, 5*
Fortuna Humboldt Beacon & Advance - Fortuna, CA - *BaconPubCkNews 84*

Fortune [of Time Inc.] - New York, NY - *BaconPubCkMag 84; Folio 83; LitMarPl 83, 84; MagDir 84; MagIndMarPl 82-83; NewsBur 6; WritMar 84*
Fortune Book Club - *See* Book-of-the-Month Club Inc.
Fortune Records - Detroit, MI - *BillIntBG 83-84*
Fortune Systems Corp. - Redwood City, CA - *MicrocomMPl 84*
Fortune Systems Corp. - San Carlos, CA - *WhoWMicrocom 83*
Fortville Tribune - Fortville, IN - *Ed&PubIntYB 82*
Fortville Tribune News - Fortville, IN - *AyerDirPub 83*
44 Press Inc. - Brooklyn, NY - *LitMag&SmPr 83-84*
40-Mile County Commentator, The - Bow Island, AB, Canada - *AyerDirPub 83; Ed&PubIntYB 82*
Forum [of Feal United] - Tallahassee, FL - *MagDir 84; NewsDir 84*
Forum - Denver, IA - *AyerDirPub 83; Ed&PubIntYB 82*
Forum - Eldon, IA - *AyerDirPub 83*
Forum - Floodwood, MN - *AyerDirPub 83; Ed&PubIntYB 82*
Forum - Fairfax, MO - *AyerDirPub 83*
Forum [of Penthouse International Ltd.] - New York, NY - *Folio 83; MagIndMarPl 82-83*
Forum - Fargo, ND - *AyerDirPub 83; BaconPubCkNews 84; Ed&PubIntYB 82; LitMarPl 84; NewsDir 84*
Forum - Don Mills, ON, Canada - *BaconPubCkMag 84*
Forum-80 [of Small Business Systems Group] - Westford, MA - *TeleSy&SerDir 2-84*
Forum-80 Headquarters - Kansas City, MO - *MicrocomMPl 83, 84*
Forum of South Queens [of Wave Publishing Co.] - Rockaway Beach, NY - *AyerDirPub 83; NewsDir 84*
Forum Press Inc. [Subs. of Harlan Davidson Inc.] - Arlington Heights, IL - *LitMarPl 83, 84*
Forum Publishing Co. - Denver, CO - *BoPubDir 4 Sup, 5*
Forum Publishing Co. - Fargo, ND - *BrCabYB 84; Ed&PubIntYB 82; Tel&CabFB 84S*
Forum School Foundation Inc. - Waldwick, NJ - *BoPubDir 4, 5*
Forum Sixty-Eight [of Remarkable Software] - Muskegon, MI - *MicrocomMPl 84*
Forum, The - Hackettstown, NJ - *AyerDirPub 83; Ed&PubIntYB 82*
Forus Communications - St. Petersburg, FL - *BrCabYB 84*
Forward [of Africa Research & Publications Project] - Trenton, NJ - *LitMag&SmPr 83-84*
Forward Association Inc. - New York, NY - *BrCabYB 84*
Forward Communications - Wausau, WI - *BrCabYB 84; Tel&CabFB 84S*
Forward Movement Publications [Aff. of Episcopal Church] - Cincinnati, OH - *BoPubDir 4 Sup, 5*
Forward Press - Arcadia, CA - *BoPubDir 5*
Forward Technology Inc. - Santa Clara, CA - *MicrocomMPl 84*
Forward Times - Houston, TX - *AyerDirPub 83; Ed&PubIntYB 82*
Forzaglia Inc., John - New York, NY - *HBIndAd&MS 82-83*
Foscoe Songs - *See* Kenwon Music
Foss, Edward G. - Charlottesville, VA - *MagIndMarPl 82-83*
Fossil Community TV Inc. - Fossil, OR - *BrCabYB 84; Tel&CabFB 84C*
Fossil Energy Information Center [of U.S. Dept. of Energy] - Oak Ridge, TN - *EISS 83*
Fosston Cable - Fosston, MN - *Tel&CabFB 84C*
Fosston Thirteen Towns - Fosston, MN - *BaconPubCkNews 84; NewsDir 84*
Foster Advertising Ltd. - Toronto, ON, Canada - *StaDirAdAg 2-84*
Foster & Associates Inc., Robert A. - Tampa, FL - *StaDirAdAg 2-84*
Foster & Davies Inc. - Cleveland, OH - *StaDirAdAg 2-84; TelAl 83, 84*
Foster & Green Inc. - Baltimore, MD - *StaDirAdAg 2-84*
Foster Associates, Trufant - University City, MO - *LitMarPl 83, 84*
Foster Broadcasters Inc., The - San Angelo, TX - *BrCabYB 84*
Foster City Islander - San Mateo, CA - *AyerDirPub 83*
Foster City Progress - Foster City, CA - *BaconPubCkNews 84; Ed&PubIntYB 82*
Foster City Progress - San Mateo, CA - *AyerDirPub 83; NewsDir 84*
Foster City United Cable Television Corp. [of United Cable TV Corp.] - Foster City, CA - *BrCabYB 84; Tel&CabFB 84C*
Foster County Independent - Carrington, ND - *Ed&PubIntYB 82*
Foster, Lee - Oakland, CA - *LitMarPl 83, 84; MagIndMarPl 82-83*
Foster Music Co., Mark - Champaign, IL - *BillIntBG 83-84; BoPubDir 4, 5*
Foster Peterson & Kostopoulos - Boston, MA - *AdAge 3-28-84; StaDirAdAg 2-84*
Foster Photography, Lee - Oakland, CA - *MagIndMarPl 82-83*
Foster, Thelma H. - Milden, SK, Canada - *BoPubDir 4, 5*
Foster, Young, Ross, Anthony & Associates Ltd. - Vancouver, BC, Canada - *StaDirAdAg 2-84*
Foster's Democrat - Dover, NH - *AyerDirPub 83; BaconPubCkNews 84; Ed&PubIntYB 82*
Fostex Corp. of America - Norwalk, CA - *AvMarPl 83*
Fostoria Review Times [of Spenley Inc.] - Fostoria, OH - *BaconPubCkNews 84; NewsDir 84*
Fotheringham & Associates - Salt Lake City, UT - *AdAge 3-28-84; StaDirAdAg 2-84*
Fotis, Denise E. - Pacific Grove, CA - *MagIndMarPl 82-83*
Foto-Comm Corp. of Chicago - Chicago, IL - *AvMarPl 83*
Foto-Kem Industries Inc. - Burbank, CA - *AvMarPl 83*
Fotofolio Inc. - New York, NY - *LitMag&SmPr 83-84*
Fotomat Corp. - Wilton, CT - *HomeVid&CabYB 82-83*
Fotos International - Studio City, CA - *Ed&PubIntYB 82*
Fotos International - New York, NY - *MagIndMarPl 82-83*
Fotouhi Alonso Inc. - Los Angeles, CA - *StaDirAdAg 2-84*
FoU-Indeks [of Norsk Senter for Informatikk] - Oslo, Norway - *CompReadDB 82; DirOnDB Spring 84*
Foundation Center - New York, NY - *CompReadDB 82; DataDirOnSer 84; EISS 83; InfIndMarPl 83; LitMag&SmPr 83-84; LitMarPl 83, 84; MicroMarPl 82-83*
Foundation Center National Database - New York, NY - *DataDirOnSer 84*
Foundation Directory Database [of The Foundation Center] - New York, NY - *CompReadDB 82; DataDirOnSer 84; DBBus 82*
Foundation for Economic Education Inc. - Irvington-on-Hudson, NY - *BoPubDir 4, 5*
Foundation for Human Understanding - Athens, GA - *BoPubDir 4, 5*
Foundation for Inner Peace - Tiburon, CA - *BoPubDir 4, 5*
Foundation for the Advancement of Artists - Philadelphia, PA - *BoPubDir 4, 5*
Foundation for the Advancement of Man - Carlsbad, CA - *BoPubDir 4 Sup, 5*
Foundation for the Community of Artists - New York, NY - *BoPubDir 4, 5; LitMag&SmPr 83-84*
Foundation Grants Index Database [of Foundation Center] - New York, NY - *CompReadDB 82; DataDirOnSer 84*
Foundation News - Washington, DC - *MagIndMarPl 82-83; WritMar 84*
Foundation of Human Understanding - Los Angeles, CA - *BoPubDir 4, 5*
Foundation Press Inc., The - Mineola, NY - *LitMarPl 83, 84*
Foundation Publications Inc. - Anaheim, CA - *BoPubDir 4, 5*
Foundation Publishing - Burlington, VT - *BoPubDir 4, 5*
Foundations - New York, NY - *DirOnDB Spring 84*
Foundry Management & Technology - Cleveland, OH - *BaconPubCkMag 84; MagDir 84; WritMar 84*
Foundry World - Stratford, CT - *MagDir 84*
Fountain Books [Aff. of Fountainhead Business Agency Ltd.] - Vancouver, BC, Canada - *BoPubDir 4, 5*
Fountain County Star - Covington, IN - *Ed&PubIntYB 82*
Fountain County Star - Kingman, IN - *AyerDirPub 83*
Fountain Hills Times - Fountain Hills, AZ - *BaconPubCkNews 84*
Fountain House East - Jeffersontown, KY - *BoPubDir 4, 5*
Fountain of Life Music - Bradenton, FL - *BillIntBG 83-84*
Fountain Records - Chicago, IL - *BillIntBG 83-84*
Fountain Security & Fountain Valley Advertiser News - Fountain, CO - *NewsDir 84*
Fountain Valley CATV - Colorado Springs, CO - *BrCabYB 84*
Fountain Valley News - Fountain, CO - *BaconPubCkNews 84*
Fountain Warren Messenger - Attica, IN - *Ed&PubIntYB 82*
Four Aces Music Inc. - *See* Special Rider Music
Four Arrows [of The School of Living] - York, PA - *LitMag&SmPr 83-84*
Four Buddies - Los Angeles, CA - *BillIntBG 83-84*

Four by Four [of Villeneuve Publications] - Montreal, PQ, Canada - *LitMag&SmPr 83-84*
Four Continent Book Corp. - New York, NY - *MagIndMarPl 82-83; MicroMarPl 82-83*
Four-County Agricultural News - Sandy Creek, NY - *MagDir 84*
Four Dogs Mountain Songs [of Doggeral Press] - Santa Barbara, CA - *LitMag&SmPr 83-84*
415 Records Ltd. - San Francisco, CA - *BillIntBG 83-84*
Four Flags Cable TV [of TCI-Taft Cablevision Associates] - Niles, MI - *BrCabYB 84; Tel&CabFB 84C*
Four Flags Cablevision Inc. [of TCI-Taft Cablevision Associates] - St. Joseph, MI - *Tel&CabFB 84C*
Four Girls Publishing Co. - New York, NY - *BillIntBG 83-84*
4-K Radio Inc. - Lewiston, ID - *BrCabYB 84*
Four Moons Music Publishing Group - New York, NY - *BillIntBG 83-84*
Four Oaks News - Four Oaks, NC - *AyerDirPub 83*
Four Oaks News - *See* County Press Publishers
Four-Phase Systems Inc. [Subs. of Motorola Inc.] - Cupertino, CA - *DataDirSup 7-83; DirInfWP 82; InfIndMarPl 83; WhoWMicrocom 83*
Four Seasons Foundation - San Francisco, CA - *BoPubDir 4, 5; LitMag&SmPr 83-84*
Four Star Entertainment Corp. [Subs. of Four Star International Inc.] - Northridge, CA - *AvMarPl 83*
Four Star International Inc. - Northridge, CA - *BillIntBG 83-84; TelAl 83, 84; Tel&CabFB 84C*
4 Wheel & Off Road [of Petersen Publishing Co.] - Los Angeles, CA - *Folio 83*
Four Wheeler - Canoga Park, CA - *ArtMar 84; BaconPubCkMag 84; MagDir 84; MagIndMarPl 82-83; WritMar 84*
Four Winds [of Hundred Arrows Press] - Austin, TX - *WritMar 84*
Four Winds Press - Locust Valley, NY - *BoPubDir 4, 5*
Four Winds Press - New York, NY - *LitMarPl 83*
4X Network - Minot, ND - *BrCabYB 84*
Four Zoas Journal of Poetry & Letters, The [of Four Zoas Night House Ltd.] - Ashuelot, NH - *LitMag&SmPr 83-84*
Four Zoas Night House Ltd. - Ashuelot, NH - *BoPubDir 4, 5; LitMag&SmPr 83-84*
Fournier & Associates Inc., Winston - Dallas, TX - *DirPRFirms 83*
Fournier Newspapers - *See* Donrey Media Group
Fournies & Associates Inc., F. - Bridgewater, NJ - *BoPubDir 4, 5*
Foursquare Press - Lancaster, NY - *LitMag&SmPr 83-84*
14 Karat Records - Raleigh, NC - *BillIntBG 83-84*
Fourtel Music Publishing Co. - *See* Four Star International Inc.
Fourth Allegheny Advertising - McMurray, PA - *StaDirAdAg 2-84*
Fourth Corner Registry - Bellingham, WA - *BoPubDir 4, 5*
Fourth Dimension [of Samisdat Associates] - Richford, VT - *LitMag&SmPr 83-84*
Fourth Floor Music Inc. - Bearsville, NY - *BillIntBG 83-84*
Fouts & Son Advertising/Promotion Inc. - Richmond, VA - *StaDirAdAg 2-84*
Fowler & Associates - Los Angeles, CA - *StaDirAdAg 2-84*
Fowler Benton Review - Fowler, IN - *BaconPubCkNews 84; NewsDir 84*
Fowler Cable TV - Fowler, CO - *Tel&CabFB 84C*
Fowler Ensign - Fowler, CA - *BaconPubCkNews 84; Ed&PubIntYB 82*
Fowler Master Antenna Systems Inc. - Rosedale, MS - *BrCabYB 84; Tel&CabFB 84C*
Fowler, Mel - New York, NY - *LitMarPl 83, 84*
Fowler Music Enterprises - Lakewood, CO - *BoPubDir 5*
Fowler News - *See* Meade Globe-Press
Fowler Services Co. - Wytheville, VA - *WhoWMicrocom 83*
Fowler Tribune - Fowler, CO - *BaconPubCkNews 84; Ed&PubIntYB 82*
Fowlerville Review [of Sliger/Livingston Publications] - Howell, MI - *AyerDirPub 83; NewsDir 84*
Fowlerville Review - *See* Sliger Livingston Publications
Fowlerville Review, The - Fowlerville, MI - *Ed&PubIntYB 82*
Fox & Associates Inc. - Cleveland, OH - *StaDirAdAg 2-84*
Fox & Co. - Denver, CO - *DataDirSup 7-83*
Fox & Geller Associates Inc. - Elmwood Park, NJ - *MicrocomSwDir 1*
Fox & Geller Associates Inc. - Teaneck, NJ - *MicrocomMPl 83; WhoWMicrocom 83*
Fox Chase Agency Inc., The - New York, NY - *LitMarPl 83, 84*
Fox Hills Press - Annapolis, MD - *BoPubDir 4, 5; LitMag&SmPr 83-84*
Fox Hills-Raintree Today [of Santa Monica Independent-Journal Newspapers] - Santa Monica, CA - *AyerDirPub 83; NewsDir 84*
Fox Lake Press - Fox Lake, IL - *AyerDirPub 83; Ed&PubIntYB 82*
Fox Lake Press [of Lakeland Publishers Inc.] - Grayslake, IL - *NewsDir 84*
Fox Lake Press - *See* Lakeland Publishers Inc.
Fox Lake Representative - Fox Lake, WI - *Ed&PubIntYB 82*
Fox Lake Representative - *See* Journal Co., The
Fox Lake Representative, The - Berlin, WI - *AyerDirPub 83*
Fox Music, Jenny - *See* Cornelius Music, Stan
Fox Music Publications - *See* Bock Music Co., Fred
Fox Point-Bayside-River Hills Herald - Oak Creek, WI - *AyerDirPub 83*
Fox Point-Bayside-River Hills Herald - *See* Community Newspapers Inc.
Fox Point Herald - Fox Point, WI - *Ed&PubIntYB 82*
Fox Public Relations Inc. - New York, NY - *DirPRFirms 83*
Fox Publishing - East Northport, NY - *BoPubDir 4, 5*
Fox Publishing Co. Inc., Sam - Palm Desert, CA - *AvMarPl 83; BillIntBG 83-84*
Fox, Rachel - Brookline, MA - *BoPubDir 4, 5*
Fox Reading Research Co. - Coeur d'Alene, ID - *BoPubDir 4, 5*
Fox River Patriot [of Fox River Publishing Co.] - Princeton, WI - *MagIndMarPl 82-83; WritMar 84*
Fox, Sanford - Fairlawn, NJ - *BoPubDir 4, 5*
Fox, Sweeney & True Inc. - Denver, CO - *StaDirAdAg 2-84*
Fox TV Cable Co. - Gilbert, WV - *BrCabYB 84; Tel&CabFB 84C*
Fox 20 [of Foxfire Systems Inc.] - Pasadena, TX - *MicrocomMPl 84*
Fox Valley Countryside - Algonquin, IL - *Ed&PubIntYB 82*
Fox Valley Countryside - Barrington, IL - *AyerDirPub 83*
Fox Valley Countryside North - Fox River Grove, IL - *Ed&PubIntYB 82*
Fox Valley Countryside South - Carpentersville, IL - *Ed&PubIntYB 82*
Fox Valley Shopping News - Yorkville, IL - *AyerDirPub 83*
Fox, Wesley - Brisbane, CA - *BoPubDir 4*
Fox, Wesley - Naperville, IL - *BoPubDir 5*
Foxboro Reporter - Foxboro, MA - *BaconPubCkNews 84; Ed&PubIntYB 82; NewsDir 84*
Foxfire Press [Aff. of The Foxfire Fund Inc.] - Rabun Gap, GA - *BoPubDir 4, 5; MagIndMarPl 82-83*
Foxworthy-Stevens & Associates Inc. - Lauderdale by the Sea, FL - *ArtMar 84*
Foxx & Geller Associates Inc. - Elmwood Park, NJ - *MicrocomMPl 84*
F.P. Color Separations Inc. - New York, NY - *MagIndMarPl 82-83*
Fradkin Bradlee Inc. - New York, NY - *StaDirAdAg 2-84*
Fralix Inc. - Austin, TX - *StaDirAdAg 2-84*
Fram, Michal - Yonkers, NY - *LitMarPl 84*
Frames - San Fernando, CA - *MagDir 84*
Framingham Middlesex News, The - Framingham, MA - *NewsDir 84*
Frammis Records - Minneapolis, MN - *BillIntBG 83-84*
Fran Mar Greeting Cards Ltd. - Mt. Vernon, NY - *WritMar 84*
Franas Press - Mantoloking, NY - *BoPubDir 4, 5*
France [of Chase Econometrics/Interactive Data Corp.] - Waltham, MA - *DataDirOnSer 84*
France - Bala Cynwyd, PA - *DirOnDB Spring 84*
France-Actualite [of Microfor Inc.] - Quebec, PQ, Canada - *CompReadDB 82*
France-Amerique - New York, NY - *Ed&PubIntYB 82*
France-Expansion - Paris, France - *MicroMarPl 82-83*
France Telecom Inc. - New York, NY - *InfoS 83-84*
Francesco Enterprises Inc., Steven - Brooklyn, NY - *MicrocomMPl 83, 84*
Francesville Tribune - Francesville, IN - *BaconPubCkNews 84; Ed&PubIntYB 82*
Franchise Advertising Co. - Atlanta, GA - *StaDirAdAg 2-84*
Franchise Group Publishers - Phoenix, AZ - *BoPubDir 4, 5*

Franchising/Investments Around the World [of Sutton Place Publications Inc.] - Hollywood, FL - *MagDir 84*
FRANCIS [of Questel Inc.] - Washington, DC - *DataDirOnSer 84*
FRANCIS [of Centre National de la Recherche Scientifique] - Paris, France - *OnBibDB 3*
FRANCIS: Art et Archeologie - Paris, France - *DirOnDB Spring 84*
FRANCIS: Bibliographie Internationale de Science Administrative - Paris, France - *DirOnDB Spring 84*
FRANCIS: CEGET - Paris, France - *DirOnDB Spring 84*
FRANCIS: DOGE - Paris, France - *DirOnDB Spring 84*
FRANCIS: Droits Antiques - Paris, France - *DirOnDB Spring 84*
FRANCIS: Ecodoc - Paris, France - *DirOnDB Spring 84*
FRANCIS: Economie de l'Energie - Paris, France - *DirOnDB Spring 84*
FRANCIS: Emploi et Formation - Paris, France - *DirOnDB Spring 84*
FRANCIS: Ethnologie - Paris, France - *DirOnDB Spring 84*
FRANCIS: Histoire des Sciences et des Techniques - Paris, France - *DirOnDB Spring 84*
FRANCIS: Histoire et Sciences des Religions - Paris, France - *DirOnDB Spring 84*
FRANCIS: Informatique et Sciences Juridiques - Paris, France - *DirOnDB Spring 84*
Francis, Philip A. - Galveston, TX - *LitMarPl 83, 84*
FRANCIS: Philosophie - Paris, France - *DirOnDB Spring 84*
FRANCIS: Prehistoire et Protohistoire - Paris, France - *DirOnDB Spring 84*
FRANCIS: Repertoire d'Art et d'Archeologie - Paris, France - *DirOnDB Spring 84*
FRANCIS: Reshus - Paris, France - *DirOnDB Spring 84*
FRANCIS: Sciences de l'Education - Paris, France - *DirOnDB Spring 84*
FRANCIS: Sciences du Langage - Paris, France - *DirOnDB Spring 84*
FRANCIS: Sociologie - Paris, France - *DirOnDB Spring 84*
Francis, Williams & Johnson Ltd. - Calgary, AB, Canada - *DirPRFirms 83; StaDirAdAg 2-84*
Franciscan Communications - Los Angeles, CA - *AvMarPl 83*
Franciscan Herald Press - Chicago, IL - *LitMarPl 83, 84; MagIndMarPl 82-83; WritMar 84*
Franciscan Marytown Press - *See* Prow Books/Franciscan Marytown Press
Franco Inc., Anthony M. - Detroit, MI - *DirPRFirms 83; StaDirAdAg 2-84*
Franco-London Music Publishing Corp. - *See* Plaza Sweet Music Inc.
Francom Advertising Inc. - Murray, UT - *StaDirAdAg 2-84*
Francom Advertising Inc. - Salt Lake City, UT - *ArtMar 84*
Frandoro Music Inc. - St. Louis, MO - *BillIntBG 83-84*
Frango-Yuro Inc. - White Plains, NY - *DirPRFirms 83*
Franje Inc. - Vista, CA - *BoPubDir 4 Sup, 5*
Frank Advertising Inc., Clinton E. [Subs. of The Interpublic Group of Cos. Inc.] - Chicago, IL - *StaDirAdAg 2-84*
Frank & Associates, Don - Marina del Rey, CA - *StaDirAdAg 2-84*
Frank & Associates Inc., Alan - Salt Lake City, UT - *AdAge 3-28-84; ArtMar 84; StaDirAdAg 2-84*
Frank Associates, Ethyl - Kew Gardens, NY - *IntDirMarRes 83*
Frank Book Corp. - New York, NY - *BoPubDir 4, 5*
Frank FCB Inc., Albert [Subs. of Foote, Cone & Belding] - New York, NY - *LitMarPl 83, 84*
Frank Film Syndication Inc., Sandy - New York, NY - *AvMarPl 83; TelAl 83, 84; Tel&CabFB 84C*
Frank-Guenther Law, Albert [Subs. of Foote, Cone & Belding Communications Inc.] - New York, NY - *ArtMar 84; BrCabYB 84; DirMarMP 83; DirPRFirms 83; TelAl 83, 84*
Frank Inc., Clinton E. - Chicago, IL - *BrCabYB 84*
Frank/James Direct Marketing Co. Inc. - St. Louis, MO - *StaDirAdAg 2-84*
Frank, Leonard Roy - San Francisco, CA - *BoPubDir 4, 5*
Frank Promotion Corp., The - New York, NY - *LitMarPl 83, 84*
Frank, Sandi - Montrose, NY - *LitMarPl 83, 84*
Frank, Sibyl Boughton - Washington, DC - *LitMarPl 83*
Frankel & Co. - Chicago, IL - *DirMarMP 83; StaDirAdAg 2-84*
Frankel Manufacturing Co. - Denver, CO - *DirInfWP 82*
Frankel, Norman - Kalamazoo, MI - *LitMarPl 84*
Frankel Productions, Karen - New York, NY - *AvMarPl 83*
Franken Public Relations, Al - Beverly Hills, CA - *DirPRFirms 83*
Frankenberry, Laughlin & Constable - Milwaukee, WI - *AdAge 3-28-84; StaDirAdAg 2-84*
Frankenmuth News - Frankenmuth, MI - *BaconPubCkNews 84; Ed&PubIntYB 82; NewsDir 84*
Frankford News Gleaner - *See* News Gleaner Publications
Frankfort Benzie County Advisor - Frankfort, MI - *BaconPubCkNews 84; NewsDir 84*
Frankfort Benzie Record-Patriot - Frankfort, MI - *BaconPubCkNews 84*
Frankfort Cable Communications Inc. [of Frankfort Times Inc.] - Frankfort, IN - *BrCabYB 84; Tel&CabFB 84C*
Frankfort Index - Frankfort, KS - *BaconPubCkNews 84; Ed&PubIntYB 82*
Frankfort-Mokena Star [of Oak Forest Star Herald Publications] - Oak Forest, IL - *Ed&PubIntYB 82; NewsDir 84*
Frankfort-Mokena Star Herald - *See* Star Publications
Frankfort-Star Herald - Frankfort, IL - *AyerDirPub 83*
Frankfort State Journal - Frankfort, KY - *NewsDir 84*
Frankfort Times - Frankfort, IN - *BaconPubCkNews 84; NewsDir 84*
Frankfurt Communications International - New York, NY - *HBIndAd&MS 82-83*
Frankfurt International - *See* K & E Holdings Inc.
Franklin Advertising Associates Inc. - Newton Highlands, MA - *LitMarPl 83, 84; MagIndMarPl 82-83; StaDirAdAg 2-84*
Franklin Advertising Inc., Ben - Santa Monica, CA - *DirMarMP 83; StaDirAdAg 2-84*
Franklin Advocate - Meadville, MS - *AyerDirPub 83; Ed&PubIntYB 82*
Franklin & Associates - San Diego, CA - *AdAge 3-28-84; StaDirAdAg 2-84*
Franklin & Associates, Ray - Ft. Lauderdale, FL - *AvMarPl 83*
Franklin & Co. Inc., Burt [Div. of Lenox Hill Publishing & Distributing Corp.] - New York, NY - *LitMarPl 83, 84*
Franklin & Joseph Inc. - White Plains, NY - *DirMarMP 83; StaDirAdAg 2-84*
Franklin & Marshall College Reporter - Lancaster, PA - *NewsDir 84*
Franklin-Baldwin Cable TV [of TCA Cable TV Inc.] - Franklin, LA - *Tel&CabFB 84C*
Franklin Banner [of Morgan City Newspapers Inc.] - Franklin, LA - *BaconPubCkNews 84; NewsDir 84*
Franklin Cable TV [of Teleservice Corp. of America Inc.] - Franklin, LA - *BrCabYB 84*
Franklin Cablevision Corp. [of Masada Corp.] - Ft. Bliss, TX - *BrCabYB 84*
Franklin Cablevision Inc. [of US Cable Corp.] - Royston, GA - *Tel&CabFB 84C*
Franklin Chronicle - Franklin, OH - *BaconPubCkNews 84; Ed&PubIntYB 82; NewsDir 84*
Franklin Computer Corp. - Cherry Hill, NJ - *WhoWMicrocom 83*
Franklin County CATV Inc. [of Marsh Media Inc.] - Winchester, TN - *BrCabYB 84; Tel&CabFB 84C*
Franklin County Citizen - Lavonia, GA - *Ed&PubIntYB 82*
Franklin County Courier [of Enosburg Falls O'Shea Publishing Co. Inc.] - Enosburg Falls, VT - *NewsDir 84*
Franklin County Courier-Leader - St. Albans, VT - *AyerDirPub 83*
Franklin County Graphic - Connell, WA - *AyerDirPub 83; Ed&PubIntYB 82*
Franklin County News - Carrabelle, FL - *NewsDir 84*
Franklin County Sentinel - Franklin, NE - *BaconPubCkNews 84; Ed&PubIntYB 82*
Franklin County Times - Russellville, AL - *AyerDirPub 83; Ed&PubIntYB 82; NewsDir 84*
Franklin County Times - Rocky Mt., VA - *AyerDirPub 83; Ed&PubIntYB 82*
Franklin County Tribune - Union, MO - *AyerDirPub 83; Ed&PubIntYB 82*
Franklin Distributors Corp. - Denville, NJ - *AvMarPl 83*
Franklin-Douglas Recording Studios Inc. - Port Washington, NY - *AvMarPl 83*
Franklin Electric (Programmed Power Div.) - Sunnyvale, CA - *DirInfWP 82*

Franklin Favorite [of Portmann, Stone, Dear Publications] - Franklin, KY - *BaconPubCkNews 84; BrCabYB 84; Ed&PubIntYB 82; NewsDir 84*
Franklin Greenwood News - Franklin, IN - *BaconPubCkNews 84*
Franklin-Hales Corners Hub - Hales Corners, WI - *Ed&PubIntYB 82*
Franklin-Hales Corners Hub - Oak Creek, WI - *AyerDirPub 83*
Franklin/Hales Corners Hub - *See* Community Newspapers Inc.
Franklin House Publishing Inc. - *See* Alexandria House Inc.
Franklin Institute Press, The [Div. of Franklin Research Center] - Philadelphia, PA - *LitMarPl 83, 84*
Franklin Journal & Farmington Chronicle - Farmington, ME - *AyerDirPub 83; Ed&PubIntYB 82*
Franklin Journal Transcript - Franklin, NH - *BaconPubCkNews 84*
Franklin Library, The [Div. of The Franklin Mint] - New York, NY - *LitMarPl 83, 84*
Franklin Limestone Music - *See* Hat Band Music
Franklin Literary & Medical Society, Benjamin (Children's Better Health Institute) - Indianapolis, IN - *MagIndMarPl 82-83*
Franklin, Lynn C. - New York, NY - *LitMarPl 83, 84*
Franklin Mint Almanac, The - Franklin Center, PA - *WritMar 84*
Franklin News & Banner - Franklin, GA - *BaconPubCkNews 84*
Franklin News-Herald - Franklin, PA - *BaconPubCkNews 84; NewsDir 84*
Franklin News-Post - Rocky Mt., VA - *AyerDirPub 83; Ed&PubIntYB 82*
Franklin News-Record [of Princeton Packet Inc.] - Princeton, NJ - *NewsDir 84*
Franklin News-Record - Somerset, NJ - *AyerDirPub 83*
Franklin News-Record, The - Franklin Township, NJ - *Ed&PubIntYB 82*
Franklin News Weekly - Franklin, TX - *BaconPubCkNews 84; Ed&PubIntYB 82*
Franklin Park Herald - Franklin Park, IL - *Ed&PubIntYB 82*
Franklin Park Herald [of Pioneer Press Inc.] - Wilmette, IL - *AyerDirPub 83; NewsDir 84*
Franklin Park Herald - *See* Pioneer Press Inc.
Franklin Park Journal [of Franklin Park Publishing Co.] - Franklin Park, IL - *Ed&PubIntYB 82; NewsDir 84*
Franklin Park Journal - Wilmette, IL - *AyerDirPub 83*
Franklin Park Post [of Elmwood Park Post Newspapers] - Chicago, IL - *NewsDir 84*
Franklin Park Post - Elmwood Park, IL - *AyerDirPub 83*
Franklin Park Post - Franklin Park, IL - *Ed&PubIntYB 82*
Franklin Park Post - *See* Meese' Newspaper Group
Franklin Park Times - Chicago, IL - *AyerDirPub 83*
Franklin Park Times - Franklin Park, IL - *Ed&PubIntYB 82*
Franklin Park Times - *See* Lerner Times Newspapers
Franklin Pendleton Times - Franklin, WV - *BaconPubCkNews 84; NewsDir 84*
Franklin Post - Franklin, LA - *Ed&PubIntYB 82; NewsDir 84*
Franklin Press [of Community Newspapers Inc.] - Franklin, NC - *BaconPubCkNews 84; Ed&PubIntYB 82; NewsDir 84*
Franklin Press, Chas. - Edmonds, WA - *BoPubDir 4, 5; LitMag&SmPr 83-84*
Franklin Printing Co. [Subs. of Williams & Marcus] - Primos, PA - *LitMarPl 83, 84*
Franklin Publishing Co. - Rockland, MA - *BaconPubCkNews 84*
Franklin Publishing Co. - East Millstone, NJ - *BoPubDir 4, 5*
Franklin Publishing Co. Inc. - Palisade, NJ - *BoPubDir 4, 5*
Franklin Readers' Service Inc. - Washington, DC - *DirMarMP 83*
Franklin Research Center [of Science Information Services Organization] - Philadelphia, PA - *FBInfSer 80; InfIndMarPl 83*
Franklin Research Center (Information Management Dept.) - Philadelphia, PA - *InfIndMarPl 83*
Franklin Research Center (Science Information Services Organization) - *See* Franklin Research Center (Information Management Dept.)
Franklin Review-Appeal - Franklin, TN - *BaconPubCkNews 84; NewsDir 84*
Franklin Ribbon & Carbon Co. Inc. - Hicksville, NY - *DirInfWP 82*
Franklin, Roberts, Carlyle Inc. - Gainesville, FL - *StaDirAdAg 2-84*
Franklin-Simpson Cablevision [of Owensboro On The Air Inc.] - Franklin, KY - *Tel&CabFB 84C*
Franklin-Southampton Cablevision Co. - Franklin, VA - *Tel&CabFB 84C*
Franklin Spier - New York, NY - *AdAge 3-28-84*
Franklin Square Bulletin - Franklin Square, NY - *Ed&PubIntYB 82; NewsDir 84*
Franklin Square Bulletin - *See* Nassau Border Papers Inc.
Franklin Square Pennysaver - Rockville Centre, NY - *AyerDirPub 83*
Franklin Sun - Winnsboro, LA - *AyerDirPub 83; Ed&PubIntYB 82*
Franklin Systems Corp. - Westlake Village, CA - *DirInfWP 82*
Franklin Telephone Co. - Meadville, MS - *TelDir&BG 83-84*
Franklin Telephone Co. - Franklin, VT - *TelDir&BG 83-84*
Franklin Tidewater News - Franklin, VA - *BaconPubCkNews 84*
Franklin Times - Franklin, IL - *Ed&PubIntYB 82*
Franklin Times - Louisburg, NC - *AyerDirPub 83; Ed&PubIntYB 82*
Franklin Trumpeter, The - Franklin, NH - *NewsDir 84*
Franklin Williamson Leader - Franklin, TN - *BaconPubCkNews 84*
Franklinton Enterprise - Franklinton, LA - *BaconPubCkNews 84*
Franklinton Era-Leader - Franklinton, LA - *BaconPubCkNews 84*
Franklintown Cable TV [of GS Communications Inc.] - Frederick, MD - *BrCabYB 84*
Franklinville Penny Saver - Springville, NY - *AyerDirPub 83*
Franklinville Sentinel - Franklinville, NJ - *BaconPubCkNews 84; NewsDir 84*
Frank's Features - Dayton, OH - *LitMarPl 83*
Franks Publishing Ranch, Ray - Amarillo, TX - *BoPubDir 4, 5*
Frankston Citizen - Frankston, TX - *BaconPubCkNews 84; Ed&PubIntYB 82*
Franson & Associates Public Relations - San Jose, CA - *DirPRFirms 83*
Franson Publications - San Diego, CA - *LitMag&SmPr 83-84*
Frantz & Co., V. M. - New York, NY - *DirPRFirms 83; LitMarPl 83, 84*
Franzak & Foster Co. - Cleveland, OH - *BoPubDir 5*
Franznick & Cusatis Advertising - New York, NY - *AdAge 3-28-84; StaDirAdAg 2-84*
Fraser Advertising - Atlanta, GA - *AdAge 3-28-84; StaDirAdAg 2-84*
Fraser Cablevision Ltd. [of Rogers Cablesystems Inc.] - Coquitlam, BC, Canada - *BrCabYB 84*
Fraser Canada Ltd., W. B. - Vancouver, BC, Canada - *BoPubDir 4, 5*
Fraser Computer Co. - Grand Blanc, MI - *MicrocomMPl 83*
Fraser Institute - Vancouver, BC, Canada - *BoPubDir 4, 5; LitMarPl 83, 84*
Fraser Lake Bugle - Vanderhoof, BC, Canada - *AyerDirPub 83*
Fraser Paper Ltd. - Greenwich, CT - *MagIndMarPl 82-83*
Fraser Paper Ltd. [Subs. of Fraser Inc.] - Madawaska, ME - *LitMarPl 83, 84*
Fraser Publishing Co. - Cos Cob, CT - *LitMarPl 84*
Fraser Publishing Co. [Aff. of Fraser Management Associates Inc.] - Burlington, VT - *BoPubDir 4, 5*
Fraser Records - *See* Jacobson, Jeffrey E.
Fraser Valley Broadcasters Ltd. - Chilliwack, BC, Canada - *BrCabYB 84*
Fraser Valley Record - Mission, BC, Canada - *AyerDirPub 83; Ed&PubIntYB 82*
Fraser Valley Today - Langley, BC, Canada - *AyerDirPub 83; Ed&PubIntYB 82*
Fraser Videotex Services - Waterloo, ON, Canada - *EISS 5-84 Sup*
Fraser Williams Group Ltd. - Liverpool, England - *MicrocomSwDir 1*
Fraser's Trade Directories Co. Ltd. - Toronto, ON, Canada - *BoPubDir 5*
Fraternal Monitor - Indianapolis, IN - *BaconPubCkMag 84; MagDir 84*
Fraternity Recording Group - Cincinnati, OH - *BillIntBG 83-84*
Fraydas, Stan - Baldwin, NY - *MagIndMarPl 82-83*
Fraydas, Stan - New Rochelle, NY - *LitMarPl 83, 84*
Frazee Forum - Frazee, MN - *BaconPubCkNews 84; Ed&PubIntYB 82*
Frazer Irby Synder Inc. - Little Rock, AR - *StaDirAdAg 2-84*

Frazier, David R. - Boise, ID - *MagIndMarPl 82-83*
Frazier, Gross & Kadlec Inc. - Washington, DC - *CabTVFinDB 83; InterCabHB 3*
FRC Research Corp. - New York, NY - *IntDirMarRes 83*
Freak Brothers Comix/Rip Off Comix [of Rip Off Press Inc.] - San Francisco, CA - *LitMag&SmPr 83-84*
Freas Communications - Santa Barbara, CA - *BoPubDir 4, 5*
Frebar Music Co. - Brentwood, TN - *BillIntBG 83-84*
Freberg Ltd. - Los Angeles, CA - *Tel&CabFB 84C*
Freckle Records - Seattle, WA - *BillIntBG 83-84*
Fred & Barney Press - Venice, CA - *LitMag&SmPr 83-84*
Freddie Records - Corpus Christi, TX - *BillIntBG 83-84*
Frederic Inter-County-Leader [of Inter-County Cooperative Publishing Association] - Frederic, WI - *BaconPubCkNews 84; NewsDir 84*
Frederic Telephone Co. [Aff. of Universal Telephone Inc.] - Frederic, WI - *TelDir&BG 83-84*
Frederick & Brown Inc. - Ezel, KY - *BrCabYB 84*
Frederick & Brown Inc. - Frenchburg, KY - *BrCabYB 84*
Frederick & Brown Inc. - Hazel Green, KY - *BrCabYB 84*
Frederick & Brown Inc. - West Liberty, KY - *Tel&CabFB 84C*
Frederick Brown County News - *See* Maple River Publishing Inc.
Frederick Cablevision Inc. [of Great Southern Printing & Manufacturing Co.] - Frederick, MD - *BrCabYB 84; Tel&CabFB 84C p.1680*
Frederick Cablevision Inc. - Frederick, OK - *BrCabYB 84; Tel&CabFB 84C*
Frederick Daily Leader [of Donrey Media Group] - Frederick, OK - *BaconPubCkNews 84; NewsDir 84*
Frederick Farmer & Miner - Frederick, CO - *BaconPubCkNews 84; Ed&PubIntYB 82*
Frederick News - Frederick, MD - *BaconPubCkNews 84*
Frederick Post [of Great Southern Printing & Manufacturing Co.] - Frederick, MD - *AyerDirPub 83; BaconPubCkNews 84; Ed&PubIntYB 82; NewsDir 84*
Frederick Press - Frederick, OK - *BaconPubCkNews 84; Ed&PubIntYB 82*
Fredericks Associates, Larry - New York, NY - *StaDirAdAg 2-84*
Fredericks Kullberg Amato Pisacane Inc. - New York, NY - *BrCabYB 84; StaDirAdAg 2-84*
Fredericks Publishing Co. - Mertztown, PA - *BoPubDir 4, 5*
Fredericksburg Cable Corp. - Fredericksburg, TX - *BrCabYB 84; Tel&CabFB 84C*
Fredericksburg Free Lance-Star - Fredericksburg, VA - *BaconPubCkNews 84; NewsDir 84*
Fredericksburg Radio Post - Fredericksburg, TX - *NewsDir 84*
Fredericksburg Radio Post - *See* Radio Post Inc.
Fredericksburg Review - Fredericksburg, IA - *Ed&PubIntYB 82*
Fredericksburg Standard [of Fredericksburg Publishing Co. Inc.] - Fredericksburg, TX - *BaconPubCkNews 84; Ed&PubIntYB 82; NewsDir 84*
Frederickson/Hounshell Associates Inc. - Omaha, NE - *StaDirAdAg 2-84*
Fredericktown Democrat-News - Fredericktown, MO - *BaconPubCkNews 84; NewsDir 84*
Fredericktown Knox County Citizen - *See* Knox Printing Co.
Fredericton Cablevision Ltd. - Fredericton, NB, Canada - *BrCabYB 84*
Fredericton Daily Gleaner - Fredericton, NB, Canada - *LitMarPl 83*
Fredola Music Publishing Co. - Auburn, NY - *BillIntBG 83-84*
Fredonia Cable TV Inc. [of Tele-Communications Inc.] - Fredonia, KS - *BrCabYB 84; Tel&CabFB 84C*
Fredonia Cablevision [of Tribune Cable Communications Inc.] - Fredonia, NY - *Tel&CabFB 84C*
Fredonia Daily Herald - Fredonia, KS - *NewsDir 84*
Fredonia Penny Saver - Fredonia, NY - *AyerDirPub 83*
Fredonia Wilson County Citizen - Fredonia, KS - *BaconPubCkNews 84; NewsDir 84*
Fredricks Marketing Research Inc., Joan - St. Louis, MO - *IntDirMarRes 83*
Free - Houston, TX - *LitMag&SmPr 83-84*
Free & Show Music - Marina del Rey, CA - *BillIntBG 83-84*
Free-Bass Press - Eugene, OR - *BoPubDir 4, 5*
Free Enterprise - Geneva, OH - *AyerDirPub 83*
Free Enterprise - Warren, OH - *AyerDirPub 83*
Free Inquiry - Buffalo, NY - *BaconPubCkMag 84*
Free Lance - Hollister, CA - *AyerDirPub 83*
Free-Lance - Henryetta, OK - *AyerDirPub 83*
Free Lance Ink - Royal Oak, MI - *MicrocomMPl 84*
Free Lance Photographers Guild Inc. - New York, NY - *LitMarPl 83, 84*
Free Lance-Star - Fredericksburg, VA - *AyerDirPub 83; Ed&PubIntYB 82*
Free Library of Philadelphia - Philadelphia, PA - *MagIndMarPl 82-83*
Free Market Books - Dobbs Ferry, NY - *BoPubDir 4, 5*
Free People Press - Tyler, TX - *LitMag&SmPr 83-84*
Free Press - Bristol, FL - *Ed&PubIntYB 82*
Free Press - Mayo, FL - *AyerDirPub 83; Ed&PubIntYB 82*
Free Press - Tampa, FL - *AyerDirPub 83; Ed&PubIntYB 82*
Free Press - Quitman, GA - *AyerDirPub 83*
Free Press - Park Forest, IL - *AyerDirPub 83*
Free Press - Colby, KS - *AyerDirPub 83*
Free Press - Boston, MA - *AyerDirPub 83*
Free Press - Melrose, MA - *AyerDirPub 83*
Free Press - Detroit, MI - *AyerDirPub 83*
Free Press - Chisholm, MN - *AyerDirPub 83*
Free Press - Mankato, MN - *AyerDirPub 83; Ed&PubIntYB 82*
Free Press - Cuba, MO - *AyerDirPub 83*
Free Press - Marionville, MO - *AyerDirPub 83*
Free Press - Elko, NV - *AyerDirPub 83*
Free Press - Phillipsburg, NJ - *AyerDirPub 83; Ed&PubIntYB 82*
Free Press - Beacon, NY - *AyerDirPub 83*
Free Press - Trumansburg, NY - *AyerDirPub 83*
Free Press - Kinston, NC - *AyerDirPub 83*
Free Press - Leipsic, OH - *AyerDirPub 83*
Free Press - Garber, OK - *AyerDirPub 83*
Free Press - Kingfisher, OK - *AyerDirPub 83*
Free Press - Midwest City, OK - *AyerDirPub 83*
Free Press - Braddock, PA - *AyerDirPub 83; Ed&PubIntYB 82*
Free Press - Emmaus, PA - *AyerDirPub 83; Ed&PubIntYB 82*
Free Press - Quakertown, PA - *AyerDirPub 83; Ed&PubIntYB 82*
Free Press - Dickson, TN - *AyerDirPub 83*
Free Press - Diboll, TX - *AyerDirPub 83; Ed&PubIntYB 82*
Free Press - Haskell, TX - *AyerDirPub 83*
Free Press - Lehi, UT - *Ed&PubIntYB 82*
Free Press - Amery, WI - *AyerDirPub 83*
Free Press - Fernie, BC, Canada - *AyerDirPub 83; Ed&PubIntYB 82*
Free Press - Nanaimo, BC, Canada - *AyerDirPub 83*
Free Press - Winnipeg, MB, Canada - *AyerDirPub 83*
Free Press - Dartmouth, NS, Canada - *AyerDirPub 83*
Free Press - Acton, ON, Canada - *Ed&PubIntYB 82*
Free Press - Essex, ON, Canada - *AyerDirPub 83; Ed&PubIntYB 82*
Free Press - London, ON, Canada - *AyerDirPub 83*
Free Press - Whitby, ON, Canada - *AyerDirPub 83*
Free Press (East Penn Edition) - Emmaus, PA - *NewsDir 84*
Free Press & Economist - Shelburne, ON, Canada - *AyerDirPub 83; Ed&PubIntYB 82*
Free Press & Herald - Tupper Lake, NY - *AyerDirPub 83*
Free Press & The Tribune Press - Chisholm, MN - *Ed&PubIntYB 82*
Free Press-Courier - Westfield, PA - *AyerDirPub 83*
Free Press Inc. - Carpentersville, IL - *BaconPubCkNews 84*
Free Press Journal - Quakertown, PA - *AyerDirPub 83*
Free Press-Progress - Nokomis, IL - *AyerDirPub 83; Ed&PubIntYB 82*
Free Press-Standard - Carrollton, OH - *AyerDirPub 83; Ed&PubIntYB 82*
Free Press, The [Div. of Macmillan Publishing Corp.] - New York, NY - *LitMarPl 83, 84; WritMar 84*
Free Press, The - Midland, ON, Canada - *AyerDirPub 83; Ed&PubIntYB 82*
Free Text Search [of Dow Jones News/Retrieval Service] - Princeton, NJ - *DataDirOnSer 84*
Free University Network - Manhattan, KS - *BoPubDir 4, 5*
Free Venice Beachhead - Venice, CA - *LitMag&SmPr 83-84*
Freebies - Santa Barbara, CA - *MagIndMarPl 82-83*
Freeborn Telephone Co. - Freeborn, MN - *TelDir&BG 83-84*
Freeburg Tribune - Freeburg, IL - *BaconPubCkNews 84; Ed&PubIntYB 82*

Freeburn Cable TV - Freeburn, KY - *BrCabYB 84; Tel&CabFB 84C*
Freed-Crown Publishing Co. Inc. - Van Nuys, CA - *BoPubDir 4, 5*
Freed, Roy N. - Boston, MA - *BoPubDir 4, 5*
Freedeeds Associates [Aff. of Multimedia Publishing Corp.] - Blauvelt, NY - *BoPubDir 4*
Freedeeds Books [Aff. of Garber Communications Inc.] - Blauvelt, NY - *BoPubDir 5*
Freedman Advertising Inc. - Cincinnati, OH - *StaDirAdAg 2-84*
Freedman Brandt & Brandt Dramatic Dept. Inc., Harold - New York, NY - *LitMarPl 83, 84*
Freedman Liturgy Research Foundation Publishers, Jacob - Springfield, MA - *BoPubDir 4, 5*
Freedman Productions, Hal - New York, NY - *AvMarPl 83*
Freedmen's Organization - Los Angeles, CA - *LitMarPl 83, 84; MagIndMarPl 82-83*
Freedom Call - Freedom, OK - *Ed&PubIntYB 82*
Freedom House - New York, NY - *BoPubDir 4, 5*
Freedom Micro-Systems Inc. - Wytheville, VA - *MicrocomMPl 84*
Freedom Network [of Graphnet Inc.] - Teaneck, NJ - *TeleSy&SerDir 7-83*
Freedom Newspapers - Santa Ana, CA - *AdAge 6-28-84; BrCabYB 84; Ed&PubIntYB 82; KnowInd 83; Tel&CabFB 84S*
Freedom Press - Land O'Lakes, FL - *AyerDirPub 83*
Freedom Press - London, England - *LitMag&SmPr 83-84*
Freedom Records Ltd. - Easley, SC - *BillIntBG 83-84*
Freedom 79 Publications Inc. - Vancouver, BC, Canada - *BoPubDir 4, 5*
Freedom Technology International - Philadelphia, PA - *MicrocomSwDir 1*
Freedom University Press - Orlando, FL - *BoPubDir 4 Sup, 5*
Freedoms' Journal - Dallas, TX - *Ed&PubIntYB 82*
Freedomways - New York, NY - *LitMag&SmPr 83-84; MagIndMarPl 82-83*
Freedonia Gazette, The - New Hope, PA - *LitMag&SmPr 83-84*
Freefield, Sandra - Miami, FL - *LitMarPl 83*
Freehold Central Jersey Leader - Freehold, NJ - *NewsDir 84*
Freehold News Transcript - Freehold, NJ - *BaconPubCkNews 84; NewsDir 84*
Freelance Art Monthly - Northfield, IL - *MagIndMarPl 82-83*
Freelance Inc. - Houston, TX - *DirInfWP 82*
Freelance Network - Pasadena, CA - *BoPubDir 4, 5*
Freelance Photographers Guild Inc. - New York, NY - *AvMarPl 83; Ed&PubIntYB 82*
Freelance Press Services - Manchester, England - *LitMag&SmPr 83-84*
Freelance Publications - Bayport, NY - *BoPubDir 4, 5; LitMarPl 83, 84*
Freelance Research Service - Houston, TX - *EISS 83; FBInfSer 80*
Freelance Writer's Report [of Cassell Communications Inc.] - Port St. Lucie, FL - *LitMag&SmPr 83-84; WritMar 84*
Freelance Writing [of Freelance Press Services] - Manchester, England - *LitMag&SmPr 83-84*
Freelancenter Inc. - New York, NY - *HBIndAd&MS 82-83*
Freelancer - Mayerthorpe, AB, Canada - *AyerDirPub 83*
Freelancer's Newsletter - Austin, TX - *MagIndMarPl 82-83*
Freeland Publications - Philadelphia, PA - *BoPubDir 4 Sup, 5*
Freeman - Kingston, NY - *AyerDirPub 83*
Freeman - Waukesha, WI - *AyerDirPub 83*
Freeman & Co., W. H. - San Francisco, CA - *LitMarPl 83*
Freeman & Co., W. H. [Subs. of Scientific American] - New York, NY - *LitMarPl 84*
Freeman & Doff Inc. - Los Angeles, CA - *DirPRFirms 83*
Freeman, Cooper & Co. - San Francisco, CA - *LitMarPl 83, 84*
Freeman Courier - Freeman, SD - *BaconPubCkNews 84; Ed&PubIntYB 82*
Freeman Graphics, Einson - Fairlawn, NJ - *MagIndMarPl 82-83*
Freeman Huenick Zilbert Inc. - Brookfield, WI - *StaDirAdAg 2-84*
Freeman, James - Headland, AL - *Tel&CabFB 84C p.1680*
Freeman-Journal - Webster City, IA - *AyerDirPub 83*
Freeman Newspapers - Pine Bluff, AR - *Ed&PubIntYB 82*
Freeman Public Relations Inc., Gerald - New York, NY - *DirPRFirms 83*
Freeman Publications Inc., Miller - San Francisco, CA - *LitMarPl 83; MagIndMarPl 82-83*
Freeman Systems - Menlo Park, CA - *MicrocomMPl 84*
Freeman, The - Irvington-on-Hudson, NY - *BaconPubCkMag 84; MagDir 84; MagIndMarPl 82-83; WritMar 84*
Freeman, William - Headland, AL - *Tel&CabFB 84C p.1680*
Freeman's, Jack - Tampa, FL - *AvMarPl 83*
Freeman's Journal - Cooperstown, NY - *AyerDirPub 83*
Freeperson Press [Aff. of TH-EC Inc.] - Novato, CA - *BoPubDir 4 Sup, 5*
Freeport Journal Standard [of Howard Publications] - Freeport, IL - *BaconPubCkNews 84; Ed&PubIntYB 82; NewsDir 84*
Freeport Leader - Freeport, NY - *Ed&PubIntYB 82*
Freeport Long Island Graphic [of Lawrence Bi-County Publishers Inc.] - Lawrence, NY - *NewsDir 84*
Freeport Long Island Graphic - *See* Richner Publications Inc.
Freeport Long Island Graphic-Roosevelt Press - Freeport, NY - *Ed&PubIntYB 82*
Freeport News - Freeport, MI - *BaconPubCkNews 84; Ed&PubIntYB 82*
Freeport Pennysaver - Freeport, NY - *AyerDirPub 83*
Freer, Bonnie M. - New City, NY - *MagIndMarPl 82-83*
Freer Gallery of Art [Aff. of Smithsonian Institution] - Washington, DC - *BoPubDir 4, 5*
Freeson Advertising Agency - Hialeah, FL - *StaDirAdAg 2-84*
Freestone Publishing Collective - Monroe, UT - *BoPubDir 4, 5; LitMag&SmPr 83-84*
Freeway - Glen Ellyn, IL - *WritMar 84*
Freiman & Co., Ray - Stamford, CT - *LitMarPl 83, 84*
Fremantle International Inc. - New York, NY - *Tel&CabFB 84C*
Fremerman, Malcy & Associates Inc. - Kansas City, MO - *ArtMar 84*
Fremerman, Malcy, Spivak, Rosenfield Inc. - Kansas City, MO - *StaDirAdAg 2-84*
Fremont Argus [of Sparks Newspapers Inc.] - Fremont, CA - *BaconPubCkNews 84; NewsDir 84*
Fremont Cable TV Inc. [of Tele-Communications Inc.] - Fremont, CA - *BrCabYB 84; Tel&CabFB 84C*
Fremont Cablevision [of MetroVision Inc.] - Fremont, NE - *Tel&CabFB 84C*
Fremont Cablevision [of Wolfe Broadcasting Corp.] - Fremont, OH - *BrCabYB 84*
Fremont CATV [of Wolfe Broadcasting Corp.] - Fremont, OH - *Tel&CabFB 84C*
Fremont County Chronicle-News - St. Anthony, ID - *AyerDirPub 83; Ed&PubIntYB 82*
Fremont County Chronicle News - *See* Standard-Journal Inc.
Fremont County Sun - Canon City, CO - *AyerDirPub 83; Ed&PubIntYB 82*
Fremont Gazette - Fremont, IA - *Ed&PubIntYB 82*
Fremont Gazette - *See* Quad County Newspapers
Fremont-Mills Beacon Enterprise - Tabor, IA - *AyerDirPub 83*
Fremont-Mundelin Patriot - *See* Lakeland Publishers Inc.
Fremont News-Messenger [of Gannett Co. Inc.] - Fremont, OH - *BaconPubCkNews 84; NewsDir 84*
Fremont Patriot - Wauconda, IL - *AyerDirPub 83*
Fremont Patriot, The - Mundelein, IL - *Ed&PubIntYB 82*
Fremont Times Indicator - Fremont, MI - *BaconPubCkNews 84; Ed&PubIntYB 82; NewsDir 84*
Fremont Trader [of Canon City Fremont County Sun] - Canon City, CO - *AyerDirPub 83; NewsDir 84*
Fremont Tribune [of Gannett Co. Inc.] - Fremont, NE - *BaconPubCkNews 84; Ed&PubIntYB 82; NewsDir 84*
Frenaye, Frances - New York, NY - *LitMarPl 83, 84*
French Agency Ltd., F. John - London, England - *StaDirAdAg 2-84*
French American Cultural Services & Educational Aid - New York, NY - *AvMarPl 83*
French & European Publications Inc. - New York, NY - *AvMarPl 83*
French & Partners Inc., Paul - LaGrange, GA - *AvMarPl 83; WritMar 84*
French & Preston Div. [of Manning, Selvange & Lee Inc.] - New York, NY - *StaDirAdAg 2-84*
French & Spanish Book Corp. [Aff. of French & European Publications Inc.] - New York, NY - *BoPubDir 4, 5; LitMarPl 83, 84; MagIndMarPl 82-83*

French Book Co. - Washington, DC - *BoPubDir 4, 5*
French Book Guild - Long Island City, NY - *LitMarPl 83*
French Federation of Data Base Producers - Orleans, France - *EISS 83*
French Forum Publisher Inc. - Lexington, KY - *BoPubDir 4, 5; LitMarPl 84*
French Inc., Samuel - New York, NY - *LitMarPl 83, 84; WritMar 84*
French Institute/Alliance Francaise - New York, NY - *BoPubDir 4, 5*
French Lick Springs Valley Herald - French Lick, IN - *BaconPubCkNews 84*
French Ltd., Samuel - Toronto, ON, Canada - *LitMarPl 83*
French Literature Publications Co. Inc. - York, SC - *BoPubDir 4, 5*
French Market Music - New Orleans, LA - *BillIntBG 83-84*
French National Readership Survey [of Interactive Market Systems Inc.] - New York, NY - *DataDirOnSer 84*
French, Peggy Lois - Sun City, CA - *LitMarPl 83, 84*
French Retrieval Automated Network for Current Information... [of Centre de Documentation Sciences Humaines] - Paris, France - *CompReadDB 82*
French Review - Chapel Hill, NC - *MagIndMarPl 82-83*
French Review, The - Champaign, IL - *MagDir 84*
French Silk - Cannon Falls, MN - *MicrocomMPl 84; MicrocomSwDir 1*
French Sullivan Inc. - Troy, MI - *StaDirAdAg 2-84*
Frenchtown Delaware Valley News - *See* Hunterdon County Democrat Inc.
Freneau Press, Philip - Monmouth Beach, NJ - *BoPubDir 4, 5*
Frequent Flyer [of Dun & Bradstreet] - New York, NY - *BaconPubCkMag 84; Folio 83; WritMar 84*
Fresh Air Music Co. - *See* Son-Ton Music Co.
Fresh Fruit [of Brown Daily Herald Inc.] - Providence, RI - *NewsDir 84*
Fresh Meadows Pennysaver - Rockville Centre, NY - *AyerDirPub 83*
Fresh Press - Palo Alto, CA - *BoPubDir 4, 5; LitMag&SmPr 83-84*
Freshcut Press - Ukiah, CA - *BoPubDir 4, 5*
Freshwater & Marine Aquarium - Sierra Madre, CA - *BaconPubCkMag 84*
Freshwater Press Inc. - Cleveland, OH - *BoPubDir 4, 5*
Fresno Bee [of McClatchy Newspapers Inc.] - Fresno, CA - *BaconPubCkNews 84; Ed&PubIntYB 82; LitMarPl 83, 84; NewsBur 6; NewsDir 84*
Fresno Cable TV Ltd. [of McClatchy Newspapers] - Fresno, CA - *BrCabYB 84; Tel&CabFB 84C*
Fresno California Advocate - Fresno, CA - *BaconPubCkNews 84*
Fresno California Courier - Fresno, CA - *BaconPubCkNews 84*
Fresno County Reporter - Fresno, CA - *AyerDirPub 83; Ed&PubIntYB 82*
Fresno Daily Legal Report - Fresno, CA - *Ed&PubIntYB 82; NewsDir 84*
Fresno Guide, The - Fresno, CA - *NewsDir 84*
Fresno MDS Co. - New York, NY - *Tel&CabFB 84C*
Freson Associates Inc. - Fairfax, VA - *DirPRFirms 83*
Frets [of GPI Publications] - Cupertino, CA - *BaconPubCkMag 84; MagDir 84; MagIndMarPl 82-83; WritMar 84*
Freund, Yvonne R. - New York, NY - *LitMarPl 83, 84; MagIndMarPl 82-83*
Freundlich Books [Div. of Lawrence Freundlich Publications Inc.] - New York, NY - *LitMarPl 84*
Frevert & Hall Research Associates Inc. - Spring Park, MN - *IntDirMarRes 83*
Frey & Co., Donald R. - Ft. Thomas, KY - *ADAPSOMemDir 83-84; MicrocomMPl 84*
Frey Enterprises - Nashville, TN - *BoPubDir 4, 5*
Frezzolini Electronics Inc. [Div. of General Research Laboratories] - Hawthorne, NJ - *AvMarPl 83*
FRI Information Services Ltd. - Montreal, PQ, Canada - *DataDirOnSer 84; EISS 83*
Frick Art Museum - Pittsburgh, PA - *BoPubDir 4, 5*
Frick Collection - New York, NY - *BoPubDir 4, 5*
Fricke 3 Inc. - Raleigh, NC - *AdAge 3-28-84; StaDirAdAg 2-84*
Fricon Entertainment Co. Inc., The - Los Angeles, CA - *BillIntBG 83-84*
Fricon Music Co. - *See* Fricon Entertainment Co. Inc., The
Fricout Music Co. - *See* Fricon Entertainment Co. Inc., The
Friday - North Oklahoma City, OK - *Ed&PubIntYB 82*
Friday - Philadelphia, PA - *WritMar 84*
Friday Harbor Journal - Friday Harbor, WA - *BaconPubCkNews 84; Ed&PubIntYB 82*
Friday Records - Nashville, TN - *BillIntBG 83-84*
Friday Report - Garden City, NY - *BaconPubCkMag 84*
Fridley Sun - Fridley, MN - *Ed&PubIntYB 82*
Fridley Sun - *See* Sun Newspapers
Fridley Sun & Columbia Heights Sun - Edina, MN - *AyerDirPub 83*
Fried Productions - Farmington, CT - *AvMarPl 83; WritMar 84*
Friede Books, Eleanor - New York, NY - *LitMarPl 84*
Friede Inc., Eleanor - New York, NY - *LitMarPl 83, 84*
Friede Publications - Davison, MI - *BoPubDir 5*
Friedland Enterprises - New York, NY - *LitMarPl 83, 84*
Friedlander Communications Ltd. - Bannockburn, IL - *ArtMar 84; DirPRFirms 83*
Friedman Advertising Inc., C. D. - Santa Monica, CA - *StaDirAdAg 2-84*
Friedman Associates Advertising - West Orange, NJ - *StaDirAdAg 2-84*
Friedman Associates, Herbert N. - Middletown, NY - *LitMarPl 83, 84*
Friedman, Gaby E. - Fair Lawn, NJ - *LitMarPl 83; MagIndMarPl 82-83*
Friedman, Gene - Wainscott, NY - *AvMarPl 83*
Friedman Inc., A. I. - New York, NY - *LitMarPl 83*
Friedman, Irene - New York, NY - *LitMarPl 83, 84; MagIndMarPl 82-83*
Friedman Marketing Services Inc., E. - Southfield, MI - *IntDirMarRes 83*
Friedman Photo Retouch, Estelle - New York, NY - *AvMarPl 83; LitMarPl 83*
Friedman/Uniphoto, Ron - Baltimore, MD - *AvMarPl 83; MagIndMarPl 82-83*
Friedrich Typography - Santa Barbara, CA - *LitMarPl 83, 84*
Friedrichs & Associates Inc., N. K. - Minneapolis, MN - *IntDirMarRes 83*
Friend Sentinel - Friend, NE - *BaconPubCkNews 84; Ed&PubIntYB 82*
Friend, The - Salt Lake City, UT - *ArtMar 84; MagIndMarPl 82-83; WritMar 84*
Friendly Exchange [of Webb Co.] - St. Paul, MN - *BaconPubCkMag 84; MagIndMarPl 82-83; WritMar 84*
Friendly Fairways of America - Royal Oak, MI - *BoPubDir 4, 5*
Friendly Farm Computer Newsletter [of FBS System Inc.] - Aledo, IL - *MicrocomMPl 84*
Friendly Press [Aff. of Leona Tyler Center] - Eugene, OR - *BoPubDir 4 Sup, 5*
Friendly Publications - New York, NY - *BoPubDir 4, 5*
Friendly TV Cable [of Consolidated Cable Co.] - Friendly, WV - *BrCabYB 84*
FriendlySoft Inc. - Arlington, TX - *MicrocomMPl 84*
Friends Journal - Philadelphia, PA - *MagIndMarPl 82-83*
Friends Magazine [of Ceco Publishing Co.] - Warren, MI - *WritMar 84*
Friends of Freedom Foundation - Waco, TX - *BoPubDir 4, 5*
Friends of Israel Gospel Ministry Inc. (Spearhead Press) - West Collingswood, NJ - *BoPubDir 4, 5*
Friends of Malatesta Inc. - Ellsworth, ME - *BoPubDir 4, 5*
Friends of Photography - Carmel, CA - *BoPubDir 4, 5; LitMarPl 84*
Friends of Poetry - Whitewater, WI - *LitMag&SmPr 83-84*
Friends of the Earth - San Francisco, CA - *LitMag&SmPr 83-84; LitMarPl 83*
Friends of Wine, The - Silver Spring, MD - *BaconPubCkMag 84; MagIndMarPl 82-83*
Friends of World Teaching - San Diego, CA - *BoPubDir 4, 5*
Friends Software - Berkeley, CA - *MicrocomMPl 83, 84; MicrocomSwDir 1*
Friends United Press - Richmond, IN - *LitMarPl 83, 84*
Friendship Circle Press - Boulder, CO - *BoPubDir 4, 5*

Friendship Press [Subs. of National Council of the Churches of Christ U.S.A.] - New York, NY - *AvMarPl 83; LitMarPl 83, 84*
Friendship Publications Inc. - Spokane, WA - *BoPubDir 5*
Friendship Records Inc. - Ft. Myers, FL - *BillIntBG 83-84*
Friendship Reporter - Adams, WI - *BaconPubCkNews 84*
Friendship Reporter, The - Friendship, WI - *Ed&PubIntYB 82*
Friendship Tri-County News - *See* Alamo Crockett Times
Friendship Videon - Friendship, NY - *BrCabYB 84; Tel&CabFB 84C*
Friendswood Journal - Friendswood, TX - *Ed&PubIntYB 82*
Friendswood Journal - *See* Fig Leaf Publishing Co.
Friendswood News - Friendswood, TX - *BaconPubCkNews 84*
Friendswood Pearland Reporter - Friendswood, TX - *BaconPubCkNews 84*
Frieze Advertising Inc. - East Brunswick, NJ - *StaDirAdAg 2-84*
Friis, Erik J. - Montvale, NJ - *LitMarPl 83, 84; MagIndMarPl 82-83*
Friis, Erik J. - New York, NY - *LitMarPl 83*
Frio-Nueces Publications Ltd. - Pearsall, TX - *BaconPubCkNews 84*
Friona Cablevision [of Ameritex Communications Inc.] - Friona, TX - *BrCabYB 84; Tel&CabFB 84C*
Friona Star - Friona, TX - *BaconPubCkNews 84; Ed&PubIntYB 82*
Fripp Island Cable Co. - Fripp Island, SC - *Tel&CabFB 84C*
Frisbie/Communications, Richard - Chicago, IL - *LitMarPl 83, 84; MagIndMarPl 82-83*
Frisch & Co., B. W. - New York, NY - *StaDirAdAg 2-84*
Frisco Enterprise - Frisco, TX - *BaconPubCkNews 84; Ed&PubIntYB 82*
Friske, Gary - Enosburg Falls, VT - *Tel&CabFB 84C p.1680*
Frith & Associates, Lew - Anaheim, CA - *TeleSy&SerDir 2-84*
Frith Films - Carmel Valley, CA - *AvMarPl 83*
Fritsche Co., W. J. - Lima, OH - *StaDirAdAg 2-84*
Fritz Creative Services - Merion, PA - *MagIndMarPl 82-83*
Fritz, Gerard - Charlotte, NC - *LitMarPl 83; MagIndMarPl 82-83*
Fritz, Larry & Helen - Merion, PA - *LitMarPl 83, 84*
Frizinghall Consultants Ltd. - Islington, ON, Canada - *WhoWMicrocom 83*
Frizzell Advertising Agency Inc. - Minneapolis, MN - *StaDirAdAg 2-84*
FRM Weekly - Garden City, NY - *BaconPubCkMag 84*
Frobber, The [of FROBCO] - Santa Cruz, CA - *MicrocomMPl 84*
Frobco [Div. of Tri-Comp Polytechnical] - Santa Cruz, CA - *MicrocomMPl 84*
Froehlich Advertising Services Inc. - Mahwah, NJ - *LitMarPl 83, 84; MagIndMarPl 82-83; StaDirAdAg 2-84*
Frog in the Well - East Palo Alto, CA - *BoPubDir 4, 5; LitMag&SmPr 83-84*
Frog Software Co. - Albany, NY - *MicrocomMPl 84*
Frogpond [of Haiku Society of America Inc.] - New York, NY - *LitMag&SmPr 83-84*
Frolics [of Frolics Publications Inc.] - Ithaca, NY - *ArtMar 84*
From Here Press - Fanwood, NJ - *BoPubDir 4, 5; LitMag&SmPr 83-84*
Fromer Writing & Editing Service - Washington, DC - *LitMarPl 83, 84*
Fromholz Publishing, Steve - *See* Prophecy Publishing Inc.
Fromm International Publishing Corp. - New York, NY - *LitMarPl 83, 84; WritMar 84*
Frommer/Pasmantier Publishers [Div. of Simon & Schuster] - New York, NY - *LitMarPl 83, 84*
Frommer Price Literary Agency Inc., The - New York, NY - *LitMarPl 83, 84*
Frompovich Publications, C. J. - Coopersburg, PA - *ArtMar 84; BoPubDir 4, 5; LitMag&SmPr 83-84; LitMarPl 83, 84; WritMar 84*
Front Hall Enterprises Inc. - Voorheesville, NY - *BillIntBG 83-84*
Front Line [of Merck, Sharp & Dohme] - West Point, PA - *ArtMar 84*
Front Musical Literature, Theodore - Beverly Hills, CA - *MagIndMarPl 82-83*
Front Page Detective [of RGH Publications] - New York, NY - *ArtMar 84; MagIndMarPl 82-83; WritMar 84*
Front Page Inc. - Buffalo, NY - *BaconPubCkNews 84*
Front Page News, The - Del City, OK - *Ed&PubIntYB 82*
Front Page, The - Lackawanna, NY - *AyerDirPub 83*
Front Press - Kingston, ON, Canada - *BoPubDir 4, 5*
Front Range Journal - Idaho Springs, CO - *AyerDirPub 83; Ed&PubIntYB 82*
Front Row Experience - Byron, CA - *BoPubDir 4, 5; WritMar 84*
Front Royal Warren Sentinel - Front Royal, VA - *BaconPubCkNews 84*
Front Street Publishers - New York, NY - *BoPubDir 4, 5*
Front Street Publishers - Poughkeepsie, NY - *LitMag&SmPr 83-84*
Front Street Trolley [of Trolley Inc.] - Nashville, TN - *LitMag&SmPr 83-84*
Frontal Lobe - Los Altos, CA - *BoPubDir 4, 5*
Frontier & Holt County Independent - O'Neill, NE - *AyerDirPub 83; Ed&PubIntYB 82*
Frontier Cable TV Co. - Boulder City, NV - *BrCabYB 84*
Frontier Cablevision [of American Television & Communications Corp.] - Stillwater, OK - *BrCabYB 84; Tel&CabFB 84C*
Frontier Enterprise - Lake Zurich, IL - *AyerDirPub 83*
Frontier Magazine - Aurora, CO - *MagDir 84*
Frontier Magazine - St. Paul, MN - *BaconPubCkMag 84; MagIndMarPl 82-83*
Frontier News Service - Massapequa, NY - *LitMarPl 83, 84*
Frontier Press - Santa Rosa, CA - *BoPubDir 4, 5; LitMag&SmPr 83-84*
Frontier Press Co., The - Columbus, OH - *LitMarPl 83, 84*
Frontier Publishing Corp. - Lake Zurich, IL - *BaconPubCkNews 84*
Frontier Software [Div. of ASYST Design Services] - Cortland, NY - *MicrocomMPl 83, 84*
Frontier TV Cable Co. [of Landmark Cablevision Associates] - Colorado City, TX - *BrCabYB 84; Tel&CabFB 84C*
Frontiers: A Journal of Women Studies - Boulder, CO - *LitMag&SmPr 83-84*
Frontiers in Immunoassay - Anaheim, CA - *MagDir 84*
Frontiers of Science - Baltimore, MD - *MagIndMarPl 82-83*
Frontiersman [of Skagit Valley Publishing Co.] - Palmer, AK - *AyerDirPub 83; Ed&PubIntYB 82; NewsDir 84*
Frontline Publications - El Toro, CA - *LitMag&SmPr 83-84*
Frontlines - Santa Barbara, CA - *LitMag&SmPr 83-84*
Frontpage [of Newspaper Guild of New York] - New York, NY - *NewsDir 84*
Frontrunners Syndications - Schaumberg, IL - *Ed&PubIntYB 82*
Frost & Sullivan Inc. - New York, NY - *CompReadDB 82; DataDirOnSer 84; EISS 83; InfIndMarPl 83; InfoS 83-84; IntDirMarRes 83; Tel&CabFB 84C; TeleSy&SerDir 2-84*
Frost & Sullivan Research Report Abstracts - New York, NY - *DirOnDB Spring 84*
Frost, David - Plainfield, NJ - *LitMarPl 83, 84*
Frost Enterprise - Frost, TX - *Ed&PubIntYB 82*
Frost, O. W. - Anchorage, AK - *BoPubDir 4, 5*
Frost Telephone Co. - Frost, MN - *TelDir&BG 83-84*
Frostburg Citizen - Frostburg, MD - *BaconPubCkNews 84*
Frostburg Guardian, The - Frostburg, MD - *NewsDir 84*
Frostproof News - Frostproof, FL - *BaconPubCkNews 84*
Frozen Food Age - New York, NY - *BaconPubCkMag 84; MagDir 84*
Frozen Waffles Press & Tapes - Bloomington, IN - *LitMag&SmPr 83-84*
FRSS - Washington, DC - *DirOnDB Spring 84*
Fruit & Vegetable Reporter - New York, NY - *Ed&PubIntYB 82*
Fruit by Telegraph [of Fruit Telegraphic Delivery Service] - Atlantic City, NJ - *MagDir 84*
Fruit Jar Music - *See* Terrace Music Group Inc.
Fruit Music - *See* Boxer Music
Fruit South - Atlanta, GA - *MagDir 84*
Fruita Times - Fruita, CO - *BaconPubCkNews 84; Ed&PubIntYB 82*
Fruitdale Telephone Co. Inc. [Aff. of Mississippi Telephone Corp.] - Fruitdale, AL - *TelDir&BG 83-84*
Fruitful Yield Newsletter - Villa Park, IL - *WritMar 84*
Fruition [of The Plan] - Santa Cruz, CA - *ArtMar 84; LitMag&SmPr 83-84; WritMar 84*
Frutkin, Mark - Ottawa, ON, Canada - *BoPubDir 4, 5*
Fry Agency Inc., The - New York, NY - *MagIndMarPl 82-83*
Fry Associates Inc. - Tulsa, OK - *StaDirAdAg 2-84*
Fry Consultants Inc. - Atlanta, GA - *IntDirMarRes 83*

Fry/Hammond/Barr Inc. - Orlando, FL - *StaDirAdAg 2-84*
Fry, L. John - Santa Barbara, CA - *BoPubDir 4, 5*
FRY9 [of Control Data Corp.] - Greenwich, CT - *DataDirOnSer 84*
Fryan Audio Visual Equipment Co. Inc. - Willoughby, OH - *AvMarPl 83*
Fryatt, Norma R. - Rockport, MA - *LitMarPl 83, 84; MagIndMarPl 82-83*
Frye Copystems (Copying Products Div.) - Cincinnati, OH - *DirInfWP 82*
Frye Syndicate - New York, NY - *Ed&PubIntYB 82*
Frye Typesetting, Pam - Mt. Prospect, IL - *LitMarPl 83, 84; MagIndMarPl 82-83*
Fryman, E. H. - Portsmouth, OH - *Tel&CabFB 84C p.1680*
Fry's - Perris, CA - *BoPubDir 4, 5*
FSTA - Frankfurt, West Germany - *DirOnDB Spring 84*
FSU Search [of Florida State University] - Tallahassee, FL - *FBInfSer 80*
Ft. Atkinson Daily Jefferson County Union [of W. D. Hoard & Sons Co.] - Ft. Atkinson, WI - *NewsDir 84*
Ft. Atkinson Telephone Co. - Ft. Atkinson, IA - *TelDir&BG 83-84*
Ft. Belvoir Castle - Ft. Belvoir, VA - *BaconPubCkNews 84; NewsDir 84*
Ft. Bend Advertiser - Alief, TX - *AyerDirPub 83*
Ft. Bend Cable Television Inc. - Richmond, TX - *BrCabYB 84; Tel&CabFB 84C*
Ft. Bend Mirror - Missouri City, TX - *Ed&PubIntYB 82*
Ft. Bend Telephone Co. - Rosenberg, TX - *TelDir&BG 83-84*
Ft. Benning Bayonet - Ft. Benning, GA - *BaconPubCkNews 84*
Ft. Benton Cable TV - Ft. Benton, MT - *Tel&CabFB 84C*
Ft. Benton River Press - Ft. Benton, MT - *BaconPubCkNews 84; NewsDir 84*
Ft. Bragg Advocate News [of Mendocino Publishing Co.] - Ft. Bragg, CA - *BaconPubCkNews 84; Ed&PubIntYB 82; NewsDir 84*
Ft. Bragg Paraglide - Fayetteville, NC - *AyerDirPub 83*
Ft. Branch Times - Ft. Branch, IN - *BaconPubCkNews 84; Ed&PubIntYB 82*
Ft. Cablevision Inc. - Ft. Scott, KS - *BrCabYB 84; Tel&CabFB 84C*
Ft. Cobb News - Ft. Cobb, OK - *BaconPubCkNews 84; Ed&PubIntYB 82*
Ft. Collins Triangle Review - Ft. Collins, CO - *AyerDirPub 83; BaconPubCkNews 84*
Ft. Covington Sun - Ft. Covington, NY - *BaconPubCkNews 84; Ed&PubIntYB 82*
Ft. Davis TV Cable - Ft. Davis, TX - *BrCabYB 84; Tel&CabFB 84C*
Ft. Deposit Lowndes Signal - Ft. Deposit, AL - *BaconPubCkNews 84*
Ft. Devens Dispatch [of East Pepperell Times-Free Press] - East Pepperell, MA - *AyerDirPub 83; BaconPubCkNews 84; NewsDir 84*
Ft. Devens Sentry [of The Public Spirit Publishing Co. Inc.] - Ayer, MA - *AyerDirPub 83; NewsDir 84*
Ft. Dix Post - Ft. Dix, NJ - *BaconPubCkNews 84*
Ft. Dix Post - Mt. Holly, NJ - *AyerDirPub 83*
Ft. Dodge Messenger [of Ogden Newspapers Inc.] - Ft. Dodge, IA - *NewsDir 84*
Ft. Dodge Messenger & Chronicle - Ft. Dodge, IA - *BaconPubCkNews 84*
Ft. Fairfield Review - Ft. Fairfield, ME - *BaconPubCkNews 84; Ed&PubIntYB 82*
Ft. Frances Times - Ft. Frances, ON, Canada - *Ed&PubIntYB 82*
Ft. Garry Pioneer - Winnipeg, MB, Canada - *Ed&PubIntYB 82*
Ft. Gateway Guide - Waynesville, MO - *AyerDirPub 83; BaconPubCkNews 84*
Ft. Gibson Times - Ft. Gibson, OK - *BaconPubCkNews 84*
Ft. Gordon Cablevision - Pensacola, FL - *BrCabYB 84*
Ft. Hill Cable TV [of Video Properties Ltd.] - Pickens, SC - *BrCabYB 84*
Ft. Hill Cable TV - Seneca, SC - *BrCabYB 84*
Ft. Hill Cable TV [of Video Properties Ltd.] - Walhalla, SC - *BrCabYB 84*
Ft. Hood Cable TV Inc. [of TeleNational Communications Inc.] - FT. Hood, TX - *BrCabYB 84; Tel&CabFB 84C*
Ft. Hood Sentinel - Temple, TX - *AyerDirPub 83*
Ft. Jackson Leader, The - Columbia, SC - *AyerDirPub 83*
Ft. Jennings Telephone Co. - Ft. Jennings, OH - *TelDir&BG 83-84*
Ft. Jones Pioneer Press - Ft. Jones, CA - *Ed&PubIntYB 82*
Ft. Knox Inside the Turret [of The News-Enterprise Corp.] - Elizabethtown, KY - *NewsDir 84*
Ft. Knox Music Co. - Broadway, NY - *BillIntBG 83-84*
Ft. Lauderdale East Broward Tribune - Ft. Lauderdale, FL - *BaconPubCkNews 84*
Ft. Lauderdale Hi-Riser - Ft. Lauderdale, FL - *BaconPubCkNews 84*
Ft. Lauderdale Magazine - Ft. Lauderdale, FL - *BaconPubCkMag 84*
Ft. Lauderdale News [of Tribune Co.] - Ft. Lauderdale, FL - *BaconPubCkNews 84; Ed&PubIntYB 82; NewsBur 6; NewsDir 84*
Ft. Lauderdale News & Sun Sentinel - Ft. Lauderdale, FL - *Ed&PubIntYB 82; NewsDir 84*
Ft. Lauderdale Shopper - Margate, FL - *NewsDir 84*
Ft. Lauderdale Shopper East - Pompano Beach, FL - *AyerDirPub 83*
Ft. Lauderdale Shopper West - Pompano Beach, FL - *AyerDirPub 83*
Ft. Lauderdale Westside Gazette - Ft. Lauderdale, FL - *BaconPubCkNews 84; NewsDir 84*
Ft. Lee Free Press - *See* West New Yorker Inc.
Ft. Lee Sun Bulletin - *See* Bergen News Publishing Corp.
Ft. Lee/Sun-Bulletin, The [of News Publishing Co.] - Palisades Park, NJ - *NewsDir 84*
Ft. Leonard Wood USACT-E [of Satellite Cable TV Corp.] - Ft. Leonard Wood, MO - *BrCabYB 84*
Ft. Lewis Ranger - Ft. Lewis, WA - *BaconPubCkNews 84*
Ft. Lewis Ranger - Tacoma, WA - *AyerDirPub 83; NewsDir 84*
Ft. Lupton Communications Corp. [of Scripps-Howard Cable Co.] - Ft. Lupton, CO - *Tel&CabFB 84C*
Ft. Lupton Press [of Brighton Newspapers Inc.] - Brighton, CO - *NewsDir 84*
Ft. Lupton Press - Ft. Lupton, CO - *AyerDirPub 83; BaconPubCkNews 84; Ed&PubIntYB 82*
Ft. Madison Daily Democrat - Ft. Madison, IA - *BaconPubCkNews 84; NewsDir 84*
Ft. Mason TV Improvement Co. Inc. - Mason, TX - *BrCabYB 84; Tel&CabFB 84C*
Ft. McMurray Today - Ft. McMurray, AB, Canada - *AyerDirPub 83; BaconPubCkNews 84; Ed&PubIntYB 82*
Ft. Meade Democrat & Leader - Ft. Meade, FL - *BaconPubCkNews 84*
Ft. Mill Telephone Co. - Ft. Mill, SC - *TelDir&BG 83-84*
Ft. Mill Times [of The Camden Co.] - Ft. Mill, SC - *BaconPubCkNews 84; Ed&PubIntYB 82; NewsDir 84*
Ft. Morgan Cable TV [of Tele-Communications Inc.] - Ft. Morgan, CO - *BrCabYB 84*
Ft. Morgan Times - Ft. Morgan, CO - *BaconPubCkNews 84; Ed&PubIntYB 82; NewsDir 84*
Ft. Myers Beach Bulletin - Ft. Myers Beach, FL - *BaconPubCkNews 84*
Ft. Myers Lee County Suburban Reporter - Ft. Myers, FL - *BaconPubCkNews 84*
Ft. Myers News-Press - Ft. Myers, FL - *BaconPubCkNews 84; Ed&PubIntYB 82; NewsDir 84*
Ft. Nelson News, The - Ft. Nelson, BC, Canada - *Ed&PubIntYB 82*
Ft. Orange Press Inc. - Albany, NY - *LitMarPl 83, 84; MagIndMarPl 82-83*
Ft. Ord Panorama - Pacific Grove, CA - *AyerDirPub 83*
Ft. Payne Times-Journal, The - Ft. Payne, AL - *NewsDir 84*
Ft. Pierce Chronicle - Ft. Pierce, FL - *BaconPubCkNews 84*
Ft. Pierce News-Tribune - Ft. Pierce, FL - *BaconPubCkNews 84*
Ft. Pierre Times - Ft. Pierre, SD - *Ed&PubIntYB 82*
Ft. Plain Courier-Standard-Enterprise - Ft. Plain, NY - *BaconPubCkNews 84*
Ft. Riley Post - Junction City, KS - *AyerDirPub 83*
Ft. Riley Post - *See* Montgomery Publications Inc.
Ft. Sackville House - Bedford, NS, Canada - *BoPubDir 4, 5*

Ft. Sam Houston News Leader - San Antonio, TX - *AyerDirPub 83*
Ft. Scott Tribune - Ft. Scott, KS - *AyerDirPub 83; BaconPubCkNews 84; Ed&PubIntYB 82; NewsDir 84*
Ft. Sheridan Tower [of Lakeland Publishers Inc.] - Grayslake, IL - *NewsDir 84*
Ft. Sheridan Tower - Highland Park, IL - *AyerDirPub 83*
Ft. Sheridan Tower - *See* Lakeland Publishers Inc.
Ft. Smith Southwest Times-Record [of Donrey Inc.] - Ft. Smith, AR - *NewsDir 84*
Ft. Smith TV Cable [of Rogers UA Cablesystems Inc.] - Ft. Smith, AR - *BrCabYB 84; Tel&CabFB 84C*
Ft. Stockton Pioneer - Ft. Stockton, TX - *BaconPubCkNews 84; Ed&PubIntYB 82; NewsDir 84*
Ft. Sumner de Baca County News - Ft. Sumner, NM - *BaconPubCkNews 84*
Ft. Thomas Campbell County Recorder - *See* Recorder Newspapers
Ft. Valley Leader-Tribune - Ft. Valley, GA - *BaconPubCkNews 84; NewsDir 84*
Ft. Walton Beach Playground News - Ft. Walton Beach, FL - *BaconPubCkNews 84*
Ft. Walton Beach Playground News - Pensacola, FL - *NewsDir 84*
Ft. Wayne Frost Illustrated - Ft. Wayne, IN - *Ed&PubIntYB 82*
Ft. Wayne Journal Gazette - Ft. Wayne, IN - *BaconPubCkNews 84; NewsDir 84*
Ft. Wayne MDS - Indianapolis, IN - *Tel&CabFB 84C*
Ft. Wayne News-Sentinel [of Knight-Ridder Newspapers Inc.] - Ft. Wayne, IN - *BaconPubCkNews 84; LitMarPl 83; NewsDir 84*
Ft. Wood Cable TV [of Satellite Cable TV Corp.] - Ft. Leonard Wood, MO - *Tel&CabFB 84C*
Ft. Worth Como Monitor - Ft. Worth, TX - *BaconPubCkNews 84; Ed&PubIntYB 82; NewsDir 84*
Ft. Worth Eastside News - Ft. Worth, TX - *BaconPubCkNews 84; NewsDir 84*
Ft. Worth Genealogical Society - Ft. Worth, TX - *BoPubDir 4, 5*
Ft. Worth La Vida News - Ft. Worth, TX - *BaconPubCkNews 84; NewsDir 84*
Ft. Worth Mind - Ft. Worth, TX - *Ed&PubIntYB 82*
Ft. Worth News Tribune - Ft. Worth, TX - *BaconPubCkNews 84; NewsDir 84*
Ft. Worth North News - *See* Suburban Newspapers Inc.
Ft. Worth South County Advertiser - *See* B & B Publishing Inc.
Ft. Worth Star-Telegram [of Carter Publications Co. Inc.] - Ft. Worth, TX - *AyerDirPub 83; BaconPubCkNews 84; Ed&PubIntYB 82; LitMarPl 83, 84; NewsBur 6; NewsDir 84; VideoDir 82-83*
Ft. Worth Times - Ft. Worth, TX - *BaconPubCkNews 84*
FTC: Watch - Springfield, VA - *MagIndMarPl 82-83*
FTCCommunications Inc. - New York, NY - *TeleSy&SerDir 2-84*
FTCData [of General Electric Information Services Co.] - Rockville, MD - *DBBus 82; DirOnDB Spring 84*
FTD News - Southfield, MI - *BaconPubCkMag 84*
FTG Data Systems - Stanton, CA - *MicrocomMPl 84; WhoWMicrocom 83*
Fuel Oil News - Morristown, NJ - *WritMar 84*
Fuel Oil News [of Publex Corp.] - Whitehouse, NJ - *BaconPubCkMag 84; MagDir 84*
Fuel Oil News - New York, NY - *MagIndMarPl 82-83*
Fuel Oil/Oil Heat & Solar Systems [of Industry Publications INC.] - Cedar Grove, NJ - *BaconPubCkMag 84; MagDir 84; WritMar 84*
Fuel Systems Information Center [of Westinghouse Hanford Co.] - Richland, WA - *EISS 83*
Fuente Music Co. - Santa Monica, CA - *BillIntBG 83-84*
Fuji Corp. - Tokyo, Japan - *InfoS 83-84*
Fuji Photo Film USA Inc. - New York, NY - *HomeVid&CabYB 82-83; Tel&CabFB 84C*
Fujii Associates Inc. - Chicago, IL - *LitMarPl 83, 84*
Fujitsu America Inc. [Subs. of Fujitsu Ltd.] - Santa Clara, CA - *WhoWMicrocom 83*
Fujitsu Ltd. - Tokyo, Japan - *ElecNews 7-25-83*
Fujitsu Microelectronics [Subs. of Fujitsu Ltd.] - Santa Clara, CA - *WhoWMicrocom 83*
Fujitsu Systems of America [Subs. of Fujitsu Ltd.] - Los Angeles, CA - *DataDirSup 7-83; MicrocomSwDir 1; WhoWMicrocom 83*
Ful Serv Reps - Rumson, NJ - *LitMarPl 84*
Fulda Free Press - Fulda, MN - *BaconPubCkNews 84; Ed&PubIntYB 82*
Fulfill - Silver Spring, MD - *BaconPubCkMag 84*
Fulfillment Associates Inc. - Farmingdale, NY - *MagIndMarPl 82-83*
Fulfillment Corp. of America - Marion, OH - *MagIndMarPl 82-83*
Full Channel TV Inc. - Warren, RI - *BrCabYB 84; Tel&CabFB 84C*
Full Circle Communications Inc. - San Luis Obispo, CA - *AvMarPl 83*
Full Circle Productions Inc. - Santa Fe, NM - *BillIntBG 83-84*
Full Count Press - Edmond, OK - *LitMag&SmPr 83-84*
Full Court Press Inc. - New York, NY - *BoPubDir 4, 5; LitMag&SmPr 83-84*
Full Cry - Boody, IL - *BaconPubCkMag 84; MagDir 84*
Full Cycle Music Publishing Co. - Santa Fe, NM - *BillIntBG 83-84*
Full-Line Research Inc. - Huntington Station, NY - *IntDirMarRes 83*
Full Service Accounting & Processing - Springfield, VA - *WhoWMicrocom 83*
Full VU TV [of Vincennes University] - Vincennes, IN - *BrCabYB 84; Tel&CabFB 84C p.1680*
Fuller Associates - Boulder, CO - *LitMarPl 83, 84*
Fuller Biety Connell Inc. - Milwaukee, WI - *StaDirAdAg 2-84*
Fuller Co., H. B. - St. Paul, MN - *LitMarPl 83, 84*
Fuller-Jeffrey Group - Cumberland, ME - *BrCabYB 84*
Fuller Productions, Charles - La Grange, IL - *AvMarPl 83*
Fuller Software - Grand Prairie, TX - *WhoWMicrocom 83*
Fullers TV - Fedscreek, KY - *BrCabYB 84*
Fullerton Daily News Tribune - Fullerton, CA - *BaconPubCkNews 84; NewsDir 84*
Fullerton Nance County Journal - Fullerton, NE - *BaconPubCkNews 84*
Fullmer & Associates, M. D. - San Jose, CA - *MicrocomMPl 84*
Fully Distributed Data Processing Systems Research Center [of Georgia Institute of Technology] - Atlanta, GA - *EISS 83*
Fulmore Music Productions - Placerville, CA - *BillIntBG 83-84*
Fulton CATV [of Tele-Communications Inc.] - Canton, IL - *BrCabYB 84*
Fulton Community Antenna TV System Inc. [of Community Tele-Communications Inc.] - Canton, IL - *Tel&CabFB 84C*
Fulton County Daily Report - Atlanta, GA - *Ed&PubIntYB 82; NewsDir 84*
Fulton County Expositor [of Gazette Publishing Co.] - Wauseon, OH - *AyerDirPub 83; BaconPubCkNews 84; NewsDir 84*
Fulton County Journal - McConnellsburg, PA - *AyerDirPub 83; Ed&PubIntYB 82*
Fulton County News - Fulton County, PA - *Ed&PubIntYB 82*
Fulton County News - McConnellsburg, PA - *AyerDirPub 83*
Fulton Daily Sun-Gazette - Fulton, MO - *NewsDir 84*
Fulton Democrat - Lewistown, IL - *AyerDirPub 83; Ed&PubIntYB 82*
Fulton-Hall Publishing Co. - San Francisco, CA - *BoPubDir 4, 5*
Fulton Inc., Richard - New York, NY - *LitMarPl 83, 84*
Fulton Itawamba County Times - Fulton, MS - *BaconPubCkNews 84*
Fulton Journal - Fulton, IL - *BaconPubCkNews 84; Ed&PubIntYB 82; NewsDir 84*
Fulton Leader - Fulton, KY - *BaconPubCkNews 84; Ed&PubIntYB 82; NewsDir 84*
Fulton NewChannels [of NewChannels Corp.] - Fulton, NY - *BrCabYB 84; Tel&CabFB 84C*
Fulton Patriot - Fulton, NY - *Ed&PubIntYB 82; NewsDir 84*
Fulton Patriot News - Fulton, NY - *BaconPubCkNews 84*
Fulton, Stanley E. - Hancock, MD - *BrCabYB 84 p.D-301*
Fulton Telecom Inc. [of Southern Telecom Inc.] - Fulton County, GA - *Tel&CabFB 84C*
Fulton Telephone Co. Inc. - Fulton, MS - *TelDir&BG 83-84*
Fulton TV Cable Co. Inc. - Fulton, MS - *BrCabYB 84; Tel&CabFB 84C*
Fulton Valley News - Fulton, NY - *BaconPubCkNews 84*
Fultone-Colortone - Louisville, KY - *AvMarPl 83*
Fultz, Debbie - Painesville, OH - *LitMarPl 83, 84*
Fun Publishing Co. - Scottsdale, AZ - *BoPubDir 4, 5*

Functional Photography - Hempstead, NY - *MagDir 84*
Functional Photography - Woodbury, NY - *BaconPubCkMag 84; MagIndMarPl 82-83*
Fund I Ltd. Partnership - Centralia, KS - *Tel&CabFB 84C p.1680*
Fund Pricing [of Interactive Data Services] - New York, NY - *DataDirOnSer 84; DirOnDB Spring 84*
Fund Raising Management [of Hoke Communications Inc.] - Garden City, NY - *BaconPubCkMag 84; MagDir 84*
Fund II Ltd. Partnership - Centralia, KS - *Tel&CabFB 84C p.1680*
Fundamental & Applied Toxicology - Akron, OH - *BaconPubCkMag 84*
Fundamental Constants Data Center [of U.S. National Bureau of Standards] - Washington, DC - *EISS 7-83 Sup*
Fundamental Data Bank [of FRI Information Services Ltd.] - Montreal, PQ, Canada - *DataDirOnSer 84*
Fundamental Photographs - New York, NY - *LitMarPl 83, 84*
Fundamental Research Press - Piedmont, CA - *BoPubDir 4, 5*
Funding Exchange - New York, NY - *BoPubDir 4, 5*
Fundmonitor - Cambridge, England - *DirOnDB Spring 84*
Fundmonitor Unit Trusts & Insurance Bonds [of I. P. Sharp Associates Ltd.] - Toronto, ON, Canada - *DataDirOnSer 84*
Fundy Cablevision Ltd. - Edmundston, NB, Canada - *BrCabYB 84*
Fundy Cablevision Ltd. - Newcastle, NB, Canada - *BrCabYB 84*
Fundy Cablevision Ltd. - St. John, NB, Canada - *BrCabYB 84*
Funk & Wagnalls [Subs. of Dun & Bradstreet Cos. Inc.] - New York, NY - *DirMarMP 83; InfoS 83-84; LitMarPl 83, 84*
Funk & Wagnalls New Encyclopedia [of Funk & Wagnalls Inc.] - New York, NY - *EISS 5-84 Sup*
Funk Dungeon Music - Philadelphia, PA - *BillIntBG 83-84*
Funk Software Inc. - Cambridge, MA - *MicrocomSwDir 1*
Funk Telephone Co. - Funk, NE - *TelDir&BG 83-84*
Funkstown Trans-Video Corp. [of Hallmark Cable Associates] - Funkstown, MD - *BrCabYB 84; Tel&CabFB 84C*
Funky Acres Music Co. - New York, NY - *BillIntBG 83-84*
Funky but Music Inc. - Hendersonville, TN - *BillIntBG 83-84*
Funky, Punky & Chic - New York, NY - *ArtMar 84; BoPubDir 4, 5*
Funnyworld Productions Inc. - Hollywood, CA - *Tel&CabFB 84C*
Funnyworld, The Magazine of Animation & Comic Art [of Association for the Study of Animated & Comic Art Inc.] - New York, NY - *ArtMar 84; LitMag&SmPr 83-84; MagDir 84; WritMar 84*
Funsoft Inc. - Agoura, CA - *MicrocomMPl 84*
Funtastic Inc. - Drexel Hill, PA - *MicrocomMPl 84*
Fuqua Industries Inc. - Atlanta, GA - *HomeVid&CabYB 82-83*
Fuquay Varina Independent - Fuquay-Varina, NC - *BaconPubCkNews 84; Ed&PubIntYB 82*
Fur Age Weekly [of Fur Vogue Publishing Co.] - New York, NY - *BaconPubCkMag 84; BoPubDir 4 Sup, 5; MagDir 84*
Fur-Fish-Game [Aff. of A. R. Harding Publishing Co.] - Columbus, OH - *ArtMar 84; BaconPubCkMag 84; BoPubDir 4, 5; MagDir 84; MagIndMarPl 82-83; WritMar 84*
Fur Music - Newton, MA - *BillIntBG 83-84*
Fur Rancher [of Communications Marketing Inc.] - Brookfield, WI - *BaconPubCkMag 84; MagDir 84*
Fur Trade Journal - Bewdley, ON, Canada - *BaconPubCkMag 84*
Furgurson Advertising Inc., Clif - Fresno, CA - *StaDirAdAg 2-84*
Furman Advertising Co. Inc., The - Eastchester, NY - *StaDirAdAg 2-84*
Furman & Associates Inc., Anthony M. - *See* Hill & Knowlton Inc.
Furman, Feiner & Co. Inc. - Englewood, NJ - *StaDirAdAg 2-84*
Furman Films Inc. - San Francisco, CA - *AvMarPl 83*
Furman Roth Advertising - New York, NY - *AdAge 3-28-84; DirMarMP 83; StaDirAdAg 2-84*
Furman University Bookstore - Greenville, SC - *BoPubDir 4, 5*
Furniture - New York, NY - *MagDir 84*
Furniture Design & Manufacturing [of Delta Communications] - Chicago, IL - *BaconPubCkMag 84; MagDir 84*
Furniture Manufacturing Management - Germantown, TN - *BaconPubCkMag 84*
Furniture Manufacturing Management [of Associations Publications Inc.] - Memphis, TN - *MagDir 84*
Furniture Production [of Production Publishing Co.] - Nashville, TN - *BaconPubCkMag 84; MagDir 84*
Furniture Production & Design - Montreal, PQ, Canada - *BaconPubCkMag 84*
Furniture/Today - High Point, NC - *BaconPubCkMag 84; MagDir 84*
Furniture Wood Digest - Ft. Aktinson, WI - *BaconPubCkMag 84*
Furniture/Woodworking Product News [of Johnson Hill Press Inc.] - Ft. Atkinson, WI - *MagDir 84; MagIndMarPl 82-83*
Furniture Workers Press - New York, NY - *NewsDir 84*
Furniture Workers Press [of United Furniture Workers, AFL-CIO] - Nashville, TN - *MagDir 84*
Furniture World [of Towse Publishing Co.] - New York, NY - *BaconPubCkMag 84; MagDir 84; WritMar 84*
Furr Stations, J. W. - *See* Gulf Central Radio Network
Furrow, The - Moline, IL - *WritMar 84*
Furst Analytic Center Inc. - New York, NY - *IntDirMarRes 83*
Fusco Entertainment Inc. - New York, NY - *Tel&CabFB 84C*
Fusion [of Fusion Energy Foundation] - New York, NY - *BaconPubCkMag 84; MagIndMarPl 82-83; WritMar 84*
Futu - Copenhagen, Denmark - *DirOnDB Spring 84*
Futura Publishing Co. Inc. - Mt. Kisco, NY - *LitMarPl 83, 84*
Futura Software - Ft. Worth, TX - *MicrocomMPl 83, 84*
Future - Tulsa, OK - *BaconPubCkMag 84; MagDir 84; MagIndMarPl 82-83*
Future Cablevision of North Carolina [of Univision Cable Systems Inc.] - Benson, NC - *Tel&CabFB 84C*
Future Gold Records Inc. - Philadelphia, PA - *BillIntBG 83-84*
Future Homemakers of America - Washington, DC - *MagIndMarPl 82-83*
Future Press [Aff. of Cultural Council Foundation] - New York, NY - *BoPubDir 4, 5; LitMag&SmPr 83-84*
Future Projects Corp. - Hawleyville, CT - *MicrocomSwDir 1*
Future Science Research Publishing Co. - Portland, OR - *BoPubDir 5*
Future Shop - Ventura, CA - *BoPubDir 4 Sup, 5*
Future Solutions Inc. - Costa Mesa, CA - *MicrocomMPl 83*
Future Step Sirkle - Philadelphia, PA - *BillIntBG 83-84*
Future Systems Technology Inc. - Marlboro, NJ - *DirInfWP 82*
Future Views - Bridgeport, MI - *NewsDir 84*
Futurecomm Publications - Fairfax, VA - *EISS 5-84 Sup*
Futures - Cedar Falls, IA - *BaconPubCkMag 84*
Futures [of FRI Information Services Ltd.] - Montreal, PQ, Canada - *DataDirOnSer 84; DirOnDB Spring 84*
Futures-Flash - Chicago, IL - *DirOnDB Spring 84*
Futures Group Inc. - Glastonbury, CT - *BoPubDir 4 Sup, 5; DataDirOnSer 84; InfIndMarPl 83*
Futures Information Service [of Institute for Futures Studies] - Copenhagen, Denmark - *EISS 5-84 Sup*
Futures Magazine [of Commodities Magazine] - Chicago, IL - *MagDir 84*
FutureScan - Chicago, IL - *DirOnDB Spring 84*
FutureSoft - Orange Park, FL - *MicrocomMPl 83*
Futureview - Joplin, MO - *MicrocomMPl 84*
Futurevision Cable Enterprises Inc. [of Storer Cable Communications] - Bordentown, NJ - *Tel&CabFB 84C*
Futurevision Cable Enterprises Inc. [of Storer Cable Communications] - Ft. Monmouth, NJ - *Tel&CabFB 84C*
Futurevision Cable Enterprises Inc. [of Storer Cable Communications] - Hightstown, NJ - *BrCabYB 84; Tel&CabFB 84C*
Futurevision Cable Enterprises Inc. [of Storer Cable Communications] - Washington, NJ - *Tel&CabFB 84C*
Futurevision Cable Enterprises Inc. [of Storer Cable Communications] - Willingboro, NJ - *BrCabYB 84; InterCabHB 3; Tel&CabFB 84C*
Futurex Security Systems - Fair Oaks, CA - *MicrocomMPl 84*
Futurific Magazine - New York, NY - *ArtMar 84; BaconPubCkMag 84; WritMar 84*
Futurist, The [of World Future Society] - Bethesda, MD - *ArtMar 84; BaconPubCkMag 84; LitMarPl 83, 84; MagIndMarPl 82-83; WritMar 84*
Futurs [of the Univas Network] - Neuilly sur Seine, France - *StaDirAdAg 2-84*
Futurscan [of The Futures Group Inc.] - Glastonbury, CT - *EISS 83*
Futurum Forlag - Oslo, Norway - *LitMag&SmPr 83-84*
Fuyo Data Processing & Systems Development Ltd. - Gardena, CA - *ADAPSOMemDir 83-84*

FX - Ann Arbor, MI - *DirOnDB Spring 84*
FXL Sound Studios Inc. - Sunrise, FL - *BillIntBG 83-84*
FYDAQ Music - Claremont, CA - *BillIntBG 83-84*
FYI Inc. - Austin, TX - *MicrocomMPl 83, 84; MicrocomSwDir 1; WhoWMicrocom 83*
FYI Information Specialists - Worcester, MA - *EISS 7-83 Sup*
FYI News Service [of Western Union Telegraph Co.] - Upper Saddle River, NJ - *DirOnDB Spring 84; EISS 83*

G

G & C Learning - Maitland, FL - *BoPubDir 4, 5*
G & D Communications Corp. - Troy, MI - *StaDirAdAg 2-84*
G & G Engineering - San Leandrok, CA - *MicrocomMPl 83*
G & G Market Research - Charleston, SC - *IntDirMarRes 83*
G & G Publishers Inc. - Hopewell Junction, NY - *BoPubDir 4, 5*
G & G Publishing - Atlanta, GA - *BoPubDir 5*
G & G Software Inc. - Austin, TX - *MicrocomMPl 84*
G & J Press Information Bank [of Gruner & Jahr AG & Co.] - Hamburg, West Germany - *EISS 83*
G & P Cable Consultants - Lakewood, CO - *CabTVFinDB 83*
G & P Records Inc. - New York, NY - *BillIntBG 83-84*
G & R Electronics Inc. - Brewster, MN - *Tel&CabFB 84C*
G/C/T - Mobile, AL - *MagIndMarPl 82-83*
G Cam-Serveur A - Paris, France - *InfIndMarPl 83*
G Cam-Serveur B - Bordeaux, France - *InfIndMarPl 83*
G/D Advertising Inc. - Miami, FL - *StaDirAdAg 2-84*
G-F Cable TV Inc. [of Community Tele-Communications Inc.] - Grand Forks, ND - *Tel&CabFB 84C*
G-String Beat - Gays Mills, WI - *WritMar 84*
Gabbro Press - Toronto, ON, Canada - *BoPubDir 4, 5*
Gabel Advertising - Colorado Springs, CO - *AdAge 3-28-84; StaDirAdAg 2-84*
Gable Agency, The - San Diego, CA - *AdAge 3-28-84; StaDirAdAg 2-84*
Gabriel Advertising Agency - Ownings Mills, MD - *StaDirAdAg 2-84*
Gabriel Creative Services, Gil - New York, NY - *MagIndMarPl 82-83*
Gabriel Graphics Inc. - New York, NY - *Ed&PubIntYB 82*
Gabriel Graphics News Bureau - New York, NY - *Ed&PubIntYB 82*
Gabriel House Inc. - Evanston, IL - *BoPubDir 4*
Gabriel House Inc. - Skokie, IL - *BoPubDir 5; LitMarPl 83, 84*
Gabriel Literary Agency, Marlene - New York, NY - *LitMarPl 84*
Gabriel Press - Phoenix, AZ - *BoPubDir 4, 5; LitMag&SmPr 83-84*
Gabriel Press - Ithaca, NY - *LitMarPl 84*
Gabriel Press - Valois, NY - *LitMarPl 83*
Gabriel's Horn Publishing Co. - Bowling Green, OH - *BoPubDir 5*
GAC Properties Inc. - Coral Gables, FL - *BrCabYB 84 p.D-301; Tel&CabFB 84C p.1680*
GAD Marketing Services - Springfield, VA - *StaDirAdAg 2-84*
Gadsby Pioneers Association - Gadsby, AB, Canada - *BoPubDir 4 Sup, 5*
Gadsden County Times - Quincy, FL - *AyerDirPub 83; Ed&PubIntYB 82*
Gadsden Times - Gadsden, AL - *BaconPubCkNews 84; Ed&PubIntYB 82; NewsDir 84*
Gadsden Times Publishing Corp. - Gadsden, AL - *Ed&PubIntYB 82*
Gaffe Inc., J. Ronald - Okemos, MI - *AdAge 3-28-84; StaDirAdAg 2-84*
Gaffigan & Associates, James - New York, NY - *LitMarPl 83*
Gaffney Ledger - Gaffney, SC - *AyerDirPub 83; BaconPubCkNews 84; Ed&PubIntYB 82; NewsDir 84*
Gage County Cable TV Inc. - Wymore, NE - *BrCabYB 84*
Gage Publishing Ltd. - Agincourt, ON, Canada - *LitMarPl 83, 84*
Gage Record - Gage, OK - *BaconPubCkNews 84; Ed&PubIntYB 82*
Gagen Associates, J. Wilfred - New York, NY - *DirPRFirms 83*
Gage's Editing Services - New Orleans, LA - *LitMarPl 83*
Gagnon TV Ltee. - St. Felicien, PQ, Canada - *BrCabYB 84*
Gahan Studio, Nancy Lou - New York, NY - *LitMarPl 83, 84; MagIndMarPl 82-83*
Gahanna Rocky Fork Enterprise - Gahanna, OH - *BaconPubCkNews 84*
Gai Saber Monographs [Aff. of Gay Academic Union] - New York, NY - *BoPubDir 4 Sup, 5; LitMag&SmPr 83-84*
Gaia [of Evolutionary Press] - San Francisco, CA - *LitMag&SmPr 83-84*
Gail Borden Star - Gail, TX - *BaconPubCkNews 84*
Gain Publications - Van Nuys, CA - *LitMag&SmPr 83-84*
Gaines Co., P. - Oak Park, IL - *BoPubDir 4 Sup, 5; LitMag&SmPr 83-84*
Gaines County News - Seagraves, TX - *AyerDirPub 83; Ed&PubIntYB 82*
Gaines Dog Research Center - Kankakee, IL - *BoPubDir 5*
Gainesboro Jackson County Sentinel - Gainesboro, TN - *BaconPubCkNews 84*
Gainesboro Jackson County Times - Gainesboro, TN - *BaconPubCkNews 84; NewsDir 84*
Gainesville Cable TV [of Northeast Georgia Broadcasting Co.] - Gainesville, GA - *BrCabYB 84*
Gainesville Daily Register - Gainesville, TX - *BaconPubCkNews 84; Ed&PubIntYB 82; NewsDir 84*
Gainesville Individual Farmer & Rancher - Gainesville, FL - *BaconPubCkNews 84*
Gainesville Ozark County Times - Gainesville, MO - *BaconPubCkNews 84*
Gainesville Sun - Gainesville, FL - *BaconPubCkNews 84; Ed&PubIntYB 82; NewsDir 84*
Gainesville Times [of Southland Publishing] - Gainesville, GA - *NewsDir 84*
Gainesville Tribune - Gainesville, GA - *BaconPubCkNews 84; Ed&PubIntYB 82; NewsDir 84*
Gainor & Shiefman Associates - Detroit, MI - *DirPRFirms 83*
Gairm Publications - Glasgow, Scotland - *LitMag&SmPr 83-84*
Gaither International Inc. - Stamford, CT - *IntDirMarRes 83*
Gaither Music - *See* Paragon/Benson Publishing Group
Gaithersburg Gazette - Gaithersburg, MD - *AyerDirPub 83; BaconPubCkNews 84; Ed&PubIntYB 82; NewsDir 84*
Gaithersburg/Germantown - Damascus, MD - *AyerDirPub 83*
Gaithersburg-Up-County Advertiser - Bethesda, MD - *AyerDirPub 83*
Gajda, George J. [Aff. of S.M. Technical Book Publishing] - Santa Monica, CA - *BoPubDir 4, 5*
Gala Books - Laguna Beach, CA - *BoPubDir 4, 5*
Galactic Software - Warwick, RI - *MicrocomSwDir 1*

Galahad Books [Div. of A & W Publishers Inc.] - New York, NY - *LitMarPl 83*
Galahad Music Inc. - *See* September Music Corp.
Galahand Press - Austin, TX - *BoPubDir 4 Sup, 5*
Galak Software - Elyria, OH - *MicrocomMPl 84*
Galanco Music - Newton Square, PA - *BillIntBG 83-84*
Galavision [of Spanish Television Network] - New York, NY - *BrCabYB 84; CabTVPrDB 83; HomeVid&CabYB 82-83; Tel&CabFB 84C*
Galax Gazette [of Landmark Community Newspapers] - Galax, VA - *BaconPubCkNews 84; NewsDir 84*
Galaxie Cablevision Corp. - Montgomery, WV - *BrCabYB 84 p.D-301*
Galaxie Productions Inc. - Washington, DC - *TelAl 83, 84*
Galaxie III Studios - Taylorsville, NC - *BillIntBG 83-84*
Galaxy - San Diego, CA - *MicrocomMPl 83, 84; MicrocomSwDir 1; WhoWMicrocom 83*
Galaxy Cablevision Inc. - Carriers Mills, IL - *BrCabYB 84*
Galaxy Cablevision Inc. - Clinton, KY - *BrCabYB 84*
Galaxy Cablevision Inc. - Eddyville, KY - *BrCabYB 84*
Galaxy Cablevision Inc. - Hickman, KY - *BrCabYB 84; Tel&CabFB 84C*
Galaxy Cablevision Inc. - Wickliffe, KY - *BrCabYB 84*
Galaxy Cablevision Inc. - Sikeston, MO - *Tel&CabFB 84C p.1681*
Galaxy Cablevision Inc. [of Robert Wall & Associates Inc.] - Snow Hill, NC - *Tel&CabFB 84C*
Galaxy Music Corp. - New York, NY - *BillIntBG 83-84; BoPubDir 4, 4 Sup, 5*
Galaxy Press - Tweed Heads, Australia - *LitMag&SmPr 83-84*
Galaxy Publications [Subs. of Ideal Opportunities Corp.] - Miami Beach, FL - *BoPubDir 5; WritMar 84*
Galaxy Studios - Richmond, VA - *LitMarPl 83, 84*
Gale Associates Inc., Saul - Flushing, NY - *LitMarPl 83, 84; MagIndMarPl 82-83*
Gale Cabinets & Shelves Unltd., Naomi - New York, NY - *DirInfWP 82*
Gale, H. R. - Sierra Madre, CA - *BoPubDir 4, 5*
Gale Research Co. - Detroit, MI - *CompReadDB 82; DataDirOnSer 84; DirMarMP 83; EISS 83; InfIndMarPl 83; InfoS 83-84; LitMarPl 83, 84; ProGuPRSer 4*
Galella Ltd., Ron - Yonkers, NY - *LitMarPl 83, 84*
Galena CATV System Inc. [of Jerico Cable TV Inc.] - Galena, KS - *Tel&CabFB 84C*
Galena Gazette & Advertiser - Galena, IL - *BaconPubCkNews 84; Ed&PubIntYB 82*
Galena Gazette Publications Inc. - Galena, IL - *NewsDir 84*
Galena Sentinel-Times - Galena, KS - *BaconPubCkNews 84; Ed&PubIntYB 82*
Galesburg Argus - Galesburg, MI - *BaconPubCkNews 84*
Galesburg Broadcasting Co. - Galesburg, IL - *BrCabYB 84; Tel&CabFB 84C*
Galesburg Labor News [of The Labor News Co. Inc.] - Galesburg, IL - *NewsDir 84*
Galesburg Post - Galesburg, IL - *Ed&PubIntYB 82; NewsDir 84*
Galesburg Post - *See* Galesburg Post Publishing Co.
Galesburg Post Publishing Co. - Galesburg, IL - *BaconPubCkNews 84*
Galesburg Printing & Publishing Co. - *See* Galesburg Broadcasting Co.
Galesville Republican - Galesville, WI - *BaconPubCkNews 84; Ed&PubIntYB 82*
Galeton TV Antenna Inc. - Galeton, PA - *BrCabYB 84; Tel&CabFB 84C*
Galien River Gazette - Three Oaks, MI - *Ed&PubIntYB 82*
Galileo Press, The - Baltimore, MD - *LitMag&SmPr 83-84*
Galion Inquirer - Galion, OH - *BaconPubCkNews 84; Ed&PubIntYB 82; NewsDir 84*
Gall Astronomical Publications - Toronto, ON, Canada - *BoPubDir 4, 5; LitMarPl 83*
Gallagher & Associates, James - Sunset Beach, CA - *WhoWMicrocom 83*
Gallagher Group Inc. - New York, NY - *StaDirAdAg 2-84*
Gallagher Organization, The - Reading, PA - *StaDirAdAg 2-84*
Gallagher Report, The - New York, NY - *BaconPubCkMag 84; MagDir 84; MagIndMarPl 82-83*
Gallaghur Communications Associates, Elizabeth - New York, NY - *ProGuPRSer 4*
Gallatin Cable-Vision Inc. - Gallatin, MO - *BrCabYB 84*
Gallatin County News - Warsaw, KY - *AyerDirPub 83; Ed&PubIntYB 82*
Gallatin Democrat, The - Shawneetown, IL - *Ed&PubIntYB 82*
Gallatin News-Examiner - Gallatin, TN - *BaconPubCkNews 84*
Gallatin North Missourian - Gallatin, MO - *BaconPubCkNews 84; Ed&PubIntYB 82*
Gallaudet College Press - Washington, DC - *LitMarPl 83, 84*
Gallaudet Information Retrieval Service [of Gallaudet College Library] - Washington, DC - *EISS 83*
Gallen & Co., Richard - New York, NY - *LitMarPl 83, 84*
Galleon Entertainment Ltd. - Riverside, CA - *BillIntBG 83-84*
Galleon Music Inc. - *See* Gallico Music Corp., Al
Gallery [of Montcalm Publishing Corp.] - New York, NY - *ArtMar 84; BaconPubCkMag 84; Folio 83; LitMarPl 83, 84; MagDir 84; MagIndMarPl 82-83; WritMar 84*
Gallery Enterprises - Bethlehem, PA - *ArtMar 84*
Gallery Graphics Press - Carmel, CA - *BoPubDir 5*
Gallery Press - Essex, CT - *BoPubDir 4, 5*
Gallery Series/Poets [of Harper Square Press] - Chicago, IL - *LitMag&SmPr 83-84*
Gallery Works - Bronx, NY - *LitMag&SmPr 83-84*
Galliard Ltd. - *See* Galaxy Music Corp.
Gallico Music Corp., Al - New York, NY - *BillIntBG 83-84*
Gallie Computer - Chicago, IL - *MicrocomMPl 84*
Gallie Microcomputer - Chicago, IL - *MicrocomSwDir 1*
Gallipolis Tribune [of Ohio Valley Publishing Co.] - Gallipolis, OH - *BaconPubCkNews 84; Ed&PubIntYB 82; NewsDir 84*
Gallo, Cristino [Aff. of Book Service of Puerto Rico] - Santurce, PR - *BoPubDir 4, 5*
Gallopade Publishing Group - Tryon, NC - *BoPubDir 4, 5*
Galloping Dog Press - London, England - *LitMag&SmPr 83-84*
Galloway, Ewing - New York, NY - *LitMarPl 83, 84; MagIndMarPl 82-83*
Galloway Field Service Inc. - San Antonio, TX - *IntDirMarRes 83*
Galloway Publications Inc. - Corvallis, OR - *BoPubDir 4, 5*
Galloway-Wallace Advertising Agency Inc. - Oklahoma City, OK - *StaDirAdAg 2-84*
Gallup & Robinson Inc. - Princeton, NJ - *HBIndAd&MS 82-83; IntDirMarRes 83; MagIndMarPl 82-83*
Gallup Independent - Gallup, NM - *BaconPubCkNews 84; Ed&PubIntYB 82; NewsDir 84*
Gallup International - London, England - *IntDirMarRes 83*
Gallup London - London, England - *IntDirMarRes 83*
Gallup Organization Inc., The - Princeton, NJ - *AdAge 5-17-84 p.37; IntDirMarRes 83; Tel&CabFB 84C*
Gallup Report, The - Princeton, NJ - *ProGuPRSer 4*
Gallup Voice of the Southwest, The - San Fidel, NM - *NewsDir 84*
Galt Herald - Galt, CA - *AyerDirPub 83; BaconPubCkNews 84; Ed&PubIntYB 82; NewsDir 84*
Galub, Jack - New York, NY - *LitMarPl 83, 84; MagIndMarPl 82-83*
Galusha & Associates - Westminster, CA - *StaDirAdAg 2-84*
Galva News - Galva, IL - *BaconPubCkNews 84; Ed&PubIntYB 82*
Galveston Daily News - Galveston, TX - *BaconPubCkNews 84; Ed&PubIntYB 82; NewsDir 84*
GAMA Communications [Aff. of Graphic Arts Marketing Associates] - Salem, NH - *BoPubDir 4, 5*
Gambit - Marietta, OH - *LitMag&SmPr 83-84*
Gambit Inc. - Ipswich, MA - *LitMarPl 83, 84*
Gambit 2 - New York, NY - *DirOnDB Spring 84*
Gambler's Book Club/GBC Press Inc. - Las Vegas, NV - *DirMarMP 83; LitMarPl 83, 84; WritMar 84*
Gamblers Edge Computing - Kansas City, MO - *MicrocomMPl 84*
Gambling Scene West - Stanford, CA - *WritMar 84*
Gambling Times [Aff. of Scientific Research Services] - Hollywood, CA - *ArtMar 84; BaconPubCkMag 84; BoPubDir 4, 5; LitMarPl 83, 84; MagIndMarPl 82-83; WritMar 84*
Gambling Times - Los Angeles, CA - *LitMarPl 83, 84; MagDir 84*
Gambol & Cain Advertising [Subs. of Caroline House Publishers Inc.] - Aurora, IL - *DirMarMP 83*

Gamco Industries Inc. [Div. of Siboney Corp.] - Big Spring, TX - *AvMarPl 83*
Game Merchandising [of Boynton & Associates Inc.] - Clifton, VA - *WritMar 84*
Gamecock - Harford, AR - *MagDir 84*
Gamecock [of University of South Carolina Student Newspaper] - Columbia, SC - *NewsDir 84*
GameLine - Vienna, VA - *DirOnDB Spring 84*
Gamelon Press [Aff. of P.R.O. Canada] - Toronto, ON, Canada - *BoPubDir 4, 5*
Gameplay - Crystal Lake, IL - *BaconPubCkMag 84*
Games [of Playboy Enterprises Inc.] - New York, NY - *ArtMar 84; BaconPubCkMag 84; DirMarMP 83; LitMarPl 83, 84; MagDir 84; MagIndMarPl 82-83; WritMar 84*
Games Network, The - Los Angeles, CA - *CabTVPrDB 83*
Games People - Los Angeles, CA - *BaconPubCkMag 84*
Gamestar Inc. - Santa Barbara, CA - *MicrocomMPl 84*
Gaminde, Richard - Iaeger, WV - *Tel&CabFB 84C p.1681*
Gaminde, Vareda - Iaeger, WV - *Tel&CabFB 84C p.1681*
Gaming Business [of BMT Publications Inc.] - New York, NY - *BaconPubCkMag 84; MagDir 84*
Gamma Books - Ithaca, NY - *LitMag&SmPr 83-84; LitMarPl 83, 84*
Gamma-Liaison Photo News Agency - New York, NY - *Ed&PubIntYB 82; LitMarPl 84*
Gamma Photo Labs Inc. - Chicago, IL - *AvMarPl 83*
Gamma Technology - Palo Alto, CA - *DataDirSup 7-83; MicrocomMPl 84*
Gammacolor Inc. - Miami, FL - *AvMarPl 83*
Gammill Murphy Music - Lubbock, TX - *BillIntBG 83-84*
Gams Chicago Inc. - Chicago, IL - *DirPRFirms 83*
Gamut [of Kyogen Publications] - Toronto, ON, Canada - *WritMar 84*
Gamut-Mitchell Inc. - Hempstead, NY - *StaDirAdAg 2-84*
Gamut Music Co. - Dedham, MA - *BoPubDir 4, 5*
Gan-Tone Publishing Co. [Aff. of Gan-Tone Productions] - New York, NY - *BoPubDir 4 Sup, 5*
Ganado Telephone Co. Inc. - Ganado, TX - *TelDir&BG 83-84*
Ganado Tribune - Edna, TX - *BaconPubCkNews 84*
Ganado Tribune - Ganado, TX - *Ed&PubIntYB 82*
Gananoque Cablevision [of Brockville Cable Telecommunications Inc.] - Brockville, ON, Canada - *BrCabYB 84*
Gancom Inc. [Subs. of Gannett Fleming Affiliates Inc.] - Harrisburg, PA - *DataDirOnSer 84*
Gancom Inc. (Computing Div.) - Harrisburg, PA - *ADAPSOMemDir 83-84*
Gandalf Data Inc. [Subs. of Gandalf Tech Inc.] - Wheeling, IL - *DataDirSup 7-83; MicrocomMPl 84*
Gandalf Data Ltd. - Ottawa, ON, Canada - *VideoDir 82-83*
Gander Beacon, The - Gander, NF, Canada - *Ed&PubIntYB 82*
Gandolf's Report - Bayside, NY - *DirOnDB Spring 84*
Gane Brothers & Lane Inc. - Elk Grove, IL - *LitMarPl 83, 84*
Ganglia Press - Toronto, ON, Canada - *LitMag&SmPr 83-84*
Ganis & Harris Inc. - New York, NY - *LitMarPl 83, 84*
Gann-Dawson - Scranton, PA - *AdAge 3-28-84; StaDirAdAg 2-84*
Gann Law Books Inc. - Newark, NJ - *BoPubDir 4, 5*
Gannett Advertising & Marketing Inc. - Dallas, TX - *StaDirAdAg 2-84*
Gannett Books, Guy [Subs. of Guy Gannett Publishing Co.] - Portland, ME - *WritMar 84*
Gannett Broadcasting Group [Div. of Gannett Co. Inc.] - Atlanta, GA - *BrCabYB 84; Tel&CabFB 84S*
Gannett Broadcasting Services, Guy - Portland, ME - *BrCabYB 84; Tel&CabFB 84S*
Gannett Co. - Rochester, NY - *AdAge 6-28-84; BrCabYB 84; HomeVid&CabYB 82-83; KnowInd 83; NewsBur 6*
Gannett News Service - Washington, DC - *BaconPubCkNews 84; Ed&PubIntYB 82; NewsBur 6*
Gannett News Service - Rochester, NY - *Ed&PubIntYB 82*
Gannett Newspapers - Rochester, NY - *Ed&PubIntYB 82*
Gannett Newspapers Advertising Sales [Div. of The Gannett Co.] - New York, NY - *LitMarPl 83, 84*
Gannett Publishing Co., Guy - Portland, ME - *BoPubDir 4, 5; Ed&PubIntYB 82*
Gannett Satellite Information Network - Arlington, VA - *BrCabYB 84*
Gannett Westchester Newspapers - White Plains, NY - *LitMarPl 83, 84*
Gannon, William - Santa Fe, NM - *BoPubDir 4, 5*
Gans & Co., Joe - New York, NY - *StaDirAdAg 2-84*
Gans, Joseph S. - Hazleton, PA - *BrCabYB 84 p.D-301; Tel&CabFB 84C p.1681*
Ganster Agency Inc. - Limekiln, PA - *StaDirAdAg 2-84*
Gant Enterprises, Don - Nashville, TN - *BillIntBG 83-84*
Gant, Margaret Elizabeth - Raleigh, NC - *BoPubDir 4, 5*
Ganus & Associates, S. S. - Champaign, IL - *DirInfWP 82*
Ganz, A. J. - Los Angeles, CA - *AvMarPl 83*
Gaphyor [of University of Paris-South] - Orsay, France - *DirOnDB Spring 84; EISS 83*
Gapset - Paris, France - *InfoS 83-84*
Garabed Books - New York, NY - *BoPubDir 4, 5*
Garage No. Three - Stanwood, WA - *BoPubDir 4, 5*
Garber & Philipson Inc. - Carle Place, NY - *StaDirAdAg 2-84*
Garber Communications Inc. - Blauvelt, NY - *BoPubDir 4; LitMarPl 83, 84; WritMar 84*
Garber Free Press - Garber, OK - *BaconPubCkNews 84; Ed&PubIntYB 82*
Garber, Goodman & Rothchild - Miami, FL - *AdAge 3-28-84; StaDirAdAg 2-84*
Garber Group, The - New York, NY - *LitMarPl 83, 84*
Garberville Cable TV - Garberville, CA - *BrCabYB 84; Tel&CabFB 84C*
Garberville Redwood Record - Garberville, CA - *BaconPubCkNews 84*
Garbutt Productions, Robert - Toronto, ON, Canada - *BoPubDir 4, 5*
Garcia & Associates, Emmanuel B. Jr. - Chicago, IL - *MicrocomMPl 83, 84; MicrocomSwDir 1; WhoWMicrocom 83*
Garcia & Associates, Lou - New York, NY - *DirPRFirms 83*
Garcia River Press - Point Arena, CA - *BoPubDir 4, 5; LitMag&SmPr 83-84*
Garden [of New York Botanical Garden] - Bronx, NY - *ArtMar 84; BaconPubCkMag 84; MagDir 84; MagIndMarPl 82-83; WritMar 84*
Garden City Cable TV [of Community Tele-Communications Inc.] - Garden City, KS - *BrCabYB 84; Tel&CabFB 84C*
Garden City-Mineola Ad World - Great Neck, NY - *AyerDirPub 83*
Garden City-Mineola Pennysaver - Jericho, NY - *AyerDirPub 83*
Garden City News - Garden City, NY - *Ed&PubIntYB 82*
Garden City News - *See* Litmore Publications
Garden City Newsday - Huntington Station, NY - *NewsDir 84*
Garden City Observer - Garden City, MI - *Ed&PubIntYB 82*
Garden City Observer [of Suburban Communications Corp.] - Livonia, MI - *AyerDirPub 83; NewsDir 84*
Garden City Observer - *See* Observer & Eccentric Newspapers
Garden City Telegram - Garden City, KS - *BaconPubCkNews 84; Ed&PubIntYB 82; NewsDir 84*
Garden County News - Oshkosh, NE - *AyerDirPub 83; Ed&PubIntYB 82*
Garden Design [of American Society of Landscape Architects] - Louisville, KY - *ArtMar 84; BaconPubCkMag 84; WritMar 84*
Garden Glories - Lisle, IL - *BaconPubCkMag 84*
Garden Grove Orange County News - *See* West Orange Publishing Co.
Garden Island, The - Kauai, HI - *Ed&PubIntYB 82*
Garden Island, The - Lahaina, HI - *AyerDirPub 83*
Garden Island, The - Lihue, HI - *NewsDir 84*
Garden, Mary-Stuart - New York, NY - *LitMarPl 83, 84; MagIndMarPl 82-83*
Garden State Arts Center Program - Trenton, NJ - *MagDir 84*
Garden State Audiovisual Co. Inc. - New Brunswick, NJ - *AvMarPl 83*
Garden State CATV Inc. [of Service Electric Cable TV Inc.] - Sparta, NJ - *BrCabYB 84; Tel&CabFB 84C*
Garden State TV Cable Corp. - Hopewell, NJ - *BrCabYB 84*
Garden State TV Cable Corp. [of Cablentertainment Inc.] - Vineland, NJ - *BrCabYB 84*
Garden Supply Retailer [of Miller Publications Co.] - Minneapolis, MN - *BaconPubCkMag 84; MagDir 84; WritMar 84*
Garden Valley Telephone Co. - Erskine, MN - *Tel&CabFB 84C p.1681; TelDir&BG 83-84*
Garden Valley Telephone Co. - McIntosh, MN - *BrCabYB 84*

Garden Way Marketing - Troy, NY - *Tel&CabFB 84C*
Garden Way Publishing [Div. of Garden Way Inc.] - Charlotte, VT - *LitMag&SmPr 83-84; LitMarPl 83; WritMar 84*
Garden Way Publishing Co. [Div. of Storey Communication Inc.] - Pownal, VT - *LitMarPl 84*
Gardena Breeze Advertiser [of Torrance Press-Herald] - Torrance, CA - *NewsDir 84*
Gardena-Valley News - Gardena, CA - *AyerDirPub 83; BaconPubCkNews 84; Ed&PubIntYB 82; NewsDir 84*
Gardendale North Jefferson News - Gardendale, AL - *BaconPubCkNews 84*
Gardener, The - Des Moines, IA - *MagDir 84*
Gardener, The - Johnston, IA - *BaconPubCkMag 84*
Gardens for All News - Burlington, VT - *BoPubDir 4, 5; WritMar 84*
Gardenshore Press - Toronto, ON, Canada - *BoPubDir 4, 5*
Gardiner Advertising Agency - Salt Lake City, UT - *AdAge 3-28-84; StaDirAdAg 2-84*
Gardiner Television Corp. - Gardiner, OR - *BrCabYB 84; Tel&CabFB 84C*
Gardner Advertising - St. Louis, MO - *ArtMar 84; BrCabYB 84; HBIndAd&MS 82-83; StaDirAdAg 2-84*
Gardner Advertising Inc., Donald W. - Beverly, MA - *AdAge 3-28-84*
Gardner Advertising Inc., Donald W. - Boston, MA - *StaDirAdAg 2-84*
Gardner Advertising, Ralph D. - New York, NY - *StaDirAdAg 2-84*
Gardner & Associates Inc., Jan - Memphis, TN - *StaDirAdAg 2-84*
Gardner Chronicle - Gardner, IL - *Ed&PubIntYB 82*
Gardner Chronicle - *See* G.W. Communications
Gardner Communications Inc. - San Francisco, CA - *StaDirAdAg 2-84*
Gardner, George F. & Marian - Carlisle, PA - *Tel&CabFB 84C p.1681*
Gardner, Jones & Co. Inc. - *See* Hill & Knowlton Inc.
Gardner Museum, Isabella Stewart - Boston, MA - *BoPubDir 4, 5*
Gardner News - Gardner, KS - *BaconPubCkNews 84; Ed&PubIntYB 82*
Gardner News - Gardner, MA - *BaconPubCkNews 84; Ed&PubIntYB 82; NewsDir 84*
Gardner Press Inc. - New York, NY - *LitMarPl 83, 84*
Gardner Publications Inc. - Cincinnati, OH - *BoPubDir 5*
Gardner, Savage Associates - Middlesex, NJ - *IntDirMarRes 83*
Gardner, Stein & Frank Inc. - Chicago, IL - *StaDirAdAg 2-84*
Gardnerville Record-Courier - Gardnerville, NV - *BaconPubCkNews 84; NewsDir 84*
Gardnor House - Spring, TX - *BoPubDir 5*
Gardo & Associates Inc., T. - Hilton Head Island, SC - *DirPRFirms 83*
Gardonville Cooperative Telephone Association - Brandon, MN - *TelDir&BG 83-84*
Garfield Book Production, Irv - Alexandria, VA - *LitMarPl 83, 84*
Garfield County News - Panguitch, UT - *AyerDirPub 83; Ed&PubIntYB 82*
Garfield Grossi & Pustarfi - Roselle, NJ - *MicrocomMPl 83, 84; WhoWMicrocom 83*
Garfield-Hasbrouck Heights-Lodi-Rochelle Park Shopper - Fair Lawn, NJ - *AyerDirPub 83*
Garfield Heights Leader - Cleveland, OH - *AyerDirPub 83; NewsDir 84*
Garfield Heights Leader - Garfield Heights, OH - *Ed&PubIntYB 82*
Garfield-Linn & Co. - Chicago, IL - *ArtMar 84; StaDirAdAg 2-84*
Garfield-Lodi-Maywood-Rochelle Park-Hasbrouck Heights Shopper - Garfield, NJ - *Ed&PubIntYB 82*
Garfield-Maple Heights Sun - Garfield Heights, OH - *Ed&PubIntYB 82*
Garfield Maple Heights Sun - *See* Sun Newspapers
Garfield Messenger - Garfield, NJ - *BaconPubCkNews 84*
Gargoyle [of Paycock Press] - Washington, DC - *LitMag&SmPr 83-84; WritMar 84*
Gargoyle - Jamaica Plain, MA - *LitMag&SmPr 83-84*
Garin Agency, The - Hollywood, CA - *StaDirAdAg 2-84*
Garland News - Farmers Branch, TX - *Ed&PubIntYB 82*
Garland News [of News Texan Inc.] - Garland, TX - *BaconPubCkNews 84; NewsDir 84*
Garland Publishing Inc. - New York, NY - *LitMarPl 83, 84; MicrocomMPl 84; MicrocomSwDir 1; WritMar 84*
Garland Way Advertising Inc. - Pittsburgh, PA - *StaDirAdAg 2-84*
Garlic Press - Rochester, NY - *BoPubDir 4, 5; LitMag&SmPr 83-84; LitMarPl 84*
Garlic Times [of Lovers of the Stinking Rose/Aris Books] - Berkeley, CA - *LitMag&SmPr 83-84*
Garlin, Emily - New York, NY - *LitMarPl 84*
Garlin, M. - Boulder, CO - *LitMarPl 83, 84; MagIndMarPl 82-83*
Garlinghouse Co. - Topeka, KS - *WritMar 84*
Garner & Associates Inc. - Charlotte, NC - *ArtMar 84; StaDirAdAg 2-84*
Garner Associates Inc., Ralph - New York, NY - *EISS 83; LitMarPl 83, 84; MagIndMarPl 82-83*
Garner Industries - Lincoln, NE - *AvMarPl 83*
Garner Leader & Signal - Garner, IA - *BaconPubCkNews 84*
Garner Leader, The - Garner, IA - *Ed&PubIntYB 82*
Garner News [of Roanoke Valley Publishing Co.] - Garner, NC - *AyerDirPub 83; BaconPubCkNews 84; NewsDir 84*
Garner, Robert M. - Canton, MS - *Tel&CabFB 84C p.1681*
Garner, Tom A. Jr. - *See* Rhodes, George F.
Garnett Anderson Countian - *See* Garnett Publishing Co.
Garnett Anderson Countian - Garnett, KS - *NewsDir 84*
Garnett Cable TV Co. [of Tele-Communications Inc.] - Garnett, KS - *BrCabYB 84; Tel&CabFB 84C*
Garnett Publishing Co. - Garnett, KS - *BaconPubCkNews 84*
Garnett Review - Garnett, KS - *Ed&PubIntYB 82; NewsDir 84*
Garnett Review - *See* Garnett Publishing Co.
Garon-Brooke Associates Inc., Jay - New York, NY - *LitMarPl 83, 84*
Garrard County News - Lancaster, KY - *Ed&PubIntYB 82*
Garrard Publishing Co. - Champaign, IL - *LitMarPl 83, 84*
Garratt Baulcombe Associates Ltd. - *See* Foote, Cone & Belding Communications Inc.
Garretson Weekly - Garretson, SD - *AyerDirPub 83; BaconPubCkNews 84; Ed&PubIntYB 82*
Garrett Buchanan Co. [Div. of Alco Standard Corp.] - Philadelphia, PA - *LitMarPl 83, 84; MagIndMarPl 82-83*
Garrett Clipper, The - Garrett, IN - *Ed&PubIntYB 82*
Garrett Coaxial TV Tower Co. Inc. [of TCA Cable TV Inc.] - Siloam Springs, AR - *Tel&CabFB 84C*
Garrett Communications - Atlanta, GA - *ArtMar 84*
Garrett De Kalb County Advertiser - Garrett, IN - *BaconPubCkNews 84*
Garrett Enterprises Inc. - New York, NY - *Ed&PubIntYB 82*
Garrett-Far North Distributors, Cecil - Anchorage, AK - *WhoWMicrocom 83*
Garrett Music Enterprises - Hollywood, CA - *BillIntBG 83-84*
Garrett Park Press - Garrett Park, MD - *AvMarPl 83; BoPubDir 4, 5; LitMag&SmPr 83-84*
Garrett, Phillip - Seattle, WA - *LitMarPl 83, 84*
Garrett Telephone Co. Inc. [Aff. of GTE Service Corp.] - Garrett, IN - *TelDir&BG 83-84*
Garrison Cable TV - Garrison, ND - *BrCabYB 84; Tel&CabFB 84C*
Garrison/Elliot Inc. - New York, NY - *HBIndAd&MS 82-83; StaDirAdAg 2-84*
Garrison, Jasper, Rose & Co. - Indianapolis, IN - *DirPRFirms 83; StaDirAdAg 2-84*
Garrison McLean County Independent - Garrison, ND - *BaconPubCkNews 84; NewsDir 84*
Garrison News - Garrison, TX - *BaconPubCkNews 84; Ed&PubIntYB 82*
Garrison Telephone Co. Inc. [Aff. of Central Telephone Co. of Texas] - West Columbia, TX - *TelDir&BG 83-84*
Garryowen Stations, The - *See* Montana Television Network
Garsas - Wilkes-Barre, PA - *Ed&PubIntYB 82; NewsDir 84*
Garsen Research Inc. - Woodland Hills, CA - *IntDirMarRes 83*
Garson & Associates Inc., Walter Jr. - Phildelphia, PA - *MagIndMarPl 82-83*
Gartenberg, Max - New York, NY - *LitMarPl 83, 84*
Gartner & Associates Inc. - Chicago, IL - *DirMarMP 83*
Gartner Group Inc. - Stamford, CT - *EISS 83; InfoS 83-84; InterCabHB 3; VideoDir 82-83*
Garvan, Fran - Harvard, MA - *AvMarPl 83*

Garver Advertising Service Inc. - New York, NY - *StaDirAdAg 2-84*
Garvey, Martin & Sampson Inc. - Cincinnati, OH - *WhoWMicrocom 83*
Garwood Telephone Co. Inc. - Garwood, TX - *TelDir&BG 83-84*
Gary American - Gary, IN - *BaconPubCkNews 84; NewsDir 84*
Gary Associates, Gayle - New York, NY - *DirPRFirms 83*
Gary Camera Co. - Merrillville, IN - *AvMarPl 83*
Gary Communications Group Inc. - Gary, IN - *BrCabYB 84; Tel&CabFB 84C*
Gary Crusader - Gary, IN - *BaconPubCkNews 84; Ed&PubIntYB 82; NewsDir 84*
Gary Group, The - Venice, CA - *DirMarMP 83*
Gary Info - Gary, IN - *BaconPubCkNews 84; NewsDir 84*
Gary Interstate - Gary, SD - *BaconPubCkNews 84; Ed&PubIntYB 82*
Gary Post-Tribune [of Knight-Ridder Newspapers Inc.] - Gary, IN - *NewsDir 84*
Gary Productions, Martin - Richmond, VA - *BillIntBG 83-84*
Gary Telephone Co. - Gary, TX - *TelDir&BG 83-84*
Gas Chromatography Service [of Preston Publications Inc.] - Niles, IL - *MicroMarPl 82-83*
Gas City Twin City Journal Reporter - Gas City, IN - *BaconPubCkNews 84*
Gas Digest [of Tri Plek Productions] - Houston, TX - *BaconPubCkMag 84; MagDir 84; WritMar 84*
Gas Industries [of Gas Industries Equipment & Appliance News Inc.] - Woodland Hills, CA - *BaconPubCkMag 84; MagDir 84; MagIndMarPl 82-83*
Gas Records - Los Angeles, CA - *BillIntBG 83-84*
Gas Turbine World News - Southport, CT - *BaconPubCkMag 84; MagDir 84*
Gasconade County Republican - Owensville, MO - *AyerDirPub 83*
Gaskill-Oertel Advertising Inc. - Boynton Beach, FL - *ArtMar 84; StaDirAdAg 2-84*
Gaslight Publications - Bloomington, IN - *BoPubDir 4, 5; LitMag&SmPr 83-84; LitMarPl 84; WritMar 84*
Gasoline News - Columbus, OH - *MagDir 84*
Gasparo Records - Nashville, TN - *BillIntBG 83-84*
Gaspe Peninsula SPEC - Gaspe Coast, PQ, Canada - *Ed&PubIntYB 82*
Gasser Inc., Adolph - San Francisco, CA - *AvMarPl 83*
Gaste Music Inc. - Las Vegas, NV - *BillIntBG 83-84*
Gaston Cable TV Inc. [of American TV & Communications Corp.] - Belmont, NC - *Tel&CabFB 84C*
Gaston Cable TV Inc. - Catawba Heights, NC - *BrCabYB 84*
Gastonia Gazette [of Freedom Newspapers] - Gastonia, NC - *BaconPubCkNews 84; Ed&PubIntYB 82; NewsDir 84*
Gastroenterology - San Francisco, CA - *BaconPubCkMag 84*
Gastroenterology - New York, NY - *MagDir 84*
Gate City Budget Saver - Keokuk, IA - *AyerDirPub 83*
Gate City Journal - Nyssa, OR - *AyerDirPub 83*
Gate Music Inc. - *See* Fox Publishing Co. Inc., Sam
Gateavisa [of Futurum Forlag] - Oslo, Norway - *LitMag&SmPr 83-84*
Gateford Publications - Collingswood, NJ - *BoPubDir 4, 5*
Gates Acoustinet Inc. - Santa Rosa, CA - *DirInfWP 82*
Gates Co., The W. N. - Berea, OH - *StaDirAdAg 2-84*
Gates Corp. Inc., V. - St. Regis, MT - *BrCabYB 84*
Gates County Index [of Parker Bros. Inc.] - Gatesville, NC - *AyerDirPub 83; Ed&PubIntYB 82; NewsDir 84*
Gates Energy Products Inc. - Denver, CO - *DirInfWP 82*
Gates International Photographer, Ralph - Short Hills, NJ - *MagIndMarPl 82-83*
Gates Music Inc. - Rochester, NY - *BillIntBG 83-84*
Gatesville Cable-Vision Inc. [of TCA Cable TV Group] - Gatesville, TX - *Tel&CabFB 84C*
Gatesville Gates County Index - Gatesville, NC - *BaconPubCkNews 84*
Gatesville Messenger - Gatesville, TX - *NewsDir 84*
Gatesville Messenger & Star-Forum - Gatesville, TX - *BaconPubCkNews 84; Ed&PubIntYB 82*
Gateway Cable Ltd. - Port-aux-Basques, NF, Canada - *BrCabYB 84*
Gateway Cablevision Corp. [of Antenna Engineering Inc.] - Gateway Village, CA - *Tel&CabFB 84C*
Gateway Cablevision Corp. - Leon County, FL - *BrCabYB 84; Tel&CabFB 84C*
Gateway Cablevision Corp. - Amsterdam, NY - *BrCabYB 84; Tel&CabFB 84C*
Gateway Cablevision Corp. - Plattsburgh, NY - *Tel&CabFB 84C*
Gateway Cablevision Corp. - Belfield, ND - *Tel&CabFB 84C*
Gateway Communications Inc. [of Storer Cable Communications] - Florissant, MO - *BrCabYB 84; Tel&CabFB 84C*
Gateway Communications Inc. - Cherry Hill, NJ - *BrCabYB 84; Tel&CabFB 84S*
Gateway Films - Lansdale, PA - *Tel&CabFB 84C*
Gateway Golfer - St. Louis, MO - *BaconPubCkMag 84*
Gateway Papers - Mahopac, NY - *BaconPubCkNews 84*
Gateway Presentation People [Div. of Gateway Studios Inc.] - Pittsburgh, PA - *AvMarPl 83*
Gateway Press Inc. [Aff. of Genealogical Publishing Co.] - Baltimore, MD - *BoPubDir 4, 5*
Gateway Press Inc. - Monroeville, PA - *BaconPubCkNews 84*
Gateway Productions Inc. - New Orleans, LA - *AvMarPl 83*
Gateway Productions Inc. [Subs. of The Gannett Co.] - New York, NY - *AvMarPl 83; Tel&CabFB 84C; WritMar 84*
Gateway, The - Floral Park, NY - *AyerDirPub 83; Ed&PubIntYB 82*
Gatewood, Charles - New York, NY - *MagIndMarPl 82-83*
Gatherfacts Group, The - Louisville, KY - *EISS 83; FBInfSer 80*
Gathering Post - St. Peter, MN - *LitMag&SmPr 83-84*
Gatineau Jones Ltd. - Ottawa, ON, Canada - *BoPubDir 4, 5*
Gatlinburg Mountain Visitor - Pigeon Forge, TN - *NewsDir 84*
Gatlinburg Press - Pigeon Forge, TN - *AyerDirPub 83; BaconPubCkNews 84*
Gatlinburg Press, The - Gatlinburg, TN - *Ed&PubIntYB 82*
GATT - Hellerup, Denmark - *DirOnDB Spring 84*
Gatto Communications Ltd. - Forest Hills, NY - *StaDirAdAg 2-84*
Gaucho Music - New York, NY - *BillIntBG 83-84*
Gauger Sparks Silva Inc. - San Francisco, CA - *StaDirAdAg 2-84*
Gaunt & Sons Inc., Wm. W. - Holmes Beach, FL - *BoPubDir 4, 5; MagIndMarPl 82-83; MicroMarPl 82-83*
Gauntlet Books - Franklin, MA - *BoPubDir 4, 5*
Gaus Ltd., Theo - Brooklyn, NY - *BoPubDir 4, 5*
Gautier Independent - Gautier, MS - *Ed&PubIntYB 82*
Gavel Computing Systems Inc. - Alachua, FL - *MicrocomMPl 84*
Gavilan Communications - Gilroy, CA - *Tel&CabFB 84C*
Gawthrop, H. Gene - Tampa, FL - *Tel&CabFB 84C p.1681*
Gay/Bell Stations - Lexington, KY - *BrCabYB 84*
Gay Community News [of Bromfield Sy. Educational Foundation] - Boston, MA - *LitMag&SmPr 83-84; MagIndMarPl 82-83; MicroMarPl 82-83*
Gay Insurgent [of Lavender Archives] - Philadelphia, PA - *LitMag&SmPr 83-84*
Gay, Mike - Panama City, FL - *Tel&CabFB 84C p.1681*
Gay News [of Masco Communications] - Philadelphia, PA - *ArtMar 84; WritMar 84*
Gay 90's Village Inc. - Sikeston, MO - *BillIntBG 83-84*
Gay Presses of New York - New York, NY - *BoPubDir 4, 5*
Gay Sunshine Journal - San Francisco, CA - *ArtMar 84; LitMag&SmPr 83-84*
Gay Sunshine Press - San Francisco, CA - *LitMag&SmPr 83-84; LitMarPl 83, 84; WritMar 84*
Gayellow Pages [of Renaissance House] - New York, NY - *LitMag&SmPr 83-84*
Gayle's Force Inc. - Tulsa, OK - *IntDirMarRes 83*
Gaylord Broadcasting Co. [Subs. of Oklahoma Publishing Co.] - Oklahoma City, OK - *BrCabYB 84; Tel&CabFB 84S*
Gaylord Brothers Inc. - Syracuse, NY - *AvMarPl 83*
Gaylord Circulation Control System [of Gaylord Bros. Inc.] - Syracuse, NY - *EISS 83*
Gaylord Herald Times - Gaylord, MI - *BaconPubCkNews 84*
Gaylord Hub - Gaylord, MN - *BaconPubCkNews 84; Ed&PubIntYB 82*
Gaylord Northern Star [of Weeklies Inc.] - Gaylord, MI - *NewsDir 84*
Gaylord Otsego County Herald Times - Gaylord, MI - *NewsDir 84*
Gaylord Professional Publications - Syracuse, NY - *BoPubDir 4, 5*
Gaynes Productions Ltd. - Hollywood, CA - *Tel&CabFB 84C*
Gaynor & Ducas - New York, NY - *HBIndAd&MS 82-83*

Gaynor, Falcone & Associates [Aff. of Gaynor & Co. Inc.] - New York, NY - *ArtMar 84; BrCabYB 84; StaDirAdAg 2-84*
Gaynor Media Corp. - New York, NY - *StaDirAdAg 2-84*
Gays Cable TV Service - Oneida, KY - *Tel&CabFB 84C p.1681*
Gays Mills Crawford County Independent - *See* Boscobel Publishers Inc.
Gazelle Publications - Auburn, CA - *BoPubDir 5; LitMag&SmPr 83-84*
Gazelle Publications - Colfax, CA - *BoPubDir 4*
Gazette - Phoenix, AZ - *AyerDirPub 83*
Gazette - Texarkana, AR - *AyerDirPub 83*
Gazette - Berkeley, CA - *BaconPubCkNews 84*
Gazette - Lindsay, CA - *AyerDirPub 83*
Gazette - Mariposa, CA - *AyerDirPub 83*
Gazette - Rocky Ford, CO - *AyerDirPub 83*
Gazette - New Castle, DE - *AyerDirPub 83*
Gazette - Ft. Lauderdale, FL - *Ed&PubIntYB 82*
Gazette - Kissimmee, FL - *AyerDirPub 83*
Gazette - Ashton, IL - *AyerDirPub 83*
Gazette - Elmwood, IL - *AyerDirPub 83*
Gazette - Girard, IL - *AyerDirPub 83*
Gazette - Glasford, IL - *AyerDirPub 83*
Gazette - Saybrook, IL - *AyerDirPub 83*
Gazette - Spring Valley, IL - *AyerDirPub 83*
Gazette - Sterling, IL - *AyerDirPub 83*
Gazette - Danville, IN - *AyerDirPub 83*
Gazette - Hobart, IN - *AyerDirPub 83*
Gazette - Oxford, IN - *AyerDirPub 83*
Gazette - Bagley, IA - *AyerDirPub 83*
Gazette - Cedar Rapids, IA - *AyerDirPub 83*
Gazette - Fremont, IA - *AyerDirPub 83*
Gazette - Neola, IA - *AyerDirPub 83*
Gazette - Sumner, IA - *AyerDirPub 83*
Gazette - Augusta, KS - *AyerDirPub 83*
Gazette - Emporia, KS - *AyerDirPub 83*
Gazette - Farmerville, LA - *AyerDirPub 83*
Gazette - Ville Platte, LA - *AyerDirPub 83*
Gazette - Dexter, ME - *AyerDirPub 83; Ed&PubIntYB 82; NewsDir 84*
Gazette - Haverhill, MA - *AyerDirPub 83; Ed&PubIntYB 82*
Gazette - Middleboro, MA - *AyerDirPub 83*
Gazette - Taunton, MA - *AyerDirPub 83*
Gazette - Worcester, MA - *AyerDirPub 83*
Gazette - Bellevue, MI - *AyerDirPub 83*
Gazette - Carson City, MI - *AyerDirPub 83*
Gazette - Kalamazoo, MI - *AyerDirPub 83*
Gazette - Gibbon, MN - *AyerDirPub 83*
Gazette - Red Lake Falls, MN - *AyerDirPub 83; Ed&PubIntYB 82*
Gazette - Stillwater, MN - *AyerDirPub 83*
Gazette - Wheaton, MN - *AyerDirPub 83*
Gazette - St. Joseph, MO - *AyerDirPub 83; Ed&PubIntYB 82*
Gazette - Billings, MT - *AyerDirPub 83*
Gazette - Ashland, NE - *AyerDirPub 83*
Gazette - Butte, NE - *AyerDirPub 83*
Gazette - McCook, NE - *AyerDirPub 83*
Gazette - Nelson, NE - *AyerDirPub 83*
Gazette - Wausa, NE - *AyerDirPub 83*
Gazette - Reno, NV - *AyerDirPub 83*
Gazette - Livonia, NY - *AyerDirPub 83*
Gazette - Monroe, NY - *AyerDirPub 83*
Gazette - New Berlin, NY - *AyerDirPub 83*
Gazette - Niagara Falls, NY - *AyerDirPub 83*
Gazette - Schenectady, NY - *AyerDirPub 83*
Gazette - Gastonia, NC - *AyerDirPub 83*
Gazette - LaGrange, NC - *AyerDirPub 83*
Gazette - Bloomville, OH - *AyerDirPub 83*
Gazette - Centerburg, OH - *AyerDirPub 83*
Gazette - Chillicothe, OH - *AyerDirPub 83*
Gazette - Delaware, OH - *AyerDirPub 83*
Gazette - Jefferson, OH - *AyerDirPub 83; Ed&PubIntYB 82*
Gazette - Xenia, OH - *AyerDirPub 83*
Gazette - Rush Springs, OK - *AyerDirPub 83*
Gazette - Wynnewood, OK - *AyerDirPub 83*
Gazette - Ambler, PA - *AyerDirPub 83*
Gazette - Bedford, PA - *AyerDirPub 83*
Gazette - Indiana, PA - *AyerDirPub 83; Ed&PubIntYB 82*
Gazette - Monroeville, PA - *AyerDirPub 83*
Gazette - New Hope, PA - *AyerDirPub 83*
Gazette - Wellsboro, PA - *AyerDirPub 83*
Gazette - Beaufort, SC - *AyerDirPub 83*
Gazette - Burke, SD - *AyerDirPub 83*
Gazette - South Shore, SD - *AyerDirPub 83*
Gazette - Pittsburg, TX - *AyerDirPub 83*
Gazette - Shiner, TX - *AyerDirPub 83*
Gazette - Alexandria, VA - *AyerDirPub 83*
Gazette - Galax, VA - *AyerDirPub 83; Ed&PubIntYB 82*
Gazette - Colfax, WA - *AyerDirPub 83*
Gazette - Charleston, WV - *AyerDirPub 83*
Gazette - Janesville, WI - *AyerDirPub 83*
Gazette - Kemmerer, WY - *AyerDirPub 83*
Gazette - Olds, AB, Canada - *AyerDirPub 83; Ed&PubIntYB 82*
Gazette - St. Albert, AB, Canada - *Ed&PubIntYB 82*
Gazette - Golden, BC, Canada - *Ed&PubIntYB 82*
Gazette - Grand Forks, BC, Canada - *AyerDirPub 83; Ed&PubIntYB 82*
Gazette - Baldur, MB, Canada - *AyerDirPub 83*
Gazette - Glenboro, MB, Canada - *AyerDirPub 83; Ed&PubIntYB 82*
Gazette - Almonte, ON, Canada - *AyerDirPub 83*
Gazette - Norwich, ON, Canada - *AyerDirPub 83; Ed&PubIntYB 82*
Gazette - Parkhill, ON, Canada - *AyerDirPub 83; Ed&PubIntYB 82*
Gazette - Picton, ON, Canada - *AyerDirPub 83; Ed&PubIntYB 82*
Gazette - Tavistock, ON, Canada - *Ed&PubIntYB 82*
Gazette [of Southam Inc.] - Montreal, PQ, Canada - *AyerDirPub 83; BaconPubCkNews 84; Ed&PubIntYB 82; LitMarPl 84*
Gazette-Advertiser - Galena, IL - *AyerDirPub 83*
Gazette-Advertiser [of Taconic Press Inc.] - Rhinebeck, NY - *AyerDirPub 83; Ed&PubIntYB 82; NewsDir 84*
Gazette-Chesterfield, The - Chesterfield County, VA - *Ed&PubIntYB 82*
Gazette-Chronicle - St. Clairsville, OH - *AyerDirPub 83*
Gazette-Democrat - Anna, IL - *AyerDirPub 83; Ed&PubIntYB 82*
Gazette-Enterprise - Seguin, TX - *AyerDirPub 83; Ed&PubIntYB 82*
Gazette Leader - Cape May County, NJ - *Ed&PubIntYB 82*
Gazette-Leader [of Worrell Newspapers Inc.] - Wildwood, NJ - *AyerDirPub 83; NewsDir 84*
Gazette-Mail - Charleston, WV - *AyerDirPub 83*
Gazette News - Kendrick, ID - *AyerDirPub 83; Ed&PubIntYB 82*
Gazette-News - Bunker Hill, IL - *AyerDirPub 83; Ed&PubIntYB 82*
Gazette-News - Jacksboro, TX - *AyerDirPub 83*
Gazette Newspapers - Janesville, WI - *Ed&PubIntYB 82*
Gazette-Patriot - Carrollton, IL - *AyerDirPub 83; Ed&PubIntYB 82*
Gazette-Post-News - Carnduff, SK, Canada - *AyerDirPub 83*
Gazette Printing Co. - Glasford, IL - *BaconPubCkNews 84*
Gazette Printing Co. - Janesville, WI - *BrCabYB 84*
Gazette Publishing Co. [Aff. of Prospector's & Treasure Hunter's Guild] - Segundo, CO - *BoPubDir 4*
Gazette Publishing Co. Inc., The - Winchester, IN - *NewsDir 84*
Gazette-Record - St. Maries, ID - *AyerDirPub 83; Ed&PubIntYB 82*
Gazette Register - Troy, PA - *AyerDirPub 83*
Gazette-Reporter - Rivers, MB, Canada - *AyerDirPub 83; Ed&PubIntYB 82*
Gazette Shopper - Parkville, MO - *AyerDirPub 83*
Gazette Shopping Guide - Tifton, GA - *AyerDirPub 83*
Gazette Telegraph - Colorado Springs, CO - *AyerDirPub 83*
Gazette, The - Old Greenwich, CT - *NewsDir 84*
Gazette, The - Old Lyme, CT - *AyerDirPub 83; Ed&PubIntYB 82*
Gazette, The - Sibley, IA - *AyerDirPub 83*
Gazette, The - Stanley, KS - *AyerDirPub 83*
Gazette, The - Magnolia, MS - *AyerDirPub 83*
Gazette, The - New Bern, NC - *AyerDirPub 83*
Gazette, The - Wilkinsburg, PA - *Ed&PubIntYB 82*
Gazette, The - Goodlettsville, TN - *Ed&PubIntYB 82*
Gazette, The - Chatham, VA - *NewsDir 84*
Gazette, The - Goochland, VA - *Ed&PubIntYB 82*
Gazette, The - Gretna, VA - *AyerDirPub 83; Ed&PubIntYB 82*

Gazette, The - Manakin, VA - *Ed&PubIntYB 82*
Gazette, The - Oromocto, NB, Canada - *AyerDirPub 83*
Gazette, The - Kinistino, SK, Canada - *Ed&PubIntYB 82*
Gazette Times - Virginia, IL - *Ed&PubIntYB 82*
Gazette-Times - Corvallis, OR - *AyerDirPub 83*
Gazette-Times - Heppner, OR - *AyerDirPub 83*
Gazette Virginian - South Boston, VA - *AyerDirPub 83*
Gazette Virginian Shopper - South Boston, VA - *AyerDirPub 83*
Gazin, Patricia A. - Hermosa Beach, CA - *BoPubDir 4, 5*
GB Associates - Granada Hills, CA - *MicrocomMPl 84; WhoWMicrocom 83*
GB Publishing - Calgary, AB, Canada - *BoPubDir 4, 5*
GBBA Horizons [of Glass Bottles Blowers Association] - Media, PA - *NewsDir 84*
GBC Closed Circuit TV Corp. - New York, NY - *AvMarPl 83*
GBC Press - Las Vegas, NV - *LitMag&SmPr 83-84*
GBC Press - *See* Gamblers Book Club/GBC Press Inc.
GCS Music Publications - Memphis, TN - *BillIntBG 83-84*
GCS Video - Green Cove Springs, FL - *BrCabYB 84*
G.D. Television Enrg. - Marsoui, PQ, Canada - *BrCabYB 84*
GDA Advertising Inc. - Lyndhurst, NJ - *StaDirAdAg 2-84*
GE-PS Cancer Memorial - Park Ridge, IL - *BoPubDir 4 Sup, 5*
GEAC Computer Corp. Ltd. - Markham, ON, Canada - *DataDirSup 7-83*
GEAC Computers Inc. - Woodland Hills, CA - *DataDirSup 7-83*
GEAC Library Information System [of GEAC Inc.] - Los Angeles, CA - *EISS 83*
Geankoplis, Christie J. - Columbus, OH - *BoPubDir 4, 5*
Gearhead Press - Grand Rapids, MI - *BoPubDir 4, 5; LitMag&SmPr 83-84*
Geary Star - Geary, OK - *BaconPubCkNews 84; Ed&PubIntYB 82*
Geauga Times Leader - Chardon, OH - *AyerDirPub 83; BaconPubCkNews 84*
Gebbie Press Inc. - New Paltz, NY - *BoPubDir 5; DirMarMP 83*
Gebelli Software Inc. - Sacto, CA - *MicrocomMPl 84*
Gebhardt, Chuck - San Jose, CA - *BoPubDir 4, 5*
GEC Viewdata Systems [of General Electric Co. Ltd.] - London, England - *EISS 83*
Geddes Charles Mix County News - Geddes, SD - *BaconPubCkNews 84*
Gediman Research Group Inc., The - Stamford, CT - *IntDirMarRes 83*
Gee, Elizabeth - New York, NY - *LitMarPl 83, 84; MagIndMarPl 82-83*
Gee Tee Bee - Los Angeles, CA - *BoPubDir 4, 5*
Geegery Software Works, The - Des Moines, IA - *MicrocomSwDir 1*
Geer, Corinne C. - Albany, GA - *BoPubDir 4, 5*
Geer, DuBois - New York, NY - *AdAge 3-28-84; ArtMar 84; StaDirAdAg 2-84*
Geer-Murray Inc. - Oshkosh, WI - *StaDirAdAg 2-84*
Geer Public Relations, Abbot - Armonk, NY - *DirPRFirms 83*
Geers Gross Advertising - New York, NY - *AdAge 3-28-84; BrCabYB 84*
Geers Gross Ltd. - London, England - *StaDirAdAg 2-84*
Geetingsville Telephone Co. Inc. - Frankfort, IN - *TelDir&BG 83-84*
Geffen Records - Los Angeles, CA - *BillIntBG 83-84*
Gefter, Judith - Jacksonville, FL - *MagIndMarPl 82-83*
Gehrung Associates University Relations Counselors Inc. - Keene, NH - *DirPRFirms 83*
Geiger Brothers - Lewiston, ME - *LitMarPl 83, 84*
Geis Associates Inc., Bernard - New York, NY - *LitMarPl 83, 84*
Geiser Productions Ltd. - London, England - *Ed&PubIntYB 82*
Geisz & Rose Advertising Inc. [Div. of Geisz International] - Los Angeles, CA - *StaDirAdAg 2-84*
Gelder Software, Allen - San Francisco, CA - *MicrocomMPl 84*
Gelfond Associates Inc., Gordon - Beverly Hills, CA - *StaDirAdAg 2-84*
Gelia, Wells & Mohr Advertising Inc. - Buffalo, NY - *StaDirAdAg 2-84*
Gelinas Associates Inc., John G. - New York, NY - *DirPRFirms 83*
Geller, Albert D. - Morton Grove, IL - *LitMarPl 83, 84; MagIndMarPl 82-83*
Geller, Bonnie S. - New York, NY - *LitMarPl 83, 84; MagIndMarPl 82-83*
Geller Computer Systems, H. - Riverdale, NY - *WhoWMicrocom 83*
Geller Inc., Stephen L. - New York, NY - *DirMarMP 83*
Gelman Advertising, Murray - New York, NY - *StaDirAdAg 2-84*
Gelman Feature Syndicate, The - Brooklyn, NY - *Ed&PubIntYB 82*
Geltzer & Co. Inc. - New York, NY - *DirPRFirms 83*
Gelula & Associates Inc., Abner J. - Atlantic City, NJ - *ArtMar 84; StaDirAdAg 2-84*
Gelula & Associates Inc., Abner J. (Resort & Travel Div.) - Atlantic City, NJ - *StaDirAdAg 2-84*
Gelwicks Co., Harry R. - Long Island City, NY - *StaDirAdAg 2-84*
Gem City College Press - Quincy, IL - *BoPubDir 4, 5*
Gem Guides Book Co. - Pico Rivera, CA - *BoPubDir 4, 4 Sup, 5; LitMag&SmPr 83-84; LitMarPl 84*
Gem Publications - Melbourne, FL - *BoPubDir 4, 5*
Gem State Utilities Corp. [Aff. of Telephone Utilities Inc.] - Portland, OR - *TelDir&BG 83-84*
Gem, The - New York, NY - *NewsDir 84*
Gemaia Press - Sequim, WA - *BoPubDir 4, 5*
Gemco Courier [of Lucky Stores Inc.] - Buena Park, CA - *WritMar 84*
Gemcon Inc. - Ft. Lauderdale, FL - *BillIntBG 83-84*
Geme Art Gallery - Vancouver, WA - *ArtMar 84*
Gemini Books - Eugene, OR - *BoPubDir 4, 5*
Gemini Books/Transemantics Publications [Aff. of Transemantics Inc.] - Washington, DC - *BoPubDir 4, 5*
Gemini Computer Products - Piscataway, NJ - *MicrocomMPl 83*
Gemini Information Systems - Englewood, CO - *MicrocomSwDir 1*
Gemini News Service - New York, NY - *Ed&PubIntYB 82*
Gemini Press - Oakmont, PA - *BoPubDir 4, 5*
Gemini Publishing Co. - Houston, TX - *BoPubDir 4, 5; LitMag&SmPr 83-84*
Gemini Smith Inc. - La Jolla, CA - *ArtMar 84; LitMarPl 83*
Gemming, Klaus - New Haven, CT - *LitMarPl 83, 84; MagIndMarPl 82-83*
Gemological Institute of America - Santa Monica, CA - *BoPubDir 4, 5*
Gems & Gemology - Santa Monica, CA - *MagDir 84; MagIndMarPl 82-83*
Gems & Minerals - Mentone, CA - *WritMar 84*
Gena Rose Press - Denver, CO - *BoPubDir 4, 5*
Genasys Corp. - Rockville, MD - *ADAPSOMemDir 83-84*
GenBank - Cambridge, MA - *DirOnDB Spring 84*
Genco Publishers - Hamilton, ON, Canada - *BoPubDir 4 Sup, 5*
Gendel Marketing Research Co. - Jericho, NY - *IntDirMarRes 83*
Genealogical Association of Southwestern Michigan [Aff. of Ft. Miami Heritage Society] - St. Joseph, MI - *BoPubDir 4, 5*
Genealogical Books in Print - Springfield, VA - *BoPubDir 4, 5*
Genealogical Computing - Fairfax, VA - *BaconPubCkMag 84*
Genealogical Enterprises - Jonesboro, GA - *BoPubDir 4, 5*
Genealogical Helper, The - Nibley, UT - *MagIndMarPl 82-83*
Genealogical Institute - Salt Lake City, UT - *BoPubDir 4, 5*
Genealogical Library [of Church of Jesus Christ of the Latter-Day Saints] - Salt Lake City, UT - *EISS 83*
Genealogical Publishing Co. Inc. - Baltimore, MD - *LitMarPl 83, 84; WritMar 84*
Genealogical Referral Service - Albany, NY - *BoPubDir 5*
Genealogical Referral Service - Moravia, NY - *BoPubDir 4*
Genealogical Sources Unltd. - Knoxville, TX - *BoPubDir 5*
Genealogy Digest - Salt Lake City, UT - *MagDir 84*
Genealogy Research - Sacramento, CA - *BoPubDir 4*
Genelco Inc. - St. Louis, MO - *ADAPSOMemDir 83-84*
Genelle Music Co. - Tifton, GA - *BillIntBG 83-84*
General Advertising Service Inc. - New York, NY - *LitMarPl 83, 84*
General Agreement on Tariffs & Trade [of United Nations] - Geneva, Switzerland - *InfIndMarPl 83*
General & Practical Data Base - Oak Ridge, TN - *DirOnDB Spring 84*
General & Technical On-Line Retrieval Service [of University of Florida Libraries] - Gainesville, FL - *InfIndMarPl 83*
General Atlantic Corp. - New York, NY - *ADAPSOMemDir 83-84*
General Audio-Visual Inc. - Valley Stream, NY - *AvMarPl 83*

General Automation - Anaheim, CA - *DataDirSup 7-83; Datamation 6-83; InfIndMarPl 83; Top100Al 83; WhoWMicrocom 83*
General Aviation Business - Snyder, TX - *MagDir 84*
General Aviation News - Carrollton, TX - *BaconPubCkMag 84*
General Aviation News - Snyder, TX - *ArtMar 84; MagDir 84; MagIndMarPl 82-83; WritMar 84*
General Aviation Press - Snyder, TX - *BoPubDir 4, 5*
General Binding Corp. - Northbrook, IL - *AvMarPl 83; DataDirSup 7-83*
General Broadcasting Service - Nashville, TN - *BillIntBG 83-84*
General Business Computer Applications Inc. - Pomona, CA - *WhoWMicrocom 83*
General Business Computers Inc. - Cherry Hill, NJ - *MicrocomMPl 83, 84; WhoWMicrocom 83*
General Business Magazine - Dallas, TX - *ArtMar 84*
General Cartography Inc. - Croton-on-Hudson, NY - *LitMarPl 83, 84; MagIndMarPl 82-83*
General Chemical Indicators - Mt. Kisco, NY - *DirOnDB Spring 84*
General Cinema Corp. - Chestnut Hill, MA - *HomeVid&CabYB 82-83; KnowInd 83*
General Communications & Entertainment Co. Inc. - Parma, ID - *BrCabYB 84*
General Communications Co. of America - Los Angeles, CA - *LitMarPl 83, 84*
General Communications Inc. - Rockville, MD - *DirInfWP 82*
General Computer Management Corp. - Bethesda, MD - *DataDirOnSer 84*
General Computer Services Inc. - San Juan, PR - *ADAPSOMemDir 83-84*
General Computer Systems Inc. - Addison, TX - *InfIndMarPl 83*
General Council of the Assemblies of God - Springfield, MO - *MagIndMarPl 82-83*
General Data Communications Industries Inc. - Danbury, CT - *MicrocomMPl 84*
General Data Consultants - Memphis, TN - *MicrocomMPl 84*
General DataComm Industries Inc. - Danbury, CT - *DataDirSup 7-83*
General Delivery Records - Antioch, TN - *BillIntBG 83-84*
General Dentistry - Chicago, IL - *BaconPubCkMag 84; MagIndMarPl 82-83*
General Digital Corp. - East Hartford, CT - *DataDirSup 7-83*
General Dynamics Communications Corp. - St. Louis, MO - *DirInfWP 82*
General Dynamics Communications Corp. (Data Systems Div.) - St. Louis, MO - *ADAPSOMemDir 83-84*
General Eclectics [Subs. of Golemics] - Berkeley, CA - *WhoWMicrocom 83*
General Educational Development Institute [Aff. of The Adult Learning Association] - Waterville, WA - *BoPubDir 4, 5*
General Educational Media Inc. - Wilmington, DE - *ArtMar 84; AvMarPl 83*
General Educational Publications - San Francisco, CA - *BoPubDir 4, 5*
General Electric Broadcasting Co. Inc. - Westport, CT - *TelAl 84*
General Electric Broadcasting Co. Inc. - Schenectady, NY - *TelAl 83*
General Electric Cablevision - Tracy, CA - *BrCabYB 84; Tel&CabFB 84C*
General Electric Cablevision [of General Electric Co.] - Schenectady, NY - *BrCabYB 84 p.D-301; CabTVFinDB 83; HomeVid&CabYB 82-83; LitMarPl 84; Tel&CabFB 84C p.1681*
General Electric Cablevision Corp. - Merced, CA - *BrCabYB 84; Tel&CabFB 84C*
General Electric Cablevision Corp. - Vacaville, CA - *BrCabYB 84; Tel&CabFB 84C*
General Electric Cablevision Corp. - Walnut Creek, CA - *BrCabYB 84; InterCabHB 3; Tel&CabFB 84C*
General Electric Cablevision Corp. - Westport, CT - *TelAl 84*
General Electric Cablevision Corp. - Decatur, IL - *BrCabYB 84; Tel&CabFB 84C*
General Electric Cablevision Corp. - Peoria, IL - *BrCabYB 84; InterCabHB 3; Tel&CabFB 84C*
General Electric Cablevision Corp. - Anderson, IN - *BrCabYB 84; Tel&CabFB 84C*
General Electric Cablevision Corp. - Grand Rapids, MI - *BrCabYB 84; HomeVid&CabYB 82-83; InterCabHB 3; Tel&CabFB 84C*
General Electric Cablevision Corp. - Wyoming, MI - *BrCabYB 84*
General Electric Cablevision Corp. - Biloxi, MS - *BrCabYB 84; Tel&CabFB 84C*
General Electric Cablevision Corp. - Hattiesburg, MS - *BrCabYB 84; Tel&CabFB 84C*
General Electric Cablevision Corp. - Schnectady, NY - *TelAl 83*
General Electric Cablevision Corp. - Watertown, NY - *BrCabYB 84; Tel&CabFB 84C*
General Electric Co. - Fairfield, CT - *AdAge 6-28-84; Datamation 6-83; ElecNews 7-25-83; HomeVid&CabYB 82-83; KnowInd 83; Top100Al 83*
General Electric Co. - Syracuse, NY - *AvMarPl 83*
General Electric Co. - Waynesboro, VA - *DataDirSup 7-83; MicrocomMPl 84*
General Electric Co. - London, England - *ElecNews 7-25-83*
General Electric Co. (Advertising & Sales Promotion Operations) - Norwalk, CT - *DirMarMP 83*
General Electric Co. (Consumer Products Sector) - Fairfield, CT - *CabTVFinDB 83*
General Electric Co. (Data Communications Products Dept.) - Waynesboro, VA - *DirInfWP 82; InfIndMarPl 83; WhoWMicrocom 83*
General Electric Co. (Technology Marketing Operation) - Schenectady, NY - *BoPubDir 4, 5*
General Electric Co. (Video Productions Div.) - Portsmouth, VA - *BillIntBG 83-84*
General Electric Credit Corp. - Stamford, CT - *DataDirSup 7-83*
General Electric Information Services [Subs. of General Electric Co.] - Rockville, MD - *ADAPSOMemDir 83-84; DataDirOnSer 84; DataDirSup 7-83*
General Exhibits & Displays Inc. - Chicago, IL - *AvMarPl 83*
General Graphic Services Inc. [Div. of Commonwealth Communication Services] - York, PA - *LitMarPl 83, 84*
General Hall Inc. - Bayside, NY - *ArtMar 84; LitMag&SmPr 83-84; LitMarPl 83, 84; WritMar 84*
General Health Inc. - Washington, DC - *WhoWMicrocom 83*
General Indicator Corp. - Ann Arbor, MI - *DirInfWP 82*
General Information File [of Standard & Poor's Compustat Services Inc.] - Englewood, CO - *DataDirOnSer 84*
General Information Processing System [of University of Oklahoma] - Norman, OK - *EISS 83*
General Information Programme [of United Nations Educational, Scientific, & Cultural Organization] - Paris, France - *EISS 83*
General Instrument Corp. - New York, NY - *Datamation 6-83; ElecNews 7-25-83; HomeVid&CabYB 82-83; Top100Al 83*
General Instrument Corp. - Westbury, NY - *DirInfWP 82*
General Instrument Corp. - Hatboro, PA - *HomeVid&CabYB 82-83*
General Instrument Corp. (Jerrold Div.) - Hatboro, PA - *CabTVFinDB 83; VideoDir 82-83*
General Interviewing Surveys - Southfield, MI - *IntDirMarRes 83*
General Kinetics Inc. - Rockville, MD - *AvMarPl 83; DataDirSup 7-83*
General Means Inc. - City of Industry, CA - *BoPubDir 5*
General Microfilm Co. - Watertown, MA - *MagIndMarPl 82-83; MicroMarPl 82-83*
General Motors Corp. - Detroit, MI - *ElecNews 7-25-83*
General Music Corp. - Los Angeles, CA - *Tel&CabFB 84C*
General Music Corp. - Nolensville, TN - *BillIntBG 83-84*
General Music Inc. - Detroit, MI - *BillIntBG 83-84*
General Music Publishing Corp. - Dobbs Ferry, NY - *BillIntBG 83-84*
General Offset Co. Inc. - New York, NY - *LitMarPl 83, 84; MagIndMarPl 82-83*
General Paperbacks [Div. of General Publishing Co. Ltd.] - Don Mills, ON, Canada - *LitMarPl 84*
General Paperbacks [Div. of General Publishing Co. Ltd.] - Markham, ON, Canada - *LitMarPl 83*
General Polymeric - West Reading, PA - *DirInfWP 82*
General Power Systems [Subs. of A-L-S Electronics Corp.] - Anaheim, CA - *MicrocomMPl 84; WhoWMicrocom 83*
General Press Features - New York, NY - *Ed&PubIntYB 82*
General Production Services Inc. - Anaheim, CA - *AvMarPl 83*

General Programmed Teaching [Div. of Career Education Associates] - Baltimore, MD - *AvMarPl 83*
General Publishing Co. Ltd. - Don Mills, ON, Canada - *LitMarPl 83, 84*
General Research Associates - Bryn Mawr, PA - *IntDirMarRes 83*
General Ribbon Corp. - Chatsworth, CA - *DirInfWP 82*
General Roll Leaf Manufacturing Co. - Long Island City, NY - *LitMarPl 83, 84*
General Signal Corp. - Stamford, CT - *ElecNews 7-25-83*
General Society of Mayflower Descendants - Plymouth, MA - *BoPubDir 4, 5*
General Software Inc. - Palo Alto, CA - *MicrocomMPl 83*
General Software Inc. - Terre Haute, IN - *MicrocomMPl 84*
General Technical Services Inc. - Upper Darby, PA - *BoPubDir 4, 5*
General Telephone & Electronics Corp. - Stamford, CT - *HomeVid&CabYB 82-83; KnowInd 83*
General Telephone Co. [Aff. of GTE Corp.] - Sun Prairie, WI - *TelDir&BG 83-84*
General Telephone Co. of Alaska [Aff. of GTE Corp.] - Everett, WA - *TelDir&BG 83-84*
General Telephone Co. of California [Aff. of GTE Corp.] - Santa Monica, CA - *TelDir&BG 83-84*
General Telephone Co. of Florida [Aff. of GTE Corp.] - Tampa, FL - *TelDir&BG 83-84*
General Telephone Co. of Illinois [Aff. of GTE Corp.] - Bloomington, IL - *TelDir&BG 83-84*
General Telephone Co. of Indiana [Aff. of GTE Corp.] - Ft. Wayne, IN - *TelDir&BG 83-84*
General Telephone Co. of Kentucky [Aff. of GTE Corp.] - Lexington, KY - *TelDir&BG 83-84*
General Telephone Co. of Michigan [Aff. of GTE Corp.] - Muskegon, MI - *TelDir&BG 83-84*
General Telephone Co. of Ohio [Aff. of GTE Corp.] - Marion, OH - *TelDir&BG 83-84*
General Telephone Co. of Pennsylvania [Aff. of GTE Corp.] - Erie, PA - *TelDir&BG 83-84*
General Telephone Co. of the Midwest [Aff. of GTE Corp.] - Grinnell, IA - *TelDir&BG 83-84*
General Telephone Co. of the Northwest Inc. [Aff. of GTE Corp.] - Everett, WA - *TelDir&BG 83-84*
General Telephone Co. of the Southeast [Aff. of GTE Corp.] - Durham, NC - *TelDir&BG 83-84*
General Telephone Co. of the Southwest [Aff. of GTE Corp.] - San Angelo, TX - *TelDir&BG 83-84*
General Television Network - Montgomery, AL - *BrCabYB 84*
General Television Network - Oak Park, MI - *AvMarPl 83; Tel&CabFB 84C; TeleSy&SerDir 2-84*
General Television of Delaware Inc. [of Storer Cable Communications] - Dover, DE - *BrCabYB 84; Tel&CabFB 84C*
General Television of Delaware Inc. [of Storer Cable Communications] - Georgetown, DE - *Tel&CabFB 84C*
General Television of Delaware Inc. - Rehoboth Beach, DE - *BrCabYB 84*
General Television of Delaware Inc. [of Storer Cable Communications] - Seaford, DE - *Tel&CabFB 84C*
General Television of Maryland Inc. [of Storer Cable Communications] - Salisbury, MD - *BrCabYB 84; Tel&CabFB 84C*
General Television of Michigan Inc. [of American Television & Communications Corp.] - Oscoda, MI - *BrCabYB 84; Tel&CabFB 84C*
General Television of Michigan Inc. [of American Television & Communications Corp.] - Tawas, MI - *BrCabYB 84*
General Television of Minnesota Inc. [of Storer Cable Communications] - Fridley, MN - *Tel&CabFB 84C*
General Television of Minnesota Inc. [of Storer Cable Communications] - St. Cloud, MN - *Tel&CabFB 84C*
General Terminal Corp. - Tustin, CA - *DataDirSup 7-83; InfIndMarPl 83; WhoWMicrocom 83*
General Tire & Rubber Co., The - Akron, OH - *HomeVid&CabYB 82-83*
General TV Co-Operative Society - Genelle, BC, Canada - *BrCabYB 84*
General Videotex Corp. - Cambridge, MA - *DataDirOnSer 84; MicrocomMPl 83; VideoDir 82-83*
General Welfare Publications - Sacramento, CA - *BoPubDir 4, 5*
General Words & Music Co. - *See* Kjos Music Co., Neil A.
Generalist Association Inc., The - New York, NY - *LitMag&SmPr 83-84*
Generation News/Continuum Inc. - New York, NY - *Ed&PubIntYB 82*
Generic Records - Wilkes Barre, PA - *BillIntBG 83-84*
Genes Inc. - Sheboygan, WI - *AvMarPl 83*
Genesee Computer Center Inc. - Rochester, NY - *DataDirOnSer 84*
Genesee Country Express - Dansville, NY - *AyerDirPub 83; Ed&PubIntYB 82*
Genesee County Herald - Mt. Morris, MI - *Ed&PubIntYB 82*
Genesee County Video Corp. [of Cablevision Industries Inc.] - Attica, NY - *Tel&CabFB 84C*
Genesee County Video Corp. [of Cablevision Industries Inc.] - Avon, NY - *Tel&CabFB 84C*
Genesee County Video Corp. - Batavia, NY - *BrCabYB 84*
Genesee County Video Corp. [of Cablevision Industries Inc.] - Bergen, NY - *Tel&CabFB 84C*
Genesee County Video Corp. [of Cablevision Industries Inc.] - Covington, NY - *Tel&CabFB 84C*
Genesee Valley Chemunications [of American Chemical Society] - Rochester, NY - *MagDir 84*
Geneseo Galaxy - Geneseo, KS - *BaconPubCkNews 84; Ed&PubIntYB 82*
Geneseo Livingston Republican - Geneseo, NY - *BaconPubCkNews 84*
Geneseo Republic - Geneseo, IL - *BaconPubCkNews 84; Ed&PubIntYB 82; NewsDir 84*
Geneseo Shopper - Geneseo, IL - *AyerDirPub 83*
Geneseo Telephone Co. - Geneseo, IL - *TelDir&BG 83-84*
Genesis [of Cycle Guide Publications Inc.] - New York, NY - *ArtMar 84; BaconPubCkMag 84; Folio 83; MagDir 84; MagIndMarPl 82-83; WritMar 84*
Genesis Information Systems Inc. - Duluth, MN - *MicrocomMPl 84*
Genesis Marketing Group Inc. - Greenville, SC - *LitMarPl 83, 84*
Genesis Network - Columbia, SC - *BrCabYB 84*
Genesis I Builders - Salt Lake City, UT - *BoPubDir 5*
Genesis Records - Detroit, MI - *BillIntBG 83-84*
Genessee County Video Corp. - Churchville, NY - *BrCabYB 84*
Genesys Group, The - Ottawa, ON, Canada - *VideoDir 82-83*
Genet [of Intersil Systems Inc.] - Sunnyvale, CA - *TeleSy&SerDir 7-83*
Genetic Engineering News - New York, NY - *BaconPubCkMag 84; WritMar 84*
Genetic Technology News - Ft. Lee, NJ - *BaconPubCkMag 84*
Genetics - Chapel Hill, NC - *MagIndMarPl 82-83*
Genetics Abstracts [of Information Retrieval Ltd.] - London, England - *CompReadDB 82*
Geneva Chronicle - Geneva, IL - *Ed&PubIntYB 82; NewsDir 84*
Geneva Chronicle - *See* Chronicle Publishing Co.
Geneva Consultants Registry Ltd. - Shelbyville, IN - *EISS 5-84 Sup*
Geneva County Reaper - Geneva, AL - *AyerDirPub 83; BaconPubCkNews 84; Ed&PubIntYB 82*
Geneva Divinity School Press - Tyler, TX - *ArtMar 84; BoPubDir 4, 5*
Geneva Nebraska Signal - Geneva, NE - *BaconPubCkNews 84; NewsDir 84*
Geneva Republican [of Republican Printing Co.] - Geneva, IL - *BaconPubCkNews 84; Ed&PubIntYB 82; NewsDir 84*
Geneva Review, The - Avenches, Switzerland - *WritMar 84*
Geneva Series [of CompuServe Inc.] - Columbus, OH - *DataDirOnSer 84*
Geneva Times - Geneva, NY - *NewsDir 84*
Geneva Times - Orem, UT - *Ed&PubIntYB 82*
Genevieve's - Milwaukee, WI - *MagIndMarPl 82-83*
Genie Computer Corp. - Westlake Village, CA - *MicrocomMPl 84; WhoWMicrocom 83*
Genie-Construction - Montreal, PQ, Canada - *BaconPubCkMag 84*
Genisco Computers Corp. - Costa Mesa, CA - *DataDirSup 7-83*
Genkins, Arnold - New York, NY - *LitMarPl 83, 84; MagIndMarPl 82-83*
Genoa-Kingston-Kirkland News [of Free Press Inc.] - Genoa, IL - *AyerDirPub 83; NewsDir 84*

Genoa-Kingston-Kirkland News - *See* Free Press Inc.
Genoa Leader-Times - Genoa, NE - *BaconPubCkNews 84; Ed&PubIntYB 82*
Genoa Suburban Press - Genoa, OH - *BaconPubCkNews 84; Ed&PubIntYB 82; NewsDir 84*
Genographics Corp. - Liverpool, NY - *DataDirSup 7-83*
Genotype - Cupertino, CA - *BoPubDir 4, 5*
GenRad/Futuredata - Culver City, CA - *WhoWMicrocom 83*
Gensheimer, Keith P. - *See* MacVay-Gensheimer Stations
Gent [of Dugent Publishing Co.] - Coral Gables, FL - *ArtMar 84; WritMar 84*
Gentian Electronics Inc. - Stittsville, ON, Canada - *DataDirSup 7-83*
Gentle Wind Publishing Co. - Sacramento, CA - *BillIntBG 83-84*
Gentleman's Companion [of Larry Flynt Publications] - Los Angeles, CA - *ArtMar 84; WritMar 84*
Gentlemen's Quarterly [of Conde Nast] - New York, NY - *ArtMar 84; BaconPubCkMag 84; Folio 83; MagDir 84; MagIndMarPl 82-83; WritMar 84*
Gentry & Pinkham Advertising Inc. - Wayne, NJ - *StaDirAdAg 2-84*
Gentry Cable TV - Gentry, AR - *BrCabYB 84*
Gentry, Helen - Santa Fe, NM - *LitMarPl 83, 84*
Gentry Journal-Advance - Gentry, AR - *BaconPubCkNews 84*
Gentry Publications - *See* Bock Music Co., Fred
Gentry Software - Chatsworth, CA - *MicrocomMPl 84*
GEO [of Knapp Communications Corp.] - Los Angeles, CA - *DirMarMP 83*
GEO [of Knapp Communications Corp.] - New York, NY - *BaconPubCkMag 84; Folio 83; MagIndMarPl 82-83; WritMar 84*
Geo Abstracts Ltd. - Norwich, England - *CompReadDB 82; EISS 83; InfIndMarPl 83*
Geo Science Analytical Inc. - Santa Monica, CA - *BoPubDir 5*
Geoarchive [of Dialog Information Services Inc.] - Palo Alto, CA - *DataDirOnSer 84*
Geoarchive [of Geosystems] - Cambridge, MA - *OnBibDB 3*
Geoarchive [of Geosystems] - London, England - *CompReadDB 82; DBBus 82; DirOnDB Spring 84*
Geobooks - San Francisco, CA - *BoPubDir 4, 5*
Geocentre Project [of Distribution Sciences Inc.] - Chicago, IL - *EISS 83; InfIndMarPl 83*
Geodata Corp. - Tulsa, OK - *EISS 83*
Geode [of Questel Inc.] - Washington, DC - *DataDirOnSer 84*
Geode - Orleans, France - *DirOnDB Spring 84*
Geode Cablevision [of Liberty Communications] - New London, IA - *BrCabYB 84; Tel&CabFB 84C*
Geodex International Inc. - Sonoma, CA - *EISS 83*
Geodial [of University of Alberta] - Edmonton, AB, Canada - *DataDirOnSer 84*
Geographic Data File [of List Processing Co.] - Addison, IL - *EISS 83*
Geographic Data Technology Inc. - Lyme, NH - *EISS 83*
Geographic Information System [of U.S. Fish & Wildlife Service] - Ft. Collins, CO - *EISS 83*
Geographic Systems Analysis - Athens, OH - *EISS 83*
Geographic Systems Inc. - Reading, MA - *EISS 83*
Geographical Analysis [of Ohio State University Press] - Columbus, OH - *MagDir 84*
Geographical Review - New York, NY - *MagDir 84*
Geographics - Easton, CT - *BoPubDir 4, 5*
Geographix Inc. - Philadelphia, PA - *DataDirSup 7-83*
Geography Div. [of U.S. Bureau of the Census] - Washington, DC - *EISS 83*
GeoIPOD - Brest, France - *DirOnDB Spring 84*
Geoline - Hannover, West Germany - *DirOnDB Spring 84*
Geologic Names of the United States [of U.S. Geological Survey] - Reston, VA - *EISS 83*
Geological & Geochemical Aspects of Uranium Deposits - Oak Ridge, TN - *DirOnDB Spring 84*
Geological Data Center [of University of California, San Diego] - La Jolla, CA - *EISS 83*
Geological Reference File [of American Geological Institute] - Falls Church, VA - *CompReadDB 82; DataDirOnSer 84; DBBus 82*
Geological Society of America - Boulder, CO - *LitMarPl 83, 84*
Geology - Boulder, CO - *BaconPubCkMag 84*
Geomatrix Associates Inc. - Milford, CT - *AvMarPl 83*
Geomechanics Abstracts [of Rock Mechanics Information Service] - London, England - *CompReadDB 82; DataDirOnSer 84; DirOnDB Spring 84; OnBibDB 3*
Geophysical Directory Inc. - Houston, TX - *BoPubDir 4 Sup, 5*
Geophysics [of Society of Exploration Geophysicists] - Tulsa, OK - *ArtMar 84; BaconPubCkMag 84; MagDir 84; MagIndMarPl 82-83*
GeoRef Information System [of American Geological Institute] - Falls Church, VA - *DirOnDB Spring 84; EISS 83; OnBibDB 3*
George & Glover Advertising Agency - Atlanta, GA - *StaDirAdAg 2-84*
George County Times - Lucedale, MS - *AyerDirPub 83; Ed&PubIntYB 82*
George, Gibbs, Hammerman & Myers Advertising Co. - St. Louis, MO - *AdAge 3-28-84; BrCabYB 84; StaDirAdAg 2-84*
George Lithograph - San Francisco, CA - *MagIndMarPl 82-83*
George Lyon County News - George, IA - *BaconPubCkNews 84*
George, Richard - San Marino, CA - *MagIndMarPl 82-83*
George William Associates - Chicago, IL - *StaDirAdAg 2-84*
Georgeson & Co. Inc. - New York, NY - *DirPRFirms 83*
Georgetown - Alexandria, VA - *BaconPubCkMag 84*
Georgetown Cable TV - Georgetown, KY - *BrCabYB 84*
Georgetown Gazette & Town Crier - Georgetown, CA - *AyerDirPub 83; Ed&PubIntYB 82*
Georgetown Graphic - Georgetown, KY - *BaconPubCkNews 84*
Georgetown Independent News - Georgetown, IL - *BaconPubCkNews 84*
Georgetown News & Times [of Scripps League Newspapers] - Georgetown, KY - *BaconPubCkNews 84; Ed&PubIntYB 82; NewsDir 84*
Georgetown News Democrat - Georgetown, OH - *BaconPubCkNews 84; Ed&PubIntYB 82*
Georgetown Press - San Francisco, CA - *BoPubDir 4, 5*
Georgetown Sunday Sun - *See* Williamson County Sun Inc.
Georgetown Sussex Countian - Georgetown, DE - *BaconPubCkNews 84; NewsDir 84*
Georgetown Telephone Co. - Georgetown, MS - *TelDir&BG 83-84*
Georgetown Times - Georgetown, SC - *BaconPubCkNews 84; Ed&PubIntYB 82; NewsDir 84*
Georgetown University (Center for Strategic & International Studies) - Washington, DC - *BoPubDir 4, 5*
Georgetown University (International Law Institute) - Washington, DC - *BoPubDir 4, 5*
Georgetown University (Kennedy Institute of Ethics) - Washington, DC - *DataDirOnSer 84*
Georgetown University (School of Languages & Linguistics) - Washington, DC - *BoPubDir 4*
Georgetown University Press - Washington, DC - *BoPubDir 5; LitMarPl 84*
Georgetown Williamson County Sun - *See* Williamson County Sun Inc.
Georgia Bulletin, The - Atlanta, GA - *NewsDir 84*
Georgia Cattleman - Macon, GA - *BaconPubCkMag 84*
Georgia Comic Group - Augusta, GA - *Ed&PubIntYB 82*
Georgia Dept. of Archives & History - Atlanta, GA - *BoPubDir 4, 5*
Georgia Engineer, The [of Georgia Architectural & Engineering Society Inc.] - Decatur, GA - *MagDir 84*
Georgia Farm Bureau News - Macon, GA - *BaconPubCkMag 84; MagDir 84*
Georgia Gazette, The - Savannah, GA - *AyerDirPub 83; Ed&PubIntYB 82*
Georgia Grocer [of Georgia Grocers Association] - Atlanta, GA - *BaconPubCkMag 84; MagDir 84*
Georgia Institute of Technology (Georgia Tech Libraries) - Atlanta, GA - *MicroMarPl 82-83*
Georgia-Pacific Corp. (Printing & Specialty Paper Div.) - Darien, CT - *LitMarPl 83, 84; MagIndMarPl 82-83*
Georgia Pioneers Publications - Albany, GA - *BoPubDir 4, 5*
Georgia Post, The - Roberta, GA - *AyerDirPub 83; Ed&PubIntYB 82*
Georgia Press Association - Atlanta, GA - *ProGuPRSer 4*
Georgia Review - Athens, GA - *LitMag&SmPr 83-84; LitMarPl 83, 84; MagIndMarPl 82-83*
Georgia Sportsman - Marietta, GA - *BaconPubCkMag 84; WritMar 84*
Georgia State Bar Journal - Atlanta, GA - *MagDir 84*

Georgia State University College of Business Administration (Business Publishing Div.) - Atlanta, GA - *LitMarPl 83, 84*
Georgia Straight - Vancouver, BC, Canada - *AyerDirPub 83*
Georgia Telecommunications Network [of Georgia Hospital Association] - Atlanta, GA - *TeleSy&SerDir 7-83*
Georgia Telephone Corp. - Blakely, GA - *TelDir&BG 83-84*
Georgia Visual Aids [Div. of Dixie Theatre Service & Supply Co. Inc.] - Albany, GA - *AvMarPl 83*
Georgian Bay West Muskoka Beacon - MacTier, ON, Canada - *Ed&PubIntYB 82*
Georgian Press Co. - Portland, OR - *BoPubDir 4, 5*
Georgian, The - Stephenville, NF, Canada - *Ed&PubIntYB 82*
Georgiana Butler County News - Georgiana, AL - *BaconPubCkNews 84*
Georgiana Cablevision Inc. - Georgiana, AL - *BrCabYB 84; Tel&CabFB 84C*
GeoRoad [of National Swedish Road & Traffic Research Institute] - Linkoping, Sweden - *CompReadDB 82*
Geosat Cable - Cedar Grove, TN - *Tel&CabFB 84C*
Geoscience Data Centre [of Ontario Ministry of Natural Resources] - Toronto, ON, Canada - *EISS 83*
Geoscience Data Index for Alberta [of Alberta Research Council] - Edmonton, AB, Canada - *EISS 83*
Geoscience Information Service [of Geological Publishing Co.] - Chico, CA - *EISS 83; FBInfSer 80*
Geoscience Information Society - Falls Church, VA - *EISS 83*
Geoscience Literature Information Service [of Federal Institute for Geosciences & Natural Resources] - Hannover, West Germany - *EISS 83*
GeoSciTech [of Institute for Scientific Information] - Philadelphia, PA - *DataDirOnSer 84*
Geosystems - Cambridge, MA - *DataDirOnSer 84; MicrocomMPl 84*
Geosystems [Div. of Lea Associates Ltd.] - London, England - *CompReadDB 82; EISS 83; FBInfSer 80; InfIndMarPl 83*
Geotechnical Abstracts [of German National Society for Soil Mechanics & Foundation Engineering] - Essen, West Germany - *EISS 83*
Geotherm Information System [of U.S. Geological Survey] - Menlo Park, CA - *EISS 83*
Geothermal Energy - Camarillo, CA - *BaconPubCkMag 84; MagDir 84; MagIndMarPl 82-83*
Geothermal Resources Council - Davis, CA - *BoPubDir 4, 5*
Geothermal World - Camarillo, CA - *BoPubDir 5*
Geotimes - Alexandria, VA - *BaconPubCkMag 84; MagDir 84*
Geotimes - Falls Church, VA - *MagIndMarPl 82-83*
Geppetto Enterprises - Westminister, CA - *MicrocomMPl 84*
Gerald Star - Gerald, MO - *BaconPubCkNews 84; Ed&PubIntYB 82*
Geraldton Times Star - Geraldton, ON, Canada - *Ed&PubIntYB 82*
Gerard Co., The - Linthicum, MD - *DirMarMP 83*
Gerard, Fritz - Charlotte, NC - *LitMarPl 84*
Gerard, John H. - Alton, IL - *LitMarPl 83, 84; MagIndMarPl 82-83*
Geraventure Corp. - Melbourne, FL - *BoPubDir 4, 5; LitMag&SmPr 83-84*
Gerber Advertising Agency - Portland, OR - *AdAge 3-28-84; StaDirAdAg 2-84; TelAl 83, 84*
Gerber/Carter Communications Inc. - New York, NY - *StaDirAdAg 2-84*
Gerber Publications - Ormond Beach, FL - *BoPubDir 4, 5*
Gerber Scientific Inc. - South Windsor, CT - *Datamation 6-83; Top100Al 83*
Gerber Systems Technology Inc. - South Windsor, CT - *DataDirSup 7-83*
Gerbig, Snell, Weisheimer & Associates Inc. - Dublin, OH - *StaDirAdAg 2-84*
Gerbino Advertising Inc., John Nicholas - Ft. Lauderdale, FL - *StaDirAdAg 2-84*
Gerbrands Corp. - Arlington, MA - *AvMarPl 83*
Gerdes Advertising Inc., Richard H. - Des Moines, IA - *LitMarPl 83, 84; StaDirAdAg 2-84*
Geriatric Medicine Today - Morganville, NJ - *BaconPubCkMag 84*
Geriatric Nursing - New York, NY - *BaconPubCkMag 84*
Geriatric Press Inc. - Bend, OR - *BoPubDir 4, 5*
Geriatrics - New York, NY - *MagDir 84; MagIndMarPl 82-83*
Geriatrics - Cleveland, OH - *BaconPubCkMag 84*
Geriatrics - Middleburg Heights, OH - *ArtMar 84*
Gering Courier - Gering, NE - *BaconPubCkNews 84; Ed&PubIntYB 82; NewsDir 84*
Gerity Cablevision [of Gerity Broadcasting Co.] - Bay City, MI - *BrCabYB 84; Tel&CabFB 84C*
Gerity Cablevision - Midland, MI - *BrCabYB 84*
Gerity Estate, James Jr. - Essexville, MI - *Tel&CabFB 84C p.1681*
Gerlach, Kathryn - Shaftsbury, VT - *LitMarPl 83, 84*
Gerlach Photography, John - Fresno, CA - *LitMarPl 84*
Gerlinger, Lorena - Hadley, MI - *BoPubDir 4, 5*
Germainbooks - San Francisco, CA - *BoPubDir 4, 5*
German Bundesbank Monthly [of I. P. Sharp Associates Ltd.] - Toronto, ON, Canada - *DataDirOnSer 84*
German Bundesbank Monthly - Frankfurt, West Germany - *DirOnDB Spring 84*
German Business Readership Survey [of Interactive Market Systems Inc.] - New York, NY - *DataDirOnSer 84*
German Business Readership Survey - Hamburg, West Germany - *DirOnDB Spring 84*
German Foreign Trade Information Office [of Ministry of Economics] - Cologne, West Germany - *EISS 83*
German Information Center for Technical Rules [of German Standards Institute] - Berlin, West Germany - *EISS 83*
German Institute for Medical Documentation & Information [of Ministry of Youth, Family, & Health] - Cologne, West Germany - *EISS 83*
German, Mark F. - Chevy Chase, MD - *FBInfSer 80*
German Online User Group - Frankfurt, West Germany - *EISS 83*
German Statistical Data - Toronto, ON, Canada - *DirOnDB Spring 84*
German Tymnet/Telenet Node [of Deutsche Bundespost, Telegrafenamt BD] - Frankfurt, West Germany - *InfIndMarPl 83*
Germans from Russia Heritage Society - Bismarck, ND - *BoPubDir 4, 5*
Germantown Banner Press - Oak Creek, WI - *AyerDirPub 83*
Germantown Banner Press - *See* Community Newspapers Inc.
Germantown Cablevision [of Dowden Communications Inc.] - Germantown, TN - *BrCabYB 84; Tel&CabFB 84C*
Germantown Courier - Germantown, PA - *Ed&PubIntYB 82*
Germantown Courier - Philadelphia, PA - *AyerDirPub 83; NewsDir 84*
Germantown Independent Telephone Co. [Aff. of Gitco Sales Inc.] - Germantown, OH - *TelDir&BG 83-84*
Germantown News Banner [of Menomonee Falls Publishing Co.] - Menomonee Falls, WI - *NewsDir 84*
Germantown News, The - Memphis, TN - *NewsDir 84*
Germantown Paper [of Inter County Publishing Co.] - Philadelphia, PA - *AyerDirPub 83; NewsDir 84*
Germantown Press - Germantown, OH - *BaconPubCkNews 84; Ed&PubIntYB 82*
Germantown Telephone Co. Inc. [Subs. of Hilltop Communications Corp.] - Germantown, NY - *TelDir&BG 83-84*
Germany [of Chase Econometrics/Interactive Data Corp.] - Waltham, MA - *DataDirOnSer 84*
Germany - Bala Cynwyd, PA - *DirOnDB Spring 84*
Germinal Press - San Francisco, CA - *BoPubDir 4, 5*
Germplasm Resources Information Network [of U.S. Dept. of Agriculture] - Beltsville, MD - *EISS 5-84 Sup*
Gerngross & Co. Inc., H. O. - New York, NY - *StaDirAdAg 2-84*
Gero Advertising, George - West Caldwell, NJ - *StaDirAdAg 2-84*
Gero & Bierstein Inc. - Hackensack, NJ - *StaDirAdAg 2-84*
Gerontologist - Washington, DC - *BaconPubCkMag 84; MagDir 84; MagIndMarPl 82-83*
Gerrard Tribune - Toronto/Gerrard, ON, Canada - *Ed&PubIntYB 82*
Gerry, Alan - Liberty, NY - *BrCabYB 84 p.D-301*
Gerry, Alan - *See* Cablevision Industries Inc.
Gerry, Roberta - New York, NY - *DirPRFirms 83*
Gersh Associates, Richard - New York, NY - *DirPRFirms 83*
Gerstman Advertising & Art Services Inc., Milt - Westbury, NY - *DirMarMP 83*

Gerstman & Meyers Inc. - New York, NY - *HBIndAd&MS 82-83*
Gervais Telephone Co. - Gervais, OR - *TelDir&BG 83-84*
Gervasi Records & Publishing Co. - Redding, CA - *BillIntBG 83-84*
Gesar-Buddhist Perspectives [of Dharma Publishing] - Berkeley, CA - *LitMag&SmPr 83-84*
Gescan 2 [of General Electric Co.] - Arlington, VA - *EISS 7-83 Sup*
GESCO Corp. [Subs. of Guarantee Financial Corp.] - Fresno, CA - *DataDirOnSer 84*
Gescom - Scottsdale, AZ - *Tel&CabFB 84C*
Gesellschaft Deutscher Chemiker eV - *See* Fachinformationszentrum Chemie GmbH
Gesellschaft fur Information und Dokumentation - Frankfurt, West Germany - *InfIndMarPl 83*
Gesellschaft fur Information und Dokumentation (Informationszentrum fur Informationswissenschaft und -praxis) - Frankfurt, West Germany - *CompReadDB 82; InfIndMarPl 83*
Gesellschaft fur Information und Dokumentation (Sektion fur Technik) - Frankfurt, West Germany - *InfIndMarPl 83*
Gessler Publishing Co. - New York, NY - *AvMarPl 83; BoPubDir 4 Sup, 5; LitMarPl 83, 84; WritMar 84*
Gestetner Corp. - Yonkers, NY - *AvMarPl 83; DirInfWP 82*
Get Rich Book Club - Middle Island, NY - *LitMarPl 83, 84*
Getschal Co. Inc., The - Greenwich, CT - *StaDirAdAg 2-84*
Gettler, John M. - New York, NY - *LitMarPl 83, 84*
Getty Museum, J. Paul - Malibu, CA - *BoPubDir 4, 5*
Getty Museum, J. Paul - Santa Monica, CA - *WritMar 84*
Getty Oil Co. - Los Angeles, CA - *HomeVid&CabYB 82-83*
Gettysburg Area Merchandiser - Lebanon, PA - *AyerDirPub 83*
Gettysburg Cable TV Service [of Midcontinent Cable Systems Co.] - Gettysburg, SD - *BrCabYB 84; Tel&CabFB 84C*
Gettysburg Potter County News - Gettysburg, SD - *BaconPubCkNews 84*
Gettysburg Times - Gettysburg, PA - *BaconPubCkNews 84; Ed&PubIntYB 82; NewsDir 84*
Geudeker Oerlemans & Needham Advertising & Marketing BV - *See* Needham, Harper & Steers Inc.
Geyer-McAllister Publishing - New York, NY - *MagIndMarPl 82-83*
Geyer's Dealer Topics - New York, NY - *BaconPubCkMag 84; MagDir 84; WritMar 84*
Geyserville Press - Geyserville, CA - *Ed&PubIntYB 82*
Gezetzgebungsstand - Bonn, West Germany - *CompReadDB 82*
GF Business Equipment Inc. - Youngstown, OH - *DirInfWP 82*
GFE Translation Co. - Annandale, VA - *LitMarPl 83, 84; MagIndMarPl 82-83*
GFLM Data Bank [of Graphic Arts Research Laboratory] - Stockholm, Sweden - *EISS 83*
GfM Research Institute - Hergiswil, Switzerland - *IntDirMarRes 83*
GFWC Clubwoman - Washington, DC - *BaconPubCkMag 84; MagDir 84; MagIndMarPl 82-83*
G.G. Communications Inc. - Boston, MA - *Tel&CabFB 84C*
GGK - Basel, Switzerland - *StaDirAdAg 2-84*
GHA Communications - New York, NY - *AvMarPl 83*
Ghan, Leonard - White Rock, BC, Canada - *BoPubDir 4, 5*
Ghana Music Corp. - *See* Goodman Group, The
Ghana News Agency - New York, NY - *Ed&PubIntYB 82*
GHB Broadcasting - Decatur, GA - *BrCabYB 84*
Ghent Cable TV [of DeSutter Cable TV] - Ghent, MN - *BrCabYB 84*
GHG Information & Library Services Co. [of Gothard House Group of Companies Ltd.] - Henley-on-Thames, England - *EISS 83*
Ghost Dance Press [Aff. of Ghost Dance Syndicate] - East Lansing, MI - *BoPubDir 4, 5; LitMag&SmPr 83-84*
Ghost Dance: The International Quarterly of Experimental Poetry - East Lansing, MI - *LitMag&SmPr 83-84*
Ghost Pony Press - Madison, WI - *BoPubDir 4, 5; LitMag&SmPr 83-84*
Ghost Records - Kalamazoo, MI - *BillIntBG 83-84*
Ghost Town Publications - Carmel, CA - *BoPubDir 4, 5*
G.I.A. Publications Inc. - Chicago, IL - *BoPubDir 4, 5*
Gianaris & Associates Inc., Harry - Greensboro, NC - *StaDirAdAg 2-84*
Gianettino & Meredith Advertising - Mountainside, NJ - *StaDirAdAg 2-84*
Gianfagna & Associates Inc. - Marietta, OH - *StaDirAdAg 2-84*
Giardini/Russell - Watertown, MA - *AdAge 3-28-84; DirPRFirms 83; StaDirAdAg 2-84*
Gibbon Gazette - Gibbon, MN - *BaconPubCkNews 84; Ed&PubIntYB 82*
Gibbon Reporter - Gibbon, NE - *BaconPubCkNews 84; Ed&PubIntYB 82*
Gibbs & Soell Inc. - New York, NY - *DirPRFirms 83*
Gibbs Consulting Group - New York, NY - *DirInfWP 82*
Gibbs-Inman Co. - Louisville, KY - *MagIndMarPl 82-83*
Gibbs, Raymond - Partridge, KY - *BrCabYB 84*
Gibney Associates Inc. - Springfield, MA - *StaDirAdAg 2-84*
Gibraltor News-Herald - Wyandotte, MI - *AyerDirPub 83*
Gibson Associates Inc., D. Parke - New York, NY - *DirPRFirms 83*
Gibson City Courier [of East Central Communications Inc.] - Gibson City, IL - *BaconPubCkNews 84; Ed&PubIntYB 82; NewsDir 84*
Gibson Co., The C. R. - Norwalk, CT - *LitMarPl 83, 84*
Gibson-Hiller Co. - Dayton, OH - *BoPubDir 4, 5; LitMag&SmPr 83-84*
Gibson Inc., R. J. - Palm Beach, FL - *StaDirAdAg 2-84*
Gibson Laboratories - Laguna Hills, CA - *MicrocomMPl 84*
Gibson Record & Guide - Gibson, GA - *BaconPubCkNews 84; Ed&PubIntYB 82*
Gibson, Rev. Theo. T. - Anacaster, ON, Canada - *BoPubDir 4, 5*
GID Music Inc. - *See* Pride Music Group
Giday Publishing Co., Gil - North Miami Beach, FL - *BillIntBG 83-84*
Giddings & Lewis Electronics Co. [Subs. of Giddings & Lewis Inc.] - Fond du Lac, WI - *WhoWMicrocom 83*
Giddings Times & News - Giddings, TX - *BaconPubCkNews 84; NewsDir 84*
Giddyup Press - San Diego, CA - *LitMag&SmPr 83-84*
Gideon-Clarkton Journal - Gideon, MO - *AyerDirPub 83; Ed&PubIntYB 82*
GIDEP - Corona, CA - *DirOnDB Spring 84*
Gielow, Fred C. Jr. - Woodstock, NY - *BoPubDir 4, 5*
Gieseking & Clive Inc. - Bronxville, NY - *HBIndAd&MS 82-83*
Gifford Memorial Fund, George E. - Rising Sun, MD - *BoPubDir 4, 5*
Gift Digest [of Market Place Publications] - Dallas, TX - *MagDir 84*
Gift Magazine - Downsview, ON, Canada - *BaconPubCkMag 84*
Gifted Children Newsletter - Sewell, NJ - *WritMar 84*
Gifts - Los Angeles, CA - *BaconPubCkMag 84*
Gifts & Decorative Accessories [of Geyer-McAllister Publications] - New York, NY - *BaconPubCkMag 84; MagDir 84; WritMar 84*
Gifts & Tableware [of Gralla Publications] - New York, NY - *MagDir 84*
Gifts & Tablewares - Don Mills, ON, Canada - *BaconPubCkMag 84*
Giftware Business [of Gralla Publications] - New York, NY - *BaconPubCkMag 84; MagDir 84; MagIndMarPl 82-83; WritMar 84*
Giftware News [of Talcott Communications] - Des Plaines, IL - *MagDir 84*
Giftware News - Deptford, NJ - *BaconPubCkMag 84*
Gig Harbor Peninsula Gateway - Gig Harbor, WA - *BaconPubCkNews 84*
Giga - Chicago, IL - *WhoWMicrocom 83*
Gil Music Corp. - New York, NY - *BillIntBG 83-84*
Gila Bend Herald - Gila Bend, AZ - *AyerDirPub 83; Ed&PubIntYB 82*
Gila Bend Herald - *See* Casa Grande Valley Newspapers Inc.
Gila Communications of Paonia Inc. - Paonia, CO - *BrCabYB 84*
Gilbert & Co. Inc., Susan - Coral Gables, FL - *StaDirAdAg 2-84*
Gilbert & Gilbert Advertising Ltd. - Phoenix, AZ - *ArtMar 84*
Gilbert Color Systems Inc. - Hudson, NH - *MagIndMarPl 82-83*
Gilbert, Felix & Sharf Inc. - New York, NY - *DirPRFirms 83*
Gilbert Herald - Gilbert, MN - *BaconPubCkNews 84*
Gilbert, Mel Z. - *See* Snyder Community Antenna TV Co. Inc.
Gilbert, Whitney & Johns - Whippany, NJ - *AdAge 3-28-84; DirPRFirms 83; StaDirAdAg 2-84*

Gilby Telephone Co. - Gilby, ND - *TelDir&BG 83-84*
Gilchem Inc. - Charlotte, NC - *BoPubDir 4, 5*
Gilchrist County Journal - Trenton, FL - *AyerDirPub 83; Ed&PubIntYB 82*
Gilcom Stations - Altoona, PA - *BrCabYB 84*
Gilderbloom, Mary Ann - Oakland, CA - *LitMarPl 84*
Giles CATV Inc. - Narrows, VA - *BrCabYB 84*
Giles County Shopper & Entertainer, The - Pulaski, TN - *NewsDir 84*
Giles Free Press - Pulaski, TN - *AyerDirPub 83; Ed&PubIntYB 82*
Gillette News-Record, The - Gillette, WY - *NewsDir 84*
Gilfer Associates Inc. - Park Ridge, NJ - *BoPubDir 4, 5*
Gilgamesh Press Ltd. - Chicago, IL - *BoPubDir 4, 5; LitMag&SmPr 83-84*
Gill Cable TV [of Gill Industries] - San Jose, CA - *BrCabYB 84; CabTVFinDB 83; HomeVid&CabYB 82-83; InterCabHB 3; TelAl 83; Tel&CabFB 84C*
Gill Management Services - San Jose, CA - *InterCabHB 3*
Gill-Perna Inc. - New York, NY - *TelAl 83, 84*
Gill, Vernon R. - Mulberry, FL - *Tel&CabFB 84C p.1681*
Gillen & Gillen, Consultants - Belfry, MT - *TeleSy&SerDir 7-83*
Gillespie Advertising Inc. - Princeton, NJ - *DirMarMP 83; StaDirAdAg 2-84*
Gillespie Area News - Gillespie, IL - *BaconPubCkNews 84; NewsDir 84*
Gillett Group Inc. - Nashville, TN - *BrCabYB 84; Tel&CabFB 84S*
Gillette, Galen G. - Redfield, SD - *Tel&CabFB 84C p.1681*
Gillette News-Record - Gillette, WY - *BaconPubCkNews 84*
Gillette Research Institute - Rockville, MD - *IntDirMarRes 83*
Gillham Advertising Inc. - Salt Lake City, UT - *StaDirAdAg 2-84; TelAl 83, 84*
Gilliam Communications Inc. - Washington, DC - *HBIndAd&MS 82-83*
Gilliam's Publishing - Encinitas, CA - *BoPubDir 4, 5*
Gillies Bay Community Television Associates - Gillies Bay, BC, Canada - *BrCabYB 84*
Gillis Advertising - Columbia, SC - *StaDirAdAg 2-84*
Gillis, Townsend & Riley Advertising Inc. - Birmingham, AL - *StaDirAdAg 2-84*
Gilman Star - Gilman, IL - *BaconPubCkNews 84; Ed&PubIntYB 82*
Gilmer Cable Television Co. Inc. - Gilmer, TX - *BrCabYB 84; Tel&CabFB 84C*
Gilmer Mirror [of Greeneway Enterprises] - Gilmer, TX - *BaconPubCkNews 84; Ed&PubIntYB 82; NewsDir 84*
Gilmore Advertising of Miami - Miami, FL - *BrCabYB 84*
Gilmore Associates Inc., Robert - Dedham, MA - *AvMarPl 83; WritMar 84*
Gilmore Broadcasting - Kalamazoo, MI - *BrCabYB 84 p.D-301; Tel&CabFB 84C p.1681*
Gilmore Heying & Associates - San Diego, CA - *DirPRFirms 83*
Gilmore, James S. Jr. - Kalamazoo, MI - *Tel&CabFB 84S*
Gilmore Leather Products Inc. - Ward Hill, MA - *LitMarPl 83, 84*
Gilmour, Audrey C. - Morristown, NJ - *LitMarPl 83, 84; MagIndMarPl 82-83*
Gilpin, Peyton & Pierce Inc. - Orlando, FL - *StaDirAdAg 2-84*
Gilroy Dispatch - Gilroy, CA - *BaconPubCkNews 84*
Gilson International - Sherman Oaks, CA - *TelAl 84*
Giltronix Inc. - Palo Alto, CA - *MicrocomMPl 84; WhoWMicrocom 83*
Gimix Inc. - Chicago, IL - *MicrocomMPl 83, 84*
Gimli Women's Institute - Gimli, MB, Canada - *BoPubDir 4, 5*
Gingery Publishing, David J. - Springfield, MO - *BoPubDir 4, 5*
Ginia Music - New York, NY - *BillIntBG 83-84*
Giniger Co. Inc., The K. S. - New York, NY - *LitMarPl 83, 84; WritMar 84*
Ginkgo Hut - Lincroft, NJ - *BoPubDir 4, 5*
Ginn & Co. [Div. of Xerox Publishing Group] - Lexington, MA - *LitMarPl 83, 84; WritMar 84*
Ginn & Co. [Div. of Xerox Canada Inc.] - Scarborough, ON, Canada - *LitMarPl 83, 84*
Ginnie Mae Data Base [of Lloyd Bush & Associates] - New York, NY - *DataDirOnSer 84*
Ginnie Mae Data Base - *See* Government Securities Management System
Ginsburg, Michael - New York, NY - *MagIndMarPl 82-83*
Ginsburg, Theodore M. - Wynnewood, PA - *Ed&PubIntYB 82*
Ginseng Press - Franklin, NC - *LitMag&SmPr 83-84*
Giorno Poetry Systems Records - New York, NY - *LitMag&SmPr 83-84*
Gips & Balkind & Associates Inc. - New York, NY - *HBIndAd&MS 82-83*
Giraffics - Rolla, MO - *LitMarPl 83, 84*
Girard & Girard Creative Concepts - Canoga Park, CA - *IntDirMarRes 83*
Girard Cosmopolite-Herald [of Brown-Thompson Newspapers] - Girard, PA - *NewsDir 84*
Girard Cosmopolite Herald - *See* Brown Thompson Newspapers
Girard Gazette - Girard, IL - *BaconPubCkNews 84; Ed&PubIntYB 82*
Girard Home News - Philadelphia, PA - *AyerDirPub 83*
Girard News - Girard, OH - *Ed&PubIntYB 82*
Girard News [of Phoenix Publications Inc.] - Niles, OH - *AyerDirPub 83; NewsDir 84*
Girard News - *See* Phoenix Publications Inc.
Girard Press-News - Girard, KS - *BaconPubCkNews 84*
Girard Press, The - Girard, KS - *Ed&PubIntYB 82; NewsDir 84*
Girl Scout Leader - New York, NY - *BaconPubCkMag 84; MagDir 84; MagIndMarPl 82-83*
Girl Scouts of U.S.A. - New York, NY - *BoPubDir 4, 5*
Girling Wade Marketing Inc. - Toronto, ON, Canada - *BoPubDir 4, 5*
Girls Clubs of America - New York, NY - *BoPubDir 5*
Girvin, Conrad & Girvin - Rancho Cordova, CA - *StaDirAdAg 2-84*
Gish, Sherwood & Friends Inc. - Nashville, TN - *ArtMar 84; DirMarMP 83; StaDirAdAg 2-84*
Giusti, George - West Redding, CT - *LitMarPl 83, 84; MagIndMarPl 82-83*
Giustizia [of ILGWU] - New York, NY - *NewsDir 84*
Givaudan Advertising Inc. - New York, NY - *StaDirAdAg 2-84*
Giveaway - Scottsburg, IN - *AyerDirPub 83; Ed&PubIntYB 82; NewsDir 84*
Giving Music - Memphis, TN - *BillIntBG 83-84*
GK & A Advertising Inc. - Dallas, TX - *StaDirAdAg 2-84*
GKD Advertising - Oklahoma City, OK - *AdAge 3-28-84; StaDirAdAg 2-84*
GL Advertising & Public Relations - Woodland Hills, CA - *StaDirAdAg 2-84*
G.L. Studios - Calgary, AB, Canada - *BoPubDir 4, 5*
G.L.A. Press - Irving, TX - *BoPubDir 4, 5*
Glacier Inventory of Canada [of Environment Canada] - Ottawa, ON, Canada - *EISS 83*
Glacier Photo Index File [of Cooperative Institute for Research in Environmental Sciences] - Boulder, CO - *CompReadDB 82*
Glacier Reporter - Browning, MT - *AyerDirPub 83; Ed&PubIntYB 82*
Glacier State Telephone Co. [Aff. of Contel Service Corp.] - Anchorage, AK - *TelDir&BG 83-84*
Glaciology Data Base [of Cooperative Institute for Research in Environmental Sciences] - Boulder, CO - *CompReadDB 82*
Glad Hag Books - Washington, DC - *BoPubDir 4 Sup, 5*
Glad Hamp Music Inc. - New York, NY - *BillIntBG 83-84*
Glad Music Co. - Houston, TX - *BillIntBG 83-84*
Gladbrook Northern-Sun Print - Gladbrook, IA - *BaconPubCkNews 84*
Glade Spring Cablesystems [of American Cablesystems Corp.] - Glade Spring, VA - *Tel&CabFB 84C*
Glades County Democrat - Moore Haven, FL - *AyerDirPub 83; Ed&PubIntYB 82*
Gladewater Cable TV [of Texas Community Antennas Inc.] - Gladewater, TX - *BrCabYB 84*
Gladewater Mirror - Gladewater, TX - *BaconPubCkNews 84; Ed&PubIntYB 82; NewsDir 84*
Gladewater-White Oak Cable TV Inc. [of TCA Cable TV Group] - Gladewater, TX - *Tel&CabFB 84C*
Gladjack Music - *See* Ca-Song Music
Gladstone, Daniel - New York, NY - *LitMarPl 83; MagIndMarPl 82-83*

Gladstone Delta Reporter [of Menominee Publishing Co. Inc.] - Gladstone, MI - *BaconPubCkNews 84; NewsDir 84*
Gladstone Graphics Inc. - New York, NY - *LitMarPl 83; MagIndMarPl 82-83*
Gladstone, M. J. - New York, NY - *LitMarPl 83*
Gladstone-Norwood News - Chicago, IL - *AyerDirPub 83*
Gladwin County Record & Beaverton Clarion - Gladwin, MI - *AyerDirPub 83; BaconPubCkNews 84; Ed&PubIntYB 82; NewsDir 84*
Glamour [of Conde Nast] - New York, NY - *ArtMar 84; BaconPubCkMag 84; Folio 83; LitMarPl 83, 84; MagDir 84; MagIndMarPl 82-83; WritMar 84*
Glamourous Music Inc. - *See* Helios Music Corp.
Glandorf Telephone Co. Inc. - Glandorf, OH - *TelDir&BG 83-84*
Glankoff & Wishner Communications Ltd. - *See* Wishner Communications Ltd.
Glanmire Electronics Ltd. - Watergrasshill, Ireland - *MicrocomSwDir 1*
Glanville Publishers Inc. [of The Oceana Group] - Dobbs Ferry, NY - *LitMarPl 83, 84*
Glanze Word Books Associates, Walter - New York, NY - *LitMarPl 83, 84*
Glas Kanadskih Srba - Windsor, ON, Canada - *AyerDirPub 83; Ed&PubIntYB 82*
Glasco Sun - Glasco, KS - *BaconPubCkNews 84; Ed&PubIntYB 82*
Glaser, Anton - Southampton, PA - *BoPubDir 4, 5*
Glaser Inc., George - Los Altos, CA - *DirInfWP 82*
Glasford Gazette - *See* Gazette Printing Co.
Glasford Gazette, The - Glasford, IL - *Ed&PubIntYB 82*
Glasford Telephone Co. - Glasford, IL - *TelDir&BG 83-84*
Glasgow Cable TV System Inc. - Glasgow, KY - *BrCabYB 84*
Glasgow Cable TV System Inc. - Horse Cave, KY - *BrCabYB 84*
Glasgow Cablevision [of Daniels & Associates] - Glasgow, MT - *BrCabYB 84; Tel&CabFB 84C*
Glasgow Cablevision - Glasgow, VA - *Tel&CabFB 84C*
Glasgow Cablevision Inc. [of Tennessee-Kentucky Cable TV Co.] - Glasgow, KY - *Tel&CabFB 84C*
Glasgow Courier - Glasgow, MT - *BaconPubCkNews 84; Ed&PubIntYB 82; NewsDir 84*
Glasgow Daily Times - Glasgow, KY - *BaconPubCkNews 84*
Glasgow Missourian - Glasgow, MO - *BaconPubCkNews 84; Ed&PubIntYB 82*
Glasgow Republican - Glasgow, KY - *BaconPubCkNews 84; Ed&PubIntYB 82; NewsDir 84*
Glasgow Times - Glasgow, KY - *NewsDir 84*
Glasgow TV Cable Co. - Glasgow, VA - *BrCabYB 84*
Glasheen Advertising - New York, NY - *AdAge 3-28-84; StaDirAdAg 2-84*
Glass & Associates - Los Angeles, CA - *DirInfWP 82*
Glass Bell Press - Royal Oak, MI - *BoPubDir 5*
Glass Dealer, The [of National Glass Dealers Association] - Washington, DC - *MagDir 84*
Glass Dealer, The - McLean, VA - *BaconPubCkMag 84*
Glass Digest [of Ashlee Publishing Co. Inc.] - New York, NY - *ArtMar 84; BaconPubCkMag 84; MagDir 84; MagIndMarPl 82-83; WritMar 84*
Glass Industry [of Ashlee Publishing Co. Inc.] - New York, NY - *BaconPubCkMag 84; MagDir 84*
Glass Packaging Institute - Washington, DC - *BoPubDir 5*
Glass Records - New York, NY - *BillIntBG 83-84*
Glass Studio - Portland, OR - *WritMar 84*
Glass Workers News [of United Glass & Ceramic Workers of NA] - Columbus, OH - *NewsDir 84*
Glass Works Press - San Diego, CA - *BoPubDir 4, 5*
Glassbooks Inc. - Ozark, MO - *BoPubDir 4, 5*
Glassboro Enterprise - Blackwood, NJ - *NewsDir 84*
Glassboro Enterprise - *See* Cam-Glo Newspapers Inc.
Glassboro State College (Kronos Press) - Glassboro, NJ - *BoPubDir 4, 5*
Glasser, Howard T. - Assonet, MA - *LitMarPl 83, 84; MagIndMarPl 82-83*
Glasserfied Directory - Brooklyn, NY - *Ed&PubIntYB 82*
Glassman Advertising, Daniel - Fairfield, NJ - *AdAge 3-28-84; StaDirAdAg 2-84*
Glastonbury Citizen - Glastonbury, CT - *BaconPubCkNews 84; Ed&PubIntYB 82; NewsDir 84*
Glastonbury River East News Bulletin - Glastonbury, CT - *BaconPubCkNews 84*
Glatfelter Co., P. H. - Spring Grove, PA - *LitMarPl 83, 84*
Glattauer, Ned - New York, NY - *LitMarPl 83, 84; MagIndMarPl 82-83*
Glazer Associates Inc., Luanne - Stamford, CT - *IntDirMarRes 83*
Glazer, Malcolm I. - Albany, GA - *Tel&CabFB 84S*
Glazer Marketing, Monroe - Chicago, IL - *DirMarMP 83*
Glazer Stations, Malcolm I. - Rochester, NY - *BrCabYB 84*
Glazier Inc., Michael - Wilmington, DE - *LitMarPl 83, 84; MicroMarPl 82-83*
Glazier Publications - Seattle, WA - *LitMag&SmPr 83-84*
GLC Publishers Ltd. [Subs. of Silver Burdett Co.] - Agincourt, ON, Canada - *LitMarPl 83, 84*
GLC Research Library [of Greater London Council] - London, England - *InfIndMarPl 83*
G.L.C. TV Inc. [of TCI-Taft Cablevision Associates] - Petoskey, MI - *BrCabYB 84*
Gleaner - Northwood, ND - *AyerDirPub 83; Ed&PubIntYB 82*
Gleaner - Cannington, ON, Canada - *Ed&PubIntYB 82*
Gleaner - Huntingdon, PQ, Canada - *AyerDirPub 83*
Gleaner & Journal - Henderson, KY - *AyerDirPub 83*
Gleaner, The - Henderson, KY - *Ed&PubIntYB 82*
Gleanings in Bee Culture - Medina, OH - *BaconPubCkMag 84; MagDir 84; WritMar 84*
Gleason Associates - San Francisco, CA - *StaDirAdAg 2-84*
Gleason Inc., Harold V. - New York, NY - *DirPRFirms 83*
Gleason, Martha & Dennis - Boothbay Harbor, ME - *LitMarPl 83, 84; MagIndMarPl 82-83*
Gleason, Tom - *See* Galaxy Cablevision Inc.
Gleckler & Spiegel Advertising - New York, NY - *AdAge 3-28-84; StaDirAdAg 2-84*
Gleckner, Dorothy S. - Paramus, NJ - *DirInfWP 82*
Glen Allan Telephone Co. - Glen Allan, MS - *TelDir&BG 83-84*
Glen-Bartlett Publishing Co. - Westboro, MA - *BoPubDir 4, 5*
Glen Burnie Maryland Gazette - Glen Burnie, MD - *BaconPubCkNews 84; NewsDir 84*
Glen Cove Guardian - Glen Cove, NY - *AyerDirPub 83; BaconPubCkNews 84; Ed&PubIntYB 82*
Glen Cove Guardian [of Oyster Bay-Syosset Guardian] - Oyster Bay, NY - *NewsDir 84*
Glen Cove Pennysaver - Huntington, NY - *AyerDirPub 83*
Glen Cove Record Pilot [of Community Newspapers Inc.] - Glen Cove, NY - *Ed&PubIntYB 82; NewsDir 84*
Glen Cove Record Pilot - *See* Community Newspapers Inc.
Glen Cove-Sea Cliff Guardian - Glen Cove, NY - *Ed&PubIntYB 82*
Glen Eagle Music - Garden City, NY - *BillIntBG 83-84*
Glen Ellyn News - Glen Ellyn, IL - *Ed&PubIntYB 82; NewsDir 84*
Glen Ellyn News - *See* Glen News Printing Co.
Glen Ellyn Times Press [of Elmhurst Press Publications] - Elmhurst, IL - *AyerDirPub 83; NewsDir 84*
Glen Ellyn Times-Press - Glen Ellyn, IL - *Ed&PubIntYB 82*
Glen Ellyn Times-Press - *See* Preee Publications
Glen Glenn Sound Co. [Div. of Republic Corp.] - Hollywood, CA - *TelAl 83*
Glen L. Marine Designs - Bellflower, CA - *BoPubDir 4, 5*
Glen Lake Cable TV [of Booth American Co.] - Empire, MI - *BrCabYB 84*
Glen News Printing Co. - Glen Ellyn, IL - *BaconPubCkNews 84*
Glen Press - Berkeley, CA - *BoPubDir 4 Sup, 5*
Glen Ridge Paper - Glen Ridge, NJ - *AyerDirPub 83; Ed&PubIntYB 82*
Glen Ridge Paper - *See* Worrall Publications
Glen Ridge Paper, The [of Worrall Publishing Co.] - Bloomfield, NJ - *NewsDir 84*
Glen Rose Reporter - Glen Rose, TX - *BaconPubCkNews 84; Ed&PubIntYB 82; NewsDir 84*
Glen Ullin Times - Glen Ullin, ND - *BaconPubCkNews 84; Ed&PubIntYB 82*
Glen Views - Glenview, IL - *AyerDirPub 83*
Glenar Studios - Burbank, CA - *TelAl 83, 84*
Glenbow Museum - Calgary, AB, Canada - *BoPubDir 4, 5; LitMarPl 83*
Glenburn Cable TV - Grand Forks, ND - *BrCabYB 84*
Glenburn Cable TV Inc. - Glenburn, ND - *Tel&CabFB 84C*

Glencoe-Alvinston Transcript & Free Press - Glencoe, ON, Canada - *AyerDirPub 83*
Glencoe Cablevision - Glencoe, MN - *Tel&CabFB 84C*
Glencoe Enterprise - Glencoe, MN - *BaconPubCkNews 84; Ed&PubIntYB 82; NewsDir 84*
Glencoe Mail-Advertiser - Glencoe, IL - *Ed&PubIntYB 82*
Glencoe Mail-Advertiser - *See* Singer Printing & Publishing Co.
Glencoe News - Glencoe, IL - *Ed&PubIntYB 82*
Glencoe News - Glendale Heights, IL - *AyerDirPub 83*
Glencoe News [of Pioneer Press Inc.] - Wilmette, IL - *NewsDir 84*
Glencoe News - *See* Pioneer Press Inc.
Glencoe News Advertiser - Highland Park, IL - *AyerDirPub 83*
Glencoe Publishing Co. Inc. [Aff. of Macmillan Publishing Co. Inc.] - Encino, CA - *LitMarPl 83, 84*
Glendale Adventist Medical Center - Glendale, CA - *BoPubDir 4*
Glendale Cablesystems Corp. [of American Cablesystems Corp.] - Cameron, WV - *Tel&CabFB 84C*
Glendale Cablesystems Corp. [of American Cablesystems Corp.] - Glen Dale, WV - *BrCabYB 84*
Glendale Cablesystems Corp. [of American Cablesystems Corp.] - Glendale, WV - *Tel&CabFB 84C*
Glendale Heights Examiner - *See* Examiner Newspapers
Glendale Heights Examiner, The - Glendale Heights, IL - *Ed&PubIntYB 82*
Glendale Heights Press [of Press Publications] - Elmhurst, IL - *AyerDirPub 83; NewsDir 84*
Glendale Heights Press - Glendale Heights, IL - *Ed&PubIntYB 82*
Glendale Heights Press - *See* Press Publications
Glendale Heights Star - Glendale Heights, IL - *Ed&PubIntYB 82*
Glendale Heights Voice - *See* Voice Newspapers
Glendale Herald - Glendale, WI - *Ed&PubIntYB 82*
Glendale Herald - Oak Creek, WI - *AyerDirPub 83*
Glendale Herald - *See* Community Newspapers Inc.
Glendale News Press - Glendale, CA - *BaconPubCkNews 84; Ed&PubIntYB 82; NewsDir 84*
Glendale Newspapers Inc. - *See* Ingersoll Publications Co.
Glendale Register - Flushing, NY - *AyerDirPub 83*
Glendale Register - Glendale, NY - *Ed&PubIntYB 82*
Glendale Register - *See* Conglor Publishing Inc.
Glendale Star - Glendale, AZ - *BaconPubCkNews 84; Ed&PubIntYB 82*
Glendale Tallyho - Glendale, AZ - *BaconPubCkNews 84*
Glendinning Associates - Westport, CT - *HBIndAd&MS 82-83*
Glendive Cable TV [of Community Tele-Communications Inc.] - Glendive, MT - *BrCabYB 84; Tel&CabFB 84C*
Glendive Ranger Review - Glendive, MT - *BaconPubCkNews 84; Ed&PubIntYB 82; NewsDir 84*
Glendora Press - Azusa, CA - *AyerDirPub 83*
Glendora Press - Glendora, CA - *Ed&PubIntYB 82*
Glendosa Research Centre - Minnedosa, MB, Canada - *BoPubDir 4, 5*
Glengarry News - Alexandria, ON, Canada - *AyerDirPub 83; Ed&PubIntYB 82*
Glenhurst Publications Inc. - St. Louis Park, MN - *LitMag&SmPr 83-84*
Gleniffer Press - Castlehead, Scotland - *LitMag&SmPr 83-84*
Glenmar Associates Inc. - Philadelphia, PA - *StaDirAdAg 2-84*
Glenmary Research Center [Aff. of Glenmary Missioners] - Atlanta, GA - *BoPubDir 4, 5*
Glenmont Cable TV - Glenmont, OH - *BrCabYB 84; Tel&CabFB 84C*
Glenn Associates - Westfield, NJ - *LitMarPl 83, 84; MagIndMarPl 82-83*
Glenn/Cliff Associates - Scottsdale, AZ - *MicrocomMPl 84*
Glenn Productions & Promotions Inc. - New York, NY - *BillIntBG 83-84*
Glenn Publications Ltd., Peter - New York, NY - *LitMarPl 83, 84*
Glenn Sound Co., Glen [Div. of Republic Corp.] - Hollywood, CA - *AvMarPl 83; TelAl 84*
Glenns Ferry Pilot - Glenns Ferry, ID - *Ed&PubIntYB 82*
Glennville Sentinel - Glennville, GA - *BaconPubCkNews 84; Ed&PubIntYB 82*
Glenrock Independent - Glenrock, WY - *BaconPubCkNews 84; Ed&PubIntYB 82*
Glens Falls Post-Star [of Glens Falls Newspapers Inc.] - Glens Falls, NY - *BaconPubCkNews 84; NewsDir 84*
Glenside News - Glenside, PA - *Ed&PubIntYB 82*
Glenside News [of Montgomery Publishing Co.] - Jenkintown, PA - *NewsDir 84*
Glenside News - *See* Montgomery Publishing Co.
GlenTan Music - *See* Campbell Music Inc., Glen
Glenview Announcements - Glenview, IL - *Ed&PubIntYB 82*
Glenview Announcements [of Pioneer Press Inc.] - Wilmette, IL - *AyerDirPub 83; NewsDir 84*
Glenview Announcements - *See* Pioneer Press Inc.
Glenview Glenviews [of Lakeland Publishers Inc.] - Grayslake, IL - *NewsDir 84*
Glenview Glenviews - *See* Lakeland Publishers Inc.
Glenview Life - Deerfield, IL - *AyerDirPub 83*
Glenview Life - Glenview, IL - *Ed&PubIntYB 82*
Glenview Life - *See* Lerner Life Newspapers
Glenview News Advertiser - Highland Park, IL - *AyerDirPub 83*
Glenview Times & News-Advertiser - Glenview, IL - *Ed&PubIntYB 82*
Glenview Times & News-Advertiser - *See* Singer Printing & Publishing
Glenville Cablesystems Corp. [of American Cablesystems Corp.] - Glenville, NY - *BrCabYB 84*
Glenville Democrat - Glenville, WV - *Ed&PubIntYB 82; NewsDir 84*
Glenville Democrat - *See* Glenville Democrat Publishing Inc.
Glenville Democrat Publishing Inc. - Glenville, WV - *BaconPubCkNews 84*
Glenville Pathfinder [of Glenville Gilmer Graphics Inc.] - Glenville, WV - *Ed&PubIntYB 82; NewsDir 84*
Glenville Pathfinder - *See* Glenville Democrat Publishing Inc.
Glenwood Cable TV [of TCA Cable TV Inc.] - Glenwood, AR - *Tel&CabFB 84C*
Glenwood Cable TV [of Community Tele-Communications Inc.] - Glenwood Springs, CO - *BrCabYB 84; Tel&CabFB 84C*
Glenwood City Tribune - Glenwood City, WI - *BaconPubCkNews 84*
Glenwood Herald - Glenwood, AR - *AyerDirPub 83; BaconPubCkNews 84; Ed&PubIntYB 82*
Glenwood Music - *See* Windham Hill Music
Glenwood Opinion Tribune - Glenwood, IA - *BaconPubCkNews 84; NewsDir 84*
Glenwood Pope County Tribune - Glenwood, MN - *BaconPubCkNews 84; NewsDir 84*
Glenwood Post - Glenwood Springs, CO - *AyerDirPub 83; BaconPubCkNews 84; Ed&PubIntYB 82; NewsDir 84*
Glenwood Springs Weekly - Glenwood Springs, CO - *BaconPubCkNews 84*
Glenwood Telephone Co. of the Southeast - Glenwood, GA - *TelDir&BG 83-84*
Glenwood Telephone Membership Corp., The - Blue Hill, NE - *TelDir&BG 83-84*
Glenwood-Thornton Economist [of Chicago Daily Southtown Economist Newspapers] - Chicago, IL - *NewsDir 84*
Glenwood-Thornton Pointer Economist - South Holland, IL - *AyerDirPub 83*
Glenwood/Thornton Pointer-Economist - *See* Pointer-Economist Newspapers
Glick & Lorwin Inc. - New York, NY - *DirPRFirms 83*
Glickman Research Associates Inc. - Roslyn Heights, NY - *IntDirMarRes 83*
Glidden Cable TV Inc. - Glidden, WI - *BrCabYB 84*
Glidden Enterprise - Glidden, WI - *BaconPubCkNews 84; Ed&PubIntYB 82*
Glidden Graphic - Glidden, IA - *BaconPubCkNews 84; Ed&PubIntYB 82*
Glider Rider Magazine - Chattanooga, TN - *BaconPubCkMag 84*
Glimpse & Co., Warren - Alexandria, VA - *EISS 83*
Glimpses of Micronesia - Agana, GU - *WritMar 84*
Glisson Inc., John L. - Richmond, VA - *AvMarPl 83*
Global Cable TV - Lancaster, NY - *BrCabYB 84*
Global Cable TV of Orchard Park - Orchard Park, NY - *Tel&CabFB 84C*
Global Church Growth Book Club [Div. of The William Carey Library] - Pasadena, CA - *LitMarPl 84*
Global Communications - Englewood, CO - *BaconPubCkMag 84*

Global Communications Ltd. - Don Mills, ON, Canada - *BrCabYB 84*
Global Computer Supplies [Div. of Global Equipment Co.] - Hempstead, NY - *MicrocomMPl 84*
Global Data Corp. (Midwest Div.) - Harvey, IL - *ADAPSOMemDir 83-84*
Global Digest Inc. - New Haven, CT - *LitMarPl 84*
Global Digest Inc. - Falls Church, VA - *Ed&PubIntYB 82*
Global Engineering Documentation Services Inc. - Santa Ana, CA - *FBInfSer 80*
Global Engineering Documents [Aff. of Information Handling Services] - Santa Ana, CA - *BoPubDir 4, 5; EISS 83*
Global Engineering Documents (Information Handling Services) - Santa Ana, CA - *InfIndMarPl 83*
Global Finance Information - New York, NY - *DirOnDB Spring 84*
Global Information Services Inc. - Flushing, NY - *EISS 83; TeleSy&SerDir 2-84*
Global Lending & Overseas Banking Evaluator [of Chase Econometrics/Interactive Data Corp.] - Waltham, MA - *DataDirOnSer 84*
Global Library Marketing Services Inc. [Subs. of Yankee Book Peddler Inc.] - Contoocook, NH - *LitMarPl 83, 84*
Global Oral Data Bank [of World Health Organization] - Geneva, Switzerland - *EISS 83*
Global Parameters - Brooklyn, NY - *WhoWMicrocom 83*
Global Press - Hollywood, CA - *Ed&PubIntYB 82*
Global Press - Denver, CO - *BoPubDir 5; LitMag&SmPr 83-84*
Global Publications - Milwaukee, WI - *BoPubDir 4, 5*
Global Sciences Corp. - New York, NY - *ADAPSOMemDir 83-84*
Global Software Inc. - Raleigh, NC - *ADAPSOMemDir 83-84*
Global Syndication & Literary Agency Ltd. - Fullerton, CA - *Ed&PubIntYB 82*
Global Tapestry Journal [of BB Books] - Blackburn, England - *LitMag&SmPr 83-84*
Global Television Network - Don Mills, ON, Canada - *BrCabYB 84*
Global Video Communications Corp. - Orlando, FL - *Tel&CabFB 84C*
Global Vision Corp. - Hollywood, CA - *Tel&CabFB 84C*
Globe [of Globe International Inc.] - West Palm Beach, FL - *Folio 83; WritMar 84*
Globe - Port Byron, IL - *AyerDirPub 83; Ed&PubIntYB 82*
Globe - Atchison, KS - *AyerDirPub 83*
Globe - Dodge City, KS - *AyerDirPub 83*
Globe - Boston, MA - *AyerDirPub 83*
Globe - Wayland, MI - *AyerDirPub 83*
Globe - Joplin, MO - *AyerDirPub 83*
Globe - Shelby, OH - *AyerDirPub 83*
Globe - Bala Cynwyd, PA - *DirOnDB Spring 84*
Globe - New Wilmington, PA - *AyerDirPub 83*
Globe - Corsica, SD - *AyerDirPub 83*
Globe - Lacombe, AB, Canada - *AyerDirPub 83*
Globe Advertising - Mt. Clemens, MI - *ArtMar 84*
Globe-Advocate - Houston, TX - *Ed&PubIntYB 82*
Globe & Mail - Toronto, ON, Canada - *AyerDirPub 83; BaconPubCkNews 84; Ed&PubIntYB 82; LitMarPl 83, 84*
Globe & Mail Database [of Info Globe] - Toronto, ON, Canada - *CompReadDB 82; DataDirOnSer 84*
Globe & Mail Online - Toronto, ON, Canada - *DirOnDB Spring 84*
Globe & Mail Report on Business, The - Toronto, ON, Canada - *Ed&PubIntYB 82*
Globe Arizona Silver Belt [of Copper Belt Printing & Publishing Co.] - Globe, AZ - *BaconPubCkNews 84; NewsDir 84*
Globe Book Co. Inc. [Subs. of Esquire Inc.] - New York, NY - *LitMarPl 83, 84*
Globe-Democrat - St. Louis, MO - *AyerDirPub 83*
Globe-Free Press, The - Grand Junction, IA - *Ed&PubIntYB 82*
Globe-Gazette - Mason City, IA - *AyerDirPub 83; Ed&PubIntYB 82*
Globe Mackay Cable & Radio Corp. - Manila, Philippines - *TeleSy&SerDir 2-84*
Globe Mail Agency - New York, NY - *MagIndMarPl 82-83*
Globe Mini Mags - West Palm Beach, FL - *WritMar 84*
Globe Music Corp. - Hollywood, CA - *Tel&CabFB 84C*
Globe-News - Auburn, WA - *AyerDirPub 83*
Globe Pequot Press Inc., The - Chester, CT - *LitMag&SmPr 83-84; LitMarPl 83, 84; WritMar 84*
Globe Photos Inc. - New York, NY - *AvMarPl 83; Ed&PubIntYB 82; LitMarPl 83, 84; MagIndMarPl 82-83*
Globe Press International - New York, NY - *Ed&PubIntYB 82*
Globe Recording Studio - Nashville, TN - *AvMarPl 83*
Globe Research Corp. - Melville, NY - *IntDirMarRes 83*
Globe Syndicate - Strasburg, VA - *Ed&PubIntYB 82; LitMarPl 84*
Globe, The - Huntingdon Valley, PA - *AyerDirPub 83; Ed&PubIntYB 82*
Globe, The [of Montgomery Publishing Co.] - Jenkintown, PA - *NewsDir 84*
Globe Ticket Co. - Horsham, PA - *DataDirSup 7-83*
Globe-Times - Bethlehem, PA - *AyerDirPub 83; Ed&PubIntYB 82*
Globe-Times - Amarillo, TX - *AyerDirPub 83*
Globedat Switched Data Service [of Teleglobe Canada] - Montreal, PQ, Canada - *TeleSy&SerDir 7-83*
Globedata [of The New York Times Information Services Inc.] - Parsippany, NJ - *CompReadDB 82; DataDirOnSer 84; EISS 83*
Globetrotter - Redlands, CA - *AyerDirPub 83*
Globus Advertising, L. J. - Los Angeles, CA - *StaDirAdAg 2-84*
Glockner, E. L. - Dalton, GA - *Tel&CabFB 84C p.1681*
Glolite Publishing Co. - Memphis, TN - *BillIntBG 83-84*
Glolite Records - Memphis, TN - *BillIntBG 83-84*
Glori Gospel Music - Belmore, NY - *BillIntBG 83-84*
Glory Patri Publishers - Lexington, KY - *BoPubDir 5; LitMag&SmPr 83-84*
GlorySound - *See* Shawnee Press Inc.
Glos Ludowy - Detroit, MI - *Ed&PubIntYB 82; NewsDir 84*
Glos Narodu - Jamesburg, NJ - *Ed&PubIntYB 82*
Glos Polski-Gazeta Polska - Toronto, ON, Canada - *Ed&PubIntYB 82*
Gloster Wilk-Amite Record - Gloster, MS - *BaconPubCkNews 84*
Glot - Cinnaminson, NJ - *LitMag&SmPr 83-84*
Gloucester Cablevision [of First Commonwealth Communications Inc.] - Gloucester, VA - *BrCabYB 84; Tel&CabFB 84C*
Gloucester City News - Gloucester City, NJ - *Ed&PubIntYB 82; NewsDir 84*
Gloucester City News - *See* Gloucester City News Publishers
Gloucester City News Publishers - Gloucester, NJ - *BaconPubCkNews 84*
Gloucester City Tele-Communications Inc. - Gloucester, NJ - *Tel&CabFB 84C*
Gloucester Computer Co. Inc. - Glouchester, MA - *MicrocomMPl 84*
Gloucester County Sentinel - Franklinville, NJ - *AyerDirPub 83*
Gloucester County Times - Woodbury, NJ - *AyerDirPub 83; BaconPubCkNews 84; Ed&PubIntYB 82*
Gloucester Daily Times [of Essex County Newspapers Inc.] - Gloucester, MA - *BaconPubCkNews 84; NewsDir 84*
Gloucester-Mathews Gazette-Journal [of Tidewater Newspapers Inc.] - Gloucester, VA - *AyerDirPub 83; BaconPubCkNews 84; Ed&PubIntYB 82; NewsDir 84*
Glouchester Press - Fairmont, WV - *BoPubDir 4, 5*
Gloversville Leader-Herald - Gloversville, NY - *NewsDir 84*
Glovertown Cable TV - Glovertown, NF, Canada - *BrCabYB 84*
Glue Fast Equipment Co. Inc. - Carlstadt, NJ - *LitMarPl 83, 84*
Gluten Co. Inc. - Provo, UT - *BoPubDir 4, 5*
Gluxlit Press - Redlands, CA - *BoPubDir 4, 5*
Glyn Group Inc., The - New York, NY - *AvMarPl 83*
Glynn Publicity & Public Relations Inc., Diane - New York, NY - *LitMarPl 83, 84*
Glyphic Press - Morgantown, WV - *BoPubDir 4, 5*
G.M. Communications - New York, NY - *StaDirAdAg 2-84*
GM Dubois Corp. - *See* BBDO International Inc.
GM Enterprises - Roselle, IL - *MicrocomMPl 84*
GMA Audio/Visual Inc. - St. Charles, IL - *AvMarPl 83*
GMA Research Corp. - Bellevue, WA - *IntDirMarRes 83*
GMA Software - Chicago, IL - *WhoWMicrocom 83*
Gmelin Institute for Inorganic Chemistry & Related Fields - Frankfurt, West Germany - *EISS 83*
GMG Publishing - New York, NY - *ArtMar 84; LitMarPl 83, 84; WritMar 84*
GMI Publications - Jacksonville, FL - *BoPubDir 4, 5*
GML Corp. - Lexington, MA - *BoPubDir 5; CompReadDB 82*
GML Information Services [of GML Corp.] - Lexington, MA - *DirOnDB Spring 84; EISS 83*

GMS Software - Baltimore, MD - *MicrocomMPl 83, 84*
GMS Systems Inc. - New York, NY - *ADAPSOMemDir 83-84; DataDirOnSer 84; EISS 7-83 Sup*
Gnam Consultation Corp., Rene - Clearwater, FL - *LitMarPl 83, 84; MagIndMarPl 82-83*
Gnam Consultation Corp., Rene - *See* Response Group Inc.
GNAT Computers Inc. - San Diego, CA - *MicrocomMPl 83*
Gnau, Carter, Jacobsen & Associates Inc. - Washington, DC - *DirPRFirms 83*
Gneiss Books - Spring Grove, PA - *BoPubDir 4 Sup, 5*
GNMAX [of Control Data Corp.] - Greenwich, CT - *DataDirOnSer 84*
Gnome Baker [of Tongue Press] - Great River, NY - *LitMag&SmPr 83-84*
Gnomon Press - Frankfort, KY - *LitMarPl 83, 84*
Gnosis - Philadelphia, PA - *MicrocomMPl 83, 84; MicrocomSwDir 1*
GNP Crescendo Records - Los Angeles, CA - *BillIntBG 83-84*
Go - Charlotte, NC - *BaconPubCkMag 84; MagDir 84*
G.O. Enterprises Inc. [of United Broadcasting Co.] - Bradford, VT - *BrCabYB 84; Tel&CabFB 84C*
G.O. Enterprises Inc. [of United Broadcasting Co.] - Chelsea, VT - *Tel&CabFB 84C*
G.O. Enterprises Inc. [of United Cable Co.] - South Royalton, VT - *BrCabYB 84; Tel&CabFB 84C*
GO Graphics Inc. - Lexington, MA - *DirInfWP 82*
Go Greyhound [of The Greyhound Corp.] - Phoenix, AZ - *WritMar 84*
GO Radio Inc. - Webster City, IA - *BrCabYB 84*
Go: The Authentic Guide to New Orleans - New Orleans, LA - *MagDir 84; MagIndMarPl 82-83*
Go West - Burlingame, CA - *BaconPubCkMag 84; MagDir 84; WritMar 84*
Goal Productions - Alta Dena, CA - *ArtMar 84*
Goal Productions - Pasadena, CA - *AvMarPl 83*
Goal Systems International Inc. - Columbus, OH - *DataDirSup 7-83*
Gobbles - St. Paul, MN - *BaconPubCkMag 84; MagDir 84*
Gober Advance Inc. - Albuquerque, NM - *BrCabYB 84*
Goble & Associates - Chicago, IL - *AdAge 3-28-84; StaDirAdAg 2-84*
Goblen, Peter - Davis, CA - *BoPubDir 4, 5*
Gobles News - Gobles, MI - *BaconPubCkNews 84; Ed&PubIntYB 82*
Goblets [of 22 Press] - Wilmington, DE - *LitMag&SmPr 83-84*
GOCI Software - Edina, MN - *MicrocomMPl 83*
Goddard, Jane Bennett - Grafton, ON, Canada - *BoPubDir 4 Sup, 5*
Goddard, Ragna Tischler - Higganum, CT - *LitMarPl 83, 84; MagIndMarPl 82-83*
Goddard, Tom - Higganum, CT - *LitMarPl 83, 84; MagIndMarPl 82-83*
Goddard West Sedgwick County News-Sentinel - Goddard, KS - *BaconPubCkNews 84*
Goderich Signal-Star, The - Goderich, ON, Canada - *Ed&PubIntYB 82*
Godfrey Advertising - Lancaster, PA - *StaDirAdAg 2-84*
Godfrey Memorial Library - Middletown, CT - *LitMarPl 83, 84; MagIndMarPl 82-83; MicroMarPl 82-83*
Godine Publisher Inc., David R. - Boston, MA - *LitMarPl 83, 84*
God's World - *See* Johnson, Stephen Enoch
Godson Publishing, David - Caledon, ON, Canada - *BoPubDir 4, 5*
Godwin Advertising Agency Inc. - Jackson, MS - *StaDirAdAg 2-84*
Godwin Music - *See* Briarmeade Music Unltd.
Goehringer & Sons Associates - Pittsburgh, PA - *BoPubDir 4, 5*
Goetz Broadcasting Corp. - Marshfield, WI - *BrCabYB 84*
Goff Communications - Corning, NY - *AdAge 3-28-84; DirPRFirms 83; StaDirAdAg 2-84*
Goffstown News - Goffstown, NH - *BaconPubCkNews 84; Ed&PubIntYB 82*
Goggin & Associates - San Diego, CA - *DirPRFirms 83*
Golconda Herald-Enterprise - Golconda, IL - *BaconPubCkNews 84*
Gold Beach Cable TV Associates [of Northland Communications Corp.] - Gold Beach, OR - *Tel&CabFB 84C*
Gold Beach Curry County Reporter - Gold Beach, OR - *BaconPubCkNews 84; NewsDir 84*
Gold Circle Productions - Nevada City, CA - *BoPubDir 5*
Gold Coast Entertainment - Lincolnwood, IL - *BillIntBG 83-84*
Gold Coast Life - Ft. Lauderdale, FL - *ArtMar 84; BaconPubCkMag 84*
Gold Coast of Florida - Ft. Lauderdale, FL - *MagDir 84*
Gold Co., H. J. - New York, NY - *StaDirAdAg 2-84*
Gold Corp., David E. - San Jose, CA - *ADAPSOMemDir 83-84*
Gold Crest Publishing - Deerfield, IL - *BoPubDir 5; LitMag&SmPr 83-84*
Gold Crest Publishing [Subs. of Children's World of Wilkes Inc.] - North Wilkesboro, NC - *BoPubDir 4; DirMarMP 83*
Gold Disk Quality Microwave of America - Glen Arm, MD - *MicrocomMPl 84*
Gold Dust Records - Strausstown, PA - *BillIntBG 83-84*
Gold Enterprises, Melvin L. - New York, NY - *TelAl 83, 84*
Gold Guitar Records - Beaumont, TX - *BillIntBG 83-84*
Gold, Hadassah - New York, NY - *LitMarPl 83, 84; MagIndMarPl 82-83*
Gold Hill Music Inc. - North Hollyood, CA - *BillIntBG 83-84*
Gold Key Entertainment - Hollywood, CA - *TelAl 84; Tel&CabFB 84C*
Gold Key Entertainment [Div. of Vidtronics Co. Inc.] - New York, NY - *TelAl 83*
Gold Leaf Farmer - Wendell, NC - *AyerDirPub 83; Ed&PubIntYB 82*
Gold Leaf, The - Hahira, GA - *Ed&PubIntYB 82*
Gold Music, Eugene [Div. of 3'G Industries] - Kansas City, MO - *BillIntBG 83-84*
Gold Music Publisher, Manny - Brooklyn, NY - *BillIntBG 83-84*
Gold Penny Press - Canoga Park, CA - *LitMarPl 83*
Gold Productions Inc., Jeff - New York, NY - *Tel&CabFB 84C*
Gold Records - Stevens Point, WI - *BillIntBG 83-84*
Gold Rush - Cripple Creek, CO - *Ed&PubIntYB 82*
Gold Seal Stations - *See* Hubbard Broadcasting Inc.
Gold Sheet Technical Report [of NewsNet Inc.] - Bryn Mawr, PA - *DataDirOnSer 84*
Gold Sheet Technical Report - Redmond, WA - *DirOnDB Spring 84*
Gold Sovereign Music - *See* Ahlert Music Corp., Fred
Gold Star News - Deerfield Beach, FL - *Ed&PubIntYB 82*
Gold Star Publications - Sioux Falls, SD - *BoPubDir 5*
Gold Street Music Co. - Kirbyville, TX - *BillIntBG 83-84*
Goldband Recording Studio - Lake Charles, LA - *BillIntBG 83-84*
Goldberg Advertising Ltd. - Auckland, New Zealand - *StaDirAdAg 2-84*
Goldberg & Associates, Lynn C. - New York, NY - *LitMarPl 84*
Goldberg Brothers [Subs. of J & R Film Co. Inc.] - Hollywood, CA - *AvMarPl 83*
Goldberg Inc., Melvin A. - Great Neck, NY - *BrCabYB 84*
Goldberg, James M. - Washington, DC - *BoPubDir 4, 5*
Goldberg Literary Agents Inc., Lucianne - New York, NY - *LitMarPl 83, 84*
Goldberg, Lynn C. - New York, NY - *LitMarPl 83*
Goldberg/Marchesano & Associates Inc. - Washington, DC - *StaDirAdAg 2-84*
Goldberg Public Relations Co., Manny - Boston, MA - *DirPRFirms 83*
Goldberg Public Relations Counsel, Gerald M. - New York, NY - *DirPRFirms 83*
Goldberger/Uniphoto, Edward - St. Louis, MO - *AvMarPl 83*
Golde Music, Franne - *See* MizMo Enterprises
Golden Advertiser [of Golden Jeffco Publications Inc.] - Golden, CO - *NewsDir 84*
Golden Advertising & Public Relations, William F. - Stockton, CA - *StaDirAdAg 2-84*
Golden Age Living - Ft. Lauderdale, FL - *AyerDirPub 83*
Golden & Associates Inc., Joyce - New York, NY - *StaDirAdAg 2-84*
Golden Bell Press - Denver, CO - *BoPubDir 4 Sup, 5*
Golden Belt Telephone Association - Rush Center, KS - *TelDir&BG 83-84*
Golden Books [of Western Publishing Co. Inc.] - New York, NY - *WritMar 84*
Golden Bridge Music - *See* Gant Enterprises, Don
Golden Bridle Research - Doylestown, PA - *EISS 7-83 Sup*

Golden Coast Publishing Co. - Savannah, GA - *BoPubDir 4, 5*
Golden Colorado Transcript - Golden, CO - *BaconPubCkNews 84*
Golden Crest Records Inc. - Huntington Station, NY - *BillIntBG 83-84*
Golden Dawn Music - Taylor, MI - *BillIntBG 83-84*
Golden Dog Press - Ottawa, ON, Canada - *BoPubDir 4, 5*
Golden Dome Productions - South Bend, IN - *TeleSy&SerDir 2-84*
Golden East Broadcasting Corp. - Hampton, VA - *BrCabYB 84*
Golden Egg Music Inc. - *See* Kaplan Productions Inc., A.
Golden Evening Star - Golden, CO - *BaconPubCkNews 84*
Golden Fleece Music Publishing Co. - Philadelphia, PA - *BillIntBG 83-84*
Golden Gate Features - Kentfield, CA - *Ed&PubIntYB 82*
Golden Gate Systems - Honolulu, HI - *WhoWMicrocom 83*
Golden Gater [of San Francisco State University] - San Francisco, CA - *NewsDir 84*
Golden Glow Publishing - Sturgeon Bay, WI - *BoPubDir 4, 5*
Golden Grain - Shelbyville, MI - *BoPubDir 4, 5*
Golden Guitar Music Publishing - Tucson, AZ - *BillIntBG 83-84*
Golden Hills Cablevision [of Western Savings & Loan Association] - East Mesa, AZ - *Tel&CabFB 84C*
Golden Hills Cablevision - Leisure World, AZ - *BrCabYB 84*
Golden Horizon Music Corp. - Burbank, CA - *BillIntBG 83-84*
Golden Image Motion Picture Corp. - Los Angeles, CA - *WritMar 84*
Golden, Jim - Steamboat Springs, CO - *Tel&CabFB 84C p.1681*
Golden Keys Success Seminar Inc. - Salt Lake City, UT - *BoPubDir 5*
Golden-Lee Book Distributors Inc. - Brooklyn, NY - *LitMarPl 83, 84*
Golden Light Press - Miller Place, NY - *BoPubDir 4 Sup, 5*
Golden Lodge News - Canton, OH - *NewsDir 84*
Golden Moon Records - Mooresville, IN - *BillIntBG 83-84*
Golden New Era - *See* Taylor Publishing Co.
Golden Nugget - Hempstead, TX - *AyerDirPub 83*
Golden Outlook [of Jeffco Publications] - Golden, CO - *NewsDir 84*
Golden Outlook - *See* Jeffco Publications
Golden Owl Publishers Inc. - Lexington Park, MD - *BoPubDir 4, 5*
Golden Pacific Group, The - San Jose, CA - *BrCabYB 84*
Golden Peso - Compton, CA - *Tel&CabFB 84C*
Golden Prairie News - Assumption, IL - *AyerDirPub 83; Ed&PubIntYB 82*
Golden Publishing Shopper's Guide - Lake Park, FL - *AyerDirPub 83*
Golden Puffer Press - Tucson, AZ - *BoPubDir 5*
Golden Pyramid Records - Fanwood, NJ - *BillIntBG 83-84*
Golden Quill Press, The - Francestown, NH - *LitMarPl 83, 84; WritMar 84*
Golden Quill Publishers Inc. - Colton, CA - *BoPubDir 4, 5*
Golden Rule Records Inc. - Memphis, TN - *BillIntBG 83-84*
Golden Sails Press - Birmingham, AL - *LitMag&SmPr 83-84*
Golden, Sandra N. - Teaneck, NJ - *IntDirMarRes 83*
Golden Scepter Press - Lancaster, NH - *BoPubDir 4, 5*
Golden Seal Research Headquarters - Hollywood, CA - *BoPubDir 4, 5*
Golden Southwest Inc. - Johnson City, KS - *BrCabYB 84*
Golden Southwest Inc. - Ulysses, KS - *BrCabYB 84; Tel&CabFB 84C p.1681*
Golden Spread Cablevision - Groom, TX - *Tel&CabFB 84C*
Golden Spread Cablevision - LeFors, TX - *Tel&CabFB 84C*
Golden State Recorders - San Francisco, CA - *AvMarPl 83*
Golden Television Ltd. - Golden, BC, Canada - *BrCabYB 84*
Golden Torch Music - *See* Golden Horizon Music Corp.
Golden Touch Enterprises - West Palm Beach, FL - *BoPubDir 4, 5*
Golden Triangle Communications - Denton, TX - *BrCabYB 84; Tel&CabFB 84C*
Golden TV - Los Angeles, CA - *Tel&CabFB 84C*
Golden Unltd. Music - *See* Schroeder International Ltd., A.
Golden Valley News - Beach, ND - *AyerDirPub 83; BaconPubCkNews 84; Ed&PubIntYB 82*
Golden Valley Post - Golden Valley, MN - *Ed&PubIntYB 82*
Golden Valley Post [of Minneapolis Post Newspapers] - Minneapolis, MN - *AyerDirPub 83; NewsDir 84*
Golden Valley Post - *See* Post Publications Inc.
Golden West Books - San Marino, CA - *ArtMar 84; LitMag&SmPr 83-84; LitMarPl 83, 84; WritMar 84*
Golden West Broadcasters - Los Angeles, CA - *BrCabYB 84; HomeVid&CabYB 82-83; KnowInd 83*
Golden West Broadcasting Ltd. - Altona, MB, Canada - *BrCabYB 84*
Golden West Historical Publications - Ventura, CA - *BoPubDir 4, 5; LitMag&SmPr 83-84*
Golden West Melodies Inc. - New York, NY - *BillIntBG 83-84*
Golden West Publishers - Phoenix, AZ - *BoPubDir 4, 5; WritMar 84*
Golden West Purchasor - Los Angeles, CA - *MagDir 84*
Golden West Purchasor - Palos Verdes Peninsula, CA - *BaconPubCkMag 84*
Golden West Subscription TV [of Golden West Broadcasters] - Los Angeles, CA - *CabTVPrDB 83*
Golden West Telecommunications Cooperative Inc. - Wall, SD - *Tel&CabFB 84C p.1681*
Golden West Telephone Co. - Wood, SD - *TelDir&BG 83-84*
Golden West Telephone Cooperative Inc. - Wall, SD - *TelDir&BG 83-84*
Golden West Television - Los Angeles, CA - *AdAge 6-28-84*
Golden West Videotape - Hollywood, CA - *Tel&CabFB 84C*
Golden West Videotape [Div. of Golden West Television] - Los Angeles, CA - *AvMarPl 83*
Golden Years - Melbourne, FL - *BaconPubCkMag 84; MagDir 84*
Golden Years Club of Bezanson - Bezanson, AB, Canada - *BoPubDir 4 Sup, 5*
Goldendale Cablevision Inc. - Goldendale, WA - *BrCabYB 84; Tel&CabFB 84C*
Goldendale Sentinel [of Easle Newspapers Inc.] - Goldendale, WA - *BaconPubCkNews 84; Ed&PubIntYB 82; NewsDir 84*
Golder Interviewing Service, Ruth - Wilmington, DE - *IntDirMarRes 83*
Goldfarb Hoff & Co. Inc. - Southfield, MI - *StaDirAdAg 2-84*
Goldfield Telephone Co. - Goldfield, IA - *TelDir&BG 83-84*
Goldfin Associates - Miami, FL - *StaDirAdAg 2-84*
Goldfinch Press - Iowa City, IA - *LitMag&SmPr 83-84*
Goldfox International Records & Videoworks - Tempe, AZ - *BillIntBG 83-84*
Goldgresh Music - Hollywood, CA - *BillIntBG 83-84*
Goldin, Frances - New York, NY - *LitMarPl 83, 84*
Goldman Advertising Agency, Frederick - Philadelphia, PA - *StaDirAdAg 2-84*
Goldman Associates Inc., Neal - New York, NY - *IntDirMarRes 83*
Goldman Associates Inc., Warren - River Vale, NJ - *IntDirMarRes 83*
Goldman-Daniels Advertising Inc. - Brookline, MA - *StaDirAdAg 2-84*
Goldman Group - Jamestown, NY - *BrCabYB 84*
Goldman, Sachs & Co. (Investment Research Div.) - New York, NY - *ADAPSOMemDir 83-84*
Goldman, Stanley - Stoughton, MA - *BoPubDir 4 Sup, 5; LitMarPl 83, 84*
Goldmark Group Inc., The - New York, NY - *DirMarMP 83*
Goldsboro Music Inc., Bobby - *See* Warner Bros. Music
Goldsboro News-Argus [of Wayne Printing Co. Inc.] - Goldsboro, NC - *BaconPubCkNews 84; Ed&PubIntYB 82; NewsDir 84*
Goldsholl Associates - Northfield, IL - *AvMarPl 83; WritMar 84*
Goldsmith, The - San Francisco, CA - *BaconPubCkMag 84; MagDir 84*
Goldsmith's Music Shop - Great Neck, NY - *AvMarPl 83*
Goldstar Telecommunications Inc. - East Rutherford, NJ - *DataDirSup 7-83*
Goldstein Ad Agency Inc., S. H. - Great Neck, NY - *StaDirAdAg 2-84*
Goldstein/Krall Marketing Resources Inc. - Stamford, CT - *IntDirMarRes 83*
Goldstein Public Relations Inc., Joe - New York, NY - *DirPRFirms 83*
Goldstream Gazette - Victoria, BC, Canada - *AyerDirPub 83*
Goldthwaite Eagle - Goldthwaite, TX - *BaconPubCkNews 84; Ed&PubIntYB 82*
Goldust Records Co. - Las Cruces, NM - *BillIntBG 83-84*
Goldweb Publications - Ione, CA - *BaconPubCkNews 84*
Goldwyn Co., The Samuel - Los Angeles, CA - *LitMarPl 83*

Goldwyn Television Co., The Samuel - Los Angeles, CA - *Tel&CabFB 84C*
GOLEM [of Siemens AG] - Munich, West Germany - *EISS 83*
Golem Press - Boulder, CO - *BoPubDir 4, 5*
Golembe Associates Inc. - Washington, DC - *BoPubDir 5*
Goleta Sun - Goleta, CA - *BaconPubCkNews 84*
Goleta Valley News - Goleta, CA - *AyerDirPub 83; Ed&PubIntYB 82*
Golf Associates - Pebble Beach, CA - *BoPubDir 5*
Golf Course Management - Lawrence, KS - *BaconPubCkMag 84; MagDir 84; WritMar 84*
Golf Digest [of Golf Digest/Tennis Inc.] - Norwalk, CT - *ArtMar 84; BaconPubCkMag 84; Folio 83; LitMarPl 83, 84; MagDir 84; MagIndMarPl 82-83; WritMar 84*
Golf Digest/Tennis Inc. [Aff. of The New York Times] - Norwalk, CT - *BoPubDir 4; DirMarMP 83*
Golf Illustrated - Temecula, CA - *MagDir 84*
Golf Illustrated - Danbury, CT - *BaconPubCkMag 84*
Golf Industry - North Miami, FL - *BaconPubCkMag 84; MagDir 84; WritMar 84*
Golf Journal [of Golf House] - Far Hills, NJ - *ArtMar 84; BaconPubCkMag 84; MagDir 84*
Golf Magazine [of Times Mirror Magazines] - New York, NY - *ArtMar 84; BaconPubCkMag 84; Folio 83; LitMarPl 84; MagDir 84; MagIndMarPl 82-83; WritMar 84*
Golf Manor Cable TV [of Community Tele-Communications Inc.] - Golf Manor, OH - *BrCabYB 84; Tel&CabFB 84C*
Golf Mill East Maine Bugle - *See* Bugle Publications
Golf Mill Journal [of Des Plaines Journal-News Publications] - Des Plaines, IL - *NewsDir 84*
Golf Mill Park Ridge Journal - *See* Journal & Topics Newspapers
Golf Shop Operations - Norwalk, CT - *ArtMar 84; BaconPubCkMag 84; MagDir 84; WritMar 84*
Golf World - Southern Pines, NC - *BaconPubCkMag 84; MagDir 84; MagIndMarPl 82-83*
Goliad Advance-Guard - Goliad, TX - *BaconPubCkNews 84*
Golin/Harris Communications Inc. - Chicago, IL - *DirPRFirms 83*
Goll, Reinhold W. - Elkins Park, PA - *BoPubDir 4, 5*
Gollancz, Victor - North Pomfret, VT - *LitMarPl 83, 84*
Gollihugh/Sullivan Inc. - Cincinnati, OH - *StaDirAdAg 2-84*
Golnick Advertising Inc., Leon Shaffer [Div. of Golnick Co.] - Ft. Lauderdale, FL - *StaDirAdAg 2-84*
Golway Computer Enterprises - Flushing, NY - *MicrocomSwDir 1*
Golway Computer Enterprises - Staten Island, NY - *WhoWMicrocom 83*
Gomes Loew - New York, NY - *Tel&CabFB 84C*
Gomez Group, The - Albuquerque, NM - *BrCabYB 84*
Gonsor & Wilson Communications - Westport, CT - *AdAge 3-28-84; StaDirAdAg 2-84*
Gonvick Leader Record - *See* Richards Publications Co. Inc.
Gonzales Cable TV Service Inc. [of Communications Services Inc.] - Gonzales, TX - *BrCabYB 84; Tel&CabFB 84C*
Gonzales Community Mirror [of The Gonzales Weekly Inc.] - Gonzales, LA - *NewsDir 84*
Gonzales Inquirer - Gonzales, TX - *BaconPubCkNews 84; Ed&PubIntYB 82; NewsDir 84*
Gonzales Tribune - Gonzales, CA - *Ed&PubIntYB 82*
Gonzales Tribune - *See* Casey Newspapers Inc.
Gonzales Weekly - Gonzales, LA - *AyerDirPub 83; BaconPubCkNews 84; Ed&PubIntYB 82*
Goochland Gazette - Goochland, VA - *AyerDirPub 83*
Good [of Partial Publishing] - San Francisco, CA - *LitMag&SmPr 83-84*
Good Apple Inc. - Carthage, IL - *BoPubDir 4, 5*
Good Book Press - Santa Cruz, CA - *BoPubDir 5*
Good Books - Intercourse, PA - *BoPubDir 4, 5*
Good Cable Co. - Falls City, OR - *BrCabYB 84; Tel&CabFB 84C*
Good Earth Press - Villa Park, IL - *LitMag&SmPr 83-84*
Good Enterprises - New York, NY - *Ed&PubIntYB 82*
Good Flavor Songs Inc. - *See* Buttermilk Sky Music Publishing Corp.
Good Food Books - Maplewood, NJ - *BoPubDir 4, 5*
Good Gay Poets - Boston, MA - *BoPubDir 4, 5; LitMag&SmPr 83-84*
Good Health - Don Mills, ON, Canada - *BaconPubCkMag 84*
Good Housekeeping [of Hearst Corp.] - New York, NY - *ArtMar 84; BaconPubCkMag 84; Folio 83; LitMarPl 83, 84; MagDir 84; MagIndMarPl 82-83; WritMar 84*
Good Housekeeping Needlecraft - New York, NY - *MagDir 84*
Good Ideas Co. - Berea, OH - *BoPubDir 4, 5*
Good Life Productions - *See* Alexandria House Inc.
Good Life Publishers - Chesterfield, VA - *BoPubDir 4, 5*
Good-Lookin' Productions - Encino, CA - *AvMarPl 83*
Good-Lyddon Data Systems - Chino, CA - *MicrocomSwDir 1*
Good Medicine Books - Canada - *BoPubDir 4, 5*
Good Neighbors - Columbus, GA - *AyerDirPub 83*
Good News [of The Forum for Scriptural Christianity Inc.] - Wilmore, KY - *WritMar 84*
Good News Broadcaster - Lincoln, NE - *ArtMar 84; MagIndMarPl 82-83; WritMar 84*
Good News Broadcasting Co. - Crane, MO - *BrCabYB 84*
Good News Inc. - New Orleans, LA - *StaDirAdAg 2-84*
Good News Publishers - Westchester, IL - *LitMarPl 83, 84*
Good Packaging - San Jose, CA - *BaconPubCkMag 84; MagDir 84*
Good Parenting - Westport, CT - *MagDir 84*
Good Product Music - New York, NY - *BillIntBG 83-84*
Good Reading [of Henry F. Henrichs Publications] - Litchfield, IL - *ArtMar 84; WritMar 84*
Good Shepherd Records - Philadelphia, PA - *BillIntBG 83-84*
Good Software - Dallas, TX - *MicrocomMPl 84; MicrocomSwDir 1*
Good Sound Factory, The - Golden Valley, MN - *BillIntBG 83-84*
Good Sounds Records Inc. [Subs. of Criteria Recording Studios] - Miami, FL - *BillIntBG 83-84*
Good Stuff - Bloomington, IN - *BrCabYB 84*
Good Thing Inc., A - New York, NY - *LitMarPl 83, 84*
Good Token Music - *See* Tutt Music, Scott
Good-Vue CATV Inc. [of Cable Information Systems Inc.] - Spring Valley, NY - *BrCabYB 84*
Good-Vue CATV Inc. [of TKR Cable Inc.] - West Nyack, NY - *Tel&CabFB 84C*
Good Works [Subs. of Graphic Artists Guild] - New York, NY - *LitMarPl 83, 84*
Goodchild & Eidson Inc. - *See* LaChance Goodchild Eidson Inc.
Goodfellow Catalog of Wonderful Things - Berkeley, CA - *BoPubDir 4, 5*
Goodfellow Review of Crafts [of Goodfellow Catalog Press] - Berkeley, CA - *BaconPubCkMag 84; MagIndMarPl 82-83; WritMar 84*
Goodfruit Grower - Yakima, WA - *BaconPubCkMag 84; MagDir 84*
Goodheart-Willcox Co. - South Holland, IL - *LitMarPl 83, 84*
Goodhue County Tribune - Goodhue, MN - *BaconPubCkNews 84*
Gooding County Leader [of O.I. Publishing Inc.] - Gooding, ID - *BaconPubCkNews 84; Ed&PubIntYB 82; NewsDir 84*
Goodis-Wolf Inc. - Toronto, ON, Canada - *StaDirAdAg 2-84*
Goodkin Inc., M. P. - Irvington, NJ - *AvMarPl 83*
Goodkind, Herbert K. - Larchmont, NY - *BoPubDir 4, 5*
Goodkind, Larney - New York, NY - *LitMarPl 83, 84*
Goodland Cable TV Co. [of KAYS Inc.] - Goodland, KS - *BrCabYB 84; Tel&CabFB 84C*
Goodland Chronicle - Goodland, KS - *BaconPubCkNews 84*
Goodland Daily News [of McCants Publishing Co. Inc.] - Goodland, KS - *BaconPubCkNews 84; Ed&PubIntYB 82; NewsDir 84*
Goodland Sherman County Herald - Goodland, KS - *BaconPubCkNews 84*
Goodlettsville Gazette - Goodlettsville, TN - *NewsDir 84*
Goodman & Associates - Ft. Worth, TX - *ArtMar 84; StaDirAdAg 2-84*
Goodman Associates - New York, NY - *LitMarPl 83, 84*
Goodman Associates, Marvin - New York, NY - *Tel&CabFB 84C*
Goodman Communications - Ossining, NY - *DirPRFirms 83*
Goodman Group Inc., The - Dallas, TX - *WhoWMicrocom 83*
Goodman Group, The - New York, NY - *BillIntBG 83-84*
Goodman, Henry Gaines Jr. - Greenville, SC - *Ed&PubIntYB 82*
Goodman Literary Agency, Irene - New York, NY - *LitMarPl 83, 84*
Goodman Productions Inc., Dan - Deerfield Beach, FL - *Tel&CabFB 84C*

Goodman Telephone Co. - Goodman, MO - *TelDir&BG 83-84*
Goodman Theatre - San Francisco, CA - *MagDir 84*
Goodren Products Corp. - Englewood, NJ - *StaDirAdAg 2-84*
Goodson-Todman Productions - New York, NY - *TelAl 83, 84; Tel&CabFB 84C*
Goodstay [of Hart Inc.] - Freehold, NJ - *WritMar 84*
Goodtime Books Paperback Book Club [of Xerox Education Publications] - Middletown, CT - *LitMarPl 83, 84*
Goodway Marketing Inc. [Subs. of Goodway Graphics Inc.] - Jenkintown, PA - *CabTVFinDB 83; DirMarMP 83*
Goodwill Messenger Service - New York, NY - *MagIndMarPl 82-83*
Goodwin & Associates, Dave - Surfside, FL - *Ed&PubIntYB 82*
Goodwin & Associates, Dave - New York, NY - *LitMarPl 84*
Goodwin, Dannenbaum, Littman & Wingfield Inc. - Houston, TX - *DirPRFirms 83; StaDirAdAg 2-84*
Goodwin/Tacker & Associates Inc. - Englewood, CO - *DirPRFirms 83*
Goodwood Data Systems Ltd. - Carleton Place, ON, Canada - *InfIndMarPl 83*
Goody Mirror, The - Manchester, GA - *ArtMar 84*
Goodyear Westsider - Goodyear, AZ - *BaconPubCkNews 84*
Goose Creek Gazette - Goose Creek, SC - *AyerDirPub 83; BaconPubCkNews 84*
Goosebump Music [Div. of The Record Co.] - Los Angeles, CA - *BillIntBG 83-84*
Goosepimple Music - Myerstown, PA - *BillIntBG 83-84*
Gooth Software - Clayton, MO - *MicrocomMPl 84*
Gooth Software - St. Louis, MO - *MicrocomMPl 83; WhoWMicrocom 83*
Gopam Enterprises Inc. - New York, NY - *BillIntBG 83-84*
Gorchov Advertising Inc. - Miami Beach, FL - *StaDirAdAg 2-84*
Gordetsky Telecommunications & General Management Consulting, G. R. - San Diego, CA - *TeleSy&SerDir 2-84*
Gordian Press Inc. - Staten Island, NY - *LitMarPl 83, 84*
Gordon & Associates, Bernard - Glencoe, IL - *MagIndMarPl 82-83*
Gordon & Breach Science Publishers Inc. - New York, NY - *LitMarPl 83, 84; MagIndMarPl 82-83*
Gordon & Breach Science Publishers Ltd. - London, England - *MicroMarPl 82-83*
Gordon & Shortt Inc. - White Plains, NY - *StaDirAdAg 2-84*
Gordon, Andrew - New York, NY - *LitMarPl 83, 84; MagIndMarPl 82-83*
Gordon Associates - New York, NY - *LitMarPl 83, 84*
Gordon, B. Douglas - New Milford, CT - *Tel&CabFB 84C p.1682*
Gordon, Bob - Kooskia, ID - *Tel&CabFB 84C p.1681*
Gordon Cablevision [of TeleNational Communications Inc.] - Ft. Gordon, GA - *BrCabYB 84; Tel&CabFB 84C*
Gordon Cablevision [of Communications Systems Inc.] - Gordon, NE - *BrCabYB 84*
Gordon, Carol - Santa Monica, CA - *BoPubDir 4, 5*
Gordon Computers, Mark [Subs. of Mark Gordon Associates Inc.] - Charlestown, MA - *WhoWMicrocom 83*
Gordon, Ellen - Larchmont, NY - *LitMarPl 83, 84; MagIndMarPl 82-83*
Gordon Enterprises Inc., Alan - North Hollywood, CA - *AvMarPl 83; Tel&CabFB 84C*
Gordon Group - Grand Rapids, MI - *AdAge 3-28-84; StaDirAdAg 2-84*
Gordon Group Inc., The - Norcross, GA - *ArtMar 84; DirPRFirms 83*
Gordon Inc., Martin - New York, NY - *BoPubDir 4, 5*
Gordon Journal - Gordon, NE - *BaconPubCkNews 84; Ed&PubIntYB 82*
Gordon, Julie Ann - New York, NY - *LitMarPl 83, 84*
Gordon Music Co. Inc. - North Hollywood, CA - *BillIntBG 83-84*
Gordon Newsfilms - San Francisco, CA - *AvMarPl 83*
Gordon Photography, Joel - New York, NY - *LitMarPl 83, 84; MagIndMarPl 82-83*
Gordon Press - New York, NY - *BoPubDir 4, 5*
Gordon Productions Inc., Marc - Los Angeles, CA - *BillIntBG 83-84*
Gordon Publications & Reproductions - Ottawa, ON, Canada - *BoPubDir 4 Sup, 5*
Gordon Publishing Inc. - Chatham, NJ - *DirMarMP 83*
Gordon, Richard W. - New London, NH - *LitMarPl 83, 84*
Gordon-Rushville Cablevision [of Scott Cable Communications Inc.] - Gordon, NE - *Tel&CabFB 84C*
Gordon Simmons Research Ltd. - Surrey, England - *IntDirMarRes 83*
Gordon, Thomas J. - Champaign, IL - *Tel&CabFB 84C*
Gordon, William Reed - Rochester, NY - *BoPubDir 4, 5*
Gordon's Books Inc. - Denver, CO - *BoPubDir 4 Sup, 5; LitMarPl 83, 84*
Gordonstown Press - Dillon, CO - *BoPubDir 4, 5*
Gordonsville Cable TV Inc. [of Equity Management] - Gordonsville, VA - *Tel&CabFB 84C*
Gore Advertising Ltd. - *See* Royds Advertising Group Ltd., The
Gore Bay Community Cable TV - Gore Bay, ON, Canada - *BrCabYB 84*
Gore Co., Chester - New York, NY - *AdAge 3-28-84; StaDirAdAg 2-84*
Gore, Gary - Nashville, TN - *LitMarPl 83, 84; MagIndMarPl 82-83*
Gorham Genealogy & History - Fullerton, CA - *ArtMar 84*
Gorham Genealogy & History [of Axios Newletter Inc.] - Los Angeles, CA - *LitMag&SmPr 83-84; WritMar 84*
Gorham International Inc. - Gorham, ME - *BoPubDir 5*
Gorham Telephone Co. - Gorham, KS - *TelDir&BG 83-84*
Gorman Advertising Agency - Chicago, IL - *StaDirAdAg 2-84*
Gorman Multimedia Communications Inc. - New York, NY - *AvMarPl 83*
Gorman Progress - Gorman, TX - *BaconPubCkNews 84; Ed&PubIntYB 82*
Gorman Publishing Co. - Chicago, IL - *BoPubDir 5; MagIndMarPl 82-83*
Gormezano & Associates, Keith S. - Iowa City, IA - *BrCabYB 84*
Gormezano Effective Public Relations, Keith - Seattle, WA - *DirPRFirms 83*
Gormezano's Book Review [of Le Beacon Presse] - Seattle, WA - *LitMag&SmPr 83-84*
Gormly, Walter - Mt. Vernon, IA - *Ed&PubIntYB 82*
Gornick Film Productions/Environmental Marine Enterprises - Los Angeles, CA - *AvMarPl 83*
Goro, Fritz - Chappaqua, NY - *MagIndMarPl 82-83*
Gorski, Roman - North Brunswick, NJ - *LitMarPl 83*
Gorsuch Scarisbrick Publishers - Dubuque, IA - *LitMarPl 83, 84*
Gorzek Films, Don - Menomonee Falls, WI - *AvMarPl 83*
Gorzkowska, Regina A. - Tuscaloosa, AL - *LitMarPl 83; MagIndMarPl 82-83*
Gorzkowska, Regina A. - Scranton, PA - *LitMarPl 84*
G.O.S. Inc. - Missoula, MT - *BoPubDir 5*
Goshen Independent Republican - Goshen, NY - *BaconPubCkNews 84; NewsDir 84*
Goshen Litho Inc. - Chester, NY - *LitMarPl 83, 84*
Goshen News - Goshen, IN - *BaconPubCkNews 84; Ed&PubIntYB 82; NewsDir 84*
Goshen Telephone Co. - Goshen, AL - *TelDir&BG 83-84*
Gospel Advocate Bookstore - Nashville, TN - *BoPubDir 4, 5*
Gospel Carrier [of Messenger Publishing House] - Joplin, MO - *WritMar 84*
Gospel Clef Publishing Co. - Brooklyn, NY - *BillIntBG 83-84*
Gospel Films Inc. - Muskegon, MI - *Tel&CabFB 84C*
Gospel International Publications - *See* Ellebie Music Publishing Co.
Gospel Media - South San Francisco, CA - *BillIntBG 83-84*
Gospel Publishing House [Div. of General Council of the Assemblies of God] - Springfield, MO - *LitMarPl 83, 84*
Gospel Truth & Publications - Wapakoneta, OH - *BoPubDir 4, 5*
Gossage Regan Associates Inc. - New York, NY - *EISS 83*
Gosub International Inc. - Wichita, KS - *MicrocomMPl 83, 84*
Gotebo Record-Times - Gotebo, OK - *BaconPubCkNews 84; Ed&PubIntYB 82*
Gotham Audio Corp. - New York, NY - *AvMarPl 83*
Gotham Book Mart Inc. - New York, NY - *BoPubDir 4, 5*
Gotham Film Productions Inc. - New York, NY - *Tel&CabFB 84C*
Gotham Video Tape [Subs. of Gotham Film Productions Inc.] - New York, NY - *AvMarPl 83*
Gothenburg Times - Gothenburg, NE - *BaconPubCkNews 84; Ed&PubIntYB 82*
Gothic Press - Baton Rouge, LA - *LitMag&SmPr 83-84*

Gothic Records Inc. - Tustin, CA - *BillIntBG 83-84*
Gotown Publishing Co. - Leesville, LA - *BillIntBG 83-84*
Gottfried, Chet & Susan - Kew Gardens, NY - *LitMarPl 83, 84; MagIndMarPl 82-83*
Gottlieb Associates, David - Scarsdale, NY - *DirPRFirms 83*
Gottschalk Publishing Co., E. J. - Lorain, OH - *BaconPubCkNews 84*
Gotuit Enterprises - Seal Beach, CA - *BoPubDir 4, 5*
Gouchenour-Pontius Inc. - Altamonte Springs, FL - *ArtMar 84; StaDirAdAg 2-84*
Gould Advertising, Irving - Philadelphia, PA - *StaDirAdAg 2-84*
Gould & Portmans Ltd. - London, England - *StaDirAdAg 2-84*
Gould Associates, J. Sutherland - Yorktown Heights, NY - *DirPRFirms 83*
Gould Enterprises, Jay - Ft. Wayne, IN - *BoPubDir 5*
Gould Entertainment Corp. - New York, NY - *Tel&CabFB 84C*
Gould, Gerald - Englewood, NJ - *LitMarPl 83*
Gould Inc. - Rolling Meadows, IL - *Datamation 6-83; ElecNews 7-25-83*
Gould Inc. (Biomation Div.) - Santa Clara, CA - *DataDirSup 7-83*
Gould Inc. (De Anza Imaging & Graphics Div.) - San Jose, CA - *DataDirSup 7-83*
Gould Inc. (Factory Automation Div.) - Nashua, NH - *DataDirSup 7-83*
Gould Inc. (Modicon Programmable Control Div.) - Andover, MA - *DataDirSup 7-83*
Gould Inc. (S.E.L. Computer Systems Div.) - Ft. Lauderdale, FL - *DataDirSup 7-83; Top100Al 83*
Gould Paper Co. Inc., Stephen - Florham Park, NJ - *LitMarPl 83, 84*
Gould Paper Corp. - New York, NY - *LitMarPl 83, 84; MagIndMarPl 82-83*
Gould Publications - Binghamton, NY - *LitMarPl 83, 84*
Gould Publications, Bruce - Seattle, WA - *BoPubDir 4, 5; LitMag&SmPr 83-84*
Gould, Stanley R. [Subs. of The Ron Smith Group] - San Francisco, CA - *LitMarPl 83, 84*
Goulder Advertising, Robert - Cleveland, OH - *StaDirAdAg 2-84*
Goulding, Catherine T. - Larchmont, NY - *LitMarPl 83*
Goulding-Elliott-Greybar Productions Inc. - New York, NY - *TelAl 83, 84; Tel&CabFB 84C*
Goulet Advertising, John E. - Cleveland, OH - *StaDirAdAg 2-84*
Gourmet - New York, NY - *BaconPubCkMag 84; Folio 83; MagDir 84; MagIndMarPl 82-83; WritMar 84*
Gourmet Guides - San Francisco, CA - *BoPubDir 4, 5; LitMag&SmPr 83-84*
Gourmet Retailer - North Miami, FL - *BaconPubCkMag 84; MagIndMarPl 82-83*
Gourmet Software - San Jose, CA - *MicrocomMPl 84*
Gourmet Today - New York, NY - *BaconPubCkMag 84*
Gousha/Chek-Chart Service Bulletin - San Jose, CA - *ArtMar 84*
Gousha Co., H. M. [Aff. of The Times Mirror Co.] - San Jose, CA - *BoPubDir 4, 5*
Gouverneur Cable Television Inc. [of Dix Newspapers] - Gouverneur, NY - *BrCabYB 84*
Gouverneur Tribune-Press [of MRS Printing Inc.] - Gouverneur, NY - *BaconPubCkNews 84; NewsDir 84*
Govatos/Dunn Inc. - Alexandria, VA - *DirPRFirms 83; StaDirAdAg 2-84*
Gove County Advocate, The - Quinter, KS - *Ed&PubIntYB 82*
Gove, Geoffrey - New York, NY - *LitMarPl 83, 84*
Government Accountants Journal, The [of Association of Government Accountants] - Arlington, VA - *BaconPubCkMag 84; MagDir 84*
Government Computer News [of US Professional Development Institute] - Silver Spring, MD - *BaconPubCkMag 84; MicrocomMPl 84*
Government Counselling Ltd. - Alexandria, VA - *DirInfWP 82*
Government Data Publications - Brooklyn, NY - *BoPubDir 5*
Government Data Systems [of United Business Publications] - New York, NY - *BaconPubCkMag 84; MagDir 84*
Government Employee, The - Washington, DC - *NewsDir 84*
Government Executive [of Executive Publications Inc.] - Washington, DC - *BaconPubCkMag 84; MagDir 84; MagIndMarPl 82-83*
Government Finance Statistics [of International Monetary Fund] - Washington, DC - *DataDirOnSer 84; DirOnDB Spring 84*
Government Finance Statistics [of Chase Econometrics/Interactive Data Corp.] - Waltham, MA - *DataDirOnSer 84*
Government-Industry Data Exchange Program [of U.S. Navy] - Corona, CA - *DataDirOnSer 84; EISS 83*
Government Information Services - Arlington, VA - *InfIndMarPl 83*
Government Institutes Inc. - Rockville, MD - *LitMarPl 83, 84*
Government of Alberta Publications [of University of Alberta] - Edmonton, AB, Canada - *DataDirOnSer 84*
Government of Israel Trade Center - New York, NY - *BoPubDir 5*
Government Printing Office (Library Div.) - Alexandria, VA - *CompReadDB 82*
Government Product News [of Penton/IPC Inc.] - Cleveland, OH - *BaconPubCkMag 84; MagDir 84; MagIndMarPl 82-83*
Government R & D Report - Cambridge, MA - *BoPubDir 4, 5*
Government Research Corp. - Washington, DC - *EISS 83*
Government Research Publications - Newton Center, MA - *BoPubDir 4, 5*
Government Sales Consultants Inc. - Annandale, VA - *ADAPSOMemDir 83-84*
Government Securities Management System - New York, NY - *DirOnDB Spring 84*
Government Standard [of American Federation of Government Employees] - Washington, DC - *MagDir 84; NewsDir 84*
Government Systems Div. [of RCA Corp.] - Cherry Hill, NJ - *Tel&CabFB 84C*
Governmental Finance [of Municipal Finance Officers Association of U.S. & Canada] - Chicago, IL - *MagDir 84*
Governmental Guides Inc. - Madison, TN - *BoPubDir 5*
Governmental Research Association Inc. - Austin, TX - *BoPubDir 4, 5*
Govett, David - Berkeley, CA - *LitMarPl 83, 84; MagIndMarPl 82-83*
Gow, Jack - Wyckoff, NJ - *DirPRFirms 83*
Gowan, J. C. - Westlake Village, CA - *BoPubDir 4, 5*
Gowanda News - Gowanda, NY - *BaconPubCkNews 84*
Gowanda News & Observer - Gowanda, NY - *NewsDir 84*
Gowanda Penny Saver - Granville, NY - *AyerDirPub 83*
Gowdy Broadcasting, Curt - Lawrence, MA - *BrCabYB 84*
Gowe Printing Co. [Subs. of Post Corp.] - Medina, OH - *MagIndMarPl 82-83*
Gower Medical Publishing Ltd. - New York, NY - *BoPubDir 4 Sup, 5*
Gower Publishing Co. - Brookfield, VT - *BoPubDir 4 Sup, 5; LitMarPl 83, 84*
Gowrie News - Gowrie, IA - *BaconPubCkNews 84; Ed&PubIntYB 82*
Goydish Music & Publishing Co. - Somerville, NJ - *BillIntBG 83-84*
GP Enterprises/Job Hunter's Forum - Annapolis, MD - *BoPubDir 4, 5*
GP Industries - Somerville, NJ - *DirInfWP 82*
G.P. Slide Co. Inc. - Houston, TX - *Tel&CabFB 84C*
GP Venture Marketing Associates Inc. - New York, NY - *HBIndAd&MS 82-83*
GPA Electronics Inc. - Laytonville, CA - *WhoWMicrocom 83*
GPN - Lincoln, NE - *Tel&CabFB 84C*
GPO Monthly Catalog Data Base [of Dialog Information Services Inc.] - Palo Alto, CA - *DataDirOnSer 84*
GPO Monthly Catalog Data Base [of U.S. Government Printing Office] - Alexandria, VA - *DBBus 82; DirOnDB Spring 84; EISS 83; OnBibDB 3*
GPO Monthly Catalog, MARC Distribution Service [of U.S. Government Printing Office] - Alexandria, VA - *CompReadDB 82*
GPO Publications Reference File [of Dialog Information Services Inc.] - Palo Alto, CA - *DataDirOnSer 84*
GPO Publications Reference File [of U.S. Government Printing Office] - Washington, DC - *DirOnDB Spring 84; EISS 83; OnBibDB 3*
G.R. Electronics Ltd. - Santa Monica, CA - *WhoWMicrocom 83*
Graber & Cohen Inc. - New York, NY - *StaDirAdAg 2-84*
Grace & Co., W. R. (Polyfibron Div.) - Quakertown, PA - *LitMarPl 83, 84*
Grace Citizen - Grace, ID - *Ed&PubIntYB 82*
Grace Citizen - Preston, ID - *AyerDirPub 83*

Grace Citizen - *See* Citizen Publishing Co. Inc.
GraCeba Telephone Co. - Ashford, AL - *TelDir&BG 83-84*
Graceville News - Graceville, FL - *BaconPubCkNews 84; Ed&PubIntYB 82*
Graceway Publishing Co. - Flushing, NY - *BoPubDir 4, 5*
Grade Finders Inc. - Bala Cynwyd, PA - *DirMarMP 83*
Grade Finders Inc. - Berwyn, PA - *BoPubDir 4, 5*
Graduate Management Admission Council - Princeton, NJ - *BoPubDir 4, 5*
Graduate Woman [of American Association of University Women] - Washington, DC - *BaconPubCkMag 84; LitMarPl 83, 84; MagDir 84; MagIndMarPl 82-83*
Graduating Engineer [of McGraw-Hill Inc.] - New York, NY - *MagDir 84; MagIndMarPl 82-83; WritMar 84*
Graduation Music Inc. - St. Louis, MO - *BillIntBG 83-84*
Graduation Records Inc. - St. Louis, MO - *BillIntBG 83-84*
Graettinger Cooperative Telephone Association - Graettinger, IA - *TelDir&BG 83-84*
Graettinger Times - Graettinger, IA - *BaconPubCkNews 84; Ed&PubIntYB 82*
Graf, Angelia - Chapel Hill, NC - *LitMarPl 83, 84*
Grafacon Inc. [Subs. of Harcourt Brace Jovanovich] - Hudson, MA - *LitMarPl 83, 84*
Grafcon Corp. - Tulsa, OK - *DataDirSup 7-83*
Grafdesley - *See* Henderson Friedlich Graf & Doyle Inc.
Graffcom Systems Ltd. - London, England - *MicrocomSwDir 1*
Grafox Ltd. - Oxford, England - *MicrocomSwDir 1*
Grafrica News - East Orange, NJ - *AyerDirPub 83; Ed&PubIntYB 82*
Graftek Press Inc. - Crystal Lake, IL - *MagIndMarPl 82-83*
Grafton Cable Communications Co. - Grafton, OH - *Tel&CabFB 84C*
Grafton Cable Co. Inc. [of Westover TV Cable Co.] - Grafton, WV - *Tel&CabFB 84C*
Grafton Cable TV [of Midcontinent Cable Systems Co.] - Grafton, ND - *BrCabYB 84*
Grafton News, The - North Grafton, MA - *Ed&PubIntYB 82*
Grafton Record [of Morgan Publishing Co.] - Grafton, ND - *BaconPubCkNews 84; Ed&PubIntYB 82; NewsDir 84*
Grafton Telephone Co. - Grafton, IL - *TelDir&BG 83-84*
Graham Agency - New York, NY - *LitMarPl 83, 84*
Graham Alamance News - Graham, NC - *BaconPubCkNews 84; NewsDir 84*
Graham Associates, David - Decorah, IA - *Ed&PubIntYB 82; LitMarPl 84*
Graham Cable TV/FM [of Cablecasting Ltd.] - Toronto, ON, Canada - *BrCabYB 84*
Graham-Henry Photography, Diane - Chicago, IL - *LitMarPl 84*
Graham Historical Society Inc. - Graham, MO - *BoPubDir 4, 5*
Graham House Review - Andover, MA - *LitMag&SmPr 83-84*
Graham Interviewing Service, Polly - Birmingham, AL - *IntDirMarRes 83*
Graham Leader - Graham, TX - *AyerDirPub 83; BaconPubCkNews 84; Ed&PubIntYB 82*
Graham Magnetics - Ft. Worth, TX - *DirInfWP 82*
Graham Magnetics Inc. - North Richland Hills, TX - *DataDirSup 7-83*
Graham Music Publisher, Roger - Carney, MI - *BillIntBG 83-84*
Graham-O-Tunes Music Inc. - *See* MizMo Enterprises
Graham, Paula Royce - Brooklyn, NY - *Ed&PubIntYB 82*
Graham Press, C. P. - Keswick, VA - *BoPubDir 4, 5*
Graham Research Service Inc. - New York, NY - *IntDirMarRes 83; Tel&CabFB 84C*
Graham Star, The - Graham, NC - *Ed&PubIntYB 82*
Graham Stations, James Alvin - Baxley, GA - *BrCabYB 84*
Grahman Software - Castleton, VT - *MicrocomMPl 84*
Grain Age - Hopkins, MN - *MagDir 84*
Grain Age - Brookfield, WI - *BaconPubCkMag 84*
Grain & Farm Service Centers - Chicago, IL - *MagDir 84*
Grain & Feed Journals - Chicago, IL - *BaconPubCkMag 84*
Grain & Feed Merchant [of Nebraska Grain & Feed Dealers' Association] - Lincoln, NE - *BaconPubCkMag 84; MagDir 84*
Grain & Feed Review [of Iowa Grain & Feed Association] - Des Moines, IA - *BaconPubCkMag 84; MagDir 84*
Grain Industries Plants - Chicago, IL - *MagDir 84*
Grain Journal - Decatur, IL - *BaconPubCkMag 84*
Grain Sorghum News - Lubbock, TX - *MagDir 84*
Grain Storage & Handling - Kansas City, MO - *BaconPubCkMag 84*
Grainfield Cap Sheaf - Grainfield, KS - *Ed&PubIntYB 82*
Grainger County News - Grainger County, TN - *Ed&PubIntYB 82*
Grajonca - San Francisco, CA - *BillIntBG 83-84*
Gralla Publications - New York, NY - *KnowInd 83; MagIndMarPl 82-83; NewsBur 6*
Gramatu Draugs - Brooklyn, NY - *BoPubDir 4, 5*
Gramavision Inc. - New York, NY - *BillIntBG 83-84*
Gramavision Music Co. - New York, NY - *BillIntBG 83-84*
Grambling Cable Television Inc. [of Action Communications Co. Inc.] - Grambling, LA - *BrCabYB 84; Tel&CabFB 84C*
Gramco Inc. - Minneapolis, MN - *ADAPSOMemDir 83-84*
Gramercy Community Herald - *See* Community Herald
Grammarphone [of Frostburg State College] - Frostburg, MD - *LitMarPl 83, 84*
GramOphone Music Co. - *See* Hall of Fame Music Co.
Gramophone Records [Div. of Audio International Inc.] - Beverly Hills, CA - *BillIntBG 83-84*
Granada Hills Times - *See* Associated Valley Publications
Granada Hills Valley View - *See* San Fernando Valley Sun Publishers
Granada Records - Westminster, CA - *BillIntBG 83-84*
Granada Telephone Co. - Castle Rock, MN - *TelDir&BG 83-84*
Granada Television International - New York, NY - *TelAl 84; Tel&CabFB 84C*
Granada Television International Ltd. - London, England - *Tel&CabFB 84C*
Granbury Hood County News - Granbury, TX - *BaconPubCkNews 84*
Granby Newton County News - Granby, MO - *BaconPubCkNews 84*
Granby Sky-Hi News - Granby, CO - *BaconPubCkNews 84*
Granby Telephone & Telegraph Co. - Granby, MA - *TelDir&BG 83-84*
Granby Telephone Co. - Granby, MO - *TelDir&BG 83-84*
Grand Artists Music [Div. of Paul Stevens Associates Inc.] - Miami, FL - *BillIntBG 83-84*
Grand Blanc News - Grand Blanc, MI - *AyerDirPub 83; BaconPubCkNews 84; Ed&PubIntYB 82; NewsDir 84*
Grand Book Inc. - Brooklyn, NY - *ProGuPRSer 4*
Grand Canyon Natural History Association - Grand Canyon, AZ - *BoPubDir 4, 5*
Grand Centre-Cold Lake Bonnyville Sun - Grand Centre, AB, Canada - *AyerDirPub 83*
Grand Coulee Star & Almira Herald - Grand Coulee, WA - *BaconPubCkNews 84; Ed&PubIntYB 82*
Grand Falls Advertiser, The - Grand Falls, NF, Canada - *Ed&PubIntYB 82*
Grand Forks Cable TV [of Tele-Communications Inc.] - Grand Forks, ND - *BrCabYB 84*
Grand Forks Herald [of Knight-Ridder Newspapers] - Grand Forks, ND - *BaconPubCkNews 84; Ed&PubIntYB 82; LitMarPl 83, 84; NewsBur 6; NewsDir 84*
Grand Haven Tribune - Grand Haven, MI - *BaconPubCkNews 84; Ed&PubIntYB 82; NewsDir 84*
Grand Haven West Michigan News Review - Grand Haven, MI - *BaconPubCkNews 84*
Grand Island Dispatch - Grand Island, NY - *BaconPubCkNews 84*
Grand Island Heartland Advertiser - Grand Island, NE - *BaconPubCkNews 84*
Grand Island Independent [of Stauffer Communications Inc.] - Grand Island, NE - *BaconPubCkNews 84; NewsDir 84*
Grand Island Penny Saver - Grand Island, NY - *AyerDirPub 83*
Grand Junction Daily Sentinel - Grand Junction, CO - *BaconPubCkNews 84*
Grand Junction Globe-Free Press - Grand Junction, IA - *BaconPubCkNews 84*
Grand Lake Cablevision Inc. - Monkey Island, OK - *BrCabYB 84*
Grand Lake Shopper's Guide - Grove, OK - *AyerDirPub 83*
Grand Ledge Independent - Grand Ledge, MI - *AyerDirPub 83; BaconPubCkNews 84; Ed&PubIntYB 82; NewsDir 84*
Grand Ledge Portland Review & Observer - Grand Ledge, MI - *BaconPubCkNews 84*
Grand Marais Cook County News-Herald - Grand Marais, MN - *BaconPubCkNews 84*

Grand Mound Cooperative Telephone Association - Grand Mound, IA - *TelDir&BG 83-84*
Grand National Illustrated - Harrisburg, NC - *BaconPubCkMag 84*
Grand Pasha Publisher, The - Hollywood, CA - *BillIntBG 83-84*
Grand Prairie Daily News - Farmers Branch, TX - *Ed&PubIntYB 82*
Grand Prairie Daily News [of News Texan Inc.] - Grand Prairie, TX - *BaconPubCkNews 84; NewsDir 84*
Grand Prairie Herald - Hazen, AR - *AyerDirPub 83; Ed&PubIntYB 82*
Grand Prix Publishing Co. - Memphis, TN - *BillIntBG 83-84*
Grand Prix Record Co. - Memphis, TN - *BillIntBG 83-84*
Grand Rapids Cadence - Grand Rapids, MI - *BaconPubCkNews 84*
Grand Rapids Herald-Review - Grand Rapids, MN - *BaconPubCkNews 84; Ed&PubIntYB 82; NewsDir 84*
Grand Rapids Magazine [of Gemini Communications] - Grand Rapids, MI - *ArtMar 84; BaconPubCkMag 84; WritMar 84*
Grand Rapids Press [of Booth Newspapers Inc.] - Grand Rapids, MI - *AyerDirPub 83; BaconPubCkNews 84; Ed&PubIntYB 82; LitMarPl 83, 84; NewsDir 84*
Grand Rapids Times - Grand Rapids, MI - *BaconPubCkNews 84; Ed&PubIntYB 82*
Grand Ridge Cable Co. Inc. - Grand Ridge, IL - *BrCabYB 84; Tel&CabFB 84C*
Grand River Mutual Telephone Co. - Grand River, IA - *TelDir&BG 83-84*
Grand River Mutual Telephone Co. - Princeton, MO - *TelDir&BG 83-84*
Grand River Sachem - Caledonia, ON, Canada - *AyerDirPub 83; Ed&PubIntYB 82*
Grand Saline Cable TV [of Texas Community Antennas Inc.] - Grand Saline, TX - *BrCabYB 84*
Grand Saline Sun - *See* Howard Publishing Co. Inc.
Grand Saline Sun, The - Grand Saline, TX - *Ed&PubIntYB 82*
Grand Stage Lighting Co. - Chicago, IL - *AvMarPl 83*
Grand Telephone Co. Inc. - Jay, OK - *TelDir&BG 83-84*
Grand Valley Advance - Jenison, MI - *AyerDirPub 83; Ed&PubIntYB 82*
Grand Valley Ledger, The - Lowell, MI - *Ed&PubIntYB 82*
Grande Cache Mountaineer - Grande Cache, AB, Canada - *Ed&PubIntYB 82*
Grande Prairie This Week - Grande Prairie, AB, Canada - *AyerDirPub 83; Ed&PubIntYB 82*
Grande Records - Houston, TX - *BillIntBG 83-84*
Grandfield Big Pasture News - Grandfield, OK - *BaconPubCkNews 84*
Grandview Exponet - Grandview, MB, Canada - *Ed&PubIntYB 82*
Grandview Herald - Grandview, WA - *Ed&PubIntYB 82*
Grandview Herald - *See* Prosser-Granview Publishers
Grandview Jackson County Advocate - Grandview, MO - *BaconPubCkNews 84*
Grandview Tribune [of Townsend Communications Inc.] - Kansas City, MO - *NewsDir 84*
Grandview Tribune - Grandview, TX - *BaconPubCkNews 84; Ed&PubIntYB 82*
Grandville Records Inc. - Chicago, IL - *BillIntBG 83-84*
Grandy Broadcasting Broker, W. John - San Luis Obispo, CA - *CabTVFinDB 83*
Grange Advocate for Rural Pennsylvania - Harrisburg, PA - *BaconPubCkMag 84; MagDir 84*
Grange News, The - Seattle, WA - *BaconPubCkMag 84; MagDir 84*
Granger Book Co. Inc. [Aff. of Core Collection Books Inc.] - Great Neck, NY - *LitMarPl 83, 84*
Granger Collection, The - New York, NY - *AvMarPl 83; LitMarPl 83, 84; MagIndMarPl 82-83*
Granger News - Granger, TX - *Ed&PubIntYB 82*
Granger News - *See* Taylor Newspapers Inc.
Grangeville Idaho County Free Press [of Eagle Newspapers Inc.] - Grangeville, ID - *BaconPubCkNews 84; NewsDir 84*
Granirer, Martus - New York, NY - *LitMarPl 83, 84*
Granite City Press-Record - Granite City, IL - *BaconPubCkNews 84*
Granite Enterprise - Granite, OK - *Ed&PubIntYB 82*
Granite Falls Press - Granite Falls, NC - *BaconPubCkNews 84; Ed&PubIntYB 82*
Granite Falls Tribune - Granite Falls, MN - *BaconPubCkNews 84; Ed&PubIntYB 82; NewsDir 84*
Granite Gazette/Mascoma Week - Lebanon, NH - *Ed&PubIntYB 82*
Granite Rock Music - Studio City, CA - *BillIntBG 83-84*
Granite State Marketing & Research - Londonderry, NH - *IntDirMarRes 83*
Granite State News - Wolfeboro, NH - *AyerDirPub 83; Ed&PubIntYB 82*
Granite State News/Carroll County Independent - Wolfeboro, NH - *NewsDir 84*
Granite State Telephone - South Weare, NH - *TelDir&BG 83-84*
Granite Televue - Granite, OK - *BrCabYB 84; Tel&CabFB 84C*
Granny Soot Publications - Vancouver, BC, Canada - *LitMag&SmPr 83-84*
Grant & Pollack Advertising - Denver, CO - *AdAge 3-28-84; StaDirAdAg 2-84*
Grant Associates, Jason - Providence, RI - *StaDirAdAg 2-84*
Grant Cable TV - Grant, NE - *Tel&CabFB 84C*
Grant City Cablevision Inc. - Grant City, MO - *BrCabYB 84; Tel&CabFB 84C*
Grant City Times-Tribune - Grant City, MO - *BaconPubCkNews 84*
Grant County Herald - Elbow Lake, MN - *AyerDirPub 83; Ed&PubIntYB 82*
Grant County Herald Independent - Lancaster, WI - *AyerDirPub 83; Ed&PubIntYB 82*
Grant County Journal - Ephrata, WA - *Ed&PubIntYB 82*
Grant County News [of Scripps-Howard] - Williamstown, KY - *AyerDirPub 83; Ed&PubIntYB 82; NewsDir 84*
Grant County News - Hyannis, NE - *AyerDirPub 83; Ed&PubIntYB 82*
Grant County News - Elgin, ND - *AyerDirPub 83; BaconPubCkNews 84; Ed&PubIntYB 82*
Grant County Press - Petersburg, WV - *AyerDirPub 83; Ed&PubIntYB 82; NewsDir 84*
Grant County Review - Milbank, SD - *AyerDirPub 83; Ed&PubIntYB 82*
Grant, Dorothy [Aff. of Consolidated Amethyst Communications Inc.] - Scarborough, ON, Canada - *BoPubDir 4, 5*
Grant Enterprises Inc., Sherry - Encino, CA - *Tel&CabFB 84C*
Grant Heilman Photography - Lititz, PA - *LitMarPl 84*
Grant Inc., David M. - New York, NY - *DirPRFirms 83*
Grant Inc., Donald M. - West Kingston, RI - *BoPubDir 4, 5*
Grant Inc., M. L. - New York, NY - *AdAge 3-28-84; StaDirAdAg 2-84*
Grant Information System [of The Oryx Press] - Phoenix, AZ - *CompReadDB 82; DBBus 82; EISS 83*
Grant/Jacoby Inc. - Chicago, IL - *AdAge 3-28-84; StaDirAdAg 2-84*
Grant Marketing Communications Inc. - Philadelphia, PA - *StaDirAdAg 2-84*
Grant Paper Co. - Philadelphia, PA - *LitMarPl 83, 84; MagIndMarPl 82-83*
Grant Park Gazette - *See* Russell Publications
Grant/Tandy Advertising - *See* K & E Holdings Inc.
Grant Tribune Sentinel - Grant, NE - *BaconPubCkNews 84; Ed&PubIntYB 82*
Grants [of The Oryx Press] - Phoenix, AZ - *DataDirOnSer 84; DirOnDB Spring 84*
Grants & Contracts Alert [of NewsNet Inc.] - Bryn Mawr, PA - *DataDirOnSer 84*
Grants & Contracts Weekly [of NewsNet Inc.] - Bryn Mawr, PA - *DataDirOnSer 84*
Grants & Contracts Weekly - Arlington, VA - *DirOnDB Spring 84*
Grants Beacon - Grants, NM - *BaconPubCkNews 84; Ed&PubIntYB 82; NewsDir 84*
Grants Pass Courier - Grants Pass, OR - *BaconPubCkNews 84; Ed&PubIntYB 82; NewsDir 84*
Grantsburg Burnett County Sentinel - Grantsburg, WI - *BaconPubCkNews 84*
Grantsmanship Center News, The - Los Angeles, CA - *WritMar 84*

Grantsville Calhoun Chronicle - Grantsville, WV - *BaconPubCkNews 84*
Grantsville News - Grantsville, WV - *BaconPubCkNews 84; Ed&PubIntYB 82*
Granum History Book Club - Granum, AB, Canada - *BoPubDir 4, 5*
Granville Cablevision Inc. - Granville, NY - *BrCabYB 84*
Granville CATV Inc. - Granville, PA - *BrCabYB 84; Tel&CabFB 84C*
Granville Putnam County Record - Granville, IL - *BaconPubCkNews 84*
Granville Sentinel - Granville, NY - *BaconPubCkNews 84; Ed&PubIntYB 82; NewsDir 84*
Granville Sentinel - Granville, OH - *Ed&PubIntYB 82*
Grape Belt - Dunkirk, NY - *AyerDirPub 83*
Grape Belt, The - Northern Chatauqua, NY - *Ed&PubIntYB 82*
Grapeland Cable TV Co. - Grapeland, TX - *BrCabYB 84; Tel&CabFB 84C*
Grapeland Messenger - Grapeland, TX - *BaconPubCkNews 84; Ed&PubIntYB 82*
Grapetree Productions Inc. - Key Biscayne, FL - *BoPubDir 5; LitMag&SmPr 83-84*
Grapevine Advertiser - Cheyenne, WY - *AyerDirPub 83*
Grapevine Productions Ltd. - Tucson, AZ - *AvMarPl 83*
Grapevine Sun - Grapevine, TX - *BaconPubCkNews 84; Ed&PubIntYB 82*
Grapevine, The - Fayetteville, AR - *AyerDirPub 83*
Grapevine, The - Tisbury, MA - *Ed&PubIntYB 82*
Grapevine, The - West Tisbury, MA - *AyerDirPub 83*
Grapevine TV - Hazard, KY - *Tel&CabFB 84C p.1682*
Graph Music - Woodstock, NY - *BillIntBG 83-84*
GraphCom Systems Inc. [Subs. of International Computaprint Corp.] - Ft. Washington, PA - *MagIndMarPl 82-83*
Graphic - Tuscaloosa, AL - *Ed&PubIntYB 82*
Graphic - Glidden, IA - *AyerDirPub 83*
Graphic - Lake Mills, IA - *AyerDirPub 83*
Graphic - Oakley, KS - *AyerDirPub 83*
Graphic - Osawatomie, KS - *AyerDirPub 83*
Graphic - Waltham, MA - *AyerDirPub 83*
Graphic - Lake City, MN - *AyerDirPub 83*
Graphic - Tryon, NE - *AyerDirPub 83*
Graphic - Brooklyn, NY - *AyerDirPub 83*
Graphic - Nashville, NC - *AyerDirPub 83*
Graphic - Spiro, OK - *AyerDirPub 83*
Graphic - Newberg, OR - *AyerDirPub 83*
Graphic - Portage La Prairie, MB, Canada - *AyerDirPub 83*
Graphic - Campbellton, NB, Canada - *AyerDirPub 83; Ed&PubIntYB 82*
Graphic Arts Buyer - New York, NY - *MagIndMarPl 82-83*
Graphic Arts Center Publishing Co. - Portland, OR - *LitMarPl 83, 84; WritMar 84*
Graphic Arts Consulting Service Inc. - Minneapolis, MN - *LitMarPl 83*
Graphic Arts Employment Service Inc. - Cincinnati, OH - *InfIndMarPl 83; LitMarPl 83, 84; MagIndMarPl 82-83*
Graphic Arts Finishers Inc. - Charlestown, MA - *LitMarPl 83, 84; MagIndMarPl 82-83*
Graphic Arts Information Service [of Rochester Institute of Technology] - Rochester, NY - *EISS 83*
Graphic Arts Monthly & the Printing Industry [of Technical Publishing Co.] - New York, NY - *BaconPubCkMag 84; LitMarPl 83, 84; MagDir 84; MagIndMarPl 82-83*
Graphic Arts Product News - Chicago, IL - *BaconPubCkMag 84*
Graphic Arts Technical Foundation - Pittsburgh, PA - *BoPubDir 4, 5*
Graphic Arts Trade Journals International Inc. - Farmingdale, NY - *BoPubDir 4, 5*
Graphic-Clarion - Arthur, IL - *Ed&PubIntYB 82*
Graphic Communication Services - Mt. Vernon, NY - *LitMarPl 83, 84*
Graphic Communications - Waltham, MA - *DataDirSup 7-83; MicrocomMPl 84*
Graphic Communications - Port Edwards, WI - *StaDirAdAg 2-84*
Graphic Communications Association - Arlington, VA - *EISS 83*
Graphic Communications World - Tallahassee, FL - *BaconPubCkMag 84*
Graphic Communicator - Washington, DC - *BaconPubCkMag 84*
Graphic Composition Inc. [Div. of The Heritage Group] - Athens, GA - *LitMarPl 83, 84; MagIndMarPl 82-83*
Graphic Controls Corp. - Buffalo, NY - *DirInfWP 82*
Graphic Crafts Inc. - Willow Street, PA - *BoPubDir 4, 5*
Graphic Curriculum, The - New York, NY - *AvMarPl 83*
Graphic Design Ad Group, The - Chattanooga, TN - *StaDirAdAg 2-84*
Graphic Dimensions - Pittsford, NY - *BoPubDir 4, 5*
Graphic Enterprise Inc. - Canton, OH - *DirInfWP 82*
Graphic Experience Inc., The - New York, NY - *ArtMar 84; DirMarMP 83*
Graphic Films Ltd. [Subs. of Crawley Films Ltd.] - Ottawa, ON, Canada - *AvMarPl 83*
Graphic House Inc., The - Englishtown, NJ - *DirMarMP 83*
Graphic I Inc., The - Lynn, MA - *DirMarMP 83*
Graphic Image Publications - La Jolla, CA - *BoPubDir 5; LitMag&SmPr 83-84; LitMarPl 84; WritMar 84*
Graphic Impressions Inc. - Denver, CO - *BoPubDir 4 Sup, 5*
Graphic International - Margate, FL - *MagDir 84*
Graphic International - Pompano Beach, FL - *MagIndMarPl 82-83*
Graphic Laminating Inc. - Cleveland, OH - *AvMarPl 83*
Graphic Litho - Lawrence, MA - *LitMarPl 83, 84; MagIndMarPl 82-83*
Graphic Marketing Enterprises - Cerritos, CA - *BoPubDir 4, 5*
Graphic Media Corp. [Subs. of Graphic Media Inc.] - Fairfield, NJ - *AvMarPl 83*
Graphic Media S/E [Subs. of Graphic Media Corp.] - Winston-Salem, NC - *AvMarPl 83*
Graphic Method Inc., A - Oceanside, NY - *LitMarPl 83, 84; MagIndMarPl 82-83*
Graphic Microfilm [Div. of Spaulding Co. Inc.] - Stoughton, MA - *MicroMarPl 82-83*
Graphic Monthly, The - Toronto, ON, Canada - *BaconPubCkMag 84; WritMar 84*
Graphic News Bureau - New York, NY - *Ed&PubIntYB 82; LitMarPl 84*
Graphic Originals Inc. - New York, NY - *ArtMar 84*
Graphic Persuasion Inc. - Boca Raton, FL - *StaDirAdAg 2-84*
Graphic Products Corp. - Bloomfield, CT - *DirInfWP 82*
Graphic Ribbon Inc. [Subs. of Franz Buettner] - Franklin, TN - *DirInfWP 82*
Graphic Scanning Corp. - Englewood, NJ - *BrCabYB 84*
Graphic Scanning Corp. - Teaneck, NJ - *HomeVid&CabYB 82-83; TeleSy&SerDir 7-83*
Graphic Services Corp. - Belleville, NJ - *MagIndMarPl 82-83*
Graphic Software Inc. - Boston, MA - *MicrocomMPl 84*
Graphic Software Inc. - Cambridge, MA - *MicrocomSwDir 1*
Graphic Software Systems - Wilsonville, OR - *DataDirSup 7-83; MicrocomMPl 84; WhoWMicrocom 83*
Graphic Technique Inc. - New York, NY - *LitMarPl 83, 84*
Graphic Technique Inc. - Lancaster, PA - *MagIndMarPl 82-83*
Graphic Technology Inc. - Newburgh, NY - *AvMarPl 83*
Graphic, The - Richmond, IN - *AyerDirPub 83*
Graphic, The - Georgetown, KY - *Ed&PubIntYB 82*
Graphic Workshop Inc. - Emerson, NJ - *StaDirAdAg 2-84*
Graphic World - St. Louis, MO - *LitMarPl 84; MagIndMarPl 82-83*
Graphical Software Ltd. - Cambridge, England - *MicrocomSwDir 1*
Graphicomposition Inc. - New York, NY - *LitMarPl 83*
GraphicProfile [of Donnelley Marketing Information Services] - Stamford, CT - *DataDirOnSer 84; DirOnDB Spring 84*
Graphics-Communication Associates - Tallahassee, FL - *BoPubDir 5*
Graphics Concepts Inc. - Worthington, OH - *DataDirSup 7-83*
Graphics Design: USA - New York, NY - *BaconPubCkMag 84; MagDir 84*
Graphics Etcetera - Boston, MA - *LitMarPl 83, 84*
Graphics for Management - Columbus, OH - *MicrocomMPl 84*
Graphics Institute [Div. of Creamer Dickson Basford] - New York, NY - *LitMarPl 83, 84; ProGuPRSer 4*
Graphics International Inc. - Albany, NY - *LitMarPl 84*
Graphics International Inc. (Merlin Equipment Div.) - Winter Park, FL - *DataDirSup 7-83*
Graphics Network News - Fairfax, VA - *BaconPubCkMag 84*
Graphics One Fifty Co. - Morris Plains, NJ - *AvMarPl 83*
Graphics Press - Santa Monica, CA - *BoPubDir 4, 5*

Graphics Software Inc. - Anaheim, CA - *MicrocomMPl 84*
Graphics Team, The - New York, NY - *LitMarPl 83, 84; MagIndMarPl 82-83*
Graphics Today - New York, NY - *MagDir 84*
Graphics West - Colorado Springs, CO - *LitMarPl 84*
Graphnet Inc. - Teaneck, NJ - *DataDirSup 7-83*
Graphophile Associates - Tappan, NY - *BoPubDir 4, 5*
Grappe [of Questel Inc.] - Washington, DC - *DataDirOnSer 84*
Grappe - Lorient, France - *DirOnDB Spring 84*
Grass & Grain [of Ag Press Inc.] - Manhattan, KS - *Ed&PubIntYB 82; NewsDir 84*
Grass-Hooper Press - St. Louis, MO - *BoPubDir 4, 5*
Grass Mountain Publishing - Ft. Worth, TX - *BillIntBG 83-84*
Grass Roots [of Night Owl Publishers] - Shepparton, Australia - *LitMag&SmPr 83-84*
Grass Valley Computer Systems - Rough & Ready, CA - *WhoWMicrocom 83*
Grass Valley-Union [of Nevada County Publishing Co.] - Grass Valley, CA - *NewsDir 84*
Grassdale Publishers Inc. - Norman, OK - *BoPubDir 4, 5*
Grassland Advertiser - Swift Current, SK, Canada - *Ed&PubIntYB 82*
Grassland Media - Madison, WI - *AvMarPl 83*
Grassroots Project Unltd. - San Francisco, CA - *BillIntBG 83-84*
Gratiot County Herald - Ithaca, MI - *AyerDirPub 83; Ed&PubIntYB 82*
Grattan Advertising & Public Relations - Palm Springs, CA - *DirPRFirms 83*
Grau-Aybar Associates Inc. - Deer Park, NY - *WhoWMicrocom 83*
Grauer & Fingerote - *See* Fingerote & Grauer/Grauer & Fingerote
Grauer, Jack - Gresham, OR - *BoPubDir 4, 5*
Graunke, Raymond - Albuquerque, NM - *LitMarPl 83, 84; MagIndMarPl 82-83*
Gravelbourg Gazette - Gravelbourg, SK, Canada - *AyerDirPub 83*
Gravelle Graphic Design, Marian - Jackson Heights, NY - *LitMarPl 83, 84*
Gravenhurst Cable System Ltd. - Bracebridge, ON, Canada - *BrCabYB 84*
Gravenhurst Music - Beaver, PA - *BillIntBG 83-84*
Gravenhurst News, The - Gravenhurst, ON, Canada - *Ed&PubIntYB 82*
Graves & Associates Inc. - Tacoma, WA - *DirPRFirms 83; StaDirAdAg 2-84*
Gravesend Press - Syracuse, NY - *BoPubDir 5*
Gravette News Herald - Gravette, AR - *BaconPubCkNews 84; Ed&PubIntYB 82*
Gravida - Bayville, NY - *LitMag&SmPr 83-84*
Gravity Cafe - New York, NY - *LitMag&SmPr 83-84*
Gray & Associates - Tampa, FL - *DirPRFirms 83*
Gray & Co. - Washington, DC - *DirPRFirms 83*
Gray & Kilgore [Subs. of Ross Roy Inc.] - Troy, MI - *ArtMar 84; StaDirAdAg 2-84*
Gray & Rogers - Philadelphia, PA - *AdAge 3-28-84; BrCabYB 84; DirPRFirms 83; StaDirAdAg 2-84*
Gray Associates, Relta - Seattle, WA - *DirPRFirms 83*
Gray Baumgarten Layport Inc. - Pittsburgh, PA - *StaDirAdAg 2-84*
Gray Beard Publications - Seattle, WA - *BoPubDir 4, 5*
Gray Communications Systems Inc. - Albany, GA - *AvMarPl 83; BrCabYB 84; Tel&CabFB 84S*
Gray/Compton Public Relations, Thelma [Subs. of Compton Advertising Inc.] - Philadelphia, PA - *DirPRFirms 83*
Gray Consulting Group Inc., The - New York, NY - *DirPRFirms 83*
Gray Family, Gordon - *See* Summit Communications Inc.
Gray, Herbi - Olympia, WA - *BoPubDir 5*
Gray Inc., R. A. - San Diego, CA - *AvMarPl 83*
Gray Jones County News - Gray, GA - *BaconPubCkNews 84*
Gray Moose Press - Rye, NY - *BoPubDir 4, 5*
Gray Publications, Edgar - Kalamazoo, MI - *BoPubDir 4, 5*
Gray-Schwartz Enterprises Inc. - Woodland Hills, CA - *TelAl 83; Tel&CabFB 84C*
Gray-Schwartz Enterprises Inc. (Teleflix Div.) - Woodland Hills, CA - *TelAl 84*
Gray Welsh Gray & Associates Inc. - Houston, TX - *MicrocomMPl 84*
Grayling Cable Services - Grayling, MI - *BrCabYB 84; Tel&CabFB 84C*
Grayling Crawford County Avalanche - Grayling, MI - *BaconPubCkNews 84*
Grays Harbor Paper Co. - Hoquiam, WA - *MagIndMarPl 82-83*
Gray's Publishing Ltd. - Sidney, BC, Canada - *BoPubDir 4 Sup, 5; LitMarPl 83, 84; WritMar 84*
Gray's Sporting Journal - Hamilton, MA - *ArtMar 84; BaconPubCkMag 84; WritMar 84*
Grayslake Times - Grayslake, IL - *Ed&PubIntYB 82; NewsDir 84*
Grayslake Times - *See* Lakeland Publishers Inc.
Grayson Associates Inc. - Ft. Lee, NJ - *HBIndAd&MS 82-83*
Grayson Cable TV Co. Inc. - Grayson, KY - *BrCabYB 84*
Grayson County News-Gazette - Leitchfield, KY - *AyerDirPub 83; Ed&PubIntYB 82; NewsDir 84*
Grayson Journal Enquirer - Grayson, KY - *BaconPubCkNews 84; Ed&PubIntYB 82; NewsDir 84*
Grayson TV Cable Co. Inc. - Grayson, KY - *Tel&CabFB 84C*
Grayson Unltd. - Glen Head, NY - *HBIndAd&MS 82-83*
Grayville Cablevision Inc. [of Omni Cable TV Corp.] - Grayville, IL - *BrCabYB 84; Tel&CabFB 84C*
Grayville Mercury-Independent - Grayville, IL - *BaconPubCkNews 84*
Graywolf Press - Port Townsend, WA - *BoPubDir 4, 5; LitMag&SmPr 83-84; LitMarPl 84*
Gre-Jac Music - Memphis, TN - *BillIntBG 83-84*
Great Alps Publishing - North Miami Beach, FL - *BillIntBG 83-84*
Great American Books - Beverly Hills, CA - *BoPubDir 4, 5*
Great American Cinema Co. - Los Angeles, CA - *Tel&CabFB 84C*
Great American Productions - Houston, TX - *AvMarPl 83*
Great American Publishing Co. - Atlanta, GA - *BillIntBG 83-84*
Great Amwell Co. - New York, NY - *LitMarPl 83*
Great Barrington Berkshire Courier - Great Barrington, MA - *BaconPubCkNews 84*
Great Basin Press - Reno, NV - *LitMag&SmPr 83-84*
Great Bend Tribune [of Morris Newspaper Corp.] - Great Bend, KS - *BaconPubCkNews 84; Ed&PubIntYB 82; NewsDir 84*
Great Britain Public Record Office (Photo-Ordering Section) - Richmond, England - *MicroMarPl 82-83*
Great Canadian Print Co. Ltd. - Winnipeg, MB, Canada - *ArtMar 84*
Great Circle News - Dallas, TX - *Ed&PubIntYB 82*
Great Circle Productions - Southwest Harbor, ME - *BoPubDir 4 Sup, 5*
Great Circle Productions - West Somerville, MA - *LitMag&SmPr 83-84*
Great Divide Software - Lakewood, CO - *MicrocomMPl 84*
Great Eastern Book Co. [Subs. of Shambhala Publications Inc.] - Boulder, CO - *LitMag&SmPr 83-84; LitMarPl 83, 84*
Great Expeditions - Vancouver, BC, Canada - *WritMar 84*
Great Falls Cablevision Inc. - Great Falls, SC - *BrCabYB 84; Tel&CabFB 84C*
Great Falls Montana Catholic Register - Great Falls, MT - *NewsDir 84*
Great Falls Tribune - Great Falls, MT - *BaconPubCkNews 84; Ed&PubIntYB 82; NewsDir 84*
Great Honesty Music Inc. - Larkspur, CA - *BillIntBG 83-84*
Great Lake Sportsman Group - Oshkosh, WI - *ArtMar 84*
Great Lakes Aviation [of Data Publications Inc.] - Brookfield, CT - *MagDir 84*
Great Lakes Books - Brighton, MI - *BoPubDir 4 Sup, 5*
Great Lakes Broadcasting Co. - Lorain, OH - *BrCabYB 84*
Great Lakes Bulletin [of Lakeland Publishers Inc.] - Grayslake, IL - *NewsDir 84*
Great Lakes Bulletin - Great Lakes, IL - *Ed&PubIntYB 82*
Great Lakes Bulletin - North Chicago, IL - *AyerDirPub 83*
Great Lakes Bulletin - *See* Lakeland Publishers Inc.
Great Lakes Cable [of The Essex Group] - Alanson, MI - *Tel&CabFB 84C*
Great Lakes Cable [of The Essex Group] - Beulah, MI - *Tel&CabFB 84C*
Great Lakes Cable [of The Essex Group] - Elk Rapids, MI - *BrCabYB 84*

Great Lakes Cable [of The Essex Group] - Kalkaska, MI - *Tel&CabFB 84C*
Great Lakes Cable [of The Essex Group] - Lapeer, MI - *BrCabYB 84*
Great Lakes Cable [of The Essex Group] - Manistee, MI - *BrCabYB 84*
Great Lakes Cable [of The Essex Group] - Manton, MI - *Tel&CabFB 84C*
Great Lakes Cable [of The Essex Group] - Mayfield Township, MI - *Tel&CabFB 84C*
Great Lakes Cable [of The Essex Group] - Onekama, MI - *Tel&CabFB 84C*
Great Lakes Cable [of The Essex Group] - Pentwater, MI - *Tel&CabFB 84C*
Great Lakes CATV - Milford, IA - *BrCabYB 84*
Great Lakes/Chicagoland Boating - Chicago, IL - *BaconPubCkMag 84*
Great Lakes Digital Resources - Detroit, MI - *MicrocomMPl 83*
Great Lakes Fisherman - Columbus, OH - *WritMar 84*
Great Lakes Fruit Growers News - Sparta, MI - *BaconPubCkMag 84; MagDir 84*
Great Lakes Information Systems Ltd. - Ann Arbor, MI - *WhoWMicrocom 83*
Great Lakes Marketing Associates Inc. - Toledo, OH - *IntDirMarRes 83*
Great Lakes Sports/Michigan - Rochester, MI - *BaconPubCkMag 84*
Great Lakes Vegetable Growers News - Sparta, MI - *BaconPubCkMag 84; MagDir 84*
Great Lander News - Anchorage, AK - *BaconPubCkNews 84*
Great Lander Shopping News & Sourdough Saver Classified - Anchorage, AK - *AyerDirPub 83*
Great Neck News - Great Neck, NY - *BaconPubCkNews 84; Ed&PubIntYB 82; NewsDir 84*
Great Neck Pennysaver - Great Neck, NY - *AyerDirPub 83*
Great Neck Record - Glen Cove, NY - *AyerDirPub 83; NewsDir 84*
Great Neck Record - Great Neck, NY - *Ed&PubIntYB 82*
Great Neck Record - *See* Community Newspapers Inc.
Great Neck Shopping News/North & South - Jericho, NY - *AyerDirPub 83*
Great Northern/Design Printing Co. - Skokie, IL - *LitMarPl 83, 84*
Great Northern Paper [Div. of Great Northern Nekoosa Corp.] - Stamford, CT - *MagIndMarPl 82-83*
Great Northwest Publishing & Distributing Co. - Anchorage, AK - *BoPubDir 5*
Great Northwest Publishing & Distributing Co. - Spokane, WA - *BoPubDir 4*
Great Nothern Data Systems Inc. - Minneapolis, MN - *MicrocomMPl 84*
Great Oak Press of Virginia - Falls Church, VA - *BoPubDir 4 Sup, 5*
Great Oak Publications Inc. - North Reading, MA - *BaconPubCkNews 84*
Great Ocean Publishers - Arlington, VA - *BoPubDir 4; LitMarPl 83, 84; WritMar 84*
Great Outdoors Publishing Co. - St. Petersburg, FL - *LitMarPl 83; WritMar 84*
Great Outdoors Trading Co. - Marshall, CA - *BoPubDir 4, 5*
Great People Music - *See* Good Product Music
Great Plains Communications Inc. - Wichita, KS - *Tel&CabFB 84C p.1682*
Great Plains Computer Co. - Idaho Falls, ID - *MicrocomMPl 84; MicrocomSwDir 1*
Great Plains National Instructional Television Library - Lincoln, NE - *AvMarPl 83; Tel&CabFB 84C*
Great Plains Software - Fargo, ND - *MicrocomMPl 84; MicrocomSwDir 1*
Great Plains Telephone Co. - Keystone, SD - *TelDir&BG 83-84*
Great Pyramid Ltd. Music - San Francisco, CA - *BillIntBG 83-84*
Great Recipes of the World [of Great Recipes Publishing Associates] - Englewood Cliffs, NJ - *BaconPubCkMag 84; Folio 83; MagIndMarPl 82-83; WritMar 84*
Great River Review - Winona, MN - *LitMag&SmPr 83-84; WritMar 84*
Great River Translation Service - Quincy, IL - *LitMarPl 83*
Great Scott Advertising Co. Inc. - New York, NY - *StaDirAdAg 2-84*
Great Scott Stations - Pottstown, PA - *BrCabYB 84*
Great Society Press - Phillipsburg, NJ - *BoPubDir 4, 5; LitMag&SmPr 83-84*
Great South Bay Poetry Co-Op - Central Islip, NY - *LitMag&SmPr 83-84*
Great Southern Printing & Manufacturing Co. - *See* GS Communications Inc.
Great Southern Record Co. Inc. - New Orleans, LA - *BillIntBG 83-84*
Great Star Press - Berkeley, CA - *BoPubDir 4, 5*
Great Trails Broadcasting Corp. - Dayton, OH - *BrCabYB 84; Tel&CabFB 84S*
Great West Books Inc. - Denver, CO - *BoPubDir 4, 5*
Great Western Advertising - San Diego, CA - *StaDirAdAg 2-84*
Great Western Properties - Tri-Palm Estates, CA - *BrCabYB 84*
Great Western Publications [Aff. of Weiler Printing & Publishing] - Gardena, CA - *BoPubDir 4, 5*
Great Western Publishing Co. Inc. - Glendale, CA - *LitMag&SmPr 83-84*
Great Western Software Co. Inc., The - Ft. Lauderdale, FL - *MicrocomMPl 83*
Great Western Software Co., The - Euless, TX - *MicrocomMPl 84*
Great White Whale Advertising Inc. - New York, NY - *StaDirAdAg 2-84*
Greater Amusements - Sunnyside, NY - *MagDir 84*
Greater Boston Cable Corp. [of Colony Communications Inc.] - Woburn, MA - *BrCabYB 84; Tel&CabFB 84C*
Greater Boston Chamber of Commerce - Boston, MA - *BoPubDir 5*
Greater Charleston Trading Post - Charleston, SC - *AyerDirPub 83*
Greater Chicopee Cablevision Inc. [of Greater Media Inc.] - Chicopee, MA - *BrCabYB 84; Tel&CabFB 84C*
Greater Colonie Townsman - Latham, NY - *Ed&PubIntYB 82*
Greater Easthampton Cablevision Inc. - Easthampton, MA - *BrCabYB 84*
Greater Fall River Cable TV [of Colony Communications Inc.] - Fall River, MA - *BrCabYB 84; Tel&CabFB 84C*
Greater Grafton Cablevision - Grafton, MA - *BrCabYB 84*
Greater Hartford CATV Inc. [of Cox Cable Communications Inc.] - Manchester, CT - *BrCabYB 84*
Greater Humboldt-Dakota City CATV [of Cable Communications of Iowa] - Humboldt, IA - *BrCabYB 84*
Greater Lafayette TV Cable Co. [of Times Mirror Cable Television Inc.] - Lafayette, IN - *BrCabYB 84; Tel&CabFB 84C*
Greater Lafourche Gazette, The - Larose, LA - *AyerDirPub 83*
Greater London Council (Research Library) - London, England - *CompReadDB 82*
Greater Media Inc. - Easthampton, MA - *Tel&CabFB 84C*
Greater Media Inc. - East Brunswick, NJ - *BrCabYB 84 p.D-301; Tel&CabFB 84C p.1682*
Greater Millbury Cablevision [of Greater Media Inc.] - Millbury, MA - *BrCabYB 84*
Greater Minneapolis Magazine - Minneapolis, MN - *MagDir 84*
Greater New England Cablevision Co. Inc. [of Greater Media Inc.] - Ludlow, MA - *BrCabYB 84*
Greater Northbridge Cablevision Inc. - East Brunswick, NJ - *BrCabYB 84*
Greater Oxford Cablevision Inc. [of Greater Media Inc.] - Webster, MA - *BrCabYB 84*
Greater Philadelphia Chamber of Commerce - Philadelphia, PA - *BoPubDir 4, 5*
Greater Philadelphia Economist, The - Philadelphia, PA - *BaconPubCkMag 84*
Greater Plaquemine Post, The - Plaquemine, LA - *Ed&PubIntYB 82*
Greater Portland - Portland, ME - *BaconPubCkMag 84*
Greater Portland Landmarks Inc. - Portland, ME - *BoPubDir 4, 5*
Greater Reading Area Merchandiser Zone I - Lebanon, PA - *AyerDirPub 83*
Greater Reading Area Merchandiser Zone II - Lebanon, PA - *AyerDirPub 83*
Greater Reading Area Merchandiser Zone III - Lebanon, PA - *AyerDirPub 83*

Greater Renovo TV Corp. - Renovo, PA - *BrCabYB 84; Tel&CabFB 84C*
Greater W-D Cablevision Co. [of Greater Media Inc.] - Webster, MA - *BrCabYB 84; Tel&CabFB 84C*
Greater Winnipeg Cablevision Ltd. - Winnipeg, MB, Canada - *BrCabYB 84*
Greater Worcester Cablevision Inc. [of Greater Media Inc.] - Worcester, MA - *Tel&CabFB 84C*
Greatest Editorial Services on Earth, The - Burbank, CA - *LitMarPl 83*
Greatest Fights of the Century Inc. - New York, NY - *TelAl 83, 84*
Greatland Publishing Co. - Front Royal, VA - *DirMarMP 83*
Greaves Typing Service - New York, NY - *LitMarPl 83, 84*
Greece Pennysaver - Rochester, NY - *AyerDirPub 83*
Greece Post [of Pittsford Wolfe Publications Inc.] - Pittsford, NY - *NewsDir 84*
Greece Post - Spencerport, NY - *AyerDirPub 83*
Greece Post, The - Greece, NY - *Ed&PubIntYB 82*
Greek Accent [of Greek Accent Publishing Corp.] - Long Island City, NY - *WritMar 84*
Greek Canadian Action - Montreal, PQ, Canada - *Ed&PubIntYB 82*
Greek Canadian Reportage - Montreal, PQ, Canada - *Ed&PubIntYB 82*
Greek Canadian Tribune - Montreal, PQ, Canada - *Ed&PubIntYB 82*
Greek Press - Chicago, IL - *Ed&PubIntYB 82*
Greek Press - Des Plaines, IL - *NewsDir 84*
Greek Star - Chicago, IL - *Ed&PubIntYB 82*
Greek Sunday News - Boston, MA - *AyerDirPub 83; Ed&PubIntYB 82; NewsDir 84*
Greeley Booster - Greeley, CO - *BaconPubCkNews 84*
Greeley Citizen - Greeley, NE - *BaconPubCkNews 84; Ed&PubIntYB 82*
Greeley County Republican - Tribune, KS - *AyerDirPub 83; Ed&PubIntYB 82*
Greeley Tribune - Greeley, CO - *Ed&PubIntYB 82; NewsDir 84*
Greeley Tribune & Republican - Greeley, CO - *BaconPubCkNews 84*
Greeley Video Inc. [of Daniels & Associates Inc.] - Greeley, CO - *BrCabYB 84*
Green Advertects Inc. - Richmond, VA - *StaDirAdAg 2-84*
Green & Associates Inc., Howard L. - Birmingham, MI - *IntDirMarRes 83*
Green & Partners - Atlanta, GA - *StaDirAdAg 2-84*
Green/Associates Advertising Inc. - Eugene, OR - *ArtMar 84; AvMarPl 83*
Green Associates Inc., George - New York, NY - *DirPRFirms 83*
Green Baron Book & Film Co. - Colorado Springs, CO - *WritMar 84*
Green Bay News-Chronicle [of Metropolitan Newspaper Corp.] - Green Bay, WI - *BaconPubCkNews 84; Ed&PubIntYB 82; NewsDir 84*
Green Bay Press-Gazette - Green Bay, WI - *BaconPubCkNews 84; Ed&PubIntYB 82; NewsDir 84*
Green, Bill - De Quincy, LA - *Tel&CabFB 84C p.1682*
Green Books, Wayne - Peterborough, NH - *BoPubDir 4 Sup, 5; DirMarMP 83*
Green City Press - Green City, MO - *Ed&PubIntYB 82*
Green City Press - Milan, MO - *BaconPubCkNews 84*
Green Country Cable of Bristow [of Mid West Communications Inc.] - Bristow, OK - *BrCabYB 84; Tel&CabFB 84C*
Green Country Cable of Maysville [of Mid West Communications Inc.] - Maysville, OK - *BrCabYB 84*
Green Country Cable of Wagoner - Wagoner, OK - *Tel&CabFB 84C*
Green Country Cable Systems Inc. - Purcell, OK - *Tel&CabFB 84C p.1682*
Green Country Cable Systems Inc. [of Mid West Communications Inc.] - Sapulpa, OK - *BrCabYB 84; Tel&CabFB 84C*
Green County Democrat - Eutaw, AL - *Ed&PubIntYB 82*
Green Cove Springs & Orange Park Clay County Crescent - Green Cove Springs, FL - *BaconPubCkNews 84; NewsDir 84*
Green Door Music - Ft. Worth, TX - *BillIntBG 83-84*
Green Eagle Press - New York, NY - *BoPubDir 4, 5*
Green Feather [of Quality Publications Inc.] - Lakewood, OH - *LitMag&SmPr 83-84; WritMar 84*
Green Forest Carroll County Tribune - Green Forest, AR - *NewsDir 84*
Green Forest Carroll County Tribune - *See* Larimer Publications Inc.
Green Group, Howard - Elmira, NY - *Tel&CabFB 84S*
Green Group, The - Linwood, NJ - *BrCabYB 84*
Green Hill Publishers - Aurora, IL - *LitMarPl 83*
Green Hill Publishers - Ottawa, IL - *LitMarPl 84; WritMar 84*
Green Hills Press - Eugene, OR - *BoPubDir 4, 5*
Green Hills Telephone Cooperative - Breckenridge, MO - *TelDir&BG 83-84*
Green Horizons Press - Kerrville, TX - *BoPubDir 4 Sup, 5*
Green Horse Press - Aromas, CA - *BoPubDir 4, 5; LitMag&SmPr 83-84*
Green Hut Press - Valencia Hills, CA - *BoPubDir 4, 5; LitMag&SmPr 83-84*
Green Inc., Paula - New York, NY - *StaDirAdAg 2-84*
Green Inc., Warren H. - St. Louis, MO - *DirMarMP 83; LitMarPl 83, 84; MagIndMarPl 82-83; WritMar 84*
Green Key Press [Aff. of Power Communications Corp.] - Toronto, ON, Canada - *BoPubDir 4 Sup, 5*
Green Knight Press - Amherst, MA - *LitMag&SmPr 83-84*
Green Lake County Cablevision Inc. - Montello, WI - *Tel&CabFB 84C*
Green Lake County Cablevision Inc. - Princeton, WI - *Tel&CabFB 84C*
Green Lake County Reporter - Berlin, WI - *AyerDirPub 83*
Green Lake Reporter - *See* Journal Co., The
Green Leaf Press - Alhambra, CA - *LitMarPl 84*
Green Leaf Press - Campbell, CA - *LitMag&SmPr 83-84; LitMarPl 83*
Green, Lind & McNulty Inc. - Union, NJ - *StaDirAdAg 2-84*
Green Linnet Records Inc. - New Canaan, CT - *BillIntBG 83-84*
Green Menu Music Co. [Div. of Green Menu Music Factory Inc.] - New Rochelle, NY - *BillIntBG 83-84*
Green Menu Records [Div. of Green Menu Music Factory Inc.] - New Rochelle, NY - *BillIntBG 83-84*
Green Mountain Post Films - Turners Falls, MA - *AvMarPl 83*
Green Oak Press - Brighton, MI - *BoPubDir 4, 5*
Green Oak Township Historical Society - Brighton, MI - *BoPubDir 4 Sup, 5*
Green Productions Inc., Bob - Houston, TX - *AvMarPl 83*
Green Publishers Inc. - Orange, VA - *BaconPubCkNews 84*
Green River Cable TV Co. [of Sweetwater Cable TV Co. Inc.] - Green River, WY - *BrCabYB 84; Tel&CabFB 84C*
Green River Cablevision Ltd. - Green River, UT - *Tel&CabFB 84C*
Green River Press - University Center, MI - *BoPubDir 4 Sup, 5*
Green River Republican - Morgantown, KY - *AyerDirPub 83; Ed&PubIntYB 82*
Green River Star - Green River, WY - *BaconPubCkNews 84; Ed&PubIntYB 82*
Green River Systems - Auburn, WA - *MicrocomMPl 83*
Green River Trading Co. - Millerton, NY - *ArtMar 84*
Green, Robert Alan - Key West, FL - *BoPubDir 4, 5*
Green Sheet - Pittsburgh, PA - *AyerDirPub 83*
Green Sheet Shopper - East Lansing, MI - *AyerDirPub 83*
Green Sheet-Shopping News - Fairfield, CA - *AyerDirPub 83*
Green Shutters Cookbook - Halifax, NS, Canada - *BoPubDir 4, 5*
Green Spring Inc. - Sharon, CT - *LitMarPl 83, 84*
Green Syndicate, The Arthur S. - Beverly Hills, CA - *BaconPubCkNews 84; Ed&PubIntYB 82*
Green Tab [of Westmoreland Journals Inc.] - Pittsburgh, PA - *AyerDirPub 83; NewsDir 84*
Green Thumb, The - Naples, NY - *Ed&PubIntYB 82*
Green Tiger Press - San Diego, CA - *LitMarPl 83, 84; WritMar 84*
Green Tree Records - Palo Alto, CA - *BillIntBG 83-84*
Green Valley Cable TV [of Listronics Corp.] - El Rancho Green Valley, CA - *BrCabYB 84*
Green Valley Lake TV Cable - Green Valley Lake, CA - *BrCabYB 84; Tel&CabFB 84C*
Green Valley News - Green Valley, AZ - *NewsDir 84*
Green Valley News & Sun - Green Valley, AZ - *AyerDirPub 83; Ed&PubIntYB 82*

Green, Walter J. - New York, NY - *LitMarPl 83; MagIndMarPl 82-83*
Green, Wilson Floyd - Winnipeg, MB, Canada - *BoPubDir 4, 5*
Greenbar Music Corp. - Los Angeles, CA - *BillIntBG 83-84*
Greenbelt News-Review [of Greenbelt Cooperative Publishing Association] - Greenbelt, MD - *BaconPubCkNews 84; Ed&PubIntYB 82; NewsDir 84*
Greenberg Public Relations, Donna - Philadelphia, PA - *DirPRFirms 83*
Greenberg Publishing Co. - Sykesville, MD - *BoPubDir 4, 5*
Greenberg, Tony - Malibu, CA - *LitMarPl 84*
Greenbriar Cable TV Co. - Cocke County, TN - *Tel&CabFB 84C*
Greenbriar Cable TV Co. [of National Telecommunications Inc.] - Pigeon Forge, TN - *Tel&CabFB 84C p.1682*
Greenbrier Cable Corp. - Caldwell, WV - *BrCabYB 84*
Greenbrier Cable Corp. - Hillsboro, WV - *BrCabYB 84*
Greenbrier Cable Corp. - Lewisburg, WV - *BrCabYB 84*
Greenbrier Marketing International - Tempe, AZ - *MicrocomMPl 84*
Greenburg, Tony - Malibu, CA - *LitMarPl 83*
Greenburger Associates Inc., Sanford J. - New York, NY - *LitMarPl 83, 84*
Greenbush Area News - East Greenbush, NY - *AyerDirPub 83*
Greenbush Area News - Greenbush, NY - *Ed&PubIntYB 82*
Greenbush Tribune - Greenbush, MN - *BaconPubCkNews 84; Ed&PubIntYB 82*
Greencastle Banner-Graphic - Greencastle, IN - *BaconPubCkNews 84*
Greencastle Echo-Pilot - Greencastle, PA - *BaconPubCkNews 84*
Greencastle Putnam County Banner-Graphic - Greencastle, IN - *NewsDir 84*
Greencrest Press Inc. - Winston-Salem, NC - *BoPubDir 4 Sup, 5; LitMag&SmPr 83-84*
Greendale Village Life - *See* Community Newspapers Inc.
Greene Advertising Agency - Snow Hill, NC - *StaDirAdAg 2-84*
Greene & Claire - New York, NY - *AdAge 3-28-84; StaDirAdAg 2-84*
Greene & Dewar New Wilderness Productions - Santa Monica, CA - *Tel&CabFB 84C*
Greene Associates, Stephen I. - Huntington, NY - *StaDirAdAg 2-84*
Greene, Berne - Portland, OR - *LitMarPl 83, 84; MagIndMarPl 82-83*
Greene, Bill Tycoon - Mill Valley, CA - *BoPubDir 4, 5*
Greene Cablevision Co. - Greene, NY - *BrCabYB 84; Tel&CabFB 84C*
Greene Chemango American Reporter - *See* Twin Valley Publishers Inc.
Greene Chenage American - Greene, NY - *NewsDir 84*
Greene County Democrat - Eutaw, AL - *AyerDirPub 83*
Greene County Herald - Leakesville, MS - *Ed&PubIntYB 82*
Greene County News - Catskill, NY - *AyerDirPub 83; Ed&PubIntYB 82*
Greene County Record - Stanardsville, VA - *AyerDirPub 83; Ed&PubIntYB 82*
Greene Inc./Communications - New York, NY - *DirPRFirms 83*
Greene, Paulette - Rockville Centre, NY - *BoPubDir 4, 5*
Greene Press, The Stephen - Brattleboro, VT - *DirMarMP 83; LitMarPl 83, 84; WritMar 84*
Greene Productions Inc., Larry - Los Angeles, CA - *Tel&CabFB 84C*
Greene Publishing, Agnes - Hamilton, ON, Canada - *BoPubDir 4 Sup, 5*
Greene, R. E. - Washington, DC - *BoPubDir 4, 5*
Greene Recorder - Greene, IA - *BaconPubCkNews 84; Ed&PubIntYB 82*
Greene Whitney Point Reporter - Greene, NY - *NewsDir 84*
Greenemont Books - Brattleboro, VT - *LitMarPl 83*
Greeneville Sun - Greeneville, TN - *BaconPubCkNews 84; Ed&PubIntYB 82; NewsDir 84*
Greenfield Adair County Free Press - Greenfield, IA - *BaconPubCkNews 84*
Greenfield Advertiser - Greenfield, MO - *Ed&PubIntYB 82*
Greenfield Argus - Greenfield, IL - *BaconPubCkNews 84; Ed&PubIntYB 82*
Greenfield Associates Inc., Martin - Great Neck, NY - *StaDirAdAg 2-84*
Greenfield Cable TV Inc. [of Tele-Communications Inc.] - Greenfield, IN - *BrCabYB 84; Tel&CabFB 84C*
Greenfield Co., Arthur - Los Angeles, CA - *Tel&CabFB 84C*
Greenfield Daily Reporter [of Home News Enterprises] - Greenfield, IN - *NewsDir 84*
Greenfield Hancock Advertiser - Greenfield, IN - *BaconPubCkNews 84*
Greenfield News - Greenfield, CA - *Ed&PubIntYB 82*
Greenfield News - King City, CA - *AyerDirPub 83*
Greenfield News - *See* Casey Newspapers Inc.
Greenfield Observer - Greenfield, WI - *Ed&PubIntYB 82*
Greenfield Observer - Oak Creek, WI - *AyerDirPub 83*
Greenfield Printing & Publishing Co., The - Greenfield, OH - *MagIndMarPl 82-83*
Greenfield Recorder - Greenfield, MA - *BaconPubCkNews 84; Ed&PubIntYB 82; NewsDir 84*
Greenfield Review Press - Greenfield Center, NY - *BoPubDir 4, 5; LitMag&SmPr 83-84*
Greenfield Times - Greenfield, OH - *BaconPubCkNews 84; Ed&PubIntYB 82; NewsDir 84*
Greenfield Vedette - Greenfield, MO - *BaconPubCkNews 84*
Greengage Associates - New York, NY - *AdAge 3-28-84; StaDirAdAg 2-84*
Greengiels Music - Greensboro, NC - *BillIntBG 83-84*
Greenhaven Press Inc. - St. Paul, MN - *BoPubDir 4; LitMarPl 83, 84*
Greenhorn Valley News - Rye, CO - *Ed&PubIntYB 82*
Greenhouse Grower - Willoughby, OH - *BaconPubCkMag 84*
Greenhouse Manager - Ft. Worth, TX - *BaconPubCkMag 84*
Greenhouse Review Press - Santa Cruz, CA - *BoPubDir 4, 5; LitMag&SmPr 83-84*
Greenleaf Books - Weare, NH - *BoPubDir 4 Sup, 5*
Greenleaf Classics Inc. [Subs. of Reed Enterprises Inc.] - San Diego, CA - *LitMarPl 83, 84; WritMar 84*
Greenleaf Music Inc. - *See* Kaye Publications, Richard
Greenleaf Press/Red Rose Books - Evanston, IL - *BoPubDir 4, 5*
Greenleaf Sentinel - *See* Record Publishing Co.
Greenman Advertising Associates Inc. - Hollywood, FL - *StaDirAdAg 2-84*
Greenmaster, The - Toronto, ON, Canada - *BaconPubCkMag 84*
Greeno, Hadden & Co. Ltd. - Winchendon, MA - *BoPubDir 4, 5*
Greenpoint Gazette - Brooklyn, NY - *AyerDirPub 83*
Greenport Suffolk Times - Greenport, NY - *BaconPubCkNews 84*
Green's Commodity Market Comments [of Economic News Agency] - Princeton, NJ - *NewsDir 84*
Green's Magazine [of Green's Educational Publishing] - Regina, SK, Canada - *LitMag&SmPr 83-84; WritMar 84*
Greensboro A & T Register - Greensboro, NC - *NewsDir 84*
Greensboro Carolina Peacemaker - Greensboro, NC - *BaconPubCkNews 84; NewsDir 84*
Greensboro Daily News [of Landmark Communications Co.] - Greensboro, NC - *BaconPubCkNews 84; Ed&PubIntYB 82; LitMarPl 83, 84; NewsBur 6; NewsDir 84*
Greensboro Herald-Journal - Greensboro, GA - *BaconPubCkNews 84*
Greensboro Record [of Greensboro News Co.] - Greensboro, NC - *BaconPubCkNews 84; Ed&PubIntYB 82; LitMarPl 83, 84; NewsDir 84*
Greensboro Times - Greensboro, NC - *BaconPubCkNews 84; Ed&PubIntYB 82; NewsDir 84*
Greensboro Watchman - Greensboro, AL - *BaconPubCkNews 84; Ed&PubIntYB 82*
Greensburg Cable TV - Greensburg, KY - *Tel&CabFB 84C*
Greensburg Catholic Accent, The [of Greensburg Catholic Publishing Associates Inc.] - Greensburg, PA - *NewsDir 84*
Greensburg Daily News - Greensburg, IN - *BaconPubCkNews 84; Ed&PubIntYB 82; NewsDir 84*
Greensburg Kiowa County Signal - Greensburg, KS - *BaconPubCkNews 84*
Greensburg Record-Herald - Greensburg, KY - *BaconPubCkNews 84; Ed&PubIntYB 82*
Greensburg St. Helena Echo - Greensburg, LA - *BaconPubCkNews 84*
Greensburg Times - Greensburg, IN - *BaconPubCkNews 84; Ed&PubIntYB 82*
Greensburg Tribune Review - Greensburg, PA - *NewsDir 84*
Greenshadow Music - *See* Windham Hill Music

Greensheet - Houston, TX - *AyerDirPub 83*
Greenspan & Kushlin Engraving Corp. - New York, NY - *LitMarPl 83, 84*
Greenstein, Mina - New York, NY - *LitMarPl 83, 84*
Greenstone & Rabasca Advertising - Melville, NY - *AdAge 3-28-84; ArtMar 84; StaDirAdAg 2-84*
Greenstripe Media Inc. - Newport Beach, CA - *StaDirAdAg 2-84*
Greensward Foundation Inc. - New York, NY - *BoPubDir 4 Sup, 5*
Greentree Group, The - Moraga, CA - *BrCabYB 84*
Greenup County Sentinel, The - Greenup, KY - *Ed&PubIntYB 82*
Greenup News - Greenup, KY - *AyerDirPub 83; BaconPubCkNews 84; Ed&PubIntYB 82; NewsDir 84*
Greenup Press - Greenup, IL - *BaconPubCkNews 84; Ed&PubIntYB 82*
Greenvale Marketing Corp. - East Hills, NY - *StaDirAdAg 2-84*
Greenvale Press - Kopperl, TX - *BoPubDir 4, 5*
Greenview Menard County Review - Greenview, IL - *BaconPubCkNews 84*
Greenview Publications - Chicago, IL - *BoPubDir 5; LitMag&SmPr 83-84*
Greenville Advocate - Greenville, AL - *BaconPubCkNews 84; Ed&PubIntYB 82; NewsDir 84*
Greenville Advocate - Greenville, IL - *BaconPubCkNews 84; Ed&PubIntYB 82; NewsDir 84*
Greenville Black Star - Columbia, SC - *AyerDirPub 83*
Greenville Black Star - *See* Juju Publishing Co.
Greenville Cable TV Inc. [of Multimedia Cablevision Inc.] - Greenville, NC - *BrCabYB 84; Tel&CabFB 84C*
Greenville Cable TV Inc. - Parmele, NC - *Tel&CabFB 84C*
Greenville Cablevision [of MetroVision Inc.] - Greenville, TX - *BrCabYB 84; Tel&CabFB 84C*
Greenville Daily Advocate - Greenville, OH - *BaconPubCkNews 84*
Greenville Daily News - Greenville, MI - *BaconPubCkNews 84; Ed&PubIntYB 82*
Greenville Daily Reflector - Greenville, NC - *Ed&PubIntYB 82; NewsDir 84*
Greenville Delta Democrat Times [of Freedom Newspapers Inc.] - Greenville, MS - *BaconPubCkNews 84; NewsDir 84*
Greenville Herald Banner - Greenville, TX - *NewsDir 84*
Greenville Indian Valley Record - *See* Feather Publishing Co. Inc.
Greenville Leader Central City News - Greenville, KY - *BaconPubCkNews 84; NewsDir 84*
Greenville Local - Greenville, NY - *AyerDirPub 83; Ed&PubIntYB 82*
Greenville Local [of Ravena News-Herald Inc.] - Ravena, NY - *NewsDir 84*
Greenville Local - *See* Ravena News-Herald Publishers
Greenville Magazine - Greenville, SC - *BaconPubCkMag 84; WritMar 84*
Greenville Meriwether Vindicator - *See* Tri-County Newspapers Inc.
Greenville News [of Fairview West New Yorker Inc.] - Fairview, NJ - *NewsDir 84*
Greenville News - Greenville, SC - *BaconPubCkNews 84; Ed&PubIntYB 82; LitMarPl 83, 84; NewsBur 6; NewsDir 84*
Greenville News-Piedmont - Greenville, SC - *Ed&PubIntYB 82; LitMarPl 83, 84*
Greenville Observer - Greenville, RI - *BaconPubCkNews 84*
Greenville Piedmont - Greenville, SC - *BaconPubCkNews 84; Ed&PubIntYB 82; LitMarPl 83, 84; NewsBur 6; NewsDir 84*
Greenville Record-Argus - Greenville, PA - *BaconPubCkNews 84; Ed&PubIntYB 82; NewsDir 84*
Greenville Shopper - Greenville, MS - *AyerDirPub 83*
Greenwald/Christian Advertising - Philadelphia, PA - *AdAge 3-28-84; StaDirAdAg 2-84*
Greenway Advertising Agency Inc. - Chesterfield, MO - *StaDirAdAg 2-84*
Greenwich Design Publications - Hopkins, MN - *BoPubDir 4, 5*
Greenwich Enterprise Review - Greenwich, OH - *BaconPubCkNews 84; Ed&PubIntYB 82*
Greenwich Journal & Salem Press - Greenwich, NY - *AyerDirPub 83; BaconPubCkNews 84; NewsDir 84*
Greenwich-Meridian - Saskatoon, SK, Canada - *BoPubDir 4, 5; LitMag&SmPr 83-84*
Greenwich Time [of Connecticut Newspapers Inc.] - Greenwich, CT - *BaconPubCkNews 84; Ed&PubIntYB 82; NewsDir 84*
Greenwich Village Gazette, The - Old Greenwich, CT - *Ed&PubIntYB 82*
Greenwillow Books [Div. of William Morrow & Co. Inc.] - New York, NY - *LitMarPl 83, 84*
Greenwood Cable TV Co. Inc. - Greenwood, AR - *BrCabYB 84*
Greenwood-Cherry Hills Village Squire - Castle Rock, CO - *AyerDirPub 83*
Greenwood-Cherry Hills Village Squire - *See* Douglas County News Publishing
Greenwood Commonwealth [of Emmerich Enterprises Inc.] - Greenwood, MS - *BaconPubCkNews 84; Ed&PubIntYB 82; NewsDir 84*
Greenwood Democrat - Greenwood, AR - *Ed&PubIntYB 82*
Greenwood Index-Journal - Greenwood, SC - *BaconPubCkNews 84; NewsDir 84*
Greenwood Lake News [of Executive Associates] - Greenwood Lake, NY - *BaconPubCkNews 84; Ed&PubIntYB 82; NewsDir 84*
Greenwood News, The - Greenwood, IN - *Ed&PubIntYB 82*
Greenwood Press [Div. of Congressional Information Service Inc.] - Westport, CT - *AvMarPl 83; DirMarMP 83; InfoS 83-84; LitMarPl 83; MagIndMarPl 82-83; MicroMarPl 82-83; WritMar 84*
Greenwood Press [Div. of Congressional Information Service Inc.] - New York, NY - *LitMarPl 84*
Greenwood Telephone Co. Inc. [Aff. of Telephone & Data Systems Inc.] - Greenwood, WI - *TelDir&BG 83-84*
Greenwood Video Ltd. [of Arnie's TV & Radio Service Ltd.] - Greenwood, BC, Canada - *BrCabYB 84*
Greer & Hartman Agency, The - Santa Ana, CA - *StaDirAdAg 2-84*
Greer Associates Corp. - Spartanburg, SC - *BrCabYB 84*
Greer Cablevision - Greer, SC - *BrCabYB 84; Tel&CabFB 84C*
Greer Citizen - Greer, SC - *BaconPubCkNews 84; Ed&PubIntYB 82; NewsDir 84*
Greer Music, Dan - *See* Gre-Jac Music
Greer Sontag Associates Inc. - New York, NY - *ADAPSOMemDir 83-84*
Greetings Magazine [of Mackay Publishing Corp.] - New York, NY - *BaconPubCkMag 84; MagDir 84*
Greey de Pencier Books [Div. of Key Publishers Ltd.] - Toronto, ON, Canada - *LitMarPl 84*
Greger, Margaret - Richland, WA - *BoPubDir 4 Sup, 5*
Gregg Corp. - Waltham, MA - *DataDirOnSer 84; EISS 5-84 Sup; InfoS 83-84*
Gregg Div. [of McGraw-Hill Book Co.] - New York, NY - *WritMar 84*
Gregg-Hamilton - Aberdeen, MS - *BoPubDir 4, 5*
Gregg International [of Avebury Publishing Co.] - Amersham, England - *MicroMarPl 82-83*
Gregg Music Sources [of Newton K. Gregg/Publisher Inc.] - Novato, CA - *MicroMarPl 82-83*
Gregg, Nancy J. - Chatham, IL - *LitMarPl 84*
Gregg Press [Div. of G. K. Hall & Co.] - Boston, MA - *LitMarPl 83, 84*
Gregor Woods - La Puente, CA - *LitMarPl 84*
Gregorich, Barbara - Chicago, IL - *LitMarPl 83, 84*
Gregory & Clyburne - New Canaan, CT - *AdAge 3-28-84; StaDirAdAg 2-84*
Gregory Associates, Howard - Redondo Beach, CA - *BoPubDir 4 Sup, 5*
Gregory Associates, Maia - New York, NY - *LitMarPl 83, 84*
Gregory House Advertising - Cape Coral, FL - *StaDirAdAg 2-84*
Gregory Inc. - Cleveland, OH - *AdAge 3-28-84; StaDirAdAg 2-84*
Gregory Inc., Blanche C. - New York, NY - *LitMarPl 83, 84*
Gregory Publishing Co. - Itasca, IL - *BoPubDir 4, 5*
Gregory, Stephen E. - Rock Hill, SC - *MicrocomSwDir 1*
Gregory Times-Advocate - Gregory, SD - *BaconPubCkNews 84*
Greif-Associates Inc. - Chappaqua, NY - *DirPRFirms 83*
Greiner Harries MacLean Ltd. - Westmount, PQ, Canada - *StaDirAdAg 2-84*
Gremaud Associates Inc., Michael - Hillsdale, NJ - *StaDirAdAg 2-84*
Grenada Lake Herald - Grenada, MS - *BaconPubCkNews 84*

Grenada Sentinel-Star - Grenada, MS - *BaconPubCkNews 84; NewsDir 84*
Grenada Video Inc. - Grenada, MS - *BrCabYB 84; Tel&CabFB 84C*
Grenadilla Enterprises Inc. - Kew Gardens, NY - *BillIntBG 83-84*
Grenier Corp., Donald - New York, NY - *DataDirOnSer 84; MagIndMarPl 82-83*
Greninger, Dorothy M. - Watkins Glen, NY - *FBInfSer 80*
Gresham Gazette - Gresham, NE - *AyerDirPub 83; BaconPubCkNews 84; Ed&PubIntYB 82*
Gresham Outlook [of Capital Cities Communications Inc.] - Gresham, OR - *AyerDirPub 83; BaconPubCkNews 84; Ed&PubIntYB 82; NewsDir 84*
Gresham Productions Inc., David - Hollywood, CA - *BillIntBG 83-84*
Greshler Productions Inc., Abner J. - Los Angeles, CA - *Tel&CabFB 84C*
Gretczko Graphic Design Inc., Robert - New York, NY - *StaDirAdAg 2-84*
Gretna Breeze - Gretna, NE - *BaconPubCkNews 84; Ed&PubIntYB 82*
Gretna Gazette [of Womack Publishing Co. Inc.] - Gretna, VA - *BaconPubCkNews 84; NewsDir 84*
Gretna Guide & News - Gretna, NE - *BaconPubCkNews 84*
Gretna West Bank Guide - *See* Guide Newspaper Corp.
Greve Marketing Communications - St. Paul, MN - *StaDirAdAg 2-84*
Grey Advertising - New York, NY - *AdAge 3-28-84, 6-25-84; ArtMar 84; Br 1-23-84; BrCabYB 84; HomeVid&CabYB 82-83; StaDirAdAg 2-84; TelAl 83, 84*
Grey Advertising Ltd. - Toronto, ON, Canada - *ArtMar 84*
Grey & Davis Inc. [Subs. of Grey Advertising Inc.] - New York, NY - *DirPRFirms 83*
Grey Direct International [Subs. of Grey Advertising] - New York, NY - *DirMarMP 83; StaDirAdAg 2-84*
Grey Eagle Gazette - Grey Eagle, MN - *Ed&PubIntYB 82*
Grey Fox Press - San Francisco, CA - *LitMarPl 83, 84*
Grey House Publishing Inc. - New York, NY - *BoPubDir 4, 5; EISS 83; InfIndMarPl 83*
Grey Lyon & King Advertising Inc. - New York, NY - *StaDirAdAg 2-84*
Grey Ronalds Smith Ltd. - Toronto, ON, Canada - *StaDirAdAg 2-84*
Grey Whale Press - Portland, OR - *BoPubDir 4, 5; LitMag&SmPr 83-84*
Greybull Standard - Greybull, WY - *BaconPubCkNews 84*
Greyfalcon House - *See* Grifalconi/Greyfalcon House, Ann
Greyhound Exposition Services (Creative Services Div.) - Las Vegas, NV - *AvMarPl 83*
Greyhound Racing Record - Miami, FL - *MagDir 84*
Greyhound Review, The [of National Greyhound Association] - Abilene, KS - *WritMar 84*
Greylock Publishers - Stamford, CT - *BoPubDir 4, 5*
GRF Ltd. - Roosevelt, UT - *LitMag&SmPr 83-84*
Grid Publishing Inc. - Columbus, OH - *LitMarPl 83, 84*
Grid Systems Corp. - Mountain View, CA - *MicrocomMPl 84; WhoWMicrocom 83*
Gridgraffiti Press - Brooklyn, NY - *BoPubDir 4, 5*
Gridley Cable Inc. - Gridley, IL - *Tel&CabFB 84C*
Gridley Herald - Gridley, CA - *BaconPubCkNews 84; Ed&PubIntYB 82; NewsDir 84*
Gridley News - Gridley, IL - *AyerDirPub 83; Ed&PubIntYB 82*
Gridley News - *See* Cornbelt Press Inc.
Gridley Telephone Co. - Gridley, IL - *TelDir&BG 83-84*
Grier's Almanac - Atlanta, GA - *MagDir 84*
Griesinger & Associates Inc., Frank K. - Cleveland, OH - *TeleSy&SerDir 7-83*
Grifalconi/Greyfalcon House, Ann - New York, NY - *AvMarPl 83; LitMarPl 83, 84; MagIndMarPl 82-83*
Griffin & Associates, Marianne - Lawrence, KS - *FBInfSer 80*
Griffin, Arthur - Winchester, MA - *LitMarPl 83, 84; MagIndMarPl 82-83*
Griffin Bacal Inc. - New York, NY - *StaDirAdAg 2-84*
Griffin Books Inc. - Oklahoma City, OK - *BoPubDir 4, 5; LitMag&SmPr 83-84*
Griffin Communications Inc. - Chesterton, IN - *AvMarPl 83; WritMar 84*
Griffin, George D. - New York, NY - *LitMarPl 83, 84; MagIndMarPl 82-83*
Griffin Group Radio, Merv - New York, NY - *BrCabYB 84*
Griffin, Hamilton & Thompson Inc. - Baltimore, MD - *StaDirAdAg 2-84*
Griffin House - Toronto, ON, Canada - *LitMarPl 83, 84*
Griffin Inc., Boyd - New York, NY - *BoPubDir 5*
Griffin News - Greenville, GA - *NewsDir 84*
Griffin News - Griffin, GA - *BaconPubCkNews 84; Ed&PubIntYB 82*
Griffin Report of Food Marketing [of Griffin Publishing Co. Inc.] - South Weymouth, MA - *BaconPubCkMag 84; MagDir 84*
Griffith & Associates Inc., Richard C. - Chicago, IL - *DirPRFirms 83*
Griffith & Rowland - Jamestown, NY - *StaDirAdAg 2-84*
Griffith & Somers Advertising Agency - Sioux City, IA - *ArtMar 84; StaDirAdAg 2-84*
Griffith, Bob D. - Ft. Smith, AR - *Tel&CabFB 84C p.1682*
Griffith Data Services - Peoria, IL - *MicrocomMPl 84*
Griffith News Feature Service - New York, NY - *Ed&PubIntYB 82; LitMarPl 84*
Griffith Park News [of Los Angeles Meredith Newspapers] - Los Angeles, CA - *AyerDirPub 83; NewsDir 84*
Griffith Shopper, The - Griffith, IN - *AyerDirPub 83*
Griffiths Royds Ltd., Creighton - *See* Royds Advertising Group Ltd., The
Griffon House Publications - Whitestone, NY - *BoPubDir 4, 5; LitMag&SmPr 83-84*
Grifo Enterprises Inc./The Dow Beaters Inc. - Summit, NJ - *BoPubDir 4 Sup, 5*
Griggs, Carl L. - Dalton, GA - *Tel&CabFB 84C p.1682*
Griggs County Telephone Co. - Cooperstown, ND - *TelDir&BG 83-84*
Griggs, Georgia - Santa Monica, CA - *LitMarPl 83, 84; MagIndMarPl 82-83*
Griggs Stations, C. R. - Decatur, IL - *BrCabYB 84*
Grimes & Co., Stan - *See* Stockton West Burkhart Inc.
Grimes Publications - Opelika, AL - *Ed&PubIntYB 82*
Grimes, Russell H. - Beatrice, NE - *MagIndMarPl 82-83*
Grimes, William J. - Hingham, MA - *LitMarPl 83, 84; MagIndMarPl 82-83*
Grimm & Co., W. T. - Chicago, IL - *BoPubDir 4 Sup, 5*
Grimoire - Westland, MI - *LitMag&SmPr 83-84*
Grimsby Cable TV Ltd. - Grimsby, ON, Canada - *BrCabYB 84*
Grimshaw Mile Zero News - Grimshaw, AB, Canada - *AyerDirPub 83*
Grinberg Film Libraries Inc., Sherman - Hollywood, CA - *Tel&CabFB 84C*
Grinnell Cablevision Inc. - Grinnell, IA - *BrCabYB 84*
Grinnell Herald Register - Grinnell, IA - *AyerDirPub 83; BaconPubCkNews 84; Ed&PubIntYB 82; NewsDir 84*
Grinning Idiot - Brooklyn, NY - *LitMag&SmPr 83-84*
Grinstead/Feik - New York, NY - *LitMarPl 83, 84*
Grise Audio Visual Center - Erie, PA - *AvMarPl 83*
Grissom Pacesetter - Kokomo, IN - *BaconPubCkNews 84*
Grist Business Services Ltd. - Southampton, England - *MicrocomSwDir 1*
Grist Mill - Eliot, ME - *BoPubDir 4, 5*
Griswold Advertising Inc. - Sacramento, CA - *StaDirAdAg 2-84*
Griswold American - Griswold, IA - *BaconPubCkNews 84; Ed&PubIntYB 82*
Griswold Cooperative Telephone Co. - Griswold, IA - *TelDir&BG 83-84*
Griswold-Eshleman Co. - Cleveland, OH - *ArtMar 84; BrCabYB 84; DirPRFirms 83; TelAl 83, 84*
Griswold Inc. - Cleveland, OH - *AdAge 3-28-84; StaDirAdAg 2-84*
Griswold, Lynch Advertising Agency - Orange, CT - *StaDirAdAg 2-84*
Grit [of Stauffer Communications Inc.] - Williamsport, PA - *BaconPubCkMag 84; Ed&PubIntYB 82; Folio 83; LitMarPl 83, 84; MagDir 84; MagIndMarPl 82-83; WritMar 84*
Grit & Steel - Gaffney, SC - *BaconPubCkMag 84; MagDir 84*
Grit Family Bookshelf [Subs. of Grit Publishing Co.] - Chappaqua, NY - *LitMarPl 83, 84*
Grit Publishing Co. [Div. of Advo Inc.] - Williamsport, PA - *DirMarMP 83*

Grizzard Advertising Inc. - Atlanta, GA - *DirMarMP 83; StaDirAdAg 2-84*
Grizzly Giant Publishing - *See* Granite Rock Music
Gro Com Group - Barrington, RI - *BoPubDir 5*
Grocers Journal of California [of Southern California Grocers Association] - Los Angeles, CA - *BaconPubCkMag 84; MagDir 84*
Grocers' Spotlight [of Shamie Publishing Co.] - St. Clair Shores, MI - *BaconPubCkMag 84; MagDir 84; WritMar 84*
Grocers' Spotlight West [of Shamie Publications Inc.] - Los Angeles, CA - *MagDir 84*
Grocery Communications [of Gro-Com Group] - Barrington, RI - *BaconPubCkMag 84; MagDir 84; MagIndMarPl 82-83*
Grocery Distribution Magazine [of Food Industry Publications] - Chicago, IL - *BaconPubCkMag 84; MagDir 84; MagIndMarPl 82-83; WritMar 84*
Grody/Tellem Communications Inc. - Los Angeles, CA - *DirPRFirms 83*
Groel, Campbell C. Jr. - New Milford, CT - *Tel&CabFB 84C p.1682*
Groesbeck Journal - Groesbeck, TX - *BaconPubCkNews 84; Ed&PubIntYB 82; NewsDir 84*
Groffsky Literary Agency, Maxine - New York, NY - *LitMarPl 83, 84*
Groleau TV Cable Enrg. - Ste. Thecle, PQ, Canada - *BrCabYB 84*
Grolier Educational Corp. [Subs. of Grolier Inc.] - Danbury, CT - *AvMarPl 83; LitMarPl 83, 84*
Grolier Electronic Publishing Inc. [Subs. of Grolier Inc.] - New York, NY - *AvMarPl 83; DataDirOnSer 84; InfoS 83-84; LitMarPl 83, 84*
Grolier Enterprises Inc. [Subs. of Grolier Inc.] - Danbury, CT - *LitMarPl 83, 84*
Grolier Inc. - Danbury, CT - *KnowInd 83; LitMarPl 83, 84*
Grolier International Inc. [Subs. of Grolier Inc.] - Danbury, CT - *LitMarPl 83, 84*
Grolier Ltd./Grolier Ltee. [Subs. of Grolier Inc.] - Toronto, ON, Canada - *LitMarPl 83, 84*
Grolier TeleMarketing Inc. [Subs. of Grolier Inc.] - Danbury, CT - *LitMarPl 83, 84*
Groom & Board - Chicago, IL - *BaconPubCkMag 84*
Groom News - Groom, TX - *BaconPubCkNews 84; Ed&PubIntYB 82*
Groome Center - Washington, DC - *BoPubDir 4, 5*
Groot Organization, The - San Francisco, CA - *AvMarPl 83*
Groove Time Records & Enterprises - San Bernardino, CA - *BillIntBG 83-84*
Groove II Music - *See* Sugarvine Music
Groovesonic Music - *See* Sugarvine Music
Groovesville Music - Detroit, MI - *BillIntBG 83-84*
Gropper Packaging [Div. of Vision Packaging Co. Inc.] - Brooklyn, NY - *LitMarPl 83, 84*
Groseclose & Poindexter Advertising - Roanoke, VA - *AdAge 3-28-84; StaDirAdAg 2-84*
Gross & Associates Inc., Myra - Ft. Lauderdale, FL - *LitMarPl 84*
Gross & Associates/Public Relations Inc. - New York, NY - *DirPRFirms 83*
Gross & Co., Herb - Rochester, NY - *AdAge 3-28-84; StaDirAdAg 2-84*
Gross & Fry Advertising Agency Inc. - Norfolk, VA - *StaDirAdAg 2-84*
Gross Associates Inc., Robert - Stamford, CT - *CabTVFinDB 83*
Gross Product Originating [of Wharton Econometric Forecasting Associates] - Philadelphia, PA - *DataDirOnSer 84*
Gross Stamp Co. Inc. - New York, NY - *BoPubDir 4, 5*
Gross, Stuart - New York, NY - *LitMarPl 83, 84*
Gross Telecasting Inc. - Lansing, MI - *BrCabYB 84; Tel&CabFB 84S*
Gross Townsend Frank - New York, NY - *AdAge 3-28-84; DirPRFirms 83; HBIndAd&MS 82-83; StaDirAdAg 2-84*
Grosscup, Jeffrey - Minneapolis, MN - *LitMarPl 83, 84*
Grosse Ile Camera - Grosse Ile, MI - *BaconPubCkNews 84*
Grosse Ile Downriver News Herald - *See* News-Herald Newspapers
Grosse Pointe Cable Inc. - Grosse Pointe, MI - *BrCabYB 84*
Grosse Pointe Cable Inc. - Grosse Pointe Woods, MI - *Tel&CabFB 84C*
Grosse Pointe Guardian [of Northeast Detroiter] - Detroit, MI - *NewsDir 84*
Grosse Pointe Guardian - *See* Harper Woods Herald
Grosse Pointe News [of Antebo Publishers] - Detroit, MI - *NewsDir 84*
Grosse Pointe News - Grosse Pointe, MI - *AyerDirPub 83; BaconPubCkNews 84; Ed&PubIntYB 82*
Grosset & Dunlap Inc. [Subs. of Putnam Publishing Group] - New York, NY - *DirMarMP 83*
Grosset & Dunlap Inc. - *See* Putnam Publishing Group
Grossman, Frances R. - West Tremont, ME - *LitMarPl 83; MagIndMarPl 82-83*
Grossman, Henry - New York, NY - *LitMarPl 83, 84; MagIndMarPl 82-83*
Grossman, Judith S. - Merion, PA - *LitMarPl 83, 84; MagIndMarPl 82-83*
Grossner, Isabel S. - Montclair, NJ - *LitMarPl 83, 84*
Grossup Tables [of On-Line Research Inc.] - Greenwich, CT - *DataDirOnSer 84*
Grote Deutsch & Co. [of The Jonathan Group] - Madison, WI - *StaDirAdAg 2-84*
Grotell Underwater Photography, Al - New York, NY - *LitMarPl 83, 84; MagIndMarPl 82-83*
Groton Independent - Groton, SD - *BaconPubCkNews 84; Ed&PubIntYB 82*
Groton Journal & Courier - Groton, NY - *Ed&PubIntYB 82*
Groton Journal & Courier - *See* Community Newspapers
Ground Under Press - Berkeley, CA - *BoPubDir 4, 5; LitMag&SmPr 83-84*
Ground Water Age [of Scott Periodicals] - Elmhurst, IL - *ArtMar 84; BaconPubCkMag 84; MagDir 84; MagIndMarPl 82-83*
Ground Water Energy Newsletter - Worthington, OH - *BaconPubCkMag 84*
Ground Water Monitoring Review - Worthington, OH - *BaconPubCkMag 84*
Ground Water Newsletter - Syosset, NY - *BaconPubCkMag 84; MagDir 84*
Groundhog Press - Toronto, ON, Canada - *BoPubDir 4, 5*
Grounds Maintenance - Overland Park, KS - *BaconPubCkMag 84*
Grounds Maintenance [of Intertec Publishing Corp.] - Shawnee Misson, KS - *MagDir 84*
Groundstar Software - Capitola, CA - *MicrocomMPl 84; MicrocomSwDir 1*
Groundwater Documentation Section [of Geological Survey of Sweden] - Uppsala, Sweden - *EISS 83*
Groundwater Press - New York, NY - *BoPubDir 4, 5; LitMag&SmPr 83-84*
Groundwater Survey [of Netherlands Organization for Applied Scientific Research] - Delft, Netherlands - *EISS 83*
Groundwood Books [Aff. of Douglas & McIntyre Ltd.] - Toronto, ON, Canada - *BoPubDir 4; LitMarPl 83, 84*
Group [of Thom Schultz Publications] - Loveland, CO - *ArtMar 84; BaconPubCkMag 84; WritMar 84*
Group Artec [Div. of Kimbal International] - Jaspar, IN - *DirInfWP 82*
Group Attitudes Corp. - New York, NY - *IntDirMarRes 83*
Group Books - Loveland, CO - *BoPubDir 4, 5*
Group Dynamics in Focus Inc. - Bala Cynwyd, PA - *IntDirMarRes 83*
Group 88 Music - Universal City, CA - *BillIntBG 83-84*
Group Five Communications Inc. - Manchester, NH - *AvMarPl 83*
Group for Applied Macroeconomic Analysis [of University of Paris-Nanterre] - Nanterre, France - *EISS 5-84 Sup*
Group One Broadcasting Co. - Akron, OH - *BrCabYB 84*
Group One Productions - San Francisco, CA - *AvMarPl 83; Tel&CabFB 84C*
Group Practice Journal - New York, NY - *MagIndMarPl 82-83*
Group Practice Journal - Alexandria, VA - *BaconPubCkMag 84; MagDir 84*
Group Sessions for Market Research Inc. - Eastchester, NY - *IntDirMarRes 83*
Group 3hree Advertising - Pompano Beach, FL - *AdAge 3-28-84; StaDirAdAg 2-84*

Group Two Advertising - Philadelphia, PA - *AdAge 3-28-84; StaDirAdAg 2-84*
Group Visionary Productions Inc. - North Hollywood, CA - *TeleSy&SerDir 2-84*
Group W - *See* Westinghouse Broadcasting & Cable Inc.
Group W Cable - Gadsden, AL - *BrCabYB 84; Tel&CabFB 84C*
Group W Cable - Huntsville, AL - *BrCabYB 84; Tel&CabFB 84C*
Group W Cable - Prescott, AZ - *Tel&CabFB 84C*
Group W Cable - Buena Park, CA - *Tel&CabFB 84C*
Group W Cable - Camarillo, CA - *BrCabYB 84*
Group W Cable - El Monte, CA - *Tel&CabFB 84C*
Group W Cable - Fontana, CA - *Tel&CabFB 84C*
Group W Cable - Fullerton, CA - *BrCabYB 84; Tel&CabFB 84C*
Group W Cable - Gardena, CA - *BrCabYB 84; Tel&CabFB 84C*
Group W Cable - Los Angeles, CA - *BrCabYB 84; Tel&CabFB 84C*
Group W Cable - Newport Beach, CA - *Tel&CabFB 84C*
Group W Cable - Reedley, CA - *Tel&CabFB 84C*
Group W Cable - Santa Ana, CA - *BrCabYB 84*
Group W Cable - Santa Cruz, CA - *Tel&CabFB 84C*
Group W Cable - Santa Maria, CA - *Tel&CabFB 84C*
Group W Cable [of Westinghouse Broadcasting & Cable Co.] - Sierra Madre, CA - *BrCabYB 84; Tel&CabFB 84C*
Group W Cable - South Gate, CA - *Tel&CabFB 84C*
Group W Cable - Yucca Valley, CA - *Tel&CabFB 84C*
Group W Cable - Trinidad, CO - *BrCabYB 84; Tel&CabFB 84C*
Group W Cable - Danbury, CT - *BrCabYB 84; Tel&CabFB 84C*
Group W Cable - Middletown, CT - *BrCabYB 84*
Group W Cable - Boca Raton, FL - *BrCabYB 84; Tel&CabFB 84C*
Group W Cable - DeBary, FL - *BrCabYB 84*
Group W Cable - Haines City, FL - *BrCabYB 84; Tel&CabFB 84C*
Group W Cable - Hillsborough County, FL - *BrCabYB 84*
Group W Cable - Holly Hill, FL - *BrCabYB 84*
Group W Cable - Largo, FL - *BrCabYB 84*
Group W Cable - Manatee, FL - *BrCabYB 84*
Group W Cable - Marianna, FL - *BrCabYB 84; Tel&CabFB 84C*
Group W Cable - New Port Richey, FL - *BrCabYB 84; Tel&CabFB 84C*
Group W Cable - New Smyrna Beach, FL - *BrCabYB 84*
Group W Cable - Palm Beach County, FL - *BrCabYB 84*
Group W Cable - Panama City, FL - *Tel&CabFB 84C*
Group W Cable - Plant City, FL - *BrCabYB 84*
Group W Cable - Plantation, FL - *BrCabYB 84; Tel&CabFB 84C*
Group W Cable - Quincy, FL - *Tel&CabFB 84C*
Group W Cable - Riviera Beach, FL - *Tel&CabFB 84C*
Group W Cable - St. Petersburg, FL - *BrCabYB 84; Tel&CabFB 84C*
Group W Cable - Tallahassee, FL - *BrCabYB 84; Tel&CabFB 84C*
Group W Cable - West Palm Beach, FL - *BrCabYB 84; Tel&CabFB 84C*
Group W Cable - Winter Garden, FL - *BrCabYB 84; Tel&CabFB 84C*
Group W Cable - Dublin, GA - *Tel&CabFB 84C*
Group W Cable - Milledgeville, GA - *Tel&CabFB 84C*
Group W Cable - Swainsboro, GA - *Tel&CabFB 84C*
Group W Cable - Thomasville, GA - *BrCabYB 84; Tel&CabFB 84C*
Group W Cable - Lewiston, ID - *Tel&CabFB 84C*
Group W Cable - Pocatello, ID - *BrCabYB 84; Tel&CabFB 84C*
Group W Cable - Galena, IL - *BrCabYB 84*
Group W Cable - Glen Ellyn, IL - *Tel&CabFB 84C*
Group W Cable - Rock Island, IL - *BrCabYB 84; Tel&CabFB 84C*
Group W Cable - Maquoketa, IA - *BrCabYB 84; Tel&CabFB 84C*
Group W Cable - Baker, LA - *Tel&CabFB 84C*
Group W Cable - Caribou, ME - *BrCabYB 84; Tel&CabFB 84C*
Group W Cable - Calumet, MI - *BrCabYB 84; Tel&CabFB 84C*
Group W Cable - Escanaba, MI - *BrCabYB 84; Tel&CabFB 84C*
Group W Cable - Iron Mountain, MI - *BrCabYB 84*
Group W Cable - Ironwood, MI - *Tel&CabFB 84C*
Group W Cable - Sault Ste. Marie, MI - *BrCabYB 84; Tel&CabFB 84C*
Group W Cable - Anoka, MN - *Tel&CabFB 84C*
Group W Cable - Brainerd, MN - *BrCabYB 84; Tel&CabFB 84C*
Group W Cable - Duluth, MN - *BrCabYB 84*
Group W Cable - Stewartville, MN - *BrCabYB 84*
Group W Cable - Winona, MN - *BrCabYB 84*
Group W Cable - Ballwin, MO - *Tel&CabFB 84C*
Group W Cable - Bridgeton, MO - *BrCabYB 84; Tel&CabFB 84C*
Group W Cable - Columbia, MO - *Tel&CabFB 84C*
Group W Cable - Kirkwood, MO - *BrCabYB 84; Tel&CabFB 84C*
Group W Cable - St. Charles, MO - *Tel&CabFB 84C*
Group W Cable - Cut Bank, MT - *Tel&CabFB 84C*
Group W Cable - Great Falls, MT - *BrCabYB 84; Tel&CabFB 84C*
Group W Cable - Hamilton, MT - *BrCabYB 84*
Group W Cable - Kalispell, MT - *Tel&CabFB 84C*
Group W Cable - Missoula, MT - *BrCabYB 84; Tel&CabFB 84C*
Group W Cable - Shelby, MT - *BrCabYB 84*
Group W Cable - Stevensville, MT - *BrCabYB 84*
Group W Cable - Whitefish, MT - *BrCabYB 84*
Group W Cable - Fallon, NV - *BrCabYB 84; Tel&CabFB 84C*
Group W Cable - Reno, NV - *BrCabYB 84; Tel&CabFB 84C*
Group W Cable - Yerington, NV - *BrCabYB 84*
Group W Cable - Keene, NH - *BrCabYB 84; Tel&CabFB 84C*
Group W Cable - Wildwood, NJ - *Tel&CabFB 84C*
Group W Cable - Brockport, NY - *Tel&CabFB 84C*
Group W Cable - Hamilton, NY - *Tel&CabFB 84C*
Group W Cable - Islip Town, NY - *BrCabYB 84*
Group W Cable - Jamestown, NY - *Tel&CabFB 84C*
Group W Cable [of Westinghouse Broadcasting & Cable Co.] - New York, NY - *BrCabYB 84 p.D-301; CabTVFinDB 83; HomeVid&CabYB 82-83; Tel&CabFB 84C p.1682, 84S*
Group W Cable - North Ridgeville, OH - *Tel&CabFB 84C*
Group W Cable - Portsmouth, OH - *BrCabYB 84*
Group W Cable - Coquille, OR - *BrCabYB 84; Tel&CabFB 84C*
Group W Cable - Eugene, OR - *BrCabYB 84; Tel&CabFB 84C*
Group W Cable - La Grande, OR - *Tel&CabFB 84C*
Group W Cable - Commerce, TX - *BrCabYB 84; Tel&CabFB 84C*
Group W Cable - El Paso, TX - *BrCabYB 84*
Group W Cable - Galveston, TX - *BrCabYB 84*
Group W Cable - Graham, TX - *BrCabYB 84*
Group W Cable - Grapevine, TX - *Tel&CabFB 84C*
Group W Cable - Irving, TX - *BrCabYB 84; Tel&CabFB 84C*
Group W Cable - Lewisville, TX - *BrCabYB 84; Tel&CabFB 84C*
Group W Cable - Palestine, TX - *BrCabYB 84*
Group W Cable - Grundy, VA - *BrCabYB 84*
Group W Cable - Keen Mountain, VA - *BrCabYB 84*
Group W Cable - Richlands, VA - *BrCabYB 84*
Group W Cable - Tazewell, VA - *BrCabYB 84*
Group W Cable - Auburn, WA - *Tel&CabFB 84C*
Group W Cable - Walla Walla, WA - *BrCabYB 84; Tel&CabFB 84C*
Group W Cable - Wenatchee, WA - *BrCabYB 84; Tel&CabFB 84C*
Group W Cable - Clarksburg, WV - *BrCabYB 84; Tel&CabFB 84C*
Group W Cable - Fairmont, WV - *BrCabYB 84*
Group W Cable - La Crosse, WI - *BrCabYB 84; Tel&CabFB 84C*
Group W Cable - Rawlins, WY - *BrCabYB 84*
Group W Cable (Middletown Div.) - Middletown, CT - *Tel&CabFB 84C*
Group W Cable (Rochester Div.) - Rochester, MN - *BrCabYB 84*
Group W Cable Inc. - Lakeland, FL - *BrCabYB 84*
Group W Cable Inc. - Port Richey, FL - *BrCabYB 84*
Group W Cable of Dearborn - Dearborn, MI - *Tel&CabFB 84C*
Group W Cable of Dothan - Dothan, AL - *BrCabYB 84; Tel&CabFB 84C*
Group W Cable of Dubuque - Dubuque, IA - *BrCabYB 84; Tel&CabFB 84C*
Group W Cable of Dubuque Corp. - Asbury, IA - *BrCabYB 84*
Group W Cable of El Paso - El Paso, TX - *Tel&CabFB 84C*
Group W Cable of Fairmont - Fairmont, WV - *Tel&CabFB 84C*
Group W Cable of Farmington - Farmington, NM - *BrCabYB 84; Tel&CabFB 84C*
Group W Cable of Florida Inc. - De Land, FL - *BrCabYB 84*
Group W Cable of Ft. Bragg - Ft. Bragg, CA - *BrCabYB 84; Tel&CabFB 84C*
Group W Cable of Galena - Galena, IL - *Tel&CabFB 84C*
Group W Cable of Galveston - Galveston, TX - *Tel&CabFB 84C*
Group W Cable of Graham - Graham, TX - *Tel&CabFB 84C*

Group W Cable of Greenwood - Greenwood, SC - *BrCabYB 84; Tel&CabFB 84C*
Group W Cable of Ironwood - Ironwood, MI - *BrCabYB 84*
Group W Cable of Jamestown - Jamestown, NY - *BrCabYB 84*
Group W Cable of Leesville - Leesville, LA - *BrCabYB 84; Tel&CabFB 84C*
Group W Cable of Liberal - Liberal, KS - *BrCabYB 84; Tel&CabFB 84C*
Group W Cable of Lompoc [of Group W Cable Inc.] - Lompoc, CA - *BrCabYB 84; Tel&CabFB 84C*
Group W Cable of Los Gatos - Los Gatos, CA - *BrCabYB 84*
Group W Cable of Lovington - Lovington, NM - *BrCabYB 84; Tel&CabFB 84C*
Group W Cable of Manatee - Manatee County, FL - *Tel&CabFB 84C*
Group W Cable of Manhattan [of Group W Cable Inc.] - New York, NY - *HomeVid&CabYB 82-83; Tel&CabFB 84C*
Group W Cable of Milpitas - Milpitas, CA - *BrCabYB 84*
Group W Cable of Mobile - Mobile, AL - *Tel&CabFB 84C*
Group W Cable of Mohawk Valley - Ilion, NY - *BrCabYB 84; Tel&CabFB 84C*
Group W Cable of Muscle Shoals - Florence, AL - *BrCabYB 84; Tel&CabFB 84C*
Group W Cable of Newark [of Group W Cable Inc.] - Newark, CA - *Tel&CabFB 84C*
Group W Cable of Newburgh - Newburgh, NY - *BrCabYB 84*
Group W Cable of Newport Beach - Newport Beach, CA - *BrCabYB 84*
Group W Cable of North Ridgeville [of Westinghouse Broadcasting & Cable] - North Ridgeville, OH - *BrCabYB 84*
Group W Cable of Oswego - Oswego, NY - *BrCabYB 84; Tel&CabFB 84C*
Group W Cable of Palestine - Palestine, TX - *Tel&CabFB 84C*
Group W Cable of Portales - Portales, NM - *BrCabYB 84; Tel&CabFB 84C*
Group W Cable of Portsmouth - Portsmouth, OH - *Tel&CabFB 84C*
Group W Cable of Prescott - Prescott, AZ - *BrCabYB 84*
Group W Cable of Quincy - Quincy, FL - *BrCabYB 84*
Group W Cable of Rawlins - Rawlins, WY - *Tel&CabFB 84C*
Group W Cable of Richland - Richland, WA - *Tel&CabFB 84C*
Group W Cable of Rochester - Rochester, MN - *Tel&CabFB 84C*
Group W Cable of San Bernardino - Loma Linda, CA - *Tel&CabFB 84C*
Group W Cable of San Bernardino - San Bernardino, CA - *BrCabYB 84; Tel&CabFB 84C*
Group W Cable of Santa Clara - Santa Clara, CA - *BrCabYB 84*
Group W Cable of Santa Cruz - Santa Cruz, CA - *BrCabYB 84*
Group W Cable of Santa Maria - Santa Maria, CA - *BrCabYB 84*
Group W Cable of Seal Beach - Seal Beach, CA - *BrCabYB 84*
Group W Cable of Seattle [of Group W Cable Inc.] - Seattle, WA - *HomeVid&CabYB 82-83; Tel&CabFB 84C*
Group W Cable of Sherman Oaks - Sherman Oaks, CA - *BrCabYB 84*
Group W Cable of Silver City - Silver City, NM - *BrCabYB 84; Tel&CabFB 84C*
Group W Cable of Simi - Simi, CA - *Tel&CabFB 84C*
Group W Cable of Simi - Simi Valley, CA - *BrCabYB 84; Tel&CabFB 84C*
Group W Cable of Tacoma - Tacoma, WA - *BrCabYB 84; Tel&CabFB 84C*
Group W Cable of Torrance - Torrance, CA - *BrCabYB 84*
Group W Cable of Tucumcari - Tucumcari, NM - *BrCabYB 84; Tel&CabFB 84C*
Group W Cable of Tuscaloosa - Tuscaloosa, AL - *Tel&CabFB 84C*
Group W Cable of Ukiah - Ukiah, CA - *BrCabYB 84; Tel&CabFB 84C*
Group W Cable of Virginia - Richlands, VA - *Tel&CabFB 84C*
Group W Cable of Willits - Willits, CA - *BrCabYB 84; Tel&CabFB 84C*
Group W Cable of Winona - Winona, MN - *Tel&CabFB 84C*
Group W Cable of Winona - Fountain City, WI - *Tel&CabFB 84C*
Group W Cable of Worcester [of Westinghouse Broadcasting & Cable] - Worcester, MA - *BrCabYB 84*
Group W Cable of Yucca Valley - Yucca Valley, CA - *BrCabYB 84*
Group W Cable Southeast Inc. - Mobile, AL - *BrCabYB 84*
Group W Cable Southeast Inc. - Tuscaloosa, AL - *BrCabYB 84*
Group W Productions [of Westinghouse Broadcasting & Cable Inc.] - Universal City, CA - *TelAl 83, 84; Tel&CabFB 84C*
Group W Productions [of Westinghouse Broadcasting & Cable Inc.] - Pittsburgh, PA - *AvMarPl 83*
Group W Satellite Communications - Stamford, CT - *BrCabYB 84*
Group W Television Sales - New York, NY - *TelAl 83, 84*
Group West - Albuquerque, NM - *DirPRFirms 83*
Groupe des Editions UFAP - Trappes, France - *InfIndMarPl 83*
Groupe Marceau/French Online User Group [of Association Nationale de la Recherche Technique] - Paris, France - *InfIndMarPl 83*
Grouped Enterprise Census [of Computer Sciences of Australia Pty. Ltd.] - St. Leonards, Australia - *DataDirOnSer 84*
Grouped Enterprises Data Base - St. Leonards, Australia - *DirOnDB Spring 84*
Groups-in-Focus - Manhasset, NY - *IntDirMarRes 83*
Groupwork Today Inc. - South Plainfield, NJ - *BoPubDir 4, 5; WritMar 84*
Grove Associates Inc. - Atlanta, GA - *TeleSy&SerDir 7-83*
Grove City Allied News - Grove City, PA - *BaconPubCkNews 84*
Grove City Edition of the Columbus Messenger, The - Grove City, OH - *Ed&PubIntYB 82*
Grove City Record - Grove City, OH - *BaconPubCkNews 84; NewsDir 84*
Grove Examiner, The - Spruce Grove, AB, Canada - *Ed&PubIntYB 82*
Grove Hill Clarke County Democrat - Grove Hill, AL - *BaconPubCkNews 84; NewsDir 84*
Grove Hill Telecable Inc. - Grove Hill, AL - *BrCabYB 84; Tel&CabFB 84C*
Grove Hill Telephone Corp. [Aff. of Colonial Telephone Co.] - Grove Hill, AL - *TelDir&BG 83-84*
Grove Press Inc. - New York, NY - *LitMarPl 83, 84; WritMar 84*
Grove Press Inc. (Film Div.) - New York, NY - *AvMarPl 83*
Grove Sun - Grove, OK - *BaconPubCkNews 84; Ed&PubIntYB 82; NewsDir 84*
Grove, The [of Naturist Foundation] - Orpington, England - *LitMag&SmPr 83-84*
Grove Video Inc. [of UltraCom Inc.] - Grove, OK - *BrCabYB 84; Tel&CabFB 84C*
Grover & Carroll Inc. - Boston, MA - *StaDirAdAg 2-84*
Grover Telephone Exchange - Grover, CO - *TelDir&BG 83-84*
Groves & Associates Inc. - Muncie, IN - *ArtMar 84; DirPRFirms 83; StaDirAdAg 2-84*
Groves Chronicle - Groves, TX - *Ed&PubIntYB 82*
Grove's Dictionaries of Music Inc. [of Peninsula Publishers Ltd.] - New York, NY - *LitMarPl 83, 84*
Groveton News - Groveton, TX - *Ed&PubIntYB 82*
Groveton News - *See* Polk County Publishing
Grower Talks - West Chicago, IL - *BaconPubCkMag 84*
Grower, The - Toronto, ON, Canada - *BaconPubCkMag 84*
Growing Room Collective - Vancouver, BC, Canada - *LitMag&SmPr 83-84*
Growing Together Press - Stanford, CA - *BoPubDir 4, 5*
Growth Associates - Rochester, NY - *BoPubDir 4, 5*
Growth Unltd. Inc. - Battle Creek, MI - *BoPubDir 5*
GRP Records - New York, NY - *BillIntBG 83-84*
GRS Communications Inc. - New York, NY - *DirPRFirms 83*
GRT Book Printing - Oakland, CA - *LitMarPl 83, 84*
Grubb-Cleland Corp., The - Minneapolis, MN - *StaDirAdAg 2-84*
Grubb, Graham & Wilder Inc. - Champaign, IL - *BrCabYB 84; StaDirAdAg 2-84; TelAl 83, 84*
Grubbs Cable TV [of Teleservice Corp. of America] - Tyler, TX - *BrCabYB 84*
Gruber Associates, Art - Minneapolis, MN - *TelAl 83, 84*
Gruber Products Co. - Toledo, OH - *AvMarPl 83*
Gruber's Hagerstown Town & Country Almanack, J. - Hagerstown, MD - *MagDir 84*
Gruenwald Associates, Dick - Palm Beach Gardens, FL - *DirPRFirms 83*
Gruetzmacher Associates - Menominee, MI - *StaDirAdAg 2-84*

Grumbacher Inc., M. [Aff. of Times-Mirror Corp.] - New York, NY - *BoPubDir 4; LitMarPl 83*
Grundy Center Register - Grundy Center, IA - *BaconPubCkNews 84; Ed&PubIntYB 82; NewsDir 84*
Grundy County Herald - Tracy City, TN - *AyerDirPub 83; Ed&PubIntYB 82*
Grundy Virginia Mountaineer - Grundy, VA - *BaconPubCkNews 84; NewsDir 84*
Grune & Stratton Inc. [Subs. of Harcourt Brace Jovanovich Inc.] - Orlando, FL - *LitMarPl 84*
Grune & Stratton Inc. [Subs. of Harcourt Brace Jovanovich Inc.] - New York, NY - *LitMarPl 83; MagIndMarPl 82-83*
Grunwald & Lester G. Bensch, Charles - Fergus Falls, MN - *Tel&CabFB 84C*
Grushkin Inc., Philip - Englewood, NJ - *LitMarPl 83, 84*
Gruver Statesman - Gruver, TX - *Ed&PubIntYB 82*
Gruver Statesman - *See* Spearman Reporter Publishers
Gruwell Publications/Class Action - Decatur, GA - *BoPubDir 4, 5*
Grygla Eagle - *See* Richards Publishing Co. Inc.
Grygla Eagle, The - Grygla, MN - *Ed&PubIntYB 82*
Gryphon - Tampa, FL - *LitMag&SmPr 83-84*
Gryphon Editions Ltd. - Birmingham, AL - *LitMarPl 83, 84*
Gryphon House Inc. - Mt. Rainier, MD - *BoPubDir 4, 5; WritMar 84*
Gryphon Microproducts - Silver Spring, MD - *MicrocomMPl 83, 84; MicrocomSwDir 1*
Gryphon Press - Highland Park, NJ - *BoPubDir 4, 5*
Gryphon Systems - Cardiff by the Sea, CA - *MicrocomMPl 83, 84; MicrocomSwDir 1*
G.S. Communications Inc. [of Great Southern Printing & Manufacturing Co.] - Frederick, MD - *BrCabYB 84 p.D-301; Tel&CabFB 84C p.1682*
G.S. Communications Inc. - Sharpsburg, MD - *BrCabYB 84*
G.S. Communications Inc. - Glen Rock, PA - *Tel&CabFB 84C*
GS Data Corp. - Denver, CO - *MicrocomMPl 84*
G.S. Lithographers [Div. of Beatrice Foods Co.] - Carlstadt, NJ - *LitMarPl 83, 84; MagIndMarPl 82-83*
GSB Fabrics Corp. - Elizabeth, NJ - *LitMarPl 83, 84*
Gscheidle, Gerhard - New York, NY - *MagIndMarPl 82-83*
GSD & M - Austin, TX - *AdAge 3-28-84; StaDirAdAg 2-84*
GSE Publications - Los Angeles, CA - *BoPubDir 4, 5*
GSI-ECO - Paris, France - *EISS 7-83 Sup*
GSI-USA [of Transcomm Data Systems Inc.] - Pittsburgh, PA - *ADAPSOMemDir 83-84*
GSII - Golden, CO - *MicrocomMPl 84*
GSM News Service/Garden State Media Inc. - Oradell, NJ - *Ed&PubIntYB 82*
GTCO Corp. - Rockville, MD - *DataDirSup 7-83; DirInfWP 82; MicrocomMPl 84; WhoWMicrocom 83*
GTE Automatic Electric - Northlake, IL - *DirInfWP 82*
GTE Corp. - Stamford, CT - *ElecNews 7-25-83; TelDir&BG 83-84*
GTE Financial System One Quotation Service [of GTE Information Systems Inc.] - Mt. Laurel, NJ - *DBBus 82*
GTE Satellite Corp. [Subs. of General Telephone & Electronics Corp.] - Stamford, CT - *BrCabYB 84*
GTE Spacenet Corp. - McLean, VA - *BrCabYB 84*
GTE Sylvania [Subs. of GTE Corp.] - Danvers, MA - *AvMarPl 83*
GTE Telenet Communications Corp. [Subs. of General Telephone & Electronics Corp.] - Vienna, VA - *DataDirOnSer 84; DataDirSup 7-83; EISS 83; TeleSy&SerDir 7-83*
GTE Telenet Information Service - Mt. Laurel, NJ - *EISS 7-83 Sup; InfIndMarPl 83*
GTE Telenet Medical Information Network [of GTE Telenet Communications Corp.] - Vienna, VA - *MicrocomMPl 84; TeleSy&SerDir 2-84*
GTE Telenet Report [of GTE Telenet Communications Corp.] - Vienna, VA - *MagIndMarPl 82-83; MicrocomMPl 84*
GTI Advertising [Div. of GTI Corp.] - San Diego, CA - *StaDirAdAg 2-84*
GTM Music - *See* Sugarvine Music
GTR Coated Fabrics Co. [Subs. of General Tire & Rubber Co.] - Toledo, OH - *LitMarPl 83, 84*
Guadalupe Valley Cable Vision Inc. [of Guadalupe Telephone Cooperative] - Boerne, TX - *BrCabYB 84; Tel&CabFB 84C*
Guadalupe Valley Telephone Cooperative Inc. - Smithson Valley, TX - *TelDir&BG 83-84*
Guajiro Records Inc. - New York, NY - *BillIntBG 83-84*
Guam Cable TV [of Western Systems Inc.] - Agana, GU - *BrCabYB 84; Tel&CabFB 84C*
Guappone Publishers - McClellandtown, PA - *BoPubDir 4 Sup, 5*
Guard - Batesville, AR - *AyerDirPub 83*
Guard the North [of Les Recherches Daniel Say Cie.] - Vancouver, BC, Canada - *LitMag&SmPr 83-84*
Guardian [of Institute for Independent Social Journalism] - New York, NY - *AyerDirPub 83; LitMag&SmPr 83-84; MagIndMarPl 82-83; NewsDir 84; WritMar 84*
Guardian - Brampton, ON, Canada - *AyerDirPub 83*
Guardian - Charlottetown, PE, Canada - *AyerDirPub 83; BaconPubCkNews 84; Ed&PubIntYB 82*
Guardian Automated Systems - Buffalo, NY - *MicrocomMPl 84*
Guardian-Journal - Homer, LA - *AyerDirPub 83*
Guardian, The - Little Rock, AR - *NewsDir 84*
Guardian, The - Frostburg, MD - *Ed&PubIntYB 82*
Guardian, The - Flat Rock, MI - *Ed&PubIntYB 82*
Guardian, The [of Wright State University] - Dayton, OH - *NewsDir 84*
Guarionex Press Ltd. - New York, NY - *BoPubDir 4, 5; LitMag&SmPr 83-84*
Gudehus, Lesley - Hasbrouck Heights, NJ - *LitMarPl 84*
Guelph Historical Society - Guelph, ON, Canada - *BoPubDir 4, 5*
Guelph This Week - Guelph, ON, Canada - *Ed&PubIntYB 82*
Guerette, Patrick - Campbellton, NB, Canada - *BrCabYB 84*
Guerette Television Communautaire Ltee. - Kedgwick, NB, Canada - *BrCabYB 84*
Guerin Communications, Polly - New York, NY - *DirPRFirms 83; LitMarPl 83, 84*
Guerin Editeur Ltee. - Montreal, PQ, Canada - *LitMarPl 83, 84*
Guerin Inc., Judy - New York, NY - *DirPRFirms 83*
Guerneville Russian River News - Guerneville, CA - *BaconPubCkNews 84*
Guernica Editions - Montreal, PQ, Canada - *BoPubDir 4; LitMag&SmPr 83-84; LitMarPl 83, 84; WritMar 84*
Guernica Review - Montreal, PQ, Canada - *LitMag&SmPr 83-84*
Guernsey Breeders' Journal - Columbus, OH - *BaconPubCkMag 84; MagDir 84*
Guernsey Community Television System - Guernsey, WY - *BrCabYB 84; Tel&CabFB 84C*
Guernsey Gazette - Guernsey, WY - *Ed&PubIntYB 82*
Guernsey Gazette - *See* Lindsey Publishing
Guest, Steven - *See* Central Oklahoma Telephone Co.
Gugenheimer, C. & K. - Edgewater, NJ - *AvMarPl 83*
Guggenheim & Bell Associates Inc. - *See* Weiss Advertising Inc., Michael B.
Guida Associates, Pat - Pine Brook, NJ - *EISS 7-83 Sup*
Guida Productions Network - Norfolk, VA - *BillIntBG 83-84*
Guida Publishing Co., Frank - *See* Guida Productions Network
Guidance Associates Inc. - Mt. Kisco, NY - *AvMarPl 83*
Guidance Centre [of University of Toronto] - Toronto, ON, Canada - *LitMarPl 83, 84; WritMar 84*
Guidance Information System [of Time Share Corp.] - Avon, CT - *DirOnDB Spring 84; EISS 83*
Guidance Information System [of Time Share Corp.] - West Hartford, CT - *DBBus 82*
Guidance Information System [of TSE/Houghton Mifflin] - Hanover, NH - *DataDirOnSer 84*
Guide - Washington, DC - *WritMar 84*
Guide - Port Chester, NY - *AyerDirPub 83*
Guide - Willow Grove, PA - *AyerDirPub 83*
Guide - Killarney, MB, Canada - *AyerDirPub 83*
Guide - Arnprior, ON, Canada - *AyerDirPub 83; Ed&PubIntYB 82*
Guide - Port Hope, ON, Canada - *AyerDirPub 83; Ed&PubIntYB 82*
Guide Advocate - Watford, ON, Canada - *Ed&PubIntYB 82*
Guide & News - Gretna, NE - *AyerDirPub 83; Ed&PubIntYB 82*
Guide Democrat - Waynesville, MO - *AyerDirPub 83*
Guide Mont-Royal - Montreal, PQ, Canada - *Ed&PubIntYB 82*
Guide News Inc., The - Port Chester, NY - *Ed&PubIntYB 82*
Guide Newspaper Corp. - Gretna, LA - *BaconPubCkNews 84*
Guide Newspapers - Philadelphia, PA - *AyerDirPub 83*

Guide-Post Research Inc. - Sewickley, PA - *BrCabYB 84; IntDirMarRes 83*
Guide Press - Bethesda, MD - *BoPubDir 4, 5*
Guide, The [of Brownsburg Mid-State Newspapers Inc.] - Brownsburg, IN - *AyerDirPub 83; Ed&PubIntYB 82; NewsDir 84*
Guide, The - Harrisburg, PA - *Ed&PubIntYB 82*
Guide, The - Mechanicsburg, PA - *AyerDirPub 83*
Guide, The - Rapid City, SD - *AyerDirPub 83*
Guide, The - Grafton, WI - *AyerDirPub 83*
Guide, The - Lingle, WY - *Ed&PubIntYB 82*
Guide, The - Salmon Arm, BC, Canada - *AyerDirPub 83*
Guide, The - Cowansville, PQ, Canada - *AyerDirPub 83*
Guide to Cross Country Skiing - New York, NY - *MagDir 84*
Guide to Reprints Inc. - Kent, CT - *BoPubDir 4, 5*
Guide to Shopping & Entertainment - Boutte, LA - *AyerDirPub 83*
Guideline Publishing Co. - Los Angeles, CA - *BoPubDir 4, 5*
Guideline Research Corp. - New York, NY - *IntDirMarRes 83*
Guidepost - Falls Church, VA - *MagDir 84*
Guideposts [of Guideposts Associates Inc.] - New York, NY - *ArtMar 84; LitMarPl 83, 84; MagIndMarPl 82-83; WritMar 84*
Guideposts Associates Inc. - Carmel, NY - *DirMarMP 83*
Guideposts Book Service [Div. of Guideposts Associates Inc.] - New York, NY - *LitMarPl 83, 84*
Guidry Music, Randy - *See* Funky but Music Inc.
Guild Advertising Agency - New York, NY - *StaDirAdAg 2-84*
Guild Books - New York, NY - *BoPubDir 4, 5*
Guild Co., The [Div. of Mail Marketing Inc.] - Haworth, NJ - *MagIndMarPl 82-83*
Guild for the Blind - Chicago, IL - *BoPubDir 4, 5*
Guild Galleries - Monroe, CT - *StaDirAdAg 2-84*
Guild Information Network - Nashville, TN - *EISS 5-84 Sup*
Guild News - San Francisco, CA - *BaconPubCkMag 84*
Guild Press [Aff. of North Hennepin Writers' Guild] - Robbinsdale, MN - *BoPubDir 4, 5; LitMarPl 84*
Guild Reporter [of The Newspaper Guild AFL-CIO, CLC] - Washington, DC - *NewsDir 84*
Guilford Group, The - Guilford, CT - *LitMarPl 83, 84*
Guilford Poets Press - Woking, England - *LitMag&SmPr 83-84*
Guilford Press, The [Div. of Guilford Publications Inc.] - New York, NY - *LitMarPl 83, 84*
Guilford Shore Line Times - Guilford, CT - *BaconPubCkNews 84*
Guinea Hollow Press - New York, NY - *BoPubDir 4, 5*
Guiney, Louise - Storrs, CT - *LitMarPl 83, 84*
Guinn Printing Co. Inc. - Hoboken, NJ - *LitMarPl 83, 84*
Guinness Publishing Ltd. - Vancouver, BC, Canada - *LitMarPl 83*
Guion TV Cable [of TCA Cable TV Inc.] - Guion, AR - *Tel&CabFB 84C*
Guitar Man Music Corp. - *See* Drake Music Group
Guitar Player - Cupertino, CA - *BaconPubCkMag 84; MagDir 84; MagIndMarPl 82-83; WritMar 84*
Guitar World - New York, NY - *BaconPubCkMag 84*
Guitarchitect Enterprises Inc. - New York, NY - *BillIntBG 83-84*
Guitargraphy Music Inc. - New York, NY - *BillIntBG 83-84*
Guldberg Agency Inc., The Carl - Ann Arbor, MI - *AdAge 3-28-84; StaDirAdAg 2-84*
Gule Records - Hollywood, CA - *BillIntBG 83-84*
Gulf & Western Industries Inc. - New York, NY - *HomeVid&CabYB 82-83; KnowInd 83*
Gulf Breeze Cablevision [of The Essex Group] - Atmore, AL - *Tel&CabFB 84C*
Gulf Breeze Cablevision [of The Essex Group] - Evergreen, AL - *Tel&CabFB 84C*
Gulf Breeze Sentinel - Gulf Breeze, FL - *BaconPubCkNews 84*
Gulf Broadcast Group - St. Petersburg, FL - *BrCabYB 84; Tel&CabFB 84S*
Gulf Cable-Vision Co. - Port St. Joe, FL - *BrCabYB 84; Tel&CabFB 84C*
Gulf Central Radio Network - Columbus, MS - *BrCabYB 84*
Gulf Coast Broadcasting Co. - Corpus Christi, TX - *Tel&CabFB 84S*
Gulf Coast Cable Television - Houston, TX - *BrCabYB 84 p.D-301; Tel&CabFB 84C*
Gulf Coast Cable Television - Memorial Villages, TX - *BrCabYB 84*
Gulf Coast Cable Television - Missouri City, TX - *BrCabYB 84*
Gulf Coast Cablevision [of National Cable Systems Inc.] - Pascagoula, MS - *BrCabYB 84; Tel&CabFB 84C*
Gulf Coast Cattleman - San Antonio, TX - *BaconPubCkMag 84; MagDir 84*
Gulf Coast History & Humanities Conference [Aff. of Historic Pensacola Preservation Board] - Pensacola, FL - *BoPubDir 4, 5*
Gulf Coast Horizon - Gulfport, MS - *AyerDirPub 83*
Gulf Coast Lumberman & Building Distributor - Houston, TX - *BaconPubCkMag 84; MagDir 84*
Gulf Coast Oil Reporter - Denver, CO - *BaconPubCkMag 84*
Gulf Coast Oil Reporter [of Hart Publications Inc.] - Houston, TX - *MagDir 84*
Gulf Coast Plumbing-Heating-Cooling News - Brookshire, TX - *BaconPubCkMag 84; MagDir 84*
Gulf Coast Research Corp. - St. Petersburg, FL - *IntDirMarRes 83*
Gulf Coast Retail Grocer [of Gulf Publishing Co.] - Houston, TX - *BaconPubCkMag 84; MagDir 84*
Gulf Coast Television of Lee County [of Palmer Broadcasting Co.] - Pine Island, FL - *BrCabYB 84*
Gulf Coast Television of Lee County [of Palmer Broadcasting Co.] - Sanibel Island, FL - *BrCabYB 84*
Gulf Coast Tribune - Needville, TX - *AyerDirPub 83; Ed&PubIntYB 82*
Gulf Coast Weekly - Long Beach, MS - *Ed&PubIntYB 82*
Gulf Communicators Inc. [of GAC Properties Inc.] - Barefoot Bay, FL - *BrCabYB 84*
Gulf Communicators Inc. [of GAC Properties Inc.] - Cape Coral, FL - *BrCabYB 84*
Gulf County Breeze - Wewahitchka, FL - *AyerDirPub 83; Ed&PubIntYB 82*
Gulf Islands Driftwood - Ganges, BC, Canada - *AyerDirPub 83; Ed&PubIntYB 82*
Gulf News, The - Port Aux Basques, NF, Canada - *Ed&PubIntYB 82*
Gulf Publishing Co. - Houston, TX - *CompReadDB 82; DirMarMP 83; MicrocomMPl 84; WritMar 84*
Gulf Publishing Co. (Book Div.) - Houston, TX - *LitMarPl 83, 84*
Gulf Shores Islander - Gulf Shores, AL - *BaconPubCkNews 84*
Gulf South Broadcasters Ltd. - Metairie, LA - *BrCabYB 84*
Gulf State Advertising Agency - Houston, TX - *AdAge 3-28-84; ArtMar 84; StaDirAdAg 2-84*
Gulf Telephone Co. - Foley, AL - *TelDir&BG 83-84*
Gulf Telephone Co. - Perry, FL - *TelDir&BG 83-84*
Gulf Times, The - Sophia, WV - *AyerDirPub 83*
Gulf United Corp. - Dallas, TX - *KnowInd 83*
Gulfcoast Weekly - Long Beach, MS - *AyerDirPub 83*
Gulfport Star Journal - Gulfport, MS - *BaconPubCkNews 84*
Gulfshore Life [of Gulfshore Publishing Co. Inc.] - Naples, FL - *BaconPubCkMag 84; MagDir 84; WritMar 84*
Gulfstream Cablevision - Williston, FL - *Tel&CabFB 84C*
Gulfstream Cablevision Inc. [of Storer Cable Communications Inc.] - Dunedin, FL - *BrCabYB 84; Tel&CabFB 84C*
Gulfstream Cablevision Inc. [of Storer Cable Communications] - Pasco County (Western), FL - *BrCabYB 84*
Gulfstream Cablevision Inc. [of Storer Cable Communications] - Port Richey, FL - *Tel&CabFB 84C*
Gulfstream Cablevision Inc. [of Storer Cable Communications] - Tarpon Springs, FL - *BrCabYB 84*
Gulfstream Cablevision Inc. - *See* Gawthrop, H. Gene
Gulfstream Vision Inc. [Aff. of Storer Cable Communications] - Dunedin, FL - *InterCabHB 3*
Gulftron Inc. [of Cardiff Cablevision Inc.] - Goliad, TX - *BrCabYB 84; Tel&CabFB 84C*
Gull Books - Brooklyn, NY - *BoPubDir 4, 5; LitMag&SmPr 83-84*
Gull Lake Advance - Gull Lake, SK, Canada - *Ed&PubIntYB 82*
Gulley Computer Associates Inc. - Tulsa, OK - *DataDirOnSer 84*
Gullmasters: Children's Books - Winnipeg, MB, Canada - *BoPubDir 4 Sup, 5*
Gulmohr Books - Los Altos, CA - *LitMarPl 83, 84*
Gulton Graphics (Instrumentation Div.) - East Greenwich, RI - *WhoWMicrocom 83*
Gulton Industries Inc. - East Greenwich, RI - *DirInfWP 82*
Gumpertz/Bentley/Fried - Los Angeles, CA - *AdAge 3-28-84; ArtMar 84; StaDirAdAg 2-84*

Gun Barrel City News [of Malakoff Territory Times Publishing Co.] - Malakoff, TX - *NewsDir 84*
Gun Dog - Adel, IA - *BaconPubCkMag 84; MagDir 84; WritMar 84*
Gun Report, The - Aledo, IL - *BaconPubCkMag 84; MagDir 84; MagIndMarPl 82-83*
Gun Room Press - Highland Park, NJ - *BoPubDir 4, 5*
Gun Week - Buffalo, NY - *ArtMar 84; BaconPubCkMag 84*
Gun Week - Dayton, OH - *MagDir 84*
Gun World - Capistrano Beach, CA - *ArtMar 84; BaconPubCkMag 84; MagDir 84; MagIndMarPl 82-83; WritMar 84*
Gung Ho - Westminster, CO - *BaconPubCkMag 84*
Gunness Advertising - Janesville, WI - *StaDirAdAg 2-84*
Gunnison Cablevision - Gunnison, CO - *BrCabYB 84; Tel&CabFB 84C*
Gunnison Country Times - Gunnison, CO - *AyerDirPub 83; BaconPubCkNews 84; Ed&PubIntYB 82; NewsDir 84*
Gunnison Telephone Co. - Gunnison, UT - *TelDir&BG 83-84*
Gunnison Valley News - Gunnison, UT - *Ed&PubIntYB 82*
Gunnison Valley News - *See* Richfield Reaper
Guns - San Diego, CA - *BaconPubCkMag 84; MagDir 84; MagIndMarPl 82-83*
Guns & Ammo [of Petersen Publishing Co.] - Los Angeles, CA - *BaconPubCkMag 84; Folio 83; MagDir 84; MagIndMarPl 82-83; WritMar 84*
Guntersville Advertiser Gleam - Guntersville, AL - *BaconPubCkNews 84; NewsDir 84*
Guntersville Cablevision Inc. [of McDonald Group] - Guntersville, AL - *Tel&CabFB 84C*
Gunzendorfer & Associates, Wilt - Belmont, CA - *BrCabYB 84; CabTVFinDB 83*
Gupta-Humphrey Advertising Inc. - Omaha, NE - *StaDirAdAg 2-84*
Gura Public Relations Inc. - New York, NY - *DirPRFirms 83*
Gurasich, Spence, Darilek & McClure - *See* GSD & M
Guravich, Dan - Greenville, MS - *MagIndMarPl 82-83*
Gurdon Times - Gurdon, AR - *BaconPubCkNews 84; Ed&PubIntYB 82*
Guren, Peter - Huntsburg, OH - *Ed&PubIntYB 82*
Gurnee Press [of Lakeland Publishers Inc.] - Grayslake, IL - *NewsDir 84*
Gurnee Press - Gurnee, IL - *AyerDirPub 83; Ed&PubIntYB 82*
Gurnee Press - *See* Lakeland Publishers Inc.
Gurney's Gardening News [of Gurney Seed & Nursery Co.] - Yankton, SD - *WritMar 84*
Gurren Music, E. J. - Los Angeles, CA - *BillIntBG 83-84*
Gurrier Co., The - Hollis, NH - *DirPRFirms 83*
Gurtman & Murtha Associates Inc. - New York, NY - *DirPRFirms 83*
Gurze Books - Santa Barbara, CA - *BoPubDir 4 Sup, 5*
Gus Productions Inc. - Los Angeles, CA - *TelAl 83*
Gusman Co. - Savannah, GA - *BillIntBG 83-84*
Gustine Standard - Gustine, CA - *BaconPubCkNews 84; Ed&PubIntYB 82*
Gusto Records Inc. - Nashville, TN - *BillIntBG 83-84*
Gutenberg Press - San Francisco, CA - *BoPubDir 4, 5; LitMag&SmPr 83-84*
Guthman Americana [Aff. of American Society of Arms Collectors] - Westport, CT - *BoPubDir 4, 5*
Guthrian, The - Guthrie Center, IA - *AyerDirPub 83; Ed&PubIntYB 82*
Guthrie, Al - Carmichael, CA - *BoPubDir 4, 5*
Guthrie & Associates, Jack - Louisville, KY - *DirPRFirms 83*
Guthrie Antenna Co. - Guthrie, TX - *Tel&CabFB 84C*
Guthrie Center Guthrie - *See* Times Guthrian Publishing Co. Inc.
Guthrie Center Times - Guthrie Center, IA - *AyerDirPub 83; Ed&PubIntYB 82; NewsDir 84*
Guthrie County Vedette - Panora, IA - *Ed&PubIntYB 82*
Guthrie Leader [of Logan Publishing Co.] - Guthrie, OK - *BaconPubCkNews 84; Ed&PubIntYB 82; NewsDir 84*
Guthrie Publications Inc., Woody - *See* Sanga Music Inc.
Guthrie Publishing Co. - Maple Grove, MN - *LitMag&SmPr 83-84*
Guthrie Register-News - Guthrie, OK - *BaconPubCkNews 84; Ed&PubIntYB 82*
Guthrie Times - *See* Times Guthrian Publishing Co. Inc.
Gutman Advertising Agency - Wheeling, WV - *ArtMar 84; StaDirAdAg 2-84*
Gutman Inc., Leo A. - New York, NY - *StaDirAdAg 2-84; TelAl 83, 84; Tel&CabFB 84C*
Guttenberg Associates Inc. - Washington, DC - *DirPRFirms 83*
Guttenberg Press - Guttenberg, IA - *BaconPubCkNews 84; Ed&PubIntYB 82*
Guttenberg TV Cable Systems - Guttenberg, IA - *BrCabYB 84; Tel&CabFB 84C*
Guttmacher Institute, Alan - New York, NY - *BoPubDir 4, 5*
Guttman & Pam Ltd. - Beverly Hills, CA - *DirPRFirms 83*
Guymark Studios Inc. - Hamden, CT - *AvMarPl 83; TelAl 83, 84*
Guymon Herald [of Donrey Media Group] - Guymon, OK - *BaconPubCkNews 84; NewsDir 84*
Guymon Observer - Guymon, OK - *BaconPubCkNews 84; Ed&PubIntYB 82*
Guynes Printing Co. - El Paso, TX - *MagIndMarPl 82-83*
Guyot Hand Bookbinding, Don - Seattle, WA - *LitMarPl 83, 84*
Guzman & Associates Inc., Joseph - Palatine, IL - *TeleSy&SerDir 2-84*
G.W. Communications - Wilmington, IL - *BaconPubCkNews 84*
G.W. Computers Ltd. - London, England - *MicrocomSwDir 1*
G.W. Review - Washington, DC - *LitMag&SmPr 83-84*
Gwen Record Service - Albany, GA - *BillIntBG 83-84*
Gwiazda - Philadelphia, PA - *Ed&PubIntYB 82*
Gwiazda Polarna - Stevens Point, WI - *Ed&PubIntYB 82; NewsDir 84*
Gwinnett Cable TV - Snellville, GA - *BrCabYB 84*
Gwinnett Cablevision Corp., N. E. - Lawrenceville, GA - *BrCabYB 84*
Gwinnett Focus - Lawrenceville, GA - *AyerDirPub 83*
Gwinnett News - Lawrenceville, GA - *AyerDirPub 83; Ed&PubIntYB 82*
GWJ Music Inc. - *See* Remick, Lloyd Zane
GWN Industries Inc. - New York, NY - *LitMarPl 84*
GWP Corp. - Cambridge, MA - *InfIndMarPl 83*
Gwynn Advertising Inc. - Erie, PA - *StaDirAdAg 2-84*
Gypsum Advocate - Gypsum, KS - *Ed&PubIntYB 82*
Gypsum Association - Evanston, IL - *AvMarPl 83*
Gypsy Press - Philadelphia, PA - *LitMag&SmPr 83-84*

H

H & B Cable Service Inc. - Claflin, KS - *BrCabYB 84*
H & B Communications - Holyrood, KS - *Tel&CabFB 84C; TelDir&BG 83-84*
H & C Communications - Houston, TX - *AdAge 6-28-84; KnowInd 83; Tel&CabFB 84S*
H & E Computronics - Spring Valley, NY - *MicrocomMPl 83, 84; WhoWMicrocom 83*
H & H Enterprises Inc. - Lawrence, KS - *BoPubDir 4, 5; LitMarPl 84*
H & H Publications - Redwood City, CA - *BoPubDir 4 Sup, 5*
H & H Scientific - Ft. Washington, MD - *MicrocomMPl 83, 84*
H & H Trading Co. - Clayton, CA - *MicrocomMPl 83; MicrocomSwDir 1*
H & H Trading Co. - Concord, CA - *MicrocomMPl 84*
H & H Trading Co. - Pleasant Hill, CA - *WhoWMicrocom 83*
H & H Typing Specialists - Breinigsville, PA - *MagIndMarPl 82-83*
H & M ADP Security - Falls Church, VA - *MicrocomMPl 84*
H & R Advertising - Wheeling, IL - *DirMarMP 83*
H & T Cable TV - Finley, ND - *Tel&CabFB 84C*
H/R Net - Covington, LA - *DirOnDB Spring 84*
H-R Productions Inc. - New York, NY - *TelAl 83, 84; Tel&CabFB 84C*
Haan Graphic Publishing Services Ltd. - Middletown, CT - *LitMarPl 84*
Haas Enterprises - Ashland, NH - *BoPubDir 4 Sup, 5*
Haas Enterprises Ltd. - Hanalei, HI - *BoPubDir 4, 5*
Haas Group Inc., The - New York, NY - *DirPRFirms 83*
Haas, Irvin - Roslyn Estates, NY - *LitMarPl 83, 84*
Haas, M. - Jeffersonville, NY - *LitMarPl 83, 84; MagIndMarPl 82-83*
Haas Photography, Ken - New York, NY - *LitMarPl 83, 84; MagIndMarPl 82-83*
Haas-Reed Inc. - Milwaukee, WI - *StaDirAdAg 2-84*
Haber Inc., Alfred - Palisades Park, NJ - *Tel&CabFB 84C*
Haberbeck Associates - Naperville, IL - *ADAPSOMemDir 83-84*
Haberman, John M. - Lakewood, OH - *LitMarPl 83*
Habersham Corp. - New Orleans, LA - *BoPubDir 4 Sup, 5*
Habicht, Michael - Howell, NJ - *MagIndMarPl 82-83*
Hach, Phila R. - Clarksville, TN - *BoPubDir 4 Sup, 5*
Hachette Inc. - New York, NY - *LitMarPl 83, 84*
Hachiyo Electric Sound Co. Ltd. - New York, NY - *AvMarPl 83*
Hacienda Heights Highlander - *See* Highlander Publications Inc.
Hacienda Heights Highlander Publications [of Media General Inc.] - La Puente, CA - *NewsDir 84*
Hacienda Recording Studio - Corpus Christi, TX - *BillIntBG 83-84*
Hacker Art Books Inc. - New York, NY - *LitMarPl 83, 84*
Hacker Inc., Gene - Hackensack, NJ - *AvMarPl 83*
Hackercolor - Sacramento, CA - *AvMarPl 83*
Hackett Photo Archives, Gabriel D. [Div. of General Press Features] - New York, NY - *Ed&PubIntYB 82; LitMarPl 83, 84; MagIndMarPl 82-83*
Hackett Publishing Co. Inc. - Indianapolis, IN - *LitMarPl 83, 84*
Hackettstown Forum - Hackettstown, NJ - *NewsDir 84*
Hackettstown Forum & Star Gazette - Hackettstown, NJ - *BaconPubCkNews 84*
Hadassah Magazine - New York, NY - *ArtMar 84; LitMarPl 83, 84; MagDir 84; MagIndMarPl 82-83; WritMar 84*
Haddad Advertising, Lawrence - Studio City, CA - *AdAge 3-28-84; StaDirAdAg 2-84*
Haddad's Fine Arts Inc. - Anaheim, CA - *ArtMar 84; BoPubDir 4, 5*
Haddon Advertising - Chicago, IL - *AdAge 3-28-84; StaDirAdAg 2-84*
Haddon Craftsmen Inc. - Scranton, PA - *LitMarPl 83, 84*
Haddon Gazette [of Cherry Hill Suburban Newspaper Group] - Cherry Hill, NJ - *AyerDirPub 83; NewsDir 84*
Haddon Gazette-Suburban, The - Haddonfield, NJ - *Ed&PubIntYB 82*
Haddon, Lynch & Baughman Public Relations Inc. - Chicago, IL - *DirPRFirms 83*
Haddonfield Haddon Gazette-Suburban - *See* Suburban Newspapers
Haddonfield Suburban - *See* Suburban Newspapers
Hades International, Micky - Calgary, AB, Canada - *BoPubDir 4, 5*
Hadle Agency, The - New York, NY - *LitMarPl 83, 84; MagIndMarPl 82-83*
Hadley Co., R. G. - Salem, OR - *BoPubDir 4, 5*
Hadley School for the Blind Inc. - Winnetka, IL - *LitMarPl 83, 84*
Hadley Telephone Co. Inc. [Aff. of Century Telephone Enterprises Inc.] - Hadley, MI - *TelDir&BG 83-84*
Hadoar Hebrew Weekly - New York, NY - *Ed&PubIntYB 82; NewsDir 84*
Haft Group Inc., The - New York, NY - *DirPRFirms 83*
Hagadone Corp., The - Coeur d'Alene, ID - *BrCabYB 84*
Hagadone Newspapers - Coeur d'Alene, ID - *Ed&PubIntYB 82*
Hagarman Star Tribune - Hagarman, NM - *BaconPubCkNews 84*
Hagedorn Communications - New York, NY - *BaconPubCkNews 84*
Hagen Systems Inc. - Minneapolis, MN - *WhoWMicrocom 83*
Hagenhofer, Robert - Flemington, NJ - *LitMarPl 83, 84; MagIndMarPl 82-83*
Hager City Telephone Co. - Hager City, WI - *TelDir&BG 83-84*
Hager, Sharp & Abramson Inc. - Washington, DC - *DirPRFirms 83*
Hagerstown Bookbinding & Printing Co. Inc. - Hagerstown, MD - *MagIndMarPl 82-83*
Hagerstown Daily Mail - Hagerstown, MD - *BaconPubCkNews 84*
Hagerstown Exponent - Hagerstown, IN - *BaconPubCkNews 84; Ed&PubIntYB 82*
Hagerstown Herald-Mail [of Schurz Communications Inc.] - Hagerstown, MD - *NewsDir 84*
Hagerstown Morning Herald - Hagerstown, MD - *BaconPubCkNews 84*
Hagerty, Lockenvitz, Ginzkey & Associates Inc. - Bloomington, IL - *StaDirAdAg 2-84*
Hagglund & Associates - Minneapolis, MN - *StaDirAdAg 2-84*

Hagin Ministries, Kenneth - Tulsa, OK - *BoPubDir 4, 5*
Hagstrom Map Co. Inc. [Subs. of American Map Corp.] - Maspeth, NY - *LitMarPl 83, 84*
Hague & Co. - Northbrook, IL - *CabTVFinDB 83*
Hahn, Basinger & Associates Inc. - Chicago, IL - *MagIndMarPl 82-83*
Hahn, Crane & Associates Inc. - Chicago, IL - *DirMarMP 83; LitMarPl 83, 84*
Hahn, Crane & Associates Inc. - *See* Haddon Advertising
Hahn Inc., Marvin - Birmingham, MI - *StaDirAdAg 2-84*
HAI - Whippany, NJ - *DataDirSup 7-83*
Haifa On-Line Bibliographic Text System [of University of Haifa Library] - Haifa, Israel - *EISS 7-83 Sup*
Haight-Ashbury Publications [Aff. of Haight-Ashbury Free Clinic] - San Francisco, CA - *BoPubDir 4 Sup, 5; LitMag&SmPr 83-84*
Haiku Society of America Inc. - New York, NY - *LitMag&SmPr 83-84*
Hail Bibliography [of Illinois State Water Survey Library] - Champaign, IL - *EISS 83*
Hail Bibliography [of Illinois State Water Survey Library] - Urbana, IL - *CompReadDB 82*
Hailey Wood River Journal - Hailey, ID - *BaconPubCkNews 84; NewsDir 84*
Haileyville Cable TV - Haileyville, OK - *BrCabYB 84*
Haim, Ernie - Warwick, NY - *LitMarPl 83, 84*
Haimo, Oscar - New York, NY - *BoPubDir 4, 5*
Hain Associates Inc., Robert - Scotch Plains, NJ - *HBIndAd&MS 82-83*
Hain, Harry & Anna A. - Lewistown, PA - *Tel&CabFB 84C p.1682*
Haines, Ben M. - Lawrence, KS - *BoPubDir 4 Sup, 5*
Haines Cable TV - Haines, AK - *BrCabYB 84*
Haines-Camron Inc. - Ottawa, ON, Canada - *AvMarPl 83*
Haines City Herald - Haines City, FL - *BaconPubCkNews 84; Ed&PubIntYB 82; NewsDir 84*
Haines Lynn Canal News - Haines, AK - *BaconPubCkNews 84*
Haines Network Inc. [of E.D. & D. Inc.] - Haines, AK - *Tel&CabFB 84C*
Haines Telephone Co. - Haines, OR - *TelDir&BG 83-84*
Hairdo & Beauty - New York, NY - *BaconPubCkMag 84; MagDir 84*
Hairenik - Boston, MA - *AyerDirPub 83; Ed&PubIntYB 82; NewsDir 84*
Hairstylist, The [of Service Publications Inc.] - New York, NY - *ArtMar 84; BaconPubCkMag 84; MagDir 84*
Hajar Associates Inc. - Needham Heights, MA - *MagIndMarPl 82-83*
Hakuhodo Inc. - Tokyo, Japan - *AdAge 6-25-84; StaDirAdAg 2-84*
Hal-Nat Music Publishing Co. - Cincinnati, OH - *BillIntBG 83-84*
Hal Systems & Services Inc. - Dallas, TX - *ADAPSOMemDir 83-84*
Halbleib & Moll Associates Inc. - Louisville, KY - *StaDirAdAg 2-84*
Halcyon Associates - Brooklyn, NY - *EISS 5-84 Sup*
Halcyon Press of Ithaca - Ithaca, NY - *BoPubDir 4, 5*
Haldimand Press - Hagersville, ON, Canada - *AyerDirPub 83*
Haldimand Press, The - Haldimard, ON, Canada - *Ed&PubIntYB 82*
Hale, Barbara - New York, NY - *LitMarPl 83*
Hale Center American - Hale Center, TX - *BaconPubCkNews 84; Ed&PubIntYB 82*
Hale Leader - Hale, MO - *BaconPubCkNews 84; Ed&PubIntYB 82*
Hale Systems Inc. (Remote Computing Div.) - Palo Alto, CA - *DataDirOnSer 84*
Haley & Associates Inc., Russ - Durham, NH - *IntDirMarRes 83*
Haley & Ruckle Advertising - Boston, MA - *AdAge 3-28-84; StaDirAdAg 2-84*
Haley, Charles W. - Canton, MS - *Tel&CabFB 84C p.1683*
Haley Cos. Inc., The Martin - New York, NY - *DirPRFirms 83*
Haley, Kiss & Dowd Inc. - New York, NY - *DirPRFirms 83*
Haleyville Northwest Alabamian - Haleyville, AL - *BaconPubCkNews 84; NewsDir 84*
Haleyville TV Cable Corp. - Haleyville, AL - *BrCabYB 84; Tel&CabFB 84C*
Half Moon Bay Review - Half Moon Bay, CA - *BaconPubCkNews 84; Ed&PubIntYB 82; NewsDir 84*
Half Moon Bay Review & Pescadero Pebble - Half Moon Bay, CA - *AyerDirPub 83*
Halhalla Enterprises - Sumner, WA - *MicrocomMPl 84*
Halhed, Dick - Islington, ON, Canada - *BoPubDir 4 Sup, 5*
Haliburton County Echo & Minden Recorder - Haliburton, ON, Canada - *AyerDirPub 83; Ed&PubIntYB 82*
Halifax Cable TV Inc. [of Athena Communications Corp.] - Daytona Beach, FL - *BrCabYB 84; Tel&CabFB 84C*
Halifax Cablevision Ltd. - Halifax, NS, Canada - *BrCabYB 84*
Halifax Chronicle-Herald - Halifax, NS, Canada - *LitMarPl 83*
Halifax County This Week [of Parker Bros. Inc.] - Ahoskie, NC - *NewsDir 84*
Halifax County This Week - Scotland Neck, NC - *AyerDirPub 83; Ed&PubIntYB 82*
Halifax Mail-Star - Halifax, NS, Canada - *LitMarPl 83*
Halker Group - Ishpeming, MI - *BrCabYB 84*
Hall Advertising, Ray - Austin, TX - *StaDirAdAg 2-84*
Hall & Co., G. K. [Div. of ITT] - Boston, MA - *DirMarMP 83; LitMarPl 83, 84; MicroMarPl 82-83*
Hall & Co. Inc., John T. - Drexel Hill, PA - *StaDirAdAg 2-84*
Hall Associates - Chicago, IL - *DirPRFirms 83*
Hall Associates Inc., Benn [Div. of Jones, Brakeley & Rockwell Inc.] - New York, NY - *LitMarPl 83, 84*
Hall Associates Inc., Everett - Stamford, CT - *AvMarPl 83*
Hall Associates, Ron - Lakewood, OH - *BoPubDir 4, 5*
Hall, C. Mitchel - Washington, DC - *BoPubDir 4, 5*
Hall Communications Inc. - Norwich, CT - *BrCabYB 84*
Hall Decker McKibbin [of Kornhauser & Calene Inc.] - New York, NY - *DirPRFirms 83; StaDirAdAg 2-84*
Hall Design - Wilmette, IL - *MicrocomMPl 84*
Hall, Eva Litchfield - Rochester, NY - *BoPubDir 4, 5*
Hall, Floyd W. - Lindsay, ON, Canada - *BoPubDir 4, 5*
Hall, Haerr, Peterson & Harney - Peoria, IL - *AdAge 3-28-84; BrCabYB 84; StaDirAdAg 2-84*
Hall Inc., W. F. - Chicago, IL - *LitMarPl 83, 84*
Hall Industrial Publicity Inc. - Troy, MI - *DirPRFirms 83*
Hall, Marie J. - Bar Harbor, ME - *LitMarPl 83, 84*
Hall Music Inc., Rick - *See* Fame Publishing Co. Inc.
Hall Music, John - Ft. Worth, TX - *BillIntBG 83-84*
Hall of Fame Music Co. - Beverly Hills, CA - *BillIntBG 83-84*
Hall Press - San Bernardino, CA - *BoPubDir 4, 5*
Hall Properties, James H. - Albany, GA - *Tel&CabFB 84C*
Hall Records Inc., John - Ft. Worth, TX - *BillIntBG 83-84*
Halladay Advertising Inc. - East Providence, RI - *StaDirAdAg 2-84*
Hallandale Digest - Hallandale, FL - *BaconPubCkNews 84; Ed&PubIntYB 82; NewsDir 84*
Hallandale Sun Reporter - Ft. Lauderdale, FL - *AyerDirPub 83*
Hallberg & Co. Inc., Chas. - Delavan, WI - *BoPubDir 4, 5*
Halleck Advertising Inc., Mark - Lexington, KY - *StaDirAdAg 2-84*
Hallen Co., E. S. - Salt Lake City, UT - *StaDirAdAg 2-84*
Hallen Publishing Co. - San Jose, CA - *BoPubDir 4, 5*
Hallenbeck & Riley - Albany, NY - *AvMarPl 83*
Haller Schwarz - Los Angeles, CA - *AdAge 3-28-84; StaDirAdAg 2-84*
Hallettsville Publishing Co. - Hallettsville, TX - *BaconPubCkNews 84*
Hallettsville Tribune-Herald - Hellettsville, TX - *NewsDir 84*
Hallettsville Tribune-Herald - *See* Hallettsville Publishing Co.
Halliday Lithograph [Div. of Arcata Graphics Co.] - West Hanover, MA - *LitMarPl 84*
Hallmark Advertising Inc. - Pittsburgh, PA - *StaDirAdAg 2-84*
Hallmark Cable Associates/Telecable Communications Corp. - Baltimore, MD - *Tel&CabFB 84C p.1683*
Hallmark Cards Inc. - Kansas City, MO - *WritMar 84*
Hallmark Data Systems Inc. - Skokie, IL - *MagIndMarPl 82-83*
Hallmark Films & Recordings Inc. - Owings Mills, MD - *AvMarPl 83*
Hallmark Press Inc. - Long Island City, NY - *LitMarPl 83, 84*
Hallmarque Musical Works Ltd. - *See* Aljoni Music Co.
Hallmundsson, Hallberg - New York, NY - *LitMarPl 83, 84; MagIndMarPl 82-83*
Hallock Cable TV Inc. - Hallock, MN - *BrCabYB 84*

Hallock Kittson County Enterprise - Hallock, MN - *BaconPubCkNews 84*
Hall's Compute Center - San Jose, CA - *MicrocomMPl 84*
Halls Graphic - Halls, TN - *Ed&PubIntYB 82*
Halls Graphic - *See* Lauderdale County Enterprise
Halls of Ivy Press - Simi Valley, CA - *BoPubDir 4, 5; LitMag&SmPr 83-84*
Hall's Radio Forum, Claude - San Diego, CA - *MagDir 84*
Hallsville Herald - Hallsville, TX - *Ed&PubIntYB 82*
Hallum, Boen - Columbus, OH - *BoPubDir 5*
Hally Services, Arlene - Augusta, GA - *IntDirMarRes 83*
Halpern Sounds Records & Tapes - Belmont, CA - *BillIntBG 83-84*
Halsey Agency, Reece - Los Angeles, CA - *LitMarPl 83, 84*
Halstad Cable Co. - Halstad, MN - *Tel&CabFB 84C*
Halstad Telephone Co. - Halstad, MN - *TelDir&BG 83-84*
Halstad Valley Journal - Halstad, MN - *BaconPubCkNews 84*
Halstead Independent - Halstead, KS - *BaconPubCkNews 84; Ed&PubIntYB 82*
Halsted Press [Div. of John Wiley & Sons Inc.] - New York, NY - *LitMarPl 83, 84*
Halton Cable Systems - Georgetown, ON, Canada - *BrCabYB 84*
Halton Hills Herald - Georgetown, ON, Canada - *AyerDirPub 83; Ed&PubIntYB 82*
Halwill Music - *See* Harlem Music
Ham Radio Horizons - Greenville, NH - *ArtMar 84; MagDir 84*
Ham Radio Magazine - Greenville, NH - *BaconPubCkMag 84; MagDir 84; MagIndMarPl 82-83*
Ham-Sem Records Inc. - Los Angeles, CA - *BillIntBG 83-84*
Hamaker-Weaver Publishers - Potterville, MI - *BoPubDir 4 Sup, 5*
Hamba Books - Conway, AR - *BoPubDir 4 Sup, 5*
Hambro International Venture Fund - Boston, MA - *ADAPSOMemDir 83-84*
Hambro Productions Inc., Lenny - Linwood, NJ - *AvMarPl 83*
Hamburg Ashley County Ledger - Hamburg, AR - *BaconPubCkNews 84*
Hamburg Item - Hamburg, PA - *BaconPubCkNews 84; Ed&PubIntYB 82; NewsDir 84*
Hamburg Penny Saver - Hamburg, NY - *AyerDirPub 83*
Hamburg Reporter - Hamburg, IA - *BaconPubCkNews 84; Ed&PubIntYB 82*
Hamburg Sun - Hamburg, NY - *NewsDir 84*
Hamburg Sun & Erie County Independent - Hamburg, NY - *BaconPubCkNews 84; Ed&PubIntYB 82*
Hamburg TV Cable [of Lenfest Communications Inc.] - Hamburg, PA - *BrCabYB 84; Tel&CabFB 84C*
Hamden Chronicle - Hamden, CT - *AyerDirPub 83; BaconPubCkNews 84; Ed&PubIntYB 82*
Hamden Chronicle [of West Hartford Imprint Newspapers] - West Hartford, CT - *NewsDir 84*
Hamden Community TV Club Inc. - Hamden, NY - *BrCabYB 84; Tel&CabFB 84C*
Hamel & Worden News - Hamel/Worden, IL - *Ed&PubIntYB 82*
Hamelfarb Public Relations, Rena - New York, NY - *DirPRFirms 83*
Hamer Advertising & Marketing Concepts - New York, NY - *HBIndAd&MS 82-83; StaDirAdAg 2-84*
Hameroff/Milenthal Inc. - Columbus, OH - *ArtMar 84; StaDirAdAg 2-84*
Hames Video - Ashville, AL - *Tel&CabFB 84C*
Hamilburg Agency, Mitchell J. - Beverly Hills, CA - *LitMarPl 83*
Hamilton Advocate-Hamiltonian - Hamilton, MO - *BaconPubCkNews 84*
Hamilton & Associates Inc. - Washington, DC - *DirPRFirms 83*
Hamilton & Region Arts Council - Hamilton, ON, Canada - *BoPubDir 4 Sup, 5*
Hamilton & Staff Inc., William R. - Chevy Chase, MD - *BrCabYB 84; Tel&CabFB 84C*
Hamilton Associates Inc. - Galveston, TX - *StaDirAdAg 2-84*
Hamilton Cablevision Associates Ltd. - Hamilton Township, NJ - *BrCabYB 84*
Hamilton Co-Axial [of Rogers Cable Systems Inc.] - Hamilton, ON, Canada - *BrCabYB 84*
Hamilton County CATV Inc. [of Horizon Communications Corp.] - Carmel, IN - *BrCabYB 84; Tel&CabFB 84C*
Hamilton County Herald - Chattanooga, TN - *AyerDirPub 83; Ed&PubIntYB 82*
Hamilton County News [of Elizabethtown Denton Publications Inc.] - Elizabethtown, NY - *NewsDir 84*
Hamilton County News - Speculator, NY - *AyerDirPub 83; Ed&PubIntYB 82*
Hamilton County Telephone Co-Operative - Dahlgren, IL - *TelDir&BG 83-84*
Hamilton Electronics Corp. - Chicago, IL - *AvMarPl 83*
Hamilton Gary Sardina O'Hara Inc. - Oak Brook, IL - *StaDirAdAg 2-84*
Hamilton, George C. & Ann - Hominy, OK - *Tel&CabFB 84C p.1683*
Hamilton, Hamish - North Pomfret, VT - *LitMarPl 83, 84*
Hamilton Harris County Journal - *See* Tri-County Newspapers Inc.
Hamilton Herald-News [of Hamilton Publishing Co. Inc.] - Hamilton, TX - *BaconPubCkNews 84; NewsDir 84*
Hamilton House - Philadelphia, PA - *BoPubDir 4, 5*
Hamilton Institute, Alexander - New York, NY - *BoPubDir 4 Sup, 5; DirMarMP 83*
Hamilton Journal-News [of Harte-Hanks Communications Inc.] - Hamilton, OH - *NewsDir 84*
Hamilton Journal-Record - Hamilton, AL - *BaconPubCkNews 84; NewsDir 84*
Hamilton Magazine [of Hamilton Publishing Inc.] - Hamilton, ON, Canada - *BaconPubCkMag 84; WritMar 84*
Hamilton Mid-York Weekly - Hamilton, NY - *BaconPubCkNews 84; NewsDir 84*
Hamilton Mountain News - Hamilton, ON, Canada - *Ed&PubIntYB 82*
Hamilton News - Hamilton, IN - *AyerDirPub 83; Ed&PubIntYB 82*
Hamilton News, The - Edgerton, OH - *AyerDirPub 83*
Hamilton Printing Co. - Rensselaer, NY - *LitMarPl 83, 84*
Hamilton Ravalli Republic - Hamilton, MT - *BaconPubCkNews 84*
Hamilton Recorder - Hamilton, ON, Canada - *AyerDirPub 83*
Hamilton Recorder News Magazine - Hamilton, ON, Canada - *Ed&PubIntYB 82*
Hamilton Sorter Co. Inc. - Fairfield, OH - *DirInfWP 82*
Hamilton Sun - Hamilton, OH - *Ed&PubIntYB 82*
Hamilton Telephone Co. - Aurora, NE - *TelDir&BG 83-84*
Hamilton Township's Area Reporter [of Area Auto Racing News Inc.] - Trenton, NJ - *NewsDir 84*
Hamilton TV Cable Co. [of Group W Cable Inc.] - Hamilton, MT - *Tel&CabFB 84C*
Hamilton TV Cable Co. - Hamilton, TX - *BrCabYB 84; Tel&CabFB 84C*
Hamilton-Wenham Chronicle [of North Shore Weeklies Inc.] - Ipswich, MA - *AyerDirPub 83; Ed&PubIntYB 82; NewsDir 84*
Hamilton-Wenham Chronicle - *See* North Shore Weeklies Inc.
Hamiota Echo - Hamiota, MB, Canada - *Ed&PubIntYB 82*
Hamlet News-Messenger - Hamlet, NC - *BaconPubCkNews 84*
Hamlet News, The - Hamlet, NC - *Ed&PubIntYB 82*
Hamlin County Herald-Enterprise - Hayti, SD - *AyerDirPub 83*
Hamlin County Republican - Castlewood, SD - *AyerDirPub 83; Ed&PubIntYB 82*
Hamlin Herald - Hamlin, TX - *BaconPubCkNews 84; Ed&PubIntYB 82*
Hamlin Weekly News Sentinel - Hamlin, WV - *Ed&PubIntYB 82*
Hamlin Weekly News Sentinel - *See* Lincoln Publishing Co.
Hamlin Williams & Associates - Memphis, TN - *DataDirSup 7-83; MicrocomMPl 83, 84; WhoWMicrocom 83*
Hamm Publications Inc. - Pasadena, CA - *BaconPubCkNews 84*
Hammack, Calvin J. Sr. - Hooker, OK - *Tel&CabFB 84C p.1683*
Hammell Newspapers of Florida Inc. - Clewiston, FL - *BaconPubCkNews 84*
Hammell Newspapers of Florida Inc. - Tequesta, FL - *Ed&PubIntYB 82*
Hammermill Papers Group [Div. of Hammermill Paper Co.] - Erie, PA - *LitMarPl 83, 84*
Hammersmith-Breithaupt Printing Corp. - Milwaukee, WI - *MagIndMarPl 82-83*
Hammett Co., J. L. - Braintree, MA - *MicrocomMPl 83, 84*
Hammill, J. H. III - Pleasant Hill, CA - *BoPubDir 4, 5*
Hammon Community TV - Hammon, OK - *BrCabYB 84; Tel&CabFB 84C*

Hammond Central St. Croix News - Hammond, WI - *BaconPubCkNews 84*
Hammond Daily Star - Hammond, LA - *BaconPubCkNews 84; NewsDir 84*
Hammond Farrell - New York, NY - *AdAge 3-28-84; DirPRFirms 83; StaDirAdAg 2-84*
Hammond-Harwood House Association - Annapolis, MD - *BoPubDir 4, 5*
Hammond Inc. - Maplewood, NJ - *AvMarPl 83; DirMarMP 83; LitMarPl 83, 84; WritMar 84*
Hammond/Keehn Inc. - New York, NY - *StaDirAdAg 2-84*
Hammond Lake County Globe-Ledger - Hammond, IN - *BaconPubCkNews 84*
Hammond Media Corp. [Subs. of Hammond & Dubs Direct] - New York, NY - *DirMarMP 83*
Hammond Music, Albert - *See* MizMo Enterprises
Hammond Newspapers - Millvale, PA - *BrCabYB 84*
Hammond Photography, Rick - Visalia, CA - *BoPubDir 4, 5*
Hammond Sun [of Hammond Murray-Huber Publishing Inc.] - Hammond, LA - *NewsDir 84*
Hammond Telephone Co. [Aff. of Universal Telephone Inc.] - Hammond, WI - *TelDir&BG 83-84*
Hammond Times - Hammond, IN - *BaconPubCkNews 84*
Hammond Vindicator - Hammond, LA - *BaconPubCkNews 84; Ed&PubIntYB 82; NewsDir 84*
Hammond-Wright Communications Inc. - New York, NY - *StaDirAdAg 2-84*
Hammonton News [of Times Graphics Inc.] - Hammonton, NJ - *BaconPubCkNews 84; Ed&PubIntYB 82; NewsDir 84*
Hamoroh Press - Los Angeles, CA - *BoPubDir 4, 5*
Hamparian, Arthur - Demarest, NJ - *LitMarPl 83, 84*
Hampden Papers Inc. - Hackensack, NY - *LitMarPl 84*
Hampden Telephone Co. - Hampden, ME - *TelDir&BG 83-84*
Hampshire Gazette - Northampton, MA - *AyerDirPub 83; BaconPubCkNews 84; LitMarPl 83*
Hampshire Group, The - Bridgeport, CT - *Ed&PubIntYB 82*
Hampshire House Publishing Corp. - *See* TRO
Hampshire Register [of Free Press Inc.] - Hampshire, IL - *AyerDirPub 83; Ed&PubIntYB 82; NewsDir 84*
Hampshire Register - *See* Free Press Inc.
Hampshire Review [of Cornwell & Ailes Inc.] - Romney, WV - *AyerDirPub 83; Ed&PubIntYB 82; NewsDir 84*
Hampstead Herald [of Ellicott City Stromberg Publishing Inc.] - Ellicott City, MD - *NewsDir 84*
Hampton, Bates & Associates Inc. - Arlington, VA - *DirPRFirms 83; ProGuPRSer 4*
Hampton Cablesystems [of American Cablesystems Corp.] - Hampton, TN - *Tel&CabFB 84C*
Hampton Chronicle - Hampton, IA - *BaconPubCkNews 84; Ed&PubIntYB 82*
Hampton Chronicle & Times - Hampton, IA - *NewsDir 84*
Hampton Chronicle-News - Westhampton Beach, NY - *AyerDirPub 83; Ed&PubIntYB 82; NewsDir 84*
Hampton Chronicle-News - *See* Southampton Press Publishing Co.
Hampton County Cablevision Co. Inc. - Hampton, SC - *BrCabYB 84; Tel&CabFB 84C*
Hampton County Guardian - Hampton, SC - *AyerDirPub 83; Ed&PubIntYB 82*
Hampton Court Publishers - Lake Mahopac, NY - *LitMag&SmPr 83-84*
Hampton Roads Advertising Inc. - Norfolk, VA - *DirPRFirms 83*
Hampton Roads Cablevision [of The Daily Press Inc.] - Newport News, VA - *Tel&CabFB 84C*
Hampton South Arkansas Accent - Hampton, AR - *BaconPubCkNews 84*
Hampton Times - Hampton, IA - *BaconPubCkNews 84; Ed&PubIntYB 82*
Hampton Union - *See* Exeter News-Letter Co.
Hampton Union, The [of Ottaway Newspapers] - Hampton, NH - *Ed&PubIntYB 82; NewsDir 84*
Hamtramck Citizen - Hamtramck, MI - *BaconPubCkNews 84; NewsDir 84*
Hamtramck-North Detroit Citizen - Detroit, MI - *AyerDirPub 83*
Hanceville Herald - Hanceville, AL - *BaconPubCkNews 84; Ed&PubIntYB 82*
Hancock Advertising Inc., Ross - Miami, FL - *StaDirAdAg 2-84*
Hancock Clarion - Hawesville, KY - *AyerDirPub 83; Ed&PubIntYB 82*
Hancock Community Cable Inc. - Bay St. Louis, MS - *BrCabYB 84*
Hancock Community Cable Inc. [of The Essex Group] - Waveland, MS - *BrCabYB 84; Tel&CabFB 84C*
Hancock County Cablevision [of Kentuckiana Cablevision Inc.] - Hawesville, KY - *BrCabYB 84; Tel&CabFB 84C*
Hancock County Courier - New Cumberland, WV - *Ed&PubIntYB 82*
Hancock County Journal Pilot - Carthage, IL - *AyerDirPub 83; Ed&PubIntYB 82*
Hancock County Quill - La Harpe, IL - *AyerDirPub 83; Ed&PubIntYB 82*
Hancock Herald - *See* Twin Valley Publishers Inc.
Hancock Herald, The - Hancock, NY - *Ed&PubIntYB 82*
Hancock House Publishers Ltd. - Blaine, WA - *BoPubDir 4 Sup, 5; WritMar 84*
Hancock News [of Berkeley Springs Morgan Messenger] - Hancock, MD - *BaconPubCkNews 84; Ed&PubIntYB 82; NewsDir 84*
Hancock, Paul M. - New Milford, CT - *Tel&CabFB 84C p.1683*
Hancock Record - Hancock, MN - *BaconPubCkNews 84; Ed&PubIntYB 82*
Hancock Rural Telephone Corp. - Maxwell, IN - *TelDir&BG 83-84*
Hancock Technology - Hancock, MD - *MicrocomMPl 84*
Hancock Techtronics - Hancock, MD - *WhoWMicrocom 83*
Hancock Telephone Co. - Hancock, MN - *TelDir&BG 83-84*
Hancock Telephone Co. - Hancock, NY - *TelDir&BG 83-84*
Hancock Video Inc. [of Pencor Services Inc.] - Hancock, NY - *BrCabYB 84; Tel&CabFB 84C*
Hand Associates - Berkeley, CA - *LitMarPl 83, 84*
Hand Book - New York, NY - *LitMag&SmPr 83-84*
Hand, Jack C. - *See* Combined Cable Corp.
Hand, Richard - *See* Oconee Cablevision Inc.
Handball - Skokie, IL - *MagIndMarPl 82-83*
Handel Film Corp. - Hollywood, CA - *AvMarPl 83; TelAl 83, 84; Tel&CabFB 84C*
Handicapped Education Exchange [of Amateur Radio Research & Development Corp.] - Silver Spring, MD - *EISS 5-84 Sup*
Handle Corp. - Tahoe City, CA - *MicrocomSwDir 1*
Handley & Miller Inc. - Indianapolis, IN - *ArtMar 84; DirPRFirms 83; StaDirAdAg 2-84*
Handling & Shipping Management [of Penton/IPC Inc.] - Cleveland, OH - *BaconPubCkMag 84; MagDir 84; MagIndMarPl 82-83*
Handloader - Prescott, AZ - *BaconPubCkMag 84; MagDir 84*
Handmade [of Lark Communications] - Asheville, NC - *BaconPubCkMag 84; WritMar 84*
Handrail Music - *See* Paragon/Benson Publishing Corp.
Hands On! [of Microcomputers in Education] - Cambridge, MA - *MicrocomMPl 84*
Hands On! [of Shopsmith Inc.] - Vandalia, OH - *ArtMar 84; WritMar 84*
Hands-On Information Ltd. - Wellington, New Zealand - *EISS 7-83 Sup; InfIndMarPl 83*
Hands On Publications - Long Beach, CA - *BoPubDir 5*
Handshake Editions - Paris, France - *LitMag&SmPr 83-84*
Handwoven [of Interweave Press] - Loveland, CO - *MagIndMarPl 82-83; WritMar 84*
Handy Co., Drucilla - New York, NY - *DirPRFirms 83*
Handy Organization, The Jam - Detroit, MI - *TelAl 83, 84; Tel&CabFB 84C*
Hane Industrial Seminars Inc. - Terre Haute, IN - *WhoWMicrocom 83*
Haney & Associates - Woodland Hills, CA - *ADAPSOMemDir 83-84*
Hanff, Konstanty Z. - New York, NY - *LitMarPl 83, 84*
Hanford Sentinel - Hanford, CA - *BaconPubCkNews 84; Ed&PubIntYB 82; NewsDir 84*
Hang Gliding [of United States Hang Gliding Association] - Los Angeles, CA - *WritMar 84*
Hang Gliding Press - San Diego, CA - *BoPubDir 4, 5*
Hanging Loose - Brooklyn, NY - *LitMag&SmPr 83-84; WritMar 84*

Hanging Loose Press - Brooklyn, NY - *LitMag&SmPr 83-84; LitMarPl 83, 84*
Hankey, Paulus & Co. Inc. - Pittsburgh, PA - *DirPRFirms 83*
Hankinson News - Hankinson, ND - *Ed&PubIntYB 82*
Hankinson News - *See* Richland Publishing Co.
Hankinson Studio Inc. - New York, NY - *TelAl 83, 84; Tel&CabFB 84C*
Hanley Audio Systems Inc., Terry - Cambridge, MA - *AvMarPl 83*
Hanna-Barbera Productions Inc. [Div. of The Taft Entertainment Co.] - Hollywood, CA - *ArtMar 84; TelAl 83, 84; Tel&CabFB 84C*
Hanna City-Trivoli Index - Hanna City, IL - *AyerDirPub 83; Ed&PubIntYB 82*
Hanna City-Trivoli Index - *See* Gazette Printing Co.
Hanna Co. Inc., R. D. - Dallas, TX - *CabTVFinDB 83*
Hanna Herald - Hanna, WY - *BaconPubCkNews 84*
Hanna North Book Club - Hanna, AB, Canada - *BoPubDir 4, 5*
Hannaford Co. Inc., The - Los Angeles, CA - *DirPRFirms 83*
Hannagan & Associates Inc. - Schaumburg, IL - *TeleSy&SerDir 7-83*
Hannan-Phillips Music - Chicago, IL - *BillIntBG 83-84*
Hannibal Cable TV [of Community Tele-Communications Inc.] - Hannibal, MO - *BrCabYB 84; Tel&CabFB 84C*
Hannibal Cable TV [of Community Tele-Communications Inc.] - Monroe City, MO - *Tel&CabFB 84C*
Hannibal Courier-Post [of Stauffer Communications Inc.] - Hannibal, MO - *BaconPubCkNews 84; Ed&PubIntYB 82; NewsDir 84*
Hannibal Figliola Inc. - *See* Figliola & Partner Inc.
Hannibal Records - New York, NY - *BillIntBG 83-84*
Hannibal TV Cable Co. - Hannibal, OH - *BrCabYB 84*
Hannover Branch - *See* Bulletin Publishing Co.
Hannum, Hunter G. - Old Lyme, CT - *LitMarPl 83, 84; MagIndMarPl 82-83*
Hanover Advertising - Palo Alto, CA - *StaDirAdAg 2-84*
Hanover & District Advertiser News - Hanover, ON, Canada - *AyerDirPub 83*
Hanover Area Merchandiser - Lebanon, PA - *AyerDirPub 83*
Hanover Cable TV Inc. [of OVC Telecommunications Inc.] - Hanover, IN - *BrCabYB 84*
Hanover Cable TV Inc. - Hanover, PA - *BrCabYB 84; Tel&CabFB 84C*
Hanover Evening Sun [of Thomson Newspapers] - Hanover, PA - *NewsDir 84*
Hanover Herald-Progress - Ashland, VA - *NewsDir 84*
Hanover-Horton Local - Hanover, MI - *BaconPubCkNews 84; Ed&PubIntYB 82*
Hanover Music Corp. - Beverly Hills, CA - *BillIntBG 83-84*
Hanover News - Hanover, KS - *BaconPubCkNews 84; Ed&PubIntYB 82*
Hanover Park Herald - *See* Paddock Publications
Hanover Park Star - Hanover Park, IL - *Ed&PubIntYB 82*
Hanover Park Township Times - Roselle, IL - *AyerDirPub 83*
Hanover Park Township Times - *See* Copley Newspaper Group
Hanover Post - Hanover, ON, Canada - *Ed&PubIntYB 82*
Hanover South Shore News - Hanover, MA - *NewsDir 84*
Hanover Sun - Hanover, PA - *BaconPubCkNews 84*
Hanover Voice - *See* Voice Newspapers
Hans Film Productions, Charles - New York, NY - *ArtMar 84; AvMarPl 83*
Hansard Oral Questions [of QL Systems Ltd.] - Ottawa, ON, Canada - *CompReadDB 82; DataDirOnSer 84; DBBus 82; DirOnDB Spring 84*
Hansard Questions Ecrites [of QL Systems Ltd.] - Ottawa, ON, Canada - *CompReadDB 82; DataDirOnSer 84; DirOnDB Spring 84*
Hansard Questions Orales [of House of Commons] - Ottawa, ON, Canada - *CompReadDB 82; DataDirOnSer 84; DirOnDB Spring 84*
Hansard Written Questions [of QL Systems Ltd.] - Ottawa, ON, Canada - *CompReadDB 82; DataDirOnSer 84; DirOnDB Spring 84*
Hansco Data Processing - Wilbraham, MA - *WhoWMicrocom 83*
Hansconian [of Minute-Man Publications Inc.] - Lexington, MA - *NewsDir 84*
Hansconian-Hanscom Air Force Base - *See* Minute-Man Publications Inc.
Hansconian, The - Acton, MA - *AyerDirPub 83*
Hansen Advertising, Don - Westport, CT - *AdAge 3-28-84; StaDirAdAg 2-84*
Hansen & Hughes - Hohokus, NJ - *WhoWMicrocom 83*
Hansen & Miller [Aff. of Miller Associates] - Lower Lake, CA - *BoPubDir 4, 5*
Hansen, Gerald - *See* Barron Cable Co. Inc.
Hansen Inc., John L. - New York, NY - *StaDirAdAg 2-84*
Hansen International Advertising - *See* Miller Meester Advertising Inc.
Hansen, Nigro & Wulfhorst Inc. - New York, NY - *StaDirAdAg 2-84*
Hansen Photography Inc., Steve - Boston, MA - *MagIndMarPl 82-83*
Hansen Publishing Co. - East Lansing, MI - *BoPubDir 4, 5*
Hansen Research & Development Corp. - Houston, TX - *MicrocomMPl 84*
Hansford Plainsman - Spearman, TX - *AyerDirPub 83; Ed&PubIntYB 82*
Hansi Ministries Inc. - Garden Grove, CA - *BoPubDir 4, 5*
Hanska Herald - Hanska, MN - *BaconPubCkNews 84; Ed&PubIntYB 82*
Hanson Co., Clem T. - Moline, IL - *StaDirAdAg 2-84*
Hanson County Telephone Co. - Alexandria, SD - *TelDir&BG 83-84*
Hanson Fassler & Associates Inc. - New York, NY - *StaDirAdAg 2-84*
Hanson, Gerald - *See* Barron Cable Co.
Hanson, Margaret Brock - Kaycee, WY - *BoPubDir 4, 5*
Hanson Music, Rick - *See* Ric Rac Music
Hanter Productions Inc. - Westwood, NJ - *BillIntBG 83-84*
Hants Journal - Windsor, NS, Canada - *AyerDirPub 83; Ed&PubIntYB 82*
Hapi Press - Portland, OR - *BoPubDir 4, 5*
Happ Electronics Inc. - Oshkosh, WI - *WhoWMicrocom 83*
HAPPI - Ramsey, NJ - *BaconPubCkMag 84*
Happiness Holding Tank [of Stone Press] - Okemos, MI - *LitMag&SmPr 83-84; WritMar 84*
Happiness Press - Magalia, CA - *BoPubDir 4, 5*
Happy Day Music Co. - *See* Keene Music Co., Joe
Happy Day Records - Oak Park, IL - *BillIntBG 83-84*
Happy Eye Enterprises [Aff. of Right On Foundation] - Glendale, CA - *BoPubDir 4, 5*
Happy Health Publishers - Seal Beach, CA - *BoPubDir 4, 5*
Happy History Inc. - Boca Raton, FL - *BoPubDir 4, 5*
Happy Press - Iowa City, IA - *BoPubDir 4, 5; LitMag&SmPr 83-84*
Happy Stepchild Music Publishing Corp. - *See* Big Seven Music Corp.
Happy Valley Music - Cambridge, MA - *BillIntBG 83-84*
Happy Valley Telephone Co. - Anderson, CA - *TelDir&BG 83-84*
Happy Wanderer, The - Skokie, IL - *BaconPubCkMag 84*
Haralson County Tribune - Buchanan, GA - *Ed&PubIntYB 82*
Harambee African News Service - London, England - *Ed&PubIntYB 82*
Harant Soghigian Advertising - Washington, DC - *ArtMar 84*
Harbeck & Associates Ltd. - Winnipeg, MB, Canada - *BoPubDir 4, 5*
Harben Publishing Co. - Safety Harbor, FL - *BoPubDir 5*
Harbor Beach Times - Harbor Beach, MI - *BaconPubCkNews 84; Ed&PubIntYB 82; NewsDir 84*
Harbor Benedetti - Los Angeles, CA - *DirInfWP 82*
Harbor Hill Books Inc. - Harrison, NY - *BoPubDir 4, 5*
Harbor Light - Harbor Springs, MI - *Ed&PubIntYB 82*
Harbor Lights Magazine - Hallandale, FL - *BaconPubCkMag 84*
Harbor Properties Inc. - Seattle, WA - *BrCabYB 84 p.D-301; Tel&CabFB 84C p.1683*
Harbor Publishing - San Francisco, CA - *DirMarMP 83; LitMarPl 83, 84; WritMar 84*
Harbor Review - Boston, MA - *LitMag&SmPr 83-84*
Harbor Springs Harbor Light - Harbor Springs, MI - *BaconPubCkNews 84*
Harbor Videocable [of Harbor Properties Inc.] - Leavenworth, WA - *BrCabYB 84; Tel&CabFB 84C*

Harbor Videocable [of Harbor Properties Inc.] - Montesano, WA - *BrCabYB 84; Tel&CabFB 84C*
Harbor Videocable [of Harbor Properties Inc.] - Shelton, WA - *BrCabYB 84; Tel&CabFB 84C*
Harbor Videocable [of Harbor Properties Inc.] - Westport, WA - *BrCabYB 84; Tel&CabFB 84C*
Harbor Vue Cable TV Inc. [of Adelphia Communications Corp.] - Dunkirk, NY - *BrCabYB 84; Tel&CabFB 84C*
Harbot Music - Nashville, TN - *BillIntBG 83-84*
Harbour & Shipping - Vancouver, BC, Canada - *BaconPubCkMag 84*
Harbour Cable Inc. [of Simmons Communications Inc.] - Anne Arundel County, MD - *Tel&CabFB 84C*
Harbour Cable Inc. - Fairfax, VA - *BrCabYB 84*
Harbour Lights Press - Margaree Harbour, NS, Canada - *BoPubDir 4, 5*
Harbour Publishing - Madeira Park, BC, Canada - *BoPubDir 4; LitMarPl 83, 84*
Harco Industries Inc. - Phoenix, AZ - *DataDirSup 7-83*
Harcourt Bindery Inc. - Boston, MA - *LitMarPl 83, 84*
Harcourt Brace Jovanovich Inc. - San Diego, CA - *WritMar 84*
Harcourt Brace Jovanovich Inc. - New York, NY - *AdAge 6-28-84; DirMarMP 83; KnowInd 83; LitMarPl 83, 84; MagIndMarPl 82-83; MicrocomMPl 84*
Harcourt Brace Jovanovich Inc. - *See* Channel 10 Inc.
Harcourt Brace Jovanovich Legal & Professional Publications Inc. [Subs. of Harcourt Brace Jovanovich Inc.] - Gardena, CA - *WritMar 84*
Hard Hat Records - Daytona Beach, FL - *BillIntBG 83-84*
Hard Press - New York, NY - *BoPubDir 4, 5; LitMag&SmPr 83-84*
Hard Pressed/Sun Ridge Press - Point Arena, CA - *BoPubDir 4, 5*
Hardcopy - Placentia, CA - *BaconPubCkMag 84; WritMar 84*
Hardcopy - Houston, TX - *MicrocomMPl 84*
Hardcore Computing [of Softkey Publishing] - Tacoma, WA - *MicrocomMPl 84*
Harden/Bob Page Communications Inc., John (Advertising Div.) - Greensboro, NC - *StaDirAdAg 2-84*
Hardhat Software - San Francisco, CA - *WhoWMicrocom 83*
Hardin Cable TV Inc. [of Communications Investment Corp.] - Hardin, MT - *Tel&CabFB 84C*
Hardin Calhoun Herald - Hardin, IL - *BaconPubCkNews 84*
Hardin Calhoun News - Hardin, IL - *BaconPubCkNews 84*
Hardin County Independent - Elizabethtown, IL - *AyerDirPub 83; Ed&PubIntYB 82*
Hardin County Index [of Eldora Herald-Index Publishing Co.] - Eldora, IA - *AyerDirPub 83; Ed&PubIntYB 82; NewsDir 84*
Hardin County News - Lumberton, TX - *AyerDirPub 83*
Hardin County Telephone Co. - Rosiclare, IL - *TelDir&BG 83-84*
Hardin County Times - Iowa Falls, IA - *AyerDirPub 83; Ed&PubIntYB 82*
Hardin Herald - Hardin, MT - *AyerDirPub 83; BaconPubCkNews 84; Ed&PubIntYB 82; NewsDir 84*
Hardin Journal - Hardin, MO - *BaconPubCkNews 84; Ed&PubIntYB 82*
Harding & Robinson - Memphis, TN - *StaDirAdAg 2-84*
Harding University (Student Association Press) - Memphis, TN - *BoPubDir 4 Sup, 5*
Hardinsburg Breckinridge Herald-News - Hardinsburg, KY - *BaconPubCkNews 84*
Hardlines Wholesaling [of Irving-Cloud Publishing Co.] - Chicago, IL - *MagDir 84*
Hardman Eastman Studios Inc. - Pittsburgh, PA - *AvMarPl 83*
Hardscrabble - Coos Bay, OR - *LitMag&SmPr 83-84*
Hardware Age - Radnor, PA - *BaconPubCkMag 84; MagIndMarPl 82-83; WritMar 84*
Hardware & Farm Equipment [of Western Retail Implement & Hardware Association] - Kansas City, MO - *BaconPubCkMag 84; MagDir 84*
Hardware Merchandiser - Lincolnwood, IL - *BaconPubCkMag 84; MagIndMarPl 82-83; NewsBur 6; WritMar 84*
Hardware Merchandiser [of Irving-Cloud Publishing Co.] - Indianapolis, IN - *MagDir 84*
Hardware Merchandising - Toronto, ON, Canada - *BaconPubCkMag 84; WritMar 84*
Hardware Retailing [of National Retail Hardware Association] - Indianapolis, IN - *BaconPubCkMag 84; MagDir 84; MagIndMarPl 82-83; NewsBur 6; WritMar 84*
Hardwick Associates, Bryan - Palos Verdes Estates, CA - *StaDirAdAg 2-84*
Hardwick Cable TV [of Emco CATV Inc.] - Hardwick, VT - *BrCabYB 84*
Hardwick Gazette [of Hardwick Publishing Co. Inc.] - Hardwick, VT - *AyerDirPub 83; BaconPubCkNews 84; Ed&PubIntYB 82; NewsDir 84*
Hardwick Research Inc., Elizabeth - New York, NY - *IntDirMarRes 83*
Hardwood Plywood Manufacturers Association - Reston, VA - *BoPubDir 5*
Hardy & Associates, Arthur - New Orleans, LA - *BoPubDir 4, 5*
Hardy, Max - Hawthorne, CA - *BoPubDir 4 Sup, 5; LitMarPl 84*
Hardy Spring River Times - Hardy, AR - *BaconPubCkNews 84*
Hardy Telephone Co. Inc. - Mathias, WV - *TelDir&BG 83-84*
Hare Editions - New York, NY - *BoPubDir 4, 5*
HARFAX [of HARFAX Database Publishing] - Cambridge, MA - *DBBus 82*
HARFAX Database Publishing [Subs. of Harper & Row Publishers Inc.] - Cambridge, MA - *CompReadDB 82; DataDirOnSer 84; InfIndMarPl 83; InfoS 83-84*
HARFAX Industry Data Sources [of HARFAX Database Publishing] - Cambridge, MA - *CompReadDB 82; DataDirOnSer 84; DirOnDB Spring 84; EISS 83*
Harford Democrat-Aberdeen Enterprise [of Aberdeen Harford Press Publishing Inc.] - Aberdeen, MD - *AyerDirPub 83; NewsDir 84*
Harford Herald [of Dell Rapids Tribune Inc.] - Dell Rapids, SD - *NewsDir 84*
Hargail Music Press - Saugerties, NY - *BillIntBG 83-84*
Hargood Associates Inc. - Provincetown, MA - *StaDirAdAg 2-84*
Hargray Telephone Co. Inc. - Hilton Head Island, SC - *TelDir&BG 83-84*
Harian Creative Press-Books [Subs. of Harian Creative Enterprises] - Ballston Spa, NY - *LitMarPl 83, 84*
Harian Creative Press-Books - Clifton Park, NY - *WritMar 84*
Haring, Jennifer - New York, NY - *LitMarPl 83*
Harkavy Publishing Service - New York, NY - *LitMarPl 83, 84; MagIndMarPl 82-83*
Harker's Information Retrieval Systems [of Harker's Specialist Book Importers] - Glebe, Australia - *EISS 7-83 Sup*
Harkins, Harry H. Jr. - Chapel Hill, NC - *Tel&CabFB 84C p.1683*
Harkins, Harry H. Sr. - Sarasota, FL - *BrCabYB 84 p.D-301*
Harkins, Harry H. Sr. - *See* Ohio Valley Cable Corp.
Harkins, Jefferson - Tampa, FL - *Tel&CabFB 84C p.1683*
Harkins, Scott - Sarasota, FL - *Tel&CabFB 84C p.1683*
Harkleroad Literary Agency, Caroline - Atlanta, GA - *LitMarPl 83, 84*
Harlan Community Television Inc. - Harlan, KY - *BrCabYB 84; Tel&CabFB 84C*
Harlan County Journal - Alma, NE - *AyerDirPub 83; Ed&PubIntYB 82*
Harlan Enterprise [of TSP Newspapers] - Harlan, KY - *BaconPubCkNews 84; Ed&PubIntYB 82; NewsDir 84*
Harlan News Advertiser - Harlan, IA - *Ed&PubIntYB 82; NewsDir 84*
Harlan News Advertiser - *See* Harlan Newspapers
Harlan Newspapers - Harlan, IA - *BaconPubCkNews 84*
Harlan Telephone Co. - Pleasant Plain, OH - *TelDir&BG 83-84*
Harlan Tribune - Harlan, IA - *Ed&PubIntYB 82; NewsDir 84*
Harlan Tribune - *See* Harlan Newspapers
Harland O'Connor Tine & White - Hartford, CT - *AdAge 3-28-84; StaDirAdAg 2-84*
Harlem Cable TV - Harlem, MT - *BrCabYB 84; Tel&CabFB 84C*
Harlem-Foster Times - Chicago, IL - *AyerDirPub 83; Ed&PubIntYB 82*
Harlem-Irving Leader [of Chicago Leader Newspapers-Leader Papers Inc.] - Chicago, IL - *AyerDirPub 83; NewsDir 84*
Harlem-Irving Times - Chicago, IL - *AyerDirPub 83; Ed&PubIntYB 82*
Harlem Music - Buffalo, NY - *BillIntBG 83-84*
Harlem News - Harlem, MT - *AyerDirPub 83; BaconPubCkNews 84; Ed&PubIntYB 82*

Harlem Valley Times - Amenia, NY - *AyerDirPub 83; Ed&PubIntYB 82; NewsDir 84*
Harlequin Books Ltd. [Subs. of Harlequin Enterprises Ltd.] - Don Mills, ON, Canada - *LitMarPl 83, 84; WritMar 84*
Harlequin Enterprises Ltd. [Subs. of Torstar Corp.] - Don Mills, ON, Canada - *LitMarPl 83, 84*
Harlequin Publications - Palos Verdes, CA - *BoPubDir 5*
Harlequin Publishing Corp. - Hollywood, CA - *LitMarPl 83*
Harlequin Sales Corp. [Subs. of Harlequin Books Ltd.] - Tarrytown, NY - *LitMarPl 84*
Harley Music - *See* Brunswick Music Publishing Co.
Harlin Jacque Inc. - Hempstead, NY - *BoPubDir 4, 5*
Harlingen Valley Morning Star - Harlingen, TX - *BaconPubCkNews 84; NewsDir 84*
Harlo Press [Aff. of Harlo Printing Co.] - Detroit, MI - *BoPubDir 4, 5*
Harlo Printing Co. - Detroit, MI - *LitMarPl 83, 84*
Harloff Inc. - Wilmington, DE - *MicrocomMPl 84*
Harlowton Times-Clarion - Harlowton, MT - *BaconPubCkNews 84*
Harmless Flirtation with Wealth - San Diego, CA - *BoPubDir 4, 5*
Harmon & Co. - Englewood, CO - *BrCabYB 84 p.D-301; CabTVFinDB 83; Tel&CabFB 84C p.1683*
Harmon Football Forecast, The Bob - Middletown, NY - *Ed&PubIntYB 82*
Harmon Pictures Corp., Larry - Hollywood, CA - *TelAl 83, 84; Tel&CabFB 84C*
Harmon Smith - Kansas City, MO - *AdAge 3-28-84; StaDirAdAg 2-84*
Harmon True Pruitt - Shawnee Mission, KS - *ArtMar 84*
Harmonia Mundi USA - Los Angeles, CA - *BillIntBG 83-84*
Harmonizer, The - Kenosha, WI - *BaconPubCkMag 84; MagDir 84*
Harmony Books [Div. of Crown Publishers] - New York, NY - *LitMarPl 83, 84; WritMar 84*
Harmony Highlights [of Local No. 831 IAMAW AFL-CIO] - Cedar Rapids, IA - *NewsDir 84*
Harmony News - Harmony, MN - *Ed&PubIntYB 82*
Harmony Records Inc. - Encino, CA - *BillIntBG 83-84*
Harmony Society Press - Worcester, MA - *BoPubDir 4 Sup, 5*
Harmony Telephone Co. - Harmony, MN - *TelDir&BG 83-84*
Harnett County News - Lillington, NC - *AyerDirPub 83; Ed&PubIntYB 82*
Harney Advertising Corp. - Lincoln, NE - *StaDirAdAg 2-84*
Harnish Group, The - Columbus, OH - *VideoDir 82-83*
Harold Telephone Co. Inc. - Harold, KY - *TelDir&BG 83-84*
Harold's TV & Appliances - Salisbury, MD - *Tel&CabFB 84C*
Harold's TV & Appliances - Salisbury, PA - *BrCabYB 84*
Harper Advocate - Harper, KS - *BaconPubCkNews 84; Ed&PubIntYB 82*
Harper & Associates, William L. - Dallas, TX - *StaDirAdAg 2-84*
Harper & Co. - Miami, FL - *StaDirAdAg 2-84*
Harper & Row Publishers Inc. - New York, NY - *KnowInd 83; LitMarPl 83, 84; WritMar 84*
Harper & Row Publishers Inc. - Philadelphia, PA - *MagIndMarPl 82-83*
Harper & Row Publishers Inc. (Electronic & Technical Publishing) - New York, NY - *MicrocomMPl 84*
Harper & Row Publishers Inc. (Junior Books Group) - New York, NY - *WritMar 84*
Harper Communications Inc. - New York, NY - *DirPRFirms 83*
Harper County Journal - Buffalo, OK - *AyerDirPub 83; Ed&PubIntYB 82*
Harper, Hellams & Paige Inc. - Columbia, SC - *StaDirAdAg 2-84*
Harper Herald - Fredericksburg, TX - *AyerDirPub 83*
Harper Herald - *See* Radio Post Inc.
Harper Herald, The - Harper, TX - *Ed&PubIntYB 82*
Harper Horticultural Slide Library - Seaford, VA - *LitMarPl 83, 84*
Harper Square Press - Chicago, IL - *BoPubDir 4, 5; LitMag&SmPr 83-84*
Harper Woods Herald [of Detroit Northeast Detroiter] - Detroit, MI - *BaconPubCkNews 84; NewsDir 84*
Harper's Bazaar [of The Hearst Corp.] - New York, NY - *BaconPubCkMag 84; Folio 83; LitMarPl 83, 84; MagDir 84; MagIndMarPl 82-83; NewsBur 6; WritMar 84*
Harpers Ferry Cable TV - Harpers Ferry, IA - *BrCabYB 84; Tel&CabFB 84C*
Harper's Graphic Services - Kansas City, MO - *MagIndMarPl 82-83*
Harper's Magazine [of Harper Magazine Foundation] - New York, NY - *DirMarMP 83; Folio 83; LitMarPl 83, 84; MagDir 84; MagIndMarPl 82-83; WritMar 84*
Harper's Today - New York, NY - *BaconPubCkMag 84*
Harpham Co., The - Chicago, IL - *StaDirAdAg 2-84*
Harrah Herald - Harrah, OK - *AyerDirPub 83; BaconPubCkNews 84; Ed&PubIntYB 82*
Harrah News - Harrah, OK - *BaconPubCkNews 84; Ed&PubIntYB 82*
Harral Music - *See* Amestoy Music
Harrell, John & Mary - Berkeley, CA - *ArtMar 84*
Harrick Music Inc. - Miami, FL - *BillIntBG 83-84*
Harriet's Kitchen - Forest Hills, NY - *BoPubDir 4, 5*
Harriett - New York, NY - *LitMarPl 83, 84; MagIndMarPl 82-83*
Harriman & Hill Pty. Ltd. - *See* Needham, Harper & Steers Inc.
Harriman Record [of The Oak Ridger] - Harriman, TN - *AyerDirPub 83; BaconPubCkNews 84; NewsDir 84*
Harriman TV Cable Co. [of National Telecommunications] - Harriman, TN - *BrCabYB 84; Tel&CabFB 84C*
Harriman TV Cable Co. [of National TV Cable Co.] - Kingston, TN - *BrCabYB 84*
Harrington Associates, Don - Wilton, CT - *StaDirAdAg 2-84*
Harrington-Jackson Inc. - Boston, MA - *StaDirAdAg 2-84*
Harrington, Joseph Denis - Carmel, CA - *LitMarPl 83, 84; MagIndMarPl 82-83*
Harrington Journal - Harrington, DE - *BaconPubCkNews 84; Ed&PubIntYB 82*
Harris & Associates - *See* Le Ance Public Relations
Harris & Associates Advertising Agency - Minnetonka, MN - *StaDirAdAg 2-84*
Harris & Associates Inc., Louis [Subs. of Gannett Co.] - New York, NY - *AdAge 5-17-84 p.33; IntDirMarRes 83*
Harris & Associates Publishing - Logan, UT - *Ed&PubIntYB 82*
Harris & Co. Inc., H. E. - Boston, MA - *BoPubDir 4, 5*
Harris & Drutt Inc. - Philadelphia, PA - *StaDirAdAg 2-84*
Harris & Harris Public Relations - El Paso, TX - *DirPRFirms 83*
Harris & Love - Salt Lake City, UT - *AdAge 3-28-84; StaDirAdAg 2-84; TelAl 83, 84*
Harris, Arthur S. Jr. - Arlington, VT - *LitMarPl 83; MagIndMarPl 82-83*
Harris, Burt I. - *See* Harris Cable Corp.
Harris, Burt I. - *See* Harriscope Broadcasting Corp.
Harris Cable Corp. - Los Angeles, CA - *BrCabYB 84 p.D-301; CabTVFinDB 83; LitMarPl 84; Tel&CabFB 84C p.1683*
Harris Co. Inc., The - Coral Gables, FL - *StaDirAdAg 2-84*
Harris Consultive Services - Mt. Horeb, WI - *EISS 7-83 Sup*
Harris Controls & Composition [Div. of Harris Corp.] - Melbourne, FL - *LitMarPl 83, 84*
Harris Corp. - Melbourne, FL - *Datamation 6-83; ElecNews 7-25-83; HomeVid&CabYB 82-83; Top100Al 83*
Harris Corp. (Computer Systems Div.) - Ft. Lauderdale, FL - *DataDirSup 7-83*
Harris Corp. (Information Terminals Group) - Dallas, TX - *InfIndMarPl 83*
Harris County Cablevision [of Television Access Inc.] - Humble, TX - *BrCabYB 84; Tel&CabFB 84C*
Harris County Journal - Hamilton, GA - *Ed&PubIntYB 82*
Harris, Drury & Associates Advertising - Ft. Lauderdale, FL - *AdAge 3-28-84; DirPRFirms 83; StaDirAdAg 2-84*
Harris Electronic News [Subs. of Harris Enterprises Inc.] - Hutchinson, KS - *DataDirOnSer 84; DirOnDB Spring 84; EISS 7-83 Sup; MicrocomMPl 84; VideoDir 82-83*
Harris Enterprises - Garden City, KS - *BrCabYB 84*
Harris Enterprises Inc. - Hutchinson, KS - *BrCabYB 84*
Harris Graphics Corp. (Bindery Systems Div.) - Champlain, NY - *LitMarPl 83, 84*
Harris Inc., Barbara [Aff. of Microwave Cooking Consulting Service] - Portland, OR - *BoPubDir 4, 5*
Harris Media Systems Ltd. - Toronto, ON, Canada - *EISS 7-83 Sup*
Harris Music Co. Ltd., Frederick - Oakville, ON, Canada - *BoPubDir 4 Sup, 5*

Harris Newspapers Inc. - Starkville, MS - *Ed&PubIntYB 82*
Harris Newspapers, John P. - Hutchinson, KS - *Ed&PubIntYB 82*
Harris Publications, Ron - *See* Alexandria House Inc.
Harris Publishing Co. - Twinsburg, OH - *BoPubDir 4, 5; EISS 7-83 Sup*
Harris Technical School - Lincoln, NE - *WhoWMicrocom 83*
Harris Technical Systems - Lincoln, NE - *MicrocomMPl 84*
Harris-Tuchman Productions Inc. - Burbank, CA - *AvMarPl 83; TelAl 83, 84; Tel&CabFB 84C*
Harris Video Systems [Div. of Harris Corp.] - Sunnyvale, CA - *AvMarPl 83*
Harris, Walter J. - Fayetteville, AR - *BoPubDir 4 Sup, 5*
Harris/Wolfram Productions Inc. - New York, NY - *AvMarPl 83*
Harris Word Processing - Melbourne, FL - *DirInfWP 82*
Harrisburg Bulletin - Harrisburg, OR - *BaconPubCkNews 84; Ed&PubIntYB 82*
Harrisburg Catholic Witness, The [of Roman Catholic Diocese of Harrisburg] - Harrisburg, PA - *NewsDir 84*
Harrisburg Evening Post - Harrisburg, PA - *LitMarPl 83*
Harrisburg Modern News - Harrisburg, AR - *BaconPubCkNews 84; Ed&PubIntYB 82*
Harrisburg Patriot - Harrisburg, PA - *LitMarPl 83*
Harrisburg Pennsylvania Beacon - Harrisburg, PA - *BaconPubCkNews 84*
Harrisburg Register - Harrisburg, IL - *BaconPubCkNews 84; NewsDir 84*
Harrisburg Sunday Patriot-News - Harrisburg, PA - *LitMarPl 83*
Harriscope Broadcasting Corp. - Los Angeles, CA - *BrCabYB 84; TelAl 83, 84; Tel&CabFB 84C, 84S*
Harrison Advertising Inc. - Yorkville, IL - *StaDirAdAg 2-84*
Harrison & Associates, Elaine - Bedeque, PE, Canada - *BoPubDir 4, 5*
Harrison Associates [Div. of Movie/Entertainment Book Club] - Harrison, NY - *DirMarMP 83; LitMarPl 83, 84; MagIndMarPl 82-83; StaDirAdAg 2-84*
Harrison Associates Inc., Claire - San Francisco, CA - *StaDirAdAg 2-84*
Harrison Boone County Headlight - Harrison, AR - *BaconPubCkNews 84*
Harrison Clare County Cleaver - Harrison, MI - *BaconPubCkNews 84*
Harrison Color Process [Div. of Harrison Art Advertising Inc.] - Willow Grove, PA - *LitMarPl 83, 84*
Harrison Co. Inc., E. Bruce - Washington, DC - *DirPRFirms 83*
Harrison County Press - Corydon, IN - *AyerDirPub 83; Ed&PubIntYB 82*
Harrison, Daniel J. - Hillsborough, NY - *LitMarPl 84*
Harrison Higgins [Div. of Al Paul Lefton Co. Inc.] - New York, NY - *DirPRFirms 83; StaDirAdAg 2-84*
Harrison House - Tulsa, OK - *BoPubDir 4, 5*
Harrison Independent - Armonk, NY - *AyerDirPub 83*
Harrison Independent - Harrison, NY - *BaconPubCkNews 84; Ed&PubIntYB 82; NewsDir 84*
Harrison, John - Ellijay, GA - *Tel&CabFB 84C p.1683*
Harrison, John C. - Pine Bluffs, WY - *BrCabYB 84 p.D-301; Tel&CabFB 84C p.1683*
Harrison Marketing Counsel Ltd. - Toronto, ON, Canada - *StaDirAdAg 2-84*
Harrison Music Corp. - Hollywood, CA - *BillIntBG 83-84*
Harrison News-Herald - Cadiz, OH - *AyerDirPub 83; Ed&PubIntYB 82*
Harrison Post - Indianapolis, IN - *AyerDirPub 83*
Harrison Press - Harrison, OH - *BaconPubCkNews 84; Ed&PubIntYB 82*
Harrison Public Relations/Advertising, H. Duane - Muncie, IN - *DirPRFirms 83*
Harrison Publishing Co. - Norcross, GA - *BoPubDir 4, 5*
Harrison Record - Harrison, OH - *BaconPubCkNews 84; Ed&PubIntYB 82; NewsDir 84*
Harrison Records Management, Trevor - Toronto, ON, Canada - *DirInfWP 82*
Harrison Schoolbook Publishing - Oklahoma City, OK - *BoPubDir 4, 5*
Harrison Sun - Harrison, NE - *Ed&PubIntYB 82*
Harrison Times [of Times Publishing Co.] - Harrison, AR - *BaconPubCkNews 84; Ed&PubIntYB 82; NewsDir 84*
Harrisonburg Daily News-Record [of Rockingham Publishing Co. Inc.] - Harrisonburg, VA - *BaconPubCkNews 84; NewsDir 84*
Harrisonville Cass County Democrat Missourian - Harrisonville, MO - *BaconPubCkNews 84; NewsDir 84*
Harrisonville Telephone Co. - Waterloo, IL - *TelDir&BG 83-84*
Harriston Review, The - Harriston, ON, Canada - *Ed&PubIntYB 82*
Harrisville Alcona County Review - Harrisville, MI - *BaconPubCkNews 84*
Harrisville Ritchie Gazette - Harrisville, WV - *BaconPubCkNews 84; NewsDir 84*
Harrodsburg Herald - Harrodsburg, KY - *BaconPubCkNews 84; Ed&PubIntYB 82; NewsDir 84*
Harron Cable Interconnect - Paoli, PA - *CabTVPrDB 83*
Harron Cable of New Jersey [Div. of Harron Communications Corp.] - Millville, NJ - *BrCabYB 84*
Harron Cable of New York - Utica, NY - *BrCabYB 84; Tel&CabFB 84C*
Harron Cable TV - Port Huron, MI - *BrCabYB 84; Tel&CabFB 84C*
Harron Cable TV - Millville, NJ - *Tel&CabFB 84C*
Harron Cable TV [of Harron Communications Corp.] - Greensburg, PA - *BrCabYB 84; Tel&CabFB 84C*
Harron Cable TV - Malvern, PA - *BrCabYB 84; Tel&CabFB 84C*
Harron Cable TV of Chesterfield [of Harron Communications Corp.] - Chesterfield, MI - *BrCabYB 84*
Harron Communications Corp. - Paoli, PA - *BrCabYB 84 p.D-301; CabTVFinDB 83; LitMarPl 84; Tel&CabFB 84C p.1683, 84S*
Harrow News - Harrow, ON, Canada - *Ed&PubIntYB 82*
Harrowood Books - Newtown Square, PA - *BoPubDir 4, 5*
Harrowsmith [of Camden House Publishing Ltd.] - Camden, ON, Canada - *ArtMar 84; WritMar 84*
Harry Browne Special Reports - Austin, TX - *BaconPubCkMag 84*
Hart Advertising Inc., Drennan W. - Indianapolis, IN - *StaDirAdAg 2-84*
Hart Advertising Inc., Les - Nashville, TN - *StaDirAdAg 2-84*
Hart Associates - Minneapolis, MN - *TeleSy&SerDir 2-84*
Hart Beat - Hart, TX - *AyerDirPub 83; Ed&PubIntYB 82*
Hart/Conway - Rochester, NY - *AdAge 3-28-84; StaDirAdAg 2-84; TelAl 83, 84*
Hart County Herald - Horse Cave, KY - *AyerDirPub 83; Ed&PubIntYB 82*
Hart County News - Munfordville, KY - *AyerDirPub 83; Ed&PubIntYB 82*
Hart County Telephone Co. - Hartwell, GA - *TelDir&BG 83-84*
Hart Graphics - Austin, TX - *BoPubDir 4*
Hart Literary Enterprises, Thomas S. - Boston, MA - *LitMarPl 84*
Hart, Norman - Apollo Beach, FL - *Tel&CabFB 84C p.1683*
Hart Oceana's Herald-Journal - Hart, MI - *BaconPubCkNews 84*
Hart Press Inc., The - Long Prairie, MN - *MagIndMarPl 82-83*
Hart Publishing Co. - New York, NY - *LitMarPl 84*
Hart, R. S. - Elkridge, MD - *BoPubDir 4, 5*
Hart Research Associates Inc., Peter D. - Washington, DC - *BrCabYB 84*
Hart Services Inc. - Chicago, IL - *DirPRFirms 83; StaDirAdAg 2-84*
Hart TV Cable Co. [of CATV Inc.] - Hart, TX - *Tel&CabFB 84C*
Harte-Hanks Communications - Bremen, GA - *BaconPubCkNews 84*
Harte-Hanks Communications - Dallas, TX - *Ed&PubIntYB 82*
Harte-Hanks Communications - Pasadena, TX - *BrCabYB 84*
Harte-Hanks Communications - San Antonio, TX - *AdAge 6-28-84; BrCabYB 84 p.D-301; CabTVFinDB 83; Ed&PubIntYB 82; HomeVid&CabYB 82-83; KnowInd 83; Tel&CabFB 84C p.1683, 84S*
Harte-Hanks Communications (Interactive Services) - San Antonio, TX - *InfoS 83-84*
Harte-Hanks Communications (Marketing Services Group) - River Edge, NJ - *AdAge 5-17-84 p.35*
Harte-Hanks Communications (Television Group) - San Antonio, TX - *BrCabYB 84*
Harte-Hanks Radio Inc. - Phoenix, AZ - *BrCabYB 84*
Harter Corp. - Sturgis, MI - *DirInfWP 82*

Hartford Advocate - Hartford, CT - *Ed&PubIntYB 82; NewsDir 84*
Hartford Advocate - Springfield, MA - *NewsDir 84*
Hartford Advocate - *See* Advocate Publishing
Hartford Automobiler - West Hartford, CT - *BaconPubCkMag 84; MagDir 84*
Hartford Bindery Inc. - Hartford, CT - *LitMarPl 83, 84*
Hartford CATV Inc. [of Times Mirror Cable TV] - Hartford, CT - *BrCabYB 84; Tel&CabFB 84C*
Hartford CATV Inc. [of Times Mirror Cable Television] - West Hartford, CT - *HomeVid&CabYB 82-83*
Hartford City News-Times - Hartford City, IN - *BaconPubCkNews 84; NewsDir 84*
Hartford Courant - Hartford, CT - *AyerDirPub 83; BaconPubCkNews 84; Ed&PubIntYB 82; LitMarPl 83, 84; NewsBur 6; NewsDir 84*
Hartford Democrat & Aberdeen Enterprise - Aberdeen, MD - *Ed&PubIntYB 82*
Hartford Herald - Hartford, SD - *Ed&PubIntYB 82*
Hartford Herald - *See* Prairie Publications
Hartford Inquirer Newspaper Group - Hartford, CT - *NewsDir 84*
Hartford MDS Co. - Pensacola, FL - *Tel&CabFB 84C*
Hartford News-Herald - Hartford, AL - *BaconPubCkNews 84; Ed&PubIntYB 82*
Hartford Ohio County News - Beaver Dam, KY - *NewsDir 84*
Hartford Ohio County Times News - Hartford, KY - *BaconPubCkNews 84*
Hartford Ohio County Times, The - Hartford, KY - *NewsDir 84*
Hartford Publications Inc. - Enfield, CT - *BaconPubCkNews 84*
Hartford Times-Press - Hartford, WI - *AyerDirPub 83; NewsDir 84*
Hartford Times-Press - *See* Lake Country Reporter Publishers
Harthun Engineering & Research Inc. - Albany, KY - *WritMar 84*
Hartington Cedar County News - Hartington, NE - *BaconPubCkNews 84*
Hartington Telephone Co. - Hartington, NE - *TelDir&BG 83-84*
Hartland & St. Albans Telephone Co. [Aff. of Telephone & Data Systems Inc.] - Hartland, ME - *TelDir&BG 83-84*
Hartland/Brighton Sun Herald, The - Hartland, MI - *Ed&PubIntYB 82*
Hartland Herald - *See* Sliger/Livingston Publications
Hartland Herald, The [of Sliger/Livingston Publications] - Howell, MI - *NewsDir 84*
Hartland Lake County Reporter - *See* Lake County Reporter Publishers
Hartley & Marks Inc. - Point Roberts, WA - *LitMarPl 84*
Hartley Courseware - Dimondale, MI - *AvMarPl 83; MicrocomMPl 83, 84; WhoWMicrocom 83*
Hartley Data Services Inc. - Glenview, IL - *ADAPSOMemDir 83-84; DataDirOnSer 84*
Hartley Data Systems Ltd. - Glenview, IL - *DataDirOnSer 84*
Hartley Film Foundation - Cos Cob, CT - *AvMarPl 83; TelAl 83, 84; Tel&CabFB 84C*
Hartley Sentinel - Hartley, IA - *BaconPubCkNews 84; Ed&PubIntYB 82*
Hartman Advertising Agency Inc., W. C. - Syracuse, NY - *StaDirAdAg 2-84*
Hartman & Co. Inc., Jack L. - Roanoke, VA - *AvMarPl 83*
Hartman & Sons Inc., Lee - Roanoke, VA - *AvMarPl 83*
Hartman Cable Inc. - Franklin, WV - *BrCabYB 84; Tel&CabFB 84C*
Hartman, Dennis - Glen Ullin, ND - *Tel&CabFB 84C p.1683*
Hartman, James E. - Clearwater, FL - *LitMarPl 83, 84*
Hartman, James E. - New York, NY - *MagIndMarPl 82-83*
Hartman Newspapers Inc. - Rosenberg, TX - *Ed&PubIntYB 82*
Hartman Newspapers, W. H. - Waterloo, IA - *Ed&PubIntYB 82*
Hartman Telephone Exchanges Inc. - Danbury, NE - *TelDir&BG 83-84*
Hartmann Advertising, Jurgen - New York, NY - *StaDirAdAg 2-84*
Hartmann, Erich - New York, NY - *MagIndMarPl 82-83*
Hartmus Press - Mill Valley, CA - *BoPubDir 4, 5; LitMag&SmPr 83-84*
Hartnell Publications - Sacramento, CA - *BoPubDir 4, 5*
Hart's Spring Works - San Francisco, CA - *BoPubDir 5*
Hartsdale Greenburgh Inquirer - Hartsdale, NY - *BaconPubCkNews 84*
Hartselle Enquirer - Hartselle, AL - *AyerDirPub 83; BaconPubCkNews 84; Ed&PubIntYB 82; NewsDir 84*
Hartselle TV Cable Co. - Hartselle, AL - *BrCabYB 84*
Hartshorn Stations - Gouverneur, NY - *BrCabYB 84*
Hartshorne Sun - Hartshorne, OK - *BaconPubCkNews 84; Ed&PubIntYB 82*
Hartsock & Co., Con - Los Angeles, CA - *Tel&CabFB 84C*
Hartsville Cable TV Co. [of Marsh Media Inc.] - Hartsville, TN - *Tel&CabFB 84C*
Hartsville Messenger - Hartsville, SC - *BaconPubCkNews 84; Ed&PubIntYB 82; NewsDir 84*
Hartsville Vidette - Hartsville, TN - *BaconPubCkNews 84*
Hartsville Vidette, The - Trousdale County, TN - *Ed&PubIntYB 82*
Hartung, Emilie C. - Philadelphia, PA - *LitMarPl 83, 84*
Hartung, Marion T. - Emporia, KS - *BoPubDir 4, 5*
Hartville News - Hartville, OH - *BaconPubCkNews 84; Ed&PubIntYB 82*
Hartwell Cable Co. [of Tele-Media Corp.] - Hartwell, GA - *Tel&CabFB 84C*
Hartwell Sun - Hartwell, GA - *BaconPubCkNews 84; Ed&PubIntYB 82*
Hartwick/Przyborski Productions - Pittsburgh, PA - *AvMarPl 83*
Harvard Advocate, The - Cambridge, MA - *LitMag&SmPr 83-84*
Harvard Associates - Harvard, MA - *DirInfWP 82; MagIndMarPl 82-83*
Harvard Business Review [of Harvard University] - Boston, MA - *BaconPubCkMag 84; DataDirOnSer 84; DBBus 82; DirMarMP 83; Folio 83; InfoS 83-84; MagDir 84; MagIndMarPl 82-83; WritMar 84*
Harvard Business Review [of John Wiley & Sons Inc.] - New York, NY - *OnBibDB 3*
Harvard Business Review Database [of Harvard University] - Boston, MA - *EISS 83*
Harvard Business Review/Online [of Bibliographic Retrieval Services Inc.] - Latham, NY - *DataDirOnSer 84*
Harvard Common Press - Boston, MA - *LitMag&SmPr 83-84; LitMarPl 84; WritMar 84*
Harvard Common Press, The - Harvard, MA - *LitMarPl 83*
Harvard Data Equipment Inc. - Harvard, MA - *WhoWMicrocom 83*
Harvard Educational Review - Cambridge, MA - *MagIndMarPl 82-83*
Harvard Features Syndicate - Cambridge, MA - *Ed&PubIntYB 82*
Harvard Group Inc. - Cambridge, MA - *BoPubDir 5*
Harvard Herald - Harvard, IL - *BaconPubCkNews 84; Ed&PubIntYB 82*
Harvard Herald & Shopper's Service - Harvard, IL - *NewsDir 84*
Harvard Industries Manufacturing Co. Inc. - St. Louis, MO - *DirInfWP 82*
Harvard Law Review - Cambridge, MA - *MagIndMarPl 82-83*
Harvard Magazine - Cambridge, MA - *LitMarPl 83, 84; MagDir 84; MagIndMarPl 82-83*
Harvard Medical School Health Letter, The [of Harvard University] - Cambridge, MA - *DirMarMP 83*
Harvard Student Agencies - Cambridge, MA - *BoPubDir 4, 5*
Harvard University (Busch-Reisinger Museum) - Cambridge, MA - *BoPubDir 4, 5*
Harvard University (Dept. of Printing & Graphic Arts) - Cambridge, MA - *BoPubDir 4, 5*
Harvard University (Fogg Art Museum) - Cambridge, MA - *BoPubDir 4, 5*
Harvard University (Graduate School of Business) - Boston, MA - *BoPubDir 4 Sup, 5; InfIndMarPl 83*
Harvard University (Harvard Business Review) - Boston, MA - *BoPubDir 5*
Harvard University (Harvard-Danforth Center for Teaching & Learning) - Cambridge, MA - *BoPubDir 4, 5*
Harvard University (Harvard Law School International Tax Program) - Cambridge, MA - *BoPubDir 4, 5*
Harvard University (Harvard Law School Library Microform Project) - Cambridge, MA - *MicroMarPl 82-83*
Harvard University (Harvard Law School Library, Publications Dept.) - Cambridge, MA - *BoPubDir 4, 5*

Harvard University (Program on Information Resources Policy) - Cambridge, MA - *InterCabHB 3*
Harvard University (Ukrainian Research Institute) - Cambridge, MA - *BoPubDir 4, 5*
Harvard University Library (Photographic Services Div.) - Cambridge, MA - *MicroMarPl 82-83*
Harvard University Press - Cambridge, MA - *AvMarPl 83; LitMarPl 83, 84; MicroMarPl 82-83; WritMar 84*
Harvast Computer Systems - Alexandria, IN - *MicrocomMPl 84*
Harvest Book Series - Goleta, CA - *LitMag&SmPr 83-84*
Harvest Educational Laboratories - Newport, RI - *AvMarPl 83*
Harvest Films Inc. - New York, NY - *AvMarPl 83*
Harvest House Ltd. - Montreal, PQ, Canada - *ArtMar 84; LitMarPl 83*
Harvest House Press [Aff. of Intercom International Inc.] - Princeton, NJ - *BoPubDir 4, 5*
Harvest House Publishers Inc. - Eugene, OR - *LitMarPl 83, 84; WritMar 84*
Harvest Moon Books - Riverside, CA - *BoPubDir 4, 5*
Harvest Press - Oakland, CA - *BoPubDir 5*
Harvest Publishers - Goleta, CA - *BoPubDir 5; LitMag&SmPr 83-84*
Harvest Publishers - Santa Barbara, CA - *BoPubDir 4*
Harvest Publishing Co. [Subs. of Harcourt Brace Jovanovich Inc.] - Lansing, MI - *DirMarMP 83*
Harvester Press Microform Publications Ltd. - Brighton, England - *MicroMarPl 82-83*
Harvestman & Associates - Menlo Park, CA - *BoPubDir 4, 5; LitMag&SmPr 83-84*
Harvey Associates, Arnold - Commack, NY - *BoPubDir 4, 5*
Harvey Cable TV [of NoDaKable Inc.] - Harvey, ND - *BrCabYB 84*
Harvey for Loving People - New York, NY - *ArtMar 84*
Harvey Herald - Harvey, ND - *BaconPubCkNews 84; Ed&PubIntYB 82; NewsDir 84*
Harvey House Publishers - New York, NY - *LitMarPl 83, 84; WritMar 84*
Harvey Publications Inc. - New York, NY - *MagIndMarPl 82-83*
Harvey Research Organization Inc. - Rochester, NY - *IntDirMarRes 83; MagIndMarPl 82-83*
Harvey Star Tribune - Chicago Heights, IL - *NewsDir 84*
Harvey Star Tribune - Harvey, IL - *AyerDirPub 83; Ed&PubIntYB 82*
Harvey Star Tribune - *See* Star Publications
Harvey's Space Ship Repair - Las Cruces, NM - *WhoWMicrocom 83*
Harwal Publishing Co. - Media, PA - *BoPubDir 4, 5*
Harwell Central Information Service [of Atomic Energy Authority] - Didcot, England - *EISS 83*
Harwick Word Processing Consultants Ltd. - Edmonton, AB, Canada - *DirInfWP 82*
Harwood Academic Publishers GmbH - New York, NY - *LitMarPl 83, 84; MicroMarPl 82-83*
Harwood Heights Citizen - *See* Pioneer Press Inc.
Harwood Heights-Norridge Harlem & Irving Passage - Chicago, IL - *AyerDirPub 83*
Harwood Manufacturing Co. [Subs. of Elgin National Industries Inc.] - Chicago, IL - *AvMarPl 83*
Harwood/Noridge Park/Edison Park Citizen - Wilmette, IL - *AyerDirPub 83*
Harwyn Medical Photographers - Philadelphia, PA - *ArtMar 84; AvMarPl 83*
Hasbrouck Heights Observer - Hasbrouck Heights, NJ - *BaconPubCkNews 84*
Hase/Schannen Research Associates Inc. - Princeton, NJ - *IntDirMarRes 83*
Haselmire Advertising Inc., William F. - West Palm Beach, FL - *StaDirAdAg 2-84*
Haselow & Associates - Cleveland, OH - *AdAge 3-28-84; DirPRFirms 83; StaDirAdAg 2-84*
Hashomer Hatzair - New York, NY - *BoPubDir 4, 5*
Haskell & Associates, E. F. - Phoenix, AZ - *WhoWMicrocom 83*
Haskell County Monitor-Chief - Sublette, KS - *AyerDirPub 83; Ed&PubIntYB 82*
Haskell Free Press - Haskell, TX - *BaconPubCkNews 84; Ed&PubIntYB 82*
Haskell House Publishers Ltd. - Brooklyn, NY - *LitMarPl 83, 84*
Haskell News - Haskell, OK - *BaconPubCkNews 84; Ed&PubIntYB 82*
Haskell Newspapers - *Ed&PubIntYB 82*
Haskell of Pittsburgh Inc. - Pittsburgh, PA - *DirInfWP 82*
Hass, Rose - Brooklyn, NY - *LitMarPl 83, 84*
Hassavampa Shopper News - Wickenburg, AZ - *AyerDirPub 83*
Hasselblad Inc., Victor [Subs. of Hasselblad AB] - Fairfield, NJ - *AvMarPl 83*
Hastech Inc. - Manchester, NH - *DataDirSup 7-83; InfIndMarPl 83*
Hasting Star - Marmora, ON, Canada - *AyerDirPub 83*
Hastings Banner [of J-Ad Graphics Inc.] - Hastings, MI - *BaconPubCkNews 84; Ed&PubIntYB 82; NewsDir 84*
Hastings Cable TV Co. [of Telephone & Data Systems Inc.] - Hastings, MN - *Tel&CabFB 84C*
Hastings Cable Vision Ltd. - Madoc, ON, Canada - *BrCabYB 84*
Hastings Center [of Institute of Society, Ethics, & the Life Sciences] - Hastings-on-Hudson, NY - *BoPubDir 4, 5*
Hastings Center Report - Hastings-on-Hudson, NY - *MagIndMarPl 82-83*
Hastings Clearview Cable TV - Hastings, FL - *BrCabYB 84*
Hastings Daily Tribune - Hastings, NE - *Ed&PubIntYB 82; NewsDir 84*
Hastings-Doyle & Co. Inc. - Milwaukee, WI - *StaDirAdAg 2-84*
Hastings Gazette - Hastings, MN - *NewsDir 84*
Hastings House Publishers Inc. - New York, NY - *LitMarPl 83, 84; WritMar 84*
Hastings Star - Hastings, MN - *NewsDir 84*
Hastings Star Gazette - Hastings, MN - *BaconPubCkNews 84; Ed&PubIntYB 82*
Hastings Tribune - Hastings, NE - *BaconPubCkNews 84*
Hastings Westchester County Press - Hastings-On-Hudson, NY - *BaconPubCkNews 84*
Hat Band Music - Nashville, TN - *BillIntBG 83-84*
Hat Island Telephone Co. - Langley, WA - *TelDir&BG 83-84*
Hatboro Progress Newspapers - Horsham, PA - *NewsDir 84*
Hatboro-Warminster Today's Spirit - Hatboro, PA - *NewsDir 84*
Hatch Associates Inc., Denison - Stamford, CT - *LitMarPl 83, 84*
Hatch, James A. - North Olmsted, OH - *MagIndMarPl 82-83*
Hatch Stations, George C. & Wilda Gene - Salt Lake City, UT - *BrCabYB 84*
Hatcher Agency, Alexandria - New York, NY - *DirPRFirms 83; LitMarPl 83, 84*
Hatfield Associates - Silver Spring, MD - *BrCabYB 84*
Hatfield Cable TV Service Inc. - Hatfield, AR - *BrCabYB 84 p.D-301; Tel&CabFB 84C p.1683*
Hatfield Cable TV Service Inc. - Mineral Springs, AR - *BrCabYB 84*
Hatfield Cable TV Service Inc. - Wickes, AR - *BrCabYB 84*
Hatfield, Mary - Fremont, CA - *LitMarPl 83, 84*
Hatfield Penn Valley Times - *See* Souderton Independent Inc.
Hathaway Publishing Corp. - Dartmouth, MA - *BaconPubCkNews 84*
Hattiesburg American - Hattiesburg, MS - *BaconPubCkNews 84; NewsDir 84*
Hatton Free Press - Hatton, ND - *AyerDirPub 83; BaconPubCkNews 84*
Hauck & Associates - Washington, DC - *DirPRFirms 83*
Haug Associates - Los Angeles, CA - *IntDirMarRes 83*
Haughey, Albert P. - Watkins Glen, NY - *Tel&CabFB 84C p.1683*
Haughey Co. Inc., W. J. [Subs. of Berk & Co. Inc.] - Boston, MA - *StaDirAdAg 2-84*
Haughey, John A. - Watkins Glen, NY - *Tel&CabFB 84C p.1684*
Haunted Book Shop - Mobile, AL - *BoPubDir 4, 5*
Hauppauge-Nesconset Pennysaver - Huntington, NY - *AyerDirPub 83*
Hauptman, Don - New York, NY - *HBIndAd&MS 82-83; MagIndMarPl 82-83*
Hauser & Associates Inc. - New York, NY - *DirPRFirms 83*
Hauser Associates - New York, NY - *IntDirMarRes 83*
Hauser Webb & Wykoff - Portland, OR - *DirPRFirms 83*
Hauserman Inc. - Cleveland, OH - *DirInfWP 82*
Havana Herald - Havana, FL - *BaconPubCkNews 84; Ed&PubIntYB 82*
Havana Mason County Democrat [of Martin Publishing Co. Inc.] - Havana, IL - *BaconPubCkNews 84; NewsDir 84*

Havana Moon Music - *See* Kentucky Colonel Music
Havana Shopper News [of Havana Mason County Publishing Co. Inc.] - Havana, IL - *NewsDir 84*
Havas Conseil [of the Univas Network) - Neuilly sur Seine, France - *StaDirAdAg 2-84*
Have Computer Will Travel - Pacoima, CA - *MicrocomMPl 84*
Havelock Citizen - Havelock, ON, Canada - *AyerDirPub 83*
Havelock Progress - Havelock, NC - *AyerDirPub 83; BaconPubCkNews 84; Ed&PubIntYB 82*
Haven Corp., The - Evanston, IL - *LitMag&SmPr 83-84*
Haven Journal - Haven, KS - *AyerDirPub 83; Ed&PubIntYB 82*
Haven, Mark - New York, NY - *MagIndMarPl 82-83*
Haven Publications - Flushing, NY - *LitMarPl 83*
Haven Publications - New York, NY - *LitMarPl 84*
Haverford House - Wayne, PA - *BoPubDir 4, 5*
Haverhill Gazette - Haverhill, MA - *BaconPubCkNews 84; NewsDir 84*
Haverhill Independent - *See* Exeter News-Letter Co.
Haverstraw Rockland County Times - Haverstraw, NY - *BaconPubCkNews 84; NewsDir 84*
Havertown Leader - Newtown Square, PA - *NewsDir 84*
Havertown Leader - *See* Marple Publishing Co. Inc.
Havertown Leader, The - Havertown, PA - *Ed&PubIntYB 82*
Haviland Telephone Co. - Haviland, KS - *TelDir&BG 83-84*
Havre Cable TV [of Tele-Communications Inc.] - Havre, MT - *Tel&CabFB 84C*
Havre Daily News - Havre, MT - *AyerDirPub 83; BaconPubCkNews 84; Ed&PubIntYB 82; NewsDir 84*
Havre De Grace Record - Havre De Grace, MD - *BaconPubCkNews 84; NewsDir 84*
Hawaii AFL-CIO Nupepa [of SB Printers] - Honolulu, HI - *NewsDir 84*
Hawaii Beverage Guide - Honolulu, HI - *BaconPubCkMag 84; MagDir 84*
Hawaii Business [of Hawaii Business Publishing Corp.] - Honolulu, HI - *BaconPubCkMag 84; MagDir 84*
Hawaii Business Directory Inc. - Honolulu, HI - *BoPubDir 4 Sup, 5*
Hawaii Carpenter, The [of TONGG Publishing] - Honolulu, HI - *NewsDir 84*
Hawaii Chamber of Commerce - Honolulu, HI - *BoPubDir 5*
Hawaii Clipping Service - Honolulu, HI - *ProGuPRSer 4*
Hawaii Educational Dissemination Diffusion System [of Hawaii State Dept. of Education] - Honolulu, HI - *EISS 83*
Hawaii Hochi [of Shizioka Shimbum Ltd.] - Honolulu, HI - *Ed&PubIntYB 82; NewsDir 84*
Hawaii Hotel Network, The - Honolulu, HI - *MagIndMarPl 82-83*
Hawaii Kai Sun Press - Hawaii Kai, HI - *Ed&PubIntYB 82*
Hawaii Kai Sun-Press - Kaneohe, HI - *AyerDirPub 83*
Hawaii Legislative Reference Bureau [Aff. of Hawaii State Legislature] - Honolulu, HI - *BoPubDir 5*
Hawaii Literary Arts Council Newsletter - Honolulu, HI - *LitMag&SmPr 83-84*
Hawaii Marine - Kaneohe, HI - *AyerDirPub 83*
Hawaii Medical Journal - Honolulu, HI - *BaconPubCkMag 84; MagDir 84*
Hawaii Navy News - Kaneohe, HI - *AyerDirPub 83*
Hawaii Newspaper Agency Inc. - Honolulu, HI - *Ed&PubIntYB 82*
Hawaii Opinion Inc. - Honolulu, HI - *IntDirMarRes 83*
Hawaii Sun Press Newspapers - Kanoehe, HI - *NewsDir 84*
Hawaii Times - Honolulu, HI - *BrCabYB 84; Ed&PubIntYB 82*
Hawaii Tribune-Herald - Hilo, HI - *AyerDirPub 83; BaconPubCkNews 84; Ed&PubIntYB 82*
Hawaiian Cable Vision Co. [of Global Telecommunications Corp.] - Lahaina, HI - *BrCabYB 84; Tel&CabFB 84C*
Hawaiian Falcon - Kaneohe, HI - *AyerDirPub 83*
Hawaiian Realtor, The - Honolulu, HI - *BaconPubCkMag 84*
Hawaiian Sugar Planters' Association - Aiea, HI - *BoPubDir 5*
Hawaiian Telephone Co. [Aff. of General Telephone & Electronics Corp.] - Honolulu, HI - *TelDir&BG 83-84*
Hawaiian Tropic Advertising - Daytona Beach, FL - *StaDirAdAg 2-84*
Hawaiian Tropic Advertising - Ormond Beach, FL - *AdAge 3-28-84*
Hawarden Independent - Hawarden, IA - *BaconPubCkNews 84; Ed&PubIntYB 82*
Hawesville Hancock Clarion - Hawesville, KY - *BaconPubCkNews 84; NewsDir 84*
Hawk Eye - Burlington, IA - *AyerDirPub 83; BaconPubCkNews 84; Ed&PubIntYB 82*
Hawk Photo Systems - Northbrook, IL - *AvMarPl 83*
Hawkes Publishing Inc. - Salt Lake City, UT - *LitMarPl 83, 84; WritMar 84*
Hawkeye Booster - Hawkeye, IA - *BaconPubCkNews 84*
Hawkeye Cablevision [of American TV & Communications Corp.] - Iowa City, IA - *BrCabYB 84; Tel&CabFB 84C*
Hawkeye Communications Inc. - Greenfield, IA - *BrCabYB 84*
Hawkeye Engineer [of Associated Students of Engineering] - Iowa City, IA - *MagDir 84*
Hawkeye Grafix - Canoga Park, CA - *MicrocomMPl 83, 84; MicrocomSwDir 1; WhoWMicrocom 83*
Hawkeye Telephone Co. - Hawkeye, IA - *TelDir&BG 83-84*
Hawkins Broadcasting Inc. - Marble Falls, TX - *BrCabYB 84*
Hawkins, Robert L. - Lexington, MO - *BoPubDir 4, 5*
Hawkinsville Dispatch & News - Hawkinsville, GA - *AyerDirPub 83; BaconPubCkNews 84; Ed&PubIntYB 82*
Hawkinsville Telephone Co. - Hawkinsville, GA - *TelDir&BG 83-84*
Hawkline Music - *See* Coal Miners Music Inc.
Hawley Communications Inc. - Hawley, MN - *Tel&CabFB 84C*
Hawley, Cooke & Orr - Louisville, KY - *BoPubDir 4, 5*
Hawley Herald - Hawley, MN - *BaconPubCkNews 84; Ed&PubIntYB 82*
Hawley News Eagle - Hawley, PA - *BaconPubCkNews 84*
Haworth Group Inc., The - Minnetonka, MN - *HBIndAd&MS 82-83; StaDirAdAg 2-84*
Haworth Inc. - Holland, MI - *DirInfWP 82*
Haworth, James A. - Katonah, NY - *MagIndMarPl 82-83*
Haworth Press - New York, NY - *LitMarPl 83, 84; MagIndMarPl 82-83*
Haws Corp. - Elkhart, IN - *DirInfWP 82*
Haws, Mary Frances - Willowdale, ON, Canada - *BoPubDir 4, 5*
Hawthorne Advertising [Subs. of Colonial Penn Group] - Philadelphia, PA - *DirMarMP 83*
Hawthorne Cable TV Inc. [of American Communications & Television Inc.] - Hawthorne, FL - *BrCabYB 84*
Hawthorne Cable TV Inc. [of Tele-Communications Inc.] - Hawthorne, NV - *Tel&CabFB 84C*
Hawthorne Community News - Culver City, CA - *NewsDir 84*
Hawthorne Community News, Lawndale Tribune - Culver City, CA - *AyerDirPub 83*
Hawthorne Community News/Press Tribune - Hawthorne, CA - *Ed&PubIntYB 82*
Hawthorne-El Segundo Beacon - El Segundo, CA - *Ed&PubIntYB 82*
Hawthorne-Glen Rock-Ridgewood Shopper - Fair Lawn, NJ - *AyerDirPub 83*
Hawthorne-Glen Rock-Ridgewood Shopper - Glen Rock, NJ - *Ed&PubIntYB 82*
Hawthorne Mineral County Independent News - Hawthorne, NV - *BaconPubCkNews 84*
Hawthorne Press - Hawthorne, NJ - *BaconPubCkNews 84; Ed&PubIntYB 82*
Hawthorne Press - Paterson, NJ - *NewsDir 84*
Hawthorne Press Tribune [of Coast Media Newspapers] - Culver City, CA - *NewsDir 84*
Hawthorne Press Tribune - *See* Coast Media Newspapers
Hawthorne Wave - *See* Central News-Wave Publications
Haxtun Herald - Haxtun, CO - *BaconPubCkNews 84; Ed&PubIntYB 82*
Haxtun Telephone Co. [Aff. of Continental Telephone Corp.] - Haxtun, CO - *TelDir&BG 83-84*
Hay Communications - Dallas, TX - *DirPRFirms 83*
Hayastanyaitz Yegeghetzy - New York, NY - *Ed&PubIntYB 82*
Haycox Photoramic Inc. - Norfolk, VA - *ArtMar 84; AvMarPl 83*
Hayden Advertising Inc. - Montclair, NJ - *StaDirAdAg 2-84*
Hayden & Associates Inc. - Lakewood, OH - *StaDirAdAg 2-84*
Hayden Book Co. - Lowell, MA - *MicrocomMPl 84*
Hayden Book Co. [Aff. of Hayden Publishing Co. Inc.] - Rochelle Park, NJ - *ArtMar 84; LitMarPl 83, 84; MicrocomMPl 83; WhoWMicrocom 83; WritMar 84*

Hayden Cable TV - Hayden, CO - *Tel&CabFB 84C*
Hayden, Harry - Beach, ND - *Tel&CabFB 84C p.1684*
Hayden Publications Co. Inc. - Rochelle Park, NJ - *DirMarMP 83*
Hayden Valley Press - Hayden, CO - *Ed&PubIntYB 82*
Hayden Valley Press - *See* Northwest Colorado Press
Hayes Center Times Republican - Hayes Center, NE - *BaconPubCkNews 84; Ed&PubIntYB 82*
Hayes Co., Charles Elwyn - Chicago, IL - *StaDirAdAg 2-84*
Hayes Co. Inc., John E. - Buffalo, NY - *StaDirAdAg 2-84*
Hayes, Edward N. - Newport Beach, CA - *BoPubDir 4 Sup, 5*
Hayes Microcomputer Products Inc. - Norcross, GA - *DataDirSup 7-83; MicrocomMPl 84; MicrocomSwDir 1; WhoWMicrocom 83*
Hayes Productions, Bruce - San Francisco, CA - *AvMarPl 83*
Hayes Productions Inc. - San Antonio, TX - *AvMarPl 83*
Hayes Publishing Co. Inc. - Cincinnati, OH - *ArtMar 84; AvMarPl 83; BoPubDir 4, 5*
Hayes Publishing Co. Inc., T. I. - Ft. Mitchell, KY - *BoPubDir 5*
Hayes Publishing Co., T. I. - Hueysville, KY - *BoPubDir 4*
Hayes Publishing Ltd. - Burlington, ON, Canada - *LitMarPl 83, 84*
Hayes School Publishing Co. Inc. - Wilkinsburg, PA - *AvMarPl 83; BoPubDir 4, 5; WritMar 84*
Hayes-Williams Inc. - New York, NY - *DirPRFirms 83*
Hayett Inc., William - New York, NY - *AvMarPl 83*
Hayfield Herald - Hayfield, MN - *BaconPubCkNews 84; Ed&PubIntYB 82*
Hayhurst Advertising Ltd. - Toronto, ON, Canada - *StaDirAdAg 2-84*
Hayhurst Communications Alberta Ltd. - Calgary, AB, Canada - *StaDirAdAg 2-84*
Hayhurst Communications B.C. Ltd. - Vancouver, BC, Canada - *StaDirAdAg 2-84*
Hayman Cash Register Co. - Washington, DC - *DataDirSup 7-83*
Haymark Publishing Co. Inc. - Fredericksburg, VA - *BoPubDir 4, 5*
Haynes Advertising - Macon, GA - *ArtMar 84; StaDirAdAg 2-84*
Haynes, Fred - Westbury, NY - *MagIndMarPl 82-83*
Haynes Music Inc., Walter - Nashville, TN - *BillIntBG 83-84*
Haynes Publications Inc. - Newbury Park, CA - *BoPubDir 4, 5; LitMarPl 83, 84*
Haynesville News - Haynesville, LA - *AyerDirPub 83; BaconPubCkNews 84; Ed&PubIntYB 82*
Hayneville Telephone Co. - Hayneville, AL - *TelDir&BG 83-84*
Hays Cable TV Co. [of KAYS Inc.] - Hays, KS - *BrCabYB 84; Tel&CabFB 84C*
Hays Daily News - Hays, KS - *BaconPubCkNews 84; Ed&PubIntYB 82; NewsDir 84*
Hays Ellis County Star - Hays, KS - *BaconPubCkNews 84*
Hays, Jim - Irvine, KY - *Tel&CabFB 84C p.1684*
Hays, Jim - McKee, KY - *BrCabYB 84 p.D-302*
Hays, Rolfes & Associates - Memphis, TN - *BoPubDir 4; LitMarPl 83, 84*
Hayseed Publishing - Shreveport, LA - *BillIntBG 83-84*
Haysi Cable Co. - Haysi, VA - *Tel&CabFB 84C*
Hayslett & Associates Inc., Dan - Dallas, TX - *CabTVFinDB 83*
Haystack Cablevision Inc. [of TCI-Taft Cablevision Associates] - Lanaan, CT - *BrCabYB 84*
Haystack Cablevision Inc. [of TCI-Taft Cablevision Associates] - Salisbury, CT - *Tel&CabFB 84C*
Hayti Hamlin County Herald-Enterprise - Hayti, SD - *BaconPubCkNews 84*
Hayti Missouri Herald - Hayti, MO - *BaconPubCkNews 84*
Hayward Cable Television Inc. [of United Cable Television Corp.] - Hayward, CA - *BrCabYB 84*
Hayward Castro Valley Observer - San Leandro, CA - *AyerDirPub 83*
Hayward Daily Review - Hayward, CA - *BaconPubCkNews 84*
Hayward Sawyer County Record - Hayward, WI - *NewsDir 84*
Hayward Sawyer County Record/Republican - Hayward, WI - *BaconPubCkNews 84*
Haywire Press - New York, NY - *BoPubDir 4, 5*
Hazard - Rockville, MD - *BaconPubCkMag 84*
Hazard Advertising Co. - New York, NY - *AdAge 3-28-84; StaDirAdAg 2-84*
Hazard Herald-Voice - Hazard, KY - *BaconPubCkNews 84; Ed&PubIntYB 82; NewsDir 84*
Hazard Television Cable Co. - Hazard, KY - *BrCabYB 84; Tel&CabFB 84C*
Hazardline [of Occupational Health Services Inc.] - New York, NY - *DataDirOnSer 84; DirOnDB Spring 84*
Hazardous Materials & Waste Management - Kutztown, PA - *BaconPubCkMag 84*
Hazardous Materials Control Research Institute - Silver Spring, MD - *BoPubDir 5*
Hazardous Waste News - Silver Spring, MD - *DirOnDB Spring 84*
Hazardous Waste News [of NewsNet Inc.] - Bryn Mawr, PA - *DataDirOnSer 84*
Hazardous Waste Report - Rockville, MD - *BaconPubCkMag 84*
Hazel Crest-Country Club Hills Star - Chicago Heights, IL - *NewsDir 84*
Hazel Crest-Country Club Hills Star - Hazel Crest, IL - *AyerDirPub 83; Ed&PubIntYB 82*
Hazel Crest-Country Club Hills Star - *See* Star Publications
Hazel Dell News - Hazel Dell, WA - *Ed&PubIntYB 82*
Hazel Dell News [of Vancouver East County News] - Vancouver, WA - *Ed&PubIntYB 82; NewsDir 84*
Hazel Dell Post - Camas, WA - *NewsDir 84*
Hazelden Educational Materials [Aff. of Hazelden Foundation] - Center City, MN - *BoPubDir 5*
Hazelden Educational Services [Aff. of Hazelden Foundation] - Center City, MN - *BoPubDir 4*
Hazelden Foundation - Center City, MN - *WritMar 84*
Hazelden Foundation (Research Dept.) - Center City, MN - *CompReadDB 82*
Hazeltine Corp. - Greenlawn, NY - *InfIndMarPl 83*
Hazelton White River News - Hazelton, IN - *BaconPubCkNews 84*
Hazen Cable TV Inc. - Hazen, ND - *BrCabYB 84; Tel&CabFB 84C*
Hazen De Valls Bluff Times - Hazen, AR - *BaconPubCkNews 84*
Hazen, Dean - El Granada, CA - *Tel&CabFB 84C p.1684*
Hazen Grand Prairie Herald - Hazen, AR - *BaconPubCkNews 84*
Hazen Star - Hazen, ND - *BaconPubCkNews 84; Ed&PubIntYB 82*
Hazlehurst Copiah County Courier - Hazlehurst, MS - *BaconPubCkNews 84*
Hazlehurst Jeff Davis County Ledger - Hazlehurst, GA - *BaconPubCkNews 84; NewsDir 84*
Hazleton Standard-Speaker - Hazleton, PA - *BaconPubCkNews 84; NewsDir 84*
Hazlett, Robert C. Jr. - Wheeling, WV - *Tel&CabFB 84C p.1684*
H.B.C. - Lansing, IL - *BoPubDir 4, 5*
HBJ Newsletters Inc. [Subs. of Harcourt Brace Jovanovich Inc.] - New York, NY - *DirMarMP 83*
HBM/Creamer Inc. - New York, NY - *AdAge 3-28-84; Br 1-23-84*
HBM/Stiefel Public Relations - New York, NY - *DirPRFirms 83*
HBO Studio Productions [Div. of Home Box Office] - New York, NY - *Tel&CabFB 84C*
HBR/Online - New York, NY - *DirOnDB Spring 84*
HBW Associates Inc. - Dallas, TX - *EISS 83*
HCM Graphic Systems Inc. - Great Neck, NY - *DirInfWP 82*
HD Manufacturing Inc. - Leverett, MA - *MicrocomMPl 84*
Hdok - Bromma, Sweden - *DirOnDB Spring 84*
HDP Inc. - Santa Barbara, CA - *MicrocomMPl 83*
HDR Systems Inc. - Omaha, NE - *ADAPSOMemDir 83-84; DataDirOnSer 84; DataDirSup 7-83*
He-Rose Records & Publishing - El Centro, CA - *BillIntBG 83-84*
Heacock Literary Agency - Santa Monica, CA - *LitMarPl 83, 84*
Head Newspapers - Liberal, KS - *Ed&PubIntYB 82*
Headache - Chicago, IL - *BaconPubCkMag 84*
Headen, Horrell & Wentsel Inc. - Hinsdale, IL - *StaDirAdAg 2-84*
Headland Cablevision Inc. - Headland, AL - *Tel&CabFB 84C*
Headland Observer - Headland, AL - *BaconPubCkNews 84; Ed&PubIntYB 82*
Headland Press - Headland, England - *MicroMarPl 82-83*

Headlands Press Inc. - Tiburon, CA - *BoPubDir 4, 5; MicrocomMPl 84*
Headlight - Wrightsville, GA - *AyerDirPub 83*
Headlight - Horton, KS - *AyerDirPub 83*
Headlight - Terry, MS - *AyerDirPub 83*
Headlight - Stanberry, MO - *AyerDirPub 83*
Headlight - Stromsburg, NE - *AyerDirPub 83; Ed&PubIntYB 82*
Headlight - Deming, NM - *AyerDirPub 83*
Headlight - Eagle Lake, TX - *AyerDirPub 83*
Headlight Herald - Tracy, MN - *AyerDirPub 83*
Headlight Herald - Tillamook, OR - *AyerDirPub 83; Ed&PubIntYB 82*
Headliner, The - Portage, MI - *Ed&PubIntYB 82*
Headlines, Ink - Studio City, CA - *StaDirAdAg 2-84*
Headnotes of the Federal Courts of Canada Reports [of Federal Dept. of Justice] - Ottawa, ON, Canada - *CompReadDB 82*
Headnotes of the Supreme Court of Canada Reports [of Federal Dept. of Justice] - Ottawa, ON, Canada - *CompReadDB 82*
Headquarters Cos. - San Francisco, CA - *TeleSy&SerDir 7-83*
Headquarters Detective [of Detective Files Group] - Montreal, PQ, Canada - *WritMar 84*
Headquarters News Service - New York, NY - *Ed&PubIntYB 82*
Headstack Music - *See* Televox Music
Headwaters Telephone Co. [Aff. of Rhinelander Telephone Co.] - Rhinelander, WI - *TelDir&BG 83-84*
Headway Publications - Newport Beach, CA - *BoPubDir 4, 5*
Heahstan Press - Denton, TX - *BoPubDir 4, 5*
Healdsburg Tribune - Healdsburg, CA - *BaconPubCkNews 84; Ed&PubIntYB 82*
Healdsburg Tribune, Enterprise & Scimitar - Healdsburg, CA - *NewsDir 84*
Healdton Herald - Healdton, OK - *BaconPubCkNews 84; Ed&PubIntYB 82*
Healey/Healey Advertising Research Services (AM-MAS Analytic Multi-Media Advertising System Div.) - New York, NY - *IntDirMarRes 83*
Healing Yourself - Vashon, WA - *BoPubDir 4 Sup, 5*
Health [of Family Media Inc.] - New York, NY - *ArtMar 84; BaconPubCkMag 84; Folio 83; LitMarPl 83, 84; MagIndMarPl 82-83; WritMar 84*
Health Administration Press - Ann Arbor, MI - *LitMarPl 83, 84*
Health & Care - Costa Mesa, CA - *BaconPubCkMag 84*
Health & Education Multimedia Inc. - New York, NY - *AvMarPl 83*
Health & Habitation Inc. - Sumter, SC - *MicrocomMPl 84*
Health & Longevity Report [of Agora Publishing] - Baltimore, MD - *WritMar 84*
Health & Safety Analysis Center [of U.S. Dept. of Labor] - Denver, CO - *EISS 83*
Health & Safety Executive - Sheffield, England - *InfIndMarPl 83*
Health & Social Work - New York, NY - *MagDir 84; MagIndMarPl 82-83*
Health & Vitality Book Guild [of Prentice-Hall Inc.] - Englewood, NJ - *LitMarPl 83, 84*
Health & Welfare Materials Center Inc. - New York, NY - *Tel&CabFB 84C*
Health Audio-Visual Online Catalog [of Bibliographic Retrieval Services Inc.] - Latham, NY - *DataDirOnSer 84*
Health Audiovisual Online Catalog [of Northeastern Ohio Universities] - Rootstown, OH - *DirOnDB Spring 84; EISS 7-83 Sup*
Health Benefit Cost Containment [of NewsNet Inc.] - Bryn Mawr, PA - *DataDirOnSer 84*
Health Benefit Cost Containment Newsletter - Virginia Beach, VA - *DirOnDB Spring 84*
Health Care Conference Planner - Stamford, CT - *MagDir 84*
Health Care in Canada - Don Mills, ON, Canada - *BaconPubCkMag 84*
Health Care Literature Information Network - Berlin, West Germany - *EISS 83*
Health Care Management Review - Gaithersburg, MD - *BaconPubCkMag 84*
Health Care News - Detroit, MI - *BaconPubCkMag 84; MagDir 84*
Health Care Product News [of Gralla Publications] - New York, NY - *MagDir 84; MagIndMarPl 82-83*
Health Care Systems - New York, NY - *BaconPubCkMag 84*
Health City Sun - Albuquerque, NM - *AyerDirPub 83; Ed&PubIntYB 82*
Health Communications Inc. - Hollywood, FL - *BoPubDir 4, 5*
Health Communications Network - New York, NY - *DirPRFirms 83*
Health Communications Network [of Medical University of South Carolina] - Charleston, SC - *TeleSy&SerDir 7-83*
Health-Comp Inc. - Pittsburgh, PA - *ADAPSOMemDir 83-84*
Health Data Products Inc. - Santa Barbara, CA - *MicrocomMPl 83, 84*
Health Devices Program [of Emergency Care Research Institute] - Plymouth Meeting, PA - *EISS 83*
Health Education - Reston, VA - *MagIndMarPl 82-83*
Health Education & Life Expansion Research - Los Angeles, CA - *BoPubDir 4, 5*
Health Education Reports - Washington, DC - *BaconPubCkMag 84*
Health Education Services [Div. of Social Studies School Service] - Culver City, CA - *AvMarPl 83*
Health Education Technologies & PRISM - *See* Doremus & Co. Public Relations
Health Explorer [of Children's Better Health Institute] - Indianapolis, IN - *ArtMar 84; WritMar 84*
Health Express - Huntington Beach, CA - *BaconPubCkMag 84*
Health Foods Business [of Howmark Publishing Corp.] - Elizabeth, NJ - *BaconPubCkMag 84; MagDir 84; WritMar 84*
Health Foods Retailing [of Communication Channels Inc.] - New York, NY - *BaconPubCkMag 84; MagDir 84*
Health Industry Today - Union, NJ - *ArtMar 84; BaconPubCkMag 84; MagDir 84; WritMar 84*
Health Insurance Underwriter, The - Hartland, WI - *BaconPubCkMag 84; MagDir 84*
Health/Pac Bulletin - New York, NY - *LitMag&SmPr 83-84*
Health, Physical Education, & Recreation Microform Publications [of University of Oregon] - Eugene, OR - *LitMarPl 83, 84*
Health Physics - Elmsford, NY - *BaconPubCkMag 84*
Health Planning & Administration Data Base [of National Library of Medicine] - Bethesda, MD - *CompReadDB 82; DataDirOnSer 84; DBBus 82; DirOnDB Spring 84; EISS 83; OnBibDB 3*
Health Plus Publishers - Phoenix, AZ - *BoPubDir 4, 5*
Health Policy Week - Chevy Chase, MD - *BaconPubCkMag 84*
Health Profession Publishing [of McGraw-Hill Publishing Co.] - New York, NY - *WritMar 84*
Health Quarterly (Plus Two), The - New Canaan, CT - *MagIndMarPl 82-83*
Health-Related Information Data Base [of Onondaga County Public Library] - Syracuse, NY - *EISS 5-84 Sup*
Health Research - Las Vegas, NV - *BoPubDir 5*
Health Science [Aff. of Live Food Products Inc.] - Santa Barbara, CA - *BoPubDir 4, 5; LitMag&SmPr 83-84*
Health Science - Bridgeport, CT - *BaconPubCkMag 84; MagIndMarPl 82-83*
Health Sciences Consortium - Carrboro, NC - *MicrocomSwDir 1*
Health Sciences Consortium - Chapel Hill, NC - *BoPubDir 4 Sup, 5*
Health Services Manager [of American Management Association] - New York, NY - *MagIndMarPl 82-83*
Health Team - Bellevue, WV - *MagDir 84*
Health-Tex - Washington, DC - *DirOnDB Spring 84*
Health Values - Thorofare, NJ - *BaconPubCkMag 84*
Healthcare Communications Inc. - Ft. Washington, PA - *IntDirMarRes 83*
Healthcare Financial Management [of Healthcare Financial Management Association] - Hinsdale, IL - *MagDir 84*
Healthcare Financial Management - Oak Brook, IL - *ArtMar 84; BaconPubCkMag 84*
Healthcare Financial Management Association - Oak Brook, IL - *BoPubDir 5*
Healthcare Horizons - San Pedro, CA - *WritMar 84*
Healthmark Communications [Div. of Ruvane-Leverte] - New York, NY - *StaDirAdAg 2-84*
Healthways - Des Moines, IA - *MagDir 84*
Healy, Dixcy & Forbes - Montclair, NJ - *StaDirAdAg 2-84*
Healy-Schutte & Comstock Advertising - Buffalo, NY - *AdAge 3-28-84; ArtMar 84; StaDirAdAg 2-84*
Hear No Evil Music - *See* Espy Music Group

Hearing Aid Journal - Harvard, MA - *BoPubDir 4, 5; MagDir 84*
Hearing & Speech Action - Rockville, MD - *MagDir 84*
Hearing Instruments - Duluth, MN - *BaconPubCkMag 84; MagDir 84; MagIndMarPl 82-83*
Hearing Journal - Chicago, IL - *BaconPubCkMag 84*
Hearne Associates Inc., Ted - Chicago, IL - *DirPRFirms 83*
Hearne Cablevision [of Star CATV Investment Corp.] - Hearne, TX - *BrCabYB 84; Tel&CabFB 84C*
Hearne Democrat - Hearne, TX - *BaconPubCkNews 84; Ed&PubIntYB 82*
Hearst/ABC Video Services - New York, NY - *BrCabYB 84*
Hearst Advertising Inc. - Milwaukee, WI - *StaDirAdAg 2-84*
Hearst Advertising Service Inc. [Subs. of The Hearst Corp.] - New York, NY - *LitMarPl 83, 84*
Hearst Basic Power Package - *Folio 83*
Hearst Books [Div. of The Hearst Corp.] - New York, NY - *LitMarPl 83, 84*
Hearst Broadcasting Inc. - Pittsburgh, PA - *BrCabYB 84*
Hearst Business Communications Inc. (UTP Div.) - Garden City, NY - *MagIndMarPl 82-83*
Hearst Business Media Corp. (IMN Div.) - Southfield, MI - *BoPubDir 5; MagDir 84*
Hearst Cablevision of Santa Clara [of Hearst Corp.] - Santa Clara, CA - *Tel&CabFB 84C*
Hearst Community Newspapers - South Gate, CA - *BaconPubCkNews 84*
Hearst Corp. - Santa Clara, CA - *Tel&CabFB 84C p.1684*
Hearst Corp. - New York, NY - *AdAge 6-28-84; BrCabYB 84; DirMarMP 83; KnowInd 83; MagIndMarPl 82-83; NewsBur 6*
Hearst Corp. of Los Gatos - Los Gatos, CA - *Tel&CabFB 84C*
Hearst Corp. of Milpitas - Milpitas, CA - *Tel&CabFB 84C*
Hearst Gold Power Package - *Folio 83*
Hearst Magazines [Div. of Hearst Corp.] - New York, NY - *DirMarMP 83*
Hearst ManPower Package - *Folio 83*
Hearst Marine Books [Aff. of Hearst Corp.] - Cos Cob, CT - *BoPubDir 4 Sup, 5*
Hearst Metrotone News - New York, NY - *Tel&CabFB 84C*
Hearst Newspapers - Washington, DC - *NewsBur 6*
Hearst Newspapers - New York, NY - *BaconPubCkNews 84; Ed&PubIntYB 82*
Hearst Stations - New York, NY - *Tel&CabFB 84S*
Heart & Lung: The Journal of Critical Care - St. Louis, MO - *BaconPubCkMag 84; MagDir 84; MagIndMarPl 82-83*
Heart of America Press - Kansas City, MO - *BoPubDir 4, 5*
Heart of America Purchaser - Kansas City, MO - *MagDir 84*
Heart of Dixie Broadcasting Corp. - Manfield, LA - *BrCabYB 84*
Heart of Iowa Telephone Cooperative - Union, IA - *TelDir&BG 83-84*
Heart of Music Publishing - Alameda, CA - *BillIntBG 83-84*
Heart of Texas Computer Systems Inc. - Arlington, TX - *MicrocomMPl 84*
Heart of the Lakes Publishing - Interlaken, NY - *BoPubDir 4, 5; WritMar 84*
Heartbeat Media Corp. - New York, NY - *BrCabYB 84*
Heartbeat Media Network - New York, NY - *BrCabYB 84*
Hearthstone Press - Broderick, CA - *BoPubDir 4, 5; LitMag&SmPr 83-84*
Heartland Communications - Shreve, OH - *DataDirOnSer 84; EISS 5-84 Sup*
Heartland Press Inc. - Minneapolis, MN - *MagIndMarPl 82-83*
Heartland Records Co. - Altamonte Springs, FL - *BillIntBG 83-84*
Heartland Software - Cleveland, OH - *MicrocomMPl 84*
Heartland Transcript - Little Falls, MN - *AyerDirPub 83*
Heat Press - Philadelphia, PA - *LitMag&SmPr 83-84*
Heat Transfer Engineering - Washington, DC - *BaconPubCkMag 84; MagIndMarPl 82-83*
Heat Treating - Hinsdale, IL - *MagDir 84*
Heat Treating - New York, NY - *BaconPubCkMag 84; MagIndMarPl 82-83*
Heath Ace News - Heath, OH - *Ed&PubIntYB 82*
Heath Ace News - *See* Heath Ace News Publishers
Heath Ace News Publishers - Heath, OH - *BaconPubCkNews 84*
Heath & Co., D. C. [Div. of Raytheon] - Lexington, MA - *ArtMar 84; AvMarPl 83; LitMarPl 83, 84; WritMar 84*
Heath Canada Ltd., D. C. - Don Mills, ON, Canada - *LitMarPl 84*
Heath Canada Ltd., D. C. - Toronto, ON, Canada - *LitMarPl 83*
Heath Co. [Subs. of Zenith Radio Corp.] - Benton Harbor, MI - *WhoWMicrocom 83*
Heath Co. [Subs. of Zenith Radio Corp.] - St. Joseph, MI - *WritMar 84*
Heath on Target - *See* Heath Ace News Publishers
Heathcote Publishers - Monmouth Junction, NJ - *BoPubDir 4, 5*
Heather Foundation - San Pedro, CA - *BoPubDir 4, 5*
Heathkit Online Catalog - Benton Harbor, MI - *DirOnDB Spring 84*
Heathsville Northumberland Echo - *See* Atlantic Publications
Heating & Plumbing Product News [of Gordon Publications Inc.] - Dover, NJ - *BaconPubCkMag 84; MagDir 84*
Heating & Plumbing Product News - Morristown, NJ - *MagIndMarPl 82-83*
Heating/Combustion Equipment News - New York, NY - *BaconPubCkMag 84; MagDir 84*
Heating/Piping/Air Conditioning [of Reinhold Publishing] - Chicago, IL - *BaconPubCkMag 84; MagDir 84*
Heating, Plumbing, Air Conditioning - Don Mills, ON, Canada - *BaconPubCkMag 84; WritMar 84*
Heavener Ledger - Heavener, OK - *BaconPubCkNews 84; Ed&PubIntYB 82*
Heavenly Romances Book Club [Subs. of JSD Corp.] - New York, NY - *LitMarPl 84*
Heavy Construction News - Toronto, ON, Canada - *BaconPubCkMag 84*
Heavy-Duty Distribution - Deerfield, IL - *BaconPubCkMag 84; MagDir 84*
Heavy Duty Marketing [of Babcox Publications] - Akron, OH - *BaconPubCkMag 84; MagIndMarPl 82-83; WritMar 84*
Heavy Duty Trucking [of HIC Corp.] - Newport Beach, CA - *BaconPubCkMag 84; MagDir 84; MagIndMarPl 82-83*
Heavy Evidence Press - Menomonie, WI - *LitMag&SmPr 83-84*
Heavy Evidence Press - Milwaukee, WI - *BoPubDir 4, 5*
Heavy Evidence/Soft Times - Milwaukee, WI - *LitMag&SmPr 83-84*
Heavy Fuel Oils [of I. P. Sharp Associates Ltd.] - Toronto, ON, Canada - *DataDirOnSer 84*
Heavy Jamin' Music - Nashville, TN - *BillIntBG 83-84*
Heavy Metal - New York, NY - *ArtMar 84*
Heavy Oil/Enhanced Recovery Index [of QL Systems Ltd.] - Ottawa, ON, Canada - *DataDirOnSer 84*
Heavyduty Marketing - Akron, OH - *MagDir 84*
Hebbronville Enterprise - Hebbronville, TX - *Ed&PubIntYB 82*
Hebbronville Jim Hogg County Enterprise - Hebbronville, TX - *BaconPubCkNews 84*
Hebdo Comiques - Ottawa, ON, Canada - *Ed&PubIntYB 82*
Hebdo de Portneuf - Donnacona, PQ, Canada - *Ed&PubIntYB 82*
Hebdo du Cap - Cap-de-la-Madeleine, PQ, Canada - *Ed&PubIntYB 82*
Hebdo du St. Maurice - Shawinigan, PQ, Canada - *Ed&PubIntYB 82*
Hebdo Flambeau - Montreal, PQ, Canada - *Ed&PubIntYB 82*
Hebdo Guide du Nord - Montreal, PQ, Canada - *Ed&PubIntYB 82*
Hebdo Journal de Rosemont - Montreal, PQ, Canada - *Ed&PubIntYB 82*
Hebdo l'Avenir de l'Est - Montreal, PQ, Canada - *Ed&PubIntYB 82*
Hebdo Nouvelles de l'Est - Montreal, PQ, Canada - *Ed&PubIntYB 82*
Hebdo St. Leonard & New Rosemont - Montreal, PQ, Canada - *Ed&PubIntYB 82*
Heber Springs Arkansas Sun - Heber Springs, AR - *BaconPubCkNews 84*
Heber Springs Cleburne County Times - Heber Springs, AR - *BaconPubCkNews 84*
Heber Wasatch Wave - Heber, UT - *BaconPubCkNews 84*
Hebert, Henry - Caribou, ME - *Tel&CabFB 84C p.1684*
Hebrew Journal - Toronto, ON, Canada - *Ed&PubIntYB 82*
Hebrew Publishing Co. - Brooklyn, NY - *LitMarPl 83, 84*
Hebrew Translation Service - New York, NY - *MagIndMarPl 82-83*
Hebrew Union College Press - Cincinnati, OH - *BoPubDir 5*
Hebron Cable TV Inc. - Belleville, NE - *BrCabYB 84*

Hebron Herald - Hebron, ND - *BaconPubCkNews 84; Ed&PubIntYB 82*
Hebron Journal Register - Hebron, NE - *BaconPubCkNews 84; Ed&PubIntYB 82*
Hebron Porter County Herald - *See* Porter County Publishing Co.
Hecate - St. Lucia, Australia - *LitMag&SmPr 83-84*
Hecate Press - St. Lucia, Australia - *LitMag&SmPr 83-84*
Hecht & Partners Inc., Arthur - New York, NY - *StaDirAdAg 2-84*
Hecht Communications Group - Chicago, IL - *DirPRFirms 83*
Hecht Production & Direction Services, Albert D. - West Orange, NJ - *AvMarPl 83*
Heck, Delmer - Armstrong, IA - *Tel&CabFB 84C p.1684*
Heckman Bindery Inc., The - North Manchester, IN - *LitMarPl 83, 84*
Hecla Independent - *See* Maple River Publishing Inc.
Heclinet - Berlin, West Germany - *DirOnDB Spring 84*
HECOM Corp. - Trinton Falls, NJ - *DirInfWP 82*
Hector Agency, Shirley - New York, NY - *LitMarPl 83, 84*
Hector Mirror - Hector, MN - *Ed&PubIntYB 82*
Hector News Mirror - Hector, MN - *BaconPubCkNews 84*
Hedberg Broadcasting Group - Blue Earth, MN - *BrCabYB 84*
Hedge & Associates Inc., Michael - Troy, MI - *DirPRFirms 83*
Hedgepeth Re-Views - Lansing, KS - *LitMarPl 83, 84*
Hedgerow House Publishing Co. Inc. - New York, NY - *ArtMar 84*
Hedges Music, Michael - *See* Windham Hill Music
Hedley Informer - Hedley, TX - *Ed&PubIntYB 82*
Hedrick Journal - Hedrick, IA - *Ed&PubIntYB 82*
Hedrick Journal - *See* Quad County Newspapers
Heffernan Press Inc. - Worcester, MA - *LitMarPl 83, 84; MagIndMarPl 82-83*
Heffernan School Supply Co. Inc. - San Antonio, TX - *AvMarPl 83*
Heffner & Cook Inc. - Richmond, VA - *StaDirAdAg 2-84*
Heflin Cable Vision - Heflin, AL - *BrCabYB 84*
Heflin Cleburne News - Heflin, AL - *BaconPubCkNews 84; NewsDir 84*
Heftel Broadcasting Corp. - Honolulu, HI - *BrCabYB 84*
Hege, Middleton & Neal Inc. - Greensboro, NC - *StaDirAdAg 2-84*
Hegeler Institute, The - LaSalle, IL - *LitMag&SmPr 83-84*
Hegewisch News, The - Chicago, IL - *AyerDirPub 83*
HEH Associates - Weston, CT - *EISS 7-83 Sup*
Heian International Inc. - South San Francisco, CA - *LitMarPl 83, 84*
Heico [Div. of Whittaker Corp.] - Delaware Water Gap, PA - *AvMarPl 83*
Heidelberg - San Francisco, CA - *LitMag&SmPr 83-84*
Heidelberg Eastern Inc. [Subs. of The East Asiatic Co. Inc.] - Glendale, NY - *LitMarPl 83, 84*
Heidelberg Graphics - Chico, CA - *BoPubDir 4 Sup, 5; LitMag&SmPr 83-84; LitMarPl 83, 84*
Heidelberg Publishers Inc. - Austin, TX - *BoPubDir 4, 5*
Heidenreich House - Fair Oaks, CA - *BoPubDir 4, 5*
Heidrick & Struggles - Chicago, IL - *BoPubDir 5*
Heights Herald - Peoria Heights, IL - *AyerDirPub 83; Ed&PubIntYB 82*
Heights Information Technology Services Inc. - Elmsford, NY - *ADAPSOMemDir 83-84*
Heilman Photography, Grant - Lititz, PA - *AvMarPl 83; LitMarPl 83; MagIndMarPl 82-83*
Heiltsuk Cable Commission - Bella Bella, BC, Canada - *BrCabYB 84*
Hein & Co. Inc., William S. - Buffalo, NY - *BoPubDir 4, 5; MicroMarPl 82-83*
Heine, Robert A. - New York, NY - *MagIndMarPl 82-83*
Heinecken & Associates Ltd. - Chicago, IL - *LitMarPl 83, 84*
Heineman Inc., James H. - New York, NY - *BoPubDir 4, 5*
Heinemann Educational Books Inc. [Subs. of Heinemann Holdings Inc.] - Exeter, NH - *LitMarPl 83, 84*
Heinemann Publisher's Ltd. - Auckland, New Zealand - *LitMag&SmPr 83-84*
Heinemann, William - North Pomfret, VT - *LitMarPl 83, 84*
Heinle & Heinle Enterprises - Concord, MA - *LitMarPl 83, 84*
Heinle & Heinle Publishers Inc. [Subs. of Science Books International Inc.] - Boston, MA - *LitMarPl 83, 84; WritMar 84*
Heinman Imported Books, W. S. - New York, NY - *LitMarPl 83, 84*
Heinold Commodity Reports - Chicago, IL - *DirOnDB Spring 84*
Heinrichshofen Editor, New York - *See* Peters Corp., C. F.
Heins Publications - Eau Claire, WI - *Ed&PubIntYB 82*
Heins Telephone Co. Inc. [Aff. of The Heins Co.] - Sanford, NC - *TelDir&BG 83-84*
Heintz Interviewing Service, Carol J. - Erie, PA - *IntDirMarRes 83*
Heirs International - San Francisco, CA - *BoPubDir 4, 5*
Heising & Wilhelm - Concord, CA - *BoPubDir 4 Sup, 5*
Heitner/Uniphoto, Marty - New York, NY - *AvMarPl 83*
Heitz Inc., Karl - New York, NY - *DirInfWP 82*
Heitz Inc., Karl - Woodside, NY - *AvMarPl 83*
Heitzman Advertising - Seattle, WA - *StaDirAdAg 2-84*
Hekimian Laboratories Inc. - Gaithersburg, MD - *DataDirSup 7-83*
Helaine Victoria Press Inc. - Martinsville, IN - *LitMag&SmPr 83-84*
Helander, Joel E. - Guilford, CT - *BoPubDir 4, 5*
Heldref Publications [Subs. of Helen Dwight Reid Educational Foundation] - Washington, DC - *DirMarMP 83; MagIndMarPl 82-83*
Helena Cable TV [of Community Tele-Communications Inc.] - Helena, MT - *BrCabYB 84; Tel&CabFB 84C*
Helena Cable TV [of Teleservice Corp. of America] - Tyler, TX - *BrCabYB 84*
Helena Independent Record - Helena, MT - *BaconPubCkNews 84*
Helena-West Helena World [of Park Newspapers] - Helena, AR - *BaconPubCkNews 84; Ed&PubIntYB 82; NewsDir 84*
Helicon Corp. - Englewood Cliffs, NJ - *BrCabYB 84 p.D-302; Tel&CabFB 84C p.1684*
Helicon Music Corp. - *See* European American Corp.
Helicon Nine - Kansas City, MO - *LitMag&SmPr 83-84*
Helicopter Association International - Washington, DC - *BoPubDir 4, 5*
Helicopter News - Bethesda, MD - *BaconPubCkMag 84*
Helikon Press - New York, NY - *BoPubDir 4, 5; LitMag&SmPr 83-84*
Helios [of Questel Inc.] - Washington, DC - *DataDirOnSer 84*
Helios - Paris, France - *DirOnDB Spring 84*
Helios Book Publishing Co. Inc. - New York, NY - *BoPubDir 4, 5*
Helios Music Corp. - New York, NY - *BillIntBG 83-84*
Helix House Publishers - La Mesa, CA - *BoPubDir 4, 5; LitMag&SmPr 83-84*
Helix Telephone Co. - Helix, OR - *TelDir&BG 83-84*
Hellenic Chronicle - Boston, MA - *AyerDirPub 83; Ed&PubIntYB 82*
Hellenic College (Holy Cross Orthodox Press) - Brookline, MA - *BoPubDir 4, 5*
Hellenic Free Press - Toronto, ON, Canada - *Ed&PubIntYB 82*
Hellenic Postman, The - Montreal, PQ, Canada - *Ed&PubIntYB 82*
Hellenic Times - New York, NY - *AyerDirPub 83; Ed&PubIntYB 82; NewsDir 84*
Hellenic View - Vancouver, BC, Canada - *Ed&PubIntYB 82*
Heller & Co. Inc., Lee - Melville, NY - *StaDirAdAg 2-84*
Heller & Son Inc., Richard - New Rochelle, NY - *LitMarPl 83, 84*
Heller Corp. - North Hollywood, CA - *Tel&CabFB 84C*
Heller, Marjorie K. - Bayside, NY - *BoPubDir 4, 5*
Heller Research Corp., Harry - Port Washington, NY - *HBIndAd&MS 82-83; IntDirMarRes 83*
Hellinger Enterprises - West Hollywood, CA - *BoPubDir 4, 5*
Hellman Animates Ltd. - Waterloo, IA - *AvMarPl 83*
Hello Love Music - New York, NY - *BillIntBG 83-84*
Hello There! Music Publishing - *See* Ahlert Music Corp., Fred
Helm Data Processing Inc. - Arcata, CA - *ADAPSOMemDir 83-84*
Helm Publishing - Las Vegas, NV - *BoPubDir 4, 5*
Helminthological Abstracts-A & B [of Commonwealth Institute of Helminthology] - St. Albans, England - *CompReadDB 82*
H.E.L.P. Books Inc. - Tucson, AZ - *BoPubDir 4, 5*

Help! Company's Coming - Newport Beach, CA - *BoPubDir 5*
Help Wanted Advertising Corp. - Boston, MA - *StaDirAdAg 2-84*
Helpis - London, England - *DirOnDB Spring 84*
Helsingin Kauppakorkeakoulu Kirjaston - Helsinki, Finland - *InfIndMarPl 83*
Helsingin Teknillisen Korkeakoulun Kirjasto - Espoo, Finland - *InfIndMarPl 83*
Helsinki School of Economics Library - Helsinki, Finland - *CompReadDB 82*
Helsinki University of Technology Library - Espoo, Finland - *EISS 83*
Helu Corp. - Aiea, HI - *MicrocomMPl 83*
Helu Corp. - Honolulu, HI - *MicrocomMPl 84*
Hemdale Leisure Corp. - New York, NY - *Tel&CabFB 84C*
Hemenway Corp. - Boston, MA - *MicrocomMPl 83, 84; MicrocomSwDir 1; WhoWMicrocom 83*
Hemet East Pennysaver - Mission Viejo, CA - *AyerDirPub 83*
Hemet News - Hemet, CA - *BaconPubCkNews 84; Ed&PubIntYB 82; NewsDir 84*
Hemet North San Jose Jacinto Pennysaver - Mission Viejo, CA - *AyerDirPub 83*
Hemet South Pennysaver - Mission Viejo, CA - *AyerDirPub 83*
Heminger Advertising - Michigan City, IN - *StaDirAdAg 2-84*
Hemingford Cooperative Telephone Co., The - Hemingford, NE - *TelDir&BG 83-84*
Hemingford Ledger - Hemingford, NE - *BaconPubCkNews 84*
Hemingway Weekly Observer - Hemingway, SC - *BaconPubCkNews 84*
Heminway Corp. [Subs. of Design-Pak Inc.] - Waterbury, CT - *LitMarPl 83, 84*
Hemisphere House Books - Corpus Christi, TX - *LitMarPl 83*
Hemisphere Publishing Corp. - Washington, DC - *MagIndMarPl 82-83*
Hemisphere Publishing Corp. - New York, NY - *LitMarPl 83*
Hemisphere Publishing Corp. (Acquisitions, Marketing, & Book Sales Div.) - New York, NY - *LitMarPl 84*
Hemisphere Steel Products Corp. (Port-A-Wall Div.) - Brooklyn, NY - *DirInfWP 82*
Hemlock Quarterly - Los Angeles, CA - *LitMag&SmPr 83-84*
Hemlocks & Balsams - Banner Elk, NC - *LitMag&SmPr 83-84*
Hemming & Gilman Inc. - New York, NY - *DirPRFirms 83*
Hemmings Motor News [of Watering Inc.] - Bennington, VT - *BoPubDir 4, 5; DirMarMP 83*
Hemphill Music - *See* Paragon/Benson Publishing Group
Hemphill Sabine County Reporter - Hemphill, TX - *BaconPubCkNews 84*
Hempstead Beacon [of Nassau County Publication] - Hempstead, NY - *NewsDir 84*
Hempstead Beacon - *See* Nassau County Publication
Hempstead Courier - Uniondale, NY - *NewsDir 84*
Hempstead Long Island Examiner - Hempstead, NY - *BaconPubCkNews 84*
Hempstead News, The - Hempstead, TX - *Ed&PubIntYB 82*
Hempstead Pennysaver - Freeport, NY - *AyerDirPub 83*
Hempstead Waller County News-Citizen - Hempstead, TX - *BaconPubCkNews 84*
Hempstone Syndicate, The - Bethesda, MD - *Ed&PubIntYB 82; LitMarPl 84*
Hemsing Advertising - Ferndale, MI - *StaDirAdAg 2-84*
Henco Software Inc. - Waltham, MA - *DataDirSup 7-83*
Hendershot & Associates - South Bend, IN - *StaDirAdAg 2-84*
Hendershot Bibliography - Bay City, MI - *BoPubDir 4, 5*
Henderson Advertising - Greenville, SC - *AdAge 3-28-84; StaDirAdAg 2-84; TelAl 83, 84*
Henderson, Albert - Bridgeport, CT - *LitMarPl 83, 84*
Henderson Books, T. Emmett - Middletown, NY - *ArtMar 84; BoPubDir 4, 5*
Henderson Cable TV [of Group W Cable Inc.] - Henderson, TN - *BrCabYB 84; Tel&CabFB 84C*
Henderson Cable TV [of Texas Community Antenna Inc.] - Henderson, TX - *BrCabYB 84*
Henderson CATV Inc. - Henderson, NC - *Tel&CabFB 84C*
Henderson CATV Inc. - Oxford, NC - *BrCabYB 84*
Henderson Chester County Independent - Henderson, TN - *BaconPubCkNews 84*
Henderson County Quill - Stronghurst, IL - *AyerDirPub 83; Ed&PubIntYB 82*
Henderson Daily Dispatch - Henderson, NC - *BaconPubCkNews 84; Ed&PubIntYB 82; NewsDir 84*
Henderson Direct [Subs. of Henderson Advertising Inc.] - Greenville, SC - *DirMarMP 83*
Henderson Friedlich Graf & Doyle Inc. - New York, NY - *StaDirAdAg 2-84*
Henderson Gleaner - Henderson, KY - *BaconPubCkNews 84; NewsDir 84*
Henderson Home News - Henderson, NV - *AyerDirPub 83; BaconPubCkNews 84; Ed&PubIntYB 82*
Henderson Inc., Dale - Houston, TX - *DirPRFirms 83*
Henderson Independent - Henderson, MN - *BaconPubCkNews 84; Ed&PubIntYB 82*
Henderson, Linda V. [Div. of The Complete Satellite Office for Creative & Technical Writers] - Fresno, CA - *LitMarPl 84*
Henderson News - Henderson, NE - *BaconPubCkNews 84; Ed&PubIntYB 82*
Henderson News - Henderson, TX - *BaconPubCkNews 84; Ed&PubIntYB 82; NewsDir 84*
Henderson Telephone Co. - Henderson, NE - *TelDir&BG 83-84*
Henderson Telephone Co. (CATV Div.) - Henderson, NE - *Tel&CabFB 84C*
Hendersonville Free Press - Hendersonville, TN - *AyerDirPub 83; NewsDir 84*
Hendersonville Star-News - Hendersonville, TN - *BaconPubCkNews 84; NewsDir 84*
Hendersonville Times-News - Hendersonville, NC - *NewsDir 84*
Hendra Associates Inc., Barbara J. - New York, NY - *DirPRFirms 83; LitMarPl 83, 84*
Hendrick-Long Publishing Co. - Dallas, TX - *BoPubDir 4 Sup, 5*
Hendricks Advertising - Atlanta, GA - *StaDirAdAg 2-84*
Hendricks Cable TV Inc. - Hendricks, MN - *BrCabYB 84*
Hendricks County Flyer - Plainfield, IN - *Ed&PubIntYB 82*
Hendricks House Inc. - Putney, VT - *BoPubDir 4, 5*
Hendricks Pioneer - Hendricks, MN - *BaconPubCkNews 84; Ed&PubIntYB 82*
Hendrix Electronics - Manchester, NH - *DataDirSup 7-83; DirInfWP 82*
Hendrix Electronics - *See* HASTECH Inc.
Hendrix Enterprises, James - Nashville, TN - *BillIntBG 83-84*
Heninger, John M. - Bristol, VA - *LitMarPl 83, 84*
Henkle Audio-Visuals - Lincoln, NE - *AvMarPl 83*
Henlein, L. - Cambridge, MA - *LitMarPl 83, 84*
Henley Centre for Forecasting - London, England - *EISS 83*
Henley Productions, Arthur - New York, NY - *TelAl 83, 84*
Hennepin County Library Cataloging Bulletin - Minnetonka, MN - *LitMag&SmPr 83-84*
Hennessey Clipper - Hennessey, OK - *BaconPubCkNews 84; Ed&PubIntYB 82*
Hennessey Co., D. L. - Berkeley, CA - *BoPubDir 4, 5*
Hennessy, Eileen B. - New York, NY - *LitMarPl 83, 84; MagIndMarPl 82-83*
Henning Advocate - Henning, MN - *BaconPubCkNews 84; Ed&PubIntYB 82*
Henning Cable TV - Henning, MN - *BrCabYB 84*
Henning, William L. - *See* Cameron Telephone Co.
Hennok Ltd., Jim A. - Toronto, ON, Canada - *BoPubDir 4, 5*
Henrickson-Renner, Jeanne - New York, NY - *DirInfWP 82*
Henrietta Clay County Leader - Henrietta, TX - *BaconPubCkNews 84*
Henrietta Post - Henrietta, NY - *AyerDirPub 83; Ed&PubIntYB 82*
Henrietta Post [of Wolfe Publications Inc.] - Pittsford, NY - *NewsDir 84*
Henrietta Post - *See* Wolfe Publications Inc.
Henry County Herald, The - McDonough, GA - *AyerDirPub 83*
Henry County Journal [of Eastern Shore News Inc.] - Accomac, VA - *NewsDir 84*
Henry County Local - New Castle, KY - *AyerDirPub 83; Ed&PubIntYB 82*
Henry County News Republican - New Castle, IN - *AyerDirPub 83*
Henry County Review - Holgate, OH - *AyerDirPub 83; Ed&PubIntYB 82*
Henry County Telephone Co. - Geneseo, IL - *TelDir&BG 83-84*
Henry-Gill Inc. - Denver, CO - *StaDirAdAg 2-84*

Henry Herald, The [of Henry County Newspapers Inc.] - McDonough, GA - *Ed&PubIntYB 82; NewsDir 84*
Henry Inc., Leon - Scarsdale, NY - *MagIndMarPl 82-83*
Henry Neighbor - Henry, GA - *Ed&PubIntYB 82*
Henry Neighbor - Marietta, GA - *AyerDirPub 83*
Henry News-Republican - Henry, IL - *BaconPubCkNews 84; Ed&PubIntYB 82; NewsDir 84*
Henry Photography, Diana Mara - New York, NY - *LitMarPl 83, 84; MagIndMarPl 82-83*
Henry Printing Co., Charles M. - Greensburg, PA - *MagIndMarPl 82-83*
Henryetta Free-Lance [of Times Publishing Co.] - Henryetta, OK - *BaconPubCkNews 84; Ed&PubIntYB 82; NewsDir 84*
Henschel Manufacturing Co., C. B. - New Berlin, WI - *LitMarPl 83, 84*
Hensley, Charles W. - Waco, TX - *LitMarPl 83, 84*
Henson Broadcasting Co. - Louisville, KY - *BrCabYB 84*
Henson, J. M. - *See* Lillenas Publishing Co.
Hepburn Co., The Ted - Cincinnati, OH - *CabTVFinDB 83*
Heppner Gazette-Times - Heppner, OR - *BaconPubCkNews 84; Ed&PubIntYB 82*
Heppner TV Inc. - Heppner, OR - *BrCabYB 84; Tel&CabFB 84C*
Heptangle Books - Berkeley Heights, NJ - *BoPubDir 4, 5*
Hepworth Advertising Co. - Dallas, TX - *ArtMar 84; StaDirAdAg 2-84*
Her Majesty's Stationery Office - Norwich, England - *MicroMarPl 82-83*
Her Publishing - Gretna, LA - *BoPubDir 4, 5*
Her Say News Service - San Francisco, CA - *BrCabYB 84*
Her Street Journal, The - Ft. Collins, CO - *LitMag&SmPr 83-84*
Herald - Abbeville, AL - *AyerDirPub 83*
Herald - Union Springs, AL - *AyerDirPub 83*
Herald - Wetumpka, AL - *AyerDirPub 83*
Herald - Lake Havasu City, AZ - *AyerDirPub 83*
Herald - Nogales, AZ - *AyerDirPub 83; BaconPubCkNews 84; Ed&PubIntYB 82*
Herald - Calipatria, CA - *AyerDirPub 83*
Herald - Carpinteria, CA - *AyerDirPub 83*
Herald - El Segundo, CA - *AyerDirPub 83*
Herald - Fillmore, CA - *AyerDirPub 83*
Herald - Gridley, CA - *AyerDirPub 83*
Herald - Linden, CA - *AyerDirPub 83*
Herald - Mt. Shasta, CA - *AyerDirPub 83*
Herald - Sanger, CA - *AyerDirPub 83*
Herald - Westminster, CA - *AyerDirPub 83*
Herald - Durango, CO - *AyerDirPub 83*
Herald - Haxtun, CO - *AyerDirPub 83*
Herald - Meeker, CO - *AyerDirPub 83*
Herald - Cheshire, CT - *AyerDirPub 83*
Herald - New Britain, CT - *AyerDirPub 83; BaconPubCkNews 84; Ed&PubIntYB 82*
Herald - Bradenton, FL - *AyerDirPub 83*
Herald - Englewood, FL - *AyerDirPub 83*
Herald - Haines City, FL - *AyerDirPub 83*
Herald - Havana, FL - *AyerDirPub 83*
Herald - High Springs, FL - *AyerDirPub 83*
Herald - Jacksonville, FL - *AyerDirPub 83; Ed&PubIntYB 82*
Herald - Miami, FL - *AyerDirPub 83*
Herald - Sanford, FL - *AyerDirPub 83*
Herald - Albany, GA - *AyerDirPub 83; Ed&PubIntYB 82*
Herald - Augusta, GA - *AyerDirPub 83; Ed&PubIntYB 82; LitMarPl 84*
Herald - Savannah, GA - *AyerDirPub 83*
Herald - Springfield, GA - *AyerDirPub 83; Ed&PubIntYB 82*
Herald - Ashton, ID - *AyerDirPub 83*
Herald - Buhl, ID - *AyerDirPub 83*
Herald - Atwood, IL - *AyerDirPub 83*
Herald - Chicago, IL - *AyerDirPub 83; Ed&PubIntYB 82*
Herald - Collinsville, IL - *AyerDirPub 83*
Herald - Crystal Lake, IL - *AyerDirPub 83*
Herald - Elburn, IL - *AyerDirPub 83*
Herald - Harvard, IL - *AyerDirPub 83*
Herald - Hutsonville, IL - *AyerDirPub 83*
Herald - Marshall, IL - *AyerDirPub 83*
Herald - Mascoutah, IL - *AyerDirPub 83*
Herald - Metamora, IL - *AyerDirPub 83; Ed&PubIntYB 82*
Herald - Morris, IL - *AyerDirPub 83; Ed&PubIntYB 82*
Herald - Park Ridge, IL - *AyerDirPub 83*
Herald - Anderson, IN - *AyerDirPub 83*
Herald - Columbus, IN - *AyerDirPub 83*
Herald - Indianapolis, IN - *Ed&PubIntYB 82*
Herald - Liberty, IN - *AyerDirPub 83*
Herald - Madison, IN - *AyerDirPub 83*
Herald - Montpelier, IN - *AyerDirPub 83*
Herald - Clinton, IA - *AyerDirPub 83*
Herald - Hudson, IA - *AyerDirPub 83*
Herald - Jefferson, IA - *AyerDirPub 83*
Herald - Oskaloosa, IA - *Ed&PubIntYB 82*
Herald - Pomeroy, IA - *AyerDirPub 83*
Herald - Postville, IA - *AyerDirPub 83*
Herald - Seymour, IA - *AyerDirPub 83*
Herald - Swea City, IA - *AyerDirPub 83*
Herald - Dighton, KS - *AyerDirPub 83*
Herald - Oberlin, KS - *AyerDirPub 83*
Herald - Ottawa, KS - *AyerDirPub 83; Ed&PubIntYB 82*
Herald - Sabetha, KS - *AyerDirPub 83*
Herald - St. Francis, KS - *AyerDirPub 83*
Herald - Harrodsburg, KY - *AyerDirPub 83*
Herald - Lexington, KY - *AyerDirPub 83*
Herald - Paintsville, KY - *AyerDirPub 83*
Herald - Kaplan, LA - *AyerDirPub 83*
Herald - Hagerstown, MD - *AyerDirPub 83*
Herald - Belmont, MA - *AyerDirPub 83*
Herald - Fennville, MI - *AyerDirPub 83*
Herald - Minden City, MI - *AyerDirPub 83*
Herald - Ontonagon, MI - *AyerDirPub 83*
Herald - South Lyon, MI - *AyerDirPub 83*
Herald - Tecumseh, MI - *AyerDirPub 83*
Herald - Amboy, MN - *AyerDirPub 83*
Herald - Austin, MN - *AyerDirPub 83*
Herald - Bertha, MN - *AyerDirPub 83*
Herald - Clara City, MN - *AyerDirPub 83*
Herald - Duluth, MN - *AyerDirPub 83*
Herald - Hanska, MN - *AyerDirPub 83*
Herald - Hawley, MN - *AyerDirPub 83*
Herald - Hayfield, MN - *AyerDirPub 83*
Herald - Howard Lake, MN - *AyerDirPub 83*
Herald - New York Mills, MN - *AyerDirPub 83*
Herald - Oklee, MN - *AyerDirPub 83*
Herald - Sauk Centre, MN - *AyerDirPub 83*
Herald - Spring Grove, MN - *AyerDirPub 83*
Herald - St. Peter, MN - *AyerDirPub 83*
Herald - Biloxi, MS - *AyerDirPub 83*
Herald - Yazoo City, MS - *AyerDirPub 83*
Herald [of Nevada Publishing Co.] - Nevada, MO - *AyerDirPub 83; NewsDir 84*
Herald - Ste. Genevieve, MO - *AyerDirPub 83*
Herald - Plentywood, MT - *AyerDirPub 83*
Herald - Ansley, NE - *AyerDirPub 83*
Herald - Chester, NE - *AyerDirPub 83*
Herald - Springview, NE - *AyerDirPub 83*
Herald - Mt. Holly, NJ - *Ed&PubIntYB 82*
Herald - Summit, NJ - *AyerDirPub 83*
Herald - Truth or Consequences, NM - *AyerDirPub 83; Ed&PubIntYB 82*
Herald - Hancock, NY - *AyerDirPub 83*
Herald - Red Creek, NY - *AyerDirPub 83*
Herald - Durham, NC - *AyerDirPub 83*
Herald - Roanoke Rapids, NC - *AyerDirPub 83*
Herald - Robersonville, NC - *AyerDirPub 83*
Herald - Sanford, NC - *AyerDirPub 83*
Herald - Smithfield, NC - *AyerDirPub 83*
Herald - Grand Forks, ND - *AyerDirPub 83*
Herald - Harvey, ND - *AyerDirPub 83*
Herald - Williston, ND - *AyerDirPub 83*
Herald - Ada, OH - *AyerDirPub 83*
Herald - Barberton, OH - *AyerDirPub 83*
Herald - Cincinnati, OH - *AyerDirPub 83*
Herald - Circleville, OH - *AyerDirPub 83; Ed&PubIntYB 82*
Herald - Delphos, OH - *AyerDirPub 83*
Herald - Fairborn, OH - *AyerDirPub 83*
Herald - Louisville, OH - *AyerDirPub 83*
Herald - Loveland, OH - *AyerDirPub 83*
Herald - New Washington, OH - *AyerDirPub 83*

Herald - Tipp City, OH - *AyerDirPub 83*
Herald - Utica, OH - *AyerDirPub 83*
Herald - Carnegie, OK - *AyerDirPub 83*
Herald - Fletcher, OK - *AyerDirPub 83*
Herald - Guymon, OK - *AyerDirPub 83; Ed&PubIntYB 82*
Herald - Sapulpa, OK - *AyerDirPub 83*
Herald - Wakita, OK - *AyerDirPub 83*
Herald - Walters, OK - *AyerDirPub 83*
Herald - Myrtle Point, OR - *AyerDirPub 83*
Herald - Sharon, PA - *AyerDirPub 83; Ed&PubIntYB 82*
Herald - Sharpsburg, PA - *AyerDirPub 83; Ed&PubIntYB 82*
Herald - Shenandoah, PA - *AyerDirPub 83*
Herald - Titusville, PA - *AyerDirPub 83*
Herald - Clover, SC - *AyerDirPub 83*
Herald - Dillon, SC - *AyerDirPub 83*
Herald - Rock Hill, SC - *AyerDirPub 83*
Herald - Spartanburg, SC - *AyerDirPub 83*
Herald - Alexandria, SD - *AyerDirPub 83*
Herald - Canova, SD - *AyerDirPub 83*
Herald - Montrose, SD - *AyerDirPub 83*
Herald - Collierville, TN - *AyerDirPub 83*
Herald - Columbia, TN - *AyerDirPub 83*
Herald - Alto, TX - *AyerDirPub 83*
Herald - Big Spring, TX - *AyerDirPub 83*
Herald - Brady, TX - *AyerDirPub 83*
Herald - Cameron, TX - *AyerDirPub 83*
Herald - Canton, TX - *AyerDirPub 83*
Herald - Denison, TX - *AyerDirPub 83*
Herald - Dilley, TX - *AyerDirPub 83*
Herald - Edna, TX - *AyerDirPub 83*
Herald - Hamlin, TX - *AyerDirPub 83*
Herald - Kaufman, TX - *AyerDirPub 83*
Herald - Mart, TX - *AyerDirPub 83*
Herald - Panhandle, TX - *AyerDirPub 83*
Herald - Perryton, TX - *AyerDirPub 83*
Herald - Plainview, TX - *AyerDirPub 83*
Herald - San Antonio, TX - *Ed&PubIntYB 82*
Herald - Universal City, TX - *AyerDirPub 83*
Herald - Provo, UT - *AyerDirPub 83*
Herald - Springville, UT - *AyerDirPub 83*
Herald - Rutland, VT - *AyerDirPub 83*
Herald - Farmville, VA - *AyerDirPub 83*
Herald - Bellingham, WA - *AyerDirPub 83*
Herald - Concrete, WA - *AyerDirPub 83*
Herald - Grandview, WA - *AyerDirPub 83*
Herald - Pullman, WA - *AyerDirPub 83*
Herald - Piedmont, WV - *AyerDirPub 83*
Herald - Iola, WI - *AyerDirPub 83*
Herald - Markesan, WI - *AyerDirPub 83*
Herald - Park Falls, WI - *AyerDirPub 83*
Herald - Sparta, WI - *AyerDirPub 83*
Herald - Wausau, WI - *AyerDirPub 83*
Herald - Hanna, WY - *AyerDirPub 83*
Herald - Lusk, WY - *AyerDirPub 83*
Herald - Calgary, AB, Canada - *AyerDirPub 83*
Herald - Hanna, AB, Canada - *AyerDirPub 83; Ed&PubIntYB 82*
Herald - Lethbridge, AB, Canada - *AyerDirPub 83*
Herald - Ponoka, AB, Canada - *AyerDirPub 83*
Herald - Merritt, BC, Canada - *AyerDirPub 83*
Herald - Penticton, BC, Canada - *AyerDirPub 83*
Herald - Dauphin, MB, Canada - *AyerDirPub 83; Ed&PubIntYB 82*
Herald - Miniota, MB, Canada - *Ed&PubIntYB 82*
Herald - Alliston, ON, Canada - *AyerDirPub 83; Ed&PubIntYB 82*
Herald - Dundalk, ON, Canada - *Ed&PubIntYB 82*
Herald - Marmora, ON, Canada - *Ed&PubIntYB 82*
Herald - Pelham, ON, Canada - *Ed&PubIntYB 82*
Herald - Thamesville, ON, Canada - *Ed&PubIntYB 82*
Herald - Herbert, SK, Canada - *AyerDirPub 83*
Herald - Oxbow, SK, Canada - *AyerDirPub 83; Ed&PubIntYB 82*
Herald - Prince Albert, SK, Canada - *AyerDirPub 83*
Herald - Spiritwood, SK, Canada - *AyerDirPub 83*
Herald - Whitewood, SK, Canada - *AyerDirPub 83; Ed&PubIntYB 82*
Herald-Advance - Milbank, SD - *AyerDirPub 83*
Herald-Advertiser - Holly, MI - *AyerDirPub 83*
Herald Advocate - Wauchula, FL - *AyerDirPub 83; Ed&PubIntYB 82*
Herald/Aerial - Millington, MI - *Ed&PubIntYB 82*
Herald American - Boston, MA - *AyerDirPub 83*
Herald-American-Post-Standard [of The Syracuse Newspapers Inc.] - Syracuse, NY - *AyerDirPub 83; Ed&PubIntYB 82; LitMarPl 84*
Herald & Adirondack Tourist - Boonville, NY - *AyerDirPub 83*
Herald & Botetourt County News - Fincastle, VA - *AyerDirPub 83*
Herald & Coastal Observer - Lake Worth, FL - *AyerDirPub 83*
Herald & News - Klamath Falls, OR - *AyerDirPub 83; Ed&PubIntYB 82*
Herald & Review - Decatur, IL - *AyerDirPub 83; Ed&PubIntYB 82*
Herald & Ruralite - Sylva, NC - *AyerDirPub 83*
Herald & Zeitung - New Braunfels, TX - *AyerDirPub 83*
Herald-Argus - La Porte, IN - *AyerDirPub 83*
Herald-Banner - Greenville, TX - *AyerDirPub 83; BaconPubCkNews 84; Ed&PubIntYB 82*
Herald Book Club - Chicago, IL - *LitMarPl 83, 84*
Herald-Chronicle - Winchester, TN - *Ed&PubIntYB 82*
Herald-Citizen - Cookeville, TN - *AyerDirPub 83; BaconPubCkNews 84; Ed&PubIntYB 82*
Herald Coaster - Rosenberg, TX - *AyerDirPub 83; Ed&PubIntYB 82*
Herald-Courier - Bristol, VA - *AyerDirPub 83; Ed&PubIntYB 82*
Herald Courier & Virginia-Tennessean [of Bristol Newspapers Inc.] - Bristol, VA - *Ed&PubIntYB 82; NewsDir 84*
Herald Democrat - Siloam Springs, AR - *AyerDirPub 83; Ed&PubIntYB 82*
Herald-Democrat - Leadville, CO - *AyerDirPub 83; Ed&PubIntYB 82*
Herald-Democrat - Beaver, OK - *AyerDirPub 83*
Herald-Dispatch - Sierra Vista, AZ - *AyerDirPub 83*
Herald Dispatch - Los Angeles, CA - *AyerDirPub 83; Ed&PubIntYB 82*
Herald Dispatch - Denver, CO - *AyerDirPub 83; Ed&PubIntYB 82*
Herald-Dispatch - Sleepy Eye, MN - *AyerDirPub 83*
Herald-Dispatch [of Huntington Publishing Co.] - Huntington, WV - *AyerDirPub 83; Ed&PubIntYB 82; LitMarPl 84*
Herald Dispatch & Bisbee Review - Sierra Vista, AZ - *BaconPubCkNews 84*
Herald-Enterprise - Golconda, IL - *AyerDirPub 83; Ed&PubIntYB 82*
Herald-Enterprise - Hayti, SD - *Ed&PubIntYB 82*
Herald-Examiner - Los Angeles, CA - *AyerDirPub 83*
Herald-Free Press - Bolivar, MO - *Ed&PubIntYB 82*
Herald-Gazette - Trenton, TN - *AyerDirPub 83; Ed&PubIntYB 82*
Herald-Gazette - Bracebridge, ON, Canada - *AyerDirPub 83; Ed&PubIntYB 82*
Herald-Gazette, The - Barnesville, GA - *AyerDirPub 83*
Herald Green Sheet - Sapulpa, OK - *AyerDirPub 83*
Herald House - Independence, MO - *LitMarPl 83, 84*
Herald-Independent - Winnsboro, SC - *AyerDirPub 83*
Herald Information Services [of Wilson & Horton Ltd.] - Auckland, New Zealand - *EISS 83; InfIndMarPl 83*
Herald-Journal - Monticello, IN - *Ed&PubIntYB 82*
Herald-Journal - Clarinda, IA - *AyerDirPub 83*
Herald-Journal - Syracuse, NY - *AyerDirPub 83*
Herald-Journal - Newkirk, OK - *AyerDirPub 83*
Herald-Journal [of Newspaper Management] - Spartanburg, SC - *AyerDirPub 83; NewsDir 84*
Herald-Journal - Logan, UT - *AyerDirPub 83; Ed&PubIntYB 82*
Herald Journal, The - Greensboro, GA - *Ed&PubIntYB 82*
Herald-Leader - Fitzgerald, GA - *AyerDirPub 83; Ed&PubIntYB 82; NewsDir 84*
Herald-Leader - Bellevue, IA - *AyerDirPub 83; Ed&PubIntYB 82*
Herald-Leader - Lexington, KY - *AyerDirPub 83; Ed&PubIntYB 82*
Herald-Leader - Menominee, MI - *AyerDirPub 83; Ed&PubIntYB 82*
Herald-Ledger - Eldora, IA - *AyerDirPub 83*
Herald Ledger - Eddyville, KY - *AyerDirPub 83; Ed&PubIntYB 82*
Herald-Mail - Fairport, NY - *Ed&PubIntYB 82*

Herald-News - Fontana, CA - *AyerDirPub 83; Ed&PubIntYB 82*
Herald-News - Punta Gorda, FL - *AyerDirPub 83*
Herald-News - Joliet, IL - *AyerDirPub 83; Ed&PubIntYB 82*
Herald-News - Milford, IL - *AyerDirPub 83*
Herald-News - Stockton, IL - *AyerDirPub 83*
Herald News - Cayuga, IN - *Ed&PubIntYB 82*
Herald News - Clinton, IN - *AyerDirPub 83*
Herald-News - Edmonton, KY - *AyerDirPub 83*
Herald-News [of Northeast Publishing Inc.] - Fall River, MA - *AyerDirPub 83; Ed&PubIntYB 82; LitMarPl 84*
Herald-News - Roscommon, MI - *AyerDirPub 83*
Herald-News - Wolf Point, MT - *AyerDirPub 83; Ed&PubIntYB 82*
Herald-News - Passaic, NJ - *AyerDirPub 83; BaconPubCkNews 84; Ed&PubIntYB 82*
Herald-News - Dayton, TN - *AyerDirPub 83; NewsDir 84*
Herald News - Hamilton, TX - *AyerDirPub 83; Ed&PubIntYB 82*
Herald-News - Mondovi, WI - *AyerDirPub 83*
Herald News Advertiser - Fontana, CA - *AyerDirPub 83*
Herald-News Publishers Inc. - Wolf Point, MT - *BaconPubCkNews 84; NewsDir 84*
Herald-Observer - Belle Glade, FL - *AyerDirPub 83; Ed&PubIntYB 82*
Herald-Observer - Logan, IA - *AyerDirPub 83*
Herald-Palladium - St. Joseph, MI - *AyerDirPub 83; BaconPubCkNews 84; Ed&PubIntYB 82*
Herald-Patriot - Chariton, IA - *AyerDirPub 83*
Herald-Picture - Florence, AL - *NewsDir 84*
Herald-Post - El Paso, TX - *AyerDirPub 83*
Herald Press - Azusa, CA - *AyerDirPub 83*
Herald-Press - Huntington, IN - *AyerDirPub 83; Ed&PubIntYB 82*
Herald Press [of Mennonite Publishing House] - Scottdale, PA - *LitMarPl 83, 84; WritMar 84*
Herald Press [of Mennonite Publishing House] - Kitchener, ON, Canada - *LitMarPl 83, 84*
Herald-Progress - Ashland, VA - *AyerDirPub 83*
Herald Progress - Hanover County, VA - *Ed&PubIntYB 82*
Herald Publishing Co. - Belmont, MA - *BaconPubCkNews 84*
Herald Publishing Co. - Jacksboro, TX - *BaconPubCkNews 84*
Herald Publishing Corp. - Vinton, VA - *BaconPubCkNews 84*
Herald Record - West Union, WV - *AyerDirPub 83; Ed&PubIntYB 82*
Herald-Republic - Yakima, WA - *AyerDirPub 83*
Herald-Republican - Angola, IN - *AyerDirPub 83; Ed&PubIntYB 82*
Herald-Republican - Houston, MO - *AyerDirPub 83*
Herald-Review - Grand Rapids, MN - *AyerDirPub 83*
Herald-Standard - Uniontown, PA - *AyerDirPub 83; BaconPubCkNews 84; Ed&PubIntYB 82*
Herald-Star - Edinburg, IL - *AyerDirPub 83; Ed&PubIntYB 82*
Herald-Star - Steubenville, OH - *AyerDirPub 83; Ed&PubIntYB 82*
Herald Sun [of Cleveland Sun Newspapers] - Cleveland, OH - *AyerDirPub 83; NewsDir 84*
Herald-Telegram - Chippewa Falls, WI - *AyerDirPub 83; BaconPubCkNews 84*
Herald-Telephone - Bloomington, IN - *AyerDirPub 83; Ed&PubIntYB 82; LitMarPl 84*
Herald, The - Bourbonnais, IL - *Ed&PubIntYB 82*
Herald, The - Melrose Park, IL - *Ed&PubIntYB 82*
Herald, The - Jasper, IN - *AyerDirPub 83; Ed&PubIntYB 82*
Herald, The - Honey Brook, PA - *AyerDirPub 83; Ed&PubIntYB 82*
Herald, The - Monongahela, PA - *AyerDirPub 83*
Herald, The - Oxford, PA - *AyerDirPub 83*
Herald, The - Everett, WA - *AyerDirPub 83; BaconPubCkNews 84; Ed&PubIntYB 82; NewsDir 84*
Herald, The - Whitefish Bay, WI - *Ed&PubIntYB 82*
Herald-Times - Bloomington, IN - *AyerDirPub 83; NewsDir 84*
Herald Times - Gaylord, MI - *AyerDirPub 83; Ed&PubIntYB 82*
Herald-Times - Yoakum, TX - *Ed&PubIntYB 82*
Herald-Times - Walkerton, ON, Canada - *AyerDirPub 83; Ed&PubIntYB 82*
Herald-Times-Reporter - Manitowoc, WI - *AyerDirPub 83; Ed&PubIntYB 82*
Herald-Tribune - Sarasota, FL - *AyerDirPub 83; Ed&PubIntYB 82*
Herald-Tribune [of Cartersville Newspapers Inc.] - Cartersville, GA - *AyerDirPub 83; Ed&PubIntYB 82; NewsDir 84*
Herald-Tribune - Batesville, IN - *AyerDirPub 83; Ed&PubIntYB 82*
Herald-Tribune - Edgemont, SD - *AyerDirPub 83*
Herald Tribune [of Jonesboro Publishing Co. Inc.] - Jonesboro, TN - *AyerDirPub 83; Ed&PubIntYB 82; NewsDir 84*
Herald-Tribune - Grande Prairie, AB, Canada - *AyerDirPub 83; BaconPubCkNews 84*
Herald-Voice - Hazard, KY - *AyerDirPub 83*
Herald-Voice - Belle Center, OH - *AyerDirPub 83; Ed&PubIntYB 82*
Herald-Whig - Quincy, IL - *AyerDirPub 83*
Herb Quarterly - Newfane, VT - *ArtMar 84; WritMar 84*
Herbage Abstracts [of Commonwealth Bureau of Pastures & Field Crops] - Maidenhead, England - *CompReadDB 82*
Herbert Herald - Herbert, SK, Canada - *Ed&PubIntYB 82*
Herbst Investment Trust Fund, Lawrence - Milford, PA - *BillIntBG 83-84*
Herbst, Margaret - New York, NY - *DirPRFirms 83*
Herder, Swanson, Van Hercke - Eden Prairie, MN - *StaDirAdAg 2-84*
Here & Now [of 22 Press] - Wilmington, DE - *LitMag&SmPr 83-84*
Hereford Brand - Hereford, TX - *BaconPubCkNews 84; Ed&PubIntYB 82; NewsDir 84*
Hereford Cablevision Co. - Hereford, TX - *BrCabYB 84; Tel&CabFB 84C*
Hereford Music - Oakland, CA - *BillIntBG 83-84*
Hereld Organization - Lawrenceville, NJ - *BoPubDir 4 Sup, 5*
Here's Life Publishers [Aff. of Campus Crusade for Christ] - San Bernardino, CA - *BoPubDir 4, 5; WritMar 84*
Heresies: A Feminist Publicaton on Art & Politics - New York, NY - *LitMag&SmPr 83-84*
Heresy Press - Newport News, VA - *BoPubDir 4 Sup, 5; LitMag&SmPr 83-84*
Herff Jones - Montgomery, AL - *LitMarPl 83*
HERI - Edmonton, AB, Canada - *DirOnDB Spring 84*
Herington Cablevision [of Multimedia Inc.] - Herington, KS - *BrCabYB 84; Tel&CabFB 84C*
Herington Times - Herington, KS - *BaconPubCkNews 84; Ed&PubIntYB 82*
Herion, Rosalie - Paramus, NJ - *LitMarPl 83, 84; MagIndMarPl 82-83*
Heritage & Destiny - London, England - *LitMag&SmPr 83-84*
Heritage & Southwest Jewish Press - Los Angeles, CA - *AyerDirPub 83*
Heritage Architectural Guides - Victoria, BC, Canada - *BoPubDir 4*
Heritage Books Inc. - Bowie, MD - *BoPubDir 4, 5; WritMar 84*
Heritage Cable TV Inc. - Bedford, IN - *Tel&CabFB 84C*
Heritage Cablevision [of Heritage Communications Inc.] - Red Bay, AL - *BrCabYB 84*
Heritage Cablevision - Buena Vista, CO - *BrCabYB 84*
Heritage Cablevision [of Heritage Communications Inc.] - Frisco, CO - *BrCabYB 84*
Heritage Cablevision [of Heritage Communications Inc.] - Hot Sulphur Springs, CO - *BrCabYB 84*
Heritage Cablevision [of Heritage Communications Inc.] - Lamar, CO - *BrCabYB 84; Tel&CabFB 84C*
Heritage Cablevision [of Heritage Communications Inc.] - Walsenburg, CO - *BrCabYB 84; Tel&CabFB 84C*
Heritage Cablevision [of Heritage Communications Inc.] - Albia, IA - *BrCabYB 84; Tel&CabFB 84C*
Heritage Cablevision [of Heritage Communications Inc.] - Ames, IA - *BrCabYB 84*
Heritage Cablevision [of Heritage Communications Inc.] - Boone, IA - *BrCabYB 84; Tel&CabFB 84C*
Heritage Cablevision [of Heritage Communications Inc.] - Clarinda, IA - *BrCabYB 84*
Heritage Cablevision [of Heritage Communications Inc.] - Clarion, IA - *BrCabYB 84; Tel&CabFB 84C*
Heritage Cablevision [of Heritage Communications Inc.] - Clinton, IA - *BrCabYB 84; Tel&CabFB 84C*
Heritage Cablevision [of Heritage Communications Inc.] - Colfax, IA - *BrCabYB 84; Tel&CabFB 84C*
Heritage Cablevision [of Heritage Communications Inc.] - Corning, IA - *BrCabYB 84*

Heritage Cablevision [of Heritage Communications Inc.] - Creston, IA - *BrCabYB 84*
Heritage Cablevision [of Heritage Communications Inc.] - Denison, IA - *BrCabYB 84*
Heritage Cablevision [of Heritage Communications Inc.] - Des Moines, IA - *BrCabYB 84; Tel&CabFB 84C*
Heritage Cablevision [of Heritage Communications Inc.] - Dexter, IA - *BrCabYB 84*
Heritage Cablevision [of Heritage Communications Inc.] - Eldora, IA - *Tel&CabFB 84C*
Heritage Cablevision [of Heritage Communications Inc.] - Forest City, IA - *BrCabYB 84*
Heritage Cablevision [of Heritage Communications Inc.] - Ft. Dodge, IA - *BrCabYB 84*
Heritage Cablevision - Guthrie Center, IA - *BrCabYB 84*
Heritage Cablevision [of Heritage Communications Inc.] - Indianola, IA - *BrCabYB 84*
Heritage Cablevision [of Heritage Communications Inc.] - Knoxville, IA - *BrCabYB 84*
Heritage Cablevision [of Heritage Communications Inc.] - Lavinia, IA - *Tel&CabFB 84C*
Heritage Cablevision [of Heritage Communications Inc.] - Leon, IA - *BrCabYB 84*
Heritage Cablevision [of Heritage Communications Inc.] - Marshalltown, IA - *BrCabYB 84*
Heritage Cablevision - Mason City, IA - *BrCabYB 84*
Heritage Cablevision [of Heritage Communications Inc.] - Mt. Ayr, IA - *BrCabYB 84*
Heritage Cablevision - Newton, IA - *BrCabYB 84*
Heritage Cablevision [of Heritage Communications Inc.] - Northwood, IA - *BrCabYB 84*
Heritage Cablevision [of Heritage Communications Inc.] - Parkersburg, IA - *Tel&CabFB 84C*
Heritage Cablevision [of Heritage Communications Inc.] - Red Oak, IA - *BrCabYB 84*
Heritage Cablevision [of Heritage Communications Inc.] - Sac City, IA - *BrCabYB 84*
Heritage Cablevision [of Heritage Communications Inc.] - Storm Lake, IA - *BrCabYB 84*
Heritage Cablevision [of Heritage Communications Inc.] - Webster City, IA - *BrCabYB 84*
Heritage Cablevision - Winterset, IA - *BrCabYB 84*
Heritage Cablevision [of Heritage Communications Inc.] - Benson, MN - *BrCabYB 84*
Heritage Cablevision [of Heritage Communications Inc.] - Willmar, MN - *BrCabYB 84*
Heritage Cablevision [of Heritage Communications Inc.] - Amory, MS - *BrCabYB 84*
Heritage Cablevision [of Heritage Communications Inc.] - Baldwyn, MS - *BrCabYB 84*
Heritage Cablevision [of Heritage Communications Inc.] - Booneville, MS - *Tel&CabFB 84C*
Heritage Cablevision [of Heritage Communications Inc.] - Charleston, MS - *BrCabYB 84*
Heritage Cablevision [of Heritage Communications Inc.] - Columbia, MS - *BrCabYB 84*
Heritage Cablevision [of Heritage Communications Inc.] - Tarkio, MO - *BrCabYB 84*
Heritage Cablevision - West Point, NE - *BrCabYB 84*
Heritage Cablevision [of Heritage Communications Inc.] - Bartlett, TN - *BrCabYB 84*
Heritage Cablevision [of Heritage Communications Inc.] - Collierville, TN - *Tel&CabFB 84C*
Heritage Cablevision [of Heritage Communications Inc.] - Alice, TX - *BrCabYB 84*
Heritage Cablevision [of Heritage Communications Inc.] - Brownsville, TX - *BrCabYB 84*
Heritage Cablevision [of Heritage Communications Inc.] - Falfurrias, TX - *BrCabYB 84*
Heritage Cablevision [of Heritage Communications Inc.] - Harlingen, TX - *Tel&CabFB 84C*
Heritage Cablevision - Los Fresnos, TX - *BrCabYB 84*
Heritage Cablevision [of Heritage Communications Inc.] - Pharr, TX - *BrCabYB 84*
Heritage Cablevision [of Heritage Communications Inc.] - Port Isabel, TX - *BrCabYB 84*
Heritage Cablevision [of Heritage Communications Inc.] - Raymondville, TX - *BrCabYB 84*
Heritage Cablevision [of Heritage Communications Inc.] - Baraboo, WI - *BrCabYB 84; Tel&CabFB 84C*
Heritage Cablevision Inc. [of Heritage Communications Inc.] - Lake Delton, WI - *BrCabYB 84*
Heritage Cablevision Inc. [of Heritage Communications Inc.] - Reedsburg, WI - *BrCabYB 84*
Heritage Cablevision of Tennessee [of Heritage Communications Inc.] - Collierville, TN - *BrCabYB 84*
Heritage Communications Inc. - Avon, CO - *Tel&CabFB 84C*
Heritage Communications Inc. - Elkhart, IN - *Tel&CabFB 84C*
Heritage Communications Inc. - Plymouth, IN - *Tel&CabFB 84C*
Heritage Communications Inc. - Rochester, IN - *Tel&CabFB 84C*
Heritage Communications Inc. - Roseland, IN - *Tel&CabFB 84C*
Heritage Communications Inc. - Des Moines, IA - *BrCabYB 84 p.D-302; CabTVFinDB 83; HomeVid&CabYB 82-83; KnowInd 83; LitMarPl 84; TelAl 83, 84; Tel&CabFB 84C p.1684*
Heritage Communications of Tennessee - Bartlett, TN - *Tel&CabFB 84C*
Heritage Computer Corp. [Subs. of Heritage Mutual Insurance Co.] - Sheboygan, WI - *DataDirOnSer 84*
Heritage Conservation & Recreation Service [Aff. of U.S. Dept. of the Interior] - Washington, DC - *BoPubDir 4, 5*
Heritage Enterprises Inc. - Los Angeles, CA - *Tel&CabFB 84C*
Heritage Features Syndicate - Washington, DC - *BaconPubCkNews 84; Ed&PubIntYB 82*
Heritage Foundation - Washington, DC - *BoPubDir 4*
Heritage Music Press - *See* Lorenz Creative Services
Heritage of Hawarden [of Heritage Communications Inc.] - Ft. Dodge, IA - *BrCabYB 84*
Heritage Press - Baltimore, MD - *BoPubDir 4, 5; LitMag&SmPr 83-84*
Heritage Printers Inc. - Charlotte, NC - *LitMarPl 83, 84*
Heritage Printers Inc. - Sewanee, TN - *LitMag&SmPr 83-84*
Heritage Publications [Aff. of Heritage Store Inc.] - Virginia Beach, VA - *BoPubDir 4, 5*
Heritage Records & Music Corp. - Southampton, PA - *BillIntBG 83-84*
Heritage Records & Recording Studio - Galax, VA - *BillIntBG 83-84*
Heritage Singers - Placerville, CA - *BillIntBG 83-84*
Heritage, The - Amherstview, ON, Canada - *Ed&PubIntYB 82*
Herkimer Evening Telegram - Herkimer, NY - *Ed&PubIntYB 82; NewsDir 84*
Herman & Rosner Enterprises - New York, NY - *AdAge 3-28-84; StaDirAdAg 2-84*
Herman Associates Inc. - New York, NY - *StaDirAdAg 2-84*
Herman/Pangborn Inc. - Detroit, MI - *StaDirAdAg 2-84*
Herman Publishing - Boston, MA - *LitMarPl 83; WritMar 84*
Herman Publishing Co., H. & A. - Cameron, SC - *BoPubDir 4, 5*
Herman Publishing Inc. - Boston, MN - *LitMarPl 84*
Herman Review - Herman, MN - *BaconPubCkNews 84; Ed&PubIntYB 82*
Hermann Advertiser-Courier - Hermann, MO - *BaconPubCkNews 84; NewsDir 84*
Hermann, Irene A. - New York, NY - *LitMarPl 83, 84; MagIndMarPl 82-83*
Hermantown Star - Hermantown, MN - *BaconPubCkNews 84*
Hermes - Hugoton, KS - *AyerDirPub 83*
Hermes [of Dept. of Industry] - London, England - *EISS 7-83 Sup*
Hermes House Press Inc. - Oakland, CA - *BoPubDir 4, 5*
Hermes House Press Inc. - Niles, IL - *LitMag&SmPr 83-84*
Hermes Products Inc. - *DirInfWP 82*
Hermes Zeitungsausschnittburo - Bonn, West Germany - *ProGuPRSer 4*
Hermesch Public Relations, Alan - Washington, DC - *DirPRFirms 83*
Hermiston Herald - Hermiston, OR - *AyerDirPub 83; BaconPubCkNews 84; Ed&PubIntYB 82; NewsDir 84*
Hermitage - Ann Arbor, MI - *LitMarPl 84*
Hermitage Index - Hermitage, MO - *BaconPubCkNews 84; NewsDir 84*
Hermitage Publishing Co. - Ann Arbor, MI - *BoPubDir 5*

Hermosa Beach Review - Hermosa Beach, CA - *AyerDirPub 83; Ed&PubIntYB 82; NewsDir 84*
Hermosa Beach Review - *See* Argonaut Newspapers
Hermosa Cablevision - Hermosa, CO - *Tel&CabFB 84C*
Hernandez, A. - Portland, ME - *LitMarPl 84*
Hernando Cable Management Co. - Hernando County, FL - *BrCabYB 84*
Hernando De Soto Times - Hernando, MS - *BaconPubCkNews 84*
Hernando Free Press - Brooksville, FL - *AyerDirPub 83*
Herndon House - Brooklyn, NY - *BoPubDir 4, 5*
Herne Sales & Film Library, Gary [Div. of Christian Audio Visual Specialists Inc.] - Ferndale, MI - *AvMarPl 83*
Herner & Co. - Arlington, VA - *EISS 83; InfIndMarPl 83*
Hernreich Broadcasting Stations - Ft. Smith, AR - *BrCabYB 84; Tel&CabFB 84S*
Hero Press - New York, NY - *BoPubDir 4, 5; LitMag&SmPr 83-84*
Heron Books - Portland, OR - *BoPubDir 4, 5*
Heron Lake News - Heron Lake, MN - *Ed&PubIntYB 82*
Heron Lake Tri County News - Heron Lake, MN - *BaconPubCkNews 84*
Heron, Michal - New York, NY - *LitMarPl 83, 84; MagIndMarPl 82-83*
Heron Press - Boston, MA - *BoPubDir 4, 5*
Herr Cable Co. - Barbours, PA - *Tel&CabFB 84C*
Herr Cable Co. - Bodines, PA - *Tel&CabFB 84C*
Herr Cable Co. - Brookside, PA - *Tel&CabFB 84C*
Herr Cable Co. - Hillsgrove, PA - *Tel&CabFB 84C*
Herr Cable Co. - Montoursville, PA - *BrCabYB 84 p.D-302*
Herr Cable Co. - Waterville, PA - *Tel&CabFB 84C*
Herr, Ralph & Rita - Montoursville, PA - *Tel&CabFB 84C p.1684*
Herrera, D. J. - Fountain Valley, CA - *LitMarPl 83, 84*
Herrick Associates Inc., C. J. - New York, NY - *BrCabYB 84; StaDirAdAg 2-84*
Herricks-Searingtown Pennysaver - Jericho, NY - *AyerDirPub 83*
Herring Cove Press - Herring Cove, NS, Canada - *BoPubDir 4, 5*
Herring-Hall-Marvin - Canton, OH - *DirInfWP 82*
Herron Associates Inc. - Greenwood, IN - *IntDirMarRes 83*
Herr's Indexing Service - Washington, VT - *LitMarPl 83, 84; MagIndMarPl 82-83*
Herscher Press - Herscher, IL - *AyerDirPub 83; Ed&PubIntYB 82*
Hersh Productions, Stuart - New York, NY - *ArtMar 84; AvMarPl 83*
Hershenhorn Frankel - St. Louis, MO - *DirPRFirms 83*
Hershey Area Merchandiser - Lebanon, PA - *AyerDirPub 83*
Hershey Cooperative Telephone Co. - Hershey, NE - *TelDir&BG 83-84*
Hershey, Virginia Sharpe - Santa Rosa, CA - *BoPubDir 4 Sup, 5*
Hershfield, Leible - Winnipeg, MB, Canada - *BoPubDir 4 Sup, 5*
Herst Litho Inc. - New York, NY - *LitMarPl 83, 84*
Hertel Bible Publishers - Wichita, KS - *BoPubDir 4, 5*
Hertford Perquimans Weekly - Hertford, NC - *BaconPubCkNews 84*
Hertz Corp., The [Subs. of RCA Corp.] - New York, NY - *Tel&CabFB 84C*
Hertzberg & Sons Monastery Hill Bindery, Ernst - Chicago, IL - *LitMarPl 83, 84*
Hertzberg-New Method-Perma-Bound Co. - Jacksonville, IL - *LitMarPl 83, 84*
Hervic Corp. - Van Nuys, CA - *AvMarPl 83*
Herwood, Norman - New York, NY - *HBIndAd&MS 82-83*
Herzl Press [Aff. of World Zionist Organization] - New York, NY - *BoPubDir 4, 5; LitMarPl 84*
HES Data Products Inc. - Willow Grove, PA - *DataDirSup 7-83*
HESCO [Div. of Hesston Corp.] - Hesston, KS - *DirInfWP 82*
Hesketh-Pope Lease Historical Society - Carbon, AB, Canada - *BoPubDir 4, 5*
Hesperia Resorter [of California News Service Inc.] - Hesperia, CA - *NewsDir 84*
Hesperian Foundation [Aff. of Archives of Alchemical Texts] - Palo Alto, CA - *BoPubDir 5*
Hesperidian Press [Aff. of Archives of Alchemical Texts] - New York, NY - *BoPubDir 4 Sup, 5*
Hess & Hunt Inc. - Chicago, IL - *DirPRFirms 83; HBIndAd&MS 82-83*
Hess Co., The D. B. - Woodstock, IL - *LitMarPl 83, 84*
Hess, Dr. W. C. - Pasadena, CA - *BoPubDir 4, 5*
Hess Productions [Div. of J. E. G. Hess Productions] - New York, NY - *AvMarPl 83*
Hesse Advertising Inc., B. M. - New York, NY - *StaDirAdAg 2-84*
Hesselbart & Mitten Inc. - Fairlawn, OH - *StaDirAdAg 2-84*
Hesselbart & Mitten/Watt Inc. - Cleveland, OH - *DirPRFirms 83*
Hessische Bibliographie [of Arbeitsgemeinschaft Hessische Bibliographie] - Frankfurt, West Germany - *CompReadDB 82*
Hesston Record - Hesston, KS - *BaconPubCkNews 84; Ed&PubIntYB 82*
Hessville-Woodmar Lite - Hammond, IN - *Ed&PubIntYB 82*
Hester, George M. - New York, NY - *MagIndMarPl 82-83*
Hetra Computer & Communications Industries Inc. - Melbourne, FL - *DataDirSup 7-83; InfIndMarPl 83*
Hettinger Adams County Record - Hettinger, ND - *BaconPubCkNews 84*
Hettinger Cablevision [of Tioga Cablevision Inc.] - Hettinger, ND - *BrCabYB 84; Tel&CabFB 84C*
Hettinger Record - Hettinger, ND - *Ed&PubIntYB 82*
Hetu & Lukstat Inc. - Washington, DC - *DirPRFirms 83*
Heuer Publishing Co. - Cedar Rapids, IA - *BoPubDir 4, 5*
Heuristicus Publishing Co. - Brea, CA - *BoPubDir 4, 5*
Hevacomp Ltd. - Sheffield, England - *MicrocomSwDir 1*
Hewlett-Packard Co. - Palo Alto, CA - *AvMarPl 83; DataDirSup 7-83; Datamation 6-83; ElecNews 7-25-83; HomeVid&CabYB 82-83; Top100Al 83; WhoWMicrocom 83*
Hewlett-Packard Co. (Boise Div.) - Boise, ID - *DirInfWP 82*
Hewlett Packard Co. (General Systems Div.) - Sunnyvale, CA - *InfIndMarPl 83; MicrocomMPl 84*
Hewlett-Packard Co. (GSD Div.) - Cupertino, CA - *DirInfWP 82; WhoWMicrocom 83*
Hewlett South Shore Record - Hewlett, NY - *BaconPubCkNews 84*
Hewson, Edward - Ocean Shores, WA - *Tel&CabFB 84C p.1684*
Hex Data Services Inc. - New York, NY - *ADAPSOMemDir 83-84*
Hexagon Co. - Asheville, NC - *BoPubDir 4, 5*
Hexagon Press - Greenacre, Australia - *LitMag&SmPr 83-84*
Hexagon Systems - Vancouver, BC, Canada - *MicrocomSwDir 1; WhoWMicrocom 83*
Hexco Inc. - Hunt, TX - *WhoWMicrocom 83*
Hexcraft Inc. - Cambridge, MA - *MicrocomMPl 84*
Hey, Mary L. - Boulder, CO - *LitMarPl 83, 84*
Heyday Books - Berkeley, CA - *BoPubDir 4, 5; LitMag&SmPr 83-84*
Heyden & Son Inc. - Philadelphia, PA - *LitMarPl 83, 84*
Heyden & Son Ltd. - London, England - *MicroMarPl 82-83*
Heye, Needham & Partner GmbH - *See* Needham, Harper & Steers Inc.
Heyeck Press - Woodside, CA - *BoPubDir 4, 5; LitMag&SmPr 83-84*
Heyer Inc. - Chicago, IL - *DirInfWP 82*
Heyward & Associates Inc. - White Plains, NY - *DirPRFirms 83*
Heyworth Star - Heyworth, IL - *BaconPubCkNews 84; Ed&PubIntYB 82*
H.F. Signalling Inc. - Kansas City, MO - *MicrocomMPl 84*
HFD-Retailing Home Furnishings [of Fairchild Publications Inc.] - New York, NY - *BaconPubCkMag 84; MagDir 84; MagIndMarPl 82-83; NewsDir 84*
HFU-TV - Walker, CA - *BrCabYB 84*
HFU-TV - Topaz Lake, NV - *BrCabYB 84*
HGM Publishing Co. Ltd. - Vancouver, BC, Canada - *BoPubDir 4, 5*
HH & D Advertising Inc. - Chicago, IL - *StaDirAdAg 2-84*
Hi Band Broadcasting Co. - Alexandria, LA - *Tel&CabFB 84C*
Hi-Country Data Systems - Woodland Park, CO - *WhoWMicrocom 83*
Hi-Desert Flyer - Victorville, CA - *AyerDirPub 83*
Hi-Desert Star - Yucca Valley, CA - *AyerDirPub 83; Ed&PubIntYB 82*
Hi-Five Audio-Video Productions - New York, NY - *BillIntBG 83-84*
Hi-G Inc. - Hartford, CT - *DataDirSup 7-83*
Hi-G Inc. - Windsor Locks, CT - *MicrocomMPl 83, 84*
Hi Ho Broadcasting Group - Orlando, FL - *BrCabYB 84; Tel&CabFB 84S*

Hi-Line Enterprise - Curtis, NE - *AyerDirPub 83; Ed&PubIntYB 82*
Hi-Lite Records - Santa Fe Springs, CA - *BillIntBG 83-84*
Hi-Lites Shoppers Guide - Buchanan, MI - *AyerDirPub 83*
Hi Oldies Music - North Hollywood, CA - *BillIntBG 83-84*
Hi-Riser - Ft. Lauderdale, FL - *AyerDirPub 83; Ed&PubIntYB 82*
Hi-Scope Research Inc. - Southfield, MI - *IntDirMarRes 83*
Hi Tech Computer Services - New City, NY - *MicrocomMPl 84*
Hi-Tech Manager's Bulletin - Waterford, CT - *WritMar 84*
Hi Tech Patents: Data Communications [of Communications Publishing Group Inc.] - Brookline, MA - *DataDirOnSer 84; DirOnDB Spring 84*
Hi Tech Patents: Fiber Optics Technology [of Communications Publishing Group Inc.] - Brookline, MA - *BaconPubCkMag 84; DataDirOnSer 84; DirOnDB Spring 84*
Hi Tech Patents: Laser Technology [of Communications Publishing Group Inc.] - Brookline, MA - *DataDirOnSer 84; DirOnDB Spring 84*
Hi Tech Patents: Telephony [of Communications Publishing Group Inc.] - Brookline, MA - *DataDirOnSer 84; DirOnDB Spring 84*
Hi-Tech Systems Inc. - Lebanon, IN - *MicrocomMPl 84*
Hi-Tek Connection, The [of Hi-Tek Publications] - North Salem, NH - *MicrocomMPl 84*
Hi Time Enterprises Buying Service - New York, NY - *StaDirAdAg 2-84*
Hi Vista Inc. [of Spacelink Ltd.] - Chester, CA - *Tel&CabFB 84C*
Hi Vista Inc. - Westwood, CA - *BrCabYB 84*
Hi-Way 15 Gazette - Semans, SK, Canada - *AyerDirPub 83*
Hi-Way's Gazette - Semans, SK, Canada - *Ed&PubIntYB 82*
Hi Willow Research & Publishing - Fayetteville, AR - *BoPubDir 4, 5*
Hialeah Home News - Hialeah, FL - *BaconPubCkNews 84*
Hialeah Home News-Las Noticias - Hialeah, FL - *NewsDir 84*
Hialeah-Miami Springs News [of Community Newspapers of Florida Inc.] - Miami, FL - *AyerDirPub 83; NewsDir 84*
Hialeah-Miami Springs News - *See* Community Newspapers of Florida Inc.
Hiawassee Towns County Herald - Hiawassee, GA - *BaconPubCkNews 84*
Hiawatha Daily World - Hiawatha, KS - *BaconPubCkNews 84; Ed&PubIntYB 82; NewsDir 84*
Hiawatha Publishing Co. - Bondurant, IA - *BoPubDir 4, 5*
Hibbert Co., The - Trenton, NJ - *LitMarPl 83, 84*
Hibbing Tribune - Hibbing, MN - *BaconPubCkNews 84; Ed&PubIntYB 82; NewsDir 84*
Hiber, Hart & Patrick Ltd. - Pebble Beach, CA - *BrCabYB 84*
Hiber Publishing Inc. - Levittown, NY - *BaconPubCkNews 84*
Hibiscus Press - Sacramento, CA - *BoPubDir 4, 5; LitMag&SmPr 83-84*
Hickey Associates, Albert E. - Portsmouth, NH - *LitMarPl 83, 84*
Hickey, Brian L. - Brooklyn, NY - *LitMarPl 84*
Hickman Cable TV Inc. - Bagdad, AZ - *Tel&CabFB 84C*
Hickman County Gazette - Clinton, KY - *AyerDirPub 83; Ed&PubIntYB 82*
Hickman County Times - Centerville, TN - *Ed&PubIntYB 82*
Hickman Courier - Hickman, KY - *BaconPubCkNews 84; Ed&PubIntYB 82*
Hickman, J. E. - Alpine, CA - *Tel&CabFB 84C p.1684*
Hickman Voice News of South Lancaster County - Hickman, NE - *BaconPubCkNews 84*
Hickory Daily Record - Hickory, NC - *BaconPubCkNews 84; Ed&PubIntYB 82; NewsDir 84*
Hickory Hill Cable TV - Bluff City, TN - *BrCabYB 84*
Hickory Hills Citizen - Hickory Hills, IL - *Ed&PubIntYB 82*
Hickory Hills Citizen [of Southwest Messenger Newspapers] - Midlothian, IL - *AyerDirPub 83; NewsDir 84*
Hickory Hills Citizen - *See* Southwest Messenger Newspapers
Hickory News - Hickory, NC - *BaconPubCkNews 84; NewsDir 84*
Hickory Records Inc. - Nashville, TN - *BillIntBG 83-84*
Hickory Telephone Co. [Aff. of Telephone & Data Systems Inc.] - Augusta, MI - *TelDir&BG 83-84*
Hickory Telephone Co. - Hickory, PA - *TelDir&BG 83-84*
Hicks Advertising, Ward - Albuquerque, NM - *StaDirAdAg 2-84*
Hicks & Co., R. Miller - Austin, TX - *CabTVFinDB 83*
Hicks & Grayson - Coral Gables, FL - *AdAge 3-28-84; StaDirAdAg 2-84*
Hicks & Greist - New York, NY - *AdAge 3-28-84; StaDirAdAg 2-84; TelAl 83, 84*
Hicks Associates, Terry [Div. of Archer-Scale Inc.] - Lynnville, TN - *LitMarPl 83, 84*
Hicks Communications Inc. - Dallas, TX - *BrCabYB 84*
Hicks, Elmer - Prince Albert, SK, Canada - *BoPubDir 4 Sup, 5*
Hicks Inc., Ray - Waco, TX - *StaDirAdAg 2-84*
Hicks, Judie - Huntington Beach, CA - *LitMarPl 83; MagIndMarPl 82-83*
Hicks, Maloof & Campbell - Atlanta, GA - *ADAPSOMemDir 83-84*
Hicksville Centre Island News [of Litmor Publications Inc.] - Hicksville, NY - *NewsDir 84*
Hicksville Mid Island Herald - Hicksville, NY - *NewsDir 84*
Hicksville Mid Island Herald - *See* Mid-Island Herald Publishers
Hicksville Mid Island Times - Hicksville, NY - *Ed&PubIntYB 82*
Hicksville Mid Island Times - *See* Litmore Publications
Hicksville News-Tribune - Hicksville, OH - *BaconPubCkNews 84*
Hicksville Pennysaver - Levittown, NY - *AyerDirPub 83*
Hico News-Review - Hico, TX - *BaconPubCkNews 84; Ed&PubIntYB 82*
Hidden Assets - Seattle, WA - *LitMag&SmPr 83-84*
Hidden Hills Times - *See* Associated Valley Publications
Hiddigeigei Books - San Francisco, CA - *BoPubDir 4, 5*
Hideaways Guide [of Hideaways International] - Concord, MA - *WritMar 84*
Hiebing Group - Madison, WI - *AdAge 3-28-84; StaDirAdAg 2-84*
Hierarchical Environmental Retrieval for Management Access & Networking (Chiroptera Section) - Riverside, CA - *CompReadDB 82*
Hierarchical Environmental Retrieval for Management Access & Networking (Marine Mammals Section) - Riverside, CA - *CompReadDB 82*
Hierarchical Environmental Retrieval for Management Access & Networking (Oceanic Birds Section) - Riverside, CA - *CompReadDB 82*
Hierarchical Environmental Retrieval for Management Access & Networking (Shorebirds Section) - Riverside, CA - *CompReadDB 82*
Hierarchical Environmental Retrieval for Management Access & Networking (Wildlife Section) - Riverside, CA - *CompReadDB 82*
HiFi Buyer's Review - Southhampton, NY - *WritMar 84*
Higbee News - *See* Huntsville Times-Herald Publishers
Higginbotham Associates Inc. - Houston, TX - *IntDirMarRes 83*
Higgins Cablevision Inc. - Higgins, TX - *Tel&CabFB 84C p.1684*
Higgins Productions Inc., Alfred - Los Angeles, CA - *AvMarPl 83*
Higgins, Shaun - Spokane, WA - *BoPubDir 4, 5*
Higginsville Advance - Higginsville, MO - *BaconPubCkNews 84; Ed&PubIntYB 82*
High Adventure - Springfield, MO - *WritMar 84*
High Blood Pressure Information Center [of U.S. Public Health Service] - Bethesda, MD - *EISS 83*
High Capacity Disks [of GML Corp.] - Lexington, MA - *CompReadDB 82*
High Chaparral Music - Nashville, TN - *BillIntBG 83-84*
High/Coo Press - Battle Ground, IN - *BoPubDir 4, 5; LitMag&SmPr 83-84; WritMar 84*
High Country Communications - Taylorsville, NC - *Tel&CabFB 84C*
High Country Films - Denver, CO - *AvMarPl 83*
High Country Microsystems - Westminster, CO - *MicrocomMPl 83*
High Country News - Bozeman, MT - *Ed&PubIntYB 82*
High Country News [of High Country Foundation] - Lander, WY - *ArtMar 84; LitMag&SmPr 83-84; MagIndMarPl 82-83; WritMar 84*
High Density Systems Inc. - New York, NY - *LitMarPl 83, 84*
High Fidelity/Musical America [of American Broadcasting Co.] - New York, NY - *BaconPubCkMag 84; LitMarPl 83, 84; MagDir 84; MagIndMarPl 82-83; WritMar 84*
High Fidelity Trade News - Atlanta, GA - *WritMar 84*

High Museum of Art [Aff. of Atlanta Arts Alliance] - Atlanta, GA - *BoPubDir 4 Sup, 5*
High Orchard Press - Dagenham, England - *LitMag&SmPr 83-84*
High Performance [of Astro Artz] - Los Angeles, CA - *LitMag&SmPr 83-84*
High Plains Advertising Agency - Dodge City, KS - *AdAge 3-28-84; StaDirAdAg 2-84*
High Plains Cablevision [of Omni Cable TV Corp.] - Idalou, TX - *BrCabYB 84*
High Plains Cablevision - Spur, TX - *BrCabYB 84*
High Plains Journal - Dodge City, KS - *BaconPubCkMag 84; MagDir 84; MagIndMarPl 82-83; NewsDir 84*
High Pockets Publishing - Buffalo, NY - *BillIntBG 83-84*
High Point Enterprise - High Point, NC - *BaconPubCkNews 84; Ed&PubIntYB 82; LitMarPl 83, 84; NewsDir 84*
High Pressure Data Center [of Brigham Young University] - Provo, UT - *EISS 83*
High Publishers - Pueblo, CO - *BoPubDir 4, 5*
High Rock Review, The - Saratoga Springs, NY - *LitMag&SmPr 83-84*
High Rockies Enterprises Inc. - Boulder, CO - *BoPubDir 4, 5*
High/Scope Press [Aff. of High/Scope Educational Research Foundation] - Ypsilanti, MI - *BoPubDir 4, 5*
High Society [of Drake Publishers Inc.] - New York, NY - *Folio 83; LitMarPl 83, 84; MagIndMarPl 82-83*
High Springs Herald - High Springs, FL - *BaconPubCkNews 84; Ed&PubIntYB 82*
High-Tech Manager's Bulletin - Waterford, CT - *ArtMar 84*
High Technology [of Goldhirsh Group Inc.] - Boston, MA - *BaconPubCkMag 84; Folio 83*
High Technology - Florissant, MO - *MicrocomMPl 84*
High Technology - Oklahoma City, OK - *MicrocomMPl 83*
High Technology Group - Darien, CT - *CabTVFinDB 83*
High Technology Growth Stocks - Concord, MA - *BaconPubCkMag 84*
High Technology Marketing Systems - *See* Madison Avenue Alliance Inc., The
High Technology Software Products Inc. - Oklahoma City, OK - *MicrocomMPl 84; MicrocomSwDir 1; WhoWMicrocom 83*
High Temperature Materials Data Bank [of Commission of the European Communities] - Petten, Niger - *EISS 83*
High Temperature Reaction Rate Data Centre [of Leeds University] - Leeds, England - *EISS 83*
High Timber Times - Conifer, CO - *AyerDirPub 83; Ed&PubIntYB 82*
High Times [of Trans-High Corp.] - New York, NY - *LitMarPl 83, 84; MagDir 84; MagIndMarPl 82-83; WritMar 84*
High Valley Press [Aff. of Monte Vista Centennial Commission] - Monte Vista, CO - *BoPubDir 5*
High Volume Printing - Northbrook, IL - *BaconPubCkMag 84; LitMarPl 83, 84; MagDir 84; WritMar 84*
High Water Recording Co. - Memphis, TN - *BillIntBG 83-84*
Higham Mirror - Scituate, MA - *AyerDirPub 83*
Highball Music - Nashville, TN - *BillIntBG 83-84*
Higher Education Center of St. Louis - St. Louis, MO - *BoPubDir 4, 5*
Higher Education Marketing Journal - Kansas City, MO - *BaconPubCkMag 84*
Highgate Press - *See* Galaxy Music Corp.
Highland Cable TV Inc. - Hillsboro, OH - *BrCabYB 84 p.D-302; Tel&CabFB 84C*
Highland Cable TV Inc. - Peebles, OH - *BrCabYB 84; Tel&CabFB 84C*
Highland Cable TV Inc. - West Union, OH - *Tel&CabFB 84C*
Highland Calumet Press - Highland, IN - *BaconPubCkNews 84*
Highland Echo - Vancouver, BC, Canada - *AyerDirPub 83; Ed&PubIntYB 82*
Highland Falls News of the Highlands - Highland Falls, NY - *BaconPubCkNews 84*
Highland Herald - Louisville, KY - *AyerDirPub 83*
Highland Herald - *See* Scripps-Howard Press
Highland Herald - *See* Ulster Offset Corp.
Highland House Publishing Inc. - Westbury, NY - *BoPubDir 4, 5*
Highland, Jean - New York, NY - *LitMarPl 83, 84*
Highland News Leader - Highland, IL - *BaconPubCkNews 84; Ed&PubIntYB 82; NewsDir 84*
Highland Park/Deerfield/Vernon Advantage - Highland Park, IL - *Ed&PubIntYB 82*
Highland Park Mail-Advertiser - Highland Park, IL - *Ed&PubIntYB 82*
Highland Park Mail Advertiser - *See* Singer Printing & Publishing Co.
Highland Park News - Highland Park, IL - *Ed&PubIntYB 82*
Highland Park News [of Wilmette Pioneer Press Inc.] - Wilmette, IL - *AyerDirPub 83; NewsDir 84*
Highland Park News - Des Moines, IA - *AyerDirPub 83; Ed&PubIntYB 82*
Highland Park News - *See* Pioneer Press Inc.
Highland Park News Advertiser - Highland Park, IL - *AyerDirPub 83*
Highland Park News-Herald & Journal [of Northeast Los Angeles Publishing Co.] - Los Angeles, CA - *AyerDirPub 83; Ed&PubIntYB 82; NewsDir 84*
Highland Park News-Herald & Journal - *See* Northeast Los Angeles Publishing Co.
Highland Park Recorder - *See* Sentinel Newspapers
Highland Press - Boerne, TX - *BoPubDir 4, 5*
Highland Telephone Co. [Aff. of Rochester Telephone Corp.] - Monroe, NY - *TelDir&BG 83-84*
Highland Telephone Cooperative - Sunbright, TN - *TelDir&BG 83-84*
Highland Telephone Cooperative - Monterey, VA - *TelDir&BG 83-84*
Highland Video Inc. [of Adelphia Communications Corp.] - Blairsville, PA - *BrCabYB 84; Tel&CabFB 84C*
Highland Video Inc. [of Adelphia Communications Corp.] - Latrobe, PA - *Tel&CabFB 84C*
Highland Video Inc. [of Adelphia Communications Corp.] - Ligonier, PA - *Tel&CabFB 84C*
Highland Vidette - Highland, KS - *BaconPubCkNews 84; Ed&PubIntYB 82*
Highlander - Lake Wales, FL - *AyerDirPub 83*
Highlander Community Newspaper - Hacienda Heights, CA - *Ed&PubIntYB 82*
Highlander Press - Nashville, IN - *LitMag&SmPr 83-84*
Highlander Publications - Hacienda Heights, CA - *BaconPubCkNews 84*
Highlander Publications - La Puente, CA - *AyerDirPub 83*
Highlander, The [of Angus J. Ray Associates Inc.] - Barrington, IL - *BaconPubCkMag 84; WritMar 84*
Highlander, The - Highlands, NC - *AyerDirPub 83; BaconPubCkNews 84; Ed&PubIntYB 82*
Highlander, The - Marble Falls, TX - *AyerDirPub 83*
Highlands Community Cable TV - Highlands, NC - *Tel&CabFB 84C*
Highlands Computer Services - Renton, WA - *MicrocomMPl 83, 84*
Highlands Herald - Sebring, FL - *AyerDirPub 83*
Highlands Ranch Cablevision [of American TV & Communications Corp.] - Highlands Ranch, CO - *Tel&CabFB 84C*
Highlands Star - Highlands, TX - *BaconPubCkNews 84; Ed&PubIntYB 82*
Highlights for Children - Columbus, OH - *DirMarMP 83; Folio 83*
Highlights for Children - Honesdale, PA - *ArtMar 84; LitMarPl 84; MagDir 84; MagIndMarPl 82-83; WritMar 84*
Highline Antenna Service [of Group W Cable] - Cut Bank, MT - *BrCabYB 84*
Highline Times - Burien, WA - *Ed&PubIntYB 82*
Highline Times [of Seattle Robinson Newspapers] - Seattle, WA - *AyerDirPub 83; NewsDir 84*
Highline TV - Colfax, WA - *Tel&CabFB 84C*
Highly Specialized Promotions - Brooklyn, NY - *MagIndMarPl 82-83*
Highmore Herald - Highmore, SD - *BaconPubCkNews 84; Ed&PubIntYB 82*
Highsmith Co. Inc. - Ft. Atkinson, WI - *AvMarPl 83; DirInfWP 82*
Hightone Records - Emeryville, CA - *BillIntBG 83-84*
Hightree - Beverly Hills, CA - *BillIntBG 83-84*
Hightstown Daily Racing Form - Hightstown, NJ - *NewsDir 84*
Hightstown Gazette - Hightstown, NJ - *BaconPubCkNews 84; Ed&PubIntYB 82*

Hightstown Windsor-Hights Herald - *See* Princeton Packet Inc.
Highwater Mark, The - Eaton Rapids, MI - *Ed&PubIntYB 82*
Highway & Heavy Construction - Barrington, IL - *BaconPubCkMag 84; MagDir 84; MagIndMarPl 82-83*
Highway & Vehicle/Safety Report - Branford, CT - *BaconPubCkMag 84*
Highway Book Shop - Cobalt, ON, Canada - *BoPubDir 4, 5; LitMag&SmPr 83-84; LitMarPl 84*
Highway Builder - Harrisburg, PA - *BaconPubCkMag 84; MagDir 84*
Highway 40 Courier - Cut Knife, SK, Canada - *AyerDirPub 83; Ed&PubIntYB 82*
Highway Loss Data Institute - Washington, DC - *BoPubDir 5*
Highway Research Information Service [of Transportation Research Board] - Washington, DC - *CompReadDB 82; DataDirOnSer 84; EISS 83; InfIndMarPl 83*
Highway Safety Films Inc. - Mansfield, OH - *AvMarPl 83*
Highway Safety Literature [of U.S. National Highway Traffic Safety Administration] - Washington, DC - *CompReadDB 82; DBBus 82*
Highway Statistics Div. [of U.S. Federal Highway Administration] - Washington, DC - *EISS 83*
Highway Traffic Safety Library [of Michigan State University] - East Lansing, MI - *EISS 83*
Highwire Magazine [of Highwire Associates] - Lowell, MA - *WritMar 84*
Higley & Associates, Don L. - Santa Barbara, CA - *ArtMar 84; AvMarPl 83*
Higley Publishing Corp. - Jacksonville, FL - *BoPubDir 4, 5*
Hignell Printing Ltd. - Winnipeg, MB, Canada - *LitMarPl 83, 84*
Hilary House Publishers Inc. - Hewlett Harbor, NY - *DirMarMP 83; LitMarPl 83, 84*
Hilbert Favorite - Hilbert, WI - *BaconPubCkNews 84; Ed&PubIntYB 82*
Hildreth Stations, Horace - *See* Community Broadcasting Service Inc.
Hilevel Technology Inc. - Irving, CA - *DataDirSup 7-83*
Hilgraeve Inc. - Monroe, MI - *MicrocomMPl 84*
Hill Advertising Ltd., Gordon - Toronto, ON, Canada - *StaDirAdAg 2-84*
Hill & Co. Publishers Inc., Lawrence - Westport, CT - *LitMag&SmPr 83-84; LitMarPl 83, 84*
Hill & Knowlton Inc. - Chicago, IL - *ArtMar 84*
Hill & Knowlton Inc. [Subs. of JWT Group Inc.] - New York, NY - *DirPRFirms 83*
Hill & Knowlton Inc. - *See* JWT Group Inc.
Hill & Wang [Div. of Farrar, Straus & Giroux Inc.] - New York, NY - *LitMarPl 83, 84*
Hill Associates, Frederick - San Francisco, CA - *LitMarPl 83, 84*
Hill City Prevalier - Hill City, SD - *Ed&PubIntYB 82*
Hill City Prevalier & Guide - Hill City, SD - *AyerDirPub 83; BaconPubCkNews 84*
Hill City Times - Hill City, KS - *BaconPubCkNews 84; Ed&PubIntYB 82*
Hill City TV Cable Co. [of CATV Inc.] - Hill City, KS - *BrCabYB 84; Tel&CabFB 84C*
Hill Co., George - Pittsburgh, PA - *StaDirAdAg 2-84*
Hill Co., W. S. - Pittsburgh, PA - *StaDirAdAg 2-84*
Hill Country Cablevision Inc. [of Times Mirror Cable Television Inc.] - Kerrville, TX - *BrCabYB 84*
Hill Country News - Cedar Park, TX - *Ed&PubIntYB 82*
Hill Country Publishing Co. Inc. - Lampasas, TX - *BaconPubCkNews 84*
Hill Country Telephone Cooperative Inc. - Ingram, TX - *TelDir&BG 83-84*
Hill-Donnelly Corp. - Tampa, FL - *DirMarMP 83*
Hill, Ed - Steamboat Springs, CO - *Tel&CabFB 84C p.1684*
Hill Hays Associates Inc. - Burlington, VT - *DirMarMP 83*
Hill Hays Associates Inc. - Randolph, VT - *AdAge 3-28-84; StaDirAdAg 2-84*
Hill, Holliday, Connors, Cosmopulos - Boston, MA - *AdAge 3-28-84; DirPRFirms 83; HBIndAd&MS 82-83; StaDirAdAg 2-84*
Hill, Isabel Louise - Fredericton, NB, Canada - *BoPubDir 4, 5*
Hill Junior College Press - Hillsboro, TX - *BoPubDir 4, 5*
Hill, Leslie C. - White Rock, BC, Canada - *BoPubDir 4 Sup, 5*
Hill/Mandelker Films - Los Angeles, CA - *Tel&CabFB 84C*
Hill Monastic Manuscript Library [of St. John's University] - Collegeville, MN - *MicroMarPl 82-83*
Hill Photography - Aspen, CO - *AvMarPl 83*
Hill Printing Co. Inc. - Keokuk, IA - *MagIndMarPl 82-83*
Hill Publications Inc. - Boca Raton, FL - *BoPubDir 4, 5*
Hill Review, The - Vankleek Hill, ON, Canada - *AyerDirPub 83*
Hill Springs Publications - South Charleston, WV - *BoPubDir 4, 5*
Hillcrest Journal - Euclid, OH - *AyerDirPub 83*
Hillcrest Pennysaver - Mission Viejo, CA - *AyerDirPub 83*
Hillebrandt Consultants Inc. - Wilton, CT - *IntDirMarRes 83*
Hiller Industries - Salt Lake City, UT - *LitMarPl 83, 84*
Hillgreen Music - *See* Folklore Music
Hilliard, Carl B. Jr. - San Diego, CA - *Tel&CabFB 84C*
Hilliard Clearview Cable TV [of Florida Clearview Inc.] - Hilliard, FL - *Tel&CabFB 84C*
Hilliard, Leslie P. - Scottsbluff, NE - *Tel&CabFB 84C p.1684*
Hilliard Music Co., Bob - *See* Better Half Music Co.
Hilliard, Russell G. - Scottsbluff, NE - *Tel&CabFB 84C p.1684*
Hilliard, William K. - Scottsbluff, NE - *Tel&CabFB 84C p.1684*
Hillman Publishing Co. Inc. - Wilsonville, OR - *LitMag&SmPr 83-84*
Hills Telephone Co. Inc. [Aff. of Ollig Utilities Co.] - Hills, MN - *TelDir&BG 83-84*
Hillsboro Aloha Breeze - *See* Hillsboro Argus Inc.
Hillsboro & Montgomery County News - Hillsboro, IL - *AyerDirPub 83; BaconPubCkNews 84; Ed&PubIntYB 82; NewsDir 84*
Hillsboro Argus - Hillsboro, OR - *BaconPubCkNews 84; Ed&PubIntYB 82*
Hillsboro Banner - Hillsboro, ND - *BaconPubCkNews 84; Ed&PubIntYB 82*
Hillsboro Cable Inc. [of Central Cable Services Inc.] - Hillsboro, KS - *BrCabYB 84; Tel&CabFB 84C*
Hillsboro Journal - Hillsboro, IL - *BaconPubCkNews 84; Ed&PubIntYB 82*
Hillsboro Messenger - Hillsboro, NH - *BaconPubCkNews 84; Ed&PubIntYB 82; NewsDir 84*
Hillsboro Press-Gazette - Hillsboro, OH - *BaconPubCkNews 84; NewsDir 84*
Hillsboro Reporter - Hillsboro, TX - *BaconPubCkNews 84*
Hillsboro Sentry-Enterprise - Hillsboro, WI, USSR - *BaconPubCkNews 84*
Hillsboro Star-Journal - Hillsboro, KS - *BaconPubCkNews 84; Ed&PubIntYB 82*
Hillsboro Telephone Co. Inc. - Hillsboro, WI - *TelDir&BG 83-84*
Hillsborough & Montgomery Telephone Co. [Aff. of United Telecommunications Inc.] - Belle Mead, NJ - *TelDir&BG 83-84*
Hillsborough Beacon - Belle Mead, NJ - *AyerDirPub 83*
Hillsborough Beacon - Hillsborough, NJ - *Ed&PubIntYB 82*
Hillsborough Beacon [of Princeton Packet Inc.] - Princeton, NJ - *NewsDir 84*
Hillsborough Boutique & Burlingame Villager - Burlingame, CA - *AyerDirPub 83*
Hillsborough Boutique & Burlingame Villager - Hillsborough, CA - *Ed&PubIntYB 82*
Hillsborough Cablevision [of Commonwealth Cable Systems Inc.] - Hillsborough Township, NJ - *BrCabYB 84; Tel&CabFB 84C*
Hillsborough Community Pub. Inc. - Plant City, FL - *BaconPubCkNews 84*
Hillsborough News of Orange County - Hillsborough, NC - *BaconPubCkNews 84*
Hillsdale Educational Publishers Inc. - Hillsdale, MI - *BoPubDir 4, 5*
Hillsdale News [of Stauffer Communications] - Hillsdale, MI - *BaconPubCkNews 84; Ed&PubIntYB 82; NewsDir 84*
Hillsdale News [of Westwood Pascack Valley Community Life] - Westwood, NJ - *NewsDir 84*
Hillside Press - Carversville, PA - *BoPubDir 4 Sup, 5*
Hillside Times - Hillside, NJ - *BaconPubCkNews 84; Ed&PubIntYB 82; NewsDir 84*
Hillsville Carroll News - Hillsville, VA - *BaconPubCkNews 84; NewsDir 84*
Hilltop Advertising Inc. - Battle Creek, MI - *StaDirAdAg 2-84*
Hilltop Messenger - Running Springs, CA - *Ed&PubIntYB 82*
Hilltop News [of Cincinnati Suburban Newspapers Inc.] - Cincinnati, OH - *AyerDirPub 83; Ed&PubIntYB 82; NewsDir 84*

Hilltop News - *See* Queen City Suburban Press Inc.
Hilltop Press - Melrose, MA - *BoPubDir 4, 5*
Hilltop Publications [Aff. of Codhill Group Inc.] - Codrington, ON, Canada - *BoPubDir 4 Sup, 5*
Hilltop Publications Inc. - New York, NY - *BoPubDir 4 Sup, 5*
Hilltopper - Austin, TX - *AyerDirPub 83*
Hilltown Press Inc. - Worthington, MA - *LitMarPl 83, 84*
Hilo Hawaii Tribune-Herald [of Donrey Media Group] - Hilo, HI - *NewsDir 84*
Hilsinger Inc., Judy - Los Angeles, CA - *LitMarPl 83, 84*
Hilstan Music - *See* Cornelius Music, Stan
Hilton Advertising Agency Inc. - Tampa, FL - *StaDirAdAg 2-84*
Hilton Head Island Packet [of News & Observer Co.] - Hilton Head Island, SC - *BaconPubCkNews 84; NewsDir 84*
Hilton Inc., Jack - New York, NY - *DirPRFirms 83; ProGuPRSer 4*
H.I.M. Advertising Public Relations - Cleveland, OH - *StaDirAdAg 2-84*
Himalayan Publishers [Div. of Himalayan International Institute of Yoga Science & Philosophy] - Westport, CT - *LitMarPl 84*
Himalayan Publishers [Div. of Himalayan International Institute of Yoga Science & Philosophy] - Honesdale, PA - *LitMag&SmPr 83-84; LitMarPl 83*
Himmah Publishing Co., Gael - Walnut Creek, CA - *BoPubDir 4, 5*
Hinchman Associates Inc., Walter - Chevy Chase, MD - *TeleSy&SerDir 7-83*
Hinckley, Clive - Redlands, CA - *BoPubDir 4, 5*
Hinckley Group, The - Houston, TX - *StaDirAdAg 2-84*
Hinckley News - Hinckley, MN - *BaconPubCkNews 84; Ed&PubIntYB 82*
Hinckley Review - Hinckley, IL - *BaconPubCkNews 84*
Hinckley Review, The - Lincoln, IL - *Ed&PubIntYB 82*
Hindall & Associates - Columbus, OH - *StaDirAdAg 2-84*
Hinderliter Management Systems - Tulsa, OK - *EISS 7-83 Sup*
Hinds County Gazette - Raymond, MS - *Ed&PubIntYB 82*
Hindsight Records - Burbank, CA - *BillIntBG 83-84*
Hines, Diane Casella - Malibu, CA - *LitMarPl 83, 84*
Hines Legal Directory Inc. - Glen Ellyn, IL - *BoPubDir 4, 5*
Hinesville Coastal Courier - Hinesville, GA - *BaconPubCkNews 84*
Hingham Journal - Hingham, MA - *BaconPubCkNews 84; Ed&PubIntYB 82*
Hingham Mirror - Hingham, MA - *Ed&PubIntYB 82*
Hinkle-Brown-Bloyed Inc. - Tulsa, OK - *StaDirAdAg 2-84*
Hinsdale Doings - Hinsdale, IL - *AyerDirPub 83; Ed&PubIntYB 82; NewsDir 84*
Hinsdale Doings - *See* Doings Newspapers, The
Hinsdale Music - *See* Temar Music
Hinsdale Suburban Life Graphic - *See* Life Printing & Publishing Co.
Hinsdale Suburban Trib - Hinsdale, IL - *NewsDir 84*
Hinton News - Hinton, WV - *AyerDirPub 83; Ed&PubIntYB 82; NewsDir 84*
Hinton Progress - Hinton, IA - *BaconPubCkNews 84; Ed&PubIntYB 82*
Hinton Record - Hinton, OK - *BaconPubCkNews 84; Ed&PubIntYB 82*
Hinton, Steel & Nelson Inc. - Seattle, WA - *AdAge 3-28-84; StaDirAdAg 2-84*
Hinton Telephone Co. Inc. - Hinton, OK - *TelDir&BG 83-84*
Hinton Television Corp. - Hinton, WV - *BrCabYB 84; Tel&CabFB 84C*
Hinz Lithographing Co. - Mt. Prospect, IL - *MagIndMarPl 82-83*
Hipolit Music Co. - *See* Memnon Ltd.
Hippocrates Worldhealth Organization [Aff. of Rising Sun Publications] - Boston, MA - *BoPubDir 4, 5*
Hippocrene Books Inc. - New York, NY - *LitMarPl 83, 84*
Hippodrome Theatre - Gainesville, FL - *WritMar 84*
Hippopotamus Press - Sutton, England - *LitMag&SmPr 83-84*
Hiram Poetry Review - Hiram, OH - *LitMag&SmPr 83-84; WritMar 84*
Hirsch & Associates, Jerome - St. Louis, MO - *StaDirAdAg 2-84*
Hirsch & Associates, Sherrie - Baltimore, MD - *DirPRFirms 83*
Hirsch Communications Services - Stamford, CT - *CabTVFinDB 83*
Hirsch Consulting Group, The - Dallas, TX - *DirInfWP 82*
Hirsch Elliott Inc. - New York, NY - *AdAge 3-28-84; StaDirAdAg 2-84*
Hirsch-Pressey Stations - Statesboro, GA - *BrCabYB 84*
Hirsch Public Relations, Susan - Chicago, IL - *DirPRFirms 83; MagIndMarPl 82-83*
Hirsch Publishers Services, Susan [Subs. of Surrey Books Inc.] - Chicago, IL - *LitMarPl 83, 84*
Hirschberg Co. Inc., The Robert S. - New York, NY - *StaDirAdAg 2-84*
Hirshfield, James A. Jr. - Bellevue, WA - *BrCabYB 84 p.D-302; Tel&CabFB 84C p.1684*
Hirst Co., The - Albuquerque, NM - *DirPRFirms 83*
His - Downers Grove, IL - *ArtMar 84; MagIndMarPl 82-83; WritMar 84*
H.I.S. Computermation - Melbourne, FL - *MicrocomMPl 83, 84*
HIS Marketing & Advertising - Cuyahoga Falls, OH - *StaDirAdAg 2-84*
His Singing Seven Publishing Co. - Etobicoke, ON, Canada - *BoPubDir 4 Sup, 5*
Hiscabeq [of Microfor Inc.] - Quebec City, PQ, Canada - *CompReadDB 82; DirOnDB Spring 84*
Hisong Records [Div. of Musedco Publishing] - Richardson, TX - *BillIntBG 83-84*
Hispania - Cincinnati, OH - *MagDir 84; MagIndMarPl 82-83*
Hispania Advertising Inc. - New York, NY - *StaDirAdAg 2-84*
Hispanic-American News Service/Servicio Hispano de Noticias - Washington, DC - *BrCabYB 84*
Hispanic Business - Santa Barbara, CA - *BaconPubCkMag 84*
Hispanic Link News Service - Washington, DC - *Ed&PubIntYB 82; LitMarPl 84*
Hispanic Seminary of Medieval Studies - Madison, WI - *BoPubDir 4, 5*
Hispanic Society of America - New York, NY - *BoPubDir 4, 5*
Hispanicmark Advertising Inc. - New York, NY - *StaDirAdAg 2-84*
Histline [of National Library of Medicine] - Bethesda, MD - *DirOnDB Spring 84; EISS 83; OnBibDB 3*
Historian, The - Albuquerque, NM - *MagIndMarPl 82-83*
Historic Baltimore Society Inc. - Randallstown, MD - *BoPubDir 5*
Historic Cherry Hill - Albany, NY - *BoPubDir 4, 5*
Historic Kansas City Foundation - Kansas City, MO - *BoPubDir 5*
Historic Key West Preservation Board - Key West, FL - *BoPubDir 5*
Historic New Orleans Collection, The - New Orleans, LA - *MagIndMarPl 82-83*
Historic Photos - St. Helena, CA - *BoPubDir 4, 5*
Historic Preservation [of National Trust for Historic Preservation] - Washington, DC - *MagIndMarPl 82-83; WritMar 84*
Historic Publications of Fredericksburg - Fredericksburg, VA - *BoPubDir 5*
Historic Trails Society of Alberta - Lethbridge, AB, Canada - *BoPubDir 5*
Historical Abstracts [of ABC-Clio Inc.] - Santa Barbara, CA - *CompReadDB 82; DataDirOnSer 84; DirOnDB Spring 84; OnBibDB 3*
Historical Averages [of Dow Jones News/Retrieval Service] - Princeton, NJ - *DataDirOnSer 84*
Historical Aviation Album - Temple City, CA - *BoPubDir 4, 5*
Historical Paper Money Research Institute - Bridgeport, PA - *BoPubDir 4, 5*
Historical Pictures Service Inc. - Chicago, IL - *AvMarPl 83; LitMarPl 83, 84; MagIndMarPl 82-83*
Historical Preservations of America Inc. - Raleigh, NC - *DirMarMP 83*
Historical Quotes [of Dow Jones News/Retrieval Service] - Princeton, NJ - *DataDirOnSer 84*
Historical Society of Alberta - Calgary, AB, Canada - *BoPubDir 4, 5; LitMag&SmPr 83-84*
Historical Society of Ottawa - Ottawa, ON, Canada - *BoPubDir 4 Sup, 5*
Historical Society of Pennsylvania - Philadelphia, PA - *MicroMarPl 82-83*
Historical Society of Rockland County - New City, NY - *BoPubDir 4, 5*

Historical Society of the Gatineau - Old Chelsea, PQ, Canada - *BoPubDir 4, 5*
Historical Society of Western Pennsylvania - Pittsburgh, PA - *BoPubDir 4 Sup, 5*
Historical Studies in the Physical Sciences [of University of California Press] - Berkeley, CA - *LitMag&SmPr 83-84*
Historical Times Inc. - Harrisburg, PA - *DirMarMP 83*
Historical Well Data On-Line - Littleton, CO - *DirOnDB Spring 84*
History & Science of Literature [of Centre de Documentation Sciences Humaines] - Paris, France - *CompReadDB 82*
History & Science of Religions [of Centre de Documentation Sciences Humaines] - Paris, France - *CompReadDB 82*
History Book Club Inc., The [Div. of HBJ Communications & Services] - Stamford, CT - *LitMarPl 83, 84*
History of Medicine Online [of National Library of Medicine] - Bethesda, MD - *CompReadDB 82; DataDirOnSer 84*
History of Science & Techniques [of Centre de Documentation Sciences Humaines] - Paris, France - *CompReadDB 82*
Historyland Journal, The - King George, VA - *Ed&PubIntYB 82*
Hit & Run Press - Berkeley, CA - *BoPubDir 4 Sup, 5*
Hit Machine Music Co., The [Div. of Diversified Management Group] - San Diego, CA - *BillIntBG 83-84*
Hit Machine Records [Div. of Diversified Management Group] - San Diego, CA - *BillIntBG 83-84*
Hit Man Record Co. - Las Vegas, NV - *BillIntBG 83-84*
Hit Parader - Derby, CT - *BaconPubCkMag 84; MagDir 84; MagIndMarPl 82-83*
Hitachi America Ltd. - Doraville, GA - *DataDirSup 7-83; DirInfWP 82*
Hitachi Denshi America Ltd. - Woodbury, NY - *AvMarPl 83; BillIntBG 83-84*
Hitachi Ltd. - Tokyo, Japan - *ElecNews 7-25-83*
Hitachi Sales Corp. of America - Compton, CA - *BillIntBG 83-84; HomeVid&CabYB 82-83*
Hitchcock County News - Trenton, NE - *AyerDirPub 83; Ed&PubIntYB 82*
Hitchcock Publishing Co. [Subs. of ABC] - Wheaton, IL - *BoPubDir 5; DirMarMP 83; MagIndMarPl 82-83*
HitKit Music - *See* Music Craftshop Inc.
Hitman Music - *See* Williams Music Group, Don
Hitstown-Disko Record Corp. - Washington, DC - *BillIntBG 83-84*
Hitzig Agency, Karen - New York, NY - *LitMarPl 83, 84*
Hive Publishing Co. - Easton, PA - *LitMarPl 83, 84*
H.K. Associates - Jenkintown, PA - *StaDirAdAg 2-84*
Hladun & Sons, John - Toronto, ON, Canada - *BoPubDir 4 Sup, 5*
Hlasatel - Berwyn, IL - *AyerDirPub 83*
HLS Duplication Inc. - Sunnyvale, CA - *MicrocomMPl 84*
HMB Publications - Hammond, IN - *BoPubDir 4, 5*
HMC Records - Charlotte, NC - *BillIntBG 83-84*
HMK Advertising - Chestnut Hill, MA - *AdAge 3-28-84; StaDirAdAg 2-84*
HN Engineering Inc. - Burnaby, BC, Canada - *TeleSy&SerDir 2-84*
Hoard's Dairyman - Ft. Atkinson, WI - *BaconPubCkMag 84; MagDir 84; MagIndMarPl 82-83*
Hoarty Corp., The - Raleigh, NC - *CabTVFinDB 83*
Hob & Nob Music Publishers - New York, NY - *BillIntBG 83-84*
Hob-Nob - Lancaster, PA - *LitMag&SmPr 83-84*
Hoban, Frank - Bensalem, PA - *DirInfWP 82*
Hobart Corp. - Troy, OH - *DataDirSup 7-83*
Hobart Democrat-Chief - Hobart, OK - *BaconPubCkNews 84; NewsDir 84*
Hobart Gazette - Hobart, IN - *BaconPubCkNews 84; Ed&PubIntYB 82; NewsDir 84*
Hobart Kiowa County Star Review - Hobart, OK - *BaconPubCkNews 84*
Hobart-McIntosh Paper Co. [Div. of Unijax Inc.] - Elk Grove Village, IL - *LitMarPl 83, 84*
Hobart Music - *See* Cornelius Music, Stan
Hobbies: The Magazine for Collectors - Chicago, IL - *BaconPubCkMag 84; MagIndMarPl 82-83*
Hobbs Cablevision [of Cable Information Systems Inc.] - Hobbs, NM - *BrCabYB 84; Tel&CabFB 84C*
Hobbs Flare - Hobbs, NM - *AyerDirPub 83; BaconPubCkNews 84; Ed&PubIntYB 82; NewsDir 84*
Hobbs Literary Agency, Ronald - New York, NY - *LitMarPl 83, 84*
Hobbs News-Sun - Hobbs, NM - *BaconPubCkNews 84; Ed&PubIntYB 82; NewsDir 84*
Hobby Artist News - Ft. Atkinson, IA - *BoPubDir 4, 5*
Hobby Horse AV Aids Service Inc., The - Easton, MD - *AvMarPl 83*
Hobby House Press Inc. - Cumberland, MD - *BoPubDir 4, 5; LitMarPl 84*
Hobby Merchandiser - Englishtown, NJ - *BaconPubCkMag 84*
Hobby Merchandiser - New York, NY - *MagIndMarPl 82-83*
Hobby Publishing Service - Albuquerque, NM - *BoPubDir 4, 5*
Hobbyworld Electronics - Northridge, CA - *WhoWMicrocom 83*
Hoboken Pictorial [of West New Yorker Inc.] - Fairview, NJ - *NewsDir 84*
Hoboken Pictorial - Hoboken, NJ - *Ed&PubIntYB 82*
Hoboken Pictorial - *See* West New Yorker Inc.
Hochberg, Bette - Santa Cruz, CA - *BoPubDir 4, 5*
Hochman Associates, Harry W. - New York, NY - *MagIndMarPl 82-83*
Hochman, Steve - New York, NY - *MagIndMarPl 82-83*
Hochmann Books, John L. - New York, NY - *LitMarPl 83, 84*
Hockey Digest - Evanston, IL - *MagIndMarPl 82-83*
Hockey News, The - Toronto, ON, Canada - *BaconPubCkMag 84*
Hodag Shopper - Rhinelander, WI - *AyerDirPub 83*
Hodder & Stoughton Ltd. - Agincourt, ON, Canada - *LitMarPl 83*
Hoddypoll Press - San Francisco, CA - *BoPubDir 4, 5; LitMag&SmPr 83-84*
Hodel, Pat - San Jose, CA - *LitMarPl 83, 84*
Hodes Advertising, Bernard [Div. of Doyle Dane Bernbach Advertising Inc.] - New York, NY - *BrCabYB 84; HBIndAd&MS 82-83; StaDirAdAg 2-84*
Hodgenville La Rue County Herald News - Hodgenville, KY - *BaconPubCkNews 84*
Hodges Advertising, Thomas V. - Bryn Mawr, PA - *StaDirAdAg 2-84*
Hodges & Associates Inc. - Richmond, VA - *IntDirMarRes 83*
Hodges Communications Inc., Jack III - Shreveport, LA - *StaDirAdAg 2-84*
Hodges, Diane - New York, NY - *LitMarPl 83, 84; MagIndMarPl 82-83*
Hodgkins Citizen [of La Grange Suburban Life/Citizen] - La Grange, IL - *NewsDir 84*
Hodolog Music - *See* Windham Hill Music
Hodson, Robert A. - Hillsboro, OH - *Tel&CabFB 84C p.1684*
Hoefer/Amidei Associates Inc. - San Francisco, CA - *DirPRFirms 83*
Hoeft Associates - Arlington, VA - *DataDirOnSer 84; EISS 7-83 Sup*
Hoehler Publishing, Robert - Conifer, CO - *BoPubDir 4, 5*
Hoeppner Advertising - Sioux City, IA - *StaDirAdAg 2-84*
Hoff, William - Dobbs Ferry, NY - *HBIndAd&MS 82-83*
Hoffman Associates Inc., Clive - Los Angeles, CA - *DirPRFirms 83*
Hoffman Camera - Farmingdale, NY - *AvMarPl 83*
Hoffman Co., Raymond A. - *See* Bock Music Co., Fred
Hoffman Educational Systems - Duarte, CA - *AvMarPl 83*
Hoffman Estates-Schaumburg Herald [of Paddock Publications] - Arlington Heights, IL - *NewsDir 84*
Hoffman Estates/Schaumburg Herald - *See* Paddock Publications
Hoffman Estates-Schaumburg Record - Wheaton, IL - *NewsDir 84*
Hoffman Estates/Schaumburg Record - *See* Copley Newspaper Group
Hoffman Estates Voice - *See* Voice Newspapers
Hoffman, Ivan - Los Angeles, CA - *BillIntBG 83-84*
Hoffman, Lee M. - Lauderhill, FL - *LitMarPl 83, 84*
Hoffman Literary Agency, Berenice - New York, NY - *LitMarPl 83, 84*
Hoffman, Paul S. - Croton-on-Hudson, NY - *ADAPSOMemDir 83-84*
Hoffman Research Services - Rillton, PA - *BoPubDir 5*
Hoffman Tribune - Hoffman, MN - *BaconPubCkNews 84; Ed&PubIntYB 82*
Hoffman Unltd. - Westbury, NY - *Tel&CabFB 84C*

Hoffman York & Compton - Milwaukee, WI - *AdAge 3-28-84; ArtMar 84; BrCabYB 84; DirPRFirms 83; StaDirAdAg 2-84*
Hofheimer Inc., Fritz S. - Mineola, NY - *LitMarPl 83, 84*
Hofmann Genealogical & Historical Research, Margaret M. - Roanoke Rapids, NC - *BoPubDir 4 Sup, 5*
Hofstra University (School of Business) - Hempstead, NY - *BoPubDir 4 Sup, 5*
Hog Digest - Columbia, MO - *BaconPubCkMag 84*
Hog Farm Management - Minneapolis, MN - *BaconPubCkMag 84; MagDir 84*
Hog Market Place Quarterly - Toronto, ON, Canada - *BaconPubCkMag 84*
Hogan & Co. Inc., J. P. - Knoxville, TN - *AdAge 3-28-84; StaDirAdAg 2-84*
Hogan & Vecchio Advertising Inc. - Riverside, CA - *StaDirAdAg 2-84*
Hogan-Feldmann Inc. - Encino, CA - *CabTVFinDB 83*
Hogan, Nolan & Stites Inc. - Cincinnati, OH - *StaDirAdAg 2-84*
Hogan Systems Inc. - Dallas, TX - *ADAPSOMemDir 83-84; DataDirSup 7-83*
Hogansville Herald - Hogansville, GA - *Ed&PubIntYB 82*
Hogansville Troup County Herald - *See* Tri-County Newspapers Inc.
Hogarth Press Hawaii Inc. - Honolulu, HI - *BoPubDir 4, 5*
Hoge & Sons Advertising Inc., Huber - James, NY - *StaDirAdAg 2-84*
Hoger, Donald - Grand Forks Air Force Base, ND - *Tel&CabFB 84C p.1684*
Hogeye Records - Evanston, IL - *BillIntBG 83-84*
Hoglund, Verner - Darrington, WA - *Tel&CabFB 84C p.1685*
Hogrefe Inc., C. J. - Toronto, ON, Canada - *BoPubDir 4 Sup, 5*
Hohenwald Lewis County Herald - Hohenwald, TN - *BaconPubCkNews 84*
Hohman Telephone Co. - Pelican Rapids, MN - *TelDir&BG 83-84*
Hohmann, Hinton & Associates Inc. - Vero Beach, FL - *StaDirAdAg 2-84*
Hoisington Dispatch - Hoisington, KS - *Ed&PubIntYB 82*
Hoisington Dispatch - *See* Dispatch Publishing Co.
Hokar Corp. - New York, NY - *StaDirAdAg 2-84*
Hoke Communications Inc. - Garden City, NY - *DirMarMP 83*
Hokubei Mainichi - San Francisco, CA - *AyerDirPub 83; Ed&PubIntYB 82; NewsDir 84*
Hokushin [Div. of Rangertone Research Inc.] - Belleville, NJ - *AvMarPl 83*
Hol-Land Books - Bonita Springs, FL - *BoPubDir 4, 5*
Holbrook Observer - Holbrook, NE - *Ed&PubIntYB 82*
Holbrook Observer - *See* Arapahoe Public Mirror
Holbrook Research Institute - Oxford, MA - *BoPubDir 4, 5*
Holbrook Sun - Holbrook, MA - *BaconPubCkNews 84; Ed&PubIntYB 82*
Holbrook Times - Holbrook, MA - *Ed&PubIntYB 82*
Holbrook Times - *See* Bulletin Publishing Co.
Holbrook Tribune News - Holbrook, AZ - *BaconPubCkNews 84; Ed&PubIntYB 82*
Holbrook Tribune News & Snowflake Herald - Holbrook, AZ - *NewsDir 84*
Holden Cable Co. Inc. - Holden, MO - *BrCabYB 84*
Holden-Day Inc. - Oakland, CA - *ArtMar 84; LitMarPl 83, 84*
Holden Progress - Holden, MO - *BaconPubCkNews 84; Ed&PubIntYB 82*
Holdenville Cable Co. - Holdenville, OK - *Tel&CabFB 84C*
Holdenville News - Holdenville, OK - *BaconPubCkNews 84; NewsDir 84*
Holder, Kennedy & Co. Inc. - Nashville, TN - *DirPRFirms 83*
Holderby Associates - Oklahoma City, OK - *ArtMar 84; StaDirAdAg 2-84*
Holdrege Citizen - Holdrege, NE - *BaconPubCkNews 84; Ed&PubIntYB 82; NewsDir 84*
Holdworth & Associates Inc., W. G. - Mt. Prospect, IL - *MagIndMarPl 82-83*
Holechek Associates Inc., James - Baltimore, MD - *DirPRFirms 83*
Holechek Communications - Baltimore, MD - *ArtMar 84*
Holiday Broadcasting Co. - Salt Lake City, UT - *BrCabYB 84*
Holiday Cablevision - Mason City, IA - *Tel&CabFB 84C p.1685*
Holiday Herald - Tarpon Springs, FL - *AyerDirPub 83; Ed&PubIntYB 82*
Holiday House - New York, NY - *ArtMar 84; LitMarPl 83, 84; WritMar 84*
Holiday Inn Hi-Net Communications Inc. - Memphis, TN - *DataDirSup 7-83*
Holiday Inn Video Network [of Holiday Inns Inc.] - Memphis, TN - *TeleSy&SerDir 7-83*
Holiday Leader - Holiday, FL - *Ed&PubIntYB 82*
Holiday Leader - Tarpon Springs, FL - *AyerDirPub 83*
Holistic Press - Downsview, ON, Canada - *BoPubDir 4 Sup, 5*
Holladay-Tyler Printing Corp. - Rockville, MD - *LitMarPl 83, 84; MagIndMarPl 82-83*
Holland & Callaway Advertising Inc. - New York, NY - *StaDirAdAg 2-84*
Holland & Partners Ltd., Brian - New York, NY - *DirMarMP 83*
Holland Automation USA Inc. - Costa Mesa, CA - *WhoWMicrocom 83*
Holland Automation USA Inc. - Santa Ana, CA - *MicrocomMPl 84; MicrocomSwDir 1*
Holland Co., William F. - Cincinnati, OH - *TelAl 83, 84*
Holland Flashes - Allegan, MI - *AyerDirPub 83*
Holland House Press - Northville, MI - *BoPubDir 4, 5*
Holland, James R. - Boston, MA - *MagIndMarPl 82-83*
Holland Productions Inc. - Dallas, TX - *AvMarPl 83*
Holland Progress - Holland, TX - *Ed&PubIntYB 82*
Holland Sentinel - Holland, MI - *BaconPubCkNews 84; Ed&PubIntYB 82; NewsDir 84*
Hollander Associates Inc., Kenneth - Atlanta, GA - *BrCabYB 84; IntDirMarRes 83*
Hollander, Cohen Associates Inc. - Baltimore, MD - *IntDirMarRes 83*
Hollandia News - Chatham, ON, Canada - *Ed&PubIntYB 82*
Holleger, Roger - Baton Rouge, LA - *Tel&CabFB 84C p.1685*
Hollenbeck Music - *See* India Music Ink
Hollenbeck Photography, Cliff - Seattle, WA - *LitMarPl 83, 84; MagIndMarPl 82-83*
Holley/Thomas Inc. - Williston Park, NY - *StaDirAdAg 2-84*
Holliday Software - San Diego, CA - *MicrocomMPl 83; MicrocomSwDir 1; WhoWMicrocom 83*
Hollidaysburg Altoona Catholic Register, The - Hollidaysburg, PA - *NewsDir 84*
Hollidaysburg Blair Press - Roaring Spring, PA - *NewsDir 84*
Hollinger Corp. - Arlington, VA - *DirInfWP 82*
Hollingsworth & Associates Inc., E. R. - Rockford, IL - *StaDirAdAg 2-84*
Hollingsworth, Larry D. - Plains, KS - *BrCabYB 84*
Hollingsworth, Larry D. - Hammon, OK - *Tel&CabFB 84C p.1685*
Hollins Critic, The - Hollins College, VA - *LitMag&SmPr 83-84*
Hollins Radio Data - Los Angeles, CA - *BoPubDir 5*
Hollis Cablevision [of Communication Systems Inc.] - Hollis, OK - *BrCabYB 84; Tel&CabFB 84C*
Hollis-Holliswood & Jamaica Estates Pennysaver - Rockville Centre, NY - *AyerDirPub 83*
Hollis Music Inc. - *See* TRO
Hollis News - Hollis, OK - *BaconPubCkNews 84; Ed&PubIntYB 82*
Hollister Advance - Hollister, CA - *Ed&PubIntYB 82*
Hollister Free Lance - Hollister, CA - *BaconPubCkNews 84; NewsDir 84*
Holliston Mills Inc., The - Hyannis, MA - *LitMarPl 83, 84*
Hollman, Stephen N. - Palo Alto, CA - *ADAPSOMemDir 83-84*
Hollow Spring Press - Chester, MA - *LitMag&SmPr 83-84*
Hollow Spring Review of Poetry - Chester, MA - *LitMag&SmPr 83-84*
Holloway House Publishing Co. - Los Angeles, CA - *WritMar 84*
Holly Chieftain - Holly, CO - *BaconPubCkNews 84; Ed&PubIntYB 82*
Holly Herald-Advertiser - Holly, MI - *BaconPubCkNews 84; Ed&PubIntYB 82*
Holly Hill Publishers - Saluda, NC - *BoPubDir 4, 5*
Holly, Marcia - New Haven, CT - *LitMarPl 83, 84*
Holly Springs South Reporter - Holly Springs, MS - *BaconPubCkNews 84; NewsDir 84*
Hollym International Corp. - Elizabeth, NJ - *BoPubDir 4, 5*
Hollyman Inc., Tom - New York, NY - *AvMarPl 83; LitMarPl 83, 84; MagIndMarPl 82-83*

Hollyrock Records - Pico Rivera, CA - *BillIntBG 83-84*
Hollytree Music - Nashville, TN - *BillIntBG 83-84*
Hollywood Cablevision - Hollywood, FL - *BrCabYB 84; Tel&CabFB 84C*
Hollywood Center for the Audio-Visual Arts [of the Los Angeles Recreation & Parks Dept.] - Los Angeles, CA - *TelAl 83, 84*
Hollywood Citizen News - Hollywood, CA - *BaconPubCkNews 84*
Hollywood Citizen News - Los Angeles, CA - *LitMarPl 83*
Hollywood Citizen News & Associated Publications - Los Angeles, CA - *NewsDir 84*
Hollywood Film Archive - Hollywood, CA - *BoPubDir 4, 5; DirMarMP 83; LitMag&SmPr 83-84*
Hollywood General Studios - Hollywood, CA - *Tel&CabFB 84C*
Hollywood Home Theatre - New York, NY - *TelAl 83*
Hollywood Home Theatre - *See* Budget Video Inc./Hollywood Home Theatre
Hollywood Hotline - Burbank, CA - *DirOnDB Spring 84; EISS 5-84 Sup*
Hollywood Hotline [of CompuServe Inc.] - Columbus, OH - *DataDirOnSer 84*
Hollywood Image International, The - Los Angeles, CA - *LitMarPl 84*
Hollywood Image, The - Los Angeles, CA - *LitMarPl 83*
Hollywood Independent - Hollywood, CA - *Ed&PubIntYB 82*
Hollywood Independent [of Los Angeles Meredith Newspapers] - Los Angeles, CA - *AyerDirPub 83; NewsDir 84*
Hollywood Inside Syndicate [Div. of International Hollywood Image] - Los Angeles, CA - *Ed&PubIntYB 82; LitMarPl 83, 84; MagIndMarPl 82-83*
Hollywood Mirror - Ft. Lauderdale, FL - *AyerDirPub 83*
Hollywood Mirror, The - West Hollywood, FL - *Ed&PubIntYB 82*
Hollywood Newsreel Syndicate Inc. - Hollywood, CA - *Tel&CabFB 84C*
Hollywood Reporter [of H.R. Industries] - Hollywood, CA - *BaconPubCkMag 84; Ed&PubIntYB 82; LitMarPl 83, 84; NewsBur 6; WritMar 84*
Hollywood Reporter - Los Angeles, CA - *MagDir 84; NewsDir 84*
Hollywood Songs Inc. - *See* Fox Publishing Co. Inc., Sam
Hollywood Squares - New York, NY - *MagDir 84*
Hollywood Sun Tattler - Hollywood, FL - *BaconPubCkNews 84; Ed&PubIntYB 82; NewsBur 6; NewsDir 84*
Hollywood U.S.A. - Hollywood, CA - *BaconPubCkNews 84*
Holman Bible Publishers [Div. of Baptist Sunday School Board] - Nashville, TN - *LitMarPl 83, 84*
Holman Data Processing - Oroville, CA - *MicrocomSwDir 1*
Holmes, Adrienne E. - Greenwich, CT - *LitMarPl 83, 84*
Holmes & Co. Inc., Michael - New York, NY - *AdAge 3-28-84; StaDirAdAg 2-84*
Holmes & Meier Publishers Inc. - Brunswick, NJ - *LitMag&SmPr 83-84*
Holmes & Meier Publishers Inc. [Div. of IUB Inc.] - New York, NY - *LitMarPl 83, 84; WritMar 84*
Holmes & Shaw Inc. - San Antonio, TX - *ADAPSOMemDir 83-84; DataDirOnSer 84*
Holmes Book Co. - Oakland, CA - *BoPubDir 4, 5*
Holmes, Burnham - New York, NY - *LitMarPl 83, 84*
Holmes County Advertiser - Bonifay, FL - *Ed&PubIntYB 82*
Holmes County Farmer-Hub [of Wooster Republican Co.] - Millersburg, OH - *AyerDirPub 83; Ed&PubIntYB 82; NewsDir 84*
Holmes County Herald - Lexington, MS - *AyerDirPub 83; Ed&PubIntYB 82*
Holmes Engineering Inc. - Murray, UT - *MicrocomMPl 84*
Holmes Enterprise, Stacy - Hollywood, CA - *BoPubDir 4 Sup, 5*
Holmes Features, Venice - Saginaw, MI - *Ed&PubIntYB 82*
Holmes Laboratories Inc., Frank - San Fernando, CA - *AvMarPl 83*
Holmes, Lee M. & Joan S. - Agana, GU - *Tel&CabFB 84C p.1685*
Holmes Protection Inc. - New York, NY - *DirInfWP 82*
Holmgangers Press - Whitethorn, CA - *BoPubDir 4, 4 Sup, 5; LitMag&SmPr 83-84*
Holographic Concepts Inc. - New York, NY - *CabTVFinDB 83; InterCabHB 3*
Holosphere - New York, NY - *BaconPubCkMag 84; MagDir 84*
Holstein Advance - Holstein, IA - *BaconPubCkNews 84; Ed&PubIntYB 82*
Holstein Journal - Don Mills, ON, Canada - *BaconPubCkMag 84*
Holstein World - Sandy Creek, NY - *BaconPubCkMag 84; MagDir 84*
Holt & Co. Inc., T. J. - Westport, CT - *DirMarMP 83*
Holt Broadcasting Service - Hattiesburg, MS - *BrCabYB 84*
Holt, Rinehart & Winston [Div. of CBS Inc.] - New York, NY - *AvMarPl 83; MicrocomMPl 83, 84; MicrocomSwDir 1; Tel&CabFB 84C*
Holt, Rinehart & Winston General Book Div. [of CBS Educational & Professional Publishing] - New York, NY - *LitMarPl 83, 84*
Holt, Rinehart & Winston of Canada Ltd. - Toronto, ON, Canada - *LitMarPl 83; WritMar 84*
Holton Cable Inc. [of Central Cable Services Inc.] - Holton, KS - *BrCabYB 84; Tel&CabFB 84C*
Holton Recorder - Holton, KS - *BaconPubCkNews 84; Ed&PubIntYB 82; NewsDir 84*
Holtville Tribune - Holtville, CA - *BaconPubCkNews 84; Ed&PubIntYB 82*
Holtzman-Kain Advertising Inc. - Chicago, IL - *StaDirAdAg 2-84*
Holub & Associates - North Stonington, CT - *LitMarPl 83, 84*
Holway Telephone Co. [Aff. of Century Telephone Enterprises Inc.] - Maitland, MO - *TelDir&BG 83-84*
Holy Cow! Press - Minneapolis, MN - *BoPubDir 4, 5; LitMag&SmPr 83-84*
Holy Spirit Corp. - Inkster, MI - *BillIntBG 83-84*
Holy Spirit Music - Edmonton, KY - *BillIntBG 83-84*
Holy Terror - Toronto, ON, Canada - *BoPubDir 4 Sup, 5*
Holyoke Coated & Printed Paper Co. [Div. of Millen Industries Inc.] - New York, NY - *LitMarPl 83*
Holyoke Enterprise - Holyoke, CO - *BaconPubCkNews 84; Ed&PubIntYB 82*
Homaco Inc. - Chicago, IL - *DataDirSup 7-83*
Home - Talladega, AL - *AyerDirPub 83*
Home - Mankato, MN - *AyerDirPub 83*
Home [of Knapp Communications Corp.] - Oradell, NJ - *BaconPubCkMag 84; MagDir 84; MagIndMarPl 82-83; WritMar 84*
Home [of Knapp Communications Corp.] - New York, NY - *Folio 83*
Home & Auto [of Harcourt Brace Jovanovich Inc.] - New York, NY - *BaconPubCkMag 84; MagDir 84*
Home & Away Connecticut - Hamden, CT - *MagDir 84*
Home & Away Magazine - Omaha, NE - *MagDir 84*
Home & Away North Dakota - Fargo, NV - *MagDir 84*
Home & School Institute Inc. - Washington, DC - *BoPubDir 4, 5*
Home & School Press - Sun City, AZ - *BoPubDir 4, 5*
Home & Store News, The - Ramsey, NJ - *AyerDirPub 83; Ed&PubIntYB 82*
Home Arts Guild Research Center - Chicago, IL - *IntDirMarRes 83*
Home Banking & Information Service [of Horizon Bancorp] - Morristown, NJ - *EISS 5-84 Sup*
Home Box Office [of Time Inc.] - New York, NY - *BrCabYB 84; CabTVPrDB 83; HomeVid&CabYB 82-83; TelAl 83; Tel&CabFB 84C*
Home Builder News [of Eneguess Publishing Co.] - Peterborough, NH - *BaconPubCkMag 84; MagDir 84*
Home Business Press - Chicago, IL - *BoPubDir 4 Sup, 5*
Home Buyers Guide [of Bryan Publications Inc.] - Newport Beach, CA - *WritMar 84*
Home Cable Co. [of TCA Cable TV Inc.] - Mountain Home, AR - *BrCabYB 84; Tel&CabFB 84C*
Home Cablevision Co. - Madelia, MN - *Tel&CabFB 84C*
Home CATV Co. Inc. [of Telephone & Data Systems] - Barnwell, SC - *BrCabYB 84*
Home CATV Co. Inc. [of Telephone & Data Systems Inc.] - Williston, SC - *Tel&CabFB 84C*
Home Center Magazine [of Vance Publishing Corp.] - Chicago, IL - *MagDir 84*
Home Center Magazine - Lincolnshire, IL - *BaconPubCkMag 84*
Home Communications - New York, NY - *BaconPubCkMag 84*
Home Computer News - Bethesda, MD - *BaconPubCkMag 84*

Home Computer News [of NewsNet Inc.] - Bryn Mawr, PA - *DataDirOnSer 84*
Home Data Vision Inc. - San Francisco, CA - *VideoDir 82-83*
Home Economic Theses [of University of Alberta] - Edmonton, AB, Canada - *DataDirOnSer 84*
Home Economics Education Association - Washington, DC - *BoPubDir 4, 5*
Home Economics Reading Service Inc. - Washington, DC - *ProGuPRSer 4*
Home Economics School Service [Div. of Social Studies School Service] - Culver City, CA - *AvMarPl 83*
Home Electronics & Entertainment [of Harris Publications Inc.] - New York, NY - *BaconPubCkMag 84; MicrocomMPl 84*
Home Electronics Products News - Dover, NJ - *BaconPubCkMag 84*
Home Electronics Products News [of Gordon Publications Inc.] - Randolph, NJ - *MicrocomMPl 84*
Home Entertainment - Carle Place, NY - *BaconPubCkMag 84*
Home Entertainment Marketing - Waltham, MA - *BaconPubCkMag 84; WritMar 84*
Home Entertainment Network [Subs. of United Cable Television Corp.] - Cincinnati, OH - *CabTVPrDB 83; HomeVid&CabYB 82-83*
Home Entertainment Productions - Huntington Station, NY - *TelAl 83*
Home Fashions Textiles - New York, NY - *BaconPubCkMag 84; MagIndMarPl 82-83*
Home Financial Services Program [of Electronic Banking Inc.] - Atlanta, GA - *TeleSy&SerDir 7-83*
Home Furnishings [of Southwest Homefurnishings Association] - Dallas, TX - *BaconPubCkMag 84; MagDir 84; WritMar 84*
Home Furnishings Services - Washington, DC - *DirPRFirms 83*
Home Goods Retailing - Toronto, ON, Canada - *BaconPubCkMag 84*
Home Grown Books Librarians' Browser [of The Carolina Wren Press] - Austin, TX - *LitMag&SmPr 83-84*
Home Happenings - Willowdale, ON, Canada - *BoPubDir 4 Sup, 5*
Home Health Care Business [of Cassak Publications Inc.] - Union, NJ - *ArtMar 84; MagDir 84; MagIndMarPl 82-83; WritMar 84*
Home Improvement Contractor - Chicago, IL - *MagIndMarPl 82-83*
Home Journal - Lacon, IL - *AyerDirPub 83; Ed&PubIntYB 82*
Home Life - Chicago, IL - *BaconPubCkMag 84; MagDir 84*
Home Life [of Sunday School Board] - Nashville, TN - *ArtMar 84; MagIndMarPl 82-83; WritMar 84*
Home Lighting & Accessories - Clifton, NJ - *BaconPubCkMag 84; MagDir 84; MagIndMarPl 82-83; WritMar 84*
Home Management Systems Inc. - Winnipeg, MB, Canada - *DataDirOnSer 84*
Home Music Store [of Digital Music Co.] - Washington, DC - *BrCabYB 84; HomeVid&CabYB 82-83*
Home News - Hialeah, FL - *AyerDirPub 83; Ed&PubIntYB 82*
Home News - Secaucus, NJ - *AyerDirPub 83; Ed&PubIntYB 82*
Home News - Bath, PA - *AyerDirPub 83; Ed&PubIntYB 82*
Home News & Times - Yonkers, NY - *AyerDirPub 83*
Home News Enterprises - Columbus, IN - *Ed&PubIntYB 82*
Home News Publishing Co. - New Brunswick, NJ - *BrCabYB 84; Tel&CabFB 84S*
Home News Publishing Co. - *See* Perkiomen Home-Vue Inc.
Home News, The - New Brunswick, NJ - *AyerDirPub 83; Ed&PubIntYB 82*
Home of Frosted Sunshine - Shermans Dale, PA - *BoPubDir 4, 5*
Home Paper - Waelder, TX - *AyerDirPub 83; Ed&PubIntYB 82*
Home Planet News - New York, NY - *LitMag&SmPr 83-84*
Home Planet Publications - New York, NY - *BoPubDir 4, 5; LitMag&SmPr 83-84*
Home Planners Inc. - Farmington Hills, MI - *BoPubDir 4, 5; DirMarMP 83*
Home Plans & Products/Custom Home Plans Guide - Mineola, NY - *MagDir 84*
Home-Record, The - Livingston, AL - *Ed&PubIntYB 82*
Home Reporter & Sunset News - Brooklyn, NY - *AyerDirPub 83; BaconPubCkNews 84; Ed&PubIntYB 82*
Home Satellite Entertainment - Sacramento, CA - *Tel&CabFB 84C*
Home Shop Machinist, The - Traverse City, MI - *MagIndMarPl 82-83; WritMar 84*
Home Showtime Inc. - Southfield, MI - *Tel&CabFB 84C*
Home Sports Entertainment Network [of Warner Amex Satellite Entertainment Co.] - New York, NY - *CabTVPrDB 83*
Home Telephone Co. - St. Jacob, IL - *TelDir&BG 83-84*
Home Telephone Co. [Aff. of Telephone & Data Systems Inc.] - Waldron, IN - *TelDir&BG 83-84*
Home Telephone Co. - Galva, KS - *TelDir&BG 83-84*
Home Telephone Co. - Grand Meadow, MN - *TelDir&BG 83-84*
Home Telephone Co. [Aff. of Century Telephone Enterprises Inc.] - Olive Branch, MS - *TelDir&BG 83-84*
Home Telephone Co. [Aff. of Telephone & Data Systems Inc.] - Condon, OR - *TelDir&BG 83-84*
Home Telephone Co. - Moncks Corner, SC - *TelDir&BG 83-84*
Home Telephone Co. of Nebraska - Brady, NE - *TelDir&BG 83-84*
Home Telephone Co. of Pittsboro Inc. [Aff. of Telephone & Data Systems Inc.] - Pittsboro, IN - *TelDir&BG 83-84*
Home Testing Institute - Garden City Park, NY - *IntDirMarRes 83*
Home Textiles Today - New York, NY - *BaconPubCkMag 84*
Home Theater Inc. - Astoria, OR - *Tel&CabFB 84C*
Home Theater Network Plus [of Westinghouse Broadcasting] - Portland, ME - *BrCabYB 84; HomeVid&CabYB 82-83; TelAl 83; Tel&CabFB 84C*
Home Times - Flanagan, IL - *AyerDirPub 83*
Home Town Flavor - Pasadena, CA - *Ed&PubIntYB 82*
Home Video & Cable Report, The - White Plains, NY - *BaconPubCkMag 84*
Home-Vue Cable TV - Doylestown, PA - *Tel&CabFB 84C*
Home-Vue Cable TV - King of Prussia, PA - *Tel&CabFB 84C*
Home Weekly - Lawrenceville, GA - *AyerDirPub 83; Ed&PubIntYB 82*
Homebase Computer Systems - Durham, NC - *MicrocomMPl 84*
Homebound/Teleteaching [of Tucson Unified School District] - Tucson, AZ - *TeleSy&SerDir 7-83*
Homebrew Records - Hazelwood, MO - *BillIntBG 83-84*
Homebuilt Aircraft [of Werner & Werner Corp.] - Encino, CA - *WritMar 84*
Homebuilt Aircraft - Van Nuys, CA - *BaconPubCkMag 84*
Homecare Rehab/Product News - Los Angeles, CA - *BaconPubCkMag 84*
Homecare Rental/Sales - Los Angeles, CA - *BaconPubCkMag 84*
HomeComputer Software - Sunnyvale, CA - *MicrocomMPl 84*
Homedale Owyhee Chronicle - Homedale, ID - *BaconPubCkNews 84*
Homefront Graphics - Santa Barbara, CA - *BoPubDir 4, 5*
Homeland Publishing Co. - Lemon Grove, CA - *BaconPubCkNews 84*
Homemaker - Springfield, IL - *MagDir 84*
Homemaker, The - Rapid City, SD - *BaconPubCkMag 84*
Homemaker's Magazine - Toronto, ON, Canada - *BaconPubCkMag 84*
Homeowner, The How To Magazine - New York, NY - *MagDir 84; WritMar 84*
Homeowners How to Handbook - New York, NY - *MagIndMarPl 82-83*
Homeoye Falls/Lima Avon Shopping News - Canandaigua, NY - *AyerDirPub 83*
Homer [of Mars Group Services] - Slough, England - *EISS 7-83 Sup*
Homer & Durham Advertising - New York, NY - *AdAge 3-28-84; HBIndAd&MS 82-83; StaDirAdAg 2-84*
Homer Guardian-Journal - Homer, LA - *BaconPubCkNews 84; Ed&PubIntYB 82*
Homer Index - Homer, MI - *AyerDirPub 83; BaconPubCkNews 84; Ed&PubIntYB 82*
Homer News - Homer, AK - *BaconPubCkNews 84; Ed&PubIntYB 82*
Homerville Clinch County News - Homerville, GA - *BaconPubCkNews 84*
Homesewing Trade News - Rockville Centre, NY - *BaconPubCkMag 84; MagDir 84*
Homestead - Napoleon, ND - *AyerDirPub 83*

Homestead Books - Brookfield, NY - *BoPubDir 4, 5*
Homestead CATV Associates [of Tele-Communications Inc.] - Homestead Air Force Base, FL - *BrCabYB 84; Tel&CabFB 84C*
Homestead Computer Co. Inc. - Evanston, IL - *MicrocomMPl 84*
Homestead Daily Messenger - Homestead, PA - *NewsDir 84*
Homestead-Florida City News [of South Miami Community Newspapers] - Miami, FL - *AyerDirPub 83; NewsDir 84*
Homestead-Florida City News - *See* Community Newspapers of Florida Inc.
Homestead Publishing - Moose, WY - *BoPubDir 5*
Homestead Records - Chicago, IL - *BillIntBG 83-84*
Homestead Squirrel Hill News - Homestead, PA - *NewsDir 84*
Hometown Computer Services - Salt Lake City, UT - *MicrocomSwDir 1*
Hometown Music Co. - Jackson Heights, NY - *BillIntBG 83-84*
Homeward Press - Berkeley, CA - *BoPubDir 4, 5*
Homeware - Ruston, LA - *MicrocomMPl 84*
Homewood Bruston News - Pittsburgh, PA - *Ed&PubIntYB 82*
Homewood Flossmoor Economist [of Chicago Daily Southtown Economist Newspapers] - Chicago, IL - *NewsDir 84*
Homewood Flossmoor-Olympia Field Pointer Economist - South Holland, IL - *AyerDirPub 83*
Homewood/Flossmoor Pointer-Economist - *See* Pointer-Economist Newspapers
Homewood-Flossmoor Star - Chicago Heights, IL - *NewsDir 84*
Homewood Flossmoor Star - Homewood, IL - *AyerDirPub 83; Ed&PubIntYB 82*
Homewood/Flossmoor Star - *See* Star Publications
Homewood House Music - Beverly Hills, CA - *BillIntBG 83-84*
Homewood Sun [of Birmingham Sun Newspapers South & West] - Birmingham, AL - *NewsDir 84*
Homiletic & Pastoral Review, The - New York, NY - *MagDir 84*
Homin Ukrainy - Toronto, ON, Canada - *Ed&PubIntYB 82*
Hominy Cablevision [of Community Cablevision Co.] - Hominy, OK - *BrCabYB 84; Tel&CabFB 84C*
Hominy News-Progress - Hominy, OK - *BaconPubCkNews 84; Ed&PubIntYB 82; NewsDir 84*
Hommel Associates Inc., Dennis - Redwood City, CA - *AvMarPl 83*
Homosexual Information Center Inc. [Aff. of The Tangent Group] - Los Angeles, CA - *BoPubDir 4, 5*
Homserv Inc. - Greenwich, CT - *EISS 7-83 Sup; InterCabHB 3; TeleSy&SerDir 7-83; VideoDir 82-83*
Homunculus Press - Deadwood, OR - *LitMag&SmPr 83-84*
Honaker Cablesystems [of American Cablesystems Corp.] - Honaker, VA - *Tel&CabFB 84C*
Hondale Inc. - Akron, OH - *BoPubDir 4 Sup, 5*
Honders Inc. - Middletown, NY - *WhoWMicrocom 83*
Hondo Anvil Herald [of Associated Texas Newspapers Inc.] - Hondo, TX - *Ed&PubIntYB 82; NewsDir 84*
Hondo Anvil Herald - *See* Associated Texas Newspapers Inc.
Honea Path Chronicle - Honea Path, SC - *Ed&PubIntYB 82*
Honeoye Falls Times - *See* Brador Publications Inc.
Honeoye Falls Times, The - Honeoye Falls, NY - *Ed&PubIntYB 82*
Honeoye Lake Courier - Honeoye, NY - *AyerDirPub 83; Ed&PubIntYB 82*
Honeoye Lake Courier - *See* Brador Publications Inc.
Honesdale TV Service - Honesdale, PA - *BrCabYB 84; Tel&CabFB 84C*
Honesdale TV Service - Paupack Township, PA - *BrCabYB 84*
Honesdale Wayne Independent - Honesdale, PA - *BaconPubCkNews 84*
Honey Bee Records - Santa Monica, CA - *BillIntBG 83-84*
Honey Grove Signal-Citizen - *See* News Publishing Co.
Honey Man Publishing Co. - *See* Drake Music Group
Honeywell Datanetwork - Minneapolis, MN - *DataDirOnSer 84*
Honeywell Inc. - Minneapolis, MN - *Datamation 6-83; ElecNews 7-25-83; Top100Al 83*
Honeywell Information Systems Inc. - Newton, MA - *ADAPSOMemDir 83-84*
Honeywell Information Systems Inc. - Waltham, MA - *DataDirSup 7-83; DirInfWP 82; InfIndMarPl 83*
Honeywell Optoelectronics - Richardson, TX - *DataDirSup 7-83*
Hong Kong Stock Exchange [of I. P. Sharp Associates Ltd.] - Toronto, ON, Canada - *DataDirOnSer 84; DirOnDB Spring 84*
Hong Kong Telephone Viewdata [of Hong Kong Telephone Co. Ltd.] - Hong Kong, Hong Kong - *EISS 7-83 Sup; TeleSy&SerDir 7-83*
Hong Kong Tymnet/Telenet Node [of Cable & Wireless Ltd.] - Wanchai, Hong Kong - *InfIndMarPl 83*
Hong, W. M. - Quesnel, BC, Canada - *BoPubDir 4 Sup, 5*
Honickman & Associates Ltd., Howard - Willowdale, ON, Canada - *DataDirSup 7-83*
Honig Associates Inc., Peter - White Plains, NY - *IntDirMarRes 83*
Honolulu [of Honolulu Publishing Co. Ltd.] - Honolulu, HI - *BaconPubCkMag 84; MagDir 84; WritMar 84*
Honolulu Advertiser - Honolulu, HI - *BaconPubCkNews 84; Ed&PubIntYB 82; LitMarPl 83, 84; NewsBur 6; NewsDir 84*
Honolulu Hawaii Times [of Don R. Pickens Co.] - Honolulu, HI - *NewsDir 84*
Honolulu Star-Bulletin [of Gannett Pacific Corp.] - Honolulu, HI - *BaconPubCkNews 84; Ed&PubIntYB 82; LitMarPl 83; NewsBur 6; NewsDir 84*
Honolulu Waikiki Beach Press - Honolulu, HI - *BaconPubCkNews 84*
Hoo-Doo - Galveston, TX - *BoPubDir 4, 5*
Hood Book Services, Alan C. - Brattleboro, VT - *LitMarPl 83, 84*
Hood Canal Cable [of Hood Canal Telephone Co.] - Union, WA - *Tel&CabFB 84C*
Hood Canal Telephone Co. Inc. - Union, WA - *TelDir&BG 83-84*
Hood County Cable TV [of Teltran Inc.] - Granbury, TX - *Tel&CabFB 84C*
Hood County News - Granbury, TX - *AyerDirPub 83; Ed&PubIntYB 82; NewsDir 84*
Hood, Hope & Associates - Tulsa, OK - *AdAge 3-28-84; ArtMar 84; StaDirAdAg 2-84*
Hood Light & Geise - Harrisburg, PA - *ArtMar 84; StaDirAdAg 2-84*
Hood Music Co., Robin - Hollywood, CA - *BillIntBG 83-84*
Hood River News - Hood River, OR - *BaconPubCkNews 84; Ed&PubIntYB 82; NewsDir 84*
Hood Stone & Hogarty - Philadelphia, PA - *DirPRFirms 83; StaDirAdAg 2-84*
Hoodswamp Records - Greenville, NC - *BillIntBG 83-84*
Hoof & Horn - Walsenburg, CO - *MagDir 84*
Hoof Beats [of United States Trotting Association] - Columbus, OH - *BaconPubCkMag 84; MagDir 84; WritMar 84*
Hook Advertising, Henry - Detroit, MI - *ArtMar 84*
Hook, Roth E. - Aliceville, AL - *BrCabYB 84 p.D-302; Tel&CabFB 84C p.1685*
Hook Stations - Aliceville, AL - *BrCabYB 84*
Hooked on Music - *See* Cornelius Music, Stan
Hookem Music - *See* Terrace Music Group Inc.
Hooker Advance - Hooker, OK - *BaconPubCkNews 84; Ed&PubIntYB 82*
Hooker County Tribune - Mullen, NE - *AyerDirPub 83; Ed&PubIntYB 82*
Hooker TV Cable - Hooker, OK - *BrCabYB 84; Tel&CabFB 84C*
Hookit Music - *See* Terrace Music Group Inc.
Hooks, Duffy III - *See* Shamba Publishing Co.
Hooks, Jerry - *See* Shamba Publishing Co.
Hooks Reporter - Hooks, TX - *BaconPubCkNews 84; Ed&PubIntYB 82*
Hooks Telephone Co. [Aff. of Century Telephone Enterprises Inc.] - Hooks, TX - *TelDir&BG 83-84*
Hoonah Cable TV - Hoonah, AK - *Tel&CabFB 84C*
Hoop [of Professional Sports Publications] - New York, NY - *WritMar 84*
Hooper Holmes Inc. - Basking Ridge, NJ - *IntDirMarRes 83*
Hooper Inc., C. E. - Mamaroneck, NY - *Tel&CabFB 84C*
Hooper Inc., Starch Inra - Mamaroneck, NY - *BrCabYB 84*
Hooper Sentinel - Hooper, NE - *BaconPubCkNews 84; Ed&PubIntYB 82*
Hooper Telephone Co. - Hooper, NE - *TelDir&BG 83-84*
Hoopeston Cable TV Co. [of Omega Communications Inc.] - Hoopeston, IL - *BrCabYB 84; Tel&CabFB 84C*
Hoopeston Chronicle - Hoopeston, IL - *BaconPubCkNews 84*
Hoopeston Chronicle-Herald [of Mills Publications Inc.] - Hoopeston, IL - *NewsDir 84*

Hoosharar - Saddle Brook, NJ - *Ed&PubIntYB 82; MagIndMarPl 82-83*
Hoosharar - New York, NY - *NewsDir 84*
Hoosick Falls Standard Press - *See* Banner Publishing Co.
Hoosier Banker [of Indiana Bankers Association] - Indianapolis, IN - *BaconPubCkMag 84; MagDir 84*
Hoosier Buckeye Cable TV Co. Inc. - Hicksville, OH - *Tel&CabFB 84C*
Hoosier Farmer - Indianapolis, IN - *BaconPubCkMag 84; MagDir 84; MagIndMarPl 82-83*
Hoosier Graphic - Kirklin, IN - *AyerDirPub 83*
Hoosier Graphic - Thorntown, IN - *Ed&PubIntYB 82*
Hoosier Hills Cable Co. [of Omega Communications Inc.] - Mitchell, IN - *BrCabYB 84; Tel&CabFB 84C*
Hoosier Hills Publishing - Sellersburg, IN - *BillIntBG 83-84*
Hoosier Independent [of Indiana Oil Marketers Association Inc.] - Indianapolis, IN - *BaconPubCkMag 84; MagDir 84*
Hoosier Motorist Home & Away - Indianapolis, IN - *BaconPubCkMag 84*
Hoosier Music - *See* Drake Music Group
Hoosier Purchasor - Indianapolis, IN - *BaconPubCkMag 84; MagDir 84*
Hootstein, Ann - New York, NY - *LitMarPl 83, 84*
Hoover Brothers Inc. - Kansas City, MO - *AvMarPl 83*
Hoover Institution Press [of Stanford University] - Stanford, CA - *LitMarPl 83, 84; MagIndMarPl 82-83; MicroMarPl 82-83*
Hoover, Peggy - Philadelphia, PA - *LitMarPl 83, 84; MagIndMarPl 82-83*
Hoover, Ruth H. - Canoga Park, CA - *LitMarPl 83, 84*
Hoover Universal (Omni Furniture Div.) - Vernon, AL - *DirInfWP 82*
Hope & Allen Publishing Co. - Belmont, CA - *BoPubDir 4, 5*
Hope Cable Television Ltd. - Hope, BC, Canada - *BrCabYB 84*
Hope Community TV Inc. [of WEHCO Video Inc.] - Hope, AR - *BrCabYB 84; Tel&CabFB 84C*
Hope Enterprises Inc. - Burbank, CA - *Tel&CabFB 84C*
Hope Enterprises of Jacksonville, FL, Inc. - Jacksonville, FL - *BoPubDir 4, 5*
Hope Express - Hope, AR - *BaconPubCkNews 84*
Hope Farm Press - Cornwallville, NY - *BoPubDir 4, 5*
Hope Productions, Harry [Subs. of Harry Hope Inter-Associates] - Hollywood, CA - *AvMarPl 83*
Hope Publishing Co. - Carol Stream, IL - *BillIntBG 83-84; BoPubDir 4, 5*
Hope Reports Inc. - Rochester, NY - *BoPubDir 4 Sup, 5*
Hope Standard Publications Ltd. - Hope, BC, Canada - *Ed&PubIntYB 82*
Hope Star - Hope, AR - *BaconPubCkNews 84; Ed&PubIntYB 82; NewsDir 84*
Hope Star Journal - Hope, IN - *BaconPubCkNews 84*
Hope Tracks - Hope, AR - *LitMag&SmPr 83-84*
Hopewell Cable Systems Inc. - Struthers, OH - *BrCabYB 84; Tel&CabFB 84C*
Hopewell News - Hopewell, VA - *BaconPubCkNews 84; NewsDir 84*
Hopewell/Prince George Cablevision [of Cable Management Associates Inc.] - Hopewell, VA - *BrCabYB 84; Tel&CabFB 84C*
Hopewell Valley News - Hopewell, NJ - *BaconPubCkNews 84*
Hopewood Press - Minneapolis, MN - *BoPubDir 4, 5*
Hopi Sound Music - *See* De Walden Music
Hopkins & Associates Inc. - Avon, CT - *StaDirAdAg 2-84*
Hopkins Bagot - Potomac, MD - *LitMarPl 83, 84*
Hopkins County Echo - Sulphur Springs, TX - *AyerDirPub 83; Ed&PubIntYB 82*
Hopkins Journal - Hopkins, MO - *BaconPubCkNews 84; Ed&PubIntYB 82*
Hopkins-Minnetonka Eden Prairie - *See* Sun Newspapers
Hopkins Minnetonka Sun - Edina, MN - *AyerDirPub 83*
Hopkins-Minnetonka Sun - Hopkins, MN - *Ed&PubIntYB 82*
Hopkins-Minnetonka Sun & Free Section [of Minnesota Suburban Newspapers Inc.] - Minneapolis, MN - *NewsDir 84*
Hopkins, Patwell & Associates [Div. of National Bakers Services Inc.] - Hollywood, FL - *StaDirAdAg 2-84*
Hopkins Syndicate Inc. - Mellott, IN - *BoPubDir 4, 5; Ed&PubIntYB 82; LitMarPl 84*
Hopkinson & Blake Publishers Inc. - New York, NY - *LitMarPl 83, 84*
Hopkinson & Co., T. M. - New York, NY - *DirPRFirms 83*
Hopkinsville Cable TV Inc. [of Times Mirror Cable TV] - Hopkinsville, KY - *BrCabYB 84; Tel&CabFB 84C*
Hopkinsville Kentucky New Era - Hopkinsville, KY - *NewsDir 84*
Hopkinton Leader - Hopkinton, IA - *BaconPubCkNews 84*
Hoppe Analysis, Donald J. - Crystal Lake, IL - *BaconPubCkMag 84*
Hoppenstedt - Darmstadt, West Germany - *DirOnDB Spring 84*
Hoppenstedt Austria - Darmstadt, West Germany - *DirOnDB Spring 84*
Hoppenstedt Netherlands - Haarlem, Netherlands - *DirOnDB Spring 84*
Hopper Co., The Schulyler - Altoona, FL - *StaDirAdAg 2-84*
Hopper Telecommunications Co. Inc. - Altoona, AL - *TelDir&BG 83-84*
Hoppmann Corp. - Chantilly, VA - *AvMarPl 83*
Horatio Community TV - Horatio, AR - *BrCabYB 84; Tel&CabFB 84C*
Horicon Reporter - Horicon, WI - *BaconPubCkNews 84; Ed&PubIntYB 82*
Horist & Associates Inc., L. P. - Evanston, IL - *DirPRFirms 83*
Horizon [of Boone Inc.] - Tuscaloosa, AL - *BaconPubCkMag 84; MagDir 84; MagIndMarPl 82-83; WritMar 84*
Horizon Air - Portland, OR - *BaconPubCkMag 84*
Horizon Books - Fremont, CA - *BoPubDir 4, 5*
Horizon Cablevision [of Horizon Communications Corp.] - Hazelwood, MO - *Tel&CabFB 84C*
Horizon Communications Corp. - Arab, AL - *Tel&CabFB 84C*
Horizon Communications Corp. - Denver, CO - *Tel&CabFB 84C p.1685*
Horizon Communications Corp. [of Tele-Communications Inc.] - Linton, IN - *BrCabYB 84*
Horizon Communications Corp. [of Tele-Communications Inc.] - Alexandria, MN - *BrCabYB 84*
Horizon Communications Corp. [of Tele-Communications Inc.] - Browerville, MN - *BrCabYB 84*
Horizon Communications Corp. [of Tele-Communications Inc.] - Glenwood, MN - *BrCabYB 84*
Horizon Communications Corp. - Kearney, NE - *Tel&CabFB 84C*
Horizon Communications Corp. - North Platte, NE - *Tel&CabFB 84C*
Horizon Communications Corp. - *See* Added Attractions Inc.
Horizon Communications Corp. - *See* Tele-Communications Inc.
Horizon Communications Corp. of Alabama - Boaz, AL - *BrCabYB 84; Tel&CabFB 84C*
Horizon Communications Corp. of Alabama - Centre, AL - *BrCabYB 84*
Horizon Communications Corp. of Alabama - Hartselle, AL - *BrCabYB 84*
Horizon Communications Corp. of Alabama - Jacksonville, AL - *BrCabYB 84; Tel&CabFB 84C*
Horizon Communications Corp. of Alabama - Piedmont, AL - *BrCabYB 84; Tel&CabFB 84C*
Horizon Communications Corp. of Broken Bow - Broken Bow, NE - *Tel&CabFB 84C*
Horizon Communications Corp. of Fulton - Fulton, KY - *BrCabYB 84*
Horizon Communications Corp. of Greencastle [of Tele-Communications Inc.] - Greencastle, IN - *BrCabYB 84*
Horizon Communications Corp. of Henderson - Henderson, KY - *Tel&CabFB 84C*
Horizon Communications Corp. of Indiana [of Tele-Communications Inc.] - Bloomington, IN - *BrCabYB 84*
Horizon Communications Corp. of Indiana [of Tele-Communications Inc.] - Boonville, IN - *BrCabYB 84*
Horizon Communications Corp. of Indiana [of Tele-Communications Inc.] - Elwood, IN - *BrCabYB 84*
Horizon Communications Corp. of Indiana - Franklin, IN - *BrCabYB 84*
Horizon Communications Corp. of Indiana - Greensburg, IN - *Tel&CabFB 84C*
Horizon Communications Corp. of Indiana [of Tele-Communications Inc.] - Martinsville, IN - *BrCabYB 84*
Horizon Communications Corp. of Indiana [of Tele-Communications Inc.] - Mt. Vernon, IN - *BrCabYB 84*

Horizon Communications Corp. of Indiana [of Tele-Communications Inc.] - Sullivan, IN - *BrCabYB 84*
Horizon Communications Corp. of Kansas - Topeka, KS - *BrCabYB 84*
Horizon Communications Corp. of Kearney - Kearney, NE - *BrCabYB 84*
Horizon Communications Corp. of Kentucky - Dawson Springs, KY - *BrCabYB 84*
Horizon Communications Corp. of Kentucky - Henderson, KY - *BrCabYB 84*
Horizon Communications Corp. of Kentucky - Princeton, KY - *BrCabYB 84*
Horizon Communications Corp. of Kentucky - Providence, KY - *BrCabYB 84; Tel&CabFB 84C*
Horizon Communications Corp. of Metro-East - East St. Louis, IL - *Tel&CabFB 84C*
Horizon Communications Corp. of Minnesota - Moorhead, MN - *Tel&CabFB 84C*
Horizon Communications Corp. of Missouri - Clinton, MO - *BrCabYB 84*
Horizon Communications Corp. of Missouri - Knob Noster, MO - *BrCabYB 84*
Horizon Communications Corp. of Nebraska - Grand Island, NE - *BrCabYB 84*
Horizon Communications Corp. of Nebraska - Hastings, NE - *BrCabYB 84; Tel&CabFB 84C*
Horizon Communications Corp. of Nebraska - Lexington, NE - *Tel&CabFB 84C*
Horizon Communications Corp. of Nebraska - McCook, NE - *BrCabYB 84*
Horizon Communications Corp. of Nebraska - North Platte, NE - *BrCabYB 84*
Horizon Communications Corp. of Nebraska - O'Neill, NE - *BrCabYB 84*
Horizon Communications Corp. of Tennessee - Manchester, TN - *Tel&CabFB 84C*
Horizon House Publishers [Aff. of Evangelistic Enterprises Society] - Beaverlodge, AB, Canada - *BoPubDir 4, 5*
Horizon Paper Co. Inc. - New York, NY - *LitMarPl 83, 84; MagIndMarPl 82-83*
Horizon Press Publishers Ltd. - New York, NY - *BoPubDir 4 Sup, 5; LitMarPl 83, 84; WritMar 84*
Horizon Publishers & Distributors Inc. - Bountiful, UT - *BoPubDir 4, 5; LitMarPl 84*
Horizon Software - Philadelphia, PA - *MicrocomMPl 84*
Horizon Software Ltd. - Leicester, England - *MicrocomSwDir 1*
Horizon Tele-Communications - Arab, AL - *BrCabYB 84*
Horizon Tele-Communications Inc. - Albany, MN - *BrCabYB 84*
Horizon Tele-Communications Inc. - Long Prairie, MN - *BrCabYB 84*
Horizon Tele-Communications Inc. - Hermann, MO - *BrCabYB 84*
Horizon Telecommunications Inc. [of Telecommunications Inc.] - Bloomfield, IN - *BrCabYB 84*
Horizons - Toronto, ON, Canada - *Ed&PubIntYB 82*
Horizons Software [Subs. of Case Technology] - Springfield, MO - *MicrocomMPl 84; WhoWMicrocom 83*
Horizons Unltd. - Edwards, CA - *MicrocomMPl 84*
Horizontal Editing Studios - Burbank, CA - *AvMarPl 83*
Horlick Levin Hodges Advertising Inc. - Los Angeles, CA - *AdAge 3-28-84; StaDirAdAg 2-84*
Horn Book - Boston, MA - *BaconPubCkMag 84; LitMarPl 83, 84; MagDir 84; MagIndMarPl 82-83*
Hornbeam Press Inc. - Columbia, SC - *BoPubDir 4, 5*
Hornell Evening Tribune [of Greenhow Newspapers Inc.] - Hornell, NY - *NewsDir 84*
Hornell Television Service Inc. - Hornell, NY - *BrCabYB 84; Tel&CabFB 84C*
Hornell Tribune-Spectator - Hornell, NY - *BaconPubCkNews 84*
Horner, Tom - New Orleans, LA - *LitMarPl 83; MagIndMarPl 82-83*
Hornitos Telephone Co. - Anderson, CA - *TelDir&BG 83-84*
Horological Times - Cincinnati, OH - *BaconPubCkMag 84*
Horoscope [of Dell Publishing Co. Inc.] - New York, NY - *MagDir 84; WritMar 84*
Horoscope Guide - West Springfield, MA - *WritMar 84*
Horowitz & Associates, Harve C. - Columbia, MD - *LitMarPl 83, 84; MagIndMarPl 82-83*
Horowitz & Sons, A. - Fairfield, NJ - *LitMarPl 83, 84*
Horowitz, Paltiel - New York, NY - *LitMarPl 83*
Horowitz Studio, David K. - Philadelphia, PA - *LitMarPl 84*
Horowitz, Ted - New York, NY - *MagIndMarPl 82-83*
Horror Show, The [of Phantasm Press] - Oak Run, CA - *WritMar 84*
Horry Cable TV Inc. - Pine Lands, SC - *BrCabYB 84*
Horry Telephone Cablevision - Loris, SC - *BrCabYB 84*
Horry Telephone Cooperative Inc. - Conway, SC - *TelDir&BG 83-84*
Horse [of Bloodstock Research Information Services Inc.] - Lexington, KY - *DataDirOnSer 84; DirOnDB Spring 84*
Horse Action Magazine - Temecula, CA - *BaconPubCkMag 84*
Horse & Bird Press - Los Angeles, CA - *BoPubDir 4 Sup, 5; LitMag&SmPr 83-84*
Horse & Horseman - Capistrano Beach, CA - *BaconPubCkMag 84; MagDir 84; MagIndMarPl 82-83; WritMar 84*
Horse & Rider - Temecula, CA - *BaconPubCkMag 84; MagDir 84; MagIndMarPl 82-83*
Horse Cave-Cave City Cable TV [of Tennessee-Kentucky Cable TV Co.] - Horse Cave, KY - *Tel&CabFB 84C*
Horse Cave Hart County Herald - *See* Cave Country Newspapers Inc.
Horse Data Bank [of Bloodstock Research Information Services Inc.] - Lexington, KY - *DBBus 82*
Horse Digest, The - Gaithersburg, MD - *BaconPubCkMag 84*
Horse Illustrated [of Fancy Publications Inc.] - San Clemente, CA - *ArtMar 84; BaconPubCkMag 84; WritMar 84*
Horse Lover's National Magazine - Menlo Park, CA - *MagDir 84*
Horse Lover's National Magazine - Temecula, CA - *BaconPubCkMag 84*
Horse of Course - Temple, NH - *MagDir 84; MagIndMarPl 82-83*
Horse Women [of Rich Publishing Inc.] - Temecula, CA - *BaconPubCkMag 84; WritMar 84*
Horse World - Shelbyville, TN - *BaconPubCkMag 84; MagDir 84*
Horsecare - Temecula, CA - *BaconPubCkMag 84*
Horseheads Chemung Valley Reporter - Horseheads, NY - *BaconPubCkNews 84*
Horseman - Houston, TX - *BaconPubCkMag 84; MagDir 84; MagIndMarPl 82-83; WritMar 84*
Horseman & Fair World - Lexington, KY - *BaconPubCkMag 84; MagDir 84*
Horsemen's Book Society - New York, NY - *LitMarPl 83, 84*
Horsemen's Journal - Rockville, MD - *BaconPubCkMag 84; MagDir 84*
Horsemen's Yankee Pedlar Newspaper - Auburn, MA - *WritMar 84*
Horseplay - Gaithersburg, MD - *ArtMar 84; BaconPubCkMag 84; MagDir 84; WritMar 84*
Horses - Encinitas, CA - *BaconPubCkMag 84*
Horses All [of Rocky Top Holdings Ltd.] - Nanton, AB, Canada - *WritMar 84*
Horses & Horsemanship [of Iowa State University Library] - Ames, IA - *CompReadDB 82*
Horseshoe Bay Cable Systems Inc. - Horseshoe Bay, TX - *Tel&CabFB 84C*
Horseshoe Valley Ltd. - Barrie, ON, Canada - *BrCabYB 84*
Horsetrader, The - Middlefield, OH - *MagDir 84*
Horsham Progress - *See* Progress Newspapers Inc.
Horst Book Room, Isaac R. - Mt. Forest, ON, Canada - *BoPubDir 4, 5*
Horticultural Abstracts [of Commonwealth Bureau of Horticulture & Plantation Crops] - Maidstone, England - *CompReadDB 82*
Horticultural Books Inc. - Stuart, FL - *BoPubDir 4, 5*
Horticultural Publications - Gainesville, FL - *BoPubDir 4 Sup, 5*
Horticulture - Boston, MA - *ArtMar 84; BaconPubCkMag 84; MagDir 84; MagIndMarPl 82-83; WritMar 84*
Horton & Associates Inc., Carolyn - New York, NY - *LitMarPl 83, 84*
Horton & Daughters, Thomas - Sun Lakes, AZ - *BoPubDir 4, 5*
Horton Associates, Thomas - Ojai, CA - *Tel&CabFB 84C*
Horton Cable Inc. - Horton, KS - *BrCabYB 84*
Horton Headlight - *See* Horton Headlight Publishers
Horton Headlight Publishers - Horton, KS - *BaconPubCkNews 84*
Horton Headlight, The - Horton, KS - *Ed&PubIntYB 82*
Horton Wathena Times - *See* Horton Headlight Publishers

Horttor Music Co. - Bakersfield, CA - *BillIntBG 83-84*
Horvath, Terri - Indianapolis, IN - *MagIndMarPl 82-83*
Horvitz Newspapers - Valley View, OH - *Ed&PubIntYB 82*
Horwitz, Mann & Bukvic Inc. - Cincinnati, OH - *StaDirAdAg 2-84*
Horwitz Organization, Robert - Granada Hills, CA - *BillIntBG 83-84*
Hosanna Press - Lawton, OK - *BoPubDir 4, 5; LitMag&SmPr 83-84*
Hoschander Inc., Emanuel - New York, NY - *AvMarPl 83*
Hoschek, Gero - Detroit, MI - *LitMarPl 83*
Hose & Nozzle [of Louisiana Oil Marketers Association] - Shreveport, LA - *BaconPubCkMag 84; MagDir 84*
Hosford Publishing Ltd. - Edmonton, AB, Canada - *BoPubDir 4, 5*
Hosiery & Underwear - New York, NY - *MagDir 84*
Hoskins, Rev. Dr. Charles L. - Savannah, GA - *BoPubDir 4 Sup, 5*
Hospers Press - Hospers, IA - *BaconPubCkNews 84*
Hospers Telephone Co. Inc. - Hospers, IA - *TelDir&BG 83-84*
Hospices Civils de Lyon (Departement Informatique) - Bron, France - *InfIndMarPl 83*
Hospital & Community Psychiatry [of American Psychiatric Association] - Washington, DC - *BaconPubCkMag 84; MagDir 84; MagIndMarPl 82-83*
Hospital & Health Services Administration [of American College of Hospital Administrators] - Chicago, IL - *BaconPubCkMag 84; MagDir 84; MagIndMarPl 82-83*
Hospital Compensation Service [Aff. of John R. Zabka Associates Inc.] - Hawthorne, NJ - *BoPubDir 4 Sup, 5*
Hospital Data Center [of American Hospital Association] - Chicago, IL - *EISS 83*
Hospital Financial Management Association - Oak Brook, IL - *BoPubDir 4*
Hospital Formulary [of Harcourt Brace Jovanovich Publications Inc.] - New York, NY - *MagDir 84; MagIndMarPl 82-83*
Hospital Forum [of Association of Western Hospitals] - San Francisco, CA - *BaconPubCkMag 84; MagDir 84*
Hospital Gift Shop Management - North Hollywood, CA - *BaconPubCkMag 84; MagDir 84*
Hospital Information Manager - Los Angeles, CA - *MagIndMarPl 82-83*
Hospital Information Systems Sharing Group - Salt Lake City, UT - *EISS 83*
Hospital Medicine - New York, NY - *BaconPubCkMag 84; MagDir 84; MagIndMarPl 82-83*
Hospital Pharmacy - Huntingdon Valley, PA - *BaconPubCkMag 84*
Hospital Pharmacy [of J. B. Lippincott Co.] - Philadelphia, PA - *MagDir 84; MagIndMarPl 82-83*
Hospital Pharmacy News [of Academy Professional Information Services Inc.] - New York, NY - *BaconPubCkMag 84; MagDir 84*
Hospital Physician - New York, NY - *BaconPubCkMag 84; MagIndMarPl 82-83*
Hospital Practice - New York, NY - *ArtMar 84; BaconPubCkMag 84; MagDir 84; MagIndMarPl 82-83*
Hospital Progress [of Catholic Health Association] - St. Louis, MO - *BaconPubCkMag 84; MagDir 84; MagIndMarPl 82-83*
Hospital Puchasing News [of McKnight Medical Communications Inc.] - Winnetka, IL - *MagDir 84*
Hospital Research & Educational Trust - Chicago, IL - *BoPubDir 4, 5*
Hospital Research Associates Inc. - Fairfield, NJ - *IntDirMarRes 83*
Hospital Satellite Network - Los Angeles, CA - *CabTVPrDB 83*
Hospital Supervisor's Bulletin - Waterford, CT - *ArtMar 84; WritMar 84*
Hospital Topics - Sarasota, FL - *BaconPubCkMag 84; MagDir 84; MagIndMarPl 82-83; NewsBur 6*
Hospital Tribune [of Medical Tribune Inc.] - New York, NY - *MagDir 84*
Hospitality Scene - Minneapolis, MN - *BaconPubCkMag 84*
Hospitals [of American Hospital Association] - Chicago, IL - *BaconPubCkMag 84; MagDir 84; MagIndMarPl 82-83; WritMar 84*
Hospodar [of Cechoslovak Publishing Co. Inc.] - West, TX - *NewsDir 84*
Host Associates Inc., Jim - Lexington, KY - *DirPRFirms 83*
Hoster Bindery Inc. - Hatboro, PA - *LitMarPl 84*
Hot Bear Enterprises - Colorado Springs, CO - *BillIntBG 83-84*
Hot CoCo [of Wayne Green Inc.] - Peterborough, NH - *BaconPubCkMag 84; MicrocomMPl 84*
Hot Line Inc. - Ft. Dodge, IA - *DirMarMP 83*
Hot Off the Press - Canby, OR - *BoPubDir 4, 5*
Hot Press Inc. [Subs. of August Studios Inc.] - New York, NY - *LitMarPl 83, 84*
Hot Property Publishing - *See* Fricon Entertainment Co. Inc.
Hot Rod [of Petersen Publishing Co.] - Los Angeles, CA - *BaconPubCkMag 84; Folio 83; MagDir 84; MagIndMarPl 82-83; WritMar 84*
Hot Springs Gazette, The [of The Doodly-Squat Press] - Los Angeles, CA - *LitMag&SmPr 83-84*
Hot Springs Information Network - Austin, TX - *LitMag&SmPr 83-84*
Hot Springs News - Hot Springs, AR - *BaconPubCkNews 84; Ed&PubIntYB 82; NewsDir 84*
Hot Springs Newsletter [of Hot Springs Information Network] - Austin, TX - *LitMag&SmPr 83-84*
Hot Springs Sentinel-Record - Hot Springs, AR - *BaconPubCkNews 84; NewsDir 84*
Hot Springs Star - Hot Springs, SD - *BaconPubCkNews 84; Ed&PubIntYB 82*
Hot Springs Telephone Co. - Hot Springs, MT - *TelDir&BG 83-84*
Hot Transistor Tunes Inc. - *See* Iguana Music Inc.
Hotaling's News Agency Inc. - New York, NY - *ProGuPRSer 4*
Hotchkiss House Inc. - Pittsford, NY - *BoPubDir 4, 5*
Hotel & Motel Management [of Harcourt Brace Jovanovich Publications Inc.] - New York, NY - *MagDir 84; MagIndMarPl 82-83*
Hotel & Motel Management - Cleveland, OH - *BaconPubCkMag 84*
Hotel & Resort Industry - New York, NY - *BaconPubCkMag 84*
Hotel & Restaurants International - New York, NY - *MagIndMarPl 82-83*
Hotel-Bar-Restaurant Review [of HMRECB Union, Local 24] - Detroit, MI - *NewsDir 84*
Hotel Data Systems Inc. - Norwalk, CT - *DataDirSup 7-83*
Hotel-Motel Professional [of Hotel-Motel Greeters International] - Denver, CO - *BaconPubCkMag 84; MagDir 84*
Hotel Sales Management Association - Margate, NJ - *BoPubDir 5*
Hotel Voice [of Hotel Trades Council, AFL-CIO] - New York, NY - *NewsDir 84*
Hotels & Restaurants International - Des Plaines, IL - *BaconPubCkMag 84*
Hotline Energy Reports Inc. - Denver, CO - *DataDirOnSer 84*
Hotline Multi-Enterprises - Mechanicsville, VA - *BoPubDir 4, 5*
Hotspots! Entertainment Guide [of La Fray Publishing Co.] - St. Petersburg, FL - *LitMag&SmPr 83-84*
Hottman Edwards Advertising - Baltimore, MD - *ArtMar 84; StaDirAdAg 2-84*
Hotwater Review - Philadelphia, PA - *BoPubDir 4, 5*
Houck Advertising - Roanoke, VA - *TelAl 83, 84*
Houck & Harrison - Roanoke, VA - *StaDirAdAg 2-84*
Houghton Daily Mining Gazette - Houghton, MI - *BaconPubCkNews 84; NewsDir 84*
Houghton Lake Cablevision [of Whitney Cablevision of Michigan Ltd.] - West Branch, MI - *BrCabYB 84*
Houghton Lake Resorter - Houghton Lake, MI - *AyerDirPub 83; BaconPubCkNews 84; Ed&PubIntYB 82; NewsDir 84*
Houghton Mifflin Canada Ltd. - Markham, ON, Canada - *LitMarPl 83, 84*
Houghton Mifflin Co. - Boston, MA - *AvMarPl 83; DirInfWP 82; KnowInd 83; LitMarPl 83, 84; WritMar 84*
Houghton Mifflin Co. (Children's Trade Books) - Boston, MA - *WritMar 84*
Houlahan/Parker Marketing Research - Whittier, CA - *IntDirMarRes 83*
Houlgate Enterprises, Deke - Redondo Beach, CA - *DirPRFirms 83*
Houlihan, Raymond F. - New York, NY - *LitMarPl 83, 84; MagIndMarPl 82-83*

Houlton Cable TV [of New England Cablevision Inc.] - Houlton, ME - *BrCabYB 84; Tel&CabFB 84C*
Houlton Pioneer Times - Houlton, ME - *BaconPubCkNews 84; Ed&PubIntYB 82; NewsDir 84*
Houma Cablevision Inc. [of Vision Cable Communications Inc.] - Houma, LA - *Tel&CabFB 84C*
Houma Courier & Terrebonne Press [of New York Times] - Houma, LA - *BaconPubCkNews 84; Ed&PubIntYB 82; NewsDir 84*
Hound Dog Films - San Francisco, CA - *AvMarPl 83*
Hounds & Hunting - Bradford, PA - *BaconPubCkMag 84; MagDir 84*
Hounslow Press [Aff. of Anthony R. Hawke Ltd.] - Willowdale, ON, Canada - *BoPubDir 4, 5; LitMarPl 83, 84; WritMar 84*
Hour, The - Norwalk, CT - *AyerDirPub 83; BaconPubCkNews 84; Ed&PubIntYB 82*
Hourglass Systems - Glen Ellyn, IL - *MicrocomMPl 84*
Housatonic Cablevision Co. - New Milford, CT - *Tel&CabFB 84C*
Housatonic Cablevision Co. - Trumbull, CT - *BrCabYB 84*
Housatonic Valley Publishing Co. - New Milford, CT - *BaconPubCkNews 84*
House & Associates Inc., Stanley G. - Rockville, MD - *StaDirAdAg 2-84*
House & Garden [of Conde Nast Publications] - New York, NY - *ArtMar 84; BaconPubCkMag 84; Folio 83; LitMarPl 83, 84; MagDir 84; MagIndMarPl 82-83; WritMar 84*
House & Garden Plans Guide - New York, NY - *MagDir 84*
House Beautiful [of The Hearst Corp.] - New York, NY - *BaconPubCkMag 84; Folio 83; LitMarPl 83, 84; MagDir 84; MagIndMarPl 82-83; NewsBur 6; WritMar 84*
House Beautiful's Building Manual - New York, NY - *BaconPubCkMag 84; MagDir 84*
House Beautiful's Home Decorating - New York, NY - *BaconPubCkMag 84; MagDir 84*
House Beautiful's Home Remodeling - New York, NY - *BaconPubCkMag 84; MagDir 84*
House Beautiful's Houses & Plans - New York, NY - *BaconPubCkMag 84; MagDir 84*
House Beautiful's Kitchens/Baths - New York, NY - *BaconPubCkMag 84; MagDir 84*
House by the Sea Publishing Co. - Waldport, OR - *BoPubDir 4, 5*
House Co., The - Houston, TX - *MagIndMarPl 82-83*
House in the Hamptons - Remsenburg, NY - *BaconPubCkMag 84*
House Information Systems [of U.S. House of Representatives] - Washington, DC - *EISS 83*
House Market Research Inc. - Potomac, MD - *IntDirMarRes 83*
House of Anansi Press Ltd. - Toronto, ON, Canada - *LitMag&SmPr 83-84; LitMarPl 83, 84*
House of Bryant Publications - Gatlinburg, TN - *BillIntBG 83-84*
House of Cash Inc. - Hendersonville, TN - *BillIntBG 83-84*
House of Collectibles Inc. - Orlando, FL - *LitMarPl 83, 84; WritMar 84*
House of Commons (Computer Systems) - Ottawa, ON, Canada - *CompReadDB 82*
House of Diamonds - Cleburne, TX - *BillIntBG 83-84*
House of Excellence [Div. of Mohr Associated Industries Inc.] - Montclair, NJ - *DirMarMP 83*
House of Falcon Inc. - McAllen, TX - *BillIntBG 83-84*
House of Gold Music Inc. - *See* Warner Bros. Music
House of Hi Ho - Chicago, IL - *BillIntBG 83-84*
House of Keys Press & Distribution - Cincinnati, OH - *BoPubDir 4, 4 Sup, 5; LitMag&SmPr 83-84*
House of Knox - Quartz Hill, CA - *BillIntBG 83-84*
House of Marketing - Los Angeles, CA - *IntDirMarRes 83*
House of Penny - Marietta, GA - *BillIntBG 83-84*
House of Rock Music - San Bernardino, CA - *BillIntBG 83-84*
House of Talos Publishers - East Lansing, MI - *BoPubDir 4, 5*
House of York - San Jose, CA - *BoPubDir 4, 5*
Household - Costa Mesa, CA - *BaconPubCkMag 84*
Household Age/Income Forecast [of Chase Econometrics/ Interactive Data Corp.] - Waltham, MA - *DataDirOnSer 84*
Household Age/Income Forecast - Bala Cynwyd, PA - *DirOnDB Spring 84*
Household & Personal Products Industry [of Rodman Publishing Corp.] - Ramsey, NJ - *MagDir 84; WritMar 84*
Houser & Stoll Inc. - Mendham, NJ - *DirInfWP 82*
Houser, Dave G. - Ridgefield, CT - *MagIndMarPl 82-83*
Houser, Dave G. - New York, NY - *LitMarPl 83*
Housesmiths Press - Kittery Point, ME - *BoPubDir 4, 5*
Housewares [of Harcourt Brace Jovanovich] - New York, NY - *BaconPubCkMag 84; MagDir 84; MagIndMarPl 82-83*
Housewares Merchandising - New York, NY - *BaconPubCkMag 84*
Housewives' Handy Hints - Mt. Dora, FL - *LitMag&SmPr 83-84*
Housing [of McGraw-Hill Inc.] - New York, NY - *MagDir 84; MagIndMarPl 82-83*
Housing & Development Reporter, The - Washington, DC - *MagIndMarPl 82-83*
Housing & Urban Development Association of Canada - Toronto, ON, Canada - *BoPubDir 4, 5*
Housing, Construction & Finance Forecast [of Chase Econometrics/Interactive Data Corp.] - Waltham, MA - *DataDirOnSer 84*
Housing Information Center [Aff. of Foundation for National Progress] - Santa Barbara, CA - *BoPubDir 4*
Housing Information Center [Aff. of Foundation for National Progress] - Green Bay, WI - *BoPubDir 5*
Housing Publishers Inc. - Washington, DC - *DirMarMP 83*
Houston [of Houston Chamber of Commerce] - Houston, TX - *BaconPubCkMag 84; MagDir 84*
Houston Academy Library Committee - Dothan, AL - *BoPubDir 4, 5*
Houston & Associates Inc., Colin A. - Mamaroneck, NY - *IntDirMarRes 83*
Houston Business Journal [of Cordovan Corp.] - Houston, TX - *BaconPubCkMag 84; MagDir 84; NewsDir 84; WritMar 84*
Houston Cable TV [Aff. of Warner Amex Cable Communications Inc.] - Houston, TX - *InterCabHB 3; Tel&CabFB 84C*
Houston Career Digest - Houston, TX - *AyerDirPub 83*
Houston Chronicle - Houston, TX - *BaconPubCkNews 84; Ed&PubIntYB 82; LitMarPl 83, 84; NewsBur 6; NewsDir 84*
Houston Chronicle Publishing Co. - Houston, TX - *AdAge 6-28-84; KnowInd 83*
Houston City Magazine [of Southwest Media Corp.] - Houston, TX - *BaconPubCkMag 84; MagDir 84; WritMar 84*
Houston Community Cablevision Inc. [of Storer Cable Communications] - Houston, TX - *BrCabYB 84; Tel&CabFB 84C*
Houston Community News - *See* Houston Community Newspapers
Houston Community Newspapers - Channelview, TX - *BaconPubCkNews 84*
Houston County News - La Crescent, MN - *AyerDirPub 83; Ed&PubIntYB 82*
Houston Engineer - Houston, TX - *MagDir 84*
Houston Fire Fighter - Houston, TX - *NewsDir 84*
Houston Forward Times - Houston, TX - *BaconPubCkNews 84; NewsDir 84*
Houston Gazette & Country Journal - Houston, MN - *BaconPubCkNews 84; Ed&PubIntYB 82*
Houston Globe Advocate - Houston, TX - *BaconPubCkNews 84*
Houston Herald - Houston, MO - *Ed&PubIntYB 82*
Houston Herald-Republican - Houston, MO - *BaconPubCkNews 84*
Houston Home & Garden [of Metro Home & Garden] - Houston, TX - *BaconPubCkMag 84; Folio 83; MagDir 84; MagIndMarPl 82-83*
Houston Home Journal, The - Perry, GA - *Ed&PubIntYB 82*
Houston Informer - Houston, TX - *BaconPubCkNews 84; Ed&PubIntYB 82; NewsDir 84*
Houston Instrument [Div. of Bausch & Lomb] - Austin, TX - *DataDirSup 7-83; MicrocomMPl 84*
Houston Living - Dallas, TX - *MagIndMarPl 82-83*
Houston Living [of Baker Publications] - Houston, TX - *MagDir 84; WritMar 84*
Houston Monthly - Houston, TX - *BaconPubCkMag 84*
Houston Newspapers Inc. - Houston, MO - *NewsDir 84; Tel&CabFB 84C*
Houston North Magazine - Houston, TX - *MagDir 84*
Houston Photolab - Houston, TX - *AvMarPl 83*
Houston Post - Houston, TX - *BaconPubCkNews 84; Ed&PubIntYB 82; LitMarPl 83, 84; NewsBur 6; NewsDir 84*
Houston Professional Translators Forum - Bellaire, TX - *LitMarPl 83*
Houston Records Ltd. - Houston, TX - *BillIntBG 83-84*

Houston Republican - Houston, MO - *Ed&PubIntYB 82*
Houston/Ritz & Associates - Dallas, TX - *StaDirAdAg 2-84*
Houston Signal - La Crescent, MN - *AyerDirPub 83*
Houston Southwest Suburban Journal - Houston, TX - *NewsDir 84*
Houston Suburbia Reporter - *See* Houston Community Newspapers
Houston Teens - Houston, TX - *NewsDir 84*
Houston Times-Post - Houston, MS - *BaconPubCkNews 84; NewsDir 84*
Houston Trust - Toronto, ON, Canada - *BoPubDir 4 Sup, 5*
Houston Writers Guild - Houston, TX - *LitMag&SmPr 83-84*
Hovemeyer, Eric E. - Cincinnati, OH - *BoPubDir 4, 5*
Hoven Review - Hoven, SD - *AyerDirPub 83; BaconPubCkNews 84; Ed&PubIntYB 82*
Hovey's Audio Visual Sales & Service [Div. of Hovey's Inc.] - Portsmouth, NH - *AvMarPl 83*
Hovland Business Systems Ltd. - Windsor, England - *MicrocomSwDir 1*
How & Peyer Ltd. - St. Eustache, PQ, Canada - *ArtMar 84*
How Books - Toronto, ON, Canada - *LitMarPl 83, 84*
How-To Book Club [Div. of TAB Books Inc.] - Blue Ridge Summit, PA - *LitMarPl 83, 84*
Howard Agency, Marilyn [Aff. of Creative Freelancers Inc.] - New York, NY - *LitMarPl 83, 84*
Howard & Associates Inc., D. S. - Chicago, IL - *IntDirMarRes 83*
Howard & Co., Edward [Aff. of Hill & Knowlton Inc.] - Cleveland, OH - *DirPRFirms 83; StaDirAdAg 2-84*
Howard & Co. Inc., Marvin - Ft. Lee, NJ - *StaDirAdAg 2-84*
Howard Associates Inc., Lloyd S. - Millwood, NY - *ArtMar 84; StaDirAdAg 2-84*
Howard, Barney - Kansas City, MO - *BoPubDir 4, 5*
Howard Cable Television Associates Inc. [of Storer Cable Communications] - Ellicott City, MD - *Tel&CabFB 84C*
Howard Cable Television Associates Inc. - Howard County, MD - *BrCabYB 84*
Howard City Record - Howard City, MI - *BaconPubCkNews 84; Ed&PubIntYB 82*
Howard Co., E. T. [Aff. of Hicks & Greist Inc.] - New York, NY - *BrCabYB 84; DirMarMP 83; StaDirAdAg 2-84*
Howard County News - Ellicott City, MD - *Ed&PubIntYB 82*
Howard County News, The - Greentown, IN - *AyerDirPub 83; Ed&PubIntYB 82*
Howard County Times - Columbia, MD - *AyerDirPub 83*
Howard County Times [of Ellicott City Stromberg Publishing Inc.] - Ellicott City, MD - *NewsDir 84*
Howard County Times - Howard County, MD - *Ed&PubIntYB 82*
Howard Courant-Citizen - Howard, KS - *BaconPubCkNews 84; Ed&PubIntYB 82*
Howard, Daniel Lynn - Los Angeles, CA - *BoPubDir 4, 5*
Howard Enterprises - Plainview, TX - *WhoWMicrocom 83*
Howard Global Syndicate - Hartsdale, NY - *Ed&PubIntYB 82*
Howard Lake Herald - Howard Lake, MN - *BaconPubCkNews 84; Ed&PubIntYB 82*
Howard, Merrell & Partners - Raleigh, NC - *AdAge 3-28-84; StaDirAdAg 2-84*
Howard Miner County Pioneer - Howard, SD - *BaconPubCkNews 84*
Howard Music, Randy - Macon, GA - *BillIntBG 83-84*
Howard Publications - Oceanside, CA - *AdAge 6-28-84; BrCabYB 84; Ed&PubIntYB 82; KnowInd 83*
Howard Publishing Co. - West Monroe, LA - *BoPubDir 4, 5*
Howard Publishing Co. Inc. - Grand Saline, TX - *BaconPubCkNews 84*
Howard Radio-TV Productions - Lincolnwood, IL - *Tel&CabFB 84C*
Howard, Rice, Nemerovski, Canady, Robertson & Falk - San Francisco, CA - *ADAPSOMemDir 83-84*
Howard-Sloan Associates Inc. - New York, NY - *InfIndMarPl 83; LitMarPl 83, 84; MagIndMarPl 82-83*
Howard Software Services - La Jolla, CA - *MicrocomMPl 84; WhoWMicrocom 83*
Howard TV Cable - Howard, PA - *BrCabYB 84*
Howard University Press - Washington, DC - *LitMarPl 83, 84; WritMar 84*
Howard's TV Cable, Frank - Salyersville, KY - *BrCabYB 84; Tel&CabFB 84C*
Howarth & Smith Ltd. - Toronto, ON, Canada - *LitMarPl 83, 84*
Howco International - Charlotte, NC - *TelAl 83, 84*
Howe Advertising, Bob - Toronto, ON, Canada - *ArtMar 84; StaDirAdAg 2-84*
Howe Consulting Group Inc., Overlock - St. Louis, MO - *HBIndAd&MS 82-83*
Howe Enterprise - Howe, TX - *BaconPubCkNews 84; Ed&PubIntYB 82*
Howe Furniture Corp. - New York, NY - *DirInfWP 82*
Howe Institute, C. D. - Toronto, ON, Canada - *BoPubDir 5*
Howe Institute, C. D. - Montreal, PQ, Canada - *BoPubDir 4*
Howe Press of Perkins School for the Blind - Watertown, MA - *LitMarPl 83, 84*
Howe Software - New City, NY - *MicrocomMPl 83, 84; WhoWMicrocom 83*
Howe Sound & District Advertiser - Squamish, BC, Canada - *AyerDirPub 83*
Howell & Kendall Associates Inc. - Elmira, NY - *StaDirAdAg 2-84*
Howell Book House Inc. - New York, NY - *LitMarPl 83, 84*
Howell Books, John - San Francisco, CA - *BoPubDir 4 Sup*
Howell Booster-News - Howell, NJ - *BaconPubCkNews 84*
Howell Enterprises, Susan P. - Hebron, CT - *BoPubDir 4, 5*
Howell, John - San Francisco, CA - *BoPubDir 5*
Howell Livingston County Press - *See* Sliger Livingston Publications
Howell North Books [Div. of Darwin Publications Inc.] - Burbank, CA - *LitMarPl 84*
Howell-North Books [of the Oak Tree Publishing Group] - San Diego, CA - *LitMarPl 83; WritMar 84*
Howell Public Relations Inc. - Allentown, PA - *DirPRFirms 83*
Howell Publications Inc. [Aff. of Indiana Printing Co. Inc.] - Crawfordsville, IN - *BoPubDir 4 Sup, 5*
Howell Publishing Co. Inc. - Anchorage, AK - *BoPubDir 5*
Howells Journal - Howells, NE - *BaconPubCkNews 84; Ed&PubIntYB 82*
Howl - London, England - *LitMag&SmPr 83-84*
Howland Bandwagon - Howland, OH - *Ed&PubIntYB 82*
Howland Bandwagon [of Niles Phoenix Publications Inc.] - Niles, OH - *AyerDirPub 83; NewsDir 84*
Howland Bandwagon - *See* Phoenix Publications Inc.
Howlett & Gaines Inc. - *See* Jamie, Howlett & Ranney-Public Relations
Howl't [of Bactrianus Enterprises] - Asker, Norway - *LitMag&SmPr 83-84*
Howser, Martin - Spokane, WA - *Tel&CabFB 84C p.1685*
Howson Algraphy Inc. - Carlstadt, NJ - *LitMarPl 83, 84*
Hoxie Sentinel - Hoxie, KS - *BaconPubCkNews 84; Ed&PubIntYB 82*
Hoxter Inc., Curtis J. - New York, NY - *DirPRFirms 83*
Hoyle & Hoyle Software - Greensboro, NC - *MicrocomMPl 84*
Hoyt Lakes Cable TV [of North American Communications Corp.] - Hoyt Lakes, MN - *Tel&CabFB 84C*
H.P. Books [Subs. of Knight-Ridder Newspaper Inc.] - Tucson, AZ - *LitMarPl 83, 84; WritMar 84*
HP Publishing Co. Inc. - New York, NY - *BoPubDir 4, 5*
H.P.B. Lending Library - Vernon, BC, Canada - *BoPubDir 4, 5*
HPN Hospital Purchasing News - McLean, VA - *BaconPubCkMag 84*
HR & H Marketing Research International Ltd. - London, England - *IntDirMarRes 83*
HRM Software - Pleasantville, NY - *MicrocomMPl 84*
HRS:Net - Boston, MA - *DirOnDB Spring 84*
Hrvatski Glas - Acton, ON, Canada - *Ed&PubIntYB 82*
Hrvatski Put - Toronto, ON, Canada - *Ed&PubIntYB 82*
H.S. Graphics Ltd. - Keasbey, NJ - *ArtMar 84*
HSA Publications [Aff. of Unification Church of America] - New York, NY - *BoPubDir 4, 5*
HSE Library & Information Services [of Health & Safety Executive] - Sheffield, England - *EISS 83*
HSE Records Inc. - Nashville, TN - *BillIntBG 83-84*
HSELINE - Red Hill, England - *DirOnDB Spring 84*
HSELINE [of Health & Safety Executive] - Sheffield, England - *OnBibDB 3*

HSELINE [of European Space Agency] - Frascati, Italy - *DataDirOnSer 84*
HTH Publishers - Freeland, WA - *BoPubDir 4, 5*
HTN Plus - Portland, ME - *CabTVPrDB 83*
Hu Press [Aff. of Sufi Order] - Gaithersburg, MD - *BoPubDir 5*
Hu Press [Aff. of Sufi Order] - New York, NY - *BoPubDir 4*
Huachuca Scout, The - Sierra Vista, AZ - *AyerDirPub 83*
Huang, Jane - Delmar, NY - *FBInfSer 80*
Hub - Gaylord, MN - *AyerDirPub 83*
Hub - Kearney, NE - *AyerDirPub 83*
Hub - Attica, OH - *AyerDirPub 83*
Hub - Westlock, AB, Canada - *AyerDirPub 83; Ed&PubIntYB 82*
Hub City Publishing Co. Inc. - Camdenton, MO - *BaconPubCkNews 84*
Hub Rail - Columbus, OH - *BaconPubCkMag 84; MagDir 84; WritMar 84*
HUB Research Inc. - Sloatsburg, NY - *IntDirMarRes 83*
Hub, The - Hay River, NT, Canada - *AyerDirPub 83; Ed&PubIntYB 82*
Hubbard Associates of Florida Inc. - *See* Hanson Fassler & Associates Inc.
Hubbard Broadcasting Inc. - St. Paul, MN - *BrCabYB 84; Tel&CabFB 84S*
Hubbard City News - Hubbard, TX - *BaconPubCkNews 84; Ed&PubIntYB 82*
Hubbard City News [of Mexia News Publishing Co.] - Mexia, TX - *AyerDirPub 83; NewsDir 84*
Hubbard Cooperative Telephone Association - Hubbard, IA - *TelDir&BG 83-84*
Hubbard County Independent - Nevis, MN - *AyerDirPub 83; Ed&PubIntYB 82*
Hubbard, Mason, Strumlauf & Loggins Inc. - Jacksonville, FL - *StaDirAdAg 2-84*
Hubbard News - Hubbard, OH - *AyerDirPub 83; Ed&PubIntYB 82*
Hubbard News [of Phoenix Publications Inc.] - Niles, OH - *NewsDir 84*
Hubbard News - *See* Phoenix Publications Inc.
Hubbard South Hardin Signal Review - Hubbard, IA - *BaconPubCkNews 84*
Hubbert Advertising & Public Relations Co. Inc. - Costa Mesa, CA - *StaDirAdAg 2-84*
Huber & Co., M. - Pittsfield, MA - *StaDirAdAg 2-84*
Huber Heights Courier - Dayton, OH - *AyerDirPub 83*
Huber Heights Courier - Huber Heights, OH - *Ed&PubIntYB 82*
Huber Heights Courier - *See* Bowling-Moorman Publications
Huber-Hoge & Sons Advertising Inc. [Subs. of Harrison-Hoge Industries Inc.] - St. James, NY - *DirMarMP 83*
Hubert Co., F. B. - Royal Oak, MI - *StaDirAdAg 2-84*
Hubler-Roseburg Associates Inc. - Dallas, TX - *HBIndAd&MS 82-83*
Hubley Studio Inc., The - New York, NY - *TelAl 83, 84; Tel&CabFB 84C*
Hubris - Concord, NH - *LitMag&SmPr 83-84*
Huckle Newspapers - Ionia, MI - *Ed&PubIntYB 82*
HUD User [of U.S. Dept. of Housing & Urban Development] - Germantown, MD - *EISS 83*
Hudgins Publishing Co., James M. - Madison, TN - *BillIntBG 83-84*
Hudis & Associates, M. - Santa Rosa, CA - *MicrocomMPl 84*
Hudson & Associates Inc., Bill - Nashville, TN - *DirPRFirms 83; StaDirAdAg 2-84*
Hudson Audio Video Enterprises - Livingston, NY - *AvMarPl 83*
Hudson Bay Music Co. - New York, NY - *BillIntBG 83-84*
Hudson Cable Co. - Hudson, MI - *BrCabYB 84*
Hudson Cable Co. [of De-Cal Cable Inc.] - Hudson, TX - *Tel&CabFB 84C*
Hudson Cablevision Corp. [of Americable Inc.] - Hudson, NH - *BrCabYB 84; Tel&CabFB 84C*
Hudson Gazette - Hudson, PQ, Canada - *Ed&PubIntYB 82*
Hudson Group Inc., The - Pleasantville, NY - *LitMarPl 83, 84*
Hudson Herald - Hudson, IA - *BaconPubCkNews 84; Ed&PubIntYB 82*
Hudson Hills Press Inc. - New York, NY - *LitMarPl 83, 84; WritMar 84*
Hudson Hub-Times - Cuyahoga Falls, OH - *NewsDir 84*
Hudson Hub-Times - Hudson, OH - *Ed&PubIntYB 82*
Hudson Hub/Times - *See* Record Publishing Co.
Hudson Hudsonite - Hudson, SD - *BaconPubCkNews 84*
Hudson Institute - Croton-on-Hudson, NY - *BoPubDir 5*
Hudson Investment Corp. - Washington, DC - *CabTVFinDB 83*
Hudson-Mohawk Association of Colleges & Universities - Latham, NY - *BoPubDir 4 Sup, 5*
Hudson Photographic Industries Inc. - Irvington-on-Hudson, NY - *AvMarPl 83*
Hudson-Post Gazette - Hudson, MI - *BaconPubCkNews 84; Ed&PubIntYB 82*
Hudson Register-Star [of Record Printing & Publishing Co. Inc.] - Hudson, NY - *BaconPubCkNews 84; NewsDir 84*
Hudson Review Inc. - New York, NY - *BoPubDir 4, 5; LitMag&SmPr 83-84; LitMarPl 83, 84; MagIndMarPl 82-83; WritMar 84*
Hudson Star-Observer - Hudson, WI - *BaconPubCkNews 84; Ed&PubIntYB 82; NewsDir 84*
Hudson Sun - Hudson, MA - *NewsDir 84*
Hudson Sun - Marlboro, MA - *BaconPubCkNews 84; Ed&PubIntYB 82*
Hudson Valley - Poughkeepsie, NY - *MagDir 84*
Hudson Valley - Yonkers, NY - *BaconPubCkMag 84*
Hudson Valley Cablesystems Corp. [of American Cablesystems Corp.] - Peekskill, NY - *BrCabYB 84; Tel&CabFB 84C*
Hudson Valley Cablesystems Corp. [of American Cablesystems Corp.] - West Haverstraw, NY - *BrCabYB 84*
Hudson Valley Magazine - Woodstock, NY - *WritMar 84*
Hudson Valley Newspapers Inc. - Highland, NY - *BaconPubCkNews 84*
Hudsonite, The - Hudson, SD - *Ed&PubIntYB 82*
Hudspeth County Herald & Dell Valley Review - Dell City, TX - *AyerDirPub 83; Ed&PubIntYB 82*
Huemark Films Inc. - New York, NY - *AvMarPl 83*
Huenefeld Co. Inc., The - Bedford, MA - *LitMarPl 83, 84*
Huerfano World - Walsenburg, CO - *AyerDirPub 83; Ed&PubIntYB 82*
Hueytown Sun [of Birmingham Sun Newspapers South & West] - Birmingham, AL - *NewsDir 84*
Huff & Co. - Mountain View, CA - *AvMarPl 83*
Huffman Press - Alexandria, VA - *BoPubDir 4, 5; LitMag&SmPr 83-84*
Hughes Advertising - St. Louis, MO - *AdAge 3-28-84; StaDirAdAg 2-84*
Hughes Aircraft Co. - El Segundo, CA - *ElecNews 7-25-83*
Hughes Airwest Sundancer - Los Angeles, CA - *MagDir 84*
Hughes & Law Advertising - Studio City, CA - *StaDirAdAg 2-84*
Hughes Communications Inc. - Los Angeles, CA - *TeleSy&SerDir 2-84*
Hughes Communications Inc. - Rockford, IL - *DirMarMP 83*
Hughes County Publishing Co. - Wetumka, OK - *BaconPubCkNews 84*
Hughes County Times - Wetumka, OK - *AyerDirPub 83; Ed&PubIntYB 82*
Hughes, Eric - Mt. Tremper, NY - *LitMarPl 83, 84; MagIndMarPl 82-83*
Hughes, Flora D. - *See* Snyder Community Antenna TV Co. Inc.
Hughes, George L. - *See* Retel TV Cable Co.
Hughes International Rig Count - Houston, TX - *DirOnDB Spring 84*
Hughes-Martindale & Associates Inc. - Arlington Heights, IL - *ArtMar 84; DirPRFirms 83*
Hughes Press - Washington, DC - *BoPubDir 4, 5*
Hughes Printing - Burney, CA - *BoPubDir 4, 5*
Hughes Printing Co. [Div. of Monroe Printing Co.] - East Stroudsburg, PA - *MagIndMarPl 82-83*
Hughes Publishing Co. - El Paso, TX - *BoPubDir 4, 5*
Hughes, Robert W. - Austin, TX - *BrCabYB 84 p.D-302*
Hughes Rotary International Rig Report - *See* Hughes International Rig Count
Hughes Rotary Rig Report [of I. P. Sharp Associates Ltd.] - Toronto, ON, Canada - *DataDirOnSer 84*
Hughes Star-Herald - *See* Causey Printing Co., F. M.
Hughes Telephone Co. - Bailey, MS - *TelDir&BG 83-84*
Hughes Television Network - New York, NY - *BrCabYB 84; Tel&CabFB 84C; TeleSy&SerDir 2-84*
Hughes, Theodore R. - Tioga, PA - *Tel&CabFB 84C p.1685*

Hughes TV Cable Service - Tioga, PA - *BrCabYB 84; Tel&CabFB 84C*
Hughley Advertising Agency Inc., David - Meridian, MS - *StaDirAdAg 2-84*
Hugo Cablevision Inc. [of Omni Cable TV Corp.] - Hugo, OK - *BrCabYB 84; Tel&CabFB 84C*
Hugo Eastern Colorado Plainsman - Hugo, CO - *BaconPubCkNews 84*
Hugo News - Hugo, OK - *BaconPubCkNews 84; NewsDir 84*
Hugoton Cablevision [of Communications Systems Inc.] - Hugoton, KS - *BrCabYB 84; Tel&CabFB 84C*
Hugoton Hermes - Hugoton, KS - *BaconPubCkNews 84; Ed&PubIntYB 82*
Huguenot Herald - New Paltz, NY - *Ed&PubIntYB 82*
Huh??? Publications - Santa Barbara, CA - *BoPubDir 4, 5; LitMag&SmPr 83-84*
Hui Hanai [Aff. of Queen Lilioukalani Children's Center] - Honolulu, HI - *BoPubDir 4, 5*
Hula Records Inc. - Honolulu, HI - *BillIntBG 83-84*
Hula Software - Haiku, HI - *MicrocomMPl 84*
Hulcher, Charles A. - Hampton, VA - *AvMarPl 83*
Hull Inc., H. Joseph - Lancaster, PA - *DirPRFirms 83*
Hull-Nantasket Times - Hull, MA - *AyerDirPub 83; BaconPubCkNews 84; Ed&PubIntYB 82*
Hull Sioux County Index-Reporter - Hull, IA - *BaconPubCkNews 84*
Hulland Engineering - Melville, NY - *MicrocomMPl 83*
Hulland Engineering - Mineola, NY - *MicrocomMPl 84*
Hult Fritz Goehausen & Matuszak Inc. - Peoria, IL - *StaDirAdAg 2-84*
Human Designed Systems Inc. - Philadelphia, PA - *DataDirSup 7-83; InfIndMarPl 83*
Human Development Press Ltd. - Poquoson, VA - *BoPubDir 5*
Human Development Training Institute - San Diego, CA - *BoPubDir 4, 5*
Human Engineered Software - Brisbane, CA - *MicrocomMPl 84*
Human Engineered Software - Los Angeles, CA - *MicrocomMPl 83; WhoWMicrocom 83*
Human Events - Washington, DC - *DirMarMP 83; MagDir 84; MagIndMarPl 82-83*
Human Factors - St. James, NY - *BrCabYB 84*
Human Kinetics Publishers - Champaign, IL - *ArtMar 84; LitMag&SmPr 83-84; LitMarPl 83, 84*
Human Organization - Washington, DC - *MagIndMarPl 82-83*
Human Pathology - Philadelphia, PA - *BaconPubCkMag 84*
Human Potential Press - Iowa City, IA - *LitMag&SmPr 83-84*
Human Press - Detroit, MI - *BoPubDir 4 Sup, 5*
Human Relations Area Files - New Haven, CT - *EISS 83; MicroMarPl 82-83*
Human Relations Media - Pleasantville, NY - *AvMarPl 83; DirMarMP 83*
Human Resource Development Press - Amherst, MA - *LitMarPl 83, 84*
Human Resource Information Network [of Executive Telecom System Inc.] - Indianapolis, IN - *EISS 5-84 Sup*
Human Resource Network - *See* HRS:Net
Human Rights Internet - Washington, DC - *BoPubDir 4, 5*
Human Sciences of Health [of Centre de Documentation Sciences Humaines] - Paris, France - *CompReadDB 82*
Human Sciences Press - New York, NY - *LitMarPl 83, 84; MagIndMarPl 82-83*
Human Sciences Promotion - New York, NY - *LitMarPl 83, 84*
Human Services Information Center - Washington, DC - *BoPubDir 5*
Human Services Resource Bank [of Comprehensive Community Services Inc.] - Chicago, IL - *EISS 83*
Human Sexuality - Shady, NY - *DirOnDB Spring 84*
Human Sound Music - *See* Sounds Ambient Music Inc.
Human Systems Dynamics - Northridge, CA - *MicrocomMPl 83, 84; MicrocomSwDir 1; WhoWMicrocom 83; WritMar 84*
Human, The [of The Uncertified Human Publishing Co. Ltd.] - Toronto, ON, Canada - *WritMar 84*
Humana Press - Clifton, NJ - *BoPubDir 4, 5; LitMag&SmPr 83-84; LitMarPl 83, 84*
Humane Society of the United States News, The - Washington, DC - *MagIndMarPl 82-83*
Humanics - Atlanta, GA - *ArtMar 84; BoPubDir 4, 5; LitMarPl 83, 84; WritMar 84*
Humanist in Canada - Ottawa, ON, Canada - *LitMag&SmPr 83-84*
Humanist, The [of American Humanist Association] - Amherst, NY - *ArtMar 84; LitMag&SmPr 83-84; MagIndMarPl 82-83; WritMar 84*
Humanities Div./CRVR [of Morris Library, Southern Illinois University] - Carbondale, IL - *CompReadDB 82*
Humanities Press Inc. - Atlantic Highlands, NJ - *LitMarPl 83, 84*
Humanity Publications - Oakville, ON, Canada - *BoPubDir 4, 5*
HumanSoft Inc. - Arlington, MA - *MicrocomMPl 84*
Humansville Star-Leader - Humansville, MO - *BaconPubCkNews 84*
Humber Log, The - Corner Brook, NF, Canada - *Ed&PubIntYB 82*
Humber Valley Broadcasting Co. - Corner Brook, NF, Canada - *BrCabYB 84*
Humbert & Jones Inc. - Stamford, CT - *StaDirAdAg 2-84*
Humble Echo [of Houston Community Newspapers] - Humble, TX - *Ed&PubIntYB 82; NewsDir 84*
Humble Echo - *See* Houston Community Newspapers
Humble Hills Books - Kalamazoo, MI - *BoPubDir 4, 5*
Humble News-Messenger - Humble, TX - *BaconPubCkNews 84*
Humboldt Beacon & Fortuna Advance - Fortuna, CA - *AyerDirPub 83; Ed&PubIntYB 82*
Humboldt Cable Co. - Humboldt, TN - *BrCabYB 84; Tel&CabFB 84C*
Humboldt County Magazine - Eureka, CA - *WritMar 84*
Humboldt Courier-Chronicle [of The Courier Chronicle Inc.] - Humboldt, TN - *BaconPubCkNews 84; NewsDir 84*
Humboldt Independent [of Humboldt Printing Co.] - Humboldt, IA - *Ed&PubIntYB 82; NewsDir 84*
Humboldt Independent - *See* Humboldt Printing Co.
Humboldt Journal, The - Humboldt, SK, Canada - *Ed&PubIntYB 82*
Humboldt Printing Co. - Humboldt, IA - *BaconPubCkNews 84*
Humboldt Republican [of Humboldt Printing Co.] - Humboldt, IA - *Ed&PubIntYB 82; NewsDir 84*
Humboldt Republican - *See* Humboldt Printing Co.
Humboldt Standard - Humboldt, NE - *BaconPubCkNews 84; Ed&PubIntYB 82*
Humboldt Sun - Winnemucca, NV - *Ed&PubIntYB 82*
Humboldt Union - Humboldt, KS - *BaconPubCkNews 84; Ed&PubIntYB 82*
Humbug Gulch Press - Amarillo, TX - *BoPubDir 4, 5*
Hume Publishing Co. - Willowdale, ON, Canada - *BoPubDir 4 Sup, 5*
Hume Smith Mickelberry Advertising Inc. - Miami, FL - *AdAge 3-28-84; StaDirAdAg 2-84*
Humeniuk, Peter - Winnipeg, MB, Canada - *BoPubDir 4, 5*
Humeston New Era - Humeston, IA - *BaconPubCkNews 84*
Humlife Publications - Sun Valley, CA - *BoPubDir 4, 5*
Hummelstown Hershey Sun - Hummelstown, PA - *BaconPubCkNews 84; NewsDir 84*
Hummingbird Press - Albuquerque, NM - *BoPubDir 4, 5; LitMag&SmPr 83-84*
Humpal, Leftwich & Sinn - Mountain View, CA - *AdAge 3-28-84; StaDirAdAg 2-84*
Humphrey, Browning, MacDougall [of Creamer Inc.] - Boston, MA - *ArtMar 84; Br 1-23-84; StaDirAdAg 2-84*
Humphrey Democrat - Humphrey, NE - *BaconPubCkNews 84; Ed&PubIntYB 82*
Humphreys County Telephone Co. - New Johnsville, TN - *TelDir&BG 83-84*
Humpty Dumpty's Magazine - Indianapolis, IN - *ArtMar 84; MagDir 84; MagIndMarPl 82-83; WritMar 84*
Huna Research Inc. - Cape Girardeau, MO - *BoPubDir 4, 5*
Hund Inc., Robert - Farmington, MI - *DirPRFirms 83; StaDirAdAg 2-84*
100 Mile House Free Press - 100 Mile House, BC, Canada - *AyerDirPub 83; Ed&PubIntYB 82*
Hungaria Records Inc. - Teaneck, NJ - *BillIntBG 83-84*
Hungarian Central Technical Library & Documentation Centre - Budapest, Hungary - *EISS 83*
Hungarian Cultural Foundation - Stone Mountain, GA - *BoPubDir 4, 5*

Hungarian Insights - Cleveland, OH - *NewsDir 84*
Hungarian Word - New York, NY - *NewsDir 84*
Hungarica Publishing House - North Vancouver, BC, Canada - *LitMag&SmPr 83-84*
Hungexpo Advertising Agency & Publicity Publishers - Budapest, Hungary - *StaDirAdAg 2-84*
Hungness Publishing, Carl - Speedway, IN - *LitMarPl 83, 84; WritMar 84*
Hungry Horse News - Columbia Falls, MT - *AyerDirPub 83; Ed&PubIntYB 82; NewsDir 84*
Hunt, Bunker & Herbert - *See* Midwest Video Corp.
Hunt Cable Co. - Hunt, TX - *BrCabYB 84*
Hunt County Shopper - Greenville, TX - *AyerDirPub 83*
Hunt, Deborah - Alameda, CA - *InfIndMarPl 83*
Hunt, Deborah - Reno, NV - *FBInfSer 80*
Hunt, Hugh W. - Blair, NE - *Tel&CabFB 84C p.1685*
Hunt Institute for Botanical Documentation [of Carnegie-Mellon University] - Pittsburgh, PA - *EISS 83*
Hunt, Jack G. - Doniphan, MO - *Tel&CabFB 84C p.1685*
Hunt, Richard W. - Blair, NE - *Tel&CabFB 84C p.1685*
Hunt, William E. - New York, NY - *WritMar 84*
Hunter & Ready Inc. - Palo Alto, CA - *ADAPSOMemDir 83-84; MicrocomSwDir 1; WhoWMicrocom 83*
Hunter Barth Advertising - Santa Ana, CA - *AdAge 3-28-84; StaDirAdAg 2-84*
Hunter, Dard II - Chillicothe, OH - *BoPubDir 4 Sup, 5*
Hunter House Inc. [Subs. of Servire BV] - Claremont, CA - *LitMarPl 83, 84; WritMar 84*
Hunter, Janet M. - Mill Valley, CA - *LitMarPl 84*
Hunter Publishing Co. - Phoenix, AZ - *BoPubDir 4, 5; LitMag&SmPr 83-84*
Hunter Rose Co. Ltd., The - Toronto, ON, Canada - *LitMarPl 84*
Hunterdon County Democrat - Flemington, NJ - *AyerDirPub 83; BaconPubCkNews 84; Ed&PubIntYB 82*
Hunterdon Review - White House Station, NJ - *AyerDirPub 83; Ed&PubIntYB 82*
Hunter's Horn SFSB Inc. - Sand Springs, OK - *MagDir 84*
Hunting Dog - Cincinnati, OH - *MagDir 84*
Huntingdon & Centre County Telephone Co. [Aff. of Mid-Continent Telephone Corp.] - Warriors Mark, PA - *TelDir&BG 83-84*
Huntingdon Broadcasters Inc. - Huntingdon, PA - *BrCabYB 84*
Huntingdon Carroll County News - Huntingdon, TN - *BaconPubCkNews 84; NewsDir 84*
Huntingdon Daily News [of The Joseph F. Biddle Publishing Co. Inc.] - Huntingdon, PA - *BaconPubCkNews 84; NewsDir 84*
Huntingdon Gleaner - Huntingdon, PQ, Canada - *Ed&PubIntYB 82*
Huntingdon Mt. Union Times - Huntingdon, PA - *BaconPubCkNews 84*
Huntingdon Tennessee Republican - Huntingdon, TN - *BaconPubCkNews 84; NewsDir 84*
Huntingdon TV Cable Co. - Huntingdon, PA - *BrCabYB 84 p.D-302; Tel&CabFB 84C*
Huntingdon Valley Globe - *See* Montgomery Publishing Co.
Huntington, B. E. - Forsyth, MT - *Tel&CabFB 84C p.1685*
Huntington Beach Independent [of West Orange Publishing Corp.] - Garden Grove, CA - *AyerDirPub 83; NewsDir 84*
Huntington Beach Independent - *See* West Orange Publishing Co.
Huntington Beach News [of American Publishing] - Huntington Beach, CA - *Ed&PubIntYB 82; NewsDir 84*
Huntington Beach News - Long Beach, CA - *BaconPubCkNews 84*
Huntington CATV Inc. [of Century Communications Corp.] - Huntington, IN - *BrCabYB 84; Tel&CabFB 84C*
Huntington Computing - Corcoran, CA - *MicrocomMPl 83, 84; WhoWMicrocom 83*
Huntington Harbour Sun - Huntington Harbour, CA - *Ed&PubIntYB 82*
Huntington Harbour Sun - Seal Beach, CA - *AyerDirPub 83*
Huntington Herald - *See* Liberal Publishers
Huntington Herald-Dispatch [of Gannett Co. Inc.] - Huntington, WV - *BaconPubCkNews 84; NewsDir 84*
Huntington Herald-Press - Huntington, IN - *BaconPubCkNews 84; NewsDir 84*
Huntington Library & Art Gallery, Henry E. - San Marino, CA - *LitMarPl 83, 84*
Huntington Long Islander - Huntington, NY - *Ed&PubIntYB 82*
Huntington Long Islander - *See* Community Newspapers Inc.
Huntington Park Bulletin - Bell, CA - *NewsDir 84*
Huntington Park Bulletin - Huntington Park, CA - *Ed&PubIntYB 82*
Huntington Park Bulletin - Los Angeles, CA - *AyerDirPub 83*
Huntington Park Bulletin - *See* Hearst Community Newspapers
Huntington Park Daily Signal [of Downey Newspapers Inc.] - Downey, CA - *NewsDir 84*
Huntington Park Daily Signal - South Gate, CA - *BaconPubCkNews 84*
Huntington Park Davis Signal - Downey, CA - *AyerDirPub 83*
Huntington Pennysaver - Huntington, NY - *AyerDirPub 83*
Huntington Tele-Cable [of Treasure Valley Tele-Cable] - Huntington, OR - *BrCabYB 84; Tel&CabFB 84C*
Huntington TV Cable Corp. - Huntington, NY - *BrCabYB 84*
Huntington TV Cable Corp. [of Communications Systems Corp.] - Huntington Station, NY - *Tel&CabFB 84C p.1685*
Huntington-Zavalia Herald [of Kountze Liberal Publishers] - Kountze, TX - *NewsDir 84*
Huntleigh House - Oklahoma City, OK - *BoPubDir 4, 5*
Huntley Farmside - Huntley, IL - *BaconPubCkNews 84; Ed&PubIntYB 82*
Huntley Republican-News [of Free Press Inc.] - Huntley, IL - *NewsDir 84*
Huntsinger, Jeffer, Van Groesbeck Inc. - Richmond, VA - *StaDirAdAg 2-84*
Huntsville Clifton Hill Rustler - *See* Huntsville Times-Herald Publishers
Huntsville Item - Huntsville, TX - *BaconPubCkNews 84; Ed&PubIntYB 82; NewsDir 84*
Huntsville Literary Association - Huntsville, AL - *LitMag&SmPr 83-84*
Huntsville Madison County Record - Huntsville, AR - *BaconPubCkNews 84; NewsDir 84*
Huntsville News - Huntsville, AL - *AyerDirPub 83; BaconPubCkNews 84; Ed&PubIntYB 82; NewsDir 84*
Huntsville Randolph County Times Herald - *See* Huntsville Times-Herald Publishers
Huntsville Record - Huntsville, AR - *Ed&PubIntYB 82*
Huntsville Times - Huntsville, AL - *BaconPubCkNews 84; Ed&PubIntYB 82; LitMarPl 83, 84; NewsDir 84*
Huntsville Times-Herald Publishers - Huntsville, MO - *BaconPubCkNews 84*
Huntsville TV Cable Inc. [of Independence County Cable TV Inc.] - Huntsville, AR - *BrCabYB 84; Tel&CabFB 84C*
Huntsville Weekly - Huntsville, AL - *Ed&PubIntYB 82*
Hurewitz, Miriam - New York, NY - *LitMarPl 83, 84*
Hurley & Haimowitz - New York, NY - *DirPRFirms 83*
Hurley Cable TV Inc. - Bayard, NM - *BrCabYB 84; Tel&CabFB 84C*
Hurley Iron County Miner - Hurley, WI - *BaconPubCkNews 84*
Hurley Leader - Hurley, SD - *BaconPubCkNews 84; Ed&PubIntYB 82*
Hurley Screen [Subs. of Consolidated Engineering & Manufacturing Corp.] - Forest Hill, MD - *AvMarPl 83*
Hurlock Cine-World Inc. - Greenwich, CT - *AvMarPl 83*
Huron Cable Television [of Midcontinent Cable Systems Co.] - Huron, SD - *BrCabYB 84; Tel&CabFB 84C*
Huron Cablevision [of TeleNational Communications Inc.] - Oscoda, MI - *BrCabYB 84; Tel&CabFB 84C*
Huron CATV Inc. [of McVay Communications Inc.] - Huron, CA - *Tel&CabFB 84C*
Huron CATV Inc. [of Omni Cable TV Corp.] - Bad Axe, MI - *BrCabYB 84; Tel&CabFB 84C*
Huron CATV Inc. [of Omni Cable TV Corp.] - Harbor Beach, MI - *BrCabYB 84; Tel&CabFB 84C*
Huron Erie County Reporter - Huron, OH - *NewsDir 84*
Huron Expositor - Seaforth, ON, Canada - *AyerDirPub 83; Ed&PubIntYB 82*
Huron News, The - Port Austin, MI - *Ed&PubIntYB 82*
Huron Path Press - Toronto, ON, Canada - *BoPubDir 4, 5*
Huron Plainsman [of Freedom Newspapers] - Huron, SD - *BaconPubCkNews 84; Ed&PubIntYB 82; NewsDir 84*

Huron Tribune - Bad Axe, MI - *AyerDirPub 83; BaconPubCkNews 84; Ed&PubIntYB 82*
Huron Valley Graphics Inc. - Ann Arbor, MI - *LitMarPl 83, 84*
Hurricane Breeze - Hurricane, WV - *BaconPubCkNews 84; Ed&PubIntYB 82*
Hurricane Co. - Jacksonville, NC - *BoPubDir 4, 5*
Hurricane Enterprises - Albuquerque, NM - *BillIntBG 83-84*
Hurricane Laboratories - San Jose, CA - *MicrocomMPl 84; WhoWMicrocom 83*
Hurriyet - New York, NY - *Ed&PubIntYB 82*
Hurst, Earl A. - Osage City, KS - *Tel&CabFB 84C p.1685*
Hurst-Mullinax Group - LaGrange, GA - *BrCabYB 84 p.D-302*
Hurtig Publishers Ltd. - Edmonton, AB, Canada - *LitMarPl 83, 84; WritMar 84*
Huse Publishing Co. - *See* Beef Empire Stations
Huskers Illustrated - Tulsa, OK - *BaconPubCkMag 84*
Hussey Survey & Research, Mary - East Providence, RI - *IntDirMarRes 83*
Hussman, Walter E. - *See* WEHCO Video Inc.
Hustler [of Larry Flynt Publications] - Los Angeles, CA - *ArtMar 84; Folio 83; MagDir 84; WritMar 84*
Hustler - South Pittsburg, TN - *AyerDirPub 83*
Hustlers Inc. - Macon, GA - *BillIntBG 83-84*
Huston, Harvey - Winnetka, IL - *BoPubDir 4, 5*
Huston, Ondre N. - Winnetka, IL - *BoPubDir 5*
Hutchins/Young & Rubicam - Rochester, NY - *BrCabYB 84; DirPRFirms 83; StaDirAdAg 2-84; TelAl 83, 84*
Hutchinson Herald - Menno, SD - *AyerDirPub 83; Ed&PubIntYB 82*
Hutchinson Industrial Corp. - Hutchinson, MN - *DirInfWP 82*
Hutchinson Leader - Hutchinson, MN - *BaconPubCkNews 84; Ed&PubIntYB 82; NewsDir 84*
Hutchinson News - Hutchinson, KS - *BaconPubCkNews 84; Ed&PubIntYB 82; NewsDir 84*
Hutchinson Publications Inc. - West Allis, WI - *AyerDirPub 83*
Hutchinson Record - Hutchinson, KS - *BaconPubCkNews 84; Ed&PubIntYB 82*
Hutchinson Ross Publishing Co. [Subs. of Van Nostrand Reinhold Co. Inc.] - Stroudsburg, PA - *LitMarPl 83, 84*
Hutchinson, Ted - North Tarrytown, NY - *BoPubDir 4, 5*
Hutchinson Telephone Co. - Hutchinson, MN - *TelDir&BG 83-84*
Hutchinsons - Orleans, MA - *BoPubDir 5*
Hutson, Bill - *See* Tri-Star Cablevision Inc.
Hutsonville Crawford Press - Hutsonville, IL - *BaconPubCkNews 84*
Hutton & Co. Inc., E. F. - New York, NY - *ADAPSOMemDir 83-84; DataDirOnSer 84*
Huttonline [of E. F. Hutton & Co. Inc.] - New York, NY - *DataDirOnSer 84; DirOnDB Spring 84; TeleSy&SerDir 2-84*
Huwen & Davies - Chicago, IL - *AdAge 3-28-84; StaDirAdAg 2-84*
Hux, Austin - El Dorado, AR - *Tel&CabFB 84C p.1685*
Huxley Cooperative Telephone Co. - Huxley, IA - *TelDir&BG 83-84*
HVAC Product News - Elmhurst, IL - *BaconPubCkMag 84*
HVC Corp. - Dallas, TX - *EISS 7-83 Sup; VideoDir 82-83*
HVR Advertising - Amstelveen, Netherlands - *StaDirAdAg 2-84*
HW Electronics - Northridge, CA - *MicrocomMPl 83; WhoWMicrocom 83*
HW Systems Inc. - Van Nuys, CA - *DataDirOnSer 84; EISS 7-83 Sup*
H.W.H. Creative Productions Inc. - Jamaica, NY - *WritMar 84*
Hy-Speed Longhand Publishing Co. - Trenton, NJ - *BoPubDir 4, 5*
Hyannis Barnstable Patriot - Hyannis, MA - *BaconPubCkNews 84*
Hyannis Grant County News - Hyannis, NE - *BaconPubCkNews 84*
Hyattsville Prince Georges Post - Hyattsville, MD - *BaconPubCkNews 84*
Hyattsville Prince Georges Sentinel - *See* Morkap Publishing
Hybrid Circuit Technology - Libertyville, IL - *BaconPubCkMag 84*
Hybrid Microelectronics Review - Chalfont, PA - *MagDir 84*
Hybrid Records - Evanston, IL - *BillIntBG 83-84*
Hyde Communications, Christopher - Gary, ME - *DirPRFirms 83*
Hyde Park Herald - Chicago, IL - *AyerDirPub 83; NewsDir 84*
Hyde Park Herald - Hyde Park, IL - *Ed&PubIntYB 82*
Hyde Park Mattapan Tribune - Boston, MA - *AyerDirPub 83*
Hyde Park Townsman [of Taconic Press Inc.] - Hyde Park, NY - *AyerDirPub 83; Ed&PubIntYB 82; NewsDir 84*
Hyde Park Townsman - *See* Taconic Press Inc.
Hyde Park Tribune - *See* Tribune Publishing Co.
Hyde Park Tribune/Mattapan Tribune - Boston, MA - *Ed&PubIntYB 82*
Hyden Leslie County News - Hyden, KY - *NewsDir 84*
Hyden Thousandsticks News - Hyden, KY - *BaconPubCkNews 84*
Hydra Communications - Rancho Palos Verdes, CA - *Tel&CabFB 84C*
Hydraulic Engineering Information Analysis Center [of U.S. Army] - Vicksburg, VA - *EISS 83*
Hydraulics & Pneumatics - Cleveland, OH - *BaconPubCkMag 84; MagDir 84*
Hydro [of Delft Hydraulics Laboratory] - Delft, Netherlands - *OnBibDB 3*
Hydro-Air Engineering Inc. [Subs. of Moehlenpah Industries] - St. Louis, MO - *DataDirOnSer 84*
Hydro Review - Hydro, OK - *BaconPubCkNews 84; Ed&PubIntYB 82*
Hydro Telephone Co., The - Moore, OK - *TelDir&BG 83-84*
Hydrocarbon Processing [of Gulf Publishing Co.] - Houston, TX - *BaconPubCkMag 84; Folio 83; MagDir 84; WritMar 84*
Hydrocomp Inc. - Mountain View, CA - *DataDirOnSer 84; EISS 83*
Hydrogene Information - St. Martin d'Heres, France - *DirOnDB Spring 84*
Hydrological Information Storage & Retrieval System [of North Carolina State University] - Raleigh, NC - *EISS 83*
Hydrological Operational Multipurpose Subprogramme [of World Meteorological Organization] - Geneva, Switzerland - *EISS 83*
Hyena Editions - Water Mill, NY - *BoPubDir 4, 5*
Hykes, Susan S. - Colorado Springs, CO - *BoPubDir 5*
Hylands, A. F. - Downsview, ON, Canada - *BoPubDir 4*
Hylands, A. F. - Port Hope, ON, Canada - *BoPubDir 5*
Hyman Associates Inc., Mark - Philadelphia, PA - *DirPRFirms 83*
Hymn Tune Index [of University of Illinois] - Urbana, IL - *EISS 5-84 Sup*
Hymnary Press - Helena, MT - *BoPubDir 5*
Hyperdynamics - Sante Fe, NM - *BoPubDir 4, 5*
Hyperion Press Inc. - Westport, CT - *LitMarPl 83, 84*
Hyperion Press Ltd. - Winnipeg, MB, Canada - *BoPubDir 4, 5; LitMarPl 83, 84*
Hypertension - Birmingham, AL - *MagIndMarPl 82-83*
Hypertension - Dallas, TX - *BaconPubCkMag 84*
Hyphen Advertising Inc. - Newport Beach, CA - *StaDirAdAg 2-84*
Hypnos Press [Aff. of Institute of Applied Natural Science Inc.] - Washington, DC - *BoPubDir 4, 5*
Hysham Echo - Hysham, MT - *Ed&PubIntYB 82*
Hyst'ry Myst'ry House - Garnerville, NY - *LitMag&SmPr 83-84; LitMarPl 83, 84*
Hyst'ry Myst'ry Magazine [of Hyst'ry Myst'ry House] - Garnerville, NY - *LitMag&SmPr 83-84; WritMar 84*

I

I & CS - Radnor, PA - *BaconPubCkMag 84*
I & EC - Washington, DC - *BaconPubCkMag 84*
I & EC Fundamentals [of American Chemical Society] - Washington, DC - *MagDir 84*
I & EC Process Design & Development [of American Chemical Society] - Washington, DC - *MagDir 84*
I & EC Product Research & Development [of American Chemical Society] - Washington, DC - *MagDir 84*
I & G Retail Audit Research - Hergiswil, Switzerland - *IntDirMarRes 83*
I & O Publishing Co. Inc. - Las Vegas, NV - *BoPubDir 4, 5*
I Can Read Book Club [of Xerox Education Publications] - Middletown, CT - *LitMarPl 83, 84*
I Like Me Publishing Co. - Chicago, IL - *BoPubDir 5*
I Love Music - Los Angeles, CA - *BillIntBG 83-84*
I/O Controls Inc. - Langhorne, PA - *WhoWMicrocom 83*
I/S Datacentralen - Copenhagen, Denmark - *InfIndMarPl 83*
I/S Datacentralen - Valby, Denmark - *EISS 83*
I2 Interface Inc. - Canoga Park, CA - *WhoWMicrocom 83*
I Type Etc. - Studio City, CA - *DirInfWP 82*
IABC Communication World - San Francisco, CA - *BaconPubCkMag 84*
Iaconi Book Imports - San Francisco, CA - *LitMarPl 83, 84*
Iaeger Industrial News - Iaeger, WV - *BaconPubCkNews 84*
IAEI News [of International Association of Electrical Inspectors] - Park Ridge, IL - *BaconPubCkMag 84; MagDir 84*
IAL - London, England - *IntDirMarRes 83*
Ialeah Home News - Hialeah, FL - *BaconPubCkNews 84*
IALINE [of Questel Inc.] - Washington, DC - *DataDirOnSer 84*
IALINE-Pascal [of Centre de Documentation de Industries Utilisatrices de Produits Agricoles] - Massy, France - *CompReadDB 82; DirOnDB Spring 84*
IAM - Tweed, ON, Canada - *BoPubDir 4, 5*
IAM Music - Irvine, CA - *BillIntBG 83-84*
IAM Shop Talk [of Machinists District 91] - East Hartford, CT - *NewsDir 84*
Iamo Telephone Co. - Coin, IA - *TelDir&BG 83-84*
Iamonia Publishing - Tallahassee, FL - *BillIntBG 83-84*
IAO Publications [Aff. of IAO Research Centre] - Toronto, ON, Canada - *BoPubDir 4, 5*
IAPES News - Frankfort, KY - *BaconPubCkMag 84; MagDir 84*
IATA North Atlantic Traffic - Washington, DC - *DirOnDB Spring 84*
IATA North Atlantic Traffic [of I. P. Sharp Associates Ltd.] - Toronto, ON, Canada - *DataDirOnSer 84*
IATSE & MTMO [of Merkle Press] - New York, NY - *NewsDir 84*
I.B. Magazette - Shreveport, LA - *MicrocomMPl 84*
Iberia New Iberian - Iberia, MO - *BaconPubCkNews 84*
Iberian - New Iberia, LA - *AyerDirPub 83*
Iberville South, The - Iberville Parish, LA - *Ed&PubIntYB 82*
IBES Summary Statistics - New York, NY - *DirOnDB Spring 84*
IBEW Journal - Washington, DC - *NewsDir 84*
IBI Inc. - Tokyo, Japan - *IntDirMarRes 83*
Ibidinc - Hartford, CT - *MicrocomMPl 84*
IBIS Information Services Inc. - New York, NY - *LitMarPl 83, 84*
Ibis Media - Pleasantville, NY - *AvMarPl 83*
IBJ Data Service Co. - Tokyo, Japan - *DirOnDB Spring 84; EISS 5-84 Sup*
IBM Corp. - Armonk, NY - *DataDirSup 7-83; Datamation 6-83; ElecNews 7-25-83; InfoS 83-84; KnowInd 83; Top100Al 83; WhoWMicrocom 83*
IBM Corp. - New York, NY - *HomeVid&CabYB 82-83*
IBM Corp. - White Plains, NY - *ADAPSOMemDir 83-84; InfIndMarPl 83; VideoDir 82-83*
IBM Corp. (National Accounts Div.) - Harrison, NY - *DirInfWP 82*
IBM Corp. (National Marketing Center) - White Plains, NY - *DirInfWP 82*
IBM Information Network - Greenwich, CT - *DataDirOnSer 84*
IBM Information Network [of IBM Corp.] - Tampa, FL - *DataDirOnSer 84; TeleSy&SerDir 2-84*
IBM Information Network (Information/Library II) - Greenwich, CT - *DataDirOnSer 84*
IBM Information Network (Information System 2) - Greenwich, CT - *DataDirOnSer 84*
IBM PC On-Line - Virginia Beach, VA - *DirOnDB Spring 84*
IBM Technical Information Retrieval Center [of IBM Corp.] - Armonk, NY - *EISS 83*
IBMS Inc. - Hillsdale, NJ - *BoPubDir 4, 5*
IBRD World Tables Data Bank - Washington, DC - *DirOnDB Spring 84*
IBRD World Tables Data Bank [of Data Resources Inc.] - Lexington, MA - *DataDirOnSer 84*
IBS - Birmingham, AL - *DataDirSup 7-83*
Ibsedex - Bracknell, England - *DirOnDB Spring 84*
IC Publications Ltd. [Div. of International Communications] - New York, NY - *MagIndMarPl 82-83*
ICA International Review of Chiropractic - Washington, DC - *MagDir 84*
ICA Publishers [Aff. of Information Consulting Associates] - Hackensack, NJ - *BoPubDir 4 Sup, 5*
ICA Telemanagement Inc. - Willowdale, ON, Canada - *TeleSy&SerDir 7-83*
ICAO Bulletin - Montreal, PQ, Canada - *BaconPubCkMag 84*
ICAO Traffic Statistics [of I. P. Sharp Associates Ltd.] - Toronto, ON, Canada - *DataDirOnSer 84; DirOnDB Spring 84*
ICAO Traffic Statistics [of International Civil Aviation Organization] - Montreal, PQ, Canada - *DataDirOnSer 84; DBBus 82*
ICAR - Ottawa, ON, Canada - *DirOnDB Spring 84*
Icare Press Inc. - Hollis, NY - *LitMag&SmPr 83-84*
Icart Vendor Gallery - Los Angeles, CA - *ArtMar 84*
Icarus [of Zacks Investment Research] - Chicago, IL - *DataDirOnSer 84*
Icarus Films - New York, NY - *AvMarPl 83*
Icarus Press Inc. - South Bend, IN - *LitMarPl 83, 84; WritMar 84*
Icas Computer Systems Inc. - Sparta, NJ - *WhoWMicrocom 83*

ICBR Data Bank [of Institute for Child Behavior Research] - San Diego, CA - *EISS 83*
ICC-Graphcom Systems Inc. [Subs. of International Computaprint Corp.] - Horsham, PA - *LitMarPl 83, 84*
ICC Information Group Ltd. - London, England - *DirOnDB Spring 84; EISS 7-83 Sup; InfIndMarPl 83*
ICC Publishing Corp. Inc., The [Aff. of the International Chamber of Commerce] - New York, NY - *LitMarPl 83, 84*
ICE Communications Inc. - Rochester, NY - *StaDirAdAg 2-84*
Ice Records & Productions - Alta Loma, CA - *BillIntBG 83-84*
Ice Skating Institute of America - Wilmette, IL - *BoPubDir 5*
Iceberg Press - Flint, MI - *LitMag&SmPr 83-84*
ICER Press - Claremont, CA - *BoPubDir 5*
ICER Press - Laguna Beach, CA - *BoPubDir 4*
ICI (Agricultural Div.) - Billingham, England - *InfIndMarPl 83*
ICI Advertising/Public Relations - San Diego, CA - *StaDirAdAg 2-84*
ICIE Database - Oak Ridge, TN - *DirOnDB Spring 84*
ICL Computers Canada Ltd. [Subs. of International Computers Ltd.] - Toronto, ON, Canada - *WhoWMicrocom 83*
ICL Data Services - Johannesburg, South Africa - *ADAPSOMemDir 83-84*
ICL Inc. - Irving, TX - *DataDirSup 7-83*
ICM Artists Ltd. - New York, NY - *Tel&CabFB 84C*
ICM Industries - Carmel, IN - *MicrocomMPl 84*
Icom Inc. - Parsippany, NJ - *TeleSy&SerDir 2-84*
Icom Inc. - Columbus, OH - *AvMarPl 83*
Icon Communications Ltd. - New York, NY - *AvMarPl 83*
Icon Group Inc., The - Dayton, OH - *DirPRFirms 83*
Icon Press - Duck Lake, SK, Canada - *BoPubDir 5*
Icon Press - Montmartre, SK, Canada - *BoPubDir 4*
Iconica Inc. - Oakland, CA - *MicrocomMPl 84*
Iconix Corp. - Cupertino, CA - *DataDirSup 7-83*
ICONOS [of Direction de la Documentation Francaise] - Paris, France - *CompReadDB 82*
ICP Database Products Div. [of International Computer Programs Inc.] - Indianapolis, IN - *InfoS 83-84*
ICP Interface Administrative & Accounting - Indianapolis, IN - *BaconPubCkMag 84*
ICP Interface Banking Industry - Indianapolis, IN - *BaconPubCkMag 84*
ICP Interface Data Processing Management - Indianapolis, IN - *BaconPubCkMag 84*
ICP Interface Insurance Industry - Indianapolis, IN - *BaconPubCkMag 84*
ICP Interface Manufacturing & Engineering - Indianapolis, IN - *BaconPubCkMag 84*
ICP Interface Series - Indianapolis, IN - *WritMar 84*
ICP Software Business Review - Indianapolis, IN - *BaconPubCkMag 84; MagDir 84*
ICPR - Los Angeles, CA - *DirPRFirms 83*
ICR-FutureSoft - Orange Park, FL - *WhoWMicrocom 83*
ICS Books Inc. [Aff. of Indiana Camp Supply Inc.] - Merrillville, IN - *BoPubDir 4, 5; LitMag&SmPr 83-84*
ICS Computing Ltd. - Belfast, Nothern Ireland - *ADAPSOMemDir 83-84*
ICS Inc. - Addison, IL - *MicrocomMPl 84*
ICS Press [Div. of Institute for Contemporary Studies] - San Francisco, CA - *LitMarPl 83, 84*
ICU Publisher [Aff. of ICU Consultants] - Tucson, AZ - *BoPubDir 4, 5*
Ida Grove County Courier - Ida Grove, IA - *AyerDirPub 83; BaconPubCkNews 84; Ed&PubIntYB 82; NewsDir 84*
Ida Grove County Pioneer Record - Ida Grove, IA - *AyerDirPub 83; BaconPubCkNews 84; Ed&PubIntYB 82*
Ida-Ireland (International Services Div.) - Dublin, Ireland - *ADAPSOMemDir 83-84*
Idabel Cablevision Inc. - Idabel, OK - *BrCabYB 84*
Idabel McCurtain Gazette - Idabel, OK - *NewsDir 84*
IDAC - Concord, CA - *DataDirSup 7-83*
Idaho Argonaut - Moscow, ID - *NewsDir 84*
Idaho Beverage Analyst [of Bevan Inc.] - Denver, CO - *BaconPubCkMag 84; MagDir 84*
Idaho Camera Inc. - Boise, ID - *AvMarPl 83*
Idaho City World - Idaho City, ID - *BaconPubCkNews 84*
Idaho County Free Press - Grangeville, ID - *AyerDirPub 83; Ed&PubIntYB 82*
Idaho Drug Information Service [of Pocatello Regional Medical Center] - Pocatello, ID - *EISS 7-83 Sup*
Idaho Enterprise - Malad City, ID - *Ed&PubIntYB 82*
Idaho Falls Post Register - Idaho Falls, ID - *BaconPubCkNews 84; NewsDir 84*
Idaho Farmer-Stockman - Spokane, WA - *BaconPubCkMag 84; MagDir 84*
Idaho Mountain Express - Ketchum, ID - *AyerDirPub 83; Ed&PubIntYB 82*
Idaho Newspaper Association Inc. - Boise, ID - *ProGuPRSer 4*
Idaho Press Tribune [of Swift-Pioneer Newspapers] - Nampa, ID - *AyerDirPub 83; BaconPubCkNews 84; Ed&PubIntYB 82; NewsDir 84*
Idaho Records - Clayton, ID - *BillIntBG 83-84*
Idaho Register [of Roman Catholic Diocese of Boise] - Boise, ID - *NewsDir 84*
Idaho Springs Courant - Idaho Springs, CO - *BaconPubCkNews 84*
Idaho Springs Courant & Evergreen Today - Idaho Springs, CO - *BaconPubCkNews 84*
Idaho Springs Front Range Journal - Idaho Springs, CO - *BaconPubCkNews 84*
Idaho State Census Data Center [of Idaho State Div. of Economic & Community Affairs] - Boise, ID - *EISS 5-84 Sup*
Idaho State Journal - Pocatello, ID - *AyerDirPub 83; BaconPubCkNews 84; Ed&PubIntYB 82; LitMarPl 83, 84*
Idaho State University (Idaho Museum of Natural History) - Pocatello, ID - *BoPubDir 4, 5*
Idaho State University Press - Pocatello, ID - *BoPubDir 4, 5*
Idaho Statesman [of Gannett Co. Inc.] - Boise, ID - *AyerDirPub 83; Ed&PubIntYB 82; NewsBur 6; NewsDir 84*
Idaho Video Inc. [of King Videocable Co.] - Gooding, ID - *BrCabYB 84*
Idaho Video Inc. [of King Videocable Co.] - Jerome, ID - *BrCabYB 84*
Idaho Wildlife - Boise, ID - *MagDir 84*
Idaho World - Idaho City, ID - *Ed&PubIntYB 82*
Idahonian - Moscow, ID - *BaconPubCkNews 84; Ed&PubIntYB 82; NewsDir 84*
Idahonian/Palouse Empire News - Moscow, ID - *AyerDirPub 83*
IDAL - Montreal, PQ, Canada - *MicroMarPl 82-83*
Idalou Beacon - Idalou, TX - *BaconPubCkNews 84; Ed&PubIntYB 82*
IDAS [of Bahrain Telecommunications Co.] - Manama, Bahrain - *InfIndMarPl 83*
IDC Data Services Inc. - Garden City, NY - *DataDirOnSer 84*
IDC Data Services Inc. - New York, NY - *HBIndAd&MS 82-83*
IDC Inorganic Chemistry File [of Internationale Dokumentationsgesellschaft fur Chemie mbH] - Frankfurt, West Germany - *CompReadDB 82*
IDC Organic Chemistry File [of Internationale Dokumentationsgesellschaft fur Chemie mbH] - Frankfurt, West Germany - *CompReadDB 82*
IDC Patent Data File [of Internationale Dokumentationsgesellschaft fur Chemie mbH] - Frankfurt, West Germany - *CompReadDB 82*
IDC Polymer Chemistry File [of Internationale Dokumentationsgesellschaft fur Chemie mbH] - Frankfurt, West Germany - *CompReadDB 82*
IDC Services Inc. - Los Angeles, CA - *ADAPSOMemDir 83-84*
IDC Services Inc. - Chicago, IL - *BrCabYB 84; Tel&CabFB 84C*
Ide Associates Inc., J. S. - Barrington, IL - *BoPubDir 4 Sup, 5; LitMarPl 83, 84*
IDE House Inc. - Mesquite, TX - *BoPubDir 4, 5; LitMag&SmPr 83-84; LitMarPl 84*
Idea Bank Inc., The - Lathrup Village, MI - *DirMarMP 83*
IDEA Inc. - Caldwell, ID - *ArtMar 84*
Idea Publishing Corp. - Yardley, PA - *BoPubDir 4 Sup, 5*
Idea Seminars - Omaha, NE - *MagIndMarPl 82-83*
Idea Shelf Inc., The [Aff. of Kamstra Communications Inc.] - St. Paul, MN - *StaDirAdAg 2-84*
Idea Source Guide - Fairless Hill, PA - *MagIndMarPl 82-83*
Ideal Audio Visual - Milwaukee, WI - *AvMarPl 83*
Ideal Business Communications Inc. - New York, NY - *AvMarPl 83*
Ideal Field Services Inc. - Brooklyn, NY - *IntDirMarRes 83*
Ideal Publishing Corp. - New York, NY - *MagIndMarPl 82-83*

Ideal School Supply Co. [Aff. of Westinghouse Learning Corp.] - Oak Lawn, IL - *ArtMar 84; AvMarPl 83; BoPubDir 4, 5; WritMar 84*
Ideal Systems - Fairfield, IA - *MicrocomMPl 84; MicrocomSwDir 1*
Ideal World Publishing Co. - Melbourne, FL - *BoPubDir 4, 5; WritMar 84*
Ideals - Milwaukee, WI - *ArtMar 84; WritMar 84*
Ideals Publishing Corp. [Subs. of Harlequin Enterprises] - Milwaukee, WI - *DirMarMP 83; LitMarPl 83, 84; WritMar 84*
Ideas - Coral Gables, FL - *BaconPubCkMag 84*
Ideas Inc. - Philadelphia, PA - *StaDirAdAg 2-84*
Ideasmiths Co., The - Burlington, ON, Canada - *BrCabYB 84*
IDEAssociates Inc. - Bedford, MA - *MicrocomMPl 84*
Ideatech Co. - Sunnyvale, CA - *MicrocomMPl 83, 84*
Identicard Systems Inc. - Lancaster, PA - *AvMarPl 83*
Identicon Corp. - Franklin, MA - *DataDirSup 7-83*
Identification Systems - Acton, MA - *AvMarPl 83*
Identity [of Prototype] - Toronto, ON, Canada - *LitMag&SmPr 83-84*
IDHHB Publishing [Aff. of Institute for the Development of the Harmonious Human Being Inc.] - Nevada City, CA - *BoPubDir 4, 5; LitMag&SmPr 83-84*
Ido-Vivo [of International Language Society of Great Britain] - Caerdydd, Wales - *LitMag&SmPr 83-84*
IDP Report [of Knowledge Industries Publications Inc.] - White Plains, NY - *BaconPubCkMag 84; MicrocomMPl 84*
IDR System [of Reuters] - New York, NY - *EISS 83*
IDS Computer Services Ltd. - Dublin, Ireland - *MicrocomSwDir 1*
IDSI - Las Cruces, NM - *MicrocomMPl 83*
IDX-3000 [of M/A-Com Linkabit Inc.] - San Diego, CA - *TeleSy&SerDir 7-83*
Idyllwild Cable TV - Idyllwild, CA - *BrCabYB 84*
Idyllwild Cablevision - Idyllwild, CA - *Tel&CabFB 84C*
Idyllwild Town Crier - Idyllwild, CA - *Ed&PubIntYB 82*
IE Inc. - South Bend, IN - *BillIntBG 83-84*
IE Systems - Newmarket, NH - *MicrocomMPl 83, 84; MicrocomSwDir 1; WhoWMicrocom 83*
IEA Annual Energy Balances - Paris, France - *DirOnDB Spring 84*
IEA Annual Energy Statistics - Paris, France - *DirOnDB Spring 84*
IEA Annual Oil & Gas Statistics - Paris, France - *DirOnDB Spring 84*
IEA Coal Research - London, England - *CompReadDB 82*
IEA Coal Research (Technical Information Service) - London, England - *InfIndMarPl 83*
IEA Data Bank [of International Association for the Evaluation of Educational Achievement] - Stockholm, Sweden - *EISS 83*
IEA Quarterly Oil & Gas Statistics - *See* OECD Quarterly Oil Statistics
IEA Reporter - Boise, ID - *BaconPubCkMag 84; MagDir 84*
IEC - Ottawa, ON, Canada - *DirOnDB Spring 84*
IEC Books [Aff. of International Evangelism Crusades Inc.] - Van Nuys, CA - *BoPubDir 5*
IEE-File - Tokyo, Japan - *DirOnDB Spring 84*
IEEE - *See* Institute of Electrical & Electronics Engineers
IEEE Almanack [of IEEE Philadelphia Section] - Philadelphia, PA - *BaconPubCkMag 84; MagDir 84*
IEEE Communications Magazine - New York, NY - *BaconPubCkMag 84*
IEEE Computer Graphics & Applications - Los Alamitos, CA - *BaconPubCkMag 84*
IEEE Grid - Mountain View, CA - *BaconPubCkMag 84*
IEEE Grid [of San Francisco Bay Area Council, IEEE] - Palo Alto, CA - *MagDir 84*
IEEE Micro - Los Alamitos, CA - *BaconPubCkMag 84*
IEEE Spectrum [of The Institute of Electrical & Electronics Engineers] - New York, NY - *MagDir 84; MagIndMarPl 82-83; WritMar 84*
Iem-Hotep Association - Boca Raton, FL - *BoPubDir 4*
Iem-Hotep Association - Ft. Lauderdale, FL - *BoPubDir 5*
IES Publishing Co. - Washington, DC - *BoPubDir 4, 5*
IESA Development Information System [of Dept. of International Economic & Social Affairs] - New York, NY - *EISS 83*
IF Studios Inc. - New York, NY - *AvMarPl 83*
IFA Computer Services - Cranford, NJ - *ADAPSOMemDir 83-84*
IFDS Inc. - Atlanta, GA - *MicrocomMPl 84*
Iffin Music Publishing Co. - Nashville, TN - *BillIntBG 83-84*
IFI Comprehensive Data Base [of IFI/Plenum Data Co.] - Alexandria, VA - *CompReadDB 82*
I.F.I. Fabricare News - Silver Spring, MD - *MagDir 84*
IFI/Plenum Data Co. [Subs. of Plenum Publishing Co.] - Alexandria, VA - *CompReadDB 82; DataDirOnSer 84; EISS 83; InfIndMarPl 83*
IFN International Facsimile Network Inc. - Toronto, ON, Canada - *TeleSy&SerDir 2-84*
IFO Time Series Data Bank [of IFO-Institute for Economic Research] - Munich, East Germany - *EISS 83*
IFP-TH [of Questel Inc.] - Washington, DC - *DataDirOnSer 84*
IFP Thermodynamique - Rueil Malmaison, France - *DirOnDB Spring 84*
IFT Marketing Research Ltd. - Esher, England - *IntDirMarRes 83*
IGA Grocergram [of IGA Inc.] - Chicago, IL - *BaconPubCkMag 84; MagDir 84*
IGA Grocergram - Greensboro, NC - *WritMar 84*
Igaku-Shoin Medical Publishers Inc. [Subs. of Igaku-Shoin Ltd.] - New York, NY - *LitMarPl 83, 84*
Ignace Driftwood - Ignace, ON, Canada - *AyerDirPub 83*
Ignatius Press [Aff. of Guadalupe Associates Inc.] - San Francisco, CA - *BoPubDir 4, 5; LitMarPl 84*
Iguana Music Inc. - New York, NY - *BillIntBG 83-84*
IHA Institute for Market Analyses - Hergiswil, Switzerland - *IntDirMarRes 83*
I.H.G. Advertising - Bay Village, FL - *StaDirAdAg 2-84*
IHRDC - Boston, MA - *LitMarPl 83, 84*
IHS Product/Subject Index - Englewood, CO - *DirOnDB Spring 84*
IIA Friday Memo - Washington, DC - *DirOnDB Spring 84*
IIA Friday Memo [of NewsNet Inc.] - Bryn Mawr, PA - *DataDirOnSer 84*
III Systems Inc. - Cambridge, MA - *DataDirOnSer 84*
IJE Inc. - Hollywood, FL - *BillIntBG 83-84*
IJG Inc. - Upland, CA - *MicrocomMPl 83, 84*
IJK International - White Plains, NY - *BoPubDir 4 Sup, 5*
Ikegami Electronics Inc. - Maywood, NJ - *AvMarPl 83*
Ikon Corp. - Seattle, WA - *WhoWMicrocom 83*
Il Cittadino Canadese - Montreal, PQ, Canada - *Ed&PubIntYB 82*
Il Corriere Italiano - Montreal, PQ, Canada - *AyerDirPub 83*
Il Mormoratore - Calgary, AB, Canada - *Ed&PubIntYB 82*
Il Pensiero - St. Louis, MO - *NewsDir 84*
Il Progresso Italo-Americano - Emerson, NJ - *AyerDirPub 83; Ed&PubIntYB 82*
Il Progresso Italo-Americano - New York, NY - *NewsDir 84*
Il Rincontro - Montreal, PQ, Canada - *Ed&PubIntYB 82*
Il Settimanale - Toronto, ON, Canada - *Ed&PubIntYB 82*
Il Tevere - Toronto, ON, Canada - *Ed&PubIntYB 82*
I.L.A. Newsletter - New York, NY - *NewsDir 84*
ILD Marketing - Nashua, NH - *WhoWMicrocom 83*
Iles Inc., Gordon R. - Seattle, WA - *StaDirAdAg 2-84*
Ilford [Subs. of Ciba Geigy] - Paramus, NJ - *AvMarPl 83*
ILIAS [of Inforonics Inc.] - Littleton, MA - *DataDirOnSer 84*
Ilkon Press - New York, NY - *BoPubDir 4, 5*
Illiana Spirit - Watseka, IL - *AyerDirPub 83*
Illini Audio-Visual Education Service Inc. - Peoria, IL - *AvMarPl 83*
Illini Data Systems - Steger, IL - *MicrocomMPl 84*
Illini Publishing Co. - Champaign, IL - *BrCabYB 84*
Illinoian-Star - Beardstown, IL - *Ed&PubIntYB 82*
Illinois Agri-News - La Salle, IL - *BaconPubCkMag 84*
Illinois Banker - Chicago, IL - *BaconPubCkMag 84; MagDir 84; WritMar 84*
Illinois Bell Telephone Co. - Chicago, IL - *TelDir&BG 83-84*
Illinois Beverage Journal [of Illinois Beverage Media Inc.] - Chicago, IL - *BaconPubCkMag 84; MagDir 84*
Illinois Bible Institute Inc. - Carlinville, IL - *BrCabYB 84*
Illinois Building News [of Illinois Lumber & Material Dealers Association] - Springfield, IL - *BaconPubCkMag 84; MagDir 84*
Illinois Business [of Crain Communications Inc.] - Chicago, IL - *WritMar 84*
Illinois Center Market Research - Chicago, IL - *IntDirMarRes 83*
Illinois Communication Cablevision Inc. - North Utica, IL - *BrCabYB 84*

Illinois Community Cablevision Inc. - Denver, CO - *BrCabYB 84*
Illinois Community Cablevision Inc. - Chebanse, IL - *BrCabYB 84*
Illinois Community Cablevision Inc. [of Tele-Communications Inc.] - Coal City, IL - *BrCabYB 84; Tel&CabFB 84C*
Illinois Community Cablevision Inc. [of Tele-Communications Inc.] - Manteno, IL - *Tel&CabFB 84C*
Illinois Community Cablevision Inc. [of Tele-Communications Inc.] - Morris, IL - *Tel&CabFB 84C*
Illinois Community Cablevision Inc. [of Tele-Communications Inc.] - North Utica, IL - *Tel&CabFB 84C*
Illinois Community Cablevision Inc. [of Tele-Communications Inc.] - Piper City, IL - *Tel&CabFB 84C*
Illinois Community Cablevision Inc. [of Tele-Communications Inc.] - Utica, IL - *BrCabYB 84*
Illinois Community Cablevision Inc. - *See* Tele-Communications Inc.
Illinois Consolidated Telephone Co. - Mattoon, IL - *TelDir&BG 83-84*
Illinois County & Township Official [of Township Officials of Illinois] - Astoria, IL - *BaconPubCkMag 84; MagDir 84*
Illinois Dental Journal - Maywood, IL - *BaconPubCkMag 84*
Illinois Dental Journal [of Illinois State Dental Society] - Springfield, IL - *MagDir 84*
Illinois Engineer [of Illinois Graphics] - Springfield, IL - *BaconPubCkMag 84; MagDir 84*
Illinois Entertainer - Des Plaines, IL - *BaconPubCkMag 84*
Illinois Entertainer - Mt. Prospect, IL - *WritMar 84*
Illinois Floodplain Information Repository [of Illinois State Water Survey] - Champaign, IL - *CompReadDB 82; EISS 83*
Illinois Food Retailer [of Illinois Food Retailers Association] - Hinsdale, IL - *MagDir 84*
Illinois Foodservice News - Chicago, IL - *BaconPubCkMag 84*
Illinois Heartland Users Group [of Illinois State Library] - Springfield, IL - *InfIndMarPl 83*
Illinois Institute of Technology (Research Institute) - Rome, NY - *CompReadDB 82*
Illinois Issues [of Sangamon State University] - Springfield, IL - *MagIndMarPl 82-83; WritMar 84*
Illinois Labor History Society - Chicago, IL - *BoPubDir 4, 5*
Illinois Libertarian - Des Plaines, IL - *LitMag&SmPr 83-84*
Illinois Library & Information Network [of Illinois State Library] - Springfield, IL - *EISS 83; InfIndMarPl 83*
Illinois Master Plumber - Springfield, IL - *BaconPubCkMag 84; MagDir 84*
Illinois Medical Journal - Chicago, IL - *BaconPubCkMag 84; MagDir 84*
Illinois Micro Inc. - Chicago, IL - *MicrocomMPl 84*
Illinois Micro Inc. - Mt. Prospect, IL - *MicrocomMPl 83*
Illinois Municipal Review [of Illinois Municipal League] - Springfield, IL - *BaconPubCkMag 84; MagDir 84*
Illinois Pharmacist [of Illinois Pharmacists Association] - Chicago, IL - *BaconPubCkMag 84; MagDir 84*
Illinois Reporter - Springfield, IL - *BaconPubCkMag 84*
Illinois Resource & Dissemination Network [of Illinois State Board of Education] - Springfield, IL - *EISS 83*
Illinois Rural Electric News - Springfield, IL - *BaconPubCkMag 84; MagDir 84*
Illinois School Board Journal - Springfield, IL - *MagDir 84*
Illinois State Chamber of Commerce - Chicago, IL - *BoPubDir 5*
Illinois State Data Center [of Illinois State Office of Planning] - Springfield, IL - *EISS 83*
Illinois State Historical Library - Springfield, IL - *BoPubDir 4, 5; MicroMarPl 82-83*
Illinois State Historical Society - Springfield, IL - *BoPubDir 4, 5*
Illinois State Museum - Springfield, IL - *BoPubDir 4, 5*
Illinois State Water Survey - Champaign, IL - *CompReadDB 82*
Illinois State Water Survey Div. Library - Urbana, IL - *CompReadDB 82*
Illinois Technograph [of Illini Publishing Co.] - Urbana, IL - *BaconPubCkMag 84; MagDir 84*
Illinois Times - Springfield, IL - *AyerDirPub 83; Ed&PubIntYB 82; WritMar 84*
Illinois Truck News - Hillside, IL - *BaconPubCkMag 84*
Illinois Truck News - Melrose Park, IL - *MagDir 84*
Illinois Underwriter - Chicago, IL - *BaconPubCkMag 84*
Illinois Underwriter - Cincinnati, OH - *MagDir 84*
Illinois Union Teacher - Hinsdale, IL - *NewsDir 84*
Illinois Valley Cable TV - Cave Junction, OR - *BrCabYB 84; Tel&CabFB 84C*
Illinois Valley News - Cave Junction, OR - *Ed&PubIntYB 82*
Illinois Wildlife - Blue Island, IL - *MagDir 84*
Illinois Writers Inc. - Macomb, IL - *LitMag&SmPr 83-84*
Illinois Writers Review - Macomb, IL - *LitMag&SmPr 83-84*
Illiopolis Illinois County Line Observer - Illiopolis, IL - *BaconPubCkNews 84*
Illiopolis Sentinel - Illiopolis, IL - *BaconPubCkNews 84; Ed&PubIntYB 82*
Illmo Jimplicute - Illmo, MO - *BaconPubCkNews 84; Ed&PubIntYB 82*
Illott Advertising Ltd. - *See* Bates Worldwide Inc., Ted
Illuminati - Los Angeles, CA - *ArtMar 84; LitMag&SmPr 83-84; LitMarPl 83, 84; WritMar 84*
Illuminating Engineering Society - New York, NY - *BoPubDir 4, 5*
Illuminations Press [Aff. of Berkeley Trucking Co.] - Berkeley, CA - *BoPubDir 4, 5; LitMag&SmPr 83-84*
Illustrated Memory Banks - Williamstown, MA - *MicrocomMPl 83*
Illustrated Speedway News - Massapequa, NY - *BaconPubCkMag 84; MagDir 84*
ILR: Access [of Cornell University] - Ithaca, NY - *FBInfSer 80; InfIndMarPl 83*
ILR Press [Div. of New York State School of Industrial & Labor Relations] - Ithaca, NY - *LitMarPl 83, 84*
Ilson Inc., Bernie - New York, NY - *DirPRFirms 83*
Iltis Associates, John - Chicago, IL - *CabTVFinDB 83; StaDirAdAg 2-84*
Ilton, Irene R. - Irvington, NY - *LitMarPl 84*
Ilut Publications [Aff. of Lane & Associates Inc.] - Bonita, CA - *BoPubDir 4*
Ilut Publications [Aff. of Lane & Associates Inc.] - La Jolla, CA - *BoPubDir 5*
Ilwaco Pacific Tribune - Ilwaco, WA - *Ed&PubIntYB 82*
IM-Internal Medicine - Morganville, NJ - *BaconPubCkMag 84*
I.M.A. Associates [Aff. of Stark County Medical Auxiliary] - Canton, OH - *BoPubDir 4, 5*
IMA Education & Research Foundation - Newtonville, NY - *BoPubDir 4, 5*
IMAA Inc. - *See* Van Brunt & Co. Advertising-Marketing Inc.
IMAA Inc./AB Olof Isacsons Annonsbyra - Gothenburg, Sweden - *StaDirAdAg 2-84*
Imag-Dataservice [of Institute of Agricultural Engineering] - Wageningen, Netherlands - *EISS 83*
Image - Austin, TX - *BaconPubCkMag 84*
Image - Burlington, VT - *StaDirAdAg 2-84*
Image Advertising - Roanoke, VA - *AdAge 3-28-84; StaDirAdAg 2-84*
Image Advertising Group Inc. - Chicago, IL - *StaDirAdAg 2-84*
Image Associates - Santa Barbara, CA - *AvMarPl 83*
Image Associates of Indiana - Mishawaka, IN - *AvMarPl 83*
Image Awareness Corp. - Auburn, CA - *BoPubDir 4, 5*
Image Bank, The - New York, NY - *MagIndMarPl 82-83*
Image Communications Inc. - New York, NY - *HBIndAd&MS 82-83*
Image Computer Products Inc. [Subs. of The Image Producers Inc.] - Northbrook, IL - *WhoWMicrocom 83*
Image Dynamics - Baltimore, MD - *AdAge 3-28-84; ArtMar 84; DirPRFirms 83; StaDirAdAg 2-84*
Image Dynamics - Morris Plains, NJ - *AvMarPl 83*
Image Engineering - Somerville, MA - *AvMarPl 83*
Image Graphics Inc. - Fairfield, CT - *DataDirSup 7-83; WhoWMicrocom 83*
Image Group, The - Atlanta, GA - *AvMarPl 83*
Image Inc. - Washington, DC - *AvMarPl 83*
Image Innovations Inc. - Somerset, NJ - *ArtMar 84; AvMarPl 83; WritMar 84*
Image Magazine [of Cornerstone Press] - St. Louis, MO - *ArtMar 84; LitMag&SmPr 83-84; WritMar 84*
Image Magnification Inc. - New Smyrna Beach, FL - *AvMarPl 83*
Image Makers [Div. of Blakeslee-Lane Inc.] - Baltimore, MD - *AvMarPl 83*
Image Makers Inc. - Westport, CT - *AvMarPl 83*
Image Management Inc. - Milwaukee, WI - *DirPRFirms 83*
Image Marketing Services Inc. - Centerville, OH - *WritMar 84*

Image Media - Minneapolis, MN - *ArtMar 84; WritMar 84*
Image 9 Productions [Div. of The Gannett Co.] - Denver, CO - *Tel&CabFB 84C*
Image Photos - Stockbridge, MA - *AvMarPl 83; LitMarPl 83, 84; MagIndMarPl 82-83*
Image Processing Systems - Madison, WI - *MicrocomMPl 83, 84*
Image Promotion Programmers-T.A. Inc. - *See* East-West Marketing Corp.
Image Resource - Westlake Village, CA - *AvMarPl 83; DataDirSup 7-83; MicrocomMPl 84*
Image Stream - Los Angeles, CA - *ArtMar 84; AvMarPl 83*
Image Studio [Div. of Image Photos] - Stockbridge, MA - *LitMarPl 83, 84; MagIndMarPl 82-83*
Image Systems Inc. - Culver City, CA - *DirInfWP 82*
Image Technology Patent Information System [of Rochester Institute of Technology] - Rochester, NY - *EISS 83*
Image Transform Inc. - North Hollywood, CA - *AvMarPl 83*
Image Works Inc., The - Woodstock, NY - *LitMarPl 84*
ImageMatrix/Cincinnati [Subs. of ImageMatrix Inc.] - Cincinnati, OH - *AvMarPl 83*
ImageMatrix/Dallas [Subs. of ImageMatrix Inc.] - Dallas, TX - *AvMarPl 83*
ImageMatrix/Houston [Subs. of ImageMatrix Inc.] - Houston, TX - *AvMarPl 83*
ImageMatrix/Tennessee [Subs. of ImageMatrix Inc.] - Nashville, TN - *AvMarPl 83*
ImageMatrix/Washington [Subs. of ImageMatrix Inc.] - Alexandria, VA - *AvMarPl 83*
Imagen Corp. - Mountain View, CA - *ADAPSOMemDir 83-84*
Imagerie - Mamaroneck, NY - *Tel&CabFB 84C*
Images - Endicott, NY - *AvMarPl 83*
Images - Dayton, OH - *LitMag&SmPr 83-84*
Images & Concepts Inc. - Northport, NY - *StaDirAdAg 2-84*
Images & Ideas by Photomethods - New York, NY - *BaconPubCkMag 84*
Images Inc. - Jacksonville, FL - *AvMarPl 83*
Images Presentations Corp. - Jericho, NY - *AvMarPl 83*
Images Press - Berkeley, CA - *BoPubDir 4*
Images Press - Sebastopol, CA - *BoPubDir 5; LitMag&SmPr 83-84*
Images II - Lincoln, NE - *AvMarPl 83*
Imagesmith Inc. - Rochester, NY - *AvMarPl 83*
Imageworks Inc. - Naples, FL - *ArtMar 84*
Imageworks Photography - Denver, CO - *LitMarPl 83, 84; MagIndMarPl 82-83*
Imagicom Productions Inc. - Hamden, CT - *Tel&CabFB 84C*
Imaginary Entertainment Corp. - Auburn, AL - *BillIntBG 83-84*
Imaginary Press, The - Cambridge, MA - *LitMag&SmPr 83-84*
Imagine That! - Chicago, IL - *ArtMar 84*
Imago Design Co. Inc. - New York, NY - *LitMarPl 84*
Imagroup [of Don Bosco Publications] - New Rochelle, NY - *LitMag&SmPr 83-84*
Imahara & Keep - Santa Clara, CA - *AdAge 3-28-84; StaDirAdAg 2-84*
Imber Advertising, Harold - Mt. Kisco, NY - *StaDirAdAg 2-84*
Imboden Ozark Journal - Imboden, AR - *BaconPubCkNews 84*
IMC Journal - Bethesda, MD - *BaconPubCkMag 84*
IMC Journal - Minneapolis, MN - *MagDir 84*
Imes Stations, Birney Jr. - Columbus, MS - *BrCabYB 84; Tel&CabFB 84S*
IMF Balance of Payments [of International Monetary Fund] - Washington, DC - *DBBus 82*
IMF Balance of Payments [of Data Resources Inc.] - Lexington, MA - *DataDirOnSer 84*
IMF Direction of Trade Statistics [of International Monetary Fund] - Washington, DC - *DBBus 82*
IMF Direction of Trade Statistics [of Data Resources Inc.] - Lexington, MA - *DataDirOnSer 84*
IMF Government Finance Statistics [of Chase Econometrics/Interactive Data Corp.] - Waltham, MA - *DataDirOnSer 84*
IMF IFS Restated Data Bank - Washington, DC - *DirOnDB Spring 84*
IMF International Financial Statistics [of Evans Economics Inc.] - Washington, DC - *DataDirOnSer 84*
IMLAC Corp. - Needham, MA - *DataDirSup 7-83; DirInfWP 82*
Imlay City Tri-City Times - *See* Tri-City Times
Immac - Santa Clara, CA - *DirInfWP 82*
Immedia Network [of Immedia Telematics Inc.] - Hudson, PQ, Canada - *TeleSy&SerDir 2-84*
Immergut & Siolek Associates, E. H. - Brooklyn, NY - *LitMarPl 83, 84*
Immigrant City Records - Lawrence, MA - *BillIntBG 83-84*
Immigration History Research Center [of University of Minnesota] - St. Paul, MN - *MicroMarPl 82-83*
Immokalee Bulletin - Immokalee, FL - *Ed&PubIntYB 82*
Immunity Music - *See* Schabraf
Immunology Abstracts [of Information Retrieval Ltd.] - London, England - *CompReadDB 82*
Immunology & Allergy Practice - New York, NY - *BaconPubCkMag 84*
IMP Press - Buffalo, NY - *BoPubDir 4, 5*
Impac Associates - Philadelphia, PA - *StaDirAdAg 2-84*
Impact [Div. of Foote, Cone & Belding/Honig] - San Francisco, CA - *DirMarMP 83*
Impact Advertising Agency Inc. [Subs. of NCH Corp.] - Irving, TX - *StaDirAdAg 2-84*
Impact Books - Nashville, TN - *BoPubDir 4, 5*
Impact Books Inc. - Kirkwood, MO - *BoPubDir 4, 5*
Impact Communicators [Div. of JRF-Tronics Inc.] - Anaheim, CA - *AvMarPl 83*
Impact Computer Systems - Glen Wild, NY - *MicrocomMPl 83*
Impact Image Resources Inc. - Denver, CO - *DirMarMP 83*
Impact Magazine - Sunnyvale, CA - *BoPubDir 4, 5*
Impact Marketing & Communications - Boston, MA - *AdAge 3-28-84; StaDirAdAg 2-84*
Impact Press - Roseville, MI - *BoPubDir 4, 5*
Impact Press Inc. - Chicago, IL - *BoPubDir 4, 5*
Impact Promotions Inc. - *See* Bloom Cos. Inc., The
Impact Public Relations & Advertising - Whittier, CA - *StaDirAdAg 2-84*
Impact Publications [Aff. of Development Concepts Inc.] - Chicago, IL - *BoPubDir 5*
Impact Publications of Virginia [Aff. of Development Concepts Inc.] - Falls Church, VA - *BoPubDir 4 Sup, 5*
Impact Publications of Virginia - Manassas, VA - *LitMag&SmPr 83-84*
Impact Publishers Inc. - San Luis Obispo, CA - *DirMarMP 83; LitMag&SmPr 83-84; LitMarPl 83, 84*
Impact 1040 Partnership Data - Bellevue, WA - *DirOnDB Spring 84*
Impact, The Promotion & Design Co. - Chicago, IL - *StaDirAdAg 2-84*
Impartial Citizen Inc. - Syracuse, NY - *AyerDirPub 83; Ed&PubIntYB 82; NewsDir 84*
Impegno 80 [of Sicilian Antigruppo/Cross-Cultural Communications] - Trapani, Italy - *LitMag&SmPr 83-84*
Imperial Automation Inc. - Costa Mesa, CA - *DataDirSup 7-83*
Imperial Beach/Nestor Pennysaver - Mission Viejo, CA - *AyerDirPub 83*
Imperial Beach Reminder Newspaper, The - Imperial Beach, CA - *NewsDir 84*
Imperial Beach Star-News [of Chula Vista Star-News] - Chula Vista, CA - *NewsDir 84*
Imperial Beach Star-News - Imperial Beach, CA - *Ed&PubIntYB 82*
Imperial Beach Star-News - *See* Star-News Publishing Co. Inc.
Imperial Cable TV [of Burwell Cable TV Inc.] - Imperial, NE - *BrCabYB 84; Tel&CabFB 84C*
Imperial International Learning Corp. - Kankakee, IL - *ArtMar 84; AvMarPl 83; WritMar 84*
Imperial Publishing Co. - Bartow, FL - *BoPubDir 4, 5*
Imperial Republican - Imperial, NE - *BaconPubCkNews 84; Ed&PubIntYB 82*
Imperial Technology Inc. - El Segundo, CA - *WhoWMicrocom 83*
Imperial Valley Cable [of Rogers UA Cablesystems Inc.] - Brawley, CA - *BrCabYB 84*
Imperial Valley Cable Co. [of Rogers UA Cablesystems] - Calexico, CA - *BrCabYB 84*
Imperial Valley Cable Co. [of Rogers UA Cable Systems Inc.] - El Centro, CA - *BrCabYB 84*
Imperial Valley Press - El Centro, CA - *AyerDirPub 83; BaconPubCkNews 84; Ed&PubIntYB 82*
Imperial Valley Weekly - El Centro, CA - *Ed&PubIntYB 82*
Impetus Magazine - London, England - *LitMag&SmPr 83-84*

Implement & Tractor - Overland Park, KS - *BaconPubCkMag 84*
Implement & Tractor [of Intertec Publishing Corp.] - Shawnee Mission, KS - *MagDir 84*
Import Automotive Parts & Accessories [of Import Automotive Publishers] - North Hollywood, CA - *BaconPubCkMag 84; WritMar 84*
Import Daily - New York, NY - *Ed&PubIntYB 82*
Import/Export Opportunities Digest - Bellflower, CA - *MagIndMarPl 82-83*
Importcar [of Babcox Publications] - Akron, OH - *BaconPubCkMag 84; MagDir 84*
Importe/12 Records - New York, NY - *BillIntBG 83-84*
Imported Crude Oil & Petroleum Products - Washington, DC - *DirOnDB Spring 84*
Imported Publications Inc. - Chicago, IL - *LitMarPl 83, 84*
Imports [of U.S. Dept. of Energy] - Washington, DC - *DBBus 82; DirOnDB Spring 84*
Imprenta el Soplon - Detroit, MI - *BoPubDir 4, 5*
Impresora Sahuaro - Tucson, AZ - *BoPubDir 4, 5*
Impress - Hanover, NH - *DirOnDB Spring 84*
Impressions [of Gralla Communications Inc.] - Dallas, TX - *BaconPubCkMag 84; MagDir 84; WritMar 84*
Impressions - Toronto, ON, Canada - *LitMag&SmPr 83-84*
Impressions Supply Corp. - Larchmont, NY - *DirInfWP 82*
Impressions Unltd. Inc. - North Palm Beach, FL - *ArtMar 84*
Impressive Advertising & Lithography Inc. - Waynesboro, VA - *AdAge 3-28-84; StaDirAdAg 2-84*
Imprint - New York, NY - *BaconPubCkMag 84; MagDir 84*
Imprint [of Advertising Specialty Institute] - Langhorne, PA - *WritMar 84*
Imprint Capablanca - Ft. Collins, CO - *EISS 83*
Imprint Editions - Ft. Collins, CO - *BoPubDir 4 Sup, 5; CompReadDB 82; InfIndMarPl 83*
Imprint Inc. - West Hartford, CT - *BoPubDir 4, 5*
Imprint Software - Ft. Collins, CO - *EISS 83*
Imprint Software - Exeter, England - *InfIndMarPl 83*
Improvising Artists Inc. - Cherry Valley, NY - *BillIntBG 83-84*
Impulse Research Corp. - Los Angeles, CA - *IntDirMarRes 83*
IMS America Ltd. [Subs. of IMS International Ltd.] - Ambler, PA - *DataDirOnSer 84*
IMS IFS Restated [of Data Resources Inc.] - Lexington, MA - *DataDirOnSer 84*
IMS International - New York, NY - *AdAge 5-17-84 p.17; IntDirMarRes 83; KnowInd 83*
IMS Ltd. - Hong Kong - *IntDirMarRes 83*
IMS Press - Bala Cynwyd, PA - *MagIndMarPl 82-83*
IMS Press [Div. of IMS Communications Inc.] - Ft. Washington, PA - *LitMarPl 83, 84*
IMS Weekly Marketeer - Santa Monica, CA - *DirOnDB Spring 84*
IMSA Journal - Ft. Worth, TX - *BaconPubCkMag 84; MagDir 84*
IMSAUS - Melbourne, Australia - *IntDirMarRes 83*
IMSL Inc. - Houston, TX - *DataDirSup 7-83*
IMSPact [of IMS America Ltd.] - Ambler, PA - *DataDirOnSer 84; DirOnDB Spring 84*
In Between Books - Sausalito, CA - *BoPubDir 4, 5*
In Business [of The JG Press Inc.] - Emmaus, PA - *ArtMar 84; BaconPubCkMag 84; MagDir 84; MagIndMarPl 82-83; WritMar 84*
In Cider - Peterborough, NH - *BaconPubCkMag 84*
In-Dex [of Infonex Inc.] - New York, NY - *EISS 83*
In-Fact Research & Information Service - Rensselaerville, NY - *EISS 83; FBInfSer 80; InfIndMarPl 83*
In-Fisherman, The - Brainerd, MN - *BaconPubCkMag 84*
In Gear - Sacramento, CA - *BaconPubCkMag 84*
In Kentucky - Bowling Green, KY - *MagDir 84*
In-Plant Printer - Northbrook, IL - *BaconPubCkMag 84; MagDir 84; MagIndMarPl 82-83; WritMar 84*
In-Plant Reproductions - Philadelphia, PA - *BaconPubCkMag 84; MagDir 84; MagIndMarPl 82-83; WritMar 84*
In-Register Newsletter - San Francisco, CA - *BaconPubCkMag 84*
In-Search Data - *See* SRG International Ltd.
In-Situ Inc. - Laramie, WY - *DataDirOnSer 84*
In-Store Merchandising Services [Div. of Lionetti & Meyers Research Center Inc.] - New York, NY - *IntDirMarRes 83*
In-Store Services - Sewickley, PA - *IntDirMarRes 83*
In Sync Laboratories Inc. - New York, NY - *BillIntBG 83-84*
In Tech - Research Triangle Park, NC - *BaconPubCkMag 84*
In the Light - Chicago, IL - *LitMag&SmPr 83-84*
In-the-Valley-of-the-Wichitas House - Lawton, OK - *BoPubDir 5*
In These Times [of Capp Street Foundation] - Chicago, IL - *AyerDirPub 83; WritMar 84*
In Touch [of Wesleyan Publishing House] - Marion, IN - *ArtMar 84; WritMar 84*
In Transit [of Amalgamated Transit Union] - Washington, DC - *NewsDir 84*
In-Vision Inc. - Wheaton, IL - *AvMarPl 83*
In Vitro - Gaithersburg, MD - *BaconPubCkMag 84*
Inacom International - Denver, CO - *BoPubDir 5; EISS 7-83 Sup; InfoS 83-84*
INC - Fresno, CA - *EISS 5-84 Sup*
Incentive Marketing [of Bill Communications] - New York, NY - *BaconPubCkMag 84; MagDir 84; WritMar 84*
Incentive Productions [Div. of Jevert Music] - Columbus, OH - *BillIntBG 83-84*
Incentive Publications Inc. - Nashville, TN - *LitMarPl 83, 84*
Incentive Travel Manager [of Brentwood Publishing Corp.] - Los Angeles, CA - *ArtMar 84; BaconPubCkMag 84; MagDir 84; MagIndMarPl 82-83; WritMar 84*
InCider [of Wayne Green Inc.] - Peterborough, NH - *MicrocomMPl 84*
Income Opportunities - Greenwich, CT - *MagDir 84*
Income Opportunities - New York, NY - *BaconPubCkMag 84; MagIndMarPl 82-83; WritMar 84*
Incomm Inc. - Waterbury, CT - *AdAge 3-28-84; StaDirAdAg 2-84*
Inconet Corp. - New York, NY - *TeleSy&SerDir 2-84*
INC. [of Goldhirsh Group Inc.] - Boston, MA - *BaconPubCkMag 84; DirMarMP 83; Folio 83; LitMarPl 84; MagIndMarPl 82-83*
Incorporating Guide - Wilmington, DE - *DirOnDB Spring 84*
Incosan Inc. - Sparta, NJ - *WhoWMicrocom 83*
Incunabula Collection Press Ltd. - Nutley, NJ - *BoPubDir 4, 5*
INDA Newsletter - New York, NY - *BaconPubCkMag 84*
INDAX [of Cox Cable Communications Inc.] - Atlanta, GA - *EISS 83; VideoDir 82-83*
Indelible Ink Works - Montclair, NJ - *Ed&PubIntYB 82*
Indenture Covenants - Hoboken, NJ - *DirOnDB Spring 84*
Independence [of Agora Publishing] - Baltimore, MD - *WritMar 84*
Independence Broadcasting Corp., The - Des Moines, IA - *BrCabYB 84*
Independence Bulletin-Journal [of Independence Newspapers] - Independence, IA - *NewsDir 84*
Independence Bulletin-Journal - *See* Independence Newspapers
Independence Cablevision Inc. [of McDonald Group] - Independence, IA - *Tel&CabFB 84C*
Independence Conservative - Independence, IA - *NewsDir 84*
Independence Conservative - *See* Independence Newspapers
Independence County Cable TV Inc. - Batesville, AR - *BrCabYB 84 p.D-302; Tel&CabFB 84C p.1685*
Independence County Cable TV Inc. - Moorefield, AR - *BrCabYB 84*
Independence County Cable TV Inc. - Mt. Pleasant, AR - *BrCabYB 84*
Independence County Cable TV Inc. - Old Trough, AR - *BrCabYB 84*
Independence Dispatch-Tribune [of Townsend Communications Inc.] - Kansas City, MO - *NewsDir 84*
Independence Examiner [of Stauffer Communications Inc.] - Independence, MO - *BaconPubCkNews 84; NewsDir 84*
Independence Independent [of Hammond Murray-Huber Publishing Inc.] - Hammond, LA - *NewsDir 84*
Independence News - Independence, KS - *BaconPubCkNews 84; Ed&PubIntYB 82*
Independence News Wave - Independence, WI - *BaconPubCkNews 84*
Independence Newspapers - Independence, IA - *BaconPubCkNews 84*
Independence Press [Div. of Herald House] - Independence, MO - *LitMarPl 83, 84*
Independence Reporter - Independence, KS - *BaconPubCkNews 84; Ed&PubIntYB 82; NewsDir 84*
Independence Unltd. - Portsmouth, NH - *BoPubDir 4, 5*

Independent - Montgomery, AL - *AyerDirPub 83*
Independent - Carlisle, AR - *AyerDirPub 83*
Independent - Newport, AR - *AyerDirPub 83*
Independent - Corona, CA - *AyerDirPub 83*
Independent - Richmond, CA - *BaconPubCkNews 84*
Independent - Ridgecrest, CA - *AyerDirPub 83*
Independent - Santa Monica, CA - *AyerDirPub 83*
Independent - Otis, CO - *AyerDirPub 83*
Independent - St. Petersburg, FL - *AyerDirPub 83*
Independent - Roseville, IL - *AyerDirPub 83*
Independent - Belmond, IA - *AyerDirPub 83*
Independent - Humboldt, IA - *AyerDirPub 83*
Independent - Eskridge, KS - *AyerDirPub 83*
Independent - Lakin, KS - *AyerDirPub 83*
Independent - Oskaloosa, KS - *AyerDirPub 83*
Independent - Ashland, KY - *AyerDirPub 83*
Independent - Rayne, LA - *AyerDirPub 83*
Independent - Bridgewater, MA - *AyerDirPub 83*
Independent - Stoneham, MA - *AyerDirPub 83*
Independent - Fenton, MI - *AyerDirPub 83; Ed&PubIntYB 82*
Independent - Jordan, MN - *AyerDirPub 83*
Independent - Le Roy, MN - *AyerDirPub 83*
Independent - Marshall, MN - *AyerDirPub 83; Ed&PubIntYB 82*
Independent - Ortonville, MN - *AyerDirPub 83*
Independent - Grand Island, NE - *AyerDirPub 83; Ed&PubIntYB 82*
Independent - Elko, NV - *AyerDirPub 83*
Independent - Wood-Ridge, NJ - *AyerDirPub 83*
Independent - Gallup, NM - *AyerDirPub 83*
Independent - Marathon, NY - *AyerDirPub 83*
Independent - Kannapolis, NC - *AyerDirPub 83*
Independent - Enderlin, ND - *AyerDirPub 83*
Independent - Johnstown, OH - *AyerDirPub 83*
Independent - Massillion, OH - *AyerDirPub 83*
Independent - Montrose, PA - *AyerDirPub 83*
Independent - Souderton, PA - *AyerDirPub 83*
Independent - Faith, SD - *AyerDirPub 83*
Independent - Frederick, SD - *AyerDirPub 83*
Independent - Groton, SD - *AyerDirPub 83*
Independent - Lennox, SD - *AyerDirPub 83*
Independent - Wessington Springs, SD - *AyerDirPub 83; Ed&PubIntYB 82*
Independent - Appalachia, VA - *AyerDirPub 83*
Independent - Elkhorn, WI - *AyerDirPub 83*
Independent - Sun Prairie, WI - *AyerDirPub 83*
Independent - Glenrock, WY - *AyerDirPub 83*
Independent - Stettler, AB, Canada - *AyerDirPub 83*
Independent - Bobcaygeon, ON, Canada - *AyerDirPub 83*
Independent - Brighton, ON, Canada - *AyerDirPub 83; Ed&PubIntYB 82*
Independent - New Hamburg, ON, Canada - *AyerDirPub 83; Ed&PubIntYB 82*
Independent - Biggar, SK, Canada - *AyerDirPub 83; Ed&PubIntYB 82*
Independent - Grenfell, SK, Canada - *Ed&PubIntYB 82*
Independent Advertiser - Clanton, AL - *Ed&PubIntYB 82*
Independent Age - Aitkin, MN - *AyerDirPub 83*
Independent Agent - New York, NY - *BaconPubCkMag 84; MagDir 84*
Independent & Enterprise News [of Brown-Thompson Newspapers] - Edinboro, PA - *AyerDirPub 83; NewsDir 84*
Independent & Montgomery Transcript - Collegeville, PA - *AyerDirPub 83; NewsDir 84*
Independent & Republican - Oakland, NE - *AyerDirPub 83; Ed&PubIntYB 82*
Independent Appeal - Selmer, TN - *AyerDirPub 83; Ed&PubIntYB 82*
Independent Banker, The - Sauk Centre, MN - *BaconPubCkMag 84; MagDir 84*
Independent Battery Manufacturers Association Inc. - Largo, FL - *BoPubDir 4, 5*
Independent Bulletin Newspapers - Chicago, IL - *Ed&PubIntYB 82*
Independent Chemical Information Services [of I. P. Sharp Associates Ltd.] - Toronto, ON, Canada - *DataDirOnSer 84*
Independent Chemical Information Services - Guernsey, England - *EISS 5-84 Sup*
Independent Chemical Information Services - Paris, France - *DirOnDB Spring 84*
Independent Cinema Artists & Producers - New York, NY - *AvMarPl 83; Tel&CabFB 84C*
Independent Coast Observer - Gualala, CA - *AyerDirPub 83*
Independent Community Consultants Inc. - Hampton, AR - *BoPubDir 4, 5*
Independent Computer Consultants Association - St. Louis, MO - *BoPubDir 5*
Independent Computer Supply - Whittier, CA - *DataDirSup 7-83*
Independent Enterprise - Payette, ID - *AyerDirPub 83; Ed&PubIntYB 82*
Independent/Enterprise News, The - Cambridge Springs, PA - *Ed&PubIntYB 82*
Independent Farmer & Rancher - Gainesville, FL - *Ed&PubIntYB 82; NewsDir 84*
Independent Florida Alligator, The [of Campus Communications Inc.] - Gainesville, FL - *NewsDir 84*
Independent Garageman, The [of The Independent Garagemen's Association/Automotive Service Association] - Austin, TX - *MagDir 84*
Independent Georgetown, The - Georgetown, ON, Canada - *Ed&PubIntYB 82*
Independent Herald - Oneida, TN - *AyerDirPub 83*
Independent-Herald - Pineville, WV - *AyerDirPub 83; NewsDir 84*
Independent-International Entertainment [Div. of Independent-International Pictures Corp.] - East Brunswick, NJ - *TelAl 84*
Independent-International Entertainment [Div. of Independent-International Pictures Corp.] - East Brunswick, NY - *TelAl 83*
Independent-Journal [of Gannett Co. Inc.] - San Rafael, CA - *AyerDirPub 83; BaconPubCkNews 84; Ed&PubIntYB 82; LitMarPl 84*
Independent-Journal - Potosi, MO - *AyerDirPub 83; Ed&PubIntYB 82*
Independent-Journal Newspapers - Santa Monica, CA - *BaconPubCkNews 84*
Independent Journal of Philosophy, The [of The Independent Philosophy Press] - Paris, France - *LitMag&SmPr 83-84*
Independent Labour Publications - Leeds, England - *LitMag&SmPr 83-84*
Independent-Mail, The - Anderson, SC - *Ed&PubIntYB 82*
Independent Media Services - New York, NY - *StaDirAdAg 2-84*
Independent-Messenger - Emporia, VA - *AyerDirPub 83; Ed&PubIntYB 82*
Independent-Mirror - Mexico, NY - *AyerDirPub 83; Ed&PubIntYB 82; NewsDir 84*
Independent Network News [Div. of WPIX Inc.] - New York, NY - *BrCabYB 84; CabTVPrDB 83*
Independent News - Georgetown, IL - *Ed&PubIntYB 82*
Independent News - Walkerton, IN - *Ed&PubIntYB 82*
Independent News - Sullivan, MO - *AyerDirPub 83*
Independent News - Hawthorne, NV - *Ed&PubIntYB 82*
Independent News Alliance [Subs. of United Feature Syndicate] - New York, NY - *Ed&PubIntYB 82; LitMarPl 83, 84; MagIndMarPl 82-83*
Independent Observer - Conrad, MT - *AyerDirPub 83; Ed&PubIntYB 82*
Independent-Observer [of The Laurel Group Press] - Scottdale, PA - *AyerDirPub 83; Ed&PubIntYB 82; NewsDir 84*
Independent Philosophy Press, The - Paris, France - *LitMag&SmPr 83-84*
Independent Post - Live Oak, FL - *AyerDirPub 83; Ed&PubIntYB 82*
Independent Press - Bloomfield, NJ - *AyerDirPub 83*
Independent Press Shopper & West Hernando News - Brooksville, FL - *AyerDirPub 83*
Independent Press, The - Marine City, MI - *Ed&PubIntYB 82*
Independent Producers Service - Los Angeles, CA - *AvMarPl 83*
Independent Professional - Gainesville, FL - *BaconPubCkMag 84*
Independent Professional Typists Network - Huntington Beach, CA - *LitMarPl 83, 84*
Independent-Prospector, The - Clifton, NJ - *Ed&PubIntYB 82; NewsDir 84*
Independent Publications - Paterson, NJ - *BoPubDir 4, 5*
Independent Publications Inc. - Bryn Mawr, PA - *Ed&PubIntYB 82; KnowInd 83*

Independent Publishers Group [Div. of David White Inc.] - Port Washington, NY - *LitMarPl 83, 84*
Independent Publishers Services/The Gottstein Co. - San Francisco, CA - *LitMarPl 83, 84*
Independent Record [of Lee Enterprises Inc.] - Helena, MT - *AyerDirPub 83; Ed&PubIntYB 82; LitMarPl 84; NewsDir 84*
Independent Record - Thermopolis, WY - *AyerDirPub 83*
Independent-Register - Brodhead, WI - *AyerDirPub 83; Ed&PubIntYB 82*
Independent Register, The - Libertyville, IL - *Ed&PubIntYB 82*
Independent Republican - Goshen, NY - *AyerDirPub 83; Ed&PubIntYB 82*
Independent Research & Development [of Defense Technical Information Center] - Alexandria, VA - *DataDirOnSer 84*
Independent Restaurants - Madison, WI - *BaconPubCkMag 84; MagDir 84*
Independent Review - Litchfield, MN - *AyerDirPub 83; Ed&PubIntYB 82*
Independent-Review - Aztec, NM - *AyerDirPub 83; Ed&PubIntYB 82*
Independent School - Boston, MA - *BaconPubCkMag 84; MagDir 84; MagIndMarPl 82-83*
Independent School Press Inc. - Wellesley Hills, MA - *LitMarPl 83, 84*
Independent-Sentinel - Canton, PA - *AyerDirPub 83*
Independent Television News - Washington, DC - *BrCabYB 84*
Independent Television News Association Inc. - New York, NY - *Tel&CabFB 84C*
Independent, The - Robertsdale, AL - *Ed&PubIntYB 82*
Independent, The - Watkins, CO - *NewsDir 84*
Independent, The - Whitewater, KS - *Ed&PubIntYB 82*
Independent, The - Parkers Prairie, MN - *Ed&PubIntYB 82*
Independent, The - Collegeville, PA - *Ed&PubIntYB 82*
Independent, The - Deerfield, WI - *Ed&PubIntYB 82*
Independent, The - Elmira, ON, Canada - *AyerDirPub 83; Ed&PubIntYB 82*
Independent, The - Georgetown, ON, Canada - *AyerDirPub 83*
Independent, The - Grimsby, ON, Canada - *AyerDirPub 83; Ed&PubIntYB 82*
Independent, The - Kincardine, ON, Canada - *AyerDirPub 83; Ed&PubIntYB 82*
Independent-Tribune - Clovis, CA - *AyerDirPub 83*
Independent TV Sales - New York, NY - *TelAl 83, 84*
Independent United Distributors - New York, NY - *BillIntBG 83-84*
Independent Villager - Tully, NY - *AyerDirPub 83*
Indeserv Inc. - Littleton, MA - *WhoWMicrocom 83*
Indevideo Co. Inc. - Keams Canyon, AZ - *BrCabYB 84; Tel&CabFB 84C*
Indevideo Co. Inc. - Scottsdale, AZ - *BrCabYB 84*
Indevideo Co. Inc. - Shonto, AZ - *Tel&CabFB 84C*
Indevideo Co. Inc. - Tuba City, AZ - *BrCabYB 84; Tel&CabFB 84C*
Index - Chase, KS - *AyerDirPub 83*
Index - Frankfort, KS - *AyerDirPub 83*
Index - Davison, MI - *AyerDirPub 83*
Index - Bridgeport, TX - *AyerDirPub 83*
Index - Childress, TX - *AyerDirPub 83*
Index - Mineral Wells, TX - *Ed&PubIntYB 82*
Index - Dousman, WI - *AyerDirPub 83; Ed&PubIntYB 82*
Index Chemicus Online [of Institute for Scientific Information] - Philadelphia, PA - *DataDirOnSer 84; DirOnDB Spring 84*
Index Chemicus Registry System [of Institute for Scientific Information] - Philadelphia, PA - *CompReadDB 82*
Index/Directory of Women's Media [of Women's Institute for Freedom of the Press] - Washington, DC - *LitMag&SmPr 83-84*
Index-Journal - Greenwood, SC - *AyerDirPub 83; Ed&PubIntYB 82*
Index on Censorship - London, England - *LitMag&SmPr 83-84*
Index Press - O'Donnell, TX - *Ed&PubIntYB 82*
Index Systems Inc. - Cambridge, MA - *DataDirSup 7-83; WhoWMicrocom 83*
Index, The - Hermitage, MO - *AyerDirPub 83; Ed&PubIntYB 82*
Index, The - Mitchell, NE - *AyerDirPub 83; Ed&PubIntYB 82*
Index to American Banker [of Bell & Howell] - Wooster, OH - *CompReadDB 82*
Index to API Abstracts/Literature [of American Petroleum Institute] - New York, NY - *CompReadDB 82; DBBus 82*
Index to API Abstracts/Patents [of American Petroleum Institute] - New York, NY - *CompReadDB 82; DBBus 82*
Index to Black Newspapers [of Bell & Howell] - Wooster, OH - *CompReadDB 82*
Index to Energy & Environmentally Related Databases & Models... [of Lawrence Livermore National Laboratory] - Livermore, CA - *CompReadDB 82*
Index to Frost & Sullivan Market Research Reports [of Frost & Sullivan Inc.] - New York, NY - *DataDirOnSer 84*
Index to Jewish Periodicals - Cleveland Heights, OH - *BoPubDir 4, 5*
Index to Mormonism in Periodical Literature [of Church of Jesus Christ of Latter Day Saints] - Salt Lake City, UT - *CompReadDB 82*
Index to Scientific & Technical Proceedings & Books [of Institute for Scientific Information] - Philadelphia, PA - *DataDirOnSer 84*
Index to Scientific Reviews [of Institute for Scientific Information] - Philadelphia, PA - *CompReadDB 82*
Index to the Christian Science Monitor [of Bell & Howell] - Wooster, OH - *CompReadDB 82; DataDirOnSer 84*
Index to the Code of Federal Regulations [of Capitol Services Inc.] - Washington, DC - *EISS 83*
Index to U.S. Government Periodicals [of Infordata International Inc.] - Chicago, IL - *EISS 83*
Index-Tribune - Sonoma, CA - *AyerDirPub 83*
Index Veterinarius [of Commonwealth Bureau of Animal Health] - Weybridge, England - *CompReadDB 82*
India Abroad - New York, NY - *NewsDir 84*
India Book House Ltd. - Huntington Station, NY - *LitMarPl 83, 84*
India Music Ink - Los Angeles, CA - *BillIntBG 83-84*
India Navigation Co. - New York, NY - *BillIntBG 83-84*
Indian Academy of Letters - New Delhi, India - *LitMag&SmPr 83-84*
Indian Citizen - Atoka, OK - *AyerDirPub 83*
Indian Country Press [Aff. of Red School House] - St. Paul, MN - *BoPubDir 4, 5*
Indian Forest Music - *See* Chestnut Mound Music
Indian Head Park Citizen [of La Grange Suburban Life/Citizen] - La Grange, IL - *NewsDir 84*
Indian Head Software - Snow Hill, SC - *MicrocomMPl 84*
Indian Head-Wolseley News - Indian Head, SK, Canada - *AyerDirPub 83; Ed&PubIntYB 82*
Indian Historian Press [Aff. of American Indian Historical Society] - San Francisco, CA - *BoPubDir 4, 5; LitMag&SmPr 83-84*
Indian House - Taos, NM - *BillIntBG 83-84; LitMag&SmPr 83-84*
Indian Institute of Technology (Dept. of Physics) - Kanpur, India - *CompReadDB 82*
Indian Lake Advertiser [of Covington Arens Corp.] - Covington, OH - *NewsDir 84*
Indian Lake Advertising [Div. of Crestwood House Inc.] - Mankato, MN - *LitMarPl 84*
Indian Life [of Intertribal Christian Communications] - Winnipeg, MB, Canada - *WritMar 84*
Indian Literature [of Indian Academy of Letters] - New Delhi, India - *LitMag&SmPr 83-84*
Indian National Oceanographic Data Centre [of National Institute of Oceanography] - Goa, India - *EISS 83*
Indian National Satellite System [of Dept. of Space] - Bangalore, India - *TeleSy&SerDir 2-84*
Indian National Scientific Documentation Centre [of Council of Scientific & Industrial Research] - New Delhi, India - *EISS 83*
Indian Press/Publications - New York, NY - *BoPubDir 4, 4 Sup, 5; LitMag&SmPr 83-84*
Indian Press Service - New Delhi, India - *ProGuPRSer 4*
Indian River Straitsland Resorter - Indian River, MI - *BaconPubCkNews 84*
Indian Truth - Philadelphia, PA - *LitMag&SmPr 83-84*
Indian Valley Echo - Telford, PA - *AyerDirPub 83*
Indian Valley Record - Greenville, CA - *AyerDirPub 83; Ed&PubIntYB 82*
Indian Voice, The - Vancouver, BC, Canada - *LitMag&SmPr 83-84*

Indiana Architect - Indianapolis, IN - *BaconPubCkMag 84*
Indiana Architect [of Indiana Society of Architects] - Noblesville, IN - *MagDir 84*
Indiana Association of Cities & Towns - Indianapolis, IN - *BoPubDir 5*
Indiana Bell Telephone Co. Inc. - Indianapolis, IN - *TelDir&BG 83-84*
Indiana Beverage Journal - Indianapolis, IN - *BaconPubCkMag 84; MagDir 84*
Indiana Business [of BLM Inc.] - Indianapolis, IN - *BaconPubCkMag 84; MagDir 84; WritMar 84*
Indiana Cable TV Co. - Indiana, PA - *BrCabYB 84*
Indiana Cablevision - Commodore, PA - *BrCabYB 84*
Indiana Cablevision [of Adelphia Communications Corp.] - Indiana, PA - *Tel&CabFB 84C*
Indiana Cablevision Corp. [of Buford Television Inc.] - Elkhart, IN - *BrCabYB 84*
Indiana Cablevision Corp. [of Buford Television Inc.] - Plymouth, IN - *BrCabYB 84*
Indiana Cablevision Corp. [of Buford Television Inc.] - Rochester, IN - *BrCabYB 84*
Indiana Cablevision Corp. [of Buford Television Inc.] - South Bend, IN - *BrCabYB 84*
Indiana Cablevision Corp. - Tell City, IN - *BrCabYB 84*
Indiana City Press - East Chicago, IN - *Ed&PubIntYB 82*
Indiana Contractor - Indianapolis, IN - *BaconPubCkMag 84*
Indiana Cooperative Library Services Authority - Indianapolis, IN - *EISS 83; InfIndMarPl 83*
Indiana Daily Student [of Indiana University] - Bloomington, IN - *NewsDir 84*
Indiana Digital Corp. - South Bend, IN - *MicrocomMPl 84*
Indiana Gazette [of Indiana Printing & Publishing Co.] - Indiana, PA - *BaconPubCkNews 84; NewsDir 84*
Indiana Higher Education Telecommunication System - Indianapolis, IN - *TeleSy&SerDir 7-83*
Indiana Historical Society - Indianapolis, IN - *BoPubDir 4, 5*
Indiana Information Retrieval System [of Indiana University] - Bloomington, IN - *EISS 83*
Indiana Magazine of History - Bloomington, IN - *MagIndMarPl 82-83*
Indiana Newsclip - Indianapolis, IN - *ProGuPRSer 4*
Indiana Pharmacist [of Indiana Pharmaceutical Association] - Indianapolis, IN - *BaconPubCkMag 84; MagDir 84*
Indiana Plumbing-Heating-Cooling Contractor - Indianapolis, IN - *MagDir 84*
Indiana Political Data Archive & Laboratory [of Indiana University] - Bloomington, IN - *EISS 83*
Indiana Prairie Farmer - Indianapolis, IN - *WritMar 84*
Indiana Prairie Farmer - Maywood, IN - *MagDir 84*
Indiana Professional Engineer - Indianapolis, IN - *BaconPubCkMag 84; MagDir 84*
Indiana Racquet Sports - Indianapolis, IN - *WritMar 84*
Indiana Review - Bloomington, IN - *LitMag&SmPr 83-84; WritMar 84*
Indiana Sports Weekly - Indianapolis, IN - *BaconPubCkMag 84*
Indiana State Data Center [of Indiana State Library] - Indianapolis, IN - *EISS 83*
Indiana Statesman, The [of Indiana State University] - Terre Haute, IN - *NewsDir 84*
Indiana Truck Exchange - Indianapolis, IN - *MagDir 84*
Indiana Underwriter, The - Cincinnati, OH - *BaconPubCkMag 84*
Indiana University (Audio-Visual Center) - Bloomington, IN - *AvMarPl 83*
Indiana University (Chemical Information Center) - Bloomington, IN - *BoPubDir 4 Sup, 5*
Indiana University (Dept. of Health & Safety Education) - Bloomington, IN - *BoPubDir 5*
Indiana University (Indiana Review) - Bloomington, IN - *BoPubDir 4, 5*
Indiana University (Institute of German Studies) - Bloomington, IN - *BoPubDir 4, 5*
Indiana University (International Development Institute) - Bloomington, IN - *BoPubDir 4, 5*
Indiana University (Kinsey Institute for Research in Sex, Gender, & Reproduction Inc.) - Bloomington, IN - *BoPubDir 5*
Indiana University (Kinsey Institute for Sex Research Inc.) - Bloomington, IN - *BoPubDir 4*
Indiana University (Latin American Studies) - Bloomington, IN - *BoPubDir 4, 5*
Indiana University (Research Institute for Inner Asian Studies) - Bloomington, IN - *BoPubDir 4, 5*
Indiana University Press - Bloomington, IN - *LitMarPl 83, 84; WritMar 84*
Indianapolis - Indianapolis, IN - *ArtMar 84; BaconPubCkMag 84; WritMar 84*
Indianapolis Business Journal - Indianapolis, IN - *BaconPubCkMag 84*
Indianapolis Cablevision Co. Ltd. - Indianapolis, IN - *Tel&CabFB 84C*
Indianapolis Cablevision Co. Ltd. - Marion County, IN - *BrCabYB 84*
Indianapolis Commercial - Indianapolis, IN - *Ed&PubIntYB 82; NewsDir 84*
Indianapolis East Side Herald [of East Side Communications Corp.] - Indianapolis, IN - *NewsDir 84*
Indianapolis East Side Herald - *See* Eastside Suburban Newspapers
Indianapolis 500 Yearbook - Speedway, IN - *ArtMar 84*
Indianapolis Indiana Herald - Indianapolis, IN - *BaconPubCkNews 84*
Indianapolis Monthly [of Mayhill Publications Inc.] - Indianapolis, IN - *ArtMar 84; BaconPubCkMag 84; WritMar 84*
Indianapolis News - Indianapolis, IN - *BaconPubCkNews 84; Ed&PubIntYB 82; LitMarPl 83, 84; NewsBur 6; NewsDir 84*
Indianapolis North Side Topics - Indianapolis, IN - *Ed&PubIntYB 82*
Indianapolis North Side Topics - *See* Topic Newspapers Inc.
Indianapolis Northeast Reporter [of Eastside Suburban Newspaper] - Indianapolis, IN - *NewsDir 84*
Indianapolis Northeast Reporter - *See* Eastside Suburban Newspapers
Indianapolis Northern Heights Herald - Indianapolis, IN - *Ed&PubIntYB 82*
Indianapolis Northern Heights Herald - *See* Topic Newspapers Inc.
Indianapolis Recorder - Indianapolis, IN - *BaconPubCkNews 84; Ed&PubIntYB 82; NewsDir 84*
Indianapolis Research Co. Inc. - Indianapolis, IN - *IntDirMarRes 83*
Indianapolis Speedway-Northwest Suburban Press - Indianapolis, IN - *BaconPubCkNews 84*
Indianapolis Spotlight - Indianapolis, IN - *BaconPubCkNews 84; NewsDir 84*
Indianapolis Star [of Indianapolis Newspapers Inc.] - Indianapolis, IN - *BaconPubCkNews 84; Ed&PubIntYB 82; LitMarPl 83, 84; NewsBur 6; NewsDir 84*
Indianapolis Westside Enterprise - Indianapolis, IN - *BaconPubCkNews 84; NewsDir 84*
Indianhead Advertiser - Frederic, WI - *AyerDirPub 83*
Indianhead Telephone Co. Inc. [Aff. of Communications Systems Inc.] - Weyerhauser, WI - *TelDir&BG 83-84*
Indianola Enterprise-Toscin - Indianola, MS - *BaconPubCkNews 84*
Indianola News - Indianola, NE - *BaconPubCkNews 84; Ed&PubIntYB 82*
Indianola Record-Herald & Tribune - Indianola, IA - *BaconPubCkNews 84; NewsDir 84*
Indiantown Telephone System - Indiantown, FL - *TelDir&BG 83-84*
Indicator - Westville, IN - *AyerDirPub 83*
Indicator, The [of N.Y. & North Jersey Sections, American Chemical Society] - Ridgewood, NJ - *BaconPubCkMag 84; MagDir 84*
Indigenous Publications - Aptos, CA - *BoPubDir 4, 5*
Indigo Data Systems Inc. - Webster, TX - *MicrocomMPl 84*
Indigo Systems - Acton, MA - *MicrocomMPl 84*
Indio Daily News [of Desert Sun Publishing Co.] - Indio, CA - *NewsDir 84*
Indisota Publishers - Placerville, CA - *BoPubDir 4*
Individual Learning Systems Inc. [Aff. of Southwest Offset Inc.] - Dallas, TX - *BoPubDir 4, 5*
Individual liberty [Aff. of Society for Individual Liberty] - Warminster, PA - *BoPubDir 4, 5*

Individual Software Inc. - Redwood City, CA - *MicrocomMPl 84; MicrocomSwDir 1*
Individualized Books Publishing Co. - Menlo Park, CA - *BoPubDir 4, 5*
Individualized Operand - San Rafael, CA - *MicrocomMPl 84*
Indo Canadian Times - Surrey, BC, Canada - *Ed&PubIntYB 82*
Indocomp Inc. [Subs. of Newcor Inc.] - Drayton Plains, MI - *DataDirSup 7-83*
Indoor Comfort News - Los Angeles, CA - *BaconPubCkMag 84*
Industria Avicola - Mt. Morris, IL - *BaconPubCkMag 84; MagDir 84*
Industria Internacional [of Lineal Publishing Co.] - Darien, CT - *BaconPubCkMag 84; MagDir 84*
Industrial & Technological Information Bank [of United Nations Industrial Development Organization] - Vienna, Australia - *EISS 83*
Industrial Applications Centers Network [of U.S. National Aeronautics & Space Administration] - Washington, DC - *EISS 83*
Industrial Audio Video Inc. [Subs. of Home Entertainment of Texas Inc.] - Houston, TX - *AvMarPl 83*
Industrial Bank of Japan - Tokyo, Japan - *DBBus 82*
Industrial Bank of Japan - *See* IBJData
Industrial Chemical News - New York, NY - *BaconPubCkMag 84; WritMar 84*
Industrial Color Lab Inc. - Framingham, MA - *AvMarPl 83*
Industrial Communications - Bethesda, MD - *BaconPubCkMag 84*
Industrial Compustat II [of Standard & Poor's Compustat Services Inc.] - Englewood, CO - *DataDirOnSer 84*
Industrial Computer Controls - Cambridge, MA - *DataDirSup 7-83*
Industrial Control Software - West Lafayette, IN - *WhoWMicrocom 83*
Industrial Data Bank Dept. [of Gulf Organization for Industrial Consulting] - Doha, Qatar - *EISS 83*
Industrial Database [of Evans Economics Inc.] - Washington, DC - *DataDirOnSer 84*
Industrial Design [of Design Publications Inc.] - New York, NY - *BaconPubCkMag 84; MagDir 84; MagIndMarPl 82-83; WritMar 84*
Industrial Development - Atlanta, GA - *BaconPubCkMag 84; MagIndMarPl 82-83*
Industrial Development Abstracts [of United Nations Industrial Development Organization] - Vienna, Austria - *CompReadDB 82*
Industrial Development & Manufacturers Record [of Conway Data Inc.] - Chamblee, GA - *MagDir 84*
Industrial Distribution [of Morgan-Grampian Inc.] - New York, NY - *BaconPubCkMag 84; MagDir 84*
Industrial Distributor News [of Chilton Co.] - Radnor, PA - *BaconPubCkMag 84; MagDir 84*
Industrial Education - Stamford, CT - *MagDir 84*
Industrial Education - Troy, MI - *BaconPubCkMag 84*
Industrial Education - New York, NY - *MagIndMarPl 82-83*
Industrial Engineering [of Institute of Industrial Engineers] - Norcross, GA - *ArtMar 84; BaconPubCkMag 84; MagDir 84; MagIndMarPl 82-83*
Industrial Equipment News [of Thomas Publishing Co.] - New York, NY - *BaconPubCkMag 84; Folio 83; MagDir 84; MagIndMarPl 82-83*
Industrial Fabric Products Review - St. Paul, MN - *BaconPubCkMag 84; MagDir 84; WritMar 84*
Industrial Finishing - Wheaton, IL - *BaconPubCkMag 84; MagDir 84*
Industrial Health Foundation - Pittsburgh, PA - *BoPubDir 4, 5*
Industrial Heating - Pittsburgh, PA - *BaconPubCkMag 84; MagDir 84*
Industrial Hygiene News - Pittsburgh, PA - *BaconPubCkMag 84; MagDir 84; MagIndMarPl 82-83*
Industrial Information [of Alberta Research Council] - Edmonton, AB, Canada - *EISS 5-84 Sup*
Industrial Information Services [of Southern Methodist University] - Dallas, TX - *EISS 83*
Industrial Launderer - Washington, DC - *ArtMar 84; BaconPubCkMag 84; MagDir 84; WritMar 84*
Industrial Life-Technical Services [Subs. of Industrial Life Insurance Co.] - Montreal, PQ, Canada - *DataDirOnSer 84; EISS 83*
Industrial Machinery Focus [Div. of Hearst Business Media Corp.] - Southfield, MI - *ArtMar 84; MagIndMarPl 82-83*
Industrial Machinery News [Div. of Hearst Business Media Corp.] - Southfield, MI - *ArtMar 84; BaconPubCkMag 84; DirMarMP 83; MagIndMarPl 82-83; WritMar 84*
Industrial Maintenance & Plant Operation [of Chilton Co.] - Radnor, PA - *BaconPubCkMag 84; MagDir 84; MagIndMarPl 82-83*
Industrial Management - Oakville, ON, Canada - *BaconPubCkMag 84; WritMar 84*
Industrial Marketing - Chicago, IL - *MagIndMarPl 82-83; NewsBur 6*
Industrial Marketing Associates [Div. of J. M. Schrier Inc.] - Hicksville, NY - *StaDirAdAg 2-84*
Industrial Marketing Services Inc. - Chicago, IL - *StaDirAdAg 2-84*
Industrial Micro Systems - Anaheim, CA - *WhoWMicrocom 83*
Industrial Models & Patterns - Cleveland, OH - *BaconPubCkMag 84; MagDir 84*
Industrial News - Iaeger, WV - *AyerDirPub 83; Ed&PubIntYB 82*
Industrial Optics [Div. of 3M] - St. Paul, MN - *AvMarPl 83*
Industrial Photography - New York, NY - *BaconPubCkMag 84; MagDir 84; MagIndMarPl 82-83*
Industrial Post - Bell/Maywood, CA - *Ed&PubIntYB 82*
Industrial Press Inc. - New York, NY - *LitMarPl 83, 84*
Industrial Product Bulletin [of Morgan-Grampian Publishing Co.] - New York, NY - *BaconPubCkMag 84; MagDir 84; MagIndMarPl 82-83*
Industrial Product Ideas - Toronto, ON, Canada - *BaconPubCkMag 84*
Industrial Production Index [of U.S. Federal Reserve System] - Washington, DC - *EISS 83*
Industrial Products Corp. - Albuquerque, NM - *WhoWMicrocom 83*
Industrial Programming Inc. - Jericho, NY - *MicrocomMPl 84; WhoWMicrocom 83*
Industrial Purchasing Agent - Great Neck, NY - *BaconPubCkMag 84; MagDir 84*
Industrial Relations Counselors Inc. - New York, NY - *BoPubDir 4, 5*
Industrial Relations Research Association - Madison, WI - *BoPubDir 5*
Industrial Research & Development [of Technical Publishing] - Barrington, IL - *BaconPubCkMag 84; Folio 83; MagDir 84; MagIndMarPl 82-83; NewsBur 6*
Industrial Research Service Inc. - Dover, NH - *BoPubDir 4, 5*
Industrial Robots International - Ft. Lee, NJ - *BaconPubCkMag 84*
Industrial Safety & Hygiene News [of Chilton Co.] - Radnor, PA - *BaconPubCkMag 84; MagIndMarPl 82-83*
Industrial Safety Product News - Philadelphia, PA - *MagDir 84*
Industrial Sciences Inc. - Gainesville, FL - *AvMarPl 83*
Industrial Shredder & Cutter Co. - Salem, OH - *DirInfWP 82*
Industrial Supervisor - Chicago, IL - *MagDir 84*
Industrial Technical Concepts Inc. - Cherry Hill, NJ - *WhoWMicrocom 83*
Industrial Technical Information Service [of Singapore Institute of Standards & Industrial Research] - Singapore, Singapore - *EISS 83*
Industrial Training Systems Corp. - Mt. Laurel, NJ - *AvMarPl 83*
Industrial Wastes - Des Plaines, IL - *BaconPubCkMag 84; MagDir 84*
Industrial Water Engineering - New Haven, CT - *BaconPubCkMag 84*
Industrial West - El Monte, CA - *BaconPubCkMag 84*
Industrial Workers of the World - Chicago, IL - *BoPubDir 4, 5*
Industrial World [of Johnston International Publishing Corp.] - New York, NY - *BaconPubCkMag 84; MagDir 84*
Industrial World en Espanol - New York, NY - *BaconPubCkMag 84*
Industrias Lacteas [of Gorman Publishing Co.] - Chicago, IL - *BaconPubCkMag 84; MagDir 84*
Industry [of AIM Service Corp.] - Boston, MA - *BaconPubCkMag 84; MagDir 84*
Industry Analysts Inc. - Rochester, NY - *IntDirMarRes 83*
Industry & Commerce - Denver, CO - *BaconPubCkMag 84; MagDir 84*

Industry & Environment Data Base [of United Nations Environment Programme] - Paris, France - *EISS 83*
Industry & International Standards - Englewood, CO - *DirOnDB Spring 84*
Industry Forecast [of Evans Economics Inc.] - Washington, DC - *DataDirOnSer 84*
Industry International - Darien, CT - *BaconPubCkMag 84*
Industry Mart - New York, NY - *MagIndMarPl 82-83*
Industry Media Inc. - Denver, CO - *MagIndMarPl 82-83*
Industry News - Garden City, NY - *BaconPubCkMag 84*
Industry Price Index Database [of Evans Economics Inc.] - Washington, DC - *DataDirOnSer 84*
Industry Standards & Military Specifications [of Information Handling Services] - Englewood, CO - *DataDirOnSer 84*
Industry Telephone Co. Inc. - Industry, TX - *TelDir&BG 83-84*
Industry Week [of Penton/IPC Inc.] - Cleveland, OH - *ArtMar 84; BaconPubCkMag 84; Folio 83; MagDir 84; MagIndMarPl 82-83; NewsBur 6; WritMar 84*
Indy-Ware - Anderson, IN - *MicrocomMPl 84*
Inercontinental Marketing Investigations Inc. - Rancho Santa Fe, CA - *IntDirMarRes 83*
Inergi Records - Houston, TX - *BillIntBG 83-84*
INET Gateway [of Transcanada Telephone System] - Ottawa, ON, Canada - *EISS 7-83 Sup; TeleSy&SerDir 7-83*
Inet 2000 [of Telecom Canada] - Ottawa, ON, Canada - *TeleSy&SerDir 2-84*
Infant & Toddler Wear [of Columbia Communications] - New York, NY - *WritMar 84*
Infantry - Ft. Benning, GA - *BaconPubCkMag 84; WritMar 84*
Infants & Toddlers Wear - New York, NY - *BaconPubCkMag 84*
Infection Control - Thorofare, NJ - *BaconPubCkMag 84*
Infectious Diseases - New York, NY - *BaconPubCkMag 84; MagDir 84*
Infinity Broadcasting Corp. - New York, NY - *BrCabYB 84*
Infinity Color Co. Ltd. - Brookville, NY - *MagIndMarPl 82-83*
Inflation Planner Forecast [of Chase Econometrics/Interactive Data Corp.] - Waltham, MA - *DataDirOnSer 84; DBBus 82*
Inflation Planner Forecast - Bala Cynwyd, PA - *DirOnDB Spring 84*
Inflight [of Meridian Publishing Co.] - Ogden, UT - *WritMar 84*
Inflight Services Inc. - New York, NY - *HomeVid&CabYB 82-83*
Info - Gary, IN - *Ed&PubIntYB 82*
Info AAU - Indianapolis, IN - *BaconPubCkMag 84*
Info-Access - Bainbridge Island, WA - *EISS 7-83 Sup*
Info/Consult - Bala Cynwyd, PA - *DataDirOnSer 84; EISS 83; FBInfSer 80; InfIndMarPl 83*
Info-Data Services Inc. - Kansas City, MO - *ADAPSOMemDir 83-84*
Info-Designs Inc. - Birmingham, MI - *WhoWMicrocom 83*
Info Earth [Aff. of Friends of the Earth] - Ottawa, ON, Canada - *BoPubDir 4 Sup, 5*
Info Franchise Newsletter - Lewiston, NY - *BaconPubCkMag 84*
Info Franchise Newsletter - St. Catharines, ON, Canada - *WritMar 84*
Info Globe [Subs. of The Globe & Mail] - Toronto, ON, Canada - *CompReadDB 82; DataDirOnSer 84; EISS 83; InfIndMarPl 83*
Info-Ky News Retrieval System [of Dissly Research Corp.] - Louisville, KY - *EISS 83*
Info-Ky Project [of Kentucky State Library] - Frankfort, KY - *EISS 83*
Info Line [of Information & Referral Federation of Los Angeles County Inc.] - El Monte, CA - *EISS 83*
Info-Mart - Santa Barbara, CA - *DataDirOnSer 84; EISS 83; FBInfSer 80; InfIndMarPl 83; MicrocomSwDir 1*
Info-Mation - Brighton, MA - *EISS 5-84 Sup*
Info/Motion - Lenox, MA - *EISS 83; FBInfSer 80; InfIndMarPl 83*
Info Press Inc. - Lewiston, NY - *BoPubDir 4, 5*
Info Pro Systems - East Hanover, NJ - *MicrocomMPl 83*
Info-Pros Inc. - Irvine, CA - *MicrocomMPl 84; MicrocomSwDir 1*
Info/Search - Berkeley, CA - *EISS 83*
Info-Search - Bloomfield Hills, MI - *EISS 83; FBInfSer 80; InfIndMarPl 83*
Info Systems Co. - Brooklyn, NY - *MicrocomMPl 84*
INFO/Tek - Washington, DC - *EISS 7-83 Sup*
Info II [of Tulsa City-County Library] - Tulsa, OK - *EISS 83; FBInfSer 80; InfIndMarPl 83*
Info Webb - Kansas City, MO - *EISS 83*
Infoage - Willowdale, ON, Canada - *BaconPubCkMag 84*
Infobank [of Mead Data Central] - Dayton, OH - *DataDirOnSer 84*
Infobank [of Computer Sciences of Australia Pty. Ltd.] - St. Leonards, Australia - *EISS 5-84 Sup*
Infobit Inc. - Sykesville, MD - *MicrocomMPl 84; WhoWMicrocom 83*
Infocom - Cambridge, MA - *MicrocomMPl 83, 84; WhoWMicrocom 83; WritMar 84*
InfoCom Productions Inc. - Cleveland, OH - *AvMarPl 83*
Infocom Service [of Western Union Telegraph Co.] - Upper Saddle River, NJ - *TeleSy&SerDir 7-83*
Infocon Inc. - Golden, CO - *EISS 83*
Infocon Information Services Ltd. - Calgary, AB, Canada - *EISS 7-83 Sup*
Infoconversion [Div. of CallData Systems Inc.] - Woodbury, NY - *DirInfWP 82; EISS 7-83 Sup*
Infocorp - Chicago, IL - *FBInfSer 80*
Infocorp - Dallas, TX - *MicrocomSwDir 1*
Infodata [of Gesellschaft fur Information und Dokumentation] - Frankfurt, West Germany - *CompReadDB 82; DirOnDB Spring 84*
Infodata Systems Inc. - Pittsford, NY - *DataDirSup 7-83*
Infodata Systems Inc. - Falls Church, VA - *EISS 83*
Infodetics Corp. - Anaheim, CA - *DirInfWP 82*
Infodinamica SA - Bosques de Las Lomas, Mexico - *ADAPSOMemDir 83-84*
Infographics Inc. - Newport Beach, CA - *DataDirSup 7-83*
Infogrow Communications Information Exchange - Sydney, Australia - *DirOnDB Spring 84*
Infogrow Pty. Ltd. - Sydney, Australia - *InfIndMarPl 83*
Infoil Secretariat [of Norwegian Petroleum Directorate] - Stavanger, Norway - *DirOnDB Spring 84; InfIndMarPl 83*
Infolaw - Washington, DC - *DirOnDB Spring 84*
Infolex Services Ltd. - Witham, England - *EISS 83*
Infoline [of Human Services Planning Council of Schenectady County] - Schenectady, NY - *EISS 83*
Infoline - *See* Pergamon-INFOLINE
Infolink Corp. - Northbrook, IL - *DataDirSup 7-83*
Infomark Corp. - New York, NY - *ADAPSOMemDir 83-84*
Infomarketing Systems Corp. - Gainesville, FL - *EISS 5-84 Sup*
Infomart - Toronto, ON, Canada - *EISS 83; InfIndMarPl 83; VideoDir 82-83*
Infomat Inc. - Rolling Hills East, CA - *DirMarMP 83*
InfoMed - Princeton, NJ - *DataDirOnSer 84*
Infomedia Corp. - San Bruno, CA - *DataDirSup 7-83*
Infometrics Inc. - Monticello, IL - *EISS 83*
Infonet [of Computer Sciences Corp.] - El Segundo, CA - *TeleSy&SerDir 2-84*
Infonet BV - Amsterdam, Netherlands - *EISS 83*
Infoperspectives - New York, NY - *BaconPubCkMag 84*
Infoplan International [Subs. of The Interpublic Group of Cos. Inc.] - Pasadena, CA - *DirPRFirms 83*
Infopro - Los Alamitos, CA - *DirInfWP 82*
InfoPro Systems - East Hanover, NJ - *EISS 5-84 Sup*
InfoQuest [Subs. of Capital Systems Group Inc.] - Kensington, MD - *DataDirOnSer 84; EISS 83; FBInfSer 80; InfIndMarPl 83*
Infoquest [Div. of Myer Communications Pty. Ltd.] - Melbourne, Australia - *InfoS 83-84*
Inforex Inc. - Burlington, MA - *DataDirSup 7-83; InfIndMarPl 83*
Inform [of SDC Search Service] - Santa Monica, CA - *DataDirOnSer 84*
Inform [of Minneapolis Public Library & Information Center] - Minneapolis, MN - *EISS 83; FBInfSer 80; InfIndMarPl 83*
Inform - New York, NY - *LitMarPl 83, 84*
Informacoes, Microformas e Sistemas SA - Sao Paulo, Brazil - *MicroMarPl 82-83*
Informagency Inc. - New York, NY - *LitMarPl 83*
Informant - Phoenix, AZ - *Ed&PubIntYB 82*
Informatech - Montreal, PQ, Canada - *DataDirOnSer 84; EISS 83*
Informatheque-PRAUS [of Universite de Sherbrooke] - Sherbrooke, PQ, Canada - *DataDirOnSer 84*

Informatics Biblio Service [of Paris District Informatics Administration] - Creteil, France - *EISS 83*
Informatics Data Services Operations - Woodland Hills, CA - *DataDirSup 7-83*
Informatics General Corp. - Woodland Hills, CA - *ADAPSOMemDir 83-84; DataDirOnSer 84; DataDirSup 7-83; Datamation 6-83*
Informatics General Corp. - Rockville, MD - *InfoS 83-84*
Informatics Inc. - Rockville, MD - *InfIndMarPl 83; Top100Al 83*
Information Access - Thousand Oaks, CA - *MicrocomSwDir 1*
Information Access & User Assistance Branch [of U.S. Environmental Protection Agency] - Washington, DC - *EISS 83*
Information Access Co. [Subs. of Ziff-Davis Publishing Co.] - Menlo Park, CA - *CompReadDB 82; DataDirOnSer 84; EISS 83; InfIndMarPl 83; InfoS 83-84; MicroMarPl 82-83*
Information Alternative - Chicago, IL - *BoPubDir 4, 5; EISS 83; LitMag&SmPr 83-84*
Information & Analysis Inc. - Hicksville, NY - *BrCabYB 84; CabTVFinDB 83; IntDirMarRes 83; InterCabHB 3*
Information & Analysis Inc. - New York, NY - *Tel&CabFB 84C*
Information & Analysts Inc. - Hicksville, NY - *HBIndAd&MS 82-83*
Information & Communication Div. [of Coordination Council for North American Affairs] - New York, NY - *Ed&PubIntYB 82*
Information & Documentation Center [of French Stockbrokers Society] - Paris, France - *EISS 83, 7-83 Sup*
Information & Documentation Center [of Royal Institute of Technology Library] - Stockholm, Sweden - *EISS 83*
Information & Documentation Center [of Ministry for Food, Agriculture, & Forestry] - Hamburg, West Germany - *EISS 83*
Information & Documentation Dept. [of Sweden Center for Working Life] - Stockholm, Sweden - *EISS 83*
Information & Documentation Dept. [of Federal Employment Institute] - Nuremberg, West Germany - *EISS 83*
Information & Documentation Div. [of Institute of Science & Technology] - Manila, Philippines - *EISS 83*
Information & Documentation Network on Sanitary Engng. & Environmtl. Sciences [of Pan American Health Organization] - Lima, Peru - *EISS 83*
Information & Documentation Section [of Delft Hydraulics Laboratory] - Delft, Netherlands - *EISS 83*
Information & Documentation Section [of National Road & Traffic Research Institute] - Linkoping, Sweden - *EISS 83*
Information & Documentation Service [of Glass Institute] - Paris, France - *EISS 83*
Information & Documentation Services [of German Plastics Institute] - Darmstadt, West Germany - *EISS 83*
Information & Documentation System [of Federal Institute for Geosciences & Natural Resources] - Hannover, West Germany - *EISS 83*
Information & Financial Services Inc. - Philadelphia, PA - *DataDirOnSer 84*
Information & Library Services [of Leatherhead Food Research Association] - Leatherhead, England - *EISS 83*
Information & Publishing Systems Inc. - *See* CORDATUM
Information & Records Management Magazine - Woodbury, NY - *MagIndMarPl 82-83*
Information & Referral Center [of United Way of Greater Richmond] - Richmond, VA - *EISS 83*
Information & Referral Service [of United Way of the Texas Gulf Coast] - Houston, TX - *EISS 83*
Information & Research International [of East Asia Research Institute] - Washington, DC - *FBInfSer 80*
Information & Statistics Div. [of U.S. Federal Aviation Administration] - Washington, DC - *EISS 83*
Information & Technology Transfer Database [of International Research & Evaluation] - Eagan, MN - *CompReadDB 82; DataDirOnSer 84; DirOnDB Spring 84*
Information & Word Processing Report - New York, NY - *BaconPubCkMag 84*
Information Architects Inc. - Menlo Park, CA - *EISS 83*
Information Associates Ltd. - Tucson, AZ - *FBInfSer 80*
Information Associates of Ithaca - Ithaca, NY - *EISS 83*
Information Automation Corp. - Dallas, TX - *WhoWMicrocom 83*
Information Automation Inc. - White Plains, NY - *DataDirSup 7-83*
Information Bank, The [of The New York Times Information Services Inc.] - Parsippany, NJ - *CompReadDB 82; DataDirOnSer 84; DBBus 82; EISS 83; ProGuPRSer 4*
Information Bank, The - New York, NY - *DirOnDB Spring 84*
Information Brokers - Boulder, CO - *EISS 5-84 Sup*
Information Builders - New York, NY - *DataDirSup 7-83; EISS 83; MicrocomMPl 84*
Information Catalysts Inc. - New York, NY - *ADAPSOMemDir 83-84*
Information Center [of Chase Manhattan Bank N.A.] - New York, NY - *EISS 83*
Information Center [of University of Sherbrooke] - Sherbrooke, PQ, Canada - *EISS 7-83 Sup*
Information Center - Ljubljana, Yugoslavia - *InfIndMarPl 83*
Information Center Complex [of U.S. Dept. of Energy] - Oak Ridge, TN - *EISS 83*
Information Center for Building & Space Planning [of Fraunhofer Society] - Stuttgart, East Germany - *EISS 83*
Information Center for Energy, Physics, Mathematics - Eggenstein-Leopoldshafen, West Germany - *EISS 83*
Information Center for Internal Exposure [of U.S. Dept. of Energy] - Oak Ridge, TN - *EISS 83; InfIndMarPl 83*
Information Center for Spectroscopic & Physicochemical Analysis [of Group f/t Advancement of Spectroscopic Methods & Physicochemical Analysis] - Paris, France - *EISS 83*
Information Center of Hampton Roads, The - Norfolk, VA - *EISS 83*
Information Center on Children's Cultures [of U.S. Committee for UNICEF] - New York, NY - *AvMarPl 83*
Information Center on Crime & Delinquency [of National Council on Crime & Delinquency] - Hackensack, NJ - *EISS 83*
Information Center on Education [of New York State Education Dept.] - Albany, NY - *EISS 83*
Information Center on Nuclear Standards [of American Nuclear Society] - La Grange Park, IL - *EISS 83*
Information Centre [of Sports Council] - London, England - *EISS 83*
Information Centre [of Patent & Registration Office] - Stockholm, Sweden - *EISS 7-83 Sup*
Information Clearinghouse Inc., The - *See* Find/SVP
Information/Communications Industry Group [of Coopers & Lybrand USA] - New York, NY - *TeleSy&SerDir 2-84*
Information Co., The - Boston, MA - *EISS 7-83 Sup*
Information Connection - Santa Barbara, CA - *EISS 83; FBInfSer 80; InfIndMarPl 83*
Information Consultants - Rexburg, ID - *FBInfSer 80*
Information Consultants Inc. - Washington, DC - *DataDirOnSer 84; DataDirSup 7-83; EISS 83; InfoS 83-84*
Information Consulting Inc. - Columbus, OH - *EISS 83*
Information Control - Rutland, VT - *FBInfSer 80*
Information Coordinators Inc. - Detroit, MI - *EISS 83; LitMarPl 83, 84*
Information Counselors Inc. - Bethel, CT - *DirPRFirms 83*
Information Data Search Inc. - Cambridge, MA - *EISS 83*
Information Dept. [of BNF Metals Technology Centre] - Wantage, England - *EISS 83*
Information Design Inc. - Mountain View, CA - *MicroMarPl 82-83*
Information Display - Cedar Glen, CA - *BaconPubCkMag 84*
Information Displays Inc. - Armonk, NY - *DataDirSup 7-83; InfIndMarPl 83*
Information/Documentation - Washington, DC - *DataDirOnSer 84; EISS 83*
Information/Education [Div. of i/e Inc.] - Areta, CA - *AvMarPl 83*
Information Enterprises - Toronto, ON, Canada - *EISS 83*
Information Exchange Center [of Georgia Institute of Technology] - Atlanta, GA - *EISS 83*
Information Exchange Centre - *See* IEC
Information Exchange Centre for Federally Supported Research in Universities [of Canada Institute for Scientific & Technical Information] - Ottawa, ON, Canada - *CompReadDB 82*
Information Focus Inc. - New York, NY - *IntDirMarRes 83*
Information for Business Decisions Inc. - New York, NY - *EISS 83; FBInfSer 80; HBIndAd&MS 82-83; ProGuPRSer 4*
Information Futures - Pullman, WA - *EISS 83*
Information Gatekeepers - Boston, MA - *TeleSy&SerDir 2-84*

Information Gatekeepers - Brookline, MA - *BoPubDir 5; EISS 83*
Information Group, The - Kensington, MD - *EISS 83*
Information Group, The - Seattle, WA - *EISS 83*
Information Handling Services [Subs. of Information Technology Group] - Englewood, CO - *CompReadDB 82; DataDirOnSer 84; EISS 83; InfIndMarPl 83; InfoS 83-84; LitMarPl 83, 84; MicroMarPl 82-83*
Information Hotline [of Science Associates/International Inc.] - New York, NY - *BaconPubCkMag 84; EISS 83; LitMarPl 83, 84*
Information India - Bhopal, India - *EISS 83; InfIndMarPl 83*
Information Industry & Market Unit [of Commission of the European Communities] - Kirchberg, Luxembourg - *EISS 83*
Information Industry Association - Washington, DC - *BoPubDir 4 Sup, 5; EISS 83; InterCabHB 3*
Information Institute [of International Academy at Santa Barbara] - Santa Barbara, CA - *EISS 5-84 Sup*
Information Intelligence Inc. - Phoenix, AZ - *DataDirOnSer 84; EISS 83*
Information Interchange Corp. - Washington, DC - *MicroMarPl 82-83*
Information International - Culver City, CA - *DataDirSup 7-83; DirInfWP 82*
Information/Library II - Armonk, NY - *DirOnDB Spring 84*
Information London - London, ON, Canada - *EISS 83*
Information Management [of PTN Publishing Corp.] - Woodbury, NY - *BaconPubCkMag 84; MicrocomMPl 84*
Information Management Associates - Memphis, TN - *InfIndMarPl 83*
Information Management Associates Ltd. - Wembley, England - *InfIndMarPl 83*
Information Management Consultants - Oklahoma City, OK - *EISS 5-84 Sup*
Information Management Consulting - Highland Lakes, NJ - *MicrocomMPl 83*
Information Management Corp. - Green Bay, WI - *DirInfWP 82*
Information Management Dept. [of Franklin Institute] - Philadelphia, PA - *EISS 83*
Information Management International - San Jose, CA - *DataDirOnSer 84; WhoWMicrocom 83*
Information Management Press - Washington, DC - *EISS 5-84 Sup*
Information Management Report - Manhassett, NY - *BaconPubCkMag 84*
Information Management Services - South Daytona, FL - *MicrocomMPl 84*
Information Management Specialists - Denver, CO - *EISS 83; FBInfSer 80; InfIndMarPl 83*
Information Management Systems Inc. - Lawrence, KS - *MicrocomMPl 84*
Information Manager, The [of PTN Publishing Co.] - Hempstead, NY - *MagDir 84*
Information Marketing Businesses Ltd. - Boston, MA - *MicrocomMPl 84*
Information Network - Houston, TX - *EISS 7-83 Sup*
Information Network for Official Statistics [of New Zealand Dept. of Statistics] - Wellington, New Zealand - *EISS 7-83 Sup*
Information on Demand [Subs. of SCI/TEC Publishing Services Inc.] - Berkeley, CA - *DataDirOnSer 84; EISS 83; FBInfSer 80; InfIndMarPl 83; InfoS 83-84; LitMarPl 83, 84; ProGuPRSer 4*
Information People, The - Newark, OH - *MicrocomMPl 83, 84; MicrocomSwDir 1; WhoWMicrocom 83*
Information Plus - South Orange, NJ - *EISS 83; FBInfSer 80*
Information Plus - Toronto, ON, Canada - *EISS 83*
Information Processing & Delivery - New York, NY - *EISS 83*
Information Processing Corp. - Dallas, TX - *DataDirSup 7-83*
Information Processing Inc. - Winter Park, FL - *DataDirSup 7-83*
Information Processing Personnel Service - Santa Clara, CA - *DirInfWP 82*
Information Processing Society of Japan - Tokyo, Japan - *EISS 83*
Information Processing Techniques Corp. - Palo Alto, CA - *DirInfWP 82*
Information Professionals - Denver, CO - *EISS 83; FBInfSer 80; InfIndMarPl 83*
Information Reduction Research - New Canaan, CT - *BoPubDir 4 Sup, 5*
Information Reduction Research - Concord, MA - *MicrocomMPl 84*
Information Referral System for Technical Cooperation Among Developing Countries [of United Nations Development Programme] - New York, NY - *EISS 83*
Information Report, The - Washington, DC - *MagIndMarPl 82-83*
Information Research Inc. - Denver, CO - *IntDirMarRes 83*
Information Research Ltd. - London, England - *EISS 83; FBInfSer 80*
Information Researchers Inc. - Tokyo, Japan - *EISS 83; InfoS 83-84*
Information Resource Consultants - St. Louis, MO - *EISS 83; FBInfSer 80*
Information Resources - Winthrop, MA - *FBInfSer 80*
Information Resources - Manhasset, NY - *MicrocomMPl 84*
Information Resources - Toronto, ON, Canada - *EISS 83; FBInfSer 80; InfIndMarPl 83*
Information Resources Inc. - Chicago, IL - *AdAge 5-17-84 p.31*
Information Resources Inc. - Lexington, MA - *BoPubDir 4, 5*
Information Resources Press [Aff. of Herner & Co.] - Lexington, MA - *BoPubDir 4*
Information Resources Press [Aff. of Herner & Co.] - Arlington, VA - *BoPubDir 5; CompReadDB 82; InfIndMarPl 83; LitMarPl 84; MicroMarPl 82-83*
Information Resources Research - Brussels, Belgium - *EISS 83*
Information Retrieval & Library Automation - Mt. Airy, MD - *MagIndMarPl 82-83*
Information Retrieval Ltd. - London, England - *CompReadDB 82*
Information Retrieval Project (Center of Bioethics) - Washington, DC - *DataDirOnSer 84*
Information Retrieval Research Laboratory [of University of Illinois] - Urbana, IL - *EISS 83*
Information Retrieval Service [of European Space Agency] - Frascati, Italy - *EISS 83*
Information Retrieval Specialists - Morgan Hill, CA - *EISS 7-83 Sup*
Information Retrieval System for the Sociology of Leisure & Sport [of University of Waterloo] - Waterloo, ON, Canada - *CompReadDB 82; EISS 83*
Information Retriever Inc., The - Denver, CO - *EISS 83; FBInfSer 80; InfIndMarPl 83*
Information Science Abstracts [of Plenum Publishing Corp.] - New York, NY - *EISS 83*
Information Science Abstracts [of IFI/Plenum Data Co.] - Alexandria, VA - *DataDirOnSer 84*
Information Science Abstracts - Arlington, VA - *DirOnDB Spring 84*
Information Science & Technology Div. [of U.S. National Science Foundation] - Washington, DC - *EISS 83*
Information Science Inc. - Montvale, NJ - *DataDirOnSer 84; EISS 7-83 Sup*
Information Sciences [of IIT Research Institute] - Chicago, IL - *EISS 83*
Information Search & Processing - Issaquah, WA - *EISS 7-83 Sup*
Information Service [of General Telephone & Electronics] - Waltham, MA - *EISS 83*
Information Service [of British Universities Film Council Ltd.] - London, England - *EISS 83*
Information Service [of Finnish Standards Association] - Helsinki, Finland - *EISS 7-83 Sup*
Information Service in Mechanical Engineering [of Cambridge Scientific Abstracts] - Bethesda, MD - *DataDirOnSer 84; DBBus 82; EISS 83*
Information Service on Social Sciences Research [of Informationszentrum Sozialwissenschaften] - Bonn, West Germany - *CompReadDB 82*
Information Service on Toxicity & Biodegradability [of Water Research Centre] - Stevenage, England - *EISS 83*
Information Service on Toxicity & Biodegradability - *See* Water Research Centre
Information Service Program [of South Dakota State Library] - Pierre, SD - *EISS 83*
Information Services [of Illinois State Geological Society] - Champaign, IL - *EISS 83*
Information Services [of 3M Co.] - St. Paul, MN - *EISS 83*

Information Services [of American Society of Civil Engineers] - New York, NY - *EISS 83*
Information Services - Rochester, NY - *FBInfSer 80*
Information Services [of North Dakota State Legislative Council] - Bismarck, ND - *EISS 83*
Information Services [of Pennsylvania State University] - University Park, PA - *EISS 83*
Information Services - St. Croix, VI - *BoPubDir 4, 5*
Information Services [of Canadian Plains Research Center] - Regina, SK, Canada - *EISS 83*
Information Services [of World Health Organization] - Alexandria, Egypt - *EISS 83*
Information Services [of BHRA Fluid Engineering] - Bedford, England - *EISS 83*
Information Services [of The Welding Institute] - Cambridge, England - *EISS 83*
Information Services [of Society of Metaphysicians Ltd.] - Hastings, England - *EISS 83*
Information Services [of Production Engineering Research Association of Great Britain] - Melton Mowbray, England - *EISS 83*
Information Services [of Royal Society of Chemistry] - Nottingham, England - *EISS 83*
Information Services [of National Foundation for Educational Research in England & Wales] - Slough, England - *EISS 83*
Information Services [of Charities Aid Foundation] - Tonbridge, England - *EISS 83*
Information Services [of Helsinki School of Economics Library] - Helsinki, Finland - *EISS 83*
Information Services [of Export Council of Norway] - Oslo, Norway - *EISS 83*
Information Services & Research - Syracuse, NY - *FBInfSer 80*
Information Services Co. - Roanoke, VA - *EISS 7-83 Sup*
Information Services Dept. [of Community Council of Greater New York] - New York, NY - *EISS 83*
Information Services Div. [of Donnelley Marketing] - Stamford, CT - *EISS 83*
Information Services Div. [of Mississippi State Research & Development Center] - Jackson, MS - *EISS 83*
Information Services Div. [of Community Services Planning Council of Southeastern Pennsylvania] - Philadelphia, PA - *EISS 83*
Information Services Div. [of Institute of Paper Chemistry] - Appleton, WI - *EISS 83*
Information Services Div. [of Canadian Engineering Publications Ltd.] - Toronto, ON, Canada - *EISS 5-84 Sup*
Information Services Div. [of National Computing Centre Ltd.] - Manchester, England - *EISS 83*
Information Services for the Physics & Engineering Communities [of Institution of Electrical Engineers] - Hitchin, England - *CompReadDB 82*
Information Services for the Physics & Engineering Communities A (Physics) - Hitchin, England - *CompReadDB 82*
Information Services for the Physics & Engineering Communities B (Electrical & Electronic) - Hitchin, England - *CompReadDB 82*
Information Services for the Physics & Engineering Communities C (Computer & Control) - Hichin, England - *CompReadDB 82*
Information Services Group [of Greater London Council] - London, England - *EISS 83*
Information Services in Mechanical Engineering [of Cambridge Scientific Abstracts] - Washington, DC - *CompReadDB 82*
Information Services Inc. - Virginia Beach, VA - *EISS 5-84 Sup*
Information Services of Alaska - Anchorage, AK - *EISS 83*
Information Solutions Inc. - San Jose, CA - *WhoWMicrocom 83*
Information Solutions Inc. - Charlottesville, VA - *MicrocomMPl 84*
Information Sources Inc. - Glenview, IL - *EISS 5-84 Sup*
Information Specialists - Cleveland, OH - *EISS 83; FBInfSer 80; InfIndMarPl 83*
Information Store - San Francisco, CA - *BoPubDir 4 Sup, 5; DataDirOnSer 84; EISS 83; FBInfSer 80; InfIndMarPl 83; InfoS 83-84*
Information System for Occupational Safety & Health [of Federal Institute for Occupational Safety & Accident Research] - Dortmund, West Germany - *EISS 83*
Information System for the Economy [of National Institute of Statistics & Economic Studies] - Paris, France - *EISS 83*
Information/System II - Armonk, NY - *DirOnDB Spring 84*
Information Systems - Los Angeles, CA - *MicrocomMPl 84*
Information Systems & Services [of Informatics Inc.] - Rockville, MD - *EISS 83*
Information Systems & Services Div. [of U.S. Dept. of Commerce] - Washington, DC - *EISS 83*
Information Systems Consultants - Mt. Vernon, NY - *EISS 7-83 Sup; LitMarPl 84*
Information Systems Consultants Inc. - Bethesda, MD - *EISS 83*
Information Systems Dept. [of Eastern Illinois University] - Charleston, IL - *EISS 83*
Information Systems Design [Subs. of Control Data Corp.] - Santa Clara, CA - *DataDirOnSer 84; DataDirSup 7-83*
Information Systems Design - Singapore, Singapore - *EISS 5-84 Sup*
Information Systems Development - Austin, TX - *BoPubDir 4, 5*
Information Systems Div. [of Bunker Remo Corp.] - Trumbull, CT - *EISS 83*
Information Systems Div. [of Ori Inc.] - Bethesda, MD - *EISS 83*
Information Systems Group [of University of Alberta] - Edmonton, AB, Canada - *EISS 83*
Information Systems Inc. - Bristol, CT - *ADAPSOMemDir 83-84*
Information Systems Marketing Inc. - Wilton, CT - *ADAPSOMemDir 83-84; EISS 83; InfoS 83-84; VideoDir 82-83*
Information Systems News [of CMP Publications Inc.] - Manhasset, NY - *BaconPubCkMag 84; Folio 83; WritMar 84*
Information Systems of America Inc. - Norcross, GA - *MicrocomSwDir 1*
Information Systems of Arkansas - Little Rock, AR - *MicrocomMPl 83, 84*
Information Systems Programme [of University of Western Ontario] - London, ON, Canada - *EISS 5-84 Sup*
Information Systems Section [of Arthur D. Little Inc.] - Cambridge, MA - *EISS 83*
Information Technology & Libraries - Chicago, IL - *BaconPubCkMag 84; MagDir 84; MagIndMarPl 82-83*
Information Technology Centre [of Polytechnic of Central London] - London, England - *EISS 5-84 Sup*
Information Technology Group - Stamford, CT - *InfoS 83-84*
Information Technology Group - Victoria, BC, Canada - *VideoDir 82-83*
Information Technology Group (Legal & Regulatory Div.) - Alexandria, VA - *CompReadDB 82*
Information Technology Group International - Berkshire, England - *InfoS 83-84*
Information Technology Inc. - Needham, MA - *WhoWMicrocom 83*
Information Today [of Learned Information Inc.] - Medford, NJ - *EISS 5-84 Sup*
Information Transfer Inc. - Silver Spring, MD - *BoPubDir 4*
Information Transform - Madison, WI - *EISS 83*
Information Unltd. Software Inc. - Kensington, CA - *WhoWMicrocom 83*
Information Unltd. Software Inc. - Sausalito, CA - *MicrocomMPl 83, 84; MicrocomSwDir 1; WhoWMicrocom 83*
Information USA - Potomac, MD - *DataDirOnSer 84*
Information Yield - Syracuse, NY - *EISS 83; FBInfSer 80*
Informations-und Dokumentationsstelle Ernaehrung [of Institut fur Ernaehrungswissenschaft der Justus] - Giessen, West Germany - *CompReadDB 82*
Informations-und Dokumentationssystem Umwelt - Berlin, West Germany - *InfIndMarPl 83*
Informationsdienst Strassenbau und Verkehrstechnik [of Bundesversuchs-& Forschungsanstalt Arsenal/Geotechnisches Institut] - Vienna, Austria - *InfIndMarPl 83*
Informationsverbundzentrum RAUM und BAU der Fraunhofer-Gesellschaft - Stuttgart, West Germany - *CompReadDB 82; InfIndMarPl 83*
Informationszentrum Sozialwissenschaften - Bonn, West Germany - *CompReadDB 82*
Informative Data Co. - St. Louis, MO - *BoPubDir 5*
Informatron - Brooklyn, NY - *FBInfSer 80*
Informed Performer, The - New York, NY - *LitMag&SmPr 83-84*
Informed Sources - Los Angeles, CA - *EISS 83; InfIndMarPl 83*
Informedia - Ardsley-on-Hudson, NY - *InfIndMarPl 83*

Informedia - Pearl River, NY - *FBInfSer 80*
Informedia - Austin, TX - *ArtMar 84*
Informer - Washington, DC - *Ed&PubIntYB 82*
Informer Computer Terminals Inc. - Laguna Hills, CA - *DataDirSup 7-83*
Informer Inc. - Los Angeles, CA - *InfIndMarPl 83*
Informer Star - Burkburnett, TX - *AyerDirPub 83; Ed&PubIntYB 82*
Informer-Times, The - Jasper, AR - *Ed&PubIntYB 82*
Informetal [of Dobra Iron & Steel Research Institute] - Dobra, Czechoslovakia - *EISS 83*
Informetrica Ltd. - Ottawa, ON, Canada - *EISS 83*
Inforonics Inc. - Littleton, MA - *DataDirOnSer 84; EISS 83; InfIndMarPl 83; LitMarPl 83, 84; MagIndMarPl 82-83; MicrocomSwDir 1*
Inforware Systems Inc. - Denver, CO - *MicrocomMPl 84*
Infosat [of American Satellite Co.] - Rockville, MD - *TeleSy&SerDir 2-84*
Infoscan Inc. - Woodmont, CT - *EISS 83*
Infoscan Inc. - Ottawa, ON, Canada - *BoPubDir 4, 5*
Infoscribe Inc. - Santa Ana, CA - *DataDirSup 7-83; MicrocomMPl 84; WhoWMicrocom 83*
Infosense Consulting Services - Narberth, PA - *FBInfSer 80*
Infoserv [of F. W. Faxon Co. Inc.] - Westwood, MA - *DataDirOnSer 84; DirOnDB Spring 84*
Infosoft Systems Inc. - Norwalk, CT - *MicrocomMPl 84*
Infosoft Systems Inc. - Westport, CT - *MicrocomMPl 83; WhoWMicrocom 83*
Infosource Inc. - Pittsburgh, PA - *EISS 83; InfIndMarPl 83; InfoS 83-84*
Infosources Publishing - New York, NY - *BoPubDir 4 Sup, 5*
Infospec - New Orleans, LA - *EISS 7-83 Sup*
Infosystems [of Hitchcock Publishing Co.] - Wheaton, IL - *BaconPubCkMag 84; Folio 83; MagDir 84; MagIndMarPl 82-83*
Infosystems - New York, NY - *EISS 7-83 Sup*
Infotecs Inc. - Manchester, NH - *WhoWMicrocom 83*
Infotecture Group - Paris, France - *DirOnDB Spring 84; EISS 83*
Infotecture-Repertoire - Paris, France - *DirOnDB Spring 84*
Infotek Systems - Anaheim, CA - *MicrocomSwDir 1*
Infotel - Torino, Italy - *DirOnDB Spring 84*
Infoterra [of United Nations Environment Programme] - Nairobi, Kenya - *EISS 83*
Infotex [of ITT World Communications Inc.] - Secaucus, NJ - *TeleSy&SerDir 7-83*
Infoton Inc. - *See* General Terminal Corp.
Infotron Systems Corp. - Cherry Hill, NJ - *DataDirSup 7-83*
Infoware Systems Inc. - Denver, CO - *MicrocomMPl 84*
Infoworld - Menlo Park, CA - *MagDir 84*
Infoworld [of Popular Computing Inc.] - Palo Alto, CA - *BaconPubCkMag 84; MagIndMarPl 82-83; WritMar 84*
InfoWorld [of CW Communications Inc.] - Framingham, MA - *Folio 83; MicrocomMPl 84*
Infrared Information & Analysis Center [of Environmental Research Institute of Michigan] - Ann Arbor, MI - *EISS 83*
Infrared Information System - Philadelphia, PA - *DirOnDB Spring 84*
Infrared Information System [of University Computing Co.] - Dallas, TX - *DataDirOnSer 84*
Infrared Search System [of Computer Sciences Corp.] - Falls Church, VA - *DataDirOnSer 84*
Infusion - Winchester, MA - *BaconPubCkMag 84*
Ingalls Associates - Boston, MA - *AdAge 3-28-84; StaDirAdAg 2-84*
Ingalls Public Relations [Div. of Ingalls Associates] - Boston, MA - *DirPRFirms 83*
Ingelewood Hawthorne-Wave - *See* Central News-Wave Publications
Ingersoll Cable Corp. [of Ingersoll Industries] - Muskego, WI - *Tel&CabFB 84C*
Ingersoll Publications Co. - Lakeville, CT - *AdAge 6-28-84*
Ingersoll Publications Co. - Sharon, CT - *Ed&PubIntYB 82*
Ingersoll Times - Ingersoll, ON, Canada - *AyerDirPub 83; Ed&PubIntYB 82*
Ingham County News - East Lansing, MI - *AyerDirPub 83*
Ingham County News, The - Mason, MI - *Ed&PubIntYB 82*
Ingle's TV Cable Co. - Guin, AL - *BrCabYB 84; Tel&CabFB 84C*
Ingleside Index - Ingleside, TX - *AyerDirPub 83; Ed&PubIntYB 82*
Ingleside Index - *See* Richards Enterprises Inc.
Ingleside Publishing - Barrington, IL - *BoPubDir 4, 5*
Inglewood Cable Television - Inglewood, CA - *BrCabYB 84*
Inglewood Hawthorne Wave [of Central News-Wave Publications] - Los Angeles, CA - *AyerDirPub 83; NewsDir 84*
Inglewood-Ladera Breeze - Inglewood, CA - *Ed&PubIntYB 82*
Inglewood-Ladera Breeze - *See* Breeze Newspapers
Inglewood News [of Coast Media Newspapers] - Culver City, CA - *AyerDirPub 83; NewsDir 84*
Inglewood News - Inglewood, CA - *Ed&PubIntYB 82*
Inglewood News - *See* Coast Media Newspapers
Inglewood Public Library - Inglewood, CA - *BoPubDir 4, 5*
Ingraham Library, Edward - Bristol, CT - *BoPubDir 4, 5*
Ingram Book Co. [Subs. of Ingram Industries Inc.] - Nashville, TN - *BoPubDir 4 Sup, 5; LitMarPl 83, 84; MicroMarPl 82-83*
Ingram Microfiche-CRT Service [of Ingram Book Co.] - Nashville, TN - *EISS 7-83 Sup*
Ingram News - Ingram, TX - *BaconPubCkNews 84*
Ingram, Rose Sinagra - Lafayette, LA - *BoPubDir 4, 5*
Ingram Software - Nashville, TN - *MicrocomMPl 84*
Ingram Ventures Inc. [Subs. of Ingram Book Co.] - New York, NY - *LitMarPl 83*
Ingstad Broadcast Properties, Robert - Valley City, ND - *BrCabYB 84*
Ingstad Broadcasting Group - Grand Forks, ND - *BrCabYB 84*
Ingstad Broadcasting, Tom - Grand Forks, ND - *BrCabYB 84*
Inheritance Press Inc. - Trenton, NC - *BoPubDir 4, 5*
INIS Atomindex [of International Atomic Energy Agency] - Vienna, Austria - *OnBibDB 3*
Ink [of Just Buffalo Press] - Buffalo, NY - *LitMag&SmPr 83-84*
Ink Art Publications - Indianapolis, IN - *BoPubDir 4, 5*
Ink Well - Hopewell Junction, NY - *LitMarPl 84*
Ink Well Advertising - St. George, UT - *AdAge 3-28-84*
INKA Corporate in Energy, Nuclear Research & Technology, Aeronautics... [of Fachinformationszentrum Energie, Physik, Mathematik GmbH] - Eggenstein-Leopoldshaften, West Germany - *CompReadDB 82*
INKA Data Base on Conference Schedules in the Fields of Energy, Physics... [of Fachinformationszentrum Energie, Physik, Mathematik GmbH] - Eggenstein-Leopoldshaften, West Germany - *CompReadDB 82*
INKA Data Base on Data Compilations in Physics [of Fachinformationszentrum Energie, Physik, Mathematik GmbH] - Eggenstein-Leopoldshaften, West Germany - *CompReadDB 82*
Inka Dinka Ink [Aff. of Wizard Productions] - Cincinnati, OH - *BoPubDir 4, 5*
INKA Mathematical Didactics Data Base [of Fachinformationszentrum Energie, Physik, Mathematik GmbH] - Eggenstein-Leopoldshaften, West Germany - *CompReadDB 82*
INKA Mathematics & Related Subjects Data Base [of Fachinformationszentrum Energie, Physik, Mathematik GmbH] - Eggenstein-Leopoldshaften, West Germany - *CompReadDB 82*
INKA Nuclear Science Data Base [of Fachinformationszentrum Energie, Physik, Mathematik GmbH] - Eggenstein-Leopoldshaften, West Germany - *CompReadDB 82*
INKA Physics Data Base [of Fachinformationszentrum Energie, Physik, Mathematik GmbH] - Eggenstein-Leopoldshaften, West Germany - *CompReadDB 82*
Inked Specialties Corp. - Brooklyn, NY - *DirInfWP 82*
Inkling Newsletter, The - Alexandria, MN - *LitMag&SmPr 83-84*
Inkling Publications Inc. - Alexandria, MN - *LitMag&SmPr 83-84*
Inkling, The - Alexandria, MN - *LitMarPl 84; WritMar 84*
Inklings [of Mudborn Press] - Santa Barbara, CA - *LitMag&SmPr 83-84*
Inkster Ledger-Star - Wayne, MI - *AyerDirPub 83; NewsDir 84*
Inkster Ledger Star - *See* Associated Newspapers Inc.
Inkster Ledger-Star, The - Inkster, MI - *Ed&PubIntYB 82*
Inkstone [of Toronto Haiku Workshop] - Toronto, ON, Canada - *LitMag&SmPr 83-84*
Inky Trails & Time to Pause - Middleton, ID - *LitMag&SmPr 83-84*
Inky Trails Publications - Middleton, ID - *LitMag&SmPr 83-84*
Inland [of Inland Steel Co.] - Chicago, IL - *WritMar 84*
Inland Architect [of Inland Architect Press] - Chicago, IL - *BaconPubCkMag 84; MagDir 84*

Inland Audio Visual Co. - Spokane, WA - *AvMarPl 83*
Inland Bay Cable TV Associates - Attleboro, MA - *BrCabYB 84; Tel&CabFB 84C*
Inland Book Co. - East Haven, CT - *LitMarPl 84*
Inland Empire - Riverside, CA - *BaconPubCkMag 84*
Inland Industries Inc. - Lenexa, KS - *Ed&PubIntYB 82*
Inland Register - Spokane, WA - *NewsDir 84*
Inland Seas - Cleveland Heights, OH - *MagIndMarPl 82-83*
Inland Telephone Co. - Champaign, IL - *TelDir&BG 83-84*
Inland Telephone Co. - Roslyn, WA - *TelDir&BG 83-84*
Inlet - Norfolk, VA - *LitMag&SmPr 83-84*
Inline Services - Tulsa, OK - *DataDirOnSer 84*
Inlingua Translation Service - Ridgewood, NJ - *LitMarPl 84*
Inlingua Translation Service - Summit, NJ - *LitMarPl 83*
Inmac - Santa Clara, CA - *MicrocomMPl 84; WhoWMicrocom 83*
Inman Review/Bukler News - Inman, KS - *AyerDirPub 83*
Inman Review, The - Inman, KS - *Ed&PubIntYB 82*
Inman Review, The - *See* Tempro Inc.
Inman Telephone Co. [Aff. of Mid-Continent Telephone Corp.] - Inman, SC - *TelDir&BG 83-84*
Inman Times - Inman, SC - *BaconPubCkNews 84; Ed&PubIntYB 82*
Inman, W. Richard - Sunnyvale, CA - *BoPubDir 4, 5*
Inn America - San Francisco, CA - *BaconPubCkMag 84; MagIndMarPl 82-83*
Inn Business, The - Toronto, ON, Canada - *WritMar 84*
Inn-Room Movies Inc. - Mt. Laurel, NJ - *CabTVPrDB 83*
Inner Access Corp. - Belmont, CA - *MicrocomMPl 84; MicrocomSwDir 1*
Inner Circle Publishing Co. - Detroit, MI - *BoPubDir 4, 5*
Inner City Books - Toronto, ON, Canada - *BoPubDir 4, 5; LitMarPl 83, 84*
Inner City Broadcasting - New York, NY - *BrCabYB 84*
Inner City News - Mobile, AL - *AyerDirPub 83; Ed&PubIntYB 82*
Inner Loop Software - Los Angeles, CA - *MicrocomSwDir 1*
Inner Press - Inglewood, CA - *BoPubDir 4, 5*
Inner Traditions/Destiny Books - New York, NY - *LitMag&SmPr 83-84*
Inner Traditions International Ltd. - New York, NY - *LitMarPl 83, 84*
Innerline [of Bank Administration Institute] - Arlington Heights, IL - *EISS 5-84 Sup*
InnerLine [of Bank Administration Institute] - Rolling Meadows, IL - *DataDirOnSer 84; DirOnDB Spring 84*
Innes & Associates, George C. - Elyria, OH - *ArtMar 84*
Innisfail Booster - Innisfail, AB, Canada - *Ed&PubIntYB 82*
Innisfail Province - Innisfail, AB, Canada - *Ed&PubIntYB 82*
Innisfil Scope - Beeton, ON, Canada - *AyerDirPub 83*
Innkeeping World - Seattle, WA - *BaconPubCkMag 84; WritMar 84*
InnoSys Inc. - Berkeley, CA - *ADAPSOMemDir 83-84; MicrocomMPl 83, 84; VideoDir 82-83; WhoWMicrocom 83*
Innotech Corp. - Trumbull, CT - *HBIndAd&MS 82-83*
Innovation Canada Inc. - Mississauga, ON, Canada - *BoPubDir 4, 5*
Innovation Data Processing - Clifton, NJ - *DataDirSup 7-83*
Innovation Organization, The - Simi Valley, CA - *ArtMar 84*
Innovation Press - Pittsburgh, PA - *BoPubDir 4 Sup, 5*
Innovative Computer Products - Tarzana, CA - *MicrocomMPl 83; WhoWMicrocom 83*
Innovative Concepts - Farmingdale, NY - *IntDirMarRes 83*
Innovative Concepts Inc. - San Jose, CA - *AvMarPl 83*
Innovative Data Technology - San Diego, CA - *DataDirSup 7-83; MicrocomMPl 84; WhoWMicrocom 83*
Innovative Design Software Inc. - Las Cruces, NM - *MicrocomMPl 83; WhoWMicrocom 83*
Innovative Educational Affairs Inc. - Great Neck, NY - *BoPubDir 4, 5*
Innovative Electronics Inc. - Miami, FL - *WhoWMicrocom 83*
Innovative Micro Systems - Tulsa, OK - *MicrocomSwDir 1*
Innovative Programming Associates Inc. - Princeton, NJ - *MicrocomMPl 84; MicrocomSwDir 1; WhoWMicrocom 83*
Innovative Sciences Inc. - Stamford, CT - *BoPubDir 4 Sup, 5*
Innovative Software - Overland Park, KS - *MicrocomMPl 83, 84; MicrocomSwDir 1; WhoWMicrocom 83*
Innovative Software - Kansas City, MO - *DirInfWP 82*
Innovative Software Applications - Menlo Park, CA - *MicrocomMPl 83*
Innovative Software Applications - Palo Alto, CA - *WhoWMicrocom 83*
Innovative Systems Inc. - Pittsburgh, PA - *ADAPSOMemDir 83-84; DataDirSup 7-83*
Innovative Technology Inc. - McLean, VA - *WhoWMicrocom 83*
Innovative Technology Inc. - Ottawa, ON, Canada - *MicrocomSwDir 1*
Innovators - Chicago, IL - *StaDirAdAg 2-84*
Innovision - Los Altos, CA - *WhoWMicrocom 83*
Inola Independent - Inola, OK - *BaconPubCkNews 84*
Inor Publishing Co. - Sweet Springs, MO - *BoPubDir 4, 5*
Inorganic & Fertilizer Chemical Forecast Data Base - Mt. Kisco, NY - *DirOnDB Spring 84*
Inorganic & Fertilizer Chemicals - Mt. Kisco, NY - *DirOnDB Spring 84*
Inorganic Crystal Structure Data Base [of University of Bonn] - Bonn, West Germany - *DirOnDB Spring 84; EISS 83*
Inpact Wine & Spirits Newsletter - New York, NY - *BaconPubCkMag 84*
Inpadoc Data Base [of Dialog Information Services Inc.] - Palo Alto, CA - *DataDirOnSer 84*
Inpadoc Data Base [of International Patent Documentation Center] - Vienna, Austria - *CompReadDB 82; DBBus 82; DirOnDB Spring 84*
Inpadoc International Patent Documentation Center - Vienna, Austria - *DataDirOnSer 84*
Inpadoc Patente - Vienna, Austria - *DirOnDB Spring 84*
Inpanew - Vienna, Austria - *DirOnDB Spring 84*
INPI Data Bases [of National Institute for Patent Rights] - Paris, France - *EISS 83*
INPI-4 - Paris, France - *DirOnDB Spring 84*
INPI-4E [of Questel Inc.] - Washington, DC - *DataDirOnSer 84*
INPI-1 [of Questel Inc.] - Washington, DC - *DataDirOnSer 84*
INPI-I [of Institut National de la Propriete Industrielle] - Paris, France - *CompReadDB 82; DirOnDB Spring 84*
INPI-3 [of Questel Inc.] - Washington, DC - *DataDirOnSer 84*
INPI-3 - Paris, France - *DirOnDB Spring 84*
INPI-2 [of Questel Inc.] - Washington, DC - *DataDirOnSer 84*
Inprint [of Writers' Center Press] - Indianapolis, IN - *LitMag&SmPr 83-84*
Inpro Products Inc. - Tarzana, CA - *MicrocomMPl 84*
Input - Mountain View, CA - *ADAPSOMemDir 83-84*
Input - Palo Alto, CA - *BoPubDir 5*
Input Business Machines Inc. - Frederick, MD - *DataDirSup 7-83*
Input Business Machines Inc. - Rockville, MD - *DirInfWP 82*
Input-ez - Englewood, CO - *DirInfWP 82*
Input Systems Inc. - Paramount, CA - *DirInfWP 82*
Inquirer - Hartford, CT - *Ed&PubIntYB 82*
Inquirer - Atlanta, GA - *AyerDirPub 83*
Inquirer - Scarsdale, NY - *AyerDirPub 83*
Inquirer - Galion, OH - *AyerDirPub 83*
Inquirer - Bedford, PA - *AyerDirPub 83*
Inquirer - Philadelphia, PA - *AyerDirPub 83*
Inquirer - Gonzales, TX - *AyerDirPub 83*
Inquirer & Mirror - Nantucket, MA - *AyerDirPub 83; Ed&PubIntYB 82*
Inquirer Magazine [of Philadelphia Inquirer] - Philadelphia, PA - *LitMarPl 84; WritMar 84*
Inquirer, The - Hartsdale, NY - *Ed&PubIntYB 82*
Inquirer, The - London, England - *LitMag&SmPr 83-84*
Inquiry - Washington, DC - *ArtMar 84; LitMag&SmPr 83-84; MagDir 84; MagIndMarPl 82-83; WritMar 84*
Inquiry - Northampton, PA - *InfIndMarPl 83*
Inquiry Inc. - Ft. Lauderdale, FL - *EISS 83*
Inquiry Press - Midland, MI - *BoPubDir 4, 5; LitMag&SmPr 83-84*
Inquiry Reference & Information Center - Richmond, CA - *FBInfSer 80*
Inquiry Systems Inc. - *See* Hindall & Associates Advertising
INRA - *See* International Research Associates Inc.
Ins & Outs - Amsterdam, Netherlands - *LitMag&SmPr 83-84*
Ins & Outs Press - Amsterdam, Netherlands - *LitMag&SmPr 83-84*
INS-U.S. International Air Travel Statistics [of U.S. Dept. of Transportation] - Washington, DC - *DBBus 82*

Insearch Ltd./DIALOG - Haymarket, Australia - *EISS 83; InfIndMarPl 83*
Insect Music - *See* Kicking Mule Publishing Co. Inc.
Inserm Research Information Bank [of National Institute for Health & Medical Research] - Paris, France - *EISS 83*
Inside [of Federation of Jewish Agencies of Greater Philadelphia] - Philadelphia, PA - *ArtMar 84; BaconPubCkMag 84; WritMar 84*
Inside Contracting [of Ceilings & Interior Systems Contractors Association] - Glenview, IL - *BaconPubCkMag 84; MagDir 84*
Inside Detective [of RGH Publications] - New York, NY - *ArtMar 84; MagDir 84*
Inside Energy - Washington, DC - *BaconPubCkMag 84*
Inside Information [of Herner & Co.] - Arlington, VA - *EISS 83*
Inside Joke [of Pen-Elayne Enterprises] - Roselle, NJ - *LitMag&SmPr 83-84*
Inside Kung-Fu [of Unique Publications] - Hollywood, CA - *WritMar 84*
Inside Local 1082 - Beaver Falls, PA - *NewsDir 84*
Inside N.R.C. - New York, NY - *MagDir 84*
Inside/Out - New York, NY - *LitMag&SmPr 83-84*
Inside R & D - Ft. Lee, NJ - *BaconPubCkMag 84*
Inside Retailing - New York, NY - *BaconPubCkMag 84*
Inside Running - Houston, TX - *WritMar 84*
Inside Sports - Evanston, IL - *BaconPubCkMag 84*
Inside Sports - New York, NY - *MagIndMarPl 82-83*
Inside the Turret - Elizabethtown, KY - *AyerDirPub 83*
Inside Today's Sports - Detroit, MI - *MagDir 84*
Inside Travel News - Los Angeles, CA - *BaconPubCkMag 84*
Insider Trading Monitor [of FCI-Invest/Net] - North Miami, FL - *DataDirOnSer 84*
Insiders' Chronicle & Commmercial & Financial Chronicle [of National News Service] - New York, NY - *MagDir 84*
Insiders' Chronicle, The - Arlington, VA - *BaconPubCkMag 84*
Insieme - Montreal, PQ, Canada - *Ed&PubIntYB 82*
Insight - Belmont, CA - *DirOnDB Spring 84*
Insight [of The Young Calvinist Federation] - Grand Rapids, MI - *ArtMar 84; WritMar 84*
Insight Communications - Whitby, ON, Canada - *ArtMar 84*
Insight! Inc. - Chicago, IL - *AvMarPl 83; WritMar 84*
Insight Magazine [of The Journal Co.] - Milwaukee, WI - *MagIndMarPl 82-83; WritMar 84*
Insight Press - San Francisco, CA - *BoPubDir 4, 5*
Insight Press Inc. - New Orleans, LA - *BoPubDir 4, 5*
Insight Publishing Inc. - Williston Park, NY - *MagIndMarPl 82-83*
Insight Research - Tiburon, CA - *IntDirMarRes 83*
Insight Research Inc. - Hartford, CT - *IntDirMarRes 83*
Insights Books - Ann Arbor, MI - *BoPubDir 4 Sup, 5*
Insilco Corp. - Meriden, CT - *HomeVid&CabYB 82-83*
Inslaw Inc. - Washington, DC - *EISS 83; InfIndMarPl 83*
Insoft - Portland, OR - *DataDirSup 7-83; MicrocomMPl 83, 84; MicrocomSwDir 1*
Insoft O'Donnell Co. - Medford, OR - *WhoWMicrocom 83*
Inspec [Subs. of Institution of Electrical Engineers] - Hitchin, England - *DataDirOnSer 84; DirOnDB Spring 84; MicroMarPl 82-83; OnBibDB 3*
INSPEC Information Science [of Institution of Electrical Engineers] - Hitchin, England - *OnBibDB 3*
Inspiration House Publications - Vero Beach, FL - *BoPubDir 4, 5*
Inspiration House Publishers - South Windsor, CT - *BoPubDir 4, 5*
Inspirational Broadcasting Corp. - Portland, OR - *BrCabYB 84*
Inspirational Network, The - Charlotte, NC - *BrCabYB 84*
Installation & Cleaning Specialist - Encino, CA - *BaconPubCkMag 84*
Installation Services & Supply Inc. - Lawrenceville, GA - *Tel&CabFB 84C p.1685*
Installation Specialist [of Specialist Publications Inc.] - Encino, CA - *MagDir 84*
Installment Retailing - New York, NY - *MagDir 84*
Instant Computer Arbitration Search [of Labor Relations Press] - Ft. Washington, PA - *CompReadDB 82*
Instant Identification Systems [Div. of Faraday National] - Herndon, VA - *AvMarPl 83*
Instant Printer - Northbrook, IL - *ArtMar 84; BaconPubCkMag 84; MagIndMarPl 82-83; WritMar 84*
Instant Replay [Div. of Instant Replay Videocassette Magazine] - Miami, FL - *AvMarPl 83*
Instant Software [Subs. of Wayne Green Enterprises] - Peterborough, NH - *MicrocomMPl 83, 84; MicrocomSwDir 1; WhoWMicrocom 83*
Instant Update [of Professional Farmers of America] - Cedar Falls, IA - *EISS 83; TeleSy&SerDir 2-84*
Instant Web Inc. - Chanhassen, MN - *MagIndMarPl 82-83*
InstanTechEx [of Dr. Dvorkovitz & Associates] - Ormond Beach, FL - *InfIndMarPl 83*
Instead of a Magazine [of Ziesing Bros. Publishing Co.] - Willimantic, CT - *LitMag&SmPr 83-84*
Institut d'Amenagement et d'Urbanisme de la Region d'Ile de France - Paris, France - *CompReadDB 82*
Institut de Recherches sur les Fruits et Agrumes - Paris, France - *InfIndMarPl 83*
Institut de Soudure - Paris, France - *CompReadDB 82*
Institut d'Ethnologie [of Museum National d'Histoire Naturelle] - Paris, France - *MicroMarPl 82-83*
Institut du Transport Aerien - Roissy Charles de Gaulle, France - *InfIndMarPl 83*
Institut du Verre - Paris, France - *InfIndMarPl 83*
Institut Francais du Petrole (Geologie Div.) - Malmaison, France - *InfIndMarPl 83*
Institut fur Angewandte Sozialwissenschaft - Bonn, West Germany - *InfIndMarPl 83*
Institut fur Arbeitsmarkt-und Berufsforschung [of Bundesanstalt fur Arbeit] - Nuremberg, West Germany - *CompReadDB 82; InfIndMarPl 83*
Institut fur Deutsche Sprache - Mannheim, West Germany - *InfIndMarPl 83*
Institut fur Dokumentation und Information uber Sozialmedizin... - Bielefeld, West Germany - *InfIndMarPl 83*
Institut fur Ernaehrungswissenschaft [of Justus-Liebig-Universitat Giessen] - Giessen, West Germany - *CompReadDB 82; InfIndMarPl 83*
Institut Gustave-Roussy - Villejuif, France - *CompReadDB 82*
Institut Gustave-Roussy (Service de Documentation Scientifique) - Villejuif, France - *InfIndMarPl 83*
Institut International de la Communication - Montreal, PQ, Canada - *CompReadDB 82*
Institut National de la Propriete Industrielle - Paris, France - *CompReadDB 82; InfIndMarPl 83*
Institut National de la Recherche Agronomique - Paris, France - *InfIndMarPl 83*
Institut National de la Recherche Agronomique - Versailles, France - *CompReadDB 82*
Institut National de la Sante et de la Recherche Medicale - Kremlin-Bicetre, France - *InfIndMarPl 83*
Institut National de la Statistique et des Etudes Economiques - Paris, France - *InfIndMarPl 83*
Institut Textile de France - Boulogne sur Seine, France - *CompReadDB 82; InfIndMarPl 83*
Institute for Advanced Studies of World Religions, The [of State University of New York, Stony Brook] - Stony Brook, NY - *MicroMarPl 82-83*
Institute for Analysis Evaluation & Design of Human Action - Pelham, NY - *BoPubDir 4 Sup, 5*
Institute for Behavioural Research [of York University] - Downsview, ON, Canada - *EISS 83; InfIndMarPl 83*
Institute for Biomedical Informatics [of University of Ljubljana] - Ljubljana, Yugoslavia - *EISS 83; InfIndMarPl 83*
Institute for Business Planning [Div. of Prentice-Hall] - Englewood Cliffs, NJ - *MagIndMarPl 82-83; WritMar 84*
Institute for Byzantine & Modern Greek Studies Inc. - Belmont, MA - *BoPubDir 4, 5*
Institute for Childhood Resources - San Francisco, CA - *BoPubDir 4 Sup, 5*
Institute for Clinical Science Inc. [Aff. of Association of Clinical Scientists] - Philadelphia, PA - *BoPubDir 4 Sup, 5*
Institute for Communication Research [of Stanford University] - Stanford, CA - *EISS 83*
Institute for Contemporary Studies - San Francisco, CA - *LitMag&SmPr 83-84*
Institute for Cultural Progress [Aff. of National Trust for American Culture] - Washington, DC - *BoPubDir 4, 5*

Institute for Documentation & Information in Social Medicine & Public Health - Bielefeld, West Germany - *EISS 83*
Institute for Ecological Policies - Fairfax, VA - *BoPubDir 4, 5; LitMag&SmPr 83-84*
Institute for Econometric Research - Ft. lauderdale, FL - *BoPubDir 4, 5; WhoWMicrocom 83*
Institute for Economic & Financial Research - Albuquerque, NM - *BoPubDir 4, 5*
Institute for Food & Development Policy - San Francisco, CA - *BoPubDir 4, 5*
Institute for Foreign Policy Analysis Inc. - Cambridge, MA - *BoPubDir 4, 5*
Institute for German Language - Mannheim, West Germany - *EISS 83*
Institute for Historical Review - Torrance, CA - *BoPubDir 4, 5*
Institute for Human Growth & Awareness - San Jose, CA - *BoPubDir 4 Sup, 5*
Institute for Humane Studies - Menlo Park, CA - *BoPubDir 4 Sup, 5*
Institute for Independent Social Journalism - New York, NY - *BoPubDir 4, 5; LitMag&SmPr 83-84*
Institute for Industrial Research & Standards - Dublin, Ireland - *InfIndMarPl 83*
Institute for Information & Documentation in Science & Technology [of Higher Council for Scientific Reseach] - Madrid, Spain - *EISS 83*
Institute for Information & Documentation in the Social Sciences & Humanities - Madrid, Spain - *EISS 83*
Institute for Information Associates - Buffalo, NY - *EISS 7-83 Sup*
Institute for Information Studies - Falls Church, VA - *BoPubDir 4 Sup, 5; EISS 83*
Institute for Iron & Steel Studies - Green Brook, NJ - *BoPubDir 5*
Institute for Language Study - Westport, CT - *BillIntBG 83-84*
Institute for Liberian Studies - Philadelphia, PA - *BoPubDir 4, 5*
Institute for Local Self-Reliance - Washington, DC - *BoPubDir 4, 5*
Institute for Medical Information - Sokolska, Czechoslovakia - *EISS 83*
Institute for Medical Literature [of South African Medical Research Council] - Tygerberg, South Africa - *EISS 83; InfIndMarPl 83*
Institute for Personality & Ability Testing Inc. - Champaign, IL - *BoPubDir 4, 5*
Institute for Policy Studies - Washington, DC - *LitMarPl 83, 84*
Institute for Polynesian Studies [of Brigham Young University] - Guam, HI - *LitMag&SmPr 83-84*
Institute for Polynesian Studies [of Brigham Young University] - Laie, HI - *LitMarPl 83, 84*
Institute for Psychoanalysis - Chicago, IL - *BoPubDir 4, 5*
Institute for Psychohistory - New York, NY - *BoPubDir 4 Sup, 5*
Institute for Public Management - Chicago, IL - *BoPubDir 5*
Institute for Quality in Human Life - Portland, OR - *BoPubDir 4, 5*
Institute for Rehabilitation & Research, The - Houston, TX - *Tel&CabFB 84C*
Institute for Research on Public Policy - Halifax, NS, Canada - *BoPubDir 4 Sup, 5*
Institute for Responsive Education - Boston, MA - *BoPubDir 4 Sup, 5*
Institute for Scientific Analysis Inc. - Wilmington, DE - *MicrocomMPl 84; WhoWMicrocom 83*
Institute for Scientific Information - Philadelphia, PA - *CompReadDB 82; DataDirOnSer 84; EISS 83; InfIndMarPl 83; InfoS 83-84; ProGuPRSer 4*
Institute for Scientific Information GmbH - Offenbach-am-Main, West Germany - *InfIndMarPl 83*
Institute for Sex Research Inc. - *See* Kinsey Institute for Sex Research Inc. (Information Service)
Institute for Sex Research Inc. (Information Service) - Bloomington, IN - *CompReadDB 82*
Institute for Sex Research Inc. (Library Records) - Bloomington, IN - *CompReadDB 82*
Institute for Social Inquiry [of University of Connecticut] - Storrs, CT - *EISS 83*
Institute for Social Justice - Dallas, TX - *BoPubDir 4 Sup, 5*
Institute for Social Research - Ann Arbor, MI - *BoPubDir 4*
Institute for Social Welfare Research [Aff. of Community Service Society] - New York, NY - *BoPubDir 4, 5*
Institute for Socioeconomic Studies - White Plains, NY - *BoPubDir 4, 5*
Institute for Southern Studies - Durham, NC - *BoPubDir 4, 5; LitMag&SmPr 83-84*
Institute for the Development of Indian Law - Washington, DC - *BoPubDir 4, 5*
Institute for the Future - Menlo Park, CA - *EISS 83; InterCabHB 3; VideoDir 82-83*
Institute for the Improvement of Analytical & Creative Abilities - Carmel, CA - *BoPubDir 4, 5*
Institute for the Study of Animal Problems [Aff. of Humane Society of the U.S.] - Washington, DC - *BoPubDir 4, 5*
Institute for the Study of Human Issues [of ISHI Publications] - Philadelphia, PA - *ArtMar 84; LitMag&SmPr 83-84; LitMarPl 83, 84; WritMar 84*
Institute for the Study of Man - Washington, DC - *BoPubDir 4, 5*
Institute for the Study of Traditional American Indian Arts [Aff. of American Indian Basketry Magazine] - Portland, OR - *BoPubDir 4, 5; LitMag&SmPr 83-84*
Institute for World Order [Aff. of World Policy Institute] - New York, NY - *BoPubDir 4, 5*
Institute in Basic Youth Conflicts - Oak Brook, IL - *BoPubDir 4, 5*
Institute of Applied Behavior [of Washington University] - St. Louis, MO - *VideoDir 82-83*
Institute of Applied Economic & Social Research [of University of Melbourne] - Parkville, Australia - *DataDirOnSer 84*
Institute of Carmelite Studies (ICS Publications) - Washington, DC - *BoPubDir 4, 5*
Institute of Civil War Studies [Aff. of International Institute for Advanced Studies] - Clayton, MO - *BoPubDir 4, 5*
Institute of Continuing Legal Education - Ann Arbor, MI - *BoPubDir 4, 5*
Institute of Dowsing - Wilmington, NC - *BoPubDir 4, 5*
Institute of Early American History & Culture - Williamsburg, VA - *BoPubDir 4, 5; LitMarPl 84; MicroMarPl 82-83*
Institute of Economic Democracy [Aff. of The Canadian League of Rights] - Vancouver, BC, Canada - *BoPubDir 4, 5*
Institute of Electrical & Electronics Engineers Inc. - Piscataway, NJ - *MagIndMarPl 82-83*
Institute of Electrical & Electronics Engineers Inc. - New York, NY - *BoPubDir 4, 5*
Institute of Electrical & Electronics Engineers Inc. (Service Center) - Piscataway, NJ - *MicroMarPl 82-83*
Institute of Environmental Sciences - Mt. Prospect, IL - *BoPubDir 4, 5*
Institute of General Semantics - Lakeville, CT - *BoPubDir 4, 5*
Institute of Industrial Engineers - Norcross, GA - *BoPubDir 4, 5*
Institute of Information Scientists - Reading, England - *EISS 83*
Institute of International Education - New York, NY - *LitMarPl 83, 84*
Institute of International Education (Communications Div.) - New York, NY - *ArtMar 84*
Institute of Jazz Studies [of Rutgers University] - Newark, NJ - *EISS 5-84 Sup; MicroMarPl 82-83*
Institute of Linguists - London, England - *InfIndMarPl 83*
Institute of Man & Resources - Charlottetown, PE, Canada - *BoPubDir 4, 5*
Institute of Management Consultants - New York, NY - *BoPubDir 5*
Institute of Mediaeval Music Ltd. - Henryville, PA - *BoPubDir 4, 5; LitMarPl 84*
Institute of Modern Languages Inc., The - Silver Spring, MD - *LitMarPl 84*
Institute of Non-Numerical Information Processing - Rorschach, Switzerland - *EISS 83; InfIndMarPl 83*
Institute of Offshore Engineering [of Heriot-Watt University] - Edinburgh, Scotland - *InfIndMarPl 83*
Institute of Paper Chemistry - Appleton, WI - *BoPubDir 4, 5; DataDirOnSer 84; InfIndMarPl 83; MicroMarPl 82-83*

Institute of Paper Chemistry (Information Services Div.) - Appleton, WI - *CompReadDB 82*
Institute of Personnel Management [Aff. of Renouf/USA Inc.] - Brookfield, VT - *BoPubDir 4 Sup, 5*
Institute of Physics, The (Publishing Div.) - Bristol, England - *MicroMarPl 82-83*
Institute of Polar Studies [of Ohio State University] - Columbus, OH - *EISS 83; InfIndMarPl 83*
Institute of Psychological Research Inc. - Montreal, PQ, Canada - *LitMarPl 83, 84*
Institute of Public Administration of Canada - Toronto, ON, Canada - *BoPubDir 4, 5*
Institute of Real Estate Management [Aff. of National Association of Realtors] - Chicago, IL - *BoPubDir 4, 5; LitMarPl 84*
Institute of Scientific, Technical, & Economic Information - Warsaw, Poland - *EISS 83*
Institute of Social Research [of Indiana University] - Bloomington, IN - *EISS 83*
Institute of Texan Cultures, The - San Antonio, TX - *MicroMarPl 82-83*
Institute of Textile Technology - Charlottesville, VA - *CompReadDB 82; DataDirOnSer 84; InfIndMarPl 83*
Institute of the Black World - Atlanta, GA - *BoPubDir 4, 5*
Institute of United States Studies - *See* University of London Institute of United States Studies
Institute on Pluralism & Group Identity [Aff. of American Jewish Committee] - New York, NY - *BoPubDir 4, 5*
Institute on the Church in Urban-Industrial Society - Chicago, IL - *BoPubDir 4, 5*
Institute Press - Santa Monica, CA - *BoPubDir 4 Sup, 5*
Institute TNO for Mathematics, Information Processing, & Statistics [of Netherlands Organization for Applied Scientific Research] - The Hague, Netherlands - *EISS 83*
Institutet for Byggdokumentation/Swedish Institute of Building Documentation - Stockholm, Sweden - *InfIndMarPl 83*
Institution of Electrical Engineers - Piscataway, NJ - *InfIndMarPl 83*
Institution of Electrical Engineers - Hitchin, England - *CompReadDB 82; InfIndMarPl 83*
Institution of Mining & Metallurgy (North American Publications Center) - Brookfield, VT - *BoPubDir 4 Sup, 5; LitMarPl 83, 84*
Institutional Bond Quote Service [of Interactive Data Services Inc.] - New York, NY - *DataDirOnSer 84*
Institutional Brokers Estimate System [of Lynch, Jones & Ryan] - New York, NY - *DataDirOnSer 84; EISS 83*
Institutional Cinema Inc. - Saugerties, NY - *AvMarPl 83*
Institutional Distribution [of Restaurant Business Inc.] - New York, NY - *BaconPubCkMag 84; Folio 83; MagDir 84*
Institutional Investor [of Institutional Investor Systems Inc.] - New York, NY - *BaconPubCkMag 84; Folio 83; MagDir 84; MagIndMarPl 82-83; ProGuPRSer 4*
Institutional Investor (International Edition) - New York, NY - *BaconPubCkMag 84*
Institutional Management [of Institutional Management & Product News Inc.] - Philadelphia, PA - *MagDir 84*
Institutions - Chicago, IL - *NewsBur 6*
Instituto Nacional de Tecnica Aerospacial Esteban Terradas - Madrid, Spain - *InfIndMarPl 83*
Instituto per la Documentazione Giuridica - Florence, Italy - *CompReadDB 82*
Instor Corp. - Menlo Park, CA - *MicrocomMPl 84; WhoWMicrocom 83*
Instructional Aides Inc. - Plano, TX - *BoPubDir 4, 5*
Instructional Aids Inc. - Mankato, MN - *AvMarPl 83*
Instructional/Communications Technology Inc. - Huntington Station, NY - *AvMarPl 83; BoPubDir 4, 5; MicrocomMPl 83, 84*
Instructional Development Systems [Subs. of Small Business Computer Systems] - Virginia Beach, VA - *WhoWMicrocom 83*
Instructional Dynamics International Inc. [Div. of Interand Corp.] - Chicago, IL - *AvMarPl 83; WritMar 84*
Instructional Improvement Information Service [of University of California, Santa Barbara] - Santa Barbara, CA - *CompReadDB 82*
Instructional Industries Inc. - Ballston Lake, NY - *AvMarPl 83*
Instructional Innovator [of Association for Educational Communications & Technology] - Washington, DC - *BaconPubCkMag 84; MagDir 84; MagIndMarPl 82-83; MicrocomMPl 84*
Instructional Materials Laboratories Inc. - New York, NY - *AvMarPl 83; DirPRFirms 83*
Instructional Media Center - Lincoln, NE - *ArtMar 84*
Instructional Micro Systems Inc. - Narberth, PA - *WhoWMicrocom 83*
Instructional Resources Inc. - Tallahassee, FL - *BoPubDir 4, 5*
Instructional Resources Information System [of U.S. Environmental Protection Agency] - Washington, DC - *DataDirOnSer 84*
Instructional Resources Information System [of U.S. Environmental Protection Agency] - Columbus, OH - *CompReadDB 82; DataDirOnSer 84; DBBus 82; EISS 83*
Instructional Supplements Inc. - Medina, OH - *AvMarPl 83*
Instructo/McGraw-Hill [Subs. of McGraw-Hill Book Co.] - Malvern, PA - *AvMarPl 83*
Instructor [of Harcourt Brace Jovanovich Inc.] - New York, NY - *BaconPubCkMag 84; Folio 83; LitMarPl 83, 84; MagDir 84; MagIndMarPl 82-83; WritMar 84*
Instructor Book Club [Div. of HBJ Communications & Services] - Stamford, CT - *LitMarPl 83, 84*
Instructor Books - Duluth, MN - *WritMar 84*
Instrument & Apparatus News - Radnor, PA - *BaconPubCkMag 84; MagIndMarPl 82-83*
Instrument Society of America - Research Triangle Park, NC - *LitMarPl 83, 84*
Instrumentalist, The - Evanston, IL - *ArtMar 84; BaconPubCkMag 84; MagDir 84; MagIndMarPl 82-83; WritMar 84*
Instrumentation Marketing Co. - Burbank, CA - *AvMarPl 83*
Instrumentation Technology - Durham, NC - *MagDir 84*
Instrumentos y Controles Internacionales - Great Neck, NY - *BaconPubCkMag 84*
Instruments & Control Systems - Radnor, PA - *MagIndMarPl 82-83*
Insulation/Circuits - Libertyville, IL - *MagIndMarPl 82-83*
Insulation Outlook [of National Insulation Contractors Association] - Washington, DC - *BaconPubCkMag 84; MagDir 84; WritMar 84*
Insurance Abstracts [of Dialog Information Services Inc.] - Palo Alto, CA - *DataDirOnSer 84*
Insurance Abstracts [of University Microfilms International] - Ann Arbor, MI - *DirOnDB Spring 84; OnBibDB 3*
Insurance Adjuster - Seattle, WA - *BaconPubCkMag 84; MagDir 84*
Insurance Advocate - New York, NY - *BaconPubCkMag 84; MagDir 84*
Insurance Communication Service [of International Business Machines Corp.] - Tampa, FL - *TeleSy&SerDir 2-84*
Insurance Co. Director's Letter, The - St. Louis, MO - *BaconPubCkMag 84*
Insurance Forecast [of Chase Econometrics/Interactive Data Corp.] - Waltham, MA - *DataDirOnSer 84; DBBus 82*
Insurance Forecast - Bala Cynwyd, PA - *DirOnDB Spring 84*
Insurance Forum - Elletsville, IN - *BaconPubCkMag 84*
Insurance Industry Data Base - Kansas City, MO - *DirOnDB Spring 84*
Insurance Industry Data Base [of National Association of Insurance Commissioners] - Brookfield, WI - *DataDirOnSer 84; DBBus 82*
Insurance Industry Newsletter - Louisville, KY - *BaconPubCkMag 84*
Insurance Institute of America [Aff. of American Institute for Property & Liability Underwriters] - Malvern, PA - *BoPubDir 4 Sup, 5*
Insurance Institute of Canada - Toronto, ON, Canada - *BoPubDir 4, 5*
Insurance Journal, The - Los Angeles, CA - *BaconPubCkMag 84; MagDir 84*
Insurance Market Place, The - Indianapolis, IN - *MagDir 84*
Insurance Rating Systems Inc. - Universal City, TX - *MicrocomMPl 84; WhoWMicrocom 83*
Insurance Record - Dallas, TX - *BaconPubCkMag 84; MagDir 84*

Insurance Sales [of Rough Notes Publishing Co. Inc.] - Indianapolis, IN - *ArtMar 84; BaconPubCkMag 84; MagIndMarPl 82-83*
Insurance Sales - Seattle, WA - *MagDir 84*
Insurance Servicing & Information Systems Corp. - Rockville, MD - *ADAPSOMemDir 83-84*
Insurance Worker, The [of Merkle Press] - Washington, DC - *NewsDir 84*
Insuranceweek - Seattle, WA - *BaconPubCkMag 84; MagDir 84*
Insure - Oldwick, NJ - *DirOnDB Spring 84*
Insure Service [of ITT World Communications Inc.] - New York, NY - *TeleSy&SerDir 7-83*
Insurgent Sociologist, The - Eugene, OR - *LitMag&SmPr 83-84*
Insurnet - Emeryville, CA - *ADAPSOMemDir 83-84; DataDirOnSer 84*
Intec Peripherals Corp. - San Bernardino, CA - *MicrocomMPl 83, 84*
InTech - Research Triangle Park, NC - *MagIndMarPl 82-83*
Intech Advertising Inc. - Depew, NY - *StaDirAdAg 2-84*
Intechnology - New York, NY - *MicrocomMPl 83*
Intecolor Corp. - Norcross, GA - *MicrocomMPl 84*
InteCom Inc. - Allen, TX - *DataDirSup 7-83*
InteCom Systems - Dallas, TX - *DirInfWP 82*
Integral Computer Systems Inc. - Putnam, CT - *MicrocomMPl 84*
Integral Data Systems - Natick, MA - *DirInfWP 82*
Integral Data Systems - Milford, NH - *MicrocomMPl 83, 84*
Integral Quality - Seattle, WA - *MicrocomMPl 84*
Integral Yoga Publications [Aff. of Satchidananda Ashram/Integral Yoga Institutes] - Pomfret Center, CT - *BoPubDir 4, 5*
Integrand Research Corp. - Visalia, CA - *MicrocomMPl 84*
Integrated Business Computer - Chatsworth, CA - *WhoWMicrocom 83*
Integrated Circuit Magazine [of Hearst Business Communications] - Santa Clara, CA - *MagDir 84*
Integrated Circuits [of Hearst Corp.] - Garden City, NY - *BaconPubCkMag 84; MagDir 84*
Integrated Computer Services Inc. - New York, NY - *ADAPSOMemDir 83-84*
Integrated Computer Systems - Provo, UT - *MicrocomMPl 84*
Integrated Computer Systems Inc. - Santa Monica, CA - *BoPubDir 4, 5*
Integrated Computer Systems Inc. - Akron, OH - *ADAPSOMemDir 83-84*
Integrated Controls - Costa Mesa, CA - *MicrocomMPl 84*
Integrated Database [of M/A-Com Sigma Data Inc.] - Rockville, MD - *DataDirOnSer 84*
Integrated Design Engineering Inc. - St. Louis, MO - *MicrocomMPl 84*
Integrated Energy Systems [Aff. of Edith Shedd & Associates] - Monroe, GA - *BoPubDir 5*
Integrated Library System [of U.S. National Library of Medicine] - Bethesda, MD - *EISS 83*
Integrated Library System [of Siemens AG] - Munich, West Germany - *EISS 83*
Integrated Management Services - Orange, CA - *MicrocomMPl 84*
Integrated Resources Inc. - *See* American Cable TV Investors
Integrated Software Systems Corp. - San Diego, CA - *ADAPSOMemDir 83-84; DataDirSup 7-83; EISS 83*
Integrated Sound Systems Inc. - Long Island City, NY - *AvMarPl 83*
Integrated System for the University of Lausanne Libraries [of University of Lausanne Libraries] - Lausanne, Switzerland - *EISS 83*
Integrated Systems Inc. - Atlanta, GA - *MicrocomMPl 83, 84*
Integrated Technologies Inc. - Haverford, PA - *DirInfWP 82*
Integrative Learning Systems Inc. - Glendale, CA - *AvMarPl 83*
Integrex Inc. - Philadelphia, PA - *MicrocomMPl 83*
Integrity Forum - Oak Park, IL - *BoPubDir 4, 5*
Integrity Management Services Pty. Ltd. - Melbourne, Australia - *MicrocomSwDir 1*
Integrity Music Corp. - New York, NY - *BillIntBG 83-84*
Integrity Press - Columbus, OH - *BoPubDir 4, 5*
Integrity Research - Canoga Park, CA - *IntDirMarRes 83*
Integrity Systems Inc. - Cincinnati, OH - *MicrocomMPl 83; WhoWMicrocom 83*
Integrity Systems Inc. - Oxford, OH - *MicrocomMPl 84; MicrocomSwDir 1*
Integron Systems - New York, NY - *MicrocomMPl 83; MicrocomSwDir 1*
Intek Manufacturing Inc. - San Jose, CA - *MicrocomMPl 84*
Intel Corp. - Santa Clara, CA - *DataDirSup 7-83; DirInfWP 82; ElecNews 7-25-83; MicrocomMPl 84; WhoWMicrocom 83*
Intel Corp. (Data Base Operation) - Austin, TX - *ADAPSOMemDir 83-84*
Intelegence - Ottawa, ON, Canada - *EISS 7-83 Sup*
Intelfax Ltd. - Brighton, England - *TeleSy&SerDir 2-84*
Intellectron Inc. - Van Nuys, CA - *DataDirOnSer 84*
Intellectual Software - Fairfield, CT - *MicrocomMPl 84*
Intelligence Plc. - Houston, TX - *MicrocomMPl 84; MicrocomSwDir 1*
Intelligencer - Edwardsville, IL - *AyerDirPub 83*
Intelligencer - Doylestown, PA - *AyerDirPub 83*
Intelligencer [of Ogden Newspapers Inc.] - Wheeling, WV - *AyerDirPub 83; BaconPubCkNews 84; Ed&PubIntYB 82; NewsDir 84*
Intelligencer - Belleville, ON, Canada - *AyerDirPub 83; BaconPubCkNews 84; Ed&PubIntYB 82*
Intelligencer Journal - Lancaster, PA - *AyerDirPub 83; Ed&PubIntYB 82*
Intelligencer Printing Co. - Lancaster, PA - *MagIndMarPl 82-83*
Intelligent Business Systems Inc. - Saco, ME - *MicrocomSwDir 1*
Intelligent Computer Systems - Arlington, VA - *MicrocomMPl 83, 84; WhoWMicrocom 83*
Intelligent Control Systems Inc. - Minneapolis, MN - *MicrocomMPl 83*
Intelligent Controls Inc. - Saco, ME - *WhoWMicrocom 83*
Intelligent Devices - Dillon, CO - *MicrocomMPl 83, 84*
Intelligent Investor - Scottsdale, AZ - *MicrocomMPl 83*
Intelligent Software Systems - Montgomery, WV - *MicrocomMPl 84*
Intelligent Systems Corp. - Norcross, GA - *DataDirSup 7-83; InfIndMarPl 83; MicrocomMPl 83, 84; WhoWMicrocom 83*
Intelligent Terminals - Los Altos, CA - *DataDirSup 7-83*
Intelmatique - Paris, France - *EISS 83*
Intelmet Videoconferencing Service [of Inter-Continental Hotels] - Washington, DC - *TeleSy&SerDir 7-83*
Intelpost [of British Post Office] - London, England - *TeleSy&SerDir 2-84*
Intense Records - Chicago, IL - *BillIntBG 83-84*
Intentional Educations - Watertown, MA - *LitMarPl 83, 84*
Inter-America Research Associates [of Information Management Services] - Rosslyn, VA - *FBInfSer 80*
Inter-American News Services - New York, NY - *Ed&PubIntYB 82*
Inter-American Publications Inc. - New York, NY - *Ed&PubIntYB 82; TelAl 83, 84*
Inter-American Satellite Television Co. - Van Nuys, CA - *BrCabYB 84*
Inter-American Tropical Tuna Commission - La Jolla, CA - *BoPubDir 4, 5*
Inter American University Press - San Juan, PR - *LitMarPl 83, 84*
Inter & Action - New Haven, CT - *MicrocomMPl 84*
Inter-Care Systems Inc. [of Data Care Systems Inc.] - Los Angeles, CA - *DataDirOnSer 84; MicrocomMPl 84*
Inter-City Express - Covina, CA - *AyerDirPub 83*
Inter-City Express - El Monte, CA - *AyerDirPub 83*
Inter-City Express - Oakland, CA - *Ed&PubIntYB 82; NewsDir 84*
Inter-City Paper Co. - St. Paul, MN - *MagIndMarPl 82-83*
Inter Collegiate Press Inc. - Shawnee Mission, KS - *LitMarPl 83, 84*
Inter-Community Telephone Co. - Nome, ND - *TelDir&BG 83-84*
Inter-Connection - Bethesda, MD - *BaconPubCkMag 84*
Inter/Consult - Cambridge, MA - *EISS 83; InfIndMarPl 83*
Inter-Continental Advertising Agency - El Cajon, CA - *StaDirAdAg 2-84*
Inter-Continental Press Syndicate Inc. - Glendale, CA - *Ed&PubIntYB 82*
Inter-Corporate Ownership - Mississauga, ON, Canada - *DirOnDB Spring 84*
Inter-County Leader - Frederic, WI - *AyerDirPub 83; Ed&PubIntYB 82*

Inter-Crescent Publishing - Dallas, TX - *BoPubDir 4, 5; LitMarPl 84*
Inter Documentation Co. AG - Zug, Switzerland - *MicroMarPl 82-83*
Inter Documentation Co. BV - Leiden, Netherlands - *MicroMarPl 82-83*
Inter-Global Communications [Div. of Radio's Reliable Resources] - Philadelphia, PA - *Tel&CabFB 84C*
Inter-Global News [Div. of Radio's Reliable Resources] - Philadelphia, PA - *BrCabYB 84; Tel&CabFB 84C*
Inter-Hobbies Distributors - Martintown, ON, Canada - *BoPubDir 4, 5*
Inter-Image Inc. - Tokyo, Japan - *StaDirAdAg 2-84*
Inter-Island Telephone Co. Inc. [Aff. of Telephone Utilities Inc.] - Friday Harbor, WA - *TelDir&BG 83-84*
Inter Lake - Kalispell, MT - *AyerDirPub 83*
Inter-Media Art Center, The - Bayville, NY - *AvMarPl 83*
Inter/Media Inc. - Los Angeles, CA - *StaDirAdAg 2-84*
Inter Media Time Buying Corp. - Sherman Oaks, CA - *StaDirAdAg 2-84*
Inter-Mountain - Elkins, WV - *AyerDirPub 83; Ed&PubIntYB 82*
Inter Mountain News - Burney, CA - *AyerDirPub 83; Ed&PubIntYB 82*
Inter Presse de France - New York, NY - *BaconPubCkNews 84*
Inter-University Consortium for Political & Social Research [of University of Michigan] - Ann Arbor, MI - *EISS 83*
Inter Varsity Press [Div. of Inter-Varsity Christian Fellowship of the U.S.A.] - Downers Grove, IL - *LitMarPl 83, 84*
Interact - Los Altos, CA - *BaconPubCkMag 84*
Interaction Books - Heber Springs, AR - *BoPubDir 4, 5*
Interaction Systems Inc. - Newtonville, MA - *DataDirSup 7-83; WhoWMicrocom 83*
Interactive Applications Inc. - Santa Clara, CA - *ADAPSOMemDir 83-84*
Interactive Business Systems Ltd. - New York, NY - *WhoWMicrocom 83*
Interactive Coaxial Management - Northridge, CA - *InterCabHB 3*
Interactive Composition Corp. - Pleasant Hill, CA - *LitMarPl 83, 84*
Interactive Computer Systems Inc. - New York, NY - *DirInfWP 82; WhoWMicrocom 83*
Interactive Data Corp. - Waltham, MA - *DataDirSup 7-83; EISS 83; Top100Al 83*
Interactive Data Corp. - *See* Chase Econometrics/Interactive Data Corp.
Interactive Data Services Inc. [Subs. of The Chase Manhattan Bank] - New York, NY - *DataDirOnSer 84; EISS 83*
Interactive Images Inc. - Woburn, MA - *MicrocomSwDir 1*
Interactive Inc. - San Diego, CA - *DataDirSup 7-83*
Interactive Information Systems Inc. - Cincinnati, OH - *ADAPSOMemDir 83-84; DirInfWP 82*
Interactive Information Systems Inc. [Subs. of NSA Inc.] - West Reading, PA - *ADAPSOMemDir 83-84; DataDirOnSer 84*
Interactive Learning Systems Inc. - Cincinnati, OH - *AvMarPl 83*
Interactive Logic Inc. - New York, NY - *ADAPSOMemDir 83-84*
Interactive Management Systems Corp. - Colorado Springs, CO - *DataDirOnSer 84*
Interactive Market Systems Inc. - New York, NY - *DataDirOnSer 84; EISS 83; HBIndAd&MS 82-83; IntDirMarRes 83*
Interactive Microware - State College, PA - *MicrocomMPl 83, 84; MicrocomSwDir 1; WhoWMicrocom 83*
Interactive Software Systems Co. [Subs. of Software Systems Inc.] - Minneapolis, MN - *MicrocomSwDir 1; WhoWMicrocom 83*
Interactive Sports Systems - New Orleans, LA - *MicrocomMPl 84*
Interactive Structures Inc. - Bala Cynwyd, PA - *MicrocomMPl 83; WhoWMicrocom 83*
Interactive Systems Corp. - Santa Monica, CA - *ADAPSOMemDir 83-84; MicrocomMPl 83; WhoWMicrocom 83*
Interactive Systems Technology - Indianapolis, IN - *WhoWMicrocom 83*
Interactive Telecommunications Inc. - Englewood, CO - *BrCabYB 84; CabTVFinDB 83; InterCabHB 3*
Interactive Television Network [of Dartmouth-Hitchcock Medical Center] - Hanover, NH - *TeleSy&SerDir 7-83*
Interactive Video Technology - Shreve, OH - *DirOnDB Spring 84*
Interactive Video Technology [of NewsNet Inc.] - Bryn Mawr, PA - *DataDirOnSer 84*
InterAmerica Research Associates - Arlington, VA - *DataDirOnSer 84*
InterAmerican Research Ltd. - Bogota, Colombia - *IntDirMarRes 83*
Interand Corp. - Chicago, IL - *AvMarPl 83*
Interand Corp. (Instructional Dynamics Inc. Div.) - Chicago, IL - *ArtMar 84*
Interaudiovisuel - Paris, France - *InfIndMarPl 83*
Interavia Air Letter [of Interavia SA] - Los Angeles, CA - *BaconPubCkMag 84; NewsDir 84*
Interavia Magazine - Los Angeles, CA - *BaconPubCkMag 84; MagDir 84*
Interbel Telephone Cooperative Inc. - Eureka, MT - *TelDir&BG 83-84*
Interbook Inc. - New York, NY - *BoPubDir 4, 5*
InterBrand Corp. - New York, NY - *IntDirMarRes 83*
Intercept Press Ltd. - Toronto, ON, Canada - *BoPubDir 4 Sup, 5*
Interchange Inc. - Chicago, IL - *DirPRFirms 83*
Interchange Inc. [Aff. of S. H. Friedman & Associates] - St. Louis Park, MN - *BoPubDir 4, 5*
InterChart Inc. - New York, NY - *IntDirMarRes 83*
Intercim Cement Data Base [of Center for Study & Research of the Hydraulic Binders Industry] - Paris, France - *DirOnDB Spring 84; EISS 83*
Intercollegiate Review, The [of Intercollegiate Studies Institute] - Bryn Mawr, PA - *MagIndMarPl 82-83; WritMar 84*
Intercollegiate Video Clearing House - Miami, FL - *AvMarPl 83*
Intercom - Newport Beach, CA - *StaDirAdAg 2-84*
Intercom Corp. - Wilmington, MA - *BoPubDir 5*
Intercon International - *See* Medicus Intercon International Inc.
Intercon Music Corp. - Carlstadt, NJ - *BillIntBG 83-84*
Interconnect Planning Corp. - New York, NY - *DirInfWP 82*
Interconnection - Bethesda, MD - *DirOnDB Spring 84*
Intercontinental Communications Inc. - New York, NY - *Tel&CabFB 84C*
Intercontinental Enterprises Co. - Bronxville, NY - *BoPubDir 4, 5*
Intercontinental Marketing Corp. - Tokyo, Japan - *InfIndMarPl 83*
Intercontinental Media Service [Subs. of Seamark International Ltd.] - Washington, DC - *BrCabYB 84; Ed&PubIntYB 82; LitMarPl 84; MagIndMarPl 82-83*
Intercontinental Press - Auburn, AL - *BoPubDir 4, 5*
Intercontinental Press/Inprecor - New York, NY - *LitMag&SmPr 83-84*
Intercontinental Publications Inc. - Westport, CT - *MagIndMarPl 82-83*
Intercontinental Releasing Corp. - Los Angeles, CA - *Tel&CabFB 84C*
Intercontinental Televideo Inc. - New York, NY - *AvMarPl 83*
Intercontinental Translations - Houston, TX - *LitMarPl 83*
Intercounty Newspaper Group - Philadelphia, PA - *BaconPubCkNews 84*
Intercultural Press Inc. - Chicago, IL - *LitMag&SmPr 83-84; LitMarPl 83, 84; WritMar 84*
Interculture - Montreal, PQ, Canada - *LitMag&SmPr 83-84*
Interdata Computer Systems Ltd. - London, England - *MicrocomSwDir 1*
InterData Inc. - Chicago, IL - *WhoWMicrocom 83*
Interdigital Inc. - Princeton, NJ - *EISS 5-84 Sup*
Interdok Corp. - Harrison, NY - *EISS 5-84 Sup*
Interdyne Co. - Van Nuys, CA - *WhoWMicrocom 83*
Interface Age [of McPheters, Wolfe & Jones] - Artesia, CA - *MagDir 84*
Interface Age - Cerritos, CA - *BaconPubCkMag 84; BoPubDir 4, 5; MicrocomMPl 84; WritMar 84*
Interface Communications [Div. of Integrated Resources Inc.] - Englewood, CO - *StaDirAdAg 2-84*
Interface Inc. - Canoga Park, CA - *MicrocomMPl 84*
Interface Mechanisms Inc. - Lynnwood, WA - *WhoWMicrocom 83*
Interface Press - Los Angeles, CA - *LitMag&SmPr 83-84*
Interface Systems Inc. - Ann Arbor, MI - *DataDirSup 7-83*
Interface Technology - Des Plains, IA - *MicrocomMPl 84*

Interface Technology - College Park, MD - *MicrocomMPl 83, 84; WhoWMicrocom 83*
Interface Technology Inc. - St. Louis, MO - *DataDirSup 7-83*
Interface: The Computer Education Quarterly [of Mitchell Publishing] - Santa Cruz, CA - *MagDir 84; MicrocomMPl 84*
Interface 200 [of Innovative Interfaces Inc.] - Berkeley, CA - *EISS 83*
Interfaces - Providence, RI - *MagIndMarPl 82-83*
Interfaith Center on Corporate Responsibility [Aff. of National Council of Churches] - New York, NY - *BoPubDir 4, 5*
Interfield AG - Hergiswil, Switzerland - *IntDirMarRes 83*
Interfinance Corp. - Minneapolis, MN - *BoPubDir 4, 5*
Intergalactic Publishing Co. - Clementon, NJ - *BoPubDir 4, 5; WritMar 84*
Intergovernmental Bureau for Informatics - Rome, Italy - *EISS 7-83 Sup*
Intergovernmental Oceanographic Commission [of UNESCO] - Paris, France - *InfIndMarPl 83*
Intergraph Corp. - Huntsville, AL - *DataDirSup 7-83; Datamation 6-83; Top100Al 83*
Intergraphic Arts Ltd. - New York, NY - *LitMarPl 83, 84; MagIndMarPl 82-83*
Intergraphics - Alexandria, VA - *DirInfWP 82*
Interguide Publications Inc. - Burlington, ON, Canada - *BoPubDir 4 Sup, 5*
Interhouse Publishing - Elmhurst, IL - *BoPubDir 4, 5*
Interim Books - New York, NY - *BoPubDir 4, 5*
Interim Press - Devon, England - *LitMag&SmPr 83-84*
Interindustry Data Banks - Washington, DC - *DirOnDB Spring 84*
Interindustry Data Banks [of Data Resources Inc.] - Lexington, MA - *DataDirOnSer 84*
Interindustry Forecast - Bala Cynwyd, PA - *DirOnDB Spring 84*
Interior Decorators' Handbook - New York, NY - *MagDir 84*
Interior Design - New York, NY - *BaconPubCkMag 84; LitMarPl 83, 84; MagDir 84; MagIndMarPl 82-83*
Interior Design Book Club [Subs. of Interior Design] - New York, NY - *LitMarPl 83, 84*
Interior Journal - Stanford, KY - *AyerDirPub 83; Ed&PubIntYB 82; NewsDir 84*
Interior News - Smithers, BC, Canada - *AyerDirPub 83; Ed&PubIntYB 82*
Interior Telephone Co. - Anchorage, AK - *TelDir&BG 83-84*
Interior Textiles [of Columbia Communications Inc.] - New York, NY - *BaconPubCkMag 84; MagDir 84*
Interiors - New York, NY - *BaconPubCkMag 84; MagIndMarPl 82-83*
Interiors by Arden - La Mesa, CA - *BoPubDir 4, 5*
Interiorscape - Tampa, FL - *BaconPubCkMag 84*
Interlake Cable TV Ltd. - Selkirk, MB, Canada - *BrCabYB 84; Tel&CabFB 84C*
Interlake Spectator, The - Stonewall, MB, Canada - *Ed&PubIntYB 82*
Interlaken Review - *See* Odyssey Publications
Interlaken Review, The - Interlaken, NY - *Ed&PubIntYB 82*
Interlaken Technology Corp. - Minneapolis, MN - *MicrocomSwDir 1*
Interlibrary Loan & Communication System [of Central Ontario Regional Library System] - Richmond Hill, ON, Canada - *EISS 5-84 Sup*
Interlibrary Users Association - Laurel, MD - *EISS 83*
Interline Reporter [of Capital Cities Media Inc.] - New York, NY - *BaconPubCkMag 84; MagDir 84; WritMar 84*
Interlingua/Eurolarts - Washington, DC - *MagIndMarPl 82-83*
Interlingua Institute [Aff. of Union Mundial Pro Interlingua] - New York, NY - *BoPubDir 4, 5*
Interlingual Television K.K. - Tokyo, Japan - *TelAl 83, 84*
Interlink Newsline - New York, NY - *DirOnDB Spring 84*
Interlink Press Service - New York, NY - *Ed&PubIntYB 82; EISS 5-84 Sup; LitMarPl 84*
Interlinked Computerized Storage & Processing System of Food & Agricultural Data [of Food & Agriculture Organization] - Rome, Italy - *EISS 83*
Interlit [of David C. Cook Foundation] - Elgin, IL - *WritMar 84*
Interlit Agency, The - Wellesley Hills, MA - *LitMarPl 83, 84*
Intermag Productions Inc. - New York, NY - *BillIntBG 83-84*
Intermarc Group - Paris, France - *EISS 83*
Intermarco Advertising Inc. - New York, NY - *StaDirAdAg 2-84*
Intermarco-Farner - Paris, France - *StaDirAdAg 2-84*
Intermark Inc. - Salt Lake City, UT - *IntDirMarRes 83; StaDirAdAg 2-84*
Intermarket Advertising Inc. - Miami, FL - *StaDirAdAg 2-84*
Intermec Corp. - Lynnwood, WA - *DataDirSup 7-83*
Intermed Communications - Springhouse, PA - *DirMarMP 83; KnowInd 83; LitMarPl 83, 84*
Intermedia - Los Angeles, CA - *LitMag&SmPr 83-84*
Intermedia Analyses Inc. - Upper Saddle River, NJ - *BrCabYB 84*
Intermedia Communications Inc. - Pleasantville, NY - *DirMarMP 83*
Intermedia Inc. - Nassau, NY - *BoPubDir 4, 5*
Intermedia News & Feature Service - New York, NY - *BrCabYB 84; Ed&PubIntYB 82*
Intermedia Press - Vancouver, BC, Canada - *LitMag&SmPr 83-84*
Intermedia Systems - Cupertino, CA - *MicrocomMPl 84*
Intermediate Technology Development Group of North America [Aff. of Intermediate Technology Publishers] - Croton-on-Hudson, NY - *BoPubDir 4 Sup, 5*
Intermem Corp. - Poughkeepsie, NY - *DataDirSup 7-83*
Intermetrics Inc. - Cambridge, MA - *DirInfWP 82*
Interministerial Documentation Service [of National Center for the Study of Telecommunications] - Issy les Moulineaux, France - *TeleSy&SerDir 7-83*
Interministerial Mission for Scientific & Technical Information - Paris, France - *EISS 83*
Intermission Temporary Personnel Inc. [Div. of Interbases] - New York, NY - *LitMarPl 83, 84*
Intermodal News [of Truck Trends Inc.] - Chicago, IL - *MagDir 84*
Intermountain Advertising Agency - Orem, UT - *StaDirAdAg 2-84*
Intermountain Air Press - Preston, ID - *BoPubDir 4, 5*
Intermountain Cable Associates [of Metro Cable Corp.] - Homedale, ID - *Tel&CabFB 84C*
Intermountain Cablevision [of Misco Cable TV Co.] - Richfield, UT - *Tel&CabFB 84C*
Intermountain Catholic - Salt Lake City, UT - *NewsDir 84*
Intermountain CATV Inc. - Winnemucca, NV - *Tel&CabFB 84C*
Intermountain Chapter [of National Railway Historical Society Inc.] - Denver, CO - *BoPubDir 4, 5*
Intermountain Contractor - Salt Lake City, UT - *BaconPubCkMag 84; MagDir 84*
Intermountain Food Retailer [of Utah Retail Grocers Association] - Salt Lake City, UT - *BaconPubCkMag 84; MagDir 84*
Intermountain Jewish News - Denver, CO - *AyerDirPub 83*
Intermountain Music - Hollywood, CA - *BillIntBG 83-84*
Intermountain Publishing Co. - Jackson, KY - *BaconPubCkNews 84*
Intermountain Telephone & Power Co. - Billings, MT - *TelDir&BG 83-84*
Internal Auditor, The [of The Institute of Internal Auditors Inc.] - Altamonte Springs, FL - *BaconPubCkMag 84; MagDir 84*
Internal Medicine News & Cardiology News - Rockville, MD - *BaconPubCkMag 84; MagIndMarPl 82-83*
International Academy at Santa Barbara - Santa Barbara, CA - *CompReadDB 82; LitMag&SmPr 83-84*
International Academy at Santa Barbara (Environmental Studies Institute) - Santa Barbara, CA - *DataDirOnSer 84*
International Academy of Preventive Medicine - Overland Park, KS - *BoPubDir 4, 5*
International Advertiser - Oak Brook, IL - *BaconPubCkMag 84*
International Aerospace Abstracts [of American Institute of Aeronautics & Astronautics] - New York, NY - *CompReadDB 82*
International Airport Characteristics Data Bank [of International Civil Aviation Organization] - Montreal, PQ, Canada - *EISS 83*
International Anasazi Inc. - Phoenix, AZ - *WhoWMicrocom 83*
International & National Information Services in Traffic & Highway Engineering [of Federal Highway Research Institute] - Cologne, West Germany - *EISS 83*
International Art Alliance - Tampa, FL - *BoPubDir 4 Sup, 5*

International Association for Medical Assistance to Travelers [Aff. of Foundation for the Support of International Medical Training Inc.] - Lewiston, NY - *BoPubDir 5*
International Association for Social Science Information Service & Technology - Princeton, NJ - *EISS 83*
International Association for Statistical Computing - Voorburg, Netherlands - *EISS 83*
International Association of Agricultural Librarians & Documentalists - Southend-on-Sea, England - *EISS 83*
International Association of Assessing Officers - Chicago, IL - *BoPubDir 4, 5*
International Association of Chiefs of Police Inc. - Gaithersburg, MD - *BoPubDir 4, 5; MagIndMarPl 82-83*
International Association of Ice Cream Manufacturers - Washington, DC - *BoPubDir 5*
International Association of Organ Teachers USA - Hammond, IN - *BoPubDir 4, 5*
International Association of Satellite Users - McLean, VA - *TeleSy&SerDir 7-83*
International Atomic Energy Agency (INIS Section) - Vienna, Austria - *CompReadDB 82; InfIndMarPl 83*
International Atomic Energy Agency (Nuclear Data Section) - Vienna, Austria - *InfIndMarPl 83*
International Auto Data Bank - Washington, DC - *DirOnDB Spring 84*
International Auto Data Bank [of Data Resources Inc.] - Lexington, MA - *DataDirOnSer 84*
International AV Designers Inc. - New York, NY - *AvMarPl 83*
International Aviation Mechanics Journal - Basin, WY - *WritMar 84*
International Aviation Mechanics Journal - Riverton, WY - *BaconPubCkMag 84*
International Bee Research Association - Gerrards Cross City, England - *CompReadDB 82; InfIndMarPl 83*
International Bibliography of Administrative Science [of Centre de Documentation Sciences Humaines] - Paris, France - *CompReadDB 82*
International Bibliography of the Social Sciences [of QL Systems Ltd.] - Ottawa, ON, Canada - *DataDirOnSer 84*
International Bibliography of the Social Sciences [of International Committee for Social Science Information & Documentation] - Paris, France - *CompReadDB 82; DirOnDB Spring 84*
International Bio-Medical Information Service Inc. - Miami, FL - *BoPubDir 4 Sup, 5*
International Book Centre - Troy, MI - *BoPubDir 4, 5*
International Book Co. - Chicago, IL - *BoPubDir 4, 5*
International Book Marketing Ltd. - New York, NY - *LitMarPl 83, 84*
International Book Service Inc. [Subs. of Intercontinental Trailsea Corp.] - Carteret, NJ - *LitMarPl 83, 84*
International Books - Washington, DC - *BoPubDir 4, 5*
International Bulletin of Missionary Research - Ventnor, NJ - *MagIndMarPl 82-83*
International Business & Management Institute [Aff. of ICS Group] - Irvine, CA - *BoPubDir 4, 5*
International Business Equipment [of Office Publications Inc.] - Stamford, CT - *MagDir 84*
International Business Forms Industries Inc. - Arlington, VA - *BoPubDir 5*
International Business Information Syndicate [Subs. of International ICS Group] - Irvine, CA - *LitMarPl 84*
International Business Intelligence Program Index [of SRI International] - Menlo Park, CA - *DBBus 82*
International Business Machines Corp. - *See* IBM Corp.
International Business Opportunities Magazine [of U.S. International Marketing Co. Inc.] - Bellflower, CA - *MagDir 84*
International Business Publishing Consultants Inc. - San Francisco, CA - *BoPubDir 5*
International Business Supplies Inc. - Brentwood, TN - *DirInfWP 82*
International Business Unit [of University of Manchester Institute of Science & Technology] - Manchester, England - *EISS 83*
International Cable [of Prime Cable Corp.] - Erie County, NY - *BrCabYB 84; Tel&CabFB 84C*
International Cable [of Comax Telcom Corp.] - North Tonawanda, NY - *BrCabYB 84*
International Cable [of Prime Cable Corp.] - West Seneca, NY - *HomeVid&CabYB 82-83*
International Cablecasting Cos. Inc. - Los Angeles, CA - *InterCabHB 3*
International Cancer Research Data Bank [Subs. of The National Cancer Institute] - Bethesda, MD - *DataDirOnSer 84; EISS 83; InfIndMarPl 83*
International Center of Scientific & Technical Information - Moscow, Ukrainian Soviet Socialist Republic - *EISS 83*
International Childbirth Education Association Inc. - Minneapolis, MN - *BoPubDir 4, 5; LitMag&SmPr 83-84*
International Church of the Foursquare Gospel - Los Angeles, CA - *BrCabYB 84*
International Circulation Distributors - New York, NY - *MagIndMarPl 82-83*
International City Management Association - Washington, DC - *BoPubDir 4, 5; InterCabHB 3*
International Civil Aviation Organization - Montreal, PQ, Canada - *DataDirOnSer 84*
International Co-Operation in the Field of Transport Economics Documentation [of European Conference of Ministers of Transport] - Paris, France - *EISS 83*
International Coal Trade [of Chase Econometrics/Interactive Data Corp.] - Waltham, MA - *DataDirOnSer 84*
International Coden Service [of American Chemical Society] - Columbus, OH - *EISS 83*
International Coffee Organization - London, England - *CompReadDB 82*
International Collectors Library [Subs. of Doubleday & Co. Inc.] - Garden City, NY - *LitMarPl 83*
International Collectors Library - *See* Doubleday Book Clubs
International Color Image Labs Inc. - Burbank, CA - *AvMarPl 83*
International Commission on Radiation Units & Measurements - Washington, DC - *BoPubDir 4, 5*
International Committee for Social Science (Information & Documentation) - Paris, France - *CompReadDB 82; EISS 83*
International Commodities [of Chase Econometrics/Interactive Data Corp.] - Waltham, MA - *DataDirOnSer 84*
International Communications Group Inc. - Los Angeles, CA - *StaDirAdAg 2-84*
International Co. for Documentation in Chemistry - Frankfurt, West Germany - *EISS 83*
International Comparative Political Parties Project [of Northwestern University] - Evanston, IL - *EISS 83*
International Computaprint Corp. - Ft. Washington, PA - *EISS 83; LitMarPl 83, 84; MagIndMarPl 82-83*
International Computer Access Service [of Kokusai Denshin Denwa Co. Ltd.] - Tokyo, Japan - *TeleSy&SerDir 7-83*
International Computer Casting - Hollywood, CA - *EISS 7-83 Sup*
International Computer Products - Los Angeles, CA - *MicrocomMPl 83, 84*
International Computer Programs Inc. - Indianapolis, IN - *ADAPSOMemDir 83-84; BoPubDir 4, 5; EISS 83*
International Computers Inc. - Irving, TX - *InfIndMarPl 83*
International Computers Pty. Ltd. - North Sydney, Australia - *ADAPSOMemDir 83-84*
International Computing Co. - Bethesda, MD - *DirInfWP 82*
International Concept Center - Carlsbad, CA - *HBIndAd&MS 82-83*
International Construction Week - New York, NY - *BaconPubCkMag 84*
International Contact Lens Clinic - Chicago, IL - *MagDir 84; MagIndMarPl 82-83*
International Cookbook Services - White Plains, NY - *LitMarPl 83, 84; MagIndMarPl 82-83*
International Copyright Information Center - Washington, DC - *EISS 83*
International Cotton Advisory Committee - Washington, DC - *BoPubDir 4 Sup, 5*
International Council for Computer Communication - Washington, DC - *EISS 83*
International Council of Scientific Unions Abstracting Board - Paris, France - *EISS 83*
International Council of Shopping Centers - New York, NY - *BoPubDir 4, 5*

International Council on the Future of the University - New York, NY - *BoPubDir 4 Sup, 5*
International Counseling Inc. - New York, NY - *DirPRFirms 83*
International Creative Management [Subs. of Josephson International Inc.] - New York, NY - *LitMarPl 83, 84; TelAl 83, 84; Tel&CabFB 84C*
International Cultural Foundation Press - New York, NY - *BoPubDir 4, 5*
International Data & Development Inc. - Arlington, VA - *MicrocomMPl 84*
International Data Base Systems Inc. - Philadelphia, PA - *DataDirSup 7-83*
International Data Corp. - Framingham, MA - *ADAPSOMemDir 83-84; EISS 83; InfIndMarPl 83; InfoS 83-84; VideoDir 82-83*
International Data Corp. (International Data Group) - Framingham, MA - *InfIndMarPl 83*
International Data Group - Framingham, MA - *AdAge 6-28-84; KnowInd 83*
International Data Processing Inc. - Murray Hill, NJ - *ADAPSOMemDir 83-84*
International Data Sciences Inc. - Lincoln, RI - *DataDirSup 7-83*
International Data Services - New York, NY - *WhoWMicrocom 83*
International Data Technology Inc. - Chicago, IL - *DataDirSup 7-83*
International Database [of Evans Economics Inc.] - Washington, DC - *DataDirOnSer 84*
International Database Association - Leesburg, VA - *EISS 5-84 Sup*
International Datel Service [of MCI International Inc.] - Rye Brook, NY - *TeleSy&SerDir 2-84*
International Defense & Aid Fund for Southern Africa (American Committee) - Cambridge, MA - *BoPubDir 4, 5*
International Defense Review - Los Angeles, CA - *BaconPubCkMag 84; MagDir 84*
International Demographic Data Center [of U.S. Bureau of the Census] - Washington, DC - *EISS 83; InfIndMarPl 83*
International Demographics Inc. - Houston, TX - *IntDirMarRes 83*
International Development Center - Kensington, MD - *InfoS 83-84*
International Development Information Network [of Organisation for Economic Co-Operation & Development] - Paris, France - *EISS 83*
International Development Research Centre Library - Ottawa, ON, Canada - *EISS 83*
International Dialogue Press - Davis, CA - *LitMarPl 83, 84*
International Documentation Center for Industries Using Agricultural Products [of Association for the Promotion of Industry-Agriculture] - Massy, France - *EISS 83*
International Doorway Music - Lubbock, TX - *BillIntBG 83-84*
International Doorways Publications - Colorado Springs, CO - *BoPubDir 4, 5*
International Dredging Review - Long Beach, CA - *BaconPubCkMag 84*
International Eco Features Syndicate - West Hollywood, CA - *LitMarPl 84*
International Economic Appraisal Service - New York, NY - *DirOnDB Spring 84*
International Economic Indicators & Indexes [of Columbia University] - New York, NY - *DataDirOnSer 84*
International Economic Indicators Database - Newark, NJ - *DirOnDB Spring 84*
International Educational Development Inc. - Silver Spring, MD - *BoPubDir 4, 5*
International Educational Representatives - Concord, MA - *LitMarPl 83, 84*
International Electronic Post [of U.S. Postal Service] - Washington, DC - *TeleSy&SerDir 2-84*
International Electronic Publishing Research Centre - Leatherhead, England - *EISS 7-83 Sup*
International Energy Data Banks - Washington, DC - *DirOnDB Spring 84*
International Energy Data Banks [of U.S. Dept. of Energy] - Oak Ride, TN - *DBBus 82*
International Energy Data Base [of Data Resources Inc.] - Lexington, MA - *DataDirOnSer 84*
International Equity Corp. - *See* Comcast Cable Communications Inc.
International Evangelism Crusades Inc. - Van Nuys, CA - *BoPubDir 4*
International Executive - White River Junction, VT - *BaconPubCkMag 84; MagDir 84*
International Exhibitions Foundation - Washington, DC - *BoPubDir 4, 5*
International Facsimile Bureau Service [of MCI International Inc.] - Rye Brook, NY - *TeleSy&SerDir 2-84*
International Falls Journal [of North Star Publishing Co.] - International Falls, MN - *BaconPubCkNews 84; NewsDir 84*
International Family Planning Perspectives - New York, NY - *MagIndMarPl 82-83*
International Features Inc. - Malibu, CA - *Ed&PubIntYB 82*
International Features Syndicate - Santa Monica, CA - *LitMarPl 83*
International Federation for Documentation - The Hague, Netherlands - *EISS 83*
International Federation for Information Processing - Geneva, Switzerland - *EISS 83*
International Federation of Data Organizations for the Social Sciences - Cologne, West Germany - *EISS 83*
International Federation of Library Associations & Institutions - The Hague, Netherlands - *EISS 83*
International Feedstuffs Institute [of Utah State University] - Logan, UT - *EISS 5-84 Sup*
International Fertilizer [of Chase Econometrics/Interactive Data Corp.] - Waltham, MA - *DataDirOnSer 84*
International Fertilizer - Bala Cynwyd, PA - *DirOnDB Spring 84*
International Fertilizer Development Center - Muscle Shoals, AL - *BoPubDir 5*
International Fertilizer Forecast - Bala Cynwyd, PA - *DirOnDB Spring 84*
International Fiction Review, The - Fredericton, NB, Canada - *LitMag&SmPr 83-84*
International Film Bureau Inc. - Chicago, IL - *AvMarPl 83; BoPubDir 4, 5; TelAl 83, 84*
International Film Exchange Ltd. - New York, NY - *TelAl 83, 84*
International Film Foundation - New York, NY - *AvMarPl 83*
International Finance Managers Study [of Interactive Market Systems Inc.] - New York, NY - *DataDirOnSer 84*
International Finance Managers Study - Wembly, England - *DirOnDB Spring 84*
International Financial Statistics [of International Monetary Fund] - Washington, DC - *DataDirOnSer 84; DBBus 82; DirOnDB Spring 84*
International Financial Statistics Database [of Wharton Econometric Forecasting Associates] - Philadelphia, PA - *DataDirOnSer 84*
International Fire Fighter [of Kelly Press] - Washington, DC - *BaconPubCkMag 84; NewsDir 84*
International Fire Service Training Association - Stillwater, OK - *BoPubDir 4, 5*
International Flying Farmer - Wichita, KS - *BaconPubCkMag 84; MagDir 84*
International Food Information Service - Reading, England - *CompReadDB 82; InfIndMarPl 83*
International Food Information Service - Shinfield, England - *EISS 83*
International Forecast [of Evans Economics Inc.] - Washington, DC - *DataDirOnSer 84*
International Forecasts Abstracts [of Predicasts Inc.] - Cleveland, OH - *CompReadDB 82*
International Foundation for Biosocial Development & Human Health Inc. - New York, NY - *BoPubDir 4, 5*
International Foundation of Employee Benefit Plans - Brookfield, WI - *BoPubDir 4, 5*
International Franchise Association - Washington, DC - *BoPubDir 5*
International Friendship - Waxhaw, NC - *BoPubDir 4, 5*
International General [Aff. of International Mass Media Research Center] - New York, NY - *BoPubDir 4, 5*

International Geographical Bibliography [of Centre de Documentation Sciences Humaines] - Paris, France - *CompReadDB 82*
International Graphics [Subs. of Rumford National Graphics Inc.] - Hollywood, FL - *LitMarPl 83, 84; MagIndMarPl 82-83*
International Graphics - Minneapolis, MN - *EISS 83*
International Graphoanalysis Society - Chicago, IL - *BoPubDir 4, 5*
International Group of Users of Information Systems - Almere-Stad, Netherlands - *EISS 83*
International Group, The [Subs. of Communications Workshop] - Long Beach, CA - *DirPRFirms 83*
International Health Council - Berea, OH - *BoPubDir 4, 5*
International Health Physics Database [of Creative Information Systems] - Portland, OR - *DataDirOnSer 84*
International Home Entertainment Inc. - Los Angeles, CA - *Tel&CabFB 84C*
International Hospital Equipment - San Francisco, CA - *BaconPubCkMag 84*
International Human Systems Institute [Aff. of Rogoca Inc.] - Toronto, ON, Canada - *BoPubDir 4, 5*
International Ideas Inc. - Philadelphia, PA - *LitMarPl 83, 84*
International Imports - Toluca Lake, CA - *BoPubDir 4, 5*
International Info - Great Neck, NY - *BaconPubCkMag 84*
International Information Center for Terminology [of Austrian Standards Institute] - Vienna, Austria - *EISS 83*
International Information Service via a Computer-Oriented Network [of Italcable] - Rome, Italy - *TeleSy&SerDir 2-84*
International Information Services Co. - Paris, France - *EISS 83*
International Information Services for the Physics & Engineering Communities [of Institution of Electrical Engineers] - Hitchin, England - *EISS 83*
International Information Services for the Physics & Engineering Communities - *See* INSPEC
International Information System for the Agricultural Sciences & Technology [of Food & Agriculture Organization] - Rome, Italy - *EISS 83*
International Information/Word Processing Association - Willow Grove, PA - *EISS 83*
International Institute for Advanced Studies - Clayton, MO - *BoPubDir 4, 5*
International Institute of Garibaldian Studies Inc. - Sarasota, FL - *BoPubDir 4 Sup, 5*
International Institute of Preventive Psychiatry - Studio City, CA - *BoPubDir 4 Sup, 5*
International Institute of Veterinary Science - Bronxville, NY - *BoPubDir 4, 5*
International Instrumentation & Controls - Great Neck, NY - *BaconPubCkMag 84; MagDir 84*
International Instrumentation Biomedical - Great Neck, NY - *BaconPubCkMag 84*
International Insurance Monitor - New York, NY - *BaconPubCkMag 84*
International Interact Corp., The - Summit, NJ - *VideoDir 82-83*
International Intertrade Index [Aff. of Printing Consultants] - Newark, NJ - *BoPubDir 4, 5; DataDirOnSer 84; DirOnDB Spring 84; EISS 5-84 Sup*
International Irrigation Information Center - Bet Dagan, Israel - *InfIndMarPl 83*
International Jaspar Music Group, The - Manchester, NH - *BillIntBG 83-84*
International Jewish Monthly - Washington, DC - *BaconPubCkMag 84; MagDir 84*
International Journal of Aging & Human Development - Farmingdale, NY - *MagIndMarPl 82-83*
International Journal of Dermatology - Philadelphia, PA - *MagDir 84*
International Journal of Health Services - Farmingdale, NY - *MagIndMarPl 82-83*
International Journal of Instructional Media [of Baywood Publishing Co. Inc. Journals] - Farmingdale, NY - *LitMarPl 83, 84*
International Journal of Periodontics & Restorative Dentistry - Chicago, IL - *BaconPubCkMag 84*
International Journal of Powder Metallurgy & Powder Technology - Princeton, NJ - *BaconPubCkMag 84; MagDir 84*
International Journal of Radiation: Oncology-Biology-Physics - Elmsford, NY - *MagIndMarPl 82-83*
International Labor Office - Washington, DC - *BoPubDir 4, 5*
International Laboratory - Fairfield, CT - *BaconPubCkMag 84; MagDir 84*
International Labour Documentation [of International Labour Office] - Geneva, Switzerland - *CompReadDB 82*
International Labour Office (Central Library & Documentation Branch) - Geneva, Switzerland - *CompReadDB 82; InfIndMarPl 83*
International Labour Office (Publications) - Geneva, Switzerland - *MicroMarPl 82-83*
International Language Services - Beaverton, OR - *MagIndMarPl 82-83*
International Language Society of Great Britain - Caerdydd, Wales - *LitMag&SmPr 83-84*
International Lead & Zinc - Bala Cynwyd, PA - *DirOnDB Spring 84*
International Lead & Zinc Study Group [of Chase Econometrics/Interactive Data Corp.] - Waltham, MA - *DataDirOnSer 84*
International Leased Channel Service [of RCA Global Communications Inc.] - New York, NY - *TeleSy&SerDir 2-84*
International Library - Arlington, VA - *BoPubDir 4, 5*
International Library Book Publishers - Arlington, VA - *LitMarPl 83, 84*
International Linguistics Corp. - Kansas City, MO - *BoPubDir 4, 5*
International Living [of Agora Publishing] - Baltimore, MD - *WritMar 84*
International Loss Control Institute - Loganville, GA - *BoPubDir 5*
International Magnesium Association - Dayton, OH - *BoPubDir 5*
International Management [of McGraw-Hill Publishing Co.] - New York, NY - *BaconPubCkMag 84; MagDir 84*
International Management Group - Cleveland, OH - *HBIndAd&MS 82-83; LitMarPl 83*
International Management Services Inc. - Framingham, MA - *EISS 83*
International Marine Publishing Co. [Subs. of Diversified Communications Inc.] - Camden, ME - *LitMag&SmPr 83-84; LitMarPl 83, 84; WritMar 84*
International Maritime Satellite Organization - London, England - *TeleSy&SerDir 2-84*
International Marketing Concepts - New York, NY - *WhoWMicrocom 83*
International Media Service - Washington, DC - *BrCabYB 84*
International Media Services Inc. - Plainfield, NJ - *AvMarPl 83*
International Medical Informatics Association - Almere-Stad, Netherlands - *EISS 83*
International Medical Information Center - Tokyo, Japan - *EISS 83*
International Medical Tribune Syndicate - Washington, DC - *Ed&PubIntYB 82; LitMarPl 84*
International Memories Inc. - Cupertino, CA - *DataDirSup 7-83*
International Memory Products of California Inc. - Santa Monica, CA - *WhoWMicrocom 83*
International Micro Systems - Shawnee Mission, KS - *MicrocomMPl 83, 84; MicrocomSwDir 1; WhoWMicrocom 83*
International Microcomputer Software Directory [of Imprint Editions] - Ft. Collins, CO - *CompReadDB 82*
International Microform Distribution Service [Div. of Clearwater Publishing Co. Inc.] - New York, NY - *MicroMarPl 82-83*
International Micrographic Congress - Bethesda, MD - *EISS 83; MicroMarPl 82-83*
International Mobile Machines Corp. - Philadelphia, PA - *DataDirSup 7-83*
International Model Database [of Evans Economics Inc.] - Washington, DC - *DataDirOnSer 84*
International Monetary Fund - Washington, DC - *BoPubDir 4, 5; DataDirOnSer 84*
International Monetary Fund Database [of Evans Economics Inc.] - Washington, DC - *DataDirOnSer 84*
International Museum of Photography at George Eastman House - Rochester, NY - *AvMarPl 83; MicroMarPl 82-83*
International Musician [of American Federation of Musicians] - New York, NY - *BaconPubCkMag 84; MagDir 84; MagIndMarPl 82-83; NewsDir 84; WritMar 84*

International Negotiation Institute - Princeton, NJ - *ADAPSOMemDir 83-84*
International Networks - Monson, MA - *TeleSy&SerDir 2-84*
International New Product Newsletter - Boston, MA - *BaconPubCkMag 84; MagIndMarPl 82-83*
International New Products Newsletter [of U.S. International Marketing Co. Inc.] - Bellflower, CA - *MagDir 84; MagIndMarPl 82-83*
International Nuclear Information System [of International Atomic Energy Agency] - Vienna, Austria - *CompReadDB 82; DirOnDB Spring 84; EISS 83*
International Nuclear Information System [of Canada Institute for Scientific & Technical Information] - Ottawa, ON, Canada - *DataDirOnSer 84*
International Occupational Safety & Health Information Centre [of International Labour Office] - Geneva, Switzerland - *CompReadDB 82; DataDirOnSer 84; EISS 83*
International Office Equipment Inc. - Ft. Lauderdale, FL - *DirInfWP 82*
International Oil Market Information System [of Organisation for Economic Co-Operation & Development] - Paris, France - *EISS 83*
International Oil News - Stamford, CT - *BaconPubCkMag 84; MagDir 84*
International Olympic Lifter [of IOL Publications] - Los Angeles, CA - *WritMar 84*
International Online [of Chase Econometrics/Interactive Data Corp.] - Waltham, MA - *DataDirOnSer 84*
International Operating Engineer - Washington, DC - *BaconPubCkMag 84; MagDir 84; NewsDir 84*
International Organization - Stanford, CA - *MagDir 84*
International Organization - Ithaca, NY - *MagIndMarPl 82-83*
International Packet-Switched Data Transfer Service [of Kokusai Denshin Denwa Co. Ltd.] - Tokyo, Japan - *TeleSy&SerDir 7-83*
International Packet-Switching Service [of MCI International Inc.] - Rye Brook, NY - *TeleSy&SerDir 2-84*
International Packet Switching Service [of British Telecommunications International] - London, England - *InfIndMarPl 83; TeleSy&SerDir 2-84*
International Paper Co. [Subs. of White Papers Group] - New York, NY - *LitMarPl 83, 84*
International Patent Documentation Center - Vienna, Austria - *CompReadDB 82; EISS 83; InfIndMarPl 83*
International Peace Center - Floral Park, NY - *BoPubDir 5*
International Peace Center - New York, NY - *BoPubDir 4*
International Petroleum Annual - Washington, DC - *DirOnDB Spring 84*
International Petroleum Annual [of I. P. Sharp Associates Ltd.] - Toronto, ON, Canada - *DataDirOnSer 84*
International Petroleum Finance - New York, NY - *DirOnDB Spring 84*
International Pharmaceutical Abstracts [of American Society of Hospital Pharmacists] - Washington, DC - *DBBus 82; EISS 83*
International Pharmaceutical Abstracts [of American Society of Hospital Pharmacists] - Bethesda, MD - *DataDirOnSer 84; DirOnDB Spring 84; InfIndMarPl 83; OnBibDB 3*
International Photo News - West Palm Beach, FL - *LitMarPl 84*
International Photographers of the Motion Picture Industries - Chicago, IL - *AvMarPl 83*
International Photographers of the Motion Picture Industries - New York, NY - *AvMarPl 83*
International Photography Society - Capitola, CA - *BoPubDir 4 Sup, 5*
International Plastic Cards Inc. - Lawndale, CA - *DataDirSup 7-83*
International Plastics Selector Inc. [Aff. of Cordura Publications Inc.] - San Diego, CA - *BoPubDir 5; EISS 83*
International Polygonics Ltd. - New York, NY - *BoPubDir 4, 5*
International Precious Metals Institute - Bethlehem, PA - *BoPubDir 5*
International Press Associates Inc. - Los Angeles, CA - *Ed&PubIntYB 82*
International Press Clipping Bureau Inc. - New York, NY - *ProGuPRSer 4*
International Press Marketing Div. [of Hindall & Associates Advertising] - *See* Hindall & Associates Advertising
International Press Publications - Toronto, ON, Canada - *LitMarPl 83*
International Press Publications - Willowdale, ON, Canada - *LitMarPl 84*
International Product Alert - Naples, NY - *BaconPubCkMag 84*
International Production Center - New York, NY - *AvMarPl 83*
International Production Group [Div. of MPCS Video Industries Inc.] - New York, NY - *AvMarPl 83*
International Programming Laboratories Corp. - Providence, RI - *ADAPSOMemDir 83-84*
International Project Management Group Inc., The - Glyndon, MD - *TeleSy&SerDir 2-84*
International Public Relations Ltd. - Honolulu, HI - *DirPRFirms 83*
International Publications - Los Angeles, CA - *BoPubDir 4, 5*
International Publications Service [Subs. of Taylor & Francis Inc.] - New York, NY - *LitMarPl 83, 84*
International Publishers Co. Inc. - New York, NY - *LitMarPl 83, 84; WritMar 84*
International Publishing & Software - Downsview, ON, Canada - *WritMar 84*
International Publishing Services - Westlake Village, CA - *BoPubDir 4*
International Racquetball - Salt Lake City, UT - *BaconPubCkMag 84*
International Railway Journal - New York, NY - *BaconPubCkMag 84; MagDir 84*
International Reading Association - Newark, DE - *BoPubDir 4*
International Record Syndicate - Hollywood, CA - *BillIntBG 83-84*
International Recording Co. Inc. - Chicago, IL - *BillIntBG 83-84*
International Referral Centre for Information Handling Equipment [of United Nations Educational, Scientific, & Cultural Organization] - Zagreb, Yugoslavia - *EISS 83*
International Referral System for Sources of Environmental Information [of United Nations Environment Programme] - Nairobi, Kenya - *InfIndMarPl 83*
International Refugee Integration Resource Centre - Geneva, Switzerland - *EISS 5-84 Sup*
International Register of Potentially Toxic Chemicals [of United Nations Environment Programme] - Geneva, Switzerland - *EISS 83*
International Register of Research on Blindness & Visual Impairment [of University of Warwick] - Coventry, England - *EISS 83*
International Rehabilitation Review - New York, NY - *BaconPubCkMag 84; MagDir 84*
International Relations Information System [of Foundation for Science & Politics] - Ebenhausen, West Germany - *CompReadDB 82; EISS 83*
International Repertory of Music Literature/Repertoire International de Litterature Musicale [of International Association of Music Libraries] - New York, NY - *EISS 83*
International Repertory of the Literature of Art [of Clark Art Institute] - Williamstown, MA - *CompReadDB 82*
International Reports - New York, NY - *BoPubDir 4, 5*
International Rescuer - Columbus, OH - *MagDir 84*
International Research & Evaluation - Eagan, MN - *CompReadDB 82; DataDirOnSer 84; EISS 83; InfIndMarPl 83*
International Research & Evaluation (Information & Technology Transfer Database) - Eagan, MN - *InfIndMarPl 83; MicroMarPl 82-83*
International Research & Evaluation (Research Publications Div.) - Eagan, MN - *BoPubDir 4, 5*
International Research Associates Inc. - Mamaroneck, NY - *IntDirMarRes 83*
International Research Associates Ltd. - Paranaque, Philippines - *IntDirMarRes 83*
International Research Institute for Political Science - College Park, MD - *BoPubDir 4, 5*
International Research Service Inc. - Blue Bell, PA - *BoPubDir 4, 5*
International Resource Development Inc. - Norwalk, CT - *BoPubDir 4 Sup, 5; EISS 83; InfIndMarPl 83; InterCabHB 3; TeleSy&SerDir 2-84; VideoDir 82-83; WhoWMicrocom 83*
International Review - Portree, Scotland - *LitMag&SmPr 83-84*

International Review of Chiropractic - Washington, DC - *BaconPubCkMag 84*
International Review Service - New York, NY - *Ed&PubIntYB 82*
International Ribbon & Carbon - Westbury, NY - *DirInfWP 82*
International Road Research Documentation [of Organisation for Economic Cooperation & Development] - Paris, France - *CompReadDB 82; DirOnDB Spring 84; EISS 83; OnBibDB 3*
International Satellite Services [of Cardiff Cablevision Inc.] - Ft. Sill, OK - *BrCabYB 84; Tel&CabFB 84C*
International Scholarly Book Services Inc. - Beaverton, OR - *LitMarPl 83, 84*
International School Psychology - Columbus, OH - *BoPubDir 4, 5*
International Science & Technology Institute Inc. - Washington, DC - *BoPubDir 4, 5*
International Security - Cambridge, MA - *MagIndMarPl 82-83*
International Self-Counsel Press Ltd. - North Vancouver, BC, Canada - *BoPubDir 4, 5; LitMarPl 83, 84; WritMar 84*
International Serials Data System [of Centre International d'Enregistrement des Publications en Serie] - Paris, France - *CompReadDB 82; EISS 83*
International Service Co. - Indialantic, FL - *LitMarPl 83, 84*
International Services [of Satellite Business Systems] - McLean, VA - *TeleSy&SerDir 7-83*
International Socialist Review - New York, NY - *MagIndMarPl 82-83*
International Society of Ecological Modelling - Vaerlose, Denmark - *InfIndMarPl 83*
International Software Alliance - Santa Barbara, CA - *MicrocomMPl 84*
International Software Database [of Dialog Information Services Inc.] - Palo Alto, CA - *DataDirOnSer 84*
International Software Database Corp. - Ft. Collins, CO - *DataDirOnSer 84; DirOnDB Spring 84*
International Software Directory [of Imprint Editions] - Ft. Collins, CO - *DBBus 82*
International Software Enterprises Inc. - Arlington Heights, IL - *MicrocomMPl 84; WhoWMicrocom 83*
International Software Enterprises Inc. - Lafayette, IN - *DataDirSup 7-83*
International Software Marketing Ltd. - Syracuse, NY - *MicrocomMPl 84*
International Software Sales Inc. - Watervliet, NY - *MicrocomMPl 84*
International Solar Energy Society (American Section) - New York, NY - *BoPubDir 4, 5*
International SOS Newsletter [of NewsNet Inc.] - Bryn Mawr, PA - *DataDirOnSer 84*
International SOS Newsletter - Virginia Beach, VA - *DirOnDB Spring 84*
International Species Inventory System [of Minnesota Zoological Garden] - Apple Valley, MN - *EISS 83*
International Spotlite Promotions Inc. - Las Vegas, NV - *BillIntBG 83-84*
International Stock Photography Ltd. - New York, NY - *LitMarPl 84*
International Surgery - Chicago, IL - *BaconPubCkMag 84; MagDir 84*
International Survey of Management Education - New York, NY - *LitMarPl 83, 84*
International Talent Marketing Inc. - New York, NY - *AvMarPl 83*
International Technical Publications Ltd. - Sao Paulo, Brazil - *EISS 7-83 Sup*
International Tele-Film Enterprises Ltd. - Toronto, ON, Canada - *Tel&CabFB 84C*
International Telecine - Santa Ana, CA - *AvMarPl 83*
International Telecom Systems Inc. - Madison, WI - *TeleSy&SerDir 2-84*
International Telecommunication Union - Geneva, Switzerland - *EISS 83; TelDir&BG 83-84*
International Telecommunications Satellite Organization - Washington, DC - *BrCabYB 84; TelDir&BG 83-84; TeleSy&SerDir 7-83*
International Telecommunications Users Group - Otford, England - *EISS 83; TeleSy&SerDir 2-84*
International Teleconferencing Association - McLean, VA - *TeleSy&SerDir 2-84*
International Telecontrol Corp. - Edgemont, PA - *DataDirSup 7-83*
International Telegram Service [of RCA Global Communications Inc.] - New York, NY - *TeleSy&SerDir 2-84*
International Telephone & Telegraph Corp. - *See* ITT Corp.
International Television - New York, NY - *BaconPubCkMag 84*
International Television Almanac - New York, NY - *MagDir 84*
International Television Association - Berkeley Heights, NJ - *BoPubDir 5; TeleSy&SerDir 7-83*
International Television Film Distributing Co. Inc. - Hollywood, CA - *Tel&CabFB 84C*
International, The - Nogales, AZ - *AyerDirPub 83*
International Thomson Holdings [Subs. of International Thomson Organisation] - London, England - *AdAge 6-28-84*
International Thomson Information Inc. - Denver, CO - *InfoS 83-84*
International Thomson Organisation Ltd. - New York, NY - *KnowInd 83*
International Time Series [of Predicasts Inc.] - Cleveland, OH - *CompReadDB 82*
International Trade Administration [of U.S. Dept. of Commerce] - Washington, DC - *InfIndMarPl 83*
International Trade & Investment - Washington, DC - *BaconPubCkMag 84*
International Trade Centre - Geneva, Switzerland - *MicroMarPl 82-83*
International Trade Information Service - Washington, DC - *DirOnDB Spring 84*
International Trade Information Service [of Data Resources Inc.] - Lexington, MA - *DataDirOnSer 84*
International Trade Information Service Monthly Monitor - Washington, DC - *DirOnDB Spring 84*
International Training Consultants Inc. - Richmond, VA - *AvMarPl 83; BoPubDir 4, 5*
International Translations Centre - Delft, Netherlands - *CompReadDB 82; EISS 83; InfIndMarPl 83*
International Travel News - Sacramento, CA - *BaconPubCkMag 84; MagIndMarPl 82-83*
International Travel Research Institute - Paranaque, Philippines - *IntDirMarRes 83*
International Tree Crops Institute - Winters, CA - *BoPubDir 4, 5; LitMag&SmPr 83-84*
International Tree-Ring Data Bank [of University of Arizona] - Tucson, AZ - *EISS 83*
International Truck Data Bank - Washington, DC - *DirOnDB Spring 84*
International Truck Data Bank [of Data Resources Inc.] - Lexington, MA - *DataDirOnSer 84*
International Tsunami Information Center [of United Nations Educational, Scientific, & Cultural Organization] - Honolulu, HI - *EISS 83*
International TV Corp. - Pasadena, MD - *Tel&CabFB 84C*
International Universities Press Inc. - New York, NY - *LitMag&SmPr 83-84; LitMarPl 83, 84; MagIndMarPl 82-83*
International University Booksellers Inc. - New York, NY - *LitMarPl 83, 84; MagIndMarPl 82-83*
International University Poetry Quarterly, The - Independence, MO - *LitMag&SmPr 83-84*
International University Press [Subs. of The International University Foundation] - Independence, MO - *BoPubDir 4, 5; LitMag&SmPr 83-84; WritMar 84*
International Videotex Information Providers' Association - London, England - *EISS 83*
International Water Report - Syosset, NY - *BaconPubCkMag 84; MagDir 84*
International Wealth Success Inc. - Merrick, NY - *WritMar 84*
International Wealth Success Inc. - Rockville Centre, NY - *BoPubDir 4, 5*
International Wildlife [of National Wildlife Federation] - Washington, DC - *LitMarPl 83*
International Wildlife - Vienna, VA - *ArtMar 84; LitMarPl 84; WritMar 84*
International Wizard of Oz Club - Kinderhook, IL - *BoPubDir 4, 5*

International Woodworker - Portland, OR - *MagDir 84; NewsDir 84*
International Writers Service - Washington, DC - *Ed&PubIntYB 82*
International Writing Institute Inc. - Cleveland, OH - *AvMarPl 83*
Internationale Dokumentationsgesellschaft fur Chemie mbH - Frankfurt, West Germany - *CompReadDB 82; InfIndMarPl 83*
Internationale Werbegesellschaft MbH - Vienna, Austria - *StaDirAdAg 2-84*
Internews Media Services - Washington, DC - *ProGuPRSer 4*
Internist, The - Washington, DC - *BaconPubCkMag 84*
Interocean Press Syndicate - Tucson, AZ - *Ed&PubIntYB 82; LitMarPl 84*
Interpartners Communications SA - *See* Humphrey Browning MacDougall Inc.
Interpersonal Communication Programs Inc. - Minneapolis, MN - *BoPubDir 4, 5; DirInfWP 82*
Interpharm Press - Prairie View, IL - *BoPubDir 4, 5*
Interphase Corp. - Dallas, TX - *WhoWMicrocom 83*
Interphase II Productions - Merrillville, IN - *AvMarPl 83*
Interplex Communications - Homewood, IL - *DirPRFirms 83*
Interpress of London & New York - New York, NY - *DirPRFirms 83; Ed&PubIntYB 82; LitMarPl 84*
Interpretation: A Journal of Bible & Theology - Richmond, VA - *MagIndMarPl 82-83*
Interpretive Data Systems - Brookline, MA - *DataDirOnSer 84*
Interpretive Data Systems - South Burlington, VT - *ADAPSOMemDir 83-84*
Interpretive Education Inc. - Kalamazoo, MI - *MicrocomMPl 83; WhoWMicrocom 83*
Interpro Corp. - Manchester, NH - *MicrocomMPl 83; MicrocomSwDir 1*
Interproject Inc. - Brentwood, MD - *WhoWMicrocom 83*
Interpublic Group of Cos. Inc., The - New York, NY - *BrCabYB 84; StaDirAdAg 2-84*
Interracial Books for Children Bulletin [of Council on Interracial Books for Children] - New York, NY - *ArtMar 84; LitMag&SmPr 83-84; MagIndMarPl 82-83*
Interrobang Inc. - Denver, CO - *DataDirOnSer 84*
Intersearch Corp. - Horsham, PA - *IntDirMarRes 83*
Intersell - San Jose, CA - *MicrocomMPl 83*
Interservice - Washington, DC - *BaconPubCkMag 84; MagDir 84*
Interservice Publishing Co. Inc. - San Francisco, CA - *BoPubDir 4 Sup, 5*
Intersil Systems Inc. - Sunnyvale, CA - *DataDirSup 7-83*
Intersociety Committee on Pathology Information Inc. - Bethesda, MD - *BoPubDir 4, 5*
Intersong International New York - New York, NY - *BillIntBG 83-84*
Intersong Music Inc. - Hollywood, CA - *BillIntBG 83-84*
Intersound Inc. - Minneapolis, MN - *BillIntBG 83-84*
Intersputnik International Organization of Space Communications - Moscow, USSR - *TeleSy&SerDir 2-84*
Interstar Corp. - Van Nuys, CA - *WhoWMicrocom 83*
Interstate - Gary, SD - *AyerDirPub 83*
Interstate [of Noumenon Press] - Austin, TX - *ArtMar 84; LitMag&SmPr 83-84*
Interstate Book Manufacturers Inc. - Olathe, KS - *LitMarPl 83, 84*
Interstate Broadcasting Systems Inc. - Orange, CA - *BrCabYB 84*
Interstate Electronics Corp. [Subs. of A-T-O Inc.] - Anaheim, CA - *WhoWMicrocom 83*
Interstate News, The - Siloam Springs, AR - *AyerDirPub 83; Ed&PubIntYB 82*
Interstate Oil Compact Commission - Oklahoma City, OK - *BoPubDir 5*
Interstate Piano Co. - Portland, OR - *BoPubDir 4 Sup, 5*
Interstate Printers & Publishers Inc. - Danville, IL - *LitMarPl 83, 84; MagIndMarPl 82-83; WritMar 84*
Interstate Printing Co. - Omaha, NE - *LitMarPl 83, 84; MagIndMarPl 82-83*
Interstate Progress - Logansport, LA - *AyerDirPub 83*
Interstate School Supply Co. - Baton Rouge, LA - *AvMarPl 83*
Interstate Shopper - Iowa City, IA - *AyerDirPub 83*
Interstate Telephone Co. - West Point, GA - *TelDir&BG 83-84*
Interstate 35 Telephone Co. [Aff. of Southwest Telephone Exchange Inc.] - Emerson, IA - *TelDir&BG 83-84*
Intersystems Publications - Seaside, CA - *BoPubDir 5*
Intersystems Software Inc. - Jericho, NY - *MicrocomSwDir 1; WhoWMicrocom 83*
Intertec Data Systems - Columbia, SC - *DataDirSup 7-83; InfIndMarPl 83; WhoWMicrocom 83*
Intertec Publishing Corp. [Subs. of ITT Publishing] - Overland Park, KS - *DirMarMP 83; MagIndMarPl 82-83*
Intertec Publishing Corp. (Technical Publications Div.) - Overland Park, KS - *BoPubDir 4, 5*
Intertel - Washington, DC - *ProGuPRSer 4*
Intertel [of Overseas Telecommunications Commission] - Sydney, Australia - *TeleSy&SerDir 2-84*
Intertel Inc. - Andover, MA - *DataDirSup 7-83*
Intertext - Anchorage, AK - *LitMag&SmPr 83-84*
Intertie Inc. - Newport Beach, CA - *BrCabYB 84 p.D-302*
Interurban Publications - Glendale, CA - *BoPubDir 4, 5; LitMarPl 84*
Intervarsity Press - Downers Grove, IL - *WritMar 84*
Intervideo Network Inc. - Los Angeles, CA - *TeleSy&SerDir 2-84*
Interview - New York, NY - *MagIndMarPl 82-83*
Interviewers for Research Inc. - Fair Lawn, NJ - *IntDirMarRes 83*
Intervision Communications Co. - West Hollywood, CA - *ArtMar 84*
Intervision Communications Co. Inc. - *See* Paterson Productions Co.
Intervisual Communications - Los Angeles, CA - *LitMarPl 83, 84*
Interweave Press Inc. - Loveland, CO - *BoPubDir 4, 5*
InterWorld Communications Inc. - Hollywood, CA - *AvMarPl 83*
InterWorld Communications Inc. - Evanston, IL - *AvMarPl 83*
Interworld Translation Services Inc. - New York, NY - *MagIndMarPl 82-83*
Intex Micro Systems Corp. - Birmingham, MI - *MicrocomMPl 84*
Intha Univas [of the Univas Network] - Turin, Italy - *StaDirAdAg 2-84*
INTI - Providence, RI - *BoPubDir 4 Sup, 5*
Intimate Fashion News [of Mackay Publishing Corp.] - New York, NY - *BaconPubCkMag 84; MagDir 84*
Intimate Romances - New York, NY - *MagDir 84*
Intimate Secrets - New York, NY - *MagDir 84*
Intimate Story - New York, NY - *MagDir 84; MagIndMarPl 82-83*
Intimate Talk Network - Berkeley, CA - *LitMag&SmPr 83-84*
Intline [of Chase Econometrics/Interactive Data Corp.] - Waltham, MA - *DataDirOnSer 84*
Intline - Bala Cynwyd, PA - *DirOnDB Spring 84*
Intra Computer Inc. - New York, NY - *MicrocomMPl 84*
Intra-Day Analyst - New Orleans, LA - *MicrocomMPl 83, 84*
Intramed Communications Inc. - *See* Sudler & Hennessey Inc.
Intrastate Radio Telephone Inc. of San Francisco - San Francisco, CA - *Tel&CabFB 84C*
Intrepid Press - Buffalo, NY - *LitMag&SmPr 83-84*
Intrepid Records & Filmworks Inc. - Kansas City, MO - *BillIntBG 83-84*
Intresco Inc. - Worburn, MA - *DirInfWP 82*
Intrigue [of Air Crafts Ltd. Inc.] - Woodbridge, NJ - *WritMar 84*
Intrigue Associates - Woodbridge, NJ - *BrCabYB 84*
Intro [of Intro International Inc.] - Los Angeles, CA - *BaconPubCkMag 84; WritMar 84*
Intro [of Dow Jones News/Retrieval Service] - Princeton, NJ - *DataDirOnSer 84; DirOnDB Spring 84*
Intro-Logic Inc. - Southfield, MI - *MicrocomSwDir 1*
Introl Corp. - Milwaukee, WI - *MicrocomMPl 83, 84*
Inuvik Drum, The - Inuvik, NT, Canada - *AyerDirPub 83*
Invention Marketing Inc. - Pittsburgh, PA - *DirMarMP 83; EISS 83*
Inventory & Monitoring Staff [of U.S. Dept. of Agriculture] - Washington, DC - *EISS 83*
Inventory Locator Service - Memphis, TN - *DirOnDB Spring 84*
Inventory of Canadian Agricultural Research [of Canadian Agricultural Research Council] - Ottawa, ON, Canada - *EISS 5-84 Sup*
Inventory of Marriage & Family Literature [of Sage Publications Inc.] - Beverly Hills, CA - *EISS 83*
Inventory of Marriage & Family Literature [of University of Minnesota] - St. Paul, MN - *CompReadDB 82*

Inventory of Marriage & Family Literature [of Bibliographic Retrieval Services Inc.] - Latham, NY - *DataDirOnSer 84*
Inventory of Sources for History of Twentieth-Century Physics [of University of California, Berkeley] - Berkeley, CA - *CompReadDB 82; EISS 83*
Inverness Citrus County Chronicle - *See* Citrus Publishing Co.
Invest-Tech - Metuchen, NJ - *DirOnDB Spring 84*
Investdata System [of Telekurs AG] - Zurich, Switzerland - *EISS 83*
Invester Publications - Cedar Falls, IA - *LitMarPl 84*
Investext - Boston, MA - *DirOnDB Spring 84*
Investigations Institute - Chicago, IL - *BoPubDir 4, 5*
Investigative Ophthalmology & Visual Science - St. Louis, MO - *MagIndMarPl 82-83*
Investigative Radiology - Philadelphia, PA - *MagDir 84*
Investigative Resource Center (Data Center) - Oakland, CA - *BoPubDir 5*
Investigative Urology - Baltimore, MD - *MagDir 84*
Investment & Tax Publications - Orem, UT - *BoPubDir 5*
Investment Co. Institute - Washington, DC - *BoPubDir 5*
Investment Dealers Digest - New York, NY - *BaconPubCkMag 84; BoPubDir 4, 5; MagDir 84; ProGuPRSer 4*
Investment Evaluations Corp. - Golden, CO - *BoPubDir 4, 5*
Investment News & Views [of Battery Lane Publications] - Gaithersburg, MD - *DataDirOnSer 84*
Investment Property System [of Citidata Corp.] - Northridge, CA - *DataDirOnSer 84*
Investments - New York, NY - *DirOnDB Spring 84*
Investor Publications - Cedar Falls, IA - *LitMarPl 83*
Investor Relations Canada Ltd. - Toronto, ON, Canada - *DirPRFirms 83*
Investor Relations Co., The - Northbrook, IL - *DirPRFirms 83*
Investor Relations Update - Philadelphia, PA - *BaconPubCkMag 84*
Investor's Daily - Los Angeles, CA - *BaconPubCkMag 84*
Investors Software - San Francisco, CA - *MicrocomSwDir 1; WhoWMicrocom 83*
Investor's Systems Inc. - Dayton, OH - *BoPubDir 4, 5*
Investrek Publishing - Huntington Beach, CA - *ArtMar 84*
Invicta Creative Services - Winnipeg, MB, Canada - *LitMarPl 83, 84*
Invincible Metal Furniture Co. - Monitowac, WI - *DirInfWP 82*
Invisible City [of Red Hill Press] - San Francisco, CA - *BoPubDir 4, 5; LitMag&SmPr 83-84*
Invisible Theatre - Tucson, AZ - *WritMar 84*
Inwood West Lyon Herald - Inwood, IA - *BaconPubCkNews 84*
Inx Inc. - New York, NY - *Ed&PubIntYB 82*
Inyo Independent & Owens Valley Progress-Citizen [of Bishop Chalfant Press Publications] - Bishop, CA - *NewsDir 84*
Inyo Independent & Owens Valley Progress-Citizen - Independence, CA - *AyerDirPub 83*
Inyo Independent & Owens Valley Progress-Citizen - Lone Pine, CA - *Ed&PubIntYB 82*
Inyo Register [of Bishop Chalfant Press Publications] - Bishop, CA - *AyerDirPub 83; Ed&PubIntYB 82; NewsDir 84*
Inyo Register - *See* Chalfant Press Publications
Io [of North Atlantic Books] - Berkeley, CA - *LitMag&SmPr 83-84*
IOFE - St. Maries, ID - *TV&RadDir 84*
IOL & Ocular Surgery News - Thorofare, NJ - *BaconPubCkMag 84*
Iola Cable TV [of Community Tele-Communications Inc.] - Iola, KS - *BrCabYB 84; Tel&CabFB 84C*
Iola Herald - Iola, WI - *BaconPubCkNews 84; Ed&PubIntYB 82*
Iola Register - Iola, KS - *BaconPubCkNews 84; Ed&PubIntYB 82; NewsDir 84*
Iomega Corp. - Ogden, UT - *WhoWMicrocom 83*
Ion Kinetics & Energetics Data Center [of U.S. National Bureau of Standards] - Washington, DC - *EISS 83*
Ione Amador Progress News - *See* Goldweb Publications
Ione City TV Co-Op - Ione, OR - *BrCabYB 84; Tel&CabFB 84C*
Ionia Cable Service - Ionia, MI - *BrCabYB 84; Tel&CabFB 84C*
Ionia Sentinel Standard - Ionia, MI - *BaconPubCkNews 84; NewsDir 84*
Ionic Industries Inc. - Morristown, NJ - *AvMarPl 83*
Iosco County News - Tawas City, MI - *Ed&PubIntYB 82*
Iosco County News Herald - East Tawas, MI - *AyerDirPub 83*
Iota Press - East Lansing, MI - *BoPubDir 4, 5*
IOTC Inc. - Laramie, WY - *MicrocomMPl 83, 84*
Iowa AFL-CIO News - Des Moines, IA - *NewsDir 84*
Iowa Architect [of Iowa Chapter, American Institute of Architects] - Des Moines, IA - *BaconPubCkMag 84; MagDir 84*
Iowa Beverage Journal [of N.W. Beverage Journal Inc.] - Minneapolis, MN - *BaconPubCkMag 84; MagDir 84*
Iowa Bystander - West Des Moines, IA - *AyerDirPub 83*
Iowa Cable Network [of Heritage Communications Inc.] - Des Moines, IA - *CabTVPrDB 83*
Iowa Cablevision Inc. - Iowa, LA - *BrCabYB 84; Tel&CabFB 84C p.1685*
Iowa Cattleman - Ames, IA - *BaconPubCkMag 84*
Iowa City Daily Iowan [of Student Publishing Inc.] - Coralville, IA - *NewsDir 84*
Iowa City Press-Citizen - Iowa City, IA - *BaconPubCkNews 84; Ed&PubIntYB 82; NewsDir 84*
Iowa City Women's Press - Iowa City, IA - *BoPubDir 4, 5; LitMag&SmPr 83-84*
Iowa Conservationist - Des Moines, IA - *MagDir 84*
Iowa Drug Information Service [of University of Iowa] - Iowa City, IA - *CompReadDB 82; EISS 83*
Iowa Engineer [of Iowa State University Press] - Ames, IA - *BaconPubCkMag 84; MagDir 84*
Iowa Falls Citizen - Iowa Falls, IA - *Ed&PubIntYB 82; NewsDir 84*
Iowa Falls Citizen - *See* Citizen Printing Co.
Iowa Falls Hardin County Times - Iowa Falls, IA - *NewsDir 84*
Iowa Falls Hardin County Times - *See* Citizen Printing Co.
Iowa Farm Bureau Spokesman - Des Moines, IA - *MagDir 84*
Iowa Farm Bureau Spokesman - Grundy Center, IA - *BaconPubCkMag 84*
Iowa Farm/Business - Des Moines, IA - *MagDir 84*
Iowa Food Dealer [of Iowa Retail Food Dealers Association] - Des Moines, IA - *BaconPubCkMag 84; MagDir 84*
Iowa Great Lakes Recording Co. Inc. - Spirit Lake, IA - *BillIntBG 83-84*
Iowa Journal of Optometry, The - Des Moines, IA - *BaconPubCkMag 84*
Iowa Library Information Teletype Exchange [of Iowa State Library Commission] - Des Moines, IA - *EISS 83*
Iowa Municipalities [of League of Iowa Municipalities] - Des Moines, IA - *ArtMar 84*
Iowa Natural Areas Inventory [of Iowa State Conservation Commission] - Des Moines, IA - *EISS 7-83 Sup*
Iowa Oil Spout - Des Moines, IA - *BaconPubCkMag 84*
Iowa Park Leader - Iowa Park, TX - *BaconPubCkNews 84; Ed&PubIntYB 82*
Iowa Pharmacist [of West Des Moines Express] - Des Moines, IA - *BaconPubCkMag 84; MagDir 84*
Iowa Press Association - Des Moines, IA - *ProGuPRSer 4*
Iowa Rec News - Des Moines, IA - *MagDir 84*
Iowa Rec News - Urbandale, IA - *BaconPubCkMag 84; WritMar 84*
Iowa Review - Iowa City, IA - *LitMag&SmPr 83-84; WritMar 84*
Iowa Smoke-Eater [of Smoke-Eater Publications] - Pierce, NE - *MagDir 84*
Iowa State Daily [of Iowa State University] - Ames, IA - *NewsDir 84*
Iowa State Historical Dept. - Iowa City, IA - *BoPubDir 4, 5*
Iowa State University (Media Resources Center) - Ames, IA - *AvMarPl 83*
Iowa State University Library - Ames, IA - *CompReadDB 82*
Iowa State University Press - Ames, IA - *LitMag&SmPr 83-84; LitMarPl 83, 84; WritMar 84*
Iowa State University Research Foundation (Educational Studies Press) - Ames, IA - *BoPubDir 4, 5*
Iowa Trucking Lifeliner - Des Moines, IA - *BaconPubCkMag 84; MagDir 84*
Iowa Video [of American TV & Communications Corp.] - Ft. Madison, IA - *BrCabYB 84; Tel&CabFB 84C*
Iowa Water Resources Data System [of Iowa State Geological Survey] - Iowa City, IA - *EISS 83*
Iowa Woman - Iowa City, IA - *LitMag&SmPr 83-84*
Iowan [of Mid-America Publishing Corp.] - Des Moines, IA - *BaconPubCkMag 84; WritMar 84*
Iowan - Iowa City, IA - *AyerDirPub 83*

Iowan - Shenandoah, IA - *MagDir 84*
Iowegian & Citizen - Centerville, IA - *AyerDirPub 83; Ed&PubIntYB 82*
IPA Information System [of American Society of Hospital Pharmacists] - Washington, DC - *CompReadDB 82*
IPC Business Press Ltd. - New York, NY - *BoPubDir 5*
IPC Chemical Database [of ADP Network Services Inc.] - Ann Arbor, MI - *DataDirOnSer 84*
IPC Chemical Database - Sutton, England - *DirOnDB Spring 84*
IPC DataDiet [Subs. of IPC International Projects Consulting] - San Jose, CA - *MicrocomMPl 83; WhoWMicrocom 83*
IPCO Info - Pittsburgh, PA - *MicrocomMPl 84*
IPD Printing & Distributing Inc. - Chamblee, GA - *MagIndMarPl 82-83*
IPI Publishing Ltd. - Toronto, ON, Canada - *BoPubDir 4, 5*
IPL Systems Inc. - Waltham, MA - *DataDirSup 7-83*
IPMS/USA Quarterly & IPMS/USA Update - Denver, CO - *MagIndMarPl 82-83*
IPPRC Political Events - Falls Church, VA - *DirOnDB Spring 84*
IPS - Minneapolis, MN - *DirInfWP 82*
IPS Publishing Services - Westlake Village, CA - *BoPubDir 5*
IPSA SA Audits & Surveys Latinamerica - Buenos Aires, Argentina - *IntDirMarRes 83*
Ipswich Cable TV [of Midcontinent Cable Inc.] - Ipswich, SD - *BrCabYB 84; Tel&CabFB 84C*
Ipswich Chronicle - Ipswich, MA - *AyerDirPub 83; Ed&PubIntYB 82; NewsDir 84*
Ipswich Chronicle - *See* North Shore Weeklies Inc.
Ipswich Press - Ipswich, MA - *ArtMar 84; BoPubDir 4 Sup, 5*
Ipswich Today - Ipswich, MA - *Ed&PubIntYB 82; NewsDir 84*
Ipswich Tribune - Ipswich, SD - *BaconPubCkNews 84; Ed&PubIntYB 82*
IQ Films Inc. - New York, NY - *AvMarPl 83*
IQ Systems [Subs. of Applied Circuit Technology] - Anaheim, CA - *MicrocomMPl 84; WhoWMicrocom 83*
IR Publications Ltd. - New York, NY - *LitMarPl 83, 84*
Iraan News - Iraan, TX - *BaconPubCkNews 84; Ed&PubIntYB 82*
Iraan TV Cable - Iraan, TX - *BrCabYB 84; Tel&CabFB 84C*
Iran Times - Washington, DC - *Ed&PubIntYB 82; NewsDir 84*
Iranian Documentation Center [of Ministry of Culture & Higher Education] - Tehran, Iran - *EISS 83*
IRCS Medical Science Database - Lancaster, England - *DirOnDB Spring 84*
IRCS Medical Science Database [of Elsevier-IRCS Ltd.] - St. Leonardgate, England - *DataDirOnSer 84; EISS 5-84 Sup*
I.R.D. Productions-Alien Productions - New York, NY - *LitMag&SmPr 83-84*
Iredell Times - Iredell, TX - *BaconPubCkNews 84; Ed&PubIntYB 82*
Irego - New York, NY - *BoPubDir 4 Sup, 5*
Irene Tri-County News - Irene, SD - *BaconPubCkNews 84*
Ireton Booster - Ireton, IA - *Ed&PubIntYB 82*
Ireton Cable TV - Ireton, IA - *Tel&CabFB 84C*
Ireton Examiner - Ireton, IA - *BaconPubCkNews 84*
IRGO [of Tymshare Inc.] - Cupertino, CA - *DataDirOnSer 84*
Irgo [of Chemir Laboratories] - Glendale, MO - *EISS 83*
IRIS [of EPA Instructional Resources Center] - Columbus, OH - *DirOnDB Spring 84; OnBibDB 3*
Iris Films [Subs. of Best People Inc.] - New York, NY - *AvMarPl 83; Tel&CabFB 84C*
IRIS International Inc. - Landover, MD - *EISS 5-84 Sup*
Iris Press Inc. - Binghamton, NY - *BoPubDir 4, 5; LitMag&SmPr 83-84*
Irish Academic Press [Aff. of Biblio Distribution Centre] - Totowa, NJ - *BoPubDir 4, 5*
Irish Advocate - New York, NY - *AyerDirPub 83; Ed&PubIntYB 82; NewsDir 84*
Irish-American Book Society, The [Subs. of Devin-Adair Publishing Co.] - Old Greenwich, CT - *LitMarPl 84*
Irish Books & Media - St. Paul, MN - *BoPubDir 4, 5*
Irish Echo - New York, NY - *Ed&PubIntYB 82; NewsDir 84*
Irish Genealogical Foundation [Aff. of O'Laughlin Press] - Kansas City, MO - *BoPubDir 4 Sup, 5*
Irish International Advertising & Marketing Ltd. - *See* Royds Advertising Group Ltd., The
Irish Literary Supplement - Selden, NY - *LitMag&SmPr 83-84*
Irish Magnetic Industries Inc. - Plainview, NY - *AvMarPl 83*
Irish Microforms Ltd. - Dublin, Ireland - *MicroMarPl 82-83*
Irish National Media Survey [of Interactive Market Systems Inc.] - New York, NY - *DataDirOnSer 84*
Irish National Media Survey - Dublin, Ireland - *DirOnDB Spring 84*
Irish People, The - New York, NY - *Ed&PubIntYB 82*
Irish Press Cuttings Ltd. - Dublin, Ireland - *ProGuPRSer 4*
Irish Roots - London, England - *FBInfSer 80*
Irish Studies - Selden, NY - *LitMag&SmPr 83-84*
Irish Terrier Club of America [Aff. of American Kennel Club] - Bloomfield Hills, MI - *BoPubDir 4, 5*
Irish World - New York, NY - *Ed&PubIntYB 82; NewsDir 84*
IRL Life Sciences Collection [of Information Retrieval Ltd.] - London, England - *CompReadDB 82*
IRL Medical Subgroup [of Information Retrieval Ltd.] - London, England - *CompReadDB 82*
IRL Press - Arlington, VA - *BoPubDir 4, 5*
IRM Inc. - New York, NY - *IntDirMarRes 83*
Irmen Associates, Robert J. - Hinsdale, IL - *ADAPSOMemDir 83-84*
Irmo Independent News - Irmo, SC - *BaconPubCkNews 84*
Iron - Tyne & Wear, England - *LitMag&SmPr 83-84*
Iron Age - Needham Heights, MA - *NewsBur 6*
Iron Age - Cleveland, OH - *NewsBur 6*
Iron Age [of Chilton Co.] - Radnor, PA - *BaconPubCkMag 84; Folio 83; MagIndMarPl 82-83*
Iron Age Metalworking Data Bank [of Chilton Co.] - Radnor, PA - *EISS 83*
Iron Age Metalworking International - Radnor, PA - *BaconPubCkMag 84*
Iron & Steel - Bala Cynwyd, PA - *DirOnDB Spring 84*
Iron & Steel Documentation Service [of Center of Experimental Metallurgy] - Rome, Italy - *EISS 5-84 Sup*
Iron & Steel Engineer - Pittsburgh, PA - *BaconPubCkMag 84; MagDir 84; MagIndMarPl 82-83*
Iron & Steel Forecast [of Chase Econometrics/Interactive Data Corp.] - Waltham, MA - *DBBus 82*
Iron & Steelmaker - Warrendale, PA - *BaconPubCkMag 84*
Iron County Miner - Hurley, WI - *AyerDirPub 83; Ed&PubIntYB 82*
Iron County Record - Cedar City, UT - *AyerDirPub 83; Ed&PubIntYB 82*
Iron Mountain Press - Emory, VA - *BoPubDir 4, 5; LitMag&SmPr 83-84*
Iron Press - Tyne & Near, England - *LitMag&SmPr 83-84*
Iron Range Cable TV [of Cox Cable Communications Corp.] - Munising, MI - *BrCabYB 84*
Iron River Cooperative TV Antenna Corp. - Iron River, MI - *BrCabYB 84; Tel&CabFB 84C*
Iron River Pioneer - Iron River, WI - *BaconPubCkNews 84; Ed&PubIntYB 82*
Iron River Reporter - Iron County, MI - *Ed&PubIntYB 82*
Iron River Reporter - Iron River, MI - *BaconPubCkNews 84; NewsDir 84*
Ironcaster - Des Plaines, IL - *BaconPubCkMag 84; MagDir 84*
Irondequoit & Penfield Shopper - Rochester, NY - *AyerDirPub 83*
Irondequoit Press - Irondequoit, NY - *Ed&PubIntYB 82*
Irondequoit Press [of Wolfe Publications Inc.] - Pittsford, NY - *NewsDir 84*
Irondequoit Press - Rochester, NY - *AyerDirPub 83*
Irondequoit Press - *See* Wolfe Publications Inc.
Ironton Mountain Echo - Ironton, MO - *BaconPubCkNews 84; NewsDir 84*
Ironton Telephone Co. - Coplay, PA - *TelDir&BG 83-84*
Ironton Tribune - Ironton, OH - *AyerDirPub 83; BaconPubCkNews 84; Ed&PubIntYB 82; NewsDir 84*
Ironwood - Tucson, AZ - *LitMag&SmPr 83-84*
Ironwood Globe - Ironwood, MI - *AyerDirPub 83; BaconPubCkNews 84; Ed&PubIntYB 82; NewsDir 84*
Ironwood Press - Tucson, AZ - *LitMag&SmPr 83-84*
Ironworker, The [of Ironworkers International] - Washington, DC - *NewsDir 84*
Iroquois Cable Co. - Watseka, IL - *BrCabYB 84; Tel&CabFB 84C*
Iroquois County Broadcasting Corp. - Watseka, IL - *BrCabYB 84*
Iroquois County Cablevision [of Firstcable Communications Inc.] - Gilman, IL - *BrCabYB 84; Tel&CabFB 84C*
Iroquois House - Mountain Park, NM - *LitMag&SmPr 83-84*

Iroquois House - Sunspot, NM - *BoPubDir 4, 5*
Iroquois Post, The - Iroquois, ON, Canada - *Ed&PubIntYB 82*
Iroquois Telephone Co. [Aff. of Continental Telecom Inc.] - Johnstown, NY - *TelDir&BG 83-84*
Iroquois Times-Republic - Watseka, IL - *BaconPubCkNews 84*
Irregular & Mt. Washington Valley News, The - North Conway, NH - *AyerDirPub 83*
Irrigation Age [of The Webb Co.] - St. Paul, MN - *BaconPubCkMag 84; MagDir 84; MagIndMarPl 82-83*
Irrigation Association - Silver Spring, MD - *BoPubDir 4, 5*
Irrigation Journal - Tampa, FL - *BaconPubCkMag 84*
Irrigation Journal - Elm Grove, WI - *MagDir 84*
Irrigator - Patterson, CA - *AyerDirPub 83*
IRS Dialtech [of Dept. of Industry] - London, England - *InfIndMarPl 83*
IRS INFO Institut [of Gesellschaft fur Informationsvermittlung und Technologieberatung mbH] - Munich, West Germany - *EISS 83; InfIndMarPl 83*
IRS Practices & Procedures - Washington, DC - *DirOnDB Spring 84*
IRS Practices & Procedures [of NewsNet Inc.] - Bryn Mawr, PA - *DataDirOnSer 84*
IRSS - Washington, DC - *DirOnDB Spring 84*
Irvine Citizen Voice & Times - Irvine, KY - *BaconPubCkNews 84; NewsDir 84*
Irvine Community Television Inc. - Irvine, KY - *BrCabYB 84; Tel&CabFB 84C*
Irvine Today [of Corona del Mar Newport Ensign] - Corona del Mar, CA - *NewsDir 84*
Irvine Today - Irvine, CA - *AyerDirPub 83*
Irvine Today - *See* Coast Media News Group
Irvine World News - Irvine, CA - *AyerDirPub 83; BaconPubCkNews 84; Ed&PubIntYB 82*
Irvine World News - Santa Ana, CA - *NewsDir 84*
Irving Advertising & Public Relations, William S. - Kansas City, MO - *StaDirAdAg 2-84*
Irving & Associates Ltd., G. D. - Calgary, AB, Canada - *WhoWMicrocom 83*
Irving Daily News - Farmers Branch, TX - *Ed&PubIntYB 82*
Irving Daily News [of News Texan Inc.] - Irving, TX - *BaconPubCkNews 84; NewsDir 84*
Irving Music Inc. - *See* Rondor Music International Inc.
Irving Newspapers - Canada - *Ed&PubIntYB 82*
Irving Park News - Chicago, IL - *AyerDirPub 83*
Irvington Herald - Irvington, NJ - *Ed&PubIntYB 82*
Irvington Herald - Union, NJ - *AyerDirPub 83*
Irvington Publishers Inc. - New York, NY - *LitMarPl 83, 84*
Irwin/Dicarlo Advertising Inc. - Honolulu, HI - *StaDirAdAg 2-84*
Irwin Inc., Richard D. [Subs. of Dow Jones & Co. Inc.] - Homewood, IL - *LitMarPl 83, 84*
Irwin Magnetics - Ann Arbor, MI - *DataDirSup 7-83*
Irwin, Penny C. - New York, NY - *HBIndAd&MS 82-83*
Irwin Research Services Inc. - Jacksonville, FL - *IntDirMarRes 83*
Irwin Standard-Observer [of Westmoreland Journals Inc.] - Irwin, PA - *BaconPubCkNews 84; NewsDir 84*
Irwinton Publishers - Mercersburg, PA - *BoPubDir 4, 5*
Irwinton Wiikinson County News - Irwinton, GA - *BaconPubCkNews 84*
Is Five Press - Toronto, ON, Canada - *BoPubDir 4, 5; LitMarPl 83, 84*
ISA Software Inc. - Dallas, TX - *MicrocomMPl 84*
Isaac Asimov's Science Fiction Magazine [of Davis Publications Inc.] - New York, NY - *LitMarPl 83, 84; MagIndMarPl 82-83; WritMar 84*
Isabel Dakotan - Isabel, SD - *BaconPubCkNews 84; Ed&PubIntYB 82*
Isabel, Joseph - Amsterdam, NY - *Tel&CabFB 84C p.1685*
Isanti News/North American - Isanti, MN - *BaconPubCkNews 84*
Isanti News, The - Isanti, MN - *Ed&PubIntYB 82*
ISC Systems - Spokane, WA - *DataDirSup 7-83*
Isco Ltd. - Cincinnati, OH - *StaDirAdAg 2-84*
ISE - West Lafayette, IN - *MicrocomMPl 83*
Ishmaelite - Sparta, GA - *AyerDirPub 83*
Ishtar Press Inc. - Laramie, WY - *LitMag&SmPr 83-84*
ISI/Biomed [of Institute for Scientific Information] - Philadelphia, PA - *CompReadDB 82; DataDirOnSer 84; DirOnDB Spring 84; OnBibDB 3*
ISI/CompuMath [of Institute for Scientific Information] - Philadelphia, PA - *CompReadDB 82; DataDirOnSer 84; OnBibDB 3*
ISI/CompuMath - *See* ISI/Multisci
ISI/GeoSciTech [of Institute for Scientific Information] - Philadelphia, PA - *OnBibDB 3*
ISI/GeoSciTech - *See* ISI/Multisci
ISI/Index to Scientific & Technical Proceedings & Books [of Institute for Scientific Information] - Philadelphia, PA - *CompReadDB 82*
ISI Infosearch Inc. - Vancouver, BC, Canada - *EISS 83; FBInfSer 80*
ISI/ISTP & B [of Institute for Scientific Information] - Philadelphia, PA - *DirOnDB Spring 84; OnBibDB 3*
ISI/Multisci - Philadelphia, PA - *DirOnDB Spring 84*
ISI Press [Subs. of Institute for Scientific Information] - Philadelphia, PA - *LitMag&SmPr 83-84; LitMarPl 83, 84; WritMar 84*
ISI Search Network [of Institute for Scientific Information] - Philadelphia, PA - *EISS 83*
ISI Systems Inc. [Div. of Grumman Corp.] - Braintree, MA - *DataDirOnSer 84*
Isis - Philadelphia, PA - *MagIndMarPl 82-83*
ISIS - Paris, France - *DirOnDB Spring 84*
Isis Press - Amherst, MA - *BoPubDir 4, 5*
ISIS Report - Washington, DC - *BaconPubCkMag 84*
Isker & Adajian Inc. - Chicago, IL - *ArtMar 84; StaDirAdAg 2-84*
ISKRA-INDOK Center - Ljubljana, Yugoslavia - *InfIndMarPl 83*
ISL International Surveys Ltd. - Toronto, ON, Canada - *Tel&CabFB 84C*
Islam Canada - Willowdale, ON, Canada - *Ed&PubIntYB 82*
Islamic Productions International - Tucson, AZ - *BoPubDir 4 Sup, 5*
Island - Lantzville, BC, Canada - *LitMag&SmPr 83-84; LitMarPl 83*
Island Ad-Vantage - Stonington, ME - *AyerDirPub 83; Ed&PubIntYB 82*
Island Books - Duncan, BC, Canada - *BoPubDir 4, 5*
Island Cable Co. [of Tele-Communications Inc.] - Beach Haven, NJ - *BrCabYB 84*
Island Cable Co. [of TKR Cable Co.] - Long Beach Township, NJ - *Tel&CabFB 84C*
Island Cable Inc. - Grand Island, NY - *Tel&CabFB 84C*
Island Cablevision Ltd. - Charlottetown, PE, Canada - *BrCabYB 84*
Island Cybernetics - Port Aransas, TX - *WhoWMicrocom 83*
Island Dispatch - Grand Island, NY - *AyerDirPub 83; Ed&PubIntYB 82*
Island Graphics - Bethel Island, CA - *MicrocomMPl 84*
Island Life - Sanibel, FL - *WritMar 84*
Island Music Inc. - Hollywood, CA - *BillIntBG 83-84*
Island Pacific Systems Corp. - Irvine, CA - *DataDirSup 7-83*
Island Packet - Hilton Head Island, SC - *AyerDirPub 83; Ed&PubIntYB 82*
Island Pictures Inc. - New York, NY - *BillIntBG 83-84*
Island Press [Div. of Round Valley Agrarian Institute] - Covelo, CA - *LitMag&SmPr 83-84; LitMarPl 83, 84; WritMar 84*
Island Press - Ft. Myers Beach, FL - *BoPubDir 4, 5*
Island Records Inc. - New York, NY - *BillIntBG 83-84*
Island Reporter [of Sunbelt Publishing] - Sanibel, FL - *AyerDirPub 83; Ed&PubIntYB 82; NewsDir 84*
Island Software - Lake Grove, NY - *MicrocomMPl 84*
Island Telephone Co. - Beaver Island, MI - *TelDir&BG 83-84*
Island Telephone Co., The - Frenchboro, ME - *TelDir&BG 83-84*
Islander News, The - Key Biscayne, FL - *AyerDirPub 83; Ed&PubIntYB 82*
Islander, The [of The Foley Robertsdale Onlooker] - Foley, AL - *NewsDir 84*
Islander, The - Anna Maria, FL - *Ed&PubIntYB 82*
Islander, The - St. Simons Island, GA - *Ed&PubIntYB 82*
Islands - Santa Barbara, CA - *BaconPubCkMag 84*
Islands - Torbay, New Zealand - *LitMag&SmPr 83-84*
Islands Gazette, The - Savannah, GA - *AyerDirPub 83*

Isle City Records - Galveston, TX - *BillIntBG 83-84*
Isle Cove Press - Foster City, CA - *LitMag&SmPr 83-84*
Isle Mille Lacs Messenger - Isle, MN - *BaconPubCkNews 84*
Isle of Guam International Publishing & Distributing Co. - *BoPubDir 5*
Isley, Fred - Clover, SC - *DirPRFirms 83*
Islip News - Central Islip, NY - *AyerDirPub 83*
Islip News - Islip, NY - *Ed&PubIntYB 82*
Islip News [of Smithtown News Inc.] - Smithtown, NY - *NewsDir 84*
Islip Town Bulletin - Bay Shore, NY - *AyerDirPub 83*
Islip Town Bulletin - Islip Town, NY - *Ed&PubIntYB 82*
ISM Press Inc. - Seattle, WA - *BoPubDir 4 Sup, 5*
ISMEC [of Cambridge Scientific Abstracts] - Bethesda, MD - *DirOnDB Spring 84; OnBibDB 3*
ISO Communications Inc. - New York, NY - *VideoDir 82-83*
ISO Information Network [of International Organization for Standardization] - Geneva, Switzerland - *EISS 83*
ISO World [of CW Communications Inc.] - Framingham, MA - *BaconPubCkMag 84; MagDir 84*
ISOREG Corp. - Littleton, MA - *WhoWMicrocom 83*
Isotopes Project [of University of California] - Berkeley, CA - *EISS 83*
Isotopics [of Cleveland Section, American Chemical Society] - Cleveland, OH - *MagDir 84*
ISQ-FM - Squamish, BC, Canada - *BrCabYB 84*
Israel Advertising Agency Inc., Elizabeth - Downers Grove, IL - *StaDirAdAg 2-84*
Israel Associates, Barbara - New York, NY - *DirPRFirms 83*
Israel Horizons - New York, NY - *LitMag&SmPr 83-84*
Israel Information Service - New York, NY - *BrCabYB 84*
ISRANET [of Ministry of Communications] - Tel Aviv, Israel - *InfIndMarPl 83*
Issac Software - St. Paul, MN - *MicrocomMPl 84*
Issaquah Press - Issaquah, WA - *AyerDirPub 83; BaconPubCkNews 84; Ed&PubIntYB 82; NewsDir 84*
Issue Inc. - Chicago, IL - *EISS 83*
Issues [of Heidelberg] - San Francisco, CA - *LitMag&SmPr 83-84*
Issues & Images Inc. - New York, NY - *BrCabYB 84*
Issues in Radical Therapy Collective - Berkeley, CA - *BoPubDir 4, 5*
IST Inc. - Montreal, PQ, Canada - *ADAPSOMemDir 83-84*
Istituto per la Documentazione Giuridica - Florence, Italy - *InfIndMarPl 83*
ISYS Corp. - Cambridge, MA - *MicrocomMPl 84*
ISYS Information Systems - Boulder, CO - *DirOnDB Spring 84*
It Is Written Telecast, The [Div. of Adventist Media Center] - Newbury Park, CA - *Tel&CabFB 84C*
It Will Stand - Charlotte, NC - *WritMar 84*
ITA-Info - Paris, France - *DirOnDB Spring 84*
Italcable - Rome, Italy - *TeleSy&SerDir 2-84*
Italian Association for the Production & Distribution of Online Information - Rome, Italy - *EISS 7-83 Sup*
Italian Echo, The - Providence, RI - *AyerDirPub 83*
Italian News - Boston, MA - *Ed&PubIntYB 82*
Italian Reference Center for Euronet Diane [of National Research Council] - Rome, Italy - *EISS 83*
Italian Tribune - Newark, NJ - *AyerDirPub 83; NewsDir 84*
Italimuse Inc. - Colfax, WI - *BoPubDir 4, 5*
Italy News-Herald - Italy, TX - *BaconPubCkNews 84*
Itasca Chronicle, The - Itasca, IL - *Ed&PubIntYB 82*
Itasca Item - Itasca, TX - *BaconPubCkNews 84; Ed&PubIntYB 82*
Itasca Record - Itasca, IL - *Ed&PubIntYB 82*
Itasca Record [of Roselle Copley Record Newspapers] - Schaumburg, IL - *NewsDir 84*
Itasca Voice - *See* Voice Newspapers
Itawamba County Times - Fulton, MS - *AyerDirPub 83; Ed&PubIntYB 82; NewsDir 84*
ITB [of Gessler Publishing Co. Inc.] - New York, NY - *LitMarPl 83, 84*
ITC - McLean, VA - *DirInfWP 82*
ITC Entertainment - New York, NY - *TelAl 83, 84; Tel&CabFB 84C*
ITC Television/Cinema Distribution Inc. - Toronto, ON, Canada - *Tel&CabFB 84C*
ITE Journal - Washington, DC - *BaconPubCkMag 84*
ITE Journal [of Institute of Transportation Engineers] - Arlington, VA - *MagDir 84*
Itek Composition Systems [Div. of Itek Corp.] - Wilmington, MA - *DirInfWP 82; LitMarPl 83, 84*
Itek Graphic Systems [Div. of Itek Corp.] - Rochester, NY - *AvMarPl 83*
Itek Graphics Products - Nashua, NH - *DirInfWP 82*
Itel Corp. - San Francisco, CA - *ADAPSOMemDir 83-84*
Item - Clinton, MA - *AyerDirPub 83*
Item - Lynn, MA - *AyerDirPub 83*
Item - Wakefield, MA - *AyerDirPub 83; Ed&PubIntYB 82*
Item - Picayune, MS - *AyerDirPub 83*
Item - Knob Noster, MO - *AyerDirPub 83*
Item - Hamburg, PA - *AyerDirPub 83*
Item - Sunbury, PA - *AyerDirPub 83*
Item - Sumter, SC - *AyerDirPub 83*
Item - Huntsville, TX - *AyerDirPub 83*
Item - Itasca, TX - *AyerDirPub 83*
Item of Millburn & Short Hills - Millburn, NJ - *AyerDirPub 83*
Iter Leggi Statali [of Centro per la Documentazione Automatica] - Rome, Italy - *CompReadDB 82*
Ithaca Gratiot County Herald - Ithaca, MI - *BaconPubCkNews 84*
Ithaca House - Ithaca, NY - *LitMag&SmPr 83-84; LitMarPl 83, 84*
Ithaca Intersystems Inc. - Ithaca, NY - *MicrocomMPl 83, 84; WhoWMicrocom 83*
Ithaca Journal [of Gannett Co. Inc.] - Ithaca, NY - *BaconPubCkNews 84; Ed&PubIntYB 82; NewsDir 84*
Ithaca Press - Lowell, MA - *BoPubDir 4, 5; LitMag&SmPr 83-84*
Ithaca Times - Ithaca, NY - *AyerDirPub 83; Ed&PubIntYB 82*
ITI - Van Nuys, CA - *BillIntBG 83-84*
ITIS Monthly Monitor [of Data Resources Inc.] - Lexington, MA - *DataDirOnSer 84*
ITM - Lafayette, CA - *MicrocomMPl 84*
Itoh Electronics Inc., C. [Subs. of C. Itoh & Co. Ltd.] - Los Angeles, CA - *DataDirSup 7-83; Datamation 6-83; MicrocomMPl 84; Top100Al 83; WhoWMicrocom 83*
ITOM International Co. - Los Altos, CA - *VideoDir 82-83*
I.T.S. Integrated Technical Software & Services - Wyndham Vale, Australia - *MicrocomSwDir 1*
It's Me [of Happy Hands Publishing Co.] - Ft. Worth, TX - *BaconPubCkMag 84; WritMar 84*
ITT Business Communications - Dallas, TX - *DirInfWP 82*
ITT-COINS - Secaucus, NJ - *ADAPSOMemDir 83-84*
ITT-COINS - New York, NY - *InfoS 83-84*
ITT Corp. - New York, NY - *Datamation 6-83; DirInfWP 82; ElecNews 7-25-83; KnowInd 83; Top100Al 83*
ITT Courier Terminal Systems Inc. [Subs. of ITT Corp.] - Tempe, AZ - *DataDirSup 7-83; InfIndMarPl 83*
ITT Dialcom - Silver Spring, MD - *DataDirSup 7-83; MicrocomMPl 84*
ITT Power Systems Div. [of ITT Corp.] - Galion, OH - *DataDirSup 7-83*
Itta Inc., John Paul - New York, NY - *AdAge 3-28-84; StaDirAdAg 2-84*
ITTI: Microfilm & Telecommunications Ltd. - Tel Aviv, Israel - *MicroMarPl 82-83*
Itty Bitty Computers - San Jose, CA - *MicrocomSwDir 1*
IUE News - Washington, DC - *NewsDir 84*
Iuka Tishomingo County News - Iuka, MS - *BaconPubCkNews 84; NewsDir 84*
Iuka TV Cable Co. Inc. [of Heritage Communications Inc.] - Iuka, MS - *Tel&CabFB 84C*
Ivan Publishing Inc. - San Antonio, TX - *BoPubDir 4, 5*
IVANCO - Rancho Palos Verdes, CA - *MicrocomMPl 83*
Ivanhoe Times - Ivanhoe, MN - *BaconPubCkNews 84; Ed&PubIntYB 82*
I've Got the Music Co. - Muscle Shoals, AL - *BillIntBG 83-84*
Iversen Norman Associates - Tarrytown, NY - *AdAge 3-28-84; StaDirAdAg 2-84*
Iversen-Norman Associates, The - New York, NY - *DirMarMP 83*
Iverson Photographics, Bruce A. - Waban, MA - *LitMarPl 83*
Ives Street Press - Mt. Carmel, CT - *BoPubDir 4 Sup, 5*
Ivey & Co., Bill - Marietta, GA - *AvMarPl 83*
Ivory Tower Publishing Co. Inc. - Watertown, MA - *LitMarPl 83, 84*

IVS-Geowissenschaften [of Bundesanstalt fur Geowissenschaften und Rohstoffe] - Hanover, West Germany - *InfIndMarPl 83*
Ivy Hill Press - Spring Valley, CA - *BoPubDir 4, 5*
Ivy League Magazines - Jacksonville, NY - *Folio 83; MagDir 84*
Ivy Press Inc. [Aff. of Ivy Financial Corp.] - Dallas, TX - *BoPubDir 4, 5*
Iwatsu America Inc. - Carlstadt, NJ - *DataDirSup 7-83*
IWP Publishing Inc. [Div. of Eckankar] - Menlo Park, CA - *LitMarPl 83, 84*
IXO Inc. - Culver City, CA - *DataDirSup 7-83; InfoS 83-84*
IZ Information Services - Falmouth, MA - *InfIndMarPl 83*
Izatt, Chuck - Costa Mesa, CA - *LitMarPl 83*

J

J & A Enterprises - Glendale, AZ - *BoPubDir 4, 5*
J & B Publishers - Taos, NM - *BoPubDir 5; LitMag&SmPr 83-84*
J & C Transcripts - Kanona, NY - *BoPubDir 4, 5*
J & C Transcripts - Garland, TX - *LitMag&SmPr 83-84*
J & J Musical Enterprises - Kings Park, NY - *BillIntBG 83-84*
J & J Publications - Traverse City, MI - *BoPubDir 4, 5*
J & J Publishing - Reseda, CA - *BoPubDir 4, 5; LitMag&SmPr 83-84*
J & K Broadcasters - La Grange, IL - *Tel&CabFB 84C*
J & K Enterprises Ltd. - Woodstock, NB, Canada - *BrCabYB 84*
J & M Systems Ltd. - Albuquerque, NM - *MicrocomMPl 83, 84*
J & N Publishing - Dollard des Ormeaux, PQ, Canada - *BoPubDir 4 Sup, 5*
J & R Film Co. - Hollywood, CA - *AvMarPl 83*
J & S Literary Services - Brooklyn, NY - *LitMarPl 83, 84*
J & S Software - Port Washington, NY - *MicrocomMPl 83, 84; MicrocomSwDir 1*
J-B Publishing Co. - Crete, NE - *BoPubDir 4, 5*
J/C Enterprises - Cocoa, FL - *MicrocomMPl 84*
J/C Enterprises - Miami, FL - *MicrocomMPl 83*
J de S Associates Inc. - South Norwalk, CT - *LitMarPl 83, 84*
J Rad Publications - Sacramento, CA - *LitMag&SmPr 83-84*
J-TEC Associates Inc. - Cedar Rapids, IA - *AvMarPl 83*
J-Tron - San Jose, CA - *DataDirSup 7-83*
JA Micropublishing Inc. - Eastchester, NY - *LitMarPl 84*
Jaap-Orr Co. - Cincinnati, OH - *StaDirAdAg 2-84*
Jabberwocky [Subs. of AVC Corp.] - Novato, CA - *AvMarPl 83*
Jablons, J. Mitchell - New York, NY - *HBIndAd&MS 82-83*
Jablonski, Andrzej - Crestwood, NY - *LitMarPl 84*
Jablonski, Andrzej - Rego Park, NY - *LitMarPl 83*
Jac Music Co. - North Hollywood, CA - *BillIntBG 83-84*
Jacek Publishing Co. - Milford, CT - *BoPubDir 4, 5*
Jack & Jill [of The Benjamin Franklin Literary & Medical Society Inc.] - Indianapolis, IN - *ArtMar 84; LitMarPl 83, 84; MagDir 84; MagIndMarPl 82-83; WritMar 84*
Jack County Herald - Jacksboro, TX - *AyerDirPub 83; Ed&PubIntYB 82*
Jack Music Inc. - Nashville, TN - *BillIntBG 83-84*
Jackaroe Music Publishers [Div. of Vanguard Recording Society Inc.] - New York, NY - *BillIntBG 83-84*
Jackinson, Alex - New York, NY - *LitMarPl 83*
Jackpine Press - Winston-Salem, NC - *BoPubDir 4, 5; LitMag&SmPr 83-84*
Jackpot Antenna Vision [of Treasure Valley Tele-Cable Inc.] - Jackpot, NV - *BrCabYB 84; Tel&CabFB 84C*
Jackpot Magazine - Poughkeepsie, NY - *BaconPubCkMag 84*
Jackrell, Thomas - Belleville, NJ - *LitMarPl 83, 84*
Jacksboro & P-K Cable TV - Jacksboro, TX - *BrCabYB 84; Tel&CabFB 84C*
Jacksboro Campbell County News - Jacksboro, TN - *BaconPubCkNews 84*
Jacksboro Gazette-News - Jacksboro, TX - *Ed&PubIntYB 82*
Jacksboro Gazette-News - *See* Herald Publishing Co.
Jacksboro Jack County Herald - *See* Herald Publishing Co.
Jackson Advocate - Jackson, MS - *BaconPubCkNews 84; Ed&PubIntYB 82; NewsDir 84*
Jackson Agency, Melanie - New York, NY - *LitMarPl 83, 84*
Jackson Amador Dispatch - *See* Goldweb Publications
Jackson Amador Ledger - *See* Goldweb Publications
Jackson & Edwards Inc. - Philadelphia, PA - *LitMag&SmPr 83-84*
Jackson Beacon Associates [Div. of LaVigne Press Incc.] - Worcester, MA - *StaDirAdAg 2-84*
Jackson Blazer - Jackson, MI - *BaconPubCkNews 84; Ed&PubIntYB 82; NewsDir 84*
Jackson-Blum Inc. - Boston, MA - *StaDirAdAg 2-84*
Jackson Cable Systems - Eaton, OH - *Tel&CabFB 84C p.1685*
Jackson Cable Systems - Oxford, OH - *Tel&CabFB 84C*
Jackson Cable TV Inc. - Clinton, LA - *Tel&CabFB 84C*
Jackson Cable TV Inc. - Kentwood, LA - *BrCabYB 84*
Jackson Cable TV Inc. [of Wometco Cable TV Inc.] - Mandeville, LA - *Tel&CabFB 84C*
Jackson Cable TV Inc. [of Tele-Communications Inc.] - Jackson, MO - *BrCabYB 84; Tel&CabFB 84C*
Jackson Cablevision Associates [of Monmouth Cablevision Associates] - Jackson, NJ - *BrCabYB 84; Tel&CabFB 84C*
Jackson Cablevision Inc. - Butts County, GA - *Tel&CabFB 84C*
Jackson Cash-Book Journal - Jackson, MO - *BaconPubCkNews 84; NewsDir 84*
Jackson Center Record - Jackson Center, OH - *Ed&PubIntYB 82*
Jackson Center Record - *See* Daily News Printing Co.
Jackson Citizen Patriot [of Booth Newspapers Inc.] - Jackson, MI - *BaconPubCkNews 84; Ed&PubIntYB 82; NewsDir 84*
Jackson Clarion-Ledger [of Mississippi Publishers Corp.] - Jackson, MS - *BaconPubCkNews 84; Ed&PubIntYB 82; NewsBur 6; NewsDir 84*
Jackson County Advertiser & Sand Mountain Booster - Scottsboro, AL - *Ed&PubIntYB 82*
Jackson County Advocate - Grandview, MO - *Ed&PubIntYB 82*
Jackson County Floridan - Marianna, FL - *BaconPubCkNews 84; Ed&PubIntYB 82*
Jackson County Historical Society - Newport, AR - *BoPubDir 4, 5*
Jackson County Livewire - Jackson, MN - *AyerDirPub 83; BaconPubCkNews 84; NewsDir 84*
Jackson County Pilot - Jackson, MN - *AyerDirPub 83; BaconPubCkNews 84; Ed&PubIntYB 82*
Jackson County Sentinel - Gainesboro, TN - *Ed&PubIntYB 82*
Jackson County Star - Walden, CO - *Ed&PubIntYB 82*
Jackson County Sun - McKee, KY - *Ed&PubIntYB 82*
Jackson County Times - Gainesboro, TN - *Ed&PubIntYB 82*
Jackson Daily News [of Mississippi Publishers Corp.] - Jackson, MS - *BaconPubCkNews 84; Ed&PubIntYB 82; LitMarPl 84; NewsBur 6; NewsDir 84*
Jackson Herald - Ripley, WV - *AyerDirPub 83; Ed&PubIntYB 82*
Jackson Herald-Banks County News - Jefferson, GA - *AyerDirPub 83*
Jackson Herald, The - Jefferson, GA - *Ed&PubIntYB 82; NewsDir 84*

Jackson Hole Cable TV [of Prime Cable Corp.] - Jackson, WY - *BrCabYB 84; Tel&CabFB 84C*
Jackson Hole Guide - Jackson, WY - *BaconPubCkNews 84; Ed&PubIntYB 82; NewsDir 84*
Jackson Hole News - Jackson, WY - *AyerDirPub 83; BaconPubCkNews 84; Ed&PubIntYB 82; NewsDir 84*
Jackson Independent - Jonesboro, LA - *AyerDirPub 83; Ed&PubIntYB 82*
Jackson, J. G. - Kentwood, LA - *Tel&CabFB 84C p.1685*
Jackson, Jackson & Wagner - Epping, NH - *DirPRFirms 83*
Jackson Journal Herald - Jackson, OH - *Ed&PubIntYB 82; NewsDir 84*
Jackson Journal-Herald - *See* Jackson Publishing Co.
Jackson Mississippi Enterprise - Jackson, MS - *BaconPubCkNews 84*
Jackson Municipal TV System - Jackson, MN - *BrCabYB 84; Tel&CabFB 84C*
Jackson, Noel - Port Saunders, NF, Canada - *BoPubDir 4 Sup, 5*
Jackson Northampton News [of Parker Bros. Inc.] - Jackson, NC - *BaconPubCkNews 84; NewsDir 84*
Jackson Northside Sun - Jackson, MS - *BaconPubCkNews 84; NewsDir 84*
Jackson Ocean County Bulletin/Jackson Bulletin - Jackson, NJ - *NewsDir 84*
Jackson Opinion Centers Inc. [Subs. of E. Friedman Marketing Services Inc.] - Jackson, MS - *IntDirMarRes 83*
Jackson Productions, Riley - Hollywood, CA - *Tel&CabFB 84C*
Jackson Progress-Argus [of Quimby Melton & Co.] - Jackson, GA - *BaconPubCkNews 84; Ed&PubIntYB 82; NewsDir 84*
Jackson Public Relations, Sally - Boston, MA - *DirPRFirms 83; HBIndAd&MS 82-83*
Jackson Publishing Co. - Jackson, OH - *BaconPubCkNews 84*
Jackson, Reggie - New Haven, CT - *LitMarPl 83, 84; MagIndMarPl 82-83*
Jackson/Ridey & Co. - Cincinnati, OH - *AdAge 3-28-84 p.112; StaDirAdAg 2-84*
Jackson South Alabamian - Jackson, AL - *BaconPubCkNews 84*
Jackson/Summers Associates Inc. - Washington, DC - *DirPRFirms 83*
Jackson Sun - Jackson, TN - *BaconPubCkNews 84; Ed&PubIntYB 82; LitMarPl 83, 84; NewsDir 84*
Jackson Symphony League [Aff. of Jackson Symphony Orchestra Association] - Jackson, MS - *BoPubDir 4, 5*
Jackson Times - Jackson, KY - *Ed&PubIntYB 82*
Jackson Times - *See* Intermountain Publishing Co.
Jacksonian, The - Cimarron, KS - *AyerDirPub 83*
Jacksonville - Jacksonville, FL - *ArtMar 84; BaconPubCkMag 84; WritMar 84*
Jacksonville Advocate - Jacksonville, FL - *Ed&PubIntYB 82*
Jacksonville Beach Leader - Jacksonville Beach, FL - *BaconPubCkNews 84; NewsDir 84*
Jacksonville Beach Sun-Times - Jacksonville Beach, FL - *BaconPubCkNews 84*
Jacksonville Cherokee County Banner - Jacksonville, TX - *BaconPubCkNews 84*
Jacksonville Courier - Jacksonville, IL - *BaconPubCkNews 84; NewsDir 84*
Jacksonville Daily News [of Canfield Publishing Co.] - Jacksonville, AR - *BaconPubCkNews 84; NewsDir 84*
Jacksonville Daily News [of Freedom Newspapers Inc.] - Jacksonville, NC - *BaconPubCkNews 84; NewsDir 84*
Jacksonville Daily Progress [of Donrey Media Group] - Jacksonville, TX - *BaconPubCkNews 84; Ed&PubIntYB 82; NewsDir 84*
Jacksonville Florida Star News - Jacksonville, FL - *BaconPubCkNews 84*
Jacksonville Florida Times-Union - Jacksonville, FL - *NewsDir 84*
Jacksonville Herald, The - Jacksonville, FL - *NewsDir 84*
Jacksonville Journal [of Florida Publishing Co.] - Jacksonville, FL - *BaconPubCkNews 84; Ed&PubIntYB 82; LitMarPl 83; NewsBur 6; NewsDir 84*
Jacksonville Journal - Jacksonville, IL - *BaconPubCkNews 84; NewsDir 84*
Jacksonville Monthly - Jacksonville, FL - *BaconPubCkMag 84*
Jacksonville News - Jacksonville, AL - *BaconPubCkNews 84; Ed&PubIntYB 82; NewsDir 84*
Jacksonville-Quincy Camera Shop Inc. - Jacksonville, IL - *AvMarPl 83*
Jacksonville Seafarer - Jacksonville, FL - *BaconPubCkMag 84; MagDir 84*
Jacksonville Southern Jewish Weekly - Jacksonville, FL - *NewsDir 84*
Jacksonville Sunday News - Jacksonville, AR - *NewsDir 84*
Jacksonville Television Cable Co. Inc. [of Vision Cable Communications Inc.] - Jacksonville, NC - *BrCabYB 84; Tel&CabFB 84C*
Jaclyn Music - Nashville, TN - *BillIntBG 83-84*
Jacobs Advertising Agency, Tevie - Indianapolis, IN - *StaDirAdAg 2-84*
Jacobs & Gerber Inc. - Los Angeles, CA - *StaDirAdAg 2-84*
Jacobs, Anna F. - Tuscaloosa, AL - *LitMarPl 84; MagIndMarPl 82-83*
Jacobs Co., The D. Baker - New York, NY - *DirPRFirms 83*
Jacobs, Daniel - San Francisco, CA - *LitMarPl 84*
Jacobs, Daniel - Seattle, WA - *LitMarPl 83*
Jacobs Instrument Co. Ltd. - Victoria, BC, Canada - *BoPubDir 4, 5*
Jacobs, Marvin - Cleveland, OH - *BoPubDir 4, 5*
Jacobs Multi Image Programming, Lance - New York, NY - *AvMarPl 83*
Jacobs Organization Inc., Joseph - New York, NY - *StaDirAdAg 2-84*
Jacobs Publishing Co. Inc. - Phoenix, AZ - *BoPubDir 4, 5*
Jacobsen & Associates Inc. - Temple City, CA - *DataDirOnSer 84*
Jacobsen & Associates, Roy - *See* Gnau, Carter, Jacobsen & Associates Inc.
Jacobsen & Co. Inc., Ellen - New York, NY - *DirPRFirms 83*
Jacobsen, Anita - Staten Island, NY - *BoPubDir 4, 5*
Jacobsohn, Peter - Wayland, MA - *LitMarPl 83; MagIndMarPl 82-83*
Jacobson Advertising - Sheboygan, WI - *AdAge 3-28-84; StaDirAdAg 2-84*
Jacobson Advertising Agency - Missoula, MT - *StaDirAdAg 2-84*
Jacobson, Altman Associates - New York, NY - *DirPRFirms 83; LitMarPl 83, 84; MagIndMarPl 82-83*
Jacobson, Helen Saltz - Setauket, NY - *LitMarPl 83, 84*
Jacobson, Jeffrey E. - New York, NY - *BillIntBG 83-84*
Jacobson, Lynda - Ranchester, WY - *Tel&CabFB 84C p.1686*
Jacobson, Robert - Ranchester, WY - *Tel&CabFB 84C p.1686*
Jacoby & Co. - Detroit, MI - *ArtMar 84; StaDirAdAg 2-84*
Jacoby/Storm Productions Inc. - Westport, CT - *ArtMar 84; AvMarPl 83*
Jacon Music/Darnoc Music - Hollywood, CA - *BillIntBG 83-84*
Jacque & Co., Jean-Guy - Hollywood, CA - *AvMarPl 83*
Jacque et Compagnie, Jean-Guy - Hollywood, CA - *WritMar 84*
Jacuzzi Music Inc. - Little Rock, AR - *BillIntBG 83-84*
Jacys Computing Services - Steyning, England - *MicrocomSwDir 1*
Jade - Los Angeles, CA - *WritMar 84*
Jade Computer Products - Hawthorne, CA - *WhoWMicrocom 83*
Jade Publications - Brantford, ON, Canada - *BoPubDir 4 Sup, 5*
Jadee Enterprises - Charleston, IL - *MicrocomMPl 84*
J'adoube! [of Cincinnati Chess Federation] - Cincinnati, OH - *LitMag&SmPr 83-84*
Jaeger Inc. - Berea, OH - *StaDirAdAg 2-84*
Jaeger Inc., Alfred - Commack, NY - *MagIndMarPl 82-83*
Jaeger, Laurence - Brooklyn, NY - *LitMarPl 83, 84; MagIndMarPl 82-83*
Jaffe Associates - Washington, DC - *ArtMar 84; DirPRFirms 83*
Jaffe, David - Arlington, VA - *BoPubDir 4, 5*
Jaffe Enterprises Inc., Henry - Los Angeles, CA - *Tel&CabFB 84C*
Jaffe Inc., Kenneth - East Orange, NJ - *StaDirAdAg 2-84*
Jaffrey Recorder & Monadnock Breeze - Jaffrey, NH - *AyerDirPub 83*
JAG Communications Inc. - New York, NY - *BrCabYB 84*
Jagdstaffel Software - San Jose, CA - *MicrocomMPl 84; WhoWMicrocom 83*
Jaggers Ozark Cable Inc. - Ozark, AR - *BrCabYB 84*
Jahn Communications - New York, NY - *DirPRFirms 83*
JAI Press Inc. - Greenwich, CT - *LitMarPl 83, 84*
Jake-Carl Publications - Opelousas, LA - *BillIntBG 83-84*

Jakeway Advertising & Public Relations, Lloyd G. - Houston, TX - *StaDirAdAg 2-84*
JAKS Publishing Co. - Helena, MT - *BoPubDir 4, 5*
Jaksa, George A. - Flint, MI - *MagIndMarPl 82-83*
Jakubowsky - Oakland, CA - *BoPubDir 4, 5*
Jal CATV Corp. [of Cable Information Systems Inc.] - Jal, NM - *BrCabYB 84; Tel&CabFB 84C*
Jal Record - Jal, NM - *AyerDirPub 83; BaconPubCkNews 84; Ed&PubIntYB 82*
Jalamap Publications Inc. - Charleston, WV - *BoPubDir 4, 5*
Jalmar Press [Div. of B. L. Winch & Associates] - Rolling Hills Estates, CA - *LitMag&SmPr 83-84; LitMarPl 83, 84; WritMar 84*
Jam-A-Ditty Records - Greensboro, NC - *BillIntBG 83-84*
Jam-Power Inc. - Northridge, CA - *BillIntBG 83-84*
Jam To-Day - Northfield, VT - *LitMag&SmPr 83-84; WritMar 84*
Jama Books - Santa Barbara, CA - *BoPubDir 4*
Jama Books - Flint, MI - *BoPubDir 5*
JAMA, The Journal of the American Medical Association - Chicago, IL - *BaconPubCkMag 84*
Jamaica New York Voice - Jamaica, NY - *NewsDir 84*
Jamaica Plain Citizen - Boston, MA - *AyerDirPub 83*
Jamaica Plain Citizen - Jamaica, MA - *Ed&PubIntYB 82*
Jamaica Tribune [of Flushing Queens Tribune] - Flushing, NY - *NewsDir 84*
Jamaka & Felco Record Co. - Mesquite, TX - *BillIntBG 83-84*
Jamar Media - Snyder, TX - *Tel&CabFB 84C p.1686*
Jambar, The [of Youngstown State University] - Youngstown, OH - *NewsDir 84*
JAME Publishing Co. - Schaumburg, IL - *BoPubDir 4, 5*
James Agency, The - Los Angeles, CA - *DirPRFirms 83*
James & Associates, L. W. - Ft. Collins, CO - *MicrocomMPl 84; MicrocomSwDir 1*
James & Law Co., The - Clarksburg, WV - *LitMarPl 83, 84*
James & Thomas Inc. - Chicago, IL - *StaDirAdAg 2-84*
James Books, Alice - Cambridge, MA - *LitMag&SmPr 83-84*
James Boy Publishing Co. - Philadelphia, PA - *BillIntBG 83-84*
James Island Journal - *See* Community Press Inc.
James Joyce Broadsheet - London, England - *LitMag&SmPr 83-84*
James Joyce Quarterly [of Academic Publications] - Tulsa, OK - *LitMag&SmPr 83-84*
James, Kay Y. - Oakland, CA - *LitMarPl 83, 84; MagIndMarPl 82-83*
James Metal Products Co. - Chicago, IL - *WhoWMicrocom 83*
James Music, Deviny - *See* Pewter Pal Music
James Music Inc., Dick - Nashville, TN - *BillIntBG 83-84*
James Press, William - Munster, IN - *BoPubDir 4, 5*
James Publishers, Jesse [Aff. of Jesse James Bank Museum] - Liberty, MO - *BoPubDir 4, 5*
James River Co. - Hackensack, NJ - *LitMarPl 83*
James River Graphics Inc. [Subs. of James River Corp.] - South Hadley, MA - *LitMarPl 83*
James S. Enterprises - Canoga Park, CA - *BillIntBG 83-84*
James, Timothy A. [Aff. of Northeast Ohio Biblical Institute] - Cortland, OH - *BoPubDir 5*
James Tri-City Intercable Inc. [of Jones Intercable Inc.] - Jefferson County, CO - *Tel&CabFB 84C*
James Valley Cooperative Telephone Co. - Groton, SD - *Tel&CabFB 84C; TelDir&BG 83-84*
Jameson Advertising - New York, NY - *AdAge 3-28-84; DirMarMP 83; LitMarPl 83, 84; MagIndMarPl 82-83; StaDirAdAg 2-84*
Jameson, E. W. Jr. - Davis, CA - *BoPubDir 4, 5*
Jamesport Tri County Weekly - Jamesport, MO - *BaconPubCkNews 84*
Jamestown Cablevision [of Quality CATV Inc.] - Jamestown, IN - *BrCabYB 84*
Jamestown Fentress County Leader-Times - Jamestown, TN - *BaconPubCkNews 84*
Jamestown Foundation Inc. - Williamsburg, VA - *BoPubDir 4*
Jamestown News - Jamestown, NC - *AyerDirPub 83; BaconPubCkNews 84*
Jamestown Post-Journal - Jamestown, NY - *BaconPubCkNews 84*
Jamestown Press - Jamestown, IN - *BaconPubCkNews 84; Ed&PubIntYB 82*
Jamestown Publishers - Providence, RI - *LitMarPl 83, 84; MicrocomMPl 84; WritMar 84*
Jamestown Russell County News - Jamestown, KY - *BaconPubCkNews 84*
Jamestown Sun [of Hansen Bros. Inc.] - Jamestown, ND - *AyerDirPub 83; BaconPubCkNews 84; Ed&PubIntYB 82; NewsDir 84*
Jamestown-Yorktown Foundation Inc. - Williamsburg, VA - *BoPubDir 5*
Jamie/Guyden Distributing Corp. - Philadelphia, PA - *BillIntBG 83-84*
Jamie, Howlett & Ranney-Public Relations - San Francisco, CA - *DirPRFirms 83*
Jamie Music Publishing Co. - Philadelphia, PA - *BillIntBG 83-84*
Jamieson & Associates Inc. - Minneapolis, MN - *TeleSy&SerDir 2-84*
Jamieson & Associates Inc. (AVSense Productions Div.) - Minneapolis, MN - *AvMarPl 83*
Jamieson Film Co. [Subs. of Kreonite Inc.] - Dallas, TX - *AvMarPl 83*
Jamil Music - Crowley, LA - *BillIntBG 83-84*
Jan Enterprises - Oaklyn, NJ - *BoPubDir 4, 5*
Janak, Tony - West Hempstead, NY - *ProGuPRSer 4*
Jando Music Inc. - *See* Jack Music Inc.
Jandon Features - Glenwood, IA - *Ed&PubIntYB 82; LitMarPl 84*
Jandon Music - *See* Trianon Publications
Jane Publications, Margoe - Malone, NY - *BoPubDir 5*
Jane Publications, Margoe - North Bangor, NY - *BoPubDir 4*
Janell Music - *See* Tiki Enterprises Inc.
Janesville Argus - Janesville, MN - *BaconPubCkNews 84; Ed&PubIntYB 82*
Janesville Gazette - Janesville, WI - *BaconPubCkNews 84; Ed&PubIntYB 82; NewsDir 84*
Janex Word Processing - Corte Madera, CA - *DirInfWP 82*
Janex Word Processing - San Francisco, CA - *DirInfWP 82*
Janik & Associates Inc. - Los Angeles, CA - *StaDirAdAg 2-84*
Janis & Co. Inc., Martin E. - Chicago, IL - *DirPRFirms 83*
Janisch Engineering - Denver, CO - *MicrocomMPl 84*
Janklow Associates, Morton - New York, NY - *LitMarPl 84*
Janney Cable TV Co. - Coal City, WV - *BrCabYB 84*
Janova Press Inc. - Cincinnati, OH - *BoPubDir 4, 5*
Jansco Records - Northridge, CA - *BillIntBG 83-84*
Jansen Associates Inc. - Santa Ana, CA - *StaDirAdAg 2-84*
Jansen Publishing - Coarsegold, CA - *BoPubDir 4, 5*
January Productions - Hawthorne, NJ - *ArtMar 84; AvMarPl 83*
Janus Book Publishers - Hayward, CA - *ArtMar 84; LitMarPl 83, 84; WritMar 84*
Janus Films Inc. - New York, NY - *Tel&CabFB 84C*
Janus Ltd. - Dublin, Iran - *StaDirAdAg 2-84*
Janus Literary Agency [Aff. of Bertha Klausner International Literary Agency] - New Haven, CT - *LitMarPl 83, 84*
Janus Press - West Burke, VT - *BoPubDir 4, 5*
Janus Publishing Co. - Vancouver, BC, Canada - *BoPubDir 4 Sup, 5*
Januz Advertising Inc. [Subs. of Januz Marketing Communications Inc.] - Lake Forest, IL - *DirMarMP 83*
Januz & Associates Inc., Lauren R. - Lake Forest, IL - *LitMarPl 84; MagIndMarPl 82-83*
Januz Direct Marketing Letter [of Januz Marketing Communications Inc.] - Lake Forest, IL - *BaconPubCkMag 84; DirMarMP 83; MagIndMarPl 82-83*
Januz Marketing Communications Inc. - Lake Forest, IL - *BoPubDir 5; LitMarPl 83*
Janzen Associates, P. - Libertyville, IL - *BoPubDir 4, 5*
Japan Association for International Chemical Information - Tokyo, Japan - *EISS 83*
Japan Data Bank [of Data Resources Inc.] - Lexington, MA - *DataDirOnSer 84*
Japan Economic Daily - New York, NY - *DirOnDB Spring 84*
Japan Economic Daily's Kyodo News [of Dow Jones News/ Retrieval Service] - Princeton, NJ - *DataDirOnSer 84*
Japan Electronics - Los Angeles, CA - *BaconPubCkMag 84*
Japan Financial [of Data Resources Inc.] - Lexington, MA - *DataDirOnSer 84*

Japan High Tech Review - Phoenix, AZ - *DirOnDB Spring 84*
Japan High Tech Review [of NewsNet Inc.] - Bryn Mawr, PA - *DataDirOnSer 84*
Japan Information Center of Science & Technology - Tokyo, Japan - *CompReadDB 82; EISS 83*
Japan Information Center of Science & Technology (Chemistry & Chemical Industry-Foreign) - Tokyo, Japan - *CompReadDB 82*
Japan Information Center of Science & Technology (Chemistry & Chemical Industry-Japanese) - Tokyo, Japan - *CompReadDB 82*
Japan Information Center of Science & Technology (Civil Engineering & Architecture) - Tokyo, Japan - *CompReadDB 82*
Japan Information Center of Science & Technology (Earth Science, Mining, & Metallurgy) - Tokyo, Japan - *CompReadDB 82*
Japan Information Center of Science & Technology (Electronics & Electrical Engineering) - Tokyo, Japan - *CompReadDB 82*
Japan Information Center of Science & Technology (Energy) - Tokyo, Japan - *CompReadDB 82*
Japan Information Center of Science & Technology (Environmental Pollution) - Tokyo, Japan - *CompReadDB 82*
Japan Information Center of Science & Technology (Management Science & Systems Engineering) - Tokyo, Japan - *CompReadDB 82*
Japan Information Center of Science & Technology (Mechanical Engineering) - Tokyo, Japan - *CompReadDB 82*
Japan Information Center of Science & Technology (Nuclear Engineering) - Tokyo, Japan - *CompReadDB 82*
Japan Information Center of Science & Technology (On-Going Research) - Tokyo, Japan - *CompReadDB 82*
Japan Information Center of Science & Technology (Pure & Applied Physics) - Tokyo, Japan - *CompReadDB 82*
Japan Information Processing Development Center - Tokyo, Japan - *ADAPSOMemDir 83-84*
Japan/MARC [of National Diet Library] - Tokyo, Japan - *CompReadDB 82*
Japan Oceanographic Data Center [of Maritime Safety Agency] - Tokyo, Japan - *EISS 83*
Japan Patent Information Center - Tokyo, Japan - *CompReadDB 82; EISS 83*
Japan Pharmaceutical Information Center - Tokyo, Japan - *EISS 5-84 Sup*
Japan Prices Data Bank [of Data Resources Inc.] - Lexington, MA - *DataDirOnSer 84*
Japan Prices Data Bank - Tokyo, Japan - *DirOnDB Spring 84*
Japan Publications Guide Service - Tokyo, Japan - *EISS 83*
Japan Software Industry Association - Tokyo, Japan - *ADAPSOMemDir 83-84*
Japan Typesetting & Graphics - New York, NY - *LitMarPl 83*
Japanese Energy Data Bank [of Data Resources Inc.] - Lexington, MA - *DataDirOnSer 84*
Japanese Journal of Applied Physics - Tokyo, Japan - *MicroMarPl 82-83*
Japanese Language Workshop - San Francisco, CA - *MagIndMarPl 82-83*
Japanese Linguistic Service - Menlo Park, CA - *MagIndMarPl 82-83*
Japanese Patent Information Service [of Japan Patent Information Center] - Tokyo, Japan - *CompReadDB 82*
Japanophile - Okemos, MI - *WritMar 84*
Japanscan [of Mitaka] - Leamington Spa, England - *EISS 5-84 Sup*
Japlin Music - *See* Jacobson, Jeffrey E.
Jaqua Co. - Grand Rapids, MI - *AdAge 3-28-84; StaDirAdAg 2-84*
Jarak Music - *See* Buttermilk Sky Music Publishing Corp.
Jargon Society, The - East Haven, CT - *LitMarPl 83, 84*
Jarman, Spitzer & Felix - New York, NY - *AdAge 3-28-84; DirPRFirms 83; StaDirAdAg 2-84*
Jarrett Co., Richard - Chicago, IL - *Ed&PubIntYB 82*
Jarrett Ltd., Irwin M. - Springfield, IL - *DataDirSup 7-83*
Jarrin Design Inc. - New York, NY - *HBIndAd&MS 82-83*
Jarvis & Partners Ltd., Michael - New York, NY - *StaDirAdAg 2-84*
Jarvis, Braff Ltd. - Staten Island, NY - *LitMarPl 83, 84*
Jarvis Corp. - Richmond, VA - *DataDirSup 7-83*
Jarvis Ltd., Albert - Toronto, ON, Canada - *StaDirAdAg 2-84*
J.A.S. Publikationen - Frankfurt, West Germany - *LitMag&SmPr 83-84*
Jasculca/Terman & Associates - Chicago, IL - *DirPRFirms 83*
Jaseppy Music - *See* Espy Music Group
Jasin Advertising - Chicopee, MA - *StaDirAdAg 2-84*
Jasmin Electronics Ltd. - Leicester, England - *VideoDir 82-83*
Jason Data Services - Mission Viejo, CA - *DataDirSup 7-83*
Jason Group - New York, NY - *AdAge 3-28-84; StaDirAdAg 2-84*
Jasonville Leader - Jasonville, IN - *BaconPubCkNews 84; Ed&PubIntYB 82*
Jaspar Music Publishing Co. - *See* International Jaspar Music Group
Jasper Booster, The - Jasper, AB, Canada - *Ed&PubIntYB 82*
Jasper Cable Contractors Ltd. - Taber, AB, Canada - *Tel&CabFB 84C*
Jasper Cablevision Inc. [of Omni Cable TV Corp.] - Monticello, GA - *Tel&CabFB 84C*
Jasper CATV - Monticello, GA - *BrCabYB 84*
Jasper County News - Bay Springs, MS - *AyerDirPub 83; Ed&PubIntYB 82*
Jasper County News - Jasper, MO - *Ed&PubIntYB 82*
Jasper County News - Ridgeland, SC - *Ed&PubIntYB 82*
Jasper County Tribune - Colfax, IA - *Ed&PubIntYB 82*
Jasper Enterprises Inc. - Jasper, IN - *Tel&CabFB 84C*
Jasper Herald - Jasper, IN - *BaconPubCkNews 84; NewsDir 84*
Jasper Journal - Jasper, MN - *BaconPubCkNews 84; Ed&PubIntYB 82; NewsDir 84*
Jasper Journal - Jasper, TN - *BaconPubCkNews 84; Ed&PubIntYB 82; NewsDir 84*
Jasper Mountain Eagle - Jasper, AL - *BaconPubCkNews 84; NewsDir 84*
Jasper News - Jasper, FL - *BaconPubCkNews 84; Ed&PubIntYB 82*
Jasper News Boy [of The Enterprise Co.] - Jasper, TX - *BaconPubCkNews 84; NewsDir 84*
Jasper Newton County Times - Jasper, AR - *BaconPubCkNews 84*
Jasper Pickens County Progress - Jasper, GA - *BaconPubCkNews 84*
Jasper TV Cable System - Jasper, AR - *BrCabYB 84; Tel&CabFB 84C*
Jasper Video - Jasper, NY - *BrCabYB 84; Tel&CabFB 84C*
JATEX Inc. - Dallas, TX - *AvMarPl 83*
Jausch's Mule - *See* Kicking Mule Publishing Inc.
Java Herald - Java, SD - *Ed&PubIntYB 82*
Java Herald - Selby, SD - *AyerDirPub 83*
Java Herald - *See* Selby Record Publishers
Javelin Electronics Inc. [Subs. of Kidde Inc.] - Torrance, CA - *AvMarPl 83*
Javorsky, Henry V. - Holliswood, NY - *AvMarPl 83*
Jawbone Press - Seattle, WA - *BoPubDir 4*
Jawbone Press - Waldron Island, WA - *BoPubDir 5; LitMag&SmPr 83-84*
Jax Fax Travel Marketing - Darien, CT - *BaconPubCkMag 84; MagDir 84; MagIndMarPl 82-83*
Jax Interconnect - Jacksonville, FL - *CabTVPrDB 83*
Jay Advertising Inc. - Rochester, NY - *StaDirAdAg 2-84*
Jay/Barr Advertising Inc. - Evanston, IL - *StaDirAdAg 2-84*
Jay Bee Magazine Stores Inc. - New York, NY - *MagIndMarPl 82-83; ProGuPRSer 4*
Jay Corp. - Chicago, IL - *DataDirSup 7-83*
Jay Delaware County Journal - Jay, OK - *BaconPubCkNews 84*
Jay Inc. - New York, NY - *Tel&CabFB 84C*
Jay Jay Record & Tape Co. - Miami, FL - *BillIntBG 83-84*
Jay Press, John - New York, NY - *BoPubDir 4, 5*
Jay Publications - San Andreas, CA - *BoPubDir 4, 5*
Jay Six Publishing Co. - Harwich Port, MA - *BillIntBG 83-84*
Jayan Film Productions - Atlanta, GA - *Tel&CabFB 84C*
Jayco Publishing Co. - South Bend, IN - *BoPubDir 4, 5*
Jaylet Co. - Bloomfield, CT - *MicrocomMPl 83, 84*
Jayme Organization Inc., The - Beachwood, OH - *AdAge 3-28-84*
Jayme Organization Inc., The - Cleveland, OH - *StaDirAdAg 2-84*
Jaymore Music - Brighton, MI - *BillIntBG 83-84*
Jaynes, Thomas L. - Miami, FL - *BoPubDir 4, 5*
Jayton Cablevision - Jayton, TX - *BrCabYB 84*
Jayton Chronicle - Jayton, TX - *BaconPubCkNews 84; Ed&PubIntYB 82*
Jazz - Boulder Creek, CA - *LitMag&SmPr 83-84*
Jazz America Marketing - Washington, DC - *BillIntBG 83-84*
Jazz Archives Inc. - New York, NY - *BillIntBG 83-84*

Jazz Composer's Orchestra Association Inc. - New York, NY - *BillIntBG 83-84*
Jazz Discographies Unltd. - Laurel, MD - *BoPubDir 4, 5*
Jazz Hounds Records - Los Gatos, CA - *BillIntBG 83-84*
Jazz Press - Boulder Creek, CA - *BoPubDir 4, 5*
Jazz Press - Santa Cruz, CA - *LitMag&SmPr 83-84*
Jazz Times - Silver Spring, MD - *DirMarMP 83*
Jazzology-GHB Records - Decatur, GA - *BillIntBG 83-84*
JB Papers Inc. - Union, NJ - *LitMarPl 83, 84; MagIndMarPl 82-83*
JBA/Westec - San Diego, CA - *TeleSy&SerDir 7-83*
JBHS Associates Inc. - New York, NY - *StaDirAdAg 2-84*
J.B.N. Telephone Co. Inc. - Wetmore, KS - *TelDir&BG 83-84*
J.C. Datatron - Massapequa, NY - *MicrocomMPl 83*
JC/DC Cartoons Ink - Salem, OR - *BoPubDir 4, 5*
JC Music Co. - *See* Jac Music Co. Inc.
J.C. Printing Co. - College Park, GA - *BoPubDir 4, 5*
JC Systems - Milpitas, CA - *MicrocomMPl 84*
JCA Literary Agency Inc. - New York, NY - *LitMarPl 83, 84*
JCF Press - Montreal, PQ, Canada - *LitMag&SmPr 83-84*
JCI Data Processing Inc. - Philadelphia, PA - *MagIndMarPl 82-83*
JCM - Hollywood, CA - *BillIntBG 83-84*
JCO-Journal of Clinical Orthodontics - Boulder, CO - *BaconPubCkMag 84*
JCPDS International Centre for Diffraction Data - Swarthmore, PA - *EISS 83*
JD Associates - Upland, CA - *DirInfWP 82*
J.D. Press - San Diego, CA - *BoPubDir 4, 5*
JDC Records - San Pedro, CA - *BillIntBG 83-84*
JDL Features - Boca Raton, FL - *Ed&PubIntYB 82*
JDM Inc. - Seattle, WA - *StaDirAdAg 2-84*
JDM International - London, England - *StaDirAdAg 2-84*
Jean & Trox - Tempe, AZ - *AvMarPl 83*
Jeanerette Enterprise [of Teche Publishing Co. Inc.] - Jeanerette, LA - *BaconPubCkNews 84; Ed&PubIntYB 82; NewsDir 84*
Jeanne's Dreams - LaFarge, WI - *BoPubDir 4, 5*
Jeannette News-Dispatch - Jeannette, PA - *NewsDir 84*
Jeannette Spirit, The [of The Laurel Group Press] - Jeannette, PA - *NewsDir 84*
Jean's Dulcimer Shop - Cosby, TN - *BillIntBG 83-84*
J.E.D. Productions Corp. - New York, NY - *Tel&CabFB 84C*
Jedick Enterprises, Peter - Cleveland, OH - *BoPubDir 4, 5*
Jednota [of First Catholic Slovak Union] - Middletown, PA - *Ed&PubIntYB 82; NewsDir 84*
JEDO Music - Woodland Hills, CA - *BillIntBG 83-84*
Jeff Davis County Ledger - Hazlehurst, GA - *AyerDirPub 83; Ed&PubIntYB 82*
Jeffco Industries Inc. - Middlesex, NJ - *DirInfWP 82*
Jeffco Publications - Golden, CO - *BaconPubCkNews 84*
Jeffcoat Schoen & Morrell Inc. - New York, NY - *DirPRFirms 83*
Jeffers/Carr Associates - New York, NY - *BoPubDir 4 Sup, 5*
Jefferson Banner - Jefferson, WI - *BaconPubCkNews 84; Ed&PubIntYB 82*
Jefferson Bee - Jefferson, IA - *Ed&PubIntYB 82; NewsDir 84*
Jefferson Bee - *See* Bee & Herald Publishing Co.
Jefferson Business - Gretna, LA - *BaconPubCkMag 84*
Jefferson Business - Metairie, LA - *WritMar 84*
Jefferson Cable [Div. of Multi Channel TV Cable Co.] - Albemarle County, VA - *BrCabYB 84*
Jefferson Cable [of Multi-Channel TV Cable Co.] - Charlottesville, VA - *BrCabYB 84; Tel&CabFB 84C*
Jefferson Cable [of Multi-Channel TV Cable Co.] - Waynesboro, VA - *BrCabYB 84; Tel&CabFB 84C*
Jefferson City Capital News - Jefferson City, MO - *BaconPubCkNews 84; NewsDir 84*
Jefferson City Catholic Missourian, The [of Diocese of Jefferson City] - Jefferson City, MO - *NewsDir 84*
Jefferson City County Standard Banner - Jefferson City, TN - *BaconPubCkNews 84*
Jefferson City Post-Tribune - Jefferson City, MO - *BaconPubCkNews 84*
Jefferson City Standard Banner - Jefferson City, TN - *NewsDir 84*
Jefferson Communications Inc. - Reston, VA - *Ed&PubIntYB 82*
Jefferson County Cable Corp. [of Fund I Ltd. Partnership] - Meriden, KS - *Tel&CabFB 84C*
Jefferson County Cable Corp. [of Fund I Ltd. Partnership] - Oskaloosa, KS - *BrCabYB 84; Tel&CabFB 84C*
Jefferson County Cable Corp. [of Fund I Ltd. Partnership] - Ozawkie, KS - *Tel&CabFB 84C*
Jefferson County Cable Corp. [of Fund I Ltd. Partnership] - Tonganoxie, KS - *Tel&CabFB 84C*
Jefferson County Democrat-Rocket - Festus, MO - *BaconPubCkNews 84; Ed&PubIntYB 82*
Jefferson County Journal - Arnold, MO - *Ed&PubIntYB 82*
Jefferson County Journal [of St. Louis Suburban Newspapers Inc.] - St. Louis, MO - *AyerDirPub 83; NewsDir 84*
Jefferson County Journal - Adams, NY - *AyerDirPub 83; Ed&PubIntYB 82*
Jefferson County Journal - *See* St. Louis Suburban Newspapers Inc.
Jefferson County Record - Festus, MO - *AyerDirPub 83*
Jefferson County Shopper [of Golden Jeffco Publications Inc.] - Golden, CO - *NewsDir 84*
Jefferson County Star, The - Rigby, ID - *Ed&PubIntYB 82*
Jefferson County Union - Ft. Atkinson, WI - *AyerDirPub 83*
Jefferson Democrat - Gretna, LA - *AyerDirPub 83; Ed&PubIntYB 82*
Jefferson Gazette - Jefferson, OH - *NewsDir 84*
Jefferson Gazette & Sentinel - Jefferson, OH - *BaconPubCkNews 84*
Jefferson Herald - Jefferson, IA - *Ed&PubIntYB 82; NewsDir 84*
Jefferson Herald - *See* Bee & Herald Publishing Co.
Jefferson Jackson Herald - Jefferson, GA - *BaconPubCkNews 84*
Jefferson Jimplecute - Jefferson, TX - *BaconPubCkNews 84; Ed&PubIntYB 82*
Jefferson Law Book Co. [Aff. of Anderson Publishing Co.] - Washington, DC - *BoPubDir 4, 5*
Jefferson, Louise E. - Litchfield, CT - *LitMarPl 83, 84*
Jefferson-Mayfair Times - Chicago, IL - *AyerDirPub 83; Ed&PubIntYB 82*
Jefferson National Expansion Historical Association [Aff. of Jefferson National Expansion Memorial] - St. Louis, MO - *BillIntBG 83-84; BoPubDir 4, 5*
Jefferson-Norwood News - Chicago, IL - *AyerDirPub 83*
Jefferson Parish Times - Metairie, LA - *Ed&PubIntYB 82*
Jefferson Park Leader [of Chicago Leader Newspapers-Leader Papers Inc.] - Chicago, IL - *AyerDirPub 83; NewsDir 84*
Jefferson Park Passage - Chicago, IL - *AyerDirPub 83*
Jefferson-Pilot Broadcasting Co. [Subs. of Jefferson-Pilot Corp.] - Charlotte, NC - *BrCabYB 84; Tel&CabFB 84S*
Jefferson-Pilot Corp. - Greensboro, NC - *AdAge 6-28-84; BrCabYB 84; Ed&PubIntYB 82; HomeVid&CabYB 82-83; KnowInd 83*
Jefferson Productions - Charlotte, NC - *Tel&CabFB 84C*
Jefferson Reporter - Wrens, GA - *AyerDirPub 83; Ed&PubIntYB 82*
Jefferson Republic [of Marten Publications Inc.] - De Soto, MO - *AyerDirPub 83; Ed&PubIntYB 82; NewsDir 84*
Jefferson Research Center, Thomas - Pasadena, CA - *BoPubDir 4, 5*
Jefferson Review - Jefferson, OR - *BaconPubCkNews 84; Ed&PubIntYB 82*
Jefferson Standard-Banner - Jefferson City, TN - *Ed&PubIntYB 82*
Jefferson Star - Rigby, ID - *AyerDirPub 83; NewsDir 84*
Jefferson Star - *See* Standard-Journal Inc.
Jefferson Telephone Co. - Jefferson, IA - *TelDir&BG 83-84*
Jefferson Telephone Co. Inc. - Jefferson, SD - *TelDir&BG 83-84*
Jefferson Times - West Jefferson, NC - *AyerDirPub 83; Ed&PubIntYB 82*
Jefferson TV Cable Co. Inc. [of Adelphia Communications Corp.] - Reynoldsville, PA - *BrCabYB 84; Tel&CabFB 84C*
Jeffersonian - Cambridge, OH - *AyerDirPub 83*
Jeffersonian - Pryor, OK - *AyerDirPub 83*
Jeffersonian/Advisor - Croswell, MI - *AyerDirPub 83*
Jeffersonian Democrat [of The McMurray Co.] - Brookville, PA - *AyerDirPub 83; Ed&PubIntYB 82; NewsDir 84*
Jeffersonian, The [of Scripps-Howard Newspapers] - Louisville, KY - *AyerDirPub 83; NewsDir 84*

Jeffersonian, The - Towson, MD - *AyerDirPub 83; Ed&PubIntYB 82*
Jeffersonville Clark County Journal - Jeffersonville, IN - *BaconPubCkNews 84*
Jeffersonville News - Jeffersonville, IN - *BaconPubCkNews 84; NewsDir 84*
Jeffersonville Twiggs County New Era - Jeffersonville, GA - *BaconPubCkNews 84*
Jeffery City Cable TV [of Dubois CATV Inc.] - Jeffrey City, WY - *BrCabYB 84*
Jeffress Advertising Pty. Ltd., Neville - Sydney, Australia - *StaDirAdAg 2-84*
Jeffrey Alan Group Ltd. - New York, NY - *StaDirAdAg 2-84*
Jeffrey City Cable TV [of Dubois CATV Inc.] - Jeffrey City, WY - *Tel&CabFB 84C*
Jeffrey Precision Color - Ft. Wayne, IN - *AvMarPl 83*
Jeffries Report, The - Santa Barbara, CA - *BaconPubCkMag 84*
Jeffry, Alix - New York, NY - *MagIndMarPl 82-83*
Jefren Publishing Co. - San Diego, CA - *BoPubDir 4*
Jefren Publishing Co. - Rockville, MD - *BoPubDir 5*
Jefsteel Business Equipment Co. - Ridgewood, NY - *DirInfWP 82*
JEKCU Inc. - New York, NY - *EISS 83*
Jellico Advance Sentinel - Jellico, TN - *BaconPubCkNews 84*
Jellico Advance Sentinel [of La Follette Press Inc.] - La Follette, TN - *NewsDir 84*
Jellico Cablevision [of V-R Corp.] - Jellico, TN - *BrCabYB 84; Tel&CabFB 84C*
Jelm Mountain Press/West - Modesto, CA - *LitMag&SmPr 83-84*
Jelm Mountain Publications - Laramie, WY - *BoPubDir 4, 5; LitMag&SmPr 83-84*
JEM Associates - Herndon, VA - *DataDirSup 7-83*
JEM Co. - San Francisco, CA - *WhoWMicrocom 83*
Jemiah Publishing - Columbia, SC - *BillIntBG 83-84*
Jemta Press - Redford, MI - *BoPubDir 4, 5*
Jena Times Olla-Tullos Signal - Jena, LA - *Ed&PubIntYB 82; NewsDir 84*
Jena Times-Signal - Jena, LA - *BaconPubCkNews 84*
Jende-Hagan Bookcorp - Frederick, CO - *LitMarPl 83, 84*
Jenel Consultants Corp. - Dallas, TX - *InterCabHB 3; TeleSy&SerDir 2-84*
Jenin Inc. - Brattleboro, VT - *LitMag&SmPr 83-84*
Jenison Grand Valley Advance - Jenison, MI - *BaconPubCkNews 84*
Jenkins Advertising Inc., William - Philadelphia, PA - *StaDirAdAg 2-84*
Jenkins & Associates Inc., T. S. - Flint, MI - *AdAge 3-28-84; StaDirAdAg 2-84*
Jenkins, Doris - Lincoln, NE - *BoPubDir 4, 5*
Jenkins, Dorothy - Rye, NY - *HBIndAd&MS 82-83*
Jenkins Television Co. - Jenkins, KY - *BrCabYB 84; Tel&CabFB 84C*
Jenkintown Times Chronicle - *See* Montgomery Publishing Co.
Jenks Journal [of McWilliams Publications Inc.] - Broken Arrow, OK - *NewsDir 84*
Jenks Journal - Jenks, OK - *BaconPubCkNews 84; Ed&PubIntYB 82*
Jenner, Page - Kirkland, WA - *Tel&CabFB 84C p.1686*
Jenniejohn Music - Milwaukee, WI - *BillIntBG 83-84*
Jennifer Music Inc. - *See* Croma Music Co. Inc.
Jennings Daily News [of Newspaper Service Co. Inc.] - Jennings, LA - *BaconPubCkNews 84; Ed&PubIntYB 82; NewsDir 84*
Jensen & Ritchie Advertising Inc. - Los Angeles, CA - *StaDirAdAg 2-84*
Jensen Beach Mirror - Jensen Beach, FL - *BaconPubCkNews 84; Ed&PubIntYB 82*
Jensen Engineering Inc. - Santa Rosa, CA - *DirInfWP 82*
Jensen Farley Pictures Inc. - Salt Lake City, UT - *Tel&CabFB 84C*
Jensen Software - Happy, TX - *MicrocomMPl 84*
Jensen Sound Laboratories (Home Electronic Div.) - Schiller Park, IL - *BillIntBG 83-84*
Jensing/Jensong Music - Nashville, TN - *BillIntBG 83-84*
Jenson Publications Inc. - New Berlin, WI - *BillIntBG 83-84*
Jeopardy [of Western Washington University] - Bellingham, WA - *LitMag&SmPr 83-84*
Jepalana Music - *See* Print Music Co. Inc.
Jeppesen-Sanderson - Englewood, CO - *LitMarPl 83*
Jepson-Murray Advertising [Div. of AVISO Inc.] - Lansing, MI - *StaDirAdAg 2-84*
Jeree Records - New Brighton, PA - *BillIntBG 83-84*
Jeremiah Records Inc. - Hendersonville, TN - *BillIntBG 83-84*
Jericho Book Manufacturing Corp. [Div. of Exposition Press] - Smithtown, NY - *LitMarPl 83, 84*
Jericho News Journal - Hicksville, NY - *AyerDirPub 83*
Jericho News-Journal - Jericho, NY - *Ed&PubIntYB 82*
Jericho News Journal - *See* Litmore Publications
Jericho Tribune - *See* Mid-Island Herald Publishers
Jericho Tribune, The - Jericho, NY - *Ed&PubIntYB 82*
Jerico Cable TV Inc. - Oswego, KS - *Tel&CabFB 84C p.1686*
JerJoy Music [Div. of Universal-Athena Records] - Peoria, IL - *BillIntBG 83-84*
Jerlil Publishing Co. - Bakersfield, CA - *BillIntBG 83-84*
Jerma Records Co. - Chicago, IL - *BillIntBG 83-84*
Jernigan's Motion Picture Service - Gainesville, FL - *AvMarPl 83*
Jero Ltd. Publishing - Milwaukee, WI - *BillIntBG 83-84*
Jeroboam Inc. - San Francisco, CA - *LitMarPl 83, 84; MagIndMarPl 82-83*
Jerome North Side News [of Standard Humines Publishing Co.] - Jerome, ID - *BaconPubCkNews 84; NewsDir 84*
Jerome Productions Inc., Jerry - North Hills, NY - *Tel&CabFB 84C*
Jerri Mick Music - *See* JMR Enterprises
Jerryend Communications Inc. - Birdsboro, PA - *ArtMar 84; DirPRFirms 83*
Jersey Business Review [of Creative Research Group Inc.] - Ramsey, NJ - *MagDir 84*
Jersey City News - Jersey City, NJ - *Ed&PubIntYB 82*
Jersey City News & Greenville News - Fairview, NJ - *AyerDirPub 83*
Jersey City News & Greenville News - *See* West New Yorker Inc.
Jersey Coast Agents Ltd. - West Keansburg, NJ - *BillIntBG 83-84*
Jersey County American - Alton, IL - *AyerDirPub 83*
Jersey Journal [of Evening Journal Association] - Jersey City, NJ - *AyerDirPub 83; BaconPubCkNews 84; Ed&PubIntYB 82; LitMarPl 83, 84; NewsDir 84*
Jersey Journal - Columbus, OH - *BaconPubCkMag 84; MagDir 84*
Jersey Pictorial [of West New Yorker Inc.] - Fairview, NJ - *NewsDir 84*
Jersey Pictorial - North Bergen, NJ - *Ed&PubIntYB 82*
Jersey Pictorial - *See* West New Yorker Inc.
Jersey Pictorial/North Bergen Free Press - Fairview, NJ - *AyerDirPub 83*
Jersey Printing Co. - Bayonne, NJ - *LitMarPl 83, 84; MagIndMarPl 82-83*
Jersey Tab Card Corp. - Union, NJ - *DirInfWP 82*
Jerseyville Democrat News - Jerseyville, IL - *BaconPubCkNews 84*
Jerseyville Jersey County American - *See* Alton Citizen Inc.
Jervis & Associates Inc., Wayne Jr. - Los Angeles, CA - *HBIndAd&MS 82-83*
Jeryl Lynn Music - *See* Coyote Productions Inc.
J.E.S. Graphics - Tulsa, OK - *MicrocomMPl 84*
JesFine Music - Utica, MI - *BillIntBG 83-84*
Jesperson Press - St. John's, NF, Canada - *BoPubDir 4, 5*
Jessamine Journal - Nicholasville, KY - *AyerDirPub 83; Ed&PubIntYB 82*
Jessyca Russell Gaver Newsletter - Metuchen, NJ - *LitMarPl 83, 84*
Jesuit Books - Seattle, WA - *BoPubDir 4, 5*
Jesup Broadcasting Corp. - Jesup, GA - *BrCabYB 84*
Jesup Citizen Herald - Jesup, IA - *BaconPubCkNews 84*
Jesus-First Publishers Inc. - Ruskin, FL - *BoPubDir 4, 5*
Jet [of Johnson Publishing Co. Inc.] - Chicago, IL - *BaconPubCkMag 84; Folio 83; LitMarPl 83, 84; MagDir 84; MagIndMarPl 82-83; NewsBur 6; WritMar 84*
Jet Cargo News [of Cordovan Corp.] - Houston, TX - *BaconPubCkMag 84; MagDir 84; MagIndMarPl 82-83; WritMar 84*
Jet-Eye Music Inc. - Utica, MI - *BillIntBG 83-84*
Jet Gazette - Austin, TX - *AyerDirPub 83*
JET Literary Associates Inc. - New York, NY - *LitMarPl 83, 84*

Jet Messenger Service Inc. - New York, NY - *MagIndMarPl 82-83*
Jet Records Inc. - Beverly Hills, CA - *BillIntBG 83-84*
Jet Stone News - Dayton, OH - *AyerDirPub 83*
Jet Visitor, The - Jet, OK - *Ed&PubIntYB 82*
Jetaway - Auckland, New Zealand - *ArtMar 84*
Jethro Publications - Frenchtown, NJ - *BoPubDir 4 Sup, 5*
Jet'iquette - Charlevoix, MI - *BoPubDir 4, 5*
Jetmore Republican - Jetmore, KS - *BaconPubCkNews 84; Ed&PubIntYB 82*
Jetmore Telephone Co. Inc. [Aff. of Sunflower Telephone Co. Inc.] - Dodge City, IA - *TelDir&BG 83-84*
Jetsand Publishers Ltd. - West Hartford, CT - *BoPubDir 4, 5*
Jetstone News - Dayton, OH - *Ed&PubIntYB 82*
Jett Advertising Agency - West Hollywood, CA - *StaDirAdAg 2-84*
Jett Press - Flint, MI - *LitMag&SmPr 83-84*
Jetzer, Moberg, Kurpris & Associates Inc. - Grand Rapids, MI - *LitMarPl 84*
Jevert Music - Columbus, OH - *BillIntBG 83-84*
Jewel Music Publishing Co. Inc. - *See* Goodman Group, The
Jewel Publications - Ft. Wayne, IN - *BoPubDir 4, 5*
Jewel Record Corp. - Shreveport, LA - *BillIntBG 83-84*
Jewel Recording Co. - Cincinnati, OH - *BillIntBG 83-84*
Jeweler/Gem Business - El Sobrante, CA - *BaconPubCkMag 84*
Jewelers' Circular-Keystone [Aff. of Chilton Co.] - Radnor, PA - *BaconPubCkMag 84; BoPubDir 4, 5*
Jewell County Record - Mankato, KS - *AyerDirPub 83; Ed&PubIntYB 82*
Jewell County Republican - Jewell, KS - *BaconPubCkNews 84; Ed&PubIntYB 82*
Jewell Record/News - Jewell, IA - *Ed&PubIntYB 82*
Jewell South Hamilton Record-News - Jewell, IA - *BaconPubCkNews 84*
Jewellery World - Toronto, ON, Canada - *BaconPubCkMag 84*
Jewelry Appraiser, The - Scottsdale, AZ - *BaconPubCkMag 84*
Jewelry Making, Gems & Minerals - Mentone, CA - *BaconPubCkMag 84; MagDir 84*
Jewelry Newsletter International - Houston, TX - *BaconPubCkMag 84*
Jewelry Workers Bulletin [of Jewelry Workers Union Local #1-J] - New York, NY - *NewsDir 84*
Jewett Messenger - Jewett, TX - *BaconPubCkNews 84; Ed&PubIntYB 82*
Jewish Advocate - Boston, MA - *AyerDirPub 83; NewsDir 84*
Jewish Book Club, The [Div. of Jason Aronson Inc.] - New York, NY - *LitMarPl 83, 84*
Jewish Braille Institute of America Inc. - New York, NY - *LitMarPl 83, 84*
Jewish Chautauqua Society, The - New York, NY - *Tel&CabFB 84C*
Jewish Chronicle Leader - Worcester, MA - *AyerDirPub 83*
Jewish Chronicle Ltd. - London, England - *MicroMarPl 82-83*
Jewish Current Events - Elmont, NY - *ArtMar 84*
Jewish Currents - New York, NY - *BoPubDir 4 Sup, 5; LitMag&SmPr 83-84; MagIndMarPl 82-83*
Jewish Daily Forward - New York, NY - *AyerDirPub 83; Ed&PubIntYB 82*
Jewish Eagle-Kanader Adfer - Montreal, PQ, Canada - *Ed&PubIntYB 82*
Jewish Exponent - Philadelphia, PA - *MagDir 84*
Jewish Floridian - Miami, FL - *AyerDirPub 83*
Jewish Herald - Pawtucket, RI - *AyerDirPub 83*
Jewish Historical Society of New York Inc. - New York, NY - *BoPubDir 4, 5*
Jewish Journal [of Worrell Publications] - Ft. Lauderdale, FL - *NewsDir 84*
Jewish Ledger - Rochester, NY - *AyerDirPub 83*
Jewish Monthly, The [of B'nai B'rith International] - Washington, DC - *LitMarPl 83, 84; WritMar 84*
Jewish News - Southfield, MI - *AyerDirPub 83*
Jewish News - East Orange, NJ - *AyerDirPub 83; NewsDir 84*
Jewish News - Cleveland, OH - *AyerDirPub 83*
Jewish People - New York, NY - *MagDir 84*
Jewish Post - Winnipeg, MB, Canada - *AyerDirPub 83; Ed&PubIntYB 82*
Jewish Post & Opinion [of National Jewish Post Inc.] - Indianapolis, IN - *BaconPubCkMag 84; WritMar 84*
Jewish Post of New York, The - New York, NY - *MagDir 84*
Jewish Press - Omaha, NE - *AyerDirPub 83*
Jewish Press - Brooklyn, NY - *AyerDirPub 83; BaconPubCkMag 84*
Jewish Publication Society of America - Philadelphia, PA - *LitMarPl 84*
Jewish Reconstructionist Foundation - New York, NY - *BoPubDir 4, 5*
Jewish Record - Atlantic City, NJ - *AyerDirPub 83*
Jewish Review - Buffalo, NY - *AyerDirPub 83*
Jewish Standard, The - Jersey City, NJ - *AyerDirPub 83*
Jewish Telegraphic Agency Inc. - New York, NY - *Ed&PubIntYB 82*
Jewish Television Network - Los Angeles, CA - *AvMarPl 83; BrCabYB 84; Tel&CabFB 84C*
Jewish Times - Baltimore, MD - *ArtMar 84*
Jewish Times - Brookline, MA - *AyerDirPub 83*
Jewish Times - Philadelphia, PA - *AyerDirPub 83*
Jewish Week - Washington, DC - *AyerDirPub 83*
Jewish Week - New York, NY - *AyerDirPub 83*
Jewish Western Bulletin - Vancouver, BC, Canada - *AyerDirPub 83; Ed&PubIntYB 82*
Jezreel Inc. - Highland Park, IL - *BillIntBG 83-84*
J.F.P. & Associates Inc. - Duluth, MN - *DirPRFirms 83; StaDirAdAg 2-84*
JFR Communications Engineering - Middletown, NJ - *VideoDir 82-83*
J.G. Furniture [Div. of Burlington Industries] - Quakerstown, PA - *DirInfWP 82*
JG Press Inc. - Emmaus, PA - *BoPubDir 4, 5*
JH Press - New York, NY - *BoPubDir 4, 5; LitMag&SmPr 83-84; WritMar 84*
JHM Corp. - Indianapolis, IN - *MagIndMarPl 82-83*
JIA Management Corp. - Los Angeles, CA - *DirInfWP 82*
Jibaro Music Co. Inc. - Mt. Clemens, MI - *BillIntBG 83-84*
Jiffy Packaging Corp. - Murray Hill, NJ - *LitMarPl 83, 84*
Jiji Press - New York, NY - *Ed&PubIntYB 82*
Jillean Music Inc. - *See* Gopam Enterprises Inc.
Jiloty, Shipley & Associates - Holly Hill, FL - *AdAge 3-28-84; StaDirAdAg 2-84*
Jim Hogg County Enterprise - Hebbronville, TX - *AyerDirPub 83*
Jimboco Records - New York, NY - *BillIntBG 83-84*
Jimplecute - Jefferson, TX - *AyerDirPub 83*
Jimplicute, The - Scott City, MO - *AyerDirPub 83*
Jimscot Inc. - Liberal, KS - *MicrocomMPl 84*
Jini Micro-Systems Inc. - Riverdale, NY - *MicrocomMPl 83, 84; WhoWMicrocom 83*
Jinro Publishing Co. - Kansas City, MO - *BoPubDir 5*
Jiru Music Inc. - New York, NY - *BillIntBG 83-84*
JIW Needham Ltd. - *See* Needham, Harper & Steers Inc.
J.J. & L. Research Co. - Philadelphia, PA - *IntDirMarRes 83*
JJ Publishing - Hollywood, FL - *BoPubDir 4, 5*
JJV Associates - Syracuse, NY - *BoPubDir 4, 5*
JKL Entertainment Productions - Minneapolis, MN - *BillIntBG 83-84*
JL Media Inc. - Union, NJ - *StaDirAdAg 2-84*
JL Works - Newport Beach, CA - *LitMarPl 83, 84*
JLA Publications [Aff. of Jeffrey Lant Associates Inc.] - Cambridge, MA - *BoPubDir 4 Sup, 5*
JLB Systems Inc. - Portland, OR - *MicrocomSwDir 1*
JLJ Publishers - Springfield, OH - *BoPubDir 4 Sup, 5*
JLR Publications [Aff. of Junior League of Rochester Inc.] - Rochester, NY - *BoPubDir 4 Sup, 5*
JLS Language Associates - Menlo Park, CA - *LitMarPl 83, 84*
JLS Language Associates - Redwood City, CA - *EISS 5-84 Sup*
JLTC & Associates - Tucson, AZ - *DirPRFirms 83*
JM Associates - Chicago, IL - *MagIndMarPl 82-83*
JM Production Co. - San Francisco, CA - *Tel&CabFB 84C*
JM Productions - Brentwood, TN - *BoPubDir 4 Sup, 5*
JM Productions Ltd. - Chicago, IL - *LitMarPl 83*
JMB Publications - Louisville, KY - *BoPubDir 4 Sup, 5*
JMC Software Distributors - Bensenville, IL - *MicrocomMPl 84*
JMH Corp. - Indianapolis, IN - *LitMarPl 83, 84; MagIndMarPl 82-83*
JMH Records - Madison, TN - *BillIntBG 83-84*

JMH Software of Minnesota Inc. - Maple Grove, MN - *MicrocomMPl 84*
JMH Software of Minnesota Inc. - Minneapolis, MN - *MicrocomMPl 83*
JMI Software Consultants Inc. [Subs. of Joffe Marketing International] - Roslyn, PA - *MicrocomMPl 84; MicrocomSwDir 1; WhoWMicrocom 83*
JML Enterprises - Albuquerque, NM - *BoPubDir 4, 5*
J.M.O. Publishing Co. Inc. - New York, NY - *BoPubDir 5*
JMP Videoconference Group [of Jack Morton Productions Inc.] - New York, NY - *TeleSy&SerDir 2-84*
JMR Electronics Inc. - Northridge, CA - *MicrocomMPl 84*
JMR Enterprises - Nashville, TN - *BillIntBG 83-84*
JMT Publications - Camp Hill, PA - *BoPubDir 5*
JNS Communications Inc. [Div. of Transtar Productions Inc.] - Englewood, CO - *AvMarPl 83*
Jo-Cee Publishing Co. - *See* Su-Ma Publishing Co. Inc.
Jo-Jo Publications - Chesapeake, VA - *BoPubDir 4, 5*
Jo-Wee Publishing - Winston-Salem, NC - *BillIntBG 83-84*
Joanna Western Mills Co. (Bookcover Materials Div.) - Kingsport, TN - *LitMarPl 83, 84*
Job Mart Inc. - New York, NY - *LitMarPl 83, 84; MagIndMarPl 82-83*
Job Safety & Health - Washington, DC - *MagDir 84*
Job Scope [of Carlson Publications Inc.] - Bethlehem, CT - *BaconPubCkMag 84; MagDir 84*
Job Shop, The - Woods Hole, MA - *LitMarPl 83, 84*
Jobber & Warehouse Executive [of Hunter Publishing Co.] - Des Plaines, IL - *BaconPubCkMag 84; MagDir 84; MagIndMarPl 82-83*
Jobber News - Toronto, ON, Canada - *BaconPubCkMag 84*
Jobber/Retailer [of Bill Communications] - Akron, OH - *BaconPubCkMag 84; MagDir 84; WritMar 84*
Jobber Topics - Chicago, IL - *MagDir 84*
Jobber Topics - Lincolnwood, IL - *ArtMar 84; BaconPubCkMag 84; MagIndMarPl 82-83; WritMar 84*
Jobeco Books - Humble, TX - *BoPubDir 4, 5*
Jobete Music Co. Inc. - Hollywood, CA - *BillIntBG 83-84*
Jobless Newsletter, The - Los Fresnos, TX - *BaconPubCkMag 84*
Jobson Associates Inc. - New York, NY - *DirPRFirms 83*
Jobson, Jordan, Harrison & Schulz Inc. - Pasadena, CA - *MagIndMarPl 82-83*
Jobson Publishing Corp. - New York, NY - *Ed&PubIntYB 82*
Joby Books - San Rafael, CA - *BoPubDir 4, 5*
JoCher Music Co. - Canonsburg, PA - *BillIntBG 83-84*
Jockey Music Inc. - *See* Croma Music Co. Inc.
JODAV Productions - New York, NY - *TelAl 83, 84*
Jodax Music Co. - *See* Gopam Enterprises Inc.
Jodi-Pat Music - *See* Kingston International
Jody Records Inc. - Brooklyn, NY - *BillIntBG 83-84*
Joe Computer - Canoga Park, CA - *MicrocomMPl 83, 84*
Joey Records - San Antonio, TX - *BillIntBG 83-84*
JOGN Nursing - Philadelphia, PA - *MagIndMarPl 82-83*
Johannes Press [Aff. of Galerie St. Etienne] - New York, NY - *BoPubDir 4, 5*
Johannesson, Reeser & Associates Inc. - St. Petersburg, FL - *StaDirAdAg 2-84*
Johansen Bookworks Ltd. - Big Sur, CA - *LitMarPl 83, 84*
Johanson, Astrid - Hoboken, NJ - *LitMarPl 83, 84*
Johl, Virinder - Yuba City, CA - *Tel&CabFB 84C*
John & Co., Henry - Dillingham, AK - *BoPubDir 4 Sup, 5*
John Associates Inc., Michael [Subs. of The Marketing Partnership Inc.] - Greenwich, CT - *AvMarPl 83*
John Day Blue Mountain Eagle - John Day, OR - *BaconPubCkNews 84*
Johnke Manufacturing Co. Inc. - Long Island City, NY - *AvMarPl 83*
Johnny Reads Inc. - St. Petersburg, FL - *BoPubDir 4, 5*
Johns & Partners Ltd., William B. - New York, NY - *StaDirAdAg 2-84*
Johns Hopkins Medical Journal, The - Baltimore, MD - *MagIndMarPl 82-83*
Johns Hopkins University Press - Baltimore, MD - *LitMarPl 83, 84; WritMar 84*
Johns Hopkins University Press (Journal Div.) - Baltimore, MD - *MagIndMarPl 82-83*
John's Press - Rock Hill, SC - *BoPubDir 4 Sup, 5*
Johnson Ad Communications - Dallas, TX - *StaDirAdAg 2-84*
Johnson Advertising, George - St. Louis, MO - *ArtMar 84; DirMarMP 83; StaDirAdAg 2-84*
Johnson Advertising Inc., Elving - Palos Heights, IL - *ArtMar 84; StaDirAdAg 2-84*
Johnson Agency, Little Richie - Belen, NM - *BillIntBG 83-84*
Johnson All-Channels Inc. [of Horizon Communications Corp.] - Franklin, IN - *Tel&CabFB 84C*
Johnson & Associates Inc., Jim - Santa Rosa, CA - *CabTVFinDB 83*
Johnson & Associates, R. N. - Arlington Heights, IL - *StaDirAdAg 2-84*
Johnson & Co. Inc., Rick - Albuquerque, NM - *AdAge 3-28-84; StaDirAdAg 2-84*
Johnson & Co., Michael - Bedford, England - *MicrocomSwDir 1*
Johnson & Crist Advertising Inc. - Minnetonka, MN - *StaDirAdAg 2-84*
Johnson & Dean Inc. - Grand Rapids, MI - *StaDirAdAg 2-84*
Johnson & Hardin Co., The - Cincinnati, OH - *LitMarPl 83, 84*
Johnson & Hayward Inc. - New York, NY - *LitMarPl 83, 84*
Johnson & Johnson Advertising - Longwood, FL - *StaDirAdAg 2-84*
Johnson & Jordan Inc. - Wheaton, IL - *StaDirAdAg 2-84*
Johnson & Jordan Inc. - New York, NY - *BrCabYB 84*
Johnson, Arthur D. - Dallas, OR - *BrCabYB 84 p.D-302*
Johnson, Arthur D. - *See* Oregon Cablevision Inc.
Johnson Associates, Malcolm C. - New York, NY - *LitMarPl 83, 84*
Johnson Associates Software - Redding, CA - *MicrocomMPl 84; WhoWMicrocom 83*
Johnson Books [Div. of Johnson Publishing Co.] - Boulder, CO - *LitMarPl 83, 84; WritMar 84*
Johnson Cable TV [of Texas Community Antennas Inc.] - Johnson, AR - *BrCabYB 84*
Johnson City Cable Co. - Johnson City, TX - *Tel&CabFB 84C*
Johnson City Press-Chronicle - Johnson City, TN - *BaconPubCkNews 84; Ed&PubIntYB 82; LitMarPl 83, 84; NewsDir 84*
Johnson City Record-Courier - Johnson City, TX - *AyerDirPub 83; BaconPubCkNews 84*
Johnson Communications Inc. - Remer, MN - *Tel&CabFB 84C*
Johnson County Broadcasters Inc. - Warrensburg, MO - *BrCabYB 84*
Johnson County Courier [of Syracuse Maverick Media Inc.] - Syracuse, NE - *AyerDirPub 83; NewsDir 84*
Johnson County Graphic - Clarksville, AR - *AyerDirPub 83; Ed&PubIntYB 82; NewsDir 84*
Johnson County Herald [of Shawnee Mission Prairie Publishing Co. Inc.] - Shawnee Mission, KS - *Ed&PubIntYB 82; NewsDir 84*
Johnson County News - Cleburne, TX - *AyerDirPub 83*
Johnson County News - Johnson County, TX - *Ed&PubIntYB 82*
Johnson County Shopper - Shawnee Mission, KS - *AyerDirPub 83*
Johnson County Sun - Overland Park, KS - *Ed&PubIntYB 82*
Johnson County Sun [of Sun Publications] - Shawnee Mission, KS - *NewsDir 84*
Johnson County Sun - *See* Sun Publications
Johnson, Curt - Highland Park, IL - *LitMarPl 83, 84*
Johnson, Eric Glenn - New York, NY - *LitMarPl 83, 84*
Johnson Ferguson Avant Advertising & Marketing - Raleigh, NC - *StaDirAdAg 2-84*
Johnson Graphics [Div. of Johnson Press] - East Dubuque, IL - *LitMarPl 83, 84*
Johnson, Harold A. - Dallas, OR - *BrCabYB 84 p.D-302*
Johnson, Harold A. - *See* Oregon Cablevision Inc.
Johnson Inc., Cato - Cincinnati, OH - *HBIndAd&MS 82-83*
Johnson Inc., Walter J. - Norwood, NJ - *LitMarPl 83, 84; MagIndMarPl 82-83*
Johnson, Jo Ann - Westport, CT - *LitMarPl 83*
Johnson, Joe Donald - Napa, CA - *BoPubDir 4, 5*
Johnson, John - North Bennington, VT - *BoPubDir 4, 5*
Johnson-Laird Inc. - Portland, OR - *WhoWMicrocom 83*
Johnson, Melody M. [of Kidder Peabody & Co.] - New York, NY - *DirInfWP 82*
Johnson, Merwyn S. - Due West, SC - *BoPubDir 4, 5*
Johnson Music Co., Little Richie - Belen, NM - *BillIntBG 83-84*

Johnson Music Productions Inc., Paul - Woodland Hills, CA - *BillIntBG 83-84*
Johnson Music Productions Inc., Paul - *See* Sonlife Music Co.
Johnson Nyquist Productions Inc. - Mission Viejo, CA - *AvMarPl 83*
Johnson Pioneer - Johnson, KS - *BaconPubCkNews 84; Ed&PubIntYB 82*
Johnson Publishing Co. - Boulder, CO - *LitMarPl 83, 84*
Johnson Publishing Co. - Chicago, IL - *BrCabYB 84; DirMarMP 83; KnowInd 83; MagIndMarPl 82-83*
Johnson Publishing Co. - Murfreesboro, NC - *BoPubDir 4, 5*
Johnson Publishing, T. M. - Alexandria, VA - *BoPubDir 4, 5*
Johnson Raffin Inc. - Newton, MA - *DirPRFirms 83*
Johnson Reprint Corp. [Aff. of Harcourt Brace Jovanovich] - New York, NY - *BoPubDir 4 Sup, 5*
Johnson Safari Museum Press, Martin & Osa - Chanute, KS - *BoPubDir 4, 5*
Johnson, Stephen Enoch - Inkster, MI - *BillIntBG 83-84*
Johnson Systems - McLean, VA - *DataDirSup 7-83*
Johnson Telecommunications - Magalia, CA - *MicrocomMPl 83, 84*
Johnson Telephone Co. - Remer, MN - *TelDir&BG 83-84*
Johnsonburg Community TV Co. - Johnsonburg, PA - *BrCabYB 84; Tel&CabFB 84C*
Johnsonburg Press - Johnsonburg, PA - *BaconPubCkNews 84; Ed&PubIntYB 82*
Johnston Advertising & Public Relations - Dallas, TX - *AdAge 3-28-84; StaDirAdAg 2-84*
Johnston Advertising, Ernest S. - Washington, DC - *StaDirAdAg 2-84*
Johnston Advertising Inc., Frank B. - Union, NJ - *StaDirAdAg 2-84*
Johnston Advertising Inc., Jim - New York, NY - *AdAge 3-28-84; ArtMar 84; LitMarPl 83, 84; MagIndMarPl 82-83; StaDirAdAg 2-84*
Johnston Citizen-News - Johnston, SC - *BaconPubCkNews 84*
Johnston County Capital Democrat - Tishomingo, OK - *AyerDirPub 83; Ed&PubIntYB 82*
Johnston Green & Co. Ltd. - Portree, Scotland - *LitMag&SmPr 83-84*
Johnston Group, The - Denver, CO - *DirPRFirms 83*
Johnston International Publishing Corp. - New York, NY - *MagIndMarPl 82-83*
Johnston Northern Polk County News - West De Moines, IA - *BaconPubCkNews 84*
Johnston Publishing Inc. - Afton, MN - *BoPubDir 5*
Johnstonian-Sun - Selma, NC - *AyerDirPub 83*
Johnstown Advertising - *See* Consolidated Capital Advertising Inc.
Johnstown Breeze - Johnstown, CO - *BaconPubCkNews 84; Ed&PubIntYB 82*
Johnstown Cable TV [of American Television & Communications Corp.] - Johnstown, PA - *BrCabYB 84*
Johnstown Independent - Johnstown, OH - *Ed&PubIntYB 82*
Johnstown Independent - *See* Ashbrook Publishing
Johnstown Observer - Johnstown, PA - *Ed&PubIntYB 82*
Johnstown Tribune-Democrat - Johnstown, PA - *BaconPubCkNews 84; NewsDir 84*
Joiner Music - *See* Merit Music Corp.
Joint Army-Navy Force Thermochemical Tables [of Dow Chemical U.S.A.] - Midland, MI - *EISS 83*
Joint Association Survey on Drilling Costs - New York, NY - *DirOnDB Spring 84*
Joint Center for Urban Studies - Cambridge, MA - *BoPubDir 4, 5*
Joint Commission on Accreditation of Hospitals - Chicago, IL - *BoPubDir 4, 5*
Joint Development Trading Co. Ltd. - Victoria, BC, Canada - *BoPubDir 4, 5*
Joint Endeavor [of Inmate Welfare Club, Texas Dept. of Corrections] - Huntsville, TX - *BoPubDir 4, 5; LitMag&SmPr 83-84; WritMar 84*
Joint-File - Tokyo, Japan - *DirOnDB Spring 84*
Joint Industry Committee for Television Advertising Research - London, England - *DirOnDB Spring 84*
Joint Legislative Information Systems [of Iowa State Legislative Service Bureau] - Des Moines, IA - *EISS 83*
Joint Program in Transportation - Toronto, ON, Canada - *BoPubDir 4, 5*
Joint Telecommunications Project - Toronto, ON, Canada - *TeleSy&SerDir 7-83*
Joliet Farmers' Weekly Review - Joliet, IL - *BaconPubCkNews 84; NewsDir 84*
Joliet Herald-News [of The Copley Press Inc.] - Joliet, IL - *BaconPubCkNews 84; NewsDir 84*
Joliette Journal - Joliette, PQ, Canada - *Ed&PubIntYB 82*
Jolly Cheeks Music - North Hollywood, CA - *BillIntBG 83-84*
Jolly Rogers Publishing Co. - *See* Cherry Lane Music Publishing Co. Inc.
Jolly Shopper - Lockport, IL - *AyerDirPub 83*
Jolson Enterprises Inc., Al - Nashville, TN - *BillIntBG 83-84*
Jo'mil Enterprises - Mamou, LA - *Tel&CabFB 84C*
Jon Music - Church Point, LA - *BillIntBG 83-84*
Jon-R Associates Inc. - New York, NY - *DirPRFirms 83*
Jonathan Advertising Inc. - New York, NY - *StaDirAdAg 2-84*
Jonathan David Publishers - Middle Village, NY - *LitMarPl 84; WritMar 84*
Jonathan-James Books - Don Mills, ON, Canada - *BoPubDir 4, 5*
Jonathan Publishing Co. - Baton Rouge, LA - *BoPubDir 4, 5*
Jonathan, The - Los Angeles, CA - *BaconPubCkMag 84*
Jondi Music - New York, NY - *BillIntBG 83-84*
Jondi Records - New York, NY - *BillIntBG 83-84*
Jones Advertising, James O. - Kansas City, MO - *AdAge 3-28-84; StaDirAdAg 2-84*
Jones Agency, The - Palm Springs, CA - *AdAge 3-28-84; StaDirAdAg 2-84*
Jones, Anastasi & Mitchell - Erie, PA - *AdAge 3-28-84; StaDirAdAg 2-84*
Jones & Bartlett Publishers Inc. - Boston, MA - *LitMarPl 84*
Jones & Co., Calvin - Houston, TX - *DirPRFirms 83*
Jones & Morris Photo-Enlarging Ltd. - Toronto, ON, Canada - *AvMarPl 83*
Jones & Taylor Inc. - South Bend, IN - *LitMarPl 83, 84; StaDirAdAg 2-84*
Jones Associates, Bob - Nashville, TN - *BrCabYB 84*
Jones Associates Inc., Gerre L. - Washington, DC - *DirPRFirms 83*
Jones, Brakeley & Rockwell Inc. - New York, NY - *StaDirAdAg 2-84*
Jones, Brakeley & Rockwell Inc. (DeWitt Conklin Organization Div.) - New York, NY - *DirPRFirms 83*
Jones Cable TV Fund VIII-B [of Jones Intercable Inc.] - St. George, UT - *BrCabYB 84*
Jones County Living - Gray, GA - *AyerDirPub 83*
Jones County News - Gray, GA - *Ed&PubIntYB 82*
Jones County Tribune - Draper, SD - *Ed&PubIntYB 82*
Jones Direct Marketing Inc., Ed - Wayne, PA - *DirMarMP 83*
Jones Engineering Associates Inc. - Charlotte, NC - *MicrocomMPl 84; MicrocomSwDir 1*
Jones, Ernest R. - Albuquerque, NM - *BoPubDir 4, 5*
Jones Futurex Inc. - Fair Oaks, CA - *MicrocomSwDir 1*
Jones Group Ltd., The - Englewood, CO - *CabTVFinDB 83*
Jones Industries, Jesse [Subs. of Jesse Jones Box Corp.] - Philadelphia, PA - *LitMarPl 83, 84*
Jones Intercable - Glenrock, WY - *BrCabYB 84*
Jones Intercable Cable TV Fund VII-A - Torrington, WY - *BrCabYB 84*
Jones Intercable Cable TV Fund VII-A - Wheatland, WY - *BrCabYB 84*
Jones Intercable Inc. - Attalla, AL - *Tel&CabFB 84C*
Jones Intercable Inc. - Benton, AR - *Tel&CabFB 84C*
Jones Intercable Inc. - Brighton, CO - *BrCabYB 84; Tel&CabFB 84C*
Jones Intercable Inc. - Englewood, CO - *BrCabYB 84 p.D-302; CabTVFinDB 83; HomeVid&CabYB 82-83; LitMarPl 84; Tel&CabFB 84C p.1686*
Jones Intercable Inc. - Sebastian, FL - *Tel&CabFB 84C*
Jones Intercable Inc. - St. Augustine, FL - *Tel&CabFB 84C*
Jones Intercable Inc. - Jerseyville, IL - *BrCabYB 84; Tel&CabFB 84C*
Jones Intercable Inc. - Shelbyville, IN - *Tel&CabFB 84C*
Jones Intercable Inc. - Hammond, LA - *Tel&CabFB 84C*
Jones Intercable Inc. - Sulphur, LA - *Tel&CabFB 84C*
Jones Intercable Inc. - Carolina Beach, NC - *Tel&CabFB 84C*

Jones Intercable Inc. - Elizabethtown, NC - *BrCabYB 84*
Jones Intercable Inc. - North Wilkesboro, NC - *Tel&CabFB 84C*
Jones Intercable Inc. - North Myrtle Beach, SC - *Tel&CabFB 84C*
Jones Intercable TV Fund IX-B - Onalaska, WI - *Tel&CabFB 84C*
Jones Intercable TV Fund IX-C - Minden, LA - *Tel&CabFB 84C*
Jones International Ltd. - Broadway Estates, CO - *BrCabYB 84*
Jones, Joe - *See* Midway Cable Corp.
Jones, John - *See* Midway Cable Corp.
Jones Medical Publications - Greenbrae, CA - *BoPubDir 4, 5; LitMarPl 84*
Jones Micro Systems, John - Helotes, TX - *MicrocomMPl 83, 84*
Jones Newspapers, Carl A. - Johnson City, TN - *Ed&PubIntYB 82*
Jones Newspapers, John M. - Greeneville, TN - *Ed&PubIntYB 82*
Jones Oklahoma County News - Jones, OK - *BaconPubCkNews 84*
Jones Press, Anson [Aff. of Fletcher's Books] - Salado, TX - *BoPubDir 4, 5*
Jones Programming, Gordon - Scarborough, ON, Canada - *Tel&CabFB 84C*
Jones Publishing Inc., Stan - Seattle, WA - *BoPubDir 4, 5*
Jones Stations, Myron - Erie, PA - *BrCabYB 84*
Jones Thomas Carter Inc. - Decatur, IL - *StaDirAdAg 2-84*
Jones Tri-City Intercable Inc. [of Jones Intercable Inc.] - Broomfield, CO - *BrCabYB 84; Tel&CabFB 84C*
Jonesboro Clayton Neighbor, The - Jonesboro, GA - *NewsDir 84*
Jonesboro Herald & Tribune - Jonesboro, TN - *BaconPubCkNews 84*
Jonesboro-Hodge Cable TV [of TCA Cable TV Inc.] - Jonesboro, LA - *Tel&CabFB 84C*
Jonesboro Jackson Independent - Jonesboro, LA - *BaconPubCkNews 84; NewsDir 84*
Jonesboro News Daily [of WoodPrint Inc.] - Jonesboro, GA - *NewsDir 84*
Jonesboro Sun [of Troutt Bros. Inc.] - Jonesboro, AR - *BaconPubCkNews 84; Ed&PubIntYB 82; NewsDir 84*
Jonesville Cablevision Inc. [of Communications Services Inc.] - Jonesville, LA - *BrCabYB 84; Tel&CabFB 84C*
Jonesville Catahoula News Booster - Jonesville, LA - *BaconPubCkNews 84*
Jonesville Independent - Jonesville, MI - *BaconPubCkNews 84; Ed&PubIntYB 82*
Jonethis Organization, The - Akron, OH - *StaDirAdAg 2-84*
Jonos Ltd. - Anaheim, CA - *WhoWMicrocom 83*
Jonos Ltd. - Fullerton, CA - *MicrocomMPl 84*
Jonsson Communications Corp. - Santa Monica, CA - *BrCabYB 84*
Jonvis Music Co. - Los Angeles, CA - *BillIntBG 83-84*
Joplin Globe [of Ottaway Newspapers Inc.] - Joplin, MO - *BaconPubCkNews 84; Ed&PubIntYB 82; NewsDir 84*
Jordan & Jordan Advertising & Public Relations - Atlanta, GA - *DirPRFirms 83*
Jordan Associates - Oklahoma City, OK - *DirPRFirms 83; StaDirAdAg 2-84*
Jordan Books, Fred - New York, NY - *LitMarPl 83*
Jordan, Case & McGrath - New York, NY - *AdAge 3-28-84; ArtMar 84; Br 1-23-84; StaDirAdAg 2-84*
Jordan Centre for Marketing Research & Surveys - Amman, Jordan - *IntDirMarRes 83*
Jordan Co., The - Dallas, TX - *StaDirAdAg 2-84*
Jordan Frederick & Co. [Div. of United Communications Corp.] - Jenkintown, PA - *StaDirAdAg 2-84*
Jordan Guide [of Midvale Sentinel Inc.] - Midvale, UT - *NewsDir 84*
Jordan Independent - Jordan, MN - *BaconPubCkNews 84; Ed&PubIntYB 82*
Jordan Line Services - London, England - *DirOnDB Spring 84*
Jordan/Tamraz/Caruso Advertising - Chicago, IL - *AdAge 3-28-84; StaDirAdAg 2-84*
Jordan, Thomas F. - Duluth, MN - *BoPubDir 5*
Jordan Tribune - Jordan, MT - *BaconPubCkNews 84; Ed&PubIntYB 82*
Jordan Valley Heritage House Inc. - Stayton, OR - *BoPubDir 4 Sup, 5; LitMag&SmPr 83-84*
Jordan Valley Sentinel [of Midvale Sentinel Inc.] - Midvale, UT - *Ed&PubIntYB 82; NewsDir 84*
Jordans Co. Information [of Jordan & Sons Ltd.] - London, England - *EISS 83*
Jordon Soldier Valley Cooperative Telephone Co. - Soldier, IA - *TelDir&BG 83-84*
Jorg Inc., James - *See* Howard Co. Inc., E. T.
Jornal Portugues - Richmond, CA - *NewsDir 84*
JoRo Music Corp. - *See* Spier Inc., Larry
Jory Publications - St. Louis, MO - *BoPubDir 5*
Joseki Computer Corp. - Redondo Beach, CA - *MicrocomMPl 84*
Joseph & Associates, Harry - New York, NY - *AvMarPl 83*
Joseph City Cable TV - Joseph City, AZ - *BrCabYB 84; Tel&CabFB 84C*
Joseph Inc., Michael - Salem, NH - *LitMarPl 83, 84*
Joseph Publishing Co. - San Mateo, CA - *BoPubDir 4, 5*
Josephs-David E. Levy Inc., Ray - New York, NY - *DirPRFirms 83*
Josephson/Arnold & Co. - Upper Montclair, NJ - *StaDirAdAg 2-84*
Josephson Communications Inc. - Dearborn, MI - *BrCabYB 84*
Josephson, Cuffari & Co. - Montclair, NJ - *DirPRFirms 83*
Josephson, Joseph - Forest Hills, NY - *Tel&CabFB 84C*
Joshua Publishing Co. - Los Angeles, CA - *BoPubDir 5; LitMag&SmPr 83-84*
Joshua Town Publishing Associates Inc. - Lyme, CT - *LitMarPl 84*
Joshua Tribune - Joshua, TX - *AyerDirPub 83; BaconPubCkNews 84; Ed&PubIntYB 82*
Joslin/Epstein Inc. - *See* Epstein Public Relations Inc.
Jossey-Bass Inc. - San Francisco, CA - *LitMarPl 83, 84; MagIndMarPl 82-83; WritMar 84*
Jost & Kiefer Printing - Quincy, IL - *MagIndMarPl 82-83*
Josten's American Yearbook Co. [Subs. of Jostens Inc.] - Topeka, KS - *LitMarPl 83, 84*
Jotarian Productions - Detroit, MI - *BoPubDir 5*
Journal - Auburn, CA - *AyerDirPub 83*
Journal - Carlsbad, CA - *AyerDirPub 83*
Journal - Corcoran, CA - *AyerDirPub 83*
Journal - Coronado, CA - *AyerDirPub 83*
Journal - Culver City, CA - *AyerDirPub 83; Ed&PubIntYB 82*
Journal - Los Angeles, CA - *Ed&PubIntYB 82*
Journal - Paramount, CA - *AyerDirPub 83*
Journal - Turlock, CA - *AyerDirPub 83*
Journal - Ukiah, CA - *AyerDirPub 83*
Journal - Willows, CA - *AyerDirPub 83*
Journal - Monte Vista, CO - *AyerDirPub 83*
Journal - Lakeville, CT - *AyerDirPub 83*
Journal - Wilmington, DE - *AyerDirPub 83*
Journal - Daytona Beach, FL - *AyerDirPub 83; Ed&PubIntYB 82*
Journal - Lake Placid, FL - *AyerDirPub 83*
Journal - Pensacola, FL - *AyerDirPub 83*
Journal - Sarasota, FL - *AyerDirPub 83; Ed&PubIntYB 82; NewsDir 84*
Journal [of Atlanta Newspapers] - Atlanta, GA - *AyerDirPub 83; Ed&PubIntYB 82; LitMarPl 84*
Journal - Cochran, GA - *AyerDirPub 83*
Journal - Marietta, GA - *AyerDirPub 83*
Journal - Rexburg, ID - *AyerDirPub 83*
Journal - Beecher City, IL - *AyerDirPub 83*
Journal - Braidwood, IL - *AyerDirPub 83*
Journal - Breese, IL - *AyerDirPub 83*
Journal - Chicago, IL - *AyerDirPub 83*
Journal - Clinton, IL - *AyerDirPub 83*
Journal - Cuba, IL - *AyerDirPub 83*
Journal - Edwardsville, IL - *AyerDirPub 83*
Journal - Eldorado, IL - *AyerDirPub 83*
Journal - Forreston, IL - *AyerDirPub 83*
Journal - Fulton, IL - *AyerDirPub 83*
Journal - Hillsboro, IL - *AyerDirPub 83*
Journal - Jacksonville, IL - *AyerDirPub 83; Ed&PubIntYB 82*
Journal [of Small Newspapers Inc.] - Kankakee, IL - *AyerDirPub 83; Ed&PubIntYB 82; NewsDir 84*
Journal - Knoxville, IL - *AyerDirPub 83*
Journal - Macomb, IL - *AyerDirPub 83*
Journal - Piper City, IL - *AyerDirPub 83*
Journal - Tuscola, IL - *AyerDirPub 83*

Journal - Waverly, IL - *AyerDirPub 83*
Journal - Wheaton, IL - *AyerDirPub 83*
Journal - Ellettsville, IN - *AyerDirPub 83; Ed&PubIntYB 82*
Journal - Franklin, IN - *AyerDirPub 83*
Journal - Oakland City, IN - *AyerDirPub 83*
Journal - Odon, IN - *AyerDirPub 83*
Journal - Osgood, IN - *AyerDirPub 83*
Journal - Ossian, IN - *AyerDirPub 83*
Journal - Armstrong, IA - *AyerDirPub 83*
Journal - Decorah, IA - *AyerDirPub 83*
Journal - Knoxville, IA - *AyerDirPub 83*
Journal - Manson, IA - *AyerDirPub 83*
Journal - Muscatine, IA - *AyerDirPub 83*
Journal - New London, IA - *AyerDirPub 83*
Journal - Scranton, IA - *AyerDirPub 83*
Journal - Sioux City, IA - *AyerDirPub 83*
Journal - Washington, IA - *AyerDirPub 83*
Journal - Altamont, KS - *AyerDirPub 83*
Journal - Andover, KS - *AyerDirPub 83*
Journal - Coffeyville, KS - *AyerDirPub 83*
Journal - Courtland, KS - *AyerDirPub 83*
Journal - Kingman, KS - *AyerDirPub 83*
Journal - Moundridge, KS - *AyerDirPub 83*
Journal - Salina, KS - *AyerDirPub 83*
Journal - Wichita, KS - *AyerDirPub 83*
Journal - Shreveport, LA - *AyerDirPub 83*
Journal - Revere, MA - *AyerDirPub 83*
Journal - Somerville, MA - *AyerDirPub 83*
Journal - Bronson, MI - *AyerDirPub 83*
Journal - Carsonville, MI - *AyerDirPub 83*
Journal - Flint, MI - *AyerDirPub 83*
Journal - Sturgis, MI - *AyerDirPub 83*
Journal - Eden Valley, MN - *AyerDirPub 83*
Journal - Fergus Falls, MN - *AyerDirPub 83*
Journal - Fertile, MN - *AyerDirPub 83*
Journal - International Falls, MN - *AyerDirPub 83*
Journal - Jasper, MN - *AyerDirPub 83*
Journal - Lewiston, MN - *AyerDirPub 83*
Journal [of Ogden Newspapers Inc.] - New Ulm, MN - *AyerDirPub 83; BaconPubCkNews 84; Ed&PubIntYB 82; NewsDir 84*
Journal - Pine River, MN - *AyerDirPub 83*
Journal - Proctor, MN - *AyerDirPub 83*
Journal - Waseca, MN - *AyerDirPub 83*
Journal - Winsted, MN - *AyerDirPub 83*
Journal - Adrian, MO - *AyerDirPub 83*
Journal - Flat River, MO - *AyerDirPub 83*
Journal - Hardin, MO - *AyerDirPub 83*
Journal - Hopkins, MO - *AyerDirPub 83*
Journal - Lee's Summit, MO - *AyerDirPub 83*
Journal - Falls City, NE - *AyerDirPub 83; Ed&PubIntYB 82*
Journal - Howells, NE - *AyerDirPub 83*
Journal - Lincoln, NE - *AyerDirPub 83*
Journal - Palmer, NE - *AyerDirPub 83*
Journal - Plattsmouth, NE - *AyerDirPub 83*
Journal - Elizabeth, NJ - *AyerDirPub 83*
Journal - Albuquerque, NM - *AyerDirPub 83*
Journal - Cheektowaga, NY - *AyerDirPub 83*
Journal - Ellenville, NY - *AyerDirPub 83*
Journal - Ithaca, NY - *AyerDirPub 83*
Journal - Northport, NY - *AyerDirPub 83*
Journal - Ogdensburg, NY - *AyerDirPub 83; Ed&PubIntYB 82*
Journal - Pleasantville, NY - *AyerDirPub 83*
Journal - Poughkeepsie, NY - *AyerDirPub 83*
Journal - Springville, NY - *AyerDirPub 83*
Journal - Windham, NY - *AyerDirPub 83*
Journal - Andrews, NC - *AyerDirPub 83*
Journal - Wilmington, NC - *AyerDirPub 83*
Journal - Winston-Salem, NC - *AyerDirPub 83*
Journal - Devils Lake, ND - *AyerDirPub 83*
Journal - Lisbon, OH - *AyerDirPub 83*
Journal - Middletown, OH - *AyerDirPub 83*
Journal - Struthers, OH - *AyerDirPub 83; Ed&PubIntYB 82*
Journal - Drumright, OK - *AyerDirPub 83*
Journal - Perkins, OK - *AyerDirPub 83*
Journal - Perry, OK - *AyerDirPub 83; Ed&PubIntYB 82*
Journal - Sayre, OK - *AyerDirPub 83*
Journal - Vinita, OK - *AyerDirPub 83*
Journal - Corry, PA - *AyerDirPub 83*
Journal - Millheim, PA - *AyerDirPub 83*
Journal - Mt. Pleasant, PA - *AyerDirPub 83*
Journal - Providence, RI - *AyerDirPub 83; Ed&PubIntYB 82; LitMarPl 84*
Journal - Charleston, SC - *AyerDirPub 83*
Journal - Spartanburg, SC - *AyerDirPub 83*
Journal - West Columbia, SC - *AyerDirPub 83; Ed&PubIntYB 82*
Journal - Williamston, SC - *AyerDirPub 83; Ed&PubIntYB 82*
Journal - Britton, SD - *AyerDirPub 83*
Journal - Centerville, SD - *AyerDirPub 83*
Journal - Estelline, SD - *AyerDirPub 83*
Journal - Rapid City, SD - *AyerDirPub 83*
Journal - Scotland, SD - *AyerDirPub 83*
Journal - Knoxville, TN - *AyerDirPub 83*
Journal [of The Enterprise Co.] - Beaumont, TX - *AyerDirPub 83; NewsDir 84*
Journal - Belton, TX - *AyerDirPub 83*
Journal - Groesbeck, TX - *AyerDirPub 83*
Journal - La Grange, TX - *AyerDirPub 83*
Journal - Longview, TX - *AyerDirPub 83*
Journal - Muleshoe, TX - *AyerDirPub 83*
Journal - Manchester, VT - *AyerDirPub 83*
Journal - Friday Harbor, WA - *AyerDirPub 83*
Journal - Morton, WA - *AyerDirPub 83; Ed&PubIntYB 82*
Journal - Martinsburg, WV - *AyerDirPub 83*
Journal - Antigo, WI - *AyerDirPub 83*
Journal - De Pere, WI - *AyerDirPub 83*
Journal - Milwaukee, WI - *AdAge 6-28-84; AyerDirPub 83; KnowInd 83*
Journal - Niagara, WI - *AyerDirPub 83*
Journal - Platteville, WI - *AyerDirPub 83*
Journal - Prescott, WI - *AyerDirPub 83*
Journal - River Falls, WI - *AyerDirPub 83*
Journal - Stevens Point, WI - *AyerDirPub 83*
Journal - Stratford, WI - *AyerDirPub 83*
Journal - Valders, WI - *AyerDirPub 83*
Journal - Edmonton, AB, Canada - *AyerDirPub 83; Ed&PubIntYB 82*
Journal - St. Paul, AB, Canada - *AyerDirPub 83*
Journal - Oxford, NS, Canada - *AyerDirPub 83*
Journal - Prescott, ON, Canada - *AyerDirPub 83*
Journal - Warkworth, ON, Canada - *AyerDirPub 83*
Journal - Humboldt, SK, Canada - *AyerDirPub 83*
Journal - Melfort, SK, Canada - *AyerDirPub 83*
Journal - Nipawin, SK, Canada - *AyerDirPub 83; Ed&PubIntYB 82*
Journal-Advance - Gentry, AR - *AyerDirPub 83; Ed&PubIntYB 82*
Journal-Advertiser - Lee's Summit, MO - *AyerDirPub 83*
Journal-Advocate - Sterling, CO - *AyerDirPub 83*
Journal-American [of Longview Publishing Co.] - Bellevue, WA - *AyerDirPub 83; BaconPubCkNews 84; NewsDir 84*
Journal American Water Works Association - Denver, CO - *BaconPubCkMag 84; MagIndMarPl 82-83*
Journal & Austin Chronicle Inc. - Scottsburg, IN - *BaconPubCkNews 84; NewsDir 84*
Journal & Constitution [of Atlanta Newspapers] - Atlanta, GA - *Ed&PubIntYB 82; LitMarPl 84*
Journal & Courier [of Federated Publications Inc.] - Lafayette, IN - *AyerDirPub 83; Ed&PubIntYB 82; LitMarPl 84*
Journal & Footville News - Orfordville, WI - *Ed&PubIntYB 82*
Journal & Guide - Norfolk, VA - *Ed&PubIntYB 82*
Journal & Monitor-Herald - Tomah, WI - *AyerDirPub 83*
Journal & News - Luverne, AL - *AyerDirPub 83*
Journal & Noble County Leader - Caldwell, OH - *AyerDirPub 83*
Journal & Republican [of Lowville Printing & Publishing Co. Inc.] - Lowville, NY - *AyerDirPub 83; Ed&PubIntYB 82; NewsDir 84*
Journal & Topics Newspapers - Des Plaines, IL - *BaconPubCkNews 84*
Journal Argus - St. Marys, ON, Canada - *AyerDirPub 83; Ed&PubIntYB 82*
Journal-Bulletin, The - Providence, RI - *Ed&PubIntYB 82; LitMarPl 84*
Journal-Capital - Pawhuska, OK - *AyerDirPub 83*
Journal Co., The - Berlin, WI - *BaconPubCkNews 84*

Journal Co., The - *See* Teltron Cable TV
Journal Co., The - *See* WTMJ Inc.
Journal-Constitution - Atlanta, GA - *AyerDirPub 83*
Journal-Courier [of The Jackson Newspapers] - New Haven, CT - *AyerDirPub 83; Ed&PubIntYB 82; LitMarPl 84; NewsBur 6; NewsDir 84*
Journal Courier - Jacksonville, IL - *AyerDirPub 83; Ed&PubIntYB 82; NewsDir 84*
Journal de Quebec - Quebec, PQ, Canada - *AyerDirPub 83*
Journal-Democrat - Syracuse, NE - *AyerDirPub 83*
Journal-Democrat, The [of Landmark Community Newspapers Inc.] - Rockport, IN - *AyerDirPub 83; Ed&PubIntYB 82; NewsDir 84*
Journal des Rivieres - Bedford, PQ, Canada - *AyerDirPub 83*
Journal des Rivieres - Farnham, PQ, Canada - *Ed&PubIntYB 82*
Journal-Enterprise - Providence, KY - *AyerDirPub 83*
Journal Era - Berrien Springs, MI - *AyerDirPub 83; Ed&PubIntYB 82*
Journal-Express Inc. - Knoxville, IA - *BaconPubCkNews 84*
Journal Films Inc. - Evanston, IL - *AvMarPl 83*
Journal, Florida Engineering Society - Tallahassee, FL - *BaconPubCkMag 84*
Journal for Arab & Islamic Studies [of Jenin Inc.] - Brattleboro, VT - *LitMag&SmPr 83-84*
Journal for Research in Mathematics Education - Reston, VA - *MagDir 84; MagIndMarPl 82-83*
Journal Francais d'Amerique [of Le Californien Publishing Co.] - San Francisco, CA - *Ed&PubIntYB 82; NewsDir 84*
Journal-Free Press - Osage City, KS - *AyerDirPub 83; Ed&PubIntYB 82*
Journal, Free Press & News - Le Roy, IL - *AyerDirPub 83*
Journal-Gazette - Mattoon, IL - *AyerDirPub 83*
Journal-Gazette - Ft. Wayne, IN - *AyerDirPub 83; Ed&PubIntYB 82*
Journal-Gazette - Richford, VT - *Ed&PubIntYB 82*
Journal Herald - Waycross, GA - *AyerDirPub 83*
Journal Herald - Lambertville, MI - *Ed&PubIntYB 82*
Journal Herald [of Toledo Herald Newspapers] - Monroe, MI - *NewsDir 84*
Journal Herald [of Dayton Newspapers Inc.] - Dayton, OH - *AyerDirPub 83; Ed&PubIntYB 82; LitMarPl 83, 84*
Journal Herald - Jackson, OH - *AyerDirPub 83*
Journal-Herald, The - Avoca, IA - *Ed&PubIntYB 82*
Journal Herald, The - White Haven, PA - *AyerDirPub 83*
Journal Inquirer - Manchester, CT - *Ed&PubIntYB 82*
Journal le Sommet - Ste. Agathe des Monts, PQ, Canada - *AyerDirPub 83*
Journal Messenger - Manassas, VA - *AyerDirPub 83; BaconPubCkNews 84; Ed&PubIntYB 82*
Journal, National Savings & Loan League - Washington, DC - *BaconPubCkMag 84*
Journal-News - Fairbury, NE - *AyerDirPub 83*
Journal News - Hamilton, OH - *AyerDirPub 83; BaconPubCkNews 84; Ed&PubIntYB 82*
Journal News, The - Spencerville, OH - *AyerDirPub 83; Ed&PubIntYB 82*
Journal Newspapers - Ballston Spa, NY - *BaconPubCkNews 84*
Journal Newspapers - Springfield, VA - *BaconPubCkNews 84*
Journal Newspapers (Printing Div.) - Washington, DC - *MagIndMarPl 82-83*
Journal Newspapers of Southern Illinois - Fairview Heights, IL - *BaconPubCkNews 84*
Journal of Accountancy [of American Institute of Certified Public Accountants] - New York, NY - *BaconPubCkMag 84; Folio 83; MagDir 84; MagIndMarPl 82-83*
Journal of Adventist Education - Washington, DC - *MagDir 84*
Journal of Advertising Research [of Advertising Research Foundation Inc.] - New York, NY - *BaconPubCkMag 84; MagDir 84; MagIndMarPl 82-83*
Journal of African Languages & Linguistics [of Foris Publications USA-Bird-Sci Books] - Cinnaminson, NJ - *LitMag&SmPr 83-84*
Journal of Agricultural & Food Chemistry [of American Chemical Society] - Washington, DC - *BaconPubCkMag 84; MagDir 84*
Journal of Air Traffic Control [of Air Traffic Control Association Inc.] - Arlington, VA - *BaconPubCkMag 84; MagDir 84*
Journal of Aircraft - New York, NY - *BaconPubCkMag 84; MagDir 84*
Journal of Albion Publishers - Albion, MI - *AyerDirPub 83; BaconPubCkNews 84*
Journal of Allergy & Clinical Immunology - St. Louis, MO - *BaconPubCkMag 84; MagDir 84; MagIndMarPl 82-83*
Journal of Allied Health - Thorofare, NJ - *MagDir 84*
Journal of American Geriatrics Society - New York, NY - *BaconPubCkMag 84*
Journal of American Geriatrics Society - Philadelphia, PA - *MagDir 84*
Journal of American History - Bloomington, IN - *MagIndMarPl 82-83*
Journal of American Insurance - Kingston, IL - *MagDir 84*
Journal of American Insurance - Schaumburg, IL - *BaconPubCkMag 84*
Journal of American Librarianship, The [of Mountainside Publishing Co.] - Ann Arbor, MI - *LitMarPl 83, 84*
Journal of American Military History, The - Ft. Collins, CO - *MagDir 84*
Journal of American Oil Chemists Society - Champaign, IL - *BaconPubCkMag 84; MagDir 84*
Journal of Analytical Toxicology - Chicago, IL - *MagDir 84*
Journal of Analytical Toxicology - Niles, IL - *BaconPubCkMag 84*
Journal of Applied Behavior Analysis - Lawrence, KS - *MagIndMarPl 82-83*
Journal of Applied Behavioral Science - Arlington, VA - *MagIndMarPl 82-83*
Journal of Applied Nutrition - La Habra, CA - *BaconPubCkMag 84; MagDir 84*
Journal of Applied Photographic Engineering - Springfield, VA - *BaconPubCkMag 84*
Journal of Applied Physics - New York, NY - *BaconPubCkMag 84*
Journal of Applied Physiology - Washington, DC - *MagDir 84*
Journal of Applied Physiology - Bethesda, MD - *BaconPubCkMag 84*
Journal of Applied Psychology - Washington, DC - *MagDir 84*
Journal of Architectural Education - Washington, DC - *MagIndMarPl 82-83*
Journal of Arizona History, The - Tucson, AZ - *MagIndMarPl 82-83*
Journal of Asian Studies - Berkeley, CA - *MagIndMarPl 82-83*
Journal of Bacteriology - Washington, DC - *BaconPubCkMag 84; MagDir 84*
Journal of Biological Chemistry - Baltimore, MD - *MagDir 84*
Journal of Biological Chemistry - Bethesda, MD - *BaconPubCkMag 84; MagIndMarPl 82-83*
Journal of Biological Photography - LaGrange, IL - *MagDir 84*
Journal of Bone & Joint Surgery - Boston, MA - *BaconPubCkMag 84; MagDir 84*
Journal of Borderland Research [of Borderland Sciences Research Foundation] - Vista, CA - *LitMag&SmPr 83-84*
Journal of Burn Care & Rehabilitation - Spring Lake, NJ - *BaconPubCkMag 84*
Journal of Business Education [of Helen Dwight Reid Educational Foundation] - Washington, DC - *BaconPubCkMag 84; MagDir 84; MagIndMarPl 82-83*
Journal of Business Strategy, The - Boston, MA - *BaconPubCkMag 84*
Journal of Canadian Fiction [of JCF Press] - Montreal, PQ, Canada - *LitMag&SmPr 83-84*
Journal of Canadian Petroleum Technology - Montreal, PQ, Canada - *BaconPubCkMag 84*
Journal of Canadian Poetry [of Borealis Press Ltd.] - Nepean, ON, Canada - *LitMag&SmPr 83-84*
Journal of Canadian Studies/Revue d Etudes Canadiennes [of Trent University] - Peterborough, ON, Canada - *LitMag&SmPr 83-84*
Journal of Cardiac Rehabilitation - New York, NY - *BaconPubCkMag 84*
Journal of Cardiovascular Medicine, The - New York, NY - *ArtMar 84*
Journal of Cell Biology - New York, NY - *MagIndMarPl 82-83*
Journal of Cellular Plastics - Westport, CT - *MagIndMarPl 82-83*
Journal of Cellular Plastics - Lancaster, PA - *BaconPubCkMag 84; MagDir 84*

Journal of Chemical & Engineering Data [of American Chemical Society] - Washington, DC - *BaconPubCkMag 84; MagDir 84*
Journal of Chemical Education - New York, NY - *BaconPubCkMag 84; MagDir 84*
Journal of Chemical Physics - Chicago, IL - *BaconPubCkMag 84*
Journal of Christian Camping - Somonauk, IL - *MagIndMarPl 82-83*
Journal of Christian Camping [of Christian Camping International] - Wheaton, IL - *WritMar 84*
Journal of Chromatographic Science [of Preston Publications Inc.] - Chicago, IL - *MagDir 84*
Journal of Chromatographic Science - Niles, IL - *BaconPubCkMag 84; MagIndMarPl 82-83*
Journal of Chronic Diseases - Elmsford, NY - *BaconPubCkMag 84; MagDir 84*
Journal of Church Music - Philadelphia, PA - *MagIndMarPl 82-83*
Journal of Clinical Endocrinology & Metabolism - Baltimore, MD - *MagDir 84*
Journal of Clinical Endocrinology & Metabolism - Chapel Hill, NC - *BaconPubCkMag 84*
Journal of Clinical Engineering - Brea, CA - *BaconPubCkMag 84; MagDir 84*
Journal of Clinical Immunology - New York, NY - *BaconPubCkMag 84*
Journal of Clinical Investigation - Boston, MA - *MagDir 84*
Journal of Clinical Investigation - New York, NY - *BaconPubCkMag 84; MagIndMarPl 82-83*
Journal of Clinical Microbiology - Washington, DC - *MagDir 84*
Journal of Clinical Orthodontics, The - Boulder, CO - *MagDir 84*
Journal of Clinical Psychiatry, The - Memphis, TN - *BaconPubCkMag 84; MagDir 84*
Journal of Clinical Psychopharmacology - Baltimore, MD - *BaconPubCkMag 84*
Journal of Clinical Ultrasound - New York, NY - *MagDir 84; MagIndMarPl 82-83*
Journal of Coal Quality, The - Charleston, WV - *BaconPubCkMag 84*
Journal of Coated Fabrics [of Technomic Publishing Co. Inc.] - Lancaster, PA - *MagDir 84*
Journal of Coatings Technology - Philadelphia, PA - *BaconPubCkMag 84; MagDir 84*
Journal of Collective Negotiations in the Public Sector - Farmingdale, NY - *MagIndMarPl 82-83*
Journal of College Placement - Bethlehem, PA - *ArtMar 84; MagDir 84; MagIndMarPl 82-83*
Journal of College Science Teaching - Washington, DC - *MagDir 84*
Journal of Colloid & Interface Science - Potsdam, NY - *BaconPubCkMag 84*
Journal of Commerce - Boise, ID - *Ed&PubIntYB 82*
Journal of Commerce [Aff. of Knight-Ridder Newspapers] - New York, NY - *BaconPubCkMag 84; BoPubDir 5; DirMarMP 83; InfoS 83-84; NewsBur 6*
Journal of Commerce - Vancouver, BC, Canada - *BaconPubCkMag 84; WritMar 84*
Journal of Commerce & Commercial - New York, NY - *Ed&PubIntYB 82*
Journal of Commerce & Northwest Construction Record - Seattle, WA - *NewsDir 84*
Journal of Commerce Export Bulletin - New York, NY - *BaconPubCkMag 84*
Journal of Commerce Import Bulletin [of Twin Coast Newspapers Inc.] - New York, NY - *BaconPubCkMag 84; MagDir 84*
Journal of Commercial Bank Lending, The - Philadelphia, PA - *MagIndMarPl 82-83*
Journal of Commonwealth Literature, The [of Hans Zell Publishers] - London, England - *LitMag&SmPr 83-84*
Journal of Communication - Philadelphia, PA - *MagIndMarPl 82-83*
Journal of Composite Materials - Lancaster, PA - *BaconPubCkMag 84; MagDir 84*
Journal of Computer Assisted Tomography - New York, NY - *MagIndMarPl 82-83*
Journal of Consulting & Clinical Psychology - Washington, DC - *BaconPubCkMag 84*
Journal of Contemporary Studies [of Institute for Contemporary Studies] - San Francisco, CA - *LitMag&SmPr 83-84; WritMar 84*
Journal of Continuing Education in Hospital & Clinics [of Medical Digest Inc.] - Winnetka, IL - *MagDir 84*
Journal of Continuing Education in Nursing, The - Thorofare, NJ - *MagIndMarPl 82-83*
Journal of Dairy Science [of American Dairy Science Association] - Champaign, IL - *BaconPubCkMag 84; MagDir 84*
Journal of Dental Education - Washington, DC - *MagIndMarPl 82-83*
Journal of Dental Education - Zellwood, FL - *MagDir 84*
Journal of Dental Research [of American Association for Dental Research] - Washington, DC - *MagDir 84*
Journal of Dental Research - Houston, TX - *BaconPubCkMag 84*
Journal of Dentistry for Children [of American Society of Dentistry for Children] - Chicago, IL - *BaconPubCkMag 84; MagDir 84*
Journal of Dentistry for Children - Dyer, IN - *MagIndMarPl 82-83*
Journal of Dermatologic Surgery & Oncology, The - New York, NY - *MagDir 84; MagIndMarPl 82-83*
Journal of Design & Construction - Des Moines, IA - *BaconPubCkMag 84*
Journal of Developmental & Behavorial Pediatrics - Baltimore, MD - *BaconPubCkMag 84*
Journal of Dynamic Systems, Measurement & Control - New York, NY - *BaconPubCkMag 84*
Journal of Economic Entomology - College Park, MD - *MagDir 84; MagIndMarPl 82-83*
Journal of Economic History - Raleigh, NC - *MagIndMarPl 82-83*
Journal of Economic Literature [of Dialog Information Services Inc.] - Palo Alto, CA - *DataDirOnSer 84*
Journal of Economic Literature [of American Economic Association] - Pittsburgh, PA - *CompReadDB 82; DataDirOnSer 84*
Journal of Economic Literature [of American Economic Association] - Nashville, TN - *OnBibDB 3*
Journal of Educational Computer Research [of Baywood Publishing Co. Inc.] - Farmingdale, NY - *MicrocomMPl 84*
Journal of Educational Research [of Helen Dwight Reid Educational Foundation] - Washington, DC - *MagDir 84; MagIndMarPl 82-83*
Journal of Educational Technology Systems [of Baywood Publishing Co. Inc.] - Farmingdale, NY - *MagIndMarPl 82-83; MicrocomMPl 84*
Journal of Elastomers & Plastics [of Technomic Publishing Co. Inc.] - Lancaster, PA - *MagDir 84*
Journal of Emergency Medical Services - Solana Beach, CA - *BaconPubCkMag 84*
Journal of Emergency Nursing - Chicago, IL - *BaconPubCkMag 84; MagDir 84*
Journal of Emergency Nursing - St. Louis, MO - *MagIndMarPl 82-83*
Journal of Endodontics - Baltimore, MD - *BaconPubCkMag 84*
Journal of Engineering for Power - New York, NY - *MagIndMarPl 82-83*
Journal of English Teaching Techniques [of JETT Press] - Flint, MI - *LitMag&SmPr 83-84*
Journal of Enterostomal Therapy - St. Louis, MO - *BaconPubCkMag 84*
Journal of Environmental Health - Denver, CO - *BaconPubCkMag 84; MagDir 84; MagIndMarPl 82-83*
Journal of Environmental Quality - Madison, WI - *BaconPubCkMag 84; MagDir 84*
Journal of Environmental Sciences - Mt. Prospect, IL - *BaconPubCkMag 84; MagDir 84; MagIndMarPl 82-83*
Journal of Experimental Medicine - New York, NY - *MagIndMarPl 82-83*
Journal of Extension - University Park, PA - *MagIndMarPl 82-83*
Journal of Family Practice - Norwalk, CT - *BaconPubCkMag 84; MagDir 84*
Journal of Family Practice - New York, NY - *MagIndMarPl 82-83*
Journal of Fee-Based Information Services, The [of Information Alternative] - Chicago, IL - *LitMag&SmPr 83-84*

Journal of Finance - New York, NY - *MagIndMarPl 82-83*
Journal of Fire & Flammability [of Technomic Publishing Co. Inc.] - Westport, CT - *MagDir 84*
Journal of Food Protection [of International Association of Milk, Food, & Environmental Sanitarians] - Ames, IA - *MagDir 84; MagIndMarPl 82-83*
Journal of Food Protection - Madison, WI - *BaconPubCkMag 84*
Journal of Food Science [of Institute of Food Technologists] - Chicago, IL - *BaconPubCkMag 84; MagDir 84; MagIndMarPl 82-83*
Journal of Forestry - Bethesda, MD - *BaconPubCkMag 84; MagDir 84*
Journal of Freshwater [of Freshwater Foundation] - Navarre, MN - *WritMar 84*
Journal of Genealogy - Omaha, NE - *MagIndMarPl 82-83*
Journal of General Education - University Park, PA - *MagDir 84*
Journal of Geography, The - Macomb, IL - *MagDir 84*
Journal of Geology - Chicago, IL - *MagDir 84*
Journal of Geophysical Research - Washington, DC - *BaconPubCkMag 84; MagDir 84*
Journal of Gerontological Nursing - Thorofare, NJ - *BaconPubCkMag 84; MagDir 84; MagIndMarPl 82-83*
Journal of Gerontology - Washington, DC - *BaconPubCkMag 84; MagDir 84*
Journal of Graphoanalysis - Chicago, IL - *MagIndMarPl 82-83; WritMar 84*
Journal of Hand Surgery, The - St. Louis, MO - *MagDir 84; MagIndMarPl 82-83*
Journal of Health & Social Behavior - San Francisco, CA - *MagIndMarPl 82-83*
Journal of Health & Social Behavior - Washington, DC - *MagDir 84*
Journal of Heat Transfer - New York, NY - *MagIndMarPl 82-83*
Journal of Heredity - Washington, DC - *MagIndMarPl 82-83*
Journal of Higher Education - Columbus, OH - *MagDir 84*
Journal of Histochemistry & Cytochemistry - Baltimore, MD - *MagDir 84*
Journal of Histochemistry & Cytochemistry - New York, NY - *BaconPubCkMag 84*
Journal of Histotechnology - Lanham, MD - *BaconPubCkMag 84*
Journal of Home Economics [of American Home Economics Association] - Washington, DC - *BaconPubCkMag 84; MagDir 84; MagIndMarPl 82-83*
Journal of Housing [of National Association of Housing & Redevelopment Officials] - Washington, DC - *BaconPubCkMag 84; MagDir 84; MagIndMarPl 82-83*
Journal of Human Stress - Washington, DC - *MagIndMarPl 82-83*
Journal of Humanistic Psychology - Beverly Hills, CA - *MagDir 84*
Journal of Humanistic Psychology - Los Angeles, CA - *MagIndMarPl 82-83*
Journal of Immunology - San Diego, CA - *BaconPubCkMag 84*
Journal of Immunology - Baltimore, MD - *MagDir 84*
Journal of Information & Image Management - Silver Spring, MD - *BaconPubCkMag 84; MagDir 84*
Journal of Instructional Psychology - Mobile, AL - *MagDir 84*
Journal of Insurance - New York, NY - *BaconPubCkMag 84; MagDir 84; MagIndMarPl 82-83; NewsBur 6*
Journal of International Affairs - New York, NY - *MagDir 84*
Journal of Investigative Dermatology - Chicago, IL - *BaconPubCkMag 84*
Journal of Investigative Dermatology - Baltimore, MD - *MagDir 84*
Journal of Italian Linguistics [of Foris Publications USA-Bird-Sci Books] - Cinnaminson, NJ - *LitMag&SmPr 83-84*
Journal of Kansas Pharmacy [of Kansas Pharmacists Association] - Topeka, KS - *BaconPubCkMag 84; MagDir 84*
Journal of Labor, The [of Georgia State AFL-CIO] - Atlanta, GA - *NewsDir 84*
Journal of Laboratory & Clinical Medicine - Kansas City, MO - *BaconPubCkMag 84*
Journal of Laboratory & Clinical Medicine - St. Louis, MO - *MagDir 84; MagIndMarPl 82-83*
Journal of Learning Disabilities - Chicago, IL - *MagDir 84; MagIndMarPl 82-83*
Journal of Liquid Chromatography - New York, NY - *MagIndMarPl 82-83*
Journal of Livestock & Agriculture, The - St. Joseph, MO - *BaconPubCkMag 84; MagDir 84*
Journal of Long-Term Care Administration - Bethesda, MD - *BaconPubCkMag 84*
Journal of Marital & Family Therapy - Upland, CA - *MagIndMarPl 82-83*
Journal of Marketing [of American Marketing Association] - Chicago, IL - *LitMarPl 83, 84; MagDir 84; MagIndMarPl 82-83*
Journal of Marketing - Austin, TX - *BaconPubCkMag 84*
Journal of Marketing Research [of American Marketing Association] - Chicago, IL - *LitMarPl 83, 84; MagDir 84*
Journal of Marketing Research - Chapel Hill, NC - *MagIndMarPl 82-83*
Journal of Marriage & the Family - Minneapolis, MN - *MagDir 84*
Journal of Marriage & the Family - Cleveland, OH - *MagIndMarPl 82-83*
Journal of Medical Education - Washington, DC - *BaconPubCkMag 84; MagDir 84*
Journal of Metals - Warrendale, PA - *BaconPubCkMag 84; MagDir 84*
Journal of Mexican American History, The - Santa Barbara, CA - *WritMar 84*
Journal of Modern Literature [of Temple University] - Philadelphia, PA - *LitMag&SmPr 83-84; WritMar 84*
Journal of Money, Credit, & Banking [of Ohio State University Press] - Columbus, OH - *MagDir 84*
Journal of Music Therapy - Lawrence, KS - *MagIndMarPl 82-83*
Journal of Narrative Technique - Ypsilanti, MI - *LitMag&SmPr 83-84*
Journal of Nervous & Mental Disease - Baltimore, MD - *MagDir 84*
Journal of Nervous & Mental Disease - Towson, MD - *BaconPubCkMag 84*
Journal of Neurophysiology - Washington, DC - *MagDir 84*
Journal of Neurophysiology - Bethesda, MD - *BaconPubCkMag 84*
Journal of Neurosurgery - St. Louis, MO - *BaconPubCkMag 84*
Journal of Neurosurgery - Hanover, NH - *MagDir 84; MagIndMarPl 82-83*
Journal of New Jersey Poets - Madison, NJ - *LitMag&SmPr 83-84*
Journal of Nuclear Medicine - Lexington, KY - *BaconPubCkMag 84*
Journal of Nuclear Medicine - New York, NY - *MagDir 84; MagIndMarPl 82-83*
Journal of Nuclear Medicine Technology - New York, NY - *MagDir 84; MagIndMarPl 82-83*
Journal of Nursing Administration - Wakefield, MA - *BaconPubCkMag 84; MagIndMarPl 82-83*
Journal of Nursing Care - Westport, CT - *MagIndMarPl 82-83; WritMar 84*
Journal of Nursing Education - Thorofare, NJ - *MagDir 84; MagIndMarPl 82-83*
Journal of Nutrition - Gainesville, FL - *MagIndMarPl 82-83*
Journal of Nutrition - Bethesda, MD - *BaconPubCkMag 84; MagDir 84*
Journal of Nutrition Education - Oakland, CA - *MagIndMarPl 82-83*
Journal of Obstetric, Gynecologic & Neonatal Nursing - Washington, DC - *BaconPubCkMag 84; MagIndMarPl 82-83*
Journal of Obstetric, Gynecologic, & Neonatal Nursing - Philadelphia, PA - *MagDir 84*
Journal of Occupational Medicine - Chicago, IL - *BaconPubCkMag 84; MagDir 84*
Journal of Ocular Therapy & Surgery - Chicago, IL - *BaconPubCkMag 84*
Journal of Opportunity - Pineville, WV - *MagDir 84*
Journal of Oral & Maxillofacial Surgery [of American Association of Oral & Maxillofacial Surgeons] - Chicago, IL - *BaconPubCkMag 84; MagDir 84*
Journal of Organic Chemistry [of American Chemical Society] - Washington, DC - *BaconPubCkMag 84; MagDir 84*
Journal of Organizational Communication - San Francisco, CA - *MagIndMarPl 82-83*

Journal of Orthopaedic & Sports Physical Therapy - Baltimore, MD - *BaconPubCkMag 84*
Journal of Parapsychology - Durham, NC - *MagDir 84*
Journal of Parasitology [of American Society of Parasitologists] - Los Angeles, CA - *MagDir 84*
Journal of Parental & Enteral Nutrition - Baltimore, MD - *BaconPubCkMag 84*
Journal of Parenteral Science & Technology - Philadelphia, PA - *BaconPubCkMag 84*
Journal of PASCAL & ADA - Orem, UT - *BaconPubCkMag 84*
Journal of PASCAL & ADA [of West Publishing Co.] - Provo, UT - *MicrocomMPl 84*
Journal of Pastoral Care - Scituate, MA - *MagIndMarPl 82-83*
Journal of Pediatric Ophthalmology & Strabismus - Thorofare, NJ - *MagDir 84*
Journal of Pediatric Surgery - New York, NY - *MagDir 84*
Journal of Pediatrics - St. Louis, MO - *BaconPubCkMag 84; MagDir 84; MagIndMarPl 82-83*
Journal of Periodontology [of Waverley Press] - Chicago, IL - *BaconPubCkMag 84; MagDir 84*
Journal of Personality & Social Psychology - Ann Arbor, MI - *MagDir 84*
Journal of Petroleum Technology [of Society of Petroleum Engineers of AIME] - Dallas, TX - *BaconPubCkMag 84; MagDir 84*
Journal of Pharmaceutical Sciences [of American Pharmaceutical Association] - Washington, DC - *BaconPubCkMag 84; MagDir 84; MagIndMarPl 82-83*
Journal of Pharmacology & Experimental Therapeutics - Davis, CA - *BaconPubCkMag 84*
Journal of Pharmacology & Experimental Therapeutics - Baltimore, MD - *MagDir 84*
Journal of Physical Chemistry [of American Chemical Society] - Washington, DC - *BaconPubCkMag 84; MagDir 84*
Journal of Physical Education, Recreation & Dance - Reston, VA - *BaconPubCkMag 84; MagDir 84; MagIndMarPl 82-83*
Journal of Pipelines - New York, NY - *BaconPubCkMag 84*
Journal of Podiatric Medicine - Oak Park, IL - *MagDir 84*
Journal of Political Psychology - Los Angeles, CA - *MagDir 84*
Journal of Polymer Science - New York, NY - *BaconPubCkMag 84*
Journal of Practical Nursing - New York, NY - *BaconPubCkMag 84; MagDir 84; MagIndMarPl 82-83*
Journal of Property Management [of Institute of Real Estate Management] - Chicago, IL - *BaconPubCkMag 84; MagDir 84*
Journal of Prosthetic Dentistry - Augusta, GA - *BaconPubCkMag 84*
Journal of Prosthetic Dentistry [of The C. V. Mosby Co.] - St. Louis, MO - *MagDir 84; MagIndMarPl 82-83*
Journal of Psychoactive Drugs [of Haight-Ashbury Publications] - San Francisco, CA - *LitMag&SmPr 83-84*
Journal of Psychoanalytic Anthropology, The [of Psychohistory Press] - New York, NY - *LitMag&SmPr 83-84*
Journal of Psychohistory, The [of Psychohistory Press] - New York, NY - *LitMag&SmPr 83-84; MagDir 84*
Journal of Psychosocial Nursing & Mental Health Services - Thorofare, NJ - *BaconPubCkMag 84; MagIndMarPl 82-83*
Journal of Purchasing & Materials Management - Oradell, NJ - *BaconPubCkMag 84*
Journal of Quality Technology - Milwaukee, WI - *MagIndMarPl 82-83*
Journal of Range Management - Denver, CO - *MagDir 84*
Journal of Reading - Newark, DE - *BaconPubCkMag 84; MagDir 84; MagIndMarPl 82-83*
Journal of Recreational Mathematics - Farmingdale, NY - *MagIndMarPl 82-83*
Journal of Rehabilitation - Alexandria, VA - *BaconPubCkMag 84; MagDir 84*
Journal of Reproductive Medicine, The - Palatine, IL - *MagDir 84*
Journal of Respiratory Diseases - Greenwich, CT - *BaconPubCkMag 84; MagIndMarPl 82-83*
Journal of Retailing - New York, NY - *MagDir 84; MagIndMarPl 82-83*
Journal of Risk & Insurance, The - Minneapolis, MN - *MagDir 84*
Journal of School Health - Kent, OH - *BaconPubCkMag 84; MagDir 84; MagIndMarPl 82-83*
Journal of Sedimentary Petrology - Durham, NC - *MagIndMarPl 82-83*
Journal of Small Business Management - Morgantown, WV - *MagIndMarPl 82-83*
Journal of Social Issues - Champaign, IL - *MagIndMarPl 82-83*
Journal of Soil & Water Conservation - Ankeny, IA - *ArtMar 84; BaconPubCkMag 84; MagDir 84; MagIndMarPl 82-83*
Journal of South Asian Literature [of Asian Studies Center] - Rochester, MI - *LitMag&SmPr 83-84*
Journal of Southern History - Houston, TX - *MagIndMarPl 82-83*
Journal of Spacecraft & Rockets [of American Institute of Aeronautics & Astronautics] - New York, NY - *BaconPubCkMag 84; MagDir 84*
Journal of Sport Psychology [of Human Kinetics Pub. Inc.] - Champaign, IL - *LitMag&SmPr 83-84*
Journal of Studies on Alcohol - New Brunswick, NJ - *MagDir 84*
Journal of Studies on Alcohol - Piscataway, NJ - *MagIndMarPl 82-83*
Journal of Systems Management [of Association for Systems Management] - Cleveland, OH - *BaconPubCkMag 84; MagDir 84; WritMar 84*
Journal of Taxation, The - New York, NY - *BaconPubCkMag 84*
Journal of Technical Writing & Communication - Farmingdale, NY - *MagIndMarPl 82-83*
Journal of the Acoustical Society of America - New York, NY - *MagDir 84*
Journal of the Acoustical Society of America - Providence, RI - *BaconPubCkMag 84*
Journal of the Air Pollution Control Association - Pittsburgh, PA - *BaconPubCkMag 84; MagDir 84*
Journal of the American Academy of Dermatology - Augusta, GA - *BaconPubCkMag 84*
Journal of the American Academy of Dermatology - St. Louis, MO - *MagDir 84; MagIndMarPl 82-83*
Journal of the American Academy of Religion - Charlottesville, VA - *MagIndMarPl 82-83*
Journal of the American Animal Hospital Association - Mishawaka, IN - *BaconPubCkMag 84*
Journal of the American Animal Hospital Association - South Bend, IN - *MagDir 84*
Journal of the American Ceramic Society [of American Ceramic Society Inc.] - Columbus, OH - *BaconPubCkMag 84; MagDir 84*
Journal of the American Chemical Society - Washington, DC - *BaconPubCkMag 84; MagDir 84*
Journal of the American College Health Association - Washington, DC - *MagDir 84*
Journal of the American College of Dentists - San Diego, CA - *BaconPubCkMag 84*
Journal of the American Concrete Institute - Detroit, MI - *BaconPubCkMag 84; MagIndMarPl 82-83*
Journal of the American Dental Association [of American Dental Association] - Chicago, IL - *BaconPubCkMag 84; MagDir 84; MagIndMarPl 82-83*
Journal of the American Dietetic Association - Chicago, IL - *BaconPubCkMag 84; MagDir 84; MagIndMarPl 82-83*
Journal of the American Helicopter Society - Alexandria, VA - *BaconPubCkMag 84; MagDir 84*
Journal of the American Leather Chemists Association - Freedom, NH - *BaconPubCkMag 84*
Journal of the American Leather Chemists Association - Cincinnati, OH - *MagDir 84*
Journal of the American Medical Association - Chicago, IL - *LitMarPl 83, 84; MagDir 84; MagIndMarPl 82-83*
Journal of the American Medical Record Association - Chicago, IL - *BaconPubCkMag 84*
Journal of the American Medical Technologists - Park Ridge, IL - *MagDir 84; MagIndMarPl 82-83*
Journal of the American Medical Women's Association - Boston, MA - *BaconPubCkMag 84*
Journal of the American Medical Women's Association - New York, NY - *MagDir 84; MagIndMarPl 82-83*

Journal of the American Optometric Association - Pompano Beach, FL - *MagIndMarPl 82-83*
Journal of the American Optometric Association - St. Louis, MO - *ArtMar 84; MagDir 84*
Journal of the American Osteopathic Association - Chicago, IL - *BaconPubCkMag 84; MagDir 84*
Journal of the American Planning Association - Chicago, IL - *MagDir 84*
Journal of the American Planning Association - Columbus, OH - *MagIndMarPl 82-83*
Journal of the American Podiatry Association - Washington, DC - *BaconPubCkMag 84; MagDir 84*
Journal of the American Psychoanalytic Association - New York, NY - *MagIndMarPl 82-83*
Journal of the American Society for Information Science - New York, NY - *MagIndMarPl 82-83*
Journal of the American Statistical Association - Washington, DC - *BaconPubCkMag 84; MagDir 84*
Journal of the American Veterinary Medical Association - Roselle, IL - *MagDir 84*
Journal of the American Veterinary Medical Association - Schaumburg, IL - *BaconPubCkMag 84*
Journal of the Arkansas Medical Society - Ft. Smith, AR - *BaconPubCkMag 84; MagDir 84*
Journal of the Association of Official Analytical Chemists - Arlington, VA - *BaconPubCkMag 84; MagDir 84; MagIndMarPl 82-83*
Journal of the Audio Engineering Society - New York, NY - *BaconPubCkMag 84; MagDir 84*
Journal of the Canadian Dental Association - Ottawa, ON, Canada - *BaconPubCkMag 84*
Journal of the Electrochemical Society - Pennington, NJ - *BaconPubCkMag 84; MagDir 84*
Journal of the Florida Engineering Society - Tallahassee, FL - *MagDir 84*
Journal of the Florida Medical Association - Jacksonville, FL - *BaconPubCkMag 84; MagDir 84*
Journal of the Franklin Institute - Philadelphia, PA - *MagDir 84*
Journal of the Hellenic Diaspora - New York, NY - *LitMag&SmPr 83-84*
Journal of the History of Ideas - Philadelphia, PA - *MagDir 84*
Journal of the Illuminating Engineering Society - New York, NY - *BaconPubCkMag 84; MagDir 84*
Journal of the Indiana State Medical Association, The - Indianapolis, IN - *BaconPubCkMag 84; MagDir 84*
Journal of the International Union of Bricklayers & Allied Craftsmen [of International Union of Bricklayers & Allied Craftsmen] - Washington, DC - *BaconPubCkMag 84; MagDir 84*
Journal of the Iowa Medical Society - Des Moines, IA - *BaconPubCkMag 84; MagDir 84*
Journal of the Kansas Medical Society - Topeka, KS - *BaconPubCkMag 84; MagDir 84*
Journal of the Kentucky Medical Association - Louisville, KY - *BaconPubCkMag 84*
Journal of the Kipling Society - London, England - *LitMag&SmPr 83-84*
Journal of the Louisiana State Medical Society - New Orleans, LA - *BaconPubCkMag 84; MagDir 84*
Journal of the Maine Water Utilities Association - Falmouth, ME - *MagDir 84*
Journal of the Medical Association of Georgia - Atlanta, GA - *BaconPubCkMag 84; MagDir 84*
Journal of the Medical Association of the State of Alabama - Montgomery, AL - *BaconPubCkMag 84*
Journal of the Medical Society of New Jersey - Lawrenceville, NJ - *BaconPubCkMag 84*
Journal of the Medical Society of New Jersey, The - Trenton, NJ - *MagDir 84*
Journal of the Milking Shorthorn & Illawarra Breeds - Springfield, MO - *BaconPubCkMag 84; MagDir 84; MagIndMarPl 82-83*
Journal of the Mississippi State Medical Association - Jackson, MS - *BaconPubCkMag 84; MagDir 84*
Journal of the Missouri Dental Association [of Missouri Dental Association] - Jefferson City, MO - *MagDir 84*
Journal of the National Medical Association - East Norwalk, CT - *BaconPubCkMag 84*
Journal of the National Medical Association - Washington, DC - *MagDir 84*
Journal of the National Medical Association - New York, NY - *MagIndMarPl 82-83*
Journal of the New England Water Works Association - Boylston, MA - *BaconPubCkMag 84*
Journal of the New England Water Works Association - Dedham, MA - *MagDir 84*
Journal of the New York State Nurses Association - Guilderland, NY - *BaconPubCkMag 84; MagDir 84*
Journal of the Oklahoma State Medical Association - Oklahoma City, OK - *BaconPubCkMag 84; MagDir 84*
Journal of the Optical Society of America - Dearborn, MI - *BaconPubCkMag 84*
Journal of the Optical Society of America - Pittsford, NY - *MagDir 84*
Journal of the Philosophy of Sport [of Human Kinetics Pub. Inc.] - Champaign, IL - *LitMag&SmPr 83-84*
Journal of the Prestressed Concrete Institute - Chicago, IL - *BaconPubCkMag 84; MagDir 84*
Journal of the San Juans, The - Friday Harbor, WA - *NewsDir 84*
Journal of the Society of Architectural Historians [of Bibliographic Retrieval Services Inc.] - Latham, NY - *DataDirOnSer 84*
Journal of the Society of Architectural Historians - Philadelphia, PA - *DirOnDB Spring 84; EISS 7-83 Sup*
Journal of the Society of Cosmetic Chemists, The - New York, NY - *BaconPubCkMag 84; MagDir 84*
Journal of the South Carolina Medical Association - Columbia, SC - *BaconPubCkMag 84; MagDir 84*
Journal of the Tennessee Medical Association - Nashville, TN - *BaconPubCkMag 84; MagDir 84*
Journal of the Water Pollution Control Federation - Washington, DC - *MagDir 84*
Journal of the West [of Sunflower University Press] - Manhattan, KS - *ArtMar 84; LitMag&SmPr 83-84; LitMarPl 83, 84; MagIndMarPl 82-83*
Journal of the Wisconsin Optometric Association - Madison, WI - *MagDir 84*
Journal of the Wisconsin Optometric Association - Weyauwega, WI - *BaconPubCkMag 84*
Journal of Thoracic & Cardiovascular Surgery - St. Louis, MO - *BaconPubCkMag 84; MagDir 84; MagIndMarPl 82-83*
Journal of Trauma - Baltimore, MD - *MagDir 84*
Journal of 20th Century Wargaming, The - Austin, TX - *WritMar 84*
Journal of Urology - Baltimore, MD - *BaconPubCkMag 84; MagDir 84*
Journal of Vacuum Science & Technology - New York, NY - *MagDir 84*
Journal of Vacuum Science & Technology - Raleigh, NC - *BaconPubCkMag 84*
Journal of Vinyl Technology - Brookfield Center, CT - *BaconPubCkMag 84*
Journal of Visual Impairment & Blindness - New York, NY - *MagIndMarPl 82-83*
Journal of Wildlife Management, The - Ft. Collins, CO - *MagIndMarPl 82-83*
Journal Opinion - Bradford, VT - *AyerDirPub 83; Ed&PubIntYB 82; NewsDir 84*
Journal-Patriot [of Carter-Hubbard Publishing Co. Inc.] - North Wilkesboro, NC - *AyerDirPub 83; Ed&PubIntYB 82; NewsDir 84*
Journal-Pioneer - Summerside, PE, Canada - *AyerDirPub 83; BaconPubCkNews 84; Ed&PubIntYB 82*
Journal-Pollution Abstracts/Cambridge Scientific Abstracts - Louisville, KY - *MagDir 84*
Journal-Press - New Athens, IL - *AyerDirPub 83; Ed&PubIntYB 82*
Journal Press [of Lawrenceberg Register Publications] - Aurora, IN - *Ed&PubIntYB 82; NewsDir 84*
Journal-Press - Lawrenceburg, IN - *AyerDirPub 83*
Journal-Press - South Milwaukee, WI - *NewsDir 84*

Journal Press Syndicate - New York, NY - *Ed&PubIntYB 82; LitMarPl 84*
Journal-Press, The - Greenwich, NY - *Ed&PubIntYB 82*
Journal Printing Co. - Carthage, IL - *MagIndMarPl 82-83*
Journal-Record, The - Hamilton, AL - *Ed&PubIntYB 82*
Journal Record, The - Oklahoma City, OK - *NewsDir 84*
Journal-Register - Albion, IL - *AyerDirPub 83; Ed&PubIntYB 82*
Journal Register - Palmer, MA - *AyerDirPub 83*
Journal Register - Hebron, NE - *AyerDirPub 83*
Journal-Register - Medina, NY - *AyerDirPub 83; Ed&PubIntYB 82*
Journal-Reporter - Leon, IA - *AyerDirPub 83*
Journal-Republican - Columbus, WI - *AyerDirPub 83; Ed&PubIntYB 82*
Journal-Republican Shopper - Columbus, WI - *AyerDirPub 83*
Journal-Review - Crawfordsville, IN - *AyerDirPub 83*
Journal Review, The - Paterson, NJ - *Ed&PubIntYB 82*
Journal-Scene - Summerville, SC - *AyerDirPub 83*
Journal Shopping News - Hamilton, OH - *AyerDirPub 83*
Journal-Spectator - Wharton, TX - *AyerDirPub 83*
Journal-Standard - Freeport, IL - *AyerDirPub 83*
Journal Star - Peoria, IL - *AyerDirPub 83; Ed&PubIntYB 82; LitMarPl 84*
Journal-Star - Lincoln, NE - *AyerDirPub 83*
Journal Star Stations - Peoria, IL - *BrCabYB 84*
Journal Suburban, The - Maple Shade, NJ - *Ed&PubIntYB 82*
Journal, The - Poplar Bluff, MO - *AyerDirPub 83*
Journal, The [of Cherry Hill Suburban Newspaper Group] - Cherry Hill, NJ - *AyerDirPub 83; NewsDir 84*
Journal, The [of Institute for Socioeconomic Studies] - White Plains, NY - *MagIndMarPl 82-83*
Journal, The - Crosby, ND - *Ed&PubIntYB 82*
Journal, The - Lorain, OH - *AyerDirPub 83; Ed&PubIntYB 82*
Journal, The [of Knepper Press Corp.] - Pittsburgh, PA - *AyerDirPub 83; NewsDir 84*
Journal, The - White Haven, PA - *Ed&PubIntYB 82*
Journal, The - James Island, SC - *Ed&PubIntYB 82*
Journal, The - Ashcroft, BC, Canada - *Ed&PubIntYB 82*
Journal, The [of Addiction Research Foundation] - Toronto, ON, Canada - *ArtMar 84*
Journal-Times - Racine, WI - *AyerDirPub 83; BaconPubCkNews 84; Ed&PubIntYB 82*
Journal Tribune - Biddeford, ME - *BaconPubCkNews 84; Ed&PubIntYB 82; NewsDir 84*
Journal-Tribune - Marysville, OH - *AyerDirPub 83*
Journal-Tribune - Blackwell, OK - *AyerDirPub 83*
Journal-Tribune - Seneca, SC - *AyerDirPub 83*
Journal/20 - Van Alstyne, TX - *MicrocomMPl 84*
Journal Water of the Pollution Control Federation - Washington, DC - *BaconPubCkMag 84*
Journal-World - Lawrence, KS - *AyerDirPub 83*
Journalism Educator, The - Chapel Hill, NC - *WritMar 84*
Journalism Quarterly - Athens, OH - *MagIndMarPl 82-83; WritMar 84*
Journalistforbundets Avisudklips-Bureau - Copenhagen, Denmark - *ProGuPRSer 4*
Journey Press - Berkeley, CA - *BoPubDir 4, 5*
Journey Publications - Woodstock, NY - *BoPubDir 4, 5; LitMag&SmPr 83-84*
Journey Roofer & Waterproofer, The - Washington, DC - *NewsDir 84*
Journeyman Barber & Beauty Culture - Lawrence, IN - *NewsDir 84*
Journeyman Barber & Beauty Culture [of National Graphics] - Maywood, IN - *MagDir 84*
Journeyman Press, The - West Nyack, NY - *LitMag&SmPr 83-84*
Jowat Music - *See* Gopam Enterprises Inc.
Joy Newspapers - Centralia, IL - *Ed&PubIntYB 82*
Joy of Sound - Menlo Park, CA - *BillIntBG 83-84*
Joy of Travel Report - Washington, DC - *MagDir 84*
Joy Publishing Co. - Boca Raton, FL - *BoPubDir 4, 5*
Joy Stik - Skokie, IL - *BaconPubCkMag 84*
Joybug Teaching Aids Inc. - Parsons, KS - *BoPubDir 4*
Joybug Teaching Aids Inc. - Salina, KS - *BoPubDir 5*
Joyce Cable Inc. - Joliet, IL - *BrCabYB 84*
Joyce Cable Inc. - Romeoville, IL - *Tel&CabFB 84C*
Joyce Records - Los Angeles, CA - *BillIntBG 83-84*
Joyce, William J. Jr. - Romeoville, IL - *Tel&CabFB 84C p.1686*
Joyce-Winn Parish Cable TV [of Teleservice Corp. of America Inc.] - Joyce, LA - *BrCabYB 84*
Joycean Lively Arts Guild Review [of Pakka Press] - East Douglas, MA - *LitMag&SmPr 83-84*
Joyful Noise Productions International - San Francisco, CA - *BoPubDir 4 Sup, 5; LitMag&SmPr 83-84*
Joyful Wisdom Music Co. - *See* Alkatraz Corner Music Co.
Joyful World Press - San Francisco, CA - *BoPubDir 4, 5*
Joyner Hutcheson Research Inc. - Atlanta, GA - *IntDirMarRes 83*
JP Office Services Inc. - Boston, MA - *DirInfWP 82*
JP Publications - Madison, WI - *BoPubDir 4, 5*
JP Trading Inc. - Brisbane, CA - *MagIndMarPl 82-83*
JPD Television Network - Rolling Hills Estates, CA - *BrCabYB 84*
JPR Associates - Santa Fe, NM - *LitMarPl 83, 84*
JPR Software Inc. - Orlando, FL - *MicrocomMPl 84*
JQTQ-FM - Hartford, CT - *TV&RadDir 84*
JR - Peterborough, NH - *BaconPubCkMag 84*
J.R. & G. Co. - Bethlehem, PA - *BoPubDir 5*
Jr. Medical Detective [of Children's Better Health Institute] - Indianapolis, IN - *WritMar 84*
JRB Marketing & Opinion Research Inc. - Great Neck, NY - *IntDirMarRes 83*
JRH Marketing Services Inc. - Long Island City, NY - *IntDirMarRes 83*
JRL Advertising & Sales Promotion - Chester Springs, PA - *AdAge 3-28-84; StaDirAdAg 2-84*
JRP Surveys Inc. - Broomall, PA - *IntDirMarRes 83*
JS & A Advertising - Northbrook, IL - *StaDirAdAg 2-84*
JSH Music - *See* Big Heart Music Inc.
JST CATV Co. - Howardwick, TX - *BrCabYB 84*
JT International - Van Nuys, CA - *StaDirAdAg 2-84*
JTC Corp. - Union, NJ - *DataDirSup 7-83*
JTL Publications - Los Angeles, CA - *BillIntBG 83-84*
Ju-Bop Music - *See* Xanadu Records Ltd.
Juan DeFuca News - Colwood, BC, Canada - *Ed&PubIntYB 82*
Juarez & Associates Inc. - Los Angeles, CA - *IntDirMarRes 83*
Jubilation Music - *See* FYDAQ Music
Judaica Book Club [Div. of Jonathan David Publishers] - Middle Village, NY - *LitMarPl 83, 84*
Judaica Press Inc. - New York, NY - *BoPubDir 4, 5; LitMarPl 84*
Judaism - New York, NY - *MagIndMarPl 82-83*
Judd & Detwiler Inc. - Washington, DC - *MagIndMarPl 82-83*
Judge & Sons Inc., Edward E. - Westminster, MD - *BoPubDir 4 Sup, 5*
Judge Associates Inc., Jean - Hackensack, NJ - *HBIndAd&MS 82-83*
Judge Inc., James J. - Westminster, MD - *BoPubDir 5*
Judicature - Chicago, IL - *ArtMar 84; MagDir 84; MagIndMarPl 82-83*
Judicial Education Teleseminar System [of Michigan Judicial Institute] - Lansing, MI - *TeleSy&SerDir 2-84*
Judicial Information System [of Ministry of Justice] - Bonn, West Germany - *EISS 83*
Judith Basin Press - Stanford, MT - *Ed&PubIntYB 82*
Judson Press [of American Baptist Churches USA] - Valley Forge, PA - *ArtMar 84; LitMarPl 83, 84; WritMar 84*
Judsonia White County Record - Judsonia, AR - *BaconPubCkNews 84*
Juggular Records - De Kalb, IL - *BillIntBG 83-84*
Juhl Advertising Agency - Elkhart, IN - *AdAge 3-28-84; StaDirAdAg 2-84*
Juju Publishing Co. - Columbia, SC - *BaconPubCkNews 84*
Juki Industries of America Inc. - Torrance, CA - *MicrocomMPl 84*
Juldane Music Co. - Silver Spring, MD - *BillIntBG 83-84*
Julep Publishing Co. [Div. of Julep Inc.] - Nashville, TN - *BillIntBG 83-84*
Jules Verne Circle - Dagenham, England - *LitMag&SmPr 83-84*
Jules Verne Voyager [of Jules Verne Circle] - Dagenham, England - *LitMag&SmPr 83-84*
Julesburg Advocate - Julesburg, CO - *BaconPubCkNews 84; Ed&PubIntYB 82*
Julian Cablevision - Julian, CA - *BrCabYB 84; Tel&CabFB 84C*

Julie Music Corp. - *See* Sanga Music Inc.
July Child Music - Atlanta, GA - *BillIntBG 83-84*
Jump Cut - Berkeley, CA - *LitMag&SmPr 83-84*
Jump River Press Inc. - Medina, OH - *BoPubDir 5; LitMag&SmPr 83-84*
Jump River Press Inc. - Prentice, WI - *BoPubDir 4*
Jump River Review [of Jump River Press Inc.] - Medina, OH - *LitMag&SmPr 83-84; WritMar 84*
Jump Tunes - Los Angeles, CA - *BillIntBG 83-84*
Junction City Daily Union [of Montgomery Publications Inc.] - Junction City, KS - *BaconPubCkNews 84; NewsDir 84*
Junction City Ft. Riley Post [of Montgomery Publications Inc.] - Junction City, KS - *NewsDir 84*
Junction City Republic - *See* Montgomery Publications Inc.
Junction City Republic News - Junction City, KS - *BaconPubCkNews 84*
Junction City Television Inc. [of Communications Services Inc.] - Junction City, KS - *BrCabYB 84*
Junction City Times - Junction City, OR - *BaconPubCkNews 84; Ed&PubIntYB 82*
Junction City Tri-County News - *See* Tri-County Publications Inc.
Junction City TV Inc. [of Communications Services Inc.] - Junction City, KS - *Tel&CabFB 84C*
Junction Eagle - Junction, TX - *BaconPubCkNews 84; Ed&PubIntYB 82*
Junction Mag - Brooklyn, NY - *LitMag&SmPr 83-84*
Junction TV Cable Co. [of Television Enterprises Inc.] - Junction, TX - *BrCabYB 84*
June Appal Recordings - Whitesburg, KY - *BillIntBG 83-84*
Juneau & Douglas Telephone Co. [Aff. of Contel Service Corp.] - Anchorage, AK - *TelDir&BG 83-84*
Juneau County Chronicle [of Mauston Juneau County Publishers] - Mauston, WI - *AyerDirPub 83; Ed&PubIntYB 82; NewsDir 84*
Juneau County Reminder - Mauston, WI - *AyerDirPub 83*
Juneau Dodge County Independent News - *See* Royle Publishing Co. Inc.
Juneau Empire - Juneau, AK - *BaconPubCkNews 84; Ed&PubIntYB 82*
Jung Foundation for Analytical Psychology, C. G. - New York, NY - *BoPubDir 4, 5*
Jung Montreal - Montreal, PQ, Canada - *Ed&PubIntYB 82*
Jung Toronto - Montreal, PQ, Canada - *Ed&PubIntYB 82*
Junger Advertising, Mort - New York, NY - *LitMarPl 83, 84; StaDirAdAg 2-84*
Junger, Elliot - New York, NY - *LitMarPl 84*
Junger-Wellman & Co. - Los Angeles, CA - *AdAge 3-28-84*
Jungle Boy Music - *See* Kaye Publications, Richard
Jungle Garden Press - Fairfax, CA - *LitMag&SmPr 83-84*
Juniata Gazette [of Greater Philadelphia Group Inc.] - Philadelphia, PA - *NewsDir 84*
Juniata Journal - *See* American Newspapers
Juniata News - Philadelphia, PA - *AyerDirPub 83*
Juniata Sentinel - Mifflintown, PA - *AyerDirPub 83; Ed&PubIntYB 82; NewsDir 84*
Junior Charity League of Monroe, LA - Monroe, LA - *BoPubDir 4, 5*
Junior League of Charleston, SC - Charleston, SC - *BoPubDir 4, 5*
Junior League of Charleston, WV - Charleston, WV - *BoPubDir 4, 5*
Junior League of Flint Publishing - Flint, MI - *BoPubDir 4, 5*
Junior League of Ft. Lauderdale, FL - Ft. Lauderdale, FL - *BoPubDir 4 Sup, 5*
Junior League of Gainesville, FL - Gainesville, FL - *BoPubDir 4 Sup, 5*
Junior League of Greenville, SC - Greenville, SC - *BoPubDir 4, 5*
Junior League of Jackson, MS - Jackson, MS - *BoPubDir 4 Sup, 5*
Junior League of Kansas City, KS - Kansas City, KS - *BoPubDir 4, 5*
Junior League of Kansas City, MO - Kansas City, MO - *BoPubDir 4, 5*
Junior League of Lafayette, LA - Lafayette, LA - *BoPubDir 4, 5*
Junior League of Lake Charles, LA - Lake Charles, LA - *BoPubDir 4, 5*
Junior League of Little Rock, AR - Little Rock, AR - *BoPubDir 4 Sup, 5*
Junior League of Longview, TX - Longview, TX - *BoPubDir 4, 5*
Junior League of Montclair-Newark, NJ - Upper Montclair, NJ - *BoPubDir 4, 5*
Junior League of Northern Westchester, NY - Chappaqua, NY - *BoPubDir 4 Sup, 5*
Junior League of Peoria, IL - Peoria, IL - *BoPubDir 5*
Junior League of Pine Bluff, AR - Pine Bluff, AR - *BoPubDir 4 Sup, 5*
Junior League of Pueblo, CO - Pueblo, CO - *BoPubDir 4, 5*
Junior League of San Jose, CA - San Jose, CA - *BoPubDir 4, 5*
Junior League of South Bend, IN - South Bend, IN - *BoPubDir 4, 5*
Junior League of Spartanburg, SC - Spartanburg, SC - *BoPubDir 4*
Junior League of Tampa, FL - Tampa, FL - *BoPubDir 4 Sup, 5*
Junior League of the Palm Beaches, FL - Palm Beach, FL - *BoPubDir 4 Sup, 5*
Junior League of Tulsa, OK - Tulsa, OK - *BoPubDir 4, 5*
Junior League of Wilmington, NC - Wilmington, NC - *BoPubDir 4, 5*
Junior League Review - New York, NY - *BaconPubCkMag 84; MagDir 84*
Junior Literary Guild - New York, NY - *LitMarPl 83, 84*
Junior Medical Detective - Indianapolis, IN - *ArtMar 84*
Junior Scholastic - New York, NY - *BaconPubCkMag 84; MagDir 84; MagIndMarPl 82-83*
Junior Service League of McAllen Inc. - McAllen, TX - *BoPubDir 4 Sup, 5*
Junior Trails [of Gospel Publishing House] - Springfield, MO - *WritMar 84*
Juniper Books [Aff. of Renfrew Advance Ltd.] - Renfrew, ON, Canada - *BoPubDir 4 Sup, 5*
Juniper Broadcasting Inc. - *See* Capps Broadcast Group
Juniper Editions - Manitou Springs, CO - *BoPubDir 4, 5*
Juniper House - Boulder, CO - *BoPubDir 4, 5*
Juniper Press [Aff. of Betts Bookstore] - Bangor, ME - *BoPubDir 4, 5*
Juniper Press - La Crosse, WI - *BoPubDir 4 Sup, 5; LitMag&SmPr 83-84*
Juniper Publishers Inc. - Lexington, KY - *BoPubDir 4, 5*
Juniro Arts Publications - Calgary, AB, Canada - *BoPubDir 5*
Junius Inc. - Philadelphia, PA - *BoPubDir 4, 5; LitMarPl 83, 84*
Junius-Vaughn Press [Aff. of Junius Book Distributors Inc.] - Fairview, NJ - *BoPubDir 4, 5*
Junk Publishing Co., Dr. W. - Hingham, MA - *LitMarPl 83, 84*
Jupiter Courier-Journal - Jupiter, FL - *AyerDirPub 83; BaconPubCkNews 84; NewsDir 84*
Jupiter Press [Aff. of Linguistic Association of Canada & The United States] - Lake Bluff, IL - *BoPubDir 4, 5*
Jupiter Publishing - Ottawa, ON, Canada - *BoPubDir 4 Sup, 5*
Jurdem/Thomas Associates Inc. - New York, NY - *DirPRFirms 83*
Juridical Databank [of Kluwer Publishing Co.] - Deventer, Netherlands - *EISS 7-83 Sup*
Jurimetrics Journal - Chicago, IL - *MagIndMarPl 82-83*
JURINPI Data Base [of National Institute for Patent Rights] - Paris, France - *EISS 83*
Juris-Classeurs [of Questel Inc.] - Washington, DC - *DataDirOnSer 84*
Juris-Data [of Editions Techniques] - Paris, France - *CompReadDB 82; DirOnDB Spring 84; EISS 5-84 Sup; InfIndMarPl 83*
Jurney Advertising Inc., Ross - Salt Lake City, UT - *StaDirAdAg 2-84*
Just Buffalo Press [Aff. of Allentown Community Center] - Buffalo, NY - *BoPubDir 4 Sup, 5; LitMag&SmPr 83-84*
Just Clare Co. - San Francisco, CA - *BoPubDir 5*
Just for Listening - Columbus, OH - *Tel&CabFB 84C*
Just Music Corp. - *See* Laurie Publishing Group
Just Reminiscing [of Dawn Valley Press] - New Wilmington, PA - *LitMag&SmPr 83-84*
Justice [of International Ladies' Garment Workers' Union] - New York, NY - *NewsDir 84*
Justice & Peace Center - Milwaukee, WI - *BoPubDir 4, 5*

Justice Retrieval & Inquiry System [of US Dept. of Justice] - Washington, DC - *DataDirOnSer 84; EISS 83*
Justicia [of International Ladies' Garment Workers' Union] - New York, NY - *NewsDir 84*
Juta & Co. Ltd. - Kenwyn, South Africa - *MicroMarPl 82-83*
Juul Press Inc., Peter - Tucson, AZ - *BoPubDir 4, 5*
Juvenescent Research Corp. - New York, NY - *BoPubDir 4, 5*
Juvenile Merchandising [of Columbia Communications Inc.] - New York, NY - *BaconPubCkMag 84; MagDir 84*
JV Co. [Div. of Materials for Today's Learning Inc.] - Reno, NV - *LitMarPl 83, 84*
JV Software - San Jose, CA - *MicrocomMPl 84*
JVC Co. of America - Elmwood Park, NJ - *BillIntBG 83-84*
JVC Cutting Center Inc. - Hollywood, CA - *BillIntBG 83-84*
JW Organisation, The - Tucson, AZ - *DirPRFirms 83*
JWB Jewish Book Council - New York, NY - *BoPubDir 4; LitMarPl 84*
JWP International - *See* Jo-Wee Publishing
JWT Group Inc. - New York, NY - *StaDirAdAg 2-84*
JWT Music Inc. [Subs. of J. Walter Thompson USA Inc.] - New York, NY - *BillIntBG 83-84*
JWT Syndication - New York, NY - *TelAl 83, 84*
Jym Enterprises - Batavia, OH - *BoPubDir 4 Sup, 5*

K

K Advertising Agency - Huntington, NY - *StaDirAdAg 2-84*
K & E Holdings Inc. - New York, NY - *StaDirAdAg 2-84*
K & H Communications - Oak Grove Heights, AR - *Tel&CabFB 84C*
K & H Productions Inc. - Dallas, TX - *TelAl 83; Tel&CabFB 84C*
K & H Software Systems - Milwaukee, WI - *MicrocomMPl 83*
K & K Publishers - Batavia, IL - *BoPubDir 4 Sup, 5*
K & K Television Inc. - Keystone, WV - *BrCabYB 84*
K & K Television Inc. - Northfork, WV - *BrCabYB 84*
K & K Univas [of the Univas Network] - Athens, Greece - *StaDirAdAg 2-84*
K. & M. Telephone Co. - Chambers, NE - *TelDir&BG 83-84*
K & M Word Processing Systems Inc. - Oceanside, NY - *LitMarPl 83, 84; MagIndMarPl 82-83*
K & R Music Inc. - Trumansburg, NY - *BillIntBG 83-84*
K & S Systems - Drexel Hill, PA - *MicrocomSwDir 1*
K-B Advertising/Productions - Wilmington, DE - *BrCabYB 84*
K-Byte - Troy, MI - *MicrocomMPl 83, 84*
K8 Software - Canton, CT - *MicrocomMPl 84*
K-Konsult - Stockholm, Sweden - *InfIndMarPl 83*
K-M Cable TV Co. Inc. - Kenmare, ND - *Tel&CabFB 84C*
K-M Cable TV Co. Inc. - Mohall, ND - *BrCabYB 84; Tel&CabFB 84C*
K-M Cable TV Inc. - Kenmore, ND - *BrCabYB 84*
K-Pay Entertainment Inc. - Los Angeles, CA - *Tel&CabFB 84C*
K Power - New York, NY - *BaconPubCkMag 84*
K-Promotions Inc. [Subs. of Carlson Co.] - Milwaukee, WI - *DirMarMP 83*
K-Tel International Inc. - Minnetonka, MN - *BillIntBG 83-84*
K-12 Micro Media - Woodcliff Lake, NJ - *MicrocomMPl 83, 84; MicrocomSwDir 1*
K-Vision Services Ltd. - New Glasgow, NS, Canada - *BrCabYB 84*
K.A. Advertising - Culloden, WV - *BoPubDir 4, 5*
Ka-Se-Ac Monthly - Glenside, PA - *MagDir 84*
KAAA - Kingman, AZ - *BrCabYB 84; TV&RadDir 84*
KAAB - Batesville, AR - *BrCabYB 84; TV&RadDir 84*
KAAK - Great Falls, MT - *BrCabYB 84*
KAAL-TV - Austin, MN - *BrCabYB 84; TelAl 83, 84; Tel&CabFB 84S; TV&RadDir 84*
KAAL-TV - Rochester, MN - *DirUSTelSta 83*
KAAM - Dallas, TX - *BrCabYB 84; NatRadPubDir Summer 83, Spring 84; TV&RadDir 84*
KAAN - New Hampton, MO - *BrCabYB 84*
KAAN-FM - Bethany, MO - *BrCabYB 84; TV&RadDir 84*
KAAR - Vancouver, WA - *BrCabYB 84; TV&RadDir 84*
KAAT - Oakhurst, CA - *BrCabYB 84*
KAAX-FM - Great Falls, MT - *TV&RadDir 84*
KAAY - Little Rock, AR - *BrCabYB 84; NatRadPubDir Summer 83, Spring 84; TV&RadDir 84*
Kabalarian Philosophy [Aff. of Society of Kabalarians of Canada] - Vancouver, BC, Canada - *BoPubDir 4 Sup, 5*
KABC - Los Angeles, CA - *BrCabYB 84; NatRadPubDir Summer 83, Spring 84; TV&RadDir 84*
KABC-TV - Hollywood, CA - *LitMarPl 83, 84*
KABC-TV - Los Angeles, CA - *BrCabYB 84; DirUSTelSta 83; TelAl 83, 84; Tel&CabFB 84S; TV&RadDir 84*
KABD - Seattle, WA - *Tel&CabFB 84S*
KABE-FM - Orem, UT - *BrCabYB 84; TV&RadDir 84*
KABF - Little Rock, AR - *BrCabYB 84*
KABG-FM - Cambridge, MN - *TV&RadDir 84*
KABI - Abilene, KS - *BrCabYB 84; TV&RadDir 84*
KABI-FM - Abilene, KS - *BrCabYB 84; TV&RadDir 84*
KABK-FM - Augusta, AR - *BrCabYB 84; TV&RadDir 84*
KABL - Oakland, CA - *BrCabYB 84*
KABL - San Francisco, CA - *NatRadPubDir Summer 83, Spring 84; TV&RadDir 84*
KABL-FM - San Francisco, CA - *BrCabYB 84; NatRadPubDir Summer 83, Spring 84; TV&RadDir 84*
Kable News Co. - New York, NY - *BoPubDir 4 Sup, 5; MagIndMarPl 82-83*
Kable Services of Pender [of TeleNational Communications Inc.] - Pender, NE - *Tel&CabFB 84C*
KABN - Anchorage, AK - *NatRadPubDir Summer 83 p.7, Spring 84*
KABN - Long Island, AK - *BrCabYB 84*
KABN - Wasilla, AK - *TV&RadDir 84*
KABQ - Albuquerque, NM - *BrCabYB 84; NatRadPubDir Summer 83, Spring 84; TV&RadDir 84*
KABR - Alamo, NM - *BrCabYB 84*
KABS - Pine Bluff, AR - *BrCabYB 84; NatRadPubDir Spring 84*
KABY-TV - Aberdeen, SD - *BrCabYB 84; TelAl 83, 84; Tel&CabFB 84S; TV&RadDir 84*
Kabyn Books - San Diego, CA - *BoPubDir 5*
KACA-FM - Prosser, WA - *BrCabYB 84; TV&RadDir 84*
KACB-TV - San Angelo, TX - *BrCabYB 84; TelAl 83, 84; Tel&CabFB 84S; TV&RadDir 84*
KACC - Alvin, TX - *BrCabYB 84*
KACE-FM - Inglewood, CA - *BrCabYB 84*
KACE-FM - Los Angeles, CA - *TV&RadDir 84*
KACH - Preston, ID - *BrCabYB 84; TV&RadDir 84*
KACH-FM - Preston, ID - *BrCabYB 84*
KACI - The Dalles, OR - *BrCabYB 84; TV&RadDir 84*
KACJ - Greenwood, AR - *BrCabYB 84; TV&RadDir 84*
Kack Klick Inc. - Rochester, NY - *BillIntBG 83-84*
KACO - Bellville, TX - *BrCabYB 84; TV&RadDir 84*
KACQ-FM - Hot Springs, AR - *BrCabYB 84; NatRadPubDir Summer 83, Spring 84; TV&RadDir 84*
KACT - Andrews, TX - *BrCabYB 84; TV&RadDir 84*
KACT-FM - Andrews, TX - *BrCabYB 84; TV&RadDir 84*
KACV-FM - Amarillo, TX - *BrCabYB 84; NatRadPubDir Summer 83, Spring 84*
KACY - Oxnard, CA - *TV&RadDir 84*
KACY - Port Hueneme, CA - *BrCabYB 84*
KACY - Santa Barbara, CA - *NatRadPubDir Summer 83 p.33, Spring 84 p.34*
KACY-FM - Oxnard, CA - *TV&RadDir 84*
KADA - Ada, OK - *BrCabYB 84; TV&RadDir 84*
KADE - Boulder, CO - *BrCabYB 84; TV&RadDir 84*

KADI-FM - St. Louis, MO - *BrCabYB 84; NatRadPubDir Summer 83 p.143, Spring 84 p.143; TV&RadDir 84*
KADL - Pine Bluff, AR - *NatRadPubDir Summer 83; TV&RadDir 84*
KADL-FM - Pine Bluff, AR - *BrCabYB 84; NatRadPubDir Summer 83, Spring 84; TV&RadDir 84*
KADN-TV - Lafayette, LA - *BrCabYB 84; DirUSTelSta 83; TelAl 83, 84; Tel&CabFB 84S; TV&RadDir 84*
KADO - Texarkana, TX - *BrCabYB 84; NatRadPubDir Summer 83, Spring 84; TV&RadDir 84*
KADO-FM - Texarkana, TX - *BrCabYB 84; NatRadPubDir Summer 83, Spring 84; TV&RadDir 84*
Kadoka Press - Kadoka, SD - *BaconPubCkNews 84; Ed&PubIntYB 82*
Kadoka Telephone Co. - Kadoka, SD - *TelDir&BG 83-84*
KADQ-FM - Rexburg, ID - *BrCabYB 84; TV&RadDir 84*
KADR - Elkader, IA - *BrCabYB 84*
KADS - Elk City, OK - *BrCabYB 84; TV&RadDir 84*
Kaduck, John M. [Aff. of Wallace-Homestead Book Co.] - Cleveland, OH - *BoPubDir 4, 5*
KAER-FM - Sacramento, CA - *BrCabYB 84; NatRadPubDir Summer 83, Spring 84; TV&RadDir 84*
KAET-TV - Phoenix, AZ - *BrCabYB 84; Tel&CabFB 84S*
KAET-TV - Tempe, AZ - *TV&RadDir 84*
KAEZ-FM - Oklahoma City, OK - *BrCabYB 84; NatRadPubDir Summer 83, Spring 84; TV&RadDir 84*
KAFE - Santa Fe, NM - *BrCabYB 84; TV&RadDir 84*
KAFE-FM - Santa Fe, NM - *BrCabYB 84; TV&RadDir 84*
KAFF - Flagstaff, AZ - *NatRadPubDir Summer 83, Spring 84*
KAFF-FM - Flagstaff, AZ - *BrCabYB 84; TV&RadDir 84*
Kafka Public Relations Services, Leon - New York, NY - *DirPRFirms 83*
KAFM-FM - Dallas, TX - *BrCabYB 84; NatRadPubDir Summer 83, Spring 84; TV&RadDir 84*
KAFT - Fayetteville, AR - *BrCabYB 84; Tel&CabFB 84S*
KAFY - Bakersfield, CA - *BrCabYB 84; NatRadPubDir Summer 83, Spring 84; TV&RadDir 84*
Kagan Associates Inc., Paul - Carmel, CA - *BoPubDir 5; InterCabHB 3*
KAGC - Bryan, TX - *BrCabYB 84; TV&RadDir 84*
KAGE - Winona, MN - *BrCabYB 84; NatRadPubDir Summer 83, Spring 84*
KAGE-FM - Winona, MN - *BrCabYB 84; NatRadPubDir Summer 83, Spring 84*
KAGH - Crossett, AR - *BrCabYB 84; TV&RadDir 84*
KAGH-FM - Crossett, AR - *BrCabYB 84; TV&RadDir 84*
KAGI - Grants Pass, OR - *BrCabYB 84; TV&RadDir 84*
Kagi Magazine - San Francisco, CA - *MagDir 84*
KAGO - Klamath Falls, OR - *BrCabYB 84; TV&RadDir 84*
KAGO-FM - Klamath Falls, OR - *BrCabYB 84; TV&RadDir 84*
KAGT - Anacortes, WA - *BrCabYB 84; TV&RadDir 84*
KAGY - Port Sulphur, LA - *BrCabYB 84; TV&RadDir 84*
KAHI - Auburn, CA - *BrCabYB 84; NatRadPubDir Summer 83, Spring 84; TV&RadDir 84*
KAHL - North Platte, NE - *NatRadPubDir Summer 83, Spring 84*
Kahlenberg Associates - Los Angeles, CA - *LitMarPl 83, 84*
Kahlotus Enterprise - *See* Tribune Newspapers Inc.
Kahlotus-Franklin County Enterprise - Clarkston, WA - *AyerDirPub 83*
Kahlotus TV Cable System - Kahlotus, WA - *BrCabYB 84; Tel&CabFB 84C*
Kahlson Illustrator, Carol - Woodmere Village, OH - *LitMarPl 83, 84*
KAHN - Prescott, AZ - *BrCabYB 84*
Kahn & Associates, Robert - Northbrook, IL - *StaDirAdAg 2-84*
Kahn Associates Inc., Bernard D. - New York, NY - *HBIndAd&MS 82-83*
Kahn Associates Inc., Milton - Los Angeles, CA - *DirPRFirms 83*
Kahn, Hannah - Miami, FL - *BoPubDir 4, 5*
Kahn Inc., A. D. - Southfield, MI - *Ed&PubIntYB 82*
Kahoka Media - Kahoka, MO - *BaconPubCkNews 84*
KAHS-FM - Arcata, CA - *BrCabYB 84; TV&RadDir 84*
KAID-TV - Boise, ID - *Tel&CabFB 84S; TV&RadDir 84*
KAII-TV - Wailuku, HI - *BrCabYB 84; TelAl 83, 84; Tel&CabFB 84S*
KAIL - Fresno, CA - *BrCabYB 84; DirUSTelSta 83; TelAl 83, 84; Tel&CabFB 84S*
KAIM - Honolulu, HI - *BrCabYB 84; LitMarPl 83, 84; NatRadPubDir Summer 83, Spring 84; TV&RadDir 84*
KAIM-FM - Honolulu, HI - *BrCabYB 84; LitMarPl 83; NatRadPubDir Summer 83, Spring 84; TV&RadDir 84*
Kaiman & Polon Inc. - Ft. Lee, NJ - *LitMarPl 83, 84*
Kaimuki-Kahala Sun Press - Kaimuki, HI - *Ed&PubIntYB 82*
Kainai News - Standoff, AB, Canada - *Ed&PubIntYB 82*
KAIR - Tucson, AZ - *BrCabYB 84; NatRadPubDir Summer 83, Spring 84; TV&RadDir 84*
Kairos [of Hermes House Press Inc.] - Niles, IL - *LitMag&SmPr 83-84*
Kaiser Corp. (Photo & AV Equipment Div.) - Colorado Springs, CO - *AvMarPl 83*
Kaiser-Group W Cable of Hawaii Inc. - Hawaii Kai, HI - *BrCabYB 84; Tel&CabFB 84C*
Kaiser Kuhn Bennett Inc. - Atlanta, GA - *StaDirAdAg 2-84*
KAIT-TV - Jonesboro, AR - *BrCabYB 84; DirUSTelSta 83; TelAl 83, 84; Tel&CabFB 84S; TV&RadDir 84*
Kaizan Music - *See* Jacobson, Jeffrey E.
KAJ Software Inc. - Phoenix, AZ - *MicrocomMPl 84*
KAJA-FM - San Antonio, TX - *BrCabYB 84; NatRadPubDir Spring 84; TV&RadDir 84*
KAJJ - Greenwood, AR - *BrCabYB 84*
KAJN - Crowley, LA - *BrCabYB 84; TV&RadDir 84*
KAJN-FM - Crowley, LA - *BrCabYB 84; TV&RadDir 84*
KAJO - Grants Pass, OR - *BrCabYB 84; TV&RadDir 84*
Kajon Computing Co. - Juneau, AK - *WhoWMicrocom 83*
KAKA - Dermott, AR - *BrCabYB 84*
KAKC - Tulsa, OK - *BrCabYB 84; NatRadPubDir Summer 83, Spring 84; TV&RadDir 84*
Kake Productions [Subs. of Chronicle Broadcasting Co.] - Wichita, KS - *AvMarPl 83*
KAKE-TV - Wichita, KS - *BrCabYB 84; DirUSTelSta 83; LitMarPl 83, 84; TelAl 83, 84; Tel&CabFB 84S; TV&RadDir 84*
Kakeland Stations, The - Wichita, KS - *BrCabYB 84*
KAKI-FM - Benton, AR - *BrCabYB 84; TV&RadDir 84*
KAKM-TV - Anchorage, AK - *BrCabYB 84; Tel&CabFB 84S; TV&RadDir 84*
KAKZ - Wichita, KS - *BrCabYB 84; NatRadPubDir Summer 83, Spring 84; TV&RadDir 84*
Kal, Merrick & Salan Inc. - Bethesda, MD - *DirPRFirms 83; StaDirAdAg 2-84*
KALA-FM - Davenport, IA - *BrCabYB 84; NatRadPubDir Summer 83, Spring 84; TV&RadDir 84*
Kalama Telephone Co. - Kalama, WA - *TelDir&BG 83-84*
Kalamazoo County Cablevision [of Adelphia Communications Corp.] - Richland, MI - *Tel&CabFB 84C*
Kalamazoo Focus News - Kalamazoo, MI - *NewsDir 84*
Kalamazoo Gazette [of Booth Newspapers Inc.] - Kalamazoo, MI - *BaconPubCkNews 84; Ed&PubIntYB 82; NewsDir 84*
Kalamazoo Public Library - Kalamazoo, MI - *BoPubDir 4, 5*
Kalamazoo Shopper - Allegan, MI - *AyerDirPub 83*
Kalart Victor Corp. - Plainville, CT - *AvMarPl 83*
KALB - Alexandria, LA - *BrCabYB 84; NatRadPubDir Summer 83, Spring 84; TV&RadDir 84*
KALB-TV - Alexandria, LA - *BrCabYB 84; DirUSTelSta 83; TelAl 83, 84; Tel&CabFB 84S; TV&RadDir 84*
Kalba Bowen Associates - Cambridge, MA - *CabTVFinDB 83; EISS 83; InfIndMarPl 83; InfoS 83-84; InterCabHB 3; TeleSy&SerDir 7-83; VideoDir 82-83*
Kalbro Computer Repairs - Morrestown, NJ - *WhoWMicrocom 83*
Kaldor Co. - South San Francisco, CA - *AvMarPl 83*
Kaldron - Grover City, CA - *LitMag&SmPr 83-84*
KALE - Pasco, WA - *TV&RadDir 84*
KALE - Richland, WA - *BrCabYB 84*
Kalehoff Productions, Edd - New York, NY - *AvMarPl 83*
Kaleidoscope - Akron, OH - *WritMar 84*
Kaleidoscope Productions Inc. - *See* Winard Advertising Agency Inc.
Kaleidoscope Records - El Cerrito, CA - *BillIntBG 83-84*
KaLeo O. Hawaii-The Voice of Hawaii [of University of Hawaii] - Honolulu, HI - *NewsDir 84*
Kaleva Telephone Co. - Kaleva, MI - *TelDir&BG 83-84*
KALF-FM - Red Bluff, CA - *BrCabYB 84; TV&RadDir 84*
KALG-FM - La Luz, NM - *BrCabYB 84*

Kalglo Electronics Co. Inc. - Bethlehem, PA - *MicrocomMPl 83, 84; WhoWMicrocom 83*
KALI - Los Angeles, CA - *NatRadPubDir Summer 83 p.19, Spring 84 p.20; TV&RadDir 84*
KALI - San Gabriel, CA - *BrCabYB 84*
Kalida Telephone Co. - Kalida, OH - *TelDir&BG 83-84*
Kalikow Advertising Co. - Kansas City, KS - *StaDirAdAg 2-84*
Kalil & Co. Inc. - Tucson, AZ - *CabTVFinDB 83*
Kalimat Press - Los Angeles, CA - *LitMag&SmPr 83-84; LitMarPl 83, 84*
Kalischer, Clemens - Stockbridge, MA - *LitMarPl 83, 84*
Kalish & Rice - Philadelphia, PA - *AdAge 3-28-84; BrCabYB 84; StaDirAdAg 2-84*
Kalispell Cable TV [of Group W Cable] - Kalispell, MT - *BrCabYB 84*
Kalispell Daily Interlake [of Hagadone Corp.] - Kalispell, MT - *BaconPubCkNews 84; NewsDir 84*
Kalispell Livestock Weekly News, The - Kalispell, MT - *NewsDir 84*
Kalispell News - Kalispell, MT - *AyerDirPub 83*
Kalispell Weekly News - Kalispell, MT - *BaconPubCkNews 84; Ed&PubIntYB 82; NewsDir 84*
Kalium Inc. - Warren, NJ - *BoPubDir 4 Sup, 5*
KALK - Denison, TX - *BrCabYB 84*
Kalkaska Leader & Kalkaskian - Kalkaska, MI - *BaconPubCkNews 84; Ed&PubIntYB 82*
KALL - Salt Lake City, UT - *BrCabYB 84; NatRadPubDir Summer 83, Spring 84; TV&RadDir 84*
KALL-FM - Salt Lake City, UT - *NatRadPubDir Summer 83, Spring 84; TV&RadDir 84*
Kallaher Inc., David - Cincinnati, OH - *ArtMar 84*
Kalliope, A Journal of Women's Art - Jacksonville, FL - *LitMag&SmPr 83-84*
Kallir, Philips, Ross - New York, NY - *AdAge 3-28-84; StaDirAdAg 2-84*
Kallman Associates - Ridgewood, NJ - *DirPRFirms 83*
KALM - Thayer, MO - *BrCabYB 84; TV&RadDir 84*
Kalman, Rogers & Trosclair Inc. - New Orleans, LA - *DirPRFirms 83*
Kalmar Responsive Ad/Marketing Corp. - Ft. Lee, NJ - *AdAge 3-28-84; StaDirAdAg 2-84*
Kalmbach Publishing Co. - Milwaukee, WI - *LitMarPl 83, 84; WritMar 84*
Kalmus & Co. Inc., Edwin F. - Opa Locka, FL - *BillIntBG 83-84*
Kalmus Corp., The - New York, NY - *DirPRFirms 83*
KALO - Beaumont, TX - *NatRadPubDir Summer 83; TV&RadDir 84*
Kalona Cooperative Telephone Co. - Kalona, IA - *TelDir&BG 83-84*
Kalona News - Kalona, IA - *BaconPubCkNews 84; Ed&PubIntYB 82*
KALQ-FM - Alamosa, CO - *BrCabYB 84; TV&RadDir 84*
KALS-FM - Kalispell, MT - *BrCabYB 84; TV&RadDir 84*
KALT - Atlanta, TX - *BrCabYB 84; TV&RadDir 84*
Kalt & Hamlin Public Relations - San Francisco, CA - *DirPRFirms 83*
Kaltronics Distributing Inc. - Northbrook, IL - *MicrocomMPl 84*
KALU-FM - Langston, OK - *BrCabYB 84; TV&RadDir 84*
Kalum Press - El Cajon, CA - *BoPubDir 4 Sup, 5*
KALV - Alva, OK - *BrCabYB 84; TV&RadDir 84*
KALW-FM - San Francisco, CA - *BrCabYB 84; NatRadPubDir Summer 83, Spring 84; TV&RadDir 84*
KALX-FM - Berkeley, CA - *BrCabYB 84; NatRadPubDir Summer 83, Spring 84; TV&RadDir 84*
KAM Executive Records - Charlotte, NC - *BillIntBG 83-84*
KAMA - El Paso, TX - *BrCabYB 84; NatRadPubDir Summer 83, Spring 84; TV&RadDir 84*
Kamal, Shuckran - Chattanooga, TN - *LitMarPl 83, 84; MagIndMarPl 82-83*
Kaman Sciences Corp. [Subs. of Kaman Corp.] - Colorado Springs, CO - *DataDirOnSer 84*
Kamas-Woodland Telephone Co. - Kamas, UT - *TelDir&BG 83-84*
KAMB-FM - Merced, CA - *BrCabYB 84; TV&RadDir 84*
Kamber Group, The - Washington, DC - *DirPRFirms 83*
Kambrina - Newport, OR - *BoPubDir 4 Sup, 5*
KAMC-TV - Lubbock, TX - *BrCabYB 84; DirUSTelSta 83; TelAl 84; Tel&CabFB 84S; TV&RadDir 84*
Kamco - Kalamazoo, MI - *AvMarPl 83*
KAMD - Camden, AR - *BrCabYB 84; TV&RadDir 84*
KAME-TV - Reno, NV - *BrCabYB 84; DirUSTelSta 83; TelAl 84; Tel&CabFB 84S; TV&RadDir 84*
Kameny Communications Inc. - Bergenfield, NJ - *StaDirAdAg 2-84*
KAMI - Cozad, NE - *BrCabYB 84; TV&RadDir 84*
Kamiah Clearwater Progress - Kamiah, ID - *BaconPubCkNews 84*
Kamin & Co., Lester - Houston, TX - *CabTVFinDB 83*
Kaminski & Associates Inc., Conrad C. - Milwaukee, WI - *StaDirAdAg 2-84*
KAML - Kenedy, TX - *BrCabYB 84; TV&RadDir 84*
Kamloops Cablenet Ltd. [of Cablenet Ltd.] - Kamloops, BC, Canada - *BrCabYB 84*
Kamloops Museum & Archives - Kamloops, BC, Canada - *BoPubDir 4, 5*
Kamloops News - Kamloops, BC, Canada - *BaconPubCkNews 84; Ed&PubIntYB 82*
KAMO - Rogers, AR - *BrCabYB 84; TV&RadDir 84*
KAMO-FM - Rogers, AR - *BrCabYB 84; TV&RadDir 84*
KAMP - El Centro, CA - *BrCabYB 84; TV&RadDir 84*
Kampmann & Co. - New York, NY - *LitMarPl 83, 84*
Kampmann Associates, Mel - Washington, DC - *CabTVFinDB 83*
KAMQ - Carlsbad, NM - *BrCabYB 84; TV&RadDir 84*
KAMR-TV - Amarillo, TX - *BrCabYB 84; DirUSTelSta 83; TelAl 83, 84; Tel&CabFB 84S; TV&RadDir 84*
KAMS-FM - Mammoth Spring, AR - *BrCabYB 84; TV&RadDir 84*
Kamsack Times - Kamsack, SK, Canada - *AyerDirPub 83; Ed&PubIntYB 82*
Kamstra Communications - St. Paul, MN - *AdAge 3-28-84; AvMarPl 83; DirMarMP 83; StaDirAdAg 2-84*
KAMT - Tacoma, WA - *BrCabYB 84; NatRadPubDir Spring 84*
KAMU-FM - Brazos, TX - *TV&RadDir 84*
KAMU-FM - College Station, TX - *BrCabYB 84; NatRadPubDir Summer 83, Spring 84*
KAMU-TV - Brazos, TX - *TV&RadDir 84*
KAMU-TV - College Station, TX - *BrCabYB 84; Tel&CabFB 84S*
KAMX - Albuquerque, NM - *BrCabYB 84; NatRadPubDir Summer 83, Spring 84; TV&RadDir 84*
KAMZ-FM - El Paso, TX - *BrCabYB 84; NatRadPubDir Summer 83, Spring 84; TV&RadDir 84*
KANA - Anaconda, MT - *BrCabYB 84; TV&RadDir 84*
Kanab Southern Utah News - Kanab, UT - *BaconPubCkNews 84*
Kanabec County Times - Mora, MN - *Ed&PubIntYB 82; NewsDir 84*
Kanada Kurier - Winnipeg, MB, Canada - *Ed&PubIntYB 82*
Kanada Kurier - Toronto, ON, Canada - *Ed&PubIntYB 82*
Kanadi Magyarsag - Toronto, ON, Canada - *Ed&PubIntYB 82*
Kanadski Srbobran - Hamilton, ON, Canada - *Ed&PubIntYB 82*
Kanadsky Slovak - Toronto, ON, Canada - *Ed&PubIntYB 82*
Kanan, Corbin, Schupak & Aronow Inc. - New York, NY - *DirPRFirms 83*
Kanan Inc., Malcolm - Montville, NJ - *StaDirAdAg 2-84*
Kanawha Cable Television Co. [of Harmon & Co.] - St. Albans, WV - *BrCabYB 84; Tel&CabFB 84C*
Kanawha CableVision Inc. - Kanawha, WV - *Tel&CabFB 84C*
Kanawha/Klemme Reporter - Kanawha, IA - *AyerDirPub 83*
Kanawha Reporter - Kanawha, IA - *BaconPubCkNews 84; Ed&PubIntYB 82*
Kanawha Valley Leader - Nitro, WV - *Ed&PubIntYB 82*
Kancen Advertising/Public Relations - Salina, KS - *StaDirAdAg 2-84*
Kanchenjunga Press - Red Bluff, CA - *BoPubDir 4, 5*
KAND - Corsicana, TX - *BrCabYB 84; TV&RadDir 84*
KANE - New Iberia, LA - *BrCabYB 84; TV&RadDir 84*
Kane Associates Inc., Allan - New York, NY - *MagIndMarPl 82-83*
Kane Associates Inc., Robert Francis - New York, NY - *ArtMar 84; DirPRFirms 83*
Kane Communications - Philadelphia, PA - *BoPubDir 5; MagIndMarPl 82-83*
Kane, Parsons & Associates Inc. - New York, NY - *IntDirMarRes 83*
Kane Report, The [of Whitaker Newsletters] - Westfield, NJ - *BaconPubCkMag 84; MagDir 84*
Kane Republican - Kane, PA - *BaconPubCkNews 84; Ed&PubIntYB 82; NewsDir 84*

Kanegis, James - Hyattsville, MD - *BoPubDir 4, 5*
Kaneohe Windward Sun Press - Kaneohe, HI - *BaconPubCkNews 84*
Kaner Associates Inc., Walter - New York, NY - *DirPRFirms 83*
Kaneshiro Publishing Co. - Chicago, IL - *BoPubDir 4, 5*
Kangan Publishing - Kansas City, KS - *BoPubDir 4, 5*
Kangaroo Press - Sydney, Austria - *LitMag&SmPr 83-84*
KANI - Wharton, TX - *BrCabYB 84; TV&RadDir 84*
Kankakee Daily Journal - Kankakee, IL - *BaconPubCkNews 84*
Kankakee Star-News [of B & B Publishing Co. Inc.] - Bourbonnais, IL - *AyerDirPub 83; NewsDir 84*
Kankakee TV Cable Co. [of Mid America Media] - Kankakee, IL - *BrCabYB 84; Tel&CabFB 84C*
Kankakee Valley Post News - Demotte, IN - *AyerDirPub 83; Ed&PubIntYB 82*
KANN - Ogden, UT - *BrCabYB 84; TV&RadDir 84*
Kannapolis Daily Independent - Kannapolis, NC - *BaconPubCkNews 84; NewsDir 84*
KanOkla Telephone Association Inc. - Anthony, KS - *TelDir&BG 83-84*
Kanrom Inc. - North Palm Beach, FL - *BoPubDir 4, 5*
KANS - Larned, KS - *BrCabYB 84; TV&RadDir 84*
KANS-FM - Larned, KS - *BrCabYB 84; TV&RadDir 84*
Kansan - Concordia, KS - *AyerDirPub 83*
Kansan - Kansas City, KS - *AyerDirPub 83*
Kansan - Newton, KS - *AyerDirPub 83*
Kansas [of Kansas Dept. of Economic Development] - Topeka, KS - *WritMar 84*
Kansas Banker, The - Topeka, KS - *BaconPubCkMag 84; MagDir 84*
Kansas Beverage News [of Beverage News Inc.] - Wichita, KS - *MagDir 84*
Kansas Broadcasting System Inc. - Hays, KS - *Tel&CabFB 84S*
Kansas Broadcasting System Inc. - Wichita, KS - *BrCabYB 84*
Kansas Broadcasting System Inc. - *See* Beach-Schmidt Group
Kansas Business News - Lindsborg, KS - *MagDir 84*
Kansas Business News [of Kansas Business Publishing Co. Inc.] - Topeka, KS - *BaconPubCkMag 84; WritMar 84*
Kansas Cablevision Inc. - Abilene, KS - *Tel&CabFB 84C p.1686*
Kansas CATV [of American TV & Communications Corp.] - Chanute, KS - *BrCabYB 84; Tel&CabFB 84C*
Kansas Chief - Troy, KS - *AyerDirPub 83; Ed&PubIntYB 82*
Kansas City Board of Trade - Kansas City, MO - *BoPubDir 5*
Kansas City Business Journal - Kansas City, MO - *BaconPubCkMag 84*
Kansas City Call - Kansas City, MO - *BaconPubCkNews 84*
Kansas City Chiefs Football Club - Kansas City, MO - *Tel&CabFB 84C*
Kansas City Grocer - Shawnee Mission, KS - *BaconPubCkMag 84; MagDir 84*
Kansas City Interviewing Service - Kansas City, MO - *IntDirMarRes 83*
Kansas City Kansan - Kansas City, KS - *BaconPubCkNews 84; Ed&PubIntYB 82; NewsDir 84*
Kansas City Libraries Metropolitan Information Network - Kansas City, MO - *EISS 83*
Kansas City Magazine - Prairie Village, KS - *BaconPubCkMag 84; WritMar 84*
Kansas City Magazine - Shawnee Mission, KS - *MagDir 84*
Kansas City Online Users Group - Kansas City, MO - *InfIndMarPl 83*
Kansas City Posse of the Westerners [Aff. of Westerners International] - Kansas City, MO - *BoPubDir 4, 5*
Kansas City Press Dispatch - Kansas City, MO - *BaconPubCkNews 84*
Kansas City Press Inc. - Kansas City, MO - *LitMarPl 83, 84*
Kansas City Silver City Record - Kansas City, KS - *BaconPubCkNews 84; NewsDir 84*
Kansas City Star [of Capital Cities Communications Inc.] - Kansas City, MO - *BaconPubCkNews 84; Ed&PubIntYB 82; LitMarPl 83, 84; NewsBur 6; NewsDir 84*
Kansas City State Globe - Kansas City, KS - *BaconPubCkNews 84*
Kansas City Times [of Capital Cities Communications Inc.] - Kansas City, MO - *BaconPubCkNews 84; Ed&PubIntYB 82; LitMarPl 83, 84; NewsBur 6; NewsDir 84*
Kansas City Voice - Kansas City, KS - *Ed&PubIntYB 82; NewsDir 84*
Kansas City Wyandotte Echo - Kansas City, KS - *BaconPubCkNews 84; Ed&PubIntYB 82*
Kansas Country Living - Topeka, KS - *BaconPubCkMag 84; MagDir 84*
Kansas Engineer [of University of Kansas] - Lawrence, KS - *BaconPubCkMag 84; MagDir 84*
Kansas Farmer - Topeka, KS - *BaconPubCkMag 84; MagDir 84*
Kansas Genealogical Society - Dodge City, KS - *BoPubDir 4, 5*
Kansas Government Journal [of League of Kansas Municipalities] - Topeka, KS - *BaconPubCkMag 84; MagDir 84*
Kansas Heritage Center - Dodge City, KS - *AvMarPl 83*
Kansas History, A Journal of the Central Plains - Topeka, KS - *MagIndMarPl 82-83*
Kansas Insurance Dept. - Topeka, KS - *BoPubDir 5*
Kansas Journal - Kansas, IL - *Ed&PubIntYB 82*
Kansas Library Services Network [of Kansas State Library] - Topeka, KS - *EISS 83*
Kansas Oil Marketer - Topeka, KS - *BaconPubCkMag 84*
Kansas/Oklahoma Chess Associations - Wichita, KS - *LitMag&SmPr 83-84*
Kansas Optometric Journal - Topeka, KS - *BaconPubCkMag 84*
Kansas Policy Database System [of University of Kansas] - Lawrence, KS - *EISS 83*
Kansas Press Service Inc. - Topeka, KS - *ProGuPRSer 4*
Kansas Professional Engineer - Topeka, KS - *BaconPubCkMag 84*
Kansas Publisher - Topeka, KS - *BaconPubCkMag 84; MagDir 84*
Kansas Quarterly [of Kansas State University] - Manhattan, KS - *LitMag&SmPr 83-84; WritMar 84*
Kansas Regents Network - Manhattan, KS - *TeleSy&SerDir 7-83*
Kansas Restaurant - Wichita, KS - *BaconPubCkMag 84; MagDir 84*
Kansas State Collegian [of Student Publications Inc.] - Manhattan, KS - *NewsDir 84*
Kansas State Data Center [of Kansas State Library] - Topeka, KS - *EISS 7-83 Sup*
Kansas State Engineer - Manhattan, KS - *MagDir 84*
Kansas State Historical Society - Topeka, KS - *MicroMarPl 82-83*
Kansas State Network - Wichita, KS - *BrCabYB 84*
Kansas State Telephone Co., The [Subs. of Contel Inc.] - Baxter Springs, KS - *TelDir&BG 83-84*
Kansas Stockman, The - Topeka, KS - *BaconPubCkMag 84; MagDir 84*
Kansas Teacher, The - Topeka, KS - *BaconPubCkMag 84*
Kansas Transporter, The - Topeka, KS - *BaconPubCkMag 84; MagDir 84*
Kansas Weekly Journal - Wichita, KS - *AyerDirPub 83; NewsDir 84*
Kansog Typing Service, Mary R. - Kendall Park, NJ - *LitMarPl 83, 84; MagIndMarPl 82-83*
Kanthaka Press - Brookline Village, MA - *BoPubDir 4, 5; LitMag&SmPr 83-84*
KANU-FM - Lawrence, KS - *BrCabYB 84; NatRadPubDir Summer 83, Spring 84; TV&RadDir 84*
KANW-FM - Albuquerque, NM - *BrCabYB 84; NatRadPubDir Summer 83, Spring 84; TV&RadDir 84*
KANZ-FM - Garden City, KS - *BrCabYB 84; TV&RadDir 84*
KAOC-FM - Port Lavaca, TX - *BrCabYB 84*
KAOI-FM - Wailuku, HI - *BrCabYB 84; TV&RadDir 84*
KAOK - Lake Charles, LA - *BrCabYB 84; NatRadPubDir Summer 83, Spring 84; TV&RadDir 84*
KAOL - Carrollton, MO - *BrCabYB 84; TV&RadDir 84*
KAOS-FM - Olympia, WA - *BrCabYB 84; NatRadPubDir Summer 83, Spring 84; TV&RadDir 84*
KAPA - Raymond, WA - *BrCabYB 84; TV&RadDir 84*
KAPB - Marksville, LA - *BrCabYB 84; TV&RadDir 84*
Kapco Communications [Div. of K. L. Rubel & Associates Ltd.] - Elk Grove Village, IL - *DirMarMP 83*
KAPE - San Antonio, TX - *BrCabYB 84; NatRadPubDir Summer 83, Spring 84; TV&RadDir 84*
KAPI - Pueblo, CO - *NatRadPubDir Summer 83; TV&RadDir 84*
Kaplan Associates Inc., Don - Marlton, NJ - *StaDirAdAg 2-84*
Kaplan Cable TV [of Telecable Associates Inc.] - Kaplan, LA - *BrCabYB 84*
Kaplan Herald - Kaplan, LA - *BaconPubCkNews 84; Ed&PubIntYB 82*

Kaplan Inc., Jay - Closter, NJ - *DirPRFirms 83*
Kaplan, Peter B. - New York, NY - *MagIndMarPl 82-83*
Kaplan Productions Inc., A. - New York, NY - *BillIntBG 83-84*
Kaplan Telephone Co. Inc., The - Kaplan, LA - *TelDir&BG 83-84*
Kapnick, Sharon - New York, NY - *LitMarPl 83, 84*
KAPP-TV - Yakima, WA - *BrCabYB 84; DirUSTelSta 83; TelAl 83, 84; Tel&CabFB 84S; TV&RadDir 84*
Kappeler Institute Publishing [Aff. of Kappeler Institute for the Science of Being] - Wilmington, DE - *BoPubDir 5*
Kappel's Computer Store Inc. - Belleville, IL - *WhoWMicrocom 83*
KAPR - Douglas, AZ - *BrCabYB 84; TV&RadDir 84*
Kapri Records - Sun Valley, CA - *BillIntBG 83-84*
KAPS - Mt. Vernon, WA - *BrCabYB 84; TV&RadDir 84*
Kapuler & Associates - Arlington Heights, IL - *IntDirMarRes 83*
Kapuler Survey Center - Arlington Heights, IL - *IntDirMarRes 83*
Kapusi Laboratories - San Mateo, CA - *DataDirSup 7-83*
KAPV-FM - Apple Valley, CA - *BrCabYB 84; TV&RadDir 84*
KAPY - Port Angeles, WA - *BrCabYB 84; TV&RadDir 84*
KAPZ - Bald Knob, AR - *BrCabYB 84*
KAPZ - Searcy, AR - *TV&RadDir 84*
Kar-Ben Copies Inc. - Rockville, MD - *BoPubDir 4, 5; LitMarPl 83, 84*
Kar-Mel CATV Systems Inc. [of Service Electric Cable TV Inc.] - Mt. Carmel, PA - *BrCabYB 84; Tel&CabFB 84C*
KARA-FM - San Jose, CA - *NatRadPubDir Summer 83 p.32, Spring 84 p.31*
KARA-FM - Santa Clara, CA - *BrCabYB 84; TV&RadDir 84*
Kara Research - San Juan Capistrano, CA - *IntDirMarRes 83*
Karamu [of Eastern Illinois University] - Charleston, IL - *WritMar 84*
Karas, Peter - Wayne, NJ - *LitMarPl 83, 84; MagIndMarPl 82-83*
Karate Illustrated [of Rainbow Publications Inc.] - Burbank, CA - *MagDir 84; MagIndMarPl 82-83; WritMar 84*
KARB-FM - Price, UT - *BrCabYB 84; TV&RadDir 84*
KARD-TV - Wichita, KS - *LitMarPl 83, 84; TelAl 83*
KARD-TV - Monroe, LA - *DirUSTelSta 83*
KARD-TV - West Monroe, LA - *BrCabYB 84; Tel&CabFB 84S*
KARDEX Systems Inc. - Marietta, OH - *DirInfWP 82*
Kardonne Advertising Agency - East Orange, NJ - *StaDirAdAg 2-84*
KARE - Atchison, KS - *BrCabYB 84; TV&RadDir 84*
Kare Records Inc. - Columbus, OH - *BillIntBG 83-84*
Karel, Frith Associates - San Francisco, CA - *LitMarPl 83, 84*
Karen Associates Inc. - West Hartford, CT - *IntDirMarRes 83*
Karger AG, S. - Basel, Switzerland - *MicroMarPl 82-83*
Karger Libri AG - Basel, Switzerland - *InfIndMarPl 83*
Karger Publishers Inc., S. [Aff. of S. Karger AG] - New York, NY - *BoPubDir 4, 5*
KARI - Blaine, WA - *BrCabYB 84; TV&RadDir 84*
Kari Records Inc. - Austin, TX - *BillIntBG 83-84*
Karien Communications Inc. - Rochelle, NY - *BrCabYB 84*
Karjan Music Publishing Co. [Div. of Little Giant Enterprises] - White Lake, NY - *BillIntBG 83-84*
KARK-TV [Subs. of Combined Communications Corp.] - Little Rock, AR - *BrCabYB 84; DirUSTelSta 83; LitMarPl 83, 84; TelAl 83, 84; Tel&CabFB 84S; TV&RadDir 84*
Karl Inc., Walter - Armonk, NY - *MagIndMarPl 82-83*
Karl Video Corp. - Newport Beach, CA - *AvMarPl 83; BillIntBG 83-84*
Karlen, Bernard E. - Slidell, LA - *Tel&CabFB 84C p.1686*
Karlen Communications Inc. - Great Bend, KS - *BrCabYB 84; Tel&CabFB 84C*
Karlen Communications Inc. - Larned, KS - *Tel&CabFB 84C*
Karlen Communications Inc. of La Crosse - La Crosse, KS - *Tel&CabFB 84C*
Karlstad North Star News - Karlstad, MN - *BaconPubCkNews 84*
KARM - Fresno, CA - *BrCabYB 84; NatRadPubDir Summer 83, Spring 84; TV&RadDir 84*
Karmic Revenge Laundry Shop Press - Guttenberg, NJ - *BoPubDir 4, 5; LitMag&SmPr 83-84*
KARN - Little Rock, AR - *BrCabYB 84; NatRadPubDir Summer 83, Spring 84; TV&RadDir 84*
Karnack Cable TV [of Karnack Corp.] - Austin Lake Estates, TX - *Tel&CabFB 84C*
Karnack Cable TV [of Karnack Corp.] - Benavides, TX - *Tel&CabFB 84C*
Karnack Cable TV [of Karnack Corp.] - Carrizo Springs, TX - *Tel&CabFB 84C*
Karnack Cable TV [of Karnack Corp.] - Crystal City, TX - *Tel&CabFB 84C*
Karnack Cable TV [of Karnack Corp.] - Cuero, TX - *Tel&CabFB 84C*
Karnack Cable TV [of Karnack Corp.] - Freer, TX - *Tel&CabFB 84C*
Karnack Cable TV [of Karnack Corp.] - Hebbronville, TX - *Tel&CabFB 84C*
Karnack Cable TV [of Karnack Corp.] - Pearsall, TX - *Tel&CabFB 84C*
Karnack Cable TV [of Karnack Corp.] - San Marcos, TX - *BrCabYB 84; Tel&CabFB 84C*
Karnack Cable TV [of Karnack Corp.] - Smithville, TX - *Tel&CabFB 84C*
Karnack Cable TV [of Karnack Corp.] - Wimberley, TX - *Tel&CabFB 84C*
Karnack Cable TV [of Karnack Corp.] - Zapata, TX - *Tel&CabFB 84C*
Karnack Corp. [of The LBJ Co.] - Austin, TX - *BrCabYB 84 p.D-302; Tel&CabFB 84C p.1686*
Karnack Telephone Co. [Aff. of Century Telephone Enterprises Inc.] - Karnack, TX - *TelDir&BG 83-84*
Karnath Corp. - Plano, TX - *CabTVFinDB 83*
Karnes Citation, The - Karnes City, TX - *Ed&PubIntYB 82*
Karnes City Cable Co. [of De-Cal Cable Inc.] - Karnes City, TX - *BrCabYB 84; Tel&CabFB 84C*
Karnes City Citation - Karnes City, TX - *BaconPubCkNews 84; NewsDir 84*
KARO - Columbia, MO - *BrCabYB 84*
Karol Media - Paramus, NJ - *ProGuPRSer 4*
Karolinska Institute Library & Information Center - Stockholm, Sweden - *EISS 83*
Karoma Publishers Inc. - Ann Arbor, MI - *BoPubDir 4, 5; LitMarPl 84*
KARR - Great Falls, MT - *BrCabYB 84; NatRadPubDir Summer 83, Spring 84; TV&RadDir 84*
Karr & Co., Jean - Washington, DC - *LitMarPl 83, 84*
Karr Productions, Paul S. - Phoenix, AZ - *ArtMar 84; AvMarPl 83; WritMar 84*
KARS - Belen, NM - *BrCabYB 84; TV&RadDir 84*
Karsh & Hagan - Englewood, CO - *AdAge 3-28-84 p.112; StaDirAdAg 2-84*
KART - Jerome, ID - *BrCabYB 84; TV&RadDir 84*
Kartoonings Advertising - Surrey, BC, Canada - *Ed&PubIntYB 82*
KARV - Russellville, AR - *BrCabYB 84; TV&RadDir 84*
Karwin & Associates, Thomas - Santa Cruz, CA - *InterCabHB 3*
KARY - Prosser, WA - *BrCabYB 84; TV&RadDir 84*
KARZ - Phoenix, AZ - *NatRadPubDir Summer 83; TV&RadDir 84*
KARZ - Burney, CA - *BrCabYB 84*
Karz-Cohl Publishing Inc. - New York, NY - *BoPubDir 5; LitMarPl 84*
Karz Publishers - New York, NY - *BoPubDir 4*
Kas Cable TV Inc. - Dayton, OH - *BrCabYB 84*
KASA - Phoenix, AZ - *BrCabYB 84; NatRadPubDir Summer 83, Spring 84; TV&RadDir 84*
KASB-FM - Bellevue, WA - *BrCabYB 84; NatRadPubDir Summer 83, Spring 84; TV&RadDir 84*
KASC-FM - Abbeville, LA - *BrCabYB 84; TV&RadDir 84*
KASD-FM - Aberdeen, SD - *NatRadPubDir Summer 83, Spring 84*
KASE-FM - Austin, TX - *BrCabYB 84; NatRadPubDir Summer 83, Spring 84; TV&RadDir 84*
KASF-FM - Alamosa, CO - *BrCabYB 84; TV&RadDir 84*
KASH - Eugene, OR - *BrCabYB 84; NatRadPubDir Summer 83, Spring 84*
KASH - Florence, OR - *TV&RadDir 84*
Kashong Publications - Bellona, NY - *BoPubDir 4, 5*
Kashu Mainichi - Los Angeles, CA - *AyerDirPub 83; Ed&PubIntYB 82; NewsDir 84*
KASI - Ames, IA - *BrCabYB 84; TV&RadDir 84*
KASK-FM - Las Cruces, NM - *BrCabYB 84; NatRadPubDir Summer 83, Spring 84; TV&RadDir 84*
Kask Labs - Tempe, AZ - *MicrocomMPl 83, 84; MicrocomSwDir 1*

KASL - Newcastle, WY - *BrCabYB 84; TV&RadDir 84*
Kaslo Television Ltd. - Kaslo, BC, Canada - *BrCabYB 84*
KASM - Albany, MN - *BrCabYB 84; TV&RadDir 84*
KASO - Minden, LA - *BrCabYB 84; TV&RadDir 84*
KASO-FM - Minden, LA - *BrCabYB 84; TV&RadDir 84*
Kass Creative Research, Babette - Sun City, AZ - *IntDirMarRes 83*
Kassebaum Radio Group - Topeka, KS - *BrCabYB 84*
Kasson & Mantorville Telephone Co. - Kasson, MN - *TelDir&BG 83-84*
Kasson Dodge County Independent - Kasson, MN - *BaconPubCkNews 84*
KAST - Astoria, OR - *BrCabYB 84; TV&RadDir 84*
Kaste Books - Barrie, ON, Canada - *BoPubDir 5*
Kaste Books - Stroud, ON, Canada - *BoPubDir 4*
Kastlemusick Inc. - Wilmington, DE - *BoPubDir 4, 5*
KASU-FM - Arkadelphia, AR - *NatRadPubDir Summer 83 p.276, Spring 84*
KASU-FM - Jonesboro, AR - *BrCabYB 84*
KASU-FM - Stonewall, AR - *TV&RadDir 84*
KASX-FM - Ada, OK - *BrCabYB 84; TV&RadDir 84*
KASY - Auburn, WA - *BrCabYB 84; TV&RadDir 84*
Kat Family Records - Atlanta, GA - *BillIntBG 83-84*
KATA - Arcata, CA - *BrCabYB 84; TV&RadDir 84*
Katahdin Press - Campbell, CA - *BoPubDir 4 Sup, 5*
Katahdin Times - Millinocket, ME - *AyerDirPub 83; Ed&PubIntYB 82*
Katavolos, Terenia - New York, NY - *LitMarPl 84*
KATC-TV - Lafayette, LA - *BrCabYB 84; DirUSTelSta 83; TelAl 83, 84; Tel&CabFB 84S; TV&RadDir 84*
Katch Nazar Music [Div. of Rose Hill Group] - Marcellus, NY - *BillIntBG 83-84*
KATE - Albert Lea, MN - *BrCabYB 84; TV&RadDir 84*
Kate's Komputers - Sausalito, CA - *MicrocomSwDir 1*
KATH - Douglas, WY - *BrCabYB 84*
KATI - Casper, WY - *BrCabYB 84; TV&RadDir 84*
KATK-FM - Carlsbad, NM - *BrCabYB 84; TV&RadDir 84*
KATL - Miles City, MT - *BrCabYB 84; TV&RadDir 84*
KATN - Fairbanks, AK - *BrCabYB 84; Tel&CabFB 84S*
KATO - Safford, AZ - *BrCabYB 84; TV&RadDir 84*
KATO - Plentywood, MT - *BrCabYB 84*
Katolicky Sokol - Passaic, NJ - *Ed&PubIntYB 82*
Katolikus Magyarok Vasarnapja - Youngstown, OH - *Ed&PubIntYB 82*
KATQ - Plentywood, MT - *TV&RadDir 84*
KATQ-FM - Plentywood, MT - *BrCabYB 84; TV&RadDir 84*
KATR - Eugene, OR - *NatRadPubDir Summer 83*
KATS-FM - Yakima, WA - *BrCabYB 84; TV&RadDir 84*
KATT - Oklahoma City, OK - *BrCabYB 84; NatRadPubDir Summer 83, Spring 84; TV&RadDir 84*
KATT-FM - Oklahoma City, OK - *NatRadPubDir Summer 83, Spring 84; TV&RadDir 84*
KATU-TV - Portland, OR - *BrCabYB 84; DirUSTelSta 83; LitMarPl 83, 84; TelAl 83, 84; Tel&CabFB 84S; TV&RadDir 84*
KATV-TV - Little Rock, AR - *BrCabYB 84; DirUSTelSta 83; LitMarPl 83, 84; TelAl 83, 84; Tel&CabFB 84S; TV&RadDir 84*
KATX-FM - Plainview, TX - *BrCabYB 84; NatRadPubDir Summer 83, Spring 84; TV&RadDir 84*
KATY - San Luis Obispo, CA - *BrCabYB 84; TV&RadDir 84*
Katy Brookshire-Katy Times - Katy, TX - *BaconPubCkNews 84*
Katy Cable Television Inc. [of Harte-Hanks Communications Inc.] - Katy, TX - *BrCabYB 84; Tel&CabFB 84C*
Katy Times - Katy, TX - *Ed&PubIntYB 82*
Katydid Books - Rochester, MI - *BoPubDir 4 Sup, 5*
KATZ - St. Louis, MO - *BrCabYB 84; NatRadPubDir Summer 83, Spring 84; TV&RadDir 84*
Katz Agency Inc., The - New York, NY - *TelAl 83, 84*
Katz Broadcasting - Bridgeport, CT - *BrCabYB 84*
KATZ-FM - Sierra Vista, AZ - *TV&RadDir 84*
Katzenstein Associates - Larchmont, NY - *HBIndAd&MS 82-83*
Katzman, Susan Manlin - St. Louis, MO - *Ed&PubIntYB 82*
Kauai Cable TV [of The Seven Twenty Ltd. Partnership] - Kalaheo, HI - *Tel&CabFB 84C*
KAUB-FM - Auburn, NE - *BrCabYB 84*
Kauffmann & Boyce Productions - Allston, MA - *AvMarPl 83*
Kaufman & Associates Inc., Henry J. - Washington, DC - *BrCabYB 84; StaDirAdAg 2-84; TelAl 83, 84*
Kaufman & Associates Inc., Henry J. (Public Relations Div.) - Washington, DC - *ArtMar 84*
Kaufman & Co. Inc., Fran - New York, NY - *DirPRFirms 83*
Kaufman & Maraffi - New York, NY - *AdAge 3-28-84; StaDirAdAg 2-84*
Kaufman Associates Inc. - Boston, MA - *StaDirAdAg 2-84*
Kaufman Herald - Kaufman, TX - *BaconPubCkNews 84; Ed&PubIntYB 82; NewsDir 84*
Kaufman Inc., Risa - New York, NY - *LitMarPl 83, 84*
Kaufman, Lansky, Baker Advertising - San Diego, CA - *StaDirAdAg 2-84*
Kaufman Photography - New York, NY - *MagIndMarPl 82-83*
Kaufman/Public Relations [Subs. of Henry J. Kaufman & Associates] - Washington, DC - *DirPRFirms 83*
Kaufman Publishers, Alvin B. - Woodland Hills, CA - *BoPubDir 5*
Kaufman, Samuel - New York, NY - *LitMarPl 83, 84; MagIndMarPl 82-83*
Kaufman, Sonia - New York, NY - *LitMarPl 83, 84; MagIndMarPl 82-83*
Kaufmann Associates - Simons Island, GA - *ArtMar 84; StaDirAdAg 2-84*
Kaufmann Inc., William - Los Altos, CA - *LitMag&SmPr 83-84; LitMarPl 83, 84; WritMar 84*
Kaukauna Times - Kaukauna, WI - *BaconPubCkNews 84; Ed&PubIntYB 82; NewsDir 84*
KAUL - North Little Rock, AR - *BrCabYB 84; TV&RadDir 84*
KAUM - Colorado City, TX - *BrCabYB 84*
Kaumagraph Corp. - Wilmington, DE - *LitMarPl 83, 84*
Kaunitz, Robert - Mt. Vernon, NY - *InfIndMarPl 83; LitMarPl 83*
KAUR-FM - Sioux Falls, SD - *BrCabYB 84; NatRadPubDir Summer 83, Spring 84; TV&RadDir 84*
KAUS - Austin, MN - *BrCabYB 84; TV&RadDir 84*
KAUS-FM - Austin, MN - *BrCabYB 84; TV&RadDir 84*
KAUT-TV - Oklahoma City, OK - *BrCabYB 84; DirUSTelSta 83; TelAl 83, 84; Tel&CabFB 84S; TV&RadDir 84*
KAUZ-TV - Wichita Falls, TX - *BrCabYB 84; DirUSTelSta 83; TelAl 83, 84; Tel&CabFB 84S; TV&RadDir 84*
KAV Books Inc. - New York, NY - *WritMar 84*
KAVA - Burney, CA - *BrCabYB 84; TV&RadDir 84*
Kavanagh Books - Brandon, MB, Canada - *BoPubDir 4, 5*
Kavanagh Hand Press, Peter - New York, NY - *BoPubDir 4, 5*
KAVE-TV - Carlsbad, NM - *BrCabYB 84; TelAl 83, 84; Tel&CabFB 84S*
KAVI - Rocky Ford, CO - *BrCabYB 84; TV&RadDir 84*
KAVI-FM - Rocky Ford, CO - *BrCabYB 84; TV&RadDir 84*
KAVL - Lancaster, CA - *BrCabYB 84; TV&RadDir 84*
KAVO-FM - Fallbrook, CA - *BrCabYB 84; TV&RadDir 84*
KAVR - Apple Valley, CA - *BrCabYB 84; TV&RadDir 84*
KAVS-FM - Thief River Falls, MN - *BrCabYB 84; NatRadPubDir Summer 83, Spring 84; TV&RadDir 84*
KAVT-FM - Austin, MN - *BrCabYB 84; NatRadPubDir Summer 83, Spring 84; TV&RadDir 84*
KAVT-TV - Austin, MN - *BrCabYB 84; Tel&CabFB 84S; TV&RadDir 84*
KAVU-TV - Victoria, TX - *BrCabYB 84; Tel&CabFB 84S*
KAVV - Benson, AZ - *BrCabYB 84*
Kawa Systems International - Palo Alto, CA - *MicrocomMPl 84*
Kawabata Press - Millbrook, England - *LitMag&SmPr 83-84*
KAWC - Yuma, AZ - *BrCabYB 84; TV&RadDir 84*
KAWE-TV - Bemidji, MN - *BrCabYB 84; Tel&CabFB 84S; TV&RadDir 84*
Kaweah Nation Times - Riviera, AZ - *LitMag&SmPr 83-84*
Kawecki, Alicja T. - Morris Plains, NJ - *LitMarPl 83, 84; MagIndMarPl 82-83*
KAWL - York, NE - *BrCabYB 84; TV&RadDir 84*
KAWL-FM - York, NE - *BrCabYB 84; TV&RadDir 84*
KAWS - Hemphill, TX - *BrCabYB 84; TV&RadDir 84*
KAWW - Heber Springs, AR - *BrCabYB 84; TV&RadDir 84*
KAWW-FM - Heber Springs, AR - *BrCabYB 84; TV&RadDir 84*
KAWY-FM - Casper, WY - *BrCabYB 84; TV&RadDir 84*
KAXE-FM - Grand Rapids, MN - *BrCabYB 84; NatRadPubDir Summer 83, Spring 84; TV&RadDir 84*
Kay/Hubbard/Associates - Santa Cruz, CA - *StaDirAdAg 2-84*
Kay Research Inc., Herbert - West Orange, NJ - *Tel&CabFB 84C*

Kayak - Santa Cruz, CA - *LitMag&SmPr 83-84*
Kayak Books Inc. - Santa Cruz, CA - *BoPubDir 4, 5*
Kayak Press - Santa Cruz, CA - *LitMag&SmPr 83-84*
KAYC - Beaumont, TX - *BrCabYB 84; NatRadPubDir Summer 83, Spring 84; TV&RadDir 84*
KAYD-FM - Beaumont, TX - *BrCabYB 84; NatRadPubDir Summer 83, Spring 84; TV&RadDir 84*
Kaye Associates - Westmont, NJ - *TeleSy&SerDir 7-83*
KAYE-FM - Tonkawa, OK - *BrCabYB 84; NatRadPubDir Summer 83, Spring 84; TV&RadDir 84*
Kaye Publications, Richard - Studio City, CA - *BillIntBG 83-84*
Kaye-Smith Radio - Bellevue, WA - *BrCabYB 84*
Kayfetz Productions Inc., Victor - New York, NY - *ProGuPRSer 4*
KAYI-FM - Muskogee, OK - *BrCabYB 84; TV&RadDir 84*
KAYK - Pueblo, CO - *BrCabYB 84*
KAYK - Provo, UT - *NatRadPubDir Summer 83*
KAYL - Storm Lake, IA - *BrCabYB 84; TV&RadDir 84*
KAYL-FM - Storm Lake, IA - *BrCabYB 84; TV&RadDir 84*
KAYN-FM - Nogales, AZ - *BrCabYB 84; TV&RadDir 84*
KAYO - Aberdeen, WA - *BrCabYB 84; TV&RadDir 84*
Kaypro [Subs. of Non-Linear Systems Inc.] - Solana Beach, CA - *WhoWMicrocom 83*
KAYQ-FM - Warsaw, MO - *BrCabYB 84; TV&RadDir 84*
KAYR - Van Buren, AR - *BrCabYB 84; TV&RadDir 84*
KAYS - Hays, KS - *BrCabYB 84 p.D-302; Tel&CabFB 84C p.1686; TV&RadDir 84*
KAYS-TV - Hays, KS - *BrCabYB 84; DirUSTelSta 83; TelAl 83, 84; Tel&CabFB 84S; TV&RadDir 84*
Kaysam Music - New York, NY - *BillIntBG 83-84*
KAYT - Rupert, ID - *BrCabYB 84; TV&RadDir 84*
Kayteekay Music - *See* Campbell Music Inc., Glen
KAYU-TV - Seattle, WA - *TelAl 84*
KAYU-TV - Spokane, WA - *DirUSTelSta 83; Tel&CabFB 84S*
KAYY - Fairbanks, AK - *BrCabYB 84*
KAYZ-FM - El Dorado, AR - *BrCabYB 84; TV&RadDir 84*
KAZA - Gilroy, CA - *BrCabYB 84*
KAZA - San Jose, CA - *TV&RadDir 84*
KAZI-FM - Austin, TX - *BrCabYB 84; TV&RadDir 84*
Kazi Publications Inc. - Chicago, IL - *BoPubDir 4 Sup, 5*
KAZM - Sedona, AZ - *BrCabYB 84; TV&RadDir 84*
Kazma, Gerald J. - Naperville, IL - *Tel&CabFB 84C p.1686*
Kazma, Gerald J. - Halifax, NS, Canada - *BrCabYB 84; Tel&CabFB 84C*
KAZU-FM - Pacific Grove, CA - *BrCabYB 84; TV&RadDir 84*
KAZY-FM - Denver, CO - *BrCabYB 84; NatRadPubDir Summer 83, Spring 84; TV&RadDir 84*
KAZZ-FM - Sallisaw, OK - *BrCabYB 84; TV&RadDir 84*
KBAA - Ortonville, MN - *BrCabYB 84*
KBAB - Indianola, IA - *BrCabYB 84; TV&RadDir 84*
KBAD - Carlsbad, NM - *BrCabYB 84; TV&RadDir 84*
KBAI - Morro Bay, CA - *BrCabYB 84; TV&RadDir 84*
KBAK-TV - Bakersfield, CA - *BrCabYB 84; DirUSTelSta 83; TelAl 83, 84; Tel&CabFB 84S; TV&RadDir 84*
KBAL - San Saba, TX - *BrCabYB 84; TV&RadDir 84*
KBAM - Longview, WA - *BrCabYB 84; TV&RadDir 84*
KBAN - Bowie, TX - *BrCabYB 84; TV&RadDir 84*
KBAR - Burley, ID - *BrCabYB 84; TV&RadDir 84*
KBAS - Bullhead City, AZ - *BrCabYB 84; TV&RadDir 84*
KBAT-FM - Midland, TX - *BrCabYB 84; NatRadPubDir Summer 83, Spring 84; TV&RadDir 84*
KBAY-FM - San Jose, CA - *BrCabYB 84; NatRadPubDir Summer 83, Spring 84; TV&RadDir 84*
KBBA - Benton, AR - *BrCabYB 84; TV&RadDir 84*
KBBB - Borger, TX - *BrCabYB 84; TV&RadDir 84*
KBBC-FM - Lake Havasu City, AZ - *BrCabYB 84; TV&RadDir 84*
KBBC-FM - Beaver, UT - *NatRadPubDir Summer 83, Spring 84*
KBBD-FM - Beaver, UT - *BrCabYB 84; TV&RadDir 84*
KBBF-FM - Santa Rosa, CA - *BrCabYB 84; TV&RadDir 84*
KBBG-FM - Waterloo, IA - *BrCabYB 84; TV&RadDir 84*
KBBI - Homer, AK - *BrCabYB 84*
KBBJ - Tulsa, OK - *BrCabYB 84; NatRadPubDir Summer 83, Spring 84; TV&RadDir 84*
KBBK-FM - Boise, ID - *BrCabYB 84; NatRadPubDir Summer 83, Spring 84; TV&RadDir 84*
KBBL - Lubbock, TX - *BrCabYB 84; NatRadPubDir Spring 84*
KBBM-TV - Jefferson City, MO - *BrCabYB 84; Tel&CabFB 84S*
KBBN-FM - Broken Bow, NE - *BrCabYB 84*
KBBO - Yakima, WA - *BrCabYB 84; TV&RadDir 84*
KBBQ - Ventura, CA - *BrCabYB 84; NatRadPubDir Summer 83, Spring 84; TV&RadDir 84*
KBBR - North Bend, OR - *BrCabYB 84; TV&RadDir 84*
KBBS - Buffalo, WY - *BrCabYB 84; TV&RadDir 84*
KBBV - Big Bear Lake, CA - *BrCabYB 84; TV&RadDir 84*
KBBW - Waco, TX - *BrCabYB 84; NatRadPubDir Summer 83, Spring 84; TV&RadDir 84*
KBBX - Bountiful, UT - *TV&RadDir 84*
KBBX - Centerville, UT - *BrCabYB 84*
KBBX - Salt Lake City, UT - *NatRadPubDir Summer 83, Spring 84*
KBBY-FM - Ventura, CA - *BrCabYB 84; NatRadPubDir Summer 83, Spring 84; TV&RadDir 84*
KBBZ - Kalispell, MT - *BrCabYB 84*
KBC Corp. [of Metrovision Inc.] - Belton, TX - *BrCabYB 84*
KBC Corp. [of Metrovision Inc.] - Killeen, TX - *Tel&CabFB 84C*
KBCB-FM - Corpus Christi, TX - *BrCabYB 84; NatRadPubDir Summer 83, Spring 84*
KBCC - Cuba, MO - *BrCabYB 84; TV&RadDir 84*
KBCC-FM - Bakersfield, CA - *NatRadPubDir Summer 83, Spring 84*
KBCE - Boyce, LA - *BrCabYB 84*
KBCH - Lincoln City, OR - *BrCabYB 84; TV&RadDir 84*
KBCI-TV - Boise, ID - *DirUSTelSta 83; TelAl 83, 84; Tel&CabFB 84S; TV&RadDir 84*
KBCL - Shreveport, LA - *BrCabYB 84; NatRadPubDir Summer 83, Spring 84 p.110; TV&RadDir 84*
KBCM-FM - Sioux City, IA - *TV&RadDir 84*
KBCO-FM - Boulder, CO - *BrCabYB 84; NatRadPubDir Summer 83, Spring 84; TV&RadDir 84*
KBCQ - Roswell, NM - *BrCabYB 84; NatRadPubDir Summer 83, Spring 84; TV&RadDir 84*
KBCR - Steamboat Springs, CO - *BrCabYB 84; TV&RadDir 84*
KBCS-FM - Bellevue, WA - *BrCabYB 84; NatRadPubDir Summer 83, Spring 84; TV&RadDir 84*
KBCT-FM - Fairfield, IA - *BrCabYB 84; TV&RadDir 84*
KBCV - Bentonville, AR - *BrCabYB 84*
KBDF - Eugene, OR - *BrCabYB 84; NatRadPubDir Summer 83, Spring 84; TV&RadDir 84*
KBDG-FM - Turlock, CA - *BrCabYB 84; TV&RadDir 84*
KBDI-TV - Broomfield, CO - *BrCabYB 84; Tel&CabFB 84S; TV&RadDir 84*
KBDY-FM - St. Louis, MO - *BrCabYB 84; NatRadPubDir Summer 83, Spring 84; TV&RadDir 84*
KBEA - Mission, KS - *BrCabYB 84*
KBEA - Shawnee Mission, KS - *TV&RadDir 84*
KBEA - Kansas City, MO - *NatRadPubDir Summer 83 p.141, Spring 84 p.141*
KBEC - Waxahachie, TX - *BrCabYB 84; TV&RadDir 84*
KBEE - Modesto, CA - *NatRadPubDir Summer 83; TV&RadDir 84*
KBEE-FM - Modesto, CA - *BrCabYB 84; NatRadPubDir Summer 83, Spring 84; TV&RadDir 84*
KBEK-FM - Lexington, MO - *BrCabYB 84; TV&RadDir 84*
KBEL - Idabel, OK - *BrCabYB 84; TV&RadDir 84*
KBEM-FM - Minneapolis, MN - *BrCabYB 84; TV&RadDir 84*
KBEM-FM - North Minneapolis, MN - *NatRadPubDir Summer 83, Spring 84*
KBEN - Carrizo Springs, TX - *BrCabYB 84; TV&RadDir 84*
KBEQ-FM - Kansas City, MO - *BrCabYB 84; NatRadPubDir Summer 83, Spring 84; TV&RadDir 84*
KBES - Ceres, CA - *BrCabYB 84*
KBET - Reno, NV - *BrCabYB 84; NatRadPubDir Summer 83, Spring 84; TV&RadDir 84*
KBEW - Blue Earth, MN - *BrCabYB 84; TV&RadDir 84*
KBEZ-FM - Tulsa, OK - *BrCabYB 84; NatRadPubDir Summer 83, Spring 84; TV&RadDir 84*
KBFC-FM - Forrest City, AR - *BrCabYB 84; TV&RadDir 84*
KBFI - Bonners Ferry, ID - *BrCabYB 84; TV&RadDir 84*
KBFL-FM - Buffalo, MO - *BrCabYB 84; NatRadPubDir Summer 83, Spring 84; TV&RadDir 84*
KBFM-FM - Edinburg, TX - *BrCabYB 84*
KBFM-FM - McAllen, TX - *NatRadPubDir Summer 83, Spring 84; TV&RadDir 84*

KBFS - Belle Fourche, SD - *BrCabYB 84; TV&RadDir 84*
KBFW - Bellingham, WA - *BrCabYB 84; NatRadPubDir Summer 83, Spring 84; TV&RadDir 84*
KBGA - Holtville, CA - *BrCabYB 84*
KBGL-FM - Pocatello, ID - *TV&RadDir 84*
KBGN - Caldwell, ID - *BrCabYB 84; TV&RadDir 84*
KBGT-TV - Albion, NE - *BrCabYB 84*
KBGX - Alturas, CA - *BrCabYB 84*
KBHB - Sturgis, SD - *BrCabYB 84; TV&RadDir 84*
KBHC - Nashville, AR - *BrCabYB 84; TV&RadDir 84*
KBHE-TV - Rapid City, SD - *BrCabYB 84; Tel&CabFB 84S; TV&RadDir 84*
KBHI-FM - Modesto, CA - *BrCabYB 84*
KBHK-TV - San Francisco, CA - *BrCabYB 84; DirUSTelSta 83; LitMarPl 84; TelAl 83, 84; Tel&CabFB 84S; TV&RadDir 84*
KBHL-FM - Lincoln, NE - *TV&RadDir 84*
KBHM - Branson, MO - *TV&RadDir 84*
KBHP-FM - Bemidji, MN - *BrCabYB 84; TV&RadDir 84*
KBHS - Hot Springs, AR - *BrCabYB 84; NatRadPubDir Summer 83, Spring 84; TV&RadDir 84*
KBHU-FM - Spearfish, SD - *BrCabYB 84; NatRadPubDir Summer 83, Spring 84; TV&RadDir 84*
KBHV - Spanish Fork, UT - *BrCabYB 84*
KBHW - International Falls, MN - *BrCabYB 84*
KBIA-FM - Columbia, MO - *BrCabYB 84; NatRadPubDir Summer 83, Spring 84; TV&RadDir 84*
KBIC-FM - Alice, TX - *BrCabYB 84; NatRadPubDir Summer 83, Spring 84; TV&RadDir 84*
KBIF - Fresno, CA - *BrCabYB 84; NatRadPubDir Summer 83, Spring 84; TV&RadDir 84*
KBIG-FM - Los Angeles, CA - *BrCabYB 84; NatRadPubDir Summer 83, Spring 84; TV&RadDir 84*
KBIL-FM - San Angelo, TX - *BrCabYB 84*
KBIM - Roswell, NM - *BrCabYB 84; NatRadPubDir Summer 83, Spring 84; TV&RadDir 84*
KBIM-FM - Roswell, NM - *BrCabYB 84; NatRadPubDir Summer 83, Spring 84; TV&RadDir 84*
KBIM-TV - Roswell, NM - *BrCabYB 84; DirUSTelSta 83; TelAl 83, 84; Tel&CabFB 84S; TV&RadDir 84*
KBIN - Council Bluffs, IA - *BrCabYB 84; Tel&CabFB 84S*
KBIQ-FM - Edmonds, WA - *BrCabYB 84; TV&RadDir 84*
KBIQ-FM - Seattle, WA - *NatRadPubDir Summer 83, Spring 84*
KBIU-FM - Lake Charles, LA - *BrCabYB 84; NatRadPubDir Spring 84; TV&RadDir 84*
KBIX - Muskogee, OK - *BrCabYB 84; TV&RadDir 84*
KBIZ - Ottumwa, IA - *BrCabYB 84; NatRadPubDir Summer 83, Spring 84; TV&RadDir 84*
KBJC-FM - Great Bend, KS - *TV&RadDir 84*
KBJH - Tulsa, OK - *BrCabYB 84; Tel&CabFB 84S*
KBJM - Lemmon, SD - *BrCabYB 84; TV&RadDir 84*
KBJR-TV - Duluth, MN - *DirUSTelSta 83; TelAl 83, 84; Tel&CabFB 84S; TV&RadDir 84*
KBJR-TV - Superior, WI - *BrCabYB 84; Tel&CabFB 84S*
KBJT - Fordyce, AR - *BrCabYB 84; TV&RadDir 84*
KBKB - Ft. Madison, IA - *BrCabYB 84; TV&RadDir 84*
KBKB-FM - Ft. Madison, IA - *BrCabYB 84; TV&RadDir 84*
KBKG - Corning, AR - *BrCabYB 84*
KBKN-FM - Astoria, OR - *BrCabYB 84; TV&RadDir 84*
KBKR - Baker, OR - *BrCabYB 84; TV&RadDir 84*
KBKR-FM - Baker, OR - *BrCabYB 84; TV&RadDir 84*
KBL Associates - *See* Entertainment Co. Music Group, The
KBLC - Lakeport, CA - *BrCabYB 84; TV&RadDir 84*
KBLE - Seattle, WA - *BrCabYB 84; NatRadPubDir Summer 83, Spring 84; TV&RadDir 84*
KBLE Ohio Inc. - Columbus, OH - *BrCabYB 84; Tel&CabFB 84C*
KBLF - Red Bluff, CA - *BrCabYB 84; TV&RadDir 84*
KBLI - Blackfoot, ID - *TV&RadDir 84*
KBLI-FM - Blackfoot, ID - *BrCabYB 84; TV&RadDir 84*
KBLJ-FM - La Junta, CO - *BrCabYB 84; TV&RadDir 84*
KBLL - Helena, MT - *BrCabYB 84; NatRadPubDir Summer 83, Spring 84; TV&RadDir 84*
KBLL-FM - Helena, MT - *BrCabYB 84; NatRadPubDir Summer 83, Spring 84; TV&RadDir 84*
KBLQ - Logan, UT - *BrCabYB 84; TV&RadDir 84*
KBLQ-FM - Logan, UT - *BrCabYB 84; TV&RadDir 84*
KBLS - Santa Barbara, CA - *BrCabYB 84; NatRadPubDir Summer 83, Spring 84; TV&RadDir 84*
KBLT-FM - Baxter Springs, KS - *BrCabYB 84*
KBLT-FM - Galena, KS - *TV&RadDir 84*
KBLU - Yuma, AZ - *BrCabYB 84; TV&RadDir 84*
KBLX-FM - Berkeley, CA - *BrCabYB 84; TV&RadDir 84*
KBLX-FM - San Francisco, CA - *NatRadPubDir Summer 83 p.30, Spring 84 p.29*
KBM - Stamford, CT - *MagIndMarPl 82-83*
KBMC-FM - Eugene, OR - *BrCabYB 84; NatRadPubDir Summer 83, Spring 84; TV&RadDir 84*
KBME-TV - Bismarck, ND - *BrCabYB 84; Tel&CabFB 84S; TV&RadDir 84*
KBMI - Roma, TX - *BrCabYB 84*
KBMJ - Phillipsburg, KS - *BrCabYB 84*
KBMN - Bozeman, MT - *BrCabYB 84; TV&RadDir 84*
KBMO - Benson, MN - *BrCabYB 84; TV&RadDir 84*
KBMO-FM - Benson, MN - *BrCabYB 84; TV&RadDir 84*
KBMR - Bismarck, ND - *BrCabYB 84; NatRadPubDir Summer 83, Spring 84; TV&RadDir 84*
KBMT-TV - Beaumont, TX - *BrCabYB 84; DirUSTelSta 83; TelAl 83, 84; Tel&CabFB 84S; TV&RadDir 84*
KBMV-FM - Birch Tree, MO - *BrCabYB 84; TV&RadDir 84*
KBMW - Breckenridge, MN - *BrCabYB 84; TV&RadDir 84*
KBMW - Wahpeton, ND - *TV&RadDir 84*
KBMY - Billings, MT - *BrCabYB 84; TV&RadDir 84*
KBND - Bend, OR - *BrCabYB 84; TV&RadDir 84*
KBNO - Denver, CO - *BrCabYB 84; NatRadPubDir Summer 83, Spring 84; TV&RadDir 84*
KBNR - Brownsville, TX - *BrCabYB 84*
KBNY-FM - Nampa, ID - *BrCabYB 84; TV&RadDir 84*
KBOA - Kennett, MO - *BrCabYB 84; TV&RadDir 84*
KBOB-FM - La Puente, CA - *TV&RadDir 84*
KBOB-FM - West Covina, CA - *BrCabYB 84*
KBOE - Oskaloosa, IA - *BrCabYB 84; TV&RadDir 84*
KBOE-FM - Molino, FL - *TV&RadDir 84*
KBOE-FM - Oskaloosa, IA - *BrCabYB 84*
KBOI - Boise, ID - *BrCabYB 84; NatRadPubDir Summer 83, Spring 84; TV&RadDir 84*
KBOI-FM - Boise, ID - *BrCabYB 84; NatRadPubDir Summer 83, Spring 84; TV&RadDir 84*
KBOK - Malvern, AR - *BrCabYB 84; TV&RadDir 84*
KBOL - Boulder, CO - *BrCabYB 84; NatRadPubDir Summer 83, Spring 84; TV&RadDir 84*
KBOM - Colby, KS - *BrCabYB 84; Tel&CabFB 84S*
KBON-FM - Lake Arrowhead, CA - *BrCabYB 84; TV&RadDir 84*
KBON-FM - San Bernardino, CA - *NatRadPubDir Summer 83, Spring 84*
KBOO-FM - Portland, OR - *BrCabYB 84; NatRadPubDir Summer 83, Spring 84; TV&RadDir 84*
KBOP - Pleasanton, TX - *BrCabYB 84; TV&RadDir 84*
KBOP-FM - Pleasanton, TX - *BrCabYB 84; TV&RadDir 84*
KBOQ - Marina, CA - *BrCabYB 84*
KBOR - Brownsville, TX - *BrCabYB 84; TV&RadDir 84*
KBOR - McAllen, TX - *NatRadPubDir Summer 83, Spring 84 p.243*
KBOS-FM - Tulare, CA - *BrCabYB 84; NatRadPubDir Summer 83, Spring 84; TV&RadDir 84*
KBOT - Cabot, AR - *BrCabYB 84; TV&RadDir 84*
KBOW - Butte, MT - *BrCabYB 84; TV&RadDir 84*
KBOX - Little Rock, AR - *NatRadPubDir Spring 84*
KBOX - North Little Rock, AR - *BrCabYB 84*
KBOX - Dallas, TX - *TV&RadDir 84*
KBOY-FM - Medford, OR - *BrCabYB 84; TV&RadDir 84*
KBOZ - Bozeman, MT - *BrCabYB 84; TV&RadDir 84*
KBPI-FM - Denver, CO - *BrCabYB 84; NatRadPubDir Summer 83, Spring 84; TV&RadDir 84*
KBPK-FM - Buena Park, CA - *BrCabYB 84; TV&RadDir 84*
KBPS - Portland, OR - *BrCabYB 84; NatRadPubDir Summer 83, Spring 84; TV&RadDir 84*
KBQC - Bettendorf, IA - *BrCabYB 84*
KBQQ - Minot, ND - *BrCabYB 84*
KBRA-FM - Wichita, KS - *BrCabYB 84; NatRadPubDir Summer 83, Spring 84; TV&RadDir 84*
KBRB - Ainsworth, NE - *BrCabYB 84; TV&RadDir 84*
KBRB-FM - Ainsworth, NE - *BrCabYB 84*

KBRC - Mt. Vernon, WA - *BrCabYB 84; TV&RadDir 84*
KBRD-FM - Tacoma, WA - *BrCabYB 84; NatRadPubDir Summer 83, Spring 84; TV&RadDir 84*
KBRE - Cedar City, UT - *BrCabYB 84; TV&RadDir 84*
KBRE-FM - Cedar City, UT - *BrCabYB 84; TV&RadDir 84*
KBRF - Fergus Falls, MN - *BrCabYB 84; TV&RadDir 84*
KBRF-FM - Fergus Falls, MN - *BrCabYB 84; TV&RadDir 84*
KBRG-FM - San Francisco, CA - *TV&RadDir 84*
KBRI - Brinkley, AR - *BrCabYB 84; TV&RadDir 84*
KBRI-FM - Brinkley, AR - *BrCabYB 84; TV&RadDir 84*
KBRK - Brookings, SD - *BrCabYB 84; TV&RadDir 84*
KBRO - Bremerton, WA - *BrCabYB 84; TV&RadDir 84*
KBRQ - Denver, CO - *BrCabYB 84; NatRadPubDir Summer 83, Spring 84; TV&RadDir 84*
KBRQ-FM - Denver, CO - *BrCabYB 84; NatRadPubDir Summer 83, Spring 84; TV&RadDir 84*
KBRS - Springdale, AR - *BrCabYB 84; TV&RadDir 84*
KBRT - Avalon, CA - *BrCabYB 84*
KBRT - Los Angeles, CA - *TV&RadDir 84*
KBRU-FM - Ft. Morgan, CO - *BrCabYB 84; TV&RadDir 84*
KBRV - Soda Springs, ID - *BrCabYB 84; TV&RadDir 84*
KBRW - Barrow, AK - *BrCabYB 84; TV&RadDir 84*
KBRX - O'Neill, NE - *BrCabYB 84; TV&RadDir 84*
KBRX-FM - O'Neill, NE - *BrCabYB 84; TV&RadDir 84*
KBRZ - Freeport, TX - *BrCabYB 84; TV&RadDir 84*
KBSA - Ontario, CA - *Tel&CabFB 84S*
KBSB-FM - Bemidji, MN - *BrCabYB 84; NatRadPubDir Summer 83, Spring 84; TV&RadDir 84*
KBSC-TV - Corona, CA - *BrCabYB 84; Tel&CabFB 84S*
KBSC-TV - Glendale, CA - *TV&RadDir 84*
KBSC-TV - Los Angeles, CA - *DirUSTelSta 83; TelAl 83, 84*
KBSF - Springhill, LA - *BrCabYB 84; TV&RadDir 84*
KBSH - Borrego Springs, CA - *BrCabYB 84*
KBSI - Cape Girardeau, MO - *Tel&CabFB 84S*
KBST - Big Spring, TX - *BrCabYB 84; TV&RadDir 84*
KBSU - Boise, ID - *BrCabYB 84; TV&RadDir 84*
KBTA - Batesville, AR - *BrCabYB 84; TV&RadDir 84*
KBTC - Houston, MO - *BrCabYB 84; TV&RadDir 84*
KBTM - Jonesboro, AR - *BrCabYB 84; TV&RadDir 84*
KBTN - Neosho, MO - *BrCabYB 84; TV&RadDir 84*
KBTO-FM - Bottineau, ND - *BrCabYB 84; TV&RadDir 84*
KBTV-TV - Denver, CO - *BrCabYB 84; DirUSTelSta 83; LitMarPl 83, 84; TelAl 83, 84; Tel&CabFB 84S; TV&RadDir 84*
KBTX-TV - Bryan, TX - *BrCabYB 84; DirUSTelSta 83; TelAl 83, 84; Tel&CabFB 84S; TV&RadDir 84*
KBUC - San Antonio, TX - *BrCabYB 84; NatRadPubDir Summer 83, Spring 84; TV&RadDir 84*
KBUC-FM - San Antonio, TX - *BrCabYB 84; NatRadPubDir Summer 83, Spring 84; TV&RadDir 84*
KBUD - Athens, TX - *BrCabYB 84; TV&RadDir 84*
KBUF - Garden City, KS - *BrCabYB 84; TV&RadDir 84*
KBUF-FM - Garden City, KS - *BrCabYB 84; TV&RadDir 84*
KBUG - Salt Lake City, UT - *BrCabYB 84*
KBUH - Brigham City, UT - *BrCabYB 84; TV&RadDir 84*
KBUH-FM - Brigham City, UT - *TV&RadDir 84*
KBUK - Baytown, TX - *BrCabYB 84; TV&RadDir 84*
KBUK - Houston, TX - *NatRadPubDir Summer 83 p.239, Spring 84 p.240*
KBUN - Bemidji, MN - *BrCabYB 84; TV&RadDir 84*
KBUR - Burlington, IA - *BrCabYB 84; NatRadPubDir Summer 83, Spring 84; TV&RadDir 84*
KBUS - Mexia, TX - *BrCabYB 84; TV&RadDir 84*
KBUY-FM - Amarillo, TX - *BrCabYB 84; NatRadPubDir Summer 83, Spring 84; TV&RadDir 84*
KBUZ-FM - Arkansas City, KS - *BrCabYB 84; TV&RadDir 84*
KBVD - Ruidoso, NM - *BrCabYB 84*
KBVL-FM - Boulder, CO - *BrCabYB 84; TV&RadDir 84*
KBVO-TV - Austin, TX - *BrCabYB 84; Tel&CabFB 84S*
KBVR-FM - Corvallis, OR - *BrCabYB 84; NatRadPubDir Summer 83, Spring 84; TV&RadDir 84*
KBWA - Williams, AZ - *TV&RadDir 84*
KBWC-FM - Marshall, TX - *BrCabYB 84; NatRadPubDir Summer 83, Spring 84; TV&RadDir 84*
KBWD - Brownwood, TX - *BrCabYB 84; TV&RadDir 84*
KBWH-FM - Blair, NE - *BrCabYB 84; TV&RadDir 84*
KBWS - Sisseton, SD - *BrCabYB 84*
KBXL-FM - Caldwell, ID - *BrCabYB 84; TV&RadDir 84*
KBXM - Kennett, MO - *BrCabYB 84; TV&RadDir 84*
KBXN - Tremonton, UT - *BrCabYB 84*
KBXN-FM - Tremonton, UT - *BrCabYB 84*
KBYE - Oklahoma City, OK - *BrCabYB 84; TV&RadDir 84*
KBYG - Big Spring, TX - *BrCabYB 84; TV&RadDir 84*
KBYO - Tallulah, LA - *BrCabYB 84*
KBYP - Shamrock, TX - *BrCabYB 84; TV&RadDir 84*
KBYQ - Sweet Home, OR - *BrCabYB 84*
KBYR - Anchorage, AK - *BrCabYB 84; NatRadPubDir Summer 83, Spring 84; TV&RadDir 84*
KBYU-FM - Provo, UT - *BrCabYB 84; NatRadPubDir Summer 83, Spring 84; TV&RadDir 84*
KBYU-TV - Provo, UT - *BrCabYB 84; Tel&CabFB 84S; TV&RadDir 84*
KBZB - Bisbee, AZ - *BrCabYB 84; TV&RadDir 84*
KBZN-FM - Bozeman, MT - *TV&RadDir 84*
KBZT - San Diego, CA - *BrCabYB 84; NatRadPubDir Summer 83*
KBZT-FM - San Diego, CA - *NatRadPubDir Spring 84; TV&RadDir 84*
KBZY - Salem, OR - *BrCabYB 84; NatRadPubDir Summer 83, Spring 84; TV&RadDir 84*
KBZZ - La Junta, CO - *BrCabYB 84; TV&RadDir 84*
KC Corp. - New Rochelle, NY - *Tel&CabFB 84C*
KC Publications - Las Vegas, NV - *BoPubDir 4, 5; LitMarPl 84*
KC Publishing Co. - Phoenix, AZ - *BoPubDir 5*
KC Research Associates - New York, NY - *IntDirMarRes 83*
KCAA - Yuma, AZ - *BrCabYB 84; Tel&CabFB 84S*
KCAB - Dardanelle, AR - *BrCabYB 84; TV&RadDir 84*
KCAJ - El Dorado, AR - *BrCabYB 84*
KCAL - Redlands, CA - *BrCabYB 84; TV&RadDir 84*
KCAL-FM - Redlands, CA - *BrCabYB 84; TV&RadDir 84*
KCAM - Glennallen, AK - *BrCabYB 84; TV&RadDir 84*
KCAN - El Reno, OK - *BrCabYB 84; TV&RadDir 84*
KCAP - Helena, MT - *BrCabYB 84; NatRadPubDir Summer 83, Spring 84; TV&RadDir 84*
KCAP-FM - Helena, MT - *BrCabYB 84; NatRadPubDir Summer 83, Spring 84; TV&RadDir 84*
KCAQ-FM - Oxnard, CA - *BrCabYB 84*
KCAQ-FM - Ventura, CA - *NatRadPubDir Spring 84 p.34*
KCAR - Clarksville, TX - *BrCabYB 84; TV&RadDir 84*
KCAS - Slaton, TX - *BrCabYB 84; TV&RadDir 84*
KCAT - Pine Bluff, AR - *BrCabYB 84; NatRadPubDir Summer 83, Spring 84; TV&RadDir 84*
KCAU-TV - Sioux City, IA - *BrCabYB 84; DirUSTelSta 83; TelAl 83, 84; Tel&CabFB 84S; TV&RadDir 84*
KCAW - Sitka, AK - *BrCabYB 84*
KCAZ - Walnut Ridge, AR - *BrCabYB 84*
KCB Corp. [of MetroVision Inc.] - Killeen, TX - *BrCabYB 84*
KCB Publications Inc. - Ottawa, ON, Canada - *BoPubDir 4 Sup, 5*
KCBA - Salinas, CA - *BrCabYB 84; DirUSTelSta 83; Tel&CabFB 84S*
KCBC - Des Moines, IA - *BrCabYB 84; NatRadPubDir Summer 83; TV&RadDir 84*
KCBD-TV - Lubbock, TX - *BrCabYB 84; DirUSTelSta 83; TelAl 83, 84; Tel&CabFB 84S; TV&RadDir 84*
KCBF - Fairbanks, AK - *BrCabYB 84; NatRadPubDir Summer 83, Spring 84; TV&RadDir 84*
KCBI-FM - Dallas, TX - *BrCabYB 84; NatRadPubDir Summer 83, Spring 84; TV&RadDir 84*
KCBJ-TV - Columbia, MO - *BrCabYB 84; DirUSTelSta 83; TelAl 83, 84; Tel&CabFB 84S; TV&RadDir 84*
KCBN - Reno, NV - *BrCabYB 84; NatRadPubDir Summer 83, Spring 84; TV&RadDir 84*
KCBN Advertising, Public Relations & Design - *See* AHM & A Public Relations
KCBQ - San Diego, CA - *BrCabYB 84; NatRadPubDir Summer 83 p.28, Spring 84 p.28*
KCBQ - Santee, CA - *TV&RadDir 84*
KCBQ-FM - San Diego, CA - *BrCabYB 84; NatRadPubDir Summer 83 p.28, Spring 84 p.28*
KCBQ-FM - Santee, CA - *TV&RadDir 84*
KCBR - Des Moines, IA - *BrCabYB 84; TelAl 84; Tel&CabFB 84S*
KCBS - San Francisco, CA - *BrCabYB 84; LitMarPl 83, 84; NatRadPubDir Summer 83, Spring 84; TV&RadDir 84*

KCBS-FM - San Francisco, CA - *TV&RadDir 84*
KCBW-FM - Sedalia, MO - *BrCabYB 84; TV&RadDir 84*
KCBX-FM - San Luis Obispo, CA - *BrCabYB 84; TV&RadDir 84*
KCBY-TV - Coos Bay, OR - *BrCabYB 84; TelAl 83, 84; Tel&CabFB 84S; TV&RadDir 84*
KCCA - Sierra Vista, AZ - *BrCabYB 84; Tel&CabFB 84S*
KCCB - Corning, AR - *BrCabYB 84; TV&RadDir 84*
KCCC - Carlsbad, NM - *BrCabYB 84; TV&RadDir 84*
KCCI-TV - Des Moines, IA - *BrCabYB 84; DirUSTelSta 83; TelAl 83, 84; Tel&CabFB 84S; TV&RadDir 84*
KCCK-FM - Cedar Rapids, IA - *BrCabYB 84; NatRadPubDir Summer 83, Spring 84; TV&RadDir 84*
KCCL - Paris, AR - *BrCabYB 84; TV&RadDir 84*
KCCM-FM - Moorhead, MN - *BrCabYB 84; NatRadPubDir Summer 83, Spring 84; TV&RadDir 84*
KCCN - Honolulu, HI - *BrCabYB 84; NatRadPubDir Summer 83, Spring 84; TV&RadDir 84*
KCCO - Lawton, OK - *BrCabYB 84; TV&RadDir 84*
KCCQ-FM - Ames, IA - *BrCabYB 84; TV&RadDir 84*
KCCR - Pierre, SD - *BrCabYB 84; TV&RadDir 84*
KCCS - Salem, OR - *BrCabYB 84; NatRadPubDir Summer 83, Spring 84; TV&RadDir 84*
KCCT - Corpus Christi, TX - *BrCabYB 84; NatRadPubDir Summer 83, Spring 84; TV&RadDir 84*
KCCU - Columbus, KS - *BrCabYB 84*
KCCV - Independence, MO - *BrCabYB 84; TV&RadDir 84*
KCCV - Kansas City, MO - *NatRadPubDir Summer 83 p.142, Spring 84 p.142*
KCCY-FM - Pueblo, CO - *BrCabYB 84; TV&RadDir 84*
KCDC-FM - Longmont, CO - *BrCabYB 84; TV&RadDir 84*
KCDQ-FM - Belgrade, MT - *TV&RadDir 84*
KCDR - Cedar Rapids, IA - *BrCabYB 84; NatRadPubDir Summer 83, Spring 84; TV&RadDir 84*
KCDS - Angwin, CA - *BrCabYB 84*
KCED-FM - Centralia, WA - *BrCabYB 84; NatRadPubDir Summer 83, Spring 84; TV&RadDir 84*
KCEE - Tucson, AZ - *BrCabYB 84; NatRadPubDir Summer 83, Spring 84; TV&RadDir 84*
KCEL-FM - Toledo, OR - *BrCabYB 84; TV&RadDir 84*
KCEN-TV - Temple, TX - *BrCabYB 84; DirUSTelSta 83; TelAl 83, 84; Tel&CabFB 84S; TV&RadDir 84*
KCEP-FM - Las Vegas, NV - *BrCabYB 84; NatRadPubDir Summer 83, Spring 84; TV&RadDir 84*
KCEQ - Walnut Creek, CA - *BrCabYB 84*
KCES-FM - Eufaula, OK - *BrCabYB 84; TV&RadDir 84*
KCET - Los Angeles, CA - *BrCabYB 84; Tel&CabFB 84S; TV&RadDir 84; VideoDir 82-83*
KCEY - Modesto, CA - *NatRadPubDir Summer 83, Spring 84*
KCEY - Turlock, CA - *BrCabYB 84; TV&RadDir 84*
KCEZ-FM - Kansas City, MO - *NatRadPubDir Summer 83 p.142; TV&RadDir 84*
KCFI - Cedar Falls, IA - *BrCabYB 84; TV&RadDir 84*
KCFI - Waterloo, IA - *NatRadPubDir Summer 83 p.97, Spring 84 p.97*
KCFM-FM - Florissant, MO - *BrCabYB 84; TV&RadDir 84*
KCFO-FM - Tulsa, OK - *BrCabYB 84; NatRadPubDir Summer 83, Spring 84; TV&RadDir 84*
KCFR-FM - Denver, CO - *BrCabYB 84; NatRadPubDir Summer 83, Spring 84; TV&RadDir 84*
KCFS-FM - Sioux Falls, SD - *BrCabYB 84; NatRadPubDir Summer 83, Spring 84; TV&RadDir 84*
KCFV-FM - Ferguson, MO - *BrCabYB 84*
KCFV-FM - St. Louis, MO - *NatRadPubDir Summer 83, Spring 84; TV&RadDir 84*
KCFW-TV - Kalispell, MT - *BrCabYB 84; DirUSTelSta 83; TelAl 83, 84; Tel&CabFB 84S; TV&RadDir 84*
KCFW-TV - Missoula, MT - *TV&RadDir 84*
KCGB-FM - Hood River, OR - *BrCabYB 84; TV&RadDir 84*
KCGL-FM - Bountiful, UT - *TV&RadDir 84*
KCGL-FM - Centerville, UT - *BrCabYB 84*
KCGL-FM - Salt Lake City, UT - *NatRadPubDir Summer 83, Spring 84*
KCGM-FM - Scobey, MT - *BrCabYB 84; TV&RadDir 84*
KCGN - Ortonville, MN - *BrCabYB 84*
KCGS - Marshall, AR - *BrCabYB 84; TV&RadDir 84*
KCHA - Charles City, IA - *BrCabYB 84; TV&RadDir 84*
KCHA-FM - Charles City, IA - *BrCabYB 84; TV&RadDir 84*
KCHC-FM - Central Point, OR - *BrCabYB 84; NatRadPubDir Summer 83, Spring 84*
KCHC-FM - Medford, OR - *TV&RadDir 84*
KCHE - Cherokee, IA - *BrCabYB 84; TV&RadDir 84*
KCHE-FM - Cherokee, IA - *BrCabYB 84; TV&RadDir 84*
KCHF - Santa Fe, NM - *BrCabYB 84; Tel&CabFB 84S*
KCHI - Chillicothe, MO - *BrCabYB 84; TV&RadDir 84*
KCHI-FM - Chillicothe, MO - *BrCabYB 84; TV&RadDir 84*
KCHJ - Delano, CA - *BrCabYB 84; TV&RadDir 84*
KCHK - New Prague, MN - *BrCabYB 84; TV&RadDir 84*
KCHO-FM - Chico, CA - *BrCabYB 84; NatRadPubDir Summer 83, Spring 84; TV&RadDir 84*
KCHR - Charleston, MO - *BrCabYB 84; TV&RadDir 84*
KCHS - Truth or Consequences, NM - *BrCabYB 84; TV&RadDir 84*
KCHU-FM - Dallas, TX - *TV&RadDir 84*
KCHV - Coachella, CA - *BrCabYB 84*
KCHV - Indio, CA - *TV&RadDir 84*
KCIC-FM - Grand Junction, CO - *BrCabYB 84; TV&RadDir 84*
KCID - Caldwell, ID - *BrCabYB 84; TV&RadDir 84*
KCID-FM - Caldwell, ID - *BrCabYB 84*
KCIE - Fairbury, NE - *BrCabYB 84*
KCII - Washington, IA - *BrCabYB 84; TV&RadDir 84*
KCII-FM - Washington, IA - *BrCabYB 84; TV&RadDir 84*
KCIJ - Shreveport, LA - *BrCabYB 84; NatRadPubDir Summer 83, Spring 84; TV&RadDir 84*
KCIK-TV - El Paso, TX - *BrCabYB 84; DirUSTelSta 83; TelAl 83, 84; Tel&CabFB 84S; TV&RadDir 84*
KCIL-FM - Houma, LA - *BrCabYB 84; NatRadPubDir Summer 83, Spring 84; TV&RadDir 84*
KCIM - Carroll, IA - *BrCabYB 84; TV&RadDir 84*
KCIN - Victorville, CA - *BrCabYB 84; TV&RadDir 84*
KCIR - Twin Falls, ID - *BrCabYB 84*
KCIV-FM - The Dalles, OR - *BrCabYB 84; TV&RadDir 84*
KCIZ-FM - Springdale, AR - *BrCabYB 84; TV&RadDir 84*
KCJB - Minot, ND - *BrCabYB 84; NatRadPubDir Summer 83, Spring 84; TV&RadDir 84*
KCJB-FM - Minot, ND - *TV&RadDir 84*
KCJF - Kellogg, ID - *BrCabYB 84*
KCJH-FM - Stockton, CA - *BrCabYB 84; TV&RadDir 84*
KCJJ - Iowa City, IA - *BrCabYB 84; TV&RadDir 84*
KCKA - Centralia, WA - *BrCabYB 84; Tel&CabFB 84S*
KCKC - San Bernardino, CA - *BrCabYB 84; NatRadPubDir Summer 83, Spring 84; TV&RadDir 84*
KCKL - Malakoff, TX - *BrCabYB 84*
KCKO - Spokane, WA - *BrCabYB 84; TV&RadDir 84*
KCKQ - Jena, LA - *BrCabYB 84*
KCKR - Crockett, TX - *BrCabYB 84*
KCKS-FM - Concordia, KS - *BrCabYB 84; TV&RadDir 84*
KCKT - Wichita, KS - *TelAl 83*
KCKU - Tyler, TX - *BrCabYB 84; Tel&CabFB 84S*
KCKW - Jena, LA - *TV&RadDir 84*
KCKY - Coolidge, AZ - *BrCabYB 84; TV&RadDir 84*
KCLA - Pine Bluff, AR - *BrCabYB 84; NatRadPubDir Summer 83, Spring 84; TV&RadDir 84*
KCLB-FM - Santa Rosa, CA - *BrCabYB 84; TV&RadDir 84*
KCLC-FM - St. Charles, MO - *BrCabYB 84; NatRadPubDir Summer 83, Spring 84; TV&RadDir 84*
KCLD-FM - St. Cloud, MN - *BrCabYB 84; NatRadPubDir Summer 83, Spring 84; TV&RadDir 84*
KCLE - Cleburne, TX - *BrCabYB 84; TV&RadDir 84*
KCLF - New Orleans, LA - *TV&RadDir 84*
KCLF - New Roads, LA - *BrCabYB 84*
KCLG - Washington, UT - *BrCabYB 84*
KCLI-FM - Clinton, OK - *BrCabYB 84; TV&RadDir 84*
KCLK - Clarkston, WA - *BrCabYB 84; TV&RadDir 84*
KCLK-FM - Clarkston, WA - *BrCabYB 84; TV&RadDir 84*
KCLM - Redding, CA - *BrCabYB 84; TV&RadDir 84*
KCLO - Leavenworth, KS - *BrCabYB 84; TV&RadDir 84*
KCLR - Ralls, TX - *BrCabYB 84; TV&RadDir 84*
KCLS - Flagstaff, AZ - *BrCabYB 84; NatRadPubDir Summer 83, Spring 84; TV&RadDir 84*
KCLT - Lockhart, TX - *TV&RadDir 84*
KCLU - Rolla, MO - *BrCabYB 84; TV&RadDir 84*
KCLU-FM - Rolla, MO - *BrCabYB 84; TV&RadDir 84*

KCLV - Clovis, NM - *BrCabYB 84; TV&RadDir 84*
KCLV-FM - Clovis, NM - *BrCabYB 84; TV&RadDir 84*
KCLW - Hamilton, TX - *BrCabYB 84; TV&RadDir 84*
KCLX - Colfax, WA - *BrCabYB 84; TV&RadDir 84*
KCLY-FM - Clay Center, KS - *BrCabYB 84; TV&RadDir 84*
KCMA - Owasso, OK - *BrCabYB 84*
KCMC - Texarkana, TX - *BrCabYB 84; NatRadPubDir Summer 83, Spring 84*
KCME - Manitou Springs, CA - *BrCabYB 84*
KCMG - Anchorage, AK - *BrCabYB 84*
KCMI - Terrytown, NE - *BrCabYB 84*
KCMJ - Palm Springs, CA - *BrCabYB 84; NatRadPubDir Summer 83, Spring 84; TV&RadDir 84*
KCMK - Glenwood Springs, CO - *BrCabYB 84*
KCMN - Colorado Springs, CO - *BrCabYB 84; TV&RadDir 84*
KCMO - Kansas City, MO - *BrCabYB 84; NatRadPubDir Summer 83 p.142, Spring 84 p.142; TV&RadDir 84*
KCMO-FM - Kansas City, MO - *BrCabYB 84; NatRadPubDir Spring 84 p.142*
KCMO-TV - Fairway, KS - *LitMarPl 83, 84*
KCMO-TV - Kansas City, MO - *DirUSTelSta 83; TelAl 83, 84*
KCMP - Brush, CO - *BrCabYB 84; TV&RadDir 84*
KCMQ-FM - Columbia, MO - *BrCabYB 84; NatRadPubDir Summer 83; TV&RadDir 84*
KCMR-FM - Mason City, IA - *BrCabYB 84; TV&RadDir 84*
KCMS-FM - Indio, CA - *TV&RadDir 84*
KCMT-FM - Alexandria, MN - *BrCabYB 84; TV&RadDir 84*
KCMT-TV - Alexandria, MN - *BrCabYB 84; DirUSTelSta 83; TelAl 83, 84; Tel&CabFB 84S; TV&RadDir 84*
KCMU-FM - Seattle, WA - *BrCabYB 84; NatRadPubDir Spring 84*
KCMW-FM - Warrensburg, MO - *BrCabYB 84; NatRadPubDir Summer 83, Spring 84; TV&RadDir 84*
KCMX - Ashland, OR - *BrCabYB 84; TV&RadDir 84*
KCMX-FM - Ashland, OR - *BrCabYB 84; TV&RadDir 84*
KCNA-TV - Albion, NE - *TelAl 84; Tel&CabFB 84S*
KCNA-TV - Kearney, NE - *TelAl 83; TV&RadDir 84*
KCNB-FM - Waterloo, IA - *BrCabYB 84; NatRadPubDir Summer 83, Spring 84; TV&RadDir 84*
KCNC-TV - Denver, CO - *BrCabYB 84; LitMarPl 84; Tel&CabFB 84S*
KCND-FM - Bismarck, ND - *BrCabYB 84; TV&RadDir 84*
KCNI - Broken Bow, NE - *BrCabYB 84; TV&RadDir 84*
KCNN - San Diego, CA - *BrCabYB 84; NatRadPubDir Summer 83; TV&RadDir 84*
KCNO - Alturas, CA - *BrCabYB 84; TV&RadDir 84*
KCNR - Portland, OR - *BrCabYB 84; NatRadPubDir Summer 83, Spring 84; TV&RadDir 84*
KCNR-FM - Portland, OR - *BrCabYB 84; NatRadPubDir Summer 83, Spring 84; TV&RadDir 84*
KCNT - Hastings, NE - *BrCabYB 84*
KCNT-FM - Hastings, NE - *TV&RadDir 84*
KCNW - Fairway, KS - *BrCabYB 84*
KCNW - Shawnee Mission, KS - *TV&RadDir 84*
KCNW - Kansas City, MO - *NatRadPubDir Summer 83 p.142, Spring 84 p.142*
KCNY - San Antonio, TX - *NatRadPubDir Summer 83 p.244, Spring 84 p.234*
KCNY - San Marcos, TX - *BrCabYB 84; TV&RadDir 84*
KCOB - Newton, IA - *BrCabYB 84; TV&RadDir 84*
KCOE-FM - Cedar Rapids, IA - *BrCabYB 84; TV&RadDir 84*
KCOG - Centerville, IA - *BrCabYB 84; TV&RadDir 84*
KCOH - Houston, TX - *BrCabYB 84; NatRadPubDir Summer 83, Spring 84; TV&RadDir 84*
KCOK - Tulare, CA - *BrCabYB 84; NatRadPubDir Summer 83, Spring 84*
KCOK - Visalia, CA - *TV&RadDir 84*
KCOL - Ft. Collins, CO - *BrCabYB 84; NatRadPubDir Summer 83, Spring 84; TV&RadDir 84*
KCOL-FM - Ft. Collins, CO - *BrCabYB 84; NatRadPubDir Summer 83, Spring 84; TV&RadDir 84*
KCOM - Comanche, TX - *BrCabYB 84; TV&RadDir 84*
KCON - Conway, AR - *BrCabYB 84; TV&RadDir 84*
KCOP-TV [of Chris Craft Industries] - Los Angeles, CA - *BrCabYB 84; DirUSTelSta 83; TelAl 83, 84; Tel&CabFB 84S; TV&RadDir 84*
KCOR - San Antonio, TX - *BrCabYB 84; NatRadPubDir Summer 83, Spring 84; TV&RadDir 84*
KCOS-TV - El Paso, TX - *BrCabYB 84; Tel&CabFB 84S; TV&RadDir 84*
KCOT-FM - Lamesa, TX - *TV&RadDir 84*
KCOT-FM - Marana, TX - *BrCabYB 84*
KCOU-FM - Columbia, MO - *BrCabYB 84; TV&RadDir 84*
KCOW - Alliance, NE - *BrCabYB 84; TV&RadDir 84*
KCOY-TV - Santa Barbara, CA - *DirUSTelSta 83*
KCOY-TV - Santa Maria, CA - *BrCabYB 84; TelAl 83, 84; Tel&CabFB 84S; TV&RadDir 84*
KCOZ-FM - Shreveport, LA - *BrCabYB 84; TV&RadDir 84*
KCPB-FM - Thousand Oaks, CA - *BrCabYB 84; TV&RadDir 84*
KCPI-FM - Albert Lea, MN - *BrCabYB 84; TV&RadDir 84*
KCPQ-TV - Seattle, WA - *DirUSTelSta 83*
KCPQ-TV - Tacoma, WA - *BrCabYB 84; Tel&CabFB 84S; TV&RadDir 84*
KCPR-FM - San Luis Obispo, CA - *BrCabYB 84; NatRadPubDir Summer 83, Spring 84; TV&RadDir 84*
KCPS - Burlington, IA - *BrCabYB 84; TV&RadDir 84*
KCPT-TV - Kansas City, MO - *BrCabYB 84; Tel&CabFB 84S; TV&RadDir 84*
KCPX - Salt Lake City, UT - *NatRadPubDir Summer 83, Spring 84; TV&RadDir 84*
KCPX-FM - Salt Lake City, UT - *BrCabYB 84; NatRadPubDir Summer 83, Spring 84; TV&RadDir 84*
KCR - San Diego, CA - *NatRadPubDir Summer 83, Spring 84*
KCRA-TV - Sacramento, CA - *BrCabYB 84; DirUSTelSta 83; LitMarPl 83, 84; TelAl 83, 84; Tel&CabFB 84S; TV&RadDir 84*
KCRB - Bemidji, MN - *BrCabYB 84*
KCRC - Enid, OK - *BrCabYB 84; TV&RadDir 84*
KCRE - Crescent City, CA - *BrCabYB 84; TV&RadDir 84*
KCRE-FM - Crescent City, CA - *BrCabYB 84; TV&RadDir 84*
KCRF - Lincoln City, CA - *BrCabYB 84*
KCRG - Cedar Rapids, IA - *BrCabYB 84; NatRadPubDir Summer 83, Spring 84; TV&RadDir 84*
KCRG-TV - Cedar Rapids, IA - *BrCabYB 84; DirUSTelSta 83; TelAl 83, 84; Tel&CabFB 84S; TV&RadDir 84*
KCRH-FM - Hayward, CA - *TV&RadDir 84*
KCRI - Helena, AR - *TV&RadDir 84*
KCRI - West Helena, AR - *BrCabYB 84*
KCRI-FM - Helena, AR - *BrCabYB 84; TV&RadDir 84*
KCRK-FM - Colville, WA - *BrCabYB 84*
KCRL-TV - Reno, NV - *BrCabYB 84; DirUSTelSta 83; TelAl 83, 84; Tel&CabFB 84S; TV&RadDir 84*
KCRM - Cameron, TX - *BrCabYB 84*
KCRO - Omaha, NE - *BrCabYB 84; NatRadPubDir Summer 83, Spring 84; TV&RadDir 84*
KCRP - Rosamond, CA - *BrCabYB 84*
KCRS - Midland, TX - *BrCabYB 84; NatRadPubDir Summer 83, Spring 84; TV&RadDir 84*
KCRT - Trinidad, CO - *BrCabYB 84; TV&RadDir 84*
KCRT-FM - Trinidad, CO - *BrCabYB 84; TV&RadDir 84*
KCRV - Caruthersville, MO - *BrCabYB 84; TV&RadDir 84*
KCRV-FM - Caruthersville, MO - *BrCabYB 84; TV&RadDir 84*
KCRW-FM - Santa Monica, CA - *BrCabYB 84; TV&RadDir 84*
KCRX - Roswell, NM - *BrCabYB 84; TV&RadDir 84*
KCSB-FM - Santa Barbara, CA - *BrCabYB 84; NatRadPubDir Summer 83, Spring 84; TV&RadDir 84*
KCSC-FM - Edmond, OK - *BrCabYB 84; NatRadPubDir Summer 83, Spring 84; TV&RadDir 84*
KCSJ - Pueblo, CO - *BrCabYB 84; NatRadPubDir Summer 83, Spring 84; TV&RadDir 84*
KCSM - San Francisco, CA - *DirUSTelSta 83*
KCSM - San Mateo, CA - *BrCabYB 84; TV&RadDir 84*
KCSM-FM - San Mateo, CA - *NatRadPubDir Summer 83, Spring 84; TV&RadDir 84*
KCSM-TV - San Mateo, CA - *BrCabYB 84; Tel&CabFB 84S*
KCSN-FM - Northridge, CA - *BrCabYB 84; TV&RadDir 84*
KCSO-TV - Modesto, CA - *BrCabYB 84; DirUSTelSta 83; TelAl 83, 84; Tel&CabFB 84S; TV&RadDir 84*
KCSR - Chadron, NE - *BrCabYB 84; TV&RadDir 84*
KCSS-FM - Turlock, CA - *BrCabYB 84; TV&RadDir 84*
KCST-TV - San Diego, CA - *BrCabYB 84; DirUSTelSta 83; LitMarPl 83, 84; TelAl 83, 84; Tel&CabFB 84S; TV&RadDir 84*
KCSU-FM - Ft. Collins, CO - *BrCabYB 84; NatRadPubDir Summer 83, Spring 84; TV&RadDir 84*

KCTA - Corpus Christi, TX - *BrCabYB 84; NatRadPubDir Summer 83, Spring 84; TV&RadDir 84*
KCTB - Cut Bank, MT - *BrCabYB 84*
KCTC-FM - Sacramento, CA - *BrCabYB 84; NatRadPubDir Summer 83, Spring 84; TV&RadDir 84*
KCTE - South West City, MO - *BrCabYB 84; TV&RadDir 84*
KCTI - Gonzales, TX - *BrCabYB 84; TV&RadDir 84*
KCTM - Rio Grande City, TX - *BrCabYB 84*
KCTN - Garnavillo, IA - *BrCabYB 84*
KCTO - Columbia, LA - *BrCabYB 84; TV&RadDir 84*
KCTO-FM - Columbia, LA - *TV&RadDir 84*
KCTS-TV - Seattle, WA - *BrCabYB 84; Tel&CabFB 84S; TV&RadDir 84*
KCTT - Yellville, AR - *BrCabYB 84; TV&RadDir 84*
KCTV-TV - Shawnee Mission, KS - *TV&RadDir 84*
KCTV-TV - Kansas City, MO - *Tel&CabFB 84S*
KCTV-TV - San Angelo, TX - *BrCabYB 84; DirUSTelSta 83; TelAl 83, 84*
KCTX - Childress, TX - *BrCabYB 84; TV&RadDir 84*
KCTY - Salinas, CA - *BrCabYB 84; NatRadPubDir Summer 83, Spring 84; TV&RadDir 84*
KCTZ - Bozeman, MT - *BrCabYB 84; Tel&CabFB 84S*
KCUB - Tucson, AZ - *BrCabYB 84; NatRadPubDir Summer 83, Spring 84; TV&RadDir 84*
KCUE - Red Wing, MN - *BrCabYB 84; TV&RadDir 84*
KCUI-FM - Pella, IA - *BrCabYB 84; TV&RadDir 84*
KCUM-FM - Crookston, MN - *BrCabYB 84; TV&RadDir 84*
KCUR-FM - Kansas City, MO - *BrCabYB 84; NatRadPubDir Summer 83, Spring 84; TV&RadDir 84*
KCUZ - Clifton, AZ - *BrCabYB 84; TV&RadDir 84*
KCVL - Colville, WA - *BrCabYB 84; TV&RadDir 84*
KCVR - Lodi, CA - *BrCabYB 84; TV&RadDir 84*
KCVT - Shawnee, OK - *BrCabYB 84; Tel&CabFB 84S*
KCWC-FM - Riverton, WY - *BrCabYB 84; NatRadPubDir Spring 84*
KCWC-TV - Lander, WY - *BrCabYB 84; Tel&CabFB 84S*
KCWD - Harrison, AR - *BrCabYB 84*
KCWM - Victoria, TX - *BrCabYB 84; TV&RadDir 84*
KCWS - Glenwood Springs, CO - *BrCabYB 84; Tel&CabFB 84S*
KCWT - Wenatchee, WA - *BrCabYB 84*
KCWW-FM - Beeville, TX - *BrCabYB 84; TV&RadDir 84*
KCWY-TV - Casper, WY - *BrCabYB 84; DirUSTelSta 83; TelAl 83, 84; Tel&CabFB 84S; TV&RadDir 84*
KCYL - Lampasas, TX - *BrCabYB 84; TV&RadDir 84*
KCYN-FM - Pocahontas, AR - *BrCabYB 84; TV&RadDir 84*
KCYX - McMinnville, OR - *BrCabYB 84; TV&RadDir 84*
KDAA - Woodward, OK - *BrCabYB 84*
KDAB-FM - Ogden, UT - *BrCabYB 84; NatRadPubDir Summer 83, Spring 84; TV&RadDir 84*
KDAC - Ft. Bragg, CA - *BrCabYB 84; TV&RadDir 84*
KDAK - Carrington, ND - *BrCabYB 84; TV&RadDir 84*
KDAK-FM - Carrington, ND - *BrCabYB 84*
KDAL - Duluth, MN - *BrCabYB 84; NatRadPubDir Summer 83, Spring 84; TV&RadDir 84*
KDAN - Newport, MN - *TV&RadDir 84*
KDAO - Marshalltown, IA - *BrCabYB 84; TV&RadDir 84*
KDAP - Douglas, AZ - *BrCabYB 84; TV&RadDir 84*
KDAQ - Shreveport, LA - *BrCabYB 84*
KDAR-FM - Oxnard, CA - *BrCabYB 84; TV&RadDir 84*
KDAV - Davenport, IA - *BrCabYB 84; Tel&CabFB 84S*
KDAY - Los Angeles, CA - *NatRadPubDir Summer 83, Spring 84; TV&RadDir 84*
KDAY - Santa Monica, CA - *BrCabYB 84*
KDAZ - Albuquerque, NM - *BrCabYB 84; TV&RadDir 84*
KDB - Santa Barbara, CA - *BrCabYB 84; NatRadPubDir Summer 83, Spring 84; TV&RadDir 84*
KDB-FM - Santa Barbara, CA - *BrCabYB 84; NatRadPubDir Summer 83, Spring 84; TV&RadDir 84*
KDBC-TV - El Paso, TX - *BrCabYB 84; DirUSTelSta 83; TelAl 83, 84; Tel&CabFB 84S; TV&RadDir 84*
KDBH-FM - Natchitoches, LA - *BrCabYB 84; TV&RadDir 84*
KDBM - Dillon, MT - *BrCabYB 84; TV&RadDir 84*
KDBQ-FM - Pittsburg, KS - *BrCabYB 84; TV&RadDir 84*
KDBS - Alexandria, LA - *BrCabYB 84; TV&RadDir 84*
KDBX-FM - Boonville, MO - *BrCabYB 84; TV&RadDir 84*
KDCD-TV - Midland, TX - *BrCabYB 84*
KDCE - Espanola, NM - *BrCabYB 84*
KDCE - Fairview, NM - *TV&RadDir 84*
KDCI - Devine, TX - *BrCabYB 84*
KDCK-FM - Dodge City, KS - *BrCabYB 84; TV&RadDir 84*
KDCQ - Sikeston, MO - *BrCabYB 84; Tel&CabFB 84S*
KDCR-FM - Sioux Center, IA - *BrCabYB 84; NatRadPubDir Summer 83, Spring 84; TV&RadDir 84*
KDCV-FM - Blair, NE - *BrCabYB 84; NatRadPubDir Summer 83, Spring 84; TV&RadDir 84*
KDDA - Dumas, AR - *BrCabYB 84; TV&RadDir 84*
KDDA-FM - Dumas, AR - *BrCabYB 84; TV&RadDir 84*
KDDB - Paso Robles, CA - *BrCabYB 84*
KDDD - Dumas, TX - *BrCabYB 84; TV&RadDir 84*
KDDE - Los Angeles, CA - *BrCabYB 84; Tel&CabFB 84S*
KDDR - Oakes, ND - *BrCabYB 84; TV&RadDir 84*
KDEA-FM - New Iberia, LA - *BrCabYB 84; TV&RadDir 84*
KDEC - Decorah, IA - *BrCabYB 84; TV&RadDir 84*
KDEF - Albuquerque, NM - *BrCabYB 84; LitMarPl 83, 84; NatRadPubDir Summer 83, Spring 84; TV&RadDir 84*
KDEI - Alexandria, LA - *BrCabYB 84*
KDEL-FM - Arkadelphia, AR - *BrCabYB 84; TV&RadDir 84*
KDEM-FM - Deming, NM - *BrCabYB 84; TV&RadDir 84*
KDEN - Denver, CO - *BrCabYB 84; NatRadPubDir Summer 83 p.40, Spring 84 p.40*
KDEN - Englewood, CO - *TV&RadDir 84*
KDEO - Waipahu, HI - *BrCabYB 84; TV&RadDir 84*
KDES - Palm Springs, CA - *BrCabYB 84; NatRadPubDir Summer 83, Spring 84; TV&RadDir 84*
KDES-FM - Palm Springs, CA - *BrCabYB 84; NatRadPubDir Summer 83, Spring 84; TV&RadDir 84*
KDET - Center, TX - *BrCabYB 84; TV&RadDir 84*
KDEW - De Witt, AR - *BrCabYB 84; TV&RadDir 84*
KDEW-FM - De Witt, AR - *BrCabYB 84; TV&RadDir 84*
KDEX - Dexter, MO - *BrCabYB 84; TV&RadDir 84*
KDEX-FM - Dexter, MO - *BrCabYB 84; TV&RadDir 84*
KDEY-FM - Lufkin, TX - *BrCabYB 84; TV&RadDir 84*
KDEZ - Crookston, MN - *BrCabYB 84*
KDFC-FM - San Francisco, CA - *BrCabYB 84; NatRadPubDir Summer 83, Spring 84; TV&RadDir 84*
KDFM-FM - Walnut Creek, CA - *TV&RadDir 84*
KDFN - Doniphan, MO - *BrCabYB 84; TV&RadDir 84*
KDFW-TV - Dallas, TX - *BrCabYB 84; DirUSTelSta 83; LitMarPl 83, 84; TelAl 83, 84; Tel&CabFB 84S; TV&RadDir 84*
KDGO - Durango, CO - *BrCabYB 84; TV&RadDir 84*
KDHI - Twentynine Palms, CA - *BrCabYB 84; TV&RadDir 84*
KDHL - Faribault, MN - *BrCabYB 84; TV&RadDir 84*
KDHL-FM - Faribault, MN - *BrCabYB 84; TV&RadDir 84*
KDHN - Dimmitt, TX - *BrCabYB 84; TV&RadDir 84*
KDHS-FM - Modesto, CA - *BrCabYB 84; NatRadPubDir Summer 83, Spring 84; TV&RadDir 84*
KDIA - Emeryville, CA - *TV&RadDir 84*
KDIA - Oakland, CA - *BrCabYB 84*
KDIA - San Francisco, CA - *NatRadPubDir Summer 83 p.30, Spring 84 p.29*
KDIC-FM - Grinnell, IA - *BrCabYB 84; TV&RadDir 84*
KDIG - San Bernardino, CA - *BrCabYB 84; NatRadPubDir Summer 83, Spring 84; TV&RadDir 84*
KDIN-TV - Des Moines, IA - *BrCabYB 84; Tel&CabFB 84S; TV&RadDir 84*
KDIO - Ortonville, MN - *BrCabYB 84; TV&RadDir 84*
KDIQ-FM - Boise, ID - *NatRadPubDir Summer 83, Spring 84*
KDIX - Dickinson, ND - *BrCabYB 84; TV&RadDir 84*
KDIX-TV - Dickinson, ND - *DirUSTelSta 83; TelAl 83, 84; TV&RadDir 84*
KDJI - Holbrook, AZ - *BrCabYB 84; TV&RadDir 84*
KDJQ - Mesa, AZ - *BrCabYB 84; TV&RadDir 84*
KDJQ - Phoenix, AZ - *NatRadPubDir Summer 83, Spring 84 p.9*
KDJS - Willmar, MN - *BrCabYB 84*
KDJW - Amarillo, TX - *BrCabYB 84; NatRadPubDir Summer 83, Spring 84; TV&RadDir 84*
KDKA - Pittsburgh, PA - *BrCabYB 84; LitMarPl 83, 84; NatRadPubDir Summer 83, Spring 84; TV&RadDir 84*
KDKA-TV - Pittsburgh, PA - *BrCabYB 84; DirUSTelSta 83; LitMarPl 83; TelAl 83, 84; Tel&CabFB 84S; TV&RadDir 84*
KDKB-FM - Mesa, AZ - *BrCabYB 84; TV&RadDir 84*
KDKB-FM - Phoenix, AZ - *NatRadPubDir Summer 83, Spring 84 p.9*
KDKD - Clinton, MO - *BrCabYB 84; TV&RadDir 84*

KDKD-FM - Clinton, MO - *BrCabYB 84; TV&RadDir 84*
KDKO - Englewood, CO - *LitMarPl 83, 84; TV&RadDir 84*
KDKO - Littleton, CO - *BrCabYB 84*
KDKQ-FM - Borger, TX - *BrCabYB 84; TV&RadDir 84*
KDKS - Benton, LA - *BrCabYB 84*
KDLA - De Ridder, LA - *BrCabYB 84; TV&RadDir 84*
KDLF - Port Neches, TX - *BrCabYB 84; TV&RadDir 84*
KDLF-TV - Sioux Falls, SD - *TelAl 84*
KDLG-FM - Dillingham, AK - *BrCabYB 84; TV&RadDir 84*
KDLH-TV - Duluth, MN - *BrCabYB 84; DirUSTelSta 83; TelAl 83, 84; Tel&CabFB 84S; TV&RadDir 84*
KDLK - Del Rio, TX - *BrCabYB 84; TV&RadDir 84*
KDLM - Detroit Lakes, MN - *BrCabYB 84; TV&RadDir 84*
KDLN-FM - Dillon, MT - *BrCabYB 84; TV&RadDir 84*
KDLO-FM - Sioux Falls, SD - *NatRadPubDir Summer 83, Spring 84; TV&RadDir 84*
KDLO-FM - Watertown, SD - *BrCabYB 84*
KDLO-TV - Florence, SD - *BrCabYB 84; TelAl 83, 84; Tel&CabFB 84S*
KDLR - Devils Lake, ND - *BrCabYB 84; TV&RadDir 84*
KDLS - Perry, IA - *BrCabYB 84; TV&RadDir 84*
KDLS-FM - Perry, IA - *BrCabYB 84; TV&RadDir 84*
KDLT-TV - Mitchell, SD - *BrCabYB 84; Tel&CabFB 84S; TV&RadDir 84*
KDLT-TV - Sioux Falls, SD - *DirUSTelSta 83*
KDLY-FM - Lander, WY - *BrCabYB 84; TV&RadDir 84*
KDMA - Montevideo, MN - *BrCabYB 84; TV&RadDir 84*
KDMI-FM - Des Moines, IA - *BrCabYB 84; NatRadPubDir Summer 83, Spring 84; TV&RadDir 84*
KDMO - Carthage, MO - *BrCabYB 84; TV&RadDir 84*
KDMS - El Dorado, AR - *BrCabYB 84; TV&RadDir 84*
KDNA - Yakima, WA - *BrCabYB 84*
KDNG-FM - Gainesville, TX - *BrCabYB 84; TV&RadDir 84*
KDNK - Carbondale, CO - *BrCabYB 84*
KDNL-TV - St. Louis, MO - *BrCabYB 84; DirUSTelSta 83; TelAl 83, 84; Tel&CabFB 84S; TV&RadDir 84*
KDNO-FM - Delano, CA - *BrCabYB 84; TV&RadDir 84*
KDNT - Denton, TX - *BrCabYB 84; TV&RadDir 84*
KDNW - Duluth, MN - *BrCabYB 84*
KDOC-TV - Anaheim, CA - *BrCabYB 84; DirUSTelSta 83; TelAl 84; Tel&CabFB 84S*
KDOG - Nacogdoches, TX - *BrCabYB 84; Tel&CabFB 84S*
KDOK - Tyler, TX - *BrCabYB 84; TV&RadDir 84*
KDOL - Mojave, CA - *BrCabYB 84; TV&RadDir 84*
KDOL-FM - Mojave, CA - *BrCabYB 84; TV&RadDir 84*
KDOM - Windom, MN - *BrCabYB 84*
KDOM-FM - Windom, MN - *BrCabYB 84*
KDON - Salinas, CA - *BrCabYB 84; NatRadPubDir Summer 83, Spring 84; TV&RadDir 84*
KDON-FM - Salinas, CA - *BrCabYB 84; NatRadPubDir Summer 83, Spring 84; TV&RadDir 84*
KDOR - Bartlesville, OK - *BrCabYB 84; Tel&CabFB 84S*
KDOS - Fremont, CA - *BrCabYB 84*
KDOT - Provo, UT - *BrCabYB 84; NatRadPubDir Spring 84; TV&RadDir 84*
KDOV - Ashland, OR - *BrCabYB 84; TV&RadDir 84*
KDPS-FM - Des Moines, IA - *BrCabYB 84; NatRadPubDir Summer 83, Spring 84; TV&RadDir 84*
KDQN - De Queen, AR - *BrCabYB 84; TV&RadDir 84*
KDQN-FM - De Queen, AR - *BrCabYB 84; TV&RadDir 84*
KDRG - Deer Lodge, MT - *BrCabYB 84; TV&RadDir 84*
KDRK-FM - Spokane, WA - *BrCabYB 84*
KDRO - Colorado Springs, CO - *TV&RadDir 84*
KDRO - Sedalia, MO - *BrCabYB 84; TV&RadDir 84*
KDRS - Paragould, AR - *BrCabYB 84; TV&RadDir 84*
KDRV - Medford, OR - *Tel&CabFB 84S*
KDRW - Silverton, CO - *BrCabYB 84; TV&RadDir 84*
KDRW-FM - Silverton, CO - *BrCabYB 84*
KDRY - Alamo Heights, TX - *BrCabYB 84; TV&RadDir 84*
KDSD-TV - Aberdeen, SD - *BrCabYB 84; Tel&CabFB 84S*
KDSD-TV - Pierpont, SD - *TV&RadDir 84*
KDSE - Dickinson, ND - *BrCabYB 84; Tel&CabFB 84S*
KDSI-FM - Alice, TX - *BrCabYB 84; TV&RadDir 84*
KDSJ - Deadwood, SD - *BrCabYB 84; TV&RadDir 84*
KDSN - Denison, IA - *BrCabYB 84; TV&RadDir 84*
KDSN-FM - Denison, IA - *BrCabYB 84; TV&RadDir 84*
KDSQ-FM - Denison, TX - *BrCabYB 84*
KDSU-FM - Fargo, ND - *BrCabYB 84; NatRadPubDir Summer 83, Spring 84; TV&RadDir 84*
KDSX - Denison, TX - *BrCabYB 84; TV&RadDir 84*
KDTA - Delta, CO - *BrCabYB 84; TV&RadDir 84*
KDTA-FM - Delta, CO - *BrCabYB 84*
KDTH - Dubuque, IA - *BrCabYB 84; NatRadPubDir Summer 83, Spring 84; TV&RadDir 84*
KDTU-TV - Tucson, AZ - *BrCabYB 84*
KDTV-TV - San Francisco, CA - *BrCabYB 84; DirUSTelSta 83; TelAl 83, 84; Tel&CabFB 84S; TV&RadDir 84*
KDUB-TV - Cedar Rapids, IA - *DirUSTelSta 83*
KDUB-TV - Dubuque, IA - *BrCabYB 84; TelAl 83, 84; Tel&CabFB 84S; TV&RadDir 84*
KDUH-TV - Hay Springs, NE - *TelAl 83, 84*
KDUH-TV - Scottsbluff, NE - *BrCabYB 84; DirUSTelSta 83; Tel&CabFB 84S*
KDUK-FM - Honolulu, HI - *BrCabYB 84; NatRadPubDir Summer 83, Spring 84; TV&RadDir 84*
KDUN - Reedsport, OR - *BrCabYB 84; TV&RadDir 84*
KDUO-FM - Riverside, CA - *BrCabYB 84*
KDUO-FM - San Bernardino, CA - *NatRadPubDir Summer 83, Spring 84; TV&RadDir 84*
KDUR-FM - Durango, CO - *BrCabYB 84; TV&RadDir 84*
KDUV-FM - Brownsville, TX - *BrCabYB 84; TV&RadDir 84*
KDUV-FM - McAllen, TX - *NatRadPubDir Summer 83, Spring 84 p.243*
KDUX-FM - Aberdeen, WA - *BrCabYB 84; TV&RadDir 84*
KDUX-FM - Ocean Shores, WA - *BrCabYB 84*
KDUZ - Hutchinson, MN - *BrCabYB 84; TV&RadDir 84*
KDUZ-FM - Hutchinson, MN - *BrCabYB 84; TV&RadDir 84*
KDVE - Nederland, TX - *BrCabYB 84*
K.D.V.H.E. Publishers - Chicago, IL - *BoPubDir 4, 5*
KDVL-FM - Devils Lake, ND - *BrCabYB 84; TV&RadDir 84*
KDVR - Denver, CO - *BrCabYB 84; Tel&CabFB 84S*
KDVS-FM - Davis, CA - *BrCabYB 84; NatRadPubDir Summer 83, Spring 84; TV&RadDir 84*
KDVV-FM - Topeka, KS - *BrCabYB 84; NatRadPubDir Summer 83, Spring 84; TV&RadDir 84*
KDWA - Hastings, MN - *BrCabYB 84; TV&RadDir 84*
KDWB - Minneapolis, MN - *NatRadPubDir Summer 83 p.133, Spring 84 p.133*
KDWB - St. Paul, MN - *BrCabYB 84; TV&RadDir 84*
KDWB-FM - Minneapolis, MN - *NatRadPubDir Summer 83 p.134, Spring 84 p.133*
KDWB-FM - Richfield, MN - *BrCabYB 84*
KDWB-FM - St. Paul, MN - *TV&RadDir 84*
KDWD - Burlington, IA - *BrCabYB 84*
KDWN - Las Vegas, NV - *BrCabYB 84; NatRadPubDir Summer 83, Spring 84; TV&RadDir 84*
KDWT - Stamford, TX - *BrCabYB 84; TV&RadDir 84*
KDXE - Sulphur Springs, TX - *BrCabYB 84*
KDXI - Mansfield, LA - *BrCabYB 84; TV&RadDir 84*
KDXL-FM - St. Louis Park, MN - *BrCabYB 84; TV&RadDir 84*
KDXT-FM - Missoula, MT - *BrCabYB 84; TV&RadDir 84*
KDXU - St. George, UT - *BrCabYB 84; TV&RadDir 84*
KDXY - Paragould, AR - *BrCabYB 84*
KDYL - Salt Lake City, UT - *BrCabYB 84; NatRadPubDir Summer 83, Spring 84*
KDYL - Tooele, UT - *TV&RadDir 84*
KDZA - Pueblo, CO - *BrCabYB 84; NatRadPubDir Summer 83, Spring 84; TV&RadDir 84*
KEA News - Louisville, KY - *BaconPubCkMag 84; MagDir 84*
Keach Productions, Stacy - North Hollywood, CA - *AvMarPl 83; TelAl 83, 84*
KeaMed Hospital Systems [Div. of Keane Inc.] - Boston, MA - *DataDirSup 7-83*
KEAN - Abilene, TX - *BrCabYB 84; NatRadPubDir Summer 83, Spring 84; TV&RadDir 84*
Kean Agency Inc., Mabyn - Baton Rouge, LA - *AdAge 3-28-84; StaDirAdAg 2-84*
KEAN-FM - Abilene, TX - *BrCabYB 84; NatRadPubDir Summer 83, Spring 84; TV&RadDir 84*
Keane Inc. - Boston, MA - *ADAPSOMemDir 83-84; DataDirSup 7-83*
KEAP - Fresno, CA - *BrCabYB 84; NatRadPubDir Summer 83, Spring 84; TV&RadDir 84*

KEAR-FM - San Francisco, CA - *BrCabYB 84; NatRadPubDir Summer 83, Spring 84*
Kearney & Associates Inc. - Hammond, IN - *DirMarMP 83*
Kearney Cablevision [of HRM Inc.] - Kearney, NE - *BrCabYB 84; Tel&CabFB 84C*
Kearney Courier - Kearney, MO - *BaconPubCkNews 84; Ed&PubIntYB 82*
Kearney Hub - Kearney, NE - *BaconPubCkNews 84; Ed&PubIntYB 82; NewsDir 84*
Kearney Inc., A. T. - Cleveland, OH - *DirInfWP 82*
Kearney Publishing Co. - Northbrook, IL - *BoPubDir 4, 5*
Kearns Valley View News [of Roy Printing Co. Newspapers] - Roy, UT - *NewsDir 84*
Kearny Copper Basin News - Kearny, AZ - *BaconPubCkNews 84*
Kearny County News - Minden, NE - *Ed&PubIntYB 82*
Kearny Observer - *See* West Hudson Publishers
Kearny Observer, The - Kearny, NJ - *NewsDir 84*
Kearsarge Cable Communications Inc. [of Telephone & Data Systems Inc.] - New London, NH - *Tel&CabFB 84C*
Kearsarge Industries Inc. - Reston, VA - *AvMarPl 83*
Kearsarge Telephone Co. [of Telephone & Data Systems Inc.] - New London, NH - *TelDir&BG 83-84*
Keary Advertising Co. Inc. - Baltimore, MD - *DirMarMP 83*
KEAS - Eastland, TX - *BrCabYB 84*
Keaten Associates, J. C. - Englewood, CO - *TeleSy&SerDir 7-83*
Keating Productions - Pahoa, HI - *AvMarPl 83*
Keats Publishing Inc. - New Canaan, CT - *LitMarPl 83, 84; WritMar 84*
KEAZ-FM - De Ridder, LA - *BrCabYB 84; TV&RadDir 84*
KEBC-FM - Oklahoma City, OK - *BrCabYB 84; NatRadPubDir Summer 83, Spring 84; TV&RadDir 84*
KEBE - Jacksonville, TX - *BrCabYB 84; TV&RadDir 84*
KEBR-FM - Sacramento, CA - *BrCabYB 84; NatRadPubDir Summer 83, Spring 84; TV&RadDir 84*
KEBY Cable - West Liberty, WV - *BrCabYB 84; Tel&CabFB 84C*
Keca Music - *See* Creative Music Group
KECC-TV - El Centro, CA - *TelAl 83*
KECG-FM - El Cerrito, CA - *BrCabYB 84; TV&RadDir 84*
KECH - Portland, OR - *DirUSTelSta 83*
KECH - Salem, OR - *BrCabYB 84; TelAl 84; Tel&CabFB 84S*
KECI-TV - Missoula, MT - *ArtMar 84; BrCabYB 84; DirUSTelSta 83; TelAl 83, 84; Tel&CabFB 84S; TV&RadDir 84*
KECK - Lincoln, NE - *BrCabYB 84; NatRadPubDir Summer 83, Spring 84; TV&RadDir 84*
Keck Advertising Agency - Oconomowoc, WI - *StaDirAdAg 2-84*
Keckley Market Research - Nashville, TN - *IntDirMarRes 83; Tel&CabFB 84C*
KECO - Elk City, OK - *BrCabYB 84*
KECR-FM - El Cajon, CA - *BrCabYB 84; TV&RadDir 84*
KECR-FM - San Diego, CA - *NatRadPubDir Summer 83 p.28, Spring 84 p.28*
KECY-TV - Yuma, AZ - *DirUSTelSta 83*
KECY-TV - El Centro, CA - *BrCabYB 84; TelAl 84; Tel&CabFB 84S; TV&RadDir 84*
KEDA - San Antonio, TX - *BrCabYB 84; NatRadPubDir Summer 83, Spring 84; TV&RadDir 84*
KEDD - Dodge City, KS - *BrCabYB 84; TV&RadDir 84*
KEDO - Longview, WA - *BrCabYB 84; TV&RadDir 84*
KEDP-FM - Las Vegas, NM - *NatRadPubDir Summer 83, Spring 84; TV&RadDir 84*
KEDT-TV - Corpus Christi, TX - *BrCabYB 84; Tel&CabFB 84S; TV&RadDir 84*
KEDY-FM - Mt. Shasta, CA - *BrCabYB 84; TV&RadDir 84*
Keeble Press Inc. - Shaker Heights, OH - *BoPubDir 4, 5*
KEED - Eugene, OR - *BrCabYB 84; NatRadPubDir Summer 83, Spring 84; TV&RadDir 84*
Keedick Lecture Bureau Inc. - New York, NY - *LitMarPl 83, 84*
KEEE - Nacogdoches, TX - *BrCabYB 84; TV&RadDir 84*
Keegan Press - Iowa City, IA - *BoPubDir 5*
KEEL - Shreveport, LA - *BrCabYB 84; NatRadPubDir Summer 83, Spring 84; TV&RadDir 84*
Keeler - Mill Valley, CA - *BoPubDir 4, 5*
Keely/Ideational Research, Ann - New York, NY - *IntDirMarRes 83*
KEEN - San Jose, CA - *BrCabYB 84; NatRadPubDir Summer 83, Spring 84; TV&RadDir 84*
Keene, J. Calvin - Lewisburg, PA - *BoPubDir 4, 5*
Keene Music Co., Joe - Kennett, MO - *BillIntBG 83-84*
Keene Publications, Sherman - Hollywood, CA - *BoPubDir 5*
Keene Sentinel - Keene, NH - *AyerDirPub 83; BaconPubCkNews 84; Ed&PubIntYB 82; NewsDir 84*
Keene Valley Sun - Keenesburg, CO - *AyerDirPub 83; Ed&PubIntYB 82*
Keene Valley Sun - Kennesburg, CO - *BaconPubCkNews 84*
Keene Valley Video Inc. - Keene Valley, NY - *Tel&CabFB 84C*
KEEO - Pans, AR - *BrCabYB 84*
KEEP - Twin Falls, ID - *BrCabYB 84; TV&RadDir 84*
Keepin' Track of Vettes - Spring Valley, NY - *WritMar 84*
Keepsake Press - Richmond, England - *LitMag&SmPr 83-84*
KEER - Las Vegas, NV - *BrCabYB 84*
KEES - Gladewater, TX - *BrCabYB 84; TV&RadDir 84*
Kees Manufacturing Co., F. D. - Beatrice, NE - *AvMarPl 83*
Keeseville-Essex County Republican [of Denton Publications Inc.] - Elizabethtown, NY - *NewsDir 84*
Keeseville-Essex County Republican - *See* Denton Publications Inc.
Keeshan Associates Inc., Robert - New York, NY - *Tel&CabFB 84C*
KEET-TV - Eureka, CA - *BrCabYB 84; Tel&CabFB 84S; TV&RadDir 84*
Keeta Music Co. - *See* Briarmeade Music Unltd.
Keetch, Caesar & Dino Music Inc. - *See* Plaza Sweet Music Inc.
KEEY - Minneapolis, MN - *NatRadPubDir Summer 83*
KEEY-FM - Minneapolis, MN - *NatRadPubDir Summer 83, Spring 84 p.133*
KEEY-FM - St. Paul, MN - *BrCabYB 84; TV&RadDir 84*
KEEZ-FM - Blue Earth, MN - *TV&RadDir 84*
KEEZ-FM - Mankato, MN - *BrCabYB 84; NatRadPubDir Summer 83, Spring 84*
KEFM-FM - Omaha, NE - *BrCabYB 84*
KEFR - Le Grand, CA - *BrCabYB 84*
KEGG - Daingerfield, TX - *BrCabYB 84; TV&RadDir 84*
KEGL-FM - Dallas, TX - *NatRadPubDir Summer 83 p.236, Spring 84 p.237*
KEGL-FM - Ft. Worth, TX - *BrCabYB 84; TV&RadDir 84*
KEHG - Fosston, MN - *BrCabYB 84; TV&RadDir 84*
KEHG-FM - Fosston, MN - *BrCabYB 84*
Kehoe, White, Towey & Savage Inc. - New York, NY - *DirPRFirms 83*
Kehrwald, Richard - Sheridan, WY - *MagIndMarPl 82-83*
Keiler Advertising - Farmington Valley, CT - *DirPRFirms 83; StaDirAdAg 2-84*
Keim, Betty - New York, NY - *LitMarPl 83, 84; MagIndMarPl 82-83*
Keim, Leonard [Aff. of Children's Crusade for Christ] - New Orleans, LA - *BoPubDir 4 Sup, 5*
KEIN - Great Falls, MT - *BrCabYB 84; NatRadPubDir Summer 83, Spring 84; TV&RadDir 84*
Keisling, Ralph - Monterey, TN - *Tel&CabFB 84C p.1686*
Keister Advertising Service - Charlottesville, VA - *Ed&PubIntYB 82*
Keister Stations, David - Martinsville, IN - *BrCabYB 84*
Keith County News - Ogallala, NE - *Ed&PubIntYB 82*
Keithwood Publishing Co. - Philadelphia, PA - *BoPubDir 4, 5; DirMarMP 83*
KEJA - Garden City, SD - *BrCabYB 84*
KEJO-FM - Corvallis, OR - *BrCabYB 84; TV&RadDir 84*
Kejon E-Ware - Raleigh, NC - *MicrocomMPl 84*
KEKA - Eureka, CA - *BrCabYB 84; TV&RadDir 84*
KEKR-TV - Kansas City, MO - *BrCabYB 84*
Kekst & Co. - New York, NY - *DirPRFirms 83*
KELA - Centralia, WA - *BrCabYB 84; TV&RadDir 84*
KELA-FM - Centralia, WA - *TV&RadDir 84*
KELC - England, AR - *BrCabYB 84; TV&RadDir 84*
Kelcy, April Gerlitz - La Canada, CA - *FBInfSer 80*
KELD - El Dorado, AR - *BrCabYB 84; TV&RadDir 84*
KELE-FM - Aurora, MO - *BrCabYB 84; TV&RadDir 84*
KELG - Elgin, TX - *BrCabYB 84; TV&RadDir 84*
KELI - Tulsa, OK - *BrCabYB 84; NatRadPubDir Summer 83, Spring 84; TV&RadDir 84*
Kelix Software Systems - Baton Rouge, LA - *MicrocomMPl 84*

KELK - Elko, NV - *BrCabYB 84; TV&RadDir 84*
Keller & Associates Inc., J. J. - Neenah, WI - *BoPubDir 4, 5*
Keller Communications, F. M. - Sioux Falls, SD - *Tel&CabFB 84C p.1686*
Keller Communications, F. M. - Tea, SD - *Tel&CabFB 84C*
Keller-Crescent - Evansville, IN - *AdAge 3-28-84; DirMarMP 83; DirPRFirms 83; MagIndMarPl 82-83; StaDirAdAg 2-84*
Keller Haver Inc. - New York, NY - *AdAge 3-28-84; StaDirAdAg 2-84*
Keller Inc., Lee - Rosemont, PA - *StaDirAdAg 2-84*
Keller Software - Newport Beach, CA - *MicrocomMPl 84; MicrocomSwDir 1*
Kellex Data Corp. - Glen Cove, NY - *EISS 5-84 Sup*
Kelley Advertising Inc., Austin - Atlanta, GA - *StaDirAdAg 2-84*
Kelley & Wallwork - Boston, MA - *StaDirAdAg 2-84*
Kelley Inc., R. T. - Hamilton, ON, Canada - *StaDirAdAg 2-84*
Kelley Publishers, Augustus M. - Fairfield, NJ - *LitMarPl 83, 84*
Kellicutt, M. H. - Half Moon Bay, CA - *MicrocomMPl 83*
Kellijai Music Corp. - Burbank, CA - *BillIntBG 83-84*
Kellner, Hugo Maria - Caledonia, NY - *LitMarPl 83*
Kellogg Evening News - Kellogg, ID - *BaconPubCkNews 84; Ed&PubIntYB 82; NewsDir 84*
Kellogg News-Wardner - Kellogg, ID - *BaconPubCkNews 84; Ed&PubIntYB 82*
Kellogg Telephone Conferencing Service [of Kellogg Telecommunications Corp.] - Littleton, CO - *TeleSy&SerDir 7-83*
Kellogg TV System Inc. - Kellogg, ID - *BrCabYB 84*
Kelly Adams Advertising - York, PA - *StaDirAdAg 2-84 p.1686*
Kelly Advertising Inc. - Lancaster, PA - *StaDirAdAg 2-84*
Kelly, Aidan A. - Staten Island, NY - *LitMarPl 84*
Kelly & Green Inc. - Bristol, VA - *AvMarPl 83*
Kelly & Lloyd Music - *See* JMR Enterprises
Kelly Associates Inc. - Wichita Falls, TX - *CabTVFinDB 83*
Kelly Broadcasting Co. - Sacramento, CA - *BrCabYB 84; Tel&CabFB 84S*
Kelly Communications Inc. - Lakeland, FL - *BrCabYB 84*
Kelly, Leed & Ries Inc. - Cincinnati, OH - *ArtMar 84; StaDirAdAg 2-84*
Kelly Media Associates Inc. - New York, NY - *StaDirAdAg 2-84*
Kelly Michener - Valley Forge, PA - *AdAge 3-28-84*
Kelly Music Publications - *See* Country Star Music
Kelly, Nason Advertising Inc. - New York, NY - *BrCabYB 84*
Kelly, Paul - Nevada City, CA - *LitMarPl 84*
Kelly Productions, Butch - Charlotte, NC - *BillIntBG 83-84*
Kelly, Scott & Madison Inc. - Chicago, IL - *HBIndAd&MS 82-83; StaDirAdAg 2-84*
Kelly Services Inc. - Detroit, MI - *DirInfWP 82*
Kelly, Zahrndt & Kelly Inc. - St. Louis, MO - *StaDirAdAg 2-84; TelAl 83, 84*
KELN - North Platte, NE - *BrCabYB 84*
KELO - Sioux Falls, SD - *BrCabYB 84; NatRadPubDir Summer 83, Spring 84; TV&RadDir 84*
KELO-FM - Sioux Falls, SD - *BrCabYB 84; NatRadPubDir Summer 83, Spring 84; TV&RadDir 84*
KELO-TV - Sioux Falls, SD - *BrCabYB 84; DirUSTelSta 83; TelAl 83, 84; Tel&CabFB 84S; TV&RadDir 84*
Keloland - Sioux Falls, SD - *BrCabYB 84*
Kelowna Cable TV Ltd. [of Capital Cities TV Ltd.] - Kelowna, BC, Canada - *BrCabYB 84*
Kelowna Daily Courier, The - Kelowna, BC, Canada - *BaconPubCkNews 84*
Kelowna-Rutland Progress - Kelowna, BC, Canada - *AyerDirPub 83*
KELP - El Paso, TX - *BrCabYB 84; NatRadPubDir Summer 83, Spring 84*
KELS-FM - Ardmore, OK - *BrCabYB 84; TV&RadDir 84*
Kelsey Publishing - Springville, UT - *BoPubDir 4, 5*
Kelsey Street Press - Berkeley, CA - *BoPubDir 4, 5; LitMag&SmPr 83-84*
Kelseyville Lake Sun & Sun Sampler - Kelseyville, CA - *NewsDir 84*
Kelso Associates - Asheville, NC - *AdAge 3-28-84; ArtMar 84*
Kelso Manufacturing Co. - Greenville, MS - *BoPubDir 4, 5*
KELT-FM - Harlingen, TX - *BrCabYB 84; TV&RadDir 84*
KELT-FM - McAllen, TX - *NatRadPubDir Summer 83, Spring 84 p.243*
Keltner, M. R. - Alpine, CA - *Tel&CabFB 84C p.1686*
Kelty, William H. - Chappaqua, NY - *LitMarPl 84*
Kelvin/Science Graphics, George V. - Great Neck, NY - *MagIndMarPl 82-83*
Kelvington Radio, The - Kelvington, SK, Canada - *Ed&PubIntYB 82*
KELY - Ely, NV - *BrCabYB 84; TV&RadDir 84*
KELZ - Bishop, TX - *BrCabYB 84*
K.E.M. & Co. - Evanston, IL - *DirMarMP 83*
KEMB-FM - Emmetsburg, IA - *BrCabYB 84; TV&RadDir 84*
Kemble Communications Inc. - Cincinnati, OH - *DirPRFirms 83*
KEMC - Billings, MT - *BrCabYB 84; TV&RadDir 84*
KEMC-FM - Billings, MT - *NatRadPubDir Summer 83, Spring 84*
Keme-Marketing Research Centre Hellas Ltd. - Athens, Greece - *IntDirMarRes 83*
Kemenyffy Advertising, Thomas E. - Los Angeles, CA - *StaDirAdAg 2-84*
KEMM - Commerce, TX - *BrCabYB 84*
Kemmerer Gazette - Kemmerer, WY - *BaconPubCkNews 84; Ed&PubIntYB 82*
Kemp Cedar Creek Pilot - *See* Community Information Center Inc.
Kemp, Morris - Washington, DC - *LitMarPl 83, 84; MagIndMarPl 82-83*
Kemp News - Kemp, TX - *Ed&PubIntYB 82*
Kemp News [of Malakoff Territory Times Publishing Co.] - Malakoff, TX - *NewsDir 84*
Kemper County Messenger - De Kalb, MS - *AyerDirPub 83; Ed&PubIntYB 82*
Kempler Institute - Costa Mesa, CA - *BoPubDir 4, 5*
Kempner Inc., M. A. - Pompano Beach, FL - *BrCabYB 84; TelAl 83, 84; Tel&CabFB 84C*
KEMR-FM - Riverside, CA - *NatRadPubDir Summer 83, Spring 84*
KEMV - Mountain View, AR - *BrCabYB 84; Tel&CabFB 84S*
Ken-A-Vision Manufacturing Co. Inc. - Raytown, MO - *AvMarPl 83*
Ken Art Co. - Whitehouse Station, NJ - *MagIndMarPl 82-83*
Ken-Books - San Francisco, CA - *BoPubDir 4 Sup, 5*
Ken-Del Productions Inc. - Wilmington, DE - *WritMar 84*
Ken-Lab - Old Lyme, CT - *AvMarPl 83*
Ken-Ton Bee [of Bee Publications Inc.] - Williamsville, NY - *NewsDir 84*
Ken-Ton Bee - *See* Bee Publications Inc.
KENA - Mena, AR - *BrCabYB 84; TV&RadDir 84*
Kenai Peninsula Cheechako News - Kenai, AK - *BaconPubCkNews 84; NewsDir 84*
Kenai Peninsula Clarion - Kenai, AK - *BaconPubCkNews 84*
Kenansville Duplin Times Progress - Kenansville, NC - *BaconPubCkNews 84*
KENB-FM - Worland, WY - *BrCabYB 84; TV&RadDir 84*
Kenbridge Cablevision Co. [of DoKel Communications Corp.] - Kenbridge, VA - *BrCabYB 84; Tel&CabFB 84C*
Kenbridge-Victoria Dispatch - Victoria, VA - *AyerDirPub 83; Ed&PubIntYB 82*
Kenco Records - Addison, TX - *BillIntBG 83-84*
KEND - Lubbock, TX - *BrCabYB 84; NatRadPubDir Summer 83, Spring 84; TV&RadDir 84*
Kendall County Record - Yorkville, IL - *AyerDirPub 83; Ed&PubIntYB 82*
Kendall/Hunt Publishing Co. [Subs. of Wm. C. Brown Co.] - Dubuque, IA - *LitMarPl 83, 84*
Kendall Park Central Post [of Princeton Packet Inc.] - Kendall Park, NJ - *NewsDir 84*
Kendall-South Miami News [of South Miami Community Newspapers] - Miami, FL - *AyerDirPub 83; NewsDir 84*
Kendall Whaling Museum - Sharon, MA - *BoPubDir 4, 5*
Kendallville News-Sun - Kendallville, IN - *BaconPubCkNews 84; Ed&PubIntYB 82; NewsDir 84*
Kendor Music Inc. - Delevan, NY - *BillIntBG 83-84*
Kendra Co. Ltd., The - Libertyville, IL - *StaDirAdAg 2-84*
Kendrick, Clarke Inc. - Toronto, ON, Canada - *MicrocomSwDir 1*
Kendrick Gazette News - Kendrick, ID - *BaconPubCkNews 84*
KENE - Toppenish, WA - *BrCabYB 84; TV&RadDir 84*
KENE-FM - Toppenish, WA - *BrCabYB 84; TV&RadDir 84*

Kenedy Advance Times - Kenedy, TX - *AyerDirPub 83; BaconPubCkNews 84; Ed&PubIntYB 82*
Kenedy & Sons, P. J. - New York, NY - *MagIndMarPl 82-83*
Kenedy Cable Co. [of De-Cal Cable Inc.] - Kenedy, TX - *BrCabYB 84; Tel&CabFB 84C*
KENI - Anchorage, AK - *BrCabYB 84; NatRadPubDir Summer 83, Spring 84; TV&RadDir 84*
KENI-TV - Anchorage, AK - *TelAl 83*
Kenilworth Leader - Kenilworth, NJ - *Ed&PubIntYB 82*
Kenilworth Leader - Union, NJ - *AyerDirPub 83*
Kenilworth Press - Eau Claire, WI - *BoPubDir 4, 5*
KENM - Portales, NM - *BrCabYB 84; TV&RadDir 84*
Kenmare News - Kenmare, ND - *BaconPubCkNews 84; Ed&PubIntYB 82*
Kenmor Software Systems - Yonkers, NY - *MicrocomMPl 83, 84*
Kenmore/Anachronic Press - Winter Haven, FL - *BoPubDir 4, 5*
KENN - Farmington, NM - *BrCabYB 84; TV&RadDir 84*
Kennan Research & Consulting - New York, NY - *IntDirMarRes 83*
Kennebec Advocate Leader - Kennebec, SD - *BaconPubCkNews 84*
Kennebec Journal [of Guy Gannett Publishing Co.] - Augusta, ME - *AyerDirPub 83; BaconPubCkNews 84; Ed&PubIntYB 82; NewsDir 84*
Kennebec River Press Inc. - Woolwich, ME - *BoPubDir 4 Sup, 5; LitMag&SmPr 83-84*
Kennebec Telephone Co. - Kennebec, SD - *TelDir&BG 83-84*
Kennebec Video Enregistree - St. Come, PQ, Canada - *BrCabYB 84*
Kennebunk York County Coast Star [of The New York Times Co.] - Kennebunk, ME - *BaconPubCkNews 84; NewsDir 84*
Kennedale News - Kennedale, TX - *AyerDirPub 83; Ed&PubIntYB 82*
Kennedy [Subs. of Allegheny International] - Monrovia, CA - *DataDirSup 7-83; WhoWMicrocom 83*
Kennedy Advertising Inc. - Chicago, IL - *StaDirAdAg 2-84*
Kennedy & Coe - Salina, KS - *DataDirOnSer 84*
Kennedy & Coe Data Processing Services [Subs. of Kennedy & Coe] - Salina, KS - *DataDirOnSer 84*
Kennedy & Kennedy Inc. - Virginia Beach, VA - *StaDirAdAg 2-84*
Kennedy Cable Construction Inc. - Polk County, GA - *Tel&CabFB 84C*
Kennedy Cable TV [of Stephen Cable TV Inc.] - Kennedy, MN - *BrCabYB 84*
Kennedy Cablevision Inc. - Reidsville, GA - *BrCabYB 84; Tel&CabFB 84C*
Kennedy Enterprises/World International Group Inc., Gene - Nashville, TN - *BillIntBG 83-84*
Kennedy Galleries Inc. - New York, NY - *BoPubDir 4, 5*
Kennedy Inc., Frank - Croton-on-Hudson, NY - *HBIndAd&MS 82-83; IntDirMarRes 83*
Kennedy, J. Roger Jr. - Reidsville, GA - *Tel&CabFB 84C p.1686*
Kennedy/Lee Inc. - York, PA - *AvMarPl 83*
Kennedy Research Inc. - Grand Rapids, MI - *IntDirMarRes 83*
Kennedy Sinclaire Inc. - Wayne, NJ - *DirMarMP 83; StaDirAdAg 2-84*
Kennedy Systems - St. Johnsbury, VT - *WhoWMicrocom 83*
Kennel Review - Los Angeles, CA - *MagDir 84*
Kenner City News - Kenner, LA - *BaconPubCkNews 84; Ed&PubIntYB 82*
Kennesaw-Acworth-South Cherokee Neighbor - South Cherokee, GA - *Ed&PubIntYB 82*
Kennesaw Neighbor - Kennesaw, GA - *Ed&PubIntYB 82*
Kennesaw Neighbor [of Marietta Neighbor Newspapers Inc.] - Marietta, GA - *NewsDir 84*
Kennett Cablevision [of American TV & Communications Corp.] - Kennett, MO - *BrCabYB 84; Tel&CabFB 84C*
Kennett Co. - Nashua, NH - *AvMarPl 83*
Kennett Daily Dunklin Democrat [of Stapleton Publications] - Kennett, MO - *NewsDir 84*
Kennett News & Advertiser - Kennett Square, PA - *AyerDirPub 83; Ed&PubIntYB 82; NewsDir 84*
Kenney Advertising Inc., Roberta - Natick, MA - *AdAge 3-28-84; StaDirAdAg 2-84*
Kennikat Press Corp. - Port Washington, NY - *LitMarPl 83*
Kenning Productions - Newark, DE - *BillIntBG 83-84*
KENO - Las Vegas, NV - *BrCabYB 84; NatRadPubDir Summer 83, Spring 84; TV&RadDir 84*
Keno Star - Keno, OR - *AyerDirPub 83*
Kenora Cable Vision Ltd. [of Norcom Telecommunications Ltd.] - Kenora, ON, Canada - *BrCabYB 84*
Kenora Daily Miner & News - Kenora, ON, Canada - *BaconPubCkNews 84*
Kenosha Labor, The - Kenosha, WI - *NewsDir 84*
Kenosha News - Kenosha, WI - *BaconPubCkNews 84; Ed&PubIntYB 82; NewsDir 84*
KENR - Houston, TX - *TV&RadDir 84*
Kenrick Advertising - St. Louis, MO - *AdAge 3-28-84; ArtMar 84; StaDirAdAg 2-84*
Kenro [Subs. of Xenon Industries Inc.] - Cedar Knolls, NJ - *AvMarPl 83*
KENS-TV - San Antonio, TX - *BrCabYB 84; DirUSTelSta 83; LitMarPl 83, 84; TelAl 83, 84; Tel&CabFB 84S; TV&RadDir 84*
Kensington Falls - Pittsburgh, PA - *AvMarPl 83*
Kensington Gazette [of Greater Philadelphia Group Inc.] - Philadelphia, PA - *NewsDir 84*
Kensington Journal [of Lackawanna Leader Publishing Co.] - Lackawanna, NY - *NewsDir 84*
Kensington Microware Ltd. - New York, NY - *MicrocomMPl 84; WhoWMicrocom 83*
Kensington Music Service - Tenafly, NJ - *BillIntBG 83-84*
Kensington Press - San Diego, CA - *BoPubDir 4, 5*
Kensington Topics - Buffalo, NY - *AyerDirPub 83*
Kensoft - Kenosha, WI - *MicrocomMPl 84; MicrocomSwDir 1*
Kent Associates Inc. - New York, NY - *LitMarPl 83, 84; MagIndMarPl 82-83*
Kent-Barlow Information Associates - London, England - *EISS 83; InfIndMarPl 83*
Kent, C. M. [Aff. of Erespin Press] - Austin, TX - *BoPubDir 4, 5*
Kent Communications Inc. - Richardson, TX - *WhoWMicrocom 83*
Kent County News - Chestertown, MD - *AyerDirPub 83; Ed&PubIntYB 82*
Kent Island Bay Times, The - Kent Island, MD - *Ed&PubIntYB 82*
Kent Organization, Grace Teed - New York, NY - *HBIndAd&MS 82-83*
Kent Popular Press - Kent, OH - *BoPubDir 4, 5*
Kent Publications - Northridge, CA - *BoPubDir 4, 5; LitMag&SmPr 83-84*
Kent Publishing Co. [Aff. of Wadsworth Inc.] - Boston, MA - *BoPubDir 4; LitMarPl 83, 84*
Kent-Ravenna Record-Courier [of Wooster Republican Party Co.] - Ravenna, OH - *NewsDir 84*
Kent State University (Audio Visual Services) - Kent, OH - *AvMarPl 83*
Kent State University Press - Kent, OH - *LitMarPl 83, 84; WritMar 84*
Kent-Sybil Associates - New York, NY - *DirInfWP 82*
Kentland Newton County Enterprise - Kentland, IN - *BaconPubCkNews 84*
Kentland TV & Kable - Goodland, IN - *BrCabYB 84*
Kentland TV & Kable - Kentland, IN - *Tel&CabFB 84C*
Kenton County Recorder - Edgewood, KY - *AyerDirPub 83*
Kenton County Recorder - Kenton County, KY - *Ed&PubIntYB 82*
Kenton Times [of Hardin County Publishing Co.] - Kenton, OH - *BaconPubCkNews 84; NewsDir 84*
Kentuckiana Cablevision Inc. [of Dear Publications & Radio Inc.] - Hawesville, KY - *BrCabYB 84 p.D-302; Tel&CabFB 84C p.1686*
Kentuckiana Purchasor - Louisville, KY - *BaconPubCkMag 84; MagDir 84*
Kentucky Advocate [of Gleaner & Journal Publishing Co.] - Danville, KY - *AyerDirPub 83; Ed&PubIntYB 82; NewsDir 84*
Kentucky Bench & Bar - Frankfort, KY - *BaconPubCkMag 84*
Kentucky Beverage Journal [of Feature Publications Inc.] - Frankfort, KY - *BaconPubCkMag 84; MagDir 84*
Kentucky Business & Government - Frankfort, KY - *BaconPubCkMag 84*
Kentucky Business Ledger [of Executive Press] - Louisville, KY - *BaconPubCkMag 84; MagDir 84; WritMar 84*

Kentucky Cable TV Inc. [of TeleScripps Cable Co.] - Bardstown, KY - *BrCabYB 84; Tel&CabFB 84C*
Kentucky Cable TV Inc. [of Tennessee-Kentucky Cable TV Co.] - Campbellsville, KY - *BrCabYB 84; Tel&CabFB 84C*
Kentucky Cable TV Inc. [of Tennessee-Kentucky Cable TV Co.] - Greenville, KY - *BrCabYB 84; Tel&CabFB 84C*
Kentucky Cable TV Inc. [of Telescripps Cable Co.] - Hodgenville, KY - *Tel&CabFB 84C*
Kentucky Cable TV Inc. [of Scripps-Howard Cable Services Co.] - Leitchfield, KY - *Tel&CabFB 84C*
Kentucky City, The [of Kentucky Municipal League] - Lexington, KY - *BaconPubCkMag 84; MagDir 84*
Kentucky Coal Journal - Frankfort, KY - *BaconPubCkMag 84; MagDir 84; WritMar 84*
Kentucky Colonel Music - Pasadena, CA - *BillIntBG 83-84*
Kentucky Cooperative Library Information Project [of Kentucky State Library] - Frankfort, KY - *EISS 83*
Kentucky Council of Economic Advisors [of University of Kentucky] - Lexington, KY - *DataDirOnSer 84*
Kentucky Crop & Livestock Service - Louisville, KY - *BoPubDir 5*
Kentucky Dept. of Economic Development - Frankfort, KY - *BoPubDir 5*
Kentucky Economic Information System [of Center for Applied Economic Research] - Lexington, KY - *DataDirOnSer 84; DirOnDB Spring 84; EISS 83; InfIndMarPl 83; MicrocomMPl 84*
Kentucky Engineer - Frankfort, KY - *BaconPubCkMag 84*
Kentucky Farm Bureau News - Louisville, KY - *BaconPubCkMag 84; MagDir 84*
Kentucky Farmer - Bowling Green, KY - *BaconPubCkMag 84; MagDir 84*
Kentucky Historical Society - Frankfort, KY - *BoPubDir 4, 5*
Kentucky Home Television System - Seco, KY - *BrCabYB 84*
Kentucky Kernel [of Kernel Press Inc.] - Lexington, KY - *NewsDir 84*
Kentucky Labor News - Louisville, KY - *NewsDir 84*
Kentucky New Era - Hopkinsville, KY - *AyerDirPub 83; BaconPubCkNews 84; Ed&PubIntYB 82; LitMarPl 83, 84*
Kentucky Newsclip Inc. - Louisville, KY - *ProGuPRSer 4*
Kentucky Pharmacist [of The Kentucky Pharmacists Association] - Frankfort, KY - *BaconPubCkMag 84; MagDir 84*
Kentucky Plumbing, Heating, & Cooling Index [of Britemark Graphics] - Louisville, KY - *BaconPubCkMag 84; MagDir 84*
Kentucky Post - Covington, KY - *AyerDirPub 83; BaconPubCkNews 84; Ed&PubIntYB 82*
Kentucky Standard [of Scripps-Howard Inc.] - Bardstown, KY - *AyerDirPub 83; Ed&PubIntYB 82; NewsDir 84*
Kentucky State Data Center [of University of Louisville] - Louisville, KY - *EISS 7-83 Sup*
Kentucky Trucker - Frankfort, KY - *BaconPubCkMag 84*
Kentucky Vision Inc. - Brownsville, KY - *Tel&CabFB 84C*
Kentwood Commercial [of Hammond Murray-Huber Publishing Inc.] - Hammond, LA - *NewsDir 84*
Kentwood Ledger - Kentwood, LA - *BaconPubCkNews 84*
Kentwood News - Kentwood, LA - *BaconPubCkNews 84; Ed&PubIntYB 82*
Kentwood News Advocate - Wyoming, MI - *Ed&PubIntYB 82*
KENU - Enumclaw, WA - *BrCabYB 84*
Kenvad Music - Orlando, FL - *BillIntBG 83-84*
KENW-FM - Portales, NM - *BrCabYB 84; NatRadPubDir Summer 83, Spring 84; TV&RadDir 84*
KENW-TV - Portales, NM - *BrCabYB 84; Tel&CabFB 84S; TV&RadDir 84*
Kenward, Jack W. - Scarsdale, NY - *MagIndMarPl 82-83*
Kenwon Music - North Hollywood, CA - *BillIntBG 83-84*
Kenwood Advertising Inc. - Oneida, NY - *StaDirAdAg 2-84*
Kenwood Electronics Inc. - Carson, CA - *BillIntBG 83-84*
Kenwood Group - San Francisco, CA - *AvMarPl 83; Tel&CabFB 84C*
Kenyan Entertainment Corp. - Miami, FL - *BillIntBG 83-84*
Kenyon & Eckhardt [of Lorimar] - New York, NY - *AdAge 3-28-84, 6-25-84; Br 1-23-84; BrCabYB 84; HomeVid&CabYB 82-83*
Kenyon & Eckhardt - *See* K & E Holdings Inc.
Kenyon Hill Publications - Hanover, NH - *LitMag&SmPr 83-84*
Kenyon Leader - Kenyon, MN - *BaconPubCkNews 84; Ed&PubIntYB 82*
Kenyon Publications - Ft. Lauderdale, FL - *BoPubDir 4, 5*
Kenyon Review, The - Gambier, OH - *LitMag&SmPr 83-84; LitMarPl 83, 84*
KENZ - Sacramento, CA - *BrCabYB 84; NatRadPubDir Summer 83, Spring 84; TV&RadDir 84*
KEOK-FM - Tahlequah, OK - *BrCabYB 84; TV&RadDir 84*
Keokuk Daily Gate City - Keokuk, IA - *BaconPubCkNews 84; NewsDir 84*
KEOL-FM - La Grande, OR - *BrCabYB 84; NatRadPubDir Summer 83, Spring 84; TV&RadDir 84*
KEOR - Atoka, OK - *BrCabYB 84; TV&RadDir 84*
KEOR-FM - Atoka, OK - *BrCabYB 84*
Keosauqua Van Buren County Register - Keosauqua, IA - *BaconPubCkNews 84*
Keota Cable TV Inc. - Keota, OK - *Tel&CabFB 84C*
Keota Eagle - Keota, IA - *BaconPubCkNews 84; Ed&PubIntYB 82*
Keowee Courier - Walhalla, SC - *AyerDirPub 83; Ed&PubIntYB 82*
KEPC-FM - Colorado Springs, CO - *BrCabYB 84; NatRadPubDir Summer 83, Spring 84; TV&RadDir 84*
Kepes Vilaghirado - Toronto, ON, Canada - *Ed&PubIntYB 82*
KEPH-FM - Ephraim, UT - *BrCabYB 84; NatRadPubDir Summer 83, Spring 84; TV&RadDir 84*
Kephart Communications Inc. - Arlington, VA - *DirMarMP 83*
Kepley, Ray R. - Ulysses, KS - *BoPubDir 4, 5*
Kepner Associates Inc., Woody - Miami, FL - *DirPRFirms 83*
KEPO - Eagle Point, OR - *BrCabYB 84*
Kepper, Tupper & Co. Inc. - McHenry, IL - *CabTVFinDB 83*
Kepper, William - Great Lakes, IL - *Tel&CabFB 84C p.1686*
KEPR-TV - Pasco, WA - *BrCabYB 84; TelAl 83, 84; Tel&CabFB 84S; TV&RadDir 84*
KEPR-TV - Richland, WA - *DirUSTelSta 83*
KEPS - Eagle Pass, TX - *BrCabYB 84; TV&RadDir 84*
KEPT-FM - Shreveport, LA - *NatRadPubDir Summer 83; TV&RadDir 84*
KEQO - Enid, OK - *BrCabYB 84; Tel&CabFB 84S*
KERA-FM - Dallas, TX - *BrCabYB 84; NatRadPubDir Summer 83, Spring 84; TV&RadDir 84*
KERA-TV - Dallas, TX - *BrCabYB 84; Tel&CabFB 84S; TV&RadDir 84*
Keramos Books [Aff. of Westwood Ceramic Supply Co.] - Bassett, CA - *BoPubDir 4, 5*
KERB - Kermit, TX - *BrCabYB 84; TV&RadDir 84*
KERC - Eastland, TX - *TV&RadDir 84*
Kerchner & Associates Inc., C. F. - Northampton, PA - *MicrocomSwDir 1*
Keremeos Similkameen Spotlight - Keremeos, BC, Canada - *Ed&PubIntYB 82*
Kerens Tribune, The - Kerens, TX - *Ed&PubIntYB 82*
KERG - Garberville, CA - *BrCabYB 84*
Kerker & Associates Inc. - Minneapolis, MN - *AdAge 3-28-84; StaDirAdAg 2-84*
Kerker & Associates Inc. (Public Relations Group) - Minneapolis, MN - *DirPRFirms 83*
Kerkhoff Computers - Orlando, FL - *MicrocomMPl 84*
Kerkhoven Banner - Kerkhoven, MN - *AyerDirPub 83; BaconPubCkNews 84; Ed&PubIntYB 82*
Kerk's Communication Service Inc. - Amelia, LA - *BrCabYB 84; Tel&CabFB 84C*
Kerlick, Switzer & Johnson Advertising - St. Louis, MO - *AdAge 3-28-84; StaDirAdAg 2-84*
KERM - Torrington, WY - *BrCabYB 84*
Kerman News - Kerman, CA - *BaconPubCkNews 84; Ed&PubIntYB 82*
Kerman Telephone Co. - Kerman, CA - *TelDir&BG 83-84*
Kerman West Side Advance - Kerman, CA - *BaconPubCkNews 84*
Kermish Public Relations, Stanley - New York, NY - *DirPRFirms 83*
Kermit Winkler County News [of Golden West Free Press Inc.] - Kermit, TX - *BaconPubCkNews 84; NewsDir 84*
KERN - Bakersfield, CA - *BrCabYB 84; NatRadPubDir Summer 83, Spring 84; TV&RadDir 84*
Kern & Associates, Walter - New York, NY - *LitMarPl 84*
Kern & Associates, Walter - Riverdale, NY - *LitMarPl 83*

Kern County Historical Society - Bakersfield, CA - *BoPubDir 5*
Kern Publications [Subs. of Data Dynamics Inc.] - Duxbury, MA - *BoPubDir 5; MicrocomMPl 83, 84; WritMar 84*
Kern Valley Cable TV [of Booth American Co.] - Kern River Valley, CA - *Tel&CabFB 84C*
Kern Valley Cable TV [of Booth American Co.] - River Valley, CA - *BrCabYB 84*
Kernersville News - Kernersville, NC - *BaconPubCkNews 84; Ed&PubIntYB 82; NewsDir 84*
Kerning Arts Press - Champaign, IL - *BoPubDir 5*
Kerns & Associates Inc. - Orlando, FL - *StaDirAdAg 2-84*
Kernville Kern Valley Sun - Kernville, CA - *BaconPubCkNews 84; NewsDir 84*
KERO-TV - Bakersfield, CA - *BrCabYB 84; DirUSTelSta 83; TelAl 83, 84; Tel&CabFB 84S; TV&RadDir 84*
Keroff & Rosenberg Advertising - Chicago, IL - *AdAge 3-28-84; DirMarMP 83; StaDirAdAg 2-84*
KERR - Polson, MT - *BrCabYB 84; TV&RadDir 84*
Kerr & Associates, Dorothy - *See* DKA Advertising
Kerr Associates Inc. - Minneapolis, MN - *BoPubDir 4, 5*
Kerr Enterprises Inc., Charles - New Hope, PA - *BoPubDir 4, 5*
Kerr Industrial Applications Center [of Southeastern Oklahoma State University] - Durant, OK - *EISS 83; InfIndMarPl 83*
Kerr Publishing Co., Charles H. - Chicago, IL - *BoPubDir 4, 5; LitMag&SmPr 83-84*
Kerr, West & Gish Inc. - Nashville, TN - *StaDirAdAg 2-84; TelAl 83*
Kerr, West & Gish Inc. - North Nashville, TN - *TelAl 84*
Kerrobert Citizen - Kerrobert, SK, Canada - *AyerDirPub 83; Ed&PubIntYB 82*
Kerrville Daily Times [of Kerr Publications Inc.] - Kerrville, TX - *BaconPubCkNews 84; Ed&PubIntYB 82; NewsDir 84*
Kerrville Mountain Sun - Kerrville, TX - *BaconPubCkNews 84; Ed&PubIntYB 82; NewsDir 84*
Kerrville Music Foundation - Kerrville, TX - *BillIntBG 83-84*
Kerrville Telephone Co. - Kerrville, TX - *TelDir&BG 83-84*
Kershaw News-Era, The - Kershaw, SC - *Ed&PubIntYB 82*
Kerstein Advertising, Duke - Albuquerque, NM - *StaDirAdAg 2-84*
Kerth, A. L. - Massapequa Park, NY - *BoPubDir 4*
Kerth, A. L. - Washington Crossing, PA - *BoPubDir 5*
KERV - Kerrville, TX - *BrCabYB 84; TV&RadDir 84*
KERV-FM - Kerrville, TX - *BrCabYB 84; TV&RadDir 84*
KESD-FM - Brookings, SD - *BrCabYB 84; NatRadPubDir Summer 83, Spring 84; TV&RadDir 84*
KESD-TV - Brookings, SD - *BrCabYB 84; Tel&CabFB 84S; TV&RadDir 84*
KESE - Monterey, CA - *TV&RadDir 84*
Kesend Publishing Ltd., Michael - New York, NY - *LitMag&SmPr 83-84; LitMarPl 83, 84*
Kesher Press - Nashville, TN - *BoPubDir 4, 5*
Keshin & Co. Inc., Mort - Roslyn, NY - *StaDirAdAg 2-84*
KESI-FM - San Antonio, TX - *NatRadPubDir Summer 83, Spring 84; TV&RadDir 84*
KESI-FM - Terrell Hills, TX - *BrCabYB 84*
Kesler, Arthur A. - La Verne, CA - *AvMarPl 83*
KESM - El Dorado Springs, MO - *BrCabYB 84; TV&RadDir 84*
KESM—FM - El Dorado Springs, MO - *BrCabYB 84; TV&RadDir 84*
KESQ-TV - Cathedral City, CA - *TV&RadDir 84*
KESQ-TV - Palm Springs, CA - *BrCabYB 84; DirUSTelSta 83; TelAl 83, 84; Tel&CabFB 84S*
KESR - Independence, CA - *BrCabYB 84*
KESS-FM - Dallas, TX - *NatRadPubDir Summer 83, Spring 84 p.237*
KESS-FM - Ft. Worth, TX - *BrCabYB 84; TV&RadDir 84*
Kesslinger & Associates, J. M. - Newark, NJ - *ArtMar 84; StaDirAdAg 2-84*
KEST - San Francisco, CA - *BrCabYB 84; NatRadPubDir Summer 83, Spring 84; TV&RadDir 84*
Kester, John J. - Scotch Plains, NJ - *BoPubDir 4, 5*
KESY-FM - Omaha, NE - *BrCabYB 84; NatRadPubDir Summer 83, Spring 84; TV&RadDir 84*
KETA-TV - Oklahoma City, OK - *BrCabYB 84; Tel&CabFB 84S; TV&RadDir 84*
KETC-TV - St. Louis, MO - *BrCabYB 84; Tel&CabFB 84S; TV&RadDir 84*
Ketch Pen Newsletter - Ellensburg, WA - *BaconPubCkMag 84*
Ketchikan News [of Pioneer Printing Co.] - Ketchikan, AK - *AyerDirPub 83; BaconPubCkNews 84; Ed&PubIntYB 82; NewsDir 84*
Ketchikan Public Utilities - Ketchikan, AK - *TelDir&BG 83-84*
Ketchum Advertising/Houston - Houston, TX - *ArtMar 84*
Ketchum Communications - Pittsburgh, PA - *AdAge 3-28-84; Br 1-23-84; StaDirAdAg 2-84*
Ketchum Direct [of Ketchum Communications Inc.] - New York, NY - *DirMarMP 83*
Ketchum International - Pittsburgh, PA - *AdAge 6-25-84*
Ketchum International Ltd. - London, England - *BrCabYB 84*
Ketchum Public Relations [of Ketchum Communications Inc.] - New York, NY - *DirPRFirms 83*
KETG-TV - Arkadelphia, AR - *BrCabYB 84; Tel&CabFB 84S*
KETG-TV - Conway, AR - *TV&RadDir 84*
KETH - Ketchikan, AK - *BrCabYB 84*
KETR-FM - Commerce, TX - *BrCabYB 84; NatRadPubDir Summer 83, Spring 84; TV&RadDir 84*
Ketron-Davis Publishing Co. - Lovelock, NV - *BoPubDir 4, 5*
KETS - Conway, AR - *TV&RadDir 84*
KETS - Little Rock, AR - *BrCabYB 84; Tel&CabFB 84S*
Kettering-Oakwood Times - Dayton, OH - *AyerDirPub 83*
Kettering-Oakwood Times [of Kettering Publishing Corp.] - Kettering, OH - *NewsDir 84*
Kettering-Oakwood Times - *See* Kettering Publishing Corp.
Kettering/Oakwood Times & Times Advertiser - Kettering, OH - *Ed&PubIntYB 82*
Kettering Publishing Corp. - Kettering, OH - *BaconPubCkNews 84*
Kettering-Times Advertiser - Dayton, OH - *AyerDirPub 83*
KETV-TV - Omaha, NE - *BrCabYB 84; DirUSTelSta 83; TelAl 83, 84; Tel&CabFB 84S; TV&RadDir 84*
KETX - Livingston, TX - *BrCabYB 84; TV&RadDir 84*
KETX-FM - Livingston, TX - *BrCabYB 84; TV&RadDir 84*
KETZ-FM - Ames, IA - *TV&RadDir 84*
Keuffel & Esser/Kratos [Subs. of Education/AV Products Div.] - Morristown, NJ - *AvMarPl 83; DataDirSup 7-83*
Keuka TV Cable - Hammondsport, NY - *BrCabYB 84; Tel&CabFB 84C*
KEUN - Eunice, LA - *BrCabYB 84; TV&RadDir 84*
KEVA - Evanston, WY - *BrCabYB 84; TV&RadDir 84*
Kevex Corp. - Foster City, CA - *WhoWMicrocom 83*
KEVN-TV - Bethlehem, SD - *TV&RadDir 84*
KEVN-TV - Rapid City, SD - *BrCabYB 84; DirUSTelSta 83; TelAl 83, 84; Tel&CabFB 84S*
KEVR-FM - Espanola, NM - *BrCabYB 84*
KEVR-FM - Fairview, NM - *TV&RadDir 84*
Kew Gardens Hills Pennysaver - Rockville Centre, NY - *AyerDirPub 83*
Kewanee Star-Courier [of Lee Enterprises Inc.] - Kewanee, IL - *BaconPubCkNews 84; NewsDir 84*
Kewanna Observer - Kewanna, IN - *BaconPubCkNews 84*
Kewaskum Statesman - Kewaskum, WI - *BaconPubCkNews 84; Ed&PubIntYB 82*
Kewaunee Cablevision Inc. - Kawaunee, WI - *BrCabYB 84*
Kewaunee Enterprise - Kewaunee, WI - *BaconPubCkNews 84; Ed&PubIntYB 82*
KEWB - Anderson, CA - *BrCabYB 84*
KEWC-FM - Cheney, WA - *BrCabYB 84; NatRadPubDir Summer 83, Spring 84; TV&RadDir 84*
KEWE-FM - Oroville, CA - *BrCabYB 84; TV&RadDir 84*
KEWI - Cape Girardeau, MO - *BrCabYB 84; NatRadPubDir Summer 83, Spring 84; TV&RadDir 84*
Kewill Systems Ltd. - Walton-on-Thames, England - *WhoWMicrocom 83*
KEWQ - Paradise, CA - *BrCabYB 84; TV&RadDir 84*
KEWS - Cuero, TX - *BrCabYB 84; TV&RadDir 84*
KEWT-FM - Sacramento, CA - *BrCabYB 84; NatRadPubDir Summer 83, Spring 84; TV&RadDir 84*
KEX - Portland, OR - *BrCabYB 84; LitMarPl 83, 84; NatRadPubDir Summer 83, Spring 84; TV&RadDir 84*
KEXI - Walla Walla, WA - *BrCabYB 84*
KEXL-FM - Norfolk, NE - *BrCabYB 84; TV&RadDir 84*
KEXO - Grand Junction, CO - *BrCabYB 84; NatRadPubDir Summer 83, Spring 84; TV&RadDir 84*
KEXS - Excelsior Springs, MO - *BrCabYB 84; TV&RadDir 84*

KEXX-FM - Corpus Christi, TX - *BrCabYB 84;*
NatRadPubDir Spring 84; TV&RadDir 84

KEXY - Anaheim, CA - *NatRadPubDir Summer 83*

Key Biscayne Islander News - Key Biscayne, FL -
BaconPubCkNews 84

Key Bits Inc. - Miami, FL - *MicrocomMPl 83, 84;*
WhoWMicrocom 83

Key Book Service Inc. - Bridgeport, CT - *LitMarPl 83, 84*

Key Books International - Bridgeport, CT - *LitMarPl 83, 84*

Key British Enterprises - New York, NY - *DirOnDB Spring 84*

Key Curriculum Project Inc. - Berkeley, CA - *BoPubDir 4, 5*

Key Financial Systems Inc. - Pine Brook, NJ -
ADAPSOMemDir 83-84; DataDirSup 7-83

Key Issues Tracking [of The New York Times Information
Service Inc.] - Parsippany, NJ - *CompReadDB 82; DBBus 82*

Key Magazine - New York, NY - *MagDir 84*

Key Magazine/This Week in Chicago - Chicago, IL -
BaconPubCkMag 84

Key Magazine/This Week in Reno & Lake Tahoe - Reno, NV -
MagDir 84

Key Magazine/This Week in San Francisco - San Francisco,
CA - *MagDir 84*

Key Micro Systems - Coventry, RI - *MicrocomMPl 84*

Key Newsletter [of Voice Publications] - Goreville, IL -
ArtMar 84; WritMar 84

Key of David Publications - Holland, PA - *BoPubDir 5*

Key Porter Books - Toronto, ON, Canada - *BoPubDir 4 Sup, 5*

Key Publications, K. [of Council for Research on Turkish History
& Civilization Inc.] - Washington, DC - *BoPubDir 4, 5*

Key Software - Des Plaines, IL - *MicrocomSwDir 1*

Key Software - Oak Ridge, TN - *MicrocomMPl 83, 84*

Key Systems Inc. - Marathon, FL - *MicrocomMPl 83, 84;*
WhoWMicrocom 83

Key Systems Inc. - Louisville, KY - *WhoWMicrocom 83*

Key, The - Florence, SC - *Ed&PubIntYB 82*

Key to Christian Education [of Standard Publishing] - Cincinnati,
OH - *WritMar 84*

Key to Toronto [of Key Publishers Co. Ltd.] - Toronto, ON,
Canada - *BaconPubCkMag 84; WritMar 84*

Key Tronic Corp. - Spokane, WA - *DataDirSup 7-83;*
MicrocomMPl 84

Key Tronic Corp. (OCR Div.) - Spokane, WA -
WhoWMicrocom 83

Key West Citizen [of Thomson Newspapers Inc.] - Key West,
FL - *BaconPubCkNews 84; Ed&PubIntYB 82; NewsDir 84*

Key Word - Longview, WA - *BoPubDir 4, 5*

KEYA-FM - Belcourt, ND - *BrCabYB 84; TV&RadDir 84*

Keyan Industries Inc. - Middleboro, MA - *AvMarPl 83*

Keyboard - Cupertino, CA - *BaconPubCkMag 84; MagDir 84;*
MagIndMarPl 82-83; WritMar 84

Keyboard Classics Magazine - Katonah, NY -
MagIndMarPl 82-83

Keyboard Communications Inc. - Carle Place, NY - *DirInfWP 82*

Keyboard Workshop - Medford, OR - *LitMag&SmPr 83-84*

Keyboard World - Downey, CA - *MagIndMarPl 82-83*

Keyborad Communications Inc. - Malden, MA - *LitMarPl 84*

Keybrook Business Systems Inc. - Hayward, CA -
WhoWMicrocom 83

KEYC-TV - Mankato, MN - *BrCabYB 84; DirUSTelSta 83;*
TelAl 83, 84; Tel&CabFB 84S; TV&RadDir 84

Keycom Electronic Publishing - Schaumburg, IL - *InterCabHB 3;*
VideoDir 82-83

KEYD - Durant, OK - *BrCabYB 84*

Keydata Corp. - Watertown, MA - *DataDirOnSer 84*

KEYE - Perryton, TX - *BrCabYB 84; TV&RadDir 84*

Keye Advertising - Brooklyn, NY - *ArtMar 84; StaDirAdAg 2-84*

Keye/Donna/Pearlstein - Beverly Hills, CA - *StaDirAdAg 2-84*

KEYE-FM - Perryton, TX - *BrCabYB 84; TV&RadDir 84*

Keyes Martin - Springfield, NJ - *AdAge 3-28-84; ArtMar 84;*
DirPRFirms 83; StaDirAdAg 2-84; TelAl 83, 84

KEYF - Grand Coulee, WA - *BrCabYB 84*

Keyfax [of Field Electronic Publishing Inc.] - Elk Grove Village,
IL - *EISS 83*

Keyfax - Schaumburg, IL - *CabTVPrDB 83*

KEYG - Grand Coulee, WA - *BrCabYB 84*

KEYH - Houston, TX - *BrCabYB 84;*
NatRadPubDir Summer 83, Spring 84; TV&RadDir 84

KEYI-FM - Austin, TX - *NatRadPubDir Summer 83, Spring 84;*
TV&RadDir 84

KEYI-FM - San Marcos, TX - *BrCabYB 84*

KEYJ - Jamestown, ND - *NatRadPubDir Summer 83, Spring 84*

KEYL - Long Prairie, MN - *BrCabYB 84; TV&RadDir 84*

Keyline Publishers [Aff. of Area Keys Genealogical Research
Foundation] - Billings, MT - *BoPubDir 4, 5*

Keymarket Group, The - Aiken, SC - *BrCabYB 84*

KEYN-FM - Wichita, KS - *BrCabYB 84;*
NatRadPubDir Summer 83, Spring 84; TV&RadDir 84

Keynote Magazine - New York, NY - *BaconPubCkMag 84*

Keynote Marketing Inc. - New York, NY - *LitMarPl 84*

Keynote Records - Youngstown, OH - *BillIntBG 83-84*

Keynoter [of Kiwanis International] - Indianapolis, IN -
ArtMar 84

Keynoter Publishing Co. Inc. - Marathon, FL - *NewsDir 84*

KEYR - Scottsbluff, NE - *TV&RadDir 84*

KEYR - Terrytown, NE - *BrCabYB 84*

KEYS - Corpus Christi, TX - *BrCabYB 84;*
NatRadPubDir Summer 83, Spring 84; TV&RadDir 84

Keyser Daily News Tribune - Keyser, WV - *NewsDir 84*

Keyser, James W. - Kenova, WV - *BrCabYB 84 p.D-302*

Keyser, James W. - *See* C-K Video Inc.

Keyser Mountain Echo-News Tribune - Keyser, WV -
BaconPubCkNews 84

Keyser News-Tribune - Keyser, WV - *BaconPubCkNews 84*

Keyser Productions Inc., Kay - Dayton, OH - *AvMarPl 83*

Keyser Television Co. - Allegany County, MD - *BrCabYB 84*

Keyser Television Co. - Keyser, WV - *BrCabYB 84*

Keystone Arthur Telephone Co. - Keystone, NE -
TelDir&BG 83-84

Keystone Cable TV - Kutztown, PA - *BrCabYB 84;*
Tel&CabFB 84C

Keystone Camera Corp. [Subs. of Amicor Inc.] - Clifton, NJ -
AvMarPl 83

Keystone Communicable Inc. [of Tele-Communications Inc.] - Mt.
Wolf, PA - *Tel&CabFB 84C*

Keystone Communicable Inc. - Oxford, PA - *BrCabYB 84*

Keystone Communicable Inc. [of Tele-Communications Inc.] -
Quarryville, PA - *Tel&CabFB 84C*

Keystone Communicable Inc. [of Tele-Communications Inc.] - Red
Lion, PA - *BrCabYB 84*

Keystone Computer Associates Inc. - Ft. Washington, PA -
DataDirSup 7-83

Keystone Distributing Co. - Norwood, MA - *MicrocomMPl 84*

Keystone Farmers Cooperative Telephone Co. - Keystone, IA -
TelDir&BG 83-84

Keystone Heights Lake Region Monitor - Keystone Heights, FL -
BaconPubCkNews 84

Keystone Motorist - Philadelphia, PA - *BaconPubCkMag 84;*
MagDir 84

Keystone Press Agency Inc. - New York, NY - *AvMarPl 83;*
Ed&PubIntYB 82; LitMarPl 83, 84; MagIndMarPl 82-83

Keystone Publications Inc. - New York, NY - *BoPubDir 4, 5*

Keystone-Wilcox Cable TV - Wilcox, PA - *BrCabYB 84;*
Tel&CabFB 84C

KEYT-TV - Santa Barbara, CA - *BrCabYB 84; DirUSTelSta 83;*
TelAl 83, 84; Tel&CabFB 84S; TV&RadDir 84

KeyTek Instrument Corp. - Burlington, MA - *DirInfWP 82*

Keytesville Chariton Courier - Keytesville, MO -
BaconPubCkNews 84

Keytime Inc. - Pennsauken, NJ - *ADAPSOMemDir 83-84*

Keytronic Corp. (OCE Div.) - Spokane, WA - *DirInfWP 82*

KEYY - Provo, UT - *BrCabYB 84; TV&RadDir 84*

KEYZ - Williston, ND - *BrCabYB 84;*
NatRadPubDir Summer 83, Spring 84; TV&RadDir 84

KEZB-FM - El Paso, TX - *BrCabYB 84;*
NatRadPubDir Summer 83, Spring 84

KEZC-FM - Glendale, AZ - *BrCabYB 84*

KEZC-FM - Phoenix, AZ - *NatRadPubDir Summer 83, Spring 84*

KEZE-FM - Spokane, WA - *BrCabYB 84;*
NatRadPubDir Summer 83, Spring 84; TV&RadDir 84

KEZG - Green Valley, AZ - *BrCabYB 84*

KEZH-FM - Hastings, NE - *BrCabYB 84; TV&RadDir 84*

KEZI-TV - Eugene, OR - *BrCabYB 84; DirUSTelSta 83;*
TelAl 83, 84; Tel&CabFB 84S; TV&RadDir 84

KEZJ - Twin Falls, ID - *BrCabYB 84*

KEZK-FM - St. Louis, MO - *BrCabYB 84; NatRadPubDir Summer 83, Spring 84; TV&RadDir 84*
KEZL-FM - Oceanside, CA - *BrCabYB 84*
KEZM - Sulphur, LA - *BrCabYB 84; TV&RadDir 84*
KEZN - Palm Desert, CA - *BrCabYB 84*
KEZO-FM - Omaha, NE - *BrCabYB 84; NatRadPubDir Summer 83, Spring 84; TV&RadDir 84*
KEZQ-FM - Jacksonville, AR - *BrCabYB 84; TV&RadDir 84*
KEZQ-FM - Little Rock, AR - *NatRadPubDir Summer 83, Spring 84*
KEZR-FM - San Jose, CA - *BrCabYB 84; NatRadPubDir Summer 83, Spring 84; TV&RadDir 84*
KEZS-FM - Liberal, KS - *BrCabYB 84; TV&RadDir 84*
KEZS-FM - Cape Girardeau, MO - *NatRadPubDir Spring 84*
KEZT-FM - Ames, IA - *BrCabYB 84; NatRadPubDir Summer 83, Spring 84*
KEZU - Scott City, KS - *BrCabYB 84*
KEZV - Spearfish, SD - *BrCabYB 84*
KEZW - Aurora, CO - *BrCabYB 84*
KEZW - Denver, CO - *NatRadPubDir Summer 83, Spring 84*
KEZW - Wheat Ridge, CO - *TV&RadDir 84*
KEZX-FM - Seattle, WA - *BrCabYB 84; LitMarPl 83, 84; NatRadPubDir Summer 83, Spring 84; TV&RadDir 84*
KEZY-FM - Anaheim, CA - *BrCabYB 84; NatRadPubDir Summer 83, Spring 84; TV&RadDir 84*
KEZZ-FM - Aitkin, MN - *BrCabYB 84; TV&RadDir 84*
KFAB - Omaha, NE - *BrCabYB 84; NatRadPubDir Summer 83, Spring 84; TV&RadDir 84*
KFAB Broadcasting Co. - Omaha, NE - *BrCabYB 84*
KFAC - Los Angeles, CA - *BrCabYB 84; LitMarPl 83, 84; NatRadPubDir Summer 83, Spring 84; TV&RadDir 84*
KFAC-FM - Los Angeles, CA - *BrCabYB 84; LitMarPl 83; NatRadPubDir Summer 83, Spring 84; TV&RadDir 84*
KFAE-FM - Richland, WA - *BrCabYB 84*
KFAI-FM - Minneapolis, MN - *BrCabYB 84; TV&RadDir 84*
KFAL - Fulton, MO - *BrCabYB 84; TV&RadDir 84*
KFAM - Bountiful, UT - *TV&RadDir 84*
KFAM - North Salt Lake City, UT - *BrCabYB 84*
KFAN-FM - Fredericksburg, TX - *BrCabYB 84; TV&RadDir 84*
KFAR - Fairbanks, AK - *BrCabYB 84; NatRadPubDir Summer 83, Spring 84; TV&RadDir 84*
KFAR-TV - Fairbanks, AK - *TelAl 83*
KFAT-FM - Gilroy, CA - *BrCabYB 84; TV&RadDir 84*
KFAX - San Francisco, CA - *BrCabYB 84; LitMarPl 83, 84; NatRadPubDir Summer 83, Spring 84; TV&RadDir 84*
KFAY - Fayetteville, AR - *BrCabYB 84; TV&RadDir 84*
KFBA - Floydada, TX - *BrCabYB 84; TV&RadDir 84*
KFBB-TV - Great Falls, MT - *BrCabYB 84; DirUSTelSta 83; TelAl 83, 84; Tel&CabFB 84S; TV&RadDir 84*
KFBC - Cheyenne, WY - *BrCabYB 84; NatRadPubDir Summer 83, Spring 84; TV&RadDir 84*
KFBD - Waynesville, MO - *BrCabYB 84; TV&RadDir 84*
KFBD-FM - Waynesville, MO - *BrCabYB 84; TV&RadDir 84*
KFBK - Sacramento, CA - *BrCabYB 84; NatRadPubDir Summer 83, Spring 84; TV&RadDir 84*
KFBQ-FM - Cheyenne, WY - *BrCabYB 84; NatRadPubDir Summer 83, Spring 84; TV&RadDir 84*
KFBR - Nogales, AZ - *BrCabYB 84; TV&RadDir 84*
KFCB - Concord, CA - *BrCabYB 84; Tel&CabFB 84S*
KFCF-FM - Fresno, CA - *BrCabYB 84; TV&RadDir 84*
KFCM - Cherokee Village, AR - *BrCabYB 84*
KFDA-TV - Amarillo, TX - *BrCabYB 84; DirUSTelSta 83; TelAl 83, 84; Tel&CabFB 84S; TV&RadDir 84*
KFDF - Van Buren, AR - *BrCabYB 84; TV&RadDir 84*
KFDI - Wichita, KS - *BrCabYB 84; NatRadPubDir Summer 83, Spring 84; TV&RadDir 84*
KFDI-FM - Wichita, KS - *BrCabYB 84; NatRadPubDir Summer 83, Spring 84; TV&RadDir 84*
KFDM-TV - Beaumont, TX - *BrCabYB 84; DirUSTelSta 83; TelAl 83, 84; Tel&CabFB 84S; TV&RadDir 84*
KFDX-TV - Wichita Falls, TX - *BrCabYB 84; DirUSTelSta 83; TelAl 83, 84; Tel&CabFB 84S; TV&RadDir 84*
KFEL - Pueblo, CO - *BrCabYB 84; TV&RadDir 84*
KFEQ - St. Joseph, MO - *BrCabYB 84; NatRadPubDir Summer 83, Spring 84; TV&RadDir 84*
KFFA - Helena, AR - *BrCabYB 84; TV&RadDir 84*
KFFB - Fairfield Bay, AR - *BrCabYB 84*
KFFM-FM - Yakima, WA - *BrCabYB 84; TV&RadDir 84*
KFFR - Hooks, TX - *BrCabYB 84*
KFGO - Fargo, ND - *BrCabYB 84; NatRadPubDir Summer 83, Spring 84; TV&RadDir 84*
KFGQ - Boone, IA - *BrCabYB 84; TV&RadDir 84*
KFGQ-FM - Boone, IA - *BrCabYB 84; TV&RadDir 84*
KFH - Wichita, KS - *BrCabYB 84; NatRadPubDir Summer 83, Spring 84; TV&RadDir 84*
KFHM - San Antonio, TX - *BrCabYB 84; TV&RadDir 84*
KFI - Los Angeles, CA - *BrCabYB 84; LitMarPl 83, 84; NatRadPubDir Summer 83, Spring 84; TV&RadDir 84*
KFIA - Carmichael, CA - *BrCabYB 84; TV&RadDir 84*
KFIG-FM - Fresno, CA - *BrCabYB 84; NatRadPubDir Summer 83, Spring 84; TV&RadDir 84*
KFIL - Preston, MN - *BrCabYB 84; TV&RadDir 84*
KFIL-FM - Preston, MN - *BrCabYB 84; TV&RadDir 84*
KFIM-FM - El Paso, TX - *BrCabYB 84; TV&RadDir 84*
KFIN-FM - Jonesboro, AR - *BrCabYB 84; TV&RadDir 84*
KFIO-FM - Ridgecrest, CA - *BrCabYB 84; TV&RadDir 84*
KFIR - Sweet Home, OR - *BrCabYB 84; TV&RadDir 84*
KFIS - Soda Springs, ID - *BrCabYB 84*
KFIV - Modesto, CA - *BrCabYB 84; NatRadPubDir Summer 83, Spring 84; TV&RadDir 84*
KFIV-FM - Modesto, CA - *BrCabYB 84; NatRadPubDir Summer 83, Spring 84; TV&RadDir 84*
KFIX-FM - Laredo, TX - *BrCabYB 84*
KFIZ - Fond du Lac, WI - *BrCabYB 84*
KFJB - Marshalltown, IA - *BrCabYB 84; TV&RadDir 84*
KFJB-FM - Marshalltown, IA - *BrCabYB 84; TV&RadDir 84*
KFJC-FM - Los Altos, CA - *BrCabYB 84; NatRadPubDir Summer 83, Spring 84; TV&RadDir 84*
KFJM - Grand Forks, ND - *BrCabYB 84; NatRadPubDir Summer 83, Spring 84; TV&RadDir 84*
KFJM-FM - Grand Forks, ND - *BrCabYB 84; NatRadPubDir Summer 83, Spring 84; TV&RadDir 84*
KFJZ - Ft. Worth, TX - *TV&RadDir 84*
KFKA - Greeley, CO - *BrCabYB 84; NatRadPubDir Summer 83, Spring 84; TV&RadDir 84*
KFKF - Kansas City, KS - *BrCabYB 84; NatRadPubDir Spring 84*
KFKF-FM - Kansas City, KS - *NatRadPubDir Summer 83, Spring 84; TV&RadDir 84*
KFKU - Lawrence, KS - *BrCabYB 84; NatRadPubDir Summer 83, Spring 84; TV&RadDir 84*
KFKU-FM - Lawrence, KS - *TV&RadDir 84*
KFLA - Scott City, KS - *BrCabYB 84; TV&RadDir 84*
KFLB-FM - Corpus Christi, TX - *BrCabYB 84*
KFLG - Flagstaff, AZ - *BrCabYB 84; TV&RadDir 84*
KFLG-FM - Flagstaff, AZ - *NatRadPubDir Spring 84*
KFLI - Mountain Home, ID - *TV&RadDir 84*
KFLJ - Walsenburg, CO - *BrCabYB 84; TV&RadDir 84*
KFLN - Baker, MT - *BrCabYB 84; TV&RadDir 84*
KFLN-FM - Baker, MT - *BrCabYB 84*
KFLO - Shreveport, LA - *BrCabYB 84; TV&RadDir 84*
KFLQ - Albuquerque, NM - *BrCabYB 84*
KFLR - Phoenix, AZ - *BrCabYB 84; TV&RadDir 84*
KFLS - Klamath Falls, OR - *BrCabYB 84; TV&RadDir 84*
KFLT - Tucson, AZ - *BrCabYB 84; NatRadPubDir Summer 83, Spring 84; TV&RadDir 84*
KFLY - Corvallis, OR - *BrCabYB 84; TV&RadDir 84*
KFLZ-FM - Bishop, TX - *TV&RadDir 84*
KFM-FM - Las Vegas, NV - *TV&RadDir 84*
KFMA-FM - Jerome, ID - *BrCabYB 84; TV&RadDir 84*
KFMB - San Diego, CA - *BrCabYB 84; NatRadPubDir Summer 83, Spring 84; TV&RadDir 84*
KFMB-FM - San Diego, CA - *BrCabYB 84; NatRadPubDir Summer 83, Spring 84*
KFMB-TV - San Diego, CA - *BrCabYB 84; DirUSTelSta 83; LitMarPl 83, 84; TelAl 83, 84; Tel&CabFB 84S; TV&RadDir 84*
KFMC-FM - Fairmont, MN - *BrCabYB 84; TV&RadDir 84*
KFMD-FM - Dubuque, IA - *BrCabYB 84; TV&RadDir 84*
KFME-TV - Fargo, ND - *BrCabYB 84; Tel&CabFB 84S; TV&RadDir 84*
KFMF-FM - Chico, CA - *BrCabYB 84; TV&RadDir 84*
KFMG-FM - Albuquerque, NM - *BrCabYB 84; NatRadPubDir Summer 83, Spring 84; TV&RadDir 84*

KFMH-FM - Muscatine, IA - *BrCabYB 84; NatRadPubDir Summer 83, Spring 84; TV&RadDir 84*
KFMI-FM - Arcata, CA - *TV&RadDir 84*
KFMI-FM - Eureka, CA - *BrCabYB 84*
KFMJ - Grants Pass, OR - *BrCabYB 84*
KFMK-FM - Houston, TX - *BrCabYB 84; NatRadPubDir Summer 83, Spring 84; TV&RadDir 84*
KFML - Whitehouse, TX - *BrCabYB 84*
KFMM-FM - Safford, AZ - *TV&RadDir 84*
KFMM-FM - Thatcher, AZ - *BrCabYB 84*
KFMN - Abilene, TX - *BrCabYB 84; NatRadPubDir Spring 84; TV&RadDir 84*
KFMN-FM - Abilene, TX - *BrCabYB 84; NatRadPubDir Summer 83, Spring 84; TV&RadDir 84*
KFMO - Flat River, MO - *BrCabYB 84; TV&RadDir 84*
KFMP-FM - Cape Girardeau, MO - *NatRadPubDir Summer 83; TV&RadDir 84*
KFMQ-FM - Lincoln, NE - *BrCabYB 84; NatRadPubDir Summer 83, Spring 84; TV&RadDir 84*
KFMR-FM - Stockton, CA - *BrCabYB 84; TV&RadDir 84*
KFMS-FM - Las Vegas, NV - *BrCabYB 84; NatRadPubDir Summer 83, Spring 84; TV&RadDir 84*
KFMT - Pendleton, OR - *BrCabYB 84*
KFMU-FM - Oak Creek, CO - *BrCabYB 84; TV&RadDir 84*
KFMV-FM - Magnolia, AR - *TV&RadDir 84*
KFMW-FM - Waterloo, IA - *BrCabYB 84; NatRadPubDir Summer 83, Spring 84*
KFMX-FM - Lubbock, TX - *BrCabYB 84; NatRadPubDir Summer 83, Spring 84*
KFMY-FM - Provo, UT - *BrCabYB 84; NatRadPubDir Summer 83, Spring 84; TV&RadDir 84*
KFMZ-FM - Columbia, MO - *BrCabYB 84; NatRadPubDir Summer 83, Spring 84; TV&RadDir 84*
KFNF - Oberlin, KS - *BrCabYB 84*
KFNK-FM - Oberlin, KS - *TV&RadDir 84*
KFNV - Ferriday, LA - *BrCabYB 84; TV&RadDir 84*
KFNV-FM - Ferriday, LA - *BrCabYB 84; TV&RadDir 84*
KFNW - Fargo, ND - *BrCabYB 84; NatRadPubDir Summer 83, Spring 84; TV&RadDir 84*
KFNW-FM - Fargo, ND - *BrCabYB 84; NatRadPubDir Summer 83, Spring 84*
KFOG-FM - San Francisco, CA - *BrCabYB 84; NatRadPubDir Summer 83, Spring 84; TV&RadDir 84*
KFOR - Lincoln, NE - *BrCabYB 84; NatRadPubDir Summer 83, Spring 84; TV&RadDir 84*
KFOX-FM - Redondo Beach, CA - *BrCabYB 84; TV&RadDir 84*
KFPS - Salem, MO - *BrCabYB 84*
KFPW - Ft. Smith, AR - *BrCabYB 84; NatRadPubDir Summer 83, Spring 84; TV&RadDir 84*
KFPW-FM - Ft. Smith, AR - *BrCabYB 84; NatRadPubDir Summer 83, Spring 84*
KFPW-TV - Ft. Smith, AR - *DirUSTelSta 83; TelAl 83, 84; TV&RadDir 84*
KFQD - Anchorage, AK - *BrCabYB 84; NatRadPubDir Summer 83, Spring 84; TV&RadDir 84*
KFQX - Llano, TX - *BrCabYB 84*
KFRA - Franklin, LA - *BrCabYB 84; TV&RadDir 84*
KFRA-FM - Franklin, LA - *BrCabYB 84; TV&RadDir 84*
KFRC - San Francisco, CA - *BrCabYB 84; LitMarPl 83, 84; NatRadPubDir Summer 83, Spring 84; TV&RadDir 84*
KFRD - Rosenberg, TX - *BrCabYB 84; TV&RadDir 84*
KFRD-FM - Rosenberg, TX - *BrCabYB 84; TV&RadDir 84*
KFRE - Fresno, CA - *BrCabYB 84; NatRadPubDir Summer 83, Spring 84; TV&RadDir 84*
KFRM - Salina, KS - *BrCabYB 84; TV&RadDir 84*
KFRN - Long Beach, CA - *BrCabYB 84*
KFRO - Longview, TX - *BrCabYB 84; NatRadPubDir Summer 83, Spring 84; TV&RadDir 84*
KFRU - Columbia, MO - *BrCabYB 84; NatRadPubDir Summer 83, Spring 84; TV&RadDir 84*
KFRX-FM - Lincoln, NE - *BrCabYB 84; NatRadPubDir Summer 83, Spring 84; TV&RadDir 84*
KFRY-FM - Fresno, CA - *BrCabYB 84; NatRadPubDir Summer 83, Spring 84; TV&RadDir 84*
KFRZ - Brigham City, UT - *BrCabYB 84*
KFSA - Ft. Smith, AR - *BrCabYB 84; NatRadPubDir Summer 83, Spring 84; TV&RadDir 84*
KFSB - Joplin, MO - *BrCabYB 84; NatRadPubDir Summer 83, Spring 84; TV&RadDir 84*
KFSD-FM - San Diego, CA - *BrCabYB 84; NatRadPubDir Summer 83, Spring 84; TV&RadDir 84*
KFSG-FM - Los Angeles, CA - *BrCabYB 84; NatRadPubDir Summer 83, Spring 84; TV&RadDir 84*
KFSH - Hilo, HI - *BrCabYB 84*
KFSI - Rochester, MN - *BrCabYB 84*
KFSK-FM - Petersburg, AK - *BrCabYB 84; TV&RadDir 84*
KFSM-TV - Ft. Smith, AR - *BrCabYB 84; DirUSTelSta 83; TelAl 83, 84; Tel&CabFB 84S; TV&RadDir 84*
KFSN-TV - Fresno, CA - *BrCabYB 84; DirUSTelSta 83; TelAl 83, 84; Tel&CabFB 84S; TV&RadDir 84*
KFSR - Fresno, CA - *BrCabYB 84; NatRadPubDir Summer 83, Spring 84*
KFSR-FM - Fresno, CA - *NatRadPubDir Summer 83, Spring 84*
KFST - Ft. Stockton, TX - *BrCabYB 84; TV&RadDir 84*
KFTM - Ft. Morgan, CO - *BrCabYB 84; TV&RadDir 84*
KFTN - Provo, UT - *BrCabYB 84; NatRadPubDir Summer 83, Spring 84; TV&RadDir 84*
KFTV-TV - Hanford, CA - *BrCabYB 84; DirUSTelSta 83; TelAl 83, 84; Tel&CabFB 84S; TV&RadDir 84*
KFTW - Fredericktown, MO - *BrCabYB 84; TV&RadDir 84*
KFTY-TV - San Francisco, CA - *DirUSTelSta 83*
KFTY-TV - Santa Rosa, CA - *BrCabYB 84; TelAl 83, 84; Tel&CabFB 84S*
KFUN - Las Vegas, NM - *BrCabYB 84; TV&RadDir 84*
KFUO - Clayton, MO - *BrCabYB 84*
KFUO - St. Louis, MO - *NatRadPubDir Summer 83, Spring 84; TV&RadDir 84*
KFUO-FM - Clayton, MO - *BrCabYB 84*
KFUO-FM - St. Louis, MO - *NatRadPubDir Summer 83, Spring 84; TV&RadDir 84*
KFVS-TV - Cape Girardeau, MO - *BrCabYB 84; TelAl 83, 84; Tel&CabFB 84S; TV&RadDir 84*
KFVS-TV - Kansas City, MO - *DirUSTelSta 83*
KFWB - Los Angeles, CA - *BrCabYB 84; NatRadPubDir Summer 83, Spring 84; TV&RadDir 84*
KFWJ - Lake Havasu City, AZ - *BrCabYB 84; TV&RadDir 84*
KFWY - Auburn, WA - *TV&RadDir 84*
KFWY - Summer-Puyallup, WA - *BrCabYB 84*
KFXD - Boise, ID - *NatRadPubDir Summer 83, Spring 84; TV&RadDir 84*
KFXD - Nampa, ID - *BrCabYB 84*
KFXD-FM - Boise, ID - *NatRadPubDir Summer 83, Spring 84; TV&RadDir 84*
KFXD-FM - Nampa, ID - *BrCabYB 84*
KFXE-FM - Pine Bluff, AR - *BrCabYB 84; NatRadPubDir Summer 83, Spring 84; TV&RadDir 84*
KFXM - San Bernardino, CA - *BrCabYB 84; NatRadPubDir Summer 83, Spring 84; TV&RadDir 84*
KFXY-FM - Morgan City, LA - *TV&RadDir 84*
KFYE-FM - Fresno, CA - *BrCabYB 84; NatRadPubDir Summer 83, Spring 84; TV&RadDir 84*
KFYN - Bonham, TX - *BrCabYB 84; TV&RadDir 84*
KFYO - Lubbock, TX - *BrCabYB 84; NatRadPubDir Summer 83, Spring 84; TV&RadDir 84*
KFYR - Bismarck, ND - *BrCabYB 84; NatRadPubDir Summer 83, Spring 84; TV&RadDir 84*
KFYR-TV - Bismarck, ND - *BrCabYB 84; DirUSTelSta 83; TelAl 83, 84; Tel&CabFB 84S; TV&RadDir 84*
KFYX - Morgan City, LA - *BrCabYB 84*
KFYZ-FM - Bonham, TX - *BrCabYB 84; TV&RadDir 84*
KGA - Spokane, WA - *BrCabYB 84; NatRadPubDir Summer 83, Spring 84; TV&RadDir 84*
KGAA - Kirkland, WA - *BrCabYB 84; TV&RadDir 84*
KGAF - Gainesville, TX - *BrCabYB 84; TV&RadDir 84*
KGAK - Gallup, NM - *BrCabYB 84; TV&RadDir 84*
KGAL - Albany, OR - *TV&RadDir 84*
KGAL - Lebanon, OR - *BrCabYB 84*
KGAN-TV - Cedar Rapids, IA - *BrCabYB 84; DirUSTelSta 83; TelAl 84; Tel&CabFB 84S; TV&RadDir 84*
KGAS - Carthage, TX - *BrCabYB 84; TV&RadDir 84*
KGAY - Salem, OR - *BrCabYB 84; NatRadPubDir Summer 83, Spring 84; TV&RadDir 84*

KGB-FM - San Diego, CA - *BrCabYB 84; NatRadPubDir Summer 83, Spring 84; TV&RadDir 84*
KGBC - Galveston, TX - *BrCabYB 84; TV&RadDir 84*
KGBI-FM - Omaha, NE - *BrCabYB 84; NatRadPubDir Summer 83, Spring 84; TV&RadDir 84*
KGBM-FM - Oakdale, LA - *BrCabYB 84*
KGBR - Gold Beach, OR - *BrCabYB 84*
KGBS-FM - Greeley, CO - *BrCabYB 84; NatRadPubDir Summer 83, Spring 84; TV&RadDir 84*
KGBT - Harlingen, TX - *BrCabYB 84; NatRadPubDir Summer 83, Spring 84 p.243; TV&RadDir 84*
KGBT-TV - Harlingen, TX - *BrCabYB 84; DirUSTelSta 83; TelAl 83, 84; Tel&CabFB 84S; TV&RadDir 84*
KGBX - Springfield, MO - *BrCabYB 84; NatRadPubDir Summer 83, Spring 84; TV&RadDir 84*
KGCA - Rugby, ND - *BrCabYB 84; TV&RadDir 84*
KGCC-FM - Denison, TX - *BrCabYB 84; NatRadPubDir Summer 83, Spring 84; TV&RadDir 84*
KGCG-FM - Henryetta, OK - *BrCabYB 84; TV&RadDir 84*
KGCH-FM - Sidney, MT - *BrCabYB 84; TV&RadDir 84*
KGCI - Grundy Center, IA - *BrCabYB 84*
KGCT-TV - Tulsa, OK - *BrCabYB 84; DirUSTelSta 83; TelAl 84; Tel&CabFB 84S; TV&RadDir 84*
KGCX - Sidney, MT - *BrCabYB 84; TV&RadDir 84*
KGDN - Edmonds, WA - *BrCabYB 84; TV&RadDir 84*
KGDN - Seattle, WA - *NatRadPubDir Summer 83, Spring 84*
KGDP - Santa Ynez, CA - *BrCabYB 84*
KGED-FM - Batesville, AR - *BrCabYB 84; TV&RadDir 84*
KGEE - Monahans, TX - *BrCabYB 84*
KGEM - Boise, ID - *BrCabYB 84; NatRadPubDir Summer 83, Spring 84; TV&RadDir 84*
KGEN - Tulare, CA - *BrCabYB 84; NatRadPubDir Summer 83, Spring 84; TV&RadDir 84*
KGEO - Bakersfield, CA - *BrCabYB 84; NatRadPubDir Spring 84; TV&RadDir 84*
KGER - Long Beach, CA - *BrCabYB 84; NatRadPubDir Summer 83, Spring 84; TV&RadDir 84*
KGEZ - Kalispell, MT - *BrCabYB 84; TV&RadDir 84*
KGFE-TV - Fargo, ND - *TV&RadDir 84*
KGFE-TV - Grand Forks, ND - *BrCabYB 84; Tel&CabFB 84S*
KGFF - Shawnee, OK - *BrCabYB 84; TV&RadDir 84*
KGFJ - Los Angeles, CA - *BrCabYB 84; LitMarPl 83, 84; NatRadPubDir Summer 83, Spring 84; TV&RadDir 84*
KGFL - Clinton, AR - *BrCabYB 84; TV&RadDir 84*
KGFM-FM - Bakersfield, CA - *BrCabYB 84; NatRadPubDir Summer 83, Spring 84; TV&RadDir 84*
KGFT - Carpinteria, CA - *BrCabYB 84*
KGFW - Kearney, NE - *BrCabYB 84; TV&RadDir 84*
KGFX - Pierre, SD - *BrCabYB 84; TV&RadDir 84*
KGGF - Coffeyville, KS - *BrCabYB 84*
KGGG-FM - Rapid City, SD - *BrCabYB 84; TV&RadDir 84*
KGGI-FM - Riverside, CA - *BrCabYB 84*
KGGI-FM - San Bernardino, CA - *TV&RadDir 84*
KGGM-TV - Albuquerque, NM - *BrCabYB 84; DirUSTelSta 83; TelAl 83, 84; Tel&CabFB 84S; TV&RadDir 84*
KGGN - Valdez, AK - *BrCabYB 84*
KGGO-FM - Des Moines, IA - *BrCabYB 84; NatRadPubDir Summer 83, Spring 84; TV&RadDir 84*
KGGR - Opportunity, WA - *BrCabYB 84*
KGGR - Spokane, WA - *TV&RadDir 84*
KGHL - Billings, MT - *BrCabYB 84; NatRadPubDir Summer 83, Spring 84; TV&RadDir 84*
KGHM - Brookfield, MO - *BrCabYB 84; TV&RadDir 84*
KGHO - Hoquiam, WA - *BrCabYB 84; TV&RadDir 84*
KGHO-FM - Hoquiam, WA - *BrCabYB 84; TV&RadDir 84*
KGHS - International Falls, MN - *BrCabYB 84; TV&RadDir 84*
KGHX - Fairbanks, AK - *BrCabYB 84*
KGIL - Los Angeles, CA - *NatRadPubDir Summer 83 p.20, Spring 84 p.20*
KGIL - San Fernando, CA - *BrCabYB 84; TV&RadDir 84*
KGIL-FM - Los Angeles, CA - *NatRadPubDir Summer 83 p.20, Spring 84 p.20*
KGIL-FM - San Fernando, CA - *BrCabYB 84*
KGIM - Aberdeen, SD - *BrCabYB 84*
KGIN-TV - Grand Island, NE - *BrCabYB 84; TelAl 83, 84; Tel&CabFB 84S*
KGIN-TV - Lincoln, NE - *TV&RadDir 84*
KGIR - Cape Girardeau, MO - *BrCabYB 84; TV&RadDir 84*
KGIW - Alamosa, CO - *BrCabYB 84; TV&RadDir 84*
KGKG-FM - Brookings, SD - *BrCabYB 84; TV&RadDir 84*
KGKL - San Angelo, TX - *BrCabYB 84; NatRadPubDir Summer 83, Spring 84; TV&RadDir 84*
KGKL-FM - San Angelo, TX - *BrCabYB 84; TV&RadDir 84*
KGKO - Benton, AR - *BrCabYB 84; TV&RadDir 84*
KGKS-FM - Goodland, MN - *BrCabYB 84*
KGLA - Gretna, LA - *BrCabYB 84*
KGLA - Marrero, LA - *TV&RadDir 84*
KGLC - Centrahoma, OK - *TV&RadDir 84*
KGLC - Miami, OK - *BrCabYB 84*
KGLD - Golden Valley, MN - *BrCabYB 84*
KGLD - Minneapolis, MN - *NatRadPubDir Summer 83 p.134, Spring 84; TV&RadDir 84*
KGLD-TV - Wichita, KS - *TelAl 83*
KGLE - Glendive, MT - *BrCabYB 84; TV&RadDir 84*
KGLI - Sioux City, IA - *BrCabYB 84*
KGLM-FM - Anaconda, MT - *BrCabYB 84; TV&RadDir 84*
KGLN - Glenwood Springs, CO - *BrCabYB 84; TV&RadDir 84*
KGLO - Mason City, IA - *BrCabYB 84; NatRadPubDir Summer 83, Spring 84; TV&RadDir 84*
KGLS-FM - Pratt, KS - *BrCabYB 84*
KGLT-FM - Big Sky, MT - *TV&RadDir 84*
KGLT-FM - Billings, MT - *TV&RadDir 84*
KGLT-FM - Bozeman, MT - *BrCabYB 84; NatRadPubDir Summer 83, Spring 84*
KGMB-TV - Honolulu, HI - *BrCabYB 84; DirUSTelSta 83; TelAl 83, 84; Tel&CabFB 84S; TV&RadDir 84*
KGMC-TV - Oklahoma City, OK - *BrCabYB 84; DirUSTelSta 83; TelAl 83, 84; Tel&CabFB 84S; TV&RadDir 84*
KGMD-TV - Hilo, HI - *BrCabYB 84; TelAl 83, 84; Tel&CabFB 84S; TV&RadDir 84*
KGMI - Bellingham, WA - *BrCabYB 84; NatRadPubDir Summer 83, Spring 84; TV&RadDir 84*
KGMO-FM - Cape Girardeau, MO - *BrCabYB 84; NatRadPubDir Summer 83, Spring 84; TV&RadDir 84*
KGMQ - Pueblo, CO - *TV&RadDir 84*
KGMS - Sacramento, CA - *BrCabYB 84; NatRadPubDir Summer 83, Spring 84; TV&RadDir 84*
KGMT - Fairbury, NE - *BrCabYB 84; TV&RadDir 84*
KGMV-TV - Kahului, HI - *TV&RadDir 84*
KGMV-TV - Wailuku, HI - *BrCabYB 84; TelAl 83, 84; Tel&CabFB 84S*
KGNB - New Braunfels, TX - *BrCabYB 84; TV&RadDir 84*
KGNC - Amarillo, TX - *BrCabYB 84; NatRadPubDir Summer 83, Spring 84; TV&RadDir 84*
KGNC-FM - Amarillo, TX - *BrCabYB 84; NatRadPubDir Summer 83, Spring 84; TV&RadDir 84*
KGNM - St. Joseph, MO - *BrCabYB 84; NatRadPubDir Summer 83, Spring 84; TV&RadDir 84*
KGNO - Dodge City, KS - *BrCabYB 84; TV&RadDir 84*
KGNQ - Lincoln, NE - *BrCabYB 84; Tel&CabFB 84S*
KGNR - Sacramento, CA - *BrCabYB 84; NatRadPubDir Summer 83, Spring 84; TV&RadDir 84*
KGNS-TV - Laredo, TX - *BrCabYB 84; DirUSTelSta 83; TelAl 83, 84; Tel&CabFB 84S; TV&RadDir 84*
KGNU-FM - Boulder, CO - *BrCabYB 84; TV&RadDir 84*
KGNZ-FM - Abilene, TX - *BrCabYB 84; TV&RadDir 84*
KGO - San Francisco, CA - *BrCabYB 84; LitMarPl 83, 84; NatRadPubDir Summer 83, Spring 84; TV&RadDir 84*
KGO-FM - San Francisco, CA - *BrCabYB 84; LitMarPl 83; TV&RadDir 84*
KGO-TV - San Francisco, CA - *BrCabYB 84; DirUSTelSta 83; LitMarPl 83, 84; TelAl 83, 84; Tel&CabFB 84S; TV&RadDir 84*
KGOE - Thousand Oaks, CA - *BrCabYB 84; TV&RadDir 84*
KGOK-FM - Pauls Valley, OK - *BrCabYB 84; TV&RadDir 84*
KGOL-FM - Houston, TX - *TV&RadDir 84*
KGOL-FM - Lake Jackson, TX - *BrCabYB 84*
KGON-FM - Milwaukie, OR - *TV&RadDir 84*
KGON-FM - Portland, OR - *BrCabYB 84; NatRadPubDir Summer 83, Spring 84*
KGOR-FM - Omaha, NE - *BrCabYB 84; NatRadPubDir Summer 83, Spring 84; TV&RadDir 84*
KGOS - Torrington, WY - *BrCabYB 84; TV&RadDir 84*
KGOT-FM - Anchorage, AK - *BrCabYB 84; NatRadPubDir Summer 83, Spring 84; TV&RadDir 84*

KGOU-FM - Chickasha, OK - *TV&RadDir 84*
KGOU-FM - Norman, OK - *BrCabYB 84; NatRadPubDir Summer 83, Spring 84*
KGPC - Lawton, OK - *TelAl 84; Tel&CabFB 84S*
KGRA-FM - Lake Charles, LA - *NatRadPubDir Summer 83*
KGRB - La Puente, CA - *TV&RadDir 84*
KGRB - West Covina, CA - *BrCabYB 84*
KGRC-FM - Hannibal, MO - *BrCabYB 84; TV&RadDir 84*
KGRE-FM - Greeley, CO - *BrCabYB 84; TV&RadDir 84*
KGRG-FM - Auburn, WA - *BrCabYB 84; NatRadPubDir Summer 83, Spring 84; TV&RadDir 84*
KGRI - Henderson, TX - *BrCabYB 84; TV&RadDir 84*
KGRI-FM - Henderson, TX - *BrCabYB 84*
KGRL - Bend, OR - *BrCabYB 84; TV&RadDir 84*
KGRM-FM - Grambling, LA - *BrCabYB 84; TV&RadDir 84*
KGRN - Grinnell, IA - *BrCabYB 84; TV&RadDir 84*
KGRO - Pampa, TX - *BrCabYB 84; TV&RadDir 84*
KGRS-FM - Burlington, IA - *BrCabYB 84; TV&RadDir 84*
KGRT - Las Cruces, NM - *BrCabYB 84; TV&RadDir 84*
KGRT-FM - Las Cruces, NM - *BrCabYB 84; TV&RadDir 84*
KGRV - Winston, OR - *BrCabYB 84*
KGRZ - Missoula, MT - *BrCabYB 84; TV&RadDir 84*
KGSF - Kellogg, ID - *BrCabYB 84*
KGSP-FM - Kansas City, MO - *TV&RadDir 84*
KGSP-FM - Parkville, MO - *BrCabYB 84; NatRadPubDir Summer 83, Spring 84*
KGST - Fresno, CA - *BrCabYB 84; NatRadPubDir Summer 83, Spring 84; TV&RadDir 84*
KGSU-FM - Cedar City, UT - *BrCabYB 84; TV&RadDir 84*
KGSW-TV - Albuquerque, NM - *BrCabYB 84; DirUSTelSta 83; TelAl 83, 84; Tel&CabFB 84S; TV&RadDir 84*
KGTF - Agana, GU - *BrCabYB 84; Tel&CabFB 84S*
KGTL-FM - Homer, AK - *BrCabYB 84; TV&RadDir 84*
KGTN - Georgetown, TX - *BrCabYB 84; TV&RadDir 84*
KGTN-FM - Georgetown, TX - *BrCabYB 84; TV&RadDir 84*
KGTO - Tulsa, OK - *BrCabYB 84; TV&RadDir 84*
KGTS-FM - College Place, WA - *BrCabYB 84; NatRadPubDir Summer 83, Spring 84; TV&RadDir 84*
KGTV-TV - San Diego, CA - *BrCabYB 84; DirUSTelSta 83; LitMarPl 83, 84; TelAl 83, 84; Tel&CabFB 84S; TV&RadDir 84*
KGU - Honolulu, HI - *BrCabYB 84; NatRadPubDir Summer 83, Spring 84; TV&RadDir 84*
KGUC - Gunnison, CO - *BrCabYB 84; TV&RadDir 84*
KGUC-FM - Gunnison, CO - *BrCabYB 84; TV&RadDir 84*
KGUD - Banning, CA - *BrCabYB 84; TV&RadDir 84*
KGUL - Port Lavaca, TX - *BrCabYB 84; TV&RadDir 84*
KGUL-FM - Port Neches, TX - *TV&RadDir 84*
KGUM - Agana, Gambia - *BrCabYB 84*
KGUN-TV - Tucson, AZ - *BrCabYB 84; DirUSTelSta 83; TelAl 83, 84; Tel&CabFB 84S; TV&RadDir 84*
KGUS - Florence, AZ - *BrCabYB 84*
KGUS-FM - Hot Springs, AR - *TV&RadDir 84*
KGUY - Palm Desert, CA - *BrCabYB 84; TV&RadDir 84*
KGVE-FM - Grove, OK - *TV&RadDir 84*
KGVH-FM - Gunnison, UT - *BrCabYB 84; NatRadPubDir Summer 83 p.323, Spring 84 p.322; TV&RadDir 84*
KGVL - Greenville, TX - *BrCabYB 84; TV&RadDir 84*
KGVO - Missoula, MT - *BrCabYB 84; NatRadPubDir Summer 83, Spring 84; TV&RadDir 84*
KGVS - Grove, OK - *BrCabYB 84*
KGVW - Belgrade, MT - *BrCabYB 84; TV&RadDir 84*
KGVY - Green Valley, AZ - *BrCabYB 84; TV&RadDir 84*
KGW - Portland, OR - *BrCabYB 84; LitMarPl 83, 84; NatRadPubDir Summer 83, Spring 84; TV&RadDir 84*
KGW-FM - Portland, OR - *LitMarPl 83*
KGW-TV - Portland, OR - *BrCabYB 84; DirUSTelSta 83; LitMarPl 83, 84; TelAl 83, 84; Tel&CabFB 84S; TV&RadDir 84*
KGWA - Enid, OK - *BrCabYB 84; TV&RadDir 84*
KGWY - Gillette, WY - *BrCabYB 84*
KGY - Olympia, WA - *BrCabYB 84; TV&RadDir 84*
KGY - Seattle, WA - *NatRadPubDir Summer 83 p.259, Spring 84 p.261*
KGYN - Guymon, OK - *BrCabYB 84; TV&RadDir 84*
KHAA - Port Sulphur, LA - *BrCabYB 84*
KHAC - Window Rock, AZ - *BrCabYB 84; TV&RadDir 84*
KHAD - De Soto, MO - *BrCabYB 84; TV&RadDir 84*
KHAI-TV - Honolulu, HI - *BrCabYB 84; Tel&CabFB 84S*
KHAK - Cedar Rapids, IA - *BrCabYB 84; NatRadPubDir Summer 83, Spring 84; TV&RadDir 84*
KHAK-FM - Cedar Rapids, IA - *BrCabYB 84; NatRadPubDir Summer 83, Spring 84; TV&RadDir 84*
Khalsa & Dharm Darshan Kaur Khalsa, Vikram Kaur - San Diego, CA - *BoPubDir 4 Sup, 5*
KHAM - Horseshoe Bend, AR - *BrCabYB 84; TV&RadDir 84*
Khaneghah & Maktab of Maleknia Naseralishah - Palisades, NY - *BoPubDir 4, 5*
Khaniqahi-Nimatullahi Publications - New York, NY - *BoPubDir 4, 5*
KHAR - Anchorage, AK - *BrCabYB 84; NatRadPubDir Summer 83, Spring 84; TV&RadDir 84*
KHAS - Hastings, NE - *BrCabYB 84; TV&RadDir 84*
KHAS-TV - Hastings, NE - *BrCabYB 84; DirUSTelSta 83; TelAl 83, 84; Tel&CabFB 84S; TV&RadDir 84*
KHAT-FM - Lincoln, NE - *BrCabYB 84; NatRadPubDir Summer 83, Spring 84; TV&RadDir 84*
KHAW-TV - Hilo, HI - *BrCabYB 84; TelAl 83, 84; Tel&CabFB 84S*
KHAY-FM - Ventura, CA - *BrCabYB 84; NatRadPubDir Summer 83, Spring 84; TV&RadDir 84*
KHBC - Wickenburg, AZ - *BrCabYB 84*
KHBJ - Canyon, TX - *BrCabYB 84; TV&RadDir 84*
KHBM - Monticello, AR - *BrCabYB 84; TV&RadDir 84*
KHBM-FM - Monticello, AR - *BrCabYB 84; TV&RadDir 84*
KHBQ-FM - Canyon, TX - *BrCabYB 84; TV&RadDir 84*
KHBR - Hillsboro, TX - *BrCabYB 84; TV&RadDir 84*
KHBR-FM - Hillsboro, TX - *TV&RadDir 84*
KHBS - Ft. Smith, AR - *BrCabYB 84; Tel&CabFB 84S*
KHBT-FM - Humboldt, IA - *BrCabYB 84; TV&RadDir 84*
KHCA - Searcy, AR - *NatRadPubDir Summer 83, Spring 84*
KHCB-FM - Houston, TX - *BrCabYB 84; NatRadPubDir Summer 83, Spring 84; TV&RadDir 84*
KHCC-FM - Hutchinson, KS - *BrCabYB 84; NatRadPubDir Summer 83, Spring 84; TV&RadDir 84*
KHCR - Paauilo, HI - *BrCabYB 84*
KHCS-FM - Round Rock, TX - *BrCabYB 84; TV&RadDir 84*
KHDN - Hardin, MT - *BrCabYB 84; TV&RadDir 84*
KHDN-FM - Hardin, MT - *BrCabYB 84; TV&RadDir 84*
KHDX-FM - Conway, AR - *BrCabYB 84; TV&RadDir 84*
KHEF-FM - El Paso, TX - *BrCabYB 84*
KHEI - Kahului, HI - *TV&RadDir 84*
KHEI - Kihei, HI - *BrCabYB 84*
KHEN - Henryetta, OK - *BrCabYB 84; TV&RadDir 84*
KHEP - Phoenix, AZ - *BrCabYB 84; NatRadPubDir Summer 83, Spring 84; TV&RadDir 84*
KHEP-FM - Phoenix, AZ - *BrCabYB 84; NatRadPubDir Summer 83, Spring 84; TV&RadDir 84*
KHER - Crystal City, TX - *BrCabYB 84*
KHET-TV - Honolulu, HI - *BrCabYB 84; Tel&CabFB 84S; TV&RadDir 84*
KHEY - El Paso, TX - *BrCabYB 84; TV&RadDir 84*
KHEY-FM - El Paso, TX - *TV&RadDir 84*
KHEZ-FM - Lake Charles, LA - *NatRadPubDir Summer 83, Spring 84; TV&RadDir 84*
KHFI-FM - Austin, TX - *BrCabYB 84; NatRadPubDir Summer 83, Spring 84; TV&RadDir 84*
KHFM-FM - Albuquerque, NM - *BrCabYB 84; NatRadPubDir Summer 83, Spring 84; TV&RadDir 84*
KHFO-FM - Osceola, AR - *BrCabYB 84; TV&RadDir 84*
KHFT - Hobbs, NM - *BrCabYB 84; Tel&CabFB 84S*
KHGI-TV - Kearney, NE - *BrCabYB 84; DirUSTelSta 83; TelAl 83, 84; Tel&CabFB 84S; TV&RadDir 84*
KHIB-FM - Durant, OK - *BrCabYB 84; NatRadPubDir Summer 83, Spring 84; TV&RadDir 84*
KHIG-FM - Paragould, AR - *TV&RadDir 84*
KHIL - Willcox, AZ - *BrCabYB 84; TV&RadDir 84*
KHIN - Red Oak, IA - *BrCabYB 84; Tel&CabFB 84S*
KHIP-FM - Hollister, CA - *BrCabYB 84; TV&RadDir 84*
Khiralla, T. W. - Studio City, CA - *BoPubDir 4, 5*
KHIS - Bakersfield, CA - *BrCabYB 84; TV&RadDir 84*
KHIS-FM - Bakersfield, CA - *TV&RadDir 84*
KHIT - Walla Walla, WA - *BrCabYB 84; TV&RadDir 84*
KHJ - Los Angeles, CA - *BrCabYB 84; NatRadPubDir Summer 83, Spring 84; TV&RadDir 84*

KHJ-TV - Hollywood, CA - *Tel&CabFB 84C*
KHJ-TV [Div. of RKO General Inc.] - Los Angeles, CA - *BrCabYB 84; DirUSTelSta 83; TelAl 83, 84; Tel&CabFB 84S; TV&RadDir 84*
KHJK - Lockhart, TX - *BrCabYB 84*
KHKE-FM - Cedar Falls, IA - *BrCabYB 84; NatRadPubDir Summer 83, Spring 84; TV&RadDir 84*
KHLB - Burnet, TX - *BrCabYB 84; TV&RadDir 84*
KHLO - Hilo, HI - *BrCabYB 84; TV&RadDir 84*
KHLS-FM - Blytheville, AR - *BrCabYB 84; TV&RadDir 84*
KHME - Comanche, OK - *BrCabYB 84*
KHMO - Hannibal, MO - *BrCabYB 84; NatRadPubDir Summer 83, Spring 84; TV&RadDir 84*
KHND - Harvey, ND - *BrCabYB 84*
KHNE-TV - Hastings, NE - *BrCabYB 84; Tel&CabFB 84S*
KHNL - Honolulu, HI - *BrCabYB 84*
KHNS - Haines, AK - *BrCabYB 84; TV&RadDir 84*
KHNY-FM - Riverside, CA - *NatRadPubDir Summer 83; TV&RadDir 84*
KHOB - Hobbs, NM - *BrCabYB 84; TV&RadDir 84*
KHOC-FM - Levelland, TX - *BrCabYB 84; TV&RadDir 84*
KHOF-FM - Glendale, CA - *TV&RadDir 84*
KHOF-FM - Los Angeles, CA - *BrCabYB 84; NatRadPubDir Summer 83 p.21, Spring 84 p.20*
KHOF-TV - Hanford, CA - *TV&RadDir 84*
KHOF-TV - Los Angeles, CA - *TelAl 83, 84*
KHOF-TV - San Bernardino, CA - *BrCabYB 84; Tel&CabFB 84S*
KHOG - Fayetteville, AR - *BrCabYB 84; TV&RadDir 84*
KHOK-FM - Hoisington, KS - *BrCabYB 84; TV&RadDir 84*
KHOL - Beulah, ND - *BrCabYB 84; TV&RadDir 84*
KHOM-FM - Houma, LA - *BrCabYB 84; TV&RadDir 84*
KHOM-FM - Thibodaux, LA - *NatRadPubDir Summer 83 p.110, Spring 84*
KHON-TV - Honolulu, HI - *BrCabYB 84; DirUSTelSta 83; TelAl 83, 84; Tel&CabFB 84S; TV&RadDir 84*
KHOO-FM - Waco, TX - *BrCabYB 84; NatRadPubDir Summer 83, Spring 84; TV&RadDir 84*
KHOP-FM - Modesto, CA - *BrCabYB 84; NatRadPubDir Summer 83, Spring 84; TV&RadDir 84*
KHOS - San Angelo, TX - *BrCabYB 84; NatRadPubDir Summer 83, Spring 84; TV&RadDir 84*
KHOT - Madera, CA - *BrCabYB 84; TV&RadDir 84*
KHOU-TV - Houston, TX - *BrCabYB 84; DirUSTelSta 83; LitMarPl 83, 84; TelAl 83, 84; Tel&CabFB 84S; TV&RadDir 84*
KHOW - Denver, CO - *BrCabYB 84; LitMarPl 83, 84; NatRadPubDir Summer 83, Spring 84; TV&RadDir 84*
KHOZ - Harrison, AR - *BrCabYB 84; TV&RadDir 84*
KHOZ-FM - Harrison, AR - *BrCabYB 84; TV&RadDir 84*
KHPA-FM - Hope, AR - *BrCabYB 84; TV&RadDir 84*
KHPE-FM - Albany, OR - *BrCabYB 84; TV&RadDir 84*
KHPQ - Clinton, AR - *BrCabYB 84*
KHPR - Honolulu, HI - *BrCabYB 84*
KHQ - Spokane, WA - *BrCabYB 84; NatRadPubDir Summer 83, Spring 84; TV&RadDir 84*
KHQ-FM - Spokane, WA - *BrCabYB 84; NatRadPubDir Summer 83, Spring 84; TV&RadDir 84*
KHQ-TV - Spokane, WA - *BrCabYB 84; DirUSTelSta 83; TelAl 83, 84; Tel&CabFB 84S; TV&RadDir 84*
KHQA-TV - Quincy, IL - *DirUSTelSta 83*
KHQA-TV - Hannibal, MO - *BrCabYB 84; TelAl 83, 84; Tel&CabFB 84S; TV&RadDir 84*
KHRT - Minot, ND - *BrCabYB 84; NatRadPubDir Summer 83, Spring 84; TV&RadDir 84*
KHRU-FM - Clayton, MO - *BrCabYB 84; NatRadPubDir Summer 83, Spring 84*
KHSD-TV - Bethlehem, SD - *TV&RadDir 84*
KHSD-TV - Lead, SD - *BrCabYB 84; TelAl 83, 84; Tel&CabFB 84S*
KHSJ - Hemet, CA - *BrCabYB 84; TV&RadDir 84*
KHSL - Chico, CA - *BrCabYB 84; TV&RadDir 84*
KHSL-TV - Chico, CA - *BrCabYB 84; DirUSTelSta 83; TelAl 83, 84; Tel&CabFB 84S; TV&RadDir 84*
KHSN - Coos Bay, OR - *BrCabYB 84; TV&RadDir 84*
KHSP - Hesperia, CA - *BrCabYB 84*
KHSU-FM - Arcata, CA - *BrCabYB 84; NatRadPubDir Summer 83, Spring 84; TV&RadDir 84*
KHTC-FM - Helena, MT - *BrCabYB 84; NatRadPubDir Summer 83, Spring 84; TV&RadDir 84*
KHTN - Placerville, CA - *BrCabYB 84*
KHTR-FM - St. Louis, MO - *BrCabYB 84; LitMarPl 84; NatRadPubDir Summer 83, Spring 84; TV&RadDir 84*
KHTT - San Jose, CA - *BrCabYB 84; NatRadPubDir Summer 83, Spring 84; TV&RadDir 84*
KHTV-TV - Houston, TX - *BrCabYB 84; DirUSTelSta 83; TelAl 83, 84; Tel&CabFB 84S; TV&RadDir 84*
KHTX-FM - Carnelian Bay, CA - *BrCabYB 84*
KHTX-FM - Kings Beach, CA - *TV&RadDir 84*
KHTZ-FM - Los Angeles, CA - *BrCabYB 84; LitMarPl 83, 84; NatRadPubDir Summer 83, Spring 84; TV&RadDir 84*
KHUB - Fremont, NE - *BrCabYB 84; TV&RadDir 84*
KHUB-FM - Fremont, NE - *BrCabYB 84; TV&RadDir 84*
KHUG - Medford, OR - *BrCabYB 84; TV&RadDir 84*
KHUM - Denver, CO - *BrCabYB 84*
KHUN-FM - Huntsville, TX - *BrCabYB 84; TV&RadDir 84*
KHUQ - Hugoton, KS - *BrCabYB 84*
KHUT-FM - Hutchinson, KS - *BrCabYB 84; TV&RadDir 84*
KHVH - Honolulu, HI - *BrCabYB 84; NatRadPubDir Summer 83, Spring 84; TV&RadDir 84*
KHVO-TV - Hilo, HI - *BrCabYB 84; TelAl 83, 84; Tel&CabFB 84S*
KHVO-TV - Honolulu, HI - *TV&RadDir 84*
KHWK-FM - Kennewick, WA - *TV&RadDir 84*
KHWK-FM - Richland, WA - *BrCabYB 84*
KHYE-FM - Hemet, CA - *BrCabYB 84; TV&RadDir 84*
KHYL-FM - Auburn, CA - *BrCabYB 84; NatRadPubDir Summer 83, Spring 84; TV&RadDir 84*
KHYM - Gilmer, TX - *BrCabYB 84; TV&RadDir 84*
KHYS-FM - Beaumont, TX - *NatRadPubDir Summer 83, Spring 84 p.235*
KHYS-FM - Port Arthur, TX - *BrCabYB 84; TV&RadDir 84*
KHYT - Tucson, AZ - *BrCabYB 84; NatRadPubDir Summer 83, Spring 84; TV&RadDir 84*
KHYV - Modesto, CA - *BrCabYB 84; NatRadPubDir Spring 84*
KIAE-FM - Aurora, NE - *BrCabYB 84; TV&RadDir 84*
KIAG - Mountain View, MO - *BrCabYB 84*
KIAH-FM - Ukiah, CA - *BrCabYB 84; TV&RadDir 84*
KIAK - Fairbanks, AK - *BrCabYB 84; NatRadPubDir Summer 83, Spring 84; TV&RadDir 84*
KIAL - Unalaska, AK - *BrCabYB 84*
KIAM-FM - Wenatchee, WA - *BrCabYB 84*
Kianka, Frances - Reston, VA - *LitMarPl 83, 84*
KIBE - Palo Alto, CA - *BrCabYB 84*
KIBE - San Francisco, CA - *NatRadPubDir Summer 83, Spring 84; TV&RadDir 84*
KIBL - Beeville, TX - *BrCabYB 84; TV&RadDir 84*
KIBQ-FM - Idaho Falls, ID - *BrCabYB 84; TV&RadDir 84*
KIBS - Bishop, CA - *BrCabYB 84; TV&RadDir 84*
KICA - Clovis, NM - *BrCabYB 84; TV&RadDir 84*
KICA-FM - Clovis, NM - *BrCabYB 84*
KICB-FM - Ft. Dodge, IA - *BrCabYB 84; NatRadPubDir Summer 83, Spring 84; TV&RadDir 84*
KICC-FM - International Falls, MN - *BrCabYB 84; TV&RadDir 84*
KICD - Spencer, IA - *BrCabYB 84; TV&RadDir 84*
KICD-FM - Spencer, IA - *BrCabYB 84; TV&RadDir 84*
KICE-FM - Bend, OR - *BrCabYB 84; TV&RadDir 84*
Kici, Gasper - Washington, DC - *BoPubDir 4, 5*
KICK - Springfield, MO - *BrCabYB 84; NatRadPubDir Summer 83, Spring 84; TV&RadDir 84*
Kick Illustrated [of Unique Publications] - Hollywood, CA - *WritMar 84*
Kick Records - Beverly Hills, CA - *BillIntBG 83-84*
Kickapoo Antennavision Inc. - Marquette, IA - *BrCabYB 84*
Kickapoo Antennavision Inc. - Gays Mills, WI - *BrCabYB 84*
Kickapoo Antennavision Inc. - Mauston, WI - *BrCabYB 84*
Kickapoo Antennavision Inc. - Prairie du Chien, WI - *BrCabYB 84 p.D-302; Tel&CabFB 84C p.1686*
Kickapoo Scout, The - Soldiers Grove, WI - *Ed&PubIntYB 82*
Kickdrum Music - *See* Espy Music Group
Kicking Mule Publishing Inc. - Alderpoint, CA - *BillIntBG 83-84*
Kicking Mule Records Inc. - Alderpoint, CA - *BillIntBG 83-84*
KICN-FM - Spokane, WA - *BrCabYB 84; NatRadPubDir Summer 83, Spring 84; TV&RadDir 84*

KICO - Calexico, CA - *BrCabYB 84*
KICO - El Centro, CA - *TV&RadDir 84*
KICR-FM - Coos Bay, OR - *TV&RadDir 84*
KICS - Hastings, NE - *BrCabYB 84; TV&RadDir 84*
KICT-FM - Wichita, KS - *BrCabYB 84; NatRadPubDir Summer 83, Spring 84; TV&RadDir 84*
KICU-TV - Salinas, CA - *DirUSTelSta 83*
KICU-TV - San Jose, CA - *BrCabYB 84; TelAl 83, 84; Tel&CabFB 84S; TV&RadDir 84*
KICX - McCook, NE - *BrCabYB 84; TV&RadDir 84*
KICX-FM - McCook, NE - *BrCabYB 84; TV&RadDir 84*
KICY - Nome, AK - *BrCabYB 84; TV&RadDir 84*
KICY-FM - Nome, AK - *BrCabYB 84; TV&RadDir 84*
KID - Idaho Falls, ID - *BrCabYB 84; TV&RadDir 84*
Kid Cuz'n Record Co. - Brooklyn, NY - *BillIntBG 83-84*
KID-FM - Idaho Falls, ID - *BrCabYB 84; TV&RadDir 84*
KID-TV - Idaho Falls, ID - *BrCabYB 84; DirUSTelSta 83; TelAl 83, 84; Tel&CabFB 84S; TV&RadDir 84*
Kidbits - Philadelphia, PA - *MagIndMarPl 82-83*
KIDD - Monterey, CA - *BrCabYB 84; TV&RadDir 84*
KIDD - Salinas, CA - *NatRadPubDir Summer 83, Spring 84 p.26*
Kidd Productions Inc., Richard - Dallas, TX - *AvMarPl 83*
Kidd, Virginia - Milford, PA - *LitMarPl 83, 84*
Kidde, Hoyt & Picard - New York, NY - *LitMarPl 83, 84*
Kiddie Camera - Philadelphia, PA - *Tel&CabFB 84C*
KIDE-FM - Hoopa, CA - *BrCabYB 84; TV&RadDir 84*
Kiderian Record Productions - Chicago, IL - *BillIntBG 83-84*
KIDN - Pueblo, CO - *BrCabYB 84; NatRadPubDir Summer 83, Spring 84; TV&RadDir 84*
Kidney International - New York, NY - *MagIndMarPl 82-83*
KIDO - Boise, ID - *BrCabYB 84; TV&RadDir 84*
KIDQ - Boise, ID - *BrCabYB 84; NatRadPubDir Summer 83, Spring 84*
Kids Can Press - Toronto, ON, Canada - *BoPubDir 4, 5; LitMag&SmPr 83-84; LitMarPl 83, 84*
Kids Come in Special Flavors Co. - Dayton, OH - *BoPubDir 4, 5*
Kids Fashions [of Larkin-Pluznick-Larkin] - Chestnut Hill, MA - *BaconPubCkMag 84; WritMar 84*
KIDS-FM - Palmyra, MO - *BrCabYB 84*
Kids on the Block Inc. - Washington, DC - *AvMarPl 83*
KidVid [of ARP Films] - New York, NY - *BrCabYB 84; CabTVPrDB 83*
KIDX-FM - Billings, MT - *BrCabYB 84; TV&RadDir 84*
KIDY-TV - San Angelo, TX - *BrCabYB 84; Tel&CabFB 84S*
KIDZ-TV - Wichita Falls, TX - *Tel&CabFB 84S*
KIEA-FM - Ethete, WY - *BrCabYB 84*
KIEE-FM - Harrisonville, MO - *BrCabYB 84; TV&RadDir 84*
KIEL - Jacksonville, AR - *BrCabYB 84; TV&RadDir 84*
KIEL - Little Rock, AR - *NatRadPubDir Summer 83*
Kiel Tri-County Record - Kiel, WI - *BaconPubCkNews 84*
KIEM-TV - Eureka, CA - *BrCabYB 84; DirUSTelSta 83; TelAl 83, 84; Tel&CabFB 84S; TV&RadDir 84*
Kier Photo Service - Cleveland, OH - *AvMarPl 83*
Kiester Courier-Sentinel - Kiester, MN - *BaconPubCkNews 84*
KIEV - Glendale, CA - *BrCabYB 84; LitMarPl 84*
KIEV - Los Angeles, CA - *NatRadPubDir Summer 83 p.21, Spring 84 p.21; TV&RadDir 84*
KIEZ - Beaumont, TX - *BrCabYB 84; NatRadPubDir Spring 84*
KIFG - Iowa Falls, IA - *BrCabYB 84; TV&RadDir 84*
KIFG-FM - Iowa Falls, IA - *BrCabYB 84; TV&RadDir 84*
KIFI-TV - Idaho Falls, ID - *BrCabYB 84; DirUSTelSta 83; TelAl 83, 84; Tel&CabFB 84S; TV&RadDir 84*
KIFM-FM - San Diego, CA - *BrCabYB 84; NatRadPubDir Summer 83, Spring 84; TV&RadDir 84*
KIFW - Sitka, AK - *BrCabYB 84; TV&RadDir 84*
KIFW-TV - Sitka, AK - *DirUSTelSta 83; TelAl 83, 84; TV&RadDir 84*
KIGC-FM - Oskaloosa, IA - *BrCabYB 84; NatRadPubDir Summer 83, Spring 84; TV&RadDir 84*
KIGO - St. Anthony, ID - *BrCabYB 84; TV&RadDir 84*
KIHN - Hugo, OK - *BrCabYB 84; TV&RadDir 84*
KIHR - Hood River, OR - *BrCabYB 84; TV&RadDir 84*
KIHS-TV - Los Angeles, CA - *BrCabYB 84*
KIII-TV - Corpus Christi, TX - *DirUSTelSta 83; TelAl 84; Tel&CabFB 84S; TV&RadDir 84*
KIIK-FM - Davenport, IA - *BrCabYB 84; NatRadPubDir Summer 83, Spring 84; TV&RadDir 84*
KIIN-TV - Iowa City, IA - *BrCabYB 84; Tel&CabFB 84S*
KIIQ - Manitou Springs, CO - *BrCabYB 84; NatRadPubDir Spring 84*
KIIQ-FM - Manitou Springs, CO - *BrCabYB 84; NatRadPubDir Summer 83, Spring 84; TV&RadDir 84*
KIIS-FM - Fresno, CA - *TV&RadDir 84*
KIIS-FM - Los Angeles, CA - *BrCabYB 84; NatRadPubDir Summer 83 p.21, Spring 84 p.21; TV&RadDir 84*
KIIX - Ft. Collins, CO - *BrCabYB 84; NatRadPubDir Summer 83, Spring 84; TV&RadDir 84*
KIIZ - Killeen, TX - *BrCabYB 84; TV&RadDir 84*
KIJK-FM - Prineville, OR - *BrCabYB 84; TV&RadDir 84*
KIJN - Farwell, TX - *TV&RadDir 84*
KIJN-FM - Farwell, TX - *BrCabYB 84*
KIJV - Huron, SD - *BrCabYB 84; TV&RadDir 84*
KIK-FM - Orange, CA - *TV&RadDir 84*
KIKC - Forsyth, MT - *BrCabYB 84; TV&RadDir 84*
KIKF-FM - Garden Grove, CA - *BrCabYB 84*
KIKF-FM - Orange, CA - *TV&RadDir 84*
KIKI - Honolulu, HI - *BrCabYB 84; NatRadPubDir Summer 83, Spring 84; TV&RadDir 84*
Kikimora Publishing Co. - Los Altos, CA - *BoPubDir 4, 5*
KIKK - Houston, TX - *NatRadPubDir Summer 83, Spring 84; TV&RadDir 84*
KIKK - Pasadena, TX - *BrCabYB 84*
KIKK-FM - Houston, TX - *BrCabYB 84; NatRadPubDir Summer 83, Spring 84; TV&RadDir 84*
KIKM - Sherman, TX - *BrCabYB 84; TV&RadDir 84*
KIKM-FM - Sherman, TX - *BrCabYB 84; TV&RadDir 84*
KIKN - Corpus Christi, TX - *NatRadPubDir Summer 83, Spring 84; TV&RadDir 84*
KIKN - Sinton, TX - *BrCabYB 84*
KIKO - Globe, AZ - *TV&RadDir 84*
KIKO - Miami, AZ - *BrCabYB 84*
KIKO-FM - Globe, AZ - *BrCabYB 84; TV&RadDir 84*
KIKR - Conroe, TX - *BrCabYB 84; TV&RadDir 84*
KIKS - Iola, KS - *BrCabYB 84; TV&RadDir 84*
KIKT-FM - Greenville, TX - *BrCabYB 84; TV&RadDir 84*
KIKU-TV - Honolulu, HI - *BrCabYB 84; DirUSTelSta 83; TelAl 83, 84; Tel&CabFB 84S; TV&RadDir 84*
KIKZ - Seminole, TX - *BrCabYB 84; TV&RadDir 84*
KIKZ-FM - Seminole, TX - *BrCabYB 84*
KILA-FM - Henderson, NV - *BrCabYB 84*
KILA-FM - Las Vegas, NV - *NatRadPubDir Summer 83, Spring 84; TV&RadDir 84*
Kilby Associates Inc. - Pendleton, OR - *BoPubDir 4, 5*
KILE - Galveston, TX - *BrCabYB 84; NatRadPubDir Summer 83, Spring 84; TV&RadDir 84*
Kilgore Cable Television Co. - Kilgore, TX - *BrCabYB 84; Tel&CabFB 84C*
Kilgore News Herald [of Donrey Inc.] - Kilgore, TX - *AyerDirPub 83; BaconPubCkNews 84; Ed&PubIntYB 82; NewsDir 84*
Kilgore Records Inc. - Leesville, LA - *BillIntBG 83-84*
KILI-FM - Porcupine, SD - *BrCabYB 84*
KILJ-FM - Mt. Pleasant, IA - *BrCabYB 84; TV&RadDir 84*
Killaly Press - London, ON, Canada - *BoPubDir 4, 5*
Killarney Guide Ltd. - Killarney, MB, Canada - *Ed&PubIntYB 82*
Killdeer Dunn County Herald - Killdeer, ND - *BaconPubCkNews 84*
Killdeer Herald - Killdeer, ND - *Ed&PubIntYB 82*
Killeen Herald - Killeen, TX - *AyerDirPub 83; BaconPubCkNews 84; NewsDir 84*
Killiam Shows Inc. - New York, NY - *TelAl 83, 84; Tel&CabFB 84C*
Killingsworth, Molly M. - Socorro, NM - *LitMarPl 83*
Killy-Moon Press - Torrance, CA - *BoPubDir 4, 5*
Kilmarnock Rappahannock Record - Kilmarnock, VA - *BaconPubCkNews 84*
Kilo Corp. - Ann Arbor, MI - *MicrocomMPl 83*
KILO-FM - Colorado Springs, CO - *BrCabYB 84; NatRadPubDir Summer 83, Spring 84; TV&RadDir 84*
KILR - Estherville, IA - *BrCabYB 84; TV&RadDir 84*
KILR-FM - Estherville, IA - *BrCabYB 84; TV&RadDir 84*
KILT - Houston, TX - *BrCabYB 84; NatRadPubDir Summer 83, Spring 84; TV&RadDir 84*
KILT-FM - Houston, TX - *BrCabYB 84; TV&RadDir 84*

Kiltie & Co., O. - Ft. Wayne, IN - *BoPubDir 4, 5*
Kilynn Music Publishing Co. Inc. - *See* Mietus Copyright Management
Kim & Gifford Productions Inc. - New York, NY - *AvMarPl 83*
KIM Productions Inc. - Boston, MA - *AvMarPl 83*
KIMA-TV - Yakima, WA - *BrCabYB 84; DirUSTelSta 83; TelAl 83, 84; Tel&CabFB 84S; TV&RadDir 84*
Kimac Co., The - Guilford, CT - *AvMarPl 83*
KIMB - Kimball, NE - *BrCabYB 84; TV&RadDir 84*
Kimball Brule County News - Kimball, SD - *BaconPubCkNews 84*
Kimball Cable TV [of Community Tele-Communications Inc.] - Kimball, NE - *BrCabYB 84*
Kimball Community TV [of Community Tele-Communications Inc.] - Kimball, NE - *Tel&CabFB 84C*
Kimball Group Inc., The - Wayne, PA - *StaDirAdAg 2-84*
Kimball Office Furniture Co. - Jasper, IN - *DirInfWP 82*
Kimball Systems - Paramus, NJ - *DataDirSup 7-83*
Kimball Tri-County News - Kimball, MN - *BaconPubCkNews 84*
Kimball Western Nebraska Observer - Kimball, NE - *BaconPubCkNews 84*
Kimballton Review - Elk Horn, IA - *Ed&PubIntYB 82*
Kimbell Art Museum - Ft. Worth, TX - *BoPubDir 4, 5*
Kimberling City-Green Forest Table Rock Gazette - Kimberling City, MO - *NewsDir 84*
Kimberling City Southwest Missourian - Branson, MO - *BaconPubCkNews 84*
Kimberling City Table Rock Gazette - Green Forest, AR - *Ed&PubIntYB 82*
Kimberling City Table Rock Gazette - *See* Larimer Publications Inc.
Kimberly - Omaha, NE - *LitMag&SmPr 83-84*
Kimberly Advertiser - Kimberly, ID - *AyerDirPub 83; Ed&PubIntYB 82*
Kimberly-Clark Corp. - Neenah, WI - *LitMarPl 83, 84*
Kimberly, Jones Publishing Co. - Omaha, NE - *BoPubDir 4, 5*
Kimberly Press Inc. - Goleta, CA - *LitMarPl 83, 84*
Kimble Terminals & Computers Inc. - Troy, MI - *WhoWMicrocom 83*
Kimbo Educational [Div. of United Sound Arts Inc.] - Long Branch, NJ - *AvMarPl 83; WritMar 84*
Kimbo Records [Div. of United Sound Arts Inc.] - Long Branch, NJ - *BillIntBG 83-84*
Kimchuk Inc. - Brookfield, CT - *AvMarPl 83*
Kimel Broadcast Group Inc. - St. Albans, VT - *BrCabYB 84*
KIMI-FM - Keokuk, IA - *BrCabYB 84; TV&RadDir 84*
KIML - Gillette, WY - *BrCabYB 84; TV&RadDir 84*
Kimlyn Music Co. - *See* Big Seven Music Corp.
KIMM - Rapid City, SD - *BrCabYB 84*
KIMN - Denver, CO - *BrCabYB 84; NatRadPubDir Summer 83, Spring 84; TV&RadDir 84*
KIMO-TV - Anchorage, AK - *BrCabYB 84; DirUSTelSta 83; TelAl 83, 84; Tel&CabFB 84S; TV&RadDir 84*
KIMP - Mt. Pleasant, TX - *BrCabYB 84; TV&RadDir 84*
KIMT-TV - Cedar Rapids, IA - *DirUSTelSta 83*
KIMT-TV - Mason City, IA - *BrCabYB 84; TelAl 83, 84; Tel&CabFB 84S; TV&RadDir 84*
Kimtra Music - *See* Hat Band Music
Kimtron Corp. - Santa Clara, CA - *DataDirSup 7-83; MicrocomMPl 84*
Kin-O-Lux - New York, NY - *AvMarPl 83*
KINA - Salina, KS - *BrCabYB 84; TV&RadDir 84*
KINB-FM - Poteau, OK - *BrCabYB 84; TV&RadDir 84*
KINB-FM - Memphis, TN - *NatRadPubDir Spring 84*
Kincaid Consulting - Mill Valley, CA - *MicrocomMPl 84*
Kincardine Cable TV Ltd. - Kincardine, ON, Canada - *BrCabYB 84*
Kincardine News, The - Kincardine, ON, Canada - *Ed&PubIntYB 82*
KIND - Independence, KS - *TV&RadDir 84*
KIND-FM - Independence, KS - *BrCabYB 84; TV&RadDir 84*
Kinder Courier-News - Kinder, LA - *BaconPubCkNews 84*
Kinder News - Kinder, LA - *Ed&PubIntYB 82*
Kindler, Leonard I. - Philadelphia, PA - *BoPubDir 5*
Kindred Joy Publications - Coquille, OR - *LitMag&SmPr 83-84*
Kindred Press [Aff. of Mennonite Brethren Conference] - Hillsboro, KS - *BoPubDir 4 Sup, 5*
Kindred Press [Aff. of Mennonite Brethren Churches of Canada] - Winnipeg, MB, Canada - *BoPubDir 4 Sup, 5*
Kindred Spirit, The [of Gray Cat Publications] - Great Bend, KS - *LitMag&SmPr 83-84; WritMar 84*
KINE - Kingsville, TX - *BrCabYB 84; TV&RadDir 84*
KINE-FM - Kingsville, TX - *TV&RadDir 84*
Kiner Cable Inc. - San Manuel, AZ - *Tel&CabFB 84C*
Kiner, Dean V. - Hot Springs, CA - *Tel&CabFB 84C p.1687*
Kiner Music Co. - Redmond, WA - *BillIntBG 83-84*
Kinetic Designs - Jacksonville, FL - *MicrocomMPl 83; WhoWMicrocom 83*
Kinetic Film Enterprises Ltd. - Toronto, ON, Canada - *AvMarPl 83*
KineticSystems Corp. - Lockport, IL - *DataDirSup 7-83*
Kinetronics Corp. - Lake Bluff, IL - *AvMarPl 83*
Kinex Corp. [Subs. of Nokia Corp.] - Largo, FL - *DataDirSup 7-83*
Kinex Corp. - Rochester, NY - *AvMarPl 83*
KINF-FM - Dodge City, KS - *BrCabYB 84*
KING - Seattle, WA - *BrCabYB 84; LitMarPl 83, 84; NatRadPubDir Summer 83, Spring 84; TV&RadDir 84*
King Advertising & Public Relations - Newport Beach, CA - *DirPRFirms 83*
King Advertising Inc., Mackay - *See* K & E Holdings Inc.
King & Associates, Jean - Mobile, AL - *DirPRFirms 83*
King & Co. Inc., D. F. - New York, NY - *DirPRFirms 83*
King & Cowen Books - Teaneck, NJ - *LitMag&SmPr 83-84*
King & Cowen Books (Bravo Editions) - Teaneck, NJ - *BoPubDir 5*
King & Cowen Books (Bravo Editions) - New York, NY - *BoPubDir 4*
King & Partners Inc., Lee - Chicago, IL - *BrCabYB 84*
King Associates, Victor - Virginia Beach, VA - *StaDirAdAg 2-84*
King Broadcasting Co. - Seattle, WA - *BrCabYB 84; Tel&CabFB 84S*
King-Casey Inc. - New Canaan, CT - *HBIndAd&MS 82-83*
King City CATV Inc. [of Communications Systems Inc.] - Pine Canyon, CA - *BrCabYB 84*
King City Rustler - King City, CA - *NewsDir 84*
King City Rustler - *See* Casey Newspapers Inc.
King City Tri-County News - King City, MO - *BaconPubCkNews 84*
King Coal Music Inc. - *See* Coal Miners Music Inc.
King Concept Corp. - Minneapolis, MN - *AvMarPl 83*
King Features - New York, NY - *NewsBur 6*
King Features Entertainment - New York, NY - *TelAl 83, 84; Tel&CabFB 84C*
King Features Syndicate [Div. of Hearst Corp.] - New York, NY - *BaconPubCkNews 84; Ed&PubIntYB 82; LitMarPl 83, 84; MagIndMarPl 82-83*
King Features Television [Div. of The Hearst Corp.] - New York, NY - *AvMarPl 83*
King Film Laboratory [Div. of King Broadcasting Co.] - Portland, OR - *AvMarPl 83*
KING-FM - Seattle, WA - *BrCabYB 84; NatRadPubDir Summer 83, Spring 84; TV&RadDir 84*
King Inc., D. - Monterey, VA - *BrCabYB 84*
King Instrument Corp. - Westboro, MA - *AvMarPl 83*
King International Corp. - Beverly Hills, CA - *TelAl 83, 84*
King, James - Harbor City, CA - *BoPubDir 4, 5*
King Kong Music - *See* Publishing Ventures Inc.
King, Leroy O. Jr. - Dallas, TX - *BoPubDir 4, 5*
King Lithographers Inc. - Tuckahoe, NY - *LitMarPl 83, 84; MagIndMarPl 82-83*
King Mail Corp. - Tuckahoe, NY - *MagIndMarPl 82-83*
King Mountain Cable Corp. - Williamsburg, KY - *BrCabYB 84; Tel&CabFB 84C*
King Music House, K. L. - *See* Barnhouse Co., C. L.
King of Kings/LA International Records - Palmdale, CA - *BillIntBG 83-84*
King of Prussia Courier - King of Prussia, PA - *AyerDirPub 83; Ed&PubIntYB 82*
King of Prussia Courier - *See* Suburban Publications Inc.
King of Prussia Today's Post - King of Prussia, PA - *BaconPubCkNews 84*
King of Prussia Today's Post [of Montgomery Publishing Co.] - Norristown, PA - *NewsDir 84*

King of Video Inc. - Las Vegas, NV - *HomeVid&CabYB 82-83*
King Public Relations, Lis - Mahwah, NJ - *DirPRFirms 83; StaDirAdAg 2-84*
King Publications - Washington, DC - *BoPubDir 4, 5; LitMag&SmPr 83-84*
King Publishing Co., Joseph & Betty - Lafayette, CA - *BoPubDir 5*
King Publishing, Phil - Erie, PA - *BoPubDir 4, 5*
King Research Inc. - Rockville, MD - *BoPubDir 5; EISS 83; InfIndMarPl 83*
King, Richard L. - Cerritos, CA - *FBInfSer 80; InfIndMarPl 83*
King Software - Lowell, MA - *MicrocomMPl 84*
King Software - Red Bank, NJ - *MicrocomMPl 84*
King Sports & Entertainment Network, Don - Rolling Hills Estates, CA - *CabTVPrDB 83*
King Sports & Entertainment Network, Don - New York, NY - *BrCabYB 84*
King Times News - King, NC - *AyerDirPub 83; BaconPubCkNews 84*
King Times-News [of Lindsay Publishing Co.] - Winston-Salem, NC - *NewsDir 84*
KING-TV - Seattle, WA - *BrCabYB 84; DirUSTelSta 83; LitMarPl 83, 84; TelAl 83, 84; Tel&CabFB 84S; TV&RadDir 84*
King Typographic Service [Div. of Typographic Communications] - New York, NY - *LitMarPl 83, 84; MagIndMarPl 82-83*
King Videocable Co. - Angels Camp, CA - *BrCabYB 84*
King Videocable Co. - Lake Elsinore, CA - *BrCabYB 84; Tel&CabFB 84C*
King Videocable Co. - Lodi, CA - *BrCabYB 84*
King Videocable Co. - Los Angeles, CA - *BrCabYB 84*
King Videocable Co. - Mt. Shasta, CA - *BrCabYB 84; Tel&CabFB 84C*
King Videocable Co. - Newhall, CA - *Tel&CabFB 84C*
King Videocable Co. - Placerville, CA - *BrCabYB 84; Tel&CabFB 84C*
King Videocable Co. - San Andreas, CA - *BrCabYB 84*
King Videocable Co. - Turlock, CA - *BrCabYB 84*
King Videocable Co. - Valley Springs, CA - *Tel&CabFB 84C*
King Videocable Co. - Twin Falls, ID - *Tel&CabFB 84C*
King Videocable Co. - Ellensburg, WA - *BrCabYB 84; Tel&CabFB 84C*
King Videocable Co. [of King Broadcasting Co.] - Seattle, WA - *BrCabYB 84 p.D-302; CabTVFinDB 83; Tel&CabFB 84C p.1687*
King Weekly - King Township, ON, Canada - *Ed&PubIntYB 82*
King World Productions Inc. - Summit, NJ - *TelAl 83, 84; Tel&CabFB 84C*
Kingdom Daily Sun-Gazette [of Waters Publications Inc.] - Fulton, MO - *BaconPubCkNews 84; Ed&PubIntYB 82; NewsDir 84*
Kingdom News - Fulton, MO - *AyerDirPub 83*
Kingdom Press - Amherst, NH - *BoPubDir 4, 5*
Kingdom Telephone Co. - Auxvasse, MO - *TelDir&BG 83-84*
Kingdom Television Inc. - Fulton, MO - *BrCabYB 84*
Kingfisher Cable TV Inc. - Kingfisher, OK - *BrCabYB 84; Tel&CabFB 84C*
Kingfisher Free Press - Kingfisher, OK - *Ed&PubIntYB 82*
Kingfisher Free Press - *See* Kingfisher Newspapers Inc.
Kingfisher Newspapers Inc. - Kingfisher, OK - *BaconPubCkNews 84*
Kingfisher Press - Red Deer, AB, Canada - *BoPubDir 4, 5*
Kingfisher Times [of Kingfisher Free Press] - Kingfisher, OK - *Ed&PubIntYB 82; NewsDir 84*
Kingfisher Times - *See* Kingfisher Newspapers Inc.
Kingman Daily Miner [of Mohave County Miner Inc.] - Kingman, AZ - *BaconPubCkNews 84; Ed&PubIntYB 82; NewsDir 84*
Kingman Journal - Kingman, KS - *Ed&PubIntYB 82; NewsDir 84*
Kingman Journal - *See* Leader-Courier/Kingman Journal
Kingman Leader-Courier - Kingman, KS - *Ed&PubIntYB 82; NewsDir 84*
Kingman Leader-Courier - *See* Leader-Courier/Kingman Journal
Kings Bay Cable Vision Inc. - St. Marys, GA - *BrCabYB 84; Tel&CabFB 84C*
Kings Bay Clearview Cable TV - Kings Bay Navy Base, GA - *BrCabYB 84*
Kings County Cable Ltd. - Sussex, NB, Canada - *BrCabYB 84*
Kings County News - Hanford, CA - *AyerDirPub 83*
Kings County Record - Sussex, NB, Canada - *AyerDirPub 83; Ed&PubIntYB 82*
Kings Courier [of Courier-Life Inc.] - Brooklyn, NY - *AyerDirPub 83; Ed&PubIntYB 82; NewsDir 84*
Kings Courier - *See* Courier-Life Inc.
Kings Crown Music Press - *See* Galaxy Music Corp.
King's Inc., D. - Monterey, VA - *Tel&CabFB 84C*
Kings Kable Ltd. - Wolfville, NS, Canada - *BrCabYB 84*
Kings Mountain Herald - Kings Mountain, NC - *BaconPubCkNews 84*
Kings Mountain Mirror-Herald - Kings Mountain, NC - *Ed&PubIntYB 82; NewsDir 84*
Kingsbridge Media & Marketing Inc. - Van Nuys, CA - *StaDirAdAg 2-84*
Kingsburg Recorder - Kingsburg, CA - *BaconPubCkNews 84; Ed&PubIntYB 82*
Kingsburg Telephone Co. - Kingsburg, CA - *TelDir&BG 83-84*
Kingsland Southeast Georgian - Kingsland, GA - *BaconPubCkNews 84*
Kingsley Colton & Associates Inc. - Beverly Hills, CA - *Tel&CabFB 84C*
Kingsley Communications Inc. - New York, NY - *StaDirAdAg 2-84*
Kingsley News-Times - Kingsley, IA - *BaconPubCkNews 84; Ed&PubIntYB 82*
Kingsley Telephone Co. - Kingsley, MI - *TelDir&BG 83-84*
Kingsport Creek Music - Burbank, CA - *BillIntBG 83-84*
Kingsport Daily News - Kingsport, TN - *BaconPubCkNews 84*
Kingsport Post-News - Kingsport, TN - *NewsDir 84*
Kingsport Press [Subs. of Arcata] - Kingsport, TN - *LitMarPl 84*
Kingsport Times News [of Kingsport Publishing Co.] - Kingsport, TN - *BaconPubCkNews 84; Ed&PubIntYB 82; LitMarPl 83, 84; NewsDir 84*
Kingston Cablenet - Kingston, ON, Canada - *BrCabYB 84*
Kingston Cablevision Inc. [of TCI Growth Inc.] - Kingston, NY - *BrCabYB 84; Tel&CabFB 84C*
Kingston Cablevision Inc. [of Tele-Communications Inc.] - Rhinebeck, NY - *Tel&CabFB 84C*
Kingston Cablevision Inc. [of Tele-Communications Inc.] - Woodstock, NY - *Tel&CabFB 84C*
Kingston Enterprise, The - Kingston, MI - *Ed&PubIntYB 82*
Kingston Freeman [of Mid-Hudson Publications] - Kingston, NY - *BaconPubCkNews 84; NewsDir 84*
Kingston International - Smithtown, NY - *BillIntBG 83-84*
Kingston Roane County News - Kingston, TN - *BaconPubCkNews 84; NewsDir 84*
Kingston Texoman - Kingston, OK - *BaconPubCkNews 84*
Kingston TV Cable Co. [of National Telecommunications] - Kingston, TN - *Tel&CabFB 84C*
Kingston Whig-Standard - Kingston, ON, Canada - *BaconPubCkNews 84; LitMarPl 83*
Kingstree News - Kingstree, SC - *BaconPubCkNews 84*
Kingsville Record - Kingsville, TX - *BaconPubCkNews 84; Ed&PubIntYB 82; NewsDir 84*
Kingsville Record & Bishop News - Kingsville, TX - *AyerDirPub 83*
Kingsville Reporter, The - Kingsville, ON, Canada - *Ed&PubIntYB 82*
Kingsville Telephone Co. - Kingsville OH - *TelDir&BG 83-84*
Kingtron Corp. - Santa Clara, CA - *DataDirSup 7-83*
Kingwood Cablevision [Aff. of Moffat International Corp.] - Kingwood, TX - *InterCabHB 3; Tel&CabFB 84C*
Kingwood Echo - *See* Houston Community Newspapers
Kingwood Observer - Humble, TX - *BaconPubCkNews 84*
Kingwood Preston County Journal - Kingwood, WV - *BaconPubCkNews 84; NewsDir 84*
KINI-FM - Crookston, NE - *BrCabYB 84*
KINI-FM - St. Francis, SD - *TV&RadDir 84*
Kinistino Post - Kinistino, SK, Canada - *AyerDirPub 83; Ed&PubIntYB 82*
KINK-FM - Portland, OR - *BrCabYB 84; NatRadPubDir Summer 83, Spring 84; TV&RadDir 84*
KINL-FM - Eagle Pass, TX - *BrCabYB 84; TV&RadDir 84*
Kinmundy Express - Kinmundy, IL - *BaconPubCkNews 84; Ed&PubIntYB 82*
KINN - Alamogordo, NM - *BrCabYB 84; TV&RadDir 84*

KINN-FM - Alamogordo, NM - *BrCabYB 84; TV&RadDir 84*
Kinneloa Television Systems [of KTS Corp.] - Pasadena, CA - *BrCabYB 84; Tel&CabFB 84C*
KINO - Winslow, AZ - *BrCabYB 84; TV&RadDir 84*
Kino Publications [Aff. of Kino Learning Center Inc.] - Tucson, AZ - *ArtMar 84; BoPubDir 5*
Kinokuniya Co. Ltd. - Tokyo, Japan - *EISS 83; InfIndMarPl 83*
Kinotone Inc. - Paterson, NJ - *AvMarPl 83*
KINQ-FM - Walnut Creek, CA - *BrCabYB 84*
KINS - Eureka, CA - *BrCabYB 84; TV&RadDir 84*
Kinsey Institute for Sex Research Inc. (Information Service) - Bloomington, IN - *InfIndMarPl 83*
Kinship Krafts Publications [Aff. of Kinship Krafts Inc.] - Montclair, NJ - *BoPubDir 4, 5*
Kinsley Advertising Inc. - Worthington, OH - *ArtMar 84*
Kinsley Cable TV Service [of Communications Services Inc.] - Kinsley, KS - *BrCabYB 84; Tel&CabFB 84C*
Kinsley Mercury - Kinsley, KS - *BaconPubCkNews 84; Ed&PubIntYB 82*
Kinsman Mutual Telephone Co. - Kinsman, IL - *TelDir&BG 83-84*
Kinston Cable TV Inc. [of Tar River Communications Inc.] - Kinston, NC - *Tel&CabFB 84C*
Kinston Free Press [of Freedom Newspapers Inc.] - Kinston, NC - *BaconPubCkNews 84; Ed&PubIntYB 82; NewsDir 84*
KINT-FM - El Paso, TX - *NatRadPubDir Summer 83*
KINT-TV - El Paso, TX - *BrCabYB 84; Tel&CabFB 84S*
KINY - Juneau, AK - *BrCabYB 84; NatRadPubDir Summer 83, Spring 84; TV&RadDir 84*
KINY-TV - Juneau, AK - *TelAl 83, 84; TV&RadDir 84*
Kinzie & Green - Wausau, WI - *AdAge 3-28-84; StaDirAdAg 2-84*
KIOA - Des Moines, IA - *BrCabYB 84; NatRadPubDir Summer 83, Spring 84; TV&RadDir 84*
KIOA-FM - Des Moines, IA - *NatRadPubDir Summer 83*
KIOB-FM - Coeur d'Alene, ID - *TV&RadDir 84*
KIOC-FM - Beaumont, TX - *NatRadPubDir Summer 83 p.235, Spring 84 p.235*
KIOC-FM - Orange, TX - *BrCabYB 84*
KIOC-FM - Vidor, TX - *TV&RadDir 84*
KIOE - Honolulu, HI - *NatRadPubDir Summer 83; TV&RadDir 84*
KIOF-FM - Lamesa, TX - *BrCabYB 84*
KIOI-FM - San Francisco, CA - *BrCabYB 84; NatRadPubDir Summer 83, Spring 84; TV&RadDir 84*
KIOK-FM - Pasco, WA - *TV&RadDir 84*
KIOK-FM - Richland, WA - *BrCabYB 84*
KIOL-FM - Iola, KS - *BrCabYB 84; TV&RadDir 84*
KIOO-FM - Porterville, CA - *BrCabYB 84; TV&RadDir 84*
KIOQ-FM - Bishop, CA - *BrCabYB 84; TV&RadDir 84*
KIOS-FM - Omaha, NE - *BrCabYB 84; NatRadPubDir Summer 83, Spring 84; TV&RadDir 84*
KIOT - Barstow, CA - *BrCabYB 84; TV&RadDir 84*
KIOU-FM - Corpus Christi, TX - *BrCabYB 84; NatRadPubDir Summer 83, Spring 84; TV&RadDir 84*
KIOV-FM - Sioux Falls, SD - *BrCabYB 84; NatRadPubDir Summer 83, Spring 84; TV&RadDir 84*
KIOW-FM - Forest City, IA - *BrCabYB 84; TV&RadDir 84*
Kiowa County Democrat - Snyder, OK - *AyerDirPub 83; Ed&PubIntYB 82*
Kiowa County Press - Eads, CO - *AyerDirPub 83*
Kiowa County Signal - Greensburg, KS - *AyerDirPub 83; Ed&PubIntYB 82*
Kiowa County Star Review - Hobart, OK - *AyerDirPub 83; Ed&PubIntYB 82*
Kiowa Elbert County News - *See* Douglas County News Publishing
Kiowa News - Kiowa, KS - *BaconPubCkNews 84; Ed&PubIntYB 82*
KIOX - Bay City, TX - *BrCabYB 84; TV&RadDir 84*
KIOZ-FM - Laramie, WY - *BrCabYB 84; NatRadPubDir Summer 83, Spring 84; TV&RadDir 84*
Kip-Lee CATV Inc. [of Harte-Hanks Communications Inc.] - Deer Park, TX - *BrCabYB 84; Tel&CabFB 84C*
Kip-Lee CATV Inc. [of Harte-Hanks Communications Inc.] - Highlands, TX - *BrCabYB 84*
KIP USA Inc. - Millbrae, CA - *DirInfWP 82*
KIPA - Hilo, HI - *BrCabYB 84; NatRadPubDir Summer 83, Spring 84; TV&RadDir 84*
Kipahulu Music Co. - Hollywood, CA - *BillIntBG 83-84*
KIPC-FM - Albuquerque, NM - *NatRadPubDir Summer 83, Spring 84*
Kipen Publishing Corp. - Chicago, IL - *DirMarMP 83*
Kipling Journal, The [of The Kipling Society] - London, England - *LitMag&SmPr 83-84*
Kiplinger California Letter, The - Washington, DC - *BaconPubCkMag 84*
Kiplinger Computer & Mailing Services - Hyattsville, MD - *MagIndMarPl 82-83*
Kiplinger Florida Letter, The - Washington, DC - *BaconPubCkMag 84*
Kiplinger Texas Letter, The - Washington, DC - *BaconPubCkMag 84*
Kiplinger Washington Editors Inc., The - Washington, DC - *KnowInd 83*
Kiplinger Washington Letter, The - Washington, DC - *BaconPubCkMag 84*
KIPO - Lihue, HI - *BrCabYB 84; TV&RadDir 84*
KIPO-FM - Lihue, HI - *BrCabYB 84*
KIPR - Diboll, TX - *BrCabYB 84; TV&RadDir 84*
KIPR-FM - Diboll, TX - *BrCabYB 84; TV&RadDir 84*
Kips Bay Music - *See* Raybird Music
KIQI - Hayward, CA - *BrCabYB 84*
KIQI - San Francisco, CA - *NatRadPubDir Summer 83, Spring 84; TV&RadDir 84*
KIQO-FM - Atascadero, CA - *BrCabYB 84*
KIQQ-FM - Los Angeles, CA - *BrCabYB 84; NatRadPubDir Summer 83 p.21, Spring 84 p.21; TV&RadDir 84*
KIQS - Willows, CA - *BrCabYB 84; TV&RadDir 84*
KIQS-FM - Willows, CA - *BrCabYB 84*
KIQY-FM - Lebanon, OR - *BrCabYB 84; TV&RadDir 84*
KIQZ-FM - Rawlins, WY - *BrCabYB 84*
Kirby Cable TV - Boron, CA - *Tel&CabFB 84C*
Kirby Co., A. J. - London, ON, Canada - *BoPubDir 4, 5*
Kirby Co. Inc., Nona - Boston, MA - *TelAl 83, 84*
Kirbyville Banner - Kirbyville, TX - *AyerDirPub 83; BaconPubCkNews 84; Ed&PubIntYB 82*
Kircher, Helton & Collett Inc. - Dayton, OH - *ArtMar 84; StaDirAdAg 2-84*
Kirchman Corp., The - Orlando, FL - *ADAPSOMemDir 83-84*
Kirchner TV Co. - Meyersdale, PA - *BrCabYB 84 p.D-302; Tel&CabFB 84C*
Kirchoff/Wohlberg Inc. - New York, NY - *LitMarPl 83, 84*
Kirin Books & Art - Alexandria, VA - *BoPubDir 4, 5*
Kirk Associates, H. L. - New York, NY - *LitMarPl 83, 84; MagIndMarPl 82-83*
Kirk Broadcasting Inc. - Moultrie, GA - *BrCabYB 84*
KIRK-FM - Branson, MO - *TV&RadDir 84*
Kirk/Marsland Advertising - New York, NY - *DirMarMP 83*
Kirk-Othmer Encyclopedia [of Bibliographic Retrieval Services Inc.] - Latham, NY - *DataDirOnSer 84*
Kirk-Othmer/Online - New York, NY - *DirOnDB Spring 84*
Kirk Press - Superior, WI - *BoPubDir 4, 5*
Kirkbride Bible Co. Inc., B. B. - Indianapolis, IN - *BoPubDir 4, 5*
Kirke-Van Orsdel Computer Services - Des Moines, IA - *ADAPSOMemDir 83-84*
Kirkland Lake Northern Daily News - Kirkland Lake, ON, Canada - *LitMarPl 83*
Kirkland News - Genoa, IL - *Ed&PubIntYB 82*
Kirkland Review - Kirkland, WA - *AyerDirPub 83*
Kirkley Press Inc. - Baltimore, MD - *WritMar 84*
Kirkman/3hree/Advertising Inc. - Delmar, NY - *StaDirAdAg 2-84*
Kirkpatrick & Associates Inc., Jim - Dallas, TX - *StaDirAdAg 2-84*
Kirkpatrick, Howard B. - Woodstock, NB, Canada - *Tel&CabFB 84C*
Kirksville Crier - Kirksville, MO - *AyerDirPub 83*
Kirksville Express & News - Kirksville, MO - *BaconPubCkNews 84; Ed&PubIntYB 82; NewsDir 84*
Kirkus Reviews - New York, NY - *MagIndMarPl 82-83*
Kirkwood Co. Ltd., The - London, England - *StaDirAdAg 2-84*
KIRL - St. Charles, MO - *BrCabYB 84; TV&RadDir 84*

KIRL - St. Louis, MO - *NatRadPubDir Summer 83 p.143, Spring 84 p.143*
KIRO - Seattle, WA - *BrCabYB 84; LitMarPl 83, 84; NatRadPubDir Summer 83, Spring 84; TV&RadDir 84; VideoDir 82-83*
KIRO-TV - Seattle, WA - *BrCabYB 84; DirUSTelSta 83; TelAl 83, 84; Tel&CabFB 84S; TV&RadDir 84*
Kirshner Cable Television, Don - New York, NY - *Tel&CabFB 84C*
Kirshner/CBS Music Publishing - Nashville, TN - *BillIntBG 83-84*
KIRT - McAllen, TX - *NatRadPubDir Summer 83, Spring 84; TV&RadDir 84*
KIRT - Mission, TX - *BrCabYB 84*
KIRV - Fresno, CA - *BrCabYB 84; NatRadPubDir Summer 83, Spring 84; TV&RadDir 84*
KIRX - Kirksville, MO - *BrCabYB 84; TV&RadDir 84*
KISA - Honolulu, HI - *BrCabYB 84; NatRadPubDir Summer 83, Spring 84; TV&RadDir 84*
KISD - Medford, OR - *BrCabYB 84; TV&RadDir 84*
Kish, Henriette - New York, NY - *Ed&PubIntYB 82*
Kish Music Publishing Co., Jimmy - Nashville, TN - *BillIntBG 83-84*
Kiski News - Vandergrift, PA - *AyerDirPub 83*
Kislingbury Public Relations Advertising, Graham - San Francisco, CA - *DirPRFirms 83*
KISM-FM - Bellingham, WA - *BrCabYB 84; NatRadPubDir Summer 83, Spring 84; TV&RadDir 84*
KISN-FM - Farwell, TX - *BrCabYB 84*
KISN-FM - Salt Lake City, UT - *BrCabYB 84; NatRadPubDir Summer 83, Spring 84; TV&RadDir 84*
KISO - El Paso, TX - *BrCabYB 84; NatRadPubDir Summer 83, Spring 84; TV&RadDir 84*
KISR - Ft. Smith, AR - *BrCabYB 84; TV&RadDir 84*
KISR-FM - Ft. Smith, AR - *NatRadPubDir Summer 83, Spring 84*
KISR-FM - Clewiston, FL - *TV&RadDir 84*
Kisron Elyon - Los Angeles, CA - *BillIntBG 83-84*
KISS-FM - San Antonio, TX - *BrCabYB 84; NatRadPubDir Summer 83, Spring 84; TV&RadDir 84*
Kissimmee Cablevision [of American TV & Communications Corp.] - Kissimmee, FL - *Tel&CabFB 84C*
Kissimmee Gazette - Kissimmee, FL - *Ed&PubIntYB 82*
Kissinger, Millman & Gerendasy - Panorama City, CA - *WhoWMicrocom 83*
KIST - Santa Barbara, CA - *BrCabYB 84; NatRadPubDir Summer 83, Spring 84; TV&RadDir 84*
KISU - Pocatello, ID - *TV&RadDir 84*
KISU-TV - Pocatello, ID - *BrCabYB 84; Tel&CabFB 84S*
KISW-FM - Seattle, WA - *BrCabYB 84; NatRadPubDir Summer 83, Spring 84; TV&RadDir 84*
KISZ-FM - Cortez, CO - *BrCabYB 84; TV&RadDir 84*
KIT - Yakima, WA - *BrCabYB 84; TV&RadDir 84*
Kit Car Quarterly - San Jose, CA - *WritMar 84*
KITA - Little Rock, AR - *BrCabYB 84; TV&RadDir 84*
Kitaab Press - Waynesburg, PA - *BoPubDir 4, 5*
Kitaeff Public Relations, Adrienne - Sag Harbor, NY - *DirPRFirms 83*
Kitazawa, Emiko - Berkeley, CA - *LitMarPl 83, 84; MagIndMarPl 82-83*
Kitchen & Bath Business [of Gralla Publications] - New York, NY - *BaconPubCkMag 84; MagDir 84; MagIndMarPl 82-83*
Kitchen Harvest Press - St. Charles, IL - *BoPubDir 4, 5*
Kitchen Planning - New York, NY - *MagDir 84*
Kitchen Sink Art Studio [Div. of Kitchen Sink Press Inc.] - Princeton, WI - *LitMarPl 84*
Kitchen Sink Press [Subs. of Krupp Comic Works Inc.] - Princeton, WI - *ArtMar 84; BoPubDir 4, 5; LitMag&SmPr 83-84; LitMarPl 83, 84*
Kitchen Table: Women of Color Press - Brooklyn, NY - *BoPubDir 4 Sup, 5; LitMag&SmPr 83-84*
Kitchener-Waterloo Art Gallery - Kitchener, ON, Canada - *BoPubDir 4, 5*
Kitchener-Waterloo Record - Kitchener, ON, Canada - *AyerDirPub 83; BaconPubCkNews 84; Ed&PubIntYB 82; LitMarPl 83, 84*
Kitching, Jessie - Forest Hills, NY - *LitMarPl 83, 84; MagIndMarPl 82-83*
KITE-FM - Portland, TX - *BrCabYB 84*
Kite Lines [of Aeolus Press Inc.] - Baltimore, MD - *LitMag&SmPr 83-84; MagIndMarPl 82-83*
KITF - International Falls, MN - *BrCabYB 84; Tel&CabFB 84S*
KITI - Centralia, WA - *TV&RadDir 84*
KITI - Chehalis, WA - *BrCabYB 84*
KITM-FM - Mission, TX - *BrCabYB 84*
KITO-FM - Vinita, OK - *BrCabYB 84; TV&RadDir 84*
KITR-FM - Creston, IA - *BrCabYB 84; TV&RadDir 84*
KITS-FM - San Francisco, CA - *BrCabYB 84; NatRadPubDir Summer 83, Spring 84*
Kitsap County Herald - Poulsbo, WA - *AyerDirPub 83; Ed&PubIntYB 82*
Kitsap Journal - Silverdale, WA - *Ed&PubIntYB 82*
KITT - Las Vegas, NV - *BrCabYB 84*
Kittanning Leader Times [of Thomson Newspapers] - Kittanning, PA - *BaconPubCkNews 84; NewsDir 84*
Kitten Records - Pittsburgh, PA - *BillIntBG 83-84*
Kittle Inc., Clare Adams - Dallas, TX - *DirMarMP 83*
Kittson County Enterprise - Hallock, MN - *AyerDirPub 83; Ed&PubIntYB 82*
KITV-TV - Honolulu, HI - *BrCabYB 84; DirUSTelSta 83; TelAl 83, 84; Tel&CabFB 84S; TV&RadDir 84*
KITX - Hugo, OK - *BrCabYB 84*
KITY-FM - San Antonio, TX - *BrCabYB 84; NatRadPubDir Summer 83, Spring 84; TV&RadDir 84*
Kitzmiller Systems - Los Angeles, CA - *WhoWMicrocom 83*
KIUL - Garden City, KS - *BrCabYB 84; TV&RadDir 84*
KIUN - Pecos, TX - *BrCabYB 84; TV&RadDir 84*
KIUP - Durango, CO - *BrCabYB 84; TV&RadDir 84*
KIVA-TV - Farmington, NM - *DirUSTelSta 83; TelAl 83, 84; Tel&CabFB 84S; TV&RadDir 84*
KIVE-FM - Glendive, MT - *BrCabYB 84; TV&RadDir 84*
KIVI-TV - Boise, ID - *DirUSTelSta 83*
KIVI-TV - Lewiston, ID - *TelAl 83, 84*
KIVI-TV - Nampa, ID - *BrCabYB 84; Tel&CabFB 84S; TV&RadDir 84*
KIVR - Cave Junction, OR - *BrCabYB 84*
KIVV-TV - Lead, SD - *BrCabYB 84; Tel&CabFB 84S*
KIVV-TV - Rapid City, SD - *TelAl 83, 84*
KIVY - Crockett, TX - *BrCabYB 84; TV&RadDir 84*
KIVY-FM - Crockett, TX - *BrCabYB 84; TV&RadDir 84*
KIWA - Sheldon, IA - *BrCabYB 84; TV&RadDir 84*
KIWA-FM - Sheldon, IA - *BrCabYB 84; TV&RadDir 84*
Kiwanis Magazine - Chicago, IL - *MagIndMarPl 82-83*
Kiwanis Magazine - Indianapolis, IN - *ArtMar 84; BaconPubCkMag 84; MagDir 84; WritMar 84*
Kiwi [Div. of Northern Mercantile Inc.] - Hialeah, FL - *AvMarPl 83*
KIWR - Council Bluffs, IA - *BrCabYB 84*
KIWW-FM - Harlingen, TX - *BrCabYB 84; TV&RadDir 84*
KIXC - Quanah, TX - *BrCabYB 84; TV&RadDir 84*
KIXC-FM - Quanah, TX - *BrCabYB 84*
KIXE-TV - Redding, CA - *BrCabYB 84; Tel&CabFB 84S; TV&RadDir 84*
KIXI - Seattle, WA - *BrCabYB 84; NatRadPubDir Summer 83, Spring 84; TV&RadDir 84*
KIXI-FM - Seattle, WA - *BrCabYB 84; NatRadPubDir Summer 83, Spring 84; TV&RadDir 84*
KIXK - Denton, TX - *BrCabYB 84*
KIXL - Austin, TX - *BrCabYB 84; NatRadPubDir Summer 83, Spring 84; TV&RadDir 84*
KIXS-FM - Killeen, TX - *BrCabYB 84; TV&RadDir 84*
KIXV-FM - Brady, TX - *BrCabYB 84; TV&RadDir 84*
KIXX-FM - Watertown, SD - *BrCabYB 84; TV&RadDir 84*
KIXY-FM - San Angelo, TX - *BrCabYB 84; NatRadPubDir Summer 83, Spring 84; TV&RadDir 84*
KIXZ - Amarillo, TX - *BrCabYB 84; NatRadPubDir Summer 83, Spring 84; TV&RadDir 84*
Kizer Creative Services, Dennis King - New York, NY - *HBIndAd&MS 82-83*
KIZN - New Plymouth, ID - *BrCabYB 84*
KIZZ-FM - Minot, ND - *BrCabYB 84; NatRadPubDir Summer 83, Spring 84; TV&RadDir 84*

KJAA-TV - Lubbock, TX - *BrCabYB 84; DirUSTelSta 83; TelAl 84; Tel&CabFB 84S; TV&RadDir 84*
KJAC-TV - Abilene, TX - *TelAl 83*
KJAC-TV - Beaumont, TX - *DirUSTelSta 83*
KJAC-TV - Port Arthur, TX - *BrCabYB 84; TelAl 84; Tel&CabFB 84S; TV&RadDir 84*
KJAD - Lihue, HI - *BrCabYB 84*
KJAE-FM - Leesville, LA - *BrCabYB 84; TV&RadDir 84*
KJAK-FM - Lubbock, TX - *TV&RadDir 84*
KJAK-FM - Slaton, TX - *BrCabYB 84*
KJAM - Madison, SD - *BrCabYB 84; TV&RadDir 84*
KJAM-FM - Madison, SD - *BrCabYB 84; TV&RadDir 84*
KJAN - Atlantic, IA - *BrCabYB 84; TV&RadDir 84*
KJAN-FM - Atlantic, IA - *BrCabYB 84; TV&RadDir 84*
KJAQ-FM - Gordonville, MO - *BrCabYB 84; TV&RadDir 84*
KJAS - Jackson, MO - *BrCabYB 84; TV&RadDir 84*
KJAV-FM - Alamo, TX - *BrCabYB 84; TV&RadDir 84*
KJAX-FM - Stockton, CA - *BrCabYB 84; NatRadPubDir Summer 83, Spring 84; TV&RadDir 84*
KJAY - Sacramento, CA - *BrCabYB 84; NatRadPubDir Summer 83*
KJAY - West Sacramento, CA - *NatRadPubDir Spring 84; TV&RadDir 84*
KJAZ-FM - Alameda, CA - *BrCabYB 84; TV&RadDir 84*
KJAZ-FM - San Francisco, CA - *NatRadPubDir Summer 83 p.31, Spring 84 p.30*
KJBA - Bethel, AK - *BrCabYB 84*
KJBC - Midland, TX - *BrCabYB 84; TV&RadDir 84*
KJBQ-FM - Jennings, LA - *BrCabYB 84*
KJBQ-FM - Jonesboro, LA - *TV&RadDir 84*
KJBR-FM - Jonesboro, AR - *BrCabYB 84; TV&RadDir 84*
KJBS-FM - Bastrop, LA - *BrCabYB 84; TV&RadDir 84*
KJCF - Festus, MO - *BrCabYB 84; TV&RadDir 84*
KJCH - Cleveland, TX - *BrCabYB 84; TV&RadDir 84*
KJCK - Junction City, KS - *BrCabYB 84; TV&RadDir 84*
KJCK-FM - Junction City, KS - *BrCabYB 84; TV&RadDir 84*
KJCO-FM - Yuma, CO - *BrCabYB 84; TV&RadDir 84*
KJCS-FM - Nacogdoches, TX - *BrCabYB 84; TV&RadDir 84*
KJCT-TV - Grand Junction, CO - *BrCabYB 84; DirUSTelSta 83; TelAl 83, 84; Tel&CabFB 84S; TV&RadDir 84*
KJCY - Mountain Home, ID - *BrCabYB 84*
KJDY - John Day, OR - *BrCabYB 84; TV&RadDir 84*
KJEF - Jennings, LA - *BrCabYB 84; TV&RadDir 84*
KJEF-FM - Jennings, LA - *BrCabYB 84; TV&RadDir 84*
KJEL - Lebanon, MO - *BrCabYB 84; TV&RadDir 84*
KJEL-FM - Lebanon, MO - *BrCabYB 84; TV&RadDir 84*
Kjellbert & Sons Inc. - Wheaton, IL - *BoPubDir 4, 5*
KJEM - Bentonville, AR - *BrCabYB 84; TV&RadDir 84*
KJEO-TV - Fresno, CA - *BrCabYB 84; DirUSTelSta 83; TelAl 83, 84; Tel&CabFB 84S; TV&RadDir 84*
KJET - Beaumont, TX - *NatRadPubDir Summer 83*
KJET - Seattle, WA - *BrCabYB 84; NatRadPubDir Summer 83, Spring 84; TV&RadDir 84*
KJEZ-FM - Poplar Bluff, MO - *BrCabYB 84; TV&RadDir 84*
KJFM - Oceanside, CA - *BrCabYB 84*
KJFP - Yakutat, AK - *BrCabYB 84*
KJHK-FM - Lawrence, KS - *BrCabYB 84; NatRadPubDir Summer 83, Spring 84; TV&RadDir 84*
KJIB-FM - Portland, OR - *BrCabYB 84; NatRadPubDir Summer 83, Spring 84; TV&RadDir 84*
KJIC-FM - Pasadena, TX - *BrCabYB 84; TV&RadDir 84*
KJIL-FM - Bethany, OK - *BrCabYB 84*
KJIL-FM - Oklahoma City, OK - *NatRadPubDir Summer 83, Spring 84; TV&RadDir 84*
KJIM - Dallas, TX - *NatRadPubDir Summer 83, Spring 84 p.237*
KJIM - Ft. Worth, TX - *BrCabYB 84; TV&RadDir 84*
KJIN - Houma, LA - *BrCabYB 84; TV&RadDir 84*
KJIN - Thibodaux, LA - *NatRadPubDir Summer 83 p.110, Spring 84*
KJJB - Eunice, LA - *BrCabYB 84*
KJJC - Osceola, IA - *BrCabYB 84*
KJJJ - Phoenix, AZ - *BrCabYB 84; NatRadPubDir Summer 83, Spring 84; TV&RadDir 84*
KJJJ-FM - Phoenix, AZ - *TV&RadDir 84*
KJJK - Fergus Falls, MN - *BrCabYB 84*
KJJO-FM - Hopkins, MN - *TV&RadDir 84*
KJJO-FM - Minneapolis, MN - *NatRadPubDir Summer 83 p.134, Spring 84 p.134*
KJJO-FM - St. Louis Park, MN - *BrCabYB 84*
KJJR - Whitefish, MT - *BrCabYB 84; TV&RadDir 84*
KJJT - Odessa, TX - *BrCabYB 84; TV&RadDir 84*
KJJY-FM - Ankeny, IA - *BrCabYB 84; TV&RadDir 84*
KJJZ - Denver, CO - *BrCabYB 84; NatRadPubDir Summer 83 p.40, Spring 84 p.40*
KJJZ - Englewood, CO - *TV&RadDir 84*
KJKK - Murfreesboro, AR - *BrCabYB 84*
KJLA - Kansas City, MO - *BrCabYB 84; NatRadPubDir Summer 83, Spring 84; TV&RadDir 84*
KJLC - Lewiston, ID - *BrCabYB 84*
KJLH-FM - Compton, CA - *BrCabYB 84*
KJLH-FM - Los Angeles, CA - *TV&RadDir 84*
KJLS-FM - Hays, KS - *BrCabYB 84; TV&RadDir 84*
KJLT - North Platte, NE - *BrCabYB 84*
KJLY - Blue Earth, MN - *BrCabYB 84*
KJMB-FM - Blythe, CA - *BrCabYB 84; TV&RadDir 84*
KJMD-FM - Aberdeen, WA - *BrCabYB 84; TV&RadDir 84*
KJMM - Needles, CA - *BrCabYB 84*
KJMO-FM - Jefferson City, MO - *BrCabYB 84; TV&RadDir 84*
KJNA-FM - Jena, LA - *BrCabYB 84; TV&RadDir 84*
KJNE-FM - Hillsboro, TX - *BrCabYB 84*
KJNO - Juneau, AK - *BrCabYB 84; NatRadPubDir Summer 83, Spring 84; TV&RadDir 84*
KJNP - North Pole, AK - *BrCabYB 84; TV&RadDir 84*
KJNP-FM - North Pole, AK - *BrCabYB 84; TV&RadDir 84*
KJNP-TV - North Pole, AK - *BrCabYB 84; DirUSTelSta 83; Tel&CabFB 84S*
KJOE - Shreveport, LA - *BrCabYB 84; NatRadPubDir Summer 83, Spring 84; TV&RadDir 84*
KJOI-FM - Beverly Hills, CA - *TV&RadDir 84*
KJOI-FM - Los Angeles, CA - *BrCabYB 84; NatRadPubDir Summer 83 p.21, Spring 84 p.21*
KJOJ-FM - Conroe, TX - *BrCabYB 84; TV&RadDir 84*
KJOK-FM - Yuma, AZ - *BrCabYB 84; TV&RadDir 84*
KJOL - Grand Junction, CO - *BrCabYB 84*
KJON - Booneville, AR - *BrCabYB 84*
KJOP - Lemoore, CA - *BrCabYB 84; TV&RadDir 84*
Kjos Music Co., Neil A. - San Diego, CA - *BillIntBG 83-84*
KJOT-FM - Boise, ID - *BrCabYB 84; NatRadPubDir Summer 83, Spring 84; TV&RadDir 84*
KJOY - Stockton, CA - *BrCabYB 84; NatRadPubDir Summer 83, Spring 84; TV&RadDir 84*
KJOY-FM - Tucson, AZ - *NatRadPubDir Spring 84*
KJOY-FM - San Diego, CA - *TV&RadDir 84*
KJPW - Waynesville, MO - *BrCabYB 84; TV&RadDir 84*
KJPW-FM - Waynesville, MO - *BrCabYB 84; TV&RadDir 84*
KJQN - Ogden, UT - *BrCabYB 84; TV&RadDir 84*
KJQN-FM - Ogden, UT - *BrCabYB 84*
KJQY-FM - San Diego, CA - *BrCabYB 84; NatRadPubDir Summer 83, Spring 84*
KJR - Seattle, WA - *BrCabYB 84; NatRadPubDir Summer 83, Spring 84; TV&RadDir 84*
KJRB - Spokane, WA - *BrCabYB 84; NatRadPubDir Summer 83, Spring 84; TV&RadDir 84*
KJRG - Newton, KS - *BrCabYB 84; TV&RadDir 84*
KJRH-TV - Tulsa, OK - *BrCabYB 84; DirUSTelSta 83; LitMarPl 83, 84; TelAl 83, 84; Tel&CabFB 84S; TV&RadDir 84*
KJSA - Mineral Wells, TX - *BrCabYB 84*
KJSK - Columbus, NE - *BrCabYB 84; TV&RadDir 84*
KJSN-FM - Klamath Falls, OR - *BrCabYB 84; TV&RadDir 84*
KJTA - Pharr, TX - *BrCabYB 84*
KJTV - Amarillo, TX - *BrCabYB 84; Tel&CabFB 84S*
KJUD - Juneau, AL - *BrCabYB 84; Tel&CabFB 84S*
KJUG-FM - Tulare, CA - *BrCabYB 84; TV&RadDir 84*
KJUN - Puyallup, WA - *BrCabYB 84*
KJVC-FM - Mansfield, LA - *BrCabYB 84; TV&RadDir 84*
KJWH - Camden, AR - *BrCabYB 84; TV&RadDir 84*
KJYE-FM - Honolulu, HI - *NatRadPubDir Summer 83*
KJYK-FM - Tucson, AZ - *BrCabYB 84; NatRadPubDir Summer 83; TV&RadDir 84*
KJYO-FM - Oklahoma City, OK - *BrCabYB 84; NatRadPubDir Summer 83, Spring 84; TV&RadDir 84*
KJZZ - Bellevue, WA - *BrCabYB 84; TV&RadDir 84*

KKAA - Aberdeen, SD - *BrCabYB 84; NatRadPubDir Summer 83, Spring 84; TV&RadDir 84*
KKAF - Arizona City, AZ - *BrCabYB 84*
KKAI - Honolulu, HI - *NatRadPubDir Summer 83*
KKAJ-FM - Ardmore, OK - *BrCabYB 84; TV&RadDir 84*
KKAL - Arroyo Grande, CA - *BrCabYB 84; TV&RadDir 84*
KKAL - San Luis Obispo, CA - *NatRadPubDir Spring 84 p.32*
KKAM - Lubbock, TX - *TV&RadDir 84*
KKAN - Phillipsburg, KS - *BrCabYB 84; TV&RadDir 84*
KKAQ - Thief River Falls, MN - *BrCabYB 84*
KKAS - Silsbee, TX - *BrCabYB 84; TV&RadDir 84*
KKAY - Donaldsonville, LA - *TV&RadDir 84*
KKAY - White Castle, LA - *BrCabYB 84*
KKAZ-FM - Cheyenne, WY - *BrCabYB 84; NatRadPubDir Summer 83, Spring 84; TV&RadDir 84*
KKB/Direct [Subs. of Kaiser Kuhn Bennett & Sharp Inc.] - Atlanta, GA - *DirMarMP 83*
KKBB - Denver, CO - *BrCabYB 84; NatRadPubDir Summer 83, Spring 84; TV&RadDir 84*
KKBC-FM - Carson City, NV - *BrCabYB 84; TV&RadDir 84*
KKBC-FM - Reno, NV - *NatRadPubDir Summer 83*
KKBG-FM - Hilo, HI - *BrCabYB 84; TV&RadDir 84*
KKBI - Broken Bow, OK - *BrCabYB 84*
KKBJ - Bemidji, MN - *BrCabYB 84; TV&RadDir 84*
KKBK - Aztec, NM - *BrCabYB 84; TV&RadDir 84*
KKBL-FM - Monett, MO - *BrCabYB 84; TV&RadDir 84*
KKBQ - Houston, TX - *BrCabYB 84; NatRadPubDir Spring 84; TV&RadDir 84*
KKBQ-FM - Houston, TX - *NatRadPubDir Summer 83, Spring 84; TV&RadDir 84*
KKBQ-FM - Pasadena, TX - *BrCabYB 84*
KKBS - Guyman, OK - *BrCabYB 84*
KKBZ - Santa Paula, CA - *BrCabYB 84*
KKBZ - Ventura, CA - *NatRadPubDir Summer 83, Spring 84 p.34; TV&RadDir 84*
KKBZ-FM - Santa Paula, CA - *BrCabYB 84*
KKBZ-FM - Ventura, CA - *NatRadPubDir Summer 83, Spring 84 p.34; TV&RadDir 84*
KKCA-FM - Fulton, MO - *BrCabYB 84; TV&RadDir 84*
KKCC - Clinton, OK - *BrCabYB 84; TV&RadDir 84*
KKCC-FM - Clinton, OK - *BrCabYB 84; TV&RadDir 84*
KKCI - Kansas City, MO - *NatRadPubDir Spring 84*
KKCI - Liberty, MO - *BrCabYB 84; TV&RadDir 84*
KKCI-FM - Kansas City, MO - *NatRadPubDir Summer 83, Spring 84; TV&RadDir 84*
KKCI-FM - Liberty, MO - *BrCabYB 84*
KKCK-FM - Marshall, MN - *BrCabYB 84; TV&RadDir 84*
KKCM - Waite Park, MN - *BrCabYB 84*
KKCS-FM - Colorado Springs, CO - *BrCabYB 84; NatRadPubDir Summer 83, Spring 84; TV&RadDir 84*
KKDA - Dallas, TX - *NatRadPubDir Summer 83 p.236, Spring 84 p.237*
KKDA - Grand Prairie, TX - *BrCabYB 84; TV&RadDir 84*
KKDA-FM - Dallas, TX - *BrCabYB 84; NatRadPubDir Summer 83 p.236, Spring 84 p.237*
KKDA-FM - Grand Prairie, TX - *TV&RadDir 84*
KKDI-FM - Sheridan, AR - *BrCabYB 84*
KKDJ - Fresno, CA - *BrCabYB 84*
KKDY - West Plains, MO - *BrCabYB 84*
KKEB - Belle Fourche, SD - *BrCabYB 84*
KKED-FM - Corpus Christi, TX - *BrCabYB 84*
KKEE-FM - Alamogordo, NM - *BrCabYB 84; TV&RadDir 84*
KKEG-FM - Fayetteville, AR - *BrCabYB 84; TV&RadDir 84*
KKEO - Phoenix, AZ - *TV&RadDir 84*
KKER - Spokane, WA - *NatRadPubDir Spring 84*
KKEY - Portland, OR - *BrCabYB 84; NatRadPubDir Summer 83, Spring 84; TV&RadDir 84*
KKEZ-FM - Ft. Dodge, IA - *BrCabYB 84; TV&RadDir 84*
KKFM-FM - Colorado Springs, CO - *BrCabYB 84; NatRadPubDir Summer 83, Spring 84; TV&RadDir 84*
KKFX - Seattle, WA - *BrCabYB 84; NatRadPubDir Summer 83, Spring 84; TV&RadDir 84*
KKGO-FM - Los Angeles, CA - *BrCabYB 84; NatRadPubDir Summer 83, Spring 84; TV&RadDir 84*
KKHI - San Francisco, CA - *BrCabYB 84; NatRadPubDir Summer 83, Spring 84; TV&RadDir 84*
KKHI-FM - San Francisco, CA - *BrCabYB 84; NatRadPubDir Summer 83, Spring 84; TV&RadDir 84*
KKHJ-FM - Bethlehem, SD - *TV&RadDir 84*
KKHR-FM - Los Angeles, CA - *BrCabYB 84; NatRadPubDir Spring 84*
KKIC - Boise, ID - *BrCabYB 84; NatRadPubDir Summer 83, Spring 84; TV&RadDir 84*
KKID - Sallisaw, OK - *BrCabYB 84; TV&RadDir 84*
KKIK - Big Spring, TX - *BrCabYB 84; TV&RadDir 84*
KKIM - Albuquerque, NM - *BrCabYB 84; NatRadPubDir Summer 83, Spring 84; TV&RadDir 84*
KKIN - Aitkin, MN - *BrCabYB 84; TV&RadDir 84*
KKIO - Santa Barbara, CA - *NatRadPubDir Summer 83*
KKIQ-FM - Livermore, CA - *BrCabYB 84; TV&RadDir 84*
KKIQ-FM - Los Angeles, CA - *NatRadPubDir Summer 83 p.21, Spring 84 p.30*
KKIS - Pittsburg, CA - *BrCabYB 84*
KKIS - Walnut Creek, CA - *TV&RadDir 84*
KKIT - Taos, NM - *BrCabYB 84; TV&RadDir 84*
KKIX - Fayetteville, AR - *BrCabYB 84*
KKJO - St. Joseph, MO - *BrCabYB 84; NatRadPubDir Summer 83, Spring 84; TV&RadDir 84*
KKJY-FM - Albuquerque, NM - *BrCabYB 84; NatRadPubDir Summer 83, Spring 84; TV&RadDir 84*
KKKC - Anoka, MN - *BrCabYB 84; TV&RadDir 84*
KKKC - Minneapolis, MN - *NatRadPubDir Summer 83 p.134*
KKKK-FM - Midland, TX - *NatRadPubDir Summer 83, Spring 84; TV&RadDir 84*
KKKK-FM - Odessa, TX - *BrCabYB 84*
KKKX-FM - Ottawa, KS - *BrCabYB 84; TV&RadDir 84*
KKLB - Chubbuck, ID - *BrCabYB 84*
KKLR-FM - Edmond, OK - *BrCabYB 84; NatRadPubDir Summer 83, Spring 84; TV&RadDir 84*
KKLS - Bethlehem, SD - *TV&RadDir 84*
KKLS - Rapid City, SD - *BrCabYB 84*
KKLS-FM - Rapid City, SD - *BrCabYB 84*
KKLT-FM - Phoenix, AZ - *BrCabYB 84; NatRadPubDir Summer 83, Spring 84; TV&RadDir 84*
KKLV-FM - Anchorage, AK - *BrCabYB 84; NatRadPubDir Summer 83, Spring 84; TV&RadDir 84*
KKMC - Gonzales, CA - *BrCabYB 84*
KKMG-FM - Pueblo West, CO - *BrCabYB 84; NatRadPubDir Spring 84*
KKNG-FM - Oklahoma City, OK - *BrCabYB 84; NatRadPubDir Summer 83, Spring 84; TV&RadDir 84*
KKNU-FM - Fresno, CA - *BrCabYB 84; NatRadPubDir Summer 83, Spring 84; TV&RadDir 84*
KKNW - Mountlake Terrace, WA - *BrCabYB 84; TV&RadDir 84*
KKNX - Huntsville, TX - *BrCabYB 84*
KKOA - Minot, ND - *BrCabYB 84; NatRadPubDir Summer 83, Spring 84; TV&RadDir 84*
KKOJ - Jackson, MN - *BrCabYB 84; TV&RadDir 84*
KKOK-FM - Morris, MN - *BrCabYB 84; TV&RadDir 84*
KKOL - El Paso, TX - *TV&RadDir 84*
KKON - Kealakekua, HI - *BrCabYB 84; TV&RadDir 84*
KKOS-FM - Carlsbad, CA - *BrCabYB 84; TV&RadDir 84*
KKOW - Pittsburg, KS - *BrCabYB 84; TV&RadDir 84*
KKOY - Chanute, KS - *BrCabYB 84; TV&RadDir 84*
KKOZ - Ava, MO - *TV&RadDir 84*
KKOZ-FM - Billings, MT - *NatRadPubDir Summer 83*
KKPL-FM - Opportunity, WA - *BrCabYB 84*
KKPL-FM - Spokane, WA - *TV&RadDir 84*
KKQT-FM - Rexburg, ID - *BrCabYB 84; TV&RadDir 84*
KKQV-FM - Wichita Falls, TX - *BrCabYB 84; NatRadPubDir Summer 83, Spring 84; TV&RadDir 84*
KKRB - Klamath Falls, OR - *BrCabYB 84*
KKRC-FM - Sioux Falls, SD - *BrCabYB 84; TV&RadDir 84*
KKRD-FM - Wichita, KS - *BrCabYB 84; NatRadPubDir Summer 83, Spring 84; TV&RadDir 84*
KKRK-FM - Douglas, AZ - *BrCabYB 84; TV&RadDir 84*
KKRL-FM - Carroll, IA - *BrCabYB 84; TV&RadDir 84*
KKRQ-FM - Iowa City, IA - *BrCabYB 84; TV&RadDir 84*
KKRZ-FM - Portland, OR - *NatRadPubDir Spring 84*
KKRZ-FM - Sioux Falls, SD - *NatRadPubDir Summer 83, Spring 84*
KKSD - Gregory, SD - *BrCabYB 84*
KKSG - Carlsbad, NM - *BrCabYB 84; Tel&CabFB 84S*

KKSI - Mt. Pleasant, IA - *BrCabYB 84; TV&RadDir 84*
KKSN - Portland, OR - *TV&RadDir 84*
KKSN - Vancouver, WA - *BrCabYB 84*
KKSS - Minneapolis, MN - *NatRadPubDir Summer 83 p.134, Spring 84 p.134*
KKSS - New Brighton, MN - *TV&RadDir 84*
KKSS - Richfield, MN - *BrCabYB 84*
KKTV-TV - Colorado Springs, CO - *BrCabYB 84; DirUSTelSta 83; TelAl 83, 84; Tel&CabFB 84S; TV&RadDir 84*
KKTX - Kilgore, TX - *BrCabYB 84; TV&RadDir 84*
KKUA - Honolulu, HI - *BrCabYB 84; NatRadPubDir Summer 83, Spring 84; TV&RadDir 84*
KKUB - Brownfield, TX - *BrCabYB 84; TV&RadDir 84*
KKUP-FM - Cupertino, CA - *BrCabYB 84; TV&RadDir 84*
KKUS - San Luis Obispo, CA - *BrCabYB 84*
KKUZ-FM - Joplin, MO - *BrCabYB 84; TV&RadDir 84*
KKVC - Valley City, ND - *BrCabYB 84*
KKWB-FM - Breckenridge, MN - *BrCabYB 84*
KKWB-FM - Wahpeton, ND - *TV&RadDir 84*
KKWS - Wadena, MN - *BrCabYB 84*
KKWZ-FM - Richfield, UT - *BrCabYB 84; TV&RadDir 84*
KKXK-FM - Montrose, CO - *BrCabYB 84; TV&RadDir 84*
KKXL - Grand Forks, ND - *BrCabYB 84; NatRadPubDir Summer 83, Spring 84; TV&RadDir 84*
KKXL-FM - Grand Forks, ND - *BrCabYB 84; TV&RadDir 84*
KKXX-FM - Bakersfield, CA - *BrCabYB 84; NatRadPubDir Summer 83, Spring 84; TV&RadDir 84*
KKYA - Yankton, SD - *BrCabYB 84*
KKYK-FM - Little Rock, AR - *BrCabYB 84; NatRadPubDir Summer 83, Spring 84; TV&RadDir 84*
KKYL-FM - Brownwood, TX - *BrCabYB 84*
KKYN - Plainview, TX - *BrCabYB 84; TV&RadDir 84*
KKYR - Marshall, TX - *BrCabYB 84; TV&RadDir 84*
KKYS-FM - Hanford, CA - *BrCabYB 84; TV&RadDir 84*
KKYX - San Antonio, TX - *BrCabYB 84; NatRadPubDir Summer 83, Spring 84; TV&RadDir 84*
KKZZ - Lancaster, CA - *BrCabYB 84; NatRadPubDir Summer 83; TV&RadDir 84*
KKZZ-FM - Lancaster, CA - *NatRadPubDir Spring 84*
KLAA - Monroe, LA - *TelAl 83, 84*
Klaassen & Associates - New Orleans, LA - *MicrocomMPl 83, 84; WhoWMicrocom 83*
KLAC - Los Angeles, CA - *BrCabYB 84; NatRadPubDir Summer 83 p.21, Spring 84 p.21; TV&RadDir 84*
KLAD - Klamath Falls, OR - *BrCabYB 84; TV&RadDir 84*
KLAF - Murray, UT - *BrCabYB 84*
KLAK - Denver, CO - *NatRadPubDir Summer 83, Spring 84; TV&RadDir 84*
KLAK - Lakewood, CO - *BrCabYB 84*
KLAM - Cordova, AK - *BrCabYB 84; TV&RadDir 84*
Klamath Cable Television [of D & B Communications Inc.] - Klamath, CA - *BrCabYB 84; Tel&CabFB 84C*
Klamath Falls Herald & News - Klamath Falls, OR - *BaconPubCkNews 84; NewsDir 84*
KLAN-FM - Glasgow, MT - *BrCabYB 84*
Klanak Press '74 - West Vancouver, BC, Canada - *BoPubDir 4, 5*
Klang, Joan - Irvine, CA - *LitMarPl 83, 84*
Klapper Associates Inc., Stanford - Hato Rey, PR - *IntDirMarRes 83*
KLAQ-FM - El Paso, TX - *BrCabYB 84; LitMarPl 84; NatRadPubDir Spring 84; TV&RadDir 84*
KLAR - Laredo, TX - *BrCabYB 84; TV&RadDir 84*
KLAS-TV - Las Vegas, NV - *BrCabYB 84; DirUSTelSta 83; TelAl 83, 84; Tel&CabFB 84S; TV&RadDir 84*
Klass Advertising Agency - Atlanta, GA - *StaDirAdAg 2-84*
Klassen & Foster Publications - Barriere, BC, Canada - *BoPubDir 4, 5*
KLAT - Houston, TX - *BrCabYB 84; NatRadPubDir Summer 83, Spring 84; TV&RadDir 84*
Klausner International Literary Agency Inc., Bertha - New York, NY - *LitMarPl 83, 84*
KLAV - Las Vegas, NV - *BrCabYB 84; TV&RadDir 84*
Klavier Record Co. - Sun Valley, CA - *BillIntBG 83-84*
KLAW-FM - Lawton, OK - *BrCabYB 84; TV&RadDir 84*
KLAX-TV - Alexandria, LA - *BrCabYB 84; TelAl 84; Tel&CabFB 84S*
KLAY - Tacoma, WA - *BrCabYB 84; NatRadPubDir Summer 83, Spring 84*
KLAZ-FM - Little Rock, AR - *BrCabYB 84; NatRadPubDir Summer 83, Spring 84; TV&RadDir 84*
KLBA - Albia, IA - *BrCabYB 84; TV&RadDir 84*
KLBB - Minneapolis, MN - *NatRadPubDir Spring 84 p.134*
KLBB - St. Paul, MN - *BrCabYB 84; TV&RadDir 84*
KLBC - Durant, OK - *BrCabYB 84*
KLBJ - Austin, TX - *BrCabYB 84; NatRadPubDir Summer 83, Spring 84; TV&RadDir 84*
KLBJ-FM - Austin, TX - *BrCabYB 84; NatRadPubDir Summer 83, Spring 84; TV&RadDir 84*
KLBK-FM - Lubbock, TX - *TV&RadDir 84*
KLBK-TV - Lubbock, TX - *BrCabYB 84; DirUSTelSta 83; TelAl 83, 84; Tel&CabFB 84S; TV&RadDir 84*
KLBM - La Grande, OR - *BrCabYB 84; TV&RadDir 84*
KLBM-FM - La Grande, OR - *BrCabYB 84; TV&RadDir 84*
KLBO-FM - El Dorado, AR - *TV&RadDir 84*
KLBQ - El Dorado, AR - *BrCabYB 84*
KLBS - Los Banos, CA - *BrCabYB 84; TV&RadDir 84*
KLCB - Libby, MT - *BrCabYB 84; TV&RadDir 84*
KLCC-FM - Eugene, OR - *BrCabYB 84; NatRadPubDir Summer 83, Spring 84; TV&RadDir 84*
KLCD-FM - Decorah, IA - *BrCabYB 84*
KLCD-FM - Chester, MN - *TV&RadDir 84*
KLCJ-FM - Bayard, NM - *BrCabYB 84*
KLCJ-FM - Silver City, NM - *TV&RadDir 84*
KLCK - Goldendale, WA - *BrCabYB 84*
KLCL - Lake Charles, LA - *BrCabYB 84; NatRadPubDir Summer 83, Spring 84; TV&RadDir 84*
KLCL-FM - Lake Charles, LA - *BrCabYB 84*
KLCM-FM - Lewistown, MT - *BrCabYB 84; TV&RadDir 84*
KLCN - Blytheville, AR - *BrCabYB 84; TV&RadDir 84*
KLCO - Branson, MO - *BrCabYB 84*
KLCQ-FM - Monroe City, MO - *BrCabYB 84; TV&RadDir 84*
KLCR-FM - Center, TX - *BrCabYB 84; TV&RadDir 84*
KLCS-TV - Los Angeles, CA - *BrCabYB 84; Tel&CabFB 84S; TV&RadDir 84*
KLCY - Salt Lake City, UT - *BrCabYB 84*
KLDH - Topeka, KS - *BrCabYB 84; Tel&CabFB 84S*
KLDN-FM - Eldon, MO - *BrCabYB 84; TV&RadDir 84*
KLDR - Denver, CO - *BrCabYB 84*
KLEA - Lovington, NM - *BrCabYB 84; TV&RadDir 84*
KLEA-FM - Lovington, NM - *BrCabYB 84; TV&RadDir 84*
KLEB - Golden Meadow, LA - *BrCabYB 84*
KLEE - Ottumwa, IA - *BrCabYB 84; TV&RadDir 84*
KLEE-FM - Ottumwa, IA - *BrCabYB 84; TV&RadDir 84*
Kleeberg Associates Inc., Fred M. - New York, NY - *LitMarPl 83, 84*
Kleen Strike Manufacturing Co. Inc. - Columbia, MD - *DirInfWP 82*
Kleer Kable Co. [of Tele-Media Corp.] - Mt. Morris, PA - *BrCabYB 84*
Kleer Kable Co. [of Tele-Media Corp.] - Waynesburg, PA - *BrCabYB 84*
Kleer-Vu Cable TV Inc. [of South Bevins] - Bell County, KY - *Tel&CabFB 84C*
KLEF-FM - Houston, TX - *BrCabYB 84; NatRadPubDir Summer 83, Spring 84; TV&RadDir 84*
KLEH - Anamosa, IA - *BrCabYB 84*
KLEI - Kailua, HI - *BrCabYB 84; TV&RadDir 84*
Kleid Co. Inc., The - New York, NY - *LitMarPl 83, 84*
Kleiman Co. Inc., The Harlan - Los Angeles, CA - *Tel&CabFB 84C*
Klein Advertising Inc. - Beverly Hills, CA - *StaDirAdAg 2-84*
Klein & - Los Angeles, CA - *HBIndAd&MS 82-83; Tel&CabFB 84C*
Klein & Associates, Anne - Mt. Laurel, NJ - *DirPRFirms 83*
Klein & Co., Ted - New York, NY - *DirPRFirms 83*
Klein Associates, Charlotte C. - New York, NY - *DirPRFirms 83*
Klein Associates Inc., Murray - Westbury, NY - *ArtMar 84*
Klein Communications Inc., Wayne - Bloomfield Hills, MI - *DirPRFirms 83*
Klein Communications, J. Edward - New York, NY - *DirPRFirms 83*
Klein Co. Ltd., Walter J. - Charlotte, NC - *AvMarPl 83; ProGuPRSer 4; TelAl 83, 84; Tel&CabFB 84C*

Klein Newsletter on Computer Graphics, S. - Sudbury, MA - *BaconPubCkMag 84; DirOnDB Spring 84*
Klein Newsletter on Computer Graphics, S. [of NewsNet Inc.] - Bryn Mawr, PA - *DataDirOnSer 84*
Klein Publications, B. - Coral Springs, FL - *ArtMar 84; LitMarPl 83, 84; WritMar 84*
Klein/Ray Broadcasting - Riverside, CA - *BrCabYB 84*
Klein/Richardson - Beverly Hills, CA - *AdAge 3-28-84; StaDirAdAg 2-84*
Klein-Sieb Advertising & Public Relations Inc. - Atlanta, GA - *StaDirAdAg 2-84*
Kleiner Music Enterprises, Sid - Naples, FL - *BillIntBG 83-84*
Kleinfeld Inc., Leonard F. - Woodside, NY - *AvMarPl 83*
Kleinschmidt Div. [of SCM Corp.] - Deerfield, IL - *DataDirSup 7-83*
Kleitz Associates Inc., George - Wheaton, IL - *StaDirAdAg 2-84*
KLEL-FM - San Jose, CA - *BrCabYB 84; TV&RadDir 84*
KLEM - Le Mars, IA - *BrCabYB 84; TV&RadDir 84*
Klemtner Advertising - New York, NY - *AdAge 3-28-84; BrCabYB 84; StaDirAdAg 2-84*
KLEO - Caulksville, AR - *BrCabYB 84*
KLEO - Wichita, KS - *BrCabYB 84; NatRadPubDir Spring 84; TV&RadDir 84*
KLEP - Newark, AR - *BrCabYB 84; Tel&CabFB 84S*
Klepper Associates Inc., Michael - New York, NY - *DirPRFirms 83*
KLER - Orofino, ID - *BrCabYB 84; TV&RadDir 84*
KLER-FM - Orofino, ID - *BrCabYB 84; TV&RadDir 84*
Kler View Cable Co. - Anadarko, OK - *BrCabYB 84; Tel&CabFB 84C*
KLEU - Waterloo, IA - *BrCabYB 84; NatRadPubDir Summer 83, Spring 84; TV&RadDir 84*
Kleven Communications Group - Sturgis, SD - *BrCabYB 84*
Klevens Publications Inc. - Littlerock, CA - *BoPubDir 4, 5*
KLEW-TV - Lewiston, ID - *BrCabYB 84; DirUSTelSta 83; TelAl 83, 84; Tel&CabFB 84S; TV&RadDir 84*
KLEX - Lexington, MO - *BrCabYB 84; TV&RadDir 84*
KLEY - Wellington, KS - *BrCabYB 84; TV&RadDir 84*
KLFA - King City, CA - *BrCabYB 84*
KLFB - Lubbock, TX - *BrCabYB 84; NatRadPubDir Summer 83, Spring 84; TV&RadDir 84*
KLFD - Litchfield, MN - *BrCabYB 84; TV&RadDir 84*
KLFD-FM - Litchfield, NM - *BrCabYB 84*
KLFF - Glendale, AZ - *BrCabYB 84*
KLFF - Phoenix, AZ - *NatRadPubDir Summer 83, Spring 84; TV&RadDir 84*
KLFJ - Springfield, MO - *BrCabYB 84; TV&RadDir 84*
KLFM - Great Falls, MT - *BrCabYB 84*
KLFQ - Lyons, KS - *BrCabYB 84*
KLFY-TV - Lafayette, LA - *BrCabYB 84; DirUSTelSta 83; TelAl 83, 84; Tel&CabFB 84S; TV&RadDir 84*
KLG Advertising [Div. of Gladney Communications Ltd.] - New York, NY - *StaDirAdAg 2-84*
KLGA - Algona, IA - *BrCabYB 84; TV&RadDir 84*
KLGA-FM - Algona, IA - *BrCabYB 84; TV&RadDir 84*
KLGM - Buffalo, WY - *BrCabYB 84*
KLGR - Redwood Falls, MN - *BrCabYB 84; TV&RadDir 84*
KLGR-FM - Redwood Falls, MN - *BrCabYB 84; TV&RadDir 84*
KLGT - Breckenridge, CO - *BrCabYB 84*
KLHS-FM - Lewiston, ID - *BrCabYB 84; TV&RadDir 84*
KLHT - Spokane, WA - *NatRadPubDir Spring 84*
KLHT-FM - San Francisco, CA - *NatRadPubDir Spring 84; TV&RadDir 84*
KLIB - Liberal, KS - *TV&RadDir 84*
KLIC - Monroe, LA - *BrCabYB 84; NatRadPubDir Summer 83, Spring 84; TV&RadDir 84*
Klickitat Cable - Mossyrock, WA - *Tel&CabFB 84C*
Klickitat Music - Portland, OR - *BillIntBG 83-84*
KLID - Poplar Bluff, MO - *BrCabYB 84; TV&RadDir 84*
KLIF - Arlington, TX - *TV&RadDir 84*
KLIF - Dallas, TX - *BrCabYB 84*
KLIK - Jefferson City, MO - *BrCabYB 84; TV&RadDir 84*
KLIL-FM - Moreauville, LA - *BrCabYB 84; TV&RadDir 84*
KLIN - Lincoln, NE - *BrCabYB 84; NatRadPubDir Summer 83, Spring 84; TV&RadDir 84*
KLIN-FM - Lincoln, NE - *BrCabYB 84; NatRadPubDir Summer 83, Spring 84; TV&RadDir 84*
Kline & Co. Inc., Charles H. - Fairfield, NJ - *BoPubDir 4, 5; IntDirMarRes 83*
Kline Communications Corp. - Los Angeles, CA - *Tel&CabFB 84C*
Kline, Don - Kinsley, KS - *Tel&CabFB 84C p.1687*
Kline's TV & Two Way - Lewis, KS - *BrCabYB 84*
Kline's TV & 2-Way - Offerie, KS - *BrCabYB 84*
Klinger Inc., Harvey - New York, NY - *LitMarPl 83, 84*
Klingler & Associates - Ocala, FL - *StaDirAdAg 2-84*
Klinski, Dr. Albert R. - Chicago, IL - *LitMag&SmPr 83-84*
KLIP - Fowler, CA - *BrCabYB 84; TV&RadDir 84*
KLIQ - Portland, OR - *BrCabYB 84; NatRadPubDir Summer 83, Spring 84; TV&RadDir 84*
KLIR-FM - Denver, CO - *BrCabYB 84; NatRadPubDir Summer 83, Spring 84; TV&RadDir 84*
KLIS-FM - Palestine, TX - *BrCabYB 84; TV&RadDir 84*
KLIT - Pomona, PA - *TV&RadDir 84*
KLIV - San Jose, CA - *BrCabYB 84; NatRadPubDir Summer 83, Spring 84; TV&RadDir 84*
KLIX - Twin Falls, ID - *BrCabYB 84; TV&RadDir 84*
KLIZ - Brainerd, MN - *BrCabYB 84; TV&RadDir 84*
KLIZ-FM - Brainerd, MN - *BrCabYB 84; TV&RadDir 84*
KLJB - Davenport, IA - *BrCabYB 84*
KLJC-FM - Kansas City, MO - *BrCabYB 84; TV&RadDir 84*
KLKC - Parsons, KS - *BrCabYB 84; TV&RadDir 84*
KLKC-FM - Parsons, KS - *BrCabYB 84; TV&RadDir 84*
KLKE-FM - Del Rio, TX - *BrCabYB 84; TV&RadDir 84*
KLKK-TV - Albuquerque, NM - *TelAl 83*
KLKO - Elko, NV - *BrCabYB 84*
KLKS - Breezy Point, MN - *BrCabYB 84*
KLKT - Incline Village, NV - *BrCabYB 84*
KLLA - Leesville, LA - *BrCabYB 84; TV&RadDir 84*
KLLB - Lompoc, CA - *BrCabYB 84*
KLLB-FM - Portland, OR - *TV&RadDir 84*
KLLH - Quincy, WA - *BrCabYB 84*
KLLK - Willits, CA - *BrCabYB 84*
KLLL - Corpus Christi, TX - *BrCabYB 84; TelAl 83*
KLLL - Lubbock, TX - *BrCabYB 84; NatRadPubDir Summer 83*
KLLL-FM - Lubbock, TX - *BrCabYB 84; NatRadPubDir Summer 83, Spring 84; TV&RadDir 84*
KLLM - Forks, WA - *BrCabYB 84*
KLLN - Newark, AR - *BrCabYB 84*
KLLR - Walker, MN - *BrCabYB 84*
KLLS - San Antonio, TX - *TV&RadDir 84*
KLLS - Terrell Hills, TX - *BrCabYB 84*
KLLS-FM - San Antonio, TX - *BrCabYB 84; TV&RadDir 84*
KLM Royal Dutch Airlines - New York, NY - *MagIndMarPl 82-83*
K.L.M. Telephone Co. - Rich Hill, MO - *TelDir&BG 83-84*
KLMB-TV - Houston, TX - *BrCabYB 84*
KLMC - Leadville, CO - *BrCabYB 84*
KLME-FM - Battle Mountain, NV - *BrCabYB 84; TV&RadDir 84*
KLMG-TV - Longview, TX - *BrCabYB 84; Tel&CabFB 84S*
KLMN-TV - Ft. Smith, AR - *TelAl 83; TV&RadDir 84*
KLMO - Longmont, CO - *BrCabYB 84; TV&RadDir 84*
KLMO-FM - Longmont, CO - *BrCabYB 84; TV&RadDir 84*
KLMR - Lamar, CO - *BrCabYB 84; TV&RadDir 84*
KLMS - Lincoln, NE - *BrCabYB 84; NatRadPubDir Summer 83, Spring 84; TV&RadDir 84*
KLMT-FM - Marlin, TX - *BrCabYB 84; TV&RadDir 84*
KLMX - Clayton, NM - *BrCabYB 84; TV&RadDir 84*
KLNE-TV - Holdrege, NE - *TV&RadDir 84*
KLNE-TV - Lexington, NE - *BrCabYB 84; Tel&CabFB 84S*
KLNG - Council Bluffs, IA - *BrCabYB 84; TV&RadDir 84*
KLNG - Omaha, NE - *NatRadPubDir Summer 83, Spring 84*
KLNI - Pearl City, HI - *BrCabYB 84*
KLNK - Oklahoma City, OK - *BrCabYB 84*
KLNT - Clinton, IA - *BrCabYB 84; TV&RadDir 84*
KLNX - Lufkin, TX - *BrCabYB 84; TV&RadDir 84*
KLO - Ogden, UT - *BrCabYB 84; NatRadPubDir Summer 83, Spring 84; TV&RadDir 84*
KLOA - Ridgecrest, CA - *BrCabYB 84; TV&RadDir 84*
KLOC - Ceres, CA - *BrCabYB 84*
KLOC - Modesto, CA - *TV&RadDir 84*
KLOE - Goodland, KS - *BrCabYB 84; TV&RadDir 84*

KLOE-TV - Goodland, KS - *BrCabYB 84; TelAl 83, 84; Tel&CabFB 84S; TV&RadDir 84*
Kloeti Advertising Agency Ltd. [of Saatchi & Saatchi Compton Worldwide] - Zurich, Switzerland - *StaDirAdAg 2-84*
KLOG - Kelso, WA - *BrCabYB 84; TV&RadDir 84*
KLOH - Pipestone, MN - *BrCabYB 84; TV&RadDir 84*
KLOH-FM - Pipestone, MN - *BrCabYB 84; TV&RadDir 84*
KLOI - Grover City, CA - *BrCabYB 84*
KLOK - San Jose, CA - *BrCabYB 84; NatRadPubDir Summer 83, Spring 84; TV&RadDir 84*
KLOL-FM - Houston, TX - *BrCabYB 84; NatRadPubDir Summer 83, Spring 84; TV&RadDir 84*
KLOM - Lompoc, CA - *BrCabYB 84; TV&RadDir 84*
KLON-FM - Long Beach, CA - *BrCabYB 84; NatRadPubDir Summer 83, Spring 84; TV&RadDir 84*
KLOO - Corvallis, OR - *BrCabYB 84; TV&RadDir 84*
KLOO-FM - Corvallis, OR - *BrCabYB 84; TV&RadDir 84*
Kloppenburg Switzer & Teich Inc. - Milwaukee, WI - *StaDirAdAg 2-84*
KLOQ - Merced, CA - *BrCabYB 84; TV&RadDir 84*
KLOQ-FM - Lyons, KS - *TV&RadDir 84*
KLOR-FM - Ponca City, OK - *BrCabYB 84; NatRadPubDir Summer 83, Spring 84; TV&RadDir 84*
KLOS - Los Angeles, CA - *BrCabYB 84; TV&RadDir 84*
KLOS-FM - Los Angeles, CA - *NatRadPubDir Summer 83, Spring 84; TV&RadDir 84*
Kloster, Henry - Chicago, IL - *LitMarPl 83, 84*
KLOU - Lake Charles, LA - *BrCabYB 84; NatRadPubDir Spring 84; TV&RadDir 84*
KLOV - Loveland, CO - *BrCabYB 84; TV&RadDir 84*
KLOV-FM - Loveland, CO - *BrCabYB 84; TV&RadDir 84*
KLOZ-FM - El Paso, TX - *BrCabYB 84; NatRadPubDir Summer 83, Spring 84; TV&RadDir 84*
KLPA-TV - Alexandria, LA - *BrCabYB 84; Tel&CabFB 84S*
KLPB-TV - Lafayette, LA - *BrCabYB 84; Tel&CabFB 84S*
KLPC-FM - Lompoc, CA - *BrCabYB 84; TV&RadDir 84*
KLPH-TV - Paris, TX - *BrCabYB 84; Tel&CabFB 84S*
KLPI-FM - Ruston, LA - *BrCabYB 84; NatRadPubDir Summer 83, Spring 84; TV&RadDir 84*
KLPL - Lake Providence, LA - *BrCabYB 84; TV&RadDir 84*
KLPL-FM - Lake Providence, LA - *TV&RadDir 84*
KLPQ-FM - Little Rock, AR - *BrCabYB 84; NatRadPubDir Summer 83, Spring 84; TV&RadDir 84*
KLPR - Oklahoma City, OK - *NatRadPubDir Summer 83*
KLPW - Union, MO - *BrCabYB 84; TV&RadDir 84*
KLPW-FM - Union, MO - *BrCabYB 84; TV&RadDir 84*
KLPX-FM - Tucson, AZ - *NatRadPubDir Summer 83, Spring 84; TV&RadDir 84*
KLPX-FM - Tuscon, AZ - *BrCabYB 84*
KLQL - Luverne, MN - *BrCabYB 84*
KLQP - Madison, MN - *BrCabYB 84*
KLQZ - Paragould, AR - *BrCabYB 84*
KLRA - Little Rock, AR - *BrCabYB 84; NatRadPubDir Summer 83, Spring 84; TV&RadDir 84*
KLRB-FM - Carmel, CA - *TV&RadDir 84*
KLRB-FM - Salinas, CA - *NatRadPubDir Summer 83 p.27*
KLRC - Siloam Springs, AR - *BrCabYB 84*
KLRE-FM - Little Rock, AR - *BrCabYB 84; NatRadPubDir Summer 83, Spring 84; TV&RadDir 84*
KLRF-FM - Emporia, KS - *BrCabYB 84; TV&RadDir 84*
KLRN-TV - Austin, TX - *TV&RadDir 84*
KLRN-TV - San Antonio, TX - *BrCabYB 84; Tel&CabFB 84S*
KLRR - Leadville, CO - *BrCabYB 84; TV&RadDir 84*
KLRS - Mountain Grove, MO - *BrCabYB 84; TV&RadDir 84*
KLRS-FM - Mountain Grove, MO - *BrCabYB 84; TV&RadDir 84*
KLRT - Little Rock, AR - *BrCabYB 84; Tel&CabFB 84S*
KLRU-TV - Austin, TX - *BrCabYB 84; Tel&CabFB 84S; TV&RadDir 84*
KLRZ-FM - Provo, UT - *BrCabYB 84; TV&RadDir 84*
KLSC - Watertown, SD - *BrCabYB 84; TV&RadDir 84*
KLSE - Rochester, MN - *TV&RadDir 84*
KLSE-FM - Rushford, MN - *BrCabYB 84*
KLSI-FM - Kansas City, MO - *BrCabYB 84; NatRadPubDir Summer 83, Spring 84; TV&RadDir 84*
KLSM - Springfield, MO - *BrCabYB 84; NatRadPubDir Summer 83, Spring 84; TV&RadDir 84*
KLSR - Memphis, TX - *BrCabYB 84; TV&RadDir 84*
KLSS-FM - Mason City, IA - *BrCabYB 84; TV&RadDir 84*
KLST-TV - San Angelo, TX - *BrCabYB 84; Tel&CabFB 84S; TV&RadDir 84*
KLSU - Baton Rouge, LA - *BrCabYB 84*
KLSX - Rochester, MN - *BrCabYB 84*
KLSY - Bellevue, WA - *BrCabYB 84*
KLTA-FM - Dinuba, CA - *TV&RadDir 84*
KLTC - Dickinson, ND - *BrCabYB 84; TV&RadDir 84*
KLTD-FM - Lampasas, TX - *BrCabYB 84; TV&RadDir 84*
KLTE-FM - Oklahoma City, OK - *BrCabYB 84; NatRadPubDir Summer 83, Spring 84; TV&RadDir 84*
KLTF - Little Falls, MN - *BrCabYB 84; TV&RadDir 84*
KLTI - Macon, MO - *BrCabYB 84; TV&RadDir 84*
KLTJ - Irving, TX - *BrCabYB 84; Tel&CabFB 84S*
KLTL-TV - Lake Charles, LA - *BrCabYB 84; Tel&CabFB 84S*
KLTM-TV - Monroe, LA - *BrCabYB 84; Tel&CabFB 84S*
KLTN - Albuquerque, NM - *BrCabYB 84*
KLTR - Blackwell, OK - *BrCabYB 84; TV&RadDir 84*
KLTS-TV - Shreveport, LA - *BrCabYB 84; Tel&CabFB 84S*
KLTT - Brighton, CO - *BrCabYB 84; TV&RadDir 84*
KLTV-TV - Tyler, TX - *BrCabYB 84; DirUSTelSta 83; TelAl 83, 84; Tel&CabFB 84S; TV&RadDir 84*
KLTZ - Glasgow, MT - *BrCabYB 84; TV&RadDir 84*
KLUB - Salt Lake City, UT - *BrCabYB 84; NatRadPubDir Summer 83, Spring 84; TV&RadDir 84*
KLUC-FM - Las Vegas, NV - *BrCabYB 84; NatRadPubDir Summer 83, Spring 84; TV&RadDir 84*
KLUE - Longview, TX - *BrCabYB 84; NatRadPubDir Summer 83, Spring 84; TV&RadDir 84*
Kluge Communications Inc. - Milwaukee, WI - *Tel&CabFB 84C*
Kluge, John W. - *See* Metromedia Inc.
KLUJ - Harlingen, TX - *BrCabYB 84; Tel&CabFB 84S*
KLUK - Knob Noster, MO - *BrCabYB 84*
KLUM-FM - Jefferson City, MO - *BrCabYB 84; NatRadPubDir Summer 83, Spring 84; TV&RadDir 84*
Klungness Electronic Supply Inc. - Iron Mountain, MI - *InterCabHB 3*
KLUP-FM - Poteau, OK - *BrCabYB 84; TV&RadDir 84*
KLUR-FM - Wichita Falls, TX - *BrCabYB 84; NatRadPubDir Summer 83, Spring 84; TV&RadDir 84*
Klutz Enterprises - Stanford, CA - *LitMag&SmPr 83-84*
Klutz Press - Stanford, CA - *BoPubDir 4, 5*
KLUV - Haynesville, LA - *BrCabYB 84; TV&RadDir 84*
KLUV-FM - Haynesville, LA - *BrCabYB 84*
Kluwer Academic Publishers [Subs. of Kluwer NV] - Hingham, MA - *LitMarPl 84*
Kluwer Boston Inc. [Subs. of Kluwer NV] - Hingham, MA - *LitMarPl 83*
Kluwer Nijhoff Publishers - Hingham, MA - *LitMarPl 83*
Kluwer Nijhoff Publishers - *See* Kluwer Boston Inc.
KLVE-FM - Los Angeles, CA - *BrCabYB 84; NatRadPubDir Summer 83 p.21, Spring 84 p.21; TV&RadDir 84*
KLVF-FM - Las Vegas, NM - *BrCabYB 84; TV&RadDir 84*
KLVI - Beaumont, TX - *BrCabYB 84; NatRadPubDir Summer 83, Spring 84; TV&RadDir 84*
KLVL - Houston, TX - *NatRadPubDir Summer 83, Spring 84; TV&RadDir 84*
KLVL - Pasadena, TX - *BrCabYB 84*
KLVN-FM - Newton, IA - *BrCabYB 84; TV&RadDir 84*
KLVR - Heber City, UT - *BrCabYB 84*
KLVT - Levelland, TX - *BrCabYB 84; TV&RadDir 84*
KLVU-FM - Dallas, TX - *BrCabYB 84; NatRadPubDir Summer 83, Spring 84; TV&RadDir 84*
KLVV - Lompoc, CA - *TV&RadDir 84*
KLVX - Las Vegas, NV - *BrCabYB 84; Tel&CabFB 84S*
KLVX-TV - Las Vegas, NV - *TV&RadDir 84*
KLWD - Sheridan, WY - *BrCabYB 84*
KLWJ - Umatilla, OR - *BrCabYB 84; TV&RadDir 84*
KLWN - Lawrence, KS - *BrCabYB 84; TV&RadDir 84*
KLWT - Lebanon, MO - *BrCabYB 84; TV&RadDir 84*
KLWT-FM - Lebanon, MO - *BrCabYB 84; TV&RadDir 84*
KLWY - Cheyenne, WY - *BrCabYB 84; Tel&CabFB 84S*
KLXL-FM - Dubuque, IA - *BrCabYB 84; TV&RadDir 84*
KLXV-TV - San Jose, CA - *BrCabYB 84; Tel&CabFB 84S*
KLXX - Bismarck, ND - *BrCabYB 84; NatRadPubDir Summer 83, Spring 84; TV&RadDir 84*

KLYC - Laurel, MT - *BrCabYB 84*
KLYD - Bakersfield, CA - *BrCabYB 84; NatRadPubDir Summer 83, Spring 84; TV&RadDir 84*
KLYD-FM - Bakersfield, CA - *NatRadPubDir Spring 84; TV&RadDir 84*
KLYF-FM - Des Moines, IA - *BrCabYB 84; NatRadPubDir Summer 83, Spring 84; TV&RadDir 84*
KLYK-FM - Longview, WA - *BrCabYB 84; TV&RadDir 84*
KLYN-FM - Lynden, WA - *BrCabYB 84; TV&RadDir 84*
KLYQ - Hamilton, MT - *BrCabYB 84; TV&RadDir 84*
KLYQ-FM - Hamilton, MT - *BrCabYB 84; TV&RadDir 84*
KLYR - Clarksville, AR - *BrCabYB 84; TV&RadDir 84*
KLYR-FM - Clarksville, AR - *BrCabYB 84; TV&RadDir 84*
KLYT-FM - Albuquerque, NM - *BrCabYB 84; TV&RadDir 84*
KLYV-FM - Dubuque, IA - *BrCabYB 84; TV&RadDir 84*
KLYX-FM - Sioux Falls, SD - *TV&RadDir 84*
KLYX-FM - Thermopolis, WY - *BrCabYB 84*
KLZ - Denver, CO - *BrCabYB 84; NatRadPubDir Summer 83, Spring 84; TV&RadDir 84*
KLZR-FM - Lawrence, KS - *BrCabYB 84; TV&RadDir 84*
KM & G International Inc. - Pittsburgh, PA - *BrCabYB 84; TelAl 83, 84*
KMA - Shenandoah, IA - *BrCabYB 84; TV&RadDir 84*
KMAC - San Antonio, TX - *BrCabYB 84; NatRadPubDir Summer 83, Spring 84; TV&RadDir 84*
KMAD - Madill, OK - *BrCabYB 84; TV&RadDir 84*
KMAG-FM - Ft. Smith, AR - *BrCabYB 84; NatRadPubDir Spring 84; TV&RadDir 84*
KMAH-FM - Menlo Park, CA - *TV&RadDir 84*
KMAI-FM - Honolulu, HI - *BrCabYB 84; NatRadPubDir Summer 83, Spring 84; TV&RadDir 84*
KMAJ-FM - Topeka, KS - *BrCabYB 84; NatRadPubDir Spring 84; TV&RadDir 84*
KMAK - Fresno, CA - *BrCabYB 84; NatRadPubDir Summer 83, Spring 84; TV&RadDir 84*
KMAL-FM - Malden, MO - *BrCabYB 84; TV&RadDir 84*
KMAM - Butler, MO - *BrCabYB 84; TV&RadDir 84*
KMAN - Manhattan, KS - *BrCabYB 84; NatRadPubDir Summer 83, Spring 84; TV&RadDir 84*
KMAP - Newport, MN - *NatRadPubDir Summer 83 p.134*
KMAP - South St. Paul, MN - *BrCabYB 84*
KMAQ - Maquoketa, IA - *BrCabYB 84; TV&RadDir 84*
KMAQ-FM - Maquoketa, IA - *BrCabYB 84; TV&RadDir 84*
KMAR - Winnsboro, LA - *BrCabYB 84; TV&RadDir 84*
KMAR-FM - Winnsboro, LA - *BrCabYB 84; TV&RadDir 84*
KMAS - Shelton, WA - *BrCabYB 84; TV&RadDir 84*
KMAU - Wailuku, HI - *TelAl 84; Tel&CabFB 84S*
KMAU - Waliuku, HI - *BrCabYB 84*
KMAV - Wailuku, HI - *TelAl 83*
KMAV - Mayville, ND - *BrCabYB 84; TV&RadDir 84*
KMAV-FM - Mayville, ND - *BrCabYB 84; TV&RadDir 84*
KMAX-FM - Arcadia, CA - *BrCabYB 84*
KMAX-FM - Los Angeles, CA - *NatRadPubDir Summer 83 p.21, Spring 84 p.21*
KMAX-FM - Pasadena, CA - *TV&RadDir 84*
KMAY - Riverside, CA - *BrCabYB 84; TV&RadDir 84*
KMAY - San Bernardino, CA - *NatRadPubDir Summer 83, Spring 84 p.27*
KMAZ-FM - Beatrice, NE - *BrCabYB 84; TV&RadDir 84*
KMBC-TV - Kansas City, MO - *BrCabYB 84; DirUSTelSta 83; LitMarPl 83, 84; TelAl 83, 84; Tel&CabFB 84S; TV&RadDir 84*
KMBI - Spokane, WA - *BrCabYB 84; NatRadPubDir Summer 83, Spring 84; TV&RadDir 84*
KMBI-FM - Spokane, WA - *BrCabYB 84; NatRadPubDir Summer 83, Spring 84; TV&RadDir 84*
KMBL - Junction, TX - *BrCabYB 84; TV&RadDir 84*
KMBQ-FM - Shreveport, LA - *BrCabYB 84; NatRadPubDir Summer 83, Spring 84; TV&RadDir 84*
KMBR-FM - Shawnee Mission, KS - *TV&RadDir 84*
KMBR-FM - Kansas City, MO - *BrCabYB 84; NatRadPubDir Summer 83 p.142, Spring 84 p.142*
KMBY-FM - Seaside, CA - *BrCabYB 84; TV&RadDir 84*
KMBZ - Kansas City, MO - *BrCabYB 84; NatRadPubDir Summer 83 p.142, Spring 84 p.142; TV&RadDir 84*
KMC Records Corp. - Ridgefield, CT - *BillIntBG 83-84*
KMC Records Corp. - Seattle, WA - *BillIntBG 83-84*
KMCC - Clovis, NM - *BrCabYB 84; DirUSTelSta 83; TelAl 83, 84; Tel&CabFB 84S*
KMCC-TV - Clovis, NM - *TV&RadDir 84*
KMCC-TV - Lubbock, TX - *TelAl 83*
KMCD - Fairfield, IA - *BrCabYB 84; TV&RadDir 84*
KMCK-FM - Siloam Springs, AR - *BrCabYB 84; TV&RadDir 84*
KMCK-FM - St. Ignace, MI - *TV&RadDir 84*
KMCL - McCall, ID - *BrCabYB 84; TV&RadDir 84*
KMCM-FM - Miles City, MT - *BrCabYB 84*
KMCO-FM - McAlester, OK - *BrCabYB 84; TV&RadDir 84*
KMCR-FM - Mesa, AZ - *TV&RadDir 84*
KMCR-FM - Phoenix, AZ - *BrCabYB 84; NatRadPubDir Summer 83, Spring 84 p.9*
KMCT-TV - West Monroe, LA - *BrCabYB 84; Tel&CabFB 84S*
KMCW - Augusta, AR - *BrCabYB 84; TV&RadDir 84*
KMCX-FM - Ogallala, NE - *BrCabYB 84; TV&RadDir 84*
KMD Media Services Inc. - Arlington, VA - *ArtMar 84*
KMDL - Kaplan, LA - *BrCabYB 84*
KMDO - Ft. Scott, KS - *BrCabYB 84; TV&RadDir 84*
KMDX-FM - Parker, AZ - *BrCabYB 84; TV&RadDir 84*
KMEB - Wailuku, HI - *BrCabYB 84*
KMEB-TV - Wailuku, HI - *Tel&CabFB 84S*
KMED - Medford, OR - *BrCabYB 84; TV&RadDir 84*
KMEG-TV - Sioux City, IA - *BrCabYB 84; DirUSTelSta 83; TelAl 83, 84; Tel&CabFB 84S; TV&RadDir 84*
KMEL-FM - San Francisco, CA - *BrCabYB 84; NatRadPubDir Summer 83, Spring 84; TV&RadDir 84*
KMEM-FM - Memphis, MO - *BrCabYB 84*
KMEN - San Bernardino, CA - *BrCabYB 84; NatRadPubDir Summer 83, Spring 84; TV&RadDir 84*
KMEO - Phoenix, AZ - *BrCabYB 84; NatRadPubDir Summer 83, Spring 84*
KMEO-FM - Phoenix, AZ - *BrCabYB 84; NatRadPubDir Summer 83, Spring 84; TV&RadDir 84*
KMER - Kemmerer, WY - *BrCabYB 84; TV&RadDir 84*
KMET-FM - Los Angeles, CA - *BrCabYB 84; NatRadPubDir Summer 83 p.22, Spring 84 p.21; TV&RadDir 84*
KMEX-TV - Los Angeles, CA - *BrCabYB 84; DirUSTelSta 83; TelAl 83, 84; Tel&CabFB 84S; TV&RadDir 84*
KMEZ - Dallas, TX - *BrCabYB 84; NatRadPubDir Summer 83, Spring 84*
KMEZ-FM - Dallas, TX - *BrCabYB 84; NatRadPubDir Summer 83, Spring 84; TV&RadDir 84*
KMFA-FM - Austin, TX - *BrCabYB 84; NatRadPubDir Summer 83, Spring 84; TV&RadDir 84*
KMFB-FM - Ft. Bragg, CA - *TV&RadDir 84*
KMFB-FM - Mendicino, CA - *BrCabYB 84*
KMFE-FM - Emmett, ID - *BrCabYB 84; TV&RadDir 84*
KMFK-FM - Manhattan, KS - *BrCabYB 84*
KMFL-FM - Marshall, MO - *BrCabYB 84; TV&RadDir 84*
KMFM - San Antonio, TX - *BrCabYB 84*
KMFO - Aptos, CA - *BrCabYB 84; TV&RadDir 84*
KMGC-FM - Dallas, TX - *BrCabYB 84; NatRadPubDir Summer 83, Spring 84; TV&RadDir 84*
KMGG-FM - Los Angeles, CA - *BrCabYB 84; NatRadPubDir Summer 83, Spring 84; TV&RadDir 84*
KMGH-TV - Denver, CO - *BrCabYB 84; DirUSTelSta 83; LitMarPl 83, 84; TelAl 83, 84; Tel&CabFB 84S; TV&RadDir 84*
KMGK-FM - Des Moines, IA - *BrCabYB 84; NatRadPubDir Spring 84; TV&RadDir 84*
KMGM - Montevideo, MN - *BrCabYB 84*
KMGN - Shafter, CA - *BrCabYB 84*
KMGO-FM - Centerville, IA - *BrCabYB 84; TV&RadDir 84*
KMGQ - Goleta, CA - *BrCabYB 84*
KMGX-FM - Fresno, CA - *TV&RadDir 84*
KMGX-FM - Hanford, CA - *BrCabYB 84*
KMGZ - Lawton, OK - *BrCabYB 84*
KMH Multi-Media - Los Angeles, CA - *AvMarPl 83*
KMHA - Four Bears, ND - *BrCabYB 84*
KMHD - Gresham, OR - *BrCabYB 84*
KMHL - Marshall, MN - *BrCabYB 84; TV&RadDir 84*
KMHT - Marshall, TX - *BrCabYB 84; NatRadPubDir Summer 83, Spring 84; TV&RadDir 84*
KMHT-FM - Marshall, TX - *BrCabYB 84; NatRadPubDir Summer 83, Spring 84; TV&RadDir 84*
KMID-TV - Midland, TX - *BrCabYB 84; TelAl 83, 84; Tel&CabFB 84S; TV&RadDir 84*

KMID-TV - Odessa, TX - *DirUSTelSta 83*
KMIH-FM - Mercer Island, WA - *BrCabYB 84; NatRadPubDir Summer 83, Spring 84; TV&RadDir 84*
KMIL - Cameron, TX - *BrCabYB 84; TV&RadDir 84*
KMIN - Grants, NM - *BrCabYB 84; TV&RadDir 84*
KMIO - Merkel, TX - *BrCabYB 84; TV&RadDir 84*
KMIO-FM - Merkel, TX - *BrCabYB 84*
KMIR-TV - Palm Desert, CA - *TV&RadDir 84*
KMIR-TV - Palm Springs, CA - *BrCabYB 84; DirUSTelSta 83; TelAl 83, 84; Tel&CabFB 84S*
KMIS - Portageville, MO - *BrCabYB 84; TV&RadDir 84*
KMIS-FM - Portageville, MO - *BrCabYB 84; TV&RadDir 84*
KMIT-FM - Mitchell, SD - *BrCabYB 84; TV&RadDir 84*
KMIX-FM - Modesto, CA - *NatRadPubDir Summer 83, Spring 84; TV&RadDir 84*
KMIX-FM - Turlock, CA - *BrCabYB 84*
KMJ - Fresno, CA - *BrCabYB 84; NatRadPubDir Summer 83, Spring 84; TV&RadDir 84*
KMJC - El Cajon, CA - *BrCabYB 84*
KMJC - San Diego, CA - *NatRadPubDir Summer 83, Spring 84; TV&RadDir 84*
KMJD-TV - Pine Bluff, AR - *BrCabYB 84*
KMJJ - Las Vegas, NV - *BrCabYB 84; NatRadPubDir Summer 83, Spring 84; TV&RadDir 84*
KMJK-FM - Lake Oswego, OR - *BrCabYB 84*
KMJK-FM - Portland, OR - *TV&RadDir 84*
KMJM-FM - St. Louis, MO - *BrCabYB 84; NatRadPubDir Summer 83, Spring 84; TV&RadDir 84*
KMJQ-FM - Clear Lake City, TX - *BrCabYB 84*
KMJQ-FM - Houston, TX - *NatRadPubDir Summer 83, Spring 84; TV&RadDir 84*
KMJX-FM - Conway, AR - *BrCabYB 84; TV&RadDir 84*
KMKF-FM - Manhattan, KS - *NatRadPubDir Summer 83, Spring 84; TV&RadDir 84*
KMKR - Meeker, CO - *BrCabYB 84*
KMLA-FM - Ashdown, AR - *BrCabYB 84; NatRadPubDir Summer 83, Spring 84; TV&RadDir 84*
KMLB - Monroe, LA - *BrCabYB 84; NatRadPubDir Summer 83, Spring 84; TV&RadDir 84*
KMLB-FM - Monroe, LA - *TV&RadDir 84*
KMLE-FM - Chandler, AZ - *BrCabYB 84; TV&RadDir 84*
KMLO - Vista, CA - *BrCabYB 84; TV&RadDir 84*
KMLT-TV - Marshall, TX - *BrCabYB 84; Tel&CabFB 84S*
KMLW - Belen, NM - *BrCabYB 84*
KMMJ - Grand Island, NE - *BrCabYB 84; TV&RadDir 84*
KMMK-FM - McKinney, TX - *BrCabYB 84; TV&RadDir 84*
KMML-FM - Amarillo, TX - *BrCabYB 84; NatRadPubDir Summer 83, Spring 84; TV&RadDir 84*
KMMM - Austin, TX - *BrCabYB 84; NatRadPubDir Spring 84; TV&RadDir 84*
KMMM-FM - Austin, TX - *BrCabYB 84*
KMMO - Marshall, MO - *BrCabYB 84; TV&RadDir 84*
KMMR - Malta, MT - *BrCabYB 84*
KMMT-FM - Mammoth Lakes, CA - *BrCabYB 84; TV&RadDir 84*
KMND - Midland, TX - *BrCabYB 84; NatRadPubDir Summer 83, Spring 84; TV&RadDir 84*
KMNE-TV - Bassett, NE - *BrCabYB 84; Tel&CabFB 84S*
KMNR-FM - Rolla, MO - *BrCabYB 84; NatRadPubDir Summer 83, Spring 84; TV&RadDir 84*
KMNS - Sioux City, IA - *BrCabYB 84; TV&RadDir 84*
KMNT - Centralia, WA - *BrCabYB 84*
KMO - Tacoma, WA - *NatRadPubDir Summer 83; TV&RadDir 84*
KMOC - McCook, NE - *TelAl 83, 84*
KMOD-FM - Tulsa, OK - *BrCabYB 84; NatRadPubDir Summer 83, Spring 84; TV&RadDir 84*
KMOE-FM - Butler, MO - *BrCabYB 84; TV&RadDir 84*
KMOG - Payson, AZ - *BrCabYB 84*
KMOJ-FM - Minneapolis, MN - *BrCabYB 84; TV&RadDir 84*
KMOK - Lewiston, ID - *BrCabYB 84*
KMOL-TV - San Antonio, TX - *BrCabYB 84; DirUSTelSta 83; LitMarPl 83, 84; TelAl 83, 84; Tel&CabFB 84S; TV&RadDir 84*
KMOM - Monticello, MN - *BrCabYB 84*
KMON - Great Falls, MT - *BrCabYB 84; NatRadPubDir Summer 83, Spring 84; TV&RadDir 84*
KMOO - Mineola, TX - *BrCabYB 84; TV&RadDir 84*
KMOO-FM - Mineola, TX - *BrCabYB 84; TV&RadDir 84*
KMOR - Scottbluff, MT - *BrCabYB 84*
KMOS-TV - Sedalia, MO - *BrCabYB 84; Tel&CabFB 84S*
KMOS-TV - Warrensburg, MO - *TV&RadDir 84*
KMOT - Minot, ND - *BrCabYB 84; TelAl 83, 84; Tel&CabFB 84S*
KMOX - St. Louis, MO - *BrCabYB 84; LitMarPl 83, 84; NatRadPubDir Summer 83, Spring 84; TV&RadDir 84*
KMOX-FM - St. Louis, MO - *LitMarPl 83*
KMOX-TV - St. Louis, MO - *BrCabYB 84; DirUSTelSta 83; LitMarPl 83, 84; TelAl 83, 84; Tel&CabFB 84S; TV&RadDir 84*
KMP Partnership Ltd. - *See* Saatchi & Saatchi Compton Worldwide
K.M.P. Telephone Co. - Kerkhoven, MN - *TelDir&BG 83-84*
KMPC - Los Angeles, CA - *BrCabYB 84; NatRadPubDir Summer 83 p.22, Spring 84 p.22; TV&RadDir 84*
KMPG - Hollister, CA - *BrCabYB 84; TV&RadDir 84*
KMPH-TV - Fresno, CA - *DirUSTelSta 83; TV&RadDir 84*
KMPH-TV - Tulare, CA - *TelAl 83, 84*
KMPH-TV - Visalia, CA - *BrCabYB 84; Tel&CabFB 84S*
KMPL - Sikeston, MO - *BrCabYB 84; TV&RadDir 84*
KMPO - Modesto, CA - *BrCabYB 84*
KMPR - Minot, ND - *BrCabYB 84*
KMPS - Seattle, WA - *BrCabYB 84; NatRadPubDir Summer 83, Spring 84; TV&RadDir 84*
KMPS-FM - Seattle, WA - *BrCabYB 84; NatRadPubDir Summer 83, Spring 84; TV&RadDir 84*
KMRB-FM - Burnet, TX - *BrCabYB 84; TV&RadDir 84*
KMRC - Morgan City, LA - *BrCabYB 4; TV&RadDir 84*
KMRE-FM - Dumas, TX - *BrCabYB 84; TV&RadDir 84*
KMRN - Cameron, MO - *BrCabYB 84; TV&RadDir 84*
KMRS - Morris, MN - *BrCabYB 84; TV&RadDir 84*
KMRY - Des Moines, IA - *NatRadPubDir Spring 84*
KMS Press - Denver, CO - *BoPubDir 4, 5*
KMSA-FM - Grand Junction, CO - *BrCabYB 84; TV&RadDir 84*
KMSC-FM - Sioux City, IA - *BrCabYB 84; TV&RadDir 84*
KMSD - Milbank, SD - *BrCabYB 84; TV&RadDir 84*
KMSL - Stamps, AR - *BrCabYB 84*
KMSM-FM - Butte, MT - *BrCabYB 84; TV&RadDir 84*
KMSP-TV - Minneapolis, MN - *BrCabYB 84; DirUSTelSta 83; TelAl 83, 84; Tel&CabFB 84S; TV&RadDir 84*
KMSR - Sauk Centre, MN - *BrCabYB 84*
KMST-TV - Monterey, CA - *BrCabYB 84; TelAl 83, 84; Tel&CabFB 84S; TV&RadDir 84*
KMST-TV - Salinas, CA - *DirUSTelSta 83*
KMSU-FM - Mankato, MN - *BrCabYB 84; NatRadPubDir Summer 83, Spring 84; TV&RadDir 84*
KMTC-TV - Springfield, MO - *BrCabYB 84; DirUSTelSta 83; TelAl 83, 84; Tel&CabFB 84S; TV&RadDir 84*
KMTF-TV - Fresno, CA - *BrCabYB 84; Tel&CabFB 84S; TV&RadDir 84*
KMTI - Manti, UT - *BrCabYB 84; TV&RadDir 84*
KMTL - Sherwood, AR - *BrCabYB 84*
KMTN-FM - Jackson, WY - *BrCabYB 84; TV&RadDir 84*
KMTP-FM - Mt. Pleasant, UT - *BrCabYB 84; NatRadPubDir Summer 83, Spring 84; TV&RadDir 84*
KMTR-TV - Eugene, OR - *BrCabYB 84; DirUSTelSta 83; TelAl 84; Tel&CabFB 84S*
KMTS-FM - Glenwood Springs, CO - *BrCabYB 84; TV&RadDir 84*
KMTV-TV - Omaha, NE - *BrCabYB 84; DirUSTelSta 83; TelAl 83, 84; Tel&CabFB 84S; TV&RadDir 84*
KMTW-FM - Twin Falls, ID - *BrCabYB 84; TV&RadDir 84*
KMTX - Helena, MT - *BrCabYB 84; TV&RadDir 84*
KMUL - Muleshoe, TX - *BrCabYB 84; TV&RadDir 84*
KMUL-FM - Muleshoe, TX - *BrCabYB 84; TV&RadDir 84*
KMUN - Astoria, OR - *BrCabYB 84*
KMUS - Muskogee, OK - *BrCabYB 84; TV&RadDir 84*
KMUW-FM - Wichita, KS - *BrCabYB 84; NatRadPubDir Summer 83, Spring 84; TV&RadDir 84*
KMUZ-FM - La Grange, TX - *BrCabYB 84; TV&RadDir 84*
KMVC-FM - Burley, ID - *BrCabYB 84; TV&RadDir 84*
KMVI - Wailuku, HI - *BrCabYB 84; TV&RadDir 84*
KMVT-TV - Twin Falls, ID - *BrCabYB 84; DirUSTelSta 83; TelAl 83, 84; Tel&CabFB 84S; TV&RadDir 84*
KMWR - Vandalia, MO - *BrCabYB 84*

KMWX - Yakima, WA - *BrCabYB 84; TV&RadDir 84*
KMXL-FM - Logan, UT - *BrCabYB 84; TV&RadDir 84*
KMXT-FM - Kodiak, AK - *BrCabYB 84; TV&RadDir 84*
KMXU-FM - Manti, UT - *BrCabYB 84; TV&RadDir 84*
KMXX-FM - Austin, TX - *TV&RadDir 84*
KMYC - Marysville, CA - *BrCabYB 84; TV&RadDir 84*
KMYT-FM - Merced, CA - *BrCabYB 84; TV&RadDir 84*
KMYZ - Pryor, OK - *BrCabYB 84; TV&RadDir 84*
KMYZ-FM - Pryor, OK - *BrCabYB 84; TV&RadDir 84*
KMZK - Belgrade, MT - *BrCabYB 84*
KMZQ-FM - Henderson, NV - *BrCabYB 84*
KMZU-FM - Carrollton, MO - *BrCabYB 84; TV&RadDir 84*
KNAA - Sparks, NV - *BrCabYB 84*
KNAB - Burlington, CO - *BrCabYB 84; TV&RadDir 84*
KNAB-FM - Burlington, CO - *BrCabYB 84; TV&RadDir 84*
KNAC-FM - Long Beach, CA - *BrCabYB 84; NatRadPubDir Summer 83, Spring 84; TV&RadDir 84*
KNAF - Fredericksburg, TX - *BrCabYB 84; TV&RadDir 84*
KNAK - Delta, UT - *BrCabYB 84; TV&RadDir 84*
KNAL - Victoria, TX - *BrCabYB 84; TV&RadDir 84*
KNAN-FM - Monroe, LA - *BrCabYB 84*
KNAN-FM - West Monroe, LA - *TV&RadDir 84*
Knapp Associates Inc., S. R. - Libertyville, IL - *DirMarMP 83*
Knapp Communications - Los Angeles, CA - *AdAge 6-28-84; DirMarMP 83; KnowInd 83*
Knapp Enterprises - Fairfield, CT - *DataDirSup 7-83*
Knapp Inc., Malcolm M. - New York, NY - *IntDirMarRes 83*
Knapp Press, The [Subs. of Knapp Communications Corp.] - Los Angeles, CA - *LitMarPl 83, 84*
KNAQ-FM - Rupert, ID - *BrCabYB 84; TV&RadDir 84*
KNAS-FM - Nashville, AR - *BrCabYB 84; TV&RadDir 84*
KNAT-TV - Albuquerque, NM - *BrCabYB 84; DirUSTelSta 83; TelAl 84; Tel&CabFB 84S; TV&RadDir 84*
KNAU-FM - Flagstaff, AZ - *BrCabYB 84; NatRadPubDir Summer 83, Spring 84; TV&RadDir 84*
KNAX-FM - Fresno, CA - *BrCabYB 84; NatRadPubDir Summer 83, Spring 84; TV&RadDir 84*
KNAZ-TV - Flagstaff, AZ - *BrCabYB 84; DirUSTelSta 83; TelAl 83; Tel&CabFB 84S; TV&RadDir 84*
KNAZ-TV - Tucson, AZ - *TelAl 84*
KNBA - Vallejo, CA - *BrCabYB 84; TV&RadDir 84*
KNBC-TV - Burbank, CA - *LitMarPl 83, 84; TV&RadDir 84; VideoDir 82-83*
KNBC-TV - Los Angeles, CA - *BrCabYB 84; DirUSTelSta 83; TelAl 83, 84; Tel&CabFB 84S*
KNBN-TV - Dallas, TX - *BrCabYB 84; DirUSTelSta 83; TelAl 83, 84; Tel&CabFB 84S; TV&RadDir 84*
KNBO - New Boston, TX - *BrCabYB 84; TV&RadDir 84*
KNBQ - Tacoma, WA - *BrCabYB 84; NatRadPubDir Summer 83, Spring 84*
KNBQ-FM - Tacoma, WA - *TV&RadDir 84*
KNBR - San Francisco, CA - *BrCabYB 84; LitMarPl 83, 84; NatRadPubDir Summer 83, Spring 84; TV&RadDir 84*
KNBT-FM - New Braunfels, TX - *BrCabYB 84; TV&RadDir 84*
KNBU-FM - Baldwin City, KS - *BrCabYB 84; NatRadPubDir Summer 83, Spring 84; TV&RadDir 84*
KNBY - Newport, AR - *BrCabYB 84; TV&RadDir 84*
KNCB - Vivian, LA - *BrCabYB 84; TV&RadDir 84*
KNCC-FM - Tsaile, AZ - *BrCabYB 84; TV&RadDir 84*
KNCI - Boerne, TX - *BrCabYB 84; TV&RadDir 84*
KNCK - Concordia, KS - *BrCabYB 84; TV&RadDir 84*
KNCN-FM - Corpus Christi, TX - *TV&RadDir 84*
KNCN-FM - Sinton, TX - *BrCabYB 84*
KNCO - Grass Valley, CA - *BrCabYB 84; TV&RadDir 84*
KNCO-FM - Grass Valley, CA - *BrCabYB 84*
KNCR - Fortuna, CA - *BrCabYB 84; TV&RadDir 84*
KNCT - Belton, TX - *BrCabYB 84; Tel&CabFB 84S*
KNCT - Eastland, TX - *TV&RadDir 84*
KNCT-FM - Killeen, TX - *BrCabYB 84; NatRadPubDir Summer 83, Spring 84; TV&RadDir 84*
KNCW - Grand Coulee, WA - *TV&RadDir 84*
KNCY - Nebraska City, NE - *BrCabYB 84; TV&RadDir 84*
KNCY-FM - Nebraska City, NE - *BrCabYB 84; TV&RadDir 84*
KNDC - Hettinger, ND - *BrCabYB 84; TV&RadDir 84*
KNDE-FM - Tucson, AZ - *BrCabYB 84; NatRadPubDir Summer 83, Spring 84; TV&RadDir 84*
KNDI - Honolulu, HI - *BrCabYB 84; NatRadPubDir Summer 83, Spring 84; TV&RadDir 84*
KNDK - Langdon, ND - *BrCabYB 84; TV&RadDir 84*
KNDN - Farmington, NM - *BrCabYB 84; TV&RadDir 84*
KNDO-TV - Yakima, WA - *BrCabYB 84; DirUSTelSta 83; TelAl 83, 84; Tel&CabFB 84S; TV&RadDir 84*
KNDR-FM - Mandan, ND - *BrCabYB 84; TV&RadDir 84*
KNDU-TV - Pasco, WA - *TV&RadDir 84*
KNDU-TV - Richland, WA - *BrCabYB 84; DirUSTelSta 83; TelAl 83, 84; Tel&CabFB 84S*
KNDX - Dickinson, ND - *BrCabYB 84; Tel&CabFB 84S*
KNDY - Marysville, KS - *BrCabYB 84; TV&RadDir 84*
KNDY-FM - Marysville, KS - *BrCabYB 84; TV&RadDir 84*
KNEA - Jonesboro, AR - *BrCabYB 84; TV&RadDir 84*
KNEB - Scottsbluff, NE - *BrCabYB 84; NatRadPubDir Summer 83, Spring 84; TV&RadDir 84*
KNEB-FM - Scottsbluff, NE - *BrCabYB 84; NatRadPubDir Summer 83, Spring 84; TV&RadDir 84*
KNED - McAlester, OK - *BrCabYB 84; TV&RadDir 84*
Knees Paperback Publishing Co. - Dallas, TX - *ArtMar 84; BoPubDir 4, 5*
KNEI - Waukon, IA - *BrCabYB 84; TV&RadDir 84*
KNEI-FM - Waukon, IA - *BrCabYB 84; TV&RadDir 84*
Kneisley Electric Co. - Toledo, OH - *AvMarPl 83*
KNEK - Washington, LA - *BrCabYB 84; TV&RadDir 84*
KNEL - Brady, TX - *BrCabYB 84; TV&RadDir 84*
KNEM - Nevada, MO - *BrCabYB 84; TV&RadDir 84*
KNEN - Norfolk, NE - *BrCabYB 84; TV&RadDir 84*
Kneptune International Records Inc. - North Hollywood, CA - *BillIntBG 83-84*
KNES - Fairfield, TX - *BrCabYB 84*
KNET - Palestine, TX - *BrCabYB 84; TV&RadDir 84*
KNEU - Roosevelt, UT - *BrCabYB 84; TV&RadDir 84*
KNEV-FM - Reno, NV - *BrCabYB 84; NatRadPubDir Summer 83, Spring 84; TV&RadDir 84*
KNEW - Oakland, CA - *BrCabYB 84; TV&RadDir 84*
KNEW - San Francisco, CA - *NatRadPubDir Summer 83 p.31, Spring 84 p.31*
KNEX - McPherson, KS - *BrCabYB 84; TV&RadDir 84*
KNEX-FM - McPherson, KS - *BrCabYB 84; TV&RadDir 84*
KNEY-FM - Pierre, SD - *BrCabYB 84; TV&RadDir 84*
KNEZ - Lompoc, CA - *BrCabYB 84; TV&RadDir 84*
KNFB - Nowata, OK - *BrCabYB 84*
KNFM-FM - Midland, TX - *BrCabYB 84; NatRadPubDir Summer 83, Spring 84; TV&RadDir 84*
KNFO-FM - Waco, TX - *BrCabYB 84; NatRadPubDir Summer 83, Spring 84; TV&RadDir 84*
KNFT - Bayard, NM - *BrCabYB 84*
KNFT - Silver City, NM - *TV&RadDir 84*
KNGS - Hanford, CA - *BrCabYB 84; TV&RadDir 84*
KNGT-FM - Jackson, CA - *BrCabYB 84; TV&RadDir 84*
KNGX-FM - Claremore, OK - *BrCabYB 84; TV&RadDir 84*
KNHC-FM - Seattle, WA - *BrCabYB 84; NatRadPubDir Summer 83, Spring 84; TV&RadDir 84*
KNHS-FM - Torrance, CA - *BrCabYB 84; TV&RadDir 84*
KNIA - Knoxville, IA - *BrCabYB 84; TV&RadDir 84*
KNIC - Winfield, KS - *BrCabYB 84; TV&RadDir 84*
Knickerbocker News [of The Hearst Corp.] - Albany, NY - *AyerDirPub 83; Ed&PubIntYB 82; LitMarPl 84; NewsBur 6; NewsDir 84*
KNID-FM - Enid, OK - *BrCabYB 84; TV&RadDir 84*
Kniep Associates - Randolph, NJ - *StaDirAdAg 2-84*
KNIF-FM - Gilmer, TX - *BrCabYB 84; TV&RadDir 84*
Knife World Books - Knoxville, TN - *BoPubDir 5*
Knight Advertising, Austin - New York, NY - *StaDirAdAg 2-84*
Knight Advertising Communications Inc. - Minneapolis, MN - *StaDirAdAg 2-84*
Knight Coaxial Services - Troy, MI - *InterCabHB 3*
Knight Co. Ltd., P. S. - Richmond, BC, Canada - *BoPubDir 4, 5*
Knight Editorial Services - Antioch, TN - *LitMarPl 83, 84*
Knight, Jeffrey B. - Charlotte Amalie, VI - *Tel&CabFB 84C p.1687*
Knight Ltd., Austin - London, England - *StaDirAdAg 2-84*
Knight, N. Scott - Charlotte Amalie, VI - *Tel&CabFB 84C p.1687*
Knight, Nancy H. - Fairfax, VA - *LitMarPl 83; MagIndMarPl 82-83*
Knight News Wire - Washington, DC - *BaconPubCkNews 84*

Knight Quality Stations - Boston, MA - *BrCabYB 84*
Knight, Randolph H. - Charlotte Amalie, VI - *Tel&CabFB 84C p.1687*
Knight-Ridder Broadcasting - Miami, FL - *BrCabYB 84; Tel&CabFB 84S*
Knight-Ridder Newspaper Sales Inc. [Subs. of Knight-Ridder Newspapers Inc.] - New York, NY - *LitMarPl 83, 84*
Knight-Ridder Newspapers - Miami, FL - *AdAge 6-28-84; BrCabYB 84; Ed&PubIntYB 82; HomeVid&CabYB 82-83; KnowInd 83; NewsBur 6*
Knight-Ridder Newspapers - *See* TKR Cable Co.
Knight, Robert A. - Charlotte Amalie, VI - *Tel&CabFB 84C p.1687*
Knight Ward Associates Inc. - Hartsdale, NY - *LitMarPl 83*
Knight Ward Associates Inc. - White Plains, NY - *LitMarPl 84*
Knight's Library Inc. - San Diego, CA - *AvMarPl 83*
Knights of Christ - Long Beach, CA - *BoPubDir 4, 5*
Knightstown Tri-County Banner - *See* Mayhill Publications
Knightstown Tri-State Trader - *See* Mayhill Publications
Knighttime Publications - Cupertino, CA - *BoPubDir 5*
KNIK-FM - Anchorage, AK - *BrCabYB 84; NatRadPubDir Summer 83, Spring 84; TV&RadDir 84*
KNIM - Maryville, MO - *BrCabYB 84; TV&RadDir 84*
KNIM-FM - Maryville, MO - *BrCabYB 84; TV&RadDir 84*
KNIN - Wichita Falls, TX - *BrCabYB 84; NatRadPubDir Summer 83, Spring 84; TV&RadDir 84*
KNIN-FM - Wichita Falls, TX - *BrCabYB 84; TV&RadDir 84*
Knippa Telephone Co. - Knippa, TX - *TelDir&BG 83-84*
KNIR - New Iberia, LA - *BrCabYB 84; TV&RadDir 84*
KNIS-FM - Carson City, NV - *BrCabYB 84; NatRadPubDir Summer 83, Spring 84; TV&RadDir 84*
KNIT-FM - Portales, NM - *BrCabYB 84; TV&RadDir 84*
Knitovations - New York, NY - *BaconPubCkMag 84*
Knitting Industry - New York, NY - *MagDir 84*
Knitting Times [of National Knitted Outerwear Association] - New York, NY - *ArtMar 84; BaconPubCkMag 84; MagDir 84; WritMar 84*
Knitting Times Newsweekly - New York, NY - *ArtMar 84*
KNIX - Phoenix, AZ - *NatRadPubDir Summer 83 p.10, Spring 84 p.10*
KNIX - Tempe, AZ - *BrCabYB 84; TV&RadDir 84*
KNIX-FM - Phoenix, AZ - *BrCabYB 84; NatRadPubDir Summer 83 p.10, Spring 84 p.10*
KNIX-FM - Tempe, AZ - *TV&RadDir 84*
KNJO-FM - Thousand Oaks, CA - *BrCabYB 84; TV&RadDir 84*
KNJY-FM - Clinton, IA - *BrCabYB 84; TV&RadDir 84*
KNLB - Lake Havasu City, AZ - *BrCabYB 84*
KNLC - St. Louis, MO - *BrCabYB 84; Tel&CabFB 84S*
KNLU-FM - Monroe, LA - *BrCabYB 84; NatRadPubDir Summer 83, Spring 84; TV&RadDir 84*
KNLV - Ord, NE - *BrCabYB 84; TV&RadDir 84*
KNLV-FM - Ord, NE - *BrCabYB 84; TV&RadDir 84*
KNME-TV - Albuquerque, NM - *BrCabYB 84; Tel&CabFB 84S; TV&RadDir 84*
KNMI-FM - Farmington, NM - *BrCabYB 84; TV&RadDir 84*
KNMO-FM - Nevada, MO - *BrCabYB 84*
KNMP Drug Databank [of Royal Netherlands Pharmaceutical Society] - The Hague, Netherlands - *EISS 83*
KNMQ-FM - Santa Fe, NM - *BrCabYB 84*
KNMT-TV - Hackensack, MN - *TV&RadDir 84*
KNMT-TV - Walker, MN - *BrCabYB 84; TelAl 83, 84; Tel&CabFB 84S*
KNMX - Las Vegas, NM - *BrCabYB 84; TV&RadDir 84*
KNNB-FM - Whiteriver, AZ - *BrCabYB 84*
KNND - Cottage Grove, OR - *BrCabYB 84; TV&RadDir 84*
KNNN-FM - Phoenix, AZ - *BrCabYB 84*
KNNS-FM - Grand Rapids, MN - *BrCabYB 84; TV&RadDir 84*
KNOB-FM - Anaheim, CA - *NatRadPubDir Summer 83, Spring 84; TV&RadDir 84*
KNOB-FM - Long Beach, CA - *BrCabYB 84*
Knob Hill TV Cable Co. - Port Matilda, PA - *BrCabYB 84; Tel&CabFB 84C*
Knob Noster Cable Inc. [of Horizon Communications Corp.] - Knob Noster, MO - *Tel&CabFB 84C*
Knob Noster Item - Knob Noster, MO - *BaconPubCkNews 84; Ed&PubIntYB 82*
Knobler Co. Inc., William - Manhasset, NY - *IntDirMarRes 83*
KNOC - Natchitoches, LA - *BrCabYB 84; TV&RadDir 84*
KNOD-FM - Harlan, IA - *BrCabYB 84; TV&RadDir 84*
KNOE - Monroe, LA - *BrCabYB 84; NatRadPubDir Summer 83, Spring 84; TV&RadDir 84*
KNOE-FM - Monroe, LA - *BrCabYB 84; TV&RadDir 84*
KNOE-TV - Monroe, LA - *BrCabYB 84; DirUSTelSta 83; TelAl 83, 84; Tel&CabFB 84S; TV&RadDir 84*
Knoedler & Co. Inc., M. - New York, NY - *MicroMarPl 82-83*
KNOF-FM - St. Paul, MN - *BrCabYB 84; TV&RadDir 84*
KNOG-FM - Havre, MT - *BrCabYB 84; TV&RadDir 84*
KNOI - Deer Park, WA - *BrCabYB 84*
KNOI - Pullman, WA - *TV&RadDir 84*
KNOK-FM - Dallas, TX - *NatRadPubDir Summer 83, Spring 84 p.237*
KNOK-FM - Ft. Worth, TX - *BrCabYB 84; TV&RadDir 84*
Knoll International - New York, NY - *DirInfWP 82*
Knollwood Music Corp. - *See* Ahlert Music Corp., Fred
Knollwood Publishing Co. - Wilmar, MN - *BoPubDir 4, 5; LitMag&SmPr 83-84*
KNOM - Nome, AK - *BrCabYB 84; TV&RadDir 84*
KNON-FM - Dallas, TX - *BrCabYB 84; TV&RadDir 84*
KNOP-TV - North Platte, NE - *BrCabYB 84; DirUSTelSta 83; TelAl 83, 84; Tel&CabFB 84S; TV&RadDir 84*
Knopf Inc., Alfred A. [Subs. of Random House Inc.] - New York, NY - *LitMarPl 83, 84; WritMar 84*
Knopik, Jerome - Beach, ND - *Tel&CabFB 84C p.1687*
KNOR - Norman, OK - *BrCabYB 84; TV&RadDir 84*
KNOS-FM - Marshall, MO - *BrCabYB 84; TV&RadDir 84*
Knossos Inc. - Corte Madera, CA - *MicrocomMPl 84*
KNOT - Prescott, AZ - *BrCabYB 84; TV&RadDir 84*
KNOT-FM - Prescott, AZ - *BrCabYB 84; TV&RadDir 84*
Knoth & Meads Co. - San Diego, CA - *DirPRFirms 83; StaDirAdAg 2-84*
Knott County News - Hindman, KY - *AyerDirPub 83; Ed&PubIntYB 82*
KNOW - Austin, TX - *BrCabYB 84; NatRadPubDir Summer 83, Spring 84; TV&RadDir 84*
Know-How Publications - Berkeley, CA - *BoPubDir 4, 5*
Know Inc. - Pittsburgh, PA - *LitMag&SmPr 83-84*
Know News - Pittsburgh, PA - *LitMag&SmPr 83-84*
Knowledge [of RSC Publishers] - Ft. Worth, TX - *MagDir 84; WritMar 84*
Knowledge Index [of Dialog Information Services Inc.] - Palo Alto, CA - *EISS 7-83 Sup; MicrocomMPl 84*
Knowledge Industry Publications - White Plains, NY - *EISS 83; LitMarPl 83, 84; WritMar 84*
Knowledge Network - Victoria, BC, Canada - *TeleSy&SerDir 2-84*
Knowledge News & Feature Syndicate - Kenilworth, IL - *LitMarPl 84*
Knowledge News & Feature Syndicate - Wilmette, IL - *BaconPubCkNews 84; Ed&PubIntYB 82*
Knowledge on Tap - Highland Park, NJ - *EISS 83; InfIndMarPl 83*
Knowledge Sciences Inc. - White Plains, NY - *LitMarPl 83, 84*
Knowledge Tree Group Inc., The - Lime, CT - *LitMarPl 83*
Knowledge Tree Group Inc., The - New York, NY - *MagIndMarPl 82-83*
Knowlogy - Wilsonville, OR - *MicrocomMPl 83, 84*
KNOX - Grand Forks, ND - *BrCabYB 84; TV&RadDir 84*
Knox Associates - Millwood, NY - *LitMarPl 83, 84*
Knox City Knox County News - Knox City, TX - *BaconPubCkNews 84*
Knox County Citizen - Fredericktown, OH - *AyerDirPub 83; Ed&PubIntYB 82*
Knox County News - Bicknell, IN - *AyerDirPub 83; BaconPubCkNews 84; Ed&PubIntYB 82*
Knox County News - Knox City, TX - *AyerDirPub 83; Ed&PubIntYB 82*
Knox Manufacturing Co. - Wood Dale, IL - *AvMarPl 83*
Knox, Nimick & Harwood Inc. - Stowe, VT - *StaDirAdAg 2-84*
Knox Press, John [Div. of Presbyterian Publishing House] - Atlanta, GA - *LitMarPl 83, 84; WritMar 84*
Knox Printing Co. - Fredericktown, OH - *BaconPubCkNews 84*
Knox Public Relations - Longview, TX - *ArtMar 84*
Knox Starke County Democrat - Knox, IN - *NewsDir 84*
Knox Starke County Leader - Knox, IN - *BaconPubCkNews 84*

Knox Video Products [Div. of Computer Operations Inc.] - Lanham, MD - *AvMarPl 83*
Knoxville Express - Knoxville, IA - *Ed&PubIntYB 82; NewsDir 84*
Knoxville Express - *See* Journal-Express Inc.
Knoxville Journal - Knoxville, IL - *Ed&PubIntYB 82*
Knoxville Journal - Knoxville, IA - *Ed&PubIntYB 82; NewsDir 84*
Knoxville Journal [of Gannett Co. Inc.] - Knoxville, TN - *BaconPubCkNews 84; Ed&PubIntYB 82; LitMarPl 84; NewsDir 84*
Knoxville Journal - *See* Galesburg Post Publishing Co.
Knoxville Journal - *See* Journal-Express Inc.
Knoxville News-Sentinel - Knoxville, TN - *BaconPubCkNews 84; Ed&PubIntYB 82; LitMarPl 83, 84; NewsDir 84*
Knoxville West Side Story - Knoxville, TN - *BaconPubCkNews 84*
KNPB - Reno, NV - *BrCabYB 84; Tel&CabFB 84S*
KNPR-FM - Las Vegas, NV - *TV&RadDir 84*
KNPT - Newport, OR - *BrCabYB 84; TV&RadDir 84*
KNPT-FM - Newport, OR - *BrCabYB 84; TV&RadDir 84*
KNRY - Monterey, CA - *BrCabYB 84*
KNRY - Salinas, CA - *NatRadPubDir Summer 83, Spring 84 p.26*
KNS Type Network - New York, NY - *LitMarPl 83*
KNSE - Ontario, CA - *BrCabYB 84; TV&RadDir 84*
KNSE - San Bernardino, CA - *NatRadPubDir Summer 83, Spring 84 p.27*
KNSI - St. Cloud, MN - *BrCabYB 84; NatRadPubDir Summer 83, Spring 84; TV&RadDir 84*
KNSP - Staples, MN - *BrCabYB 84*
KNST - Tucson, AZ - *BrCabYB 84; NatRadPubDir Spring 84; TV&RadDir 84*
KNSX - Steelville, MO - *BrCabYB 84*
KNT News Wire - Washington, DC - *Ed&PubIntYB 82*
KNTA - San Jose, CA - *NatRadPubDir Summer 83 p.32, Spring 84 p.32*
KNTA - Santa Clara, CA - *BrCabYB 84; TV&RadDir 84*
KNTF-FM - Ontario, CA - *BrCabYB 84; TV&RadDir 84*
KNTF-FM - San Bernardino, CA - *NatRadPubDir Summer 83, Spring 84 p.27*
KNTO - Delhi, CA - *BrCabYB 84*
KNTU-FM - Denton, TX - *BrCabYB 84; NatRadPubDir Summer 83, Spring 84; TV&RadDir 84*
KNTV-TV - Salinas, CA - *DirUSTelSta 83*
KNTV-TV - San Jose, CA - *BrCabYB 84; TelAl 83, 84; Tel&CabFB 84S; TV&RadDir 84*
Knud-Feldt Music Co. - Woodhaven, NY - *BillIntBG 83-84*
Knudsen & Associates, Arvid - Hackensack, NJ - *LitMarPl 83, 84; MagIndMarPl 82-83*
Knudsen, Gardner & Howe Inc. - Cleveland, OH - *StaDirAdAg 2-84*
Knudsen-Moore Public Relations [Subs. of Knudsen-Moore Inc.] - Norwalk, CT - *DirPRFirms 83*
Knudsen Moore Schropfer - Stamford, CT - *AdAge 3-28-84; StaDirAdAg 2-84*
KNUE-FM - Tyler, TX - *BrCabYB 84; NatRadPubDir Summer 83, Spring 84; TV&RadDir 84*
KNUI - Kahului, HI - *BrCabYB 84; TV&RadDir 84*
KNUJ - New Ulm, MN - *BrCabYB 84; TV&RadDir 84*
KNUR-FM - Paradise, CA - *TV&RadDir 84*
KNUS - Denver, CO - *BrCabYB 84; NatRadPubDir Summer 83, Spring 84; TV&RadDir 84*
Knuth Multimedia, Charles - San Francisco, CA - *AvMarPl 83*
KNUU - Las Vegas, NV - *BrCabYB 84; NatRadPubDir Summer 83, Spring 84; TV&RadDir 84*
KNUW-FM - Great Falls, MT - *BrCabYB 84; NatRadPubDir Summer 83, Spring 84; TV&RadDir 84*
KNUZ - Houston, TX - *BrCabYB 84; NatRadPubDir Summer 83, Spring 84; TV&RadDir 84*
KNVR-FM - Paradise, CA - *BrCabYB 84*
KNWA-FM - Fayetteville, AR - *TV&RadDir 84*
KNWC - Sioux Falls, SD - *BrCabYB 84; NatRadPubDir Summer 83, Spring 84; TV&RadDir 84*
KNWC-FM - Sioux Falls, SD - *BrCabYB 84; NatRadPubDir Summer 83, Spring 84; TV&RadDir 84*
KNWD-FM - Natchitoches, LA - *BrCabYB 84; NatRadPubDir Summer 83, Spring 84; TV&RadDir 84*
KNWR-FM - Bellingham, WA - *BrCabYB 84; TV&RadDir 84*
KNWS - Waterloo, IA - *BrCabYB 84; NatRadPubDir Summer 83, Spring 84*
KNWS-FM - Waterloo, IA - *BrCabYB 84; NatRadPubDir Summer 83, Spring 84; TV&RadDir 84*
KNWY - Powell, WY - *BrCabYB 84*
KNWZ - Anaheim, CA - *BrCabYB 84; NatRadPubDir Spring 84*
KNX - Los Angeles, CA - *BrCabYB 84; NatRadPubDir Summer 83 p.22, Spring 84 p.22; TV&RadDir 84*
KNX-FM - Hollywood, CA - *LitMarPl 83, 84*
KNX-FM - Los Angeles, CA - *NatRadPubDir Summer 83; TV&RadDir 84*
KNXN - Quincy, CA - *BrCabYB 84*
KNXR-FM - Rochester, MN - *BrCabYB 84; TV&RadDir 84*
KNXT-TV - Los Angeles, CA - *BrCabYB 84; DirUSTelSta 83; TelAl 83, 84; Tel&CabFB 84S; TV&RadDir 84; VideoDir 82-83*
KNXV-TV - Phoenix, AZ - *BrCabYB 84; DirUSTelSta 83; TelAl 83, 84; Tel&CabFB 84S; TV&RadDir 84*
KNYD - Lone Pine, CA - *TV&RadDir 84*
KNYN-FM - Santa Fe, NM - *BrCabYB 84; TV&RadDir 84*
KNZA-FM - Hiawatha, KS - *BrCabYB 84; TV&RadDir 84*
Ko-Rec-Type [Div. of Barouh Eaton Allen] - Brooklyn, NY - *DirInfWP 82*
KOA - Denver, CO - *BrCabYB 84; NatRadPubDir Summer 83, Spring 84; TV&RadDir 84*
KOA-TV - Denver, CO - *DirUSTelSta 83; LitMarPl 83; TelAl 83, 84; TV&RadDir 84*
KOAA-TV - Colorado Springs, CO - *TelAl 83, 84*
KOAA-TV - Pueblo, CO - *BrCabYB 84; DirUSTelSta 83; Tel&CabFB 84S; TV&RadDir 84*
KOAB-TV - Bend, OR - *BrCabYB 84; Tel&CabFB 84S*
KOAC - Corvallis, OR - *BrCabYB 84; NatRadPubDir Summer 83, Spring 84; TV&RadDir 84*
KOAC-TV - Corvallis, OR - *BrCabYB 84; Tel&CabFB 84S; TV&RadDir 84*
KOAK - Red Oak, IA - *BrCabYB 84; TV&RadDir 84*
KOAK-FM - Red Oak, IA - *BrCabYB 84; TV&RadDir 84*
KOAL - Price, UT - *BrCabYB 84; TV&RadDir 84*
Koala Books of Canada Ltd. - Edmonton, AB, Canada - *LitMarPl 83, 84*
Koala Music Inc. - *See* Music Music Music Inc.
Koala Record Co. - Hendersonville, TN - *BillIntBG 83-84*
Koala Records Inc. - Los Angeles, CA - *BillIntBG 83-84*
KOAM-TV - Pittsburg, KS - *BrCabYB 84; TelAl 83, 84; Tel&CabFB 84S; TV&RadDir 84*
KOAM-TV - Joplin, MO - *DirUSTelSta 83*
KOAP-FM - Portland, OR - *BrCabYB 84; NatRadPubDir Summer 83, Spring 84; TV&RadDir 84*
KOAP-TV - Portland, OR - *BrCabYB 84; Tel&CabFB 84S; TV&RadDir 84*
KOAQ-FM - Denver, CO - *BrCabYB 84; NatRadPubDir Summer 83, Spring 84; TV&RadDir 84*
KOAS - Kealakekua, HI - *BrCabYB 84*
KOAT-TV - Albuquerque, NM - *BrCabYB 84; DirUSTelSta 83; TelAl 83, 84; Tel&CabFB 84S; TV&RadDir 84*
KOAV - Denison, TX - *BrCabYB 84; Tel&CabFB 84S*
KOAW - Ruidoso Downs, NM - *BrCabYB 84*
KOAX-FM - Dallas, TX - *BrCabYB 84; NatRadPubDir Summer 83, Spring 84; TV&RadDir 84*
KOB - Albuquerque, NM - *BrCabYB 84; NatRadPubDir Summer 83, Spring 84; TV&RadDir 84*
KOB-FM - Albuquerque, NM - *BrCabYB 84; NatRadPubDir Summer 83, Spring 84*
KOB-TV - Albuquerque, NM - *BrCabYB 84; DirUSTelSta 83; TelAl 83, 84; Tel&CabFB 84S; TV&RadDir 84*
Kobak Inc., James B. - Darien, CT - *LitMarPl 83; MagIndMarPl 82-83*
KOBC - Joplin, MO - *BrCabYB 84; TV&RadDir 84*
KOBC-FM - Joplin, MO - *NatRadPubDir Summer 83, Spring 84; TV&RadDir 84*
KOBE - Las Cruces, NM - *BrCabYB 84; NatRadPubDir Summer 83, Spring 84; TV&RadDir 84*
Kober & Associates Inc., Art - Pleasantville, NY - *DirMarMP 83*
Kober Press - San Francisco, CA - *BoPubDir 4, 5*
KOBH - Hot Springs, SD - *BrCabYB 84; TV&RadDir 84*
KOBH-FM - Hot Springs, SD - *BrCabYB 84; TV&RadDir 84*

KOBI-TV - Medford, OR - *BrCabYB 84; DirUSTelSta 83; TelAl 83, 84; Tel&CabFB 84S; TV&RadDir 84*

KOBK - Walla Walla, WA - *BrCabYB 84; Tel&CabFB 84S*

KOBO - Yuba City, CA - *BrCabYB 84; TV&RadDir 84*

KOBR - Brainerd, MN - *TV&RadDir 84*

Kobro Publications Inc. - New York, NY - *BoPubDir 4 Sup, 5*

Kobs & Brady Advertising - Chicago, IL - *AdAge 3-28-84; DirMarMP 83; StaDirAdAg 2-84*

KOBY - Reno, NV - *BrCabYB 84; NatRadPubDir Summer 83; TV&RadDir 84*

KOCA - Kilgore, TX - *BrCabYB 84; TV&RadDir 84*

KOCC-FM - Oklahoma City, OK - *BrCabYB 84; TV&RadDir 84*

KOCE-TV - Huntington Beach, CA - *BrCabYB 84; Tel&CabFB 84S; TV&RadDir 84*

Koch/Marschall Productions Inc. - Chicago, IL - *AvMarPl 83; WritMar 84*

Kochel, Timothy F. - Mott, ND - *Tel&CabFB 84C p.1687*

KOCM-FM - Newport Beach, CA - *BrCabYB 84; TV&RadDir 84*

KOCN-FM - Pacific Grove, CA - *BrCabYB 84; TV&RadDir 84*

KOCO-TV - Oklahoma City, OK - *BrCabYB 84; DirUSTelSta 83; LitMarPl 83, 84; TelAl 83, 84; Tel&CabFB 84S; TV&RadDir 84*

KOCV-FM - Odessa, TX - *BrCabYB 84; NatRadPubDir Summer 83, Spring 84; TV&RadDir 84*

KOCY - Oklahoma City, OK - *NatRadPubDir Summer 83; TV&RadDir 84*

KODA-FM - Houston, TX - *BrCabYB 84; NatRadPubDir Summer 83, Spring 84; TV&RadDir 84*

Kodansha International USA Ltd. [Div. of Kodansha Ltd.] - New York, NY - *LitMarPl 83, 84*

KODE - Joplin, MO - *BrCabYB 84; NatRadPubDir Summer 83, Spring 84; TV&RadDir 84*

KODE-TV - Joplin, MO - *BrCabYB 84; DirUSTelSta 83; TelAl 83, 84; Tel&CabFB 84S; TV&RadDir 84*

KODI - Cody, WY - *BrCabYB 84; TV&RadDir 84*

Kodiak Cablevision [of Alaska Cablevision Inc.] - Kodiak, AK - *BrCabYB 84; Tel&CabFB 84C*

Kodiak Daily Mirror - Kodiak, AK - *AyerDirPub 83; Ed&PubIntYB 82; NewsDir 84*

KODK - Kingsville, TX - *BrCabYB 84*

KODL - The Dalles, OR - *BrCabYB 84; TV&RadDir 84*

KODY - North Platte, NE - *BrCabYB 84; NatRadPubDir Summer 83, Spring 84; TV&RadDir 84*

KODY-FM - North Platte, NE - *BrCabYB 84; TV&RadDir 84*

KOEA-FM - Doniphan, MO - *BrCabYB 84; TV&RadDir 84*

Koechling, William - Orrs Island, ME - *LitMarPl 83, 84*

KOED-TV - Tulsa, OK - *BrCabYB 84; Tel&CabFB 84S; TV&RadDir 84*

Koehler Counselors Inc. - Yellow Springs, OH - *StaDirAdAg 2-84*

Koehler Iversen - New York, NY - *AdAge 3-28-84; StaDirAdAg 2-84*

KOEL - Oelwein, IA - *BrCabYB 84; TV&RadDir 84*

KOEL-FM - Oelwein, IA - *BrCabYB 84; TV&RadDir 84*

Koen Book Distributors Inc. - Cinnaminson, NJ - *BoPubDir 4 Sup, 5*

Koenig, Bill - Kirkland, WA - *Tel&CabFB 84C p.1687*

Koenig Inc., Julian - New York, NY - *StaDirAdAg 2-84*

Koepenick International - Atlanta, GA - *StaDirAdAg 2-84*

Koester Books, Arthur R. - Burbank, CA - *BoPubDir 4, 5*

KOET - Eufaula, OK - *BrCabYB 84; Tel&CabFB 84S*

KOEZ-FM - Newton, KS - *BrCabYB 84; TV&RadDir 84*

KOFE - St. Maries, ID - *BrCabYB 84*

KOFI - Kalispell, MT - *BrCabYB 84; TV&RadDir 84*

KOFM-FM - Oklahoma City, OK - *BrCabYB 84; NatRadPubDir Summer 83, Spring 84; TV&RadDir 84*

KOFO - Ottawa, KS - *BrCabYB 84; TV&RadDir 84*

Kofoed Inc., Bill - North Miami, FL - *DirPRFirms 83*

KOFY - Burlingame, CA - *TV&RadDir 84*

KOFY - San Mateo, CA - *BrCabYB 84*

KOGA - Ogallala, NE - *BrCabYB 84; TV&RadDir 84*

KOGA-FM - Ogallala, NE - *BrCabYB 84*

Kogan & Co., Irving Smith - New York, NY - *DirPRFirms 83*

KOGM-FM - Opelousas, LA - *BrCabYB 84; TV&RadDir 84*

KOGO - San Diego, CA - *BrCabYB 84; NatRadPubDir Summer 83, Spring 84; TV&RadDir 84*

KOGT - Orange, TX - *BrCabYB 84; TV&RadDir 84*

KOH - Reno, NV - *BrCabYB 84; NatRadPubDir Summer 83, Spring 84; TV&RadDir 84*

KOHA-TV - Hilo, HI - *BrCabYB 84; Tel&CabFB 84S*

Kohaw Music Inc. - *See* Bicycle Music Co., The

KOHI - St. Helens, OR - *BrCabYB 84; TV&RadDir 84*

KOHL - Fremont, CA - *BrCabYB 84*

Kohl, James - Cleveland, OH - *LitMarPl 83, 84*

Kohlenberger Designs - Orange, CA - *MicrocomMPl 84*

Kohler Co. Inc., The - Riverside, CT - *StaDirAdAg 2-84*

Kohler Microforms Ltd. - Dorking, England - *MicroMarPl 82-83*

Kohler/Twin Cities Inc. - Minneapolis, MN - *StaDirAdAg 2-84*

KOHM-FM - Lubbock, TX - *BrCabYB 84; TV&RadDir 84*

KOHO - Honolulu, HI - *BrCabYB 84; NatRadPubDir Summer 83, Spring 84; TV&RadDir 84*

KOHS-FM - Orem, UT - *BrCabYB 84; NatRadPubDir Summer 83, Spring 84; TV&RadDir 84*

KOHU - Hermiston, OR - *TV&RadDir 84*

KOHU-FM - Hermiston, OR - *BrCabYB 84; TV&RadDir 84*

KOIL - Omaha, NE - *BrCabYB 84; NatRadPubDir Summer 83, Spring 84; TV&RadDir 84*

KOIN-TV - Portland, OR - *BrCabYB 84; DirUSTelSta 83; LitMarPl 83, 84; TelAl 83, 84; Tel&CabFB 84S; TV&RadDir 84*

KOIR-FM - Edinburg, TX - *BrCabYB 84*

KOIT - San Francisco, CA - *BrCabYB 84*

KOIT-FM - San Francisco, CA - *NatRadPubDir Summer 83, Spring 84; TV&RadDir 84*

KOJC - Cedar Rapids, IA - *BrCabYB 84*

KOJM - Havre, MT - *BrCabYB 84; TV&RadDir 84*

KOJO - Laramie, WY - *BrCabYB 84; NatRadPubDir Summer 83, Spring 84; TV&RadDir 84*

KOJY - Dinuba, CA - *BrCabYB 84*

KOKA - Shreveport, LA - *BrCabYB 84; NatRadPubDir Summer 83, Spring 84; TV&RadDir 84*

KOKC - Guthrie, OK - *BrCabYB 84; TV&RadDir 84*

KOKE - Austin, TX - *NatRadPubDir Summer 83*

KOKE-FM - Austin, TX - *NatRadPubDir Summer 83, Spring 84; TV&RadDir 84*

KOKF-FM - Edmond, OK - *BrCabYB 84; TV&RadDir 84*

KOKH-TV - Oklahoma City, OK - *BrCabYB 84; DirUSTelSta 83; TelAl 83, 84; Tel&CabFB 84S; TV&RadDir 84*

KOKI-TV - Tulsa, OK - *BrCabYB 84; DirUSTelSta 83; TelAl 83, 84; Tel&CabFB 84S; TV&RadDir 84*

KOKK - Huron, SD - *BrCabYB 84; TV&RadDir 84*

KOKL - Okmulgee, OK - *BrCabYB 84; TV&RadDir 84*

KOKL-FM - Okmulgee, OK - *BrCabYB 84; TV&RadDir 84*

KOKN - Claremore, OK - *BrCabYB 84*

KOKO - Warrensburg, MO - *BrCabYB 84; TV&RadDir 84*

Koko Music - *See* Boxer Music

Kokomo Tribune [of Thomson Newspapers Inc.] - Kokomo, IN - *BaconPubCkNews 84; Ed&PubIntYB 82; NewsDir 84*

Kokono - Byron, CA - *BoPubDir 4, 5*

KOKQ - Oakdale, CA - *BrCabYB 84*

KOKR-FM - Newport, AR - *BrCabYB 84; TV&RadDir 84*

KOKX - Keokuk, IA - *BrCabYB 84; TV&RadDir 84*

KOKY - Little Rock, AR - *BrCabYB 84; NatRadPubDir Summer 83, Spring 84; TV&RadDir 84*

KOLA-FM - Riverside, CA - *TV&RadDir 84*

KOLA-FM - San Bernardino, CA - *BrCabYB 84; NatRadPubDir Summer 83, Spring 84 p.27*

Kolb & Bauman Advertising Inc. - Chicago, IL - *StaDirAdAg 2-84*

Kolber Advertising Inc., Gene K. - Willow Grove, PA - *AdAge 3-28-84; StaDirAdAg 2-84*

KOLD-TV - Tucson, AZ - *BrCabYB 84; DirUSTelSta 83; TelAl 83, 84; Tel&CabFB 84S; TV&RadDir 84*

KOLE - Beaumont, TX - *NatRadPubDir Spring 84*

KOLE - Port Arthur, TX - *BrCabYB 84; NatRadPubDir Summer 83; TV&RadDir 84*

Kolesar & Hartwell Inc. - Minneapolis, MN - *StaDirAdAg 2-84*

Koleszar-Fenneman Advertising Inc. - Evansville, IN - *StaDirAdAg 2-84*

KOLI - Coalinga, CA - *BrCabYB 84; TV&RadDir 84*

Kolker, Talley, Hermann - New York, NY - *AdAge 3-28-84; StaDirAdAg 2-84*

KOLL-FM - Gillette, WY - *BrCabYB 84; TV&RadDir 84*

Kollmorgen Corp. (Photo Research Div.) - Burbank, CA - *AvMarPl 83*

KOLM - Rochester, MN - *BrCabYB 84; TV&RadDir 84*

Kolmer Enterprises, Lloyd - New York, NY - *HBIndAd&MS 82-83*
KOLN-TV - Lincoln, NE - *BrCabYB 84; DirUSTelSta 83; TelAl 83, 84; Tel&CabFB 84S; TV&RadDir 84*
KOLO - Reno, NV - *BrCabYB 84; NatRadPubDir Summer 83, Spring 84; TV&RadDir 84*
KOLO-TV - Reno, NV - *BrCabYB 84; DirUSTelSta 83; TelAl 83, 84; Tel&CabFB 84S; TV&RadDir 84*
Kolody Inc., John F. - New York, NY - *StaDirAdAg 2-84*
Kolon, Bittker & Desmond - Troy, MI - *AdAge 3-28-84; StaDirAdAg 2-84*
Kolor-Krome Inc. - Milwaukee, WI - *AvMarPl 83*
Kolpin, Ruth I. - Carthage, MO - *BrCabYB 84 p.D-303*
Kolpin, Ruth I. - *See* Southwest Missouri Cable TV Inc.
Kolpin, Ruth I. - *See* TDS Engineering Co.
KOLR-TV - Springfield, MO - *BrCabYB 84; DirUSTelSta 83; TelAl 83, 84; Tel&CabFB 84S; TV&RadDir 84*
KOLS - DeSoto, MO - *BrCabYB 84*
KOLT - Scottsbluff, NE - *BrCabYB 84; NatRadPubDir Summer 83, Spring 84; TV&RadDir 84*
KOLU-FM - Pasco, WA - *BrCabYB 84; NatRadPubDir Summer 83, Spring 84; TV&RadDir 84*
KOLV - Olivia, MN - *BrCabYB 84*
KOLY - Mobridge, SD - *BrCabYB 84; TV&RadDir 84*
KOLY-FM - Mobridge, SD - *BrCabYB 84; TV&RadDir 84*
KOMA - Oklahoma City, OK - *BrCabYB 84; NatRadPubDir Summer 83, Spring 84; TV&RadDir 84*
Komanoff Energy Associates - New York, NY - *BoPubDir 4 Sup, 5*
KOMB-FM - Ft. Scott, KS - *BrCabYB 84; TV&RadDir 84*
KOME-FM - San Jose, CA - *BrCabYB 84; NatRadPubDir Summer 83, Spring 84; TV&RadDir 84*
KOME-FM - Manitou Springs, CO - *TV&RadDir 84*
KOMO - Seattle, WA - *BrCabYB 84; LitMarPl 83, 84; NatRadPubDir Summer 83, Spring 84; TV&RadDir 84*
KOMO-TV - Seattle, WA - *BrCabYB 84; DirUSTelSta 83; LitMarPl 83, 84; TelAl 83, 84; Tel&CabFB 84S; TV&RadDir 84*
KOMP-FM - Las Vegas, NV - *BrCabYB 84; NatRadPubDir Summer 83, Spring 84; TV&RadDir 84*
Komp Information Services - Louisville, KY - *CompReadDB 82; DataDirOnSer 84; InfIndMarPl 83*
Kompass [of Croner Publications Inc.] - Queens Village, NY - *EISS 83*
Kompass Data Base [of Industrial News Publishing Co.] - Paris, France - *EISS 83*
Kompass Data Base - Stockholm, Sweden - *DirOnDB Spring 84*
KOMR-FM - St. Louis, MO - *BrCabYB 84; TV&RadDir 84*
KOMU-TV - Columbia, MO - *BrCabYB 84; DirUSTelSta 83; TelAl 83, 84; Tel&CabFB 84S; TV&RadDir 84*
KOMW - Omak, WA - *BrCabYB 84; TV&RadDir 84*
KOMW-FM - Omak, WA - *BrCabYB 84; TV&RadDir 84*
KOMX-FM - Pampa, TX - *BrCabYB 84; TV&RadDir 84*
KOMY - Watsonville, CA - *BrCabYB 84; TV&RadDir 84*
KONA - Kennewick, WA - *BrCabYB 84*
KONA - Pasco, WA - *TV&RadDir 84*
KONA-FM - Kennewick, WA - *BrCabYB 84*
KONA-FM - Pasco, WA - *TV&RadDir 84*
Konan Corp. - Phoenix, AZ - *WhoWMicrocom 83*
Konawa Leader - Konawa, OK - *Ed&PubIntYB 82*
Konawa Leader - *See* Konawa Newspapers
Konawa Newspapers - Konawa, OK - *BaconPubCkNews 84*
KONE - Reno, NV - *BrCabYB 84; NatRadPubDir Summer 83, Spring 84; TV&RadDir 84*
Konecky Associates Inc., William S. - New York, NY - *LitMarPl 83, 84*
Konecky Co. Inc., Gerald M. - Port Washington, NY - *LitMarPl 83, 84*
KONG - Tulare, CA - *NatRadPubDir Summer 83, Spring 84 p.34*
KONG - Visalia, CA - *BrCabYB 84; TV&RadDir 84*
KONG-FM - Tulare, CA - *NatRadPubDir Summer 83, Spring 84 p.34*
KONG-FM - Visalia, CA - *BrCabYB 84; TV&RadDir 84*
Konglomerati Press [Div. of Konglomerati Florida Foundation for Literature & the Book Arts Inc.] - Gulfport, FL - *LitMag&SmPr 83-84; LitMarPl 83, 84*
Kongsberg North America Inc. - Houston, TX - *DataDirSup 7-83*
Kongsberg/Sysscan - Houston, TX - *DataDirSup 7-83*
KONI - Spanish Fork, UT - *BrCabYB 84; TV&RadDir 84*
Koninklijk Instituut voor de Tropen/Royal Tropical Institute - Amsterdam, Netherlands - *InfIndMarPl 83*
Koninklijk Nederlands Meteorologisch Instituut - De Bildt, Netherlands - *InfIndMarPl 83*
Koninklijke Nederlandse Akademie van Wetenschappen - Amsterdam, Netherlands - *InfIndMarPl 83*
Koninklijke Vermande BV - Ijmuiden, Netherlands - *EISS 5-84 Sup*
KONO - San Antonio, TX - *BrCabYB 84; NatRadPubDir Summer 83, Spring 84; TV&RadDir 84*
Konocti Books/Cannonade Press - Winters, CA - *BoPubDir 4, 5; LitMag&SmPr 83-84*
Konocti TV Inc. [of Jones Intercable Inc.] - Clearlake Oaks, CA - *BrCabYB 84*
Konocti TV Inc. [of Jones Intercable Inc.] - Cobb Mountain, CA - *Tel&CabFB 84C*
KONP - Port Angeles, WA - *BrCabYB 84; TV&RadDir 84*
Konrad Public Relations, Evelyn - New York, NY - *DirPRFirms 83*
Kontexts Publications - Amsterdam, Netherlands - *LitMag&SmPr 83-84*
Kontron Electronics - Redwood City, CA - *DataDirSup 7-83*
KONY - Thief River Falls, MN - *BrCabYB 84; Tel&CabFB 84S*
KOOC - Cozad, NE - *BrCabYB 84*
KOOD - Hays, KS - *BrCabYB 84; Tel&CabFB 84S*
KOOG-TV - Ogden, UT - *BrCabYB 84; Tel&CabFB 84S*
KOOI-FM - Jacksonville, TX - *BrCabYB 84; TV&RadDir 84*
KOOK - Billings, MT - *BrCabYB 84; NatRadPubDir Summer 83, Spring 84; TV&RadDir 84*
KOOK-FM - Billings, MT - *BrCabYB 84; NatRadPubDir Summer 83, Spring 84; TV&RadDir 84*
KOOL-FM - Phoenix, AZ - *BrCabYB 84; NatRadPubDir Summer 83, Spring 84; TV&RadDir 84*
Kool Kat Music [Div. of Kool Kat Productions Inc.] - Monsey, NY - *BillIntBG 83-84*
Kool Kat Productions Inc. - Monsey, NY - *BillIntBG 83-84*
Kool Music Inc. - *See* Buttermilk Sky Music Publishing Corp.
KOOL-TV - Phoenix, AZ - *LitMarPl 83; TelAl 83*
KOOO - Omaha, NE - *BrCabYB 84; NatRadPubDir Summer 83, Spring 84; TV&RadDir 84*
KOOQ - North Platte, NE - *BrCabYB 84; TV&RadDir 84*
KOOS-FM - Coos Bay, OR - *TV&RadDir 84*
KOOS-FM - North Bend, OR - *BrCabYB 84*
Kooskia Cable Systems - Elk City, ID - *BrCabYB 84; Tel&CabFB 84C*
Koota Publishing - *See* Seltzer, Ralph L.
Kootenai Communications Inc. - Sandpoint, ID - *BrCabYB 84*
Kootenay Advertiser - Cranbrook, BC, Canada - *AyerDirPub 83; Ed&PubIntYB 82*
Kootenay Cable Ltd. - Fernie, BC, Canada - *BrCabYB 84; Tel&CabFB 84C*
KOOV-FM - Copperas Cove, TX - *BrCabYB 84; TV&RadDir 84*
KOOZ-FM - Great Falls, MT - *BrCabYB 84; TV&RadDir 84*
KOPA - Scottsdale, AZ - *BrCabYB 84; TV&RadDir 84*
KOPA-FM - Scottsdale, AZ - *BrCabYB 84; TV&RadDir 84*
Kopak Creations Inc. - Union City, NJ - *MicrocomMPl 84*
KOPE-FM - Las Cruces, NM - *NatRadPubDir Summer 83, Spring 84*
KOPE-FM - Mesilla Park, NM - *BrCabYB 84*
Kopf & Isaacson Advertising - Melville, NY - *AdAge 3-28-84; StaDirAdAg 2-84*
Koplar Communications Center [of Koplar Communications Inc.] - St. Louis, MO - *Tel&CabFB 84C; TeleSy&SerDir 2-84*
Koplar Communications Inc. - St. Louis, MO - *BrCabYB 84; Tel&CabFB 84S*
KOPN-FM - Columbia, MO - *BrCabYB 84; TV&RadDir 84*
KOPO - Marana, AZ - *BrCabYB 84*
Koppe & Co. Inc., S. S. - Lyndhurst, NJ - *Ed&PubIntYB 82*
Koppelman-Bandier Music Corp. - *See* Entertainment Co. Music Group, The
Kopplemann Inc., H. P. - Hartford, CT - *LitMarPl 83, 84*
KOPR - Butte, MT - *BrCabYB 84; TV&RadDir 84*
KOPY - Alice, TX - *BrCabYB 84; TV&RadDir 84*
Kopy Katz Kwik Typing Service - Long Beach, CA - *LitMarPl 83, 84*
KOQT - Bellingham, WA - *BrCabYB 84*

KOQT - Ferndale, WA - *TV&RadDir 84*
KOQZ - Waynesville, MO - *BrCabYB 84*
KORA-FM - Bryan, TX - *BrCabYB 84; TV&RadDir 84*
Korakas, Roberts & Kirby - Oklahoma City, OK - *BoPubDir 4 Sup, 5*
Korchnoy Ltd., E. A. - New York, NY - *StaDirAdAg 2-84*
KORD - Pasco, WA - *BrCabYB 84; TV&RadDir 84*
Korda Rand Levine Inc. - New York, NY - *HBIndAd&MS 82-83*
Kordet Graphics Inc. - Oceanside, NY - *MagIndMarPl 82-83*
KORE - Springfield, OR - *BrCabYB 84; TV&RadDir 84*
Korea Advanced Institute of Science & Technology Library - Seoul, South Korea - *InfIndMarPl 83*
Korea Institute for Industrial Economics & Technology - Seoul, South Korea - *EISS 7-83 Sup*
Korea News - Long Island City, NY - *Ed&PubIntYB 82*
Korea Times, The - Toronto, ON, Canada - *AyerDirPub 83; Ed&PubIntYB 82*
Korean Journal - Willowdale, ON, Canada - *Ed&PubIntYB 82*
Koreanna, The - Port Coquitlam, BC, Canada - *Ed&PubIntYB 82*
Kores-Canada Ltd. - St. Laurent, PQ, Canada - *DirInfWP 82*
Korey, Kay & Partners - New York, NY - *StaDirAdAg 2-84*
KORK - Las Vegas, NV - *BrCabYB 84; NatRadPubDir Summer 83, Spring 84; TV&RadDir 84*
KORK-FM - Las Vegas, NV - *NatRadPubDir Summer 83, Spring 84; TV&RadDir 84*
KORL - Honolulu, HI - *BrCabYB 84; NatRadPubDir Summer 83, Spring 84; TV&RadDir 84*
KORN - Mitchell, SD - *BrCabYB 84; TV&RadDir 84*
Korn, Alfred Jr. - Kenilworth, NJ - *BoPubDir 4, 5*
Kornfeld Recording Inc., Dan - New York, NY - *AvMarPl 83*
Kornhauser & Calene - New York, NY - *AdAge 3-28-84; Br 1-23-84; BrCabYB 84; StaDirAdAg 2-84*
Kornhauser, Ellen - New York, NY - *LitMarPl 83*
KORO-TV - Corpus Christi, TX - *BrCabYB 84; DirUSTelSta 83; TelAl 83, 84; Tel&CabFB 84S; TV&RadDir 84*
KORQ-FM - Abilene, TX - *BrCabYB 84; NatRadPubDir Summer 83, Spring 84; TV&RadDir 84*
Korshak Associates, Margie - Chicago, IL - *DirPRFirms 83*
KORT - Grangeville, ID - *BrCabYB 84; TV&RadDir 84*
KORT-FM - Grangeville, ID - *BrCabYB 84; TV&RadDir 84*
KORV - Oroville, CA - *BrCabYB 84; TV&RadDir 84*
KORV - Medford, OR - *BrCabYB 84*
KOSA-TV - Odessa, TX - *BrCabYB 84; DirUSTelSta 83; LitMarPl 83, 84; TelAl 83, 84; Tel&CabFB 84S; TV&RadDir 84*
KOSC - Marshfield, MO - *BrCabYB 84; TV&RadDir 84*
KOSC-FM - Marshfield, MO - *BrCabYB 84; TV&RadDir 84*
Kosciusko Star-Herald - Kosciusko, MS - *BaconPubCkNews 84; NewsDir 84*
Kosciuszko Foundation Inc. - New York, NY - *BoPubDir 4, 5*
KOSE - Osceola, AR - *BrCabYB 84; TV&RadDir 84*
KOSG-FM - Osage, IA - *TV&RadDir 84*
Kosho-Shorei Publishing Co. - Sacramento, CA - *BoPubDir 4 Sup, 5*
KOSI-FM - Denver, CO - *BrCabYB 84*
KOSI-FM - Wheat Ridge, CO - *TV&RadDir 84*
Kosikowski & Associates, Frank - Brooktondale, NY - *BoPubDir 4, 5*
Kosmos - San Francisco, CA - *BoPubDir 4, 5; LitMag&SmPr 83-84*
KOSO-FM - Modesto, CA - *NatRadPubDir Summer 83, Spring 84; TV&RadDir 84*
KOSO-FM - Patterson, CA - *BrCabYB 84*
Kosoy Travel Guides - Toronto, ON, Canada - *BoPubDir 4, 5*
Koss Corp. - Milwaukee, WI - *AvMarPl 83*
Koss, Mayburn - Greenwich, CT - *MagIndMarPl 82-83*
Kossack Advertising Associates Inc. - Tucson, AZ - *StaDirAdAg 2-84*
Kossdorf & Partner, Dr. - *See* Needham, Harper & Steers Inc.
Kossuth County Advance [of Algona Publishing Co.] - Algona, IA - *AyerDirPub 83; NewsDir 84*
KOST-FM - Los Angeles, CA - *BrCabYB 84; LitMarPl 84; NatRadPubDir Summer 83, Spring 84; TV&RadDir 84*
Kostanski, Michael - Winnipeg, MB, Canada - *BoPubDir 4 Sup, 5*
Koster Music, Iren - *See* Snugglebush Music Co.
Kostka & Associates Inc., William - Denver, CO - *DirPRFirms 83; StaDirAdAg 2-84*
Kostman/Schmid & Associates - Chicago, IL - *AdAge 3-28-84; StaDirAdAg 2-84*
Kostyniuk Publishing, R. - Canada - *BoPubDir 4 Sup, 5*
KOSU-FM - Stillwater, OK - *BrCabYB 84; LitMarPl 83; NatRadPubDir Summer 83, Spring 84; TV&RadDir 84*
KOSY - Texarkana, TX - *BrCabYB 84; TV&RadDir 84*
KOSY-FM - Texarkana, TX - *BrCabYB 84; TV&RadDir 84*
KOTA - Bethlehem, SD - *TV&RadDir 84*
KOTA - Rapid City, SD - *BrCabYB 84*
KOTA Cable TV Co. [of Northern Communications Associates] - Brookings, SD - *Tel&CabFB 84C*
KOTA-TV - Bethlehem, SD - *TV&RadDir 84*
KOTA-TV - Rapid City, SD - *BrCabYB 84; DirUSTelSta 83; TelAl 83, 84; Tel&CabFB 84S*
KOTB - Evanston, WY - *BrCabYB 84*
KOTD - Plattsmouth, NE - *BrCabYB 84; TV&RadDir 84*
KOTE - Lancaster, CA - *BrCabYB 84; NatRadPubDir Spring 84*
KOTE-FM - Lancaster, CA - *NatRadPubDir Summer 83; TV&RadDir 84*
KOTI-TV - Klamath Falls, OR - *BrCabYB 84; DirUSTelSta 83; TelAl 83, 84; Tel&CabFB 84S; TV&RadDir 84*
KOTN - Pine Bluff, AR - *BrCabYB 84; NatRadPubDir Summer 83, Spring 84; TV&RadDir 84*
KOTO-FM - Telluride, CO - *BrCabYB 84; TV&RadDir 84*
KOTS - Deming, NM - *BrCabYB 84; TV&RadDir 84*
Kotula Co. Inc., The - Greenwich, CT - *StaDirAdAg 2-84*
KOTV-TV - Tulsa, OK - *BrCabYB 84; DirUSTelSta 83; LitMarPl 83, 84; TelAl 83, 84; Tel&CabFB 84S; TV&RadDir 84*
KOTY - Kennewick, WA - *BrCabYB 84; TV&RadDir 84*
KOTZ - Kotzebue, AK - *BrCabYB 84; TV&RadDir 84*
Kotzebue Cablevision [of Alaska Cablevision Inc.] - Kotzebue, AK - *BrCabYB 84; Tel&CabFB 84C*
KOUH-TV - Hay Springs, NE - *TV&RadDir 84*
KOUL-FM - Corpus Christi, TX - *NatRadPubDir Summer 83, Spring 84; TV&RadDir 84*
KOUL-FM - Sinton, TX - *BrCabYB 84*
Kountry Kable - Mecca, CA - *BrCabYB 84*
Kountry Kablevision North Carolina Inc. - Johnston County, NC - *Tel&CabFB 84C*
Kountze News-Visitor - Kountze, TX - *Ed&PubIntYB 82*
Kountze News Visitor - *See* Liberal Publishers
KOUR - Independence, IA - *BrCabYB 84; TV&RadDir 84*
KOUR-FM - Independence, IA - *BrCabYB 84; TV&RadDir 84*
Kourier, The - Willow Creek, CA - *AyerDirPub 83*
KOUS-TV - Hardin, MT - *BrCabYB 84; DirUSTelSta 83; TelAl 83, 84; Tel&CabFB 84S; TV&RadDir 84*
Kouts Times - Kouts, IN - *Ed&PubIntYB 82*
Kouts Times - *See* Porter County Publishing Co.
KOVA-FM - Ojai, CA - *BrCabYB 84; TV&RadDir 84*
Kovacs & Relf - New York, NY - *LitMarPl 83*
Kovar, Milo [Aff. of Astro Psychology Institute] - San Francisco, CA - *BoPubDir 5*
KOVC - Valley City, ND - *BrCabYB 84; NatRadPubDir Summer 83, Spring 84; TV&RadDir 84*
KOVE - Lander, WY - *BrCabYB 84; TV&RadDir 84*
Kovics Creative Service, Stan - New York, NY - *HBIndAd&MS 82-83*
KOVO-FM - Gallup, NM - *BrCabYB 84; TV&RadDir 84*
KOVR - Sacramento, CA - *DirUSTelSta 83*
KOVR-TV - Sacramento, CA - *LitMarPl 83, 84; TV&RadDir 84*
KOVR-TV - Stockton, CA - *BrCabYB 84; TelAl 83, 84; Tel&CabFB 84S*
KOWB - Laramie, WY - *BrCabYB 84; NatRadPubDir Summer 83, Spring 84; TV&RadDir 84*
KOWL - South Lake Tahoe, CA - *BrCabYB 84; NatRadPubDir Summer 83, Spring 84*
KOWL - Stateline, CA - *TV&RadDir 84*
KOWN - Escondido, CA - *BrCabYB 84; TV&RadDir 84*
KOWN-FM - Escondido, CA - *BrCabYB 84; TV&RadDir 84*
KOWO - Waseca, MN - *BrCabYB 84*
KOWY - Lander, WY - *BrCabYB 84; Tel&CabFB 84S*
KOXE-FM - Brownwood, TX - *BrCabYB 84; TV&RadDir 84*
KOXI-FM - Columbus, NE - *BrCabYB 84; TV&RadDir 84*
KOXR - Oxnard, CA - *BrCabYB 84; TV&RadDir 84*
KOXR - Ventura, CA - *NatRadPubDir Summer 83, Spring 84 p.34*

KOY - Phoenix, AZ - *BrCabYB 84; NatRadPubDir Summer 83, Spring 84; TV&RadDir 84*
KOYE-FM - Laredo, TX - *BrCabYB 84; TV&RadDir 84*
Koyemsi Press - Santa Fe, NM - *BoPubDir 4 Sup, 5*
KOYL - Midland, TX - *NatRadPubDir Summer 83, Spring 84 p.244*
KOYL - Odessa, TX - *BrCabYB 84; TV&RadDir 84*
KOYN - Billings, MT - *BrCabYB 84; NatRadPubDir Summer 83, Spring 84; TV&RadDir 84*
KOYT-FM - Phoenix, AZ - *TV&RadDir 84*
KOYY - El Dorado, KS - *BrCabYB 84; NatRadPubDir Summer 83, Spring 84; TV&RadDir 84*
KOZA - Midland, TX - *NatRadPubDir Summer 83, Spring 84 p.244*
KOZA - Odessa, TX - *BrCabYB 84; TV&RadDir 84*
Kozak, Maria - Toronto, ON, Canada - *BoPubDir 4, 5*
KOZE - Lewiston, ID - *BrCabYB 84; TV&RadDir 84*
KOZE-FM - Lewiston, ID - *BrCabYB 84; TV&RadDir 84*
KOZI - Chelan, WA - *BrCabYB 84; TV&RadDir 84*
KOZI-FM - Chelan, WA - *BrCabYB 84*
KOZK-TV - Springfield, MO - *BrCabYB 84; Tel&CabFB 84S; TV&RadDir 84*
Kozmik Press Centre - London, England - *LitMag&SmPr 83-84*
KOZN - Imperial, CA - *BrCabYB 84*
KOZT - Ft. Bragg, CA - *BrCabYB 84*
KOZY - Grand Rapids, MN - *BrCabYB 84; TV&RadDir 84*
KOZZ - Reno, NV - *BrCabYB 84; TV&RadDir 84*
KOZZ-FM - Reno, NV - *NatRadPubDir Summer 83, Spring 84*
KPAC - Port Arthur, TX - *NatRadPubDir Summer 83*
KPAC-FM - San Antonio, TX - *BrCabYB 84*
KPAG - Pagosa Springs, CO - *BrCabYB 84; TV&RadDir 84*
KPAH - Tonopah, NV - *BrCabYB 84*
KPAL - Pineville, LA - *BrCabYB 84; TV&RadDir 84*
KPAM - Portland, OR - *TV&RadDir 84*
KPAN - Hereford, TX - *BrCabYB 84; TV&RadDir 84*
KPAN-FM - Hereford, TX - *BrCabYB 84; TV&RadDir 84*
KPAR - Granbury, TX - *BrCabYB 84; TV&RadDir 84*
KPAS-FM - El Paso, TX - *NatRadPubDir Summer 83, Spring 84*
KPAS-FM - Fabens, TX - *BrCabYB 84*
KPAT-FM - Sioux Falls, SD - *BrCabYB 84; NatRadPubDir Summer 83, Spring 84; TV&RadDir 84*
KPAU - Covelo, CA - *BrCabYB 84*
KPAX-TV - Missoula, MT - *BrCabYB 84; DirUSTelSta 83; TelAl 83, 84; Tel&CabFB 84S; TV&RadDir 84*
KPAY - Chico, CA - *BrCabYB 84; TV&RadDir 84*
KPAY-FM - Chico, CA - *BrCabYB 84; TV&RadDir 84*
Kpay-TV Corp. - *See* K-Pay Entertainment Inc.
KPAZ-TV - Phoenix, AZ - *BrCabYB 84; DirUSTelSta 83; TelAl 83, 84; Tel&CabFB 84S; TV&RadDir 84*
KPBC - Dallas, TX - *BrCabYB 84; NatRadPubDir Summer 83 p.237, Spring 84*
KPBC - Irving, TX - *TV&RadDir 84*
KPBM-FM - Poplar Bluff, MO - *BrCabYB 84*
KPBS-FM - San Diego, CA - *BrCabYB 84; NatRadPubDir Summer 83, Spring 84; TV&RadDir 84*
KPBS-TV - San Diego, CA - *BrCabYB 84; Tel&CabFB 84S; TV&RadDir 84*
KPBX-FM - Spokane, WA - *BrCabYB 84; TV&RadDir 84*
KPCA - Marked Tree, AR - *BrCabYB 84; TV&RadDir 84*
KPCC-FM - Los Angeles, CA - *NatRadPubDir Summer 83 p.22, Spring 84*
KPCC-FM - Pasadena, CA - *BrCabYB 84; TV&RadDir 84*
KPCO - Quincy, CA - *BrCabYB 84; TV&RadDir 84*
KPCQ - Powell, WY - *BrCabYB 84*
KPCR - Bowling Green, MO - *BrCabYB 84; TV&RadDir 84*
KPCR-FM - Bowling Green, MO - *BrCabYB 84; TV&RadDir 84*
KPCS-FM - Pasadena, CA - *NatRadPubDir Summer 83*
KPCW-FM - Park City, UT - *BrCabYB 84; TV&RadDir 84*
KPDQ - Portland, OR - *BrCabYB 84; NatRadPubDir Summer 83, Spring 84; TV&RadDir 84*
KPDQ-FM - Portland, OR - *BrCabYB 84; NatRadPubDir Summer 83, Spring 84; TV&RadDir 84*
KPDX - Vancouver, WA - *BrCabYB 84; Tel&CabFB 84S*
KPEC-FM - Tacoma, WA - *NatRadPubDir Summer 83, Spring 84; TV&RadDir 84*
KPEL - Lafayette, LA - *BrCabYB 84; NatRadPubDir Summer 83, Spring 84; TV&RadDir 84*
KPEN-FM - Los Altos, CA - *BrCabYB 84*
KPEN-FM - Mountain View, CA - *TV&RadDir 84*
KPEP-FM - Gatesville, TX - *BrCabYB 84; TV&RadDir 84*
KPER-FM - Hobbs, NM - *BrCabYB 84; TV&RadDir 84*
KPET - Lamesa, TX - *BrCabYB 84; TV&RadDir 84*
KPEZ - Austin, TX - *BrCabYB 84*
KPFA - Berkeley, CA - *BrCabYB 84; TV&RadDir 84*
KPFA-FM - Berkeley, CA - *LitMarPl 83, 84*
KPFA-FM - San Francisco, CA - *NatRadPubDir Summer 83 p.31, Spring 84 p.31*
KPFB-FM - Berkeley, CA - *BrCabYB 84; LitMarPl 83, 84; TV&RadDir 84*
KPFK-FM - Los Angeles, CA - *BrCabYB 84; NatRadPubDir Summer 83 p.22, Spring 84 p.22*
KPFK-FM - North Hollywood, CA - *LitMarPl 83, 84; TV&RadDir 84*
KPFT-FM - Houston, TX - *BrCabYB 84; LitMarPl 83, 84; NatRadPubDir Summer 83, Spring 84; TV&RadDir 84*
KPGA-FM - Pismo Beach, CA - *BrCabYB 84; TV&RadDir 84*
KPGE - Page, AZ - *BrCabYB 84; TV&RadDir 84*
KPGR-FM - American Fork, UT - *TV&RadDir 84*
KPGR-FM - Pleasant Grove, UT - *BrCabYB 84*
KPGY-FM - Ames, IA - *NatRadPubDir Summer 83, Spring 84; TV&RadDir 84*
KPHO-TV [Div. of Meredith Corp.] - Phoenix, AZ - *BrCabYB 84; DirUSTelSta 83; TelAl 83, 84; Tel&CabFB 84S; TV&RadDir 84*
KPHX - Phoenix, AZ - *BrCabYB 84; NatRadPubDir Summer 83, Spring 84; TV&RadDir 84*
KPIA - Ironton, MO - *BrCabYB 84; TV&RadDir 84*
KPIC-TV [Aff. of KVAL-TV] - Roseburg, OR - *BrCabYB 84; TelAl 83, 84; Tel&CabFB 84S; TV&RadDir 84*
KPIK - Colorado Springs, CO - *BrCabYB 84; NatRadPubDir Summer 83, Spring 84; TV&RadDir 84*
KPIN - Casa Grande, AZ - *BrCabYB 84; TV&RadDir 84*
KPIP - Roseville, CA - *BrCabYB 84*
KPIX-TV - San Francisco, CA - *BrCabYB 84; DirUSTelSta 83; LitMarPl 83, 84; TelAl 83, 84; Tel&CabFB 84S; TV&RadDir 84; VideoDir 82-83*
KPJH-FM - Ft. Stockton, TX - *BrCabYB 84; TV&RadDir 84*
KPKE-FM - Denver, CO - *BrCabYB 84; TV&RadDir 84*
KPKJ - Eureka, CA - *BrCabYB 84*
KPKY-FM - Boise, ID - *NatRadPubDir Summer 83 p.77, Spring 84*
KPKY-FM - Pocatello, ID - *BrCabYB 84*
KPLC-TV - Lake Charles, LA - *BrCabYB 84; DirUSTelSta 83; TelAl 83, 84; Tel&CabFB 84S; TV&RadDir 84*
KPLE-FM - Temple, TX - *BrCabYB 84; TV&RadDir 84*
KPLM - Palm Springs, CA - *BrCabYB 84*
KPLN-FM - Plains, TX - *BrCabYB 84; TV&RadDir 84*
KPLO-TV - Reliance, SD - *BrCabYB 84; TelAl 83, 84; Tel&CabFB 84S*
KPLR-TV - St. Louis, MO - *BrCabYB 84; DirUSTelSta 83; TelAl 83, 84; Tel&CabFB 84S; TV&RadDir 84*
KPLS - Santa Rosa, CA - *BrCabYB 84; TV&RadDir 84*
KPLT - Paris, TX - *BrCabYB 84; TV&RadDir 84*
KPLU-FM - Tacoma, WA - *BrCabYB 84; NatRadPubDir Summer 83, Spring 84; TV&RadDir 84*
KPLV - Pueblo, CO - *NatRadPubDir Summer 83, Spring 84*
KPLX-FM - Arlington, TX - *TV&RadDir 84*
KPLX-FM - Dallas, TX - *NatRadPubDir Summer 83 p.237, Spring 84 p.238*
KPLX-FM - Ft. Worth, TX - *BrCabYB 84*
KPLZ-FM - Seattle, WA - *BrCabYB 84; NatRadPubDir Summer 83, Spring 84; TV&RadDir 84*
KPMA - Tacoma, WA - *BrCabYB 84; NatRadPubDir Summer 83, Spring 84*
KPMB-FM - Poplar Bluff, MO - *TV&RadDir 84*
KPMC - Bakersfield, CA - *BrCabYB 84; NatRadPubDir Summer 83, Spring 84; TV&RadDir 84*
KPMO - Ft. Bragg, CA - *TV&RadDir 84*
KPMO - Mendicino, CA - *BrCabYB 84*
KPNC-FM - Ponca City, OK - *BrCabYB 84*
KPND-FM - Sandpoint, ID - *BrCabYB 84; TV&RadDir 84*
KPNE-TV - North Platte, NE - *BrCabYB 84; Tel&CabFB 84S*
KPNT-FM - Pittsburgh, PA - *NatRadPubDir Summer 83*

KPNW - Eugene, OR - *BrCabYB 84; NatRadPubDir Summer 83, Spring 84*
KPNW - Florence, OR - *TV&RadDir 84*
KPNW-FM - Eugene, OR - *BrCabYB 84; NatRadPubDir Summer 83, Spring 84*
KPNW-FM - Florence, OR - *TV&RadDir 84*
KPNX-TV - Mesa, AZ - *BrCabYB 84*
KPNX-TV - Phoenix, AZ - *DirUSTelSta 83; LitMarPl 83, 84; TelAl 83, 84; Tel&CabFB 84S; TV&RadDir 84*
KPNY-FM - Alliance, NE - *BrCabYB 84; TV&RadDir 84*
KPOB-TV - Poplar Bluff, MO - *BrCabYB 84; TelAl 83, 84; Tel&CabFB 84S; TV&RadDir 84*
KPOC - Pocahontas, AR - *BrCabYB 84; TV&RadDir 84*
KPOD - Crescent City, CA - *TV&RadDir 84*
KPOF - Denver, CO - *BrCabYB 84; TV&RadDir 84*
KPOI - Honolulu, HI - *BrCabYB 84; NatRadPubDir Summer 83, Spring 84; TV&RadDir 84*
KPOI-FM - Honolulu, HI - *BrCabYB 84*
KPOK - Bowman, ND - *BrCabYB 84; TV&RadDir 84*
KPOL - Crescent City, CA - *BrCabYB 84*
KPOM-TV - Ft. Smith, AR - *BrCabYB 84; DirUSTelSta 83; TelAl 84; Tel&CabFB 84S*
KPOO-FM - San Francisco, CA - *BrCabYB 84; TV&RadDir 84*
KPOP-FM - Roseville, CA - *BrCabYB 84; TV&RadDir 84*
KPOS - Post, TX - *BrCabYB 84; TV&RadDir 84*
KPOW - Powell, WY - *BrCabYB 84; TV&RadDir 84*
KPPC - Los Angeles, CA - *NatRadPubDir Summer 83 p.23, Spring 84 p.23*
KPPC - Pasadena, CA - *BrCabYB 84; TV&RadDir 84*
KPPL-FM - Denver, CO - *NatRadPubDir Summer 83, Spring 84; TV&RadDir 84*
KPPL-FM - Lakewood, CO - *BrCabYB 84*
KPQ - Wenatchee, WA - *BrCabYB 84; TV&RadDir 84*
KPQ-FM - Wenatchee, WA - *BrCabYB 84; TV&RadDir 84*
KPQP - San Diego, CA - *NatRadPubDir Spring 84*
KPQX-FM - Havre, MT - *BrCabYB 84; TV&RadDir 84*
KPR/Infor/Media Corp. - *See* Kallir, Philips, Ross Inc.
KPRA-FM - Paso Robles, CA - *TV&RadDir 84*
KPRB - Redmond, OR - *BrCabYB 84; TV&RadDir 84*
KPRB-FM - Redmond, OR - *BrCabYB 84; TV&RadDir 84*
KPRC - Houston, TX - *BrCabYB 84; NatRadPubDir Summer 83, Spring 84; TV&RadDir 84*
KPRC-TV - Houston, TX - *BrCabYB 84; DirUSTelSta 83; LitMarPl 83, 84; TelAl 83, 84; Tel&CabFB 84S; TV&RadDir 84*
KPRD - Barstow, CA - *BrCabYB 84*
KPRE - Paris, TX - *BrCabYB 84; TV&RadDir 84*
KPRI-FM - San Diego, CA - *BrCabYB 84; NatRadPubDir Summer 83, Spring 84; TV&RadDir 84*
KPRK - Livingston, MT - *BrCabYB 84; TV&RadDir 84*
KPRL - Paso Robles, CA - *BrCabYB 84; TV&RadDir 84*
KPRM - Park Rapids, MN - *BrCabYB 84; TV&RadDir 84*
KPRM-FM - Park Rapids, MN - *BrCabYB 84; TV&RadDir 84*
KPRN-FM - Angwin, CA - *BrCabYB 84; NatRadPubDir Summer 83, Spring 84; TV&RadDir 84*
KPRO - Riverside, CA - *BrCabYB 84; TV&RadDir 84*
KPRO - San Bernardino, CA - *NatRadPubDir Summer 83, Spring 84 p.27*
KPRQ - Salt Lake City, UT - *TV&RadDir 84*
KPRR-TV - Honolulu, HI - *BrCabYB 84; Tel&CabFB 84S*
KPRS-FM - Kansas City, MO - *BrCabYB 84; NatRadPubDir Summer 83, Spring 84; TV&RadDir 84*
KPRT - Kansas City, MO - *BrCabYB 84; NatRadPubDir Summer 83, Spring 84; TV&RadDir 84*
KPRY-TV - Pierre, SD - *BrCabYB 84; TelAl 83, 84; Tel&CabFB 84S*
KPRZ - Los Angeles, CA - *BrCabYB 84; NatRadPubDir Summer 83, Spring 84; TV&RadDir 84*
KPSA - Alamogordo, NM - *BrCabYB 84; TV&RadDir 84*
KPSA-FM - Alamogordo, NM - *BrCabYB 84*
KPSD-TV - Eagle Butte, SD - *BrCabYB 84; Tel&CabFB 84S*
KPSH-FM - Palm Springs, CA - *BrCabYB 84; TV&RadDir 84*
KPSI - Palm Springs, CA - *BrCabYB 84; NatRadPubDir Summer 83, Spring 84; TV&RadDir 84*
KPSI-FM - Palm Springs, CA - *BrCabYB 84; NatRadPubDir Summer 83, Spring 84*
KPSM-FM - Brownwood, TX - *BrCabYB 84; TV&RadDir 84*
KPSN-FM - Payson, AZ - *BrCabYB 84*
KPSO - Falfurrias, TX - *BrCabYB 84; TV&RadDir 84*
KPSO-FM - Falfurrias, TX - *BrCabYB 84*
KPSU-FM - Goodwell, OK - *BrCabYB 84; TV&RadDir 84*
KPTL - Carson City, NV - *BrCabYB 84; TV&RadDir 84*
KPTS - Hutchinson, KS - *BrCabYB 84*
KPTS - Wichita, KS - *Tel&CabFB 84S; TV&RadDir 84*
KPTV-TV - Portland, OR - *BrCabYB 84; DirUSTelSta 83; TelAl 83, 84; Tel&CabFB 84S; TV&RadDir 84*
KPTW - Wichita, KS - *BrCabYB 84*
KPTX - Pecos, TX - *BrCabYB 84*
KPUA - Hilo, HI - *BrCabYB 84; TV&RadDir 84*
KPUB - Winters, TX - *BrCabYB 84*
KPUG - Bellingham, WA - *BrCabYB 84; NatRadPubDir Summer 83, Spring 84; TV&RadDir 84*
KPUP - Redmond, OR - *BrCabYB 84*
KPUR - Amarillo, TX - *BrCabYB 84; NatRadPubDir Summer 83, Spring 84; TV&RadDir 84*
KPVI-TV - Pocatello, ID - *BrCabYB 84; DirUSTelSta 83; TelAl 83, 84; Tel&CabFB 84S; TV&RadDir 84*
KPVU-FM - Prairie View, TX - *BrCabYB 84*
KPWB - Piedmont, MO - *BrCabYB 84; TV&RadDir 84*
KPWN-FM - Cedar City, UT - *NatRadPubDir Summer 83, Spring 84*
KPWN-FM - Parowan, UT - *BrCabYB 84*
KPWR-TV - Bakersfield, CA - *BrCabYB 84; DirUSTelSta 83; TelAl 83, 84; Tel&CabFB 84S; TV&RadDir 84*
KPXE - Liberty, TX - *BrCabYB 84; TV&RadDir 84*
KPXI-FM - Mt. Pleasant, TX - *BrCabYB 84; TV&RadDir 84*
KPYN - Atlanta, TX - *BrCabYB 84*
KQAA-FM - Aberdeen, SD - *BrCabYB 84; NatRadPubDir Summer 83, Spring 84; TV&RadDir 84*
KQAD - Luverne, MN - *BrCabYB 84; TV&RadDir 84*
KQAD-FM - Luverne, MN - *TV&RadDir 84*
KQAK-FM - San Francisco, CA - *BrCabYB 84; NatRadPubDir Summer 83, Spring 84; TV&RadDir 84*
KQAL-FM - Winona, MN - *BrCabYB 84; NatRadPubDir Summer 83, Spring 84; TV&RadDir 84*
KQAM - Wichita, KS - *BrCabYB 84; NatRadPubDir Summer 83, Spring 84*
KQAM-FM - Wichita, KS - *TV&RadDir 84*
KQAQ - Austin, MN - *BrCabYB 84; TV&RadDir 84*
KQAY-FM - Tucumcari, NM - *TV&RadDir 84*
KQBE - Ellensburg, WA - *BrCabYB 84*
KQBR - Brainerd, MN - *BrCabYB 84*
KQCA-FM - Canton, MO - *BrCabYB 84; TV&RadDir 84*
KQCD-TV - Dickinson, ND - *BrCabYB 84; DirUSTelSta 83; TelAl 83, 84; Tel&CabFB 84S; TV&RadDir 84*
KQCR-FM - Cedar Rapids, IA - *BrCabYB 84; NatRadPubDir Summer 83, Spring 84; TV&RadDir 84*
KQCV - Oklahoma City, OK - *BrCabYB 84; NatRadPubDir Summer 83, Spring 84; TV&RadDir 84*
KQDB - Volga, SD - *BrCabYB 84*
KQDE-FM - Waseca, MN - *BrCabYB 84*
KQDI - Great Falls, MT - *BrCabYB 84; NatRadPubDir Summer 83, Spring 84; TV&RadDir 84*
KQDJ - Jamestown, ND - *BrCabYB 84; TV&RadDir 84*
KQDJ-FM - Jamestown, ND - *BrCabYB 84*
KQDQ - Eugene, OR - *BrCabYB 84; NatRadPubDir Spring 84; TV&RadDir 84*
KQDS - Duluth, MN - *NatRadPubDir Summer 83*
KQDS-FM - Duluth, MN - *BrCabYB 84; NatRadPubDir Summer 83, Spring 84; TV&RadDir 84*
KQDY-FM - Bismarck, ND - *BrCabYB 84; NatRadPubDir Summer 83, Spring 84; TV&RadDir 84*
KQEC-TV - San Francisco, CA - *BrCabYB 84; Tel&CabFB 84S; TV&RadDir 84*
KQED-FM - San Francisco, CA - *BrCabYB 84; TV&RadDir 84*
KQED-TV - San Francisco, CA - *BrCabYB 84; Tel&CabFB 84S; TV&RadDir 84*
KQEE - West Helena, AR - *BrCabYB 84*
KQEN - Roseburg, OR - *BrCabYB 84; TV&RadDir 84*
KQEO - Albuquerque, NM - *BrCabYB 84; NatRadPubDir Summer 83, Spring 84; TV&RadDir 84*
KQEU - Olympia, WA - *BrCabYB 84; TV&RadDir 84*
KQEW - Fordyce, AR - *BrCabYB 84*
KQEZ - Coolidge, AZ - *BrCabYB 84*
KQFB - Tacoma, WA - *BrCabYB 84; Tel&CabFB 84S*

KQFM-FM - Portland, OR - *BrCabYB 84; NatRadPubDir Summer 83; TV&RadDir 84*
KQHJ - Key West, FL - *Tel&CabFB 84S*
KQHU-FM - Yankton, SD - *BrCabYB 84; NatRadPubDir Summer 83, Spring 84; TV&RadDir 84*
KQIC - Willmar, MN - *BrCabYB 84*
KQID-FM - Alexandria, LA - *BrCabYB 84; TV&RadDir 84*
KQIK - Lakeview, OR - *BrCabYB 84; TV&RadDir 84*
KQIL - Grand Junction, CO - *BrCabYB 84; NatRadPubDir Summer 83, Spring 84; TV&RadDir 84*
KQIN - Burien, WA - *BrCabYB 84*
KQIN - Seattle, WA - *TV&RadDir 84*
KQIP-FM - Odessa, TX - *BrCabYB 84; TV&RadDir 84*
KQIQ - Hanford, CA - *TV&RadDir 84*
KQIQ - Lemoore, CA - *BrCabYB 84*
KQIS - Clarinda, IA - *BrCabYB 84*
KQIX-FM - Grand Junction, CO - *BrCabYB 84; NatRadPubDir Summer 83, Spring 84; TV&RadDir 84*
KQIZ - Amarillo, TX - *BrCabYB 84; NatRadPubDir Summer 83, Spring 84; TV&RadDir 84*
KQIZ-FM - Amarillo, TX - *BrCabYB 84; NatRadPubDir Summer 83, Spring 84; TV&RadDir 84*
KQJA - Winnemucca, NV - *BrCabYB 84; Tel&CabFB 84S*
KQKD - Redfield, SD - *BrCabYB 84; TV&RadDir 84*
KQKI-FM - Bayou Vista, LA - *BrCabYB 84*
KQKI-FM - Morgan City, LA - *TV&RadDir 84*
KQKK-FM - Manteca, CA - *BrCabYB 84; TV&RadDir 84*
KQKQ-FM - Council Bluffs, IA - *BrCabYB 84; TV&RadDir 84*
KQKQ-FM - Omaha, NE - *NatRadPubDir Summer 83, Spring 84*
KQKY-FM - Kearney, NE - *BrCabYB 84; TV&RadDir 84*
KQKZ - Mountain Home, ID - *BrCabYB 84*
KQLH-FM - Los Angeles, CA - *NatRadPubDir Summer 83 p.23, Spring 84 p.23*
KQLH-FM - San Bernardino, CA - *BrCabYB 84; TV&RadDir 84*
KQLS-FM - Colby, KS - *BrCabYB 84; NatRadPubDir Summer 83, Spring 84*
KQLT - Casper, WY - *BrCabYB 84*
KQMO - Brookfield, MO - *BrCabYB 84*
KQMQ-FM - Honolulu, HI - *BrCabYB 84; NatRadPubDir Summer 83, Spring 84; TV&RadDir 84*
KQMS - Redding, CA - *BrCabYB 84; TV&RadDir 84*
KQNK - Norton, KS - *BrCabYB 84; TV&RadDir 84*
KQNM-FM - Gallup, NM - *BrCabYB 84; TV&RadDir 84*
KQOK-FM - Kenai, AK - *BrCabYB 84; TV&RadDir 84*
KQOL-TV - Lawton, OK - *BrCabYB 84*
KQOT - Yakima, WA - *BrCabYB 84; TV&RadDir 84*
KQPD-FM - Ogden, UT - *BrCabYB 84; TV&RadDir 84*
KQPI-FM - Idaho Falls, ID - *BrCabYB 84; TV&RadDir 84*
KQPM - Glencoe, MN - *BrCabYB 84*
KQQF-FM - Coffeyville, KS - *BrCabYB 84*
KQQQ - Pullman, WA - *BrCabYB 84*
KQQQ-FM - Pullman, WA - *BrCabYB 84; TV&RadDir 84*
KQRK-FM - Bandera, TX - *BrCabYB 84*
KQRN-FM - Mitchell, SD - *BrCabYB 84; TV&RadDir 84*
KQRR - Ronan, MT - *BrCabYB 84*
KQRS-FM - Golden Valley, MN - *BrCabYB 84*
KQRS-FM - Minneapolis, MN - *NatRadPubDir Summer 83 p.134, Spring 84; TV&RadDir 84*
KQRX-FM - Bakersfield, CA - *NatRadPubDir Summer 83*
KQRZ - Fairbanks, AK - *BrCabYB 84*
KQSA - San Angelo, TX - *BrCabYB 84; NatRadPubDir Summer 83, Spring 84; TV&RadDir 84*
KQSD-TV - Lowry, SD - *BrCabYB 84; Tel&CabFB 84S*
KQSD-TV - Vermillion, SD - *TV&RadDir 84*
KQSK-FM - Chadron, NE - *BrCabYB 84; TV&RadDir 84*
KQSM-FM - Chanute, KS - *BrCabYB 84; TV&RadDir 84*
KQST - Sedona, AZ - *BrCabYB 84*
KQSW-FM - Rock Springs, WY - *BrCabYB 84; TV&RadDir 84*
KQTE - Santa Rosa, CA - *BrCabYB 84; TV&RadDir 84*
KQTI - Edna, TX - *BrCabYB 84*
KQTV-TV - Kansas City, MO - *DirUSTelSta 83*
KQTV-TV - St. Joseph, MO - *BrCabYB 84; TelAl 83, 84; Tel&CabFB 84S; TV&RadDir 84*
KQTY - Borger, TX - *BrCabYB 84; TV&RadDir 84*
KQTZ-FM - Hobart, OK - *BrCabYB 84; TV&RadDir 84*
KQUE-FM - Houston, TX - *BrCabYB 84; NatRadPubDir Summer 83, Spring 84; TV&RadDir 84*
KQUY-FM - Butte, MT - *BrCabYB 84; TV&RadDir 84*
KQV - Pittsburgh, PA - *BrCabYB 84; NatRadPubDir Summer 83, Spring 84; TV&RadDir 84*
KQVO - Calexico, CA - *BrCabYB 84*
KQWB - Fargo, ND - *BrCabYB 84; NatRadPubDir Summer 83, Spring 84; TV&RadDir 84*
KQWB-FM - Moorhead, MN - *BrCabYB 84*
KQWB-FM - Fargo, ND - *NatRadPubDir Summer 83; Spring 84; TV&RadDir 84*
KQWC - Webster City, IA - *BrCabYB 84; TV&RadDir 84*
KQWC-FM - Webster City, IA - *BrCabYB 84; TV&RadDir 84*
KQXI - Arvada, CO - *BrCabYB 84*
KQXI - Denver, CO - *NatRadPubDir Summer 83 p.41, Spring 84 p.41*
KQXI - Englewood, CO - *TV&RadDir 84*
KQXK - Springdale, AR - *BrCabYB 84; TV&RadDir 84*
KQXL - New Roads, LA - *TV&RadDir 84*
KQXL-FM - New Roads, LA - *BrCabYB 84; TV&RadDir 84*
KQXR-FM - Bakersfield, CA - *BrCabYB 84; NatRadPubDir Spring 84*
KQXT-FM - San Antonio, TX - *BrCabYB 84; NatRadPubDir Summer 83, Spring 84; TV&RadDir 84*
KQXX-FM - McAllen, TX - *BrCabYB 84; NatRadPubDir Summer 83, Spring 84; TV&RadDir 84*
KQXY-FM - Beaumont, TX - *BrCabYB 84; NatRadPubDir Summer 83, Spring 84; TV&RadDir 84*
KQYB-FM - Spring City, MN - *BrCabYB 84*
KQYN-FM - Twentynine Palms, CA - *BrCabYB 84; TV&RadDir 84*
KQYT-FM - Phoenix, AZ - *BrCabYB 84; NatRadPubDir Summer 83, Spring 84*
KQYX - Joplin, MO - *BrCabYB 84; NatRadPubDir Summer 83, Spring 84; TV&RadDir 84*
KQYZ - Lemoore, CA - *BrCabYB 84*
KQZQ - Caldwell, ID - *BrCabYB 84*
KRAB-FM - Seattle, WA - *BrCabYB 84; TV&RadDir 84*
KRAE - Cheyenne, WY - *BrCabYB 84; NatRadPubDir Summer 83, Spring 84; TV&RadDir 84*
Kraft & Kraft - Newburyport, MA - *LitMarPl 83, 84*
Kraft Smith - Seattle, WA - *AdAge 3-28-84; StaDirAdAg 2-84*
Kraft Systems Co. [Subs. of Carlisle Corp.] - Vista, CA - *MicrocomMPl 84; WhoWMicrocom 83*
KRAI - Craig, CO - *BrCabYB 84; TV&RadDir 84*
KRAK - Sacramento, CA - *BrCabYB 84; NatRadPubDir Summer 83, Spring 84; TV&RadDir 84*
Kraken Press - New Haven, CT - *BoPubDir 4*
Kraken Press - Milwaukee, WI - *BoPubDir 5*
KRAL - Rawlins, WY - *BrCabYB 84; TV&RadDir 84*
Krall Management Inc. - King of Prussia, PA - *MicrocomSwDir 1*
KRAM - Las Vegas, NV - *BrCabYB 84; NatRadPubDir Summer 83, Spring 84; TV&RadDir 84*
Kramer Advertising Inc., Arthur - Jericho, NY - *StaDirAdAg 2-84*
Kramer & Co., Arthur - Philadelphia, PA - *ADAPSOMemDir 83-84*
Kramer Broadcasting Inc. - Portage, WI - *BrCabYB 84*
Kramer et al Inc. - Rolling Meadows, IL - *StaDirAdAg 2-84*
Kramer Inc., Justin - Los Angeles, CA - *BoPubDir 4, 5*
Kramer Printing - Detroit, MI - *MagIndMarPl 82-83*
Kramer Research Services Inc. - Canton, OH - *EISS 5-84 Sup*
Kramer, Sidney B. - Westport, CT - *LitMarPl 83, 84*
Kramer Verlag GmbH & Co., Karl - Stuttgart, West Germany - *WritMar 84*
KRAN - Morton, TX - *BrCabYB 84; TV&RadDir 84*
Krank Enterprises - Baltimore, MD - *BoPubDir 4 Sup, 5*
Krantz Co. Publishers Inc., The - Chicago, IL - *LitMarPl 83, 84; WritMar 84*
Kranz Associates Inc., Walter - Denver, CO - *StaDirAdAg 2-84*
Krasner Associates Inc., Harvey J. - Great Neck, NY - *WhoWMicrocom 83*
Krasney Associates Inc., Samuel (SK Group) - New York, NY - *DirPRFirms 83*
Krasny, M. Cristina - Research Triangle Park, NC - *LitMarPl 83, 84*
Kraszeski, Julia - Newburgh, NY - *LitMarPl 83, 84*
Krate/Huber Associates Inc. - *See* Huber & Co., H.

Kraus Electronic Systems - Joliet, IL - *BrCabYB 84 p.D-303*
Kraus Marketing & Business Research, Richard - Sea Bright, NJ - *IntDirMarRes 83*
Kraus Microform [Div. of Kraus-Thomson Organization Ltd.] - Millwood, NY - *LitMarPl 83, 84; MagIndMarPl 82-83; MicroMarPl 82-83*
Kraus Periodicals Co. - Millwood, NY - *MagIndMarPl 82-83*
Kraus-Thomson Organization Ltd. - Millwood, NY - *LitMarPl 83, 84*
Krause & Remal Music - San Francisco, CA - *BillIntBG 83-84*
Krause, Arthur J. - Seneca, IL - *Tel&CabFB 84C p.1687*
Krause Publications - Iola, WI - *BoPubDir 4, 5; DirMarMP 83; MagIndMarPl 82-83*
Krauss Advertising Inc., Oscar - New York, NY - *StaDirAdAg 2-84*
Kraut Co. Inc., G. A. - New York, NY - *DirPRFirms 83*
KRAV-FM - Tulsa, OK - *BrCabYB 84; NatRadPubDir Summer 83, Spring 84; TV&RadDir 84*
Kravetz Media Corp. - Englewood, CO - *Tel&CabFB 84C*
Krax - Leeds, England - *LitMag&SmPr 83-84*
KRAY-FM - Salinas, CA - *BrCabYB 84; NatRadPubDir Summer 83, Spring 84; TV&RadDir 84*
KRAZ-FM - Farmington, NM - *BrCabYB 84; TV&RadDir 84*
Krazeski, Julia - Newburgh, NY - *MagIndMarPl 82-83*
KRBA - Lufkin, TX - *BrCabYB 84; TV&RadDir 84*
KRBC - Abilene, TX - *BrCabYB 84; NatRadPubDir Summer 83, Spring 84; TV&RadDir 84*
KRBC-TV - Abilene, TX - *BrCabYB 84; DirUSTelSta 83; TelAl 83, 84; Tel&CabFB 84S; TV&RadDir 84*
KRBD-FM - Ketchikan, AK - *BrCabYB 84; TV&RadDir 84*
KRBE - Houston, TX - *BrCabYB 84; NatRadPubDir Summer 83, Spring 84*
KRBE-FM - Houston, TX - *NatRadPubDir Summer 83, Spring 84; TV&RadDir 84*
KRBI-FM - St. Peter, MN - *BrCabYB 84*
KRBK-TV - Sacramento, CA - *BrCabYB 84; DirUSTelSta 83; TelAl 83, 84; Tel&CabFB 84S; TV&RadDir 84*
KRBM-FM - Pendleton, OR - *BrCabYB 84; NatRadPubDir Summer 83, Spring 84; TV&RadDir 84*
KRBN - Red Lodge, MT - *BrCabYB 84; TV&RadDir 84*
KRBQ - Red Bluff, CA - *BrCabYB 84*
KRBU-FM - Pocatello, ID - *BrCabYB 84; NatRadPubDir Summer 83, Spring 84; TV&RadDir 84*
KRC Development Council - New Canaan, CT - *BoPubDir 4 Sup, 5*
KRCB-TV - Cotati, CA - *BrCabYB 84; Tel&CabFB 84S*
KRCC-FM - Colorado Springs, CO - *BrCabYB 84; NatRadPubDir Summer 83, Spring 84; TV&RadDir 84*
KRCG-TV - Jefferson City, MO - *BrCabYB 84; DirUSTelSta 83; TelAl 83, 84; Tel&CabFB 84S; TV&RadDir 84*
KRCH-FM - Rochester, MN - *BrCabYB 84; TV&RadDir 84*
KRCK-FM - Portland, OR - *NatRadPubDir Summer 83, Spring 84*
KRCL-FM - Salt Lake City, UT - *TV&RadDir 84*
KRCO - Prineville, OR - *BrCabYB 84; TV&RadDir 84*
KRCQ - Indio, CA - *BrCabYB 84; TV&RadDir 84*
KRCR-TV - Redding, CA - *BrCabYB 84; DirUSTelSta 83; TelAl 83, 84; Tel&CabFB 84S; TV&RadDir 84*
KRCS-FM - Sturgis, SD - *BrCabYB 84; TV&RadDir 84*
KRCT-FM - Ozona, TX - *BrCabYB 84; TV&RadDir 84*
KRCU-FM - Cape Girardeau, MO - *BrCabYB 84; NatRadPubDir Summer 83, Spring 84*
KRDC-FM - St. George, UT - *BrCabYB 84; NatRadPubDir Summer 83, Spring 84; TV&RadDir 84*
KRDD - Roswell, NM - *BrCabYB 84; TV&RadDir 84*
KRDF-FM - Spearman, TX - *BrCabYB 84; TV&RadDir 84*
KRDG - Redding, CA - *BrCabYB 84*
KRDK-FM - Spokane, WA - *TV&RadDir 84*
KRDO - Colorado Springs, CO - *BrCabYB 84; NatRadPubDir Summer 83, Spring 84*
KRDO-FM - Colorado Springs, CO - *BrCabYB 84; NatRadPubDir Summer 83, Spring 84; TV&RadDir 84*
KRDO-TV - Colorado Springs, CO - *BrCabYB 84; DirUSTelSta 83; TelAl 83, 84; Tel&CabFB 84S; TV&RadDir 84*
KRDR - Gresham, OR - *BrCabYB 84; TV&RadDir 84*
KRDS - Phoenix, AZ - *NatRadPubDir Summer 83, Spring 84; TV&RadDir 84*
KRDS - Tolleson, AZ - *BrCabYB 84*
KRDU - Dinuba, CA - *BrCabYB 84; TV&RadDir 84*
KRDZ - Hayden, CO - *BrCabYB 84*
KRE - Berkeley, CA - *BrCabYB 84; TV&RadDir 84*
KRE - San Francisco, CA - *NatRadPubDir Summer 83 p.31, Spring 84 p.31*
Krebs & Associates Inc., F. J. - St. Louis, MO - *StaDirAdAg 2-84*
KRED - Eureka, CA - *BrCabYB 84; TV&RadDir 84*
Kregel Publications [Div. of Kregel Inc.] - Grand Rapids, MI - *LitMarPl 83, 84*
KREH - Oakdale, LA - *BrCabYB 84; TV&RadDir 84*
Krehbiel Co., C. J. - Cincinnati, OH - *LitMarPl 83, 84*
KREI - Farmington, MO - *BrCabYB 84; TV&RadDir 84*
Kreicker & Meloan Inc. - Northfield, IL - *StaDirAdAg 2-84*
Kreimers Music Inc. - *See* Kaye Publications, Richard
KREK-FM - Bristow, OK - *BrCabYB 84; TV&RadDir 84*
Krell Software Corp. - Stony Brook, NY - *MicrocomSwDir 1*
KREM - Spokane, WA - *BrCabYB 84; NatRadPubDir Summer 83; TV&RadDir 84*
KREM-FM - Spokane, WA - *BrCabYB 84; NatRadPubDir Summer 83, Spring 84; TV&RadDir 84*
KREM-TV - Spokane, WA - *BrCabYB 84; DirUSTelSta 83; TelAl 83, 84; Tel&CabFB 84S; TV&RadDir 84*
Krementz, Jill - New York, NY - *LitMarPl 83, 84*
Kremer, Merrill Inc. - Memphis, TN - *StaDirAdAg 2-84*
Kremitske, John - New York, NY - *LitMarPl 84*
Kremmling Middle Park Times - Kremmling, CO - *BaconPubCkNews 84*
KREN-TV - Reno, NV - *BrCabYB 84; Tel&CabFB 84S*
KREO-FM - Healdsburg, CA - *BrCabYB 84; TV&RadDir 84*
Kreonite Inc. - Wichita, KS - *AvMarPl 83*
KRER-FM - Billings, MT - *BrCabYB 84; NatRadPubDir Summer 83, Spring 84*
KRES-FM - Moberly, MO - *BrCabYB 84; TV&RadDir 84*
Kress & Associates, J. - Knoxville, TN - *StaDirAdAg 2-84*
Kress Chronicle, The - Kress, TX - *Ed&PubIntYB 82*
Kresser, Robbins & Associates - Los Angeles, CA - *DirPRFirms 83; StaDirAdAg 2-84*
KREW - Sunnyside, WA - *BrCabYB 84; TV&RadDir 84*
KREW-FM - Sunnyside, WA - *BrCabYB 84; TV&RadDir 84*
KREX - Grand Junction, CO - *BrCabYB 84; NatRadPubDir Summer 83, Spring 84; TV&RadDir 84*
KREX-FM - Grand Junction, CO - *BrCabYB 84; NatRadPubDir Summer 83, Spring 84; TV&RadDir 84*
KREX-TV - Grand Junction, CO - *BrCabYB 84; DirUSTelSta 83; TelAl 83, 84; Tel&CabFB 84S; TV&RadDir 84*
KREY-TV - Montrose, CO - *BrCabYB 84; TelAl 83, 84; Tel&CabFB 84S; TV&RadDir 84*
KREZ-TV - Durango, CO - *BrCabYB 84; TelAl 83, 84; Tel&CabFB 84S; TV&RadDir 84*
KRFD-FM - Marysville, CA - *BrCabYB 84; TV&RadDir 84*
KRFG-FM - Greenfield, MO - *BrCabYB 84; TV&RadDir 84*
KRFM - Show Low, AZ - *BrCabYB 84*
KRFO - Owatonna, MN - *BrCabYB 84; TV&RadDir 84*
KRFO-FM - Owatonna, MN - *BrCabYB 84; TV&RadDir 84*
KRFS - Superior, NE - *BrCabYB 84; TV&RadDir 84*
KRFS-FM - Superior, NE - *BrCabYB 84; TV&RadDir 84*
KRGI - Grand Island, NE - *BrCabYB 84; TV&RadDir 84*
KRGI-FM - Grand Island, NE - *BrCabYB 84; TV&RadDir 84*
KRGK-FM - Carthage, MO - *BrCabYB 84; TV&RadDir 84*
KRGO - Salt Lake City, UT - *NatRadPubDir Summer 83, Spring 84; TV&RadDir 84*
KRGO - West Valley City, UT - *BrCabYB 84*
KRGO-FM - Roy, UT - *BrCabYB 84*
KRGS-FM - Spencer, IA - *BrCabYB 84; TV&RadDir 84*
KRGT-FM - Austin, TX - *TV&RadDir 84*
KRGT-FM - Taylor, TX - *BrCabYB 84*
KRGV - Weslaco, TX - *BrCabYB 84; TV&RadDir 84*
KRGV-TV - Harlingen, TX - *DirUSTelSta 83*
KRGV-TV - Weslaco, TX - *BrCabYB 84; TelAl 83, 84; Tel&CabFB 84S; TV&RadDir 84*
KRHD - Duncan, OK - *BrCabYB 84; TV&RadDir 84*
KRHD-FM - Duncan, OK - *BrCabYB 84; TV&RadDir 84*
KRHS-FM - Bullhead City, AZ - *BrCabYB 84; TV&RadDir 84*
K.R.I. Publications [Aff. of Kundalini Research Institute] - Pomona, CA - *BoPubDir 4, 5*

KRIB - Mason City, IA - *BrCabYB 84; NatRadPubDir Summer 83, Spring 84; TV&RadDir 84*
KRIC-FM - Rexburg, ID - *BrCabYB 84; TV&RadDir 84*
Krieger Publishing Co. Inc., R. E. - Melbourne, FL - *LitMarPl 83, 84*
KRIG - Midland, TX - *NatRadPubDir Summer 83, Spring 84 p.244*
KRIG - Odessa, TX - *BrCabYB 84; TV&RadDir 84*
KRIJ - Paradise, CA - *BrCabYB 84*
Krikorian-Miller Associates - Chestnut Hill, MA - *BoPubDir 4 Sup, 5; LitMarPl 83, 84*
KRIM - Winslow, AZ - *BrCabYB 84*
KRIN - Waterloo, IA - *BrCabYB 84; Tel&CabFB 84S*
KRIO - Brownsville, TX - *NatRadPubDir Summer 83*
KRIO - McAllen, TX - *BrCabYB 84; NatRadPubDir Spring 84; TV&RadDir 84*
KRIS-TV - Corpus Christi, TX - *BrCabYB 84; DirUSTelSta 83; TelAl 83, 84; Tel&CabFB 84S; TV&RadDir 84*
Krishane Music Co. [Div. of Kris Stevens Enterprises Inc.] - Sherman Oaks, CA - *BillIntBG 83-84*
Krishna Press [Aff. of Gordon Press] - New York, NY - *BoPubDir 4, 5*
Kristaus Karaliaus Laivas - Chicago, IL - *Ed&PubIntYB 82*
Kristjan Enterprises Ltd. - Bowen Island, BC, Canada - *BrCabYB 84*
Kristofferson Productions - Hollywood, CA - *AvMarPl 83*
KRIT-FM - Clarinda, IA - *TV&RadDir 84*
KRIT-FM - Clarion, IA - *BrCabYB 84*
KRIV-TV - Houston, TX - *BrCabYB 84; DirUSTelSta 83; TelAl 83, 84; Tel&CabFB 84S; TV&RadDir 84*
KRIX-FM - Brownsville, TX - *BrCabYB 84; TV&RadDir 84*
KRIZ-FM - Roswell, NM - *BrCabYB 84; TV&RadDir 84*
KRJB-FM - Monte Rio, CA - *BrCabYB 84; TV&RadDir 84*
KRJC-FM - Elko, NV - *BrCabYB 84; TV&RadDir 84*
KRJH - Hallettsville, TX - *BrCabYB 84; TV&RadDir 84*
KRKA - Alva, OK - *BrCabYB 84*
KRKC - King City, CA - *BrCabYB 84; TV&RadDir 84*
KRKE - Albuquerque, NM - *BrCabYB 84; NatRadPubDir Summer 83, Spring 84; TV&RadDir 84*
KRKK - Rock Springs, WY - *BrCabYB 84; TV&RadDir 84*
KRKN-FM - Anchorage, AK - *BrCabYB 84; NatRadPubDir Summer 83, Spring 84; TV&RadDir 84*
KRKO - Everett, WA - *BrCabYB 84; TV&RadDir 84*
KRKO - Seattle, WA - *NatRadPubDir Summer 83 p.260, Spring 84 p.262*
KRKR - Kansas City, MO - *NatRadPubDir Summer 83; TV&RadDir 84*
KRKS - Denver, CO - *BrCabYB 84; NatRadPubDir Summer 83, Spring 84; TV&RadDir 84*
KRKT - Albany, OR - *BrCabYB 84; TV&RadDir 84*
KRKT-FM - Albany, OR - *BrCabYB 84*
KRKY-FM - Castle Rock, CO - *BrCabYB 84; TV&RadDir 84*
KRLA - Los Angeles, CA - *NatRadPubDir Summer 83 p.23, Spring 84 p.23*
KRLA - Pasadena, CA - *BrCabYB 84; TV&RadDir 84*
KRLB - Lubbock, TX - *BrCabYB 84; NatRadPubDir Summer 83, Spring 84; TV&RadDir 84*
KRLB-FM - Lubbock, TX - *BrCabYB 84; NatRadPubDir Summer 83, Spring 84; TV&RadDir 84*
KRLC - Lewiston, ID - *BrCabYB 84; TV&RadDir 84*
KRLD - Dallas, TX - *BrCabYB 84; NatRadPubDir Summer 83, Spring 84; TV&RadDir 84*
KRLG-FM - Lawton, OK - *BrCabYB 84; TV&RadDir 84*
KRLN - Canon City, CO - *BrCabYB 84; TV&RadDir 84*
KRLN-FM - Canon City, CO - *TV&RadDir 84*
KRLQ - Muskogee, OK - *BrCabYB 84*
KRLR - Las Vegas, NV - *BrCabYB 84; Tel&CabFB 84S*
KRLS - Knoxville, IA - *BrCabYB 84*
KRLT-FM - South Lake Tahoe, CA - *BrCabYB 84; NatRadPubDir Summer 83, Spring 84; TV&RadDir 84*
KRLW - Walnut Ridge, AR - *BrCabYB 84; TV&RadDir 84*
KRLX-FM - Northfield, MN - *BrCabYB 84; NatRadPubDir Summer 83, Spring 84; TV&RadDir 84*
KRLY-FM - Houston, TX - *BrCabYB 84; NatRadPubDir Summer 83, Spring 84; TV&RadDir 84*
KRMA-TV - Denver, CO - *BrCabYB 84; Tel&CabFB 84S; TV&RadDir 84*
KRMC - Midwest City, OK - *BrCabYB 84*
KRMC - Oklahoma City, OK - *TV&RadDir 84*
KRMD - Shreveport, LA - *BrCabYB 84; NatRadPubDir Summer 83, Spring 84; TV&RadDir 84*
KRMD-FM - Shreveport, LA - *BrCabYB 84; NatRadPubDir Summer 83, Spring 84; TV&RadDir 84*
KRME - Hondo, TX - *BrCabYB 84; TV&RadDir 84*
KRMG - Tulsa, OK - *BrCabYB 84; NatRadPubDir Summer 83, Spring 84; TV&RadDir 84*
KRML - Carmel, CA - *BrCabYB 84; TV&RadDir 84*
KRML - Salinas, CA - *NatRadPubDir Summer 83 p.27, Spring 84 p.27*
KRMO - Monett, MO - *BrCabYB 84; TV&RadDir 84*
KRMS - Osage Beach, MO - *BrCabYB 84; TV&RadDir 84*
KRMS-FM - Osage Beach, MO - *TV&RadDir 84*
KRMW - Silt, CO - *BrCabYB 84*
KRMX-FM - Pueblo, CO - *BrCabYB 84*
KRNA - Iowa City, IA - *BrCabYB 84; CabTVFinDB 83*
KRNA-FM - Iowa City, IA - *TV&RadDir 84*
KRNB-FM - Memphis, TN - *BrCabYB 84; TV&RadDir 84*
KRND - Moab, UT - *BrCabYB 84*
KRNE-TV - Gordon, NE - *TV&RadDir 84*
KRNE-TV - Merriman, NE - *BrCabYB 84; Tel&CabFB 84S*
KRNL-FM - Mt. Vernon, IA - *BrCabYB 84; NatRadPubDir Summer 83, Spring 84; TV&RadDir 84*
KRNO-FM - Reno, NV - *BrCabYB 84; NatRadPubDir Summer 83, Spring 84; TV&RadDir 84*
KRNQ-FM - Des Moines, IA - *BrCabYB 84; NatRadPubDir Summer 83, Spring 84; TV&RadDir 84*
KRNR - Roseburg, OR - *BrCabYB 84; TV&RadDir 84*
KRNS - Burns, OR - *BrCabYB 84; TV&RadDir 84*
KRNT - Des Moines, IA - *BrCabYB 84; NatRadPubDir Summer 83, Spring 84; TV&RadDir 84*
KRNU-FM - Lincoln, NE - *BrCabYB 84; NatRadPubDir Summer 83, Spring 84; TV&RadDir 84*
KRNY - Kearney, NE - *BrCabYB 84; TV&RadDir 84*
KRNY-FM - Kearney, NE - *BrCabYB 84; TV&RadDir 84*
KROA-FM - Grand Island, NE - *BrCabYB 84; TV&RadDir 84*
KROB - Robstown, TX - *BrCabYB 84; TV&RadDir 84*
KROB-FM - Robstown, TX - *BrCabYB 84; TV&RadDir 84*
KROC - Rochester, MN - *BrCabYB 84; NatRadPubDir Summer 83, Spring 84; TV&RadDir 84*
KROC-FM - Rochester, MN - *BrCabYB 84; NatRadPubDir Summer 83, Spring 84; TV&RadDir 84*
KROD - El Paso, TX - *BrCabYB 84; LitMarPl 83, 84; NatRadPubDir Summer 83, Spring 84; TV&RadDir 84*
KROE - Sheridan, WY - *BrCabYB 84; TV&RadDir 84*
KROE-FM - Sheridan, WY - *BrCabYB 84; TV&RadDir 84*
KROF - Abbeville, LA - *BrCabYB 84; TV&RadDir 84*
KROF-FM - Abbeville, LA - *TV&RadDir 84*
KROG-FM - Sonora, CA - *BrCabYB 84; TV&RadDir 84*
Krohm International - Troy, MI - *LitMarPl 83, 84*
Krohn & Associates, Barbara - Seattle, WA - *DirPRFirms 83*
Krohne Advertising, Robert - Shawnee Mission, KS - *StaDirAdAg 2-84*
KROI - Reno, NV - *NatRadPubDir Summer 83 p.154, Spring 84 p.154; TV&RadDir 84*
KROI - Sparks, NV - *BrCabYB 84*
KROK-FM - Shreveport, LA - *BrCabYB 84; NatRadPubDir Summer 83, Spring 84; TV&RadDir 84*
Kroll Agency, Lucy - New York, NY - *LitMarPl 83, 84*
Kroll, Edite - New York, NY - *LitMarPl 83, 84*
Kroloff, Marshall & Associates - Washington, DC - *ArtMar 84*
KRON-TV - San Francisco, CA - *BrCabYB 84; DirUSTelSta 83; LitMarPl 83, 84; TelAl 83, 84; Tel&CabFB 84S; TV&RadDir 84*
Krone & Associates, I. - New York, NY - *HBIndAd&MS 82-83*
Krone-Olim Advertising Inc. - New York, NY - *StaDirAdAg 2-84*
Kronos Computacion y Teleproceso SA - Mexico City, Mexico - *ADAPSOMemDir 83-84*
Kronos Inc. - Boston, MA - *WhoWMicrocom 83*
KROO - Breckenridge, TX - *BrCabYB 84*
KROP - Brawley, CA - *BrCabYB 84; TV&RadDir 84*
Kropotkin's Lighthouse Publications - London, England - *LitMag&SmPr 83-84*
KROQ - Burbank, CA - *BrCabYB 84*
KROQ - Pasadena, CA - *TV&RadDir 84*

KROQ-FM - Pasadena, CA - *BrCabYB 84; TV&RadDir 84*
KROR - Myrtle Creek, OR - *BrCabYB 84; TV&RadDir 84*
KROS - Clinton, IA - *BrCabYB 84; TV&RadDir 84*
KROW - Reno, NV - *BrCabYB 84; NatRadPubDir Summer 83, Spring 84; TV&RadDir 84*
Krown Advertising Agency - Cinnaminson, NJ - *StaDirAdAg 2-84*
Krown Enterprises - Scotts Valley, CA - *MicrocomMPl 83; WhoWMicrocom 83*
KROX - Crookston, MN - *BrCabYB 84; TV&RadDir 84*
KROY - Sacramento, CA - *TV&RadDir 84*
KROY-FM - Sacramento, CA - *BrCabYB 84; NatRadPubDir Summer 83, Spring 84; TV&RadDir 84*
Kroy Industries Inc. - St. Paul, MN - *AvMarPl 83*
Kroy Industries Inc. (Graphic Div.) - Scottsdale, AZ - *LitMarPl 84*
Kroy Industries Inc. (Graphic Div.) - St. Paul, MN - *LitMarPl 83*
KROZ-FM - Tyler, TX - *BrCabYB 84; TV&RadDir 84*
KRPC-FM - Owatonna, MN - *BrCabYB 84; TV&RadDir 84*
KRPCO Music [Div. of Kiderian Records Productions] - Chicago, IL - *BillIntBG 83-84*
KRPL - Moscow, ID - *BrCabYB 84; TV&RadDir 84*
KRPL-FM - Moscow, ID - *BrCabYB 84; TV&RadDir 84*
KRPM-FM - Tacoma, WA - *BrCabYB 84; NatRadPubDir Summer 83, Spring 84; TV&RadDir 84*
KRPR-FM - Rochester, MN - *BrCabYB 84; NatRadPubDir Summer 83, Spring 84; TV&RadDir 84*
KRPT - Anadarko, OK - *BrCabYB 84; TV&RadDir 84*
KRPT-FM - Anadarko, OK - *TV&RadDir 84*
KRPX - Price, UT - *BrCabYB 84; TV&RadDir 84*
KRQK - Lompoc, CA - *BrCabYB 84*
KRQQ-FM - Tucson, AZ - *BrCabYB 84; NatRadPubDir Summer 83, Spring 84; TV&RadDir 84*
KRQR-FM - San Francisco, CA - *BrCabYB 84; LitMarPl 84; NatRadPubDir Summer 83, Spring 84; TV&RadDir 84*
KRQX - Dallas, TX - *BrCabYB 84; NatRadPubDir Spring 84*
KRQY-FM - Pueblo, CO - *NatRadPubDir Summer 83; TV&RadDir 84*
KRQZ - Wray, CO - *BrCabYB 84; TV&RadDir 84*
KRQZ-FM - Wray, CO - *BrCabYB 84*
KRRB - Dickinson, ND - *BrCabYB 84*
KRRC-FM - Portland, OR - *BrCabYB 84; NatRadPubDir Summer 83, Spring 84; TV&RadDir 84*
KRRG - Laredo, TX - *BrCabYB 84*
KRRI - Boulder City, NV - *BrCabYB 84*
KRRK - East Grand Forks, MN - *BrCabYB 84; TV&RadDir 84*
KRRK-FM - East Grand Forks, MN - *BrCabYB 84; TV&RadDir 84*
KRRP - Coushatta, LA - *BrCabYB 84*
KRRR - Ruidoso, NM - *BrCabYB 84; TV&RadDir 84*
KRRV - Alexandria, LA - *BrCabYB 84*
KRS Communications - Hempstead, NY - *AdAge 3-28-84; StaDirAdAg 2-84*
KRSA - Petersburg, AK - *BrCabYB 84*
KRSB-FM - Roseburg, OR - *BrCabYB 84; TV&RadDir 84*
KRSC - Othello, WA - *BrCabYB 84; TV&RadDir 84*
KRSE-FM - Yakima, WA - *BrCabYB 84; TV&RadDir 84*
KRSH-FM - Overland, MO - *BrCabYB 84*
KRSH-FM - St. Louis, MO - *TV&RadDir 84*
KRSI - Hopkins, MN - *TV&RadDir 84*
KRSI - Minneapolis, MN - *NatRadPubDir Summer 83 p.134, Spring 84 p.134*
KRSI - St. Louis Park, MN - *BrCabYB 84*
KRSJ-FM - Durango, CO - *BrCabYB 84; TV&RadDir 84*
KRSL - Russell, KS - *BrCabYB 84; TV&RadDir 84*
KRSL-FM - Russell, KS - *BrCabYB 84; TV&RadDir 84*
KRSM-FM - Dallas, TX - *BrCabYB 84; NatRadPubDir Summer 83, Spring 84; TV&RadDir 84*
KRSN - Los Alamos, NM - *BrCabYB 84; TV&RadDir 84*
KRSN-FM - Los Alamos, NM - *BrCabYB 84; TV&RadDir 84*
KRSP - Salt Lake City, UT - *NatRadPubDir Summer 83, Spring 84; TV&RadDir 84*
KRSP - South Salt Lake, UT - *BrCabYB 84*
KRSP-FM - Salt Lake City, UT - *BrCabYB 84; NatRadPubDir Summer 83, Spring 84; TV&RadDir 84*
KRSS - Sioux Falls, SD - *BrCabYB 84; TV&RadDir 84*
KRST-FM - Albuquerque, NM - *BrCabYB 84; NatRadPubDir Summer 83, Spring 84; TV&RadDir 84*
KRSW-FM - Pipestone, MN - *BrCabYB 84; TV&RadDir 84*
KRSY - Roswell, NM - *BrCabYB 84; TV&RadDir 84*
KRTH-FM - Los Angeles, CA - *BrCabYB 84; NatRadPubDir Summer 83, Spring 84; TV&RadDir 84*
KRTM - Temecula, CA - *TV&RadDir 84*
KRTN - Raton, NM - *BrCabYB 84; TV&RadDir 84*
KRTN-FM - Raton, NM - *BrCabYB 84*
KRTR - Thermopolis, WY - *BrCabYB 84*
KRTS - Manitou Springs, CO - *NatRadPubDir Summer 83; TV&RadDir 84*
KRTU - San Antonio, TX - *BrCabYB 84; TV&RadDir 84*
KRTU-FM - San Antonio, TX - *NatRadPubDir Summer 83, Spring 84*
KRTV-TV - Great Falls, MT - *BrCabYB 84; DirUSTelSta 83; TelAl 83, 84; Tel&CabFB 84S; TV&RadDir 84*
KRUC-FM - Cape Girardeau, MO - *TV&RadDir 84*
Krueger Associates Inc., Joseph A. - San Rafael, CA - *StaDirAdAg 2-84*
Krueger Co., W. A. - Scottsdale, AZ - *MagIndMarPl 82-83*
Krueger Co., W. A. - New Berlin, WI - *LitMarPl 83, 84*
Krug & Associates Inc., Herbert - Evanston, IL - *DirMarMP 83; StaDirAdAg 2-84*
Kruger Literary Services, Bill - St. Petersburg, FL - *LitMarPl 83, 84*
Kruhm & Associates, Robert H. - Fulton, MD - *MagIndMarPl 82-83*
Krumwiede, Grace I. - Falls Church, VA - *BoPubDir 4, 5*
KRUN - Ballinger, TX - *BrCabYB 84; TV&RadDir 84*
KRUN-FM - Ballinger, TX - *BrCabYB 84; TV&RadDir 84*
Krupnick & Associates Inc. - St. Louis, MO - *StaDirAdAg 2-84; TelAl 83, 84*
Krupp, Carl E. - Chicago, IL - *MagIndMarPl 82-83*
KRUS - Ruston, LA - *BrCabYB 84; TV&RadDir 84*
Kruse Berberet Associates Inc. - Rockford, IL - *DirPRFirms 83*
KRUX - Lubbock, TX - *BrCabYB 84*
KRUZ-FM - Santa Barbara, CA - *BrCabYB 84; NatRadPubDir Summer 83, Spring 84; TV&RadDir 84*
Kruzas Associates, Anthony T. - Ann Arbor, MI - *BoPubDir 4 Sup, 5*
KRV - Nampa, ID - *BrCabYB 84*
KRVC - Medford, OR - *BrCabYB 84*
KRVE-FM - Los Gatos, CA - *BrCabYB 84; TV&RadDir 84*
KRVH-FM - Rio Vista, CA - *BrCabYB 84; TV&RadDir 84*
KRVM-FM - Eugene, OR - *BrCabYB 84; NatRadPubDir Summer 83, Spring 84; TV&RadDir 84*
KRVN - Lexington, NE - *BrCabYB 84; TV&RadDir 84*
KRVN-FM - Lexington, NE - *BrCabYB 84; TV&RadDir 84*
KRVR-FM - Davenport, IA - *BrCabYB 84; TV&RadDir 84*
KRVS-FM - Lafayette, LA - *BrCabYB 84; NatRadPubDir Summer 83, Spring 84; TV&RadDir 84*
KRVV - Vail, CO - *BrCabYB 84*
KRWA-FM - Waldron, AR - *BrCabYB 84*
KRWB - Roseau, MN - *BrCabYB 84; TV&RadDir 84*
KRWC - Buffalo, MN - *BrCabYB 84; TV&RadDir 84*
KRWG-FM - Las Cruces, NM - *BrCabYB 84; NatRadPubDir Summer 83, Spring 84; TV&RadDir 84*
KRWG-TV - Las Cruces, NM - *BrCabYB 84; Tel&CabFB 84S; TV&RadDir 84*
KRWN-FM - Farmington, NM - *BrCabYB 84; TV&RadDir 84*
KRWQ-FM - Gold Hill, OR - *BrCabYB 84*
KRWY - Rawlins, WY - *BrCabYB 84; Tel&CabFB 84S*
KRXA - Seward, AK - *BrCabYB 84; TV&RadDir 84*
KRXK - Rexburg, ID - *BrCabYB 84; TV&RadDir 84*
KRXL-FM - Kirksville, MO - *BrCabYB 84; TV&RadDir 84*
KRXV - Yermo, CA - *BrCabYB 84*
KRYK - Chinook, MT - *BrCabYB 84*
KRYS - Corpus Christi, TX - *BrCabYB 84; NatRadPubDir Summer 83, Spring 84; TV&RadDir 84*
KRYT - Colorado Springs, CO - *TV&RadDir 84*
KRYZ - Springville, AZ - *BrCabYB 84*
KRZA - Alamosa, CO - *BrCabYB 84*
KRZE - Farmington, NM - *BrCabYB 84; TV&RadDir 84*
KRZI - Waco, TX - *BrCabYB 84; NatRadPubDir Summer 83, Spring 84; TV&RadDir 84*
KRZK-FM - Branson, MO - *BrCabYB 84*

KRZN - Englewood, CO - *TV&RadDir 84*
KRZY - Albuquerque, NM - *BrCabYB 84; NatRadPubDir Summer 83, Spring 84; TV&RadDir 84*
KSAA-FM - Casa Grande, AZ - *BrCabYB 84; TV&RadDir 84*
KSAC - Manhattan, KS - *BrCabYB 84; NatRadPubDir Summer 83, Spring 84; TV&RadDir 84*
KSAF-TV - Santa Fe, NM - *BrCabYB 84; Tel&CabFB 84S*
KSAK-FM - Walnut, CA - *BrCabYB 84; TV&RadDir 84*
KSAL - Salina, KS - *BrCabYB 84; TV&RadDir 84*
KSAM - Huntsville, TX - *BrCabYB 84; TV&RadDir 84*
KSAN-FM - San Francisco, CA - *BrCabYB 84; NatRadPubDir Summer 83 p.31, Spring 84 p.31; TV&RadDir 84*
KSAR-FM - Salem, AR - *BrCabYB 84; TV&RadDir 84*
KSAT-TV - San Antonio, TX - *BrCabYB 84; DirUSTelSta 83; LitMarPl 83, 84; TelAl 83, 84; Tel&CabFB 84S; TV&RadDir 84*
KSAU-FM - Nacogdoches, TX - *BrCabYB 84; NatRadPubDir Summer 83, Spring 84*
KSAX - Dallas, TX - *NatRadPubDir Summer 83, Spring 84 p.238*
KSAX - Ft. Worth, TX - *BrCabYB 84; TV&RadDir 84*
KSAY-FM - Clinton, IA - *BrCabYB 84; TV&RadDir 84*
KSBI - Oklahoma City, OK - *BrCabYB 84; Tel&CabFB 84S*
KSBJ - Humble, TX - *BrCabYB 84*
KSBQ - Santa Maria, CA - *BrCabYB 84; NatRadPubDir Summer 83, Spring 84; TV&RadDir 84*
KSBR-FM - Mission Viejo, CA - *BrCabYB 84*
KSBR-FM - Mission View, SC - *TV&RadDir 84*
KSBT-FM - Steamboat Springs, CO - *BrCabYB 84; TV&RadDir 84*
KSBW-TV - Salinas, CA - *BrCabYB 84; DirUSTelSta 83; TelAl 83, 84; Tel&CabFB 84S; TV&RadDir 84*
KSBY-TV - San Luis Obispo, CA - *BrCabYB 84; TelAl 83, 84; Tel&CabFB 84S; TV&RadDir 84*
KSBY-TV - Santa Barbara, CA - *DirUSTelSta 83*
KSCA - Santa Barbara, CA - *BrCabYB 84*
KSCB - Liberal, KS - *BrCabYB 84; TV&RadDir 84*
KSCB-FM - Liberal, KS - *BrCabYB 84*
KSCC-FM - Berryville, AR - *BrCabYB 84; TV&RadDir 84*
KSCG - St. Peter, MN - *BrCabYB 84*
KSCH-TV - Stockton, CA - *BrCabYB 84; Tel&CabFB 84S*
KSCI-TV - Los Angeles, CA - *DirUSTelSta 83; TelAl 83, 84; TV&RadDir 84*
KSCI-TV - San Bernardino, CA - *BrCabYB 84; Tel&CabFB 84S*
KSCJ - Sioux City, IA - *BrCabYB 84; TV&RadDir 84*
KSCL-FM - Shreveport, LA - *BrCabYB 84; NatRadPubDir Summer 83, Spring 84; TV&RadDir 84*
KSCM-FM - Houston, MO - *BrCabYB 84; TV&RadDir 84*
KSCO - Santa Cruz, CA - *BrCabYB 84; TV&RadDir 84*
KSCO-FM - Santa Cruz, CA - *BrCabYB 84; TV&RadDir 84*
KSCR - Renton, WA - *BrCabYB 84*
KSCS-FM - Dallas, TX - *NatRadPubDir Summer 83, Spring 84 p.238*
KSCS-FM - Ft. Worth, TX - *BrCabYB 84; TV&RadDir 84*
KSCU - Santa Clara, CA - *BrCabYB 84*
KSCV - Kearney, NE - *BrCabYB 84; TV&RadDir 84*
KSCV-FM - Kearney, NE - *TV&RadDir 84*
KSD - St. Louis, MO - *BrCabYB 84; NatRadPubDir Summer 83, Spring 84; TV&RadDir 84*
KSD-FM - St. Louis, MO - *BrCabYB 84; NatRadPubDir Summer 83, Spring 84; TV&RadDir 84*
KSD-TV - St. Louis, MO - *TelAl 83*
KSDA-FM - Wichita, KS - *TV&RadDir 84*
KSDB-FM - Manhattan, KS - *BrCabYB 84; TV&RadDir 84*
KSDK-TV - St. Louis, MO - *BrCabYB 84; DirUSTelSta 83; LitMarPl 83, 84; TelAl 84; Tel&CabFB 84S; TV&RadDir 84*
KSDM-FM - International Falls, MN - *BrCabYB 84; TV&RadDir 84*
KSDN - Aberdeen, SD - *BrCabYB 84; NatRadPubDir Summer 83, Spring 84; TV&RadDir 84*
KSDN-FM - Aberdeen, SD - *BrCabYB 84; NatRadPubDir Summer 83, Spring 84; TV&RadDir 84*
KSDO - San Diego, CA - *BrCabYB 84; NatRadPubDir Summer 83, Spring 84; TV&RadDir 84*
KSDO-FM - San Diego, CA - *BrCabYB 84; NatRadPubDir Summer 83, Spring 84; TV&RadDir 84*
KSDP - Sand Point, AK - *BrCabYB 84*
KSDS-FM - San Diego, CA - *BrCabYB 84; NatRadPubDir Summer 83, Spring 84; TV&RadDir 84*
KSDW-FM - Sulphur, OK - *BrCabYB 84; TV&RadDir 84*
KSDY - Sidney, MT - *BrCabYB 84*
KSDZ-FM - Gordon, NE - *BrCabYB 84; TV&RadDir 84*
KSEA-FM - Seattle, WA - *BrCabYB 84; NatRadPubDir Summer 83, Spring 84; TV&RadDir 84*
KSEC-FM - Lamar, CO - *BrCabYB 84; TV&RadDir 84*
KSEE-TV - Fresno, CA - *BrCabYB 84; DirUSTelSta 83; TelAl 83, 84; Tel&CabFB 84S; TV&RadDir 84*
KSEI - Pocatello, ID - *BrCabYB 84; LitMarPl 83, 84; NatRadPubDir Summer 83, Spring 84; TV&RadDir 84*
KSEK - Pittsburg, KS - *BrCabYB 84; TV&RadDir 84*
KSEL - Lubbock, TX - *BrCabYB 84; NatRadPubDir Summer 83, Spring 84; TV&RadDir 84*
KSEL-FM - Lubbock, TX - *BrCabYB 84; NatRadPubDir Summer 83, Spring 84; TV&RadDir 84*
KSEM - Moses Lake, WA - *BrCabYB 84; TV&RadDir 84*
KSEM-FM - Moses Lake, WA - *BrCabYB 84*
KSEN - Shelby, MT - *BrCabYB 84; TV&RadDir 84*
KSEO - Durant, OK - *TV&RadDir 84*
KSEO-FM - Durant, OK - *BrCabYB 84; TV&RadDir 84*
KSER-FM - Searcy, AR - *BrCabYB 84; TV&RadDir 84*
KSES - Yucca Valley, CA - *BrCabYB 84*
KSET - El Paso, TX - *BrCabYB 84; NatRadPubDir Summer 83, Spring 84*
KSET-FM - El Paso, TX - *BrCabYB 84; NatRadPubDir Summer 83, Spring 84; TV&RadDir 84*
KSEY - Seymour, TX - *BrCabYB 84; TV&RadDir 84*
KSEY-FM - Seymour, TX - *BrCabYB 84; TV&RadDir 84*
KSEZ-FM - Sioux City, IA - *BrCabYB 84; TV&RadDir 84*
KSFA - Nacogdoches, TX - *BrCabYB 84; TV&RadDir 84*
KSFC-FM - Spokane, WA - *BrCabYB 84; NatRadPubDir Summer 83, Spring 84; TV&RadDir 84*
KSFE - Needles, CA - *BrCabYB 84; TV&RadDir 84*
KSFH-FM - Mountain View, CA - *BrCabYB 84; TV&RadDir 84*
KSFI-FM - Salt Lake City, UT - *BrCabYB 84; NatRadPubDir Summer 83, Spring 84; TV&RadDir 84*
KSFM-FM - Sacramento, CA - *NatRadPubDir Summer 83 p.26, Spring 84 p.26; TV&RadDir 84*
KSFM-FM - Woodland, CA - *BrCabYB 84; TV&RadDir 84*
KSFO - San Francisco, CA - *BrCabYB 84; LitMarPl 84; NatRadPubDir Summer 83, Spring 84; TV&RadDir 84*
KSFT-FM - St. Joseph, MO - *BrCabYB 84; NatRadPubDir Summer 83, Spring 84; TV&RadDir 84*
KSFX-FM - San Francisco, CA - *NatRadPubDir Summer 83*
KSFY-TV - Sioux Falls, SD - *BrCabYB 84; DirUSTelSta 83; TelAl 83, 84; Tel&CabFB 84S; TV&RadDir 84*
KSGL - Wichita, KS - *BrCabYB 84; TV&RadDir 84*
KSGM - Chester, IL - *BrCabYB 84; TV&RadDir 84*
KSGM-FM - Chester, IL - *TV&RadDir 84*
KSGM-FM - Ste. Genevieve, MO - *BrCabYB 84; TV&RadDir 84*
KSGN-FM - Riverside, CA - *BrCabYB 84; NatRadPubDir Summer 83, Spring 84; TV&RadDir 84*
KSGR - Windsor, CO - *BrCabYB 84; TV&RadDir 84*
KSGT - Jackson, WY - *BrCabYB 84; TV&RadDir 84*
KSGW-TV - Bethlehem, SD - *TV&RadDir 84*
KSGW-TV - Sheridan, WY - *BrCabYB 84; TelAl 83, 84; Tel&CabFB 84S*
KSHA - Redding, CA - *BrCabYB 84*
KSHB-TV - Kansas City, MO - *BrCabYB 84; DirUSTelSta 83; Tel&CabFB 84S; TV&RadDir 84*
KSHE-FM - Crestwood, MO - *BrCabYB 84*
KSHE-FM - St. Louis, MO - *NatRadPubDir Summer 83, Spring 84; TV&RadDir 84*
KSHI-FM - Zuni, NM - *BrCabYB 84; TV&RadDir 84*
KSHO - Honolulu, HI - *BrCabYB 84; Tel&CabFB 84S*
KSHO-FM - Honolulu, HI - *NatRadPubDir Spring 84 p.75*
KSHO-FM - Kailua, HI - *BrCabYB 84; TV&RadDir 84*
KSHR - Coquille, OR - *BrCabYB 84; TV&RadDir 84*
KSHR-FM - Coquille, OR - *BrCabYB 84*
KSHU-FM - Huntsville, TX - *BrCabYB 84; NatRadPubDir Summer 83, Spring 84; TV&RadDir 84*
KSHY - Cheyenne, WY - *BrCabYB 84; TV&RadDir 84*
KSIB - Creston, IA - *BrCabYB 84; TV&RadDir 84*
KSID - Sidney, NE - *BrCabYB 84; TV&RadDir 84*
KSID-FM - Sidney, NE - *BrCabYB 84; TV&RadDir 84*
KSIG - Crowley, LA - *BrCabYB 84; TV&RadDir 84*
KSIL - Silver City, NM - *BrCabYB 84; TV&RadDir 84*

KSIM - Sikeston, MO - *BrCabYB 84; TV&RadDir 84*
KSIN - Sioux City, IA - *BrCabYB 84; Tel&CabFB 84S*
KSIQ - Brawley, CA - *BrCabYB 84*
KSIR - Estes Park, CO - *BrCabYB 84; TV&RadDir 84*
KSIS - Sedalia, MO - *BrCabYB 84; TV&RadDir 84*
KSIT - Rock Springs, WY - *BrCabYB 84*
KSIV - Clayton, MO - *BrCabYB 84*
KSIV - St. Louis, MO - *TV&RadDir 84*
KSIW - Woodward, OK - *BrCabYB 84; TV&RadDir 84*
KSIW-FM - Woodward, OK - *BrCabYB 84; TV&RadDir 84*
KSIX - Corpus Christi, TX - *BrCabYB 84; NatRadPubDir Summer 83, Spring 84; TV&RadDir 84*
KSIX-FM - Corpus Christi, TX - *NatRadPubDir Summer 83*
KSJB - Jamestown, ND - *BrCabYB 84; TV&RadDir 84*
KSJC-FM - Stockton, CA - *BrCabYB 84; NatRadPubDir Summer 83, Spring 84; TV&RadDir 84*
KSJL - San Antonio, TX - *BrCabYB 84*
KSJM-FM - Jamestown, ND - *BrCabYB 84; TV&RadDir 84*
KSJN - Minneapolis, MN - *BrCabYB 84*
KSJN - St. Paul, MN - *TV&RadDir 84*
KSJN-FM - Minneapolis, MN - *BrCabYB 84*
KSJN-FM - St. Paul, MN - *TV&RadDir 84*
KSJO-FM - San Jose, CA - *BrCabYB 84; NatRadPubDir Summer 83, Spring 84; TV&RadDir 84*
KSJR-FM - Collegeville, MN - *BrCabYB 84; TV&RadDir 84*
KSJS-FM - San Jose, CA - *BrCabYB 84; NatRadPubDir Summer 83, Spring 84; TV&RadDir 84*
KSJU-FM - Collegeville, MN - *BrCabYB 84; TV&RadDir 84*
KSJV-FM - Fresno, CA - *BrCabYB 84; TV&RadDir 84*
KSKA-FM - Anchorage, AK - *BrCabYB 84; NatRadPubDir Summer 83, Spring 84*
KSKD-FM - Salem, OR - *BrCabYB 84; NatRadPubDir Summer 83, Spring 84; TV&RadDir 84*
KSKG-FM - Salina, KS - *BrCabYB 84; TV&RadDir 84*
KSKI - Hailey, ID - *BrCabYB 84; TV&RadDir 84*
KSKI-FM - Hailey, ID - *TV&RadDir 84*
KSKI-FM - Sun Valley, ID - *BrCabYB 84*
KSKN - Spokane, WA - *BrCabYB 84; Tel&CabFB 84S*
KSKO - McGrath, AK - *BrCabYB 84*
KSKS - Conroe, TX - *BrCabYB 84; TV&RadDir 84*
KSKU-FM - Hutchinson, KS - *BrCabYB 84; TV&RadDir 84*
KSKX - Topeka, KS - *BrCabYB 84; NatRadPubDir Summer 83, Spring 84; TV&RadDir 84*
KSKY - Dallas, TX - *BrCabYB 84; NatRadPubDir Summer 83, Spring 84; TV&RadDir 84*
KSL - Salt Lake City, UT - *BrCabYB 84; NatRadPubDir Summer 83, Spring 84; TV&RadDir 84; VideoDir 82-83*
KSL Media Inc. - New York, NY - *StaDirAdAg 2-84*
KSL-TV - Salt Lake City, UT - *BrCabYB 84; DirUSTelSta 83; LitMarPl 83; TelAl 83, 84; Tel&CabFB 84S; TV&RadDir 84*
KSLA-TV - Shreveport, LA - *BrCabYB 84; DirUSTelSta 83; LitMarPl 83, 84; TelAl 83, 84; Tel&CabFB 84S; TV&RadDir 84*
KSLC-FM - McMinnville, OR - *BrCabYB 84; NatRadPubDir Summer 83, Spring 84; TV&RadDir 84*
KSLE-FM - Seminole, OK - *BrCabYB 84; TV&RadDir 84*
KSLH-FM - St. Louis, MO - *BrCabYB 84; NatRadPubDir Summer 83, Spring 84; TV&RadDir 84*
KSLL - Richardson, TX - *BrCabYB 84*
KSLM - Salem, OR - *BrCabYB 84; NatRadPubDir Summer 83, Spring 84; TV&RadDir 84*
KSLO - Opelousas, LA - *BrCabYB 84; TV&RadDir 84*
KSLR-FM - San Antonio, TX - *BrCabYB 84; NatRadPubDir Summer 83, Spring 84; TV&RadDir 84*
KSLS - Liberal, KS - *BrCabYB 84*
KSLT - Spearfish, ND - *BrCabYB 84*
KSLU-FM - Hammond, LA - *BrCabYB 84; NatRadPubDir Summer 83, Spring 84*
KSLV - Monte Vista, CO - *BrCabYB 84; TV&RadDir 84*
KSLY - San Luis Obispo, CA - *BrCabYB 84; TV&RadDir 84*
KSMA - Santa Maria, CA - *BrCabYB 84; TV&RadDir 84*
KSMB-FM - Lafayette, LA - *BrCabYB 84; NatRadPubDir Summer 83, Spring 84; TV&RadDir 84*
KSMC-FM - Cottonwood, AZ - *TV&RadDir 84*
KSMC-FM - Moraga, CA - *BrCabYB 84; TV&RadDir 84*
KSME-FM - Manti, UT - *BrCabYB 84; NatRadPubDir Summer 83, Spring 84; TV&RadDir 84*
KSMI-FM - Donaldsonville, LA - *BrCabYB 84; TV&RadDir 84*
KSMK-FM - Cottonwood, AZ - *BrCabYB 84*
KSML - Globe, AZ - *BrCabYB 84; TV&RadDir 84*
KSMM - Minneapolis, MN - *NatRadPubDir Summer 83, Spring 84 p.134*
KSMM - Shakopee, MN - *BrCabYB 84*
KSMN - Mason City, IA - *BrCabYB 84*
KSMN - Shakopee, IA - *TV&RadDir 84*
KSMO - Salem, MO - *BrCabYB 84; TV&RadDir 84*
KSMO-FM - Salem, MO - *BrCabYB 84; TV&RadDir 84*
KSMR - Winona, MN - *BrCabYB 84*
KSMU - Springfield, MO - *BrCabYB 84*
KSMU - Dallas, TX - *NatRadPubDir Summer 83, Spring 84*
KSMU-FM - Springfield, MO - *TV&RadDir 84*
KSMX-FM - Ft. Dodge, IA - *BrCabYB 84; TV&RadDir 84*
KSNB-TV - Kearney, NE - *TelAl 83*
KSNB-TV - Superior, NE - *BrCabYB 84; TelAl 84; Tel&CabFB 84S*
KSNC-TV - Great Bend, KS - *BrCabYB 84; TelAl 84; Tel&CabFB 84S; TV&RadDir 84*
KSND-FM - Florence, OR - *TV&RadDir 84*
KSND-FM - Springfield, OR - *BrCabYB 84*
KSNE - Broken Arrow, OK - *BrCabYB 84*
KSNF-TV - Joplin, MO - *BrCabYB 84; DirUSTelSta 83; TelAl 84; Tel&CabFB 84S; TV&RadDir 84*
KSNG-TV - Garden City, KS - *BrCabYB 84; TelAl 84; Tel&CabFB 84S; TV&RadDir 84*
KSNI-FM - Los Banos, CA - *BrCabYB 84*
KSNI-FM - Santa Maria, CA - *BrCabYB 84; TV&RadDir 84*
KSNK - McCook, NE - *BrCabYB 84; Tel&CabFB 84S*
KSNN-FM - Los Banos, CA - *TV&RadDir 84*
KSNN-FM - Pocatello, ID - *TV&RadDir 84*
KSNO - Aspen, CO - *BrCabYB 84; TV&RadDir 84*
KSNR - Thief River Falls, MN - *BrCabYB 84*
KSNT-TV - Topeka, KS - *BrCabYB 84; DirUSTelSta 83; TelAl 84; Tel&CabFB 84S; TV&RadDir 84*
KSNW-TV - Great Bend, KS - *TelAl 84*
KSNW-TV - Wichita, KS - *BrCabYB 84; DirUSTelSta 83; Tel&CabFB 84S; TV&RadDir 84*
KSNY - Snyder, TX - *BrCabYB 84; TV&RadDir 84*
KSNY-FM - Snyder, TX - *BrCabYB 84; TV&RadDir 84*
KSO - Des Moines, IA - *BrCabYB 84; NatRadPubDir Summer 83, Spring 84; TV&RadDir 84*
KSOA - Ava, MO - *BrCabYB 84*
KSOF-FM - Wichita, KS - *BrCabYB 84; TV&RadDir 84*
KSoft Co. - Naperville, IL - *MicrocomMPl 84*
KSOH - Little Rock, AR - *BrCabYB 84*
KSOH - North Little Rock, AR - *NatRadPubDir Summer 83, Spring 84; TV&RadDir 84*
KSOJ-FM - Flagstaff, AZ - *BrCabYB 84; TV&RadDir 84*
KSOK - Arkansas City, KS - *BrCabYB 84; TV&RadDir 84*
KSOL-FM - San Mateo, CA - *BrCabYB 84; TV&RadDir 84*
KSON - San Diego, CA - *BrCabYB 84; NatRadPubDir Summer 83, Spring 84; TV&RadDir 84*
KSON-FM - San Diego, CA - *BrCabYB 84; NatRadPubDir Summer 83, Spring 84; TV&RadDir 84*
KSOO - Sioux Falls, SD - *BrCabYB 84; NatRadPubDir Summer 83, Spring 84; TV&RadDir 84*
KSOP - Salt Lake City, UT - *NatRadPubDir Summer 83, Spring 84; TV&RadDir 84*
KSOP - South Salt Lake, UT - *BrCabYB 84*
KSOP-FM - Salt Lake City, UT - *BrCabYB 84; NatRadPubDir Summer 83, Spring 84; TV&RadDir 84*
KSOR-FM - Ashland, OR - *BrCabYB 84; NatRadPubDir Summer 83, Spring 84; TV&RadDir 84*
KSOX - Raymondville, TX - *BrCabYB 84; TV&RadDir 84*
KSOX-FM - Raymondville, TX - *BrCabYB 84; TV&RadDir 84*
KSOZ-FM - Point Lookout, MO - *BrCabYB 84; NatRadPubDir Summer 83, Spring 84; TV&RadDir 84*
KSPA-FM - Hot Springs, AR - *BrCabYB 84; NatRadPubDir Spring 84; TV&RadDir 84*
KSPB - Pebble Beach, CA - *BrCabYB 84*
KSPC-FM - Claremont, CA - *BrCabYB 84; NatRadPubDir Summer 83, Spring 84; TV&RadDir 84*
KSPC-FM - Pebble Beach, CA - *TV&RadDir 84*
KSPD - Boise, ID - *BrCabYB 84; NatRadPubDir Summer 83, Spring 84; TV&RadDir 84*

KSPG-FM - El Dorado, KS - *BrCabYB 84; NatRadPubDir Summer 83, Spring 84; TV&RadDir 84*
KSPI - Stillwater, OK - *BrCabYB 84; TV&RadDir 84*
KSPI-FM - Stillwater, OK - *BrCabYB 84; TV&RadDir 84*
KSPL - Seattle, WA - *BrCabYB 84; NatRadPubDir Summer 83, Spring 84; TV&RadDir 84*
KSPN-FM - Aspen, CO - *BrCabYB 84; TV&RadDir 84*
KSPO - Spokane, WA - *BrCabYB 84; NatRadPubDir Summer 83; TV&RadDir 84*
KSPR - Springfield, MO - *BrCabYB 84; TelAl 84; Tel&CabFB 84S*
KSPS-TV - Spokane, WA - *BrCabYB 84; Tel&CabFB 84S; TV&RadDir 84*
KSPT - Sandpoint, ID - *BrCabYB 84; TV&RadDir 84*
KSPZ-FM - Colorado Springs, CO - *BrCabYB 84; NatRadPubDir Summer 83, Spring 84; TV&RadDir 84*
KSQU - Weed, CA - *BrCabYB 84*
KSQY - Deadwood, SD - *BrCabYB 84*
KSRA - Salmon, ID - *BrCabYB 84; TV&RadDir 84*
KSRA-FM - Salmon, ID - *BrCabYB 84; TV&RadDir 84*
KSRB - Hardy, AR - *BrCabYB 84; TV&RadDir 84*
KSRC - Socorro, NM - *BrCabYB 84; TV&RadDir 84*
KSRD - Seward, NE - *BrCabYB 84*
KSRE - Minot, ND - *BrCabYB 84; Tel&CabFB 84S*
KSRF-FM - Los Angeles, CA - *NatRadPubDir Summer 83 p.23, Spring 84 p.23*
KSRF-FM - Santa Monica, CA - *BrCabYB 84; TV&RadDir 84*
KSRH-FM - San Rafael, CA - *BrCabYB 84; TV&RadDir 84*
KSRM - Soldotna, AK - *BrCabYB 84; TV&RadDir 84*
KSRN-FM - Reno, NV - *BrCabYB 84; TV&RadDir 84*
KSRO - Santa Rosa, CA - *BrCabYB 84; TV&RadDir 84*
KSRR-FM - Houston, TX - *BrCabYB 84; NatRadPubDir Summer 83, Spring 84; TV&RadDir 84*
KSRV - Ontario, OR - *BrCabYB 84; TV&RadDir 84*
KSSA - Ft. Worth, TX - *BrCabYB 84*
KSSK - Honolulu, HI - *BrCabYB 84; NatRadPubDir Summer 83, Spring 84; TV&RadDir 84*
KSSM-FM - Centrahoma, OK - *TV&RadDir 84*
KSSM-FM - Miami, OK - *BrCabYB 84*
KSSN-FM - Little Rock, AR - *BrCabYB 84; NatRadPubDir Summer 83, Spring 84; TV&RadDir 84*
KSSS - Colorado Springs, CO - *BrCabYB 84; NatRadPubDir Summer 83, Spring 84; TV&RadDir 84*
KSST - Sulphur Springs, TX - *BrCabYB 84; TV&RadDir 84*
KSTA - San Jose, CA - *TelAl 84*
KSTA - Coleman, TX - *BrCabYB 84; TV&RadDir 84*
KSTA-FM - Coleman, TX - *BrCabYB 84; TV&RadDir 84*
KSTB - Breckenridge, TX - *BrCabYB 84; TV&RadDir 84*
KSTC - Sterling, CO - *BrCabYB 84; TV&RadDir 84*
KSTC-FM - Sterling, CO - *BrCabYB 84; TV&RadDir 84*
KSTF-TV - Scottsbluff, NE - *BrCabYB 84; TelAl 83, 84; Tel&CabFB 84S; TV&RadDir 84*
KSTG-FM - Sikeston, MO - *BrCabYB 84; TV&RadDir 84*
KSTI-FM - Springfield, SD - *BrCabYB 84; NatRadPubDir Summer 83, Spring 84; TV&RadDir 84*
KSTK-FM - Wrangell, AK - *BrCabYB 84; TV&RadDir 84*
KSTL - St. Louis, MO - *BrCabYB 84; NatRadPubDir Summer 83, Spring 84; TV&RadDir 84*
KSTM-FM - Apache Junction, AZ - *BrCabYB 84; TV&RadDir 84*
KSTN - Stockton, CA - *BrCabYB 84; NatRadPubDir Summer 83, Spring 84; TV&RadDir 84*
KSTN-FM - Stockton, CA - *BrCabYB 84; NatRadPubDir Summer 83, Spring 84; TV&RadDir 84*
KSTO - Agana, GU - *BrCabYB 84*
KSTP - Minneapolis, MN - *NatRadPubDir Summer 83, Spring 84 p.134*
KSTP - St. Paul, MN - *BrCabYB 84; TV&RadDir 84*
KSTP-FM - Minneapolis, MN - *NatRadPubDir Summer 83, Spring 84; TV&RadDir 84*
KSTP-FM - St. Paul, MN - *BrCabYB 84*
KSTP-TV - Minneapolis, MN - *DirUSTelSta 83; TelAl 83, 84; Tel&CabFB 84S*
KSTP-TV - St. Paul, MN - *BrCabYB 84; LitMarPl 83, 84; TV&RadDir 84*
KSTR - Grand Junction, CO - *BrCabYB 84; NatRadPubDir Summer 83, Spring 84; TV&RadDir 84*
KSTS - Salinas, CA - *DirUSTelSta 83*
KSTS - San Jose, CA - *BrCabYB 84; Tel&CabFB 84S*
KSTT - Davenport, IA - *BrCabYB 84; NatRadPubDir Summer 83, Spring 84; TV&RadDir 84*
KSTU-TV - Salt Lake City, UT - *BrCabYB 84; DirUSTelSta 83; TelAl 83, 84; Tel&CabFB 84S; TV&RadDir 84*
KSTV - Stephenville, TX - *BrCabYB 84; TV&RadDir 84*
KSTW-TV - Seattle, WA - *DirUSTelSta 83*
KSTW-TV - Tacoma, WA - *BrCabYB 84; TelAl 83, 84; Tel&CabFB 84S; TV&RadDir 84*
KSUA - Fairbanks, AK - *NatRadPubDir Summer 83, Spring 84*
KSUB - Cedar City, UT - *BrCabYB 84; TV&RadDir 84*
KSUB-FM - Cedar City, UT - *BrCabYB 84; TV&RadDir 84*
KSUC-FM - Keene, TX - *BrCabYB 84; NatRadPubDir Summer 83, Spring 84; TV&RadDir 84*
KSUD - West Memphis, AR - *BrCabYB 84; TV&RadDir 84*
KSUE - Susanville, CA - *BrCabYB 84; TV&RadDir 84*
KSUE-FM - Susanville, CA - *BrCabYB 84; TV&RadDir 84*
KSUI-FM - Coralville, IA - *TV&RadDir 84*
KSUI-FM - Iowa City, IA - *BrCabYB 84*
KSUM - Fairmont, MN - *BrCabYB 84; TV&RadDir 84*
KSUN - Phoenix, AZ - *BrCabYB 84; TV&RadDir 84*
KSUT-FM - Ignacio, CO - *BrCabYB 84; TV&RadDir 84*
KSUZ-TV - Abilene, TX - *BrCabYB 84*
KSVA - Sierra Vista, AZ - *BrCabYB 84; TV&RadDir 84*
KSVC - Richfield, UT - *BrCabYB 84; TV&RadDir 84*
KSVN - Ogden, UT - *BrCabYB 84; TV&RadDir 84*
KSVN - Riverdale, UT - *NatRadPubDir Summer 83*
KSVP - Artesia, NM - *BrCabYB 84; TV&RadDir 84*
KSVR-FM - Mt. Vernon, WA - *BrCabYB 84; NatRadPubDir Summer 83, Spring 84; TV&RadDir 84*
KSW & G Advertising Inc. - New York, NY - *BrCabYB 84*
KSWA - Graham, TX - *BrCabYB 84; TV&RadDir 84*
KSWB - Seaside, OR - *BrCabYB 84; TV&RadDir 84*
KSWC-FM - Winfield, KS - *BrCabYB 84; NatRadPubDir Summer 83, Spring 84; TV&RadDir 84*
KSWH-FM - Arkadelphia, AR - *BrCabYB 84; NatRadPubDir Summer 83, Spring 84; TV&RadDir 84*
KSWK-TV - Garden City, KS - *Tel&CabFB 84S*
KSWM - Aurora, MO - *BrCabYB 84; TV&RadDir 84*
KSWN - McCook, NE - *BrCabYB 84; TV&RadDir 84*
KSWO - Lawton, OK - *BrCabYB 84; TV&RadDir 84*
KSWO-TV - Lawton, OK - *BrCabYB 84; TelAl 83, 84; Tel&CabFB 84S; TV&RadDir 84*
KSWO-TV - Wichita Falls, TX - *DirUSTelSta 83*
KSWS-TV - Roswell, NM - *BrCabYB 84; TelAl 83, 84; Tel&CabFB 84S*
KSWT-FM - Topeka, KS - *NatRadPubDir Summer 83*
KSXO - Redding, CA - *BrCabYB 84; TV&RadDir 84*
KSXT-FM - Walla Walla, WA - *BrCabYB 84; TV&RadDir 84*
KSYC - Yreka, CA - *BrCabYB 84; TV&RadDir 84*
KSYL - Alexandria, LA - *BrCabYB 84; NatRadPubDir Summer 83, Spring 84; TV&RadDir 84*
KSYM-FM - San Antonio, TX - *BrCabYB 84; NatRadPubDir Summer 83, Spring 84; TV&RadDir 84*
KSYN-FM - Joplin, MO - *BrCabYB 84; TV&RadDir 84*
KSYS-TV - Medford, OR - *BrCabYB 84; Tel&CabFB 84S; TV&RadDir 84*
KSYV - Solvang, CA - *BrCabYB 84*
KSYX - Santa Rosa, NM - *BrCabYB 84; TV&RadDir 84*
KSYZ - Grand Island, NE - *BrCabYB 84*
KSZN - Pampa, TX - *BrCabYB 84; TV&RadDir 84*
KSZU-FM - Stanford, CA - *TV&RadDir 84*
KTAA - California, MO - *BrCabYB 84*
KTAB-TV - Abilene, TX - *BrCabYB 84; DirUSTelSta 83; TelAl 83, 84; Tel&CabFB 84S; TV&RadDir 84*
KTAC - Tacoma, WA - *BrCabYB 84; NatRadPubDir Summer 83, Spring 84; TV&RadDir 84*
KTAD - St. Louis, MO - *BrCabYB 84*
KTAE - Taylor, TX - *BrCabYB 84; TV&RadDir 84*
KTAG - Cody, WY - *BrCabYB 84*
KTAH - Portland, OR - *Tel&CabFB 84S*
KTAI-FM - Kingsville, TX - *BrCabYB 84; NatRadPubDir Summer 83, Spring 84; TV&RadDir 84*
KTAJ - St. Joseph, MO - *BrCabYB 84*
KTAK-FM - Riverton, WY - *BrCabYB 84; TV&RadDir 84*
KTAL-FM - Texarkana, TX - *BrCabYB 84; TV&RadDir 84*

KTAL-TV - Shreveport, LA - *DirUSTelSta 83; TelAl 83, 84; Tel&CabFB 84S; TV&RadDir 84*
KTAL-TV - Texarkana, TX - *BrCabYB 84; LitMarPl 83, 84; TV&RadDir 84*
KTAM - Bryan, TX - *BrCabYB 84; TV&RadDir 84*
KTAN - Sierra Vista, AZ - *BrCabYB 84; TV&RadDir 84*
KTAP-FM - Crete, NE - *BrCabYB 84; TV&RadDir 84*
KTAR - Phoenix, AZ - *BrCabYB 84; NatRadPubDir Summer 83, Spring 84; TV&RadDir 84*
KTAT - Frederick, OK - *BrCabYB 84; TV&RadDir 84*
KTAV-FM - Knoxville, IA - *BrCabYB 84; TV&RadDir 84*
Ktav Publishing House Inc. - New York, NY - *LitMarPl 83, 84*
KTAW - College Station, TX - *BrCabYB 84*
KTAZ-FM - Sierra Vista, AZ - *BrCabYB 84*
KTBA - Tuba City, AZ - *BrCabYB 84*
KTBB - Tyler, TX - *BrCabYB 84; NatRadPubDir Summer 83, Spring 84; TV&RadDir 84*
KTBC-FM - Nacogdoches, TX - *BrCabYB 84; TV&RadDir 84*
KTBC-TV - Austin, TX - *BrCabYB 84; DirUSTelSta 83; TelAl 83, 84; Tel&CabFB 84S; TV&RadDir 84*
KTBI - Ephrata, WA - *BrCabYB 84*
KTBN-TV - Fontana, CA - *TelAl 83, 84; Tel&CabFB 84S*
KTBN-TV - Santa Ana, CA - *TV&RadDir 84*
KTBO-TV - Oklahoma City, OK - *BrCabYB 84; DirUSTelSta 83; Tel&CabFB 84S*
KTBS-TV - Shreveport, LA - *BrCabYB 84; DirUSTelSta 83; LitMarPl 83, 84; TelAl 83, 84; Tel&CabFB 84S; TV&RadDir 84*
KTBY - Anchorage, AK - *BrCabYB 84; Tel&CabFB 84S*
KTCA-TV - St. Paul, MN - *BrCabYB 84; Tel&CabFB 84S; TV&RadDir 84*
KTCB - Malden, MO - *BrCabYB 84; TV&RadDir 84*
KTCC - Colby, KS - *BrCabYB 84*
KTCH - Wayne, NE - *BrCabYB 84; TV&RadDir 84*
KTCH-FM - Wayne, NE - *BrCabYB 84; TV&RadDir 84*
KTCI-TV - St. Paul, MN - *BrCabYB 84; Tel&CabFB 84S; TV&RadDir 84*
KTCL-FM - Ft. Collins, CO - *BrCabYB 84; NatRadPubDir Summer 83, Spring 84; TV&RadDir 84*
KTCR - Minneapolis, MN - *BrCabYB 84; NatRadPubDir Summer 83, Spring 84; TV&RadDir 84*
KTCR-FM - Minneapolis, MN - *BrCabYB 84; NatRadPubDir Summer 83, Spring 84; TV&RadDir 84*
KTCS - Ft. Smith, AR - *BrCabYB 84; NatRadPubDir Summer 83, Spring 84; TV&RadDir 84*
KTCS-FM - Ft. Smith, AR - *BrCabYB 84; NatRadPubDir Summer 83, Spring 84; TV&RadDir 84*
KTCU-FM - Ft. Worth, TX - *BrCabYB 84; NatRadPubDir Summer 83, Spring 84; TV&RadDir 84*
KTDB - Ramah, NM - *BrCabYB 84*
KTDL - Farmerville, LA - *BrCabYB 84; TV&RadDir 84*
KTDO - Toledo, OR - *BrCabYB 84; TV&RadDir 84*
KTDY-FM - Lafayette, LA - *BrCabYB 84; NatRadPubDir Summer 83, Spring 84; TV&RadDir 84*
KTDZ - Portland, OR - *BrCabYB 84*
KTEC-FM - Klamath Falls, OR - *BrCabYB 84; TV&RadDir 84*
KTED - Fowler, CA - *BrCabYB 84*
KTEE - Idaho Falls, ID - *BrCabYB 84; TV&RadDir 84*
KTEH-TV - San Jose, CA - *BrCabYB 84; Tel&CabFB 84S; TV&RadDir 84*
KTEI - Poggott, AR - *BrCabYB 84*
KTEJ-TV - Bono, AR - *TV&RadDir 84*
KTEJ-TV - Jonesboro, AR - *BrCabYB 84; Tel&CabFB 84S*
KTEK - Alvin, TX - *BrCabYB 84*
KTEL - Walla Walla, WA - *BrCabYB 84; TV&RadDir 84*
KTEM - Temple, TX - *BrCabYB 84; TV&RadDir 84*
KTEN-FM - Ada, OK - *BrCabYB 84; TV&RadDir 84*
KTEN-TV - Ada, OK - *BrCabYB 84; DirUSTelSta 83; TelAl 83, 84; Tel&CabFB 84S; TV&RadDir 84*
KTEO - San Angelo, TX - *BrCabYB 84; NatRadPubDir Summer 83, Spring 84; TV&RadDir 84*
KTEP-FM - El Paso, TX - *BrCabYB 84; NatRadPubDir Summer 83, Spring 84; TV&RadDir 84*
KTEQ-FM - Rapid City, SD - *BrCabYB 84; NatRadPubDir Summer 83, Spring 84; TV&RadDir 84*
KTER - Terrell, TX - *BrCabYB 84; TV&RadDir 84*
KTEW - Poteau, OK - *BrCabYB 84; TV&RadDir 84*
KTEZ-FM - Lubbock, TX - *BrCabYB 84; NatRadPubDir Summer 83, Spring 84; TV&RadDir 84*
KTFA - Groves, TX - *BrCabYB 84*
KTFC-FM - Sioux City, IA - *BrCabYB 84; TV&RadDir 84*
KTFM-FM - San Antonio, TX - *BrCabYB 84; NatRadPubDir Summer 83, Spring 84; TV&RadDir 84*
KTFS - Texarkana, TX - *BrCabYB 84; TV&RadDir 84*
KTFX-FM - Tulsa, OK - *BrCabYB 84; NatRadPubDir Summer 83, Spring 84; TV&RadDir 84*
KTGC - Nederland, TX - *BrCabYB 84; Tel&CabFB 84S*
KTGO - Tioga, ND - *BrCabYB 84; TV&RadDir 84*
KTGR - Columbia, MO - *BrCabYB 84; NatRadPubDir Summer 83, Spring 84; TV&RadDir 84*
KTHE - Thermopolis, WY - *BrCabYB 84; TV&RadDir 84*
KTHI-TV - Fargo, ND - *BrCabYB 84; DirUSTelSta 83; TelAl 83, 84; Tel&CabFB 84S; TV&RadDir 84*
KTHO - South Lake Tahoe, CA - *BrCabYB 84; NatRadPubDir Summer 83, Spring 84; TV&RadDir 84*
KTHS - Berryville, AR - *BrCabYB 84; TV&RadDir 84*
KTHV-TV - Little Rock, AR - *BrCabYB 84; DirUSTelSta 83; LitMarPl 83, 84; TelAl 83, 84; Tel&CabFB 84S; TV&RadDir 84*
KTI Inc. - Fulton, MO - *Tel&CabFB 84C*
KTIA - Ft. Worth, TX - *BrCabYB 84*
KTIB - Thibodaux, LA - *BrCabYB 84; TV&RadDir 84*
KTIE - Oxnard, CA - *BrCabYB 84; Tel&CabFB 84S*
KTIG-FM - Pequot Lakes, MN - *BrCabYB 84; TV&RadDir 84*
KTIL - Tillamook, OR - *BrCabYB 84; TV&RadDir 84*
KTIL-FM - Tillamook, OR - *BrCabYB 84*
KTIM - San Rafael, CA - *BrCabYB 84; NatRadPubDir Summer 83, Spring 84; TV&RadDir 84*
KTIM-FM - San Rafael, CA - *BrCabYB 84; NatRadPubDir Summer 83, Spring 84; TV&RadDir 84*
KTIN - Ft. Dodge, IA - *BrCabYB 84; Tel&CabFB 84S*
KTIP - Porterville, CA - *BrCabYB 84; TV&RadDir 84*
KTIS - Minneapolis, MN - *BrCabYB 84; NatRadPubDir Summer 83 p.294, Spring 84 p.296*
KTIS - St. Paul, MN - *TV&RadDir 84*
KTIS-FM - Minneapolis, MN - *BrCabYB 84; NatRadPubDir Summer 83 p.294, Spring 84 p.296*
KTIV-TV - Sioux City, IA - *BrCabYB 84; DirUSTelSta 83; TelAl 83, 84; Tel&CabFB 84S; TV&RadDir 84*
KTIX - Pendleton, OR - *BrCabYB 84; TV&RadDir 84*
KTIZ-FM - Alexandria, LA - *BrCabYB 84; TV&RadDir 84*
KTJA - Beaverton, OR - *BrCabYB 84*
KTJJ-FM - Farmington, MO - *BrCabYB 84; TV&RadDir 84*
KTJO-FM - Ottawa, KS - *BrCabYB 84; NatRadPubDir Summer 83, Spring 84; TV&RadDir 84*
KTJS - Hobart, OK - *BrCabYB 84; TV&RadDir 84*
KTKC-FM - Springhill, LA - *BrCabYB 84; TV&RadDir 84*
KTKN - Ketchikan, AK - *BrCabYB 84; TV&RadDir 84*
KTKR - Taft, CA - *BrCabYB 84; TV&RadDir 84*
KTKT - Tucson, AZ - *BrCabYB 84; NatRadPubDir Summer 83, Spring 84; TV&RadDir 84*
KTLA-TV - Los Angeles, CA - *BrCabYB 84; DirUSTelSta 83; LitMarPl 84; TelAl 83, 84; Tel&CabFB 84S; TV&RadDir 84*
KTLB-FM - Rockwell City, IA - *TV&RadDir 84*
KTLB-FM - Twin Lakes, IA - *BrCabYB 84*
KTLC - Twin Falls, ID - *BrCabYB 84; TV&RadDir 84*
KTLE - Tooele, UT - *BrCabYB 84; TV&RadDir 84*
KTLE-FM - Tooele, UT - *TV&RadDir 84*
KTLK - Beaumont, TX - *TV&RadDir 84*
KTLO - Mountain Home, AR - *BrCabYB 84; TV&RadDir 84*
KTLO-FM - Mountain Home, AR - *BrCabYB 84; TV&RadDir 84*
KTLQ - Tahlequah, OK - *TV&RadDir 84*
KTLQ-FM - Tahlequah, OK - *BrCabYB 84*
KTLR-FM - Terrell, TX - *BrCabYB 84; TV&RadDir 84*
KTLU - Rusk, TX - *BrCabYB 84; TV&RadDir 84*
KTLX-FM - Columbus, NE - *BrCabYB 84; NatRadPubDir Summer 83, Spring 84; TV&RadDir 84*
KTMA-TV - Minneapolis, MN - *BrCabYB 84; TelAl 84; Tel&CabFB 84S*
KTMC - McAlester, OK - *BrCabYB 84; TV&RadDir 84*
KTMG - Deer Trail, CO - *BrCabYB 84*
KTMO-FM - Kennett, MO - *BrCabYB 84; TV&RadDir 84*
KTMP-FM - Spanish Fork, UT - *TV&RadDir 84*

KTMS - Santa Barbara, CA - *BrCabYB 84; NatRadPubDir Summer 83, Spring 84; TV&RadDir 84*
KTMS-FM - Santa Barbara, CA - *BrCabYB 84; NatRadPubDir Summer 83, Spring 84; TV&RadDir 84*
KTMT-FM - Eugene, OR - *TV&RadDir 84*
KTMT-FM - Medford, OR - *BrCabYB 84*
KTNC - Falls City, NE - *BrCabYB 84; TV&RadDir 84*
KTNC-FM - Falls City, NE - *BrCabYB 84*
KTNE-TV - Alliance, NE - *BrCabYB 84; Tel&CabFB 84S*
KTNL - Sitka, AK - *BrCabYB 84; Tel&CabFB 84S*
KTNM - Tucumcari, NM - *BrCabYB 84; TV&RadDir 84*
KTNM-FM - Tucumcari, NM - *BrCabYB 84*
KTNQ - Los Angeles, CA - *BrCabYB 84; NatRadPubDir Summer 83 p.23, Spring 84 p.23; TV&RadDir 84*
KTNR - Kenedy, TX - *BrCabYB 84*
KTNT - Tacoma, WA - *TV&RadDir 84*
KTNV-TV - Las Vegas, NV - *BrCabYB 84; DirUSTelSta 83; TelAl 83, 84; Tel&CabFB 84S; TV&RadDir 84*
KTNW-TV - Riverton, WY - *BrCabYB 84; DirUSTelSta 83; TelAl 83, 84; Tel&CabFB 84S; TV&RadDir 84*
KTNX - Anchorage, AK - *BrCabYB 84; NatRadPubDir Summer 83, Spring 84; TV&RadDir 84*
KTOB - Petaluma, CA - *BrCabYB 84; TV&RadDir 84*
KTOC - Jonesboro, LA - *BrCabYB 84; TV&RadDir 84*
KTOD - Conway, AR - *BrCabYB 84; TV&RadDir 84*
KTOE - Mankato, MN - *BrCabYB 84; NatRadPubDir Summer 83, Spring 84; TV&RadDir 84*
KTOF-FM - Cedar Rapids, IA - *BrCabYB 84; NatRadPubDir Summer 83, Spring 84; TV&RadDir 84*
KTOK - Oklahoma City, OK - *BrCabYB 84; NatRadPubDir Summer 83, Spring 84; TV&RadDir 84*
KTOL - Lacey, WA - *BrCabYB 84*
KTOM - Salinas, CA - *BrCabYB 84; NatRadPubDir Summer 83, Spring 84; TV&RadDir 84*
KTON - Belton, TX - *BrCabYB 84; TV&RadDir 84*
KTON-FM - Belton, TX - *BrCabYB 84; TV&RadDir 84*
KTOO-FM - Juneau, AK - *BrCabYB 84; TV&RadDir 84*
KTOO-TV - Juneau, AK - *BrCabYB 84; Tel&CabFB 84S*
KTOP - Topeka, KS - *BrCabYB 84; NatRadPubDir Summer 83, Spring 84; TV&RadDir 84*
KTOQ - Rapid City, SD - *BrCabYB 84; TV&RadDir 84*
KTOT-FM - Big Bear Lake, CA - *BrCabYB 84; TV&RadDir 84*
KTOW - Sand Springs, OK - *BrCabYB 84*
KTOW - Tulsa, OK - *NatRadPubDir Summer 83, Spring 84; TV&RadDir 84*
KTOX - Boise, ID - *BrCabYB 84*
KTOY-FM - Tacoma, WA - *BrCabYB 84; NatRadPubDir Summer 83, Spring 84; TV&RadDir 84*
KTPA - Prescott, AR - *BrCabYB 84; TV&RadDir 84*
KTPI - Tehachapi, CA - *BrCabYB 84*
KTPK-FM - Topeka, KS - *BrCabYB 84; NatRadPubDir Summer 83, Spring 84; TV&RadDir 84*
KTPR-FM - Ft. Dodge, IA - *BrCabYB 84; TV&RadDir 84*
KTPS-TV - Tacoma, WA - *BrCabYB 84; Tel&CabFB 84S; TV&RadDir 84*
KTPX-TV - Monahans, TX - *BrCabYB 84; TelAl 83, 84*
KTPX-TV - Odessa, TX - *DirUSTelSta 83; Tel&CabFB 84S*
KTQM-FM - Clovis, NM - *BrCabYB 84; TV&RadDir 84*
KTQQ-FM - Sulphur, LA - *BrCabYB 84; TV&RadDir 84*
KTRB - Modesto, CA - *BrCabYB 84; NatRadPubDir Summer 83, Spring 84; TV&RadDir 84*
KTRC - Santa Fe, NM - *BrCabYB 84; NatRadPubDir Summer 83, Spring 84; TV&RadDir 84*
KTRE-TV - Lufkin, TX - *BrCabYB 84; TelAl 83, 84; Tel&CabFB 84S; TV&RadDir 84*
KTRF - Thief River Falls, MN - *BrCabYB 84*
KTRH - Houston, TX - *BrCabYB 84; NatRadPubDir Summer 83, Spring 84; TV&RadDir 84*
KTRI-FM - Mansfield, MO - *BrCabYB 84; TV&RadDir 84*
KTRK-TV - Houston, TX - *BrCabYB 84; DirUSTelSta 83; LitMarPl 83, 84; TelAl 83, 84; Tel&CabFB 84S; TV&RadDir 84*
KTRM - Beaumont, TX - *BrCabYB 84; NatRadPubDir Summer 83, Spring 84*
KTRM - Ephrata, WA - *BrCabYB 84*
KTRN - Wichita Falls, TX - *BrCabYB 84; NatRadPubDir Summer 83, Spring 84; TV&RadDir 84*
KTRQ - Ephrata, WA - *TV&RadDir 84*
KTRS - Casper, WY - *BrCabYB 84*
KTRT - Truckee, CA - *BrCabYB 84; TV&RadDir 84*
KTRU-FM - Houston, TX - *BrCabYB 84; NatRadPubDir Summer 83, Spring 84; TV&RadDir 84*
KTRV-TV - Boise, ID - *DirUSTelSta 83*
KTRV-TV - Nampa, ID - *TelAl 84; Tel&CabFB 84S; TV&RadDir 84*
KTRW - East Wenatchee, WA - *BrCabYB 84*
KTRX-FM - Tarkio, MO - *BrCabYB 84; TV&RadDir 84*
KTRY - Bastrop, LA - *BrCabYB 84; TV&RadDir 84*
KTRY-FM - Bastrop, LA - *BrCabYB 84; TV&RadDir 84*
KTS Information Systems - Munich, West Germany - *EISS 7-83 Sup*
KTSA - San Antonio, TX - *BrCabYB 84; NatRadPubDir Summer 83, Spring 84; TV&RadDir 84*
KTSB - Topeka, KS - *TelAl 83*
KTSC-FM - Pueblo, CO - *BrCabYB 84; NatRadPubDir Summer 83, Spring 84; TV&RadDir 84*
KTSC-TV - Pueblo, CO - *BrCabYB 84; Tel&CabFB 84S; TV&RadDir 84*
KTSD-FM - Reliance, SD - *BrCabYB 84*
KTSD-TV - Pierre, SD - *BrCabYB 84; Tel&CabFB 84S*
KTSF-TV - San Francisco, CA - *BrCabYB 84; DirUSTelSta 83; TelAl 83, 84; Tel&CabFB 84S; TV&RadDir 84*
KTSJ - Pomona, CA - *BrCabYB 84*
KTSM - El Paso, TX - *BrCabYB 84; NatRadPubDir Summer 83, Spring 84; TV&RadDir 84*
KTSM-FM - El Paso, TX - *BrCabYB 84; NatRadPubDir Summer 83, Spring 84; TV&RadDir 84*
KTSM-TV - El Paso, TX - *BrCabYB 84; DirUSTelSta 83; TelAl 83, 84; Tel&CabFB 84S; TV&RadDir 84*
KTSP-TV - Phoenix, AZ - *BrCabYB 84; DirUSTelSta 83; LitMarPl 84; TelAl 84; Tel&CabFB 84S; TV&RadDir 84*
KTSR-FM - Kansas City, MO - *BrCabYB 84; TV&RadDir 84*
KTSU-FM - Houston, TX - *BrCabYB 84; NatRadPubDir Summer 83, Spring 84; TV&RadDir 84*
KTTC - Rochester, MN - *BrCabYB 84; DirUSTelSta 83; Tel&CabFB 84S*
KTTC-TV - Rochester, MN - *BrCabYB 84; TelAl 83, 84; TV&RadDir 84*
KTTH - Naknek, AK - *BrCabYB 84*
KTTI-FM - Yuma, AZ - *BrCabYB 84; TV&RadDir 84*
KTTL-FM - Dodge City, KS - *BrCabYB 84; TV&RadDir 84*
KTTN - Trenton, MO - *BrCabYB 84; TV&RadDir 84*
KTTN-FM - Trenton, MO - *BrCabYB 84; TV&RadDir 84*
KTTR - Rolla, MO - *BrCabYB 84; TV&RadDir 84*
KTTS - Springfield, MO - *BrCabYB 84; NatRadPubDir Summer 83, Spring 84; TV&RadDir 84*
KTTS-FM - Springfield, MO - *BrCabYB 84; NatRadPubDir Summer 83, Spring 84; TV&RadDir 84*
KTTT - Columbus, NE - *BrCabYB 84; TV&RadDir 84*
KTTT-FM - Columbus, NE - *BrCabYB 84; TV&RadDir 84*
KTTU-TV - Fairbanks, AK - *BrCabYB 84; DirUSTelSta 83; TelAl 84; Tel&CabFB 84S; TV&RadDir 84*
KTTV-TV - Hollywood, CA - *LitMarPl 83, 84*
KTTV-TV - Los Angeles, CA - *BrCabYB 84; DirUSTelSta 83; TelAl 83, 84; Tel&CabFB 84S; TV&RadDir 84*
KTTX - Brenham, TX - *BrCabYB 84; TV&RadDir 84*
KTTY - San Diego, CA - *BrCabYB 84; Tel&CabFB 84S*
KTTZ - Oracle, AZ - *BrCabYB 84*
KTUC - Tucson, AZ - *BrCabYB 84; NatRadPubDir Summer 83, Spring 84; TV&RadDir 84*
KTUE - Tulia, TX - *BrCabYB 84; TV&RadDir 84*
KTUF - Kirksville, MO - *BrCabYB 84*
KTUH-FM - Honolulu, HI - *BrCabYB 84; NatRadPubDir Summer 83, Spring 84; TV&RadDir 84*
KTUI - Sullivan, MO - *BrCabYB 84; TV&RadDir 84*
KTUI-FM - Sullivan, MO - *BrCabYB 84*
KTUL-TV - Tulsa, OK - *BrCabYB 84; DirUSTelSta 83; LitMarPl 83, 84; TelAl 83, 84; Tel&CabFB 84S; TV&RadDir 84*
KTUN - Humble, TX - *BrCabYB 84*
KTUO-FM - Sonora, CA - *BrCabYB 84; TV&RadDir 84*
KTUS - Snowmass Village, CO - *BrCabYB 84*

KTUU-TV - Anchorage, AK - *BrCabYB 84; DirUSTelSta 83; TelAl 84; Tel&CabFB 84S; TV&RadDir 84*
KTUX - Rock Springs, WY - *TelAl 83*
KTVA-TV - Anchorage, AK - *BrCabYB 84; DirUSTelSta 83; TelAl 83, 84; Tel&CabFB 84S; TV&RadDir 84*
KTVB-TV - Boise, ID - *BrCabYB 84; DirUSTelSta 83; TelAl 83, 84; Tel&CabFB 84S; TV&RadDir 84*
KTVC-TV - Dodge City, KS - *DirUSTelSta 83; TV&RadDir 84*
KTVC-TV - Ensign, KS - *BrCabYB 84; TelAl 83, 84; Tel&CabFB 84S*
KTVE-TV - El Dorado, AR - *Tel&CabFB 84S; TV&RadDir 84*
KTVE-TV - Monroe, LA - *BrCabYB 84; DirUSTelSta 83; TelAl 83, 84*
KTVF-TV - Fairbanks, AK - *BrCabYB 84; DirUSTelSta 83; TelAl 83, 84; Tel&CabFB 84S; TV&RadDir 84*
KTVG-TV - Helena, MT - *BrCabYB 84; DirUSTelSta 83; TelAl 83, 84; Tel&CabFB 84S; TV&RadDir 84*
KTVH-TV - Wichita, KS - *DirUSTelSta 83; LitMarPl 83; TelAl 83; TV&RadDir 84*
KTVI-TV - St. Louis, MO - *BrCabYB 84; DirUSTelSta 83; LitMarPl 83, 84; TelAl 83, 84; Tel&CabFB 84S; TV&RadDir 84*
KTVJ - Boulder, CO - *BrCabYB 84; Tel&CabFB 84S*
KTVJ - Joplin, MO - *TelAl 83*
KTVK-TV - Phoenix, AZ - *BrCabYB 84; DirUSTelSta 83; LitMarPl 83, 84; TelAl 83, 84; Tel&CabFB 84S; TV&RadDir 84*
KTVL-TV - Medford, OR - *BrCabYB 84; DirUSTelSta 83; TelAl 83, 84; Tel&CabFB 84S; TV&RadDir 84*
KTVM-TV - Butte, MT - *BrCabYB 84; DirUSTelSta 83; TelAl 84; Tel&CabFB 84S*
KTVM-TV - Missoula, MT - *TelAl 83; TV&RadDir 84*
KTVN-TV - Reno, NV - *BrCabYB 84; DirUSTelSta 83; TelAl 83, 84; Tel&CabFB 84S; TV&RadDir 84*
KTVO-TV - Ottumwa, IA - *DirUSTelSta 83; TelAl 83, 84*
KTVO-TV - Kirksville, MO - *BrCabYB 84; Tel&CabFB 84S; TV&RadDir 84*
KTVP-TV - Fayetteville, AR - *BrCabYB 84; TelAl 83, 84; Tel&CabFB 84S; TV&RadDir 84*
KTVQ-TV - Billings, MT - *BrCabYB 84; DirUSTelSta 83; TelAl 83, 84; Tel&CabFB 84S; TV&RadDir 84*
KTVR-TV - La Grande, OR - *BrCabYB 84; Tel&CabFB 84S*
KTVS-TV - Sterling, CO - *BrCabYB 84; TelAl 83, 84; Tel&CabFB 84S; TV&RadDir 84*
KTVT-TV - Dallas, TX - *DirUSTelSta 83*
KTVT-TV - Ft. Worth, TX - *BrCabYB 84; TelAl 83, 84; Tel&CabFB 84S; TV&RadDir 84*
KTVU-TV - Oakland, CA - *BrCabYB 84; Tel&CabFB 84S; TV&RadDir 84*
KTVU-TV - San Francisco, CA - *DirUSTelSta 83; TelAl 83, 84*
KTVV-TV - Austin, TX - *BrCabYB 84; DirUSTelSta 83; TelAl 83, 84; Tel&CabFB 84S; TV&RadDir 84*
KTVW-TV - Phoenix, AZ - *BrCabYB 84; DirUSTelSta 83; TelAl 83, 84; Tel&CabFB 84S; TV&RadDir 84*
KTVX-TV - Salt Lake City, UT - *BrCabYB 84; DirUSTelSta 83; LitMarPl 83, 84; TelAl 83, 84; Tel&CabFB 84S; TV&RadDir 84*
KTVY-TV - Oklahoma City, OK - *BrCabYB 84; DirUSTelSta 83; LitMarPl 83, 84; TelAl 84; Tel&CabFB 84S; TV&RadDir 84*
KTVZ-TV - Bend, OR - *BrCabYB 84; DirUSTelSta 83; TelAl 83, 84; Tel&CabFB 84S; TV&RadDir 84*
KTWA - Ottumwa, IA - *BrCabYB 84*
KTWG - Agana, GU - *BrCabYB 84*
KTWN-FM - Anoka, MN - *BrCabYB 84; TV&RadDir 84*
KTWN-FM - Minneapolis, MN - *NatRadPubDir Summer 83 p.134, Spring 84 p.134*
KTWO - Casper, WY - *BrCabYB 84; NatRadPubDir Summer 83, Spring 84; TV&RadDir 84*
KTWO-TV - Casper, WY - *BrCabYB 84; DirUSTelSta 83; TelAl 83, 84; Tel&CabFB 84S; TV&RadDir 84*
KTWS-TV - Dallas, TX - *BrCabYB 84; DirUSTelSta 83; TelAl 84; Tel&CabFB 84S; TV&RadDir 84*
KTWU-TV - Topeka, KS - *BrCabYB 84; Tel&CabFB 84S; TV&RadDir 84*
KTXA-TV - Arlington, TX - *TV&RadDir 84*
KTXA-TV - Dallas, TX - *DirUSTelSta 83; TelAl 83, 84*
KTXA-TV - Ft. Worth, TX - *BrCabYB 84; Tel&CabFB 84S*
KTXC - Port Arthur, TX - *BrCabYB 84; TV&RadDir 84*
KTXH - Houston, TX - *BrCabYB 84; DirUSTelSta 83; TelAl 84; Tel&CabFB 84S*
KTXI - Mercedes, TX - *BrCabYB 84*
KTXJ - Jasper, TX - *BrCabYB 84; TV&RadDir 84*
KTXK - Texarkana, TX - *BrCabYB 84*
KTXL-TV - Sacramento, CA - *BrCabYB 84; DirUSTelSta 83; TelAl 83, 84; Tel&CabFB 84S; TV&RadDir 84*
KTXN-FM - Victoria, TX - *BrCabYB 84; TV&RadDir 84*
KTXO - Sherman, TX - *BrCabYB 84; TV&RadDir 84*
KTXQ - Dallas, TX - *NatRadPubDir Summer 83, Spring 84*
KTXQ - Ft. Worth, TX - *BrCabYB 84*
KTXQ-FM - Dallas, TX - *TV&RadDir 84*
KTXR-FM - Springfield, MO - *BrCabYB 84; NatRadPubDir Summer 83, Spring 84; TV&RadDir 84*
KTXS-TV - Abilene, TX - *DirUSTelSta 83; TelAl 83, 84; TV&RadDir 84*
KTXS-TV - Sweetwater, TX - *BrCabYB 84; Tel&CabFB 84S*
KTXT-FM - Lubbock, TX - *BrCabYB 84; NatRadPubDir Summer 83, Spring 84; TV&RadDir 84*
KTXT-TV - Lubbock, TX - *BrCabYB 84; Tel&CabFB 84S; TV&RadDir 84*
KTXU-FM - Paris, TX - *BrCabYB 84; TV&RadDir 84*
KTXX - Whitefish, MT - *BrCabYB 84; TV&RadDir 84*
KTXY-FM - Jefferson City, MO - *BrCabYB 84; TV&RadDir 84*
KTXZ - West Lake Hills - *BrCabYB 84*
KTYD-FM - Santa Barbara, CA - *BrCabYB 84; NatRadPubDir Summer 83, Spring 84; TV&RadDir 84*
KTYE - Tye, TX - *BrCabYB 84*
KTYL - Tyler, TX - *BrCabYB 84; NatRadPubDir Summer 83, Spring 84; TV&RadDir 84*
KTYL-FM - Tyler, TX - *NatRadPubDir Summer 83, Spring 84; TV&RadDir 84*
KTYM - Inglewood, CA - *BrCabYB 84; TV&RadDir 84*
KTYM - Los Angeles, CA - *NatRadPubDir Summer 83 p.23, Spring 84 p.23*
KTYN - Minot, ND - *BrCabYB 84; NatRadPubDir Summer 83, Spring 84; TV&RadDir 84*
KTZA-FM - Artesia, NM - *BrCabYB 84; TV&RadDir 84*
KTZO-TV - San Francisco, CA - *BrCabYB 84; DirUSTelSta 83; TelAl 83, 84; Tel&CabFB 84S; TV&RadDir 84*
KTZZ - Seattle, WA - *BrCabYB 84*
KUAC-FM - Fairbanks, AK - *BrCabYB 84; NatRadPubDir Summer 83, Spring 84; TV&RadDir 84*
KUAC-TV - Fairbanks, AK - *BrCabYB 84; Tel&CabFB 84S; TV&RadDir 84*
KUAD-FM - Windsor, CO - *BrCabYB 84; TV&RadDir 84*
KUAF-FM - Fayetteville, AR - *BrCabYB 84; TV&RadDir 84*
KUAI - Eleele, HI - *BrCabYB 84; TV&RadDir 84*
KUAL-FM - Enid, OK - *BrCabYB 84; TV&RadDir 84*
KUAM-FM - Agana, GU - *BrCabYB 84*
KUAM-TV - Agana, GU - *BrCabYB 84; Tel&CabFB 84S*
KUAR - Little Rock, AR - *BrCabYB 84*
KUAT - Tucson, AZ - *BrCabYB 84; NatRadPubDir Summer 83, Spring 84; TV&RadDir 84*
KUAT-FM - Tucson, AZ - *BrCabYB 84; NatRadPubDir Summer 83, Spring 84; TV&RadDir 84*
KUAT-TV - Tucson, AZ - *BrCabYB 84; Tel&CabFB 84S; TV&RadDir 84*
KUBA - Yuba City, CA - *BrCabYB 84; TV&RadDir 84*
Kubaney Publishing Corp. - Miami Lakes, FL - *BillIntBG 83-84*
Kubasek & Associates Inc., John R. - Staten Island, NY - *DirPRFirms 83*
Kubasik Inc., Ben - New York, NY - *DirPRFirms 83*
KUBB-FM - Mariposa, CA - *BrCabYB 84; TV&RadDir 84*
KUBC - Montrose, CO - *BrCabYB 84; TV&RadDir 84*
KUBE-FM - Seattle, WA - *BrCabYB 84; NatRadPubDir Summer 83, Spring 84; TV&RadDir 84*
KUBO - Chualar, CA - *BrCabYB 84*
KUBS-FM - Newport, WA - *BrCabYB 84; NatRadPubDir Summer 83, Spring 84; TV&RadDir 84*
K.U.C. Cable TV [of Northern Communications Associates] - Brookings, SD - *BrCabYB 84*
KUCA-FM - Conway, AR - *TV&RadDir 84*
KUCB-FM - Des Moines, IA - *BrCabYB 84*
KUCI-FM - Irvine, CA - *BrCabYB 84; NatRadPubDir Summer 83, Spring 84; TV&RadDir 84*
KUCR-FM - Riverside, CA - *BrCabYB 84; TV&RadDir 84*
KUCR-FM - San Bernardino, CA - *NatRadPubDir Summer 83, Spring 84 p.28*

KUCU-TV - St. Louis, MO - *BrCabYB 84; Tel&CabFB 84S*
KUCV-FM - Lincoln, NE - *BrCabYB 84; NatRadPubDir Summer 83, Spring 84; TV&RadDir 84*
KUDE - Oceanside, CA - *TV&RadDir 84*
KUDE-FM - Oceanside, CA - *TV&RadDir 84*
Kudelka, Mark - East Meadow, NY - *LitMarPl 83, 84*
KUDL-FM - Kansas City, KS - *BrCabYB 84*
KUDL-FM - Shawnee Mission, KS - *TV&RadDir 84*
KUDL-FM - Kansas City, MO - *NatRadPubDir Summer 83 p.143, Spring 84 p.143*
KUDO-FM - Las Vegas, NV - *BrCabYB 84; NatRadPubDir Summer 83, Spring 84; TV&RadDir 84*
Kudos - Leeds, England - *LitMag&SmPr 83-84*
KUDY - Spokane, WA - *BrCabYB 84; NatRadPubDir Summer 83, Spring 84; TV&RadDir 84*
KUED-TV - Salt Lake City, UT - *BrCabYB 84; Tel&CabFB 84S; TV&RadDir 84*
KUEN - Wenatchee, WA - *BrCabYB 84; TV&RadDir 84*
KUER-FM - Salt Lake City, UT - *BrCabYB 84; NatRadPubDir Summer 83, Spring 84; TV&RadDir 84*
KUET - Black Canyon City, AZ - *BrCabYB 84*
KUEV-TV - Everett, WA - *BrCabYB 84*
KUFM-FM - Missoula, MT - *BrCabYB 84; NatRadPubDir Summer 83, Spring 84; TV&RadDir 84*
KUFO-FM - Midland, TX - *NatRadPubDir Spring 84 p.244; TV&RadDir 84*
KUFO-FM - Odessa, TX - *BrCabYB 84; NatRadPubDir Summer 83*
KUGN - Eugene, OR - *BrCabYB 84; NatRadPubDir Summer 83, Spring 84; TV&RadDir 84*
KUGN-FM - Eugene, OR - *BrCabYB 84; NatRadPubDir Summer 83, Spring 84*
KUGN-FM - Florence, OR - *TV&RadDir 84*
KUGR - Green River, WY - *BrCabYB 84; TV&RadDir 84*
KUGS-FM - Bellingham, WA - *BrCabYB 84; NatRadPubDir Summer 83, Spring 84; TV&RadDir 84*
KUHF-FM - Houston, TX - *BrCabYB 84; NatRadPubDir Summer 83, Spring 84; TV&RadDir 84*
KUHL - Santa Maria, CA - *BrCabYB 84; TV&RadDir 84*
Kuhn & Co., James - Brussels, Belgium - *DirPRFirms 83*
KUHT-TV - Houston, TX - *BrCabYB 84; Tel&CabFB 84S; TV&RadDir 84*
KUIB - Vernal, UT - *BrCabYB 84*
KUIC-FM - Vacaville, CA - *BrCabYB 84; TV&RadDir 84*
KUID-FM - Moscow, ID - *BrCabYB 84; NatRadPubDir Summer 83, Spring 84; TV&RadDir 84*
KUID-TV - Moscow, ID - *BrCabYB 84; Tel&CabFB 84S; TV&RadDir 84*
KUIK - Hillsboro, OR - *BrCabYB 84; TV&RadDir 84*
KUIN-FM - Vernal, UT - *BrCabYB 84; TV&RadDir 84*
Kuiper Stations - Grand Rapids, MI - *BrCabYB 84*
KUJ - Walla Walla, WA - *BrCabYB 84; TV&RadDir 84*
KUKA - San Antonio, TX - *NatRadPubDir Summer 83*
KUKD - Phoenix, AZ - *TV&RadDir 84*
KUKI - Ukiah, CA - *BrCabYB 84*
KUKQ - Phoenix, AZ - *NatRadPubDir Summer 83, Spring 84*
KUKQ - Tempe, AZ - *BrCabYB 84*
Kuksu: Journal of Backcountry Writing - Nevada City, CA - *LitMag&SmPr 83-84*
KUKU - Willow Springs, MO - *BrCabYB 84; TV&RadDir 84*
KULA-FM - Waipahu, HI - *BrCabYB 84; TV&RadDir 84*
Kulchur Foundation - New York, NY - *BoPubDir 4, 5; LitMag&SmPr 83-84*
KULL-FM - Scott City, KS - *TV&RadDir 84*
KULM-FM - Columbus, TX - *BrCabYB 84; TV&RadDir 84*
Kulm Messenger - Kulm, ND - *BaconPubCkNews 84; Ed&PubIntYB 82*
KULP - El Campo, TX - *BrCabYB 84; TV&RadDir 84*
KULR-TV - Billings, MT - *BrCabYB 84; DirUSTelSta 83; TelAl 83, 84; Tel&CabFB 84S; TV&RadDir 84*
KULY - Ulysses, KS - *BrCabYB 84; TV&RadDir 84*
KUMA - Pendleton, OR - *BrCabYB 84; TV&RadDir 84*
KUMA-FM - Pendleton, OR - *BrCabYB 84; TV&RadDir 84*
Kumarian Press - West Hartford, CT - *BoPubDir 4, 5; LitMarPl 84; WritMar 84*
KUMD-FM - Duluth, MN - *BrCabYB 84; NatRadPubDir Summer 83, Spring 84; TV&RadDir 84*
KUMM-FM - Morris, MN - *BrCabYB 84; NatRadPubDir Summer 83, Spring 84; TV&RadDir 84*
KUMR-FM - Rolla, MO - *BrCabYB 84; TV&RadDir 84*
KUMS - Roosevelt, UT - *BrCabYB 84*
KUMU - Honolulu, HI - *BrCabYB 84; NatRadPubDir Summer 83, Spring 84; TV&RadDir 84*
KUMU-FM - Honolulu, HI - *BrCabYB 84; NatRadPubDir Summer 83, Spring 84; TV&RadDir 84*
KUMV-TV - Bismarck, ND - *TelAl 83*
KUMV-TV - Williston, ND - *BrCabYB 84; TelAl 84; Tel&CabFB 84S; TV&RadDir 84*
KUNA-FM - San Luis Obispo, CA - *BrCabYB 84; TV&RadDir 84*
KUNC-FM - Greeley, CO - *BrCabYB 84; NatRadPubDir Summer 83, Spring 84; TV&RadDir 84*
KUNF - La Canada, CA - *BrCabYB 84*
Kunglige Tekniska Hogskolana Bibliotek - *See* Royal Institute of Technology Library
KUNI-FM - Cedar Falls, IA - *BrCabYB 84; NatRadPubDir Summer 83, Spring 84; TV&RadDir 84*
Kunis & Co. Inc., S. R. - Bellerose, NY - *DirPRFirms 83*
KUNM-FM - Albuquerque, NM - *BrCabYB 84; NatRadPubDir Summer 83, Spring 84; TV&RadDir 84*
KUNO - Corpus Christi, TX - *BrCabYB 84; NatRadPubDir Summer 83, Spring 84; TV&RadDir 84*
KUNR-FM - Reno, NV - *BrCabYB 84; NatRadPubDir Summer 83, Spring 84; TV&RadDir 84*
KUNV-FM - Las Vegas, NV - *BrCabYB 84; TV&RadDir 84*
KUOA - Siloam Springs, AR - *BrCabYB 84; TV&RadDir 84*
KUOI-FM - Moscow, ID - *BrCabYB 84; NatRadPubDir Summer 83, Spring 84; TV&RadDir 84*
KUOL-FM - Mena, AR - *BrCabYB 84; TV&RadDir 84*
KUOM - Minneapolis, MN - *BrCabYB 84; NatRadPubDir Summer 83, Spring 84; TV&RadDir 84*
KUON-TV - Lincoln, NE - *BrCabYB 84; Tel&CabFB 84S; TV&RadDir 84*
KUOP-FM - Stockton, CA - *BrCabYB 84; TV&RadDir 84*
KUOR-FM - Redlands, CA - *BrCabYB 84; NatRadPubDir Summer 83, Spring 84; TV&RadDir 84*
KUOW-FM - Seattle, WA - *BrCabYB 84; NatRadPubDir Summer 83, Spring 84; TV&RadDir 84*
KUPD-FM - Phoenix, AZ - *NatRadPubDir Summer 83, Spring 84; TV&RadDir 84*
KUPD-FM - Tempe, AZ - *BrCabYB 84*
KUPI - Idaho Falls, ID - *BrCabYB 84; TV&RadDir 84*
KUPK-TV - Copeland, KS - *TV&RadDir 84*
KUPK-TV - Garden City, KS - *BrCabYB 84; TelAl 83, 84; Tel&CabFB 84S*
KUPL - Portland, OR - *BrCabYB 84; NatRadPubDir Summer 83, Spring 84; TV&RadDir 84*
KUPL-FM - Portland, OR - *BrCabYB 84; NatRadPubDir Summer 83, Spring 84*
Kupper Advertising Inc. - St. Louis, MO - *StaDirAdAg 2-84*
Kuppinger, Roger P. - Arcadia, CA - *BoPubDir 4, 5*
KUPS-FM - Tacoma, WA - *BrCabYB 84; NatRadPubDir Summer 83, Spring 84; TV&RadDir 84*
KUQQ - Dallas, TX - *NatRadPubDir Summer 83, Spring 84 p.238*
KUQQ - Ft. Worth, TX - *BrCabYB 84; TV&RadDir 84*
KURA - Moab, UT - *BrCabYB 84; TV&RadDir 84*
Kurian Reference Books, George - Baldwin Place, NY - *LitMarPl 83, 84*
Kurios Press - Bryn Mawr, PA - *BoPubDir 4, 5; LitMag&SmPr 83-84*
KURL - Billings, MT - *BrCabYB 84; NatRadPubDir Summer 83, Spring 84; TV&RadDir 84*
KURM - Rogers, AR - *BrCabYB 84; TV&RadDir 84*
KURN - Sonora, TX - *TV&RadDir 84*
KURO-FM - Huron, SD - *BrCabYB 84; TV&RadDir 84*
Kurtz & Friends - Hollywood, CA - *AvMarPl 83*
Kurtz, Ellie - North Miami, FL - *LitMarPl 83, 84; MagIndMarPl 82-83*
KURU - San Antonio, TX - *BrCabYB 84*

KURV - Edinburg, TX - *BrCabYB 84; TV&RadDir 84*
KURV - McAllen, TX - *NatRadPubDir Summer 83, Spring 84 p.243*
KURY - Brookings, OR - *BrCabYB 84; TV&RadDir 84*
KURY-FM - Brookings, OR - *BrCabYB 84; TV&RadDir 84*
Kurzweil Computer Products - Cambridge, MA - *DataDirSup 7-83; DirInfWP 82; EISS 83*
KUSC-FM - Los Angeles, CA - *BrCabYB 84; LitMarPl 84; NatRadPubDir Summer 83, Spring 84; TV&RadDir 84*
KUSD - Vermillion, SD - *BrCabYB 84; NatRadPubDir Summer 83, Spring 84; TV&RadDir 84*
KUSD-FM - Vermillion, SD - *BrCabYB 84; NatRadPubDir Summer 83, Spring 84; TV&RadDir 84*
KUSD-TV - Vermillion, SD - *BrCabYB 84; Tel&CabFB 84S; TV&RadDir 84*
Kuser, R. George Jr. - Troy, OH - *Ed&PubIntYB 82*
KUSF - San Francisco, CA - *BrCabYB 84; NatRadPubDir Summer 83, Spring 84*
KUSF-FM - San Francisco, CA - *NatRadPubDir Summer 83, Spring 84; TV&RadDir 84*
KUSH - Cushing, OK - *BrCabYB 84; TV&RadDir 84*
KUSI-TV - San Diego, CA - *BrCabYB 84; DirUSTelSta 83; TelAl 84; Tel&CabFB 84S*
KUSK - Phoenix, AZ - *DirUSTelSta 83*
KUSK - Prescott, AZ - *BrCabYB 84; TelAl 84; Tel&CabFB 84S*
KUSP-FM - Santa Cruz, CA - *BrCabYB 84; TV&RadDir 84*
KUSR - Ames, IA - *BrCabYB 84*
Kussmaul Encyclopedia [of General Videotex Corp.] - Cambridge, MA - *DataDirOnSer 84*
Kustom Electronics Inc. - Lenexa, KS - *InfIndMarPl 83*
Kustom Quality - El Paso, TX - *MagIndMarPl 82-83*
KUSU-FM - Logan, UT - *BrCabYB 84; NatRadPubDir Summer 83, Spring 84; TV&RadDir 84*
KUT-FM - Austin, TX - *BrCabYB 84; NatRadPubDir Summer 83, Spring 84; TV&RadDir 84*
KUTA - Blanding, UT - *BrCabYB 84; TV&RadDir 84*
KUTE-FM - Glendale, CA - *BrCabYB 84; TV&RadDir 84*
KUTE-FM - Los Angeles, CA - *LitMarPl 84; NatRadPubDir Summer 83, Spring 84*
KUTI - Yakima, WA - *BrCabYB 84; TV&RadDir 84*
KUTI Communicators Inc. - Yakima, WA - *BrCabYB 84*
Kutt Inc. - Boulder, CO - *MagIndMarPl 82-83*
Kuttner & Kuttner Inc. - Chicago, IL - *StaDirAdAg 2-84; TelAl 83, 84*
KUTV-TV - Salt Lake City, UT - *BrCabYB 84; CabTVPrDB 83; DirUSTelSta 83; LitMarPl 83, 84; TelAl 83, 84; Tel&CabFB 84S; TV&RadDir 84*
KUTY - Palmdale, CA - *BrCabYB 84; TV&RadDir 84*
Kutztown Patriot - Kutztown, PA - *BaconPubCkNews 84; NewsDir 84*
KUUK - Wickenburg, AZ - *BrCabYB 84; TV&RadDir 84*
KUUL-FM - Madera, CA - *BrCabYB 84; TV&RadDir 84*
KUUU - Neola, UT - *BrCabYB 84*
KUUX - Hobbs, NM - *BrCabYB 84; TV&RadDir 84*
KUUY - Cheyenne, WY - *BrCabYB 84; NatRadPubDir Summer 83, Spring 84; TV&RadDir 84*
KUUZ-FM - Lake Village, AR - *BrCabYB 84*
KUUZ-FM - Portland, AR - *TV&RadDir 84*
KUVR - Holdrege, NE - *BrCabYB 84; TV&RadDir 84*
KUVR-FM - Holdrege, NE - *BrCabYB 84; TV&RadDir 84*
KUWR-FM - Laramie, WY - *BrCabYB 84; NatRadPubDir Spring 84; TV&RadDir 84*
KUXL - Golden Valley, MN - *BrCabYB 84*
KUXL - Minneapolis, MN - *NatRadPubDir Summer 83 p.135, Spring 84; TV&RadDir 84*
Kuzel Computer Services - Chicago, IL - *MicrocomMPl 84*
KUZN - West Monroe, LA - *BrCabYB 84; TV&RadDir 84*
KUZZ - Bakersfield, CA - *BrCabYB 84; NatRadPubDir Summer 83, Spring 84; TV&RadDir 84*
KV Industries - Brownsville, TX - *DirInfWP 82*
KV33 Corp. - Tuscon, AZ - *MicrocomMPl 83, 84*
KVAA - Volga, SD - *BrCabYB 84; TV&RadDir 84*
KVAC - Forks, WA - *BrCabYB 84; TV&RadDir 84*
KVAK - Valdez, AK - *BrCabYB 84*
KVAL-TV - Eugene, OR - *BrCabYB 84; DirUSTelSta 83; TelAl 83, 84; Tel&CabFB 84S*
KVAL-TV - Florence, OR - *TV&RadDir 84*
KVAN - Vancouver, WA - *BrCabYB 84; NatRadPubDir Summer 83, Spring 84; TV&RadDir 84*
KVAR - San Antonio, TX - *BrCabYB 84; TV&RadDir 84*
KVAR-FM - San Antonio, TX - *TV&RadDir 84*
KVAS - Astoria, OR - *BrCabYB 84; TV&RadDir 84*
KVBC-TV - Las Vegas, NV - *BrCabYB 84; DirUSTelSta 83; TelAl 83, 84; Tel&CabFB 84S; TV&RadDir 84*
KVCA - Conway, AR - *BrCabYB 84*
KVCK - Wolf Point, MT - *BrCabYB 84; TV&RadDir 84*
KVCL - Winnfield, LA - *BrCabYB 84; TV&RadDir 84*
KVCL-FM - Winnfield, LA - *BrCabYB 84; TV&RadDir 84*
KVCM-FM - Montgomery City, MO - *BrCabYB 84; TV&RadDir 84*
KVCO - Concordia, KS - *BrCabYB 84; TV&RadDir 84*
KVCR-FM - San Bernardino, CA - *BrCabYB 84; NatRadPubDir Summer 83, Spring 84; TV&RadDir 84*
KVCR-TV - San Bernardino, CA - *BrCabYB 84; Tel&CabFB 84S; TV&RadDir 84*
KVDB - Sioux Center, IA - *BrCabYB 84; TV&RadDir 84*
KVDB-FM - Sioux Center, IA - *BrCabYB 84; TV&RadDir 84*
KVEC - San Luis Obispo, CA - *BrCabYB 84; NatRadPubDir Summer 83, Spring 84; TV&RadDir 84*
KVEG - Henderson, NV - *BrCabYB 84*
KVEG - Las Vegas, NV - *NatRadPubDir Summer 83, Spring 84; TV&RadDir 84*
KVEL - Vernal, UT - *BrCabYB 84; TV&RadDir 84*
Kvell, Ene-Mai - Washington, DC - *LitMarPl 84*
KVEN - Ventura, CA - *BrCabYB 84; NatRadPubDir Summer 83; TV&RadDir 84*
KVEN-FM - Tyler, TX - *BrCabYB 84*
KVEO-TV - Brownsville, TX - *TelAl 84; Tel&CabFB 84S*
KVEO-TV - Harlingen, TX - *DirUSTelSta 83*
KVEO-TV - McAllen, TX - *BrCabYB 84*
KVET - Austin, TX - *BrCabYB 84; NatRadPubDir Summer 83, Spring 84; TV&RadDir 84*
KVEW - Kennewick, WA - *Tel&CabFB 84S*
KVEW-TV - Kennewick, WA - *BrCabYB 84*
KVEW-TV - Pasco, WA - *TV&RadDir 84*
KVEW-TV - Richland, WA - *TelAl 83, 84*
KVEZ - Smithfield, UT - *BrCabYB 84*
KVFC - Cortez, CO - *BrCabYB 84; TV&RadDir 84*
KVFD - Ft. Dodge, IA - *BrCabYB 84; TV&RadDir 84*
KVFD-TV - Ft. Dodge, IA - *TelAl 83*
KVFG-FM - Thibodaux, LA - *BrCabYB 84; TV&RadDir 84*
KVGB - Great Bend, KS - *BrCabYB 84; TV&RadDir 84*
KVGB-FM - Great Bend, KS - *BrCabYB 84; TV&RadDir 84*
KVGM - Yakima, WA - *TV&RadDir 84*
KVHP - Lake Charles, LA - *BrCabYB 84; Tel&CabFB 84S*
KVHS-FM - Concord, CA - *BrCabYB 84; TV&RadDir 84*
KVI - Seattle, WA - *BrCabYB 84; NatRadPubDir Summer 83, Spring 84; TV&RadDir 84*
KVIA-TV - El Paso, TX - *BrCabYB 84; DirUSTelSta 83; TelAl 83, 84; Tel&CabFB 84S; TV&RadDir 84*
KVIB-FM - Kahului, HI - *TV&RadDir 84*
KVIB-FM - Makawao, HI - *BrCabYB 84*
KVIC-FM - Victoria, TX - *BrCabYB 84; TV&RadDir 84*
KVIE-TV [Subs. of Central California Educational Television] - Sacramento, CA - *AvMarPl 83; BrCabYB 84; Tel&CabFB 84S; TeleSy&SerDir 2-84; TV&RadDir 84*
KVII-TV - Amarillo, TX - *BrCabYB 84; DirUSTelSta 83; TelAl 83, 84; Tel&CabFB 84S; TV&RadDir 84*
KVIJ-TV - Sayre, OK - *BrCabYB 84; TelAl 83, 84; Tel&CabFB 84S; TV&RadDir 84*
KVIK-FM - Travis Air Force Base, CA - *BrCabYB 84; TV&RadDir 84*
KVIL - Dallas, TX - *NatRadPubDir Summer 83, Spring 84; TV&RadDir 84*
KVIL - Highland Park, TX - *BrCabYB 84*
KVIL-FM - Dallas, TX - *NatRadPubDir Summer 83, Spring 84; TV&RadDir 84*
KVIL-FM - Highland Park, TX - *BrCabYB 84*
KVIM-FM - Coachella, CA - *BrCabYB 84*
KVIM-FM - Indio, CA - *TV&RadDir 84*
KVIN - Vinita, OK - *BrCabYB 84; TV&RadDir 84*
KVIP-FM - Redding, CA - *BrCabYB 84; TV&RadDir 84*
KVIQ-TV - Eureka, CA - *BrCabYB 84; DirUSTelSta 83; TelAl 83, 84; Tel&CabFB 84S; TV&RadDir 84*

KVKG - Solvang, CA - *BrCabYB 84*
KVKI-FM - Shreveport, LA - *BrCabYB 84; NatRadPubDir Spring 84*
KVKM - Monahans, TX - *BrCabYB 84; TV&RadDir 84*
KVLD - Valdez, AK - *BrCabYB 84*
KVLE-FM - Gunnison, CO - *BrCabYB 84; TV&RadDir 84*
KVLF - Alpine, TX - *BrCabYB 84; TV&RadDir 84*
KVLG - La Grange, TX - *BrCabYB 84; TV&RadDir 84*
KVLH - Pauls Valley, OK - *BrCabYB 84; TV&RadDir 84*
KVLI - Lake Isabella, CA - *BrCabYB 84; TV&RadDir 84*
KVLL - Woodville, TX - *BrCabYB 84; TV&RadDir 84*
KVLR-FM - Detroit Lakes, MN - *BrCabYB 84; TV&RadDir 84*
KVLU-FM - Beaumont, TX - *BrCabYB 84; NatRadPubDir Summer 83, Spring 84; TV&RadDir 84*
KVLV - Fallon, NV - *BrCabYB 84; TV&RadDir 84*
KVLV-FM - Fallon, NV - *BrCabYB 84; TV&RadDir 84*
KVLY-FM - Edinburg, TX - *BrCabYB 84; TV&RadDir 84*
KVLY-FM - McAllen, TX - *NatRadPubDir Summer 83, Spring 84 p.243*
KVMA - Magnolia, AR - *BrCabYB 84; TV&RadDir 84*
KVMA-FM - Magnolia, AR - *BrCabYB 84*
KVMC - Colorado City, TX - *BrCabYB 84; TV&RadDir 84*
KVMC - Texarkana, TX - *TV&RadDir 84*
KVML - Sonora, CA - *BrCabYB 84; TV&RadDir 84*
KVMR-FM - Nevada City, CA - *BrCabYB 84; TV&RadDir 84*
KVMT-FM - Vail, CO - *BrCabYB 84; TV&RadDir 84*
KVMV-FM - McAllen, TX - *BrCabYB 84; NatRadPubDir Summer 83, Spring 84*
KVMV-FM - Pharr, TX - *TV&RadDir 84*
KVMX - Eastland, TX - *BrCabYB 84*
KVNF-FM - Paonia, CO - *BrCabYB 84; TV&RadDir 84*
KVNI - Coeur d'Alene, ID - *BrCabYB 84; TV&RadDir 84*
KVNJ-TV - Fargo, ND - *BrCabYB 84; Tel&CabFB 84S*
KVNM-FM - Taos, NM - *BrCabYB 84; TV&RadDir 84*
KVNO-FM - Omaha, NE - *BrCabYB 84; NatRadPubDir Summer 83, Spring 84*
KVNU - Logan, UT - *BrCabYB 84; TV&RadDir 84*
KVOA-TV - Tucson, AZ - *BrCabYB 84; DirUSTelSta 83; TelAl 83, 84; Tel&CabFB 84S; TV&RadDir 84*
KVOB - Bastrop, LA - *BrCabYB 84; TV&RadDir 84*
KVOC - Casper, WY - *BrCabYB 84; NatRadPubDir Summer 83, Spring 84; TV&RadDir 84*
KVOD-FM - Denver, CO - *BrCabYB 84; NatRadPubDir Summer 83, Spring 84; TV&RadDir 84*
KVOE - Emporia, KS - *BrCabYB 84; TV&RadDir 84*
KVOF-TV - San Francisco, CA - *BrCabYB 84; TelAl 83, 84; Tel&CabFB 84S; TV&RadDir 84*
KVOI - Tucson, AZ - *BrCabYB 84; TV&RadDir 84*
KVOK - Kodiak, AK - *BrCabYB 84; TV&RadDir 84*
KVOL - Lafayette, LA - *BrCabYB 84; NatRadPubDir Summer 83, Spring 84; TV&RadDir 84*
KVOM - Morrilton, AR - *BrCabYB 84; TV&RadDir 84*
KVOM-FM - Morrilton, AR - *BrCabYB 84*
KVON - Napa, CA - *BrCabYB 84; NatRadPubDir Summer 83, Spring 84; TV&RadDir 84*
KVOO - Tulsa, OK - *BrCabYB 84; NatRadPubDir Summer 83, Spring 84; TV&RadDir 84*
KVOP - Plainview, TX - *BrCabYB 84; NatRadPubDir Summer 83, Spring 84; TV&RadDir 84*
KVOR - Colorado Springs, CO - *BrCabYB 84; NatRadPubDir Summer 83, Spring 84; TV&RadDir 84*
KVOS - Bellingham, WA - *TV&RadDir 84*
KVOS-TV - Bellingham, WA - *BrCabYB 84; DirUSTelSta 83; LitMarPl 83, 84; TelAl 83, 84; Tel&CabFB 84S*
KVOS-TV - Vancouver, BC, Canada - *Tel&CabFB 84S*
KVOU - Uvalde, TX - *BrCabYB 84; TV&RadDir 84*
KVOV - Henderson, NV - *BrCabYB 84; TV&RadDir 84*
KVOW - Riverton, WY - *BrCabYB 84; TV&RadDir 84*
KVOX - Moorhead, MN - *BrCabYB 84; TV&RadDir 84*
KVOX - Fargo, ND - *NatRadPubDir Summer 83, Spring 84 p.187*
KVOX-FM - Moorhead, MN - *TV&RadDir 84*
KVOX-FM - Fargo, ND - *NatRadPubDir Summer 83, Spring 84 p.187*
KVOY - Yuma, AZ - *BrCabYB 84; TV&RadDir 84*
KVOZ - Laredo, TX - *BrCabYB 84; TV&RadDir 84*
KVPI - Ville Platte, LA - *BrCabYB 84; TV&RadDir 84*
KVPI-FM - Ville Platte, LA - *BrCabYB 84; TV&RadDir 84*
KVPR-FM - Fresno, CA - *BrCabYB 84; TV&RadDir 84*
KVRA - Vermillion, SD - *BrCabYB 84; TV&RadDir 84*
KVRC - Arkadelphia, AR - *BrCabYB 84; TV&RadDir 84*
KVRD - Cottonwood, AZ - *BrCabYB 84; TV&RadDir 84*
KVRE-FM - Santa Rosa, CA - *BrCabYB 84; TV&RadDir 84*
KVRF-FM - Vermillion, SD - *BrCabYB 84; TV&RadDir 84*
KVRH - Salida, CO - *BrCabYB 84*
KVRH - Security, CO - *TV&RadDir 84*
KVRH-FM - Salida, CO - *BrCabYB 84*
KVRH-FM - Security, CO - *TV&RadDir 84*
KVRN-FM - Sonora, TX - *BrCabYB 84; TV&RadDir 84*
KVRO-FM - Stillwater, OK - *BrCabYB 84; TV&RadDir 84*
KVRP-FM - Haskell, TX - *BrCabYB 84; TV&RadDir 84*
KVRS - Sterling, CO - *BrCabYB 84*
KVSA - McGehee, AR - *BrCabYB 84; TV&RadDir 84*
KVSC-FM - St. Cloud, MN - *BrCabYB 84; NatRadPubDir Summer 83, Spring 84; TV&RadDir 84*
KVSF - Santa Fe, NM - *BrCabYB 84; NatRadPubDir Summer 83, Spring 84; TV&RadDir 84*
KVSH - Valentine, NE - *BrCabYB 84; TV&RadDir 84*
KVSI - Montpelier, ID - *BrCabYB 84; TV&RadDir 84*
KVSL - Show Low, AZ - *BrCabYB 84; TV&RadDir 84*
KVSO - Ardmore, OK - *BrCabYB 84; TV&RadDir 84*
KVSR-FM - Rapid City, SD - *BrCabYB 84; TV&RadDir 84*
KVSV-FM - Beloit, KS - *BrCabYB 84*
KVT-FM - Brattleboro, VT - *BrCabYB 84*
KVTI - Tacoma, WA - *BrCabYB 84*
KVTT-FM - Dallas, TX - *BrCabYB 84; NatRadPubDir Summer 83, Spring 84; TV&RadDir 84*
KVTV-TV - Laredo, TX - *BrCabYB 84; DirUSTelSta 83; TelAl 83, 84; Tel&CabFB 84S; TV&RadDir 84*
KVTX - Victoria, TX - *BrCabYB 84; Tel&CabFB 84S*
KVUE-TV - Austin, TX - *BrCabYB 84; DirUSTelSta 83; TelAl 83, 84; Tel&CabFB 84S; TV&RadDir 84*
KVVA - Phoenix, AZ - *BrCabYB 84; NatRadPubDir Summer 83, Spring 84; TV&RadDir 84*
KVVC-FM - Cabool, MO - *BrCabYB 84; TV&RadDir 84*
KVVP-FM - Leesville, LA - *BrCabYB 84; TV&RadDir 84*
KVVQ-FM - Victorville, CA - *BrCabYB 84; TV&RadDir 84*
KVVU-TV - Henderson, NV - *BrCabYB 84; TelAl 83, 84; Tel&CabFB 84S; TV&RadDir 84*
KVVU-TV - Las Vegas, NV - *DirUSTelSta 83*
KVWC - Vernon, TX - *BrCabYB 84; TV&RadDir 84*
KVWC-FM - Vernon, TX - *BrCabYB 84; TV&RadDir 84*
KVWG - Pearsall, TX - *BrCabYB 84; TV&RadDir 84*
KVWG-FM - Pearsall, TX - *BrCabYB 84*
KVWM - Show Low, AZ - *BrCabYB 84; TV&RadDir 84*
KVWM-FM - Show Low, AZ - *BrCabYB 84; TV&RadDir 84*
KVYL - Holdenville, OK - *BrCabYB 84; TV&RadDir 84*
KVYN-FM - Napa, CA - *NatRadPubDir Summer 83, Spring 84; TV&RadDir 84*
KVYN-FM - St. Helena, CA - *BrCabYB 84*
KWAB-TV - Big Spring, TX - *BrCabYB 84; TelAl 83, 84; Tel&CabFB 84S*
KWAC - Bakersfield, CA - *BrCabYB 84; NatRadPubDir Summer 83, Spring 84; TV&RadDir 84*
KWAD - Wadena, MN - *BrCabYB 84*
KWAK - Stuttgart, AR - *BrCabYB 84; TV&RadDir 84*
KWAL - Osburn, ID - *TV&RadDir 84*
KWAL - Wallace, ID - *BrCabYB 84*
KWAM - Memphis, TN - *BrCabYB 84; NatRadPubDir Summer 83, Spring 84; TV&RadDir 84*
KWAM-FM - Memphis, TN - *NatRadPubDir Summer 83*
KWAO-FM - Sun City, AZ - *TV&RadDir 84*
KWAP - Atherton, CA - *BrCabYB 84*
KWAR-FM - Waverly, IA - *BrCabYB 84; NatRadPubDir Summer 83, Spring 84; TV&RadDir 84*
KWAS-FM - Amarillo, TX - *BrCabYB 84; TV&RadDir 84*
KWAT - Watertown, SD - *BrCabYB 84; TV&RadDir 84*
KWAV-FM - Monterey, CA - *BrCabYB 84; TV&RadDir 84*
KWAV-FM - Salinas, CA - *NatRadPubDir Summer 83, Spring 84 p.27*
KWAX - St. James, MN - *BrCabYB 84*
KWAX-FM - Eugene, OR - *BrCabYB 84; NatRadPubDir Summer 83, Spring 84; TV&RadDir 84*
KWAY - Waverly, IA - *BrCabYB 84; TV&RadDir 84*

KWAY-FM - Waverly, IA - *BrCabYB 84; TV&RadDir 84*
KWAZ - Lubbock, TX - *TV&RadDir 84*
KWAZ - Lufkin, TX - *BrCabYB 84*
KWBA - Pembina, ND - *BrCabYB 84; Tel&CabFB 84S*
KWBC - Navasota, TX - *BrCabYB 84; TV&RadDir 84*
KWBE - Beatrice, NE - *BrCabYB 84; TV&RadDir 84*
KWBG - Boone, IA - *BrCabYB 84; TV&RadDir 84*
KWBG-FM - Boone, IA - *BrCabYB 84; TV&RadDir 84*
KWBI-FM - Morrison, CO - *BrCabYB 84; TV&RadDir 84*
KWBJ-FM - Payette, ID - *BrCabYB 84*
KWBJ-FM - Ontario, OR - *TV&RadDir 84*
KWBN-TV - Hayes Center, NE - *TelAl 84*
KWBO-FM - Hot Springs, AR - *BrCabYB 84; NatRadPubDir Summer 83, Spring 84; TV&RadDir 84*
KWBU-FM - Waco, TX - *BrCabYB 84; NatRadPubDir Summer 83, Spring 84; TV&RadDir 84*
KWBW - Hutchinson, KS - *BrCabYB 84; TV&RadDir 84*
KWBZ - Englewood, CO - *BrCabYB 84*
KWCB-FM - Floresville, TX - *BrCabYB 84; TV&RadDir 84*
KWCH-TV - Hutchinson, KS - *BrCabYB 84; Tel&CabFB 84S*
KWCH-TV - Wichita, KS - *LitMarPl 84; TelAl 84*
KWCK - Searcy, AR - *BrCabYB 84; TV&RadDir 84*
KWCL - Oak Grove, LA - *BrCabYB 84; TV&RadDir 84*
KWCL-FM - Oak Grove, LA - *BrCabYB 84; TV&RadDir 84*
KWCM-TV - Appleton, MN - *BrCabYB 84; Tel&CabFB 84S; TV&RadDir 84*
KWCO - Chickasha, OK - *BrCabYB 84; NatRadPubDir Summer 83, Spring 84; TV&RadDir 84*
KWCR-FM - Ogden, UT - *BrCabYB 84; NatRadPubDir Summer 83, Spring 84; TV&RadDir 84*
KWCS - Bridgeport, TX - *BrCabYB 84*
KWCW-FM - Walla Walla, WA - *BrCabYB 84; TV&RadDir 84*
KWCX-FM - Willcox, AZ - *BrCabYB 84; TV&RadDir 84*
KWDE-FM - Montrose, CO - *BrCabYB 84; TV&RadDir 84*
KWDG-FM - Idabel, OK - *BrCabYB 84; TV&RadDir 84*
KWDJ-FM - Riverside, CA - *BrCabYB 84*
KWDJ-FM - San Bernardino, CA - *NatRadPubDir Spring 84 p.28*
KWDM-FM - West Des Moines, IA - *BrCabYB 84; TV&RadDir 84*
KWDX-FM - Silsbee, TX - *BrCabYB 84; TV&RadDir 84*
KWEB - Rochester, MN - *BrCabYB 84; TV&RadDir 84*
KWEB-FM - Claremont, CA - *NatRadPubDir Summer 83, Spring 84*
KWED - Seguin, TX - *BrCabYB 84; NatRadPubDir Summer 83, Spring 84; TV&RadDir 84*
KWED-FM - Seguin, TX - *BrCabYB 84; NatRadPubDir Summer 83, Spring 84; TV&RadDir 84*
KWEF-FM - Weatherford, OK - *BrCabYB 84*
KWEH-FM - Camden, AR - *BrCabYB 84; TV&RadDir 84*
KWEI - Weiser, ID - *BrCabYB 84; TV&RadDir 84*
KWEI-FM - Weiser, ID - *BrCabYB 84*
KWEL - Midland, TX - *BrCabYB 84; TV&RadDir 84*
KWEN-FM - Tulsa, OK - *BrCabYB 84; NatRadPubDir Summer 83, Spring 84; TV&RadDir 84*
KWES - Monahans, TX - *BrCabYB 84*
KWET - Cheyenne, OK - *BrCabYB 84; Tel&CabFB 84S*
KWEX-TV - San Antonio, TX - *BrCabYB 84; DirUSTelSta 83; TelAl 83, 84; Tel&CabFB 84S; TV&RadDir 84*
KWEY - Weatherford, OK - *BrCabYB 84; TV&RadDir 84*
KWEY-FM - Weatherford, OK - *TV&RadDir 84*
KWEZ - Monroe, LA - *BrCabYB 84*
KWFC-FM - Springfield, MO - *BrCabYB 84; NatRadPubDir Summer 83, Spring 84; TV&RadDir 84*
KWFM-FM - Tucson, AZ - *BrCabYB 84; NatRadPubDir Summer 83, Spring 84; TV&RadDir 84*
KWFT - Wichita Falls, TX - *BrCabYB 84; NatRadPubDir Summer 83, Spring 84; TV&RadDir 84*
KWG - Stockton, CA - *BrCabYB 84; NatRadPubDir Summer 83, Spring 84; TV&RadDir 84*
KWGF-FM - Stockton, CA - *NatRadPubDir Summer 83, Spring 84; TV&RadDir 84*
KWGG - Hampton, IA - *BrCabYB 84*
KWGH - Big Lake, TX - *BrCabYB 84; TV&RadDir 84*
KWGN-TV - Denver, CO - *BrCabYB 84; DirUSTelSta 83; TelAl 83, 84; Tel&CabFB 84S*
KWGN-TV - Englewood, CO - *TV&RadDir 84*
KWGS-FM - Tulsa, OK - *BrCabYB 84; TV&RadDir 84*
KWHI-FM - Brenham, TX - *BrCabYB 84; TV&RadDir 84*
KWHK - Hutchinson, KS - *BrCabYB 84; NatRadPubDir Summer 83, Spring 84; TV&RadDir 84*
KWHK Broadcasting Co. - Hutchinson, KS - *BrCabYB 84*
KWHL - Anchorage, AK - *BrCabYB 84*
KWHN - Ft. Smith, AR - *BrCabYB 84; NatRadPubDir Summer 83, Spring 84; TV&RadDir 84*
KWHO - Salt Lake City, UT - *BrCabYB 84; NatRadPubDir Summer 83, Spring 84; TV&RadDir 84*
KWHO-FM - Salt Lake City, UT - *BrCabYB 84; NatRadPubDir Summer 83, Spring 84; TV&RadDir 84*
KWHP - Boise, ID - *BrCabYB 84; Tel&CabFB 84S*
KWHW - Altus, OK - *BrCabYB 84; TV&RadDir 84*
KWHW-FM - Altus, OK - *BrCabYB 84; TV&RadDir 84*
KWHY-TV - Los Angeles, CA - *BrCabYB 84; DirUSTelSta 83; TelAl 83, 84; Tel&CabFB 84S; TV&RadDir 84*
KWIC-FM - Beaumont, TX - *BrCabYB 84; NatRadPubDir Summer 83, Spring 84; TV&RadDir 84*
KWIC Index to Ontario Government Services [of Ontario Ministry of Government Services] - Toronto, ON, Canada - *EISS 83*
KWIK - Pocatello, ID - *BrCabYB 84; NatRadPubDir Summer 83, Spring 84; TV&RadDir 84*
Kwik Sew Pattern Co. Inc. - Minneapolis, MN - *BoPubDir 4 Sup, 5*
Kwik Software - Bolivar, MO - *MicrocomMPl 84*
KWIL - Albany, OR - *BrCabYB 84; TV&RadDir 84*
KWIN-FM - Lodi, CA - *BrCabYB 84*
KWIN-FM - Stockton, CA - *TV&RadDir 84*
KWINDEX [of Golden Gate Systems] - Honolulu, HI - *EISS 83*
KWIP - Dallas, OR - *BrCabYB 84; TV&RadDir 84*
KWIP - Salem, OR - *NatRadPubDir Summer 83 p.207, Spring 84 p.207*
KWIQ - Moses Lake, WA - *BrCabYB 84; TV&RadDir 84*
KWIQ-FM - Moses Lake, WA - *BrCabYB 84; TV&RadDir 84*
KWIT-FM - Sioux City, IA - *BrCabYB 84; TV&RadDir 84*
KWIV - Douglas, WY - *BrCabYB 84; TV&RadDir 84*
KWIX - Moberly, MO - *BrCabYB 84; TV&RadDir 84*
KWIZ - Anaheim, CA - *NatRadPubDir Summer 83, Spring 84 p.17*
KWIZ - Santa Ana, CA - *BrCabYB 84; TV&RadDir 84*
KWIZ-FM - Anaheim, CA - *NatRadPubDir Summer 83, Spring 84 p.17*
KWIZ-FM - Santa Ana, CA - *BrCabYB 84; TV&RadDir 84*
KWJJ - Portland, OR - *BrCabYB 84; NatRadPubDir Summer 83, Spring 84; TV&RadDir 84*
KWJM-FM - Farmerville, LA - *BrCabYB 84; TV&RadDir 84*
KWJS-FM - Arlington, TX - *BrCabYB 84; TV&RadDir 84*
KWJS-FM - Dallas, TX - *NatRadPubDir Summer 83 p.238, Spring 84 p.238*
KWK - St. Louis, MO - *BrCabYB 84; NatRadPubDir Summer 83, Spring 84*
KWK-FM - Granite City, IL - *BrCabYB 84*
KWK-FM - St. Louis, MO - *NatRadPubDir Summer 83, Spring 84; TV&RadDir 84*
KWKA - Clovis, NM - *BrCabYB 84; TV&RadDir 84*
KWKC - Abilene, TX - *BrCabYB 84; NatRadPubDir Summer 83, Spring 84; TV&RadDir 84*
KWKH - Shreveport, LA - *BrCabYB 84; NatRadPubDir Summer 83, Spring 84; TV&RadDir 84*
KWKI - Big Spring, TX - *BrCabYB 84*
KWKK-FM - Dardanelle, AR - *BrCabYB 84; TV&RadDir 84*
KWKN - Wichita, KS - *NatRadPubDir Summer 83*
KWKQ-FM - Graham, TX - *BrCabYB 84; TV&RadDir 84*
KWKR - Leoti, KS - *BrCabYB 84*
KWKS-FM - Winfield, KS - *BrCabYB 84; TV&RadDir 84*
KWKW - Los Angeles, CA - *NatRadPubDir Summer 83 p.24, Spring 84 p.23; TV&RadDir 84*
KWKW - Pasadena, CA - *BrCabYB 84*
KWKY - Des Moines, IA - *BrCabYB 84; NatRadPubDir Summer 83, Spring 84; TV&RadDir 84*
KWLA - Many, LA - *BrCabYB 84; TV&RadDir 84*
KWLB-FM - Marksville, LA - *BrCabYB 84; TV&RadDir 84*
KWLC - Decorah, IA - *BrCabYB 84; TV&RadDir 84*
KWLD-FM - Plainview, TX - *BrCabYB 84; NatRadPubDir Summer 83, Spring 84*
KWLL - Casa Grande, AZ - *BrCabYB 84*

KWLM - Willmar, MN - *BrCabYB 84*
KWLO - Waterloo, IA - *BrCabYB 84; NatRadPubDir Summer 83, Spring 84; TV&RadDir 84*
KWLS - Pratt, KS - *BrCabYB 84; TV&RadDir 84*
KWLS-FM - Pratt, KS - *TV&RadDir 84*
KWLV - Many, LA - *BrCabYB 84*
KWLW-FM - San Angelo, TX - *BrCabYB 84; NatRadPubDir Summer 83, Spring 84; TV&RadDir 84*
KWMB - Wabasha, MN - *BrCabYB 84*
KWMC - Del Rio, TX - *BrCabYB 84; TV&RadDir 84*
KWMJ-FM - Midland, TX - *BrCabYB 84; NatRadPubDir Summer 83, Spring 84 p.244; TV&RadDir 84*
KWMR-FM - Cedar Rapids, IA - *BrCabYB 84; TV&RadDir 84*
KWMT - Ft. Dodge, IA - *BrCabYB 84; TV&RadDir 84*
KWMU-FM - St. Louis, MO - *BrCabYB 84; LitMarPl 83, 84; NatRadPubDir Summer 83, Spring 84; TV&RadDir 84*
KWNA - Winnemucca, NV - *BrCabYB 84; TV&RadDir 84*
KWNA-FM - Winnemucca, NV - *BrCabYB 84*
KWNB-TV - Hayes Center, NE - *BrCabYB 84; Tel&CabFB 84S*
KWNB-TV - Kearney, NE - *TelAl 83; TV&RadDir 84*
KWNC - Quincy, WA - *BrCabYB 84; TV&RadDir 84*
KWND - Saratoga, WY - *BrCabYB 84*
KWNE-FM - Ukiah, CA - *BrCabYB 84; TV&RadDir 84*
KWNG-FM - Red Wing, MN - *BrCabYB 84; TV&RadDir 84*
KWNK - Simi Valley, CA - *BrCabYB 84*
KWNO - Winona, MN - *BrCabYB 84; NatRadPubDir Summer 83, Spring 84*
KWNR - Liberal, KS - *BrCabYB 84*
KWNS - Winnesboro, TX - *BrCabYB 84*
KWNT - Davenport, IA - *NatRadPubDir Summer 83*
KWOA - Worthington, MN - *BrCabYB 84; TV&RadDir 84*
KWOA-FM - Worthington, MN - *BrCabYB 84; TV&RadDir 84*
KWOC - Poplar Bluff, MO - *BrCabYB 84; TV&RadDir 84*
KWOD - Sacramento, CA - *BrCabYB 84*
KWOK - Wagoner, OK - *BrCabYB 84; TV&RadDir 84*
KWON - Bartlesville, OK - *BrCabYB 84; NatRadPubDir Summer 83, Spring 84; TV&RadDir 84*
KWOR - Worland, WY - *BrCabYB 84; TV&RadDir 84*
KWOS - Jefferson City, MO - *BrCabYB 84; TV&RadDir 84*
KWOW - Pomona, CA - *BrCabYB 84; TV&RadDir 84*
KWOX - Woodward, OK - *BrCabYB 84*
KWOZ - Mountain View, AR - *BrCabYB 84*
KWPB-FM - Kansas City, MO - *TV&RadDir 84*
KWPB-FM - Liberty, MO - *BrCabYB 84; NatRadPubDir Summer 83, Spring 84*
KWPC - Muscatine, IA - *BrCabYB 84; NatRadPubDir Summer 83, Spring 84; TV&RadDir 84*
KWPM - West Plains, MO - *BrCabYB 84; TV&RadDir 84*
KWPM-FM - West Plains, MO - *BrCabYB 84; TV&RadDir 84*
KWPR - Claremore, OK - *BrCabYB 84; TV&RadDir 84*
KWRC - Woodburn, OR - *BrCabYB 84; TV&RadDir 84*
KWRD - Henderson, TX - *BrCabYB 84; TV&RadDir 84*
KWRE - Warrenton, MO - *BrCabYB 84; TV&RadDir 84*
KWRF - Warren, AR - *BrCabYB 84; TV&RadDir 84*
KWRF-FM - Warren, AR - *BrCabYB 84; TV&RadDir 84*
KWRM - Corona, CA - *BrCabYB 84; TV&RadDir 84*
KWRM - Los Angeles, CA - *NatRadPubDir Summer 83 p.24, Spring 84 p.24*
KWRS-FM - Spokane, WA - *BrCabYB 84; NatRadPubDir Summer 83, Spring 84; TV&RadDir 84*
KWRT - Boonville, MO - *BrCabYB 84; TV&RadDir 84*
KWRW-FM - Rusk, TX - *BrCabYB 84; TV&RadDir 84*
KWSB-FM - Gunnison, CO - *BrCabYB 84; TV&RadDir 84*
KWSC-FM - Wayne, NE - *BrCabYB 84; NatRadPubDir Summer 83, Spring 84; TV&RadDir 84*
KWSD - Mt. Shasta, CA - *BrCabYB 84; TV&RadDir 84*
KWSE - Williston, ND - *BrCabYB 84; Tel&CabFB 84S*
KWSH - Wewoka, OK - *BrCabYB 84; TV&RadDir 84*
KWSI - Warm Springs, OR - *BrCabYB 84*
KWSK - Wishek, ND - *BrCabYB 84*
KWSL - Sioux City, IA - *BrCabYB 84; TV&RadDir 84*
KWSO - Wasco, CA - *BrCabYB 84; TV&RadDir 84*
KWSR - Rifle, CO - *BrCabYB 84; TV&RadDir 84*
KWSS-FM - San Jose, CA - *NatRadPubDir Summer 83, Spring 84*
KWST-FM - Carmel, CA - *BrCabYB 84*
KWST-FM - Salinas, CA - *NatRadPubDir Spring 84 p.27*
KWSU - Pullman, WA - *BrCabYB 84; NatRadPubDir Summer 83, Spring 84; TV&RadDir 84*
KWSU-TV - Pullman, WA - *BrCabYB 84; Tel&CabFB 84S; TV&RadDir 84*
KWTC - Barstow, CA - *TV&RadDir 84*
KWTD - Lonoke, AR - *BrCabYB 84*
KWTO - Springfield, MO - *BrCabYB 84; NatRadPubDir Summer 83, Spring 84; TV&RadDir 84*
KWTO-FM - Springfield, MO - *BrCabYB 84; NatRadPubDir Summer 83, Spring 84; TV&RadDir 84*
KWTS-FM - Canyon, TX - *BrCabYB 84; NatRadPubDir Summer 83, Spring 84; TV&RadDir 84*
KWTV-TV - Oklahoma City, OK - *BrCabYB 84; DirUSTelSta 83; LitMarPl 83, 84; TelAl 83, 84; Tel&CabFB 84S; TV&RadDir 84*
KWTX - Waco, TX - *BrCabYB 84; NatRadPubDir Summer 83, Spring 84; TV&RadDir 84*
KWTX Broadcasting Co. - Waco, TX - *BrCabYB 84; Tel&CabFB 84S*
KWTX-FM - Waco, TX - *BrCabYB 84; NatRadPubDir Summer 83, Spring 84; TV&RadDir 84*
KWTX-TV - Waco, TX - *BrCabYB 84; DirUSTelSta 83; TelAl 83, 84; Tel&CabFB 84S; TV&RadDir 84*
KWTY-FM - Salinas, CA - *BrCabYB 84*
KWUN - Concord, CA - *BrCabYB 84; TV&RadDir 84*
KWUR-FM - Montgomery, AL - *TV&RadDir 84*
KWUR-FM - Clayton, MO - *BrCabYB 84*
KWVE-FM - San Clemente, CA - *BrCabYB 84; TV&RadDir 84*
KWVR - Enterprise, OR - *BrCabYB 84; TV&RadDir 84*
KWWA-FM - Bremerton, WA - *BrCabYB 84; TV&RadDir 84*
KWWC-FM - Columbia, MO - *BrCabYB 84; NatRadPubDir Summer 83, Spring 84; TV&RadDir 84*
KWWI-FM - Big Spring, TX - *TV&RadDir 84*
KWWK-FM - Rochester, MN - *BrCabYB 84; NatRadPubDir Summer 83, Spring 84; TV&RadDir 84*
KWWL-TV - Cedar Rapids, IA - *DirUSTelSta 83*
KWWL-TV - Waterloo, IA - *BrCabYB 84; TelAl 83, 84; Tel&CabFB 84S; TV&RadDir 84*
KWWM-FM - Stephenville, TX - *BrCabYB 84; TV&RadDir 84*
KWWR-FM - Mexico, MO - *BrCabYB 84; TV&RadDir 84*
KWWW - Wenatchee, WA - *BrCabYB 84; TV&RadDir 84*
KWWY - Rock Springs, WY - *BrCabYB 84; TelAl 84; Tel&CabFB 84S*
KWXI - Glenwood, AR - *BrCabYB 84; TV&RadDir 84*
KWXL-FM - Albuquerque, NM - *BrCabYB 84; NatRadPubDir Summer 83, Spring 84; TV&RadDir 84*
KWXY - Cathedral City, CA - *BrCabYB 84*
KWXY - Palm Springs, CA - *TV&RadDir 84*
KWXY-FM - Cathedral City, CA - *BrCabYB 84*
KWXY-FM - Palm Springs, CA - *TV&RadDir 84*
KWYD - Security, CO - *BrCabYB 84*
KWYK-FM - Aztec, NM - *BrCabYB 84; TV&RadDir 84*
KWYN - Wynne, AR - *BrCabYB 84; TV&RadDir 84*
KWYN-FM - Wynne, AR - *BrCabYB 84; TV&RadDir 84*
KWYO - Sheridan, WY - *BrCabYB 84; TV&RadDir 84*
KWYR - Winner, SD - *BrCabYB 84; TV&RadDir 84*
KWYR-FM - Winner, SD - *BrCabYB 84; TV&RadDir 84*
KWYS - West Yellowstone, MT - *BrCabYB 84; TV&RadDir 84*
KWYT-FM - Salinas, CA - *NatRadPubDir Summer 83, Spring 84; TV&RadDir 84*
KWYX-FM - Jasper, TX - *BrCabYB 84; TV&RadDir 84*
KWYZ - Everett, WA - *BrCabYB 84; TV&RadDir 84*
KWYZ - Seattle, WA - *NatRadPubDir Summer 83 p.260, Spring 84 p.262*
KWZ-FM - Boise, ID - *TV&RadDir 84*
KXA - Seattle, WA - *BrCabYB 84; NatRadPubDir Summer 83, Spring 84; TV&RadDir 84*
KXAK - Corrales, NM - *BrCabYB 84*
KXAR - Hope, AR - *BrCabYB 84; TV&RadDir 84*
KXAS-TV - Dallas, TX - *DirUSTelSta 83; TelAl 83, 84*
KXAS-TV - Ft. Worth, TX - *BrCabYB 84; LitMarPl 83, 84; Tel&CabFB 84S; TV&RadDir 84*
KXAZ - Page, AZ - *BrCabYB 84*
KXBJ - Bemidji, MN - *BrCabYB 84*
KXBQ-FM - Ontario, OR - *BrCabYB 84; TV&RadDir 84*
KXCI - Tucson, AZ - *BrCabYB 84*
KXCL - Corsicana, TX - *BrCabYB 84*
KXCV-FM - Maryville, MO - *BrCabYB 84; TV&RadDir 84*

KXDD-FM - Richland, WA - *BrCabYB 84*
KXDD-FM - Yakima, WA - *TV&RadDir 84*
KXE6S Verein Registered Press - Chapel Hill, NC - *BoPubDir 4, 5*
KXEG - Phoenix, AZ - *BrCabYB 84; NatRadPubDir Summer 83, Spring 84; TV&RadDir 84*
KXEI - Havre, MT - *BrCabYB 84*
KXEL - Waterloo, IA - *BrCabYB 84; NatRadPubDir Summer 83, Spring 84; TV&RadDir 84*
KXEM - McFarland, CA - *BrCabYB 84; TV&RadDir 84*
KXEN - St. Louis, MO - *BrCabYB 84; NatRadPubDir Summer 83, Spring 84; TV&RadDir 84*
KXEO - Mexico, MO - *BrCabYB 84; TV&RadDir 84*
KXES - Salinas, CA - *BrCabYB 84; TV&RadDir 84*
KXEW - Tucson, AZ - *BrCabYB 84; NatRadPubDir Summer 83, Spring 84; TV&RadDir 84*
KXEX - Fresno, CA - *BrCabYB 84; NatRadPubDir Summer 83, Spring 84; TV&RadDir 84*
KXEZ-FM - Yuba City, CA - *BrCabYB 84; TV&RadDir 84*
KXFM-FM - Santa Maria, CA - *BrCabYB 84; TV&RadDir 84*
KXGC-FM - El Campo, TX - *BrCabYB 84*
KXGN - Glendive, MT - *BrCabYB 84; TV&RadDir 84*
KXGN-TV - Glendive, MT - *BrCabYB 84; DirUSTelSta 83; TelAl 83, 84; Tel&CabFB 84S; TV&RadDir 84*
KXGO-FM - Arcata, CA - *BrCabYB 84; TV&RadDir 84*
KXIC - Iowa City, IA - *BrCabYB 84; TV&RadDir 84*
KXII-TV - Ardmore, OK - *BrCabYB 84; TelAl 83, 84; Tel&CabFB 84S*
KXII-TV - Sherman, TX - *DirUSTelSta 83; TV&RadDir 84*
KXIQ-FM - Bend, OR - *BrCabYB 84; TV&RadDir 84*
KXIT - Dalhart, TX - *BrCabYB 84; TV&RadDir 84*
KXIT-FM - Dalhart, TX - *BrCabYB 84; TV&RadDir 84*
KXIV - Phoenix, AZ - *NatRadPubDir Summer 83*
KXIX-TV - Corpus Christi, TX - *DirUSTelSta 83*
KXIX-TV - Victoria, TX - *BrCabYB 84; DirUSTelSta 83; TelAl 83, 84; Tel&CabFB 84S; TV&RadDir 84*
KXJB-TV - Fargo, ND - *DirUSTelSta 83; TV&RadDir 84*
KXJB-TV - Valley City, ND - *BrCabYB 84; TelAl 83, 84; Tel&CabFB 84S*
KXJK - Forrest City, AR - *BrCabYB 84; TV&RadDir 84*
KXJX-FM - Pella, IA - *BrCabYB 84; TV&RadDir 84*
KXKQ - Safford, AZ - *BrCabYB 84*
KXKS - Albuquerque, NM - *BrCabYB 84; NatRadPubDir Summer 83, Spring 84; TV&RadDir 84*
KXKW - Lafayette, LA - *BrCabYB 84; NatRadPubDir Summer 83, Spring 84; TV&RadDir 84*
KXKX-FM - Galveston, TX - *BrCabYB 84; TV&RadDir 84*
KXKZ-FM - Ruston, LA - *BrCabYB 84; TV&RadDir 84*
KXL - Portland, OR - *BrCabYB 84; NatRadPubDir Summer 83, Spring 84; TV&RadDir 84*
KXL-FM - Portland, OR - *BrCabYB 84; NatRadPubDir Summer 83, Spring 84; TV&RadDir 84*
KXLA - Rayville, LA - *BrCabYB 84; TV&RadDir 84*
KXLE - Ellensburg, WA - *BrCabYB 84; TV&RadDir 84*
KXLE-FM - Ellensburg, WA - *BrCabYB 84; TV&RadDir 84*
KXLF - Butte, MT - *BrCabYB 84; TV&RadDir 84*
KXLF-TV - Butte, MT - *BrCabYB 84; DirUSTelSta 83; TelAl 83, 84; Tel&CabFB 84S; TV&RadDir 84*
KXLI - St. Cloud, MN - *BrCabYB 84; DirUSTelSta 83; Tel&CabFB 84S*
KXLO - Lewistown, MT - *BrCabYB 84; TV&RadDir 84*
KXLP-FM - New Ulm, MN - *BrCabYB 84; TV&RadDir 84*
KXLR - Little Rock, AR - *NatRadPubDir Summer 83*
KXLR - North Little Rock, AR - *TV&RadDir 84*
KXLS-FM - Alva, OK - *TV&RadDir 84*
KXLS-FM - Enid, OK - *BrCabYB 84*
KXLT - Rochester, MN - *BrCabYB 84; Tel&CabFB 84S*
KXLU - Los Angeles, CA - *BrCabYB 84; NatRadPubDir Summer 83, Spring 84; TV&RadDir 84*
KXLU-FM - Los Angeles, CA - *NatRadPubDir Summer 83, Spring 84; TV&RadDir 84*
KXLV-FM - Cambridge, MN - *BrCabYB 84*
KXLY - Spokane, WA - *BrCabYB 84; NatRadPubDir Summer 83, Spring 84; TV&RadDir 84*
KXLY-FM - Spokane, WA - *BrCabYB 84; NatRadPubDir Summer 83, Spring 84; TV&RadDir 84*
KXLY-TV - Spokane, WA - *BrCabYB 84; DirUSTelSta 83; TelAl 83, 84; Tel&CabFB 84S; TV&RadDir 84*
KXMB-TV - Bismarck, ND - *BrCabYB 84; TelAl 83, 84; Tel&CabFB 84S; TV&RadDir 84*
KXMC-TV - Bismarck, ND - *DirUSTelSta 83*
KXMC-TV - Minot, ND - *BrCabYB 84; TelAl 83, 84; Tel&CabFB 84S; TV&RadDir 84*
KXMD-TV - Williston, ND - *BrCabYB 84; TelAl 83, 84; Tel&CabFB 84S; TV&RadDir 84*
KXMU-FM - Seattle, WA - *NatRadPubDir Summer 83*
KXNE-TV - Norfolk, NE - *BrCabYB 84; Tel&CabFB 84S*
KXNP - North Platte, NE - *BrCabYB 84*
KXO - El Centro, CA - *BrCabYB 84; TV&RadDir 84*
KXO-FM - El Centro, CA - *BrCabYB 84; TV&RadDir 84*
KXOA - Sacramento, CA - *BrCabYB 84; NatRadPubDir Summer 83, Spring 84; TV&RadDir 84*
KXOA-FM - Sacramento, CA - *BrCabYB 84; NatRadPubDir Summer 83, Spring 84; TV&RadDir 84*
KXOF - Bloomfield, IA - *BrCabYB 84*
KXOI - Corsicana, TX - *TV&RadDir 84*
KXOI - Crane, TX - *BrCabYB 84; TV&RadDir 84*
KXOJ - Sapulpa, OK - *BrCabYB 84; TV&RadDir 84*
KXOJ-FM - Sapulpa, OK - *BrCabYB 84; TV&RadDir 84*
KXOK - St. Louis, MO - *BrCabYB 84; NatRadPubDir Summer 83 p.144, Spring 84 p.144; TV&RadDir 84*
KXOL - Ft. Worth, TX - *BrCabYB 84; NatRadPubDir Summer 83, Spring 84 p.238; TV&RadDir 84*
KXON-TV - Mitchell, SD - *TelAl 83*
KXOQ - Hot Springs, AR - *BrCabYB 84*
KXOR-FM - Thibodaux, LA - *BrCabYB 84; NatRadPubDir Summer 83, Spring 84; TV&RadDir 84*
KXOW - Hot Springs, AR - *NatRadPubDir Summer 83, Spring 84*
KXOX - Sweetwater, TX - *BrCabYB 84; TV&RadDir 84*
KXOX-FM - Sweetwater, TX - *BrCabYB 84; TV&RadDir 84*
KXPO - Grafton, ND - *BrCabYB 84; TV&RadDir 84*
KXPR-FM - Sacramento, CA - *BrCabYB 84; NatRadPubDir Summer 83, Spring 84; TV&RadDir 84*
KXQR - Clovis, CA - *BrCabYB 84; TV&RadDir 84*
KXRA - Alexandria, MN - *BrCabYB 84; TV&RadDir 84*
KXRA-FM - Alexandria, MN - *BrCabYB 84; TV&RadDir 84*
KXRB - Sioux Falls, SD - *BrCabYB 84; NatRadPubDir Summer 83, Spring 84; TV&RadDir 84*
KXRC-FM - Craig, CO - *BrCabYB 84; TV&RadDir 84*
KXRK - Davenport, IA - *BrCabYB 84*
KXRM-TV - Colorado Springs, CO - *Tel&CabFB 84S*
KXRO - Aberdeen, WA - *BrCabYB 84; TV&RadDir 84*
KXRQ - Trumann, AR - *BrCabYB 84; TV&RadDir 84*
KXRX - Davenport, IA - *TV&RadDir 84*
KXSS - Lincoln, NE - *BrCabYB 84*
KXTC - Nampa, ID - *BrCabYB 84; TV&RadDir 84*
KXTC - Beaumont, TX - *NatRadPubDir Spring 84 p.236*
KXTC-FM - Beaumont, TX - *NatRadPubDir Summer 83*
KXTP - Duluth, MN - *NatRadPubDir Summer 83, Spring 84*
KXTP - Superior, WI - *BrCabYB 84*
KXTR-FM - Kansas City, MO - *BrCabYB 84; NatRadPubDir Summer 83, Spring 84; TV&RadDir 84*
KXTV-TV - Sacramento, CA - *BrCabYB 84; DirUSTelSta 83; LitMarPl 83; TelAl 83, 84; Tel&CabFB 84S; TV&RadDir 84*
KXTX-TV - Dallas, TX - *BrCabYB 84; DirUSTelSta 83; TelAl 83, 84; Tel&CabFB 84S; TV&RadDir 84*
KXTZ-FM - Henderson, NV - *BrCabYB 84; TV&RadDir 84*
KXVI - McKinney, TX - *BrCabYB 84*
KXVI - Plano, TX - *TV&RadDir 84*
KXVQ - Pawhuska, OK - *BrCabYB 84; TV&RadDir 84*
KXVR - Mountain Pass, CA - *BrCabYB 84*
KXXA - Monette, AR - *BrCabYB 84; TV&RadDir 84*
KXXE-FM - Forsyth, MT - *BrCabYB 84*
KXXE-FM - Miles City, MT - *TV&RadDir 84*
KXXI-FM - Ft. Smith, AR - *BrCabYB 84*
KXXI-FM - Van Buren, AR - *TV&RadDir 84*
KXXK-FM - Chickasha, OK - *BrCabYB 84; NatRadPubDir Summer 83, Spring 84; TV&RadDir 84*
KXXL - Bozeman, MT - *BrCabYB 84; TV&RadDir 84*
KXXN - Santa Barbara, CA - *BrCabYB 84; NatRadPubDir Spring 84; TV&RadDir 84*

KXXR - Spokane, WA - *BrCabYB 84; NatRadPubDir Summer 83, Spring 84; TV&RadDir 84*
KXXX - Colby, KS - *BrCabYB 84; NatRadPubDir Summer 83, Spring 84; TV&RadDir 84*
KXXX-FM - Colby, KS - *TV&RadDir 84*
KXXY - Oklahoma City, OK - *BrCabYB 84*
KXXY-FM - Oklahoma City, OK - *NatRadPubDir Summer 83, Spring 84; TV&RadDir 84*
KXY - Oklahoma City, OK - *NatRadPubDir Spring 84*
KXYL - Brownwood, TX - *BrCabYB 84; TV&RadDir 84*
KXYL-FM - Brownwood, TX - *TV&RadDir 84*
KXYZ - Houston, TX - *BrCabYB 84; NatRadPubDir Summer 83, Spring 84; TV&RadDir 84*
KXZL - San Antonio, TX - *BrCabYB 84*
Ky Enterprises - Long Beach, CA - *MicrocomMPl 84*
KYA - San Francisco, CA - *NatRadPubDir Summer 83, Spring 84; TV&RadDir 84*
KYA-FM - San Francisco, CA - *BrCabYB 84; TV&RadDir 84*
KYAC - Seattle, WA - *BrCabYB 84*
KYAK - Anchorage, AK - *BrCabYB 84; NatRadPubDir Summer 83, Spring 84; TV&RadDir 84*
KYBB - Tracy, CA - *BrCabYB 84*
KYBE - Frederick, OK - *BrCabYB 84*
KYBS-FM - Livingston, MT - *BrCabYB 84; TV&RadDir 84*
KYCA - Prescott, AZ - *BrCabYB 84; TV&RadDir 84*
KYCK-FM - Crookston, MN - *BrCabYB 84; TV&RadDir 84*
KYCN - Wheatland, WY - *BrCabYB 84; TV&RadDir 84*
KYCU-TV - Cheyenne, WY - *BrCabYB 84; DirUSTelSta 83; TelAl 83, 84; Tel&CabFB 84S; TV&RadDir 84*
KYCX - Mexia, TX - *BrCabYB 84*
KYDE - Pine Bluff, AR - *BrCabYB 84; NatRadPubDir Summer 83, Spring 84; TV&RadDir 84*
KYDS-FM - Sacramento, CA - *BrCabYB 84; TV&RadDir 84*
KYDZ-FM - Cody, WY - *BrCabYB 84; TV&RadDir 84*
KYEA-FM - West Monroe, LA - *BrCabYB 84; TV&RadDir 84*
KYEL-TV - Yuma, AZ - *BrCabYB 84; DirUSTelSta 83; TelAl 83, 84; Tel&CabFB 84S; TV&RadDir 84*
KYES - Roseburg, OR - *BrCabYB 84; TV&RadDir 84*
KYET - Payette, ID - *BrCabYB 84*
KYET - Ontario, OR - *TV&RadDir 84*
KYEZ - Salina, KS - *BrCabYB 84*
KYFC-TV - Shawnee Mission, KS - *TV&RadDir 84*
KYFC-TV - Kansas City, MO - *BrCabYB 84; DirUSTelSta 83; TelAl 83, 84; Tel&CabFB 84S*
KYFM-FM - Bartlesville, OK - *BrCabYB 84; NatRadPubDir Summer 83, Spring 84; TV&RadDir 84*
KYFR - Shenandoah, IA - *BrCabYB 84; TV&RadDir 84*
KYGO-FM - Denver, CO - *BrCabYB 84; NatRadPubDir Summer 83, Spring 84; TV&RadDir 84*
KYIN - Mason City, IA - *BrCabYB 84; Tel&CabFB 84S*
KYJC - Medford, OR - *BrCabYB 84; TV&RadDir 84*
KYJR-FM - Wenatchee, WA - *TV&RadDir 84*
KYKC - Sioux Falls, SD - *BrCabYB 84; NatRadPubDir Summer 83, Spring 84; TV&RadDir 84*
KYKK - Hobbs, NM - *TV&RadDir 84*
KYKK - Humble City, NM - *BrCabYB 84*
KYKN-FM - Grants, NM - *BrCabYB 84; TV&RadDir 84*
KYKR-FM - Beaumont, TX - *NatRadPubDir Summer 83, Spring 84*
KYKR-FM - Port Arthur, TX - *BrCabYB 84; TV&RadDir 84*
KYKS-FM - Lufkin, TX - *BrCabYB 84; TV&RadDir 84*
KYKX-FM - Longview, TX - *BrCabYB 84; NatRadPubDir Summer 83, Spring 84; TV&RadDir 84*
KYKY-FM - St. Louis, MO - *NatRadPubDir Summer 83, Spring 84; TV&RadDir 84*
KYKZ-FM - Lake Charles, LA - *BrCabYB 84; TV&RadDir 84*
KYLC-FM - Osage Beach, MO - *BrCabYB 84*
KYLC-FM - Albuquerque, NM - *TV&RadDir 84*
Kylix International Ltd. [Aff. of Wine Tidings Magazine] - Montreal, PQ, Canada - *BoPubDir 4 Sup, 5*
KYLO-FM - Davis, CA - *BrCabYB 84; TV&RadDir 84*
KYLT - Missoula, MT - *BrCabYB 84; NatRadPubDir Summer 83, Spring 84; TV&RadDir 84*
KYLT-FM - Missoula, MT - *BrCabYB 84*
KYLY - St. Louis, MO - *BrCabYB 84*
KYMC-FM - Ballwin, MO - *BrCabYB 84*
KYMC-FM - St. Louis, MO - *TV&RadDir 84*
KYME - Boise, ID - *NatRadPubDir Summer 83, Spring 84; TV&RadDir 84*
KYMG - Derby, KS - *BrCabYB 84*
KYMN - Northfield, MN - *BrCabYB 84; TV&RadDir 84*
KYMO - East Prairie, MO - *BrCabYB 84; TV&RadDir 84*
KYMS-FM - Anaheim, CA - *NatRadPubDir Summer 83, Spring 84 p.17*
KYMS-FM - Orange, CA - *TV&RadDir 84*
KYMS-FM - Santa Ana, CA - *BrCabYB 84*
KYND - Pasadena, TX - *BrCabYB 84*
KYNE-TV - Omaha, NE - *BrCabYB 84; Tel&CabFB 84S; TV&RadDir 84*
KYNG - Coos Bay, OR - *BrCabYB 84; TV&RadDir 84*
KYNG-FM - Coos Bay, OR - *BrCabYB 84; TV&RadDir 84*
KYNN - Omaha, NE - *BrCabYB 84; NatRadPubDir Summer 83, Spring 84; TV&RadDir 84*
KYNN-FM - Omaha, NE - *NatRadPubDir Summer 83, Spring 84; TV&RadDir 84*
KYNO - Fresno, CA - *BrCabYB 84; NatRadPubDir Summer 83, Spring 84; TV&RadDir 84*
KYNO-FM - Fresno, CA - *BrCabYB 84; NatRadPubDir Summer 83, Spring 84; TV&RadDir 84*
KYNR-FM - Kemmerer, WY - *TV&RadDir 84*
KYNT - Yankton, SD - *BrCabYB 84; NatRadPubDir Summer 83, Spring 84; TV&RadDir 84*
KYOC - Yoakum, TX - *BrCabYB 84*
Kyocera International Inc. - Warren, NJ - *BillIntBG 83-84*
Kyodo News Service - New York, NY - *Ed&PubIntYB 82*
KYOK - Houston, TX - *BrCabYB 84; NatRadPubDir Summer 83, Spring 84; TV&RadDir 84*
KYOO - Bolivar, MO - *BrCabYB 84; TV&RadDir 84*
KYOO-FM - Bolivar, MO - *BrCabYB 84; TV&RadDir 84*
KYOR - Blythe, CA - *TV&RadDir 84*
KYOR - Sun Valley, NV - *BrCabYB 84*
KYOS - Merced, CA - *BrCabYB 84; TV&RadDir 84*
KYOT-FM - Refugio, TX - *BrCabYB 84; TV&RadDir 84*
KYOU - Greeley, CO - *BrCabYB 84; NatRadPubDir Summer 83, Spring 84; TV&RadDir 84*
KYRE - Yreka, CA - *BrCabYB 84*
KYRO - Potosi, MO - *BrCabYB 84; TV&RadDir 84*
KYRS-FM - Chariton, IA - *BrCabYB 84; TV&RadDir 84*
KYSC-FM - Yakima, WA - *BrCabYB 84; TV&RadDir 84*
KYSM - Mankato, MN - *BrCabYB 84; NatRadPubDir Summer 83; TV&RadDir 84*
KYSM - North Mankato, MN - *NatRadPubDir Spring 84*
KYSM-FM - Mankato, MN - *BrCabYB 84; NatRadPubDir Summer 83; TV&RadDir 84*
KYSM-FM - North Mankato, MN - *NatRadPubDir Spring 84*
KYSN - Colorado Springs, CO - *BrCabYB 84; NatRadPubDir Summer 83, Spring 84; TV&RadDir 84*
KYSP - El Paso, TX - *BrCabYB 84*
KYSR - El Paso, TX - *TV&RadDir 84*
KYSR-FM - El Paso, TX - *BrCabYB 84; NatRadPubDir Spring 84*
KYSS - Missoula, MT - *BrCabYB 84; TV&RadDir 84*
KYSS-FM - Missoula, MT - *BrCabYB 84; TV&RadDir 84*
KYST - Texas City, TX - *BrCabYB 84; NatRadPubDir Summer 83 p.246, Spring 84; TV&RadDir 84*
KYTE - Portland, OR - *BrCabYB 84; NatRadPubDir Summer 83, Spring 84; TV&RadDir 84*
KYTN-FM - Grand Forks, ND - *BrCabYB 84; TV&RadDir 84*
KYTT-FM - Coos Bay, OR - *BrCabYB 84*
KYTV-TV - Springfield, MO - *BrCabYB 84; DirUSTelSta 83; TelAl 83, 84; Tel&CabFB 84S; TV&RadDir 84*
KYUF-FM - Uvalde, TX - *BrCabYB 84; TV&RadDir 84*
KYUK-TV - Bethel, AK - *BrCabYB 84; Tel&CabFB 84S; TV&RadDir 84*
KYUS-TV - Miles City, MT - *BrCabYB 84; DirUSTelSta 83; TelAl 83, 84; Tel&CabFB 84S*
KYUU-FM - San Francisco, CA - *BrCabYB 84; LitMarPl 83, 84; NatRadPubDir Summer 83, Spring 84; TV&RadDir 84*
KYVA - Gallup, NM - *BrCabYB 84; TV&RadDir 84*
KYVE-TV - Yakima, WA - *BrCabYB 84; Tel&CabFB 84S; TV&RadDir 84*
KYVY - Oklahoma City, OK - *TelAl 83*

KYW - Philadelphia, PA - *BrCabYB 84; LitMarPl 83, 84; NatRadPubDir Summer 83, Spring 84*
KYW-TV - Philadelphia, PA - *BrCabYB 84; DirUSTelSta 83; LitMarPl 83, 84; TelAl 83, 84; Tel&CabFB 84S; TV&RadDir 84*
KYXE - Selah, WA - *BrCabYB 84*
KYXI - Clackamas, OR - *TV&RadDir 84*
KYXI - Oregon City, OR - *BrCabYB 84*
KYXI - Portland, OR - *NatRadPubDir Summer 83, Spring 84*
KYXS - Mineral Wells, TX - *TV&RadDir 84*
KYXS-FM - Mineral Wells, TX - *BrCabYB 84; TV&RadDir 84*
KYXX - Odessa, TX - *BrCabYB 84; TV&RadDir 84*
KYXY-FM - San Diego, CA - *BrCabYB 84; NatRadPubDir Summer 83, Spring 84; TV&RadDir 84*
KYYA-FM - Billings, MT - *BrCabYB 84; TV&RadDir 84*
KYYK-FM - Palestine, TX - *BrCabYB 84; TV&RadDir 84*
KYYS-FM - Kansas City, MO - *BrCabYB 84; NatRadPubDir Summer 83, Spring 84; TV&RadDir 84*
KYYX-FM - Seattle, WA - *BrCabYB 84; NatRadPubDir Summer 83, Spring 84; TV&RadDir 84*
KYYY-FM - Bismarck, ND - *BrCabYB 84; NatRadPubDir Summer 83, Spring 84; TV&RadDir 84*
KYYZ-FM - Williston, ND - *TV&RadDir 84*
KYZZ - Wolf Point, MT - *BrCabYB 84*
KZAM-FM - Bellevue, WA - *BrCabYB 84; TV&RadDir 84*
KZAN-FM - Ogden, UT - *BrCabYB 84; TV&RadDir 84*
KZAP-FM - Sacramento, CA - *BrCabYB 84; NatRadPubDir Summer 83, Spring 84; TV&RadDir 84*
KZAZ-TV - Nogales, AZ - *BrCabYB 84; TelAl 83, 84*
KZAZ-TV - Tucson, AZ - *DirUSTelSta 83; Tel&CabFB 84S; TV&RadDir 84*
KZBA - Pocatello, ID - *TV&RadDir 84*
KZBQ - Pocatello, ID - *BrCabYB 84; NatRadPubDir Summer 83, Spring 84*
KZBQ-FM - Pocatello, ID - *BrCabYB 84; NatRadPubDir Summer 83, Spring 84; TV&RadDir 84*
KZBS-FM - Oklahoma City, OK - *TV&RadDir 84*
KZDO - Copperopolis, CA - *BrCabYB 84*
KZED-FM - Wellington, KS - *BrCabYB 84; TV&RadDir 84*
KZEE - Weatherford, TX - *BrCabYB 84; TV&RadDir 84*
KZEL-FM - Eugene, OR - *BrCabYB 84; NatRadPubDir Summer 83, Spring 84; TV&RadDir 84*
KZEN-FM - Redwood City, CA - *TV&RadDir 84*
KZEU - Victoria, TX - *BrCabYB 84*
KZEV-FM - Clear Lake, IA - *BrCabYB 84; TV&RadDir 84*
KZEW-FM - Dallas, TX - *BrCabYB 84; LitMarPl 84; NatRadPubDir Summer 83, Spring 84; TV&RadDir 84*
KZEY - Tyler, TX - *BrCabYB 84; TV&RadDir 84*
KZEZ-FM - St. George, UT - *BrCabYB 84; TV&RadDir 84*
KZFM-FM - Corpus Christi, TX - *BrCabYB 84; NatRadPubDir Summer 83, Spring 84; TV&RadDir 84*
KZFR-FM - South Lake Tahoe, CA - *BrCabYB 84; NatRadPubDir Summer 83, Spring 84; TV&RadDir 84*
KZHI - Honolulu, HI - *BrCabYB 84*
KZIA - Albuquerque, NM - *BrCabYB 84; NatRadPubDir Summer 83, Spring 84; TV&RadDir 84*
KZIG-FM - Cave City, AR - *BrCabYB 84; TV&RadDir 84*
KZIN-FM - Shelby, MT - *BrCabYB 84; TV&RadDir 84*
KZIO-FM - Duluth, MN - *TV&RadDir 84*
KZIO-FM - Superior, WI - *BrCabYB 84*
KZIP - Amarillo, TX - *BrCabYB 84; NatRadPubDir Summer 83, Spring 84; TV&RadDir 84*
KZIQ - Ridgecrest, CA - *BrCabYB 84; TV&RadDir 84*
KZIQ-FM - Ridgecrest, CA - *BrCabYB 84; TV&RadDir 84*
KZJO - Salt Lake City, UT - *NatRadPubDir Summer 83, Spring 84*
KZJO - Sandy, UT - *BrCabYB 84*
KZJO-FM - Salt Lake City, UT - *TV&RadDir 84*
KZKZ - Flagstaff, AZ - *BrCabYB 84; NatRadPubDir Summer 83, Spring 84; TV&RadDir 84*
KZLA - Los Angeles, CA - *BrCabYB 84; NatRadPubDir Summer 83, Spring 84; TV&RadDir 84*
KZLA-FM - Los Angeles, CA - *BrCabYB 84; NatRadPubDir Summer 83, Spring 84; TV&RadDir 84*
KZLE - Batesville, AR - *BrCabYB 84*
KZLN-TV - Harlingen, TX - *BrCabYB 84; Tel&CabFB 84S*
KZLN-TV - San Benito, TX - *TV&RadDir 84*
KZLO-FM - Pueblo, CO - *BrCabYB 84; TV&RadDir 84*
KZLS-FM - Billings, MT - *BrCabYB 84; NatRadPubDir Spring 84*
KZMC-FM - McCook, NE - *BrCabYB 84*
KZMK-FM - Bisbee, AZ - *BrCabYB 84; TV&RadDir 84*
KZMO-FM - California, MO - *BrCabYB 84*
KZMQ - Greybull, WY - *BrCabYB 84*
KZMQ-FM - Columbia, MO - *NatRadPubDir Spring 84*
KZNG - Hot Springs, AR - *BrCabYB 84; NatRadPubDir Summer 83, Spring 84; TV&RadDir 84*
KZNN-FM - Rolla, MO - *BrCabYB 84; TV&RadDir 84*
KZNS-FM - Barstow, CA - *BrCabYB 84; TV&RadDir 84*
KZOC - Osage City, KS - *BrCabYB 84*
KZOK-FM - Seattle, WA - *BrCabYB 84; NatRadPubDir Summer 83, Spring 84; TV&RadDir 84*
KZOM-FM - Beaumont, TX - *NatRadPubDir Spring 84*
KZOM-FM - Orange, TX - *BrCabYB 84; NatRadPubDir Summer 83; TV&RadDir 84*
KZON - Santa Maria, CA - *BrCabYB 84; TV&RadDir 84*
KZOO - Honolulu, HI - *BrCabYB 84; NatRadPubDir Summer 83, Spring 84; TV&RadDir 84*
KZOQ-FM - Missoula, MT - *TV&RadDir 84*
KZOR-FM - Hobbs, NM - *BrCabYB 84; TV&RadDir 84*
KZOT - Marianna, AR - *BrCabYB 84; TV&RadDir 84*
KZOZ-FM - Carmel, CA - *TV&RadDir 84*
KZOZ-FM - San Luis Obispo, CA - *BrCabYB 84; NatRadPubDir Summer 83 p.33, Spring 84 p.32*
KZPR - Minot, ND - *BrCabYB 84*
KZRK - Ozark, AR - *BrCabYB 84; TV&RadDir 84*
KZRK-FM - Ozark, AR - *BrCabYB 84; TV&RadDir 84*
KZRO - Marshall, AR - *BrCabYB 84*
KZSC-FM - Santa Cruz, CA - *BrCabYB 84; TV&RadDir 84*
KZSD-TV - Martin, SD - *BrCabYB 84; Tel&CabFB 84S*
KZST-FM - Santa Rosa, CA - *BrCabYB 84; TV&RadDir 84*
KZSU-FM - Stanford, CA - *BrCabYB 84; NatRadPubDir Summer 83, Spring 84*
KZTR-FM - Camarillo, CA - *BrCabYB 84*
KZTR-FM - Ventura, CA - *TV&RadDir 84*
KZTV-TV - Corpus Christi, TX - *BrCabYB 84; DirUSTelSta 83; TelAl 83, 84; Tel&CabFB 84S; TV&RadDir 84*
KZUL - Parker, AZ - *BrCabYB 84; TV&RadDir 84*
KZUM - Lincoln, NE - *BrCabYB 84*
KZUU-FM - Pullman, WA - *BrCabYB 84; TV&RadDir 84*
KZYM - Cape Girardeau, MO - *BrCabYB 84; NatRadPubDir Summer 83, Spring 84; TV&RadDir 84*
KZZA - Glenwood, MN - *BrCabYB 84*
KZZB-FM - Beaumont, TX - *BrCabYB 84; NatRadPubDir Summer 83, Spring 84; TV&RadDir 84*
KZZC-FM - Leavenworth, KS - *BrCabYB 84; TV&RadDir 84*
KZZI - West Jordan, UT - *BrCabYB 84*
KZZK-FM - Pasco, WA - *TV&RadDir 84*
KZZK-FM - Richland, WA - *BrCabYB 84*
KZZL-FM - Le Mars, IA - *BrCabYB 84; TV&RadDir 84*
KZZM - Tallulah, LA - *BrCabYB 84; TV&RadDir 84*
KZZN - Littlefield, TX - *BrCabYB 84; TV&RadDir 84*
KZZP - Mesa, AZ - *BrCabYB 84*
KZZP - Phoenix, AZ - *NatRadPubDir Summer 83, Spring 84 p.11; TV&RadDir 84*
KZZP-FM - Mesa, AZ - *BrCabYB 84; TV&RadDir 84*
KZZP-FM - Phoenix, AZ - *NatRadPubDir Summer 83, Spring 84 p.11*
KZZQ-FM - Golden Meadow, LA - *BrCabYB 84; TV&RadDir 84*
KZZX-FM - Albuquerque, NM - *BrCabYB 84; TV&RadDir 84*
KZZY-FM - Devils Lake, ND - *BrCabYB 84*
KZZY-FM - San Antonio, TX - *NatRadPubDir Summer 83*
KZZZ-FM - Kingman, AZ - *BrCabYB 84; TV&RadDir 84*

L

L/A House Editorial - Los Angeles, CA - *LitMarPl 84*
L/A House Productions - Los Angeles, CA - *LitMarPl 83; MagIndMarPl 82-83*
L & J Cablevision [of Star CATV Investment Corp.] - Olson Green Acres, TX - *Tel&CabFB 84C*
L & J Technical Services Trading - Mountainside, NJ - *ADAPSOMemDir 83-84*
L & M Enterprises - Rushville, IN - *Tel&CabFB 84C*
L & M Productions Inc. - Cleveland, OH - *WritMar 84*
L & M Stagecraft - Cleveland, OH - *AvMarPl 83*
L & S Computerware - Sunnyvale, CA - *MicrocomMPl 83*
L C-Liquid Chromatography & HPLC Magazine - Springfield, OR - *BaconPubCkMag 84*
L-Com Inc. - North Andover, MA - *MicrocomMPl 84*
L-W Communications Systems Inc. - Granite Shoals, TX - *BrCabYB 84 p.D-303*
La Agencia de McCann-Erikson - Los Angeles, CA - *StaDirAdAg 2-84*
LA Air Force - Long Beach, CA - *AvMarPl 83*
La Bell Music Publishing - *See* Brunswick Music Publishing Co.
La Belle Caloosa Belle - *See* Hammel Newspapers of Florida Inc.
La Belle Industries Inc. - Oconomowoc, WI - *AvMarPl 83*
La Belle Star - La Belle, MO - *BaconPubCkNews 84; Ed&PubIntYB 82*
La Belle Vision Inc. [of Cogeco] - Montmagny, PQ, Canada - *BrCabYB 84*
La Belle Vision Inc. - Shawinigan, PQ, Canada - *BrCabYB 84*
La Belle Vision Inc. - Trois-Rivieres, PQ, Canada - *BrCabYB 84; Tel&CabFB 84C*
La Canada Valley Sun - La Canada, CA - *BaconPubCkNews 84; Ed&PubIntYB 82; NewsDir 84*
La Compagnie de Television de Sept-Iles Ltee. - Sept-Iles, PQ, Canada - *BrCabYB 84*
La Concorde - Mirabel, PQ, Canada - *Ed&PubIntYB 82*
La Conner Cable TV - La Conner, WA - *Tel&CabFB 84C*
La Cosecha/The Harvest - Albuquerque, NM - *MagDir 84*
La Costa Community Antenna System - Carlsbad, CA - *BrCabYB 84; Tel&CabFB 84C*
La Costa Community Antenna System [of Rancho La Costa Inc.] - Rancho La Costa, CA - *Tel&CabFB 84C*
La Costa Products International - Carlsbad, CA - *HBIndAd&MS 82-83*
La Crescent Apple - La Crescent, MN - *AyerDirPub 83*
La Crescent Houston County News - La Crescent, MN - *BaconPubCkNews 84*
La Crosse Citibusiness - La Crosse, WI - *BaconPubCkMag 84*
La Crosse County Countryman - La Crosse County, WI - *Ed&PubIntYB 82*
La Crosse County Countryman - West Salem, WI - *AyerDirPub 83*
La Crosse Regional News - La Crosse, IN - *BaconPubCkNews 84*
La Crosse Rush County News - La Crosse, KS - *BaconPubCkNews 84*
La Crosse Telephone Corp. [Aff. of Century Telephone Enterprises Inc.] - La Crosse, WI - *TelDir&BG 83-84*
La Crosse Times-Review [of Diocese of La Crosse] - La Crosse, WI - *NewsDir 84*
La Crosse Tribune [of Lee Enterprises Inc.] - La Crosse, WI - *BaconPubCkNews 84; Ed&PubIntYB 82; NewsDir 84*
La Crosse Union Herald - La Crosse, WI - *NewsDir 84*
La Crosse-Winona Comic Unit - La Crosse, WI - *Ed&PubIntYB 82*
La Documentation Francaise - Paris, France - *InfIndMarPl 83; MicroMarPl 82-83*
La Dynamique de la Mauricie - St. Tite, PQ, Canada - *Ed&PubIntYB 82*
La Farge River & Hills Epitaph - La Farge, WI - *BaconPubCkNews 84*
La Fayette Press-Journal - *See* St. Louis Suburban Newspapers Inc.
La Fayette Walker County Messenger - La Fayette, GA - *BaconPubCkNews 84*
La Feria News - La Feria, TX - *BaconPubCkNews 84; Ed&PubIntYB 82*
La Feuille d'Erable - Plessisville, PQ, Canada - *Ed&PubIntYB 82*
LA 5 Inc. - Beverly Hills, CA - *BillIntBG 83-84*
La Follette Press - La Follette, TN - *AyerDirPub 83; BaconPubCkNews 84; Ed&PubIntYB 82; NewsDir 84*
La Fountaine, Susan - Maumee, OH - *LitMarPl 83, 84*
La Fray Publishing Co. - St. Petersburg, FL - *LitMag&SmPr 83-84*
La Frontiere - Rouyn, PQ, Canada - *Ed&PubIntYB 82*
La Gaceta - Tampa, FL - *AyerDirPub 83; Ed&PubIntYB 82*
La Gatineau - Maniwaki, PQ, Canada - *Ed&PubIntYB 82*
La Gazette - Maniwaki, PQ, Canada - *Ed&PubIntYB 82*
La Gazzetta - Windsor, ON, Canada - *Ed&PubIntYB 82*
La Gran Cadena Network - Santurce, PR - *BrCabYB 84*
La Grande Observer - La Grande, OR - *BaconPubCkNews 84*
La Grande Union County Review - La Grande, OR - *Ed&PubIntYB 82*
La Grange Cable TV [of Tar River Communications Inc.] - La Grange, NC - *Tel&CabFB 84C*
La Grange Citizen - La Grange, IL - *NewsDir 84*
La Grange Countian - La Grange, IN - *AyerDirPub 83*
La Grange Countian - *See* La Grange Publishing Co.
La Grange Countryside Citizen - La Grange, IL - *NewsDir 84*
La Grange Fayette County Record - La Grange, TX - *BaconPubCkNews 84; NewsDir 84*
La Grange Independent [of Mahopac Putnam County Press] - Mahopac, NY - *AyerDirPub 83; NewsDir 84*
La Grange Journal - La Grange, TX - *BaconPubCkNews 84; Ed&PubIntYB 82*
La Grange-La Grange Park Sun - La Grange, IL - *AyerDirPub 83*
La Grange News - La Grange, GA - *BaconPubCkNews 84; Ed&PubIntYB 82; NewsDir 84*
La Grange News - *See* La Grange Publishing Co.
La Grange Oldham Era - La Grange, KY - *BaconPubCkNews 84*
La Grange Park Citizen - La Grange, IL - *NewsDir 84*

La Grange Park Suburban Life - *See* Life Printing & Publishing Co.
La Grange Press - Citrus Heights, CA - *BoPubDir 4, 5*
La Grange Publishing Co. - La Grange, IN - *BaconPubCkNews 84*
La Grange Standard - *See* La Grange Publishing Co.
La Grange Suburban Life Citizen - *See* Life Printing & Publishing Co.
La Grange Sun Newspapers - La Grange, IL - *NewsDir 84*
La Grange Weekly Gazette - La Grange, NC - *BaconPubCkNews 84*
La Grave Klipfel Inc. - Des Moines, IA - *ArtMar 84*
La Guadeloupe Television Inc. - St. Evariste, PQ, Canada - *BrCabYB 84*
La Habra-Brea Daily Star Progress [of Freedom Newspapers Inc.] - La Habra, CA - *NewsDir 84*
La Habra-Brea Highlander - *See* Highlander Publications Inc.
La Habra Daily Star-Progress - La Habra, CA - *BaconPubCkNews 84*
La Hacienda - North Miami, FL - *BaconPubCkMag 84; MagDir 84*
La Harpe Hancock County Quill - La Harpe, IL - *BaconPubCkNews 84*
LA House Editorial - Los Angeles, CA - *LitMarPl 83*
La Jara Conejos County Citizen - La Jara, CO - *BaconPubCkNews 84*
La Jicarita Rural Telephone Cooperative - Mora, NM - *TelDir&BG 83-84*
La Jolla Light [of Harte-Hanks Communications] - La Jolla, CA - *AyerDirPub 83; BaconPubCkNews 84; Ed&PubIntYB 82; NewsDir 84*
La Jolla Museum of Contemporary Art - La Jolla, CA - *BoPubDir 4, 5*
La Jolla Pennysaver - Mission Viejo, CA - *AyerDirPub 83*
La Junta Arkansas Valley Journal - La Junta, CO - *BaconPubCkNews 84*
La Junta Tribune-Democrat - La Junta, CO - *BaconPubCkNews 84; NewsDir 84*
La Leche League International Inc. - Franklin Park, IL - *BoPubDir 4, 5*
La Liberte - St. Boniface, MB, Canada - *Ed&PubIntYB 82*
La Luz Press Inc. - La Luz, NM - *BoPubDir 4 Sup, 5; LitMag&SmPr 83-84*
La Marque Times [of Galveston Newspapers Inc.] - La Marque, TX - *BaconPubCkNews 84; Ed&PubIntYB 82; NewsDir 84*
La Mars Daily Sentinel - Le Mars, IA - *BaconPubCkNews 84*
La Mesa Courier - La Mesa, CA - *AyerDirPub 83; BaconPubCkNews 84; Ed&PubIntYB 82*
La Mesa Courier & Scout Newspaper [of La Mesa Publishing Co.] - La Mesa, CA - *NewsDir 84*
La Mesa Life-News [of Chula Vista Star-News] - Chula Vista, CA - *NewsDir 84*
La Mesa North Pennysaver - Mission Viejo, CA - *AyerDirPub 83*
La Mesa South Pennysaver - Mission Viejo, CA - *AyerDirPub 83*
La Mirada Lamplighter [of Garden Grove West Orange Publishing Corp.] - Garden Grove, CA - *AyerDirPub 83; NewsDir 84*
La Monte Cable Services Inc. - Topeka, KS - *BrCabYB 84*
La Morenita Publishers Inc. - San Francisco, CA - *ArtMar 84; BoPubDir 5*
La Moure Cable TV Inc. - La Moure, ND - *BrCabYB 84; Tel&CabFB 84C*
La Moure Chronicle - La Moure, ND - *BaconPubCkNews 84; Ed&PubIntYB 82*
La Nacion Americana/La Tribuna - Franklin Park, NJ - *Ed&PubIntYB 82*
La Nouvelle - Victoriaville, PQ, Canada - *Ed&PubIntYB 82*
La Nouvelle Revue - Granby, PQ, Canada - *Ed&PubIntYB 82*
La Oficina - Stamford, CT - *MagDir 84*
La Opinion [of Lozano Enterprises Inc.] - Los Angeles, CA - *AyerDirPub 83; Ed&PubIntYB 82; NewsDir 84*
L.A. Parent/Pony Ride Magazine [of Pony Publications] - Los Angeles, CA - *WritMar 84*
La Parole - Drummondville, PQ, Canada - *Ed&PubIntYB 82*
La Patrie Video Inc. - La Patrie, PQ, Canada - *BrCabYB 84*
La Penseede Bagot - Acton Vale, PQ, Canada - *Ed&PubIntYB 82*
La Petite Nation/le Bulletin - St. Andre-Avellin, PQ, Canada - *Ed&PubIntYB 82*
La Pharillon Voyageur - Rimouski, PQ, Canada - *Ed&PubIntYB 82*
La Pice, Margaret - San Francisco, CA - *BoPubDir 4, 5*
La Place l'Observateur - La Place, LA - *BaconPubCkNews 84*
La Plata Macon County Home Press - La Plata, MO - *BaconPubCkNews 84*
La Plata Times-Crescent - La Plata, MD - *BaconPubCkNews 84*
La Playa Cable TV Inc. - Oxnard, CA - *Tel&CabFB 84C*
La Porte Bayshore Sun - La Porte, TX - *NewsDir 84*
La Porte-Bayshore Sun Broadcaster - La Porte, TX - *BaconPubCkNews 84*
La Porte City Progress Review - La Porte City, IA - *BaconPubCkNews 84*
La Porte Herald-Argus - La Porte, IN - *BaconPubCkNews 84; Ed&PubIntYB 82; NewsDir 84*
La Presse - Montreal, PQ, Canada - *AyerDirPub 83; BaconPubCkNews 84; Ed&PubIntYB 82*
La Puente West Covina Highlander - *See* Highlander Publications Inc.
La Reina Press - Cincinnati, OH - *LitMag&SmPr 83-84*
La Revue - Terrebonne, PQ, Canada - *Ed&PubIntYB 82*
La Salle Audio Visual Aids Inc. - St. Clair Shores, MI - *AvMarPl 83*
La Salle County Broadcasting Corp. - La Salle, IL - *BrCabYB 84*
La Salle Daily News-Tribune - La Salle, IL - *BaconPubCkNews 84; NewsDir 84*
La Salle Letter Co. - New York, NY - *LitMarPl 83, 84; MagIndMarPl 82-83*
La Salle Litho - New York, NY - *LitMarPl 83, 84*
La Salle Messinger Paper Co. [Div. of Unisource Corp.] - Broadview, IL - *LitMarPl 83, 84; MagIndMarPl 82-83*
La Seigneurie - Boucherville, PQ, Canada - *Ed&PubIntYB 82*
La Sentinelle - Chibougamau, PQ, Canada - *Ed&PubIntYB 82*
La Siesta Press - Glendale, CA - *BoPubDir 4, 5*
La Stampa Calligrafica - Detroit, MI - *BoPubDir 4, 5*
La Terr Broadcasting Corp. - Houma, LA - *BrCabYB 84*
La Tribuna de North Jersey - Newark, NJ - *Ed&PubIntYB 82; NewsDir 84*
La Tribuna Italiana - Montreal, PQ, Canada - *Ed&PubIntYB 82*
La Tribune - Sherbrooke, PQ, Canada - *AyerDirPub 83; BaconPubCkNews 84; Ed&PubIntYB 82*
La Val Record Co. - Kalamazoo, MI - *BillIntBG 83-84*
La Vallee de la Chaudiere - St. Joseph-de-Beauce, PQ, Canada - *Ed&PubIntYB 82*
La Velle Telephone Co-Operative - La Valle, WI - *TelDir&BG 83-84*
La Verne Courier [of Claremont Courier Graphics Corp.] - Claremont, CA - *NewsDir 84*
La Verne Courier - *See* Claremont Courier Graphics Corp.
La Verne Leader - La Verne, CA - *Ed&PubIntYB 82*
La Verne Leader [of Ontario Bonita Publishing Co.] - Ontario, CA - *AyerDirPub 83; NewsDir 84*
La Verne Leader - *See* Pomona Progress Bulletin
La Vernia News - La Vernia, TX - *BaconPubCkNews 84; Ed&PubIntYB 82*
La Victoire - St. Eustache, PQ, Canada - *Ed&PubIntYB 82*
La Voce d'Italia - Montreal, PQ, Canada - *Ed&PubIntYB 82*
La Voce Italiana - Paterson, NJ - *Ed&PubIntYB 82*
La Voix Acadienne - Summerside, PE, Canada - *Ed&PubIntYB 82*
La Voix de l'Est - Granby, PQ, Canada - *AyerDirPub 83; BaconPubCkNews 84; Ed&PubIntYB 82*
La Voix des Mille-Iles - Ste. Therese, PQ, Canada - *Ed&PubIntYB 82*
La Voix du Samedi - Sorel, PQ, Canada - *Ed&PubIntYB 82*
La Voix du Sud - Lac Etchemin, PQ, Canada - *Ed&PubIntYB 82*
La Voix Gaspesienne - Matane, PQ, Canada - *Ed&PubIntYB 82*
La Voix Metropolitaine - Sorel, PQ, Canada - *Ed&PubIntYB 82*
La Voz - Elizabeth, NJ - *Ed&PubIntYB 82*
La Voz Hispana de Colorado - Denver, CO - *Ed&PubIntYB 82; NewsDir 84*
L.A. West Advertising Inc. - Los Angeles, CA - *StaDirAdAg 2-84*
Lab Animal - New York, NY - *BaconPubCkMag 84; MagDir 84*
Lab Technicians - New York, NY - *AvMarPl 83*
Lab World - Philadelphia, PA - *MagDir 84; MagIndMarPl 82-83*

Label Letter [of Union Label & Service Trades Dept., AFL-CIO] - Washington, DC - *NewsDir 84*
Label X Music Corp. - Walnut Creek, CA - *BillIntBG 83-84*
LaBelle & Shallbetter - Minneapolis, MN - *AdAge 3-28-84; StaDirAdAg 2-84*
Labelon Corp. - Canandaigua, NY - *AvMarPl 83*
Labinfo - Paris, France - *DirOnDB Spring 84*
Labonte, Claude - St. Evariste de Forsythe, PQ, Canada - *Tel&CabFB 84C*
Labor Arts Books - Buffalo, NY - *BoPubDir 4, 5; LitMag&SmPr 83-84*
Labor Beacon - Michigan City, IN - *NewsDir 84*
Labor Herald - Baltimore, MD - *AyerDirPub 83*
Labor Journal [of Central Labor Council] - Bakersfield, CA - *NewsDir 84*
Labor Market Information Systems [of University of Michigan] - Ann Arbor, MI - *EISS 83*
Labor News - Galesburg, IL - *AyerDirPub 83*
Labor News - Indianapolis, IN - *NewsDir 84*
Labor Newspaper - Washington, DC - *NewsDir 84*
Labor Paper, The [of West Central Illinois Building & Construction Trades Council] - Peoria, IL - *NewsDir 84*
Labor Press Association - Washington, DC - *Ed&PubIntYB 82*
Labor Relations Digest & Index [of Bureau of National Affairs Inc.] - Washington, DC - *CompReadDB 82*
Labor Relations Press - Ft. Washington, PA - *CompReadDB 82; EISS 83*
Labor Research Association Inc. - New York, NY - *BoPubDir 4, 5*
Labor Statistics [of U.S. Dept. of Labor] - Washington, DC - *CompReadDB 82*
Labor Times [of Amalgamated Clothing & Textile Workers Union] - Chicago, IL - *NewsDir 84*
Labor Unity - Boston, MA - *NewsDir 84*
Labor Unity [of Amalgamated Clothing & Textile Workers Union] - New York, NY - *MagIndMarPl 82-83; NewsDir 84*
Labor World [of The Duluth Central Labor Body] - Duluth, MN - *NewsDir 84*
Labor World, The [of Chattanooga Area Labor Council AFL-CIO] - Chattanooga, TN - *NewsDir 84*
Laboratoire d'Anthropologie-Appliquee - Paris, France - *InfIndMarPl 83*
Laboratoire de Science du Sol et Service d'Etude des Sols [of Institut National de la Recherche Agronomique] - Montpellier, France - *InfIndMarPl 83*
Laboratory Animal Data Bank - McLean, VA - *DirOnDB Spring 84*
Laboratory Animal Data Bank [of Battelle Memorial Institute] - Vienna, VA - *EISS 83*
Laboratory Animal Science - Joliet, IL - *MagDir 84*
Laboratory Animal Science - Ames, IA - *BaconPubCkMag 84*
Laboratory Computer Systems Inc. - Cambridge, MA - *MicrocomMPl 83, 84; MicrocomSwDir 1; WhoWMicrocom 83*
Laboratory Consulting Inc. - Madison, WI - *WhoWMicrocom 83*
Laboratory Equipment [of Gordon Publications Inc.] - Dover, NJ - *BaconPubCkMag 84; Folio 83; MagDir 84*
Laboratory Equipment - Morristown, NJ - *MagIndMarPl 82-83*
Laboratory for Applied Behavioral Science Inc. - Westfield, NJ - *BoPubDir 5*
Laboratory for Computer Graphics & Spatial Analysis [of Harvard University] - Cambridge, MA - *EISS 83*
Laboratory for Information Systems [of Boris Kidric Institute of Nuclear Sciences] - Belgrade, Yugoslavia - *EISS 83*
Laboratory Hazards Bulletin [of Pergamon International Information Corp.] - McLean, VA - *DataDirOnSer 84*
Laboratory Hazards Bulletin - Nottingham, England - *DirOnDB Spring 84*
Laboratory Investigation - Baltimore, MD - *BaconPubCkMag 84; MagDir 84*
Laboratory Management - New York, NY - *BaconPubCkMag 84; MagDir 84*
Laboratory Medicine - Chicago, IL - *BaconPubCkMag 84; MagDir 84*
Laboratory Medicine - Philadelphia, PA - *MagIndMarPl 82-83*
Laboratory Microsystems - Los Angeles, CA - *MicrocomMPl 83, 84; WhoWMicrocom 83*
Laboratory Product News - Don Mills, ON, Canada - *BaconPubCkMag 84*
Labordoc [of International Labour Office] - Geneva, Switzerland - *DBBus 82; DirOnDB Spring 84; OnBibDB 3*
Laborer, The - Washington, DC - *NewsDir 84*
Laborlaw [of The Bureau of National Affairs] - Washington, DC - *DataDirOnSer 84; DirOnDB Spring 84; EISS 7-83 Sup*
Labour College of Canada - Ottawa, ON, Canada - *BoPubDir 4 Sup, 5*
Labour Information Database [of International Labour Office] - Geneva, Switzerland - *EISS 83*
Labour Leader [of Independent Labour Publications] - Leeds, England - *LitMag&SmPr 83-84*
Labourdoc [of SDC Search Service] - Santa Monica, CA - *DataDirOnSer 84*
Labrys [of Bran's Head at the Hunting Raven Press] - Frome, England - *LitMag&SmPr 83-84*
LaBuick & Associates Media Inc. - Palm Springs, CA - *StaDirAdAg 2-84*
Labyrinth Press, The - Durham, NC - *LitMarPl 83, 84*
LACC News & Alumni Report - Whittier, CA - *BaconPubCkMag 84*
Lacebark Publications - Stillwater, OK - *BoPubDir 5*
Lacey Leader - Olympia, WA - *NewsDir 84*
LaChance Goodchild Eidson Inc. - Providence, RI - *DirPRFirms 83*
LaChance Productions Inc. - Providence, RI - *StaDirAdAg 2-84*
Lachine Messenger - Lachine, PQ, Canada - *Ed&PubIntYB 82*
Lacis - Berkeley, CA - *BoPubDir 4, 5*
Lack & Associates Ltd., Francesca - New York, NY - *DirPRFirms 83*
Lackawanna Front Page - Lackawanna, NY - *Ed&PubIntYB 82; NewsDir 84*
Lackawanna Front Page - *See* Front Page Inc.
Lackawanna Leader - Lackawanna, NY - *Ed&PubIntYB 82; NewsDir 84*
Lackawaxen Telephone Co. - Rowland, PA - *TelDir&BG 83-84*
Lackey Group - Henderson, KY - *BrCabYB 84*
Laclede Communication Service Inc. - St. Louis, MO - *AvMarPl 83*
LACMA Physician - Los Angeles, CA - *ArtMar 84; BaconPubCkMag 84; MagDir 84*
Lacombe Globe - Lacombe, AB, Canada - *Ed&PubIntYB 82*
Lacon Home Journal - *See* Marshall County Publishing Co.
Lacon Illinois Valley Peach - *See* Marshall County Publishing Co.
Lacon Lake Wildwood Sunbeam - *See* Marshall County Publishing Co.
Laconia Citizen - Laconia, NH - *BaconPubCkNews 84; NewsDir 84*
Lacquer-Mat - Syracuse, NY - *AvMarPl 83*
Lacret Publishing Co. Inc. - Union City, NJ - *BoPubDir 5*
Lacrosse - Baltimore, MD - *BaconPubCkMag 84*
L'Actualite - Toronto, ON, Canada - *BaconPubCkMag 84*
L'Actualite [of Maclean Hunter] - Montreal, PQ, Canada - *WritMar 84*
Lacy & Associates, Wm. - *See* Fellers, Lacy & Gaddis
Lacy/Associates Ltd., N. Lee - Los Angeles, CA - *Tel&CabFB 84C*
Lacy/Associates Ltd., N. Lee - New York, NY - *HBIndAd&MS 82-83*
Lacy, Susana B. - Miami, FL - *LitMarPl 83, 84*
Ladco Development Co. Inc. - Olean, NY - *MicrocomMPl 83, 84; WhoWMicrocom 83*
Ladd Cablevision - Albion, PA - *BrCabYB 84*
Ladd Communications [of Tele-Media Corp.] - Albion, PA - *Tel&CabFB 84C*
Ladd, Elizabeth - Holliston, MA - *LitMarPl 84*
Ladd Music Co. - Scranton, PA - *BillIntBG 83-84*
Ladd/Wells/Presba Advertising Inc. - Chicago, IL - *StaDirAdAg 2-84*
Laddin & Co. Inc. - New York, NY - *ArtMar 84; StaDirAdAg 2-84*
Ladel - Metairie, LA - *AvMarPl 83*
Ladera Music Publishing - Los Angeles, CA - *BillIntBG 83-84*
Ladies' Home Journal [of Charter Corp.] - New York, NY - *BaconPubCkMag 84; Folio 83; LitMarPl 83, 84; MagDir 84; MagIndMarPl 82-83; WritMar 84*

Ladies' Home Journal Needle & Craft - New York, NY - *MagDir 84*
Ladies' Home Journal Prime Showcase - New York, NY - *MagDir 84*
Ladner, Edna G. - Burnaby, BC, Canada - *BoPubDir 4, 5*
Ladonia News - Ladonia, TX - *Ed&PubIntYB 82*
Ladonia News - *See* News Publishing Co.
Lady Jane Music - Tahoe City, CA - *BillIntBG 83-84*
Lady Lois Music - *See* Hello Love Music
Lady Love Records - Philadelphia, PA - *BillIntBG 83-84*
Ladycom [of Downey Communications Inc.] - Washington, DC - *BaconPubCkMag 84; MagDir 84; MagIndMarPl 82-83; WritMar 84*
Lady's Circle [of Lopez Publications Inc.] - New York, NY - *BaconPubCkMag 84; MagDir 84; MagIndMarPl 82-83; WritMar 84*
Lady's Circle Knitting & Crochet Guide - New York, NY - *MagDir 84*
Ladysmith Chemainus Chronicle - Ladysmith, BC, Canada - *AyerDirPub 83; Ed&PubIntYB 82*
Ladysmith News - Ladysmith, WI - *BaconPubCkNews 84; Ed&PubIntYB 82; NewsDir 84*
LAE News - Baton Rouge, LA - *BaconPubCkMag 84; MagDir 84*
Lafayette Advertiser [of Thomson Newspapers Inc.] - Lafayette, LA - *BaconPubCkNews 84; NewsDir 84*
Lafayette Cable TV Inc. - Lafayette, AL - *BrCabYB 84; Tel&CabFB 84C*
Lafayette Cable TV Inc. [of TCA Cable TV Inc.] - Lafayette, LA - *BrCabYB 84; Tel&CabFB 84C*
Lafayette Communications Corp. [of Scripps-Howard Cable Services Co.] - Lafayette, CO - *Tel&CabFB 84C*
Lafayette Contra Costa Sun - Lafayette, CA - *BaconPubCkNews 84; NewsDir 84*
Lafayette County Democrat - Lewisville, AR - *AyerDirPub 83; Ed&PubIntYB 82*
Lafayette Instrument Co. - Lafayette, IN - *AvMarPl 83*
Lafayette Journal & Courier [of Gannett Co. Inc.] - Lafayette, IN - *BaconPubCkNews 84; LitMarPl 83; NewsDir 84*
Lafayette Leader - Lafayette, IN - *BaconPubCkNews 84; Ed&PubIntYB 82; NewsDir 84*
Lafayette Macon County Times - Lafayette, TN - *BaconPubCkNews 84; NewsDir 84*
Lafayette MDS Co. - New York, NY - *Tel&CabFB 84C*
Lafayette Morning Star [of Diocese of Lafayette] - Lafayette, LA - *NewsDir 84*
Lafayette News - Lafayette, CO - *BaconPubCkNews 84; Ed&PubIntYB 82*
Lafayette-Nicollet Ledger - Lafayette, MN - *AyerDirPub 83; BaconPubCkNews 84; Ed&PubIntYB 82*
Lafayette Press Journal - Lafayette, MO - *Ed&PubIntYB 82*
Lafayette Press-Journal - St. Louis, MO - *AyerDirPub 83*
Lafayette Sun - Lafayette, AL - *BaconPubCkNews 84; Ed&PubIntYB 82*
Lafayette Sun - Lafayette, CA - *Ed&PubIntYB 82*
Lafayette Visitor - Lafayette, IN - *NewsDir 84*
Lafayette-Walker County Messenger - Lafayette, GA - *NewsDir 84*
Laffan Public Relations Systems, Robert - New York, NY - *DirPRFirms 83*
LaFollette Cable TV Inc. [of Athena Communications Corp.] - LaFollette, TN - *Tel&CabFB 84C*
LaFollette-Livingston Cable TV Inc. - Leitchfield, KY - *BrCabYB 84*
Lafourche Communications Inc. [of Wometco Cable TV Inc.] - Napoleonville, LA - *BrCabYB 84*
Lafourche Communications Inc. [of Wometco Cable TV Inc.] - St. James Parish, LA - *Tel&CabFB 84C*
Lafourche Communications Inc. [of Wometco Cable TV Inc.] - Thibodaux, LA - *BrCabYB 84; Tel&CabFB 84C*
Lafourche Telephone Co. Inc. - Larose, LA - *TelDir&BG 83-84*
Lafray Publishing Co. - St. Petersburg, FL - *BoPubDir 5*
Lager & Associates, Thelma - Los Angeles, CA - *StaDirAdAg 2-84*
Lagrange Ledger - *See* Taconic Press Inc.
Lagrange News - Lagrange, IN - *Ed&PubIntYB 82*
Lagrange Standard - Lagrange, IN - *Ed&PubIntYB 82*
Lagrange Standard News - Lagrange, IN - *NewsDir 84*
Lagrangeville La Grange Independent - Lagrangeville, NY - *Ed&PubIntYB 82*
Lagrangeville La Grange Independent - *See* Gateway Papers
LaGuardia Automated Library System [of LaGuardia Community College] - Long Island, NY - *EISS 83*
Laguna Beach Pennysaver - Mission Viejo, CA - *AyerDirPub 83*
Laguna Hills News Post - Laguna Hills, CA - *BaconPubCkNews 84*
Laguna Hills North/South Pennysaver - Mission Viejo, CA - *AyerDirPub 83*
Laguna News-Post - Laguna Beach, CA - *Ed&PubIntYB 82*
Laguna Niguel News [of Media General Inc.] - Laguna Beach, CA - *NewsDir 84*
LaHarpe Telephone Co. - LaHarpe, KS - *TelDir&BG 83-84*
LaHarpe Telephone Co. Inc. - LaHarpe, IL - *TelDir&BG 83-84*
Lahontan Valley News - Fallon, NV - *AyerDirPub 83; Ed&PubIntYB 82*
Laib PR/Publicity, Janet [Subs. of Edward Gottlieb Inc.] - New York, NY - *DirPRFirms 83; LitMarPl 83, 84*
Laidlaw Brothers [Div. of Doubleday & Co. Inc.] - River Forest, IL - *LitMarPl 83, 84*
Laikin Optical - Los Angeles, CA - *AvMarPl 83*
Laiks - Brooklyn, NY - *Ed&PubIntYB 82*
Laird Productions Inc. - Mechanicsburg, PA - *AvMarPl 83*
Laird Telemedia Inc. - Salt Lake City, UT - *AvMarPl 83*
Laird Unltd. - Haverford, PA - *DirPRFirms 83*
Laissez Faire Books Inc. - New York, NY - *BoPubDir 4, 5*
Laisve - Ozone Park, NY - *Ed&PubIntYB 82; NewsDir 84*
Laitin Enterprises, Julie A. - New York, NY - *DirPRFirms 83*
LaJoie, Raymond A. - Worcester, MA - *MagIndMarPl 82-83*
LaJolla Music Publishing - *See* Kjos Music Co., Neil S.
Lakco Record Co. - Chicago, IL - *BillIntBG 83-84*
Lake Andes Wave - Lake Andes, SD - *BaconPubCkNews 84; Ed&PubIntYB 82*
Lake Arrowhead Mountain News & Mountaineer - Lake Arrowhead, CA - *BaconPubCkNews 84*
Lake Arrowhead Mountain News, The [of Anderson Publications] - Lake Arrowhead, CA - *NewsDir 84*
Lake Arrowhead Timberline Journal - Lake Arrowhead, CA - *BaconPubCkNews 84*
Lake Arthur Jeff Davis Revue - Lake Arthur, LA - *AyerDirPub 83; Ed&PubIntYB 82*
Lake Benton Lincoln County Valley Journal - Lake Benton, MN - *BaconPubCkNews 84*
Lake Book/John F. Cuneo Inc. - Melrose Park, IL - *LitMarPl 84*
Lake Butler Clearview Cable Television - Lake Butler, FL - *BrCabYB 84*
Lake Butler Union County Times - Lake Butler, FL - *BaconPubCkNews 84*
Lake Champlain Communications Corp. - South Burlington, VT - *Tel&CabFB 84C*
Lake Champlain Press - Redford, NY - *Ed&PubIntYB 82; NewsDir 84*
Lake Charles American Press - Lake Charles, LA - *BaconPubCkNews 84; Ed&PubIntYB 82; LitMarPl 83, 84; NewsDir 84*
Lake Charlevoix Cable TV Co. [of Tele-Communications Inc.] - Charlevoix, MI - *BrCabYB 84; Tel&CabFB 84C p.1687*
Lake Charlevoix Cable TV Co. - Gaylord, MI - *Tel&CabFB 84C*
Lake Cities Cable Vision [of Rust Capital Ltd.] - Corinth, TX - *BrCabYB 84; Tel&CabFB 84C*
Lake City Cable TV Inc. [of Wometco Cable TV Inc.] - Lake City, SC - *BrCabYB 84*
Lake City Graphic - Lake City, IA - *BaconPubCkNews 84; Ed&PubIntYB 82*
Lake City Graphic - Lake City, MN - *BaconPubCkNews 84; Ed&PubIntYB 82*
Lake City Journal - Lake City, WA - *Ed&PubIntYB 82*
Lake City Reporter [of The New York Times] - Lake City, FL - *BaconPubCkNews 84; Ed&PubIntYB 82; NewsDir 84*
Lake City Silver World - Lake City, CO - *AyerDirPub 83*
Lake City Town Crier - Lake City, TN - *BaconPubCkNews 84*
Lake City Waterfront - Lake City, MI - *BaconPubCkNews 84; NewsDir 84*
Lake Country Music - Graham, TX - *BillIntBG 83-84*

Lake County Banner - Tiptonville, TN - *AyerDirPub 83; Ed&PubIntYB 82*
Lake County Cablevision [of Scripps-Howard Cable Co.] - Silver Springs Shores, FL - *Tel&CabFB 84C*
Lake County Citizen - Pueblo, CO - *AyerDirPub 83*
Lake County Citizen - Tavares, FL - *Ed&PubIntYB 82*
Lake County Examiner - Lakeview, OR - *AyerDirPub 83; Ed&PubIntYB 82*
Lake County Express - Willoughby, OH - *AyerDirPub 83*
Lake County Globe Ledger - Hammond, IN - *Ed&PubIntYB 82*
Lake County News-Chronicle - Two Harbors, MN - *Ed&PubIntYB 82; NewsDir 84*
Lake County News-Herald - Willoughby, OH - *AyerDirPub 83; Ed&PubIntYB 82*
Lake County Record-Bee - Lakeport, CA - *AyerDirPub 83*
Lake County Record-Bee, The - Lake County, CA - *Ed&PubIntYB 82*
Lake County Reporter - Hartland, WI - *AyerDirPub 83; Ed&PubIntYB 82*
Lake County Reporter Publishers - Hartland, WI - *BaconPubCkNews 84*
Lake County Shopper, The - Somerset, KY - *AyerDirPub 83*
Lake County Star - Crown Point, IN - *AyerDirPub 83; Ed&PubIntYB 82*
Lake County Star - Baldwin, MI - *Ed&PubIntYB 82*
Lake Cowichan News, The - Lake Cowichan, BC, Canada - *Ed&PubIntYB 82*
Lake Crystal Tribune - Lake Crystal, MN - *BaconPubCkNews 84; Ed&PubIntYB 82*
Lake Dallas Cities Sun - Lake Dallas, TX - *BaconPubCkNews 84*
Lake Dallas Telephone Co. Inc. - Lake Dallas, TX - *TelDir&BG 83-84*
Lake District News - Burns Lake, BC, Canada - *AyerDirPub 83*
Lake Elsinore Valley Sun - Lake Elsinore, CA - *AyerDirPub 83; NewsDir 84*
Lake End Graphics Ltd. - New York, NY - *LitMarPl 83, 84; MagIndMarPl 82-83*
Lake Erie College Press - Painesville, OH - *BoPubDir 4, 5*
Lake Forest-Lake Bluff News-Advertiser - Lake Forest, IL - *Ed&PubIntYB 82*
Lake Forest-Lake Bluff News-Advertiser - *See* Singer Printing & Publishing Co.
Lake Forest/Lake Forester - Wilmette, IL - *AyerDirPub 83*
Lake Forest/Lake Forester - *See* Pioneer Press Inc.
Lake Forest News Advertiser - Highland Park, IL - *AyerDirPub 83*
Lake Forester - Lake Forest, IL - *Ed&PubIntYB 82*
Lake Forester - Wilmette, IL - *NewsDir 84*
Lake Geneva Regional News - Lake Geneva, WI - *BaconPubCkNews 84; NewsDir 84*
Lake Havasu City Herald [of Western Newspapers Inc.] - Lake Havasu City, AZ - *BaconPubCkNews 84; Ed&PubIntYB 82; NewsDir 84*
Lake House Books - Bethesda, MD - *BoPubDir 4 Sup, 5*
Lake Hughes Television Cable Service - Lake Hughes, CA - *BrCabYB 84; Tel&CabFB 84C*
Lake Huron Broadcasting Corp. - Saginaw, MI - *BrCabYB 84*
Lake Jackson Brazorian News - Lake Jackson, TX - *BaconPubCkNews 84*
Lake Keystone News - Mannford, OK - *AyerDirPub 83; Ed&PubIntYB 82*
Lake Land Cablevision Inc. - Detroit Lakes, MN - *BrCabYB 84*
Lake Lillian Crier - Lake Lillian, MN - *Ed&PubIntYB 82*
Lake Line Cable TV - Montpelier, ID - *BrCabYB 84; Tel&CabFB 84C*
Lake Livingston Progress - *See* Polk County Publishing
Lake Mills Graphic - Lake Mills, IA - *BaconPubCkNews 84; Ed&PubIntYB 82*
Lake Mills Leader - Lake Mills, WI - *BaconPubCkNews 84; Ed&PubIntYB 82*
Lake Minnetonka Sun - Edina, MN - *AyerDirPub 83*
Lake Minnetonka Sun - Wayzata, MN - *Ed&PubIntYB 82*
Lake Minnetonka Sun - *See* Sun Newspapers
Lake Minnetonka Sun & Free Section [of Minnesota Suburban Newspapers Inc.] - Minneapolis, MN - *NewsDir 84*
Lake Murray/Del Cerro/Allied Gardens Life-News [of Chula Vista Star-News] - Chula Vista, CA - *NewsDir 84*
Lake News - Leesburg, FL - *AyerDirPub 83; NewsDir 84*
Lake News - Lake Cowichan, BC, Canada - *AyerDirPub 83*
Lake Odessa Wave - Lake Odessa, MI - *BaconPubCkNews 84; Ed&PubIntYB 82*
Lake of Two Mountains Gazette, The - Hudson, PQ, Canada - *AyerDirPub 83*
Lake Office, Candace - Los Angeles, CA - *LitMarPl 83, 84*
Lake Orion Review - Lake Orion, MI - *BaconPubCkNews 84; Ed&PubIntYB 82*
Lake Oswego Review - Lake Oswego, OR - *BaconPubCkNews 84; Ed&PubIntYB 82*
Lake Park Journal - Lake Park, MN - *BaconPubCkNews 84; Ed&PubIntYB 82*
Lake Park News - Lake Park, IA - *AyerDirPub 83; BaconPubCkNews 84; Ed&PubIntYB 82*
Lake Placid Journal - Lake Placid, FL - *BaconPubCkNews 84; Ed&PubIntYB 82; NewsDir 84*
Lake Placid News - Lake Placid, NY - *BaconPubCkNews 84; Ed&PubIntYB 82; NewsDir 84*
Lake Powell Chronicle - Page, AZ - *AyerDirPub 83; Ed&PubIntYB 82*
Lake Preston Times - Lake Preston, SD - *BaconPubCkNews 84; Ed&PubIntYB 82*
Lake Providence East Carroll Delta News - Lake Providence, LA - *BaconPubCkNews 84*
Lake Publishing Corp. - Libertyville, IL - *BoPubDir 5*
Lake Region Echo - Alexandria, MN - *AyerDirPub 83; Ed&PubIntYB 82; NewsDir 84*
Lake Region Echo - *See* Alexandria Newspapers Inc.
Lake Region Life - Waterville, MN - *AyerDirPub 83; Ed&PubIntYB 82*
Lake Region Monitor - Keystone Heights, FL - *Ed&PubIntYB 82*
Lake Region Press - Alexandria, MN - *AyerDirPub 83; Ed&PubIntYB 82; NewsDir 84*
Lake Region Press - *See* Alexandria Newspapers Inc.
Lake Region Telephone Co. - Pelican Rapids, MN - *TelDir&BG 83-84*
Lake Region Times - Madison Lake, MN - *AyerDirPub 83; Ed&PubIntYB 82*
Lake San Marcos Outlook - Lake San Marcos, CA - *Ed&PubIntYB 82*
Lake San Marcos Outlook - San Marcos, CA - *NewsDir 84*
Lake Shore Master Antenna Corp. [of New Channels Corp.] - Eufaula, AL - *BrCabYB 84*
Lake Shore Master Antenna Corp. [of New Channels Corp.] - Wetumpka, AL - *BrCabYB 84*
Lake Shore News [of Chicago Downtown News Inc.] - Chicago, IL - *NewsDir 84*
Lake Shore Radio & TV - Heber Springs, AR - *BrCabYB 84; Tel&CabFB 84C*
Lake Shore Visitor [of Roman Catholic Diocese of Erie] - Erie, PA - *NewsDir 84*
Lake-Spiro-Shurman - Memphis, TN - *StaDirAdAg 2-84*
Lake Star - Shoal Lake, MB, Canada - *AyerDirPub 83*
Lake Street Review - Minneapolis, MN - *LitMag&SmPr 83-84; WritMar 84*
Lake Sun - Kelseyville, CA - *Ed&PubIntYB 82*
Lake Superior Cablevision - Sault Ste. Marie, ON, Canada - *BrCabYB 84*
Lake Tahoe News - South Lake Tahoe, CA - *AyerDirPub 83; Ed&PubIntYB 82; NewsDir 84*
Lake Telephone Co. [of CATV Systems Inc.] - Livingston, TX - *BrCabYB 84; Tel&CabFB 84C p.1687; TelDir&BG 83-84*
Lake Telephone Co. [of United Savings Association] - Memorial Point Community, TX - *BrCabYB 84*
Lake Telephone Co. Inc. [of United Savings Association] - April Sound, TX - *BrCabYB 84*
Lake Texoma Cable TV Associates [of Northland Communications Corp.] - Tishomingo, OK - *BrCabYB 84; Tel&CabFB 84C*
Lake TV Cable - Big Lake, WA - *BrCabYB 84; Tel&CabFB 84C*
Lake TV Cable - Lake Goodwin, WA - *Tel&CabFB 84C*
Lake TV Cable - Lakewood, WA - *BrCabYB 84*
Lake TV Cable - Seven Lakes, WA - *BrCabYB 84*
Lake Video Service Ltd. - Lake Cowichan, BC, Canada - *BrCabYB 84*
Lake View Press - Chicago, IL - *ArtMar 84; BoPubDir 4, 5; LitMag&SmPr 83-84; WritMar 84*

Lake View Resort - Lake View, IA - *BaconPubCkNews 84; Ed&PubIntYB 82*
Lake Villa Record [of Grayslake Lakeland Publishers Inc.] - Grayslake, IL - *NewsDir 84*
Lake Villa Record - Lake Villa, IL - *AyerDirPub 83; Ed&PubIntYB 82*
Lake Villa Record - *See* Lakeland Publishers Inc.
Lake Village Chicot Spectator - Lake Village, AR - *BaconPubCkNews 84*
Lake Village Northern Star - Lake Village, IN - *BaconPubCkNews 84*
Lake Wales Highlander - Lake Wales, FL - *BaconPubCkNews 84; NewsDir 84*
Lake Wales News [of Brice Printing Co.] - Lake Wales, FL - *BaconPubCkNews 84; Ed&PubIntYB 82; NewsDir 84*
Lake Windermere Valley Echo, The - Invermere, BC, Canada - *AyerDirPub 83*
Lake Worth Coastal Observer - *See* Lake Worth Herald Press Inc.
Lake Worth Herald - *See* Lake Worth Herald Press Inc.
Lake Worth Herald & Coastal Observer - Lake Worth, FL - *Ed&PubIntYB 82; NewsDir 84*
Lake Worth Herald Press Inc. - Lake Worth, FL - *BaconPubCkNews 84*
Lake Worth News [of Suburban Newspapers Inc.] - Ft. Worth, TX - *AyerDirPub 83; NewsDir 84*
Lake Worth News - *See* Suburban Newspapers Inc.
Lake Zurich Frontier Enterprise - Lake Zurich, IL - *Ed&PubIntYB 82; NewsDir 84*
Lake Zurich Frontier Enterprise - *See* Frontier Publishing Corp.
Lake Zurich Herald - Lake Zurich, IL - *Ed&PubIntYB 82*
Lake Zurich Herald [of Mundelein Paddock Circle Newspapers Inc.] - Mundelein, IL - *NewsDir 84*
Lake Zurich Herald - *See* Paddock Publications
Lakedale Telephone Co. [Aff. of Communications Sales & Leasing Inc.] - Annandale, MN - *TelDir&BG 83-84*
Lakefield Standard - Lakefield, MN - *BaconPubCkNews 84; Ed&PubIntYB 82*
Lakefield Telephone Co. - Newton, WI - *TelDir&BG 83-84*
Lakehead Living - Thunder Bay, ON, Canada - *AyerDirPub 83; Ed&PubIntYB 82*
Lakeland Boating - Chicago, IL - *BaconPubCkMag 84*
Lakeland Boating [of Petersen Publishing Co.] - Ann Arbor, MI - *ArtMar 84; MagDir 84; MagIndMarPl 82-83; WritMar 84*
Lakeland Cable TV Inc. [of Canadian Valley Telephone Co.] - Canadian, OK - *Tel&CabFB 84C*
Lakeland Cablevision Inc. - Detroit Lakes, MN - *Tel&CabFB 84C p.1687*
Lakeland Computing Service Inc. - Fontana, WI - *ADAPSOMemDir 83-84*
Lakeland Lanier County News - Lakeland, GA - *BaconPubCkNews 84*
Lakeland Publishers Inc. - Grayslake, IL - *BaconPubCkNews 84*
Lakeland Shopper - Alexandria, MN - *AyerDirPub 83*
Lakeland Times - Minocqua, WI - *AyerDirPub 83; Ed&PubIntYB 82*
Lakeland Today - *See* Today Newspapers
Lakeport Lake County Record-Bee - Lakeport, CA - *BaconPubCkNews 84; NewsDir 84*
Lakeridge Press - Forest, VA - *BoPubDir 4, 5*
Lakes Cable TV Inc. - Lakefield, MN - *BrCabYB 84*
Lakes Cablevision Inc. - McHenry, IL - *BrCabYB 84; Tel&CabFB 84C*
Lakes Cablevision Inc. - Round Lake Beach, IL - *BrCabYB 84*
Lakes Countryside [of Barrington Press Inc.] - Barrington, IL - *AyerDirPub 83; NewsDir 84*
Lakes Countryside - Island Lake, IL - *Ed&PubIntYB 82*
Lakes District News - Burns Lake, BC, Canada - *Ed&PubIntYB 82*
Lakes Publishing Co. Inc. - Detroit Lakes, MN - *BaconPubCkNews 84*
Lakeshore Cablevision - Iva, SC - *Tel&CabFB 84C*
Lakeshore Cablevision - Two Rivers, WI - *BrCabYB 84; Tel&CabFB 84C*
Lakeshore Chronicle - Manitowoc, WI - *Ed&PubIntYB 82*
Lakeshore Chronicle - Two Rivers, WI - *AyerDirPub 83*
Lakeshore Communications - La Porte, IN - *Tel&CabFB 84C*
Lakeshore Community Television Ltd. - Terrace Bay, ON, Canada - *BrCabYB 84*
Lakeshore Courier - Stevensville, MI - *AyerDirPub 83*
Lakeshore Flashes - Allegan, MI - *AyerDirPub 83*
Lakeshore Master Antenna Corp. [of New Channels Corp.] - Greenville, AL - *BrCabYB 84*
Lakeshore Penny Saver - Fredonia, NY - *AyerDirPub 83*
Lakeshore Telephone Co. - Cecil, WI - *TelDir&BG 83-84*
Lakeside Cable TV Inc. [of Tar River Communications Inc.] - Mooresville, NC - *Tel&CabFB 84C*
Lakeside Cablevision - Fond du Lac, WI - *BrCabYB 84; Tel&CabFB 84C*
Lakeside Cablevision - Sheboygan, WI - *BrCabYB 84; Tel&CabFB 84C*
Lakeside Leader - Slave Lake, AB, Canada - *AyerDirPub 83; Ed&PubIntYB 82*
Lakeside Pennysaver - Mission Viejo, CA - *AyerDirPub 83*
Lakeside Review, The - Roy, UT - *Ed&PubIntYB 82*
Lakeside Telephone Co. Inc. [Aff. of Continental Telecom Inc.] - Whitehouse, TX - *TelDir&BG 83-84*
Lakeview Cable TV - Runaway Bay, TX - *Tel&CabFB 84C*
Lakeview Enterprise - Lakeview, MI - *Ed&PubIntYB 82; NewsDir 84*
Lakeview Lake County Examiner - Lakeview, OR - *BaconPubCkNews 84*
Lakeview Pennysaver - Rockville Centre, NY - *AyerDirPub 83*
Lakeview Times-Enterprise - Lakeview, MI - *BaconPubCkNews 84*
Lakeview TV Inc. - Lakeview, OR - *BrCabYB 84; Tel&CabFB 84C*
Lakeville Journal - Lakeville, CT - *BaconPubCkNews 84; Ed&PubIntYB 82; NewsDir 84*
Lakeway Cablevision Inc. - Lake Brownwood, TX - *BrCabYB 84; Tel&CabFB 84C*
Lakewood Books Inc. - Clearwater, FL - *LitMarPl 83, 84*
Lakewood Books Inc. - New York, NY - *WritMar 84*
Lakewood Cable TV [of Community Tele-Communications Inc.] - Lakewood, CO - *Tel&CabFB 84C*
Lakewood Clarion [of The Paramount Journal] - Paramount, CA - *NewsDir 84*
Lakewood Herald American - Lakewood, CA - *Ed&PubIntYB 82*
Lakewood Herald American - South Gate, CA - *AyerDirPub 83*
Lakewood Herald American - *See* Hearst Community Newspapers
Lakewood Publications Inc. - Minneapolis, MN - *DirMarMP 83*
Lakewood Rural Telephone Co. - Barnesville, PA - *TelDir&BG 83-84*
Lakewood Sentinel - *See* Sentinel Newspapers
Lakewood South Jefferson Sun [of Jeffco Publications Inc.] - Golden, CO - *NewsDir 84*
Lakewood South Jefferson Sun - *See* Jeffco Publications
Lakewood Sun Post [of Sun Newspapers] - Cleveland, OH - *AyerDirPub 83; NewsDir 84*
Lakewood Sun Post - Lakewood, OH - *Ed&PubIntYB 82*
Lakewood Sun Post - *See* Sun Newspapers
Lakewood Television Inc. [of Storer Cable Communications Inc.] - Point Clear, AL - *BrCabYB 84*
Lakewood Town News - Lakewood, NJ - *Ed&PubIntYB 82*
Lakin Independent - Lakin, KS - *BaconPubCkNews 84; Ed&PubIntYB 82; NewsDir 84*
Lakota American - Lakota, ND - *BaconPubCkNews 84; Ed&PubIntYB 82*
Lakside Telephone Co. - Champaign, IL - *TelDir&BG 83-84*
Lakstun Press - Bensalem, PA - *BoPubDir 4, 5*
L'Alimentation au Quebec - Montreal, PQ, Canada - *BaconPubCkMag 84*
Lally, McFarland & Pantello - New York, NY - *AdAge 3-28-84; StaDirAdAg 2-84*
LAMA Books [Aff. of Leo A. Meyer Associates Inc.] - Hayward, CA - *BoPubDir 5*
Lamagna, Joseph - Yonkers, NY - *BoPubDir 5*
Lamar Cable TV Inc. [of Bailey Cable TV Inc.] - Mendenhall, MS - *Tel&CabFB 84C*
Lamar CablePartners [of Lamar Communications Inc.] - Crystal Springs, MS - *BrCabYB 84*
Lamar Cablepartners Nineteen Eighty - Hazlehurst, MS - *BrCabYB 84*
Lamar Cablesystems Inc. - Apalachicola, FL - *BrCabYB 84*
Lamar Communications Inc. - Jackson, MS - *BrCabYB 84 p.D-303*

Lamar County Echo - Paris, TX - *AyerDirPub 83; Ed&PubIntYB 82; NewsDir 84*
Lamar County Leader - Sulligent, AL - *AyerDirPub 83; Ed&PubIntYB 82*
Lamar County News - Purvis, MS - *AyerDirPub 83; Ed&PubIntYB 82*
Lamar County Telephone Co. Inc. [Aff. of Mid-South Telephone Co. Inc.] - Millport, AL - *TelDir&BG 83-84*
Lamar Daily News [of Betz Publishing Co. Inc.] - Lamar, CO - *NewsDir 84*
Lamar Daily News & Holly Chieftain - Lamar, CO - *BaconPubCkNews 84*
Lamar Democrat - Vernon, AL - *AyerDirPub 83; Ed&PubIntYB 82*
Lamar Democrat - Lamar, MO - *AyerDirPub 83; BaconPubCkNews 84; Ed&PubIntYB 82; NewsDir 84*
Lamar Instruments - Redondo Beach, CA - *MicrocomMPl 83, 84*
Lamar Leader - Sulligent, AL - *NewsDir 84*
Lamar Tri State Daily News - Lamar, CO - *AyerDirPub 83*
Lamar Tri State Trader, The - Lamar, CO - *AyerDirPub 83*
LaMarca Direct Marketing [Div. of LaMarca Group Inc.] - New York, NY - *StaDirAdAg 2-84*
Lamarca Group Inc. - New York, NY - *StaDirAdAg 2-84*
Lamb - London, England - *LitMag&SmPr 83-84*
Lamb & Associates Inc. - Shreveport, LA - *StaDirAdAg 2-84*
Lamb County Leader-News [of Roberts Publishing Co.] - Littlefield, TX - *AyerDirPub 83; Ed&PubIntYB 82; NewsDir 84*
Lamb Enterprises Inc. - Toledo, OH - *Tel&CabFB 84S*
Lambda Rising Inc. - Washington, DC - *BoPubDir 4, 5*
Lambe Advertising Agency, Laura - Virginia Beach, VA - *StaDirAdAg 2-84*
Lambert & Feasley Inc. - New York, NY - *StaDirAdAg 2-84*
Lambert, Charles S. - Destrehan, LA - *Tel&CabFB 84C p.1687*
Lambert Marketing Services, William - New York, NY - *HBIndAd&MS 82-83*
Lambert Studios, Harold M. - Philadelphia, PA - *MagIndMarPl 82-83*
Lamberton Cable TV - Lamberton, MN - *BrCabYB 84*
Lamberton News - Lamberton, MN - *BaconPubCkNews 84; Ed&PubIntYB 82*
Lambertville Beacon-Record - Lambertville, NJ - *BaconPubCkNews 84*
Lambertville Journal Herald - Lambertville, MI - *BaconPubCkNews 84*
Lambesis & Associates Inc. - Phoenix, AZ - *StaDirAdAg 2-84*
Lambeth, James - Fayetteville, AR - *BoPubDir 4, 5*
Lambeth Press - New York, NY - *BoPubDir 4 Sup, 5*
Lambrecht Publications - Duncan, BC, Canada - *BoPubDir 4, 5*
Lambton County Gazette - Sarnia, ON, Canada - *AyerDirPub 83*
Lambton County Historical Society - Sarnia, ON, Canada - *BoPubDir 4, 5*
Lame Johnny Press - Hermosa, SD - *BoPubDir 4, 5; LitMag&SmPr 83-84; WritMar 84*
Lamesa Cable TV - Lamesa, TX - *BrCabYB 84; Tel&CabFB 84C*
Lamesa Press-Reporter - Lamesa, TX - *BaconPubCkNews 84; Ed&PubIntYB 82; NewsDir 84*
Laminex Inc. - Charlotte, NC - *AvMarPl 83*
Lamishpaha - New York, NY - *NewsDir 84*
Lamm-Morada Publishing Co. Inc. [Aff. of Lotsa Watts Video Productions] - Stockton, CA - *BoPubDir 4, 5*
Lamon Records - Charlotte, NC - *BillIntBG 83-84*
Lamoni Chronicle - Lamoni, IA - *BaconPubCkNews 84; Ed&PubIntYB 82*
Lamont Leader - Lamont, IA - *BaconPubCkNews 84; Ed&PubIntYB 82*
Lamont Reporter - Lamont, CA - *AyerDirPub 83; BaconPubCkNews 84; Ed&PubIntYB 82; NewsDir 84*
LaMonte Cable Services Inc. [of Comm Management Inc.] - Concordia, MO - *BrCabYB 84*
Lampack Agency Inc., Peter - New York, NY - *LitMarPl 83, 84*
Lampasas Dispatch - Lampasas, TX - *Ed&PubIntYB 82*
Lampasas Dispatch - *See* Hill Country Publishing Co. Inc.
Lampasas Record - Lampasas, TX - *Ed&PubIntYB 82*
Lampasas Record - *See* Hill Country Publishing Co. Inc.
Lampe Communications Inc. - Orchard Lake, MI - *DirPRFirms 83*
Lampe Communications Inc. - West Bloomfield, MI - *ArtMar 84*
Lampkin Associates Inc. - Chicago, IL - *DirPRFirms 83*
Lamplighters-Opera West Foundation - San Francisco, CA - *BoPubDir 4 Sup, 5*
Lamplighters Roadway Press - Freestone, CA - *BoPubDir 4, 5*
Lampus Press - Cape May, NJ - *BoPubDir 5*
LAN - Boston, MA - *DirOnDB Spring 84*
Lancaster Antelope Valley Ledger-Gazette - Lancaster, CA - *NewsDir 84*
Lancaster Cable [of Communications Systems Inc.] - Lancaster, KY - *Tel&CabFB 84C*
Lancaster Central Record - Lancaster, KY - *BaconPubCkNews 84; Ed&PubIntYB 82*
Lancaster Coos County Democrat - Lancaster, NH - *BaconPubCkNews 84*
Lancaster County Fireman's Association - Lancaster, PA - *BoPubDir 4 Sup, 5*
Lancaster Eagle-Gazette - Lancaster, OH - *BaconPubCkNews 84; Ed&PubIntYB 82; NewsDir 84*
Lancaster Enterprise [of Bee Publications Inc.] - Williamsville, NY - *NewsDir 84*
Lancaster Enterprise - *See* Bee Publications Inc.
Lancaster Enterprise & Journal - Lancaster, NY - *Ed&PubIntYB 82*
Lancaster Excelsior - Lancaster, MO - *BaconPubCkNews 84; Ed&PubIntYB 82*
Lancaster Fairfield Advertiser - Lancaster, OH - *AyerDirPub 83*
Lancaster Farming [of Lititz Record Express] - Lititz, PA - *AyerDirPub 83; BaconPubCkMag 84; Ed&PubIntYB 82; MagDir 84; NewsDir 84; WritMar 84*
Lancaster Grant County Herald Independent - Lancaster, WI - *BaconPubCkNews 84; NewsDir 84*
Lancaster Intelligencer Journal - Lancaster, PA - *BaconPubCkNews 84; NewsDir 84*
Lancaster Journal [of DeSoto Journal Publishing Co.] - De Soto, TX - *NewsDir 84*
Lancaster Leader - Dallas, TX - *AyerDirPub 83*
Lancaster Leader & Courier - Dallas, TX - *NewsDir 84*
Lancaster Leader & Courier - *See* Zauber Publishing
Lancaster, Miller & Schnobrich Publishers - Berkeley, CA - *LitMarPl 84; WritMar 84*
Lancaster-Miller Publishers - Berkeley, CA - *ArtMar 84; LitMarPl 83*
Lancaster New Era - Lancaster, PA - *BaconPubCkNews 84; Ed&PubIntYB 82*
Lancaster News - Lancaster, SC - *BaconPubCkNews 84; Ed&PubIntYB 82; NewsDir 84*
Lancaster News [of Duncanville Suburban] - Duncanville, TX - *NewsDir 84*
Lancaster News - Lancaster, TX - *AyerDirPub 83; BaconPubCkNews 84*
Lancaster Newspapers Inc. - *See* Steinman Stations
Lancaster Press Inc. - Lancaster, PA - *MagIndMarPl 82-83*
Lancaster Telephone Co. - Lancaster, SC - *TelDir&BG 83-84*
Lance - Elmvale, ON, Canada - *Ed&PubIntYB 82*
Lance Studios - New York, NY - *AvMarPl 83*
Lance, The - Winnipeg, MB, Canada - *AyerDirPub 83*
Lancelot Press - Hantsport, NS, Canada - *BoPubDir 4, 5; LitMarPl 83, 84; WritMar 84*
Lancer Communications [Div. of Dittman Communications Ltd.] - New York, NY - *ArtMar 84; AvMarPl 83*
Lancer Militaria - Sims, AR - *LitMag&SmPr 83-84*
Lancet - Boston, MA - *BaconPubCkMag 84; MagDir 84; MagIndMarPl 82-83*
Lancet - London, England - *DirOnDB Spring 84*
Lanco Data Processing Services Inc. - Tempe, AZ - *ADAPSOMemDir 83-84*
Land & Water [of Rasch Publishing] - Ft. Dodge, IA - *BaconPubCkMag 84; MagDir 84*
Land Economics - Madison, WI - *MagIndMarPl 82-83*
Land Educational Associates Foundation Inc. - Stevens Point, WI - *BoPubDir 4, 5*
Land Innovation - Maple Plain, MN - *MicrocomMPl 84*
Land-Line - Grain Valley, MO - *MagDir 84*
Land-Line - Oak Grove, MO - *BaconPubCkMag 84*
Land Mobile Product News - Overland Park, KS - *BaconPubCkMag 84*
Land O' Jazz Records - New Orleans, LA - *BillIntBG 83-84*

Land Research Group Inc., T. H. - Mt. Kisco, NY - *IntDirMarRes 83*
Land, The - Mankato, MN - *BaconPubCkMag 84; MagDir 84*
Land Use & Ownership Data Base [of San Francisco Planning & Urban Research Association] - San Francisco, CA - *EISS 5-84 Sup*
Land Use Planning Report - Silver Spring, MD - *DirOnDB Spring 84*
Land Use Planning Report [of NewsNet Inc.] - Bryn Mawr, PA - *DataDirOnSer 84*
Landart Systems Inc. [Subs. of CM & M Group Inc.] - New York, NY - *DataDirOnSer 84; EISS 83*
Landau Book Co. Inc. - Long Beach, NY - *BoPubDir 4 Sup, 5; LitMarPl 83, 84*
Lande Promotions Inc., M. - New York, NY - *LitMarPl 84*
Landeck Productions, Philip - New York, NY - *Tel&CabFB 84C*
Lander & Associates - Sherman Oaks, CA - *StaDirAdAg 2-84*
Lander & Associates Ltd., R. - Vancouver, BC, Canada - *DirInfWP 82*
Lander Cable TV [of Community Tele-Communications Inc.] - Lander, WY - *BrCabYB 84; Tel&CabFB 84C*
Lander Wyoming State Journal [of Swift-Pioneer Newspapers] - Lander, WY - *BaconPubCkNews 84; NewsDir 84*
Landers & Partners Inc. - St. Petersburg, FL - *StaDirAdAg 2-84*
Landes, Burton R. - Trappe, PA - *BoPubDir 4, 5*
Landfall Press Inc. - Dayton, OH - *BoPubDir 5*
Landis, George E. - Cromwell, CT - *LitMarPl 84*
Landmann Associates Inc. - Madison, WI - *LitMarPl 83, 84*
Landmark - Platte City, MO - *AyerDirPub 83; Ed&PubIntYB 82*
Landmark Advertising & Public Relations - Whippany, NJ - *StaDirAdAg 2-84*
Landmark Book Co. - New York, NY - *BoPubDir 4 Sup, 5*
Landmark Books - Minneapolis, MN - *LitMarPl 83, 84; WritMar 84*
Landmark Cablevision - Olathe, KS - *BrCabYB 84*
Landmark Cablevision - Independence, MO - *BrCabYB 84; Tel&CabFB 84C*
Landmark Cablevision Associates - New York, NY - *BrCabYB 84 p.D-303; Tel&CabFB 84C p.1687*
Landmark Cablevision Associates - Brownfield, TX - *BrCabYB 84*
Landmark Cablevision Associates - Littlefield, TX - *BrCabYB 84*
Landmark Cablevision Associates - Morton, TX - *BrCabYB 84*
Landmark Cablevision of Brownfield - Brownfield, TX - *Tel&CabFB 84C*
Landmark Cablevision of Levelland [of Landmark Cablevision Associates] - Levelland, TX - *Tel&CabFB 84C*
Landmark Cablevision of Littlefield - Littlefield, TX - *Tel&CabFB 84C*
Landmark Cablevision of Morton - Morton, TX - *Tel&CabFB 84C*
Landmark Communications - Norfolk, VA - *AdAge 6-28-84; BrCabYB 84 p.D-303; Ed&PubIntYB 82; KnowInd 83; Tel&CabFB 84S*
Landmark Enterprises - Rancho Cordova, CA - *BoPubDir 5*
Landmark Group Inc. - Tinton Falls, NJ - *DirMarMP 83*
Landmark Publishing Corp. - South Hero, VT - *BoPubDir 4, 5*
Landon Associates Inc. - New York, NY - *LitMarPl 83, 84*
Landon Radio Stations, Alf M. - Topeka, KS - *BrCabYB 84*
Landor Associates - San Francisco, CA - *HBIndAd&MS 82-83*
Landrum News Leader - Landrum, SC - *BaconPubCkNews 84; NewsDir 84*
Landry, Bolder - Buena Park, CA - *BoPubDir 4, 5*
Lands End Books - Gloucester, VA - *BoPubDir 4, 5*
Landsburg Productions, Alan - Los Angeles, CA - *TelAl 83, 84; Tel&CabFB 84C*
Landscape - Berkeley, CA - *LitMag&SmPr 83-84*
Landscape & Irrigation - Encino, CA - *BaconPubCkMag 84; MagDir 84*
Landscape Architecture [of American Society of Landscape Architects] - Louisville, KY - *BaconPubCkMag 84; MagDir 84; MagIndMarPl 82-83*
Landscape Architecture Foundation - Washington, DC - *BoPubDir 5*
Landscape Contractor, The [of Illinois Landscape Contractors Association] - Batavia, IL - *BaconPubCkMag 84; MagDir 84; WritMar 84*
Landscape Industry [of Brantwood Publications Inc.] - Elm Grove, WI - *MagDir 84*
Landscape Ontario - Mississauga, ON, Canada - *BaconPubCkMag 84*
Landscape Trades - Mississauga, ON, Canada - *BaconPubCkMag 84*
Landscaping Lawns & Gardens - Amawalk, NY - *BaconPubCkMag 84*
Landslide Records Inc. - Atlanta, GA - *BillIntBG 83-84*
Landsman Media - New York, NY - *BrCabYB 84*
Lane Advertising Inc., David J. - Philadelphia, PA - *StaDirAdAg 2-84*
Lane & Associates Inc. - La Jolla, CA - *WritMar 84*
Lane & Associates Inc. - San Diego, CA - *BoPubDir 4, 5*
Lane & Associates Inc. - Cheyenne, WY - *DirPRFirms 83*
Lane & Associates Inc., E. B. - Phoenix, AZ - *StaDirAdAg 2-84*
Lane & Coady Public Relations - New York, NY - *DirPRFirms 83*
Lane & Huff Advertising - San Diego, CA - *StaDirAdAg 2-84*
Lane & Leslie Advertising Agency Inc. - Wichita, KS - *ArtMar 84; StaDirAdAg 2-84*
Lane & Young - Jersey City, NJ - *AvMarPl 83*
Lane County Cablevision Inc. - Veneta, OR - *Tel&CabFB 84C*
Lane Inc., J. J. - New York, NY - *DirPRFirms 83*
Lane Music, Christy - Madison, TN - *BillIntBG 83-84*
Lane Pictures Inc., Don - New York, NY - *ArtMar 84; AvMarPl 83; TelAl 83, 84; Tel&CabFB 84C*
Lane Press Inc., The - Burlington, VT - *LitMarPl 83, 84; MagIndMarPl 82-83*
Lane Publishing Co. - Menlo Park, CA - *KnowInd 83; LitMarPl 83, 84*
Lane Publishing, Joe - Evergreen, CO - *BoPubDir 4, 5*
Lane Scientific Systems Ltd. - Petersfield, England - *MicrocomSwDir 1*
Lane Syndicate, Lydia - Burbank, CA - *Ed&PubIntYB 82*
Lane Video Enterprises Inc., Philip J. - Los Angeles, CA - *StaDirAdAg 2-84*
Lanesboro Leader - Lanesboro, MN - *Ed&PubIntYB 82*
Lanett Valley Times-News [of Valley Newspapers Inc.] - Lanett, AL - *BaconPubCkNews 84; NewsDir 84*
Laney-Smith Inc. - Charlotte, NC - *StaDirAdAg 2-84*
Lanford Estate, T. B. - Shreveport, LA - *Tel&CabFB 84S*
Lanford Stations, T. B. - Alexandria, LA - *BrCabYB 84*
LanFranco Corp. - San Francisco, CA - *MagIndMarPl 82-83*
Lang Advertising Associates Inc. - Vineland, NJ - *StaDirAdAg 2-84*
Lang Advertising Inc., Raymond I. - San Carlos, CA - *AdAge 3-28-84; StaDirAdAg 2-84*
Lang, Fisher & Stashower Advertising - Cleveland, OH - *AdAge 3-28-84; ArtMar 84; BrCabYB 84; StaDirAdAg 2-84*
Lang Inc., Ed - Dayton, OH - *ArtMar 84; AvMarPl 83*
Lang Systems Inc. - Menlo Park, CA - *WhoWMicrocom 83*
Lang TV Ltd., Fred - Kirkland Lake, ON, Canada - *BrCabYB 84*
Langdale Press - Gananoque, ON, Canada - *BoPubDir 4, 5*
Langdon Cable TV - Langdon, ND - *BrCabYB 84; Tel&CabFB 84C*
Langdon Cable TV Inc. - Carrington, ND - *BrCabYB 84*
Langdon Cavalier County Republican - Langdon, ND - *BaconPubCkNews 84; NewsDir 84*
Langdon, Eleanor - Chicago, IL - *LitMarPl 83, 84*
Langdon Publications, Larry - Cottage Grove, OR - *BoPubDir 4 Sup, 5; LitMag&SmPr 83-84*
Langdon Republican - Langdon, ND - *Ed&PubIntYB 82*
Lange Medical Publications [Subs. of Wadsworth Inc.] - Los Altos, CA - *LitMarPl 83, 84*
Langer Associates Inc., Judith - New York, NY - *IntDirMarRes 83*
Langerman Co., Hal - Center Square, PA - *AdAge 3-28-84; DirMarMP 83; StaDirAdAg 2-84*
Langford Bugle - Langford, SD - *BaconPubCkNews 84; Ed&PubIntYB 82*
Langhorne Bucks County Advance - *See* Intercounty Newspaper Group
Langie Audio Visual Co. Inc. - East Rochester, NY - *AvMarPl 83*
Langley Music Co. - New York, NY - *BillIntBG 83-84*
Langley South Whidbey Record - Langley, WA - *BaconPubCkNews 84*

Langley-St. Clair Instrumentation Systems Inc. - New York, NY - *MicrocomMPl 84*
Langley Times - Langley, BC, Canada - *AyerDirPub 83*
Langman, Ida K. - Atlantic City, NJ - *LitMarPl 83, 84; MagIndMarPl 82-83*
Langton Information Systems Ltd. - London, England - *EISS 83; InfIndMarPl 83*
Language - Los Angeles, CA - *MagDir 84*
Language - Washington, DC - *MagIndMarPl 82-83*
Language - New York, NY - *BoPubDir 4, 5; LitMag&SmPr 83-84*
Language & Language Behavior Abstracts [of Dialog Information Services Inc.] - Palo Alto, CA - *DataDirOnSer 84*
Language & Language Behavior Abstracts [of Sociological Abstracts Inc.] - San Diego, CA - *CompReadDB 82; DirOnDB Spring 84; EISS 83; OnBibDB 3*
Language Arts [of National Council of Teachers of English] - Urbana, IL - *BaconPubCkMag 84; LitMarPl 83, 84*
Language Catalog [of University of Alberta] - Edmonton, AB, Canada - *DataDirOnSer 84*
Language Center Inc., The - South Orange, NJ - *LitMarPl 84; MagIndMarPl 82-83*
Language Guild Institute Inc. - New York, NY - *MagIndMarPl 82-83*
Language Learning Systems Inc. - Alexandria, VA - *BoPubDir 4, 5*
Language Service Inc., The - Hasting-on-Hudson, NY - *MagIndMarPl 82-83*
Lanier Business Products - Atlanta, GA - *DataDirSup 7-83; Datamation 6-83; Top100Al 83; WhoWMicrocom 83*
Lanier Business Systems - Atlanta, GA - *DirInfWP 82*
Lanier County News - Lakeland, GA - *Ed&PubIntYB 82*
Laning/Magnone Media - Pasadena, MD - *Tel&CabFB 84C*
Lanis Music Inc., Stuart - Los Angeles, CA - *BillIntBG 83-84*
Lankenau Associates Advertising - Indianapolis, IN - *MagIndMarPl 82-83*
Lankford & Associates - Indianapolis, IN - *DirInfWP 82*
Lanman Cos., The - Washington, DC - *MagIndMarPl 82-83*
Lanor Records - Church Point, LA - *BillIntBG 83-84*
Lansdale, Carr & Baum - Irvine, CA - *AdAge 3-28-84; StaDirAdAg 2-84*
Lansdale Reporter, The [of The Gannett Co.] - Lansdale, PA - *NewsDir 84*
Lansdale Town & Country - Lansdale, PA - *BaconPubCkNews 84*
Lansdowne & Partners, David K. [Aff. of Consortium Group Ltd.] - London, ON, Canada - *BoPubDir 4 Sup, 5*
Lansdowne Press Inc. [Subs. of The Rigby Group] - New York, NY - *LitMarPl 83, 84*
L'Anse Sentinel - L'Anse, MI - *BaconPubCkNews 84; Ed&PubIntYB 82; NewsDir 84*
Lansford Publishing Co. Inc. - San Jose, CA - *AvMarPl 83*
Lansing Allamakee Journal & Mirror - Lansing, IA - *BaconPubCkNews 84*
Lansing Catholic Weekly, The - Flint, MI - *NewsDir 84*
Lansing Computer Institute - East Lansing, MI - *MicrocomMPl 83, 84; WhoWMicrocom 83*
Lansing Labor News [of United Auto Workers Lansing Locals] - Lansing, MI - *NewsDir 84*
Lansing Leader - Lansing, KS - *NewsDir 84*
Lansing Magazine - Lansing, MI - *BaconPubCkMag 84*
Lansing Pointer-Economist - South Holland, IL - *AyerDirPub 83*
Lansing Pointer-Economist - *See* Pointer-Economist Newspapers
Lansing, Raymond - Cheyenne, WY - *DirPRFirms 83*
Lansing State Journal [of Federated Publications Inc.] - Lansing, MI - *BaconPubCkNews 84; Ed&PubIntYB 82; LitMarPl 83, 84; NewsDir 84*
Lansing Suburban Newspapers [of Suburban Communications] - Grand Ledge, MI - *NewsDir 84*
Lansing Sun Journal [of Liverpool Daily Post & Echo] - Lansing, IL - *BaconPubCkNews 84; Ed&PubIntYB 82; NewsDir 84*
Lanson/Tremaine - Tigard, OR - *LitMarPl 83, 84*
Lantech Systems Inc. - Dallas, TX - *MicrocomMPl 84*
Lantern Books - Farwell, MN - *BoPubDir 4 Sup, 5*
Lantern Light Music - Chillicothe, OH - *BillIntBG 83-84*
Lantern Press Inc. - Mt. Vernon, NY - *BoPubDir 4, 5*
Lanting, Frans - Santa Cruz, CA - *LitMarPl 84*
Lantz Office Inc., The - New York, NY - *LitMarPl 83, 84*
Lantz Productions Inc., Walter - Hollywood, CA - *Tel&CabFB 84C*
Lapeer County Press - Lapeer, MI - *AyerDirPub 83; BaconPubCkNews 84; Ed&PubIntYB 82; NewsDir 84*
Lapel Review - Lapel, IN - *Ed&PubIntYB 82*
Lapidary Journal - San Diego, CA - *BaconPubCkMag 84; MagDir 84; MagIndMarPl 82-83; WritMar 84*
Lapidary Journal (Book Dept.) - San Diego, CA - *BoPubDir 5*
Lapin & Associates, Jackie - Woodland Hills, CA - *DirPRFirms 83*
Lapine Inc., Mike - Cleveland, OH - *DirPRFirms 83*
Lapis [of Lapis Educational Association Inc.] - Homewood, IL - *LitMag&SmPr 83-84*
Lapis Educational Association Inc. - Homewood, IL - *LitMag&SmPr 83-84*
Laplace L'Observateur - Laplace, LA - *Ed&PubIntYB 82; NewsDir 84*
LaPointe Schott & Smith Inc. - San Francisco, CA - *StaDirAdAg 2-84*
Lapolla Publishing Properties, Paul - Del Mar, CA - *LitMarPl 83, 84*
LaPorte City Telephone Co. - LaPorte City, IA - *TelDir&BG 83-84*
Lapp Associates Inc. - Birmingham, MI - *DirPRFirms 83*
Lapp Princess Press Ltd. - New York, NY - *BoPubDir 4 Sup, 5*
L'Appel - Ste. Foy, PQ, Canada - *Ed&PubIntYB 82*
Laramie Boomerang - Laramie, WY - *BaconPubCkNews 84; Ed&PubIntYB 82; NewsDir 84*
Laramie Community TV Co. [of Community Tele-Communications Inc.] - Laramie, WY - *BrCabYB 84; Tel&CabFB 84C*
Laranmark Inc. - Neshkoro, WI - *LitMag&SmPr 83-84*
Laranmark Press - Neshkoro, WI - *WritMar 84*
Larchmont Books [Aff. of Communication Channels Inc.] - New York, NY - *BoPubDir 4, 5*
Lardas Advertising, Christopher - New York, NY - *StaDirAdAg 2-84*
Lardis, McCurdy & Co. - Meriden, CT - *AdAge 3-28-84*
Lardis, McCurdy & Co. - New Haven, CT - *StaDirAdAg 2-84*
Lareau, George A. - Urbana, IL - *MagIndMarPl 82-83*
Laredo Citizen - Laredo, TX - *AyerDirPub 83; BaconPubCkNews 84; Ed&PubIntYB 82; NewsDir 84*
Laredo Morning Times - Laredo, TX - *BaconPubCkNews 84; NewsDir 84*
Laredo News - Laredo, TX - *BaconPubCkNews 84; Ed&PubIntYB 82; NewsDir 84*
Laredo Systems Inc. - Santa Clara, CA - *MicrocomMPl 84*
Laredo Times - Laredo, TX - *Ed&PubIntYB 82; NewsDir 84*
Larence County Record, The - Mt. Vernon, MO - *Ed&PubIntYB 82*
Large Lakes Research Laboratory [of U.S. Environmental Protection Agency] - Grosse Ile, MI - *EISS 83*
L'Argenteuil - Lachute, PQ, Canada - *Ed&PubIntYB 82*
Largo & Florida Sentinel - Largo, FL - *NewsDir 84*
Largo Buyers Guide - Largo, FL - *AyerDirPub 83*
L'Argo della Stampa - Milan, Italy - *ProGuPRSer 4*
Largo Music Inc. - New York, NY - *BillIntBG 83-84*
Largo Sentinel - Largo, FL - *Ed&PubIntYB 82*
Laridae Press - Ocean City, NJ - *BoPubDir 4 Sup, 5; LitMag&SmPr 83-84*
Larimer Publications Inc. - Green Forest, AR - *BaconPubCkNews 84*
Larimi Communications Inc. - New York, NY - *BoPubDir 4, 5*
Larimore Leader - Larimore, ND - *Ed&PubIntYB 82*
Larimore Leader - *See* Ness Press Inc.
Larimore Pioneer, The - Larimore, ND - *Ed&PubIntYB 82*
Larimore Pioneer, The - *See* Community News Inc.
Lark Books [Aff. of Lark Communications] - Asheville, NC - *BoPubDir 4, 5*
Larksdale - Houston, TX - *LitMarPl 84; WritMar 84*
Larksdale Press, The - Houston, TX - *LitMag&SmPr 83-84; LitMarPl 83*
Larkspur - Monterey, KY - *BoPubDir 4, 5*
Larkspur Music Publishing Co. - Soquel, CA - *BillIntBG 83-84*
Larkspur Publications - Bowmansville, NY - *BoPubDir 4 Sup, 5; WritMar 84*
Larkspur Records - Soquel, CA - *BillIntBG 83-84*
Larlin Corp. - Marietta, GA - *LitMarPl 83, 84*

Larned Tiller & Toiler - Larned, KS - *BaconPubCkNews 84; NewsDir 84*
LaRose Productions Ltd. - New York, NY - *Tel&CabFB 84C*
Larousse & Co. Inc. [Aff. of Librairie Larousse USA Inc.] - New York, NY - *LitMarPl 83, 84*
Larratt & Associates Ltd., Richard - Demorestville, ON, Canada - *EISS 83; VideoDir 82-83*
Larsen/Elizabeth Pomada, Michael - San Francisco, CA - *LitMarPl 83, 84*
Larsen, Marjorie S. - Stockton, CA - *AvMarPl 83*
Larsen Publishing, J. - Deer Lodge, MT - *BoPubDir 4, 5*
Larsen-Readfield Telephone Co. [Aff. of Universal Telephone Inc.] - Larsen, WI - *TelDir&BG 83-84*
Larson Advertising Inc., William K. - Jamestown, NY - *StaDirAdAg 2-84*
Larson, Bateman & McAllister - Santa Barbara, CA - *AdAge 3-28-84; StaDirAdAg 2-84*
Larson Enterprises - Fountain Valley, CA - *AvMarPl 83*
Larson, Gene - Windom, MN - *Tel&CabFB 84C p.1687*
Larson Group, Brent - Ogden, UT - *BrCabYB 84*
Larson, Margaret - New York, NY - *DirPRFirms 83*
Larson Publications Inc. - Osseo, MN - *BaconPubCkNews 84*
Larson Publications Inc. [Subs. of Bokforlaget Robert Larson AB] - Burdett, NY - *LitMarPl 84*
L'Artisan - Repentigny, PQ, Canada - *Ed&PubIntYB 82*
LARU - Toronto, ON, Canada - *BoPubDir 4, 5*
LaRue County Herald News, The - Hodgenville, KY - *AyerDirPub 83; Ed&PubIntYB 82; NewsDir 84*
LaRue, H. B. - San Francisco, CA - *CabTVFinDB 83*
Larwin/Livers Associated - Huntingdon Valley, PA - *AdAge 3-28-84; StaDirAdAg 2-84*
Laryngoscope, The - St. Louis, MO - *BaconPubCkMag 84; MagDir 84*
Las Americas Publishing Co. Inc. - New York, NY - *LitMarPl 83, 84*
Las Animas Bent County Democrat - Las Animas, CO - *BaconPubCkNews 84*
Las Campanas Publications - Bernalillo, NM - *BoPubDir 5*
Las Colinas Association - Las Colinas, TX - *BrCabYB 84*
Las Cruces Bulletin - Las Cruces, NM - *Ed&PubIntYB 82*
Las Cruces MDS Co. - Las Cruces, NM - *Tel&CabFB 84C*
Las Cruces Sun-News - Las Cruces, NM - *BaconPubCkNews 84; Ed&PubIntYB 82; NewsDir 84*
Las Cruces TV Cable [of Western Communications Inc.] - Las Cruces, NM - *BrCabYB 84; Tel&CabFB 84C*
Las Noticias de Hialeah - Hialeah, FL - *AyerDirPub 83; Ed&PubIntYB 82*
Las Palmas Music - *See* Amestoy Music
LAS Systems Inc. - Lake Zurich, IL - *MicrocomMPl 84*
Las Vegas Insider, The - Henderson, NV - *LitMag&SmPr 83-84*
Las Vegas Look [of Las Vegas Valley Publishing Co.] - North Las Vegas, NV - *NewsDir 84*
Las Vegas Optic - Las Vegas, NM - *BaconPubCkNews 84; NewsDir 84*
Las Vegas Recording Studio Inc. - Las Vegas, NV - *BillIntBG 83-84*
Las Vegas Review-Journal [of Donrey Inc.] - Las Vegas, NV - *BaconPubCkNews 84; Ed&PubIntYB 82; LitMarPl 84; NewsBur 6; NewsDir 84*
Las Vegas Sun - Las Vegas, NV - *BaconPubCkNews 84; NewsDir 84*
Las Vegas Today [of Las Vegas Valley Publishing Co.] - North Las Vegas, NV - *NewsDir 84*
Las Vegas Valley Times - North Las Vegas, NV - *BaconPubCkNews 84*
Las Vegas Voice - Las Vegas, NV - *NewsDir 84*
Las Virg Agoura Valley News - Agoura, CA - *Ed&PubIntYB 82*
Las Virgenes News Enterprise - Calabasas, CA - *AyerDirPub 83; BaconPubCkNews 84; Ed&PubIntYB 82*
LaSalle Computing Inc. [Subs. of Brown Associates Inc.] - Blue Bell, PA - *WhoWMicrocom 83*
LaSalle Leader - LaSalle, CO - *Ed&PubIntYB 82*
LaSalle Messenger - Montreal, PQ, Canada - *AyerDirPub 83*
Lase Co., The - Chicago, IL - *AvMarPl 83*
Lasenda Publishers - South Laguna, CA - *BoPubDir 4, 5*
Laser Fantasy Labs - Redmond, WA - *LitMarPl 83*
Laser Focus with Fiberoptic Technology [of Advanced Technical Publishing Inc.] - Littleton, MA - *BaconPubCkMag 84; MagDir 84; WritMar 84*
Laser Focus with Fiberoptic Technology - Newton, MA - *MagIndMarPl 82-83*
Laser Media Inc. - Los Angeles, CA - *AvMarPl 83*
Laser Professional Typing, Connie J. - Long Beach, CA - *LitMarPl 83, 84*
Laser Report - Littleton, MA - *BaconPubCkMag 84*
LaserColor Laboratories [Subs. of Photo Electronics Corp.] - West Palm Beach, FL - *AvMarPl 83*
Lasers & Applications - Torrance, CA - *BaconPubCkMag 84; WritMar 84*
Lasher Agency, The Maureen - Pacific Palisades, CA - *LitMarPl 83, 84*
Lasky Associates Inc., Burton - New York, NY - *LitMarPl 83, 84; MagIndMarPl 82-83*
Lassen Advocate - Susanville, CA - *AyerDirPub 83; Ed&PubIntYB 82*
Lassen County Times - Susanville, CA - *Ed&PubIntYB 82*
L'Association pour la Teledistribution et Radio La Minerve Inc. - La Minerve, PQ, Canada - *BrCabYB 84*
Lastauto Omnibus [of Vereinigte Motor-verlage GmbH & Co. KG] - Palos Verdes Peninsula, CA - *MagDir 84*
Latah County Historical Society - Moscow, ID - *BoPubDir 4, 5*
Latah Observer - Latah, WA - *Ed&PubIntYB 82*
Late Music Co. - Berlin, NY - *BillIntBG 83-84*
Lateiner Publishing - Palm Beach, FL - *BoPubDir 4 Sup, 5*
Latham Foundation, The - Alameda, CA - *Tel&CabFB 84C*
Latham Process Corp. - New York, NY - *LitMarPl 83, 84*
Lathrop Enterprises, Norman - Wooster, OH - *BoPubDir 4, 5*
Lathrop Optimist - Lathrop, MO - *BaconPubCkNews 84; Ed&PubIntYB 82*
Lathrop Telephone Co. - Lathrop, MO - *TelDir&BG 83-84*
Latimer County News-Tribune - Wilburton, OK - *AyerDirPub 83*
Latimer County Today - Wilburton, OK - *AyerDirPub 83*
Latin Admerica Inc. - Miami, FL - *Ed&PubIntYB 82*
Latin America Data Bank [of Data Resources Inc.] - Lexington, MA - *DBBus 82*
Latin America Forecast [of Chase Econometrics/Interactive Data Corp.] - Waltham, MA - *DataDirOnSer 84*
Latin America Forecast - Bala Cynwyd, PA - *DirOnDB Spring 84*
Latin American Center for Economic & Social Documentation [of Economic Commission for Latin America] - Santiago, Chile - *EISS 83*
Latin American Energy Report [of NewsNet Inc.] - Bryn Mawr, PA - *DataDirOnSer 84*
Latin American Literary Review - Pittsburgh, PA - *LitMag&SmPr 83-84*
Latin American Literary Review Press - Pittsburgh, PA - *LitMag&SmPr 83-84*
Latin American Music Co. - *See* TIM
Latin American Music Review - Austin, TX - *MagDir 84*
Latin American Newsletters Ltd. - London, England - *EISS 83*
Latin American Perspectives - Riverside, CA - *LitMag&SmPr 83-84*
Latin American Population Documentation System [of United Nations Latin American Demographic Center] - Santiago, Chile - *CompReadDB 82; EISS 83*
Latin New York Magazine - New York, NY - *MagIndMarPl 82-83*
Latin News - Miami, FL - *Ed&PubIntYB 82*
Latin Percussion Ventures Inc. - Garfield, NJ - *BillIntBG 83-84*
Latin Sound Inc., The - New York, NY - *AvMarPl 83; HBIndAd&MS 82-83*
Latona Press - Ellsworth, ME - *BoPubDir 4, 5; LitMag&SmPr 83-84*
Latrobe Bulletin - Latrobe, PA - *BaconPubCkNews 84; Ed&PubIntYB 82; NewsDir 84*
Latron Computer Systems Inc. (Software Services Div.) - Mountainside, NJ - *ADAPSOMemDir 83-84*
Latsec Inc. - La Jolla, CA - *EISS 83*
Latta Observer, The - Latta, SC - *AyerDirPub 83*
Latter End Music - *See* Campbell Music Inc., Glen
Latto Group of Northland Radio Stations, Lew - Duluth, MN - *BrCabYB 84*
Latvian News Laiks - Brooklyn, NY - *NewsDir 84*

Latvija-Amerika - Toronto, ON, Canada - *Ed&PubIntYB 82*
Lauderdale County Enterprise - Ripley, TN - *AyerDirPub 83; BaconPubCkNews 84; Ed&PubIntYB 82; NewsDir 84*
Lauer, Annette J. - Chevy Chase, MD - *LitMarPl 83, 84*
Lauer Associates Inc. - McLean, VA - *DirPRFirms 83; StaDirAdAg 2-84*
Lauerer Markin Gibbs - Toledo, OH - *AdAge 3-28-84; StaDirAdAg 2-84*
Lauf Associates Inc., Walter - Bethel, CT - *StaDirAdAg 2-84*
Laufman & Co., Herbert S. - Skokie, IL - *TelAl 83, 84*
Laugh Factory, The - Teaneck, NJ - *LitMag&SmPr 83-84*
Laughing Bear - San Jose, CA - *LitMag&SmPr 83-84*
Laughing Bear Press - San Jose, CA - *BoPubDir 4, 5; LitMag&SmPr 83-84*
Laughing Bird Songs - *See* Roman Enterprises, Angelo
Laughing Man, The [of The Dawn Horse Press] - Clearlake, CA - *LitMag&SmPr 83-84*
Laughing Waters Press - Boulder, CO - *BoPubDir 4 Sup, 5*
Laughlin Enterprises - Newcastle, CA - *BoPubDir 4 Sup, 5*
Laumic Co. Inc. - New York, NY - *AvMarPl 83*
Laundry News - New York, NY - *BaconPubCkMag 84; MagDir 84*
Launey, Hachmann & Harris - New York, NY - *AdAge 3-28-84; DirMarMP 83; StaDirAdAg 2-84*
Laura Books - Davenport, FL - *LitMarPl 83, 84*
Laureate Learning Systems Inc. - Burlington, VT - *MicrocomMPl 84; MicrocomSwDir 1*
Laurel Advocate - Laurel, NE - *BaconPubCkNews 84; Ed&PubIntYB 82*
Laurel Cable TV - Laurel, MT - *BrCabYB 84; Tel&CabFB 84C*
Laurel Cablevision [of American TV & Communications Corp.] - Torrington, CT - *BrCabYB 84; Tel&CabFB 84C*
Laurel Cablevision Co. - Somerset, PA - *BrCabYB 84*
Laurel Community Antenna System [of Comcast Corp.] - Laurel, MS - *BrCabYB 84; Tel&CabFB 84C*
Laurel Entertainment Corp. - Los Angeles, CA - *Tel&CabFB 84C*
Laurel Highland Television Co. - Indian Creek, PA - *BrCabYB 84*
Laurel Highland Television Co. - Stahlstown, PA - *Tel&CabFB 84C; TelDir&BG 83-84*
Laurel Highlands Scene, The [of The Laurel Group Press] - Scottdale, PA - *NewsDir 84*
Laurel Leader - Laurel, MD - *AyerDirPub 83; Ed&PubIntYB 82*
Laurel Leader-Call [of The Independent Inc.] - Laurel, MS - *BaconPubCkNews 84; Ed&PubIntYB 82; NewsDir 84*
Laurel News Leader - Laurel, MD - *BaconPubCkNews 84; Ed&PubIntYB 82; NewsDir 84*
Laurel Outlook - Laurel, MT - *BaconPubCkNews 84; Ed&PubIntYB 82*
Laurel Review, The - Buckhannon, WV - *LitMag&SmPr 83-84*
Laurel Sentinel - Laurel, MD - *AyerDirPub 83*
Laurel Sentinel [of Rockville Sentinel Newspapers] - Rockville, MD - *NewsDir 84*
Laurel State Register - Laurel, DE - *BaconPubCkNews 84; Ed&PubIntYB 82*
Laurel State Register & BiState Weekly - Laurel, DE - *NewsDir 84*
Laurel Telephone Co. - Laurel, IA - *TelDir&BG 83-84*
Lauren Kim Music - Stanford, CT - *BillIntBG 83-84*
Lauren, Ward - Los Angeles, CA - *DirPRFirms 83*
Laurence, Charles & Free [Subs. of Mickelberry Corp.] - New York, NY - *AdAge 3-28-84; ArtMar 84; Br 1-23-84; StaDirAdAg 2-84*
Laurens Cablevision - Laurens, SC - *BrCabYB 84*
Laurens County Advertiser - Laurens, SC - *AyerDirPub 83; BaconPubCkNews 84; Ed&PubIntYB 82; NewsDir 84*
Laurens County Communications Inc. - Clinton, SC - *BrCabYB 84*
Laurens County News - Dublin, GA - *Ed&PubIntYB 82*
Laurens Sun - Laurens, IA - *BaconPubCkNews 84; Ed&PubIntYB 82*
Laurida Books Publishing Co. - Hollywood, CA - *BoPubDir 4, 5*
Laurie & Associates, Bob - New York, NY - *LitMarPl 83, 84; MagIndMarPl 82-83*
Laurie Publishing Group - Monsey, NY - *BillIntBG 83-84*
Laurie Records - Monsey, NY - *BillIntBG 83-84*
Laurie Studios Inc., Bob - New York, NY - *LitMarPl 83, 84; MagIndMarPl 82-83*
Laurinburg Exchange - Laurinburg, NC - *BaconPubCkNews 84; Ed&PubIntYB 82; NewsDir 84*
Laursen Custom Color Lab - Irvine, CA - *AvMarPl 83*
Lautard, Guy [Aff. of Lautard Tool Works] - West Vancouver, BC, Canada - *BoPubDir 4, 5*
Laux Advertising Inc. - Ithaca, NY - *StaDirAdAg 2-84*
Lava Mt. Talking Books - New York, NY - *BoPubDir 4, 5*
LaVaca County Tribune-Herald - Hallettsville, TX - *Ed&PubIntYB 82*
Lavaca Telephone Co. Inc. - Lavaca, AR - *TelDir&BG 83-84*
Lavaca TV Cable Co. - Lavaca, AR - *BrCabYB 84*
L'Avant-Poste Gaspesien - Amqui, PQ, Canada - *Ed&PubIntYB 82*
L'Avant Studios - Tallahassee, FL - *BoPubDir 4 Sup, 5*
Lave Marketing, Martin A. - Indianapolis, IN - *AdAge 3-28-84; StaDirAdAg 2-84*
Laven, Fuller & Perkins Advertising & Marketing Inc. - Chicago, IL - *AdAge 3-28-84; StaDirAdAg 2-84*
Lavender Archives - Philadelphia, PA - *LitMag&SmPr 83-84*
L'Avenir de Brome Missisquoi - Farnham, PQ, Canada - *Ed&PubIntYB 82*
Laventhol & Horwath - Philadelphia, PA - *DataDirSup 7-83*
Laverne Leader-Tribune - Laverne, OK - *BaconPubCkNews 84; Ed&PubIntYB 82*
Laverne TV Cable Co. Inc. - Laverne, OK - *BrCabYB 84; Tel&CabFB 84C*
Lavery Co., The - Joliet, IL - *DirPRFirms 83; StaDirAdAg 2-84*
Lavey/Wolff/Swift [of BBDO International] - New York, NY - *AdAge 3-28-84; StaDirAdAg 2-84*
Lavidge & Associates Inc. - Knoxville, TN - *BrCabYB 84; StaDirAdAg 2-84*
Lavine Newspaper Group - Chippewa Falls, WI - *Ed&PubIntYB 82*
L'Aviron - Campbellton, NB, Canada - *Ed&PubIntYB 82*
Lavonia Franklin County Citizen - Lavonia, GA - *BaconPubCkNews 84; NewsDir 84*
Lavsky's Music House, Dick - New York, NY - *Tel&CabFB 84C*
Law & Capital Dynamics - Beverly Hills, CA - *BoPubDir 4*
Law & Capital Dynamics - Los Angeles, CA - *BoPubDir 5*
Law & Order - Chicago, IL - *BaconPubCkMag 84; MagDir 84; WritMar 84*
Law & Psychology Press - Venice, CA - *BoPubDir 4 Sup, 5*
Law & Technology Press - Manhattan Beach, CA - *BoPubDir 5*
Law-Arts Publishers - Santa Monica, CA - *WritMar 84*
Law Distributors [Aff. of Harcourt Brace Jovanovich Legal & Professional Publications Inc.] - Gardena, CA - *BoPubDir 4, 5*
Law Education Institute - Valley Stream, NY - *Ed&PubIntYB 82*
Law Enforcement & Criminal Justice Information Database [of International Research & Evaluation] - Eagan, MN - *CompReadDB 82; DataDirOnSer 84; DirOnDB Spring 84*
Law Enforcement Communications - Gaithersburg, MD - *MagDir 84*
Law Enforcement Communications - New York, NY - *BaconPubCkMag 84*
Law Enforcement Ordnance Co. - Athens, GA - *BoPubDir 5*
Law, John - Miami, FL - *Ed&PubIntYB 82*
Law Journal Seminars-Press - New York, NY - *BoPubDir 4 Sup, 5; DirMarMP 83*
Law Library Journal - Chicago, IL - *MagDir 84*
Law Library Microform Consortium - Honolulu, HI - *MicroMarPl 82-83*
Law Office Economics & Management - Croton-on-Hudson, NY - *BaconPubCkMag 84; MagDir 84*
Law Publications Inc. - Los Angeles, CA - *DirMarMP 83*
Law Publishing Co. - Satsuma, AL - *BillIntBG 83-84*
Law Reform Div. [of Dept. of Justice] - Fredericton, NB, Canada - *CompReadDB 82*
Law Reprints Inc. - *See* BNA's Law Reprints
Laward Telephone Exchange Inc. - Laward, TX - *TelDir&BG 83-84*
Lawhead Press Inc., The - Athens, OH - *MagIndMarPl 82-83*
Lawler Ballard Advertising - Norfolk, VA - *AdAge 3-28-84; StaDirAdAg 2-84*
Lawler, Matusky & Skelly Engineers - Pearl River, NY - *DataDirSup 7-83*

Lawn & Garden Marketing - Overland Park, KS - *BaconPubCkMag 84*
Lawn & Garden Marketing [of Intertec Publishing Corp.] - Shawnee Mission, KS - *MagDir 84*
Lawn & Garden Trade - Montreal, PQ, Canada - *BaconPubCkMag 84*
Lawn Care Industry [of HBJ Publications] - Cleveland, OH - *BaconPubCkMag 84; MagDir 84; WritMar 84*
Lawn Care Professional - Cleveland, OH - *BaconPubCkMag 84*
Lawn Servicing - Overland Park, KS - *BaconPubCkMag 84*
Lawndale News - Chicago, IL - *AyerDirPub 83; Ed&PubIntYB 82*
Lawndale News - *See* West Town Publications
Lawndale Tribune [of Coast Media Newspapers] - Culver City, CA - *NewsDir 84*
Lawndale Tribune - Lawndale, CA - *Ed&PubIntYB 82*
Lawndale Tribune - *See* Coast Media Newspapers
Lawrad - Portland, OR - *StaDirAdAg 2-84*
Lawren Productions Inc. - Mendocino, CA - *AvMarPl 83; Tel&CabFB 84C*
Lawrence, Alan - New York, NY - *AvMarPl 83*
Lawrence & Schiller Inc. - Sioux Falls, SD - *StaDirAdAg 2-84*
Lawrence Associates - New York, NY - *DirPRFirms 83*
Lawrence Associates Inc., Stewart - Clark, NJ - *DirInfWP 82*
Lawrence Berkeley Laboratory [of University of California] - Berkeley, CA - *CompReadDB 82*
Lawrence Co., The - Santa Monica, CA - *StaDirAdAg 2-84*
Lawrence Corp., Bruce [Aff. of Leicester House Ltd.] - Jericho, NY - *BoPubDir 5*
Lawrence Corp., Bruce [Aff. of Leicester House Ltd.] - North Woodmere, NY - *BoPubDir 4*
Lawrence County News - Lawrenceville, IL - *AyerDirPub 83; Ed&PubIntYB 82*
Lawrence County Press - Monticello, MS - *AyerDirPub 83; Ed&PubIntYB 82*
Lawrence County Record - Mt. Vernon, MO - *AyerDirPub 83*
Lawrence, Detrick - Duxbury, MA - *AvMarPl 83*
Lawrence Eagle-Tribune - Lawrence, MA - *BaconPubCkNews 84; Ed&PubIntYB 82*
Lawrence Eagle-Tribune - North Andover, MA - *NewsDir 84*
Lawrence, Frank - New York, NY - *MagIndMarPl 82-83*
Lawrence, Frank D. - Montclair, NJ - *LitMarPl 83*
Lawrence Inc., Merloyd - Boston, MA - *LitMarPl 84*
Lawrence Inc., Seymour - Boston, MA - *LitMarPl 83*
Lawrence Inc., Seymour - New York, NY - *LitMarPl 84*
Lawrence Journal World - Lawrence, KS - *BaconPubCkNews 84; Ed&PubIntYB 82; NewsDir 84*
Lawrence Ledger - Lawrenceville, NJ - *AyerDirPub 83*
Lawrence Ledger [of Princeton Packet Inc.] - Trenton, NJ - *NewsDir 84*
Lawrence Ledger, The - Lawrence Township, NJ - *Ed&PubIntYB 82*
Lawrence, Legters, Borden Inc. - New York, NY - *StaDirAdAg 2-84*
Lawrence Livermore National Laboratory - Livermore, CA - *CompReadDB 82*
Lawrence Livermore National Laboratory (Criticality Safety Office) - Livermore, CA - *CompReadDB 82*
Lawrence Locomotive - Lawrence, NE - *BaconPubCkNews 84; Ed&PubIntYB 82*
Lawrence Nassau Herald [of Bi-County Publishers Inc.] - Lawrence, NY - *NewsDir 84*
Lawrence Nassau Herald - *See* Richner Publications Inc.
Lawrence Newspapers Inc. (Lawrence Microfilming Service) - Fuquay-Varina, NC - *MicroMarPl 82-83*
Lawrence Productions, Donna - Louisville, KY - *AvMarPl 83*
Lawrence Productions Inc., Robert - New York, NY - *TelAl 83, 84; Tel&CabFB 84C*
Lawrence Publications, H. R. - University Park, PA - *MicroMarPl 82-83*
Lawrence Review, The D. H. - Fayetteville, AR - *LitMag&SmPr 83-84*
Lawrence Sunday Sun - Lawrence, MA - *NewsDir 84*
Lawrence Times [of Pace Publishing Inc.] - Indianapolis, IN - *NewsDir 84*
Lawrence Times - Lawrence, IN - *Ed&PubIntYB 82*
Lawrence Times - *See* Topic Newspapers Inc.
Lawrence Township Journal - Indianapolis, IN - *AyerDirPub 83*
Lawrence Township Journal - Lawrence, IN - *Ed&PubIntYB 82; NewsDir 84*
Lawrence Township Journal & Harrison Post - Lawrence, IN - *BaconPubCkNews 84*
Lawrenceburg Anderson News - Lawrenceburg, KY - *BaconPubCkNews 84; Ed&PubIntYB 82; NewsDir 84*
Lawrenceburg Cable TV [of Rogers UA Cablesystems Inc.] - Lawrenceburg, TN - *BrCabYB 84; Tel&CabFB 84C*
Lawrenceburg Dearborn County Register - *See* Register Publications Inc.
Lawrenceburg Democrat Union - Lawrenceburg, TN - *BaconPubCkNews 84; NewsDir 84*
Lawrenceburg Rising Sun Recorder & News - *See* Register Publications Inc.
Lawrenceville Brunswick Times-Gazette - Lawrenceville, VA - *BaconPubCkNews 84*
Lawrenceville Cable TV [of DoKel Communications Corp.] - Lawrenceville, VA - *BrCabYB 84*
Lawrenceville Cablevision Co. [of DoKel Communications Corp.] - Lawrenceville, VA - *Tel&CabFB 84C*
Lawrenceville Daily Record - Lawrenceville, IL - *BaconPubCkNews 84; NewsDir 84*
Lawrenceville Gwinnett News - Lawrenceville, GA - *BaconPubCkNews 84; NewsDir 84*
Lawrenceville Home Weekly, The - Lawrenceville, GA - *NewsDir 84*
Lawrenceville Lawrence County News - Lawrenceville, IL - *BaconPubCkNews 84*
Lawrenceville Lawrence Ledger - *See* Princeton Packet Inc.
Lawrimore Communications Inc. - Charlotte, NC - *DirPRFirms 83*
Lawson Books - Seneca Falls, NY - *BoPubDir 4, 5*
Lawson Graphics - Toronto, ON, Canada - *LitMarPl 83, 84*
Lawson Review - Lawson, MO - *AyerDirPub 83; BaconPubCkNews 84; Ed&PubIntYB 82*
Lawton Cablevision - Lawton, OK - *BrCabYB 84; Tel&CabFB 84C*
Lawton Cache Times Weekly - Lawton, OK - *BaconPubCkNews 84*
Lawton Constitution - Lawton, OK - *Ed&PubIntYB 82; NewsDir 84*
Lawton, Elise Timmons - Houston, TX - *BoPubDir 5*
Lawton Morning Press - Lawton, OK - *BaconPubCkNews 84; Ed&PubIntYB 82; NewsDir 84*
Lawton-Teague Publications - Oakland, CA - *BoPubDir 4, 5*
Lawyers & Judges Publishing Co. - La Jolla, CA - *LitMarPl 83, 84*
Lawyer's Book Club [of Prentice-Hall Inc.] - Englewood, NJ - *LitMarPl 83, 84*
Lawyers Co-Operative Publishing Co. - Rochester, NY - *CompReadDB 82; KnowInd 83; LitMarPl 83, 84*
Lawyers Diary & Manual [Aff. of New Jersey Law Journal] - Newark, NJ - *BoPubDir 4, 5*
Lawyers' Literary Club [of North American Book Clubs Inc.] - Dover, NH - *LitMarPl 83, 84*
Lawyer's Microcomputer, The [of RPW Publishing Corp.] - Lexington, SC - *BaconPubCkMag 84; MicrocomMPl 84*
Lawyer's PC, The [of RPW Publishing Corp.] - Lexington, SC - *MicrocomMPl 84*
Lawyers Publishing Co. [Aff. of Let the People Know Law Book Store Inc.] - New Concord, OH - *BoPubDir 4, 5*
Lawyer's Weekly Publications - Boston, MA - *DirMarMP 83*
Lawyers Word Processing Ltd. - Chicago, IL - *DirInfWP 82*
Lay, Elizabeth - Oakland, CA - *LitMarPl 83, 84*
Layback Music Inc. - Baton Rouge, LA - *BillIntBG 83-84*
Layla Productions - New York, NY - *LitMarPl 83, 84*
Layman Associates Inc. - Dedham, MA - *ArtMar 84; StaDirAdAg 2-84*
Laymond Publishing Co. Inc. - Charlotte, NC - *BillIntBG 83-84*
Lazar Agency, Irving Paul - Beverly Hills, CA - *LitMarPl 83*
Lazar Associates, N. - New York, NY - *StaDirAdAg 2-84*
Lazarus Associates Inc., A. J. - New York, NY - *DirPRFirms 83*
Lazer Music Publishing Co. - Center Square, PA - *BillIntBG 83-84*
Lazer Records - Philadelphia, PA - *BillIntBG 83-84*
Lazy Brown Associates - Washington, DC - *LitMarPl 84*
LBJ Co., The - Austin, TX - *BrCabYB 84*
LBJ Co., The - *See* Karnack Corp.

LBS Entertainment Network - New York, NY - *BrCabYB 84*
LC/Line [of SDC Search Service] - Santa Monica, CA - *DataDirOnSer 84; DirOnDB Spring 84*
LC MARC [of Dialog Information Services Inc.] - Palo Alto, CA - *DataDirOnSer 84*
LC MARC [of Library of Congress] - Washington, DC - *DirOnDB Spring 84; OnBibDB 3*
LC Typesetting Co. Inc. - South Bend, IN - *LitMarPl 83, 84*
LCA Video/Films [Div. of Learning Corp. of America] - New York, NY - *AvMarPl 83*
LCS Industries Inc. - Clifton, NJ - *LitMarPl 83, 84; MagIndMarPl 82-83*
LD & A Advertising Corp. - Batavia, IL - *StaDirAdAg 2-84*
LDA Publishing - Bayside, NY - *LitMag&SmPr 83-84*
LDC Africa/Middle East Data Bank - Washington, DC - *DirOnDB Spring 84*
LDC Africa/Middle East Data Bank [of Data Resources Inc.] - Lexington, MA - *DataDirOnSer 84*
LDC Asia/Australia Data Bank - Washington, DC - *DirOnDB Spring 84*
LDC Asia/Australia Data Bank [of Data Resources Inc.] - Lexington, MA - *DataDirOnSer 84*
LDC Latin America Data Bank - Washington, DC - *DirOnDB Spring 84*
LDC Latin America Data Bank [of Data Resources Inc.] - Lexington, MA - *DataDirOnSer 84*
LDM Inc. - Covina, CA - *InterCabHB 3*
LDX Broadcast Inc. - East Peoria, IL - *BrCabYB 84*
Le Ance Public Relations - Costa Mesa, CA - *DirPRFirms 83*
Le Beacon Presse - Seattle, WA - *BoPubDir 4, 5; LitMag&SmPr 83-84; WritMar 84*
Le Beacon Review - Seattle, WA - *LitMag&SmPr 83-84*
Le Bill Music Inc. - Ft. Worth, TX - *BillIntBG 83-84*
Le Biocreux Inc. - Montreal, PQ, Canada - *BoPubDir 4, 5*
Le Bureau - Montreal, PQ, Canada - *ArtMar 84; WritMar 84*
Le Cable de Riviere-du-Loup Ltee. - Riviere du Loup, PQ, Canada - *BrCabYB 84*
Le Canada Francais - St. Jean, PQ, Canada - *Ed&PubIntYB 82*
Le Carillon - Hawkesbury, ON, Canada - *Ed&PubIntYB 82*
Le Center Leader - Le Center, MN - *BaconPubCkNews 84; Ed&PubIntYB 82; NewsDir 84*
Le Cercle du Livre de France [Subs. of French Book Club] - Long Island City, NY - *LitMarPl 83, 84*
Le Cercle du Livre de France Ltee. - Montreal, PQ, Canada - *LitMarPl 83, 84*
Le Citoyen - Asbestos, PQ, Canada - *Ed&PubIntYB 82*
Le Courier - Trois Pistoles, PQ, Canada - *Ed&PubIntYB 82*
Le Courrier de la Nouvelle-Ecosse - Yarmouth, NS, Canada - *Ed&PubIntYB 82*
Le Courrier de St. Hyacinthe - St. Hyacinthe, PQ, Canada - *Ed&PubIntYB 82*
Le Courrier du Sud - Longueuil, PQ, Canada - *AyerDirPub 83; Ed&PubIntYB 82*
Le Courrier Metropolitan - Montreal, PQ, Canada - *Ed&PubIntYB 82*
Le Courrier Riviera - Sorel, PQ, Canada - *Ed&PubIntYB 82*
Le Devoir - Montreal, PQ, Canada - *AyerDirPub 83; BaconPubCkNews 84; Ed&PubIntYB 82*
Le Droit - Ottawa, ON, Canada - *AyerDirPub 83; BaconPubCkNews 84; Ed&PubIntYB 82*
Le Flore County Sun [of Poteau Publishing Co.] - Poteau, OK - *NewsDir 84*
Le Franco-Albertain - Edmonton, AB, Canada - *Ed&PubIntYB 82*
Le Gourmet Microwave [of Creative Resources] - Cincinnati, OH - *LitMag&SmPr 83-84*
Le Groupe BST Inc. - Montreal, PQ, Canada - *WhoWMicrocom 83*
Le Guide - Cowansville, PQ, Canada - *Ed&PubIntYB 82*
Le Guide - Ste. Marie, PQ, Canada - *Ed&PubIntYB 82*
Le Guide de Montreal-Nord - Montreal, PQ, Canada - *Ed&PubIntYB 82*
Le Guide Mont-Royal - Montreal, PQ, Canada - *AyerDirPub 83*
Le Jacq Publishing Inc. - New York, NY - *LitMarPl 83, 84*
Le Journal - Cornwall, ON, Canada - *Ed&PubIntYB 82*
Le Journal Chaleur - Rimouski, PQ, Canada - *AyerDirPub 83; Ed&PubIntYB 82*
Le Journal de Montreal - Montreal, PQ, Canada - *AyerDirPub 83; BaconPubCkNews 84; Ed&PubIntYB 82*
Le Journal de Quebec [of Dee Quebecor Inc.] - Quebec, PQ, Canada - *Ed&PubIntYB 82*
Le Journal de Quebec - Ville Vanier, PQ, Canada - *BaconPubCkNews 84*
Le Journal de St. Bruno - St. Bruno, PQ, Canada - *Ed&PubIntYB 82*
Le Journal des Pays d'en Haut - Ste. Adele, PQ, Canada - *Ed&PubIntYB 82*
Le Journal-l'Action - Joliette, PQ, Canada - *Ed&PubIntYB 82*
Le Lac St. Jean - Alma, PQ, Canada - *Ed&PubIntYB 82*
Le Madawaska - Edmundston, NB, Canada - *AyerDirPub 83; Ed&PubIntYB 82*
Le Mars Cablevision [of Heritage Communications Inc.] - Le Mars, IA - *BrCabYB 84; Tel&CabFB 84C*
Le Mars Daily Sentinel - Le Mars, IA - *Ed&PubIntYB 82; NewsDir 84*
Le Messager - Lachine, PQ, Canada - *AyerDirPub 83*
Le Messager Regional - St. Jovite, PQ, Canada - *Ed&PubIntYB 82*
Le-Mo Cable TV Co. [of Communications Systems Inc.] - Lebanon, MO - *BrCabYB 84*
Le Moniteur & The Echo Discount - Hawkesbury, ON, Canada - *Ed&PubIntYB 82*
Le Nor-Info - St. Therese, PQ, Canada - *Ed&PubIntYB 82*
Le Nord - Hearst, ON, Canada - *Ed&PubIntYB 82*
Le Nordic - Baie Comeau, PQ, Canada - *Ed&PubIntYB 82*
Le Nordic Regional - Sept-Isles, PQ, Canada - *Ed&PubIntYB 82*
Le Nordic Regional - Shefferville, PQ, Canada - *Ed&PubIntYB 82*
Le Nouveau Clairon - St. Hyacinthe, PQ, Canada - *Ed&PubIntYB 82*
Le Nouvelliste - Trois Rivieres, PQ, Canada - *AyerDirPub 83; BaconPubCkNews 84; Ed&PubIntYB 82*
Le Peuple-Tribune - Levis, PQ, Canada - *Ed&PubIntYB 82*
Le Pharillion Voyageur - Rimouski, PQ, Canada - *AyerDirPub 83*
Le Pharillon Voyageur - Gaspe, PQ, Canada - *Ed&PubIntYB 82*
Le Pharmacien - Montreal, PQ, Canada - *BaconPubCkMag 84*
Le Point - Dolbeau, PQ, Canada - *Ed&PubIntYB 82*
Le Progres - Ste. Therese, PQ, Canada - *Ed&PubIntYB 82*
Le Progres-Carrousel de Thetford - Thetford, PQ, Canada - *Ed&PubIntYB 82*
Le Progres de Coaticook - Coaticook, PQ, Canada - *Ed&PubIntYB 82*
Le Progres de Magog - Magog, PQ, Canada - *AyerDirPub 83; Ed&PubIntYB 82*
Le Progres de Villeray - Montreal, PQ, Canada - *Ed&PubIntYB 82*
Le Progres du Nord - Monreal, PQ, Canada - *Ed&PubIntYB 82*
Le Progres-Echo - Rimouski, PQ, Canada - *Ed&PubIntYB 82*
Le Quebec Industriel - Montreal, PQ, Canada - *BaconPubCkMag 84*
Le Quotidien - Chicoutimi, PQ, Canada - *AyerDirPub 83; BaconPubCkNews 84*
Le Quotidien du Saguenay-Lac St. Jean - Chicoutimi, PQ, Canada - *Ed&PubIntYB 82*
Le Radar - Cap-aux-Meules, PQ, Canada - *AyerDirPub 83*
Le Reflet - Laprairie, PQ, Canada - *Ed&PubIntYB 82*
Le Regional de Loutaouais - Hull, PQ, Canada - *Ed&PubIntYB 82*
Le Reveil a Chicoutimi - Chicoutimi, PQ, Canada - *Ed&PubIntYB 82*
Le Reveil a Jonquiere - Jonquiere, PQ, Canada - *Ed&PubIntYB 82*
Le Reveil a La Baie - La Baie, PQ, Canada - *Ed&PubIntYB 82*
Le Rimouskois - Rimouski, PQ, Canada - *Ed&PubIntYB 82*
Le Roux International Inc. - New Bedford, MA - *WhoWMicrocom 83*
Le Roy Gazette-News - Le Roy, NY - *Ed&PubIntYB 82*
Le Roy Gazette News & Batavie County Post - *See* Sanders Publications
Le Roy Independent - Le Roy, MN - *BaconPubCkNews 84; Ed&PubIntYB 82*
Le Roy Journal - Le Roy, IL - *BaconPubCkNews 84; Ed&PubIntYB 82*
Le Roy Motion Picture Production Studios [Subs. of Le Roy Associates Inc.] - Philadelphia, PA - *AvMarPl 83*

Le-Ru Telephone Co. - Stella, MO - *TelDir&BG 83-84*
Le Soleil - Quebec, PQ, Canada - *AyerDirPub 83; BaconPubCkNews 84; Ed&PubIntYB 82*
Le Soleil de Colombie - Vancouver, BC, Canada - *Ed&PubIntYB 82*
Le Sommet Echo des Laurentides - Ste. Agathe-des-Monts, PQ, Canada - *Ed&PubIntYB 82*
Le St.-Laurent Echo du Grand-Portage - Riviere-du-Loup, PQ, Canada - *Ed&PubIntYB 82*
Le Sueur News-Herald - Le Sueur, MN - *BaconPubCkNews 84*
Le Temiscamien - Ville-Marie, PQ, Canada - *Ed&PubIntYB 82*
Le Travailleur - Linwood, MA - *Ed&PubIntYB 82*
Le Van Enterprises Inc. - Chicago, IL - *Tel&CabFB 84C*
Le Verdad - Corpus Christi, TX - *Ed&PubIntYB 82*
Le Volilier - Caraquet, NB, Canada - *Ed&PubIntYB 82*
Le Voltigeur - Drummondville, PQ, Canada - *Ed&PubIntYB 82*
Le Voyageur - Sudbury, ON, Canada - *Ed&PubIntYB 82*
Lea & Febiger - Philadelphia, PA - *LitMarPl 83, 84*
Lea Pocket Scores - New York, NY - *BillIntBG 83-84*
Lea Publishing Co. - Nashville, TN - *BillIntBG 83-84*
Leach, Douglas R. - Imperial, NE - *Tel&CabFB 84C p.1687*
Leach, Lonnie L. - Imperial, NE - *Tel&CabFB 84C p.1687*
Leach Research Inc. - Santa Fe, NM - *DirPRFirms 83*
Leachville Cable TV [of Spectrum Teltronics Inc.] - Leachville, AR - *BrCabYB 84*
Leaco Music - *See* Lea Publishing Co.
Leaco Rural Telephone Cooperative Inc. - Lovington, NM - *TelDir&BG 83-84*
Leacom Cablevision [of Communications Systems Inc.] - Truth or Consequences, NM - *BrCabYB 84; Tel&CabFB 84C*
Leacom Cablevision Inc. [of Heritage Communications Inc.] - Buena Vista, CO - *Tel&CabFB 84C*
Leacom Cablevision Inc. [of Heritage Communications Inc.] - Frisco, CO - *Tel&CabFB 84C*
Leacom Cablevision Inc. [of Heritage Communications Inc.] - Kremmling, CO - *Tel&CabFB 84C*
Leacom Music - *See* Lea Publishing Co.
Lead - New York, NY - *BaconPubCkMag 84; MagDir 84*
Lead Belt News - Flat River, MO - *AyerDirPub 83; Ed&PubIntYB 82*
Lead Black Hills Weekly - Lead, SD - *BaconPubCkNews 84*
Lead Call [of Seaton Publishing Co.] - Lead, SD - *BaconPubCkNews 84; NewsDir 84*
Lead Forecast [of Chase Econometrics/Interactive Data Corp.] - Waltham, MA - *DataDirOnSer 84*
Lead Forecast - Bala Cynwyd, PA - *DirOnDB Spring 84*
Lead Industries Association Inc. - New York, NY - *BoPubDir 5*
Leader - Roanoke, AL - *AyerDirPub 83*
Leader - Lincoln, AR - *AyerDirPub 83*
Leader - Lucerne Valley, CA - *AyerDirPub 83*
Leader - Oakdale, CA - *AyerDirPub 83*
Leader - La Salle, CO - *AyerDirPub 83*
Leader - Limon, CO - *AyerDirPub 83*
Leader - Jacksonville Beach, FL - *AyerDirPub 83*
Leader - Tarpon Springs, FL - *AyerDirPub 83*
Leader - Blue Mound, IL - *AyerDirPub 83*
Leader - Earlville, IL - *AyerDirPub 83*
Leader - Pontiac, IL - *AyerDirPub 83*
Leader - Rochelle, IL - *AyerDirPub 83*
Leader - Walnut, IL - *AyerDirPub 83*
Leader - Washburn, IL - *AyerDirPub 83*
Leader - Jasonville, IN - *AyerDirPub 83*
Leader - Lafayette, IN - *AyerDirPub 83*
Leader - Chariton, IA - *AyerDirPub 83*
Leader - Lamont, IA - *AyerDirPub 83*
Leader - Malvern, IA - *AyerDirPub 83*
Leader [of MPC Newspapers] - Oxford, IA - *AyerDirPub 83; NewsDir 84*
Leader - Schleswig, IA - *AyerDirPub 83*
Leader - Tripoli, IA - *AyerDirPub 83*
Leader - Winona, KS - *AyerDirPub 83*
Leader - Lexington, KY - *AyerDirPub 83*
Leader - Princeton, KY - *AyerDirPub 83*
Leader - Leesville, LA - *AyerDirPub 83*
Leader - Ruston, LA - *AyerDirPub 83; Ed&PubIntYB 82*
Leader - Dexter, MI - *AyerDirPub 83*
Leader - Oxford, MI - *AyerDirPub 83*
Leader - Hutchinson, MN - *AyerDirPub 83*
Leader - Kenyon, MN - *AyerDirPub 83*
Leader - Le Center, MN - *AyerDirPub 83*
Leader - Long Prairie, MN - *AyerDirPub 83*
Leader - Silver Lake, MN - *AyerDirPub 83*
Leader - Brookhaven, MS - *AyerDirPub 83*
Leader - Hale, MO - *AyerDirPub 83*
Leader - New Haven, MO - *AyerDirPub 83*
Leader - Scobey, MT - *AyerDirPub 83*
Leader - Bellevue, NE - *AyerDirPub 83*
Leader - Blue Hill, NE - *AyerDirPub 83*
Leader - Westfield, NJ - *AyerDirPub 83*
Leader - Wrightstown, NJ - *AyerDirPub 83*
Leader - Corning, NY - *AyerDirPub 83; Ed&PubIntYB 82*
Leader - Lackawanna, NY - *AyerDirPub 83*
Leader - Locust Valley, NY - *AyerDirPub 83; Ed&PubIntYB 82*
Leader - Washburn, ND - *AyerDirPub 83*
Leader [of The Order of United Commercial Travelers of America] - Columbus, OH - *MagDir 84; WritMar 84*
Leader - East Palestine, OH - *AyerDirPub 83; Ed&PubIntYB 82*
Leader - Minerva, OH - *AyerDirPub 83*
Leader - New Concord, OH - *AyerDirPub 83*
Leader - St. Marys, OH - *AyerDirPub 83*
Leader - Frederick, OK - *AyerDirPub 83*
Leader - Guthrie, OK - *AyerDirPub 83*
Leader - Ryan, OK - *AyerDirPub 83*
Leader - Sand Springs, OK - *AyerDirPub 83*
Leader - Sentinel, OK - *AyerDirPub 83*
Leader - Drexel Hill, PA - *AyerDirPub 83*
Leader - Havertown, PA - *AyerDirPub 83*
Leader - Lemmon, SD - *AyerDirPub 83*
Leader - Madison, SD - *AyerDirPub 83*
Leader - Covington, TN - *AyerDirPub 83*
Leader - Lewisville, TX - *AyerDirPub 83*
Leader - Orange, TX - *AyerDirPub 83*
Leader - Round Rock, TX - *AyerDirPub 83*
Leader - Wellington, TX - *AyerDirPub 83*
Leader - Staunton, VA - *AyerDirPub 83*
Leader - Port Townsend, WA - *AyerDirPub 83*
Leader - Lake Mills, WI - *AyerDirPub 83*
Leader - Shawano, WI - *AyerDirPub 83*
Leader - Tomahawk, WI - *AyerDirPub 83*
Leader - Woodville, WI - *AyerDirPub 83*
Leader - Moorcroft, WY - *AyerDirPub 83*
Leader - Edson, AB, Canada - *AyerDirPub 83*
Leader - Surrey, BC, Canada - *AyerDirPub 83; Ed&PubIntYB 82*
Leader - Morrisburg, ON, Canada - *AyerDirPub 83; Ed&PubIntYB 82*
Leader - Davidson, SK, Canada - *AyerDirPub 83; Ed&PubIntYB 82*
Leader & Kalkaskian - Kalkaska, MI - *AyerDirPub 83*
Leader & Press [of Gannett Co. Inc.] - Springfield, MO - *AyerDirPub 83; NewsDir 84*
Leader-Call - Laurel, MS - *AyerDirPub 83*
Leader-Central City News - Greenville, KY - *AyerDirPub 83*
Leader-Courier - Kingman, KS - *AyerDirPub 83; BaconPubCkNews 84*
Leader-Courier, The - Elk Point, SD - *AyerDirPub 83; Ed&PubIntYB 82*
Leader Enterprise [of Bryan Publishing Co.] - Montpelier, OH - *NewsDir 84*
Leader-Free Press - East Rutherford, NJ - *Ed&PubIntYB 82*
Leader Free Press - Lyndhurst, NJ - *AyerDirPub 83*
Leader-Garland Times - Tremonton, UT - *AyerDirPub 83; Ed&PubIntYB 82*
Leader-Herald - Gloversville, NY - *AyerDirPub 83; BaconPubCkNews 84; Ed&PubIntYB 82*
Leader-Herald & News Gazette - Everett, MA - *AyerDirPub 83*
Leader in Lancaster, The - Lancaster, TX - *Ed&PubIntYB 82*
Leader-Journal - Pierce City, MO - *Ed&PubIntYB 82*
Leader-Journal - St. James, MO - *AyerDirPub 83*
Leader-News - Greenville, KY - *Ed&PubIntYB 82*
Leader-News - Uvalde, TX - *AyerDirPub 83*
Leader-News - Waupun, WI - *AyerDirPub 83; Ed&PubIntYB 82*
Leader News - Leader, SK, Canada - *AyerDirPub 83*
Leader Newspapers Inc. - Lyndhurst, NJ - *BaconPubCkNews 84*
Leader Observer - Jamaica, NY - *AyerDirPub 83*

Leader Observer - Woodhaven, NY - *Ed&PubIntYB 82; NewsDir 84*
Leader Papers Inc. - Chicago, IL - *BaconPubCkNews 84*
Leader-Post - Regina, SK, Canada - *AyerDirPub 83; Ed&PubIntYB 82*
Leader Press - Emmons, MN - *AyerDirPub 83*
Leader-Press & Laddonia Herald - Vandalia, MO - *AyerDirPub 83*
Leader Publishing - Tarpon Springs, FL - *BaconPubCkNews 84*
Leader Publishing Co. - Salem, IN - *BaconPubCkNews 84*
Leader Record - Gonvick, MN - *AyerDirPub 83; Ed&PubIntYB 82*
Leader-Review - Onarga, IL - *AyerDirPub 83*
Leader-Statesman - Versailles, MO - *AyerDirPub 83*
Leader-Telegram [of Eau Claire Press Co.] - Eau Claire, WI - *AyerDirPub 83; Ed&PubIntYB 82; NewsDir 84*
Leader, The - Stuttgart, AR - *AyerDirPub 83*
Leader, The - Seaford, DE - *AyerDirPub 83; Ed&PubIntYB 82*
Leader, The - Lancing, KS - *Ed&PubIntYB 82*
Leader, The - Point Pleasant Beach, NJ - *Ed&PubIntYB 82*
Leader, The - Freeport, NY - *AyerDirPub 83; NewsDir 84*
Leader, The - Jamaica, NY - *NewsDir 84*
Leader, The - Clinton, OK - *AyerDirPub 83*
Leader, The - Philadelphia, PA - *AyerDirPub 83; Ed&PubIntYB 82*
Leader, The - Houston, TX - *AyerDirPub 83; Ed&PubIntYB 82*
Leader, The - Hinton, WV - *Ed&PubIntYB 82*
Leader, The - Evansville, WI - *AyerDirPub 83*
Leader, The - Lakefield, ON, Canada - *Ed&PubIntYB 82*
Leader-Times - Bridgeport, IL - *AyerDirPub 83; Ed&PubIntYB 82*
Leader-Times - Genoa, NE - *AyerDirPub 83*
Leader-Times - Kittanning, PA - *AyerDirPub 83; Ed&PubIntYB 82*
Leader-Tribune - Ft. Valley, GA - *AyerDirPub 83; Ed&PubIntYB 82*
Leader-Tribune - Laverne, OK - *AyerDirPub 83*
Leader Union - Vandalia, IL - *AyerDirPub 83*
Leader-Vindicator, The [of Southern Clarion County Newspapers Inc.] - New Bethlehem, PA - *AyerDirPub 83; Ed&PubIntYB 82; NewsDir 84*
Leaders - New York, NY - *BaconPubCkMag 84; MagDir 84*
Leadership - Marion, OH - *BaconPubCkMag 84*
Leadership: A Practical Journal for Church Leaders - Carol Stream, IL - *MagIndMarPl 82-83*
Leadership Cablevision Associates [of Fairbanks Broadcasting Co. Inc.] - Delray Beach, FL - *Tel&CabFB 84C*
Leadership Network, The - *Folio 83*
Leadership 100 [of Christianity Today] - Carol Stream, IL - *WritMar 84*
Leadership Press - Claremont, CA - *BoPubDir 4 Sup, 5*
Leading Edge Bulletin [of Interface Press] - Los Angeles, CA - *LitMag&SmPr 83-84*
Leading Edge Products - Canton, MA - *MicrocomMPl 83, 84*
Leading Edge Products Inc. - Needham Heights, MA - *MicrocomMPl 84*
Leading Edge Products Inc. - Norwood, MA - *MicrocomMPl 84*
Leading Edge, The [of Society of Exploration Geophysicists] - Tulsa, OK - *WritMar 84*
Leading National Advertisers Inc. - Norwalk, CT - *MagIndMarPl 82-83*
Leadville Cable TV [of Tele-Communications Inc.] - Leadville, CO - *BrCabYB 84; Tel&CabFB 84C*
Leadville Herald Democrat [of Continental Divide Press Inc.] - Leadville, CO - *BaconPubCkNews 84; NewsDir 84*
Leaf-Chronicle [of Multimedia Inc.] - Clarksville, TN - *AyerDirPub 83; Ed&PubIntYB 82; NewsDir 84*
Leaf River Valley Telephone Co. - Leaf River, IL - *TelDir&BG 83-84*
League Books - Cleveland, OH - *LitMag&SmPr 83-84*
League City News [of Sun Publishing] - League City, TX - *NewsDir 84*
League for Ecological Democracy - San Pedro, CA - *BoPubDir 4 Sup, 5*
League of Arab States Documentation & Information Center - Tunis, Tunisia - *EISS 5-84 Sup*
League of Minnesota Cities - St. Paul, MN - *BoPubDir 4, 5*
League of Women Voters of Minnesota - St. Paul, MN - *BoPubDir 4 Sup, 5*
League of Women Voters of the City of New York - New York, NY - *BoPubDir 4, 5*
League of Women Voters of the United States - Washington, DC - *BoPubDir 4, 5*
Leahy Press Inc., The - Montpelier, VT - *MagIndMarPl 82-83*
Leakesville Greene County Herald - Leakesville, MS - *BaconPubCkNews 84*
Leakey County American - Leakey, TX - *BaconPubCkNews 84*
Leamington Post - Leamington, ON, Canada - *Ed&PubIntYB 82*
Leamington Shopper - Leamington, ON, Canada - *AyerDirPub 83*
Lean County News, The - Woodville, FL - *NewsDir 84*
Leander Records - Yonkers, NY - *BillIntBG 83-84*
Leanin' Tree Publishing Co. - Boulder, CO - *WritMar 84*
Leap Inc. - Hamden, CT - *EISS 5-84 Sup*
Leapac Services - Sacramento, CA - *MicrocomMPl 83, 84*
Lear Data - Napa, CA - *MicrocomMPl 83, 84*
Lear Inc., A. E. - Pipersville, PA - *BoPubDir 4, 5*
Lear Music Inc. - Los Angeles, CA - *BillIntBG 83-84*
Lear Siegler Inc. - Anaheim, CA - *Datamation 6-83; DirInfWP 82; MicrocomMPl 83*
Lear Siegler Inc. - Santa Monica, CA - *Top100Al 83*
Lear Siegler Inc. (Data Products Div.) - Anaheim, CA - *DataDirSup 7-83; InfIndMarPl 83; WhoWMicrocom 83*
Learmonth & Burchett Management Systems Inc. - Houston, TX - *ADAPSOMemDir 83-84*
Learn/Alaska Network [of Alaska Instructional Communications Consortium] - Anchorage, AK - *TeleSy&SerDir 7-83*
Learn Inc. - Mt. Laurel, NJ - *BoPubDir 4, 5; DirMarMP 83; Tel&CabFB 84C*
Learned Information Inc. - Medford, NJ - *BoPubDir 4 Sup, 5; DataDirOnSer 84; InfoS 83-84*
Learned Information Ltd. - Oxford, England - *EISS 83; InfIndMarPl 83; MicroMarPl 82-83*
Learned Publications Inc. [Aff. of Nawealaerts Editions] - Jamaica, NY - *BoPubDir 4, 5*
Learning [of Pitman Learning Inc.] - Belmont, CA - *BaconPubCkMag 84; Folio 83; LitMarPl 84; MagDir 84; WritMar 84*
Learning [of Pitman Learning Inc.] - Palo Alto, CA - *LitMarPl 83; MagIndMarPl 82-83*
Learning Achievements Inc. - Reading, PA - *DirInfWP 82*
Learning & Information Inc. - New York, NY - *AvMarPl 83*
Learning Arts - Wichita, KS - *MicrocomMPl 84*
Learning Center Books [Div. of Conrad Lilly Co.] - Newburyport, MA - *LitMarPl 84*
Learning Channel, The - Washington, DC - *BrCabYB 84*
Learning Co., The - Menlo Park, CA - *MicrocomMPl 84*
Learning Co., The - Portola Valley, CA - *MicrocomSwDir 1*
Learning Concepts Inc. - San Diego, CA - *LitMarPl 83, 84*
Learning Corp. of America - New York, NY - *Tel&CabFB 84C*
Learning Endeavors - Apple Valley, MN - *WritMar 84*
Learning House Publishers - Roslyn Heights, NY - *BoPubDir 4 Sup, 5*
Learning Inc. - Manset, ME - *BoPubDir 4, 5*
Learning Line, The - Palo Alto, CA - *LitMarPl 83, 84*
Learning Publications Inc. - Holmes Beach, FL - *LitMarPl 83, 84; WritMar 84*
Learning Resources in International Studies - New York, NY - *BoPubDir 4 Sup, 5*
Learning Resources Network - Manhattan, KS - *BoPubDir 4 Sup, 5*
Learning Source Inc. - Irvine, CA - *MicrocomMPl 84*
Learning Systems Inc. - Fenton, MO - *AvMarPl 83*
Learning Systems Ltd. Corp. - Ft. Collins, CO - *MicrocomMPl 84*
Learning Tools - Cambridge, MA - *MicrocomMPl 83, 84; MicrocomSwDir 1*
Learning Tree Publishing - Englewood, CO - *AvMarPl 83*
Learning Unltd. - Research Triangle Park, NC - *AvMarPl 83*
Learning Well - Roslyn Heights, NY - *MicrocomMPl 84; MicrocomSwDir 1*
Learning Works Inc., The - Santa Barbara, CA - *DirMarMP 83*
Learnxs Press [Aff. of Toronto Board of Education] - Toronto, ON, Canada - *BoPubDir 4, 5*
Lease Sale History [of Computer Sciences Corp.] - El Segundo, CA - *DataDirOnSer 84*

Lease Sale History - Reston, VA - *DirOnDB Spring 84*
Leased Telegraph Service [of Teleglobe Canada] - Montreal, PQ, Canada - *TeleSy&SerDir 7-83*
Leased Voicegrace Service [of Teleglobe Canada] - Montreal, PQ, Canada - *TeleSy&SerDir 7-83*
Leather & Shoes - Des Plaines, IL - *BaconPubCkMag 84; MagDir 84*
Leather Manufacturer, The - Cambridge, MA - *BaconPubCkMag 84; MagDir 84*
Leather Stocking Books - West Allis, WI - *WritMar 84*
Leatherhead Food Research Association - Leatherhead, England - *InfIndMarPl 83*
Leatherneck Magazine - Quantico, VA - *ArtMar 84; BaconPubCkMag 84; MagDir 84; MagIndMarPl 82-83; WritMar 84*
Leavell, Wise & Turner Advertising - Montgomery, AL - *DirPRFirms 83; StaDirAdAg 2-84*
Leavenworth Cable TV [of Tele-Communications Inc.] - Lansing, KS - *Tel&CabFB 84C*
Leavenworth Cable TV [of Tele-Communications Inc.] - Leavenworth, KS - *BrCabYB 84*
Leavenworth Echo - Leavenworth, WA - *BaconPubCkNews 84; Ed&PubIntYB 82*
Leavenworth Times - Leavenworth, KS - *BaconPubCkNews 84; Ed&PubIntYB 82; NewsDir 84*
Leaves of Grass Press - San Rafael, CA - *BoPubDir 4, 5*
Leavitt Advertising Agency - New York, NY - *DirMarMP 83*
Leawood Sun [of Sun Newspapers] - Shawnee Mission, KS - *NewsDir 84*
Leawood Sun - *See* Sun Publications
Lebanese Cuisine - Portland, OR - *BoPubDir 4 Sup, 5*
Lebanon Advertiser - Lebanon, IL - *BaconPubCkNews 84; Ed&PubIntYB 82*
Lebanon Area Merchandiser - Lebanon, PA - *AyerDirPub 83*
Lebanon Cable TV [of Centel Cable Television Co.] - Lebanon, KY - *BrCabYB 84*
Lebanon Cable TV [of National Telecommunications Corp.] - Lebanon, TN - *BrCabYB 84*
Lebanon Cablesystems [of American Cablesystems Corp.] - Lebanon, VA - *Tel&CabFB 84C*
Lebanon CATV Inc. [of Horizon Communications Corp.] - Lebanon, IN - *BrCabYB 84; Tel&CabFB 84C*
Lebanon Connecticut Valley Reporter - Lebanon, NH - *NewsDir 84*
Lebanon Daily Record - Lebanon, MO - *AyerDirPub 83; BaconPubCkNews 84; Ed&PubIntYB 82; NewsDir 84*
Lebanon Democrat - Lebanon, TN - *BaconPubCkNews 84; Ed&PubIntYB 82; NewsDir 84*
Lebanon Enterprise - Lebanon, KY - *BaconPubCkNews 84; Ed&PubIntYB 82; NewsDir 84*
Lebanon Express - Lebanon, OR - *BaconPubCkNews 84; Ed&PubIntYB 82; NewsDir 84*
Lebanon News - Lebanon, PA - *BaconPubCkNews 84; NewsDir 84*
Lebanon News - Lebanon, VA - *BaconPubCkNews 84; NewsDir 84*
Lebanon News-Aim, The - Lebanon, VA - *Ed&PubIntYB 82*
Lebanon Reporter [of Lebanon Newspapers Inc.] - Lebanon, IN - *BaconPubCkNews 84; Ed&PubIntYB 82; NewsDir 84*
Lebanon Star [of Brown Publishing Co.] - Lebanon, OH - *BaconPubCkNews 84; Ed&PubIntYB 82; NewsDir 84*
Lebanon Times - Lebanon, KS - *BaconPubCkNews 84; Ed&PubIntYB 82*
Lebanon TV Cable [of Liberty Communications Inc.] - Lebanon, OR - *BrCabYB 84*
Lebanon Valley Cable TV Co. Inc. [of Lenfest Communications Inc.] - Lebanon, PA - *BrCabYB 84; Tel&CabFB 84C*
Lebanon Western Star - Lebanon, OH - *BaconPubCkNews 84*
Lebanon Wilson World - Lebanon, TN - *BaconPubCkNews 84*
LeBaron, Mae M. - Livonia, MI - *DirInfWP 82*
LeBeau & Associates, Herbert - South Milwaukee, WI - *BoPubDir 4, 5*
LeBeau Santangini Inc. - Rumford, RI - *StaDirAdAg 2-84*
Lebel Enterprises Ltd., J. M. - Edmonton, AB, Canada - *BoPubDir 4, 5*
Leber Katz Partners - New York, NY - *AdAge 3-28-84; StaDirAdAg 2-84*
Lebhar-Friedman Inc. [Subs. of Chain Store Publishing Corp.] - New York, NY - *IntDirMarRes 83; KnowInd 83; LitMarPl 83, 84; MagIndMarPl 82-83; WritMar 84*
Lebo Cable TV Co. - Lebo, KS - *BrCabYB 84; Tel&CabFB 84C*
Lebo Enterprise, The - Burlington, KS - *AyerDirPub 83*
Lebo Enterprise, The - Lebo, KS - *Ed&PubIntYB 82*
LeBoutillier, Joanne B. - Philadelphia, PA - *DirInfWP 82*
LeBow Advertising Co. - Rockville Centre, NY - *BrCabYB 84*
L.E.C. Bookbinders - Lynbrook, NY - *LitMarPl 83, 84; MagIndMarPl 82-83*
Lechner & Charles Huffman, Judith - Saugerties, NY - *LitMarPl 84*
Lechner & Charles Huffman, Judith - Shady, NY - *LitMarPl 83*
L'Echo - Dorion, PQ, Canada - *Ed&PubIntYB 82*
L'Echo de Frontenac - Lac Megantic, PQ, Canada - *Ed&PubIntYB 82*
L'Echo de la Lievre - Mont Laurier, PQ, Canada - *Ed&PubIntYB 82*
L'Echo de La Tuque - La Tuque, PQ, Canada - *Ed&PubIntYB 82*
L'Echo de Louiseville/Berthier - Louiseville, PQ, Canada - *Ed&PubIntYB 82*
L'Echo de Vaudreuil-Soulanges - Dorion, PQ, Canada - *AyerDirPub 83*
L'Echo de Vaudreuil Soulanges - Vaudreuil, PQ, Canada - *Ed&PubIntYB 82*
L'Echo du Nord - St. Jerome, PQ, Canada - *Ed&PubIntYB 82*
L'Eclaireur-Progres - St. Georges, PQ, Canada - *Ed&PubIntYB 82*
L'Eco d'Italia - San Francisco, CA - *NewsDir 84*
L'Eco d'Italia - Vancouver, BC, Canada - *Ed&PubIntYB 82*
Leco Photo Service Inc. - New York, NY - *LitMarPl 83*
Lector [of California Spanish Language Data Base] - Berkeley, CA - *LitMag&SmPr 83-84*
Lectorum Publications Inc. - New York, NY - *LitMarPl 83, 84*
Lectrosonics Inc. - Albuquerque, NM - *AvMarPl 83*
LED Systems Inc. - Mechanicsburg, PA - *TeleSy&SerDir 7-83*
LEDA2 - Frascati, Italy - *DirOnDB Spring 84*
Lederer Enterprises - Lake Oswego, OR - *BoPubDir 5*
Lederer, Wolfgang - Mill Valley, CA - *LitMarPl 83, 84; MagIndMarPl 82-83*
Ledger - Enterprise, AL - *AyerDirPub 83*
Ledger - Antioch, CA - *AyerDirPub 83*
Ledger - Columbus, GA - *AyerDirPub 83*
Ledger - Canton, IL - *AyerDirPub 83*
Ledger - Steeleville, IL - *AyerDirPub 83*
Ledger - Noblesville, IN - *AyerDirPub 83*
Ledger - Fairfield, IA - *AyerDirPub 83*
Ledger - Cawker City, KS - *AyerDirPub 83*
Ledger - Kentwood, LA - *AyerDirPub 83*
Ledger - Albany, MO - *AyerDirPub 83*
Ledger - Mexico, MO - *AyerDirPub 83*
Ledger - Hemingford, NE - *AyerDirPub 83; Ed&PubIntYB 82*
Ledger - Columbiana, OH - *AyerDirPub 83*
Ledger - Broken Arrow, OK - *AyerDirPub 83*
Ledger - Heavener, OK - *AyerDirPub 83*
Ledger - Ellwood City, PA - *AyerDirPub 83*
Ledger - Tripp, SD - *AyerDirPub 83*
Ledger - Ballinger, TX - *AyerDirPub 83*
Ledger & Times - Murray, KY - *AyerDirPub 83*
Ledger & Tribune [of Thomson Newspapers Inc.] - New Albany, IN - *AyerDirPub 83; Ed&PubIntYB 82; NewsDir 84*
Ledger Enquirer [of R. W. Page Corp.] - Columbus, GA - *AyerDirPub 83; NewsDir 84*
Ledger Gazette - Lancaster, CA - *AyerDirPub 83*
Ledger-Independent, The [of Maysville Newspaper Inc.] - Maysville, KY - *AyerDirPub 83; Ed&PubIntYB 82; NewsDir 84*
Ledger-Messenger - Oakland, IL - *Ed&PubIntYB 82*
Ledger-Sentinel - Oswego, IL - *Ed&PubIntYB 82*
Ledger Star [of Landmark Communications Inc.] - Norfolk, VA - *AyerDirPub 83; BaconPubCkNews 84; Ed&PubIntYB 82; LitMarPl 83, 84; NewsBur 6*
Ledger, The - Montrose, CA - *Ed&PubIntYB 82*
Ledger, The - Lakeland, FL - *AyerDirPub 83; BaconPubCkNews 84; Ed&PubIntYB 82*
Ledger-Tribune - Attica, IN - *AyerDirPub 83*
Ledgewood West Morris Star Journal - Ledgewood, NJ - *BaconPubCkNews 84; NewsDir 84*

Leduc Representative - Leduc, AB, Canada - *Ed&PubIntYB 82*
Lee & Associates Inc. - Los Angeles, CA - *DirPRFirms 83; StaDirAdAg 2-84*
Lee & Co., Brian - Milwaukee, WI - *WritMar 84*
Lee & Co., John - Los Angeles, CA - *StaDirAdAg 2-84*
Lee & Young Communications Inc. - New York, NY - *HBIndAd&MS 82-83*
Lee/Baader & Rose Inc. - East Orange, NJ - *StaDirAdAg 2-84*
Lee Booksellers, J. & L. - Lincoln, NE - *BoPubDir 4 Sup, 5*
Lee Co. Inc. - Terre Haute, IN - *AvMarPl 83*
Lee Co., Norma A. - New York, NY - *DirPRFirms 83*
Lee Co., Norma A. - *See* Fitzgerald Gardner Advertising Inc.
Lee County CATV - Beattyville, KY - *Tel&CabFB 84C*
Lee County Messenger - Bishopville, SC - *Ed&PubIntYB 82*
Lee County Shopper - Cape Coral, FL - *AyerDirPub 83*
Lee County Sun News - Tupelo, MS - *AyerDirPub 83*
Lee County TV - Beattyville, KY - *BrCabYB 84*
Lee County TV - Heidelburg, KY - *BrCabYB 84*
Lee Data Corp. - Eden Prairie, MN - *DataDirSup 7-83; WhoWMicrocom 83*
Lee Enterprises - Davenport, IA - *AdAge 6-28-84; BrCabYB 84; KnowInd 83*
Lee Enterprises (Broadcast Div.) - Davenport, IA - *Tel&CabFB 84S*
Lee Inc., J. Richard - Los Angeles, CA - *BrCabYB 84; StaDirAdAg 2-84*
Lee, Kenneth W. - Glendale, CA - *BoPubDir 4, 5*
Lee Lighting America Ltd. - New York, NY - *AvMarPl 83*
Lee Myles Associates Inc. - New York, NY - *StaDirAdAg 2-84*
Lee Newspapers - Davenport, IA - *Ed&PubIntYB 82*
Lee Photography, Robert II - St. Louis, MO - *LitMarPl 83, 84; MagIndMarPl 82-83*
Lee Publications Inc. - Cambridge, MA - *BoPubDir 5*
Lee Publishers Group Inc. - New York, NY - *BoPubDir 4, 5*
Lee Publishing, Walt - Potter Valley, CA - *BoPubDir 4, 5*
Lee Town News - Des Moines, IA - *AyerDirPub 83; NewsDir 84*
Lee Town News - East Des Moines, IA - *Ed&PubIntYB 82*
Lee TV Cable Co. Inc. - Pennington Gap, VA - *BrCabYB 84; Tel&CabFB 84C*
Lee Valley Tools Ltd. - Ottawa, ON, Canada - *BoPubDir 5*
Lee Words/Graphics - Lee, MA - *LitMarPl 83, 84; MagIndMarPl 82-83*
Leechburg Advance - Leechburg, PA - *BaconPubCkNews 84; Ed&PubIntYB 82*
Leedal Inc. (Matrix Div.) - Chicago, IL - *AvMarPl 83*
Leedey Star - Leedey, OK - *Ed&PubIntYB 82*
Leeds Advertising Inc. - Miami, FL - *StaDirAdAg 2-84*
Leeds & Associates Inc., Barry - New York, NY - *HBIndAd&MS 82-83; IntDirMarRes 83*
Leeds & Northrup Co. - North Wales, PA - *DataDirSup 7-83*
Leeds Cable TV Inc. - Lansford, ND - *BrCabYB 84*
Leeds Cable TV Inc. - Leeds, ND - *Tel&CabFB 84C*
Leeds Cablevision Inc. - Leeds, AL - *BrCabYB 84; Tel&CabFB 84C*
Leeds Music Corp. - *See* MCA Music
Leeds News - Leeds, AL - *BaconPubCkNews 84; Ed&PubIntYB 82; NewsDir 84*
Leeds Polytechnic School of Librarianship - Leeds, England - *MicroMarPl 82-83*
Leeds Telephone Co. Inc. [Aff. of Mid-Continent Telephone Corp.] - Leeds, AL - *TelDir&BG 83-84*
Leelanau Enterprise [of Leelanau Publishing Co. Inc.] - Leland, MI - *AyerDirPub 83; NewsDir 84*
Leelanau Enterprise & Tribune, The - Leland, MI - *Ed&PubIntYB 82*
Lee's ABC of the Telephone - Geneva, IL - *BoPubDir 4*
Lee's Books for Young Readers - Wellington, TX - *WritMar 84*
Lees-McRae College (Puddingstone Press) - Banner Elk, NC - *BoPubDir 4, 5*
Lee's Summit Journal - Lee's Summit, MO - *BaconPubCkNews 84; Ed&PubIntYB 82; NewsDir 84*
Leesburg Cablevision Inc. [of Scripps-Howard Cable Co.] - Leesburg, FL - *Tel&CabFB 84C*
Leesburg Citizen - Leesburg, OH - *AyerDirPub 83; Ed&PubIntYB 82*
Leesburg Citizen - *See* Greenfield Times Publishers
Leesburg Commercial [of New York Times Co.] - Leesburg, FL - *AyerDirPub 83; BaconPubCkNews 84; Ed&PubIntYB 82; NewsDir 84*
Leesburg Lake News - Leesburg, FL - *BaconPubCkNews 84*
Leesburg Lakeshore Mobile Home Park Inc. - Leesburg, FL - *BrCabYB 84; Tel&CabFB 84C*
Leesburg Loudoun Times-Mirror - *See* Loudoun Times Publishing Co. Inc.
Leeser & Associates Inc., Lew - Los Angeles, CA - *StaDirAdAg 2-84*
Leeson, Tom & Pat - Vancouver, WA - *LitMarPl 84*
Leesville Leader - Leesville, LA - *BaconPubCkNews 84; Ed&PubIntYB 82; NewsDir 84*
Leete's Island Books - New Haven, CT - *BoPubDir 4 Sup, 5; LitMag&SmPr 83-84*
LeFan Features, Mike - Temple, TX - *Ed&PubIntYB 82*
LeFebure Corp. - Cedar Rapids, IA - *DataDirSup 7-83*
Leferman Associates Inc. - Stamford, CT - *IntDirMarRes 83*
Leff & Co. Inc., Murray - New York, NY - *StaDirAdAg 2-84*
Leff Associates Inc., Jerry - New York, NY - *LitMarPl 83, 84; MagIndMarPl 82-83*
Leff, Perry B. - *See* National Telecommunications
Lefkoff Innovation Corp. - Atlanta, GA - *WhoWMicrocom 83*
Left Bank Books - Seattle, WA - *BoPubDir 5; LitMag&SmPr 83-84*
Left Curve Publications - Oakland, CA - *BoPubDir 4 Sup, 5*
Lefton Co., Al Paul - New York, NY - *AdAge 3-28-84; HBIndAd&MS 82-83; StaDirAdAg 2-84*
Lefton Co. Inc., Al Paul - Philadelphia, PA - *BrCabYB 84*
Legacy Books - Hatboro, PA - *LitMag&SmPr 83-84*
Legal Administrator, The - Glenview, IL - *BaconPubCkMag 84*
Legal Advocate [of Daily Court Review Inc.] - Houston, TX - *NewsDir 84*
Legal Book Co. - Los Angeles, CA - *BoPubDir 4, 5*
Legal Economics - Columbia, SC - *ArtMar 84; BaconPubCkMag 84; WritMar 84*
Legal Forum - East Setauket, NY - *DirOnDB Spring 84*
Legal Information & Reference Services [of U.S. General Accounting Office] - Washington, DC - *EISS 83*
Legal Intelligencer [of Packard Press] - Philadelphia, PA - *Ed&PubIntYB 82; NewsDir 84*
Legal Management Services Inc. - New York, NY - *BoPubDir 4 Sup, 5; LitMag&SmPr 83-84*
Legal Marketing Research - Evanston, IL - *IntDirMarRes 83*
Legal News - Detroit, MI - *Ed&PubIntYB 82*
Legal News - Cleveland, OH - *Ed&PubIntYB 82*
Legal News - Toledo, OH - *Ed&PubIntYB 82; NewsDir 84*
Legal Publications Inc. - Van Nuys, CA - *BoPubDir 4, 5*
Legal Register Publishing Co. - Washington, DC - *BoPubDir 5*
Legal Resource Index [of Information Access Corp.] - Los Altos, CA - *DBBus 82*
Legal Resource Index [of Information Access Co.] - Menlo Park, CA - *CompReadDB 82; DataDirOnSer 84; DirOnDB Spring 84; EISS 83; OnBibDB 3*
Legal Secretaries Newsletter, The - Denver, CO - *BaconPubCkMag 84*
Legal Systems Development - Placerville, CA - *MicrocomMPl 84*
Legal Systems Letter - New York, NY - *BaconPubCkMag 84*
Legal Technology Group - London, England - *EISS 5-84 Sup*
Legal Times [of Harcourt Brace Jovanovich Inc.] - Washington, DC - *BaconPubCkMag 84; LitMarPl 83, 84*
Legal Translating Service, The - Cambridge, MA - *LitMarPl 83, 84*
Legalvision Inc. - New York, NY - *BillIntBG 83-84*
Legasse Associates Advertising Inc. - Walpole, NH - *StaDirAdAg 2-84*
Legend Industries Ltd. - Pontiac, MI - *MicrocomMPl 84; MicrocomSwDir 1*
Legend Records & Promotions - Lenoir, NC - *BillIntBG 83-84*
Legey Associates - Albuquerque, NM - *WhoWMicrocom 83*
Leggett & Lustig Research Inc. - New York, NY - *IntDirMarRes 83*
Leggett, Harry F. - Victoria, BC, Canada - *BoPubDir 4 Sup, 5*

Leggi Regionali [of Centro per la Documentazione Automatica] - Rome, Italy - *CompReadDB 82*
Legi-Slate [Subs. of The Washington Post Co.] - Washington, DC - *DataDirOnSer 84; DirOnDB Spring 84; EISS 83; MicrocomMPl 84*
Legi-Slate - Dallas, TX - *CompReadDB 82; InfIndMarPl 83*
Legi-Tech - Sacramento, CA - *DirOnDB Spring 84*
Legion - Ottawa, ON, Canada - *ArtMar 84; BaconPubCkMag 84*
Legion Software - Joplin, MO - *WhoWMicrocom 83*
Legislative Administrative Committee [of Oregon Legislature] - Salem, OR - *DataDirOnSer 84*
Legislative Authorization Program Information System [of U.S. General Accounting Office] - Washington, DC - *EISS 83*
Legislative Bill Status System - Springfield, IL - *DirOnDB Spring 84*
Legislative Data Processing Services [of Alaska State Legislative Affairs Agency] - Juneau, AK - *EISS 83*
Legislative Data Processing Systems [of Georgia State Legislature] - Atlanta, GA - *EISS 83*
Legislative Information Office [of Maine State Legislature] - Augusta, ME - *EISS 83*
Legislative Information Processing Systems [of Rhode Island State General Assembly] - Providence, RI - *EISS 83*
Legislative Information System [of National Conference of State Legislatures] - Denver, CO - *EISS 83*
Legislative Information System [of Illinois General Assembly] - Springfield, IL - *DataDirOnSer 84; EISS 83*
Legislative Information System [of Kansas State Legislature] - Topeka, KS - *EISS 83*
Legislative Information System [of Mississippi State Central Data Processing Authority] - Jackson, MS - *EISS 83*
Legislative Information System [of Washington State Legislature] - Olympia, WA - *EISS 83*
Legislative Information Systems [of South Dakota State Legislative Research Council] - Pierre, SD - *EISS 83*
Legislative Intelligence Week - Washington, DC - *DirOnDB Spring 84*
Legislative Intelligence Week [of NewsNet Inc.] - Bryn Mawr, PA - *DataDirOnSer 84*
Legislative Reference Bureau [Aff. of Hawaii State Legislature] - Honolulu, HI - *BoPubDir 4 Sup*
Legislative Reference Bureau [of Wisconsin State Legislature] - Madison, WI - *EISS 83*
Legislative Services Office [of North Carolina State Legislature] - Raleigh, NC - *EISS 83*
Legist Automation - Arlington, TX - *MicrocomMPl 84*
Legrand Records International - Norfolk, VA - *BillIntBG 83-84*
Legs Music Inc. - *See* Abkco Music Inc.
Legz Music - *See* Ciano Publishing Co.
Lehi Free Press - Lehi, UT - *AyerDirPub 83*
Lehi Free Press - *See* Newtah News Group
Lehi Publishing Co. [Aff. of Law Enforcement Hypnosis Institute Inc.] - Los Angeles, CA - *BoPubDir 4 Sup, 5*
Lehigh Acres News - Lehigh Acres, FL - *BaconPubCkNews 84*
Lehigh Acres Suburban Reporter, The - Ft. Myers, FL - *NewsDir 84*
Lehigh Electronic Color [Subs. of Lehigh Press] - Elk Grove Village, IL - *LitMarPl 83, 84; MagIndMarPl 82-83*
Lehigh Information Service [of Lehigh University Libraries] - Bethlehem, PA - *EISS 7-83 Sup*
Lehigh-Leopold Furniture - Burlington, IA - *DirInfWP 82*
Lehigh News - Lehigh Acres, FL - *AyerDirPub 83; Ed&PubIntYB 82; NewsDir 84*
Lehigh Press Inc. - Pennsauken, NJ - *LitMarPl 83, 84; MagIndMarPl 82-83*
Lehigh/Rocappi [Div. of Lehigh Press Inc.] - Pennsauken, NJ - *InfoS 83-84; LitMarPl 84*
Lehigh Valley Cooperative Telephone Association - Lehigh, IA - *TelDir&BG 83-84*
Lehigh Valley Motor Club News - Allentown, PA - *MagDir 84*
Lehighton Times News [of Pencor Services Inc.] - Lehighton, PA - *BaconPubCkNews 84; NewsDir 84*
Lehman Brothers Kuhn Loeb (Research Dept.) - New York, NY - *ADAPSOMemDir 83-84*
Lehman Newspapers - Longmont, CO - *Ed&PubIntYB 82*
Lehmann & Associates Inc., Ernest K. - Minneapolis, MN - *EISS 5-84 Sup*
Lehua Music Co. - Honolulu, HI - *BillIntBG 83-84*
Leibfried, John E. Jr. - Gladwyne, PA - *LitMarPl 83, 84*
Leibowitz Market Research Associates Inc. - Charlotte, NC - *IntDirMarRes 83*
Leibson, Lightle & Associates Inc. - Chicago, IL - *StaDirAdAg 2-84*
Leiffer Bureau of Social & Religious Research [Aff. of Garrett-Evangelical Theological Seminary] - Evanston, IL - *BoPubDir 4 Sup, 5*
Leigh-Bell & Associates Ltd., Peter - Burlington, ON, Canada - *EISS 83; InfoS 83-84*
Leigh Group Inc. - Lakewood, NJ - *BillIntBG 83-84*
Leigh Inc., W. Colston - Princeton, NJ - *LitMarPl 83, 84*
Leigh World - Leigh, NE - *BaconPubCkNews 84; Ed&PubIntYB 82*
Leighton & Associates Inc., Joe - Dana Point, CA - *StaDirAdAg 2-84*
Leighton Enterprises Inc. - St. Cloud, MN - *BrCabYB 84*
Leighton, Estella R. - Oswego, NY - *LitMarPl 83, 84*
Leighton, Thomas G. - New York, NY - *DirPRFirms 83*
Leinwand, Freda - New York, NY - *LitMarPl 83, 84*
Leipsic Free Press - Leipsic, OH - *Ed&PubIntYB 82*
Leisner & Associates, Abe - New York, NY - *IntDirMarRes 83*
Leisure Beverage Insider Newsletter - New York, NY - *BaconPubCkMag 84*
Leisure Business - Washington, DC - *BaconPubCkMag 84*
Leisure Press [Subs. of SJ Books Inc.] - Oakland, CA - *LitMarPl 84*
Leisure Press [Subs. of SJ Books Inc.] - West Point, NY - *BoPubDir 4; LitMarPl 83*
Leisure, Recreation, & Tourism Abstracts [of Commonwealth Bureau of Agricultural Economics] - Oxford, England - *CompReadDB 82*
Leisure Studies Data Bank [of University of Waterloo] - Waterloo, ON, Canada - *EISS 83*
Leisure Time Electronics [of Charleson Publishing] - New York, NY - *BaconPubCkMag 84; MicrocomMPl 84; WritMar 84*
Leisure Ways - Toronto, ON, Canada - *BaconPubCkMag 84*
Leisure World News [of Golden West Publishing Inc.] - Laguna Hills, CA - *NewsDir 84*
Leisure World News - San Juan Capistrano, CA - *AyerDirPub 83*
Leisureguide - Agoura, CA - *MagDir 84; WritMar 84*
Leisureguide International - London, England - *WritMar 84*
Leitchfield Grayson County News-Gazette - Leitchfield, KY - *BaconPubCkNews 84*
Leitchfield Grayson County News-Gazette - *See* Smith Communications Inc., Al
Leitchfield News-Gazette [of Russellville Logan Ink Inc.] - Russellville, KY - *NewsDir 84*
LeJan Advertising Agency - Los Angeles, CA - *ArtMar 84*
Lekas & Associates Inc. - New York, NY - *IntDirMarRes 83*
Lektra Laboratories - College Point, NY - *AvMarPl 83*
Leland Advertising Inc. - New York, NY - *StaDirAdAg 2-84*
Leland Leelanau Enterprise Tribune - Leland, MI - *BaconPubCkNews 84*
Leland Progress - Leland, MS - *BaconPubCkNews 84; Ed&PubIntYB 82*
Leland Young Co. - Bay Pines, FL - *MicrocomSwDir 1*
Leland Young Co. - Tampa, FL - *MicrocomMPl 84*
Lem Associates Inc., Dean - Los Angeles, CA - *BoPubDir 4, 5*
Lemand & Co. Inc. - Orlando, FL - *StaDirAdAg 2-84*
LeMans Record Co. - Somerville, NJ - *BillIntBG 83-84*
LeMarche Manufacturing Co. - Des Plaines, IL - *DataDirSup 7-83*
LEMCOM Systems Inc. - Phoenix, AZ - *DataDirSup 7-83*
Lemhi Telephone Co. [Aff. of Century Telephone Enterprises Inc.] - Salmon, ID - *TelDir&BG 83-84*
Lemko News - Toronto, ON, Canada - *Ed&PubIntYB 82*
Lemley Music, Ty - *See* Tymena Music
Lemmon Cable TV [of Midcontinent Cable Inc.] - Lemmon, SD - *BrCabYB 84; Tel&CabFB 84C*
Lemmon Leader - Lemmon, SD - *BaconPubCkNews 84; Ed&PubIntYB 82*
Lemon Grove Pennysaver - Mission Viejo, CA - *AyerDirPub 83*
Lemon Grove Review [of Homeland Publishing Co.] - Lemon Grove, CA - *Ed&PubIntYB 82; NewsDir 84*
Lemon Grove Review - *See* Homeland Publishing Co.

Lemont Consulting Group - New York, NY - *HBIndAd&MS 82-83*
Lemont Metropolitan - Lemont, IL - *Ed&PubIntYB 82*
Lemonweir Valley Telephone Co. - Camp Douglas, WI - *TelDir&BG 83-84*
Lemoore Advance - Lemoore, CA - *BaconPubCkNews 84; Ed&PubIntYB 82*
Lemoore Leader - Lemoore, CA - *Ed&PubIntYB 82*
Lempert Co. - Belleville, NJ - *AdAge 3-28-84*
Lempert Design & Marketing - Belleville, NJ - *StaDirAdAg 2-84*
Lemrac CATV - Bear Valley, CA - *BrCabYB 84; Tel&CabFB 84C*
Lemur Musical Research Corp. - Bloomington, IN - *BoPubDir 4 Sup, 5*
Len-Lon Music Publishing Co. - Los Angeles, CA - *BillIntBG 83-84*
Lena Northwestern Illinois Farmer - Lena, IL - *BaconPubCkNews 84*
Lenac, Warford, Stone Inc. - Newport Beach, CA - *DirPRFirms 83; StaDirAdAg 2-84*
Lenchamps Publishers - Washington, DC - *BoPubDir 4, 5*
Lenco Inc. - Jackson, MO - *AvMarPl 83*
Lending Div. [of British Library] - Wetherby, England - *EISS 83*
Lenexa Sun [of Sun Newspapers] - Shawnee Mission, KS - *NewsDir 84*
Lenexa Sun - *See* Sun Publications
Lenfest Berks Cable TV Inc. [of Lenfest Communications Inc.] - Boyertown, PA - *Tel&CabFB 84C*
Lenfest Communications Inc. - Abington, PA - *Tel&CabFB 84C p.1687*
Lenfest Communications Inc. - Huntingdon Valley, PA - *BrCabYB 84 p.D-303*
Lenmac Music - *See* De Walden Music
Lenniger Payne Literary Agency Inc. - New York, NY - *LitMarPl 83, 84*
Lenninger, Sharon K. - Milwaukee, WI - *LitMarPl 83, 84*
Lennon Telephone Co. - Lennon, MI - *TelDir&BG 83-84*
Lennox Citizen - *See* Coast Media Newspapers
Lennox Independent - Lennox, SD - *BaconPubCkNews 84; Ed&PubIntYB 82*
Lennoxville Transvision Inc. - Lennoxville, PQ, Canada - *BrCabYB 84; Tel&CabFB 84C*
Lenny Publishing Co. - *See* Su-Ma Publishing Co. Inc.
Lenoir City News - Lenoir City, TN - *NewsDir 84*
Lenoir City News-Herald - Lenoir City, TN - *BaconPubCkNews 84*
Lenoir News-Topic - Lenoir, NC - *BaconPubCkNews 84; Ed&PubIntYB 82; NewsDir 84*
Lenoir TV Cable Inc. [of McDonald Group Inc.] - Lenoir, NC - *BrCabYB 84*
Lenora TV Cable Co. [of CATV Inc.] - Lenora, KS - *Tel&CabFB 84C*
Lenora TV Cable Co. [of CATV Inc.] - Lenora, TX - *BrCabYB 84*
Lenox Cablevision - Lenox, IA - *BrCabYB 84; Tel&CabFB 84C*
Lenox Hill Publishing & Distributing Corp. [Aff. of Burt Franklin & Co. Inc.] - New York, NY - *LitMarPl 83, 84*
Lenox Time-Table - Lenox, IA - *BaconPubCkNews 84; Ed&PubIntYB 82*
Lenroy Music - *See* Tridex Music Co.
Lens - Garden City, NY - *BaconPubCkMag 84; MagDir 84; MagIndMarPl 82-83*
Lens & Repro Equipment Corp. - New York, NY - *AvMarPl 83*
Lens' on Campus - Garden City, NY - *MagDir 84*
Lent, Max - Rochester, NY - *LitMarPl 84*
Leo Animation - New York, NY - *AvMarPl 83*
L.E.O. Broadcasting Inc. - St. Cloud, MN - *BrCabYB 84*
Leola McPherson County Herald - Leola, SD - *BaconPubCkNews 84*
Leoleen-Durck Creations [Subs. of Leonard Bruce Designs] - Jackson, TN - *LitMarPl 84*
Leon Co. Inc., S. R. - Great Neck, NY - *AdAge 3-28-84; StaDirAdAg 2-84*
Leon County News, The - Centerville, TX - *Ed&PubIntYB 82*
Leon Journal-Reporter - Leon, IA - *BaconPubCkNews 84; Ed&PubIntYB 82; NewsDir 84*
Leon News - Leon, KS - *Ed&PubIntYB 82*
Leonard AV Communications [Div. of Jack Hodges III Communications] - New Orleans, LA - *AvMarPl 83*
Leonard Enterprises Inc., Herbert - Van Nuys, CA - *TelAl 83, 84*
Leonard Financial Planning Systems Inc. - Raleigh, NC - *WhoWMicrocom 83*
Leonard Graphic - Leonard, TX - *BaconPubCkNews 84; Ed&PubIntYB 82*
Leonard, Isabel A. - Hingham, MA - *LitMarPl 83, 84; MagIndMarPl 82-83*
Leonard Monahan Saabye - Providence, RI - *AdAge 3-28-84; StaDirAdAg 2-84*
Leonard Productions Inc. - Gainesville, TX - *BillIntBG 83-84*
Leonard Publishing Corp., Hal - Milwaukee, WI - *BillIntBG 83-84; BoPubDir 4 Sup, 5*
Leonarda Productions - New York, NY - *BillIntBG 83-84*
Leonardo Literary Typesetting - Santa Monica, CA - *LitMarPl 84*
Leonardo Literary Typesetting - Kailua, HI - *LitMarPl 83*
Leonardtown St. Mary's Beacon - Mechanicsville, MD - *NewsDir 84*
Leone Agency Inc., The Adele - New York, NY - *LitMarPl 83, 84*
Leonine Press - Kalamazoo, MI - *BoPubDir 4, 5*
Leonore Mutual Telephone Co. - Leonore, IL - *TelDir&BG 83-84*
Leoti Standard - Leoti, KS - *BaconPubCkNews 84; Ed&PubIntYB 82*
Leousis Advertising SA, J. N. - Athens, Greece - *StaDirAdAg 2-84*
Lepanto Cable TV [of Spectrum Teltronics Inc.] - Jonesboro, AR - *BrCabYB 84*
Lepanto News Record - Lepanto, AR - *BaconPubCkNews 84; Ed&PubIntYB 82*
L'Epervier Press - Seattle, WA - *BoPubDir 4, 5; LitMag&SmPr 83-84*
Lepi Graphics - Albany, NY - *LitMarPl 83*
Leposky, George - Coral Gables, FL - *Ed&PubIntYB 82*
Lepp & Associates - Los Osos, CA - *AvMarPl 83*
Leprechaun Books - Fulford, BC, Canada - *BoPubDir 4, 5*
Leprechaun Press - New York, NY - *BoPubDir 5*
Lerch & Co. Inc., Donald - Washington, DC - *DirPRFirms 83*
Lerner, Abe - New York, NY - *LitMarPl 83, 84*
Lerner Communications Inc. - Elmwood Park, IL - *BrCabYB 84*
Lerner Life Newspapers - Skokie, IL - *BaconPubCkNews 84*
Lerner Publications Co. - Minneapolis, MN - *LitMarPl 83, 84*
Lerner Scott Corp. - Wilmette, IL - *DirMarMP 83*
Lerner Times Newspapers - Chicago, IL - *BaconPubCkNews 84*
Leroy Coffey County Reporter - Leroy, KS - *BaconPubCkNews 84*
Leroy Gazette-News & Country Post - Geneseo, NY - *AyerDirPub 83*
Les Cables de Nord - Roberval, PQ, Canada - *BrCabYB 84*
Les Echos Abitbien - Val d'Or, PQ, Canada - *Ed&PubIntYB 82*
Les Editions Bellarmin Enr. - Montreal, PQ, Canada - *LitMarPl 83, 84*
Les Editions de l'Homme [Div. of Dogides] - Montreal, PQ, Canada - *LitMarPl 83, 84*
Les Editions du Richelieu Ltee. - St. Jean, PQ, Canada - *LitMarPl 83, 84*
Les Editions Francaises Inc. - Boucherville, PQ, Canada - *LitMarPl 83, 84*
Les Editions Internationales Alain Stanke Ltd. - Montreal, PQ, Canada - *LitMarPl 83, 84*
Les Editions la Presse Ltee. [Subs. of La Presse Ltee.] - Montreal, PQ, Canada - *LitMarPl 83, 84*
Les Editions Projets Inc. - Sherbrooke, PQ, Canada - *LitMarPl 83, 84*
Les Presses de la Fondation Nationale des Sciences Politiques - Paris, France - *MicroMarPl 82-83*
Les Presses de l'Universite de Montreal - Montreal, PQ, Canada - *LitMarPl 83, 84; MicroMarPl 82-83*
Les Presses de l'Universite du Quebec - Ste-Foy, PQ, Canada - *LitMarPl 83, 84*
Les Presses de l'Universite Laval - Ste-Foy, PQ, Canada - *LitMarPl 83, 84*

Les Rapports de la Cour Federale du Canada [of QL Systems Ltd.] - Ottawa, ON, Canada - *DataDirOnSer 84; DirOnDB Spring 84*
Les Rapports de la Cour Supreme du Canada [of QL Systems Ltd.] - Ottawa, ON, Canada - *DataDirOnSer 84; DirOnDB Spring 84*
Les Recherches Daniel Say Cie - Vancouver, BC, Canada - *LitMag&SmPr 83-84*
Les Statutus Revises du Canada [of QL Systems Ltd.] - Ottawa, ON, Canada - *DataDirOnSer 84*
Lesansky Inc., Doris - Bonita Springs, FL - *IntDirMarRes 83*
Lesbian Connection - East Lansing, MI - *LitMag&SmPr 83-84*
Lesbian Voices - San Jose, CA - *LitMag&SmPr 83-84*
Lescarboura Advertising Inc. - Briarcliff Manor, NY - *StaDirAdAg 2-84*
Lescher & Lescher Ltd. - New York, NY - *LitMarPl 83, 84*
Lescron Enterprises Inc. - Johnson City, NY - *LitMarPl 83*
LeSea Broadcasting Network - Indianapolis, IN - *Tel&CabFB 84C*
Lesemann, Gloria - New York, NY - *MagIndMarPl 82-83*
LeShell Music - *See* Brunswick Music Publishing Co.
Lesher Associates, Stephan - Washington, DC - *DirPRFirms 83*
Lesher Communications Inc. - Walnut Creek, CA - *BrCabYB 84*
Lesher Newspapers - Walnut Creek, CA - *Ed&PubIntYB 82*
Lesko Inc. - Pittsburgh, PA - *DirPRFirms 83; StaDirAdAg 2-84*
Leslie Advertising Agency - Greenville, SC - *AdAge 3-28-84; StaDirAdAg 2-84*
Leslie & Hoover Advertising Inc. - El Paso, TX - *StaDirAdAg 2-84*
Leslie & Leslie Inc. - New York, NY - *DirPRFirms 83*
Leslie & Martin Advertising - Charlotte, NC - *StaDirAdAg 2-84*
Leslie County News, The - Hyden, KY - *AyerDirPub 83; Ed&PubIntYB 82*
Leslie County Telephone Co. - Hyden, KY - *TelDir&BG 83-84*
Leslie Local Independent - Jackson, MI - *NewsDir 84*
Leslie Local Independent - Leslie, MI - *AyerDirPub 83; BaconPubCkNews 84; Ed&PubIntYB 82*
Leslie Local Independent Shopping Guide - Leslie, MI - *AyerDirPub 83*
Leslie Music Supply - Oakville, ON, Canada - *BoPubDir 4, 5*
Leslie Paper Co. - Minneapolis, MN - *DirInfWP 82*
Lesly Associates Inc. - New York, NY - *StaDirAdAg 2-84*
Lesly Co., The Philip - Chicago, IL - *DirPRFirms 83*
Less is More Advertising & Promotions Inc. - New York, NY - *HBIndAd&MS 82-83*
Lesser, Robert - Weymouth, MA - *Tel&CabFB 84C p.1687*
Lessing-Flynn Advertising Co. - Des Moines, IA - *AdAge 3-28-84; StaDirAdAg 2-84*
Lessner Slossberg Gahl & Partners - Avon, CT - *AdAge 3-28-84; StaDirAdAg 2-84*
Lesso Inc. - Wichita, KS - *BrCabYB 84*
Lester & Orpen Dennys Ltd. - Toronto, ON, Canada - *LitMarPl 83, 84; WritMar 84*
Lester Associates - New Haven, CT - *StaDirAdAg 2-84*
Lester, Marilyn - New York, NY - *LitMarPl 83*
Lester Prairie Journal - Lester Prairie, MN - *BaconPubCkNews 84*
Lester Productions, Gene - North Hollywood, CA - *AvMarPl 83; Tel&CabFB 84C*
Lester Syndicate - Cupertino, CA - *Ed&PubIntYB 82*
Lestock Historical Committee - Lestock, SK, Canada - *BoPubDir 4 Sup, 5*
Letcher County Community Press - Cromona, KY - *AyerDirPub 83*
Letcher County Community Press, The - Jenkins, KY - *Ed&PubIntYB 82*
Letcher Offshore Design - Southwest Harbor, ME - *MicrocomMPl 84*
Leterman-Gortz Corp., The - Stamford, CT - *ADAPSOMemDir 83-84*
Lethbridge Cablenet [of Cablenet Ltd.] - Lethbridge, AB, Canada - *BrCabYB 84*
Lethbridge Herald, The [of Canadian Newspaper Co. Ltd.] - Lethbridge, AB, Canada - *BaconPubCkNews 84; Ed&PubIntYB 82*
Lethbridge, Jackson - St. Thomas, ON, Canada - *LitMarPl 83*
L'Etincelle - Windsor, PQ, Canada - *Ed&PubIntYB 82*
Letna Music Co. - *See* Draw Music Co.
L'Etoile de l'Outaouais-St.-Laurent - Dorion, PQ, Canada - *Ed&PubIntYB 82*
L'Etoile du Lac - Roberval, PQ, Canada - *Ed&PubIntYB 82*
Letraset USA Inc. [Div. of Esselte Business Systems Group] - Paramus, NJ - *AvMarPl 83; LitMarPl 83*
Let's Cook It Metric - Tulsa, OK - *BoPubDir 4, 5*
Let's Flaunt It! - Ames, IA - *LitMag&SmPr 83-84*
Let's Have Lunch Music - *See* Danoff Music Co.
Let's Live [of Oxford Industries Inc.] - Los Angeles, CA - *BaconPubCkMag 84; MagDir 84; MagIndMarPl 82-83; WritMar 84*
Let's Read [Div. of Bibliotech Corp.] - Framingham, MA - *LitMarPl 83, 84*
Letter Among Friends, A - Groton, CT - *LitMag&SmPr 83-84*
Letter Graphics/CPC Inc. - Kansas City, MO - *LitMarPl 83, 84*
Letter Guild Inc., The - New York, NY - *LitMarPl 83, 84; MagIndMarPl 82-83*
Letter Space, The - New York, NY - *LitMarPl 83*
Letterex Communications Inc. - Elmwood Park, NJ - *ADAPSOMemDir 83-84*
Letterguide - Lincoln, NE - *AvMarPl 83*
Letters [of Mainespring Press] - Stonington, ME - *LitMag&SmPr 83-84; WritMar 84*
Letters [of The Country Press] - New York, NY - *LitMag&SmPr 83-84*
Letters Inc. [Subs. of Garvey Inc.] - Wichita, KS - *LitMarPl 83, 84; MagIndMarPl 82-83*
Lettersmith - Marblehead, MA - *DirInfWP 82*
Lettick Inc. - Bridgeport, CT - *LitMarPl 83, 84; MagIndMarPl 82-83*
Lettres from Limerick [of The Limerick League Inc.] - Philadelphia, PA - *ArtMar 84; LitMag&SmPr 83-84; WritMar 84*
L'Evangeline - Moncton, NB, Canada - *AyerDirPub 83; Ed&PubIntYB 82*
L'Eveil des Marchands Unis - St. Eustache, PQ, Canada - *Ed&PubIntYB 82*
Level IV Products Inc. - Livonia, MI - *MicrocomMPl 83, 84; WhoWMicrocom 83*
Levelland & Hockley County News-Press - Levelland, TX - *AyerDirPub 83; Ed&PubIntYB 82; NewsDir 84*
Levelland Cable Co. [of Landmark Cablevision Associates] - Levelland, TX - *BrCabYB 84*
Levelland News Press - Levelland, TX - *BaconPubCkNews 84*
Levenson & Levenson Inc. - Dallas, TX - *DirPRFirms 83; StaDirAdAg 2-84*
Levenson, Levenson & Hill - Dallas, TX - *AdAge 3-28-84*
Levenson Press - Los Angeles, CA - *BoPubDir 4, 5*
Leventhal Inc., Oscar [Div. of Charles Henricks Inc.] - New York, NY - *LitMarPl 83, 84*
Levey Co. Inc., Mervin N. - Toledo, OH - *StaDirAdAg 2-84*
Levi Publishing Co. Inc. - Sumter, SC - *BoPubDir 4, 5*
Levie & Associates, Harold M. - Chicago, IL - *StaDirAdAg 2-84*
Levien International Productions - London, England - *Tel&CabFB 84C*
Levin Productions, Lear - New York, NY - *AvMarPl 83; Tel&CabFB 84C*
Levine, Abby B. - Evanston, IL - *LitMarPl 83; MagIndMarPl 82-83*
Levine & Associates Inc., William V. - New York, NY - *ArtMar 84; AvMarPl 83; WritMar 84*
Levine & Rudd Inc. - Washington, DC - *DirPRFirms 83*
Levine, Huntley, Schmidt & Beaver - New York, NY - *AdAge 3-28-84; BrCabYB 84; StaDirAdAg 2-84*
Levine, Huntley, Schmidt, Plapler & Beaver Inc. - New York, NY - *HBIndAd&MS 82-83*
Levine Literary Agency Inc., Barry - Stony Creek, CT - *LitMarPl 83, 84*
Levine Literary Agency Inc., Ellen - New York, NY - *LitMarPl 83, 84*
Levine, Michael - Hollywood, CA - *DirPRFirms 83*
Levine, Nathan A. - Dallas, TX - *BrCabYB 84 p.D-303; Tel&CabFB 84C p.1688*
Levine Public Relations, Bambe - New York, NY - *DirPRFirms 83*

Levine, Samuel P. - Canoga Park, CA - *BoPubDir 4, 5; Ed&PubIntYB 82; LitMag&SmPr 83-84*
Levine Screened Mailing Lists Inc., Ceil - New York, NY - *MagIndMarPl 82-83*
Levine's Information Machine, Dr. - Milwaukee, WI - *EISS 7-83 Sup*
Levings Communications Inc. - Miami, FL - *IntDirMarRes 83*
Levinson Acoustic Recordings Ltd., Mark - Hamden, CT - *BillIntBG 83-84*
Levinson Associates Inc. - Los Angeles, CA - *DirPRFirms 83; LitMarPl 83, 84*
Levinson Communications, Peter - New York, NY - *DirPRFirms 83*
Levinson Institute Inc. - Cambridge, MA - *BoPubDir 4, 5*
Levit & Sherman Advertising - New York, NY - *DirMarMP 83; StaDirAdAg 2-84*
Levitt & Associates Inc., James K. - North Hollywood, CA - *MagIndMarPl 82-83*
Levitt Associates Inc., Ronald L. - Coral Gables, FL - *DirPRFirms 83*
Levitt Enterprises, Rod - Bedford Hills, NY - *AvMarPl 83*
Levittown Bucks County Courier Times - Levittown, PA - *NewsDir 84*
Levittown Pennysaver - Levittown, NY - *AyerDirPub 83*
Levittown Tribune - Levittown, NY - *Ed&PubIntYB 82; NewsDir 84*
Levittown Tribune - *See* Hiber Publishing Inc.
Levy Advertising Associates - New York, NY - *AdAge 3-28-84; StaDirAdAg 2-84*
Levy Advertising Inc., Milton - Danville, CA - *BoPubDir 5*
Levy & Associates Inc., Jack - Chicago, IL - *AdAge 3-28-84; StaDirAdAg 2-84*
Levy & Associates, William V. - Cleveland, OH - *DirPRFirms 83*
Levy & Father Enterprises Inc., Adam R. - *See* Big Seven Music Corp.
Levy County Journal - Bronson, FL - *Ed&PubIntYB 82*
Levy, Flaxman & Associates - New York, NY - *AdAge 3-28-84; StaDirAdAg 2-84*
Levy, Karen - New York, NY - *LitMarPl 83, 84*
Levy, King & White - Buffalo, NY - *AdAge 3-28-84*
Levy Productions, Lawrence - Santa Monica, CA - *AvMarPl 83; LitMarPl 83, 84*
Levy, Stan - Bellmore, NY - *LitMarPl 83, 84; MagIndMarPl 82-83*
Levy, Sussman & Levine Inc. - New York, NY - *StaDirAdAg 2-84*
Levy's Film & Projection Service [Subs. of Crepho Corp.] - Cincinnati, OH - *AvMarPl 83*
Lewandowski Enterprises Inc. - New York, NY - *StaDirAdAg 2-84*
Lewcor International Inc. - New York, NY - *HBIndAd&MS 82-83*
Lewin Bookbinding Co., J. [Subs. of Keeler Morris Printing Co.] - Hazelwood, MO - *LitMarPl 84*
Lewin Bookbinding Co., J. - St. Louis, MO - *LitMarPl 83*
Lewin, Cynthia - New York, NY - *LitMarPl 83, 84*
Lewin, Ted - Brooklyn, NY - *LitMarPl 83, 84; MagIndMarPl 82-83*
Lewis Advertising Agency - Newark, NJ - *StaDirAdAg 2-84*
Lewis Advertising Agency Inc., J. H. - Mobile, AL - *AdAge 3-28-84; ArtMar 84; StaDirAdAg 2-84*
Lewis Advertising Co. Inc. - Baltimore, MD - *DirMarMP 83; MagIndMarPl 82-83*
Lewis Advertising Inc. - Rocky Mt., NC - *StaDirAdAg 2-84*
Lewis & Associates, Richard - West Covina, CA - *StaDirAdAg 2-84*
Lewis & Co., A. F. - New York, NY - *BoPubDir 4, 5*
Lewis & Gilman Inc. - Philadelphia, PA - *BrCabYB 84; DirPRFirms 83; TelAl 83, 84*
Lewis & Gilman Inc. (Directcom Div.) - Philadelphia, PA - *DirMarMP 83*
Lewis & Neale Inc. - New York, NY - *DirPRFirms 83; LitMarPl 83, 84*
Lewis Associates Inc., Lorrie - New York, NY - *LitMarPl 83; MagIndMarPl 82-83*
Lewis Broadcasting Corp. - Savannah, GA - *ArtMar 84; BrCabYB 84; Tel&CabFB 84S*
Lewis-Clark State College (Confluence Press Inc.) - Lewiston, ID - *BoPubDir 4, 5*
Lewis/Coffin/Associates - Los Angeles, CA - *DirPRFirms 83; StaDirAdAg 2-84*
Lewis Co. Ltd., The - Los Angeles, CA - *DirPRFirms 83*
Lewis County Cable Vision - Garrison, KY - *Tel&CabFB 84C*
Lewis County Cable Vision - Vanceburg, KY - *BrCabYB 84*
Lewis County Herald - Nezperce, ID - *AyerDirPub 83; Ed&PubIntYB 82*
Lewis County Herald - Vanceburg, KY - *AyerDirPub 83; Ed&PubIntYB 82*
Lewis County Herald - Hohenwald, TN - *AyerDirPub 83; Ed&PubIntYB 82*
Lewis County News - Winlock, WA - *Ed&PubIntYB 82*
Lewis, Edith - New York, NY - *LitMarPl 83*
Lewis Film Service - Wichita, KS - *AvMarPl 83*
Lewis, Gilman & Kynett Inc. - Philadelphia, PA - *StaDirAdAg 2-84*
Lewis Graphics Inc. - New York, NY - *LitMarPl 83, 84; MagIndMarPl 82-83*
Lewis Inc., Frederic - New York, NY - *AvMarPl 83; LitMarPl 83, 84; MagIndMarPl 82-83*
Lewis Inc., Robert F. - Woodstock, VT - *LitMarPl 83, 84*
Lewis, Nell - Chicago, IL - *MagIndMarPl 82-83*
Lewis Newspapers, Kent V. - Lawrenceville, IL - *Ed&PubIntYB 82*
Lewis Paper Corp., Richard - Northfield, IL - *LitMarPl 83, 84*
Lewis, Patricia - New York, NY - *LitMarPl 83, 84*
Lewis Press - Lewis, KS - *BaconPubCkNews 84; Ed&PubIntYB 82*
Lewis Publishing Co. Inc. - Belle, MO - *BaconPubCkNews 84*
Lewis Publishing Co., The [Div. of The Stephen Greene Press] - Lexington, MA - *LitMarPl 83, 84; WritMar 84*
Lewis, Ralph L. - Wilmore, KY - *BoPubDir 4 Sup, 5*
Lewis, Richard - Brooklyn, NY - *LitMarPl 83, 84; MagIndMarPl 82-83*
Lewis River News - Woodland, WA - *AyerDirPub 83; Ed&PubIntYB 82*
Lewis River News & Kalama Bulletin [of Lafromboise Newspapers Inc.] - Woodland, WA - *NewsDir 84*
Lewis River Telephone Co. Inc. - Lacenter, WA - *TelDir&BG 83-84*
Lewis, Robert - New York, NY - *LitMarPl 83, 84*
Lewis, Robert D. - San Rafael, CA - *Tel&CabFB 84C p.1688*
Lewis, Robert D. - Towson, MD - *Tel&CabFB 84C*
Lewis-Sloan Publishing Co. - Charleston, SC - *BoPubDir 4, 5*
Lewis, Sol - New York, NY - *BoPubDir 4, 5*
Lewisboro Ledger - Lewisboro, CT - *Ed&PubIntYB 82*
Lewisboro Ledger [of Acorn Press Inc.] - Ridgefield, CT - *NewsDir 84*
Lewisboro Ledger - *See* Acorn Press Inc.
Lewisburg CATV - Lewisburg, PA - *BrCabYB 84; Tel&CabFB 84C*
Lewisburg Greenbrier Independent - Lewisburg, WV - *NewsDir 84*
Lewisburg Leader - Lewisburg, OH - *AyerDirPub 83; BaconPubCkNews 84; Ed&PubIntYB 82*
Lewisburg Marshall Gazette - *See* Lewisburg Tribune Inc.
Lewisburg Star Independent - Lewisburg, WV - *BaconPubCkNews 84*
Lewisburg Tribune - Lewisburg, TN - *BaconPubCkNews 84; Ed&PubIntYB 82; NewsDir 84*
Lewisburg Union County Journal - Lewisburg, PA - *BaconPubCkNews 84*
Lewisburg West Virginia Daily News - Lewisburg, WV - *NewsDir 84*
Lewisport Cable Co. - Lewisport, KY - *Tel&CabFB 84C*
Lewisport Telephone Co. Inc. - Lewisport, KY - *TelDir&BG 83-84*
Lewiston Daily Sun - Lewiston, ME - *AyerDirPub 83; BaconPubCkNews 84; Ed&PubIntYB 82; LitMarPl 83, 84; NewsDir 84*
Lewiston Evening Journal - Lewiston, ME - *BaconPubCkNews 84; LitMarPl 83*
Lewiston Journal - Lewiston, ME - *AyerDirPub 83; Ed&PubIntYB 82; LitMarPl 84*
Lewiston Journal - Lewiston, MN - *Ed&PubIntYB 82*
Lewiston Journal - *See* Mack Publishing Co.

Lewiston Morning Tribune - Lewiston, ID - *NewsDir 84*
Lewiston Tribune - Lewiston, ID - *BaconPubCkNews 84; LitMarPl 83*
Lewistown Cable TV [of Community Tele-Communications Inc.] - Lewistown, MT - *BrCabYB 84; Tel&CabFB 84C*
Lewistown Fulton Democrat [of Martin Publishing Co. Inc.] - Lewistown, IL - *BaconPubCkNews 84; NewsDir 84*
Lewistown News-Argus - Lewistown, MT - *BaconPubCkNews 84; Ed&PubIntYB 82; NewsDir 84*
Lewistown Sentinel - Lewistown, PA - *BaconPubCkNews 84; NewsDir 84*
Lewisville Democrat - Lewisville, AR - *BaconPubCkNews 84*
Lewisville Leader [of Taylor Communications Inc.] - Lewisville, TX - *BaconPubCkNews 84; NewsDir 84*
Lewisville News-Advertiser - Lewisville, TX - *Ed&PubIntYB 82*
Lewmar Paper Co. - Newark, NJ - *LitMarPl 83, 84*
Lewmark TV Network - Los Angeles, CA - *Tel&CabFB 84C*
Lewy Film & Sound Service Inc. - Baltimore, MD - *AvMarPl 83*
LEX [of Questel Inc.] - Washington, DC - *DataDirOnSer 84*
Lex - Paris, France - *DirOnDB Spring 84*
Lex Par Cable Video Inc. [of Prime Cable Corp.] - Lexington Park, MD - *BrCabYB 84*
Lexcom Inc. - Dallas, TX - *DirMarMP 83; StaDirAdAg 2-84*
Lexicon Corp. - Ft. Lauderdale, FL - *DataDirSup 7-83; MicrocomMPl 84*
Lexicon Corp. - Miami, FL - *WhoWMicrocom 83*
Lexicon Inc. - Waltham, MA - *AvMarPl 83; DataDirSup 7-83*
Lexicon Publications Inc. [Subs. of Grolier Inc.] - New York, NY - *LitMarPl 83*
Lexidata Corp. - Billerica, MA - *DataDirSup 7-83*
Lexigraphics Inc. - New York, NY - *LitMarPl 83, 84; MagIndMarPl 82-83*
Lexik House Publishers - Cold Spring, NY - *BoPubDir 4, 5; LitMag&SmPr 83-84*
Lexikon Inc. - Bannockburn, IL - *DirPRFirms 83*
Lexikos - San Francisco, CA - *BoPubDir 4; LitMag&SmPr 83-84; LitMarPl 83, 84*
Lexington Advertiser, The - Lexington, MS - *Ed&PubIntYB 82*
Lexington Book Co. - San Diego, CA - *BoPubDir 4 Sup, 5*
Lexington Books [Aff. of D. C. Heath & Co.] - Lexington, MA - *LitMarPl 83, 84*
Lexington Broadcast Services - New York, NY - *TelAl 83, 84; Tel&CabFB 84C*
Lexington Cable Co. [of Mid-Atlantic Network Inc.] - Lexington, VA - *BrCabYB 84; Tel&CabFB 84C*
Lexington Cable Television - Lexington, OR - *BrCabYB 84*
Lexington Cablevision [of Group W Cable Inc.] - Lexington, TN - *Tel&CabFB 84C*
Lexington Clipper - Lexington, NE - *BaconPubCkNews 84; Ed&PubIntYB 82*
Lexington Data Inc. - Ashland, MA - *BoPubDir 4, 5*
Lexington Dawson County Herald - Lexington, NE - *BaconPubCkNews 84; NewsDir 84*
Lexington Dispatch [of New York Times Co.] - Lexington, NC - *NewsDir 84*
Lexington Dispatch-News - Lexington, SC - *BaconPubCkNews 84*
Lexington Henderson County Times - Lexington, TN - *BaconPubCkNews 84*
Lexington Herald-Leader [of Knight-Ridder Newspapers Inc.] - Lexington, KY - *BaconPubCkNews 84; DataDirOnSer 84; DirOnDB Spring 84; LitMarPl 84; NewsDir 84*
Lexington Herald-Leader [of VU/Text Information Services] - Philadelphia, PA - *DataDirOnSer 84*
Lexington Herald, The - Lexington, KY - *Ed&PubIntYB 82*
Lexington Holmes County Herald - Lexington, MS - *BaconPubCkNews 84*
Lexington Independent - Acton, MA - *Ed&PubIntYB 82*
Lexington Journal - *See* Cornbelt Press Inc.
Lexington Leader, The - Lexington, KY - *Ed&PubIntYB 82*
Lexington Minute-Man - Acton, MA - *AyerDirPub 83*
Lexington Minute-Man - Lexington, MA - *Ed&PubIntYB 82; NewsDir 84*
Lexington Minute-Man - *See* Minute-Man Publications Inc.
Lexington News - Lexington, MO - *AyerDirPub 83; BaconPubCkNews 84; NewsDir 84*
Lexington News-Gazette - Lexington, VA - *BaconPubCkNews 84; NewsDir 84*
Lexington Oglethoppe Echo - Lexington, GA - *BaconPubCkNews 84*
Lexington Park Enterprise - *See* Lexleon Inc.
Lexington Park St. Mary's Beacon - Lexington Park, MD - *BaconPubCkNews 84*
Lexington Press Inc., The - Lexington, MA - *LitMarPl 83, 84*
Lexington Progress - Lexington, TN - *BaconPubCkNews 84; Ed&PubIntYB 82; NewsDir 84*
Lexington Telephone Co. - Lexington, NC - *TelDir&BG 83-84*
LexIntellect Inc. - Kokomo, IN - *MicrocomMPl 83*
Lexis [of Mead Data Central] - Chicago, IL - *MicrocomMPl 84*
Lexis [of Mead Data Central] - New York, NY - *CompReadDB 82; DBBus 82; EISS 83*
Lexis [of Mead Data Central] - Dayton, OH - *DataDirOnSer 84; DirOnDB Spring 84*
Lexisoft Inc. - Davis, CA - *MicrocomMPl 83, 84; MicrocomSwDir 1; WhoWMicrocom 83*
Lexleon Inc. - Lexington Park, MD - *BaconPubCkNews 84*
Lexor Corp. - Van Nuys, CA - *DirInfWP 82; WhoWMicrocom 83*
LexPar Cable Video Inc. - Lexington Park, MD - *Tel&CabFB 84C*
Lexpat [of Mead Data Central] - Dayton, OH - *DataDirOnSer 84; DirOnDB Spring 84; EISS 5-84 Sup*
L'Express - Toronto, ON, Canada - *Ed&PubIntYB 82*
L'Express - Drummondville, PQ, Canada - *Ed&PubIntYB 82*
Leyden Communications Inc. - New York, NY - *DirPRFirms 83*
Leyden Star-Sentinel - Leyden, IL - *Ed&PubIntYB 82*
Leyden Star-Sentinel [of West Suburban Press Inc.] - Melrose Park, IL - *AyerDirPub 83; NewsDir 84*
Leyden Star Sentinel - *See* West Suburban Press Inc.
Leyerle Publications - Geneseo, NY - *BoPubDir 4, 5*
LFP Inc. - Los Angeles, CA - *KnowInd 83*
LH Advertising Agency Inc. - Scarsdale, NY - *StaDirAdAg 2-84*
LH Management - Scarsdale, NY - *MagIndMarPl 82-83*
L'Hebdo - Trois Rivieres, PQ, Canada - *Ed&PubIntYB 82*
L'Hebdo de la Rouge - L'Annonciation, PQ, Canada - *Ed&PubIntYB 82*
L'Hospitalite - Montreal, PQ, Canada - *BaconPubCkMag 84*
LI Business Newsweekly - Plainview, NY - *MagDir 84*
Li Inc./Pflaum Press, Peter [Div. of Peter Li Inc.] - Dayton, OH - *AvMarPl 83; MagIndMarPl 82-83*
L.I. TV-News - East Norwich, NY - *Tel&CabFB 84C*
Liaison Agency Inc,/Gamma-Liaison Inc. - New York, NY - *MagIndMarPl 82-83*
Liaison Agency Inc. - New York, NY - *DirPRFirms 83*
Liban au Canada - Montreal, PQ, Canada - *Ed&PubIntYB 82*
Libbin, Lois M. - Albuquerque, NM - *LitMarPl 84*
Libby Cablevision - Libby, MT - *BrCabYB 84; Tel&CabFB 84C*
Libby Western News - Libby, MT - *BaconPubCkNews 84*
Libcon [of SDC Search Service] - Santa Monica, CA - *CompReadDB 82; DataDirOnSer 84*
Liberal News - Liberal, MO - *BaconPubCkNews 84; Ed&PubIntYB 82*
Liberal News - London, England - *LitMag&SmPr 83-84*
Liberal Publishers - Kountze, TX - *BaconPubCkNews 84*
Liberal Southwest Daily Times - Liberal, KS - *NewsDir 84*
Liberation Publications Inc. [Aff. of The Advocate] - San Mateo, CA - *BoPubDir 4 Sup, 5*
Liberator Music - *See* Two Fifty Nine Music
Liberator Press - Chicago, IL - *BoPubDir 4, 5*
Libertarian Books Ltd. - Tampa, FL - *BoPubDir 4, 5*
Libertarian Digest - Berkeley, CA - *LitMag&SmPr 83-84*
Libertarian Microfiche Publishing - Berrima, Australia - *MicroMarPl 82-83*
Liberty - Washington, DC - *ArtMar 84; MagIndMarPl 82-83; WritMar 84*
Liberty Bee-Times - Liberty, IL - *BaconPubCkNews 84; Ed&PubIntYB 82*
Liberty Bell Associates - Franklin Park, NJ - *BoPubDir 4, 5*
Liberty Book Co. - Albany, NY - *BoPubDir 4 Sup, 5*
Liberty Broadcasting Inc. - Eugene, OR - *Tel&CabFB 84S*
Liberty Broadcasting Inc. - Madison, WI - *BrCabYB 84*
Liberty Cable TV - Macomb, IL - *Tel&CabFB 84C*
Liberty Cable TV [of Liberty Communications Inc.] - Bangor, MI - *BrCabYB 84*
Liberty Cable TV - South Haven, MI - *Tel&CabFB 84C*

Liberty Cable TV [of Liberty Communications Inc.] - Corvallis, OR - *Tel&CabFB 84C*
Liberty Cable TV [of Liberty Communications Inc.] - Lebanon, OR - *Tel&CabFB 84C*
Liberty Cable TV [of Liberty Communications Inc.] - Portland, OR - *BrCabYB 84; Tel&CabFB 84C*
Liberty Cable TV [of Liberty Communications Inc.] - Sweet Home, OR - *Tel&CabFB 84C*
Liberty Cable TV - Washington County, OR - *BrCabYB 84*
Liberty Cable TV [of Liberty Communications Inc.] - West Linn, OR - *BrCabYB 84*
Liberty Casey County News - Liberty, KY - *BaconPubCkNews 84; NewsDir 84*
Liberty Center Press - *See* Ohioprint Publications Inc.
Liberty College Corner News - Liberty, IN - *BaconPubCkNews 84*
Liberty Communications - Iowa City, IA - *BrCabYB 84 p.D-303; Tel&CabFB 84C p.1688*
Liberty Communications - Mt. Vernon, IA - *BrCabYB 84*
Liberty Communications - West Liberty, IA - *BrCabYB 84*
Liberty Communications [of Tele-Communications Inc.] - Eugene, OR - *BrCabYB 84 p.D-303; CabTVFinDB 83; HomeVid&CabYB 82-83; KnowInd 83; LitMarPl 84; TelAl 83, 84; Tel&CabFB 84C p.1688*
Liberty Communications - Newberg, OR - *Tel&CabFB 84C*
Liberty Corp., The - Greenville, SC - *KnowInd 83*
Liberty County Times - Chester, MT - *AyerDirPub 83; Ed&PubIntYB 82*
Liberty-Dayton CATV Inc. [of Liberty Communications Inc.] - Liberty, TX - *Tel&CabFB 84C*
Liberty Electronics USA - San Francisco, CA - *DataDirSup 7-83; MicrocomMPl 84*
Liberty Fund Inc. - Indianapolis, IN - *LitMarPl 83, 84*
Liberty Herald - Liberty, IN - *BaconPubCkNews 84; Ed&PubIntYB 82*
Liberty Hill Country News - *See* Taylor Newspapers Inc.
Liberty Library Corp. - New York, NY - *DirMarMP 83*
Liberty Monitor - Liberty, SC - *BaconPubCkNews 84*
Liberty News - Liberty, NC - *BaconPubCkNews 84*
Liberty News [of Phoenix Publications Inc.] - Niles, OH - *AyerDirPub 83; NewsDir 84*
Liberty News - *See* Phoenix Publications Inc.
Liberty News International - Detroit, MI - *Ed&PubIntYB 82*
Liberty News, The - Miami, FL - *Ed&PubIntYB 82*
Liberty News, The - Liberty, OH - *Ed&PubIntYB 82*
Liberty Opinion Research Inc. - Independence, OH - *IntDirMarRes 83*
Liberty Press, The - Liberty Center, OH - *AyerDirPub 83; Ed&PubIntYB 82*
Liberty Publishing Co. - St. Louis, MO - *BoPubDir 4 Sup, 5*
Liberty Publishing Co. Inc. - Cockeysville, MD - *BoPubDir 4 Sup, 5; LitMag&SmPr 83-84; LitMarPl 83, 84; WritMar 84*
Liberty Shopper News - Liberty, MO - *Ed&PubIntYB 82*
Liberty Software Co., The - Washington, DC - *MicrocomMPl 83*
Liberty Southern Herald - Liberty, MS - *BaconPubCkNews 84; NewsDir 84*
Liberty Studios Inc. - New York, NY - *TelAl 83, 84*
Liberty Telephone & Communications Inc. [Aff. of Century Telephone Enterprises Inc.] - Hardy, AR - *TelDir&BG 83-84*
Liberty Tribune [of Townsend Communications Inc.] - Kansas City, MO - *AyerDirPub 83; NewsDir 84*
Liberty Tribune - Liberty, MO - *Ed&PubIntYB 82*
Liberty Tribune - *See* Townsend Communications Inc.
Liberty TV Cable Inc. [of Liberty Communications Inc.] - Novato, CA - *BrCabYB 84*
Liberty TV Cable Inc. [of Liberty Communications Inc.] - San Bernardino, CA - *BrCabYB 84*
Liberty TV Cable Inc. [of Liberty Communications Inc.] - Sun City, CA - *BrCabYB 84*
Liberty TV Cable Inc. [of Liberty Communications Inc.] - Athens, GA - *BrCabYB 84; Tel&CabFB 84C*
Liberty TV Cable Inc. [of Liberty Communications Inc.] - Eastman, GA - *BrCabYB 84; Tel&CabFB 84C*
Liberty TV Cable Inc. [of Liberty Communications Inc.] - Fitzgerald, GA - *BrCabYB 84; Tel&CabFB 84C*
Liberty TV Cable Inc. [of Liberty Communications Inc.] - Hazlehurst, GA - *BrCabYB 84; Tel&CabFB 84C*
Liberty TV Cable Inc. [of Liberty Communications Inc.] - McRae, GA - *BrCabYB 84; Tel&CabFB 84C*
Liberty TV Cable Inc. [of Liberty Communications Inc.] - Sandersville, GA - *BrCabYB 84; Tel&CabFB 84C*
Liberty TV Cable Inc. [of Liberty Communications Inc.] - Toccoa, GA - *BrCabYB 84; Tel&CabFB 84C*
Liberty TV Cable Inc. [of Liberty Communications Inc.] - Vidalia, GA - *BrCabYB 84; Tel&CabFB 84C*
Liberty TV Cable Inc. [of Liberty Communications Inc.] - Blandinsville, IL - *BrCabYB 84*
Liberty TV Cable Inc. [of Liberty Communications Inc.] - Charleston, IL - *BrCabYB 84; Tel&CabFB 84C*
Liberty TV Cable Inc. [of Liberty Communications Inc.] - Colchester, IL - *BrCabYB 84*
Liberty TV Cable Inc. [of Liberty Communications Inc.] - Macomb, IL - *BrCabYB 84*
Liberty TV Cable Inc. [of Liberty Communications Inc.] - Angola, IN - *BrCabYB 84*
Liberty TV Cable Inc. [of Liberty Communications Inc.] - Winchester, IN - *BrCabYB 84; Tel&CabFB 84C*
Liberty TV Cable Inc. [of Liberty Communications Inc.] - Adrian, MI - *BrCabYB 84; Tel&CabFB 84C*
Liberty TV Cable Inc. [of Liberty Communications Inc.] - South Haven, MI - *BrCabYB 84*
Liberty TV Cable Inc. [of Liberty Communications Inc.] - Junction City, OR - *BrCabYB 84*
Liberty TV Cable Inc. [of Liberty Communications Inc.] - Vandergrift, PA - *BrCabYB 84*
Liberty TV Cable Inc. [of Liberty Communications Inc.] - Beaumont, TX - *Tel&CabFB 84C*
Liberty TV Cable Inc. [of Liberty Communications Inc.] - Liberty, TX - *BrCabYB 84*
Liberty TV Cable Inc. [of Liberty Communications Inc.] - Orange, TX - *Tel&CabFB 84C*
Liberty TV Cable Inc. [of Liberty Communications Inc.] - Port Arthur, TX - *BrCabYB 84; Tel&CabFB 84C*
Liberty TV Cable Inc. [of Liberty Communications Inc.] - Port Neches, TX - *Tel&CabFB 84C*
Liberty TV Cable Inc. [of Liberty Communications Inc.] - Arlington, WA - *Tel&CabFB 84C*
Liberty TV Cable Inc. [of Liberty Communications Inc.] - Edmonds, WA - *BrCabYB 84*
Liberty TV Cable Inc. [of Liberty Communications Inc.] - Marysville, WA - *BrCabYB 84*
Liberty TV Cable Inc. [of Liberty Communications Inc.] - Richmond Beach, WA - *BrCabYB 84*
Liberty TV Co. Inc. [of Basil Cable Systems Inc.] - Dunnville, KY - *Tel&CabFB 84C*
Liberty TV Co. Inc. [of Basil Cable Systems Inc.] - Liberty, KY - *BrCabYB 84; Tel&CabFB 84C*
Liberty Video Corp. - Fallsburg, NY - *BrCabYB 84*
Liberty Video Corp. - Liberty, NY - *BrCabYB 84*
Liberty Video Corp. - Neversink, NY - *BrCabYB 84*
Liberty Video Corp. - Woodbourne, NY - *BrCabYB 84*
Liberty Vindicator - Liberty, TX - *BaconPubCkNews 84; Ed&PubIntYB 82*
Libertyville Herald - Libertyville, IL - *Ed&PubIntYB 82*
Libertyville Herald [of Paddock Circle Newspapers Inc.] - Mundelein, IL - *NewsDir 84*
Libertyville Herald - *See* Paddock Publications
Libertyville Independent Register - Libertyville, IL - *BaconPubCkNews 84; NewsDir 84*
Libertyville Review - Wilmette, IL - *AyerDirPub 83*
Libertyville Review - *See* Pioneer Press Inc.
Libov Associates, Ed - Chicago, IL - *DirMarMP 83*
Libov Associates, Ed - New York, NY - *StaDirAdAg 2-84*
Libra Graphics Inc. - New York, NY - *LitMarPl 83, 84*
Libra Laboratories Inc. - Metuchen, NJ - *MicrocomMPl 83, 84; MicrocomSwDir 1*
Libra Press - Wataga, IL - *LitMag&SmPr 83-84*
Libra Programming Inc. - Salt Lake City, UT - *MicrocomMPl 83, 84; WhoWMicrocom 83*
Libra Publishers Inc. - Roslyn Heights, NY - *LitMag&SmPr 83-84; LitMarPl 83, 84; WritMar 84*
Librairie Beauchemin Ltee. - Montreal, PQ, Canada - *LitMarPl 83*
Librairie Droz SA - Geneva, Switzerland - *LitMag&SmPr 83-84*

Librairie Garneau Ltee. [Subs. of Librairie Dussault] - Montreal, PQ, Canada - *LitMarPl 83*
Librairie LSC - Montreal, PQ, Canada - *LitMarPl 83*
Librairie Rouge - Montreal, PQ, Canada - *BoPubDir 4, 5*
Librarian [of Eurotec Consultants Ltd.] - Colchester, England - *EISS 7-83 Sup*
Librarians for Social Change - Brighton, England - *LitMag&SmPr 83-84*
Librarians of Institutes & Schools of Education - *See* LISE Publications
Libraries Unltd. - Littleton, CO - *LitMarPl 83, 84; WritMar 84*
Library [of University of Alberta] - Edmonton, AB, Canada - *DataDirOnSer 84*
Library & Abstracting Service [of Zinc Development Association/ Lead Development Association/Cadmium Association] - London, England - *EISS 83*
Library & Archival Services Div. [of American Medical Association] - Chicago, IL - *EISS 83*
Library & Information Centre [of Transport Canada] - Ottawa, ON, Canada - *EISS 83*
Library & Information Centre [of House of Lords] - London, England - *EISS 83*
Library & Information Consultants Ltd. - Edmonton, AB, Canada - *EISS 83*
Library & Information Research Group - Loughborough, England - *EISS 83*
Library & Information Science Abstracts [of Dialog Information Services Inc.] - Palo Alto, CA - *DataDirOnSer 84*
Library & Information Science Abstracts [of The Library Association] - London, England - *CompReadDB 82; DBBus 82; EISS 83; OnBibDB 3*
Library & Information Services [of Institution of Mining & Metallurgy] - London, England - *EISS 7-83 Sup*
Library & Information Services [of Water Research Centre] - Stevenage, England - *EISS 83*
Library & Information Technology Association - Chicago, IL - *EISS 83*
Library & Technical Information Dept. [of Israel Atomic Energy Commission] - Yavne, Israel - *EISS 83*
Library Association - London, England - *CompReadDB 82; InfIndMarPl 83*
Library Automation & Data Base Program [of Brown University Libraries] - Providence, RI - *EISS 83*
Library Automation Inc. - Columbus, OH - *EISS 83*
Library Automation Program [of Union Theological Seminary Library] - New York, NY - *EISS 83*
Library Automation Program [of University of Pittsburgh Library] - Pittsburgh, PA - *EISS 83*
Library Automation Program [of Brigham Young University Library] - Provo, UT - *EISS 83*
Library Automation System [of National Diet Library] - Tokyo, Japan - *EISS 83*
Library Binding Service - Des Moines, IA - *LitMarPl 83, 84*
Library Bookseller, The - West Orange, NJ - *LitMarPl 83*
Library Bureau Inc. - Herkimer, NY - *AvMarPl 83*
Library Co. of Philadelphia - Philadelphia, PA - *BoPubDir 4 Sup, 5*
Library Computer System [of University of Illinois Libraries] - Urbana, IL - *EISS 83*
Library Council of Metropolitan Milwaukee - Milwaukee, WI - *EISS 83*
Library Development Consultants Inc. - Washington, DC - *EISS 83*
Library Div. [of U.S. Dept. of Housing & Urban Development] - Washington, DC - *EISS 83*
Library Documentation Centre [of National Library of Canada] - Ottawa, ON, Canada - *EISS 83*
Library Filmstrip Center - Wichita, KS - *AvMarPl 83*
Library Hi Tech [of Pierian Press Inc.] - Ann Arbor, MI - *EISS 5-84 Sup*
Library Hi Tech - Armonk, NY - *BaconPubCkMag 84*
Library Imagination Paper, The - Charleston, WV - *LitMag&SmPr 83-84*
Library Information Access System [of Pennsylvania State University Libraries] - University Park, PA - *EISS 83*
Library Information & On-Line Network Service [of New York Public Library] - New York, NY - *EISS 83*
Library Information & Research Service - Pittsburgh, PA - *FBInfSer 80*
Library/Information Consultant - Cerritos, CA - *EISS 83*
Library/Information Program [of Center for Population & Family Health] - New York, NY - *DataDirOnSer 84*
Library Information Retrieval System [of California Institute of Technology] - Pasadena, CA - *EISS 83*
Library Information Service - Honolulu, HI - *FBInfSer 80*
Library Information Services - Oakland, CA - *EISS 83; FBInfSer 80; InfIndMarPl 83*
Library Information Services [of Informatics Inc.] - Rockville, MD - *EISS 83*
Library Information System [of Royal Library] - Stockholm, Sweden - *EISS 83; InfIndMarPl 83*
Library Instruction Materials Bank [of Loughborough University of Technology Library] - Loughborough, England - *EISS 5-84 Sup*
Library Integrated & Automated Retrieval System [of Brigham Young University, Hawaii Campus] - Laie, HI - *EISS 5-84 Sup*
Library Journal - New York, NY - *BaconPubCkMag 84; MagDir 84; MagIndMarPl 82-83; WritMar 84*
Library Management & Retrieval System [of U.S. Navy] - San Diego, CA - *EISS 83*
Library Management & Services - Austin, TX - *FBInfSer 80*
Library Management Network Inc. - Huntsville, AL - *EISS 5-84 Sup*
Library Microfilms [Div. of Bay Microfilm Inc.] - Palo Alto, CA - *LitMarPl 83, 84; MicroMarPl 82-83*
Library Microfilms & Materials Co. - Inglewood, CA - *AvMarPl 83*
Library of America, The - New York, NY - *LitMarPl 84*
Library of Computer & Information Sciences [of Macmillan Book Clubs Inc.] - New York, NY - *LitMarPl 83, 84*
Library of Congress - Washington, DC - *BoPubDir 4, 5*
Library of Congress (Cataloging Distribution Service) - Washington, DC - *CompReadDB 82*
Library of Congress (Geography & Map Div.) - Washington, DC - *CompReadDB 82*
Library of Congress (Information System) - Washington, DC - *EISS 83*
Library of Congress (Motion Picture, Broadcasting, & Recorded Sound Div.) - Washington, DC - *AvMarPl 83; BillIntBG 83-84*
Library of Congress (National Library Service for the Blind & Physically Handicapped) - Washington, DC - *AvMarPl 83*
Library of Congress (Photoduplication Service) - Washington, DC - *MicroMarPl 82-83*
Library of Congress (Prints & Photographs Div.) - Washington, DC - *LitMarPl 83, 84*
Library of Human Behavior Ltd. [Div. of International Universities Press] - New York, NY - *LitMarPl 83, 84*
Library of Parliament - Ottawa, ON, Canada - *EISS 83*
Library of Science [of Macmillan Book Clubs Inc.] - New York, NY - *LitMarPl 83, 84*
Library of Social Science - New York, NY - *LitMarPl 83, 84*
Library of Special Education [of Macmillan Book Clubs Inc.] - New York, NY - *LitMarPl 83, 84*
Library of Urban Affairs [of Macmillan Book Clubs Inc.] - New York, NY - *LitMarPl 83*
Library of Vehicles - Garden Grove, CA - *MagIndMarPl 82-83*
Library of World History [of Macmillan Book Clubs Inc.] - New York, NY - *LitMarPl 83*
Library Program [of Consortium of Universities of the Washington Metropolitan Area] - Washington, DC - *EISS 83*
Library Publicity Clippings - Santa Ana, CA - *LitMarPl 83, 84*
Library Quarterly, The [of The University of Chicago Press] - Chicago, IL - *LitMarPl 83, 84*
Library Reports & Research Service Inc. - Denver, CO - *EISS 83; FBInfSer 80; InfIndMarPl 83*
Library Research Associates - Monroe, NY - *BoPubDir 4, 5; LitMag&SmPr 83-84*
Library Research Center [of University of Illinois] - Urbana, IL - *EISS 83*
Library Resources & Technical Services - Chicago, IL - *BaconPubCkMag 84; MagDir 84*
Library Resources Inc. [Div. of Encyclopaedia Britannica Inc.] - Chicago, IL - *LitMarPl 83, 84; MagIndMarPl 82-83; MicroMarPl 82-83*

Library/Safety Research Information Service [of National Safety Council] - Chicago, IL - *EISS 83*
Library Services - Denver, CO - *FBInfSer 80*
Library Software Co., The - Pleasant Hill, CA - *MicrocomMPl 84*
Library Store Ltd., The - Bethesda, MD - *EISS 83*
Library System [of U.S. Dept. of Energy] - Oak Ridge, TN - *EISS 83*
Library Systems Office [of University of California, Berkeley] - Berkeley, CA - *EISS 83*
Library Systems Services [of General Research Corp.] - Santa Barbara, CA - *EISS 83*
Library Trends - Champaign, IL - *MagIndMarPl 82-83*
Libraryworks, The [Div. of Neal-Schuman Publishers Inc.] - New York, NY - *LitMarPl 83*
Libris - Stockholm, Sweden - *DirOnDB Spring 84*
Libris II - Somerville, NJ - *DirOnDB Spring 84*
Libros Espanoles SA - Miami, FL - *LitMarPl 83, 84*
LIBS 100 System [of CL Systems Inc.] - Newtonville, MA - *EISS 83*
Licensable Technology - Ormond Beach, FL - *DirOnDB Spring 84*
Licensed Beverage Journal - Bronx, NY - *BaconPubCkMag 84; MagDir 84*
Licensing Today - New York, NY - *BaconPubCkMag 84*
Licensure Information System [of U.S. Public Health Service] - Hyattsville, MD - *EISS 83*
Lichelle Music Co. Inc. - Burbank, CA - *BillIntBG 83-84*
Lichtenberg, Al - New York, NY - *LitMarPl 83, 84; MagIndMarPl 82-83*
Lichtenberg Graphic Advertising - New York, NY - *LitMarPl 83; MagIndMarPl 82-83*
Lichtman Co. Inc., Jerry - New York, NY - *StaDirAdAg 2-84*
Licking Cable Inc. - Licking, MO - *BrCabYB 84; Tel&CabFB 84C*
Licking Countian - Newark, OH - *AyerDirPub 83; Ed&PubIntYB 82*
Licking News - Licking, MO - *BaconPubCkNews 84; Ed&PubIntYB 82*
Licking Valley Courier - West Liberty, KY - *AyerDirPub 83; Ed&PubIntYB 82*
Lida Enterprises Inc. - *See* Notable Music Co. Inc.
Lidec Inc. - Montreal, PQ, Canada - *LitMarPl 83, 84*
Lidgerwood/Wyndmere Monitor - Lidgerwood, ND - *BaconPubCkNews 84*
Lidiraven Books - Sherman Oaks, CA - *BoPubDir 4, 5; LitMarPl 83, 84*
Lieb Productions Inc., Jack - Chicago, IL - *AvMarPl 83; TelAl 83, 84; Tel&CabFB 84C*
Lieb/Schott Publications - Bourbonnais, IL - *LitMag&SmPr 83-84*
Lieber-Atherton Inc. - New York, NY - *LitMarPl 83, 84*
Lieber Attitude Research Inc. - New York, NY - *IntDirMarRes 83*
Lieberman-Appalucci - Allentown, PA - *AdAge 3-28-84; StaDirAdAg 2-84*
Lieberman Freelance Services, Cindy - Northridge, CA - *LitMarPl 83, 84*
Lieberman Research East Inc. - Great Neck, NY - *IntDirMarRes 83*
Lieberman Research Inc. - New York, NY - *HBIndAd&MS 82-83; IntDirMarRes 83*
Lieberman Research West Inc. - Los Angeles, CA - *IntDirMarRes 83*
Liebert Corp. - Columbus, OH - *DataDirSup 7-83; WhoWMicrocom 83*
Liebert, Norma - New York, NY - *LitMarPl 83, 84; MagIndMarPl 82-83*
Liebling Associates Corp. - New York, NY - *IntDirMarRes 83*
Liederbach, Robert J. - Winston-Salem, NC - *BoPubDir 4, 5*
Lief & Associates, Philip - Southfield, MA - *ArtMar 84; LitMarPl 83; WritMar 84*
Lief & Associates, Philip - New York, NY - *LitMarPl 84*
Life - Bellmore, NY - *AyerDirPub 83*
Life - Merrick, NY - *AyerDirPub 83*
Life [of Time Inc.] - New York, NY - *Folio 83; LitMarPl 83, 84; MagDir 84; MagIndMarPl 82-83; WritMar 84*
Life & Health - Washington, DC - *MagIndMarPl 82-83*
Life & Health Insurance [of Chase Econometrics/Interactive Data Corp.] - Waltham, MA - *DataDirOnSer 84*
Life & Health Insurance - Bala Cynwyd, PA - *DirOnDB Spring 84*
Life Association News - Washington, DC - *BaconPubCkMag 84; MagDir 84; MagIndMarPl 82-83*
Life Enrichment Publishers - Canton, OH - *LitMarPl 83; WritMar 84*
Life Insurance Index [of University Microfilms International] - Ann Arbor, MI - *EISS 83*
Life Insurance Marketing & Research Association Inc. - Hartford, CT - *BoPubDir 5*
Life Insurance Selling - St. Louis, MO - *BaconPubCkMag 84; MagDir 84*
Life Insurers Conference - Richmond, VA - *BoPubDir 5*
Life Magazine - New York, NY - *BaconPubCkMag 84*
Life Newspapers - Berwyn, IL - *AyerDirPub 83*
Life Office Management Association Inc. - Atlanta, GA - *BoPubDir 4, 5*
Life Picture Service [Div. of Time Inc.] - New York, NY - *LitMarPl 83, 84; MagIndMarPl 82-83*
Life Printing & Publishing Co. - Berwyn, IL - *BaconPubCkNews 84*
Life Printing & Publishing Co. - Downers Grove, IL - *BaconPubCkNews 84*
Life Printing & Publishing Co. - La Grange, IL - *BaconPubCkNews 84*
Life Publishers International [Aff. of General Council of the Assemblies of God] - Miami, FL - *BoPubDir 4, 5*
Life Rates & Data [of National Underwriter Co.] - Cincinnati, OH - *EISS 83*
Life Science Associates - Bayport, NY - *MicrocomSwDir 1*
Life Sciences - Elmsford, NY - *MagIndMarPl 82-83*
Life Sciences Associates - Bayport, NY - *WhoWMicrocom 83*
Life Sciences Collection [of Cambridge Scientific Abstracts] - Bethesda, MD - *DataDirOnSer 84; DirOnDB Spring 84; EISS 83; OnBibDB 3*
Life Signs: Words & Images - El Cerrito, CA - *BoPubDir 5*
Life Skills Program - Toronto, ON, Canada - *BoPubDir 4, 5*
Life Song Music Press - *See* Paragon/Benson Publishing Group
Life-Study Fellowship Foundation Inc. - Darien, CT - *DirMarMP 83*
Life-Style Market Segmentation System [of Old American Insurance Co.] - Kansas City, MO - *EISS 83*
Life Style Publications - Stanford, CA - *LitMag&SmPr 83-84*
Life Support Nursing - Tempe, AZ - *BaconPubCkMag 84*
Life Understanding Foundation (El Cariso Publications) - Santa Barbara, CA - *BoPubDir 4, 5*
Life Underwriters Association of Canada - Don Mills, ON, Canada - *BoPubDir 4, 5*
Lifeboat Associates [Subs. of Intersoft Corp.] - New York, NY - *DataDirSup 7-83; MicrocomMPl 83, 84; MicrocomSwDir 1; WhoWMicrocom 83*
Lifelines - New York, NY - *BaconPubCkMag 84*
Lifelong Learning: The Adult Years - Washington, DC - *MagDir 84; MagIndMarPl 82-83*
Life:Net - Boston, MA - *DirOnDB Spring 84*
Lifesong Records Inc. - Englewood, NJ - *BillIntBG 83-84*
Lifestyle - San Francisco, CA - *BaconPubCkMag 84; LitMag&SmPr 83-84*
Lifestyle - Raleigh, NC - *BrCabYB 84*
Lifestyle [of United Video] - Tulsa, OK - *BrCabYB 84; HomeVid&CabYB 82-83*
Lifestyle Book Society, The [Subs. of Horchow Mail Order Inc.] - New York, NY - *LitMarPl 83, 84*
Lifestyle Guide - Orange, CA - *BaconPubCkMag 84*
Lifestyle Selector, The - Denver, CO - *MagIndMarPl 82-83*
Lifetime - New York, NY - *Tel&CabFB 84C*
Lifetime Apple Software Technology - Montgomery, AL - *WhoWMicrocom 83*
Lifetime Learning Publications [Div. of Wadsworth Inc.] - Belmont, CA - *LitMarPl 83, 84*
Lifetime Recordings - Rochester, NY - *BillIntBG 83-84*
Lifetimes - Nashville, TN - *BaconPubCkMag 84; MagDir 84*
Lifetree Software Inc. - Monterey, CA - *MicrocomMPl 84*
Lifeway Home Shopping Service [Div. of Southern Baptist Sunday School Board] - Nashville, TN - *DirMarMP 83*
Lifson, Herrmann, Blackmarr & Harris - Dallas, TX - *DataDirSup 7-83; DirInfWP 82*

Lift-Off Corp. - Hickory, NC - *DirInfWP 82*
Lifton, Bernice - Pasadena, CA - *LitMarPl 83, 84; MagIndMarPl 82-83*
Ligature Inc. - Chicago, IL - *LitMarPl 83, 84*
Liggett Broadcast Group, The - Williamston, MI - *BrCabYB 84*
Light [of UWUA, AFL-CIO] - Washington, DC - *NewsDir 84*
Light - San Antonio, TX - *AyerDirPub 83*
Light - Waxahachie, TX - *AyerDirPub 83*
Light: A Poetry Review - New York, NY - *LitMag&SmPr 83-84; WritMar 84*
Light & Life [of Free Methodist Publishing House] - Winona Lake, IN - *ArtMar 84; WritMar 84*
Light & Life Press [Aff. of Free Methodist Publishing House] - Winona Lake, IN - *BoPubDir 4, 5*
Light & Life Publishing Co. - Minneapolis, MN - *BoPubDir 4, 5*
Light & Sunlight Shopper - Corsicana, TX - *AyerDirPub 83*
Light-House Publications - Vancouver, BC, Canada - *BoPubDir 4, 5*
Light Impressions Corp. - Rochester, NY - *AvMarPl 83; BoPubDir 4, 5*
Light Inc. - Honolulu, HI - *AvMarPl 83*
Light Interviewing Services Inc., Jean M. - Miami, FL - *IntDirMarRes 83*
Light Metal Age - San Francisco, CA - *BaconPubCkMag 84; MagDir 84*
Light Star Press - Victoria, BC, Canada - *BoPubDir 4, 5*
Light, The - North Ridgeville, OH - *Ed&PubIntYB 82*
Light Year [of Bits Press] - Cleveland, OH - *WritMar 84*
Lightbooks - Twain Harte, CA - *BoPubDir 4, 5; LitMag&SmPr 83-84; WritMar 84*
Lightfoot Broadcast Group - Lyme, CT - *BrCabYB 84*
Lighthouse Hill Publishing - Staten Island, NY - *BoPubDir 5*
Lighthouse Press - Honolulu, HI - *BoPubDir 4, 5*
Lighthouse Productions - San Rafael, CA - *BillIntBG 83-84*
Lighting Design & Application - New York, NY - *ArtMar 84; BaconPubCkMag 84; MagDir 84; WritMar 84*
Lighting Dimensions - Laguna Beach, CA - *ArtMar 84; BaconPubCkMag 84; MagDir 84; WritMar 84*
Lighting Systems - Milwaukee, WI - *MagDir 84*
Lightman Inc., H. Allen - New York, NY - *StaDirAdAg 2-84*
Lightner & Associates Inc., Richard - Columbus, OH - *DirPRFirms 83*
Lightning Software - Palo Alto, CA - *MicrocomMPl 83, 84; WhoWMicrocom 83*
Lightning Tree - Sante Fe, NM - *BoPubDir 4, 5; LitMarPl 84*
Lightship Press Ltd. - Victoria, BC, Canada - *BoPubDir 4 Sup, 5*
Lightwave - Chestnut Hill, MA - *BaconPubCkMag 84*
Lightworks Magazine - Birmingham, MI - *LitMag&SmPr 83-84*
Lightyear Press Inc. - Laurel, NY - *BoPubDir 4, 5*
Ligo Research Inc. - Harvey, IL - *MicrocomMPl 84*
Ligonier Advance Leader [of Kendallville Publishing] - Ligonier, IN - *BaconPubCkNews 84; NewsDir 84*
Ligonier Cable Communications [of Adelphia Communications Corp.] - Ligonier, PA - *BrCabYB 84*
Ligonier Echo [of The Laurel Group Press] - Ligonier, PA - *BaconPubCkNews 84; Ed&PubIntYB 82; NewsDir 84*
Ligonier Telephone Co. Inc. - Ligonier, IN - *TelDir&BG 83-84*
Liguori Publications - Liguori, MO - *DirMarMP 83; LitMarPl 83, 84*
Liguori Publications (Book & Pamphlet Dept.) - Liguori, MO - *WritMar 84*
Liguorian [of The Redemptorist Fathers] - Liguori, MO - *LitMarPl 83, 84; MagDir 84; MagIndMarPl 82-83; WritMar 84*
Lihue Garden Island - Lihue, HI - *BaconPubCkNews 84*
Lilbourn Semo News - Lilbourn, MO - *BaconPubCkNews 84*
Lilco Productions - Harrisburg, PA - *AvMarPl 83*
Lilith - New York, NY - *LitMag&SmPr 83-84*
Lillenas Program Builders [of Lillenas Publishing Co.] - Kansas City, MO - *WritMar 84*
Lillenas Publishing Co. - Kansas City, MO - *BillIntBG 83-84*
Liller Neal Inc. - Atlanta, GA - *AdAge 3-28-84; BrCabYB 84; DirPRFirms 83; StaDirAdAg 2-84*
Lilley & Son Inc., J. P. - Harrisburg, PA - *AvMarPl 83*
Lillie Suburban Newspapers - St. Paul, MN - *BaconPubCkNews 84; NewsDir 84*
Lillington Harnett County News - Lillington, NC - *BaconPubCkNews 84*
Lilly & Co., Eli - New York, NY - *BoPubDir 5*
Lilval Inc. - Lincoln Village West, CA - *Tel&CabFB 84C*
Lim Press - Belmont, CA - *BoPubDir 5*
Lima Communications Corp. - Lima, OH - *BrCabYB 84*
Lima News - Lima, OH - *BaconPubCkNews 84; Ed&PubIntYB 82; NewsDir 84*
Lima Recorder, The - Lima, NY - *Ed&PubIntYB 82*
Lima Recorder, The - *See* Brador Publications Inc.
Lima Sentinel, The - Cridersville, OH - *NewsDir 84*
Limberlost Review, The - Pocatello, ID - *LitMag&SmPr 83-84*
Limbo Bar & Grill Books - Melrose Park, PA - *LitMag&SmPr 83-84*
Lime Rock Press Inc. - Salisbury, CT - *BoPubDir 4, 5*
Lime Springs Herald - Lime Springs, IA - *AyerDirPub 83; BaconPubCkNews 84; Ed&PubIntYB 82; NewsDir 84*
Limelite, The - Loring Air Force Base, ME - *NewsDir 84*
Limerick League Inc., The - Philadelphia, PA - *LitMag&SmPr 83-84*
Limestone - Arlington, VA - *BaconPubCkMag 84*
Limestone Cable TV - Groesbeck, TX - *BrCabYB 84; Tel&CabFB 84C*
Limestone Cable Vision Inc. [of Standard Tobacco Co. Inc.] - Maysville, KY - *BrCabYB 84; Tel&CabFB 84C*
Limestone Press - Kingston, ON, Canada - *BoPubDir 4, 5*
Limited Edition Press - Darlington, MD - *BoPubDir 4 Sup, 5*
Limited Editions Club - New York, NY - *BoPubDir 4 Sup, 5; LitMarPl 83, 84*
Limited Editions Press - Northridge, CA - *BoPubDir 5*
Limits Book Co. - Toronto, ON, Canada - *BoPubDir 4, 5*
Limnology & Oceanography - Seattle, WA - *BaconPubCkMag 84*
Limon Leader - Limon, CO - *BaconPubCkNews 84; Ed&PubIntYB 82*
Limousine & Chauffeur - Costa Mesa, CA - *BaconPubCkMag 84*
Lin Broadcasting - New York, NY - *AdAge 6-28-84; BrCabYB 84; KnowInd 83; Tel&CabFB 84S*
LINA [of Informationsverbundzentrum RAUM und BAU der Fraunhofer-Gesellschaft] - Stuttgart, West Germany - *CompReadDB 82; DirOnDB Spring 84*
Linberg Systems - Worcester, MA - *MicrocomMPl 83*
Linburg & Associates Inc. - Dallas, TX - *WhoWMicrocom 83*
Linc Associates Inc. - Columbus, OH - *LitMarPl 83, 84*
Linc Resources Inc. - Columbus, OH - *InfoS 83-84; MagIndMarPl 82-83*
Linc Service [of Memphis & Shelby County Public Library & Information Center] - Memphis, TN - *EISS 83*
Linch Corp. - Orlando, FL - *LitMarPl 84*
Linck, Tony - Ft. Lee, NJ - *LitMarPl 84*
Linco - Newtonville, MA - *MicrocomSwDir 1*
Lincoln Arc Welding Foundation, James F. - Cleveland, OH - *BoPubDir 4, 5*
Lincoln-Belmont Booster [of Chicago Lerner Newspapers] - Chicago, IL - *AyerDirPub 83; Ed&PubIntYB 82; NewsDir 84*
Lincoln-Belmont Publishing Co. - Chicago, IL - *BaconPubCkNews 84*
Lincoln Bulletin - Culloden, WV - *AyerDirPub 83; NewsDir 84*
Lincoln Cable Television Inc. - Kemmerer, WY - *BrCabYB 84*
Lincoln Cable TV - Lincoln, AL - *Tel&CabFB 84C*
Lincoln Cable TV [of Great Plains Communications Systems Inc.] - Lincoln, KS - *BrCabYB 84; Tel&CabFB 84C*
Lincoln Cablevision [of MetroVision Inc.] - Lincoln, NE - *Tel&CabFB 84C*
Lincoln Cablevision Inc. - Lincolnton, NC - *Tel&CabFB 84C*
Lincoln Center for the Performing Arts Inc. - New York, NY - *DirMarMP 83*
Lincoln City News Guard - Lincoln City, OR - *BaconPubCkNews 84*
Lincoln Closed-Circuit Inc. - San Francisco, CA - *Tel&CabFB 84C*
Lincoln County Journal - Shoshone, ID - *AyerDirPub 83; Ed&PubIntYB 82*
Lincoln County Leader - Toledo, OR - *AyerDirPub 83; Ed&PubIntYB 82*
Lincoln County News - Damariscotta, ME - *AyerDirPub 83; Ed&PubIntYB 82*
Lincoln County News - Newcastle, ME - *NewsDir 84*
Lincoln County News - Carrizozo, NM - *AyerDirPub 83; Ed&PubIntYB 82*

Lincoln County News - Chandler, OK - *AyerDirPub 83; Ed&PubIntYB 82*
Lincoln County Record - Caliente, NV - *AyerDirPub 83; Ed&PubIntYB 82*
Lincoln County Telephone System Inc. - Pioche, NV - *TelDir&BG 83-84*
Lincoln County Valley Journal - Lake Benton, MN - *AyerDirPub 83; Ed&PubIntYB 82*
Lincoln Courier [of Logan County Publishing Co.] - Lincoln, IL - *BaconPubCkNews 84; Ed&PubIntYB 82; NewsDir 84*
Lincoln-Cumberland Observer-News Leader [of Greenville Observer Publications Inc.] - Greenville, RI - *NewsDir 84*
Lincoln-Cumberland Observer, The - Cumberland, RI - *Ed&PubIntYB 82*
Lincoln Farm Camp [Div. of Ardsley Advertising Agency] - Ardsley, NY - *LitMarPl 83, 84; MagIndMarPl 82-83*
Lincoln Graphic Arts Inc. - Farmingdale, NY - *LitMarPl 83, 84; MagIndMarPl 82-83*
Lincoln Heights Bulletin-News [of Northeast Los Angeles Publishing Co.] - Los Angeles, CA - *AyerDirPub 83; Ed&PubIntYB 82; NewsDir 84*
Lincoln Heights Bulletin-News - *See* Northeast Los Angeles Publishing Co.
Lincoln Herald - Lincoln Park, NJ - *Ed&PubIntYB 82*
Lincoln Institute of Land Policy [Aff. of Lincoln Foundation] - Cambridge, MA - *BoPubDir 4, 5*
Lincoln Journal - Lincoln, NE - *BaconPubCkNews 84; Ed&PubIntYB 82; LitMarPl 83, 84; NewsBur 6*
Lincoln Journal - Hamlin, WV - *Ed&PubIntYB 82*
Lincoln Journal - *See* Lincoln Publishing Co.
Lincoln Journal-Star - Lincoln, NE - *NewsDir 84*
Lincoln Journal, The - Lincolnton, GA - *Ed&PubIntYB 82*
Lincoln Leader - Lincoln, AR - *BaconPubCkNews 84; Ed&PubIntYB 82*
Lincoln Ledger - Star City, AR - *AyerDirPub 83; Ed&PubIntYB 82; NewsDir 84*
Lincoln Lincolnland Sun - *See* Sun Newspapers of Lincoln Inc.
Lincoln Literary Agency, Ray [Div. of Lincoln Associates Inc.] - Melrose Park, PA - *LitMarPl 83, 84*
Lincoln Log - Raymond, IL - *LitMag&SmPr 83-84*
Lincoln New Era - Lincoln, MO - *AyerDirPub 83; BaconPubCkNews 84; Ed&PubIntYB 82*
Lincoln News - Lincoln, ME - *AyerDirPub 83; BaconPubCkNews 84; Ed&PubIntYB 82; NewsDir 84*
Lincoln News - Sheldonville, MA - *NewsDir 84*
Lincoln News Messenger - Lincoln, CA - *AyerDirPub 83; BaconPubCkNews 84; Ed&PubIntYB 82*
Lincoln Northeast Sun - *See* Sun Newspapers of Lincoln Inc.
Lincoln Northwest Sun - *See* Sun Newspapers of Lincoln Inc.
Lincoln Park Herald Inc. - Fairfield, NJ - *BaconPubCkNews 84*
Lincoln Park-Lakeview Booster - Chicago, IL - *AyerDirPub 83*
Lincoln Park-Lakeview-Sheridan Center Booster [of Chicago Lerner Newspapers] - Chicago, IL - *NewsDir 84*
Lincoln Parker [of Mellus Newspapers Inc.] - Lincoln Park, MI - *AyerDirPub 83; Ed&PubIntYB 82; NewsDir 84*
Lincoln Parker - *See* Mellus Newspapers Inc.
Lincoln Picture Studio - Dayton, OH - *LitMarPl 83, 84; MagIndMarPl 82-83*
Lincoln, Pitt & Associates Inc. - Jericho, NY - *StaDirAdAg 2-84*
Lincoln Post Express - Beamsville, ON, Canada - *AyerDirPub 83*
Lincoln Post-Express - Lincoln, ON, Canada - *Ed&PubIntYB 82*
Lincoln Publishers - Palo Alto, CA - *BoPubDir 4, 5*
Lincoln Publishing Co. - Palo Alto, CA - *LitMag&SmPr 83-84*
Lincoln Publishing Co. - Hamlin, WV - *BaconPubCkNews 84*
Lincoln Records - Cambridge, MA - *BillIntBG 83-84*
Lincoln Road Music Co. - *See* Keene Music Co., Joe
Lincoln Sentinel-Republican - Lincoln, KS - *BaconPubCkNews 84; Ed&PubIntYB 82*
Lincoln Southeast Sun - *See* Sun Newspapers of Lincoln Inc.
Lincoln Southwest Sun - *See* Sun Newspapers of Lincoln Inc.
Lincoln Star - Lincoln, NE - *BaconPubCkNews 84; Ed&PubIntYB 82; LitMarPl 83, 84*
Lincoln Sunday Journal & Star - Lincoln, NE - *Ed&PubIntYB 82*
Lincoln Telephone Co. - Lincoln, MT - *TelDir&BG 83-84*
Lincoln Telephone Co., The [Aff. of Lincoln Telecommunications Co.] - Lincoln, NE - *TelDir&BG 83-84*
Lincoln Television System Inc. - Hebo, OR - *BrCabYB 84*
Lincoln Television System Inc. - Lincoln City, OR - *BrCabYB 84; Tel&CabFB 84C*
Lincoln Times-News - Lincolnton, NC - *AyerDirPub 83; Ed&PubIntYB 82*
Lincolnland Shopping Guide - Tell City, IN - *AyerDirPub 83*
Lincolnland Sun - Lincoln, NE - *AyerDirPub 83; Ed&PubIntYB 82; NewsDir 84*
Lincoln's Leadership Library [Aff. of Professional Real Estate Publishers] - Tulsa, OK - *BoPubDir 4 Sup, 5*
Lincolnton Lincoln Journal - Lincolnton, GA - *BaconPubCkNews 84*
Lincolnton Times-News [of Western Carolina Publishing Co.] - Lincolnton, NC - *BaconPubCkNews 84; NewsDir 84*
Lincolnville Telephone Co. - Lincolnville, ME - *TelDir&BG 83-84*
Lincolnwood Life [of Lerner Newspapers] - Chicago, IL - *NewsDir 84*
Lincolnwood Life - Skokie, IL - *AyerDirPub 83*
Lincolnwood Life - *See* Myers Publishing Co.
Lincolnwood Life, The - Lincolnwood, IL - *Ed&PubIntYB 82*
Lind Leader - Clarkston, WA - *AyerDirPub 83*
Lind Leader - *See* Tribune Newspapers Inc.
Lind Leader, The - Lind, WA - *Ed&PubIntYB 82*
Lind Organization, The - New York, NY - *AvMarPl 83*
Lind TV Service Inc. - Lind, WA - *Tel&CabFB 84C*
Lindahl, Judy - Portland, OR - *BoPubDir 4, 5*
Lindale News - Lindale, TX - *BaconPubCkNews 84; Ed&PubIntYB 82*
Lindberg Productions Inc. - New York, NY - *AvMarPl 83*
Lindberg Records - Glenview, IL - *BillIntBG 83-84*
Lindbergh Systems - Holden, MA - *MicrocomMPl 84; MicrocomSwDir 1*
Lindell-Keys Co. - Dallas, TX - *DirPRFirms 83; StaDirAdAg 2-84*
Lindell Publishers - Springtown, PA - *BoPubDir 4, 5*
Lindemann, Barbara M. - Los Angeles, CA - *FBInfSer 80*
Linden Advertising Agency Inc. - Virginia Beach, VA - *DirMarMP 83; StaDirAdAg 2-84*
Linden Buffalo River Review - Linden, TN - *BaconPubCkNews 84*
Linden Cass County Sun - Linden, TX - *BaconPubCkNews 84*
Linden Color Laboratories - Linden, NJ - *AvMarPl 83*
Linden Democrat-Reporter - Linden, AL - *BaconPubCkNews 84; NewsDir 84*
Linden, Elaine - Santa Monica, CA - *LitMarPl 83, 84*
Linden Herald - Linden, CA - *BaconPubCkNews 84; Ed&PubIntYB 82*
Linden Leader - Linden, NJ - *Ed&PubIntYB 82*
Linden Leader - Union, NJ - *AyerDirPub 83*
Linden Press [Subs. of Simon & Schuster] - New York, NY - *LitMarPl 83, 84*
Linden Press Baltimore - Baltimore, MD - *LitMag&SmPr 83-84*
Linden Publishers - Hollywood, CA - *BoPubDir 4, 5*
Linden Publishing Co. - Fresno, CA - *LitMag&SmPr 83-84*
Lindenhurst-Copiague Pennysaver - Levittown, NY - *AyerDirPub 83*
Lindenhurst South Bay's Newspaper - Lindenhurst, NY - *BaconPubCkNews 84*
Lindenmeyr Paper Corp. - Rutherford, NJ - *DirInfWP 82*
Lindenmeyr Paper Corp. - Long Island City, NY - *LitMarPl 83, 84; MagIndMarPl 82-83*
Linder Co., William A. - Lindsborg, KS - *BoPubDir 4, 5*
Linder, Herbert - New York, NY - *BoPubDir 4 Sup, 5*
Linder Radio Group - Willmar, MN - *BrCabYB 84*
Lindgren Associates - Chicago, IL - *StaDirAdAg 2-84*
Lindisfarne Letter, The - West Stockbridge, MA - *LitMag&SmPr 83-84*
Lindisfarne Press [Aff. of Lindisfarne Association] - West Stockbridge, MA - *BoPubDir 4 Sup, 5; LitMag&SmPr 83-84*
Lindley-Presho Cable TV - Lindley, NY - *BrCabYB 84; Tel&CabFB 84C*
Lindsay CATV System Ltd. - Lindsay, ON, Canada - *BrCabYB 84*
Lindsay Daily Post, The - Lindsay, ON, Canada - *AyerDirPub 83; BaconPubCkNews 84*
Lindsay Gazette - Lindsay, CA - *BaconPubCkNews 84; Ed&PubIntYB 82; NewsDir 84*
Lindsay News - Lindsay, OK - *BaconPubCkNews 84; Ed&PubIntYB 82*

Lindsay Publications - Bradley, IL - *BoPubDir 4 Sup, 5*
Lindsay Specialty - Buffalo, NY - *HomeVid&CabYB 82-83*
Lindsay This Week - Lindsay, ON, Canada - *AyerDirPub 83*
Lindsay Voice, The - Lindsay, TX - *Ed&PubIntYB 82*
Lindsborg Cable TV [of Great Plains Communications Systems Inc.] - Lindsborg, KS - *BrCabYB 84; Tel&CabFB 84C*
Lindsborg News Record - Lindsborg, KS - *AyerDirPub 83*
Lindsborg News-Record - McPherson, KS - *Ed&PubIntYB 82*
Lindsborg News-Record - *See* Montgomery Publications Inc.
Lindsey Publishing - Torrington, WY - *BaconPubCkNews 84*
Lindsey Unroe & Harbin Marketing Services - Zionsville, IN - *StaDirAdAg 2-84*
Lindstrom & Jett of Arizona Inc. - Phoenix, AZ - *StaDirAdAg 2-84*
Lindstrom Chisago County Press - Lindstrom, MN - *BaconPubCkNews 84*
Line One Video - New York, NY - *AvMarPl 83*
Line Printers [of GML Corp.] - Lexington, MA - *CompReadDB 82*
Lineage Publishing Co. - East Prairie, MO - *BillIntBG 83-84*
Lineal Lois & Peters Inc. - Darien, CT - *StaDirAdAg 2-84*
Lineal Publishing Co. - Darien, CT - *BoPubDir 4, 5*
Linear Electronics - Inglewood, CA - *HomeVid&CabYB 82-83*
Linear Software Co. - Westminster, CA - *MicrocomMPl 83, 84*
Linen, Fortinberry & Associates - Greenwich, CT - *DirPRFirms 83*
Linens, Domestics & Bath Products [of Columbia Communications Inc.] - New York, NY - *BaconPubCkMag 84; MagDir 84; WritMar 84*
Lines Magazine - Philadelphia, PA - *WritMar 84*
Lines of Vision - Atlanta, GA - *BoPubDir 4, 5*
Linesville Herald [of Gazette Printing Co. Inc.] - Jefferson, OH - *NewsDir 84*
Linesville Herald - Linesville, PA - *AyerDirPub 83; BaconPubCkNews 84; Ed&PubIntYB 82*
Lineville Tribune - Lineville, AL - *BaconPubCkNews 84; Ed&PubIntYB 82*
L'Information - Mont-Joli, PQ, Canada - *Ed&PubIntYB 82*
L'Information Regionale - Chateauguay, PQ, Canada - *AyerDirPub 83*
Lingle Guide - *See* Lindsey Publishing
Lingua House - Pasadena, CA - *BoPubDir 4, 5*
Lingua Press - Ramona, CA - *BoPubDir 4, 5*
Linguadex Publications - San Diego, CA - *BoPubDir 4, 5*
Linguamundi Publications - McClean, VA - *MagIndMarPl 82-83*
Linguistic Review [of Foris Publications USA-Bird-Sci Books] - Cinnaminson, NJ - *LitMag&SmPr 83-84*
Linguistic Systems Inc. - Cambridge, MA - *LitMarPl 83, 84; MagIndMarPl 82-83*
Linguistics [of Centre de Documentation Sciences Humaines] - Paris, France - *CompReadDB 82*
Linguistics Research Center [of University of Texas, Austin] - Austin, TX - *EISS 83*
Linhoff Color Photo - Edina, MN - *AvMarPl 83*
Linick, Andrew S. - Middle Island, NY - *LitMarPl 83, 84; MagIndMarPl 82-83*
Linju-Ryu Karate Association Inc. - Middle Island, NY - *BoPubDir 4, 5*
Link - New York, NY - *InterCabHB 3; VideoDir 82-83*
Link House Communications - Poole, England - *InfIndMarPl 83*
Link News Briefs - New York, NY - *DirOnDB Spring 84*
Link News Briefs [of NewsNet Inc.] - Bryn Mawr, PA - *DataDirOnSer 84*
Link Resources Corp. [Subs. of International Data Corp.] - New York, NY - *EISS 83; InfIndMarPl 83; InfoS 83-84*
Link Systems - Santa Monica, CA - *MicrocomMPl 83, 84; MicrocomSwDir 1; WhoWMicrocom 83; WritMar 84*
Link Up [of On Line Communications] - St. Louis Park, MN - *MicrocomMPl 84*
Linker Productions, Hal - Encino, CA - *Tel&CabFB 84C*
Linkhorn, Forbes - New York, NY - *LitMarPl 83, 84*
Linkline [of Freeman Hospital] - Joplin, MO - *EISS 5-84 Sup*
Links Inc. - Medway, MA - *Tel&CabFB 84C*
Linkup [of Information Technologies Inc.] - Scottsdale, AZ - *TeleSy&SerDir 2-84*
Linn County Historical Society - Pleasanton, KS - *BoPubDir 4 Sup, 5*
Linn County News - Pleasanton, KS - *AyerDirPub 83; Ed&PubIntYB 82*
Linn, Mrs. Stahle Jr. - Salisbury, NC - *BoPubDir 4, 5*
Linn Music, Roger - *See* Williams Music Group, Don
Linn News-Letter - Central City, IA - *AyerDirPub 83; Ed&PubIntYB 82*
Linn-Palmer Record - Linn, KS - *Ed&PubIntYB 82*
Linn Rural Telephone Co. - Linn, KS - *TelDir&BG 83-84*
Linn Unterrified Democrat - Linn, MO - *BaconPubCkNews 84; NewsDir 84*
Linn's Stamp News - Dayton, OH - *MagDir 84*
Linn's Stamp News - Sidney, OH - *MagIndMarPl 82-83*
Linq [of English Language Literature Association] - Townsville, Australia - *LitMag&SmPr 83-84*
Linscott, William D. - Mill Valley, CA - *BoPubDir 4, 5*
Linsman Film & Tape - Scottsdale, AZ - *AvMarPl 83; Tel&CabFB 84C*
L'Institut National des Viandes Inc. - Montreal, PQ, Canada - *BoPubDir 5*
Linstok Press - Silver Spring, MD - *BoPubDir 4, 5*
Lintel - St. George, NY - *BoPubDir 4; LitMag&SmPr 83-84*
Lintel - Roanoke, VA - *BoPubDir 5*
Linthurst Books, Randolph - West Trenton, NJ - *BoPubDir 4, 5*
Lintlaw Historical Society [Aff. of Lintlaw Chamber of Commerce] - Lintlaw, SK, Canada - *BoPubDir 4, 5*
Linton Cable TV Inc. [of Horizon Communications Corp.] - Linton, IN - *Tel&CabFB 84C*
Linton Citizen [of Hammell Newspapers of Indiana Inc.] - Linton, IN - *BaconPubCkNews 84; Ed&PubIntYB 82; NewsDir 84*
Linton Emmons County Record - Linton, ND - *BaconPubCkNews 84; NewsDir 84*
Linton, Shafer & Co. - Frederick, MD - *WhoWMicrocom 83*
Linweave Inc. - Holyoke, MA - *LitMarPl 83, 84*
Linwood Publishers - North Charleston, SC - *LitMag&SmPr 83-84*
Linzer, Elliot - Flushing, NY - *LitMarPl 83, 84*
Lion & the Unicorn - Brooklyn, NY - *LitMag&SmPr 83-84*
Lion Books [of Sayre Publishing Inc.] - New York, NY - *LitMarPl 83*
Lion Books - Scarsdale, NY - *LitMarPl 84*
Lion Cub Music - *See* Paragon/Benson Publishing Group
Lion Enterprises - Walkerton, IN - *BoPubDir 4, 5; LitMag&SmPr 83-84*
Lion Services Co. - Coranado, CA - *BoPubDir 4, 5*
Lion, The - Naperville, IL - *MagDir 84*
Lion, The - Oak Brook, IL - *BaconPubCkMag 84; MagIndMarPl 82-83; WritMar 84*
Lioness Records - Philadelphia, PA - *BillIntBG 83-84*
Lionetti & Meyers Research Center Inc. - New York, NY - *IntDirMarRes 83*
Lionhead Publishing/Roar Recording - Shorewood, WI - *BoPubDir 4 Sup, 5; LitMag&SmPr 83-84*
Lionheart Television International - New York, NY - *Tel&CabFB 84C*
Lions Bay Cablevision Ltd. - Lions Bay, BC, Canada - *BrCabYB 84*
Lion's Gate Films Inc. - Los Angeles, CA - *BillIntBG 83-84*
Lion's Head Publishing Co. - Ft. Wayne, IN - *BoPubDir 4, 5*
Lipan Telephone Co. - Lipan, TX - *TelDir&BG 83-84*
Lipids [of American Oil Chemists Society] - Champaign, IL - *BaconPubCkMag 84; MagDir 84*
Lipkind Agency, Wendy - New York, NY - *LitMarPl 83, 84*
Liplop Press - Berkeley, CA - *BoPubDir 4, 5*
Lipman Advertising - New York, NY - *AdAge 3-28-84; StaDirAdAg 2-84*
Lipman Publishing Inc. - Toronto, ON, Canada - *ArtMar 84*
Lipper Communications - New York, NY - *Tel&CabFB 84C*
Lipper-LaRue Inc. - Stockton, CA - *Tel&CabFB 84C*
Lippin & Grant Inc. - Los Angeles, CA - *DirPRFirms 83*
Lippincott Co., J. B. [Subs. of Harper & Row Inc.] - New York, NY - *DirMarMP 83*
Lippincott Co., J. B. [Subs. of Harper & Row Inc.] - Philadelphia, PA - *AvMarPl 83; LitMarPl 83, 84; MagIndMarPl 82-83; WritMar 84*
Lippincott Co., J. B. (Media Development/Health Services Div.) - Philadelphia, PA - *ArtMar 84*
Lippincott Junior Books - *See* Harper & Row (Junior Books Group)

Lippisch Advertising/Design Inc. - Cedar Rapids, IA - *StaDirAdAg 2-84*
Lips - Montclair, NJ - *LitMag&SmPr 83-84*
Lipscomb County Limelight - Follett, TX - *Ed&PubIntYB 82*
Lipservices [Div. of T.S.E.C. Inc.] - New York, NY - *BillIntBG 83-84*
Lipsey & Associates, J. - Omaha, NE - *StaDirAdAg 2-84*
Lipsman & Associates Inc., Arnold - Los Angeles, CA - *DirPRFirms 83*
Lipsner-Smith Co. [Subs. of Research Technology International] - Lincolnwood, IL - *AvMarPl 83*
Lipson Public Relations, Benjamin - New York, NY - *DirPRFirms 83*
Lipson's Co., Charlotte - New York, NY - *DirPRFirms 83*
Lipton, E. Trina - New York, NY - *LitMarPl 83, 84; MagIndMarPl 82-83*
Liquified Petroleum Gas Report - New York, NY - *DirOnDB Spring 84*
Liquified Petroleum Gas Report [of I. P. Sharp Associates Ltd.] - Toronto, ON, Canada - *DataDirOnSer 84*
Liquor Store Magazine [of Jobson Publishing Corp.] - New York, NY - *BaconPubCkMag 84; WritMar 84*
Lirol TV Productions - Los Angeles, CA - *WritMar 84*
LIRS Classics - Brooklyn, NY - *BillIntBG 83-84*
Lis-Ti Publishing - *See* Mietus Copyright Management
LISA - London, England - *DirOnDB Spring 84*
Lisa's Interviewing Service Inc. - Miami, FL - *IntDirMarRes 83*
Lisas Theme Music Inc. - St. Petersburg, FL - *BillIntBG 83-84*
Lisboa Associates Inc. - Washington, DC - *DirPRFirms 83*
Lisbon Canfield Courier - Lisbon, OH - *BaconPubCkNews 84*
Lisbon Falls Post Enterprise - Lisbon Falls, ME - *BaconPubCkNews 84*
Lisbon Morning Journal [of Buckeye Publishing Co.] - Lisbon, OH - *NewsDir 84*
Lisbon Ransom County Gazette & Enterprise - Lisbon, ND - *BaconPubCkNews 84; NewsDir 84*
LISE Publications - Lancaster, England - *MicroMarPl 82-83*
Lisher & Co. Inc. - New York, NY - *HBIndAd&MS 82-83; StaDirAdAg 2-84*
Lisle Township Sun - Lisle, IL - *AyerDirPub 83; BaconPubCkNews 84; Ed&PubIntYB 82; NewsDir 84*
Lismore Cooperative Telephone Co. - Lismore, MN - *TelDir&BG 83-84*
Liss, Eli & Gail - Woodstock, NY - *LitMarPl 83, 84*
Liss Inc., Alan R. - New York, NY - *LitMarPl 83, 84; MagIndMarPl 82-83*
List [of Redgate Publishing Co.] - Vero Beach, FL - *BaconPubCkMag 84; MicrocomMPl 84*
List Maintenance Corp. - Armonk, NY - *MagIndMarPl 82-83*
List Services Corp. - Ridgefield, CT - *EISS 7-83 Sup*
Listen - Washington, DC - *MagDir 84; WritMar 84*
Listeners' Network - Quincy, MA - *BrCabYB 84*
Listening Inc. - Gary, IN - *Ed&PubIntYB 82*
Listening Library - Old Greenwich, CT - *ArtMar 84; AvMarPl 83; BillIntBG 83-84*
Lister Butler Inc. - New York, NY - *HBIndAd&MS 82-83*
Lister Hill National Center for Biomedical Communications [of U.S. National Library of Medicine] - Bethesda, MD - *EISS 83*
Lister Publications, Mosie - Tampa, FL - *BillIntBG 83-84*
Listowel Banner, The - Listowel, ON, Canada - *Ed&PubIntYB 82*
Listronics Inc. - El Rancho Green Valley, CA - *Tel&CabFB 84C*
Lists International Inc. - New York, NY - *MagIndMarPl 82-83*
L'Italo-Americano - Sun Valley, CA - *Ed&PubIntYB 82*
Litchfield Broadcasting Co. - Minneapolis, MN - *BrCabYB 84*
Litchfield Cablevision [of Metro Cable Inc.] - Litchfield, MN - *BrCabYB 84; Tel&CabFB 84C*
Litchfield Enquirer - Litchfield, CT - *Ed&PubIntYB 82*
Litchfield Enquirer [of New Milford Housatonic Valley Publishing Co.] - New Milford, CT - *AyerDirPub 83; NewsDir 84*
Litchfield Enquirer - *See* Housatonic Valley Publishing Co.
Litchfield Independent-Review - Litchfield, MN - *BaconPubCkNews 84; NewsDir 84*
Litchfield News-Herald - Litchfield, IL - *BaconPubCkNews 84; NewsDir 84*
Litchfield-Pawleys Island CATV - Georgetown County, SC - *BrCabYB 84*
Litchville Bulletin - Litchville, ND - *BaconPubCkNews 84; Ed&PubIntYB 82*
Literary Art Press Newsletter [of Wash 'n Press] - Seattle, WA - *LitMag&SmPr 83-84*
Literary/Business Associates/Shelley Gross - Hollywood, CA - *LitMarPl 83, 84*
Literary Cavalcade - New York, NY - *MagIndMarPl 82-83*
Literary Classics of the United States Inc. - New York, NY - *LitMarPl 83*
Literary Consultants [Subs. of Author Aid Associates] - New York, NY - *LitMarPl 83, 84; MagIndMarPl 82-83*
Literary Guild of America - New York, NY - *LitMarPl 83*
Literary Guild of America - *See* Doubleday Book Clubs
Literary Guild of America (Young Adults' Div.) - New York, NY - *LitMarPl 83*
Literary Herald Press - Danville, IL - *BoPubDir 4, 5*
Literary Lantern, The - Chapel Hill, NC - *LitMarPl 83, 84*
Literary Magazine Review - Manhattan, KS - *LitMag&SmPr 83-84*
Literary Markets - Richmond, BC, Canada - *LitMag&SmPr 83-84*
Literary Research Newsletter - Bronx, NY - *LitMag&SmPr 83-84*
Literary Review [of Fairleigh Dickinson University] - Madison, NJ - *LitMag&SmPr 83-84; WritMar 84*
Literary Services Institute - Towson, MD - *LitMarPl 84*
Literary Services Unltd. - Dallas, TX - *LitMarPl 83, 84*
Literary Sketches - Williamsburg, VA - *LitMag&SmPr 83-84; WritMar 84*
Literary Supplement, The - London, England - *LitMag&SmPr 83-84*
Literations - Pittsfield, MA - *BoPubDir 5*
Literaturdienst Medizin/Literature Service in Medicine [of Osterreichisches Bundesinstitut fur Gesundheitswesen] - Vienna, Austria - *InfIndMarPl 83*
Literaturdokumentation zur Arbeitsmarkt-und Berufsforschung [of Institut fur Arbeitsmarkt-und Berufsforschung] - Nuremberg, West Germany - *CompReadDB 82*
Literature Analysis System on Road Safety - Dickson, Australia - *DirOnDB Spring 84*
Literature Information System [of Institute for Air Pollution Control in North Rhine-Westphalia] - Essen, West Germany - *EISS 83*
Literature Research Section [of SRI International] - Menlo Park, CA - *EISS 83*
Literature Service in Medicine [of Austrian National Institute for Public Health] - Vienna, Austria - *EISS 83*
Literaturinformation aus Raumordnung, Stadtebau, Wohnungswesen, Bauwesen [of Informationsverbundzentrum RAUM und BAU der Fraunhofer-Gesellschaft] - Stuttgart, West Germany - *CompReadDB 82*
Literaturinformation zur Orts-, Regional-, und Landesplanung [of Deutsches Institut fuer Urbanistik] - Berlin, West Germany - *CompReadDB 82*
Literistic Ltd. - New York, NY - *LitMarPl 83, 84*
Lithium Information Center [of University of Wisconsin] - Madison, WI - *DataDirOnSer 84*
Lithium Library [of University of Wisconsin] - Madison, WI - *DataDirOnSer 84; DirOnDB Spring 84; EISS 83*
Litho Prepsters Inc. - New York, NY - *MagIndMarPl 82-83*
Litho Prestige [Div. of Uniprimerie Inc.] - Drummondville, PQ, Canada - *LitMarPl 83*
Litho Productions Inc. - Madison, WI - *MagIndMarPl 82-83*
Lithonia Observer [of Decatur News Publishing Co. Inc.] - Lithonia, GA - *BaconPubCkNews 84; Ed&PubIntYB 82; NewsDir 84*
Lithuanian Daily News Naujienos - Chicago, IL - *NewsDir 84*
Lithuanian Folk Art Institute - Toronto, ON, Canada - *BoPubDir 5*
Lithuanian Historical Society - Oak Lawn, IL - *BoPubDir 4, 5*
Lithuanian Institute of Education - Chicago, IL - *BoPubDir 4, 5*
Lithuanian Library Press Inc. - Chicago, IL - *BoPubDir 4, 5*
LITIR Database - Edmonton, AB, Canada - *BoPubDir 4 Sup, 5*
Lititz Record-Express - Lititz, PA - *BaconPubCkNews 84; Ed&PubIntYB 82*
Litmore Publications - Hicksville, NY - *BaconPubCkNews 84*
Litmus Inc. - Walla Walla, WA - *BoPubDir 4 Sup, 5*
Lito Music - North Hollywood, CA - *BillIntBG 83-84*
Littauer Condensed - Westwood, NJ - *MagDir 84*

Little A Music Inc. - *See* Schroeder International Ltd., A.
Little & Associates - Atlanta, GA - *StaDirAdAg 2-84*
Little, B. J. - Tuscola, TX - *Tel&CabFB 84C p.1688*
Little Balkans Press Inc. - Pittsburg, KS - *BoPubDir 4 Sup, 5*
Little Balkans Review [of Little Balkans Press Inc.] - Pittsburg, KS - *WritMar 84*
Little Bee Educational Programs - Massillon, OH - *MicrocomMPl 83*
Little Books & Co. - Denver, CO - *BoPubDir 4, 5*
Little Brick House - Vandalia, IL - *BoPubDir 4, 5*
Little Brick Schoolhouse - Mississauga, ON, Canada - *BoPubDir 5*
Little Brown & Co. - Boston, MA - *LitMarPl 83, 84; MicrocomMPl 84; MicrocomSwDir 1; WritMar 84*
Little, Brown & Co. (Adult Trade Div.) - Boston, MN - *ArtMar 84*
Little, Brown & Co. Ltd. - Toronto, ON, Canada - *LitMarPl 84*
Little Caesar - New York, NY - *LitMag&SmPr 83-84*
Little Caesar Press - Los Angeles, CA - *BoPubDir 4, 5*
Little Caesar Press - New York, NY - *LitMag&SmPr 83-84*
Little Cajun Books - Baton Rouge, LA - *BoPubDir 4, 5*
Little Chief Broadcasting Co. - Fayetteville, AR - *BrCabYB 84*
Little Courier, The - Littleton, NH - *AyerDirPub 83*
Little, Dan L. - Tuscola, TX - *Tel&CabFB 84C p.1688*
Little Dania's Juvenile Promotions - New York, NY - *LitMarPl 84*
Little Darlin Music - *See* Cooper Music, Martin
Little David Music Inc. - *See* Shetland Enterprises International
Little David Records - Los Angeles, CA - *BillIntBG 83-84*
Little Elm Colony Courier - Little Elm, TX - *BaconPubCkNews 84*
Little Falls Evening Times - Little Falls, NY - *NewsDir 84*
Little Falls Transcript [of St. Cloud Newspapers Inc.] - Little Falls, MN - *Ed&PubIntYB 82; NewsDir 84*
Little Feat - Water Mill, NY - *BoPubDir 4 Sup, 5*
Little Free Press - Minneapolis, MN - *LitMag&SmPr 83-84*
Little Giant Records - White Lake, NY - *BillIntBG 83-84*
Little Giant Records - Nashville, TN - *BillIntBG 83-84*
Little Glass Shack - Sacramento, CA - *BoPubDir 4, 5*
Little Inc., Arthur D. - Cambridge, MA - *CabTVFinDB 83; DataDirOnSer 84; DirInfWP 82; InfIndMarPl 83; InterCabHB 3*
Little Joe Music - Johnstown, PA - *BillIntBG 83-84*
Little K [of Poundfoolish Publishing] - Dubuque, IA - *MicrocomMPl 84*
Little King Publishing & Novelty Co. - Cleveland, OH - *LitMarPl 83, 84*
Little London Press - Colorado Springs, CO - *BoPubDir 4, 5*
Little Neck/Glen Oaks Ledger, The - Little Neck, NY - *Ed&PubIntYB 82*
Little Nickel Want Ads - Bremerton, WA - *AyerDirPub 83*
Little/Online, Arthur D. [of Arthur D. Little Inc.] - Cambridge, MA - *DirOnDB Spring 84; EISS 5-84 Sup*
Little Otis Music - Port Chester, NY - *BillIntBG 83-84*
Little Papers [of Inter County Publishing Co.] - Philadelphia, PA - *NewsDir 84*
Little/Probe, Arthur D. - Cambridge, MA - *FBInfSer 80*
Little Red Filmhouse, The - Los Angeles, CA - *AvMarPl 83*
Little Red Hen Inc. - Pocatello, ID - *BoPubDir 4, 5; LitMag&SmPr 83-84*
Little Red Hen's Co. Inc. - Portland, OR - *BoPubDir 5*
Little Review, The - Huntington, WV - *LitMag&SmPr 83-84*
Little River News - Ashdown, AR - *AyerDirPub 83; Ed&PubIntYB 82*
Little River Press - Westfield, MA - *BoPubDir 4, 5; LitMag&SmPr 83-84*
Little River Rice County Monitor Journal - *See* Ellsworth Reporter
Little Rock AFB Cable TV Co. [of Satellite Cable TV Corp.] - Jacksonville, AR - *Tel&CabFB 84C*
Little Rock AFB Cable TV Co. [of Satellite Cable TV Corp.] - Little Rock Air Force Base, AR - *BrCabYB 84*
Little Rock Arkansas Democrat [of Little Rock Newspapers Inc.] - Little Rock, AR - *BaconPubCkNews 84; NewsDir 84*
Little Rock Arkansas Gazette - Little Rock, AR - *BaconPubCkNews 84; LitMarPl 83*
Little Rock Signal Corp. - Birmingham, AL - *Tel&CabFB 84C*
Little Rock South Antelope Valley News - Little Rock, CA - *BaconPubCkNews 84*
Little Rock Southern Mediator - Little Rock, AR - *BaconPubCkNews 84; NewsDir 84*
Little Roger Music - *See* July Child Music
Little Silver Records - Red Bank, NJ - *BillIntBG 83-84*
Little Star Records [Div. of Barnum Entertainment] - Los Angeles, CA - *BillIntBG 83-84*
Little Telecommunications, Arthur D. - Cambridge, MA - *TeleSy&SerDir 7-83*
Little Things - Winnipeg, MB, Canada - *LitMag&SmPr 83-84*
Little Things Music - *See* July Child Music
Little Treasures Publications Inc. - Fruitland Park, FL - *BoPubDir 4, 5*
Little Wing Publishing - Lund, BC, Canada - *BoPubDir 4*
Little Wing Publishing - Powell River, BC, Canada - *BoPubDir 5*
Little Wizard Manufacturing - Wales, WI - *MicrocomMPl 84*
Little Word Machine, The - Bradford, England - *LitMag&SmPr 83-84*
Littlebird Publications - New York, NY - *BoPubDir 4 Sup, 5*
Littlefield, Adams & Co. - Totowa, NJ - *LitMarPl 83, 84*
Littlefield Lamb County Leader-News - Littlefield, TX - *BaconPubCkNews 84*
Littlefork Times - Littlefork, MN - *BaconPubCkNews 84; Ed&PubIntYB 82*
Littlejohn Productions, William - Malibu, CA - *AvMarPl 83*
Littleman Press - Seattle, WA - *BoPubDir 5*
Littlestown Cable Corp. [of Telecable Communications Corp.] - Littlestown, PA - *BrCabYB 84; Tel&CabFB 84C*
Littlestown Cable TV - Bonneauville, PA - *Tel&CabFB 84C*
Littlestown Cable TV - East Berlin, PA - *Tel&CabFB 84C*
Littleton Courier - Littleton, NH - *BaconPubCkNews 84; Ed&PubIntYB 82; NewsDir 84*
Littleton Independent - Littleton, CO - *AyerDirPub 83; BaconPubCkNews 84; Ed&PubIntYB 82*
Littleton Independent - Littleton, MA - *Ed&PubIntYB 82*
Littleton Independent - *See* Minute-Man Publications Inc.
Littleton Independent, The - Acton, MA - *AyerDirPub 83; NewsDir 84*
Littleton Observer [of Nashville Wilson Newspapers Inc.] - Littleton, NC - *BaconPubCkNews 84; Ed&PubIntYB 82; NewsDir 84*
Littleton Sentinel - *See* Sentinel Newspapers
Littlewood, Barbara S. - Madison, WI - *LitMarPl 83, 84*
Litton Computer Services [Subs. of Litton Industries] - Reston, VA - *ADAPSOMemDir 83-84; DataDirOnSer 84*
Litton Industries Inc. - Beverly Hills, CA - *DataDirSup 7-83; ElecNews 7-25-83*
Litton Industries Inc. (Cole Business Furniture Div.) - Beverly Hills, CA - *DirInfWP 82*
Litton Industries Inc. (Royal Business Machines Div.) - Hartford, CT - *DirInfWP 82*
Litton Mellonics Information Center [Div. of Litton Industries Inc.] - Canoga Park, CA - *DataDirOnSer 84*
Littoral Development Co. - Philadelphia, PA - *BoPubDir 4, 5*
Lituanus Quarterly Journal of Arts & Sciences - Chicago, IL - *MagIndMarPl 82-83*
Liturgical Conference - Washington, DC - *BoPubDir 4, 5*
Liturgical Press [Aff. of The Order of St. Benedict Inc.] - Collegeville, MN - *BoPubDir 4, 5; LitMarPl 83, 84*
Live - Springfield, MO - *WritMar 84*
Live Free Inc. - Harvey, IL - *BoPubDir 4, 5*
Live Line Inc. - Jasper, AL - *BrCabYB 84; Tel&CabFB 84C p.1688*
Live Music Publishing Corp. - *See* Live Music Publishing Group
Live Music Publishing Group - Ridgewood, NJ - *BillIntBG 83-84*
Live Oak Cable TV - Live Oak, CA - *Tel&CabFB 84C*
Live Oak Cablevision [of Cardiff Cablevision Inc.] - Three Rivers, TX - *BrCabYB 84; Tel&CabFB 84C*
Live Oak County Progress - *See* Beeville Publishing Co. Inc.
Live Oak Independent Post - Live Oak, FL - *BaconPubCkNews 84; NewsDir 84*
Live Oak Media - Somers, NY - *AvMarPl 83*
Live Oak Publications - Boulder, CO - *LitMag&SmPr 83-84*
Live Oak Suwannee Democrat - Live Oak, FL - *BaconPubCkNews 84*

Live Steam - Traverse City, MI - *BaconPubCkMag 84; MagIndMarPl 82-83; WritMar 84*
Live Writers! [of La Reina Press] - Cincinnati, OH - *LitMag&SmPr 83-84*
Lively Arts & Fine Arts - Watsonville, CA - *BaconPubCkMag 84*
Livengood Cable Co. - Alstead, NH - *Tel&CabFB 84C p.1688*
Livermore Cablevision Ltd. - Livermore, IA - *Tel&CabFB 84C*
Livermore Falls Advertiser - Livermore Falls, ME - *AyerDirPub 83; BaconPubCkNews 84; Ed&PubIntYB 82; NewsDir 84*
Livermore Newspapers - Sapulpa, OK - *Ed&PubIntYB 82*
Livermore Tri Valley Herald & News [of Bay Area Publishing Co.] - Livermore, CA - *NewsDir 84*
Liverpool Polytechnic School of Librarianship & Information Studies - Liverpool, England - *InfIndMarPl 83*
Liverpool-Salina Review [of Baldwinsville Onon-Town Publishing Co. Inc.] - Liverpool, NY - *AyerDirPub 83; NewsDir 84*
Liverpool-Salina Review - *See* Brown Newspapers Co. Inc.
Liverpool-Salina Shopping News - Syracuse, NY - *AyerDirPub 83*
Liverpool University Press - Liverpool, England - *LitMag&SmPr 83-84*
Livesay Group, J. R. - Mattoon, IL - *BrCabYB 84*
Livestock Breeder Journal - Macon, GA - *MagDir 84*
Livestock Magazine - Clovis, CA - *MagDir 84*
Livestock Market Digest - Kansas City, MO - *MagDir 84*
Livewire - Vinton, IA - *AyerDirPub 83*
Living Abroad - New York, NY - *MagDir 84*
Living Arts Inc. - New York, NY - *ArtMar 84*
Living Blues - Chicago, IL - *LitMag&SmPr 83-84; MagIndMarPl 82-83*
Living Books Inc. - Riverside, CA - *BoPubDir 4 Sup, 5*
Living Church - Milwaukee, WI - *BaconPubCkMag 84; MagDir 84; MagIndMarPl 82-83*
Living Color Productions - Elmira, NY - *LitMag&SmPr 83-84*
Living Color, The [of Living Color Productions] - Elmira, NY - *LitMag&SmPr 83-84; WritMar 84*
Living Flame Press - Locust Valley, NY - *BoPubDir 4, 5; LitMarPl 84*
Living Free - Buffalo, NY - *LitMag&SmPr 83-84*
Living in South Carolina - Cayce, SC - *BaconPubCkMag 84; MagDir 84*
Living Love Publications - Coos Bay, OR - *BoPubDir 5*
Living Magazine - Dallas, TX - *ArtMar 84*
Living Montgomery [of Rockville Sentinel Newspapers] - Rockville, MD - *NewsDir 84*
Living Music Records Inc. - Litchfield, CT - *BillIntBG 83-84*
Living Off the Land: Subtropic Newsletter [of Geraventure Corp.] - Melbourne, FL - *LitMag&SmPr 83-84*
Living Single [of The Dispatch Printing Co.] - Columbus, OH - *BaconPubCkMag 84; WritMar 84*
Living Water Record Co. - Inglewood, CA - *BillIntBG 83-84*
Living West - Fullerton, CA - *BoPubDir 4*
Living West - San Bernadino, CA - *BoPubDir 5*
Living Wilderness, The - Washington, DC - *MagIndMarPl 82-83*
Living With Teenagers [of Baptist Sunday School Board] - Nashville, TN - *WritMar 84*
Livingston & Associates Inc. - Honolulu, HI - *StaDirAdAg 2-84*
Livingston & Co. - Seattle, WA - *StaDirAdAg 2-84*
Livingston & Evans - *See* Shayne Enterprises, Larry
Livingston Associates, Peter - Boulder, CO - *LitMarPl 83, 84*
Livingston Business News & Photo Service, Guy - Boston, MA - *Ed&PubIntYB 82*
Livingston Cable TV [of Community Tele-Communications Inc.] - Livingston, MT - *BrCabYB 84; Tel&CabFB 84C*
Livingston Cable TV Inc. [of Athena Communications Corp.] - Livingston, TN - *Tel&CabFB 84C*
Livingston Chronicle - Livingston, CA - *BaconPubCkNews 84*
Livingston County Leader - Geneseo, NY - *AyerDirPub 83; Ed&PubIntYB 82*
Livingston County Leader - *See* Sanders Publications
Livingston County Press - Howell, MI - *AyerDirPub 83; Ed&PubIntYB 82*
Livingston East Texas Eye - Livingston, TX - *NewsDir 84*
Livingston Enterprise [of Yellowstone Newspapers] - Livingston, MT - *BaconPubCkNews 84; NewsDir 84*
Livingston Enterprise - Livingston, TN - *BaconPubCkNews 84; Ed&PubIntYB 82; NewsDir 84*
Livingston Home Record - Livingston, AL - *BaconPubCkNews 84*
Livingston Lake Livingston Progress - Livingston, TX - *BaconPubCkNews 84*
Livingston Ledger - Smithland, KY - *AyerDirPub 83; Ed&PubIntYB 82*
Livingston Overton County News - Livingston, TN - *BaconPubCkNews 84*
Livingston Polk County Enterprise - Livingston, TX - *NewsDir 84*
Livingston Polk County Enterprise - *See* Polk County Publishing
Livingston Productions, Peter - Boulder, CO - *LitMarPl 83*
Livingston Public Relations - Livingston, NJ - *DirPRFirms 83*
Livingston Publishing Inc. - Boulder, CO - *LitMarPl 84*
Livingston Telephone Co. [Aff. of Evans Telephone Co.] - Patterson, CA - *TelDir&BG 83-84*
Livingston Telephone Co. - Livingston, TX - *TelDir&BG 83-84*
Livingston West Essex Tribune - Livingston, NJ - *BaconPubCkNews 84; NewsDir 84*
Livonia Gazette, The - Livonia, NY - *Ed&PubIntYB 82*
Livonia Gazette, The - *See* Brador Publications Inc.
Livonia News - *See* Suburban Newspapers
Livonia Observer [of Livonia Suburban Communications Corp.] - Livonia, MI - *AyerDirPub 83; Ed&PubIntYB 82; NewsDir 84*
Livonia Observer - *See* Observer & Eccentric Newspapers
Lizcon Trading - Salt Lake City, UT - *MicrocomMPl 84; MicrocomSwDir 1*
L.J. Publishing - Edmonton, AB, Canada - *BoPubDir 4 Sup, 5*
LJB Music - Jersey City, NJ - *BillIntBG 83-84*
LJK Enterprises Inc. - St. Louis, MO - *MicrocomMPl 83, 84; MicrocomSwDir 1*
Ljus - Brussels, Belgium - *DirOnDB Spring 84*
L.K. Advertising Agency - Middle Island, NY - *LitMarPl 83, 84; MagIndMarPl 82-83*
LK Graphics [Div. of LK Direct Inc.] - Middle Island, NY - *LitMarPl 83, 84*
LL Co. - Los Angeles, CA - *BoPubDir 4, 5*
Llano News - Llano, TX - *BaconPubCkNews 84; Ed&PubIntYB 82; NewsDir 84*
Llano TV Cable Co. [of L-W Communications Systems Inc.] - Llano, TX - *BrCabYB 84*
LLBA - *See* Language & Language Behavior Abstracts
Llen Cymru [of University of Wales Press] - Cardiff, Wales - *LitMag&SmPr 83-84*
Llewellyn Publications [Div. of Chester Kent Inc.] - St. Paul, MN - *ArtMar 84; LitMarPl 83, 84; WritMar 84*
Lloyd Books, Lela Latch - Cisco, TX - *BoPubDir 5*
Lloyd, Du Vall & Miller Inc. - New York, NY - *StaDirAdAg 2-84*
Lloyd Film Loader Co. - Madera, PA - *AvMarPl 83*
Lloyd Inc., Darryl - North Hollywood, CA - *DirPRFirms 83*
Lloyd Music, Mick - *See* JMR Enterprises
Lloyd Personnel Consultants Inc. - Great Neck, NY - *DirInfWP 82*
Lloyd Publications of Canada [Aff. of Lloyd's Local Directories Div.] - West Hill, ON, Canada - *BoPubDir 4, 5; LitMarPl 84*
Lloydminster Daily Times - Lloydminster, SK, Canada - *Ed&PubIntYB 82*
Lloydminster Meridian Booster - Lloydminster, SK, Canada - *AyerDirPub 83*
Lloyds Radio & TV - McGregor, IA - *BrCabYB 84*
Lloyds TV & Cable Co. - McGregor, IA - *Tel&CabFB 84C*
LM Systems Inc. - Anaheim, CA - *MicrocomMPl 84*
LMC - Chicago, IL - *MicrocomMPl 84*
LMC-400 [of Loral Corp.] - San Diego, CA - *TeleSy&SerDir 7-83*
LMD Service for Publishers - New York, NY - *LitMarPl 83, 84*
LMR Books - Lexington, KY - *BoPubDir 4, 5*
LMS/Barrett Public Relations - Providence, RI - *DirPRFirms 83*
LMTA News - Baton Rouge, LA - *BaconPubCkMag 84*
LNW Computers [Subs. of LNW Research Corp.] - Tustin, CA - *WhoWMicrocom 83*
LNW Research Corp. - Tustin, CA - *MicrocomMPl 83, 84*
LNW User - Grand Island, NE - *MicrocomMPl 84*
Lo Gatto Bookbinding - East Rutherford, NJ - *LitMarPl 83, 84*
L.O.A. Advertising Agency - Malden, MA - *StaDirAdAg 2-84*
Loadstone & Open Record Co. - San Francisco, CA - *BillIntBG 83-84*
Loaves & Fishes Music Co. Inc. - *See* Bicycle Music Co., The

Lobo Drives International - Goleta, CA - *MicrocomMPl 83; WhoWMicrocom 83*
Lobo Systems Inc. - Goleta, CA - *DataDirSup 7-83; MicrocomMPl 84*
Lobsenz-Stevens Inc. - New York, NY - *DirPRFirms 83*
L'Observateur - Laplace, LA - *AyerDirPub 83*
Local - Sylvester, GA - *AyerDirPub 83*
Local - Clinton, MI - *AyerDirPub 83*
Local - Ennis, TX - *AyerDirPub 83*
Local Area Data Distribution System [of Printer Terminal Communications Corp.] - Ramona, CA - *EISS 83*
Local Area Networks [of NewsNet Inc.] - Bryn Mawr, PA - *DataDirOnSer 84*
Local Communications Inc. [Subs. of Interpublic Group of Cos. Inc.] - New York, NY - *StaDirAdAg 2-84*
Local Drizzle - Carnation, WA - *LitMag&SmPr 83-84*
Local 880 News & Views - Cleveland, OH - *NewsDir 84*
Local 876 - Madison Heights, MI - *NewsDir 84*
Local 11 [of Hotel & Restaurant Employees & Bartenders Union] - Los Angeles, CA - *NewsDir 84*
Local Exchange, The - Ft. Qu'Appelle, SK, Canada - *AyerDirPub 83*
Local 50 News [of Liberal Press] - New York, NY - *NewsDir 84*
Local 4757 News USWA - Babbitt, MN - *NewsDir 84*
Local 1470 Journal - Kearny, NJ - *NewsDir 84*
Local Government Information Network [of Control Data Corp.] - Minneapolis, MN - *CompReadDB 82; DataDirOnSer 84; EISS 83*
Local I-S News [of Local 1-5] - New York, NY - *NewsDir 84*
Local News - Green Ridge, MO - *AyerDirPub 83; Ed&PubIntYB 82*
Local News - West Chester, PA - *AyerDirPub 83*
Local 138 News - Farmingdale, NY - *NewsDir 84*
Local Press - Claresholm, AB, Canada - *AyerDirPub 83; Ed&PubIntYB 82*
Local Review - Park Ridge, NJ - *AyerDirPub 83*
Local Review, The - Pascack Valley, NJ - *Ed&PubIntYB 82*
Local Review, The [of RNI Publications Inc.] - Ridgewood, NJ - *NewsDir 84*
Local 717 News - Warren, OH - *NewsDir 84*
Local 73 Journal [of Service Employees Local 73] - Chicago, IL - *NewsDir 84*
Local 69 Reporter - New York, NY - *NewsDir 84*
Local Storms: A Review of Georgia Poetry [of Ali Baba Press] - Gainesville, GA - *LitMag&SmPr 83-84*
Local 1010 Steelworker [of USWA Local 1010] - East Chicago, IN - *NewsDir 84*
Local 37 News [of California Offset Printers] - Los Angeles, CA - *NewsDir 84*
Local 3 Bakery Workers News - Long Island City, NY - *NewsDir 84*
Local 324 Reporter - Buena Park, CA - *NewsDir 84*
Local 2483 Monthly News [of Mimeo] - Gary, IN - *NewsDir 84*
Local 22 New York Culinarian - New York, NY - *NewsDir 84*
Local 234 Bulletin - New York, NY - *NewsDir 84*
Localnetter Newsletter, The [of Architecture Technology Corp.] - Minneapolis, MN - *BaconPubCkMag 84; MicrocomMPl 84*
Locare Research Group - Los Angeles, CA - *BoPubDir 4, 5*
Location Register of Twentieth Century English Literary Manuscripts & Letters [of University of Reading Library] - Reading, England - *EISS 5-84 Sup*
Loch Arbour Direct - Allenhurst, NJ - *DirMarMP 83; StaDirAdAg 2-84*
Lock City Cable [of Global Cable Inc.] - Lockport, NY - *BrCabYB 84*
Lock Haven Express - Lock Haven, PA - *NewsDir 84*
Lockard's TV Cable Service - Sand Fork, WV - *Tel&CabFB 84C*
Locke Systems & Software - Montgomery, AL - *MicrocomMPl 84*
Lockeford-Clements News - Lockeford, CA - *AyerDirPub 83; BaconPubCkNews 84; Ed&PubIntYB 82; NewsDir 84*
Lockhart & Pettus - New York, NY - *AdAge 3-28-84; DirPRFirms 83; StaDirAdAg 2-84*
Lockhart Cable TV Services Inc. [of Communications Services Inc.] - Lockhart, TX - *BrCabYB 84; Tel&CabFB 84C*
Lockhart Post-Register [of Garrett Newspapers Inc.] - Lockhart, TX - *BaconPubCkNews 84; Ed&PubIntYB 82; NewsDir 84*
Lockhart Power Co. - Lockhart, SC - *TelDir&BG 83-84*
Lockhart Press, The - Port Townsend, WA - *LitMag&SmPr 83-84*
Lockheed Corp. - Burbank, CA - *KnowInd 83*
Lockheed Dataplan Inc. - Los Gatos, CA - *EISS 7-83 Sup*
Lockheed Information Systems - Palo Alto, CA - *CompReadDB 82; ProGuPRSer 4*
Lockney Beacon - Lockney, TX - *BaconPubCkNews 84; Ed&PubIntYB 82*
Lockport Tri-County News - Lockport, NY - *BaconPubCkNews 84; NewsDir 84*
Lockport Union Sun & Journal - Lockport, NY - *BaconPubCkNews 84; NewsDir 84*
Locksmith Ledger [of Nickerson & Collins Co.] - Des Plaines, IL - *BaconPubCkMag 84; MagDir 84*
Lockwood Association Inc., The - San Antonio, TX - *ADAPSOMemDir 83-84*
Lockwood Communications, Chris - New York, NY - *DirPRFirms 83*
Lockwood Indexers - New York, NY - *LitMarPl 83, 84; MagIndMarPl 82-83*
Loco Book Club [Subs. of Sky Books International Inc.] - New York, NY - *LitMarPl 83, 84*
Locom Corp. - San Jose, CA - *DataDirSup 7-83*
Locomotive - Lawrence, NE - *AyerDirPub 83*
Locomotive Engineer, The - Cleveland, OH - *BaconPubCkMag 84; MagDir 84*
Locus Communications - New York, NY - *AvMarPl 83*
Locus Press - Oakland, CA - *LitMag&SmPr 83-84*
Locus: The Newspaper of the Science Fiction Field - Oakland, CA - *LitMag&SmPr 83-84; LitMarPl 83, 84; MagIndMarPl 82-83*
Locust Valley Leader - Locust Valley, NY - *BaconPubCkNews 84; NewsDir 84*
Loda Times - Loda, IL - *Ed&PubIntYB 82*
Loda Times - Paxton, IL - *AyerDirPub 83*
Lodestar [of Ali Baba Press] - Gainesville, GA - *LitMag&SmPr 83-84*
Lodestar Books [Div. of E. P. Dutton] - New York, NY - *ArtMar 84; WritMar 84*
Lodestar Computer Services - Roseville, CA - *MicrocomMPl 84*
Lodestar Productions - Pacific Palisades, CA - *AvMarPl 83*
Lodging - New York, NY - *BaconPubCkMag 84; MagDir 84*
Lodging & Food-Service East [of HSI Inc.] - Boston, MA - *BaconPubCkMag 84; MagDir 84*
Lodging Hospitality [of Penton/IPC Inc.] - Cleveland, OH - *BaconPubCkMag 84; MagDir 84*
Lodi Advertiser - Lodi, OH - *BaconPubCkNews 84; Ed&PubIntYB 82*
Lodi Cable Service Co. - Leroy, OH - *BrCabYB 84*
Lodi Cable Service Co. - Lodi, OH - *BrCabYB 84 p.D-303*
Lodi Cable TV [of King Videocable Co.] - Lodi, CA - *Tel&CabFB 84C*
Lodi Enterprise - Lodi, WI - *BaconPubCkNews 84; Ed&PubIntYB 82*
Lodi Messenger - Lodi, NJ - *Ed&PubIntYB 82*
Lodi News-Sentinel - Lodi, CA - *BaconPubCkNews 84; Ed&PubIntYB 82; NewsDir 84*
Lodi Weekly News - Lodi, NJ - *BaconPubCkNews 84*
Lodima Press - Revere, PA - *BoPubDir 4, 5*
Loebel Productions - New York, NY - *Tel&CabFB 84C*
Loeffler Marley Mountjoy - Charlotte, NC - *AdAge 3-28-84; StaDirAdAg 2-84*
L'Oeil Regional - Beloeil, PQ, Canada - *Ed&PubIntYB 82*
Loersch Corp. of PA - Allentown, PA - *AvMarPl 83*
Loewenthal Press - New York, NY - *BoPubDir 4, 5*
Loewy Stempel Zabin Inc. - Hempstead, NY - *StaDirAdAg 2-84*
Log Book - Lemont, IL - *NewsDir 84*
Log Boom Brewing - Boulder, CO - *BoPubDir 4, 5*
Log Cabin Democrat - Conway, AR - *BaconPubCkNews 84; Ed&PubIntYB 82*
Log Cabin Publishers - Allentown, PA - *BoPubDir 4, 5; LitMag&SmPr 83-84*
Log Etronics - Springfield, VA - *AvMarPl 83*
Log Home & Alternative Housing Builder [of Log Home Builder] - Corry, PA - *BaconPubCkMag 84; WritMar 84*
Log Home Guide for Builders & Buyers [of Muir Publishing Co. Ltd.] - Gardenvale, PQ, Canada - *BaconPubCkMag 84; WritMar 84*

Log House Magazine - Prince George, BC, Canada - *WritMar 84*
Log House Publishing Co. Ltd. - Prince George, BC, Canada - *BoPubDir 4, 5*
Log P Database - Claremont, CA - *DirOnDB Spring 84*
Log, The - Annapolis, MD - *BaconPubCkMag 84; MagDir 84*
Log, The - Dallas, TX - *ArtMar 84*
Logan, Auralie Phillips - Peekskill, NY - *LitMarPl 83, 84*
Logan Banner - Logan, WV - *BaconPubCkNews 84; Ed&PubIntYB 82; NewsDir 84*
Logan Cable Television - Logan, NM - *BrCabYB 84; Tel&CabFB 84C*
Logan Cable Television Co. [of Intertie Inc.] - Bellefontaine, OH - *BrCabYB 84*
Logan Cablevision [of Tele-Communications Inc.] - Logan, WV - *BrCabYB 84; Tel&CabFB 84C*
Logan Cablevision [of Tele-Communications Inc.] - Sharples, WV - *Tel&CabFB 84C*
Logan Cablevision Co. - Snow Shoe, PA - *BrCabYB 84; Tel&CabFB 84C*
Logan Cache Citizen - Logan, UT - *BaconPubCkNews 84*
Logan County News - Crescent, OK - *AyerDirPub 83; Ed&PubIntYB 82*
Logan Design Group - North Hollywood, CA - *BoPubDir 4, 5*
Logan Electric Specialty Manufacturing Co. - Chicago, IL - *AvMarPl 83*
Logan Herald Journal [of Pioneer Newspapers Inc.] - Logan, UT - *BaconPubCkNews 84; NewsDir 84*
Logan Herald-Observer - Logan, IA - *BaconPubCkNews 84; Ed&PubIntYB 82*
Logan Hill Press - Ithaca, NY - *BoPubDir 4, 5*
Logan Lake Leader - Ashcroft, BC, Canada - *AyerDirPub 83*
Logan Lake Leader - Logan Lake, BC, Canada - *Ed&PubIntYB 82*
Logan Leader - Russellville, KY - *AyerDirPub 83; Ed&PubIntYB 82*
Logan News [of Wayne Newspaper Co.] - Logan, OH - *BaconPubCkNews 84; Ed&PubIntYB 82; NewsDir 84*
Logan News - Logan, WV - *Ed&PubIntYB 82*
Logan News - West Logan, WV - *BaconPubCkNews 84*
Logan Republican - Logan, KS - *BaconPubCkNews 84; Ed&PubIntYB 82*
Logan Square News - Chicago, IL - *AyerDirPub 83*
Logan Square Times - Chicago, IL - *AyerDirPub 83*
Logan Telephone Cooperative Inc. - Auburn, KY - *TelDir&BG 83-84*
Logan Times [of Greater Philadelphia Group Inc.] - Philadelphia, PA - *NewsDir 84*
Logan TV Cable Co. [of CATV Inc.] - Logan, KS - *Tel&CabFB 84C*
Logansport Interstate Progress - Logansport, LA - *BaconPubCkNews 84; Ed&PubIntYB 82*
Logansport Pharos-Tribune [of Logansport Newspapers Inc.] - Logansport, IN - *NewsDir 84*
Loganton TV Cable Association Inc. - Loganton, PA - *BrCabYB 84; Tel&CabFB 84C*
Logberg Heimskringla - Winnipeg, MB, Canada - *AyerDirPub 83*
Logbridge-Rhodes Inc. - Durango, CO - *BoPubDir 4, 5; LitMag&SmPr 83-84*
LogE/Dunn Instruments - San Francisco, CA - *DataDirSup 7-83*
Logger & Lumberman - Wadley, GA - *BaconPubCkMag 84; MagDir 84*
Loggers World - Chehalis, WA - *BaconPubCkMag 84; MagDir 84*
Logic Associates Inc. - White River Junction, VT - *DataDirOnSer 84*
Logic Inc. - Dallas, TX - *ADAPSOMemDir 83-84*
Logica Inc. - New York, NY - *DataDirSup 7-83; InterCabHB 3; TeleSy&SerDir 7-83; VideoDir 82-83*
Logica Ltd. - London, England - *DirInfWP 82; EISS 83; MicrocomSwDir 1*
Logical Business Machines - Sunnyvale, CA - *DataDirSup 7-83; MicrocomMPl 84*
Logical Choice Inc., The - Fair Oaks, CA - *MicrocomMPl 84*
Logical Machines Corp. - Sunnyvale, CA - *WhoWMicrocom 83*
Logical Systems Inc. - Los Altos, CA - *MicrocomMPl 84*
Logical Systems Inc. - Mequon, WI - *MicrocomMPl 83*
Logical Systems Inc. - Milwaukee, WI - *MicrocomMPl 84*
Login - Minneapolis, MN - *DirOnDB Spring 84*
Login Brothers Book Co. Inc. - Chicago, IL - *LitMarPl 83, 84*
Login Brothers/Eliot Books - Jersey City, NJ - *LitMarPl 83*
Login Brothers New Jersey - Fairfield, NJ - *LitMarPl 84*
Logistics Management Engineering Inc. - Annapolis, MD - *TeleSy&SerDir 2-84*
Logitech Inc. - Palo Alto, CA - *MicrocomMPl 84*
Logix Corp. - Rochester, NY - *MicrocomMPl 84*
Logoptics A-V - Rutland, VT - *ArtMar 84*
LOGOS [of Questel Inc.] - Washington, DC - *DataDirOnSer 84*
Logos - Paris, France - *DirOnDB Spring 84*
Logos Broadcast Group Ltd. - Oklahoma City, OK - *BrCabYB 84*
Logos Films [Div. of W. Whitticar Co.] - Wilmington, DE - *AvMarPl 83*
Logsys (U.S.A.) Inc. - New York, NY - *ADAPSOMemDir 83-84*
Lohman Organization Inc., J. P. - New York, NY - *StaDirAdAg 2-84*
Lohmann Films - West Lafayette, IN - *AvMarPl 83*
Lohmeyer Simpson Communications Inc. - Morristown, NJ - *StaDirAdAg 2-84*
Lohre & Associates - Cincinnati, OH - *ArtMar 84; StaDirAdAg 2-84*
Loiry Consulting Service - Sarasota, FL - *LitMarPl 84*
Loiry Publishing House - Sarasota, FL - *LitMag&SmPr 83-84; WritMar 84*
Lois Pitts Gershon - New York, NY - *AdAge 3-28-84; BrCabYB 84; StaDirAdAg 2-84*
Loizeaux Brothers Inc. - Neptune, NJ - *LitMarPl 83, 84*
Loken/Alaskaphoto, Marty - Seattle, WA - *LitMarPl 83, 84*
LOL [of Y'lolfa] - Dyfed, Wales - *LitMag&SmPr 83-84*
Lollipop Music Corp. - New York, NY - *BillIntBG 83-84*
Lollipop Power Inc. - Chapel Hill, NC - *BoPubDir 4, 5; LitMag&SmPr 83-84*
Lollipop Productions Inc. - New York, NY - *BillIntBG 83-84*
LOM Press Inc. - St. Petersburg, FL - *BoPubDir 4, 5*
Loma Cable Co. [of Mickelson Media Inc.] - Hatch, NM - *BrCabYB 84*
Loma Linda University School of Medicine (Woman's Auxiliary of Alumni Association) - Loma Linda, CA - *BoPubDir 4, 5*
Lomas Associates, Stanley - Pound Ridge, NY - *HBIndAd&MS 82-83; IntDirMarRes 83*
Lomas Data Products Inc. - Westboro, MA - *MicrocomMPl 84*
Lombard Historical Society Inc. - Lombard, IL - *BoPubDir 4, 5*
Lombard Interuniversity Consortium for Data Processing - Milan, Italy - *EISS 83*
Lombard Lombardian - Lombard, IL - *NewsDir 84*
Lombard Lombardian - *See* MacKay Enterprises Inc., E. A.
Lombard Spectator [of Press Publications] - Elmhurst, IL - *AyerDirPub 83; NewsDir 84*
Lombard Spectator - *See* Press Publications
Lombard Spectator, The - Lombard, IL - *Ed&PubIntYB 82*
Lombard Villa Park Review - Lombard, IL - *NewsDir 84*
Lombardi Advertising Inc., Robert - New York, NY - *StaDirAdAg 2-84*
Lombardi Indexing Information Services - Santa Cruz, CA - *LitMarPl 83, 84*
Lombardian - Lombard, IL - *AyerDirPub 83; Ed&PubIntYB 82*
Lometa Cable TV - Lometa, TX - *BrCabYB 84*
Lomita News - Lomita, CA - *Ed&PubIntYB 82*
Lomond Press, The - Kinnesswood, Scotland - *LitMag&SmPr 83-84*
Lomond Publications - Mt. Airy, MD - *BoPubDir 4, 5; EISS 83; MicroMarPl 82-83*
Lompoc Record - Lompoc, CA - *BaconPubCkNews 84; Ed&PubIntYB 82; NewsDir 84*
Lond Publications - Pomona, NY - *BoPubDir 4, 5*
Londe-Parker-Michels Inc. - St. Louis, MO - *MicrocomMPl 83; WhoWMicrocom 83*
London Advertising, Allen - West Caldwell, NJ - *StaDirAdAg 2-84*
London & South Eastern Library Region - London, England - *EISS 7-83 Sup*
London Associates, Michael - New York, NY - *DirPRFirms 83*
London Cable TV [of Centel Cable Television Co. of Kentucky] - Keavy, KY - *BrCabYB 84*
London Cable TV [of Canadian Cablesystems Ltd.] - London, ON, Canada - *BrCabYB 84*
London Community Television Inc. [of OVC Telecommunications Inc.] - London, KY - *BrCabYB 84*

London Daily Mail - New York, NY - *Ed&PubIntYB 82*
London Daily Mirror - New York, NY - *Ed&PubIntYB 82*
London Daily Telegraph - New York, NY - *Ed&PubIntYB 82*
London Free Press - London, ON, Canada - *BaconPubCkNews 84; Ed&PubIntYB 82; LitMarPl 83, 84*
London International Financial Futures Exchange Ltd., The - London, England - *EISS 5-84 Sup*
London Madison Press [of Central Ohio Printing Corp.] - London, OH - *BaconPubCkNews 84; NewsDir 84*
London Magazine - London, ON, Canada - *BaconPubCkMag 84*
London Mills Times [of Roseville Carlberg Publishing Co.] - Roseville, IL - *NewsDir 84*
London Mt. Sterling Tribune - London, OH - *BaconPubCkNews 84*
London Northwest - Olympia, WA - *BoPubDir 4, 5*
London Over the Counter Market - London, England - *EISS 5-84 Sup*
London Progressive Advertising Ltd. - *See* Royds Advertising Group Ltd., The
London Publishing Co. - Bethesda, MD - *BoPubDir 4, 5*
London Researchers - London, England - *FBInfSer 80*
London Sentinel-Echo - London, KY - *BaconPubCkNews 84; NewsDir 84*
London Software - Piedmont, CA - *MicrocomMPl 84*
London South Charleston Sentinel - London, OH - *BaconPubCkNews 84*
London Stage 1800-1900: A Documentary Record & Calendar of Performances, The [of University of Massachusetts, Amherst] - Amherst, MA - *EISS 83*
London Stage Information Bank [of Lawrence University] - Appleton, WI - *EISS 83*
London Sun - New York, NY - *Ed&PubIntYB 82*
London Times - London, IL - *Ed&PubIntYB 82*
London TV Service - London, England - *Tel&CabFB 84C*
Lone Lake Songs Inc. - Elmsford, NY - *BillIntBG 83-84*
Lone, Lord & Schon - Mountain View, CA - *StaDirAdAg 2-84*
Lone Oak Books - Bethesda, MD - *BoPubDir 4, 5*
Lone Pine Progress Citizen/Inyo Industries - *See* Chalfant Press Publications
Lone Pine TV Inc. - Lone Pine, CA - *BrCabYB 84; Tel&CabFB 84C*
Lone Raven Publishing Co. Inc. - Anchorage, AK - *BoPubDir 4 Sup, 5*
Lone Rock Cooperative Telephone Co. - Lone Rock, IA - *TelDir&BG 83-84*
Lone Runner Sports Inc. - Long Island City, NY - *BoPubDir 4, 5*
Lone Star [of Lone Star Publications of Humor] - San Antonio, TX - *LitMag&SmPr 83-84; WritMar 84*
Lone Star Book of Texas Records Inc. - Ft. Worth, TX - *BoPubDir 4 Sup, 5*
Lone Star Comedy Monthly, The - Houston, TX - *LitMag&SmPr 83-84*
Lone Star Comedy Monthly, The - San Antonio, TX - *WritMar 84*
Lone Star Publishers Inc. - Austin, TX - *BoPubDir 4, 5; WritMar 84*
Lone Star Video Inc. - Champions, TX - *BrCabYB 84*
Lone Star Video Inc. [Aff. of Centel Communications] - Houston, TX - *InterCabHB 3*
Lone Tree Reporter - Lone Tree, IA - *BaconPubCkNews 84; Ed&PubIntYB 82*
Lonely Planet Publications - South Yarra, Australia - *LitMag&SmPr 83-84*
LoneStar Micro Inc. - Dallas, TX - *MicrocomMPl 84*
Long Advertising Agency, The W. E. - Chicago, IL - *StaDirAdAg 2-84; TelAl 83, 84*
Long & Associates, Maury - Chevy Chase, MD - *CabTVFinDB 83*
Long Beach Argus - Long Beach, CA - *Ed&PubIntYB 82; NewsDir 84*
Long Beach Cablevision - Long Beach, CA - *Tel&CabFB 84C*
Long Beach Chinook Observer - Long Beach, WA - *BaconPubCkNews 84; NewsDir 84*
Long Beach Gulf Coast Weekly - Long Beach, MS - *BaconPubCkNews 84*
Long Beach Hometown News - Long Beach, CA - *Ed&PubIntYB 82*
Long Beach Independent [of Knight-Ridder Publications Inc.] - Long Beach, CA - *NewsBur 6; NewsDir 84*
Long Beach Independent Voice - Long Beach, NY - *AyerDirPub 83; BaconPubCkNews 84; Ed&PubIntYB 82; NewsDir 84*
Long Beach Long Island Journal [of Long Beach Publications Inc.] - Long Beach, NY - *NewsDir 84*
Long Beach Marina News - Long Beach, CA - *BaconPubCkNews 84; NewsDir 84*
Long Beach Nassau Star - Long Beach, NY - *NewsDir 84*
Long Beach Pennysaver - Rockville Centre, NY - *AyerDirPub 83*
Long Beach Press Telegram - Long Beach, CA - *BaconPubCkNews 84; NewsBur 6*
Long Beach Publications - Long Beach, CA - *BoPubDir 5*
Long Beach Reporter - Long Beach, CA - *BaconPubCkNews 84; Ed&PubIntYB 82*
Long-Distance Letter - Bethesda, MD - *BaconPubCkMag 84*
Long Distance/USA Inc. - Honolulu, HI - *TeleSy&SerDir 2-84*
Long Haul Press - Brooklyn, NY - *BoPubDir 4, 5*
Long, Haymes & Carr - Winston-Salem, NC - *AdAge 3-28-84; StaDirAdAg 2-84*
Long House - New Canaan, CT - *BoPubDir 4, 5*
Long Island Advance - Patchogue, NY - *AyerDirPub 83*
Long Island Builder - Huntington Station, NY - *MagDir 84*
Long Island Business Newsweekly [of Long Island Commercial Review Inc.] - Plainview, NY - *BaconPubCkMag 84; NewsDir 84*
Long Island Cablevision Corp. [of Times Mirror Cable Television Inc.] - East Quogue, NY - *BrCabYB 84*
Long Island Cablevision Corp. [of Times Mirror Cable Television Inc.] - Greenport, NY - *BrCabYB 84*
Long Island Cablevision Corp. [of Times Mirror Cable Television Inc.] - Sag Harbor, NY - *BrCabYB 84*
Long Island Cablevision Corp. [of Times Mirror Cable TV] - Southampton, NY - *BrCabYB 84*
Long Island Cablevision Corp. of Greenport [of Times Mirror Cable TV] - Greenport, NY - *Tel&CabFB 84C*
Long Island Cablevision Corp. of Riverhead [of Times Mirror Cable TV] - Riverhead, NY - *Tel&CabFB 84C*
Long Island Cablevision Corp. of Sag Harbor [of Times Mirror Cable TV] - Sag Harbor, NY - *Tel&CabFB 84C*
Long Island Cablevision Corp. of Southampton [of Times Mirror Cable TV] - East Quogue, NY - *Tel&CabFB 84C*
Long Island Cablevision Corp. of Southampton [of Times Mirror Cable TV] - Southampton, NY - *Tel&CabFB 84C*
Long Island Catholic [of Catholic Press Association Diocese Rockville Centre Inc.] - Hempstead, NY - *NewsDir 84*
Long Island City Woodside Herald - Long Island City, NY - *BaconPubCkNews 84*
Long Island Examiner - Hempstead, NY - *Ed&PubIntYB 82*
Long Island Fisherman, The - Sag Harbor, NY - *BaconPubCkMag 84*
Long Island Graphic & Roosevelt Press - Freeport, NY - *AyerDirPub 83*
Long Island Heritage [of Community Newspapers Inc.] - Glen Cove, NY - *WritMar 84*
Long Island Journal Newspapers - Nassau County, NY - *Ed&PubIntYB 82*
Long Island Journal, The - Long Beach, NY - *AyerDirPub 83*
Long Island Library Resources Council - Bellport, NY - *EISS 83*
Long Island Life - Mamaroneck, NY - *MagDir 84*
Long Island Life - Manhasset, NY - *BaconPubCkMag 84*
Long Island Local News - Malverne, NY - *AyerDirPub 83*
Long Island News - Coram, NY - *AyerDirPub 83; Ed&PubIntYB 82*
Long Island News & Owl, The - Rockville Centre, NY - *AyerDirPub 83; Ed&PubIntYB 82*
Long Island News East - Coram, NY - *NewsDir 84*
Long Island News North - Coram, NY - *NewsDir 84*
Long Island News West - Coram, NY - *NewsDir 84*
Long Island Poetry Collective - Huntington, NY - *BoPubDir 4, 5; LitMag&SmPr 83-84*
Long Island Sports Network [of Cablevision Program Services] - Woodbury, NY - *CabTVPrDB 83*

Long Island Traveler-Watchman - Southold, NY - *AyerDirPub 83; Ed&PubIntYB 82; NewsDir 84*
Long Island University Press - Brooklyn, NY - *BoPubDir 4, 5*
Long Islander, The - Huntington, NY - *AyerDirPub 83*
Long, Kathye Pettebone - Crownsville, MD - *LitMarPl 83, 84; MagIndMarPl 82-83*
Long Marketing Inc., W. H. - Greensboro, NC - *IntDirMarRes 83; StaDirAdAg 2-84*
Long Pond Review - Selden, NY - *LitMag&SmPr 83-84*
Long Prairie Leader - Long Prairie, MN - *BaconPubCkNews 84; Ed&PubIntYB 82; NewsDir 84*
Long River Productions [Subs. of Inland Book Co.] - East Haven, CT - *LitMarPl 84*
Long, Robert P. - Cutchogue, NY - *BoPubDir 4, 5*
Long Story, The - North Andover, MA - *LitMag&SmPr 83-84*
Long Survival Publications - Wamego, KS - *BoPubDir 4, 5*
Long-Term Interindustry Forecast [of Chase Econometrics/ Interactive Data Corp.] - Waltham, MA - *DataDirOnSer 84*
Long-Term Personal Consumption Expenditure Forecast [of Chase Econometrics/Interactive Data Corp.] - Waltham, MA - *DataDirOnSer 84*
Longacre Press Inc., The - New Rochelle, NY - *LitMarPl 83, 84*
Longbow Publications - Redditt, ON, Canada - *BoPubDir 4 Sup, 5*
Longendyke/Loreque - Santa Ana, CA - *AvMarPl 83*
Longest Revolution, The - San Diego, CA - *ArtMar 84; LitMag&SmPr 83-84*
Longhair Music - *See* Budd Music Corp.
Longhorn Ballroom Inc. - Dallas, TX - *BillIntBG 83-84*
Longhorn Press - Cisco, TX - *BoPubDir 4, 5*
Longhouse - Brattleboro, VT - *BoPubDir 4, 5; LitMag&SmPr 83-84*
Longland, Jean R. - New York, NY - *LitMarPl 83, 84*
Longman Group Ltd. - Harlow, England - *MicroMarPl 82-83*
Longman Inc. [Aff. of Churchill Livingstone Inc.] - New York, NY - *LitMarPl 83, 84; WritMar 84*
Longmeadow News [of Enfield Hartford Publications Inc.] - Enfield, CT - *AyerDirPub 83; Ed&PubIntYB 82; NewsDir 84*
Longmeadow News - Longmeadow, MA - *BaconPubCkNews 84*
Longmont Communications Corp. [of Scripps-Howard Cable Services Co.] - Longmont, CO - *BrCabYB 84; Tel&CabFB 84C*
Longmont Scene - Longmont, CO - *NewsDir 84*
Longmont Times-Call - Longmont, CO - *BaconPubCkNews 84; Ed&PubIntYB 82; NewsDir 84*
Longshanks Book - Mystic, CT - *BoPubDir 4, 5*
Longship Press - West Peterborough, NH - *BoPubDir 4 Sup, 5; LitMag&SmPr 83-84*
Longshot Music - *See* Tyner International Inc., Harrison
Longspoon Press - Edmonton, AB, Canada - *BoPubDir 4 Sup; LitMarPl 83, 84*
Longton Elk City News-Sun - Sedan, KS - *Ed&PubIntYB 82*
Longton-Elk City News-Sun - *See* Star Publications
Longview Cable TV Co. Inc. [of WEHCO Video Inc.] - Longview, TX - *BrCabYB 84; Tel&CabFB 84C*
Longview Daily News - Longview, WA - *BaconPubCkNews 84; NewsDir 84*
Longview Morning Journal - Longview, TX - *BaconPubCkNews 84; Ed&PubIntYB 82; NewsDir 84*
Longview News - Longview, TX - *BaconPubCkNews 84; Ed&PubIntYB 82*
Longview Shopper - Longview, TX - *AyerDirPub 83*
Longview Sunday Journal - Longview, TX - *Ed&PubIntYB 82*
Longwood Press Ltd. - Dover, NH - *LitMarPl 83*
Longwood Publishing Group Inc. - Dover, NH - *LitMarPl 84*
Longyear Research Library, J. M. [Aff. of Marquette County Historical Society] - Marquette, MI - *BoPubDir 4*
Lonoke Democrat - Lonoke, AR - *BaconPubCkNews 84; Ed&PubIntYB 82*
Lonsdale Advertising Ltd. - London, England - *StaDirAdAg 2-84*
Lonsdale Telephone Co. - Lonsdale, MN - *TelDir&BG 83-84*
Lonstein Publications - Ellenville, NY - *BoPubDir 4, 5*
Loo Associates Inc., Beverly Jane [Aff. of The Hamlyn Publishing Group Ltd.] - New York, NY - *LitMarPl 83, 84*
Loogootee Cable [of Welbal Cable TV Corp.] - Loogootee, IN - *Tel&CabFB 84C*
Loogootee Cablevision [of Omni Cable TV Corp.] - Loogootee, IN - *BrCabYB 84*
Loogootee Tribune - Loogootee, IN - *BaconPubCkNews 84*
Look & Chapin - New York, NY - *Tel&CabFB 84C*
Look Hear Music - Southfield, MI - *BillIntBG 83-84*
Look-Listen-Learn Inc. - Tujunga, CA - *AvMarPl 83*
Look Quick [of Quick Books] - Pueblo, CO - *LitMag&SmPr 83-84*
Lookout Cable Services Inc. - Rossville, GA - *Tel&CabFB 84C p.1688*
Lookout Music - *See* Excellorec Music Co. Inc.
Lookout, The - Cincinnati, OH - *ArtMar 84; WritMar 84*
Looks Like Music - *See* Delvy Enterprises Inc., Richard
Loomis News - Loomis, CA - *BaconPubCkNews 84; Ed&PubIntYB 82*
Loompanics Unltd. - Mason, MI - *BoPubDir 4*
Loompanics Unltd. - Port Townsend, WA - *BoPubDir 5*
Loonan Advertising Inc., Matthew - Piscataway, NJ - *StaDirAdAg 2-84*
LoonBooks - Northeast Harbor, ME - *LitMag&SmPr 83-84*
Loonfeather: Minnesota North Country Art [of Bemidji Arts Center] - Bemidji, MN - *LitMag&SmPr 83-84; WritMar 84*
Loop Music Co. - *See* Kjos Music Co., Neil A.
Loop Press - Keene, CA - *BoPubDir 4, 5*
Loos, Edwards & Sexauer Inc. - Akron, OH - *StaDirAdAg 2-84*
Loose Change [of Mead Publishing Corp.] - Long Beach, CA - *BaconPubCkMag 84; WritMar 84*
Loose Leaf Industries - South Plainfield, NJ - *AvMarPl 83*
Loot - Peterborough, England - *LitMag&SmPr 83-84*
Lopatin Productions Inc., Ralph - Philadelphia, PA - *AvMarPl 83*
Lopez Publications - New York, NY - *ArtMar 84*
Lopez Stations, Pirallo - San Juan, PR - *BrCabYB 84*
L'Ora di Ottawa - Ottawa, ON, Canada - *Ed&PubIntYB 82*
Lorain Cable TV Inc. - Lorain, OH - *BrCabYB 84; Tel&CabFB 84C*
Lorain County Printing & Publishing Co. - Elyria, OH - *Ed&PubIntYB 82*
Lorain County Times - Lorain, OH - *AyerDirPub 83*
Lorain County Times - *See* Gottschalk Publishing Co., E. J.
Lorain County Westlaker Times - Lorain, OH - *NewsDir 84*
Lorain Journal - Lorain, OH - *BaconPubCkNews 84; NewsDir 84*
Lorain Journal Co. - *See* Multi-Channel TV Cable Co.
Lorain Labor Leader - Lorain, OH - *NewsDir 84*
Lorain Products - Lorain, OH - *DataDirSup 7-83; DirInfWP 82*
Loral Terra Com - San Diego, CA - *DataDirSup 7-83*
Lorance & Associates Inc., Richard - Phoenix, AZ - *MicrocomMPl 83*
Lorant, Jean A. - Captain Cook, HI - *IntDirMarRes 83*
Loras College Press - Dubuque, IA - *BoPubDir 4, 5*
Lord Agency Inc., The Sterling - New York, NY - *LitMarPl 83, 84*
Lord Americana & Research Inc. - West Columbia, SC - *BoPubDir 4, 5*
Lord & Emerson Co. - Jackson, MI - *StaDirAdAg 2-84*
Lord, Geller, Federico, Einstein [Subs. of JWT Group] - New York, NY - *AdAge 3-28-84; StaDirAdAg 2-84*
Lord John Press - Northridge, CA - *BoPubDir 4, 5; LitMarPl 84*
Lord Publishing - Dover, MA - *BoPubDir 4 Sup, 5*
Lord, Sullivan & Yoder - Marion, OH - *AdAge 3-28-84; StaDirAdAg 2-84*
Lord, William H. - Indianapolis, IN - *BoPubDir 4, 5*
Lordsburg Liberal - Lordsburg, NM - *BaconPubCkNews 84; Ed&PubIntYB 82*
Lore & Language - Sheffield, England - *LitMag&SmPr 83-84*
Loreburn Historical Committee - Loreburn, SK, Canada - *BoPubDir 4, 5*
Lorell Advertising Ltd. - West Hempstead, NY - *StaDirAdAg 2-84*
Lorell Press - Avon, MA - *MagIndMarPl 82-83*
Lorenz & Co., William T. - Boston, MA - *BoPubDir 4 Sup, 5*
Lorenz & Herweg - Long Beach, CA - *BoPubDir 4, 5*
Lorenz Creative Services - Nashville, TN - *BillIntBG 83-84*
Lorenz Publishing Co. - *See* Lorenz Creative Services
Lorenzo Leader - Lorenzo, TX - *Ed&PubIntYB 82*
Loretto CATV Inc. - Loretto, TN - *BrCabYB 84*
Loretto Telephone Co. Inc. - Loretto, TN - *TelDir&BG 83-84*
Lori Productions Inc. - Hollywood, CA - *ArtMar 84; AvMarPl 83; WritMar 84*
Lorian Press - Middleton, WI - *BoPubDir 4, 5*

Lorien House - Black Mountain, NC - *BoPubDir 4, 5; LitMag&SmPr 83-84*
Lorimar Productions - Culver City, CA - *TelAl 83, 84; Tel&CabFB 84C*
Lorimar Television - Culver City, CA - *TelAl 84*
Lorimer Advertising, John A. - Warwick, RI - *StaDirAdAg 2-84*
Lorimer & Co., James - Toronto, ON, Canada - *BoPubDir 4, 5; LitMarPl 84*
Loring Corporate Services Inc. - New York, NY - *DirPRFirms 83*
Loring Music Co. - Los Angeles, CA - *BillIntBG 83-84*
Loris Data Corp. - New York, NY - *MicrocomMPl 84*
Loris Sentinel - Loris, SC - *BaconPubCkNews 84; Ed&PubIntYB 82*
Lorraine Publishing Inc. - Bordentown, NJ - *BaconPubCkNews 84*
Lorsch Co., The Bob [Div. of The Lorsch Group] - Los Angeles, CA - *StaDirAdAg 2-84*
Lorsch Group - Los Angeles, CA - *AdAge 3-28-84*
Lorville Music - *See* Terrace Music Group Inc.
Los Alamitos Community Advocate - *See* Hearst Community Newspapers
Los Alamitos News-Enterprise - Los Alamitos, CA - *BaconPubCkNews 84; NewsDir 84*
Los Alamos Cable TV Co. [of Mickelson Media Inc.] - Los Alamos, NM - *BrCabYB 84; Tel&CabFB 84C*
Los Alamos Monitor - Los Alamos, NM - *BaconPubCkNews 84; Ed&PubIntYB 82; NewsDir 84*
Los Altos Town Crier [of Meredith Corp.] - Cupertino, CA - *AyerDirPub 83; NewsDir 84*
Los Altos Town Crier - Los Altos, CA - *Ed&PubIntYB 82*
Los Altos Town Crier - *See* Meredith Newspapers
Los Angeles Brooklyn-Belvedere Comet [of Eastern Group Publications Inc.] - Los Angeles, CA - *NewsDir 84*
Los Angeles Business Journal [of Cordovan Corp.] - Los Angeles, CA - *BaconPubCkMag 84; WritMar 84*
Los Angeles Canyon Crier News - North Hollywood, CA - *NewsDir 84*
Los Angeles Canyon Crier News, The - Beverly Hills, CA - *Ed&PubIntYB 82*
Los Angeles Canyon Crier News/Tolucan - Toluca Lake, CA - *BaconPubCkNews 84*
Los Angeles Center for Educational Resource Services [of Los Angeles County Superintendent of Schools Office] - Downey, CA - *EISS 83*
Los Angeles Central News - Los Angeles, CA - *NewsDir 84*
Los Angeles Central News - *See* Central News-Wave Publications
Los Angeles City News - Los Angeles, CA - *AyerDirPub 83; Ed&PubIntYB 82*
Los Angeles City News - *See* Meredith Newspapers
Los Angeles City Press - Los Angeles, CA - *AyerDirPub 83; Ed&PubIntYB 82*
Los Angeles City Press - *See* Meredith Newspapers
Los Angeles City Terrace Comet [of Eastern Group Publications Inc.] - Los Angeles, CA - *NewsDir 84*
Los Angeles City Terrace Comet - *See* Eastern Group Publications Inc.
Los Angeles Conference Center - Los Angeles, CA - *IntDirMarRes 83*
Los Angeles County Museum of Art - Los Angeles, CA - *BoPubDir 4, 5*
Los Angeles Daily Journal, The - Los Angeles, CA - *NewsDir 84*
Los Angeles Daily Racing Form Inc. - Los Angeles, CA - *NewsDir 84*
Los Angeles Eastside Journal - Los Angeles, CA - *Ed&PubIntYB 82*
Los Angeles Eastside Journal - *See* Northeast Los Angeles Publishing Co.
Los Angeles Eastside Sun [of Eastern Group Publications Inc.] - Los Angeles, CA - *NewsDir 84*
Los Angeles Eastside Sun - *See* Eastern Group Publications Inc.
Los Angeles Enterprise - Los Angeles, CA - *MagDir 84; NewsDir 84*
Los Angeles Firefighter [of United Firefighters of L.A. Local 112] - Los Angeles, CA - *NewsDir 84*
Los Angeles Firestone Park News - *See* Los Angeles Herald Dispatch Publishers
Los Angeles Griffith Park News - Los Angeles, CA - *Ed&PubIntYB 82*
Los Angeles Griffith Park News - *See* Meredith Newspapers
Los Angeles Happenings - Sacramento, CA - *Ed&PubIntYB 82*
Los Angeles Herald Dispatch - *See* Los Angeles Herald Dispatch Publishers
Los Angeles Herald Dispatch Publishers - Los Angeles, CA - *BaconPubCkNews 84*
Los Angeles Herald-Examiner [of Hearst Corp. Inc.] - Los Angeles, CA - *BaconPubCkNews 84; Ed&PubIntYB 82; LitMarPl 83, 84; NewsBur 6; NewsDir 84*
Los Angeles Hollywood Independent - *See* Meredith Newspapers
Los Angeles IEEE Bulletin - Torrance, CA - *BaconPubCkMag 84*
Los Angeles La Opinion [of Lozano Enterprises Inc.] - Los Angeles, CA - *NewsDir 84*
Los Angeles Lawyer - Los Angeles, CA - *BaconPubCkMag 84*
Los Angeles Literary Agency, The - Los Angeles, CA - *LitMarPl 84*
Los Angeles Los Feliz Hills News - *See* Meredith Newspapers
Los Angeles Magazine [of American Broadcasting Co.] - Los Angeles, CA - *ArtMar 84; BaconPubCkMag 84; Folio 83; LitMarPl 83, 84; MagDir 84; MagIndMarPl 82-83; WritMar 84*
Los Angeles Marketing Research Associates - North Hollywood, CA - *IntDirMarRes 83*
Los Angeles Mesa-Wave - *See* Central News-Wave Publications
Los Angeles Metropolitan Gazette - Pasadena, CA - *AyerDirPub 83; NewsDir 84*
Los Angeles Mexican American Sun [of Eastern Group Publications Inc.] - Los Angeles, CA - *NewsDir 84*
Los Angeles Mexican American Sun - *See* Eastern Group Publications Inc.
Los Angeles Nor Or - Los Angeles, CA - *BaconPubCkNews 84*
Los Angeles Northeast Star-Review - Los Angeles, CA - *Ed&PubIntYB 82*
Los Angeles Northeast Star-Review - *See* Northeast Los Angeles Publishing Co.
Los Angeles Northwest Leader - Los Angeles, CA - *Ed&PubIntYB 82*
Los Angeles Northwest Leader - *See* Meredith Newspapers
Los Angeles Parkside Journal - Los Angeles, CA - *Ed&PubIntYB 82*
Los Angeles Parkside Journal - *See* Meredith Newspapers
Los Angeles/Pasadena Metro Gazette - Pasadena, CA - *Ed&PubIntYB 82*
Los Angeles Post Newspaper Group - Los Angeles, CA - *Ed&PubIntYB 82*
Los Angeles Reader - Los Angeles, CA - *WritMar 84*
Los Angeles Reporter [of Los Angeles Waxman Publishing] - Los Angeles, CA - *AyerDirPub 83; Ed&PubIntYB 82; NewsDir 84*
Los Angeles Scoop - Los Angeles, CA - *BaconPubCkNews 84*
Los Angeles Sentinel - Los Angeles, CA - *BaconPubCkNews 84; Ed&PubIntYB 82; NewsDir 84*
Los Angeles Soul Newsmagazine - Los Angeles, CA - *NewsDir 84*
Los Angeles Southeast News-Press - Los Angeles, CA - *BaconPubCkNews 84; Ed&PubIntYB 82*
Los Angeles Southside Journal - Los Angeles, CA - *NewsDir 84*
Los Angeles Southside Journal - *See* Central News-Wave Publications
Los Angeles Southwest News - *See* Central News-Wave Publications
Los Angeles Southwest Topics-Wave - *See* Central News-Wave Publications
Los Angeles Southwest Wave - *See* Central News-Wave Publications
Los Angeles Southwest Wave-Star - *See* Central News-Wave Publications
Los Angeles Southwestern Sun - *See* Central News-Wave Publications
Los Angeles Star Review - Los Angeles, CA - *NewsDir 84*
Los Angeles Sunday Green Sheet - Los Angeles, CA - *Ed&PubIntYB 82*
Los Angeles Tidings, The - Los Angeles, CA - *NewsDir 84*
Los Angeles Times [of Times Mirror Co.] - Los Angeles, CA - *BaconPubCkNews 84; Ed&PubIntYB 82; LitMarPl 83, 84; NewsBur 6; NewsDir 84*
Los Angeles Times Book Review - Los Angeles, CA - *WritMar 84*

Los Angeles Times Syndicate - Los Angeles, CA - *BaconPubCkNews 84; Ed&PubIntYB 82; LitMarPl 83, 84; MagIndMarPl 82-83*
Los Angeles Times/Washington Post News Service - Washington, DC - *BaconPubCkNews 84; Ed&PubIntYB 82*
Los Angeles Tribune News Wave - *See* Central News-Wave Publications
Los Angeles T.V. Journal & News Magazine - Los Angeles, CA - *NewsDir 84*
Los Angeles Watts Star Review - *See* Los Angeles Herald Dispatch Publishers
Los Angeles Wave Newspapers - Los Angeles, CA - *Ed&PubIntYB 82*
Los Angeles Westlake Post - *See* Meredith Newspapers
Los Angeles Wilshire Independent - *See* Meredith Newspapers
Los Angeles Wilshire Press - Los Angeles, CA - *Ed&PubIntYB 82*
Los Angeles Wilshire Press - *See* Meredith Newspapers
Los Angeles Wyvernwood Chronicle [of Eastern Group Publications Inc.] - Los Angeles, CA - *NewsDir 84*
Los Angeles Wyvernwood Chronicle - *See* Eastern Group Publications Inc.
Los Arboles Publications - Redondo Beach, CA - *BoPubDir 4 Sup, 5*
Los Banos Enterprise - Los Banos, CA - *BaconPubCkNews 84; NewsDir 84*
Los Feliz Hills News [of Los Angeles Meredith Newspapers] - Los Angeles, CA - *AyerDirPub 83; Ed&PubIntYB 82; NewsDir 84*
Los Gatos Magazine [of Pelican Advertising & Publishing] - Campbell, CA - *LitMag&SmPr 83-84*
Los Gatos Times-Observer [of Meredith Corp.] - Los Gatos, CA - *Ed&PubIntYB 82; NewsDir 84*
Los Gatos Times-Saratoga Observer - *See* Meredith Newspapers
Los Lunas Valencia County News - Belen, NM - *BaconPubCkNews 84*
Los Penasquitos Pennysaver - Mission Viejo, CA - *AyerDirPub 83*
Lost & Found Times [of Luna Bisonte Prods] - Columbus, OH - *LitMag&SmPr 83-84*
Lost Cause Press - Louisville, KY - *LitMarPl 83, 84; MicroMarPl 82-83*
Lost Creek CATV Inc. - Shady Cove, OR - *BrCabYB 84; Tel&CabFB 84C*
Lost Data Press - Austin, TX - *BoPubDir 4, 5*
Lost in the Fog Players, The - Mendocino, CA - *WritMar 84*
Lost Music Network - Olympia, WA - *LitMag&SmPr 83-84*
Lost Nation-Elwood Telephone Co. - Lost Nation, IA - *TelDir&BG 83-84*
Lost Pleiade Press - Lake Oswego, OR - *BoPubDir 4, 5*
Lost River Star - Merrill City, OR - *AyerDirPub 83*
Lost Roads Publishers - Eureka Springs, AR - *BoPubDir 5; WritMar 84*
Lost Roads Publishers - San Francisco, CA - *BoPubDir 4*
Lost Roads Publishers - Providence, RI - *LitMag&SmPr 83-84*
Lost Treasure - Bixby, OK - *ArtMar 84; BaconPubCkMag 84; MagIndMarPl 82-83; WritMar 84*
Lothlorien - Edinburgh, Scotland - *LitMag&SmPr 83-84*
Lothrop, Lee & Shepard Books [Div. of William Morrow & Co. Inc.] - New York, NY - *LitMarPl 83, 84; WritMar 84*
Lott Video Productions - Santa Monica, CA - *TelAl 83, 84*
Lott Walker Advertising Inc. - Jackson, MS - *StaDirAdAg 2-84*
Lottery Player's Magazine [of Intergalactic Publishing Co.] - Clementon, NJ - *ArtMar 84; WritMar 84*
Lotus Ashram Inc. - Goose Creek, SC - *BoPubDir 4, 5*
Lotus Communications Corp. - Las Vegas, NV - *BrCabYB 84*
Lotus Development Corp. - Cambridge, MA - *MicrocomMPl 84; MicrocomSwDir 1*
Lotus Light Publications - Wilmot, WI - *BoPubDir 5*
Lotus Press Inc. - Detroit, MI - *LitMag&SmPr 83-84; LitMarPl 83, 84*
Lou-Lee Music Co. - *See* Alexis Music Inc.
Loud Consulting Corp., The - Garden City, NY - *ADAPSOMemDir 83-84*
Louderback, Ann - Staten Island, NY - *LitMarPl 83*
Loudon County Cable TV Inc. [of Matrix Enterprises Inc.] - Lenoir City, TN - *Tel&CabFB 84C*
Loudon Herald - Loudon, TN - *Ed&PubIntYB 82*
Loudon News-Herald - Loudon, TN - *BaconPubCkNews 84*
Loudonville Times - Loudonville, OH - *BaconPubCkNews 84; Ed&PubIntYB 82*
Loudoun Times-Mirror - Leesburg, VA - *AyerDirPub 83; Ed&PubIntYB 82; NewsDir 84*
Loudoun Times Publishing Co. Inc. - Leesburg, VA - *BaconPubCkNews 84*
Loughborough University of Technology Library - Loughborough, England - *MicroMarPl 82-83*
Lougheed Women's Institute - Lougheed, AB, Canada - *BoPubDir 4, 5*
Louis & Saul Advertising - Santa Monica, CA - *AdAge 3-28-84; StaDirAdAg 2-84*
Louis-Rowe Enterprises Inc. - New Rochelle, NY - *DirPRFirms 83*
Louisa Big Sandy News - Louisa, KY - *BaconPubCkNews 84; NewsDir 84*
Louisa Central Virginian - Louisa, VA - *BaconPubCkNews 84*
Louisburg Franklin Times - Louisburg, NC - *BaconPubCkNews 84; NewsDir 84*
Louisburg Herald - Louisburg, KS - *BaconPubCkNews 84; Ed&PubIntYB 82*
Louise Jack Publishing Inc. - *See* Sumac Music Inc.
Louise Sentinel-Courier - Pilot Mound, MB, Canada - *Ed&PubIntYB 82*
Louisiana Banker [of Louisiana Bankers Association] - Baton Rouge, LA - *BaconPubCkMag 84; MagDir 84*
Louisiana Cable TV Fund VII-B [of Jones Intercable Inc.] - Hammond, LA - *BrCabYB 84*
Louisiana Cablevision - De Quincy, LA - *BrCabYB 84*
Louisiana Cablevision - Kinder, LA - *Tel&CabFB 84C*
Louisiana Cablevision - Moss Bluff, LA - *BrCabYB 84*
Louisiana Cablevision - Welsh, LA - *BrCabYB 84*
Louisiana Cablevision - Westlake, LA - *BrCabYB 84*
Louisiana Cattleman - Port Allen, LA - *BaconPubCkMag 84*
Louisiana CATV [of American TV & Communications Corp.] - West Monroe, LA - *BrCabYB 84; Tel&CabFB 84C*
Louisiana Community Cablevision Ltd. [of Firstcable Communications Inc.] - Louisiana, MO - *BrCabYB 84; Tel&CabFB 84C*
Louisiana Cos. (Computer Services Div.) - Baton Rouge, LA - *ADAPSOMemDir 83-84*
Louisiana Contractor [of Rhodes Publishing Co. Inc.] - Baton Rouge, LA - *BaconPubCkMag 84; MagDir 84; WritMar 84*
Louisiana Dept. of Commerce - Baton Rouge, LA - *BoPubDir 4 Sup, 5*
Louisiana Game & Fish [of Game & Fish Publications Inc.] - Marietta, GA - *BaconPubCkMag 84; WritMar 84*
Louisiana Government Information Network [of Louisiana State Library] - Baton Rouge, LA - *EISS 83*
Louisiana Grocer [of N.O. Retail Grocers Association] - Metairie, LA - *BaconPubCkMag 84; MagDir 84*
Louisiana Journal, The - Baton Rouge, LA - *MagDir 84*
Louisiana Life - New Orleans, LA - *ArtMar 84; BaconPubCkMag 84*
Louisiana Motor Transport Association News - Baton Rouge, LA - *MagDir 84*
Louisiana Municipal Review - Baton Rouge, LA - *BaconPubCkMag 84*
Louisiana Numerical Register [of Louisiana State Library] - Baton Rouge, LA - *EISS 83*
Louisiana Press-Journal - Louisiana, MO - *BaconPubCkNews 84; Ed&PubIntYB 82; NewsDir 84*
Louisiana State University (College of Arts & Sciences) - Baton Rouge, LA - *DataDirOnSer 84*
Louisiana State University Press - Baton Rouge, LA - *LitMarPl 83, 84; WritMar 84*
Louisiana Suburban Press - Zachary, LA - *BaconPubCkNews 84*
Louisiana Technical Engineer - Ruston, LA - *BaconPubCkMag 84; MagDir 84*
Louisiana Weekly - New Orleans, LA - *AyerDirPub 83; Ed&PubIntYB 82*
Louisiana Western Telephone Co. [Aff. of Century Telephone Enterprises Inc.] - Breaux Bridge, LA - *TelDir&BG 83-84*
Louisville [of Louisville Area Chamber of Commerce] - Louisville, KY - *BaconPubCkMag 84; MagDir 84*

Louisville American Baptist - Louisville, KY - *BaconPubCkNews 84*
Louisville Cardinal, The - Louisville, KY - *AyerDirPub 83*
Louisville Clay County Republican - Louisville, IL - *BaconPubCkNews 84*
Louisville Communications Co. - Louisville, GA - *Tel&CabFB 84C*
Louisville Computer Literature Searchers [of University of Louisville Library] - Louisville, KY - *InfIndMarPl 83*
Louisville Courier-Journal - Louisville, KY - *LitMarPl 83, 84*
Louisville Defender - Louisville, KY - *BaconPubCkNews 84; Ed&PubIntYB 82; NewsDir 84*
Louisville Herald - Louisville, OH - *BaconPubCkNews 84; Ed&PubIntYB 82; NewsDir 84*
Louisville Jeffersonian - *See* Scripps-Howard Press
Louisville Messenger - Louisville, NE - *Ed&PubIntYB 82*
Louisville Messenger [of Maverick Media Inc.] - Syracuse, NE - *NewsDir 84*
Louisville Messenger - *See* Maverick Media Inc.
Louisville News & Farmer & Wadley Herald - Louisville, GA - *BaconPubCkNews 84*
Louisville Orchestra First Edition Records - Louisville, KY - *BillIntBG 83-84*
Louisville Record, The - Louisville, KY - *NewsDir 84*
Louisville Review, The - Louisville, KY - *LitMag&SmPr 83-84*
Louisville Times - Louisville, CO - *BaconPubCkNews 84*
Louisville Times - Louisville, KY - *AyerDirPub 83; BaconPubCkNews 84; Ed&PubIntYB 82; LitMarPl 83, 84; NewsBur 6*
Louisville Voice - *See* Scripps-Howard Press
Louisville/Wadley Cablevision Inc. - Louisville, GA - *BrCabYB 84*
Louisville Winston County Journal - Louisville, MS - *BaconPubCkNews 84; NewsDir 84*
Loup City Sherman County Times - Loup City, NE - *BaconPubCkNews 84*
Love Printing Service Ltd. - Canada - *BoPubDir 4, 5*
Love Productions Inc., James - New York, NY - *Tel&CabFB 84C*
Love Publishing Co. - Denver, CO - *LitMarPl 83, 84*
Love Street Books - Louisville, KY - *BoPubDir 4, 5; LitMag&SmPr 83-84*
Love Street Publishing - Des Moines, IA - *BillIntBG 83-84*
Lovejoy, John M. - Wilbraham, MA - *LitMarPl 83, 84*
Lovejoy Press, The - Washington, DC - *LitMag&SmPr 83-84*
Loveland Herald [of Queen City Suburban Press] - Cincinnati, OH - *NewsDir 84*
Loveland Herald - Loveland, OH - *Ed&PubIntYB 82*
Loveland Herald - *See* Queen City Suburban Press Inc.
Loveland Reporter-Herald - Loveland, CO - *BaconPubCkNews 84; Ed&PubIntYB 82; NewsDir 84*
Lovell Associates, Brent - Pleasanton, CA - *LitMarPl 83, 84*
Lovell Cable TV Co. - Lovell, WY - *BrCabYB 84; Tel&CabFB 84C*
Lovell Chronicle - Lovell, WY - *BaconPubCkNews 84; Ed&PubIntYB 82*
Lovell, Emily Kalled - Stockton, CA - *BoPubDir 4, 5*
Lovelock Review-Miner - Lovelock, NV - *BaconPubCkNews 84; Ed&PubIntYB 82*
Lovely Communications Ltd. - New York, NY - *BillIntBG 83-84*
Lovers of the Stinking Rose/Aris Books - Berkeley, CA - *LitMag&SmPr 83-84*
Loves Park Post - Loves Park, IL - *BaconPubCkNews 84*
Loves Park Post & Buyers Guide - Rockford, IL - *NewsDir 84*
Lovinger, Tardio, Melsky Inc. - New York, NY - *Tel&CabFB 84C*
Lovingston Nelson County Times - *See* Amherst-Nelson Publishing Co.
Lovington Leader - Lovington, NM - *BaconPubCkNews 84; Ed&PubIntYB 82; NewsDir 84*
Lovio-George Public Relations - Detroit, MI - *DirPRFirms 83*
Low Bidder, The - Albany, NY - *BaconPubCkMag 84; MagDir 84*
Low Down to Hull & Back News, The - Hull, PQ, Canada - *Ed&PubIntYB 82*
Low, Joseph - Chilmark, MA - *LitMarPl 83, 84*
Low-Priced Stock Alert [of NewsNet Inc.] - Bryn Mawr, PA - *DataDirOnSer 84*
Low-Priced Stock Alert - Yardley, PA - *DirOnDB Spring 84*
Low Speed Data Service [of RCA Global Communications Inc.] - New York, NY - *TeleSy&SerDir 2-84*
Low-Tech Press - Long Island City, NY - *BoPubDir 5; LitMag&SmPr 83-84*
Lowden Sun-News - Lowden, IA - *BaconPubCkNews 84*
Lowe & Hall Advertising Inc. - Greenville, SC - *ArtMar 84; StaDirAdAg 2-84; TelAl 83, 84*
Lowe, George L. - Chicago, IL - *BoPubDir 4 Sup, 5*
Lowel-Light Manufacturing - New York, NY - *AvMarPl 83*
Lowell Cable TV Co. Inc. [of Colony Communications Inc.] - Lowell, MA - *BrCabYB 84; InterCabHB 3; Tel&CabFB 84C*
Lowell Community TV Corp. - Lowell, OH - *BrCabYB 84; Tel&CabFB 84C*
Lowell Co. Inc., Mortimer - Great Neck, NY - *StaDirAdAg 2-84*
Lowell Conference on Industrial History - Lowell, MA - *BoPubDir 5*
Lowell Grand Valley Ledger - Lowell, MI - *BaconPubCkNews 84; NewsDir 84*
Lowell Museum - Lowell, MA - *BoPubDir 5*
Lowell Press Inc. - Kansas City, MO - *BoPubDir 4, 5; WritMar 84*
Lowell Sun - Lowell, MA - *BaconPubCkNews 84; NewsDir 84*
Lowell Tribune [of Lowell Pilcher Publishing Co.] - Lowell, IN - *AyerDirPub 83; BaconPubCkNews 84; Ed&PubIntYB 82; NewsDir 84*
Lowell TV Cable - Lowell, AR - *BrCabYB 84; Tel&CabFB 84C*
Lowengard & Brotherhood Inc. - Hartford, CT - *DirPRFirms 83*
Lowenstein Associates Inc., Barbara - New York, NY - *LitMarPl 83, 84*
Lowenthal, Jeff - Chicago, IL - *MagIndMarPl 82-83*
Lower Bucks Cablevision Inc. [of American Television & Communications Corp.] - Levittown, PA - *BrCabYB 84; Tel&CabFB 84C*
Lower Cape Publishing - Orleans, MA - *BoPubDir 4, 5*
Lower Delaware CATV Inc. [of Simmons Communications Inc.] - Selbyville, DE - *Tel&CabFB 84C*
Lower Horton United Church Women [Aff. of Covenanter Church] - Grand Pre, NS, Canada - *BoPubDir 4, 5*
Lower Peace Publishing Co. Ltd. - High Level, AB, Canada - *BoPubDir 4, 5*
Lower Township Lantern - Cape May, NJ - *AyerDirPub 83*
Lower Township Lantern - Lower Township, NJ - *Ed&PubIntYB 82*
Lower Turkeyfoot Cable TV [of Belisle Enterprises] - Confluence, PA - *BrCabYB 84; Tel&CabFB 84C*
Lowery Group of Music Publishing Cos. - Atlanta, GA - *BillIntBG 83-84*
Lowlands Review - New Orleans, LA - *LitMag&SmPr 83-84*
Lowman, Hubert A. - Arroyo Grande, CA - *AvMarPl 83*
Lowndes Signal - Ft. Deposit, AL - *Ed&PubIntYB 82*
Lowry Airman - *See* Sentinel Newspapers
Lowry & Partners Inc. - San Francisco, CA - *DirPRFirms 83; StaDirAdAg 2-84*
Lowry Associates Inc., Thomas - New York, NY - *LitMarPl 83, 84*
Lowry Telephone Co. Inc. - Lowry, MN - *TelDir&BG 83-84*
Lowville Journal & Republican - Lowville, NY - *BaconPubCkNews 84*
Lowy Publishing - Houston, TX - *BoPubDir 4, 5; LitMag&SmPr 83-84*
Loyal Colonies Press - Kingston, ON, Canada - *BoPubDir 4, 5*
Loyal Tribune-Record-Gleaner - Loyal, WI - *BaconPubCkNews 84; NewsDir 84*
Loyola University - New Orleans, LA - *BrCabYB 84; Tel&CabFB 84S*
Loyola University Press - Chicago, IL - *LitMarPl 83, 84*
LP-Gas [of Harcourt Brace Jovanovich Inc.] - Duluth, MN - *BaconPubCkMag 84; MagDir 84*
LP Masters Inc. - Cambridge, WI - *BillIntBG 83-84*
LP Publications [Aff. of The Love Project] - San Diego, CA - *BoPubDir 4, 5; LitMag&SmPr 83-84*
LPA Tech Corp. - Springtown, PA - *MicrocomMPl 83*
LPG/PON Inc. - New York, NY - *StaDirAdAg 2-84*
LPI (Data Processing Div.) - Grandview, MO - *ADAPSOMemDir 83-84*
LPTV - Prairie Village, KS - *BaconPubCkMag 84*

LR & Associates Publishing Ltd. - Agincourt, ON, Canada - *LitMarPl 83, 84*
LR & Associates Publishing Ltd. - Scarborough, ON, Canada - *BoPubDir 4, 5*
L.R.H. Enterprises - New Beford, MA - *MicrocomMPl 84*
LS Records - Madison, TN - *BillIntBG 83-84*
LSC Cable Systems Ltd. - Keswick, ON, Canada - *BrCabYB 84*
LSF Media Services Inc. - New York, NY - *StaDirAdAg 2-84*
LSI Enterprises - Woodhaven, NY - *MicrocomMPl 83, 84*
LSM Press - Oakland, CA - *BoPubDir 4, 5*
LST-Language Specialists & Translators Inc. - Washington, DC - *LitMarPl 83, 84*
LT Data Inc. - Wheatridge, CO - *MicrocomMPl 83*
LTM Corp. of America [Subs. of LTM France] - Hollywood, CA - *AvMarPl 83*
Lubavitch Women's Organization Publications - Brooklyn, NY - *BoPubDir 4, 5*
Lubbock Avalanche-Journal [of Southwestern Newspapers Corp.] - Lubbock, TX - *BaconPubCkNews 84; Ed&PubIntYB 82; LitMarPl 83, 84; NewsDir 84*
Lubbock County Cablevision - Reese Air Force Base, TX - *BrCabYB 84*
Lubbock Digest - Lubbock, TX - *Ed&PubIntYB 82*
Lubbock MDS Co. - New York, NY - *Tel&CabFB 84C*
Lubbock Southwest Digest - Lubbock, TX - *BaconPubCkNews 84*
Lubell Laboratories Inc. - Columbus, OH - *AvMarPl 83*
Lubliner/Saltz Inc. - New York, NY - *HBIndAd&MS 82-83; StaDirAdAg 2-84*
Lubow Advertising Inc. - Chicago, IL - *StaDirAdAg 2-84*
Lubrecht & Cramer [Aff. of J. Cramer Verlag] - Monticello, NY - *BoPubDir 4, 5*
Lubrication Engineering [of American Society of Lubrication Engineers] - Park Ridge, IL - *BaconPubCkMag 84; MagDir 84*
Lucas/Guinn Corp. - Hoboken, NJ - *MagIndMarPl 82-83*
Lucas Heights Research Laboratories Library [of Australian Atomic Energy Commission] - Sutherland, Australia - *EISS 83*
Lucas Litho Inc. [Subs. of John D. Lucas Printing Co. Inc.] - New York, NY - *LitMarPl 83*
Lucas/McFaul - New York, NY - *HBIndAd&MS 82-83; Tel&CabFB 84C*
Lucas Printing Co., John D. - Baltimore, MD - *LitMarPl 84*
Lucas-Sylvan News - Lucas, KS - *AyerDirPub 83; BaconPubCkNews 84; Ed&PubIntYB 82*
Luce Cable Systems Inc. - Kilbourne, LA - *Tel&CabFB 84C*
Luce Inc., Robert B. [Subs. of M & B Fulfillment Service Inc.] - Bridgeport, CT - *LitMarPl 83, 84*
Luce Press Clippings - Mesa, AZ - *ProGuPRSer 4*
Luce Press Clippings - New York, NY - *LitMarPl 83, 84*
Lucedale George County Times - Lucedale, MS - *BaconPubCkNews 84; NewsDir 84*
Lucerne Films Inc. - Morris Plains, NJ - *AvMarPl 83*
Lucerne Valley Leader - Lucerne Valley, CA - *BaconPubCkNews 84; Ed&PubIntYB 82*
Lucey Art & Design, Jack - San Rafael, CA - *LitMarPl 83, 84; MagIndMarPl 82-83*
Lucha/Struggle - New York, NY - *LitMag&SmPr 83-84*
Lucifer Records Inc. - Hasbrouck Heights, NJ - *BillIntBG 83-84*
Lucis Publishing Co. [Aff. of Lucis Trust] - New York, NY - *BoPubDir 4, 5*
Luck Telephone Co. - Luck, WI - *TelDir&BG 83-84*
Luckie & Forney Advertising Inc. - Birmingham, AL - *AdAge 3-28-84; BrCabYB 84; StaDirAdAg 2-84*
Lucky Book Club [of Scholastic Book Services] - New York, NY - *LitMarPl 83, 84*
Lucky Charoi Music - *See* Jiru Music Inc.
Lucky Heart Books [of Salt Lick Press] - Austin, TX - *LitMag&SmPr 83-84*
Lucky Star [of The Erie Street Press] - Oak Park, IL - *LitMag&SmPr 83-84*
Lucky's Kum-Ba-Ya Publishing Co. - Brohman, MI - *BillIntBG 83-84*
Luckyu Music - Los Angeles, CA - *BillIntBG 83-84*
Lucy's Store Music - Yonkers, NY - *BillIntBG 83-84*
Ludcke Associates - Minneapolis, MN - *Ed&PubIntYB 82*
Ludd's Mill [of Eight Miles High Products] - Ossett, England - *LitMag&SmPr 83-84*
Luddy Conceptions, Tim J. - New York, NY - *LitMarPl 83, 84*
Ludington Daily News - Ludington, MI - *BaconPubCkNews 84; NewsDir 84*
Ludix Publishing Co. Inc. - *See* Mietus Copyright Management
Ludlow Advertising - Minneapolis, MN - *StaDirAdAg 2-84*
Ludlow Composites [Div. of Ludlow Corp.] - Fremont, OH - *WhoWMicrocom 83*
Ludlow News Enterprise - Covington, KY - *NewsDir 84*
Ludlow News Enterprise - Ludlow, KY - *BaconPubCkNews 84; Ed&PubIntYB 82*
Ludlow, Norman H. - Rochester, NY - *BoPubDir 4, 5*
Ludlow Register [of Palmer Pioneer Enterprises Inc.] - Palmer, MA - *NewsDir 84*
Ludlow Telephone Co. - Ludlow, VT - *TelDir&BG 83-84*
Ludove Noviny - Chicago, IL - *Ed&PubIntYB 82*
Ludowici News - Ludowici, GA - *AyerDirPub 83; BaconPubCkNews 84; Ed&PubIntYB 82; NewsDir 84*
Ludwig, Billy Jack - Dallas, TX - *BoPubDir 4, 5*
Ludwig Periodica, Fred - Tucson, AZ - *MagIndMarPl 82-83*
Luebbers, David J. - Denver, CO - *BoPubDir 4, 5*
Lueders Telephone Cooperative Inc. [Aff. of Taylor Telephone Co. Inc.] - Lueders, TX - *TelDir&BG 83-84*
Luedke & Associates, Walter P. - Rockford, IL - *AdAge 3-28-84; ArtMar 84; StaDirAdAg 2-84*
Luery & Associates Inc., Rodney - Brunswick, NJ - *StaDirAdAg 2-84*
Luff, Moe - Spring Valley, NY - *BoPubDir 4, 5*
Lufkin-Conroe Communications Co. - Lufkin, TX - *TelDir&BG 83-84*
Lufkin News [of Cox Enterprises Inc.] - Lufkin, TX - *BaconPubCkNews 84; Ed&PubIntYB 82; NewsDir 84*
Luggage & Leathergoods News - Downsview, ON, Canada - *BaconPubCkMag 84*
Luggage & Travelware - Norwalk, CT - *BaconPubCkMag 84; MagDir 84; WritMar 84*
Luhrs & Lange Inc. - Stillwater, MN - *StaDirAdAg 2-84*
Luhrs Marketing Research Corp. - Chicago, IL - *IntDirMarRes 83*
Lui Associates - Southfield, MI - *Ed&PubIntYB 82*
Lukman Inc., Mphahlele K. - Brooklyn, NY - *BoPubDir 4, 5*
Luling Cablevision Corp. - Bryan, TX - *BrCabYB 84*
Luling Cablevision Corp. - Luling, TX - *Tel&CabFB 84C*
Luling Newsboy & Signal [of Luling Publishing Co. Inc.] - Luling, TX - *BaconPubCkNews 84; Ed&PubIntYB 82; NewsDir 84*
Lumber City Log, The - Lumber City, GA - *Ed&PubIntYB 82*
Lumber City Log, The - *See* Suburban Printing Corp.
Lumber Co-Operator, The - Rochester, NY - *BaconPubCkMag 84; MagDir 84*
Lumberton Lamar County Head Block - Lumberton, MS - *BaconPubCkNews 84*
Lumberton Robesonian - Lumberton, NC - *BaconPubCkNews 84; NewsDir 84*
Lumby Historians - Lumby, BC, Canada - *BoPubDir 4 Sup, 5*
Lumedyne Inc. - Port Richey, FL - *AvMarPl 83*
Lumeli Press - San Carlos, CA - *BoPubDir 4 Sup, 5*
Lumen Christi Press - Houston, TX - *BoPubDir 4, 5*
Luminary - Muncy, PA - *AyerDirPub 83; Ed&PubIntYB 82*
Luminos Photo Corp. - Yonkers, NY - *AvMarPl 83*
Luna - Kew, Australia - *LitMag&SmPr 83-84*
Luna Bisonte Productions - Columbus, OH - *BoPubDir 4, 5; LitMag&SmPr 83-84*
Luna Software Inc. - San Jose, CA - *MicrocomMPl 84*
Luna Tack [of Dog Hair Press] - Iowa City, IA - *LitMag&SmPr 83-84*
Lunan-Ferguson Library - San Francisco, CA - *BoPubDir 4, 5*
Lunan Hoffman Advertising Ltd. - Montreal, PQ, Canada - *StaDirAdAg 2-84*
Lunar & Planetary Bibliography [of Lunar & Planetary Institute] - Houston, TX - *CompReadDB 82; EISS 83*
Lunar & Planetary Institute [Aff. of Universities Space Research Association] - Houston, TX - *BoPubDir 5*
Lunar & Planetary Institute (Library/Information Center) - Houston, TX - *CompReadDB 82*
Lunar Power - *See* Aristos Music
Lunchbox Theatre - Calgary, AB, Canada - *WritMar 84*
Lunchroom Press - Grosse Pointe Farms, MI - *BoPubDir 4 Sup, 5; LitMag&SmPr 83-84*
Lund & Lommer A/S - *See* Dancer Fitzgerald Sample Inc.

Lund-Heitman-Smith Advertising - Honolulu, HI - *StaDirAdAg 2-84*
Lund, John J. - Jacksonville, OR - *MagIndMarPl 82-83*
Lundberg Share of Market [of I. P. Sharp Associates Ltd.] - Toronto, ON, Canada - *DataDirOnSer 84*
Lundberg Survey Dealer Buying Price - *See* Lundberg Survey Wholesale Petroleum Price Diary
Lundberg Survey Inc. - North Hollywood, CA - *DataDirOnSer 84*
Lundberg Survey Share of Market - North Hollywood, CA - *DirOnDB Spring 84*
Lundberg Survey Wholesale Petroleum Price Diary - North Hollywood, CA - *DirOnDB Spring 84*
Lundgren Publishing Co. - Elkton, SD - *BaconPubCkNews 84*
Lundia - *See* MII Lundia Inc.
Lundmark Advertising & Design - Kansas City, MO - *AdAge 3-28-84; StaDirAdAg 2-84*
Lundy Electronics & Systems Inc. - Glen Head, NY - *DataDirSup 7-83; DirInfWP 82*
Lundy's Lane Historical Society - Niagara Falls, ON, Canada - *BoPubDir 4, 5*
Luning Prak Associates Inc. - Montvale, NJ - *BoPubDir 4 Sup, 5; IntDirMarRes 83*
L'Union [of Union Saint-Jean-Baptiste] - Woonsocket, RI - *NewsDir 84*
L'Union des Cantons de l'Est - Victoriaville, PQ, Canada - *Ed&PubIntYB 82*
Luongo Co., C. Paul - Boston, MA - *DirPRFirms 83*
Lupfer & Long Inc. - Hanover, NH - *MicrocomMPl 84; MicrocomSwDir 1*
Luray Page News & Courier [of Page-Shenandoah Newspaper Corp. Inc.] - Luray, VA - *BaconPubCkNews 84; NewsDir 84*
Lurie, William - Bellevue, WA - *LitMarPl 83, 84; MagIndMarPl 82-83*
Lusion - Los Angeles, CA - *BillIntBG 83-84*
Lusitano - Montreal, PQ, Canada - *Ed&PubIntYB 82*
Lusk Herald - Lusk, WY - *BaconPubCkNews 84; Ed&PubIntYB 82*
Lusky Associates Inc., Sam - Denver, CO - *ArtMar 84; StaDirAdAg 2-84*
Luso-Americano - Newark, NJ - *AyerDirPub 83; Ed&PubIntYB 82; NewsDir 84*
Lust Publications, Benedict - Greenwich, CT - *BoPubDir 4, 5*
Lustrum Press Inc. - New York, NY - *BoPubDir 4, 5*
Lutcher News Examiner - Lutcher, LA - *BaconPubCkNews 84; Ed&PubIntYB 82*
Luth & Katz - New York, NY - *HBIndAd&MS 82-83*
Luth Research Inc. - San Diego, CA - *IntDirMarRes 83*
Luther College Press - Decorah, IA - *BoPubDir 4, 5*
Luther Co. Inc., The Frederic - Indianapolis, IN - *MicroMarPl 82-83*
Lutheran Academy for Scholarship Inc. - Valparaiso, IN - *BoPubDir 4 Sup, 5*
Lutheran Braille Evangelism Association - St. Paul, MN - *LitMarPl 83, 84*
Lutheran Braille Workers Inc. (Sight-Saving Div.) - San Francisco, CA - *BoPubDir 4, 5*
Lutheran Church in America - New York, NY - *Tel&CabFB 84C*
Lutheran Church in America (Dept. of News & Information) - New York, NY - *Ed&PubIntYB 82*
Lutheran Education - Forest, IL - *MagIndMarPl 82-83*
Lutheran Film Associates - New York, NY - *AvMarPl 83*
Lutheran Forum - New York, NY - *MagIndMarPl 82-83; WritMar 84*
Lutheran Journal, The - Edina, MN - *ArtMar 84; WritMar 84*
Lutheran Layman, The - St. Louis, MO - *MagDir 84*
Lutheran Standard [of Augsburg Publishing House] - Minneapolis, MN - *ArtMar 84; BaconPubCkMag 84; LitMarPl 83, 84; MagDir 84; MagIndMarPl 82-83; WritMar 84*
Lutheran Television - St. Louis, MO - *Tel&CabFB 84C*
Lutheran, The [of Lutheran Church in America] - Philadelphia, PA - *ArtMar 84; BaconPubCkMag 84; LitMarPl 83, 84; MagDir 84; MagIndMarPl 82-83; WritMar 84*
Lutheran Women - Philadelphia, PA - *WritMar 84*
Lutz & Sheinkman [Div. of Einson, Freeman & De Troy Corp.] - Fairlawn, NJ - *LitMarPl 83, 84; MagIndMarPl 82-83*
Lutz Party Line [of Tampa Suburban Newspapers] - Tampa, FL - *NewsDir 84*
Lutz Party Line - *See* Tampa Suburban Newspapers Inc.
Lutzker Advertising, Steve - Phoenix, AZ - *AdAge 3-28-84*
Luverne Cable TV [of Zylstra Communications Corp.] - Luverne, MN - *Tel&CabFB 84C*
Luverne Journal & News - Luverne, AL - *BaconPubCkNews 84*
Luverne Journal, The - Luverne, AL - *Ed&PubIntYB 82*
Luverne Rock County Star Herald - Luverne, MN - *BaconPubCkNews 84*
Luverne TV Cable Service - Luverne, AL - *BrCabYB 84; Tel&CabFB 84C*
Lux-Jornal Recortes Ltda. - Rio de Janeiro, Brazil - *ProGuPRSer 4*
Luxemburg News - Luxemburg, WI - *BaconPubCkNews 84; Ed&PubIntYB 82*
Luxor Corp. - Waukegan, IL - *AvMarPl 83; DataDirSup 7-83; DirInfWP 82*
Lyceum Books Inc. - Wilton, CT - *BoPubDir 4, 5*
Lyceum Productions - La Puente, CA - *AvMarPl 83*
Lyco Computer Marketing & Consultants - Montoursville, PA - *MicrocomMPl 83*
Lycoming Data Services Inc. - Montoursville, PA - *ADAPSOMemDir 83-84*
Lydette Publishing Co. - Cedar Falls, IA - *BoPubDir 4, 5*
Lykens TV Co. - Lykens, PA - *BrCabYB 84; Tel&CabFB 84C*
Lyles, Patricia & William - Greenfield, MA - *LitMarPl 83; MagIndMarPl 82-83*
Lyman Associates, E. W. - Chicago, IL - *DirPRFirms 83*
Lyman Bridger Valley Pioneer - Lyman, WY - *BaconPubCkNews 84*
Lyman County Herald - Presho, SD - *Ed&PubIntYB 82*
Lyman Publications - Middlefield, CT - *BoPubDir 4, 5*
Lymburner & Sons Ltd., James R. - Toronto, ON, Canada - *BoPubDir 4 Sup, 5; DataDirOnSer 84*
Lyn-Lou Music Inc. - Memphis, TN - *BillIntBG 83-84*
Lynbrook News [of Lawrence Bi-County Publishers Inc.] - Lawrence, NY - *AyerDirPub 83; NewsDir 84*
Lynbrook News - *See* Richner Publications Inc.
Lynbrook Pennysaver - Rockville Centre, NY - *AyerDirPub 83*
Lynch & Rockey Advertising - San Francisco, CA - *StaDirAdAg 2-84*
Lynch Co., M. - New York, NY - *IntDirMarRes 83*
Lynch Data Processing - Cary, IL - *ADAPSOMemDir 83-84; DataDirOnSer 84*
Lynch, Jones & Ryan - New York, NY - *DataDirOnSer 84*
Lynch, Sheila - New York, NY - *LitMarPl 83, 84*
Lynch Studio - New York, NY - *MagIndMarPl 82-83*
Lynch Television Inc. - Lynch, KY - *BrCabYB 84; Tel&CabFB 84C*
Lynch Transcription Service - Smithtown, NY - *ProGuPRSer 4*
Lynchburg Cable Television - Lynchburg, TN - *BrCabYB 84; Tel&CabFB 84C*
Lynchburg Cablevision [of American TV & Communications Corp.] - Lynchburg, VA - *BrCabYB 84; Tel&CabFB 84C*
Lynchburg Daily Advance - Lynchburg, VA - *BaconPubCkNews 84*
Lynchburg Moore County News - Lynchburg, TN - *BaconPubCkNews 84*
Lynchburg News - Lynchburg, OH - *AyerDirPub 83; Ed&PubIntYB 82*
Lynchburg News [of Worrell Newspapers Inc.] - Lynchburg, VA - *BaconPubCkNews 84; NewsDir 84*
Lynchburg News - *See* Greenfield Times Publishers
Lyncourt Pennysaver - Syracuse, NY - *AyerDirPub 83*
Lynd Cable TV [of DeSutter Cable Inc.] - Minneota, MN - *BrCabYB 84*
Lynden Tribune [of Lewis Publishing Co. Inc.] - Lynden, WA - *BaconPubCkNews 84; Ed&PubIntYB 82; NewsDir 84*
Lyndhurst Commercial Leader - *See* Leader Newspapers Inc.
Lyndon Cable TV - Lyndon, KS - *BrCabYB 84*
Lyndon House Publishing - Fredericton, NB, Canada - *LitMarPl 83, 84*
Lyndon News-Herald - Lyndon, KS - *BaconPubCkNews 84; Ed&PubIntYB 82*
Lynn & Associates - Heidelburg, PA - *CabTVFinDB 83*
Lynn Associates Inc. - White Plains, NY - *DirPRFirms 83*
Lynn Canal News - Haines, AK - *AyerDirPub 83*
Lynn Computer Service - Tinley Park, IL - *MicrocomMPl 83, 84*

Lynn Computer Services, Joe - Plainfield, IL - *MicrocomSwDir 1*
Lynn County CATV - O'Donnell, TX - *BrCabYB 84*
Lynn County News - Tahoka, TX - *AyerDirPub 83; Ed&PubIntYB 82*
Lynn Daily Evening Item - Lynn, MA - *BaconPubCkNews 84*
Lynn Enterprises, Richard - Lagro, IN - *Ed&PubIntYB 82*
Lynn, Erwin - Plainview, NY - *Ed&PubIntYB 82*
Lynn-Free Enterprise - *See* B & R Publishing
Lynn Organization Inc., The - Wilkes-Barre, PA - *StaDirAdAg 2-84*
Lynn Publishing Co. - Regina, SK, Canada - *BoPubDir 4, 5*
Lynn Sonberg Book Services - New York, NY - *LitMarPl 83*
Lynn Sunday Post - Lynn, MA - *BaconPubCkNews 84; NewsDir 84*
Lynn Times - Lynn, MA - *NewsDir 84*
Lynn TV Cable Co. [of Ind Co. TV Cable Inc.] - Lynn, AR - *BrCabYB 84*
Lynnal Music - *See* Buttermilk Sky Music Publishing Corp.
Lynnfield Villager, The - Lynnfield, MA - *AyerDirPub 83; Ed&PubIntYB 82*
Lynnfield Villager, The - *See* Great Oak Publications Inc.
Lynn's Radio & Appliance - Protection, KS - *BrCabYB 84; Tel&CabFB 84C*
Lynnville Community Telephone Co. Inc. - Lynnville, IA - *TelDir&BG 83-84*
Lynnwood Enterprise - Lynnwood, WA - *BaconPubCkNews 84; Ed&PubIntYB 82; NewsDir 84*
Lynnwood Music - *See* Espy Music Group
Lynwood Press & Tribune - Lynwood, CA - *BaconPubCkNews 84; Ed&PubIntYB 82; NewsDir 84*
Lynx House Press - Amherst, MA - *BoPubDir 4, 5; LitMag&SmPr 83-84; WritMar 84*
Lyon & Kurz - Washington, DC - *ADAPSOMemDir 83-84*
Lyon County News - George, IA - *AyerDirPub 83; Ed&PubIntYB 82*
Lyon County Reporter - Rock Rapids, IA - *AyerDirPub 83; Ed&PubIntYB 82*
Lyon-Davis Research Inc. - Forest Hills, NY - *EISS 7-83 Sup; InfIndMarPl 83; LitMarPl 83; MagIndMarPl 82-83*
Lyon Inc., David G. - Greens Farms, CT - *StaDirAdAg 2-84*
Lyon Metal Products Inc. - Aurora, IL - *DirInfWP 82*
Lyon Metal Products Inc. - Montgomery, IL - *AvMarPl 83*
Lyon Pictures, Fred - San Francisco, CA - *AvMarPl 83*
Lyons Advertising Inc. - Attleboro Falls, MA - *StaDirAdAg 2-84*
Lyons & Associates, Walter - Amesbury, MA - *StaDirAdAg 2-84*
Lyons Associates Inc. - Aspen, CO - *DirPRFirms 83*
Lyons Books, Nick [Div. of Benn Brothers Inc.] - New York, NY - *LitMarPl 83, 84*
Lyons CATV Inc. [of Multimedia Cablevision Inc.] - Lyons, KS - *Tel&CabFB 84C*
Lyons Citizen [of La Grange Suburban Life/Citizen] - La Grange, IL - *NewsDir 84*
Lyons, David - Merrimack, NH - *BoPubDir 4 Sup, 5*
Lyons/Graphics Inc. - New York, NY - *StaDirAdAg 2-84*
Lyons Mirror Sun - Lyons, NE - *BaconPubCkNews 84; Ed&PubIntYB 82*
Lyons News - Lyons, KS - *BaconPubCkNews 84; Ed&PubIntYB 82; NewsDir 84*
Lyons Progress - Lyons, GA - *BaconPubCkNews 84; Ed&PubIntYB 82*
Lyons Recorder - Lyons, CO - *BaconPubCkNews 84*
Lyons Studios - Wilmington, DE - *AdAge 3-28-84; ArtMar 84; AvMarPl 83; StaDirAdAg 2-84; WritMar 84*
Lyons Suburban Life Citizen - *See* Life Printing & Publishing Co.
Lyons Times [of Lyons Enterprise Publishing Co.] - Lyons, IL - *BaconPubCkNews 84; NewsDir 84*
Lyons Visualization Series - Marshall, CA - *BoPubDir 4, 5*
Lyons Wayne County Star - Lyons, NY - *BaconPubCkNews 84; NewsDir 84*
Lyra Music Co. - New York, NY - *BillIntBG 83-84*
Lyresong Inc. - Atlanta, GA - *BillIntBG 83-84*
Lyric, The - Blacksburg, VA - *WritMar 84*
Lyrichord Discs Inc. - New York, NY - *BillIntBG 83-84*
Lytton Publishing Co. - College Station, TX - *BoPubDir 4, 5*

M

M [of Fairchild Publications] - New York, NY - *ArtMar 84; BaconPubCkMag 84; Folio 83*
M/A-COM Comm/Scope Inc. - Catawba, NC - *CabTVFinDB 83*
M/A-COM DCC Inc. - Germantown, MD - *DataDirSup 7-83*
M/A-COM Inc. - Burlington, MA - *Datamation 6-83; ElecNews 7-25-83; HomeVid&CabYB 82-83; Top100Al 83*
M/A COM Linkabit Inc. - San Diego, CA - *DataDirSup 7-83*
M/A-COM Office Systems Inc. - Bedford, MA - *WhoWMicrocom 83*
M/A-COM Sigma Data Inc. [Div. of M/A-COM Inc.] - Rockville, MD - *DataDirOnSer 84*
M/A Press - Beaverton, OR - *BoPubDir 4, 5*
M & A Database [of ADP Network Services] - Ann Arbor, MI - *DataDirOnSer 84; DirOnDB Spring 84*
M & B Consulting - Idaho Falls, ID - *WhoWMicrocom 83*
M & Co. - New York, NY - *StaDirAdAg 2-84*
M & E - New York, NY - *BillIntBG 83-84*
M & E Cable TV - Fergus Falls, MN - *Tel&CabFB 84C p.1688*
M & G TV - Waynesburg, PA - *BrCabYB 84*
M & M Advertising Inc. - Appleton, WI - *StaDirAdAg 2-84*
M & M Cable Co. Inc. - Sunset-Whitney Ranch, CA - *BrCabYB 84*
M & R Cablevision Inc. - Cabin Creek, WV - *BrCabYB 84 p.D-304; Tel&CabFB 84C p.1688*
M & R Cablevision Inc. - Knollwood, WV - *BrCabYB 84*
M & R Cablevision Inc. - Ridgeview, WV - *BrCabYB 84*
M & R Cablevision Inc. - Rumble, WV - *BrCabYB 84*
M & R Productions Inc. - New York, NY - *AvMarPl 83; Tel&CabFB 84C*
M & R Publications - Turlock, CA - *BoPubDir 5*
M & S Press Inc. [Aff. of M & S Rare Books Inc.] - Weston, MA - *BoPubDir 4, 5*
M-C Publications - Burbank, CA - *BoPubDir 4, 5*
M-Cubed Publications - Garland, TX - *MicrocomMPl 83*
M/D/A List Brokerage Co. - New York, NY - *MagIndMarPl 82-83*
M/D/A List Management Co. - Croton Falls, NY - *MagIndMarPl 82-83*
M-E Music Co. - New York, NY - *BillIntBG 83-84*
M-P Software - Cumming, GA - *MicrocomMPl 84*
M-R Cable TV Inc. - Ridgeland, MS - *BrCabYB 84*
M-R-K Publishing - Petaluma, CA - *BoPubDir 4, 5; LitMag&SmPr 83-84*
M/T/M Publishing Co. [Aff. of Moore/Taylor/Moore] - Washougal, WA - *BoPubDir 4, 5*
M-Tec Computer Services - Norwich, England - *MicrocomSwDir 1*
M-3 Music Co. - *See* Cherry Lane Music Publishing Co. Inc.
MA/AH Publishing Series - Manhattan, KS - *LitMarPl 83, 84*
Maarjamaa - Scarborough, ON, Canada - *BoPubDir 5*
Maaroufa Press Inc. - Chicago, IL - *BoPubDir 4, 5*
Mabank Banner [of Malakoff Territory Times Publishing Co.] - Malakoff, TX - *NewsDir 84*
Mabank Tri-County News - Mabank, TX - *BaconPubCkNews 84*
Mabel Cooperative Telephone Co. - Mabel, MN - *TelDir&BG 83-84*
Mabel Record - Mabel, MN - *BaconPubCkNews 84; Ed&PubIntYB 82*
Mableton Neighbor - Mableton, GA - *Ed&PubIntYB 82*
Mableton Neighbor [of Marietta Neighbor Newspapers Inc.] - Marietta, GA - *AyerDirPub 83; NewsDir 84*
Mableton South Cobb Today - Mableton, GA - *NewsDir 84*
Mabton Press - Clarkston, WA - *AyerDirPub 83*
Mabton Press - *See* Tribune Newspapers Inc.
MAC - Los Angeles, CA - *MagDir 84*
MAC Cable Ltd. - McAdam, NB, Canada - *BrCabYB 84*
M.A.C. Gopher - Minneapolis, MN - *BaconPubCkMag 84; MagDir 84*
MAC Panel Co. - High Point, NC - *DataDirSup 7-83*
MacAlester Park Publishing Co. - St. Paul, MN - *BoPubDir 4, 5*
Macanudo Music - *See* Sound Column Cos., The
Macaroni Journal [of National Pasta Association] - Palatine, IL - *BaconPubCkMag 84; MagDir 84*
Macaroni Music - *See* Harlem Music
MacArthur Memorial - Norfolk, VA - *BoPubDir 4, 5*
MacArthur Music - Palmdale, CA - *BillIntBG 83-84*
MacCampbell Inc., Donald - New York, NY - *LitMarPl 83, 84*
MacClenny Baker County Press - MacClenny, FL - *BaconPubCkNews 84*
Macco Communications Inc. - Blanchard, LA - *Tel&CabFB 84C*
Macco Communications Inc. - Caddo Parish, LA - *BrCabYB 84*
MacDonald & Sons Inc., Harrison C. - Lafayette, IN - *Ed&PubIntYB 82*
MacDonald Broadcasting Co. - Saginaw, MI - *BrCabYB 84*
MacDonald, J. E. - Thessalon, ON, Canada - *BoPubDir 4 Sup, 5*
MacDonald Journal - St. Anne de Bellevue, PQ, Canada - *BaconPubCkMag 84*
Mace Advertising Agency Inc. - Morton, IL - *AdAge 3-28-84; StaDirAdAg 2-84*
Macfadden Holdings Inc. - New York, NY - *KnowInd 83*
MacFadden Women's Group - New York, NY - *Folio 83; MagIndMarPl 82-83; NewsBur 6*
MacFarland, Aveyard & Co. - Chicago, IL - *StaDirAdAg 2-84; TelAl 83, 84*
MacFarland Co., The - Middlesex, NJ - *LitMarPl 83, 84*
MacFarlane & Co. Inc. - Atlanta, GA - *IntDirMarRes 83*
MacGibbon & Kobasic Advertising Inc. - Portland, OR - *AdAge 3-28-84; StaDirAdAg 2-84*
MacGill Johnson Hargreaves - Indianapolis, IN - *StaDirAdAg 2-84*
MacGown Advertising Inc., John - Valley Stream, NY - *StaDirAdAg 2-84*
MacGregor Publications, Scotty - Smithtown, NY - *BoPubDir 4, 5*
MacHarmony Music [Div. of Date Line International Records] - New York, NY - *BillIntBG 83-84*
Machias Valley News Observer - Machias, ME - *AyerDirPub 83; BaconPubCkNews 84; Ed&PubIntYB 82; NewsDir 84*
Machinability Data Center [of Metcut Research Associates Inc.] - Cincinnati, OH - *CompReadDB 82; EISS 83; InfIndMarPl 83*

Machine & Tool Blue Book - Wheaton, IL - *BaconPubCkMag 84; MagDir 84; MagIndMarPl 82-83*
Machine-Assisted Reference Section [of American Library Association] - Chicago, IL - *EISS 7-83 Sup*
Machine Composition Co. - Boston, MA - *LitMarPl 83*
Machine Design [of Penton/IPC] - Cleveland, OH - *BaconPubCkMag 84; Folio 83; MagDir 84; MagIndMarPl 82-83*
Machine Readable Archives Branch [of U.S. General Services Administration] - Washington, DC - *EISS 83*
Machine Readable Archives Div. [of Public Archives of Canada] - Ottawa, ON, Canada - *EISS 83*
Machine Readable Cataloging-Books [of Library of Congress] - Washington, DC - *CompReadDB 82*
Machine Readable Cataloging-Films [of Library of Congress] - Washington, DC - *CompReadDB 82*
Machine Readable Cataloging-Maps [of Library of Congress] - Washington, DC - *CompReadDB 82*
Machine Readable Cataloging-Name Authorities [of Library of Congress] - Washington, DC - *CompReadDB 82*
Machine Readable Cataloging-Serials [of Library of Congress] - Washington, DC - *CompReadDB 82*
Machine Readable Cataloging-Subject Authorities [of Library of Congress] - Washington, DC - *CompReadDB 82*
Machine Readable Data Archives [of Western Kentucky University] - Bowling Green, KY - *EISS 83*
Machinist, The - Washington, DC - *BaconPubCkMag 84; MagDir 84; NewsDir 84*
Macia, Rafael - New York, NY - *LitMarPl 83, 84; MagIndMarPl 82-83*
MacIntosh Communications Inc., Rob - Boston, MA - *LitMarPl 83, 84; MagIndMarPl 82-83*
Macintyre, Venka V. - Falls Church, VA - *LitMarPl 83*
Mack Allied Corp. [Subs. of Mack Chicago Co.] - Long Island City, NY - *LitMarPl 83, 84*
Mack Book Review Service, Jerry - San Angelo, TX - *LitMarPl 83, 84*
Mack Information & Composition System [of Mack Printing Co.] - Easton, PA - *EISS 83*
Mack, Jerry - San Angelo, TX - *LitMarPl 83, 84*
Mack Printing Co. - Easton, PA - *LitMarPl 83, 84; MagIndMarPl 82-83*
Mack Publishing Co. - Plainview, MN - *BaconPubCkNews 84*
Mack Publishing Co. - Easton, PA - *BoPubDir 4, 5*
MacKay Enterprises Inc., E. A. - Lombard, IL - *BaconPubCkNews 84*
MacKay United Church - Ottawa, ON, Canada - *BoPubDir 4, 5*
Mackenzie & Associates, Malcolm L. - Wilmington, DE - *ArtMar 84; AvMarPl 83*
MacKenzie Books - Christmas Island, NS, Canada - *BoPubDir 4, 5*
Mackenzie Laboratories Inc. - Arcadia, CA - *AvMarPl 83*
Mackenzie Media Ltd. - Yellowknife, NT, Canada - *BrCabYB 84*
Mackerodt Inc., Fred - New York, NY - *DirPRFirms 83*
Mackey Publishing, Cleo - Dallas, TX - *BoPubDir 5*
Mackinac Island State Park Commission - Mackinac Island, MI - *BoPubDir 4, 5*
Mackinac Island Town Crier - Mackinac Island, MI - *AyerDirPub 83*
Macksville Enterprise - Macksville, KS - *BaconPubCkNews 84; Ed&PubIntYB 82*
MacLachlan & Associates Inc., J. - Wayzata, MN - *AdAge 3-28-84; StaDirAdAg 2-84*
MacLaren Advertising - Toronto, ON, Canada - *StaDirAdAg 2-84*
MacLaren Associates, Donald - Bowie, MD - *LitMarPl 84*
Maclay & Associates - Baltimore, MD - *BoPubDir 4; LitMarPl 83, 84; WritMar 84*
Maclean Hunter Cable TV - Rexdale, ON, Canada - *BrCabYB 84; CabTVFinDB 83; LitMarPl 84; Tel&CabFB 84C*
Maclean Hunter Cable TV Ltd. - Garden City, MI - *Tel&CabFB 84C*
Maclean Hunter Cable TV Ltd. - East Orange, NJ - *Tel&CabFB 84C p.1688*
Maclean Hunter Cable TV Ltd. - Ajax, ON, Canada - *BrCabYB 84*
Maclean Hunter Cable TV Ltd. - Collingwood, ON, Canada - *BrCabYB 84*
Maclean Hunter Cable TV Ltd. - Guelph, ON, Canada - *BrCabYB 84*
Maclean Hunter Cable TV Ltd. - Hamilton, ON, Canada - *BrCabYB 84*
Maclean Hunter Cable TV Ltd. - Huntsville, ON, Canada - *BrCabYB 84*
Maclean Hunter Cable TV Ltd. - London, ON, Canada - *BrCabYB 84*
Maclean Hunter Cable TV Ltd. - Midland, ON, Canada - *BrCabYB 84*
Maclean Hunter Cable TV Ltd. - Mississauga, ON, Canada - *BrCabYB 84*
Maclean Hunter Cable TV Ltd. - North Bay, ON, Canada - *BrCabYB 84*
Maclean Hunter Cable TV Ltd. - Owen Sound, ON, Canada - *BrCabYB 84*
Maclean Hunter Cable TV Ltd. - Peterborough, ON, Canada - *BrCabYB 84*
Maclean Hunter Cable TV Ltd. - Sarnia, ON, Canada - *BrCabYB 84*
Maclean Hunter Cable TV Ltd. - St. Catharines, ON, Canada - *BrCabYB 84*
Maclean Hunter Cable TV Ltd. - Thunder Bay, ON, Canada - *BrCabYB 84*
Maclean Hunter Cable TV Ltd. - Wallaceburg, ON, Canada - *BrCabYB 84*
Maclean Hunter Communications - Toronto, ON, Canada - *AdAge 6-28-84*
Maclean Hunter Learning Resources [Subs. of Maclean Hunter Media Inc.] - New York, NY - *DirMarMP 83*
Maclean Hunter Micropublishing Co. - Toronto, ON, Canada - *MicroMarPl 82-83*
MacLean Hunter Publishing Corp. - Chicago, IL - *MagIndMarPl 82-83*
Maclean's - Toronto, ON, Canada - *BaconPubCkMag 84; WritMar 84*
Macleod Gazette - Ft. Macleod, AB, Canada - *AyerDirPub 83; Ed&PubIntYB 82*
MacMahon Advertising Inc. - Orlando, FL - *StaDirAdAg 2-84*
MacManiman Inc. - Fall City, WA - *BoPubDir 4, 5*
Macmillan Book Clubs Inc. - New York, NY - *LitMarPl 84*
Macmillan Inc. - New York, NY - *KnowInd 83*
Macmillan of Canada [Div. of Gage Publishing Ltd.] - Toronto, ON, Canada - *LitMarPl 83, 84; WritMar 84*
Macmillan Publishing Corp. [Div. of Macmillan Inc.] - New York, NY - *ArtMar 84; LitMarPl 83, 84; MicroMarPl 82-83; WritMar 84*
Macmillan Publishing Corp. (Professional Books Div.) - New York, NY - *ArtMar 84*
MacMurray Society, John - Toronto, ON, Canada - *BoPubDir 4, 5*
MacNab Circle - Hamilton, ON, Canada - *BoPubDir 4, 5*
MacNair-Dorland Co. - New York, NY - *BoPubDir 5; MagIndMarPl 82-83*
MacNamara, Clapp & Klein Inc. - New York, NY - *StaDirAdAg 2-84*
MacNeal-Schwendler Corp., The - Los Angeles, CA - *ADAPSOMemDir 83-84*
Macomb Daily - Mt. Clemens, MI - *AyerDirPub 83; BaconPubCkNews 84; Ed&PubIntYB 82*
Macomb Journal [of Park Newspapers of Illinois Inc.] - Macomb, IL - *BaconPubCkNews 84; Ed&PubIntYB 82; NewsDir 84*
Macomber Research & Information Services - Modesto, CA - *EISS 7-83 Sup*
Macomnet Inc. - Germantown, MD - *TeleSy&SerDir 7-83, 2-84*
Macon Beacon - Macon, MS - *BaconPubCkNews 84; Ed&PubIntYB 82; NewsDir 84*
Macon Cablevision Inc. [of Cotton Hill Cablevision Inc.] - Macon, MO - *Tel&CabFB 84C*
Macon Cablevision Inc. [of Mills Communications Inc.] - Franklin, NC - *Tel&CabFB 84C*
Macon Chronicle-Herald - Macon, MO - *BaconPubCkNews 84; Ed&PubIntYB 82; NewsDir 84*
Macon County Historical Society - Decatur, IL - *BoPubDir 4, 5*
Macon County Home Press - La Plata, MO - *AyerDirPub 83; Ed&PubIntYB 82*

Macon County Times - Lafayette, TN - *AyerDirPub 83; Ed&PubIntYB 82*
Macon Courier - Macon, GA - *BaconPubCkNews 84*
Macon News [of The Macon Telegraph Publishing Co.] - Macon, GA - *Ed&PubIntYB 82; LitMarPl 83, 84; NewsDir 84*
Macon Telegraph - Macon, GA - *Ed&PubIntYB 82; LitMarPl 83, 84; NewsDir 84*
Macon Telegraph & News - Macon, GA - *BaconPubCkNews 84; Ed&PubIntYB 82; LitMarPl 83, 84*
Macon Times - Macon, GA - *BaconPubCkNews 84; Ed&PubIntYB 82*
Macon Video Co. [of Heritage Communications Inc.] - Macon, MS - *BrCabYB 84; Tel&CabFB 84C*
Macoupin County Cablevision - Carlinville, IL - *BrCabYB 84; Tel&CabFB 84C*
Macoupin County Cablevision - Staunton, IL - *BrCabYB 84*
Macoupin County Enquirer - Carlinville, IL - *AyerDirPub 83; Ed&PubIntYB 82*
Macoupin County Shopper [of Hillsboro Journal] - Hillsboro, IL - *NewsDir 84*
Macoy Publishing & Masonic Supply Co. Inc. - Richmond, VA - *BoPubDir 5*
MacRae Publications - Enumelaw, WA - *BoPubDir 4, 5*
Macro Books [Aff. of Macro Society] - Tempe, AZ - *BoPubDir 4, 5*
Macro Forecasts [of Evans Economics Inc.] - Washington, DC - *DataDirOnSer 84*
Macro 4 Inc. - Mt. Freedom, NJ - *DataDirSup 7-83*
Macro Long-Term Database [of Evans Economics Inc.] - Washington, DC - *DataDirOnSer 84*
Macro Micro Systems Inc. - St. Petersburg, FL - *MicrocomMPl 83, 84*
Macro Model Standard Forecast Database [of Evans Economics Inc.] - Washington, DC - *DataDirOnSer 84*
Macrodare, Allen - Redondo Beach, CA - *MicrocomMPl 84*
Macroeconomic Forecast [of Chase Econometrics/Interactive Data Corp.] - Waltham, MA - *DataDirOnSer 84*
Macrolink Inc. - Anaheim, CA - *MicrocomMPl 84*
Macrolink Inc. - Westboro, MA - *MicrocomMPl 84*
Macromedia Inc. - Hackensack, NJ - *AdAge 6-28-84*
Macrotel Inc. - Buffalo, NY - *VideoDir 82-83*
Macrotronics Inc. - Turlock, CA - *MicrocomMPl 83, 84*
MacVay-Gensheimer Stations - Grand Blanc, MI - *BrCabYB 84*
MacVay, Robert Dana - Grand Blanc, MI - *BrCabYB 84*
Macy, Dan - Warm Springs, OR - *Tel&CabFB 84C p.1688*
Macy Foundation, Josiah Jr. - New York, NY - *BoPubDir 4, 5*
M.A.D. about Marketing - New York, NY - *HBIndAd&MS 82-83*
M.A.D. Advertising Ltd. - Syosset, NY - *StaDirAdAg 2-84*
Mad Ave East - Melville, NY - *AdAge 3-28-84; StaDirAdAg 2-84*
Mad Computer Inc. - Santa Clara, CA - *MicrocomMPl 84; WhoWMicrocom 83*
M.A.D. House - Sanford, FL - *BoPubDir 4, 5*
Mad Magazine - New York, NY - *MagIndMarPl 82-83; WritMar 84*
Mad Monkey Music - North Hollywood, CA - *BillIntBG 83-84*
Mad River Press - Eureka, CA - *BoPubDir 4, 5*
Madawaska St. John Valley Times - Madawaska, ME - *BaconPubCkNews 84; NewsDir 84*
Madden & Goodrum & Associates Inc. - Nashville, TN - *StaDirAdAg 2-84*
Madden Associates, Chris Casson - New York, NY - *LitMarPl 83; MagIndMarPl 82-83*
Madden Associates, Chris Casson - Rye, NY - *LitMarPl 84*
Maddock Cable TV [of Maddock Area Development Corp.] - Maddock, ND - *Tel&CabFB 84C*
Maddox & McArthur Inc. - Roanoke, VA - *DirMarMP 83*
Maddox Group, The - Dallas, TX - *StaDirAdAg 2-84*
Made in Mexico Magazine [of Trade America Inc.] - Denver, CO - *MagDir 84*
Madelia Telephone Co. - Madelia, MN - *TelDir&BG 83-84*
Madelia Times-Messenger - Madelia, MN - *BaconPubCkNews 84*
Madeline Island Telephone Co. - La Pointe, WI - *TelDir&BG 83-84*
Madelon Music - *See* Audio Arts Publishing Co.
Mademoiselle [of Conde Nast Publications] - New York, NY - *BaconPubCkMag 84; Folio 83; LitMarPl 83, 84; MagDir 84; MagIndMarPl 82-83; WritMar 84*
Madera Shopper - Madera, CA - *AyerDirPub 83*
Madera Tribune [of Madera Newspapers Inc.] - Madera, CA - *BaconPubCkNews 84; Ed&PubIntYB 82; NewsDir 84*
Madhatter Press - Minneapolis, MN - *BoPubDir 4, 5; LitMag&SmPr 83-84*
Madigan & Associates, Joseph V. - Cleveland, OH - *DirPRFirms 83*
Madill Record - Madill, OK - *BaconPubCkNews 84; Ed&PubIntYB 82; NewsDir 84*
Madison Academic Computing Center [of University of Wisconsin] - Madison, WI - *DataDirOnSer 84; EISS 83*
Madison & Polk - Asheville, NC - *BoPubDir 5*
Madison Avenue - New York, NY - *BaconPubCkMag 84; MagDir 84*
Madison Avenue Alliance Inc., The - New York, NY - *StaDirAdAg 2-84*
Madison Business Forms Inc. - Fairfield, NJ - *DataDirSup 7-83*
Madison Cable TV [of Action CATV Inc.] - Madison, KS - *BrCabYB 84*
Madison Cable TV Inc. [of Tele-Media Corp.] - Madison, OH - *BrCabYB 84*
Madison Cablevision Inc. - Old Fort, CO - *BrCabYB 84*
Madison Cablevision Inc. [of Tele-Communications Inc.] - Elkton, MD - *BrCabYB 84; Tel&CabFB 84C*
Madison Cablevision Inc. [of Tele-Communications Inc.] - Marion, NC - *BrCabYB 84; Tel&CabFB 84C*
Madison Cablevision Inc. [of Tele-Communications Inc.] - Morganton, NC - *BrCabYB 84; Tel&CabFB 84C*
Madison Cablevision Inc. [of Tele-Communications Inc.] - Bennettsville, SC - *BrCabYB 84; Tel&CabFB 84C*
Madison Cablevision Inc. [of Tele-Communications Inc.] - Culpeper, VA - *BrCabYB 84*
Madison Cablevision Inc. [of Tele-Communications Inc.] - Orange, VA - *BrCabYB 84; Tel&CabFB 84C*
Madison Capital Times - Madison, WI - *BaconPubCkNews 84; NewsDir 84*
Madison Coal Valley News - Danville, WV - *NewsDir 84*
Madison Coal Valley News - Madison, WV - *BaconPubCkNews 84*
Madison Computer - Madison, WI - *MicrocomMPl 83, 84*
Madison County Carrier - Madison, FL - *AyerDirPub 83; BaconPubCkNews 84; NewsDir 84*
Madison County Eagle - Madison, VA - *AyerDirPub 83; Ed&PubIntYB 82; NewsDir 84*
Madison County Eagle - *See* Green Publishers Inc.
Madison County Herald [of Mississippi Publishers Corp.] - Canton, MS - *AyerDirPub 83; Ed&PubIntYB 82; NewsDir 84*
Madison County History Association - Sheridan, MT - *BoPubDir 4, 5*
Madison County Newsweek - Richmond, KY - *Ed&PubIntYB 82*
Madison County Post/Advertiser, The - Richmond, KY - *Ed&PubIntYB 82*
Madison County Record - Huntsville, AL - *AyerDirPub 83*
Madison County Record - Madison, AL - *BaconPubCkNews 84; Ed&PubIntYB 82; NewsDir 84*
Madison County Telephone Co. Inc. - Huntsville, AR - *TelDir&BG 83-84*
Madison Courier - Madison, IN - *BaconPubCkNews 84; Ed&PubIntYB 82; NewsDir 84*
Madison Eagle - Madison, NJ - *AyerDirPub 83; Ed&PubIntYB 82*
Madison Enterprise-Recorder - Madison, FL - *BaconPubCkNews 84; Ed&PubIntYB 82*
Madison Fielding Inc. - Los Angeles, CA - *DirPRFirms 83*
Madison-Florham Park Eagle - Madison, NJ - *BaconPubCkNews 84; NewsDir 84*
Madison International Group Inc. - New York, NY - *Tel&CabFB 84C*
Madison Journal - Madison Parish, LA - *Ed&PubIntYB 82*
Madison Journal - Tallulah, LA - *AyerDirPub 83*
Madison Lake Region Times - Madison Lake, MN - *BaconPubCkNews 84*
Madison Leader [of Hunter Publishing Inc.] - Madison, SD - *BaconPubCkNews 84; Ed&PubIntYB 82; NewsDir 84*
Madison Madisonian - Madison, GA - *BaconPubCkNews 84; NewsDir 84*
Madison Magazine - Madison, WI - *MagDir 84; WritMar 84*
Madison MDS Co. - New York, NY - *Tel&CabFB 84C*

Madison Messenger - Madison, NC - *BaconPubCkNews 84; NewsDir 84*
Madison News - Madison, KS - *BaconPubCkNews 84; Ed&PubIntYB 82*
Madison Pacific Inc. - Sherman Oaks, CA - *Tel&CabFB 84C*
Madison Press - London, OH - *AyerDirPub 83; Ed&PubIntYB 82*
Madison Press Books - Toronto, ON, Canada - *LitMarPl 83, 84*
Madison Press Connection [of Photo/Type Co-Op] - Madison, WI - *NewsDir 84*
Madison Press, The - Madison, OH - *Ed&PubIntYB 82*
Madison Research Associates - New York, NY - *IntDirMarRes 83*
Madison Research Inc. - Danbury, CT - *IntDirMarRes 83*
Madison Review, The - Madison, WI - *LitMag&SmPr 83-84*
Madison Square Garden Network [of Gulf & Western] - New York, NY - *CabTVPrDB 83; Tel&CabFB 84C*
Madison Square Garden Television - New York, NY - *TelAl 83, 84*
Madison Star-Mail - Madison, NE - *BaconPubCkNews 84; Ed&PubIntYB 82*
Madison Symphony Orchestra League [Aff. of Madison Civic Music Association] - Madison, WI - *BoPubDir 4, 5*
Madison Telephone Co. - Hamel, IL - *TelDir&BG 83-84*
Madison Telephone Co. Inc. - Madison, KS - *TelDir&BG 83-84*
Madison Type - New York, NY - *MagIndMarPl 82-83*
Madison Weekly Herald - Madison, IN - *BaconPubCkNews 84*
Madison West Advertising & Marketing Associates Inc. [Subs. of Shiffman/Fergusson/Stone Advertising Inc.] - Ft. Lee, NJ - *StaDirAdAg 2-84*
Madison Western Guard - Madison, MN - *BaconPubCkNews 84; NewsDir 84*
Madison Wisconsin State Journal - Madison, WI - *NewsDir 84*
Madisonian - Madison, GA - *AyerDirPub 83; Ed&PubIntYB 82*
Madisonian - Winterset, IA - *AyerDirPub 83*
Madisonian - Virginia City, MT - *AyerDirPub 83; Ed&PubIntYB 82*
Madison's Canadian Lumber - Vancouver, BC, Canada - *BoPubDir 5*
Madisonville Cablevision [of American TV & Communications Corp.] - Madisonville, KY - *BrCabYB 84; Tel&CabFB 84C*
Madisonville Messenger - Madisonville, KY - *BaconPubCkNews 84; NewsDir 84*
Madisonville Meteor - Madisonville, TX - *BaconPubCkNews 84; Ed&PubIntYB 82*
Madisonville Tri-County Observer - Madisonville, TN - *BaconPubCkNews 84; NewsDir 84*
Madoc Review - Madoc, ON, Canada - *AyerDirPub 83*
Madras Pioneer [of Eagle Newspapers Inc.] - Madras, OR - *BaconPubCkNews 84; Ed&PubIntYB 82; NewsDir 84*
Madrid Music Co. - Bonita, CA - *BillIntBG 83-84*
Madrid Register-News - Madrid, IA - *BaconPubCkNews 84; Ed&PubIntYB 82*
Madrona Publishers Inc. - Seattle, WA - *BoPubDir 4 Sup, 5; LitMarPl 83, 84; WritMar 84*
Madwest Software - Athens, GA - *MicrocomMPl 84*
Madwest Software - Madison, WI - *MicrocomMPl 83*
Madzar Corp. - Fremont, CA - *DataDirSup 7-83*
Maelstrom Press - Long Beach, CA - *BoPubDir 4, 5*
Maelstrom Press - Cape Elizabeth, ME - *LitMag&SmPr 83-84*
Maelstrom Review - Cape Elizabeth, ME - *LitMag&SmPr 83-84*
Maenad: A Women's Literary Journal - Gloucester, MA - *LitMag&SmPr 83-84*
Maercklein Advertising Inc. [Div. of Conrad C. Kaminski & Associates Inc.] - Milwaukee, WI - *StaDirAdAg 2-84*
Maescher Advertising Inc., Al - Clayton, MO - *StaDirAdAg 2-84*
Maezon [Div. of Konan Corp.] - Phoenix, AZ - *MicrocomMPl 84*
Mafdet Press [Aff. of W. D. Firestone Press] - Springfield, MO - *BoPubDir 4, 5*
Mafex Associates Inc. - Johnstown, PA - *AvMarPl 83; LitMarPl 83, 84; MicrocomMPl 84*
Mag-a-Book - New York, NY - *MagIndMarPl 82-83*
Mag City - New York, NY - *LitMag&SmPr 83-84*
MAG Inc. - Athens, GA - *MicrocomMPl 84*
MAG Software Inc. - Canoga Park, CA - *MicrocomMPl 84*
Mag-Tek Inc. - Carson, CA - *DataDirSup 7-83*
Magary Editorial/Design, Alan - San Francisco, CA - *LitMarPl 83*
Magatar [of Programmer's Institute] - Chapel Hill, NC - *MicrocomMPl 84*
Magazine [of Beyond Baroque Foundation Publications] - Venice, CA - *LitMag&SmPr 83-84*
Magazine Age - New York, NY - *BaconPubCkMag 84; MagIndMarPl 82-83; WritMar 84*
Magazine & Bookseller [of North American Publishing] - New York, NY - *BaconPubCkMag 84; LitMarPl 83, 84; MagDir 84; MagIndMarPl 82-83*
Magazine Antiques, The [of Straight Enterprises Inc.] - New York, NY - *MagDir 84; MagIndMarPl 82-83; WritMar 84*
Magazine ASAP [of Information Access Co.] - Belmont, CA - *DataDirOnSer 84; DirOnDB Spring 84*
Magazine Buyers' Service - Stamford, CT - *MagIndMarPl 82-83*
Magazine Center - New York, NY - *ProGuPRSer 4*
Magazine Index [of Information Access Co.] - Menlo Park, CA - *CompReadDB 82; DataDirOnSer 84; DBBus 82; DirOnDB Spring 84; EISS 83; OnBibDB 3*
Magazine of Bank Administration [of Bank Administration Institute] - Arlington Heights, IL - *MagDir 84*
Magazine of Fantasy & Science Fiction, The - Cornwall, CT - *MagDir 84; MagIndMarPl 82-83*
Magazine of New York Business - New York, NY - *MagDir 84*
Magazine of Sigma Chi, The - Evanston, IL - *BaconPubCkMag 84; MagDir 84*
Magazine of the Midlands - Omaha, NE - *MagIndMarPl 82-83*
Magazine Publishers Association Inc. - New York, NY - *BrCabYB 84*
Magazine Subscription Service - Worcester, MA - *MagIndMarPl 82-83*
Magazine Supply House Inc. - Worcester, MA - *MagIndMarPl 82-83*
Magazine Telephone Co. - Magazine, AR - *TelDir&BG 83-84*
Magazine, The - San Francisco, CA - *MagIndMarPl 82-83*
Magazine, The - St. Louis, MO - *MagIndMarPl 82-83*
Magazine, The - Dayton, OH - *WritMar 84*
Magazines for Industry Inc. - New York, NY - *MagIndMarPl 82-83*
Magder Studios - Toronto, ON, Canada - *LitMarPl 83*
Magee Courier - Magee, MS - *BaconPubCkNews 84; Ed&PubIntYB 82*
Magee Inc., John [Aff. of Buttonwood Securities Corp. of Massachusetts] - Boston, MA - *BoPubDir 4, 5*
Maggie's Place [of Pikes Peak Library District] - Colorado Springs, CO - *EISS 83*
Magi Books Inc. - Albany, NY - *BoPubDir 4, 5*
Magic Carpet Software - Phoenix, AZ - *MicrocomMPl 83*
Magic Changes - Chicago, IL - *LitMag&SmPr 83-84*
Magic Circle Press - Weston, CT - *LitMag&SmPr 83-84*
Magic City Free Press - Moberly, MO - *AyerDirPub 83*
Magic Key - Baltimore, MD - *Tel&CabFB 84C*
Magic Lantern - Madison, WI - *MicrocomMPl 83*
Magic Ltd./Lloyd E. Jones - Oakland, CA - *BoPubDir 4, 5; LitMarPl 84*
Magic Theatre Inc. - San Francisco, CA - *WritMar 84*
Magic Touch Music - *See* Delvy Enterprises Inc., Richard
Magic Typewriter, The - Brooklyn, NY - *LitMarPl 83, 84*
Magic Unicorn Publications - Fairfax, CA - *BoPubDir 4, 5*
Magic Valley Cable Vision Inc. - Aberdeen, ID - *BrCabYB 84*
Magic Valley Cable Vision Inc. [of King Videocable Co.] - Twin Falls, ID - *BrCabYB 84*
Magic Window Cable TV Inc. [of McLoud Telecommunications Inc.] - Harrah, OK - *Tel&CabFB 84C*
Magicable - New York, NY - *CabTVPrDB 83*
Magical Blend - San Francisco, CA - *ArtMar 84; LitMag&SmPr 83-84; WritMar 84*
Magickal Childe Inc. - New York, NY - *BoPubDir 4, 5*
Magicom - Minneapolis, MN - *Tel&CabFB 84C*
Magid Associates Inc., Frank N. - Marion, IA - *BrCabYB 84; IntDirMarRes 83; Tel&CabFB 84C*
Magid Inc., Lee - Malibu, CA - *AvMarPl 83; BillIntBG 83-84*
Magna Carta Book Co. - Baltimore, MD - *BoPubDir 4, 5*
Magna Mundi Music Co. Inc. - *See* Print Music Co. Inc.
Magna-Tech Electronic Co. Inc. - New York, NY - *AvMarPl 83*
Magna Times [of Magna Valley View News] - Magna, UT - *AyerDirPub 83; Ed&PubIntYB 82; NewsDir 84*

Magna Times [of Roy Printing Co. Newspapers] - Roy, UT - *NewsDir 84*
Magnagraph Magnetic Visual Control Systems [Div. of Astro Mobile Products Corp.] - Long Island City, NY - *AvMarPl 83*
Magnamusic Distributors Inc. - Sharon, CT - *BoPubDir 4, 5*
Magnaplan Corp. [Div. of NIL] - Champlain, NY - *AvMarPl 83*
Magnasync/Moviola Corp. [Subs. of Craig Corp.] - North Hollywood, CA - *AvMarPl 83*
Magnaverde Productions [Div. of Spanish International Network] - New York, NY - *Tel&CabFB 84C*
Magnavox - *See* NAP Consumer Electronics
Magnavox CATV Systems Inc. [of North American Philips Corp.] - Manlius, NY - *CabTVFinDB 83; HomeVid&CabYB 82-83*
Magnavox Co., The - New York, NY - *TelAl 83*
Magnavox Consumer Electronics Co., The - Ft. Wayne, IN - *TelAl 84*
Magnavox/NAP Consumer Electronics - Knoxville, TN - *BillIntBG 83-84*
Magnes Advertising Inc., William - Washington, DC - *StaDirAdAg 2-84*
Magnes Museum, Judah L. - Berkeley, CA - *BoPubDir 4, 5*
Magnesium Forecasts [of Chase Econometrics/Interactive Data Corp.] - Waltham, MA - *DataDirOnSer 84*
Magnesium Forecasts - Bala Cynwyd, PA - *DirOnDB Spring 84*
Magnet Sales & Manufacturing Co. - Santa Monica, CA - *AvMarPl 83*
Magnetic Media - Farmingdale, NY - *AvMarPl 83*
Magnetic Memory Corp. - Berkeley, CA - *MicrocomMPl 84*
Magnetic Shield Div. [of Perfection Mica Co.] - Bensenville, IL - *WhoWMicrocom 83*
Magnetic Tape Drives [of GML Corp.] - Lexington, MA - *CompReadDB 82*
Magnetic Technologies Inc. - Rockville Centre, NY - *DirInfWP 82*
Magnetix Corp. - Winter Garden, FL - *WritMar 84*
Magno - New York, NY - *AvMarPl 83*
Magnolia Banner-News - Magnolia, AR - *BaconPubCkNews 84; NewsDir 84*
Magnolia Cable TV [of Big Spring Cable TV] - Magnolia, AR - *BrCabYB 84*
Magnolia Clipping Service - Jackson, MS - *ProGuPRSer 4*
Magnolia Gazette - Magnolia, MS - *BaconPubCkNews 84; Ed&PubIntYB 82*
Magnolia Microsystems - Seattle, WA - *MicrocomMPl 83, 84*
Magnolia News - Seattle, WA - *AyerDirPub 83*
Magnolia Press - Dallas, TX - *BoPubDir 5*
Magnolia Press - Houston, TX - *BoPubDir 4*
Magnolia Publishers - Baldwyn, MS - *BoPubDir 4, 5*
Magnolia-Waldo Cable TV [of TCA Cable TV Inc.] - Magnolia, AR - *Tel&CabFB 84C*
Magnum Computer Corp. - Tucson, AZ - *ADAPSOMemDir 83-84*
Magnum Photos Inc. - New York, NY - *Ed&PubIntYB 82; LitMarPl 83, 84*
Magnum Records Inc. - Metairie, LA - *BillIntBG 83-84*
Magnussen Advertising Agency Inc. - Ft. Worth, TX - *StaDirAdAg 2-84*
Magreeable Software Inc. - Plymouth, MN - *MicrocomMPl 84; MicrocomSwDir 1*
Maguey Press/Friends of Tucson Public Library, The - Tucson, AZ - *LitMag&SmPr 83-84*
Magus Cartoons - Vancouver, BC, Canada - *BoPubDir 4 Sup, 5*
Magyar Elet - Toronto, ON, Canada - *Ed&PubIntYB 82*
Magyar Herald - New Brunswick, NJ - *Ed&PubIntYB 82*
Magyar Hirdeto-Sajtofigyelo - Budapest, Hungary - *ProGuPRSer 4*
Magyar Hirlap - Toronto, ON, Canada - *Ed&PubIntYB 82*
Magyar Naplo - Toronto, ON, Canada - *Ed&PubIntYB 82*
Magyarsag - Pittsburgh, PA - *Ed&PubIntYB 82*
Mahaffey Enterprises Inc. - Springfield, MO - *BrCabYB 84*
Mahanoy & Mahantango Telephone Co. - Herndon, PA - *TelDir&BG 83-84*
Mahaska Cablevision [of McDonald Group] - Oskaloosa, IA - *Tel&CabFB 84C*
Maher, David W. - Chicago, IL - *ADAPSOMemDir 83-84*
Maher/Greenwich Inc. - Greenwich, CT - *StaDirAdAg 2-84*
Maher/Hartford Inc. - Hartford, CT - *StaDirAdAg 2-84*
Maher Inc. - Hartford, CT - *AdAge 3-28-84; StaDirAdAg 2-84*
Maher Kaump & Clark - Hollywood, CA - *StaDirAdAg 2-84*
Maheux, Guy - Montreal, PQ, Canada - *BoPubDir 4 Sup, 5*
Mahnomen Pioneer - Mahnomen, MN - *BaconPubCkNews 84; Ed&PubIntYB 82*
Mahomet Citizen, The - Mahomet, IL - *Ed&PubIntYB 82*
Mahon, Ronald A. - *See* Video Link Ltd.
Mahoney & Associates Inc., H. E. - New York, NY - *StaDirAdAg 2-84*
Mahoney & Mitchell Inc. - Philadelphia, PA - *DirPRFirms 83*
Mahoney Associates, Thomas P. - Rockford, IL - *MagIndMarPl 82-83*
Mahoney/Wasserman & Associates - Los Angeles, CA - *DirPRFirms 83*
Mahoning Valley Cablevision Associates [of Tele-Communications Inc.] - Warren, OH - *BrCabYB 84; Tel&CabFB 84C*
Mahoning Valley Cablevision Inc. [of Tele-Communications Inc.] - Cortland, OH - *Tel&CabFB 84C*
Mahoning Valley Cablevision Inc. - Girard, OH - *BrCabYB 84*
Mahopac Press - Mahopac, NY - *AyerDirPub 83; Ed&PubIntYB 82*
Mahopac Press - *See* Gateway Papers
MAI/Basic Four Business Products Corp. - Albuquerque, NM - *MicrocomMPl 84; MicrocomSwDir 1*
MAI-Sorbus Service Div. [of Management Assistance Inc.] - Frazer, PA - *WhoWMicrocom 83*
Maiden Books [Aff. of The Maiden Co. Inc.] - Newark, NJ - *BoPubDir 4, 5*
Maiden Music - Trevilians, VA - *BillIntBG 83-84*
Maiden Times - Maiden, NC - *BaconPubCkNews 84*
Maiden Voyage Records - San Fernando, CA - *BillIntBG 83-84*
Maidstone Mirror, The - Maidstone, SK, Canada - *Ed&PubIntYB 82*
Maier Advertising Inc. - Farmington, CT - *StaDirAdAg 2-84*
Maier-Hancock [SU J & R Film Co. Inc.] - Hollywood, CA - *AvMarPl 83*
Maierhofer Stations, Louis J. - Altoona, PA - *BrCabYB 84*
Mail - Winslow, AZ - *AyerDirPub 83*
Mail - Sheldon, IA - *AyerDirPub 83*
Mail - Hagerstown, MD - *AyerDirPub 83*
Mail - Marshfield, MO - *AyerDirPub 83*
Mail - Nevada, MO - *AyerDirPub 83*
Mail - Phillipsburg, MT - *AyerDirPub 83*
Mail - Catskill, NY - *AyerDirPub 83*
Mail - Myrtle Creek, OR - *AyerDirPub 83; Ed&PubIntYB 82*
Mail - Stayton, OR - *AyerDirPub 83*
Mail [of Harte-Hanks Communications] - Anderson, SC - *NewsDir 84*
Mail - Merkel, TX - *AyerDirPub 83*
Mail - Charleston, WV - *AyerDirPub 83*
Mail - Mt. Horeb, WI - *AyerDirPub 83*
Mail - Drumheller, AB, Canada - *AyerDirPub 83*
Mail-Dairy Panel - Cranford, NJ - *IntDirMarRes 83*
Mail-Journal [of The Papers Inc.] - Milford, IN - *AyerDirPub 83; NewsDir 84*
Mail-Journal, The - Syracuse, IN - *Ed&PubIntYB 82*
Mail Marketing Inc. - Haworth, NJ - *MagIndMarPl 82-83*
Mail Marketing Materials Inc. - South Bend, IN - *LitMarPl 83, 84*
Mail Order Business - Welch, WV - *MagDir 84*
Mail Order Buying Guide, The [Div. of American Theatre Press Inc.] - New York, NY - *DirMarMP 83*
Mail Order Digest - Los Angeles, CA - *MagIndMarPl 82-83*
Mail Order Product Newsletter - Goreville, IL - *BaconPubCkMag 84*
Mail Order USA - Washington, DC - *BoPubDir 4, 5*
Mail-Star, The - Halifax, NS, Canada - *AyerDirPub 83; BaconPubCkNews 84; Ed&PubIntYB 82*
Mail Trade Enterprises - New Berlin, WI - *BoPubDir 4 Sup, 5*
Mail Tribune, The - Medford, OR - *AyerDirPub 83*
Mailbag Inc. - Philadelphia, PA - *LitMarPl 83, 84; MagIndMarPl 82-83*
MAILeader - Valley Stream, NY - *AyerDirPub 83*
Mailhandler, The - Washington, DC - *NewsDir 84*

Mailing Data Services East Inc. - Waldorf, MD - *MagIndMarPl 82-83*
Mailing List Marketing [Subs. of International Thomson] - Oradell, NJ - *DirMarMP 83*
Mailmen Inc. - New York, NY - *MagIndMarPl 82-83*
Mailnet [of Edunet] - Princeton, NJ - *TeleSy&SerDir 7-83*
Maimes, Steven L. - Oakland, CA - *BoPubDir 4, 5*
Main Economic Indicators/Quarterly National Accounts [of ADP Network Services] - Ann Arbor, MI - *DataDirOnSer 84*
Main Electronics Inc. - Wichita, KS - *WhoWMicrocom 83*
Main Hurdman - New York, NY - *TeleSy&SerDir 7-83*
Main Kanning Systems Inc. - Columbus, OH - *MicrocomMPl 84*
Main Line Chronicle - Ardmore, PA - *AyerDirPub 83*
Main Line Chronicle, The - Lower Merion Township, PA - *Ed&PubIntYB 82*
Main Line Times - Ardmore, PA - *AyerDirPub 83; Ed&PubIntYB 82*
Main Stream Music - *See* Hope Publishing Co.
Main Street - Zionsville, IN - *AyerDirPub 83*
Main Street Press - Patchogue, NY - *AyerDirPub 83; Ed&PubIntYB 82*
Main Street Press [of Wooster Republican Printing Co.] - Rittman, OH - *NewsDir 84*
Main Street Press, The - Pittstown, NJ - *LitMarPl 83, 84*
Main Street Records & Tapes - New York, NY - *BillIntBG 83-84*
Main Track Publications - Studio City, CA - *LitMag&SmPr 83-84*
Main Trend - New York, NY - *LitMag&SmPr 83-84*
MainData - Portland, ME - *MicrocomMPl 83, 84*
Maine Antique Digest Inc. - Waldoboro, ME - *BoPubDir 4, 5*
Maine Broadcasting System - Portland, ME - *BrCabYB 84; Tel&CabFB 84S*
Maine Cable Co. - Milo, ME - *Tel&CabFB 84C p.1688*
Maine Cable Television Inc. [of A-R Telecommunications] - Dexter, ME - *BrCabYB 84*
Maine Data & Financial Systems Inc. - Orland, ME - *MicrocomMPl 84*
Maine Dept. of Human Services (Bureau of Health Planning) - Augusta, ME - *BoPubDir 5*
Maine Dept. of Manpower Affairs (Research Div.) - Augusta, ME - *BoPubDir 5*
Maine Historical Society - Portland, ME - *BoPubDir 4, 5*
Maine Labor News - Brewer, ME - *NewsDir 84*
Maine Life - Freedom, ME - *ArtMar 84; MagDir 84; WritMar 84*
Maine Line Co. - Rockport, ME - *WritMar 84*
Maine Manufacturing Co. - Nashua, NH - *WhoWMicrocom 83*
Maine Microband - New York, NY - *Tel&CabFB 84C*
Maine Motor Transport News - Hallowell, ME - *BaconPubCkMag 84; MagDir 84*
Maine-New Hampshire-Vermont Beverage Journal [of New England Beverage Publications Inc.] - Avon, MA - *BaconPubCkMag 84; MagDir 84*
Maine News Service Inc. - Augusta, ME - *BrCabYB 84*
Maine Sportsman, The - Augusta, ME - *BaconPubCkMag 84; WritMar 84*
Maine State Grocers Bulletin [of Maine State Grocers Association Inc.] - Portland, ME - *MagDir 84*
Maine State Museum Publications - Augusta, ME - *BoPubDir 4, 5*
Maine Sunday Telegram [of Guy Gannett Publishing Co.] - Portland, ME - *AyerDirPub 83; Ed&PubIntYB 82; LitMarPl 83, 84; NewsDir 84*
Maine Teacher, The - Augusta, ME - *BaconPubCkMag 84*
Maine Times [of Peter Cox Maine Times Inc.] - Topsham, ME - *AyerDirPub 83; BaconPubCkNews 84; Ed&PubIntYB 82; NewsDir 84*
Maine Townsman [of Maine Municipal Association] - Augusta, ME - *BaconPubCkMag 84; MagDir 84*
Maine Trail, The - Augusta, ME - *BaconPubCkMag 84; MagDir 84*
Mainespring Press [Aff. of Maine Writers Workshop] - Stonington, ME - *BoPubDir 4, 5; LitMag&SmPr 83-84*
Mainland Journal - Pleasantville, NJ - *AyerDirPub 83; Ed&PubIntYB 82*
Mainline Modeler - Edmonds, WA - *BaconPubCkMag 84*
Mainliner - New York, NY - *MagDir 84*
Mainliner - Portage, PA - *AyerDirPub 83*
Mainly Marketing [Aff. of Schoonmaker Associates] - Coram, NY - *BoPubDir 4, 5*
Mainspring Advertising Inc. - *See* WLK Cos. Inc.
Mainspring Music Corp. - *See* Gallico Music Corp., Al
Mainspring Watchworks Music - San Francisco, CA - *BillIntBG 83-84*
Mainstay Music Inc. - *See* Gallico Music Corp., Al
Mainstream - Sacramento, CA - *MagIndMarPl 82-83*
Mainstream - San Diego, CA - *BaconPubCkMag 84*
Mainstream News, The - Northampton, MA - *DirOnDB Spring 84*
Maintenance & Modernization Supervisor - Olney, MD - *BaconPubCkMag 84*
Maintenance Automation Corp. - Hallandale, FL - *MicrocomMPl 84*
Maintenance Supplies - New York, NY - *BaconPubCkMag 84; MagDir 84*
Mainville, Richard - Harrisburg, OR - *LitMarPl 84*
Maish Co., The Jay H. - Marion, OH - *StaDirAdAg 2-84*
Maize: Notebooks of Xicano Art & Literature - San Diego, CA - *LitMag&SmPr 83-84*
Maize Press [Aff. of Centro Cultural de la Raza] - San Diego, CA - *BoPubDir 4, 5; LitMag&SmPr 83-84*
Maize This Week - Maize, KS - *Ed&PubIntYB 82*
Maizner & Franklin Inc. - Ft. Lauderdale, FL - *DirPRFirms 83*
Majega Records - Claremont, CA - *BillIntBG 83-84*
Majers Corp. - Omaha, NE - *HBIndAd&MS 82-83*
Majestic Advertising Agency Inc. - Pewaukee, WI - *StaDirAdAg 2-84*
Majestic Industries - Teterboro, NJ - *DirInfWP 82*
Majewski, Kasmir - Wellsburg, WV - *Tel&CabFB 84C p.1688*
Major Label Record Co. - Worthington, OH - *BillIntBG 83-84*
Major League Baseball Productions - New York, NY - *Tel&CabFB 84C*
Major News Service - Chesterfield, MO - *Ed&PubIntYB 82; LitMarPl 83*
Major News Service - New Bremen, OH - *LitMarPl 84*
Major Pacific Records/Domino Inc. - Orange, CA - *BillIntBG 83-84*
Major Press Inc. [Subs. of Metro Associated Services Inc.] - New York, NY - *LitMarPl 83, 84; MagIndMarPl 82-83*
Major Recording Co. - Waynesboro, VA - *BillIntBG 83-84*
Majors Co., J. A. - Irving, TX - *LitMarPl 83, 84*
Majors Scientific Books Inc. - Irving, TX - *LitMarPl 83*
Majors Scientific Books Inc. (Journals Div.) - Irving, TX - *MagIndMarPl 82-83*
Makapu'u Press - Honolulu, HI - *BoPubDir 4, 5*
Makara, Frank - Jericho, NY - *BoPubDir 4, 5*
Make It with Leather [Aff. of Tandycrafts Inc.] - Ft. Worth, TX - *ArtMar 84; BaconPubCkMag 84; BoPubDir 4 Sup, 5; MagDir 84; MagIndMarPl 82-83; WritMar 84*
Makedonska Tribuna - Indianapolis, IN - *AyerDirPub 83; Ed&PubIntYB 82; NewsDir 84*
Makepeace/Barry Books Ltd. - Chicago, IL - *BoPubDir 4, 5*
Makepeace Colony Inc. - Stevens Point, WI - *BoPubDir 4, 5*
Making It! - New York, NY - *BaconPubCkMag 84; MagDir 84; MagIndMarPl 82-83; WritMar 84*
Mako Data Products - Anaheim, CA - *MicrocomMPl 83, 84*
Makovsky & Co. Inc. - New York, NY - *DirPRFirms 83*
Makrotest - *See* Cegmark International Inc.
Malaco Music Co. - Jackson, MS - *BillIntBG 83-84*
Malaco Records - Jackson, MS - *BillIntBG 83-84*
Malad City Idaho Enterprise - Malad City, ID - *BaconPubCkNews 84*
Malaga, Rose Colombo - Babylon, NY - *BoPubDir 4, 5*
Malahat Review, The [of The University of Victoria] - Victoria, BC, Canada - *LitMag&SmPr 83-84; WritMar 84*
Malakoff News [of Community Information Center Inc.] - Malakoff, TX - *Ed&PubIntYB 82; NewsDir 84*
Malakoff News - *See* Community Information Center Inc.
Malarkey-Taylor Associates - Washington, DC - *CabTVFinDB 83*
Malave, George - New York, NY - *MagIndMarPl 82-83*
Malaysian Rubber Bureau, U.S.A. - Washington, DC - *BoPubDir 4 Sup, 5*
MALCO Systems - Owing Mills, MD - *DataDirSup 7-83*
Malcolm & Associates Inc., R. - Evansville, IN - *StaDirAdAg 2-84*
Malcolm-Howard - Chicago, IL - *TelAl 83, 84*

Malcolm Music Ltd. - *See* Shawnee Press Inc.
Malcolm Video Services, Charles - Costa Mesa, CA - *AvMarPl 83*
Maldeau Graphic Designer, Michele - New York, NY - *MagIndMarPl 82-83*
Malden Evening News - Malden, MA - *NewsDir 84*
Malden News - Malden, MA - *BaconPubCkNews 84; LitMarPl 83, 84*
Malden Press-Merit - Malden, MO - *BaconPubCkNews 84; Ed&PubIntYB 82; NewsDir 84*
Maledicta Press [Aff. of Maledicta: The International Research Center for Verbal Aggression Inc.] - Waukesha, WI - *BoPubDir 4, 5; LitMag&SmPr 83-84*
Maledicta: The International Journal of Verbal Aggression - Waukesha, WI - *LitMag&SmPr 83-84*
Malek Group - New York, NY - *AdAge 3-28-84; StaDirAdAg 2-84*
Maler Inc., Roger - Arlington, NJ - *StaDirAdAg 2-84*
Maleson Advertising Inc. - Owings Mills, MD - *StaDirAdAg 2-84*
Malheur Enterprise - Vale, OR - *AyerDirPub 83; Ed&PubIntYB 82*
Malheur Home Telephone Co. - Ontario, OR - *TelDir&BG 83-84*
Malibu Electronics Corp. [Subs. of Datametrics Corp.] - Westlake Village, CA - *WhoWMicrocom 83*
Malibu Surfside News - Malibu, CA - *BaconPubCkNews 84; Ed&PubIntYB 82; NewsDir 84*
Malibu Times - Malibu, CA - *AyerDirPub 83; BaconPubCkNews 84; NewsDir 84*
Malini - Claremont, CA - *WritMar 84*
Malki Museum Press - Banning, CA - *BoPubDir 4, 5*
Malkin Public Relations, Seymour F. - Washington Township, NJ - *DirPRFirms 83*
Mall Surveys Inc. - Englewood Cliffs, NJ - *IntDirMarRes 83*
Mallama Press - Houston, TX - *BoPubDir 4, 5; LitMag&SmPr 83-84*
Mallard Music - *See* Kicking Mule Publishing Inc.
Mallof, Abruzino & Nash Marketing - Lombard, IL - *StaDirAdAg 2-84*
Mallon Inc., Irv - Lexington, NY - *MagIndMarPl 82-83*
Mallon Inc., Peter F. - Long Island City, NY - *LitMarPl 83, 84*
Mallory Factor Associates Inc. - *See* Factor Associates Inc., Mallory
Malloy Lithographing Inc. - Ann Arbor, MI - *LitMarPl 83, 84; MagIndMarPl 82-83*
Malmo Advertising Inc., John - Memphis, TN - *AdAge 3-28-84; StaDirAdAg 2-84*
Maloff, Abruzino & Nash - Lombard, IL - *AdAge 3-28-84*
Malone - Akron, OH - *AdAge 3-28-84; StaDirAdAg 2-84*
Malone/Dill - Charlotte, NC - *StaDirAdAg 2-84*
Malone Evening Telegram - Malone, NY - *NewsDir 84*
Malone NewChannels [of NewChannels Corp.] - Malone, NY - *BrCabYB 84; Tel&CabFB 84C*
Malone Public Relations - Akron, OH - *DirPRFirms 83*
Malone Telegram - Malone, NY - *BaconPubCkNews 84; Ed&PubIntYB 82*
Malpractice Reporter, The - New York, NY - *MagDir 84*
Malrite Communications Group - Cleveland, OH - *BrCabYB 84; Tel&CabFB 84S*
Malta Cable TV - Malta, MT - *Tel&CabFB 84C*
Malta Phillips County News - Malta, MT - *BaconPubCkNews 84*
Malvern Cable TV [of TCA Cable TV Inc.] - Malvern, AR - *BrCabYB 84; Tel&CabFB 84C*
Malvern Community News [of Alliance Publishing Co.] - Malvern, OH - *Ed&PubIntYB 82; NewsDir 84*
Malvern Daily Record [of Record Publications Inc.] - Malvern, AR - *AyerDirPub 83; BaconPubCkNews 84; Ed&PubIntYB 82; NewsDir 84*
Malvern Leader - Malvern, IA - *BaconPubCkNews 84; Ed&PubIntYB 82*
Malvern Meteor-Journal - Malvern, AR - *BaconPubCkNews 84*
Malvern News - *See* Alliance Publishing Co.
MAM Corp. - Los Angeles, CA - *BillIntBG 83-84*
Mamaroneck Times [of Westchester Rockland Newspapers] - Mamaroneck, NY - *NewsDir 84*
Mamaroneck Times - *See* Westchester-Rockland Newspapers
Mamaroneck Times, The - White Plains, NY - *Ed&PubIntYB 82*
Mamlish Records - New York, NY - *BillIntBG 83-84*
Mammoth Electric Cable TV [of Mammoth Electric Corp.] - Mammoth Lakes, CA - *BrCabYB 84; Tel&CabFB 84C*
Mammoth Lakes Mono Herald/Chronicle - *See* Chalfant Press Publications
Mammoth Spring Democrat - Mammoth Spring, AR - *Ed&PubIntYB 82*
Mamou Acadian Press - Mamou, LA - *BaconPubCkNews 84; Ed&PubIntYB 82; NewsDir 84*
Man-Computer Systems Inc. - Jamaica, NY - *MagIndMarPl 82-83*
Man-Ken Music Ltd. - Old Westbury, NY - *BillIntBG 83-84*
Man-Nen-Sha Inc. - Osaka, Japan - *StaDirAdAg 2-84*
Man Quin - *See* Beneditti Music, Quint
Man/Society/Technology - Washington, DC - *MagDir 84*
Manage [of United Color Press] - Dayton, OH - *BaconPubCkMag 84; MagDir 84; MagIndMarPl 82-83; WritMar 84*
Management Accountability Group Inc. - Athens, GA - *MicrocomSwDir 1; WhoWMicrocom 83*
Management Accounting [of National Association of Accountants] - New York, NY - *ArtMar 84; BaconPubCkMag 84; MagDir 84; MagIndMarPl 82-83*
Management Advisory Publications - Wellesley Hills, MA - *BoPubDir 4, 5*
Management Analysis & Control Inc. - Auburn, WA - *WhoWMicrocom 83*
Management Analysis by Computer Inc. - Guttenberg, NJ - *DataDirOnSer 84*
Management & Computer Services Inc. [Subs. of Pentamation Enterprises Inc.] - Valley Forge, PA - *DataDirOnSer 84*
Management & Marketing Abstracts [of Pergamon International Information Corp.] - McLean, VA - *DataDirOnSer 84*
Management & Marketing Abstracts [of PIRA] - Leatherhead, England - *DirOnDB Spring 84; OnBibDB 3*
Management & Systems Consultants Inc. - Tucson, AZ - *BoPubDir 4, 5*
Management Assistance Inc. - New York, NY - *DataDirSup 7-83; Datamation 6-83; InfIndMarPl 83; Top100Al 83*
Management Books Institute [of Prentice-Hall Inc.] - Englewood, NJ - *LitMarPl 83, 84*
Management Communications Consultants Inc. - Cincinnati, OH - *ADAPSOMemDir 83-84*
Management Computer Services - Cape Town, South Africa - *ADAPSOMemDir 83-84*
Management Computer Services Inc. - Columbus, OH - *DataDirOnSer 84*
Management Concepts Inc. - Atlanta, GA - *DataDirOnSer 84*
Management Consortium, The - Ft. Lauderdale, FL - *CabTVFinDB 83*
Management Consultants International Inc. - Toronto, ON, Canada - *EISS 83; VideoDir 82-83*
Management Contents [Subs. of Ziff-Davis Publishing Co.] - Northbrook, IL - *BoPubDir 5; CompReadDB 82; DataDirOnSer 84; DBBus 82; DirOnDB Spring 84; EISS 83; InfIndMarPl 83; InfoS 83-84; OnBibDB 3*
Management Contents Data Base - Northbrook, IL - *CompReadDB 82; DataDirOnSer 84*
Management Control Concepts Inc. - Boston, MA - *WhoWMicrocom 83*
Management Control Systems Inc. [Subs. of Informatics Inc.] - Atlanta, GA - *WhoWMicrocom 83*
Management Control Systems Inc. - Ft. Worth, TX - *ADAPSOMemDir 83-84*
Management Data Corp. - Rapid City, SD - *MicrocomMPl 84; MicrocomSwDir 1*
Management Decision Systems - Waltham, MA - *AdAge 5-17-84 p.37; ADAPSOMemDir 83-84; DataDirOnSer 84; HBIndAd&MS 82-83; IntDirMarRes 83*
Management Directions Inc. - Ft. Worth, TX - *StaDirAdAg 2-84*
Management Graphics - Minneapolis, MN - *AvMarPl 83; DataDirSup 7-83*
Management Horizons - Columbus, OH - *BoPubDir 5; IntDirMarRes 83*
Management Information System [of Prince George's County Memorial Library] - Hyattsville, MD - *EISS 83*
Management/Marketing Associates Inc. - Portland, OR - *IntDirMarRes 83*
Management of World Wastes, The - Atlanta, GA - *MagDir 84*

Management Personal Time Network - Cleveland, OH - *Folio 83; MagDir 84*
Management Recruiters of Wall Street - New York, NY - *LitMarPl 83, 84; MagIndMarPl 82-83*
Management Reporting Services Inc. - Denver, CO - *ADAPSOMemDir 83-84*
Management Resources Inc. - New York, NY - *DirMarMP 83; LitMarPl 83, 84*
Management Review [of American Management Associations] - New York, NY - *BaconPubCkMag 84; LitMarPl 84; MagDir 84; MagIndMarPl 82-83*
Management Science [of The Institute of Management Sciences] - Providence, RI - *MagDir 84*
Management Science America - Atlanta, GA - *ADAPSOMemDir 83-84; DataDirSup 7-83; Datamation 6-83; Top100Al 83*
Management Science Associates Inc. - Pittsburgh, PA - *DataDirOnSer 84; EISS 83; IntDirMarRes 83*
Management Sciences Inc. - Albuquerque, NM - *ADAPSOMemDir 83-84*
Management Services - Longview, TX - *MicrocomMPl 83, 84; WhoWMicrocom 83*
Management Software Inc. - Tenafly, NJ - *MicrocomSwDir 1*
Management System for Astronomical Data in Machine-Readable Form [of Academy of Sciences of the USSR] - Moscow, USSR - *EISS 83*
Management Systems Corp. - Salt Lake City, UT - *DataDirOnSer 84; WhoWMicrocom 83*
Management Systems Dept. [of General Physics Corp.] - Columbia, MD - *EISS 5-84 Sup*
Management Systems Engineering - Southfield, MI - *MicrocomSwDir 1*
Management Systems Inc. - Ft. Collins, CO - *WhoWMicrocom 83*
Management Systems Software Inc. - St. Petersburg, FL - *MicrocomMPl 83, 84; MicrocomSwDir 1; WhoWMicrocom 83*
Management Technologies Inc. - Boston, MA - *MicrocomMPl 84*
Management Technology [of International Thomson Tech Information Inc.] - Norwalk, CT - *BaconPubCkMag 84; MicrocomMPl 84*
Management Technology JNCD Inc. - Denver, CO - *MicrocomMPl 83, 84*
Management, The - Aledo, TX - *MicrocomMPl 83, 84*
Management III Music - Los Angeles, CA - *BillIntBG 83-84*
Management Training Systems Inc. - Springfield, VA - *AvMarPl 83*
Management World - Willow Grove, PA - *ArtMar 84; BaconPubCkMag 84; MagIndMarPl 82-83*
Manager Software Products Inc. - Lexington, MA - *ADAPSOMemDir 83-84; DataDirSup 7-83*
Manager's Magazine - Farmington, CT - *MagDir 84*
Manager's Magazine - Hartford, CT - *BaconPubCkMag 84*
Managing [of University of Pittsburgh] - Pittsburgh, PA - *ArtMar 84; WritMar 84*
Managing Change Inc. - Barrington, IL - *HBIndAd&MS 82-83*
Managing Resources for University Libraries [of University of Georgia Libraries] - Athens, GA - *EISS 83*
Managing: The Entrepreneur's Guide To Success - New York, NY - *MagIndMarPl 82-83*
Managing the Leisure Facility - Nashville, TN - *MagIndMarPl 82-83*
Managistics Inc. - New York, NY - *MicrocomSwDir 1*
Managistics Inc. - Woodside, NY - *DataDirOnSer 84*
Manahawkin Beach Haven Times - Manahawkin, NJ - *BaconPubCkNews 84*
Manakin Sabot Gazette of Goochland & Powhatan - Manakin Sabot, VA - *NewsDir 84*
Manas Publications - St. Petersburg, FL - *BoPubDir 4, 5*
Manasett Inc. - *See* Community CATV Corp.
Manasquan Coast Star - Manasquan, NJ - *BaconPubCkNews 84*
Manassas Journal Messenger [of Prince William Publishing Co.] - Manassas, VA - *NewsDir 84*
Manassas Review: Essays on Contemporary American Poetry - Manassas, VA - *LitMag&SmPr 83-84*
Manatt, Phelps, Rothenberg & Tunney - Los Angeles, CA - *BillIntBG 83-84*
Manawa Advocate - Manawa, WI - *BaconPubCkNews 84; Ed&PubIntYB 82*
Manawa Telephone Co. Inc. - Manawa, WI - *TelDir&BG 83-84*
Manbeck Pictures Corp. - Des Moines, IA - *Tel&CabFB 84C*
Manchester Cable TV [of Regional Cable Corp.] - Manchester, MD - *BrCabYB 84; Tel&CabFB 84C*
Manchester Cricket - Manchester, MA - *AyerDirPub 83; BaconPubCkNews 84; Ed&PubIntYB 82*
Manchester Democrat Radio [of Manchester Publishing Co.] - Manchester, IA - *NewsDir 84*
Manchester Democrat Radio - *See* Manchester Publishing Co.
Manchester Democrat, The - Manchester, IA - *Ed&PubIntYB 82*
Manchester Enfield Journal Inquirer - Manchester, CT - *AyerDirPub 83*
Manchester Enterprise - Manchester, KY - *BaconPubCkNews 84; Ed&PubIntYB 82; NewsDir 84*
Manchester Enterprise - Manchester, MI - *BaconPubCkNews 84; Ed&PubIntYB 82*
Manchester-Hartland Telephone Co. - Manchester, MN - *TelDir&BG 83-84*
Manchester Herald [of Scripps League Newspapers Inc.] - Manchester, CT - *AyerDirPub 83; BaconPubCkNews 84; Ed&PubIntYB 82; NewsDir 84*
Manchester Journal - Manchester, VT - *BaconPubCkNews 84; Ed&PubIntYB 82*
Manchester Journal Inquirer - Manchester, CT - *BaconPubCkNews 84; NewsDir 84*
Manchester Journal, The - Manchester, NH - *AyerDirPub 83; Ed&PubIntYB 82*
Manchester Press [of Manchester Publishing Co.] - Manchester, IA - *Ed&PubIntYB 82; NewsDir 84*
Manchester Press - *See* Manchester Publishing Co.
Manchester Public Libraries - Manchester, England - *MicroMarPl 82-83*
Manchester Publishing Co. - Manchester, IA - *BaconPubCkNews 84*
Manchester Signal - Manchester, OH - *BaconPubCkNews 84; NewsDir 84*
Manchester Signal, The - Adams County, OH - *Ed&PubIntYB 82*
Manchester Star-Mercury [of Tri-County Newspaper Inc.] - Manchester, GA - *Ed&PubIntYB 82; NewsDir 84*
Manchester Star-Mercury - *See* Tri-County Newspapers Inc.
Manchester Times - Manchester, TN - *BaconPubCkNews 84; Ed&PubIntYB 82; NewsDir 84*
Manchester Union Leader - Manchester, NH - *Ed&PubIntYB 82; NewsBur 6*
Mancos Times-Tribune [of Cortez Newspapers Inc.] - Mancos, CO - *BaconPubCkNews 84; Ed&PubIntYB 82; NewsDir 84*
Mandabach & Simms - Chicago, IL - *AdAge 3-28-84; ArtMar 84; BrCabYB 84; StaDirAdAg 2-84*
Mandabach & Simms - New York, NY - *StaDirAdAg 2-84*
Mandabach & Simms/Currier - Mansfield, OH - *StaDirAdAg 2-84*
Mandabach & Simms/Pacific - Emeryville, CA - *StaDirAdAg 2-84*
Mandala [Aff. of Association for Holistic Health] - Del Mar, CA - *BoPubDir 5*
Mandala Books - Vershire, VT - *BoPubDir 4, 5*
Mandala International - Nashville, TN - *BillIntBG 83-84*
Mandarin Offset Inc. - New York, NY - *LitMarPl 84*
Mandekic Enterprise, A. V. - Wrightwood, CA - *BoPubDir 5*
Mandel & Co., M. - New York, NY - *StaDirAdAg 2-84*
Mandel, Bette - New York, NY - *LitMarPl 83, 84; MagIndMarPl 82-83*
Mandell Associates, Irving - New York, NY - *DirPRFirms 83*
Mandell Co., Lee - New York, NY - *StaDirAdAg 2-84*
Manderino Associates, Ned - Los Angeles, CA - *BoPubDir 4, 5*
Mandeville Press, The - Hitchin, England - *LitMag&SmPr 83-84*
Mandeville Publishing Associates Inc., J. T. - Ossining, NY - *LitMarPl 83, 84*
Mandeville St. Tammany News-Banner - Mandeville, LA - *NewsDir 84*
Mandorla Publications - Wyong, Australia - *LitMag&SmPr 83-84*
Mandy Advertising [Div. of Shopsmith Inc.] - Dayton, OH - *StaDirAdAg 2-84*
Maneater, The [of University of Missouri-Columbia] - Columbia, MO - *NewsDir 84*
Manessier Publishing Co. - Bryn Mawr, CA - *BoPubDir 4, 5*
Manet Guild [Aff. of Talco Corp.] - Boston, MA - *BoPubDir 4, 5*
Manfield Music - *See* Johnson, Stephen Enoch

Manfile [of University of Manitoba] - Winnipeg, MB, Canada - *EISS 83*
Mangan Books - El Paso, TX - *BoPubDir 4, 5*
Mangan Rains Ginnaven Holcomb - Little Rock, AR - *ArtMar 84; StaDirAdAg 2-84*
Manganese Forecast [of Chase Econometrics/Interactive Data Corp.] - Waltham, MA - *DataDirOnSer 84*
Manganese Forecast - Bala Cynwyd, PA - *DirOnDB Spring 84*
Mangio Professional Communications - San Diego, CA - *StaDirAdAg 2-84*
Mango & Co. - St. Louis, MO - *DirPRFirms 83; StaDirAdAg 2-84*
Mangum Star-News - Mangum, OK - *BaconPubCkNews 84; Ed&PubIntYB 82*
Manhasset Mail [of Carr Communications Inc.] - Manhasset, NY - *AyerDirPub 83; NewsDir 84*
Manhasset Mail - *See* Carr Communications Inc.
Manhasset Press [of Community Newspapers Inc.] - Glen Cove, NY - *AyerDirPub 83; Ed&PubIntYB 82; NewsDir 84*
Manhasset Press - Great Neck, NY - *Ed&PubIntYB 82*
Manhasset Press - *See* Community Newspapers Inc.
Manhattan Advertising Inc. - New York, NY - *StaDirAdAg 2-84*
Manhattan American - Manhattan, IL - *Ed&PubIntYB 82*
Manhattan American - *See* Russell Publications
Manhattan Beach Messenger - *See* Breeze Newspapers
Manhattan Beach News - Hermosa Beach, CA - *NewsDir 84*
Manhattan Beach News - Manhattan Beach, CA - *AyerDirPub 83; Ed&PubIntYB 82*
Manhattan Beach News - *See* Argonaut Newspapers
Manhattan Beach Reporter, The - Manhattan Beach, CA - *NewsDir 84*
Manhattan Business - New York, NY - *BaconPubCkMag 84*
Manhattan Cable TV - Manhattan, IL - *BrCabYB 84; Tel&CabFB 84C*
Manhattan Cable TV Inc. [of American Television & Communications Corp.] - New York, NY - *AvMarPl 83; BrCabYB 84; HomeVid&CabYB 82-83; InterCabHB 3; TelAl 83, 84; Tel&CabFB 84C*
Manhattan Cable TV Services Inc. [of Communications Services Inc.] - Manhattan, KS - *BrCabYB 84; Tel&CabFB 84C*
Manhattan College Engineer - Bronx, NY - *MagDir 84*
Manhattan College Engineer - New York, NY - *BaconPubCkMag 84*
Manhattan Elwood Express - Wilmington, IL - *AyerDirPub 83*
Manhattan Elwood Express - *See* G.W. Communications
Manhattan Grass & Grain - Manhattan, KS - *BaconPubCkNews 84*
Manhattan Ltd. [Aff. of C. C. Cribb World Outreach] - Raleigh, NC - *BoPubDir 4, 5*
Manhattan Mercury [of Seaton Publishing Co. Inc.] - Manhattan, KS - *BaconPubCkNews 84; Ed&PubIntYB 82; NewsDir 84*
Manhattan Messenger - Torrance, CA - *AyerDirPub 83*
Manhattan Review Press - New York, NY - *LitMag&SmPr 83-84*
Manhattan Review, The - New York, NY - *LitMag&SmPr 83-84*
Manhattan Software - Woodland Hills, CA - *MicrocomMPl 84*
Manhattan Theatre Club - New York, NY - *WritMar 84*
Manhattan Video Productions - New York, NY - *AvMarPl 83*
Manheim Advertising Inc. - Beachwood, OH - *BrCabYB 84*
Manheim, Michael Philip - Marblehead, MA - *LitMarPl 83, 84; MagIndMarPl 82-83*
Manheim Stiegel News - Manheim, PA - *Ed&PubIntYB 82*
Manifest [of Alternate Publishing] - San Francisco, CA - *WritMar 84*
Manila Northeast Arkansas Town Crier - Manila, AR - *BaconPubCkNews 84*
Manilla Municipal Cable - Manilla, IA - *Tel&CabFB 84C*
Manilla Telephone Co. - Manilla, IA - *TelDir&BG 83-84*
Manilla Times - Manilla, IA - *BaconPubCkNews 84; Ed&PubIntYB 82*
Manion Public Relations, Waltona - San Diego, CA - *DirPRFirms 83*
Manistee Cable TV Co. [of The Essex Group] - Manistee, MI - *Tel&CabFB 84C*
Manistee County Pioneer Press - Bear Lake, MI - *AyerDirPub 83; Ed&PubIntYB 82*
Manistee News-Advocate - Manistee, MI - *BaconPubCkNews 84; Ed&PubIntYB 82*
Manistique Pioneer Tribune - Manistique, MI - *BaconPubCkNews 84; NewsDir 84*
Manistique TV Cable Co. - Manistique, MI - *BrCabYB 84; Tel&CabFB 84C*
Manitoba Beaver - Beausejour, MB, Canada - *AyerDirPub 83; Ed&PubIntYB 82*
Manitoba Business - Winnipeg, MB, Canada - *ArtMar 84; BaconPubCkMag 84*
Manitoba Co-Operator - Winnipeg, MB, Canada - *BaconPubCkMag 84*
Manitoba Historical Society - Winnipeg, MB, Canada - *BoPubDir 4, 5*
Manitoba Legislative Counsel Office - Winnipeg, MB, Canada - *DataDirOnSer 84*
Manitoba Museum of Man & Nature - Winnipeg, MB, Canada - *BoPubDir 4, 5*
Manitoba Naturalists Society - Winnipeg, MB, Canada - *BoPubDir 4 Sup, 5*
Manitoba School Library Audio Visual Association - Winnipeg, MB, Canada - *BoPubDir 4 Sup, 5*
Manitoba Superintendent of Insurance - Winnipeg, MB, Canada - *BoPubDir 5*
Manitoba Teacher, The - Winnipeg, MB, Canada - *ArtMar 84*
Manitoba Telephone System - Winnipeg, MB, Canada - *VideoDir 82-83*
Manitou - Watrous, SK, Canada - *AyerDirPub 83*
Manitou Springs Pikes Peak Journal - Manitou Springs, CO - *BaconPubCkNews 84; NewsDir 84*
Manitoulin Expositor - Little Current, ON, Canada - *AyerDirPub 83; Ed&PubIntYB 82*
Manitoulin Recorder - Gore Bay, ON, Canada - *AyerDirPub 83; Ed&PubIntYB 82*
Manitowoc Herald Times & Reporter - Manitowoc, WI - *BaconPubCkNews 84; NewsDir 84*
Maniwaki Television Ltee. - Maniwaki, PQ, Canada - *BrCabYB 84*
Mankato Citizens Telephone Co. [Aff. of Mid Communications Inc.] - Mankato, MN - *TelDir&BG 83-84*
Mankato Free Press [of Ottaway Newspapers Inc.] - Mankato, MN - *BaconPubCkNews 84; NewsDir 84*
Mankato Jewell County Record - Mankato, KS - *BaconPubCkNews 84*
Mankind Magazine - Los Angeles, CA - *MagDir 84*
Mankind Publishing Co. - Los Angeles, CA - *BoPubDir 4, 5*
Manko Associates, R. M. - New York, NY - *IntDirMarRes 83*
Mankota Television Co-Operative Association Ltd. - Mankota, SK, Canada - *BrCabYB 84*
ManLabs-NPL Materials Data Bank - Cambridge, MA - *DirOnDB Spring 84*
Manley Data Processing Co. Inc. - Paramus, NJ - *ADAPSOMemDir 83-84*
Manley Film Productions Inc., Ray - Tucson, AZ - *AvMarPl 83*
Manley Photography Inc., Ray - Tucson, AZ - *BoPubDir 4, 5*
Manley Productions Inc. - New York, NY - *TelAl 83, 84*
Manly Signal - Manly, IA - *BaconPubCkNews 84; Ed&PubIntYB 82*
Mann Advertising Inc., David H. - New York, NY - *StaDirAdAg 2-84*
Mann & Associates, Charles - Yucca Valley, CA - *MicrocomMPl 83, 84*
Mann & Associates, Jim - Gales Ferry, CT - *LitMag&SmPr 83-84; MagIndMarPl 82-83*
Mann Endless Cassette Industries - San Francisco, CA - *AvMarPl 83*
Mann Film Laboratories, Hal - Hollywood, CA - *AvMarPl 83*
Mann Inc., R. M. - Armonk, NY - *StaDirAdAg 2-84*
Mann Literary Agency, Carol - Brooklyn, NY - *LitMarPl 83, 84*
Mann Media - High Point, NC - *BrCabYB 84*
Mann Music Corp., Herbie - *See* Mietus Copyright Management
Mann Publishers - Jersey City, NJ - *BoPubDir 4, 5*
Manna - Charlotte, NC - *MicrocomMPl 84*
Manna - Sanford, NC - *LitMag&SmPr 83-84; WritMar 84*
Manna Music & Records - Burbank, CA - *BillIntBG 83-84*
Manna Music Inc. - Burbank, CA - *BillIntBG 83-84*
Manna Publications Inc. - Camas, WA - *BoPubDir 4 Sup, 5*
Manna Publishing - St. Jean, PQ, Canada - *BoPubDir 4, 5*
Manners Co. Inc., David X. - Norwalk, CT - *DirPRFirms 83*

Mannesmann Tally - Kent, WA - *DataDirSup 7-83; Datamation 6-83; DirInfWP 82; InfIndMarPl 83; MicrocomMPl 84; WhoWMicrocom 83*
Mannford News Derrick Journal - Mannford, OK - *BaconPubCkNews 84*
Manning & Associates Inc. - San Diego, CA - *StaDirAdAg 2-84*
Manning, Earl - Roanoke, AL - *Tel&CabFB 84C p.1688*
Manning Monitor - Manning, IA - *BaconPubCkNews 84; Ed&PubIntYB 82*
Manning Municipal Cable TV - Manning, IA - *Tel&CabFB 84C*
Manning, Selvage & Lee Inc. - Washington, DC - *ArtMar 84*
Manning, Selvage & Lee Inc. [Div. of Benton & Bowles] - New York, NY - *ArtMar 84; DirPRFirms 83*
Manning, Selvage & Lee Inc. - *See* Benton & Bowles Inc.
Manning, Selvage & Lee/Mid America [Div. of Benton & Bowles] - Chicago, IL - *ArtMar 84; LitMarPl 83, 84*
Manning Times, The - Manning, SC - *Ed&PubIntYB 82*
Mannington TV Corp. - Mannington, WV - *BrCabYB 84; Tel&CabFB 84C*
Mannmark - Northfield, IL - *DirMarMP 83*
Manoa Press Inc. - Honolulu, HI - *BoPubDir 4 Sup, 5*
Manor Publishing - Staten Island, NY - *BoPubDir 4, 5*
Manpower & Training Research Information System [of U.S. Dept. of Defense] - San Diego, CA - *EISS 7-83 Sup*
Manpower Inc. - Milwaukee, WI - *DirInfWP 82*
Manroot Books - San Francisco, CA - *LitMag&SmPr 83-84*
Man's Magazine - New York, NY - *MagDir 84*
Mansell Publishing - London, England - *MicroMarPl 82-83*
Mansfield Cable TV - Mansfield, LA - *BrCabYB 84*
Mansfield Cablevision - Logansport, LA - *Tel&CabFB 84C*
Mansfield Citizen - Mansfield, AR - *BaconPubCkNews 84*
Mansfield Co. Inc., Lloyd - Buffalo, NY - *ArtMar 84; StaDirAdAg 2-84*
Mansfield Enterprise - Mansfield, LA - *Ed&PubIntYB 82*
Mansfield Enterprise Journal - Mansfield, LA - *BaconPubCkNews 84; NewsDir 84*
Mansfield-Huntingdon TV Cable Co. - Mansfield, AR - *BrCabYB 84*
Mansfield Journal - Mansfield, LA - *AyerDirPub 83; Ed&PubIntYB 82*
Mansfield Journal Co. - *See* Multi-Channel TV Cable Co. of Mansfield
Mansfield Mirror-Republican - Mansfield, MO - *BaconPubCkNews 84*
Mansfield Mirror, The - Mansfield, MO - *Ed&PubIntYB 82*
Mansfield News - Mansfield, MA - *BaconPubCkNews 84; Ed&PubIntYB 82*
Mansfield News - North Billerica, MA - *NewsDir 84*
Mansfield News Journal - Mansfield, OH - *BaconPubCkNews 84; NewsDir 84*
Mansfield News-Mirror - Mansfield, TX - *BaconPubCkNews 84; Ed&PubIntYB 82*
Mansfield TV Cable Co. - Mansfield, AR - *Tel&CabFB 84C*
Mansfield Video System Inc. - Mansfield, PA - *BrCabYB 84; Tel&CabFB 84C*
Manship Stations - Baton Rouge, LA - *BrCabYB 84; Tel&CabFB 84S*
Manson International - Hollywood, CA - *AvMarPl 83*
Manson Journal - Manson, IA - *BaconPubCkNews 84; Ed&PubIntYB 82*
Manson Productions Inc. & Margery Music Inc., Eddy - Los Angeles, CA - *Tel&CabFB 84C*
Manson Video - Hollywood, CA - *AvMarPl 83*
Manston Associates Inc., Freya - New York, NY - *LitMarPl 83, 84*
Manteca Bulletin [of Morris Newspapers] - Manteca, CA - *BaconPubCkNews 84; Ed&PubIntYB 82; NewsDir 84*
ManTech International - Annapolis, MD - *DataDirOnSer 84*
Mantek Services Inc. - Rye, NY - *LitMarPl 83*
Manteno-News - Manteno, IL - *BaconPubCkNews 84; Ed&PubIntYB 82*
Manteo Coastland Times - Manteo, NC - *BaconPubCkNews 84; Ed&PubIntYB 82; NewsDir 84*
Manti Messenger - Manti, UT - *BaconPubCkNews 84; Ed&PubIntYB 82*
Manti Telephone Co. - Manti, UT - *TelDir&BG 83-84*
Mantice Advertising, Jim - Chicago, IL - *DirMarMP 83*
Mantronics Software Designs - North Mankato, MN - *MicrocomMPl 84*
Mantua Streetsboro Record News - Streetsboro, OH - *Ed&PubIntYB 82*
Manufactured Housing Dealer - Chicago, IL - *MagDir 84*
Manufacturers' Agent Publishing Co. Inc. - New York, NY - *BoPubDir 4, 5*
Manufacturers' Equipment Repair Group - Ann Arbor, MI - *WhoWMicrocom 83*
Manufacturers' Mart - Fairfield, CT - *BaconPubCkMag 84*
Manufacturers' News Inc. - Chicago, IL - *BoPubDir 4 Sup, 5*
Manufacturing & Consulting Services Inc. - Irvine, CA - *DataDirSup 7-83*
Manufacturing Confectioner - Glen Rock, NJ - *BaconPubCkMag 84; MagDir 84*
Manufacturing Confectioner Publishing Co. - Glen Rock, NJ - *BoPubDir 5*
Manufacturing Data Systems Inc. [Div. of Schlumberger Technology Corp.] - Ann Arbor, MI - *DataDirOnSer 84*
Manufacturing Engineering [of Society of Manufacturing Engineers] - Dearborn, MI - *BaconPubCkMag 84; MagDir 84; MagIndMarPl 82-83*
Manufacturing Midwest - Bartlett, IL - *MagDir 84*
Manufacturing Midwest - Streamwood, IL - *BaconPubCkMag 84*
Manufacturing Technology Horizons - Naperville, IL - *BaconPubCkMag 84*
Manus Literary Agency Inc., Janet Wilkens - New York, NY - *LitMarPl 83, 84*
Manus Services Corp. - Seattle, WA - *ADAPSOMemDir 83-84; DataDirOnSer 84*
Manuscript Press - Kingston, NJ - *BoPubDir 4, 5*
Manville News [of Princeton Packet Inc.] - Princeton, NJ - *NewsDir 84*
Manville News - Somerville, NJ - *Ed&PubIntYB 82*
Manville News - *See* Princeton Packet Inc.
Manville Research Inc., Richard [Div. of Commercial Analysts Co.] - New York, NY - *IntDirMarRes 83; Tel&CabFB 84C*
Manwin Music - Los Angeles, CA - *BillIntBG 83-84*
Manx Software Systems - Shrewsbury, NJ - *MicrocomMPl 83*
Many Hats Music - *See* Lorenz Creative Services
Many Sabine Index - Many, LA - *BaconPubCkNews 84*
Many Smokes Earth Awareness Magazine - Spokane, WA - *LitMag&SmPr 83-84*
Many Voices Press - Wollaston, MA - *BoPubDir 4, 5*
Many West Louisiana Star - Many, LA - *BaconPubCkNews 84*
Manyland Books Inc. - Woodhaven, NY - *ArtMar 84; BoPubDir 4, 5; WritMar 84*
Manz Datenbanken [of Manz Info Datenvermittlung] - Vienna, Austria - *EISS 7-83 Sup*
Manzanita Press - San Rafael, CA - *BoPubDir 4, 5; LitMag&SmPr 83-84*
MAP Advertising Agency Inc. - Springfield, MO - *AdAge 3-28-84; StaDirAdAg 2-84*
Map Information & Records Unit [of U.S. Tennessee Valley Authority] - Chattanooga, TN - *EISS 83*
Mapes & Ross Inc. - Princeton, NJ - *IntDirMarRes 83*
Maple Creek News, The - Maple Creek, SK, Canada - *Ed&PubIntYB 82*
Maple Heights Press - Bedford, OH - *AyerDirPub 83*
Maple Heights Press [of Cuyahoga Falls News] - Cuyahoga Falls, OH - *NewsDir 84*
Maple Heights Press - Maple Heights, OH - *Ed&PubIntYB 82*
Maple Heights Press - *See* Record Publishing Co.
Maple Lake Messenger - Maple Lake, MN - *BaconPubCkNews 84; Ed&PubIntYB 82*
Maple Leaf - Port Dover, ON, Canada - *Ed&PubIntYB 82*
Maple Leaf Music - *See* Webman & Co., H. W.
Maple Leaf Press - Gilbert Plains, MB, Canada - *AyerDirPub 83; Ed&PubIntYB 82*
Maple Music Co. Inc. - *See* Sure-Fire Music Co. Inc.
Maple Ridge Pitt Meadows Gazette - Maple Ridge, BC, Canada - *AyerDirPub 83; Ed&PubIntYB 82*
Maple River Publishing Inc. - Frederick, SD - *BaconPubCkNews 84*
Maple Shade Cable Co. - Maple Shade, NJ - *BrCabYB 84; Tel&CabFB 84C*
Maple Shade Progress - Maple Shade, NJ - *Ed&PubIntYB 82*

Maple Shade Progress - *See* Progress Publications Inc.
Maple Shade Progress/Mt. Laurel Progress-Press - Maple Shade, NJ - *NewsDir 84*
Maple Syrup Journal - St. Andre East, PQ, Canada - *BaconPubCkMag 84*
Maple Telephone Cooperative Inc. - Maple, WI - *TelDir&BG 83-84*
Maple-Vail Book Manufacturing Group, The - York, PA - *LitMarPl 83, 84*
Maple Valley News [of J-Ad Graphics Inc.] - Hastings, MI - *AyerDirPub 83; NewsDir 84*
Maple Valley News - Nashville, MI - *Ed&PubIntYB 82*
Maplegrove & Montgrove Press - Chicago, IL - *BoPubDir 4, 5*
Maplesville Music Publishing Inc. - *See* Crescent Music Group
Mapleton Enterprise - Mapleton, MN - *AyerDirPub 83; BaconPubCkNews 84*
Mapleton House Books Inc. - Brooklyn, NY - *MagIndMarPl 82-83*
Mapleton Press - Mapleton, IA - *BaconPubCkNews 84; Ed&PubIntYB 82*
Maplewood News Record - *See* Worrall Publications
Maplewood Press - Meadville, PA - *BoPubDir 4, 5*
Maplewood Review - Maplewood, MN - *Ed&PubIntYB 82*
Maplewood Review - *See* Lillie Suburban Newspapers
Maquoketa Community Press [of Maquoketa Newspapers Inc.] - Burlington, IA - *NewsDir 84*
Maquoketa Sentinel Press [of Maquoketa Newspapers Inc.] - Maquoketa, IA - *AyerDirPub 83; BaconPubCkNews 84; Ed&PubIntYB 82; NewsDir 84*
Mar Car Advertising Agency - Tampa, FL - *StaDirAdAg 2-84*
Mar/Chuck Film Industries Inc. - Mt. Prospect, IL - *AvMarPl 83*
Mar-Tec - Dana Point, CA - *MicrocomMPl 84*
Mar-Tel Communications Inc. - Bergenfield, NJ - *MagIndMarPl 82-83*
Mar Vista Publishing Co. - Los Angeles, CA - *BoPubDir 4, 5; LitMag&SmPr 83-84*
Mar Vista Westside News - *See* Coast Media Newspapers
Mara Books - Santa Monica, CA - *BoPubDir 4, 5*
Mara Press - Marblehead, MA - *BoPubDir 4, 5*
Maran Publishing Co. - Baltimore, MD - *BoPubDir 4, 5*
Maranatha Baptist Press [Aff. of Marantha Baptist Bible College] - Watertown, WI - *BoPubDir 4, 5*
Maranatha Distributors - San Diego, CA - *BoPubDir 4, 5*
Maranatha! Music Inc. - Santa Ana, CA - *BillIntBG 83-84*
Marantz Co. Inc. - Chatsworth, CA - *BillIntBG 83-84*
Maras Inc. - Sharon, CT - *BoPubDir 4, 5*
Marathon Entertainment - New York, NY - *Tel&CabFB 84C*
Marathon Florida Keys Keynoter - Marathon, FL - *BaconPubCkNews 84*
Marathon Independent - Marathon, NY - *BaconPubCkNews 84; Ed&PubIntYB 82; NewsDir 84*
Marathon International Productions - New York, NY - *BrCabYB 84; TelAl 83, 84; Tel&CabFB 84C*
Marathon International Publishing Co. - Louisville, KY - *BoPubDir 5; WritMar 84*
Marathon Mercury, The - Marathon, ON, Canada - *Ed&PubIntYB 82*
Marathon Press - Long Island City, NY - *BoPubDir 5*
Marathon Press [Aff. of Sanford J. Durst] - New York, NY - *BoPubDir 4*
Marathon Secretarial Service - Forest Hills, NY - *LitMarPl 83*
Marathon Software - Jacksonville, TX - *MicrocomMPl 84*
Marathon TV Cable - Marathon, TX - *BrCabYB 84; Tel&CabFB 84C*
Marathon Typing & Word Processing Service - Forest Hills, NY - *LitMarPl 84*
Marathon World [of Marathon Oil Co.] - Findlay, OH - *WritMar 84*
Marble Falls Highlander - Marble Falls, TX - *BaconPubCkNews 84; Ed&PubIntYB 82; NewsDir 84*
Marble Hill Bollinger County Banner-Press, The - Marble Hill, MO - *NewsDir 84*
Marble Music Publishing - *See* Brunswick Music Publishing Co.
Marblehead Reporter - Ipswich, MA - *AyerDirPub 83*
Marblehead Reporter - Marblehead, MA - *Ed&PubIntYB 82; NewsDir 84*
Marblehead Reporter - *See* North Shore Weeklies Inc.
Marboro Books Corp. [Div. of Barnes & Noble] - Moonachie, NJ - *LitMarPl 83, 84*
Marbridge Printing Co. Inc. [Div. of The Adams Group Inc.] - New York, NY - *LitMarPl 83, 84*
Marbro Advertising - Columbus, OH - *AdAge 3-28-84; StaDirAdAg 2-84*
Marburger Publications - Plandome, NY - *BoPubDir 4, 5*
MARC - Dallas, TX - *Tel&CabFB 84C*
MARC - *See* Marketing & Research Counselors Inc.
Marc & Co. - Pittsburgh, PA - *AdAge 3-28-84; ArtMar 84; StaDirAdAg 2-84*
MARC Applied Research Co. [Div. of the Library Corp.] - Washington, DC - *MicroMarPl 82-83*
Marc Associates Inc. - Mansfield, OH - *StaDirAdAg 2-84*
Marc Ed [Subs. of George F. Cram Co.] - Indianapolis, IN - *MicrocomMPl 84*
Marc I Communications - Lithonia, GA - *Tel&CabFB 84C p.1688*
MARC Records Distribution Service [of National Library of Canada] - Ottawa, ON, Canada - *EISS 83*
Marc Roll Leaf Inc. - Elk Grove Village, IL - *LitMarPl 83, 84*
Marc Software International Inc. - Palo Alto, CA - *DirInfWP 82; MicrocomMPl 83*
Marceline Press - Marceline, MO - *BaconPubCkNews 84; Ed&PubIntYB 82; NewsDir 84*
Marcella Press - Palm Desert, CA - *BoPubDir 4, 5*
Marcellus News - Marcellus, MI - *BaconPubCkNews 84; Ed&PubIntYB 82*
Marcellus Observer - Marcellus, NY - *Ed&PubIntYB 82*
Marcellus Observer - Skaneateles, NY - *LitMarPl 83, 84*
Marcellus Observer - *See* Wobo Corp.
Marcfiche [of Marc Applied Research Co.] - Washington, DC - *EISS 83*
March & Green - Wayne, IL - *DirInfWP 82*
March Direct Marketing [Div. of McCann-Erickson Inc.] - New York, NY - *BrCabYB 84; DirMarMP 83; LitMarPl 83, 84; StaDirAdAg 2-84*
March Five Inc. - New York, NY - *DirPRFirms 83*
Marcil Literary Agency Inc., Denise - New York, NY - *LitMarPl 83, 84*
Marcinik, Roger - Palm Bay, FL - *LitMarPl 83, 84; MagIndMarPl 82-83*
Marcive Inc. - San Antonio, TX - *EISS 83*
Marck - Bramford, CT - *MicrocomMPl 83, 84*
Marclay Cable TV [of Belisle Enterprises] - Markleysburg, PA - *BrCabYB 84; Tel&CabFB 84C*
Marco Associates Inc. - New York, NY - *LitMarPl 83, 84*
Marco Book Co. Inc. - Brooklyn, NY - *LitMarPl 83, 84*
Marco Island Eagle - Marco Island, FL - *BaconPubCkNews 84; Ed&PubIntYB 82; NewsDir 84*
Marcoa Direct Advertising - Chicago, IL - *AdAge 3-28-84; DirMarMP 83; StaDirAdAg 2-84*
Marcom - Scotts Valley, CA - *TeleSy&SerDir 2-84*
Marcom/Day Advertising Inc. - Houston, TX - *StaDirAdAg 2-84*
Marcom Inc. - East Windsor, CT - *AdAge 3-28-84; StaDirAdAg 2-84*
Marcon Public Relations [Div. of Marcon Communications Inc.] - Westport, CT - *DirPRFirms 83*
Marconi & Others - Northbrook, IL - *StaDirAdAg 2-84*
Marcontur-Gabinete de Marketing e Publicidade Lda. - Lisbon, Portugal - *StaDirAdAg 2-84*
Marcum, Nellie - Switzer, WV - *Tel&CabFB 84C p.1688*
Marcus Advertising Inc. - Cleveland, OH - *BrCabYB 84; StaDirAdAg 2-84*
Marcus Books - Toronto, ON, Canada - *BoPubDir 4 Sup, 5*
Marcus Communications Inc. - Greenwich, CT - *BrCabYB 84 p.D-303; Tel&CabFB 84C p.1688*
Marcus Communications Inc. - Babbitt, MN - *BrCabYB 84*
Marcus Communications Inc. - Fergus Falls, MN - *BrCabYB 84*
Marcus Communications Inc. - Little Falls, MN - *BrCabYB 84*
Marcus Communications Inc. - Ashland, WI - *BrCabYB 84; Tel&CabFB 84C*
Marcus Communications Inc. - Cornell, WI - *BrCabYB 84*
Marcus Communications Inc. - Ladysmith, WI - *BrCabYB 84; Tel&CabFB 84C*
Marcus Communications Inc. - Spooner, WI - *BrCabYB 84; Tel&CabFB 84C*
Marcus Communications Inc. - Tomah, WI - *Tel&CabFB 84C*

Marcus Group Inc., The - Atlanta, GA - *AdAge 3-28-84; StaDirAdAg 2-84*
Marcus Group Inc., The - Newark, NJ - *DirPRFirms 83*
Marcus, Helen - New York, NY - *MagIndMarPl 82-83*
Marcus Hook Press [of Press Publishing Co.] - Drexel Hill, PA - *NewsDir 84*
Marcus Hook Press - Marcus Hook, PA - *AyerDirPub 83; Ed&PubIntYB 82*
Marcus Hook Press - *See* Press Publishing Co.
Marcus News - Marcus, IA - *BaconPubCkNews 84; Ed&PubIntYB 82*
Marcuse, David - Takoma Park, MD - *LitMarPl 83*
Mardata - Stamford, CT - *DirOnDB Spring 84*
Marden-Kane Inc. - New York, NY - *DirMarMP 83; StaDirAdAg 2-84*
Marden-Sheridan, Laurel - Corinth, VT - *LitMarPl 83*
Marder Associates Inc., Eric - New York, NY - *IntDirMarRes 83*
Mardikian-Farr-Snell Stations - *See* Golden Pacific Group, The
Marengo Beacon-News - Marengo, IL - *BaconPubCkNews 84; NewsDir 84*
Marengo Newspapers of Iowa County - Marengo, IA - *NewsDir 84*
Marengo Pioneer-Republican - Marengo, IA - *Ed&PubIntYB 82*
Marengo Pioneer Republican - *See* Newspapers of Iowa County
Marengo Republican-News [of Free Press Inc.] - Marengo, IL - *Ed&PubIntYB 82; NewsDir 84*
Marengo Republican News - *See* Free Press Inc.
Marer Associates, H. K. - Weston, CT - *LitMarPl 83; MagIndMarPl 82-83*
Maresco Research Inc. - Great Neck, NY - *IntDirMarRes 83*
Marfa Big Bend Sentinel - Marfa, TX - *BaconPubCkNews 84*
Marfa TV Cable Co. - Marfa, TX - *BrCabYB 84; Tel&CabFB 84C*
Margaret Records - Chicago, IL - *BillIntBG 83-84*
Margaretville Catskill Mountain News - *See* Catskill Mountain Publishing Corp.
Margaretville Tel-Viz Inc. - Andes, NY - *Tel&CabFB 84C*
Margaretville Tel-Viz Inc. - Margaretville, NY - *BrCabYB 84*
Margaretville Telephone Co. Inc. - Margaretville, NY - *TelDir&BG 83-84*
Margarine Maypole Orangoutang Express, The [of Anonymous Owl Press] - Albuquerque, NM - *LitMag&SmPr 83-84*
Margenia Music - *See* Gopam Enterprises Inc.
Margeotes/Fertitta & Weiss - New York, NY - *AdAge 3-28-84; StaDirAdAg 2-84*
Marginal Media - Fredonia, NY - *BoPubDir 5*
Marginal Politics [of On the Move Press] - San Francisco, CA - *LitMag&SmPr 83-84*
Marginal Press - San Francisco, CA - *BoPubDir 4, 5*
Margolis Marketing & Research Co. - New York, NY - *BoPubDir 4 Sup, 5*
Margreno, John - Watkins Glen, NY - *Tel&CabFB 84C*
Margrill Advertising Inc., Herbert - New York, NY - *DirPRFirms 83*
Mariah Productions - New York, NY - *AvMarPl 83*
Marian Helpers Bulletin - Stockbridge, MA - *WritMar 84*
Marianist Communication Center [Aff. of Society of Mary] - St. Louis, MO - *BoPubDir 5*
Marianna & Scenery Hill Telephone Co. - Marianna, PA - *TelDir&BG 83-84*
Marianna Courier Index - Marianna, AR - *BaconPubCkNews 84; NewsDir 84*
Marianna Jackson County Floridian - Marianna, FL - *AyerDirPub 83; NewsDir 84*
Marich Inc. - Oldsmar, FL - *BoPubDir 4, 5*
Marielle Music Publishing Corp. - New York, NY - *BillIntBG 83-84*
Maries County Gazette-Adviser - Vienna, MO - *AyerDirPub 83; Ed&PubIntYB 82*
Marietta Journal [of Times-Journal Inc.] - Marietta, GA - *BaconPubCkNews 84; Ed&PubIntYB 82; LitMarPl 83, 84; NewsDir 84*
Marietta Monitor - Marietta, OK - *BaconPubCkNews 84; Ed&PubIntYB 82*
Marietta Times [of Gannett Co. Inc.] - Marietta, OH - *BaconPubCkNews 84; Ed&PubIntYB 82; NewsDir 84*
Marigold Advertising/Marketing - New York, NY - *StaDirAdAg 2-84*
Marilee Publications - Bonita Springs, FL - *BoPubDir 4, 5; LitMag&SmPr 83-84*
Marin County Independent Journal [of Gannett Co. Inc.] - Novato, CA - *NewsDir 84*
Marin Shopping News - Mill Valley, CA - *AyerDirPub 83*
Marin Suburban Newspapers Inc. - San Rafael, CA - *BaconPubCkNews 84*
Marina Advertising Inc., Sam - Phillipsburg, NJ - *StaDirAdAg 2-84*
Marina del Rey Argonaut, The - Venice, CA - *NewsDir 84*
Marina del Rey Mail - *See* Independent-Journal Newspapers
Marina Mail - Marina del Rey, CA - *Ed&PubIntYB 82*
Marina Mail [of Santa Monica Independent Journal Newspapers] - Santa Monica, CA - *NewsDir 84*
Marina Management/Marketing - New Orleans, LA - *MagDir 84*
Marina News - Long Beach, CA - *AyerDirPub 83; Ed&PubIntYB 82*
Marinchip Systems - Mill Valley, CA - *MicrocomMPl 83, 84*
Marine Advisory Service [of U.S. National Oceanic & Atmospheric Administration] - Rockville, MD - *EISS 83*
Marine & Coastal Technology Information Service [of Ocean Economics & Technology Branch] - New York, NY - *EISS 83*
Marine & Recreation News - St. Clair Shores, MI - *BaconPubCkMag 84; MagDir 84*
Marine Biological Association of the United Kingdon (Library & Information Services) - Plymouth, England - *InfIndMarPl 83*
Marine Business - Boston, MA - *MagDir 84*
Marine City Independent Press - *See* Sommerville Communications Corp.
Marine City St. Clair County Independent Press [of Sommerville Communications Corp.] - Marine City, MI - *NewsDir 84*
Marine Corps Gazette - Quantico, VA - *BaconPubCkMag 84; MagDir 84; MagIndMarPl 82-83*
Marine Digest - Seattle, WA - *BaconPubCkMag 84; MagDir 84*
Marine Education Textbooks - Houma, LA - *BoPubDir 4, 5*
Marine Engineering/Log - New York, NY - *BaconPubCkMag 84; MagIndMarPl 82-83*
Marine Environmental Data Information Referral System [of United Nations Educational, Scientific, & Cultural Organization] - Paris, France - *EISS 83*
Marine Information & Advisory Service [of Natural Environment Research Council] - Godalming, England - *EISS 83*
Marine Pollution Information Centre [of Marine Biological Association of the United Kingdom] - Plymouth, England - *EISS 83*
Marine Technology Society - Washington, DC - *BoPubDir 4, 5*
Marine Technology Society Journal - Washington, DC - *MagIndMarPl 82-83*
Marine Trades - Mississauga, ON, Canada - *BaconPubCkMag 84*
Marineland of Florida Inc. - St. Augustine, FL - *Tel&CabFB 84C*
Mariner - Norwell, MA - *AyerDirPub 83*
Mariner Books - Flat Rock, NC - *BoPubDir 5*
Mariner Books - Hendersonville, NC - *BoPubDir 4*
Mariner Chart Shop - Tobermory, ON, Canada - *BoPubDir 4, 5*
Mariner Publishing Co. Inc. - Tampa, FL - *LitMarPl 83, 84; WritMar 84*
Mariner Typographers - Tampa, FL - *LitMarPl 84*
Mariners - Marshfield, MA - *AyerDirPub 83*
Marinette Eagle-Star - Marinette, WI - *BaconPubCkNews 84; NewsDir 84*
Marinoff Publications, Abraham - Brooklyn, NY - *BoPubDir 4, 5*
Marion Advertiser - Marion, WI - *BaconPubCkNews 84; Ed&PubIntYB 82*
Marion Cable TV [of American Television & Communications Corp.] - Marion, IN - *BrCabYB 84; Tel&CabFB 84C*
Marion Cable TV - Marion, KY - *Tel&CabFB 84C*
Marion Cable TV - Marion, LA - *Tel&CabFB 84C*
Marion Cablevision [of Cable Information Systems Inc.] - Marion, IL - *BrCabYB 84; Tel&CabFB 84C*
Marion CableVision - Marion, MT - *Tel&CabFB 84C*
Marion CATV [of Community Tele-Communications Inc.] - Marion, OH - *BrCabYB 84; Tel&CabFB 84C*
Marion Chronicle Tribune [of Federated Publication Inc.] - Marion, IN - *BaconPubCkNews 84; NewsDir 84*
Marion Computer Services - Oxnard, CA - *EISS 83*

Marion County News - Pleasantville, IA - *Ed&PubIntYB 82*
Marion County Record - Marion, KS - *AyerDirPub 83; BaconPubCkNews 84; Ed&PubIntYB 82; NewsDir 84*
Marion Crittenden Press - Marion, KY - *BaconPubCkNews 84*
Marion Leader, The - Ocala, FL - *AyerDirPub 83*
Marion Leader, The [of Pinellas Park Post] - Pinellas Park, FL - *NewsDir 84*
Marion McDowell News - Marion, NC - *BaconPubCkNews 84*
Marion Messenger, The - Marion, AL - *Ed&PubIntYB 82*
Marion Municipal Cablevision - Marion, KS - *BrCabYB 84*
Marion News Herald - Marion, IN - *BaconPubCkNews 84; Ed&PubIntYB 82*
Marion Newslife - Marion, OH - *AyerDirPub 83*
Marion Press - Marion, MI - *BaconPubCkNews 84; Ed&PubIntYB 82*
Marion Record - Marion, SD - *BaconPubCkNews 84; Ed&PubIntYB 82*
Marion Republican - Marion, IL - *BaconPubCkNews 84; Ed&PubIntYB 82; NewsDir 84*
Marion Sentinel - Marion, IA - *BaconPubCkNews 84; Ed&PubIntYB 82*
Marion Sippican Sentinel - *See* MPG Communications
Marion Smyth County News [of Worrell Newspapers Inc.] - Marion, VA - *BaconPubCkNews 84; NewsDir 84*
Marion Star - Marion, OH - *BaconPubCkNews 84; Ed&PubIntYB 82; NewsDir 84*
Marion Star - Marion, SC - *AyerDirPub 83; BaconPubCkNews 84; Ed&PubIntYB 82; NewsDir 84*
Marion Times-Standard - Marion, AL - *BaconPubCkNews 84; Ed&PubIntYB 82*
Marionville Free Press - Marionville, MO - *BaconPubCkNews 84; Ed&PubIntYB 82*
Mariotti Inc., Robert - Glastonbury, CT - *MicrocomMPl 83*
Mariposa Cable TV - Mariposa, CA - *BrCabYB 84; Tel&CabFB 84C*
Mariposa County Telephone Co. Inc. [Aff. of Sierra Telephone Co. Inc.] - Oakhurst, CA - *TelDir&BG 83-84*
Mariposa Gazette - Mariposa, CA - *BaconPubCkNews 84; Ed&PubIntYB 82; NewsDir 84*
Maris, West & Baker - Jackson, MS - *AdAge 3-28-84; StaDirAdAg 2-84*
Marissa Messenger - Marissa, IL - *BaconPubCkNews 84; Ed&PubIntYB 82*
Maritime [of Maritime Trades Dept.. AFL-CIO] - Washington, DC - *NewsDir 84*
Maritime Communications [of Overseas Telecommunications Commission] - Sydney, Australia - *TeleSy&SerDir 2-84*
Maritime Computer Corp. - Cranford, NJ - *ADAPSOMemDir 83-84*
Maritime Data Network [of Marine Management Systems Inc.] - Stamford, CT - *DataDirOnSer 84; EISS 83; InfIndMarPl 83*
Maritime Information Centre - Rotterdam, Netherlands - *CompReadDB 82; EISS 7-83 Sup; InfIndMarPl 83*
Maritime Law Book Co. Ltd. - Frederickton, NB, Canada - *CompReadDB 82*
Maritime Municipal Training & Development Board - Halifax, NS, Canada - *BoPubDir 4 Sup, 5*
Maritime Reporter & Engineering News - New York, NY - *BaconPubCkMag 84; MagDir 84*
Maritime Research Information Service [of Transportation Research Board] - Washington, DC - *CompReadDB 82; InfIndMarPl 83*
Maritime Review - Novato, CA - *BaconPubCkMag 84*
Maritimes - Kingston, RI - *MagIndMarPl 82-83*
Maritz Communications Co. - Stamford, CT - *AvMarPl 83*
Maritz Communications Co. - Fenton, MO - *ArtMar 84*
Maritz Market Research [Subs. of Maritz Inc.] - Fenton, MO - *AdAge 5-17-84 p.31; IntDirMarRes 83*
Marjon International Records - Hermitage, PA - *BillIntBG 83-84*
Mark-Age Inc. - Ft. Lauderdale, FL - *BoPubDir 4, 5*
Mark Data Products - Mission Viejo, CA - *MicrocomMPl 83, 84*
Mark 56 Records - Anaheim, CA - *BillIntBG 83-84*
Mark Five Studio - Greenville, SC - *BillIntBG 83-84*
Mark IV Advertising Inc. - Peoria, IL - *StaDirAdAg 2-84*
Mark IV Resources Inc. [Subs. of Peter Li Inc.] - Dayton, OH - *AvMarPl 83*
Mark IV User Group - Canoga Park, CA - *EISS 83*
Mark Media Group - *See* Sink Stations, J. Ardell
Mark of Aries Music - New York, NY - *BillIntBG 83-84*
Mark of the Unicorn - Arlington, MA - *MicrocomMPl 84; MicrocomSwDir 1; WhoWMicrocom 83*
Mark of the Unicorn - Belmont, MA - *MicrocomMPl 83*
Mark I Greeting Card Co. - Chicago, IL - *WritMar 84*
Mark/Ops [Subs. of Northeastern Systems Associates Inc.] - Boston, MA - *DataDirOnSer 84*
Mark Three Graphics Inc. - Providence, RI - *TelAl 83, 84*
Mark III Service [of General Electric Co.] - Rockville, MD - *EISS 83*
Mark Video Enterprises Inc. - Ann Arbor, MI - *AvMarPl 83*
Markco - Battle Creek, NE - *BoPubDir 4 Sup, 5*
Markdale Standard, The - Markdale, ON, Canada - *Ed&PubIntYB 82*
Marke Communications - New York, NY - *DirMarMP 83*
Marked Tree Tribune - Marked Tree, AR - *BaconPubCkNews 84; Ed&PubIntYB 82*
Markem Corp. - Keene, NH - *DataDirSup 7-83*
Marken Communications Associates - Palo Alto, CA - *DirPRFirms 83*
Marker, Robert S. - New York, NY - *HBIndAd&MS 82-83*
Markesan Herald - Markesan, WI - *BaconPubCkNews 84; Ed&PubIntYB 82*
Market - Storden, MN - *AyerDirPub 83*
Market Aides Ltd. - Toronto, ON, Canada - *IntDirMarRes 83*
Market Analysis Systems Inc. - Minneapolis, MN - *EISS 83*
Market Analytics Inc. - Narberth, PA - *IntDirMarRes 83*
Market & Opinion Research International - London, England - *IntDirMarRes 83*
Market Audits [Div. of Burke Marketing Services Inc.] - Cincinnati, OH - *IntDirMarRes 83*
Market Behavior Inc. - New York, NY - *IntDirMarRes 83*
Market Builders Inc. - Princeton, NJ - *DirMarMP 83; StaDirAdAg 2-84*
Market Buy Market [Subs. of Golden West Broadcasters] - Los Angeles, CA - *DataDirOnSer 84; EISS 5-84 Sup*
Market Chronicle, The [of William B. Dana Co.] - New York, NY - *BaconPubCkMag 84; MagDir 84*
Market Communication Associates - Chicago, IL - *DirPRFirms 83*
Market Communications Inc. - Milwaukee, WI - *BoPubDir 4, 5*
Market Compilation & Research Bureau Inc. - North Hollywood, CA - *LitMarPl 83, 84*
Market Consensus Alert [of NewsNet Inc.] - Bryn Mawr, PA - *DataDirOnSer 84*
Market Consensus Alert - Yardley, PA - *DirOnDB Spring 84*
Market Data Retrieval - Westport, CT - *CompReadDB 82; DataDirOnSer 84; EISS 83; InfIndMarPl 83; LitMarPl 83, 84; MagIndMarPl 82-83*
Market Data Systems Inc. - Memphis, TN - *DataDirOnSer 84; EISS 7-83 Sup*
Market Decision System 7 [of Bunker Ramo Information Systems] - Trumbull, CT - *DataDirOnSer 84; DirOnDB Spring 84*
Market Decisions Corp. - Portland, OR - *IntDirMarRes 83*
Market Development Corp. - Hazlewood, MO - *MagIndMarPl 82-83*
Market Development Group International Inc. - Orlando, FL - *StaDirAdAg 2-84*
Market Development Inc. - San Diego, CA - *IntDirMarRes 83*
Market-Direct Advertising - El Toro, CA - *ArtMar 84; DirMarMP 83; StaDirAdAg 2-84*
Market Discovery-I. M. Olson Associates - Alexandria, VA - *IntDirMarRes 83*
Market Dynamics Inc. - Falls Church, VA - *IntDirMarRes 83*
Market Facts - Chicago, IL - *AdAge 5-17-84 p.26; IntDirMarRes 83*
Market Facts - New York, NY - *IntDirMarRes 83; MagIndMarPl 82-83*
Market Facts of Canada Ltd. - Toronto, ON, Canada - *IntDirMarRes 83*
Market Focus Inc. - Chicago, IL - *IntDirMarRes 83*
Market Focus Inc. - Bogota, NJ - *IntDirMarRes 83*
Market Information Bank - Stockholm, Sweden - *DirOnDB Spring 84*
Market Intelligence A/S - Hovik, Norway - *CompReadDB 82*
Market Interviews - Southfield, MI - *IntDirMarRes 83*

Market Location - Leamington Spa, England - *EISS 5-84 Sup*
Market Navigation Inc. - Orangeburg, NY - *IntDirMarRes 83*
Market Opinion Research - Detroit, MI - *AdAge 5-17-84 p.39; BrCabYB 84; IntDirMarRes 83*
Market Perceptions Co. - Cranston, RI - *BrCabYB 84*
Market Place Advertiser, The - Ramona, CA - *AyerDirPub 83*
Market Place, The - Vandalia, OH - *AyerDirPub 83*
Market Place, The - Dallas, TX - *BaconPubCkMag 84; MagDir 84*
Market-Pro Inc. - Chicago, IL - *IntDirMarRes 83*
Market Probe International Inc. - New York, NY - *IntDirMarRes 83*
Market Program [of Marshall & Swift Publication Co.] - Los Angeles, CA - *DBBus 82*
Market Research Abstracts [of Market Research Society] - London, England - *EISS 7-83 Sup*
Market Research & Analysis Field Staff Inc. - Houston, TX - *IntDirMarRes 83*
Market Research Bureau Inc. - Washington, DC - *IntDirMarRes 83*
Market Research Corp. of America - Stamford, CT - *IntDirMarRes 83; Tel&CabFB 84C*
Market Research Interviewing Inc. - Phoenix, AZ - *IntDirMarRes 83*
Market Research of Toledo - Toledo, OH - *IntDirMarRes 83*
Market Research Services Inc. - Cleveland, OH - *IntDirMarRes 83*
Market Research Services of Dallas - Mesquite, TX - *IntDirMarRes 83*
Market Research Unltd. Inc. - South Portland, ME - *IntDirMarRes 83*
Market-Rite Advertising Agency - Pembroke Pines, FL - *StaDirAdAg 2-84*
Market Science Associates Inc. - Chicago, IL - *IntDirMarRes 83*
Market Statistics - New York, NY - *EISS 83; IntDirMarRes 83; Tel&CabFB 84C*
Market Structure Insights Inc. - Minneapolis, MN - *IntDirMarRes 83*
Market Trends Inc. - New York, NY - *IntDirMarRes 83*
Market Trends Inc. - Kirkland, WA - *IntDirMarRes 83*
Market Watch - New York, NY - *BaconPubCkMag 84; MagDir 84*
Marketaide - Salina, KS - *AdAge 3-28-84; ArtMar 84; StaDirAdAg 2-84*
MarketBase [of Urban Decision Systems Inc.] - Los Angeles, CA - *DBBus 82; DirOnDB Spring 84*
Marketeam Associates - St. Louis, MO - *IntDirMarRes 83*
MarkeTechs Inc. - York, PA - *AvMarPl 83*
Marketest - New York, NY - *IntDirMarRes 83*
Marketfacts - Farmington, CT - *BaconPubCkMag 84*
Marketfax - Toronto, ON, Canada - *DirOnDB Spring 84*
Marketfax Professional Stock Charting System [of Marketfax Information Services Ltd.] - Toronto, ON, Canada - *DataDirOnSer 84*
Marketfax Stock Market Charting Service [of Faxtel Information Systems Ltd.] - Toronto, ON, Canada - *DataDirOnSer 84*
Marketforce Communications Corp. [Subs. of Hughes Advertising Inc.] - St. Louis, MO - *DirMarMP 83*
Marketing - Toronto, ON, Canada - *BaconPubCkMag 84*
Marketing & Creative Services Inc. - Richmond, IN - *StaDirAdAg 2-84*
Marketing & Media Decisions [of Decision Publications Inc.] - New York, NY - *BaconPubCkMag 84; MagDir 84*
Marketing & Research Counselors [Subs. of Allcom Inc.] - Dallas, TX - *AdAge 5-17-84 p.26; IntDirMarRes 83*
Marketing Centre, The - St. Petersburg, FL - *HBIndAd&MS 82-83*
Marketing Centre, The - New York, NY - *LitMarPl 83, 84*
Marketing Communications [of United Business Publications Inc.] - New York, NY - *BaconPubCkMag 84; MagDir 84; MagIndMarPl 82-83; WritMar 84*
Marketing Communications - Dayton, OH - *AvMarPl 83*
Marketing Communications Group Inc., The - Toledo, OH - *StaDirAdAg 2-84*
Marketing Communications Management Inc. - Philadelphia, PA - *DirMarMP 83*
Marketing Concepts Inc. [Subs. of Gulf & Western Industries Inc.] - New York, NY - *AvMarPl 83*
Marketing Consultants Associated - Trenton, NJ - *StaDirAdAg 2-84*
Marketing Coordinators Inc. - New York, NY - *HBIndAd&MS 82-83*
Marketing Decisions Inc. - Minneapolis, MN - *IntDirMarRes 83*
Marketing Directions - Newport Beach, CA - *AdAge 3-28-84; StaDirAdAg 2-84*
Marketing Directions Associates Inc. - New Fairfield, CT - *IntDirMarRes 83*
Marketing, Directory & Yellow Pages Service [Div. of Moss & Co. Inc.] - New York, NY - *StaDirAdAg 2-84*
Marketing Dynamax Inc. - Deerfield, IL - *HBIndAd&MS 82-83*
Marketing East Inc. - Norwalk, CT - *StaDirAdAg 2-84*
Marketing Economics Institute Ltd. - New York, NY - *BoPubDir 4, 5; EISS 83*
Marketing Evaluations/TVQ Inc. - Port Washington, NY - *BrCabYB 84; IntDirMarRes 83; Tel&CabFB 84C*
Marketing Executive's Digest - New York, NY - *BaconPubCkMag 84; MagIndMarPl 82-83*
Marketing Fact Book - Chicago, IL - *DirOnDB Spring 84*
Marketing Facts & Sales - Hamilton, MT - *BrCabYB 84*
Marketing Group - Horsham, PA - *AdAge 3-28-84; StaDirAdAg 2-84*
Marketing Group Inc., The - Boston, MA - *StaDirAdAg 2-84*
Marketing IMPAI - Houston, TX - *Tel&CabFB 84C*
Marketing Information Data Systems - Dallas, TX - *DataDirOnSer 84; EISS 83*
Marketing Information Institute Inc. - La Mesa, CA - *IntDirMarRes 83*
Marketing Information Systems Inc. - San Diego, CA - *EISS 83*
Marketing Information Systems Inc. - Englewood Cliffs, NJ - *IntDirMarRes 83*
Marketing Innovations - Scottsdale, AZ - *StaDirAdAg 2-84*
Marketing Insights Inc. - East Brunswick, NJ - *IntDirMarRes 83*
Marketing Intelligence Corp. - Tokyo, Japan - *EISS 5-84 Sup*
Marketing Intelligence Services Inc. - Blue Bell, PA - *MagIndMarPl 82-83*
Marketing Investigations Inc. - Sewickley, PA - *IntDirMarRes 83*
Marketing Letter, The - New York, NY - *MagIndMarPl 82-83*
Marketing Logistics Inc. - Deerfield, IL - *HBIndAd&MS 82-83*
Marketing Mechanics - New York, NY - *IntDirMarRes 83*
Marketing News [of American Marketing Association] - Chicago, IL - *BaconPubCkMag 84; MagDir 84; MagIndMarPl 82-83*
Marketing Programs & Services Group Inc. - Gaithersburg, MD - *TeleSy&SerDir 2-84*
Marketing Pros Inc. - New York, NY - *DirPRFirms 83*
Marketing Research Div. [of Doane-Western Inc.] - St. Louis, MO - *EISS 83*
Marketing Research Services - Utica, KY - *IntDirMarRes 83*
Marketing Research Services Inc. - Cincinnati, OH - *IntDirMarRes 83*
Marketing Research Workshop Inc. - Ft. Lee, NJ - *IntDirMarRes 83*
Marketing Resources Inc. - Overland Park, KS - *StaDirAdAg 2-84*
Marketing Results Corp. - St. Paul, MN - *DirMarMP 83*
Marketing Service Associates Inc. - Hartsdale, NY - *IntDirMarRes 83*
Marketing Services Co. Inc. - West Hartford, CT - *IntDirMarRes 83*
Marketing Services of New Mexico [Div. of Marketing Research of New Mexico Inc.] - Albuquerque, NM - *IntDirMarRes 83*
Marketing Shop, The - London, England - *FBInfSer 80*
Marketing Solutions Inc. - New York, NY - *IntDirMarRes 83*
Marketing Strategies for Industry Ltd. - Mitcham, England - *IntDirMarRes 83*
Marketing Support - Chicago, IL - *AdAge 3-28-84; ArtMar 84; StaDirAdAg 2-84*
Marketing Support Services Inc. - Dallas, TX - *IntDirMarRes 83*
Marketing Three - Peekskill, NY - *DirMarMP 83*
Marketing Times [of Sales & Marketing Executives International Inc.] - New York, NY - *BaconPubCkMag 84; MagDir 84; MagIndMarPl 82-83*
Marketing Trends [of Midwest Petroleum Marketers] - Des Plaines, IL - *MagDir 84*
Marketing Trends - Rosemont, IL - *BaconPubCkMag 84*

Marketing Viewpoints Inc. - White Plains, NY - *IntDirMarRes 83*
Marketing Workshop Inc., The - Norcross, GA - *HBIndAd&MS 82-83; IntDirMarRes 83*
Marketline Systems Inc. - Southampton, PA - *MicrocomMPl 84; WhoWMicrocom 83*
Marketmath Inc. - New York, NY - *IntDirMarRes 83*
Marketnews - Scarborough, ON, Canada - *BaconPubCkMag 84*
Marketnews - Toronto, ON, Canada - *WritMar 84*
Marketplace, The - Marianna, FL - *AyerDirPub 83*
MarketPotential - Stamford, CT - *DirOnDB Spring 84*
MarketPotential [of Control Data Corp.] - Minneapolis, MN - *DataDirOnSer 84*
Marketreach Inc. - Seattle, WA - *AdAge 3-28-84; StaDirAdAg 2-84*
Marketron - Menlo Park, CA - *DataDirOnSer 84*
Marketronics Inc. [Subs. of Interactive Market Systems Inc.] - New York, NY - *MagIndMarPl 82-83*
Markets Advisory - Racine, WI - *DirOnDB Spring 84*
Marketscan [of Info Globe] - Toronto, ON, Canada - *DataDirOnSer 84; DirOnDB Spring 84*
Marketscope [of Standard & Poor's Corp.] - New York, NY - *EISS 5-84 Sup*
MarketSearch Inc. - Thiensville, WI - *IntDirMarRes 83*
MarketStat - New York, NY - *IntDirMarRes 83*
MarketVision Research - Cincinnati, OH - *IntDirMarRes 83*
Marketware - Richmond, VA - *MicrocomMPl 84*
Markewich, Reese - Pleasantville, NY - *BoPubDir 4, 5*
Markgraf & Wells Marketing & Advertising Inc. - Minneapolis, MN - *StaDirAdAg 2-84*
Markham Historical Society - Markham, ON, Canada - *BoPubDir 4, 5*
Markham, Jim - San Antonio, TX - *LitMarPl 83, 84; MagIndMarPl 82-83*
Markham/Novell Communications Ltd. - New York, NY - *DirPRFirms 83*
Markham Review, The - Staten Island, NY - *LitMag&SmPr 83-84*
Markham Star-Tribune [of Oak Forest Star Herald Publications] - Chicago Heights, IL - *Ed&PubIntYB 82; NewsDir 84*
Markham Star-Tribune - Markham, IL - *AyerDirPub 83*
Markham Star-Tribune - *See* Star Publications
Markham/Thornhill Economist & Sun - Markham, ON, Canada - *Ed&PubIntYB 82*
Marking Industry [of Marking Devices Publishing Co.] - Chicago, IL - *BaconPubCkMag 84; MagDir 84; WritMar 84*
Markinor - Pinegowrie, South Africa - *IntDirMarRes 83*
Markkinointi Viherjuuri Oy - Helsinki, Finland - *StaDirAdAg 2-84*
Markland Corp. [Aff. of Smith/Greenland Co. Inc.] - New York, NY - *StaDirAdAg 2-84*
Marklin Advertising Ltd. - Hong Kong, Hong Kong - *StaDirAdAg 2-84*
Markmakers Inc. - South Bend, IN - *StaDirAdAg 2-84*
Marko Enterprises [Aff. of Mark O. Haroldsen Inc.] - Salt Lake City, UT - *BoPubDir 4, 5*
Markow, Herbert L. - Miami, FL - *BoPubDir 4, 5*
Marks Advertising, Howard - New York, NY - *StaDirAdAg 2-84*
Marks & Co. Inc., Gordon - Jackson, MS - *DirPRFirms 83; StaDirAdAg 2-84*
Marks, Betty - New York, NY - *LitMarPl 83, 84; MagIndMarPl 82-83*
Marks Cablevision of Ohio Inc. [of Capital Cities Communications Inc.] - Franklin Township, OH - *Tel&CabFB 84C*
Marks Cablevision of Ohio Inc. [of Capitol Cities Cable Inc.] - Green, OH - *BrCabYB 84*
Marks Enterprises, M. H. - Pittsburgh, PA - *MicrocomMPl 84*
Marks, Frank H. - Chicago, IL - *LitMarPl 83, 84; MagIndMarPl 82-83*
Marks, Joseph - New York, NY - *LitMarPl 83, 84*
Mark's Publishing Co. Ltd. - Halifax, NS, Canada - *BoPubDir 4, 5*
Marks Quitman County Democrat - Marks, MS - *BaconPubCkNews 84*
Markson Literary Agency Inc., Elaine - New York, NY - *LitMarPl 83, 84*
Marktime Features Inc. - Lakewood, CO - *Ed&PubIntYB 82*
Markus, Tom - Richmond, VA - *WritMar 84*
Marlboro Compass - Marlboro, MA - *BaconPubCkNews 84*
Marlboro Enterprise - Marlboro, MA - *BaconPubCkNews 84; Ed&PubIntYB 82; NewsDir 84*
Marlboro Herald-Advocate - Bennettsville, SC - *AyerDirPub 83; Ed&PubIntYB 82*
Marlboro Press - Marlboro, VT - *BoPubDir 5; LitMag&SmPr 83-84; LitMarPl 84*
Marlboro Southern Ulster Pioneer - *See* Hudson Valley Newspapers Inc.
Marlborough Press [Aff. of Brooke Evan Associates] - Morganville, NJ - *BoPubDir 4 Sup, 5*
Marlborough Publications - San Diego, CA - *BoPubDir 4, 5; LitMag&SmPr 83-84*
Marlborough Southern Ulster Pioneer - Marlborough, NY - *Ed&PubIntYB 82*
Marle Art Inc. - Smithtown, NY - *StaDirAdAg 2-84*
Marlen Music Co. - *See* Gordon Music Co. Inc.
Marlette Leader - Marlette, MI - *BaconPubCkNews 84; Ed&PubIntYB 82*
Marley Music Ltd., Bob - *See* Rondor Music International Inc.
Marlin Daily Democrat - Marlin, TX - *BaconPubCkNews 84; Ed&PubIntYB 82; NewsDir 84*
Marlin Publishers, E. & R. - Ottawa, ON, Canada - *BoPubDir 4, 5*
Marlin TV Cable Co. Inc. [of Times Mirror Cable Television Inc.] - Marlin, TX - *BrCabYB 84*
Marlin Weekly Democrat - Marlin, TX - *BaconPubCkNews 84; Ed&PubIntYB 82*
Marlinton Pocahontas Times - Marlinton, WV - *BaconPubCkNews 84; Ed&PubIntYB 82*
Marlow Review - Marlow, OK - *BaconPubCkNews 84; Ed&PubIntYB 82*
Marmac Publishing Co. Inc. - Atlanta, GA - *BoPubDir 4 Sup, 5*
Marmarth Slope Messenger - *See* New England Herald Publishers
Marmora Herald - Marmora, ON, Canada - *AyerDirPub 83*
Marna [of Samson Data Systemen BV] - Alphen, Netherlands - *DataDirOnSer 84*
Marna [of The Maritime Information Centre] - Rotterdam, Netherlands - *CompReadDB 82; DirOnDB Spring 84; OnBibDB 3*
Marnay Sales & Manufacturing Co. Inc. - New York, NY - *DirInfWP 82*
Marne & Elk Horn Telephone Co. - Elk Horn, IA - *TelDir&BG 83-84*
Maro Verlag - Augsburg, West Germany - *LitMag&SmPr 83-84*
Maroa Prairie Post - Maroa, IL - *BaconPubCkNews 84*
Maromaty & Scotto Software Corp. - Floral Park, NY - *MicrocomMPl 83*
Marotta, Tom - New York, NY - *LitMarPl 83, 84*
Marplan Research Inc. - *See* McCann-Erickson Worldwide
Marplan Research International - New York, NY - *IntDirMarRes 83*
Marple Publishing Co. Inc. - Newtown Square, PA - *BaconPubCkNews 84*
Marquardt & Co. Inc. - New York, NY - *LitMarPl 83, 84; MagIndMarPl 82-83*
Marquardt & Roche - Stamford, CT - *AdAge 3-28-84; DirPRFirms 83; StaDirAdAg 2-84*
Marquardt, Frank N. - Montgomery, PA - *BrCabYB 84 p.D-303*
Marquee - Coral Gables, FL - *BaconPubCkMag 84*
Marquee - Springfield, PA - *LitMag&SmPr 83-84*
Marquest Colorguide Books - Palos Verdes Estates, CA - *BoPubDir 4, 5*
Marquest/Message Factors - Beaufort, NC - *BrCabYB 84*
Marquette-Adams Telephone Cooperative Inc. - Oxford, WI - *TelDir&BG 83-84*
Marquette Cablevision Inc. - Marquette, MI - *Tel&CabFB 84C p.1689*
Marquette County Historical Society - Marquette, MI - *BoPubDir 4, 5*
Marquette County Tribune - Montello, WI - *AyerDirPub 83; Ed&PubIntYB 82*
Marquette-Deane Systems Inc. - Arlington, VA - *MicrocomMPl 84*
Marquette Mining Journal [of Thomson Newspapers] - Marquette, MI - *BaconPubCkNews 84; NewsDir 84*

Marquette Paper Co. [Div. of Jim Walter Papers] - Maywood, IL - *LitMarPl 83, 84; MagIndMarPl 82-83*
Marquette Tribune - Marquette, KS - *Ed&PubIntYB 82*
Marquette Tribune [of Marquette University] - Milwaukee, WI - *NewsDir 84*
Marquette Tribune - *See* Ellsworth Reporter
Marquette University Press - Milwaukee, WI - *BoPubDir 4 Sup, 5*
Marquis/Bennett Associates Inc. - Warwick, RI - *StaDirAdAg 2-84*
Marquis' Custer Publications, Dr. - Lodi, CA - *BoPubDir 4, 5*
Marquis Online Pro-Files [of Marquis Who's Who Inc.] - Chicago, IL - *DirOnDB Spring 84; EISS 5-84 Sup*
Marquis Who's Who [of Dialog Information Services Inc.] - Palo Alto, CA - *DataDirOnSer 84*
Marquis Who's Who [Subs. of ITT Publishing] - Chicago, IL - *DataDirOnSer 84; DirMarMP 83; DirOnDB Spring 84; InfoS 83-84; LitMarPl 83, 84*
Marquis Who's Who Database [of Marquis Who's Who Inc.] - Chicago, IL - *EISS 7-83 Sup*
Marr Publications - New York, NY - *BoPubDir 4, 5*
Marr Publishing Co., Jack J. - Hauppauge, NY - *BoPubDir 4, 5*
Marracino, Paola - New York, NY - *LitMarPl 83, 84*
Marriage & Divorce Today - New York, NY - *DirOnDB Spring 84*
Marriage & Divorce Today [of NewsNet Inc.] - Bryn Mawr, PA - *DataDirOnSer 84*
Marriage & Family Living [of Abbey Press] - St. Meinrad, IN - *ArtMar 84; MagIndMarPl 82-83; WritMar 84*
Marriott Stations - *See* First Media Corp.
Marriott Teleconference Network [of Marriott Corp.] - Washington, DC - *TeleSy&SerDir 2-84*
Marron Carrel Inc. - Tempe, AZ - *AvMarPl 83*
Mars Advertising Co. - Southfield, MI - *StaDirAdAg 2-84*
Mars Bars Studio Music - *See* Hat Band Music
Mar's Surveys - Cinnaminson, NJ - *IntDirMarRes 83*
MARSAC - Spring Valley, CA - *AvMarPl 83*
Marsaint Music Inc. - New Orleans, LA - *BillIntBG 83-84*
Marsal Productions Inc. - San Antonio, TX - *BillIntBG 83-84*
Marschalk Campbell-Ewald Worldwide [Subs. of The Interpublic Group of Cos. Inc.] - Warren, MI - *StaDirAdAg 2-84*
Marschalk Campbell-Ewald Worldwide - New York, NY - *AdAge 3-28-84, 6-25-84*
Marschalk Co. Inc., The [Div. of Marschalk Campbell-Ewald Worldwide] - New York, NY - *Br 1-23-84; BrCabYB 84; StaDirAdAg 2-84*
Marschalk Co. Inc., The - Cleveland, OH - *ArtMar 84*
Marschalk DM/DR [Div. of The Marschalk Co. Inc.] - Cleveland, OH - *DirMarMP 83*
Marseilles Telephone Co. - Marseilles, IL - *TelDir&BG 83-84*
Marsh Media - Amarillo, TX - *BrCabYB 84; Tel&CabFB 84C p.1689, 84S*
Marsh Media Cable Television [of Marsh Media Ltd.] - Murfreesboro, TN - *BrCabYB 84 p.D-303*
Marsh Point Press - Orono, ME - *LitMag&SmPr 83-84*
Marshall/Altman Advertising Inc. - Great Neck, NY - *StaDirAdAg 2-84*
Marshall & Swift Computerized Cost Programs - Los Angeles, CA - *DataDirOnSer 84; DirOnDB Spring 84*
Marshall Associates - Huntsville, AL - *MicrocomMPl 83, 84*
Marshall Cable TV [of American Television & Communications Corp.] - Marshall, MN - *BrCabYB 84; Tel&CabFB 84C*
Marshall Cable TV [of American Television & Communications Corp.] - Marshall, MO - *BrCabYB 84; Tel&CabFB 84C*
Marshall Cablevision Inc. [of Horizon Communications Corp.] - Arab, AL - *BrCabYB 84*
Marshall Cavendish Corp. [Subs. of Marshall Cavendish Ltd.] - Freeport, NY - *LitMarPl 83, 84*
Marshall Chronicle - Marshall, MI - *BaconPubCkNews 84*
Marshall Community Advisor - Marshall, MI - *BaconPubCkNews 84; NewsDir 84*
Marshall County Green Tab - Moundsville, WV - *AyerDirPub 83*
Marshall County Publishing Co. - Lacon, IL - *BaconPubCkNews 84*
Marshall Democrat-News, The - Marshall, MO - *NewsDir 84*
Marshall Electric Co. - Marshalltown, IA - *BrCabYB 84*
Marshall Evening Chronicle - Marshall, MI - *Ed&PubIntYB 82; NewsDir 84*
Marshall Gazette [of Lewisburg Tribune Inc.] - Lewisburg, TN - *AyerDirPub 83; Ed&PubIntYB 82; NewsDir 84*
Marshall Herald - Marshall, IL - *BaconPubCkNews 84*
Marshall Independent - Marshall, IL - *BaconPubCkNews 84*
Marshall Independent - Marshall, MN - *BaconPubCkNews 84; NewsDir 84*
Marshall, John E. - Orangeville, ON, Canada - *BoPubDir 4, 5*
Marshall Mountain Wave - Marshall, AR - *BaconPubCkNews 84; Ed&PubIntYB 82; NewsDir 84*
Marshall News Messenger - Marshall, TX - *BaconPubCkNews 84; Ed&PubIntYB 82*
Marshall News-Record - Marshall, NC - *BaconPubCkNews 84*
Marshall, Roberts & Co. - New York, NY - *DirInfWP 82*
Marshall Songs Music - Riverside, CA - *BillIntBG 83-84*
Marshall Street Melodies - Minneapolis, MN - *BillIntBG 83-84*
Marshall's Creative Ideas Newsletter [of Creative Book Co.] - Van Nuys, CA - *LitMag&SmPr 83-84*
Marshall's TV Cable Co. - Florence, MT - *BrCabYB 84*
Marshall's TV Cable Co. - Milltown, MT - *BrCabYB 84; Tel&CabFB 84C*
Marshalltown Times-Republican - Marshalltown, IA - *BaconPubCkNews 84; NewsDir 84*
Marshe Infoservices Inc. - Roslyn, NY - *EISS 83*
Marshe Infoservices Inc. - Wantagh, NY - *FBInfSer 80*
Marshfield Mail - Marshfield, MO - *BaconPubCkNews 84; Ed&PubIntYB 82; NewsDir 84*
Marshfield Mariner - Marshfield, MA - *Ed&PubIntYB 82*
Marshfield News-Herald [of Forward Communications] - Marshfield, WI - *BaconPubCkNews 84; Ed&PubIntYB 82; NewsDir 84*
Marshfield Shoppinguide - Plymouth, MA - *AyerDirPub 83*
Marshfilm Enterprises Inc. - Shawnee Mission, KS - *AvMarPl 83; WritMar 84*
Marshville Union News & Home - Marshville, NC - *BaconPubCkNews 84; NewsDir 84*
Marsing Owyhee Nugget - Marsing, ID - *BaconPubCkNews 84*
Marsmith Music - *See* Amestoy Music
Marson Inc. - Nashville, TN - *BillIntBG 83-84*
Marstellar - Englewood, CO - *ArtMar 84*
Marsteller Inc. [Subs. of Young & Rubicam] - New York, NY - *AdAge 3-28-84, 6-25-84; BrCabYB 84; StaDirAdAg 2-84*
Marston & Associates Inc., Robert - New York, NY - *DirPRFirms 83; LitMarPl 84*
Marstons Inc. - Tempe, AZ - *AvMarPl 83*
Marstrat Inc. - Chicago, IL - *AdAge 3-28-84; StaDirAdAg 2-84*
Mart Herald - Mart, TX - *BaconPubCkNews 84; Ed&PubIntYB 82; NewsDir 84*
Mart Magazine [of Morgan-Grampian Publishing Co.] - New York, NY - *BaconPubCkMag 84; MagDir 84; MagIndMarPl 82-83*
Martcoa - *See* Cooper Music, Martin
Martcom Inc. - Columbus, OH - *StaDirAdAg 2-84*
Martel & Freres Television Enrg. - Notre-Dame-des-Anges, PQ, Canada - *BrCabYB 84*
Martel Electronics - Anaheim, CA - *AvMarPl 83*
Martell Research - Springfield, MO - *IntDirMarRes 83*
Martelle Cooperative Telephone Association - Martelle, IA - *TelDir&BG 83-84*
Marten Publications Inc. - De Soto, MO - *BaconPubCkNews 84*
Marthasville Record - Marthasville, MO - *BaconPubCkNews 84; Ed&PubIntYB 82*
Martik Music - *See* Armstrong Associates, Pat
Martin Agency - Richmond, VA - *AdAge 3-28-84; StaDirAdAg 2-84*
Martin Agency (Product & Services Div.) - Baltimore, MD - *DirMarMP 83*
Martin, Alan F. - Toms River, NJ - *Tel&CabFB 84C*
Martin & Associates - Sacramento, CA - *WhoWMicrocom 83*
Martin & Associates Inc., Louis J. - New York, NY - *LitMarPl 83*
Martin & Benedict Inc. - Santa Monica, CA - *StaDirAdAg 2-84*
Martin & Stefanacci Associates - Lancaster, PA - *EISS 83*
Martin/Arnold Color Systems - New York, NY - *ArtMar 84; AvMarPl 83*

Martin Associates, David - Richmond, England - *MicrocomSwDir 1*
Martin Associates Inc., J. P. - New York, NY - *StaDirAdAg 2-84*
Martin Associates, Peppy - Louisville, KY - *HBIndAd&MS 82-83*
Martin Associates, Peter - New York, NY - *ArtMar 84; DirPRFirms 83*
Martin Audio/Video Corp. - New York, NY - *AvMarPl 83*
Martin Co., R. J. - Palisades Park, NJ - *AvMarPl 83*
Martin Countian, The - Inez, KY - *AyerDirPub 83; Ed&PubIntYB 82; NewsDir 84*
Martin-Daylor Advertising Inc. - Des Plaines, IL - *StaDirAdAg 2-84*
Martin, Edward A. - Grand Junction, CO - *BoPubDir 4, 5*
Martin, Frances - New York, NY - *LitMarPl 83, 84; MagIndMarPl 82-83*
Martin, George - New York, NY - *LitMarPl 83, 84*
Martin-Hamblin Research Ltd. - London, England - *IntDirMarRes 83*
Martin Interviewing Services Inc., J. B. - Bridgeport, CT - *IntDirMarRes 83*
Martin Lithographers - Plainview, NY - *LitMarPl 83, 84; MagIndMarPl 82-83*
Martin Marietta Corp. - Bethesda, MD - *Datamation 6-83*
Martin Marietta Data Systems [Div. of Martin Marietta Corp.] - Bethesda, MD - *ADAPSOMemDir 83-84; Top100Al 83*
Martin Marietta Data Systems [Div. of Martin Marietta Corp.] - Greenbelt, MD - *DataDirOnSer 84; DataDirSup 7-83*
Martin Music, Pete - *See* Vaam Music
Martin Press - Torrance, CA - *BoPubDir 4 Sup, 5*
Martin Publishing, B. B. [Aff. of Ralph McElroy Co.] - Austin, TX - *BoPubDir 4, 5*
Martin Publishing Co. - Ft. Wayne, IN - *BoPubDir 4 Sup, 5*
Martin, Remick, Moore Inc. - Richmond, VA - *StaDirAdAg 2-84*
Martin, Sturtevant, Silverman & Marshall - New York, NY - *AdAge 3-28-84; StaDirAdAg 2-84*
Martin Video Productions - Freeport, NY - *AvMarPl 83*
Martin Weakley County Press - Martin, TN - *BaconPubCkNews 84; NewsDir 84*
Martin-Williams Inc. - Minneapolis, MN - *AdAge 3-28-84; StaDirAdAg 2-84*
Martindale Drug Data Bank [of Pharmaceutical Society of Great Britain] - London, England - *EISS 83*
Martindale-Hubbell Inc. - Summit, NJ - *BoPubDir 4, 5*
Martineau Corp. - Bethesda, MD - *DirMarMP 83*
Martinez, Arthur D. & Barbara - Silver City, NM - *BoPubDir 4, 5*
Martinez-Columbia News - Augusta, GA - *NewsDir 84*
Martinez Columbia News - Martinez, GA - *BaconPubCkNews 84*
Martinez News-Gazette [of Gibson Publishing] - Martinez, CA - *AyerDirPub 83; BaconPubCkNews 84; Ed&PubIntYB 82; NewsDir 84*
Martinez, Poosh - Huntsville, AR - *LitMarPl 83*
Martingale Manuscripts - North Pitcher, NY - *BoPubDir 4, 5*
Martins Ferry-Bellaire Times-Leader [of Dix News Media] - Martins Ferry, OH - *NewsDir 84*
Martins, William P. - Bradenton, FL - *Tel&CabFB 84C p.1689*
Martinsburg Evening Journal - Martinsburg, WV - *BaconPubCkNews 84*
Martinsburg Morrisons Cove Herald - Martinsburg, PA - *BaconPubCkNews 84; NewsDir 84*
Martinsburg News - Martinsburg, WV - *BaconPubCkNews 84; Ed&PubIntYB 82*
Martinsville Bulletin - Martinsville, VA - *BaconPubCkNews 84; NewsDir 84*
Martinsville Cablevision [of Multi-Channel TV Cable Co.] - Martinsville, VA - *BrCabYB 84; Tel&CabFB 84C*
Martinsville Planet - Martinsville, IL - *Ed&PubIntYB 82*
Martinsville Planet - *See* Martinsville Review Publishers
Martinsville Reporter - Martinsville, IN - *BaconPubCkNews 84; NewsDir 84*
Martinsville Review Publishers - Martinsville, IL - *BaconPubCkNews 84*
Martinsville Westfield Review - *See* Martinsville Review Publishers
Martinus Nijhoff Medical Publishers - *See* Kluwer Boston Inc.
Martiny & Co. - Cincinnati, OH - *StaDirAdAg 2-84*
Marton, Elisabeth - New York, NY - *LitMarPl 83, 84*
Marton, Ruth - New York, NY - *LitMarPl 83, 84*
Martu Music Inc. - *See* Marsaint Music Inc.
Martz & Associates - Scottsdale, AZ - *StaDirAdAg 2-84*
Marullo Music, A. W. - Galveston, TX - *BillIntBG 83-84*
Marullo Productions Inc. - Galveston, TX - *BillIntBG 83-84*
Maruzen Co. Ltd. - Tokyo, Japan - *InfIndMarPl 83*
Maruzen International Co. Ltd. [Subs. of Maruzen Co. Ltd.] - New York, NY - *LitMarPl 83, 84*
Maruzen Online Network [of Maruzen Co. Ltd.] - Tokyo, Japan - *InfIndMarPl 83*
Maruzen Scientific Information Service Center [of Maruzen Co. Ltd.] - Tokyo, Japan - *EISS 83*
Marvanco Enterprizes - Peekskill, NY - *BoPubDir 4, 5*
Marvel Comics Group [Div. of Cadence Industries Corp.] - New York, NY - *MagIndMarPl 82-83*
Marvel Inc. - Boca Raton, FL - *StaDirAdAg 2-84*
Marvel Music, Andy - East Norwich, NY - *BillIntBG 83-84*
Marvell Messenger - Hazen, AR - *Ed&PubIntYB 82*
Marvelle Music Co. - *See* Alexis Music Inc.
Marvelwood Music - Nashville, TN - *BillIntBG 83-84*
Marvelwood Records & Tapes - Nashville, TN - *BillIntBG 83-84*
Marvin & Leonard Advertising Co. Inc. - Boston, MA - *StaDirAdAg 2-84*
Marvin Gardens Music - New York, NY - *BillIntBG 83-84*
Marx & Associates Inc., Dick - Chicago, IL - *AvMarPl 83*
Marx, Engels, Lenin, Stalin Institute - Toronto, ON, Canada - *BoPubDir 4, 5; LitMag&SmPr 83-84*
Marx, Knoll & Mangels Inc. - Portland, OR - *StaDirAdAg 2-84*
Marx Music Co., Josef - *See* McGinnis & Marx Music Publishers
Marxist Educational Press - Minneapolis, MN - *BoPubDir 4*
Marxist-Leninist Publications - Chicago, IL - *BoPubDir 4, 5*
Mary Ellen Enterprises Inc. - St. Louis Park, MN - *BoPubDir 4 Sup, 5*
Maryben Books - Rockville, MD - *BoPubDir 4, 5*
Marycords - Powers Lake, ND - *BillIntBG 83-84*
Maryknoll Films - Maryknoll, NY - *Tel&CabFB 84C*
Maryknoll Magazine [of Maryknoll Fathers] - Maryknoll, NY - *MagIndMarPl 82-83; WritMar 84*
Maryland Automated Geographic Information System [of Maryland Dept. of State Planning] - Baltimore, MD - *EISS 83*
Maryland Beachcomber [of Atlantic Publications Inc.] - Ocean City, MD - *AyerDirPub 83; NewsDir 84*
Maryland Business Journal - Baltimore, MD - *BaconPubCkMag 84*
Maryland Center for Public Broadcasting - Owings Mills, MD - *AvMarPl 83*
Maryland Coast Press - Ocean City, MD - *Ed&PubIntYB 82*
Maryland Composition Co. Inc. - Glen Burnie, MD - *LitMarPl 83, 84; MagIndMarPl 82-83*
Maryland Dept. of Economic & Community Development (Business Directories Office) - Annapolis, MD - *BoPubDir 4 Sup, 5*
Maryland Gazette - Glen Burnie, MD - *AyerDirPub 83; Ed&PubIntYB 82*
Maryland Genealogical Society Inc. - Baltimore, MD - *BoPubDir 4, 5*
Maryland Hall of Records [Aff. of Maryland Dept. of General Services] - Annapolis, MD - *BoPubDir 4, 5; MicroMarPl 82-83*
Maryland Historical Press [Aff. of Energy Forum Inc.] - Lanham, MD - *BoPubDir 4, 5; LitMag&SmPr 83-84*
Maryland Historical Society - Baltimore, MD - *BoPubDir 4, 5; MicroMarPl 82-83*
Maryland Home & Apartment Journal [of HBAM Publications Inc.] - Baltimore, MD - *MagDir 84*
Maryland Home & Apartment Journal - Towson, MD - *BaconPubCkMag 84*
Maryland Independent - Waldorf, MD - *AyerDirPub 83; Ed&PubIntYB 82*
Maryland Interlibrary Organization - Baltimore, MD - *EISS 83*
Maryland Magazine [of Dept. of Economic & Community Development] - Annapolis, MD - *MagDir 84; WritMar 84*
Maryland Master Plumber [of Associated Plumbing Contractors of Maryland Inc.] - Baltimore, MD - *BaconPubCkMag 84; MagDir 84*
Maryland Model II Games - Temple Hills, MD - *MicrocomMPl 84*

Maryland Motorist - Baltimore, MD - *BaconPubCkMag 84; MagDir 84*
Maryland Pharmacist [of Maryland Pharmaceutical Association] - Baltimore, MD - *MagDir 84*
Maryland Purchasing - Baltimore, MD - *BaconPubCkMag 84*
Maryland State Medical Journal - Baltimore, MD - *BaconPubCkMag 84; MagDir 84*
Maryland State News - Dover, DE - *Ed&PubIntYB 82*
Maryland-Washington-Delaware Beverage Journal [of The Beverage Journal Inc.] - Baltimore, MD - *BaconPubCkMag 84; MagDir 84*
Marylander & Herald - Princess Anne, MD - *AyerDirPub 83; Ed&PubIntYB 82*
Marylander Marketing Research Inc. - Encino, CA - *IntDirMarRes 83*
Marymae Industries Inc. - Katy, TX - *MicrocomMPl 83, 84*
Marysville Advocate - Marysville, KS - *BaconPubCkNews 84; Ed&PubIntYB 82; NewsDir 84*
Marysville Appeal Democrat [of Freedom Newspapers Inc.] - Marysville, CA - *NewsDir 84*
Marysville Cable TV Co. [of United Artists Cablesystems Corp.] - Marysville, KS - *Tel&CabFB 84C*
Marysville Globe - Marysville, WA - *BaconPubCkNews 84; Ed&PubIntYB 82*
Marysville Journal Tribune - Marysville, OH - *BaconPubCkNews 84; Ed&PubIntYB 82; NewsDir 84*
Maryville-Alcoa Times - Maryville, TN - *LitMarPl 83; NewsDir 84*
Maryville Cable TV [of American TV & Communications Corp.] - Maryville, MO - *BrCabYB 84; Tel&CabFB 84C*
Maryville Daily Forum, The - Maryville, MO - *NewsDir 84*
Maryville Enterprise - Maryville, TN - *BaconPubCkNews 84; Ed&PubIntYB 82*
Marzique Music - Los Angeles, CA - *BillIntBG 83-84*
Marzola & Associates, Ed - Studio City, CA - *AvMarPl 83; WritMar 84*
Mas TV de Caguas Inc. - Caguas, PR - *Tel&CabFB 84C*
Masa Records - San Juan, PR - *BillIntBG 83-84*
Masada Corp. - Birmingham, AL - *Tel&CabFB 84C p.1689*
Masaoka-Ishikawa & Associates Inc. - Washington, DC - *DirPRFirms 83*
Mascot, The - Minneota, MN - *Ed&PubIntYB 82*
Mascoutah County Journal - Mascoutah, IL - *Ed&PubIntYB 82*
Mascoutah County Journal - *See* Journal Newspapers of Southern Illinois
Mascoutah Herald [of Yelvington Publications] - Mascoutah, IL - *NewsDir 84*
Mascoutah Herald - *See* Yelvington Enterprises Inc., Rube
Masculines [of Earl Barron Publications Inc.] - New York, NY - *BaconPubCkMag 84; MagDir 84*
Maserek, Luverne - Sleepy Eye, MN - *Tel&CabFB 84C p.1689*
Maserek, Magdalen - Sleepy Eye, MN - *Tel&CabFB 84C p.1689*
Mashell Telephone Co. Inc. - Eatonville, WA - *TelDir&BG 83-84*
Masheris Associates Inc., R. - Deerfield, IL - *LitMarPl 83, 84*
Mask-O-Neg [Subs. of Metro Associated Services Inc.] - New York, NY - *MagIndMarPl 82-83*
Maslow, Gold & Rothschild Direct [Subs. of Maslow, Gold & Rothschild Inc.] - Boston, MA - *DirMarMP 83*
Maslow, Gold & Rothschild Inc. - Boston, MA - *StaDirAdAg 2-84*
Mason & Madison - Bethany, CT - *AdAge 3-28-84; DirPRFirms 83; StaDirAdAg 2-84*
Mason City Banner Times - Mason City, IL - *BaconPubCkNews 84; Ed&PubIntYB 82*
Mason City Globe-Gazette [of Lee Enterprises Inc.] - Mason City, IA - *BaconPubCkNews 84; NewsDir 84*
Mason City Shoppers News - Mason City, IA - *AyerDirPub 83*
Mason County Courier - Mason, MI - *Ed&PubIntYB 82*
Mason County Democrat - Havana, IL - *AyerDirPub 83; Ed&PubIntYB 82*
Mason County News - Mason, TX - *AyerDirPub 83; BaconPubCkNews 84; Ed&PubIntYB 82*
Mason County News - Mason, WV - *BaconPubCkNews 84; Ed&PubIntYB 82*
Mason, Elda - Nanaimo, BC, Canada - *BoPubDir 4, 5*
Mason Ingham County News - Mason, MI - *BaconPubCkNews 84; NewsDir 84*
Mason, James H. - Gardena, CA - *BoPubDir 5*
Mason Publishing Co. [Aff. of Butterworth & Co. Ltd.] - St. Paul, MN - *BoPubDir 4, 5*
Mason-Relkin Co. - New York, NY - *StaDirAdAg 2-84*
Mason Valley News - Yerington, NV - *AyerDirPub 83; Ed&PubIntYB 82*
Masonite Corp. (Commercial Div.) - Dover, OH - *DirInfWP 82*
Masonry - Oakbrook Terrace, IL - *BaconPubCkMag 84*
Masonry [of Mason Contractors Association of America] - Villa Park, IL - *MagDir 84*
Masonry Design West - Pleasanton, CA - *BaconPubCkMag 84*
Masonry Industry [of Building News Inc.] - Los Angeles, CA - *MagDir 84*
Masontown Sentinel - Masontown, PA - *BaconPubCkNews 84*
Maspeth Queens Ledger - Maspeth, NY - *NewsDir 84*
Maspeth Queens Ledger - *See* Conglor Publishing Inc.
Mass Cablevision [Aff. of Colony Communications Inc.] - Falmouth, MA - *InterCabHB 3*
Mass High Tech - Burlington, MA - *ArtMar 84; BaconPubCkMag 84; WritMar 84*
Mass Media Booknotes - Annandale, VA - *MagIndMarPl 82-83*
Mass Media Ministries Inc. - Baltimore, MD - *AvMarPl 83*
Mass Press - Washington, DC - *BoPubDir 5*
Mass Spectral Search System [of Computer Sciences Corp.] - Falls Church, VA - *DataDirOnSer 84*
Mass Spectrometry Bulletin [of Pergamon International Information Corp.] - McLean, VA - *DataDirOnSer 84*
Mass Spectrometry Bulletin [of Mass Spectrometry Data Centre] - Nottingham, England - *CompReadDB 82; DirOnDB Spring 84; OnBibDB 3*
Mass Spectrometry Data Centre [of The Royal Society of Chemistry] - Nottingham, England - *CompReadDB 82; EISS 83*
Mass Spectroscopy Literature [of Iowa State University] - Ames, IA - *CompReadDB 82*
Mass Transit - Washington, DC - *BaconPubCkMag 84; MagDir 84*
Massachusetts & New Hampshire Out-of-Doors - Littleton, MA - *BaconPubCkMag 84*
Massachusetts Beverage Journal [of New England Beverage Publications Inc.] - Avon, MA - *BaconPubCkMag 84; MagDir 84*
Massachusetts Cable Co. [of Adelphia Communications Corp.] - Falmouth, MA - *Tel&CabFB 84C*
Massachusetts Cablevision Inc. - Falmouth, MA - *BrCabYB 84*
Massachusetts Cablevision Systems Inc. - Medway, MA - *BrCabYB 84*
Massachusetts CPA Review [of Massachusetts Society of CPA's] - Boston, MA - *BaconPubCkMag 84; MagDir 84*
Massachusetts Health Data Consortium Inc. - Waltham, MA - *EISS 83*
Massachusetts Historical Society - Boston, MA - *BoPubDir 4, 5; LitMarPl 83, 84; MicroMarPl 82-83*
Massachusetts Institute of Technology - Cambridge, MA - *AvMarPl 83*
Massachusetts Institute of Technology (Electronics Research Laboratory) - Cambridge, MA - *CompReadDB 82*
Massachusetts Labor Leader - Boston, MA - *NewsDir 84*
Massachusetts Lawyers Weekly - Boston, MA - *BaconPubCkMag 84; MagDir 84*
Massachusetts Natural Heritage Program [of Massachusetts State Dept. of Environmental Management] - Boston, MA - *EISS 7-83 Sup*
Massachusetts Poverty Law Center Inc. [Aff. of Massachusetts Law Reform Institute] - Boston, MA - *BoPubDir 4 Sup, 5*
Massachusetts Review, The - Amherst, MA - *LitMag&SmPr 83-84; WritMar 84*
Massachusetts Teacher, The - Boston, MA - *MagDir 84*
Massapequa Massapequan Observer - *See* Hiber Publishing Inc.
Massapequa North Pennysaver - Levittown, NY - *AyerDirPub 83*
Massapequa Post - Massapequa Park, NY - *AyerDirPub 83; BaconPubCkNews 84; Ed&PubIntYB 82; NewsDir 84*
Massapequa South Pennysaver - Levittown, NY - *AyerDirPub 83*
Massapequan Observer [of Levittown Observer/Tribune Community Newspapers] - Massapequa Park, NY - *AyerDirPub 83; Ed&PubIntYB 82; NewsDir 84*
Massena NewChannels [of NewChannels Corp.] - Massena, NY - *BrCabYB 84; Tel&CabFB 84C*

Massena Observer - Massena, NY - *BaconPubCkNews 84; Ed&PubIntYB 82; NewsDir 84*
Massena Telephone Co. - Massena, IA - *TelDir&BG 83-84*
Massey, Blanche - New York, NY - *LitMarPl 83, 84*
Massillon Cable TV Inc. - Massillon, OH - *BrCabYB 84; Tel&CabFB 84C p.1689*
Massillon Evening Independent - Massillon, OH - *BaconPubCkNews 84; NewsDir 84*
MassMarket Books - Somerville, MA - *LitMarPl 84*
Masson Publishing USA Inc. - New York, NY - *LitMarPl 83, 84*
Masspac Publishing Co. - Mt. Clemens, MI - *BoPubDir 4, 5*
Mast Advertising Associates Inc. - New York, NY - *StaDirAdAg 2-84*
Mast & Associates, C. L. Jr. - Flossmoor, IL - *BoPubDir 4, 5*
Mast Development Co. - Davenport, IA - *AvMarPl 83*
Masta Plan Inc. - *See* Van Brunt & Co. Advertising-Marketing Inc.
Mastbaum Marketing - Dayton, OH - *IntDirMarRes 83*
Master Cable Corp. - Velma, OK - *Tel&CabFB 84C*
Master Designer - Chicago, IL - *BoPubDir 4, 5*
Master Detective [of R.G.H. Publishing Corp.] - New York, NY - *MagDir 84; MagIndMarPl 82-83; WritMar 84*
Master Eagle Photoengraving Co. - New York, NY - *LitMarPl 83*
Master Electronics Inc. - Raymondville, TX - *MicrocomMPl 84*
Master Gator Software - Alachua, FL - *MicrocomMPl 83*
Master Key - Baltimore, MD - *Tel&CabFB 84C*
Master Key Publications - Bonita, CA - *BoPubDir 4, 5*
Master Lists [Div. of of Phelon, Sheldon & Marsar Inc.] - New York, NY - *MagIndMarPl 82-83*
Master, Mate & Pilot, The - New York, NY - *NewsDir 84*
Master Media Inc. - Atlanta, GA - *WritMar 84*
Master Media Inc. - Tucker, GA - *AvMarPl 83*
Master Menu [of Dow Jones News/Retrieval Service] - Princeton, NJ - *DataDirOnSer 84*
Master Motion Picture Co. - Boston, MA - *Tel&CabFB 84C*
Master Press - Dayton, OH - *BoPubDir 4, 5*
Master Salesmanship [of MWL Inc.] - Westlake Village, CA - *MicrocomMPl 84*
Master Slide Inc. - Webster Grove, MO - *AvMarPl 83*
Master Specialties Co. - Costa Mesa, CA - *DataDirSup 7-83*
Master Teacher - Manhattan, KS - *BoPubDir 5*
Master Telecable Inc. - Matoaka, WV - *BrCabYB 84; Tel&CabFB 84C*
Master Telecable Inc. - Peterstown, WV - *Tel&CabFB 84C p.1689*
Master Telecable Inc. [of Phoenix Communications] - Racine, WV - *BrCabYB 84*
Master Telecable Inc. - Rupert, WV - *BrCabYB 84; Tel&CabFB 84C*
Master Thoughts [of Dominion Press] - San Marcos, CA - *LitMag&SmPr 83-84*
Master-Trak Sound Recorders - Crowley, LA - *BillIntBG 83-84*
Master Z Music - Little Rock, AR - *BillIntBG 83-84*
Masterco Press Inc. - Ann Arbor, MI - *BoPubDir 4, 5*
MasterComputing Inc. - Greenville, SC - *MicrocomMPl 84*
Mastercraft Music - *See* Brown & Associates Inc., J. Aaron
Masterfile - Toronto, ON, Canada - *Ed&PubIntYB 82*
Masterlease Music Publications - St. Louis, MO - *BillIntBG 83-84*
Master's Press Inc. - Kalamazoo, MI - *BoPubDir 4, 5*
Masters Publications, Jim - Berkeley, CA - *BoPubDir 5*
Masters Publications, Jim - Brooklyn, NY - *BoPubDir 4*
Masters Software Co. - Sandy, UT - *MicrocomSwDir 1; WhoWMicrocom 83*
Masters Speech & Voice - New York, NY - *ProGuPRSer 4*
Masters Touch Recording Studio Inc. - Nashville, TN - *BillIntBG 83-84*
Masterspec 2 [of Production Systems for Architects & Engineers] - Washington, DC - *DataDirOnSer 84; EISS 83*
Masterview Music Publishing Corp. - Perkasie, PA - *BillIntBG 83-84*
MasterVision - New York, NY - *AvMarPl 83*
MasterVision - Bentley Creek, PA - *Tel&CabFB 84C*
Masterwork Press - Pottersville, NJ - *BoPubDir 4, 5*
Masterworks Software - Lomita, CA - *MicrocomMPl 83, 84; MicrocomSwDir 1; WritMar 84*
Matador Tribune - Matador, TX - *BaconPubCkNews 84; Ed&PubIntYB 82*
Matagiri - Mt. Tremper, NY - *BoPubDir 4, 5; LitMag&SmPr 83-84; LitMarPl 83, 84*
Matamoras Video Cable Corp. - Matamoras, PA - *BrCabYB 84; Tel&CabFB 84C*
Matanuska Telephone Association Inc. - Palmer, AK - *TelDir&BG 83-84*
Matawan Sentinel - *See* Sentinel Newspapers
Matches, G. Alex - North Vancouver, BC, Canada - *BoPubDir 4, 5*
Matchless Systems - Gardena, CA - *DirInfWP 82*
Matchless Systems - Long Beach, CA - *MicrocomMPl 84*
Matell Associates Inc., Robin - Miami, FL - *DirPRFirms 83*
Mater Dei Provincialate [Aff. of Daughters of Charity of Indiana Inc.] - Evansville, IN - *BoPubDir 4, 5*
Material Handling Engineering [of Penton/IPC Inc.] - Cleveland, OH - *BaconPubCkMag 84; MagDir 84; MagIndMarPl 82-83*
Material Handling Institute Inc. [Aff. of Shea Management Inc.] - Pittsburgh, PA - *BoPubDir 5*
Material Handling Product News - Dover, NJ - *BaconPubCkMag 84*
Material Handling Wholesaler - Owings Mills, MD - *BaconPubCkMag 84*
Material Information System for Iron & Steel [of German Iron & Steel Association] - Dusseldorf, West Germany - *EISS 83*
Materials & Components Plant Performance Data Center [of U.S. National Bureau of Standards] - Washington, DC - *EISS 83*
Materials Data Retrieval System [of European Space Agency] - Noordwijk, Netherlands - *EISS 83*
Materials Engineering [of Penton/IPC Inc.] - Cleveland, OH - *BaconPubCkMag 84; MagDir 84; MagIndMarPl 82-83*
Materials Evaluation - Columbus, OH - *BaconPubCkMag 84; MagDir 84; MagIndMarPl 82-83*
Materials Management & Distribution - Toronto, ON, Canada - *BaconPubCkMag 84*
Materials of Music [of University of Georgia] - Athens, GA - *CompReadDB 82*
Materials Performance - Houston, TX - *BaconPubCkMag 84; MagDir 84*
Materials Properties Data Center [of U.S. National Bureau of Standards] - Washington, DC - *EISS 83*
Maternity Center Association - New York, NY - *BoPubDir 4, 5*
Matex Inc. - Torrance, CA - *MicrocomMPl 83*
Math - Eggenstein-Leopoldshafen, West Germany - *DirOnDB Spring 84*
Math Counseling Institute Press - Seattle, WA - *BoPubDir 4, 5; LitMag&SmPr 83-84*
Math Group Inc., The - Minneapolis, MN - *DirMarMP 83*
Math House [Aff. of Mosaic Media Inc.] - Glen Ellyn, IL - *AvMarPl 83; BoPubDir 4, 5*
Math Sci Press - Brookline, MA - *BoPubDir 4, 5*
Math Software - Deerfield, IL - *MicrocomMPl 83, 84; WhoWMicrocom 83*
Mathco - Rockport, MA - *BoPubDir 4, 5*
Mathdi - Eggenstein-Leopoldshafen, West Germany - *DirOnDB Spring 84*
Mathematica Products Group - Princeton, NJ - *DataDirSup 7-83*
Mathematical Reviews - Ann Arbor, MI - *MagDir 84*
Mathematical Reviews Titles [of American Mathematical Society] - Providence, RI - *CompReadDB 82*
Mathematical Software Co. - El Cajon, CA - *MicrocomMPl 84*
Mathematical Spectrum [of Applied Probability Trust] - Sheffield, England - *LitMag&SmPr 83-84*
Mathematics & Computer Education - Old Bethpage, NY - *BaconPubCkMag 84; MagDir 84*
Mathematics Teacher - Reston, VA - *BaconPubCkMag 84; MagDir 84; MagIndMarPl 82-83*
Mather Air Force-Wingtips [of Sacramento Suburban Newspapers Inc.] - Fair Oaks, CA - *NewsDir 84*
Mather Editorial Services, Anne D. - Atlanta, GA - *LitMarPl 83*
Mather Editorial Services, Anne D. - Marietta, GA - *LitMarPl 84*
Mathews & Clark Communications - Palo Alto, CA - *DirPRFirms 83*

Mathews & Co. - Darien, CT - *ADAPSOMemDir 83-84*
Mathews Associates, Walter - New York, NY - *HBIndAd&MS 82-83*
Mathfile [of American Mathematical Society] - Providence, RI - *DataDirOnSer 84; DirOnDB Spring 84; EISS 83; OnBibDB 3*
Mathiesen Editions - Providence, RI - *BoPubDir 4, 5*
Mathis Advertising, Jack - Libertyville, IL - *AdAge 3-28-84; StaDirAdAg 2-84*
Mathis & Co., J. D. - Baltimore, MD - *StaDirAdAg 2-84*
Mathis Cable TV Inc. [of Tele-Communications Inc.] - Mathis, TX - *Tel&CabFB 84C*
Mathis, Dale - Del Rio, TX - *Tel&CabFB 84C p.1689*
Mathis, James E. - Gainesville, GA - *Tel&CabFB 84C*
Mathis News, The - Mathis, TX - *Ed&PubIntYB 82*
Mathis News, The - *See* San Patricio Publishing Co.
Mathis Stations - Magee, MS - *BrCabYB 84*
Mathom Publishing Co. - Oswego, NY - *BoPubDir 4, 5*
Mathware - Hermosa Beach, CA - *WhoWMicrocom 83*
Mathware/Math City - Rolling Hills Estate, CA - *MicrocomMPl 83, 84*
Mati [of Ommation Press] - Chicago, IL - *BoPubDir 4, 5; LitMag&SmPr 83-84*
Matic Data Systems - Arcadia, CA - *MicrocomMPl 84*
Matilda Literary & Arts Magazine - Melbourne, Australia - *LitMag&SmPr 83-84*
Matilda Publications - Melbourne, Australia - *LitMag&SmPr 83-84*
Matkovich, Walter - Wellsburg, WV - *Tel&CabFB 84C p.1689*
Matlin Co. - Washington Crossing, PA - *AdAge 3-28-84; StaDirAdAg 2-84*
Matlock Communications Inc. - Eagle, IA - *BrCabYB 84*
Matra (Telecommunications Branch) - New York, NY - *VideoDir 82-83*
Matri Satsang - Nevada City, CA - *BoPubDir 4, 5*
Matrix [of Red Herring Press] - Urbana, IL - *LitMag&SmPr 83-84*
Matrix - Lennoxville, PQ, Canada - *LitMag&SmPr 83-84*
Matrix [of British Science Fiction Association Ltd.] - Reading, England - *LitMag&SmPr 83-84*
Matrix-Cablevision Entertainment Services Inc. - Bedford Heights, OH - *BrCabYB 84*
Matrix Cablevision Entertainment Services Inc. [of Matrix Enterprises Inc.] - North Royalton, OH - *Tel&CabFB 84C*
Matrix Cablevision Entertainment Services Inc. [of Matrix Enterprises Inc.] - Solon, OH - *Tel&CabFB 84C*
Matrix Computer Co. - Oakland, CA - *WhoWMicrocom 83*
Matrix Enterprises Inc. - Franklin, TN - *BrCabYB 84 p.D-303; Tel&CabFB 84C p.1689*
Matrix Instruments Inc. [Subs. of Matrix Corp.] - Northvale, NJ - *AvMarPl 83; DataDirSup 7-83*
Matrix Press - Palo Alto, CA - *BoPubDir 4, 5; LitMag&SmPr 83-84*
Matrix Publications Inc. - Providence, RI - *BoPubDir 4 Sup, 5*
Matrix Publishers Inc. [of Dilithium Press] - Beaverton, OR - *LitMarPl 83*
Matrix Publishing Co. - Memphis, TN - *BillIntBG 83-84*
Matrix Research Group - Berkeley, CA - *IntDirMarRes 83*
Matrix Software - Big Rapids, MI - *MicrocomMPl 83, 84*
Matrix Transaction Exchange - Berkeley, CA - *DirOnDB Spring 84*
Matrix Transaction Exchange [of Cross Information Co.] - Boulder, CO - *TeleSy&SerDir 7-83*
Matrix Video Services Inc. - New York, NY - *AvMarPl 83*
Matrix Vision [of Matrix Enterprises Inc.] - Maryville, TN - *Tel&CabFB 84C*
Matrix Vision of Evarts Inc. - Evarts, KY - *Tel&CabFB 84C*
Matrix Vision of Harlan County Inc. - Putney, KY - *BrCabYB 84*
Matrix Vision of Loudon County Inc. [of Matrix Enterprises Inc.] - Lenoir City, TN - *BrCabYB 84*
Matrix Vision of Suburban Toledo Inc. [of Matrix Enterprises Inc.] - Allen Township, OH - *Tel&CabFB 84C*
Matrix Vision of Wilmette Inc. [of Matrix Enterprises Inc.] - Wilmette, IL - *Tel&CabFB 84C*
Matson Co. Inc., Harold [Aff. of McIntosh, McKee & Dodds Inc.] - New York, NY - *LitMarPl 83, 84*
Matson Multi-Media - San Antonio, TX - *AvMarPl 83*
Matsumoto-Herzog Advertising - Los Angeles, CA - *StaDirAdAg 2-84*
Matsushita - Osaka, Japan - *ElecNews 7-25-83*
Matsushita Electric Industrial Co. Ltd. - Secaucus, NJ - *HomeVid&CabYB 82-83*
Mattapan Tribune - Mattapan, MA - *Ed&PubIntYB 82*
Mattel Electronics [Subs. of Mattel Inc.] - Hawthorne, CA - *MicrocomMPl 84; WhoWMicrocom 83*
Mattel Inc. - Hawthorne, CA - *HomeVid&CabYB 82-83; KnowInd 83*
Matteson-Richton Park Star - Chicago Heights, IL - *NewsDir 84*
Matteson-Richton Park Star - Matteson, IL - *AyerDirPub 83; Ed&PubIntYB 82*
Matteson-Richton Park Star - *See* Star Publications
Matthew, J. M. - Bloomington, IN - *LitMarPl 83, 84*
Matthew Publishers - Houston, TX - *BoPubDir 5*
Matthews, Allan F. - McLean, VA - *BoPubDir 4, 5*
Matthews & Associates Inc., J. - Grass Valley, CA - *EISS 83*
Matthews & Partners Ltd. - Pointe Claire, PQ, Canada - *BoPubDir 4, 5*
Matthews Book Co. - Maryland Heights, MO - *LitMarPl 83, 84*
Matthews Corp., J. L. - Mt. Prospect, IL - *HBIndAd&MS 82-83*
Matthews, Robert T. - West Friendship, MD - *BoPubDir 4, 5*
Mattice TV System - Hearst, ON, Canada - *BrCabYB 84*
Mattingly & Butler Publishers Ltd. - Atlanta, GA - *BoPubDir 4, 5*
Mattole Press - San Francisco, CA - *BoPubDir 4, 5*
Mattoon Cablevision Inc. [of Tele-Communications Inc.] - Mattoon, IL - *BrCabYB 84; Tel&CabFB 84C*
Mattoon Journal-Gazette - Mattoon, IL - *BaconPubCkNews 84; Ed&PubIntYB 82; NewsDir 84*
Mattox Corp., S. E. - San Pedro, CA - *BoPubDir 4, 5*
Mattson, Marie - San Francisco, CA - *Ed&PubIntYB 82*
Mattydale-North Syracuse Pennysaver - Syracuse, NY - *AyerDirPub 83*
Mature Living [of The Southern Baptist Convention] - Nashville, TN - *MagIndMarPl 82-83; WritMar 84*
Mature Years - Nashville, TN - *MagIndMarPl 82-83; WritMar 84*
Maturity Magazines Group [of NRTA/AARP] - New York, NY - *MagIndMarPl 82-83*
Matz Associates, Joyce - New York, NY - *DirPRFirms 83*
Matz Associates, Mortimer - New York, NY - *DirPRFirms 83*
Maud News-Recorder - *See* Konawa Newspapers
Maud Record - Maud, OK - *Ed&PubIntYB 82*
Maui News - Wailuku, HI - *AyerDirPub 83; Ed&PubIntYB 82; NewsDir 84*
Mauldin Cablevision Associates - Mauldin, SC - *BrCabYB 84*
Mauldin Tribune-Times - Mauldin, SC - *BaconPubCkNews 84*
Maumee Cable TV [of Times Mirror Cable Television Inc.] - Napoleon, OH - *BrCabYB 84*
Maumee Valley Herald [of Toledo Herald Newspapers] - Toledo, OH - *AyerDirPub 83; BaconPubCkNews 84; NewsDir 84*
Maumee Valley News - Maumee, OH - *Ed&PubIntYB 82*
Maunders Co. Inc., The - Birmingham, MI - *DirPRFirms 83*
Maurer, Fleisher, Anderson & Conway Inc. - Washington, DC - *StaDirAdAg 2-84*
Maurizi Associates - Sacramento, CA - *MicrocomMPl 84*
Mauston Juneau County Star-Times - Mauston, WI - *BaconPubCkNews 84*
Mauston Star [of Mauston Juneau County Publishers] - Mauston, WI - *Ed&PubIntYB 82; NewsDir 84*
Maverick Media Inc. - Syracuse, NE - *BaconPubCkNews 84*
Maverick Publications - Bend, OR - *LitMarPl 84*
Maverick Records - Dickens, TX - *BillIntBG 83-84*
Maverick, The - Excelsior, MN - *Ed&PubIntYB 82*
Mavora Publications Inc. - Woodbridge, ON, Canada - *BoPubDir 4 Sup, 5*
Max [of Lexitel Communications] - Birmingham, MI - *TeleSy&SerDir 7-83*
Max Area Evaluation & Modeling System - Ithaca, NY - *DirOnDB Spring 84*
Max Business Machines Corp. - Lake Success, NY - *DataDirSup 7-83*
Max Marketing Services Inc., Carol - St. Louis, MO - *IntDirMarRes 83*
Max Media - Los Angeles, CA - *Tel&CabFB 84C*
Max Promotions - Beaumont, TX - *BillIntBG 83-84*

Maxell Corp. of America - Hasbrouck Heights, NJ - *WhoWMicrocom 83*
Maxell Corp. of America [Subs. of Hitachi Maxell Ltd.] - Moonachie, NJ - *AvMarPl 83; DataDirSup 7-83; DirInfWP 82*
Maxfield Co., Joseph - Providence, RI - *StaDirAdAg 2-84*
Maxfilms Inc. - Los Angeles, CA - *ArtMar 84; WritMar 84*
Maxim Music Inc. - *See* Croma Music Co. Inc.
Maxima Corp. - Bethesda, MD - *EISS 83; InfoS 83-84*
Maximum Exposure Advertising - Scarsdale, NY - *DirMarMP 83; StaDirAdAg 2-84*
Maxtek Inc. - Torrance, CA - *MicrocomMPl 84; MicrocomSwDir 1; WhoWMicrocom 83*
Maxton Lock Co. Inc. - New York, NY - *DirInfWP 82*
Maxtone-Graham, Katrina - New York, NY - *LitMarPl 83*
Maxtor Corp. - Santa Clara, CA - *DataDirSup 7-83; MicrocomMPl 84*
Maxway Data Corp. - New York, NY - *LitMarPl 83, 84; MagIndMarPl 82-83*
Maxwell/Ashley Associates Inc. - Chestertown, MD - *StaDirAdAg 2-84*
Maxwell, Diana - Chicago, IL - *LitMarPl 83*
Maxwell Library Systems - Cambridge, MA - *EISS 7-83 Sup*
Maxwell Publications, Fay [Aff. of Eternal Light Information Center] - Columbus, OH - *BoPubDir 4, 5*
Maxwell Scientific International [Div. of Pergamon Press Inc.] - Elmsford, NY - *LitMarPl 83, 84; MagIndMarPl 82-83*
Maxwell Telephone Exchange - Maxwell, NM - *TelDir&BG 83-84*
May Broadcasting Co. - Shenandoah, IA - *BrCabYB 84*
May Broadcasting Co. - Omaha, NE - *Tel&CabFB 84S*
May Communications Inc. - Matawan, NJ - *DirPRFirms 83*
May Co. [Subs. of May Dept. Stores] - Los Angeles, CA - *DirMarMP 83*
May Day Pictorial News - San Francisco, CA - *BaconPubCkMag 84; MagDir 84*
May Day Press - Bellflower, CA - *BoPubDir 4, 5*
May, E. J. [Aff. of Independent Bar of Michigan] - Roseville, MI - *BoPubDir 4, 5*
May-Murdock Publications - Ross, CA - *BoPubDir 4, 5*
May/Partners Inc. - Seattle, WA - *StaDirAdAg 2-84*
May-Tal Associated Advertising Services Ltd. - Tel Aviv, Israel - *StaDirAdAg 2-84*
May Trends - Park Ridge, IL - *WritMar 84*
Maya Press - San Francisco, CA - *BoPubDir 5*
Mayapple Press - Kent, OH - *BoPubDir 4 Sup, 5; LitMag&SmPr 83-84*
Mayborn Enterprises Inc., Frank - Temple, TX - *Ed&PubIntYB 82*
Maycon Records Co. - Philadelphia, PA - *BillIntBG 83-84*
Mayday Software - Phillips, WI - *MicrocomMPl 84*
Mayer Advertising Inc., Peter A. - New Orleans, LA - *StaDirAdAg 2-84*
Mayer Color Laboratories Inc., Kurt - New York, NY - *AvMarPl 83*
Mayer Inc., Terry - New York, NY - *DirPRFirms 83*
Mayer Studios, Charles - Akron, OH - *ArtMar 84; AvMarPl 83*
Mayeri Research Inc., Harriet - Napa Valley, CA - *IntDirMarRes 83*
Mayers & Co. Inc., Joseph - Newark, NJ - *BoPubDir 4, 5*
Mayerson Interviewing Service, B. J. - Milwaukee, WI - *IntDirMarRes 83*
Mayes Stations, Wendell - Austin, TX - *BrCabYB 84*
Mayfair-Irving Park Passage - Chicago, IL - *AyerDirPub 83*
Mayfair Leader [of Leader Newspapers] - Chicago, IL - *AyerDirPub 83; NewsDir 84*
Mayfair News - Chicago, IL - *AyerDirPub 83*
Mayfair-Northeast News - *See* News Gleaner Publications
Mayfield Cablevision [of American TV & Communications Corp.] - Mayfield, KY - *BrCabYB 84; Tel&CabFB 84C*
Mayfield Messenger - Mayfield, KY - *BaconPubCkNews 84; Ed&PubIntYB 82; NewsDir 84*
Mayfield Publishing Co. - Palo Alto, CA - *DirMarMP 83; LitMarPl 83, 84*
Mayfield Smith Park Advertising Inc. - Honolulu, HI - *StaDirAdAg 2-84*
Mayflower Music Corp. - Wilton, CT - *BillIntBG 83-84*
Mayflower Warehouseman, The - Indianapolis, IN - *BaconPubCkMag 84*
Mayhew, H. Carl - Ayer's Cliff, PQ, Canada - *BoPubDir 4, 5*
Mayhill Publications - Knightstown, IN - *BaconPubCkNews 84; BoPubDir 4, 5*
Maylayalee - Toronto, ON, Canada - *Ed&PubIntYB 82*
Maynard Electronics - Casselberry, FL - *MicrocomMPl 84*
Maynard News - Maynard, MN - *BaconPubCkNews 84; Ed&PubIntYB 82*
Maynard's Cable Service - Inez, KY - *Tel&CabFB 84C*
Maynardville Union News Leader - Luttrell, TN - *BaconPubCkNews 84*
Mayne Agency Inc., The - Glendale, CA - *StaDirAdAg 2-84*
Mayo Alumnus, The - Rochester, MN - *WritMar 84*
Mayo Cable TV [of Cable Specialties Ltd.] - Mayo, FL - *Tel&CabFB 84C*
Mayo Clinic Medical Library [of Mayo Foundation] - Rochester, MN - *EISS 83*
Mayo Clinic Proceedings - Rochester, MN - *BaconPubCkMag 84; MagDir 84*
Mayo Free Press - Mayo, FL - *BaconPubCkNews 84*
Mayo Infurna Design Inc. - *See* Compton Communications Inc.
Mayor, Bruni - New York, NY - *LitMarPl 83, 84; MagIndMarPl 82-83*
Mayor Editorial Services, Adrienne - Bozeman, MT - *LitMarPl 83, 84*
Mayport Mirror, The - Jacksonville Beach, FL - *AyerDirPub 83*
Mays Landing Atlantic County Record - Mays Landing, NJ - *BaconPubCkNews 84*
Maysles Films Inc. - New York, NY - *AvMarPl 83; Tel&CabFB 84C*
Maysville De Kalb County Record-Herald - Maysville, MO - *BaconPubCkNews 84*
Maysville Ledger Independent - Maysville, KY - *BaconPubCkNews 84*
Maysville News - Maysville, OK - *BaconPubCkNews 84; Ed&PubIntYB 82*
Mayville Monitor - Mayville, MI - *BaconPubCkNews 84; Ed&PubIntYB 82*
Mayville News - Mayville, WI - *BaconPubCkNews 84; Ed&PubIntYB 82; NewsDir 84*
Mayville Sentinel - Mayville, NY - *Ed&PubIntYB 82*
Mayville Sentinel - *See* Ogden Newspapers Inc.
Mayville Traill County Tribune - Mayville, ND - *BaconPubCkNews 84*
Maywood Herald - Maywood, IL - *Ed&PubIntYB 82*
Maywood Herald [of Pioneer Press Inc.] - Melrose Park, IL - *NewsDir 84*
Maywood Herald - Wilmette, IL - *AyerDirPub 83*
Maywood Herald - *See* Pioneer Press Inc.
Maywood Journal - Bell, CA - *AyerDirPub 83*
Maywood Journal - Maywood, CA - *Ed&PubIntYB 82*
Maywood Our Town - Maywood, NJ - *BaconPubCkNews 84; NewsDir 84*
Mazda Publishers - Lexington, KY - *BoPubDir 4, 5; LitMag&SmPr 83-84*
Mazeppa Journal - Mazeppa, MN - *BaconPubCkNews 84; Ed&PubIntYB 82*
Mazeppa Telephone Co. - Mazeppa, MN - *TelDir&BG 83-84*
Mazer Corp., The - Dayton, OH - *LitMarPl 83, 84*
Maznaim Publishing Corp. - Brooklyn, NY - *BoPubDir 4, 5*
Mazner & Associates - Studio City, CA - *DirPRFirms 83*
Mazomanie Sickle Cross Plains Arrow - *See* News Publishing Co. Inc.
MB News [of Monument Builders of North America] - Evanston, IL - *BaconPubCkMag 84; MagDir 84*
MB Productions Inc. - New York, NY - *AvMarPl 83*
MBA Information Corp. - Memphis, TN - *DataDirOnSer 84*
MBA Magazine - New York, NY - *MagDir 84*
MBA Systems Automation - Columbus, OH - *DataDirOnSer 84*
MBAA Technical Quarterly - Madison, WI - *BaconPubCkMag 84*
MBM Associates/Advertising Inc. - Bethesda, MD - *StaDirAdAg 2-84*
MBM Productions Inc. - Dallas, TX - *AvMarPl 83*
MBO Inc. - Westfield, MA - *BoPubDir 4, 5*
MBP/Information Research [of H. Prim Co. Inc.] - Bergenfield, NJ - *EISS 83; FBInfSer 80*
MBP Software & Systems Technology - Oakland, CA - *MicrocomMPl 83, 84; MicrocomSwDir 1*

MBS Cable of Rittman - Rittman, OH - *BrCabYB 84*
MBS Cable TV Inc. - Minerva, OH - *BrCabYB 84; Tel&CabFB 84C p.1689*
MBS Cable TV Inc. - Newton Falls, OH - *BrCabYB 84*
MBS Cable TV Inc. - Salineville, OH - *BrCabYB 84*
MBS Cable TV Inc. - Scio, OH - *BrCabYB 84*
MBS Cable TV Inc. - Windham Village, OH - *BrCabYB 84*
MBS Cable TV Inc. [of Audio Associates Inc.] - Pittsburgh, PA - *BrCabYB 84 p.D-303*
M.C. Software Inc. - Denver, CO - *WhoWMicrocom 83*
MCA Advertising [Subs. of Marketing Corp. of America] - New York, NY - *AdAge 3-28-84; Br 1-23-84; StaDirAdAg 2-84*
MCA Corporate Films - Universal City, CA - *ProGuPRSer 4*
MCA Home Video Inc. - Universal City, CA - *BillIntBG 83-84*
MCA Inc. - Universal City, CA - *HomeVid&CabYB 82-83; KnowInd 83*
MCA Music [Div. of MCA Inc.] - New York, NY - *BillIntBG 83-84*
MCA Records Inc. - Universal City, CA - *BillIntBG 83-84*
MCA TV [Subs. of MCA Inc.] - New York, NY - *TelAl 83, 84; Tel&CabFB 84C*
MCA-TV Canada [Div. of MCA International BV] - Willowdale, ON, Canada - *Tel&CabFB 84C*
MCA TV International - Universal City, CA - *Tel&CabFB 84C*
MCA TV International - New York, NY - *TelAl 83, 84*
MCA Universal Corporate Film Div. [of MCA Inc.] - Universal City, CA - *Tel&CabFB 84C*
McAdams & Ong - Philadelphia, PA - *AdAge 3-28-84; StaDirAdAg 2-84*
McAdams Inc., William Douglas - New York, NY - *AdAge 3-28-84; StaDirAdAg 2-84*
McAfee, Lynn - North Hollywood, CA - *LitMarPl 83, 84; MagIndMarPl 82-83*
McAinsh & Co. Ltd. - Toronto, ON, Canada - *LitMarPl 83*
McAlester Cable TV Co. [of Rogers Cablesystems Inc.] - McAlester, OK - *BrCabYB 84; Tel&CabFB 84C*
McAlester Democrat - McAlester, OK - *NewsDir 84*
McAlester News-Capital - McAlester, OK - *NewsDir 84*
McAlester News Capital & Democrat - McAlester, OK - *BaconPubCkNews 84; Ed&PubIntYB 82*
McAlinden Associates Inc. - New York, NY - *ProGuPRSer 4*
McAllen Monitor [of Freedom Newspapers] - McAllen, TX - *BaconPubCkNews 84; NewsDir 84*
McAllen Valley Town Crier - McAllen, TX - *BaconPubCkNews 84; NewsDir 84*
McAllister-Barker Associates Inc. - Orlando, FL - *StaDirAdAg 2-84*
McAllister Books - Waukegan, IL - *BoPubDir 4, 5*
McAllister of Denver - Denver, CO - *MagIndMarPl 82-83*
McAndrew Advertising - Bronx, NY - *AdAge 3-28-84; ArtMar 84; StaDirAdAg 2-84*
McArdle Printing Co. Inc. - Silver Spring, MD - *MagIndMarPl 82-83*
McArthur Vinton County Courier - McArthur, OH - *BaconPubCkNews 84; NewsDir 84*
McArthur, William G. - Shippensburg, PA - *MicrocomSwDir 1*
McAuto Health Services Div. [of McDonnell Douglas Automation Co.] - Hazelwood, MO - *DataDirOnSer 84*
McAvoy Publications International Inc. - Englewood Cliffs, NJ - *MagIndMarPl 82-83*
MCB Cable Co. Inc. - Marlinton, WV - *BrCabYB 84; Tel&CabFB 84C*
MCBA - Montrose, CA - *DataDirSup 7-83; MicrocomMPl 84*
McBooks Press - Ithaca, NY - *BoPubDir 4, 5*
McBride Accounting Service - Star, NC - *MicrocomMPl 84*
McBride Literary Agency, Margaret - La Jolla, CA - *LitMarPl 84*
McBride Literary Agency, Margaret - San Diego, CA - *LitMarPl 83*
McBride/Publisher - Hartford, CT - *BoPubDir 4, 5*
McBride Publishing Co., Dale - Lampasas, TX - *BillIntBG 83-84*
MCC Software - Johnston, IA - *MicrocomSwDir 1*
M.C.C.A. Service Corp. - Jackson, MS - *Tel&CabFB 84C*
McCabe, Kevin - Hamilton, ON, Canada - *BoPubDir 4, 5*
McCabe, Newton & Associates Inc. - Providence, RI - *StaDirAdAg 2-84*
McCaffery & Ratner Inc. - New York, NY - *StaDirAdAg 2-84*
McCaffrey & McCall - New York, NY - *AdAge 3-28-84; Br 1-23-84; BrCabYB 84; HomeVid&CabYB 82-83; StaDirAdAg 2-84*
McCaffrey & McCall Direct Marketing Inc. [Subs. of McCaffrey & McCall Inc.] - New York, NY - *DirMarMP 83*
McCaffrey Enterprises - Harrison, NY - *MagIndMarPl 82-83*
McCain Publishers - Ft. Recovery, OH - *BoPubDir 4 Sup, 5*
McCall Central Idaho Star News - McCall, ID - *BaconPubCkNews 84; NewsDir 84*
McCall Publishing Co. - New York, NY - *AdAge 6-28-84; DirMarMP 83; KnowInd 83*
McCallister Co., R. J. - Youngstown, OH - *StaDirAdAg 2-84*
McCall's [of McCall Publishing Co.] - New York, NY - *BaconPubCkMag 84; Folio 83; LitMarPl 83, 84; MagDir 84; MagIndMarPl 82-83; NewsBur 6; WritMar 84*
McCall's Christmas - New York, NY - *MagDir 84*
McCall's Needlework & Crafts [Subs. of American Broadcasting Co.] - New York, NY - *DirMarMP 83; MagDir 84; MagIndMarPl 82-83; WritMar 84*
McCall's Working Mother - New York, NY - *MagIndMarPl 82-83*
McCamey Cable TV Service [of CMI Cable Communications Inc.] - McCamey, TX - *BrCabYB 84; Tel&CabFB 84C*
McCamey News - McCamey, TX - *BaconPubCkNews 84; Ed&PubIntYB 82*
McCann-Erickson Advertising of Canada - Toronto, ON, Canada - *ArtMar 84*
McCann-Erickson Inc. - New York, NY - *Br 1-23-84; TelAl 83, 84; Tel&CabFB 84C*
McCann-Erickson, Louisville - Louisville, KY - *ArtMar 84*
McCann-Erickson Worldwide [Subs. of The Interpublic Group of Cos. Inc.] - New York, NY - *AdAge 3-28-84, 6-25-84; BrCabYB 84; HomeVid&CabYB 82-83; StaDirAdAg 2-84*
McCann-Erickson Worldwide - Houston, TX - *ArtMar 84*
McCanse & Associates, Ross - Hollywood, CA - *Tel&CabFB 84C*
McCarron, Kane Inc. - Pasadena, CA - *StaDirAdAg 2-84*
McCartan & Root - New York, NY - *BoPubDir 4*
McCartan, Edward F. - New York, NY - *LitMarPl 83, 84*
McCartan Maritime Publishers - New York, NY - *BoPubDir 5*
McCarter, Renate B. - New York, NY - *LitMarPl 83, 84*
McCarter Theatre Co. - Princeton, NJ - *WritMar 84*
McCarthy Information Ltd. - Warminster, England - *EISS 83*
McCartney-Gray of Dallas - Dallas, TX - *StaDirAdAg 2-84*
McCartney, Susan - New York, NY - *MagIndMarPl 82-83*
McCarty Co., F. M. - Austin, TX - *BoPubDir 4, 5*
McCauley Agency Inc., Gerard - New York, NY - *LitMarPl 83, 84*
McCauley Ltd., Kirby - New York, NY - *LitMarPl 83, 84*
McCausland Associates Inc., William - Pitman, NJ - *MagIndMarPl 82-83*
McCaw Cablevision/Cascade [of McCaw Communications Cos. Inc.] - Fall City, WA - *BrCabYB 84; Tel&CabFB 84C*
McCaw Cablevision/Cascade [of McCaw Communications Cos. Inc.] - North Bend, WA - *BrCabYB 84; Tel&CabFB 84C*
McCaw Cablevision/Cle Elum [of McCaw Communications Cos. Inc.] - Cle Elum, WA - *BrCabYB 84; Tel&CabFB 84C*
McCaw Cablevision/Florence [of McCaw Communications Cos. Inc.] - Florence, OR - *Tel&CabFB 84C*
McCaw Cablevision/Frontier [of McCaw Communications Cos.] - Fairbanks, AK - *BrCabYB 84*
McCaw Cablevision/Frontier [of McCaw Communications Cos. Inc.] - North Pole, AK - *BrCabYB 84; Tel&CabFB 84C*
McCaw Cablevision/Grants Pass [of McCaw Communications Cos. Inc.] - Grants Pass, OR - *BrCabYB 84; Tel&CabFB 84C*
McCaw Cablevision/Ketchikan [of McCaw Communications Cos. Inc.] - Ketchikan, AK - *BrCabYB 84; Tel&CabFB 84C*
McCaw Cablevision/Klamath Falls [of McCaw Communications Cos. Inc.] - Klamath Falls, OR - *BrCabYB 84; Tel&CabFB 84C*
McCaw Cablevision/Medford [of McCaw Communications Cos. Inc.] - Medford, OR - *BrCabYB 84; Tel&CabFB 84C*
McCaw Cablevision/Okanogan Valley [of McCaw Communications Cos. Inc.] - Omak, WA - *BrCabYB 84; Tel&CabFB 84C*
McCaw Cablevision/Okanogan Valley [of McCaw Communications Cos. Inc.] - Oroville, WA - *BrCabYB 84*
McCaw Cablevision/Okanogan Valley [of McCaw Communications Cos. Inc.] - Tonasket, WA - *BrCabYB 84; Tel&CabFB 84C*

McCaw Cablevision/Redmond - Redmond, OR - *BrCabYB 84; Tel&CabFB 84C*
McCaw Cablevision/Roseburg [of McCaw Communications Cos. Inc.] - Roseburg, OR - *BrCabYB 84; Tel&CabFB 84C*
McCaw Cablevision/Sitka [of McCaw Communications Cos. Inc.] - Sitka, AK - *BrCabYB 84; Tel&CabFB 84C*
McCaw Cablevision/St. Helens & Scappoose [of McCaw Communications Cos. Inc.] - St. Helens, OR - *BrCabYB 84; Tel&CabFB 84C*
McCaw Cablevision/Twin City [of McCaw Communications Cos. Inc.] - Centralia, WA - *BrCabYB 84; Tel&CabFB 84C*
McCaw Cablevision/Twin City [of McCaw Communications Cos. Inc.] - Oakville, WA - *BrCabYB 84; Tel&CabFB 84C*
McCaw Cablevision/Twin City [of McCaw Communications Cos. Inc.] - Tenino, WA - *BrCabYB 84; Tel&CabFB 84C*
McCaw Cablevision/Twin City [of McCaw Communications Cos. Inc.] - Winlock, WA - *BrCabYB 84*
McCaw Cablevision/Whatcom County [of McCaw Communications Cos. Inc.] - Blaine, WA - *BrCabYB 84; Tel&CabFB 84C*
McCaw Cablevision/Whatcom County [of McCaw Communications Cos. Inc.] - Everson, WA - *BrCabYB 84; Tel&CabFB 84C*
McCaw Cablevision/Whatcom County [of McCaw Communications Cos. Inc.] - Ferndale, WA - *Tel&CabFB 84C*
McCaw Cablevision/Whatcom County [of McCaw Communications Cos. Inc.] - Lynden, WA - *BrCabYB 84; Tel&CabFB 84C*
McCaw Cablevision/Whatcom County [of McCaw Communications Cos. Inc.] - Sudden Valley, WA - *BrCabYB 84; Tel&CabFB 84C*
McCaw Cablevision/Whidbey Island [of McCaw Communications Cos. Inc.] - Coupeville, WA - *Tel&CabFB 84C*
McCaw Cablevision/Whidbey Island [of McCaw Communications Cos. Inc.] - Freeland, WA - *BrCabYB 84; Tel&CabFB 84C*
McCaw Cablevision/Whidbey Island [of McCaw Communications Cos. Inc.] - Langley, WA - *BrCabYB 84; Tel&CabFB 84C*
McCaw Cablevision/Yakima Valley [of McCaw Communications Cos. Inc.] - Grandview, WA - *BrCabYB 84; Tel&CabFB 84C*
McCaw Cablevision/Yakima Valley [of McCaw Communications Cos. Inc.] - Prosser, WA - *BrCabYB 84; Tel&CabFB 84C*
McCaw Cablevision/Yakima Valley [of McCaw Communications Cos. Inc.] - Selah, WA - *Tel&CabFB 84C*
McCaw Cablevision/Yakima Valley [of McCaw Communications Cos. Inc.] - Yakima, WA - *Tel&CabFB 84C*
McCaw Cablevision/Yakima Valley [of McCaw Communications Cos. Inc.] - Yakima County, WA - *BrCabYB 84*
McCaw Communications Cos. Inc. - Bellevue, WA - *BrCabYB 84 p.D-303; CabTVFinDB 83; Tel&CabFB 84C p.1689*
McClain Productions Inc., B. F. - Asheville, NC - *AvMarPl 83*
McClatchy Broadcasting Stations - Sacramento, CA - *BrCabYB 84*
McClatchy Newspapers - Sacramento, CA - *AdAge 6-28-84; BrCabYB 84 p.D-303; Ed&PubIntYB 82; KnowInd 83; Tel&CabFB 84C p.1689*
McClellan A.F.B.-Spacemaker [of Sacramento Suburban Newspapers Inc.] - Fair Oaks, CA - *NewsDir 84*
McClelland & Stewart Bantam Ltd. - Toronto, ON, Canada - *LitMarPl 83, 84; WritMar 84*
McClelland Newspapers - Longview, WA - *Ed&PubIntYB 82*
McClellanville Telephone Co. Inc. [Aff. of Telephone & Data Systems Inc./SE] - McClellanville, SC - *TelDir&BG 83-84*
McClendon, Judson D. - Birmingham, AL - *MicrocomSwDir 1*
McClernan, James - Madison, WI - *BoPubDir 5*
McClintock Corp. - Miami, FL - *MicrocomMPl 83, 84; MicrocomSwDir 1; WhoWMicrocom 83*
McCluney/Brewer Inc. - Overland, KS - *StaDirAdAg 2-84*
McClure CATV - McClure, PA - *BrCabYB 84; Tel&CabFB 84C*
McClure Furniture - Milton, PA - *DirInfWP 82*
McClure, Mike - Redfield, SD - *Tel&CabFB 84C p.1689*
McClure Research Co. - Seattle, WA - *IntDirMarRes 83*
McClure Stations, C. A. - Columbus, GA - *BrCabYB 84*
McClure Telephone Co. - McClure, OH - *TelDir&BG 83-84*
McClusky Gazette - McClusky, ND - *BaconPubCkNews 84; Ed&PubIntYB 82*
McColl Messenger - Bennettsville, SC - *AyerDirPub 83*
McColl Messenger, The - McColl, SC - *Ed&PubIntYB 82*
McColloch, Bryan, Cipriano Inc. - Miami, FL - *StaDirAdAg 2-84*
McColl's Ltd., Ann - London, ON, Canada - *BoPubDir 4, 5*
McCollum/Spielman & Co. Inc. - Great Neck, NY - *HBIndAd&MS 82-83; IntDirMarRes 83*
McCollum/Spielman Research - Great Neck, NY - *AdAge 5-17-84 p.36; Tel&CabFB 84C*
McComb Enterprise Journal [of J. O. Emmerich & Associates Inc.] - McComb, MS - *BaconPubCkNews 84; NewsDir 84*
McConnell Co., The - Seattle, WA - *DirPRFirms 83*
McConnell, Duane - Lakeland, FL - *Tel&CabFB 84C*
McConnellsburg Fulton County News - McConnellsburg, PA - *BaconPubCkNews 84; NewsDir 84*
McConnellsburg Fulton Journal - McConnellsburg, PA - *BaconPubCkNews 84*
McConnelsville Morgan County Herald - McConnelsville, OH - *BaconPubCkNews 84*
McCook Citizen [of La Grange Suburban Life/Citizen] - La Grange, IL - *NewsDir 84*
McCook Co-Operative Telephone Co. - Salem, SD - *TelDir&BG 83-84*
McCook Gazette - McCook, NE - *BaconPubCkNews 84; Ed&PubIntYB 82; NewsDir 84*
McCorkle Co. Inc., Joe - Whitesville, KY - *Tel&CabFB 84C p.1689*
McCorkle Research Services Inc. - Los Angeles, CA - *IntDirMarRes 83*
McCormack & Dodge Corp. - Needham Heights, MA - *ADAPSOMemDir 83-84; DataDirSup 7-83*
McCormick Advertising Agency - Amarillo, TX - *StaDirAdAg 2-84*
McCormick-Armstrong Advertising Agency Inc. - Wichita, KS - *StaDirAdAg 2-84*
McCormick Communications Inc. - Boston, MA - *BrCabYB 84*
McCormick Messenger - McCormick, SC - *AyerDirPub 83; BaconPubCkNews 84; Ed&PubIntYB 82*
McCosh, Melvin - Excelsior, MN - *BoPubDir 4, 5*
McCown, Edna - New York, NY - *LitMarPl 83, 84*
McCoy, James A. - Caco, MI - *Tel&CabFB 84C p.1689*
McCoy Music, Jim - Winchester, VA - *BillIntBG 83-84*
McCracken Computer Inc. - Lexington, MA - *DataDirSup 7-83*
McCraken Newspapers - Cheyenne, WY - *Ed&PubIntYB 82*
McCreary County Record [of Commonwealth Journal Inc.] - Whitley City, KY - *AyerDirPub 83; Ed&PubIntYB 82; NewsDir 84*
McCreary Software, Dann - San Diego, CA - *MicrocomSwDir 1; WhoWMicrocom 83*
McCrory Cable TV [of TCA Cable TV Inc.] - McCrory, AR - *Tel&CabFB 84C*
McCrory Leader - McCrory, AR - *BaconPubCkNews 84; Ed&PubIntYB 82*
McCubbins, Charles L. - Williamston, MI - *Tel&CabFB 84C p.1689*
McCue Advertising & Public Relations - Binghamton, NY - *ArtMar 84; StaDirAdAg 2-84*
McCullough & Associates - Excelsior Springs, MO - *MicrocomMPl 83, 84; MicrocomSwDir 1; WhoWMicrocom 83*
McCune Audio-Visual-Video - San Francisco, CA - *AvMarPl 83*
McCune Sound Service, Harry - San Francisco, CA - *ProGuPRSer 4*
McCurdy, Michael - Great Barrington, MA - *LitMarPl 83, 84*
McCurtain Gazette - Idabel, OK - *AyerDirPub 83; BaconPubCkNews 84; Ed&PubIntYB 82*
McCutchan Publishing Corp. - Berkeley, CA - *LitMarPl 83, 84*
McDaniel & Hillard - Georgetown, TX - *Tel&CabFB 84C p.1689*
McDaniel & Tate - Houston, TX - *DirPRFirms 83*
McDaniel Studio, J. W. - Greenwich, CT - *LitMarPl 83, 84; MagIndMarPl 82-83*
McDaniel Telephone Co. - Salkum, WA - *TelDir&BG 83-84*
McDaniels & Co. Advertising Inc., E. W. - Pekin, IL - *StaDirAdAg 2-84*
McDarrah, Fred W. - New York, NY - *LitMarPl 83, 84; MagIndMarPl 82-83*
McDonald, Allan J. - *See* McDonald Group
McDonald & Little [Subs. of Ted Bates Co.] - Atlanta, GA - *AdAge 3-28-84; StaDirAdAg 2-84*
McDonald Associates Inc., Roy - Emeryville, CA - *MagIndMarPl 82-83*

McDonald, Babb & Clarkson Inc. - Portland, OR - *StaDirAdAg 2-84*
McDonald County News-Gazette - Pineville, MO - *AyerDirPub 83*
McDonald County Press - Noel, MO - *AyerDirPub 83; Ed&PubIntYB 82*
McDonald County Telephone Co. - Pineville, MO - *TelDir&BG 83-84*
McDonald Davis & Associates Inc. - Milwaukee, WI - *StaDirAdAg 2-84*
McDonald Group - Birmingham, AL - *BrCabYB 84; CabTVFinDB 83; Tel&CabFB 84C p.1690*
McDonald Media Services - Los Angeles, CA - *DirPRFirms 83*
McDonald Music Co. - *See* Alkatraz Corner Music Co.
McDonald Record-Outlook - McDonald, PA - *BaconPubCkNews 84*
McDonald, William W. - *See* McDonald Group
McDonnell Douglas Automation Co. [Subs. of McDonnell Douglas Corp.] - St. Louis, MO - *DataDirOnSer 84; DataDirSup 7-83; EISS 83*
McDonnell Douglas Automation Co. (Health Services Div.) - Hazelwood, MO - *DataDirOnSer 84*
McDonnell Douglas Automation Co. (Market Planning Div.) - Hazelwood, MO - *ADAPSOMemDir 83-84*
McDonnell Douglas Communications Systems & Services Inc. [Subs. of McDonnell Douglas Corp.] - Denver, CO - *DataDirOnSer 84*
McDonnell Douglas Corp. - Long Beach, CA - *AvMarPl 83*
McDonnell Douglas Corp. - St. Louis, MO - *Datamation 6-83; Top100Al 83*
McDonnell Douglas Corp. (Film & TV Communications) - Long Beach, CA - *Tel&CabFB 84C*
McDonough-Democrat - Bushnell, IL - *Ed&PubIntYB 82*
McDonough Henry Herald - McDonough, GA - *BaconPubCkNews 84*
McDonough Telephone Cooperative Inc. - Colchester, IL - *TelDir&BG 83-84*
McDougal, Littell & Co. - Evanston, IL - *LitMarPl 83, 84*
McDougal, Littell & Co. - Skokie, IL - *MicrocomMPl 84*
McDougall Associates - Salem, MA - *AdAge 3-28-84; StaDirAdAg 2-84*
McDougall, Sheila - Calgary, AB, Canada - *BoPubDir 4 Sup, 5*
McDowell Express - Marion, NC - *Ed&PubIntYB 82*
McDowell News [of Park Newspapers of Marion Inc.] - Marion, NC - *AyerDirPub 83; Ed&PubIntYB 82; NewsDir 84*
McDuffie Progress - Thomson, GA - *AyerDirPub 83; Ed&PubIntYB 82*
MCE Inc. - Kalamazoo, MI - *AvMarPl 83; MicrocomMPl 84*
McElderry Books, Margaret K. - New York, NY - *WritMar 84*
McElroy Advertising, Edward J. - Los Angeles, CA - *StaDirAdAg 2-84; TelAl 83, 84*
McElroy Co. Inc., The Ralph - Austin, TX - *LitMarPl 83, 84*
McEvoy, Hogan, Day & Associates - East Norwich, NY - *StaDirAdAg 2-84*
McFarland & Co. Inc. - Jefferson, NC - *BoPubDir 4, 5; LitMag&SmPr 83-84; LitMarPl 83, 84; WritMar 84*
McFarland & Drier Inc. - Miami, FL - *StaDirAdAg 2-84*
McFarland Co., The - Harrisburg, PA - *LitMarPl 83, 84*
McFarland Group Inc., The - Elm Grove, WI - *StaDirAdAg 2-84*
McFarland Life - *See* Community Herald Newpapers Inc.
McFarland Press - McFarland, CA - *BaconPubCkNews 84; Ed&PubIntYB 82*
McFarlane Mobilvision - Saratoga, CA - *AvMarPl 83; Tel&CabFB 84C*
McFrank & Williams Advertising Agency Inc. - New York, NY - *StaDirAdAg 2-84*
McGaw, Lisa - Chapel Hill, NC - *LitMarPl 83, 84; MagIndMarPl 82-83*
McGee, Barbara - Greenbelt, MD - *MagIndMarPl 82-83*
McGee Creek Cable TV Associates [of Northland Communications Corp.] - Atoka, OK - *Tel&CabFB 84C*
McGehee Times - McGehee, AR - *Ed&PubIntYB 82*
McGehee Times-News - McGehee, AR - *BaconPubCkNews 84*
McGiffert/Mueller Associates - Washington, DC - *DirPRFirms 83*
McGiffin Newspapers, W. J. - Downey, CA - *Ed&PubIntYB 82*
McGill, J. S. - Toronto, ON, Canada - *BoPubDir 4, 5*
McGill/Jensen Inc. - St. Paul, MN - *LitMarPl 83, 84*
McGill Publications Inc. - Flanders, NJ - *BoPubDir 5*
McGill-Queens University Press - Montreal, PQ, Canada - *LitMarPl 83, 84*
McGill University (Centre for Developing-Area Studies) - Montreal, PQ, Canada - *BoPubDir 5*
McGill University (Centre for Northern Studies & Research) - Montreal, PQ, Canada - *BoPubDir 4, 5*
McGill University (Graduate School of Library Science) - Montreal, PQ, Canada - *CompReadDB 82; DataDirOnSer 84*
McGill University (McGill University Libraries) - Montreal, PQ, Canada - *BoPubDir 4 Sup, 5*
McGilvery, Laurence - La Jolla, CA - *BoPubDir 4, 5*
McGinley, Robert F. Sr. - Collegeville, PA - *Tel&CabFB 84C p.1690*
McGinnis & Marx Music Publishers - New York, NY - *BillIntBG 83-84; BoPubDir 4, 5*
McGlynn, June A. - Great Falls, MT - *BoPubDir 4, 5*
McGrath & Associates, Helen - Concord, CA - *LitMarPl 83, 84*
McGrath & Co. - Indianapolis, IN - *StaDirAdAg 2-84*
McGrath/Power Associates Inc. - New York, NY - *DirPRFirms 83*
McGrath Publishing Co. - Wilmington, NC - *LitMarPl 83*
McGrath Publishing Co. - Falls Church, VA - *LitMarPl 84*
McGravie, Anne V. - Chicago, IL - *LitMarPl 83, 84*
McGraw-Hill Book Co. [Div. of McGraw-Hill Inc.] - New York, NY - *InfoS 83-84; LitMarPl 83, 84; MicrocomMPl 84*
McGraw-Hill Book Co. (College Books Div.) - New York, NY - *ArtMar 84; WritMar 84*
McGraw-Hill Book Co. (Continuing Education Center) - Washington, DC - *LitMarPl 84*
McGraw Hill Book Co. (DM Dept.) - New York, NY - *DirMarMP 83*
McGraw-Hill Book Co. (General Div.) - New York, NY - *WritMar 84*
McGraw-Hill Book Co. (Professional & Reference Div.) - New York, NY - *WritMar 84*
McGraw-Hill Broadcasting Co. [Subs. of McGraw-Hill Inc.] - New York, NY - *BrCabYB 84; InfoS 83-84; Tel&CabFB 84S*
McGraw-Hill Inc. - New York, NY - *AdAge 6-28-84; HomeVid&CabYB 82-83; KnowInd 83; LitMarPl 83, 84; MagIndMarPl 82-83; Top100Al 83*
McGraw-Hill Inc. (Export Subscription Agency) - Hightstown, NJ - *MagIndMarPl 82-83*
McGraw-Hill Inc. (Marketing Information Center) - New York, NY - *FBInfSer 80*
McGraw-Hill Inc. (World News Service) - New York, NY - *NewsBur 6*
McGraw-Hill Inc. (World News Service) - Dallas, TX - *BaconPubCkNews 84*
McGraw-Hill Information Systems Co. [Div. of McGraw-Hill Inc.] - New York, NY - *InfoS 83-84*
McGraw-Hill Information Systems Co. (Cost Information Systems Div.) - Princeton, NJ - *DataDirOnSer 84*
McGraw-Hill International Book Co. [Div. of McGraw-Hill Inc.] - New York, NY - *InfoS 83-84; LitMarPl 84*
McGraw-Hill Publications Co. [Div. of McGraw-Hill Inc.] - New York, NY - *DataDirOnSer 84; DirMarMP 83; InfoS 83-84*
McGraw-Hill Publications Co. (Research Div.) - New York, NY - *IntDirMarRes 83*
McGraw-Hill Ryerson Ltd. - Scarborough, ON, Canada - *ArtMar 84; LitMarPl 83, 84*
McGregor & Werner Inc. - Washington, DC - *LitMarPl 83, 84*
McGregor Magazine Agency - Mt. Morris, IL - *MagIndMarPl 82-83*
McGregor Mirror - McGregor, TX - *BaconPubCkNews 84; Ed&PubIntYB 82*
McGregor North Iowa Times - McGregor, IA - *BaconPubCkNews 84*
McGuane Studio - New York, NY - *AvMarPl 83; Tel&CabFB 84C*
McGuffey Lane Music - *See* Hat Band Music
McGuire Airtides - Pemberton, NJ - *AyerDirPub 83*
McHargue, Woodrow & Maribelle - Lexington, MO - *Tel&CabFB 84C p.1690*
McHenry County Citizen - McHenry, IL - *AyerDirPub 83; BaconPubCkNews 84*
McHenry County Journal-Register - Velva, ND - *AyerDirPub 83; Ed&PubIntYB 82*

McHenry Herald [of Free Press Inc.] - McHenry, IL - *NewsDir 84*
McHenry Herald - *See* Free Press Inc.
McHenry Plain Dealer - McHenry, IL - *BaconPubCkNews 84; Ed&PubIntYB 82; NewsDir 84*
McHugh & Hoffman Inc. - Fairfax, VA - *CabTVFinDB 83*
McHugh Music Inc., Jimmy - Beverly Hills, CA - *BillIntBG 83-84*
MCI Advantage Service [of MCI Telecommunications Corp.] - Washington, DC - *TeleSy&SerDir 2-84*
MCI Corporate Account Service [of MCI Telecommunications Corp.] - Washington, DC - *TeleSy&SerDir 2-84*
MCI Credit Card Service [of MCI Telecommunications Corp.] - Washington, DC - *TeleSy&SerDir 2-84*
MCI Leased Channel Service [of MCI International Inc.] - Rye Brook, NY - *TeleSy&SerDir 2-84*
MCI Mail [of MCI Digital Information Service Corp.] - Washington, DC - *TeleSy&SerDir 2-84*
MCI Network Service [of MCI Telecommunications Corp.] - Washington, DC - *TeleSy&SerDir 2-84*
MCI Productions - Houston, TX - *Tel&CabFB 84C*
MCI Residential Services [of MCI Telecommunications Corp.] - Washington, DC - *TeleSy&SerDir 2-84*
MCI School of Telecommunications Management [of MCI Telecommunications Corp.] - Washington, DC - *TeleSy&SerDir 2-84*
MCI Telecommunications Corp. - Washington, DC - *DataDirSup 7-83; TeleSy&SerDir 2-84*
MCI WATS [of MCI Telecommunications Corp.] - Washington, DC - *TeleSy&SerDir 2-84*
McIlhenny-Humphrey - Pittsburgh, PA - *AdAge 3-28-84; StaDirAdAg 2-84*
McIlvaine Co. - Northbrook, IL - *BoPubDir 5*
McInerney, Christina - New York, NY - *LitMarPl 83, 84*
McIntosh & Otis Inc. - New York, NY - *LitMarPl 83, 84*
McIntosh County Democrat - Checotah, OK - *Ed&PubIntYB 82*
McIntosh Times - McIntosh, MN - *Ed&PubIntYB 82*
McIntosh Times - *See* Richards Publishing Co. Inc.
McIntyre, Jane - Cape Coral, FL - *LitMarPl 83, 84*
McKamy & Partners Inc. - New York, NY - *DirPRFirms 83*
McKay, Al - Port Arthur, TX - *Tel&CabFB 84C p.1690*
McKay Co. Inc., David [Subs. of Morgan-Grampian Inc.] - New York, NY - *LitMarPl 83, 84; WritMar 84*
McKean County Miner [of McKean County Press Inc.] - Bradford, PA - *AyerDirPub 83; NewsDir 84*
McKean County Miner - Smethport, PA - *Ed&PubIntYB 82*
McKean County Press Inc. - Bradford, PA - *BaconPubCkNews 84*
McKee Advertising - Elmhurst, IL - *AdAge 3-28-84; StaDirAdAg 2-84*
McKee Jackson County Sun - McKee, KY - *BaconPubCkNews 84*
McKee Television Enterprises Inc. - McKee, KY - *BrCabYB 84*
McKees Rocks Suburban Gazette - McKees Rocks, PA - *BaconPubCkNews 84*
McKeesport Daily News - McKeesport, PA - *NewsDir 84*
McKelvie Programs - Willingboro, NJ - *MicrocomMPl 84*
McKenna, Cleora - *See* Blue Mountain TV Cable Co.
McKenna, Jack C. - Chelan, WA - *Tel&CabFB 84C p.1690*
McKenna, Jack C. - *See* Blue Mountain TV Cable Co.
McKenna Public Relations, Regis - Palo Alto, CA - *DirPRFirms 83*
McKenna Radio Stations - Washington, DC - *BrCabYB 84*
McKenzie & Associates, Karl - St. Louis, MO - *StaDirAdAg 2-84*
McKenzie Banner - McKenzie, TN - *BaconPubCkNews 84; Ed&PubIntYB 82; NewsDir 84*
McKenzie Bridge River Reflections - McKenzie Bridge, OR - *BaconPubCkNews 84*
McKenzie County Farmer & Watford Guide - Watford City, ND - *AyerDirPub 83*
McKenzie County Farmer, The - Watford City, ND - *Ed&PubIntYB 82*
McKenzie, King & Gordon - Hollywood, CA - *StaDirAdAg 2-84; TelAl 83, 84*
McKenzie River TV & Cable Co. Inc. - Sedona, AZ - *BrCabYB 84*
McKenzie River TV & Cable Co. Inc. - McKenzie Bridge, OR - *BrCabYB 84*
McKericher Advertising Inc. - Charlotte, NC - *StaDirAdAg 2-84*
McKettner Publishing - Seattle, WA - *LitMag&SmPr 83-84*
McKilligan Supply Corp. - Johnson City, NY - *MicrocomMPl 84*
McKim Advertising Ltd. - Toronto, ON, Canada - *StaDirAdAg 2-84*
McKim & Co. Inc., Robert - Los Angeles, CA - *AdAge 3-28-84; StaDirAdAg 2-84*
McKinlay Advertising - Simsbury, CT - *StaDirAdAg 2-84*
McKinney Courier-Gazette - McKinney, TX - *BaconPubCkNews 84; Ed&PubIntYB 82; NewsDir 84*
McKinney/Gulf Coast - Bellaire, TX - *ArtMar 84*
McKinney/New England - Boston, MA - *ArtMar 84*
McKinney Public Relations Inc. - Philadelphia, PA - *AdAge 3-28-84; DirPRFirms 83; StaDirAdAg 2-84*
McKinney Silver & Rockett - Raleigh, NC - *AdAge 3-28-84; StaDirAdAg 2-84*
McKinnon Broadcasting Co. - Corpus Christi, TX - *BrCabYB 84; Tel&CabFB 84S*
McKinzie Publishing Co. [Aff. of Aaims Inc.] - Los Angeles, CA - *BoPubDir 4 Sup, 5*
McKnight Medical Communications Inc. - Northfield, IL - *BoPubDir 5; MagIndMarPl 82-83*
McKnight Publishing Co. - Bloomington, IL - *AvMarPl 83; LitMarPl 83, 84; WritMar 84*
McKone & Co. Inc. - Dallas, TX - *DirPRFirms 83*
McKone & Co. Inc. - Ft. Worth, TX - *StaDirAdAg 2-84*
MCL Associates - McLean, VA - *BoPubDir 4, 5*
MCL Unltd. - Cresco, PA - *BoPubDir 4 Sup, 5*
McLain Family Bank - Berea, KY - *BillIntBG 83-84*
McLane Advertising Inc., Bonner - Austin, TX - *StaDirAdAg 2-84*
McLaren, Lynn - Boston, MA - *LitMarPl 83, 84*
McLaren Micropublishing Ltd. - Toronto, ON, Canada - *MicroMarPl 82-83*
McLaren, Thomas A. - Camrose, AB, Canada - *Tel&CabFB 84C*
McLaughlin, DelVecchio & Casey - New Haven, CT - *AdAge 3-28-84; StaDirAdAg 2-84*
McLaughlin Messenger - McLaughlin, SD - *Ed&PubIntYB 82*
McLaughlin, Tom - Chicago, IL - *MagIndMarPl 82-83*
McLauglin & Reilly Co. - *See* Birch Tree Group Ltd.
McLean Cable Associates - Tarrytown, NY - *BrCabYB 84*
McLean Cargo Specialists Inc. - Jamaica, NY - *MagIndMarPl 82-83*
McLean County Cablevision [of Kentuckiana Cablevision Inc.] - Livermore, KY - *Tel&CabFB 84C*
McLean County Historical Society - Bloomington, IL - *BoPubDir 5*
McLean County Independent - Garrison, ND - *AyerDirPub 83; Ed&PubIntYB 82*
McLean County Journal - Turtle Lake, ND - *AyerDirPub 83; Ed&PubIntYB 82*
McLean County News - Calhoun, KY - *AyerDirPub 83; Ed&PubIntYB 82*
McLean, Michael J. - *See* Interlake Cable TV Ltd.
McLean News - McLean, TX - *BaconPubCkNews 84; Ed&PubIntYB 82*
McLean Providence Journal & Fairfax Herald - McLean, VA - *BaconPubCkNews 84; Ed&PubIntYB 82*
McLean Trucking Co. - Indianapolis, IN - *LitMarPl 83*
McLean Trucking Co. - Winston-Salem, NC - *MagIndMarPl 82-83*
McLeansboro Times-Leader [of Thomson Newspapers Inc.] - McLeansboro, IL - *AyerDirPub 83; BaconPubCkNews 84; Ed&PubIntYB 82; NewsDir 84*
McLeod Advertising Co. - Detroit, MI - *StaDirAdAg 2-84*
McLoud Telephone Co. - McLoud, OK - *TelDir&BG 83-84*
MCM Enterprises - Oakland, CA - *MicrocomMPl 84*
MCM Medical - *See* Muir Cornelius Moore
McMahon Publishing Co. - Georgetown, CT - *MagIndMarPl 82-83*
McManus Co., The - Greens Farms, CT - *ArtMar 84; StaDirAdAg 2-84; WritMar 84*
McManus Co., The - Westport, CT - *HBIndAd&MS 82-83*
McManus, Michael J. - Stamford, CT - *Ed&PubIntYB 82*
McMaster University Library Press - Hamilton, ON, Canada - *BoPubDir 4, 5*
McMasters Associates Public Relations - Troy, MI - *DirPRFirms 83*
McMillan, Bruce A. - Shapleigh, ME - *LitMarPl 84*

McMillan Computing Services - Reading, England - *MicrocomSwDir 1*
McMillan Publications - Woodridge, IL - *BoPubDir 4, 5*
McMillen, Belfour R. - Ft. Worth, TX - *LitMarPl 83, 84*
McMillion Publications [Aff. of Five Senses Inc.] - Denton, TX - *BoPubDir 5*
McMinnville News-Register - McMinnville, OR - *BaconPubCkNews 84*
McMinnville Southern Standard - McMinnville, TN - *BaconPubCkNews 84*
McMinnville TV Cable Co. [of National Telecommunications] - McMinnville, TN - *BrCabYB 84; Tel&CabFB 84C*
McMinnville Warren County News - McMinnville, TN - *BaconPubCkNews 84*
McMoran Associates Inc. - Greenwich, CT - *DirPRFirms 83; StaDirAdAg 2-84*
McMullen Advertising Inc. - Gardena, CA - *StaDirAdAg 2-84*
McMurray Advertiser - *See* Publix Publications
McMurray Co. - Brookville, PA - *BaconPubCkNews 84*
McMurtie Ltd. - *See* Stewart & Associates Ltd./IMAA Inc., Rex
MCN, American Journal of Maternal Child Nursing - New York, NY - *BaconPubCkMag 84*
M.C.N. Press - Tulsa, OK - *BoPubDir 4, 5*
McNabb & Co., M. J. - Houston, TX - *StaDirAdAg 2-84*
McNabb Telephone Co. - McNabb, IL - *TelDir&BG 83-84*
McNairy County Publishing Co. - Selmer, TN - *BaconPubCkNews 84*
McNally & Loftin - Santa Barbara, CA - *LitMag&SmPr 83-84; LitMarPl 83, 84*
McNamara Advertising Inc., John - New York, NY - *StaDirAdAg 2-84*
McNaught Syndicate Inc. - Greenwich, CT - *BaconPubCkNews 84; LitMarPl 84*
McNaught Syndicate Inc. - New York, NY - *Ed&PubIntYB 82; LitMarPl 83; MagIndMarPl 82-83; NewsBur 6*
McNaughton & Gunn Inc. - Ann Arbor, MI - *LitMarPl 83, 84*
McNaughton Newspapers - Effingham, IL - *Ed&PubIntYB 82*
McNaughton Stations - Effingham, IL - *BrCabYB 84*
McNee Photo Communications Inc. - Houston, TX - *ArtMar 84; AvMarPl 83*
McNees, Pat - Washington, DC - *LitMarPl 83, 84*
McNeil Cable TV - El Dorado, AR - *Tel&CabFB 84C*
McNulty, Nancy G. - New York, NY - *MagIndMarPl 82-83*
McNutt Publications, Randy - Fairfield, OH - *BoPubDir 4, 5*
MCP Books - Germantown, MD - *BoPubDir 4, 5*
MCP/DaviSound - Newberry, SC - *BillIntBG 83-84*
MCP Microsystems - Rainhill, England - *MicrocomSwDir 1*
McPherson & Co. - New Paltz, NY - *LitMag&SmPr 83-84; LitMarPl 84; WritMar 84*
McPherson Cablevision [of Multimedia Cablevision Inc.] - McPherson, KS - *Tel&CabFB 84C*
McPherson County Herald - Leola, SD - *AyerDirPub 83; Ed&PubIntYB 82*
McPherson Sentinel - McPherson, KS - *BaconPubCkNews 84; Ed&PubIntYB 82; NewsDir 84*
McQuerry, Mary Noble - Jacksonville, FL - *BoPubDir 5*
McQuien & Lawson - Dallas, TX - *StaDirAdAg 2-84*
McQuown & Co. Inc., Judith H. - New York, NY - *LitMarPl 83, 84*
McQuown & Co. Inc., Judith H. - Staten Island, NY - *MagIndMarPl 82-83*
McRae & Co. Inc., Floyd - Atlanta, GA - *StaDirAdAg 2-84*
McRae Telfair Enterprise - McRae, GA - *BaconPubCkNews 84*
McRon Music Co. - New York, NY - *BillIntBG 83-84*
MCS Enterprises - Eugene, OR - *BoPubDir 5*
MCSA - Kirkland, WA - *BoPubDir 4, 5*
McTaggart, Kenneth D. - London, ON, Canada - *BoPubDir 4, 5*
McVay Communications Inc. - King City, CA - *Tel&CabFB 84C p.1690*
McVay Systems Inc. - King City, CA - *CabTVFinDB 83*
McVille Messenger - *See* Ness Press Inc.
MD Magazine - New York, NY - *BaconPubCkMag 84; LitMarPl 83, 84; MagDir 84; MagIndMarPl 82-83; WritMar 84*
MDA Publications [Aff. of Management Development Associates] - Temple Terrace, FL - *BoPubDir 4 Sup, 5*
MDB Systems Inc. - Orange, CA - *DataDirSup 7-83; WhoWMicrocom 83*
MDC Enterprises - Tijeras, NM - *BoPubDir 4 Sup, 5*
MDCR Inc. - East Brunswick, NJ - *MicrocomMPl 84; MicrocomSwDir 1*
MDDC Press Clips Inc. - Baltimore, MD - *ProGuPRSer 4*
MDF/I - Metals Park, OH - *DirOnDB Spring 84*
MDK Inc. - Chapel Hill, NC - *BoPubDir 5*
MDM Systems Inc. - Warren, MI - *MicrocomSwDir 1*
MDR Compiled Business File [of Market Data Retrieval Inc.] - Westport, CT - *DataDirOnSer 84*
MDR Inc. - Houston, TX - *StaDirAdAg 2-84*
MDR Telecom - Marina del Rey, CA - *DataDirOnSer 84; EISS 5-84 Sup*
MDS Associates - Orchard Park, NY - *MicrocomMPl 84*
MDS Communications Inc. - New York, NY - *Tel&CabFB 84C*
MDS Enterprises - Waterville, OH - *BillIntBG 83-84*
MDS Inc. - New Orleans, LA - *Tel&CabFB 84C*
MDS Qantel Inc. - Hayward, CA - *DataDirSup 7-83; MicrocomSwDir 1; WhoWMicrocom 83*
MDS Service Co. - New York, NY - *Tel&CabFB 84C*
MDS Services of Cape Coral Inc. - Lake Worth, FL - *Tel&CabFB 84C*
MDS Services of Clewiston Inc. - Lake Worth, FL - *Tel&CabFB 84C*
MDS Services of Englewood Inc. - Lake Worth, FL - *Tel&CabFB 84C*
MDS Services of Homestead Inc. - Lake Worth, FL - *Tel&CabFB 84C*
MDS Services of Melbourne Inc. - Lake Worth, FL - *Tel&CabFB 84C*
MDS Services of Okeechobee Inc. - Lake Worth, FL - *Tel&CabFB 84C*
MDS Services of Stuart Inc. - Lake Worth, FL - *Tel&CabFB 84C*
MDS Systems - Anchorage, AK - *Tel&CabFB 84C*
MDS Trivex [of Mohawk Data Sciences] - Costa Mesa, CA - *DataDirSup 7-83; DirInfWP 82; InfIndMarPl 83; MicrocomMPl 83*
Me-Benish Music Inc. - *See* Schroeder International Ltd., A.
Me Books - Encino, CA - *LitMarPl 83*
Me-Books Publishing Co. Inc. - Westlake Village, CA - *DirMarMP 83*
Me Magazine [of Pittore Euforico] - New York, NY - *LitMag&SmPr 83-84*
ME Publications [Aff. of Minne Ha! Ha!] - Minneapolis, MN - *BoPubDir 4, 5*
MEA Advocate - St. Paul, MN - *NewsDir 84*
MEA Records [Div. of Antell Data Systems] - Waterford, PA - *BillIntBG 83-84*
MEA Today - Helena, MT - *BaconPubCkMag 84; MagDir 84*
Mead Advertising Ltd., Godfrey J. - Vancouver, BC, Canada - *StaDirAdAg 2-84*
Mead Corp., The - Dayton, OH - *KnowInd 83*
Mead Corp., The (Paperboard Products Div.) - Dayton, OH - *LitMarPl 83, 84*
Mead Data Central - New York, NY - *CompReadDB 82; ProGuPRSer 4*
Mead Data Central [Div. of The Mead Corp.] - Dayton, OH - *DataDirOnSer 84; InfIndMarPl 83; InfoS 83-84*
Mead Enterprises, Jerry D. - San Francisco, CA - *Ed&PubIntYB 82*
Mead, Florence - Kenora, ON, Canada - *BoPubDir 4 Sup, 5*
Mead Newspapers - Erie, PA - *Ed&PubIntYB 82*
Mead Paper (Publishing Paper Div.) - Escanaba, MI - *LitMarPl 83, 84; MagIndMarPl 82-83*
Meade County Messenger - Brandenburg, KY - *AyerDirPub 83; Ed&PubIntYB 82*
Meade County Times-Tribune [of Allison Publishing Inc.] - Sturgis, SD - *AyerDirPub 83; Ed&PubIntYB 82; NewsDir 84*
Meade Globe-Press - Meade, KS - *BaconPubCkNews 84; Ed&PubIntYB 82*
Meades, Kenneth R. - Beverly Hills, CA - *AvMarPl 83; LitMarPl 83, 84*
Meadow Grove News - Meadow Grove, NE - *BaconPubCkNews 84; Ed&PubIntYB 82*
Meadow Lake Progress - Meadow Lake, SK, Canada - *Ed&PubIntYB 82*

Meadow Lane Publications - Escondido, CA - *BoPubDir 5*
Meadow Lane Publications - Provo, UT - *BoPubDir 4*
Meadow Press - San Francisco, CA - *BoPubDir 4, 5*
Meadow Press - Port Jefferson, NY - *BoPubDir 4, 5*
Meadow River Post - Rainelle, WV - *AyerDirPub 83; Ed&PubIntYB 82; NewsDir 84*
Meadowbrook Press - Deephaven, MN - *LitMarPl 83, 84; WritMar 84*
Meadowbrook Times - East Meadow, NY - *Ed&PubIntYB 82*
Meadowbrook Times - Lawrence, NY - *AyerDirPub 83*
Meadowee Music - Sacramento, CA - *BillIntBG 83-84*
Meadowgreen Music - *See* Tree International
Meadowlander & Secaucus Press, The - Fairview, NJ - *AyerDirPub 83*
Meadowlands Cablevision - Lyndhurst Township, NJ - *Tel&CabFB 84C*
Meadowlands Cablevision Corp. [of Comcast Cablevision Corp.] - Lyndhurst, NJ - *BrCabYB 84*
Meadowlane Enterprises Inc. - Van Nuys, CA - *Tel&CabFB 84C*
Meadowlark Press - Prairie Village, KS - *BoPubDir 4, 5; LitMag&SmPr 83-84*
Meadowvale Review - Meadowvale, ON, Canada - *Ed&PubIntYB 82*
Meadville Franklin County Advocate - Meadville, MS - *BaconPubCkNews 84*
Meadville Master Antenna Inc. - Meadville, PA - *BrCabYB 84 p.D-303; Tel&CabFB 84C p.1690*
Meadville Tribune - Meadville, PA - *BaconPubCkNews 84; Ed&PubIntYB 82; NewsDir 84*
Meagher County News - White Sulphur Springs, MT - *AyerDirPub 83; Ed&PubIntYB 82*
Mealer & Emerson Inc. - Costa Mesa, CA - *StaDirAdAg 2-84*
Mealink [of Interactive Market Systems Inc.] - New York, NY - *DataDirOnSer 84*
Mealink - London, England - *DirOnDB Spring 84*
MEAMCO - *See* Middle East Advertising & Marketing Corp.
Mean Mountain Music - Milwaukee, WI - *BillIntBG 83-84*
Meanjin Quarterly - Parkville, Australia - *LitMag&SmPr 83-84*
Means Co. Inc., R. S. - Kingston, MA - *BoPubDir 4, 5*
Measurement Concept Corp. - Rome, NY - *MicrocomSwDir 1; WhoWMicrocom 83*
Measurement of Mechanical Quantities Documentation [of Federal Institute for Materials Testing] - Berlin, West Germany - *EISS 83*
Measurement Systems & Controls Inc. - Orange, CA - *WhoWMicrocom 83*
Measurements & Control/Measurements & Control News - Pittsburgh, PA - *BaconPubCkMag 84; MagDir 84; MagIndMarPl 82-83*
Meat Industry - Mill Valley, CA - *BaconPubCkMag 84; MagDir 84*
Meat Plant Magazine - St. Louis, MO - *BaconPubCkMag 84; MagDir 84; WritMar 84*
Meat, Poultry, & Seafood Digest - Shawnee Mission, KS - *MagDir 84*
Meat Processing International - Hinsdale, IL - *BaconPubCkMag 84; MagDir 84*
Mebane Alamance-Orange Enterprise - Mebane, NC - *BaconPubCkNews 84; NewsDir 84*
Mebane Home Telephone Co. - Mebane, NC - *TelDir&BG 83-84*
MEC Information Services [of Merrimack Education Center] - Chelmsford, MA - *EISS 83*
Meca - Yucca Valley, CA - *WhoWMicrocom 83*
Meca Corp., The - Alvin, TX - *BrCabYB 84*
Meca Corp., The [of Storer Cable Communications Inc.] - Clear Lake City, TX - *BrCabYB 84*
Meca Corp., The [of Storer Cable Communications] - Houston, TX - *BrCabYB 84; Tel&CabFB 84C p.1690*
Meca Corp., The - Kemah, TX - *Tel&CabFB 84C*
Meca Corp., The [of Storer Cable Communications Inc.] - La Marque, TX - *BrCabYB 84; Tel&CabFB 84C*
Meca Corp., The [of Storer Cable Communications] - League City, TX - *BrCabYB 84*
Meca Corp., The [of Storer Cable Communications Inc.] - Nassau Bay, TX - *BrCabYB 84*
Meca Corp., The [of Storer Cable Communications Inc.] - Tomball, TX - *BrCabYB 84*
Mecanica Popular - Miami, FL - *MagDir 84*
Mecanica Popular - Virginia Gardens, FL - *BaconPubCkMag 84*
Mechanical Engineering [of American Society of Mechanical Engineers] - New York, NY - *BaconPubCkMag 84; MagDir 84; MagIndMarPl 82-83*
Mechanical Engineering [of Royal Institute of Technology Library] - Stockholm, Sweden - *CompReadDB 82*
Mechanical Engineering & Metalworking Documentation [of Technical Information Center] - Frankfurt, West Germany - *EISS 83*
Mechanical Engineers' Book Club [of McGraw-Hill Book Club] - New York, NY - *LitMarPl 83, 84*
Mechanical Music Center Inc. - Darien, CT - *BoPubDir 4, 5*
Mechanical Properties Data Center [of Battelle Columbus Laboratories] - Columbus, OH - *CompReadDB 82; EISS 83*
Mechanical Properties Data Center - *See* Metals & Ceramics Information Center
Mechanical Secretary Inc. - New York, NY - *LitMarPl 83, 84*
Mechanics - Hyde Park, NY - *WritMar 84*
Mechanicsburg Telegram - London, OH - *BaconPubCkNews 84*
Mechanicsburg West Shore Times - Mechanicsburg, PA - *BaconPubCkNews 84*
Mechanicsville Pioneer Herald - Mechanicsville, IA - *BaconPubCkNews 84*
Mechanicsville Telephone Co. - Mechanicsville, IA - *TelDir&BG 83-84*
Mechanix Illustrated [of CBS Publications Inc.] - New York, NY - *BaconPubCkMag 84; Folio 83; LitMarPl 84; MagDir 84; MagIndMarPl 82-83; NewsBur 6; WritMar 84*
Mechanix Illustrated Computers 83 - New York, NY - *BaconPubCkMag 84*
Mechanized Information Center [of Ohio State University Libraries] - Columbus, OH - *CompReadDB 82; DataDirOnSer 84; EISS 83; FBInfSer 80; InfIndMarPl 83*
Mecke Associates Inc., Herbert E. - New York, NY - *IntDirMarRes 83*
Mecklenburg Gazette [of Park Newspapers Inc.] - Davidson, NC - *AyerDirPub 83; NewsDir 84*
Mecklenburg Gazette, The - Mecklenburg, NC - *Ed&PubIntYB 82*
Mecklenburg Times, The - Charlotte, NC - *NewsDir 84*
Meckler Publishing - Westport, CT - *EISS 83; LitMarPl 83, 84; MagIndMarPl 82-83; MicroMarPl 82-83*
Meckler Publishing - New York, NY - *InfoS 83-84*
Meczka, Michael A. - Los Angeles, CA - *IntDirMarRes 83*
Med-Com Advertising Group Inc. - Memphis, TN - *StaDirAdAg 2-84*
M.E.D. Communications - Woodbridge, NJ - *AdAge 3-28-84; StaDirAdAg 2-84*
Med-Data Resources Inc. - Columbus, OH - *MicrocomMPl 84*
Med Ed Communications - Pittsburgh, PA - *AvMarPl 83*
Med/Mail [of GTE Telenet Communications Corp.] - Vienna, VA - *TeleSy&SerDir 2-84*
Med-Psych Publications - West Allis, WI - *WritMar 84*
Med Systems - Chapel Hill, NC - *MicrocomMPl 83, 84*
Meda Record Co. - Detroit, MI - *BillIntBG 83-84*
Medallion TV Enterprises Inc. - West Hollywood, CA - *TelAl 83, 84; Tel&CabFB 84C*
Medberry Associates Inc., Lynn - Los Angeles, CA - *StaDirAdAg 2-84*
Medcom Products [Div. of Medcom Inc.] - New York, NY - *AvMarPl 83*
Medcom Systems Inc. - Newport Beach, CA - *MicrocomMPl 83*
Medcomp - New York, NY - *BaconPubCkMag 84*
Medfield Computer Software - Medfield, MA - *MicrocomMPl 83*
Medfield Suburban Press - Medfield, MA - *Ed&PubIntYB 82*
Medfield Suburban Press [of Suburban World Inc.] - Needham, MA - *AyerDirPub 83; NewsDir 84*
Medfield Suburban Press - *See* Suburban World Inc.
Medford Cable TV Inc. - Medford, OK - *BrCabYB 84; Tel&CabFB 84C p.1690*
Medford Central Record - Medford, NJ - *BaconPubCkNews 84; NewsDir 84*
Medford Mail Tribune [of Ottaway Newspapers Inc.] - Medford, OR - *BaconPubCkNews 84; Ed&PubIntYB 82; LitMarPl 83, 84; NewsDir 84*

Medford Mercury [of Malden Publications Inc.] - Malden, MA - *BaconPubCkNews 84; Ed&PubIntYB 82; LitMarPl 83, 84; NewsDir 84*
Medford Patriot-Star & Grant County Journal - Medford, OK - *BaconPubCkNews 84; Ed&PubIntYB 82*
Medford Star-News - Medford, WI - *BaconPubCkNews 84; NewsDir 84*
Medi Comp Press - Berkeley, CA - *BoPubDir 4, 5*
Medi-Publishing Group - Ft. Lauderdale, FL - *BoPubDir 4, 5*
Medi-Sim Inc. - Kansas City, MO - *MicrocomMPl 83, 84; MicrocomSwDir 1*
Media Action Research Center Inc. - New York, NY - *BoPubDir 4, 5*
Media Advertising Ltd. - Montreal, PQ, Canada - *ArtMar 84; StaDirAdAg 2-84*
Media Alliance - San Francisco, CA - *BoPubDir 4 Sup, 5*
Media & Methods [of American Society of Educators] - Philadelphia, PA - *BaconPubCkMag 84; LitMarPl 83, 84; MagDir 84; MagIndMarPl 82-83; WritMar 84*
Media Awards Handbook - Danville, CA - *BoPubDir 4, 5*
Media Books [Div. of Westwood Enterprises] - Woodstock, CT - *LitMarPl 83, 84*
Media Broadcasting Inc. - Toledo, OH - *Tel&CabFB 84C*
Media Bureau International Inc., The - Chicago, IL - *HBIndAd&MS 82-83; StaDirAdAg 2-84*
Media Buying Services International Inc. - Los Angeles, CA - *HBIndAd&MS 82-83*
Media Buying Services International Inc. - New York, NY - *StaDirAdAg 2-84*
Media Central Inc. - Chattanooga, TN - *Tel&CabFB 84S*
Media Communications Inc. - New York, NY - *HBIndAd&MS 82-83; StaDirAdAg 2-84*
Media Communications Inc. - Austin, TX - *ArtMar 84*
Media Communications Inc. - Houston, TX - *DirPRFirms 83; StaDirAdAg 2-84*
Media Concepts Press - Philadelphia, PA - *AvMarPl 83; BoPubDir 4, 5*
Media Consultants - Columbus, GA - *StaDirAdAg 2-84*
Media Consultants Group - Seattle, WA - *HBIndAd&MS 82-83*
Media Control Co. Inc. - Hartford, CT - *DirInfWP 82*
Media Control Inc. - Schiller Park, IL - *AvMarPl 83*
Media Dept. Inc. - St. Charles, IL - *ArtMar 84; AvMarPl 83*
Media Dept. Inc. - New York, NY - *StaDirAdAg 2-84*
Media Design Group - Winter Park, FL - *ArtMar 84; AvMarPl 83*
Media Distributing [Subs. of Magmedia Corp.] - Foster City, CA - *WhoWMicrocom 83*
Media Distributing - Scotts Valley, CA - *MicrocomMPl 83, 84*
Media Distribution Services - New York, NY - *LitMarPl 83, 84; MagIndMarPl 82-83*
Media Fabricators Inc. - Los Angeles, CA - *AvMarPl 83*
Media for Childbirth Education - Castro Valley, CA - *AvMarPl 83*
Media Forum International - Mt. Vernon, NY - *AvMarPl 83; BoPubDir 4, 5; LitMarPl 83, 84*
Media Four Productions - Hollywood, CA - *AvMarPl 83*
Media General Braodcast Services Inc. - Memphis, TN - *StaDirAdAg 2-84*
Media General Cable of Fairfax County Inc. [of Media General Inc.] - Fairfax County, VA - *BrCabYB 84; Tel&CabFB 84C*
Media General Data Base [of Media General Financial Services] - Richmond, VA - *DataDirOnSer 84; DBBus 82; DirOnDB Spring 84*
Media General Financial Services Inc. [Subs. of Media General Inc.] - Richmond, VA - *DataDirOnSer 84; EISS 83*
Media General Financial Weekly [of Media General Inc.] - Richmond, VA - *BaconPubCkMag 84; MagDir 84*
Media General Inc. - Tampa, FL - *Tel&CabFB 84S*
Media General Inc. - Richmond, VA - *AdAge 6-28-84; BrCabYB 84; Ed&PubIntYB 82; HomeVid&CabYB 82-83; InfoS 83-84; KnowInd 83; Tel&CabFB 84C p.1690*
Media Graphics Corp. [Subs. of Spectrum Industries] - Chicago, IL - *MagIndMarPl 82-83*
Media Group Inc., The - Columbus, OH - *AvMarPl 83*
Media Group Television - Moline, IL - *AvMarPl 83*
Media Guild, The - San Diego, CA - *AvMarPl 83*
Media History Digest [of Media Digest History Corp.] - New York, NY - *WritMar 84*
Media History Digest - Philadelphia, PA - *LitMag&SmPr 83-84*
Media Home Entertainment - Los Angeles, CA - *BillIntBG 83-84; Tel&CabFB 84C*
Media House Ltd. - Wilton, CT - *StaDirAdAg 2-84*
Media Inc. - Juneau, AK - *BrCabYB 84*
Media Index Survey - *DirOnDB Spring 84*
Media Index Survey-Hong Kong [of Interactive Market Systems Inc.] - New York, NY - *DataDirOnSer 84*
Media Index Survey-Indonesia [of Interactive Market Systems Inc.] - New York, NY - *DataDirOnSer 84*
Media Index Survey-Malaysia [of Interactive Market Systems Inc.] - New York, NY - *DataDirOnSer 84*
Media Index Survey-Singapore [of Interactive Market Systems Inc.] - New York, NY - *DataDirOnSer 84*
Media Index Survey-Thailand [of Interactive Market Systems Inc.] - New York, NY - *DataDirOnSer 84*
Media Industry Newsletter - New York, NY - *BaconPubCkMag 84; MagIndMarPl 82-83*
Media Institute - Washington, DC - *BoPubDir 4 Sup, 5; LitMag&SmPr 83-84*
Media Interstellar Music [Div. of Clay Pigeon International] - Chicago, IL - *BillIntBG 83-84*
Media Investment Services - *See* Local Communications Inc.
Media Lab Inc. - Boston, MA - *AvMarPl 83*
Media Law Reporter - Washington, DC - *MagIndMarPl 82-83*
Media Learning Systems - Pasadena, CA - *AvMarPl 83*
Media: Library Services Journal [of Sunday School Board of Southern Baptist Convention] - Nashville, TN - *LitMarPl 83, 84; WritMar 84*
Media Loft Inc. - Minneapolis, MN - *AvMarPl 83*
Media Magazine - Toronto, ON, Canada - *BaconPubCkMag 84*
Media Man Inc., The - Teaneck, NJ - *AvMarPl 83*
Media Management Consultants Inc. - Abilene, TX - *StaDirAdAg 2-84*
Media Management Inc. - Westport, CT - *StaDirAdAg 2-84*
Media Management Inc. - Kansas City, MO - *StaDirAdAg 2-84*
Media Management Monographs [of Jim Mann & Associates] - Gales Ferry, CT - *LitMag&SmPr 83-84; MagIndMarPl 82-83*
Media/Marketing Service Center Inc. - Western Springs, IL - *StaDirAdAg 2-84*
Media Marketing Services Inc. - Yonkers, NY - *StaDirAdAg 2-84*
Media Materials Inc. - Baltimore, MD - *ArtMar 84; AvMarPl 83; WhoWMicrocom 83*
Media Measurement Services Inc. - Toronto, ON, Canada - *Tel&CabFB 84C*
Media Methods - Montville, NJ - *DirPRFirms 83*
Media Monitors Inc. - Indianapolis, IN - *BrCabYB 84*
Media Networks Inc. - *Folio 83*
Media News Keys [of Television Index Inc.] - New York, NY - *MagDir 84; MagIndMarPl 82-83*
Media P - Paris, France - *DirOnDB Spring 84*
Media/Pac Inc. - Chicago, IL - *StaDirAdAg 2-84*
Media People - New York, NY - *BaconPubCkMag 84*
Media Productions & Marketing Inc. - Lincoln, NE - *BoPubDir 4, 5*
Media Profiles: The AV Marketing Newsletter - Hoboken, NJ - *WritMar 84*
Media Profiles: The Career Development Edition - Hoboken, NJ - *WritMar 84*
Media Profiles: The Health Sciences Edition - Hoboken, NJ - *WritMar 84*
Media Profiles: The Whole Earth Edition - Hoboken, NJ - *WritMar 84*
Media Projects Inc. - New York, NY - *LitMarPl 83, 84*
Media Publications - Phoenix, AZ - *BoPubDir 5*
Media Records Inc. - New York, NY - *BrCabYB 84*
Media Referral Service - Minneapolis, MN - *BoPubDir 5*
Media Report to Women [of Women's Institute for Freedom of the Press] - Washington, DC - *BoPubDir 4, 5; LitMag&SmPr 83-84*
Media Research Associates Inc. - Salem, OR - *AvMarPl 83*
Media Resource Associates - New York, NY - *InfIndMarPl 83*
Media Sales Associates - Capistrano Beach, CA - *MagIndMarPl 82-83*

Media Science Newsletter [of NewsNet Inc.] - Bryn Mawr, PA - *DataDirOnSer 84*
Media Science Reports - New York, NY - *DirOnDB Spring 84*
Media Selection Corp. - Goleta, CA - *StaDirAdAg 2-84*
Media Service Concepts - Chicago, IL - *MicrocomMPl 83, 84; MicrocomSwDir 1*
Media Services Corp. - San Francisco, CA - *StaDirAdAg 2-84*
Media Services Corp. [Subs. of Publishing Corp. of America] - Canton, OH - *DirMarMP 83*
Media Specialists Inc. - New York, NY - *StaDirAdAg 2-84*
Media Spotlight [of Wordland] - Costa Mesa, CA - *LitMag&SmPr 83-84*
Media Statistics Inc. - Silver Spring, MD - *Tel&CabFB 84C*
Media Systems Nineteen Eighty Ltd. - Allen, TX - *BrCabYB 84*
Media Systems Nineteen Eighty Ltd. - Farmersville, TX - *BrCabYB 84*
Media Systems Nineteen Eighty Ltd. - McKinney, TX - *BrCabYB 84*
Media Systems Nineteen Eighty Ltd. - Richardson, TX - *BrCabYB 84*
Media Systems Nineteen Eighty Ltd. - Sachse, TX - *BrCabYB 84*
Media Systems Nineteen Eighty Ltd. - Wylie, TX - *BrCabYB 84*
Media Technology Associates - Bethesda, MD - *InterCabHB 3; VideoDir 82-83*
Media Texas Inc. - Abilene, TX - *StaDirAdAg 2-84*
Media, The - Kahoka, MO - *Ed&PubIntYB 82*
Media Town Talk - Media, PA - *BaconPubCkNews 84*
Media Unltd. - Alameda, CA - *BoPubDir 4, 5*
Media Ventures Inc. - Princeton, NJ - *LitMarPl 84*
Media Ventures Inc. - Cincinnati, OH - *BoPubDir 4, 5*
Media West - Redondo Beach, CA - *BoPubDir 4, 5*
Media West - Vancouver, BC, Canada - *BaconPubCkMag 84*
Media West Group Inc., The - Aspen, CO - *StaDirAdAg 2-84*
Media Works Inc., The - Chicago, IL - *AvMarPl 83*
Mediafile - San Francisco, CA - *LitMag&SmPr 83-84*
Mediaforce - New York, NY - *StaDirAdAg 2-84*
Medial - Chambourcy, France - *DirOnDB Spring 84*
Mediamark Research Inc. [Subs. of Mills & Allen International PLC] - New York, NY - *AdAge 5-17-84 p.39; BrCabYB 84; DataDirOnSer 84; EISS 83; InfIndMarPl 83; IntDirMarRes 83; MagIndMarPl 82-83*
Median Co., The - North River, NY - *StaDirAdAg 2-84*
Medianalysis Monitoring Reports - Washington, DC - *BrCabYB 84*
Mediaor - Prineville, OR - *BoPubDir 4, 5*
Mediapolis New Era - Mediapolis, IA - *BaconPubCkNews 84; Ed&PubIntYB 82*
Mediapolis Telephone Co. - Mediapolis, IA - *TelDir&BG 83-84*
Mediaprint Inc. - New York, NY - *LitMarPl 83, 84; MagIndMarPl 82-83*
Mediastat [of Media Statistics Inc.] - Silver Spring, MD - *BrCabYB 84*
Mediatech - Chicago, IL - *Tel&CabFB 84C*
Mediatech - Dallas, TX - *HBIndAd&MS 82-83*
Mediatech Software - Wembley, England - *MicrocomSwDir 1*
Mediators Inc., The - New York, NY - *HBIndAd&MS 82-83; StaDirAdAg 2-84*
Mediavision Inc. - Toronto, ON, Canada - *Tel&CabFB 84C*
Mediawerks - Winona, MN - *StaDirAdAg 2-84*
Mediawire [of VU/TEXT Information Services] - Philadelphia, PA - *DataDirOnSer 84; DirOnDB Spring 84*
Mediaworks - Albuquerque, NM - *StaDirAdAg 2-84*
Mediax Inc. - Westport, CT - *BoPubDir 4, 5*
Medic Data Base [of Central Medical Library] - Helsinki, Finland - *CompReadDB 82; DirOnDB Spring 84; EISS 83*
Medic Publishing Co. - Issaquah, WA - *BoPubDir 4*
Medic Publishing Co. - Redmond, WA - *BoPubDir 5; LitMag&SmPr 83-84*
Medical Abstracts Newsletter - Teaneck, NJ - *DirOnDB Spring 84*
Medical & Pharmaceutical Information Bureau Inc. - New York, NY - *DirPRFirms 83*
Medical & Scientific Literature Research - Seattle, WA - *EISS 7-83 Sup*
Medical & Technical Books Inc. - Los Angeles, CA - *BoPubDir 4 Sup, 5; LitMarPl 83, 84*
Medical Aspects of Human Sexuality - New York, NY - *MagDir 84; MagIndMarPl 82-83*
Medical/Behavioral Associates Inc. - Mansfield, OH - *BoPubDir 4, 5*
Medical Care - Philadelphia, PA - *MagDir 84*
Medical Care Products - Dover, NJ - *BaconPubCkMag 84*
Medical Communications - Richmond, VA - *WritMar 84*
Medical Computer Journal - East Hampton, CT - *MicrocomMPl 84*
Medical Data Processing Corp. - Glastonbury, CT - *ADAPSOMemDir 83-84*
Medical Data Research - Norcross, GA - *WhoWMicrocom 83*
Medical Data Services - San Diego, CA - *MicrocomMPl 84*
Medical Device & Diagnostic Industry - Santa Monia, CA - *BaconPubCkMag 84*
Medical Documentation Service [of College of Physicians] - Philadelphia, PA - *EISS 83; FBInfSer 80; InfIndMarPl 83*
Medical Documentation Systems [of Eli Lilly & Co.] - Indianapolis, IN - *EISS 83*
Medical Documents [of University of Utah] - Salt Lake City, UT - *CompReadDB 82; DBBus 82*
Medical Economics Books [Div. of Medical Economics Co.] - Oradell, NJ - *LitMarPl 83, 84; WritMar 84*
Medical Economics Co. [Subs. of Mailing List Marketing] - Oradell, NJ - *ArtMar 84; BaconPubCkMag 84; LitMarPl 83, 84; MagDir 84; MagIndMarPl 82-83; NewsBur 6*
Medical Education Consultants - Los Angeles, CA - *BoPubDir 4, 5*
Medical Electronic Educational Services Inc. - Tucson, AZ - *AvMarPl 83*
Medical Electronics - Pittsburgh, PA - *BaconPubCkMag 84*
Medical Electronics & Equipment News - Park Ridge, IL - *BaconPubCkMag 84; MagDir 84*
Medical Electronics/Medical Electronic Products - Pittsburgh, PA - *MagDir 84*
Medical Equipment Classified - Minneapolis, MN - *MagDir 84*
Medical Examination Publishing Co. Inc. [Subs. of Excerpta Medica] - New Hyde Park, NY - *LitMarPl 83, 84; WritMar 84*
Medical Gazette [of Taylor Communications Inc.] - Universal City, TX - *NewsDir 84*
Medical Grand Rounds - New York, NY - *BaconPubCkMag 84*
Medical Group Management - Denver, CO - *BaconPubCkMag 84; MagDir 84*
Medical Group News - Glencoe, IL - *BaconPubCkMag 84; MagDir 84; MagIndMarPl 82-83*
Medical History - London, England - *LitMag&SmPr 83-84*
Medical Hotline - New York, NY - *BaconPubCkMag 84*
Medical Illustrations Co. - New York, NY - *AvMarPl 83*
Medical Information Center [of Ayerst Laboratories] - New York, NY - *EISS 83*
Medical Information Centre [of Karolinska Institutet Library & Information Center] - Stockholm, Sweden - *CompReadDB 82; InfIndMarPl 83*
Medical Information System [of American Rheumatism Association] - Palo Alto, CA - *EISS 83*
Medical Information System [of Reference & Index Services Inc.] - Indianapolis, IN - *EISS 5-84 Sup*
Medical Information Technology Inc. - Cambridge, MA - *DataDirOnSer 84*
Medical Instrumentation - Arlington, VA - *BaconPubCkMag 84; MagDir 84*
Medical Laboratory Observer - Oradell, NJ - *BaconPubCkMag 84*
Medical Library Association - Chicago, IL - *BoPubDir 4, 5; EISS 83*
Medical Library Center of New York - New York, NY - *CompReadDB 82; EISS 83*
Medical Literature Information Center [of St. Mary's Hospital Medical Education & Research Foundation] - Kansas City, MO - *EISS 83*
Medical Logic International - Sumter, SC - *MicrocomMPl 84*
Medical Marketing & Media - Ridgefield, CT - *ArtMar 84; BaconPubCkMag 84; MagIndMarPl 82-83*
Medical Marketing & Media [of Technomic Publishing Corp.] - Westport, CT - *MagDir 84*
Medical Media Corp. - Flemington, NJ - *BoPubDir 4, 5*
Medical Media Publishers [Aff. of American Hospital Publishing Inc.] - Pittsburgh, PA - *BoPubDir 4, 5*

Medical Meetings [of The Laux Co. Inc.] - Harvard, MA - *BaconPubCkMag 84; MagDir 84*
Medical Meetings - New York, NY - *MagIndMarPl 82-83*
Medical Month - New York, NY - *BaconPubCkMag 84*
Medical/Mrs. - Rye, NY - *MagDir 84; MagIndMarPl 82-83*
Medical Multimedia Corp. - New York, NY - *ArtMar 84; AvMarPl 83; WritMar 84*
Medical Office Management - Miami, FL - *BoPubDir 4 Sup, 5*
Medical-Pharmaceutical Publishing Co. - Paris, France - *EISS 83*
Medical Physics - New York, NY - *BaconPubCkMag 84; MagDir 84*
Medical Plastics Laboratory Inc. - Gatesville, TX - *AvMarPl 83*
Medical Post, The - Toronto, ON, Canada - *BaconPubCkMag 84; WritMar 84*
Medical Products Sales - Winnetka, IL - *MagDir 84*
Medical Products Sales - McLean, VA - *BaconPubCkMag 84*
Medical Record News - Chicago, IL - *MagDir 84*
Medical Reference Services Quarterly [of Haworth Press Journals] - New York, NY - *LitMarPl 83, 84*
Medical Research Bureau - Minneapolis, MN - *IntDirMarRes 83*
Medical Research Bureau - New York, NY - *IntDirMarRes 83*
Medical Research Council - Harrow, England - *InfIndMarPl 83*
Medical Research Engineering - Little Falls, NJ - *MagDir 84*
Medical School Rounds - Miami, FL - *MagDir 84*
Medical Self-Care - Inverness, CA - *BaconPubCkMag 84; LitMag&SmPr 83-84*
Medical Software Co. - Center Moriches, NY - *MicrocomMPl 84*
Medical Software Consortium - Hopkinsville, KY - *MicrocomMPl 84*
Medical Subject Headings Vocabulary File [of National Library of Medicine] - Bethesda, MD - *CompReadDB 82; DataDirOnSer 84*
Medical Times - Port Washington, NY - *ArtMar 84; BaconPubCkMag 84; MagDir 84; MagIndMarPl 82-83; WritMar 84*
Medical Tribune - New York, NY - *BaconPubCkMag 84; MagDir 84; MagIndMarPl 82-83*
Medical World News - New York, NY - *MagDir 84; MagIndMarPl 82-83*
Medical World News - Houston, TX - *BaconPubCkMag 84*
Medice Penny Saver - Medina, NY - *AyerDirPub 83*
Medicindata [of University of Goteborg] - Goteborg, Sweden - *EISS 83; InfIndMarPl 83*
Medicine & Computer - White Plains, NY - *BaconPubCkMag 84*
Medicine Bow Cable TV [of Dubois CATV Inc.] - Medicine Bow, WY - *BrCabYB 84; Tel&CabFB 84C*
Medicine Bow Post - Medicine Bow, WY - *AyerDirPub 83; BaconPubCkNews 84*
Medicine Bow Telephone Co. - Medicine Bow, WY - *TelDir&BG 83-84*
Medicine Hat News, The - Medicine Hat, AB, Canada - *BaconPubCkNews 84*
Medicine Lodge Barber County Index - Medicine Lodge, KS - *BaconPubCkNews 84*
Medicine Lodge Cablevision [of Multimedia Cablevision Inc.] - Medicine Lodge, KS - *BrCabYB 84; Tel&CabFB 84C*
Medicine North America - Westmount, PQ, Canada - *BaconPubCkMag 84*
Medicine Park Cablevision [of Transwestern Video Inc.] - Medicine Park, OK - *BrCabYB 84; Tel&CabFB 84C*
Medicine Park Telephone Co. - Medicine Park, OK - *TelDir&BG 83-84*
Medicom [of McDonnell Douglas Automation Co.] - St. Louis, MO - *DataDirOnSer 84*
Medicus Affiliates Inc. [Subs. of Whittaker Corp.] - Evanston, IL - *WhoWMicrocom 83*
Medicus Intercon International [Subs. of Benton & Bowles] - New York, NY - *AdAge 3-28-84; DirMarMP 83; StaDirAdAg 2-84*
Medieval Academy of America - Cambridge, MA - *BoPubDir 4 Sup, 5*
Medill News Service - Washington, DC - *NewsBur 6*
Medina Cablevision Inc. - Medina, ND - *Tel&CabFB 84C*
Medina County Gazette - Medina, OH - *AyerDirPub 83; BaconPubCkNews 84; Ed&PubIntYB 82; NewsDir 84*
Medina Journal-Register - Medina, NY - *BaconPubCkNews 84; NewsDir 84*
Medina Press - Santa Ana, CA - *LitMag&SmPr 83-84*
Medina Sun - Cleveland, OH - *AyerDirPub 83*
Medina Sun Sentinel - Medina, OH - *Ed&PubIntYB 82*
Medina Sun Sentinel - *See* Sun Newspapers
Medina University Press International - Wilmette, IL - *BoPubDir 4, 5*
Medina Valley Times - Medina Valley, TX - *Ed&PubIntYB 82*
MediSoft - Santa Cruz, CA - *MicrocomMPl 84*
Meditec - Frankfurt, West Germany - *DirOnDB Spring 84*
Medium - Seattle, WA - *Ed&PubIntYB 82*
Medium & Heavy Truck Forecast [of Chase Econometrics/ Interactive Data Corp.] - Waltham, MA - *DataDirOnSer 84*
Medium Well Done - Minneapolis, MN - *AvMarPl 83*
MEDLARS [of National Library of Medicine] - Bethesda, MD - *CompReadDB 82; EISS 83; MicrocomMPl 84*
MEDLINE [of National Library of Medicine] - Bethesda, MD - *DataDirOnSer 84; DBBus 82; DirOnDB Spring 84; EISS 83; OnBibDB 3*
Medmaster Inc. - North Miami Beach, FL - *BoPubDir 4, 5*
MEDOC [of University of Utah] - Salt Lake City, UT - *DataDirOnSer 84; EISS 83; OnBibDB 3*
M.E.D.S. Corp. - Bloomfield, NJ - *AvMarPl 83; BoPubDir 5*
M.E.D.S. Corp. - Newark, NJ - *BoPubDir 4*
Medso Inc. - Cincinnati, OH - *ADAPSOMemDir 83-84*
Medtrac Inc. [of Burke Marketing Services Inc.] - Teaneck, NJ - *IntDirMarRes 83*
Meeker County Advertiser - Litchfield, MN - *AyerDirPub 83*
Meeker Herald - Meeker, CO - *BaconPubCkNews 84; Ed&PubIntYB 82*
Meeker-Mayer Public Relations Inc. - Akron, OH - *DirPRFirms 83*
Meeker Publishing Co. - Albuquerque, NM - *BoPubDir 4, 5*
Meese' Newspaper Group - Chicago, IL - *BaconPubCkNews 84*
Meeting [of Questel Inc.] - Washington, DC - *DataDirOnSer 84*
Meeting Agenda - Gif sur Yvette, France - *DirOnDB Spring 84*
Meeting Makers Inc. - New York, NY - *WritMar 84*
Meeting News [of Gralla Publications] - New York, NY - *BaconPubCkMag 84; MagDir 84; MagIndMarPl 82-83*
Meeting Services [Div. of Communications Co. Inc.] - San Diego, CA - *AvMarPl 83*
Meetings & Conventions [of Ziff-Davis Publishing] - New York, NY - *BaconPubCkMag 84; MagDir 84; MagIndMarPl 82-83; WritMar 84*
Meetings & Incentive Travel - Don Mills, ON, Canada - *BaconPubCkMag 84*
Mefford Weir Inc. - Denver, CO - *StaDirAdAg 2-84*
Mega-Data Computer Products Inc. - Overland Park, KS - *MicrocomMPl 84*
Mega Media Associates Inc. - Fountain Valley, CA - *DirMarMP 83; StaDirAdAg 2-84*
Mega Music Corp. - New York, NY - *AvMarPl 83*
Mega-Star Music - *See* Yearwood Music Inc.
Mega Vision Co. - Detroit, MI - *BrCabYB 84 p.D-303; Tel&CabFB 84C p.1690*
Megabild Press - Walkertown, NC - *BoPubDir 4, 5*
Megadata Corp. - Bohemia, NY - *DataDirSup 7-83; DirInfWP 82; InfIndMarPl 83*
Megalon Publications - Goleta, CA - *BoPubDir 4, 5*
Megalon Publications - Santa Maria, CA - *LitMag&SmPr 83-84*
Megan Marketing Inc. - Teaneck, NJ - *StaDirAdAg 2-84*
Megan's World - Fullerton, CA - *BoPubDir 5*
Megantic Transvision Inc. - Lac Megantic, PQ, Canada - *BrCabYB 84*
Megantic Transvision Inc. - Woburn, PQ, Canada - *BrCabYB 84*
Megasoft Computer Corp. - San Jose, CA - *MicrocomMPl 84*
Megasynthesis Ltd. - Edmonton, AB, Canada - *BoPubDir 4 Sup, 5*
MegaTape Corp. - Duarte, CA - *MicrocomMPl 84*
Megatek Corp. - San Diego, CA - *DataDirSup 7-83; WhoWMicrocom 83*
Megatherium Press - Cupertino, CA - *LitMag&SmPr 83-84*
Megatone Records - San Francisco, CA - *BillIntBG 83-84*
Megavault - Woodland Hills, CA - *DataDirSup 7-83*
Megden Publishing Co. - Huntington Beach, CA - *BoPubDir 4, 5*
Meher Baba Information - Berkeley, CA - *BoPubDir 4, 5*
Mehetabel & Co. - San Rafael, CA - *BoPubDir 4, 5*
Mehl Cable Systems - Tucson, AZ - *Tel&CabFB 84C*

Meidinger Inc. - Louisville, KY - *BoPubDir 4 Sup, 5; DirPRFirms 83*
Meie Elu - Toronto, ON, Canada - *Ed&PubIntYB 82*
Meier Advertising Inc. - New York, NY - *StaDirAdAg 2-84*
Meier Productions, Don - Chicago, IL - *Tel&CabFB 84C*
Meiklejohn Civil Liberties Institute - Berkeley, CA - *BoPubDir 4, 5; MicroMarPl 82-83*
Meilach Features, Dona Z. - Carlsbad, CA - *Ed&PubIntYB 82; LitMarPl 83, 84; MagIndMarPl 82-83*
Meincke, Pearce & Co. - Weehawken, NJ - *DataDirOnSer 84*
Meister Publishing Co. - Willoughby, OH - *DirMarMP 83; MagIndMarPl 82-83*
Mekel Engineering Inc. - Walnut, CA - *AvMarPl 83*
Mekler/Ansell Associates Inc. - New York, NY - *DirPRFirms 83*
Mel-View Cable TV - Melstone, MT - *BrCabYB 84; Tel&CabFB 84C*
Melanson Associates, Donya - Boston, MA - *LitMarPl 83, 84*
Melbourne House Software Inc. - New York, NY - *AvMarPl 83*
Melbourne Music Publishing Co. - *See* International Jaspar Music Group
Melbourne Record - Melbourne, IA - *BaconPubCkNews 84; Ed&PubIntYB 82*
Melbourne South Brevard Shopping News - Melbourne, FL - *AyerDirPub 83*
Melbourne Times - Melbourne, AR - *BaconPubCkNews 84*
Melbourne Times - Melbourne, FL - *BaconPubCkNews 84; NewsDir 84*
Melbourne TV Cable Co. - Melbourne, AR - *BrCabYB 84; Tel&CabFB 84C*
Melcher & Associates, Daniel - Charlottesville, VA - *LitMarPl 83, 84; MagIndMarPl 82-83*
Melco Laboratories Inc. - Bellevue, WA - *DataDirSup 7-83*
Meldrum & Campbell Advertising Inc. - Cleveland, OH - *AdAge 3-28-84; StaDirAdAg 2-84*
Meldrum & Fewsmith - Cleveland, OH - *AdAge 3-28-84; BrCabYB 84; DirPRFirms 83; StaDirAdAg 2-84; TelAl 83, 84*
Mele, Barbara A. - Bronx, NY - *LitMarPl 83, 84*
Mele Loke Publishing Co. - Honolulu, HI - *BoPubDir 4, 5*
Melear Multi-Media [Div. of Lifeplan Communications Corp.] - Marietta, GA - *AvMarPl 83*
Melfort Journal, The - Melfort, SK, Canada - *Ed&PubIntYB 82*
Melgar Nordlinger Inc. - New York, NY - *AdAge 3-28-84; StaDirAdAg 2-84*
Mellekas & Sevieri Advertising Inc. - Albuquerque, NM - *StaDirAdAg 2-84*
Mellen Cable TV Inc. - Mellen, WI - *BrCabYB 84; Tel&CabFB 84C*
Mellen Press, Edwin - Lewiston, NY - *BoPubDir 4, 5; LitMarPl 84*
Mellen Weekly-Record - Mellen, WI - *BaconPubCkNews 84*
Mellers Publishing Services, Tom - New York, NY - *LitMarPl 83, 84; MagIndMarPl 82-83*
Mellette County News - White River, SD - *AyerDirPub 83; Ed&PubIntYB 82*
Mellifluous Voice - Hollywood, CA - *LitMag&SmPr 83-84*
Mellonics Information Center [of Litton Systems Inc.] - Canoga Park, CA - *EISS 83*
Mellordata Ltd. - Colchester, England - *InfIndMarPl 83*
Mellus Newspapers Inc. - Lincoln Park, MI - *BaconPubCkNews 84*
Melman, Ned - Ossining, NY - *LitMarPl 83, 84*
Melodee Records - Nashville, TN - *BillIntBG 83-84*
Melomusic Publications - *See* Graham Music Publisher, Roger
Melrose - East Devon, England - *LitMag&SmPr 83-84*
Melrose Beacon - Melrose, MN - *BaconPubCkNews 84; Ed&PubIntYB 82; NewsDir 84*
Melrose Chronicle - Melrose, WI - *BaconPubCkNews 84; Ed&PubIntYB 82*
Melrose Evening News - Malden, MA - *AyerDirPub 83; Ed&PubIntYB 82; LitMarPl 83*
Melrose Free Press - Melrose, MA - *BaconPubCkNews 84; Ed&PubIntYB 82; NewsDir 84*
Melrose News [of Eastern Middlesex Publications] - Malden, MA - *BaconPubCkNews 84; LitMarPl 84; NewsDir 84*
Melrose Park Herald - Wilmette, IL - *AyerDirPub 83*
Melrose Park Herald - *See* Pioneer Press Inc.
Melrose Publishing Co. [Aff. of Al Berkman Studio] - Los Angeles, CA - *BoPubDir 4, 5*
Melrose Shoppers News [of The Stoneham Independent] - Stoneham, MA - *AyerDirPub 83; NewsDir 84*
Melrose Telephone Co. - Melrose, MN - *TelDir&BG 83-84*
Melstep Music - *See* Woodrich Publishing Co.
Melton Peninsula Inc. [Aff. of MacMillan Ltd.] - Dallas, TX - *BoPubDir 4, 5*
Meltzer, Aron & Lemen Inc. - San Francisco, CA - *TelAl 83*
Melvin Ford County Press - Melvin, IL - *BaconPubCkNews 84*
Melvin Paper Enterprises - Brooklyn, NY - *LitMarPl 83, 84*
Melvindale Messenger [of The Mellus Newspapers] - Lincoln Park, MI - *AyerDirPub 83; NewsDir 84*
Melvindale Messenger - *See* Mellus Newspapers Inc.
Melvindale Messenger, The - Melvindale, MI - *Ed&PubIntYB 82*
Membership Services Inc. [Subs. of National Chemsearch] - Irving, TX - *DataDirOnSer 84*
Membrane Press - Milwaukee, WI - *BoPubDir 4 Sup, 5; LitMag&SmPr 83-84*
Memco News - Appleton, WI - *ArtMar 84*
Memento Publications Inc. - Wilmington, DE - *BoPubDir 4, 5*
Memex Books Inc. [Subs. of Michael Roger Press Inc.] - Middlesex, NJ - *LitMarPl 83, 84*
Memnon Ltd. - Forrest Hills, NY - *BillIntBG 83-84*
Memodyne Corp. - Needham Heights, MA - *DataDirSup 7-83*
Memorex Corp. - Santa Clara, CA - *DataDirSup 7-83; DirInfWP 82*
Memorex Corp. (Communications Group) - Cupertino, CA - *InfIndMarPl 83*
Memorial Dose Distribution Computation Service [of Memorial Sloan-Kettering Cancer Center] - New York, NY - *EISS 83*
Memorial University of Newfoundland (Extension Service) - St. John's, NF, Canada - *BoPubDir 4, 5*
Memorial University of Newfoundland (Folklore & Language Publications) - St. John's, NF, Canada - *BoPubDir 4, 5*
Memorial University of Newfoundland (Institute of Social & Economic Research) - St. John's, NF, Canada - *BoPubDir 4, 5*
Memory Lane Music Corp. - *See* Spier Inc., Larry
Memory Machine Records - Pittsburgh, PA - *BillIntBG 83-84*
Memory Systems Inc. - Skokie, IL - *MicrocomMPl 84*
Memory Technologies Inc. - Logansport, IN - *MicrocomMPl 84*
Memory Technologies Inc. - Twelve Mile, IN - *MicrocomMPl 84*
Memotec Data Inc. - St. Laurent, PQ, Canada - *DataDirSup 7-83*
Memotech Corp. - Denver, CO - *MicrocomMPl 84; MicrocomSwDir 1*
Memphis [of Towery Press] - Memphis, TN - *BaconPubCkMag 84; MagDir 84; WritMar 84*
Memphis Cablevision [of American TV & Communications Corp.] - Memphis, TN - *Tel&CabFB 84C*
Memphis CATV Inc. - Memphis, TN - *BrCabYB 84*
Memphis Commercial Appeal - Memphis, TN - *BaconPubCkNews 84; LitMarPl 83; NewsDir 84*
Memphis Communications Corp. - Memphis, TN - *AvMarPl 83*
Memphis Democrat - Memphis, MO - *BaconPubCkNews 84; Ed&PubIntYB 82*
Memphis Democrat - Memphis, TX - *BaconPubCkNews 84; Ed&PubIntYB 82*
Memphis Junior League Publications Inc. - Memphis, TN - *BoPubDir 4, 5*
Memphis Press-Scimitar [of Memphis Publishing Co.] - Memphis, TN - *BaconPubCkNews 84; Ed&PubIntYB 82; LitMarPl 83, 84; NewsBur 6; NewsDir 84*
Memphis State Review - Memphis, TN - *LitMag&SmPr 83-84*
Memphis State University Press - Memphis, TN - *LitMarPl 83, 84; WritMar 84*
Memphis Town Publishing Co. - *See* Beckie Publishing Co.
Memphis Tri-State Defender - Memphis, TN - *BaconPubCkNews 84*
M.E.M.R.B. - *See* Middle East Marketing Research Bureau Ltd.
M.E.M.R.B. Co. - Al-Kuwait, Kuwait - *IntDirMarRes 83*
M.E.M.R.B. Co. - Sharjah, United Arab Emirates - *IntDirMarRes 83*
Memtec Corp. - Salem, NH - *MicrocomMPl 84*
Men - New York, NY - *MagDir 84*
Mena Enterprises Inc. - Santurce, PR - *BillIntBG 83-84*
Mena Evening Star [of The Enterprise Group Inc.] - Mena, AR - *Ed&PubIntYB 82; NewsDir 84*

Mena Star - Mena, AR - *BaconPubCkNews 84*
Mena Weekly Star [of Enterprise Group Inc.] - Mena, AR - *BaconPubCkNews 84; Ed&PubIntYB 82; NewsDir 84*
Menaid Press International - Colorado Springs, CO - *BoPubDir 4, 5*
Menaker & Wright - Chicago, IL - *AdAge 3-28-84; HBIndAd&MS 82-83; StaDirAdAg 2-84*
Menard County Review - Greenview, IL - *AyerDirPub 83; Ed&PubIntYB 82*
Menard News - Menard, TX - *Ed&PubIntYB 82*
Menard News & Messenger - Menard, TX - *BaconPubCkNews 84*
Menard Press - Berkeley, CA - *BoPubDir 5*
Menard Press - Kensington, CA - *BoPubDir 4*
Menard Press, The - London, England - *LitMag&SmPr 83-84*
Mendel, Carol - San Diego, CA - *BoPubDir 4, 5*
Mendelsohn Media Research [Div. of Monroe Mendelsohn Research Inc.] - New York, NY - *IntDirMarRes 83; MagIndMarPl 82-83*
Mendelson Film Productions, Lee - Burlingame, CA - *Tel&CabFB 84C*
Mendenhall Simpson County News - Mendenhall, MS - *BaconPubCkNews 84*
Mendenhall, Wedder & Leistra - Grand Rapids, MI - *StaDirAdAg 2-84*
Menderson Co., Ted - Cincinnati, OH - *StaDirAdAg 2-84*
Mendez, Carmen Medina - New York, NY - *BoPubDir 4, 5*
Mendez Inc., Toni - New York, NY - *LitMarPl 83, 84*
Mendham Observer Tribune [of Recorder Publishing Co.] - Chester, NJ - *NewsDir 84*
Mendham Observer Tribune - *See* Recorder Publishing Co.
Mendocino Beacon - Mendocino, CA - *BaconPubCkNews 84; Ed&PubIntYB 82; NewsDir 84*
Mendocino Graphics - Mendocino, CA - *LitMag&SmPr 83-84*
Mendocino Publishing Co. - Palos Verdes, CA - *Ed&PubIntYB 82*
Mendocino Review [of Mendocino Graphics] - Mendocino, CA - *LitMag&SmPr 83-84*
Mendocino Software - Willits, CA - *MicrocomMPl 84; WhoWMicrocom 83*
Mendon Dispatch-Times - *See* Taylor Publishing Co.
Mendota Reporter - Mendota, IL - *BaconPubCkNews 84; Ed&PubIntYB 82; NewsDir 84*
Mendota Shopping Guide - Mendota, IL - *AyerDirPub 83*
Mendoza, Dillon & Asociados - Newport Beach, CA - *AdAge 3-28-84; StaDirAdAg 2-84*
Mendte Associates, J. Robert - Lansdowne, PA - *StaDirAdAg 2-84*
Mendy Enterprises - New York, NY - *BoPubDir 4 Sup, 5*
Menell Co., Jerome [Div. of Media Facilities Corp.] - New York, NY - *AvMarPl 83*
Meneough & Associates Inc. - Des Moines, IA - *StaDirAdAg 2-84*
Menges, Roger - Johnsburg, NY - *LitMarPl 83; MagIndMarPl 82-83*
Menhaden Information Data Bank [of Gulf States Marine Fisheries Commission] - Ocean Springs, MS - *EISS 5-84 Sup*
Menifee County News - Morehead, KY - *Ed&PubIntYB 82*
Menlo Atherton Recorder [of Menlo Park Nowels Publishing] - Menlo Park, CA - *AyerDirPub 83; Ed&PubIntYB 82; NewsDir 84*
Menlo Cable TV - Summerville, GA - *Tel&CabFB 84C*
Menlo Park Atherton Recorder - *See* Regal Publishing Co.
Menlo Park Black Times - Menlo Park, CA - *NewsDir 84*
Mennick, James - San Rafael, CA - *LitMarPl 83, 84; MagIndMarPl 82-83*
Menno Hutchinson Herald - Menno, SD - *BaconPubCkNews 84*
Mennonite Brethren Herald - Winnipeg, MB, Canada - *WritMar 84*
Mennonite Heritage Centre [Aff. of Conference of Mennonites in Canada] - Winnipeg, MB, Canada - *BoPubDir 4, 5*
Mennonite Literary Society Inc. - Winnipeg, MB, Canada - *BoPubDir 4, 5*
Mennonite Media Services - Harrisonburg, VA - *Tel&CabFB 84C*
Mennonite Weekly Review - Newton, KS - *AyerDirPub 83; NewsDir 84*
Mennonitische Rundschau - Winnipeg, MB, Canada - *Ed&PubIntYB 82*
Menominee County Journal - Stephenson, MI - *Ed&PubIntYB 82*
Menominee Herald-Leader - Menominee, MI - *BaconPubCkNews 84; NewsDir 84*
Menomonee Falls News - Menomonee Falls, WI - *Ed&PubIntYB 82*
Menomonee Falls News - Oak Creek, WI - *AyerDirPub 83*
Menomonee Falls News - *See* Community Newspapers Inc.
Menomonee Falls Post [of Suburban Milwaukee Post Newspapers] - Milwaukee, WI - *NewsDir 84*
Menomonie Dunn County News - Menomonie, WI - *NewsDir 84*
Menomonie Review - Menomonie, WI - *LitMag&SmPr 83-84*
Menorah-Egyenloseg - Toronto, ON, Canada - *Ed&PubIntYB 82*
Menorah Institute library - Brooklyn, NY - *BoPubDir 4, 5*
Menorah Publishing Co. Inc. - New York, NY - *BoPubDir 4, 5*
Men's Apparel News [of California Fashion Publications] - Los Angeles, CA - *BaconPubCkMag 84; MagDir 84*
Men's Wear [of Fairchild Publications Inc.] - New York, NY - *MagDir 84; MagIndMarPl 82-83*
Men's Wear of Canada - Downsview, ON, Canada - *BaconPubCkMag 84*
Menschenfreund, Joan - New York, NY - *MagIndMarPl 82-83*
Mental Health [of National Clearinghouse for Mental Health Information] - Rockville, MD - *OnBibDB 3*
Mental Health Abstracts [of Plenum Publishing Corp.] - Wilmington, DE - *EISS 5-84 Sup*
Mental Health Abstracts [of Bibliographic Retrieval Services Inc.] - Latham, NY - *DataDirOnSer 84*
Mental Health Materials Center Inc. - New York, NY - *BoPubDir 4, 5*
Mental Health Scope - Washington, DC - *MagDir 84*
Mental Measurements Yearbook [of University of Nebraska-Lincoln] - Lincoln, NE - *DirOnDB Spring 84; EISS 5-84 Sup*
Mental Measurements Yearbook [of Bibliographic Retrieval Services Inc.] - Latham, NY - *DataDirOnSer 84*
Mental Retardation - Washington, DC - *MagIndMarPl 82-83*
Mention Music Inc. - *See* Music Music Music Inc.
Mentken, Robert - New York, NY - *LitMarPl 83, 84*
Mentor/Mail [of Mentor Consultants Inc.] - Concordville, PA - *TeleSy&SerDir 2-84*
Mentor Music Inc. - Brookfield, CT - *BillIntBG 83-84*
Mentor Systems Inc. - Lexington, KY - *WhoWMicrocom 83*
Mentors Inc. - Spring Valley, CA - *BoPubDir 4, 5*
MEP Publications [of University of Minnesota] - Minneapolis, MN - *BoPubDir 5*
Mequon Herald - Oak Creek, WI - *AyerDirPub 83*
M.E.R. & Associates - Lexington, KY - *StaDirAdAg 2-84*
Meramec Community Press [of St. Louis Suburban Newspapers Inc.] - St. Louis, MO - *NewsDir 84*
Meramec Community Press - *See* St. Louis Suburban Newspapers Inc.
Meramec Journal - Meramec, MO - *Ed&PubIntYB 82*
Meramec Journal - St. Louis, MO - *AyerDirPub 83*
Meramec Valley Communications Inc. - St. Clair, MO - *BrCabYB 84*
Meramec Valley Communications Inc. - St. James, MO - *BrCabYB 84; Tel&CabFB 84C*
Meramec Valley Communications Inc. - Steelville, MO - *Tel&CabFB 84C p.1690*
Meramec Valley Communications Inc. - Sullivan, MO - *Tel&CabFB 84C*
Meramec Valley Transcript - Pacific, MO - *AyerDirPub 83; Ed&PubIntYB 82*
Meranza Press - Riverside, CA - *BoPubDir 4, 5*
Mercadotecnia Consulting - Southfield, MI - *IntDirMarRes 83*
Mercantile Music - Palm Springs, CA - *BillIntBG 83-84*
Mercantile Records - Palm Springs, CA - *BillIntBG 83-84*
Mercantine Press - Lincoln, NE - *BoPubDir 4, 5; LitMag&SmPr 83-84*
Mercatis [of Society for the Study of Economic & Social Development] - Paris, France - *DirOnDB Spring 84; EISS 5-84 Sup*
Mercator Business Systems - Sunnyvale, CA - *MicrocomMPl 83, 84; WhoWMicrocom 83*
Merced Guide - Merced, CA - *Ed&PubIntYB 82; NewsDir 84*
Merced Guide - *See* Waterford News Publishers
Merced Sun Star [of Lesher Newspapers Inc.] - Merced, CA - *BaconPubCkNews 84; Ed&PubIntYB 82; NewsDir 84*
Mercedes Book Distributors - Brooklyn, NY - *LitMarPl 83, 84*

Mercedes Enterprise - Mercedes, TX - *BaconPubCkNews 84; Ed&PubIntYB 82*
Mercedes Shipping Service [Div. of Mercedes Book Distributors] - Brooklyn, NY - *LitMarPl 83, 84*
Mercer Business [of Mercer County Chamber of Commerce] - Trenton, NJ - *BaconPubCkMag 84; MagDir 84*
Mercer County Chronicle - Coldwater, OH - *AyerDirPub 83; Ed&PubIntYB 82*
Mercer County Messenger - Hamilton, NJ - *Ed&PubIntYB 82*
Mercer County Messenger - Trenton, NJ - *NewsDir 84*
Mercer County Messenger & Hamilton Life - Trenton, NJ - *AyerDirPub 83*
Mercer House Press - Kennebunkport, ME - *BoPubDir 4, 5; LitMag&SmPr 83-84*
Mercer Island Reporter [of Longview Publishing Co.] - Mercer Island, WA - *BaconPubCkNews 84; Ed&PubIntYB 82; NewsDir 84*
Mercer Systems Inc. - Hicksville, NY - *MicrocomMPl 83, 84; MicrocomSwDir 1; WhoWMicrocom 83*
Mercer University Press - Macon, GA - *LitMarPl 83, 84; WritMar 84*
Mercersburg Journal - Franklin County, PA - *Ed&PubIntYB 82*
Mercersburg Journal - Mercersburg, PA - *BaconPubCkNews 84*
Merchandise Dynamics Inc. - New York, NY - *DirMarMP 83; LitMarPl 83*
Merchandiser - Mt. Joy, PA - *AyerDirPub 83*
Merchandising [of Gralla Publications] - New York, NY - *BaconPubCkMag 84; MagDir 84; MagIndMarPl 82-83; NewsBur 6*
Merchandising & Promotion Associates - New York, NY - *HBIndAd&MS 82-83*
Merchandising Consultants International - New York, NY - *HBIndAd&MS 82-83*
Merchandising Factory - San Francisco, CA - *AdAge 3-28-84; ArtMar 84; StaDirAdAg 2-84*
Merchandising Group Inc., The - New York, NY - *StaDirAdAg 2-84*
Merchant Magazine, The - Newport Beach, CA - *BaconPubCkMag 84; MagDir 84*
Merchants & Farmers Telephone Co. - Hillsboro, IN - *TelDir&BG 83-84*
Merchants & Farmers Telephone Co. - Montpelier, VA - *TelDir&BG 83-84*
Merchants Broadcasting Systems [of MBS Cable TV Inc.] - Carrollton, PA - *BrCabYB 84*
Merchant's Directory - Mullinville, KS - *Ed&PubIntYB 82*
Merchants Messenger - Warrensburg, MO - *AyerDirPub 83*
Merchants News - Mt. Pleasant, IA - *AyerDirPub 83*
Merchants Paper Co. Inc. - Cincinnati, OH - *MagIndMarPl 82-83*
Mercier, Louis - New York, NY - *LitMarPl 83, 84; MagIndMarPl 82-83*
Mercure Telecommunications Inc. - Albuquerque, NM - *Tel&CabFB 84C p.1690*
Mercurio Consultants - New York, NY - *AdAge 3-28-84; StaDirAdAg 2-84*
Mercury [of Astronomical Society of the Pacific] - San Francisco, CA - *ArtMar 84; MagIndMarPl 82-83*
Mercury - San Jose, CA - *AyerDirPub 83; Ed&PubIntYB 82; LitMarPl 84*
Mercury - Kinley, KS - *AyerDirPub 83*
Mercury - Manhattan, KS - *AyerDirPub 83*
Mercury - Carlisle, KY - *AyerDirPub 83*
Mercury - Medford, MA - *AyerDirPub 83*
Mercury - Pottstown, PA - *AyerDirPub 83*
Mercury - Weimar, TX - *AyerDirPub 83*
Mercury - Tofield, AB, Canada - *AyerDirPub 83*
Mercury - Guelph, ON, Canada - *AyerDirPub 83*
Mercury - Marathon, ON, Canada - *AyerDirPub 83*
Mercury - Renfrew, ON, Canada - *AyerDirPub 83*
Mercury - Rodney, ON, Canada - *AyerDirPub 83*
Mercury - Estevan, SK, Canada - *AyerDirPub 83; Ed&PubIntYB 82*
Mercury & News - Newport, RI - *AyerDirPub 83*
Mercury Bird Music - *See* Hoffman, Ivan
Mercury Broadcasting Corp. - Middlebury, CT - *BrCabYB 84*
Mercury-Independent - Grayville, IL - *AyerDirPub 83; Ed&PubIntYB 82*
Mercury Mailers Inc. - Washington, DC - *MagIndMarPl 82-83*
Mercury Markets Inc. - Barrington, IL - *StaDirAdAg 2-84*
Mercury-News - San Jose, CA - *AyerDirPub 83; Ed&PubIntYB 82; LitMarPl 84*
Mercury-Register - Oroville, CA - *AyerDirPub 83*
Mercury Service Systems Inc. - New York, NY - *MagIndMarPl 82-83*
Mercury Tri County Market Place - Pottstown, PA - *AyerDirPub 83*
Meredith & Brothers - Kansas City, MO - *ArtMar 84; StaDirAdAg 2-84*
Meredith Associates Inc. - Sea Bright, NJ - *DirPRFirms 83*
Meredith/Burda Inc. - Lynchburg, VA - *MagIndMarPl 82-83*
Meredith Corp. - Des Moines, IA - *AdAge 6-28-84; BrCabYB 84; InfoS 83-84; KnowInd 83; LitMarPl 83, 84; MagIndMarPl 82-83*
Meredith Corp. (Broadcasting Group) - Des Moines, IA - *BrCabYB 84; Tel&CabFB 84S*
Meredith Corp. (Printing Group) - Des Moines, IA - *MagIndMarPl 82-83*
Meredith Fulfillment Services - Des Moines, IA - *MagIndMarPl 82-83*
Meredith Literary Agency Inc., Scott - New York, NY - *LitMarPl 83, 84*
Meredith News - Meredith, NH - *BaconPubCkNews 84; Ed&PubIntYB 82*
Meredith Newspapers - Cupertino, CA - *BaconPubCkNews 84*
Meredith Newspapers - Los Angeles, CA - *BaconPubCkNews 84*
Meredith Newspapers - Albuquerque, NM - *Ed&PubIntYB 82*
Meredith Video Publishing - Des Moines, IA - *InterCabHB 3*
Meredosia Budget, The - Meredosia, IL - *Ed&PubIntYB 82*
Mereweather Press Inc. - New York, NY - *LitMarPl 83*
Merganzer Press - Lake Forest, IL - *BoPubDir 4, 5*
Mergenthaler Linotype Co. - Melville, NY - *DirInfWP 82*
Mergenthaler Mycro-Tek Co. [Div. of Eltra Corp.] - Wichita, KS - *LitMarPl 83, 84*
Merger Stat Review - Chicago, IL - *MagIndMarPl 82-83*
Mergers & Acquisitions [of Securities Data Co.] - New York, NY - *DataDirOnSer 84; DBBus 82; DirOnDB Spring 84*
Mergers & Acquisitions - Philadelphia, PA - *WritMar 84*
Merging Media - Westfield, NJ - *BoPubDir 4, 5; LitMag&SmPr 83-84*
Meriden Gravure Co. [Div. of Meridan-Stinehour Inc.] - Meriden, CT - *LitMarPl 83, 84; MagIndMarPl 82-83*
Meriden Record-Journal - Meriden, CT - *BaconPubCkNews 84*
Meriden Telephone Co. Inc. [Aff. of Telephone & Data Systems Inc.] - Meriden, NH - *TelDir&BG 83-84*
Meridian Booster - Lloydminster, AB, Canada - *Ed&PubIntYB 82*
Meridian Cable - Meridian, OK - *BrCabYB 84*
Meridian Consulting - Ellisville, MO - *ADAPSOMemDir 83-84*
Meridian Editions - Silver Spring, MD - *BoPubDir 4, 5*
Meridian Mississippi Memo Digest - Meridian, MS - *BaconPubCkNews 84*
Meridian Publishing - Utica, NY - *BoPubDir 4, 5*
Meridian Star - Meridian, MS - *BaconPubCkNews 84; BrCabYB 84; Ed&PubIntYB 82; NewsDir 84*
Meridian Systems Inc. - Windsor, CT - *ADAPSOMemDir 83-84*
Meridian Systems Ltd. - Calabasas, CA - *WhoWMicrocom 83*
Meridian Tribune - Meridian, TX - *BaconPubCkNews 84; Ed&PubIntYB 82*
Meridian Valley News [of Tribune Publishing Inc.] - Meridian, ID - *BaconPubCkNews 84; NewsDir 84*
Meridional - Abbeville, LA - *AyerDirPub 83; Ed&PubIntYB 82*
Meridional Publications - Wake Forest, NC - *BoPubDir 5; LitMag&SmPr 83-84*
Merilees Associates Inc. - Toronto, ON, Canada - *EISS 83*
Merims Communications, Art - Cleveland, OH - *ArtMar 84; DirPRFirms 83*
Merion Associates - Meadowbrook, PA - *CabTVFinDB 83; InterCabHB 3*
MERIP - Washington, DC - *BoPubDir 4, 5*
MERIP Reports - Washington, DC - *LitMag&SmPr 83-84; MagIndMarPl 82-83*
Merit Computer Network - Ann Arbor, MI - *EISS 83*
Merit Engraving Co. - New York, NY - *LitMarPl 83, 84*
Merit Micro Software Corp. - Oklahoma City, OK - *MicrocomMPl 84*
Merit Music Corp. - Nashville, TN - *BillIntBG 83-84*

Merit Research Ltd. - Houston, TX - *IntDirMarRes 83*
Meritakis, S. - Oakleigh, Australia - *Ed&PublIntYB 82*
Meriwether Inc., Arthur - Downers Grove, IL - *AvMarPl 83; HBIndAd&MS 82-83; WritMar 84*
Meriwether Publishing Ltd. - Colorado Springs, CO - *BoPubDir 5; LitMarPl 84*
Meriwether Publishing Ltd. - Downers Grove, IL - *BoPubDir 4; WritMar 84*
Meriwether Vindicator - Greenville, GA - *AyerDirPub 83; Ed&PublIntYB 82*
Merix Chemical - Chicago, IL - *AvMarPl 83*
Merkel Mail - Merkel, TX - *BaconPubCkNews 84; Ed&PublIntYB 82*
Merkel TV Cable Co. [of The Vinegarroon Corp.] - Merkel, TX - *BrCabYB 84*
Merlan Scientific Ltd. - Georgetown, ON, Canada - *WhoWMicrocom 83*
Merle Distributing Co. - Detroit, MI - *LitMarPl 83, 84*
Merlin [of Remote Computing Corp.] - Palo Alto, CA - *DirOnDB Spring 84; EISS 83*
Merlin Communications Inc. - New York, NY - *LitMarPl 83, 84*
Merlin-Eco - Grenoble, France - *DirOnDB Spring 84*
Merlin Engine Works - San Bruno, CA - *BoPubDir 4, 5*
Merlin Equipment Inc. - Winter Park, FL - *DataDirSup 7-83*
Merlin-Tech - Grenoble, France - *DirOnDB Spring 84*
Merling, Marx & Seidman Inc. - New York, NY - *StaDirAdAg 2-84*
Mernee Music - *See* Woodrich Publishing Co.
Merrell Enterprises - Washington, DC - *Ed&PublIntYB 82*
Merriam Co., G. & C. [Subs. of Encyclopaedia Britannica Inc.] - Springfield, MA - *LitMarPl 83*
Merriam-Eddy Co. Inc., The - South Waterford, ME - *LitMarPl 83*
Merriam, Robert L. - Greenfield, MA - *BoPubDir 4, 5*
Merriam Sun [of Sun Newspapers] - Shawnee Mission, KS - *NewsDir 84*
Merriam Sun - *See* Sun Publications
Merriam-Webster Inc. [Subs. of Encyclopaedia Britannica Inc.] - Springfield, MA - *LitMarPl 84*
Merrian Center Library - Chicago, IL - *BoPubDir 4, 5*
Merrick Beacon [of Nassau County Publication] - Hempstead, NY - *NewsDir 84*
Merrick Beacon - *See* Nassau County Publication
Merrick Life - Merrick, NY - *BaconPubCkNews 84; Ed&PublIntYB 82; NewsDir 84*
Merrick Pennysaver - Geneseo, NY - *AyerDirPub 83*
Merrill Anderson Co. Inc., The - Westport, CT - *ArtMar 84; StaDirAdAg 2-84*
Merrill, Bruce - Phoenix, AZ - *BrCabYB 84 p.D-303*
Merrill Co., K. F. - St. Paul, MN - *LitMarPl 83, 84*
Merrill, Helen - New York, NY - *LitMarPl 83, 84*
Merrill-Hemlock Monitor-Herald - Merrill, MI - *Ed&PublIntYB 82*
Merrill Lynch Economics Inc. [Subs. of Merrill Lynch & Co.] - New York, NY - *ADAPSOMemDir 83-84; DataDirOnSer 84; DirOnDB Spring 84; EISS 83*
Merrill Lynch Economics National Data Base - New York, NY - *DBBus 82*
Merrill Lynch Economics Regional Data Base - New York, NY - *DBBus 82*
Merrill, McEnroe, Fox & Associates Inc. - Chicago, IL - *StaDirAdAg 2-84*
Merrill Monitor-Herald - Merrill, MI - *NewsDir 84*
Merrill Photo Supply Co. Inc. - Charleston, WV - *AvMarPl 83*
Merrill Photos Corp. - New York, NY - *AvMarPl 83*
Merrill Publishing Co., Charles E. [Div. of Bell & Howell Co.] - Columbus, OH - *LitMarPl 83; WritMar 84*
Merrill Publishing Co., Charles E. [Div. of Bell & Howell Co.] - Westerville, OH - *LitMarPl 84*
Merrill Valley News - *See* Saginaw Valley News Inc.
Merrillville/Crown Point Town & Country - Hammond, IN - *AyerDirPub 83*
Merrillville Herald - Gary, IN - *NewsDir 84*
Merrillville Herald - Merrillville, IN - *BaconPubCkNews 84*
Merrimac Music Corp. - *See* Goodman Group, The
Merrimack Book Service Inc. - Salem, NH - *LitMarPl 83*
Merrimack College - North Andover, MA - *BoPubDir 4, 5*
Merrimack County Telephone Co. - Contoocook, NH - *TelDir&BG 83-84*
Merrimack Publishers' Circle - Salem, NH - *LitMarPl 84*
Merrimack Systems - Redwood City, CA - *WhoWMicrocom 83*
Merrimack Valley Advertiser - Tewksbury, MA - *AyerDirPub 83; Ed&PublIntYB 82*
Merrimack Valley Textile Museum - North Andover, MA - *BoPubDir 4, 5*
Merriman Studio, The - Albuquerque, NM - *LitMarPl 84*
Merrin Public Relations, Bruce - Los Angeles, CA - *LitMarPl 83; MagIndMarPl 82-83*
Merrin Public Relations, Bruce - Woodland Hills, CA - *LitMarPl 84*
Merritt Advertising, Stan - New York, NY - *AdAge 3-28-84; HBIndAd&MS 82-83; StaDirAdAg 2-84*
Merritt Cablevision Ltd. - Merritt, BC, Canada - *BrCabYB 84*
Merritt Co. - Santa Monica, CA - *BoPubDir 4, 5*
Merritt Creative Services, Dick - Los Angeles, CA - *HBIndAd&MS 82-83*
Merritt Editions Ltd. - Toronto, ON, Canada - *BoPubDir 5*
Merritt Herald - Merritt, BC, Canada - *Ed&PublIntYB 82*
Merritt News-Advertiser Focus - Merritt, BC, Canada - *AyerDirPub 83*
Merritt Public Relations, Russ - Anderson, IN - *DirPRFirms 83*
Merritt Publishers - Richardson, TX - *BoPubDir 4, 5*
Merritt Publishing Co. Ltd. - Toronto, ON, Canada - *BoPubDir 4*
Merrittonian - Merritt, BC, Canada - *Ed&PublIntYB 82*
Merriwell Inc., Frank [Subs. of National Learning Corp.] - Syosset, NY - *LitMarPl 83, 84*
Merry Bee Communications - Omaha, NE - *MicrocomMPl 84; MicrocomSwDir 1*
Merry Sounds [Div. of Lisa Sue Music] - Bronx, NY - *BillIntBG 83-84*
Merry Thoughts Inc. - Bedford Hills, NY - *LitMarPl 83, 84*
Merson Associates, Irving - Dobbs Ferry, NY - *IntDirMarRes 83*
Mertis Music Co. - Detroit, MI - *BillIntBG 83-84*
Merton House Publishing Co. - Wheaton, IL - *BoPubDir 4*
Merton House Travel & Tourism Publishers Inc. - Wheaton, IL - *LitMarPl 83, 84*
Mertzer & Co. Inc., William - Forest Hills, NY - *StaDirAdAg 2-84*
Mervap Cold Light Products - Los Angeles, CA - *AvMarPl 83*
Mervyn Peake Review, The - Vaud, Switzerland - *LitMag&SmPr 83-84*
Mesa Broadcasting Co. - Chicago, IL - *BrCabYB 84*
Mesa Cable Inc. [of Rock Associates] - Raton, NM - *BrCabYB 84; Tel&CabFB 84C*
Mesa Community Cable [of Camelback Cablevision Inc.] - Mesa, AZ - *BrCabYB 84; Tel&CabFB 84C*
Mesa Missilier [of Lompoc Record Publications] - Lompoc, CA - *AyerDirPub 83; NewsDir 84*
Mesa News - Los Angeles, CA - *AyerDirPub 83*
Mesa Publications - Tucson, AZ - *BoPubDir 4, 5*
Mesa Records - Nashville, TN - *BillIntBG 83-84*
Mesa Research Inc. - Waco, TX - *MicrocomMPl 84*
MESA Technology Corp. - Gaithersburg, MD - *DataDirSup 7-83*
Mesa Tribune [of Cox Arizona Publications] - Mesa, AZ - *BaconPubCkNews 84; NewsDir 84*
Mesa Verde Press - Santa Fe, NM - *BoPubDir 5*
Mesabi News - Virginia, MN - *AyerDirPub 83; BaconPubCkNews 84; Ed&PublIntYB 82*
Mesaros, Ron - Topanga, CA - *MagIndMarPl 82-83*
Meshoppen Video - Meshoppen, PA - *BrCabYB 84*
Meshugah Music - *See* Xanadu Records Ltd.
Mesick Telephone Co. [Aff. of National Communications Systems Inc.] - Mesick, MI - *TelDir&BG 83-84*
Mesorah Publications - Brooklyn, NY - *LitMarPl 83, 84*
Mesquite News [of Taylor Communications Inc.] - Mesquite, TX - *BaconPubCkNews 84; Ed&PublIntYB 82; NewsDir 84*
Message - Moberly, MO - *AyerDirPub 83*
Message Post - Philomath, OR - *LitMag&SmPr 83-84*
Message, The [of Sufi Order Publications/Omega Press] - Tucson, AZ - *LitMag&SmPr 83-84*
Messenger - Troy, AL - *AyerDirPub 83*
Messenger - Manhattan Beach, CA - *Ed&PublIntYB 82*
Messenger - Montebello, CA - *AyerDirPub 83*
Messenger - Eatonton, GA - *AyerDirPub 83*

Messenger - Plainfield, IN - *AyerDirPub 83; Ed&PubIntYB 82*
Messenger - Cedar Vale, KS - *AyerDirPub 83*
Messenger - Minneapolis, KS - *AyerDirPub 83*
Messenger - Madisonville, KY - *AyerDirPub 83; Ed&PubIntYB 82*
Messenger - Mayfield, KY - *AyerDirPub 83*
Messenger - Maple Lake, MN - *AyerDirPub 83*
Messenger - Montgomery, MN - *AyerDirPub 83*
Messenger - Morgan, MN - *AyerDirPub 83*
Messenger - Okolona, MS - *AyerDirPub 83*
Messenger - Louisville, NE - *AyerDirPub 83*
Messenger - Hillsboro, NH - *AyerDirPub 83*
Messenger - Garfield, NJ - *AyerDirPub 83; Ed&PubIntYB 82*
Messenger - Baldwinsville, NY - *AyerDirPub 83; Ed&PubIntYB 82*
Messenger - Canandaigua, NY - *AyerDirPub 83*
Messenger - Smithtown, NY - *AyerDirPub 83*
Messenger - Madison, NC - *AyerDirPub 83; Ed&PubIntYB 82*
Messenger - Athens, OH - *AyerDirPub 83; Ed&PubIntYB 82*
Messenger - Cherokee, OK - *AyerDirPub 83*
Messenger - Homestead, PA - *AyerDirPub 83*
Messenger - Clemson, SC - *AyerDirPub 83; Ed&PubIntYB 82*
Messenger - Hartsville, SC - *AyerDirPub 83*
Messenger - Union City, TN - *AyerDirPub 83*
Messenger - Forney, TX - *AyerDirPub 83*
Messenger - Jewett, TX - *AyerDirPub 83*
Messenger - Miles, TX - *AyerDirPub 83*
Messenger - Waco, TX - *AyerDirPub 83*
Messenger - Whitney, TX - *AyerDirPub 83*
Messenger - Manti, UT - *AyerDirPub 83*
Messenger - St. Albans, VT - *AyerDirPub 83*
Messenger - Radford, VA - *AyerDirPub 83*
Messenger - Wytheville, VA - *AyerDirPub 83*
Messenger - Colfax, WI - *AyerDirPub 83*
Messenger - Monticello, WI - *AyerDirPub 83*
Messenger - La Salle, PQ, Canada - *Ed&PubIntYB 82*
Messenger - Verdun, PQ, Canada - *Ed&PubIntYB 82*
Messenger Advertiser - Smithtown, NY - *AyerDirPub 83*
Messenger & Advertiser [of Torrance Press-Herald] - Torrance, CA - *NewsDir 84*
Messenger & Star Forum - Gatesville, TX - *AyerDirPub 83*
Messenger Banner - Stephen, MN - *Ed&PubIntYB 82*
Messenger Graphics [Subs. of Messenger Corp.] - Phoenix, AZ - *LitMarPl 83, 84*
Messenger-Index - Emmett, ID - *AyerDirPub 83; Ed&PubIntYB 82*
Messenger-Inquirer - Owensboro, KY - *AyerDirPub 83; Ed&PubIntYB 82*
Messenger of the Sacred Heart, The - Toronto, ON, Canada - *WritMar 84*
Messenger-Press - Allentown, NJ - *AyerDirPub 83; Ed&PubIntYB 82*
Messenger Review - Homestead, PA - *AyerDirPub 83*
Messenger, The - Ft. Dodge, IA - *AyerDirPub 83; Ed&PubIntYB 82*
Messenger, The - Covington, KY - *NewsDir 84*
Messer & Susslin & Others Inc. - Pearl River, NY - *StaDirAdAg 2-84*
Messerschmidt/Uniphoto, Al - Miami, FL - *AvMarPl 83*
Messina Enterprises Inc. - New York, NY - *AvMarPl 83*
Messmer, Victor - Mott, ND - *Tel&CabFB 84C p.1690*
Messner, Julian [of Simon & Schuster] - New York, NY - *ArtMar 84; LitMarPl 83, 84; WritMar 84*
Mester Music Publishing - *See* Hendrix Enterprises, James
Meszaros Associates Inc. - Buffalo, NY - *ADAPSOMemDir 83-84*
Met Richmond Latin Record Sales - Brooklyn, NY - *BillIntBG 83-84*
Meta Software Engineering Inc. - Albuquerque, NM - *MicrocomMPl 83*
Metabolism - New York, NY - *MagDir 84*
Metacom Press - Worcester, MA - *LitMag&SmPr 83-84*
Metacrafts Ltd. - Crewe, England - *MicrocomSwDir 1*
Metadata Inc. - New York, NY - *BoPubDir 4, 5*
Metadex [of American Society for Metals] - Metals Park, OH - *DataDirOnSer 84; DirOnDB Spring 84; OnBibDB 3*
Metairie East Bank Guide [of Cox Communications] - Metairie, LA - *Ed&PubIntYB 82; NewsDir 84*
Metairie East Bank Guide - *See* Guide Newspaper Corp.
Metal Building News - Chicago, IL - *BaconPubCkMag 84*
Metal Building Review [of Nickerson & Collins] - Des Plaines, IL - *BaconPubCkMag 84; MagIndMarPl 82-83; WritMar 84*
Metal/Center News - New York, NY - *BaconPubCkMag 84; MagDir 84; MagIndMarPl 82-83*
Metal Fabricating News - Rockford, IL - *BaconPubCkMag 84; MagDir 84; MagIndMarPl 82-83*
Metal Fabricator - Wakefield, RI - *BaconPubCkMag 84; MagDir 84*
Metal Finishing - Hackensack, NJ - *BaconPubCkMag 84; MagDir 84*
Metal Matrix Composites Information Analysis Center [of Kaman Tempo] - Santa Barbara, CA - *EISS 83*
Metal Powder Industries Federation - Princeton, NJ - *BoPubDir 4, 5*
Metal Producing - New York, NY - *BaconPubCkMag 84*
Metal Progress - Metals Park, OH - *BaconPubCkMag 84; MagDir 84; MagIndMarPl 82-83*
Metal Stamping - Cleveland, OH - *MagDir 84*
Metal Stamping - Richmond Heights, OH - *BaconPubCkMag 84*
Metaletter - Washington, DC - *NewsDir 84*
Metallgesellschaft AG - Frankfurt, West Germany - *InfIndMarPl 83*
Metallurgical & Thermochemical Data Service [of Dept. of Industry] - Teddington, England - *EISS 83*
Metallurgical Society of AIME [Aff. of American Institute of Mining, Metallurgical, & Petroleum Engineers] - Warrendale, PA - *BoPubDir 4, 5*
Metallurgical Transactions - Warrendale, PA - *MagDir 84*
Metals Abstracts [of QL Systems Ltd.] - Ottawa, ON, Canada - *DataDirOnSer 84*
Metals Abstracts Index [of American Society for Metals] - Metals Park, OH - *CompReadDB 82*
Metals & Ceramics Information Center [of Battelle Columbus Laboratories] - Columbus, OH - *CompReadDB 82; EISS 83; InfIndMarPl 83*
Metals & Plastics Publications Inc. - Hackensack, NJ - *BoPubDir 5*
Metals Data Centre - Ottawa, ON, Canada - *EISS 7-83 Sup*
Metals Database [of Evans Economics Inc.] - Washington, DC - *DataDirOnSer 84*
Metals Datafile [of Metals Information] - Metals Park, OH - *EISS 5-84 Sup*
Metals Information [of American Society for Metals] - Metals Park, OH - *EISS 83; InfIndMarPl 83*
Metals Information [of The Metals Society] - London, England - *InfIndMarPl 83*
Metals Information Data File [of SDC Search Service] - Santa Monica, CA - *DataDirOnSer 84*
Metals Information Designations & Specifications [of SDC Search Service] - Santa Monica, CA - *DataDirOnSer 84*
Metals Information Service [of The Metals Society] - London, England - *FBInfSer 80*
Metals Week [of Data Resources Inc.] - Lexington, MA - *DataDirOnSer 84*
Metals Week [of McGraw-Hill Inc.] - New York, NY - *BaconPubCkMag 84; DBBus 82; DirOnDB Spring 84; EISS 83; MagDir 84*
Metalsmith [of Society of North American Goldsmiths] - Green Bay, WI - *BaconPubCkMag 84; WritMar 84*
Metalwork - New York, NY - *MagIndMarPl 82-83*
Metalworking Digest - Dover, NJ - *BaconPubCkMag 84*
Metalworking Digest - Morristown, NJ - *MagDir 84; MagIndMarPl 82-83*
Metalworking News Edition American Metal Market [of Fairchild Publications Inc.] - New York, NY - *BaconPubCkMag 84; MagIndMarPl 82-83; NewsDir 84*
Metalworking Production & Purchasing - Milliken, ON, Canada - *BaconPubCkMag 84*
Metamicro Library Systems Inc. - San Antonio, TX - *EISS 83; InfIndMarPl 83*
Metamora Herald - *See* Woodford Publishing Co.
Metamora Telephone Co. - Metamora, IL - *TelDir&BG 83-84*
Metamorphics Inc. - Bala Cynwyd, PA - *MicrocomMPl 84; MicrocomSwDir 1; WhoWMicrocom 83*
Metamorphous Press [Subs. of Metamorphosis Enterprises Inc.] - Lake Oswego, OR - *LitMag&SmPr 83-84; LitMarPl 83, 84; WritMar 84*

Metaphysical Science Association - Los Angeles, CA - *BoPubDir 4, 5*
Metaresearch Inc. - Portland, OR - *MicrocomSwDir 1*
Metascience Corp. - Franklin, NC - *BoPubDir 4, 5*
Metasoft Corp. - Casa Grande, AZ - *MicrocomMPl 83, 84; MicrocomSwDir 1; WhoWMicrocom 83*
Metatron Press - Milwaukee, WI - *BoPubDir 4, 5*
Metax Inc. - Bethesda, MD - *ADAPSOMemDir 83-84*
Metcalfe-Cook & Smith Inc. - Nashville, TN - *ArtMar 84; StaDirAdAg 2-84*
Metcut Research Associates Inc. - Cincinnati, OH - *BoPubDir 4, 5*
Meteor - Crystal Springs, MS - *AyerDirPub 83; Ed&PubIntYB 82*
Meteor & Times - Madisonville, TX - *AyerDirPub 83*
Meteor-Journal - Malvern, AR - *AyerDirPub 83; Ed&PubIntYB 82*
Meteor Music - *See* S & R Music Publishing Co.
Meteor Photo Co. - Troy, MI - *AvMarPl 83*
Meteorological & Geoastrophysical Abstracts [of American Meteorological Society] - Rockville, MD - *OnBibDB 3*
Meteorological & Geoastrophysical Abstracts [of American Meteorological Society] - Boston, MA - *CompReadDB 82; DataDirOnSer 84; DBBus 82; DirOnDB Spring 84; EISS 83*
Methods Research - Farmingdale, NJ - *AvMarPl 83*
Methow Valley News - The Methow Valley, WA - *Ed&PubIntYB 82*
Methow Valley News - Twisp, WA - *AyerDirPub 83*
Methuen Inc. [Subs. of Associated Book Publishers Ltd.] - New York, NY - *LitMarPl 83, 84*
Methuen News [of Ayer Public Spirit Publishing Co. Inc.] - Ayer, MA - *NewsDir 84*
Methuen Publications [Div. of Carswell Co. Ltd.] - Toronto, ON, Canada - *LitMarPl 83, 84*
Metier - San Jose, CA - *MicrocomMPl 83, 84*
Metier Industrial Inc./Jean Callan King - New York, NY - *LitMarPl 84*
Metis Association of the Northwest Territories - Yellowknife, NT, Canada - *BoPubDir 4, 5*
Metis Press Inc. - Chicago, IL - *BoPubDir 4, 5; LitMag&SmPr 83-84*
Metlfax Magazine - Cleveland, OH - *MagDir 84*
Metlfax Magazine - Solon, OH - *BaconPubCkMag 84; MagIndMarPl 82-83*
Metorion Music Corp. - New York, NY - *BillIntBG 83-84*
Metra Consulting Group Ltd. - London, England - *IntDirMarRes 83*
Metra Consulting Group Ltd. (Information Dept.) - London, England - *FBInfSer 80*
Metrek Div. [of Mitre Corp.] - McLean, VA - *EISS 83*
Metric Splicer & Film Co. Inc. - Yorba Linda, CA - *AvMarPl 83*
Metricomp Inc. - Grundy Center, IA - *LitMarPl 83, 84*
Metrics Inc. - Atlanta, GA - *EISS 83*
Metrics Research Corp. - Atlanta, GA - *EISS 83; InfoS 83-84*
Metro America Records - Detroit, MI - *BillIntBG 83-84*
Metro Associated Services Inc. - New York, NY - *Ed&PubIntYB 82*
Metro Cable - Richfield, MN - *BrCabYB 84*
Metro Cable Corp. - Payette, ID - *Tel&CabFB 84C*
Metro Cable Corp. - Afton, WY - *Tel&CabFB 84C*
Metro Cable Corp. - Meeteetse, WY - *Tel&CabFB 84C*
Metro Cable Corp. - Riverton, WY - *CabTVFinDB 83; Tel&CabFB 84C p.1690*
Metro Cable Inc. - Rosemount, MN - *BrCabYB 84 p.D-303; Tel&CabFB 84C p.1690*
Metro Cablevision [of Maclean Hunter Cable TV Ltd.] - East Detroit, MI - *InterCabHB 3; LitMarPl 84; Tel&CabFB 84C*
Metro Cities News - Ft. Worth, TX - *Ed&PubIntYB 82*
Metro Data Co. Inc. - Minneapolis, MN - *ADAPSOMemDir 83-84*
Metro East Cable TV Co. [of Satellite Cable TV Corp.] - Mascoutah, IL - *Tel&CabFB 84C*
Metro Enterprises - Bayard, NE - *BrCabYB 84; Tel&CabFB 84C*
Metro Enterprises - Minatare, NE - *BrCabYB 84*
Metro Enterprises Inc. - Minden, NE - *Tel&CabFB 84C*
Metro Enterprises Inc. - Mitchell, NE - *BrCabYB 84*
Metro Enterprises Inc. - Scottsbluff, NE - *BrCabYB 84 p.D-303*
Metro Expansion - St. Lambert, PQ, Canada - *Ed&PubIntYB 82*
Metro Food Service News - New York, NY - *BaconPubCkMag 84; MagDir 84*
Metro-Goldwyn-Mayer Film Co. [Subs. of MGM/UA Entertainment Co.] - Culver City, CA - *HomeVid&CabYB 82-83; LitMarPl 83*
Metro Home & Garden Magazines - *Folio 83*
Metro Magazine - Norfolk, VA - *MagDir 84*
Metro Market Pennysavers - Buffalo, NY - *AyerDirPub 83*
Metro Newark - Jersey City, NJ - *BaconPubCkMag 84*
Metro-Newark [of Greater Newark Chamber of Commerce] - Newark, NJ - *MagDir 84*
Metro Newsfeatures - White Plains, NY - *LitMarPl 84*
Metro One: St. James - Winnipeg, MB, Canada - *AyerDirPub 83*
Metro One: The Herald - Winnipeg, MB, Canada - *AyerDirPub 83*
Metro Reporter Group - San Francisco, CA - *AyerDirPub 83*
Metro Salon News - New York, NY - *MagDir 84*
Metro Shopper - Marysville, CA - *AyerDirPub 83*
Metro Star Group - Quartz Hill, CA - *Ed&PubIntYB 82*
Metro Sunday Comics Network - New York, NY - *Ed&PubIntYB 82*
Metro Survey Service Inc. - Feasterville, PA - *IntDirMarRes 83*
Metro Systems Inc. - Tulsa, OK - *ADAPSOMemDir 83-84*
Metro-Tel Corp. - Gardena, CA - *Tel&CabFB 84C*
Metro Toronto News Co. (Library & Educational Div.) - Scarborough, ON, Canada - *LitMarPl 83, 84*
Metro Translation Service - Brooklyn, NY - *LitMarPl 83, 84*
Metro Weather Service Inc. - Jamaica, NY - *BrCabYB 84*
Metrocable [of Business Development Services Inc.] - Arlington, VA - *Tel&CabFB 84C*
Metrocenter YMCA [Aff. of Seattle YMCA] - Seattle, WA - *BoPubDir 4, 5*
Metrofone [of Western Union Telegraph Co.] - Upper Saddle River, NJ - *TeleSy&SerDir 2-84*
Metrographics Ltd. - New York, NY - *LitMarPl 83, 84*
Metrolina Publishing Co. Inc. - Pineville, NC - *BillIntBG 83-84*
Metromark Market Research Inc. - Columbia, SC - *IntDirMarRes 83*
Metromedia - Secaucus, NJ - *AdAge 6-28-84; BrCabYB 84; HomeVid&CabYB 82-83; KnowInd 83; TelAl 83, 84; Tel&CabFB 84S*
Metromedia News - Washington, DC - *Tel&CabFB 84C*
Metromedia Producers Corp. [Subs. of Metromedia Inc.] - Hollywood, CA - *LitMarPl 83; WritMar 84*
Metromedia Producers Corp. - Needham, MA - *AvMarPl 83; Tel&CabFB 84C*
Metromedia Producers Corp. - New York, NY - *TelAl 84*
Metron Publications - Princeton, NJ - *BoPubDir 4 Sup, 5*
Metronome Music Publishing Co. - Philadelphia, PA - *BillIntBG 83-84*
Metroplex Advertising Agency Inc. - Ft. Worth, TX - *StaDirAdAg 2-84*
Metroplex Communications - Cleveland, OH - *BrCabYB 84*
Metropol-Gesellschaft - Berlin, West Germany - *ProGuPRSer 4*
Metropolis - New York, NY - *BaconPubCkMag 84*
Metropolis Music Publishing Inc. - Beverly Hills, CA - *BillIntBG 83-84*
Metropolis Planet - Metropolis, IL - *BaconPubCkNews 84; Ed&PubIntYB 82; NewsDir 84*
Metropolis Records Inc. - Beverly Hills, CA - *BillIntBG 83-84*
Metropolitan - Redondo Beach, CA - *BaconPubCkMag 84; MagDir 84; MagIndMarPl 82-83*
Metropolitan Almanac - New York, NY - *MagDir 84*
Metropolitan Council on Housing - New York, NY - *BoPubDir 4, 5*
Metropolitan Home [of Meredith Corp.] - Des Moines, IA - *Folio 83; MagDir 84*
Metropolitan Home [of Meredith Corp.] - New York, NY - *BaconPubCkMag 84; LitMarPl 83, 84; MagIndMarPl 82-83; WritMar 84*
Metropolitan Library Service Agency - St. Paul, MN - *MicroMarPl 82-83*
Metropolitan Magazine - Germantown, MD - *WritMar 84*
Metropolitan Microforms Ltd. - Cranford, NJ - *DirInfWP 82*
Metropolitan Museum of Art - New York, NY - *LitMarPl 83, 84*
Metropolitan Museum of Art (Photograph Library) - New York, NY - *MagIndMarPl 82-83*

Metropolitan Music Co. - Houston, TX - *BillIntBG 83-84*
Metropolitan-National - Yeadon, PA - *MagIndMarPl 82-83*
Metropolitan News - Los Angeles, CA - *BaconPubCkMag 84; Ed&PubIntYB 82; MagDir 84; NewsDir 84*
Metropolitan Newspapers - Bolingbrook, IL - *BaconPubCkNews 84*
Metropolitan Pittsburgh Public Broadcasting Inc. - Pittsburgh, PA - *AvMarPl 83*
Metropolitan Press Clipping Bureau of Louisiana - Baton Rouge, LA - *ProGuPRSer 4*
Metropolitan Publishers Representatives - Lincolnwood, IL - *MagIndMarPl 82-83*
Metropolitan Purchasor - Trenton, NJ - *BaconPubCkMag 84; MagDir 84*
Metropolitan Research Co. - New York, NY - *LitMarPl 83, 84*
Metropolitan Ribbon & Carbon - Springfield, VA - *DirInfWP 82*
Metropolitan Satellite Corp. - Independence, OH - *Tel&CabFB 84C*
Metropolitan Sunday Newspapers Inc. - New York, NY - *DirMarMP 83; LitMarPl 83, 84*
Metropolitan Toronto Business Journal - Toronto, ON, Canada - *BaconPubCkMag 84*
Metropolitan Toronto Library Board - Toronto, ON, Canada - *BoPubDir 4, 5*
Metrosoft Inc. - Los Angeles, CA - *MicrocomMPl 84*
Metrosports [Div. of Metro Communications Inc.] - Rockville, MD - *BrCabYB 84; Tel&CabFB 84C*
Metrotape [Div. of Metromedia Inc.] - New York, NY - *Tel&CabFB 84C*
MetroVision Inc. [of Newhouse] - Atlanta, GA - *BrCabYB 84 p.D-303; CabTVFinDB 83; LitMarPl 84; Tel&CabFB 84C p.1690*
Metrovision Ltd. - Bedford, NS, Canada - *BrCabYB 84*
MetroVision of Glendale Heights Inc. [of MetroVision Inc.] - Glendale Heights, IL - *Tel&CabFB 84C*
MetroVision of Green Township Inc. [of MetroVision Inc.] - Green Township, OH - *BrCabYB 84; Tel&CabFB 84C*
Metrovision of Indiana II Inc. [of MetroVision Inc.] - Portage, IN - *BrCabYB 84; Tel&CabFB 84C*
MetroVision of Livonia Inc. [of MetroVision Inc.] - Livonia, MI - *Tel&CabFB 84C*
MetroVision of Oakland County Inc. [of MetroVision Inc.] - Farmington Hills, MI - *Tel&CabFB 84C*
MetroVision of Redford Inc. [of MetroVision Inc.] - Redford, MI - *Tel&CabFB 84C*
MetroVision of Wisconsin Inc. [of MetroVision Inc.] - Menomonee, WI - *BrCabYB 84*
MetroVision of Wisconsin Inc. - Menomonee Falls, WI - *Tel&CabFB 84C*
MetroVision Southwest Cook County Inc. [of MetroVision Inc.] - Hickory Hills, IL - *BrCabYB 84*
MetroVision Southwest Cook County Inc. - Palos Hills, IL - *Tel&CabFB 84C*
Metroweb Corp. - Erlanger, KY - *MagIndMarPl 82-83*
Metter Cable Co. [of Tele-Media Corp.] - Metter, GA - *BrCabYB 84*
Metter News & Advertiser - Metter, GA - *AyerDirPub 83; BaconPubCkNews 84; Ed&PubIntYB 82*
Mettler Studios Inc./Tucson Creative Dance Center - Tucson, AZ - *BoPubDir 4, 5*
Metuchen Criterion News-Advertiser - Metuchen, NJ - *BaconPubCkNews 84*
Metuchen Weekend Sentinel - *See* Sentinel Newspapers
Metzdorf Advertising Agency - Houston, TX - *ArtMar 84; DirPRFirms 83*
Metzer, Aron & Lemen Inc. - San Francisco, CA - *TelAl 84*
Metzner Productions, Jeffrey - New York, NY - *Tel&CabFB 84C*
MEW Advertising Agency - Columbus, OH - *StaDirAdAg 2-84*
Mexia News - Mexia, TX - *AyerDirPub 83; BaconPubCkNews 84; Ed&PubIntYB 82; NewsDir 84*
Mexican American Sun - East Los Angeles, CA - *Ed&PubIntYB 82*
Mexican American Sun - Los Angeles, CA - *AyerDirPub 83*
Mexican Music Centre Inc. - New York, NY - *BillIntBG 83-84*
Mexico Independent Mirror - *See* Oswego County Weeklies
Mexico Ledger - Mexico, MO - *BaconPubCkNews 84; Ed&PubIntYB 82; NewsDir 84*
Mexico Oswego County Weeklies - Mexico, NY - *NewsDir 84*
Mexico Parish Town & Country News [of Gouverneur Town & Country News of Jefferson County] - Gouverneur, NY - *NewsDir 84*
Meyer Advertising & Promotions Inc., R. L. - Milwaukee, WI - *AdAge 3-28-84; StaDirAdAg 2-84*
Meyer Advertising Ltd., Samuel H. - New York, NY - *StaDirAdAg 2-84*
Meyer & Associates Inc., N. Dean - Ridgefield, CT - *TeleSy&SerDir 2-84*
Meyer & Associates Inc., Robert H. - Minneapolis, MN - *StaDirAdAg 2-84*
Meyer & Son Inc., John C. - Philadelphia, PA - *LitMarPl 83, 84; MagIndMarPl 82-83*
Meyer Associates Inc., Hank - Miami, FL - *DirPRFirms 83*
Meyer Broadcasting Co. - Bismarck, ND - *BrCabYB 84*
Meyer Communications Inc. - Springfield, MO - *BrCabYB 84*
Meyer/Fredericks & Associates Ltd. - Chicago, IL - *StaDirAdAg 2-84*
Meyer Inc., Fred - Portland, OR - *ArtMar 84*
Meyer, Rosalind - Milwaukee, WI - *LitMarPl 83, 84*
Meyer, William E. - Shrub Oak, NY - *DirPRFirms 83*
Meyerbooks - Glenwood, IL - *BoPubDir 4, 5*
Meyerhoff Associates Inc., Arthur [Div. of BBDO International Inc.] - Chicago, IL - *BrCabYB 84*
Meyerhoff, Rich - Joseph City, AZ - *Tel&CabFB 84C p.1691*
Meyers & Associates Inc., Michael - Chicago, IL - *StaDirAdAg 2-84*
Meyers, Roger A. - Gardnerville, NV - *Tel&CabFB 84C*
Meyersdale Republic - Meyersdale, PA - *BaconPubCkNews 84*
Mezperce Lewis County Herald - Nezperce, ID - *BaconPubCkNews 84*
MFAS Associates [Div. of Pearl Data Systems Inc.] - Wayne, PA - *DataDirSup 7-83*
MFC News - Madison, MS - *ArtMar 84; BaconPubCkMag 84; MagDir 84*
MFE Corp. - Salem, NH - *WhoWMicrocom 83*
MFE Corp. (Computer Peripheral Div.) - Salem, NH - *DataDirSup 7-83*
MFG Computer Systems - West Covina, CA - *MicrocomMPl 84*
MFJ Electro-Enterprises - Kanata, ON, Canada - *MicrocomSwDir 1*
MFJ Enterprises Inc. - Starkville, MS - *MicrocomMPl 83, 84; WhoWMicrocom 83*
MFRC Publishing [Aff. of Institute for Nonprofit Organizations] - Toronto, ON, Canada - *BoPubDir 4, 5*
MG & Casey Inc. - Detroit, MI - *DirPRFirms 83*
M.G. Features - Marlton, NJ - *Ed&PubIntYB 82*
MG Films Inc. - New York, NY - *Tel&CabFB 84C*
MG Media - New York, NY - *StaDirAdAg 2-84*
MGLS Publishing [Aff. of Minnesota Glassblowing & Laboratory Supply] - Marshall, MN - *BoPubDir 4, 5*
MGM/UA (Home Entertainment Group) - New York, NY - *TelAl 83, 84; Tel&CabFB 84C*
MGM/UA (Home Video Div.) - New York, NY - *BillIntBG 83-84; TelAl 83*
MGM/UA (Television Distribution) - New York, NY - *TelAl 83, 84*
MGM/UA (Television Productions) - Culver City, CA - *TelAl 83, 84; Tel&CabFB 84C*
MGM/UA Entertainment Co. - Culver City, CA - *KnowInd 83*
M'Godolim [of Le Beacon Presse] - Seattle, WA - *LitMag&SmPr 83-84*
MGR Direct [Subs. of Maslow, Gold & Rothschild Inc.] - Boston, MA - *DirMarMP 83*
MGS Services [Subs. of Viacom International Inc.] - New York, NY - *TelAl 83, 84; Tel&CabFB 84C*
MH Builders News - Chicago, IL - *BaconPubCkMag 84; MagDir 84*
MHBusiness [of TL Enterprises Inc.] - Agoura, CA - *WritMar 84*
Mho & Mho Works - San Diego, CA - *BoPubDir 4, 5; LitMag&SmPr 83-84*
MHT Services Inc. - Hackensack, NJ - *ADAPSOMemDir 83-84*
Mi Kom Business System Inc. - Denver, CO - *MicrocomMPl 83*
Miami Beach Star - Miami Beach, FL - *BaconPubCkNews 84*
Miami Beach Sun-Reporter - Miami Beach, FL - *AyerDirPub 83; BaconPubCkNews 84; Ed&PubIntYB 82; NewsDir 84*

Miami Beach Times - Miami Beach, FL - *Ed&PubIntYB 82; NewsDir 84*
Miami Business Journal - Miami, FL - *BaconPubCkMag 84*
Miami Chief, The - Miami, TX - *Ed&PubIntYB 82*
Miami County Communications [of Valley Antenna Systems Inc.] - Tipp City, OH - *BrCabYB 84; Tel&CabFB 84C*
Miami County Communications Inc. [of Valley Antenna Systems] - Bradford, OH - *BrCabYB 84*
Miami County Publishing Co. - Paola, KS - *BaconPubCkNews 84*
Miami-Dade Community College - Miami, FL - *AvMarPl 83*
Miami Florida Courier - Opa Locka, FL - *BaconPubCkNews 84*
Miami Herald [of Knight-Ridder Newspapers Inc.] - Miami, FL - *BaconPubCkNews 84; DirOnDB Spring 84; Ed&PubIntYB 82; LitMarPl 83, 84; NewsBur 6; NewsDir 84*
Miami Herald [of VU/Text Information Services] - Philadelphia, PA - *DataDirOnSer 84*
Miami Hurricane, The [of The University of Miami] - Miami, FL - *NewsDir 84*
Miami Liberty News - Miami, FL - *NewsDir 84*
Miami Magazine - Coral Gables, FL - *WritMar 84*
Miami Magazine - Miami, FL - *MagDir 84*
Miami Mensual [of Quintus Communications Group] - Miami, FL - *WritMar 84*
Miami News - Miami, FL - *BaconPubCkNews 84; Ed&PubIntYB 82; NewsDir 84*
Miami News Record - Miami, OK - *BaconPubCkNews 84; Ed&PubIntYB 82; NewsDir 84*
Miami Paper Corp. [Subs. of Pentair Inc.] - West Carrollton, OH - *LitMarPl 83, 84; MagIndMarPl 82-83*
Miami Records Distributing Corp. - Miami, FL - *BillIntBG 83-84*
Miami Republican - Paola, KS - *AyerDirPub 83; Ed&PubIntYB 82*
Miami Review [of Review Printing Co.] - Miami, FL - *BaconPubCkMag 84; NewsDir 84*
Miami Review & Daily Record - Miami, FL - *Ed&PubIntYB 82*
Miami Shore News [of South Miami Community Newspapers] - Miami, FL - *AyerDirPub 83; NewsDir 84*
Miami Shore News - *See* Community Newspapers of Florida Inc.
Miami/South Florida - Miami, FL - *BaconPubCkMag 84*
Miami Springs News - Hialeah Gardens, FL - *BaconPubCkNews 84*
Miami Star - Miami, FL - *NewsDir 84*
Miami Student [of Miami University] - Oxford, OH - *NewsDir 84*
Miami Times - Miami, FL - *BaconPubCkNews 84; BrCabYB 84; Ed&PubIntYB 82; NewsDir 84*
Miami Valley Business Journal [of Gramarye Communications Inc.] - Dayton, OH - *BaconPubCkMag 84; WritMar 84*
Miami Valley Cable Inc. [of Community Tele-Communications Inc.] - Hamilton, OH - *BrCabYB 84; Tel&CabFB 84C*
Miami Valley Cable Inc. [of Community Tele-Communications Inc.] - Middletown, OH - *BrCabYB 84; Tel&CabFB 84C*
Miami Valley Paper [Div. of Millen Industries Inc.] - Franklin, OH - *LitMarPl 83, 84*
Miami Valley Sunday News - Troy, OH - *Ed&PubIntYB 82*
Miami Whitewater Press - *See* Queen City Suburban Press Inc.
Miamisburg News [of Brown Publishing Co.] - Miamisburg, OH - *BaconPubCkNews 84; Ed&PubIntYB 82; NewsDir 84*
Mibar Enterprises Ltd. - New York, NY - *ADAPSOMemDir 83-84*
Micah - Sausalito, CA - *MicrocomMPl 84*
Micah Publications - Marblehead, MA - *BoPubDir 4, 5; LitMag&SmPr 83-84*
Micanopy Cable TV Inc. [of Coaxial Associates of Florida Ltd.] - Alachua, FL - *BrCabYB 84; Tel&CabFB 84C*
Micanopy Cable TV Inc. [of Coaxial Associates of Florida Ltd.] - Branford, FL - *BrCabYB 84; Tel&CabFB 84C*
Micanopy Cable TV Inc. [of Coaxial Associates of Florida Ltd.] - Chiefland, FL - *Tel&CabFB 84C*
Micanopy Cable TV Inc. [of Coaxial Associates of Florida Ltd.] - Cross City, FL - *BrCabYB 84; Tel&CabFB 84C*
Micanopy Cable TV Inc. [of Coaxial Associates of Florida Ltd.] - High Springs, FL - *BrCabYB 84*
Micanopy Cable TV Inc. [of Tele-Media Corp.] - Jasper, FL - *BrCabYB 84*
Micanopy Cable TV Inc. [of Coaxial Associates of Florida Ltd.] - Micanopy, FL - *BrCabYB 84; Tel&CabFB 84C*
Micanopy Cable TV Inc. [of Coaxial Associates of Florida Ltd.] - Sarasota, FL - *BrCabYB 84 p.D-303*
Michael, Pansy D. - South Whitley, IN - *BoPubDir 4, 5*
Michael, Prudence Groff - Lakeville, IN - *BoPubDir 4, 5*
Michael-Sellers Advertising - San Francisco, CA - *ArtMar 84; StaDirAdAg 2-84*
Michaeljay Audio-Visual Services Inc. - St. Petersburg, FL - *AvMarPl 83*
Michaels Inc., Kaye - Casselberry, FL - *StaDirAdAg 2-84*
Michaels Music, Jill - *See* Kaye Publications, Richard
Michalak, Ingeborg - Detroit, MI - *LitMarPl 83, 84*
Michavin Music - Pensacola, FL - *BillIntBG 83-84*
Michel Software, Arthur - Chicago, IL - *MicrocomMPl 83*
Michele Audio Corp. - Massena, NY - *BillIntBG 83-84*
Michelin Guides & Maps [Aff. of Michelin Tire Corp.] - Lake Success, NY - *BoPubDir 4, 5*
Michell Manuals Inc. [Aff. of Cordura Publishing Inc.] - San Diego, CA - *BoPubDir 4*
Michelson Advertising & Public Relations - Los Angeles, CA - *DirPRFirms 83*
Michelson Inc., Charles - Beverly Hills, CA - *Tel&CabFB 84C*
Michener Associates Inc., Edward C. - Harrisburg, PA - *StaDirAdAg 2-84*
Michener Co., The - Valley Forge, PA - *StaDirAdAg 2-84*
Michiana - South Bend, IN - *WritMar 84*
Michiana Cablevision Corp. - Three Oaks, MI - *Tel&CabFB 84C p.1691*
Michie Co. Law Publishing, The [Subs. of ITT Publishing] - Charlottesville, VA - *LitMarPl 83, 84; MicroMarPl 82-83*
Michigan [of The Detroit News] - Detroit, MI - *LitMarPl 83, 84; WritMar 84*
Michigan Accident Location Index [of Michigan State Police] - Lansing, MI - *EISS 7-83 Sup*
Michigan AFL-CIO News - Lansing, MI - *NewsDir 84*
Michigan Banking & Business News - Lansing, MI - *BaconPubCkMag 84*
Michigan Banking & Business News - Okemos, MI - *MagDir 84*
Michigan Bell Telephone Co. - Detroit, MI - *TelDir&BG 83-84*
Michigan Beverage News - Southfield, MI - *BaconPubCkMag 84; MagDir 84*
Michigan Cable Corp. - Three Oaks, MI - *BrCabYB 84*
Michigan CATV Co. - Sturgis, MI - *BrCabYB 84; Tel&CabFB 84C*
Michigan Christian Advocate - Adrian, MI - *BaconPubCkMag 84; MagDir 84*
Michigan Chronicle - Detroit, MI - *AyerDirPub 83; Ed&PubIntYB 82; NewsDir 84*
Michigan Chronicle - New York, NY - *AyerDirPub 83*
Michigan City News-Dispatch - Michigan City, IN - *BaconPubCkNews 84; NewsDir 84*
Michigan Contractor & Builder [of Contractor Publishing Co.] - Detroit, MI - *BaconPubCkMag 84; MagDir 84*
Michigan Cooperative Health Information System [of Michigan State Dept. of Public Health] - Lansing, MI - *EISS 83*
Michigan Daily, The [of Board for Student Publications] - Ann Arbor, MI - *NewsDir 84*
Michigan Data Base User Group [of The Upjohn Co.] - Kalamazoo, MI - *InfIndMarPl 83*
Michigan Dept. of State (Michigan History Div.) - Lansing, MI - *BoPubDir 4, 5*
Michigan Diver - Grand Rapids, MI - *WritMar 84*
Michigan Dry Bean Digest - Saginaw, MI - *BaconPubCkMag 84*
Michigan Education Resources Information Center [of Michigan State Library] - Lansing, MI - *EISS 7-83 Sup*
Michigan Farm News Rural Living - Lansing, MI - *BaconPubCkMag 84; MagDir 84*
Michigan Farmer - Lansing, MI - *BaconPubCkMag 84; MagDir 84; WritMar 84*
Michigan Fisherman - East Lansing, MI - *BaconPubCkMag 84*
Michigan Florist, The [of Michigan State Florists Association] - Okemos, MI - *BaconPubCkMag 84; MagDir 84*
Michigan Food News [of Michigan Food Dealers Service Corp.] - Lansing, MI - *BaconPubCkMag 84; MagDir 84*
Michigan Hospitality - Southfield, MI - *BaconPubCkMag 84*
Michigan Information Center [of Michigan State Dept. of Management & Budget] - Lansing, MI - *EISS 83*

Michigan Information Transfer Source [of University of Michigan Libraries] - Ann Arbor, MI - *EISS 83; InfIndMarPl 83*
Michigan Interviews - Lansing, MI - *IntDirMarRes 83*
Michigan Investor [of Contractor Publishing Co.] - Detroit, MI - *BaconPubCkMag 84; MagDir 84*
Michigan Law Review - Ann Arbor, MI - *MagDir 84*
Michigan Library Association - Lansing, MI - *BoPubDir 4 Sup, 5*
Michigan Library Consortium - Lansing, MI - *EISS 83; InfIndMarPl 83*
Michigan Living [of Automobile Club of Michigan] - Dearborn, MI - *BaconPubCkMag 84; MagDir 84; WritMar 84*
Michigan Master Plumber & Mechanical Contractor - Lansing, MI - *BaconPubCkMag 84; MagDir 84*
Michigan Media - Ann Arbor, MI - *AvMarPl 83*
Michigan Medicine - East Lansing, MI - *BaconPubCkMag 84; MagDir 84*
Michigan Memorial-Phoenix Project [of University of Michigan] - Ann Arbor, MI - *InfIndMarPl 83*
Michigan Metropolitan Information Center [of Wayne State University] - Detroit, MI - *EISS 83*
Michigan Milk Messenger [of Michigan Milk Producer's Association] - Southfield, MI - *BaconPubCkMag 84; MagDir 84*
Michigan Municipal League - Ann Arbor, MI - *BoPubDir 4, 5*
Michigan Municipal Review [of Michigan Municipal League] - Ann Arbor, MI - *BaconPubCkMag 84; MagDir 84*
Michigan Natural Resources Magazine [Aff. of Michigan Dept. of Natural Resources] - Lansing, MI - *BoPubDir 5; WritMar 84*
Michigan Nelson County Arena - *See* Ness Press Inc.
Michigan Occasional Papers in Women's Studies - Ann Arbor, MI - *LitMag&SmPr 83-84*
Michigan Occupational Information System [of Michigan State Dept. of Education] - Lansing, MI - *EISS 7-83 Sup*
Michigan Optometrist, The - Lansing, MI - *BaconPubCkMag 84; MagDir 84*
Michigan Out-of-Doors - Lansing, MI - *ArtMar 84; BaconPubCkMag 84; MagDir 84; MagIndMarPl 82-83; WritMar 84*
Michigan Pharmacist [of Michigan Pharmacists Association] - Lansing, MI - *BaconPubCkMag 84; MagDir 84*
Michigan Plant & Equipment - Detroit, MI - *BaconPubCkMag 84; MagDir 84*
Michigan Press Reading Service - Williamston, MI - *ProGuPRSer 4*
Michigan Project for Computer-Assisted Biblical Studies [of University of Michigan] - Ann Arbor, MI - *EISS 83*
Michigan Purchasing Management - Detroit, MI - *MagDir 84*
Michigan Quarterly Review - Ann Arbor, MI - *LitMag&SmPr 83-84*
Michigan Roads & Construction [of Baker Publishing Co.] - Lansing, MI - *BaconPubCkMag 84; MagDir 84*
Michigan Snowmobiler - East Jordan, MI - *BaconPubCkMag 84; MagDir 84*
Michigan Sportsman - Oshkosh, WI - *BaconPubCkMag 84*
Michigan Sportwoman [Subs. of American Sportswoman] - San Jose, CA - *WritMar 84*
Michigan State University (Abrams Planetarium) - East Lansing, MI - *BoPubDir 4 Sup, 5*
Michigan State University (African Studies Center) - East Lansing, MI - *BoPubDir 4, 5*
Michigan State University (Community Development/Lifelong Education Programs) - East Lansing, MI - *BoPubDir 4, 5*
Michigan State University (Dept. of Telecommunication) - East Lansing, MI - *InterCabHB 3*
Michigan State University (Graduate School of Business Administration) - East Lansing, MI - *BoPubDir 4, 5*
Michigan State University (Philosophy of Science Association) - East Lansing, MI - *BoPubDir 4*
Michigan State University Press - East Lansing, MI - *LitMarPl 83, 84*
Michigan Technic - Ann Arbor, MI - *BaconPubCkMag 84; MagDir 84*
Michigan Trucking Today - Lansing, MI - *MagDir 84*
Michigan United Conservation Clubs - Lansing, MI - *BoPubDir 4, 5*
Michigan's Oil & Gas News - Mt. Pleasant, MI - *MagDir 84*
Michilander Industries - St. Joseph, MI - *BoPubDir 4, 5*
Michlin & Co. Inc. - New York, NY - *HBIndAd&MS 82-83*
Mickaelian & Newman Inc. - Los Angeles, CA - *StaDirAdAg 2-84*
Mickelson Media Inc. - Hastings, MN - *BrCabYB 84 p.D-304*
Mickelson Media Inc. - Santa Fe, NM - *Tel&CabFB 84C p.1691*
Mickelson Media Inc. - *See* Ogden Newspapers, The
Mickey Records - Dover, NJ - *BillIntBG 83-84*
Mickle Street Review, The - Lewisville, TX - *LitMag&SmPr 83-84*
Mickler House [Aff. of Florida Breezes Inc.] - Chuluota, FL - *BoPubDir 4, 5*
Micoa Corp. - Indianapolis, IN - *ADAPSOMemDir 83-84*
Micom Automated Storage & Retrieval System [of U.S. Army] - Redstone Arsenal, AL - *EISS 83*
Micom Electronics Corp. (Norcom Div.) - New York, NY - *DirInfWP 82*
Micom Systems - Chatsworth, CA - *DataDirSup 7-83; Datamation 6-83; DirInfWP 82; WhoWMicrocom 83*
Micor Advertising Agency - New York, NY - *StaDirAdAg 2-84*
Micro [of Micro Ink Inc.] - Amherst, NH - *BaconPubCkMag 84; MicrocomMPl 84; WritMar 84*
Micro Advisor [of Battery Lane Publications] - Gaithersburg, MD - *DataDirOnSer 84*
Micro Alliance Corp. - Pacific Grove, CA - *MicrocomMPl 84*
Micro-Ap - Dublin, CA - *MicrocomMPl 83, 84; MicrocomSwDir 1; WhoWMicrocom 83*
Micro Applications & Hardware - Kentfield, CA - *WhoWMicrocom 83*
Micro Applications Group - Canoga Park, CA - *MicrocomMPl 83; MicrocomSwDir 1; WhoWMicrocom 83*
Micro Architect - Arlington, MA - *DirInfWP 82; MicrocomMPl 83, 84; MicrocomSwDir 1; WhoWMicrocom 83*
Micro-Art Programmers - Cayucos, CA - *MicrocomMPl 84*
Micro Associates Inc. - Metairie, LA - *WhoWMicrocom 83*
Micro Banking Report - Atlanta, GA - *BaconPubCkMag 84*
Micro Blajak Systems - Flagstaff, AZ - *MicrocomMPl 83*
Micro Book Manufacturing Co. - Chicago, IL - *LitMarPl 83, 84*
Micro Business Applications [Subs. of Datametrics Corp.] - San Diego, CA - *WhoWMicrocom 83*
Micro Business Applications - Burnsville, MN - *MicrocomMPl 84; MicrocomSwDir 1*
Micro Business Software - Clearwater, FL - *WhoWMicrocom 83*
Micro Business Software - Chichester, NH - *MicrocomMPl 83, 84; MicrocomSwDir 1*
Micro Business Systems Inc. - Merrillville, IN - *MicrocomMPl 83, 84; MicrocomSwDir 1*
Micro Business World [Subs. of Quarish International] - Tarzana, CA - *WhoWMicrocom 83*
Micro-Call Services - Laurel, MD - *WhoWMicrocom 83*
Micro Center, The - Pleasantville, NY - *MicrocomMPl 83, 84*
Micro Communications - San Francisco, CA - *BaconPubCkMag 84*
Micro Computer Devices Inc. - Anaheim, CA - *WhoWMicrocom 83*
Micro Computer Distributing - Williamsport, PA - *MicrocomMPl 83*
Micro Computer Industries Ltd. - Ft. Collins, CO - *MicrocomMPl 83; WhoWMicrocom 83*
Micro Computer Management Inc. - Ft. Collins, CO - *MicrocomMPl 83, 84; WhoWMicrocom 83*
Micro Computer Planning Systems - Wayland, MA - *MicrocomMPl 84*
Micro-Computer Sales Corp./The Software Terminal - Fayetteville, NC - *MicrocomSwDir 1*
Micro Computer Service Inc. - Boulder, CO - *WhoWMicrocom 83*
Micro Computer Store of Puerto Rico, The - Caparra Heights Station, PR - *WhoWMicrocom 83*
Micro Computer Systems - Ft. Collins, CO - *WhoWMicrocom 83*
Micro Computers of New Orleans Inc. - New Orleans, LA - *WhoWMicrocom 83*
Micro Concepts - Dallas, TX - *MicrocomMPl 84*
Micro Control Systems - Vernon, CT - *MicrocomMPl 84; MicrocomSwDir 1*
Micro Cornucopia - Bend, OR - *BaconPubCkMag 84; MicrocomMPl 84*
Micro Craft - Huntsville, AL - *MicrocomMPl 84*
Micro Craft - Dallas, TX - *WhoWMicrocom 83*
Micro Craft Systems Inc. - Ann Arbor, MI - *MicrocomMPl 83, 84*

Micro D Inc. - Fountain Valley, CA - *MicrocomMPl 84*
Micro Data Base Systems Inc. - Lafayette, IN - *DataDirSup 7-83; MicrocomMPl 83, 84; MicrocomSwDir 1; WhoWMicrocom 83*
Micro Data Business Forms & Systems - Olympia, WA - *MicrocomMPl 83, 84; MicrocomSwDir 1; WhoWMicrocom 83*
Micro Data Collection - Novato, CA - *MicrocomMPl 84; MicrocomSwDir 1*
Micro Data Supplies - Euclid, OH - *MicrocomMPl 84*
Micro Decision Systems - Lakeland, FL - *WhoWMicrocom 83*
Micro Decision Systems - Pittsburgh, PA - *MicrocomMPl 84*
Micro Decisionware - Boulder, CO - *MicrocomMPl 83; MicrocomSwDir 1*
Micro-Design - Austin, TX - *MicrocomMPl 84*
Micro-Design - Manchaca, TX - *MicrocomMPl 83*
Micro-Design - Hartford, WI - *DirInfWP 82*
Micro Discovery [of Micro Digest Inc.] - Los Alamitos, CA - *ArtMar 84; BaconPubCkMag 84; MicrocomMPl 84; WritMar 84*
Micro Discovery - Bergenfield, NJ - *MagDir 84*
Micro Display Systems Inc. - Hastings, MN - *MicrocomMPl 84; WhoWMicrocom 83*
Micro Distributed Systems - Lyme, CT - *WhoWMicrocom 83*
Micro Distributors Inc. - Santa Ana, CA - *WhoWMicrocom 83*
Micro Distributors Inc. - Rockville, MD - *MicrocomMPl 84*
Micro-Ed Inc. - Edina, MN - *MicrocomMPl 83, 84*
Micro-80 Inc. - Oak Harbor, WA - *MicrocomMPl 83, 84*
Micro-Fantastic Programming - New York, NY - *MicrocomMPl 83*
Micro Five Corp. - Irvine, CA - *WhoWMicrocom 83*
Micro Focus - Swindon, England - *MicrocomSwDir 1*
Micro Focus Inc. - Palo Alto, CA - *MicrocomMPl 84*
Micro Focus Inc. - Santa Clara, CA - *MicrocomMPl 83; WhoWMicrocom 83*
Micro Futures - Livonia, MI - *MicrocomMPl 84*
Micro General Corp. - Irvine, CA - *MicrocomMPl 84*
Micro Grafx - Dallas, TX - *MicrocomMPl 84; MicrocomSwDir 1*
Micro-Grip Ltd. - San Bernardino, CA - *MicrocomMPl 83, 84*
Micro-Images Industries Inc. - Flushing, NY - *MicrocomMPl 83, 84*
Micro Information Systems Inc. - Wayne, NJ - *MicrocomMPl 84*
Micro Information Systems Inc. - Montgomeryville, PA - *MicrocomMPl 83; MicrocomSwDir 1; WhoWMicrocom 83*
Micro Ink - Chelmsford, MA - *BoPubDir 4 Sup, 5; MicrocomMPl 83*
Micro Ink - Amherst, NH - *MicrocomMPl 84*
Micro-Integration Inc. - Friendsville, MD - *MicrocomMPl 83, 84; MicrocomSwDir 1; WhoWMicrocom 83*
Micro Investment Software - Stockton, CA - *MicrocomMPl 83, 84; MicrocomSwDir 1*
Micro Lab - Highland Park, IL - *MicrocomMPl 83, 84; MicrocomSwDir 1; WhoWMicrocom 83*
Micro-Labs Inc. - Richardson, TX - *MicrocomMPl 83, 84; WhoWMicrocom 83*
Micro Learningware - North Mankato, MN - *MicrocomMPl 83, 84; MicrocomSwDir 1; WhoWMicrocom 83*
Micro Magic Cooking Co. - Lincoln, NE - *BoPubDir 4, 5*
Micro Mainframe - Rancho Cordova, CA - *MicrocomMPl 84*
Micro Management Ltd. - New York, NY - *ADAPSOMemDir 83-84*
Micro Management Systems - Cairo, GA - *MicrocomMPl 84*
Micro-Managers Inc. - Madison, WI - *WhoWMicrocom 83*
Micro Manufacturing Systems - Columbus, OH - *WhoWMicrocom 83*
Micro Manufacturing Systems - Westerville, OH - *MicrocomMPl 83, 84; MicrocomSwDir 1*
Micro Market Examiner [of Morgan Point Press] - Eureka Springs, AR - *MicrocomMPl 84*
Micro Match - Tujunga, CA - *MicrocomMPl 84*
Micro Matrix - Daly City, CA - *MicrocomMPl 83, 84*
Micro Matrix - Pacifica, CA - *MicrocomMPl 83*
Micro Med Inc. - Cincinnati, OH - *MicrocomMPl 84*
Micro Media Inc. - New Haven, CT - *LitMarPl 83, 84*
Micro Media Inc. - North Branford, CT - *MagIndMarPl 82-83*
Micro Memory Inc. - Chatsworth, CA - *DataDirSup 7-83*
Micro Mike's Inc. - Amarillo, TX - *MicrocomMPl 83, 84; MicrocomSwDir 1; WhoWMicrocom 83*
Micro Mode Inc. - San Antonio, TX - *MicrocomMPl 83, 84; MicrocomSwDir 1; WhoWMicrocom 83*
Micro Money - Washington, IL - *BaconPubCkMag 84*
Micro Moonlighter [of NewsNet Inc.] - Bryn Mawr, PA - *DataDirOnSer 84*
Micro Moonlighter - Nashville, TN - *DirOnDB Spring 84; MicrocomMPl 83*
Micro Moonlighter Newsletter - Lewisville, TX - *LitMag&SmPr 83-84; MicrocomMPl 84; WritMar 84*
Micro MRP - Foster City, CA - *MicrocomMPl 84*
Micro Music Inc. - Normac, IL - *WhoWMicrocom 83*
Micro Music Inc. - Bellevue, WA - *MicrocomMPl 83, 84*
Micro-Net Systems - Latham, NY - *MicrocomMPl 84*
Micro Notes - St. Cloud, MN - *NewsDir 84*
Micro Peripherals Inc. - Chatsworth, CA - *DataDirSup 7-83*
Micro Peripherals Inc. - Salt Lake City, UT - *MicrocomMPl 83, 84; WhoWMicrocom 83*
Micro Photo Div. [of Bell & Howell Co.] - Wooster, OH - *EISS 83*
Micro Planning Services - Bristol, England - *MicrocomSwDir 1*
Micro Plus Inc. - Minneapolis, MN - *WhoWMicrocom 83*
Micro Power & Light Co. - Dallas, TX - *MicrocomMPl 83, 84; WhoWMicrocom 83*
Micro Pro Systems - Cumming, GA - *MicrocomMPl 83*
Micro Products - Wilmington, DE - *WhoWMicrocom 83*
Micro Program Designs - Wilmington, DE - *MicrocomMPl 84*
Micro Programs Association - Sanford, FL - *MicrocomSwDir 1; WhoWMicrocom 83*
Micro Programs Inc. - Syosset, NY - *MicrocomSwDir 1; WhoWMicrocom 83*
Micro Projects Engineering Co. - Culver City, CA - *MicrocomMPl 84*
Micro Research Inc. - Littleton, CO - *MicrocomMPl 84; MicrocomSwDir 1*
Micro School Programs [of Betamax Inc.] - Seattle, WA - *MicrocomMPl 83*
Micro-Sci [Div. of Standun Controls Inc.] - Santa Ana, CA - *MicrocomMPl 84; WhoWMicrocom 83*
Micro-Sci - Tustin, CA - *MicrocomMPl 83*
Micro Software - Ft. Walton Beach, FL - *MicrocomMPl 84*
Micro Software Distributors - Grand Blanc, MI - *MicrocomMPl 84*
Micro Software Inc. - Minneapolis, MN - *WhoWMicrocom 83*
Micro Software International Inc. - Newton Upper Falls, MA - *MicrocomMPl 84*
Micro Software Marketing - Congers, NY - *MicrocomMPl 84*
Micro Software Systems - Salt Lake City, UT - *WhoWMicrocom 83*
Micro-Solutions Inc. [Subs. of The A. H. Pugh Printing Co.] - Cincinnati, OH - *WhoWMicrocom 83*
Micro Solutions Inc. - Richmond, VA - *MicrocomMPl 84; MicrocomSwDir 1*
Micro Source Inc. - New Lebanon, OH - *MicrocomMPl 84; WhoWMicrocom 83*
Micro-Sparc Systems - Lincoln, MA - *MicrocomMPl 83; WhoWMicrocom 83*
Micro Star Computers - Torrance, CA - *MicrocomMPl 83*
Micro/Sys 80 - Southampton, PA - *MicrocomMPl 84; MicrocomSwDir 1; WhoWMicrocom 83*
Micro Systems Technology - Phoenixville, PA - *MicrocomMPl 83, 84*
Micro-Tax - Mountain View, CA - *MicrocomMPl 83*
Micro-Tax - Woodland Hills, CA - *MicrocomMPl 83; WhoWMicrocom 83*
Micro Tech Exports Inc. - Palo Alto, CA - *DataDirSup 7-83*
Micro Technical Products Inc. - Mesa, AZ - *MicrocomMPl 84*
Micro Technology Unltd. [Subs. of Consolidated Sciences Inc.] - Raleigh, NC - *MicrocomMPl 83; WhoWMicrocom 83*
Micro-Term Inc. - St. Louis, MO - *DataDirSup 7-83; InfIndMarPl 83; WhoWMicrocom 83*
Micro-Trak Corp. - Holyoke, MA - *AvMarPl 83*
Micro TV Inc. [of Community Tele-Communications Inc.] - Miles City, MT - *BrCabYB 84; Tel&CabFB 84C*
Micro TV Inc. - Philadelphia, PA - *EISS 83; Tel&CabFB 84C*
Micro-Urba - Aix en Provence, France - *MicroMarPl 82-83*
Micro Video - Ann Arbor, MI - *MicrocomMPl 83, 84; MicrocomSwDir 1*
Micro Vision - Lindenhurst, NY - *MicrocomMPl 84*

Micro-Ware Distributing Inc. - Butler, NJ - *MicrocomMPl 83, 84; MicrocomSwDir 1*
Micro Works - Del Mar, CA - *MicrocomMPl 83, 84; MicrocomSwDir 1*
Micro World [of CW Communications Inc.] - Farmingham, MA - *MicrocomMPl 84*
Micro World Computer Store Inc. - Johnson City, NY - *WhoWMicrocom 83*
Micro-World Inc. - Roanoke, VA - *MicrocomMPl 84*
Micro-Z Co. - Monrovia, CA - *DataDirSup 7-83*
Micro-Z Co. - Rolling Hills, CA - *MicrocomSwDir 1*
MicroAmerica Distributing [Subs. of New England Electronics Co. Inc.] - Needham, MA - *WhoWMicrocom 83*
MicroAmerica Distributing - Richardson, TX - *MicrocomMPl 84*
MicroAPL Ltd. - London, England - *MicrocomSwDir 1*
MicroArt Corp. - Portland, OR - *MicrocomMPl 84; MicrocomSwDir 1*
Microband Buffalo Corp. - New York, NY - *Tel&CabFB 84C*
Microband Corp. of America - New York, NY - *Tel&CabFB 84C*
Microband National System Inc. - New York, NY - *EISS 83*
Microband of Virginia Inc. - New York, NY - *Tel&CabFB 84C*
Microband Pacific Corp. - New York, NY - *Tel&CabFB 84C*
Microband United Corp. - New York, NY - *Tel&CabFB 84C*
Microbanker - Schaumburg, IL - *BaconPubCkMag 84*
Microbase Software Inc. - Indianapolis, IN - *MicrocomMPl 84*
Microbial Ecology Data Base [of University of Maryland] - College Park, MD - *EISS 83*
Microbiological Reviews - Washington, DC - *BaconPubCkMag 84; MagDir 84*
Microbiology Abstracts (Section A: Industrial & Applied Microbiology) - London, England - *CompReadDB 82*
Microbiology Abstracts (Section B: Bacteriology) - London, England - *CompReadDB 82*
Microbiology Abstracts (Section C: Algology, Mycology, & Protozoology) - London, England - *CompReadDB 82*
Microbiotic Computing Inc. - Albuquerque, NM - *WhoWMicrocom 83*
Microbits Peripheral Products Inc. - Albany, OR - *MicrocomMPl 84*
MicroCALL Services - Laurel, MD - *MicrocomMPl 84*
Microchart Systems Inc. - San Rafael, CA - *MicroMarPl 82-83*
Microcircuit Device Reliability [of Reliability Analysis Center] - Franklin Springs, NY - *CompReadDB 82*
Microcode Corp. - Fremont, CA - *MicrocomMPl 84*
Microcode Corp. - Columbus, OH - *MicrocomMPl 84*
Microcom Inc. - Norwood, MA - *DataDirSup 7-83; MicrocomMPl 83, 84*
Microcom Inc. - Boise City, OK - *BrCabYB 84; Tel&CabFB 84C*
Microcomp - Solana Beach, CA - *MicrocomMPl 83, 84*
Microcomp - Southampton, England - *MicrocomSwDir 1*
MicroComPac Inc. - Golden, CO - *MicrocomMPl 83*
Microcomputer Applications [of ACTA Press] - Anaheim, CA - *MicrocomMPl 84*
Microcomputer Applications - Suisun City, CA - *BoPubDir 4, 5*
Microcomputer Business Application Consultants - Fountain Valley, CA - *MicrocomSwDir 1*
Microcomputer Business Industries Corp. - Golden, CO - *MicrocomMPl 83, 84*
Microcomputer Business International - Irvine, CA - *MicrocomMPl 84*
Microcomputer Business Systems Ltd. - London, England - *MicrocomSwDir 1*
Microcomputer Consultants - Davis, CA - *MicrocomMPl 83, 84; MicrocomSwDir 1; WhoWMicrocom 83*
Microcomputer Courseware [of Minnesota Educational Computing Consortium] - St. Paul, MN - *DataDirOnSer 84*
Microcomputer Development Services - Seattle, WA - *MicrocomSwDir 1*
Microcomputer Digest - Old Bridge, NJ - *BaconPubCkMag 84*
Microcomputer Games [Div. of Avalon Hill] - Baltimore, MD - *MicrocomMPl 84; WhoWMicrocom 83*
Microcomputer Index [of Microcomputer Information Services] - Santa Clara, CA - *CompReadDB 82; DataDirOnSer 84; DBBus 82; DirOnDB Spring 84; EISS 83*
Microcomputer Information Services - Santa Clara, CA - *CompReadDB 82; DataDirOnSer 84; InfIndMarPl 83*
Microcomputer Interlibrary Loan Network [of Montana State Library] - Helena, MT - *EISS 7-83 Sup*
MicroComputer Investors Association - Fredericksburg, VA - *MicrocomMPl 83, 84*
Microcomputer Products International Ltd. - Barking, England - *MicrocomSwDir 1*
Microcomputer Resources Inc. - Clearwater, FL - *WhoWMicrocom 83*
Microcomputer Software Letter [of Scarborough Systems Inc.] - Tarrytown, NY - *MicrocomMPl 84*
Microcomputer Software Systems Inc. - Metairie, LA - *MicrocomMPl 84*
MicroComputer Specialists - Elkins Park, PA - *MicrocomSwDir 1; WhoWMicrocom 83*
MicroComputer Specialists - Philadelphia, PA - *MicrocomMPl 84*
Microcomputer Systems Corp. - Sunnyvale, CA - *WhoWMicrocom 83*
Microcomputer Taxsystems Inc. - Woodland Hills, CA - *MicrocomSwDir 1*
Microcomputer Technology Inc. - Santa Ana, CA - *MicrocomMPl 83, 84; WhoWMicrocom 83*
Microcomputer Workshops - Port Chester, NY - *MicrocomMPl 83, 84*
Microcomputers Corp. [of GML Corp.] - Lexington, MA - *CompReadDB 82*
Microcomputers Corp. - Armonk, NY - *MicrocomMPl 83, 84; MicrocomSwDir 1*
Microcomputers in Education [of Queue Inc.] - Fairfield, CT - *MicrocomMPl 84*
Microcomputers in Information Handling Atindex - Brighton, England - *LitMag&SmPr 83-84*
Microcomputing [of Wayne Green Inc.] - Peterborough, NH - *BaconPubCkMag 84; Folio 83; MagDir 84; MicrocomMPl 84; WritMar 84*
MicroComputing Research - Marana, AZ - *MicrocomMPl 83, 84; MicrocomSwDir 1*
Microcon Inc. - Watertown, MA - *MicrocomMPl 83*
Microcontamination - Santa Monica, CA - *BaconPubCkMag 84*
Microdata Corp. [Subs. of McDonnell-Douglas Corp.] - Irvine, CA - *DataDirSup 7-83; DirInfWP 82*
Microdigital/Tech2 Software Inc. - Webster, NY - *MicrocomMPl 84*
MICRODOC - Philadelphia, PA - *EISS 83; InfIndMarPl 83*
Microdome - Denville, NJ - *MicrocomMPl 83, 84*
Microdyne Corp. - Ocala, FL - *CabTVFinDB 83; HomeVid&CabYB 82-83*
Microed - San Diego, CA - *MicrocomMPl 83; WhoWMicrocom 83*
Microeditions Hachette - Paris, France - *MicroMarPl 82-83*
Microelectronic Manufacturing & Testing [of Lake Publishing Corp.] - Libertyville, IL - *BaconPubCkMag 84; MagDir 84; MagIndMarPl 82-83*
Microelectronics Journal - Luton, England - *WritMar 84*
Microelectronics News - Pacific Grove, CA - *BaconPubCkMag 84*
Microfiche Foundation - Delft, Netherlands - *MicroMarPl 82-83*
Microfiche Publications [Div. of Microfiche Systems Corp.] - Queens Village, NY - *LitMarPl 83, 84*
Microfiche Systems Corp. - New York, NY - *EISS 83*
Microfile Pty. Ltd. - Johannesburg, South Africa - *MicroMarPl 82-83*
Microfilm Center Inc. - *See* Microplex Inc.
Microfilm Corp. of Pennsylvania - Pittsburgh, PA - *MicroMarPl 82-83*
Microfilm Enterprises Corp. - East Brunswick, NJ - *DirInfWP 82*
Microfilm Products Co. - New York, NY - *DirInfWP 82*
Microfilm Publishing Inc. - New Rochelle, NY - *BoPubDir 4, 5; EISS 83*
Microfilm Sciences Corp. - New York, NY - *EISS 83*
Microfilming Corp. of America [of New York Times Co.] - Sanford, NC - *DirMarMP 83; EISS 83; InfoS 83-84; LitMarPl 83, 84; MagIndMarPl 82-83; MicroMarPl 82-83*
Microfin Systems Ltd. - Weybridge, England - *MicrocomSwDir 1*
Microfinancial Corp. - Industry, CA - *MicrocomMPl 84*
Microfor Inc. - Quebec, PQ, Canada - *CompReadDB 82; EISS 83; InfIndMarPl 83*
Microform Association of Great Britain - Chesham, England - *MicroMarPl 82-83*
Microform Biblios - Lethbridge, AB, Canada - *BoPubDir 4 Sup, 5*

Microform Ltd. - East Ardsley, England - *MicroMarPl 82-83*
Microform Review - Westport, CT - *BaconPubCkMag 84; LitMarPl 83; MagDir 84*
Microform Review - *See* Meckler Publishing
Microforms International Marketing Corp. [Subs. of Pergamon Press Inc.] - Elmsford, NY - *LitMarPl 83, 84; MagIndMarPl 82-83; MicroMarPl 82-83; ProGuPRSer 4*
Microft Inc. - East Falmouth, MA - *WhoWMicrocom 83*
MicroGnome [Subs. of Fireside Computing Inc.] - Elkridge, MD - *MicrocomMPl 83; WhoWMicrocom 83*
MicroGram Systems Group - San Diego, CA - *MicrocomMPl 83; WhoWMicrocom 83*
Micrograms Inc. - Loves Park, IL - *MicrocomMPl 83, 84*
Micrographics Newsletter - New Rochelle, NY - *BaconPubCkMag 84; MagIndMarPl 82-83*
Microhatch - Dewitt, NY - *MicrocomMPl 84*
Microhouse - Bethlehem, PA - *MicrocomMPl 83, 84*
Microinfo Ltd. - Alton, England - *EISS 83; InfIndMarPl 83; MicroMarPl 82-83*
Microinfo Ltd. - Hampshire, England - *InfoS 83-84*
Microline [of Source Telecomputing Corp.] - McLean, VA - *DataDirOnSer 84*
Microline - Pacific Grove, Canada - *DirOnDB Spring 84*
Microlithics Inc. - Oklahoma City, OK - *WhoWMicrocom 83*
MICROLOG [of Canada Institute for Scientific & Technical Information] - Ottawa, ON, Canada - *DataDirOnSer 84*
MICROLOG [of Micromedia Ltd.] - Toronto, ON, Canada - *CompReadDB 82; DirOnDB Spring 84*
Microlog Inc. - Suffern, NY - *MicrocomMPl 84*
Micrologue Inc. - Denver, CO - *MicroMarPl 82-83*
Micromark Inc. [Subs. of Credicom Corp.] - San Jose, CA - *WhoWMicrocom 83*
Micromatic Checks & Forms Inc. - Jersey City, NJ - *DataDirSup 7-83*
Micromatic Programming Co. - Georgetown, CT - *MicrocomMPl 83, 84*
Micromatics Inc. - Bountiful, UT - *MicrocomSwDir 1*
Micromation Inc. - San Francisco, CA - *MicrocomMPl 83, 84; WhoWMicrocom 83*
Micromax - Glastonbury, CT - *MicrocomMPl 84*
Micromedex Inc. - Englewood, CO - *MicroMarPl 82-83*
Micromedia Ltd. - Toronto, ON, Canada - *CompReadDB 82; DataDirOnSer 84; EISS 83; FBInfSer 80; InfIndMarPl 83; LitMarPl 83, 84; MicroMarPl 82-83*
MicroMedx - East Northport, NY - *MicrocomMPl 84*
MicroMethods - Warrenton, OR - *MicrocomMPl 83, 84*
Micromint Inc. - Cedarhurst, NY - *MicrocomMPl 84*
Micromint Inc. - Woodmere, NY - *MicrocomMPl 83*
Micromize Inc. - Ashland, OR - *MicrocomMPl 84*
MicroMotion - Los Angeles, CA - *MicrocomMPl 83, 84*
Micron Corp. - Iron Ridge, WI - *DirInfWP 82*
Micron Inc. - Ellicott City, MD - *MicrocomMPl 84; WhoWMicrocom 83*
Micron Word Processing Supplies - Inglewood, CA - *DataDirSup 7-83; DirInfWP 82*
Micronesia Support Committee - Honolulu, HI - *BoPubDir 4 Sup, 5*
Micronet 800 [of EMAP Business & Computer Publications Ltd.] - London, England - *EISS 5-84 Sup*
Micronet Services Inc. - Arlington, VA - *EISS 83*
Micronetics - Hollywood, FL - *MicrocomMPl 83, 84; MicrocomSwDir 1*
Micronomics Business Systems Inc. - Brooklyn, NY - *WhoWMicrocom 83*
Micropad - La Grange, IL - *ADAPSOMemDir 83-84*
MicroPeripheral Corp. (Kole Business Center) - Redmond, WA - *VideoDir 82-83*
MicroPeripheral Corp., The - Mercer Island, WA - *WhoWMicrocom 83*
MicroPeripheral Corp., The - Redmond, WA - *MicrocomMPl 83, 84; WhoWMicrocom 83*
Microphys Programs Inc. - Brooklyn, NY - *MicrocomMPl 83, 84; MicrocomSwDir 1; WhoWMicrocom 83*
Micropi - Bellingham, WA - *MicrocomMPl 83, 84*
Micropi - Lummi Island, WA - *WhoWMicrocom 83*
Microplex Inc. [Subs. of West Canadian Graphic Industries Ltd.] - Dallas, TX - *LitMarPl 83; MicroMarPl 82-83*
Micropolis Corp. - Chatsworth, CA - *DataDirSup 7-83; WhoWMicrocom 83*
MicroPro International - San Rafael, CA - *ADAPSOMemDir 83-84; DirInfWP 82; MicrocomMPl 83, 84; MicrocomSwDir 1; WhoWMicrocom 83*
Microprocessor Developments Ltd. - London, England - *MicrocomSwDir 1*
Microproducts - Ramona, CA - *MicrocomMPl 84*
Microproducts [Subs. of Elecromancy Inc.] - Rancho Palos Verdes, CA - *MicrocomMPl 83; WhoWMicrocom 83*
Microproducts Software Ltd. - London, England - *MicrocomSwDir 1*
MicroProse Software - Parkton, MD - *MicrocomMPl 84*
Micropsychology Newsletter, The [of Microsphere Enterprises] - New York, NY - *WritMar 84*
Micropublications Dept. [of General Microfilm Co.] - Watertown, MA - *EISS 83*
Micropublishers International - New York, NY - *MicroMarPl 82-83*
Micropublishing International Ltd. - London, England - *MicroMarPl 82-83*
Micropute Ltd. - Macclesfield, England - *MicrocomSwDir 1*
MicroQ Inc. - Fairfax, VA - *MicrocomMPl 84*
MicroQuote - Waltham, MA - *DirOnDB Spring 84*
MicroQuote [of CompuServe Inc.] - Columbus, OH - *DataDirOnSer 84; DBBus 82*
MicroRIM Inc. - Bellevue, WA - *MicrocomMPl 84; MicrocomSwDir 1; WhoWMicrocom 83*
Micros Systems Inc. - Beltsville, MD - *DataDirSup 7-83*
Microsave - Bristol, England - *MicrocomSwDir 1*
Microscience International Corp. - Mountain View, CA - *MicrocomMPl 84*
Microscope Publications [of Elexpro Enterprises Inc.] - Aurora, IL - *MagDir 84*
Microscope Publications [Aff. of McCrone Research Institute] - Chicago, IL - *BoPubDir 4, 5*
Microscopical Society of Canada [of University of Toronto] - Toronto, ON, Canada - *BoPubDir 5*
Microsearch [of Source Telecomputing Corp.] - McLean, VA - *DataDirOnSer 84*
Microserve Inc. - New York, NY - *WhoWMicrocom 83*
Microsignal - Santa Barbara, CA - *WhoWMicrocom 83*
Microsoft - Bellevue, WA - *MicrocomMPl 84; MicrocomSwDir 1; WhoWMicrocom 83*
Microsoft Newsletter - Bellevue, WA - *DirOnDB Spring 84*
Microsoft Structural Control Systems Ltd. - Altrincham, England - *MicrocomSwDir 1*
Microsoftware Services - Harrisonburg, VA - *MicrocomMPl 84; MicrocomSwDir 1*
MicroSource [Subs. of Phoenix Group Inc.] - Tempe, AZ - *WhoWMicrocom 83*
MicroSPARC Inc. - Lincoln, MA - *MicrocomMPl 84*
MicroSpec - Plano, TX - *MicrocomMPl 83, 84*
Microstuf Inc. - Atlanta, GA - *MicrocomMPl 84; MicrocomSwDir 1; WhoWMicrocom 83*
Microstuf Inc. - Marietta, GA - *MicrocomMPl 83*
Microsym Inc. - Wayne, PA - *MicrocomSwDir 1*
Microsystems - Morris Plains, NJ - *MagIndMarPl 82-83*
Microsystems [of AHL Computing Inc.] - New York, NY - *BaconPubCkMag 84; MicrocomMPl 84*
Microsystems - Mercer Island, WA - *WhoWMicrocom 83*
Microsystems Development Corp. - Teaneck, NJ - *WhoWMicrocom 83*
Microsystems Engineering Corp. - Hoffman Estates, IL - *MicrocomMPl 83, 84*
Microtaure Inc. - Ottawa, ON, Canada - *MicrocomSwDir 1*
Microtax - Woodland Hills, CA - *MicrocomMPl 84*
Microtec - Sunnyvale, CA - *MicrocomMPl 84*
Microtech Business Systems - Costa Mesa, CA - *DataDirSup 7-83; WhoWMicrocom 83*
MicroTech Exports Inc. - Palo Alto, CA - *MicrocomMPl 83, 84; MicrocomSwDir 1; WhoWMicrocom 83*
Microtek - San Diego, CA - *MicrocomMPl 84; WhoWMicrocom 83*
Microtex Communications Co. - New York, NY - *Tel&CabFB 84C*

Microthought, The Journal of Financial Software - Santa Monica, CA - *BaconPubCkMag 84*
Microtime [Subs. of Andersen Group Inc.] - Bloomfield, CT - *AvMarPl 83*
Microtraining Associates Inc. - North Amherst, MA - *BoPubDir 4, 5*
Microtran Co. Inc. - Valley Stream, NY - *AvMarPl 83*
Microtrend Inc. - Jamul, CA - *WritMar 84*
Microvision Corp. - San Diego, CA - *Tel&CabFB 84C*
Microware Distributors Inc. - Portland, OR - *WhoWMicrocom 83*
MicroWare Inc. - Kingston, MA - *MicrocomSwDir 1*
Microware Systems Corp. - Des Moines, IA - *MicrocomMPl 83, 84; MicrocomSwDir 1; WhoWMicrocom 83*
Microwave Communications Association - Washington, DC - *TeleSy&SerDir 2-84*
Microwave Distribution Services Inc. - Lynn, MA - *Tel&CabFB 84C*
Microwave Helps - Minneapolis, MN - *BoPubDir 4, 5*
Microwave Journal [of Horizon House-Microwave Inc.] - Dedham, MA - *BaconPubCkMag 84; MagDir 84; MagIndMarPl 82-83*
Microwave Movies Inc. - Osage Beach, MO - *Tel&CabFB 84C*
Microwave News - New York, NY - *BaconPubCkMag 84*
Microwave Service Co. - Tupelo, MS - *Tel&CabFB 84C*
Microwave Style [of Creative Resources] - Cincinnati, OH - *LitMag&SmPr 83-84*
Microwave Systems News [of EW Communications] - Palo Alto, CA - *BaconPubCkMag 84; MagDir 84*
Microwave TV Inc. - Jesup, GA - *BrCabYB 84; Tel&CabFB 84C*
Microwaves & RF [of Hayden Publishing] - Rochelle Park, NJ - *BaconPubCkMag 84; MagDir 84; WritMar 84*
Microwaves Computer Products - Antrim, NH - *MicrocomMPl 84*
MicroWest Software - El Cajon, CA - *MicrocomMPl 84*
MicroXchange - Santa Barbara, CA - *MicrocomMPl 84*
Microzine [of Scholastic Inc.] - New York, NY - *MicrocomMPl 84*
Mid-America CATV Systems Inc. [of W.W. Communications] - Carrollton, MO - *BrCabYB 84 p.D-304; Tel&CabFB 84C*
Mid-America CATV Systems Inc. [of W.W. Communications] - Excelsior Springs, MO - *Tel&CabFB 84C*
Mid-America CATV Systems Inc. [of W.W. Communications] - Marceline, MO - *BrCabYB 84; Tel&CabFB 84C*
Mid-America CATV Systems Inc. [of W.W. Communications] - Salisbury, MO - *BrCabYB 84; Tel&CabFB 84C*
Mid-America Commerce & Industry - Topeka, KS - *BaconPubCkMag 84; MagDir 84*
Mid-America Communications - Bloomington, IN - *VideoDir 82-83*
Mid-America Insurance - Kansas City, MO - *BaconPubCkMag 84; MagDir 84*
Mid-America Marketing Inc. - Indianapolis, IN - *DirMarMP 83*
Mid America Media - Kankakee, IL - *BrCabYB 84; Tel&CabFB 84C p.1691*
Mid-America Music Publishing [Div. of Ozark Opry Inc.] - Osage Beach, MO - *BillIntBG 83-84*
Mid America Plastics - Reseda, CA - *AvMarPl 83*
Mid-America Publishing Corp. - Des Moines, IA - *Ed&PubIntYB 82*
Mid-America Research - Mt. Prospect, IL - *IntDirMarRes 83*
Mid-America Telephone Inc. [Aff. of Universal Telephone Inc.] - Stonewall, OK - *TelDir&BG 83-84*
Mid-America Television Co. [Subs. of Kansas City Southern Industries] - Peoria, IL - *Tel&CabFB 84S*
Mid-American Review [of Bowling Green State University] - Bowling Green, OH - *LitMag&SmPr 83-84; WritMar 84*
Mid-Ark Cablevision Inc. - Shannon Hills, AR - *BrCabYB 84*
Mid-Atlantic Book Service Inc. - Bloomfield, NJ - *LitMarPl 83, 84*
Mid-Atlantic Graphic Arts Review - Philadephia, PA - *MagDir 84*
Mid Atlantic Network - Front Royal, VA - *Tel&CabFB 84C p.1691*
Mid Atlantic Network - Winchester, VA - *BrCabYB 84 p.D-304*
Mid-Atlantic Newspaper Services Inc. - Harrisburg, PA - *ProGuPRSer 4*
Mid Atlantic Purchasing - Philadelphia, PA - *BaconPubCkMag 84; MagDir 84*
Mid-Atlantic Solar Energy Association [Aff. of American Section of the International Solar Energy Society Inc.] - Philadelphia, PA - *BoPubDir 4, 5*
Mid-Atlantic Trucker - Chatham, NJ - *MagDir 84*
Mid-Canada Communications - Timmins, ON, Canada - *BrCabYB 84*
Mid-Carolina Telephone Co. [Aff. of Mid-Continent Telephone Corp.] - Matthews, NC - *TelDir&BG 83-84*
Mid Century Telephone Cooperative - Canton, IL - *TelDir&BG 83-84*
Mid-Cities Daily News - Farmers Branch, TX - *Ed&PubIntYB 82*
Mid-Cities News [of News Texan Inc.] - Hurst, TX - *AyerDirPub 83; BaconPubCkNews 84; NewsDir 84*
Mid-City Copying Products Inc. - Vandrevil, PQ, Canada - *DirInfWP 82*
Mid-City Lithographers Inc. - Northfield, IL - *LitMarPl 83, 84*
Mid-Coast Cable Television - Bay City, TX - *BrCabYB 84; Tel&CabFB 84C*
Mid-Coast Cable Television - El Campo, TX - *BrCabYB 84; Tel&CabFB 84C*
Mid-Coast Cable Television - Sweeny, TX - *BrCabYB 84; Tel&CabFB 84C*
Mid-Coast Cable Television - Wharton, TX - *BrCabYB 84; Tel&CabFB 84C*
Mid Communications Inc. [Aff. of Mankato Citizens Telephone Co.] - Mankato, MN - *TelDir&BG 83-84*
Mid-Continent Banker - St. Louis, MO - *BaconPubCkMag 84*
Mid-Continent Banker - Milwaukee, WI - *MagDir 84*
Mid-Continent Bottler - Overland Park, KS - *BaconPubCkMag 84; WritMar 84*
Mid-Continent Bottler [of Fan Publications Inc.] - Shawnee Mission, KS - *MagDir 84*
Mid-Continent Cable Corp. - Victoria, KS - *Tel&CabFB 84C*
Mid-Continent Cable Corp. - Wichita, KS - *Tel&CabFB 84C p.1691*
Mid-Continent Computer Services Inc. - Englewood, CO - *DataDirSup 7-83*
Mid-Continent/Paulus Feature Syndicate - Pittsburgh, PA - *Ed&PubIntYB 82; LitMarPl 83, 84; MagIndMarPl 82-83*
Mid-Continent Purchasor - Kansas City, MO - *MagDir 84*
Mid-Continent Surveys Inc. - Minneapolis, MN - *IntDirMarRes 83*
Mid-Continent Telephone Corp. - Hudson, OH - *TelDir&BG 83-84*
Mid-County Times - Pardeeville, WI - *AyerDirPub 83; Ed&PubIntYB 82*
Mid East Publishing Co. - Chicago, IL - *BoPubDir 4, 5*
Mid-Empire Music Publishing Co. - Carlisle, IA - *BillIntBG 83-84*
Mid-Georgia Telephone Corp. [Aff. of Mid-Continent Telephone Corp.] - Byron, GA - *TelDir&BG 83-84*
Mid-Georgia Telephone Corp. [Aff. of Mid-Continent Telephone Corp.] - Cairo, GA - *TelDir&BG 83-84*
Mid-Georgia Telephone Corp. [Aff. of Mid-Continent Telephone Corp.] - Commerce, GA - *TelDir&BG 83-84*
Mid-Hudson Cablevision Inc. - Catskill, NY - *BrCabYB 84; Tel&CabFB 84C*
Mid-Hudson Cablevision Inc. - *See* Catskill Mountain Video Inc.
Mid-Hudson Herald - Poughkeepsie, NY - *Ed&PubIntYB 82*
Mid-Hudson Post - Highland, NY - *AyerDirPub 83*
Mid-Hudson Post - *See* Hudson Valley Newspapers Inc.
Mid-Indiana Telephone Co. of Indiana Inc. [Aff. of Mid-Continent Telephone Corp.] - Ossian, IN - *TelDir&BG 83-84*
Mid Iowa Telephone Cooperative - Gilman, IA - *TelDir&BG 83-84*
Mid-Island Herald - Hicksville, NY - *AyerDirPub 83; Ed&PubIntYB 82*
Mid-Island Herald Publishers - Hicksville, NY - *BaconPubCkNews 84*
Mid-Island News - Centereach, NY - *AyerDirPub 83; Ed&PubIntYB 82*
Mid-Island News [of Smithtown News Inc.] - Smithtown, NY - *NewsDir 84*
Mid-Island Times - Hicksville, NY - *AyerDirPub 83*
Mid Island Yankee Trader - *See* Yankee Trader
Mid-Kansas Cable Services Inc. - Moundridge, KS - *Tel&CabFB 84C*
Mid-Kentucky Cable Television Inc. [of Centel Communications Co.] - Albany, KY - *Tel&CabFB 84C*
Mid-Kentucky Cable Television Inc. - Burkesville, KY - *BrCabYB 84*

Mid-Kentucky Cable Television Inc. - Glasgow, KY - *Tel&CabFB 84C p.1691*
Mid Kentucky Cable Television Inc. - Munfordville, KY - *BrCabYB 84*
Mid Kentucky Cable Television Inc. - Somerset, KY - *BrCabYB 84 p.D-304*
Mid-Kentucky Cable Television Inc. - Tompkinsville, KY - *BrCabYB 84*
Mid-Michigan Telephone Corp. [Aff. of Mid-Continent Telephone Corp.] - Stockbridge, MI - *TelDir&BG 83-84*
Mid-Missouri System Inc. - Bunceton, MO - *Tel&CabFB 84C*
Mid-Missouri System Inc. - Pilot Grove, MO - *Tel&CabFB 84C p.1691*
Mid-Missouri Telephone Co. - Pilot Grove, MO - *TelDir&BG 83-84*
Mid-Nebraska Telecommunications Inc. - Kearney, NE - *Tel&CabFB 84C*
Mid-North Monitor - Espanola, ON, Canada - *AyerDirPub 83; Ed&PubIntYB 82*
Mid-Ocean News - Hamilton, Bermuda - *AyerDirPub 83*
Mid-Ohio Farmer - Wayne, OH - *Ed&PubIntYB 82*
Mid-Ohio Telephone Corp. [Aff. of Mid-Continent Telephone Corp.] - Kenton, OH - *TelDir&BG 83-84*
Mid-Penn Telephone Corp. [Aff. of Mid-Continent Telephone Corp.] - Kittanning, PA - *TelDir&BG 83-84*
Mid Pinellas Sun - Largo, FL - *AyerDirPub 83*
Mid-Plains Rural Telephone Cooperative Inc. - Tulia, TX - *TelDir&BG 83-84*
Mid-Plains Telephone Inc. - Middleton, WI - *TelDir&BG 83-84*
Mid-Rivers Telephone Cooperative Inc. - Circle, MT - *Tel&CabFB 84C p.1691; TelDir&BG 83-84*
Mid-Shore CATV Inc. - Federalsburg, MD - *BrCabYB 84*
Mid-Shore CATV Inc. - Fairfax, VA - *BrCabYB 84*
Mid-South Business [of Mid-South Communications Inc.] - Memphis, TN - *BaconPubCkMag 84; WritMar 84*
Mid South Cablevision Inc. - Pearl, MS - *BrCabYB 84*
Mid-South Express - Memphis, TN - *Ed&PubIntYB 82*
Mid South Magazine - Memphis, TN - *WritMar 84*
Mid-South Magazine Agency Inc. - Jackson, MS - *MagIndMarPl 82-83*
Mid-South Mississippi Dailies - New York, NY - *LitMarPl 83*
Mid-South Online User's Group [of Memphis State University Libraries] - Memphis, TN - *InfIndMarPl 83*
Mid-South Publishing Co. - Amelia, VA - *BoPubDir 4, 5*
Mid-South Scientific Publishers - Mississippi State, MS - *BoPubDir 4, 5*
Mid-South Stockman/Farmer - Jackson, MS - *MagDir 84*
Mid-State Community TV Co. - Sargent, NE - *BrCabYB 84*
Mid-State Community TV Inc. - Aurora, NE - *BrCabYB 84; Tel&CabFB 84C p.1691*
Mid State Newspapers Inc. - Brownsburg, IN - *BaconPubCkNews 84*
Mid-State Publishing Co. Inc. - Winona, MS - *BaconPubCkNews 84*
Mid-State Telephone Co. [Aff. of Telephone Data Systems Inc.] - Spicer, MN - *TelDir&BG 83-84*
Mid-State Telephone Co. [Aff. of Central Telephone Co. of Texas] - Killeen, TX - *TelDir&BG 83-84*
Mid-States Cablevision Inc. - Cuba, MO - *BrCabYB 84; Tel&CabFB 84C p.1691*
Mid States Visual - Jacksonville, IL - *AvMarPl 83*
Mid-Valley Cablevision Ltd. - Kingston, NS, Canada - *BrCabYB 84*
Mid-Valley Gazette [of Dallas Pennaprint Inc.] - Dallas, PA - *NewsDir 84*
Mid-Valley News - Weslaco, TX - *AyerDirPub 83*
Mid Valley Press - Sanger, CA - *AyerDirPub 83*
Mid West Communications Inc. - Walnut Creek, CA - *BrCabYB 84 p.D-304*
Mid-West Contractor [of Construction Digest] - Kansas City, MO - *BaconPubCkMag 84; MagDir 84; WritMar 84*
Mid-West Family Stations - Madison, WI - *BrCabYB 84*
Mid-West Herald & Near West Side Herald - Chicago, IL - *AyerDirPub 83*
Mid West Outdoors - Hinsdale, IL - *BaconPubCkMag 84; MagIndMarPl 82-83; WritMar 84*
Mid-West Tennessee Genealogical Society - Jackson, TN - *BoPubDir 4, 5*
Mid-West Truckman, The - Topeka, KS - *MagDir 84*
Mid-Western Banker [of Bankers Publishing Co.] - Milwaukee, WI - *MagDir 84*
Mid-Willamette Cable TV - Jefferson, OR - *BrCabYB 84; Tel&CabFB 84C*
Mid-York Weekly - Hamilton, NY - *AyerDirPub 83; Ed&PubIntYB 82*
MidArk Cablevision Inc. [of Combined Cable Corp.] - Shannon Hills, AR - *Tel&CabFB 84C*
MIDAS [of Overseas Telecommunications Commission] - Sydney, Australia - *InfIndMarPl 83*
Midas [of IMS AG] - Zug, Switzerland - *EISS 83*
MiDavAnMar - *See* Benedetti Music, Quint
Midcoast Publications - St. Louis, MO - *BoPubDir 4 Sup, 5*
Midcontinent Broadcasting Cable Systems of North Dakota [of Midcontinent Cable Inc.] - Grafton, ND - *Tel&CabFB 84C*
Midcontinent Broadcasting Co. - Sioux Falls, SD - *BrCabYB 84; Tel&CabFB 84S*
Midcontinent Cable Inc. - Devils Lake, ND - *Tel&CabFB 84C*
Midcontinent Cable Systems Co. - Aberdeen, SD - *BrCabYB 84 p.D-304; Tel&CabFB 84C p.1691*
Middle Atlantic Press - Wallingford, PA - *LitMag&SmPr 83-84; LitMarPl 83, 84*
Middle Earth Books Inc. - Philadelphia, PA - *BoPubDir 4, 5*
Middle East: Abstracts & Index, The [of Northumberland Press] - Pittsburgh, PA - *DirOnDB Spring 84; EISS 7-83 Sup*
Middle East Advertising & Marketing Co. - New York, NY - *HBIndAd&MS 82-83; StaDirAdAg 2-84*
Middle East Data Base [of New York Times Information Service] - Parsippany, NJ - *CompReadDB 82; DBBus 82; EISS 83*
Middle East Institute - Washington, DC - *BoPubDir 4, 5*
Middle East Journal, The - Washington, DC - *MagIndMarPl 82-83*
Middle East Marketing Research Bureau Ltd. - Nicosia, Cyprus - *IntDirMarRes 83*
Middle Park Times - Kremmling, CO - *AyerDirPub 83; Ed&PubIntYB 82*
Middle Point Home Telephone Co. - Middle Point, OH - *TelDir&BG 83-84*
Middle River Record - *See* Record Printing Co.
Middleberg Middleton Inc. - New York, NY - *DirPRFirms 83*
Middleboro Gazette [of Somerset Spectator Publishing Corp.] - Fall River, MA - *NewsDir 84*
Middleboro Gazette - Middleboro, MA - *Ed&PubIntYB 82*
Middleboro Gazette - *See* Hathaway Publishing Corp.
Middleborough Municipal Gas & Electric Dept. - Middleborough, MA - *BrCabYB 84*
Middlebourne TV Cable - Middlebourne, WV - *BrCabYB 84; Tel&CabFB 84C*
Middleburg Post - Middleburg, PA - *BaconPubCkNews 84; Ed&PubIntYB 82; NewsDir 84*
Middleburg Press - Orange City, IA - *BoPubDir 4, 5; LitMag&SmPr 83-84*
Middleburgh News-Schoharie Review, The - Middleburgh, NY - *Ed&PubIntYB 82*
Middleburgh Telephone Co. - Middleburgh, NY - *TelDir&BG 83-84*
Middlebury Addison County Independent - Middlebury, VT - *BaconPubCkNews 84; NewsDir 84*
Middlebury Independent - Middlebury, IN - *AyerDirPub 83; BaconPubCkNews 84; Ed&PubIntYB 82*
Middlefork Journal - Potomac, IL - *AyerDirPub 83; Ed&PubIntYB 82*
Middlesboro Daily News - Middlesboro, KY - *BaconPubCkNews 84; Ed&PubIntYB 82; NewsDir 84*
Middlesex Cablevision Inc. [of Storer Communications Inc.] - Brunswick, NJ - *BrCabYB 84*
Middlesex Cablevision Inc. [of Storer Cable Communications] - East Brunswick, NJ - *Tel&CabFB 84C*
Middlesex Chronicle [of Somerset Press] - Middlesex, NJ - *NewsDir 84*
Middlesex Chronicle - *See* Somerset Press
Middlesex News - Framingham, MA - *AyerDirPub 83; BaconPubCkNews 84; Ed&PubIntYB 82*

Middleton Times-Tribune - Middleton, WI - *Ed&PubIntYB 82*
Middleton Times Tribune - *See* News Publishing Co. Inc.
Middletown Advisor - Middletown, NJ - *BaconPubCkNews 84*
Middletown Courier [of Bayshore Press Inc.] - Middletown, NJ - *BaconPubCkNews 84; NewsDir 84*
Middletown Echo - Middletown, IL - *Ed&PubIntYB 82*
Middletown Journal [of Thomson Newspapers Inc.] - Middletown, OH - *BaconPubCkNews 84; Ed&PubIntYB 82; NewsDir 84*
Middletown Mirror - Louisville, KY - *AyerDirPub 83*
Middletown Mirror - *See* Scripps-Howard Press
Middletown News - Middletown, IN - *BaconPubCkNews 84; Ed&PubIntYB 82*
Middletown Press - Middletown, CT - *BaconPubCkNews 84; Ed&PubIntYB 82; LitMarPl 83, 84; NewsDir 84*
Middletown Press & Journal - Middletown, PA - *BaconPubCkNews 84; NewsDir 84*
Middletown Times Herald-Record - Middletown, NY - *BaconPubCkNews 84*
Middletown Times Star - Middletown, CA - *BaconPubCkNews 84*
Middletown Transcript - Middletown, DE - *BaconPubCkNews 84; Ed&PubIntYB 82*
Middletown Valley Register - *See* Valley Register Inc.
Middleville Sun & Caledonia News - Middleville, MI - *BaconPubCkNews 84; Ed&PubIntYB 82*
Mideast Business Exchange [of The News Circle Publishers] - Glendale, CA - *BaconPubCkMag 84; MagDir 84*
Mideast File [of Dialog Information Services Inc.] - Palo Alto, CA - *DataDirOnSer 84*
Mideast File - Abingdon, England - *DirOnDB Spring 84*
Mideast File [of Tel-Aviv University] - Tel-Aviv, Israel - *EISS 83*
Midesco Ltd. - Hermosa Beach, CA - *InfIndMarPl 83*
Midget Music - *See* Widget Publishing
Midland Advertising Agency Inc. - Cincinnati, OH - *StaDirAdAg 2-84*
Midland Cablevision Systems Inc. - Bettendorf, IA - *Tel&CabFB 84C p.1691*
Midland Cooperator - Minneapolis, MN - *MagDir 84*
Midland Daily News - Midland, MI - *BaconPubCkNews 84; Ed&PubIntYB 82; NewsDir 84*
Midland Gazette - Granville, IL - *Ed&PubIntYB 82*
Midland Gazette - Spring Valley, IL - *AyerDirPub 83*
Midland News, The - Midland (PA), OH - *Ed&PubIntYB 82*
Midland News, The - Midland, PA - *AyerDirPub 83*
Midland Paper Co. - Chicago, IL - *LitMarPl 83, 84*
Midland Publishing Co. - Sister Bay, WI - *BoPubDir 4, 5*
Midland Reporter-Telegram - Midland, TX - *BaconPubCkNews 84; Ed&PubIntYB 82; NewsDir 84*
Midland Telephone Co. - Champaign, IL - *TelDir&BG 83-84*
Midland Television Corp. - Springfield, MO - *Tel&CabFB 84S*
Midlands Cable Systems Inc. - Papillion, NE - *Tel&CabFB 84C p.1691*
Midlen Trust, John H. - Washington, DC - *BrCabYB 84 p.D-304*
Midlothian-Bremen Messenger [of Midlothian Southwest Messenger Newspapers] - Midlothian, IL - *AyerDirPub 83; Ed&PubIntYB 82; NewsDir 84*
Midlothian Bremen Messenger - *See* Southwest Messenger Newspapers
Midlothian Cable Communications - Midlothian, TX - *BrCabYB 84*
Midlothian Mirror - Midlothian, TX - *BaconPubCkNews 84; Ed&PubIntYB 82*
Midlothian Penny Saver Newspapers Inc. - Midlothian, IL - *NewsDir 84*
Midlothian Reporter [of Duncanville Suburban] - Duncanville, TX - *NewsDir 84*
Midlothian Reporter - Midlothian, TX - *BaconPubCkNews 84; Ed&PubIntYB 82*
Midlothian Southtown Economist - Chicago, IL - *AyerDirPub 83*
Midlothian Southtown Economist - *See* Southtown Economist Inc.
Midlothian Star-Herald - Midlothian, IL - *AyerDirPub 83; Ed&PubIntYB 82*
Midlothian Star-Herald - Oak Forest, IL - *NewsDir 84*
Midlothian Star-Herald - *See* Star Publications
Midmarch Associates - New York, NY - *BoPubDir 4, 5; LitMag&SmPr 83-84*
Midnight Gold Publishing Co. - Berwick, LA - *BillIntBG 83-84*
Midnight Gold Record Co. - Berwick, LA - *BillIntBG 83-84*
Midnight-Oil - Beaverton, OR - *MicrocomMPl 84*
Midnite/Paper Magazine [of Midnite Software Inc.] - Lincoln, IL - *MicrocomMPl 84*
Midori Book Store Co. - Osaka, Japan - *EISS 83; InfIndMarPl 83*
MIDS/Agriculture [of Marketing Information Data Systems] - Dallas, TX - *DataDirOnSer 84; DirOnDB Spring 84*
MIDS/Banking & Finance [of Marketing Information Data Systems] - Dallas, TX - *DataDirOnSer 84; DirOnDB Spring 84*
MIDS/Construction & Building Permits [of Marketing Information Data Systems] - Dallas, TX - *DataDirOnSer 84; DirOnDB Spring 84*
MIDS Database [of Marketing Information Data Systems] - Dallas, TX - *DataDirOnSer 84*
MIDS/Marketing [of Marketing Information Data Systems] - Dallas, TX - *DataDirOnSer 84; DirOnDB Spring 84*
MIDS/Medical [of Marketing Information Data Systems] - Dallas, TX - *DataDirOnSer 84; DirOnDB Spring 84*
MIDS/1980 Census [of Marketing Information Data Systems] - Dallas, TX - *DataDirOnSer 84; DirOnDB Spring 84*
MIDS/1980-1970 Census Comparison [of Marketing Information Data Systems] - Dallas, TX - *DataDirOnSer 84; DirOnDB Spring 84*
Midsouthwest Foodservice Magazine - Oklahoma City, OK - *MagDir 84*
Midsouthwest Restaurant - Shawnee Mission, KS - *BaconPubCkMag 84*
Midstate Cable of Perry [of United Cable Co. Inc.] - Perry, GA - *BrCabYB 84; Tel&CabFB 84C*
Midstate Cable TV [of United Cable Co. Inc.] - Hawkinsville, GA - *BrCabYB 84; Tel&CabFB 84C*
Midstate Telephone Co. - Stanley, ND - *TelDir&BG 83-84*
Midstate Telephone Co. - Kimball, SD - *TelDir&BG 83-84*
Midstate Telephone Corp. (Fulton District) - Fulton, NY - *TelDir&BG 83-84*
Midstate Telephone Corp. (Jamestown District) - Jamestown, NY - *TelDir&BG 83-84*
Midstate Telephone Corp. (Red Jacket District) - Fulton, NY - *TelDir&BG 83-84*
Midstream - New York, NY - *MagIndMarPl 82-83; WritMar 84*
Midstream Music Publishers - Winchester, VA - *BillIntBG 83-84*
Midtec Paper Corp. - Kimberly, WI - *LitMarPl 83, 84*
Midtec Sales Inc. - New York, NY - *LitMarPl 83, 84*
Midtown Video [Subs. of Miller Mermell Inc.] - Denver, CO - *AvMarPl 83*
Midvale Jordan Valley Sentinel - Midvale, UT - *BaconPubCkNews 84*
Midvale Telephone Exchange Inc. - Midvale, ID - *TelDir&BG 83-84*
Midway - Naples, FL - *BoPubDir 4, 5*
Midway Cable - Stroud, OK - *BrCabYB 84*
Midway Cable Corp. - Lockney, TX - *Tel&CabFB 84C p.1691*
Midway Cable TV [of Centel Cable Television Co.] - Midway, KY - *BrCabYB 84*
Midway Cablevision - Marengo, IL - *Tel&CabFB 84C p.1691*
Midway Cablevision [of Combined Cable Corp.] - Whitewater, WI - *BrCabYB 84; Tel&CabFB 84C*
Midway Driller - Taft, CA - *AyerDirPub 83*
Midway Mutual Telephone Co., The [Aff. of Mid-Continent Telephone Corp.] - Midway, PA - *TelDir&BG 83-84*
Midway Telephone Co. - Watton, MI - *TelDir&BG 83-84*
Midway Telephone Co. [Aff. of Telephone & Data Systems Inc.] - Medford, WI - *TelDir&BG 83-84*
Midweek - Xenia, OH - *AyerDirPub 83*
Midweek Eagle - West Fargo, ND - *AyerDirPub 83; NewsDir 84*
Midweek Plus - West Fargo, ND - *NewsDir 84*
Midweek, The - De Kalb, IL - *AyerDirPub 83*
Midweek, The - West Fargo, ND - *AyerDirPub 83*
Midwest Arts & Literature - Jefferson City, MO - *LitMag&SmPr 83-84*
Midwest Automotive News [of Automotive Publishing Co.] - Chicago, IL - *BaconPubCkMag 84; MagDir 84*
Midwest Bookwatch, The - Oregon, WI - *LitMag&SmPr 83-84*
Midwest Cable Communications Inc. - Bemidji, MN - *BrCabYB 84; Tel&CabFB 84C*
Midwest Cable Communications Inc. - Cass Lake, MN - *BrCabYB 84*

Midwest Cable Corp. - Keokuk, IA - *Tel&CabFB 84C p.1691*
Midwest Cable Inc. - Mt. Carmel, IL - *BrCabYB 84; Tel&CabFB 84C*
Midwest Cable Television Inc. - Haxtun, CO - *BrCabYB 84*
Midwest Cable TV Inc. - Holyoke, CO - *Tel&CabFB 84C*
Midwest Cable TV Inc. - Halliday, ND - *Tel&CabFB 84C p.1692*
Midwest Cablevision Inc. [of Metro Cable Corp.] - Hamburg, IA - *Tel&CabFB 84C*
Midwest Cablevision Inc. - Sidney, IA - *Tel&CabFB 84C*
Midwest Chaparral - Waverly, IA - *LitMag&SmPr 83-84*
Midwest City Greensheet - Midwest City, OK - *AyerDirPub 83*
Midwest City Sun - Midwest City, OK - *AyerDirPub 83; BaconPubCkNews 84; Ed&PubIntYB 82*
Midwest Commerce Data Corp. [Subs. of Midwest Commerce Corp.] - Elkhart, IN - *DataDirOnSer 84*
Midwest Communications Inc. - Minneapolis, MN - *BrCabYB 84; Tel&CabFB 84S*
Midwest Communications Stations - Green Bay, WI - *BrCabYB 84*
Midwest Computer Center - Johnston, IA - *MicrocomMPl 84; WhoWMicrocom 83*
Midwest Corp. - Charleston, WV - *Tel&CabFB 84C*
Midwest Data Systems Inc. [Subs. of Celina Financial Corp.] - Celina, OH - *ADAPSOMemDir 83-84; DataDirOnSer 84*
Midwest Distributors - Kansas City, MO - *BoPubDir 4 Sup, 5*
Midwest Diversified Communications Inc. - Osage Beach, MO - *BrCabYB 84; Tel&CabFB 84C*
Midwest Editing - Indianapolis, IN - *LitMarPl 84*
Midwest Engineer [of The Western Society of Engineers] - Chicago, IL - *BaconPubCkMag 84; MagDir 84*
Midwest Film Studios - Chicago, IL - *AvMarPl 83; Tel&CabFB 84C*
Midwest Fleet Management - Indianapolis, IN - *BaconPubCkMag 84; MagDir 84*
Midwest Flyer Magazine - Oregon, WI - *BaconPubCkMag 84*
Midwest Heritage Publishing Co. - Iowa City, IA - *BoPubDir 4, 5*
Midwest Laboratories Inc. - Watertown, WI - *TeleSy&SerDir 2-84*
Midwest Library Service - Bridgeton, MO - *LitMarPl 83, 84*
Midwest Mailers & Distributors - South Bend, IN - *LitMarPl 83, 84; MagIndMarPl 82-83*
Midwest Metro Inc. - Julesburg, CO - *BrCabYB 84; Tel&CabFB 84C*
Midwest Metro Inc. - Ovid, CO - *BrCabYB 84*
Midwest Metro Inc. - Big Spring, NE - *BrCabYB 84*
Midwest Metro Inc. - Chappell, NE - *BrCabYB 84*
Midwest Micro-Tek Inc. - Brooklyn Center, MN - *MicrocomMPl 84*
Midwest Microsystems - Omaha, NE - *DataDirSup 7-83*
Midwest Motor Transport News - Minneapolis, MN - *MagDir 84*
Midwest Motor Transport News - St. Paul, MN - *BaconPubCkMag 84*
Midwest Motorist [of The Auto Club of Missouri] - St. Louis, MO - *BaconPubCkMag 84; MagDir 84; MagIndMarPl 82-83; WritMar 84*
Midwest Newsclip Inc. - Chicago, IL - *ProGuPRSer 4*
Midwest Oil Register Inc. - Tulsa, OK - *BoPubDir 5*
Midwest Photo Co. - Omaha, NE - *AvMarPl 83*
Midwest Plan Service - Ames, IA - *BoPubDir 4, 5*
Midwest Playwrights' Program - Minneapolis, MN - *WritMar 84*
Midwest Poetry Review [of River City Publishers] - Rock Island, IL - *WritMar 84*
Midwest Publications Co. Inc. - Pacific Grove, CA - *BoPubDir 4, 5*
Midwest Publishing Co. - Ceresco, NE - *BoPubDir 4, 5*
Midwest Publishing Co. - Columbus, OH - *BillIntBG 83-84*
Midwest Purchasing - Cleveland, OH - *BaconPubCkMag 84; MagDir 84*
Midwest Quarterly, The - Pittsburg, KS - *LitMag&SmPr 83-84*
Midwest Racing News - Milwaukee, WI - *BaconPubCkMag 84; MagDir 84*
Midwest Radio Co. - Fargo, ND - *BrCabYB 84*
Midwest Region Library Network - Chicago, IL - *EISS 83; InfIndMarPl 83*
Midwest Retailer - Bloomington, MN - *BaconPubCkMag 84*
Midwest Roto - Cleveland, OH - *MagIndMarPl 82-83*
Midwest Satellite Cablevision Inc. - Halliday, ND - *Tel&CabFB 84C p.1692*
Midwest Scientific Instruments - Olathe, KS - *MicrocomMPl 83, 84*
Midwest Software Associates - St. Louis, MO - *MicrocomMPl 84*
Midwest Survey Inc. - Omaha, NE - *IntDirMarRes 83*
Midwest Taekwon-Do Association - Grand Blanc, MI - *BoPubDir 4, 5*
Midwest Technology - University Center, MI - *BaconPubCkMag 84*
Midwest Telephone Co. - Parkers Prairie, MN - *TelDir&BG 83-84*
Midwest Telephone Supply Inc. - Appleton, WI - *DataDirSup 7-83*
Midwest Television Inc. - Champaign, IL - *BrCabYB 84; Tel&CabFB 84S*
Midwest Video [Div. of Home Theatres Inc.] - Little Rock, AR - *BrCabYB 84 p.D-304; CabTVFinDB 83; KnowInd 83; LitMarPl 84; TelAl 83, 84; Tel&CabFB 84C p.1692*
Midwest Video Corp. - Dexter, MO - *BrCabYB 84*
Midwest Video Corp. - Poplar Bluff, MO - *BrCabYB 84; Tel&CabFB 84C*
Midwest Video Corp. - Clovis, NM - *BrCabYB 84; Tel&CabFB 84C*
Midwest Video Corp. - Bryan, TX - *Tel&CabFB 84C*
Midwest Video Corp. - College Station, TX - *BrCabYB 84*
Midwest Video Corp. - Farwell, TX - *BrCabYB 84*
Midwest Video Corp. - Paris, TX - *BrCabYB 84; Tel&CabFB 84C*
Midwest Video Electronics Inc. - Rhinelander, WI - *BrCabYB 84; Tel&CabFB 84C*
Midwest Video Electronics of Tomahawk, Wisconsin Inc. - Rochester, MN - *BrCabYB 84*
Midwest Video Electronics of Tomahawk, Wisconsin Inc. - Crandon, WI - *Tel&CabFB 84C*
Midwest Video Electronics of Tomahawk, Wisconsin Inc. - Tomahawk, WI - *Tel&CabFB 84C*
Midwest Visual Equipment - Chicago, IL - *AvMarPl 83*
Midwest Visuals Inc. - Brimson, MN - *AvMarPl 83*
Midwestern Broadcasting Co. - *See* Bunyan Network, Paul
Midwestern Telephone Co. Inc. - Sentinel, OK - *TelDir&BG 83-84*
Miehle Sales & Services (Graphic Systems Div.) - Westmont, IL - *LitMarPl 83, 84*
Mier-Collins/WLK Public Relations - Buffalo, NY - *DirPRFirms 83*
Mietus Copyright Management - Union, NJ - *BillIntBG 83-84*
Mifflinburg Telegraph - Mifflinburg, PA - *BaconPubCkNews 84; Ed&PubIntYB 82*
Mifflintown Juniata Sentinel - Mifflintown, PA - *BaconPubCkNews 84*
Mighty Byte Computer Inc. - Phoenix, AZ - *MicrocomMPl 84*
Mighty Byte Computer Inc. - Ho Ho Kus, NJ - *WhoWMicrocom 83*
Mighty M Music Inc. - *See* Lipservices
Mighty Matthew Music - Cleveland, OH - *BillIntBG 83-84*
Mighty Minute Programs - San Francisco, CA - *Tel&CabFB 84C*
Mighty Pretty Music - *See* Gant Enterprises, Don
Mighty Three Music Group - Philadelphia, PA - *BillIntBG 83-84*
Migliara/Kaplan Associates - Towson, MD - *IntDirMarRes 83*
MIH Publications - Silver Spring, MD - *BoPubDir 4, 5*
MII Lundia Inc. - Jacksonville, IL - *DirInfWP 82*
Mika Publishing Co. [Div. of Mika Silk Screening Ltd.] - Belleville, ON, Canada - *BoPubDir 4; LitMarPl 83, 84*
Mike Shayne Mystery Magazine [of Renown Publications Inc.] - Reseda, CA - *ArtMar 84; MagIndMarPl 82-83; WritMar 84*
Mike's TV Inc. - Morton, WA - *BrCabYB 84; Tel&CabFB 84C*
Mikesell, Gordon G. & Maxine - Clearwater, KS - *Tel&CabFB 84C p.1692*
Mikesell, Stephen R. & Evelyn L. - Clearwater, KS - *Tel&CabFB 84C p.1692*
Miklos Research Associates Inc. - New York, NY - *IntDirMarRes 83*
Miko's Pacific News Services - Stratford, CT - *Ed&PubIntYB 82*
Mikro-Cerid - Boulogne sur Seine, France - *EISS 83*
Mikrofilmarchiv der Deutschsprachigen Presse eV - Dortmund, West Germany - *MicroMarPl 82-83*
Mikropress GmbH - Bonn, West Germany - *MicroMarPl 82-83*
Mil-Mor Media Inc. - Richmond, VA - *StaDirAdAg 2-84*
MIL Research Inc. - Chicago, IL - *IntDirMarRes 83*

Milaca Mille Lacs County Times - Milaca, MN - *BaconPubCkNews 84*
Milady Publishing Corp. - New York, NY - *ArtMar 84; BoPubDir 4, 5; LitMarPl 84*
Milagro Press - Santa Fe, NM - *BoPubDir 5; LitMag&SmPr 83-84*
Milan Area Leader - Milan, MI - *AyerDirPub 83; BaconPubCkNews 84; Ed&PubIntYB 82*
Milan Cablevision Inc. - Milan, GA - *BrCabYB 84*
Milan Cablevision Inc. - Milan, MO - *BrCabYB 84*
Milan Leader - Milan, MI - *NewsDir 84*
Milan Mirror-Exchange - Milan, TN - *BaconPubCkNews 84; Ed&PubIntYB 82; NewsDir 84*
Milan Standard - Milan, MO - *BaconPubCkNews 84; Ed&PubIntYB 82; NewsDir 84*
Milan Standard-Watson Journal - Milan, MN - *AyerDirPub 83; BaconPubCkNews 84; Ed&PubIntYB 82*
Milanese Associates Inc. - Philadelphia, PA - *AvMarPl 83*
Milbank Grant County Review - Milbank, SD - *BaconPubCkNews 84; NewsDir 84*
Milbank Herald Advance - Milbank, SD - *BaconPubCkNews 84; Ed&PubIntYB 82*
Milbank Memorial Fund Quarterly/Health & Society - New York, NY - *MagIndMarPl 82-83*
Milberg Theatrical Productions Inc. - East Norwalk, CT - *Tel&CabFB 84C*
Milbrae Sun-Leader & Burlingame Leader - Milbrae, CA - *Ed&PubIntYB 82*
Milch, Adele - Stony Brook, NY - *LitMarPl 83, 84*
Milch, Robert J. - Stony Brook, NY - *LitMarPl 83, 84; MagIndMarPl 82-83*
Mildoba Publishing Corp. - Brooklyn, NY - *BillIntBG 83-84*
Mile Hi Cablevision Associates Ltd. - Denver, CO - *BrCabYB 84; Tel&CabFB 84C*
Miles & Weir Ltd. - San Pedro, CA - *LitMag&SmPr 83-84; LitMarPl 83, 84*
Miles City Hysham Echo - Miles City, MT - *BaconPubCkNews 84*
Miles City Star - Miles City, MT - *BaconPubCkNews 84; Ed&PubIntYB 82; NewsDir 84*
Miles City Star - *See* Star Printing Co.
Miles Computing - Van Nuys, CA - *MicrocomMPl 84; MicrocomSwDir 1*
Miles Cooperative Telephone Association - Miles, IA - *TelDir&BG 83-84*
Miles, J. Todd [Aff. of Ford Fergie Farmer Magazine] - Millbury, MA - *BoPubDir 4, 5*
Miles Messenger - Miles, TX - *BaconPubCkNews 84; Ed&PubIntYB 82*
Miles Publishing Co., Earl - Stockton, CA - *BillIntBG 83-84*
Miles, R. & E. - San Pedro, CA - *BoPubDir 4 Sup, 5; LitMag&SmPr 83-84*
Milestone Mail, The - Milestone, SK, Canada - *Ed&PubIntYB 82*
Miley, Edward G. - Alturas, CA - *BrCabYB 84 p.D-304*
Miley, Edward G. - *See* Cal-Nor Cableview Inc.
Milford Advertiser [of Queen City Suburban Press Inc.] - Cincinnati, OH - *NewsDir 84*
Milford Advertiser - Milford, OH - *Ed&PubIntYB 82*
Milford Advertiser - *See* Queen City Suburban Press Inc.
Milford Beaver County News - Milford, UT - *BaconPubCkNews 84*
Milford Cabinet - Milford, NH - *BaconPubCkNews 84; Ed&PubIntYB 82*
Milford Cabinet & Wilton Journal - Milford, NH - *AyerDirPub 83; NewsDir 84*
Milford Cablevision Corp. [of Americable Inc.] - Milford, NH - *BrCabYB 84; Tel&CabFB 84C*
Milford Chronicle - Milford, DE - *BaconPubCkNews 84; NewsDir 84*
Milford Citizen - Milford, CT - *BaconPubCkNews 84; Ed&PubIntYB 82; NewsDir 84*
Milford Herald-News - Milford, IL - *BaconPubCkNews 84; Ed&PubIntYB 82*
Milford-Highland Spinal Column [of Union Lake Spinal Column] - Union Lake, MI - *NewsDir 84*
Milford, Kenneth - New York, NY - *LitMarPl 83, 84*
Milford-Loveland Area Mailer, The [of The Batavia Buying Guide] - Batavia, OH - *NewsDir 84*
Milford Mail - Milford, IA - *AyerDirPub 83; BaconPubCkNews 84; Ed&PubIntYB 82*
Milford Mail-Journal - Milford, IN - *BaconPubCkNews 84*
Milford News - Milford, MA - *BaconPubCkNews 84; Ed&PubIntYB 82; NewsDir 84*
Milford Pike County Dispatch - Milford, PA - *BaconPubCkNews 84*
Milford Reporter - Milford, CT - *Ed&PubIntYB 82*
Milford Spinal Column Newsweekly - *See* Spinal Column Newsweekly
Milford Sunday Citizen - Milford, CT - *NewsDir 84*
Milford Times - Milford, MI - *AyerDirPub 83; BaconPubCkNews 84; Ed&PubIntYB 82; NewsDir 84*
Milford Times - Milford, NE - *BaconPubCkNews 84; Ed&PubIntYB 82*
Milford, Toni - New York, NY - *LitMarPl 83*
Milici/Valenti Advertising Inc. - Honolulu, HI - *ArtMar 84; BrCabYB 84; StaDirAdAg 2-84*
Militant, The - New York, NY - *AyerDirPub 83; LitMag&SmPr 83-84*
Military Aircraft Publications - Chillicothe, OH - *BoPubDir 4, 5*
Military & Federal Specifications & Standards - Englewood, CO - *DirOnDB Spring 84*
Military Book Club [Subs. of Doubleday & Co. Inc.] - Garden City, NY - *LitMarPl 83*
Military Book Club - *See* Doubleday Book Clubs
Military Chaplain, The - Washington, DC - *MagDir 84*
Military Clubs & Recreation - Alexandria, VA - *BaconPubCkMag 84*
Military Collector's Journal - Trexlertown, PA - *WritMar 84*
Military Collectors News Press - Tulsa, OK - *ArtMar 84; LitMarPl 84*
Military Electronics/Countermeasures [of ICDM of North America Inc.] - Santa Clara, CA - *BaconPubCkMag 84; MagDir 84; WritMar 84*
Military Engineer, The [of The Society of American Military Engineers] - Alexandria, VA - *BaconPubCkMag 84; MagDir 84; MagIndMarPl 82-83; WritMar 84*
Military Images Magazine - Whitehall, PA - *LitMag&SmPr 83-84*
Military Living - Arlington, VA - *WritMar 84*
Military Living R & R Report - Arlington, VA - *WritMar 84*
Military Market - Washington, DC - *ArtMar 84; BaconPubCkMag 84; MagDir 84*
Military Marketing Services Inc. - Arlington, VA - *BoPubDir 4, 5*
Military Medicine - Kensington, MD - *BaconPubCkMag 84; MagDir 84*
Military Outdoors Magazine - Ft. Monroe, VA - *BaconPubCkMag 84*
Military Review [of US Army Command & General Staff College] - Ft. Leavenworth, KS - *BaconPubCkMag 84; MagDir 84; WritMar 84*
Military Specifications & Standards [of Information Handling Services] - Englewood, CO - *DataDirOnSer 84*
Military Technology - McLean, VA - *BaconPubCkMag 84*
Milk & Liquid Food Transporter [of Dairy Marketing Communications] - Menomonee Falls, WI - *BaconPubCkMag 84; MagDir 84; WritMar 84*
Milk Marketer [of Milk Marketing Inc.] - Cleveland, OH - *MagDir 84*
Milk Marketer - Strongsville, OH - *BaconPubCkMag 84*
Milk River Cable Club - Milk River, AB, Canada - *BrCabYB 84*
Milkweed Chronicle - Minneapolis, MN - *LitMag&SmPr 83-84; WritMar 84*
Milkweeditions [Aff. of Milkweed Chronicle] - Minneapolis, MN - *BoPubDir 5*
Mill City Enterprise - Mill City, OR - *BaconPubCkNews 84; Ed&PubIntYB 82*
Mill City Records - Minneapolis, MN - *BillIntBG 83-84*
Mill Creek Antennae Co. - Mill Creek, PA - *BrCabYB 84*
Mill Hall Cable Co. Inc. - Mill Hall, PA - *BrCabYB 84; Tel&CabFB 84C*
Mill Valley Pacific Sun - Mill Valley, CA - *NewsDir 84*
Mill Valley Record - Mill Valley, CA - *BaconPubCkNews 84; Ed&PubIntYB 82; NewsDir 84*

Millan/Detroit Repertory Theatre, Bruce E. - Detroit, MI - *WritMar 84*
Millar & Co. Inc., George W. - New York, NY - *DirInfWP 82; LitMarPl 83; MagIndMarPl 82-83*
Millar, Clare - Canada - *BoPubDir 4, 5*
Millar Publications - Exshaw, AB, Canada - *BoPubDir 4, 5*
Millard County Chronicle - Delta, UT - *Ed&PubIntYB 82*
Millard County Progress - Fillmore, UT - *AyerDirPub 83; Ed&PubIntYB 82*
Millard Literary Agency, Martha - New York, NY - *LitMarPl 83, 84*
Millbrae Leader - Millbrae, CA - *AyerDirPub 83*
Millbrae Recorder-Progress - *See* San Mateo Times Group Newspapers
Millbrae Sun & Leader - Millbrae, CA - *BaconPubCkNews 84*
Millbrook Community Press - Millbrook, AL - *BaconPubCkNews 84*
Millbrook Round Table [of Taconic Press Inc.] - Millbrook, NY - *Ed&PubIntYB 82; NewsDir 84*
Millbrook Round Table - *See* Taconic Press Inc.
Millburn & Short Hills Item [of Item Publishing Co. Inc.] - Millburn, NJ - *BaconPubCkNews 84; Ed&PubIntYB 82; NewsDir 84*
Millburn Short Hills Independent - *See* Passaic Valley Independent Press
Millbury Journal - Millbury, MA - *BaconPubCkNews 84; Ed&PubIntYB 82*
Millcreek Press [Subs. of M.W.H. Ltd.] - Bath, ON, Canada - *WritMar 84*
Millcreek Sun - *See* Brown Thompson Newspapers
Millcreek Valley News [of Cincinnati Suburban Newspapers Inc.] - Cincinnati, OH - *AyerDirPub 83; Ed&PubIntYB 82; NewsDir 84*
Millcreek Valley News - *See* Queen City Suburban Press Inc.
Mille Lacs County Times - Milaca, MN - *AyerDirPub 83; Ed&PubIntYB 82; NewsDir 84*
Mille Lacs Messenger - Isle, MN - *AyerDirPub 83; Ed&PubIntYB 82*
Milledgeville Union Recorder - Milledgeville, GA - *BaconPubCkNews 84*
Millen Industries Inc. - New York, NY - *LitMarPl 83*
Millen News - Millen, GA - *BaconPubCkNews 84; Ed&PubIntYB 82*
Millenium House [Aff. of Millenium House Branch U.L.C.] - Agoura, CA - *BoPubDir 4, 5*
Millennium Design Communications Inc. - New York, NY - *StaDirAdAg 2-84*
Millennium Records - New York, NY - *BillIntBG 83-84*
Millennium Systems Inc. [Subs. of American Microsystems Inc.] - Cupertino, CA - *WhoWMicrocom 83*
Miller Accounting Publications Inc. [Subs. of Harcourt Brace Jovanovich Inc.] - New York, NY - *LitMarPl 83, 84*
Miller, Addison, Steele - New York, NY - *AdAge 3-28-84; StaDirAdAg 2-84*
Miller Advertising Agency - New York, NY - *AdAge 3-28-84; BrCabYB 84; StaDirAdAg 2-84*
Miller Agency Inc., The Peter [Subs. of Lion Entertainment Inc.] - New York, NY - *LitMarPl 83, 84*
Miller-Alpine Photography, Len - Ephraim, UT - *LitMarPl 83, 84; MagIndMarPl 82-83*
Miller & Kreisel Sound Corp. - Culver City, CA - *BillIntBG 83-84*
Miller Associates - DeKalb Junction, NY - *DirPRFirms 83*
Miller Associates, Dick - New York, NY - *Tel&CabFB 84C*
Miller Associates, Howard - Lancaster, PA - *AdAge 3-28-84; StaDirAdAg 2-84*
Miller Books - Alhambra, CA - *BoPubDir 4, 5; WritMar 84*
Miller Cable TV [of Midcontinent Cable Systems Co.] - Miller, SD - *BrCabYB 84; Tel&CabFB 84C*
Miller Co., T. A. - Clifton, NJ - *IntDirMarRes 83*
Miller County Autogran Sentinel - Tuscumbia, MO - *Ed&PubIntYB 82*
Miller County Liberal - Colquitt, GA - *AyerDirPub 83; Ed&PubIntYB 82*
Miller, David - New York, NY - *LitMarPl 83, 84*
Miller Enterprises, Nann - Los Angeles, CA - *DirPRFirms 83*
Miller, Eric - New York, NY - *LitMarPl 83, 84*
Miller Filmaker Inc., Robin - Bethlehem, PA - *AvMarPl 83*
Miller Films, Warren - Hermosa Beach, CA - *Tel&CabFB 84C*
Miller Freeman Publications - San Francisco, CA - *DirMarMP 83; MagIndMarPl 82-83*
Miller Friendt Ludemann Inc. - Lincoln, NE - *ArtMar 84; StaDirAdAg 2-84*
Miller Group, The Bruce - Chicago, IL - *LitMarPl 83, 84*
Miller, Henry S. Jr. - Somerville, MA - *MagIndMarPl 82-83*
Miller Inc., Herman - Zealand, MI - *DirInfWP 82*
Miller, J. Kit - Toronto, ON, Canada - *BoPubDir 4, 5*
Miller, J. McCarthy & June J. - Pensacola, FL - *Tel&CabFB 84C*
Miller, Joan M. - Erie, PA - *LitMarPl 83, 84*
Miller, L. Matthew - New York, NY - *AvMarPl 83*
Miller, Marjorie L. - New York, NY - *LitMarPl 83, 84*
Miller Marketeer, Harold - Miami, FL - *AdAge 3-28-84; StaDirAdAg 2-84*
Miller Media (Spee-d Print) Inc. - Ft. Meyers, FL - *AvMarPl 83*
Miller Meester Advertising - Minneapolis, MN - *AdAge 3-28-84; StaDirAdAg 2-84*
Miller Microcomputer Services - Natick, MA - *MicrocomMPl 83, 84; MicrocomSwDir 1; WhoWMicrocom 83*
Miller News Service - Glencoe, IL - *Ed&PubIntYB 82*
Miller Newspapers - Pittsfield, MA - *Ed&PubIntYB 82*
Miller, O. D. - *See* Total TV Inc.
Miller Pond Books - Thetford Center, VT - *BoPubDir 4, 5*
Miller Press - Miller, MO - *BaconPubCkNews 84; Ed&PubIntYB 82*
Miller Press - Miller, SD - *BaconPubCkNews 84; Ed&PubIntYB 82*
Miller Productions, E. - Cardiff by the Sea, CA - *AvMarPl 83*
Miller Productions Inc. - Austin, TX - *Tel&CabFB 84C*
Miller Productions, Warren - Hermosa, CA - *ArtMar 84*
Miller Publishers Projects Inc., Hughes - New York, NY - *LitMarPl 83, 84*
Miller Publishing Co. - Minneapolis, MN - *DirMarMP 83; MagIndMarPl 82-83*
Miller-Reid Group - Chattanooga, TN - *AdAge 3-28-84; ArtMar 84; StaDirAdAg 2-84*
Miller Research Group - Little Rock, AR - *IntDirMarRes 83*
Miller, Richard A. - York, PA - *Ed&PubIntYB 82*
Miller Services Ltd. - Toronto, ON, Canada - *BaconPubCkNews 84; Ed&PubIntYB 82*
Miller Telephone Co. - Miller, IA - *TelDir&BG 83-84*
Miller Telephone Co. Inc. - Miller, MO - *TelDir&BG 83-84*
Millers Enterprises - Boulder Creek, CA - *BoPubDir 4 Sup, 5*
Miller's Inc., Barney - Lexington, KY - *AvMarPl 83*
Miller's TV Cable Corp. - Watertown, OH - *BrCabYB 84; Tel&CabFB 84C*
Millersburg Cable TV [of Centel Cable Television Co.] - Millersburg, KY - *BrCabYB 84*
Millersburg Community TV System Inc. - Millersburg, OH - *BrCabYB 84 p.D-304; Tel&CabFB 84C*
Millersburg Holmes County Farmer-Hub - Millersburg, OH - *BaconPubCkNews 84*
Millersburg TV Co. - Millersburg, PA - *BrCabYB 84; Tel&CabFB 84C*
Millersburg Upper Dauphin Sentinel - Millersburg, PA - *BaconPubCkNews 84*
Millerton News - Millerton, NY - *BaconPubCkNews 84; Ed&PubIntYB 82*
Millheim Journal - Millheim, PA - *BaconPubCkNews 84; Ed&PubIntYB 82*
Millheim TV Transmission Co. - Millheim, PA - *BrCabYB 84; Tel&CabFB 84C*
Milliagan News Co. Inc. - San Jose, CA - *LitMarPl 83*
Milligan, Harry J. - Sarnia, ON, Canada - *BoPubDir 4, 5*
Milligan, J. G. - Fergus, ON, Canada - *Tel&CabFB 84C*
Milligan News Co. Inc. - San Jose, CA - *LitMarPl 83, 84*
Milligan Syndicate, Patsy - Dundee, IL - *Ed&PubIntYB 82*
Milliken Publishing Co. - St. Louis, MO - *AvMarPl 83; MicrocomMPl 83, 84; MicrocomSwDir 1; WhoWMicrocom 83*
Millimeter - New York, NY - *BaconPubCkMag 84; MagDir 84*
Milling & Baking News [of Sosland Cos. Inc.] - Kansas City, MO - *BaconPubCkMag 84; MagDir 84*
Millington CATV Inc. - Millington, TN - *Tel&CabFB 84C*
Millington, Dale E. - *See* Progressive Communications Inc.

Millington Herald & Lakeville Aerial - Millington, MI - *AyerDirPub 83; BaconPubCkNews 84; NewsDir 84*
Millington Star [of H & C Publications] - Millington, TN - *AyerDirPub 83; BaconPubCkNews 84; Ed&PubIntYB 82; NewsDir 84*
Millington Star Shopper - Millington, TN - *AyerDirPub 83*
Millington Telephone Co. Inc. - Millington, TN - *TelDir&BG 83-84*
Millinocket Katahdin Times - Millinocket, ME - *BaconPubCkNews 84*
Million Dollar Directory [of Dun's Marketing Services] - Parsippany, NJ - *DataDirOnSer 84*
Million Market Newspapers Inc. - New York, NY - *LitMarPl 83, 84*
Millionaire Pastimes - Missouri City, TX - *MicrocomMPl 83, 84*
Millport West Alabama Gazette - Millport, AL - *BaconPubCkNews 84*
Millry Telephone Co. Inc. - Millry, AL - *TelDir&BG 83-84*
Mills Advertising - Los Angeles, CA - *AdAge 3-28-84*
Mills Advertising Inc. - Rancho Dominguez, CA - *StaDirAdAg 2-84*
Mills Agency Inc., The - New York, NY - *DirMarMP 83*
Mills & Associates - Beverly Hills, CA - *DirPRFirms 83*
Mills & Associates, Arnold - Los Angeles, CA - *BillIntBG 83-84*
Mills & Associates, William - Atlanta, GA - *StaDirAdAg 2-84*
Mills & Co. Inc., Richard - Boston, MA - *StaDirAdAg 2-84*
Mills, Charles P. - Huntingdon Valley, PA - *BoPubDir 4, 5*
Mills Communications Inc. - Chicago, IL - *StaDirAdAg 2-84*
Mills Communications Inc. - Oak Brook, IL - *AdAge 3-28-84*
Mills Hall Walborn & Associates - Cleveland, OH - *StaDirAdAg 2-84*
Mills, Ivor J. - Vancouver, BC, Canada - *BoPubDir 4, 5*
Mills Ltd., Robert P. - New York, NY - *LitMarPl 83, 84*
Mills Publishing Co. - Santa Ana, CA - *BoPubDir 4, 5*
Millsboro County Post [of Independent Newspapers Inc.] - Millsboro, DE - *BaconPubCkNews 84; NewsDir 84*
Millsboro Delmarva News - Millsboro, DE - *BaconPubCkNews 84*
Millstadt Enterprise - Millstadt, IL - *BaconPubCkNews 84*
Milltown Mutual Telephone Co. - Milltown, WI - *TelDir&BG 83-84*
Millville Daily [of Times Graphics Inc.] - Millville, NJ - *BaconPubCkNews 84; Ed&PubIntYB 82; NewsDir 84*
Milne Miniatures - New York, NY - *AvMarPl 83*
Milne, Robert Scott - New York, NY - *DataDirOnSer 84*
Milner, Craig S. - Wellesley, MA - *MagIndMarPl 82-83*
Milner-Fenwick Inc. - Timonium, MD - *AvMarPl 83; TelAl 83, 84; Tel&CabFB 84C*
Milner Inc., George - Ponca City, OK - *CabTVFinDB 83*
Milnor Teller - Milnor, ND - *BaconPubCkNews 84*
Milor [of SIA Computer Services] - London, England - *EISS 7-83 Sup*
Milpitas Post [of Meredith Corp.] - Cupertino, CA - *NewsDir 84*
Milpitas Post - Milpitas, CA - *AyerDirPub 83; Ed&PubIntYB 82*
Milpitas Post - *See* Meredith Newspapers
Milprint - Milwaukee, WI - *LitMarPl 83, 84; MagIndMarPl 82-83*
Milroy Cable TV [of De Sutter Cable Inc.] - Milroy, MN - *BrCabYB 84*
Milstadt Enterprise - Milstadt, IL - *Ed&PubIntYB 82*
Milton Cabell Record - Milton, WV - *BaconPubCkNews 84*
Milton Canadian Champion - Milton, ON, Canada - *AyerDirPub 83*
Milton CATV - Milton, PA - *BrCabYB 84; Tel&CabFB 84C*
Milton Courier - Milton, WI - *BaconPubCkNews 84; Ed&PubIntYB 82*
Milton-Freewater Valley Herald - Milton-Freewater, OR - *BaconPubCkNews 84; Ed&PubIntYB 82*
Milton Paper Co. Inc. - New York, NY - *LitMarPl 83, 84*
Milton Press Gazette - Milton, FL - *BaconPubCkNews 84; NewsDir 84*
Milton Record-Transcript - Milton, MA - *Ed&PubIntYB 82*
Milton Record-Transcript - Milton Village, MA - *NewsDir 84*
Milton Record Transcript - *See* Tribune Publishing Co.
Milton Santa Rose Free Press - Milton, FL - *BaconPubCkNews 84*
Milton Society for the Blind, John - New York, NY - *LitMarPl 84*
Milton Standard - Milton, PA - *BaconPubCkNews 84; Ed&PubIntYB 82; NewsDir 84*
Miltonvale Record - Miltonvale, KS - *BaconPubCkNews 84; Ed&PubIntYB 82*
Miltope Corp. - Melville, NY - *DataDirSup 7-83; WhoWMicrocom 83*
Milwaukee Books - Milwaukee, WI - *BoPubDir 5*
Milwaukee Community Journal - Milwaukee, WI - *AyerDirPub 83; BaconPubCkNews 84; NewsDir 84*
Milwaukee County Historical Society - Milwaukee, WI - *BoPubDir 4, 5*
Milwaukee County News - Milwaukee, WI - *NewsDir 84*
Milwaukee Courier [of Courier Communications Corp.] - Milwaukee, WI - *BrCabYB 84; Ed&PubIntYB 82; NewsDir 84*
Milwaukee Courier - *See* Courier Communications Group
Milwaukee Deutsche Zeitung - Milwaukee, WI - *AyerDirPub 83; Ed&PubIntYB 82; NewsDir 84*
Milwaukee Herold - Glendale, WI - *Ed&PubIntYB 82*
Milwaukee Herold - Milwaukee, WI - *NewsDir 84*
Milwaukee Journal [of Newspapers Inc.] - Milwaukee, WI - *ArtMar 84; BaconPubCkNews 84; Ed&PubIntYB 82; LitMarPl 83, 84; NewsBur 6; NewsDir 84*
Milwaukee Labor Press - West Allis, WI - *MagDir 84*
Milwaukee L'Italia Italian News - Milwaukee, WI - *NewsDir 84*
Milwaukee Magazine - Milwaukee, WI - *BaconPubCkMag 84*
Milwaukee MDS Co. - Pasadena, MD - *Tel&CabFB 84C*
Milwaukee Public Museum - Milwaukee, WI - *BoPubDir 4, 5*
Milwaukee Repertory Theatre - Milwaukee, WI - *WritMar 84*
Milwaukee Sentinel [of The Journal Co.] - Milwaukee, WI - *BaconPubCkNews 84; Ed&PubIntYB 82; LitMarPl 83, 84; NewsBur 6; NewsDir 84*
Milwaukee South Side Bay Viewer [of South Milwaukee Voice-Journal] - South Milwaukee, WI - *NewsDir 84*
Milwaukee Star [of Courier Communications Corp.] - Milwaukee, WI - *AyerDirPub 83; NewsDir 84*
Milwaukee Star - *See* Courier Communications Group
Milwaukie Clackamas County Review - Milwaukie, OR - *BaconPubCkNews 84*
Mimic Music - Smyrna, GA - *BillIntBG 83-84*
Mimir Publishers Inc. - Madison, WI - *BoPubDir 4, 5; WritMar 84*
Mimsa Music - Phoenixville, PA - *AvMarPl 83*
Min Microcomputer Software Inc. - Norcross, GA - *MicrocomMPl 83; WhoWMicrocom 83*
Mina Press - Sebastopol, CA - *BoPubDir 4 Sup, 5; LitMag&SmPr 83-84*
Minburn Telephone Co. - Minburn, IA - *TelDir&BG 83-84*
Minco Minstrel - Minco, OK - *Ed&PubIntYB 82*
Minco Minstrel - *See* Star Publishing Co.
Mincron SBC Corp. - New York, NY - *ADAPSOMemDir 83-84*
Mind Over Matter - Black Mountain, NC - *LitMag&SmPr 83-84*
Mind Over Matter Newsletter - Black Mountain, NC - *LitMag&SmPr 83-84*
Mind Systems Corp. - Northampton, MA - *MicrocomMPl 84*
Mind to Sound - *See* McGinnis & Marx Music Publishers
Mind Your Own Business at Home - Chicago, IL - *LitMag&SmPr 83-84*
Mindata Ltd. - London, England - *MicroMarPl 82-83*
Minden City Herald - Minden City, MI - *BaconPubCkNews 84; Ed&PubIntYB 82*
Minden Courier - Minden, NE - *AyerDirPub 83; BaconPubCkNews 84*
Minden Press-Herald - Minden, LA - *BaconPubCkNews 84; Ed&PubIntYB 82; NewsDir 84*
Mindlin, Leon - New York, NY - *MagIndMarPl 82-83*
Mind's Eye Music - Raleigh, NC - *BillIntBG 83-84*
Mine & Quarry - London, England - *WritMar 84*
Mine & Quarry Trader - Indianapolis, IN - *MagDir 84*
Mine Development Monthly - Boulder, CO - *BaconPubCkMag 84*
Mine-Equip - Lakewood, CO - *DirOnDB Spring 84*
Mine-Equip [of CompuServe Inc.] - Columbus, OH - *DataDirOnSer 84*
Mineola American - Mineola, NY - *BaconPubCkNews 84; Ed&PubIntYB 82; NewsDir 84*

Mineola Cable TV [of Texas Community Antennas Inc.] - Mineola, TX - *BrCabYB 84*
Mineola Monitor - Mineola, TX - *BaconPubCkNews 84; Ed&PubIntYB 82*
Mineola Williston Times - *See* Litmore Publications
Miner - Kingman, AZ - *AyerDirPub 83*
Miner - Ely, MN - *AyerDirPub 83*
Miner - Newport, WA - *AyerDirPub 83*
Miner & News - Kenora, ON, Canada - *AyerDirPub 83*
Miner County Pioneer - Howard, SD - *AyerDirPub 83; Ed&PubIntYB 82*
Miner, The - Clarks Summit, PA - *AyerDirPub 83*
Mineral Area Cablevision Co. [of Omega Communications Inc.] - Flat River, MO - *BrCabYB 84; Tel&CabFB 84C*
Mineral County Independent-News - Hawthorne, NV - *AyerDirPub 83*
Mineral County Miner - Creede, CO - *Ed&PubIntYB 82*
Mineral Daily News Tribune - Keyser, WV - *AyerDirPub 83; Ed&PubIntYB 82*
Mineral Independent - Superior, MT - *AyerDirPub 83; Ed&PubIntYB 82*
Mineral Information Section [of Natural Environment Research Council] - London, England - *EISS 5-84 Sup*
Mineral King Publishing - Exeter, CA - *BaconPubCkNews 84*
Mineral Point Iowa County Democrat Tribune - Mineral Point, WI - *BaconPubCkNews 84*
Mineral Processing [of Canada Centre for Mineral & Energy Technology] - Ottawa, ON, Canada - *DataDirOnSer 84*
Mineral Processing Technology [of QL Systems Ltd.] - Ottawa, ON, Canada - *DataDirOnSer 84*
Mineral River Records - Dover, NH - *BillIntBG 83-84*
Mineral Wells Index - Mineral Wells, TX - *AyerDirPub 83; BaconPubCkNews 84; NewsDir 84*
Mineral Wells Palo Pinto County Star - Mineral Wells, TX - *BaconPubCkNews 84*
Mineral Wells Reporter - Mineral Wells, TX - *AyerDirPub 83; BaconPubCkNews 84; Ed&PubIntYB 82*
Mineralogical Abstracts [of Mineralogical Society of Great Britain] - London, England - *EISS 7-83 Sup*
Minerals Data System [of University of Oklahoma] - Norman, OK - *DataDirOnSer 84; DirOnDB Spring 84*
Minerals Information & Analysis Directorate [of U.S. Bureau of Mines] - Washington, DC - *EISS 83*
Mineroff Electronics - Valley Stream, NY - *DirInfWP 82*
Minerva [of Overseas Telecommunications Commission] - Sydney, Australia - *TeleSy&SerDir 2-84*
Minerva Books Ltd. - New York, NY - *LitMarPl 83, 84*
Minerva Consulting Group Inc. - New York, NY - *BoPubDir 4, 5; LitMarPl 83, 84*
Minerva Leader - Minerva, OH - *Ed&PubIntYB 82; NewsDir 84*
Minerva Leader - *See* Alliance Publishing Co.
Minerva Mikrofilm A/S - Ehlersvej, Denmark - *MicroMarPl 82-83*
Minerva Valley Telephone Co. Inc. - Zearing, IA - *TelDir&BG 83-84*
Mines Magazine, The - Golden, CO - *BaconPubCkMag 84; MagDir 84*
Minesearch - Boulder, CO - *DirOnDB Spring 84*
MINET [of GTE Telenet] - Vienna, VA - *DataDirOnSer 84*
Minford Telephone Co. - Minford, OH - *TelDir&BG 83-84*
Mingo-Jones Advertising Inc. - New York, NY - *StaDirAdAg 2-84*
Mini Business Systems Inc. - Southfield, MI - *MicrocomMPl 84; WhoWMicrocom 83*
Mini-Computer Systems Inc. - Elmsford, NY - *DirInfWP 82*
Mini/Micro Advisor [of Alexander Hamilton Institute Inc.] - New York, NY - *MicrocomMPl 84*
Mini/Micro Bulletin [of Averbach Publishers Inc.] - Pennsauken, NJ - *DirOnDB Spring 84; MicrocomMPl 84*
Mini-Micro Computer Report - Annandale, VA - *BaconPubCkMag 84*
Mini-Micro Systems [of Cahners Publishing Inc.] - Boston, MA - *BaconPubCkMag 84; Folio 83; MagDir 84; MagIndMarPl 82-83; WritMar 84*
Mini Movie Reviews [of Cineman Syndicate] - Middletown, NY - *DataDirOnSer 84*
Mini-Probe Corp. - Rego Park, NY - *ADAPSOMemDir 83-84; DataDirOnSer 84*
Mini Records Inc. [Div. of Prospo Records] - Brooklyn, NY - *BillIntBG 83-84*
Mini-Truck - Costa Mesa, CA - *BaconPubCkMag 84*
Mini-Word Editions - Champaign, IL - *BoPubDir 4 Sup, 5*
Miniature Collector [of Acquire Publishing Co. Inc.] - New York, NY - *WritMar 84*
Miniature Magazine, The - Newton, NJ - *MagIndMarPl 82-83*
Miniatures & Doll Dealer [of Boynton & Associates Inc.] - Clifton, VA - *ArtMar 84; MagDir 84; WritMar 84*
Minicom - Walnut Creek, CA - *AvMarPl 83*
Minicom - Cherry Hill, NJ - *WhoWMicrocom 83*
Minicom Data Corp. - Willowdale, ON, Canada - *DataDirSup 7-83*
Minicomputer Co. of Maryland Inc., The - Linthicum, MD - *ADAPSOMemDir 83-84*
Minicomputer Modeling Inc. - Seattle, WA - *MicrocomSwDir 1*
Minicomputer Press - Richboro, PA - *BoPubDir 4, 5*
Minicomputer Systems Inc. - Boulder, CO - *WhoWMicrocom 83*
Minidata Ltd. - Mississauga, ON, Canada - *DataDirOnSer 84*
Minidata Services Inc. - Parsippany, NJ - *ADAPSOMemDir 83-84*
Minidoka County News - Rupert, ID - *AyerDirPub 83; Ed&PubIntYB 82*
Minier Olympia Review - Minier, IL - *BaconPubCkNews 84*
Minimal-Input Cataloguing System [of Loughborough University of Technology Library] - Loughborough, England - *EISS 83*
Minimax Research Corp. - Berkeley, CA - *ADAPSOMemDir 83-84*
Mining Association of Canada - Toronto, ON, Canada - *BoPubDir 4, 5*
Mining Congress Journal - Washington, DC - *MagIndMarPl 82-83*
Mining Engineering - Littleton, CO - *BaconPubCkMag 84; MagDir 84*
Mining Equipment International - New York, NY - *BaconPubCkMag 84; MagDir 84; MagIndMarPl 82-83*
Mining Gazette - Houghton, MI - *AyerDirPub 83*
Mining Journal - Chicago, IL - *MagDir 84*
Mining Journal - Marquette, MI - *AyerDirPub 83; Ed&PubIntYB 82*
Mining Magazine - Chicago, IL - *BaconPubCkMag 84; MagDir 84*
Mining News - Florence, WI - *AyerDirPub 83; Ed&PubIntYB 82*
Mining/Processing Equipment - Dover, NJ - *BaconPubCkMag 84; MagDir 84*
Mining Record - Denver, CO - *BaconPubCkMag 84; MagDir 84*
Mining Review - Rich Hill, MO - *AyerDirPub 83*
Mining Technology [of Canada Centre for Mineral & Energy Technology] - Ottawa, ON, Canada - *CompReadDB 82; DataDirOnSer 84*
Mining Technology Clearing House [of Organisation for Economic Co-Operation & Development] - Tamworth, England - *EISS 83*
MiniScribe Corp. - Longmont, CO - *DataDirSup 7-83; MicrocomMPl 84*
Minisis [of Systemhouse Ltd.] - Ottawa, ON, Canada - *EISS 83*
Ministere de l'Agriculture - *See* Reseau de Documentation en Economie Agricole
Ministere des Affaires Economiques (Bibliotheque-Fonds Quetelet) - Brussels, Belgium - *CompReadDB 82*
Ministry of Communications - Jerusalem, Israel - *TeleSy&SerDir 2-84*
Ministry of Culture & Recreation (Citizen's Inquiry Bureau) - Toronto, ON, Canada - *CompReadDB 82*
Minitab Project - University Park, PA - *ADAPSOMemDir 83-84; DataDirSup 7-83; MicrocomSwDir 1*
Miniware Inc. - Annapolis, MD - *MicrocomMPl 84; MicrocomSwDir 1*
Mink, Randy - Bolingbrook, IL - *Ed&PubIntYB 82*
Minkus Publications Inc. - New York, NY - *BoPubDir 4 Sup, 5*
Minkus Stamp & Coin Journal - New York, NY - *MagIndMarPl 82-83*
Minn-Kota Cable TV [of Northern Communications Associates] - Wahpeton, ND - *BrCabYB 84; Tel&CabFB 84C*
Minne Ha! Ha! - Minneapolis, MN - *ArtMar 84; LitMag&SmPr 83-84*
Minneapolis Institute of Arts [Aff. of Minneapolis Society of Fine Arts] - Minneapolis, MN - *BoPubDir 4, 5*

Minneapolis Labor Review [of Minneapolis Central Labor Union Council] - Minneapolis, MN - *NewsDir 84*
Minneapolis MDS Co. - New York, NY - *Tel&CabFB 84C*
Minneapolis Messenger - Minneapolis, KS - *BaconPubCkNews 84; Ed&PubIntYB 82*
Minneapolis Public Library & Information Center - Minneapolis, MN - *DataDirOnSer 84*
Minneapolis Spokesman - Minneapolis, MN - *AyerDirPub 83; BaconPubCkNews 84*
Minneapolis Spokesman & Recorder - Minneapolis, MN - *Ed&PubIntYB 82*
Minneapolis-St. Paul Magazine - Minneapolis, MN - *ArtMar 84; BaconPubCkMag 84; LitMarPl 83, 84; MagDir 84; MagIndMarPl 82-83; WritMar 84*
Minneapolis St. Paul Recorder, The - St. Paul, MN - *NewsDir 84*
Minneapolis Star - Minneapolis, MN - *Ed&PubIntYB 82; NewsBur 6*
Minneapolis Star & Tribune [of Cowles Media Co.] - Minneapolis, MN - *AyerDirPub 83; BaconPubCkNews 84; InfoS 83-84; LitMarPl 83, 84; NewsDir 84*
Minneapolis Tribune - Minneapolis, MN - *BoPubDir 4, 5; Ed&PubIntYB 82; NewsBur 6; NewsDir 84*
Minneapolis Tribune Sunday Picture - Minneapolis, MN - *MagIndMarPl 82-83*
Minneapolis Twin Cities Courier - Minneapolis, MN - *BaconPubCkNews 84; NewsDir 84*
Minneapolis Valley Telephone Co. [Aff. of Larson Utilities Inc.] - Franklin, MN - *TelDir&BG 83-84*
Minnedosa Tribune - Minnedosa, MB, Canada - *Ed&PubIntYB 82*
Minneola Record - Minneola, KS - *BaconPubCkNews 84*
Minneota Cable TV - Minneota, MN - *BrCabYB 84*
Minneota Mascot - Minneota, MN - *BaconPubCkNews 84*
Minnesota AAA Motorist - Burnsville, MN - *MagDir 84*
Minnesota All-Channel Cablevision Inc. [of Horizon Communications Corp.] - Alexandria, MN - *Tel&CabFB 84C*
Minnesota All-Channel Cablevision Inc. [of Horizon Communications Corp.] - Clarissa, MN - *Tel&CabFB 84C*
Minnesota All-Channel Cablevision Inc. [of Horizon Communications Corp.] - Glenwood, MN - *Tel&CabFB 84C*
Minnesota All-Channel Cablevision Inc. [of Horizon Communications Corp.] - Long Prairie, MN - *Tel&CabFB 84C*
Minnesota All-Channel Cablevision Inc. [of Horizon Communications Corp.] - Melrose, MN - *Tel&CabFB 84C*
Minnesota All-Channel Cablevision Inc. [of Horizon Communications Corp.] - Osakis, MN - *Tel&CabFB 84C*
Minnesota All-Channel Cablevision Inc. [of Horizon Communications Corp.] - Park Rapids, MN - *Tel&CabFB 84C*
Minnesota All-Channel Cablevision Inc. [of Horizon Communications Corp.] - Sauk Centre, MN - *Tel&CabFB 84C*
Minnesota All-Channel Cablevision Inc. [of Horizon Communications Corp.] - Staples, MN - *Tel&CabFB 84C*
Minnesota All-Channel Cablevision Inc. [of Horizon Communications Corp.] - Wadena, MN - *Tel&CabFB 84C*
Minnesota Business Journal [of Update Publications Service Inc.] - Minneapolis, MN - *BaconPubCkMag 84; MagDir 84*
Minnesota Cable Enterprises [of Harmon & Co. Inc.] - Balaton, MN - *BrCabYB 84; Tel&CabFB 84C*
Minnesota Cable Enterprises [of Harmon & Co. Inc.] - Tracy, MN - *BrCabYB 84; Tel&CabFB 84C*
Minnesota Cablesystems Southwest - Eden Prairie, MN - *BrCabYB 84; Tel&CabFB 84C*
Minnesota CATV [of American TV & Communications Corp.] - Mankato, MN - *BrCabYB 84; Tel&CabFB 84C*
Minnesota Chemist [of Sexton Printing Inc.] - Minneapolis, MN - *BaconPubCkMag 84; MagDir 84*
Minnesota Cities [of League of Minnesota Cities] - St. Paul, MN - *BaconPubCkMag 84; MagDir 84*
Minnesota Daily, The - Minneapolis, MN - *NewsDir 84*
Minnesota Educational Computing Consortium - St. Paul, MN - *DataDirOnSer 84; EISS 83; MicrocomMPl 84; WhoWMicrocom 83*
Minnesota Food Guide [of Minnesota Food Retailers Association] - St. Paul, MN - *BaconPubCkMag 84; MagDir 84*
Minnesota Historical Society (Archives & Manuscripts Div.) - St. Paul, MN - *MicroMarPl 82-83*
Minnesota Historical Society Press - St. Paul, MN - *LitMarPl 83, 84*
Minnesota History - St. Paul, MN - *MagIndMarPl 82-83*
Minnesota Horticulturist, The - St. Paul, MN - *MagDir 84*
Minnesota Interconnect - Bloomington, MN - *CabTVPrDB 83*
Minnesota Interlibrary Telecommunications Exchange [of Minnesota Higher Education Coordinating Board] - Minneapolis, MN - *EISS 83; InfIndMarPl 83*
Minnesota Lake Telephone Co. - Minnesota Lake, MN - *TelDir&BG 83-84*
Minnesota Lake Tribune - Minnesota Lake, MN - *BaconPubCkNews 84; Ed&PubIntYB 82*
Minnesota Land Management Information System [of Minnesota State Planning Agency] - St. Paul, MN - *EISS 83*
Minnesota Library Association - Rosemount, MN - *BoPubDir 5*
Minnesota Literature Newsletter - Minneapolis, MN - *LitMag&SmPr 83-84*
Minnesota Medicine - Minneapolis, MN - *BaconPubCkMag 84; MagDir 84*
Minnesota Mining & Manufacturing Co. - St. Paul, MN - *HomeVid&CabYB 82-83*
Minnesota Motorist Home & Away - Burnsville, MN - *BaconPubCkMag 84*
Minnesota Natural Heritage Program [of Minnesota State Dept. of Natural Resources] - St. Paul, MN - *EISS 7-83 Sup*
Minnesota Newspaper Association - Minneapolis, MN - *ProGuPRSer 4*
Minnesota P-H-C Contractor [of Minnesota Master Plumber Publishing Co.] - Minneapolis, MN - *MagDir 84*
Minnesota Pharmacist - Minneapolis, MN - *BaconPubCkMag 84*
Minnesota Pharmacist [of Minnesota State Pharmaceutical Association] - St. Paul, MN - *MagDir 84*
Minnesota Plumbing-Heating-Cooling Contractor - Minneapolis, MN - *BaconPubCkMag 84*
Minnesota Public Employee [of Minnesota State Employees Union] - St. Paul, MN - *NewsDir 84*
Minnesota Public Radio - St. Paul, MN - *LitMarPl 83*
Minnesota Public Television Association - St. Paul, MN - *BrCabYB 84*
Minnesota Review Press, The - Corvallis, OR - *LitMag&SmPr 83-84*
Minnesota Review, The - Corvallis, OR - *LitMag&SmPr 83-84*
Minnesota Scholarly Press Inc. - Mankato, MN - *LitMarPl 83, 84; MagIndMarPl 82-83*
Minnesota Smoke-Eater [of Smoke-Eater Publications] - Pierce, NE - *MagDir 84*
Minnesota Software Inc. - White Bear Lake, MN - *MicrocomMPl 83*
Minnesota Sportsman - Oshkosh, WI - *BaconPubCkMag 84*
Minnesota State Demography Unit [of Minnesota State Dept. of Energy, Planning & Development] - St. Paul, MN - *EISS 7-83 Sup*
Minnesota State Documents Center [Aff. of Minnesota State Dept. of Administration] - St. Paul, MN - *BoPubDir 4 Sup, 5*
Minnesota State University System (Project for Automation of Library Systems) - Mankato, MN - *EISS 83*
Minnesota Technolog - Minneapolis, MN - *BaconPubCkMag 84*
Minnesota Tooling & Machining Association Journal - Minneapolis, MN - *BaconPubCkMag 84; MagDir 84*
Minnesota Valley/Burnsville Sun - *See* Sun Newspapers
Minnesotan Science Fiction Reader, The - Golden Valley, MN - *WritMar 84*
Minnewaukan Benson County Farmers Press - Minnewaukan, ND - *BaconPubCkNews 84*
Minnewaukan Cable TV Inc. - Minnewaukan, ND - *BrCabYB 84; Tel&CabFB 84C*
Minnick & Associates Inc., W. F. - Pittsburgh, PA - *StaDirAdAg 2-84*
Minnie Music Inc. - Las Vegas, NV - *BillIntBG 83-84*
Minocqua Lakeland Times - Minocqua, WI - *BaconPubCkNews 84; NewsDir 84*
Minolta Corp. - Ramsey, NJ - *AvMarPl 83*
Minolta Corp. (Business Equipment Div.) - Ramsey, NJ - *DirInfWP 82*
Minonk News-Dispatch - Minonk, IL - *BaconPubCkNews 84*
Minor, Bruce K. - Leawood, KS - *TeleSy&SerDir 2-84*
Minor Planets, Comets, & Satellites Dept. [of Academy of Sciences of the USSR] - Leningrad, USSR - *EISS 83*

Minority Builder [of C. J. Kent Enterprises Inc.] - Reston, VA - *MagDir 84*
Minority Engineer - Greenlawn, NY - *BaconPubCkMag 84*
Minority Features Syndicate Inc. - Farrell, PA - *Ed&PubIntYB 82*
Minority Rights Group Inc. - New York, NY - *BoPubDir 4 Sup, 5*
Minority Rights Group Reports - London, England - *LitMag&SmPr 83-84*
Minority Vendor Information Service [of National Minority Supplier Development Council Inc.] - New York, NY - *EISS 83*
Minos SA - Athens, Greece - *StaDirAdAg 2-84*
Minot Daily News - Grand Forks, ND - *NewsDir 84*
Minot Daily News - Minot, ND - *BaconPubCkNews 84; Ed&PubIntYB 82*
Minotaur - Burlingame, CA - *LitMag&SmPr 83-84*
Minproc - Ottawa, ON, Canada - *DirOnDB Spring 84*
Minster Community Post - Minster, OH - *BaconPubCkNews 84*
Minstrel - Chickasha, OK - *AyerDirPub 83*
MinSys [of Geosystems] - Cambridge, MA - *DataDirOnSer 84*
MinSys [of Geosystems] - London, England - *DBBus 82; DirOnDB Spring 84*
Mint Productions - New York, NY - *BoPubDir 4, 5*
Mint Software Inc. - Baton Rouge, LA - *MicrocomMPl 83, 84*
Mintec - Ottawa, ON, Canada - *DirOnDB Spring 84*
Mintmark Press Ltd. - Toronto, ON, Canada - *BoPubDir 4, 5*
Minton Communications Inc. - New York, NY - *BrCabYB 84*
Minturn Advertising Inc. - Kansas City, MO - *StaDirAdAg 2-84*
Mintz & Hoke - Avon, CT - *AdAge 3-28-84; DirPRFirms 83; StaDirAdAg 2-84*
Mintz Opinion Sampling, Gloria - North Miami Beach, FL - *IntDirMarRes 83*
Mintz/Public Relations Advertising, Bennett J. - Encino, CA - *ArtMar 84; DirPRFirms 83*
Minute Mail Electronic Message Service [of Mail Boxes Etc. USA] - Carlsbad, CA - *TeleSy&SerDir 2-84*
Minute-Man Publications Inc. - Lexington, MA - *BaconPubCkNews 84*
Minute Messages - Raleigh, NC - *Ed&PubIntYB 82*
Minuteman - Great Falls, MT - *AyerDirPub 83*
Minzer, Karen [Aff. of Paris & Co.] - Dallas, TX - *BoPubDir 4, 5*
Mio Oscoda County News - Mio, MI - *BaconPubCkNews 84*
Miorita - Rochester, NY - *LitMag&SmPr 83-84*
Miprog - Minneapolis, MN - *MicrocomMPl 83, 84*
MIR, PA - Pittsburgh, PA - *BoPubDir 4, 5*
MIR Publication Society - Grand Forks, BC, Canada - *BoPubDir 4, 5*
MIRA Corp. - Birmingham, MI - *BrCabYB 84*
Mira Mesa Pennysaver/East & West - Mission Viejo, CA - *AyerDirPub 83*
Miracle Computing - Lawrence, KS - *MicrocomMPl 84; MicrocomSwDir 1*
Miracle-Joy Publications - Hackensack, NJ - *BillIntBG 83-84*
Miracle Mile Music - *See* Respect Music Co.
Miraculous Medal, The - Philadelphia, PA - *WritMar 84*
Mirage Concepts Inc. - Fresno, CA - *MicrocomMPl 84*
Mirage Records Inc. - Stamford, CT - *BillIntBG 83-84*
Miraleste Music - *See* Delvy Enterprises Inc., Richard
Miramar Mirror - Ft. Lauderdale, FL - *AyerDirPub 83*
Miramar Mirror, The - Miramar, FL - *Ed&PubIntYB 82*
Miramichi Leader - Newcastle, NB, Canada - *AyerDirPub 83; Ed&PubIntYB 82*
Miramichi Weekend - Chatham, NB, Canada - *AyerDirPub 83; Ed&PubIntYB 82*
Miriam Press Inc. - Alexandria, VA - *LitMag&SmPr 83-84*
Miricott Music - *See* Espy Music Group
Mirisch Corp. - Culver City, CA - *LitMarPl 83*
Miro Music Inc. - New York, NY - *BillIntBG 83-84*
Miro Packaging Corp. - Ft. Lee, NJ - *LitMarPl 83, 84*
Mirror - Jensen Beach, FL - *AyerDirPub 83; NewsDir 84*
Mirror - Monroe, IA - *AyerDirPub 83*
Mirror - Newell, IA - *AyerDirPub 83*
Mirror - Richland, MO - *AyerDirPub 83*
Mirror - Altoona, PA - *AyerDirPub 83*
Mirror - Cranston, RI - *AyerDirPub 83*
Mirror - Gilmer, TX - *AyerDirPub 83*
Mirror - Gladewater, TX - *AyerDirPub 83*
Mirror - McGregor, TX - *AyerDirPub 83*
Mirror - Midlothian, TX - *AyerDirPub 83*
Mirror - Wolfe City, TX - *AyerDirPub 83*
Mirror - Sooke, BC, Canada - *AyerDirPub 83; Ed&PubIntYB 82*
Mirror - Macklin, SK, Canada - *AyerDirPub 83*
Mirror - Maidstone, SK, Canada - *AyerDirPub 83*
Mirror-Democrat - Mt. Carroll, IL - *Ed&PubIntYB 82*
Mirror-Exchange - Milan, TN - *AyerDirPub 83*
Mirror Images Software Inc. - Troy, NY - *MicrocomMPl 84; MicrocomSwDir 1*
Mirror News [of Market Power Inc.] - Hopkins, MN - *BaconPubCkMag 84; MagDir 84*
Mirror-Recorder - Stamford, NY - *AyerDirPub 83*
Mirror Records Inc. - Rochester, NY - *BillIntBG 83-84*
Mirror-Republican - Mansfield, MO - *AyerDirPub 83*
Mirror-Sun - Lyons, NE - *AyerDirPub 83*
Mirror, The - Milan, IL - *Ed&PubIntYB 82*
Mirror, The [of Scripps-Howard Newspapers] - Louisville, KY - *NewsDir 84*
Mirror, The - Springfield, MO - *NewsDir 84*
Mirror, The - Missouri City, TX - *AyerDirPub 83*
Mirror, The - Halifax, NS, Canada - *AyerDirPub 83*
Mirror, The - Middleton, NS, Canada - *Ed&PubIntYB 82*
Mirsky, Mike - Santa Monica, CA - *LitMarPl 83, 84*
Mirus Music Inc. - Cleveland, OH - *BillIntBG 83-84*
Mirus Publishing Corp. - Cleveland, OH - *BillIntBG 83-84*
MIS - Boulder Creek, CA - *MicrocomMPl 83, 84*
MIS Syndications/Interpublic Television - New York, NY - *Tel&CabFB 84C*
MIS Week [of Fairchild Publications] - New York, NY - *BaconPubCkMag 84; MagIndMarPl 82-83; MicrocomMPl 84*
Misamore Advertising & Public Relations - Grand Rapids, MI - *DirPRFirms 83; StaDirAdAg 2-84*
Misar Industries - Irvine, CA - *DataDirSup 7-83*
Miscellaneous Graphics - Chicago, IL - *LitMarPl 83, 84*
Misco Cable TV Co. - Draper, UT - *Tel&CabFB 84C p.1692*
Misco Computer Services - Miami, FL - *ADAPSOMemDir 83-84*
Misco-Draper Ltd. [of Misco Cable TV Co.] - Draper, UT - *Tel&CabFB 84C*
Misco Inc. - Marlboro, NJ - *MicrocomMPl 84; WhoWMicrocom 83*
Misco-Kuna Ltd. [of Misco Cable TV Co.] - Kuna, ID - *Tel&CabFB 84C*
Misco-Morgan Ltd. [of Misco Cable TV Co.] - Morgan, UT - *Tel&CabFB 84C*
Mishawaka Enterprise Record - Mishawaka, IN - *AyerDirPub 83; BaconPubCkNews 84*
Mishawaka Enterprise-Record - North Liberty, IN - *NewsDir 84*
Misol Inc. - Austin, TX - *MicrocomSwDir 1*
Misosys - Alexandria, VA - *MicrocomMPl 83, 84; MicrocomSwDir 1*
Miss Jackie Music - Overland Park, KS - *BoPubDir 4, 5*
Missco Shoppers Guide, The - Osceola, AR - *AyerDirPub 83*
Missile - Wyndmere, ND - *AyerDirPub 83*
Missing Links Products - Colorado Springs, CO - *MicrocomMPl 84*
Missiology, An International Review - Pasadena, CA - *MagIndMarPl 82-83*
Mission Argyle Productions Inc. - Los Angeles, CA - *StaDirAdAg 2-84*
Mission Associates - San Juan Capistrano, CA - *StaDirAdAg 2-84*
Mission Aviation Fellowship - Redland, CA - *ArtMar 84*
Mission Bay/Crown Point Pennysaver - Mission Viejo, CA - *AyerDirPub 83*
Mission Computers - Billerica, MA - *MicrocomMPl 83, 84*
Mission Dolores Publishers - Burlingame, CA - *BoPubDir 4, 5*
Mission Hills Pennysaver - Mission Viejo, CA - *AyerDirPub 83*
Mission Hills Sun [of Overland Park Sun Newspapers] - Shawnee Mission, KS - *NewsDir 84*
Mission Hills Sun - *See* Sun Publications
Mission Press - Kenwood, CA - *BoPubDir 4, 5*
Mission Publishing Co. - Greenwich, CT - *BoPubDir 4, 5*
Mission Todd County Tribune - Mission, SD - *BaconPubCkNews 84*

Mission Upper Valley Progress - Mission, TX - *BaconPubCkNews 84*
Mission Valley News - Ronan, MT - *Ed&PubIntYB 82*
Mission Valley Review - Lompoc, CA - *AyerDirPub 83*
Mission Valley/Santa Ynez Valley Review - Lompoc, CA - *Ed&PubIntYB 82*
Mission Viejo North/North Park South Pennysaver - Mission Viejo, CA - *AyerDirPub 83*
Mission Viejo Pennysaver/North & South - Mission Viejo, CA - *AyerDirPub 83*
Missions Advanced Research & Communication Center [Aff. of World Vision International] - Monrovia, CA - *BoPubDir 4, 5; EISS 83*
Missisquoi Historical Society - Stanbridge East, PQ, Canada - *BoPubDir 4, 5*
Mississauga News - Mississauga, ON, Canada - *AyerDirPub 83; Ed&PubIntYB 82*
Mississauga Times, The - Mississauga, ON, Canada - *Ed&PubIntYB 82*
Mississippi Banker [of Mississippi Banker's Association] - Jackson, MS - *BaconPubCkMag 84; MagDir 84*
Mississippi Educator, The - Jackson, MS - *BaconPubCkMag 84; MagDir 84*
Mississippi EPA News - Jackson, MS - *BaconPubCkMag 84; MagDir 84*
Mississippi Farm Bureau News - Jackson, MS - *BaconPubCkMag 84; MagDir 84*
Mississippi Game & Fish [of Game & Fish Publications Inc.] - Marietta, GA - *BaconPubCkMag 84; WritMar 84*
Mississippi Grocers Guide - Jackson, MS - *BaconPubCkMag 84; MagDir 84*
Mississippi Magazine - Jackson, MS - *BaconPubCkMag 84; MagDir 84*
Mississippi Memo Digest - Meridian, MS - *AyerDirPub 83; Ed&PubIntYB 82*
Mississippi Mud [of Mud Press] - Portland, OR - *LitMag&SmPr 83-84*
Mississippi Pharmacist - Jackson, MS - *BaconPubCkMag 84*
Mississippi Press - Pascagoula, MS - *AyerDirPub 83; Ed&PubIntYB 82*
Mississippi Press Register - Pascagoula, MS - *AyerDirPub 83; BaconPubCkNews 84; Ed&PubIntYB 82; NewsDir 84*
Mississippi Research & Development Center - Jackson, MS - *BoPubDir 4, 5*
Mississippi Review [of University of Southern Mississippi] - Hattiesburg, MS - *LitMag&SmPr 83-84; WritMar 84*
Mississippi River Music Publishing - *See* Ahlert Music Corp., Fred
Mississippi State University Alumnus [of Mississippi State University] - Mississippi State, MS - *WritMar 84*
Mississippi Telephone & Communications Inc. [Aff. of Century Telephone Enterprises Inc.] - Olive Branch, MS - *TelDir&BG 83-84*
Mississippi Telephone Corp. - Leakesville, MS - *TelDir&BG 83-84*
Mississippi Valley Review [of Western Illinois University] - Macomb, IL - *LitMag&SmPr 83-84; WritMar 84*
Missoulian [of Lee Enterprises Inc.] - Missoula, MT - *AyerDirPub 83; BaconPubCkNews 84; Ed&PubIntYB 82; NewsDir 84*
Missouri Beef Cattleman - Kansas City, MO - *BaconPubCkMag 84; MagDir 84*
Missouri Beverage Journal [of N.W. Beverage Journal Inc.] - Minneapolis, MN - *BaconPubCkMag 84; MagDir 84*
Missouri Business - Jefferson City, MO - *BaconPubCkMag 84*
Missouri City Mirror - Missouri City, TX - *BaconPubCkNews 84*
Missouri Div. of Geology & Land Survey [of Missouri Dept. of Natural Resources] - Rolla, MO - *BoPubDir 4, 5*
Missouri Engineer [of Missouri Society of Professional Engineers] - Jefferson City, MO - *BaconPubCkMag 84; MagDir 84*
Missouri Farm Bureau News - Jefferson City, MO - *BaconPubCkMag 84; MagDir 84*
Missouri Grocer - Springfield, MO - *BaconPubCkMag 84*
Missouri Herald - Hayti, MO - *AyerDirPub 83; Ed&PubIntYB 82*
Missouri Life - Columbia, MO - *BaconPubCkMag 84; MagDir 84; MagIndMarPl 82-83; WritMar 84*
Missouri Life Publishing Co. - Columbia, MO - *DirMarMP 83*
Missouri Medicine - Jefferson City, MO - *BaconPubCkMag 84; MagDir 84*
Missouri Municipal Review [of Missouri Municipal League] - Jefferson City, MO - *BaconPubCkMag 84; MagDir 84*
Missouri Oil Jobber [of Missouri Oil Jobbers Association] - Jefferson City, MO - *BaconPubCkMag 84; MagDir 84*
Missouri Pharmacist [of Missouri Pharmaceutical Association] - Jefferson City, MO - *BaconPubCkMag 84; MagDir 84*
Missouri Press Clipping Bureau - Columbia, MO - *ProGuPRSer 4*
Missouri Press News - Columbia, MO - *BaconPubCkMag 84; MagDir 84*
Missouri Realtor, The [of Missouri Association of Realtors] - Columbia, MO - *BaconPubCkMag 84; MagDir 84*
Missouri Restaurant, The - Kansas City, MO - *BaconPubCkMag 84*
Missouri Review, The - Columbia, MO - *LitMag&SmPr 83-84*
Missouri Ruralist [of Harcourt Brace Jovanovich Inc.] - Columbia, MO - *ArtMar 84; BaconPubCkMag 84; MagDir 84; MagIndMarPl 82-83; WritMar 84*
Missouri Shamrock - Columbia, MO - *BaconPubCkMag 84; MagDir 84*
Missouri State Data Center [of Missouri State Library] - Jefferson City, MO - *EISS 7-83 Sup*
Missouri Statewide Interlibrary Loan Network [of Missouri State Library] - Jefferson City, MO - *EISS 83*
Missouri Telephone Co. - Bolivar, MO - *Tel&CabFB 84C p.1692*
Missouri Telephone Co. - Columbia, MO - *TelDir&BG 83-84*
Missouri Union List of Serial Publications [of St. Louis Public Library] - St. Louis, MO - *EISS 83*
Missouri Valley Cable TV - Chamberlain, SD - *BrCabYB 84; Tel&CabFB 84C*
Missouri Valley Times News [of Enterprise Publishing] - Missouri Valley, IA - *BaconPubCkNews 84; NewsDir 84*
Missourian - Columbia, MO - *AyerDirPub 83; LitMarPl 83*
Missourian - Glasgow, MO - *AyerDirPub 83*
Missourian - Portageville, MO - *AyerDirPub 83*
Missourian - Washington, MO - *AyerDirPub 83*
Missourian Publishing Co. - Washington, MO - *BaconPubCkNews 84*
Missourian Weekly - Columbia, MO - *AyerDirPub 83*
Mistaire Laboratories - Millburn, NJ - *BoPubDir 4, 5*
Mister B Greeting Card Co. - Miami, FL - *WritMar 84*
Mister Moose Music - *See* Funky but Music Inc.
Mist'er Rain Inc. - Puyallup, WA - *BoPubDir 4, 5*
Mister Sunshine Music Inc. - *See* Armstrong Associates Inc., Pat
Misti II [of Control Data Corp.] - Greenwich, CT - *DataDirOnSer 84*
MIT Outing Club Inc. - Cambridge, MA - *BoPubDir 4, 5*
MIT Press - Cambridge, MA - *LitMarPl 83, 84; MicrocomSwDir 1; WritMar 84*
MIT Press (Journals Dept.) - Cambridge, MA - *MagIndMarPl 82-83*
MIT Textile Information System [of Massachusetts Institute of Technology] - Cambridge, MA - *CompReadDB 82*
Mita Copystar America Inc. - Hasbrouk Heights, NJ - *DirInfWP 82*
Mitchell Advertising, Howard E. Jr. - Findlay, OH - *StaDirAdAg 2-84*
Mitchell Advocate, The - Mitchell, ON, Canada - *Ed&PubIntYB 82*
Mitchell & Associates - Oceanside, CA - *StaDirAdAg 2-84*
Mitchell & Associates Inc., X. W. - Ottawa, IL - *CabTVFinDB 83*
Mitchell & Co. - Jenkintown, PA - *AdAge 3-28-84; StaDirAdAg 2-84*
Mitchell & Co. - Dallas, TX - *DirMarMP 83*
Mitchell & Gauthier Associates Inc. - Concord, MA - *ADAPSOMemDir 83-84*
Mitchell & Manning Advertising Inc. - Dallas, TX - *StaDirAdAg 2-84*
Mitchell & Webb Inc. - Boston, MA - *DirMarMP 83; DirPRFirms 83*
Mitchell, Benn - New York, NY - *LitMarPl 83, 84*

Mitchell Cable TV [of Sioux Falls Cable Television] - Mitchell, SD - *BrCabYB 84; Tel&CabFB 84C*
Mitchell Christian Features Inc., Phyllis - Strathroy, ON, Canada - *Ed&PubIntYB 82*
Mitchell Co. Inc., John H. - Los Angeles, CA - *HBIndAd&MS 82-83*
Mitchell County Press-News - Osage, IA - *AyerDirPub 83; Ed&PubIntYB 82*
Mitchell, Erwin - Dalton, GA - *Tel&CabFB 84C p.1692*
Mitchell, Frederick C. - Berkeley, CA - *LitMarPl 83*
Mitchell Guide - Princeton, NJ - *BoPubDir 5*
Mitchell, Helen - Dalton, GA - *Tel&CabFB 84C p.1692*
Mitchell Inc., Harold M. - New York, NY - *StaDirAdAg 2-84*
Mitchell Index - Mitchell, NE - *BaconPubCkNews 84*
Mitchell Manuals Inc. [Aff. of Cordura Publications Inc.] - San Diego, CA - *BoPubDir 5; DirMarMP 83*
Mitchell Press Ltd. - Vancouver, BC, Canada - *LitMarPl 83, 84*
Mitchell Publishing Inc. - Santa Cruz, CA - *LitMarPl 83, 84*
Mitchell, Ralph - Kenosha, WI - *BoPubDir 4, 5*
Mitchell Republic - Mitchell, SD - *BaconPubCkNews 84; NewsDir 84*
Mitchell Seaforth Cable TV - Mitchell, ON, Canada - *BrCabYB 84*
Mitchell Software Associates - Palo Alto, CA - *MicrocomSwDir 1*
Mitchell Tribune - Mitchell, IN - *BaconPubCkNews 84; Ed&PubIntYB 82*
Mitchems TV & Refrigeration Service - Brenton, WV - *Tel&CabFB 84C*
Mitec Computer Business Systems - Woodland Hills, CA - *MicrocomSwDir 1; WhoWMicrocom 83*
Mitel - Boca Raton, FL - *DataDirSup 7-83*
Mitel Inc. - Washington, DC - *DirInfWP 82*
Mithoff Advertising Inc. - El Paso, TX - *StaDirAdAg 2-84*
Mitkus-Wolkenheim Inc. - Milwaukee, WI - *LitMarPl 83, 84*
Mitron Systems Corp. - Columbia, MD - *DataDirSup 7-83; InfIndMarPl 83*
Mitsubishi Electric Sales America Inc. - Compton, CA - *BillIntBG 83-84*
Mitsubishi Electronics America Inc. [Subs. of Mitsubishi Electric Corp.] - Torrance, CA - *DataDirSup 7-83; WhoWMicrocom 83*
Mitsui U.S.A. Inc. [Subs. of Sord Computer Systems of Japan] - New York, NY - *WhoWMicrocom 83*
Mittenthal, Joseph - Sherman Oaks, CA - *LitMarPl 83, 84*
MIW Associates - Belmont, MA - *BoPubDir 5; EISS 5-84 Sup; InfoS 83-84*
Mix - Berkeley, CA - *BaconPubCkMag 84*
Mixner/Scott Inc. - Los Angeles, CA - *DirPRFirms 83*
Mizan Press - Berkeley, CA - *BoPubDir 4, 5*
MizMo Enterprises - North Hollywood, CA - *BillIntBG 83-84*
Mizzy Music - *See* Espy Music Group
MJ Recording Inc. - Dodge, NE - *BillIntBG 83-84*
MJA Public Relations/Marketing Services - Chicago, IL - *DirPRFirms 83*
MJB Publisher - Paradise, CA - *BoPubDir 4, 5*
MJG Co. - Midland, TX - *BoPubDir 4, 5*
MJG Music Inc. - *See* Fox Publishing Co. Inc., Sam
MJK Associates - Santa Clara, CA - *DataDirOnSer 84; InfIndMarPl 83*
MJK Commodity Database [of MJK Associates] - Santa Clara, CA - *DataDirOnSer 84*
MJK Data Retrieval Service [of MJK Associates] - Santa Clara, CA - *MicrocomMPl 84*
MJN Publishing - Chicago, IL - *LitMag&SmPr 83-84*
MJQ Music Inc. - New York, NY - *BillIntBG 83-84*
MKG Systems Inc. - Fridley, MN - *WhoWMicrocom 83*
MKTG Inc. - Farmingdale, NY - *IntDirMarRes 83*
MLA Bibliography [of Dialog Information Services Inc.] - Palo Alto, CA - *DataDirOnSer 84*
MLA Bibliography [of Modern Language Association] - New York, NY - *DirOnDB Spring 84; EISS 83*
MLA International Bibliography [of Modern Language Association of America] - New York, NY - *CompReadDB 82*
MLD - Manati, PR - *BrCabYB 84*
MLO/Medical Laboratory Observer - Oradell, NJ - *MagDir 84*
MLP Enterprises - San Francisco, CA - *BoPubDir 4*
MLP Enterprises - Philadelphia, PA - *BoPubDir 5; LitMag&SmPr 83-84*
MLVW-FM - Moncks Corner, SC - *TV&RadDir 84*
MM Computer Club - Downers Grove, IL - *MicrocomSwDir 1*
MM Editing Systems Inc. - New York, NY - *AvMarPl 83*
MMG Micro Software - Marlboro, NJ - *MicrocomMPl 84; MicrocomSwDir 1*
MMI Corp. - Baltimore, MD - *AvMarPl 83*
MMLX - Cincinnati, OH - *TV&RadDir 84*
MMM Advertising Inc. - Charlotte, NC - *StaDirAdAg 2-84*
MMO Music Group Inc. - New York, NY - *BillIntBG 83-84*
MMT Sales Inc. - New York, NY - *Tel&CabFB 84S*
M.N. Publishers - Bonnerdale, AR - *BoPubDir 4, 5*
Mnemonics Inc. - Norwalk, CT - *DataDirSup 7-83; IntDirMarRes 83*
MNH-Applied Electronics Inc. - Alexandria, VA - *WhoWMicrocom 83*
MNP Star Enterprises - San Francisco, CA - *BoPubDir 4 Sup, 5*
Mo-Kan Dial Inc. [Aff. of K.M. Dial] - Louisburg, KS - *TelDir&BG 83-84*
Moab Times-Independent - Moab, UT - *BaconPubCkNews 84*
Moapa Valley Telephone - Overton, NV - *TelDir&BG 83-84*
Moberg, Verne - Brooklyn, NY - *LitMarPl 83, 84*
Moberly Magic City Free Press - Moberly, MO - *NewsDir 84*
Moberly Monitor Index [of Donrey Media Group] - Moberly, MO - *NewsDir 84*
Moberly Monitor-Index & Democrat - Moberly, MO - *BaconPubCkNews 84; Ed&PubIntYB 82*
Mobil Oil Corp. - Fairfax, VA - *DataDirOnSer 84*
Mobil Travel Guide [of Mobil Oil Corp.] - Fairfax, VA - *DataDirOnSer 84; DirOnDB Spring 84; EISS 7-83 Sup*
Mobile Azalea City News - Mobile, AL - *NewsDir 84*
Mobile Azalea City News & Review - Mobile, AL - *BaconPubCkNews 84*
Mobile Beacon - Mobile, AL - *BaconPubCkNews 84; NewsDir 84*
Mobile Beacon & Alabama Citizen - Mobile, AL - *BaconPubCkNews 84; Ed&PubIntYB 82*
Mobile County News - Bayou La Batre, AL - *AyerDirPub 83; Ed&PubIntYB 82; NewsDir 84*
Mobile Fidelity Sound Laboratory - Chatsworth, CA - *BillIntBG 83-84*
Mobile Home News - Altamonte Springs, FL - *BaconPubCkMag 84; MagDir 84*
Mobile Inner City News - Mobile, AL - *BaconPubCkNews 84; NewsDir 84*
Mobile Junior League Publications - Mobile, AL - *BoPubDir 4, 5*
Mobile Living - Sarasota, FL - *BaconPubCkMag 84; MagDir 84*
Mobile Magazine - Mobile, AL - *BaconPubCkMag 84*
Mobile/Manufactured Home Merchandiser - Chicago, IL - *BaconPubCkMag 84; MagDir 84*
Mobile Messenger [of Arizona Mobile Publications] - Phoenix, AZ - *Ed&PubIntYB 82*
Mobile Park Properties Inc. - Bay Indies Mobile Home Park, FL - *Tel&CabFB 84C*
Mobile Phone News - Bethesda, MD - *BaconPubCkMag 84; DirOnDB Spring 84*
Mobile Phone News [of NewsNet Inc.] - Bryn Mawr, PA - *DataDirOnSer 84*
Mobile Press - Mobile, AL - *BaconPubCkNews 84; LitMarPl 83, 84*
Mobile Press-Register - Mobile, AL - *LitMarPl 83*
Mobile Radio System of San Jose Inc. - San Jose, CA - *Tel&CabFB 84C*
Mobile Radio Technology - Littleton, CO - *BaconPubCkMag 84; MagDir 84*
Mobile Register - Mobile, AL - *BaconPubCkNews 84; LitMarPl 83, 84; NewsDir 84*
Mobile Source Emissions Control Data Base System [of U.S. Environmental Protection Agency] - Washington, DC - *EISS 83*
Mobile-Video Productions Inc. - Bethesda, MD - *AvMarPl 83*
Mobile Visual Productions Inc. - Garden Grove, CA - *AvMarPl 83*
MobileSoft - Aberdeen, NJ - *MicrocomMPl 84*
Mobiletimes - Denver, CO - *MagDir 84*
Mobility - Washington, DC - *BaconPubCkMag 84*
Mobility Systems Inc. - Cabin John, MD - *MicrocomMPl 84*
Mobility Trends - Chicago, IL - *BaconPubCkMag 84*
Mobius [of University of California Press] - Berkeley, CA - *LitMag&SmPr 83-84*

Mobridge Cable Television Inc. - Mobridge, SD - *BrCabYB 84; Tel&CabFB 84C*
Mobridge Tribune - Mobridge, SD - *BaconPubCkNews 84; Ed&PubIntYB 82*
Moby Dick Publishing - San Francisco, CA - *BillIntBG 83-84*
Moby Dick Records - San Francisco, CA - *BillIntBG 83-84*
Mochson, Sondra - Port Washington, NY - *LitMarPl 83, 84; MagIndMarPl 82-83*
Mockel Gallery, Henry R. - Twenty-Nine Palms, CA - *BoPubDir 4, 5*
Mockingbird Books - St. Simons Island, GA - *LitMarPl 83, 84*
Mockingbird Press - Alpine, TX - *BoPubDir 4, 5*
Mockingbird Press Inc. - Tallahassee, FL - *BoPubDir 4, 5*
Mocksville Davie County Enterprise-Record [of Davie County Publishing Co. Inc.] - Mocksville, NC - *BaconPubCkNews 84; NewsDir 84*
Mod-Art Records [Div. of Mod-Art Producing Co. Inc.] - Chicago, IL - *BillIntBG 83-84*
Mode-Art Pictures - Pittsburgh, PA - *TelAl 83, 84; Tel&CabFB 84C; WritMar 84*
Model Airplane News - Darien, CT - *BaconPubCkMag 84; MagDir 84; MagIndMarPl 82-83*
Model Builder - Costa Mesa, CA - *BaconPubCkMag 84*
Model Railroader - Milwaukee, WI - *BaconPubCkMag 84; MagDir 84; MagIndMarPl 82-83; WritMar 84*
Model Retailer [of Clifton House] - Clifton, VA - *ArtMar 84; BaconPubCkMag 84; MagDir 84; WritMar 84*
Model II A Regular 16 Newsletter [of Computronics Inc.] - Spring Valley, NY - *MicrocomMPl 84*
Models Data Base [of Solar Energy Research Institute] - Golden, CO - *CompReadDB 82*
Modern Age - Bryn Mawr, PA - *MagIndMarPl 82-83*
Modern Applications News for Design & Manufacturing - Highland Park, IL - *BaconPubCkMag 84; MagDir 84*
Modern Aviation Library - Blue Ridge Summit, PA - *LitMarPl 83*
Modern Books & Crafts Inc. - Green Farm, CT - *LitMarPl 83, 84*
Modern Brewery Age - Norwalk, CT - *BaconPubCkMag 84; MagDir 84; WritMar 84*
Modern Bride [of Ziff-Davis Publishing Co.] - New York, NY - *BaconPubCkMag 84; Folio 83; MagDir 84; MagIndMarPl 82-83; WritMar 84*
Modern Bulk Transporter - Houston, TX - *BaconPubCkMag 84; MagDir 84; MagIndMarPl 82-83*
Modern Cable Network [Div. of Modern Talking Picture Service] - St. Petersburg, FL - *TelAl 83*
Modern Camera Center Inc. - Hilo, HI - *AvMarPl 83*
Modern Cartooning - North Kingstown, RI - *MagIndMarPl 82-83*
Modern Casting - Des Plaines, IL - *BaconPubCkMag 84; MagDir 84*
Modern Communications [of C.E.D. Enterprises Inc.] - Rock Rapids, IA - *BrCabYB 84; Tel&CabFB 84C*
Modern Computer Systems Inc. - Sarasota, FL - *MicrocomMPl 84*
Modern Cooperative Telephone Co. - South English, IA - *TelDir&BG 83-84*
Modern Curriculum Press [Subs. of Esquire Inc.] - Cleveland, OH - *ArtMar 84; LitMarPl 83, 84; WritMar 84*
Modern Dairy - Toronto, ON, Canada - *BaconPubCkMag 84*
Modern Dentalab - Stamford, CT - *BaconPubCkMag 84*
Modern Drummer - Clifton, NJ - *ArtMar 84; BaconPubCkMag 84; MagDir 84; WritMar 84*
Modern Fiction Studies - West Lafayette, IN - *MagIndMarPl 82-83*
Modern Floor Coverings [of Charleson Publishing Co.] - New York, NY - *BaconPubCkMag 84; MagDir 84; WritMar 84*
Modern Graphics Inc. - Randolph, MA - *LitMarPl 83, 84; MagIndMarPl 82-83*
Modern Grocer [of Grocers Publishing Co. Inc.] - New York, NY - *BaconPubCkMag 84; MagDir 84*
Modern Haiku - Madison, WI - *LitMag&SmPr 83-84; WritMar 84*
Modern Handcraft Inc. - Kansas City, MO - *DirMarMP 83; LitMarPl 83, 84*
Modern Healthcare [of Crain Communications Inc.] - Chicago, IL - *BaconPubCkMag 84; MagDir 84; MagIndMarPl 82-83*
Modern Images - Mattoon, IL - *LitMag&SmPr 83-84*
Modern Imaging - Philadelphia, PA - *InfoS 83-84*
Modern Industrial Energy [of Publishing Dynamics Inc.] - Stamford, CT - *MagDir 84; MagIndMarPl 82-83*
Modern Jeweler - Overland Park, KS - *BaconPubCkMag 84*
Modern Jeweler - Kansas City, MO - *MagDir 84*
Modern Knitting Management - Coral Springs, FL - *BaconPubCkMag 84*
Modern Knitting Management - New York, NY - *MagDir 84*
Modern Language Association of America [of Bibliographic Retrieval Services Inc.] - Latham, NY - *DataDirOnSer 84*
Modern Language Association of America - New York, NY - *CompReadDB 82; DataDirOnSer 84; InfIndMarPl 83; LitMarPl 83, 84; OnBibDB 3*
Modern Language Journal - Columbus, OH - *LitMag&SmPr 83-84; MagIndMarPl 82-83*
Modern Language Quarterly - Seattle, WA - *LitMag&SmPr 83-84*
Modern Light - Columbus, KS - *AyerDirPub 83; Ed&PubIntYB 82*
Modern Liturgy [of Resource Publications Inc.] - Saratoga, CA - *ArtMar 84; LitMag&SmPr 83-84; WritMar 84*
Modern Machine Shop - Cincinnati, OH - *ArtMar 84; BaconPubCkMag 84; MagDir 84; MagIndMarPl 82-83; WritMar 84*
Modern Marketing Inc. - Huntingdon Valley, PA - *DirInfWP 82; MagIndMarPl 82-83*
Modern Mass Media Inc. - Florham Park, NJ - *AvMarPl 83*
Modern Mass Media Inc. - New York, NY - *AvMarPl 83*
Modern Masters Ltd. - Frankfort, IL - *ArtMar 84*
Modern Materials Handling [of Cahners Publishing Co.] - Boston, MA - *BaconPubCkMag 84; MagDir 84; MagIndMarPl 82-83*
Modern Maturity [of American Association of Retired Persons] - Long Beach, CA - *ArtMar 84; BaconPubCkMag 84; Folio 83; MagDir 84; MagIndMarPl 82-83; WritMar 84*
Modern Media Institute - St. Petersburg, FL - *BoPubDir 4, 5*
Modern Medicine - New York, NY - *MagDir 84*
Modern Medicine - Cleveland, OH - *BaconPubCkMag 84*
Modern Medicine of Canada - Don Mills, ON, Canada - *BaconPubCkMag 84*
Modern Metals - Chicago, IL - *BaconPubCkMag 84; MagDir 84*
Modern Microcomputers - Westbury, NY - *MicrocomMPl 84; MicrocomSwDir 1; WhoWMicrocom 83*
Modern Music Publishing Inc. - Los Angeles, CA - *BillIntBG 83-84*
Modern News - Harrisburg, AR - *AyerDirPub 83*
Modern Office Procedures - Cleveland, OH - *BaconPubCkMag 84; MagDir 84; MagIndMarPl 82-83*
Modern Packaging Encyclopedia - Des Plaines, IL - *MagDir 84*
Modern Paint & Coatings - Atlanta, GA - *BaconPubCkMag 84; MagDir 84*
Modern Photography [of ABC Leisure Magazine Inc.] - New York, NY - *BaconPubCkMag 84; LitMarPl 84; MagDir 84; MagIndMarPl 82-83*
Modern Plant Operation & Maintenance [of Publishing Dynamics] - Stamford, CT - *MagDir 84*
Modern Plastics - New York, NY - *BaconPubCkMag 84; MagDir 84; MagIndMarPl 82-83*
Modern Plastics International - New York, NY - *MagIndMarPl 82-83*
Modern Poetry Studies - Buffalo, NY - *LitMag&SmPr 83-84*
Modern Printing & Lithography Inc. - Brookfield, CT - *MagIndMarPl 82-83*
Modern Promotions/Publishers [Div. of Unisystems Inc.] - New York, NY - *LitMarPl 83, 84*
Modern Purchasing - Toronto, ON, Canada - *BaconPubCkMag 84*
Modern Radio & TV Systems - Geraldton, ON, Canada - *BrCabYB 84*
Modern Railroads - Des Plaines, IL - *BaconPubCkMag 84; MagDir 84*
Modern Railroads Rail Transit - Chicago, IL - *MagIndMarPl 82-83*
Modern Recording & Music [of MR & M Publishing Corp.] - Plainview, NY - *BaconPubCkMag 84; WritMar 84*
Modern Recording & Music - Port Washington, NY - *MagDir 84; MagIndMarPl 82-83*
Modern Records - New York, NY - *BillIntBG 83-84*
Modern Ribbon & Carbon Co. - Philadelphia, PA - *DirInfWP 82*

Modern Romances [of Macfadden Women's Group] - New York, NY - *MagDir 84; MagIndMarPl 82-83; WritMar 84*
Modern Salon - Chicago, IL - *MagDir 84; MagIndMarPl 82-83; NewsBur 6*
Modern Salon - Lincolnshire, IL - *BaconPubCkMag 84*
Modern Satellite Network [of Modern Talking Picture Service] - St. Petersburg, FL - *AvMarPl 83*
Modern Satellite Network [of Modern Talking Picture Service] - New York, NY - *HomeVid&CabYB 82-83*
Modern Screen - New York, NY - *BaconPubCkMag 84; MagDir 84*
Modern Signs Press - Los Alamitos, CA - *BoPubDir 4, 5*
Modern Software Design - Tarzana, CA - *MicrocomMPl 83, 84*
Modern Sound Pictures Inc. - Omaha, NE - *AvMarPl 83; TelAl 83, 84; Tel&CabFB 84C*
Modern Sports Book Club [Subs. of Sky Books International Inc.] - New York, NY - *LitMarPl 83, 84*
Modern Stores & Offices [of B. J. Martin Co. Inc.] - Glencoe, IL - *MagDir 84*
Modern Talking Picture Service Inc. [Aff. of Modern Telecommunications Inc.] - St. Petersburg, FL - *AvMarPl 83; TelAl 83, 84*
Modern Talking Picture Service Inc. - New York, NY - *ProGuPRSer 4*
Modern Talking Picture Service Inc. (Modern Cable Network Div.) - St. Petersburg, FL - *TelAl 83, 84*
Modern Talking Picture Service Inc. (Modern Satellite Network Div.) - St. Petersburg, FL - *TelAl 83, 84*
Modern Talking Picture Service Inc. (Modern TV Div.) - St. Petersburg, FL - *TelAl 83, 84*
Modern Textile Business - Coral Springs, FL - *BaconPubCkMag 84*
Modern Textiles Magazine - New York, NY - *MagDir 84*
Modern Tire Dealer [of Rubber & Automotive Communications] - Akron, OH - *BaconPubCkMag 84; MagDir 84; WritMar 84*
Modern TV [Div. of Modern Talking Picture Service Inc.] - St. Petersburg, FL - *Tel&CabFB 84C*
Modern Veterinary Practice - Santa Barbara, CA - *BaconPubCkMag 84; MagDir 84; WritMar 84*
Modern Woodmen, The - Rock Island, IL - *BaconPubCkMag 84; WritMar 84*
Modern World Publishing Co. - Los Angeles, CA - *BoPubDir 4, 5*
Modernage Photo Services Inc. - New York, NY - *AvMarPl 83*
Modernart Editions Inc. - New York, NY - *ArtMar 84*
Modernfold - New Castle, IN - *DirInfWP 82*
Modernismo Publications Ltd. - New York, NY - *BoPubDir 4, 5*
Modersmaalet - Oakville, ON, Canada - *Ed&PubIntYB 82*
Modesto Bee [of McClatchy Newspapers] - Modesto, CA - *AyerDirPub 83; BaconPubCkNews 84; Ed&PubIntYB 82; NewsDir 84*
Modesto MDS Co. - Pasadena, MD - *Tel&CabFB 84C*
Modney, David - Tucson, AZ - *MicrocomMPl 83; WhoWMicrocom 83*
Modoc County Record - Alturas, CA - *AyerDirPub 83; Ed&PubIntYB 82*
Modoc Music - *See* Penny Pincher Music
Modtec - Tucson, AZ - *MicrocomMPl 83, 84; MicrocomSwDir 1*
Modular Computer Systems - Ft. Lauderdale, FL - *DataDirSup 7-83; Datamation 6-83; Top100Al 83; VideoDir 82-83*
Modular Information Systems - Orlando, FL - *ADAPSOMemDir 83-84; DataDirSup 7-83*
Modular Integration Inc. - Issaquah, WA - *WhoWMicrocom 83*
Modular Marketing Inc. - New York, NY - *HBIndAd&MS 82-83; StaDirAdAg 2-84*
Modular Media - Miami, FL - *MicrocomMPl 83, 84*
Modulo 2 Co. - Tukwila, WA - *WhoWMicrocom 83*
Modway [of Gould Inc.] - Andover, MA - *TeleSy&SerDir 7-83*
Moeck - *See* European American Music Corp.
Moffat Communications Ltd. - Winnipeg, MB, Canada - *BrCabYB 84*
Moffat Communications Ltd. - *See* Urban TV Cable Systems Inc.
Moffat Publishing Co. Inc. - Nutley, NJ - *BoPubDir 5*
Moffat Publishing Co. Inc. - New York, NY - *BoPubDir 4*
Moffitt-Lee Productions - Hollywood, CA - *Tel&CabFB 84C*
Moffitt Newspapers - Lewisburg, WV - *Ed&PubIntYB 82*
Mogg TV, James - Cheyenne, OK - *BrCabYB 84; Tel&CabFB 84C*
Mogollon Cable TV - Pine, AZ - *BrCabYB 84 p.D-304; Tel&CabFB 84C p.1692*
Mogollon Cable TV - Saddle Mountain, AZ - *BrCabYB 84*
Mogollon Cable TV Co. - Christopher Creek, AZ - *BrCabYB 84*
Mogul Book & Film Works - Pittsburgh, PA - *LitMag&SmPr 83-84*
Mogull Film Co. - Plainfield, NJ - *Tel&CabFB 84C*
Mogull Music Corp., Ivan - New York, NY - *BillIntBG 83-84*
Mohair Weekly - Rocksprings, TX - *Ed&PubIntYB 82*
Mohall Renville County Farmer - Mohall, ND - *BaconPubCkNews 84*
Mohan Enterprises - Rochester, NY - *BoPubDir 4, 5*
Mohave Cable Co. [of American Cable TV Inc.] - Bulkhead City, AZ - *Tel&CabFB 84C*
Mohave Cable Co. [of American Cable Television Inc.] - Bullhead City, AZ - *BrCabYB 84*
Mohave Cable Co. [of American Cable TV Inc.] - Lake Havasu City, AZ - *BrCabYB 84; Tel&CabFB 84C*
Mohave Valley News - Bullhead City, AZ - *Ed&PubIntYB 82*
Mohawk Advertising - Mason City, IA - *AdAge 3-28-84; ArtMar 84; StaDirAdAg 2-84*
Mohawk Data Sciences - Parsippany, NJ - *DataDirSup 7-83; Datamation 6-83; InfIndMarPl 83; MicrocomSwDir 1; Top100Al 83; WhoWMicrocom 83*
Mohawk Leader - Sycamore, OH - *AyerDirPub 83; Ed&PubIntYB 82*
Mohawk Paper Mills Inc. - Cohoes, NY - *LitMarPl 83, 84; MagIndMarPl 82-83*
Mohawk Printing Corp. - Rochester, NY - *MagIndMarPl 82-83*
Mohawk Valley Democrat - Fonda, NY - *AyerDirPub 83; Ed&PubIntYB 82*
Mohr, R. L. - Redondo Beach, CA - *Tel&CabFB 84C*
Moise Music - *See* Bob & Ethel Music
Mojave Books - Reseda, CA - *BoPubDir 4, 5; LitMag&SmPr 83-84*
Mojave Desert News - Mojave, CA - *BaconPubCkNews 84; Ed&PubIntYB 82*
Mojo Navigatore [of Cat's Pajamas Press] - Oak Park, IL - *LitMag&SmPr 83-84*
Mokin Productions Inc., Arthur - Santa Rosa, CA - *AvMarPl 83*
Molalla Pioneer - Molalla, OR - *BaconPubCkNews 84; Ed&PubIntYB 82*
Molalla Telephone Co. - Molalla, OR - *TelDir&BG 83-84*
Molders' Journal - Cincinnati, OH - *NewsDir 84*
Mole Publishing Co. - Bonners Ferry, ID - *BoPubDir 4 Sup, 5*
Mole-Richardson Co. - Hollywood, CA - *AvMarPl 83*
Molecular Computer - San Jose, CA - *WhoWMicrocom 83*
Molecular Design Ltd. - Hayward, CA - *EISS 5-84 Sup*
Molecular Spectra Data Center [of U.S. National Bureau of Standards] - Washington, DC - *EISS 83*
Molek Inc., M. - Dover, DE - *BoPubDir 4, 5*
Moler Research Associates - Cincinnati, OH - *IntDirMarRes 83*
Moleres, Bobby - Grants, NM - *Tel&CabFB 84C p.1692*
Moline Advance - Moline, KS - *BaconPubCkNews 84; Ed&PubIntYB 82*
Moline Advance, The - Howard, KS - *AyerDirPub 83*
Moline Daily Dispatch - Moline, IL - *BaconPubCkNews 84; NewsDir 84*
Moll Advertising Inc., George - Abington, PA - *StaDirAdAg 2-84*
Mollica Stained Glass Press - Oakland, CA - *BoPubDir 4, 5*
Molly Yes Press - New Berlin, NY - *BoPubDir 4, 5; LitMag&SmPr 83-84*
Molner & Co. Advertising Inc. - Oak Park, MI - *ArtMar 84; StaDirAdAg 2-84*
Moloda Ukraina - Toronto, ON, Canada - *Ed&PubIntYB 82*
Molten Salts Data Center [of Rensselaer Polytechnic Institute] - Troy, NY - *EISS 83*
Molton Advertising, Ellis - Hendersonville, NC - *BrCabYB 84*
Molybdenum Forecast [of Chase Econometrics/Interactive Data Corp.] - Waltham, MA - *DataDirOnSer 84*
Molybdenum Forecast - Bala Cynwyd, PA - *DirOnDB Spring 84*
Mom & Dad Music - *See* Funky but Music Inc.
Momence Community Cablevision [of Firstcable Communications Inc.] - Momence, IL - *BrCabYB 84; Tel&CabFB 84C*

Momence Progress-Reporter - Momence, IL - *BaconPubCkNews 84; Ed&PubIntYB 82*
Moment Magazine - Boston, MA - *ArtMar 84; MagIndMarPl 82-83; WritMar 84*
Moment Productions - Austin, TX - *BillIntBG 83-84*
Moment Record Co. - St. Petersburg, FL - *BillIntBG 83-84*
Momentum - Washington, DC - *MagIndMarPl 82-83; WritMar 84*
Momentum Computer Systems International - Sunnyvale, CA - *MicrocomMPl 84; WhoWMicrocom 83*
Momentum Press [Aff. of Century City Educational Arts Project] - Los Angeles, CA - *BoPubDir 4, 5*
Momentum Press - Santa Monica, CA - *LitMag&SmPr 83-84*
Momo's Press - San Francisco, CA - *BoPubDir 5*
Mon-Cre Telephone Co-Operative Inc. - Ramer, AL - *TelDir&BG 83-84*
Mon-Dak Cablevision - Fairview, MT - *Tel&CabFB 84C*
Mona & Associates Inc., David L. - Minneapolis, MN - *DirPRFirms 83*
Mona Lisa Precision - Port Chester, NY - *BoPubDir 5*
Monaco - Wilton, CT - *AvMarPl 83*
Monaco & Co., James - New York, NY - *LitMarPl 83, 84*
Monad Press [of the Anchor Foundation Inc.] - New York, NY - *LitMarPl 83, 84*
Monad Trainer's Aide - Whitestone, NY - *DirInfWP 82*
Monadnock Cable Co. - Springfield, VT - *BrCabYB 84 p.D-304*
Monadnock Cable Co. Inc. [of Young's Community TV Corp.] - Alstead, NH - *Tel&CabFB 84C*
Monadnock Cable Co. Inc. [of Young's Community TV Corp.] - Charlestown, NH - *Tel&CabFB 84C*
Monadnock Cablevision Co. - Peterborough, NH - *BrCabYB 84*
Monadnock Ledger - Peterborough, NH - *AyerDirPub 83; Ed&PubIntYB 82; LitMarPl 83, 84*
Monadnock Paper Mills Inc. - Bennington, NH - *LitMarPl 83, 84*
Monaghan Associates, H. I. [Aff. of H. I. Monaghan Advertising] - Hatboro, PA - *DirPRFirms 83; StaDirAdAg 2-84*
Monahan-Ross Inc. Advertising - Kansas City, MO - *ArtMar 84*
Monahans News - Monahans, TX - *BaconPubCkNews 84; Ed&PubIntYB 82; NewsDir 84*
Monarch Furniture Corp. - High Point, NC - *DirInfWP 82*
Monarch Marking Systems Inc. - Dayton, OH - *DataDirSup 7-83*
Monarch Press [Div. of Simon & Schuster] - New York, NY - *LitMarPl 83, 84*
Monarch Publishing - *See* Lorenz Creative Services
Monard Music - Tujunga, CA - *BillIntBG 83-84*
Monchik-Weber Corp. - New York, NY - *ADAPSOMemDir 83-84; DataDirOnSer 84; DataDirSup 7-83; EISS 83; InfIndMarPl 83*
Monchik-Weber Datasharing Service [of Monchik-Weber Corp.] - New York, NY - *DataDirOnSer 84*
Monchik-Weber Datasharing Service - *See* Monchik-Weber Price Access Service
Monchik-Weber Options Monitor Service [of Monchik-Weber Corp.] - New York, NY - *DataDirOnSer 84; DirOnDB Spring 84*
Monchik-Weber Price Access Service [of Monchik-Weber Corp.] - New York, NY - *DirOnDB Spring 84*
Monchik-Weber Wall Street Concepts [of Monchik-Weber Corp.] - New York, NY - *DataDirOnSer 84; DataDirSup 7-83*
Moncton Times-Transcript - Moncton, NB, Canada - *BaconPubCkNews 84*
Mondadori-AME Publishing Ltd. [Subs. of Arnoldo Mondadori Editore] - New York, NY - *LitMarPl 83, 84*
Monday Green Sheet - Howell, MI - *AyerDirPub 83*
Monday Morning Newspapers - Detroit, MI - *BaconPubCkNews 84*
Monday Morning Press [Aff. of Margins] - Fairwater, WI - *BoPubDir 4, 5*
Monday Sentinel - Cortez, CO - *Ed&PubIntYB 82*
Monday's Pub - Anna, IL - *AyerDirPub 83*
Mondo Hunkamooga - Toronto, ON, Canada - *LitMag&SmPr 83-84*
Mondovi Herald News - Mondovi, WI - *BaconPubCkNews 84; Ed&PubIntYB 82*
Mondovi Telephone Co. - Mondovi, WI - *TelDir&BG 83-84*
Monee Moniter - Monee, IL - *Ed&PubIntYB 82*
Monee Monitor - *See* Russell Publications
Monegon Ltd. Future Systems Inc. - Gaithersburg, MD - *BoPubDir 5*
Monessen Valley Independent [of Thomson Newspapers Inc.] - Monessen, PA - *NewsDir 84*
Monett Media Inc. - Atlanta, GA - *StaDirAdAg 2-84*
Monett Times - Monett, MO - *BaconPubCkNews 84; Ed&PubIntYB 82; NewsDir 84*
Money [of Time Inc.] - New York, NY - *BaconPubCkMag 84; Folio 83; MagDir 84; MagIndMarPl 82-83; WritMar 84*
Money Disk - Richland, WA - *WhoWMicrocom 83*
Money for Food Press - New York, NY - *BoPubDir 4, 5*
Money Mailer - Westminster, CA - *DirMarMP 83*
Money Maker [of Consumers Digest Inc.] - Chicago, IL - *BaconPubCkMag 84; MagDir 84; MagIndMarPl 82-83; WritMar 84*
Money Making Opportunities - Hollywood, CA - *MagDir 84*
Money Making Opportunities - Studio City, CA - *BaconPubCkMag 84*
Money Management Letter - New York, NY - *BaconPubCkMag 84*
Money Management Systems Inc. - Waltham, MA - *DataDirOnSer 84*
Money Manager, The [of The Bond Buyer] - New York, NY - *Ed&PubIntYB 82; MagDir 84*
Money Market Directories Inc. - Charlottesville, VA - *EISS 83*
Money Market Monitor [of Whittle Raddon Motley & Hanks Inc.] - Chicago, IL - *EISS 5-84 Sup*
Money Market Rates [of I. P. Sharp Associates Ltd.] - Toronto, ON, Canada - *DataDirOnSer 84; DBBus 82; DirOnDB Spring 84*
Money Market Services Inc. - Belmont, CA - *DataDirOnSer 84; EISS 83; InfIndMarPl 83*
Money Market Services Inc. [of Dow Jones News/Retrieval Service] - Princeton, NJ - *DataDirOnSer 84*
Money Markets Data Base - Bala Cynwyd, PA - *DirOnDB Spring 84*
Money Saver - Mobile, AL - *AyerDirPub 83*
Money Tree - Newport Beach, CA - *ArtMar 84*
Money Tree Software - Corvallis, OR - *MicrocomMPl 84*
Money Watch - Goleta, CA - *BoPubDir 4 Sup, 5*
Moneyfax - Ischua, NY - *WritMar 84*
Moneyhun Advertising Inc. - Dallas, TX - *StaDirAdAg 2-84*
Moneysaver - Randolph, MA - *AyerDirPub 83*
Moneysaver [of Journal Newspapers Inc.] - Ballston Spa, NY - *AyerDirPub 83; NewsDir 84*
Moneysaver Shopping Guide - Bolivar, NY - *AyerDirPub 83*
Moneysaver Shopping News - Bolivar, NY - *AyerDirPub 83*
Moneysworth [of Avant-Garde Media Inc.] - New York, NY - *BaconPubCkMag 84; DirMarMP 83; Folio 83; LitMarPl 83, 84; MagDir 84; MagIndMarPl 82-83*
Moneywatch - New York, NY - *DirOnDB Spring 84*
Mongolia Society Inc. - Bloomington, IN - *BoPubDir 4, 5*
Monist, The [of The Hegeler Institute] - La Salle, IL - *LitMag&SmPr 83-84*
Monitan Information Consultants Ltd. - Consett, England - *EISS 5-84 Sup*
Moniter, The [of Sooner Publishing Co. Inc.] - Oklahoma City, OK - *NewsDir 84*
Monitor [of SDC Search Service] - Santa Monica, CA - *DataDirOnSer 84*
Monitor - Danielsville, GA - *AyerDirPub 83*
Monitor - East St. Louis, IL - *Ed&PubIntYB 82*
Monitor - Manning, IA - *AyerDirPub 83*
Monitor - Mayville, MI - *AyerDirPub 83*
Monitor - Boulder, MT - *AyerDirPub 83*
Monitor - Bloomfield, NE - *AyerDirPub 83*
Monitor - Springfield, NE - *AyerDirPub 83*
Monitor - Concord, NH - *AyerDirPub 83*
Monitor [of Bell & Howell Co.] - Wooster, OH - *DirOnDB Spring 84; OnBibDB 3*
Monitor - Naples, TX - *AyerDirPub 83; Ed&PubIntYB 82*
Monitor - Bridgetown, NS, Canada - *AyerDirPub 83; Ed&PubIntYB 82*
Monitor - Montreal, PQ, Canada - *AyerDirPub 83; Ed&PubIntYB 82*
Monitor Book Co. Inc. - Beverly Hills, CA - *BoPubDir 4, 5; WritMar 84*

Monitor Cooperative Telephone Co. - Woodburn, OR - *TelDir&BG 83-84*
Monitor-Herald - Calhoun City, MS - *AyerDirPub 83; Ed&PubIntYB 82*
Monitor-Index & Democrat - Moberly, MO - *AyerDirPub 83*
Monitor News & Feature Services - Montreal, PQ, Canada - *BaconPubCkNews 84; Ed&PubIntYB 82*
Monitor Recordings Inc. - New York, NY - *AvMarPl 83; BillIntBG 83-84*
Monitor Review - Stacyville, IA - *AyerDirPub 83; Ed&PubIntYB 82*
Monitor Review - Adams, MN - *Ed&PubIntYB 82*
Monitor, The - Marianna, FL - *AyerDirPub 83*
Monitor, The - Perryville, MO - *AyerDirPub 83*
Monitor, The - Lidgerwood, ND - *AyerDirPub 83; Ed&PubIntYB 82*
Monitor, The - Liberty, SC - *Ed&PubIntYB 82*
Monitor, The - McAllen, TX - *Ed&PubIntYB 82*
Monitor Trade Publications - New York, NY - *BoPubDir 4, 5*
Monk & Associates Inc., Howard H. - Rockford, IL - *StaDirAdAg 2-84*
Monkey Man Press - Los Angeles, CA - *BoPubDir 4, 5*
Monkey Music - Nashville, TN - *BillIntBG 83-84*
Monkey Sisters - Laguna Niguel, CA - *BoPubDir 4, 5*
Monkman-Rumsey - Wilmington, DE - *BoPubDir 5*
Monkmeyer Press Photo Service - New York, NY - *MagIndMarPl 82-83*
Monks & Co., W. E. - Columbus, OH - *MicrocomMPl 84*
Monks Associates Inc., Arthur - Milton, MA - *DirPRFirms 83*
Monks of New Skete - Cambridge, NY - *BoPubDir 4, 5*
Monmouth Cablevision Associates - Monmouth County, NJ - *Tel&CabFB 84C*
Monmouth Cablevision Associates - Wall, NJ - *BrCabYB 84*
Monmouth Cablevision Inc. [of Storer Cable Communications] - Middletown Township, NJ - *BrCabYB 84*
Monmouth County Eagle - Long Branch, NJ - *AyerDirPub 83*
Monmouth-Evergreen Records - New York, NY - *BillIntBG 83-84*
Monmouth-Independence Sun-Enterprise - Independence, OR - *NewsDir 84*
Monmouth-Independence Sun-Enterprise - Monmouth, OR - *AyerDirPub 83; BaconPubCkNews 84*
Monmouth Review Atlas - Monmouth, IL - *BaconPubCkNews 84; NewsDir 84*
Mono County TV Corp. - June Lake, CA - *Tel&CabFB 84C*
Mono Herald & Bridgeport Chronicle-Union [of Bishop Chalfant Press Publications] - Bishop, CA - *NewsDir 84*
Mono Herald & Bridgeport Chronicle-Union - Mammoth Lakes, CA - *AyerDirPub 83; Ed&PubIntYB 82*
Mono Lake Committee - Lee Vining, CA - *BoPubDir 4, 5*
Mono Lino Typesetting Co. Ltd. - Toronto, ON, Canada - *DirInfWP 82*
Monogram Aviation Publications - Boylston, MA - *BoPubDir 4, 5*
Monolithic Memories Inc. - Sunnyvale, CA - *DataDirSup 7-83*
Monolithic Systems Corp. - Englewood, CO - *DataDirSup 7-83; WhoWMicrocom 83*
Monon News - Monon, IN - *BaconPubCkNews 84; Ed&PubIntYB 82*
Monon Telephone Co. Inc. - Monon, IN - *TelDir&BG 83-84*
Monona Billboard - Monona, IA - *BaconPubCkNews 84; Ed&PubIntYB 82*
Monona Community Herald - Madison, WI - *AyerDirPub 83*
Monona Community Herald - Monona, WI - *Ed&PubIntYB 82*
Monona Driver Book Co. - Madison, WI - *BoPubDir 4, 5*
Monona Herald - *See* Community Herald Newspapers Inc.
Monongahela Bentleyville Courier - Monongahela, PA - *BaconPubCkNews 84*
Monongahela-Charleroi-Donora Herald [of Pioneer Newspapers] - Monongahela, PA - *NewsDir 84*
Monongahela Daily Herald - Monongahela, PA - *BaconPubCkNews 84*
Mono's Press - San Francisco, CA - *LitMag&SmPr 83-84*
Monoson Microsystems - Watertown, MA - *MicrocomMPl 83*
Monosson on Dec - Boston, MA - *BaconPubCkMag 84*
Monotype Composition Co. Inc. - Baltimore, MD - *LitMarPl 83, 84; MagIndMarPl 82-83*
Monroe Advertiser Photo News - *See* Advertiser Photo News Group
Monroe All-Channel Cablevision Inc. [of Horizon Communications Corp.] - Bloomington, IN - *Tel&CabFB 84C*
Monroe Cable TV [of American TV & Communications Corp.] - Monroe, NC - *Tel&CabFB 84C*
Monroe Cablevision Inc. [of The Cablesystem] - Monroe, MI - *BrCabYB 84*
Monroe City Cable TV [of Tele-Communications Inc.] - Monroe City, MO - *BrCabYB 84*
Monroe City News - Monroe City, MO - *BaconPubCkNews 84; Ed&PubIntYB 82*
Monroe County Advocate - Sweetwater, TN - *AyerDirPub 83*
Monroe County Advocate, The - Monroe County, TN - *Ed&PubIntYB 82*
Monroe County Appeal - Monroe County, MO - *Ed&PubIntYB 82*
Monroe County Appeal - Paris, MO - *NewsDir 84*
Monroe County Appeal & Madison Times - Paris, MO - *AyerDirPub 83*
Monroe County Beacon - Woodsfield, OH - *AyerDirPub 83; Ed&PubIntYB 82*
Monroe County Clarion - Columbia, IL - *AyerDirPub 83; Ed&PubIntYB 82*
Monroe County Democrat [of Sparta Monroe County Publishers Inc.] - Sparta, WI - *AyerDirPub 83; Ed&PubIntYB 82; NewsDir 84*
Monroe County News - Albia, IA - *AyerDirPub 83; Ed&PubIntYB 82*
Monroe County Publishers Inc. - Sparta, WI - *BaconPubCkNews 84*
Monroe County Reporter - Forsyth, GA - *AyerDirPub 83; Ed&PubIntYB 82*
Monroe County Sun, The - Clarendon, AR - *Ed&PubIntYB 82*
Monroe County Telephone Co. [Aff. of Universal Telephone Inc.] - Sparta, WI - *TelDir&BG 83-84*
Monroe Courier - Monroe, CT - *Ed&PubIntYB 82; NewsDir 84*
Monroe Courier - *See* Trumbull Times Publishers
Monroe Dispatch - Monroe, LA - *BaconPubCkNews 84; NewsDir 84*
Monroe Distributing Inc. - Cleveland, OH - *MicrocomMPl 84*
Monroe Enterprise - Glassboro, NJ - *Ed&PubIntYB 82*
Monroe Evening News - Monroe, MI - *BaconPubCkNews 84; Ed&PubIntYB 82; NewsDir 84*
Monroe Evening Times - Monroe, WI - *Ed&PubIntYB 82; NewsDir 84*
Monroe Gazette - Monroe, NY - *Ed&PubIntYB 82*
Monroe, James A. - Scottsdale, AZ - *Tel&CabFB 84C p.1692*
Monroe, John F. - Lake Geneva, WI - *Tel&CabFB 84C p.1692*
Monroe Journal - Monroeville, AL - *AyerDirPub 83; BrCabYB 84; Ed&PubIntYB 82*
Monroe, LaJunta K. - Scottsdale, AZ - *Tel&CabFB 84C p.1692*
Monroe MDS Inc. - *See* Miller, J. McCarthy & June J.
Monroe Mendelsohn College Study - New York, NY - *DirOnDB Spring 84*
Monroe Mendelsohn Research Inc. - New York, NY - *EISS 7-83 Sup; IntDirMarRes 83*
Monroe Mirror - Monroe, IA - *BaconPubCkNews 84; Ed&PubIntYB 82*
Monroe Monitor - Monroe, WA - *AyerDirPub 83; BaconPubCkNews 84; Ed&PubIntYB 82*
Monroe News-Star-World - Monroe, LA - *BaconPubCkNews 84; LitMarPl 83*
Monroe Systems for Business [Subs. of Litton Business Systems Inc.] - Morris Plains, NJ - *DirInfWP 82; MicrocomMPl 84; WhoWMicrocom 83*
Monroe Telephone Co. - Monroe, OR - *TelDir&BG 83-84*
Monroe Times - Monroe, WI - *BaconPubCkNews 84*
Monroe Township Enterprise [of Cam-Glo Newspapers Inc.] - Blackwood, NJ - *NewsDir 84*
Monroe Township Enterprise - *See* Cam-Glo Newspapers Inc.
Monroe Walton Tribune - Monroe, GA - *BaconPubCkNews 84; NewsDir 84*
Monroe Watchman - Union, WV - *Ed&PubIntYB 82*
Monroe-Woodbury Photo News [of Turnell Publishing Co. Inc.] - Monroe, NY - *AyerDirPub 83; Ed&PubIntYB 82; NewsDir 84*

Monroeville Monroe Journal [of Southwest ACA Publishing Co. Inc.] - Monroeville, AL - *BaconPubCkNews 84; NewsDir 84*
Monroeville News - Monroeville, IN - *BaconPubCkNews 84; Ed&PubIntYB 82*
Monroeville South Hills Record - *See* Gateway Press Inc.
Monroeville Spectator - Monroeville, OH - *BaconPubCkNews 84; Ed&PubIntYB 82*
Monroeville Telephone Co. Inc. - Monroeville, AL - *TelDir&BG 83-84*
Monroeville Times Express - Monroeville, PA - *Ed&PubIntYB 82*
Monroeville Times-Express - *See* Gateway Press Inc.
Monroeville Westmoreland Star - *See* Gateway Press Inc.
Monrovia Highlander - *See* Sun Independent Newspapers
Monrovia News-Post [of Foothill Inter-City Newspapers] - Arcadia, CA - *AyerDirPub 83; NewsDir 84*
Monrovia News-Post - Monrovia, CA - *Ed&PubIntYB 82*
Monrovia News-Post - *See* Foothill Inter-City Newspapers
Monrovia Telephone Corp., The [Aff. of Clay County Rural Telephone Cooperative Inc.] - Cloverdale, IN - *TelDir&BG 83-84*
Monsapec Music Inc. - *See* Helios Music Corp.
Mont Alto Cable [of Telecable Communications Corp.] - Mont Alto, PA - *BrCabYB 84; Tel&CabFB 84C*
Mont Clare News - Chicago, IL - *AyerDirPub 83*
Mont Clare Post [of Meese' Newspapers Inc.] - Chicago, IL - *NewsDir 84*
Mont Clare Post - Elmwood Park, IL - *AyerDirPub 83*
Mont Clare Post - *See* Meese' Newspaper Group
Mont St. Pierre TV Engr. - Gaspe, PQ, Canada - *BrCabYB 84*
Montachusett Cable Television Inc. [of Adams-Russell Co. Inc.] - Fitchburg, MA - *Tel&CabFB 84C*
Montachusett Cable Television Inc. [of Adams-Russell Co. Inc.] - Gardner, MA - *Tel&CabFB 84C*
Montachusett Cable Television Inc. [of Adams-Russell Inc.] - Leominster, MA - *BrCabYB 84*
Montachusett Review - Fitchburg, MA - *AyerDirPub 83; NewsDir 84*
Montage Communications - Los Angeles, CA - *AvMarPl 83; WritMar 84*
Montage Publishing - Culver City, CA - *DirMarMP 83*
Montage Records Inc. - Philadelphia, PA - *BillIntBG 83-84*
Montague Township Corp. - Smiths Falls, ON, Canada - *BoPubDir 4 Sup, 5*
Montague White Laker Observer/Oceana County News - Montague, MI - *NewsDir 84*
Montaigne Publishing Co. - Orinda, CA - *BoPubDir 4, 5*
Montana Agriculture - Bozeman, MT - *BaconPubCkMag 84; MagDir 84*
Montana Beverage Analyst [of Bevan Inc.] - Denver, CO - *BaconPubCkMag 84; MagDir 84*
Montana Beverage News - Billings, MT - *BaconPubCkMag 84; MagDir 84*
Montana Books Publishers Inc. - Seattle, WA - *BoPubDir 4, 5*
Montana Color Comic Group - Billings, MT - *Ed&PubIntYB 82*
Montana Council for Indian Education - Billings, MT - *BoPubDir 4, 5*
Montana Farmer-Stockman - Billings, MT - *MagDir 84*
Montana Farmer-Stockman - Spokane, WA - *BaconPubCkMag 84*
Montana Folklife Project - Missoula, MT - *BillIntBG 83-84*
Montana Food Distributor - Helena, MT - *BaconPubCkMag 84*
Montana Food Distributor [of Montana Food Distributors Association] - Missoula, MT - *MagDir 84*
Montana Historical Society Press - Helena, MT - *BoPubDir 4, 5*
Montana Kaimin [of University of Montana] - Missoula, MT - *NewsDir 84*
Montana League of Cities & Towns - Helena, MT - *BoPubDir 5*
Montana Music, Vincent Jr. - Cherry Hill, NJ - *BillIntBG 83-84*
Montana Oil Journal - Billings, MT - *MagDir 84*
Montana Review, The [of Owl Creek Press] - Missoula, MT - *LitMag&SmPr 83-84*
Montana Rural Electric News - Great Falls, MT - *MagDir 84*
Montana Standard - Butte, MT - *AyerDirPub 83; BaconPubCkNews 84; Ed&PubIntYB 82*
Montana Stockgrower, The - Helena, MT - *MagDir 84*
Montana Television Network - Billings, MT - *BrCabYB 84; Tel&CabFB 84S*
Montana: The Magazine of Western History - Helena, MT - *BaconPubCkMag 84; MagDir 84; MagIndMarPl 82-83; WritMar 84*
Montana Video Inc. [of Community Tele-Communications Inc.] - Billings, MT - *BrCabYB 84; Tel&CabFB 84C*
Montana/West Advertising Inc. - Helena, MT - *StaDirAdAg 2-84*
Montana Wool Grower - Helena, MT - *BaconPubCkMag 84; MagDir 84*
Montaque White Lake Observer - Montaque, MI - *BaconPubCkNews 84*
Montauk Music Inc. - *See* Webman & Co., H. B.
Montbello News [of Southern California Publishing Co.] - Los Angeles, CA - *NewsDir 84*
Montclair Courier [of Claremont Courier Graphics Corp.] - Claremont, CA - *Ed&PubIntYB 82; NewsDir 84*
Montclair Courier - *See* Claremont Courier Graphics Corp.
Montclair Piedmont Pines Oakland American [of Oakland Neighborhood Journal] - Oakland, CA - *NewsDir 84*
Montclair Press [of Oakland Press Publications] - Oakland, CA - *NewsDir 84*
Montclair Times - Montclair, NJ - *BaconPubCkNews 84; Ed&PubIntYB 82; NewsDir 84*
Montclair Tribune - Montclair, CA - *Ed&PubIntYB 82*
Montclair Tribune [of Ontario Bonita Publishing Co.] - Ontario, CA - *AyerDirPub 83; NewsDir 84*
Montclair Tribune - *See* Ontario Daily Report
Montclarion, The - Oakland, CA - *AyerDirPub 83; Ed&PubIntYB 82*
Monte Cable [of American TV & Communications Corp.] - Montevideo, MN - *BrCabYB 84; Tel&CabFB 84C*
Monte Publishing Co. - Underwood, WA - *BoPubDir 5*
Monte Vista Cable TV [of Tele-Communications Inc.] - Monte Vista, CO - *BrCabYB 84; Tel&CabFB 84C*
Monte Vista Journal - Monte Vista, CO - *BaconPubCkNews 84; Ed&PubIntYB 82*
Monteagle TV Cable Co. [of National Telecommunications] - Monteagle, TN - *Tel&CabFB 84C*
Montealegre Inc., Marcelo - New York, NY - *ArtMar 84; AvMarPl 83*
Montebello Comet [of Eastern Group Publications Inc.] - Los Angeles, CA - *AyerDirPub 83; NewsDir 84*
Montebello Comet - Montebello, CA - *Ed&PubIntYB 82*
Montebello Comet - *See* Eastern Group Publications Inc.
Montebello Messenger - Montebello, CA - *BaconPubCkNews 84; Ed&PubIntYB 82*
Montebello News - *See* Southern California Publishing Co.
Monteleone Associates, John - Rocky Hill, NJ - *MagIndMarPl 82-83*
Montello Marquette County Tribune - Montello, WI - *BaconPubCkNews 84*
Montello Music - Madison, WI - *BillIntBG 83-84*
Montemora Foundation Inc., The - New York, NY - *LitMag&SmPr 83-84*
Monterey Cable Service - Monterey, TN - *BrCabYB 84; Tel&CabFB 84C*
Monterey Home Video - Canoga Park, CA - *BillIntBG 83-84*
Monterey Life - Monterey, CA - *BaconPubCkMag 84; WritMar 84*
Monterey Observer - Monterey, CA - *NewsDir 84*
Monterey Park Comet [of Eastern Group Publications Inc.] - Los Angeles, CA - *AyerDirPub 83; NewsDir 84*
Monterey Park Comet - Monterey Park, CA - *Ed&PubIntYB 82*
Monterey Park Comet - *See* Eastern Group Publications Inc.
Monterey Park Independent - San Gabriel, CA - *Ed&PubIntYB 82*
Monterey Park Independent - *See* Sun Independent Newspapers
Monterey Park Progress - Monterey Park, CA - *Ed&PubIntYB 82*
Monterey Park Progress - *See* Southern California Publishing Co.
Monterey Peninsula Herald - Monterey, CA - *BaconPubCkNews 84; Ed&PubIntYB 82; NewsDir 84*
Monterey Peninsula Review - *See* Brown & Wilson Corp.
Monterey Peninsula TV Cable [of Western Communications Inc.] - Monterey, CA - *BrCabYB 84; Tel&CabFB 84C*
Monterey Recorder - Monterey, VA - *BaconPubCkNews 84*
Monterey Records - Universal City, CA - *BillIntBG 83-84*

Montesano-Grays Harbor County Vidette - Montesano, WA - *BaconPubCkNews 84; Ed&PubIntYB 82*
Montessori Workshop - Ithaca, NY - *BoPubDir 4*
Montevideo American News [of Pan Publications] - Montevideo, MN - *BaconPubCkNews 84; Ed&PubIntYB 82; NewsDir 84*
Montevideo Shopper - Montevideo, MN - *AyerDirPub 83*
Montezuma Cable TV Co. [of Tele-Media Corp.] - Montezuma, GA - *BrCabYB 84; Tel&CabFB 84C*
Montezuma Citizen & Georgian - Montezuma, GA - *BaconPubCkNews 84*
Montezuma Mutual Telephone Co. - Montezuma, IA - *TelDir&BG 83-84*
Montezuma Press - Montezuma, KS - *BaconPubCkNews 84; Ed&PubIntYB 82*
Montezuma Republican - Montezuma, IA - *BaconPubCkNews 84; Ed&PubIntYB 82*
Montezuma Valley Journal - Cortez, CO - *AyerDirPub 83*
Montford Publications [Aff. of Montford Missionaries] - Bay Shore, NY - *BoPubDir 4, 5*
Montgomery Advertiser [of Advertiser Co.] - Montgomery, AL - *BaconPubCkNews 84; Ed&PubIntYB 82; LitMarPl 83; NewsDir 84*
Montgomery Alabama Journal - Montgomery, AL - *BaconPubCkNews 84*
Montgomery & Associates - Bala Cynwyd, PA - *AdAge 3-28-84; StaDirAdAg 2-84*
Montgomery & Stire Inc. - New Orleans, LA - *StaDirAdAg 2-84*
Montgomery Communications - Seattle, WA - *BoPubDir 4, 5*
Montgomery County Cablevision Inc. [of Tribune Cable Communications Inc.] - Gaithersburg, MD - *BrCabYB 84; Tel&CabFB 84C*
Montgomery County CATV Inc. [of Communications Systems Inc.] - Montgomery County, TX - *Tel&CabFB 84C*
Montgomery County CATV Inc. [of Communications Systems Inc.] - Shenandoah, TX - *BrCabYB 84*
Montgomery County Daily Courier - Conroe, TX - *BaconPubCkNews 84*
Montgomery County Government (Publications Office) - Rockville, MD - *BoPubDir 4, 5*
Montgomery County News - Mt. Ida, AR - *AyerDirPub 83; Ed&PubIntYB 82*
Montgomery County News - Clarksville, TN - *AyerDirPub 83*
Montgomery County Observer - Center Square, PA - *AyerDirPub 83*
Montgomery County Observer, The - Norristown, PA - *Ed&PubIntYB 82*
Montgomery County Record - Horsham, PA - *BaconPubCkNews 84*
Montgomery County Sentinel [of Rockville Sentinel Newspapers] - Rockville, MD - *AyerDirPub 83; NewsDir 84*
Montgomery Herald - Montgomery County, NC - *Ed&PubIntYB 82*
Montgomery Herald - Troy, NC - *AyerDirPub 83; NewsDir 84*
Montgomery Herald - Montgomery, WV - *BaconPubCkNews 84; Ed&PubIntYB 82; NewsDir 84*
Montgomery Independent - Montgomery, AL - *BaconPubCkNews 84; Ed&PubIntYB 82; NewsDir 84*
Montgomery Journal, The - Washington, DC - *Ed&PubIntYB 82*
Montgomery Journal, The - Bethesda, MD - *AyerDirPub 83*
Montgomery Journal, The - Rockville, MD - *NewsDir 84*
Montgomery Messenger - Montgomery, MN - *BaconPubCkNews 84; Ed&PubIntYB 82*
Montgomery Monitor, The - Mt. Vernon, GA - *Ed&PubIntYB 82*
Montgomery Museum of Fine Arts - Montgomery, AL - *BoPubDir 4, 5*
Montgomery Music Inc., Bob - Nashville, TN - *BillIntBG 83-84*
Montgomery News, The - Mt. Sterling, KY - *Ed&PubIntYB 82*
Montgomery Post - King of Prussia, PA - *Ed&PubIntYB 82*
Montgomery Publications Inc. - Junction City, KS - *BaconPubCkNews 84*
Montgomery Publishing Co. - Ft. Washington, PA - *BaconPubCkNews 84*
Montgomery Publishing Co. - Austin, TX - *BillIntBG 83-84*
Montgomery Standard - Montgomery City, MO - *AyerDirPub 83; BaconPubCkNews 84; Ed&PubIntYB 82; NewsDir 84*
Montgomery Sycamore Messenger News - Montgomery, OH - *BaconPubCkNews 84*
Montgomery/Tuskegee Times - Montgomery, AL - *Ed&PubIntYB 82*
Montgomery Video Corp. - Montgomery, PA - *BrCabYB 84; Tel&CabFB 84C*
Montgomery, Zukerman, Davis Inc. - Indianapolis, IN - *StaDirAdAg 2-84*
Montgomeryville Spirit [of Montgomery Publishing Co.] - Ft. Washington, PA - *AyerDirPub 83; NewsDir 84*
Montgomeryville Spirit - Montgomeryville, PA - *Ed&PubIntYB 82*
Montgomeryville Spirit - *See* Montgomery Publishing Co.
Monthly Bildor [of Builders Association of Metropolitan Detroit] - Manistique, MI - *MagDir 84*
Monthly Current Economic Indicators [of Chase Econometrics/ Interactive Data Corp.] - Waltham, MA - *DataDirOnSer 84*
Monthly Detroit - Detroit, MI - *ArtMar 84; BaconPubCkMag 84; MagDir 84; MagIndMarPl 82-83; WritMar 84*
Monthly Energy Review - Washington, DC - *DirOnDB Spring 84*
Monthly Energy Review [of I. P. Sharp Associates Ltd.] - Toronto, ON, Canada - *DataDirOnSer 84*
Monthly Far East [of Chase Econometrics/Interactive Data Corp.] - Waltham, MA - *DataDirOnSer 84*
Monthly Far East - *See* Far East
Monthly Latin America [of Chase Econometrics/Interactive Data Corp.] - Waltham, MA - *DataDirOnSer 84*
Monthly Latin America - Bala Cynwyd, PA - *DirOnDB Spring 84*
Monthly Magazine of Food & Wine, The - New York, NY - *MagIndMarPl 82-83*
Monthly Petroleum Statement [of I. P. Sharp Associates Ltd.] - Toronto, ON, Canada - *DataDirOnSer 84*
Monthly Petroleum Statistics Report - Washington, DC - *DirOnDB Spring 84*
Monthly Price Review [of Urner Barry Publications Inc.] - Bayville, NJ - *NewsDir 84*
Monthly Report of Heating Oil [of I. P. Sharp Associates Ltd.] - Toronto, ON, Canada - *DataDirOnSer 84*
Monthly Report of Heating Oil & Other Middle Distillate Sales by State - New York, NY - *DirOnDB Spring 84*
Monthly Review Press [Div. of Monthly Review Foundation Inc.] - New York, NY - *LitMarPl 83, 84*
Monthly Supply & Disposition Report [of I. P. Sharp Associates Ltd.] - Toronto, ON, Canada - *DataDirOnSer 84*
Monthly Tax Features - Washington, DC - *MagIndMarPl 82-83*
Monticello Advance-Monticellonian - Monticello, AR - *BaconPubCkNews 84*
Monticello Books Inc. [Aff. of Jefferson Publications Inc.] - Lake Zurich, IL - *BoPubDir 4, 5*
Monticello Cable Communications [of Centel Cable Television Co.] - Monticello, IL - *BrCabYB 84*
Monticello Cable Co. [of Cumberland Valley Cablevision Inc.] - Monticello, KY - *BrCabYB 84*
Monticello Cable TV [of Cable Specialties Ltd.] - Monticello, FL - *Tel&CabFB 84C*
Monticello Express - Monticello, IA - *BaconPubCkNews 84; Ed&PubIntYB 82; NewsDir 84*
Monticello Herald-Journal - Monticello, IN - *BaconPubCkNews 84; NewsDir 84*
Monticello Lawrence County Press - Monticello, MS - *BaconPubCkNews 84*
Monticello Messenger - Monticello, WI - *BaconPubCkNews 84; Ed&PubIntYB 82*
Monticello News - Monticello, FL - *BaconPubCkNews 84; Ed&PubIntYB 82*
Monticello News - Monticello, GA - *AyerDirPub 83; BaconPubCkNews 84; Ed&PubIntYB 82*
Monticello Piatt County Journal Republican - Monticello, IL - *BaconPubCkNews 84; NewsDir 84*
Monticello Productions - Monticello, FL - *BillIntBG 83-84*
Monticello San Juan Record - Monticello, UT - *BaconPubCkNews 84*
Monticello Times - Monticello, MN - *BaconPubCkNews 84; Ed&PubIntYB 82*
Monticello Video Corp. - Monticello, NY - *BrCabYB 84*
Monticello Wayne County Outlook - Monticello, KY - *BaconPubCkNews 84; NewsDir 84*
Montle Advertising Ltd. - Halifax, NS, Canada - *StaDirAdAg 2-84*
Montmorency County Tribune - Atlanta, MI - *AyerDirPub 83; Ed&PubIntYB 82*

Montour Computer Systems Inc. - Euclid, OH - *MicrocomMPl 84*
Montour Falls TV Corp. - Montour Falls, NY - *BrCabYB 84*
Montpelier Countyline - Montpelier, OH - *Ed&PubIntYB 82; NewsDir 84*
Montpelier Herald, The - Montpelier, IN - *Ed&PubIntYB 82*
Montpelier Leader-Enterprise - Montpelier, OH - *BaconPubCkNews 84; Ed&PubIntYB 82*
Montpelier News Examiner - Montpelier, ID - *BaconPubCkNews 84*
Montreal Gazette - Montreal, PQ, Canada - *LitMarPl 83*
Montreal Health Press Inc. - Montreal, PQ, Canada - *BoPubDir 4, 5*
Montrose Broadcasting Corp. - Montrose, PA - *BrCabYB 84*
Montrose Herald - Montrose, SD - *BaconPubCkNews 84; Ed&PubIntYB 82*
Montrose Independent [of County Publishers Corp.] - Montrose, PA - *BaconPubCkNews 84; Ed&PubIntYB 82; NewsDir 84*
Montrose Mutual Telephone Co. - Dietrich, IL - *TelDir&BG 83-84*
Montrose Press - Montrose, CO - *BaconPubCkNews 84; Ed&PubIntYB 82; NewsDir 84*
Montrose Telecable Co. Inc. [of Community Tele-Communications Inc.] - Montrose, CO - *BrCabYB 84; Tel&CabFB 84C*
Montross Westmoreland News - *See* Atlantic Publications
Montuno Records Inc. - New York, NY - *BillIntBG 83-84*
Montville Herald - *See* Lincoln Park Herald Inc.
Montwyo Agri-News - Billings, MT - *AyerDirPub 83*
Monument Computer Service - Joshua Tree, CA - *MicrocomMPl 84*
Monument El Paso County Tribune - Monument, CO - *BaconPubCkNews 84*
Monument Record Corp. - Nashville, TN - *BillIntBG 83-84*
Monumental Films & Recordings Inc. - Baltimore, MD - *AvMarPl 83*
Moody Bible Institute of Chicago, The - Chicago, IL - *BrCabYB 84*
Moody Cable TV [of Jones Intercable Inc.] - Moody Air Force Base, GA - *Tel&CabFB 84C*
Moody County Enterprise - Flandreau, SD - *AyerDirPub 83; Ed&PubIntYB 82*
Moody Courier - Moody, TX - *BaconPubCkNews 84; Ed&PubIntYB 82*
Moody District TV - Toledo, OR - *Tel&CabFB 84C*
Moody Monthly - Chicago, IL - *BaconPubCkMag 84; MagDir 84; MagIndMarPl 82-83*
Moody Music, Doug - Carlsbad, CA - *BillIntBG 83-84*
Moody Press - Chicago, IL - *LitMarPl 83, 84*
Moody Street Irregulars - Clarence Center, NY - *BoPubDir 4, 5; LitMag&SmPr 83-84*
Moody's Investors Service - New York, NY - *BoPubDir 5; InfoS 83-84*
Mook & Blanchard - La Puente, CA - *LitMarPl 83, 84*
Moon Books - Berkeley, CA - *BoPubDir 4, 5*
Moon June Music - Portland, OR - *BillIntBG 83-84*
Moon Publications - Chico, CA - *BoPubDir 4, 5; LitMag&SmPr 83-84; LitMarPl 84*
Moon Shine Records - Nashville, TN - *BillIntBG 83-84*
Moonbow Music - *See* Appalshop Inc.
Mooney, David P. - Hot Springs, AR - *Tel&CabFB 84C p.1692*
Moonlight Press, The - Troy, NY - *ArtMar 84*
Moonlight Productions - Mountain View, CA - *AvMarPl 83*
Moonlight Productions - Universal City, CA - *AvMarPl 83*
Moonlight Publications - La Jolla, CA - *BoPubDir 4, 5; LitMag&SmPr 83-84*
Moonlight Records - Chapel Hill, NC - *BillIntBG 83-84*
Moonlight Two Music - *See* Fricon Entertainment Co. Inc., The
Moonmad Press - Terre Haute, IN - *BoPubDir 4, 5*
Moonridge Music - *See* Pacific Challenger Music
Moonsquilt Press - Brattleboro, VT - *BoPubDir 4*
Moonsquilt Press & Distribution - Miami, FL - *BoPubDir 5; LitMag&SmPr 83-84*
Moonstone Press - Anaheim, CA - *BoPubDir 4, 5*
Moorcroft Leader - Moorcroft, WY - *BaconPubCkNews 84; Ed&PubIntYB 82*
Moore Advertising Inc., D. J. - Guilderland, NY - *StaDirAdAg 2-84*
Moore Agency, William - New York, NY - *InfIndMarPl 83*
Moore & Associates, Julie (Biological Information Service) - Riverside, CA - *DataDirOnSer 84*
Moore & Liberty Telephone Co. - Enderlin, ND - *TelDir&BG 83-84*
Moore-Barnes Co., The - Roseburg, OR - *MicrocomMPl 84*
Moore, Brian - Brooklyn, NY - *MagIndMarPl 82-83*
Moore Business Forms - Glenville, IL - *DirInfWP 82*
Moore Business Systems [Subs. of Moore Business Forms Inc.] - Dallas, TX - *WhoWMicrocom 83*
Moore Co., S. Spencer - Charleston, WV - *AvMarPl 83*
Moore Cookbook, Mary - Lombardy, ON, Canada - *BoPubDir 5*
Moore Cookbook, Mary - Perth, ON, Canada - *BoPubDir 4*
Moore-Cottrell Subscription Agencies Inc. - North Cohocton, NY - *EISS 83; MagIndMarPl 82-83*
Moore County News - Lynchburg, TN - *AyerDirPub 83; Ed&PubIntYB 82*
Moore County News-Press - Dumas, TX - *AyerDirPub 83; Ed&PubIntYB 82*
Moore County News, The - Carthage, NC - *Ed&PubIntYB 82*
Moore, Diane M. - New Iberia, LA - *BoPubDir 4, 5*
Moore Haven Glades County Democrat - *See* Hammel Newspapers of Florida Inc.
Moore Inc., Art - Seattle, WA - *TelAl 83, 84*
Moore Inc., Forrest W. - Dallas, TX - *ArtMar 84; DirPRFirms 83*
Moore Industries Productions Inc. - Sepulveda, CA - *AvMarPl 83*
Moore, Kyle - *See* TV Cable Co.
Moore Monitor - Moore, OK - *AyerDirPub 83*
Moore Monitor/County Line Monitor - Moore, OK - *BaconPubCkNews 84*
Moore, Nancy Kay - Smyrna, TN - *LitMarPl 83, 84*
Moore Personnel Agency Inc. - New York, NY - *LitMarPl 83*
Moore Public Relations Inc. - Phoenix, AZ - *DirPRFirms 83*
Moore Publishing Co. Inc. - Oak Park, IL - *BoPubDir 4, 5*
Moore Qualitative - New York, NY - *IntDirMarRes 83*
Moore, Woodrow - Norfolk, VA - *LitMarPl 83, 84*
Moorefield Examiner - Moorefield, WV - *AyerDirPub 83; BaconPubCkNews 84; NewsDir 84*
Moorefield Examiner & Hardy County News, The - Moorefield, WV - *Ed&PubIntYB 82*
Mooreland Leader - Mooreland, OK - *BaconPubCkNews 84; Ed&PubIntYB 82*
Mooreland Television Co. - Mooreland, OK - *BrCabYB 84*
Moorepark, Howard - New York, NY - *LitMarPl 83, 84*
Moore's Photo Service - Charleston, WV - *AvMarPl 83*
Moore's TV Cable - Tidioute, PA - *BrCabYB 84; Tel&CabFB 84C*
Moorestown News Chronicle [of Suburban Newspaper Group] - Cherry Hill, NJ - *NewsDir 84*
Moorestown News Chronicle - *See* Suburban Newspapers
Mooresville Times - Mooresville, IN - *BaconPubCkNews 84; NewsDir 84*
Mooresville Tribune - Mooresville, NC - *BaconPubCkNews 84; Ed&PubIntYB 82; NewsDir 84*
Moorex Inc. - Madison, CT - *AvMarPl 83*
Moorhead Advertising/Public Relations, John L. - Durham, NC - *AdAge 3-28-84; StaDirAdAg 2-84*
Moorhead Marketing - San Francisco, CA - *IntDirMarRes 83*
Moorlands Press/Anne Johnston, The - Leek, England - *LitMag&SmPr 83-84*
Moorlands Review, The - Leek, England - *LitMag&SmPr 83-84*
Moos Publishing, Heinz - Baltimore, MD - *LitMarPl 83, 84*
Moosbrugger Marketing Research - La Grange Park, IL - *IntDirMarRes 83*
Moose Jaw Times-Herald - Moose Jaw, SK, Canada - *BaconPubCkNews 84*
Moose Lake Star Gazette - Moose Lake, MN - *BaconPubCkNews 84; NewsDir 84*
Moose Magazine - Chicago, IL - *MagIndMarPl 82-83*
Moose Magazine - Mooseheart, IL - *BaconPubCkMag 84; MagDir 84*
Moose Magazine - Portland, OR - *LitMag&SmPr 83-84*
Moosehead Enterprises Inc. - Greenville, ME - *Tel&CabFB 84C p.1692*
Moosehead Enterprises Inc. - Jackman, ME - *BrCabYB 84*
Moosehead Review, The - Ayer's Cliff, PQ, Canada - *LitMag&SmPr 83-84*

Mooshie & Associates Advertising Inc. - Tallahassee, FL - *StaDirAdAg 2-84*
M.O.P. Press - Ft. Myers, FL - *BoPubDir 4, 5; LitMag&SmPr 83-84*
MoPro Inc. - Cincinnati, OH - *BillIntBG 83-84*
Mor-Mac Publishing Co. - Daytona Beach, FL - *BoPubDir 4, 5*
MOR Records - San Diego, CA - *BillIntBG 83-84*
Mora Advertiser - Mora, MN - *AyerDirPub 83*
Mora Kanabec County Times - Mora, MN - *BaconPubCkNews 84*
Moraga Community Telephone Association - Moraga, CA - *TelDir&BG 83-84*
Moraga Sun, The - Moraga, CA - *Ed&PubIntYB 82*
Moran Agency Inc. - New York, NY - *LitMarPl 83, 84*
Moran & Associates, Joe - Arlington, TX - *DirPRFirms 83*
Moran/Andrews Inc. - Chicago, IL - *BoPubDir 4, 5*
Moran Colorgraphic Inc. - Baton Rouge, LA - *LitMarPl 83, 84*
Moran Co., The Martin J. - New York, NY - *DirPRFirms 83*
Moran Inc. - Greenwich, CT - *IntDirMarRes 83*
Moran, Lanig & Duncan Advertising Inc. - Palo Alto, CA - *StaDirAdAg 2-84*
Moran Publishing Corp. - Baton Rouge, LA - *BoPubDir 4, 5*
Moran, Ray - Albuquerque, NM - *Tel&CabFB 84S*
Moran Stations, Richard J. - Wichita Falls, TX - *BrCabYB 84*
Moravia Republican-Register - Moravia, NY - *Ed&PubIntYB 82*
Moravia Republican Register - *See* Community Newspapers
Moravia TV Cable Service - Moravia, NY - *BrCabYB 84*
Moravia Union - Moravia, IA - *BaconPubCkNews 84; Ed&PubIntYB 82*
More Association, Thomas - Chicago, IL - *AvMarPl 83; LitMarPl 83, 84*
More Book Club, Thomas [Subs. of Thomas More Association] - Chicago, IL - *LitMarPl 83, 84*
More Business - Jerico, NY - *WritMar 84*
More, Harry W. Jr. - Santa Cruz, CA - *BoPubDir 4, 5*
More Institute of Canada for Research in Adult Liberal Studies, Thomas [Aff. of Thomas More Institute for Adult Education] - Montreal, PQ, Canada - *BoPubDir 4 Sup, 5*
More Press, Thomas [Subs. of Thomas More Association] - Chicago, IL - *LitMarPl 83, 84*
Morehead Advertising/Public Relations, Jeanne - Tampa, FL - *StaDirAdAg 2-84*
Morehead Cable TV Co. [of Centel Cable Television Co.] - Olive Hill, KY - *BrCabYB 84*
Morehead City Carteret County News-Times [of Cartevet Publishing Inc.] - Morehead City, NC - *BaconPubCkNews 84; NewsDir 84*
Morehead News - Morehead, KY - *AyerDirPub 83; BaconPubCkNews 84; Ed&PubIntYB 82; NewsDir 84*
Morehouse-Barlow Co. Inc. - Wilton, CT - *LitMarPl 83, 84; WritMar 84*
Moreillon Inc., Robert E. - Detroit, MI - *DirPRFirms 83*
Moreland Co., The Chester C. - Cincinnati, OH - *StaDirAdAg 2-84*
Morenci Observer - Morenci, MI - *BaconPubCkNews 84; Ed&PubIntYB 82; NewsDir 84*
Morency & Associates, Carolyn - Chicago, IL - *DirPRFirms 83*
Moretus Press Inc. - New York, NY - *LitMag&SmPr 83-84; LitMarPl 83, 84*
Morgan Advertising & Public Relations, Thomas E. - Pittsburgh, PA - *DirPRFirms 83*
Morgan Advertising Inc., Dick - New York, NY - *StaDirAdAg 2-84*
Morgan Advertising, Leon - Chicago, IL - *StaDirAdAg 2-84*
Morgan & Associates Advertising - Richmond, VA - *StaDirAdAg 2-84*
Morgan & Associates Inc. - Joplin, MO - *StaDirAdAg 2-84*
Morgan & Morgan Inc. - Dobbs Ferry, NY - *LitMarPl 83, 84*
Morgan Associates - Fairfield, CT - *StaDirAdAg 2-84*
Morgan Burchette Associates - Alexandria, VA - *AdAge 3-28-84; StaDirAdAg 2-84*
Morgan Cable TV Inc. - Hartselle, AL - *Tel&CabFB 84C*
Morgan City Review - Morgan City, LA - *BaconPubCkNews 84*
Morgan City St. Mary Journal - Morgan City, LA - *BaconPubCkNews 84*
Morgan, Cohen & Naish Inc. - Philadelphia, PA - *StaDirAdAg 2-84*
Morgan Communications Group Inc. - Chicago, IL - *DirPRFirms 83*
Morgan Communications, Janice - New York, NY - *LitMarPl 83, 84*
Morgan Co., John D. - Santa Barbara, CA - *StaDirAdAg 2-84*
Morgan Computer Services, Gareth - Bristol, England - *MicrocomSwDir 1*
Morgan Computing Co. Inc. - Dallas, TX - *MicrocomMPl 84*
Morgan Consultants, J. H. - Morristown, NJ - *TeleSy&SerDir 7-83*
Morgan County Cablevision Inc. - Wartburg, TN - *Tel&CabFB 84C*
Morgan County Herald - McConnelsville, OH - *AyerDirPub 83; Ed&PubIntYB 82; NewsDir 84*
Morgan County News - Morgan County, TN - *Ed&PubIntYB 82*
Morgan County News - Heber City, UT - *Ed&PubIntYB 82*
Morgan County News - Morgan, UT - *AyerDirPub 83*
Morgan County News - *See* Wave Publishing Co.
Morgan County Press - Decatur, AL - *Ed&PubIntYB 82*
Morgan County Press - Stover, MO - *Ed&PubIntYB 82*
Morgan County Tele-Cable Inc. [of Horizon Communications Corp.] - Martinsville, IN - *Tel&CabFB 84C*
Morgan-Fairfield Graphics - Seattle, WA - *MicrocomMPl 84; MicrocomSwDir 1*
Morgan-Grampian Publishing Co. - New York, NY - *MagIndMarPl 82-83*
Morgan Hill Times & San Martin News [of McClatchy Newspapers Inc.] - Morgan Hill, CA - *BaconPubCkNews 84; Ed&PubIntYB 82; NewsDir 84*
Morgan Horse, The [of American Morgan Horse Association] - Westmoreland, NY - *ArtMar 84; WritMar 84*
Morgan Inc., Mark - Newman, GA - *Ed&PubIntYB 82*
Morgan Library, Pierpont - New York, NY - *BoPubDir 4, 5*
Morgan Messenger - Morgan, MN - *BaconPubCkNews 84; Ed&PubIntYB 82*
Morgan Messenger - Berkeley Springs, WV - *AyerDirPub 83; Ed&PubIntYB 82*
Morgan Music Group - Prescott, AR - *BillIntBG 83-84*
Morgan Press - Lomita, CA - *BoPubDir 4, 5*
Morgan Press - Dobbs Ferry, NY - *LitMarPl 83, 84; MagIndMarPl 82-83*
Morgan Press - Milwaukee, WI - *BoPubDir 4, 5*
Morgan-Rand Co. - Pleasantville, NY - *BoPubDir 5*
Morgan Research Centre Pty. Ltd., Roy - Melbourne, Australia - *IntDirMarRes 83*
Morgan Sign Machine Co., The - Chicago, IL - *AvMarPl 83*
Morgan Stanley & Co. - New York, NY - *CabTVFinDB 83*
Morgan/Technical Corp., The - Modesto, CA - *MicrocomMPl 83*
Morgan/Uniphoto, Barry - Riverridge, LA - *AvMarPl 83*
Morganfield Union County Advocate - Morganfield, KY - *BaconPubCkNews 84; NewsDir 84*
Morganton News-Herald - Morganton, NC - *BaconPubCkNews 84; NewsDir 84*
Morgantown Green River Republican - Morgantown, KY - *NewsDir 84*
Morgantown Green River Republican - *See* Smith Communications Inc., Al
Morhaim Literary Agency, Howard - New York, NY - *LitMarPl 83, 84*
Moriarty Associates, Dan - Newport, MN - *BoPubDir 4, 5*
Morich Inc., Donald - Wilmette, IL - *IntDirMarRes 83*
Moriches Bay Tide - Shirley, NY - *AyerDirPub 83*
Morino Associates Inc. - Vienna, VA - *DataDirSup 7-83*
Morkap Publishing - Gaithersburg, MD - *BaconPubCkNews 84*
Morley Co. - Portsmouth, NH - *DirInfWP 82*
Morley Music Co. - New York, NY - *BillIntBG 83-84*
Morley Telephone Co. Inc. - Morley, IA - *TelDir&BG 83-84*
Morlock Advertising Agency - Chicago, IL - *StaDirAdAg 2-84*
Mormon Church - *See* Bonneville International Corp.
Mormon News Service - Salt Lake City, UT - *Tel&CabFB 84C*
Morning Call, The - Allentown, PA - *Ed&PubIntYB 82; LitMarPl 84*
Morning Call Weekender, The - Allentown, PA - *Ed&PubIntYB 82; LitMarPl 84*
Morning Freiheit - New York, NY - *Ed&PubIntYB 82*
Morning Glory Press - Buena Park, CA - *BoPubDir 4, 5*
Morning Herald, The - Hagerstown, MD - *Ed&PubIntYB 82*

Morning Journal - Lisbon, OH - *BaconPubCkNews 84; Ed&PubIntYB 82*
Morning Music Inc. - Nashville, TN - *BillIntBG 83-84*
Morning News [of The News Journal Co.] - Wilmington, DE - *BaconPubCkNews 84; Ed&PubIntYB 82; NewsDir 84*
Morning News [of Times Publishing Co.] - Erie, PA - *Ed&PubIntYB 82; LitMarPl 84*
Morning News of Southeastern Idaho, The - Blackfoot, ID - *Ed&PubIntYB 82*
Morning Press [of Press-Courier Publishing Co.] - Vista, CA - *NewsDir 84*
Morning Press-Enterprise, The - Riverside, CA - *NewsDir 84*
Morning Press, The - Bloomsburg, PA - *Ed&PubIntYB 82*
Morning Star Music Co. - *See* Robertson Music Corp., Don
Morning Star Press - Haydenville, MA - *BoPubDir 4, 5*
Morning Star Shopping Guide - Albion, MI - *AyerDirPub 83*
Morning Sun - Pittsburg, KS - *Ed&PubIntYB 82*
Morning Sun - Mt. Pleasant, MI - *BaconPubCkNews 84; Ed&PubIntYB 82*
Morning Sun News-Herald - Morning Sun, IA - *AyerDirPub 83; BaconPubCkNews 84; Ed&PubIntYB 82*
Morningside Bookshop [Div. of Morningside House Inc.] - Dayton, OH - *LitMarPl 83, 84*
Morningside Editorial Associates Inc. - Pleasantville, NY - *LitMarPl 83, 84*
Morningside House Inc. - Dayton, OH - *BoPubDir 4*
Moro Cooperative TV Club - Moro, OR - *BrCabYB 84; Tel&CabFB 84C*
Moro Sherman County Journal - Moro, OR - *BaconPubCkNews 84*
Morocco Courier - Morocco, IN - *BaconPubCkNews 84; Ed&PubIntYB 82*
Moroch & Associates Inc. - Dallas, TX - *StaDirAdAg 2-84*
Moroder Enterprises, Giorgio - Los Angeles, CA - *BillIntBG 83-84*
Morphis & Friends Inc. - Winston-Salem, NC - *ArtMar 84*
Morrilton Conway Petit Jean Headlight - Morrilton, AR - *BaconPubCkNews 84*
Morrilton Democrat - Morrilton, AR - *Ed&PubIntYB 82*
Morrilton Video Inc. [of WEHCO Video Inc.] - Morrilton, AR - *BrCabYB 84; Tel&CabFB 84C*
Morris Agency Inc., William - New York, NY - *LitMarPl 83, 84; TelAl 83, 84; Tel&CabFB 84C*
Morris & Co., Edwin H. [Div. of MPL Communications Inc.] - New York, NY - *BillIntBG 83-84*
Morris & Co. Inc., Mark - Minneapolis, MN - *StaDirAdAg 2-84*
Morris & Guthrie Marketing Communications - San Antonio, TX - *StaDirAdAg 2-84*
Morris Associates - Cincinnati, OH - *EISS 5-84 Sup*
Morris Associates Inc., Seymour - Gloversville, NY - *StaDirAdAg 2-84*
Morris Associates, Robert - Philadelphia, PA - *BoPubDir 5*
Morris Books, Victoria S. - Oakland, CA - *BoPubDir 4, 5*
Morris Cable Services Inc. - Morris, NY - *BrCabYB 84; Tel&CabFB 84C*
Morris, Carroll F. - Baxley, GA - *BrCabYB 84 p.D-304; Tel&CabFB 84C p.1692*
Morris CATV Associates [of Tele-Communications Inc.] - Morris, IL - *BrCabYB 84*
Morris Communications Co. [of OT & T Communications Inc.] - Morris, OK - *Tel&CabFB 84C*
Morris Communications Corp. - Augusta, GA - *AdAge 6-28-84; KnowInd 83*
Morris Communications Corp. - Savannah, GA - *Ed&PubIntYB 82*
Morris Communications Corp. - New Rochelle, NY - *StaDirAdAg 2-84*
Morris Co., Norman A. - Los Angeles, CA - *StaDirAdAg 2-84*
Morris County Historical Society - Morristown, NJ - *LitMag&SmPr 83-84*
Morris Genealogical Library - Allenhurst, NJ - *BoPubDir 4, 5*
Morris Harvey College Publications - Charleston, WV - *BoPubDir 4, 5*
Morris Herald [of B. F. Shaw Printing Co.] - Morris, IL - *BaconPubCkNews 84; NewsDir 84*
Morris Inc., Tom - Park Ridge, IL - *ArtMar 84; AvMarPl 83; StaDirAdAg 2-84*
Morris Information Network, Philip [of Philip Morris U.S.A.] - Richmond, VA - *EISS 5-84 Sup*
Morris, John - Walnut Creek, CA - *BoPubDir 4 Sup, 5*
Morris Music Inc. - Los Angeles, NY - *BillIntBG 83-84*
Morris Music, Steve - *See* Morris Music Inc.
Morris News - Morris, OK - *BaconPubCkNews 84; Ed&PubIntYB 82*
Morris News Bee - Morris Plains, NJ - *AyerDirPub 83; NewsDir 84*
Morris Newspaper Corp. - Savannah, GA - *BrCabYB 84; Ed&PubIntYB 82*
Morris Plains News-Bee - Morris Plains, NJ - *BaconPubCkNews 84*
Morris Productions Inc., Nelson - New York, NY - *TelAl 83, 84; Tel&CabFB 84C*
Morris Publishing Co. [Aff. of Face Metrics Inc.] - Plymouth Meeting, PA - *BoPubDir 4 Sup, 5*
Morris Software - Las Vegas, NV - *MicrocomMPl 84*
Morris Sun - Morris, MN - *Ed&PubIntYB 82; NewsDir 84*
Morris Sun - *See* Morris Tribune
Morris Tribune - Morris, MN - *BaconPubCkNews 84; Ed&PubIntYB 82; NewsDir 84*
Morris, White & Associates Inc. - Charlotte, NC - *StaDirAdAg 2-84*
Morrison Associates, Ruth - New York, NY - *ArtMar 84; DirPRFirms 83*
Morrison, Butterfield & Boyle Ltd. - Santa Barbara, CA - *BoPubDir 5*
Morrison-Gottlieb Inc. - New York, NY - *DirPRFirms 83*
Morrison Hill Music Publishing Co. - Lodi, NJ - *BillIntBG 83-84*
Morrison Inc., Henry - New York, NY - *LitMarPl 83, 84*
Morrison Museum Association - Islay, AB, Canada - *BoPubDir 4, 5*
Morrison, Raven-Hill Co. Inc. - Beverly Hills, CA - *LitMarPl 84*
Morrison Whiteside News-Sentinel - Morrison, IL - *BaconPubCkNews 84*
Morrisongs Publishing - *See* Morris Music Inc.
Morrisons Cove Herald - Martinsburg, PA - *AyerDirPub 83*
Morrisons Cove Herald - Morrisons Cove, PA - *Ed&PubIntYB 82*
Morrisonville Times - Morrisonville, IL - *BaconPubCkNews 84; Ed&PubIntYB 82*
Morrisseau Syndications [Subs. of Morrisseau Associates, Publishers] - Burlington, VT - *LitMarPl 83, 84*
Morristown Citizen Tribune [of Lakeway Publishers Inc.] - Morristown, TN - *BaconPubCkNews 84; NewsDir 84*
Morristown Daily Gazette-Mail - Morristown, TN - *NewsDir 84*
Morristown Life - Morristown, MN - *AyerDirPub 83; BaconPubCkNews 84; Ed&PubIntYB 82*
Morrisville News & Citizen - *See* News & Citizen Inc.
Morrisville Transcript, The [of Morrisville C. A. Limoge Publishers] - Morrisville, VT - *NewsDir 84*
Morrisville Transcript, The - *See* News & Citizen Inc.
Morro Bay Sun-Bulletin [of Ivanhoe Industries] - Morro Bay, CA - *BaconPubCkNews 84; NewsDir 84*
Morrow - San Leandro, CA - *MicrocomMPl 84*
Morrow & Co. Inc., William [Subs. of The Hearst Corp.] - New York, NY - *LitMarPl 83, 84; WritMar 84*
Morrow, Christopher - Arlington, MA - *MagIndMarPl 82-83*
Morrow County Independent - Cardington, OH - *AyerDirPub 83; NewsDir 84*
Morrow County Independent Register & Tri-County Star, The - Cardington, OH - *Ed&PubIntYB 82*
Morrow County Sentinel - Mt. Gilead, OH - *AyerDirPub 83; Ed&PubIntYB 82; NewsDir 84*
Morrow Designs Inc. - Richmond, CA - *MicrocomMPl 83*
Morrow Designs Inc. - San Leandro, CA - *WhoWMicrocom 83*
Morrow Junior Books [Div. of William Morrow & Co. Inc.] - New York, NY - *LitMarPl 83, 84; WritMar 84*
Morrow Lewis & Kelley - New York, NY - *AdAge 3-28-84; StaDirAdAg 2-84*
Morrow Ltd., Bradford - Santa Barbara, CA - *BoPubDir 4*
Morrow Ltd., Bradford - New York, NY - *BoPubDir 5*
Morrow Photography, Christopher - Arlington, MA - *LitMarPl 83, 84*
Morse Gallery Inc., Mitch - New York, NY - *ArtMar 84*
Morse Inc., Benjamin - Boston, MA - *LitMarPl 83, 84; MagIndMarPl 82-83; WritMar 84*

Morse Press [Div. of Cone-Heiden Printing] - Seattle, WA - *BoPubDir 4; LitMarPl 83, 84*
Mortal Press - Denver, CO - *BoPubDir 4, 5*
Morten Publishing Co. Inc. - Signal Mountain, TN - *BoPubDir 5*
Mortenson Broadcasting Co. - Lexington, KY - *BrCabYB 84*
Mortgage Banking [of Mortgage Bankers Association of America] - Washington, DC - *BaconPubCkMag 84; MagDir 84*
Mortgage Closing Associates - Ogden, UT - *DataDirSup 7-83*
Mortgage Index [of Remote Computing Corp.] - Palo Alto, CA - *DataDirOnSer 84; DirOnDB Spring 84; EISS 83*
Mortgage Insurance Cos. of America - Washington, DC - *BoPubDir 4 Sup, 5*
Morticians of the Southwest [of Farring Inc.] - Garland, TX - *BaconPubCkMag 84; MagDir 84*
Mortimer & Hurst Ltd. - Toronto, ON, Canada - *DirInfWP 82*
Morton Advertising Inc. - New York, NY - *StaDirAdAg 2-84*
Morton Advertising Inc. - Portland, OR - *ArtMar 84; StaDirAdAg 2-84*
Morton Advertising, Ira - Phoenix, AZ - *StaDirAdAg 2-84*
Morton Bay Software - Santa Barbara, CA - *MicrocomMPl 84*
Morton County & Mandan News, The - Mandan, ND - *Ed&PubIntYB 82*
Morton Grove Bugle - *See* Bugle Publications
Morton Grove Champion - Morton Grove, IL - *Ed&PubIntYB 82*
Morton Grove Champion [of Pioneer Press Inc.] - Park Ridge, IL - *NewsDir 84*
Morton Grove Champion - Wilmette, IL - *AyerDirPub 83*
Morton Grove Champion - *See* Pioneer Press Inc.
Morton Grove Life - Morton Grove, IL - *Ed&PubIntYB 82*
Morton Grove Life - Skokie, IL - *AyerDirPub 83*
Morton Grove Life - *See* Myers Publishing Co.
Morton Journal - Morton, WA - *BaconPubCkNews 84*
Morton Productions Inc., Jack - New York, NY - *AvMarPl 83*
Morton Research Corp. - Merrick, NY - *EISS 83*
Morton-Tazewell News - Morton, IL - *NewsDir 84*
Morton Tazewell News - *See* Tazewell Publishing Co.
Morton Tazewell South - *See* Tazewell Publishing Co.
Morton Tribune - Morton, TX - *BaconPubCkNews 84; Ed&PubIntYB 82*
Mortuary Management - Los Angeles, CA - *BaconPubCkMag 84; MagDir 84*
Morvay Advertising Agency - South Orange, NJ - *ArtMar 84; StaDirAdAg 2-84*
Morvue Electronic Systems [Subs. of Industrial-America Corp.] - Newberg, OR - *WhoWMicrocom 83*
Mosaic Arts Co. - Pittsburgh, PA - *Ed&PubIntYB 82*
Mosaic Electronics - Oregon City, OR - *MicrocomMPl 84*
Mosaic Enterprises Ltd. - Kelowna, BC, Canada - *BoPubDir 4 Sup, 5*
Mosaic Media Inc. - Glen Ellyn, IL - *StaDirAdAg 2-84*
Mosaic Press - Tucson, AZ - *BoPubDir 4 Sup, 5*
Mosaic Press - Cincinnati, OH - *BoPubDir 4, 5; LitMag&SmPr 83-84; WritMar 84*
Mosaic Press (Valley Editions) - Oakville, ON, Canada - *BoPubDir 4, 5; LitMag&SmPr 83-84*
Mosaic Publications - Cypress, CA - *BoPubDir 4, 5*
Mosby Co., C. V. [Subs. of The Times Mirror Co.] - St. Louis, MO - *DirMarMP 83; LitMarPl 83, 84; MagIndMarPl 82-83*
Mosby Co. Ltd., C. V. - Scarborough, ON, Canada - *LitMarPl 83, 84*
Moscow TV Cable Co. [of Pullman TV Cable Co.] - Moscow, ID - *BrCabYB 84; Tel&CabFB 84C*
Moscow Villager, The - Moscow, PA - *NewsDir 84*
Mosel & Centerville Telephone Co. [Aff. of Telephone & Data Systems Inc.] - Cleveland, WI - *TelDir&BG 83-84*
Moseley Associates Inc. - New York, NY - *LitMarPl 83, 84; MagIndMarPl 82-83*
Moses Co., Charles A. - Westlake Village, CA - *DirPRFirms 83*
Moses Engineering - Huntsville, AL - *MicrocomMPl 84*
Moses Kimicata Anshell - Phoenix, AZ - *StaDirAdAg 2-84*
Moses Lake Columbia Basin Daily Herald - Moses Lake, WA - *NewsDir 84*
Moses Poetry Collection & Book Publishing Co. Inc. [Aff. of J. Enterprises] - Hudson, NY - *BoPubDir 4, 5*
Moshannon Valley TV Cable Co. Inc. - Philipsburg, PA - *BrCabYB 84*
Mosheim Video Inc. - Mosheim, TN - *Tel&CabFB 84C*
Mosher & Associates Inc. - Wheat Ridge, CO - *StaDirAdAg 2-84*
Mosher Public Relations, Paul R. - New York, NY - *DirPRFirms 83*
Moshman Associates Inc. - Washington, DC - *EISS 83*
Mosinee Telephone Co., The - Mosinee, WI - *TelDir&BG 83-84*
Mosinee Times - Mosinee, WI - *BaconPubCkNews 84; Ed&PubIntYB 82*
Moske & Associates Advertising - Falls Church, VA - *AdAge 3-28-84; StaDirAdAg 2-84*
Moskof & Associates Inc., Martin S. - New York, NY - *ArtMar 84*
Moskowitz/Jacobs Inc. - Scarsdale, NY - *IntDirMarRes 83*
Mosquito Press - London, England - *LitMag&SmPr 83-84*
Moss Advertising Inc. - New York, NY - *BrCabYB 84; TelAl 83, 84*
Moss & Co. Inc. - New York, NY - *StaDirAdAg 2-84*
Moss Communications Inc. - Kingwood, TX - *AvMarPl 83*
Moss Inc., Jerry - New York, NY - *StaDirAdAg 2-84*
Moss Music Group Inc., The - New York, NY - *BillIntBG 83-84*
Moss Publications - Berkeley, CA - *BoPubDir 4, 5*
Moss, Richard - New York, NY - *LitMarPl 83, 84*
Mossart - Weaverville, CA - *BoPubDir 4 Sup, 5*
Mossbauer Effect Reference & Data Center [of University of North Carolina] - Asheville, NC - *CompReadDB 82; EISS 83*
Mostek Corp. [Subs. of United Technologies] - Carrollton, TX - *MicrocomMPl 84*
Motel/Hotel Insider Newsletter - New York, NY - *BaconPubCkMag 84*
Mother Bertha Music Inc. - Los Angeles, CA - *BillIntBG 83-84*
Mother Courage Press - Racine, WI - *LitMag&SmPr 83-84*
Mother Dubbers Inc. - Dallas, TX - *AvMarPl 83*
Mother Duck Press - McNeal, AZ - *BoPubDir 4, 5; LitMag&SmPr 83-84*
Mother Earth News - Hendersonville, NC - *BaconPubCkMag 84; BrCabYB 84; DirMarMP 83; Folio 83; LitMarPl 83, 84; MagDir 84; MagIndMarPl 82-83; WritMar 84*
Mother Earth Poetry - Baltimore, MD - *LitMag&SmPr 83-84*
Mother Gail Music - *See* Royal Martian Music
Mother Jones [of Foundation for National Progress] - San Francisco, CA - *BaconPubCkMag 84; LitMarPl 83, 84; MagDir 84; MagIndMarPl 82-83*
Mother Thunder Publishing Co. - Northridge, CA - *BillIntBG 83-84*
Motheral Ltd., George B. - Pittsburgh, PA - *StaDirAdAg 2-84*
Mothering - Baltimore, MD - *LitMag&SmPr 83-84*
Motheroot Journal - Pittsburgh, PA - *LitMag&SmPr 83-84*
Motheroot Publications - Pittsburgh, PA - *BoPubDir 4, 5; LitMag&SmPr 83-84*
Mothers' Manual - New York, NY - *MagIndMarPl 82-83*
Mothers Today - New York, NY - *BaconPubCkMag 84; MagDir 84; WritMar 84*
Motherway's Professional Services - Urbana, IL - *LitMarPl 84*
Motif/Arkenstone - Atlanta, GA - *LitMag&SmPr 83-84*
Motion Message Corp. - Holbrook, NY - *AvMarPl 83*
Motion Picture & Television Writing Consultants - Hollywood, CA - *LitMarPl 84*
Motion Picture Editors - New York, NY - *AvMarPl 83*
Motion Picture Enterprises Inc. - Tarrytown, NY - *Tel&CabFB 84C*
Motion Picture Laboratories Inc. - Memphis, TN - *AvMarPl 83*
Motion Picture Magazine - New York, NY - *MagDir 84*
Motion Picture Product Digest [of Quigley Publishing Co.] - New York, NY - *BaconPubCkMag 84; MagDir 84*
Motion Picture Service Co. - San Francisco, CA - *TelAl 83, 84; Tel&CabFB 84C*
Motion Picture Video Corp. - Toronto, ON, Canada - *AvMarPl 83*
Motion Technology Corp. - Aston, PA - *DirInfWP 82*
Motivation Analysis Inc. - Long Branch, NJ - *IntDirMarRes 83; Tel&CabFB 84C*
Motivation Development Inc. - Bishop, CA - *BoPubDir 4, 5*
Motivation Media Inc. - Glenview, IL - *ArtMar 84; AvMarPl 83; WritMar 84*
Motivational Aids - Endicott, NY - *BoPubDir 5*
Motivational Communications Inc. - New York, NY - *BoPubDir 5; DirPRFirms 83; HBIndAd&MS 82-83; LitMarPl 83, 84; MagIndMarPl 82-83*

Motivational Marketing Inc. - Paramus, NJ - *ADAPSOMemDir 83-84*
Motivational Media - Los Angeles, CA - *AvMarPl 83*
Motivational Programmers Inc. - New York, NY - *HBIndAd&MS 82-83*
Motivational Research - Brooklyn, NY - *IntDirMarRes 83*
Motivators Inc. - Houston, TX - *DirPRFirms 83*
Motocross Action Magazine - Encino, CA - *MagIndMarPl 82-83*
Motocross Action Magazine - Mission Hills, CA - *WritMar 84*
Motocross Action Magazine - San Fernando, CA - *MagDir 84*
Motor [of Hearst Magazines] - New York, NY - *BaconPubCkMag 84; Folio 83; MagDir 84; MagIndMarPl 82-83; NewsBur 6; WritMar 84*
Motor/Age - Radnor, PA - *BaconPubCkMag 84; MagIndMarPl 82-83*
Motor Boating & Sailing [of Hearst Corp.] - New York, NY - *BaconPubCkMag 84; MagDir 84; MagIndMarPl 82-83; NewsBur 6; WritMar 84*
Motor Club News - Newark, NJ - *BaconPubCkMag 84; MagDir 84*
Motor in Canada - Winnipeg, MB, Canada - *BaconPubCkMag 84*
Motor News - Cherry Hill, NJ - *MagDir 84*
Motor North [of Northland Publishing Corp.] - Minneapolis, MN - *BaconPubCkMag 84; MagDir 84*
Motor Service [of Hunter Publishing Co.] - Des Plaines, IL - *BaconPubCkMag 84; MagDir 84; MagIndMarPl 82-83; WritMar 84*
Motor Tech - New York, NY - *BaconPubCkMag 84*
Motor Transportation Hi-Lights - Columbia, SC - *BaconPubCkMag 84; MagDir 84*
Motor Travel - Columbus, OH - *BaconPubCkMag 84; MagDir 84*
Motor Trend [of Petersen Publishing Co.] - Los Angeles, CA - *BaconPubCkMag 84; Folio 83; MagDir 84; MagIndMarPl 82-83; WritMar 84*
Motor Truck - Toronto, ON, Canada - *BaconPubCkMag 84*
Motor Vehicle Manufacturers Association of the U.S. Inc. - Detroit, MI - *BoPubDir 5*
Motor Vehicle Registrations [of Computer Sciences of Australia Pty. Ltd.] - St. Leonards, Australia - *DataDirOnSer 84*
Motor Vehicle Safety Defect Recall Campaign [of National Highway Traffic Safety Administration] - Washington, DC - *CompReadDB 82*
Motor West [of McHenry Publishing Co.] - Orange, CA - *MagDir 84*
Motorboat - Boston, MA - *MagDir 84*
Motorbooks International Publishers & Wholesalers Inc. - Osceola, WI - *LitMarPl 83, 84; WritMar 84*
Motorcycle - St. Paul, MN - *BaconPubCkMag 84*
Motorcycle Dealer & Trade - Toronto, ON, Canada - *WritMar 84*
Motorcycle Dealer News - Irvine, CA - *BaconPubCkMag 84*
Motorcycle Dealer News - Santa Ana, CA - *MagDir 84; WritMar 84*
Motorcycle Industry Business Journal - Costa Mesa, CA - *BaconPubCkMag 84*
Motorcycle Industry Shopper - Thousand Oaks, CA - *BaconPubCkMag 84*
Motorcycle Product News - Van Nuys, CA - *BaconPubCkMag 84; MagDir 84; MagIndMarPl 82-83*
Motorcycle Weekly - Newport Beach, CA - *MagDir 84*
Motorcyclist [of Petersen Publishing Co.] - Los Angeles, CA - *ArtMar 84; BaconPubCkMag 84; MagDir 84; MagIndMarPl 82-83; WritMar 84*
Motorhome - Agoura, CA - *BaconPubCkMag 84; MagDir 84; MagIndMarPl 82-83; WritMar 84*
Motorist, The [of Northampton County Motor Club] - Columbus, OH - *BaconPubCkMag 84; MagDir 84*
Motorist, The [of Mid-State Auto Club] - Johnstown, PA - *BaconPubCkMag 84; MagDir 84*
Motorist, The [of East Penn Motor Club] - Pottstown, PA - *BaconPubCkMag 84*
Motorland [of California State Automobile Association] - San Francisco, CA - *BaconPubCkMag 84; Folio 83; MagDir 84; MagIndMarPl 82-83*
Motormatics Publications [Aff. of Beach Cities Enterprises] - Long Beach, CA - *BoPubDir 4, 5*
Motorola Inc. - Schaumburg, IL - *ElecNews 7-25-83; Top100Al 83*
Motorola Inc. (Information Systems Group) - Schaumburg, IL - *Datamation 6-83*
Motour - Cincinnati, OH - *BaconPubCkMag 84*
Motown Industries - Hollywood, CA - *KnowInd 83*
Motown Record Corp. - Los Angeles, CA - *BillIntBG 83-84*
Motrix [of Cleworth Publishing Co. Inc.] - Cos Cob, CT - *BaconPubCkMag 84; MagDir 84*
Mott Cable System Inc. [of Midcontinent Cable Systems Inc.] - Mott, ND - *Tel&CabFB 84C*
Mott Cable TV [of Midcontinent Cable Systems Inc.] - Mott, ND - *BrCabYB 84*
Mott Media [Aff. of Evangelical Book Club] - Milford, MI - *ArtMar 84; BoPubDir 4, 5; DirMarMP 83; LitMarPl 84; WritMar 84*
Mott Pioneer Press - Mott, ND - *BaconPubCkNews 84; Ed&PubIntYB 82*
Mottus, Allan - New York, NY - *HBIndAd&MS 82-83*
Moulder Trust, Rebecca Hunt - Tucson, AZ - *BoPubDir 4, 5*
Moulton Advertiser [of Slaco] - Moulton, AL - *BaconPubCkNews 84; Ed&PubIntYB 82; NewsDir 84*
Moulton Eagle, The - Moulton, TX - *Ed&PubIntYB 82*
Moulton Eagle, The - *See* Hallettsville Publishing Co.
Moulton Tribune - Moulton, IA - *Ed&PubIntYB 82*
Moulton Weekly Tribune - Moulton, IA - *BaconPubCkNews 84*
Moultrie County Cablevision Inc. - Sullivan, IL - *Tel&CabFB 84C p.1692*
Moultrie County Historical & Genealogical Society - Sullivan, IL - *BoPubDir 4, 5*
Moultrie Independent Telephone Co. - Lovington, IL - *TelDir&BG 83-84*
Moultrie News [of The Charleston Journal] - Charleston, SC - *NewsDir 84*
Moultrie News - *See* Community Press Inc.
Moultrie Observer - Moultrie, GA - *BaconPubCkNews 84; Ed&PubIntYB 82; NewsDir 84*
Moultrie Telecommunications Inc. [of Moultrie County Cablevision Inc.] - Lovington, IL - *Tel&CabFB 84C*
Moultrie Weekly Observer - Moultrie, GA - *BaconPubCkNews 84*
Mound Bayou Cable TV [of Action Communications Co.] - Mound Bayou, MS - *BrCabYB 84; Tel&CabFB 84C*
Mound City Cablevision Inc. - Mound City, MO - *BrCabYB 84*
Mound City News-Independent - Mound City, MO - *BaconPubCkNews 84; Ed&PubIntYB 82; NewsDir 84*
Mound Laker, The - Mound, MN - *Ed&PubIntYB 82*
Mound Valley Times-Journal - Mound Valley, KS - *BaconPubCkNews 84*
Moundridge Journal - Moundridge, KS - *Ed&PubIntYB 82*
Moundridge Journal - *See* Tempro Inc.
Moundridge Telephone Co. - Moundridge, KS - *TelDir&BG 83-84*
Mounds Pulaski Enterprise - Mounds, IL - *BaconPubCkNews 84; NewsDir 84*
Moundsville Echo - Moundsville, WV - *BaconPubCkNews 84; Ed&PubIntYB 82; NewsDir 84*
Moundville Telephone Co. Inc. - Moundville, AL - *TelDir&BG 83-84*
Mount & Nadler Inc. - New York, NY - *DirPRFirms 83*
Mountain Advisor - Mars Hill, NC - *Ed&PubIntYB 82*
Mountain Advocate - Barbourville, KY - *AyerDirPub 83*
Mountain Books - Santa Barbara, CA - *BoPubDir 4, 5*
Mountain Broadcasters - North Fork, CA - *Tel&CabFB 84C*
Mountain Brook Cablevision Inc. [of McDonald Group] - Mountain Brook, AL - *BrCabYB 84; Tel&CabFB 84C*
Mountain Cable Systems Inc. - Pikeville, KY - *Tel&CabFB 84C*
Mountain Cable Systems Inc. - Quicksand, KY - *BrCabYB 84*
Mountain Cablevision - Neon, KY - *BrCabYB 84*
Mountain Cablevision - Huntsville, TN - *BrCabYB 84; Tel&CabFB 84C*
Mountain Cablevision - Jamestown, TN - *BrCabYB 84*
Mountain Cablevision - Maidsville, WV - *BrCabYB 84*
Mountain Cablevision Ltd. - Hamilton, ON, Canada - *BrCabYB 84*
Mountain Cat Press - Denver, CO - *LitMag&SmPr 83-84*
Mountain Cat Review - Denver, CO - *LitMag&SmPr 83-84*
Mountain City Cablesystems [of American Cablesystems Corp.] - Mountain City, TN - *Tel&CabFB 84C*
Mountain City Tomahawk - Mountain City, TN - *BaconPubCkNews 84; NewsDir 84*

Mountain City TV Co. [of Service Electric Cable TV Inc.] - Hazleton, PA - *BrCabYB 84; Tel&CabFB 84C*
Mountain Computer Inc. - Santa Cruz, CA - *WhoWMicrocom 83*
Mountain Computer Inc. - Scotts Valley, CA - *MicrocomMPl 83, 84*
Mountain Courier - Crestline, CA - *AyerDirPub 83; Ed&PubIntYB 82; NewsDir 84*
Mountain Democrat & Placerville Times - Placerville, CA - *AyerDirPub 83; Ed&PubIntYB 82*
Mountain Eagle - Jasper, AL - *AyerDirPub 83*
Mountain Eagle - Hunter, NY - *AyerDirPub 83*
Mountain Echo - Yellville, AR - *AyerDirPub 83; Ed&PubIntYB 82*
Mountain Echo - Ironton, MO - *AyerDirPub 83; Ed&PubIntYB 82*
Mountain Echo - Keyser, WV - *AyerDirPub 83*
Mountain Echo & Daily News Tribune Weekender, The - Keyser, WV - *Ed&PubIntYB 82*
Mountain Ghost Music - Tacoma, WA - *BillIntBG 83-84*
Mountain Green Music - *See* Sound Column Cos., The
Mountain Grove Journal - Mountain Grove, MO - *Ed&PubIntYB 82*
Mountain Grove News Journal - Mountain Grove, MO - *BaconPubCkNews 84; NewsDir 84*
Mountain-Grove Williamsville Telephone Co. - Williamsville, VA - *TelDir&BG 83-84*
Mountain Home Baxter Bulletin [of Multimedia Newspaper Co. Inc.] - Mountain Home, AR - *BaconPubCkNews 84; NewsDir 84*
Mountain Home News - Mountain Home, ID - *AyerDirPub 83; Ed&PubIntYB 82; NewsDir 84*
Mountain Home News - *See* News Publishing Co. Inc.
Mountain Home Telephone Co. Inc. [Aff. of Century Telephone Enterprises Inc.] - Mountain Home, AR - *TelDir&BG 83-84*
Mountain Home Wing Spread - *See* News Publishing Co. Inc.
Mountain House Publishing Inc. [Aff. of C.P.I.] - Waitsfield, VT - *BoPubDir 4 Sup, 5*
Mountain Journal/Orange Cove News, The - Fresno County, CA - *Ed&PubIntYB 82*
Mountain Lake/Butterfield Observer/Advocate - Mountain Lake, MN - *AyerDirPub 83*
Mountain Lake Cablevision Inc. - Mountain Lake, MN - *BrCabYB 84; Tel&CabFB 84C*
Mountain Lake Observer/Advocate - Mountain Lake, MN - *BaconPubCkNews 84; Ed&PubIntYB 82*
Mountain Lion Books - Rocky Hill, NJ - *LitMarPl 83, 84*
Mountain Mail - Salida, CO - *AyerDirPub 83; BaconPubCkNews 84; Ed&PubIntYB 82*
Mountain Messenger - Downieville, CA - *AyerDirPub 83; Ed&PubIntYB 82*
Mountain News - Hiawassee, GA - *Ed&PubIntYB 82*
Mountain News & Mountaineer - Lake Arrowhead, CA - *AyerDirPub 83; Ed&PubIntYB 82*
Mountain Park Cable TV - Mountain Park, OR - *BrCabYB 84*
Mountain Park Homeowners Association - Mountain Park, OR - *Tel&CabFB 84C*
Mountain Press Publishing Co. - Missoula, MT - *DirMarMP 83; LitMag&SmPr 83-84; LitMarPl 83, 84; WritMar 84*
Mountain Railroad Music - Madison, WI - *BillIntBG 83-84*
Mountain Railroad Records Inc. - Madison, WI - *BillIntBG 83-84*
Mountain Records - North Miami Beach, FL - *BillIntBG 83-84*
Mountain Rural Telephone Cooperative Corp. Inc. - West Liberty, KY - *TelDir&BG 83-84*
Mountain Software Growers Inc. - Houston, TX - *DataDirSup 7-83*
Mountain Standard Time [of Tree Frog Press Ltd.] - Edmonton, AB, Canada - *LitMag&SmPr 83-84*
Mountain State Cable Inc. [of Wilton Holdings Inc.] - Kingwood, WV - *BrCabYB 84*
Mountain State Cable Inc. - Sophia, WV - *BrCabYB 84; Tel&CabFB 84C*
Mountain State Cable Inc. - Stephenson, WV - *Tel&CabFB 84C*
Mountain State Cable Inc. [of Mountain State Cablevision] - Tunnelton, WV - *Tel&CabFB 84C*
Mountain State Cablevision [of Omni Cable TV Corp.] - Fayetteville, WV - *BrCabYB 84*
Mountain State Cablevision [of Omni Cable TV Inc.] - Oak Hill, WV - *BrCabYB 84; Tel&CabFB 84C p.1692*
Mountain State Press [Aff. of University of Charleston] - Charleston, WV - *BoPubDir 4, 5; LitMag&SmPr 83-84; WritMar 84*
Mountain State Telephone Co. [Aff. of Mid-Continent Telephone Corp.] - Hundred, WV - *TelDir&BG 83-84*
Mountain States Banker [of Mountain States Publishing Co.] - Kansas City, MO - *BaconPubCkMag 84; MagDir 84; WritMar 84*
Mountain States Communications Inc. - Aspen, CO - *BaconPubCkNews 84*
Mountain States E/C News [of Bender Publications Inc.] - Los Angeles, CA - *MagDir 84*
Mountain States Telephone & Telegraph Co., The - Denver, CO - *TelDir&BG 83-84*
Mountain Statesman - Grafton, WV - *AyerDirPub 83; BaconPubCkNews 84; Ed&PubIntYB 82*
Mountain Sun - Kerrville, TX - *AyerDirPub 83*
Mountain Times - Hamilton, ON, Canada - *AyerDirPub 83*
Mountain View Cable TV Co. - Mountain View, AR - *BrCabYB 84*
Mountain View Enterprises Inc. - Clayton, GA - *Tel&CabFB 84C p.1692*
Mountain View News - Mountain View, OK - *BaconPubCkNews 84; Ed&PubIntYB 82*
Mountain View Press Inc. - Mountain View, CA - *MicrocomMPl 83, 84*
Mountain View Standard - Mountain View, MO - *BaconPubCkNews 84; Ed&PubIntYB 82*
Mountain View Stone County Leader - Mountain View, AR - *BaconPubCkNews 84*
Mountain View Sun [of Meredith Corp.] - Cupertino, CA - *AyerDirPub 83; NewsDir 84*
Mountain View Sun - Mountain View, CA - *Ed&PubIntYB 82*
Mountain View Sun - *See* Meredith Newspapers
Mountain View Telephone Co. - Mountain View, AR - *TelDir&BG 83-84*
Mountain View TV Cable - Mountain View, OK - *Tel&CabFB 84C*
Mountain Villager, The - Ramona, CA - *AyerDirPub 83*
Mountain Visitor, The - Pigeon Forge, TN - *AyerDirPub 83*
Mountain Wave - Marshall, AR - *AyerDirPub 83*
Mountain West Cable TV Inc. - Castle Dale, UT - *BrCabYB 84; Tel&CabFB 84C*
Mountain West Cable TV Inc. - Ephraim, UT - *Tel&CabFB 84C p.1693*
Mountain West Research-Southwest Inc. - Tempe, AZ - *DataDirOnSer 84; EISS 5-84 Sup*
Mountain Willie Music - *See* Mighty Matthew Music
Mountaineer - Colorado Springs, CO - *AyerDirPub 83*
Mountaineer - Waynesville, NC - *AyerDirPub 83; Ed&PubIntYB 82; NewsDir 84*
Mountaineer - Rocky Mountain House, AB, Canada - *AyerDirPub 83; Ed&PubIntYB 82*
Mountaineer Cablevision [of Consolidated Communications Inc.] - Arnettsville, WV - *BrCabYB 84; Tel&CabFB 84C*
Mountaineer-Herald - Ebensburg, PA - *AyerDirPub 83; Ed&PubIntYB 82; NewsDir 84*
Mountaineer Progress - Wrightwood, CA - *AyerDirPub 83; Ed&PubIntYB 82*
Mountaineers Books - Seattle, WA - *BoPubDir 4 Sup, 5; LitMarPl 83, 84; WritMar 84*
Mountains Cablevision [of The Cable TV Co. Inc.] - Fairfield Mountain, NC - *Tel&CabFB 84C*
Mountainside Echo - Mountainside, NJ - *Ed&PubIntYB 82*
Mountainside Echo [of Union Vailsburg Leader] - Union, NJ - *AyerDirPub 83; NewsDir 84*
Mountaintop Eagle [of Dallas Pennaprint Inc.] - Dallas, PA - *NewsDir 84*
Mountaintop Eagle - Mountaintop, PA - *AyerDirPub 83; Ed&PubIntYB 82*
Mountaintop Eagle - *See* Pennaprint Inc.
Mountrail County Promoter - Stanley, ND - *Ed&PubIntYB 82*
Mountrail County Record - Parshall, ND - *AyerDirPub 83; Ed&PubIntYB 82*
Mourey Associates, Richard L. - Seymour, CT - *DirPRFirms 83*

Mousaw, Vigdor, Reeves, Heilbronner & Kroll - Rochester, NY - *ADAPSOMemDir 83-84*
Mouse River Farmers Press, The - Towner, ND - *Ed&PubIntYB 82*
Mouse Systems - Santa Clara, CA - *MicrocomMPl 84*
Mouser, Robert - Ironton, MO - *Tel&CabFB 84C p.1693*
Mouton Publishers [Aff. of Walter de Gruyter Inc.] - Hawthorne, NY - *BoPubDir 4, 5; LitMarPl 83, 84*
Mouvement Publications - Ithaca, NY - *BoPubDir 4, 5*
Move 'n' Groove Records - New York, NY - *BillIntBG 83-84*
Movement Shorthand Society Press - Newport Beach, CA - *BoPubDir 4, 5*
Movers News - Albany, NY - *BaconPubCkMag 84*
Movers News [of White Eagle Printing Co.] - New York, NY - *MagDir 84*
Movie Channel, The [of Warner Amex Satellite Entertainment Co.] - New York, NY - *BrCabYB 84; CabTVPrDB 83; HomeVid&CabYB 82-83*
Movie Channel, The - *See* Showtime/The Movie Channel Inc.
Movie Channel, The - *See* Warner Amex Satellite Entertainment Co.
Movie Entertainment Book Club - Harrison, NY - *LitMarPl 83, 84*
Movie Life - New York, NY - *NewsBur 6*
Movie Mirror - New York, NY - *BaconPubCkMag 84; MagDir 84*
Movie Reviews Data Base [of Cineman Syndicate] - Middletown, NY - *EISS 7-83 Sup*
Movie Reviews Data Base - Park City, UT - *DirOnDB Spring 84*
Movie Systems Inc. - Des Moines, IA - *HomeVid&CabYB 82-83*
Movielab Inc. - New York, NY - *AvMarPl 83; Tel&CabFB 84C*
Moviemakers Inc. [Subs. of Steve Campus Productions] - New York, NY - *AvMarPl 83*
Movies, The - New York, NY - *BaconPubCkMag 84*
Movietone Music Corp. - *See* Fox Publishing Co. Inc., Sam
Movietone News Inc. - New York, NY - *TelAl 83, 84; Tel&CabFB 84C*
Moville Record - Moville, IA - *BaconPubCkNews 84; Ed&PubIntYB 82*
Moving House & Home - New York, NY - *BaconPubCkMag 84*
Moving Image - San Francisco, CA - *MagDir 84; MagIndMarPl 82-83*
Moving Images - Washington, DC - *AvMarPl 83*
Moving Out: A Feminist Literary & Arts Journal - Detroit, MI - *ArtMar 84; LitMag&SmPr 83-84; WritMar 84*
Moving Parts Press - Santa Cruz, CA - *BoPubDir 4, 5; LitMag&SmPr 83-84*
Moving to... Publications - Don Mills, ON, Canada - *BoPubDir 4; 5*
Moviola by J & R [Subs. of J & R Film Co. Inc.] - Hollywood, CA - *AvMarPl 83*
Movtady, Myrna - New York, NY - *LitMarPl 83, 84*
Mowat, Ruth D. - Williamstown, ON, Canada - *BoPubDir 4, 5*
Mowry Press - Wayland, MA - *BoPubDir 4 Sup, 5*
Moxon, Dolphin & Kerby Ltd. - *See* Bates Worldwide Inc., Ted
Moyle, Gilbert D. - *See* Corner, Sherwood L.
Moynihan Public Affairs - Newport, RI - *DirPRFirms 83*
Moza Publications - Chattanooga, TN - *BoPubDir 4 Sup, 5; LitMarPl 83, 84*
MP Audio Corp. - Easton, CT - *AvMarPl 83*
MPA Enterprises - Wyomissing, PA - *MicrocomMPl 84; MicrocomSwDir 1*
MPB/Information Research [of H. Prim Co. Inc.] - Bergenfield, NJ - *InfIndMarPl 83*
MPC Educational Publishers [Div. of Milady Publishing Corp.] - Bronx, NY - *AvMarPl 83*
MPC Educational Systems Inc. - New Haven, CT - *AvMarPl 83*
MPCS Video Industries Inc. - New York, NY - *AvMarPl 83*
MPG Communications - Plymouth, MA - *BaconPubCkNews 84*
MPL Communications Inc. - New York, NY - *BillIntBG 83-84*
MPM-Propaganda - Sao Paulo, Brazil - *StaDirAdAg 2-84*
MPO Videotronic Projector Co. [Subs. of MPO Videotronics Inc.] - New York, NY - *AvMarPl 83*
MPO Videotronics Inc. - New York, NY - *TelAl 83, 84*
MPPI Ltd. - Northbrook, IL - *MicrocomMPl 84*
MPS Co. - Addison, IL - *MicrocomMPl 84; MicrocomSwDir 1; WhoWMicrocom 83*
MPW/Univas [of the Univas Network] - Dusseldorf, West Germany - *StaDirAdAg 2-84*
MQI Computer Products - Fountain Valley, CA - *DirInfWP 82*
MR Associates - Los Angeles, CA - *DirMarMP 83*
Mr. Bones Music Publishing - *See* Ahlert Music Corp., Fred
Mr. Coach Inc. - Downers Grove, IL - *BoPubDir 5*
Mr. Cogito - Forest Grove, OR - *LitMag&SmPr 83-84*
Mr. Cogito Press - Forest Grove, OR - *LitMag&SmPr 83-84*
Mr. Cogito Press - Portland, OR - *BoPubDir 4, 5*
Mr. D's The Poetic Experience Publishing Co. - Hollywood, CA - *BoPubDir 5*
Mr. Mazoo - Saline, MI - *AyerDirPub 83*
Mr. Mort Music - Nashville, TN - *BillIntBG 83-84*
Mr. Par Music - North Hollywood, CA - *BillIntBG 83-84*
Mr. Production Enterprise - Norwalk, CA - *LitMag&SmPr 83-84*
Mr. Wizard Studio - Canoga Park, CA - *Tel&CabFB 84C*
MRA Communicators Inc. - New York, NY - *ProGuPRSer 4*
MRB International Ltd. - London, England - *IntDirMarRes 83*
MRC Films & Video [Div. of McLaughlin Research Corp.] - New York, NY - *AvMarPl 83; TelAl 83, 84; WritMar 84*
MRC Systems - Houston, TX - *WhoWMicrocom 83*
MRCA - Stamford, CT - *IntDirMarRes 83*
MRDC Educational Institute - Dallas, TX - *BoPubDir 4, 5*
MRI Business-to-Business [of Mediamark Research Inc.] - New York, NY - *DataDirOnSer 84; DirOnDB Spring 84*
MRI-Mediamarkets - New York, NY - *DirOnDB Spring 84*
MRI Music - New York, NY - *BillIntBG 83-84*
Ms. Atlas Press & Bookstore - San Jose, CA - *BoPubDir 4, 5; LitMag&SmPr 83-84*
Ms. Magazine [of Ms. Foundation for Education & Communication Inc.] - New York, NY - *BaconPubCkMag 84; Folio 83; LitMarPl 83, 84; MagDir 84; MagIndMarPl 82-83; WritMar 84*
MS Rhythm Section Music Inc. - *See* Muscle Shoals Sound Publishing Co. Inc.
MS/Smiths-Editorial Consultants - Bridgewater, CT - *LitMarPl 83; MagIndMarPl 82-83*
MS/Smiths-Editorial Consultants - Danbury, CT - *LitMarPl 84*
MS USA Microsystems - Orlando, FL - *DataDirSup 7-83*
MSA [Aff. of McCollum/Spielman Inc.] - New York, NY - *IntDirMarRes 83*
MSA Advertising - Philadelphia, PA - *AdAge 3-28-84; StaDirAdAg 2-84*
M.S.A. Cablevision Ltd. - Abbotsford, BC, Canada - *BrCabYB 84*
MSA-TAB - New York, NY - *IntDirMarRes 83*
MSB Consultants - Millburn, NJ - *MicrocomMPl 84*
MSC - Salt Lake City, UT - *MicrocomMPl 84*
MSC Inc. - Tucson, AZ - *Ed&PubIntYB 82*
MSD Advertising Agency Inc. - Clifton, NJ - *StaDirAdAg 2-84*
M.S.E. Cable Systems Inc. - Troy, MI - *Tel&CabFB 84C*
MSG Associates Inc. - Omaha, ME - *MicrocomMPl 84*
MSI Data Corp. - Costa Mesa, CA - *DataDirSup 7-83; DirInfWP 82; WhoWMicrocom 83*
M.S.I. Micrographic Systems Industries Ltd. - *See* ITTI: Microfilm & Telecommunications Ltd.
MSK Productions Inc. - Dearborn, MI - *BillIntBG 83-84*
MSN: The Information Channel [Div. of Modern Talking Picture Service Inc.] - New York, NY - *BrCabYB 84; CabTVPrDB 83; Tel&CabFB 84C*
MSP Inc. - Lexington, MA - *DataDirSup 7-83; WhoWMicrocom 83*
MSS Magazine [of SUNY Binghamton Foundation] - Binghamton, NY - *LitMag&SmPr 83-84; WritMar 84*
MSS/Manuscript Services - Galena, IL - *LitMarPl 83, 84; MagIndMarPl 82-83*
MSS Records Inc. - Sheffield, AL - *BillIntBG 83-84*
MSSS-Mass Spectral Search System - Falls Church, VA - *DirOnDB Spring 84*
Mstique - Chicago, IL - *MagDir 84*
MSU Inc. - New York, NY - *BillIntBG 83-84*
MSUSTAT [of Montana State University] - Bozeman, MT - *EISS 7-83 Sup*
Mt. Airy News [of Mid-South Management Co.] - Mt. Airy, NC - *BaconPubCkNews 84; NewsDir 84*
Mt. Airy Times - Mt. Airy, NC - *BaconPubCkNews 84; Ed&PubIntYB 82; NewsDir 84*
Mt. Angel Telephone Co. - Mt. Angel, OR - *TelDir&BG 83-84*

Mt. Ayr Record-News - Mt. Ayr, IA - *BaconPubCkNews 84; Ed&PubIntYB 82; NewsDir 84*
Mt. Carmel Republican-Register - Mt. Carmel, IL - *BaconPubCkNews 84; NewsDir 84*
Mt. Carroll County Mirror-Democrat - Mt. Carroll, IL - *BaconPubCkNews 84*
Mt. Castor Industries - Amherst, MA - *MicrocomMPl 84*
Mt. Cities TV Cable Inc. [of Rogers UA Cablesystems Inc.] - Mt. Pleasant, TX - *BrCabYB 84*
Mt. Clemens Macomb Daily [of Panax Newspapers Inc.] - Mt. Clemens, MI - *NewsDir 84*
Mt. Dora Topic - Mt. Dora, FL - *BaconPubCkNews 84; Ed&PubIntYB 82*
Mt. Enterprise Cushing News - *See* Mt. Enterprise Progress Publishers
Mt. Enterprise Progress - Mt. Enterprise, TX - *Ed&PubIntYB 82*
Mt. Enterprise Progress - *See* Mt. Enterprise Progress Publishers
Mt. Enterprise Progress Publishers - Mt. Enterprise, TX - *BaconPubCkNews 84*
Mt. Gilead Morrow County Sentinel - Mt. Gilead, OH - *BaconPubCkNews 84*
Mt. Greenwood Express [of Southwest Messenger Newspapers] - Midlothian, IL - *AyerDirPub 83; NewsDir 84*
Mt. Greenwood Express - Mt. Greenwood, IL - *Ed&PubIntYB 82*
Mt. Greenwood Express - *See* Southwest Messenger Newspapers
Mt. Holly Ft. Dix Post - Mt. Holly, NJ - *NewsDir 84*
Mt. Holly News - Mt. Holly, NC - *BaconPubCkNews 84; Ed&PubIntYB 82*
Mt. Hope Clarion, The - Mt. Hope, KS - *Ed&PubIntYB 82*
Mt. Horeb Mail - Mt. Horeb, WI - *Ed&PubIntYB 82*
Mt. Horeb Mail - *See* News Publishing Co. Inc.
Mt. Horeb Telephone Co. - Mt. Horeb, WI - *TelDir&BG 83-84*
Mt. Ida Montgomery County News - Mt. Ida, AR - *BaconPubCkNews 84*
Mt. Joy Merchandiser - Mt. Joy, PA - *BaconPubCkNews 84; NewsDir 84*
Mt. Kisco Patent Trader - Mt. Kisco, NY - *NewsDir 84*
Mt. Laurel Progress-Press - *See* Progress Publications Inc.
Mt. Lebanon Almanac - *See* Publix Publications
Mt. Lebanon Cablevision Inc. [of Adelphia Communications Corp.] - Mt. Lebanon Township, PA - *Tel&CabFB 84C*
Mt. Lebanon News - Homestead, PA - *AyerDirPub 83*
Mt. Lebanon News Review - Homestead, PA - *AyerDirPub 83*
Mt. Morris Enterprise - Geneseo, NY - *AyerDirPub 83*
Mt. Morris Enterprise - Mt. Morris, NY - *Ed&PubIntYB 82*
Mt. Morris Enterprise - *See* Sanders Publications
Mt. Morris Genesee County Herald - Mt. Morris, MI - *BaconPubCkNews 84*
Mt. Morris Times - Mt. Morris, IL - *AyerDirPub 83; BaconPubCkNews 84; Ed&PubIntYB 82*
Mt. Olive Chronicle - Budd Lake, NJ - *AyerDirPub 83*
Mt. Olive Chronicle - *See* Recorder Publishing Co.
Mt. Olive Herald - Mt. Olive, IL - *BaconPubCkNews 84*
Mt. Olive Tribune - Mt. Olive, MS - *BaconPubCkNews 84; Ed&PubIntYB 82*
Mt. Olive Tribune - Mt. Olive, NC - *BaconPubCkNews 84; Ed&PubIntYB 82; NewsDir 84*
Mt. Oliver Cable TV Corp. [of Adelphia Communications Corp.] - Mt. Oliver, PA - *BrCabYB 84; Tel&CabFB 84C*
Mt. Olivet Robertson County Review - *See* Poage Publishing Co.
Mt. Pleasant Buyer's Guide - Mt. Pleasant, MI - *AyerDirPub 83*
Mt. Pleasant Cablevision [of American TV & Communications Corp.] - Mt. Pleasant, IA - *BrCabYB 84; Tel&CabFB 84C*
Mt. Pleasant Journal - Mt. Pleasant, PA - *BaconPubCkNews 84; Ed&PubIntYB 82*
Mt. Pleasant Journal [of The Laurel Group Press] - Scottdale, PA - *NewsDir 84*
Mt. Pleasant Morning Sun [of Central Michigan Newspapers Inc.] - Mt. Pleasant, MI - *NewsDir 84*
Mt. Pleasant News - Mt. Pleasant, IA - *BaconPubCkNews 84; Ed&PubIntYB 82; NewsDir 84*
Mt. Pleasant Pyramid - *See* Art City Publishing Co.
Mt. Pleasant Record - Mt. Pleasant, TN - *BaconPubCkNews 84; Ed&PubIntYB 82*
Mt. Pleasant Tribune [of Palmer Media Inc.] - Mt. Pleasant, TX - *BaconPubCkNews 84; Ed&PubIntYB 82; NewsDir 84*
Mt. Prospect Family Journal - *See* Journal & Topics Newspapers
Mt. Prospect Journal [of Des Plaines Journal-News Publications] - Des Plaines, IL - *NewsDir 84*
Mt. Prospect Journal - *See* Journal & Topics Newspapers
Mt. Prospect/Prospect Heights Herald [of Paddock Publications] - Arlington Heights, IL - *NewsDir 84*
Mt. Prospect/Prospect Heights Herald - *See* Paddock Publications
Mt. Prospect Suburban Times - *See* Des Plaines Publishing Co.
Mt. Pulaski Telephone & Electric Co. - Lincoln, IL - *TelDir&BG 83-84*
Mt. Pulaski Times-News - Mt. Pulaski, IL - *BaconPubCkNews 84*
Mt. Shasta Herald - Mt. Shasta, CA - *Ed&PubIntYB 82; NewsDir 84*
Mt. Shasta Herald - *See* Southern Siskiyou Newspapers Inc.
Mt. Sinai Journal of Medicine, The - New York, NY - *BaconPubCkMag 84*
Mt. Soledad/Birdrock Pennysaver - Mission Viejo, CA - *AyerDirPub 83*
Mt. Sterling Advocate - Mt. Sterling, KY - *BaconPubCkNews 84; Ed&PubIntYB 82*
Mt. Sterling Antennavision [of Matrix Vision of Harlan County Inc.] - Richmond, KY - *BrCabYB 84*
Mt. Sterling Antennavision Co. [of Centel Cable Television Co.] - Jeffersonville, KY - *BrCabYB 84; Tel&CabFB 84C*
Mt. Sterling Cablevision [of Ablecom Inc.] - Mt. Sterling, OH - *Tel&CabFB 84C*
Mt. Sterling Democrat-Message - Mt. Sterling, IL - *BaconPubCkNews 84; NewsDir 84*
Mt. Sterling Tribune - Mt. Sterling, OH - *Ed&PubIntYB 82*
Mt. Tremper Video Ltd. [of Group W Cable Inc.] - Mt. Tremper, NY - *Tel&CabFB 84C*
Mt. Union Times - Mt. Union, PA - *AyerDirPub 83; Ed&PubIntYB 82*
Mt. Vernon Argus - Mt. Vernon, WA - *Ed&PubIntYB 82*
Mt. Vernon Argus - *See* Westchester-Rockland Newspapers
Mt. Vernon Cablevision [of Semo Communications Inc.] - Mt. Vernon, MO - *Tel&CabFB 84C*
Mt. Vernon Cablevision Inc. - Mt. Vernon, OH - *BrCabYB 84; Tel&CabFB 84C*
Mt. Vernon Daily Argus [of Westchester Rockland Newspapers Inc.] - Mt. Vernon, NY - *NewsDir 84*
Mt. Vernon Daily Argus, The - White Plains, NY - *Ed&PubIntYB 82*
Mt. Vernon Democrat - Mt. Vernon, IN - *BaconPubCkNews 84; Ed&PubIntYB 82; NewsDir 84*
Mt. Vernon Lawrence County Record - Mt. Vernon, MO - *BaconPubCkNews 84; NewsDir 84*
Mt. Vernon Montgomery Monitor - *See* Suburban Printing Corp.
Mt. Vernon News [of Republican Publishing Co.] - Mt. Vernon, OH - *BaconPubCkNews 84; Ed&PubIntYB 82; NewsDir 84*
Mt. Vernon Optic-Herald - Mt. Vernon, TX - *BaconPubCkNews 84; Ed&PubIntYB 82*
Mt. Vernon Register News [of Thomson Newspapers Inc.] - Mt. Vernon, IL - *NewsDir 84*
Mt. Vernon Signal - Mt. Vernon, KY - *BaconPubCkNews 84; Ed&PubIntYB 82*
Mt. Vernon Skagit Argus - Mt. Vernon, WA - *BaconPubCkNews 84*
Mt. Vernon Sun - Mt. Vernon, IA - *BaconPubCkNews 84*
Mt. Vernon Telephone Co. [Aff. of Telephone & Data Systems Inc.] - Verona, WI - *TelDir&BG 83-84*
Mt. Vernon TV Cable - Mt. Vernon, KY - *BrCabYB 84; Tel&CabFB 84C*
Mt. Washington News, The - Mt. Washington, PA - *Ed&PubIntYB 82*
Mt. Washington Press [of Cincinnati Nichols Printing Co.] - Cincinnati, OH - *AyerDirPub 83; Ed&PubIntYB 82; NewsDir 84*
Mt. Washington Star - Mt. Washington, KY - *AyerDirPub 83; BaconPubCkNews 84; Ed&PubIntYB 82*
Mt. Zion Region News, The - Mt. Zion, IL - *Ed&PubIntYB 82*
MTI Teleprograms Inc. - Northbrook, IL - *BoPubDir 4, 5*
MTI Television City - New York, NY - *AvMarPl 83*
MTM Enterprises Inc. - Studio City, CA - *TelAl 83, 84; Tel&CabFB 84C*
MTR Sales - North Vancouver, BC, Canada - *BoPubDir 4 Sup, 5*
MTS Enterprises - Niceville, FL - *MicrocomMPl 84*
MTS Inc. - Niceville, FL - *MicrocomMPl 83, 84*

MTV: Music Television [of Warner Amex Satellite Entertainment Co.] - New York, NY - *CabTVPrDB 83; HomeVid&CabYB 82-83; Tel&CabFB 84C*
Mu Publications - Dahlgren, VA - *LitMag&SmPr 83-84*
Mucci Associates Inc. - Stuart, FL - *StaDirAdAg 2-84*
Muchnick Co., Paul - Los Angeles, CA - *ArtMar 84; DirMarMP 83; LitMarPl 83, 84; MagIndMarPl 82-83; StaDirAdAg 2-84*
Mud Lake Telephone Cooperative Association Inc. - Dubois, ID - *TelDir&BG 83-84*
Mud Press - Portland, OR - *LitMag&SmPr 83-84*
Mudborn Press - Santa Barbara, CA - *LitMag&SmPr 83-84*
Mueller, Hella M. & J. J. - *See* EMCO CATV Inc.
Mueller, Hillsman & Co. - Elgin, IL - *WhoWMicrocom 83*
Mueller, Justin J. - *See* EMCO CATV Inc.
Mueller-Martini Corp. [Div. of Mueller Martini AG] - Hauppauge, NY - *LitMarPl 83, 84*
Mueller/The Firehouse Theater, Dick - Omaha, NE - *WritMar 84*
Muenster Enterprise - Muenster, TX - *BaconPubCkNews 84; Ed&PubIntYB 82*
Muenster Telephone Corp. of Texas - Muenster, TX - *TelDir&BG 83-84*
Muenzhuber, Arlen R. - *See* Armco Communications Inc.
Muffler Digest [of M.D. Publications Inc.] - Springfield, MO - *BaconPubCkMag 84; MagDir 84; WritMar 84*
Muhlenberg Music Inc. - *See* World Wide Music Inc.
Muir Cornelius Moore - New York, NY - *AdAge 3-28-84; DirMarMP 83; StaDirAdAg 2-84*
Muir Publications Inc., John - Santa Fe, NM - *LitMag&SmPr 83-84; LitMarPl 83, 84; WritMar 84*
Muir Publishing Co. Ltd. - Gardenvale, PQ, Canada - *BoPubDir 4, 5*
Muirhead Corp. - Bristol, NJ - *DirInfWP 82*
Mukluk Telephone Co. Inc. - Teller, AK - *TelDir&BG 83-84*
Mukwonago Chief - Mukwonago, WI - *Ed&PubIntYB 82; NewsDir 84*
Mul-T-Rul Co. - Ft. Morgan, CO - *BoPubDir 4, 5*
Mulberry Advance, The - Mulberry, KS - *Ed&PubIntYB 82*
Mulberry Cooperative Telephone Co. Inc. - Mulberry, IN - *TelDir&BG 83-84*
Mulberry Crawford County Bulletin - Mulberry, AR - *BaconPubCkNews 84*
Mulberry Press - Mulberry, FL - *BaconPubCkNews 84; Ed&PubIntYB 82*
Mulch Press - San Francisco, CA - *BoPubDir 4 Sup, 5*
Muldoon Marketing Inc. - New York, NY - *DirMarMP 83*
Muldoon, Nancy Dale - Brookfield Center, CT - *LitMarPl 84; MagIndMarPl 82-83*
Muldoon Public Relations, Margaret Reilly - New York, NY - *DirPRFirms 83*
Muleshoe & Bailey County Journals - Muleshoe, TX - *BaconPubCkNews 84*
Muleshoe Antenna Co. - Earth, TX - *BrCabYB 84*
Muleshoe Antenna Co. - Muleshoe, TX - *BrCabYB 84; Tel&CabFB 84C*
Muleshoe Antenna Co. - Sudan, TX - *BrCabYB 84*
Muleshoe Journal - Muleshoe, TX - *Ed&PubIntYB 82*
Mull-Ti Hit Music Co. - Nashville, TN - *BillIntBG 83-84*
Mullan Television Co. - Mullan, ID - *BrCabYB 84; Tel&CabFB 84C*
Mulle/Breen Advertising - Beverly Hills, CA - *StaDirAdAg 2-84*
Mullen Advertising - Beverly Farms, MA - *AdAge 3-28-84; StaDirAdAg 2-84*
Mullen Advertising & Public Relations Inc. - Phoenix, AZ - *DirPRFirms 83; StaDirAdAg 2-84*
Mullen Co. - Green Bay, WI - *Tel&CabFB 84C p.1693*
Mullen Computer Products Inc. - Hayward, CA - *WhoWMicrocom 83*
Mullen Hooker County Tribune - Mullen, NE - *BaconPubCkNews 84*
Mullens Advocate - Mullens, WV - *BaconPubCkNews 84; Ed&PubIntYB 82*
Muller & Associates, Margaret L. - Santa Clara, CA - *MagIndMarPl 82-83*
Muller Data [Subs. of Muller & Co.] - New York, NY - *DataDirOnSer 84; EISS 83*
Muller Jordan Weiss - New York, NY - *AdAge 3-28-84; ArtMar 84; StaDirAdAg 2-84*
Muller Media Inc. - New York, NY - *Tel&CabFB 84C*
Muller-Mugno Corp. - New York, NY - *DirInfWP 82*
Mullican Co. - Louisville, KY - *StaDirAdAg 2-84*
Mullins, Carolyn J. - Bloomington, IN - *LitMarPl 83*
Mullins, Carolyn J. [Div. of Wordworks] - Blacksburg, VA - *LitMarPl 84*
Mullins Enterprise - Mullins, SC - *BaconPubCkNews 84; Ed&PubIntYB 82*
Mullins Music, Dee - Hendersonville, TN - *BillIntBG 83-84*
Mullinville Cable TV - Mullinville, KS - *Tel&CabFB 84C*
Mullinville Development Associates Inc. - Mullinville, KS - *BrCabYB 84*
Multi-Ad Services Inc. - Peoria, IL - *Ed&PubIntYB 82*
Multi-Business Computer Systems Inc. - Portland, CT - *WhoWMicrocom 83*
Multi-Channel Cablevision Inc. - Brookville, PA - *BrCabYB 84*
Multi-Channel TV Cable Co. - Bucyrus, OH - *BrCabYB 84; Tel&CabFB 84C*
Multi-Channel TV Cable Co. - Fredericktown, OH - *BrCabYB 84*
Multi-Channel TV Cable Co. [of Mansfield Journal Co.] - Mansfield, OH - *BrCabYB 84 p.D-304; Tel&CabFB 84C p.1693*
Multi-Channel TV Cable Co. - Mt. Gilead, OH - *BrCabYB 84; Tel&CabFB 84C*
Multi-Channel TV Cable Co. - Shelby, OH - *BrCabYB 84; Tel&CabFB 84C*
Multi-Channel TV Cable Co. - Valley View, OH - *CabTVFinDB 83*
Multi-Com Inc. - Green City, MO - *Tel&CabFB 84C p.1693*
Multi-Communication Services Inc. - Pensacola, FL - *Tel&CabFB 84C*
Multi-County Cablevision Inc. - Lodi, OH - *Tel&CabFB 84C*
Multi-County Cablevision Inc. - Shreve, OH - *BrCabYB 84; Tel&CabFB 84C*
Multi County Star - Covington, GA - *AyerDirPub 83*
Multi Cultural Services - Toronto, ON, Canada - *LitMarPl 84*
Multi-Housing News [of Gralla Publications] - New York, NY - *BaconPubCkMag 84; MagDir 84; MagIndMarPl 82-83*
Multi Image Productions Inc. [Subs. of Fotomat Corp.] - San Diego, CA - *AvMarPl 83*
Multi-Level Marketing News - Fair Oaks, CA - *BaconPubCkMag 84*
Multi-List/McGraw-Hill [Subs. of McGraw-Hill] - New York, NY - *DataDirOnSer 84*
Multi-Medea Enterprises/Water Press - Minneapolis, MN - *BoPubDir 4, 5*
Multi Media Arts - Austin, TX - *BoPubDir 4, 5; LitMag&SmPr 83-84; LitMarPl 84*
Multi-Media Concepts Inc. - *See* Shaller, Rubin & Winer Inc.
Multi-Media International - Northridge, CA - *WritMar 84*
Multi-Media Presentations Inc. - Culver City, CA - *AvMarPl 83*
Multi-Media Productions Inc. - Stanford, CA - *AvMarPl 83; WritMar 84*
Multi-Media Publishing Inc. - Denver, CO - *LitMarPl 83, 84*
Multi-Media Publishing Inc. (Production Services Div.) - Denver, CO - *AvMarPl 83*
Multi-Media Works - Los Angeles, CA - *ArtMar 84; AvMarPl 83*
Multi Photon Bibliography [of Lawrence Livermore National Laboratory] - Livermore, CA - *CompReadDB 82*
Multi Pix of Idaho [of Community Tele-Communications Inc.] - Burley, ID - *Tel&CabFB 84C*
Multi-Point Communications Corp. - San Antonio, TX - *Tel&CabFB 84C*
Multi-Point Distribution System Inc. - San Antonio, TX - *Tel&CabFB 84C*
Multi-Point Distributors Inc. - San Antonio, TX - *Tel&CabFB 84C*
Multi-Spectral Press - Buffalo, NY - *BoPubDir 4, 5*
Multi-Tech Systems - New Brighton, MN - *DataDirSup 7-83; MicrocomMPl 84; WhoWMicrocom 83*
Multi-Track Magnetics Inc. [Subs. of Matrix Corp.] - Upper Saddle River, NJ - *AvMarPl 83*
Multi-View Systems of Woodland Inc. - Woodland, CA - *BrCabYB 84*
Multi-Vision Cable Systems - Birmingham, MI - *Tel&CabFB 84C*

Multicept Corp. - Rome, NY - *MicrocomMPl 84; MicrocomSwDir 1*
Multichannel Communications Inc. - Walnut Cove, NC - *Tel&CabFB 84C p.1693*
Multichannel News [of Fairchild Publications] - Denver, CO - *BaconPubCkMag 84; Folio 83; MagIndMarPl 82-83*
MultiChannel TV Inc. - Miami, TX - *BrCabYB 84; Tel&CabFB 84C*
Multicultural History Society of Ontario - Toronto, ON, Canada - *BoPubDir 4, 5*
Multicultural Resources - Stanford, CA - *BoPubDir 4, 5*
Multidex Computing Co. - Suffern, NY - *EISS 83*
Multiforms Inc. - Fairfield, CT - *DataDirSup 7-83*
Multimedia Advertising Inc. - Chattanooga, TN - *StaDirAdAg 2-84*
Multimedia Advertising Services Ltd. - *See* CM Group Ltd.
Multimedia Broadcasting Co. [Div. of Multimedia Inc.] - Cincinnati, OH - *BrCabYB 84; Tel&CabFB 84S*
Multimedia Cablevision Inc. [Div. of Multimedia Inc.] - Wichita, KS - *BrCabYB 84 p.D-304; CabTVFinDB 83; LitMarPl 84; Tel&CabFB 84C p.1693*
Multimedia Cablevision Inc. - Cushing, OK - *Tel&CabFB 84C*
Multimedia Cablevision Inc. - Lindsay, OK - *BrCabYB 84*
Multimedia Cablevision Inc. - Midwest City, OK - *Tel&CabFB 84C*
Multimedia Cablevision of Batavia - Batavia, IL - *BrCabYB 84; Tel&CabFB 84C*
Multimedia Cablevision of Bethany - Bethany, OK - *BrCabYB 84*
Multimedia Cablevision of Chickasha - Chickasha, OK - *BrCabYB 84*
Multimedia Cablevision of Del City - Del City, OK - *BrCabYB 84*
Multimedia Cablevision of Edmond - Edmond, OK - *BrCabYB 84*
Multimedia Cablevision of Guthrie - Guthrie, OK - *BrCabYB 84*
Multimedia Cablevision of Harvey - Harvey, IL - *Tel&CabFB 84C*
Multimedia Cablevision of Lisle - Lisle, IL - *BrCabYB 84; Tel&CabFB 84C*
Multimedia Cablevision of Lyons [of Multimedia Inc.] - Lyons, KS - *BrCabYB 84*
Multimedia Cablevision of McPherson [of Multimedia Inc.] - McPherson, KS - *BrCabYB 84*
Multimedia Cablevision of Moore - Moore, OK - *BrCabYB 84*
Multimedia Cablevision of Mustang - Mustang, OK - *BrCabYB 84*
Multimedia Cablevision of Nichols Hills - Nichols Hills, OK - *BrCabYB 84*
Multimedia Cablevision of Oak Forest - Oak Forest, IL - *BrCabYB 84; Tel&CabFB 84C*
Multimedia Cablevision of Oak Lawn - Oak Lawn, IL - *BrCabYB 84; Tel&CabFB 84C*
Multimedia Cablevision of The Village - The Village, OK - *BrCabYB 84*
Multimedia Cablevision of Warr Acres - Warr Acres, OK - *BrCabYB 84; Tel&CabFB 84C*
Multimedia Cablevision of Yukon - Yukon, OK - *BrCabYB 84*
Multimedia Inc. - Greenville, SC - *AdAge 6-28-84; BrCabYB 84; HomeVid&CabYB 82-83; KnowInd 83*
Multimedia Music Group - Nashville, TN - *BillIntBG 83-84*
Multimedia Newspapers - Greenville, SC - *Ed&PubIntYB 82*
Multimedia Program Productions Inc. - Nashville, TN - *TelAl 84; Tel&CabFB 84C*
Multimedia Resource Center - San Francisco, CA - *AvMarPl 83*
Multimode International Data Acquisition Service [of Overseas Telecommunications Commission] - Sydney, Australia - *EISS 83; TeleSy&SerDir 2-84*
Multinational Computer Models Inc. - Montclair, NJ - *DataDirOnSer 84; EISS 7-83 Sup*
Multinational Computer Research Corp. - New York, NY - *WhoWMicrocom 83*
Multinational Media - Scotts Valley, CA - *BoPubDir 4, 5*
Multiphase Data Systems [Subs. of Multiphase Corp.] - Brea, CA - *WhoWMicrocom 83*
Multiple Channels of Alabama Ltd. - Wetumpka, AL - *Tel&CabFB 84C p.1693*
Multiple Listing Service [of Multi-List/McGraw-Hill] - New York, NY - *DataDirOnSer 84*
Multiplex Display Fixture Co. - Fenton, MO - *AvMarPl 83*
Multiplications Inc. - Cambridge, MA - *ADAPSOMemDir 83-84*
Multipoint Information Systems Inc. - Cleveland, OH - *Tel&CabFB 84C*
Multipoint Network Corp. - Pasadena, MD - *Tel&CabFB 84C*
Multiprint Inc. - New York, NY - *LitMarPl 83, 84*
Multis - Chicago, IL - *BaconPubCkMag 84*
Multiscience Publications Ltd. - Montreal, PQ, Canada - *BoPubDir 4, 5; LitMarPl 84*
Multiservice Corp. - Hartselle, AL - *AdAge 3-28-84; StaDirAdAg 2-84*
Multisonics Inc. - Dublin, CA - *DataDirSup 7-83*
Multitech Electronics Inc. - Sunnyvale, CA - *MicrocomMPl 84; WhoWMicrocom 83*
Multivariance Data Analysts Inc. - New York, NY - *IntDirMarRes 83*
Multiview Cable Co. [of Comcast Corp.] - Aberdeen, MD - *BrCabYB 84; Tel&CabFB 84C*
Multivision - Needham, MA - *AvMarPl 83*
Multivision - Charlotte, NC - *AvMarPl 83*
MultiVision Group - Portsmouth, OH - *BrCabYB 84 p.D-304*
Multivision International - Chicago, IL - *AvMarPl 83*
MultiVision Northeast Inc. - Cornelia, GA - *BrCabYB 84; Tel&CabFB 84C*
MultiVision Northeast Inc. [of MultiVision Group] - Helen, GA - *BrCabYB 84; Tel&CabFB 84C*
MultiVision Northwest Inc. - Dalton, GA - *BrCabYB 84; Tel&CabFB 84C*
MultiVision of Commerce Inc. - Commerce, GA - *Tel&CabFB 84C*
MultiVision of Commerce Inc. - Jefferson, GA - *Tel&CabFB 84C*
Multivision Productions - South Miami, FL - *ArtMar 84; AvMarPl 83*
Multivision Systems - Honolulu, HI - *AvMarPl 83*
Multivisions Ltd. [of Pacific Telecom Inc.] - Anchorage, AK - *BrCabYB 84; Tel&CabFB 84C p.1693*
Multivue - Tempe, AZ - *AvMarPl 83*
Multnomah Press [Aff. of Multnomah School of the Bible] - Portland, OR - *BoPubDir 4, 5; LitMarPl 83, 84*
Mulvane News - Mulvane, KS - *BaconPubCkNews 84; Ed&PubIntYB 82*
Mulvey Associates - New York, NY - *LitMarPl 83, 84*
Mumford Micro Systems - Summerland, CA - *MicrocomMPl 83, 84; MicrocomSwDir 1*
MUMPS Users' Group - St. Louis, MO - *BoPubDir 4, 5*
Muncie Evening Press [of Muncie Newspapers Inc.] - Muncie, IN - *BaconPubCkNews 84; Ed&PubIntYB 82; LitMarPl 83, 84; NewsDir 84*
Muncie Star - Muncie, IN - *BaconPubCkNews 84; Ed&PubIntYB 82; LitMarPl 83; NewsDir 84*
Muncy Luminary - Muncy, PA - *BaconPubCkNews 84*
Muncy TV Corp. - Muncy, PA - *BrCabYB 84; Tel&CabFB 84C*
Munday & Collins Inc. - San Jose, CA - *AvMarPl 83*
Munday Courier - Munday, TX - *BaconPubCkNews 84; Ed&PubIntYB 82*
Mundelein Fremont Patriot [of Lakeland Publishers Inc.] - Grayslake, IL - *NewsDir 84*
Mundelein Herald [of Paddock Circle Newspapers Inc.] - Mundelein, IL - *AyerDirPub 83; Ed&PubIntYB 82; NewsDir 84*
Mundelein Herald - *See* Paddock Publications
Mundelein Review - Wilmette, IL - *AyerDirPub 83*
Mundelein Review - *See* Pioneer Press Inc.
Mundus Artium - Richardson, TX - *LitMag&SmPr 83-84*
Munfordville Hart County News - *See* Cave Country Newspapers Inc.
Munger, Keith - *See* Sanval Cablevision Inc.
Municipal Automated Geographic Information System [of District of Columbia Office of the Mayor] - Washington, DC - *EISS 83*
Municipal Bond Pricing Service [of Control Data Corp.] - Greenwich, CT - *DataDirOnSer 84*
Municipal Data Service [of International City Management Association] - Washington, DC - *EISS 83*
Municipal Debt - New York, NY - *DirOnDB Spring 84*
Municipal Index [of Morgan-Grampian Publishing Co.] - Pittsfield, MA - *MagDir 84*
Municipal TV Corp. [of Service Electric Cable TV Inc.] - Bloomsburg, PA - *BrCabYB 84; Tel&CabFB 84C*

Municipal Utilities Systems - Fairbanks, AK - *TelDir&BG 83-84*
Municipal World - St. Thomas, ON, Canada - *BaconPubCkMag 84*
Municipality, The [of League of Wisconsin Municipalities] - Madison, WI - *BaconPubCkMag 84; MagDir 84*
Munifacts - New York, NY - *DirOnDB Spring 84*
Munilease [of Interactive Data Services Inc.] - New York, NY - *DataDirOnSer 84*
Munising News - Munising, MI - *BaconPubCkNews 84; Ed&PubIntYB 82; NewsDir 84*
Munising Telephone Co. - Munising, MI - *TelDir&BG 83-84*
Muniz Stations, Ed - New Orleans, LA - *BrCabYB 84*
Munk & Co., Burt - Northbrook, IL - *AvMarPl 83; WritMar 84*
Munn & Associates Inc., E. Harold Jr. - Coldwater, MI - *InterCabHB 3; Tel&CabFB 84C p.1693*
Munro, J. Alex - Springfield, IL - *BoPubDir 4, 5*
Munsey News Service - New York, NY - *Ed&PubIntYB 82; MagIndMarPl 82-83*
Munster/Hammond/Highland Town & Country - Hammond, IN - *AyerDirPub 83*
Muppet Music Inc. - *See* Cherry Lane Music Publishing Co. Inc.
Murat, Felix - Miami, FL - *BoPubDir 4, 5*
Murchison & Bailey Inc. - Fayetteville, NC - *StaDirAdAg 2-84*
Murdo Coyote - Murdo, SD - *BaconPubCkNews 84; Ed&PubIntYB 82*
Murdock Productions Inc. - Cincinnati, OH - *Tel&CabFB 84C*
Murdocksville Telephone - Imperial, PA - *TelDir&BG 83-84*
Murfin-Harris Syndicate - Columbus, OH - *Ed&PubIntYB 82*
Murfreesboro Cable Television Co. [of Marsh Media Cable Television] - Murfreesboro, TN - *BrCabYB 84; Tel&CabFB 84C*
Murfreesboro Daily News-Journal [of Mid-South Publishing] - Murfreesboro, TN - *BaconPubCkNews 84; NewsDir 84*
Murfreesboro Diamond - Murfreesboro, AR - *BaconPubCkNews 84; Ed&PubIntYB 82*
Murfreesboro TV Cable Co. - Murfreesboro, AR - *BrCabYB 84; Tel&CabFB 84C*
Murios Publishing Inc. - *See* Mirus Publishing Corp.
Murphy & Broad Publishing Co. - Newport Beach, CA - *BoPubDir 4 Sup, 5*
Murphy & Smylie Enterprises - Brandon, MS - *Tel&CabFB 84C*
Murphy Cable TV Inc. - Murphy, NC - *BrCabYB 84; Tel&CabFB 84C*
Murphy Cherokee Scout & Andrews Journal [of Community Newspapers Inc.] - Murphy, NC - *NewsDir 84*
Murphy Cherokee Scout & Clay Progress - Murphy, NC - *BaconPubCkNews 84*
Murphy, Dennis D. - Milwaukee, WI - *BoPubDir 4, 5*
Murphy Institute, Tayloe [of University of Virginia] - Charlottesville, VA - *EISS 83*
Murphy Marketing Research, James P. - Wayne, PA - *IntDirMarRes 83*
Murphy, Merwin L. - Alhambra, CA - *BoPubDir 4, 5*
Murphy Newspapers, Morgan - Superior, WI - *Ed&PubIntYB 82*
Murphy Parker Inc. - Philadelphia, PA - *LitMarPl 83, 84*
Murphy Productions Inc., Owen - Westport, CT - *AvMarPl 83*
Murphy Publishing Co. - Timonium, MD - *BoPubDir 4, 5*
Murphy Stations, Morgan - Superior, WI - *BrCabYB 84; Tel&CabFB 84S*
Murphy, William V. - *See* Combined Cable Corp.
Murray Advertising Agency Inc., John F. - New York, NY - *BrCabYB 84; StaDirAdAg 2-84*
Murray & Associates Inc., Stanley H. - Greenwich, CT - *ArtMar 84; StaDirAdAg 2-84*
Murray Associates, John C. - Canby, OR - *LitMarPl 83, 84*
Murray Book Sales Co. Inc. - Brooklyn, NY - *LitMarPl 83*
Murray/Bradley & Peterson Inc. - Anchorage, AK - *AdAge 3-28-84; DirPRFirms 83; StaDirAdAg 2-84*
Murray Cablevision [of American TV & Communications Corp.] - Murray, KY - *BrCabYB 84; Tel&CabFB 84C*
Murray County Herald - Murray County, MN - *Ed&PubIntYB 82*
Murray County Herald - Slayton, MN - *AyerDirPub 83; NewsDir 84*
Murray County Shopper - Slayton, MN - *AyerDirPub 83*
Murray Eagle - Murray, UT - *Ed&PubIntYB 82*
Murray Eagle [of Murray Printing Inc.] - Salt Lake City, UT - *NewsDir 84*
Murray Eagle - *See* Murray Printing Co. Inc.
Murray Editing & Translation, Steven T. [Subs. of Fjord Press] - Berkeley, CA - *LitMarPl 83*
Murray Hill Center - New York, NY - *IntDirMarRes 83*
Murray Hill News - New York, NY - *LitMarPl 83, 84*
Murray Hill Pennysaver - Jericho, NY - *AyerDirPub 83*
Murray Hill Press, The - Sands Point, NY - *LitMag&SmPr 83-84*
Murray Ledger & Times - Murray, KY - *BaconPubCkNews 84; Ed&PubIntYB 82; NewsDir 84*
Murray News Advertiser East - *See* Murray Printing Co. Inc.
Murray News Advertiser West - *See* Murray Printing Co. Inc.
Murray Printing Co. - Westford, MA - *LitMarPl 83, 84*
Murray Printing Co. Inc. - Murray, UT - *BaconPubCkNews 84*
Murray Publishing Co. - Seattle, WA - *BaconPubCkNews 84*
Murray Research Center, Henry A. [of Radcliffe College] - Cambridge, MA - *EISS 83*
Murray, Steven T. [Subs. of Fjord Press] - Berkeley, CA - *LitMarPl 83, 84; MagIndMarPl 82-83*
Murray, William S. - Bismarck, ND - *BoPubDir 4, 5*
Murraysville Telephone Co., The [Aff. of Mid-Continent Telephone Corp.] - Export, PA - *TelDir&BG 83-84*
Murrysville Penn Franklin News - Murrysville, PA - *BaconPubCkNews 84*
Murton Press - Greenwich, CT - *BoPubDir 4, 5*
Murzin Publishing - Deerfield Beach, FL - *BoPubDir 5*
Musari Music - *See* Starfox Publishing
Muscadine - Boulder, CO - *LitMag&SmPr 83-84*
Muscatine Journal [of Lee Enterprises Inc.] - Muscatine, IA - *BaconPubCkNews 84; Ed&PubIntYB 82; NewsDir 84*
Muscatine TV & Communications Corp. [of American TV & Communications Corp.] - Muscatine, IA - *BrCabYB 84; Tel&CabFB 84C*
Muscle & Fitness [of Weider Health & Fitness] - Woodland Hills, CA - *BaconPubCkMag 84; WritMar 84*
Muscle Bound Bindery Inc. - Minneapolis, MN - *LitMarPl 83, 84*
Muscle Builder & Power - Woodland Hills, CA - *MagDir 84*
Muscle Digest - San Gabriel, CA - *BaconPubCkMag 84*
Muscle Digest - Whittier, CA - *MagDir 84*
Muscle Games - Norristown, PA - *BoPubDir 4, 5*
Muscle Mag International - Brampton, ON, Canada - *ArtMar 84*
Muscle Music - *See* Jo-Wee Publishing
Muscle Shoals Sound Publishing Co. Inc. - Sheffield, AL - *BillIntBG 83-84*
Muscoda Progressive - Muscoda, WI - *BaconPubCkNews 84; Ed&PubIntYB 82*
Muscular Development - York, PA - *MagIndMarPl 82-83*
Muse - Baltimore, MD - *DirInfWP 82*
Muse-Ed Co. - Van Nuys, CA - *BoPubDir 4, 5; LitMag&SmPr 83-84*
Muse-Pie - Passaic, NJ - *LitMag&SmPr 83-84*
Muse Records [Div. of Blanchris Inc.] - New York, NY - *BillIntBG 83-84*
Muse Software - Baltimore, MD - *MicrocomMPl 83, 84; MicrocomSwDir 1; WhoWMicrocom 83*
Musedco Publishing Co. [Div. of Hisong Records] - Richardson, TX - *BillIntBG 83-84*
Muses Co. - Ste. Anne de Bellevue, PQ, Canada - *BoPubDir 5*
Musetta Music Co. - *See* Loring Music Co.
Museum at Large Ltd. - New York, NY - *AvMarPl 83*
Museum Computer Network Inc. - Stony Brook, NY - *EISS 83*
Museum News - Washington, DC - *BaconPubCkMag 84; MagDir 84; MagIndMarPl 82-83*
Museum of Fine Arts - Boston, MA - *BoPubDir 4, 5*
Museum of Fine Arts (Bookstore) - Houston, TX - *BoPubDir 4, 5*
Museum of History & Industry [Aff. of Historical Society of Seattle & King County] - Seattle, WA - *BoPubDir 4, 5*
Museum of Modern Art - New York, NY - *LitMarPl 83, 84*
Museum of Modern Art (Film Stills Archive) - New York, NY - *AvMarPl 83*
Museum of Modern Art of Latin America - Washington, DC - *AvMarPl 83*
Museum of New Mexico Press - Santa Fe, NM - *LitMag&SmPr 83-84; LitMarPl 83, 84; WritMar 84*
Museum of Northern Arizona Press - Flagstaff, AZ - *BoPubDir 4, 5; WritMar 84*
Museum of Science - Boston, MA - *BoPubDir 4, 5*

Museum of Temporary Art Magazine - Washington, DC - *LitMag&SmPr 83-84*
Museum of the American Indian - New York, NY - *BoPubDir 4, 5*
Museum of the City of Mobile - Mobile, AL - *BoPubDir 4, 5*
Museum of the Great Plains [Aff. of Institute of the Great Plains] - Lawton, OK - *BoPubDir 4, 5*
Museum Press Inc. - Washington, DC - *BoPubDir 4, 5*
Museum Restoration Service - Bloomfield, ON, Canada - *BoPubDir 4, 5*
Museum Systems - Los Angeles, CA - *BoPubDir 4, 5*
Museums Collaborative Inc. - New York, NY - *BoPubDir 4, 5*
Museums New York - New York, NY - *MagDir 84*
Mushroom News, The - Kennett Square, PA - *WritMar 84*
Music Adventures Records Inc. - Cleveland, OH - *BillIntBG 83-84*
Music & Letters [of Oxford University Press] - Oxford, England - *LitMag&SmPr 83-84*
Music & Sound Output [of Testa Communications] - Carle Place, NY - *BaconPubCkMag 84; WritMar 84*
Music-Book Associates Inc. - New York, NY - *LitMarPl 83, 84; MagIndMarPl 82-83*
Music Book Society [of North American Book Clubs Inc.] - Dover, NH - *LitMarPl 83, 84*
Music City News - Nashville, TN - *BaconPubCkMag 84; MagDir 84; MagIndMarPl 82-83; WritMar 84*
Music Corp. of America Inc. - *See* MCA Music
Music Craftshop Inc. - Nashville, TN - *BillIntBG 83-84*
Music Education Publications - Fullerton, CA - *BoPubDir 5*
Music Educators' Book Society [of Prentice-Hall Inc.] - Englewood, NJ - *LitMarPl 83, 84*
Music Educators Journal - Reston, VA - *ArtMar 84; BaconPubCkMag 84; MagDir 84; MagIndMarPl 82-83; WritMar 84*
Music Educators National Conference - Reston, VA - *BoPubDir 4, 5*
Music Enterprises Inc. - Houston, TX - *BillIntBG 83-84*
Music Exchange, The - Ft. Worth, TX - *BillIntBG 83-84*
Music Express - Willowdale, ON, Canada - *BaconPubCkMag 84*
Music for Percussion - Ft. Lauderdale, FL - *BillIntBG 83-84*
Music Gig, The - New York, NY - *MagDir 84*
Music Group, The - Tulsa, OK - *Tel&CabFB 84C*
Music in the Air [of Satellite Cable Audio Networks] - Tulsa, OK - *CabTVPrDB 83*
Music Inc. - New York, NY - *BillIntBG 83-84*
Music Industry Products - Palm Springs, CA - *BaconPubCkMag 84*
Music Inn - New York, NY - *BillIntBG 83-84*
Music Journal - Southampton, NY - *MagDir 84*
Music Magazine [of Barrett & Colgrass Inc.] - Toronto, ON, Canada - *BaconPubCkMag 84; WritMar 84*
Music Makers Inc. - New York, NY - *Tel&CabFB 84C*
Music Makers Promotion Network - New York, NY - *LitMarPl 84*
Music Music Music Inc. - New York, NY - *BillIntBG 83-84*
Music of Polynesia Inc. - Honolulu, HI - *BillIntBG 83-84*
Music Phaze Magazine - Fair Oaks, CA - *MagDir 84*
Music River Publishing Co. - *See* Mississippi River Music Publishing Co.
Music Sales Corp. - New York, NY - *BillIntBG 83-84; LitMarPl 83, 84; WritMar 84*
Music Television - New York, NY - *BrCabYB 84*
Music Television - *See* Warner Amex Satellite Entertainment Co.
Music Trades - Englewood, NJ - *BaconPubCkMag 84; MagDir 84*
Music Treasure Publications - New York, NY - *BoPubDir 4, 5*
Music Type Service - Nashville, TN - *LitMarPl 83*
Music Video Retailer - Chestnut Hill, MA - *BaconPubCkMag 84; MagDir 84*
Musica Latina International Inc. - New York, NY - *BillIntBG 83-84*
Musica Publishing Co. - Edison, NJ - *BoPubDir 4 Sup, 5*
Musical Heritage Society Inc. - Tinton Falls, NJ - *BillIntBG 83-84*
Musical Merchandise Review - Chestnut Hill, MA - *BaconPubCkMag 84; MagDir 84; MagIndMarPl 82-83*
Musical Opinion - Bournemouth, England - *LitMag&SmPr 83-84*
Musical Product News/Musical Electronics - New York, NY - *MagDir 84*
Musical Properties Inc. - New York, NY - *BillIntBG 83-84*
Musical Quarterly, The - New York, NY - *BaconPubCkMag 84*
Musical Records Co. - Hialeah, FL - *BillIntBG 83-84*
Musical Signature Records - Detroit, MI - *BillIntBG 83-84*
Musicanza Corp. - Wantagh, NY - *BillIntBG 83-84*
Musicdata Inc. - Philadelphia, PA - *BoPubDir 4, 5*
Musician Magazine - Gloucester, MA - *MagDir 84*
Musician, Player & Listener - New York, NY - *MagIndMarPl 82-83*
Musicmaster Publications Inc. - New York, NY - *BillIntBG 83-84*
Musicmasters - Tinton Falls, NJ - *BillIntBG 83-84*
Musicor Records - New York, NY - *BillIntBG 83-84*
Musicprint Corp. - New York, NY - *BillIntBG 83-84; BoPubDir 4, 5*
MusicSource - Minnetonka, MN - *DirOnDB Spring 84*
Musictone Music - Santa Monica, CA - *BillIntBG 83-84*
Musicues Corp. - New York, NY - *AvMarPl 83*
Musicworks - Toronto, ON, Canada - *LitMag&SmPr 83-84*
Musifex Inc. - Arlington, VA - *Tel&CabFB 84C*
Musigram Inc. - North Miami, FL - *BillIntBG 83-84*
Musigraph - Louisville, KY - *LitMarPl 83, 84*
Musique Circle Records - Long Beach, CA - *BillIntBG 83-84*
Musique Records - Brooklyn, NY - *BillIntBG 83-84*
Musitronic Inc. - Owatonna, MN - *MicrocomMPl 83, 84*
Muskego Sun - Muskego, WI - *Ed&PubIntYB 82*
Muskego Sun - Oak Creek, WI - *AyerDirPub 83*
Muskego Sun - *See* Community Newspapers Inc.
Muskegon Cable TV [of TCI-Taft Cablevision Associates] - Fremont, MI - *Tel&CabFB 84C*
Muskegon Cable TV [of Tele-Communications Inc.] - Muskegon, MI - *BrCabYB 84; Tel&CabFB 84C*
Muskegon Chronicle [of Booth Newspapers Inc.] - Muskegon, MI - *BaconPubCkNews 84; Ed&PubIntYB 82; NewsDir 84*
Muskegon Examiner - Muskegon, MI - *BaconPubCkNews 84*
Muskegon/Norton Shores/Roosevelt Park Examiner - Muskegon, MI - *NewsDir 84*
Muskogee Phoenix & Times-Democrat [of Oklahoma Press Printing Co.] - Muskogee, OK - *BaconPubCkNews 84; NewsDir 84*
Muskogee Sunday Phoenix & Times-Democrat [of Oklahoma Press Publishing Co.] - Muskogee, OK - *NewsDir 84*
Muskoka Free Press - Huntsville, ON, Canada - *AyerDirPub 83; Ed&PubIntYB 82*
Muskoka Lakes-Georgian Bay Beacon - MacTier, ON, Canada - *AyerDirPub 83*
Muskoka Publications Ltd. - Bracebridge, ON, Canada - *BoPubDir 4, 5*
Musrad Publishing - *See* Shayne Enterprises, Larry
Musson Book Co. [Div. of General Publishing Co. Ltd.] - Don Mills, ON, Canada - *LitMarPl 83, 84*
Mustang Cable TV [of Scott Cable Communications Inc.] - Andrews, TX - *BrCabYB 84; Tel&CabFB 84C*
Mustang Daily [of California State Polytechnic University] - San Luis Obispo, CA - *NewsDir 84*
Mustang Mirror - Mustang, OK - *AyerDirPub 83; BaconPubCkNews 84; Ed&PubIntYB 82*
Mustang Press - Denver, CO - *BoPubDir 4, 5*
Mustang Telephone Co. [Aff. of Century Telephone Enterprises Inc.] - Port Aransas, TX - *TelDir&BG 83-84*
Mustard Seed Records & Publishing - Nashville, TN - *BillIntBG 83-84*
Mustard Tree Music - Nashville, TN - *BillIntBG 83-84*
Mustardseed Press [Aff. of Interuniverse] - Cocoa, FL - *BoPubDir 4, 5*
Muste Memorial Institute, A. J. - New York, NY - *BoPubDir 5*
Mustevic Sound Inc. - New York, NY - *BillIntBG 83-84*
Mustevic Sound Records Inc. - Albans, NY - *BillIntBG 83-84*
MuSYS Corp. - Irvine, CA - *MicrocomMPl 84*
MuSYS Corp. - Tustin, CA - *MicrocomMPl 83*
Mutual Broadcasting System [Subs. of Amway Communications] - Arlington, VA - *BrCabYB 84; LitMarPl 83, 84; Tel&CabFB 84C*
Mutual Broadcasting System - *See* MBS
Mutual Media - Englewood Cliffs, NJ - *AdAge 3-28-84; StaDirAdAg 2-84*

Mutual Press Clipping Service Inc. - Philadelphia, PA - *ProGuPRSer 4*
Mutual Publishing Co. - Washington, DC - *BoPubDir 4, 5*
Mutual Radio News - *See* MBS
Mutual Telephone Co. - Sioux Center, IA - *TelDir&BG 83-84*
Mutual Telephone Co. of Morning Sun - Morley, IA - *TelDir&BG 83-84*
Mutual Telephone Co., The - Little River, KS - *TelDir&BG 83-84*
Muzzelloading Artilleryman, The [of Century Publications Inc.] - Winchester, MA - *WritMar 84*
Muzzie Music - Clayton, ID - *BillIntBG 83-84*
Muzzle Blasts - Friendship, IN - *MagDir 84*
M.V. Cablevision Ltd. - Grand Falls, NB, Canada - *BrCabYB 84*
MVP Communications Inc. - New York, NY - *AvMarPl 83*
MW Software - Urbana, IL - *MicrocomMPl 84*
MWN Publications - Winnipeg, MB, Canada - *LitMag&SmPr 83-84*
My Daddy's Music Co. - *See* Schroeder International Ltd., A.
My Devotions - St. Louis, MO - *WritMar 84*
My i Svit - Niagara Falls, ON, Canada - *Ed&PubIntYB 82*
My Little Salesman - Eugene, OR - *MagDir 84*
My Way Publishing - Maui, HI - *BoPubDir 5*
My Weekly [of D. C. Thomson & Co. Ltd.] - Dundee, Scotland - *WritMar 84*
Myco Publishing House - Arcadia, CA - *BoPubDir 4, 5*
Mycologia - Bronx, NY - *MagIndMarPl 82-83*
Mycological Society of San Francisco - San Francisco, CA - *BoPubDir 4, 5*
Mycroft Labs - Tallahassee, FL - *MicrocomMPl 83, 84; WhoWMicrocom 83*
Myers, A. D. - Mountain View, CA - *BoPubDir 4, 5*
Myers Advertising Inc. - Honolulu, HI - *StaDirAdAg 2-84*
Myers, Albert E. - Harrisburg, PA - *BoPubDir 4, 5*
Myers & Associates Inc. - Stuart, FL - *StaDirAdAg 2-84*
Myers & Associates Inc., W. S. - Honolulu, HI - *BrCabYB 84*
Myers & Associates, Tom - Atlanta, GA - *BrCabYB 84*
Myers Communicounsel Inc. - New York, NY - *DirPRFirms 83*
Myers Enterprises Inc., B. J. - Big Wells, TX - *BrCabYB 84*
Myers Enterprises Inc., B. J. - La Pryor, TX - *BrCabYB 84*
Myers, J. William - Lyons, OH - *LitMarPl 83, 84; MagIndMarPl 82-83*
Myers Newspapers Group [of Chicago Lerner Newspapers] - Chicago, IL - *NewsDir 84*
Myers Public Relations, Margaret P. - Paoli, PA - *DirPRFirms 83*
Myers Publishing Co. - Chicago, IL - *BaconPubCkNews 84*
Myerstown Merchandiser - Lebanon, PA - *AyerDirPub 83*
Myette, Louise - Montreal, PQ, Canada - *LitMarPl 84*
Mylee Digital Sciences Inc. - Maryland Heights, MO - *DataDirSup 7-83; WhoWMicrocom 83*
Mynabird Publishing - Portola Valley, CA - *BoPubDir 4, 5*
Myrbeck & Co. Inc., S. Gunnar - Norwell, MA - *StaDirAdAg 2-84*
Myriad Moods - San Antonio, TX - *LitMag&SmPr 83-84*
Myriad Music Publishing Corp. - *See* Webman & Co., H. B.
Myriade Press Inc. - New Rochelle, NY - *BoPubDir 4, 5*
Myrin Institute Inc. - New York, NY - *BoPubDir 4, 5*
Myrtle Beach MDS Co. - Pasadena, MD - *Tel&CabFB 84C*
Myrtle Beach Sun News - Myrtle Beach, SC - *NewsDir 84*
Myrtle Creek Umpqua Free Press - Myrtle Creek, OR - *BaconPubCkNews 84*
Myrtle Point Herald - Myrtle Point, OR - *BaconPubCkNews 84; Ed&PubIntYB 82*
Myrtle Telephone Co. [Aff. of Century Telephone Enterprises Inc.] - Olive Branch, MS - *TelDir&BG 83-84*
Myrtle Wood - Tulsa, OK - *LitMag&SmPr 83-84*
Mysterious Press - New York, NY - *LitMag&SmPr 83-84; LitMarPl 83, 84*
Mystery Fancier, The [of Brownstone Books] - Madison, IN - *LitMag&SmPr 83-84*
Mystery Guild [Subs. of Doubleday & Co. Inc.] - Garden City, NY - *LitMarPl 83*
Mystery Guild - *See* Doubleday Book Clubs
Mystery Manor Press [Aff. of Manor House Publications Inc.] - Huntingdon Valley, PA - *BoPubDir 4, 5*
Mystery Music Inc. - Plano, TX - *BillIntBG 83-84*
Mystery Time Anthology - Coeur D'Alene, ID - *LitMag&SmPr 83-84*
Mystic Arts Book Society [Subs. of Lyle Stuart Inc.] - Secaucus, NJ - *LitMarPl 83, 84*
Mystic Records Inc. - Hollywood, CA - *BillIntBG 83-84*
Mystic Seaport Museum - Mystic, CT - *BoPubDir 4, 5; LitMarPl 84*
Mystic Software - Mystic, CT - *MicrocomMPl 83*
Mystic Valley Newspapers - Malden, MA - *Ed&PubIntYB 82*
Mytee Music - Evansville, IN - *MicrocomMPl 83*
Mythlore - Whittier, CA - *LitMag&SmPr 83-84*

N

N & N Publishing Co. - Wappinger, NY - *BoPubDir 4, 5*
N & N Resources - Troy, ID - *BoPubDir 4, 5*
N Cybernetic Frontiers Corp. - East Lansing, MI - *WhoWMicrocom 83*
N4 Transportation Systems of Canada Ltd. - Deerfield, IL - *EISS 5-84 Sup*
N-Squared Computing - Silverton, OR - *MicrocomMPl 84; MicrocomSwDir 1*
N 2 D Publishing Co. - *See* Hat Band Music
NA Hotline - Washington, DC - *DirOnDB Spring 84*
Na Pali Publishing Co. - Honolulu, HI - *BoPubDir 4, 5*
NAA Hotline [of NewsNet Inc.] - Bryn Mawr, PA - *DataDirOnSer 84*
NAARS - New York, NY - *DirOnDB Spring 84*
NABCAT Inc. [of King Videocable Co.] - Valencia, CA - *BrCabYB 84*
Nabet News [of National Association of Broadcast Employees & Technicians] - Chicago, IL - *NewsDir 84*
Naborhood Link News - St. Louis, MO - *AyerDirPub 83*
NABSCAN - Rutherford, NJ - *EISS 7-83 Sup; IntDirMarRes 83*
NABSCAN Data Base - New York, NY - *DBBus 82*
NABSCAN Supermarket Product Movement Data - Rutherford, NJ - *DirOnDB Spring 84*
NABSCAN Supermarket Product Movement Data [of Management Science Associates Inc.] - Pittsburgh, PA - *DataDirOnSer 84*
NABU Commercial Terminals Ltd. - Waterloo, ON, Canada - *DataDirSup 7-83*
Nabu Manufacturing Corp. - Wayne, PA - *ADAPSOMemDir 83-84*
NABU Manufacturing Corp. - Ottawa, ON, Canada - *DataDirSup 7-83; InfoS 83-84; VideoDir 82-83; WhoWMicrocom 83*
NABW Journal - Chicago, IL - *BaconPubCkMag 84; MagDir 84; WritMar 84*
Nachman Associates, Henry - New York, NY - *AdAge 3-28-84; StaDirAdAg 2-84*
NACLA Report on the Americas - New York, NY - *MagIndMarPl 82-83*
Naclerio & Associates Inc., Nicholas J. - Springfield, VA - *DirInfWP 82*
Nacogdoches Advertising Associates - Nacogdoches, TX - *StaDirAdAg 2-84*
Nacogdoches Cable TV [of TCA Cable TV Group] - Nacogdoches, TX - *BrCabYB 84; Tel&CabFB 84C*
Nacogdoches Sentinel [of Herald Publishing Co. Inc.] - Nacogdoches, TX - *BaconPubCkNews 84; NewsDir 84*
Nada Press - Grandville, MI - *BoPubDir 4 Sup, 5; LitMag&SmPr 83-84*
Nadeau, Louis Marie - East Broughton, PQ, Canada - *BrCabYB 84*
Nadell's Fashion Sense, Lila - New York, NY - *Ed&PubIntYB 82*
Nader & Associates Inc. - Chicago, IL - *StaDirAdAg 2-84*
Nadja - New York, NY - *BoPubDir 4, 5*
NADL Journal [of National Association of Dental Laboratories Inc.] - Alexandria, VA - *BaconPubCkMag 84; MagDir 84*
Nadler & Larimer [Subs. of Mickelberry Corp.] - New York, NY - *AdAge 3-28-84; BrCabYB 84; StaDirAdAg 2-84*
Nadller Concepts - Flushing, NY - *BoPubDir 4 Sup, 5*
NAEIR News - Northfield, IL - *BaconPubCkMag 84*
NAFA Bulletin - New York, NY - *BaconPubCkMag 84; MagDir 84*
Naftzger & Kuhe - Farmington, CT - *AdAge 3-28-84; StaDirAdAg 2-84*
Naggar Literary Agency, Jean V. - New York, NY - *LitMarPl 83, 84*
Nagle, G. S. - Duncan, BC, Canada - *Tel&CabFB 84C*
Nagra Magnetic Recorders Inc. - New York, NY - *AvMarPl 83*
NAHB-Builder [of National Association of Home Builders] - Washington, DC - *BaconPubCkMag 84; LitMag&SmPr 83-84*
NAHB County Database - Washington, DC - *DirOnDB Spring 84*
Nahser Inc., Frank C. - Chicago, IL - *AdAge 3-28-84; StaDirAdAg 2-84*
Nahsville MDS Co. - New Rochelle, NY - *Tel&CabFB 84C*
Nahunta Brantley Enterprise - Nahunta, GA - *BaconPubCkNews 84*
Nahunta Clearview Cable TV - Nahunta, GA - *BrCabYB 84; Tel&CabFB 84C*
Naiad Press Inc. - Tallahassee, FL - *BoPubDir 4, 5; LitMag&SmPr 83-84; LitMarPl 83, 84; WritMar 84*
NAIC Reporter - New York, NY - *BaconPubCkMag 84*
NAICO-Net - East Hartford, CT - *DirOnDB Spring 84*
Naigai Pressclipping Bureau Ltd. - Tokyo, Japan - *ProGuPRSer 4*
Naikoon Marine [Aff. of Allison Holdings] - Vancouver, BC, Canada - *BoPubDir 4, 5*
Naimark & Barba Inc. - Cedar Knolls, NJ - *StaDirAdAg 2-84*
Naked Man - Bowling Green, KS - *LitMag&SmPr 83-84*
Naked Man Press - Lawrence, KS - *LitMag&SmPr 83-84*
NAL Books [Div. of The New American Library Inc.] - New York, NY - *LitMarPl 83*
Nalewajk, Jerome - Stamford, CT - *MagIndMarPl 82-83*
Nallevents - Tacoma, WA - *ArtMar 84*
NAM New Age Mailing Lists [of Spiritual Community Publications] - Berkeley, CA - *LitMarPl 83, 84; MagIndMarPl 82-83*
Name Authority File [of National Library of Medicine] - Bethesda, MD - *DataDirOnSer 84*
Name Game Co. Inc., The - New York, NY - *Ed&PubIntYB 82*
Nameless Press - Jonestown, TX - *BoPubDir 4, 5*
Names & Addresses Inc. - Northbrook, IL - *LitMarPl 83, 84; MagIndMarPl 82-83*
Names Unltd. Inc. [Subs. of Computer Directions Group Inc.] - New York, NY - *LitMarPl 83, 84; MagIndMarPl 82-83*
Nanaimo Daily Free Press - Nanaimo, BC, Canada - *BaconPubCkNews 84; Ed&PubIntYB 82*
Nanaimo Historical Society - Nanaimo, BC, Canada - *BoPubDir 4, 5*
Nanaimo Times, The - Nanaimo, BC, Canada - *AyerDirPub 83*
Nance County Journal - Fullerton, NE - *Ed&PubIntYB 82*

Nance Design for Publishing, Bob & Faith - Homewood, AL - *LitMarPl 83, 84*
Nancy Jane Publishing Co. - Lenoir, NC - *BillIntBG 83-84*
Nanny Goat Productions - Laguna Beach, CA - *BoPubDir 4, 5; LitMag&SmPr 83-84*
Nanodata Computer Corp. - Buffalo, NY - *DataDirSup 7-83*
Nanogens International - Freedom, CA - *BoPubDir 4, 5*
Nanosecond Computer Services - Detroit, MI - *MicrocomMPl 84*
Nantahala Cablevision Corp. [of Omni Cable TV Corp.] - Bryson City, NC - *Tel&CabFB 84C*
Nanticoke Times - Nanticoke, ON, Canada - *Ed&PubIntYB 82*
Nanton News, The - Nanton, AB, Canada - *Ed&PubIntYB 82*
Nantucket Cablevision Corp. - Nantucket, MA - *BrCabYB 84*
Nantucket Historical Association - Nantucket, MA - *BoPubDir 5*
Nantucket Inquirer & Mirror - Nantucket, MA - *BaconPubCkNews 84; NewsDir 84*
Nantucket Review - Nantucket, MA - *BoPubDir 4, 5; LitMag&SmPr 83-84*
Nanty Glo Cable TV [of Eastern Telecom Corp.] - Nanty Glo, PA - *BrCabYB 84; Tel&CabFB 84C*
Nanty Glo Journal - Nanty Glo, PA - *Ed&PubIntYB 82*
Nanty-Glo Journal - Portage, PA - *AyerDirPub 83*
Nanty Glo Journal - *See* Sedloff Publications Inc.
Nanuet Rockland Review - Nanuet, NY - *BaconPubCkNews 84*
Naomi's Professional Clerical Services - Racine, WI - *LitMarPl 83, 84*
NAP Consumer Electronics - Knoxville, TN - *BillIntBG 83-84*
NAP Records Inc. - Abilene, TX - *BillIntBG 83-84*
Napa County Record - Napa, CA - *AyerDirPub 83; BaconPubCkNews 84; Ed&PubIntYB 82; NewsDir 84*
Napa Register [of Napa Valley Publishing Co.] - Napa, CA - *BaconPubCkNews 84; Ed&PubIntYB 82; NewsDir 84*
Napa Valley Cablevision Inc. [of Viacom International Inc.] - Napa, CA - *Tel&CabFB 84C*
Napanee-Deseronto Cablevision Ltd. - Napanee, ON, Canada - *BrCabYB 84*
Naperville Sun - Naperville, IL - *BaconPubCkNews 84; Ed&PubIntYB 82; NewsDir 84*
Naples CATV [of El-Mar Communications Co.] - Naples, NY - *BrCabYB 84*
Naples Monitor - Naples, TX - *BaconPubCkNews 84*
Naples News - Naples, FL - *AyerDirPub 83; BaconPubCkNews 84; Ed&PubIntYB 82; NewsDir 84*
Naples Now - Naples, FL - *MagDir 84*
Naples Record - Naples, NY - *Ed&PubIntYB 82; NewsDir 84*
Naples Shopping News - Canandaigua, NY - *AyerDirPub 83*
Naples Star - Naples, FL - *Ed&PubIntYB 82; NewsDir 84*
Naples Star - *See* Sunbelt Publishing Co.
Napoleon Homestead - Napoleon, ND - *BaconPubCkNews 84; Ed&PubIntYB 82*
Napoleon Northwest Signal - Napoleon, OH - *BaconPubCkNews 84; NewsDir 84*
Napoleonville Assumption Pioneer - Napoleonville, LA - *BaconPubCkNews 84*
Napp Creations Inc. - Nutley, NJ - *BoPubDir 4, 5*
Nappanee Advance News - Nappanee, IN - *BaconPubCkNews 84; Ed&PubIntYB 82*
Nappanee Cable TV - Nappanee, IN - *BrCabYB 84*
Nappo Software - Milford, CT - *MicrocomMPl 84*
NAPSAC International - Marble Hill, MO - *BoPubDir 4, 5*
N.A.P.T. Journal - Anaheim, CA - *BaconPubCkMag 84*
Narcisso-Volz - Philadelphia, PA - *StaDirAdAg 2-84*
Narcotics Education Inc. - Washington, DC - *BoPubDir 4, 5*
NARD Journal - Washington, DC - *MagIndMarPl 82-83*
NARD Journal - Alexandria, VA - *BaconPubCkMag 84; MagDir 84; WritMar 84*
NARDA News [of National Association of Retail Dealers of America] - Chicago, IL - *BaconPubCkMag 84; MagDir 84*
Naren Products Inc. [Div. of Brandess Brothers Sales Co.] - Chicago, IL - *AvMarPl 83*
NARI Newsletter - Windsor, NJ - *BaconPubCkMag 84*
NARIC - Washington, DC - *DirOnDB Spring 84*
NARIC [of Bibliographic Retrieval Services Inc.] - Latham, NY - *DataDirOnSer 84*
Narodna Volya - Detroit, MI - *Ed&PubIntYB 82; NewsDir 84*
Narodna Volya - Scranton, PA - *AyerDirPub 83*
Narodne Noviny - Pittsburgh, PA - *Ed&PubIntYB 82; NewsDir 84*
Narragansett Capital Corp. - Providence, RI - *Tel&CabFB 84C p.1693*
Narragansett Coated Papers [Div. of Ecological Fibers Inc.] - Pawtucket, RI - *LitMarPl 83, 84*
Narragansett Times - Wakefield, RI - *AyerDirPub 83*
Narragansett Times, The - Narragansett, RI - *Ed&PubIntYB 82*
Narrative Accomplishment Reporting System [of U.S. Dept. of Agriculture] - Beltsville, MD - *EISS 7-83 Sup*
Narrow Gate Music Inc. - *See* Special Rider Music
Narrow Gauge & Short Line Gazette - Los Altos, CA - *MagIndMarPl 82-83*
Narrowroad Music - *See* Sugarvine Music
Narup & Co., William J. - Northbrook, IL - *StaDirAdAg 2-84*
NASA Directory of Numerical Databases [of U.S. National Aeronautics & Space Administration] - Baltimore, MD - *DirOnDB Spring 84*
NASA/Florida State Technology Applications Center [of University of Florida] - Gainesville, FL - *EISS 83; InfIndMarPl 83*
NASA Industrial Applications Center - Los Angeles, CA - *EISS 83; InfIndMarPl 83*
NASA Industrial Applications Center [of University of Pittsburgh] - Pittsburgh, PA - *DataDirOnSer 84; EISS 83; InfIndMarPl 83*
NASA Library Network [of U.S. National Aeronautics & Space Administration] - Washington, DC - *EISS 83*
Nasa Nada - Chicago, IL - *Ed&PubIntYB 82*
Nasa Nada - Hobart, IN - *NewsDir 84*
NASA NALNET Books [of U.S. National Aeronautics & Space Administration] - Baltimore, MD - *DirOnDB Spring 84*
NASA NALNET Periodicals [of U.S. National Aeronautics & Space Administration] - Baltimore, MD - *DirOnDB Spring 84*
Nasa Novine - Toronto, ON, Canada - *Ed&PubIntYB 82*
NASA/RECON [of U.S. National Aeronautics & Space Administration] - Washington, DC - *EISS 83*
NASA Standard/Available Flight Qualified Equipment [of U.S. National Aeronautics & Space Administration] - Washington, DC - *CompReadDB 82*
NASA STI Database [of U.S. National Aeronautics & Space Administration] - Washington, DC - *CompReadDB 82; OnBibDB 3*
NASA STI Database [of U.S. National Aeronautics & Space Administration] - Baltimore, MD - *DirOnDB Spring 84*
NASA Tech Briefs [of U.S. National Aeronautics & Space Administration] - Baltimore, MD - *DirOnDB Spring 84*
NASA Technology Applications Center [of U.S. National Aeronautics & Space Administration] - Albuquerque, NM - *DataDirOnSer 84*
NASA/UK Technology Applications Program [of University of Kentucky] - Lexington, KY - *EISS 83*
NASCAR Newsletter - Daytona Beach, FL - *BaconPubCkMag 84; MagDir 84*
Nasco [Div. of Nasco International Inc.] - Ft. Atkinson, WI - *AvMarPl 83*
Nase Hlasy - Toronto, ON, Canada - *Ed&PubIntYB 82*
Nasetan Publishing Co. - Lake Charles, LA - *BillIntBG 83-84*
NASFT Showcase - New York, NY - *BaconPubCkMag 84*
Nash & Associates Inc., Helen - New York, NY - *DirPRFirms 83*
Nash Information Services Inc. - Ottawa, ON, Canada - *EISS 7-83 Sup*
Nash Information Services Inc. - Vanier, ON, Canada - *MicroMarPl 82-83*
Nash Productions Inc., Bob - New York, NY - *AvMarPl 83*
Nasha Meta - Toronto, ON, Canada - *Ed&PubIntYB 82*
Nashboro Record Co. - Nashville, TN - *BillIntBG 83-84*
Nashcal Music - *See* Fischer Music, Bobby
Nashoba Communications Inc. - Westford, MA - *BrCabYB 84; Tel&CabFB 84C p.1693*
Nashua Corp. - Nashua, NH - *DirInfWP 82; MicrocomMPl 84; Top100Al 83*
Nashua 1590 Broadcaster - Nashua, NH - *NewsDir 84*
Nashua Reporter - Nashua, IA - *BaconPubCkNews 84; Ed&PubIntYB 82*
Nashua Telegraph - Nashua, NH - *BaconPubCkNews 84; Ed&PubIntYB 82; NewsDir 84*
Nashville! - Nashville, TN - *BaconPubCkMag 84; MagDir 84*

Nashville Academy Theatre - Nashville, TN - *WritMar 84*
Nashville A.M.E. Christian Recorder - Nashville, TN - *BaconPubCkNews 84*
Nashville Amusement Business [of Billboard Publications Inc.] - Nashville, TN - *NewsDir 84*
Nashville Banner [of Music City Media Inc.] - Nashville, TN - *BaconPubCkNews 84; Ed&PubIntYB 82; LitMarPl 83, 84; NewsBur 6; NewsDir 84*
Nashville Berrien Press - Nashville, GA - *BaconPubCkNews 84; NewsDir 84*
Nashville Brown County Democrat - Nashville, IN - *BaconPubCkNews 84; NewsDir 84*
Nashville Cablevision Corp. [of Omni Cable TV Corp.] - Nashville, IL - *BrCabYB 84; Tel&CabFB 84C*
Nashville Educational Marketing [Subs. of Southwestern Co.] - Nashville, TN - *DirMarMP 83*
Nashville Graphic [of Nashville Wilson Newspapers Inc.] - Nashville, NC - *BaconPubCkNews 84; Ed&PubIntYB 82; NewsDir 84*
Nashville International Corp. - Nashville, TN - *BillIntBG 83-84*
Nashville International Music Group - Nashville, TN - *BillIntBG 83-84*
Nashville Maple Valley News - Nashville, MI - *BaconPubCkNews 84*
Nashville Network, The [of Group W Satellite Communications] - Stamford, CT - *BrCabYB 84*
Nashville Network, The - Nashville, TN - *CabTVPrDB 83; Tel&CabFB 84C*
Nashville News - Nashville, AR - *AyerDirPub 83; BaconPubCkNews 84; Ed&PubIntYB 82; NewsDir 84*
Nashville News - Nashville, IL - *BaconPubCkNews 84; Ed&PubIntYB 82; NewsDir 84*
Nashville Record - Nashville, TN - *BaconPubCkNews 84; Ed&PubIntYB 82*
Nashville Suburban News, The - Nashville, TN - *NewsDir 84*
Nashville Tennessee Register - Miami, FL - *NewsDir 84*
Nashville TV Cable Co. [of Basil Cable Systems Inc.] - Nashville, AR - *BrCabYB 84; Tel&CabFB 84C*
Nashville Westview - Nashville, TN - *BaconPubCkNews 84*
Nashwauk Eastern Itascan - Nashwauk, MN - *BaconPubCkNews 84*
Nashwauk-Keewatin Cable TV [of North American Communications Corp.] - Keewatin, MN - *Tel&CabFB 84C*
Nasinec - Granger, TX - *Ed&PubIntYB 82; NewsDir 84*
Nason, Marilyn - Asheville, NC - *MagIndMarPl 82-83*
Nason Productions Inc., Henry - New York, NY - *AvMarPl 83; WritMar 84*
Nassau Border Papers Inc. - Franklin Square, NY - *BaconPubCkNews 84*
Nassau County Library Association - Uniondale, NY - *BoPubDir 4, 5*
Nassau County Publication - Hempstead, NY - *BaconPubCkNews 84*
Nassau County Record - Callahan, FL - *AyerDirPub 83; Ed&PubIntYB 82*
Nassau Herald - Lawrence, NY - *AyerDirPub 83; Ed&PubIntYB 82*
Nassau Illustrated News - New Hyde Park, NY - *AyerDirPub 83; Ed&PubIntYB 82*
Nassau Star - Long Beach, NY - *AyerDirPub 83; Ed&PubIntYB 82*
NASSP Bulletin - Reston, VA - *MagDir 84*
Nastec Corp. - Southfield, MI - *DataDirSup 7-83*
NASW News - Silver Spring, MD - *MagDir 84*
Natasha Dawn Music Publishing - Brazil, IN - *BillIntBG 83-84*
Natasha Dawn Records - Madison, TN - *BillIntBG 83-84*
Natchez Democrat - Natchez, MS - *BaconPubCkNews 84; Ed&PubIntYB 82; NewsDir 84*
Natchitoches Cable TV [of TCA Cable TV Inc.] - Natchitoches, LA - *BrCabYB 84; Tel&CabFB 84C*
Natchitoches Times - Natchitoches, LA - *BaconPubCkNews 84; Ed&PubIntYB 82*
Natcommunication Inc. - Montreal, PQ, Canada - *StaDirAdAg 2-84*
N.A.T.E.S.A. Scope - Chicago, IL - *BaconPubCkMag 84; MagDir 84*
Nathan Associates Inc., Robert R. - Washington, DC - *CabTVFinDB 83*
Nathan Co., The - Dallas, TX - *DirPRFirms 83*
Nathan, Ruth - New York, NY - *LitMarPl 83, 84*
Nathan, Theodore Reade - New York, NY - *StaDirAdAg 2-84*
Nathanson, Marc - *See* Falcon Communications Inc.
Natick Bulletin - Natick, MA - *Ed&PubIntYB 82*
Natick Bulletin & Sun [of Suburban World Inc.] - Natick, MA - *AyerDirPub 83; BaconPubCkNews 84; NewsDir 84*
Natick Cablevision Corp. - Natick, MA - *BrCabYB 84*
Natick Sun - Natick, MA - *Ed&PubIntYB 82*
Nation, The - New York, NY - *BaconPubCkMag 84; LitMag&SmPr 83-84; LitMarPl 83, 84; MagDir 84; MagIndMarPl 82-83; WritMar 84*
Nation Wide Cablevision [of Tele-Communications Inc.] - Olympia, WA - *BrCabYB 84; Tel&CabFB 84C*
Nation Wide Cablevision Inc. [of Tele-Communications Inc.] - Grass Valley, CA - *BrCabYB 84; Tel&CabFB 84C*
Nation Wide Cablevision Inc. [of Tele-Communications Inc.] - Millbrae, CA - *BrCabYB 84*
Nation Wide Cablevision Inc. [of Tele-Communications Inc.] - San Carlos, CA - *BrCabYB 84; Tel&CabFB 84C*
Nation Wide Cablevision Inc. [of Tele-Communications Inc.] - Denver, CO - *Tel&CabFB 84C p.1693*
Nation Wide Cablevision Inc. [of Tele-Communications Inc.] - Anacortes, WA - *BrCabYB 84; Tel&CabFB 84C*
Nation Wide Cablevision Inc. [of Tele-Communications Inc.] - Bellingham, WA - *BrCabYB 84; Tel&CabFB 84C*
Nation Wide Cablevision Inc. [of Tele-Communications Inc.] - Bremerton, WA - *Tel&CabFB 84C*
Nation Wide Cablevision Inc. [of Tele-Communications Inc.] - Burlington, WA - *BrCabYB 84; Tel&CabFB 84C*
Nation Wide Cablevision Inc. - *See* Tele-Communications Inc.
Nation-Wide Sports Publications - Redmond, WA - *EISS 5-84 Sup*
National Academy of Education - Pittsburgh, PA - *BoPubDir 4, 5*
National Academy of Sciences (Transportation Research Board) - Washington, DC - *BoPubDir 4, 5*
National Academy Press [Div. of National Academy of Sciences] - Washington, DC - *LitMarPl 83, 84*
National Accreditation Council for Agencies Serving the Blind & Visually Handicapped - New York, NY - *BoPubDir 4, 5*
National Adult Education Clearinghouse/National Multimedia Center for Adult Education [of Montclair State College] - Upper Montclair, NJ - *EISS 83*
National Advanced Systems - Mountain View, CA - *ADAPSOMemDir 83-84; DataDirSup 7-83*
National Advertising & Marketing Enterprises - Los Angeles, CA - *ArtMar 84*
National Advertising Service Pvt. Ltd. - Bombay, India - *StaDirAdAg 2-84*
National Advisory Council for Danish Research Libraries [of Ministry of Cultural Affairs] - Copenhagen, Denmark - *EISS 83*
National Aeronautic Association - Washington, DC - *BoPubDir 4, 5*
National Aeronautic Association News - Washington, DC - *BaconPubCkMag 84*
National Aeronautics & Space Administration - *See* NASA
National Agricultural Library [of Dept. of Agriculture] - Beltsville, MD - *DataDirOnSer 84; EISS 83; InfIndMarPl 83*
National Air Data Branch [of U.S. Environmental Protection Agency] - Research Triangle Park, NC - *EISS 83*
National ALS Case Registry [of Amyotrophic Lateral Sclerosis Society of America] - Sherman Oaks, CA - *EISS 83*
National Analysts [Div. of Booz, Allen & Hamilton] - Philadelphia, PA - *AdAge 5-17-84 p.37; HBIndAd&MS 82-83; IntDirMarRes 83*
National Archives & Records Service [of U.S. General Services Administration] - Washington, DC - *EISS 83; LitMarPl 83; MagIndMarPl 82-83*
National Archives & Records Service (Publications Div.) - Washington, DC - *BoPubDir 4, 5*
National Archives & Records Service (Publications Sales Branch) - Washington, DC - *LitMarPl 84*
National Art Education Association - Reston, VA - *BoPubDir 4, 5*

National Assessment of Educational Progress [of Education Commission of the States] - Denver, CO - *EISS 83*
National Association for State Information Systems - Lexington, KY - *EISS 83*
National Association for the Education of Young Children - Washington, DC - *BoPubDir 4, 5*
National Association for Women Deans, Administrators, & Counselors - Washington, DC - *BoPubDir 4, 5*
National Association of Accountants - New York, NY - *BoPubDir 4, 5*
National Association of Bedding Manufacturers - Washington, DC - *BoPubDir 5*
National Association of Broadcast Engineers & Technicians - Hollywood, CA - *AvMarPl 83*
National Association of Broadcast Engineers & Technicians - New York, NY - *AvMarPl 83*
National Association of Broadcast Engineers & Technicians - Toronto, ON, Canada - *AvMarPl 83*
National Association of College & University Business Officers - Washington, DC - *BoPubDir 4, 5; WritMar 84*
National Association of Computer Stores - Stamford, CT - *WhoWMicrocom 83*
National Association of Corrosion Engineers - Houston, TX - *BoPubDir 4, 5*
National Association of Counties - Washington, DC - *BoPubDir 4, 5; Ed&PubIntYB 82; InterCabHB 3*
National Association of Credit Management - New York, NY - *BoPubDir 4, 5*
National Association of Dealers in Antiques Inc. - Rockford, IL - *BoPubDir 5*
National Association of Educational Office Personnel - Reston, VA - *BoPubDir 4, 5*
National Association of Furniture Manufacturers - Rockville, MD - *BoPubDir 5*
National Association of Home Builders - Washington, DC - *BoPubDir 4, 5*
National Association of Home Builders [of Chase Econometrics/ Interactive Data Corp.] - Waltham, MA - *DataDirOnSer 84*
National Association of Home Builders Builder Bookstore - Washington, DC - *LitMag&SmPr 83-84*
National Association of Hosiery Manufacturers - Charlotte, NC - *BoPubDir 4 Sup, 5*
National Association of Housing Cooperatives - Washington, DC - *BoPubDir 4, 5*
National Association of Independent Insurance Adjusters - Chicago, IL - *BoPubDir 5*
National Association of Independent Schools - Boston, MA - *BoPubDir 4, 5*
National Association of Industrial & Office Parks - Arlington, VA - *BoPubDir 5*
National Association of Insurance Commissioners - Brookfield, WI - *DataDirOnSer 84; InfIndMarPl 83*
National Association of Intercollegiate Athletics - Kansas City, MO - *BoPubDir 4, 5*
National Association of Real Estate Investment Trusts Inc. - Washington, DC - *BoPubDir 5*
National Association of Regulatory Utility Commissioners - Washington, DC - *BoPubDir 5*
National Association of Retail Grocers of the United States - Washington, DC - *BoPubDir 5*
National Association of Schools of Art & Design - Reston, VA - *BoPubDir 5*
National Association of Secondary School Principals - Reston, VA - *BoPubDir 4, 5*
National Association of Securities Dealers Automated Quotations - Washington, DC - *EISS 83*
National Association of Securities Dealers Inc. - Washington, DC - *BoPubDir 5*
National Association of Social Workers - New York, NY - *LitMarPl 83, 84*
National Association of Telecommunications Officers & Advisors - Seattle, WA - *TeleSy&SerDir 7-83*
National Association of the Deaf - Silver Spring, MD - *LitMarPl 83, 84*
National Association of Trade & Technical Schools - Washington, DC - *BoPubDir 5*
National Athletic Injury/Illness Reporting System [of Pennsylvania State University] - University Park, PA - *EISS 83*
National Audience Data Bank [of Interactive Market Systems Inc.] - New York, NY - *DataDirOnSer 84*
National Audio Visual Association Inc. - Fairfax, VA - *BoPubDir 4*
National Audio-Visual Supply Corp. - East Rutherford, NJ - *AvMarPl 83*
National Audiovisual Center [of U.S. General Services Administration] - Washington, DC - *AvMarPl 83; EISS 83; Tel&CabFB 84C*
National Audubon Society - New York, NY - *Tel&CabFB 84C*
National Automated Accounting Research System [of American Institute of Certified Public Accountants] - New York, NY - *CompReadDB 82; DBBus 82; EISS 83*
National Automated Accounting Research System [of Mead Data Central] - Dayton, OH - *DataDirOnSer 84*
National Automobile Dealers Association - McLean, VA - *BoPubDir 5*
National Auxiliary Publications Service - New York, NY - *LitMarPl 83*
National Auxiliary Publications Service (Microfiche Publications) - New York, NY - *LitMarPl 84*
National Baby Panel [Div. of ParaTest Marketing] - Eastchester, NY - *IntDirMarRes 83*
National Beauty News - Tulsa, OK - *BaconPubCkMag 84*
National Beauty News - Dallas, TX - *MagDir 84*
National Beauty School Journal [of Milady Publishing Corp.] - Bronx, NY - *BaconPubCkMag 84; MagDir 84*
National Behavior Systems - Granada Hills, CA - *BoPubDir 4, 5; LitMag&SmPr 83-84*
National Beta Club - Spartanburg, SC - *BoPubDir 5*
National Billiard News, The - Birmingham, MI - *BaconPubCkMag 84*
National Bindery Co. Inc. [Div. of L & BB Inc.] - Pomona, CA - *LitMarPl 83, 84*
National Biomedical Research Foundation [Aff. of Georgetown University Medical Center] - Washington, DC - *BoPubDir 4, 5*
National Black Network - New York, NY - *BrCabYB 84*
National Blood Data Center [of American Blood Commission] - Arlington, VA - *EISS 83*
National Board of Health & Welfare (Dept. of Drugs) - Uppsala, Sweden - *InfIndMarPl 83*
National Book Centre [Div. of Maclean Hunter Ltd.] - Toronto, ON, Canada - *LitMarPl 83, 84*
National Book Co. [Div. of Educational Research Associates] - Portland, OR - *LitMarPl 83, 84; WritMar 84*
National Braille Press - Boston, MA - *LitMarPl 83, 84*
National Broadcasting Co. [Subs. of RCA Corp.] - New York, NY - *BrCabYB 84; LitMarPl 83, 84; TelAl 83, 84; Tel&CabFB 84C, 84S; VideoDir 82-83*
National Bureau for Ocean Data [of National Center for Ocean Utilization] - Brest, France - *EISS 83*
National Bureau of Economic Research Inc. - Cambridge, MA - *LitMarPl 83, 84*
National Bureau of Standards (Alloy Data Center, Metallurgy Div.) - Washington, DC - *CompReadDB 82*
National Burglar & Fire Alarm Association - Washington, DC - *BoPubDir 5*
National Bus Trader - Delavan, WI - *BaconPubCkMag 84; WritMar 84*
National Business Aircraft Association - Washington, DC - *BoPubDir 5*
National Business Furniture - Milwaukee, WI - *DirInfWP 82*
National Business Institute - Eau Claire, WI - *MicrocomMPl 84*
National Business Systems Inc. - Moonachie, NJ - *DataDirSup 7-83*
National Business Woman - Washington, DC - *BaconPubCkMag 84; MagDir 84; MagIndMarPl 82-83*
National Businessmen Readership Study [of Interactive Market Systems Inc.] - New York, NY - *DataDirOnSer 84*
National Businessmen Readership Study - Wembly, England - *DirOnDB Spring 84*
National Cable Co. - *See* Tele-Media Corp.
National Cable Co. of Pennsylvania [of Tele-Media Corp.] - Ferguson Township, PA - *BrCabYB 84*

National Cable Systems Inc. - Atlanta, GA - *Tel&CabFB 84C p.1693*
National Cable Television Association - Washington, DC - *BoPubDir 5; InterCabHB 3*
National Cable Television Corp. [of Armstrong Utilities Inc.] - Connellsville, PA - *BrCabYB 84; Tel&CabFB 84C*
National Cablecasting Service Inc. - West Branch, MI - *Tel&CabFB 84C p.1693*
National Cablesystems Inc. - Atlanta, GA - *BrCabYB 84 p.D-304*
National Cablevision Ltd. - Montreal, PQ, Canada - *BrCabYB 84*
National Cablevision Ltd. - *See* Cablevision Nationale Ltee.
National Cancer Foundation Inc./Cancer Care Inc. - New York, NY - *BoPubDir 4, 5*
National Cancer Institute (International Cancer Research Data Bank Program) - Bethesda, MD - *CompReadDB 82*
National Cancer Institute/Management Information System [of U.S. Public Health Service] - Bethesda, MD - *EISS 83*
National Capital Christian Broadcasting Inc. - Manassas, VA - *BrCabYB 84*
National Capital Pharmacist - Washington, DC - *BaconPubCkMag 84*
National Captioning Institute - Falls Church, VA - *TeleSy&SerDir 2-84; VideoDir 82-83*
National Cartographic Information Center [of U.S. Geological Survey] - Reston, VA - *EISS 83*
National Catholic Development Conference - Rockville Centre, NY - *BoPubDir 4, 5*
National Catholic News Service - Washington, DC - *Ed&PubIntYB 82; LitMarPl 83, 84; MagIndMarPl 82-83*
National Catholic Register, The - Los Angeles, CA - *BaconPubCkMag 84; MagDir 84*
National Catholic Reporter - Kansas City, MO - *BaconPubCkMag 84; MagDir 84; NewsDir 84*
National Catholic Reporter Publishing Co. - Kansas City, MO - *AvMarPl 83; BoPubDir 4, 5; DirMarMP 83*
National Caves Association - McMinnville, TN - *BoPubDir 5*
National Center for a Barrier Free Environment - Washington, DC - *EISS 7-83 Sup*
National Center for Audio Tapes - Boulder, CO - *AvMarPl 83*
National Center for Automated Information Retrieval - New York, NY - *EISS 83*
National Center for Chemical Information - Paris, France - *EISS 83*
National Center for Computer Crime Data - Los Angeles, CA - *EISS 83*
National Center for Education Statistics [of U.S. Dept. of Education] - Washington, DC - *EISS 83*
National Center for Educational Brokering [Aff. of National Institute for Work & Learning] - Washington, DC - *BoPubDir 4, 5*
National Center for Health Information & Documentation - Mexico City, Mexico - *EISS 83*
National Center for Health Statistics [Aff. of Public Health Service] - Hyattsville, MD - *BoPubDir 4, 5; EISS 83; InfIndMarPl 83*
National Center for Housing Management - Washington, DC - *BoPubDir 4, 5*
National Center for Job-Market Studies - Washington, DC - *BoPubDir 4, 5*
National Center for Juvenile Justice - Pittsburgh, PA - *EISS 83*
National Center for Micrographic Development - Sao Paulo, SP, Brazil - *EISS 83*
National Center for Pedagogical Documentation - Paris, France - *EISS 7-83 Sup*
National Center for Public Productivity - New York, NY - *BoPubDir 4, 5*
National Center for Research in Vocational Education [of Ohio State University] - Columbus, OH - *CompReadDB 82; DataDirOnSer 84; EISS 83; InfIndMarPl 83*
National Center for Scientific & Technical Documentation [of Royal Library of Belgium] - Brussels, Belgium - *EISS 83*
National Center for Standards & Certification Information [of U.S. National Bureau of Standards] - Washington, DC - *InfIndMarPl 83*
National Center for State Courts - Williamsburg, VA - *BoPubDir 4, 5*
National Center for Telephone Research - New York, NY - *IntDirMarRes 83*
National Center for the Thermodynamic Data of Minerals [of U.S. Geological Survey] - Reston, VA - *EISS 83*
National Center for Urban Ethnic Affairs [Aff. of U.S. Catholic Conference] - Washington, DC - *BoPubDir 4, 5*
National Center of Scientific & Technological Information [of National Council for Research & Development] - Tel-Aviv, Israel - *EISS 83*
National Center on Child Abuse & Neglect [of US Dept. of Health & Human Services] - Washington, DC - *CompReadDB 82; DataDirOnSer 84*
National Child Labor Committee - New York, NY - *BoPubDir 4, 5*
National Christian Network - Cocoa, FL - *AvMarPl 83; BrCabYB 84; CabTVPrDB 83; HomeVid&CabYB 82-83; Tel&CabFB 84C*
National Christian Press Inc. - Algood, TN - *BoPubDir 4, 5*
National Chronicle - Hayden Lake, ID - *AyerDirPub 83*
National Citizens Committee for Broadcasting - Washington, DC - *BoPubDir 4*
National City North Pennysaver - Mission Viejo, CA - *AyerDirPub 83*
National City South Pennysaver - Mission Viejo, CA - *AyerDirPub 83*
National City Star News [of Chula Vista Star-News] - Chula Vista, CA - *NewsDir 84*
National City Star-News - National City, CA - *Ed&PubIntYB 82*
National City Star News - *See* Star-News Publishing Co. Inc.
National Civic Review [of National Municipal League Inc.] - New York, NY - *BaconPubCkMag 84; MagDir 84*
National Classical Network - Cocoa, FL - *Tel&CabFB 84C*
National Clearing House of Rehabilitation Training Materials [of Oklahoma State University] - Stillwater, OK - *EISS 83*
National Clearinghouse for Alcoholic Information [of U.S. Public Health Service] - Rockville, MD - *EISS 83*
National Clearinghouse for Bilingual Education - Arlington, VA - *CompReadDB 82*
National Clearinghouse for Bilingual Education [Aff. of InterAmerica Research Associates Inc.] - Rosslyn, VA - *BoPubDir 4, 5; EISS 83*
National Clearinghouse for Criminal Justice Information Systems - Sacramento, CA - *EISS 83*
National Clearinghouse for Drug Abuse Information [of U.S. Public Health Service] - Rockville, MD - *EISS 83*
National Clearinghouse for Human Genetic Diseases [of U.S. Public Health Service] - Washington, DC - *EISS 83*
National Clearinghouse for Mental Health Information [of U.S. Public Health Service] - Rockville, MD - *CompReadDB 82; EISS 83; InfIndMarPl 83*
National Clearinghouse for Poison Control Centers [of U.S. Public Health Service] - Rockville, MD - *EISS 83*
National Clearinghouse on Aging - Washington, DC - *CompReadDB 82*
National Clearinghouse on Election Administration [of U.S. Federal Election Commission] - Washington, DC - *EISS 83*
National Clearinghouse on Marital Rape [Aff. of Women's History Research Center] - Berkeley, CA - *BoPubDir 4 Sup, 5*
National Climatic Center [of U.S. Dept. of Commerce] - Asheville, NC - *EISS 83; MicroMarPl 82-83*
National Clothesline, The - Philadelphia, PA - *BaconPubCkMag 84*
National Coal Resources Data System [of U.S. Geological Survey] - Reston, VA - *DBBus 82; EISS 83*
National College Databank - *See* Peterson's College Database
National College of Juvenile Justice [Aff. of National Council of Juvenile & Family Court Judges] - Reno, NV - *BoPubDir 5*
National Color Laboratories Inc. - Roselle, NJ - *AvMarPl 83*
National Commercial News - San Francisco, CA - *BaconPubCkMag 84*
National Commission for Cooperative Education - Boston, MA - *BoPubDir 5*
National Committee for Citizens in Education - Columbia, MD - *BoPubDir 4, 5*
National Committee of Catholic Laymen - New York, NY - *BoPubDir 4, 5*

National Committee to Support the Marion Brothers Inc. - St. Louis, MO - *BoPubDir 4, 5*
National Communications Forum [of National Engineering Consortium Inc.] - Chicago, IL - *TeleSy&SerDir 2-84*
National Communications Institute - Bethesda, MD - *MagIndMarPl 82-83*
National Community Education Clearinghouse [of National Community Education Association] - Washington, DC - *EISS 83*
National Computer Graphics Association - Washington, DC - *EISS 83*
National Computer Network of Chicago - Chicago, IL - *ADAPSOMemDir 83-84; DataDirOnSer 84; DataDirSup 7-83; EISS 83; InfIndMarPl 83*
National Computer Program Abstract Service Inc. - Washington, DC - *EISS 83*
National Computer Systems [Subs. of Westinghouse Electric Corp.] - Iowa City, IA - *DataDirOnSer 84*
National Computer Systems Inc. - Minneapolis, MN - *DataDirSup 7-83; DirInfWP 82; WhoWMicrocom 83*
National Computer Utility Co. - Elizabeth, NJ - *ADAPSOMemDir 83-84*
National Computing Centre Ltd. (Information Services Div.) - Manchester, England - *CompReadDB 82*
National Confectioners Association - Chicago, IL - *BoPubDir 5*
National Conference of Catholic Charities - Washington, DC - *BoPubDir 4, 5*
National Conference of Standards Laboratories [Aff. of National Bureau of Standards] - Boulder, CO - *BoPubDir 4 Sup, 5*
National Consultor - San Jose, CA - *MagIndMarPl 82-83*
National Consumer Finance Association - Washington, DC - *BoPubDir 5*
National Council for Alternative Work Patterns Inc. - Washington, DC - *BoPubDir 5*
National Council for the Social Studies - Washington, DC - *BoPubDir 4, 5*
National Council for U.S.-China Trade - Washington, DC - *BoPubDir 4, 5*
National Council of Architectural Registration Boards - Washington, DC - *BoPubDir 5*
National Council of Churches - New York, NY - *AvMarPl 83*
National Council of Churches (Communication Commission) - New York, NY - *InterCabHB 3*
National Council of Farmer Cooperatives - Washington, DC - *BoPubDir 4 Sup, 5*
National Council of Teachers of English - Urbana, IL - *LitMarPl 83, 84; MagIndMarPl 82-83*
National Council of Teachers of English - Bloomington, IN - *LitMag&SmPr 83-84*
National Council of Teachers of Mathematics - Reston, VA - *LitMarPl 83, 84*
National Council of Women of Canada [Aff. of International Council of Women] - Ottawa, ON, Canada - *BoPubDir 4, 5*
National Council on Family Relations - Minneapolis, MN - *CompReadDB 82*
National Council on Family Relations [of Bibliographic Retrieval Services Inc.] - Latham, NY - *DataDirOnSer 84*
National Council on Radiation Protection & Measurements - Bethesda, MD - *BoPubDir 4, 5*
National Courier - Pittsburgh, PA - *Ed&PubIntYB 82*
National Crime Information Center [of U.S. Federal Bureau of Investigation] - Washington, DC - *EISS 83*
National Criminal Justice Reference Service [of Dialog Information Services Inc.] - Palo Alto, CA - *DataDirOnSer 84*
National Criminal Justice Reference Service [of National Institute of Justice] - Washington, DC - *CompReadDB 82*
National Criminal Justice Reference Service [of U.S. Dept. of Justice] - Rockville, MD - *EISS 83; OnBibDB 3*
National CSS [Subs. of The Dun & Bradstreet Corp.] - Wilton, CT - *ADAPSOMemDir 83-84; DataDirOnSer 84; DataDirSup 7-83; EISS 83; InfoS 83-84*
National Daily Program - New York, NY - *Ed&PubIntYB 82*
National Dairy News - Madison, WI - *BaconPubCkMag 84; WritMar 84*
National Data Base [of Merrill Lynch Economics Inc.] - New York, NY - *DataDirOnSer 84*
National Data Corp. - Atlanta, GA - *ADAPSOMemDir 83-84; DataDirOnSer 84; DataDirSup 7-83; Datamation 6-83; Top100Al 83*
National Data Corp. (Rapidata Div.) - Fairfield, NJ - *DataDirOnSer 84*
National Data Services Inc. - Chatsworth, CA - *ADAPSOMemDir 83-84; DataDirOnSer 84*
National Data Systems Inc. - Saddle Brook, NJ - *MagIndMarPl 82-83*
National Decency Reporter - Phoenix, AZ - *MagIndMarPl 82-83*
National Decision Systems - Encinitas, CA - *DataDirOnSer 84; EISS 5-84 Sup*
National Decorating Products Association - St. Louis, MO - *BoPubDir 5*
National Defense - Arlington, VA - *BaconPubCkMag 84; MagDir 84; MagIndMarPl 82-83; WritMar 84*
National Development/Modern Government [of Intercontinental Publications Inc.] - Westport, CT - *BaconPubCkMag 84; MagDir 84; WritMar 84*
National Diabetes Information Clearinghouse [of U.S. Public Health Service] - Bethesda, MD - *EISS 83*
National Diet Library (Automation Systems) - Tokyo, Japan - *CompReadDB 82*
National Digestive Diseases Education & Information Clearinghouse [of U.S. Public Health Service] - Rosslyn, VA - *EISS 83*
National Dragster - North Hollywood, CA - *BaconPubCkMag 84; MagDir 84*
National Dragster Publications [Aff. of National Hot Rod Association] - North Hollywood, CA - *BoPubDir 4, 5*
National Drug Code System [of U.S. Public Health Service] - Rockville, MD - *EISS 83*
National Dynamics Inc. - Smyrna, GA - *ADAPSOMemDir 83-84; DataDirOnSer 84*
National E-F-T Inc. - Providence, RI - *DataDirSup 7-83*
National Earth Satellite Service [of U.S. National Oceanic & Atmospheric Administration] - Suitland, MD - *EISS 83*
National Easter Seal Society - Chicago, IL - *BoPubDir 4, 5*
National Economic Research Associates Inc. - White Plains, NY - *CabTVFinDB 83*
National Edition [of Baltimore Afro-American Newspapers] - Baltimore, MD - *NewsDir 84*
National Education Association - Washington, DC - *LitMarPl 83, 84*
National Educational Aids Inc. - Columbia, SC - *LitMarPl 83, 84*
National Educational Computer Review [of National Educational Computer Library] - New Milford, CT - *MicrocomMPl 84*
National Educational Laboratory Publishers Inc. [Subs. of Southwest Educational Development Corp.] - Austin, TX - *LitMarPl 83*
National Educational Media Inc. - Chatsworth, CA - *AvMarPl 83; DirMarMP 83*
National Electrical Manufacturers Association [of General Electric Information Services Co.] - Rockville, MD - *DataDirOnSer 84*
National Electrical Manufacturers Association Data Base - Washington, DC - *DBBus 82*
National Electronic Home Services Test, The [Div. of Reymer & Gersin Associates Inc.] - Southfield, MI - *VideoDir 82-83*
National Electronic Information Corp. - New York, NY - *ADAPSOMemDir 83-84; EISS 83*
National Emergency Equipment Locator System - Ottawa, ON, Canada - *DirOnDB Spring 84*
National Emergency Equipment Locator System [of I. P. Sharp Associates Ltd.] - Toronto, ON, Canada - *DataDirOnSer 84*
National Employee Services & Recreation Association - Chicago, IL - *BoPubDir 5*
National Energy Accounts [of U.S. Dept. of Commerce] - Washington, DC - *EISS 5-84 Sup*
National Energy Information Center [of US Dept. of Energy] - Washington, DC - *CompReadDB 82; DataDirOnSer 84; EISS 83*
National Energy Information Center Affiliate [of University of New Mexico] - Albuquerque, NM - *EISS 83*
National Energy Journal, The - Glendale, AZ - *BaconPubCkMag 84*
National Energy Software Center [of U.S. Dept. of Energy] - Argonne, IL - *DirOnDB Spring 84; EISS 83*

National Engineer - Chicago, IL - *BaconPubCkMag 84; MagDir 84*
National Engineering Laboratory [of Dept. of Industry] - Glasgow, Scotland - *InfIndMarPl 83*
National Engineering Laboratory's Thermophysical Properties Package [of Dept. of Industry] - Glasgow, Scotland - *EISS 83*
National Enquirer - Lake Worth, FL - *MagDir 84; NewsDir 84*
National Enquirer - Lantana, FL - *AdAge 6-28-84; ArtMar 84; BaconPubCkMag 84; Folio 83; KnowInd 83; MagIndMarPl 82-83; NewsBur 6; WritMar 84*
National Entertainment Group Inc. - *See* American Entertainment Marketing
National Eutrophication Study Data Base [of U.S. Environmental Protection Agency] - Las Vegas, NV - *EISS 83*
National Evaluation Systems - Amherst, MA - *InfIndMarPl 83; LitMarPl 83, 84*
National Examiner [of Globe International Inc.] - West Palm Beach, FL - *Folio 83*
National Export Advertising Service Inc. - New York, NY - *TelAl 83, 84*
National Family Opinion Inc. - Toledo, OH - *EISS 83; IntDirMarRes 83*
National Farm Readership Study [of Interactive Market Systems Inc.] - New York, NY - *DataDirOnSer 84*
National Farm Readership Study - Milwaukee, WI - *DirOnDB Spring 84*
National Features Syndicate - Grand Rapids, MI - *Ed&PubIntYB 82*
National Federation of Abstracting & Information Services - Philadelphia, PA - *BoPubDir 4 Sup, 5; EISS 83*
National Federation of Temple Sisterhoods [Aff. of Union of American Hebrew Congregations] - New York, NY - *BoPubDir 4, 5*
National Field Sales Inc. - Broomall, PA - *MicrocomMPl 84*
National Film Board of Canada - New York, NY - *AvMarPl 83; Tel&CabFB 84C*
National Fire Data Center [of U.S. Fire Administration] - Washington, DC - *EISS 83*
National Fire Protection Association - Quincy, MA - *AvMarPl 83; BoPubDir 4, 5*
National Fisherman [of Diversified Communications] - Camden, ME - *BaconPubCkMag 84; MagDir 84; MagIndMarPl 82-83; WritMar 84*
National Flag Foundation - Pittsburgh, PA - *BoPubDir 4 Sup, 5*
National Fluid Power Association Inc. - Milwaukee, WI - *BoPubDir 4, 5*
National Forensic Center - Fair Lawn, NJ - *BoPubDir 4, 5*
National Forensic Center [Subs. of Forensic Services Directory Inc.] - Lawrenceville, NJ - *DataDirOnSer 84*
National Forest Products Association - Washington, DC - *BoPubDir 5*
National Forum: The Phi Kappa Phi Journal - Johnson City, TN - *WritMar 84*
National Foundations [of Dialog Information Services Inc.] - Palo Alto, CA - *DataDirOnSer 84*
National Foundations [of Foundation Center] - New York, NY - *CompReadDB 82*
National 4-H News - Washington, DC - *MagDir 84*
National 4-H News - Chevy Chase, MD - *ArtMar 84; BaconPubCkMag 84; DirMarMP 83; MagIndMarPl 82-83; WritMar 84*
National Fraternal Club News - Chicago, IL - *MagDir 84*
National Frozen Food Association Inc. - Hershey, PA - *BoPubDir 4 Sup, 5*
National FSI Inc. - Dallas, TX - *DataDirSup 7-83; WhoWMicrocom 83*
National Fuchsia Society - Oxnard, CA - *BoPubDir 4, 5*
National Future Farmer, The - Alexandria, VA - *ArtMar 84; BaconPubCkMag 84; MagDir 84; MagIndMarPl 82-83; WritMar 84*
National Gallery of Art (Dept. of Extension Program) - Washington, DC - *AvMarPl 83*
National Gallery of Australia - Canberra, Australia - *InfIndMarPl 83*
National Gallery of Canada, The (Publications Div.) - Ottawa, ON, Canada - *WritMar 84*
National Gardener - St. Louis, MO - *BaconPubCkMag 84; MagDir 84*
National Gay Task Force - New York, NY - *BoPubDir 4, 5*
National Genealogical Society - Washington, DC - *BoPubDir 4, 5*
National Geochemical Data Bank [of Natural Environment Research Council] - London, England - *EISS 83*
National Geodetic Information Center [of U.S. National Oceanic & Atmospheric Administration] - Rockville, MD - *EISS 83*
National Geographic - Washington, DC - *ArtMar 84; BaconPubCkMag 84; LitMarPl 84; MagDir 84; MagIndMarPl 82-83; NewsBur 6; WritMar 84*
National Geographic [of National Geographic Society] - New York, NY - *Folio 83*
National Geographic Society - Washington, DC - *AdAge 6-28-84; AvMarPl 83; KnowInd 83; LitMarPl 83, 84*
National Geographic Society News Service - Washington, DC - *Ed&PubIntYB 82*
National Geographic World [of National Geographic Society] - Washington, DC - *Folio 83; MagIndMarPl 82-83*
National Geophysical & Solar-Terrestrial Data Center [of U.S. National Oceanic & Atmospheric Administration] - Boulder, CO - *EISS 83*
National Geoscan Centre [of Dept. of Energy, Mines, & Resources] - Ottawa, ON, Canada - *EISS 83*
National Geothermal Information Resource [of University of California] - Berkeley, CA - *CompReadDB 82*
National Glass Budget [of LJV Inc.] - Pittsburgh, PA - *ArtMar 84; BaconPubCkMag 84; BoPubDir 5; MagDir 84; WritMar 84*
National Golf Foundation Inc. - North Palm Beach, FL - *BoPubDir 4, 5*
National Graphics Corp. - Columbus, OH - *MagIndMarPl 82-83*
National Greek Tribune - Detroit, MI - *Ed&PubIntYB 82*
National Greek Tribune - Warren, MI - *NewsDir 84*
National Ground Water Information Center [of National Water Well Association] - Worthington, OH - *DataDirOnSer 84; DirOnDB Spring 84*
National Guard - Washington, DC - *BaconPubCkMag 84; MagDir 84; MagIndMarPl 82-83; WritMar 84*
National Hardwood Magazine - Memphis, TN - *BaconPubCkMag 84; MagDir 84*
National Health Information Clearinghouse [of U.S. Public Health Service] - Rosslyn, VA - *EISS 83*
National Health Planning Information Center [of U.S. Public Health Service] - Hyattsville, MD - *EISS 83*
National Herald - New York, NY - *Ed&PubIntYB 82; NewsDir 84*
National Heritage Publishers - St. James, MI - *BoPubDir 4 Sup, 5*
National Highway Carriers Directory Inc. - Buffalo Grove, IL - *BoPubDir 4 Sup, 5*
National Highway Traffic Safety Administration - Washington, DC - *CompReadDB 82*
National Highway Traffic Safety Administration (Office of Defects Investigation) - Washington, DC - *CompReadDB 82*
National Hog Farmer [of The Webb Co.] - St. Paul, MN - *BaconPubCkMag 84; MagDir 84; MagIndMarPl 82-83*
National Home Center News [of Lebhar-Friedman Inc.] - New York, NY - *BaconPubCkMag 84; MagDir 84; WritMar 84*
National Home Furnishing Association - Chicago, IL - *BoPubDir 5*
National Homecaring Council - New York, NY - *BoPubDir 4, 5*
National Horseman, The - Louisville, KY - *MagDir 84*
National Horseman, The - Middletown, KY - *BaconPubCkMag 84*
National Housewares Manufacturers Association - Chicago, IL - *BoPubDir 5*
National Immigration Project [of the National Lawyers Guild Inc.] - Boston, MA - *BoPubDir 4, 5*
National Income & Product Accounts [of Chase Econometrics/ Interactive Data Corp.] - Waltham, MA - *DataDirOnSer 84*
National Income Forecasting Model Data Base [of Computer Sciences of Australia Pty. Ltd.] - St. Leonards, Australia - *DataDirOnSer 84; DirOnDB Spring 84*
National Income Forecasting Model of the Australian Economy - Toronto, ON, Canada - *DirOnDB Spring 84*
National Index of Computer-Readable Energy & Environmentally Related Databases - Washington, DC - *CompReadDB 82*

National Industrial Zoning Committee - Columbus, OH - *BoPubDir 4 Sup, 5*
National Information Center for Educational Media [of University of Southern California] - Los Angeles, CA - *CompReadDB 82; DataDirOnSer 84; EISS 83; InfIndMarPl 83*
National Information Center for Educational Media - *See* NICEM
National Information Center for Special Education Materials [of National Information Center for Educational Media] - Los Angeles, CA - *CompReadDB 82; DataDirOnSer 84; EISS 83; InfIndMarPl 83*
National Information Consultants Inc. - Tulsa, OK - *MicrocomMPl 84*
National Information Data Center [Subs. of MB Ltd.] - Washington, DC - *DirMarMP 83*
National Information Service for Earthquake Engineering [of University of California, Berkeley] - Richmond, CA - *EISS 83*
National Information Sources on the Handicapped [of U.S. Dept of Education] - Washington, DC - *DataDirOnSer 84*
National Information System [of Colombian Fund for Scientific Research] - Bogota, Colombia - *EISS 83*
National Information Systems Inc. - Cupertino, CA - *DataDirOnSer 84; DataDirSup 7-83; EISS 7-83 Sup*
National Information Systems Task Force [of Society of American Archivists] - Washington, DC - *EISS 83*
National Injury Information Clearinghouse [of U.S. Consumer Product Safety Commission] - Washington, DC - *EISS 83*
National Institute for Agricultural Engineering - Silsoe, England - *CompReadDB 82*
National Institute for Burn Medicine - Ann Arbor, MI - *BoPubDir 4, 5*
National Institute for Documentation Techniques [of National Conservatory of Arts & Crafts] - Paris, France - *EISS 83*
National Institute for Information & Documentation [of National Council for Science & Technology] - Bucharest, Romania - *EISS 83*
National Institute for Occupational Safety & Health - Cincinnati, OH - *CompReadDB 82*
National Institute for Occupational Safety & Health (Clearinghouse for Occupational Safety & Health Information) - Cincinnati, OH - *InfIndMarPl 83*
National Institute for Occupational Safety & Health (Technical Information Center) - Cincinnati, OH - *CompReadDB 82*
National Institute for Research in Informatics & Automation - Le Chesnay, France - *EISS 83*
National Institute for the Foodservice Industry - Chicago, IL - *BoPubDir 4, 5*
National Institute of Arthritis, Diabetes & Digestive & Kidney Diseases (Arthritis Information Clearinghouse) - Bethesda, MD - *CompReadDB 82*
National Institute of Justice [of U.S. Dept. of Justice] - Washington, DC - *CompReadDB 82*
National Institute of Justice [of U.S. Dept. of Justice] - Rockville, MD - *DataDirOnSer 84*
National Institute of Neurological & Communicative Disorders & Stroke [of National Institutes of Health] - Bethesda, MD - *CompReadDB 82; InfIndMarPl 83*
National Institute of Reboundology & Health Inc. - Edmonds, WA - *BoPubDir 4, 5*
National Institute on Mental Retardation [Aff. of Canadian Association for the Mentally Retarded] - Downsview, ON, Canada - *BoPubDir 4, 5*
National Institutes of Health (Research Grants Div., Research Documentation Section) - Bethesda, MD - *CompReadDB 82*
National Instruments - Austin, TX - *MicrocomMPl 84*
National Insurance Advertising Regulation Service [Aff. of NIARS Corp.] - Minneapolis, MN - *BoPubDir 4, 5*
National Integrated Software Services Inc. [Subs. of CSS Inc.] - Englewood, CO - *DirMarMP 83; WhoWMicrocom 83*
National Interreligious Service Board for Conscientious Objectors - Washington, DC - *BoPubDir 4, 5*
National Investment Library - New York, NY - *EISS 83; FBInfSer 80; InfIndMarPl 83; ProGuPRSer 4*
National Investor News - Chicago, IL - *BaconPubCkMag 84*
National Jazz Network [of Telecast Corp.] - Amherst, MA - *CabTVPrDB 83*
National Jeweler - New York, NY - *BaconPubCkMag 84; MagDir 84; MagIndMarPl 82-83*
National Jewish Television - Riverdale, NY - *BrCabYB 84; HomeVid&CabYB 82-83*
National Journal [of Government Research Corp.] - Washington, DC - *BaconPubCkMag 84; Folio 83; MagDir 84; MagIndMarPl 82-83; WritMar 84*
National Knife Collector, The - Chattanooga, TN - *WritMar 84*
National Lampoon - New York, NY - *BaconPubCkMag 84; MagDir 84; MagIndMarPl 82-83*
National Law Journal - New York, NY - *BaconPubCkMag 84; WritMar 84*
National Law Library Ltd. - London, England - *EISS 83*
National Lawyers Guild - New York, NY - *BoPubDir 4, 5*
National League for Nursing - New York, NY - *BoPubDir 4, 5*
National League of Cities - Washington, DC - *BoPubDir 4, 5; InterCabHB 3*
National Learning Corp. - Syosset, NY - *BoPubDir 4 Sup, 5; LitMarPl 83, 84*
National Librarian [of Oakland University] - Rochester, MI - *ArtMar 84*
National Library of Agriculture [of Ministry of Agriculture] - Brasilia, DF, Brazil - *EISS 83*
National Library of Australia - Canberra, Australia - *CompReadDB 82; EISS 83; MicroMarPl 82-83*
National Library of Australia - Parkes, Australia - *InfIndMarPl 83*
National Library of Canada - Ottawa, ON, Canada - *BoPubDir 4, 5; EISS 83; MicroMarPl 82-83*
National Library of Canada (Computer-Based Reference Service) - Ottawa, ON, Canada - *CompReadDB 82*
National Library of Economics [of Kiel Institute for World Economics] - Kiel, West Germany - *EISS 83*
National Library of Medicine [of National Institutes of Health] - Bethesda, MD - *CompReadDB 82; DataDirOnSer 84; InfIndMarPl 83*
National Library of Medicine (Toxicology Information Program) - Bethesda, MD - *CompReadDB 82*
National Library of Medicine (TSD-Audiovisuals) - Bethesda, MD - *CompReadDB 82*
National Library of Quebec - Montreal, PQ, Canada - *CompReadDB 82*
National Library of Scotland - Edinburgh, Scotland - *MicroMarPl 82-83*
National Library of Scotland - *See* Scottish Libraries Co-Operative Automation Project
National Library Service for the Blind & Physically Handicapped [of Library of Congress] - Washington, DC - *CompReadDB 82; EISS 83*
National List Council Inc. - Altamonte Springs, FL - *DirMarMP 83*
National List of Scientific Plant Names [of U.S. Dept. of Agriculture] - Washington, DC - *EISS 83*
National Locksmith, The - Bartlett, IL - *MagDir 84*
National Logo Exchange, The - Charlottesville, VA - *MicrocomMPl 84*
National Long-Term Forecast [of Merrill Lynch Economics Inc.] - New York, NY - *DataDirOnSer 84*
National Longitudinal Surveys [of Ohio State University] - Worthington, OH - *EISS 83*
National Loss Prevention - Willowdale, ON, Canada - *BaconPubCkMag 84*
National LP-Gas Association - Oak Brook, IL - *BoPubDir 5*
National Lumber & Building Material Dealers Association - Washington, DC - *BoPubDir 5*
National Mall Monitor - Clearwater, FL - *ArtMar 84; BaconPubCkMag 84; MagDir 84*
National Management Systems Ltd. - Alexandria, VA - *ADAPSOMemDir 83-84*
National Marine Electronics News - Eatontown, NJ - *MagDir 84*
National Maritime Historical Society - Brooklyn, NY - *BoPubDir 4*
National Maritime Historical Society - New York, NY - *BoPubDir 5*
National Marketing Research of California - Los Angeles, CA - *IntDirMarRes 83*
National Marketing Studies - New York, NY - *IntDirMarRes 83*
National Mass Retailing Institute - New York, NY - *BoPubDir 5*

National Master Specifications [of Construction Specifications Canada] - Toronto, ON, Canada - *EISS 83*
National Masters News [of Gain Publications] - Van Nuys, CA - *BaconPubCkMag 84; LitMag&SmPr 83-84*
National Mediarep Corp. - New York, NY - *MagIndMarPl 82-83*
National Medical Audiovisual Center [of U.S. National Library of Medicine] - Bethesda, MD - *EISS 83*
National Meteorological Center [of U.S. National Oceanic & Atmospheric Administration] - Camp Springs, MD - *EISS 83*
National Micro Distributors Inc. - Beaverton, OR - *MicrocomMPl 84*
National Micrographics Association - Silver Spring, MD - *EISS 83; LitMarPl 83; MicroMarPl 82-83*
National Microsales - Stratford, CT - *AvMarPl 83; DirInfWP 82*
National Motorist [of National Automobile Club] - San Francisco, CA - *ArtMar 84; BaconPubCkMag 84; MagDir 84; MagIndMarPl 82-83; WritMar 84*
National Multiplex Corp. - Middlesex, NJ - *WhoWMicrocom 83*
National Museums of Canada - Ottawa, ON, Canada - *BoPubDir 4, 5; LitMarPl 84*
National Music Enterprises - Houston, TX - *BillIntBG 83-84*
National Neighbors Inc. - Washington, DC - *BoPubDir 4, 5*
National Net [of NCR Telecommunication Services Inc.] - Dayton, OH - *TeleSy&SerDir 2-84*
National Network Services [of Satellite Business Systems] - McLean, VA - *TeleSy&SerDir 7-83*
National News Bureau - Philadelphia, PA - *BaconPubCkNews 84; Ed&PubIntYB 82; LitMarPl 84; StaDirAdAg 2-84*
National Newspaper Index [of Information Access Co.] - Menlo Park, CA - *CompReadDB 82; DataDirOnSer 84; DBBus 82; DirOnDB Spring 84; EISS 83; OnBibDB 3*
National Notary Association - Woodland Hills, CA - *BoPubDir 4, 5*
National Notary, The - Woodland Hills, CA - *ArtMar 84; BaconPubCkMag 84; MagDir 84; MagIndMarPl 82-83*
National NOW Times - Washington, DC - *MagIndMarPl 82-83*
National Nuclear Data Center [of U.S. Dept. of Energy] - Upton, NY - *EISS 83*
National Nuclear Data Center (Brookhaven National Laboratory) - Upton, NY - *CompReadDB 82*
National Nursing Review Inc. - Los Altos, CA - *BoPubDir 4, 5*
National Oceanic & Atmospheric Administration (Library & Information Services Div.) - Rockville, MD - *CompReadDB 82; DataDirOnSer 84; InfIndMarPl 83*
National Oceanographic Data Center [of U.S. National Oceanic & Atmospheric Administration] - Washington, DC - *EISS 83*
National Oceanographic Data Center (Environmental Data & Information Service) - Washington, DC - *InfIndMarPl 83*
National Office Products Association - Alexandria, VA - *DirInfWP 82*
National Older Workers Information System [of University of Michigan] - Ann Arbor, MI - *EISS 5-84 Sup*
National On-Campus Report - Madison, WI - *WritMar 84*
National Onderzoek Persmedia [of Interactive Market Systems Inc.] - New York, NY - *DataDirOnSer 84*
National Onderzoek Persmedia - Amsterdam, Netherlands - *DirOnDB Spring 84*
National Online Circuit [of IIT Research Institute] - Chicago, IL - *EISS 83; InfIndMarPl 83*
National Opera Association - Commerce, TX - *BoPubDir 4, 5*
National Opinion Poll - San Rafael, CA - *ProGuPRSer 4*
National Opinion Research Center - Chicago, IL - *EISS 83*
National Organization of Telecommunications Engineers & Scientists - Washington, DC - *TeleSy&SerDir 2-84*
National Organization on Legal Problems of Education - Topeka, KS - *BoPubDir 4, 5*
National Organization Service Inc. - Des Moines, IA - *MagIndMarPl 82-83*
National OTC Stock Journal - Denver, CO - *BaconPubCkMag 84*
National Pageant Association Inc. - Overland Park, KS - *ArtMar 84*
National Paperback Books Inc. - Knoxville, TN - *BoPubDir 4, 5*
National Park Service (AV Arts Div.) - Harpers Ferry, WV - *WritMar 84*
National Parks [of National Parks & Conservation Association] - Washington, DC - *ArtMar 84; BaconPubCkMag 84; MagDir 84; MagIndMarPl 82-83; WritMar 84*
National Personnel Records Center [of U.S. General Services Administration] - St. Louis, MO - *EISS 83*
National Pesticide Information Retrieval System [of Purdue University] - West Lafayette, IN - *EISS 5-84 Sup*
National Petroleum Council - Washington, DC - *BoPubDir 4, 5*
National Petroleum News - Des Plaines, IL - *BaconPubCkMag 84; MagIndMarPl 82-83; WritMar 84*
National Petroleum News [of McGraw-Hill Inc.] - New York, NY - *MagDir 84*
National Photocomposition Service Inc. - Syosset, NY - *LitMarPl 83, 84; MagIndMarPl 82-83*
National Photographic Laboratories - Houston, TX - *AvMarPl 83*
National Physical Laboratory (Materials Applications Div.) - Teddington, England - *InfIndMarPl 83*
National Piracy Data Base [of Subscription Television Association] - Washington, DC - *EISS 5-84 Sup*
National Planning Association - Washington, DC - *BoPubDir 5; DataDirOnSer 84*
National Planning Association/Demographic Data - Washington, DC - *DataDirOnSer 84; DirOnDB Spring 84*
National Planning Association Demographic Data [of I. P. Sharp Associates Ltd.] - Toronto, ON, Canada - *DataDirOnSer 84*
National Planning Association/Economic Data Base - Washington, DC - *DBBus 82; DirOnDB Spring 84; EISS 83*
National Planning Association Economic Data Base [of I. P. Sharp Associates Ltd.] - Toronto, ON, Canada - *DataDirOnSer 84*
National Planning Data Corp. - Ithaca, NY - *EISS 83; InfoS 83-84*
National Poetry Foundation - Orono, ME - *LitMag&SmPr 83-84*
National Poetry Press - Agoura, CA - *BoPubDir 4, 5*
National Poison Control Center [of Ministry of Health] - Brussels, Belgium - *EISS 83*
National Police Chiefs & Sheriffs Information Bureau - Milwaukee, WI - *BoPubDir 4, 5*
National Postal Museum [Aff. of Canada Post] - Ottawa, ON, Canada - *BoPubDir 4, 5*
National Press Service - New York, NY - *LitMarPl 84*
National Profile Ltd. - Rexdale, ON, Canada - *BoPubDir 4, 5*
National Prospector's Gazette [of Gazette Publishing] - Ames, NE - *WritMar 84*
National Provisioner, The - Chicago, IL - *BaconPubCkMag 84; MagDir 84*
National PTA - Chicago, IL - *BoPubDir 4, 5*
National Public Accountant [of National Society of Public Accountants] - Alexandria, VA - *BaconPubCkMag 84; MagDir 84; MagIndMarPl 82-83*
National Public Radio - Washington, DC - *BrCabYB 84; CabTVPrDB 83; Tel&CabFB 84C*
National Publishers of the Black Hills Inc. [of Fair Chase Publications] - Rapid City, SD - *WritMar 84*
National Publishing Co. [Subs. of Courier Corp.] - Philadelphia, PA - *LitMarPl 83, 84*
National Racquetball [of Publication Management Inc.] - Glenview, IL - *BaconPubCkMag 84; MagDir 84; MagIndMarPl 82-83; WritMar 84*
National Radio Theatre - Chicago, IL - *WritMar 84*
National Railway Information & Publishing Div. [of National Railway Publication Co.] - New York, NY - *InfoS 83-84*
National Railway Publication Co. - New York, NY - *BoPubDir 4 Sup, 5; MagIndMarPl 82-83*
National Readership Survey - Wembly, England - *DirOnDB Spring 84*
National Real Estate Investor [of Communications Channels Inc.] - Atlanta, GA - *BaconPubCkMag 84; MagDir 84*
National Records - Lubbock, TX - *BillIntBG 83-84*
National Referral Center [of Library of Congress] - Washington, DC - *CompReadDB 82; DirOnDB Spring 84; EISS 83; InfIndMarPl 83*
National Referral Center Master File - Washington, DC - *CompReadDB 82*
National Register Publishing Co. Inc. [Subs. of Macmillan Inc.] - Skokie, IL - *EISS 83; LitMarPl 83, 84*
National Rehabilitation Information Center [of Catholic University of America] - Washington, DC - *CompReadDB 82; DataDirOnSer 84; EISS 83; InfIndMarPl 83; OnBibDB 3*

National Reporter System - Fredericton, NB, Canada - *DirOnDB Spring 84*
National Reporter System [of QL Systems Ltd.] - Ottawa, ON, Canada - *DataDirOnSer 84*
National Reproductions Corp. - Detroit, MI - *LitMarPl 83, 84*
National Reprographic Centre for Documentation [of The Hatfield Polytechnic] - Hertford, England - *EISS 83; InfIndMarPl 83; MicroMarPl 82-83*
National Research & Information Center - Evanston, IL - *BoPubDir 5*
National Research Associates - Bedford, NY - *IntDirMarRes 83*
National Research Bureau Inc. - Burlington, IA - *Ed&PubIntYB 82; ProGuPRSer 4*
National Restaurant Association - Chicago, IL - *BoPubDir 4, 5*
National Retail Hardware Association - Indianapolis, IN - *BoPubDir 5; Ed&PubIntYB 82*
National Retail Merchants Association - New York, NY - *BoPubDir 4, 5*
National Retail Tracking Index Inc. - Englewood Cliffs, NJ - *IntDirMarRes 83*
National Review - New York, NY - *ArtMar 84; BaconPubCkMag 84; LitMarPl 83, 84; MagDir 84; MagIndMarPl 82-83; WritMar 84*
National Ribbon Corp. - Pennsauken, NJ - *DirInfWP 82*
National Right to Work Committee - Springfield, VA - *Ed&PubIntYB 82*
National Road Traveler - Cambridge City, IN - *AyerDirPub 83; Ed&PubIntYB 82*
National Running Data Center Inc. - Tucson, AZ - *EISS 5-84 Sup*
National Rural Letter Carrier [of National Rural Letter Carrier Association] - Washington, DC - *ArtMar 84; MagDir 84; MagIndMarPl 82-83*
National Safety Council - Chicago, IL - *BoPubDir 4, 5*
National Safety News [of National Safety Council] - Chicago, IL - *ArtMar 84; BaconPubCkMag 84; MagDir 84; MagIndMarPl 82-83*
National Sash & Door Jobbers Association - Park Ridge, IL - *BoPubDir 5*
National Savings & Loan League Journal - Washington, DC - *MagDir 84*
National Scene - New York, NY - *MagIndMarPl 82-83*
National Scholarship Research Service - San Rafael, CA - *EISS 83*
National School & Industrial Corp. - Raleigh, NC - *AvMarPl 83*
National School Boards Association - Washington, DC - *BoPubDir 4, 5*
National School Public Relations Association - Arlington, VA - *BoPubDir 4, 5; DataDirOnSer 84*
National Science Teachers Association (Publications Dept.) - Washington, DC - *BoPubDir 4, 5*
National Scientific & Technological Documentation Center - La Paz, Bolivia - *EISS 83*
National Scientific Documentation Center - Jakarta, Indonesia - *EISS 83*
National Sculpture Review - New York, NY - *MagIndMarPl 82-83*
National Semiconductor Corp. - Santa Clara, CA - *Datamation 6-83; ElecNews 7-25-83; Top100Al 83; WhoWMicrocom 83*
National Serials Data Program [of U.S. Library of Congress] - Washington, DC - *EISS 83*
National Sharegraphics Inc. - Dallas, TX - *LitMarPl 83, 84; MagIndMarPl 82-83*
National Sheriff, The - Washington, DC - *BaconPubCkMag 84; MagDir 84*
National Short-Term Forecast [of Merrill Lynch Economics Inc.] - New York, NY - *DataDirOnSer 84*
National Shorthand Reporter - Vienna, VA - *BaconPubCkMag 84; MagDir 84*
National Shorthand Reporters Association - Vienna, VA - *BoPubDir 5*
National Ski Hall of Fame Press [Aff. of United States Ski Educational Foundation] - Ishpeming, MI - *BoPubDir 4, 5*
National Society Daughters of the American Colonists - Washington, DC - *BoPubDir 4, 5*
National Society of Colonial Dames of America in the State of Alabama - Birmingham, AL - *BoPubDir 4, 5*
National Society of Public Accountants - Alexandria, VA - *ArtMar 84*
National Society to Prevent Blindness - New York, NY - *AvMarPl 83; BoPubDir 4, 5*
National Soft Drink Association - Washington, DC - *BoPubDir 5*
National Software Co., The - Baltimore, MD - *MicrocomMPl 84*
National Software Marketing Inc. - Hollywood, FL - *WhoWMicrocom 83*
National Space Science Data Center [of U.S. National Aeronautics & Space Administration] - Greenbelt, MD - *EISS 83*
National Speed Sport News - Ridgewood, NJ - *BaconPubCkMag 84; MagDir 84*
National Square Dance Directory - Jackson, MS - *BoPubDir 4 Sup, 5*
National Standard Reference Data System [of U.S. National Bureau of Standards] - Washington, DC - *EISS 83*
National Standards Association Inc. - Washington, DC - *MicroMarPl 82-83*
National Standards Association Inc. - Bethesda, MD - *CompReadDB 82; DataDirOnSer 84; EISS 83*
National Standards Council of American Embroiderers - Pendleton, OR - *BoPubDir 4, 5*
National Study of Local Newspaper Ratings [of Simmons Market Research Bureau Inc.] - New York, NY - *DataDirOnSer 84; DirOnDB Spring 84*
National Subscription TV - Glendale, CA - *TelAl 83*
National Supermarket Shopper, The - Great Neck, NY - *MagDir 84*
National Supermarket Shopper, The [of American Coupon Club Inc.] - New York, NY - *WritMar 84*
National Survey Panel [Div. of ParaTest Marketing Inc.] - Eastchester, NY - *IntDirMarRes 83*
National Survey Research Group Inc. - New York, NY - *IntDirMarRes 83*
National Swedish Road & Traffic Research Institute - Linkoping, Sweden - *CompReadDB 82*
National Switchboard, The [of Air Couriers International Inc.] - Phoenix, AZ - *TeleSy&SerDir 2-84*
National System, The - St. Louis, MO - *ProGuPRSer 4*
National Systems Analysts Inc. [Div. of NSA Inc.] - Cherry Hill, NJ - *ADAPSOMemDir 83-84*
National Systems Corp. - Cleveland, OH - *WhoWMicrocom 83*
National Systems Laboratories Inc. - Schaumburg, IL - *ADAPSOMemDir 83-84*
National Tank Truck Carriers Inc. - Washington, DC - *BoPubDir 5*
National Tax Journal - Cambridge, MA - *MagIndMarPl 82-83*
National Tax Shelter Digest - Dallas, TX - *BaconPubCkMag 84*
National Teaching Aids Inc. - Garden City Park, NY - *ArtMar 84; AvMarPl 83*
National Technical Information Service [of US Dept. of Commerce] - Springfield, VA - *DataDirOnSer 84; DBBus 82; DirMarMP 83; InfIndMarPl 83; MagIndMarPl 82-83; MicroMarPl 82-83*
National Technical Information Service (Bibliographic Data Base) - Springfield, VA - *CompReadDB 82*
National Telecommunications - Beverly Hills, CA - *BrCabYB 84; Tel&CabFB 84C p.1693*
National Telecommunications & Information Administration [of U.S. Dept. of Commerce] - Washington, DC - *EISS 83*
National Telecommunications Services Inc. [of Harte-Hanks Communications Inc.] - Akron, CO - *BrCabYB 84; Tel&CabFB 84C*
National Telecommunications Services Inc. [of Harte-Hanks Communications Inc.] - Yuma, CO - *BrCabYB 84; Tel&CabFB 84C*
National Telecommunications Services Inc. - *See* Harte-Hanks Communications Inc.
National Telefilm Associates Inc. - Los Angeles, CA - *TelAl 83, 84; Tel&CabFB 84C*
National Telemarketing Inc. - Randolph, NJ - *TeleSy&SerDir 7-83*
National Telephone Co. of Alabama [Aff. of Telephone Electronics Corp.] - Cherokee, AL - *TelDir&BG 83-84*

National Telephone Cooperative Association - Washington, DC - *TeleSy&SerDir 2-84*
National Television News Inc. - Woodland Hills, CA - *AvMarPl 83; BrCabYB 84*
National Television News Inc. - Oak Park, MI - *ArtMar 84*
National Textbook Co. - Lincolnwood, IL - *LitMarPl 84; WritMar 84*
National Textbook Co. - Skokie, IL - *LitMarPl 83*
National Theater File [of Theater Sources Inc.] - Dallas, TX - *EISS 83*
National Thrift News - New York, NY - *BaconPubCkMag 84*
National Time Sales - New York, NY - *TelAl 83, 84*
National Time Sharing [Subs. of Conbow Corp.] - Niagara Falls, NY - *ADAPSOMemDir 83-84; DataDirOnSer 84*
National Tooling & Machining Association - Ft. Washington, MD - *BoPubDir 4, 5*
National Toxicology Program (Environmental Mutagen Information Center) - Oak Ridge, TN - *CompReadDB 82*
National Toxicology Program (Environmental Teratology Information Center) - Oak Ridge, TN - *CompReadDB 82*
National Training & Information Center - Chicago, IL - *BoPubDir 4, 5*
National Transplant Communications Network [of University of California, Los Angeles] - Los Angeles, CA - *EISS 83*
National Tricor Inc. - Kalamazoo, MI - *MicrocomMPl 83*
National Truck Equipment Association - Oak Park, MI - *BoPubDir 5*
National TV Cable Co. [of National Telecommunications Corp.] - Beverly Hills, CA - *BrCabYB 84 p.D-304*
National TV Cable Co. [of National Telecommunications Corp.] - Benton, TN - *Tel&CabFB 84C*
National TV Cable Co. Inc. [of National Telecommunications] - Athens, TN - *Tel&CabFB 84C*
National Underwriter (Life & Health Insurance Edition) - Hoboken, NJ - *BaconPubCkMag 84; MagDir 84*
National Underwriter (Property & Casualty Insurance Edition) - Hoboken, NJ - *BaconPubCkMag 84; MagDir 84*
National Underwriter Co. - Cincinnati, OH - *BoPubDir 4, 5; DirMarMP 83*
National University Continuing Education Association - Washington, DC - *BoPubDir 4, 5*
National Unltd. Business Systems - Bronx, NY - *DataDirSup 7-83*
National Utilities Inc. [Aff. of Alaska Power & Telephone Co.] - Skagway, AK - *TelDir&BG 83-84*
National Utility Contractor, The - Arlington, VA - *BaconPubCkMag 84*
National Video Center Recording Studios Inc. - New York, NY - *AvMarPl 83*
National Video Clearinghouse Inc. - Syosset, NY - *BoPubDir 4, 5; EISS 83*
National Video Industries Inc. - New York, NY - *AvMarPl 83*
National Video Systems - Seaside Heights, NJ - *BrCabYB 84; Tel&CabFB 84C*
National Water Data Exchange [of U.S. Geological Survey] - Reston, VA - *EISS 83*
National Water Data System [of U.S. Geological Survey] - Reston, VA - *EISS 83*
National Water Information Center [of French Water Study Association] - Paris, France - *EISS 83*
National Water Quality Data Bank [of Environment Canada] - Ottawa, ON, Canada - *EISS 83*
National Water Well Association - Worthington, OH - *BoPubDir 5; DataDirOnSer 84*
National Waterways Conference Inc. - Washington, DC - *BoPubDir 4, 5*
National WATS Services - Fair Lawn, NJ - *IntDirMarRes 83*
National Wholesale Druggists' Association - Scarsdale, NY - *BoPubDir 5*
National Wildlife [of National Wildlife Federation] - Washington, DC - *LitMarPl 83, 84*
National Wildlife [of National Wildlife Federation] - Vienna, VA - *ArtMar 84; Folio 83; WritMar 84*
National Wildlife - Milwaukee, WI - *MagIndMarPl 82-83*
National Wildlife Federation - Washington, DC - *BoPubDir 4, 5*
National Wool Grower - Salt Lake City, UT - *BaconPubCkMag 84; MagDir 84*
National Writers Press [Aff. of National Writers Club] - Aurora, CO - *BoPubDir 5*
National Youth Work Alliance - Washington, DC - *BoPubDir 5*
Nationality Broadcasting Network [of Satellite Cable Audio Networks] - Cleveland, OH - *BrCabYB 84*
Nationality Broadcasting Network [of Satellite Cable Audio Networks] - Tulsa, OK - *CabTVPrDB 83*
Nation's Business [of U.S. Chamber of Commerce] - Washington, DC - *BaconPubCkMag 84; DirMarMP 83; Folio 83; LitMarPl 83, 84; MagDir 84; MagIndMarPl 82-83; WritMar 84*
Nation's Center News - Buffalo, SD - *Ed&PubIntYB 82*
Nation's Cities Weekly [of National League of Cities] - Washington, DC - *BaconPubCkMag 84; MagDir 84; MagIndMarPl 82-83*
Nation's Health, The - Washington, DC - *BaconPubCkMag 84; MagDir 84*
Nation's Restaurant News [of Lebhar-Friedman Inc.] - New York, NY - *BaconPubCkMag 84; Folio 83; MagDir 84; MagIndMarPl 82-83*
Nation's Schools Report - Arlington, VA - *BaconPubCkMag 84*
Nationwide Advertising Service - Cleveland, OH - *AdAge 3-28-84; HBIndAd&MS 82-83; StaDirAdAg 2-84*
Nationwide Communications Inc. - Columbus, OH - *BrCabYB 84; Tel&CabFB 84S*
Nationwide Communications Inc. - Lancaster, OH - *Tel&CabFB 84C p.1694*
Nationwide Fulfillment Systems Inc. - Ridgely, MD - *LitMarPl 84*
Nationwide Press Ltd. - Pueblo, CO - *BoPubDir 4, 5*
Nationwide Sound Distributors - Nashville, TN - *BillIntBG 83-84*
Native American Public Broadcasting Consortium Inc. - Lincoln, NE - *TeleSy&SerDir 2-84*
Native American Rights Fund Inc. - Boulder, CO - *BoPubDir 4, 5*
Native American Solidarity Committee - St. Paul, MN - *BoPubDir 4, 5*
Native Publishing Co. - Salem, OR - *BoPubDir 4, 5*
Natoma-Luray Independent - Natoma, KS - *AyerDirPub 83; BaconPubCkNews 84; Ed&PubIntYB 82*
NATO's Sixteen Nations - McLean, VA - *BaconPubCkMag 84*
NATPE Programmer - New York, NY - *BaconPubCkMag 84*
NATSO Trucker's News - Alexandria, VA - *BaconPubCkMag 84; MagIndMarPl 82-83*
Natural Dynamics Inc. - Jarvis, ON, Canada - *LitMag&SmPr 83-84*
Natural Dynamics Inc. - Scotland, ON, Canada - *BoPubDir 4, 5*
Natural Foods Merchandiser - New Hope, PA - *BaconPubCkMag 84*
Natural Health & Fitness Bulletin - Princeton, NJ - *BaconPubCkMag 84*
Natural Heritage Program [of Ohio State Dept. of Natural Resources] - Columbus, OH - *EISS 5-84 Sup*
Natural History [of American Museum of Natural History] - New York, NY - *ArtMar 84; BaconPubCkMag 84; DirMarMP 83; Folio 83; LitMarPl 83, 84; MagDir 84; MagIndMarPl 82-83; WritMar 84*
Natural History Museum of Los Angeles County - Los Angeles, CA - *BoPubDir 4, 5*
Natural History Publishing Co. - La Jolla, CA - *BoPubDir 4, 5*
Natural Hygiene Press [Aff. of American Natural Hygiene Society Inc.] - Bridgeport, CT - *BoPubDir 4, 5*
Natural Life Book Club - Brookline Village, MA - *LitMarPl 83*
Natural Press - Manitowoc, WI - *BoPubDir 4 Sup, 5*
Natural Resources Data Bank [of Nebraska State Natural Resources Commission] - Lincoln, NE - *EISS 83*
Natural Science Book Club [of Macmillan Book Clubs Inc.] - New York, NY - *LitMarPl 84*
Natural Science of Canada Ltd. - Toronto, ON, Canada - *BoPubDir 4, 5*
Natural Woodland Nursery Ltd. - Waterloo, ON, Canada - *BoPubDir 4 Sup, 5*
Natural World Press - San Mateo, CA - *LitMag&SmPr 83-84; LitMarPl 83, 84*
Nature - New York, NY - *BaconPubCkMag 84; MagIndMarPl 82-83*
Nature Alaska Photographic - Fairbanks, AK - *MagIndMarPl 82-83*

Nature Books Publishers - Jackson, MS - *BoPubDir 4, 5*
Nature Life [Aff. of McGill/Jensen Inc.] - St. Paul, MN - *BoPubDir 4, 5*
Nature Science Book Club [of Macmillan Book Clubs Inc.] - New York, NY - *LitMarPl 83*
Nature Study Guild - Berkeley, CA - *BoPubDir 4, 5*
Nature Trail Press - Palm Springs, CA - *BoPubDir 4, 5*
Naturegraph Publishers Inc. - Happy Camp, CA - *ArtMar 84; LitMag&SmPr 83-84; LitMarPl 83, 84; WritMar 84*
Naturegraphs - Golden, CO - *LitMarPl 84*
Naturist Foundation - Orpington, England - *LitMag&SmPr 83-84*
Naugatuck News - Naugatuck, CT - *BaconPubCkNews 84; Ed&PubIntYB 82; NewsDir 84*
Naujienos - Chicago, IL - *AyerDirPub 83; Ed&PubIntYB 82*
Nautical Almanac Office [of U.S. Navy] - Washington, DC - *EISS 83*
Nautical & Aviation Publishing Co. of America Inc., The - Annapolis, MD - *LitMarPl 83, 84; WritMar 84*
Nautical Music Co. - Nashville, TN - *BillIntBG 83-84*
Nautical Quarterly - New York, NY - *WritMar 84*
Nautilus [of American Malacologists Inc.] - Melbourne, FL - *MagDir 84*
Nautilus Communications Inc. - New York, NY - *LitMarPl 83, 84*
Nautilus Fund Inc. - Boston, MA - *ADAPSOMemDir 83-84*
Nautilus Recordings [of Triton Industries Inc.] - San Luis Obispo, CA - *BillIntBG 83-84*
Nauvoo Grapevine - Nauvoo, IL - *Ed&PubIntYB 82*
Nava-Hopi Observer - Tuba City, AZ - *Ed&PubIntYB 82*
NAVA, The International Communications Industries Association - Fairfax, VA - *BoPubDir 5*
Navajo Communications Co. Inc. [Aff. of CP National Corp.] - Window Rock, AZ - *TelDir&BG 83-84*
Navajo Community College Press - Tempe, AZ - *BoPubDir 4, 5*
Naval Affairs - Washington, DC - *BaconPubCkMag 84; MagDir 84; MagIndMarPl 82-83*
Naval Aviation News - Washington, DC - *MagDir 84*
Naval Book Club [Subs. of Sky Books International Inc.] - New York, NY - *LitMarPl 83, 84*
Naval Engineer's Journal - Washington, DC - *BaconPubCkMag 84*
Naval Engineer's Journal - Alexandria, VA - *MagDir 84*
Naval Facilities Engineering Command Master Specification [of Bowne Information Systems Inc.] - New York, NY - *DataDirOnSer 84*
Naval Fighter Books - Simi Valley, CA - *BoPubDir 5*
Naval Forces - McLean, VA - *BaconPubCkMag 84*
Naval Institute Press - Annapolis, MD - *DirMarMP 83; LitMarPl 83, 84; WritMar 84*
Naval Ordnance Technical Documents Dept. [of U.S. Navy] - Louisville, KY - *EISS 83*
Naval Stores Review [of The Dough Boy Inc.] - New Orleans, LA - *BaconPubCkMag 84; MagDir 84*
Navarro & Associates Inc., J. R. - Los Angeles, CA - *StaDirAdAg 2-84*
Navasota Examiner & Grimes County Review, The - Navasota, TX - *Ed&PubIntYB 82*
Navasota Examiner-Review - Navasota, TX - *BaconPubCkNews 84; NewsDir 84*
Navic Software - North Palm Beach, FL - *MicrocomMPl 84*
Navpress [Aff. of The Navigators] - Colorado Springs, CO - *BoPubDir 4, 5; LitMarPl 84*
Navtel Div. [of Associated Test Equipment] - Concord, ON, Canada - *DataDirSup 7-83*
Navy Alternate Fuel Reference File [of Battelle Memorial Institute] - Columbus, OH - *EISS 83*
Navy Mobility Fuels Reference File [of Battelle Columbus Laboratories] - Columbus, OH - *DataDirOnSer 84*
Navy News - San Diego, CA - *MagDir 84; MagIndMarPl 82-83*
Navy News [of Icarus Publishers Inc.] - Washington, DC - *NewsDir 84*
Navy News - Arlington, VA - *AyerDirPub 83*
Navy News - Virginia Beach, VA - *MagDir 84*
Navy Offices of Information - Atlanta, GA - *Tel&CabFB 84C*
Navy Times - Washington, DC - *BaconPubCkMag 84; MagDir 84; MagIndMarPl 82-83*
Nay Advertising Inc., Ken - Cincinnati, OH - *StaDirAdAg 2-84*
Nazarene Publishing House - Kansas City, MO - *LitMarPl 83; WritMar 84*
Nazarene Publishing House - *See* Lillenas Publishing Co.
NB Jackets - Woodside, NY - *DirInfWP 82*
NBC - *See* National Broadcasting Co.
NBC Enterprises [Subs. of National Broadcasting Co.] - New York, NY - *AvMarPl 83; Tel&CabFB 84C*
NBC International Ltd. [Subs. of National Broadcasting Co.] - New York, NY - *TelAl 84; Tel&CabFB 84C*
NBC Music Inc. - Brentwood, TN - *BillIntBG 83-84*
NBC Music Records - Brentwood, TN - *BillIntBG 83-84*
NBC Spot Sales [of National Broadcasting Co.] - New York, NY - *TelAl 83, 84*
NBC Teletext [of National Broadcasting Co.] - New York, NY - *EISS 5-84 Sup; TeleSy&SerDir 2-84*
NBI - Boulder, CO - *Datamation 6-83; DirInfWP 82; MicrocomMPl 84; Top100Al 83*
NBS Alloy Data Base [of National Bureau of Standards] - Washington, DC - *CompReadDB 82*
NBS Update - Washington, DC - *MagIndMarPl 82-83*
NC Broadcast News - Washington, DC - *BrCabYB 84*
NC Press - Toronto, ON, Canada - *BoPubDir 4, 5; LitMarPl 84; WritMar 84*
NC Shopowner - New York, NY - *BaconPubCkMag 84; MagIndMarPl 82-83*
NCCAN Information Clearinghouse [of U.S. Dept. of Health & Human Services] - Washington, DC - *EISS 83*
NCE of Florida Inc. - North Miami, FL - *AvMarPl 83*
NCE Supply Corp. - Carol Stream, IL - *DirInfWP 82*
NCI - Memphis, TN - *CabTVFinDB 83*
NCJRS - Washington, DC - *DirOnDB Spring 84*
NCK Organization Ltd., The - *See* Foote, Cone & Belding Communications Inc.
NCom - Aarhus, Denmark - *DirOnDB Spring 84*
NCR Comten - St. Paul, MN - *DataDirSup 7-83*
NCR Corp. - Dayton, OH - *DataDirSup 7-83; Datamation 6-83; DirInfWP 82; ElecNews 7-25-83; InfIndMarPl 83; Top100Al 83; WhoWMicrocom 83*
NCR Corp. - Kettering, OH - *MagIndMarPl 82-83*
NCR Corp. (Source Document Services Div.) - Dayton, OH - *LitMarPl 83, 84; MagIndMarPl 82-83*
NCR Data Centers Div. [of NCR Corp.] - Dayton, OH - *DataDirOnSer 84*
NCR EFT & Data Services Div. [of NCR Corp.] - Dayton, OH - *DataDirOnSer 84*
N.D. Rec Magazine - Mandan, ND - *WritMar 84*
NDEX - Wooster, OH - *DirOnDB Spring 84*
NDL Cable [of Cardiff Cablevision nc.] - Castroville, TX - *Tel&CabFB 84C*
NDL Cable [of Cardiff Cablevision Inc.] - Devine, TX - *Tel&CabFB 84C*
NDL Cable [of Cardiff Cablevision Inc.] - Lytle, TX - *Tel&CabFB 84C*
NDL Cable [if Cardiff Cablevision Inc.] - Natalia, TX - *Tel&CabFB 84C*
NDM - Chicago, IL - *StaDirAdAg 2-84*
NDX Corp. - Houston, TX - *InfoS 83-84*
NEA Data Bank [of Organisation for Economic Co-Operation & Development] - Gif-sur-Yvette, France - *EISS 83*
NEA Today - Washington, DC - *BaconPubCkMag 84; MagDir 84*
Neahtawanta Press - Traverse City, MI - *BoPubDir 4, 5*
Neal Associates, Richard - Manassas, VA - *BoPubDir 4, 5*
Neal Productions Inc., Stanley - *See* Lane Pictures Inc., Don
Neal Publications - Perrysburg, OH - *BoPubDir 5*
Neal-Schuman Publishers Inc. - New York, NY - *LitMarPl 83, 84*
Neal Slate Co., W. S. - Eden Prairie, MN - *DirInfWP 82*
Neale Advertising Associates - Toluca Lake, CA - *StaDirAdAg 2-84*
Near East Report - Washington, DC - *MagIndMarPl 82-83*
Near North News - Chicago, IL - *AyerDirPub 83*
Near North News - Near North, IL - *Ed&PubIntYB 82*
Near South Herald [of Hyde Park Herald Inc.] - Chicago, IL - *NewsDir 84*
Nearman Co. Inc., Gilbert S. - Garden City, NY - *StaDirAdAg 2-84*

Neathery, Robert F. Jr. - West Plains, MO - *BrCabYB 84 p.D-304*
Neathery, Robert F. Jr. - *See* Community Cable Co.
Neathery, Robert F. Sr. - West Plains, MO - *BrCabYB 84 p.D-304*
Neathery, Robert F. Sr. - *See* Community Cable Co.
Nebo - Russelville, AR - *LitMag&SmPr 83-84*
Nebraska Agriculture - Lincoln, NE - *MagDir 84*
Nebraska Beverage Analyst [of Bevan Inc.] - Denver, CO - *BaconPubCkMag 84; MagDir 84*
Nebraska Blue Print [of University of Nebraska] - Lincoln, NE - *BaconPubCkMag 84; MagDir 84*
Nebraska Cattleman - Alliance, NE - *BaconPubCkMag 84; MagDir 84*
Nebraska Central Telephone Co. - Gibbon, NE - *TelDir&BG 83-84*
Nebraska City News-Press [of Park Newspapers Inc.] - Nebraska City, NE - *BaconPubCkNews 84; Ed&PubIntYB 82; NewsDir 84*
Nebraska Data Center [of University of Nebraska-Lincoln] - Lincoln, NE - *EISS 83*
Nebraska Education News - Lincoln, NE - *MagDir 84*
Nebraska Farm Bureau News - Lincoln, NE - *BaconPubCkMag 84*
Nebraska Farmer - Lincoln, NE - *BaconPubCkMag 84; MagDir 84*
Nebraska History - Lincoln, NE - *MagDir 84*
Nebraska Insurance Dept. - Lincoln, NE - *BoPubDir 5*
Nebraska-Iowa Retailer - Omaha, NE - *BaconPubCkMag 84; MagDir 84*
Nebraska Journal-Leader - Ponca, NE - *AyerDirPub 83; Ed&PubIntYB 82*
Nebraska Library Commission - Lincoln, NE - *InfIndMarPl 83*
Nebraska Medical Journal - Lincoln, NE - *BaconPubCkMag 84*
Nebraska Mortar & Pestle [of Nebraska Pharmacists Association] - Lincoln, NE - *BaconPubCkMag 84; MagDir 84*
Nebraska Municipal Review - Lincoln, NE - *BaconPubCkMag 84*
Nebraska Oil Jobber [of Nebraska Petroleum Marketers Inc.] - Lincoln, NE - *BaconPubCkMag 84; MagDir 84*
Nebraska Online Users Group [of University of Nebraska at Omaha] - Omaha, NE - *InfIndMarPl 83*
Nebraska Retailer [of Nebraska & Omaha Food Retailers Association] - Omaha, NE - *BaconPubCkMag 84; MagDir 84*
Nebraska Signal - Geneva, NE - *AyerDirPub 83; Ed&PubIntYB 82*
Nebraska Smoke-Eater [of Smoke-Eater Publications] - Pierce, NE - *MagDir 84*
Nebraska State Historical Society - Lincoln, NE - *BoPubDir 4, 5; MicroMarPl 82-83*
Nebraska State Library Commission - Lincoln, NE - *EISS 83*
Nebraska Telephone Co. [Aff. of Unitel of Nebraska] - Blair, NE - *TelDir&BG 83-84*
Nebraska Trucker - Lincoln, NE - *BaconPubCkMag 84; MagDir 84*
Nebraska Union Farmer - Lincoln, NE - *MagDir 84*
Nebraskaland - Lincoln, NE - *BaconPubCkMag 84*
NEBS Computer Forms [Subs. of New England Business Service Inc.] - Groton, MA - *MicrocomMPl 83; WhoWMicrocom 83*
Nebula Press [Aff. of Nebula Magazine] - North Bay, ON, Canada - *BoPubDir 4, 5*
Nebulae Productions - Flushing, NY - *BillIntBG 83-84; Tel&CabFB 84C*
NEC America Inc. [Subs. of Nippon Electric Co. Ltd.] - Dallas, TX - *DirInfWP 82*
NEC America Inc. (Broadcast Equipment Div.) - Elk Grove Village, IL - *AvMarPl 83*
NEC Corp. - Tokyo, Japan - *ElecNews 7-25-83*
NEC Home Electronics USA [Subs. of Nippon Electric Co. Ltd.] - Elk Grove Village, IL - *BillIntBG 83-84; MicrocomMPl 84; WhoWMicrocom 83*
NEC Information Systems Inc. [Subs. of Nippon Electric Co. Ltd.] - Lexington, MA - *DataDirSup 7-83; Datamation 6-83; DirInfWP 82; WhoWMicrocom 83*
NEC Telephones Inc. - Melville, NY - *DataDirSup 7-83*
Nechako Chronicle - Vanderhoof, BC, Canada - *AyerDirPub 83; Ed&PubIntYB 82*
Nechako Valley Historical Society - Vanderhoof, BC, Canada - *BoPubDir 4 Sup, 5*
Necksaver - Oakland, CA - *AvMarPl 83*
Necronomicon Press - West Warwick, RI - *BoPubDir 4, 5*
Ned Baden Clinton County News - *See* Yelvington Enterprises Inc., Rube
NEDA Journal/Electronic Merchandising - Park Ridge, IL - *MagDir 84*
Nedco Today - Syracuse, NY - *BaconPubCkMag 84; MagDir 84*
Nederland Review - Nederland, TX - *Ed&PubIntYB 82*
Nederlandsche Organisatie voor Toegepast-Natuurwetenschappelijk Onderzoek (Centre for Scientific & Technical Information & Documentation) - Delft, Netherlands - *InfIndMarPl 83*
Nederlandse Informatie Combinatie/Netherlands Information Combine - Delft, Netherlands - *InfIndMarPl 83*
NEDRES - Washington, DC - *DirOnDB Spring 84*
Needham & Grohmann Inc. - New York, NY - *StaDirAdAg 2-84; TelAl 83, 84*
Needham Chronicle - Dedham, MA - *AyerDirPub 83*
Needham Chronicle, The - Needham, MA - *Ed&PubIntYB 82*
Needham, Harper & Steers Advertising Inc. - Los Angeles, CA - *ArtMar 84*
Needham, Harper & Steers Advertising Inc. - Chicago, IL - *AdAge 6-25-84; HomeVid&CabYB 82-83*
Needham, Harper & Steers Advertising Inc. - New York, NY - *AdAge 3-28-84; Br 1-23-84; BrCabYB 84; StaDirAdAg 2-84; TelAl 83, 84*
Needham, Harper & Steers Advertising Inc. - Dayton, OH - *ArtMar 84*
Needham Times, The - Needham, MA - *Ed&PubIntYB 82*
Needham Times, The - *See* Suburban World Inc.
Needham, William L. - Tallahassee, FL - *FBInfSer 80*
Needle - Spencer, NY - *AyerDirPub 83*
Needle & Thread [of Happy Hands Publishing] - Ft. Worth, TX - *WritMar 84*
Needlecraft for Today [of Happy Hands Publishing] - Ft. Worth, TX - *WritMar 84*
Needlemania Inc. - Franklin, MI - *BoPubDir 5*
Needlepoint News - Evanston, IL - *BaconPubCkMag 84; MagDir 84*
Needles Desert Star - Needles, CA - *BaconPubCkNews 84; Ed&PubIntYB 82; NewsDir 84*
Needle's Eye, The [of Union Special Corp.] - Chicago, IL - *BaconPubCkMag 84; MagDir 84*
Needville Gulf Coast Tribune - *See* Brazoria County News Publishers
Neely Printing Co. Inc. - Chicago, IL - *MagIndMarPl 82-83*
Neepawa Press, The - Neepawa, MB, Canada - *Ed&PubIntYB 82*
Nefertiti Head Press - Austin, TX - *BoPubDir 4, 5*
Neff & Associates, Tom - Smyrna, TN - *LitMarPl 83, 84*
Neff Lithographing Co. Inc. - New York, NY - *LitMarPl 83, 84*
Negafile Systems Inc. - Furlong, PA - *AvMarPl 83*
Negative Capability - Mobile, AL - *LitMag&SmPr 83-84; WritMar 84*
Negative Capability Press - Mobile, AL - *BoPubDir 5; LitMag&SmPr 83-84*
Negro Educational Review, The - Jacksonville, FL - *MagIndMarPl 82-83*
Negro History Bulletin, The - Washington, DC - *MagIndMarPl 82-83*
Negro Traveler & Conventioneer - Chicago, IL - *MagDir 84*
Nehalem Telephone & Telegraph Co. - Nehalem, OR - *TelDir&BG 83-84*
NEI - Roskilde, Norway - *DirOnDB Spring 84*
Neighbor, The - Louisville, KY - *NewsDir 84*
Neighborhood Journal - Oakland, CA - *AyerDirPub 83*
Neighborhood News - St. Louis, MO - *AyerDirPub 83; Ed&PubIntYB 82*
Neighborhood Publications Inc. - Mt. Kisco, NY - *DirMarMP 83*
Neighborhood Times - Florissant, MO - *AyerDirPub 83*
Neighborhood Times [of Overland Buhrman Publications] - St. Louis, MO - *NewsDir 84*
Neighborhood Works [Aff. of Center for Neighborhood Technology] - Chicago, IL - *BoPubDir 5*
Neighbors - Montgomery, AL - *BaconPubCkMag 84; MagDir 84*
Neighbors East/West - Coral Gables, FL - *Ed&PubIntYB 82*
Neighbors Inc., Charles - New York, NY - *LitMarPl 83, 84*
Neikrug Photographica Ltd. - New York, NY - *MagIndMarPl 82-83*

Neil Music Inc. - Los Angeles, CA - *BillIntBG 83-84*
Neillsville Cable Co. [of Telephone & Data Systems Inc.] - Neillsville, WI - *BrCabYB 84; Tel&CabFB 84C*
Neillsville Clark County Press - Neillsville, WI - *BaconPubCkNews 84*
Neilson & Anklam Inc. - Burbank, CA - *StaDirAdAg 2-84*
Neither/Nor Press - Ann Arbor, MI - *BoPubDir 5; LitMag&SmPr 83-84*
Nekoosa Papers Inc. [Subs. of Great Northern Nekoosa Corp.] - Port Edwards, WI - *LitMarPl 83, 84*
Nelder/Uniphoto, Oscar - Presque Isle, ME - *AvMarPl 83*
Neligh News & Leader - Neligh, NE - *BaconPubCkNews 84; Ed&PubIntYB 82*
Nelinet Inc. - Newton, MA - *EISS 83; InfIndMarPl 83*
Nellen Publishing Co. Inc. - Newton, NJ - *LitMarPl 83, 84; WritMar 84*
Neller & Kane Inc. - Dallas, TX - *HBIndAd&MS 82-83; StaDirAdAg 2-84*
Nellis AFB Bullseye [of Las Vegas Valley Publishing Co.] - North Las Vegas, NV - *NewsDir 84*
Nelso Manufacturing Co. - Plumsteadville, PA - *DirInfWP 82*
Nelson Advertising Agency - Studio City, CA - *StaDirAdAg 2-84*
Nelson Advertising, Lawrence - New York, NY - *StaDirAdAg 2-84*
Nelson & Co., Allen - Seattle, WA - *DirPRFirms 83; StaDirAdAg 2-84*
Nelson & Co., Ken - Dallas, TX - *TeleSy&SerDir 2-84*
Nelson & Siegel Research Inc. - New York, NY - *IntDirMarRes 83*
Nelson & Visel Inc. - San Pedro, CA - *DirPRFirms 83*
Nelson & Watson Associates Inc. - Santa Ana, CA - *Tel&CabFB 84C*
Nelson Associates, Dallas - Memphis, TN - *StaDirAdAg 2-84*
Nelson Associates/Graphic Press, Carl L. - Washington, DC - *BoPubDir 4, 5*
Nelson-Ball Ground Telephone Co. Inc. - Nelson, GA - *TelDir&BG 83-84*
Nelson Canada [Div. of International Thomson Ltd.] - Scarborough, ON, Canada - *LitMarPl 83, 84*
Nelson Communications Inc. - Brookline, MA - *DataDirSup 7-83; TeleSy&SerDir 7-83*
Nelson Co. - Hopkins, MN - *BoPubDir 5*
Nelson County Arena - Fordville, ND - *AyerDirPub 83*
Nelson County Arena - Michigan, ND - *Ed&PubIntYB 82*
Nelson County Cablevision Corp. - Nelson County, VA - *BrCabYB 84; Tel&CabFB 84C*
Nelson County Times - Lovingston, VA - *AyerDirPub 83; Ed&PubIntYB 82*
Nelson Daily News - Nelson, BC, Canada - *Ed&PubIntYB 82*
Nelson Data Resources Inc. - Omaha, NE - *MicrocomSwDir 1*
Nelson, Franklin W. - *See* Progressive Communications Inc.
Nelson Gazette - Nelson, NE - *BaconPubCkNews 84; Ed&PubIntYB 82*
Nelson-Hall Publishers - Chicago, IL - *ArtMar 84; DirMarMP 83; LitMarPl 83, 84; WritMar 84*
Nelson Lecture Bureau, B. K. - New York, NY - *LitMarPl 84*
Nelson Literary Agency, B. K. - New York, NY - *LitMarPl 83, 84*
Nelson Publications [Aff. of W. R. Nelson & Co.] - Rye, NY - *BoPubDir 5*
Nelson Publishers Inc., Thomas - Nashville, TN - *KnowInd 83; LitMarPl 83, 84; WritMar 84*
Nelson Publishers Inc., Thomas (Premium Marketing Div.) - Nashville, TN - *DirMarMP 83*
Nelson, Robert R. - *See* Green Group, Howard
Nelson Software Systems - Minneapolis, MN - *MicrocomMPl 83*
Nelson Software Systems - St. Paul, MN - *MicrocomMPl 84*
Nelson, Ted - South Bend, IN - *BoPubDir 4, 5; LitMag&SmPr 83-84*
Nelson Telephone Cooperative - Durand, WI - *TelDir&BG 83-84*
Nelsonville TV Cable Inc. - Nelsonville, OH - *BrCabYB 84; Tel&CabFB 84C*
NEMA - Washington, DC - *DirOnDB Spring 84*
Nemaha County Herald [of Auburn Newspapers] - Auburn, NE - *AyerDirPub 83; Ed&PubIntYB 82; NewsDir 84*
Nemaha County Journal-Leader - Centralia, KS - *Ed&PubIntYB 82*
Nemco - Rutherford, NJ - *MicrocomMPl 84*
Nemer, Fieger & Associates Inc. - Minneapolis, MN - *DirPRFirms 83*
Nemesian Associates - Jeffersonville, PA - *BoPubDir 5*
Nemeth Studios, Ted - New York, NY - *Tel&CabFB 84C*
Nemetz & Associates Inc., Jeffrey - Chicago, IL - *StaDirAdAg 2-84*
Nemiroff Productions Inc., Paul - New York, NY - *AvMarPl 83*
Nemo News Service - San Jose, CA - *BrCabYB 84*
Nemont Cablevision Inc. - Scobey, MT - *Tel&CabFB 84C p.1694*
Nemont Communication Inc. [of Nemont Telephone Cooperative Inc.] - Culbertson, MT - *BrCabYB 84*
Nemont Communication Inc. [of Nemont Telephone Cooperative Inc.] - Poplar, MT - *BrCabYB 84*
Nemont Communication Inc. [of Nemont Telephone Cooperative Inc.] - Scobey, MT - *BrCabYB 84 p.D-304*
Nemont Communications Inc. - Culbertson, MT - *Tel&CabFB 84C*
Nemont Telephone Cooperative Inc. - Scobey, MT - *TelDir&BG 83-84*
NEMS - New Haven, CT - *MicrocomMPl 84*
Neneteenth-Century Music [of University of California Press] - Berkeley, CA - *LitMag&SmPr 83-84*
NEO Records - New York, NY - *BillIntBG 83-84*
Neodata Services - New York, NY - *MagIndMarPl 82-83*
Neodesha Register - Neodesha, KS - *Ed&PubIntYB 82*
Neodesha Sun - Neodesha, KS - *Ed&PubIntYB 82*
Neodesha Sun & Register - Neodesha, KS - *BaconPubCkNews 84; NewsDir 84*
Neoga News - Neoga, IL - *BaconPubCkNews 84; Ed&PubIntYB 82*
Neola Gazette - Neola, IA - *BaconPubCkNews 84*
Neola Gazette-Reporter & Shelby News - Neola, IA - *Ed&PubIntYB 82*
Neon Sun - Berkeley, CA - *BoPubDir 4, 5*
Neosho News - Neosho, MO - *BaconPubCkNews 84; Ed&PubIntYB 82; NewsDir 84*
Neostat Music Co. - Birmingham, MI - *BillIntBG 83-84*
Neoteric Music - Los Angeles, CA - *BillIntBG 83-84*
NEP Productions Inc. - New York, NY - *AvMarPl 83*
Nepean Clarion - Ottawa, ON, Canada - *Ed&PubIntYB 82*
Nepean Review, The [of The Firebird Press] - Kingswood, Australia - *LitMag&SmPr 83-84*
Nepenthe Programs - Chula Vista, CA - *WhoWMicrocom 83*
Nepenthe Programs - National City, CA - *MicrocomMPl 83; WhoWMicrocom 83*
Nephi Times-News - Nephi, UT - *BaconPubCkNews 84*
Nephrology Nurse - Bridgewater, NJ - *BaconPubCkMag 84*
NEPLAN - West Springfield, MA - *BoPubDir 5*
Nepriklausoma Lietuva - La Salle, PQ, Canada - *Ed&PubIntYB 82*
Neptune Music Publishers - Rochester, NY - *BillIntBG 83-84*
N.E.R. Data & Business Products - Glassboro, NJ - *DirInfWP 82*
NERA - White Plains, NY - *BrCabYB 84*
NERAC [of University of Connecticut] - Storrs, CT - *DataDirOnSer 84*
Neras Systems - Beverly Hills, CA - *BoPubDir 4, 5*
Nerge Film Laboratories Inc. - Minneapolis, MN - *AvMarPl 83*
Nerve Press - Vancouver, BC, Canada - *BoPubDir 4 Sup, 5*
Nesbe Cable/Satellite Communications Inc. [of Bahakel Communications] - Crewe, VA - *BrCabYB 84*
Nesbe Cable/Satellite Communications Ltd. [of Bahakel Communications] - Blackstone, VA - *BrCabYB 84*
Neshaminy Valley Information Processing Inc. [Subs. of Combined International Corp.] - Trevose, PA - *ADAPSOMemDir 83-84; DataDirOnSer 84*
Neshoba Democrat, The - Philadelphia, MS - *Ed&PubIntYB 82*
Ness Agency, G. L. - Fargo, ND - *DirMarMP 83*
Ness & Associates, David - Calgary, AB, Canada - *DirInfWP 82*
Ness City Cable Communications - Ness City, KS - *BrCabYB 84*
Ness City Ness County News - Ness City, KS - *BaconPubCkNews 84*
Ness County News - Ness City, KS - *AyerDirPub 83; Ed&PubIntYB 82*
Ness Press Inc. - Fordville, ND - *BaconPubCkNews 84*
Nessa Records - Chicago, IL - *BillIntBG 83-84*
Nestar Systems Inc. - Palo Alto, CA - *DataDirSup 7-83; DirInfWP 82; WhoWMicrocom 83*

Nested Phrase Indexing System [of University of Western Ontario] - London, ON, Canada - *EISS 83*
Net Cable Inc. - Pulaski, WI - *Tel&CabFB 84C*
Net/One [of Ungermann-Bass Inc.] - Santa Clara, CA - *TeleSy&SerDir 7-83*
Net Profit Computers - Anaheim, CA - *MicrocomMPl 84*
Net Profit Computers - Torrance, CA - *MicrocomMPl 83*
Netarts Cable TV Inc. - Netarts, OR - *Tel&CabFB 84C*
Netarts TV Service - Netarts, OR - *BrCabYB 84*
Netcom International - San Francisco, CA - *BrCabYB 84; TeleSy&SerDir 2-84*
Netcom Star - San Francisco, CA - *BrCabYB 84*
Netcong News-Leader - Netcong, NJ - *BaconPubCkNews 84; NewsDir 84*
Netedu Co., The [Div. of Electrographic Corp.] - Benton Harbor, MI - *AvMarPl 83; StaDirAdAg 2-84*
Netherlands Association of Users of Online Information Systems - Delft, Netherlands - *EISS 83; InfIndMarPl 83*
Netherlands Bibliographical & Documentary Committee - Amsterdam, Netherlands - *EISS 83*
Netherlands Center for Informatics - Amsterdam, Netherlands - *EISS 83*
Netherlands Center for Information Policy - The Hague, Netherlands - *EISS 83*
Netherlands Information Combine - Delft, Netherlands - *EISS 83*
Netherlands Organization for Applied Scientific Research (Study & Information Centre on Environmental Research) - Delft, Netherlands - *CompReadDB 82*
Netherlands Organization for Information Policy - The Hague, Netherlands - *EISS 83*
Netherlands Society for Informatics - Amsterdam, Netherlands - *EISS 83*
Netherton, H. Eugene - West Sacramento, CA - *BoPubDir 5*
Netronics R & D Ltd. - New Milford, CT - *MicrocomMPl 83, 84*
Nettle Creek Publishing [Aff. of Bill Speidel Enterprises] - Seattle, WA - *BoPubDir 4 Sup, 5*
Nettleton News - Nettleton, MS - *Ed&PubIntYB 82*
Netwits Newsletter - Sherman Oaks, CA - *DirOnDB Spring 84*
Netword Inc. - Riverdale, MD - *MicrocomMPl 84*
Networds - Clayton, MO - *LitMag&SmPr 83-84*
Network [of National Committee for Citizens in Education] - Columbia, MD - *ArtMar 84; WritMar 84*
Network Against Psychiatric Assault - Berkeley, CA - *BoPubDir 4, 5*
Network Communications Ltd. - Edmonton, AB, Canada - *WritMar 84*
Network Communications USA - Los Angeles, CA - *DirPRFirms 83*
Network Computing Corp. [Subs. of National Spinning Co. Inc.] - Charlotte, NC - *ADAPSOMemDir 83-84; DataDirOnSer 84*
Network Connection Inc. - Delray Beach, FL - *Tel&CabFB 84C*
Network Consultants Inc. - Chicago, IL - *DataDirSup 7-83*
Network Data Processing Corp. - Cedar Rapids, IA - *DataDirOnSer 84*
Network Development Office [of U.S. Library of Congress] - Washington, DC - *EISS 83*
Network Inc. - Berkeley, CA - *LitMarPl 83, 84*
Network Messenger [of D.B. Systems Inc.] - Arlington Heights, IL - *TeleSy&SerDir 7-83*
Network News Inc. - Washington, DC - *Ed&PubIntYB 82; LitMarPl 84*
Network of Social Security Information Services, A [of Health & Welfare Canada] - Ottawa, ON, Canada - *EISS 83*
Network Production Music Library Inc. - San Diego, CA - *AvMarPl 83*
Network Products Inc. - Research Triangle Park, NC - *DataDirSup 7-83*
Network Publications [Aff. of ETR Associates] - Santa Cruz, CA - *BoPubDir 5*
Network Records - Los Angeles, CA - *BillIntBG 83-84*
Network Services [of International Business Machines Corp.] - Greenwich, CT - *TeleSy&SerDir 2-84*
Network Strategies Inc. - Burke, VA - *TeleSy&SerDir 7-83*
Network Systems Corp. - Brooklyn Park, MN - *DataDirSup 7-83; TeleSy&SerDir 7-83*
Network Systems Inc. - Minneapolis, MN - *DirInfWP 82*
Neu, Wallace I. - Alpine, TX - *BrCabYB 84 p.D-305; Tel&CabFB 84C p.1694*
Neufeld Creative Service Inc., Bert - New York, NY - *HBIndAd&MS 82-83*
Neugebauer Press USA - Natick, MA - *BoPubDir 5*
Neuger & Associates, Edwin - Minneapolis, MN - *DirPRFirms 83*
Neuhaus Features - Riverdale, MD - *Ed&PubIntYB 82*
Neulieb Photos, Robert - Theresa, NY - *LitMarPl 83, 84; MagIndMarPl 82-83*
Neumade Products Corp. - Scarsdale, NY - *AvMarPl 83*
Neuman Inc., Susan - Miami, FL - *ArtMar 84; DirPRFirms 83*
Neumann Associates Inc., Peter H. - Marblehead, MA - *LitMarPl 83, 84*
NeuroCommunication Research Laboratories Inc. - Danbury, CT - *IntDirMarRes 83*
Neurology - New York, NY - *MagDir 84*
Neurology - Cleveland, OH - *BaconPubCkMag 84*
Neuron Music - Hollywood, CA - *AvMarPl 83*
Neurosciences Abstracts [of Cambridge Scientific Abstracts] - Bethesda, MD - *EISS 7-83 Sup*
Neurosurgery - Baltimore, MD - *MagDir 84*
Neuwirth-Koller Inc. - Denver, CO - *StaDirAdAg 2-84*
Nevada Agriculture & Livestock Journal - Sparks, NV - *BaconPubCkMag 84; MagDir 84*
Nevada Appeal - Carson City, NV - *AyerDirPub 83; Ed&PubIntYB 82*
Nevada Audio Visual Services Inc. - Las Vegas, NV - *AvMarPl 83*
Nevada Beverage Index [of Nevada Publishing Co.] - Reno, NV - *BaconPubCkMag 84; MagDir 84*
Nevada City Mountain Messenger, The - Nevada City, CA - *NewsDir 84*
Nevada County Nugget - Grass Valley, CA - *AyerDirPub 83; Ed&PubIntYB 82*
Nevada County Picayune - Prescott, AR - *AyerDirPub 83; Ed&PubIntYB 82*
Nevada Daily Mail - Nevada, MO - *Ed&PubIntYB 82; NewsDir 84*
Nevada Dept. of Economic Development - Carson City, NV - *BoPubDir 5*
Nevada Evening Journal - Nevada, IA - *BaconPubCkNews 84; Ed&PubIntYB 82; NewsDir 84*
Nevada Herald - Nevada, MO - *BaconPubCkNews 84; Ed&PubIntYB 82; NewsDir 84*
Nevada Journal - Nevada, IA - *AyerDirPub 83*
Nevada Magazine - Carson City, NV - *BaconPubCkMag 84; LitMarPl 83, 84; MagDir 84; MagIndMarPl 82-83; WritMar 84*
Nevada Mail & Herald - Nevada, MO - *BaconPubCkNews 84*
Nevada News - Nevada, MO - *BaconPubCkNews 84*
Nevada Press Clipping Service - Reno, NV - *ProGuPRSer 4*
Nevada Publications - Las Vegas, NV - *BoPubDir 4, 5*
Nevada Publications - Reno, NV - *LitMag&SmPr 83-84*
Nevada Rancher - Sparks, NV - *BaconPubCkMag 84; MagDir 84*
Nevada State Journal - Reno, NV - *AyerDirPub 83; BaconPubCkNews 84; Ed&PubIntYB 82; NewsBur 6*
Nevada State Publications Distribution Center [of Nevada State Library] - Carson City, NV - *EISS 83*
Nevada Telephone & Telegraph Co. - Tonopah, NV - *TelDir&BG 83-84*
Nevada TV Cable Co. [of Communications Services Inc.] - Nevada, MO - *BrCabYB 84; Tel&CabFB 84C*
Nevadan, The - Las Vegas, NV - *ArtMar 84; WritMar 84*
Never Ending Music - Glendora, NJ - *BillIntBG 83-84*
Never Ltd./Never Editions - London, England - *LitMag&SmPr 83-84*
Neverland Music Publishing Co. - New York, NY - *BillIntBG 83-84*
New Addition Music - *See* McCoy Music, Jim
New Age Action Group - Alexandria, VA - *BoPubDir 4, 5*
New Age-Examiner - Tunkhannock, PA - *AyerDirPub 83; Ed&PubIntYB 82*
New Age Journal - Brighton, MA - *LitMarPl 84*
New Age Magazine - Washington, DC - *MagDir 84*
New Age Magazine [of New Age Communications] - Allston, MA - *ArtMar 84; LitMarPl 83; MagIndMarPl 82-83; WritMar 84*
New Age Publishing Center - Madison, WI - *BoPubDir 4, 5*

New Age Teachings - Brookfield, MA - *BoPubDir 4, 5*
New Age Video Inc. - New York, NY - *AvMarPl 83*
New Al-Hoda - New York, NY - *Ed&PubIntYB 82; NewsDir 84*
New Alaskan - Ketchikan, AK - *WritMar 84*
New Albany Cable TV Co. - New Albany, IN - *BrCabYB 84; Tel&CabFB 84C*
New Albany Cable TV Inc. [of Heritage Communications Inc.] - New Albany, MS - *Tel&CabFB 84C*
New Albany Gazette [of Landmark Community Publishing Co.] - New Albany, MS - *AyerDirPub 83; BaconPubCkNews 84; Ed&PubIntYB 82; NewsDir 84*
New Albany Music - *See* Drake Music Group
New Albany Tribune [of Thomson Newspapers Inc.] - New Albany, IN - *BaconPubCkNews 84; NewsDir 84*
New Alchemy Institute - East Falmouth, MA - *BoPubDir 4, 5*
New America - Albuquerque, NM - *LitMag&SmPr 83-84*
New American Electronics Literature & Technical Data - Daytona Beach, FL - *MagDir 84*
New American Electronics Literature & Technical Data - Holly Hill, FL - *BaconPubCkMag 84*
New American Library [Subs. of The Times Mirror Co.] - New York, NY - *LitMarPl 83, 84; WritMar 84*
New American Theater, The - Rockford, IL - *WritMar 84*
New Art Examiner [of Chicago New Art Association] - Chicago, IL - *LitMag&SmPr 83-84*
New Arts Review - Athens, GA - *LitMag&SmPr 83-84*
New Athens Journal-Press - New Athens, IL - *BaconPubCkNews 84*
New Baltimore Anchor Bay Beacon - New Baltimore, MI - *BaconPubCkNews 84*
New Bedford/Fall River - New Bedford, MA - *WritMar 84*
New Bedford Press - Los Angeles, CA - *BoPubDir 4, 5; LitMag&SmPr 83-84*
New Bedford Standard-Times - New Bedford, MA - *LitMarPl 83; NewsDir 84*
New Benjamin Franklin House Publishing Co. Inc. - New York, NY - *LitMarPl 83, 84*
New Berkeley Press - Berkeley, CA - *LitMag&SmPr 83-84*
New Berlin Bee - New Berlin, IL - *AyerDirPub 83*
New Berlin Bee - *See* Swettman Publications
New Berlin Bee-Press - New Berlin, IL - *Ed&PubIntYB 82*
New Berlin Cablevision [of American TV & Communications Corp.] - New Berlin, WI - *BrCabYB 84; Tel&CabFB 84C*
New Berlin Citizen - New Berlin, WI - *Ed&PubIntYB 82*
New Berlin Citizen - Oak Creek, WI - *AyerDirPub 83*
New Berlin Citizen - *See* Community Newspapers Inc.
New Berlin Gazette - New Berlin, NY - *BaconPubCkNews 84; Ed&PubIntYB 82*
New Berlin NewChannels [of NewChannels Corp.] - New Berlin, NY - *BrCabYB 84*
New Berlin This Week [of Hutchison Publications Inc.] - Milwaukee, WI - *NewsDir 84*
New Bern Cable TV Inc. [of Tar River Communications Inc.] - New Bern, NC - *Tel&CabFB 84C*
New Bern Sun-Journal [of Freedom Newspapers Inc.] - New Bern, NC - *BaconPubCkNews 84; NewsDir 84*
New Bethlehem Leader-Vindicator - New Bethlehem, PA - *BaconPubCkNews 84*
New Bloomfield Perry County Times - New Bloomfield, PA - *BaconPubCkNews 84; NewsDir 84*
New Body Magazine - New York, NY - *BaconPubCkMag 84*
New Boston Bowie County News - New Boston, TX - *BaconPubCkNews 84*
New Boston Citizens Tribune - New Boston, TX - *BaconPubCkNews 84*
New Boston News-Herald - Wyandotte, MI - *AyerDirPub 83*
New Boston Review - Cambridge, MA - *MagIndMarPl 82-83*
New Braunfels Cable Communications [of Communications Services Inc.] - New Braunfels, TX - *BrCabYB 84; Tel&CabFB 84C*
New Braunfels Herald & Zeitung [of Taylor Communications Inc.] - New Braunfels, TX - *BaconPubCkNews 84; Ed&PubIntYB 82; NewsDir 84*
New Breed - Nanuet, NY - *WritMar 84*
New Breze Music - *See* Gold Street Music Co.
New Brighton Bulletin - New Brighton, MN - *Ed&PubIntYB 82*
New Brighton Bulletin - *See* Bulletin Newspapers
New Britain Herald - New Britain, CT - *NewsDir 84*
New Brooklyn [of Motivational Communications] - New York, NY - *MagDir 84; WritMar 84*
New Broom Private Press - Leicester, England - *LitMag&SmPr 83-84*
New Brunswick Home News - New Brunswick, NJ - *BaconPubCkNews 84; NewsDir 84*
New Brunswick Human Rights Commission [Aff. of Canadian Human Rights Commission] - Fredericton, NB, Canada - *BoPubDir 4, 5*
New Brunswick Museum - St. John, NB, Canada - *BoPubDir 4, 5*
New Brunswick Spokesman - New Brunswick, NJ - *BaconPubCkNews 84*
New Brunswick Sun Times - *See* Sun Newspapers
New Brunswick Telephone Co. - St. John, NB, Canada - *VideoDir 82-83*
New Buffalo Times - New Buffalo, MI - *BaconPubCkNews 84; Ed&PubIntYB 82; NewsDir 84*
New Business - Lafayette, LA - *BaconPubCkMag 84*
New Business Consultant Service, The - New Canaan, CT - *HBIndAd&MS 82-83*
New Business Report - New York, NY - *MagIndMarPl 82-83*
New California Hellenic - San Francisco, CA - *Ed&PubIntYB 82*
New Canaan Advertiser [of Hersam Publishing Co.] - New Canaan, CT - *BaconPubCkNews 84; Ed&PubIntYB 82; NewsDir 84*
New Canaan Historical Society - New Canaan, CT - *BoPubDir 4, 5*
New Canadian, The - Toronto, ON, Canada - *Ed&PubIntYB 82*
New Caney Echo - *See* Houston Community Newspapers
New Capernaum Works - Portland, OR - *LitMag&SmPr 83-84*
New Carlisle Sun - New Carlisle, OH - *Ed&PubIntYB 82; NewsDir 84*
New Carlisle Sun - *See* Bowling-Moorman Publications
New Castle Cable Communications Inc. [of Community Tele-Communications Inc.] - New Castle, IN - *BrCabYB 84; Tel&CabFB 84C*
New Castle Courier-Times - New Castle, IN - *BaconPubCkNews 84; NewsDir 84*
New Castle Gazette, The - New Castle, DE - *Ed&PubIntYB 82*
New Castle Henry County Local - New Castle, KY - *NewsDir 84*
New Castle News - New Castle, PA - *BaconPubCkNews 84; Ed&PubIntYB 82*
New Castle News-Republican - New Castle, IN - *BaconPubCkNews 84; Ed&PubIntYB 82*
New Castle Record - New Castle, VA - *AyerDirPub 83; BaconPubCkNews 84; Ed&PubIntYB 82*
New Catholic World - Ramsey, NJ - *MagIndMarPl 82-83*
New Center News [of Monday Morning Newspapers Inc.] - Detroit, MI - *NewsDir 84*
New Center News-Monday Morning Sun - Detroit, MI - *AyerDirPub 83*
New Century Education Corp. - Piscataway, NJ - *LitMarPl 84*
New Century Publishers Inc. [Subs. of New Century Education Corp.] - Piscataway, NJ - *DirMarMP 83; LitMarPl 83, 84*
New Century Publishers Inc. - New York, NY - *WritMar 84*
New Chamber Music Inc. - *See* Special Rider Music
New Channels Corp. - North Syracuse, NY - *TelAl 83, 84*
New Chatham Music - Pittsburgh, PA - *BillIntBG 83-84*
New Child Music Publishing - Kailua, HI - *BillIntBG 83-84*
New Citizen, The - Stoneboro, PA - *Ed&PubIntYB 82*
New City Press [Aff. of Focolare Movement] - Brooklyn, NY - *BoPubDir 4, 5; LitMarPl 84*
New Classics Library Inc. - Gainesville, GA - *BoPubDir 4, 5*
New Classics Software - Denville, NJ - *MicrocomMPl 84; MicrocomSwDir 1; WritMar 84*
New Cleveland Woman Journal - Cleveland, OH - *WritMar 84*
New Collage Magazine - Sarasota, FL - *LitMag&SmPr 83-84; WritMar 84*
New Collage Press - Sarasota, FL - *BoPubDir 4, 5; LitMag&SmPr 83-84*
New Colony Records - Chillicothe, OH - *BillIntBG 83-84*
New Community Projects - Allston, MA - *BoPubDir 4, 5*
New Concord Leader - New Concord, OH - *BaconPubCkNews 84*
New Covenant - Ann Arbor, MI - *MagIndMarPl 82-83*
New Creation - *See* Jo-Wee Publishing

New Criterion, The [of Foundation for Cultural Review Inc.] - New York, NY - *LitMarPl 84*
New Crusader - Chicago, IL - *AyerDirPub 83; Ed&PubIntYB 82*
New Cumberland Hancock County Courier - New Cumberland, WV - *BaconPubCkNews 84*
New Dawn - New York, NY - *MagDir 84*
New Dawn Book Committee - Coronation, AB, Canada - *BoPubDir 4 Sup, 5*
New Day Press Inc. - Cleveland, OH - *BoPubDir 4, 5*
New Departures - Stroud, England - *LitMag&SmPr 83-84*
New Dimensions in Computing Inc. - DeWitt, MI - *WhoWMicrocom 83*
New Dimensions In Computing Inc. - East Lansing, MI - *WhoWMicrocom 83*
New Dimensions Marketing Inc. - *See* NDM
New Directions for Experiential Learning - San Francisco, CA - *MagIndMarPl 82-83*
New Directions for Women - Westwood, NJ - *LitMag&SmPr 83-84*
New Directions for Young Women Inc. - Tucson, AZ - *BoPubDir 5*
New Directions Publishing Corp. - New York, NY - *LitMarPl 83, 84*
New Edinburgh Review - Edinburgh, Scotland - *LitMag&SmPr 83-84*
New Egypt Press - New Egypt, NJ - *BaconPubCkNews 84; Ed&PubIntYB 82*
New Engineer - New York, NY - *MagDir 84*
New England Advertising Associates - Rowayton, CT - *AdAge 3-28-84*
New England Advertising Week - Boston, MA - *BaconPubCkMag 84; MagDir 84*
New England Book Components Inc. - Hingham, MA - *LitMarPl 83, 84*
New England Book Sales Co. - Westport, CT - *LitMarPl 83, 84*
New England Books & Arts - Framingham, MA - *LitMarPl 83, 84*
New England Bride Weekly Engagement Lists - Sudbury, MA - *MagDir 84*
New England Builder - Johnsbury, VT - *BaconPubCkMag 84*
New England Business [of Yankee Publishing Inc.] - Boston, MA - *BaconPubCkMag 84; Folio 83; MagDir 84; MagIndMarPl 82-83*
New England Cable Rep - Boston, MA - *HomeVid&CabYB 82-83*
New England Cablevision Inc. [of American TV & Communications Corp.] - Biddeford, ME - *Tel&CabFB 84C*
New England Cablevision Inc. [Div. of Diversified Communications Inc.] - Portland, ME - *BrCabYB 84 p.D-305*
New England Cablevision Inc. [of American TV & Communications Corp.] - Sanford, ME - *Tel&CabFB 84C*
New England Cablevision Inc. - Wells, ME - *BrCabYB 84*
New England Cablevision Inc. [of Diversified Communications Inc.] - Gloucester, MA - *BrCabYB 84; Tel&CabFB 84C p.1694*
New England Cablevision Inc. [of Diversified Communications Inc.] - Rochester, NH - *BrCabYB 84; Tel&CabFB 84C*
New England Cablevision Inc. - New England, ND - *BrCabYB 84; Tel&CabFB 84C*
New England Cablevision of Massachusetts Inc. [of Diversified Communications Inc.] - Amesbury, MA - *Tel&CabFB 84C*
New England Color Lab - Lynn, MA - *AvMarPl 83*
New England Construction - Lexington, MA - *BaconPubCkMag 84*
New England Economic Review - Boston, MA - *BaconPubCkMag 84*
New England Electrical Blue Book [of Trade Register & Data] - Cohasset, MA - *MagDir 84*
New England Farmer/North East Farmer - St. Johnsbury, VT - *BaconPubCkMag 84; WritMar 84*
New England Fashion Retailer [of Larkin Publications] - Chestnut Hill, MA - *MagDir 84*
New England Fisherman - Mystic, CT - *BaconPubCkMag 84; MagDir 84*
New England Free Press - Somerville, MA - *BoPubDir 4, 5*
New England Gerontology Center [Aff. of New England Center for Continuing Education] - Durham, NH - *BoPubDir 4*
New England Grocery Magazine [of Gro-Com Group] - Barrington, RI - *BaconPubCkMag 84; MagDir 84*
New England Group, The - Portland, ME - *StaDirAdAg 2-84*
New England Herald - New England, ND - *Ed&PubIntYB 82*
New England Herald Publishers - New England, ND - *BaconPubCkNews 84*
New England Hettinger County Herald - *See* New England Herald Publishers
New England Historical & Genealogical Register - Boston, MA - *MagDir 84*
New England Interviewing Inc. - Nashua, NH - *IntDirMarRes 83*
New England Journal of Medicine [of Massachusetts Medical Society] - Boston, MA - *DirMarMP 83; DirOnDB Spring 84; MagDir 84; MagIndMarPl 82-83*
New England Journal of Medicine [of Massachusetts Medical Society] - Waltham, MA - *BaconPubCkMag 84*
New England Journal of Optometry - Boston, MA - *BaconPubCkMag 84; MagDir 84*
New England Marketing Research Corp. - Danvers, MA - *IntDirMarRes 83*
New England Mobile Book Fair Inc., The - Newton Highlands, MA - *LitMarPl 83, 84*
New England Music - *See* Marvelwood Music
New England News Service - Newton, MA - *Ed&PubIntYB 82*
New England Newsclip Agency - Framingham, MA - *BoPubDir 4, 5; LitMarPl 83, 84; ProGuPRSer 4*
New England On Line Users Group [of Digital Equipment Corp.] - Hudson, MA - *InfIndMarPl 83*
New England Outdoors - Boston, MA - *MagDir 84*
New England Press - New York, NY - *BoPubDir 4, 5; LitMag&SmPr 83-84*
New England Press Inc. - Shelburne, VT - *BoPubDir 4, 5*
New England Printer & Publisher - Salem, NH - *BaconPubCkMag 84; MagDir 84*
New England Progress Plumbing-Heating-Cooling - Framingham, MA - *BaconPubCkMag 84*
New England Purchaser - Boston, MA - *BaconPubCkMag 84; MagDir 84*
New England Real Estate Journal [of East Coast Publications Inc.] - Accord, MA - *BaconPubCkMag 84*
New England Real Estate Journal [of East Coast Publications Inc.] - Norwell, MA - *MagDir 84*
New England Record Co. - Stafford, TX - *BillIntBG 83-84*
New England Research Application Center [of University of Connecticut] - Storrs, CT - *EISS 83; InfIndMarPl 83*
New England Review & Bread Loaf Quarterly [of Kenyon Hill Publications] - Hanover, NH - *LitMag&SmPr 83-84*
New England Running [of Whetstone Publishing] - Brattleboro, VT - *ArtMar 84; LitMag&SmPr 83-84*
New England Sampler - Brooks, ME - *LitMag&SmPr 83-84*
New England Science Fiction Association Inc. - Cambridge, MA - *BoPubDir 4, 5*
New England Senior Citizen [of Prime National Publishing Corp.] - Weston, MA - *ArtMar 84; BaconPubCkMag 84; MagDir 84; WritMar 84*
New England Slide Service Ltd. - Rutland, VT - *AvMarPl 83*
New England Telephone & Telegraph Co. - Boston, MA - *TelDir&BG 83-84*
New England Truck World - Lexington, MA - *BaconPubCkMag 84*
New England Typographic Service Inc. - Bloomfield, CT - *LitMarPl 83, 84*
New England Word Processing Inc. - Woburn, MA - *DirInfWP 82*
New English Art Gallery - Rochester, NH - *BoPubDir 4, 5*
New Equipment Digest [of Penton/IPC Inc.] - Cleveland, OH - *BaconPubCkMag 84; Folio 83; MagDir 84; MagIndMarPl 82-83*
New Equipment News - Toronto, ON, Canada - *BaconPubCkMag 84*
New Equipment Reporter [of DeRoche Publications] - Westminster, CA - *BaconPubCkMag 84; MagDir 84*
New Era - Ordway, CO - *AyerDirPub 83*
New Era - Golden, IL - *AyerDirPub 83; Ed&PubIntYB 82*
New Era - Humeston, IA - *Ed&PubIntYB 82*
New Era - Mediapolis, IA - *AyerDirPub 83*
New Era - South Haven, KS - *AyerDirPub 83*
New Era - Pembina, ND - *AyerDirPub 83*
New Era - Sweet Home, OR - *AyerDirPub 83; Ed&PubIntYB 82*

New Era [of Lancaster Newspaper Inc.] - Lancaster, PA - *AyerDirPub 83; NewsDir 84*
New Era - Melita, MB, Canada - *AyerDirPub 83; Ed&PubIntYB 82*
New Era Laundry & Cleaning Lines - Huntington Beach, CA - *BaconPubCkMag 84; MagDir 84*
New Era Press - Weaverville, CA - *BoPubDir 4, 5*
New Era-Progress - Amherst, VA - *AyerDirPub 83*
New Era Ribbon & Carbon Co. - West Chester, PA - *DirInfWP 82*
New Era Technologies Inc. - Washington, DC - *InfoS 83-84*
New Era, The - Davenport, OK - *AyerDirPub 83*
New Era, The - Parker, SD - *AyerDirPub 83; Ed&PubIntYB 82*
New Era, The - Salt Lake City, UT - *WritMar 84*
New Farm - Emmaus, PA - *BaconPubCkMag 84; MagDir 84; MagIndMarPl 82-83*
New Film Co. Inc., The - Boston, MA - *AvMarPl 83*
New Florence Telephone Co. - New Florence, MO - *TelDir&BG 83-84*
New Freedom Cable TV [of GS Communications Inc.] - New Freedom, PA - *BrCabYB 84*
New Freeman, The - St. John, NB, Canada - *Ed&PubIntYB 82*
New from U.S. - Scotia, NY - *BaconPubCkMag 84*
New From USA [of Arrow Press Inc.] - Boston, MA - *WritMar 84*
New Front Films Inc. - Minneapolis, MN - *AvMarPl 83*
New Frontier - Philadelphia, PA - *LitMag&SmPr 83-84*
New Frontier Communications Ltd. - Philadelphia, PA - *LitMag&SmPr 83-84*
New German Studies - Hull, England - *LitMag&SmPr 83-84*
New Glarus Post - New Glarus, WI - *BaconPubCkNews 84; Ed&PubIntYB 82*
New Grolier Interstate Inc., The [Subs. of Grolier Inc.] - White Plains, NY - *LitMarPl 83, 84*
New Guard [of Young Americans for Freedom] - Sterling, VA - *WritMar 84*
New Hampshire Attorney General (Charitable Trusts Div.) - Concord, NH - *BoPubDir 5*
New Hampshire Audio-Vue Inc. - Milford, NH - *AvMarPl 83*
New Hampshire Educator - Concord, NH - *BaconPubCkMag 84; MagDir 84*
New Hampshire Highways - Concord, NH - *BaconPubCkMag 84; MagDir 84*
New Hampshire Historical Society - Concord, NH - *BoPubDir 4, 5; MicroMarPl 82-83*
New Hampshire Profiles [of Profiles Publishing Co.] - Concord, NH - *ArtMar 84; BaconPubCkMag 84; MagDir 84; MagIndMarPl 82-83; WritMar 84*
New Hampshire Publishing Co. - Somersworth, NH - *LitMarPl 83, 84*
New Hampshire Software - Nashua, NH - *MicrocomMPl 83, 84*
New Hampshire State Legislative Information Systems - Concord, NH - *EISS 7-83 Sup*
New Hampshire Sunday News [of Union Leader Corp.] - Manchester, NH - *AyerDirPub 83; Ed&PubIntYB 82; LitMarPl 83, 84; NewsBur 6*
New Hampton Cablevision - New Hampton, IA - *Tel&CabFB 84C*
New Hampton Economist [of New Hampton Publishing Co.] - New Hampton, IA - *Ed&PubIntYB 82; NewsDir 84*
New Hampton Economist - *See* New Hampton Publishing Co.
New Hampton Publishing Co. - New Hampton, IA - *BaconPubCkNews 84*
New Hampton Tribune [of New Hampton Publishing Co.] - New Hampton, IA - *Ed&PubIntYB 82; NewsDir 84*
New Hampton Tribune - *See* New Hampton Publishing Co.
New Harbinger Publications - Oakland, CA - *BoPubDir 4, 5*
New Harmony-Mt. Vernon Times - New Harmony, IN - *BaconPubCkNews 84*
New Harmony Times - New Harmony, IN - *Ed&PubIntYB 82*
New Haven Advocate [of New Mass Media Inc.] - New Haven, CT - *AyerDirPub 83; Ed&PubIntYB 82; NewsDir 84; WritMar 84*
New Haven Advocate - *See* Advocate Publishing
New Haven Colony Historical Society - New Haven, CT - *BoPubDir 4, 5*
New Haven Info Magazine - Hamden, CT - *WritMar 84*
New Haven Journal-Courier - New Haven, CT - *BaconPubCkNews 84*
New Haven Leader - New Haven, MO - *BaconPubCkNews 84; Ed&PubIntYB 82*
New Haven Register [of The Jackson Newspapers] - New Haven, CT - *BaconPubCkNews 84; Ed&PubIntYB 82; LitMarPl 83, 84; NewsBur 6; NewsDir 84*
New Holland Clarion - New Holland, PA - *BaconPubCkNews 84; Ed&PubIntYB 82*
New Holland Leader, The - New Holland, OH - *Ed&PubIntYB 82*
New Holstein Cable-Vision [of Wisconsin Cablevision & Radio Co. Inc.] - New Holstein, WI - *Tel&CabFB 84C*
New Holstein Reporter - New Holstein, WI - *BaconPubCkNews 84; Ed&PubIntYB 82*
New Homes Magazine - Costa Mesa, CA - *BaconPubCkMag 84*
New Hope Gazette [of Inter County Publishing Co.] - Philadelphia, PA - *NewsDir 84*
New Hope Gazette - *See* Intercounty Newspaper Group
New Hope Gazette, The - New Hope, PA - *Ed&PubIntYB 82*
New Hope News [of Delaware Valley Publishing Co. Inc.] - Lambertville, NJ - *NewsDir 84*
New Hope News Bugle - New Hope, PA - *BaconPubCkNews 84*
New Hope-Plymouth Post [of Minneapolis Post Newspapers] - Minneapolis, MN - *AyerDirPub 83; NewsDir 84*
New Hope-Plymouth Post - New Hope, MN - *Ed&PubIntYB 82*
New Hope-Plymouth Post - *See* Post Publications Inc.
New Hope Telephone Co-Op - New Hope, AL - *TelDir&BG 83-84*
New Hope Telephone Co. - New Hope, VA - *TelDir&BG 83-84*
New Horizens Communications Group Press - Culver City, CA - *BoPubDir 4, 5*
New Horizons Color Corp. - Chicago, IL - *LitMarPl 84*
New Hyde Park Advertiser - Great Neck, NY - *AyerDirPub 83*
New Hyde Park Herald Courier - Hicksville, NY - *AyerDirPub 83*
New Hyde Park Herald Courier - Williston Park, NY - *AyerDirPub 83; Ed&PubIntYB 82*
New Hyde Park Herald Courier - *See* Litmore Publications
New Hyde Park Nassau Illustrated News - New Hyde Park, NY - *BaconPubCkNews 84*
New Hyde Park Pennysaver - Jericho, NY - *AyerDirPub 83*
New Iberia Cable TV [of TCA Cable TV Inc.] - New Iberia, LA - *Tel&CabFB 84C*
New Iberia Cablevision Inc. [of Telecable Associates Inc.] - New Iberia, LA - *BrCabYB 84*
New Iberia Daily Iberian & Sunday Iberian [of Teche Publishing Co. Inc.] - New Iberia, LA - *NewsDir 84*
New Ideas Music Co. - *See* NRP Music Group
New International Review, The [of Fist & Rose Publishers Inc.] - Afula, IL - *LitMag&SmPr 83-84*
New Iowa Bystander - West Des Moines, IA - *AyerDirPub 83; Ed&PubIntYB 82*
New Issues of Corporate Securities [of Securities Data Co.] - New York, NY - *DataDirOnSer 84; DBBus 82*
New Issues of Municipal Debt [of Securities Data Co.] - New York, NY - *DataDirOnSer 84; DBBus 82*
New Jersey Afro American [of Baltimore Afro-American Newspapers] - Baltimore, MD - *NewsDir 84*
New Jersey Afro-American [of Baltimore Afro-American Newspapers] - Newark, NJ - *Ed&PubIntYB 82*
New Jersey Audio-Video Inc. - Boonton, NJ - *AvMarPl 83*
New Jersey Banker [of New Jersey Bankers Association] - Princeton, NJ - *BaconPubCkMag 84; MagDir 84*
New Jersey Bell Telephone Co. - Newark, NJ - *TelDir&BG 83-84*
New Jersey Beverage Journal [of Gem Publishers Inc.] - Union, NJ - *BaconPubCkMag 84; MagDir 84*
New Jersey Business [of New Jersey Business & Industry Association] - Newark, NJ - *BaconPubCkMag 84; MagDir 84; WritMar 84*
New Jersey Clipping Service - Livingston, NJ - *LitMarPl 83, 84*
New Jersey Dept. of Labor (Planning & Research Div.) - Trenton, NJ - *BoPubDir 4 Sup, 5*
New Jersey Dept. of Labor (State Data Center) - Trenton, NJ - *BoPubDir 4 Sup, 5*
New Jersey Education Association Review - Trenton, NJ - *LitMarPl 83, 84*

New Jersey Freie Zeitung - Kenilworth, NJ - *Ed&PubIntYB 82; NewsDir 84*
New Jersey Herald - Newton, NJ - *AyerDirPub 83; BaconPubCkNews 84; Ed&PubIntYB 82; NewsDir 84*
New Jersey Historical Commission - Trenton, NJ - *BoPubDir 4, 5*
New Jersey Historical Society [Aff. of Dept. of Education] - Newark, NJ - *BoPubDir 4, 5*
New Jersey Journal of Pharmacy [of New Jersey Pharmaceutical Association] - Trenton, NJ - *BaconPubCkMag 84; MagDir 84*
New Jersey Law Journal - Newark, NJ - *AyerDirPub 83; BaconPubCkMag 84*
New Jersey Legislative Manual - Trenton, NJ - *BoPubDir 5*
New Jersey Library Network - Trenton, NJ - *EISS 83*
New Jersey Monthly - Morristown, NJ - *ArtMar 84; BaconPubCkMag 84; DirMarMP 83; MagDir 84; WritMar 84*
New Jersey Monthly - Princeton, NJ - *MagIndMarPl 82-83*
New Jersey Motor Truck Association - Brunswick, NJ - *MagDir 84*
New Jersey Municipalities [of New Jersey State League of Municipalities] - Trenton, NJ - *BaconPubCkMag 84; MagDir 84*
New Jersey Success - Hillside, NJ - *BaconPubCkMag 84*
New Jersey Telephone Co. [Aff. of United Telecommunications Inc.] - Clinton, NJ - *TelDir&BG 83-84*
New Kauri - Tucson, AZ - *LitMag&SmPr 83-84; WritMar 84*
New Kent Quarterly, The - Kent, OH - *LitMag&SmPr 83-84*
New Kingwood Cablevision Inc. - Kingwood, TX - *BrCabYB 84*
New Knoxville Telephone Co., The - New Knoxville, OH - *TelDir&BG 83-84*
New Korea - Los Angeles, CA - *Ed&PubIntYB 82; NewsDir 84*
New Korea Times - Toronto, ON, Canada - *Ed&PubIntYB 82*
New Laurel Review, The - New Orleans, LA - *LitMag&SmPr 83-84*
New Leader, The - Spencer, MA - *AyerDirPub 83; Ed&PubIntYB 82; NewsDir 84*
New Leader, The - New York, NY - *LitMarPl 83, 84*
New Leaf Distributing Co. - Atlanta, GA - *BoPubDir 4 Sup, 5*
New Leaf Press Inc. - Harrison, AR - *BillIntBG 83-84; BoPubDir 4, 5; WritMar 84*
New Letters - Kansas City, MO - *ArtMar 84; LitMag&SmPr 83-84*
New Lexington Perry County Tribune - New Lexington, OH - *BaconPubCkNews 84*
New Library Scene - Accord, MA - *BaconPubCkMag 84; MagDir 84*
New Life Foundation - Boulder City, NV - *BoPubDir 4, 5*
New Life Records [Div. of National Music Service Inc.] - Spokane, WA - *BillIntBG 83-84*
New Lifestyle Publishing - North Hollywood, CA - *BoPubDir 4, 5*
New Line Cinema Corp. - New York, NY - *AvMarPl 83*
New Line Presentations - New York, NY - *LitMarPl 83, 84*
New Lisbon Telephone Co. Inc. - New Lisbon, IN - *TelDir&BG 83-84*
New Literature & Ideology [of Norman Bethune Institute] - Toronto, ON, Canada - *LitMag&SmPr 83-84*
New London County Historical Society - New London, CT - *BoPubDir 4, 5*
New London Day - New London, CT - *BaconPubCkNews 84*
New London Day & Sun - New London, CT - *NewsDir 84*
New London Journal - New London, IA - *BaconPubCkNews 84; Ed&PubIntYB 82*
New London Press Star - New London, WI - *BaconPubCkNews 84; NewsDir 84*
New London Ralls County Herald Record - New London, MO - *BaconPubCkNews 84*
New London Record - New London, OH - *BaconPubCkNews 84; Ed&PubIntYB 82*
New London Shoppers Revue - New London, WI - *AyerDirPub 83*
New London Spicer Times - New London, MN - *AyerDirPub 83; BaconPubCkNews 84; Ed&PubIntYB 82*
New Lyons Recorder, The - Lyons, CO - *Ed&PubIntYB 82*
New Madrid Record - New Madrid, MO - *BaconPubCkNews 84*
New Madrid Weekly Record, The - New Madrid, MO - *Ed&PubIntYB 82*
New Magazine Review - North Las Vegas, NV - *LitMag&SmPr 83-84; MagIndMarPl 82-83*
New Market Cablevision - New Market, IN - *BrCabYB 84*
New Martinsville Wetzel Chronicle - New Martinsville, WV - *BaconPubCkNews 84*
New Martinsville Wetzel-Tyler Counties Green Tab [of Moundsville Marshall County Green Tab] - Moundsville, WV - *NewsDir 84*
N.E.W. Media Cablevision [of American TV & Communications Corp.] - Green Bay, WI - *BrCabYB 84; Tel&CabFB 84C*
New Media Graphics Corp. - Cambridge, MA - *MicrocomMPl 84*
New Medical Publishers - Montreal, PQ, Canada - *BoPubDir 4, 5*
New Merritt Enterprises Inc. - *See* Nicholson-Muir Productions Inc.
New Methods - San Francisco, CA - *BaconPubCkMag 84*
New Mexican - Santa Fe, NM - *AyerDirPub 83; Ed&PubIntYB 82; LitMarPl 83, 84*
New Mexico Beverage Analyst [of Bevan Inc.] - Denver, CO - *BaconPubCkMag 84; MagDir 84*
New Mexico Business Journal [of Southwest Publications Inc.] - Albuquerque, NM - *BaconPubCkMag 84; MagDir 84; WritMar 84*
New Mexico Daily Lobo [of UNM Student Publications Board] - Albuquerque, NM - *NewsDir 84*
New Mexico Farm & Ranch - Las Cruces, NM - *BaconPubCkMag 84; MagDir 84*
New Mexico Independent, The - Albuquerque, NM - *AyerDirPub 83; Ed&PubIntYB 82; NewsDir 84*
New Mexico Magazine - Santa Fe, NM - *ArtMar 84; BaconPubCkMag 84; LitMarPl 83, 84; MagDir 84; MagIndMarPl 82-83; WritMar 84*
New Mexico Media Co. - Santa Fe, NM - *Tel&CabFB 84C*
New Mexico Natural Resources Information System [of New Mexico State Dept. of Natural Resources] - Santa Fe, NM - *EISS 7-83 Sup*
New Mexico Philatelic Association Inc. - Los Alamos, NM - *BoPubDir 4, 5*
New Mexico Press Clipping Bureau - Albuquerque, NM - *ProGuPRSer 4*
New Mexico Professional Engineer - Albuquerque, NM - *BaconPubCkMag 84; MagDir 84*
New Mexico Santa Fe Reporter - Santa Fe, NM - *BaconPubCkNews 84*
New Mexico Spectrum - Albuquerque, NM - *IntDirMarRes 83*
New Mexico State Records Center & Archives - Santa Fe, NM - *MicroMarPl 82-83*
New Mexico State University (Studies in Latin American Popular Culture) - Las Cruces, NM - *BoPubDir 5*
New Mexico Stockman - Albuquerque, NM - *BaconPubCkMag 84; MagDir 84*
New Miami Entertainment Co. - Coconut Grove, FL - *BillIntBG 83-84*
New Milford Cablevision - New Milford, CT - *BrCabYB 84; Tel&CabFB 84C*
New Milford Times [of Housatonic Valley Publishing Co.] - New Milford, CT - *Ed&PubIntYB 82; NewsDir 84*
New Milford Times - *See* Housatonic Valley Publishing Co.
New Moon - Madison, WI - *LitMag&SmPr 83-84*
New Moon Communications Inc. - Stamford, CT - *BoPubDir 4, 5*
New Moon/Humble Hills Press - Kalamazoo, MI - *BoPubDir 4, 5*
New Nativity Press [Aff. of Birth at Home League] - Leawood, KS - *BoPubDir 4 Sup, 5*
New Nurse - Plattsburgh, NY - *BoPubDir 4, 5*
New Observer, The [of Black Media Inc.] - Washington, DC - *AyerDirPub 83; Ed&PubIntYB 82; NewsDir 84*
New Observer, The - Philadelphia, PA - *Ed&PubIntYB 82*
New Oregon Review [of Nor Publications] - Hillsboro, OR - *LitMag&SmPr 83-84*
New Orient Media - Dundee, IL - *ArtMar 84; AvMarPl 83; WritMar 84*
New Orleans Black Data - New Orleans, LA - *BaconPubCkNews 84*
New Orleans Clarion Herald - New Orleans, LA - *NewsDir 84*
New Orleans Daily Journal of Commerce [of Guide Publishing Co. Inc.] - Gretna, LA - *NewsDir 84*
New Orleans Guide, The - New Orleans, LA - *NewsDir 84*

New Orleans Louisiana Weekly - New Orleans, LA - *BaconPubCkNews 84; NewsDir 84*
New Orleans Magazine [of ARC Publishing Co.] - New Orleans, LA - *ArtMar 84; BaconPubCkMag 84; MagDir 84; WritMar 84*
New Orleans Poetry Journal Press Inc. - New Orleans, LA - *BoPubDir 4, 5*
New Orleans Record - New Orleans, LA - *AyerDirPub 83; NewsDir 84*
New Orleans Review - New Orleans, LA - *ArtMar 84; LitMag&SmPr 83-84; WritMar 84*
New Orleans Video Access Center Inc. - New Orleans, LA - *AvMarPl 83*
New Outlook Music Inc. - Philadelphia, PA - *BillIntBG 83-84*
New Outlook Publishers & Distributors - New York, NY - *BoPubDir 4, 5*
New Oxford Cable [of Telecable Communications Corp.] - New Oxford, PA - *BrCabYB 84; Tel&CabFB 84C*
New Pages: News & Reviews of the Progressive Booktrade [of New Pages Press] - Grand Blanc, MI - *LitMag&SmPr 83-84; WritMar 84*
New Pages Press - Grand Blanc, MI - *BoPubDir 4, 5; LitMag&SmPr 83-84*
New Paltz Cablevision Inc. [of Cablevision Industries Inc.] - New Paltz, NY - *BrCabYB 84*
New Paltz Huguenot Herald - *See* Ulster Offset Corp.
New Paltz News - New Paltz, NY - *Ed&PubIntYB 82*
New Paltz News - *See* Hudson Valley Newspapers Inc.
New Paris Telephone Inc. - New Paris, IN - *TelDir&BG 83-84*
New Pathway, The - Toronto, ON, Canada - *AyerDirPub 83*
New Petroleum Retailer, The - Barrington, IL - *BaconPubCkMag 84*
New Philadelphia Times-Reporter [of Horvitz Newspapers] - New Philadelphia, OH - *BaconPubCkNews 84; NewsDir 84*
New Physician, The - Chantilly, VA - *MagIndMarPl 82-83*
New Physician, The - Reston, VA - *ArtMar 84; BaconPubCkMag 84; MagDir 84; WritMar 84*
New Pickup Truck Buyer Marketing & Media Study [of Interactive Market Systems Inc.] - Westlake Village, CA - *DirOnDB Spring 84*
New Pickup Truck Buyer Marketing & Media Study [of Interactive Market Systems Inc.] - New York, NY - *DataDirOnSer 84*
New Pittsburgh Courier - Pittsburgh, PA - *AyerDirPub 83; Ed&PubIntYB 82*
New Pittsburgh Publications - Pittsburgh, PA - *BoPubDir 5*
New Plays Inc. - Rowayton, CT - *BoPubDir 4, 5*
New Playwrights' Theatre of Washington, The - Washington, DC - *WritMar 84*
New Poetry [of Prism Books] - Sydney, Australia - *LitMag&SmPr 83-84*
New Poets Series - Baltimore, MD - *BoPubDir 4, 5; LitMag&SmPr 83-84*
New Port Richey Suncoast News [of Sunbelt Publishing Co.] - New Port Richey, FL - *NewsDir 84*
New Port Richey West Pasco Press - New Port Richey, FL - *BaconPubCkNews 84*
New Prague Times - New Prague, MN - *AyerDirPub 83; BaconPubCkNews 84; Ed&PubIntYB 82; NewsDir 84*
New Press - Canada - *BoPubDir 4, 5*
New Price Report [of Hearst Corp.] - New York, NY - *MagDir 84*
New Prince Georges Post, The - Hyattsville, MD - *Ed&PubIntYB 82*
New Product Insights - Overland Park, KS - *AdAge 3-28-84; HBIndAd&MS 82-83*
New Product News - Sandy, UT - *MagDir 84*
New Products Resources Inc. - New York, NY - *HBIndAd&MS 82-83*
New Progress - Homestead, PA - *AyerDirPub 83*
New Providence Berkeley Heights Dispatch [of Herald Publications] - New Providence, NJ - *BaconPubCkNews 84; NewsDir 84*
New Puritan Library Inc. - Fletcher, NC - *BoPubDir 4, 5*
New Readers Press [Div. of Laubach Literacy International] - Syracuse, NY - *LitMarPl 83, 84; WritMar 84*
New Realities - San Francisco, CA - *ArtMar 84; MagIndMarPl 82-83; WritMar 84*
New Records Group - Beverly Hills, CA - *BillIntBG 83-84*
New Renaissance, The - Arlington, MA - *LitMag&SmPr 83-84; WritMar 84*
New Renaissance Workshop - Ojai, CA - *BoPubDir 4, 5*
New Republic - Washington, DC - *ArtMar 84; BaconPubCkMag 84; LitMarPl 83, 84; MagDir 84; MagIndMarPl 82-83; WritMar 84*
New Republic Chinese Daily News - Vancouver, BC, Canada - *Ed&PubIntYB 82*
New Research Publications Inc. - Greenvale, NY - *BoPubDir 5; LitMag&SmPr 83-84*
New Research Traveler & Conventioneer, The - Chicago, IL - *MagIndMarPl 82-83*
New Review Books - Toronto, ON, Canada - *BoPubDir 4, 5*
New Review, The - Milwaukie, OR - *AyerDirPub 83; Ed&PubIntYB 82*
New Richland Star - New Richland, MN - *BaconPubCkNews 84; Ed&PubIntYB 82*
New Richmond News - New Richmond, WI - *BaconPubCkNews 84; NewsDir 84*
New Rivers Press Inc. - St. Paul, MN - *BoPubDir 4, 5; LitMag&SmPr 83-84*
New Rochelle Standard-Star [of Westchester Rockland Newspapers Inc.] - New Rochelle, NY - *NewsDir 84*
New Rochelle Standard-Star - White Plains, NY - *Ed&PubIntYB 82*
New Rochelle Standard-Star - *See* Westchester-Rockland Newspapers
New Rockford Transcript - New Rockford, ND - *BaconPubCkNews 84; Ed&PubIntYB 82*
New Roots - Greenfield, MA - *MagIndMarPl 82-83*
New Salem Journal - New Salem, ND - *BaconPubCkNews 84; Ed&PubIntYB 82*
New Science Publications - London, England - *MicroMarPl 82-83*
New Seed Press - Berkeley, CA - *BoPubDir 4, 5; LitMag&SmPr 83-84*
New Sharon Star - New Sharon, IA - *Ed&PubIntYB 82*
New Sharon Star - *See* Quad County Newspapers
New Shelter [of Rodale Press] - Emmaus, PA - *BaconPubCkMag 84; Folio 83; WritMar 84*
New Sibylline Books Inc. - New York, NY - *BoPubDir 4, 5*
New Smyrna Beach News & Observer - New Smyrna Beach, FL - *BaconPubCkNews 84; NewsDir 84*
New Smyrna Beach Pelican - New Smyrna Beach, FL - *Ed&PubIntYB 82*
New Smyrna Beach Volusia - New Smyrna Beach, FL - *BaconPubCkNews 84*
New Socialist [of New Social Publications/New Socialist Committee] - Denver, CO - *BoPubDir 4, 5; WritMar 84*
New Society Publishers [Aff. of Movement for a New Society] - Philadelphia, PA - *BoPubDir 4, 5; LitMag&SmPr 83-84; LitMarPl 84*
New South Co. - Los Angeles, CA - *BoPubDir 4, 5; LitMag&SmPr 83-84*
New South Magazine, The [of New South Profile Inc.] - Lafayette, LA - *WritMar 84*
New South Radio Network - Meridian, MS - *BrCabYB 84*
New Southern Literary Messenger, The [of The Airplane Press] - Richmond, VA - *LitMag&SmPr 83-84; WritMar 84*
New Spring Publishing - *See* Brentwood Publishing Group
New Star Books Ltd. - Vancouver, BC, Canada - *BoPubDir 4; LitMarPl 83, 84*
New Tandem Music - *See* Duce Music
New Tazewell & Tazewell Observer Inc. - New Tazewell, TN - *NewsDir 84*
New Texas - Austin, TX - *BaconPubCkMag 84*
New Thought - Scottsdale, AZ - *LitMag&SmPr 83-84*
New Times - Rock Island, IL - *LitMag&SmPr 83-84*
New Times Magazine - New York, NY - *MagDir 84*
New Times Music - *See* Open End Music
New Town Music - *See* Croma Music Co. Inc.
New Town News - New Town, ND - *BaconPubCkNews 84; Ed&PubIntYB 82*
New Traditions Publications - Huntington, MA - *LitMag&SmPr 83-84*
New Trend Publishers - Toronto, ON, Canada - *BoPubDir 5; LitMarPl 84*

New Trier CATV [of Matrix Enterprises Inc.] - Wilmette, IL - *BrCabYB 84*
New Ulm Enterprise - New Ulm, TX - *Ed&PubIntYB 82*
New Ulm Enterprise - *See* New Ulm Enterprise Publishers
New Ulm Enterprise Publishers - New Ulm, TX - *BaconPubCkNews 84*
New Ulm Rural Telephone Co. - New Ulm, MN - *TelDir&BG 83-84*
New Ulm TV Signal Co. - New Ulm, MN - *BrCabYB 84; Tel&CabFB 84C*
New Unionist - Minneapolis, MN - *LitMag&SmPr 83-84*
New University [of ASUCI] - Irvine, CA - *NewsDir 84*
New University Press - Chicago, IL - *MicroMarPl 82-83*
New Valley Music Press - Northampton, MA - *BillIntBG 83-84*
New Victoria Publishers - Lebanon, NH - *BoPubDir 4, 5; LitMag&SmPr 83-84*
New Virginia Review - Richmond, VA - *LitMag&SmPr 83-84*
New Virginian, The - New Virginia, IA - *Ed&PubIntYB 82*
New Vision Cable Co. - New Martinsville, WV - *BrCabYB 84; Tel&CabFB 84C*
New Vision Publications - Homewood, IL - *BoPubDir 4 Sup, 5*
New Visions Inc. - Aspen, CO - *Tel&CabFB 84C*
New Vista Press - Sebastopol, CA - *BoPubDir 4, 5*
New Voices [of Astra Publications] - Methuen, MA - *LitMag&SmPr 83-84; WritMar 84*
New Washington Herald - New Washington, OH - *BaconPubCkNews 84; Ed&PubIntYB 82*
New West Agency - Denver, CO - *LitMarPl 83, 84; MagIndMarPl 82-83*
New Westminster Today - New Westminster, BC, Canada - *AyerDirPub 83; Ed&PubIntYB 82*
New Wilmington Borough Cable TV - New Wilmington, PA - *Tel&CabFB 84C*
New Wilmington Globe - New Wilmington, PA - *BaconPubCkNews 84; Ed&PubIntYB 82*
New Windsor Telephone Co. - New Windsor, IL - *TelDir&BG 83-84*
New Wine Productions - Lomita, CA - *BillIntBG 83-84*
New Woman - Ft. Lauderdale, FL - *MagDir 84*
New Woman - Palm Beach, FL - *BaconPubCkMag 84; Folio 83; MagIndMarPl 82-83; WritMar 84*
New Woman Press - Sunny Valley, OR - *BoPubDir 5*
New Woman Press - Wolf Creek, OR - *BoPubDir 4; LitMag&SmPr 83-84*
New Women's Times - Rochester, NY - *LitMag&SmPr 83-84; MagIndMarPl 82-83*
New World Books - Kensington, MD - *BoPubDir 4, 5*
New World Outlook - New York, NY - *MagIndMarPl 82-83; WritMar 84*
New World Press - New York, NY - *BoPubDir 4, 5*
New World Records [Div. of Recorded Anthology of American Music] - New York, NY - *BillIntBG 83-84*
New World Review - New York, NY - *MagIndMarPl 82-83*
New Worlds - Newport Beach, CA - *MagDir 84*
New Worlds Cable TV Inc. - Rockdale, TX - *BrCabYB 84*
New Worlds Unltd. - Saddle Brook, NJ - *BoPubDir 4, 5; LitMag&SmPr 83-84; WritMar 84*
New York Academy of Sciences - New York, NY - *BoPubDir 4, 5; LitMarPl 84*
New York Affairs [of New York University] - New York, NY - *WritMar 84*
New York Alive - Albany, NY - *BaconPubCkMag 84*
New York Amsterdam News - New York, NY - *BaconPubCkNews 84; Ed&PubIntYB 82*
New York Antique Almanac, The [of The New York Eye Publishing Co. Inc.] - Lawrence, NY - *BaconPubCkMag 84; WritMar 84*
New York Apparel News - New York, NY - *BaconPubCkMag 84*
New York Astrology Center [Div. of ASI Inc.] - New York, NY - *LitMarPl 83, 84*
New York Aufbau [of New World Club Inc.] - New York, NY - *NewsDir 84*
New York Auto Repair News [of Van Allen Publishing Co.] - Hicksville, NY - *BaconPubCkMag 84; MagDir 84*
New York Big Red - New York, NY - *BaconPubCkNews 84*
New York Black American - New York, NY - *BaconPubCkNews 84*
New York Botanical Garden - Bronx, NY - *BoPubDir 4, 5*
New York Bronx Co-op City News - *See* Hagedorn Communications
New York Bronx Co-op Weekender - *See* Hagedorn Communications
New York Bronx News - *See* Hagedorn Communications
New York Bronx Press-Review - New York, NY - *BaconPubCkNews 84*
New York Chelsea Clinton News - New York, NY - *BaconPubCkNews 84; NewsDir 84*
New York Chief-Leader - New York, NY - *BaconPubCkNews 84*
New York City Board of Education (Curriculum & Instruction Div.) - Brooklyn, NY - *BoPubDir 4 Sup, 5*
New York City Commission on the Status of Women - New York, NY - *BoPubDir 5*
New York City Data Bank - Washington, DC - *DirOnDB Spring 84*
New York City Model Data Bank [of Data Resources Inc.] - Lexington, MA - *DataDirOnSer 84; DBBus 82*
New York Civil Service Leader - New York, NY - *NewsDir 84*
New York Coding - Flushing, NY - *IntDirMarRes 83*
New York Communications Inc. - Bryn Mawr, PA - *BrCabYB 84*
New York Communications Inc. - Upper Darby, PA - *ArtMar 84*
New York Conference Center - New York, NY - *IntDirMarRes 83*
New York Construction News - New York, NY - *BaconPubCkMag 84; MagDir 84*
New York Consultants Group Inc., The - New York, NY - *HBIndAd&MS 82-83*
New York Crop Reporting Service [Aff. of Dept. of Agriculture & Markets] - Albany, NY - *BoPubDir 5*
New York Daily News - New York, NY - *AyerDirPub 83; BaconPubCkNews 84; Ed&PubIntYB 82; LitMarPl 83, 84*
New York Directory Co. Inc. - Huntington, NY - *BoPubDir 4 Sup, 5*
New York Downtown Herald - *See* Community Herald
New York Graphic Society Books [Div. of Little, Brown & Co.] - Boston, MA - *LitMarPl 83, 84*
New York Graphic Society Ltd. - Greenwich, CT - *ArtMar 84*
New York Guardian - New York, NY - *BaconPubCkNews 84*
New York Guide - Riverdale, NY - *DirOnDB Spring 84*
New York Heights Inwood - New York, NY - *NewsDir 84*
New York Historical Society, The - New York, NY - *AvMarPl 83*
New York Holstein News - Sandy Creek, NY - *BaconPubCkMag 84; MagDir 84*
New York India Abroad - New York, NY - *NewsDir 84*
New York International Bible Society - New York, NY - *Tel&CabFB 84C*
New York International Records - Bronx, NY - *BillIntBG 83-84*
New York Jewish Daily Forward - New York, NY - *NewsDir 84*
New York Journal of Commerce, The [of Knight-Ridder Newspapers] - New York, NY - *NewsDir 84*
New York Journal of Dentistry - New York, NY - *BaconPubCkMag 84; MagDir 84*
New York Labor News [Aff. of Socialist Labor Party] - Palo Alto, CA - *BoPubDir 4, 5*
New York Law Journal - New York, NY - *BaconPubCkMag 84; Ed&PubIntYB 82; LitMarPl 83; MagDir 84; MagIndMarPl 82-83; NewsDir 84*
New York Law Publishing Co. - New York, NY - *MicroMarPl 82-83*
New York Literary Forum - New York, NY - *BoPubDir 4, 5; LitMarPl 83, 84; MagDir 84*
New York-Long Island Courier - Hempstead, NY - *Ed&PubIntYB 82*
New York Magazine [of News Group Publications Inc.] - New York, NY - *ArtMar 84; BaconPubCkMag 84; DirMarMP 83; Folio 83; LitMarPl 83, 84; MagDir 84; MagIndMarPl 82-83; WritMar 84*
New York Mall Research - Staten Island, NY - *IntDirMarRes 83*
New York Metro News - *See* Home Reporter & Sunset News Inc.
New York Metropolitan Reference & Research Library Agency - New York, NY - *EISS 83; InfIndMarPl 83*
New York Microform Journal for Medical Archives, The - New York, NY - *MicroMarPl 82-83*

New York Mid-Hudson Transportation Corp. - Carlstadt, NJ - *LitMarPl 83*
New York Militant - New York, NY - *BaconPubCkNews 84*
New York Mills Herald - New York Mills, MN - *BaconPubCkNews 84; Ed&PubIntYB 82*
New York Motorist - New York, NY - *BaconPubCkMag 84; MagDir 84*
New York Native - New York, NY - *MagIndMarPl 82-83*
New York News [of Chicago Tribune Co.] - New York, NY - *NewsBur 6; NewsDir 84*
New York News for Kids - New York, NY - *MagDir 84*
New York Nichibei - New York, NY - *AyerDirPub 83; Ed&PubIntYB 82*
New York Opinion Centers - Middletown, NY - *IntDirMarRes 83*
New York Our Town - New York, NY - *BaconPubCkNews 84*
New York Outdoor Guide - Rochester, NY - *BoPubDir 4 Sup, 5*
New York Parkchester News - *See* Hagedorn Communications
New York Photo District News - New York, NY - *WritMar 84*
New York Poets Cooperative - Bronx, NY - *BoPubDir 4, 5*
New York Post - New York, NY - *BaconPubCkNews 84; Ed&PubIntYB 82; LitMarPl 83, 84; NewsBur 6; NewsDir 84*
New York Press Photographers Association - New York, NY - *Ed&PubIntYB 82*
New York Production Manual Inc. - New York, NY - *BoPubDir 4, 5*
New York Professional Engineer - Albany, NY - *BaconPubCkMag 84; MagDir 84*
New York Public Library - New York, NY - *BoPubDir 4, 5*
New York Public Library (Billy Rose Theatre Collection) - New York, NY - *AvMarPl 83*
New York Public Library (Photographic Service) - New York, NY - *LitMarPl 83, 84; MicroMarPl 82-83*
New York Recorder - Brooklyn, NY - *AyerDirPub 83; Ed&PubIntYB 82*
New York Regional Economic Database [of Rapidata Inc.] - Fairfield, NJ - *DataDirOnSer 84*
New York Restaurant Guide [of Applebites] - Riverdale, NY - *DataDirOnSer 84; DirOnDB Spring 84*
New York Review of Books - New York, NY - *MagDir 84; MagIndMarPl 82-83*
New York Soho Weekly News, The - New York, NY - *NewsDir 84*
New York State (Budget Div.) - Albany, NY - *BoPubDir 5*
New York State AFL-CIO News - Albany, NY - *NewsDir 84*
New York State Data Center [of New York State Dept. of Commerce] - Albany, NY - *EISS 83*
New York State Dental Journal - New York, NY - *BaconPubCkMag 84; MagDir 84*
New York State Historical Association - Cooperstown, NY - *BoPubDir 4, 5*
New York State Interlibrary Loan Program [of New York State Library] - Albany, NY - *EISS 83*
New York State Journal of Medicine - Lake Success, NY - *BaconPubCkMag 84*
New York State Journal of Medicine - New York, NY - *MagIndMarPl 82-83*
New York State Pharmacist [of Pharmaceutical Society of the State of New York] - Elmont, NY - *BaconPubCkMag 84*
New York State Pharmacist [of Pharmaceutical Society of the State of New York] - White Plains, NY - *MagDir 84*
New York State Science Service [Aff. of New York State Education Dept.] - Albany, NY - *BoPubDir 4 Sup, 5*
New York State Small Press Association [of The Montemora Foundation] - Nyack, NY - *BoPubDir 4 Sup, 5; LitMarPl 83*
New York Teacher - New York, NY - *BaconPubCkMag 84; NewsDir 84*
New York Teacher, The - Albany, NY - *MagDir 84*
New York Telephone Co. - New York, NY - *TelDir&BG 83-84*
New York Times [of New York Times Information Service] - Parsippany, NJ - *OnBibDB 3*
New York Times - New York, NY - *AdAge 6-28-84; BaconPubCkNews 84; BrCabYB 84; Ed&PubIntYB 82; HomeVid&CabYB 82-83; KnowInd 83; LitMarPl 83, 84; NewsBur 6; NewsDir 84; Tel&CabFB 84S*
New York Times Book Review - New York, NY - *ArtMar 84*
New York Times Consumer Library [of Source Telecomputing Corp.] - McLean, VA - *DataDirOnSer 84*
New York Times Full Text [of New York Times Information Service] - Parsippany, NJ - *CompReadDB 82*
New York Times Information Bank, The - *See* New York Times Information Service
New York Times Information Service - Parsippany, NJ - *CompReadDB 82; DataDirOnSer 84; EISS 83; InfIndMarPl 83; InfoS 83-84; LitMarPl 83; MicroMarPl 82-83*
New York Times Magazine - New York, NY - *Folio 83; LitMarPl 83, 84; MagIndMarPl 82-83*
New York Times News Service - Newton, MA - *Ed&PubIntYB 82*
New York Times News Service - New York, NY - *BaconPubCkNews 84; Ed&PubIntYB 82*
New York Times-Online [of New York Times Information Service Inc.] - Parsippany, NJ - *EISS 83*
New York Times-Online - New York, NY - *DirOnDB Spring 84*
New York Times-Online [of Mead Data Central] - Dayton, OH - *DataDirOnSer 84*
New York Times Syndication Sales Corp. - New York, NY - *LitMarPl 83, 84; MagIndMarPl 82-83*
New York Times Syndication Sales Corp. (Special Features) - New York, NY - *Ed&PubIntYB 82*
New York Today - Forest Hills, NY - *Ed&PubIntYB 82; MagDir 84*
New York Town & Village - New York, NY - *BaconPubCkNews 84*
New York Tribune - New York, NY - *BaconPubCkNews 84*
New York University (Film Library) - New York, NY - *AvMarPl 83*
New York University (Graduate School of Business Administration) - New York, NY - *BoPubDir 5*
New York University (Institute of Judicial Administration) - New York, NY - *BoPubDir 4, 5*
New York University (School of the Arts) - New York, NY - *InterCabHB 3*
New York University Press - New York, NY - *LitMarPl 83, 84; WritMar 84*
New York Video - New York, NY - *AvMarPl 83*
New York Village Voice - New York, NY - *BaconPubCkNews 84*
New York Villager - New York, NY - *BaconPubCkNews 84*
New York Voice, The - Flushing, NY - *AyerDirPub 83*
New York Voice, The - Queens, NY - *Ed&PubIntYB 82*
New York West Side Herald - *See* Community Herald
New York Westsider - New York, NY - *BaconPubCkNews 84*
New York Zoetrope - New York, NY - *LitMarPl 83, 84; WritMar 84*
New York Zoological Society (Photo Services Dept.) - Bronx, NY - *MagIndMarPl 82-83*
New Yorker - New York, NY - *ArtMar 84; BaconPubCkMag 84; Folio 83; KnowInd 83; LitMarPl 83, 84; MagDir 84; MagIndMarPl 82-83; WritMar 84*
New Yorker Films - New York, NY - *AvMarPl 83*
New Yorker Staats-Zeitung und Herold - Long Island City, NY - *AyerDirPub 83; NewsDir 84*
New Yorkers Anonymous - Coral Gables, FL - *StaDirAdAg 2-84*
New Yorkin Uutiset - Brooklyn, NY - *Ed&PubIntYB 82; NewsDir 84*
New Youth Connections - New York, NY - *BaconPubCkMag 84*
New Zealand Dept. of Scientific & Industrial Research (Science Information Div.) - Wellington, New Zealand - *InfIndMarPl 83*
New Zealand Dept. of Statistics - Wellington, New Zealand - *InfIndMarPl 83*
New Zealand Tymnet/Telenet Node - *See* OASIS
New Zoo Revue - Beverly Hills, CA - *Tel&CabFB 84C*
Newark Advocate [of Catholic Archdiocese of Newark] - East Orange, NJ - *NewsDir 84*
Newark Advocate [of Catholic Archdiocese of Newark] - Newark, OH - *BaconPubCkNews 84*
Newark Courier Gazette - Newark, NY - *BaconPubCkNews 84*
Newark/Essex Greater News - Newark, NJ - *Ed&PubIntYB 82*
Newark/Essex-Suburban Greater News - Newark, NJ - *BaconPubCkNews 84*
Newark Licking Advertiser - Newark, OH - *AyerDirPub 83*
Newark Licking Countian - *See* Ashbrook Publishing
Newark Museum - Newark, NJ - *BoPubDir 4, 5*

Newark New Jersey Afro-American - East Orange, NJ - *BaconPubCkNews 84*
Newark Star Ledger [of Newhouse Publications] - Newark, NJ - *BaconPubCkNews 84; LitMarPl 83; NewsDir 84*
Newark Telephone Co., The [Aff. of Mid-Continent Telephone Corp.] - Newark, OH - *TelDir&BG 83-84*
Newark Weekly Post - Newark, DE - *NewsDir 84*
Newbag Music Co. - Hanover, VA - *BillIntBG 83-84*
Newberg Graphic - Newberg, OR - *BaconPubCkNews 84; Ed&PubIntYB 82; NewsDir 84*
Newbern Dyer County Tennessean - Newbern, TN - *BaconPubCkNews 84*
Newberry Cable [of Duncannon Area Cable Co.] - Duncannon, PA - *Tel&CabFB 84C*
Newberry Cable [of Pencor Services Inc.] - Newberrytown, PA - *Tel&CabFB 84C*
Newberry Investments Ltd. - Calgary, AB, Canada - *BoPubDir 4, 5*
Newberry News - Newberry, MI - *BaconPubCkNews 84; Ed&PubIntYB 82*
Newberry Observer & Herald News, The - Newberry, SC - *BaconPubCkNews 84; Ed&PubIntYB 82*
Newberry Observer, The [of The State Record Co.] - Newberry, SC - *NewsDir 84*
Newburg Cable TV System - Newburg, MO - *BrCabYB 84; Tel&CabFB 84C*
Newburgh-Beacon News - Newburgh, NY - *Ed&PubIntYB 82*
Newburgh Evening News [of Thomson Newspapers Inc.] - Newburgh, NY - *BaconPubCkNews 84; NewsDir 84*
Newburgh Register - Newburgh, IN - *AyerDirPub 83; BaconPubCkNews 84; Ed&PubIntYB 82; NewsDir 84*
Newbury Associates - Boston, MA - *LitMarPl 83; MagIndMarPl 82-83*
Newbury Books - Topsfield, MA - *BoPubDir 4 Sup, 5*
Newbury House Publishers - Rowley, MA - *ArtMar 84; LitMarPl 83, 84*
Newburyport News [of Essex County Newspapers Inc.] - Newburyport, MA - *BaconPubCkNews 84; LitMarPl 83, 84; NewsDir 84*
Newby Book Room - Jamestown, NC - *BoPubDir 4, 5*
Newcastle Cable TV - Newcastle, WY - *BrCabYB 84; Tel&CabFB 84C*
Newcastle News - Newcastle, PA - *NewsDir 84*
Newcastle News Letter-Journal - Newcastle, WY - *BaconPubCkNews 84; Ed&PubIntYB 82*
Newcastle Publishing Co. Inc. - North Hollywood, CA - *LitMarPl 83, 84; WritMar 84*
Newcastle Reporter - Newcastle, ON, Canada - *Ed&PubIntYB 82*
Newchannels Cable TV - Canonsburg, PA - *BrCabYB 84*
NewChannels Corp. [of Newhouse Broadcasting Corp.] - Syracuse, NY - *BrCabYB 84 p.D-305; CabTVFinDB 83; LitMarPl 84; Tel&CabFB 84C p.1694*
NewChannels Corp. - Canonsburg, PA - *Tel&CabFB 84C*
NewChannels Corp. - Coraopolis, PA - *Tel&CabFB 84C*
NewCo [of Viacom International Inc.] - Oroville, CA - *Tel&CabFB 84C*
Newcomerstown News - Newcomerstown, OH - *BaconPubCkNews 84; Ed&PubIntYB 82; NewsDir 84*
Newcreature Music - Madison, TN - *BillIntBG 83-84*
Newdale Historical Society - Newdale, MB, Canada - *BoPubDir 4, 5*
Newell Buena Vista County Journal - Newell, IA - *BaconPubCkNews 84*
Newell Color Lab [Div. of Filmfair] - Los Angeles, CA - *AvMarPl 83*
Newell Color Lab - San Francisco, CA - *AvMarPl 83*
Newell Valley Irrigator - Newell, SD - *BaconPubCkNews 84*
Newest Press - Edmonton, AB, Canada - *BoPubDir 4, 5; LitMag&SmPr 83-84; LitMarPl 84*
NeWest Review - Canada - *LitMag&SmPr 83-84*
Newfield News - Newfield, NY - *AyerDirPub 83; Ed&PubIntYB 82*
Newfield News - *See* Odyssey Publications
Newfoundland Book Publishers Ltd. - St. John's, NF, Canada - *BoPubDir 4, 5*
Newfoundland Broadcasting Co. - St. John's, NF, Canada - *BrCabYB 84*
Newfoundland Gazette, The - St. John's, NF, Canada - *ArtMar 84*
Newfoundland Herald TV Week - St. John's, NF, Canada - *ArtMar 84*
Newhall Signal & Saugus Enterprise [of Morris Newspaper Corp.] - Newhall, CA - *AyerDirPub 83; BaconPubCkNews 84; Ed&PubIntYB 82; NewsDir 84*
Newhoff-Blumberg Inc. - Baltimore, MD - *StaDirAdAg 2-84*
Newhouse & Sons Inc., Samuel I. - New York, NY - *KnowInd 83*
Newhouse Broadcasting Corp. - Syracuse, NY - *HomeVid&CabYB 82-83*
Newhouse Broadcasting Corp. - *See* Eastern Microwave Inc.
Newhouse News Service - Washington, DC - *BaconPubCkNews 84; Ed&PubIntYB 82; NewsBur 6*
Newhouse Newspapers - New York, NY - *Ed&PubIntYB 82; LitMarPl 83, 84*
Newhouse Press - Los Angeles, CA - *BoPubDir 4, 5*
Newington Town Crier [of West Hartford Imprint Newspapers] - Newington, CT - *Ed&PubIntYB 82*
Newington Town Crier [of West Hartford Imprint Newspapers] - West Hartford, CT - *NewsDir 84*
Newkeys Music Inc. - Nashville, TN - *BillIntBG 83-84*
Newkirk Cable TV Service [of Communications Services Inc.] - Newkirk, OK - *BrCabYB 84; Tel&CabFB 84C*
Newkirk Herald-Journal - Newkirk, OK - *BaconPubCkNews 84; Ed&PubIntYB 82*
Newland Avery Journal - Newland, NC - *BaconPubCkNews 84; Ed&PubIntYB 82*
Newlin, Lyman W. - Lewiston, NY - *LitMarPl 84*
Newline Software - Littleton, MA - *MicrocomMPl 83, 84*
Newman Advertising, Al - Newport Beach, CA - *StaDirAdAg 2-84*
Newman Advertising, Emmet J. - Chicago, IL - *StaDirAdAg 2-84*
Newman & Associates, Rebecca - Los Angeles, CA - *LitMarPl 84*
Newman Associates Inc., Richard - Champaign, IL - *ArtMar 84*
Newman Associates, Stuart - Miami, FL - *DirPRFirms 83*
Newman Audio/Video Communications Inc. - Grand Rapids, MI - *AvMarPl 83*
Newman, Blitz & McConnell Inc. - Miami, FL - *StaDirAdAg 2-84*
Newman Group Ltd., The - San Mateo, CA - *IntDirMarRes 83*
Newman Grove Reporter - Newman Grove, NE - *BaconPubCkNews 84; Ed&PubIntYB 82*
Newman Independent - Newman, IL - *BaconPubCkNews 84; Ed&PubIntYB 82*
Newman Literary Services, Lois - Hollywood, CA - *LitMarPl 83, 84*
Newman, Marvin E. - New York, NY - *LitMarPl 83, 84; MagIndMarPl 82-83*
Newman Research, Alan - Richmond, VA - *IntDirMarRes 83*
Newman-Stein Inc. - New York, NY - *IntDirMarRes 83*
Newman Times-Herald - Newman, GA - *Ed&PubIntYB 82; NewsDir 84*
Newman West Side Index - Newman, CA - *BaconPubCkNews 84*
Newmark Advertising Agency, Nelson - Van Nuys, CA - *StaDirAdAg 2-84*
Newmark & Associates Inc., S. M. - Los Angeles, CA - *StaDirAdAg 2-84*
Newmark Coated Products Co. - New York, NY - *LitMarPl 83*
Newmark, Posner & Mitchell - New York, NY - *AdAge 3-28-84; BrCabYB 84; StaDirAdAg 2-84*
Newmarket Book Properties - New York, NY - *LitMarPl 83, 84*
Newmarket Era, The - Newmarket, ON, Canada - *Ed&PubIntYB 82*
Newmarket Press [Div. of Newmarket Publishing & Communications] - New York, NY - *LitMarPl 83, 84*
Newmark's Advertising Agency Inc. - New York, NY - *ArtMar 84; StaDirAdAg 2-84*
Newmyer Associates Inc. - Washington, DC - *DirPRFirms 83*
Newnan Junior Service League - Newnan, GA - *BoPubDir 4 Sup, 5*
Newnan Times Herald - Newnan, GA - *BaconPubCkNews 84*
Neworld Animation - South Blue Hill, ME - *ArtMar 84*
Neworld Media Music Publishers - South Blue Hill, ME - *BillIntBG 83-84*
Newport Advertising - Santa Ana, CA - *StaDirAdAg 2-84*
Newport Argus-Champion - Newport, NH - *BaconPubCkNews 84; NewsDir 84*

Newport Beach Newporter-Mesa News - Newport Beach, CA - *NewsDir 84*
Newport Beach Publisher - Newport Beach, CA - *BoPubDir 4, 5*
Newport Broadcasting Co. - *See* Sudbury Services Inc.
Newport Cable TV [of Teleservice Corp. of America] - Swifton, AR - *BrCabYB 84*
Newport Cable TV - Newport Township, PA - *BrCabYB 84; Tel&CabFB 84C*
Newport Cable TV - Newport, VT - *BrCabYB 84*
Newport Cablevision Inc. - Newport, VT - *Tel&CabFB 84C*
Newport Daily Express [of Scripps League Newspapers] - Newport, VT - *AyerDirPub 83; BaconPubCkNews 84; Ed&PubIntYB 82; NewsDir 84*
Newport Daily Independent - Newport, AR - *BaconPubCkNews 84; Ed&PubIntYB 82; NewsDir 84*
Newport Daily News [of Edward A. Sherman Publishing Co.] - Newport, RI - *BaconPubCkNews 84; Ed&PubIntYB 82; NewsDir 84*
Newport Ensign - Newport Beach, CA - *AyerDirPub 83; Ed&PubIntYB 82*
Newport Ensign - *See* Coast Media News Group
Newport Mercury - *See* Sherman Publishing Co., Edward A.
Newport Mercury & Weekly News [of E. A. Sherman Publishing] - Newport, RI - *NewsDir 84*
Newport Miner - Newport, WA - *BaconPubCkNews 84*
Newport Miner & Gem State News Miner [of Newport Publications Inc.] - Newport, WA - *Ed&PubIntYB 82; NewsDir 84*
Newport Music Co. - Boston, MA - *BillIntBG 83-84*
Newport Navalog [of Edward A. Sherman Publishing] - Newport, RI - *NewsDir 84*
Newport Navalog - *See* Sherman Publishing Co., Edward A.
Newport News Cablevision [of The Daily Press Inc.] - Newport News, VA - *BrCabYB 84*
Newport News Daily Press - Newport News, VA - *LitMarPl 83; NewsDir 84*
Newport News-Sun - Newport, PA - *BaconPubCkNews 84*
Newport News-Times [of Capital Cities Communications Inc.] - Newport, OR - *NewsDir 84*
Newport News-Times - *See* Newport News-Times Publishers
Newport News Times-Herald [of The Daily Press Inc.] - Newport News, VA - *LitMarPl 83; NewsDir 84*
Newport News-Times Publishers - Newport, OR - *BaconPubCkNews 84*
Newport Plain Talk - Cocke, TN - *Ed&PubIntYB 82*
Newport Plain Talk - Newport, TN - *BaconPubCkNews 84*
Newport Press Inc. - Brooklyn, NY - *LitMarPl 83, 84*
Newport Telephone Co. Inc. - Newport, NY - *TelDir&BG 83-84*
Newport TV Cable Inc. [of Teleservice Corp. of America] - Newport, AR - *BrCabYB 84; Tel&CabFB 84C*
Newporter Mesa News - Newport Beach, CA - *Ed&PubIntYB 82*
News - Birmingham, AL - *AyerDirPub 83*
News - Jacksonville, AL - *AyerDirPub 83*
News - Opp, AL - *AyerDirPub 83*
News - Tuscaloosa, AL - *AyerDirPub 83*
News - Anchorage, AK - *AyerDirPub 83*
News - Tempe, AZ - *Ed&PubIntYB 82*
News - Williams, AZ - *AyerDirPub 83*
News - Camden, AR - *AyerDirPub 83*
News - Jacksonville, AR - *Ed&PubIntYB 82*
News - Pine Bluff, AR - *AyerDirPub 83*
News - Springdale, AR - *AyerDirPub 83*
News - Atascadero, CA - *AyerDirPub 83*
News - Biggs, CA - *AyerDirPub 83*
News - Camarillo, CA - *AyerDirPub 83*
News - Chowchilla, CA - *AyerDirPub 83*
News - Dunsmuir, CA - *AyerDirPub 83*
News - Hemet, CA - *AyerDirPub 83*
News - Huntington Beach, CA - *AyerDirPub 83*
News - Indio, CA - *AyerDirPub 83*
News - Kerman, CA - *AyerDirPub 83*
News - Loomis, CA - *AyerDirPub 83*
News - Manteca, CA - *AyerDirPub 83*
News - Montebello, CA - *AyerDirPub 83*
News - Oildale, CA - *AyerDirPub 83*
News - Palos Verdes Peninsula, CA - *AyerDirPub 83*
News - Red Bluff, CA - *AyerDirPub 83*
News - Riverbank, CA - *AyerDirPub 83*
News - San Jose, CA - *AyerDirPub 83; Ed&PubIntYB 82; LitMarPl 84*
News - Sierra Madre, CA - *AyerDirPub 83*
News - Sun City, CA - *AyerDirPub 83*
News - Tehachapi, CA - *AyerDirPub 83*
News - Terra Bella, CA - *AyerDirPub 83*
News - Wasco, CA - *AyerDirPub 83*
News - Waterford, CA - *AyerDirPub 83*
News - Whittier, CA - *AyerDirPub 83*
News - Willits, CA - *AyerDirPub 83*
News - Flagler, CO - *AyerDirPub 83*
News - Darien, CT - *AyerDirPub 83*
News - Naugatuck, CT - *AyerDirPub 83*
News - Westport, CT - *AyerDirPub 83*
News - Wilmington, DE - *AyerDirPub 83*
News - Brandon, FL - *AyerDirPub 83*
News - Clewiston, FL - *AyerDirPub 83*
News - Daytona Beach, FL - *AyerDirPub 83; Ed&PubIntYB 82*
News - Frostproof, FL - *AyerDirPub 83; Ed&PubIntYB 82*
News - Ft. Lauderdale, FL - *AyerDirPub 83*
News - Graceville, FL - *AyerDirPub 83*
News - Lake Wales, FL - *AyerDirPub 83*
News - Miami, FL - *AyerDirPub 83*
News - Monticello, FL - *AyerDirPub 83*
News - Palatka, FL - *AyerDirPub 83*
News - Pensacola, FL - *AyerDirPub 83*
News - Sebring, FL - *AyerDirPub 83*
News - Stuart, FL - *AyerDirPub 83*
News - Zephyrhills, FL - *AyerDirPub 83*
News - Athens, GA - *AyerDirPub 83*
News - Brunswick, GA - *AyerDirPub 83*
News - Comer, GA - *AyerDirPub 83*
News - Commerce, GA - *AyerDirPub 83*
News - Covington, GA - *AyerDirPub 83*
News - Darien, GA - *AyerDirPub 83*
News - Donalsonville, GA - *AyerDirPub 83*
News - Griffin, GA - *AyerDirPub 83*
News - Macon, GA - *AyerDirPub 83*
News - Savannah, GA - *AyerDirPub 83*
News - Soperton, GA - *AyerDirPub 83*
News - Kellogg, ID - *AyerDirPub 83*
News - Altamont, IL - *AyerDirPub 83*
News - Amboy, IL - *AyerDirPub 83*
News - Ashley, IL - *AyerDirPub 83*
News - Benton, IL - *AyerDirPub 83; Ed&PubIntYB 82*
News - Cerro Gordo, IL - *AyerDirPub 83*
News - Elizabeth, IL - *AyerDirPub 83*
News - Farina, IL - *AyerDirPub 83*
News - Forrest, IL - *AyerDirPub 83*
News - Galva, IL - *AyerDirPub 83*
News - Manteno, IL - *AyerDirPub 83*
News - Nashville, IL - *AyerDirPub 83*
News - Neoga, IL - *AyerDirPub 83*
News - Raymond, IL - *AyerDirPub 83*
News - Rochelle, IL - *AyerDirPub 83*
News - Skokie, IL - *AyerDirPub 83; Ed&PubIntYB 82*
News - Sorento, IL - *AyerDirPub 83*
News - Tonica, IL - *AyerDirPub 83*
News - Villa Grove, IL - *AyerDirPub 83*
News - Westchester, IL - *AyerDirPub 83*
News - Alexandria, IN - *AyerDirPub 83*
News - Avilla, IN - *AyerDirPub 83*
News - Dale, IN - *AyerDirPub 83*
News - Farmersburg, IN - *AyerDirPub 83; Ed&PubIntYB 82*
News - Ferdinand, IN - *AyerDirPub 83*
News - Goshen, IN - *AyerDirPub 83*
News - Greensburg, IN - *AyerDirPub 83*
News - Greenwood, IN - *AyerDirPub 83*
News - Indianapolis, IN - *AyerDirPub 83*
News - La Grange, IN - *AyerDirPub 83*
News - Middletown, IN - *AyerDirPub 83*
News - Paoli, IN - *AyerDirPub 83*
News - Shelbyville, IN - *AyerDirPub 83*
News - Sheridan, IN - *AyerDirPub 83*
News - Shoals, IN - *AyerDirPub 83*
News - St. Joe, IN - *AyerDirPub 83*

News - Adair, IA - *AyerDirPub 83*
News - Bayard, IA - *AyerDirPub 83*
News - Estherville, IA - *Ed&PubIntYB 82*
News - Gowrie, IA - *AyerDirPub 83*
News - Kalona, IA - *AyerDirPub 83*
News - Mt. Pleasant, IA - *AyerDirPub 83*
News - Sioux Center, IA - *AyerDirPub 83*
News - Belle Plaine, KS - *AyerDirPub 83*
News - El Dorado, KS - *AyerDirPub 83*
News - Goodland, KS - *AyerDirPub 83*
News - Hanover, KS - *AyerDirPub 83*
News - Hays, KS - *AyerDirPub 83*
News - Hutchinson, KS - *AyerDirPub 83*
News - Independance, KS - *AyerDirPub 83*
News - Kiowa, KS - *AyerDirPub 83*
News - Lyons, KS - *AyerDirPub 83*
News - Madison, KS - *AyerDirPub 83*
News - Mulvane, KS - *AyerDirPub 83*
News - Olathe, KS - *AyerDirPub 83*
News - Parsons, KS - *AyerDirPub 83*
News - Russell, KS - *AyerDirPub 83*
News - Spearville, KS - *AyerDirPub 83*
News - Ulysses, KS - *AyerDirPub 83*
News - Yates Center, KS - *AyerDirPub 83*
News - Middlesboro, KY - *AyerDirPub 83*
News - Sturgis, KY - *AyerDirPub 83*
News - Bogalusa, LA - *AyerDirPub 83*
News - De Quincy, LA - *AyerDirPub 83*
News - Denham Springs, LA - *AyerDirPub 83*
News - Eunice, LA - *AyerDirPub 83*
News - Jennings, LA - *AyerDirPub 83*
News - Kentwood, LA - *AyerDirPub 83*
News - Vinton, LA - *AyerDirPub 83*
News - Bangor, ME - *AyerDirPub 83*
News - Cumberland, MD - *AyerDirPub 83; Ed&PubIntYB 82*
News [of Great Southern Printing & Manufacturing Co.] - Frederick, MD - *AyerDirPub 83; Ed&PubIntYB 82; NewsDir 84*
News - Athol, MA - *AyerDirPub 83*
News - Malden, MA - *AyerDirPub 83; Ed&PubIntYB 82*
News - Milford, MA - *AyerDirPub 83*
News - Newburyport, MA - *AyerDirPub 83*
News - North Billerica, MA - *AyerDirPub 83*
News - Salem, MA - *AyerDirPub 83*
News [of Nanlo Inc.] - Southbridge, MA - *AyerDirPub 83; BaconPubCkNews 84; Ed&PubIntYB 82; NewsDir 84*
News [of The Republican Co.] - Springfield, MA - *AyerDirPub 83; Ed&PubIntYB 82; LitMarPl 83, 84*
News - Alpena, MI - *AyerDirPub 83*
News - Ann Arbor, MI - *AyerDirPub 83*
News - Cadillac, MI - *AyerDirPub 83*
News - Clarkston, MI - *AyerDirPub 83*
News - Concord, MI - *AyerDirPub 83*
News - Dowagiac, MI - *AyerDirPub 83*
News - Freeport, MI - *AyerDirPub 83*
News - Greenville, MI - *AyerDirPub 83*
News - Hillsdale, MI - *AyerDirPub 83*
News - Iron Mountain, MI - *AyerDirPub 83*
News - Ludington, MI - *AyerDirPub 83; Ed&PubIntYB 82*
News - Midland, MI - *AyerDirPub 83*
News - Monroe, MI - *AyerDirPub 83*
News - Munising, MI - *AyerDirPub 83*
News - Saginaw, MI - *AyerDirPub 83*
News - Sault Ste. Marie, MI - *AyerDirPub 83*
News - Chatfield, MN - *AyerDirPub 83*
News - Claremont, MN - *AyerDirPub 83*
News - Eagle Bend, MN - *AyerDirPub 83*
News - Faribault, MN - *AyerDirPub 83*
News - Hinckley, MN - *AyerDirPub 83*
News - Lamberton, MN - *AyerDirPub 83*
News - Plainview, MN - *AyerDirPub 83*
News - Sacred Heart, MN - *AyerDirPub 83*
News - Tower, MN - *AyerDirPub 83*
News - Winona, MN - *AyerDirPub 83*
News - Wood Lake, MN - *AyerDirPub 83*
News - Jackson, MS - *AyerDirPub 83*
News - Nettleton, MS - *AyerDirPub 83*
News - Starkville, MS - *AyerDirPub 83*
News - Boonville, MO - *AyerDirPub 83*
News - Liberal, MO - *AyerDirPub 83*
News - Monroe City, MO - *AyerDirPub 83*
News - Neosho, MO - *AyerDirPub 83*
News - Richmond, MO - *AyerDirPub 83*
News - Rolla, MO - *AyerDirPub 83*
News - Salem, MO - *AyerDirPub 83*
News - Springfield, MO - *AyerDirPub 83*
News - Thayer, MO - *AyerDirPub 83*
News - Warrenton, MO - *AyerDirPub 83*
News - Willow Springs, MO - *AyerDirPub 83*
News - Albion, NE - *AyerDirPub 83*
News - Comstock, NE - *AyerDirPub 83*
News - Creighton, NE - *AyerDirPub 83*
News - Crete, NE - *AyerDirPub 83*
News - Henderson, NE - *AyerDirPub 83*
News - Indianola, NE - *AyerDirPub 83*
News - Meadow Grove, NE - *AyerDirPub 83*
News - Norfolk, NE - *AyerDirPub 83*
News - Orchard, NE - *AyerDirPub 83*
News - Plainview, NE - *AyerDirPub 83*
News - Ravenna, NE - *AyerDirPub 83*
News - West Point, NE - *AyerDirPub 83*
News - Meredith, NH - *AyerDirPub 83*
News - Belvidere, NJ - *AyerDirPub 83; Ed&PubIntYB 82*
News - Bernardsville, NJ - *AyerDirPub 83*
News - Bridgeton, NJ - *AyerDirPub 83*
News - Gloucester City, NJ - *AyerDirPub 83*
News - Hammonton, NJ - *AyerDirPub 83*
News - Lodi, NJ - *AyerDirPub 83*
News - Manville, NJ - *AyerDirPub 83*
News [of Dow Jones News/Retrieval Service] - Princeton, NJ - *DataDirOnSer 84*
News - Ridgewood, NJ - *AyerDirPub 83*
News - Swedesboro, NJ - *AyerDirPub 83; Ed&PubIntYB 82*
News - Wyckoff, NJ - *AyerDirPub 83*
News - Alamogordo, NM - *AyerDirPub 83*
News - Ruidoso, NM - *AyerDirPub 83*
News - Santa Rosa, NM - *AyerDirPub 83*
News - Taos, NM - *AyerDirPub 83*
News - Andover, NY - *AyerDirPub 83*
News - Batavia, NY - *AyerDirPub 83*
News - Buffalo, NY - *AyerDirPub 83*
News - Commack, NY - *AyerDirPub 83*
News - Garden City, NY - *AyerDirPub 83*
News - Great Neck, NY - *AyerDirPub 83*
News - Greenwood Lake, NY - *AyerDirPub 83*
News - Lake Placid, NY - *AyerDirPub 83*
News - Millerton, NY - *AyerDirPub 83*
News - New Paltz, NY - *AyerDirPub 83*
News - Newburgh, NY - *AyerDirPub 83*
News - Sherburne, NY - *AyerDirPub 83*
News - Smithtown, NY - *AyerDirPub 83*
News - Vestal, NY - *AyerDirPub 83*
News - Black Mountain, NC - *AyerDirPub 83*
News - Charlotte, NC - *AyerDirPub 83*
News - Clayton, NC - *AyerDirPub 83*
News - Greensboro, NC - *AyerDirPub 83*
News - Jacksonville, NC - *AyerDirPub 83*
News - Kernersville, NC - *AyerDirPub 83*
News - Mt. Airy, NC - *AyerDirPub 83; Ed&PubIntYB 82*
News - Valdese, NC - *AyerDirPub 83*
News - Washington, NC - *AyerDirPub 83*
News - Hankinson, ND - *AyerDirPub 83*
News - Kenmare, ND - *AyerDirPub 83*
News - Bluffton, OH - *AyerDirPub 83*
News - Dayton, OH - *AyerDirPub 83*
News - Hartville, OH - *AyerDirPub 83*
News - Lima, OH - *AyerDirPub 83*
News - Logan, OH - *AyerDirPub 83*
News - Mt. Vernon, OH - *AyerDirPub 83*
News - Newcomerstown, OH - *AyerDirPub 83*
News - North Baltimore, OH - *AyerDirPub 83*
News - Salem, OH - *AyerDirPub 83*
News - Sidney, OH - *AyerDirPub 83*
News - Sunbury, OH - *AyerDirPub 83*
News - Toledo, OH - *AyerDirPub 83*

News - Troy, OH - *AyerDirPub 83*
News - Wapakoneta, OH - *AyerDirPub 83*
News - Yellow Springs, OH - *AyerDirPub 83*
News - Ada, OK - *AyerDirPub 83*
News - Anadarko, OK - *AyerDirPub 83*
News - Billings, OK - *AyerDirPub 83*
News - Boise City, OK - *AyerDirPub 83*
News - Bristow, OK - *AyerDirPub 83*
News - Broken Bow, OK - *AyerDirPub 83*
News - Clinton, OK - *AyerDirPub 83*
News - Cyril, OK - *AyerDirPub 83*
News - Del City, OK - *AyerDirPub 83*
News - Elk City, OK - *AyerDirPub 83*
News - Enid, OK - *AyerDirPub 83; Ed&PubIntYB 82*
News - Ft. Cobb, OK - *AyerDirPub 83*
News - Harrah, OK - *AyerDirPub 83*
News - Holdenville, OK - *Ed&PubIntYB 82*
News - Hugo, OK - *AyerDirPub 83; Ed&PubIntYB 82*
News - Lindsay, OK - *AyerDirPub 83*
News - Maysville, OK - *AyerDirPub 83*
News - Ponca City, OK - *AyerDirPub 83*
News - Tonkawa, OK - *AyerDirPub 83*
News - Weatherford, OK - *AyerDirPub 83*
News - Wellston, OK - *AyerDirPub 83*
News - Yale, OK - *AyerDirPub 83*
News - Hood River, OR - *AyerDirPub 83*
News - Springfield, OR - *AyerDirPub 83*
News - Albion, PA - *AyerDirPub 83*
News [of R. A. Palket Co. Inc.] - Aliquippa, PA - *AyerDirPub 83; NewsDir 84*
News - Bangor, PA - *AyerDirPub 83; Ed&PubIntYB 82*
News - Carbondale, PA - *AyerDirPub 83*
News - Clarion, PA - *AyerDirPub 83*
News - Columbia, PA - *AyerDirPub 83*
News - Erie, PA - *AyerDirPub 83*
News - Forest City, PA - *AyerDirPub 83*
News - Glenside, PA - *AyerDirPub 83*
News - Harrisburg, PA - *AyerDirPub 83*
News - Huntingdon, PA - *AyerDirPub 83*
News - Lancaster, PA - *AyerDirPub 83*
News - McKeesport, PA - *AyerDirPub 83; Ed&PubIntYB 82*
News - New Castle, PA - *AyerDirPub 83*
News - Strasburg, PA - *AyerDirPub 83*
News - Newport, RI - *AyerDirPub 83*
News - Belton, SC - *AyerDirPub 83*
News - Calhoun Falls, SC - *AyerDirPub 83*
News - Florence, SC - *AyerDirPub 83*
News - Greenville, SC - *AyerDirPub 83*
News - Hilton Head Island, SC - *AyerDirPub 83*
News - Lancaster, SC - *AyerDirPub 83*
News - Woodruff, SC - *AyerDirPub 83*
News - Carthage, SD - *AyerDirPub 83*
News - De Smet, SD - *AyerDirPub 83*
News - Eagle Butte, SD - *AyerDirPub 83*
News - Woonsocket, SD - *AyerDirPub 83*
News - Kingsport, TN - *AyerDirPub 83*
News - Alamo, TX - *AyerDirPub 83*
News - Alvord, TX - *AyerDirPub 83*
News - Amarillo, TX - *AyerDirPub 83*
News - Arlington, TX - *AyerDirPub 83*
News - Bogata, TX - *AyerDirPub 83*
News - Booker, TX - *AyerDirPub 83*
News - Bowie, TX - *AyerDirPub 83*
News - Claude, TX - *AyerDirPub 83*
News - Ennis, TX - *AyerDirPub 83*
News - Galveston, TX - *AyerDirPub 83*
News - Garland, TX - *AyerDirPub 83*
News - Garrison, TX - *AyerDirPub 83*
News - Grand Prairie, TX - *AyerDirPub 83*
News - Groom, TX - *AyerDirPub 83*
News - Groveton, TX - *AyerDirPub 83*
News - Henderson, TX - *AyerDirPub 83*
News - Irving, TX - *AyerDirPub 83*
News - La Feria, TX - *AyerDirPub 83*
News - Laredo, TX - *AyerDirPub 83*
News - Lindale, TX - *AyerDirPub 83*
News - Llano, TX - *AyerDirPub 83*
News - Longview, TX - *AyerDirPub 83*
News - Lufkin, TX - *AyerDirPub 83*
News - Malakoff, TX - *AyerDirPub 83*
News - Mathis, TX - *AyerDirPub 83*
News - McCamey, TX - *AyerDirPub 83*
News - McLean, TX - *AyerDirPub 83*
News - Mesquite, TX - *AyerDirPub 83*
News - Monahans, TX - *AyerDirPub 83*
News - Nixon, TX - *AyerDirPub 83*
News - Nocona, TX - *AyerDirPub 83*
News - Pampa, TX - *AyerDirPub 83; Ed&PubIntYB 82*
News - Paris, TX - *AyerDirPub 83*
News - Port Arthur, TX - *AyerDirPub 83*
News - Richardson, TX - *AyerDirPub 83*
News - Rosebud, TX - *AyerDirPub 83*
News - San Antonio, TX - *AyerDirPub 83*
News - Sealy, TX - *AyerDirPub 83*
News - Snyder, TX - *AyerDirPub 83; Ed&PubIntYB 82*
News - Winnsboro, TX - *AyerDirPub 83*
News - Wylie, TX - *AyerDirPub 83*
News - Charlotte Amalie, VI - *AyerDirPub 83*
News - Hopewell, VA - *AyerDirPub 83; Ed&PubIntYB 82*
News - Lynchburg, VA - *AyerDirPub 83; Ed&PubIntYB 82*
News - Longview, WA - *AyerDirPub 83*
News - Martinsburg, WV - *AyerDirPub 83*
News - Parkersburg, WV - *AyerDirPub 83*
News - Pennsboro, WV - *AyerDirPub 83*
News - Ravenswood, WV - *AyerDirPub 83*
News - Williamson, WV - *AyerDirPub 83*
News - Beloit, WI - *AyerDirPub 83*
News - Brillion, WI - *AyerDirPub 83; Ed&PubIntYB 82*
News - Cambridge, WI - *AyerDirPub 83*
News - Campbellsport, WI - *AyerDirPub 83*
News - East Troy, WI - *AyerDirPub 83*
News - Kenosha, WI - *AyerDirPub 83*
News - Ladysmith, WI - *AyerDirPub 83*
News - Luxemburg, WI - *AyerDirPub 83*
News - Mayville, WI - *AyerDirPub 83*
News - New Richmond, WI - *AyerDirPub 83; Ed&PubIntYB 82*
News - Rhinelander, WI - *AyerDirPub 83*
News - West Bend, WI - *AyerDirPub 83*
News - Winneconne, WI - *AyerDirPub 83*
News - Nanton, AB, Canada - *AyerDirPub 83*
News - Provost, AB, Canada - *AyerDirPub 83*
News - Redwater, AB, Canada - *Ed&PubIntYB 82*
News - Sylvan Lake, AB, Canada - *AyerDirPub 83*
News - Westlock, AB, Canada - *Ed&PubIntYB 82*
News - Castlegar, BC, Canada - *AyerDirPub 83; Ed&PubIntYB 82*
News - Ft. Nelson, BC, Canada - *AyerDirPub 83*
News - Kamloops, BC, Canada - *AyerDirPub 83*
News - Nelson, BC, Canada - *AyerDirPub 83*
News - Powell River, BC, Canada - *AyerDirPub 83; Ed&PubIntYB 82*
News - Prince Rupert, BC, Canada - *AyerDirPub 83*
News - Vernon, BC, Canada - *AyerDirPub 83*
News - Belmont, MB, Canada - *Ed&PubIntYB 82*
News - Dalhousie, NB, Canada - *AyerDirPub 83*
News - St. John's, NF, Canada - *AyerDirPub 83*
News - Amherst, NS, Canada - *AyerDirPub 83*
News - New Glasgow, NS, Canada - *AyerDirPub 83*
News - Truro, NS, Canada - *AyerDirPub 83*
News - Ayr, ON, Canada - *AyerDirPub 83*
News - Gravenhurst, ON, Canada - *AyerDirPub 83*
News - Harrow, ON, Canada - *AyerDirPub 83*
News - Stoney Creek, ON, Canada - *AyerDirPub 83*
News - Tillsonburg, ON, Canada - *AyerDirPub 83*
News - Toronto/Scarborough, ON, Canada - *Ed&PubIntYB 82*
News - Tweed, ON, Canada - *AyerDirPub 83*
News - West Hill, ON, Canada - *Ed&PubIntYB 82*
News - Montreal, PQ, Canada - *AyerDirPub 83*
News - St. Laurent, PQ, Canada - *Ed&PubIntYB 82*
News - Ituna, SK, Canada - *Ed&PubIntYB 82*
News - Leader, SK, Canada - *Ed&PubIntYB 82*
News - Maple Creek, SK, Canada - *AyerDirPub 83*
News - Wadena, SK, Canada - *AyerDirPub 83*
News-A-Tron - Boston, MA - *EISS 5-84 Sup*
News Advertiser - Lake City, FL - *AyerDirPub 83*

News-Advertiser - Creston, IA - *AyerDirPub 83*
News-Advertiser - Harlan, IA - *AyerDirPub 83*
News-Advertiser - Jackson, MI - *AyerDirPub 83*
News-Advertiser - De Soto, TX - *AyerDirPub 83*
News-Advertiser - Lewisville, TX - *AyerDirPub 83*
News-Advertiser - Wetaskiwin, AB, Canada - *AyerDirPub 83*
News-Advertiser - Kitimat, BC, Canada - *Ed&PubIntYB 82*
News Advertiser - Westbank, BC, Canada - *Ed&PubIntYB 82*
News Advertiser East - Holladay, UT - *Ed&PubIntYB 82*
News Advertiser East - Murray, UT - *AyerDirPub 83*
News Advertiser East [of Murray Printing Inc.] - Salt Lake City, UT - *NewsDir 84*
News Advertiser West - Magna, UT - *Ed&PubIntYB 82*
News Advertiser West - Murray, UT - *AyerDirPub 83*
News Advertiser West [of Murray Printing Inc.] - Salt Lake City, UT - *NewsDir 84*
News-Advocate - Fordyce, AR - *AyerDirPub 83*
News America Publishing - New York, NY - *AdAge 6-28-84; Ed&PubIntYB 82*
News-American [of The Hearst Co. Inc.] - Baltimore, MD - *AyerDirPub 83; Ed&PubIntYB 82; LitMarPl 84*
News Analysis Institute, The - Pittsburgh, PA - *ProGuPRSer 4*
News & Advertiser - Northfield, VT - *Ed&PubIntYB 82*
News & Advertiser - Ponoka, AB, Canada - *Ed&PubIntYB 82*
News & Alumni Report [of Los Angeles College of Chiropractic] - Whittier, CA - *MagDir 84*
News & Banner, The - Franklin, GA - *Ed&PubIntYB 82*
News & Bryan County Democrat - Durant, OK - *AyerDirPub 83*
News & Chronicle - Montreal, PQ, Canada - *AyerDirPub 83*
News & Chronicle - West Island, PQ, Canada - *Ed&PubIntYB 82*
News & Citizen - Morrisville, VT - *AyerDirPub 83; BaconPubCkNews 84; Ed&PubIntYB 82*
News & County Press & Rockbridge Weekly, The [of Welch Daily News] - Lexington, VA - *NewsDir 84*
News & County Press, The - Buena Vista, VA - *AyerDirPub 83; Ed&PubIntYB 82*
News & Courier - Charleston, SC - *AyerDirPub 83; Ed&PubIntYB 82; LitMarPl 83, 84*
News & Courier Post - Charleston, SC - *Ed&PubIntYB 82; LitMarPl 83, 84*
News & Daily Advance, The - Lynchburg, VA - *Ed&PubIntYB 82*
News & Eagle - Enid, OK - *Ed&PubIntYB 82*
News & Farmer - Preston, MD - *AyerDirPub 83; BaconPubCkMag 84; Ed&PubIntYB 82; MagDir 84*
News & Farmer & Wadely Herald - Louisville, GA - *Ed&PubIntYB 82*
News & Food Report [of New Hampshire Retail Grocers Association] - Manchester, NH - *BaconPubCkMag 84; MagDir 84*
News & Gazette - Weymouth, MA - *AyerDirPub 83*
News & Guardian - Tullahoma, TN - *AyerDirPub 83*
News & Herald - Winnsboro, SC - *AyerDirPub 83; Ed&PubIntYB 82*
News & Leader - Springfield, MO - *AyerDirPub 83*
News & Leader - Neligh, NE - *AyerDirPub 83*
News & Letters - Detroit, MI - *BoPubDir 4, 5*
News & McHenry County Guide - Crystal Lake, IL - *AyerDirPub 83*
News & Messenger - Menard, TX - *AyerDirPub 83*
News & Observer - New Smyrna Beach, FL - *AyerDirPub 83*
News & Observer - Raleigh, NC - *AyerDirPub 83; BaconPubCkNews 84; Ed&PubIntYB 82; LitMarPl 83, 84; NewsBur 6; WritMar 84*
News & Observer Publishing Co. - Raleigh, NC - *Ed&PubIntYB 82*
News & Post - Lake City, SC - *AyerDirPub 83; Ed&PubIntYB 82*
News & Press - Darlington, SC - *AyerDirPub 83; Ed&PubIntYB 82*
News & Record - South Boston, VA - *AyerDirPub 83*
News & Reporter - Bensalem, PA - *AyerDirPub 83*
News & Reporter - Chester, SC - *AyerDirPub 83; Ed&PubIntYB 82*
News & Sentinel - Colebrook, NH - *AyerDirPub 83; Ed&PubIntYB 82*
News & Star - San Saba, TX - *AyerDirPub 83*
News & Sun - Poteau, OK - *AyerDirPub 83*
News & Sun-Sentinel - Ft. Lauderdale, FL - *AyerDirPub 83*
News & Times - Downs, KS - *AyerDirPub 83*
News & Times - Georgetown, KY - *AyerDirPub 83*
News & Tribune - Jefferson City, MO - *AyerDirPub 83; Ed&PubIntYB 82; NewsDir 84*
News & Views [of IPGCU] - Washington, DC - *NewsDir 84*
News & Views of Local 1478 - Chicago, IL - *NewsDir 84*
News & Views of Local 23, The [of UFCW Local 23] - Pittsburgh, PA - *NewsDir 84*
News-Argus - Lewistown, MT - *AyerDirPub 83*
News-Argus - Goldsboro, NC - *AyerDirPub 83*
News-Argus - Stirling, ON, Canada - *AyerDirPub 83*
News Associates - Idyllwild, CA - *Ed&PubIntYB 82; LitMarPl 84*
News-Banner - Baxley, GA - *AyerDirPub 83*
News-Banner - Bluffton, IN - *AyerDirPub 83; Ed&PubIntYB 82*
News-Banner - Wadsworth, OH - *AyerDirPub 83; Ed&PubIntYB 82*
News-Beacon & Dispatch - Fair Lawn, NJ - *Ed&PubIntYB 82*
News-Beacon, The - Fair Lawn, NJ - *AyerDirPub 83*
News-Bee - Morris Plains, NJ - *Ed&PubIntYB 82*
News-Blade - Bridgeport, NE - *AyerDirPub 83*
News Boy - Jasper, TX - *Ed&PubIntYB 82*
News-Bulletin - Sandpoint, ID - *AyerDirPub 83; Ed&PubIntYB 82*
News-Bulletin - Brookfield, MO - *AyerDirPub 83; Ed&PubIntYB 82*
News-Bulletin - Castroville, TX - *AyerDirPub 83; Ed&PubIntYB 82*
News-Capital & Democrat - McAlester, OK - *AyerDirPub 83*
News Castle Henry County Local - News Castle, KY - *BaconPubCkNews 84*
News-Chief - Winter Haven, FL - *AyerDirPub 83*
News-Chieftain - Poway, CA - *AyerDirPub 83*
News-Chronicle - Thousand Oaks, CA - *AyerDirPub 83; Ed&PubIntYB 82*
News-Chronicle - Vallejo, CA - *AyerDirPub 83*
News-Chronicle - Cherry Hill, NJ - *AyerDirPub 83*
News-Chronicle - Pawling, NY - *AyerDirPub 83*
News-Chronicle - Shippensburg, PA - *AyerDirPub 83; BaconPubCkNews 84; Ed&PubIntYB 82*
News-Chronicle - Green Bay, WI - *AyerDirPub 83*
News-Chronicle Shopper's Guide - Green Bay, WI - *AyerDirPub 83*
News-Chronicle Suburban, The - Moorestown, NJ - *Ed&PubIntYB 82*
News Circle - Glendale, CA - *ArtMar 84; BoPubDir 4, 5; NewsDir 84*
News Circle - Los Angeles, CA - *Ed&PubIntYB 82*
News Circle Magazine, The - Glendale, CA - *LitMag&SmPr 83-84*
News Circle Publishing Co., The - Glendale, CA - *LitMag&SmPr 83-84*
News-Citizen - New York, NY - *MagDir 84*
News-Citizen - Vandergrift, PA - *AyerDirPub 83; Ed&PubIntYB 82*
News-Commercial - Collins, MS - *AyerDirPub 83; Ed&PubIntYB 82*
News Corp. Ltd., The - New York, NY - *KnowInd 83*
News Courier - Athens, AL - *AyerDirPub 83*
News Daily - Jonesboro, GA - *AyerDirPub 83*
News Daily [of Standard & Poor's Corp.] - New York, NY - *DataDirOnSer 84*
News Daily of Clayton County - Jonesboro, GA - *BaconPubCkNews 84*
News-Democrat - Belleville, IL - *AyerDirPub 83; BaconPubCkNews 84; Ed&PubIntYB 82*
News-Democrat - Carrollton, KY - *AyerDirPub 83; Ed&PubIntYB 82*
News-Democrat - Russellville, KY - *AyerDirPub 83*
News-Democrat - Georgetown, OH - *AyerDirPub 83*
News-Democrat - Waurika, OK - *AyerDirPub 83*
News-Democrat - Waverly, TN - *AyerDirPub 83; Ed&PubIntYB 82*
News Diary - Donelson, TN - *Ed&PubIntYB 82*
News-Digest - Amite, LA - *AyerDirPub 83; Ed&PubIntYB 82*
News-Digest/TV Today - Texarkana, TX - *Ed&PubIntYB 82*
News-Dispatch - Minonk, IL - *AyerDirPub 83; Ed&PubIntYB 82*

News-Dispatch - Michigan City, IN - *AyerDirPub 83; Ed&PubIntYB 82*
News-Dispatch - Seneca, MO - *Ed&PubIntYB 82*
News Eagle, The [of Dyson Publications] - Hawley, PA - *AyerDirPub 83; Ed&PubIntYB 82; NewsDir 84*
News Election Service - New York, NY - *Ed&PubIntYB 82*
News-Enterprise - Los Alamitos, CA - *AyerDirPub 83; Ed&PubIntYB 82*
News-Enterprise - Covington, KY - *AyerDirPub 83*
News-Enterprise - Elizabethtown, KY - *AyerDirPub 83; Ed&PubIntYB 82*
News-Enterprise - North Creek, NY - *AyerDirPub 83*
News Era - Kershaw, SC - *AyerDirPub 83*
News-Examiner - Montpelier, ID - *AyerDirPub 83*
News-Examiner - Connersville, IN - *AyerDirPub 83*
News-Examiner [of Multi Media] - Gallatin, TN - *AyerDirPub 83; Ed&PubIntYB 82; NewsDir 84*
News-Examiner, The - Bear Lake Valley, ID - *Ed&PubIntYB 82*
News-Express - Carberry, MB, Canada - *AyerDirPub 83*
News-Free Press - Chattanooga, TN - *AyerDirPub 83; Ed&PubIntYB 82; LitMarPl 84*
News Front [of Year Inc.] - Ross, CA - *MagDir 84*
News Front Business Trends Data Bank [of Baldwin H. Ward Publications] - Petaluma, CA - *BaconPubCkMag 84; EISS 83*
News-Gazette - Champaign, IL - *AyerDirPub 83*
News-Gazette - Winchester, IN - *AyerDirPub 83; BaconPubCkNews 84; Ed&PubIntYB 82*
News-Gazette - Pineville, MO - *Ed&PubIntYB 82*
News-Gazette, The - Lexington, VA - *AyerDirPub 83; Ed&PubIntYB 82*
News Gleaner/Bustleton-Somerton Edition - Philadelphia, PA - *AyerDirPub 83*
News Gleaner/Frankford-Juniata Edition - Philadelphia, PA - *AyerDirPub 83*
News Gleaner/Mayfair-Northeast Edition - Philadelphia, PA - *AyerDirPub 83*
News Gleaner Publications - Philadelphia, PA - *BaconPubCkNews 84*
News-Globe [of Southwestern Newspapers] - Amarillo, TX - *AyerDirPub 83; NewsDir 84*
News-Graphic Pilot - Cedarburg, WI - *AyerDirPub 83; Ed&PubIntYB 82*
News Guard, The - Lincoln City, OR - *AyerDirPub 83; Ed&PubIntYB 82; NewsDir 84*
News Guide - Eagle Pass, TX - *AyerDirPub 83*
News-Herald - Gravette, AR - *AyerDirPub 83*
News-Herald - Santa Rosa, CA - *AyerDirPub 83*
News-Herald - Panama City, FL - *AyerDirPub 83; Ed&PubIntYB 82*
News-Herald - Perry, FL - *AyerDirPub 83*
News-Herald - Litchfield, IL - *AyerDirPub 83; Ed&PubIntYB 82*
News-Herald - Tama, IA - *AyerDirPub 83*
News-Herald - Riverview, MI - *Ed&PubIntYB 82*
News-Herald - Le Sueur, MN - *AyerDirPub 83; Ed&PubIntYB 82*
News-Herald - Ravena, NY - *AyerDirPub 83; Ed&PubIntYB 82*
News-Herald [of Parker Bros. Inc.] - Ahoskie, NC - *AyerDirPub 83; Ed&PubIntYB 82; NewsDir 84*
News-Herald [of Fremont Messenger Co.] - Port Clinton, OH - *AyerDirPub 83; Ed&PubIntYB 82; NewsDir 84*
News-Herald - Willoughby, OH - *BaconPubCkNews 84*
News-Herald - Franklin, PA - *AyerDirPub 83; Ed&PubIntYB 82*
News-Herald - Perkasie, PA - *AyerDirPub 83*
News-Herald [of Loudon Publishing Co.] - Lenoir City, TN - *AyerDirPub 83; NewsDir 84*
News-Herald - Loudon, TN - *AyerDirPub 83*
News-Herald - Borger, TX - *AyerDirPub 83*
News-Herald - Del Rio, TX - *AyerDirPub 83*
News-Herald - Italy, TX - *Ed&PubIntYB 82*
News-Herald - Suffolk, VA - *AyerDirPub 83; Ed&PubIntYB 82*
News-Herald - Marshfield, WI - *AyerDirPub 83*
News-Herald & Owen County Democrat - Owenton, KY - *AyerDirPub 83*
News-Herald Guardian, The - Wyandotte, MI - *NewsDir 84*
News-Herald Newspapers - Wyandotte, MI - *BaconPubCkNews 84; Ed&PubIntYB 82*
News-Herald Shopper - Tama, IA - *AyerDirPub 83*
News-Herald, The - Chickasaw, AL - *Ed&PubIntYB 82*
News-Herald, The - Saraland, AL - *NewsDir 84*
News-Herald, The - Owenton, KY - *Ed&PubIntYB 82*
News-Herald, The - Wyandotte, MI - *NewsDir 84*
News-Herald, The - Morganton, NC - *AyerDirPub 83; Ed&PubIntYB 82*
News-Herald, The - Conneaut, OH - *AyerDirPub 83; Ed&PubIntYB 82*
News-Herald, The - Loudon County, TN - *Ed&PubIntYB 82*
News Hi-Lites [of VA St. AFL-CIO] - Richmond, VA - *NewsDir 84*
News Independent - Cissna Park, IL - *AyerDirPub 83*
News Independent - Mound City, MO - *AyerDirPub 83*
News Information Weekly Service - Sherman Oaks, CA - *BrCabYB 84*
News-Item - Shamokin, PA - *AyerDirPub 83; Ed&PubIntYB 82*
News-Journal - Wilmington, DE - *AyerDirPub 83; Ed&PubIntYB 82*
News-Journal - Daytona Beach, FL - *AyerDirPub 83; Ed&PubIntYB 82; NewsDir 84*
News-Journal - Pensacola, FL - *AyerDirPub 83*
News-Journal - Ramsey, IL - *AyerDirPub 83*
News-Journal - Carmel, IN - *AyerDirPub 83*
News-Journal - Mountain Grove, MO - *AyerDirPub 83; Ed&PubIntYB 82*
News-Journal - Clovis, NM - *AyerDirPub 83*
News-Journal - Raeford, NC - *AyerDirPub 83*
News-Journal - Mansfield, OH - *AyerDirPub 83; Ed&PubIntYB 82*
News-Journal - Wilmington, OH - *AyerDirPub 83*
News-Journal - Murfreesboro, TN - *AyerDirPub 83*
News-Journal - Longview, TX - *AyerDirPub 83*
News-Journal - Radford, VA - *AyerDirPub 83; Ed&PubIntYB 82*
News-Journal - Kent, WA - *AyerDirPub 83*
News-Journal Inc. - Seattle, WA - *BaconPubCkNews 84*
News-Journal, The - North Manchester, IN - *AyerDirPub 83; Ed&PubIntYB 82*
News-Leader - Fernandina Beach, FL - *AyerDirPub 83; Ed&PubIntYB 82*
News-Leader - Highland, IL - *AyerDirPub 83*
News-Leader - Netcong, NJ - *AyerDirPub 83; Ed&PubIntYB 82*
News-Leader - Rutherford, NJ - *Ed&PubIntYB 82*
News-Leader - Okemah, OK - *AyerDirPub 83*
News-Leader - Landrum, SC - *AyerDirPub 83; Ed&PubIntYB 82*
News-Leader - Parsons, TN - *AyerDirPub 83*
News-Leader - Richmond, VA - *AyerDirPub 83*
News-Leader [of Multimedia Inc.] - Staunton, VA - *AyerDirPub 83; NewsDir 84*
News-Leader - Arcadia, WI - *AyerDirPub 83*
News-Leader, The [of North American Publications] - Royston, GA - *AyerDirPub 83; NewsDir 84*
News-Ledger - West Sacramento, CA - *AyerDirPub 83*
News-Letter - Exeter, NH - *AyerDirPub 83*
News Letter-Journal - Newcastle, WY - *AyerDirPub 83*
News Ltd. of Australia - New York, NY - *Ed&PubIntYB 82*
News Media & The Law, The - Washington, DC - *MagIndMarPl 82-83*
News Merchandiser - Lodi, CA - *AyerDirPub 83*
News-Messenger - Hamlet, NC - *AyerDirPub 83; NewsDir 84*
News-Messenger - Fremont, OH - *AyerDirPub 83; Ed&PubIntYB 82*
News-Messenger - Marshall, TX - *AyerDirPub 83*
News-Messenger - Christiansburg, VA - *BaconPubCkNews 84; Ed&PubIntYB 82*
News-Messenger - Saltville, VA - *AyerDirPub 83*
News-Messenger, The - English, IN - *Ed&PubIntYB 82*
News-Miner - Fairbanks, AK - *AyerDirPub 83*
News-Mirror - Bourbon, IN - *AyerDirPub 83*
News-Mirror - Mansfield, TX - *AyerDirPub 83*
News/North - Yellowknife, NT, Canada - *AyerDirPub 83; Ed&PubIntYB 82*
News-Observer - New Smyrna Beach, FL - *Ed&PubIntYB 82*
News-Observer - Vienna, GA - *AyerDirPub 83*
News of Chesterfield & Daleville, The - Chesterfield, IN - *Ed&PubIntYB 82*
News of Delaware County - Upper Darby, PA - *AyerDirPub 83; Ed&PubIntYB 82*
News of Mt. Laurel & Marlton, The - Cherry Hill, NJ - *AyerDirPub 83*

News of Orange County - Hillsborough, NC - *AyerDirPub 83; Ed&PubIntYB 82; NewsDir 84*
News of Orangevale - Folsom, CA - *Ed&PubIntYB 82*
News of Southern Berks, The - Birdsboro, PA - *Ed&PubIntYB 82*
News of Southern Berks, The - Boyertown, PA - *AyerDirPub 83*
News of the Highlands - Highland Falls, NY - *AyerDirPub 83; Ed&PubIntYB 82*
News of the North - Yellowknife, NT, Canada - *Ed&PubIntYB 82*
News of the World - New York, NY - *Ed&PubIntYB 82*
News Online [of Standard & Poor's Corp.] - New York, NY - *DataDirOnSer 84*
News-Optimist - North Battleford, SK, Canada - *AyerDirPub 83*
News-Optimist & Total - North Battleford, SK, Canada - *Ed&PubIntYB 82*
News Outlook [of Media of Moore Inc.] - Southern Pines, NC - *AyerDirPub 83; Ed&PubIntYB 82; NewsDir 84*
News-Palladium - Pana, IL - *AyerDirPub 83; Ed&PubIntYB 82*
News Pennsylvania - Lebanon, PA - *AyerDirPub 83*
News Photographer - Bowling Green, OH - *BaconPubCkMag 84; MagDir 84*
News-Piedmont - Greenville, SC - *AyerDirPub 83*
News Pilot - San Pedro, CA - *AyerDirPub 83; BaconPubCkNews 84; Ed&PubIntYB 82*
News-Plaindealer - Sparta, IL - *AyerDirPub 83*
News Pointer - San Rafael, CA - *AyerDirPub 83*
News Portraits Syndicate - Hackensack, NJ - *Ed&PubIntYB 82; LitMarPl 84*
News-Post [of Laguna Publishing Co.] - Laguna Hills, CA - *NewsDir 84*
News-Post Newspapers - Laguna Beach, CA - *AyerDirPub 83*
News-Press - Glendale, CA - *AyerDirPub 83*
News-Press - Santa Barbara, CA - *Ed&PubIntYB 82*
News-Press - Ft. Myers, FL - *AyerDirPub 83*
News-Press - Savannah, GA - *AyerDirPub 83*
News Press - St. Joseph, MO - *AyerDirPub 83; Ed&PubIntYB 82; NewsDir 84*
News-Press [of Overland Buhrman Publications] - St. Louis, MO - *NewsDir 84*
News-Press - Nebraska City, NE - *AyerDirPub 83*
News-Press - Stillwater, OK - *AyerDirPub 83; Ed&PubIntYB 82*
News-Press - Richlands, VA - *AyerDirPub 83*
News-Press & Gazette Co. - St. Joseph, MO - *BrCabYB 84; Tel&CabFB 84S*
News Press & Gazette Co. - *See* St. Joseph Cablevision
News-Press Publishing Co. - Santa Barbara, CA - *BrCabYB 84*
News-Progress - Sullivan, IL - *AyerDirPub 83; Ed&PubIntYB 82*
News-Progress - Hominy, OK - *AyerDirPub 83*
News-Progress - Homestead, PA - *Ed&PubIntYB 82*
News-Progress - Chase City, VA - *Ed&PubIntYB 82*
News-Progress - Clarksville, VA - *AyerDirPub 83; Ed&PubIntYB 82*
News Publishing - Crawfordville, FL - *BaconPubCkNews 84*
News Publishing Co. - Atkinson, IL - *BaconPubCkNews 84*
News Publishing Co. - Honey Grove, TX - *BaconPubCkNews 84*
News Publishing Co. Inc. - Mountain Home, ID - *BaconPubCkNews 84*
News Publishing Co. Inc. - Pittsburgh, PA - *BaconPubCkNews 84*
News Publishing Co. Inc. - Black Earth, WI - *BaconPubCkNews 84*
News-Record - Dalton, MA - *AyerDirPub 83*
News-Record - Rahway, NJ - *AyerDirPub 83*
News-Record - Marshall, NC - *AyerDirPub 83*
News-Record - Miami, OK - *AyerDirPub 83*
News-Record - Sterling City, TX - *AyerDirPub 83*
News-Record - Whitesboro, TX - *AyerDirPub 83; Ed&PubIntYB 82*
News-Record - Harrisonburg, VA - *AyerDirPub 83*
News-Record - Gillette, WY - *AyerDirPub 83; Ed&PubIntYB 82*
News-Record - Clinton, ON, Canada - *AyerDirPub 83*
News-Record - Delhi, ON, Canada - *AyerDirPub 83*
News-Record Div. [of News Printing Co.] - Pittsburgh, PA - *BaconPubCkNews 84*
News-Record of Maplewood & South Orange [of Worrall Publishing Co.] - Maplewood, NJ - *AyerDirPub 83; Ed&PubIntYB 82; NewsDir 84*
News-Record, The - Madison County, NC - *Ed&PubIntYB 82*
News-Register - Aurora, NE - *AyerDirPub 83*
News-Register - McMinnville, OR - *AyerDirPub 83; Ed&PubIntYB 82; NewsDir 84*
News-Register - Wheeling, WV - *AyerDirPub 83; Ed&PubIntYB 82*
News Report [of Blackwood Cam-Glo Newspapers Inc.] - Blackwood, NJ - *AyerDirPub 83; NewsDir 84*
News-Reporter - Tampa, FL - *Ed&PubIntYB 82*
News-Reporter - Washington, GA - *AyerDirPub 83*
News-Reporter - Whiteville, NC - *AyerDirPub 83; Ed&PubIntYB 82*
News-Republic - Baraboo, WI - *Ed&PubIntYB 82*
News-Republican - Henry, IL - *AyerDirPub 83*
News-Republican - Boone, IA - *AyerDirPub 83; Ed&PubIntYB 82*
News Research Service - San Diego, CA - *Ed&PubIntYB 82*
News/Retrieval Sports Report [of Dow Jones News/Retrieval Service] - Princeton, NJ - *DataDirOnSer 84; DirOnDB Spring 84*
News/Retrieval Symbols Directory [of Dow Jones News/Retrieval Service] - Princeton, NJ - *DirOnDB Spring 84*
News/Retrieval Weather Report [of Dow Jones News/Retrieval Service] - Princeton, NJ - *DataDirOnSer 84; DirOnDB Spring 84*
News/Retrieval World Report [of Dow Jones News/Retrieval Service] - Princeton, NJ - *DataDirOnSer 84; DirOnDB Spring 84*
News-Review - Inyokern, CA - *AyerDirPub 83*
News-Review - Augusta, GA - *Ed&PubIntYB 82*
News-Review - Sigourney, IA - *AyerDirPub 83*
News-Review - Greenbelt, MD - *AyerDirPub 83*
News-Review - Petoskey, MI - *AyerDirPub 83*
News-Review - Riverhead, NY - *AyerDirPub 83; Ed&PubIntYB 82*
News-Review - Continental, OH - *AyerDirPub 83*
News-Review - Roseburg, OR - *AyerDirPub 83; BaconPubCkNews 84; Ed&PubIntYB 82*
News-Review - Hico, TX - *AyerDirPub 83*
News-Review - Wallis, TX - *Ed&PubIntYB 82*
News-Review - Bellows Falls, VT - *AyerDirPub 83*
News-Review, The - Keokuk County, IA - *Ed&PubIntYB 82*
News-Review, The - Sumner, WA - *Ed&PubIntYB 82; NewsDir 84*
News-Rustler - Slater, MO - *AyerDirPub 83; Ed&PubIntYB 82*
News-Sentinel - Lodi, CA - *AyerDirPub 83*
News-Sentinel - Ft. Wayne, IN - *AyerDirPub 83; Ed&PubIntYB 82; LitMarPl 84*
News-Sentinel - Stigler, OK - *AyerDirPub 83*
News-Sentinel - Knoxville, TN - *AyerDirPub 83*
News-Sickle-Arrow - Black Earth, WI - *Ed&PubIntYB 82*
News-Standard - Coulee City, WA - *AyerDirPub 83; Ed&PubIntYB 82*
News-Star - Monroe, LA - *NewsDir 84*
News-Star - Shawnee, OK - *AyerDirPub 83*
News-Star - Lambeth, ON, Canada - *AyerDirPub 83; Ed&PubIntYB 82*
News-Star-World - Monroe, LA - *AyerDirPub 83; Ed&PubIntYB 82*
News Suburban, The - Marlton, NJ - *Ed&PubIntYB 82*
News-Sun - Sun City, AZ - *AyerDirPub 83*
News-Sun - Waukegan, IL - *AyerDirPub 83; BaconPubCkNews 84; Ed&PubIntYB 82*
News-Sun - Fairmount, IN - *AyerDirPub 83*
News-Sun - Kendallville, IN - *AyerDirPub 83*
News-Sun - Longton, KS - *AyerDirPub 83*
News-Sun - Hobbs, NM - *AyerDirPub 83*
News-Sun - Berea, OH - *Ed&PubIntYB 82*
News-Sun - Springfield, OH - *AyerDirPub 83*
News-Sun - Newport, PA - *AyerDirPub 83; Ed&PubIntYB 82; NewsDir 84*
News-Telegram - Sulphur Springs, TX - *AyerDirPub 83*
News-Telegraph - Atlantic, IA - *AyerDirPub 83*
News-Texan Newspapers - Farmers Branch, TX - *Ed&PubIntYB 82*
News, The - San Pablo, CA - *Ed&PubIntYB 82*
News, The - Chesterfield, IN - *AyerDirPub 83; Ed&PubIntYB 82*
News, The - Clay City, IN - *AyerDirPub 83; Ed&PubIntYB 82*
News, The - Tell City, IN - *AyerDirPub 83; Ed&PubIntYB 82*
News, The - Yorktown, IN - *Ed&PubIntYB 82*
News, The - Hancock, MD - *AyerDirPub 83*
News, The - Gardner, MA - *AyerDirPub 83*
News, The - Waverly, NE - *Ed&PubIntYB 82*

News, The [of Cherry Hill Suburban Newspaper Group] - Cherry Hill, NJ - *AyerDirPub 83; NewsDir 84*
News, The - Egg Harbor City, NJ - *AyerDirPub 83; Ed&PubIntYB 82*
News, The - Paterson, NJ - *Ed&PubIntYB 82; LitMarPl 83, 84*
News, The - Hickory, NC - *AyerDirPub 83*
News, The - Port Orford, OR - *Ed&PubIntYB 82*
News, The - Homestead, PA - *AyerDirPub 83*
News, The - Albany, TX - *AyerDirPub 83*
News, The - Friendswood, TX - *Ed&PubIntYB 82*
News, The - North Ft. Worth, TX - *Ed&PubIntYB 82*
News, The - West, TX - *AyerDirPub 83*
News, The - Port Angeles, WA - *AyerDirPub 83*
News, The - Medicine Hat, AB, Canada - *AyerDirPub 83; Ed&PubIntYB 82*
News, The - Teeswater, ON, Canada - *AyerDirPub 83*
News-Times - El Dorado, AR - *AyerDirPub 83*
News-Times - Danbury, CT - *AyerDirPub 83; Ed&PubIntYB 82*
News-Times - Hartford City, IN - *AyerDirPub 83; Ed&PubIntYB 82*
News-Times - York, NE - *AyerDirPub 83*
News-Times - Amherst, OH - *AyerDirPub 83*
News-Times - Newport, OR - *AyerDirPub 83; Ed&PubIntYB 82*
News-Times Yorba Linda Star - Placentia, CA - *NewsDir 84*
News-Topic - Lenoir, NC - *AyerDirPub 83*
News Transcript - Freehold, NJ - *AyerDirPub 83; Ed&PubIntYB 82*
News-Tribune - Fullerton, CA - *AyerDirPub 83*
News-Tribune - Brush, CO - *AyerDirPub 83*
News-Tribune [of Florida Freedom Newspapers Inc.] - Ft. Pierce, FL - *AyerDirPub 83; Ed&PubIntYB 82; NewsDir 84*
News-Tribune - La Salle, IL - *AyerDirPub 83; Ed&PubIntYB 82*
News-Tribune - Clifton, KS - *AyerDirPub 83*
News-Tribune [of Waltham Publishing Co.] - Waltham, MA - *AyerDirPub 83; Ed&PubIntYB 82; LitMarPl 83, 84*
News-Tribune - Duluth, MN - *AyerDirPub 83*
News-Tribune [of Middlesex County Publishing Co.] - Woodbridge, NJ - *AyerDirPub 83; BaconPubCkNews 84; Ed&PubIntYB 82; NewsDir 84*
News-Tribune - Portales, NM - *AyerDirPub 83*
News-Tribune - Oberlin, OH - *AyerDirPub 83*
News-Tribune - Ft. Worth, TX - *AyerDirPub 83; Ed&PubIntYB 82*
News-Tribune - Teague, TX - *Ed&PubIntYB 82*
News-Tribune - Blenheim, ON, Canada - *AyerDirPub 83*
News-Tribune & Herald [of Knight-Ridder Newspapers Inc.] - Duluth, MN - *LitMarPl 84; NewsDir 84*
News-Tribune, The - Hicksville, OH - *Ed&PubIntYB 82*
News-Virginian - Waynesboro, VA - *AyerDirPub 83; Ed&PubIntYB 82*
News-Visitor - Kountze, TX - *AyerDirPub 83*
News Watchman - Waverly, OH - *AyerDirPub 83*
News Wave - Independence, WI - *AyerDirPub 83; Ed&PubIntYB 82*
News West - Coram, NY - *AyerDirPub 83*
News World, The - New York, NY - *AyerDirPub 83; Ed&PubIntYB 82; NewsDir 84*
Newsart - New York, NY - *LitMag&SmPr 83-84*
Newsbank Inc. - New Canaan, CT - *CompReadDB 82; EISS 83; InfoS 83-84; MagIndMarPl 82-83; MicroMarPl 82-83*
Newsbank Inc. - New York, NY - *BrCabYB 84*
Newsbank Library [of Newsbank Inc.] - New Canaan, CT - *CompReadDB 82*
Newsbase [of Fintel Ltd.] - London, England - *CompReadDB 82; EISS 83*
Newsbeat [of GTE Information Systems Inc.] - Mt. Laurel, NJ - *DBBus 82; DirOnDB Spring 84*
Newsbeat [of GTE Telenet] - Vienna, VA - *DataDirOnSer 84*
Newsboy & Signal - Luling, TX - *AyerDirPub 83*
Newsclip Ltd. - London, England - *ProGuPRSer 4*
NewScript Media Services - San Francisco, CA - *BrCabYB 84*
Newsday - Long Island, NY - *BaconPubCkNews 84; Ed&PubIntYB 82; LitMarPl 83, 84; NewsBur 6; WritMar 84*
Newsday - Melville, NY - *AyerDirPub 83*
Newsearch [of Information Access Co.] - Menlo Park, CA - *CompReadDB 82; DataDirOnSer 84; DBBus 82; DirOnDB Spring 84; EISS 83; OnBibDB 3*
Newsfeed Network, The [Div. of Westinghouse Broadcasting & Cable Co.] - New York, NY - *BrCabYB 84; Tel&CabFB 84C*
Newsfilm Inc. [Aff. of Marathon International Productions Inc.] - New York, NY - *BrCabYB 84; TelAl 83, 84; Tel&CabFB 84C*
Newsfilm Lab Inc. - Los Angeles, CA - *AvMarPl 83*
Newsfilmproducers-Seacoast Film - Philadelphia, PA - *BrCabYB 84*
NewsFlash [of NewsNet Inc.] - Bryn Mawr, PA - *DataDirOnSer 84*
Newsfoto Publishing Co. [Subs. of Taylor Publishing Co.] - San Angelo, TX - *LitMarPl 83, 84*
Newsfront International [of People's Translation Service] - Oakland, CA - *LitMag&SmPr 83-84*
Newsgroup Inc. - Rockville, MD - *BrCabYB 84*
Newsletter [of Long Island Poetry Collective Inc.] - Huntington, NY - *LitMag&SmPr 83-84*
Newsletter - New York, NY - *MagIndMarPl 82-83*
Newsletter Inago - Tucson, AZ - *LitMag&SmPr 83-84*
Newsletter Management Corp. - Boca Raton, FL - *DirMarMP 83*
Newsletter of Advertising - New York, NY - *MagIndMarPl 82-83*
Newsletter of Research - New York, NY - *MagIndMarPl 82-83*
Newsletter on Newsletters - Rhinebeck, NY - *BaconPubCkMag 84; MagIndMarPl 82-83*
Newsletter, The - Los Angeles, CA - *MagIndMarPl 82-83*
Newslife - Marion, OH - *Ed&PubIntYB 82*
Newsline [of Finbury Data Services] - London, England - *DataDirOnSer 84; DirOnDB Spring 84*
Newsmaking International Inc. - *See* Madison Fielding Inc.
NewsNet Action Newsletter [of NewsNet Inc.] - Bryn Mawr, PA - *DataDirOnSer 84; DirOnDB Spring 84*
NewsNet Inc. [Subs. of Independent Publications Inc.] - Bryn Mawr, PA - *DataDirOnSer 84; EISS 83; InfIndMarPl 83; InfoS 83-84; MicrocomMPl 84*
NewsNet's On-line Bulletin [of NewsNet Inc.] - Bryn Mawr, PA - *DataDirOnSer 84*
Newsom & Co. Inc., Earl - New York, NY - *DirPRFirms 83*
Newsome & Co. Inc. - *See* Byoir & Associates Inc., Carl
Newspaper Archive Developments Ltd. - Reading, England - *MicroMarPl 82-83*
Newspaper Audience Data Bank - Toronto, ON, Canada - *DirOnDB Spring 84*
Newspaper Book Service - Columbia, SC - *BoPubDir 4, 5*
Newspaper Enterprise Association [Aff. of United Media Enterprises] - New York, NY - *BaconPubCkNews 84; Ed&PubIntYB 82; LitMarPl 83, 84; MagIndMarPl 82-83; NewsBur 6*
Newspaper Index [of Bell & Howell] - Wooster, OH - *CompReadDB 82; DataDirOnSer 84; DBBus 82; OnBibDB 3*
Newspaper Index to the Chicago Sun-Times [of Bell & Howell] - Wooster, OH - *CompReadDB 82*
Newspaper Index to the Chicago Tribune [of Bell & Howell] - Wooster, OH - *CompReadDB 82*
Newspaper Index to the Denver Post [of Bell & Howell] - Wooster, OH - *CompReadDB 82*
Newspaper Index to the Detroit News [of Bell & Howell] - Wooster, OH - *CompReadDB 82*
Newspaper Index to the Houston Post [of Bell & Howell] - Wooster, OH - *CompReadDB 82*
Newspaper Index to the Los Angeles Times [of Bell & Howell] - Wooster, OH - *CompReadDB 82*
Newspaper Index to the New Orleans Times-Picayune [of Bell & Howell] - Wooster, OH - *CompReadDB 82*
Newspaper Index to the San Francisco Chronicle [of Bell & Howell] - Wooster, OH - *CompReadDB 82*
Newspaper Index to the St. Louis Post-Dispatch [of Bell & Howell] - Wooster, OH - *CompReadDB 82*
Newspaper Index to the Washington Post [of Bell & Howell] - Wooster, OH - *CompReadDB 82*
Newspaper Production - Philadelphia, PA - *WritMar 84*
Newspaper Services - Friendship, WI - *BoPubDir 4, 5*
Newspaper Technology - Philadelphia, PA - *MagDir 84*
Newspapers of Benton County - Belle Plaine, IA - *AyerDirPub 83*
Newspapers of Iowa County - Marengo, IA - *BaconPubCkNews 84*
Newspapers of New England Inc. - Concord, NH - *Ed&PubIntYB 82*

Newsradio Ltd. - Toronto, ON, Canada - *BrCabYB 84*
Newsreal - Tucson, AZ - *LitMag&SmPr 83-84*
Newsshare [of United Press International] - New York, NY - *EISS 83*
Newstex [of QL Systems Ltd.] - Ottawa, ON, Canada - *DataDirOnSer 84*
Newstex [of Press News Ltd.] - Toronto, ON, Canada - *CompReadDB 82; DirOnDB Spring 84*
Newsweb Corp. - Chicago, IL - *BrCabYB 84; MagIndMarPl 82-83*
Newsweek [of The Washington Post Co.] - New York, NY - *BaconPubCkMag 84; DirMarMP 83; Folio 83; LitMarPl 83, 84; MagDir 84; MagIndMarPl 82-83; NewsBur 6; WritMar 84*
Newsweek Books - New York, NY - *LitMarPl 83, 84*
Newsweek Broadcasting Service - New York, NY - *Tel&CabFB 84C*
Newsweek International Editorial Service - New York, NY - *Ed&PubIntYB 82*
Newsweek, The - Shively, KY - *AyerDirPub 83; Ed&PubIntYB 82*
Newswire Central - Minneapolis, MN - *ProGuPRSer 4*
Newtah News Group - American Fork, UT - *BaconPubCkNews 84*
Newton Advertising - Los Angeles, CA - *StaDirAdAg 2-84*
Newton Associates - St. Davids, PA - *AdAge 3-28-84; StaDirAdAg 2-84*
Newton Cable TV Co. Inc. - Effingham, IL - *BrCabYB 84*
Newton Cable TV Co. Inc. [of Vandalia Cable TV Co. Inc.] - Newton, IL - *Tel&CabFB 84C*
Newton Cable TV Inc. [of Tele-Communications Inc.] - Newton, KS - *Tel&CabFB 84C*
Newton Cablevision Inc. [of Davis Enterprises] - Newton, PA - *Tel&CabFB 84C*
Newton CATV - Newton, KS - *BrCabYB 84*
Newton County Enterprise - Kentland, IN - *AyerDirPub 83; Ed&PubIntYB 82*
Newton County News - Granby, MO - *AyerDirPub 83; Ed&PubIntYB 82*
Newton County News - Newton, TX - *BaconPubCkNews 84; Ed&PubIntYB 82*
Newton Falls Herald - Newton Falls, OH - *BaconPubCkNews 84; Ed&PubIntYB 82*
Newton Falls Paper Mill Inc. - Newton Falls, NY - *LitMarPl 83, 84*
Newton-Fenderson Communications - New York, NY - *DirPRFirms 83*
Newton Graphic [of Dedham Daily Transcript] - Dedham, MA - *NewsDir 84*
Newton Graphic - *See* Transcript Newspapers Inc.
Newton Graphic, The - Newton, MA - *Ed&PubIntYB 82*
Newton Jasper Co. - Nashville, TN - *StaDirAdAg 2-84*
Newton Kansan [of Stauffer Communications Inc.] - Newton, KS - *BaconPubCkNews 84; Ed&PubIntYB 82; NewsDir 84*
Newton Marketing & Advertising, B. C. - Philadelphia, PA - *ArtMar 84*
Newton News - Newton, IA - *AyerDirPub 83; BaconPubCkNews 84; Ed&PubIntYB 82; NewsDir 84*
Newton Observer-News-Enterprise [of Mebane Printing Co. Inc.] - Newton, NC - *NewsDir 84*
Newton Press-Mentor - Newton, IL - *BaconPubCkNews 84; NewsDir 84*
Newton Record - Newton, MS - *BaconPubCkNews 84; Ed&PubIntYB 82; NewsDir 84*
Newton Square County Leader - Newton Square, PA - *BaconPubCkNews 84*
Newton Times - Newton Center, MA - *Ed&PubIntYB 82; NewsDir 84*
Newton Villager [of Belmont Offset Printing & Publishing Co. Inc.] - Belmont, MA - *Ed&PubIntYB 82; NewsDir 84*
Newton Villager - *See* Herald Publishing Co.
Newton Villager & Transcript - Belmont, MA - *AyerDirPub 83*
Newtown Bee - Newtown, CT - *AyerDirPub 83; BaconPubCkNews 84; Ed&PubIntYB 82; NewsDir 84*
Newville Valley Times-Star [of Shippensburg News-Chronicle Co. Inc.] - Newville, PA - *NewsDir 84*
Newville Valley Times-Star - *See* News Chronicle Co. Inc.
Nexis [of Mead Data Central] - Chicago, IL - *MicrocomMPl 84*
Nexis [of Mead Data Central] - New York, NY - *CompReadDB 82; DBBus 82; EISS 83*
Nexis [of Mead Data Central] - Dayton, OH - *DataDirOnSer 84; DirOnDB Spring 84*
Nexo Publicidad SA - Buenos Aires, Argentina - *StaDirAdAg 2-84*
Next Exit - Tamworth, ON, Canada - *LitMag&SmPr 83-84*
Next Move Theatre, The - Boston, MA - *WritMar 84*
Nexus - Los Angeles, CA - *WhoWMicrocom 83*
Nexus Press - Atlanta, GA - *BoPubDir 4, 5*
Nexus Press - Kirkland, WA - *BoPubDir 4, 5*
Nexus Productions - New York, NY - *AvMarPl 83*
Nexus Verlag - Frankfurt, West Germany - *LitMag&SmPr 83-84*
NF Systems Ltd. - Atlanta, GA - *MicrocomMPl 83, 84*
NFAIS Newsletter - Philadelphia, PA - *MagIndMarPl 82-83*
NFL Films Inc. - Mt. Laurel, NJ - *BillIntBG 83-84; Tel&CabFB 84C*
NFO Research [Subs. of AGB Research Group] - Toledo, OH - *AdAge 5-17-84 p.30*
NFS Press - San Francisco, CA - *ArtMar 84; BoPubDir 4, 5*
NGL Research Services Inc. - New Orleans, LA - *IntDirMarRes 83*
NGN Radio Network - San Francisco, CA - *BrCabYB 84*
NHM Publications - Cary, NC - *BoPubDir 4, 5*
NHPRC Data Base on Historical Records in the United States [of U.S. National Historical Publications & Records Commission] - Washington, DC - *EISS 83*
NHTV 21 Inc. - Concord, NH - *BrCabYB 84*
Niagara Advance - Niagara-on-the-Lake, ON, Canada - *AyerDirPub 83; Ed&PubIntYB 82*
Niagara Co-Axial Ltd. - Stoney Creek, ON, Canada - *BrCabYB 84*
Niagara Community TV Co-Op - Niagara, WI - *BrCabYB 84; Tel&CabFB 84C*
Niagara Falls Gazette - Niagara Falls, NY - *NewsDir 84*
Niagara Falls Review - Niagara Falls, ON, Canada - *BaconPubCkNews 84; Ed&PubIntYB 82*
Niagara Frontier Cable Television Inc. [of Adelphia Communications Corp.] - Niagara Falls, NY - *BrCabYB 84; Tel&CabFB 84C*
Niagara Gazette - Niagara Falls, NY - *BaconPubCkNews 84; Ed&PubIntYB 82*
Niagara Journal - Niagara, WI - *BaconPubCkNews 84; Ed&PubIntYB 82*
Niagara/Northtowns Pennysaver - Grand Island, NY - *AyerDirPub 83*
Niagara of Wisconsin Paper Corp. [Subs. of Pentair Inc.] - Niagara, WI - *LitMarPl 83, 84; MagIndMarPl 82-83*
Niagara Scientific Inc. - East Syracuse, NY - *WhoWMicrocom 83*
Niagara Telephone Co. - Niagara, WI - *TelDir&BG 83-84*
Niagara University Press - Niagara University, NY - *BoPubDir 4 Sup, 5*
Niantic News [of Guilford Shore Line Times] - Guilford, CT - *NewsDir 84*
Niantic News [of Guilford Shore Line Times] - Niantic, CT - *BaconPubCkNews 84; Ed&PubIntYB 82*
Nibble [of Micro SPARC Inc.] - Lincoln, MA - *BaconPubCkMag 84; MicrocomMPl 84; WritMar 84*
Nibble Micro Sparc Inc. - Lincoln, MA - *MicrocomMPl 83*
Niccolini Creations, Dianora - New York, NY - *LitMarPl 83, 84*
NICEM [of National Information Center for Educational Media] - Los Angeles, CA - *DataDirOnSer 84; DirOnDB Spring 84; MicroMarPl 82-83*
NICER Productions - Indianapolis, IN - *AvMarPl 83*
Nicetonian [of Greater Philadelphia Group Inc.] - Philadelphia, PA - *NewsDir 84*
Niceville Bayou Times - Crestview, FL - *BaconPubCkNews 84*
Nichi Bei Times - San Francisco, CA - *AyerDirPub 83; Ed&PubIntYB 82*
Nichol & Co., B. - New York, NY - *DirPRFirms 83*
Nicholas Chronicle - Summersville, WV - *Ed&PubIntYB 82*
Nicholas County News Leader - Richwood, WV - *AyerDirPub 83; Ed&PubIntYB 82*
Nicholas Marketing Associates - New York, NY - *StaDirAdAg 2-84*
Nicholasville Cablevision [of Centel Cable Television Co.] - Nicholasville, KY - *BrCabYB 84*
Nicholasville Jessamine Journal - Nicholasville, KY - *BaconPubCkNews 84; NewsDir 84*

Nichols Advertising Associates, Robert - Seattle, WA - *StaDirAdAg 2-84*
Nichols & Associates Inc., Robert - Decatur, IL - *StaDirAdAg 2-84*
Nichols Applied Management - Edmonton, AB, Canada - *EISS 5-84 Sup; InfIndMarPl 83*
Nichols Investment Corp. - Terre Haute, IN - *Tel&CabFB 84C p.1694*
Nichols, Joseph - Tulsa, OK - *BoPubDir 5*
Nichols Publishing Co. - New York, NY - *ArtMar 84; EISS 7-83 Sup; LitMarPl 83, 84; WritMar 84*
Nicholson Agency, The - Studio City, CA - *StaDirAdAg 2-84*
Nicholson & Co. Inc., B. A. - New York, NY - *MicrocomMPl 84; MicrocomSwDir 1*
Nicholson, Kovac, Huntley & Welsh Inc. - Kansas City, MO - *StaDirAdAg 2-84*
Nicholson-Muir Productions Inc. - Larchmont, NY - *TelAl 83, 84; Tel&CabFB 84C*
Nicholson Photography, Nick - Raleigh, NC - *AvMarPl 83; LitMarPl 83, 84; MagIndMarPl 82-83*
Nicholson Press, The - Toronto, ON, Canada - *LitMarPl 83*
Nicholson-Smith, Donald - New York, NY - *LitMarPl 83, 84*
Nicholson's Books, George - Vancouver, BC, Canada - *BoPubDir 4, 5*
Nicholstone Book Bindery - Nashville, TN - *LitMarPl 83, 84*
Nicholville Telephone Co. Inc. - Nicholville, NY - *TelDir&BG 83-84*
Nick & Dave Music - *See* Sesco Music
Nick-O-Val Music - New York, NY - *BillIntBG 83-84*
Nickel Belt News - Thompson, MB, Canada - *Ed&PubIntYB 82*
Nickel Belt Rails - Sudbury, ON, Canada - *BoPubDir 4, 5*
Nickel Forecast - Bala Cynwyd, PA - *DirOnDB Spring 84*
Nickel Record Productions - Hartford, CT - *BillIntBG 83-84*
Nickelodeon [of Warner Amex Satellite Entertainment Co.] - New York, NY - *BrCabYB 84; CabTVPrDB 83; HomeVid&CabYB 82-83; Tel&CabFB 84C; WritMar 84*
Nickle, John T. - Forsyth, MT - *Tel&CabFB 84C p.1694*
Nicklin Advertising Ltd. - London, England - *StaDirAdAg 2-84*
Nico Cable Inc. - Great Lakes, IL - *BrCabYB 84; Tel&CabFB 84C*
Nicolai TV Cable Co. - Knappa, OR - *Tel&CabFB 84C*
Nicolai TV Cable Co. - Westport, OR - *BrCabYB 84*
Nicolas-Hays Inc. - York Beach, ME - *BoPubDir 4, 5*
Nicolet Zeta Corp. [Subs. of Nicolet Instrument Corp.] - Concord, CA - *DataDirSup 7-83; MicrocomMPl 84; WhoWMicrocom 83*
Nicoletti Music Co., Joseph - Newport Beach, CA - *BillIntBG 83-84*
Nicoll-Manuscript Typing Service, Sara - New York, NY - *LitMarPl 83, 84*
Nicolls Press, Alexander - Vancouver, BC, Canada - *BoPubDir 4, 5*
Nicols, Joseph - Tulsa, OK - *BoPubDir 4*
NICSEM - Washington, DC - *DirOnDB Spring 84*
NICSEM [of Bibliographic Retrieval Services Inc.] - Latham, NY - *DataDirOnSer 84*
NICSEM [of Ontario Ministries of Education & of Colleges & Universities] - Toronto, ON, Canada - *DataDirOnSer 84*
Nida Music Publishing Co. - Sherman Oaks, CA - *BillIntBG 83-84*
Niehoff, Henry W. - *See* Barron Cable Co.
Nielsen Co., A. C. - Northbrook, IL - *AdAge 5-17-84 p.16; BrCabYB 84; EISS 83; InfoS 83-84; IntDirMarRes 83; KnowInd 83; Tel&CabFB 84C*
Nielsen Co., A. C. - New York, NY - *DataDirOnSer 84*
Nielsen Inquiry Service - Clinton, IA - *MagIndMarPl 82-83*
Nielsen Retail Index [of A. C. Nielsen Co.] - Northbrook, IL - *DBBus 82; DirOnDB Spring 84*
Nielsen Station Index [of A. C. Nielsen Co.] - Northbrook, IL - *DBBus 82; DirOnDB Spring 84*
Nielsen Station Index [of Interactive Market Systems Inc.] - New York, NY - *DataDirOnSer 84*
Nielsen Television Index [of A. C. Nielsen Co.] - Northbrook, IL - *DBBus 82; DirOnDB Spring 84*
Nielsen Television Index [of Interactive Market Systems Inc.] - New York, NY - *DataDirOnSer 84*
Niemi - Oakridge, OR - *BoPubDir 5*
Nigberg Public Relations Corp. - Framingham, MA - *DirPRFirms 83; HBIndAd&MS 82-83; StaDirAdAg 2-84*
Night Horn Books - San Francisco, CA - *BoPubDir 4 Sup, 5; LitMag&SmPr 83-84*
Night Light Magazine [of Bovincular Atavists Co.] - Santa Barbara, CA - *LitMag&SmPr 83-84*
Night Owl Publishers - Shepparton, Australia - *LitMag&SmPr 83-84*
Nighthawk Press - Forest Grove, OR - *BoPubDir 4, 5*
Nighthawk Records - St. Louis, MO - *BillIntBG 83-84*
Nightingale-Conant Corp. - Chicago, IL - *DirMarMP 83*
Nightsun [of Acheron Press] - Frostburg, MD - *LitMag&SmPr 83-84*
NIH/EPA Chemical Information System [of U.S. Environmental Protection Agency] - Washington, DC - *DataDirOnSer 84; EISS 83*
Nihom Advertising Co., Jack - Mission Viejo, CA - *StaDirAdAg 2-84*
Nihon Kagaku Gijutsu Joho Senta/Japanese Infor. Center for Science & Technology - Tokyo, Japan - *InfIndMarPl 83*
Nihon Keizai Shimbun - Tokyo, Japan - *InfIndMarPl 83*
Nikeda Music Co. - Alton, IL - *BillIntBG 83-84*
Nikkei Area & Marketing Databank - Tokyo, Japan - *DirOnDB Spring 84*
Nikkei Economic Electronic Databank Service-Information Retrieval [of Nihon Keizai Shimbun Inc.] - Tokyo, Japan - *EISS 83*
Nikkei Economic Electronic Databank Service-Time Sharing [of Nihon Keizai Shimbun Inc.] - Tokyo, Japan - *EISS 83*
Nikkei Economic Statistics - Tokyo, Japan - *DBBus 82; DirOnDB Spring 84*
Nikkei Energy Data Bank [of Data Resources Inc.] - Lexington, MA - *DBBus 82*
Nikkei Energy Data Bank - Tokyo, Japan - *DirOnDB Spring 84*
Nikkei-File - Tokyo, Japan - *DirOnDB Spring 84*
Nikkei Financials - Tokyo, Japan - *DirOnDB Spring 84*
Nikkei Stock Prices - Tokyo, Japan - *DirOnDB Spring 84*
Nikkel Saaver - Moses Lake, WA - *AyerDirPub 83*
Nikki Songs Ltd. - *See* Kellijai Music Corp.
Nikmal Publishing - Mattapan, MA - *BoPubDir 4, 5; LitMag&SmPr 83-84*
Nikon Inc. - Garden City, NY - *AvMarPl 83*
Niktek Inc. - Montville, NJ - *DirInfWP 82*
Niles Bugle - *See* Bugle Publications
Niles Bugle Publications - Chicago, IL - *NewsDir 84*
Niles Communications Centers, Fred A. - Chicago, IL - *ProGuPRSer 4; StaDirAdAg 2-84; TelAl 83, 84*
Niles Communications Centers, Fred A. - New York, NY - *ArtMar 84; Tel&CabFB 84C*
Niles Daily Times [of Phoenix Publications Inc.] - Niles, OH - *BaconPubCkNews 84; Ed&PubIntYB 82; NewsDir 84*
Niles Family Journal - *See* Journal & Topics Newspapers
Niles Journal [of Des Plaines Journal-News Publications] - Des Plaines, IL - *NewsDir 84*
Niles Journal [of Des Plaines Journal-News Publications] - Niles, IL - *Ed&PubIntYB 82*
Niles Journal - *See* Journal & Topics Newspapers
Niles Life - Niles, IL - *Ed&PubIntYB 82*
Niles Life - *See* Myers Publishing Co.
Niles Life, The - Skokie, IL - *AyerDirPub 83*
Niles Spectator - Niles, IL - *Ed&PubIntYB 82*
Niles Spectator [of Pioneer Press Inc.] - Park Ridge, IL - *NewsDir 84*
Niles Spectator - Wilmette, IL - *AyerDirPub 83*
Niles Spectator - *See* Pioneer Press Inc.
Niles Star - Niles, MI - *BaconPubCkNews 84; NewsDir 84*
Nilgiri Press - Petaluma, CA - *LitMarPl 83, 84*
Nils Publishing Co. [Subs. of American Broadcasting Cos. Inc.] - Chatsworth, CA - *DirMarMP 83*
Nilson Report, The - Los Angeles, CA - *BaconPubCkMag 84*
Nimbus Publishing Ltd. [Subs. of H. H. Marshall Ltd.] - Halifax, NS, Canada - *BoPubDir 4, 5; WritMar 84*
Nimeck, Fran Gazze - North Brunswick, NJ - *LitMarPl 83, 84*
NIMH - Arlington, VA - *DirOnDB Spring 84*
Nimitz Foundation, Admiral - Fredericksburg, TX - *BoPubDir 4, 5*
Nimrod - Tulsa, OK - *LitMag&SmPr 83-84; WritMar 84*

Nimrod Press - Boston, MA - *LitMarPl 83, 84; MagIndMarPl 82-83*
Nin-Ra Enterprises - La Canada, CA - *BoPubDir 4, 5*
1981 Canadian Census [of Statistics Canada] - Toronto, ON, Canada - *DirOnDB Spring 84*
Nineteenth-Century Fiction [of University of California Press] - Berkeley, CA - *LitMag&SmPr 83-84*
Nineteenth Century Magazine - Philadelphia, PA - *MagIndMarPl 82-83*
19th Street Music - *See* Lorenz Creative Services
99'er Home Computer [of Emerald Valley Publishing Co.] - Eugene, OR - *BaconPubCkMag 84; MicrocomMPl 84*
9200 Film Center - Minneapolis, MN - *AvMarPl 83*
Nininger Stations - Bristol, VA - *BrCabYB 84*
Ninnescah Valley Times - Pretty Prairie, KS - *Ed&PubIntYB 82*
Ninth Decade [of Shearsman Books] - London, England - *LitMag&SmPr 83-84*
Ninth Sign Publications - Hoboken, NJ - *BoPubDir 4, 5*
Niobium Forecast - Bala Cynwyd, PA - *DirOnDB Spring 84*
Niobrara Tribune - Niobrara, NE - *BaconPubCkNews 84; Ed&PubIntYB 82*
Nipigon Gazette - Nipigon, ON, Canada - *Ed&PubIntYB 82*
Nippon Electric Co. Ltd. - Melville, NY - *HomeVid&CabYB 82-83*
Nippon Gijutsu Boeki Co. Ltd. - Tokyo, Japan - *EISS 83*
Nippon Information Services - Washington, DC - *MagIndMarPl 82-83*
Nippon Kagaku Gijutsu Joho Senta - Tokyo, Japan - *CompReadDB 82*
Nippon Research Center Ltd. - Tokyo, Japan - *IntDirMarRes 83*
Nippon Technical Service - Tokyo, Japan - *MicroMarPl 82-83*
NIPS - Tokyo, Japan - *DirOnDB Spring 84*
NIR/New Infinity Review - Ironton, OH - *ArtMar 84*
Nirvana Records - Manville, NJ - *BillIntBG 83-84*
Nisbet Music Inc., Ben - *See* Special Rider Music
Nise Productions Inc. - Camden, NJ - *BillIntBG 83-84*
Nishna Valley Tribune - Audubon, IA - *AyerDirPub 83*
Nisqually Valley News - Yelm, WA - *AyerDirPub 83; Ed&PubIntYB 82*
Nisqually Valley Shopper - Yelm, WA - *AyerDirPub 83*
Nissei Sangyo America Ltd. - New York, NY - *DataDirSup 7-83*
Nissen Advertising Inc. - Lakeland, FL - *StaDirAdAg 2-84*
Nissen-Lie Consult Inc. - New York, NY - *DirPRFirms 83*
Nit & Wit - Chicago, IL - *ArtMar 84; BaconPubCkMag 84; LitMag&SmPr 83-84; MagDir 84*
NITA - Philadelphia, PA - *BaconPubCkMag 84; MagDir 84*
Nite-Beat News Service - New York, NY - *LitMarPl 84*
Nite-Line [of National Computer Network] - Chicago, IL - *MicrocomMPl 84*
Nitec/Midtec Sales Inc. - New York, NY - *MagIndMarPl 82-83*
Nitfol Music [Div. of Nitfol Enterprises] - Tulsa, OK - *BillIntBG 83-84*
Nitfol Records - Tulsa, OK - *BillIntBG 83-84*
Nittan Corp. - Des Plaines, IL - *DataDirSup 7-83*
Nitty-Gritty Cookbooks - Concord, CA - *LitMarPl 84*
Nitty-Gritty Productions - Concord, CA - *LitMarPl 83*
NIV Complete Concordance [of Zondervan Corp.] - Grand Rapids, MI - *EISS 83*
Nivram Corp. - New York, NY - *LitMarPl 83, 84*
Nixa Enterprise - Nixa, MO - *BaconPubCkNews 84; Ed&PubIntYB 82*
Nixdorf Computer AG - Paderborn, West Germany - *InfIndMarPl 83*
Nixdorf Computer Corp. - Burlington, MA - *DataDirSup 7-83; Top100Al 83; WhoWMicrocom 83*
Nixdorf Computer Corp. - Waltham, MA - *Datamation 6-83; DirInfWP 82; InfIndMarPl 83*
Nixdorf Computer Software Co. - Richmond, VA - *ADAPSOMemDir 83-84*
Nixon Cable TV [of Combined Technologies of Texas Inc.] - Nixon, TX - *Tel&CabFB 84C*
Nixon News - Nixon, TX - *Ed&PubIntYB 82*
Nixon News - *See* South Texas Newspapers Inc.
Nixon Newspapers Inc. - Wabash, IN - *Ed&PubIntYB 82*
N.J. Law Journal - Newark, NJ - *MagDir 84*
NJEA Review - Trenton, NJ - *ArtMar 84; BaconPubCkMag 84; MagDir 84*
NLADA Briefcase - Washington, DC - *ArtMar 84; MagDir 84*
NLADA Cornerstone - Washington, DC - *MagDir 84*
Nlex - Ijmuiden, Netherlands - *DirOnDB Spring 84*
NLGI Spokesman [of National Lubricating Grease Institute] - Kansas City, MO - *BaconPubCkMag 84; MagDir 84*
NMD Features - Chicago, IL - *Ed&PubIntYB 82*
NMEA News - Tinton Falls, NJ - *BaconPubCkMag 84*
NMF Inc. - Charlotte, NC - *DataDirSup 7-83*
NMI Microprocessing [Subs. of Norton-Murphy International] - Fairfield, NJ - *WhoWMicrocom 83*
NMI Productions Corp. - Kansas City, MO - *BillIntBG 83-84*
NMRLit - Bethesda, MD - *DirOnDB Spring 84*
NMU Pilot - New York, NY - *NewsDir 84*
No Club Music - *See* Southern Crescent Publishing
No Dead Lines - Portola Valley, CA - *BoPubDir 4, 5*
No Load Mutual Fund Association Inc. - New York, NY - *BoPubDir 5*
No Loose Change Music - New York, NY - *BillIntBG 83-84*
No Soap Radio/Bryan Wells Music - New York, NY - *HBIndAd&MS 82-83*
No Tickee/No Washee Enterprises Ltd. - Chicago, IL - *LitMag&SmPr 83-84*
No-Till Farmer - Brookfield, WI - *BaconPubCkMag 84*
NOAA Data Buoy Office [of National Oceanic & Atmospheric Administration] - NSTL Station, MS - *EISS 83*
NOAA Library & Information Network [of National Oceanic & Atmospheric Administration] - Rockville, MD - *InfIndMarPl 83*
NOAA National Weather Service [of National Oceanic & Atmospheric Administration] - Washington, DC - *DirOnDB Spring 84*
NOAA National Weather Service [of National Oceanic & Atmospheric Administration] - Silver Spring, MD - *BrCabYB 84*
Noakes Data Communications Inc. - Irving, TX - *DataDirSup 7-83*
Noalmark Broadcasting Corp. - El Dorado, AR - *BrCabYB 84*
Nob Hill Gazette - San Francisco, CA - *BaconPubCkMag 84*
Noble & Asociados Advertising Group - Mexico City, Mexico - *StaDirAdAg 2-84*
Noble & Associates - Springfield, MO - *AdAge 3-28-84; StaDirAdAg 2-84*
Noble Arnold & Associates - Arlington Heights, IL - *ArtMar 84*
Noble Cable of Churubusco Inc. - Churubusco, IN - *Tel&CabFB 84C*
Noble Cable TV Inc. - Albion, IN - *BrCabYB 84*
Noble Cable TV Inc. - Kendallville, IN - *BrCabYB 84; Tel&CabFB 84C p.1694*
Noble Cable TV Inc. - Lagrange, IN - *BrCabYB 84*
Noble Cable TV Inc. - Ligonier, IN - *BrCabYB 84*
Noble Cable TV Inc. - Syracuse, IN - *Tel&CabFB 84C*
Noble Cable TV Ltd. - Noble, OK - *BrCabYB 84*
Noble Cleveland County Reporter - Noble, OK - *BaconPubCkNews 84*
Noble County American, The - Albion, IN - *AyerDirPub 83; Ed&PubIntYB 82*
Noble Fulfillment Corp. - New York, NY - *MagIndMarPl 82-83*
Noble House Publishing - Beverly Hills, CA - *BoPubDir 4, 5; LitMag&SmPr 83-84*
Noble McQuerry, Mary - Jacksonville, FL - *BoPubDir 4*
Noble Offset Printers Inc. - New York, NY - *LitMarPl 83, 84*
Noble Productions Inc. - Sherman Oaks, CA - *Tel&CabFB 84C*
Noble, Tim - New York, NY - *LitMarPl 84*
Nobles County Review - Adrian, MN - *AyerDirPub 83; Ed&PubIntYB 82*
Noblesville Cablevision Inc. - Noblesville, IN - *BrCabYB 84; Tel&CabFB 84C*
Noblesville Ledger - Noblesville, IN - *BaconPubCkNews 84; Ed&PubIntYB 82; NewsDir 84*
Noblesville Telegraph [of Pace Publishing Inc.] - Noblesville, IN - *Ed&PubIntYB 82; NewsDir 84*
Noblesville Telegraph - *See* Topic Newspapers Inc.
Noblesville Times - Noblesville, IN - *BaconPubCkNews 84; Ed&PubIntYB 82*
Nobodaddy Press - Lansing, NY - *BoPubDir 4, 5; LitMag&SmPr 83-84*

Nocona News - Nocona, TX - *BaconPubCkNews 84; Ed&PubIntYB 82*
Nocona Telephone Co [Aff. of Allied Telephone Co.] - Nocona, TX - *TelDir&BG 83-84*
Nocona TV Cable System [of Dorate Interstate Inc.] - Nocona, TX - *BrCabYB 84; Tel&CabFB 84C*
Noda - Denver, CO - *AvMarPl 83*
Nodak Cablevision - Rosemount, MN - *Tel&CabFB 84C*
Nodak Cablevision - Wishek, ND - *BrCabYB 84*
NoDaKable Inc. - Bottineau, ND - *BrCabYB 84 p.D-305; Tel&CabFB 84C p.1694*
NoDaKable Inc. - Goodrich, ND - *BrCabYB 84*
Nodarse, Connie - Miami, FL - *LitMarPl 83; MagIndMarPl 82-83*
Nodin Press Inc. [Aff. of The Bookmen Inc.] - Minneapolis, MN - *BoPubDir 4, 5*
Nodlew Music - *See* Iguana Music Inc.
Nodvill Software - Ridgefield, CT - *MicrocomMPl 84*
Noel McDonald County Press - Noel, MO - *BaconPubCkNews 84*
Noell's Ark Publishers - Tarpon Springs, FL - *BoPubDir 4, 5*
Noemer, Fred - Old Tappan, NJ - *MagIndMarPl 82-83*
Noesis Computing Co. - San Francisco, CA - *DataDirOnSer 84*
Nogales International - Nogales, AZ - *BaconPubCkNews 84*
Noise Control Engineering - Poughkeepsie, NY - *BaconPubCkMag 84*
Noise Control Engineering Journal [of Institute of Noise Control Engineering] - Lafayette, IN - *MagDir 84*
Noise/News [of Noise Control Foundation] - Poughkeepsie, NY - *BaconPubCkMag 84; MagDir 84*
Noit Amrofer Publishing Co. - Seattle, WA - *BoPubDir 4, 5*
Nok Publishers International - New York, NY - *BoPubDir 4, 5; LitMarPl 84*
Nokomis Free Press-Progress - Nokomis, IL - *BaconPubCkNews 84; NewsDir 84*
Nokomis Times, The - Nokomis, SK, Canada - *Ed&PubIntYB 82*
Nola Data Systems Inc. - Lancaster, PA - *MicrocomMPl 83, 84*
Nolan & Co. Advertising & Graphics Inc. - Skokie, IL - *StaDirAdAg 2-84*
Nolan Co. Inc., Robert E. - Simsbury, CT - *WhoWMicrocom 83*
Nolan County News - Sweetwater, TX - *AyerDirPub 83; Ed&PubIntYB 82*
Nolan Family - Iron Springs, AB, Canada - *BoPubDir 4, 5*
Nolan Group Inc., The Betsy - New York, NY - *DirPRFirms 83; LitMarPl 83, 84; MagIndMarPl 82-83*
Nolan Information Management Services - Torrance, CA - *BoPubDir 4 Sup, 5*
Nolan, Kellor & Stites Inc. - *See* Hogan, Nolan & Stites Inc.
Nolan Literary Agency, The Betsy [Div. of The Betsy Nolan Group Inc.] - New York, NY - *LitMarPl 83, 84*
Nolan Market Research Service Inc., Barbara - Altamonte Springs, FL - *IntDirMarRes 83*
Nolan Publishing Co., Kenny - Los Angeles, CA - *BillIntBG 83-84*
Nolans Audio Visual Inc. - Memphis, TN - *AvMarPl 83*
Noll Printing Co. Inc. - Huntington, IN - *MagIndMarPl 82-83*
Nolo Press - Occidental, CA - *BoPubDir 4, 5; LitMag&SmPr 83-84*
NOMDA Spokesman - Wood Dale, IL - *BaconPubCkMag 84; MagDir 84*
Nome Cablevision [of Alaska Cablevision Inc.] - Nome, AK - *BrCabYB 84; Tel&CabFB 84C*
Nome Nugget - Nome, AK - *BaconPubCkNews 84; Ed&PubIntYB 82*
Nomis Publications Inc. - Poland, OH - *BoPubDir 5*
Nomura Computer Systems Co. Ltd. - Tokyo, Japan - *ADAPSOMemDir 83-84*
Nomura Research Institute [Subs. of Nomura Securities] - Tokyo, Japan - *DataDirOnSer 84*
Nomura Research Institute (Japan Economic & Business Data Bank) - Tokyo, Japan - *DirOnDB Spring 84*
Nomura Research Institute Data Base-Japan [of Chase Econometrics/Interactive Data Corp.] - Waltham, MA - *DataDirOnSer 84*
Non-Entity Press - Fredericton, NB, Canada - *BoPubDir 4 Sup, 5*
Non-Ferrous Metals Forecast [of Chase Econometrics/Interactive Data Corp.] - Waltham, MA - *DBBus 82*
Non-Foods Merchandising - New York, NY - *BaconPubCkMag 84; MagDir 84; WritMar 84*
Non-Procedural Systems - Westport, CT - *ADAPSOMemDir 83-84*
Nonagon - El Cerrito, CA - *MicrocomMPl 84*
Nondestructive Testing Documentation [of Federal Institute for Materials Testing] - Berlin, West Germany - *EISS 83*
Nondestructive Testing Information Analysis Center [of Southwest Research Institute] - San Antonio, TX - *CompReadDB 82; EISS 83; InfIndMarPl 83*
Nonferrous Metals Abstracts [of Dialog Information Services Inc.] - Palo Alto, CA - *DataDirOnSer 84*
Nonferrous Metals Abstracts - Wantage, England - *DirOnDB Spring 84*
Nongilloc Books - L'Original, ON, Canada - *BoPubDir 4 Sup, 5*
Nonnee Coan - Houston, TX - *Ed&PubIntYB 82*
Nonpareil - Council Bluffs, IA - *AyerDirPub 83*
Nonviolent Anarchist Newsletter [of Slough Press] - Austin, TX - *LitMag&SmPr 83-84*
Nonwovens Industry - Ramsey, NJ - *BaconPubCkMag 84; MagDir 84*
Noon-National Outdoor Outfitters News - Prospect Hights, IL - *BaconPubCkMag 84*
Noon Rock - Barrytown, NY - *BoPubDir 4, 5*
Noonan Farmers Telephone Co. - Noonan, ND - *TelDir&BG 83-84*
Noonan Marketing & Opinion Research, Edward J. - Ormond Beach, FL - *BrCabYB 84; Tel&CabFB 84C*
Noontide Press - Terrance, CA - *BoPubDir 4, 5*
Nooter Stock Program - New York, NY - *MicrocomMPl 84*
Nopoly Press Inc. - Wilmington, DE - *BoPubDir 4, 5*
Nor-Cal Cablevision - Alturas, CA - *BrCabYB 84*
Nor-Cal Cablevision [of McClatchy Newspapers] - Marysville, CA - *BrCabYB 84; Tel&CabFB 84C*
Nor-Cal Cablevision - *See* McClatchy Newspapers
Nor-Com Cable Investors - *See* Nor-Com Video Inc.
Nor-Com Video Inc. - Cadott, WI - *BrCabYB 84*
Nor-Com Video Inc. [of North-West Telephone Co.] - Mt. Horeb, WI - *Tel&CabFB 84C*
Nor-Com Video Inc. - Tomah, WI - *Tel&CabFB 84C p.1694*
Nor-Com Video Inc. - Wautoma, WI - *BrCabYB 84*
Nor Publications - Hillsboro, OR - *LitMag&SmPr 83-84*
Nora Springs Advertiser - Nora Springs, IA - *BaconPubCkNews 84; Ed&PubIntYB 82*
Noral Color Corp. - Chicago, IL - *LitMarPl 83, 84*
NorAmSo - Arvada, CO - *MicrocomMPl 84*
Norand Corp. - Cedar Rapids, IA - *DataDirSup 7-83*
Norand Publishing Ltd. [Aff. of Northwest Litho Ltd.] - Calgary, AB, Canada - *BoPubDir 4, 5*
Noranda Press - Rouyn, PQ, Canada - *Ed&PubIntYB 82*
NorArk Cable TV [of Pinion Corp.] - Calico Rock, AR - *Tel&CabFB 84C*
NorArk Cable TV [of Pinion Corp.] - Cotter, AR - *Tel&CabFB 84C*
NorArk Cable TV [of Pinion Corp.] - Salem, AR - *Tel&CabFB 84C*
Norborne Democrat-Leader - Norborne, MO - *BaconPubCkNews 84*
Norbu, Thinley - New York, NY - *BoPubDir 5*
Norbud Music - *See* Duce Music
Norcable Ltd. - Gagnon, PQ, Canada - *BrCabYB 84*
Norco St. Charles Herald - Norco, LA - *BaconPubCkNews 84; Ed&PubIntYB 82*
NorCom Cable Investors - Black Earth, WI - *Tel&CabFB 84C*
NorCom Cable Investors - Poynette, WI - *Tel&CabFB 84C*
NorCom Cable Investors - Spencer, WI - *Tel&CabFB 84C*
Norcom Systems Inc. - Seattle, WA - *DataDirSup 7-83*
Norcom Telecommunications Ltd. - Kenora, ON, Canada - *BrCabYB 84*
Norcom Video of Red Wing - Red Wing, MN - *BrCabYB 84*
Nord Advertising Associates - Salt Lake City, UT - *AdAge 3-28-84; StaDirAdAg 2-84*
Nordale Estate, Thomas N. - Tucson, AZ - *Tel&CabFB 84C*
Nordbye Advertising & Marketing - Missoula, MT - *StaDirAdAg 2-84*
Norden - Brooklyn, NY - *Ed&PubIntYB 82; NewsDir 84*
Nordhaus Research Inc. - Farmington Hills, MI - *IntDirMarRes 83*

Nordic Atomic Libraries Joint Secretariat [of Riso National Laboratory] - Roskilde, Denmark - *InfIndMarPl 83*
Nordic Books - Philadelphia, PA - *BoPubDir 4, 5; LitMag&SmPr 83-84*
Nordic Council for Scientific Information & Research Libraries - Espoo, Finland - *EISS 83*
Nordic Documentation Center for Mass Communication Research - Aarhus, Denmark - *EISS 83*
Nordic Energy Index [of Nordic Atomic Libraries Joint Secretariat] - Roskilde, Denmark - *EISS 83*
Nordic 1981 - Brattleboro, VT - *MagDir 84*
Nordic Systems - Williamsville, NY - *MicrocomMPl 84*
Nordic Translators - St. Paul, MN - *BoPubDir 5*
Nordic World - Mountain View, CA - *MagDir 84*
Nordisk BDI-Indeks [of Norsk Senter for Informatikk] - Oslo, Norway - *CompReadDB 82*
Nordisk Tidende - Brooklyn, NY - *Ed&PubIntYB 82; NewsDir 84*
Nordland Publishing International Inc. - Belmont, MA - *LitMarPl 83*
Nordstijernan-Svea - Brooklyn, NY - *AyerDirPub 83; Ed&PubIntYB 82*
Nordstrom/Cox Marketing Inc. - Grand Rapids, MI - *StaDirAdAg 2-84*
Noreale Music Inc. - *See* Elektra/Asylum Music Inc.
Norelco Dictation Systems - Woodbury, NY - *DirInfWP 82*
Norell Data Systems Corp. - Los Angeles, CA - *MicrocomMPl 84; MicrocomSwDir 1; WritMar 84*
Norfolk Daily News [of Huse Publishing Co.] - Norfolk, NE - *BaconPubCkNews 84; Ed&PubIntYB 82; NewsDir 84*
Norfolk Journal & Guide - Norfolk, VA - *BaconPubCkNews 84; NewsDir 84*
Norfolk Ledger-Star [of Landmark Communications Inc.] - Norfolk, VA - *NewsDir 84*
Norfolk MDS Co. - Englewood, NJ - *Tel&CabFB 84C*
Norges Eksportrad - Oslo, Norway - *CompReadDB 82*
Norges Standardiseringsforbund - Oslo, Norway - *CompReadDB 82*
Noriane [of Questel Inc.] - Washington, DC - *DataDirOnSer 84*
Noriane - Paris, France - *DirOnDB Spring 84*
Norma-Lewis Agency, The - New York, NY - *LitMarPl 83, 84*
Normal Heights/Kensington Pennysaver - Mission Viejo, CA - *AyerDirPub 83*
Normal Normalite - Normal, IL - *BaconPubCkNews 84*
Norman & Sandra - Orient, NY - *BoPubDir 4, 5*
Norman Cable Television Inc. [of American Television & Communications Corp.] - Norman, OK - *BrCabYB 84; Tel&CabFB 84C*
Norman, Carig & Kummel Inc. - New York, NY - *BrCabYB 84*
Norman County Index - Ada, MN - *AyerDirPub 83; Ed&PubIntYB 82*
Norman County Telephone Co. Inc. [Aff. of Ollig Utilities Co.] - Ada, MN - *TelDir&BG 83-84*
Norman, Lawrence, Patterson & Farrell Inc. - New York, NY - *DirPRFirms 83*
Norman Press - Toronto, ON, Canada - *BoPubDir 4 Sup, 5*
Norman Public Relations, Beverly - Kansas City, MO - *ArtMar 84; DirPRFirms 83*
Norman Publishing Co. - Wayne, NJ - *BoPubDir 4, 5*
Norman Robert Associates - Philadelphia, PA - *StaDirAdAg 2-84*
Norman Transcript - Norman, OK - *BaconPubCkNews 84; Ed&PubIntYB 82; NewsDir 84*
Normandie Publishing Co. - Los Angeles, CA - *BoPubDir 4*
Normandie Publishing Co. - New York, NY - *BoPubDir 5*
Normangee Star - Normangee, TX - *BaconPubCkNews 84; Ed&PubIntYB 82*
Norman's International Inc. - College Park, GA - *BillIntBG 83-84*
Normes et Reglements Informations Accessibles en Ligne [of Association Francaise de Normalisation] - Paris, France - *CompReadDB 82*
Noroil - Houston, TX - *BaconPubCkMag 84*
Norpak Ltd. - Kanata, ON, Canada - *VideoDir 82-83*
Norrell Systems Corp. - Atlanta, GA - *ADAPSOMemDir 83-84*
Norridge-Edison Park Citizen - Norwood Park, IL - *Ed&PubIntYB 82*
Norris Associates Inc., E. Scott - New York, NY - *StaDirAdAg 2-84*
Norris Electronics Co. - Pleasant Ridge Plantation, ME - *BrCabYB 84*
Norris Ink, Joan - Hanover, MA - *LitMarPl 83, 84*
Norris Place - St. Catharines, ON, Canada - *BoPubDir 4, 5*
Norristown Times Herald - Norristown, PA - *BaconPubCkNews 84; NewsDir 84*
Norrona - Delta, BC, Canada - *Ed&PubIntYB 82*
Norsearch International Inc. - New York, NY - *IntDirMarRes 83*
Norseman Cablevision [of McDonald Group Inc.] - Ada, OH - *BrCabYB 84; Tel&CabFB 84C*
Norseman Cablevision [of McDonald Group Inc.] - Bluffton, OH - *BrCabYB 84; Tel&CabFB 84C*
Norseman Cablevision [of McDonald Group Inc.] - Carey, OH - *BrCabYB 84; Tel&CabFB 84C*
Norseman Cablevision [of McDonald Group Inc.] - Minster, OH - *BrCabYB 84; Tel&CabFB 84C*
Norseman Cablevision [of McDonald Group Inc.] - Versailles, OH - *BrCabYB 84; Tel&CabFB 84C*
Norsk Brannvern Forening/Norwegian Fire Protection Association - Oslo, Norway - *InfIndMarPl 83*
Norsk Medieindeks - Oslo, Norway - *DirOnDB Spring 84*
Norsk Mediendeks [of Interactive Market Systems Inc.] - New York, NY - *DataDirOnSer 84*
Norsk Oseanografisk Datasenter - Bergen Nordnes, Norway - *InfIndMarPl 83*
Norsk Senter for Informatikk - Oslo, Norway - *CompReadDB 82; InfIndMarPl 83*
Norsk Skipsforskningsinstitutt - Oslo, Norway - *CompReadDB 82*
Norske Argus A/S - Oslo, Norway - *ProGuPRSer 4*
North Adams Research Institute - North Adams, MA - *IntDirMarRes 83*
North America Mica Inc. - San Diego, CA - *MicrocomMPl 83, 84; MicrocomSwDir 1; WhoWMicrocom 83*
North American Cable Systems [of North American Communications Corp.] - Appleton, MN - *BrCabYB 84; Tel&CabFB 84C*
North American Cable Systems [of North American Communications Corp.] - Aurora, MN - *BrCabYB 84*
North American Cable Systems [of North American Communications Corp.] - Clara City, MN - *BrCabYB 84; Tel&CabFB 84C*
North American Cable Systems [of Cable Communications Systems Inc.] - Clinton, MN - *Tel&CabFB 84C*
North American Cable Systems [of Cable Communications Systems Inc.] - Cloquet, MN - *BrCabYB 84*
North American Cable Systems [of North American Communications Corp.] - Eveleth, MN - *BrCabYB 84*
North American Cable Systems [of North American Communications Corp.] - Fuida, MN - *BrCabYB 84*
North American Cable Systems [of North American Communications Corp.] - Gilbert, MN - *BrCabYB 84*
North American Cable Systems [of North American Communications Corp.] - Graceville, MN - *BrCabYB 84*
North American Cable Systems - Grand Rapids, MN - *BrCabYB 84*
North American Cable Systems [of North American Communications Corp.] - Hector, MN - *BrCabYB 84*
North American Cable Systems [of North American Communications Corp.] - Hoyt Lakes, MN - *BrCabYB 84*
North American Cable Systems [of North American Communications Corp.] - Ivanhoe, MN - *BrCabYB 84*
North American Cable Systems [of North American Communications Corp.] - Lake Benton, MN - *BrCabYB 84*
North American Cable Systems - Lake City, MN - *BrCabYB 84*
North American Cable Systems [of North American Communications Corp.] - Madison, MN - *BrCabYB 84*
North American Cable Systems - Moose Lake, MN - *BrCabYB 84*
North American Cable Systems - Nashwauk-Keewatin, MN - *BrCabYB 84*
North American Cable Systems - Olivia, MN - *BrCabYB 84*
North American Cable Systems - Proctor, MN - *BrCabYB 84*
North American Cable Systems [of North American Communications Corp.] - Slayton, MN - *BrCabYB 84*
North American Cable Systems - Springfield, MN - *BrCabYB 84*
North American Cable Systems - Two Harbors, MN - *BrCabYB 84; Tel&CabFB 84C*

North American Cable Systems - Tyler, MN - *BrCabYB 84*
North American Cable Systems [of North American Communications] - Virginia, MN - *BrCabYB 84; Tel&CabFB 84C*
North American Cable Systems [of North American Communications Corp.] - Wheaton, MN - *BrCabYB 84*
North American Cable Systems [of Communications Systems Inc.] - Clear Lake, SD - *BrCabYB 84*
North American Carline Production Forecast - Bala Cynwyd, PA - *DirOnDB Spring 84*
North American Communications Corp. - Hector, MN - *Tel&CabFB 84C p.1694*
North American Communications Corp. - Pine Island, MN - *Tel&CabFB 84C*
North American Congress on Latin America - New York, NY - *BoPubDir 4, 5*
North American Controls Inc. - Portland, OR - *WhoWMicrocom 83*
North American Falconry & Hunting Hawks - Denver, CO - *BoPubDir 4, 5*
North American Hunter - Minneapolis, MN - *BaconPubCkMag 84*
North American Indian Traveling College - Cornwall Island, ON, Canada - *BoPubDir 4, 5*
North American Lily Society Inc. - Waukee, IA - *BoPubDir 4, 5*
North American Liturgy Resources [Aff. of Epoch Universal Publications] - Phoenix, AZ - *BoPubDir 4*
North American Marketing Corp. [Subs. of Environmental Educators Inc.] - Washington, DC - *DirMarMP 83*
North American Mentor [of Westburg Associates] - Fennimore, WI - *ArtMar 84; LitMag&SmPr 83-84; WritMar 84*
North American Micronics Inc. - San Clemente, CA - *DataDirSup 7-83*
North American Newstime - Atlanta, GA - *HomeVid&CabYB 82-83*
North American Philips Corp. - New York, NY - *ElecNews 7-25-83; HomeVid&CabYB 82-83*
North American Philips Lighting Corp. [Subs. of North American Philips Corp.] - Hightstown, NJ - *AvMarPl 83*
North American Post - Seattle, WA - *Ed&PubIntYB 82; NewsDir 84*
North American Precis Syndicate Inc. - New York, NY - *Ed&PubIntYB 82*
North American Publishing Co. - Philadelphia, PA - *BoPubDir 4, 5; MagIndMarPl 82-83*
North American Review [of The University of Northern Iowa] - Cedar Falls, IA - *LitMag&SmPr 83-84; LitMarPl 83, 84; MagIndMarPl 82-83; WritMar 84*
North American Software Inc. - St. Louis, MO - *WhoWMicrocom 83*
North American Stock Market Database [of I. P. Sharp Associates Ltd.] - Toronto, ON, Canada - *DataDirOnSer 84; DirOnDB Spring 84*
North American Students of Cooperation - Ann Arbor, MI - *BoPubDir 4, 5*
North American Technology Inc. - Peterborough, NH - *MicrocomMPl 83, 84*
North American Telecommunications Association - Washington, DC - *TeleSy&SerDir 7-83*
North American Teleshopping Inc. - San Mateo, CA - *VideoDir 82-83*
North American Truckline Production Forecast - Bala Cynwyd, PA - *DirOnDB Spring 84*
North American Vegetarian Society [Aff. of International Vegetarian Union] - Dolgeville, NY - *BoPubDir 4, 5*
North American Voice of Fatima - Youngstown, NY - *WritMar 84*
North American Whitetail - Marietta, GA - *BaconPubCkMag 84*
North Andover Citizen - North Andover, MA - *AyerDirPub 83*
North Area Pennysaver - Syracuse, NY - *AyerDirPub 83*
North Arlington Leader - Lyndhurst, NJ - *AyerDirPub 83*
North Arlington Leader - North Arlington, NJ - *Ed&PubIntYB 82*
North Arlington Leader - *See* Leader Newspapers Inc.
North Atlanta Neighbor - North Atlanta, GA - *Ed&PubIntYB 82*
North Atlantic Aviation [of Data Publications Inc.] - Brookfield, CT - *MagDir 84*
North Atlantic Books [Div. of Society for the Study of Native Arts & Sciences] - Berkeley, CA - *LitMag&SmPr 83-84; LitMarPl 84*
North Atlantic Books [Div. of Society for the Study of Native Arts & Sciences] - Richmond, CA - *LitMarPl 83*
North Atlantic Industries - Hauppauge, NY - *MicrocomMPl 84*
North Augusta Star - North Augusta, SC - *BaconPubCkNews 84*
North Baltimore News - North Baltimore, OH - *Ed&PubIntYB 82*
North Baltimore News - *See* Ohioprint Publications Inc.
North Bartow News - Adairsville, GA - *Ed&PubIntYB 82*
North Bay Cable Television Inc. [of Donrey Media Group] - Vallejo, CA - *BrCabYB 84*
North Bay Computers - Yountville, CA - *WhoWMicrocom 83*
North Bay Cooperative Library System - Santa Rosa, CA - *EISS 83*
North Bay Nugget, The - North Bay, ON, Canada - *BaconPubCkNews 84; Ed&PubIntYB 82*
North Bay Sun, The - North Bay, ON, Canada - *Ed&PubIntYB 82*
North Beach Beacon - Ocean Shores, WA - *AyerDirPub 83; Ed&PubIntYB 82*
North Bend Eagle - North Bend, NE - *BaconPubCkNews 84*
North Bend News - North Bend, OR - *AyerDirPub 83; BaconPubCkNews 84; Ed&PubIntYB 82; NewsDir 84*
North Bergen Cable Television Inc. [of Prime Cable Corp.] - North Bergen, NJ - *BrCabYB 84; Tel&CabFB 84C*
North Billerica News - North Billerica, MA - *BaconPubCkNews 84; NewsDir 84*
North Bonneville Community Cable TV System - North Bonneville, WA - *Tel&CabFB 84C*
North Branch Video - North Branch, NY - *Tel&CabFB 84C*
North Brooklyn News - Brooklyn, NY - *AyerDirPub 83; Ed&PubIntYB 82*
North California Electronic News [of Bender Publications Inc.] - Los Angeles, CA - *MagDir 84*
North Canton Sun - North Canton, OH - *BaconPubCkNews 84*
North Carolina - Raleigh, NC - *BaconPubCkMag 84*
North Carolina Anvil - Durham, NC - *AyerDirPub 83; NewsDir 84*
North Carolina Architect [of American Institute of Architects/ North Carolina Chapter] - Raleigh, NC - *MagDir 84*
North Carolina Catholic, The [of Roman Catholic Diocese of Raleigh] - Raleigh, NC - *NewsDir 84*
North Carolina Dept. of Cultural Resources (Historical Publications Section) - Raleigh, NC - *BoPubDir 4, 5*
North Carolina Education - Raleigh, NC - *BaconPubCkMag 84; MagDir 84*
North Carolina Historical Review [of Historical Publications Section, Archives & History] - Raleigh, NC - *WritMar 84*
North Carolina Libraries [of Meridional Publications] - Wake Forest, NC - *LitMag&SmPr 83-84*
North Carolina Medical Journal - Durham, NC - *BaconPubCkMag 84; MagDir 84*
North Carolina Museum of Art [Aff. of Dept. of Cultural Resources] - Raleigh, NC - *BoPubDir 4, 5*
North Carolina Online Users Group [of Duke University] - Durham, NC - *InfIndMarPl 83*
North Carolina Plumbing-Heating-Cooling Forum - Raleigh, NC - *BaconPubCkMag 84*
North Carolina Science & Technology Research Center - Research Triangle Park, NC - *EISS 83*
North Carolina State Agency for Public Telecommunications - Raleigh, NC - *TeleSy&SerDir 2-84*
North Carolina State Budget & Management Div. (State Data Center) - Raleigh, NC - *BoPubDir 5*
North Carolina State Data Center [of Office of State Budget & Management] - Raleigh, NC - *EISS 83*
North Carolina State Interviewing Service Inc., A - Raleigh, NC - *IntDirMarRes 83*
North Carolina State Museum of Natural History [Aff. of North Carolina Dept. of Agriculture] - Raleigh, NC - *BoPubDir 4, 5*
North Carolina State University (Industrial Extension Service) - Raleigh, NC - *BoPubDir 4, 5*
North Castle Books Inc. - Greenwich, CT - *BoPubDir 4, 5*
North Castle News - Armonk, NY - *AyerDirPub 83*
North Castle Partners - Greenwich, CT - *AdAge 3-28-84; StaDirAdAg 2-84*

North Center/Irving Park Booster [of Chicago Lerner Newspapers] - Chicago, IL - *AyerDirPub 83; NewsDir 84*
North Central Associated Publishers - Durand, IL - *BaconPubCkNews 84*
North Central Cable Co. - Rose City, MI - *Tel&CabFB 84C*
North Central Telephone Co. - Badger, IA - *TelDir&BG 83-84*
North Central Telephone Cooperative Inc. - Lafayette, TN - *TelDir&BG 83-84*
North Chicago Tribune [of Lakeland Publishers Inc.] - Grayslake, IL - *NewsDir 84*
North Chicago Tribune - North Chicago, IL - *AyerDirPub 83; Ed&PubIntYB 82*
North Chicago Tribune - *See* Lakeland Publishers Inc.
North, Christina Bolt - Long Island City, NY - *BoPubDir 4, 5*
North City Free Press [of Greater Philadelphia Group Inc.] - Philadelphia, PA - *NewsDir 84*
North Coast Press - East Machias, ME - *BoPubDir 4, 5*
North Coast Publishers Inc. - Encinitas, CA - *BaconPubCkNews 84*
North Coast Publishing - Shaker Heights, OH - *LitMag&SmPr 83-84*
North Conway Northern Light - North Conway, NH - *AyerDirPub 83*
North Conway Northern Light - *See* Rochester Courier Publishers
North Conway Reporter - North Conway, NH - *BaconPubCkNews 84*
North Country Anvil [of Anvil Press] - Millville, MN - *LitMag&SmPr 83-84*
North Country Book Express Inc. - Moscow, ID - *BoPubDir 4 Sup, 5*
North Country Books Inc. - Utica, NY - *LitMag&SmPr 83-84*
North Country Cablevision Inc. - Enosburg Falls, VT - *BrCabYB 84; Tel&CabFB 84C*
North Country Reference & Research Resources Council - Canton, NY - *EISS 83*
North Country Saver - Ely, MN - *AyerDirPub 83*
North Country Sun - Ironwood, MI - *AyerDirPub 83*
North Country TV Cable Inc. - Groveton, NH - *BrCabYB 84*
North Countryman - Rouses Point, NY - *AyerDirPub 83*
North County - Escondido, CA - *AyerDirPub 83*
North County-Baden News-Press - North St. Louis County, MO - *Ed&PubIntYB 82*
North County-Baden News-Press - St. Louis, MO - *AyerDirPub 83*
North County Cablevision [of Daniels & Associates] - Encinitas, CA - *BrCabYB 84*
North County Cablevision [of Daniels Properties Inc.] - Solana Beach, CA - *BrCabYB 84*
North County Cablevision - Squires Dam, CA - *Tel&CabFB 84C*
North County Computer Services Inc. - Escondido, CA - *DataDirOnSer 84*
North County Journal - Paso Robles, CA - *AyerDirPub 83; Ed&PubIntYB 82*
North County Journal - St. Louis, MO - *AyerDirPub 83*
North County Journal - St. Louis County, MO - *Ed&PubIntYB 82*
North County News - Red Bud, IL - *AyerDirPub 83; Ed&PubIntYB 82*
North County News [of Northern Tier Publishing Corp.] - Yorktown Heights, NY - *AyerDirPub 83; Ed&PubIntYB 82; NewsDir 84*
North County News - Vancouver, WA - *Ed&PubIntYB 82*
North County News-Castroville Times - Salinas, CA - *Ed&PubIntYB 82*
North Creek Mutual Telephone Co., The - North Creek, OH - *TelDir&BG 83-84*
North Creek News-Enterprise - North Creek, NY - *BaconPubCkNews 84; Ed&PubIntYB 82*
North Cumberland Historical Society - Pugwash, NS, Canada - *BoPubDir 4, 5*
North Dakota Cable TV Inc. - Cando, ND - *Tel&CabFB 84C*
North Dakota Journal of Education - Bismarck, ND - *BaconPubCkMag 84; MagDir 84*
North Dakota Natural Heritage Program [of North Dakota State Parks & Recreation Dept.] - Bismarck, ND - *EISS 7-83 Sup*
North Dakota Network for Knowledge [of North Dakota State Library] - Bismarck, ND - *EISS 83*
North Dakota Outdoors - Bismarck, ND - *BaconPubCkMag 84*
North Dakota Publisher - Grand Fork, ND - *MagDir 84*
North Dakota Rural Electric Magazine - Mandan, ND - *BaconPubCkMag 84; MagDir 84*
North Dakota State Center [of North Dakota State University] - Fargo, ND - *EISS 7-83 Sup*
North Dakota State Data Center [of North Dakota State Planning Div.] - Bismarck, ND - *EISS 83*
North Dakota State University (Institute for Regional Studies) - Fargo, ND - *BoPubDir 4, 5*
North Dakota Stockman, The - Bismarck, ND - *MagDir 84*
North Dakota Telephone Co. [Aff. of Continental Telephone Corp.] - Devils Lake, ND - *TelDir&BG 83-84*
North Dekalb Cable TV Co. [of Southmedia] - Chamblee, GA - *BrCabYB 84*
North East Breeze - North East, PA - *BaconPubCkNews 84; Ed&PubIntYB 82; NewsDir 84*
North East Cablevision Ltd. - Bathurst, NB, Canada - *BrCabYB 84*
North East Topics [of Indianapolis Topics Newspapers] - Indianapolis, IN - *NewsDir 84*
North-Eastern Pennsylvania Telephone Co., The - Forest City, PA - *TelDir&BG 83-84*
North Edition [of Baltimore Star Publications] - Baltimore, MD - *NewsDir 84*
North Electra Books - Toronto, ON, Canada - *BoPubDir 4, 5*
North English Corp. Telephone Co. - North English, IA - *TelDir&BG 83-84*
North English Record - North English, IA - *Ed&PubIntYB 82*
North Essex News - Belle River, ON, Canada - *AyerDirPub 83*
North Florida Telephone Co. [Aff. of Mid-Continent Telephone Corp.] - Live Oak, FL - *TelDir&BG 83-84*
North Flushing Pennysaver - Jericho, NY - *AyerDirPub 83*
North Fork Journal - Madera County, CA - *Ed&PubIntYB 82*
North Freeway Leader - Houston, TX - *AyerDirPub 83; Ed&PubIntYB 82*
North Ft. Worth News [of Suburban Newspapers Inc.] - Ft. Worth, TX - *AyerDirPub 83; Ed&PubIntYB 82; NewsDir 84*
North Georgia News - Blairsville, GA - *AyerDirPub 83; Ed&PubIntYB 82*
North Gibson CATV Associates [of U.S. Cable Corp.] - Dyer, TN - *BrCabYB 84*
North Glenn/Thornton Sentinel - *See* Sentinel Newspapers
North Greene News - Roodhouse, IL - *Ed&PubIntYB 82*
North Greene News - White Hall, IL - *AyerDirPub 83; Ed&PubIntYB 82*
North Harris County News - Spring, TX - *Ed&PubIntYB 82*
North Haven Post - North Haven, CT - *Ed&PubIntYB 82*
North Haven Post [of Walingford Post] - Wallingford, CT - *AyerDirPub 83; NewsDir 84*
North Hennepin Post [of Minneapolis Post Newspapers] - Minneapolis, MN - *AyerDirPub 83; NewsDir 84*
North Hennepin Post - North Hennepin, MN - *Ed&PubIntYB 82*
North Highlander & Football Farms Reporter [of Sacramento Suburban Newspapers Inc.] - Fair Oaks, CA - *NewsDir 84*
North Highlander & North Football Farms Reporter - North Highlands, CA - *Ed&PubIntYB 82*
North Hill News - Calgary, AB, Canada - *AyerDirPub 83*
North Hills News Record - Pittsburgh, PA - *AyerDirPub 83; Ed&PubIntYB 82*
North Hills News Record - *See* News-Record Div. [of News Printing Co.]
North-Holland Publishing Co. - Amsterdam, Netherlands - *TeleSy&SerDir 2-84*
North Hollywood Graphic - *See* Associated Valley Publications
North Hollywood Studio City Toluca Lake Graphic - Encino, CA - *AyerDirPub 83*
North Idaho Press - Wallace, ID - *BaconPubCkNews 84; Ed&PubIntYB 82*
North Iowa Times - McGregor, IA - *Ed&PubIntYB 82*
North Island Advertiser, The - Courtenay, BC, Canada - *Ed&PubIntYB 82*
North Island Gazette - Port Hardy, BC, Canada - *AyerDirPub 83; Ed&PubIntYB 82*
North Island Gazette Printers & Publishers - Port Hardy, BC, Canada - *BoPubDir 4, 5*

North Jackson Community News - Stevenson, AL - *Ed&PubIntYB 82*
North Jefferson News - Gardendale, AL - *AyerDirPub 83; Ed&PubIntYB 82*
North Jersey Suburbanite - Cresskill, NJ - *AyerDirPub 83*
North Jersey Suburbanite, The - Englewood, NJ - *Ed&PubIntYB 82*
North Kansas City Press Dispatch - *See* Townsend Communications Inc.
North Kent Advance - Sparta, MI - *Ed&PubIntYB 82; NewsDir 84*
North Kent Cable Co. Inc. - Cedar Springs, MI - *BrCabYB 84; Tel&CabFB 84C*
North Kent Leader - Dresden, ON, Canada - *AyerDirPub 83; Ed&PubIntYB 82*
North Kingstown Standard-Times [of Wakefield Narragansett Times] - Wakefield, RI - *NewsDir 84*
North Kingstown Standard-Times - *See* Wilson Publishing Co.
North Las Vegas Valley Times, The - North Las Vegas, NV - *NewsDir 84*
North Light - Fairfield, CT - *ArtMar 84; WritMar 84*
North Light Book Club [Div. of Fletcher Art Services Inc.] - Fairfield, CT - *LitMarPl 84*
North Light Book Club [Div. of Fletcher Art Services Inc.] - Westport, CT - *LitMarPl 83*
North Light Publishers [Div. of Fletcher Art Services Inc.] - Fairfield, CT - *LitMarPl 84*
North Light Publishers [Div. of Fletcher Art Services Inc.] - Westport, CT - *LitMarPl 83*
North Light Repertory - Evanston, IL - *WritMar 84*
North Little Rock Times - North Little Rock, AR - *BaconPubCkNews 84; NewsDir 84*
North Long Beach Herald American - Long Beach, CA - *Ed&PubIntYB 82*
North Long Beach Herald American - South Gate, CA - *AyerDirPub 83*
North Long Beach Herald American - *See* Hearst Community Newspapers
North Loop News - Chicago, IL - *AyerDirPub 83; Ed&PubIntYB 82; NewsDir 84*
North Manchester News-Journal [of Weller Family Publishing Co. Inc.] - North Manchester, IN - *BaconPubCkNews 84; NewsDir 84*
North Miami Beach Leader - Miami Beach, FL - *AyerDirPub 83*
North Miami Beach Leader - North Miami Beach, FL - *Ed&PubIntYB 82*
North Miami Beach News [of South Miami Community Newspapers] - Miami, FL - *AyerDirPub 83; NewsDir 84*
North Miami Beach News - *See* Community Newspapers of Florida Inc.
North Miami Neighbors Newspaper - Miami, FL - *NewsDir 84*
North Miami News [of South Miami Community Newspapers] - Miami, FL - *AyerDirPub 83; NewsDir 84*
North Miami News - *See* Community Newspapers of Florida Inc.
North Miami Sun - Miami Beach, FL - *AyerDirPub 83*
North Miami Sun - North Miami, FL - *Ed&PubIntYB 82*
North Middletown Cable TV [of Centel Cable Television Co.] - North Middletown, KY - *BrCabYB 84*
North Minneapolis & Suburban Shopping Guide - Minneapolis, MN - *AyerDirPub 83*
North Minneapolis Post [of Minneapolis Post Newspapers] - Minneapolis, MN - *Ed&PubIntYB 82; NewsDir 84*
North Mississippi Herald - Water Valley, MS - *AyerDirPub 83; Ed&PubIntYB 82*
North Mississippi Times - Hernando, MS - *Ed&PubIntYB 82*
North Missourian - Gallatin, MO - *AyerDirPub 83*
North Myrtle Beach Times - North Myrtle Beach, SC - *ArtMar 84; BaconPubCkNews 84; Ed&PubIntYB 82; NewsDir 84*
North News - New Brighton, PA - *Ed&PubIntYB 82*
North Okaloosa Bulletin - Crestview, FL - *AyerDirPub 83; Ed&PubIntYB 82*
North Omaha Sun - Omaha, NE - *AyerDirPub 83; Ed&PubIntYB 82; NewsDir 84*
North Ottawa Cablevision Inc. [of Cable Group Management Inc.] - Grand Haven, MI - *Tel&CabFB 84C*
North Pacific Publishers - Portland, OR - *BoPubDir 4, 5*
North Peace Pictorial - Peace River, AB, Canada - *AyerDirPub 83*
North Penn Chat [of Greater Philadelphia Group Inc.] - Philadelphia, PA - *NewsDir 84*
North Penn Telephone Co. - Mansfield, PA - *TelDir&BG 83-84*
North Pittsburgh Telephone Co. - Gibsonia, PA - *TelDir&BG 83-84*
North Plains Press [Aff. of Dakota North Plains Corp.] - Aberdeen, SD - *BoPubDir 4, 5*
North Platte Telegraph [of Western Publishing Co.] - North Platte, NE - *BaconPubCkNews 84; Ed&PubIntYB 82; NewsDir 84*
North Point Press - Berkeley, CA - *LitMag&SmPr 83-84; LitMarPl 83, 84*
North Port Sun Coast Times [of Venice Sun Coast Gondolier Inc.] - Venice, FL - *NewsDir 84*
North Port Sun Coast Times - *See* Sun Coast Media Group Inc.
North Ranch Music - Thousand Oaks, CA - *BillIntBG 83-84*
North Reading Transcript - North Reading, MA - *Ed&PubIntYB 82; NewsDir 84*
North Reading Transcript - *See* Great Oak Publications Inc.
North Renfrew Times - Deep River, ON, Canada - *AyerDirPub 83; Ed&PubIntYB 82*
North Ridgeville Light - Elyria, OH - *NewsDir 84*
North Ridgeville Light - North Ridgeville, OH - *BaconPubCkNews 84*
North River Press Inc. - Croton-on-Hudson, NY - *BoPubDir 4; LitMarPl 83, 84*
North River Telephone Cooperative - Dayton, VA - *TelDir&BG 83-84*
North Riverside Citizen [of La Grange Suburban Life/Citizen] - La Grange, IL - *NewsDir 84*
North Riverside Suburban Life/Citizen - *See* Life Printing & Publishing Co.
North Sacramento Sun - Fair Oaks, CA - *Ed&PubIntYB 82*
North Salem Gallery - North Salem, NY - *ArtMar 84*
North San Antonio Times - San Antonio, TX - *AyerDirPub 83; Ed&PubIntYB 82*
North San Jose Sun - San Jose, CA - *Ed&PubIntYB 82*
North Scott Press - Eldridge, IA - *AyerDirPub 83; Ed&PubIntYB 82*
North Shore - Winnetka, IL - *BaconPubCkMag 84*
North Shore Community Television Ltd. - Cambellton, NB, Canada - *BrCabYB 84*
North Shore Examiner - Evanston, IL - *Ed&PubIntYB 82*
North Shore Magazine [of Essex County Newspapers Inc.] - Beverly, MA - *LitMarPl 83, 84*
North Shore Mail - Pacific Palisades, CA - *AyerDirPub 83*
North Shore News - Roxboro, PQ, Canada - *Ed&PubIntYB 82*
North Shore News & Sunday News - North Vancouver, BC, Canada - *Ed&PubIntYB 82*
North Shore Record - Port Jefferson, NY - *Ed&PubIntYB 82*
North Shore Shopper [of Small Newspapers] - Pacific Palisades, CA - *NewsDir 84*
North Shore: Sunday - Boston, MA - *Ed&PubIntYB 82*
North Shore: Sunday - Danvers, MA - *NewsDir 84*
North Shore: Sunday - Ipswich, MA - *AyerDirPub 83*
North Shore: Sunday - Lynn, MA - *Ed&PubIntYB 82*
North Shore Weeklies Inc. - Ipswich, MA - *BaconPubCkNews 84*
North Shore Yankee Trader - *See* Yankee Trader
North Side Community News - Jennings, MO - *Ed&PubIntYB 82*
North Side Community News - St. Louis, MO - *AyerDirPub 83*
North Side Journal - St. Louis, MO - *Ed&PubIntYB 82*
North Side News - Jerome, ID - *AyerDirPub 83; Ed&PubIntYB 82*
North Side Topics [of Pace Publishing Inc.] - Indianapolis, IN - *NewsDir 84*
North Sider, The - Largo, FL - *AyerDirPub 83*
North Smithfield-Burrillville Observer [of Greenville Observer Publications Inc.] - Greenville, RI - *NewsDir 84*
North Smithfield-Burrillville Observer - North Smithfield, RI - *Ed&PubIntYB 82*
North-South Institute/Institut Nord-Sud - Ottawa, ON, Canada - *BoPubDir 4, 5; LitMarPl 84*
North South Trader - Langley Park, MD - *WritMar 84*
North St. Paul Ramsey County Review - *See* Lillie Suburban Newspapers

North Star - Parry Sound, ON, Canada - *Ed&PubIntYB 82*
North Star - Norquay, SK, Canada - *AyerDirPub 83; Ed&PubIntYB 82*
North Star Advertiser - Oklahoma City, OK - *AyerDirPub 83*
North Star Books - Brandon, MN - *BoPubDir 4, 5*
North Star Computers Inc. - San Leandro, CA - *DataDirSup 7-83; MicrocomMPl 83, 84; WhoWMicrocom 83*
North Star News - Karlstad, MN - *AyerDirPub 83; Ed&PubIntYB 82*
North Star Press - St. Cloud, MN - *BoPubDir 4, 5; LitMag&SmPr 83-84*
North-State Telephone Co. - High Point, NC - *TelDir&BG 83-84*
North-State Telephone Co. - Dufur, OR - *TelDir&BG 83-84*
North Stonington Press - Greenwich, CT - *BoPubDir 4 Sup, 5*
North Suburban Press - Vadnais Heights, MN - *Ed&PubIntYB 82*
North Suburban Press - White Bear Lake, MN - *AyerDirPub 83*
North Suburban Sentinel - Thornton, CO - *AyerDirPub 83*
North Supply Co. - Industrial Airport, KS - *DataDirSup 7-83*
North Syracuse-Cicero Scotchaman News - *See* Brown Newspapers Co. Inc.
North Syracuse Star News [of Baldwinsville Onon-Town Publishing Co. Inc.] - Baldwinsville, NY - *NewsDir 84*
North Tampa Independent - *See* Tampa Suburban Newspapers Inc.
North Texas Communications Co. - Muenster, TX - *BrCabYB 84; Tel&CabFB 84C*
North Texas Daily - Denton, TX - *NewsDir 84*
North Tonawanda Kenmore Record-Advertiser - North Tonawanda, NY - *BaconPubCkNews 84*
North Tonawanda News - North Tonawanda, NY - *BaconPubCkNews 84*
North Toronto Free Press - Toronto, ON, Canada - *Ed&PubIntYB 82*
North Torrance-Gardena-Adviser - *See* Breeze Newspapers
North Town News [of Chicago Lerner Newspapers] - Chicago, IL - *AyerDirPub 83; Ed&PubIntYB 82; NewsDir 84*
North Trade Journal - North, SC - *AyerDirPub 83*
North Utah Community TV - Logan, UT - *BrCabYB 84; Tel&CabFB 84C*
North Vernon Plain Dealer - North Vernon, IN - *Ed&PubIntYB 82*
North Vernon Plain Dealer - *See* Plain Dealer & Sun Inc.
North Vernon Sun [of North Vernon Plain Dealer] - North Vernon, IN - *Ed&PubIntYB 82; NewsDir 84*
North Vernon Sun - *See* Plain Dealer & Sun Inc.
North Warren News - Norwalk, IA - *Ed&PubIntYB 82*
North Watertown Town & Country News [of Gouverneur Town & Country News of Jefferson County] - Gouverneur, NY - *NewsDir 84*
North Weld Herald - Eaton, CO - *AyerDirPub 83*
North West Arts - Manchester, England - *LitMag&SmPr 83-84*
North West News - Chicago, IL - *AyerDirPub 83; Ed&PubIntYB 82*
North West Suburban - Chicago, IL - *AyerDirPub 83*
North-West Telephone Co. [Aff. of North-West Telecommunications Inc.] - Tomah, WI - *Tel&CabFB 84C p.1694; TelDir&BG 83-84*
North Wilkesboro Journal-Patriot - North Wilkesboro, NC - *BaconPubCkNews 84*
North Wind, The [of Beaver Lodge Press] - Vancouver, BC, Canada - *LitMag&SmPr 83-84*
North Woods Call, The - Charlevoix, MI - *BaconPubCkMag 84; MagDir 84*
North York Mirror - North York, ON, Canada - *Ed&PubIntYB 82*
North York Mirror - Willowdale, ON, Canada - *AyerDirPub 83*
North York News - Toronto/North York, ON, Canada - *Ed&PubIntYB 82*
Northampton Daily Hampshire Gazette [of H. S. Gere & Sons Inc.] - Northampton, MA - *NewsDir 84*
Northampton News - Ahoskie, NC - *Ed&PubIntYB 82*
Northampton News - Jackson, NC - *AyerDirPub 83*
Northampton Times - *See* Peerless Publications
Northbrook Life - Northbrook, IL - *Ed&PubIntYB 82*
Northbrook Life - *See* Lerner Life Newspapers
Northbrook News Advertiser - Highland Park, IL - *AyerDirPub 83*
Northbrook News-Advertiser - Northbrook, IL - *Ed&PubIntYB 82*
Northbrook News Advertiser - *See* Singer Printing & Publishing Co.
Northbrook/Northfield Life - Deerfield, IL - *AyerDirPub 83*
Northbrook Star [of Pioneer Press Inc.] - Northbrook, IL - *Ed&PubIntYB 82; NewsDir 84*
Northbrook Star - Wilmette, IL - *AyerDirPub 83*
Northbrook Star - *See* Pioneer Press Inc.
Northcenter News - Chicago, IL - *AyerDirPub 83; Ed&PubIntYB 82*
Northeast Advertiser [of Menomonee Falls Publishing Co.] - Menomonee Falls, WI - *NewsDir 84*
Northeast Advertising Group - New York, NY - *AdAge 3-28-84*
Northeast Advisor - Bensalem, PA - *AyerDirPub 83*
Northeast Advisor [of Inter County Publishing Co.] - Philadelphia, PA - *NewsDir 84*
Northeast Alabamian Shopping News - Ft. Payne, AL - *Ed&PubIntYB 82*
Northeast Breeze, The [of Inter County Publishing Co.] - Philadelphia, PA - *AyerDirPub 83; Ed&PubIntYB 82; NewsDir 84*
Northeast Buyers Guide - Gaylord, MI - *AyerDirPub 83*
Northeast Cable TV - Clarks Summit, PA - *BrCabYB 84; Tel&CabFB 84C*
Northeast Color Research - Somerville, MA - *AvMarPl 83*
Northeast Communications Corp. - Franklin, NH - *BrCabYB 84*
Northeast Communications Inc. - Ft. Devens, MA - *BrCabYB 84*
Northeast Conference on the Teaching of Foreign Languages - Middlebury, VT - *BoPubDir 4, 5*
Northeast Dallas County Record - Woodward, IA - *BaconPubCkNews 84; Ed&PubIntYB 82*
Northeast Detroiter - *See* Harper Woods Herald
Northeast Detroiter Harper Woods Herald - Detroit, MI - *AyerDirPub 83; Ed&PubIntYB 82*
Northeast Edition [of Baltimore Star Publications] - Baltimore, MD - *NewsDir 84*
Northeast Field Facts Inc. - Framingham, MA - *IntDirMarRes 83*
Northeast Florida Telephone Co. Inc. - MacClenny, FL - *TelDir&BG 83-84*
Northeast Georgia - Athens, GA - *AyerDirPub 83*
Northeast Georgian - Cornelia, GA - *AyerDirPub 83; Ed&PubIntYB 82*
Northeast Gwinnett Inc. - Lawrenceville, GA - *Tel&CabFB 84C*
Northeast Horseman [of Henley Sales Ltd.] - Hampden, ME - *WritMar 84*
Northeast Hunting & Fishing - New Hope, PA - *BaconPubCkMag 84*
Northeast Improver, The - Sandy Creek, NY - *BaconPubCkMag 84*
Northeast Iowa Telephone Co. - Monona, IA - *Tel&CabFB 84C; TelDir&BG 83-84*
Northeast Journal - Kingston, RI - *LitMag&SmPr 83-84*
Northeast/Juniper Books [of Juniper Press] - La Crosse, WI - *LitMag&SmPr 83-84*
Northeast Lincoln Sun - Lincoln, NE - *AyerDirPub 83; Ed&PubIntYB 82; NewsDir 84*
Northeast Literary Agency - Concord, NH - *LitMarPl 83, 84*
Northeast Los Angeles Publishing Co. - Los Angeles, CA - *BaconPubCkNews 84*
Northeast Louisiana Telephone Co. Inc. - Collinston, LA - *TelDir&BG 83-84*
Northeast Magazine - Hartford, CT - *ArtMar 84; WritMar 84*
Northeast Minnesota Cable TV [of Group W Cable Inc.] - Duluth, MN - *Tel&CabFB 84C*
Northeast Mississippi Daily Journal - Tupelo, MS - *AyerDirPub 83; BaconPubCkNews 84; Ed&PubIntYB 82*
Northeast Missouri Cable TV Inc. - Edina, MO - *Tel&CabFB 84C p.1694*
Northeast Missouri Rural Telephone Co. - Green City, MO - *TelDir&BG 83-84*
Northeast Missouri State University (Chariton Review Press) - Kirksville, MO - *BoPubDir 4, 5*
Northeast Nebraska Telephone Co. - Jackson, NE - *TelDir&BG 83-84*
Northeast News, The - Northeast Columbus, OH - *Ed&PubIntYB 82*
Northeast-Northland News - Columbus, OH - *AyerDirPub 83*
Northeast Ohio Major Academic Libraries - Kent, OH - *EISS 83*

Northeast Oil Reporter [of Hart Publications Inc.] - Columbus, OH - *BaconPubCkMag 84; MagDir 84*
Northeast Outdoors - Waterbury, CT - *ArtMar 84; BaconPubCkMag 84; MagDir 84; WritMar 84*
Northeast Reporter, The - Indianapolis, IN - *AyerDirPub 83*
Northeast Sales Associates - West Islip, NY - *LitMarPl 84*
Northeast Sportsman's Press - Tarrytown, NY - *BoPubDir 4 Sup, 5*
Northeast Star-Review [of Northeast Los Angeles Publishing Co.] - Los Angeles, CA - *AyerDirPub 83; NewsDir 84*
Northeast Suburban Life [of Cincinnati Suburban Newspapers Inc.] - Cincinnati, OH - *AyerDirPub 83; NewsDir 84*
Northeast Suburban Life - *See* Queen City Suburban Press Inc.
Northeast Telephone Co. - Pulaski, WI - *TelDir&BG 83-84*
Northeast Texas Online Users Group [of American Heart Association Library] - Dallas, TX - *InfIndMarPl 83*
Northeast Times - Northeast Philadelphia, PA - *Ed&PubIntYB 82*
Northeast Times - Philadelphia, PA - *AyerDirPub 83; NewsDir 84*
Northeast Times - San Antonio, TX - *AyerDirPub 83*
Northeast Update - Quincy, MA - *BaconPubCkMag 84*
Northeast Video Inc. - New York, NY - *AvMarPl 83*
Northeastern Buyers Guide [of Weeklies Inc.] - West Branch, MI - *NewsDir 84*
Northeastern Communications Systems Inc. - Green Bay, WI - *Tel&CabFB 84C*
Northeastern Pennsylvania Bibliographic Center - Wilkes-Barre, PA - *EISS 83*
Northeastern Pennsylvania TV Cable Co. - *See* Gans, Joseph S.
Northeastern Shopper - Tawas City, MI - *AyerDirPub 83*
Northeastern Telephone Co. [Aff. of Unitel of Nebraska] - Blair, NE - *TelDir&BG 83-84*
Northeastern University Press - Boston, MA - *LitMarPl 83, 84; WritMar 84*
Northern Ad-Vertiser - Gaylord, MI - *NewsDir 84*
Northern Allegany Observer & Belfast Blaze - Geneseo, NY - *AyerDirPub 83*
Northern Arkansas Telephone Co. Inc. [Aff. of Nova Business Systems] - Flippin, AR - *TelDir&BG 83-84*
Northern Berks Merchandiser - Hamburg, PA - *AyerDirPub 83*
Northern Berkshire Pennysaver - North Adams, MA - *AyerDirPub 83*
Northern Book House [Aff. of Norfacts Ltd.] - Gravenhurst, ON, Canada - *BoPubDir 4 Sup, 5*
Northern Breeze, The - Lynn Lake, MB, Canada - *Ed&PubIntYB 82*
Northern Cable Co. - Coleman, WI - *Tel&CabFB 84C*
Northern Cable Co. - Gillett, WI - *BrCabYB 84; Tel&CabFB 84C*
Northern Cable Services Ltd. - Sudbury, ON, Canada - *BrCabYB 84; Tel&CabFB 84C*
Northern Cable TV Inc. - Eagle Lake, ME - *BrCabYB 84*
Northern Cablevision Inc. [Aff. of Storer Cable Communications] - Bloomington, MN - *BrCabYB 84; InterCabHB 3; Tel&CabFB 84C*
Northern Cablevision Inc. [of Storer Cable Communications] - Fridley, MN - *BrCabYB 84; InterCabHB 3*
Northern Cablevision Inc. [of Storer Cable Communications] - St. Louis Park, MN - *BrCabYB 84; Tel&CabFB 84C*
Northern Cablevision Ltd. - Edmonton, AB, Canada - *BrCabYB 84; Tel&CabFB 84C*
Northern Cablevision Northwest Inc. [of Storer Cable Communications] - Brooklyn Park, MN - *BrCabYB 84; Tel&CabFB 84C*
Northern California Digger, The - Dublin, CA - *BaconPubCkMag 84*
Northern California Labor [of SFLCNA] - San Francisco, CA - *NewsDir 84*
Northern California Retailer - San Jose, CA - *BaconPubCkMag 84; MagDir 84*
Northern Cartographic Inc. - Burlington, VT - *BoPubDir 4, 5*
Northern Cass Review - Deer River, MN - *AyerDirPub 83*
Northern Colorado Video Inc. [of Daniels & Associates Inc.] - Greeley, CO - *Tel&CabFB 84C*
Northern Colorado Video Inc. [of Daniels & Associates Inc.] - Windsor, CO - *BrCabYB 84; Tel&CabFB 84C*
Northern Connecticut Bazaar, The - Enfield, CT - *AyerDirPub 83; Ed&PubIntYB 82*
Northern Consulting Services - Aurora, ON, Canada - *BoPubDir 5*
Northern Consulting Services - North Bay, ON, Canada - *BoPubDir 4*
Northern Data Systems Inc. - Bedford, NH - *DataDirSup 7-83; WhoWMicrocom 83*
Northern Data Systems of Northeast Inc. - Westwood, MA - *DataDirSup 7-83*
Northern Dutchess-Hyde Park Pennysaver - Yorktown Heights, NY - *AyerDirPub 83*
Northern Hardware Trade [of Master Publications Inc.] - Colorado Springs, CO - *BaconPubCkMag 84; MagDir 84*
Northern Headlight - Minneapolis, MN - *Ed&PubIntYB 82*
Northern Hills-Northwest Press - *See* Queen City Suburban Press Inc.
Northern Hills Press-Northwest Press - Cincinnati, OH - *AyerDirPub 83*
Northern House - Newcastle Upon Tyne, England - *LitMag&SmPr 83-84*
Northern Illinois Broadcasting Co. - Chicago, IL - *BrCabYB 84*
Northern Illinois Cablevision Inc. [of Storer Cable Communications] - Glendale Heights, IL - *BrCabYB 84*
Northern Illinois University (Center for Southeast Asian Studies) - De Kalb, IL - *BoPubDir 4, 5*
Northern Illinois University Press - De Kalb, IL - *LitMarPl 83, 84; WritMar 84*
Northern Iowa Telephone Co. - Sioux Center, IA - *TelDir&BG 83-84*
Northern Iowan [of University of Northern Iowa] - Cedar Falls, IA - *NewsDir 84*
Northern Journey Press - Scotsburn, NS, Canada - *BoPubDir 4, 5*
Northern Kittitas County Tribune - Cle Elum, WA - *AyerDirPub 83; Ed&PubIntYB 82*
Northern Lake-Wildwood Productions - Grand Rapids, MI - *BoPubDir 4 Sup, 5*
Northern Life - Sudbury, ON, Canada - *Ed&PubIntYB 82*
Northern Light - Winnipeg, MB, Canada - *LitMag&SmPr 83-84*
Northern Light - Bathurst, NB, Canada - *AyerDirPub 83; Ed&PubIntYB 82*
Northern Light, The - Lexington, MA - *ArtMar 84; MagIndMarPl 82-83*
Northern Lights Cable Corp. - Sayner, WI - *BrCabYB 84*
Northern Lights Cable Corp. - Vilas County, WI - *BrCabYB 84*
Northern Lights Press - Bottineau, ND - *ArtMar 84*
Northern Line [of Poetry Leeds Publications] - Leeds, England - *LitMag&SmPr 83-84*
Northern Logger & Timber Processor [of Northeastern Loggers Association Inc.] - Old Forge, NY - *ArtMar 84; BaconPubCkMag 84; MagDir 84; WritMar 84*
Northern Marianas Cable TV - Saipan, CM - *BrCabYB 84*
Northern Michigan Herald Times - Gaylord, MI - *AyerDirPub 83*
Northern Michigan News - Cadillac, MI - *AyerDirPub 83*
Northern Michigan University Press - Marquette, MI - *BoPubDir 4, 5*
Northern Micrographics - La Crosse, WI - *MicroMarPl 82-83*
Northern Miner Press Ltd. - Toronto, ON, Canada - *BoPubDir 4, 5*
Northern Miner, The - Toronto, ON, Canada - *BaconPubCkMag 84*
Northern Neck Cablevision [of First Commonwealth Communications Inc.] - Kilmarnock, VA - *BrCabYB 84*
Northern Neck News - Warsaw, VA - *AyerDirPub 83; Ed&PubIntYB 82*
Northern Neighbors - Gravenhurst, ON, Canada - *LitMag&SmPr 83-84*
Northern Network [of University of Southern Maine] - Portland, ME - *TeleSy&SerDir 7-83*
Northern New England Review - Rindge, NH - *LitMag&SmPr 83-84*
Northern New England Review Press - Amherst, MA - *LitMag&SmPr 83-84*
Northern News - Kirkland Lake, ON, Canada - *AyerDirPub 83; BaconPubCkNews 84; Ed&PubIntYB 82*
Northern Numbers Inc. - Minneapolis, MN - *ADAPSOMemDir 83-84*
Northern Nut Growers Association Inc. - Hamden, CT - *BoPubDir 4, 5*

Northern Ogle Tempo - Byron, IL - *Ed&PublntYB 82*
Northern Ogle Tempo [of Durand North Central Associated Publishers] - Durand, IL - *AyerDirPub 83; NewsDir 84*
Northern Ohio CATV Associates [of Triax Communications] - Northwood, OH - *Tel&CabFB 84C*
Northern Ohio Live - Cleveland, OH - *BaconPubCkMag 84*
Northern Ontario Business - Sudbury, ON, Canada - *BaconPubCkMag 84*
Northern Pen, The - St. Anthony, NF, Canada - *AyerDirPub 83*
Northern Pig Development Co. - Driffield, England - *MicrocomSwDir 1*
Northern Pioneer, The - Ft. Vermillion, AB, Canada - *Ed&PublntYB 82*
Northern Plains Broadcasting Group - Hardin, MT - *BrCabYB 84; Tel&CabFB 84S*
Northern Polk County News - Johnson, IA - *Ed&PublntYB 82*
Northern Polk County News [of West Des Moines Express Inc.] - West Des Moines, IA - *NewsDir 84*
Northern Press - Potsdam, NY - *BoPubDir 4 Sup, 5*
Northern Publications - Don Mills, ON, Canada - *BoPubDir 4 Sup, 5*
Northern Research Information Service [of Dept. of Indian Affairs & Northern Development] - Ottawa, ON, Canada - *CompReadDB 82*
Northern School Supply Co. - Great Falls, MT - *AvMarPl 83*
Northern Sentinel - Kitimat, BC, Canada - *AyerDirPub 83*
Northern Sonoma County Shopping Guide - Healdsburg, CA - *AyerDirPub 83*
Northern Star [of Northern Illinois University] - De Kalb, IL - *NewsDir 84*
Northern Star - Gaylord, MI - *AyerDirPub 83*
Northern Star, The - Lake Village, IN - *AyerDirPub 83*
Northern Star, The - Clinton, MN - *Ed&PublntYB 82*
Northern States Power Co. - Minot, ND - *TelDir&BG 83-84*
Northern-Sun Print - Gladbrook, IA - *AyerDirPub 83; Ed&PublntYB 82*
Northern Technologies Inc. - Markham, ON, Canada - *DataDirSup 7-83*
Northern Technology Books - Evanston, IL - *MicrocomMPl 83, 84*
Northern Telecom Inc. - Minnetonka, MN - *DataDirSup 7-83*
Northern Telecom Inc. - Nashville, TN - *Top100Al 83*
Northern Telecom Inc. (Electronic Office Systems) - Minneapolis, MN - *WhoWMicrocom 83*
Northern Telecom Ltd. - Brampton, ON, Canada - *VideoDir 82-83*
Northern Telecom Ltd. - Mississauga, ON, Canada - *Datamation 6-83; ElecNews 7-25-83*
Northern Telecom Systems Corp. - Minneapolis, MN - *DirInfWP 82; InfIndMarPl 83*
Northern Telephone Co. [Aff. of National Communications Systems Inc.] - Mesick, MI - *TelDir&BG 83-84*
Northern Telephone Co. - Wawina, MN - *TelDir&BG 83-84*
Northern Telephone Co. [Aff. of Unitel of Nebraska] - Blair, NE - *TelDir&BG 83-84*
Northern Telephone Cooperative Inc. - Sunburst, MT - *TelDir&BG 83-84*
Northern Television Systems - Whitehorse, YT, Canada - *BrCabYB 84*
Northern Times - Terrace, BC, Canada - *Ed&PublntYB 82*
Northern Times - Kapuskasing, ON, Canada - *AyerDirPub 83; Ed&PublntYB 82*
Northern Times Press - Terrace, BC, Canada - *BoPubDir 4, 5*
Northern TV Inc. - Anchorage, AK - *BrCabYB 84*
Northern Valley Green Tab [of Moundsville Marshall County Green Tab] - Moundsville, WV - *AyerDirPub 83; NewsDir 84*
Northern Video Inc. [of Tele-Communications Inc.] - Baraga Village, MI - *BrCabYB 84*
Northern Video Inc. - Carp Lake Township, MI - *BrCabYB 84*
Northern Video Inc. [of TCI-Taft Cablevision Associates] - Ontonagon, MI - *BrCabYB 84; Tel&CabFB 84C*
Northern Virginia - Vienna, VA - *WritMar 84*
Northern Virginia Daily [of Shenandoah Publishing House Inc.] - Strasburg, VA - *AyerDirPub 83; BaconPubCkNews 84; Ed&PublntYB 82; NewsDir 84*
Northern Virginia Sun - Arlington, VA - *AyerDirPub 83; BaconPubCkNews 84; Ed&PublntYB 82*
Northern Westchester-Putnam Pennysaver - Yorktown Heights, NY - *AyerDirPub 83*
Northern Wyoming Daily News - Worland, WY - *AyerDirPub 83; BaconPubCkNews 84; Ed&PublntYB 82*
Northern Yavapai Record - Ash Fork, AZ - *Ed&PublntYB 82*
Northernaire Publications - Martinex, CA - *BoPubDir 4, 5*
Northfield News - Northfield, MN - *AyerDirPub 83; BaconPubCkNews 84; Ed&PublntYB 82; NewsDir 84*
Northfield News - Northfield, VT - *AyerDirPub 83; BaconPubCkNews 84*
Northfield Telephone Co. [Aff. of Telephone & Data Systems Inc.] - Northfield, VT - *TelDir&BG 83-84*
Northgate Cable TV Ltd. - Hamilton, ON, Canada - *BrCabYB 84*
Northgate Journal - Greenwood-Northgate, WA - *Ed&PublntYB 82*
Northglenn/Thornton Sentinel [of Denver Community Publications Co.] - Denver, CO - *NewsDir 84*
Northglenn/Thornton Sentinel - Northglenn, CO - *AyerDirPub 83*
Northkent Advance - Jenison, MI - *AyerDirPub 83*
Northlake Post [of Elmwood Park Post Newspapers-Meese Newspapers Inc.] - Chicago, IL - *NewsDir 84*
Northlake Post - Elmwood Park, IL - *AyerDirPub 83*
Northlake Post - *See* Meese' Newspaper Group
Northlake Times - Chicago, IL - *AyerDirPub 83*
Northlake Times - Northlake, IL - *Ed&PublntYB 82*
Northlake Times - *See* Lerner Times Newspapers
Northland Accounting Inc. - Two Harbors, MN - *MicrocomMPl 84*
Northland Ad-Liner - West Branch, MI - *AyerDirPub 83*
Northland Cable Communications - Oakhurst, CA - *Tel&CabFB 84C*
Northland Cable Properties-I [of Northland Communications Corp.] - Reedsport, OR - *Tel&CabFB 84C*
Northland Communications Corp. - Burnet, TX - *Tel&CabFB 84C*
Northland Communications Corp. - Crockett, TX - *Tel&CabFB 84C*
Northland Communications Corp. - Mexia, TX - *Tel&CabFB 84C*
Northland Communications Corp. - Navasota, TX - *Tel&CabFB 84C*
Northland Communications Corp. - Stephenville, TX - *Tel&CabFB 84C*
Northland Communications Corp. - Seattle, WA - *Tel&CabFB 84C p.1694*
Northland News - Cedar Springs, MI - *AyerDirPub 83*
Northland News - Uranium City, SK, Canada - *AyerDirPub 83*
Northland News - *See* Suburban News Publications
Northland News, The - Northland, OH - *Ed&PublntYB 82*
Northland News, The - La Ronge, SK, Canada - *Ed&PublntYB 82*
Northland Post - Cochrane, ON, Canada - *AyerDirPub 83; Ed&PublntYB 82*
Northland Press [Div. of Justin Industries] - Flagstaff, AZ - *LitMag&SmPr 83-84; LitMarPl 83, 84; WritMar 84*
Northland Publishing Co. - Menomonie, WI - *LitMag&SmPr 83-84*
Northland Telephone Co. Inc. - Hill City, MN - *TelDir&BG 83-84*
Northlander Tribune Advertiser [of Townsend Communications Inc.] - Kansas City, MO - *NewsDir 84*
Northlich, Stolley Inc. - Cincinnati, OH - *AdAge 3-28-84; BrCabYB 84; DirPRFirms 83; StaDirAdAg 2-84*
Northliner Magazine - Minneapolis, MN - *MagDir 84*
Northnet [of North Star Computers Inc.] - San Leandro, CA - *TeleSy&SerDir 2-84*
Northome Record & Mizpah Message - Northome, MN - *BaconPubCkNews 84; Ed&PublntYB 82*
Northport-East Northport Pennysaver - Huntington, NY - *AyerDirPub 83*
Northport Journal - Northport, NY - *BaconPubCkNews 84; Ed&PublntYB 82*
Northport Observer [of Smithtown News Inc.] - Smithtown, NY - *NewsDir 84*
Northport Observer - *See* Smithtown News Inc.
Northridge Advertising - Monrovia, CA - *StaDirAdAg 2-84*
Northridge Chatsworth Valley View - *See* San Fernando Valley Sun Publishers
Northridge Times - Encino, CA - *AyerDirPub 83*

Northridge Times - *See* Associated Valley Publications
Northridger/Northridge Shopper - Northridge, CA - *AyerDirPub 83*
Northridger, The - Northridge, CA - *BaconPubCkNews 84; NewsDir 84*
Northrup & Teel - Pittsford, NY - *AdAge 3-28-84; StaDirAdAg 2-84*
Northshore Cable Services Ltd. - Sudbury, ON, Canada - *BrCabYB 84*
Northshore Citizen - Bothell, WA - *AyerDirPub 83; Ed&PubIntYB 82*
Northside Journal - St. Louis, MO - *AyerDirPub 83*
Northside Neighbor [of Marietta Neighbor Newspapers Inc.] - Atlanta, GA - *Ed&PubIntYB 82; NewsDir 84*
Northside Neighbor - Marietta, GA - *AyerDirPub 83*
Northside Recorder - San Antonio, TX - *AyerDirPub 83*
Northside Sun - Jackson, MS - *AyerDirPub 83*
Northside Sun, The - North Jackson, MS - *Ed&PubIntYB 82*
Northside TV Corp. - Iron Mountain, MI - *BrCabYB 84; Tel&CabFB 84C*
Northside Victoria Times - Sydney, NS, Canada - *AyerDirPub 83*
Northstar Counselors-Public Relations/PA - Minneapolis, MN - *DirPRFirms 83*
Northtown Books - Arcata, CA - *BoPubDir 4 Sup, 5*
Northumberland Cable TV Ltd. [of Utilities Management Group Ltd.] - Cobourg, ON, Canada - *BrCabYB 84*
Northumberland Echo [of Atlantic Publications Inc.] - Heathsville, VA - *AyerDirPub 83; NewsDir 84*
Northumberland Echo, The - Northumberland/Lancaster Counties, VA - *Ed&PubIntYB 82*
Northumberland Press - Pittsburgh, PA - *InfIndMarPl 83*
Northville Record [of Sliger/Livingston Publications Inc.] - Northville, MI - *Ed&PubIntYB 82; NewsDir 84*
Northwest - Chicago, IL - *AyerDirPub 83*
Northwest [of The Oregonian] - Portland, OR - *LitMarPl 84; MagIndMarPl 82-83; WritMar 84*
Northwest - Unity, SK, Canada - *Ed&PubIntYB 82*
Northwest Airlifter - Tacoma, WA - *AyerDirPub 83*
Northwest Alabamian - Haleyville, AL - *AyerDirPub 83; Ed&PubIntYB 82*
Northwest Analytical Inc. - Portland, OR - *MicrocomMPl 83, 84; MicrocomSwDir 1; WhoWMicrocom 83*
Northwest Arkansas Morning News [of Northwest Arkansas Publishing Co.] - Rogers, AR - *AyerDirPub 83; BaconPubCkNews 84; Ed&PubIntYB 82*
Northwest Arkansas Times - Fayetteville, AR - *AyerDirPub 83; BaconPubCkNews 84; Ed&PubIntYB 82*
Northwest Attitudes & Social Research Inc. - Portland, OR - *IntDirMarRes 83*
Northwest Beachcomber - Seattle, WA - *BoPubDir 4, 5*
Northwest Bergen Today - *See* Today Newspapers
Northwest Beverage Journal - Minneapolis, MN - *BaconPubCkMag 84; MagDir 84*
Northwest Blade - Eureka, SD - *AyerDirPub 83; Ed&PubIntYB 82*
Northwest Cable [of McCaw Communications Cos. Inc.] - Rockaway, OR - *BrCabYB 84; Tel&CabFB 84C*
Northwest Cable TV - Oakridge, OR - *Tel&CabFB 84C*
Northwest Cablevision Inc. - Winchester, CT - *BrCabYB 84; Tel&CabFB 84C*
Northwest Cablevision Inc. [of Group W Cable] - Seattle, WA - *BrCabYB 84*
Northwest Colorado Press - Craig, CO - *AyerDirPub 83; BaconPubCkNews 84; Ed&PubIntYB 82; NewsDir 84*
Northwest Columbus - *See* Suburban News Publications
Northwest Computer Services Inc. - Vancouver, WA - *WhoWMicrocom 83*
Northwest Computing - Seattle, WA - *BaconPubCkMag 84*
Northwest Construction News - Seattle, WA - *BaconPubCkMag 84*
Northwest County Journal - St. Louis, MO - *AyerDirPub 83*
Northwest County Journal - St. Louis County, MO - *Ed&PubIntYB 82*
Northwest Courier - Napoleon, OH - *AyerDirPub 83*
Northwest Dentistry [of Minnesota Dental Association] - St. Paul, MN - *BaconPubCkMag 84; MagDir 84*
Northwest Digital - West Covina, CA - *DirInfWP 82*
Northwest Farm Equipment Journal - St. Paul, MN - *BaconPubCkMag 84; MagDir 84*
Northwest Herald - Chicago, IL - *AyerDirPub 83*
Northwest Herald - Unity, SK, Canada - *AyerDirPub 83*
Northwest Houston Business News - Houston, TX - *BaconPubCkMag 84*
Northwest Illinois TV Cable Co. - Galesburg, IL - *BrCabYB 84; Tel&CabFB 84C*
Northwest Illinois TV Cable Co. - Monmouth, IL - *BrCabYB 84 p.D-305*
Northwest Indian News Association - Ft. Hall, ID - *Ed&PubIntYB 82*
Northwest Information Enterprises - Beaverton, OR - *FBInfSer 80; InfIndMarPl 83*
Northwest Insurance Journal - Minneapolis, MN - *MagDir 84*
Northwest Investment Review - Portland, OR - *WritMar 84*
Northwest Iowa Cable TV Inc. [of Metro Cable Corp.] - Sheldon, IA - *Tel&CabFB 84C*
Northwest Iowa Cable TV Inc. [of Metro Cable Corp.] - Sibley, IA - *Tel&CabFB 84C*
Northwest Iowa Herald - Spencer, IA - *AyerDirPub 83*
Northwest Iowa Review - Sheldon, IA - *Ed&PubIntYB 82*
Northwest Iowa Review - Sibley, IA - *AyerDirPub 83*
Northwest Iowa Shopper - Spencer, IA - *AyerDirPub 83*
Northwest Iowa Telephone Co. Inc. - Sergeant Bluff, IA - *TelDir&BG 83-84*
Northwest Journal [of Des Plaines Journal-News Publications] - Des Plaines, IL - *NewsDir 84*
Northwest Kansas Cable TV Co. Inc. - St. Francis, KS - *BrCabYB 84; Tel&CabFB 84C*
Northwest Leader [of Los Angeles Meredith Newspapers] - Los Angeles, CA - *AyerDirPub 83; NewsDir 84*
Northwest Leader [of Chicago Leader Newspapers] - Chicago, IL - *AyerDirPub 83; NewsDir 84*
Northwest Lincoln Sun - Lincoln, NE - *AyerDirPub 83; Ed&PubIntYB 82; NewsDir 84*
Northwest Louisiana Telephone Co. Inc. [Aff. of Century Telephone Enterprises Inc.] - Plain Dealing, LA - *TelDir&BG 83-84*
Northwest Management Services Inc. [Subs. of Northwest Administrators Inc.] - Seattle, WA - *DataDirOnSer 84*
Northwest Matrix - Eugene, OR - *BoPubDir 4, 5; LitMag&SmPr 83-84*
Northwest Media Services - Seattle, WA - *StaDirAdAg 2-84*
Northwest Microfilm Inc. - Minneapolis, MN - *DirInfWP 82*
Northwest Milwaukee Advertiser-Press [of Menomonee Falls Publishing Co.] - Menomonee Falls, WI - *NewsDir 84*
Northwest Mining Association - Spokane, WA - *BoPubDir 4, 5*
Northwest Mobile Television - Seattle, WA - *Tel&CabFB 84C*
Northwest Motor - Seattle, WA - *BaconPubCkMag 84; MagDir 84*
Northwest Mutual Aid Telephone Corp. - Powers Lake, ND - *BrCabYB 84*
Northwest Mutual Aid Telephone Corp. - Ray, ND - *Tel&CabFB 84C p.1694; TelDir&BG 83-84*
Northwest Oklahoman & Ellis County News - Shattuck, OK - *AyerDirPub 83*
Northwest Orient [of The Webb Co.] - St. Paul, MN - *BaconPubCkMag 84; WritMar 84*
Northwest Paper [Div. of Potlatch Corp.] - Cloquet, MN - *LitMarPl 83, 84*
Northwest Passage [of Chicago Passage Publications] - Chicago, IL - *Ed&PubIntYB 82; NewsDir 84*
Northwest Pennysaver - Rochester, NY - *AyerDirPub 83*
Northwest Regional Educational Laboratory - Portland, OR - *DataDirOnSer 84*
Northwest Retailer [of Retailer Services Co. Inc.] - Seattle, WA - *MagDir 84*
Northwest Review - Eugene, OR - *ArtMar 84; LitMag&SmPr 83-84; WritMar 84*
Northwest Science - Pullman, WA - *BaconPubCkMag 84; MagDir 84*
Northwest Side Sunday Press - Chicago, IL - *AyerDirPub 83*
Northwest-Signal - Napoleon, OH - *AyerDirPub 83; Ed&PubIntYB 82*
Northwest Skier & Sports - Seattle, WA - *MagDir 84*
Northwest Stage, The - Moscow, ID - *WritMar 84*
Northwest Star Inc. - Baltimore, MD - *NewsDir 84*
Northwest Suburban - Chicago, IL - *Ed&PubIntYB 82*
Northwest Sun-Journal - Woodward, OK - *AyerDirPub 83*

Northwest Sunday Times - Chicago, IL - *AyerDirPub 83*
Northwest Surveys Inc. - Seattle, WA - *IntDirMarRes 83*
Northwest Telephone Cooperative - Havelock, IA - *TelDir&BG 83-84*
Northwest Times - Chicago, IL - *AyerDirPub 83; Ed&PubIntYB 82*
Northwest Times, The - San Antonio, TX - *AyerDirPub 83*
Northwest Today - Mt. Vernon, WA - *AyerDirPub 83*
Northwest Today - *See* Today Newspapers
Northwest Trader-Advertiser [of Spooner Advocate] - Spooner, WI - *NewsDir 84*
Northwest Trails Association - Lynnwood, WA - *BoPubDir 5; LitMag&SmPr 83-84*
Northwest Translator TV Inc. - Anthony, KS - *BrCabYB 84*
Northwest Translator TV Inc. - Caldwell, KS - *BrCabYB 84*
Northwest Translator TV Inc. - Alva, OK - *BrCabYB 84; Tel&CabFB 84C p.1695*
Northwest TV Inc. - Freedom, OK - *BrCabYB 84*
Northwest TV Inc. - North Enid, OK - *BrCabYB 84*
Northwest TV Inc. - Pondcreek, OK - *BrCabYB 84*
Northwest Unit Farm Magazines [Subs. of Northwest Farmer-Stockman Inc.] - Spokane, WA - *MagIndMarPl 82-83*
Northwest Video Center - Seattle, WA - *AvMarPl 83*
Northwestern - Oshkosh, WI - *AyerDirPub 83*
Northwestern Banker - Des Moines, IA - *BaconPubCkMag 84; MagDir 84*
Northwestern Bell Telephone Co. - Omaha, NE - *TelDir&BG 83-84*
Northwestern College Radio Network - Roseville, MN - *BrCabYB 84*
Northwestern Engineer - Evanston, IL - *MagDir 84*
Northwestern Illinois Dispatch [of Savanna Times Journal Inc.] - Savanna, IL - *AyerDirPub 83; NewsDir 84*
Northwestern Illinois Farmer - Lena, IL - *Ed&PubIntYB 82; NewsDir 84*
Northwestern Inc. - Portland, OR - *Tel&CabFB 84C*
Northwestern Indiana Telephone Co., The - Hebron, IN - *TelDir&BG 83-84*
Northwestern Jeweler - Albert Lea, MN - *BaconPubCkMag 84; MagDir 84*
Northwestern Lumberman - Minneapolis, MN - *BaconPubCkMag 84; MagDir 84*
Northwestern News - Palmyra, IL - *AyerDirPub 83*
Northwestern News - Virden, IL - *Ed&PubIntYB 82*
Northwestern On-Line Total Integrated System [of Northwestern University Library] - Evanston, IL - *EISS 83*
Northwestern State University of Louisiana (Northwestern State University Press) - Natchitoches, LA - *BoPubDir 4, 5*
Northwestern Telephone Systems Inc. [Aff. of Telephone Utilities Inc.] - Kalispell, MT - *TelDir&BG 83-84*
Northwestern Telephone Systems Inc. [Aff. of Telephone Utilities Inc.] - Lebanon, OR - *TelDir&BG 83-84*
Northwestern University (Astronomy Dept.) - Evanston, IL - *BoPubDir 4, 5*
Northwestern University (Center for American Archeology Press) - Evanston, IL - *BoPubDir 5*
Northwestern University (Center for the Study of Multiple Birth) - Chicago, IL - *BoPubDir 4, 5*
Northwestern University (Traffic Institute) - Evanston, IL - *BoPubDir 4, 5*
Northwestern University (Transportation Center Publications) - Evanston, IL - *BoPubDir 4, 5*
Northwestern University Press - Evanston, IL - *LitMarPl 83, 84*
Northwestside Press - Chicago, IL - *Ed&PubIntYB 82*
Northwind Editorial Services - Pleasant Valley, NY - *LitMarPl 83, 84*
Northwood Anchor - Northwood, IA - *BaconPubCkNews 84; Ed&PubIntYB 82*
Northwood Gleaner - Northwood, ND - *NewsDir 84*
Northwood Gleaner - *See* Community News Inc.
Northwood Institute Press - Midland, MI - *BoPubDir 4, 5*
Northwoods Journal - Thomaston, ME - *LitMag&SmPr 83-84*
Northwoods Press - South Thomaston, ME - *BoPubDir 5; LitMag&SmPr 83-84*
Northwoods Press [Aff. of Romar Inc.] - Stafford, VA - *BoPubDir 4*
Northwoods Publishing Co. - Menomonee Falls, WI - *DirMarMP 83*
Northword - Madison, WI - *BoPubDir 4 Sup, 5*
Norton & Co. Inc., W. W. - New York, NY - *KnowInd 83; LitMarPl 83, 84; WritMar 84*
Norton Art Gallery, R. W. [Aff. of The R. W. Norton Art Foundation] - Shreveport, LA - *BoPubDir 4, 5*
Norton, Boyd - Evergreen, CO - *LitMarPl 83, 84*
Norton Cable TV - Norton, KS - *BrCabYB 84; Tel&CabFB 84C*
Norton Coalfield Progress - Norton, VA - *BaconPubCkNews 84; Ed&PubIntYB 82; NewsDir 84*
Norton Computing, Peter - Santa Monica, CA - *MicrocomMPl 84*
Norton Daily Telegram - Norton, KS - *BaconPubCkNews 84; NewsDir 84*
Norton, Peter - Venice, CA - *MicrocomSwDir 1*
Norton Pride - Norton, OH - *Ed&PubIntYB 82*
Norton Pride - Wadsworth, OH - *AyerDirPub 83; BaconPubCkNews 84*
Norton Public Relations, Alice - Ridgefield, CT - *DirPRFirms 83; LitMarPl 83, 84; MagIndMarPl 82-83*
Norton Publicidade SA [of the Univas Network] - Sao Paulo, Brazil - *StaDirAdAg 2-84*
Norton Publishers Inc., Jeffrey - Guilford, CT - *AvMarPl 83; LitMarPl 83, 84; MicroMarPl 82-83*
Norton Simon Communications Inc. - New York, NY - *StaDirAdAg 2-84*
Norton, Walter M. - Bath, ME - *Tel&CabFB 84C p.1695*
Norton/Wood Public Relations Services - Pasadena, CA - *DirPRFirms 83*
Nortronics Co. Inc. - Minneapolis, MN - *AvMarPl 83*
Norvik/Hauge Music Publishing Co. - Oakland, CA - *BillIntBG 83-84*
Norwalk Herald American - Norwalk, CA - *Ed&PubIntYB 82*
Norwalk Herald American - South Gate, CA - *AyerDirPub 83*
Norwalk Herald American - *See* Hearst Community Newspapers
Norwalk Hour - Norwalk, CT - *NewsDir 84*
Norwalk News - *See* Brooks Community Newspapers
Norwalk Pico Rivera Community News - Downey, CA - *AyerDirPub 83*
Norwalk Reflector - Norwalk, OH - *BaconPubCkNews 84; Ed&PubIntYB 82; NewsDir 84*
Norwalk Voice - Huron, OH - *AyerDirPub 83*
Norwalk Weekly Trader - Norwalk, CT - *Ed&PubIntYB 82*
Norwant Ltd. - Atikokan, ON, Canada - *BrCabYB 84*
Norway Advertiser Democrat - Norway, ME - *BaconPubCkNews 84; NewsDir 84*
Norway Rural Telephone Co. - Kanawha, IA - *TelDir&BG 83-84*
Norway Telephone Co. Inc. - Norway, SC - *TelDir&BG 83-84*
Norwegian Center for Informatics - Oslo, Norway - *EISS 83*
Norwegian Computing Centre for the Humanities - Bergen, Norway - *EISS 83*
Norwegian Online User Group - Oslo, Norway - *EISS 83*
Norwegian Petroleum Directorate - Stavanger, Norway - *CompReadDB 82*
Norwegian Seismic Array [of Royal Norwegian Council for Scientific & Industrial Research] - Kjeller, Norway - *EISS 7-83 Sup*
Norwegian Social Science Data Services [of Norwegian Research Council for Science & Humanities] - Bergen, Norway - *EISS 83*
Norwegian Standards Catalogue [of Norges Standardiseringsforbund] - Oslo, Norway - *CompReadDB 82*
Norwegian Telecommunications Users Group - Oslo, Norway - *TeleSy&SerDir 2-84*
Norwegian Term Bank [of University of Bergen] - Bergen, Norway - *EISS 83*
Norwegian Tymnet/Telenet Access [of Teledirektoratet] - Oslo, Norway - *InfIndMarPl 83*
Norwell Mariner - Marshfield, MA - *NewsDir 84*
Nor'wester, The - Seattle, WA - *BaconPubCkMag 84*
Norwich Bulletin - Norwich, CT - *BaconPubCkNews 84; Ed&PubIntYB 82; NewsDir 84*
Norwich Evening Sun - Norwich, NY - *NewsDir 84*
Norwich Sun - Norwich, NY - *BaconPubCkNews 84*
Norwolk Voice - *See* Erie County Reporter Co.
Norwont Ltd. - Atikokan, ON, Canada - *Tel&CabFB 84C*
Norwont Ltd. - Ft. Frances, ON, Canada - *BrCabYB 84*
Norwood Editions - Norwood, PA - *BoPubDir 4, 5*

Norwood Editions - *See* Folcraft Library Editions/Norwood Editions
Norwood Enterprise [of Cincinnati Suburban Newspapers Inc.] - Cincinnati, OH - *AyerDirPub 83; Ed&PubIntYB 82; NewsDir 84*
Norwood Enterprise - *See* Queen City Suburban Press Inc.
Norwood Park-Edison Park Passage - Chicago, IL - *AyerDirPub 83*
Norwood Register - Marmora, ON, Canada - *AyerDirPub 83*
Norwood Times - Norwood, MN - *BaconPubCkNews 84; Ed&PubIntYB 82*
Nosbooks - New York, NY - *BoPubDir 4, 5*
Nostalgia Alley/Props for Today - New York, NY - *AvMarPl 83*
Nostalgia Book Club [Div. of Crown Publishers Inc.] - New York, NY - *LitMarPl 83, 84*
Nostalgia Channel, The - East Northport, NY - *Tel&CabFB 84C*
Nostalgia Lane Inc. - New York, NY - *BillIntBG 83-84*
Nostalgia Press Inc. - Franklin Square, NY - *BoPubDir 4, 5*
Nostalgia World for Collectors & Fans - North Haven, CT - *ArtMar 84; LitMag&SmPr 83-84; WritMar 84*
Nostoc [of Arts End Books] - Newton, MA - *LitMag&SmPr 83-84*
Nostradamus Advertising [Subs. of Advocate Enterprises Inc.] - New York, NY - *ArtMar 84; LitMarPl 83, 84*
Not-for-Sale-Press - San Francisco, CA - *LitMag&SmPr 83-84*
Not Just Jazz - New York, NY - *WritMar 84*
Not Man Apart [of Friends of the Earth] - San Francisco, CA - *BaconPubCkMag 84; LitMag&SmPr 83-84; MagIndMarPl 82-83*
Not-Polyoptics [Div. of Synchronet] - Woodbridge, VA - *MicrocomMPl 84*
Nota Bene Software - Glenview, IL - *MicrocomMPl 84; MicrocomSwDir 1*
Notable Music Co. Inc. [Div. of Cy Coleman Enterprises] - New York, NY - *BillIntBG 83-84*
Note Filler Music - *See* Jamie Music Publishing Co.
Notegun Music - *See* Virginia Arts Publishing Co.
Notes - New York, NY - *MagDir 84*
Notes Advertising Associates - New Haven, CT - *StaDirAdAg 2-84*
Notes & Queries [of Oxford University Press] - Oxford, England - *LitMag&SmPr 83-84*
Noteworth Music Publishing - San Francisco, CA - *BillIntBG 83-84*
Noteworthy Co., The - Amsterdam, NY - *ArtMar 84*
Nothing New - Silver Spring, MD - *BoPubDir 4, 5*
Notice [of Computer Sciences Corp.] - El Segundo, CA - *TeleSy&SerDir 2-84*
Notices of the American Mathematical Society - Providence, RI - *MagDir 84*
Noticias de Maquinaria Industrial [Div. of Hearst Business Media Corp.] - Southfield, MI - *ArtMar 84*
Noticias Latinas [of South Miami Community Newspapers] - Miami, FL - *NewsDir 84*
Notification Services [of Interactive Data Services Inc.] - New York, NY - *DataDirOnSer 84*
Notimoda - Sherman Oaks, CA - *BaconPubCkMag 84*
Notivest - Sherman Oaks, CA - *BaconPubCkMag 84*
Notre Dame Magazine [of University of Notre Dame] - Notre Dame, IN - *ArtMar 84; WritMar 84*
Notre Dame Technical Review - Notre Dame, IN - *BaconPubCkMag 84; MagDir 84*
Nottingham Medieval Studies - Nottingham, England - *LitMag&SmPr 83-84*
Nottoway Cable TV [of Bahakel Communications Ltd.] - Blackstone, VA - *Tel&CabFB 84C*
Nottoway Cable TV [of Bahakel Communications Ltd.] - Crewe, VA - *Tel&CabFB 84C*
Noumenon [of Sagittarius Publications] - Oneroa, New Zealand - *LitMag&SmPr 83-84*
Noumenon Corp. - Alameda, CA - *MicrocomSwDir 1*
Noumenon Press [Aff. of Noumenon Foundation] - Austin, TX - *BoPubDir 4, 5; LitMag&SmPr 83-84*
Nourishing Thoughts - Stow, OH - *BoPubDir 4, 5*
Nourse-Chleboun Associates - Point Richmond, CA - *LitMarPl 83*
Nourse, Floyd L. - Portola Valley, CA - *LitMarPl 84*
Nouveau Courrier de la Presse Lit-Tout - Paris, France - *ProGuPRSer 4*
Nouveau Graphics Ltd. - New York, NY - *LitMarPl 83; MagIndMarPl 82-83*
Nouveaux Video Ltd. - Los Angeles, CA - *BillIntBG 83-84*
Nouvelle - Bonnyville, AB, Canada - *AyerDirPub 83*
Nouvelles Editions de l'Arc - Montreal, PQ, Canada - *BoPubDir 4, 5*
Nova Communications Inc. [of Midland Cablevision Systems Inc.] - Beardstown, IL - *Tel&CabFB 84C p.1695*
Nova Communications Inc. - Chapin, IL - *Tel&CabFB 84C*
Nova Communications Inc. - Roseville, IL - *Tel&CabFB 84C*
Nova Electric Manufacturing Co. - Nuttey, NJ - *DirInfWP 82*
Nova Enterprises Inc. - Falls Church, VA - *WhoWMicrocom 83*
Nova Music Ltd. - *See* Schirmer Music Co., E. C.
Nova Press - *See* Lorenz Creative Services
Nova Research Group - San Francisco, CA - *IntDirMarRes 83*
Nova Scarcity Publishers - Wolfville, NS, Canada - *BoPubDir 4, 5*
Nova Scotia Debating Society - Halifax, NS, Canada - *BoPubDir 4 Sup, 5*
Nova Scotia Museum - Halifax, NS, Canada - *BoPubDir 4, 5*
Nova Telephone Co. - Nova, OH - *TelDir&BG 83-84*
Nova Typesetting - Bellevue, WA - *LitMarPl 83, 84*
Nova Venturion - Walnut Creek, CA - *BoPubDir 4 Sup, 5*
Novak, Jack - Alexandria, VA - *LitMarPl 83, 84*
Novalis [of Headplay Press] - Pantego Station, TX - *WritMar 84*
Novamedia Corp. - Sierra Madre, CA - *AvMarPl 83*
Novatex [of Teleglobe Canada] - Montreal, PQ, Canada - *EISS 7-83 Sup; TeleSy&SerDir 7-83*
Novati Gourmet Cooking Ltd., Chef - Montreal, PQ, Canada - *BoPubDir 5*
Novation Inc. - Tarzana, CA - *DataDirSup 7-83; WhoWMicrocom 83*
Novato Advance [of Scripps League Newspapers Inc.] - Novato, CA - *BaconPubCkNews 84; Ed&PubIntYB 82; NewsDir 84*
Novatron of Dallas Inc. - Dallas, TX - *AvMarPl 83*
Noveck Productions, Fima - New York, NY - *TelAl 83, 84*
Novell Inc. - Orem, UT - *DataDirSup 7-83*
Novello & Co. - Bryn Mawr, PA - *BillIntBG 83-84*
November House Publishers - Vancouver, BC, Canada - *LitMarPl 83*
Novi & Walled Lake News [of Sliger/Livingston Publications Inc.] - Northville, MI - *BaconPubCkNews 84; Ed&PubIntYB 82; NewsDir 84*
Novi & Walled Lake News - Walled Lake, MI - *AyerDirPub 83*
Novi Spinal Column Newsweekly - *See* Spinal Column Newsweekly
Novi Sun Forum - *See* Suburban Newspapers
Novi-Wixom Spinal Column [of Union Lake Spinal Column] - Union Lake, MI - *NewsDir 84*
Novick & Associates, I. A. - Chicago, IL - *DirPRFirms 83*
Novosti Press Agency - New York, NY - *Ed&PubIntYB 82*
Novoye Russkoye Slovo - New York, NY - *AyerDirPub 83; Ed&PubIntYB 82*
Novy Domov - Scarborough, ON, Canada - *Ed&PubIntYB 82*
Novy Shliakh - Toronto, ON, Canada - *Ed&PubIntYB 82*
Novy Svet - Cleveland, OH - *Ed&PubIntYB 82*
Novy's Telephone Co. - Kendall, WI - *TelDir&BG 83-84*
Now It's Up To You Publications - Seattle, WA - *LitMag&SmPr 83-84*
Nowak Barlow Johnson - Fayetteville, NY - *DirPRFirms 83; StaDirAdAg 2-84; TelAl 83, 84*
Nowata Cable TV [of Capital Cities Cable Inc.] - Nowata, OK - *BrCabYB 84*
Nowata Star - Nowata, OK - *BaconPubCkNews 84; Ed&PubIntYB 82; NewsDir 84*
Nowata Star - Vinita, OK - *Ed&PubIntYB 82*
Nowi Dni - Toronto, ON, Canada - *Ed&PubIntYB 82*
Nowicki/Trevisan - Santa Barbara, CA - *BoPubDir 4, 5*
Nowiny Minnescockie - St. Paul, MN - *Ed&PubIntYB 82*
Nowland Organization Inc., The - Greenwich, CT - *HBIndAd&MS 82-83; IntDirMarRes 83*
Nowling & Co. Inc. - New York, NY - *DirPRFirms 83*
Nowry Antenna Service - Swastika, ON, Canada - *BrCabYB 84*
Nowy Dziennik - New York, NY - *AyerDirPub 83; Ed&PubIntYB 82*
Noxapater Telephone Co. Inc. [Aff. of Colonial Telephone Co.] - Noxapater, MS - *TelDir&BG 83-84*

Noyce, John L. - Brighton, England - *LitMag&SmPr 83-84*
Noyes Data Corp. - Park Ridge, NJ - *LitMarPl 83, 84; WritMar 84*
Noyes Newspapers - *See* Gazette Newspapers
Noyes Press - Park Ridge, NJ - *ArtMar 84*
Nozzle, The [of Greater Washington-Maryland Service Station Association] - Greenbelt, MD - *BaconPubCkMag 84; MagDir 84*
N.P. Surveys Inc. - Bryn Mawr, PA - *IntDirMarRes 83*
NPC Photo - Newton, MA - *AvMarPl 83*
NPC Publishing Co. - Granada Hills, CA - *BoPubDir 4, 5*
N.P.D. Corp. - Austin, TX - *BoPubDir 4*
N.P.D. Corp. - Ft. Stockton, TX - *BoPubDir 5*
NPD Group - Port Washington, NY - *AdAge 5-17-84 p.30; Tel&CabFB 84C*
NPD Research Inc. - Floral Park, NY - *IntDirMarRes 83*
NPM Information Services [of New Product Management Group] - London, England - *FBInfSer 80; InfIndMarPl 83*
NPO Resource Review [of NPO Management Services Inc.] - New York, NY - *WritMar 84*
NPO/Task Force Inc. - New York, NY - *DirPRFirms 83*
NPP Books - Ann Arbor, MI - *BoPubDir 5*
NPR Communications Inc. - New York, NY - *StaDirAdAg 2-84*
NPSE Newsletter & Incentive Report - Union, NJ - *BaconPubCkMag 84*
NRA News - Washington, DC - *BaconPubCkMag 84*
NRA News - Chicago, IL - *MagDir 84*
NRE Systems - Maitland, FL - *MicrocomMPl 84*
NRG [of Skydog Press] - Portland, OR - *LitMag&SmPr 83-84*
NRI/E Japan Economic & Business Data Bank [of Nomura Research Institute] - Tokyo, Japan - *DataDirOnSer 84; EISS 83*
NRIC Database [of National Rehabilitation Information Center] - Washington, DC - *DataDirOnSer 84*
NRP Music Group - New York, NY - *BillIntBG 83-84*
NSA Action Shopper - Charlevoix, MI - *AyerDirPub 83*
NSA Inc. - Cherry Hill, NJ - *ADAPSOMemDir 83-84; DataDirSup 7-83*
NSC International - Englewood Cliffs, NJ - *DirInfWP 82*
NSP Inc. - Crofton, MD - *WhoWMicrocom 83*
Nsub - Ijmuiden, Netherlands - *DirOnDB Spring 84*
NSW Motor Vehicles Registrations Data Base - St. Leonards, Australia - *DirOnDB Spring 84*
NTA Courier - Lexington, KY - *BaconPubCkMag 84*
NTC Inc. - Park Falls, WI - *BrCabYB 84; Tel&CabFB 84C*
NTDRA Dealer News [of National Tire Dealers & Retreaders Association] - Washington, DC - *BaconPubCkMag 84; MagDir 84*
NTI Inc. - Markham, ON, Canada - *DirInfWP 82*
NTIS [of U.S. Dept. of Commerce] - Springfield, VA - *DirOnDB Spring 84; OnBibDB 3*
NTIS Bibliographic Database [of Cableshare Inc.] - London, ON, Canada - *DataDirOnSer 84*
NTS Software Inc. - Rialto, CA - *MicrocomMPl 84*
NTU Bulletin - Newark, NJ - *NewsDir 84*
Nu Data Corp. - Little Silver, NJ - *DataDirSup 7-83*
Nu-Sound Records - Nashville, TN - *BillIntBG 83-84*
NU View TV Inc. - Oriskany Falls, NY - *BrCabYB 84; Tel&CabFB 84C*
Nuance Press Inc. - Columbus, OH - *BoPubDir 4, 5*
Nub Pub Music Inc. - *See* Escrow Music
NUC/Codes [of SDC Search Service] - Santa Monica, CA - *CompReadDB 82; DataDirOnSer 84*
Nucifora & Associates - Atlanta, GA - *AdAge 3-28-84; StaDirAdAg 2-84*
Nucla-Naturita Telephone Co. - Nucla, CA - *TelDir&BG 83-84*
Nucla San Miguel Basin Forum - Nucla, CO - *BaconPubCkNews 84*
Nuclear & Chemical Waste Management - Alexandria, VA - *BaconPubCkMag 84*
Nuclear Canada Nucleaire - Toronto, ON, Canada - *BaconPubCkMag 84*
Nuclear Criticality Experiments from 1943 to 1978 [of University of California] - Livermore, CA - *EISS 83*
Nuclear Data Center [of Institute of Physics & Energy] - Obinsk, Ukrainian Soviet Socialist Republic - *EISS 83*
Nuclear Data Project [of U.S. Dept. of Energy] - Oak Ridge, TN - *EISS 83*
Nuclear Data Section [of International Atomic Energy Agency] - Vienna, Austria - *EISS 83*
Nuclear Information & Documentation Center [of National Institute of Nuclear Research] - Mexico City, Mexico - *EISS 83*
Nuclear Magnetic Resonance Literature Search System [of Preston Publications Inc.] - Niles, IL - *CompReadDB 82*
Nuclear News - La Grange Park, IL - *BaconPubCkMag 84; MagDir 84*
Nuclear Plant Safety - Lombard, IL - *BaconPubCkMag 84*
Nuclear Products Co. - El Monte, CA - *AvMarPl 83*
Nuclear Regulatory Commission/Reactor Safety Research Data Bank [of U.S. Dept. of Energy] - Idaho Falls, ID - *EISS 83*
Nuclear Research Information Center [of American Nuclear Society] - La Grange Park, IL - *EISS 83*
Nuclear Safety Information Center [of Oak Ridge National Laboratory] - Oak Ridge, TN - *CompReadDB 82; DirOnDB Spring 84; EISS 83; InfIndMarPl 83*
Nuclear Science Abstracts [of U.S. Dept. of Energy] - Oak Ridge, TN - *CompReadDB 82; DirOnDB Spring 84; OnBibDB 3*
Nuclear Science & Engineering - La Grange Park, IL - *BaconPubCkMag 84; MagDir 84*
Nuclear Standards News - La Grange Park, IL - *BaconPubCkMag 84*
Nuclear Structure References [of National Nuclear Data Center] - Upton, NY - *CompReadDB 82*
Nuclear Technology - Tucson, AZ - *BaconPubCkMag 84*
Nuclear Technology - La Grange Park, IL - *MagDir 84*
Nuclear Times - New York, NY - *BaconPubCkMag 84; WritMar 84*
Nuclear Waste News - Silver Spring, MD - *BaconPubCkMag 84; DirOnDB Spring 84*
Nuclear Waste News [of NewsNet Inc.] - Bryn Mawr, PA - *DataDirOnSer 84*
NuclearFuel - New York, NY - *BaconPubCkMag 84; MagDir 84*
Nucleonics Week - New York, NY - *BaconPubCkMag 84; MagDir 84*
Nucleotide Sequence Search System [of Computer Sciences Corp.] - Bethesda, MD - *DirOnDB Spring 84*
Nucleotide Sequence Search System [of Computer Sciences Corp.] - Falls Church, VA - *DataDirOnSer 84*
Nucleus Corp. - Madison Heights, MI - *DataDirSup 7-83*
Nucleus Records - Sea Bright, NJ - *BillIntBG 83-84*
Nucleus Science Journal - Flushing, NY - *WritMar 84*
NUCO Systems Inc. - Oak Brook, IL - *ADAPSOMemDir 83-84; DataDirOnSer 84; DataDirSup 7-83*
Nueces County Cable TV Inc. - Port Aransas, TX - *BrCabYB 84; Tel&CabFB 84C*
Nuestro - New York, NY - *BaconPubCkMag 84; MagDir 84; MagIndMarPl 82-83*
Nuevo Tech Inc. - Plano, TX - *ADAPSOMemDir 83-84*
Nuffer/Smith Associates Inc. - San Diego, CA - *DirPRFirms 83*
Nugent & Co., Patrick - Boston, MA - *StaDirAdAg 2-84*
Nugget [of Dugent Publishing Co.] - Coral Gables, FL - *ArtMar 84; WritMar 84*
Nugget - North Bay, ON, Canada - *AyerDirPub 83*
Nujac Publishing Co. Inc. - *See* Jamie Music Publishing Co.
Numarc Book Corp. - Buffalo, NY - *BoPubDir 4, 5*
 # Magazine - New York, NY - *LitMag&SmPr 83-84*
Number 9 Music - New York, NY - *BillIntBG 83-84*
Number One International Inc. - McLean, VA - *DirMarMP 83*
Number One Television Network - Naples, FL - *BrCabYB 84*
Numerax IV [of Numerax Inc.] - Maywood, NJ - *DataDirOnSer 84; DirOnDB Spring 84*
Numerax Inc. - Maywood, NJ - *DataDirOnSer 84*
Numeri/Comp Inc. - Rockford, IL - *MicrocomMPl 83, 84*
Numismatic Fine Arts Inc. - Beverly Hills, CA - *BoPubDir 4 Sup, 5*
Numismatic Information Service - Pleasant Valley, NY - *Ed&PubIntYB 82; LitMarPl 84*
Numismatic News [of Krause Publications] - Iola, WI - *BaconPubCkMag 84; MagDir 84; MagIndMarPl 82-83; WritMar 84*
Numismatist, The - Colorado Springs, CO - *MagDir 84; MagIndMarPl 82-83*
Numonics Corp. - Lansdale, PA - *DataDirSup 7-83; MicrocomMPl 84*

Numsen Master Antenna Systems Inc. - De Soto, WI - *BrCabYB 84*
Numsen Master Antenna Systems Inc. - La Farge, WI - *BrCabYB 84*
Numsen Master Antenna Systems Inc. - Soldier's Grove, WI - *BrCabYB 84; Tel&CabFB 84C*
Numsen, Robert - La Crosse, WI - *Tel&CabFB 84C p.1695*
Nunaga Publishing Co. - New Westminister, BC, Canada - *BoPubDir 4, 5*
Nunatsiaq News - Frobisher Bay, NT, Canada - *Ed&PubIntYB 82*
Nunda News, The - Nunda, NY - *AyerDirPub 83; Ed&PubIntYB 82*
Nunes Publishing Co. - Kailua, HI - *BoPubDir 4, 5*
Nunn Telephone Co. - Nunn, CA - *TelDir&BG 83-84*
Nuovo Mondo - Toronto, ON, Canada - *Ed&PubIntYB 82*
Nurse Educator - Wakefield, MA - *BaconPubCkMag 84; MagIndMarPl 82-83*
Nurse Practitioner, The - Seattle, WA - *BaconPubCkMag 84; MagIndMarPl 82-83*
Nurseco Inc. - Pacific Palisades, CA - *BoPubDir 4, 5; LitMarPl 84; WritMar 84*
Nursery Business - Tampa, FL - *BaconPubCkMag 84*
Nursery Business [of Brantwood Publications Inc.] - Elm Grove, WI - *MagDir 84*
Nurse's Book Society [of Macmillan Book Clubs Inc.] - New York, NY - *LitMarPl 83, 84*
Nursing & Allied Health Literature Index - Glendale, CA - *DirOnDB Spring 84*
Nursing Dimensions - Wakefield, MA - *MagDir 84*
Nursing '83 [of Intermed Communications Inc.] - Springhouse, PA - *LitMarPl 84; MagDir 84*
Nursing '82 [of Intermed Communications Inc.] - Springhouse, PA - *BaconPubCkMag 84; Folio 83; LitMarPl 83; MagIndMarPl 82-83*
Nursing Forum - Hillsdale, NJ - *MagDir 84*
Nursing Homes [of Heldref Publications] - Washington, DC - *BaconPubCkMag 84; MagDir 84*
Nursing Leadership - Thorofare, NJ - *BaconPubCkMag 84*
Nursing Life - Springhouse, PA - *BaconPubCkMag 84*
Nursing Management - Chicago, IL - *MagIndMarPl 82-83*
Nursing Outlook - New York, NY - *BaconPubCkMag 84; MagDir 84*
Nursing Report - Westport, CT - *BaconPubCkMag 84; MagDir 84*
Nursing Research - New York, NY - *MagDir 84; MagIndMarPl 82-83*
Nursingworld Journal - Weston, MA - *ArtMar 84; BaconPubCkMag 84; MagDir 84; WritMar 84*
NUS Training Corp. - Gaithersburg, MD - *AvMarPl 83*
Nushagak Telephone Co-Operative Inc. - Dillingham, AK - *TelDir&BG 83-84*
Nussbaum Associates Inc. - Tenafly, NJ - *ADAPSOMemDir 83-84*
Nustyle Quilting Frame Co. - Stover, MO - *BoPubDir 4, 5*
Nutley Sun - Nutley, NJ - *BaconPubCkNews 84; Ed&PubIntYB 82*
Nutmeg Broadcasting Co., The - Willimantic, CT - *BrCabYB 84*
Nutmeg Music - New York, NY - *AvMarPl 83*
NuTop Record Inc. - Tempe, AZ - *BillIntBG 83-84*
Nutri-Books Corp. - Denver, CO - *BoPubDir 4 Sup, 5*
NutriQuest [of Capital Systems Group Inc.] - Kensington, MD - *InfIndMarPl 83*
Nutrition Abstracts & Reviews [of Commonwealth Bureau of Nutrition] - Aberdeen, Scotland - *CompReadDB 82*
Nutrition Action [of Center for Science in the Public Interest] - Washington, DC - *LitMag&SmPr 83-84; WritMar 84*
Nutrition Analysis System [of Pillsbury Co.] - Edina, MN - *DirOnDB Spring 84*
Nutrition Analysis System [of Pillsbury Co.] - Minneapolis, MN - *EISS 83*
Nutrition & the M.D. - Van Nuys, CA - *BaconPubCkMag 84*
Nutrition Education Association Publishing Co. - Houston, TX - *BoPubDir 4 Sup, 5*
Nutrition for Optimal Health Association - Winnetka, IL - *BoPubDir 4, 5*
Nutrition Foundation - Washington, DC - *BoPubDir 5*
Nutrition Health Review - Madison, NY - *LitMag&SmPr 83-84*
Nutrition Health Review - New York, NY - *ArtMar 84; BaconPubCkMag 84; MagDir 84; MagIndMarPl 82-83*
Nutrition Marketing Co. - Englewood, NJ - *StaDirAdAg 2-84*
Nutrition Reviews - St. Louis, MO - *MagDir 84; MagIndMarPl 82-83*
Nutrition Today - Annapolis, MD - *MagIndMarPl 82-83*
Nutritional Development Inc. - St. Petersburg Beach, FL - *BoPubDir 4, 5*
Nutritional Support Services - North Hollywood, CA - *BaconPubCkMag 84; MagDir 84; MagIndMarPl 82-83*
Nutshell - Knoxville, TN - *MagDir 84; WritMar 84*
Nutshell News [of Boynton & Associates] - Clifton, VA - *WritMar 84*
NV Advertising Inc. - *See* Cohen Okerlund Smith Advertising & Marketing Inc.
NWI Audio Visual Systems Inc. [Div. of Photo & Sound Co.] - Portland, OR - *AvMarPl 83*
N.W.R. Publications Inc. [Aff. of New World Review] - New York, NY - *BoPubDir 4, 5*
N.Y. Habitat [of The Carol Group Ltd.] - New York, NY - *LitMag&SmPr 83-84; WritMar 84*
NY Institute of Word Processing - New York, NY - *DirInfWP 82*
Nya Svenska Pressen - Vancouver, BC, Canada - *Ed&PubIntYB 82*
Nyack Gazette, The - Nyack, NY - *LitMarPl 84*
Nyack Journal-News [of Westchester Rockland Newspapers] - Nyack, NY - *NewsDir 84*
Nyack Rockland Journal-News - *See* Westchester-Rockland Newspapers
NYC War Tax Resistance & NYC People's Life Fund - New York, NY - *BoPubDir 4, 5*
Nyerges, Anton N. - Richmond, KY - *BoPubDir 4, 5*
Nyssa Gate City Journal - Nyssa, OR - *BaconPubCkNews 84; Ed&PubIntYB 82*
Nystrom [Div. of Carnation] - Chicago, IL - *ArtMar 84; AvMarPl 83; WritMar 84*
NYT Cable TV [of The New York Times] - Audubon, NJ - *BrCabYB 84; CabTVFinDB 83; HomeVid&CabYB 82-83*
NYT Pictures [of The New York Times] - New York, NY - *AvMarPl 83; Ed&PubIntYB 82; LitMarPl 83, 84*
NYT Productions [Div. of The New York Times Syndication Sales Corp.] - New York, NY - *AvMarPl 83; Tel&CabFB 84C*

O

O & A Marketing News [of McAnally & Associates Inc.] - La Canada, CA - *BaconPubCkMag 84; MagDir 84; WritMar 84*
O & B Books Inc. - Corvallis, OR - *BoPubDir 4, 5*
O & D Cable Television [of Tribune Cable Communications Inc.] - Obion, TN - *BrCabYB 84; Tel&CabFB 84C*
O-K Cable TV [of Oshtemo-Kalamazoo Associates] - Oshtemo, MI - *BrCabYB 84*
O Mensageiro - Vancouver, BC, Canada - *Ed&PubIntYB 82*
OA Software Inc. - San Jose, CA - *MicrocomMPl 84*
OAG-EE - Oak Brook, IL - *DirOnDB Spring 84*
Oak Bay Star, The - Victoria, BC, Canada - *AyerDirPub 83*
Oak Brook Doings [of Doings Newspapers] - Hinsdale, IL - *NewsDir 84*
Oak Brook Doings [of Doings Newspapers] - Oak Brook, IL - *AyerDirPub 83; Ed&PubIntYB 82*
Oak Brook Doings - *See* Doings Newspapers, The
Oak Brook Press [of Elmhurst Press Publications] - Elmhurst, IL - *AyerDirPub 83; NewsDir 84*
Oak Brook Press - *See* Press Publications
Oak Brook Suburban Life Graphic - *See* Life Printing & Publishing Co.
Oak Cable Systems Inc. - Huxley, IA - *Tel&CabFB 84C p.1695*
Oak Cliff Tribune [of Dallas Tribune Printing Co. Inc.] - Dallas, TX - *AyerDirPub 83; Ed&PubIntYB 82; NewsDir 84*
Oak Cliff Tribune Advertiser [of Dallas Tribune Printing Co. Inc.] - Dallas, TX - *AyerDirPub 83; NewsDir 84*
Oak Communications Inc. - Rancho Bernardo, CA - *HomeVid&CabYB 82-83; Tel&CabFB 84S; VideoDir 82-83*
Oak Communications Inc. - San Diego, CA - *CabTVFinDB 83; TelAl 83*
Oak Communications Inc. - Crystal Lake, IL - *HomeVid&CabYB 82-83*
Oak Creek & Caledonia Pictorial - Oak Creek, WI - *AyerDirPub 83*
Oak Creek Pictorial - Oak Creek, WI - *Ed&PubIntYB 82*
Oak Creek Pictorial - *See* Community Newspapers Inc.
Oak Forest Southtown Economist - Chicago, IL - *AyerDirPub 83*
Oak Forest Southtown Economist - Oak Forest, IL - *Ed&PubIntYB 82*
Oak Forest Southtown Economist - *See* Southtown Economist Inc.
Oak Forest Star Herald - Chicago Heights, IL - *NewsDir 84*
Oak Forest Star-Herald - Oak Forest, IL - *AyerDirPub 83; Ed&PubIntYB 82*
Oak Forest Star Herald - *See* Star Publications
Oak Grove Banner - Oak Grove, MO - *BaconPubCkNews 84; Ed&PubIntYB 82*
Oak Grove West Carroll Gazette - Oak Grove, LA - *BaconPubCkNews 84; NewsDir 84*
Oak Harbor Crosswind - Oak Harbor, WA - *Ed&PubIntYB 82*
Oak Harbor Ottawa County Exponent - Oak Harbor, OH - *BaconPubCkNews 84*
Oak Harbor Whidbey News-Times - Oak Harbor, WA - *BaconPubCkNews 84*
Oak Harbor Whidbey News Times & Whidbey Island Reporter - Oak Harbor, WA - *NewsDir 84*
Oak Hill Fayette Tribune - Oak Hill, WV - *BaconPubCkNews 84*
Oak Industries - Rancho Bernardo, CA - *AdAge 6-28-84; HomeVid&CabYB 82-83; KnowInd 83*
Oak Lawn Independent [of Southwest Messenger Newspapers] - Midlothian, IL - *AyerDirPub 83; NewsDir 84*
Oak Lawn Independent - Oak Lawn, IL - *Ed&PubIntYB 82*
Oak Lawn Independent - *See* Southwest Messenger Newspapers
Oak Lawn Reporter - *See* Reporter Publications
Oak Leaves [of Pioneer Press Inc.] - Oak Park, IL - *Ed&PubIntYB 82; NewsDir 84*
Oak Park Camera Co. - Oak Park, IL - *AvMarPl 83*
Oak Park Oak Leaves [of Pioneer Press Inc.] - Wilmette, IL - *AyerDirPub 83*
Oak Park Oak Leaves - *See* Pioneer Press Inc.
Oak Park Weekend World - Wilmette, IL - *AyerDirPub 83*
Oak Park Weekend World - *See* Pioneer Press Inc.
Oak Ridge Associated Universities - Oak Ridge, TN - *BoPubDir 4, 5*
Oak Ridge National Laboratory (Environmental Mutagen, Carcinogen & Teratogen Information Dept.) - Oak Ridge, TN - *DataDirOnSer 84*
Oak Ridge National Laboratory (Information Center Complex) - Oak Ridge, TN - *InfIndMarPl 83*
Oak Ridge National Laboratory (Radiation Shielding Information Center) - Oak Ridge, TN - *DataDirOnSer 84*
Oak Ridge National Laboratory (Toxic Materials Information Center) - Oak Ridge, TN - *BoPubDir 5*
Oak Ridger - Oak Ridge, TN - *AyerDirPub 83; BaconPubCkNews 84; Ed&PubIntYB 82; NewsDir 84*
Oak Tree Publications Inc. [of Leisure Dynamics Inc.] - San Diego, CA - *LitMarPl 83, 84; WritMar 84*
Oakdale Cablevision Inc. [of Communications Services Inc.] - Oakdale, LA - *BrCabYB 84; Tel&CabFB 84C*
Oakdale Journal - Oakdale, LA - *BaconPubCkNews 84; Ed&PubIntYB 82; NewsDir 84*
Oakdale Leader - Oakdale, CA - *Ed&PubIntYB 82; NewsDir 84*
Oakdale Weekly [of Greater Philadelphia Group Inc.] - Philadelphia, PA - *NewsDir 84*
Oakes Times - Oakes, ND - *BaconPubCkNews 84; Ed&PubIntYB 82*
Oakhurst Sierra Star - Oakhurst, CA - *BaconPubCkNews 84*
Oakland Acorn - Oakland, IA - *BaconPubCkNews 84; Ed&PubIntYB 82*
Oakland Botna Valley Times - Oakland, IA - *BaconPubCkNews 84*
Oakland California Voice - Oakland, CA - *NewsDir 84*
Oakland Catholic Voice - Oakland, CA - *NewsDir 84*
Oakland City Journal - Oakland City, IN - *BaconPubCkNews 84; Ed&PubIntYB 82*
Oakland County (Planning Div.) - Pontiac, MI - *EISS 5-84 Sup*
Oakland Independent - Oakland, NE - *BaconPubCkNews 84*
Oakland Ledger-Messenger - Oakland, IL - *BaconPubCkNews 84*
Oakland Metro Reporter - *See* Reporter Publishing Co.
Oakland Montclair Press - *See* Press Publications
Oakland Montclarion - Oakland, CA - *BaconPubCkNews 84*

Oakland Montclarion - Piedmont, CA - *NewsDir 84*
Oakland News - Oakland, PA - *Ed&PubIntYB 82*
Oakland News - Pittsburgh, PA - *AyerDirPub 83*
Oakland Piedmonter - *See* Snyder Publications
Oakland Post [of Alameda Publishing Corp.] - Oakland, CA - *AyerDirPub 83; NewsDir 84*
Oakland Post - *See* Alameda Publishing Corp.
Oakland Post Enquirer [of Oakland Neighborhood Journal] - Oakland, CA - *AyerDirPub 83; NewsDir 84*
Oakland Post Newspaper Group - Oakland, CA - *NewsDir 84*
Oakland Press - Oakland, CA - *Ed&PubIntYB 82*
Oakland Press [of Capital Cities Communications] - Pontiac, MI - *AyerDirPub 83; BaconPubCkNews 84; Ed&PubIntYB 82; NewsDir 84*
Oakland Press - *See* Press Publications
Oakland Republican - Oakland, MD - *BaconPubCkNews 84*
Oakland Seaside Post - *See* Alameda Publishing Corp.
Oakland Symphony - San Francisco, CA - *MagDir 84*
Oakland Times/Journal [of Oakland Neighborhood Journal] - Oakland, CA - *AyerDirPub 83; Ed&PubIntYB 82; NewsDir 84*
Oakland Tribune - Oakland, CA - *BaconPubCkNews 84; Ed&PubIntYB 82; LitMarPl 83, 84; NewsBur 6; NewsDir 84*
Oakley Co., The Cherri - Dallas, TX - *DirPRFirms 83*
Oakley Diablo Valley News - Oakley, CA - *BaconPubCkNews 84*
Oakley Graphic - Oakley, KS - *BaconPubCkNews 84; Ed&PubIntYB 82*
Oakman Telephone Co. Inc. - Oakman, AL - *TelDir&BG 83-84*
Oakmont Allegheny Valley Advance-Leader - *See* Gateway Press Inc.
Oakridge Dead Mountain Echo - Oakridge, OR - *BaconPubCkNews 84*
Oakridge Music Publishing Co. - Haltom City, TX - *BillIntBG 83-84*
Oakridge Music Recording Service - Ft. Worth, TX - *BillIntBG 83-84*
Oakview Book Press - Adelphi, MD - *BoPubDir 4, 5*
Oakville Beaver - Oakville, ON, Canada - *Ed&PubIntYB 82*
Oakville Cablenet - Oakville, ON, Canada - *BrCabYB 84*
Oakville Journal Record - Oakville, ON, Canada - *Ed&PubIntYB 82*
Oakwood Agency Inc. - Hauppauge, NY - *StaDirAdAg 2-84*
Oakwood Cable TV - Oakwood, IL - *BrCabYB 84; Tel&CabFB 84C*
Oakwood Mutual Telephone Co. - Oakwood, OH - *TelDir&BG 83-84*
Oakwood News - Oakwood, OH - *Ed&PubIntYB 82*
Oakwood Press [Aff. of Blodgett Enterprises Inc.] - McMinnville, OR - *BoPubDir 4, 5*
OAN Digger, The [of Oregon Association of Nurserymen] - Milwaukie, OR - *MagDir 84*
O.ARS - Cambridge, MA - *LitMag&SmPr 83-84*
OAS Music Group Inc. - Nashville, TN - *BillIntBG 83-84*
OAS Music Publishing - *See* Counterpop Music Group
OASES - Kansas City, MO - *DirOnDB Spring 84*
OASIS [of Post Office Headquarters] - Wellington, New Zealand - *InfIndMarPl 83*
Oasis Books - London, England - *LitMag&SmPr 83-84*
O.A.S.I.S. Inc. - New York, NY - *DirInfWP 82*
Oasis Press - Sunnyvale, CA - *LitMag&SmPr 83-84*
Oasis Systems - San Diego, CA - *MicrocomMPl 83, 84*
Oasys Inc. - Cambridge, MA - *MicrocomMPl 84*
Oat Willie Productions - Brooklyn, NY - *BillIntBG 83-84*
Oates TV Inc. - Petersburg, WV - *BrCabYB 84; Tel&CabFB 84C*
Oatman Computer Services Inc. - Lancaster, PA - *ADAPSOMemDir 83-84*
Oatmeal Studios - Rochester, VT - *WritMar 84*
OB-GYN News - Rockville, MD - *BaconPubCkMag 84; MagIndMarPl 82-83*
Ober Associates Inc., Harold - New York, NY - *LitMarPl 83, 84*
Ober Park Associates - Pittsburgh, PA - *BoPubDir 4, 5*
Oberlin CATV Inc. - Oberlin, KS - *BrCabYB 84; Tel&CabFB 84C*
Oberlin College (Field Translation Series) - Oberlin, OH - *BoPubDir 4, 5*
Oberlin Herald - Oberlin, KS - *BaconPubCkNews 84; Ed&PubIntYB 82*
Oberlin News-Tribune - Oberlin, OH - *BaconPubCkNews 84; Ed&PubIntYB 82*
Oberlin Printing Co. - Elyria, OH - *LitMarPl 83, 84*
Oberon Press [Div. of Michael, Hardy Ltd.] - Ottawa, ON, Canada - *LitMarPl 83, 84*
Obertunes - Warren, OH - *BillIntBG 83-84*
Obesity & Bariatric Medicine - Englewood, CO - *MagDir 84; MagIndMarPl 82-83*
Obie, Marlin T. - *See* Central Valley Cablevision Inc.
Oblates Magazine [of Missionary Association of Mary Immaculate] - Belleville, IL - *WritMar 84*
Oblique Records - New York, NY - *BillIntBG 83-84*
Oblong Oracle - Hudsonville, IL - *BaconPubCkNews 84*
Oboe [of Night Horn Books] - San Francisco, CA - *LitMag&SmPr 83-84*
Obol International [Aff. of Div. Unigraphics Inc.] - Chicago, IL - *BoPubDir 4, 5*
Obranoel Press - Franklin Square, NY - *BoPubDir 4, 5*
Obremski Studio - New York, NY - *MagIndMarPl 82-83*
O'Brien Associates, Al - *See* Baron/O'Brien Inc.
O'Brien, C. J. - Richmond, VA - *LitMarPl 83, 84*
O'Brien County Bell - Primghar, IA - *AyerDirPub 83; Ed&PubIntYB 82*
O'Brien Lapidary - Hollywood, CA - *BoPubDir 4, 5*
O'Brien Partition Co. Inc., Glen - Kansas City, MO - *DirInfWP 82*
O'Brien-Sherwood Associates Inc. - Woodside, NY - *IntDirMarRes 83*
Observer - Corning, CA - *AyerDirPub 83*
Observer - Sacramento, CA - *Ed&PubIntYB 82*
Observer - Athens, GA - *AyerDirPub 83*
Observer - Moultrie, GA - *AyerDirPub 83*
Observer - Chicago, IL - *AyerDirPub 83; Ed&PubIntYB 82*
Observer - Peoria, IL - *AyerDirPub 83; Ed&PubIntYB 82*
Observer - Petersburg, IL - *AyerDirPub 83*
Observer - De Witt, IA - *AyerDirPub 83*
Observer - Cheboygan, MI - *AyerDirPub 83*
Observer - Flushing, MI - *AyerDirPub 83*
Observer - Morenci, MI - *AyerDirPub 83*
Observer - Holbrook, NE - *AyerDirPub 83*
Observer - Salem, NH - *AyerDirPub 83*
Observer [of Blackwood Cam-Glo Newspapers Inc.] - Blackwood, NJ - *AyerDirPub 83; NewsDir 84*
Observer - Hasbrouck Heights, NJ - *AyerDirPub 83; Ed&PubIntYB 82*
Observer - Kearny, NJ - *AyerDirPub 83*
Observer - Rio Rancho, NM - *AyerDirPub 83; Ed&PubIntYB 82*
Observer - Dundee, NY - *AyerDirPub 83*
Observer - Dunkirk, NY - *AyerDirPub 83*
Observer - Massena, NY - *AyerDirPub 83*
Observer - Northport, NY - *AyerDirPub 83; Ed&PubIntYB 82*
Observer - Charlotte, NC - *AyerDirPub 83*
Observer - Fayetteville, NC - *AyerDirPub 83*
Observer - Littleton, NC - *AyerDirPub 83*
Observer [of Western Communications Inc.] - La Grande, OR - *AyerDirPub 83; Ed&PubIntYB 82; NewsDir 84*
Observer - Portland, OR - *Ed&PubIntYB 82*
Observer [of Mid State News Inc.] - Johnstown, PA - *NewsDir 84*
Observer - Philadelphia, PA - *BaconPubCkMag 84; MagDir 84*
Observer - Yankton, SD - *Ed&PubIntYB 82*
Observer - Robert Lee, TX - *AyerDirPub 83*
Observer - Oregon, WI - *AyerDirPub 83*
Observer - Vegreville, AB, Canada - *AyerDirPub 83*
Observer - Salmon Arm, BC, Canada - *AyerDirPub 83*
Observer - Hartland, NB, Canada - *Ed&PubIntYB 82*
Observer - Dryden, ON, Canada - *AyerDirPub 83*
Observer - Palmerston, ON, Canada - *AyerDirPub 83*
Observer - Pembroke, ON, Canada - *AyerDirPub 83; Ed&PubIntYB 82*
Observer - Sarnia, ON, Canada - *AyerDirPub 83; Ed&PubIntYB 82*
Observer - Carlyle, SK, Canada - *AyerDirPub 83; Ed&PubIntYB 82*
Observer - Carrot River, SK, Canada - *Ed&PubIntYB 82*
Observer-American - Clearlake Highlands, CA - *AyerDirPub 83*

Observer & Eccentric Newspapers - Livonia, MI - *BaconPubCkNews 84*
Observer & Herald & News - Newberry, SC - *AyerDirPub 83*
Observer-Dispatch - Utica, NY - *AyerDirPub 83; Ed&PubIntYB 82*
Observer GmbH - Vienna, Austria - *ProGuPRSer 4*
Observer-News Enterprise - Newton, NC - *AyerDirPub 83; BaconPubCkNews 84; Ed&PubIntYB 82*
Observer Newspapers - Bellmore, NY - *BaconPubCkNews 84*
Observer Patriot - Putnam, CT - *AyerDirPub 83; Ed&PubIntYB 82*
Observer-Reporter - Washington, PA - *AyerDirPub 83; Ed&PubIntYB 82; NewsDir 84*
Observer Sentinel - Rockville, MD - *AyerDirPub 83*
Observer, The - Southington, CT - *AyerDirPub 83*
Observer, The - Lithonia, GA - *AyerDirPub 83*
Observer, The - Kewanna, IN - *AyerDirPub 83; Ed&PubIntYB 82*
Observer, The [of Students of Notre Dame-St. Mary's College] - Notre Dame, IN - *NewsDir 84*
Observer, The - Vail, IA - *Ed&PubIntYB 82*
Observer, The - Somerset, KY - *Ed&PubIntYB 82*
Observer, The - Baker, LA - *AyerDirPub 83*
Observer, The - Belgrade, MN - *Ed&PubIntYB 82*
Observer, The - Corrales, NM - *AyerDirPub 83*
Observer, The [of Greenville Observer Publications Inc.] - Greenville, RI - *AyerDirPub 83; NewsDir 84*
Observer, The - Grand Prairie, TX - *AyerDirPub 83*
Observer-Times - Fayetteville, NC - *AyerDirPub 83*
Observer-Tribune - Mendham, NJ - *AyerDirPub 83; Ed&PubIntYB 82*
Obsidian: Black Literature in Review - Detroit, MI - *LitMag&SmPr 83-84*
Obst Advertising, Raymond - Culver City, CA - *StaDirAdAg 2-84*
Obstetrical & Gynecological Survey - Baltimore, MD - *MagDir 84*
Obstetrical & Gynecological Survey - Norfolk, VA - *BaconPubCkMag 84*
Obstetrics & Gynecology - New York, NY - *MagDir 84*
Obstetrics & Gynecology - Milwaukee, WI - *BaconPubCkMag 84*
Obywatel Amerykanski - Jamesburg, NJ - *Ed&PubIntYB 82*
O.C. Media Advertising - Syosset, NY - *StaDirAdAg 2-84*
Ocala Star-Banner - Ocala, FL - *AyerDirPub 83; BaconPubCkNews 84; Ed&PubIntYB 82; NewsDir 84*
OCAW Union News - Denver, CO - *WritMar 84*
OCB Cablevision Inc. [of National Cablesystems Inc.] - Clarke County, GA - *Tel&CabFB 84C*
OCB Cablevision Inc. [of National Cablesystems Inc.] - Watkinsville, GA - *Tel&CabFB 84C*
OCB Cablevision Inc. [of National Cablesystems Inc.] - Winder, GA - *Tel&CabFB 84C*
OCC Advertising - New York, NY - *BrCabYB 84*
Occasional Productions - Los Gatos, CA - *BoPubDir 4 Sup, 5; LitMag&SmPr 83-84*
Occasional Review [of Realities] - San Jose, CA - *LitMag&SmPr 83-84*
Occidental Press - Washington, DC - *BoPubDir 4, 5*
Occidente - Thornhill, ON, Canada - *Ed&PubIntYB 82*
Occupational Awareness - Los Alamitos, CA - *WritMar 84*
Occupational Computing Co. Inc. - Woodland Hills, CA - *MicrocomMPl 84; WhoWMicrocom 83*
Occupational Hazards - Cleveland, OH - *BaconPubCkMag 84; MagDir 84*
Occupational Health & Safety - Waco, TX - *BaconPubCkMag 84; MagDir 84*
Occupational Health Nursing - Thorofare, NJ - *BaconPubCkMag 84; MagDir 84; MagIndMarPl 82-83*
Occupational Health Services Inc. - New York, NY - *DataDirOnSer 84; EISS 7-83 Sup*
Occupational Safety & Health Database [of International Occupational Safety & Health Information Centre] - Geneva, Switzerland - *DataDirOnSer 84*
Ocean Beach Pennysaver - Mission Viejo, CA - *AyerDirPub 83*
Ocean City Eastern Shore Times - Ocean City, MD - *BaconPubCkNews 84*
Ocean City Maryland Coast Press - Ocean City, MD - *NewsDir 84*
Ocean City Sentinel-Ledger - Ocean City, NJ - *BaconPubCkNews 84*
Ocean City Week - Ocean City, MD - *Ed&PubIntYB 82*
Ocean Coast Properties Inc. - Portland, ME - *BrCabYB 84*
Ocean Construction Report - Houston, TX - *BaconPubCkMag 84; MagDir 84*
Ocean County Bulletin - Jackson, NJ - *Ed&PubIntYB 82*
Ocean County Citizen - Lakewood, NJ - *Ed&PubIntYB 82*
Ocean County Leader - Point Pleasant Beach, NJ - *AyerDirPub 83*
Ocean County Observer - Toms River, NJ - *BaconPubCkNews 84*
Ocean County Reporter - Ocean County, NJ - *Ed&PubIntYB 82*
Ocean County Reporter, The [of Bergen Evening Record Corp.] - Toms River, NJ - *AyerDirPub 83; NewsDir 84*
Ocean County Review - Seaside Heights, NJ - *AyerDirPub 83; Ed&PubIntYB 82*
Ocean County Times Observer [of Seacoast Publications] - Toms River, NJ - *AyerDirPub 83; Ed&PubIntYB 82; NewsDir 84*
Ocean Data Systems Inc. - Rockville, MD - *ADAPSOMemDir 83-84*
Ocean Engineering - Elmsford, NY - *MagDir 84*
Ocean Grove & Neptune Times - Ocean Grove, NJ - *BaconPubCkNews 84; Ed&PubIntYB 82*
Ocean Industry - Houston, TX - *BaconPubCkMag 84; MagDir 84; WritMar 84*
Ocean Living Institute - Kearney, NJ - *BoPubDir 4, 5*
Ocean Oil Weekly Report - Houston, TX - *BaconPubCkMag 84*
Ocean Realm Magazine - Miami, FL - *WritMar 84*
Ocean Realm Video Productions - Miami, FL - *WritMar 84*
Ocean Reef Cable TV - Ocean Reef Club, SD - *BrCabYB 84*
Ocean Science News - Washington, DC - *BaconPubCkMag 84; MagDir 84*
Ocean Springs Record [of Gannett] - Ocean Springs, MS - *BaconPubCkNews 84; Ed&PubIntYB 82; NewsDir 84*
Ocean View Cablevision Inc. - *See* Western Communications Inc.
Oceana County News - Montague, MI - *AyerDirPub 83; Ed&PubIntYB 82*
Oceana Publications Inc. - Dobbs Ferry, NY - *BoPubDir 4 Sup, 5; LitMarPl 83, 84*
Oceana TV Cable Co. [of Bahakel Communications Ltd.] - Oceana, WV - *BrCabYB 84; Tel&CabFB 84C*
Oceana's Herald-Journal - Hart, MI - *AyerDirPub 83; Ed&PubIntYB 82; NewsDir 84*
Oceanic Abstracts [of Cambridge Scientific Abstracts] - Washington, DC - *CompReadDB 82*
Oceanic Abstracts [of Cambridge Scientific Abstracts] - Bethesda, MD - *DataDirOnSer 84; DBBus 82; DirOnDB Spring 84; EISS 83; OnBibDB 3*
Oceanic Cablevision [of American Television & Communications Corp.] - Honolulu, HI - *HomeVid&CabYB 82-83; Tel&CabFB 84C*
Oceanic Press [Aff. of American Reflections] - Princeton, NJ - *BoPubDir 4, 5*
Oceanic Press Service - North Hollywood, CA - *Ed&PubIntYB 82*
Oceanic Society - Stamford, CT - *AvMarPl 83*
Oceanographic Literature Review - Elmsford, NY - *DirOnDB Spring 84*
Oceanographic Literature Review [of Pergamon International Information Corp.] - McLean, VA - *DataDirOnSer 84*
Oceans [of Oceanic Society] - San Francisco, CA - *ArtMar 84; BaconPubCkMag 84; MagDir 84; MagIndMarPl 82-83; WritMar 84*
Oceanside Beacon - Oceanside, NY - *AyerDirPub 83; BaconPubCkNews 84; Ed&PubIntYB 82; NewsDir 84*
Oceanside Blade-Tribune [of Southcoast Publishers] - Oceanside, CA - *NewsDir 84*
Oceanside East Pennysaver - Mission Viejo, CA - *AyerDirPub 83*
Oceanside-Island Park Herald [of Lawrence Bi-County Publishers Inc.] - Lawrence, NY - *NewsDir 84*
Oceanside-Island Park Herald [of Lawrence Bi-County Publishers Inc.] - Oceanside, NY - *AyerDirPub 83; Ed&PubIntYB 82*
Oceanside Island Park Herald - *See* Richner Publications Inc.
Oceanside North Pennysaver - Mission Viejo, CA - *AyerDirPub 83*
Oceanside Pennysaver - Rockville Centre, NY - *AyerDirPub 83*

OECD Publications & Information Center [of Organization for Economic Cooperation & Development] - Washington, DC - *MicroMarPl 82-83*
OECD Quarterly National Income Accounts [of Chase Econometrics/Interactive Data Corp.] - Waltham, MA - *DataDirOnSer 84*
OECD Quarterly National Income Accounts [of Organization for Economic Cooperation & Development] - Paris, France - *DirOnDB Spring 84*
OECD Quarterly Oil Statistics [of Organization for Economic Cooperation & Development] - Paris, France - *DBBus 82; DirOnDB Spring 84*
OECD Statistics of Foreign Trade: Series A [of Organization for Economic Cooperation & Development] - Paris, France - *DirOnDB Spring 84*
OECD Trade Series A [of Chase Econometrics/Interactive Data Corp.] - Waltham, MA - *DataDirOnSer 84*
OECD Trade Series A Data Bank [of Data Resources Inc.] - Lexington, MA - *DataDirOnSer 84*
Oelgeschlager, Gunn & Hain Inc. - Cambridge, MA - *LitMarPl 83, 84*
Oelwein Cablevision Inc. - Oelwein, IA - *Tel&CabFB 84C*
Oelwein Daily Register [of Thomson Newspapers] - Oelwein, IA - *BaconPubCkNews 84; NewsDir 84*
O'Fallon Journal - *See* Journal Newspapers of Southern Illinois
O'Fallon Progress - O'Fallon, IL - *BaconPubCkNews 84*
O'Fallon-St. Peters County Tribune [of St. Charles Community News Inc.] - O'Fallon, MO - *NewsDir 84*
O'Fallon-St. Peters Times - O'Fallon, MO - *Ed&PubIntYB 82*
O'Farrill Music Ltd. - New York, NY - *AvMarPl 83*
O.F.C. Publications [Aff. of Ottawa Folklore Centre Ltd.] - Ottawa, ON, Canada - *BoPubDir 4 Sup, 5*
Off Belay - Renton, WA - *MagDir 84*
Off Duty America - Costa Mesa, CA - *ArtMar 84; BaconPubCkMag 84; WritMar 84*
Off Hollywood Music - *See* Sleepy Deacon Ltd.
Off-Lead Dog Training - Westmoreland, NY - *BaconPubCkMag 84; MagIndMarPl 82-83*
Off Our Backs - Washington, DC - *LitMag&SmPr 83-84; MagIndMarPl 82-83*
Off-Price News - Pinellas Park, FL - *BaconPubCkMag 84*
Off-Price Retailing - New York, NY - *BaconPubCkMag 84*
Off-Road [of Argus Publishing] - Los Angeles, CA - *BaconPubCkMag 84; MagDir 84; MagIndMarPl 82-83; WritMar 84*
Off-Road Advertiser - Cypress, CA - *BaconPubCkMag 84*
Off the Land - Dell Rapids, SD - *NewsDir 84*
Off to College - Montgomery, AL - *BoPubDir 4, 5*
Offenheiser, Marilyn J. - New York, NY - *MagIndMarPl 82-83*
Office - Stamford, CT - *BaconPubCkMag 84; MagDir 84; MagIndMarPl 82-83*
Office Administration & Automation [of Geyer-McAllister Publications Inc.] - New York, NY - *BaconPubCkMag 84; MagDir 84; MicrocomMPl 84; WritMar 84*
Office Associates Inc., Philip - Dayton, OH - *StaDirAdAg 2-84*
Office Automation Inc. - Conyers, GA - *DirInfWP 82*
Office Automation News [of Office Automation Society International] - Washington, DC - *MicrocomMPl 84*
Office Automation Reporting Service - Framingham, MA - *BaconPubCkMag 84*
Office Automation Systems [Div. of N. J. Naclerio & Associates Inc.] - Springfield, VA - *DirInfWP 82*
Office Automation Update - Boca Raton, FL - *DirOnDB Spring 84*
Office Automation Update [of NewsNet Inc.] - Bryn Mawr, PA - *DataDirOnSer 84*
Office Away - Chicago, IL - *AvMarPl 83*
Office Belge du Commerce Exterieur - Brussels, Belgium - *InfIndMarPl 83*
Office Communications - Spring Valley, NY - *DirInfWP 82*
Office Data Products - Woburn, MA - *DirInfWP 82*
Office de la Recherche Scientifique et Technique Outre-Mer - Bondy, France - *InfIndMarPl 83*
Office Environment Co-Operative Inc. - Ft. Worth, TX - *DirInfWP 82*
Office Equipment & Methods - Toronto, ON, Canada - *BaconPubCkMag 84*
Office Equipment Exporter - Stamford, CT - *MagDir 84*
Office for History of Science & Technology [of University of California, Berkeley] - Berkeley, CA - *CompReadDB 82*
Office Information Resources Inc. - Santa Clara, CA - *DirInfWP 82*
Office Manager Inc., The - Seattle, WA - *DirInfWP 82; WhoWMicrocom 83*
Office of Air Force History - Washington, DC - *BoPubDir 4, 5*
Office of Development Information & Utilization [of U.S. Agency for International Development] - Washington, DC - *EISS 83*
Office of Economic Information & Forecasting - Neuilly, France - *EISS 7-83 Sup*
Office of Geographic Research [of U.S. Geological Survey] - Reston, VA - *EISS 83*
Office of Legislative Data Processing [of Massachusetts General Court] - Boston, MA - *EISS 83*
Office of Legislative Research [of Utah State Legislature] - Salt Lake City, UT - *EISS 83*
Office of Legislative Services [of New Jersey State Legislature] - Trenton, NJ - *EISS 83*
Office of Legislative Services [of Tennessee State General Assembly] - Nashville, TN - *EISS 83*
Office of Research & Development [of West Virginia University] - Morgantown, WV - *EISS 83*
Office of Research & Statistics [of U.S. Social Security Administration] - Washington, DC - *EISS 83*
Office of Technology Assessment & Forecast Data Base [of U.S. Patent & Trademark Office] - Washington, DC - *CompReadDB 82*
Office of the Revisor of Statues [of Nebraska State Legislative Council] - Lincoln, NE - *EISS 83*
Office of Trade Studies & Statistics [of U.S. Maritime Administration] - Washington, DC - *EISS 83*
Office of Water Data Coordination [of U.S. Geological Survey] - Reston, VA - *EISS 83*
Office on Smoking & Health Database - Rockville, MD - *CompReadDB 82*
Office Productivity - La Grange, IL - *BaconPubCkMag 84*
Office Products Dealer - Wheaton, IL - *BaconPubCkMag 84; MagDir 84; MagIndMarPl 82-83; NewsBur 6*
Office Products Industry Report - Alexandria, VA - *BaconPubCkMag 84*
Office Products International - Denver, CO - *DirInfWP 82*
Office Publications Inc. - Stamford, CT - *BoPubDir 4, 5*
Office Sciences International Inc. - Iselin, NJ - *DirInfWP 82*
Office Suites Inc. - Chicago, IL - *DirInfWP 82*
Office/Supplies [Div. of U.S. Toner] - Venice, CA - *DirInfWP 82*
Office Support Services - Willowdale, ON, Canada - *DirInfWP 82*
Office System Integration Inc. - La Jolla, CA - *DirInfWP 82*
Office Systems Consulting Group Inc. - Boston, MA - *DirInfWP 82*
Office Technology Management Association - Milwaukee, WI - *TeleSy&SerDir 2-84*
Office World News - Garden City, NY - *BaconPubCkMag 84; MagDir 84*
Officer, The - Washington, DC - *BaconPubCkMag 84; MagDir 84; MagIndMarPl 82-83*
Officesmiths Inc. - Ottawa, ON, Canada - *ADAPSOMemDir 83-84*
Official Airline Guides [of Dun & Bradstreet Corp.] - Oak Brook, IL - *BoPubDir 4 Sup, 5; DataDirOnSer 84; DBBus 82; EISS 83; InfIndMarPl 83; InfoS 83-84; MicrocomMPl 84*
Official Airline Guides - New York, NY - *NewsBur 6*
Official Airline Guides - London, England - *InfIndMarPl 83*
Official Airline Guides (Electronic Edition) - Oak Brook, IL - *DataDirOnSer 84*
Official Airline Guides (Travel Magazines Div.) - New York, NY - *MagIndMarPl 82-83*
Official Airline Guides (Worldwide Edition) - Hinsdale, IL - *MagDir 84*
Official Board Markets - Chicago, IL - *BaconPubCkMag 84; MagDir 84*
Official Catholic Directory Mailing Lists, The [of P. J. Kenedy & Sons] - New York, NY - *LitMarPl 83, 84*
Official Detective Stories [of R.G.H. Publishing Corp.] - New York, NY - *ArtMar 84; MagDir 84; MagIndMarPl 82-83; WritMar 84*

Official Directory of Data Processing [of Official Directories & Services Inc.] - Gresham, OR - *EISS 5-84 Sup*
Official Films Inc. - New York, NY - *TelAl 83*
Official Karate - Derby, CT - *MagIndMarPl 82-83*
Official Magazine - Los Angeles, CA - *BaconPubCkMag 84*
Official Michigan - Bridgeport, MI - *MagDir 84*
Official Motor Carrier Directory - Chicago, IL - *BoPubDir 4, 5*
Official Railway Equipment Register [of National Railway Publications Co.] - New York, NY - *EISS 83*
Official Railway Guide, Travel Edition - New York, NY - *MagDir 84*
Official Records - Summertown, TN - *BillIntBG 83-84*
Official Shippers Guide - Chicago, IL - *MagDir 84*
Offield & Brower - Los Gatos, CA - *AdAge 3-28-84*
Offield & Brower - *See* Advertising Co. of Offield & Brower, The
Offset Composition Services [Subs. of Photo Data Inc.] - Washington, DC - *LitMarPl 83, 84*
Offset Paperback Manufacturers Inc. - Dallas, PA - *LitMarPl 83, 84*
Offshore [of PennWell Publishing Co.] - Tulsa, OK - *Folio 83*
Offshore [of Petroleum Publishing Co.] - Houston, TX - *BaconPubCkMag 84; MagDir 84*
Offshore Press - Allston, MA - *BoPubDir 4, 5*
Offshore Press - Watertown, MA - *LitMag&SmPr 83-84*
Offshore Resources - North Vancouver, BC, Canada - *BaconPubCkMag 84*
Offshore Rig Newsletter, The - Houston, TX - *BaconPubCkMag 84*
Offshore Telephone Co. [Aff. of Data Com Inc.] - New Orleans, LA - *TelDir&BG 83-84*
Ogallala Community TV [of Community Tele-Communications Inc.] - Ogallala, NE - *Tel&CabFB 84C*
Ogallala Keith County News - Ogallala, NE - *BaconPubCkNews 84; NewsDir 84*
Ogden MDS Co. - New York, NY - *Tel&CabFB 84C*
Ogden Newspapers Inc. - Mayville, NY - *BaconPubCkNews 84*
Ogden Newspapers Inc. - Wheeling, WV - *BrCabYB 84; Ed&PubIntYB 82*
Ogden Reporter - Ogden, IA - *BaconPubCkNews 84; Ed&PubIntYB 82*
Ogden Standard-Examiner [of The Standard Corp.] - Ogden, UT - *BaconPubCkNews 84; Ed&PubIntYB 82; LitMarPl 83, 84; NewsDir 84*
Ogden Telephone Co. - Ogden, IA - *TelDir&BG 83-84*
Ogden Telephone Co. - Blissfield, MI - *TelDir&BG 83-84*
Ogden Telephone Co. - Spencerport, NY - *TelDir&BG 83-84*
Ogdensburg Journal [of Park Newspapers of St. Lawrence Inc.] - Ogdensburg, NY - *NewsDir 84*
Ogdensburg Journal-Advance News - Ogdensburg, NY - *BaconPubCkNews 84*
Ogdensburg NewChannels [of NewChannels Corp.] - Ogdensburg, NY - *BrCabYB 84; Tel&CabFB 84C*
Ogdensburg North Country Catholic [of Diocese of Ogdensburg] - Ogdensburg, NY - *NewsDir 84*
Ogema Telephone Co. [Aff. of Universal Telephone Co. Inc.] - Hawkins, WI - *TelDir&BG 83-84*
Ogemaw County Herald - West Branch, MI - *AyerDirPub 83; Ed&PubIntYB 82*
Ogilvie, Taylor & Associates - New York, NY - *DirPRFirms 83*
Ogilvy & Mather (Canada) Ltee. - Montreal, PQ, Canada - *ArtMar 84*
Ogilvy & Mather Direct Response Inc. [Subs. of Ogilvy & Mather Inc.] - New York, NY - *DirMarMP 83*
Ogilvy & Mather Inc. - San Francisco, CA - *ArtMar 84*
Ogilvy & Mather Inc. - New York, NY - *ArtMar 84; Br 1-23-84; BrCabYB 84; StaDirAdAg 2-84*
Ogilvy & Mather Inc. - Houston, TX - *DirMarMP 83*
Ogilvy & Mather International - New York, NY - *AdAge 3-28-84, 6-25-84; HomeVid&CabYB 82-83*
Ogilvy & Mather Public Relations [Div. of Ogilvy & Mather International] - New York, NY - *DirPRFirms 83*
Ogilvy & Mather Recruitment Advertising - Los Angeles, CA - *ArtMar 84*
Ogle County Life [of Rochelle Newspapers Inc.] - Oregon, IL - *AyerDirPub 83; Ed&PubIntYB 82; NewsDir 84*
Ogle County Life [of Rochelle Newspapers Inc.] - Rochelle, IL - *NewsDir 84*
Ogle County Life - *See* Rochelle Newspapers Inc.
Oglethorpe Echo - Lexington, GA - *AyerDirPub 83; Ed&PubIntYB 82*
O'Halloran Advertising - Wilton, CT - *StaDirAdAg 2-84*
O'Hanlon Computer Systems Inc. - Bellevue, WA - *MicrocomSwDir 1*
Ohara Publications Inc. - Burbank, CA - *LitMarPl 83, 84; WritMar 84*
O'Hare in Focus - Des Plaines, IL - *IntDirMarRes 83*
Ohio Academy of Science - Columbus, OH - *BoPubDir 4, 5*
Ohio AFL-CIO News & Views - Columbus, OH - *NewsDir 84*
Ohio & Northern Kentucky Gasoline Dealers & Garage News - Cincinnati, OH - *BaconPubCkMag 84*
Ohio Antique Review - Worthington, OH - *WritMar 84*
Ohio Banker [of OBA Service Corp. Inc.] - Columbus, OH - *BaconPubCkMag 84; MagDir 84*
Ohio Bell Telephone Co., The - Cleveland, OH - *TelDir&BG 83-84*
Ohio Beverage Journal [of Midwest Publications Inc.] - Wheeling, WV - *BaconPubCkMag 84; MagDir 84*
Ohio Business [of Business Journal Publishing Co.] - Cleveland, OH - *BaconPubCkMag 84; WritMar 84*
Ohio Cable Inc. - Aberdeen, OH - *Tel&CabFB 84C*
Ohio Chess Association - Dayton, OH - *LitMag&SmPr 83-84*
Ohio Chess Bulletin [of Ohio Chess Association] - Dayton, OH - *LitMag&SmPr 83-84*
Ohio Cities & Villages [of The Ohio Municipal League] - Columbus, OH - *BaconPubCkMag 84; MagDir 84*
Ohio Contractor - Columbus, OH - *BaconPubCkMag 84; MagDir 84*
Ohio County Cablevision [of American TV & Communications Corp.] - Hartford, KY - *BrCabYB 84; Tel&CabFB 84C*
Ohio County Messenger - Beaver Dam, KY - *AyerDirPub 83; Ed&PubIntYB 82*
Ohio County News [of Register Publications] - Rising Sun, IN - *AyerDirPub 83; Ed&PubIntYB 82; NewsDir 84*
Ohio County News - Hartford, KY - *AyerDirPub 83; Ed&PubIntYB 82*
Ohio County Times - Hartford, KY - *AyerDirPub 83; Ed&PubIntYB 82*
Ohio CPA Journal, The [of The Ohio Society of CPA's] - Dublin, OH - *BaconPubCkMag 84; MagDir 84*
Ohio Data Base - Cleveland, OH - *MicrocomSwDir 1*
Ohio Data Users Center [of Ohio State Dept. of Economic & Community Development] - Columbus, OH - *EISS 83*
Ohio Dental Journal [of Ohio Dental Association] - Columbus, OH - *BaconPubCkMag 84; MagDir 84*
Ohio Dept. of Energy - Columbus, OH - *BoPubDir 5*
Ohio Educational Broadcasting Network Commission - Columbus, OH - *BrCabYB 84*
Ohio Engineer [of Ohio Society of Professional Engineers] - Columbus, OH - *BaconPubCkMag 84; MagDir 84*
Ohio Farmer, The - Columbus, OH - *BaconPubCkMag 84; MagDir 84; WritMar 84*
Ohio Fisherman - Columbus, OH - *WritMar 84*
Ohio Flock-Cote Co. Inc. - East Cleveland, OH - *AvMarPl 83*
Ohio Genealogical Society - Mansfield, OH - *BoPubDir 4, 5*
Ohio Grange - Columbus, OH - *BaconPubCkMag 84; MagDir 84*
Ohio Graphic - Eaton, OH - *AyerDirPub 83*
Ohio Historical Society - Columbus, OH - *MicroMarPl 82-83*
Ohio Holstein News - Wooster, OH - *BaconPubCkMag 84*
Ohio Jersey News - Prospect, OH - *BaconPubCkMag 84; MagDir 84*
Ohio Journal of Science - Columbus, OH - *MagDir 84*
Ohio Journal, The [of Ohio State University] - Columbus, OH - *LitMag&SmPr 83-84; WritMar 84*
Ohio Magazine - Columbus, OH - *ArtMar 84; BaconPubCkMag 84; MagDir 84; MagIndMarPl 82-83; WritMar 84*
Ohio MDS Corp. - Dayton, OH - *Tel&CabFB 84C*
Ohio Media Newswire - Cleveland, OH - *ProGuPRSer 4*
Ohio Medical Education Network [of Ohio State University] - Columbus, OH - *TeleSy&SerDir 7-83*
Ohio Micro Systems - Kent, OH - *WhoWMicrocom 83*
Ohio Motorist - Cleveland, OH - *BaconPubCkMag 84; MagDir 84; WritMar 84*
Ohio News Bureau Co., The - Cleveland, OH - *ProGuPRSer 4*

Ohio Newspaper Service Inc. - Columbus, OH - *ProGuPRSer 4*
Ohio Pharmacist [of Lawhead Press] - Columbus, OH - *BaconPubCkMag 84; MagDir 84*
Ohio Printing Co. - Dayton, OH - *LitMarPl 83, 84*
Ohio Records - Hudson, OH - *BillIntBG 83-84*
Ohio Review, The - Athens, OH - *LitMag&SmPr 83-84; WritMar 84*
Ohio River Cable TV Inc. [of C-K Video Inc.] - Perry Township, OH - *Tel&CabFB 84C*
Ohio River Cable TV Inc. - South Point, OH - *BrCabYB 84*
Ohio Schools - Columbus, OH - *BaconPubCkMag 84; MagDir 84*
Ohio Scientific Inc. - Trumbull, CT - *DataDirSup 7-83; MicrocomMPl 84*
Ohio Scientific Inc. [Subs. of Kendata Inc.] - Bedford, MA - *MicrocomMPl 83; WhoWMicrocom 83*
Ohio Scientific Inc. - Aurora, OH - *DirInfWP 82*
Ohio State Bar Association Report - Columbus, OH - *MagDir 84*
Ohio State Contractor - Columbus, OH - *BaconPubCkMag 84*
Ohio State Daily Lantern, The - Columbus, OH - *NewsDir 84*
Ohio State Engineer - Columbus, OH - *BaconPubCkMag 84; MagDir 84*
Ohio State Legislative Service Commission - Columbus, OH - *EISS 83*
Ohio State Library - Columbus, OH - *EISS 83*
Ohio State Medical Journal - Columbus, OH - *BaconPubCkMag 84; MagDir 84*
Ohio State University (ERIC Clearinghouse for Science, Mathematics & Environmental Education) - Columbus, OH - *BoPubDir 4, 5*
Ohio State University (Libraries Publications Committee) - Columbus, OH - *BoPubDir 4, 5*
Ohio State University (Logan Elm Press & Paper Mill) - Columbus, OH - *BoPubDir 4, 5*
Ohio State University (Ohio Biological Survey) - Columbus, OH - *BoPubDir 4, 5*
Ohio State University Press - Columbus, OH - *LitMarPl 83, 84; WritMar 84*
Ohio Tavern News - Worthington, OH - *BaconPubCkMag 84; MagDir 84*
Ohio Truck Times - Columbus, OH - *BaconPubCkMag 84; MagDir 84*
Ohio Underwriter, The - Cincinnati, OH - *BaconPubCkMag 84; MagDir 84*
Ohio University (Telecommunications Center) - Athens, OH - *VideoDir 82-83*
Ohio University Press - Athens, OH - *LitMarPl 83, 84; WritMar 84*
Ohio Valley Cable Corp. - Crooksville, OH - *BrCabYB 84; Tel&CabFB 84C*
Ohio Valley Cable Corp. - Marietta, OH - *BrCabYB 84; Tel&CabFB 84C p.1695*
Ohio Valley Cable Corp. - Roseville, OH - *BrCabYB 84*
Ohio Valley Cable Corp. - Belmont, WV - *BrCabYB 84*
Ohio Valley Cablevision [of OVC Telecommunications Inc.] - Madison, IN - *BrCabYB 84*
Ohio Valley Cablevision [of Centel Cable Television Co.] - Carrollton, KY - *BrCabYB 84*
Ohio Valley Data Control Inc. - Belpre, OH - *DataDirOnSer 84*
Ohio Valley Retailer - Loveland, OH - *BaconPubCkMag 84*
Ohio Woodlands/Conservation in Action - Columbus, OH - *BaconPubCkMag 84; MagDir 84*
Ohioana Quarterly - Columbus, OH - *LitMag&SmPr 83-84*
OHIONET - Columbus, OH - *EISS 83*
Ohioprint Publications Inc. - Columbus-Grove, OH - *BaconPubCkNews 84*
Ohlmeyer Advertising - New York, NY - *AdAge 3-28-84; Br 1-23-84; StaDirAdAg 2-84*
OHM-TADS - Washington, DC - *DirOnDB Spring 84*
Ohrbach & Benjamin Inc. - New York, NY - *StaDirAdAg 2-84*
Ohsawa Macrobiotic Foundation, George - Oroville, CA - *BoPubDir 4, 5*
Oikos - Montclair, NJ - *LitMag&SmPr 83-84*
Oil - Stavanger, Norway - *DirOnDB Spring 84*
Oil & Gas Digest - Houston, TX - *BaconPubCkMag 84; WritMar 84*
Oil & Gas Directory [Aff. of Sidney Schafer & Associates] - Houston, TX - *BoPubDir 4, 5*
Oil & Gas Drilling Data Bank - Washington, DC - *DirOnDB Spring 84*
Oil & Gas Drilling Data Bank [of Data Resources Inc.] - Lexington, MA - *DataDirOnSer 84*
Oil & Gas Investor [of Hart Publications Inc.] - Denver, CO - *BaconPubCkMag 84; MagDir 84*
Oil & Gas Journal [of Pennwell Publishing Co.] - Tulsa, OK - *BaconPubCkMag 84; DirMarMP 83; Folio 83; MagDir 84; MagIndMarPl 82-83*
Oil & Gas News - Mt. Pleasant, MI - *BaconPubCkMag 84*
Oil & Gas Tax Alert - New York, NY - *BaconPubCkMag 84*
Oil & Hazardous Materials Technical Assistance Data System [of U.S. Environmental Protection Agency] - Washington, DC - *CompReadDB 82; EISS 83*
Oil & Hazardous Materials-Technical Assistance Data System [of Computer Sciences Corp.] - Falls Church, VA - *DataDirOnSer 84*
Oil Can, The [of Illinois Petroleum Marketers Association] - Springfield, IL - *BaconPubCkMag 84; MagDir 84*
Oil, Chemical & Atomic Union News - Denver, CO - *NewsDir 84*
Oil City Derrick - Oil City, PA - *BaconPubCkNews 84; NewsDir 84*
Oil City Visitor [of Kountze Liberal Publishers] - Kountze, TX - *NewsDir 84*
Oil City Visitor - Sour Lake, TX - *Ed&PubIntYB 82*
Oil Co. [of Data Resources Inc.] - Lexington, MA - *DataDirOnSer 84*
Oil Co. Data Bank - Washington, DC - *DirOnDB Spring 84*
Oil Daily, The - Washington, DC - *BaconPubCkMag 84; Ed&PubIntYB 82*
Oil, Gas & Petrochem Equipment [of The Petroleum Publishing Co.] - Tulsa, OK - *BaconPubCkMag 84; MagDir 84*
Oil Index [of Norwegian Petroleum Directorate] - Stavanger, Norway - *CompReadDB 82; EISS 83*
Oil Marketer, The - Oklahoma City, OK - *BaconPubCkMag 84*
Oil Mill Gazetteer - Houston, TX - *BaconPubCkMag 84; MagDir 84*
Oil Patch - Lafayette, LA - *BaconPubCkMag 84*
Oil Sands Researchers & Research Projects - Edmonton, AB, Canada - *DirOnDB Spring 84*
Oildale News - Oildale, CA - *BaconPubCkNews 84; Ed&PubIntYB 82*
Oilton Gusher - Oilton, OK - *BaconPubCkNews 84*
Oilweek - Calgary, AB, Canada - *BaconPubCkMag 84*
Oink! - Chicago, IL - *LitMag&SmPr 83-84*
OISE Press [Aff. of The Ontario Institute for Studies in Education] - Toronto, ON, Canada - *BoPubDir 4, 5*
Ojai Valley News - Ojai, CA - *AyerDirPub 83; BaconPubCkNews 84; Ed&PubIntYB 82; NewsDir 84*
OJG Inc. - Manchester, NH - *StaDirAdAg 2-84*
Ojibway-Cree Cultural Centre - Timmins, ON, Canada - *BoPubDir 4 Sup, 5*
Okaloosa News-Journal - Crestview, FL - *AyerDirPub 83*
Okaloosa News-Journal & Bayou Times Edition - Crestview, FL - *Ed&PubIntYB 82*
Okarche Chieftain - Okarche, OK - *BaconPubCkNews 84; Ed&PubIntYB 82*
Okawville Cablevision Co. [of Omni Cable TV Corp.] - Mt. Vernon, IL - *Tel&CabFB 84C*
Okawville Cablevision Co. [of Omni Cable TV Corp.] - Okawville, IL - *BrCabYB 84*
Okawville Times - Okawville, IL - *BaconPubCkNews 84; Ed&PubIntYB 82*
OkeAir Co. Inc. - Okeechobee, FL - *BrCabYB 84; Tel&CabFB 84C*
Okee TV - Okeechobee, FL - *AyerDirPub 83*
Okeechobee News [of Independent Newspapers Inc.] - Okeechobee, FL - *AyerDirPub 83; BaconPubCkNews 84; Ed&PubIntYB 82; NewsDir 84*
Okeechobee Shopper's Guide - Lake Park, FL - *AyerDirPub 83*
Okeechobee Shopper's Guide - Okeechobee, FL - *AyerDirPub 83*
O'Keefe & Associates - Fayetteville, NY - *MicrocomMPl 83, 84*
Okeene Record - Okeene, OK - *AyerDirPub 83; BaconPubCkNews 84; Ed&PubIntYB 82*
Okefenokee Press - Folkston, GA - *BoPubDir 4, 5*
Okema Vue Inc. - Ludlow, VT - *Tel&CabFB 84C*

Okemah News Leader - Okemah, OK - *BaconPubCkNews 84; Ed&PubIntYB 82*
Okemo Vue Inc. - Ludlow, VT - *BrCabYB 84*
OKI Electronics of America - Ft. Lauderdale, FL - *DataDirSup 7-83; DirInfWP 82*
Okidata Corp. [Subs. of Oko Electric of Japan Ltd.] - Mt. Laurel, NJ - *DataDirSup 7-83; DirInfWP 82; MicrocomMPl 84; WhoWMicrocom 83*
Okisher Publishing Co. - Oklahoma City, OK - *BillIntBG 83-84*
Okla-Western Telephone Co. - Clayton, OK - *TelDir&BG 83-84*
Okladek, John [Div. of Contemporary Studio] - Ft. Lee, NJ - *LitMarPl 83, 84; MagIndMarPl 82-83*
Oklahoma Allied Telephone Co. [Aff. of Allied Telephone Co.] - Poteau, OK - *TelDir&BG 83-84*
Oklahoma Banker [of Oklahoma Bankers Association] - Oklahoma City, OK - *BaconPubCkMag 84; MagDir 84*
Oklahoma Beverage News - Wichita, KS - *MagDir 84*
Oklahoma Business - Oklahoma City, OK - *BaconPubCkMag 84*
Oklahoma Cable System Inc. [of Transwestern Video Inc.] - Weatherford, OK - *BrCabYB 84; Tel&CabFB 84C*
Oklahoma City Black Chronicle - Oklahoma City, OK - *BaconPubCkNews 84*
Oklahoma City Capital Hill Beacon - Oklahoma City, OK - *BaconPubCkNews 84*
Oklahoma City Friday - Oklahoma City, OK - *AyerDirPub 83; BaconPubCkNews 84; NewsDir 84*
Oklahoma City North Star Advertiser - Oklahoma City, OK - *NewsDir 84*
Oklahoma City Oklahoman - Oklahoma City, OK - *BaconPubCkNews 84; NewsDir 84*
Oklahoma City Times - Oklahoma City, OK - *BaconPubCkNews 84; LitMarPl 83; NewsBur 6; NewsDir 84*
Oklahoma Communication Systems Inc. [Aff. of Telephone & Data Systems Inc.] - Choctaw, OK - *TelDir&BG 83-84*
Oklahoma County News - Jones, OK - *AyerDirPub 83; Ed&PubIntYB 82*
Oklahoma Cowman, The - Oklahoma City, OK - *BaconPubCkMag 84; MagDir 84*
Oklahoma Daily [of Publication Board of University of Oklahoma] - Chickasha, OK - *NewsDir 84*
Oklahoma Data Archive [of Oklahoma State University] - Stillwater, OK - *EISS 83*
Oklahoma Dispatch - Oklahoma City, OK - *BaconPubCkNews 84*
Oklahoma Eagle - Tulsa, OK - *Ed&PubIntYB 82*
Oklahoma Economic Development News [of Oklahoma Economic Development Dept.] - Oklahoma City, OK - *BaconPubCkMag 84; WritMar 84*
Oklahoma Electric Co-Op News - Norman, OK - *BaconPubCkMag 84*
Oklahoma Environmental Information & Media Center - Ada, OK - *InfIndMarPl 83*
Oklahoma Farm Bureau Farmer - Oklahoma City, OK - *BaconPubCkMag 84; MagDir 84*
Oklahoma Food Journal [of Oklahoma Retail Grocers Association] - Oklahoma City, OK - *BaconPubCkMag 84; MagDir 84*
Oklahoma Game & Fish Magazine - Marietta, GA - *BaconPubCkMag 84*
Oklahoma Historical Society - Oklahoma City, OK - *BoPubDir 5*
Oklahoma Home & Garden - Tulsa, OK - *BaconPubCkMag 84*
Oklahoma Home Builder - Oklahoma City, OK - *BaconPubCkMag 84*
Oklahoma Hornet - Waukomis, OK - *AyerDirPub 83*
Oklahoma Information Lines [of Oklahoma State Dept. of Libraries] - Oklahoma City, OK - *EISS 83*
Oklahoma Living Magazine - Oklahoma City, OK - *BaconPubCkMag 84*
Oklahoma Monthly - Oklahoma City, OK - *MagDir 84*
Oklahoma Motor Carrier - Oklahoma City, OK - *BaconPubCkMag 84; MagDir 84*
Oklahoma Observer - Oklahoma City, OK - *BaconPubCkNews 84*
Oklahoma Oil Marketer [of Oklahoma Oil Marketers Association Inc.] - Oklahoma City, OK - *MagDir 84*
Oklahoma Online Users Group [of Tulsa City-County Library] - Tulsa, OK - *InfIndMarPl 83*
Oklahoma Press Clipping Bureau - Oklahoma City, OK - *ProGuPRSer 4*
Oklahoma Professional Engineer - Oklahoma City, OK - *BaconPubCkMag 84; MagDir 84*
Oklahoma Publisher - Oklahoma City, OK - *BaconPubCkMag 84; MagDir 84*
Oklahoma Publishing Co. - Oklahoma City, OK - *AdAge 6-28-84; Ed&PubIntYB 82; KnowInd 83*
Oklahoma Retailer - Oklahoma City, OK - *BaconPubCkMag 84*
Oklahoma Rural News - Oklahoma City, OK - *BaconPubCkMag 84; MagDir 84*
Oklahoma State University (Audiovisual Center) - Stillwater, OK - *AvMarPl 83*
Oklahoma Teleconference Network - Enid, OK - *TeleSy&SerDir 7-83*
Oklahoma Telephone & Telegraph Inc. - Dustin, OK - *TelDir&BG 83-84*
Oklahoma Today [of Oklahoma Dept. of Tourism & Recreation] - Oklahoma City, OK - *LitMarPl 83, 84; MagIndMarPl 82-83; WritMar 84*
Oklahoma Union Farmer - Oklahoma City, OK - *BaconPubCkMag 84; MagDir 84*
Oklahoman - Oklahoma City, OK - *AyerDirPub 83*
Oklahoman & Times [of Oklahoma Publishing Co.] - Oklahoma City, OK - *Ed&PubIntYB 82; LitMarPl 83, 84*
Oklahoman City Times [of Oklahoma Publishing Co.] - Oklahoma City, OK - *Ed&PubIntYB 82; LitMarPl 84*
Oklee Herald - *See* Richards Publishing Co. Inc.
Oklee Herald, The - Oklee, MN - *Ed&PubIntYB 82*
Okmulgee County News - Okmulgee, OK - *AyerDirPub 83; BaconPubCkNews 84; Ed&PubIntYB 82; NewsDir 84*
Okmulgee Times - Okmulgee, OK - *BaconPubCkNews 84; NewsDir 84*
Okmulgee Video Inc. [of UltraCom Inc.] - Okmulgee, OK - *BrCabYB 84; Tel&CabFB 84C*
Okoboji Music - Spirit Lake, IA - *BillIntBG 83-84*
Okolona Community Antenna System [of Comcast Corp.] - Okolona, MS - *BrCabYB 84; Tel&CabFB 84C*
Okolona Messenger - Okolona, MS - *BaconPubCkNews 84; Ed&PubIntYB 82*
Oktologic Reg. - Ottawa, ON, Canada - *WhoWMicrocom 83*
Okun Productions, Lillian - New York, NY - *TelAl 83, 84*
Okun Publishing Co., Milton - *See* Cherry Lane Music Publishing Co. Inc.
O.L. Records & Productions Inc. - Santa Fe Springs, CA - *BillIntBG 83-84*
Olam Publications [Aff. of Center for Olamic Studies] - Arlington, VA - *BoPubDir 4, 5*
Olas Corp. - Van Nuys, CA - *Tel&CabFB 84C*
Olathe News - Olathe, KS - *BaconPubCkNews 84*
Olathe Sun - *See* Sun Publications
Olchak Market Research Inc. - Greenbelt, MD - *IntDirMarRes 83*
OLCTD Newsletter [of J. A. Cambron Co. Inc.] - Kansas City, MO - *MicrocomMPl 84*
Old Adobe Press - Penngrove, CA - *LitMag&SmPr 83-84*
Old Army Press - Ft. Collins, CO - *BoPubDir 4, 5; LitMarPl 83, 84; WritMar 84*
Old Boston Publishing - Cohasset, MA - *BillIntBG 83-84*
Old Bottle Magazine - Bend, OR - *ArtMar 84; WritMar 84*
Old Capital Cablevision Inc. [of Penn Communications Inc.] - Corydon, IN - *BrCabYB 84; Tel&CabFB 84C*
Old Cars [of Krause Publications Inc.] - Iola, WI - *BaconPubCkMag 84; MagDir 84; MagIndMarPl 82-83; WritMar 84*
Old Cars Price Guide [of Krause Publications] - Iola, WI - *WritMar 84*
Old Colony Memorial - Plymouth, MA - *AyerDirPub 83; Ed&PubIntYB 82; NewsDir 84*
Old Dominion Press - Alexandria, VA - *LitMag&SmPr 83-84*
Old Dreams Music - *See* Sky Riders Music
Old Dutch Post Star, The - Saugerties, NY - *Ed&PubIntYB 82*
Old Farmer's Almanac, The [of Yankee Publishing Inc.] - Dublin, NH - *MagDir 84; WritMar 84*
Old Forge Adirondack Echo - Old Forge, NY - *BaconPubCkNews 84*
Old Forge Triboro Banner - Old Forge, PA - *BaconPubCkNews 84*
Old Friends Music - *See* Gant Enterprises, Don

Old Globe Theatre - San Diego, CA - *WritMar 84*
Old Greenwich Suburbanite - Old Greenwich, CT - *BaconPubCkNews 84*
Old Greenwich Village Gazette - Old Greenwich, CT - *BaconPubCkNews 84*
Old Hat Records - Ft. Worth, TX - *BillIntBG 83-84*
Old Home Place Music - Gaithersburg, MD - *BillIntBG 83-84*
Old Homestead Records Inc. - Brighton, MI - *BillIntBG 83-84*
Old-House Journal, The - Brooklyn, NY - *BaconPubCkMag 84; MagDir 84*
Old Iron Book Co. - Atkins, IA - *BoPubDir 5*
Old Log Theater - Excelsior, MN - *WritMar 84*
Old Mill Marketing [Subs. of Renovator's Supply Inc.] - Millers Falls, MA - *DirMarMP 83; StaDirAdAg 2-84*
Old Mill Press - New York, NY - *BoPubDir 4, 5*
Old Moore's Almanack - New York, NY - *MagDir 84*
Old, Phyllis - Norwalk, CT - *LitMarPl 83*
Old Red Kimono, The - Rome, GA - *LitMag&SmPr 83-84*
Old Saybrook Pictorial - Orange, CT - *NewsDir 84*
Old Sparta Press - Raleigh, NC - *BoPubDir 5*
Old Timers Club - Mamaroneck, NY - *BoPubDir 4 Sup, 5*
Old Town Orono Times - Old Town, ME - *AyerDirPub 83; BaconPubCkNews 84; NewsDir 84*
Old Ursuline Convent Cookbook [Aff. of Parents Club of Ursuline Academy Inc.] - Metairie, LA - *BoPubDir 4, 5*
Old Violin-Art Publishing - Helena, MT - *BoPubDir 4, 5*
Old West [of Western Publications] - Iola, WI - *ArtMar 84; MagDir 84; MagIndMarPl 82-83; WritMar 84*
Old West Publishing Co. - Denver, CO - *BoPubDir 4, 5*
Oldfather, Gail E. - Walnut Creek, CA - *BrCabYB 84 p.D-305*
Oldfather, Gail E. - *See* Televents Inc.
Oldfield Davis Inc. - Dallas, TX - *StaDirAdAg 2-84*
Oldham County Cable TV Co. Inc. [of ACT 2] - Oldham County, KY - *Tel&CabFB 84C*
Oldham Era, The [of Landmark Newspapers Inc.] - La Grange, KY - *AyerDirPub 83; Ed&PubIntYB 82; NewsDir 84*
Olds, W. J. - Forsyth, MT - *Tel&CabFB 84C p.1695*
Oldsmar Herald [of Tarpon Springs Herald Newspapers] - Oldsmar, FL - *AyerDirPub 83*
Oldsmar Herald [of The Tarpon Springs Herald Newspapers] - Tarpon Springs, FL - *NewsDir 84*
Oldsmar Herald - *See* Pinellas Publishers Inc.
Oldtown Community Systems Inc. - Oldtown, MD - *Tel&CabFB 84C*
Olean Times-Herald - Olean, NY - *BaconPubCkNews 84; NewsDir 84*
Oleander Press - New York, NY - *BoPubDir 4, 5; LitMag&SmPr 83-84*
Oleander Press - Cambridge, England - *LitMag&SmPr 83-84*
Olearius Editions - Kemblesville, PA - *BoPubDir 4, 5*
Olenik Records - Clio, MI - *BillIntBG 83-84*
Olensky Brothers Inc. - Mobile, AL - *MicrocomMPl 83, 84*
Oleo Music - Redondo Beach, CA - *BillIntBG 83-84*
Olga Coal Co. - Coalwood, WV - *BrCabYB 84*
Olga Coal Co. (CATV Div.) - Coalwood, WV - *Tel&CabFB 84C*
Olian Communications, Julie - Chicago, IL - *DirPRFirms 83*
Olin Ecusta Paper & Film Group - Pesgah Forest, NC - *MagIndMarPl 82-83*
Olin Library, John M. [of Washington University] - St. Louis, MO - *EISS 83*
Olin Telephone Co. Inc. - Olin, IA - *TelDir&BG 83-84*
Olive Branch De Soto County Tribune - Olive Branch, MS - *BaconPubCkNews 84*
Olive Branch Software - Santa Barbara, CA - *MicrocomMPl 84; MicrocomSwDir 1*
Olive Hill Times - Olive Hill, KY - *AyerDirPub 83; BaconPubCkNews 84; Ed&PubIntYB 82; NewsDir 84*
Olive Press Publications, The - Los Olivos, CA - *LitMag&SmPr 83-84*
Olive/Uniphoto, Jim - Houston, TX - *AvMarPl 83*
Oliver Advanced Engineering Inc. - Glendale, CA - *WhoWMicrocom 83*
Oliver-Beckman Inc. - New York, NY - *StaDirAdAg 2-84*
Oliver Chronicle - Oliver, BC, Canada - *Ed&PubIntYB 82*
Oliver Co. Inc., Leland - Santa Ana, CA - *StaDirAdAg 2-84*
Oliver, James - San Antonio, TX - *CabTVFinDB 83*
Oliver Press - Totowa, NJ - *BoPubDir 4, 5*
Oliver Springs Cablevision Inc. - Oliver Springs, TN - *BrCabYB 84*
Oliver Tele-Vue Ltd. - Oliver, BC, Canada - *BrCabYB 84*
Olivestone Publishing Services - New York, NY - *LitMarPl 83, 84*
Olivet Optic - Olivet, MI - *BaconPubCkNews 84; Ed&PubIntYB 82*
Olivetti Corp. [Div. of Ing C. Olivetti & Co. SpA] - Tarrytown, NY - *DataDirSup 7-83; DirInfWP 82; InfIndMarPl 83*
Olivia & Hill Press - Ann Arbor, MI - *BoPubDir 4, 5*
Olivia Records Inc. - Oakland, CA - *BillIntBG 83-84*
Olivia Times-Journal - Olivia, MN - *BaconPubCkNews 84; Ed&PubIntYB 82*
Olken Publications - Livermore, CA - *BoPubDir 4, 5*
Ollig Utilities Co. - Ada, MN - *TelDir&BG 83-84*
Ollis Book Corp. - Steger, IL - *LitMarPl 83, 84*
Olms Verlag GmbH, Georg - Hildesheim, West Germany - *MicroMarPl 82-83*
Olmstead, David B. - Bowman, ND - *Tel&CabFB 84C p.1695*
Olney Cable TV Co. Inc. [of Tele-Communications Inc.] - Olney, TX - *BrCabYB 84; Tel&CabFB 84C*
Olney Daily Mail - Olney, IL - *BaconPubCkNews 84; NewsDir 84*
Olney Enterprise - Olney, TX - *BaconPubCkNews 84; Ed&PubIntYB 82*
Olney/Laytonsville Courier - Damascus, MD - *AyerDirPub 83*
Olney Times - Philadelphia, PA - *AyerDirPub 83*
Ololon Publications - Lumberton, NC - *BoPubDir 5*
Olschewski, Alfred - Acton, MA - *MagIndMarPl 82-83*
Olsen Associates, G. V. - New York, NY - *EISS 83*
Olsen's Radio & TV Repair - East Corinth, VT - *BrCabYB 84; Tel&CabFB 84C*
Olshan's Sports Features, Mort - Los Angeles, CA - *Ed&PubIntYB 82; LitMarPl 84*
Olson, Archer R. - Elbow Lake, MN - *Tel&CabFB 84C p.1695*
Olson, Arleen - Larkspur, CA - *LitMarPl 84*
Olsson Co. Inc., John B. - Orange, CA - *AvMarPl 83*
Olsten Personnel - Toronto, ON, Canada - *DirInfWP 82*
Olsten Services - New York, NY - *LitMarPl 83, 84*
Olsten Temporary Services - Westbury, NY - *DirInfWP 82*
Olton Enterprise - Olton, TX - *BaconPubCkNews 84; Ed&PubIntYB 82*
Olustee Chieftain - Olustee, OK - *BaconPubCkNews 84; Ed&PubIntYB 82*
Olympia Fields Pointer-Economist - *See* Pointer-Economist Newspapers
Olympia News - Olympia, WA - *AyerDirPub 83; Ed&PubIntYB 82*
Olympia News 52 - Olympia, WA - *BaconPubCkNews 84*
Olympia Review - Minier, IL - *Ed&PubIntYB 82; NewsDir 84*
Olympia USA Inc. - Somerville, NJ - *DirInfWP 82; MicrocomMPl 84; WhoWMicrocom 83*
Olympian [of Federated Publications Inc.] - Olympia, WA - *AyerDirPub 83; LitMarPl 84; NewsDir 84*
Olympic Computers Inc. - Port Angeles, WA - *MicrocomSwDir 1*
Olympic Labs - Los Angeles, CA - *MicrocomMPl 83*
Olympic Media Information - Hoboken, NJ - *BoPubDir 4, 5; EISS 83; MicroMarPl 82-83*
Olympic Paper Co. - New York, NY - *LitMarPl 83, 84; MagIndMarPl 82-83*
Olympic Press - Minneapolis, MN - *BoPubDir 4, 5*
Olympic TV Cable Inc. - Port Orchard, WA - *BrCabYB 84; Tel&CabFB 84C*
Olympus Camera Corp. [Subs. of Olympus Optical Co. Ltd.] - Woodbury, NY - *AvMarPl 83*
Olympus Corp. of America - New Hyde Park, NJ - *DirInfWP 82*
Olympus Publishing Co. - Salt Lake City, UT - *LitMarPl 83, 84*
Olympus Television Inc. - Sherman Oaks, CA - *Tel&CabFB 84C*
O'Lyric Music - Studio City, CA - *BillIntBG 83-84*
OMAC Records/Mark O'Connor Productions - Mountlake Terrace, WA - *BillIntBG 83-84*
Omaha Cablevision Inc. - Naples, TX - *Tel&CabFB 84C*
Omaha Catholic Voice - Omaha, NE - *NewsDir 84*
Omaha Creative Group - Omaha, NE - *AdAge 3-28-84; StaDirAdAg 2-84*
Omaha Dundee & West Omaha Sun - *See* Sun Newspapers
Omaha Magazine - Omaha, NE - *MagDir 84; WritMar 84*
Omaha North Sun - *See* Sun Newspapers

Omaha Research Service Inc. - Omaha, NE - *IntDirMarRes 83*
Omaha Sarpy County Sun - *See* Sun Newspapers
Omaha South Sun - *See* Sun Newspapers
Omaha Star - Omaha, NE - *BaconPubCkNews 84; Ed&PubIntYB 82*
Omaha World-Herald - Omaha, NE - *AyerDirPub 83; BaconPubCkNews 84; Ed&PubIntYB 82; LitMarPl 83, 84; NewsBur 6; NewsDir 84*
Omak-Okanogan County Chronicle - Omak, WA - *AyerDirPub 83; Ed&PubIntYB 82; NewsDir 84*
O'Malley, Martin J. - Passaic, NJ - *BoPubDir 4, 5*
Oman Enterprises - Carmel, CA - *BoPubDir 4, 5*
Oman Publications, Robert - Needham, MA - *BoPubDir 4, 5*
Omangod Press - Woodstock Valley, CT - *BoPubDir 4*
OMAR Inc. - Chicago, IL - *ArtMar 84; StaDirAdAg 2-84*
OMARCO - Ennis, TX - *DirInfWP 82*
Omec Publishing Co. - Great Falls, VA - *BoPubDir 4 Sup, 5*
Omega Cable Communications - Huntington City, UT - *BrCabYB 84*
Omega Cable Corp. [of Service Electric Cable TV Inc.] - Portland, PA - *BrCabYB 84; Tel&CabFB 84C*
Omega Communications Inc. - Indianapolis, IN - *BrCabYB 84 p.D-305; Tel&CabFB 84C p.1695*
Omega Communications Inc. - North Manchester, IN - *Tel&CabFB 84C*
Omega Data Systems - Stone Mountain, GA - *WhoWMicrocom 83*
Omega Electronics - Guthrie, OK - *MicrocomMPl 84*
Omega Enterprises - Los Angeles, CA - *MicrocomMPl 83*
Omega Information Systems - Lexington, KY - *MicrocomMPl 83, 84; WhoWMicrocom 83*
Omega: Journal of Death & Dying - Farmingdale, NY - *MagIndMarPl 82-83*
Omega Microware - Chicago, IL - *MicrocomMPl 83, 84; WhoWMicrocom 83*
Omega News Group - Philadelphia, PA - *BrCabYB 84*
Omega News, The - Omega, GA - *Ed&PubIntYB 82*
Omega of Indiana Cable Co. [of Omega Communications Inc.] - North Manchester, IN - *BrCabYB 84*
Omega of Michigan Cable Co. [of Omega Communications Inc.] - Three Rivers, MI - *BrCabYB 84*
Omega of Michigan Cable Co. - Vicksburg, MI - *Tel&CabFB 84C*
Omega Press [Div. of Sufi Order] - Santa Fe, NM - *LitMarPl 83, 84*
Omega Publications [Aff. of Omega Ministries] - Medford, OR - *BoPubDir 4, 5*
Omega Publishing Co. - Snohomish, WA - *BoPubDir 4, 5*
Omega Research & Development - Bakersfield, CA - *MicrocomMPl 83, 84*
Omega TV of Fortville Co. [of Omega Communications Inc.] - Fortville, IN - *Tel&CabFB 84C*
Omeganet [of Compucorp] - Santa Monica, CA - *TeleSy&SerDir 2-84*
Omegavision Corp. - Newland, NC - *BrCabYB 84; Tel&CabFB 84C*
Omenana - Roxbury, MA - *BoPubDir 5*
OMF Books [Aff. of Overseas Missionary Fellowship] - Robesonia, PA - *BoPubDir 4, 5; LitMarPl 84*
OMG Booksource [Div. of Overseas Marketing Group] - Baltimore, MD - *AvMarPl 83; LitMarPl 84*
Omicron Software - Atlanta, GA - *MicrocomSwDir 1*
Omikron Systems - Berkeley, CA - *MicrocomMPl 83, 84*
Omineca Express - Vanderhoof, BC, Canada - *AyerDirPub 83*
Omkara Press - Occidental, CA - *BoPubDir 4*
Omkara Press - Santa Rosa, CA - *BoPubDir 5*
Ommation Press - Chicago, IL - *BoPubDir 4, 5; LitMag&SmPr 83-84*
Omni [of Penthouse International] - New York, NY - *BaconPubCkMag 84; Folio 83; LitMarPl 83, 84; MagIndMarPl 82-83; WritMar 84*
Omni Cable TV Corp. - Calera, AL - *Tel&CabFB 84C*
Omni Cable TV Corp. - Norwalk, CT - *BrCabYB 84 p.D-305*
Omni Cable TV Corp. - Roswell, GA - *BrCabYB 84; Tel&CabFB 84C*
Omni Cable TV Corp. - Centralia, IL - *Tel&CabFB 84C*
Omni Cable TV Corp. - Mt. Vernon, IL - *Tel&CabFB 84C*
Omni Cable TV Corp. - Mahwah, NJ - *Tel&CabFB 84C p.1695*
Omni Communications Inc. - Carmel, IN - *AvMarPl 83*
Omni Communications Inc. - Lynn, MA - *Tel&CabFB 84C*
Omni Computer Corp. - San Juan Capistrano, CA - *WhoWMicrocom 83*
Omni Computer Systems - Chestnut Hill, MA - *MicrocomMPl 84*
Omni Computers Inc. - Joplin, MO - *MicrocomSwDir 1*
Omni Enterprises - Wheaton, IL - *DirMarMP 83*
Omni Intercommunications Inc. - Houston, TX - *MagIndMarPl 82-83*
Omni Midwest Cablevision Corp. - Chester, IL - *Tel&CabFB 84C*
Omni Midwest Cablevision Corp. - McLeansboro, IL - *Tel&CabFB 84C*
Omni Midwest Communications Corp. [of Omni Cable TV Corp.] - Cairo, IL - *Tel&CabFB 84C*
Omni Midwest Communications Corp. - Chester, IL - *BrCabYB 84*
Omni Midwest Communications Corp. - McLeansboro, IL - *BrCabYB 84*
Omni Midwest Communications Corp. [of Omni Cable TV Corp.] - Steeleville, IL - *Tel&CabFB 84C*
Omni Photo Communications Inc. - New York, NY - *LitMarPl 83, 84*
Omni Press - New York, NY - *LitMarPl 83, 84*
Omni Research - Jupiter, FL - *BrCabYB 84*
Omni Research - Portland, OR - *IntDirMarRes 83*
Omni Resources Corp. - Millbury, MA - *MicrocomMPl 83*
Omni Software Systems Inc. - Griffith, IN - *MicrocomMPl 83, 84; MicrocomSwDir 1*
Omni Systems - Doraville, GA - *MicrocomMPl 83*
Omni Systems - Elmhurst, IL - *MicrocomMPl 84*
Omnibyte Corp. - West Chicago, IL - *MicrocomMPl 84*
Omnico Promotions Ltd. - Hartsdale, NY - *StaDirAdAg 2-84*
Omnicom of Illinois - Highland Park, IL - *BrCabYB 84; Tel&CabFB 84C*
Omnicom of Michigan Inc. [of Capital Cities Communications Inc.] - Canton, MI - *InterCabHB 3*
Omnicom of Michigan Inc. [of Capital Cities Communications Inc.] - Hamtramck, MI - *BrCabYB 84*
Omnicom of Michigan Inc. [of Capital Cities Communications Inc.] - Plymouth, MI - *BrCabYB 84; Tel&CabFB 84C*
Omnicom Productions - Okemos, MI - *AvMarPl 83; Tel&CabFB 84C*
Omnicron Systems - Plaistow, NH - *MicrocomMPl 84*
Omnidata - Westlake Village, CA - *WhoWMicrocom 83*
OmniMedia Inc. - Tampa, FL - *StaDirAdAg 2-84*
Omnimusic [SU Franklin-Douglas Recording Studios Inc.] - Port Washington, NY - *AvMarPl 83*
Omninet [of Corvus Systems Inc.] - San Jose, CA - *TeleSy&SerDir 7-83*
Omnipraxis Inc. - Cliffside Park, NJ - *ADAPSOMemDir 83-84*
Omniquest Inc. - Encino, CA - *EISS 83*
OmniQuest Inc. - Chappaqua, NY - *FBInfSer 80; InfIndMarPl 83*
Omnisound Inc. [Div. of Waring Enterprises Inc.] - Delaware Water Gap, PA - *BillIntBG 83-84*
Omnitec Data Inc. - Phoenix, AZ - *DataDirSup 7-83; MicrocomMPl 84*
Omnitext Inc. - Chicago, IL - *DirInfWP 82*
Omniview Cable TV - Missouri Valley, IA - *Tel&CabFB 84C*
Omniview Cable TV - Onawa, IA - *Tel&CabFB 84C*
Omniview Cable TV - Oakland, NE - *Tel&CabFB 84C*
Omniview Inc. - Onawa, IA - *BrCabYB 84*
Omniview Inc. - Blair, NE - *BrCabYB 84; Tel&CabFB 84C p.1695*
Omniview Inc. - Tekamah, NE - *BrCabYB 84*
OmniWeather Inc. - Aberdeen, MD - *BrCabYB 84*
Omoto Advertising Agency - Littleton, CO - *StaDirAdAg 2-84*
Omric Corp. - Chaplin, CT - *MicrocomSwDir 1*
Omro Herald - Berlin, WI - *AyerDirPub 83; Ed&PubIntYB 82*
Omro Herald - *See* Journal Co., The
On Cable Magazine - Norwalk, CT - *BaconPubCkMag 84*
On Campus [of Inter-Collegiate Press Inc.] - Shawnee Mission, KS - *WritMar 84*
On Da Bayou Press & Publishing - New Orleans, LA - *LitMag&SmPr 83-84*
On Dit - Adelaide, Australia - *LitMag&SmPr 83-84*
On-Going Ideas - Starksboro, VT - *MicrocomMPl 84; MicrocomSwDir 1; WhoWMicrocom 83*

On Hand Advisory Service - Marblehead, MA - *FBInfSer 80*
On-line Acquisitions Systems [of Brodart Inc.] - Williamsport, CT - *EISS 83*
On-Line Auto Rate - Des Plaines, IL - *DirOnDB Spring 84*
On-Line Business Systems Inc. - San Francisco, CA - *DataDirOnSer 84; DataDirSup 7-83*
On Line Computer Centers - La Mesa, CA - *DataDirSup 7-83*
On-Line Computer Systems Inc. - Newport Beach, CA - *ADAPSOMemDir 83-84; DataDirOnSer 84*
On-Line Computer Telephone Directory - Kansas City, MO - *DirOnDB Spring 84*
On-Line Computer Telephone Directory [of NewsNet Inc.] - Bryn Mawr, PA - *DataDirOnSer 84*
On Line Documents & Data - Indianapolis, IN - *EISS 7-83 Sup*
On-Line Multi-User System, The [of Carlyle Systems Inc.] - Berkeley, CA - *EISS 5-84 Sup*
On-Line Research - Los Angeles, CA - *IntDirMarRes 83*
On Line Research - Greenwich, CT - *DataDirOnSer 84; EISS 83; InfIndMarPl 83; MicrocomMPl 84*
On-Line Software International - Ft. Lee, NJ - *ADAPSOMemDir 83-84; DataDirSup 7-83*
On-Line Stock Option Analysis [of Broker Services Inc.] - Englewood, CO - *DataDirOnSer 84*
On-Line Systems - Coarsegold, CA - *MicrocomMPl 83*
On-Line Tariff Guide [of The DMW Group Inc.] - Ann Arbor, MI - *DataDirOnSer 84; DirOnDB Spring 84*
On-line Training Center [of University of Pittsburgh] - Pittsburgh, PA - *EISS 7-83 Sup*
On-Line Union Catalog [of Online Computer Library Center] - Dublin, OH - *DataDirOnSer 84*
On Location - Hollywood, CA - *WritMar 84*
On Location - Los Angeles, CA - *BaconPubCkMag 84*
On Magazine [of Scott/Shannon Inc.] - Springfield, MO - *BaconPubCkMag 84; WritMar 84*
On Page - Sudbury, MA - *WritMar 84*
On Satellite TV - Rancho Bernardo, CA - *Tel&CabFB 84C*
On Site Computer Assisted Research [of OSCAR Inc.] - Bergenfield, NJ - *EISS 5-84 Sup*
On-Site Testing Inc. - New York, NY - *IntDirMarRes 83*
On Target [of Heath Ace News] - Newark, OH - *NewsDir 84*
On-Target Marketing Counselors Inc. - Hinsdale, IL - *StaDirAdAg 2-84*
On the Line [of Mennonite Publishing House] - Scottdale, PA - *WritMar 84*
On the Move Press - San Francisco, CA - *LitMag&SmPr 83-84*
On the Record - Columbus, OH - *BaconPubCkMag 84*
On the Sound - Scarsdale, NY - *MagDir 84*
On the Truck [of Astoria Press Inc.] - New York, NY - *NewsDir 84*
On the Upbeat - Fairfield, NJ - *WritMar 84*
On Time Records - New York, NY - *BillIntBG 83-84*
On-Trac Research - *See* Martell Research
On Track [of Paul Oxman Publishing] - Fountain Valley, CA - *BaconPubCkMag 84; WritMar 84*
ON-TV [of Oak Communications Systems] - Rancho Bernardo, CA - *BrCabYB 84*
ON-TV [of Oak Media Corp.] - San Diego, CA - *CabTVPrDB 83*
ON-TV [of Chartwell] - Troy, MI - *CabTVPrDB 83*
ONA Journal, The - Thorofare, NJ - *MagDir 84*
Onaga Herald - Onaga, KS - *BaconPubCkNews 84; Ed&PubIntYB 82*
Onarga Leader - *See* Cornbelt Press Inc.
Onarga Leader-Review - Onarga, IL - *Ed&PubIntYB 82*
Onawa Democrat - Onawa, IA - *AyerDirPub 83; BaconPubCkNews 84; Ed&PubIntYB 82*
Onawa Sentinel - Onawa, IA - *AyerDirPub 83; BaconPubCkNews 84; Ed&PubIntYB 82*
Onaway Outlook - Onaway, MI - *BaconPubCkNews 84; Ed&PubIntYB 82; NewsDir 84*
Onaway Publications - San Rafael, CA - *BoPubDir 4, 5*
Once Upon a Planet Inc. - Bayside, NY - *WritMar 84*
Once Upon a Planet Inc. - Fresh Meadows, NY - *ArtMar 84; BoPubDir 4*
Once Upon A Time Music - Beverly Hills, CA - *BillIntBG 83-84*
Onchiota Books - Onchiota, NY - *BoPubDir 4, 5*
Oncology Information Service [of University of Leeds] - Leeds, England - *EISS 83*
Oncology Times - New York, NY - *BaconPubCkMag 84; WritMar 84*
Ondine Press - Los Angeles, CA - *BoPubDir 5; LitMarPl 84*
One Act Theatre Co. - San Francisco, CA - *WritMar 84*
One Call [of Western Union Travel Industry Services Inc.] - Dallas, TX - *EISS 5-84 Sup*
One Candle Press - Atlanta, GA - *BoPubDir 4, 5*
One Earth [of The Findhorn Press] - Forres, Scotland - *LitMag&SmPr 83-84*
One Eye Soul Publishing Co. - *See* Jamie Music Publishing Co.
101 Productions - San Francisco, CA - *ArtMar 84; LitMarPl 83, 84; WritMar 84*
One Magazine - Kansas City, MO - *ArtMar 84; WritMar 84*
One More Music - *See* Annextra Music
One Note Beyond Music - Cardiff-by-the-Sea, CA - *BillIntBG 83-84*
One Pass Film & Video - San Francisco, CA - *AvMarPl 83; Tel&CabFB 84C*
One Pass Inc. - San Francisco, CA - *Tel&CabFB 84C; TeleSy&SerDir 2-84*
One Pass Media [Subs. of One Pass Inc.] - San Francisco, CA - *AvMarPl 83; Tel&CabFB 84C*
One Percent Publishing Co. - Boulder, CO - *LitMag&SmPr 83-84*
1,001 Decorating Ideas - New York, NY - *MagDir 84*
1001 Decorating Ideas - Montreal, PQ, Canada - *BaconPubCkMag 84*
1001 Home Ideas [of Family Media] - New York, NY - *BaconPubCkMag 84; Folio 83; MagIndMarPl 82-83; WritMar 84*
1001 Truck & Van Ideas - Los Angeles, CA - *MagDir 84*
1 Up Pharmacy Software - San Francisco, CA - *MicrocomMPl 84*
1W1 Communications [Aff. of Ontario College of Art] - Toronto, ON, Canada - *BoPubDir 4, 5*
One World - State College, PA - *LitMag&SmPr 83-84*
O'Neal & Prelle - Hartford, CT - *StaDirAdAg 2-84*
O'Neal, W. C. - Ft. Smith, AR - *Tel&CabFB 84C p.1695*
Oneida Cable TV Inc. - Oneida, TN - *BrCabYB 84; Tel&CabFB 84C*
Oneida Cablevision [of Tribune Cable Communications Inc.] - Oneida, NY - *Tel&CabFB 84C*
Oneida County Rural Telephone Co. - Holland Patent, NY - *TelDir&BG 83-84*
Oneida Dispatch - Oneida, NY - *BaconPubCkNews 84; Ed&PubIntYB 82; NewsDir 84*
Oneida Independent Herald - Oneida, TN - *BaconPubCkNews 84*
Oneida Music Publishing Co. - Utica, NY - *BillIntBG 83-84*
Oneida Scott County News - Oneida, TN - *BaconPubCkNews 84; NewsDir 84*
Oneida Telephone Exchange - Oneida, IL - *TelDir&BG 83-84*
O'Neil Jalbert & Gould Inc. - *See* OJG Inc.
O'Neil, Mildred Jean - Napanee, ON, Canada - *BoPubDir 4, 5*
O'Neill Frontier & Holt County Independent - O'Neill, NE - *BaconPubCkNews 84; NewsDir 84*
O'Neill Theater Center (National Playwrights Conference) - New York, NY - *WritMar 84*
Oneonta NewChannels [of NewChannels Corp.] - Oneonta, NY - *BrCabYB 84; Tel&CabFB 84C*
Oneonta Southern Democrat - Oneonta, AL - *BaconPubCkNews 84*
Oneonta Star [of Ottaway Newspapers] - Oneonta, NY - *BaconPubCkNews 84; NewsDir 84*
Oneonta Telephone Co. - Oneonta, AL - *BrCabYB 84; Tel&CabFB 84C; TelDir&BG 83-84*
Ong & Associates Inc. - New York, NY - *HBIndAd&MS 82-83; StaDirAdAg 2-84*
Ongoing Research Project Data Bank [of Ministry for Research & Technology] - Bonn, West Germany - *EISS 83*
Onhisown Music - *See* OAS Music Group
Onida Watchman - Onida, SD - *BaconPubCkNews 84; Ed&PubIntYB 82*
Onion Creek Free Press - Austin, TX - *Ed&PubIntYB 82*
Onley Eastern Shore News - *See* Atlantic Publications
Online - Weston, CT - *BaconPubCkMag 84; BoPubDir 4 Sup, 5; CompReadDB 82; EISS 83; InfIndMarPl 83; MagIndMarPl 82-83; MicrocomMPl 84*
Online-Benutzergruppe der Bundesrepublik Deutschland [of Industrie & Handelskammer Borsenplatz] - Frankfurt, West Germany - *InfIndMarPl 83*

Online Careers - Phoenix, AZ - *DirOnDB Spring 84*
Online Catalog System [of Dartmouth College Libraries] - Hanover, NH - *EISS 5-84 Sup*
Online Chronicle [of Dialog Information Services Inc.] - Palo Alto, CA - *DataDirOnSer 84*
Online Chronicle [of Online Inc.] - Weston, CT - *CompReadDB 82; DBBus 82; DirOnDB Spring 84*
Online Computer Library Center - Dublin, OH - *DataDirOnSer 84; VideoDir 82-83*
Online Database Report - New York, NY - *BaconPubCkMag 84; DirOnDB Spring 84*
Online Database Report [of NewsNet Inc.] - Bryn Mawr, PA - *DataDirOnSer 84*
Online Database Search Assistance Machine [of Franklin Institute] - Philadelphia, PA - *EISS 83*
Online GmbH - Heidelberg, West Germany - *EISS 7-83 Sup*
Online Hotline [of Information Intelligence Inc.] - Phoenix, AZ - *DataDirOnSer 84; DirOnDB Spring 84*
Online Information Centre - London, England - *EISS 83; InfIndMarPl 83*
Online Jobline [of Information Intelligence Inc.] - Phoenix, AZ - *DataDirOnSer 84*
Online Microcomputer Software Guide & Directory [of Online Inc.] - Georgetown, CT - *EISS 5-84 Sup*
Online Microcomputer Software Guide & Directory - Weston, CT - *DirOnDB Spring 84*
Online Microcomputer Software Guide & Directory [of Bibliographic Retrieval Services Inc.] - Latham, NY - *DataDirOnSer 84*
Online Review Training Centre - Oxford, England - *InfIndMarPl 83*
Online Site Evaluation System [of Urban Decision Systems Inc.] - Los Angeles, CA - *DBBus 82*
Online Stock & Industry Filter - Silver Spring, MD - *DirOnDB Spring 84*
Online Users' Group/Ireland - Dublin, Ireland - *EISS 83*
Online Users Group of Nebraska [of University of Nebraska] - Omaha, NE - *InfIndMarPl 83*
Onlooker, The - Foley, AL - *AyerDirPub 83*
Only Poetry - London, England - *LitMag&SmPr 83-84*
Only Poetry Publications - London, England - *LitMag&SmPr 83-84*
Onnysay Publishing Co. - Knoxville, TN - *BillIntBG 83-84*
Onondaga Valley News - Syracuse, NY - *NewsDir 84*
Onoway Tribune - Onoway, AB, Canada - *AyerDirPub 83*
Onset Publications - Ashland, OR - *BoPubDir 4, 5*
Onsite [of Urban Decision Systems Inc.] - Los Angeles, CA - *DataDirOnSer 84; DirOnDB Spring 84*
Onslow Coooperative Telephone Association - Onslow, IA - *TelDir&BG 83-84*
Ontap ABI/Inform [of Dialog Information Services Inc.] - Palo Alto, CA - *DataDirOnSer 84*
Ontap CA Search [of Dialog Information Services Inc.] - Palo Alto, CA - *DataDirOnSer 84*
Ontap Chemnane [of Dialog Information Services Inc.] - Palo Alto, CA - *DataDirOnSer 84*
Ontap Compendex [of Dialog Information Services Inc.] - Palo Alto, CA - *DataDirOnSer 84*
Ontap Dialindex [of Dialog Information Services Inc.] - Palo Alto, CA - *DataDirOnSer 84*
Ontap ERIC [of Dialog Information Services Inc.] - Palo Alto, CA - *DataDirOnSer 84*
Ontap Inspec [of Dialog Information Services Inc.] - Palo Alto, CA - *DataDirOnSer 84*
Ontap Magazine Index [of Dialog Information Services Inc.] - Palo Alto, CA - *DataDirOnSer 84*
Ontap Medline [of Dialog Information Services Inc.] - Palo Alto, CA - *DataDirOnSer 84*
Ontap PTS PROMT [of Dialog Information Services Inc.] - Palo Alto, CA - *DataDirOnSer 84*
Ontario Advertising - Chicago, IL - *StaDirAdAg 2-84*
Ontario Cable TV Inc. - Geneva, NY - *BrCabYB 84*
Ontario Crafts Council - Toronto, ON, Canada - *BoPubDir 4, 5*
Ontario Daily Argus Observer [of Malheur Publishing Co.] - Ontario, OR - *NewsDir 84*
Ontario Daily Report [of Donrey Media] - Ontario, CA - *BaconPubCkNews 84; NewsDir 84*
Ontario Education - Toronto, ON, Canada - *BaconPubCkMag 84*
Ontario Education Research Information System [of Ministry of Education] - Toronto, ON, Canada - *CompReadDB 82*
Ontario Education Resources Information [of Bibliographic Retrieval Services Inc.] - Latham, NY - *DataDirOnSer 84*
Ontario Education Resources Information System [of Ministry of Education] - Toronto, ON, Canada - *DirOnDB Spring 84; EISS 83*
Ontario Genealogical Society - Toronto, ON, Canada - *BoPubDir 4, 5*
Ontario Government Information [of QL Systems Ltd.] - Ottawa, ON, Canada - *DataDirOnSer 84*
Ontario Government Information [of Ministry of Culture & Recreation] - Toronto, ON, Canada - *CompReadDB 82; DirOnDB Spring 84*
Ontario Hospital Association - Don Mills, ON, Canada - *BoPubDir 4 Sup, 5*
Ontario Innkeeper - Toronto, ON, Canada - *BaconPubCkMag 84*
Ontario-Lexington Tribune Courier - Ontario, OH - *BaconPubCkNews 84*
Ontario Library Association - Toronto, ON, Canada - *LitMag&SmPr 83-84*
Ontario Medical Review - Toronto, ON, Canada - *BaconPubCkMag 84*
Ontario Milk Producer - Toronto, ON, Canada - *BaconPubCkMag 84; WritMar 84*
Ontario Ministries of Education & of Colleges & Universities - Toronto, ON, Canada - *DataDirOnSer 84*
Ontario Ministry of Government Services (Citizens Inquiry Bureau, Information Services Branch) - Toronto, ON, Canada - *InfIndMarPl 83*
Ontario Ministry of Government Services (Publications Services Section) - Toronto, ON, Canada - *BoPubDir 4, 5*
Ontario Out Of Doors - Toronto, ON, Canada - *ArtMar 84; WritMar 84*
Ontario Outdoor Publications - Kitchener, ON, Canada - *BoPubDir 4, 5*
Ontario Press Council - Ottawa, ON, Canada - *BoPubDir 4, 5*
Ontario Puppetry Association Publishing Co. - Willowdale, ON, Canada - *BoPubDir 4, 5*
Ontario Research Council on Leisure - Toronto, ON, Canada - *BoPubDir 4, 5*
Ontario Review Press - Princeton, NJ - *BoPubDir 4 Sup, 5; LitMag&SmPr 83-84*
Ontario Review, The - Princeton, NJ - *LitMag&SmPr 83-84*
Ontario Technologist, The - Toronto, ON, Canada - *WritMar 84*
Ontario Telephone Co. Inc. [Aff. of Trumansburg Home Telephone Co.] - Phelps, NY - *TelDir&BG 83-84*
Ontario Wayne County Mail - *See* Empire State Weeklies
Ontel Corp. - Woodbury, NY - *DataDirSup 7-83; DirInfWP 82; InfIndMarPl 83; WhoWMicrocom 83*
Ontonagon County Telephone Co. - Ontonagon, MI - *TelDir&BG 83-84*
Ontonagon Herald - Ontonagon, MI - *BaconPubCkNews 84; Ed&PubIntYB 82; NewsDir 84*
Ontyme Electronic Message Network Service [of Tymshare Inc.] - Cupertino, CA - *TeleSy&SerDir 2-84*
Onyx & IMI Inc. - San Jose, CA - *DataDirSup 7-83*
Onyx News - Columbus, OH - *AyerDirPub 83*
Onyx Systems - San Jose, CA - *DirInfWP 82; WhoWMicrocom 83*
Oolichan Books - Lantzville, BC, Canada - *BoPubDir 4, 5; LitMag&SmPr 83-84; LitMarPl 84*
OOLP Inc. - New York, NY - *BoPubDir 4, 5*
Ooltewah-Collegedale Telephone Co. - Chickamauga, GA - *TelDir&BG 83-84*
OON - Ottawa, ON, Canada - *DirOnDB Spring 84*
OONL - Ottawa, ON, Canada - *DirOnDB Spring 84*
OOT - Ottawa, ON, Canada - *DirOnDB Spring 84*
Oozle Music - Woodstock, NY - *BillIntBG 83-84*
OP: Independent Music - Olympia, WA - *LitMag&SmPr 83-84*
Opamp/Technical Books - Hollywood, CA - *WhoWMicrocom 83*
Opasquia Times - The Pas, MB, Canada - *AyerDirPub 83*
Opatow Associates Inc. - New York, NY - *HBIndAd&MS 82-83; IntDirMarRes 83*

Opelika-Auburn News [of Thomson Newspaper of Alabama Inc.] - Opelika, AL - *AyerDirPub 83; BaconPubCkNews 84; Ed&PubIntYB 82; NewsDir 84*
Opelousas Cablevision - Westlake, LA - *BrCabYB 84*
Opelousas Daily World - Opelousas, LA - *BaconPubCkNews 84; NewsDir 84*
Open Book Publications [Aff. of Station Hill Press] - Barrytown, NY - *BoPubDir 5; LitMag&SmPr 83-84*
Open Books - Berkeley, CA - *BoPubDir 4, 5*
Open Chain [of Fibar Designs] - Menlo Park, CA - *LitMag&SmPr 83-84*
Open Court Publishing Co. [Div. of Carus Corp.] - La Salle, IL - *LitMarPl 83, 84; WritMar 84*
Open Door Inc. - Charlottesville, VA - *BoPubDir 5*
Open-Door Press - Arlington, VA - *BoPubDir 4, 5; LitMarPl 83, 84*
Open End Music - Los Angeles, CA - *BillIntBG 83-84*
Open Hand Publishing Inc. - Washington, DC - *LitMag&SmPr 83-84*
Open Hand Publishing Inc. - Seattle, WA - *BoPubDir 4, 5*
Open Places - Columbia, MO - *LitMag&SmPr 83-84*
Open Road - Vancouver, BC, Canada - *LitMag&SmPr 83-84*
Open Road & the Professional Driver - Ft. Worth, TX - *MagDir 84*
Open Sky Music Publishers - Huntington Woods, MI - *BillIntBG 83-84*
Open Sky Records - Huntington Woods, MI - *BillIntBG 83-84*
Open Space Gallery - Victoria, BC, Canada - *LitMag&SmPr 83-84*
Open Studio - Rhinebeck, NY - *LitMarPl 83, 84*
Open Studios - New York, NY - *LitMag&SmPr 83-84*
Open Systems - Stamford, CT - *BaconPubCkMag 84*
Open Systems Inc. - Minneapolis, MN - *ADAPSOMemDir 83-84; MicrocomMPl 83, 84; MicrocomSwDir 1; WhoWMicrocom 83*
Open Wheel - Burlington, MA - *MagIndMarPl 82-83*
Open Wheel - Ipswich, MA - *BaconPubCkMag 84*
Openers [of American Library Association] - Chicago, IL - *WritMar 84*
Openings Press - Woodchester, England - *LitMag&SmPr 83-84*
Opera Canada - Toronto, ON, Canada - *WritMar 84*
Opera News - New York, NY - *BaconPubCkMag 84; MagDir 84; MagIndMarPl 82-83; WritMar 84*
Operational Services Div. [of Home Office Central Research Establishment] - Reading, England - *EISS 83*
Operations & Maintenance Costs [of Utility Data Institute] - Washington, DC - *DataDirOnSer 84*
Operations Data Systems Div. [of U.S. Postal Service] - Washington, DC - *EISS 83*
Operative - New York, NY - *LitMag&SmPr 83-84*
Operator Handled Services [of American Telephone & Telegraph Co.] - Bedminster, NJ - *TeleSy&SerDir 2-84*
O.P.F. Univas [of the Univas Network] - Paris, France - *StaDirAdAg 2-84*
Ophir International - Sylmar, CA - *BoPubDir 4, 5*
Ophthalmic Surgery - Thorofare, NJ - *MagIndMarPl 82-83*
Ophthalmologist, The - Philadelphia, PA - *MagIndMarPl 82-83*
Ophthalmology - Rochester, MN - *MagDir 84*
Ophthalmology - New Rochelle, NY - *BaconPubCkMag 84*
Ophthalmology - Philadelphia, PA - *MagIndMarPl 82-83*
Opie Oriental Rugs Inc., James - Portland, OR - *BoPubDir 5*
Opinion - Bloomington, IL - *WritMar 84*
Opinion Builders Inc. - *See* Meldrum & Fewsmith Inc.
Opinion Centers of Maryland - Baltimore, MD - *IntDirMarRes 83*
Opinion Centers, The - Atlanta, GA - *IntDirMarRes 83*
Opinion Centers, The - Springfield, VA - *IntDirMarRes 83*
Opinion Place, The - Farmington Hills, MI - *IntDirMarRes 83*
Opinion Research Corp. [Subs. of Arthur D. Little Inc.] - Princeton, NJ - *AdAge 5-17-84 p.35; IntDirMarRes 83; MagIndMarPl 82-83; ProGuPRSer 4*
Opinion Research Corp. - New York, NY - *Tel&CabFB 84C*
Opinion-Tribune, The - Glenwood, IA - *Ed&PubIntYB 82*
OPOC Computing Inc. - Port Washington, NY - *IntDirMarRes 83*
Opp Cablevision - Opp, AL - *BrCabYB 84; Tel&CabFB 84C*
Opp News [of Covington Publishing Co. Inc.] - Opp, AL - *BaconPubCkNews 84; Ed&PubIntYB 82; NewsDir 84*
Oppenheim Herminghausen Clarke Inc. - Dayton, OH - *StaDirAdAg 2-84*
Oppenheimer & Co. - New York, NY - *ADAPSOMemDir 83-84*
Oppenheimer, Dorothea - New York, NY - *LitMarPl 83, 84*
Oppenheimer, Evelyn - Dallas, TX - *LitMarPl 83, 84*
Oppenheimer Software - New York, NY - *MicrocomMPl 83, 84; MicrocomSwDir 1; WhoWMicrocom 83*
Opportunities for Learning - Chatsworth, CA - *BoPubDir 4, 5; MicrocomMPl 83, 84; MicrocomSwDir 1; WhoWMicrocom 83*
Opportunity - Chicago, IL - *BaconPubCkMag 84; MagDir 84*
Opportunity Books Inc. - Lakeland, FL - *BoPubDir 4, 5*
Opportunity Valley News - Orange, TX - *AyerDirPub 83; Ed&PubIntYB 82*
OPS-Oceanic Press Service [Subs. of Singer Communications Inc.] - North Hollywood, CA - *LitMarPl 83, 84; MagIndMarPl 82-83*
Opt-Tech Data Processing - Humble, TX - *MicrocomMPl 84*
Optasonics Productions - Cresskill, NJ - *AvMarPl 83*
Optdat [of National Computer Network of Chicago Inc.] - Chicago, IL - *DBBus 82; DirOnDB Spring 84*
Optel Communications Inc. - New York, NY - *DataDirSup 7-83*
Optelecom Inc. - Gaithersburg, MD - *DataDirSup 7-83*
Optex Corp. - Butler, NJ - *DirInfWP 82*
Optic - Olivet, MI - *AyerDirPub 83*
Optic - Las Vegas, NM - *AyerDirPub 83; Ed&PubIntYB 82*
Optic Graphics Inc. - Glen Burnie, MD - *LitMarPl 83, 84*
Optic-Herald - Mt. Vernon, TX - *AyerDirPub 83*
Optical Art Camera - Ottawa, ON, Canada - *AvMarPl 83*
Optical Business Machines Inc. - Melbourne, FL - *DataDirSup 7-83; DirInfWP 82*
Optical Communications Corp. - Silver Spring, MD - *DataDirSup 7-83*
Optical Engineering [of SPIE-The International Society for Opitcal Engineering] - Bellingham, WA - *BaconPubCkMag 84; MagDir 84*
Optical House Inc., The - New York, NY - *AvMarPl 83*
Optical Index - Chicago, IL - *MagDir 84; MagIndMarPl 82-83*
Optical Index - New York, NY - *BaconPubCkMag 84*
Optical Management - White Plains, NY - *MagDir 84*
Optical Memory Newsletter [of Rothchild Consultants] - San Francisco, CA - *BaconPubCkMag 84; MicrocomMPl 84*
Optical Prism - New York, ON, Canada - *BaconPubCkMag 84*
Optical Programming Associates - New York, NY - *AvMarPl 83*
Optical Publishing Co. Inc. - Pittsfield, MA - *BoPubDir 4, 5*
Optical Recording Project [Div. of 3M] - St. Paul, MN - *AvMarPl 83*
Optical Resolution Information Center - Riverdale, NY - *BoPubDir 4, 5*
Optical Society of America - Washington, DC - *MicroMarPl 82-83*
Optical Systems Corp. - Concord, CA - *TelAl 83*
Opticom Inc. - Richmond, VA - *TeleSy&SerDir 2-84*
Opticomm Group, The - St. Louis, MO - *LitMarPl 83, 84*
Optics Letters - Washington, DC - *BaconPubCkMag 84; MagDir 84*
Optics News - Washington, DC - *BaconPubCkMag 84; MagDir 84*
Optima Productions - Bountiful, UT - *Ed&PubIntYB 82*
Optimist Magazine, The [of Optimist International] - St. Louis, MO - *ArtMar 84; MagIndMarPl 82-83; WritMar 84*
Optimist, The [of Abilene Christian University] - Abilene, TX - *NewsDir 84*
Optimist, The - Redvers, SK, Canada - *AyerDirPub 83; Ed&PubIntYB 82*
Optimized Data Systems - Placentia, CA - *MicrocomMPl 83, 84; WhoWMicrocom 83*
Optimized Systems Software - Cupertino, CA - *MicrocomMPl 83, 84; WhoWMicrocom 83; WritMar 84*
Optimum - Chicago, IL - *DirOnDB Spring 84*
Optimum Applied Systems [Subs. of Ocean & Atmospheric Science Inc.] - Dobbs Ferry, NY - *WhoWMicrocom 83*
Optimum Book Marketing Co. Inc. - New York, NY - *BoPubDir 4 Sup, 5*
Optimum Publishing International Inc./Editions Optimum Internationales Inc. - Montreal, PQ, Canada - *LitMarPl 83, 84; WritMar 84*
Optimum Systems Inc. - Santa Clara, CA - *DirInfWP 82*

Optimum Tested Products Inc. - Deer Park, NY - *DataDirSup 7-83; DirInfWP 82*
Options [of FRI Information Services Ltd.] - Montreal, PQ, Canada - *DataDirOnSer 84; DirOnDB Spring 84*
Options Data [of National Computer Network of Chicago] - Chicago, IL - *DataDirOnSer 84*
Options-80 - Concord, MA - *MicrocomMPl 83, 84; MicrocomSwDir 1*
Options Price Reporting Authority - Chicago, IL - *EISS 7-83 Sup*
Options Publishing Co. - Wayne, NJ - *BoPubDir 4, 5*
Optometric Management - White Plains, NY - *BaconPubCkMag 84; MagDir 84*
Optometric Monthly - Chicago, IL - *BaconPubCkMag 84; MagDir 84; MagIndMarPl 82-83*
Optometric World - Glendale, CA - *BaconPubCkMag 84; MagDir 84*
Optosonic Press - New York, NY - *BoPubDir 4, 5*
Opus Associates Inc. - Newport, NC - *LitMag&SmPr 83-84*
Opus Mundi Canada Ltd. - Ottawa, ON, Canada - *BoPubDir 4, 5*
Opus III - Chicago, IL - *Tel&CabFB 84C*
O'Quinn Stations, Farnell - Jesup, GA - *BrCabYB 84; Tel&CabFB 84C p.1695*
OR/MS Dialogue Inc. - New York, NY - *DataDirOnSer 84; IntDirMarRes 83*
Orabona, Nadine - Los Angeles, CA - *LitMarPl 84*
Oracle - Detroit, MI - *WritMar 84*
Oracle - St. Marys, WV - *AyerDirPub 83*
Oracle [of Independent Broadcasting Authority] - London, England - *InfIndMarPl 83; VideoDir 82-83*
Oracle Corp. - Menlo Park, CA - *DataDirSup 7-83*
Oracle Teletext Ltd. - London, England - *EISS 83*
Oral Health - Don Mills, ON, Canada - *BaconPubCkMag 84*
Oral Surgery, Oral Medicine & Oral Pathology [of The C. V. Mosby Co.] - St. Louis, MO - *BaconPubCkMag 84; MagDir 84; MagIndMarPl 82-83*
Oram Group Inc., The - New York, NY - *DirPRFirms 83*
Oran Mutual Telephone Co. - Oran, IA - *TelDir&BG 83-84*
Orange Belt Shopper - Tustin, CA - *AyerDirPub 83*
Orange Cherry Media - Bedford Hills, NY - *MicrocomMPl 84*
Orange City/Alton Cable [of Zylstra Communications Corp.] - Orange City, IA - *Tel&CabFB 84C*
Orange City Democrat - Orange City, IA - *BaconPubCkNews 84*
Orange City Enterprise - Orange City, FL - *BaconPubCkNews 84*
Orange City News - Orange City, CA - *AyerDirPub 83*
Orange City Sioux County Capital - Orange City, IA - *BaconPubCkNews 84*
Orange Coast - Irvine, CA - *BaconPubCkMag 84*
Orange Coast Pilot [of Orange Coast Publishing Co.] - Costa Mesa, CA - *AyerDirPub 83; BaconPubCkNews 84; Ed&PubIntYB 82; NewsDir 84*
Orange County Apartment News [of Ed Mee Publications Inc.] - Laguna Beach, CA - *BaconPubCkMag 84; MagDir 84*
Orange County Business [of Orange County Illustrated Inc.] - Irvine, CA - *MagDir 84*
Orange County Business Journal - Santa Ana, CA - *BaconPubCkMag 84*
Orange County Cable Communications Co. [of Times Mirror Co.] - Agean Hills, CA - *BrCabYB 84*
Orange County Cable Communications Co. [of Times Mirror Co.] - Coto de Caza, CA - *BrCabYB 84; Tel&CabFB 84C*
Orange County Cable Communications Co. [of Times Mirror Cable TV] - Modjeska Canyon, CA - *Tel&CabFB 84C*
Orange County Cable Communications Co. [of Times Mirror Co.] - San Clemente, CA - *BrCabYB 84*
Orange County Cable Communications Co. [of Times Mirror Co.] - San Juan Capistrano, CA - *BrCabYB 84*
Orange County Cable Communications Co. [of Times Mirror Co.] - Silverado, CA - *BrCabYB 84*
Orange County Cable Communications Co. [of Times Mirror Cable TV] - Silverado Canyon, CA - *Tel&CabFB 84C*
Orange County Cable Communications Co. [of Times Mirror Cable TV] - Trabuco Canyon, CA - *Tel&CabFB 84C*
Orange County Cable Communications Co. [of Times Mirror Co.] - Trustin, CA - *BrCabYB 84*
Orange County Cablevision Inc. - Highland Falls, NY - *BrCabYB 84*
Orange County Cablevision Inc. - Wallkill, NY - *BrCabYB 84*
Orange County Cablevision Inc. - West Point, NY - *BrCabYB 84*
Orange County Genealogical Society - Goshen, NY - *BoPubDir 4, 5*
Orange County Gentry - Costa Mesa, CA - *BaconPubCkMag 84*
Orange County Illustrated - Newport Beach, CA - *MagDir 84*
Orange County Magazine - Costa Mesa, CA - *BaconPubCkMag 84*
Orange County News [of West Orange Publishing Co.] - Garden Grove, CA - *AyerDirPub 83; Ed&PubIntYB 82; NewsDir 84*
Orange County Pennysaver - Yorktown Heights, NY - *AyerDirPub 83*
Orange County Post - Washingtonville, NY - *AyerDirPub 83; Ed&PubIntYB 82*
Orange County Publishing Co. Inc. - Paoli, IN - *BaconPubCkNews 84*
Orange County Radiotelephone Service Inc. - Santa Ana, CA - *Tel&CabFB 84C*
Orange County Register [of Freedom Newspapers Inc.] - Santa Ana, CA - *LitMarPl 83; NewsDir 84*
Orange County Review - Orange, VA - *NewsDir 84*
Orange County's Business to Business Magazine - Costa Mesa, CA - *BaconPubCkMag 84*
Orange Duck Press - Carbondale, OH - *BoPubDir 4 Sup, 5*
Orange Leader, The - Orange, TX - *BaconPubCkNews 84; Ed&PubIntYB 82; NewsDir 84*
Orange Park Clay Today [of Thomson Newspapers Inc.] - Orange Park, FL - *BaconPubCkNews 84; NewsDir 84*
Orange Review - Orange, VA - *AyerDirPub 83; Ed&PubIntYB 82*
Orange Review - *See* Green Publishers Inc.
Orange/Seminole Cablevision [of American Television & Communications Corp.] - Orlando, FL - *HomeVid&CabYB 82-83; Tel&CabFB 84C*
Orange Transcript [of Worrall Publications] - Orange, NJ - *Ed&PubIntYB 82; NewsDir 84*
Orange Transcript - *See* Worrall Publications
Orangeburg Black Voice - Columbia, SC - *AyerDirPub 83; Ed&PubIntYB 82*
Orangeburg Black Voice - *See* Juju Publishing Co.
Orangeburg Cable TV Inc. - Orangeburg, SC - *BrCabYB 84; Tel&CabFB 84C*
Orangeburg Times & Democrat [of Howard Publications Inc.] - Orangeburg, SC - *BaconPubCkNews 84; NewsDir 84*
Orangetown Cablevision Inc. [of TKR Cable Inc.] - Orangetown, NY - *BrCabYB 84; Tel&CabFB 84C*
Orangevale News - Folsom, CA - *AyerDirPub 83*
Orangevale News, The - Orangevale, CA - *Ed&PubIntYB 82*
Orangevale Shopper - Folsom, CA - *AyerDirPub 83*
Orangeville Banner, The - Orangeville, ON, Canada - *Ed&PubIntYB 82*
Orangeville Cable-Vu Ltd. - Orangeville, ON, Canada - *BrCabYB 84*
Orangeville Citizen - Orangeville, ON, Canada - *AyerDirPub 83; Ed&PubIntYB 82*
Orb Music Co. - San Francisco, CA - *BillIntBG 83-84*
ORBA News [of Oregon Restaurant & Beverage Association] - Salem, OR - *MagDir 84*
Orban Associates Inc., Diana M. - New York, NY - *DirPRFirms 83*
Orbchem/Orbpat [of SDC Search Service] - Santa Monica, CA - *DataDirOnSer 84*
Orben's Current Comedy - Arlington, VA - *WritMar 84*
Orbi - Brussels, Belgium - *DirOnDB Spring 84*
Orbis - Philadelphia, PA - *MagIndMarPl 82-83*
Orbis - Pawtacket, RI - *DataDirOnSer 84*
Orbis - Nuneaton, England - *LitMag&SmPr 83-84; WritMar 84*
Orbis Books [Div. of Maryknoll Fathers] - Maryknoll, NY - *DirMarMP 83; LitMarPl 83, 84; WritMar 84*
Orbis Inc. - Pawtucket, RI - *ADAPSOMemDir 83-84*
Orbit - Wayland, MI - *AyerDirPub 83*
Orbit Information Retrieval [of SDC Search Service] - Santa Monica, CA - *DataDirOnSer 84; MicrocomMPl 84*
Orbit Records - Nashville, TN - *BillIntBG 83-84*
Orbob Music Ltd. - *See* Lipservices
Orbyte Software - Waterbury, CT - *MicrocomMPl 84*
ORC Enterprises Ltd. - Richmond, BC, Canada - *BoPubDir 4 Sup, 5*

Orca Sound Publishing & Design - Vancouver, BC, Canada - *BoPubDir 4, 5*
Orcable Ltd. [of Tidel Communications Inc.] - Union Park, FL - *Tel&CabFB 84C*
Orcadian, The - Kirkwall, Scotland - *LitMag&SmPr 83-84*
Orcal Cable Inc. - Cedarville, CA - *BrCabYB 84*
Orcal Cable Inc. - Happy Camp, CA - *BrCabYB 84*
Orcal Cable Inc. - Willow Creek, CA - *BrCabYB 84*
Orcal Cable Inc. - Malin, OR - *BrCabYB 84*
Orcal Cable Inc. - Merrill, OR - *BrCabYB 84; Tel&CabFB 84C p.1695*
Orcatech Inc. - Ottawa, ON, Canada - *DataDirSup 7-83*
Orchard Farm Telephone Co. - St. Charles, MO - *TelDir&BG 83-84*
Orchard House Inc. - Concord, MA - *BoPubDir 4, 5*
Orchard News - Orchard, NE - *BaconPubCkNews 84; Ed&PubIntYB 82*
Orchard Park Pennysaver - Orchard Park, NY - *AyerDirPub 83*
Orchard Park Suburban Press [of Coleman Communications Corp.] - Orchard Park, NY - *BaconPubCkNews 84; NewsDir 84*
Orchid Publishing - Shreveport, LA - *BillIntBG 83-84*
Ord Quiz - Ord, NE - *BaconPubCkNews 84; Ed&PubIntYB 82; NewsDir 84*
Ordinary Women Books - Brooklyn, NY - *BoPubDir 4, 5*
Ordway New Era - Ordway, CO - *BaconPubCkNews 84; Ed&PubIntYB 82*
Oregon Beverage Analyst [of Bevan Inc.] - Denver, CO - *BaconPubCkMag 84; MagDir 84*
Oregon Business [of MIF Publications] - Portland, OR - *BaconPubCkMag 84; WritMar 84*
Oregon Business Information System [of Oregon State Economic Development Dept.] - Salem, OR - *EISS 5-84 Sup*
Oregon Cablevision Co. - Dallas, OR - *BrCabYB 84; Tel&CabFB 84C p.1696*
Oregon Cablevision Co. - Independence-Monmouth, OR - *BrCabYB 84*
Oregon Cattleman - Portland, OR - *MagDir 84*
Oregon Cattleman - Wanatchee, WA - *BaconPubCkMag 84*
Oregon CATV [of Group W Cable Inc.] - Baker, OR - *BrCabYB 84; Tel&CabFB 84C*
Oregon CATV [of Group W Cable Inc.] - La Grande, OR - *BrCabYB 84*
Oregon CATV - Union, OR - *BrCabYB 84*
Oregon City Enterprise-Courier - Oregon City, OR - *BaconPubCkNews 84; NewsDir 84*
Oregon Contractor, The [of Oregon Plumbing-Heating-Cooling Contractors] - Salem, OR - *BaconPubCkMag 84; MagDir 84*
Oregon Daily Emerald - Eugene, OR - *AyerDirPub 83; NewsDir 84*
Oregon Economic Development Dept. - Salem, OR - *BoPubDir 4 Sup, 5*
Oregon Economic Development Dept. (International Trade Div.) - Portland, OR - *BoPubDir 5*
Oregon Education - Portland, OR - *MagDir 84*
Oregon Education - Tigard, OR - *BaconPubCkMag 84*
Oregon Farm Bureau News - Salem, OR - *BaconPubCkMag 84; MagDir 84*
Oregon Farmer-Stockman - Portland, OR - *MagDir 84*
Oregon Farmer-Stockman - Spokane, WA - *BaconPubCkMag 84*
Oregon Farmers Mutual Telephone Co. - Oregon, MO - *Tel&CabFB 84C; TelDir&BG 83-84*
Oregon Grange Bulletin - Portland, OR - *BaconPubCkMag 84; MagDir 84*
Oregon Historical Quarterly - Portland, OR - *LitMag&SmPr 83-84; MagIndMarPl 82-83*
Oregon Historical Society - Portland, OR - *BoPubDir 4, 5; LitMag&SmPr 83-84*
Oregon Industrialist, The - Portland, OR - *MagDir 84*
Oregon Journal [of Oregonian Publishing Co.] - Portland, OR - *AyerDirPub 83; Ed&PubIntYB 82; LitMarPl 84; NewsBur 6*
Oregon Legislative Information System [of Legislative Administrative Committee] - Salem, OR - *DataDirOnSer 84; DirOnDB Spring 84*
Oregon Magazine - Portland, OR - *BaconPubCkMag 84*
Oregon Motorist, The - Portland, OR - *MagDir 84*
Oregon News - Oregon, OH - *Ed&PubIntYB 82*
Oregon News - Toledo, OH - *NewsDir 84*
Oregon Observer - Oregon, WI - *BaconPubCkNews 84; Ed&PubIntYB 82*
Oregon Online Users Group [of Northwest Regional Educational Laboratory] - Portland, OR - *InfIndMarPl 83*
Oregon Professional Microsystems - Portland, OR - *WhoWMicrocom 83*
Oregon Purchasor - Portland, OR - *BaconPubCkMag 84; MagDir 84*
Oregon Republican-Reporter - Oregon, IL - *BaconPubCkNews 84*
Oregon Software Inc. - Portland, OR - *ADAPSOMemDir 83-84; MicrocomMPl 83, 84; MicrocomSwDir 1*
Oregon State Bar Bulletin - Portland, OR - *MagDir 84*
Oregon State Daily Barometer - Corvallis, OR - *NewsDir 84*
Oregon State Natural Heritage Program - Portland, OR - *EISS 7-83 Sup*
Oregon State University Press - Corvallis, OR - *LitMarPl 83, 84; WritMar 84*
Oregon Telephone Corp. - Mt. Vernon, OR - *TelDir&BG 83-84*
Oregon Times Observer - Oregon, MO - *BaconPubCkNews 84*
Oregon Total Information System - Eugene, OR - *EISS 83*
Oregon Voter [of Who's Who Publications Inc.] - Portland, OR - *MagDir 84*
Oregon Wheat - Pendleton, OR - *BaconPubCkMag 84*
Oregonian - Portland, OR - *AyerDirPub 83; Ed&PubIntYB 82; LitMarPl 83, 84; NewsBur 6*
O'Reilly Inc., Richard T. - Greenwich, CT - *HBIndAd&MS 82-83*
Oreland Springfield Sun - *See* Montgomery Publishing Co.
Orem-Geneva Times - Orem, UT - *BaconPubCkNews 84; NewsDir 84*
Orenda Publishing - Mill Valley, CA - *LitMarPl 84*
Orenda Publishing - Santa Cruz, CA - *LitMarPl 83*
Orenda/Unity Press - Berkeley, CA - *LitMag&SmPr 83-84*
Orfeon Records Inc. - Los Angeles, CA - *BillIntBG 83-84*
Orfordville Journal & Footville News - Orfordville, WI - *AyerDirPub 83; BaconPubCkNews 84*
Organ Donors Canada - Edmonton, AB, Canada - *BoPubDir 4, 5*
Organ Literature Foundation - Braintree, MA - *BillIntBG 83-84; BoPubDir 4, 5*
Organic Computing - Joshua, TX - *MicrocomMPl 84*
Organic Gardening [of Rodale Press Publications] - Emmaus, PA - *ArtMar 84; BaconPubCkMag 84; Folio 83; MagDir 84; MagIndMarPl 82-83; WritMar 84*
Organic Gardening Book Club [Subs. of Rodale Press Inc.] - Emmaus, PA - *LitMarPl 83, 84*
Organic Software - Livermore, CA - *WhoWMicrocom 83*
Organization for Economic Cooperation & Development - Washington, DC - *BoPubDir 4, 5*
Organization for Economic Cooperation & Development [of I. P. Sharp Associates Ltd.] - Toronto, ON, Canada - *DataDirOnSer 84*
Organization for Economic Cooperation & Development - *See* OECD Publications & Information Center
Organization for Economic Cooperation & Development (Economic Statistics & National Accounts Div.) - Paris, France - *InfIndMarPl 83*
Organization for Economic Cooperation & Development (Nuclear Energy Agency Data Bank) - Gif-sur-Yvette, France - *InfIndMarPl 83*
Organization for Economic Cooperation & Development (Road Research Programme) - Paris, France - *InfIndMarPl 83*
Organization for the Protection & Advancement of Small Telephone Companies - Washington, DC - *TeleSy&SerDir 7-83*
Organization Plus - Denver, CO - *FBInfSer 80*
Organizational & Human Resources Ltd. - Houston, TX - *CabTVFinDB 83*
Organizational Dynamics Inc. - Burlington, MA - *AvMarPl 83*
Organizational Dynamics Inc. - New York, NY - *MagIndMarPl 82-83*
Organizational Images Inc. - Columbus, OH - *BoPubDir 4, 5*
Organizational Measurement Systems Press - Atlanta, GA - *BoPubDir 4, 5*
ORI Inc. (Information Systems Div.) - Bethesda, MD - *DataDirOnSer 84; InfIndMarPl 83*
Oriel - Cardiff, Wales - *LitMag&SmPr 83-84*
Oriel Bibliographical Services Ltd. - Chipping Norton, England - *MicroMarPl 82-83*

Oriel Computer Services Ltd. - Chipping Norton, England - *EISS 83*
Oriel Press - Portland, OR - *BoPubDir 4 Sup, 5*
Oriental Book Store - Pasadena, CA - *BoPubDir 5; LitMarPl 83, 84*
Oriental Publishing Co. - Honolulu, HI - *BoPubDir 4, 5*
Oriental Records - New York, NY - *BillIntBG 83-84*
Oriental Research Partners - Newtonville, MA - *BoPubDir 4, 5*
Origin-Destination [of I. P. Sharp Associates Ltd.] - Toronto, ON, Canada - *DataDirOnSer 84*
Origin-Destination International - Washington, DC - *DirOnDB Spring 84*
Origin Inc. - St. Louis, MO - *WritMar 84*
Origin Jazz Library - Santa Monica, CA - *BillIntBG 83-84*
Original Art Report, The - Chicago, IL - *LitMag&SmPr 83-84; WritMar 84*
Original Cast Records - Georgetown, CT - *BillIntBG 83-84*
Original Communications - Denver, CO - *DirInfWP 82*
Original Crossword Puzzles, Easy-Timed Crossword Puzzles - New York, NY - *WritMar 84*
Original New England Guide [of New England Publications Inc.] - Camden, ME - *ArtMar 84; WritMar 84*
Original Sound Records - Hollywood, CA - *BillIntBG 83-84*
Orikomi Advertising Ltd. - *See* Bates Worldwide Inc., Ted
Orillia Cable Communications [of Trillium Cable Communications Ltd.] - Orillia, ON, Canada - *BrCabYB 84*
Orinda Sun - Orinda, CA - *Ed&PubIntYB 82*
Orion Electric Co. Ltd. - New York, NY - *BillIntBG 83-84*
Orion Group - Minneapolis, MN - *AdAge 3-28-84; StaDirAdAg 2-84*
Orion Master Recordings Inc. - Malibu, CA - *BillIntBG 83-84*
Orion Pictures International Inc. - Los Angeles, CA - *LitMarPl 83; TelAl 84*
Orion Press - Weston, CT - *LitMag&SmPr 83-84*
Orion Software - Auburn, AL - *MicrocomMPl 84*
Orion Software Associates - Ossining, NY - *MicrocomMPl 83*
Orion Telephone Exchange - Orion, IL - *TelDir&BG 83-84*
Orion Times, The - Orion, IL - *Ed&PubIntYB 82*
Orirana Press - Canoga Park, CA - *BoPubDir 4, 5*
Oriskany Falls Telephone Corp. - Oriskany Falls, NY - *TelDir&BG 83-84*
Orland Park Messenger [of Midlothian Southwest Messenger Newspapers] - Midlothian, IL - *AyerDirPub 83; NewsDir 84*
Orland Park Southtown Economist - Chicago, IL - *AyerDirPub 83*
Orland Park Southtown Economist - Orland Park, IL - *Ed&PubIntYB 82*
Orland Park Southtown Economist - *See* Southtown Economist Inc.
Orland Park Star-Herald [of Oak Forest Star Herald Publications] - Oak Forest, IL - *NewsDir 84*
Orland Park Star-Herald - Orland Park, IL - *AyerDirPub 83; Ed&PubIntYB 82*
Orland Park Star-Herald - *See* Star Publications
Orland Press-Register [of Glenn-Colusa Newspapers Inc.] - Orland, CA - *BaconPubCkNews 84; NewsDir 84*
Orland Township Messenger - Orland Park, IL - *Ed&PubIntYB 82*
Orland Township Messenger - *See* Southwest Messenger Newspapers
Orland Unit Register - Orland, CA - *Ed&PubIntYB 82*
Orlando Florida Sun Review - Orlando, FL - *BaconPubCkNews 84; NewsDir 84*
Orlando Magazine - Orlando, FL - *BaconPubCkMag 84; MagDir 84; WritMar 84*
Orlando Record Corp. - Orlando, FL - *BillIntBG 83-84*
Orlando Sentinel - Orlando, FL - *AyerDirPub 83; BaconPubCkNews 84; NewsDir 84*
Orlando Sentinel Star - Orlando, FL - *NewsBur 6*
Orlando Sun of Pine Hills [of Winter Park Sun Herald] - Winter Park, FL - *NewsDir 84*
Orlando Times - Orlando, FL - *BaconPubCkNews 84*
Orleans Cape Cod News - *See* Orleans Hughes Newspapers Inc.
Orleans Cape Cod Oracle - *See* Orleans Hughes Newspapers Inc.
Orleans Cape Codder - Orleans, MA - *BaconPubCkNews 84*
Orleans Guide, The - East New Orleans, LA - *Ed&PubIntYB 82*
Orleans Guide, The [of Gretna Guide Newspaper Corp.] - Gretna, LA - *NewsDir 84*
Orleans Hughes Newspapers Inc. - Orleans, MA - *BaconPubCkNews 84*
Orleans-Progress-Examiner - Orleans, IN - *BaconPubCkNews 84*
Orling, Alan S. - New York, NY - *MagIndMarPl 82-83*
Orlis - Stuttgart, West Germany - *DirOnDB Spring 84*
Orlook [of U.S. Dept. of Energy] - Oak Ridge, TN - *EISS 83*
Orman Guidance Research Inc. - Minneapolis, MN - *IntDirMarRes 83*
Ormonde Publishing Ltd. - London, England - *MicroMarPl 82-83*
Ornament - Los Angeles, CA - *ArtMar 84; LitMag&SmPr 83-84; MagIndMarPl 82-83*
Ornamental/Miscellaneous Metal Fabricator - Atlanta, GA - *BaconPubCkMag 84; MagDir 84*
Ornamentals South - Atlanta, GA - *MagDir 84; WritMar 84*
Ornest, Naomi - New York, NY - *LitMarPl 83, 84; MagIndMarPl 82-83*
Oro Madre - Seattle, WA - *LitMag&SmPr 83-84*
Oro Valley Voice/Call - Tucson, AZ - *AyerDirPub 83; BaconPubCkNews 84; Ed&PubIntYB 82*
Orodenker Advertising Inc., Maurie H. - Philadelphia, PA - *StaDirAdAg 2-84*
Orofino Clearwater Tribune [of Clearwater Publishing Co. Inc.] - Orofino, ID - *BaconPubCkNews 84; NewsDir 84*
Oromocto Post, The - Oromocto, NB, Canada - *Ed&PubIntYB 82*
Orono Weekly Times - Orono, ON, Canada - *Ed&PubIntYB 82*
Orovan Books [Aff. of Orovan Associates] - Honolulu, HI - *BoPubDir 4, 5*
Oroville Gazette-Tribune - Oroville, WA - *BaconPubCkNews 84; Ed&PubIntYB 82*
Oroville Mercury-Register - Oroville, CA - *BaconPubCkNews 84; Ed&PubIntYB 82; NewsDir 84*
Oroville Radio Inc. - Oroville, CA - *BrCabYB 84*
Orpheus [of Illuminati] - Los Angeles, CA - *LitMag&SmPr 83-84; WritMar 84*
Orpheus Publications [Aff. of Pacific Region Association of Alternative Schools] - San Francisco, CA - *BoPubDir 4, 5*
Orphic Lute - Newport News, VA - *LitMag&SmPr 83-84; WritMar 84*
Orr, Leonard - Sierraville, CA - *BoPubDir 4, 5*
Orr, S. - Redwood Estates, CA - *MicroMarPl 82-83*
ORR System of Construction Cost Management [of Constech Inc.] - Dallas, TX - *DataDirOnSer 84*
ORR System of Construction Cost Management [of Cost Systems Engineers Inc.] - Ft. Worth, TX - *DataDirOnSer 84; DBBus 82; DirOnDB Spring 84; EISS 83*
Orrington Economics Inc. - Arlington, VA - *EISS 7-83 Sup*
Orrox Corp. - Santa Clara, CA - *HomeVid&CabYB 82-83*
Orrville Courier-Crescent [of Dix Newspapers] - Orrville, OH - *BaconPubCkNews 84; NewsDir 84*
Orsborn Group, The - San Francisco, CA - *DirPRFirms 83*
Orseck & Associates Inc., Paul - Houston, TX - *StaDirAdAg 2-84*
Ortho Books [Div. of Chevron Chemical Co.] - San Francisco, CA - *LitMarPl 83*
Ortho Information Services [Div. of Chevron Chemical Co.] - San Francisco, CA - *LitMarPl 84*
Orthocode Corp. - Albany, CA - *MicrocomMPl 83, 84; MicrocomSwDir 1; WhoWMicrocom 83*
Orthodox Observer - New York, NY - *MagDir 84*
Orthodox Poetry Journal [of Axios Newletter Inc.] - Fullerton, CA - *LitMag&SmPr 83-84*
Orthopaedic Nursing - Pitman, NJ - *BaconPubCkMag 84*
Orthopaedic Review - New York, NY - *BaconPubCkMag 84; MagDir 84*
Orthopedic Surgery Product News - New York, NY - *BaconPubCkMag 84*
Orthopedics - Thorofare, NJ - *MagDir 84; MagIndMarPl 82-83*
Orthopedics Today - Thorofare, NJ - *BaconPubCkMag 84; MagIndMarPl 82-83*
Orthstar Enterprises Inc. - Elmira, NY - *WhoWMicrocom 83*
Orting Observer - Orting, WA - *Ed&PubIntYB 82*
Orton, Kent - Bruce, WI - *Tel&CabFB 84C p.1696*
Ortonville Independent - Ortonville, MN - *BaconPubCkNews 84; Ed&PubIntYB 82; NewsDir 84*
Ortonville Reminder - Ortonville, MI - *BaconPubCkNews 84; NewsDir 84*
Ortx Systems Inc. - Wausau, WI - *MicrocomMPl 84*
Orwell Telephone Co. - Orwell, OH - *TelDir&BG 83-84*

Orwell Valley News - Orwell, OH - *BaconPubCkNews 84*
Oryx Press - Phoenix, AZ - *ArtMar 84; CompReadDB 82; DataDirOnSer 84; EISS 83; InfIndMarPl 83; InfoS 83-84; LitMarPl 83, 84; MagIndMarPl 82-83; MicroMarPl 82-83; WritMar 84*
O.S. Publications - San Francisco, CA - *LitMag&SmPr 83-84*
OS/Tech [of Consult/DM Inc.] - Clearwater, FL - *MicrocomMPl 84*
Osage Beach Lake Sun-Leader, The [of Hub City Publishing Co. Inc.] - Osage Beach, MO - *NewsDir 84*
Osage City Cable TV Co. - Lyndon, KS - *Tel&CabFB 84C*
Osage City Cable TV Co. - Osage City, KS - *BrCabYB 84*
Osage City Journal-Free Press - Osage City, KS - *BaconPubCkNews 84*
Osage Communications Inc. - Buckner, MO - *Tel&CabFB 84C*
Osage Journal News - Pawhuska, OK - *AyerDirPub 83; Ed&PubIntYB 82*
Osage Lake Sun-Leader - *See* Hub City Publishing Co. Inc.
Osage Mitchell County Press-News - Osage, IA - *BaconPubCkNews 84; NewsDir 84*
Osakis Review - Ortonville, MN - *AyerDirPub 83*
Osakis Review - Osakis, MN - *BaconPubCkNews 84; Ed&PubIntYB 82*
Osakis Telephone Co. [Aff. of Midwest Telephone Co.] - Parkers Prairie, MN - *TelDir&BG 83-84*
Osawatomie Cable TV Inc. [of Cable TV of Paola Inc.] - Osawatomie, KS - *BrCabYB 84; Tel&CabFB 84C*
Osawatomie Graphic - Osawatomie, KS - *BaconPubCkNews 84; Ed&PubIntYB 82; NewsDir 84*
Osborne Cable Television Inc. - Osborne, KS - *BrCabYB 84; Tel&CabFB 84C*
Osborne Computer Corp. - Hayward, CA - *WhoWMicrocom 83*
Osborne County Farmer - Osborne, KS - *BaconPubCkNews 84; Ed&PubIntYB 82*
Osborne Electronics Inc. - Ashland, KS - *Tel&CabFB 84C*
Osborne/McGraw-Hill [Subs. of McGraw-Hill Book Co.] - Berkeley, CA - *LitMarPl 84; MicrocomMPl 83; WhoWMicrocom 83*
Osborne's TV Cable - Robinson Creek, KY - *Tel&CabFB 84C*
Osburn/Reynolds Group - Longview, TX - *BrCabYB 84*
Oscar Inc. - Bergenfield, NJ - *IntDirMarRes 83*
Oscard Associates Inc., Fifi - New York, NY - *LitMarPl 83, 84*
Oscarson Communications Co. - New York, NY - *DirPRFirms 83*
Osceola Cable TV - Reed City, MI - *BrCabYB 84; Tel&CabFB 84C*
Osceola County Gazette-Tribune - Sibley, IA - *NewsDir 84*
Osceola County Herald - Reed City, MI - *AyerDirPub 83; Ed&PubIntYB 82*
Osceola County Tribune - Sibley, IA - *AyerDirPub 83; Ed&PubIntYB 82*
Osceola Record - Osceola, NE - *BaconPubCkNews 84; Ed&PubIntYB 82*
Osceola Sentinel - Osceola, IA - *Ed&PubIntYB 82*
Osceola Sentinel & Tribune [of Osceola Clarke County Publishing Co.] - Osceola, IA - *BaconPubCkNews 84; NewsDir 84*
Osceola St. Clair County Courier - Osceola, MO - *BaconPubCkNews 84*
Osceola Sun - Osceola, WI - *BaconPubCkNews 84; Ed&PubIntYB 82*
Osceola Times - Osceola, AR - *BaconPubCkNews 84; Ed&PubIntYB 82; NewsDir 84*
Osceola Tribune [of Osceola Clarke County Publishing Co.] - Osceola, IA - *Ed&PubIntYB 82; NewsDir 84*
Oscher, Jon - Cartersville, GA - *BrCabYB 84 p.D-305; Tel&CabFB 84C p.1696*
Oscoda County News - Mio, MI - *AyerDirPub 83; Ed&PubIntYB 82*
Oscoda Press - Oscoda, MI - *BaconPubCkNews 84; Ed&PubIntYB 82; NewsDir 84*
Oser, Randy - *See* Tri-Star Cablevision Inc.
Oset Microcomputer Systems - Santa Cruz, CA - *MicrocomMPl 83, 84*
Osgood & Hazen - New York, NY - *StaDirAdAg 2-84*
Osgood Journal - Osgood, IN - *Ed&PubIntYB 82*
Osgood Journal [of Ripley Publishing Co. Inc.] - Versailles, IN - *NewsDir 84*
Osgood Journal - *See* Ripley Publishing Co. Inc.
Osgoode Township Historical Society - Vernon, ON, Canada - *BoPubDir 4, 5*
Oshanews - Santa Monica, CA - *BaconPubCkMag 84*
Oshawa This Week - Oshawa, ON, Canada - *Ed&PubIntYB 82*
Oshawa Times, The - Oshawa, ON, Canada - *BaconPubCkNews 84; Ed&PubIntYB 82*
Oshkosh Garden County News - Oshkosh, NE - *BaconPubCkNews 84*
Oshkosh Northwestern - Oshkosh, WI - *Ed&PubIntYB 82; NewsDir 84*
Oshkosh Outlook - Oshkosh, WI - *AyerDirPub 83*
Osiris - Deerfield, MA - *LitMag&SmPr 83-84*
Osito Music Publishing - *See* Group 88 Music
Oskaloosa Herald [of Donrey Media Group] - Oskaloosa, IA - *BaconPubCkNews 84; NewsDir 84*
Oskaloosa Independent - Oskaloosa, KS - *Ed&PubIntYB 82*
Oskaloosa Independent - *See* Wilson-Davis Publications Inc.
OSM Computer Corp. - Mountain View, CA - *DataDirSup 7-83; WhoWMicrocom 83*
Osmar Press - Modesto, CA - *BoPubDir 4, 5*
Osmond Cablevision [of Omniview Inc.] - Osmond, NE - *Tel&CabFB 84C*
Osmond Republican - Osmond, NE - *BaconPubCkNews 84; Ed&PubIntYB 82*
Osprey Books - Huntington, NY - *BoPubDir 4 Sup, 5; LitMag&SmPr 83-84*
Osprey Press Inc. - Black Diamond, WA - *BoPubDir 5*
Osprey Press Inc. - Snohomish, WA - *BoPubDir 4*
Osseo Crow River News - *See* Larson Publications Inc.
Osseo-Maple Grove Press - Osseo, MN - *AyerDirPub 83; Ed&PubIntYB 82*
Osseo-Maple Grove Press - *See* Larson Publications Inc.
Osseo Tri-County News - Osseo, WI - *BaconPubCkNews 84*
OSSI Publications - Fern Park, FL - *BoPubDir 4, 5*
Ossian Bee - Ossian, IA - *BaconPubCkNews 84; Ed&PubIntYB 82*
Ossian Journal - Ossian, IN - *BaconPubCkNews 84; Ed&PubIntYB 82*
Ossining Citizen Register - Ossining, NY - *NewsDir 84*
Ossining Citizen Register - White Plains, NY - *AyerDirPub 83; Ed&PubIntYB 82*
Ossining Citizen-Register - *See* Westchester-Rockland Newspapers
Ostberg Associates, H. D. - New York, NY - *IntDirMarRes 83*
Osteen, Ike - Springfield, CO - *BoPubDir 4, 5*
Ostego County Herald Times - Gaylord, MI - *AyerDirPub 83*
Osteopathic Annals - Williston Park, NY - *MagDir 84; MagIndMarPl 82-83*
Osteopathic Hospitals [of American Osteopathic Hospital Association] - Arlington Heights, IL - *BaconPubCkMag 84; MagDir 84*
Ostertag Cable Television Co., H. C. - Wrightsville, PA - *BrCabYB 84*
Ostertag Cable Television Co. Inc., H. C. - Columbia, PA - *BrCabYB 84; Tel&CabFB 84C*
Ostrander-Wilson Stations - Seattle, WA - *BrCabYB 84*
Ostreicher Advertising, Bernard F. - Boston, MA - *StaDirAdAg 2-84*
OSU Outreach - Stillwater, OK - *WritMar 84*
O'Sullivan, Dugan & Partners - Morristown, NJ - *AdAge 3-28-84; StaDirAdAg 2-84*
O'Sullivan, Tom - New York, NY - *LitMarPl 83, 84*
O'Sullivan Woodside & Co. - Phoenix, AZ - *LitMarPl 83, 84*
Oswayo River Telephone Co. - Shinglehouse, PA - *TelDir&BG 83-84*
Oswego County Weeklies - Mexico, NY - *BaconPubCkNews 84*
Oswego Independent-Observer - Oswego, KS - *BaconPubCkNews 84; Ed&PubIntYB 82*
Oswego Ledger-Sentinel - Oswego, IL - *BaconPubCkNews 84*
Oswego Palladium-Times - Oswego, NY - *NewsDir 84*
Oswego Valley News - Fulton, NY - *AyerDirPub 83; Ed&PubIntYB 82*
Otari Corp. [Subs. of Otari Electric Co. Ltd.] - Belmont, CA - *AvMarPl 83*
Otay Mesa/San Ysidro Pennysaver - Mission Viejo, CA - *AyerDirPub 83*
O.T.C. Review - Oreland, PA - *BaconPubCkMag 84*
Otera Cable TV Co. - Tularosa, NM - *Tel&CabFB 84C*
Othello Outlook - Othello, WA - *BaconPubCkNews 84*

Other Music Inc. - North Ferrisburg, VT - *BillIntBG 83-84*
Other Publishers - Barrytown, NY - *BoPubDir 4 Sup, 5; LitMarPl 83, 84*
Other Side, The - Philadelphia, PA - *ArtMar 84*
Other Side, The - Fredericksburg, VA - *WritMar 84*
Othergates [of Unique Graphics] - Oakland, CA - *LitMag&SmPr 83-84*
Others Marketing - Eden Prairie, MN - *StaDirAdAg 2-84*
Otis Cos. Inc., George - Edina, MN - *MicrocomMPl 84*
Otis Independent - Otis, CO - *BaconPubCkNews 84; Ed&PubIntYB 82*
OTL Productions - Maynard, MA - *BillIntBG 83-84*
O.T.O. - Nashville, TN - *BoPubDir 4, 5*
Otoao Records Co. International Ltd. - New York, NY - *BillIntBG 83-84*
Otolaryngology-Head & Neck Surgery - Washington, DC - *MagDir 84*
Otolaryngology-Head & Neck Surgery - Rochester, MN - *MagIndMarPl 82-83*
Otrona Corp. - Boulder, CO - *DataDirSup 7-83; WhoWMicrocom 83*
Ottawa Advance - Jenison, MI - *AyerDirPub 83*
Ottawa Cable TV Inc. [of Tele-Communications Inc.] - Ottawa, KS - *BrCabYB 84; Tel&CabFB 84C*
Ottawa Cablevision Ltd. - Ottawa, ON, Canada - *BrCabYB 84; Tel&CabFB 84C*
Ottawa Citizen - Ottawa, ON, Canada - *LitMarPl 83*
Ottawa County Exponent - Oak Harbor, OH - *AyerDirPub 83; Ed&PubIntYB 82; NewsDir 84*
Ottawa Herald [of Harris Enterprises] - Ottawa, KS - *BaconPubCkNews 84; NewsDir 84*
Ottawa Magazine - Ottawa, ON, Canada - *ArtMar 84; BaconPubCkMag 84*
Ottawa Putnam County Sentinel - Ottawa, OH - *BaconPubCkNews 84*
Ottawa Sentinel, The - Ottawa, ON, Canada - *AyerDirPub 83*
Ottawa Thrif-T-Nikel Weekly, The - Ottawa, IL - *Ed&PubIntYB 82*
Ottawa Times - Ottawa, IL - *BaconPubCkNews 84; NewsDir 84*
Ottawa Times - Ottawa, KS - *BaconPubCkNews 84; Ed&PubIntYB 82*
Ottaway News Service - Washington, DC - *Ed&PubIntYB 82*
Ottaway Newspapers [Subs. of Dow Jones & Co.] - Campbell Hall, NY - *Ed&PubIntYB 82; LitMarPl 83, 84*
Otte Co., The - Belmont, MA - *LitMarPl 83, 84*
Ottenheimer Publishers Inc. - Baltimore, MD - *LitMarPl 83, 84; WritMar 84*
Otter Press - Waterloo, ON, Canada - *BoPubDir 4, 5*
Otterbein Home (Program Dept.) - Lebanon, OH - *BoPubDir 4, 5*
Otterbourg & Co., Robert K. - Englewood Cliffs, NJ - *ADAPSOMemDir 83-84; DirPRFirms 83*
Ottmann Advertising Agency Inc. - Ft. Worth, TX - *StaDirAdAg 2-84*
Otto Publishing - Sunrise, FL - *BillIntBG 83-84*
Otto Telephone Co. Inc. - Duke Center, PA - *TelDir&BG 83-84*
Ottoville Mutual Telephone Co., The - Ottoville, OH - *TelDir&BG 83-84*
Ottumwa Cablevision Corp. - Eldon, IA - *BrCabYB 84*
Ottumwa Cablevision Corp. - Ottumwa, IA - *Tel&CabFB 84C*
Ottumwa Courier [of Lee Enterprises Inc.] - Ottumwa, IA - *BaconPubCkNews 84; Ed&PubIntYB 82; NewsDir 84*
Ottumwa TV & FM Inc. [of McDonald Group Inc.] - Ottumwa, IA - *BrCabYB 84*
Ouachita Citizen - West Monroe, LA - *AyerDirPub 83; NewsDir 84*
Ouachita Citizen, The - Ouachita Parish, LA - *Ed&PubIntYB 82*
Ouellette, Roger - Ferme Neuve, PQ, Canada - *BrCabYB 84*
Oui [of Laurant Publishing Ltd.] - New York, NY - *BaconPubCkMag 84; Folio 83; LitMarPl 83, 84; MagDir 84; MagIndMarPl 82-83*
Our Family [of Oblate Fathers of St. Mary's Province] - Battleford, SK, Canada - *ArtMar 84; WritMar 84*
Our Gang - Dayton, OH - *ArtMar 84*
Our Gang Entertainment Inc. - Cleveland, OH - *BillIntBG 83-84*
Our Gang Publications - Canon City, CO - *LitMag&SmPr 83-84*
Our Generation - Montreal, PQ, Canada - *LitMag&SmPr 83-84*
Our Little Friend [of Pacific Press Publishing Association] - Mountain View, CA - *WritMar 84*
Our Lively Language - Broken Arrow, OK - *Ed&PubIntYB 82*
Our Northland Diocese - Crookston, MN - *NewsDir 84*
Our Paper [of Our Projects Inc.] - San Jose, CA - *LitMag&SmPr 83-84*
Our Projects Inc. - San Jose, CA - *LitMag&SmPr 83-84*
Our Secretary - Chicago, IL - *LitMarPl 84*
Our Socialism [of O.S. Publications] - San Francisco, CA - *LitMag&SmPr 83-84*
Our Sunday Visitor - Huntington, IN - *AvMarPl 83; DirMarMP 83; LitMarPl 83, 84; MagDir 84; MagIndMarPl 82-83; WritMar 84*
Our Sunday Visitor (Dept. of Religious Education & Liturgy) - Huntington, IN - *ArtMar 84*
Our Town - Maywood, NJ - *AyerDirPub 83; Ed&PubIntYB 82*
Our Town [of East Side/West Side Communications Corp.] - New York, NY - *AyerDirPub 83; Ed&PubIntYB 82; NewsDir 84; WritMar 84*
Our Town - Pearl River, NY - *AyerDirPub 83*
Our Town - Rhinelander, WI - *AyerDirPub 83*
Ouray County Plaindealer - Ouray, CO - *BaconPubCkNews 84; Ed&PubIntYB 82*
Ouray County Plaindealer & Herald - Ouray, CO - *AyerDirPub 83*
Ouray Ridgway Sun - Ouray, CO - *BaconPubCkNews 84*
Ourobourus Institute Inc. - New York, NY - *BoPubDir 4, 5*
Out of Home Media Services Inc. - New York, NY - *StaDirAdAg 2-84*
Out of the Ashes Press - Portland, OR - *BoPubDir 4, 5*
Out of the Sky Press - Saratoga, CA - *BoPubDir 4, 5*
Outbooks Inc. - Golden, CO - *BoPubDir 4, 5; WritMar 84*
Outcrop Ltd. - Yellowknife, NT, Canada - *BoPubDir 4, 5*
Outcrop Publications - Avon, England - *LitMag&SmPr 83-84*
Outdoor America - Arlington, VA - *MagDir 84; MagIndMarPl 82-83; WritMar 84*
Outdoor Associates - Schenectady, NY - *BoPubDir 4, 5*
Outdoor Books-Nature Series Inc. - Baltimore, MD - *BoPubDir 5*
Outdoor Canada - Toronto, ON, Canada - *ArtMar 84; BaconPubCkMag 84; WritMar 84*
Outdoor Club of Victoria (Trails Information Society) - Victoria, BC, Canada - *BoPubDir 4, 5*
Outdoor Eduquip [Aff. of Wilderness Leadership International] - North Fork, CA - *BoPubDir 4 Sup, 5*
Outdoor Empire Publishing Inc. - Seattle, WA - *ArtMar 84; LitMarPl 83, 84; WritMar 84*
Outdoor Graphics - Cordova, TN - *BoPubDir 5*
Outdoor Life [of Times Mirror Co.] - New York, NY - *ArtMar 84; BaconPubCkMag 84; Folio 83; MagDir 84; MagIndMarPl 82-83; NewsBur 6*
Outdoor Life Book Club [Subs. of Times Mirror Magazines Inc.] - New York, NY - *LitMarPl 83, 84*
Outdoor Life Books [Subs. of Times Mirror Co.] - New York, NY - *WritMar 84*
Outdoor Pictures - Anacortes, WA - *AvMarPl 83; BoPubDir 4, 5*
Outdoor Power Equipment [of Quinn Publications] - Ft. Worth, TX - *BaconPubCkMag 84; MagDir 84*
Outdoor Press, The - Spokane, WA - *MagDir 84*
Outdoor Products Marketing Inc. - Northfield, IL - *HBIndAd&MS 82-83*
Outdoor Publications - Ithaca, NY - *BoPubDir 4, 5*
Outdoor Publishers [Aff. of Cobblesmith] - Freeport, ME - *BoPubDir 4, 5*
Outdoor Retailer - South Laguna, CA - *BaconPubCkMag 84*
Outdoor Skills Bookshelf - Nashville, TN - *BoPubDir 5*
Outdoors Today - St. Louis, MO - *MagDir 84*
Outer Banks Cablevision Associates [of Sutton Capital Group] - Buxton, NC - *BrCabYB 84*
Outer Banks Cablevision Associates [of Sutton Capital Group] - Kill Devil Hills, NC - *BrCabYB 84; Tel&CabFB 84C*
Outer Banks Cablevision Associates [of Sutton Capital Group Inc.] - Manteo, NC - *BrCabYB 84*
Outer Banks Video Inc. [of Sutton Capital Associates Inc.] - Manteo, NC - *Tel&CabFB 84C*
Outer Galaxie Publishers Co. Inc. - *See* Aura Love Publishing
Outer National Publishing Co. Inc. - *See* Remick, Lloyd Zane
Outerbridge - Staten Island, NY - *LitMag&SmPr 83-84*

Outlaw - Memphis, TN - *LitMag&SmPr 83-84*
Outlaw Press - Memphis, TN - *LitMag&SmPr 83-84*
Outlet Book Co. - New York, NY - *LitMarPl 83*
Outlet Book Co. - *See* Crown Publishers Inc.
Outlet Co. - Providence, RI - *AdAge 6-28-84; KnowInd 83; Tel&CabFB 84S*
Outlet Records - Ferrum, VA - *BillIntBG 83-84*
Outlook - Palo Alto, CA - *BaconPubCkMag 84; MagDir 84*
Outlook - San Marcos, CA - *AyerDirPub 83*
Outlook - Santa Monica, CA - *AyerDirPub 83*
Outlook - Falmouth, KY - *AyerDirPub 83*
Outlook - Onaway, MI - *AyerDirPub 83*
Outlook - Albuquerque, NM - *AyerDirPub 83*
Outlook - Alexandria, VA - *MagDir 84*
Outlook - Othello, WA - *AyerDirPub 83; Ed&PubIntYB 82*
Outlook & Situation Information System [of U.S. Dept. of Agriculture] - Washington, DC - *EISS 83*
Outlook in Alcohol & Drug Abuse - Arlington, VA - *MagDir 84*
Outlook, The - Washington, DC - *NewsDir 84*
Outlook, The - Outlook, SK, Canada - *Ed&PubIntYB 82*
Outpost Publications - Walton-on-Thames, England - *LitMag&SmPr 83-84*
Outposts - Walton-on-Thames, England - *LitMag&SmPr 83-84*
Outrageous Public Relations - New York, NY - *DirPRFirms 83*
Outreach Publications Inc. - Siloam Springs, AR - *ArtMar 84*
Outrigger Publishers - Hamilton, New Zealand - *LitMag&SmPr 83-84*
Outside [of Mariah Publication Corp.] - Chicago, IL - *ArtMar 84; BaconPubCkMag 84; Folio 83; LitMarPl 83, 84; MagDir 84; MagIndMarPl 82-83; WritMar 84*
Outside Enterprise Press - Pullman, WA - *BoPubDir 4, 5*
Outstanding Records - Huntington Beach, CA - *BillIntBG 83-84*
O.V.A.S. - Singapore, Singapore - *DirOnDB Spring 84*
Ovation - New York, NY - *BaconPubCkMag 84; WritMar 84*
Ovation Films Inc. - New York, NY - *AvMarPl 83*
Ovations Films Inc. - New York, NY - *ArtMar 84*
Over-the-Counter Review [of Review Publishing Co.] - Jenkintown, PA - *MagDir 84*
Over the Rainbow Music - *See* Creative Music Group
Overbeek Enterprises - Elgin, IL - *MicrocomMPl 84*
Overbrook House - Mountain Brook, AL - *BoPubDir 4 Sup, 5; LitMag&SmPr 83-84*
Overcomer Press Inc. - Owosso, MI - *BoPubDir 4 Sup, 5*
Overdrive - Los Angeles, CA - *BaconPubCkMag 84; MagDir 84*
Overflow, The - Kissimmee, FL - *BaconPubCkMag 84; MagDir 84*
Overland Baden-North County News-Press - St. Louis, MO - *NewsDir 84*
Overland Computer Services Co. - Omaha, NE - *MicrocomMPl 84*
Overland Park Sun - Shawnee Mission, KS - *NewsDir 84*
Overland Park Sun - *See* Sun Publications
Overland-St. John Community News - Overland, MO - *Ed&PubIntYB 82*
Overland West Press - Portland, OR - *BoPubDir 4, 5*
Overlook Hospital Auxiliary - Summit, NJ - *BoPubDir 4, 5*
Overlook Press, The - New York, NY - *LitMarPl 83, 84*
Overlook Press, The - Woodstock, NY - *LitMag&SmPr 83-84*
Overseas! [of Military Consumer Today Inc.] - Heidelberg, West Germany - *ArtMar 84; WritMar 84*
Overseas Datel [of Overseas Telecommunications Commission] - Sydney, Australia - *TeleSy&SerDir 2-84*
Overseas Programming Cos. Ltd. - San Francisco, CA - *Tel&CabFB 84C*
Overseas Pulp & Paper Corp. - New York, NY - *LitMarPl 83, 84*
Overseas Telecommunications Commission - Sydney, NS, Australia - *TeleSy&SerDir 2-84*
Overseas Telephone Services [of Overseas Telecommunications Commission] - Sydney, Australia - *TeleSy&SerDir 2-84*
Overseas Telex Service [of Overseas Telecommunications Commission] - Sydney, Australia - *TeleSy&SerDir 2-84*
Overseas Times, The - East Vancouver, BC, Canada - *Ed&PubIntYB 82*
Overseasfax [of Overseas Telecommunications Commission] - Sydney, Australia - *TeleSy&SerDir 2-84*
Overstock Book Co. Inc. - Farmingdale, NY - *BoPubDir 4 Sup, 5; LitMarPl 83, 84*
Overstock Book Co. Inc. - New York, NY - *LitMarPl 84*
Overton Beacon-Observer - Overton, NE - *BaconPubCkNews 84*
Overton Press - Overton, TX - *BaconPubCkNews 84; Ed&PubIntYB 82*
Overton, Tom - Baker, MT - *Tel&CabFB 84C*
Overtone Press - Philadelphia, PA - *BoPubDir 4 Sup, 5; LitMag&SmPr 83-84*
Overtone Series - Philadelphia, PA - *LitMag&SmPr 83-84*
Overture [of Musicians Union Local 47] - Los Angeles, CA - *NewsDir 84*
Overview - West Hartford, CT - *MagIndMarPl 82-83*
Ovid Gazette - Trumansburg, NY - *AyerDirPub 83*
Ovid Gazette - *See* Odyssey Publications
Ovid Gazette & Independent - Ovid, NY - *Ed&PubIntYB 82*
Oviedo Outlook - Oviedo, FL - *BaconPubCkNews 84*
Ovo Magazine - Montreal, PQ, Canada - *LitMag&SmPr 83-84*
Owasso Cable TV [of Tele-Communications Inc.] - Owasso, OK - *BrCabYB 84*
Owasso Reporter - Owasso, OK - *BaconPubCkNews 84; Ed&PubIntYB 82*
Owasso Reporter [of Tulsa Retherford Publications Inc.] - Tulsa, OK - *NewsDir 84*
Owatonna Cablevision [of Tribune Cable Communications Inc.] - Owatonna, MN - *Tel&CabFB 84C*
Owatonna People's Press [of Ottaway Newspapers Inc.] - Owatonna, MN - *BaconPubCkNews 84; NewsDir 84*
Owego CATV Associates [of Simmons Communications Inc.] - Owego, NY - *BrCabYB 84; Tel&CabFB 84C*
Owego Tioga County Gazette & Times - Owego, NY - *BaconPubCkNews 84; NewsDir 84*
Owen Co., The Edward - Avon, CT - *StaDirAdAg 2-84*
Owen Enterprise - Owen, WI - *BaconPubCkNews 84*
Owen Murphy Productions Inc. - South Westport, CT - *TelAl 83*
Owen, Peter - Salem, NH - *LitMarPl 83, 84*
Owen Wade Delmonte Ltd. - London, England - *StaDirAdAg 2-84*
Owens & Associates Advertising & Public Relations - Phoenix, AZ - *ArtMar 84; StaDirAdAg 2-84*
Owens Associates Inc., John D. - Staten Island, NY - *MicrocomMPl 83, 84; WhoWMicrocom 83*
Owens-Corning Fiberglas Corp. (Interior Products Operating Div.) - Toledo, OH - *DirInfWP 82*
Owens-Darr-Koffron Inc. - Milwaukee, WI - *StaDirAdAg 2-84*
Owens Enterprises, Buck - Bakersfield, CA - *Tel&CabFB 84C*
Owens Publishing, Bill - Livermore, CA - *BoPubDir 4, 5; MagIndMarPl 82-83*
Owens Stations, Buck - Tempe, AZ - *BrCabYB 84*
Owens Television Productions, Harry - Hollywood, CA - *TelAl 83, 84*
Owensboro Broadcasting Co. - Owensboro, KY - *BrCabYB 84*
Owensboro Cablevision [of Century Communications Corp.] - Owensboro, KY - *BrCabYB 84; Tel&CabFB 84C*
Owensboro Messenger-Inquirer - Owensboro, KY - *BaconPubCkNews 84; NewsDir 84*
Owensville Gasconade County Republican - Owensville, MO - *BaconPubCkNews 84; NewsDir 84*
Owensville Republican - Owensville, MO - *Ed&PubIntYB 82*
Owensville Star-Echo - Owensville, IN - *BaconPubCkNews 84*
Owenton News-Herald & Owen Democrat - Owenton, KY - *BaconPubCkNews 84*
Owingsville Bath County News-Outlook - Owingsville, KY - *BaconPubCkNews 84; NewsDir 84*
Owl Computers - Bishop's Stortford, England - *WhoWMicrocom 83*
Owl Computers - Sawbridgeworth, England - *InfIndMarPl 83*
Owl Creek Press - Missoula, MT - *BoPubDir 4, 5; LitMag&SmPr 83-84*
Owl Magazine [of The Young Naturalist Foundation] - Toronto, ON, Canada - *WritMar 84*
Owl Micro-Communications Ltd. - Sawbridgeworth, England - *MicrocomSwDir 1*
Owl Press Inc. - Las Vegas, NV - *BoPubDir 4, 5*
Owl Software Corp. - North Hollywood, CA - *WhoWMicrocom 83*
Owlflight [of Unique Graphics] - Oakland, CA - *LitMag&SmPr 83-84*
Owlseye Publications - Hayward, CA - *LitMag&SmPr 83-84*
Owlswick Press - Philadelphia, PA - *BoPubDir 4, 5*

Owlswood Productions Inc. - San Francisco, CA - *LitMag&SmPr 83-84; LitMarPl 83; WritMar 84*
Owner-Builder Publications - North Fork, CA - *BoPubDir 4, 5*
Owner Operator - Radnor, PA - *BaconPubCkMag 84; MagIndMarPl 82-83*
Owosso Argus-Press - Owosso, MI - *BaconPubCkNews 84*
Owosso Broadcasting Co. - Owosso, MI - *BrCabYB 84*
Owosso Cable TV [of Cox Cable Communications Inc.] - Owosso, MI - *BrCabYB 84*
Owsley County TV - Booneville, KY - *BrCabYB 84; Tel&CabFB 84C*
Owyhee Chronicle - Homedale, ID - *AyerDirPub 83; Ed&PubIntYB 82*
Owyhee Nugget - Marsing, ID - *AyerDirPub 83; Ed&PubIntYB 82*
Ox Bow Press - Woodbridge, CT - *LitMarPl 84*
Ox Head Press - Marshall, MN - *BoPubDir 4, 5; LitMag&SmPr 83-84*
Ox Products Inc. - Mamaroneck, NY - *AvMarPl 83*
Oxberry [Div. of Richmark Camera Service] - Carlstadt, NJ - *AvMarPl 83*
Oxbridge Communications Inc. - New York, NY - *LitMarPl 83, 84*
Oxfam-America - Boston, MA - *BoPubDir 4 Sup, 5*
Oxfam-Canada - Toronto, ON, Canada - *BoPubDir 4, 5*
Oxford Chester County Press [of Chester County Communications Ltd.] - Oxford, PA - *NewsDir 84*
Oxford Chester County Press - *See* Chester County Communications Ltd.
Oxford County Citizen - Bethel, ME - *AyerDirPub 83*
Oxford County Telephone & Telegraph Co. - Buckfield, ME - *TelDir&BG 83-84*
Oxford Eagle - Oxford, MS - *BaconPubCkNews 84; Ed&PubIntYB 82; NewsDir 84*
Oxford Gazette - Oxford, IN - *BaconPubCkNews 84; Ed&PubIntYB 82*
Oxford Group - Norway, ME - *LitMarPl 83*
Oxford Journal, The - Oxford, NS, Canada - *Ed&PubIntYB 82*
Oxford Leader - Oxford, IA - *BaconPubCkNews 84*
Oxford Leader - Oxford, MI - *BaconPubCkNews 84; Ed&PubIntYB 82*
Oxford Microform & Publishing Services Ltd. - Oxford, England - *EISS 83; MicroMarPl 82-83*
Oxford NewChannels - Oxford, NY - *BrCabYB 84*
Oxford Pendaflex Corp. - Garden City, NY - *DirInfWP 82*
Oxford Press - Oxford, OH - *BaconPubCkNews 84; Ed&PubIntYB 82; NewsDir 84*
Oxford Public Ledger - Oxford, NC - *BaconPubCkNews 84; Ed&PubIntYB 82; NewsDir 84*
Oxford Publishing Co. - Oxford, England - *MicroMarPl 82-83*
Oxford Register - Oxford, KS - *BaconPubCkNews 84; Ed&PubIntYB 82*
Oxford Review-Times - Oxford, NY - *Ed&PubIntYB 82*
Oxford Review Times - *See* Twin Valley Publishers Inc.
Oxford Shopping News - Woodstock, ON, Canada - *AyerDirPub 83*
Oxford Software Co. - Oxford, MS - *WhoWMicrocom 83*
Oxford Software Corp. - Hasbrouck Heights, NJ - *ADAPSOMemDir 83-84; DataDirSup 7-83*
Oxford Standard - Oxford, NE - *BaconPubCkNews 84; Ed&PubIntYB 82*
Oxford Sun - Anniston, AL - *NewsDir 84*
Oxford Sun - Oxford, AL - *BaconPubCkNews 84; Ed&PubIntYB 82*
Oxford TV Cable Co. [of CATV Inc.] - Oxford, NE - *Tel&CabFB 84C*
Oxford University Press - New York, NY - *BillIntBG 83-84; DirMarMP 83; KnowInd 83; LitMarPl 83, 84; MicroMarPl 82-83; WritMar 84*
Oxford University Press - Oxford, England - *LitMag&SmPr 83-84*
Oxford University Press (Canadian Branch) - Don Mills, ON, Canada - *LitMarPl 83, 84*
Oxford University Press (Children's Books) - Salem, NH - *LitMarPl 83, 84*
Oxford University Press (ELT Dept.) - New York, NY - *ArtMar 84*
Oxford Valley Cablevision Inc. [of Sammons Communications Inc.] - Bensalem, PA - *Tel&CabFB 84C*
Oxford Valley Cablevision Inc. [of Sammons Communications Inc.] - Falls Township, PA - *BrCabYB 84; Tel&CabFB 84C*
Oxford Video Co. [of Heritage Communications Inc.] - Oxford, MS - *Tel&CabFB 84C*
Oxmoor House [Div. of The Southern Progress Corp.] - Birmingham, AL - *ArtMar 84; DirMarMP 83; LitMarPl 83, 84; WritMar 84*
Oxmoor Press [Subs. of Stevens Graphics Inc.] - Birmingham, AL - *LitMarPl 83, 84; MagIndMarPl 82-83*
Oxnard Press-Courier - Oxnard, CA - *BaconPubCkNews 84; NewsDir 84*
Oxtoby-Smith Inc. - New York, NY - *IntDirMarRes 83*
Oxus Press - London, England - *LitMag&SmPr 83-84*
Oxymora Book Press - Venice, CA - *BoPubDir 5*
Oy Mainos Taucher Reklam AB - *See* Taucher Group
Oyen Echo - Oyen, AB, Canada - *Ed&PubIntYB 82*
Oyez - Berkeley, CA - *BoPubDir 4, 5; LitMag&SmPr 83-84*
Oyez Review - Chicago, IL - *LitMag&SmPr 83-84*
Oyster Bay & Norwich Pennysaver - Huntington, NY - *AyerDirPub 83*
Oyster Bay Enterprise Pilot - Glen Cove, NY - *AyerDirPub 83*
Oyster Bay Enterprise Pilot [of Community Newspapers Inc.] - Oyster Bay, NY - *Ed&PubIntYB 82; NewsDir 84*
Oyster Bay Enterprise Pilot - *See* Community Newspapers Inc.
Oyster Bay-Syosset Guardian - Oyster Bay, NY - *AyerDirPub 83; BaconPubCkNews 84; Ed&PubIntYB 82*
Oyster Music - *See* Open End Music
Oz Records - Hollywood, CA - *BillIntBG 83-84*
Ozark Beacon - Poplar Bluff, MO - *AyerDirPub 83*
Ozark Beacon & Journal - Poplar Bluff, MO - *Ed&PubIntYB 82*
Ozark Cable TV Inc. [of Pinion Corp.] - Horseshoe Bend, AR - *Tel&CabFB 84C*
Ozark Cable TV Inc. [of Pinion Corp.] - Salem, AR - *BrCabYB 84*
Ozark Cablevision Co. [of McDonald Group] - Ozark, AL - *BrCabYB 84; Tel&CabFB 84C*
Ozark Cablevision Co. - Ozark, AR - *Tel&CabFB 84C*
Ozark Communications Inc. - Springfield, MO - *Tel&CabFB 84C p.1696*
Ozark Community Cable TV Co. - Imboden, AR - *BrCabYB 84*
Ozark Community Cable TV Inc. - Ironton, MO - *BrCabYB 84; Tel&CabFB 84C*
Ozark County Times - Gainesville, MO - *AyerDirPub 83; Ed&PubIntYB 82*
Ozark Flightime [of East-West Network Inc.] - Los Angeles, CA - *ArtMar 84; MagIndMarPl 82-83*
Ozark Graphic Home Shopper (Carter County Edition) - Doniphan, MO - *AyerDirPub 83*
Ozark Graphic Home Shopper (Ripley County Edition) - Doniphan, MO - *AyerDirPub 83*
Ozark Graphic Weekly - Doniphan, MO - *AyerDirPub 83*
Ozark Headliner - Ozark, MO - *AyerDirPub 83; BaconPubCkNews 84; Ed&PubIntYB 82; NewsDir 84*
Ozark Journal - Imboden, AR - *Ed&PubIntYB 82*
Ozark Magazine [of East/West Network Inc.] - Los Angeles, CA - *BaconPubCkMag 84; MagDir 84; WritMar 84*
Ozark Mountain Software - Fayetteville, AR - *MicrocomMPl 83, 84*
Ozark Opry Inc. - Osage Beach, MO - *BillIntBG 83-84*
Ozark Society Books [Aff. of Ozark Society Foundation] - Little Rock, AR - *BoPubDir 5*
Ozark Southern Star - Ozark, AL - *BaconPubCkNews 84*
Ozark Spectator - Ozark, AR - *BaconPubCkNews 84; NewsDir 84*
Ozark Summit Communications Inc. - Marshfield, MO - *Tel&CabFB 84C p.1696*
Ozarks Communications Co. Inc. - Nixa, MO - *BrCabYB 84*
Ozarks Communications Co. Inc. - Ozark, MO - *BrCabYB 84*
Ozaukee Press - Port Washington, WI - *AyerDirPub 83; Ed&PubIntYB 82*
Ozer Publisher Inc., Jerome S. - Englewood, NJ - *BoPubDir 4 Sup, 5; LitMarPl 83, 84*
Ozma Broadcast Sales - Philadelphia, PA - *Tel&CabFB 84C*
Ozona Stockman - Ozona, TX - *BaconPubCkNews 84; Ed&PubIntYB 82*
Ozona TV System - Ozona, TX - *Tel&CabFB 84C*

P

P & P Engineering - Carlsbad, CA - *MicrocomSwDir 1*
P & P Studios Inc. - Stamford, CT - *AvMarPl 83*
P & W Marketing Research - Youngstown, OH - *IntDirMarRes 83*
P/E News [of American Petroleum Institute] - New York, NY - *DataDirOnSer 84; DirOnDB Spring 84; OnBibDB 3*
P80Nut Software Inc. - Lilburn, GA - *MicrocomMPl 83*
P-H Associates - Vienna, VA - *MicrocomMPl 84*
P-I Communications Inc. - Onalaska, TX - *BrCabYB 84*
P-J Promotions Inc. - New York, NY - *MagIndMarPl 82-83*
P-K Cable TV Co. - Possum Kingdom Lake, TX - *Tel&CabFB 84C*
P-M Enterprises - Hendersonville, NC - *BoPubDir 4 Sup, 5*
P/M Technology Newsletter - Princeton, NJ - *BaconPubCkMag 84*
P-ROM Software Inc. - Burlington, VT - *WhoWMicrocom 83*
PA Drug Update - New York, NY - *BaconPubCkMag 84*
PA International Management Consultants Inc. - New York, NY - *IntDirMarRes 83*
PAB Software Inc. - Ft. Wayne, IN - *MicrocomMPl 84*
Pablo Records Inc. - Beverly Hills, CA - *BillIntBG 83-84*
PAC Corp. [Subs. of Alta Summa Corp.] - Stockton, CA - *MicrocomMPl 83; WhoWMicrocom 83*
Pac Researchers Ltd. - Burke, VA - *EISS 7-83 Sup*
Pace [of Fisher-Harrison Publications] - Greensboro, NC - *BaconPubCkMag 84; MagDir 84; WritMar 84*
Pace Advertising Agency Inc. - New York, NY - *StaDirAdAg 2-84*
Pace Advertising & Public Relations [of the Pace Corp.] - Woodbridge, CT - *StaDirAdAg 2-84*
Pace Applied Technology Inc. - Manassas, VA - *ADAPSOMemDir 83-84; DataDirSup 7-83*
Pace Associates, C. L. - Wilton, CT - *MagIndMarPl 82-83*
Pace Communications Inc. - New York, NY - *DirMarMP 83*
Pace Educational Software - Falls Church, VA - *MicrocomSwDir 1*
Pace Films Inc. - New York, NY - *WritMar 84*
Pace Gallery Publications [Div. of Pace Gallery of New York Inc.] - New York, NY - *BoPubDir 4, 5; LitMag&SmPr 83-84; LitMarPl 84*
Pace, Julian V. - Weston, CT - *HBIndAd&MS 82-83*
Pace Music Co. - *See* Fox Publishing Co. Inc., Sam
Pace Publishing Inc. - Minneapolis, MN - *BoPubDir 4, 5*
Pace Research & Analysis Inc. - Melville, NY - *IntDirMarRes 83*
Pacer Co., The - Omaha, NE - *AvMarPl 83*
Pacesetter Publishing House [Div. of Pacesetter Enterprises Inc.] - Cleveland, OH - *BoPubDir 4 Sup, 5*
Pacesetting Computers Inc. - Long Beach, CA - *MicrocomMPl 83, 84*
Pach Brothers - New York, NY - *MagIndMarPl 82-83*
Pacha Books - Potsdam, NY - *BoPubDir 4, 5*
Pachart Publishing House - Tucson, AZ - *BoPubDir 4, 5; LitMag&SmPr 83-84*
Pacheco Automotive News Service - Concord, CA - *Ed&PubIntYB 82*
Pacific - Seattle, WA - *MagIndMarPl 82-83*
Pacific Arts Video Records - Carmel, CA - *BillIntBG 83-84*
Pacific/Asian American Mental Health Research Center [Aff. of University of Illinois at Chicago] - Chicago, IL - *BoPubDir 4, 5*
Pacific Automotive News [of Automotive Publishing Co.] - Laguna Beach, CA - *MagDir 84*
Pacific Automotive News - Laguna Niguel, CA - *BaconPubCkMag 84*
Pacific Bakers News - Belfair, WA - *WritMar 84*
Pacific Banker & Business [of Vernon Publications Inc.] - Seattle, WA - *BaconPubCkMag 84; MagDir 84*
Pacific Beach Pennysaver - Mission Viejo, CA - *AyerDirPub 83*
Pacific Boating Almanac - Ventura, CA - *ArtMar 84; WritMar 84*
Pacific Book Service [Div. of Pacific Freeport Warehouse] - Sparks, NV - *LitMarPl 83*
Pacific Books - Palo Alto, CA - *LitMarPl 83, 84; WritMar 84*
Pacific Builder & Engineer [of Vernon Publications Inc.] - Seattle, WA - *BaconPubCkMag 84; MagDir 84*
Pacific Business - Beaverton, OR - *BaconPubCkMag 84*
Pacific Business News - Honolulu, HI - *BaconPubCkMag 84*
Pacific Cable TV [of Capital Cities Communications Inc.] - Burlingame, CA - *BrCabYB 84; Tel&CabFB 84C*
Pacific Cablevision Corp. [of Oceanic Cable-Vision Inc.] - Honolulu, HI - *BrCabYB 84*
Pacific Challenger Music - Anaheim, CA - *BillIntBG 83-84*
Pacific Challenger Records Inc. - Anaheim, CA - *BillIntBG 83-84*
Pacific Clipping Service - Santa Ana, CA - *ProGuPRSer 4*
Pacific Coast Cable Co. - Ione, CA - *Tel&CabFB 84C*
Pacific Coast Nurseryman & Garden Supply Dealer - Arcadia, CA - *BaconPubCkMag 84; MagDir 84*
Pacific Coast Press Bureau - Huntington Beach, CA - *LitMarPl 83, 84*
Pacific Coast Software Corp. - Diamond Bab, CA - *MicrocomMPl 84*
Pacific Color Inc. - Seattle, WA - *AvMarPl 83*
Pacific Computer Supply - Redwood City, CA - *DirInfWP 82*
Pacific Data Systems - Agana, GU - *ADAPSOMemDir 83-84*
Pacific Discovery [of California Academy of Sciences] - San Francisco, CA - *MagIndMarPl 82-83; WritMar 84*
Pacific Exchanges - San Luis Obispo, CA - *MicrocomMPl 83*
Pacific Express [of Skies West Publishing Co.] - Portland, OR - *BaconPubCkMag 84; WritMar 84*
Pacific Eye & Ear - Los Angeles, CA - *StaDirAdAg 2-84*
Pacific Fast Mail [Aff. of PFM Industries Inc.] - Edmonds, WA - *BoPubDir 4, 5*
Pacific Features - Berkeley, CA - *LitMarPl 83, 84; MagIndMarPl 82-83*
Pacific Fishing - Seattle, WA - *BaconPubCkMag 84; MagDir 84; WritMar 84*
Pacific Foodservice News - Sausalito, CA - *ArtMar 84; BaconPubCkMag 84*
Pacific Gallery Publishers - Portland, OR - *LitMag&SmPr 83-84*
Pacific Grove Ft. Ord Panorama - Pacific Grove, CA - *BaconPubCkNews 84*

Pacific Grove/Pebble Beach Tribune - Pacific Grove, CA - *AyerDirPub 83; Ed&PubIntYB 82*
Pacific Home Theaters - Honolulu, HI - *Tel&CabFB 84C*
Pacific Horticulture - Berkeley, CA - *BaconPubCkMag 84; LitMag&SmPr 83-84; MagDir 84*
Pacific International Marketing Group - Los Angeles, CA - *ADAPSOMemDir 83-84*
Pacific Islands Ecosystems [of SDC Search Service] - Santa Monica, CA - *DataDirOnSer 84*
Pacific Islands Ecosystems [of U.S. Fish & Wildlife Service] - Portland, OR - *CompReadDB 82; EISS 83*
Pacific Islands Ecosystems [of U.S. Fish & Wildlife Service] - Springfield, VA - *OnBibDB 3*
Pacific Maramec Valley Transcript [of Union Franklin Publishing Co.] - Union, MO - *NewsDir 84*
Pacific Marketer [of Northwest Furniture Retailers' Association] - Seattle, WA - *BaconPubCkMag 84; MagDir 84*
Pacific Media Corp. - Palm Springs, CA - *BrCabYB 84*
Pacific Medical Systems - Simi Valley, CA - *MicrocomMPl 84*
Pacific Meramec Valley Transcript - Pacific, MO - *BaconPubCkNews 84*
Pacific Microsystems - Laguna Hills, CA - *WhoWMicrocom 83*
Pacific Motion Pictures - North Hollywood, CA - *AvMarPl 83*
Pacific Mountain Network - Denver, CO - *BrCabYB 84; Tel&CabFB 84C*
Pacific Network Communications Corp. - Dallas, TX - *TeleSy&SerDir 7-83*
Pacific News [of Chatham Publishing Co.] - Burlingame, CA - *LitMag&SmPr 83-84*
Pacific News - Long Beach, CA - *AyerDirPub 83*
Pacific News Service - San Francisco, CA - *Ed&PubIntYB 82; MagIndMarPl 82-83*
Pacific Northwest [of Pacific Search Communications] - Seattle, WA - *ArtMar 84; BaconPubCkMag 84; DirMarMP 83; MagDir 84; WritMar 84*
Pacific Northwest Agencies Inc. [Div. of Plainsman Publications Ltd.] - Vancouver, BC, Canada - *BoPubDir 4 Sup, 5; LitMarPl 83, 84*
Pacific Northwest Bell Telephone Co. - Seattle, WA - *TelDir&BG 83-84*
Pacific Northwest Bibliographic Center - Seattle, WA - *EISS 83*
Pacific Northwest E/C News [of Bender Publications Inc.] - Los Angeles, CA - *MagDir 84*
Pacific Northwest Laboratory (Seasonal Thermal Energy Program) - Richland, WA - *CompReadDB 82*
Pacific Northwest Theatre Associates Inc. - Seattle, WA - *AvMarPl 83*
Pacific Office Systems - Mountain View, CA - *MicrocomMPl 83*
Pacific Oil World [of Petroleum Publishers Inc.] - Brea, CA - *BaconPubCkMag 84; MagDir 84*
Pacific Palisades Palisadian Post - Pacific Palisades, CA - *BaconPubCkNews 84*
Pacific Press Ltd. - Vancouver, BC, Canada - *Ed&PubIntYB 82*
Pacific Press Publishing Association - Mountain View, CA - *LitMarPl 83, 84*
Pacific Press Santa Barbara - Pierce City, MO - *BoPubDir 4, 5*
Pacific Printers Pilot - Monterey Park, CA - *BaconPubCkMag 84; MagDir 84*
Pacific Productions [Subs. of ISC] - Honolulu, HI - *AvMarPl 83*
Pacific Publishing Co. - Concord, CA - *BoPubDir 4, 5*
Pacific Publishing Services - Santa Cruz, CA - *LitMarPl 83, 84; MagIndMarPl 82-83*
Pacific Purchasor - Los Angeles, CA - *BaconPubCkMag 84; MagDir 84*
Pacific Quarterly Moana [of Outrigger Publishers] - Hamilton, New Zealand - *LitMag&SmPr 83-84*
Pacific Records - Los Angeles, CA - *BillIntBG 83-84*
Pacific Science Association - Honolulu, HI - *BoPubDir 4 Sup, 5*
Pacific Scientific Press Inc. - Kelso, WA - *BoPubDir 5*
Pacific Scientific Press Inc. - Longview, WA - *LitMag&SmPr 83-84*
Pacific Search Press [Div. of Pacific Search Publications] - Seattle, WA - *LitMarPl 83, 84*
Pacific Shipper - San Francisco, CA - *BaconPubCkMag 84; MagDir 84*
Pacific Skipper - Newport Beach, CA - *MagDir 84*
Pacific Software - Berkeley, CA - *MicrocomMPl 83, 84; WhoWMicrocom 83*
Pacific Southwest Computer Systems Inc. - Northridge, CA - *MicrocomMPl 84*
Pacific Southwest Computer Systems Inc. - Panorama City, CA - *MicrocomMPl 83*
Pacific Star Records - Hollywood, CA - *BillIntBG 83-84*
Pacific Street Film Library - Franklin Lakes, NJ - *AvMarPl 83*
Pacific Studies [of Institute for Polynesian Studies] - Laie, HI - *LitMag&SmPr 83-84*
Pacific Sun - Marin County, CA - *Ed&PubIntYB 82*
Pacific Sun - Mill Valley, CA - *AyerDirPub 83*
Pacific Telecom Inc. - Vancouver, WA - *TelDir&BG 83-84*
Pacific Telecommunications Council - Honolulu, HI - *TeleSy&SerDir 2-84*
Pacific Telephone & Telegraph Co., The - San Francisco, CA - *TelDir&BG 83-84*
Pacific Trade Group - Kailua, HI - *LitMarPl 84*
Pacific Trade Group - Waipahu, HI - *BoPubDir 4 Sup, 5*
Pacific Traffic - Marina Del Rey, CA - *BaconPubCkMag 84*
Pacific Traffic [of The Knowlton Group Inc.] - Venice, CA - *MagDir 84*
Pacific Travel News - San Francisco, CA - *BaconPubCkMag 84; MagDir 84; MagIndMarPl 82-83; WritMar 84*
Pacific Tri-County Journal [of Suburban Newspapers] - Pacific, MO - *BaconPubCkNews 84; NewsDir 84*
Pacific Tri Micro Inc. - Knoxville, TN - *MicrocomMPl 84*
Pacific View Music - *See* Williams Music Group, Don
Pacific Woodworker - Santa Rosa, CA - *ArtMar 84; LitMag&SmPr 83-84; WritMar 84*
Pacific Yachting [Aff. of Special Interest Publications] - Vancouver, BC, Canada - *BaconPubCkMag 84; BoPubDir 4, 5; WritMar 84*
Pacifica Coastside Buyers Guide [of Pacifica Tribune] - Pacifica, CA - *NewsDir 84*
Pacifica Coastside Chronicle [of San Bruno Amphlett Printing Co.] - San Bruno, CA - *NewsDir 84*
Pacifica Coastside Chronicle - *See* San Mateo Times Group Newspapers
Pacifica Foundation Inc. - Los Angeles, CA - *BrCabYB 84*
Pacifica News Bureau - Washington, DC - *BrCabYB 84*
Pacifica Record - Pacifica, CA - *Ed&PubIntYB 82*
Pacifica Record [of South San Francisco Industrial City Publishing Co.] - South San Francisco, CA - *NewsDir 84*
Pacifica Tribune - Pacifica, CA - *BaconPubCkNews 84; Ed&PubIntYB 82*
Package Engineering Including Modern Packaging - Chicago, IL - *MagIndMarPl 82-83*
Package Good Music - Manville, NJ - *BillIntBG 83-84*
Package Printing - Philadelphia, PA - *BaconPubCkMag 84; MagDir 84; MagIndMarPl 82-83; WritMar 84*
Package Publicity Service Inc. - New York, NY - *BoPubDir 4, 5; DirPRFirms 83*
Packaged Facts Inc. - New York, NY - *DataDirOnSer 84; FBInfSer 80; HBIndAd&MS 82-83; InfIndMarPl 83; LitMarPl 83, 84; ProGuPRSer 4*
Packaging - Des Plaines, IL - *BaconPubCkMag 84; MagDir 84*
Packaging Digest - Chicago, IL - *BaconPubCkMag 84; MagDir 84; MagIndMarPl 82-83*
Packaging Industries Group Inc. - Hyannis, MA - *LitMarPl 83, 84*
Packaging Institute Inc. - New York, NY - *BoPubDir 5*
Packaging Letter - Westfield, NJ - *BaconPubCkMag 84*
Packaging Machinery Manufacturers Institute - Washington, DC - *BoPubDir 4 Sup, 5*
Packaging Science & Technology Abstracts [of Fraunhofer Institute for Food Technology & Packaging] - Munich, West Germany - *EISS 5-84 Sup*
Packaging Strategy Associates - Darien, CT - *IntDirMarRes 83*
Packaging Technology - Hillsdale, NJ - *BaconPubCkMag 84*
Packard Industries Inc. - Niles, MI - *DirInfWP 82*
Packer Advertising Corp. - Valley Stream, NY - *StaDirAdAg 2-84*
Packer, The - Kansas City, KS - *MagDir 84*
Packer, The - Shawnee Mission, KS - *BaconPubCkMag 84; WritMar 84*
Packet - Princeton, NJ - *AyerDirPub 83*
Packet & Times - Orillia, ON, Canada - *AyerDirPub 83*

Packet Switching Service [of British Telecommunications] - London, England - *EISS 83*
Packet Switchstream [of British Telecommunications] - London, England - *TeleSy&SerDir 7-83, 2-84*
PacketCable Inc. - Cupertino, CA - *VideoDir 82-83*
Packing & Shipping - Plainfield, NJ - *MagDir 84*
Packrat Press Books - Cambridge, ID - *BoPubDir 4, 5*
Pacnet [Subs. of I-NET Corp.] - Dallas, TX - *DataDirOnSer 84*
PACs & Lobbies - Washington, DC - *DirOnDB Spring 84*
PACS & Lobbies [of NewsNet Inc.] - Bryn Mawr, PA - *DataDirOnSer 84*
PacSoft Inc. - Kirkland, WA - *MicrocomMPl 84*
Pacucah Newspapers Inc. - Paducah, KY - *BrCabYB 84*
Paddlewheel Press - Tigard, OR - *BoPubDir 4 Sup, 5*
Paddock Publications - Arlington Heights, IL - *BaconPubCkNews 84; Ed&PubIntYB 82*
Paddock Publications - Mundelein, IL - *BaconPubCkNews 84*
Paddon Books - St. Thomas, ON, Canada - *BoPubDir 4, 5*
Padgitt Co. Inc., Tom - Austin, TX - *AvMarPl 83*
Padilla & Speer Inc. - Minneapolis, MN - *DirPRFirms 83*
Padma Press - Oatman, AZ - *BoPubDir 4, 5; LitMag&SmPr 83-84*
Padmede Computer Services - Fleet, England - *MicrocomSwDir 1*
Padre Productions - San Luis Obispo, CA - *ArtMar 84; BoPubDir 4, 5; LitMag&SmPr 83-84; WritMar 84*
Padua Music Co. - *See* Faro Music Publishing
Paducah Post - Paducah, TX - *BaconPubCkNews 84; Ed&PubIntYB 82*
Paducah Sun - Paducah, KY - *BaconPubCkNews 84; Ed&PubIntYB 82; NewsDir 84*
Pagan Press - New York, NY - *LitMag&SmPr 83-84*
Pagani & Brother Inc., O. - New York, NY - *BillIntBG 83-84*
Paganiniana Publications - Neptune, NJ - *BillIntBG 83-84; BoPubDir 4, 5; LitMarPl 84*
Page Books - Gunnison, CO - *BoPubDir 4, 5*
Page Communications Inc., Bob - *See* Harden/Bob Page Communications Inc., John
Page Lake Powell Chronicle - Page, AZ - *BaconPubCkNews 84*
Page Marketing Services Inc. - Port Charlotte, FL - *DirMarMP 83*
Page News & Courier - Luray, VA - *AyerDirPub 83; Ed&PubIntYB 82*
Page, O. D. - Bethesda, MD - *InterCabHB 3*
Page Publishers - Red Bank, NJ - *Ed&PubIntYB 82*
Page Recording Co. - Johnstown, PA - *BillIntBG 83-84*
Pageant Book Co. - New York, NY - *ProGuPRSer 4*
Pageant Publishing Co. - Cordova, TN - *BoPubDir 5*
PageCrafters Inc. - Oswego, NY - *LitMarPl 84*
Pageland Progressive-Journal - Orangeburg, SC - *AyerDirPub 83*
Pageland Progressive Journal - Pageland, SC - *BaconPubCkNews 84; Ed&PubIntYB 82*
Pages to Go!! - Escondido, CA - *LitMarPl 83; MagIndMarPl 82-83*
Pagliotti, Rick - Santa Barbara, CA - *BoPubDir 4, 5*
Pagosa Springs Sun - Pagosa Springs, CO - *BaconPubCkNews 84; Ed&PubIntYB 82*
Pagurian Corp. Ltd., The - Toronto, ON, Canada - *WritMar 84*
PAID Records - Houston, TX - *BillIntBG 83-84*
Paideia - Santa Monica, CA - *AvMarPl 83*
Paideia Press - Jordan Station, ON, Canada - *BoPubDir 4, 5*
Paideuma [of National Poetry Foundation] - Orono, ME - *LitMag&SmPr 83-84*
Paine Webber Mitchell Hutchins (Research Div.) - New York, NY - *ADAPSOMemDir 83-84*
Painesville Telegraph [of Lake-Geauga Printing Co.] - Painesville, OH - *NewsDir 84*
Paint Horse Journal [of American Paint Horse Association] - Ft. Worth, TX - *ArtMar 84; BaconPubCkMag 84; MagIndMarPl 82-83; WritMar 84*
Paint Research Association - Teddington, England - *CompReadDB 82; InfIndMarPl 83*
Paint Rock Concho Herald - Paint Rock, TX - *BaconPubCkNews 84*
Paintbrush [of Ishtar Press Inc.] - Laramie, WY - *LitMag&SmPr 83-84*
Painted Smiles Records [Subs. of Battery Records Inc.] - New York, NY - *BillIntBG 83-84*
Painter & Associates Ltd., Larry - Jackson, MS - *StaDirAdAg 2-84*
Painters & Allied Trades Journal - Washington, DC - *BaconPubCkMag 84; MagDir 84; MagIndMarPl 82-83; NewsDir 84*
Painting & Wallcovering Contractor [of Painting & Decorating Contractors of America] - Falls Church, VA - *BaconPubCkMag 84; MagDir 84; WritMar 84*
Paintsville Herald - Paintsville, KY - *BaconPubCkNews 84; Ed&PubIntYB 82; NewsDir 84*
Paintsville TV Cable Corp. - Paintsville, KY - *Tel&CabFB 84C*
Pair Records - Passaic, NJ - *BillIntBG 83-84*
PAIS Bulletin/Foreign Language Index Database [of Public Affairs Information Service] - New York, NY - *DataDirOnSer 84*
PAIS International [of Public Affairs Information Service] - New York, NY - *DirOnDB Spring 84; OnBibDB 3*
Paisano Productions - Los Angeles, CA - *Tel&CabFB 84C*
Pajarito Publications [Aff. of De Colores] - Albuquerque, NM - *BoPubDir 4, 5*
Pak Interviewing Co. - Philadelphia, PA - *IntDirMarRes 83*
Pakistan Feature Syndicate - Lahore, Pakistan - *Ed&PubIntYB 82*
Pakistan Scientific & Technological Information Centre - Islamabad, Pakistan - *EISS 83*
Pakka Press - East Douglas, MA - *LitMag&SmPr 83-84*
Paklegis [of Pergamon International Information Corp.] - McLean, VA - *DataDirOnSer 84*
Paklegis [of Pira: Research Association for the Paper & Board, Printing & Packaging Industries] - Leatherhead, England - *DirOnDB Spring 84; EISS 7-83 Sup*
Pako Corp. - Minneapolis, MN - *AvMarPl 83*
Pakre Inc. - Lakewood, CA - *MicrocomMPl 84*
Pakula Co. Inc., The - Los Angeles, CA - *TelAl 84*
Pal & Co. Inc., J. B. - Chicago, IL - *BoPubDir 4, 5*
PAL Press - San Anselmo, CA - *BoPubDir 4, 5*
Pal Publishing - Northridge, CA - *BoPubDir 4, 5*
Pal Publishing - Witter Springs, CA - *BillIntBG 83-84*
Pala Mesa Cablevision Inc. [of Daniels Properties] - Fallbrook, CA - *BrCabYB 84*
Pala Mesa Cablevision Inc. - Vista, CA - *BrCabYB 84*
Palacios Beacon - Palacios, TX - *Ed&PubIntYB 82*
Palacios Beacon - *See* Brazoria County News Publishers
Palacios TV Cable Corp. - Palacios, TX - *BrCabYB 84; Tel&CabFB 84C*
Paladin Enterprises Inc. - Boulder, CO - *LitMag&SmPr 83-84*
Paladin House Publishers - Geneva, IL - *BoPubDir 4, 5*
Paladin Press [Div. of Paladin Enterprises Inc.] - Boulder, CO - *ArtMar 84; DirMarMP 83; LitMarPl 83, 84; WritMar 84*
Paladin Public Relations Inc. - New York, NY - *DirPRFirms 83*
Palamar Music Publishers - Orlando, FL - *BillIntBG 83-84*
Palantir Software - Houston, TX - *MicrocomMPl 84*
Palatine Countryside [of Barrington Press Inc.] - Barrington, IL - *AyerDirPub 83; NewsDir 84*
Palatine Countryside - Palatine, IL - *Ed&PubIntYB 82*
Palatine Countryside - *See* Barrington Press Inc.
Palatine Herald - *See* Paddock Publications
Palatine/Inverness Daily Herald [of Paddock Publications] - Arlington Heights, IL - *NewsDir 84*
Palatine Publications Inc. - Ruston, LA - *BoPubDir 4, 5*
Palatine Topics - *See* Journal & Topics Newspapers
Palatka News - Palatka, FL - *BaconPubCkNews 84; Ed&PubIntYB 82; NewsDir 84*
Palazzo & Associates - New York, NY - *HBIndAd&MS 82-83*
Pale Fire Review, The - Providence, RI - *LitMag&SmPr 83-84*
Pale Pachyderm Publishing - San Francisco, CA - *BillIntBG 83-84*
Paleontological Research Institution - Ithaca, NY - *BoPubDir 4, 5*
Palestine Herald-Press - Palestine, TX - *AyerDirPub 83; BaconPubCkNews 84; Ed&PubIntYB 82; NewsDir 84*
Palestine Register - Palestine, IL - *Ed&PubIntYB 82*
Palimpsest, The [of State Historical Society] - Iowa City, IA - *MagIndMarPl 82-83*
PALINET & Union Library Catalogue of Pennsylvania - Philadelphia, PA - *EISS 83; InfIndMarPl 83*
Palisade Tribune - Palisade, CO - *BaconPubCkNews 84; Ed&PubIntYB 82*

Palisades Advertising & Marketing - Pacific Palisades, CA - *DirMarMP 83*
Palisades-Malibu News - Malibu, CA - *Ed&PubIntYB 82*
Palisades-Malibu News [of Santa Monica United Western Newspapers Inc.] - Santa Monica, CA - *AyerDirPub 83; NewsDir 84*
Palisades Park Bergen Bulletin - Palisades Park, NJ - *BaconPubCkNews 84; NewsDir 84*
Palisades Park Bergen News - *See* Bergen News Publishing Corp.
Palisades Park Valley Bergen News - Palisades Park, NJ - *NewsDir 84*
Palisades Publishers - Pacific Palisades, CA - *LitMarPl 83, 84*
Palisades Wildlife Film Library - Los Angeles, CA - *AvMarPl 83*
Palisadian - Cliffside Park, NJ - *AyerDirPub 83*
Palisadian-Post [of Small Newspapers] - Pacific Palisades, CA - *AyerDirPub 83; Ed&PubIntYB 82; NewsDir 84*
Palladium-Item - Richmond, IN - *AyerDirPub 83; Ed&PubIntYB 82*
Palladium Publishing Co. - St. Joseph, MI - *BrCabYB 84*
Palladium-Times - Oswego, NY - *AyerDirPub 83; BaconPubCkNews 84; Ed&PubIntYB 82*
Pallas Photo Lab - Denver, CO - *AvMarPl 83*
Palm Advertiser - Palmyra, PA - *AyerDirPub 83*
Palm & Co. Inc., Charles - Bloomfield, CT - *ArtMar 84; StaDirAdAg 2-84*
Palm Beach County Labor News - West Palm Beach, FL - *NewsDir 84*
Palm Beach Daily News - Palm Beach, FL - *BaconPubCkNews 84; Ed&PubIntYB 82; NewsDir 84*
Palm Beach Gardens Town Crier - *See* Town Crier Newspapers
Palm Beach Life - Palm Beach, FL - *ArtMar 84; BaconPubCkMag 84; MagDir 84; WritMar 84*
Palm Beach Post - West Palm Beach, FL - *BaconPubCkNews 84; NewsBur 6*
Palm Beach Social Pictorial - Palm Beach, FL - *MagDir 84*
Palm Beach Times - West Palm Beach, FL - *BaconPubCkNews 84*
Palm Books - Antioch, CA - *ArtMar 84*
Palm Cable TV Inc. [of ITT Community Development Corp.] - Palm Coast, FL - *BrCabYB 84; Tel&CabFB 84C*
Palm Desert North Pennysaver - Mission Viejo, CA - *AyerDirPub 83*
Palm Desert Post - Palm Desert, CA - *BaconPubCkNews 84*
Palm Desert South Pennysaver - Mission Viejo, CA - *AyerDirPub 83*
Palm Harbor Herald [of The Tarpon Springs Herald Newspapers] - Tarpon Springs, FL - *NewsDir 84*
Palm Harbor Leader - Tarpon Springs, FL - *AyerDirPub 83; Ed&PubIntYB 82*
Palm Harbor Leader - *See* Leader Publishing
Palm Springs Desert Sun - Palm Springs, CA - *BaconPubCkNews 84*
Palm Springs Life - Palm Springs, CA - *BaconPubCkMag 84; MagDir 84*
Palm Springs North Pennysaver - Mission Viejo, CA - *AyerDirPub 83*
Palm Springs South Pennysaver - Mission Viejo, CA - *AyerDirPub 83*
Palmdale Antelope Valley Press - Palmdale, CA - *BaconPubCkNews 84; NewsDir 84*
Palmer Agency Inc., The Lynne - New York, NY - *LitMarPl 83, 84; MagIndMarPl 82-83*
Palmer Agency, The - San Diego, CA - *StaDirAdAg 2-84*
Palmer & Co., Shelton Leigh - New York, NY - *AvMarPl 83*
Palmer & Palmer - Hampton, IA - *MicrocomMPl 84*
Palmer Cablevision [of Palmer Communications Inc.] - Naples, FL - *BrCabYB 84; Tel&CabFB 84C*
Palmer Communications Inc. - Naples, FL - *Tel&CabFB 84C*
Palmer Communications Inc. - Des Moines, IA - *BrCabYB 84 p.D-305; CabTVFinDB 83; Tel&CabFB 84C p.1696, 84S*
Palmer Co., A. N. - Schaumburg, IL - *BoPubDir 4, 5*
Palmer Enterprises - Orangevale, CA - *BoPubDir 4 Sup, 5*
Palmer Films, W. A. - San Francisco, CA - *AvMarPl 83*
Palmer Frontiersman - Palmer, AK - *BaconPubCkNews 84*
Palmer Inc., R. J. - New York, NY - *StaDirAdAg 2-84*
Palmer Journal - Palmer, NE - *BaconPubCkNews 84; Ed&PubIntYB 82*
Palmer Journal Register [of Palmer Pioneer Enterprises Inc.] - Palmer, MA - *Ed&PubIntYB 82; NewsDir 84*
Palmer Mutual Telephone Co. - Palmer, IA - *TelDir&BG 83-84*
Palmer Newspapers - Camden, AR - *Ed&PubIntYB 82*
Palmer Paper Co. - Houston, TX - *MagIndMarPl 82-83*
Palmer Photo Agency Inc., Nancy - Bantam, CT - *LitMarPl 84*
Palmer Photo Agency Inc., Nancy - New York, NY - *LitMarPl 83; MagIndMarPl 82-83*
Palmer/Pletsch Associates - Portland, OR - *BoPubDir 4, 5*
Palmer Publications Inc. - Sussex, WI - *LitMag&SmPr 83-84*
Palmer Publishers, J. - Manchester, NH - *BoPubDir 4, 5*
Palmer Record - *See* Record Publishing Co.
Palmer, Robert J. - Jamaica, NY - *LitMarPl 83*
Palmer, Robert J. - New York, NY - *LitMarPl 84*
Palmer Rustler - Ennis, TX - *AyerDirPub 83*
Palmer Rustler - Palmer, TX - *Ed&PubIntYB 82*
Palmer Rustler - *See* United Publishing Co. Inc.
Palmer State Line Shopping Guide [of Palmer Pioneer Enterprises Inc.] - Palmer, MA - *NewsDir 84*
Palmerston Observer - Palmerston, ON, Canada - *Ed&PubIntYB 82*
Palmerton - *See* Dawn Productions Ltd.
Palmerton Telephone Co. - Palmerton, PA - *TelDir&BG 83-84*
Palmetto Cable TV - Palmetto, FL - *BrCabYB 84*
Palmetto Cable TV - Ft. Mill, SC - *BrCabYB 84; Tel&CabFB 84C*
Palmetto Cable TV Inc. - Rock Hill, SC - *Tel&CabFB 84C p.1696*
Palmetto Piper [of R. L. Bryan Co.] - Columbia, SC - *BaconPubCkMag 84; MagDir 84*
Palmetto Press, The - Palmetto, FL - *Ed&PubIntYB 82*
Palmetto Rural Telephone Cooperative Inc. - Walterboro, SC - *TelDir&BG 83-84*
Palmyra Courier-Journal [of Timesaver Advertising Inc.] - Palmyra, NY - *BaconPubCkNews 84; NewsDir 84*
Palmyra Enterprise - Palmyra, WI - *BaconPubCkNews 84; Ed&PubIntYB 82*
Palmyra Northwestern News - Palmyra, IL - *BaconPubCkNews 84*
Palmyra Spectator - Palmyra, MO - *BaconPubCkNews 84; Ed&PubIntYB 82; NewsDir 84*
Palo Altan - Palo Alto, CA - *Ed&PubIntYB 82*
Palo Alto Jazz Records - Palo Alto, CA - *BillIntBG 83-84*
Palo Alto Peninsula Times Tribune [of Peninsula Newspapers Inc.] - Palo Alto, CA - *NewsDir 84*
Palo Alto Reminder - Emmetsburg, IA - *AyerDirPub 83*
Palo Alto Suburban American - Oakland, CA - *Ed&PubIntYB 82*
Palo Alto Weekly - Palo Alto, CA - *LitMarPl 83, 84*
Palo Cooperative Telephone Association - Palo, IA - *TelDir&BG 83-84*
Palo Pinto Cable TV - Palo Pinto, TX - *BrCabYB 84; Tel&CabFB 84C*
Palo Pinto County Star - Mineral Wells, TX - *AyerDirPub 83; Ed&PubIntYB 82*
Palo Pinto Telephone Co. [Aff. of United Telephone Co. of Texas Inc.] - Tyler, TX - *TelDir&BG 83-84*
Palo Publishing - Palo Alto, CA - *BillIntBG 83-84*
Palo Verde Valley Times - Blythe, CA - *AyerDirPub 83; Ed&PubIntYB 82*
Palomar Books - Palmdale, CA - *BoPubDir 4, 5*
Palomar Broadcasters Corp. - Encino, CA - *BrCabYB 84*
Palomar Records - Santa Monica, CA - *BillIntBG 83-84*
Palomino Horses - Mineral Wells, TX - *MagDir 84*
Palomino Press - Briarwood, NY - *BoPubDir 5*
Palos Citizen [of Southwest Messenger Newspapers] - Midlothian, IL - *AyerDirPub 83; NewsDir 84*
Palos Citizen - Palos Hills, IL - *Ed&PubIntYB 82*
Palos Citizen - *See* Southwest Messenger Newspapers
Palos Heights Regional News - Palos Heights, IL - *BaconPubCkNews 84*
Palos Heights Star Herald - Palos Heights, IL - *AyerDirPub 83*
Palos Park Star Herald - Palos Park, IL - *AyerDirPub 83*
Palos Southtown Economist - Chicago, IL - *AyerDirPub 83*
Palos Southtown Economist - *See* Southtown Economist Inc.
Palos Star-Herald - Chicago Heights, IL - *NewsDir 84*
Palos Star-Herald - Palos, IL - *Ed&PubIntYB 82*

Palos Star-Herald - *See* Star Publications
Palos Verdes Book Co. - Lomita, CA - *BoPubDir 4, 5*
Palos Verdes Learning Center - Palos Verdes Estates, CA - *MicrocomMPl 84*
Palos Verdes Peninsula Breeze - *See* Breeze Newspapers
Palos Verdes Peninsula Cable Communications [of Times Mirror Cable TV] - Palos Verdes Peninsula, CA - *Tel&CabFB 84C*
Palos Verdes Peninsula News - Palos Verdes Peninsula, CA - *BaconPubCkNews 84; Ed&PubIntYB 82; NewsDir 84*
Palouse Empire News - Pullman, WA - *BaconPubCkNews 84; Ed&PubIntYB 82*
Palouse Shopper - Latah County, ID - *Ed&PubIntYB 82*
Palouse Shopper [of News Review Publishing Co. Inc.] - Moscow, ID - *NewsDir 84*
Palouse Whitman Latah Record - Palouse, WA - *BaconPubCkNews 84*
Palshaw Measurement Inc. - Greens Farms, CT - *IntDirMarRes 83*
Paluszek & Leslie Associates Inc. - New York, NY - *DirPRFirms 83*
Pam Music - *See* Ralph's Radio Music
Pamco Electronics Inc. - Austin, TX - *DataDirSup 7-83*
Pampa News [of Freedom Newspapers] - Pampa, TX - *BaconPubCkNews 84; NewsDir 84*
Pan-African Documentation & Information System [of Economic Commission for Africa] - Addis Ababa, Ethiopia - *EISS 83*
Pan Am Clipper [of East/West Network Inc.] - New York, NY - *BaconPubCkMag 84; MagDir 84; WritMar 84*
Pan Am Clipper Cargo - Jamaica, NY - *MagIndMarPl 82-83*
Pan American Broadcasting Co. - New York, NY - *TelAl 83, 84*
Pan American Business Systems - Cincinnati, OH - *DirInfWP 82*
Pan American Electronics - Mission, TX - *MicrocomMPl 84*
Pan American Navigation Service Inc. - Van Nuys, CA - *LitMarPl 83, 84*
Pan-American Publishing Co. - Las Vegas, NM - *BoPubDir 4, 5*
Pan American Records Inc. - Chicago, IL - *BillIntBG 83-84*
Pan American Review [of Wade Press] - Edinburg, TX - *LitMag&SmPr 83-84*
Pan American Travel Guide - New York, NY - *DirOnDB Spring 84*
Pan Asia News Ltd. - Karachi, Pakistan - *ProGuPRSer 4*
Pan Audiovisual Ltd. - Dublin, Ireland - *ArtMar 84*
Pan European Survey [of Interactive Market Systems Inc.] - New York, NY - *DataDirOnSer 84*
Pan European Survey [of Research Services Ltd.] - Wembley, England - *DirOnDB Spring 84; EISS 83*
Pan-Eval Data Inc. - *See* SPAR Inc.
Pan Industries, Peter - Newark, NJ - *AvMarPl 83; BillIntBG 83-84*
Pan Oklahoma Communications Inc. - Oklahoma City, OK - *BrCabYB 84*
Pan Pacific & Low Ball Cable Television of Emeryville - Emeryville, CA - *BrCabYB 84*
Pan Productions - Coronado, CA - *BoPubDir 4, 5*
Pan, Richard - New York, NY - *MagIndMarPl 82-83*
Pana News-Palladium - Pana, IL - *BaconPubCkNews 84; NewsDir 84*
Panache Books - Sunderland, MA - *LitMag&SmPr 83-84*
Panache Inc. - Sunderland, MA - *BoPubDir 4, 5*
Panadero Latinoamericano - Chicago, IL - *BaconPubCkMag 84*
Panafax Corp. - Woodbury, NY - *DirInfWP 82*
Panama City Beach Cablevision Inc. [of Jones Intercable Inc.] - Panama City Beach, FL - *Tel&CabFB 84C*
Panama City Junior Service League - Panama City, FL - *BoPubDir 4 Sup, 5*
Panama City News Herald [of Freedom Newspapers Inc.] - Panama City, FL - *BaconPubCkNews 84; NewsDir 84*
Panasonic Co. [Subs. of Matsushita Electric Inc.] - Secaucus, NJ - *DataDirSup 7-83; DirInfWP 82; MicrocomMPl 84; VideoDir 82-83; WhoWMicrocom 83*
Panasonic Co. (Consumer Electronic Group) - Secaucus, NJ - *BillIntBG 83-84*
Panatec Inc. - Garden Grove, CA - *MicrocomMPl 83; WhoWMicrocom 83*
Pancake Press - San Francisco, CA - *BoPubDir 4, 5; LitMag&SmPr 83-84*
Panda Computers Inc. - Brooklyn, NY - *MicrocomMPl 84*
Panda Programs/Books - Brea, CA - *BoPubDir 4, 5*
Pandemonium Press - Encinitas, CA - *LitMag&SmPr 83-84*
Pandora [of Sproing Books] - Tampa, FL - *LitMag&SmPr 83-84*
Pandora [of Empire Books] - Murray, KY - *WritMar 84*
Pandora Music - Westover, WV - *BillIntBG 83-84*
Pandora Publishing Ltd. - Victoria, BC, Canada - *BoPubDir 4, 5*
Pandora Times - Pandora, OH - *Ed&PubIntYB 82*
Pandora Times - *See* Ohioprint Publications Inc.
Panel Concepts Inc. - Santa Ana, CA - *DirInfWP 82*
Panel Opinions Inc. - Needham, MA - *IntDirMarRes 83*
Panel Publishers [Subs. of Cantor, Fitzgerald Group Ltd.] - Greenvale, NY - *BoPubDir 4, 5; DirMarMP 83*
Pangloss Papers [of Pangloss Press] - Los Angeles, CA - *LitMag&SmPr 83-84*
Pangloss Press - Los Angeles, CA - *LitMag&SmPr 83-84*
Panhandle Cablevision - Bonifay, FL - *Tel&CabFB 84C*
Panhandle Cablevision - Abernathy, TX - *BrCabYB 84*
Panhandle Cablevision - Hale Center, TX - *BrCabYB 84*
Panhandle Herald - Panhandle, TX - *BaconPubCkNews 84; Ed&PubIntYB 82*
Panhandle Press - Farmersville, IL - *AyerDirPub 83; Ed&PubIntYB 82*
Panhandle Press [of Buckeye Publishing Co.] - Chester, WV - *AyerDirPub 83; Ed&PubIntYB 82; NewsDir 84*
Panhandle Telephone Cooperative Inc. - Guymon, OK - *TelDir&BG 83-84*
Panhandle TV & Cable Co. - Augusta, WV - *Tel&CabFB 84C*
Panhandle TV & Cable Co. - Shanks, WV - *BrCabYB 84*
Panhandler, The - Pensacola, FL - *LitMag&SmPr 83-84*
Panitch Field Service Inc. - Washington, DC - *IntDirMarRes 83*
Panjab - Toronto, ON, Canada - *Ed&PubIntYB 82*
Panjandrum Books - Los Angeles, CA - *LitMag&SmPr 83-84; LitMarPl 83, 84*
Panjandrum Poetry Journal [of Panjandrum Books] - Los Angeles, CA - *LitMag&SmPr 83-84*
Pannell Kerr Forster - Houston, TX - *BoPubDir 4 Sup, 5*
Pannonia Books - Toronto, ON, Canada - *LitMarPl 83, 84*
Panola County Post - Carthage, TX - *Ed&PubIntYB 82*
Panola Watchman - Carthage, TX - *AyerDirPub 83; Ed&PubIntYB 82*
Panolian, The - Batesville, MS - *AyerDirPub 83; Ed&PubIntYB 82*
Panopticum Press London - Upminster, England - *LitMag&SmPr 83-84*
Panora Cooperative Cablevision Association Inc. - Panora, IA - *BrCabYB 84; Tel&CabFB 84C*
Panora Cooperative Telephone Association Inc. - Panora, IA - *TelDir&BG 83-84*
Panora Guthrie County Vedette - Panora, IA - *BaconPubCkNews 84*
Panorama - Boston, MA - *BaconPubCkMag 84*
Panorama - Elizabeth, NJ - *Ed&PubIntYB 82*
Panorama - Don Mills, ON, Canada - *WritMar 84*
Panorama Cable Systems Ltd. - Invermere, BC, Canada - *BrCabYB 84*
Panorama Magazine - Rockford, IL - *MagDir 84*
Panorama Productions - Santa Clara, CA - *AvMarPl 83*
Panorama Publications Ltd. - Vancouver, BC, Canada - *BoPubDir 4 Sup, 5*
Panorama Publishers - Chewelah, WA - *BaconPubCkNews 84*
Panoramic Studios - Philadelphia, PA - *ArtMar 84*
Panquitch Garfield County News - *See* Richfield Reaper
Pansophic Systems Inc. - Oak Brook, IL - *ADAPSOMemDir 83-84; DataDirSup 7-83; EISS 83*
Pansophics Ltd. - Rockport, MA - *MicrocomMPl 83, 84*
Pantages Photos, Thomas M. - Gloucester, MA - *AvMarPl 83; LitMarPl 83, 84; MagIndMarPl 82-83*
Pantagraph - Bloomington, IL - *AyerDirPub 83; BaconPubCkNews 84*
Pantagraph - Edwardsville, IL - *LitMag&SmPr 83-84*
Pantagraph Printing - Bloomington, IL - *LitMarPl 83, 84; MagIndMarPl 82-83*
Pantego Sound - *See* Upstart Music
Pantheon Books [Div. of Random House Inc.] - New York, NY - *LitMarPl 83, 84; WritMar 84*
Pantheon Desert Publishing - Scottsdale, AZ - *BillIntBG 83-84*
Pantheon Desert Records - Scottsdale, AZ - *BillIntBG 83-84*

Pantheon Music International Inc. - New York, NY - *BillIntBG 83-84*
Pantheon Press - Fontana, CA - *LitMag&SmPr 83-84*
Panther Valley Service Inc. - Allamuchy, NJ - *BrCabYB 84; Tel&CabFB 84C*
Pantomime Pictures Inc. - North Hollywood, CA - *AvMarPl 83; Tel&CabFB 84C*
Panwar, R. S. - Houston, TX - *MicrocomMPl 84*
Paola Miami Republican [of Miami County Publishing Co.] - Paola, KS - *NewsDir 84*
Paola Republican - *See* Miami County Publishing Co.
Paola Western Spirit [of Miami County Publishing Co.] - Paola, KS - *NewsDir 84*
Paola Western Spirit - *See* Miami County Publishing Co.
Paoli News [of The Orange County Publishing Co. Inc.] - Paoli, IN - *Ed&PubIntYB 82; NewsDir 84*
Paoli News - *See* Orange County Publishing Co. Inc.
Paoli Republican [of The Orange County Publishing Co. Inc.] - Paoli, IN - *Ed&PubIntYB 82; NewsDir 84*
Paoli Republican - *See* Orange County Publishing Co. Inc.
Paolin & Sweeney - Cherry Hill, NJ - *AdAge 3-28-84; StaDirAdAg 2-84*
Paolucci Inc., B. - Larchmont, NY - *LitMarPl 83, 84; MagIndMarPl 82-83*
Paonia North Fork Times - Paonia, CO - *BaconPubCkNews 84*
Paonian-Herald - Paonia, CO - *AyerDirPub 83; Ed&PubIntYB 82; NewsDir 84*
Paper Age - Hillsdale, NJ - *BaconPubCkMag 84; MagDir 84; MagIndMarPl 82-83*
Paper Air [of Singing Horse Books] - Blue Bell, PA - *LitMag&SmPr 83-84*
Paper & Board, Printing & Packaging Industries Research Association - Surrey, England - *CompReadDB 82*
Paper & Pulp Data Bank [of Data Resources Inc.] - Lexington, MA - *DBBus 82*
Paper & Twine Journal - New York, NY - *BaconPubCkMag 84; MagDir 84*
Paper Corp. of United States [Div. of Unisource] - New York, NY - *LitMarPl 83, 84; MagIndMarPl 82-83*
Paper, Film & Foil Converter - Chicago, IL - *BaconPubCkMag 84; MagDir 84; MagIndMarPl 82-83*
Paper Manufacturers Co. - Philadelphia, PA - *DataDirSup 7-83*
Paper Merchants [Div. of Hammermill Paper Co.] - Philadelphia, PA - *LitMarPl 83, 84; MagIndMarPl 82-83*
Paper News [of Vanity Press] - New York, NY - *LitMag&SmPr 83-84*
Paper Sales - Duluth, MN - *BaconPubCkMag 84; MagDir 84*
Paper Sales Corp. - Darien, CT - *LitMarPl 83; MagIndMarPl 82-83*
Paper Sales Corp. - Norwalk, CT - *LitMarPl 84*
Paper Tape Drives [of GML Corp.] - Lexington, MA - *CompReadDB 82*
Paper, The - Sierra Vista, AZ - *AyerDirPub 83*
Paper, The - Sanger, CA - *AyerDirPub 83*
Paper, The - Milford, IN - *Ed&PubIntYB 82*
Paper, The - Wabash, IN - *AyerDirPub 83*
Paper Tiger Paperbacks Inc. - Gainesville, FL - *BoPubDir 4, 5*
Paper Trade Journal - New York, NY - *BaconPubCkMag 84; MagDir 84; MagIndMarPl 82-83; WritMar 84*
Paperback Press - Fairfield, NJ - *LitMarPl 83, 84*
Paperback Quarterly - Brownwood, TX - *LitMarPl 83*
Paperboard Packaging - New York, NY - *MagDir 84; MagIndMarPl 82-83*
Paperboard Packaging - Cleveland, OH - *BaconPubCkMag 84; WritMar 84*
Paperbook Press Inc., The - Westwood, MA - *LitMarPl 83, 84*
Paperchem [of Institute of Paper Chemistry] - Appleton, WI - *DataDirOnSer 84; DirOnDB Spring 84; OnBibDB 3*
Paperjacks Ltd. [Div. of General Publishing Co. Ltd.] - Markham, ON, Canada - *LitMarPl 83, 84*
Papert Cos., The - New York, NY - *LitMarPl 84*
Paperweight Press [Aff. of L. H. Selman Ltd.] - Santa Cruz, CA - *BoPubDir 4, 5; LitMag&SmPr 83-84*
Paperworker, The [of United Paperworkers International Union] - Nashville, TN - *MagIndMarPl 82-83; NewsDir 84*
Papillion Times - Papillion, NE - *BaconPubCkNews 84; Ed&PubIntYB 82; NewsDir 84*
Papillon Press - Carpinteria, CA - *BoPubDir 4, 5*
Papp, Joseph - New York, NY - *WritMar 84*
Pappas Telecasting Inc. - Fresno, CA - *BrCabYB 84; Tel&CabFB 84S*
PAPYRUS [of Direction de la Documentation Francaise] - Paris, France - *CompReadDB 82*
Papyrus Publishers - Yonkers, NY - *BoPubDir 4 Sup, 5; LitMag&SmPr 83-84*
Paquet, Clement - St. Sauveur des Monts, PQ, Canada - *BrCabYB 84*
PAR - *See* Product Acceptance & Research Inc.
Par Advertising Inc. - Minneapolis, MN - *StaDirAdAg 2-84*
Par Cable Inc. - Evansville, IN - *BrCabYB 84*
Par Cable Inc. - New York, NY - *Tel&CabFB 84C p.1696*
Par Cable of Ft. Campbell - Ft. Campbell, KY - *Tel&CabFB 84C*
Par Cable of K.I. Sawyer - Sawyer Air Force Base, MI - *BrCabYB 84*
Par Cable of Sumner County [of Par Cable Inc.] - Hendersonville, TN - *Tel&CabFB 84C*
Par Cable of Walkerton - Walkerton, IN - *Tel&CabFB 84C*
Par Communications Ltd. - New York, NY - *StaDirAdAg 2-84*
P.A.R. Inc. - Providence, RI - *WritMar 84*
Par-Troy Today - *See* Today Newspapers
Para Publishing - Santa Barbara, CA - *LitMag&SmPr 83-84; LitMarPl 83, 84*
Para Research - Gloucester, MA - *LitMarPl 84*
Para Research - Rockport, MA - *BoPubDir 4, 4 Sup, 5; LitMarPl 83; WritMar 84*
Parable Press - Amherst, MA - *BoPubDir 4, 5; LitMag&SmPr 83-84*
Parabola - New York, NY - *ArtMar 84; LitMag&SmPr 83-84; MagIndMarPl 82-83; WritMar 84*
Parabolic Press - Stanford, CA - *BoPubDir 4, 5*
Parabut Music Corp. - *See* Famous Music Corp.
Parachute Press Inc. - New York, NY - *LitMarPl 84*
Parachuting Resources Inc. - Richmond, IN - *BoPubDir 4*
Parachuting Resources Inc. - Dayton, OH - *BoPubDir 5; LitMag&SmPr 83-84*
Parachutist - Washington, DC - *MagIndMarPl 82-83*
Parachutist - Alexandria, VA - *BaconPubCkMag 84; LitMag&SmPr 83-84*
Paraclete Computer Corp. - New Milford, NJ - *MicrocomMPl 84*
Paraclete Press - Orleans, MA - *LitMarPl 84*
Parade [of Parade Publications Inc.] - New York, NY - *ArtMar 84; Folio 83; LitMarPl 83, 84; MagIndMarPl 82-83; NewsBur 6; WritMar 84*
Parade of Homes - Southfield, MI - *Ed&PubIntYB 82*
Parade Pictures - Hollywood, CA - *Tel&CabFB 84C*
Paradigm Consultants - Fremont, CA - *MicrocomMPl 84*
Paradigm Press - Osprey, FL - *EISS 5-84 Sup*
Paradise Hills/Bonita Pennysaver - Mission Viejo, CA - *AyerDirPub 83*
Paradise Post - Paradise, CA - *BaconPubCkNews 84; Ed&PubIntYB 82; NewsDir 84*
Paradise Press - Santa Monica, CA - *BoPubDir 4, 5; LitMag&SmPr 83-84*
Paradise Records Inc. - Hendersonville, TN - *BillIntBG 83-84*
Paradise Valley News-Progress - Scottsdale, AZ - *AyerDirPub 83*
Paradise Valley Progress - Phoenix, AZ - *Ed&PubIntYB 82*
Paradox Publishing Co. - Florissant, MO - *WritMar 84*
Paradyne Corp. - Largo, FL - *DataDirSup 7-83; Datamation 6-83; InfIndMarPl 83; Top100Al 83*
Paragold Records [Div. of Paragold Enterprises] - Lawton, OK - *BillIntBG 83-84*
Paragon Advertising - Florence, KY - *BrCabYB 84*
Paragon Advertising & Public Relations - Minneapolis, MN - *AdAge 3-28-84; StaDirAdAg 2-84*
Paragon/Benson Publishing Group - Nashville, TN - *BillIntBG 83-84*
Paragon Book Reprint Corp. - New York, NY - *BoPubDir 4, 5*
Paragon Music Corp. - *See* Paragon/Benson Publishing Group
Paragon Music Inc. - *See* Alexandria House Music
Paragon Productions - Denver, CO - *BoPubDir 4, 5*
Paragon Technology Corp. - Pacheco, CA - *DataDirSup 7-83*
Paragould Cablevision Inc. [of Adams-Russell Co. Inc.] - Paragould, AR - *BrCabYB 84; Tel&CabFB 84C*

Paragould Daily Press - Paragould, AR - *BaconPubCkNews 84; Ed&PubIntYB 82; NewsDir 84*
Paragram Sales - Vienna, VA - *DirInfWP 82*
Paragraph Press - Felton, CA - *BoPubDir 4, 5*
Parallax Studio - Stony Brook, NY - *AvMarPl 83*
Parallel Line Records - New York, NY - *BillIntBG 83-84*
Parallel Procedures Corp. - San Francisco, CA - *ADAPSOMemDir 83-84*
Parallel Publishers Ltd. - Vancouver, BC, Canada - *BoPubDir 4, 5*
Paralog - Stockholm, Sweden - *InfIndMarPl 83*
Parameters: Journal of the U.S. Army War College [of U.S. Army War College] - Carlisle Barracks, PA - *WritMar 84*
Parameters Unltd. - Albany, NY - *AvMarPl 83*
Parametrics Inc. - Wickford, RI - *MicrocomMPl 84*
Paramint Data Systems - Bakersfield, CA - *MicrocomMPl 84*
ParaMIS Corp. - Huntington Beach, CA - *MicrocomMPl 84*
Paramore, Felice - Los Angeles, CA - *MagIndMarPl 82-83*
Paramount Home Video - Hollywood, CA - *BillIntBG 83-84*
Paramount Journal - Paramount, CA - *BaconPubCkNews 84; Ed&PubIntYB 82*
Paramount Line Inc., The - Pawtucket, RI - *WritMar 84*
Paramount Music Corp. - *See* Famous Music Corp.
Paramount Pictures - New York, NY - *LitMarPl 83*
Paramount Television & Video Distribution Div. [of Paramount Pictures Corp.] - Hollywood, CA - *TelAl 83, 84*
Paramount Television & Video Distribution Div. [of Paramount Pictures Corp.] - New York, NY - *Tel&CabFB 84C*
Paramount Television Network Production - Hollywood, CA - *TelAl 83, 84; Tel&CabFB 84C*
Paramount-West Enterprises - Mira Loma, CA - *BillIntBG 83-84*
Paramus Post - *See* Ridgewood News Publishers
Paramus Sunday Post - Paramus, NJ - *NewsDir 84*
Paramus Town News South Inc. - Paramus, NJ - *NewsDir 84*
Paranoid Publications - Chicago, IL - *BoPubDir 4, 5*
Parant, Marcel - St. Justine, PQ, Canada - *BrCabYB 84*
Paraplegia News - Phoenix, AZ - *BaconPubCkMag 84; MagDir 84*
Parapsychology Foundation - New York, NY - *BoPubDir 4, 5*
Parapsychology Press [Aff. of Foundation for Research on the Nature of Man] - Durham, NC - *BoPubDir 4, 5*
ParaSac Music Corp. - *See* Famous Music Corp.
Parasitic Engineering - Albany, CA - *MicrocomMPl 83*
ParaTest Marketing Inc. - Eastchester, NY - *IntDirMarRes 83*
ParCable Inc. - New York, NY - *BrCabYB 84 p.D-305*
ParCable of Carmi - Carmi, IL - *BrCabYB 84*
ParCable of Forsyth - Gwinn, MI - *BrCabYB 84*
ParCable of Norris City - Norris City, IL - *BrCabYB 84*
ParCable of Sebree [of Matrix Vision of Robertson County Inc.] - Sebree, KY - *BrCabYB 84*
ParCable of Sumner County - Hendersonville, TN - *BrCabYB 84*
Parchment [of Woodrose Editions] - Waupaca, WI - *LitMag&SmPr 83-84*
Parchment Local 323 - Richland, MI - *NewsDir 84*
Parchment Press - Anoka, MN - *LitMag&SmPr 83-84*
Parchment Press - Chattanooga, TN - *BoPubDir 4, 5*
P.A.R.D. Bulletin [of Philadelphia Association of Retail Druggists] - Philadelphia, PA - *BaconPubCkMag 84; MagDir 84*
Pardeeville Mid-County Times - Pardeeville, WI - *BaconPubCkNews 84*
Parent Child Press - Altoona, PA - *BoPubDir 4, 5*
Parent Education Programs Press - Lubbock, TX - *BoPubDir 4, 5*
Parent, Marcel - St. Cyprien, PQ, Canada - *BrCabYB 84*
Parenting Press - Seattle, WA - *BoPubDir 4, 5; LitMag&SmPr 83-84*
Parent's Choice [of Parents' Choice Foundation] - Waban, MA - *ArtMar 84; BaconPubCkMag 84; MagDir 84; WritMar 84*
Parents for Peace - Ithaca, NY - *BoPubDir 4 Sup, 5*
Parents Magazine [of Gruner & Jahr USA Inc.] - New York, NY - *BaconPubCkMag 84; Folio 83; LitMarPl 83, 84; MagDir 84; MagIndMarPl 82-83; WritMar 84*
Parents Magazine Enterprises [Div. of Gruner & Jahr USA Inc.] - New York, NY - *DirMarMP 83; MagIndMarPl 82-83*
Parents' Magazine Enterprises (Children's Books Div.) - New York, NY - *ArtMar 84*
Parents Magazine Filmstrips - Mt. Kisco, NY - *AvMarPl 83*
Parents Magazine Press [Div. of Parents' Magazine Enterprises Inc.] - New York, NY - *LitMarPl 83, 84; WritMar 84*
Parents Magazine's Read Aloud & Easy Reading Program [Div. of Gruner & Jahr USA Inc.] - New York, NY - *LitMarPl 83, 84*
Parents Productions - San Francisco, CA - *WritMar 84*
Parex Business Journals - Worthington, OH - *WritMar 84*
Parey Scientific Publishers, Paul [Aff. of Paul Parey Verlagsbuchhandlung] - New York, NY - *BoPubDir 4, 5*
Parimco America Inc. - San Diego, CA - *LitMarPl 84*
Parimco Corp. - New York, NY - *LitMarPl 83, 84*
Parimco Products Inc. [of Paul R. McNaughton Co. Inc.] - New York, NY - *LitMarPl 83*
Parimist Funding Corp. - Jericho, NY - *DataDirSup 7-83*
Paris/Atlantic International Magazine of Poetry - Paris, France - *LitMag&SmPr 83-84*
Paris Beacon-News - Paris, IL - *BaconPubCkNews 84; Ed&PubIntYB 82; NewsDir 84*
Paris Cable Inc. - Paris, MO - *Tel&CabFB 84C*
Paris Cable TV Inc. [of Centel Cable Television Co.] - Paris, KY - *BrCabYB 84*
Paris Citizen-Advertiser - Paris, KY - *BaconPubCkNews 84*
Paris Enterprise [of Bourbon County Publishing] - Paris, KY - *BaconPubCkNews 84; NewsDir 84*
Paris Express-Progress - Paris, AR - *BaconPubCkNews 84; Ed&PubIntYB 82*
Paris Gestion Informatique [of Chambre de Commerce & d'Industrie de Paris] - Creteil, France - *InfIndMarPl 83*
Paris Lamar County Echo - Paris, TX - *BaconPubCkNews 84*
Paris Monroe County Appeal - Paris, MO - *BaconPubCkNews 84*
Paris News - Paris, TX - *BaconPubCkNews 84; Ed&PubIntYB 82; NewsDir 84*
Paris Post Intelligencer - Paris, TN - *BaconPubCkNews 84; Ed&PubIntYB 82; NewsDir 84*
Paris Records - North Hollywood, CA - *BillIntBG 83-84*
Paris Review - Flushing, NY - *LitMag&SmPr 83-84; LitMarPl 83, 84; MagIndMarPl 82-83; WritMar 84*
Paris Star - Paris, ON, Canada - *Ed&PubIntYB 82*
Parish Family Digest [of Our Sunday Visitor Inc.] - Huntington, IN - *WritMar 84*
Parish Mirror - Mexico, NY - *Ed&PubIntYB 82*
Parity - Washington, DC - *BaconPubCkMag 84*
Park Avenue Records - Seattle, WA - *BillIntBG 83-84*
Park Avenue Social Review - New York, NY - *MagDir 84*
Park Broadcasting Inc. - Ithaca, NY - *KnowInd 83; Tel&CabFB 84S*
Park Cities Cable TV [of Sammons Communications Inc.] - Dallas, TX - *BrCabYB 84*
Park Cities Cable TV [of Sammons Communications Inc.] - University Park, TX - *InterCabHB 3; Tel&CabFB 84C*
Park Cities News - Dallas, TX - *AyerDirPub 83; Ed&PubIntYB 82*
Park City Daily News - Bowling Green, KY - *Ed&PubIntYB 82*
Park Communications - Ithaca, NY - *AdAge 6-28-84; BrCabYB 84*
Park East - New York, NY - *LitMarPl 83, 84*
Park Falls Herald - Park Falls, WI - *BaconPubCkNews 84; Ed&PubIntYB 82; NewsDir 84*
Park Forest Star - Chicago Heights, IL - *NewsDir 84*
Park Forest Star - Park Forest, IL - *AyerDirPub 83; Ed&PubIntYB 82*
Park Forest Star - *See* Star Publications
Park J. Tunes [Div. of Northcoast Entertainment] - Waterville, OH - *BillIntBG 83-84*
Park Maintenance [of Madisen Publishing Div.] - Appleton, WI - *BaconPubCkMag 84; MagDir 84; MagIndMarPl 82-83*
Park Newspapers Inc. - Ithaca, NY - *Ed&PubIntYB 82*
Park Newspapers Inc. - *See* Park Broadcasting Inc.
Park Place Group Inc. - New York, NY - *StaDirAdAg 2-84*
Park Publishing Inc. - St. Paul, MN - *BoPubDir 4, 5*
Park Rapids Enterprise - Park Rapids, MN - *BaconPubCkNews 84; Ed&PubIntYB 82; NewsDir 84*
Park Record - Park City, UT - *Ed&PubIntYB 82*
Park Region Mutual Telephone Co. - Underwood, MN - *TelDir&BG 83-84*
Park Ridge Advocate [of Pioneer Press Inc.] - Park Ridge, IL - *Ed&PubIntYB 82; NewsDir 84*
Park Ridge Advocate - Wilmette, IL - *AyerDirPub 83*
Park Ridge Advocate - *See* Pioneer Press Inc.

Park Ridge Herald [of Des Plaines Publishing Co.] - Park Ridge, IL - *Ed&PubIntYB 82; NewsDir 84*
Park Ridge Herald - *See* Des Plaines Publishing Co.
Park River Walsh County Press - Park River, ND - *BaconPubCkNews 84; NewsDir 84*
Park, S. H. - Trenton, NJ - *BoPubDir 4, 5*
Park South Presentations Ltd. - New York, NY - *ArtMar 84*
Park, The - Mission Viejo, CA - *AyerDirPub 83*
Parkchester News - Bronx, NY - *Ed&PubIntYB 82; NewsDir 84*
Parkchester News - New York, NY - *AyerDirPub 83*
Parkdale TV Cooperative Inc. - Parkdale, OR - *BrCabYB 84; Tel&CabFB 84C*
Parke County Cablevision Inc. - Rockville, IN - *Tel&CabFB 84C*
Parke County Sentinel - Rockville, IN - *AyerDirPub 83; Ed&PubIntYB 82*
Parke-Randall Co. - Hollywood, CA - *WhoWMicrocom 83*
Parker Advertising Co., The - Dayton, OH - *StaDirAdAg 2-84*
Parker & Son Publications Inc. - Los Angeles, CA - *DirMarMP 83; LitMarPl 83, 84*
Parker Associates Inc., Richard - San Francisco, CA - *DirMarMP 83*
Parker Brothers Publishing - Beverly, MA - *LitMarPl 84*
Parker, Carl Allen - Port Arthur, TX - *Tel&CabFB 84C p.1696*
Parker Communications Inc. - Minneapolis, MN - *BrCabYB 84*
Parker Computer Systems - Ft. Worth, TX - *MicrocomMPl 83, 84; WhoWMicrocom 83*
Parker County News - Weatherford, TX - *Ed&PubIntYB 82*
Parker, D. C. - Springfield, IL - *BoPubDir 5*
Parker, Dorothy - Bridgewater, CT - *LitMarPl 83*
Parker Douglas County Press - Parker, CO - *Ed&PubIntYB 82*
Parker Films, Kit [Div. of Kit Parker Inc.] - Monterey, CA - *AvMarPl 83*
Parker Interviewing Service Inc., Iris - Birmingham, AL - *IntDirMarRes 83*
Parker New Era - Parker, SD - *BaconPubCkNews 84*
Parker News-Press - Castle Rock, CO - *AyerDirPub 83*
Parker Pioneer - Parker, AZ - *BaconPubCkNews 84; Ed&PubIntYB 82; NewsDir 84*
Parker Publishing Co. [Subs. of Prentice-Hall Inc.] - Englewood Cliffs, NJ - *LitMarPl 83*
Parker Publishing Co. - West Nyack, NY - *WritMar 84*
Parker-Scott Inc. - New York, NY - *ADAPSOMemDir 83-84*
Parker/Studio Three, Robert B. - Corning, NY - *MagIndMarPl 82-83*
Parker Television Productions Inc., Tom - Tarzana, CA - *AvMarPl 83; TelAl 83, 84*
Parker Theatrical Productions Inc., Tom - Tarzana, CA - *Tel&CabFB 84C*
Parker, Willox, Fairchild & Campbell Advertising Inc. - Saginaw, MI - *ArtMar 84*
Parker, Willox, Fairchild & Campbell Advertising Inc. - *See* Common Sense Communications Inc.
Parkers Prairie Independent - Parkers Prairie, MN - *BaconPubCkNews 84*
Parkersburg Eclipse-News-Review - Parkersburg, IA - *BaconPubCkNews 84; Ed&PubIntYB 82*
Parkersburg News [of Ogden Newspapers Inc.] - Parkersburg, WV - *BaconPubCkNews 84; Ed&PubIntYB 82; NewsDir 84*
Parkersburg Sentinel - Parkersburg, WV - *BaconPubCkNews 84; Ed&PubIntYB 82*
Parkes Catalogue of Radio Sources [of Australian National Radio Astronomy Observatory] - Parkes, Australia - *EISS 83*
Parkesburg Post - Parkesburg, PA - *BaconPubCkNews 84; Ed&PubIntYB 82*
Parkhurst Communications - New York, NY - *LitMarPl 84*
Parkhurst Press - Laguna Beach, CA - *BoPubDir 4, 5; LitMag&SmPr 83-84*
Parkin Cross County Times - Parkin, AR - *BaconPubCkNews 84*
Parking [of National Parking Association Inc.] - Washington, DC - *ArtMar 84; BaconPubCkMag 84; MagDir 84; MagIndMarPl 82-83; WritMar 84*
Parkland Enterprise - Dauphin, MB, Canada - *Ed&PubIntYB 82*
Parklander, The - Hinton, AB, Canada - *Ed&PubIntYB 82*
Parks & Recreation - Alexandria, VA - *BaconPubCkMag 84; MagDir 84*
Parks Music Corp. - *See* Kjos Music Co., Neil A.
Parks-Thompson Co. - St. Louis, MO - *BoPubDir 5*
Parkside Journal [of Los Angeles Meredith Newspapers] - Los Angeles, CA - *AyerDirPub 83; NewsDir 84*
Parkside Press Publishing Co. - Santa Ana, CA - *LitMag&SmPr 83-84*
Parkson Advertising Agency Inc. - New York, NY - *TelAl 83, 84*
Parkson Advertising Agency Inc. - *See* Ohlmeyer Advertising
Parkston Advance - Parkston, SD - *BaconPubCkNews 84; Ed&PubIntYB 82*
Parkston Cable TV - Parkston, SD - *BrCabYB 84; Tel&CabFB 84C*
Parksville-Qualicum Beach Progress - Parksville, BC, Canada - *Ed&PubIntYB 82*
Parkville Reporter - Baltimore, MD - *AyerDirPub 83*
Parkway Color Laboratories Inc. - Chicago, IL - *AvMarPl 83*
Parkway Press - Shawnee Mission, KS - *BoPubDir 5*
Parkway Press - Roslyn Heights, NY - *BoPubDir 5*
Parkway Transcript - Dedham, MA - *AyerDirPub 83; NewsDir 84*
Parkway Transcript - *See* Transcript Newspapers Inc.
Parliamentary Documentation & Information Printing Service - Paris, France - *EISS 7-83 Sup*
Parliamentary On-Line Information System [of House of Commons Library] - London, England - *EISS 83*
Parma News - Parma, MI - *Ed&PubIntYB 82*
Parma News - *See* Journal of Albion Publishers
Parma Review - Parma, ID - *BaconPubCkNews 84; Ed&PubIntYB 82*
Parma Sun Post [of Cleveland Sun Newspapers] - Cleveland, OH - *AyerDirPub 83; NewsDir 84*
Parma Sun Post - Parma, OH - *Ed&PubIntYB 82*
Parma Sun Post - *See* Sun Newspapers
Parnassos - New York, NY - *BoPubDir 4, 5; LitMag&SmPr 83-84*
Parnassus: Poetry in Review - New York, NY - *LitMag&SmPr 83-84*
Paroutaud, Mrs. Henri - Monterey, CA - *LitMarPl 83, 84; MagIndMarPl 82-83*
Parpinelli Tecnon SRL - Milan, Italy - *InfIndMarPl 83*
Parqueth, Carolyn - New York, NY - *MagIndMarPl 82-83*
Parr Associates, V. A. - New York, NY - *MagIndMarPl 82-83*
Parr Programming - Gary, IN - *MicrocomMPl 84*
Parr-X Corp. - Philadelphia, PA - *BillIntBG 83-84*
Parrot Communications - Brewster, NY - *Tel&CabFB 84C*
Parrott, Donald F. - Brandon, MB, Canada - *BoPubDir 4, 5*
Parry & Associates, David - Los Angeles, CA - *LitMarPl 83, 84*
Parry Associates, John - Mt. Pleasant, SC - *DirPRFirms 83*
Parry Sound Beacon - Parry Sound, ON, Canada - *Ed&PubIntYB 82*
Parsec Research - Fremont, CA - *MicrocomMPl 84*
Parshall Mountrail County Record - Parshall, ND - *BaconPubCkNews 84*
Parsippany Today [of Wayne Today Newspapers] - Wayne, NJ - *NewsDir 84*
Parsley Cable Co. - Lenore, WV - *Tel&CabFB 84C*
Parsley Cable Co. of Bias - Bias, WV - *BrCabYB 84; Tel&CabFB 84C*
Parsley Cable Co. of Crum - Crum, WV - *BrCabYB 84; Tel&CabFB 84C*
Parsley Cable Co. of Lenore - Oppy, KY - *Tel&CabFB 84C*
Parsley Cable Co. of Lenore - Lenore, WV - *BrCabYB 84*
Parsley Cable Co. of Marrowbone Creek - Marrowbone Creek, WV - *Tel&CabFB 84C*
Parsley Cable Co. of Marrowbone Creek - Williamson, WV - *BrCabYB 84*
Parsley Cable Co. of Rawl - Merrimac, WV - *BrCabYB 84*
Parsley Cable Co. of Sprigg - Sprigg, WV - *Tel&CabFB 84C*
Parsley Press - Shrewsbury, MA - *BoPubDir 5*
Parsley, Robert Lee - Williamson, WV - *Tel&CabFB 84C p.1696*
Parsons Advocate - Parsons, WV - *BaconPubCkNews 84; Ed&PubIntYB 82; NewsDir 84*
Parsons Cable TV [of The Essex Group] - Parsons, TN - *Tel&CabFB 84C*
Parsons, Friedmann & Central Inc. - Boston, MA - *StaDirAdAg 2-84*
Parsons News - Parsons, KS - *BaconPubCkNews 84; Ed&PubIntYB 82*

Parsons News-Leader - Parsons, TN - *BaconPubCkNews 84; Ed&PubIntYB 82; NewsDir 84*
Parsons Paper Div. [of NVF Co.] - Holyoke, MA - *MagIndMarPl 82-83*
Parsons, Sally J. - Chicago, IL - *MagIndMarPl 82-83*
Parsons Software - Parkersburg, WV - *MicrocomMPl 84*
Parsons Sun - Parsons, KS - *BaconPubCkNews 84; Ed&PubIntYB 82*
Parsons Sun - Warsaw, MO - *NewsDir 84*
Part-Ease Inc. - New Milford, NJ - *BoPubDir 5*
Parthenon Press - Nashville, TN - *LitMarPl 83, 84; MagIndMarPl 82-83*
Parthenon, The [of Marshall University] - Huntington, WV - *NewsDir 84*
Partial Publishing - San Francisco, CA - *LitMag&SmPr 83-84*
Participate [of Participation Systems Inc.] - Winchester, MA - *TeleSy&SerDir 2-84*
Participation Music Inc. - New York, NY - *BillIntBG 83-84*
Participation Systems Inc. - Winchester, MA - *InfoS 83-84*
Particle Science & Technology Information Service [of Loughborough University of Technology] - Loughborough, England - *EISS 83*
Particulate & Microbial Control - Santa Monica, CA - *BaconPubCkMag 84*
Partime Features - New York, NY - *Ed&PubIntYB 82*
Partington, Paul G. - Whittier, CA - *MicroMarPl 82-83*
Partisan Review - Boston, MA - *LitMag&SmPr 83-84; MagIndMarPl 82-83; WritMar 84*
Partner Press - Livonia, MI - *BoPubDir 4, 5*
Partners for Livable Places - Washington, DC - *BoPubDir 4 Sup, 5*
Partners in Publishing - Tulsa, OK - *BoPubDir 4, 5; LitMag&SmPr 83-84*
Partnership - Dallas, TX - *BoPubDir 4 Sup, 5*
Parton Catalogues, Dolly - *See* Tree International
Partridge Advertising Inc. - Minneapolis, MN - *StaDirAdAg 2-84*
Partridge Pair Inc. - Sandy Springs, SC - *BoPubDir 4, 5*
Partridge Publications of California - Beverly Hills, CA - *BoPubDir 4, 5*
Parts Pups - Atlanta, GA - *ArtMar 84*
Party Line Music - *See* Pickin' Post Publishing
Parvino, Marvin - Hughes Springs, TX - *Tel&CabFB 84C p.1696*
Parwest Ltd. - Chippenham, England - *MicrocomSwDir 1*
Paryzek Advertising & Public Relations, John F. - Aurora, OH - *DirPRFirms 83*
Parzych Publishing Inc., Cynthia - New York, NY - *LitMarPl 84*
Pasadena CATV Ltd. [of Harte-Hanks Communications Inc.] - Pasadena, TX - *Tel&CabFB 84C*
Pasadena Citizen - Pasadena, TX - *AyerDirPub 83; BaconPubCkNews 84; Ed&PubIntYB 82; NewsDir 84*
Pasadena Gazette - Pasadena, CA - *AyerDirPub 83*
Pasadena Gazette - *See* Hamm Publications Inc.
Pasadena Star-News - Pasadena, CA - *BaconPubCkNews 84; LitMarPl 83; NewsDir 84*
Pasadena Technology Press - Pasadena, CA - *MicrocomMPl 83, 84*
Pascack Valley Community Life - Westwood, NJ - *AyerDirPub 83; Ed&PubIntYB 82*
Pascack Valley News [of Westwood Pascack Valley Community Life] - Westwood, NJ - *AyerDirPub 83; NewsDir 84*
Pascack Valley News, The - Pascack Valley, NJ - *Ed&PubIntYB 82*
PASCAL [of Questel Inc.] - Washington, DC - *DataDirOnSer 84*
PASCAL [of Centre de Documentation Scientific et Technique] - Paris, France - *CompReadDB 82; DirOnDB Spring 84; OnBibDB 3*
PASCAL 101 (Information Science, Documentation) - *CompReadDB 82*
PASCAL 110 (Numerical Analysis, Computer Science, Automation, Operations Research) - *CompReadDB 82*
PASCAL 120 (Internal Geophysics, Astronomy, & Astrophysics) - *CompReadDB 82*
PASCAL 130 (Mathematical Physics, Optics, Acoustics, Mechanics, Heat) - *CompReadDB 82*
PASCAL 140 (Electrical Engineering) - *CompReadDB 82*
PASCAL 145 (Electronics) - *CompReadDB 82*
PASCAL 160 (Condensed State Physics) - *CompReadDB 82*
PASCAL 161 (Condensed State Structure, Crystallography) - *CompReadDB 82*
PASCAL 165 (Atoms & Molecules, Plasmas) - *CompReadDB 82*
PASCAL 166 (GAPHYOR Database) - *CompReadDB 82*
PASCAL 171 (General Chemistry & Physical Chemistry) - *CompReadDB 82*
PASCAL 172 (Analytical Chemistry) - *CompReadDB 82*
PASCAL 173 (Inorganic & Organic Chemistry) - *CompReadDB 82*
PASCAL 220 (Mineralogy, Geochemistry, Estraterrestrial Geology) - Orleans, France - *CompReadDB 82*
PASCAL 221 (Metallic & Non-Metallic Deposits, Mining Economics) - Orleans, France - *CompReadDB 82*
PASCAL 222 (Crystalline Rocks) - Orleans, France - *CompReadDB 82*
PASCAL 223 (Sedimentary Rocks & Marine Geology) - Orleans, France - *CompReadDB 82*
PASCAL 224 (Stratigraphy, Regional & General Geology) - Orleans, France - *CompReadDB 82*
PASCAL 225 (Tectonics) - Orleans, France - *CompReadDB 82*
PASCAL 226 (Hydrology, Engineering Geology, & Surface Formations) - Orleans, France - *CompReadDB 82*
PASCAL 227 (Paleontology) - Orleans, France - *CompReadDB 82*
PASCAL 310 (Biomedical Engineering, Biomedical Applications of Computer Science) - *CompReadDB 82*
PASCAL 320 (Biochemistry, Biophysics) - *CompReadDB 82*
PASCAL 330 (Pharmacological Science, Toxicology) - *CompReadDB 82*
PASCAL 340 (Microbiology, Virology, Immunology) - *CompReadDB 82*
PASCAL 346 (Ophthalmology) - *CompReadDB 82*
PASCAL 347 (Otorhinolaryngology, Stomatology, Pathology of the Face & Neck) - *CompReadDB 82*
PASCAL 348 (Dermatology, Venerology) - *CompReadDB 82*
PASCAL 349 (Anaesthesia, Resuscitation) - *CompReadDB 82*
PASCAL 352 (Diseases of the Respiratory Tract, Heart, & Blood Vessels) - *CompReadDB 82*
PASCAL 354 (Diseases of the Digestive Tract, Abdominal Surgery) - *CompReadDB 82*
PASCAL 355 (Diseases of the Kidneys & Urinary System, Surgery on the Urinary System) - *CompReadDB 82*
PASCAL 356 (Diseases of the Nervous System, Muscular Disorders, Neurosurgery) - *CompReadDB 82*
PASCAL 357 (Diseases of the Bones & Joints, Orthopaedic Surgery, Traumatology) - *CompReadDB 82*
PASCAL 359 (Diseases of the Blood) - *CompReadDB 82*
PASCAL 361 (Reproduction, Embryology, Endocrinology) - *CompReadDB 82*
PASCAL 362 (Diabetes, Metabolic Disorders) - *CompReadDB 82*
PASCAL 363 (Genetics) - *CompReadDB 82*
PASCAL 364 (Protozoa & Invertebrates, General & Applied Zoology) - Versailles, France - *CompReadDB 82*
PASCAL 365 (Zoology of Vertebrates, Animal Ecology, Applied Human Physiology) - *CompReadDB 82*
PASCAL 370 (Plant Biology & Physiology) - *CompReadDB 82*
PASCAL 380 (Food Stuffs) - *CompReadDB 82*
PASCAL 381 (Agricultural Science, Plant Production, Forestry) - Versailles, France - *CompReadDB 82*
PASCAL 390 (Psychology, Psychopathology, Psychiatry) - *CompReadDB 82*
PASCAL 730 (Fuels, Energy) - *CompReadDB 82*
PASCAL 740 (Metals, Metallurgy) - *CompReadDB 82*
PASCAL 745 (Welding, Brazing, etc.) - Paris, France - *CompReadDB 82*
PASCAL 761 (Electron Microscopy, Electronic Diffraction) - *CompReadDB 82*
PASCAL 780 (Polymers, Paints, Wood, Leather) - Paris, France - *CompReadDB 82*
PASCAL 880 (Chemical Engineering, Chemical & Parachemical Industries) - *CompReadDB 82*
PASCAL 885 (Pollution) - *CompReadDB 82*
PASCAL 891 (Mechanical Industries) - *CompReadDB 82*
PASCAL 892 (Building, Public Works, Transport) - *CompReadDB 82*
Pascal News - Cleveland, OH - *MicrocomMPl 84*
Pascal Publishers - Wellesley, MA - *BoPubDir 4, 5; LitMag&SmPr 83-84*

Pascal Translation Services Inc., Ivan - Wilmington, DE - *LitMarPl 83, 84; MagIndMarPl 82-83*
Pasco Cable [of Acton Corp.] - West Pasco, FL - *Tel&CabFB 84C*
Pasco Columbia Basin News - *See* Tribune Newspapers Inc.
Pasco-Kennewick-Richland Tri-City Herald [of McClatchy Newspapers] - Kennewick, WA - *NewsDir 84*
Pasco News - Dade City, FL - *AyerDirPub 83; Ed&PubIntYB 82*
Pasco Shopper - Dade City, FL - *AyerDirPub 83*
Pascoe Pty. Ltd., W & F - Milson's Point, Australia - *MicroMarPl 82-83*
Pascoe, Starling & Pollock Inc. - Seattle, WA - *TelAl 83, 84*
Pase Inc. - New Brunswick, NJ - *DirPRFirms 83*
Pasha Music Co. - *See* Grand Pasha Publisher, The
Pasha Publications - Arlington, VA - *BoPubDir 4 Sup, 5; DataDirOnSer 84; DirMarMP 83*
Paso Robles Country News - Paso Robles, CA - *AyerDirPub 83; Ed&PubIntYB 82*
Paso Robles Daily Press - Paso Robles, CA - *BaconPubCkNews 84; NewsDir 84*
Paso Robles North County Journal - Paso Robles, CA - *BaconPubCkNews 84*
Paso Sound Products Inc. - Pelham, NY - *AvMarPl 83*
Pass Christian Tarpon Beacon - Pass Christian, MS - *BaconPubCkNews 84*
Pass Herald Ltd., The - Blairmore, AB, Canada - *AyerDirPub 83; Ed&PubIntYB 82*
PASS Press [Aff. of PASS International] - New York, NY - *BoPubDir 4, 5*
Pass Promoter - Blairmore, AB, Canada - *AyerDirPub 83; Ed&PubIntYB 82*
Passage Publications Inc. - Chicago, IL - *BaconPubCkNews 84*
Passages Magazine - St. Paul, MN - *MagIndMarPl 82-83*
Passages North [of William Bonifas Fine Arts Center] - Escanaba, MI - *LitMag&SmPr 83-84; WritMar 84*
Passaic Citizen - Passaic, NJ - *BaconPubCkNews 84; Ed&PubIntYB 82; NewsDir 84*
Passaic Dateline Journal - Clifton, NJ - *BaconPubCkNews 84*
Passaic Herald-News - Passaic, NJ - *NewsDir 84*
Passaic Review - Passaic, NJ - *LitMag&SmPr 83-84*
Passaic Valley Independent Press - Summit, NJ - *BaconPubCkNews 84*
Passante Associates Inc., D. L. - Ft. Lee, NJ - *StaDirAdAg 2-84*
Passenger & Inflight Service [of International Publishing Co. of America] - Miami Springs, FL - *ArtMar 84; BaconPubCkMag 84; MagDir 84; MagIndMarPl 82-83*
Passenger Car [of Chase Econometrics/Interactive Data Corp.] - Waltham, MA - *DBBus 82*
Passenger Train Journal - Park Forest, IL - *BaconPubCkMag 84; MagDir 84*
Passenger Transport - Washington, DC - *BaconPubCkMag 84; MagDir 84*
Passin Productions, Jim - Chicago, IL - *AvMarPl 83*
Passive Solar Institute - Bascom, OH - *BoPubDir 4 Sup, 5; LitMag&SmPr 83-84*
Passive Solar News - Alexandria, VA - *BaconPubCkMag 84*
Passport [of Multinational Computer Models Inc.] - Montclair, NJ - *DataDirOnSer 84; DirOnDB Spring 84*
Passport Designs Inc. - Half Moon Bay, CA - *MicrocomMPl 84*
Passport Press - Moscow, VT - *BoPubDir 4, 5*
Past in Glass - Boulder City, NV - *BoPubDir 4, 5*
Pastarnack Associates Inc. - New York, NY - *ArtMar 84*
Pastoral Life [of Society of St. Paul] - Canfield, OH - *ArtMar 84; MagIndMarPl 82-83; WritMar 84*
P.A.T. Film Services Inc. - New York, NY - *TelAl 83, 84*
Pat Kennedy's Executive International Newsletter - Omaha, NE - *BaconPubCkMag 84*
Pata Group, The - Washington, DC - *EISS 5-84 Sup*
Pata Publications - Foresthill, CA - *BoPubDir 4 Sup, 5*
Patagonia Cable TV Co. - Patagonia, AZ - *BrCabYB 84; Tel&CabFB 84C*
Pataskala Standard - Pataskala, OH - *BaconPubCkNews 84; Ed&PubIntYB 82*
Patch & Frazzle Press [Aff. of The Boyd Co.] - Austin, TX - *BoPubDir 4, 5*
Patch as Patch Can - Port Washington, NY - *BoPubDir 5*
Patchen Brownfeld - Phoenix, AZ - *AdAge 3-28-84; StaDirAdAg 2-84*
Patchogue Long Island Advance - Patchogue, NY - *BaconPubCkNews 84; NewsDir 84*
Patchogue Main Street Press - Patchogue, NY - *BaconPubCkNews 84*
Patclass [of Pergamon International Information Corp.] - McLean, VA - *CompReadDB 82; DataDirOnSer 84; DirOnDB Spring 84*
Patdata [of Bibliographic Retrieval Services Inc.] - Latham, NY - *DataDirOnSer 84; DirOnDB Spring 84*
Patelson Music House Ltd., Joseph - New York, NY - *BillIntBG 83-84; BoPubDir 4, 5*
Patent & Trademark Review - New York, NY - *BaconPubCkMag 84; MagDir 84*
Patent Data Publications Inc. - Wheaton, IL - *BoPubDir 4, 5*
Patent Family Service/Patent Register Service - Vienna, Austria - *DirOnDB Spring 84*
Patent Office [of Dept. of Trade] - London, England - *InfIndMarPl 83*
Patent Trader - Mt. Kisco, NY - *AyerDirPub 83; BaconPubCkNews 84; Ed&PubIntYB 82*
Patents Documentation Services [of Derwent Publications Ltd.] - London, England - *EISS 83*
Patents Quarterly Digest & Index [of Bureau of National Affairs Inc.] - Washington, DC - *CompReadDB 82*
Paterson Associates Inc., Sid - Rego Park, NY - *StaDirAdAg 2-84*
Paterson News - Paterson, NJ - *BaconPubCkNews 84; NewsDir 84*
Paterson Productions Co. - West Hollywood, CA - *StaDirAdAg 2-84*
Path Press Inc. - Chicago, IL - *LitMag&SmPr 83-84; WritMar 84*
Pathe News Inc. - New York, NY - *TelAl 83, 84; Tel&CabFB 84C*
Pathe Pictures Inc. - New York, NY - *AvMarPl 83; Tel&CabFB 84C*
Pathelogical Corp., The - Beverly Hills, CA - *StaDirAdAg 2-84*
Pathescope Educational Media Inc. - Mt. Kisco, NY - *AvMarPl 83*
Pathfinder - Glenville, WV - *AyerDirPub 83*
Pathfinder Press - New York, NY - *LitMarPl 83, 84*
Pathfinder Press - Montreal, PQ, Canada - *BoPubDir 4 Sup, 5*
Pathfinder Publications Inc. - Madison, NJ - *BoPubDir 4 Sup, 5*
Pathfinders - Escondido, CA - *BoPubDir 4, 5*
Pathfinders Inc. - St. Petersburg, FL - *BillIntBG 83-84*
Pathologist - Skokie, IL - *BaconPubCkMag 84; MagDir 84*
Pathology Data System [of Case Western Reserve University] - Cleveland, OH - *EISS 83*
Pathway Books - Golden Valley, MN - *BoPubDir 4, 5; LitMag&SmPr 83-84*
Pathway Computers - Palo Alto, CA - *MicrocomMPl 84*
Pathway Press [Aff. of Church of God] - Cleveland, TN - *BoPubDir 4 Sup, 5*
Pathway Records - Matteson, IL - *BillIntBG 83-84*
Pathways [of Inky Trails Publications] - Middleton, ID - *LitMag&SmPr 83-84*
Pathways - Tulsa, OK - *MicrocomMPl 83, 84*
Pathways of Sound Inc. - Cambridge, MA - *BillIntBG 83-84*
Patient Care - Darien, CT - *MagDir 84; MagIndMarPl 82-83*
Patient Care Information System [of Datacare Inc.] - Roanoke, VA - *EISS 83*
Patient Information Library [Subs. of PAS Publishing] - Daly City, CA - *DirMarMP 83*
Patient Magazine [of American Health Publications] - Wausau, WI - *WritMar 84*
Patient Research Institute, The - Lansdale, PA - *IntDirMarRes 83*
Patio Publications - Buffalo Grove, IL - *BoPubDir 4 Sup, 5*
Patlaw [of The Bureau of National Affairs] - Washington, DC - *DataDirOnSer 84; DirOnDB Spring 84; EISS 83*
Patlis Advertising Agency Inc., Gerald - New York, NY - *AdAge 3-28-84; DirMarMP 83; MagIndMarPl 82-83; StaDirAdAg 2-84*
Patlow Publications Co. - Detroit, MI - *BillIntBG 83-84*
Patmos Press Inc. - Shepherdstown, WV - *BoPubDir 4, 5*
Paton & Associates - Kansas City, MO - *DirPRFirms 83*
Patri, Stella - San Francisco, CA - *LitMarPl 83, 84*
Patrice Press - Gerald, MO - *BoPubDir 4, 5*
Patricks & Associates - Rock Hill, SC - *Ed&PubIntYB 82*

Patriot - Waconia, MN - *AyerDirPub 83*
Patriot - Fulton, NY - *AyerDirPub 83*
Patriot [of Newhouse Newspapers] - Harrisburg, PA - *AyerDirPub 83; BaconPubCkNews 84; Ed&PubIntYB 82; LitMarPl 84; NewsBur 6; NewsDir 84*
Patriot - Kutztown, PA - *ArtMar 84; AyerDirPub 83; Ed&PubIntYB 82*
Patriot - Charlottetown, PE, Canada - *AyerDirPub 83*
Patriot & Free Press - Cuba, NY - *AyerDirPub 83*
Patriot-Citizen - Buena Vista, GA - *AyerDirPub 83*
Patriot Ledger [of Geo. W. Prescott Publishing Co. Inc.] - Quincy, MA - *AyerDirPub 83; BaconPubCkNews 84; Ed&PubIntYB 82; LitMarPl 83, 84; NewsDir 84*
Patriot-News - Harrisburg, PA - *AyerDirPub 83*
Patriot-Star & Grant County Journal - Medford, OK - *AyerDirPub 83*
Patriotic Education Inc. - Daytona Beach, FL - *BoPubDir 4, 5*
Patriotic Publishers [Aff. of Stephen Koschal Autographs] - Verona, NJ - *BoPubDir 5*
Pat's Cable TV - Lobelville, TN - *BrCabYB 84*
Pat's Cable TV Co. [of Pat's Mobilephone Inc.] - Linden, TN - *Tel&CabFB 84C*
Patsearch [of Pergamon International Information Corp.] - McLean, VA - *CompReadDB 82; DataDirOnSer 84; DirOnDB Spring 84*
Pattecky Music Publishers - College Park, MD - *BoPubDir 4, 5*
Patten Communications Corp. - Southfield, MI - *BrCabYB 84; StaDirAdAg 2-84*
Pattern Makers' Journal - Arlington, VA - *BaconPubCkMag 84*
Pattern Music - *See* Creative Music Group
Pattern Systems of New Jersey Inc. [Subs. of R. Shriver Associates] - Parsippany, NJ - *MicrocomSwDir 1; WhoWMicrocom 83*
Patterson Advertising Agency - Topeka, KS - *AdAge 3-28-84; StaDirAdAg 2-84*
Patterson & Associates, Jere - New York, NY - *HBIndAd&MS 82-83*
Patterson & Hall/The Film Works - Corte Madera, CA - *AvMarPl 83*
Patterson & Smith Inc. - Richmond, IN - *StaDirAdAg 2-84*
Patterson Cable TV [of TCA Cable TV Inc.] - Patterson, LA - *BrCabYB 84; Tel&CabFB 84C*
Patterson Communications - Jackson, MI - *LitMarPl 83*
Patterson Editorial Services - Ft. Worth, TX - *LitMarPl 83*
Patterson Irrigator - Patterson, CA - *BaconPubCkNews 84; Ed&PubIntYB 82*
Patterson, Kathleen J. - Hastings-on-Hudson, NY - *LitMarPl 83, 84*
Patterson Press, Eleanora - Putney, VT - *BoPubDir 5*
Patterson Pty. Ltd., George - *See* Bates Worldwide Inc., Ted
Patterson, Raymond L. - *See* Progressive Communications Inc.
Patterson, Richard E. - Virginia Beach, VA - *BoPubDir 4 Sup, 5*
Patterson Studios Inc. - Winter Haven, FL - *Tel&CabFB 84C*
Patterson's California Beverage Journal [of Wolfer Printing Co. Inc.] - Los Angeles, CA - *BaconPubCkMag 84; MagDir 84; WritMar 84*
Pattersonville Telephone Co. - Rotterdam Junction, NY - *TelDir&BG 83-84*
Pattis Group, The - Lincolnwood, IL - *MagIndMarPl 82-83*
Pattison, Myron - Crawfordsville, IN - *Tel&CabFB 84C p.1696*
Patton Consultants Inc. - Rochester, NY - *WhoWMicrocom 83*
Patton Union Press-Courier - Patton, PA - *BaconPubCkNews 84; Ed&PubIntYB 82*
Pattonsburg Call - Pattonsburg, MO - *BaconPubCkNews 84; Ed&PubIntYB 82*
Paubil Music Publishing Co. - Youngstown, OH - *BillIntBG 83-84*
Paul Advertising Agency Inc., Robert A. - Fairfield, CT - *StaDirAdAg 2-84*
Paul & Associates, Harry - Boston, MA - *StaDirAdAg 2-84*
Paul & Baum Inc. - Los Angeles, CA - *StaDirAdAg 2-84*
Paul, Ann Casselman - Keremeas, BC, Canada - *BoPubDir 4, 5*
Paul, Chris Hammill - Concord, MA - *LitMarPl 83, 84*
Paul, J. S. - Bakersfield, CA - *Ed&PubIntYB 82*
Paul, Margareta & David Mel - Washington, DC - *LitMarPl 83, 84; MagIndMarPl 82-83*
Paul Publishing Co. Inc./Budget Book Manufacturing Co., H. - San Diego, CA - *LitMarPl 84*
Paulding Neighbor - Marietta, GA - *AyerDirPub 83*
Paulding Neighbor - Paulding, GA - *Ed&PubIntYB 82*
Paulding Progress [of Delphos Herald Inc.] - Paulding, OH - *BaconPubCkNews 84; Ed&PubIntYB 82; NewsDir 84*
Paulette Publishing Co. - La Canada, CA - *BoPubDir 4, 5*
Paulist Communications - Los Angeles, CA - *AvMarPl 83*
Paulist Press - Ramsey, NJ - *LitMarPl 83, 84; WritMar 84*
Paulist Productions - Pacific Palisades, CA - *AvMarPl 83; Tel&CabFB 84C; WritMar 84*
Paullina Times - Paullina, IA - *BaconPubCkNews 84; Ed&PubIntYB 82*
Paulmar Inc. - Northbrook, IL - *AvMarPl 83*
Pauls Valley Democrat [of Donrey Media Group] - Pauls Valley, OK - *BaconPubCkNews 84; Ed&PubIntYB 82; NewsDir 84*
Paulsboro Record-Spirit - Blackwood, NJ - *BaconPubCkNews 84*
Paulsen Advertising Inc., Maurice - Sioux Falls, SD - *AdAge 3-28-84; StaDirAdAg 2-84*
Pauma Valley Cable TV Co. Inc. - Pauma Valley, CA - *Tel&CabFB 84C*
Paumalu Press - San Clemente, CA - *BoPubDir 4, 5*
Paunch - Buffalo, NY - *BoPubDir 4, 5; LitMag&SmPr 83-84*
Pauper Press Inc., Peter - New York, NY - *LitMarPl 84*
Pauper Press Inc., Peter - White Plains, NY - *LitMarPl 83*
PAUSA Records - Glendale, CA - *BillIntBG 83-84*
Pavan Publishers - Palo Alto, CA - *BoPubDir 4, 5*
Pavanne Music Co. - Franklin, TN - *BillIntBG 83-84*
Pavement - Iowa City, IA - *LitMag&SmPr 83-84*
Pavements & Soil Trafficability Information Analysis Center [of U.S. Army] - Vicksburg, MS - *EISS 83*
Pavese, Edith Messing - Brooklyn, NY - *LitMarPl 83, 84*
Pavlovian Journal of Biological Science, The [of J. B. Lippincott Co.] - Philadelphia, PA - *MagDir 84*
Paw Paw Courier-Leader [of Vineyard Press Inc.] - Paw Paw, MI - *NewsDir 84*
Paw Paw Lake Area Cable TV Co. [of Omega Communications] - Watervliet, MI - *BrCabYB 84; Tel&CabFB 84C*
Pawhuska Cable TV Services Inc. [of Communications Services Inc.] - Pawhuska, OK - *BrCabYB 84; Tel&CabFB 84C*
Pawhuska Journal-Capital [of Western Publishing Co.] - Pawhuska, OK - *BaconPubCkNews 84; Ed&PubIntYB 82; NewsDir 84*
Pawhuska Osage Journal News - Pawhuska, OK - *BaconPubCkNews 84*
Pawling News-Chronicle [of Housatonic Valley Publishing Co.] - Pawling, NY - *Ed&PubIntYB 82; NewsDir 84*
Pawling-Patterson News-Chronicle - Pawling, NY - *BaconPubCkNews 84*
Pawlus Associates, Bernard K. - Cincinnati, OH - *StaDirAdAg 2-84*
Pawn Review, The [of Calliope Press] - Austin, TX - *LitMag&SmPr 83-84*
Pawnee Chief - Pawnee, OK - *BaconPubCkNews 84; Ed&PubIntYB 82*
Pawnee City Pawnee Republican - Pawnee City, NE - *BaconPubCkNews 84*
Pawnee Post - Pawnee, IL - *Ed&PubIntYB 82*
Pawnee Post - *See* South County Publications
Pawnee Republican - Pawnee City, NE - *AyerDirPub 83; Ed&PubIntYB 82*
Pawson, John R. - Willow Grove, PA - *BoPubDir 4, 5*
Pawtuxet Valley Times - West Warwick, RI - *AyerDirPub 83; BaconPubCkNews 84; Ed&PubIntYB 82*
Paxson Advertising Inc., Carolin - El Paso, TX - *AdAge 3-28-84; StaDirAdAg 2-84*
Paxton Cablevision [of Combined Cable Corp.] - Paxton, IL - *Tel&CabFB 84C*
Paxton Community Antenna System Inc. - Paxton, IL - *BrCabYB 84*
Paxton Record - Paxton, IL - *BaconPubCkNews 84; Ed&PubIntYB 82; NewsDir 84*
Paxton Weekly Record - Paxton, IL - *BaconPubCkNews 84*
Pay Day Press - Scottsdale, AZ - *BoPubDir 4, 5*
Pay Dirt - Bisbee, AZ - *BaconPubCkMag 84; MagDir 84*
Pay Dirt Music - Atlanta, GA - *BillIntBG 83-84*

Pay-Fone Systems Inc. - West Los Angeles, CA - *ADAPSOMemDir 83-84*
Pay Per View Associates - Rolling Hills Estates, CA - *BrCabYB 84*
Pay Television Corp. - Manhasset, NY - *TelAl 83*
Pay TV Newsletter, The - Carmel, CA - *BaconPubCkMag 84*
Pay TV Services - Dunwoody, GA - *TelAl 83; Tel&CabFB 84C*
Paycock Press - Washington, DC - *BoPubDir 4, 5; LitMag&SmPr 83-84*
Payday - San Francisco, CA - *ADAPSOMemDir 83-84*
Payette, G. C. - Montreal, PQ, Canada - *BoPubDir 4, 5*
Payette Independent Enterprise - Payette, ID - *BaconPubCkNews 84*
Paymar, Dan - Costa Mesa, CA - *WhoWMicrocom 83*
Payment Systems Inc. - Atlanta, GA - *InterCabHB 3*
Payment Systems Newsletter - Tampa, FL - *BaconPubCkMag 84*
Payne Consultants Inc., Bruce - New York, NY - *DataDirSup 7-83*
Payne Publishing, Alex - Fallbrook, CA - *BoPubDir 4, 5; LitMag&SmPr 83-84*
Payne, Ross & Devins Advertising Inc. - Charlottesville, VA - *StaDirAdAg 2-84*
Payne Webber Jackson & Curtis Inc. - New York, NY - *DataDirOnSer 84*
Paynesville Press - Paynesville, MN - *BaconPubCkNews 84; Ed&PubIntYB 82*
Paynter & Associates, E. F. - Indianapolis, IN - *MicrocomMPl 84*
Payson Chronicle - Payson, UT - *BaconPubCkNews 84; Ed&PubIntYB 82*
Payson Roundup & Rim County News - Payson, AZ - *BaconPubCkNews 84; NewsDir 84*
Payson Roundup, The - Payson, AZ - *Ed&PubIntYB 82*
Payvision Communications Inc. - Shreveport, LA - *Tel&CabFB 84C*
Pazifische Rundschau - Blaine, WA - *Ed&PubIntYB 82; NewsDir 84*
Pazifische Rundschau - Vancouver, BC, Canada - *Ed&PubIntYB 82*
PB Consulting Service - New York, NY - *LitMarPl 83, 84*
PB Press - Dallas, TX - *ArtMar 84*
PBL Corp. - Wayzata, MN - *MicrocomMPl 84; MicrocomSwDir 1; WhoWMicrocom 83*
PBL Telecommunications Co. [of National Telecommunications Corp.] - Beverly Hills, CA - *BrCabYB 84*
PBL Telecommunications Co. - Lebanon, TN - *Tel&CabFB 84C*
PBM/STIRS - New York, NY - *DirOnDB Spring 84*
PBS Computing - St. Paul, MN - *ADAPSOMemDir 83-84; DataDirOnSer 84*
PBS Video [Div. of Public Broadcasting Service] - Washington, DC - *AvMarPl 83; Tel&CabFB 84C*
PBSoftware - Dayton, OH - *MicrocomMPl 84*
PC [of Ziff-Davis Publishing Co.] - New York, NY - *BaconPubCkMag 84; Folio 83; MicrocomMPl 84; WritMar 84*
PC Codex - Bedminister, PA - *MicrocomMPl 84*
PC Disk [of Ziff-Davis Publishing Co.] - New York, NY - *MicrocomMPl 84*
PC Innovations - Stanton, CA - *MicrocomSwDir 1*
PC News Watch - Andover, MA - *BaconPubCkMag 84*
PC Perspectives Newsletter [of Architecture Technology Corp.] - Minneapolis, MN - *BaconPubCkMag 84; MicrocomMPl 84*
PC Products - Boston, MA - *BaconPubCkMag 84*
P.C. Publishing Co. - Culloden, WV - *BaconPubCkNews 84*
PC Software of San Diego - San Diego, CA - *MicrocomMPl 84*
PC Tech Journal [of PC Tech Corp.] - Baltimore, MD - *BaconPubCkMag 84; MicrocomMPl 84*
PC Telemart [of PC Telemart Inc.] - Fairfax, VA - *DataDirOnSer 84*
PC2 - Sunnyvale, CA - *MicrocomMPl 84*
PC User, The - St. Clair Shores, MI - *BaconPubCkMag 84*
PC/W Advertising - Santa Fe Springs, CA - *StaDirAdAg 2-84*
PC Week - Newton, MA - *BaconPubCkMag 84*
PC World [of CW Communications Inc.] - San Francisco, CA - *BaconPubCkMag 84; Folio 83; MicrocomMPl 84; WritMar 84*
PCD Systems Inc. - Penn Yan, NY - *MicrocomMPl 83, 84; MicrocomSwDir 1; WhoWMicrocom 83*
PCI Journal [of Prestressed Concrete Institute] - Chicago, IL - *MagDir 84*
PCM: The Portable Computer Magazine [of Falsoft Inc.] - Prospect, KY - *MicrocomMPl 84*
PCN Inc. - Point Reyes, CA - *LitMag&SmPr 83-84*
PCNH Inc. [of Tele-Communications Inc.] - Hampton, NH - *Tel&CabFB 84C*
PCS Book Service [Div. of Paperback Catalog Service] - Putnam Valley, NY - *LitMarPl 83, 84*
PCS Data Processing Inc. - New York, NY - *ADAPSOMemDir 83-84; DataDirOnSer 84; LitMarPl 83, 84; MagIndMarPl 82-83*
PCS/Energy Data Base (API Monthly & Quarterly Drilling Reports) - Washington, DC - *DBBus 82*
PCS/Energy Data Base (API Weekly Statistical Bulletin) - Washington, DC - *DBBus 82*
PCS/Energy Data Base (DOE Energy Data Reports) - Washington, DC - *DBBus 82*
PCS/Energy Data Base (DOE Monthly Petroleum Statistics Report) - Washington, DC - *DBBus 82*
PCS/Energy Data Base (Electric Utility Information) - Washington, DC - *DBBus 82*
PCS/Energy Data Base (Federal Energy Data System) - Washington, DC - *DBBus 82*
PCS/Energy Data Base (Hughes Rig Count) - Houston, TX - *DBBus 82*
PCS/Energy Data Base (Joint Association Survey on Drilling Costs) - Washington, DC - *DBBus 82*
PCS/Energy Data Base (Reed Rock Bit Co. Rig Census) - Houston, TX - *DBBus 82*
PCS/Energy Data Base (State Energy Data System) - Washington, DC - *DBBus 82*
PCS/Spec - Washington, DC - *DBBus 82; DirOnDB Spring 84*
PCT & S Alumni Bulletin - Philadelphia, PA - *MagDir 84*
PCX - Lake Forest, CA - *MicrocomMPl 84*
PD - St. Louis, MO - *MagIndMarPl 82-83*
P.D. Cue - Lancaster, PA - *MagDir 84*
PD Review - Piscataway, NJ - *AyerDirPub 83*
PDA Engineering - Santa Ana, CA - *ADAPSOMemDir 83-84*
PDA Publishers - Mesa, AZ - *BoPubDir 5*
PDA Publishers - West Lafayette, IN - *BoPubDir 4*
PDQ [of International Cancer Research Data Bank] - Bethesda, MD - *DataDirOnSer 84; DirOnDB Spring 84*
PDQ - Arlington, VA - *MagDir 84*
PDQ Directory [of International Cancer Research Data Bank] - Bethesda, MD - *DataDirOnSer 84; DirOnDB Spring 84*
Pea Ridge Country Times - Northeast Benton County, AR - *Ed&PubIntYB 82*
Pea Ridge Country Times - Pea Ridge, AR - *BaconPubCkNews 84*
Peabody Gazette-Bulletin - Peabody, KS - *BaconPubCkNews 84; Ed&PubIntYB 82*
Peabody Museum of Salem - Salem, MA - *MagIndMarPl 82-83*
Peabody Museum Publications - Cambridge, MA - *LitMarPl 83, 84*
Peabody Reflector, The - Nashville, TN - *MagDir 84*
Peabody Times [of Essex County Newspapers] - Peabody, MA - *NewsDir 84*
Peace & Pieces Press [Aff. of San Francisco Arts & Letters] - San Francisco, CA - *BoPubDir 4, 5; LitMag&SmPr 83-84*
Peace Arch News, The - White Rock, BC, Canada - *AyerDirPub 83; Ed&PubIntYB 82*
Peace News For Non-Violent Revolution [of Russell Press] - Nottingham, England - *LitMag&SmPr 83-84*
Peace Newsletter, The [of Syracuse Peace Council] - Syracuse, NY - *LitMag&SmPr 83-84*
Peace on Earth Press - Kent, OH - *BoPubDir 5*
Peace Pipe Music - *See* Firedrum Music Publishers
Peace Press [Subs. of Citrus House Publishers] - Culver City, CA - *LitMag&SmPr 83-84; LitMarPl 83, 84*
Peace Research Abstracts [of Peace Research Institute-Dundas] - Dundas, ON, Canada - *EISS 83*
Peace Research Institute - Dundas, ON, Canada - *BoPubDir 4, 5*
Peace Research Laboratory - St. Louis, MO - *BoPubDir 4, 5*
Peace River Block News - Dawson Creek, BC, Canada - *AyerDirPub 83; Ed&PubIntYB 82*
Peace Translation & Clipping Services - Singapore, Singapore - *ProGuPRSer 4*
Peace Valley Telephone - Peace Valley, MO - *TelDir&BG 83-84*

Peaceable Music - Malibu, CA - *BillIntBG 83-84*
Peaceful Music Co. [Div. of Pacific Arts Corp. Inc.] - Carmel, CA - *BillIntBG 83-84*
Peacemaker - Greensboro, NC - *Ed&PubIntYB 82*
Peacework [of Weston Graphics] - Cambridge, MA - *LitMag&SmPr 83-84*
Peach Times - Martinsburg, WV - *BaconPubCkMag 84; MagDir 84*
Peach Tree - Monroeville, PA - *Ed&PubIntYB 82*
Peach Tree Shopping Guide/East - Monroeville, PA - *AyerDirPub 83*
Peach Tree South - Pittsburgh, PA - *AyerDirPub 83*
Peachtree Publishers Ltd. - Atlanta, GA - *LitMarPl 83, 84*
Peachtree Software [Subs. of Management Sciences of America] - Atlanta, GA - *DataDirSup 7-83; MicrocomMPl 83, 84; WhoWMicrocom 83*
Peachtree Software International Ltd. - Atlanta, GA - *MicrocomSwDir 1*
Peacock Enterprises - Nashua, NH - *MicrocomMPl 84*
Peacock Publishers Inc., F. E. - Itasca, IL - *LitMarPl 83, 84*
Peak - Boulder, CO - *MicrocomMPl 84*
Peak Delay Guide - Chesterfield, MO - *DataDirOnSer 84; DirOnDB Spring 84*
Peak Doll Enterprises - Colorado Springs, CO - *BoPubDir 4, 5*
Peak Productions Inc. - Winter Park, CO - *AvMarPl 83*
Peak Records USA - West Los Angeles, CA - *BillIntBG 83-84*
Peanut - New York, NY - *BaconPubCkMag 84*
Peanut Butter Publishing [Subs. of McGraw Mountain Inc.] - Mercer Island, WA - *LitMarPl 83, 84*
Peanut Farmer - Raleigh, NC - *BaconPubCkMag 84; MagDir 84*
Peanut Journal & Nut World - Suffolk, VA - *BaconPubCkMag 84; MagDir 84*
Pear Software [Div. of Multi Data Serv Corp.] - Ashland, OR - *MicrocomMPl 83, 84*
Pear Systems Corp. - Stamford, CT - *MicrocomMPl 83*
Pear Systems-Remote Computing Corp. - Roslyn, NY - *MicrocomSwDir 1*
Pearce, Ellen - Rolla, MO - *LitMarPl 83*
Pearisburg Virginian-Leader - Pearisburg, VA - *BaconPubCkNews 84*
Pearl City/Aiea Sun Press - Kaneohe, HI - *AyerDirPub 83*
Pearl City-Aiea Sun Press - Pearl City, HI - *Ed&PubIntYB 82*
Pearl Press - Portales, NM - *BoPubDir 4, 5*
Pearl Record Co. - Baltimore, MD - *BillIntBG 83-84*
Pearl-Win Publishing Co. - Hancock, WI - *BoPubDir 4, 5*
Pearland Journal - *See* Fig Leaf Publishing Co.
Pearland Sun Progress [of Alvin Newspapers Inc.] - Alvin, TX - *NewsDir 84*
Pearlman/Rowe/Kolomatsky - New York, NY - *AdAge 3-28-84; StaDirAdAg 2-84*
Pearlsoft [Div. of Relational Systems International Corp.] - Salem, OR - *MicrocomMPl 84; MicrocomSwDir 1*
Pearman Ltd., Alan - Mortlake Crescent, England - *MicrocomSwDir 1*
Pearsall Leader - Pearsall, TX - *Ed&PubIntYB 82*
Pearsall Leader - *See* Frio-Nueces Publications Ltd.
Pearson Advertising, John - Boston, MA - *HBIndAd&MS 82-83; StaDirAdAg 2-84*
Pearson Atkinson County Citizen - Pearson, GA - *BaconPubCkNews 84*
Pearson/Carchia Advertising - Edison, NJ - *StaDirAdAg 2-84*
Pearson Clarke & Sawyer Advertising & Public Relations - Lakeland, FL - *StaDirAdAg 2-84*
Pearson Enterprises Inc., Bob - Birmingham, AL - *BoPubDir 5*
Pearson International, John - Los Angeles, CA - *AvMarPl 83; TelAl 83, 84; Tel&CabFB 84C*
Pearson, J. Michael - Miami Beach, FL - *BoPubDir 4, 5*
Pearson Longman plc - New York, NY - *KnowInd 83*
Pearson, McGuire Associates - Coral Gables, FL - *DirPRFirms 83*
Pearson, Ralph E. - Austin, TX - *BoPubDir 4, 5*
Peat, Grace Sims - New York, NY - *LitMarPl 83*
Peat, Laurey & Associates - Dallas, TX - *DirPRFirms 83*
Peat, Marwick, Mitchell & Co. - New York, NY - *DirInfWP 82*
Pecan South - Atlanta, GA - *MagDir 84; WritMar 84*
Pecarry Press - Tucson, AZ - *BoPubDir 4, 5*
Pecatonica News [of North Central Associated Publishers] - Durand, IL - *AyerDirPub 83; NewsDir 84*
Pecatonica News - Pecatonica, IL - *Ed&PubIntYB 82*
Pecatonica News - *See* North Central Associated Publishers
Pecci Educational Publications [Aff. of Educational Book Distributors] - San Mateo, CA - *BoPubDir 4, 5*
Peck Bindery Inc. - New Haven, CT - *LitMarPl 83, 84; MagIndMarPl 82-83*
Peck Brothers Advertising - New Haven, CT - *StaDirAdAg 2-84*
Peck Magazine Agency, Walter - Galesburg, IL - *MagIndMarPl 82-83*
Peck Sims Mueller Inc. - Honolulu, HI - *StaDirAdAg 2-84*
Peck, Thomas B. Jr. - Germantown, MD - *LitMarPl 83, 84; MagIndMarPl 82-83*
Peckham Productions Inc. - White Plains, NY - *AvMarPl 83; TelAl 83, 84; Tel&CabFB 84C*
Pecos Enterprise [of Buckner News Alliance] - Pecos, TX - *BaconPubCkNews 84; Ed&PubIntYB 82; NewsDir 84*
Peddler's Wagon - Dowagiac, MI - *BoPubDir 4, 5*
Peden, Margaret Sayers - Columbia, MO - *LitMarPl 83, 84*
Pedersen Instruments - Walnut Creek, CA - *WhoWMicrocom 83*
Pederson, Herzog & Nee Inc. - Minneapolis, MN - *ArtMar 84; StaDirAdAg 2-84*
Pedestrian Research - Forest Hills, NY - *LitMag&SmPr 83-84*
Pediatric Annals - Thorofare, NJ - *MagDir 84; MagIndMarPl 82-83*
Pediatric News - Rockville, MD - *MagIndMarPl 82-83*
Pediatrics - Evanston, IL - *BaconPubCkMag 84; MagDir 84*
Pediatrics for Parents [of Pediatrics for Parents Inc.] - Bangor, ME - *WritMar 84*
Pedlar Press - Calgary, AB, Canada - *BoPubDir 4 Sup, 5*
Pedott Advertising & Marketing Inc., Joseph - San Francisco, CA - *StaDirAdAg 2-84*
Pedro Music Corp. - Westlake Village, CA - *BillIntBG 83-84*
Peduncle Enterprises Inc. - Springfield, VA - *BillIntBG 83-84*
Peebles Press International Inc. - New York, NY - *LitMarPl 83, 84*
Peek Publications - Sunnyvale, CA - *BoPubDir 4 Sup, 5*
Peek 65 - Owings Mills, MD - *MicrocomMPl 84*
Peek: The Journal of MicroAbstracts [of Environmental Services] - Morris Plains, NJ - *MicrocomMPl 84*
Peekner Literary Agency, Ray - Milwaukee, WI - *LitMarPl 83, 84*
Peekskill-Cortlandt-Putnam Valley Pennysaver - Yorktown Heights, NY - *AyerDirPub 83*
Peekskill Star - Peekskill, NY - *BaconPubCkNews 84; NewsDir 84*
Peelings II - Las Cruces, NM - *BaconPubCkMag 84; MicrocomMPl 84*
Peeples, Edwin A. - Phoenixville, PA - *BoPubDir 4, 5*
Peer-Southern Organization - New York, NY - *BillIntBG 83-84*
Peerless Engineering Service [Subs. of Peerless Land & Cattle Co.] - Soquel, CA - *MicrocomMPl 84; WhoWMicrocom 83*
Peerless Publications - Bethlehem, PA - *BaconPubCkNews 84*
Peerless Publishing Co. - New Orleans, LA - *BoPubDir 4, 5*
Peets Advertising Inc. - Jackson, MS - *StaDirAdAg 2-84*
Peetz Cooperative Telephone - Peetz, CO - *TelDir&BG 83-84*
Peg Music Co. - *See* Neverland Music Publishing Co.
Pegasus-Basis Software Inc. - Richardson, TX - *MicrocomMPl 84*
Pegasus Books/Press - Vashon, WA - *BoPubDir 5*
Pegasus Press - Van Nuys, CA - *BoPubDir 4 Sup, 5*
Pegasus Records - Dallas, TX - *BillIntBG 83-84*
Pegasus Review, The - Flanders, NJ - *LitMag&SmPr 83-84*
Pegasus Software Ltd. - Kettering, England - *MicrocomSwDir 1*
Peggy's Desk - New York, NY - *LitMarPl 83, 84*
Pegra Supply Co. - Old Tappan, NJ - *BoPubDir 4 Sup, 5*
Peguis Publishers Ltd. - Winnipeg, MB, Canada - *LitMarPl 83, 84*
Peimei News Inc., The - New York, NY - *Ed&PubIntYB 82*
Peitscher Associates Inc. - Chicago, IL - *DirPRFirms 83; StaDirAdAg 2-84*
Pejepscot Paper [Div. of The Hearst Corp.] - Brunswick, ME - *LitMarPl 83, 84*
Pejepscot Press - Brunswick, ME - *BoPubDir 4, 5*
Pekin Banner-Gazette - Pekin, IN - *BaconPubCkNews 84*
Pekin Daily Times [of Howard Publications] - Pekin, IL - *BaconPubCkNews 84; Ed&PubIntYB 82; NewsDir 84*
Pekin Today - Morton, IL - *AyerDirPub 83*

Pekin Today - Pekin, IL - *Ed&PubIntYB 82*
Pekin Today - *See* Tazewell Publishing Co.
Pel-Tek - Southampton, PA - *MicrocomMPl 84*
Pelham Journal - Pelham, GA - *BaconPubCkNews 84; Ed&PubIntYB 82; NewsDir 84*
Pelham Marketing Services - *See* Henderson Advertising Inc.
Pelham Sun - Pelham, NY - *AyerDirPub 83; BaconPubCkNews 84; Ed&PubIntYB 82*
Pelican Advertising & Publishing - Campbell, CA - *LitMag&SmPr 83-84*
Pelican Publishing Co. - Gretna, LA - *ArtMar 84; LitMarPl 83, 84; WritMar 84*
Pelican Rapids Press - Pelican Rapids, MN - *BaconPubCkNews 84; Ed&PubIntYB 82; NewsDir 84*
Pelican Telephone Co. - Pelican Rapids, MN - *TelDir&BG 83-84*
Pelikan Inc. [Subs. of Pelikan AG Podbielskistr] - Franklin, TN - *DataDirSup 7-83; MicrocomMPl 83; WhoWMicrocom 83*
Pelikan, Maria - Riverdale, NY - *LitMarPl 83, 84*
Peliperus Music Co. - Kansas City, MO - *BillIntBG 83-84*
Pell City St. Clair News-Aegis [of Bryan Publications] - Pell City, AL - *BaconPubCkNews 84; NewsDir 84*
Pell Studio - New York, NY - *LitMarPl 83, 84*
Pella Chronicle [of Marion County Publications Inc.] - Pella, IA - *BaconPubCkNews 84; Ed&PubIntYB 82; NewsDir 84*
Pella Publishing Co. - New York, NY - *BoPubDir 4, 5; LitMag&SmPr 83-84*
Pellechia, Tom [Div. of Cana Creation Inc.] - Brooklyn, NY - *AvMarPl 83*
Pellennorath [of Pandemonium Press] - Encinitas, CA - *LitMag&SmPr 83-84*
Peller & Associates Inc., A. W. - Hawthorne, NJ - *AvMarPl 83*
Pelter, Rodney - New York, NY - *LitMarPl 83, 84*
Pelton Publishing Co. - Brooklyn, NY - *BillIntBG 83-84*
Pema-2 B.S.A. - Paris, France - *StaDirAdAg 2-84*
Pemberley Press - New York, NY - *BoPubDir 4 Sup, 5*
Pemberton Pioneer Women - Pemberton, BC, Canada - *BoPubDir 4, 5*
Pembina New Era - Pembina, ND - *Ed&PubIntYB 82*
Pembina New Era - *See* Ness Press Inc.
Pembina Times - Morden, MB, Canada - *AyerDirPub 83; Ed&PubIntYB 82*
Pembroke Cable - Ahoskie, NC - *BrCabYB 84; Tel&CabFB 84C*
Pembroke Cable - Murfreesboro, NC - *BrCabYB 84*
Pembroke Cable [of WVEC Television Inc.] - Emporia, VA - *BrCabYB 84; Tel&CabFB 84C*
Pembroke Cable [of WVEC Television Inc.] - Hampton, VA - *BrCabYB 84 p.D-305; Tel&CabFB 84C p.1696*
Pembroke Cable [of WVEC Television Inc.] - South Boston, VA - *BrCabYB 84; Tel&CabFB 84C*
Pembroke Cable [of WVEC Television Inc.] - South Hill, VA - *BrCabYB 84; Tel&CabFB 84C*
Pembroke Cable Corp. [of WVEC Television Inc.] - Greensville County, VA - *BrCabYB 84*
Pembroke Cablevision Ltd. [of Ottawa Cablevision Ltd.] - Pembroke, ON, Canada - *BrCabYB 84*
Pembroke Carolina Indian Voice - Pembroke, NC - *BaconPubCkNews 84*
Pembroke Journal - Pembroke, GA - *Ed&PubIntYB 82*
Pembroke Magazine - Pembroke, NC - *LitMag&SmPr 83-84*
Pembroke Mirror - Ft. Lauderdale, FL - *AyerDirPub 83*
Pembroke Mirror - Pembroke Pines, FL - *Ed&PubIntYB 82*
Pembroke Observer, The - Pembroke, ON, Canada - *BaconPubCkNews 84*
Pembroke Silver Lake News - *See* MPG Communications
Pembroke Telephone Co. Inc. - Pembroke, GA - *TelDir&BG 83-84*
Pembroke Telephone Cooperative - Pembroke, VA - *TelDir&BG 83-84*
Pembroke Welsh Corgi Club of America Inc. [Aff. of American Kennel Club] - Pound Ridge, NY - *BoPubDir 4 Sup, 5*
Pembrook Pines Inc. - Wellsville, NY - *BrCabYB 84*
Pemiscot Journal - Caruthersville, MO - *AyerDirPub 83; Ed&PubIntYB 82*
Pemiscot Publishing Co. - Caruthersville, MO - *BaconPubCkNews 84*
Pemmican Publications - Winnipeg, MB, Canada - *BoPubDir 4, 5; LitMarPl 83, 84*
PEN American Center [Aff. of International PEN] - New York, NY - *BoPubDir 4, 5; LitMag&SmPr 83-84*
Pen & Booth - Washington, DC - *BoPubDir 4, 5*
Pen & Podium Inc. - New York, NY - *BoPubDir 4, 5*
Pen Argyl Cable TV [of Service Electric Cable TV Inc.] - Pen Argyl, PA - *BrCabYB 84*
Pen-Art Publishers - Westwood, NJ - *ArtMar 84*
Pen-Elayne Enterprises - Roselle, NJ - *LitMag&SmPr 83-84*
Pen Pusher Publications - Woodland Hills, CA - *BoPubDir 4, 5*
Pena Cable TV - Socorro, NM - *BrCabYB 84*
Pena, Eddie & Marie - Grants, NM - *Tel&CabFB 84C p.1696*
Pena, Paul - *See* Blue Mountain Cable Co.
Pena, Vicky - Stamford, CT - *LitMarPl 83, 84*
Penasco Valley Telephone Cooperative Inc. - Artesia, NM - *TelDir&BG 83-84*
Pencept Inc. - Waltham, MA - *DataDirSup 7-83; MicrocomMPl 84*
Penchina, Selkowitz - New York, NY - *AdAge 3-28-84; StaDirAdAg 2-84*
Penco Records Inc. - New Bedford, MA - *BillIntBG 83-84*
Pencor Services Inc. - Palmerton, PA - *BrCabYB 84 p.D-305; Tel&CabFB 84C p.1696*
Pencraft, M. C. - New York, NY - *LitMarPl 83*
Pend Oreille Cable TV [of Northland Communications Corp.] - Sandpoint, ID - *Tel&CabFB 84C*
Pendas Productions - Orangeville, ON, Canada - *BoPubDir 4 Sup, 5*
Pendell Publishing Co. - Midland, MI - *BoPubDir 4, 5*
Pender Chronicle - Burgaw, NC - *AyerDirPub 83; Ed&PubIntYB 82; NewsDir 84*
Pender Post - Burgaw, NC - *AyerDirPub 83; Ed&PubIntYB 82; NewsDir 84*
Pender Times - Pender, NE - *BaconPubCkNews 84; Ed&PubIntYB 82*
Pendle Hill Publications - Wallingford, PA - *BoPubDir 4, 5*
Pendleton Cable [of Rogers UA Cablesystems Inc.] - Pendleton, OR - *BrCabYB 84*
Pendleton Community TV System [of UA Cablesystems Corp.] - Pilot Rock, OR - *Tel&CabFB 84C*
Pendleton East Oregonian - Pendleton, OR - *NewsDir 84*
Pendleton Record - Pendleton, OR - *BaconPubCkNews 84; Ed&PubIntYB 82*
Pendleton Times - Pendleton, IN - *Ed&PubIntYB 82*
Pendleton Times - Franklin, WV - *Ed&PubIntYB 82*
Pendragon House Inc. - Campbell, CA - *MagIndMarPl 82-83*
Pendragon Journal of the Creative Arts [of Rocky Mountain Writers Guild Inc.] - Boulder, CO - *LitMag&SmPr 83-84*
Pendragon Press [Subs. of Camelot Publishing Co. Inc.] - New York, NY - *LitMarPl 83, 84*
Pendulum Press Inc. [Subs. of Academic Industries Inc.] - West Haven, CT - *LitMarPl 83, 84*
PENewsletter - New York, NY - *MagIndMarPl 82-83*
Penfield Post-Republican - Penfield, NY - *Ed&PubIntYB 82*
Penfield Post Republican [of Wolfe Publications Inc.] - Pittsford, NY - *NewsDir 84*
Penfield Post Republican - *See* Wolfe Publications Inc.
Penfield Press - Penfield, NY - *AyerDirPub 83; Ed&PubIntYB 82*
Penfield Press [of Empire State Weeklies] - Webster, NY - *NewsDir 84*
Penfield Press - *See* Empire State Weeklies
Penfil Public Relations, Leonore - Beverly Hills, CA - *DirPRFirms 83*
Penglase, Bill - New York, NY - *LitMarPl 83, 84; MagIndMarPl 82-83*
Pengra Co./Advertising Inc., The Marshall - Houston, TX - *StaDirAdAg 2-84*
Penguin Books [Div. of Viking Penguin Inc.] - New York, NY - *LitMarPl 83, 84; WritMar 84*
Penguin Software - Geneva, IL - *MicrocomMPl 83, 84*
Peninhand Press - Volcano, CA - *LitMag&SmPr 83-84*
Peninsula Ad-Visor - Redwood City, CA - *AyerDirPub 83*
Peninsula Artist Record Group - Newport News, VA - *BillIntBG 83-84*
Peninsula Breeze - Rolling Hills, CA - *Ed&PubIntYB 82*

Peninsula Breeze [of Torrance Press-Herald] - Torrance, CA - *AyerDirPub 83; NewsDir 84*
Peninsula Cable Television Corp. of San Mateo [of Tele-Communications Inc.] - San Mateo, CA - *BrCabYB 84*
Peninsula Cable Television Corp. of San Mateo/Millbrae [of Nation Wide Cablevision Inc.] - Millbrae, CA - *Tel&CabFB 84C*
Peninsula Cable Television Corp. of San Mateo/Millbrae [of Nation Wide Cablevision Inc.] - San Mateo, CA - *Tel&CabFB 84C*
Peninsula Cablevision Corp. [of Booth American Co.] - Madeira Beach, FL - *BrCabYB 84; Tel&CabFB 84C*
Peninsula Clarion, The [of Kenai Peninsula Newspapers Inc.] - Kenai, AK - *Ed&PubIntYB 82*
Peninsula Gateway - Gig Harbor, WA - *AyerDirPub 83; Ed&PubIntYB 82; NewsDir 84*
Peninsula Herald - Monterey, CA - *AyerDirPub 83*
Peninsula Library System - Belmont, CA - *EISS 83*
Peninsula-Metro Reporter - *See* Reporter Publishing Co.
Peninsula Publishing - Los Altos, CA - *BoPubDir 4; LitMarPl 83, 84*
Peninsula Publishing - Port Angeles, WA - *BoPubDir 4, 5*
Peninsula Telephone & Telegraph Co. - Forks, WA - *TelDir&BG 83-84*
Peninsula Telephone Co. - Old Mission, MI - *TelDir&BG 83-84*
Peninsula Times, The - Palo Alto, CA - *AyerDirPub 83*
Peninsula Times Tribune [of Peninsula Newspapers Inc.] - Palo Alto, CA - *AyerDirPub 83; BaconPubCkNews 84; Ed&PubIntYB 82; LitMarPl 83, 84*
Peninsula TV Power Inc. [of Community Tele-Communications Inc.] - Sunnyvale, CA - *Tel&CabFB 84C*
Penkevill Publishing Co., The - Greenwood, FL - *LitMarPl 84*
Penmaen Press Ltd. - Great Barrington, MA - *LitMarPl 83, 84*
Penn Cable Co., William [of M.U.S. Industries Inc.] - Murrysville, PA - *BrCabYB 84; Tel&CabFB 84C*
Penn Central Corp. - Greenwich, CT - *ElecNews 7-25-83*
Penn Communications Inc. - Middletown, DE - *BrCabYB 84*
Penn Communications Inc. - Swedesboro, NJ - *Tel&CabFB 84C*
Penn Communications Inc. - Christiana, PA - *Tel&CabFB 84C*
Penn Communications Inc. - Perryville, PA - *BrCabYB 84*
Penn Communications Inc. - York, PA - *Tel&CabFB 84C p.1696*
Penn Franklin News - Export, PA - *AyerDirPub 83*
Penn Franklin News - Murrysville, PA - *Ed&PubIntYB 82*
Penn-Grampian TV Cable Co. - Penn Township, PA - *Tel&CabFB 84C*
Penn Hills & Churchill Progress - *See* Gateway Press Inc.
Penn State Coal Data Base [of Pennsylvania State University] - University Park, PA - *EISS 83*
Penn, The [of Indiana University of Pennsylvania] - Indiana, PA - *NewsDir 84*
Penn Treaty Gazette [of Greater Philadelphia Group Inc.] - Philadelphia, PA - *NewsDir 84*
Penn Valley Times - Souderton, PA - *AyerDirPub 83*
Penn Visual Aids Center of Pittsburgh, William - Pittsburgh, PA - *AvMarPl 83*
Penn Yan Chronicle-Express - Penn Yan, NY - *BaconPubCkNews 84; Ed&PubIntYB 82*
Pennaprint Inc. - Dallas, PA - *BaconPubCkNews 84*
Pennebaker Associates Inc. - New York, NY - *Tel&CabFB 84C*
Penner Brothers Inc. - Stuart, FL - *MicrocomMPl 83*
Pennine Platform - Wetherby, England - *LitMag&SmPr 83-84*
Pennington Associates Inc. - Raleigh, NC - *DirPRFirms 83*
Pennington County Courant - Wall, SD - *AyerDirPub 83; Ed&PubIntYB 82*
Pennington Gap Powell Valley News - Pennington Gap, VA - *BaconPubCkNews 84; NewsDir 84*
Pennington Trading Post - Fremont, MO - *BoPubDir 4 Sup, 5*
Pennmarva - Southampton, PA - *BaconPubCkMag 84; MagDir 84*
Penns Grove Record - Penns Grove, NJ - *Ed&PubIntYB 82; NewsDir 84*
Penns Grove Record - Salem, NJ - *BaconPubCkNews 84*
Penns Valley Publishers - Harrisburg, PA - *BoPubDir 4, 5*
Pennsauken Community News - *See* Suburban Newspapers
Pennsboro News - Pennsboro, WV - *Ed&PubIntYB 82*
Pennsboro News - *See* St. Marys Oracle Publishers
Pennsburg Town & Country [of Equitable Publishing Co.] - Pennsburg, PA - *NewsDir 84*
Pennsylvania AFL-CIO News - Harrisburg, PA - *NewsDir 84*
Pennsylvania Angler [of Pennsylvania Fish Commission] - Harrisburg, PA - *ArtMar 84; BaconPubCkMag 84; MagDir 84; WritMar 84*
Pennsylvania Cablevision Industries - Corry, PA - *BrCabYB 84*
Pennsylvania Cablevision Industries [of Cablevision Industries Inc.] - Greenville, PA - *BrCabYB 84; Tel&CabFB 84C*
Pennsylvania Cablevision Industries - Union City, PA - *BrCabYB 84*
Pennsylvania Contractor - Harrisburg, PA - *BaconPubCkMag 84*
Pennsylvania CPA Journal - Philadelphia, PA - *BaconPubCkMag 84*
Pennsylvania CPA Spokesman [of Pennsylvania Institute of CPA's] - Philadelphia, PA - *MagDir 84*
Pennsylvania Dept. of Agriculture (Bureau of Agricultural Development) - Harrisburg, PA - *BoPubDir 5*
Pennsylvania Economy League Inc. (Eastern Div.) - Philadelphia, PA - *BoPubDir 4 Sup, 5*
Pennsylvania Farmer - Camp Hill, PA - *BaconPubCkMag 84; MagDir 84*
Pennsylvania Forests - Mechanicsburg, PA - *BaconPubCkMag 84*
Pennsylvania Game News - Harrisburg, PA - *WritMar 84*
Pennsylvania Gazette [of General Alumni Society] - Philadelphia, PA - *LitMarPl 83, 84*
Pennsylvania German Folklore Society of Ontario - Kitchener, ON, Canada - *BoPubDir 5*
Pennsylvania German Society - Breinigsville, PA - *BoPubDir 4, 5*
Pennsylvania Governor's Energy Council - Harrisburg, PA - *BoPubDir 5*
Pennsylvania Grocer - Abington, PA - *BaconPubCkMag 84; WritMar 84*
Pennsylvania Historical & Museum Commission [of William Penn Memorial Museum] - Harrisburg, PA - *BoPubDir 4, 5; MicroMarPl 82-83*
Pennsylvania Historical Association - University Park, PA - *BoPubDir 4, 5*
Pennsylvania Holstein News - Sandy Creek, NY - *BaconPubCkMag 84; MagDir 84*
Pennsylvania Law Journal [of Packard Press] - Philadelphia, PA - *NewsDir 84*
Pennsylvania Lawyer, The - Harrisburg, PA - *WritMar 84*
Pennsylvania Legislative Database - Harrisburg, PA - *DirOnDB Spring 84*
Pennsylvania Legislative Database [of VU/Text Information Services] - Philadelphia, PA - *DataDirOnSer 84*
Pennsylvania Magazine - Camp Hill, PA - *ArtMar 84; MagDir 84*
Pennsylvania Medicine - Lemoyne, PA - *BaconPubCkMag 84; MagDir 84*
Pennsylvania Natural Diversity Inventory - Middletown, PA - *EISS 5-84 Sup*
Pennsylvania Pharmacist [of Pennsylvania Pharmaceutical Association] - Harrisburg, PA - *BaconPubCkMag 84; MagDir 84*
Pennsylvania Plumbing, Heating, Cooling Contractor - Harrisburg, PA - *MagDir 84*
Pennsylvania Public Television Network - Hershey, PA - *BrCabYB 84*
Pennsylvania Regional Library Resource Program [of Pennsylvania State Library] - Harrisburg, PA - *EISS 83*
Pennsylvania Resources & Information Center for Special Education [of Montgomery County Intermediate Unit] - King of Prussia, PA - *EISS 83*
Pennsylvania Road Builder - Altoona, PA - *MagDir 84*
Pennsylvania Sportsman - Harrisburg, PA - *BaconPubCkMag 84; WritMar 84*
Pennsylvania State University (Audio Visual Services) - University Park, PA - *AvMarPl 83*
Pennsylvania State University Press - University Park, PA - *LitMag&SmPr 83-84; LitMarPl 83, 84; WritMar 84*
Pennsylvania Teacher, The - Pittsburgh, PA - *NewsDir 84*
Pennsylvania Technical Assistance Program [of Pennsylvania State University] - University Park, PA - *EISS 83*
Pennsylvania Telephone Co. - Oval, PA - *TelDir&BG 83-84*
Pennsylvania Township News [of Pennsylvania State Association of Township Supervisors] - Camp Hill, PA - *BaconPubCkMag 84; MagDir 84*

Pennsylvania Triangle [of University of Pennsylvania] - Philadelphia, PA - *MagDir 84*
Pennsylvanian - Harrisburg, PA - *BaconPubCkMag 84; MagDir 84*
Pennsylvania's Outdoor People - Monroeville, PA - *MagDir 84*
Penntech Papers Inc. - White Plains, NY - *LitMarPl 83, 84; MagIndMarPl 82-83*
Penntrux - Camp Hill, PA - *BaconPubCkMag 84; MagDir 84*
PennWell Books [Div. of PennWell Publishing Co.] - Tulsa, OK - *LitMarPl 83, 84; WritMar 84*
PennWell Books (Circulation Services) - Tulsa, OK - *MagIndMarPl 82-83*
PennWell Publishing Co. - Tulsa, OK - *DataDirOnSer 84; DirMarMP 83; MagIndMarPl 82-83*
Penny/Ohlmann/Neiman - Dayton, OH - *AdAge 3-28-84; ArtMar 84; DirPRFirms 83; StaDirAdAg 2-84*
Penny Pincher Music - Oakwood, VA - *BillIntBG 83-84*
Penny Power - Mt. Vernon, NY - *MagIndMarPl 82-83*
Penny Press - Peoria, IL - *Ed&PubIntYB 82*
Penny Saver - Mascoutah, IL - *AyerDirPub 83*
Penny Saver - Harlan, IA - *AyerDirPub 83*
Penny Saver [of Covington Arens Corp.] - Covington, OH - *NewsDir 84*
Penny-Saver - Mansfield, PA - *AyerDirPub 83*
Penny Saver Publications - Tinley Park, IL - *AyerDirPub 83*
Penny Stock Journal - New York, NY - *BaconPubCkMag 84*
Penny Stock Preview [of NewsNet Inc.] - Bryn Mawr, PA - *DataDirOnSer 84*
Penny Stock Preview - Yardley, PA - *DirOnDB Spring 84*
Penny Thoughts Music [Div. of John Penny Enterprises Inc.] - Belmont, MA - *BillIntBG 83-84*
Pennyfarthing Press - Berkeley, CA - *BoPubDir 4, 5*
Pennypower Shopping News - Topeka, KS - *AyerDirPub 83*
Pennypower Shopping News - Wichita, KS - *AyerDirPub 83*
Pennypower Shopping News - Springfield, MO - *AyerDirPub 83*
Pennypress Inc. - Seattle, WA - *BoPubDir 4 Sup, 5*
Pennysaver - Brea, CA - *AyerDirPub 83*
Pennysaver - Plymouth, NH - *AyerDirPub 83*
Pennysaver - Medford, NJ - *AyerDirPub 83*
Pennysaver - Auburn, NY - *AyerDirPub 83*
Pennysaver - Corinth, NY - *AyerDirPub 83*
Pennysaver News of Brookhaven - Medford, NY - *AyerDirPub 83*
Pennysaver Press - Bennington, VT - *AyerDirPub 83*
Pennysaver, The - Severna Park, MD - *AyerDirPub 83*
Pennysaver, The - Falmouth, MA - *AyerDirPub 83*
Pennysaver, The - Westfield, MA - *AyerDirPub 83*
Pennyshopper - Yuma, AZ - *AyerDirPub 83*
Penobscot Bay Press - Stonington, ME - *BoPubDir 4, 5*
Penobscot Broadcasting Corp. - Bangor, ME - *BrCabYB 84*
Penoragon - Boulder, CO - *LitMag&SmPr 83-84*
Penril Corp. - Rockville, MD - *DataDirSup 7-83*
Penrith Publishing Co. - Cleveland Heights, OH - *BoPubDir 4, 5*
Pensacola Escambia County Beacon - Pensacola, FL - *BaconPubCkNews 84*
Pensacola Escambia Sun-Press - Pensacola, FL - *BaconPubCkNews 84*
Pensacola Historical Society - Pensacola, FL - *BoPubDir 4, 5*
Pensacola Journal - Pensacola, FL - *BaconPubCkNews 84; Ed&PubIntYB 82; LitMarPl 83, 84; NewsDir 84*
Pensacola News - Pensacola, FL - *BaconPubCkNews 84; Ed&PubIntYB 82; LitMarPl 83, 84; NewsDir 84*
Pensacola News-Journal - Pensacola, FL - *Ed&PubIntYB 82; LitMarPl 83, 84; NewsDir 84*
Pensacola Voice - Pensacola, FL - *BaconPubCkNews 84; Ed&PubIntYB 82*
Pension World - Atlanta, GA - *BaconPubCkMag 84; MagDir 84; MagIndMarPl 82-83*
Pensions & Benefits - Toronto, ON, Canada - *BaconPubCkMag 84*
Pensions & Investment Age [of Crain Communications Inc.] - Chicago, IL - *Folio 83*
Pensions & Investment Age [of Crain Communications Inc.] - New York, NY - *BaconPubCkMag 84; MagDir 84*
Pent-R-Books - Brooklyn, NY - *BoPubDir 4, 5*
Pentagon Industries Inc. - Chicago, IL - *AvMarPl 83*
Pentagon Music Co. - *See* Jamie Music Publishing Co.
Pentagram - Markesan, WI - *BoPubDir 4, 5; LitMag&SmPr 83-84*
Pentagram Productions Inc. - Los Angeles, CA - *AvMarPl 83; WritMar 84*
Pentagramm Record Productions - Holtsville, NY - *BillIntBG 83-84*
Pentamation Enterprises Inc. - Bethlehem, PA - *ADAPSOMemDir 83-84; DataDirOnSer 84*
Pentax Corp. [Subs. of Asahi Optical Ltd.] - Englewood, CO - *AvMarPl 83*
Pentecostal Evangel [of The General Council of the Assemblies of God] - Springfield, MO - *MagDir 84; WritMar 84*
Pentecostal Messenger, The - Joplin, MO - *MagDir 84; MagIndMarPl 82-83*
Pentecostal Publishing House [Aff. of United Pentecostal Church International] - Hazelwood, MO - *BoPubDir 4 Sup, 5; LitMarPl 84*
Pentecostal Testimony, The - Toronto, ON, Canada - *WritMar 84*
Pentel of America Ltd. - Torrance, CA - *WhoWMicrocom 83*
Penthouse [of Penthouse International] - New York, NY - *BaconPubCkMag 84; Folio 83; LitMarPl 83, 84; MagDir 84; MagIndMarPl 82-83; NewsBur 6; WritMar 84*
Penthouse Entertainment Television Network [of Telemine] - New York, NY - *BrCabYB 84; HomeVid&CabYB 82-83*
Penthouse International - New York, NY - *AdAge 6-28-84; KnowInd 83; LitMarPl 83*
Penthouse Letters - New York, NY - *MagDir 84*
Penthouse Television - New York, NY - *CabTVPrDB 83*
Penthouse Variations [of Penthouse International] - New York, NY - *WritMar 84*
Penticton Cable TV Ltd. [of Capital Cable TV Ltd.] - Penticton, BC, Canada - *BrCabYB 84*
Penticton Herald - Penticton, BC, Canada - *BaconPubCkNews 84; Ed&PubIntYB 82*
Penton/IPC Inc. [Subs. of Pittway Corp.] - Cleveland, OH - *DirMarMP 83; MagIndMarPl 82-83*
Penumbra Press - Lisbon, IA - *ArtMar 84; BoPubDir 5; LitMag&SmPr 83-84*
Penumbra Press - Moonbeam, ON, Canada - *BoPubDir 4, 5; LitMarPl 83, 84*
Penzell & Associates Inc., Lawrence [Subs. of Lila Productions Ltd.] - New York, NY - *BrCabYB 84; LitMarPl 83, 84; MagIndMarPl 82-83*
People [of Time Inc.] - New York, NY - *BaconPubCkMag 84; Folio 83; LitMarPl 84; MagDir 84; NewsBur 6*
People in Action [of Meridian Publishing Co.] - Ogden, UT - *ArtMar 84; WritMar 84*
People in Places Inc. - Morristown, NJ - *LitMarPl 83, 84*
People Panel Inc., The - Port Washington, NY - *IntDirMarRes 83*
People Pleaser Music - Charlotte, NC - *BillIntBG 83-84*
People-Sentinel - Barnwell, SC - *AyerDirPub 83*
People That Love - Charlotte, NC - *HomeVid&CabYB 82-83*
People Weekly [of Time Inc.] - New York, NY - *LitMarPl 83, 84; MagIndMarPl 82-83; WritMar 84*
Peoples Broadband Communications Systems Inc. [of Peoples Consolidated Communications Services Inc.] - Pardeeville, WI - *Tel&CabFB 84C*
Peoples Cable TV - Aurelia, IA - *Tel&CabFB 84C*
People's Canada Daily News - Toronto, ON, Canada - *LitMag&SmPr 83-84*
People's Computer Co. - Menlo Park, CA - *BoPubDir 4, 5; LitMag&SmPr 83-84; MicrocomMPl 83, 84*
Peoples Consolidated Communications Services Inc. - Randolph, WI - *Tel&CabFB 84C p.1697*
People's Folk Dance Directory [Aff. of Texas International Folk Dancers Inc.] - Austin, TX - *BoPubDir 5*
People's Law School - San Francisco, CA - *BoPubDir 4, 5*
People's Light & Theatre Co. - Malvern, PA - *WritMar 84*
People's Lobby - Los Angeles, CA - *BoPubDir 4, 5*
Peoples Mutual Telephone Co. - Lacygne, KS - *TelDir&BG 83-84*
Peoples Mutual Telephone Co. - Gretna, VA - *TelDir&BG 83-84*
People's Press - Owatonna, MN - *AyerDirPub 83; Ed&PubIntYB 82*
Peoples Rural Telephone Cooperative Corp. Inc. - McKee, KY - *TelDir&BG 83-84*
Peoples Sentinel - Barnwell, SC - *Ed&PubIntYB 82*

Peoples Telephone & Telegraph Co. [Aff. of Golden West Telephone Cooperative Inc.] - Hot Springs, SD - *TelDir&BG 83-84*
Peoples Telephone Co. [Aff. of Telephone & Data Systems Inc.] - Leesburg, AL - *TelDir&BG 83-84*
Peoples Telephone Co. - Aurelia, IA - *TelDir&BG 83-84*
Peoples Telephone Co. - Lyons, OR - *TelDir&BG 83-84*
Peoples Telephone Co. [Aff. of Telephone & Data Systems Inc.] - Bloomington, WI - *TelDir&BG 83-84*
Peoples Telephone Co. [Aff. of Peoples Consolidated Communications Services Inc.] - Randolph, WI - *TelDir&BG 83-84*
Peoples Telephone Co. Inc. - Big Fork, MN - *TelDir&BG 83-84*
Peoples Telephone Co. Inc. [Aff. of Telephone Electronics Corp.] - Erin, TN - *TelDir&BG 83-84*
Peoples Telephone Co. Inc. - Coolidge, TX - *TelDir&BG 83-84*
Peoples Telephone Cooperative Inc. - Quitman, TX - *TelDir&BG 83-84*
People's Translation Service - Oakland, CA - *BoPubDir 4, 5; LitMag&SmPr 83-84*
People's Yellow Pages Press - San Francisco, CA - *LitMag&SmPr 83-84*
Peoria Daily Record [of Blaydes Record Printing Co.] - Peoria, IL - *NewsDir 84*
Peoria Heights Herald - Peoria Heights, IL - *BaconPubCkNews 84*
Peoria Journal-Star - Peoria, IL - *BaconPubCkNews 84; BrCabYB 84; LitMarPl 83; NewsDir 84*
Peoria Observer [of Tazewell Publishing Co.] - Peoria, IL - *NewsDir 84*
Peoria Observer - *See* Tazewell Publishing Co.
Peoria Penny Press, The [of Walfred Publications] - Peoria, IL - *NewsDir 84*
Peoria Times - Peoria, AZ - *BaconPubCkNews 84; Ed&PubIntYB 82*
Peotone Vedette - Peotone, IL - *Ed&PubIntYB 82*
Peotone Vedette - *See* Russell Publications
Pepe Associates Inc., Paul E. - Syosset, NY - *DirPRFirms 83*
Pepi & Associates, Vincent - Melville, NY - *LitMarPl 83, 84*
Pepin Laker - Pepin, WI - *Ed&PubIntYB 82*
Pepper & Salt Music - *See* Bee/Mor Music
Pepper Publishing - Tucson, AZ - *BoPubDir 4, 5*
Pepper Publishing Co. - Danbury, NC - *BaconPubCkNews 84*
Pepperdine University Press - Malibu, CA - *BoPubDir 4, 5; LitMarPl 84*
Peppermint Press - Toronto, ON, Canada - *BoPubDir 4, 5*
Peppertree Publishing - Newport Beach, CA - *BoPubDir 4, 5; LitMag&SmPr 83-84*
Pepys Press - New York, NY - *BoPubDir 4, 5; LitMag&SmPr 83-84*
Pequannock Herald - *See* Lincoln Park Herald Inc.
Pequod - San Francisco, CA - *LitMag&SmPr 83-84*
Pequod Press - New York, NY - *LitMag&SmPr 83-84*
Pequot Avenue Group Inc. - Larchmont, NY - *DirMarMP 83*
Pequot Lakes County Echo - Pequot Lakes, MN - *BaconPubCkNews 84; Ed&PubIntYB 82*
Per Ardua Press - Canoga Park, CA - *BoPubDir 4, 5*
Per Mar Research Services - Davenport, IA - *IntDirMarRes 83*
Peradam Publishing House - Urbana, IL - *LitMag&SmPr 83-84*
Peradam Publishing House - Bellingham, WA - *BoPubDir 4 Sup, 5*
Perception Development Techniques - New York, NY - *BoPubDir 4, 5*
Perception Research Services Inc. - Englewood Cliffs, NJ - *HBIndAd&MS 82-83; IntDirMarRes 83*
Perception Technology Corp. - Canton, MA - *DataDirSup 7-83*
Perceptive Marketers Agency Ltd. - Philadelphia, PA - *DirMarMP 83; LitMarPl 83, 84; MagIndMarPl 82-83*
Perceptual Development Laboratories - Big Spring, TX - *AvMarPl 83*
Perceptum Information AB - *See* Needham, Harper & Steers Inc.
Perceval [of Radio Television Belge de la Communaute Culturelle Francais] - Brussels, Belgium - *VideoDir 82-83*
Perchak, George J. - Stony Point, NY - *MagIndMarPl 82-83*
Perco Telephone Co. - Perryville, AR - *TelDir&BG 83-84*
Percom Data Co. Inc. - Dallas, TX - *MicrocomMPl 84; WhoWMicrocom 83*
Perdesi Panjab - Toronto, ON, Canada - *Ed&PubIntYB 82*
Perdido Bay Press - Pensacola, FL - *BoPubDir 4, 5*
Peregrine Associates - Ft. Lauderdale, FL - *BoPubDir 4, 5; LitMag&SmPr 83-84*
Peregrine Press - Old Saybrook, CT - *BoPubDir 4, 5; LitMarPl 84*
Peregrine Smith Books [of Gibbs M. Smith Inc.] - Layton, UT - *LitMag&SmPr 83-84; LitMarPl 83, 84; WritMar 84*
Perennial Education Inc. - Highland Park, IL - *AvMarPl 83*
Perennial Music - Lafayette, CA - *BillIntBG 83-84*
Perf-Fix Co., The [Div. of Hudson Photographic Industries Inc.] - Irvington-on-Hudson, NY - *AvMarPl 83*
Perfect Circle Records - Houston, TX - *BillIntBG 83-84*
Perfect Graphic Arts - Old Tappan, NJ - *BoPubDir 4, 5*
Perfect Home Magazine - Cedar Rapids, IA - *MagDir 84*
Perfect Image Materials Corp. - Hicksville, NY - *DirInfWP 82*
Perfect Page, The - Escondido, CA - *LitMarPl 84*
Perfect Plastic Printing Corp. - Addison, IL - *DataDirSup 7-83*
Perfect Productions - Larkspur, CA - *LitMag&SmPr 83-84*
Perfect Software - Canton, MA - *MicrocomMPl 84*
Perfect Solutions Inc. - Champaign, IL - *ADAPSOMemDir 83-84*
Perfect TV Co. - Manchester, KY - *BrCabYB 84; Tel&CabFB 84C*
Perfect Typing - New York, NY - *LitMarPl 83, 84*
Perfection Form Co., The - Des Moines, IA - *WritMar 84*
Performance - Ft. Worth, TX - *WritMar 84*
Performance Achievement Group Inc. - Chicago, IL - *TeleSy&SerDir 2-84*
Performance Channel [of AIM Broadcasting Corp.] - Vancouver, BC, Canada - *BrCabYB 84*
Performance Design - Evanston, IL - *DataDirSup 7-83*
Performance Designs Inc. - Woodcliff Lake, NJ - *AvMarPl 83*
Performance Development Corp. - Princeton, NJ - *ADAPSOMemDir 83-84*
Performance Horseman [of Gum Tree Store Press Inc.] - Unionville, PA - *WritMar 84*
Performance Inc. - Birmingham, AL - *IntDirMarRes 83*
Performance Management Magazine - Tucker, GA - *BaconPubCkMag 84*
Performance Plus Inc. - Framingham, MA - *IntDirMarRes 83*
Performance Promotions Inc. - Rochester, NY - *DirMarMP 83; StaDirAdAg 2-84*
Performance Publishing Co. - Elgin, IL - *LitMarPl 83, 84; WritMar 84*
Performance Services Inc. - Virginia Beach, VA - *WhoWMicrocom 83*
Performance Software Corp. - Oakland, CA - *WhoWMicrocom 83*
Performance Software Inc. - Midlothian, VA - *ADAPSOMemDir 83-84*
Performance Systems Inc. - Rockville, MD - *DataDirSup 7-83*
Performance Video - Montclair, NJ - *BillIntBG 83-84*
Performing Arts - Beverly Hills, CA - *BaconPubCkMag 84; MagDir 84*
Performing Arts Book Club Inc. - New York, NY - *LitMarPl 84*
Performing Arts in Canada - Toronto, ON, Canada - *WritMar 84*
Performing Arts Journal Publications - New York, NY - *BoPubDir 4 Sup, 5; LitMag&SmPr 83-84*
Performing Arts Network Inc. - Toronto, ON, Canada - *WritMar 84*
Perfumer & Flavorist [of Allured Publishing Corp.] - Wheaton, IL - *BaconPubCkMag 84; MagDir 84*
Pergamon-Infoline - London, England - *EISS 83, 7-83 Sup; InfIndMarPl 83*
Pergamon International Information Corp. [Subs. of Pergamon Group of Publishing Cos.] - McLean, VA - *CompReadDB 82; DataDirOnSer 84; EISS 83; InfoS 83-84*
Pergamon Press Canada Ltd. [Subs. of Pergamon Press Inc.] - Willowdale, ON, Canada - *LitMarPl 83, 84*
Pergamon Press Inc. [Subs. of Pergamon Holding Corp.] - Elmsford, NY - *ArtMar 84; AvMarPl 83; LitMarPl 83, 84; MagIndMarPl 82-83*
Pergamon Press Inc. - *See* Microforms International Marketing Corp.
Perham Enterprise Bulletin [of Parta Printers] - Perham, MN - *BaconPubCkNews 84; Ed&PubIntYB 82; NewsDir 84*
Pericomp Corp. - Natick, MA - *DataDirSup 7-83; MicrocomMPl 84; MicrocomSwDir 1*

Pericomp Corp. (Systems Div.) - Natick, MA - *WhoWMicrocom 83*
Perigee Books - *See* Putnam Publishing Group
Perihelion Corp. - Bala Cynwyd, PA - *MicrocomMPl 84*
Perilla & Associates Inc., Bob - New York, NY - *DirPRFirms 83*
Perimeter Data Systems - Boca Raton, FL - *WhoWMicrocom 83*
Perin Enterprises Inc. - New York, NY - *Tel&CabFB 84C*
Perinatology/Neonatology [of Brentwood Publishing Corp.] - Los Angeles, CA - *ArtMar 84; MagDir 84; MagIndMarPl 82-83*
Periodical [of Council on America's Military Past] - Tucson, AZ - *WritMar 84*
Periodical Abstrax [of Bibliograhic Retrieval Services Inc.] - Latham, NY - *DataDirOnSer 84*
Periodical File - Oxford, England - *DirOnDB Spring 84*
Periodical Guide for Computerists [of CompuServe Inc.] - Columbus, OH - *DataDirOnSer 84*
Periodical Guide for Computerists [of Applegate Computer Enterprises] - Grants Pass, OR - *DirOnDB Spring 84; EISS 5-84 Sup*
Periodical Periodical - Van Nuys, CA - *MagIndMarPl 82-83*
Periodical Studies Service - New York, NY - *MagIndMarPl 82-83*
Periodical Update - North Cohocton, NY - *MagIndMarPl 82-83*
Periomen Home-Vue Inc. - King of Prussia, PA - *BrCabYB 84*
Peripatetic Press - Grinnell, IA - *BoPubDir 4, 5*
Peripatos Press - Wainscott, NY - *LitMag&SmPr 83-84*
Peripheral Dynamics Inc. - Plymouth Meeting, PA - *DataDirSup 7-83; MicrocomMPl 84*
Peripheral Marketing Inc. - Fairfield, NJ - *MicrocomMPl 84*
Peripheral People, The - Mercer Island, WA - *WhoWMicrocom 83*
Peripheral People, The - Seattle, WA - *MicrocomMPl 83*
Peripheral Visions - Hillsboro, OR - *AvMarPl 83*
Peripherals - Costa Mesa, CA - *WhoWMicrocom 83*
Peripherals Digest - Annandale, VA - *BaconPubCkMag 84*
Peripherals Weekly [of EDP News Services Inc.] - Annandale, VA - *MagDir 84*
Peripherials Plus - Morris Plains, NJ - *MicrocomMPl 83*
Periphex Inc. - Southbury, CT - *MicrocomMPl 84*
Periphonics - Bohemia, NY - *DataDirSup 7-83*
Periphral Systems Inc. - Marlton, NJ - *WhoWMicrocom 83*
Periscope Music Co. - Brockton, MA - *BillIntBG 83-84*
Periscope Record Co. - Brockton, MA - *BillIntBG 83-84*
Perishable Press Ltd. - Mt. Horeb, WI - *BoPubDir 4, 5*
Peristyle - Hermosa Beach, CA - *BaconPubCkMag 84*
Periterra Music - Long Island City, NY - *BillIntBG 83-84*
Perivale Press - Van Nuys, CA - *LitMag&SmPr 83-84; WritMar 84*
Periwinkle Press - Woodland Hills, CA - *BoPubDir 4, 5*
Perkasie News-Herald [of Baum Publishing Co.] - Perkasie, PA - *BaconPubCkNews 84; Ed&PubIntYB 82; NewsDir 84*
Perkin-Elmer Corp. - Norwalk, CT - *Datamation 6-83; ElecNews 7-25-83; Top100Al 83*
Perkin-Elmer Corp. - Oceanport, NJ - *InfIndMarPl 83*
Perkin-Elmer Terminals Div. [of Perkin-Elmer Corp.] - Flanders, NJ - *DataDirSup 7-83; DirInfWP 82*
Perkins & Associates, E. Stuart - Wellington, OH - *BoPubDir 4 Sup, 5*
Perkins & Squier Co. - New York, NY - *LitMarPl 83, 84*
Perkins Associates - Savannah, GA - *MagIndMarPl 82-83*
Perkins Cable TV Inc. - Perkins, OK - *Tel&CabFB 84C*
Perkins Goodwin Co. Inc. - New York, NY - *LitMarPl 83, 84*
Perkins Journal - Perkins, OK - *BaconPubCkNews 84; Ed&PubIntYB 82*
Perkins, Judy - Louisville, KY - *LitMarPl 84*
Perkins, Percy H. Jr. - Atlanta, GA - *BoPubDir 4, 5*
Perkinsville Telephone Co. Inc. [Aff. of Telephone & Data Systems Inc.] - Perkinsville, VT - *TelDir&BG 83-84*
Perkiomen Home-Vue Inc. - King of Prussia, PA - *Tel&CabFB 84C p.1697*
Perla Music - Woodcliff Lake, NJ - *BillIntBG 83-84*
Perle Systems Ltd. - Scarborough, Canada - *DataDirSup 7-83*
Perlmutter, Barbara - Flushing, NY - *LitMarPl 83, 84*
Perlmutter Inc., Alvin H. - New York, NY - *Tel&CabFB 84C*
Perma Power Electronics Inc. - Chicago, IL - *AvMarPl 83*
Perma Products Co. - Dallas, TX - *DirInfWP 82*
Permafilm International - New York, NY - *AvMarPl 83*
Permalin Products Corp. - Port Washington, NY - *LitMarPl 83, 84*
Permanent Committee on Patent Information [of World Intellectual Property Organization] - Geneva, Switzerland - *EISS 83*
Permanent Press - London, England - *LitMag&SmPr 83-84*
Permanent Press, The - Sag Harbor, NY - *LitMag&SmPr 83-84; LitMarPl 83, 84*
Permian Basin Television Corp. - Midland, TX - *BrCabYB 84*
Permian Records Inc. - Dallas, TX - *BillIntBG 83-84*
Permit Data On-Line [of Petroleum Information Corp.] - Denver, CO - *DataDirOnSer 84*
Permit Data On-Line - Littleton, CO - *DirOnDB Spring 84*
Peroni Business Systems - Lexington, MA - *WhoWMicrocom 83*
Perpetual Motion Pictures Inc. - New York, NY - *ArtMar 84*
Perpetual Storage Inc. - Salt Lake City, UT - *MicroMarPl 82-83*
Perquimans Weekly - Hertford, NC - *AyerDirPub 83; Ed&PubIntYB 82*
Perrett Co. Inc., The - Pasadena, CA - *StaDirAdAg 2-84*
Perri Debes Looney & Crane Advertising Inc. - Rochester, NY - *StaDirAdAg 2-84*
Perrier, Patricia - Brookline, MA - *LitMarPl 83, 84*
Perris Progress - Perris, CA - *BaconPubCkNews 84; Ed&PubIntYB 82*
Perron, Robert - New York, NY - *LitMarPl 83, 84*
Perry & Associates Inc., Donald A. - Gloucester, VA - *CabTVFinDB 83*
Perry Cable TV Corp. [of Perry Cable Cos. Inc.] - Greenacres City, FL - *BrCabYB 84; Tel&CabFB 84C*
Perry Cable TV Corp. - Indiantown, FL - *BrCabYB 84*
Perry Cable TV Corp. [of Perry Cable Cos. Inc.] - Palm Beach Gardens, FL - *BrCabYB 84; Tel&CabFB 84C*
Perry Cable TV Corp. [of Perry Cable Cos. Inc.] - Riviera Beach, FL - *BrCabYB 84 p.D-305; Tel&CabFB 84C p.1697*
Perry Cable TV Corp. [of Perry Cable Cos. Inc.] - Stuart, FL - *BrCabYB 84; Tel&CabFB 84C*
Perry Cablevision - Perry, IA - *BrCabYB 84*
Perry Cablevision - Perry, KS - *Tel&CabFB 84C*
Perry Cablevision - New Lexington, OH - *BrCabYB 84; Tel&CabFB 84C*
Perry Cablevision Inc. - Junction City, OH - *BrCabYB 84*
Perry County Advocate - Pinckneyville, IL - *AyerDirPub 83; Ed&PubIntYB 82*
Perry County News - Perryville, AR - *Ed&PubIntYB 82*
Perry County Petit Jean Country Headlight - Perryville, AR - *AyerDirPub 83; BaconPubCkNews 84; Ed&PubIntYB 82*
Perry County Times - New Bloomfield, PA - *AyerDirPub 83; Ed&PubIntYB 82*
Perry County Tribune - New Lexington, OH - *AyerDirPub 83; Ed&PubIntYB 82*
Perry Daily Chief - Perry, IA - *BaconPubCkNews 84; Ed&PubIntYB 82; NewsDir 84*
Perry Data Systems Inc. - Raleigh, NC - *DataDirSup 7-83; InfIndMarPl 83*
Perry Enterprise - Perry, MO - *Ed&PubIntYB 82*
Perry Herald - Perry, NY - *AyerDirPub 83; BaconPubCkNews 84; Ed&PubIntYB 82*
Perry Houston Home Journal - Perry, GA - *BaconPubCkNews 84; NewsDir 84*
Perry Journal - Perry, OK - *BaconPubCkNews 84; NewsDir 84*
Perry News-Herald [of Live Oak Publications] - Perry, FL - *BaconPubCkNews 84; Ed&PubIntYB 82; NewsDir 84*
Perry-Omega Publishing Inc. - Escondido, CA - *BoPubDir 4, 5*
Perry Printing Corp. - Waterloo, WI - *MagIndMarPl 82-83*
Perry Shiawassee County Journal - Perry, MI - *BaconPubCkNews 84*
Perry-Spencer Rural Telephone Cooperative Inc. - Tell City, IN - *TelDir&BG 83-84*
Perry Taco Times - Perry, FL - *BaconPubCkNews 84; NewsDir 84*
Perry Twainland Enterprise - Perry, MO - *BaconPubCkNews 84*
Perrysburg Messenger-Journal - Perrysburg, OH - *AyerDirPub 83; Ed&PubIntYB 82*
Perrysburg Messenger-Journal - *See* Welch Publishing Co.
Perryton Herald - Perryton, TX - *BaconPubCkNews 84; Ed&PubIntYB 82*
Perryville Monitor - Perryville, MO - *BaconPubCkNews 84; Ed&PubIntYB 82; NewsDir 84*

Perryville Perry County Republic - Perryville, MO - *BaconPubCkNews 84; NewsDir 84*
Persbureau Vaz Dias NV - Amsterdam, Netherlands - *ProGuPRSer 4*
PerSci Inc. - West Los Angeles, CA - *DataDirSup 7-83; WhoWMicrocom 83*
Persea Books - New York, NY - *BoPubDir 4 Sup, 5; LitMarPl 83, 84; WritMar 84*
Persephone Press Inc. - Watertown, MA - *BoPubDir 4, 5; LitMag&SmPr 83-84; WritMar 84*
Persephone Review, The [of Persephone Press Inc.] - Watertown, MA - *LitMag&SmPr 83-84*
Perseverance Press - Menlo Park, CA - *BoPubDir 4, 5*
Persimmon Hill - Oklahoma City, OK - *WritMar 84*
Persimmon Software - Greensboro, NC - *MicrocomMPl 84; MicrocomSwDir 1*
Persoft Inc. - Madison, WI - *MicrocomMPl 84*
Persoft Inc. - Stoughton, WI - *WhoWMicrocom 83*
Persona Press - San Francisco, CA - *BoPubDir 4, 5*
Persona Press - New Orleans, LA - *BoPubDir 4, 5*
Personabooks - Oakland, CA - *BoPubDir 4, 5; LitMag&SmPr 83-84*
Personal Achievement Associates [of Prentice-Hall Inc.] - Englewood, NJ - *LitMarPl 83, 84*
Personal Achievement Library - New York, NY - *BoPubDir 4, 5*
Personal & Professional - Philadelphia, PA - *BaconPubCkMag 84*
Personal & Professional [of Personal Press Inc.] - Springhouse, PA - *MicrocomMPl 84; WritMar 84*
Personal Bibliographic Software Inc. - Ann Arbor, MI - *EISS 5-84 Sup*
Personal Christianity - Baldwin Park, CA - *BoPubDir 4 Sup, 5*
Personal Communications - Flushing, NY - *AvMarPl 83*
Personal Communications - Port Washington, NY - *MagDir 84*
Personal Communications - Fairfax, VA - *BaconPubCkMag 84*
Personal Computer Age - Sunland, CA - *BaconPubCkMag 84; MicrocomMPl 84*
Personal Computer Age - Tujunga, CA - *WritMar 84*
Personal Computer Journal - Spokane, WA - *MicrocomMPl 84*
Personal Computer Leasing Corp. - Boston, MA - *DataDirSup 7-83*
Personal Computer News [of PCN Inc.] - Point Reyes Station, CA - *BaconPubCkMag 84; LitMag&SmPr 83-84; MicrocomMPl 84; WritMar 84*
Personal Computer Perspectives [of Architecture Technology Corp.] - Minneapolis, MN - *MicrocomMPl 84*
Personal Computer Products Inc. - San Diego, CA - *MicrocomMPl 84*
Personal Computer Products Inc. - Santa Clara, CA - *MicrocomSwDir 1*
Personal Computer Service - Las Cruces, NM - *WhoWMicrocom 83*
Personal Computer Systems - Syracuse, NY - *MicrocomMPl 84*
Personal Computer Technology [of Architecture Technology Corp.] - Minneapolis, MN - *MicrocomMPl 84*
Personal Computers Today - Bethesda, MD - *BaconPubCkMag 84; DirOnDB Spring 84*
Personal Computers Today [of NewsNet Inc.] - Bryn Mawr, PA - *DataDirOnSer 84*
Personal Computing - Boston, MA - *MagDir 84*
Personal Computing [of Hayden Publishing Co. Inc.] - Rochelle Park, NJ - *ArtMar 84; BaconPubCkMag 84; Folio 83; MagIndMarPl 82-83; WritMar 84*
Personal Consumption Expenditure Forecast - Bala Cynwyd, PA - *DirOnDB Spring 84*
Personal Development Center Press - Windham, CT - *BoPubDir 4, 5*
Personal Electronics - Atlanta, GA - *BaconPubCkMag 84; MagDir 84*
Personal Library [Subs. of Bestsellers Inc.] - Toronto, ON, Canada - *LitMarPl 83*
Personal Micro Computers Inc. [Subs. of Recortec Inc.] - Mountain View, CA - *DataDirSup 7-83; MicrocomMPl 84; WhoWMicrocom 83*
Personal Opinion Inc. - Louisville, KY - *IntDirMarRes 83*
Personal Press - Point Reyes Station, CA - *BoPubDir 4, 5*
Personal Romances - New York, NY - *MagIndMarPl 82-83*
Personal Security Systems [Aff. of DNA] - River Forest, IL - *BoPubDir 4, 5*
Personal Software - Rochelle Park, NJ - *BaconPubCkMag 84; MicrocomMPl 84*
Personal Software Co. - Salt Lake City, UT - *MicrocomMPl 84; WhoWMicrocom 83*
Personal Systems Consulting - El Cajon, CA - *WhoWMicrocom 83*
Personal Systems Technology Inc. - Laguna Hills, CA - *MicrocomMPl 83*
Personal Tutor Associates [Div. of ExecSystems Corp.] - Clinton, MD - *MicrocomMPl 84*
Personality Photos Inc. - Brooklyn, NY - *MagIndMarPl 82-83*
Personalized Computer Systems - Arcadia, CA - *MicrocomMPl 83*
Personnel [of American Management Association] - New York, NY - *BaconPubCkMag 84; MagDir 84; MagIndMarPl 82-83*
Personnel Administrator - Berea, OH - *BaconPubCkMag 84; MagDir 84; MagIndMarPl 82-83*
Personnel Advisory Bulletin [of Bureau of Business Practice] - Waterford, CT - *ArtMar 84; WritMar 84*
Personnel & Guidance Journal, The - Washington, DC - *MagDir 84*
Personnel Communications [Div. of Ian Roberts Inc.] - Toronto, ON, Canada - *StaDirAdAg 2-84*
Personnel Journal - Costa Mesa, CA - *ArtMar 84; BaconPubCkMag 84; MagDir 84; MagIndMarPl 82-83*
Personnel Management Systems [Subs. of Midwest Computing Inc.] - Wichita, KS - *WhoWMicrocom 83*
Personnel Pool-Temporary Service [Subs. of Personnel Pool of America Inc.] - New York, NY - *LitMarPl 84*
Personnel Press [Div. of Ginn & Co.] - Lexington, MA - *BoPubDir 4, 5*
Personnel Report [of Robertson/Merrell-Information Services Group] - Hamden, CT - *WritMar 84*
Personnel Research Inc. - Durham, NC - *EISS 7-83 Sup*
Personnel Security Digest - Park Ridge, IL - *BaconPubCkMag 84*
Persons Magazine - Hattiesburg, MS - *WritMar 84*
Perspective [of Pioneer Clubs] - Wheaton, IL - *WritMar 84*
Perspective Music Co. - *See* NRP Music Group
Perspective Records - Hollywood, CA - *BillIntBG 83-84*
Perspectives - Ridgefield, CT - *ArtMar 84; BaconPubCkMag 84*
Perspectives in Psychiatric Care - Hillsdale, NJ - *MagDir 84*
Perspectives Press - Ft. Wayne, IN - *BoPubDir 5*
Perspectives Resources Inc. - Hartsdale, NY - *IntDirMarRes 83*
Perspectra Inc. - Westmount, PQ, Canada - *DirInfWP 82*
Perspectus - New York, NY - *DirPRFirms 83; StaDirAdAg 2-84*
Pert Survey Research - West Hartford, CT - *IntDirMarRes 83*
Pertec Computer Corp. [Subs. of Triumph Adler North America Inc.] - Irvine, CA - *DataDirSup 7-83; MicrocomMPl 84; WhoWMicrocom 83*
Pertec Computer Corp. - Los Angeles, CA - *InfIndMarPl 83*
Perth Courier, The - Perth, ON, Canada - *Ed&PubIntYB 82*
Peru Challenge [of Syracuse Maverick Media Inc.] - Syracuse, NE - *NewsDir 84*
Peru Tribune - Peru, IN - *BaconPubCkNews 84; Ed&PubIntYB 82; NewsDir 84*
Peruzzi & Walzer Research Services Inc. - New York, NY - *IntDirMarRes 83*
Pesante Record Co. - Norfolk, VA - *BillIntBG 83-84*
Pesca y Marina [of Editorial Pesca Marina SA] - Los Angeles, CA - *BaconPubCkMag 84; MagDir 84*
Pesce Advertising [Subs. of BP & R Inc.] - Melville, NY - *LitMarPl 84*
Pesce Advertising [Subs. of Barbini, Pesce & Noble Inc.] - New York, NY - *DirMarMP 83; LitMarPl 83, 84; MagIndMarPl 82-83; StaDirAdAg 2-84*
Peschel Instruments - Cape Coral, FL - *MicrocomMPl 83, 84; MicrocomSwDir 1*
Peshtigo Times - Peshtigo, WI - *BaconPubCkNews 84; Ed&PubIntYB 82; NewsDir 84*
Pesin, Sydney & Bernard Advertising - New York, NY - *AdAge 3-28-84; StaDirAdAg 2-84*
Pesque Isle County Advance - Rogers City, MI - *Ed&PubIntYB 82*
Pest Control - New York, NY - *MagDir 84; MagIndMarPl 82-83*
Pest Control - Cleveland, OH - *BaconPubCkMag 84; WritMar 84*

Pest Control Literature Documentation [of SDC Search Service] - Santa Monica, CA - *DataDirOnSer 84*
Pest Control Literature Documentation [of Derwent Publications Ltd.] - London, England - *DBBus 82; EISS 83*
Pest Control Technology - Cleveland, OH - *BaconPubCkMag 84; MagDir 84*
Pest Interception Database [of U.S. Dept. of Agriculture] - Hyattsville, MD - *EISS 83*
Pest Management - Dunn Loring, VA - *BaconPubCkMag 84*
Pestdoc/Pestdoc-II [of Derwent Publications Ltd.] - London, England - *DirOnDB Spring 84; OnBibDB 3*
Pesticidal Literature Documentation [of Derwent Publications Ltd.] - London, England - *CompReadDB 82*
Pesticide & Toxic Chemical News - Washington, DC - *BaconPubCkMag 84*
Pet Age - Chicago, IL - *BaconPubCkMag 84; MagDir 84; WritMar 84*
Pet Business - Miami, FL - *ArtMar 84; MagDir 84; MagIndMarPl 82-83; WritMar 84*
Pet Dealer, The - Elizabeth, NJ - *MagDir 84; WritMar 84*
Pet Gazette - Vancouver, WA - *MagDir 84*
Pet Hospital News [of Impressions Writing Service] - Indianapolis, IN - *WritMar 84*
Pet News - Brooklyn, NY - *MagDir 84*
Pet Parade, The - Universal City, CA - *Ed&PubIntYB 82*
Pet Records/Tapes - Burbank, CA - *BillIntBG 83-84*
Petaluma Argus-Courier [of Sonoma-Martin Publishing Co.] - Petaluma, CA - *BaconPubCkNews 84; NewsDir 84*
Peter Associates Inc., James - Tenafly, NJ - *LitMarPl 83, 84*
Peter Associates Inc., John - New York, NY - *MagIndMarPl 82-83*
Peter-Jan Publishing - Omaha, NE - *BillIntBG 83-84*
Peterborough Examiner - Peterborough, ON, Canada - *BaconPubCkNews 84; Ed&PubIntYB 82; LitMarPl 83, 84*
Peterborough Monadnock Ledger - Peterborough, NH - *BaconPubCkNews 84*
Peterborough Transcript - Peterborough, NH - *BaconPubCkNews 84; Ed&PubIntYB 82; NewsDir 84*
Petereins Press - Glendale, CA - *BoPubDir 4 Sup, 5*
Peters Co., Ferguson E. - Ft. Lauderdale, FL - *BoPubDir 4, 5*
Peters Corp., C. F. - New York, NY - *BillIntBG 83-84*
Peters, Griffin, Woodward Inc. - New York, NY - *TelAl 83, 84*
Peters International Inc. - New York, NY - *BillIntBG 83-84*
Peters, Marjorie - Chicago, IL - *LitMarPl 83*
Peters Marketing Research - St. Louis, MO - *IntDirMarRes 83*
Peters Music, Ben - Brentwood, TN - *BillIntBG 83-84*
Peters Productions - San Diego, CA - *Tel&CabFB 84C*
Petersburg Broadcasting Co. - Petersburg, VA - *BrCabYB 84*
Petersburg Cablevision [of Alaska Cablevision Inc.] - Petersburg, AK - *BrCabYB 84; Tel&CabFB 84C*
Petersburg Grant County Press - Petersburg, WV - *BaconPubCkNews 84*
Petersburg Observer - Petersburg, IL - *BaconPubCkNews 84; Ed&PubIntYB 82; NewsDir 84*
Petersburg Pilot - Petersburg, AK - *BaconPubCkNews 84; Ed&PubIntYB 82; NewsDir 84*
Petersburg Post - Petersburg, TX - *BaconPubCkNews 84; Ed&PubIntYB 82*
Petersburg Press - Petersburg, NE - *BaconPubCkNews 84; Ed&PubIntYB 82*
Petersburg Press Dispatch - Petersburg, IN - *BaconPubCkNews 84; NewsDir 84*
Petersburg Progress-Index [of Thomson Newspapers] - Petersburg, VA - *BaconPubCkNews 84; NewsDir 84*
Petersburg Sun - Petersburg, MI - *Ed&PubIntYB 82*
Petersburg Sun - *See* Reporter Publishing Co.
Petersburg Telephone Co. - Petersburg, NE - *TelDir&BG 83-84*
Petersen Action Group - *Folio 83*
Petersen Co., The - Hollywood, CA - *Tel&CabFB 84C*
Petersen, Dean - Carthage, MO - *Tel&CabFB 84C p.1697*
Petersen Press Inc. - Appleton, WI - *MagIndMarPl 82-83*
Petersen Prints - Los Angeles, CA - *ArtMar 84*
Petersen Publishing Co. - Los Angeles, CA - *AdAge 6-28-84; DirMarMP 83; KnowInd 83; MagIndMarPl 82-83; WritMar 84*
Petersen's 4-Wheel & Off-Road [of Petersen Publishing Co.] - Los Angeles, CA - *MagIndMarPl 82-83; WritMar 84*
Petersen's Hunting Magazine [of Petersen Publishing Co.] - Los Angeles, CA - *ArtMar 84; BaconPubCkMag 84; Folio 83; MagDir 84; MagIndMarPl 82-83; WritMar 84*
Petersen's Photographic Magazine [of Petersen Publishing Co.] - Los Angeles, CA - *BaconPubCkMag 84; MagDir 84; MagIndMarPl 82-83; WritMar 84*
Peterson, A. G. - DeBary, FL - *BoPubDir 4, 5*
Peterson Advertising Agency, Robert - Riverside, IL - *StaDirAdAg 2-84*
Peterson & Blyth Associates Inc. - New York, NY - *HBIndAd&MS 82-83*
Peterson & Dodge-Specialists In Print - San Francisco, CA - *DirPRFirms 83*
Peterson, Betty J. - Peoria, IL - *BoPubDir 4, 5*
Peterson Minerals, Helen - Bancroft, ON, Canada - *BoPubDir 4, 5*
Peterson-Morris - St. Paul, MN - *AdAge 3-28-84; StaDirAdAg 2-84*
Peterson Patriot - Peterson, IA - *BaconPubCkNews 84; Ed&PubIntYB 82*
Peterson, West F. - Forest Hills, NY - *MagIndMarPl 82-83*
Peterson's College Database - Princeton, NJ - *DirOnDB Spring 84*
Peterson's Guides Inc. - Princeton, NJ - *DataDirOnSer 84; DirMarMP 83; EISS 5-84 Sup; LitMarPl 83, 84; WritMar 84*
Peterson's National College Database [of Bibliographic Retrieval Services Inc.] - Lathan, NY - *DataDirOnSer 84*
Petervin Press - Davis, CA - *BoPubDir 4, 5*
Petervin Press Information Search Service [of The Petervin Press] - Davis, CA - *EISS 83*
Petewood Music Co. Inc. - *See* Drake Music Group
Petfood Industry - Mt. Morris, IL - *BaconPubCkMag 84; MagDir 84*
Petheric Press - Halifax, NS, Canada - *BoPubDir 4, 5*
Petit Jean CTV Co. Inc. - Danville, AR - *BrCabYB 84; Tel&CabFB 84C*
Petite Film Co. - Seattle, WA - *AvMarPl 83*
Petoskey Music Inc. - *See* Jet-Eye Music Inc.
Petoskey News Review [of Northern Michigan Review Inc.] - Petoskey, MI - *BaconPubCkNews 84; Ed&PubIntYB 82; NewsDir 84*
Petrocelli Books Inc. - Princeton, NJ - *LitMarPl 83, 84; WritMar 84*
Petrochemical Equipment News [of Gordon Publications] - Dover, NJ - *BaconPubCkMag 84; MagDir 84*
Petrochemical News - Stamford, CT - *BaconPubCkMag 84*
Petrochemicals [of Probe Economics Inc.] - Mt. Kisco, NY - *DataDirOnSer 84; DirOnDB Spring 84*
Petrochemicals Forecast Data Base [of Probe Economics Inc.] - Mt. Kisco, NY - *DataDirOnSer 84; DirOnDB Spring 84*
Petroflash! - Lakewood, NJ - *DirOnDB Spring 84*
Petroglyph Press Ltd. - Hilo, HI - *BoPubDir 4, 5*
Petroleo Internacional [of Pennwell Publishing Co.] - Tulsa, OK - *BaconPubCkMag 84; MagDir 84; WritMar 84*
Petroleum Abstracts Data Base [of University of Tulsa] - Tulsa, OK - *CompReadDB 82; DBBus 82; OnBibDB 3*
Petroleum Abstracts Information System [of University of Tulsa] - Tulsa, OK - *EISS 83*
Petroleum Argus Daily Market Report [of I. P. Sharp Associates Ltd.] - Toronto, ON, Canada - *DataDirOnSer 84*
Petroleum Argus Daily Market Report - London, England - *DirOnDB Spring 84*
Petroleum Argus Prices [of I. P. Sharp Associates Ltd.] - Toronto, ON, Canada - *DataDirOnSer 84*
Petroleum Argus Prices [of Europ-Oil Prices] - London, England - *DBBus 82; DirOnDB Spring 84*
Petroleum Argus Time Series Database [of I. P. Sharp Associates Ltd.] - Toronto, ON, Canada - *DataDirOnSer 84*
Petroleum Data System [of University of Oklahoma] - Norman, OK - *DataDirOnSer 84; DirOnDB Spring 84; EISS 83*
Petroleum/Energy Business News Index [of American Petroleum Institute] - Washington, DC - *DBBus 82*
Petroleum/Energy Business News Index [of American Petroleum Institute] - New York, NY - *CompReadDB 82*
Petroleum Engineer International [of Energy Publications] - Dallas, TX - *BaconPubCkMag 84; Folio 83; MagDir 84*
Petroleum Equipment - Morristown, NJ - *MagIndMarPl 82-83*
Petroleum Equipment - Whitehouse, NJ - *BaconPubCkMag 84*

Petroleum Equipment Suppliers Association - Houston, TX - *BoPubDir 5*
Petroleum Independent - Washington, DC - *BaconPubCkMag 84; MagDir 84; WritMar 84*
Petroleum Information [Aff. of A. C. Nielsen Co.] - Denver, CO - *BoPubDir 5; DataDirOnSer 84; InfIndMarPl 83; InfoS 83-84*
Petroleum Information International - Littleton, CO - *DirOnDB Spring 84*
Petroleum Information International [of NewsNet Inc.] - Bryn Mawr, PA - *DataDirOnSer 84*
Petroleum Intelligence Weekly - New York, NY - *BaconPubCkMag 84; DirOnDB Spring 84*
Petroleum Intelligence Weekly [of I. P. Sharp Associates Ltd.] - Toronto, ON, Canada - *DataDirOnSer 84*
Petroleum Marketer [of McKeand Publications Inc.] - West Haven, CT - *BaconPubCkMag 84; MagDir 84*
Petroleum Marketing Management - Rockville, MD - *BaconPubCkMag 84*
Petroleum Software Systems Inc. (Marketing Div.) - Oklahoma City, OK - *ADAPSOMemDir 83-84*
Petroleum Supply Monthly [of I. P. Sharp Associates Ltd.] - Toronto, ON, Canada - *DataDirOnSer 84*
Petrolia Enniskillen Gazette - Petrolia, ON, Canada - *Ed&PubIntYB 82*
Petrolia-Enniskillen Gazette, The - Sarnia, ON, Canada - *AyerDirPub 83*
Petronium Press - Honolulu, HI - *BoPubDir 4, 5; LitMag&SmPr 83-84*
PetroScan [of United Communications Group] - Silver Spring, MD - *DirOnDB Spring 84; EISS 5-84 Sup*
Petroseries - Washington, DC - *DBBus 82*
Petrulakis, Paul - Olney, MD - *LitMarPl 83, 84*
Petry & Co. Inc., Edward - New York, NY - *TelAl 83, 84*
Pets/Supplies/Marketing - Duluth, MN - *BaconPubCkMag 84; MagDir 84; WritMar 84*
Petted Micro Systems - Milwaukee, WI - *MicrocomMPl 83*
Pettigrew Enterprises Inc. - Washington, DC - *BoPubDir 4, 5*
Pettigrew Telephone Line - Oelrichs, SD - *TelDir&BG 83-84*
Pettinella Advertising Co. - Franklin Lakes, NJ - *StaDirAdAg 2-84*
Pettler Degrassi & Hill - Oakland, CA - *ArtMar 84; StaDirAdAg 2-84*
Pettus Advertising Inc. - Corpus Christi, TX - *StaDirAdAg 2-84*
Petzold Advertising Inc. - Bedford, NH - *StaDirAdAg 2-84*
Petzold & Associates - Portland, OR - *StaDirAdAg 2-84*
Peuple/Courier - Montmagny, PQ, Canada - *Ed&PubIntYB 82*
Pewter Pal Music - Ojai, CA - *BillIntBG 83-84*
Peyton Records Inc. [Div. of JPM Industries] - Northbrook, IL - *BillIntBG 83-84*
Pezzano Associates Ltd., Linda - New York, NY - *DirPRFirms 83*
Pfaff Inc., Warren - New York, NY - *HBIndAd&MS 82-83; StaDirAdAg 2-84*
P.F.C. Publishing Co. Inc. - New York, NY - *BoPubDir 4, 5*
Pfeiffer, Philip A. - Pensacola, FL - *BoPubDir 4, 5*
Pfister Communications - New York, NY - *DirPRFirms 83; ProGuPRSer 4*
Pflaum Co. Inc., The William C. - Reston, VA - *ArtMar 84; DirPRFirms 83*
Pflaum Press [Aff. of Peter Li Inc.] - Dayton, OH - *BoPubDir 4, 5*
PFM-Professional Furniture Merchant - Coral Springs, FL - *BaconPubCkMag 84*
PFMA Advisor - Erie, PA - *BaconPubCkMag 84*
PGA Book of Golf - West Palm Beach, FL - *MagDir 84*
PGA Data Base - Ponte Vedra, FL - *DirOnDB Spring 84*
PGA Magazine - Palm Beach Gardens, FL - *BaconPubCkMag 84; MagDir 84; WritMar 84*
PGI Publishing - Tempe, AZ - *MicrocomMPl 83, 84*
PGI Wholesale - Tempe, AZ - *MicrocomMPl 84*
Phaedrus Inc. - Greenwich, CT - *IntDirMarRes 83*
Phalanx Productions - London, ON, Canada - *BoPubDir 4 Sup, 5*
Phaneuf Computer Systems Inc. - West Warwick, RI - *MicrocomSwDir 1*
Phantasia Press - Huntington Woods, MI - *BoPubDir 4, 5*
Phantasm [of Heidelberg Graphics] - Chico, CA - *LitMag&SmPr 83-84; MagDir 84; WritMar 84*
Pharma Documentation Ring - Basel, Switzerland - *EISS 83*
Pharma-Documentation Ring Online User Group [of Ciba-Geigy Ltd.] - Basel, Switzerland - *InfIndMarPl 83*
Pharma Documentation Service - Frankfurt, West Germany - *EISS 83*
Pharmaceutical Executive - Springfield, OR - *BaconPubCkMag 84*
Pharmaceutical Literature Documentation [of Derwent Publications Ltd.] - London, England - *CompReadDB 82; DBBus 82; EISS 83*
Pharmaceutical Manufacturers Association - Washington, DC - *BoPubDir 5*
Pharmaceutical News Index [of Data Courier] - Louisville, KY - *CompReadDB 82; DataDirOnSer 84; DBBus 82; DirOnDB Spring 84; EISS 83; OnBibDB 3*
Pharmaceutical Prospects - Glastonbury, CT - *DBBus 82; DirOnDB Spring 84*
Pharmaceutical Representative - Northfield, IL - *BaconPubCkMag 84*
Pharmaceutical Representative [of McKnight Medical Communications] - Winnetka, IL - *MagDir 84*
Pharmaceutical Technology - Springfield, OR - *ArtMar 84; BaconPubCkMag 84*
Pharmaceutical Technology Publications [Aff. of Aster Publishing Corp.] - Springfield, OR - *BoPubDir 5*
Pharmaco-Medical Documentation Inc. - Chatham, NJ - *EISS 83*
Pharmaco-Medical Documentation Inc. - Madison, NJ - *BoPubDir 5; InfoS 83-84*
Pharmaco-Medical Documentation Inc. (Biomedical Information Sciences) - Chatham, NJ - *InfIndMarPl 83*
Pharmacy Associates - Bossier City, LA - *WhoWMicrocom 83*
Pharmacy Associates - Hampton, VA - *MicrocomMPl 84*
Pharmacy Times [of Romaine Pierson Publishing] - Port Washington, NY - *BaconPubCkMag 84; MagDir 84; MagIndMarPl 82-83*
Pharmacy West [of Western Communications Ltd.] - Los Angeles, CA - *BaconPubCkMag 84; MagDir 84*
Pharmline [of Drug Information Pharmacists Group] - London, England - *EISS 5-84 Sup*
Pharos Press - Victoria, BC, Canada - *BoPubDir 4, 5*
Pharos Tribune - Logansport, IN - *AyerDirPub 83; BaconPubCkNews 84; Ed&PubIntYB 82*
Pharr Brothers Advertising - Clarksdale, MS - *StaDirAdAg 2-84*
Pharr Cox Communications - *See* Richards Group Inc., The
Pharr News - Pharr, TX - *AyerDirPub 83*
Pharr Press - Pharr, TX - *BaconPubCkNews 84; Ed&PubIntYB 82*
Phase Diagrams for Ceramists Data Center [of U.S. National Bureau of Standards] - Washington, DC - *EISS 83*
Phase Linear [Div. of International Jensen] - Lynnwood, WA - *BillIntBG 83-84*
Phase One Systems Inc. - Oakland, CA - *MicrocomMPl 84; WhoWMicrocom 83*
Phase Seven - Boston, MA - *DirInfWP 82*
Phase Zero Ltd. - Tucson, AZ - *MicrocomMPl 83, 84*
Phasecom Corp. - Los Angeles, CA - *AvMarPl 83*
Phax Records & Filmworks Inc. - Long Beach, CA - *BillIntBG 83-84*
Phaze Information Machines Corporations - Scottsdale, AZ - *DataDirSup 7-83*
Pheasant Run Publications - St. Louis, MO - *LitMag&SmPr 83-84*
Phelan/Schreiner Productions & Associates Inc. - Denver, CO - *AvMarPl 83*
Phelon, Sheldon & Marsar Inc. - New York, NY - *BoPubDir 4, 5; MagIndMarPl 82-83*
Phelps Publishing Co. - London, ON, Canada - *BoPubDir 4, 5*
Phenix Citizen - Phenix City, AL - *BaconPubCkNews 84; Ed&PubIntYB 82*
Phenix Citizen/Citizen Extra [of Thompson Newspapers] - Phenix City, AL - *NewsDir 84*
Phenix City CATV - Phenix City, AL - *Tel&CabFB 84C*
Phi Delta Kappan - Bloomington, IN - *ArtMar 84; BoPubDir 4, 5; MagDir 84; MagIndMarPl 82-83; WritMar 84*
PHI Technologies Inc. - Oklahoma City, OK - *AvMarPl 83*
Phi Theta Pi Fraternity - Jacksonville, FL - *BoPubDir 5*

Phiebig Inc., Albert J. - White Plains, NY - *LitMarPl 83, 84; MagIndMarPl 82-83*
Phil Campbell Television Service Inc. - Phil Campbell, AL - *BrCabYB 84; Tel&CabFB 84C*
Philadelphia Afro-American [of Baltimore Afro-American Newspapers] - Baltimore, MD - *NewsDir 84*
Philadelphia Bulletin - Philadelphia, PA - *NewsBur 6; NewsDir 84*
Philadelphia Business Journal - Philadelphia, PA - *BaconPubCkMag 84*
Philadelphia Catholic Standard & Times - Philadelphia, PA - *NewsDir 84*
Philadelphia Chestnut Hill Local [of Chestnut Hill Community Association] - Philadelphia, PA - *BaconPubCkNews 84; NewsDir 84*
Philadelphia City Paper - Philadelphia, PA - *LitMag&SmPr 83-84*
Philadelphia Consulting Group Inc. - Wynnewood, PA - *MicrocomMPl 83, 84; WhoWMicrocom 83*
Philadelphia Daily News [of Philadelphia Newspapers Inc.] - Philadelphia, PA - *BaconPubCkNews 84; DirOnDB Spring 84; Ed&PubIntYB 82; LitMarPl 84; NewsDir 84*
Philadelphia Daily News Full Text [of VU/Text Information Services] - Philadelphia, PA - *DataDirOnSer 84*
Philadelphia Drummer Planet, The - Philadelphia, PA - *NewsDir 84*
Philadelphia Far Northeast Citizen Sentinel - *See* Progress Newspapers Inc.
Philadelphia Gazette-Democrat - Philadelphia, PA - *Ed&PubIntYB 82*
Philadelphia Germantown Courier - *See* Acme Newspapers Inc.
Philadelphia Germantown Paper - *See* Intercounty Newspaper Group
Philadelphia Girard Home News - Philadelphia, PA - *BaconPubCkNews 84; NewsDir 84*
Philadelphia Guide Newspapers Inc. - Philadelphia, PA - *NewsDir 84*
Philadelphia Inquirer [of Philadelphia Newspapers Inc.] - Philadelphia, PA - *BaconPubCkNews 84; DirOnDB Spring 84; Ed&PubIntYB 82; LitMarPl 83, 84; NewsBur 6; NewsDir 84*
Philadelphia Inquirer Full Text [of VU/Text Information Services] - Philadelphia, PA - *DataDirOnSer 84*
Philadelphia Inquirer Magazine-Today - Philadelphia, PA - *MagIndMarPl 82-83*
Philadelphia Insulated Wire Co. Inc. - Moorestown, NJ - *DataDirSup 7-83*
Philadelphia International Records - Philadelphia, PA - *BillIntBG 83-84*
Philadelphia Jewish Exponent [of Federation of Jewish Agencies] - Philadelphia, PA - *NewsDir 84*
Philadelphia Jewish Times of the Greater Northeast - Philadelphia, PA - *NewsDir 84*
Philadelphia Magazine [of Municipal Publications Inc.] - Philadelphia, PA - *ArtMar 84; BaconPubCkMag 84; Folio 83; MagDir 84; MagIndMarPl 82-83; WritMar 84*
Philadelphia Maritime Museum - Philadelphia, PA - *BoPubDir 4, 5*
Philadelphia Medicine - Philadelphia, PA - *BaconPubCkMag 84; MagDir 84*
Philadelphia Museum of Art - Philadelphia, PA - *BoPubDir 4, 5*
Philadelphia Museum of Art Bulletin - Philadelphia, PA - *MagIndMarPl 82-83*
Philadelphia Music Works - Bryn Mawr, PA - *AvMarPl 83*
Philadelphia National Leader - Philadelphia, PA - *BaconPubCkNews 84*
Philadelphia Neshoba Democrat - Philadelphia, MS - *BaconPubCkNews 84; NewsDir 84*
Philadelphia New Observer - Philadelphia, PA - *BaconPubCkNews 84; NewsDir 84*
Philadelphia/New York Action Newspaper [of PNS Research Inc.] - Ft. Washington, PA - *WritMar 84*
Philadelphia News Gleaner Publications - Philadelphia, PA - *NewsDir 84*
Philadelphia Nite Owl - Philadelphia, PA - *BaconPubCkNews 84*
Philadelphia Nite Scene - Philadelphia, PA - *BaconPubCkNews 84*
Philadelphia Northeast Advisor - *See* Intercounty Newspaper Group
Philadelphia Northeast Breeze - *See* Intercounty Newspaper Group
Philadelphia Northeast Times - Philadelphia, PA - *BaconPubCkNews 84*
Philadelphia Olney Times - Philadelphia, PA - *BaconPubCkNews 84*
Philadelphia Patristic Foundation Ltd. - Cambridge, MA - *BoPubDir 4, 5*
Philadelphia Poets - Darby, PA - *LitMag&SmPr 83-84*
Philadelphia Roxborough Review - *See* Intercounty Newspaper Group
Philadelphia Shlakh/The Way - Philadelphia, PA - *NewsDir 84*
Philadelphia Solidarity/Wooden Shoe - Philadelphia, PA - *BoPubDir 4, 5*
Philadelphia South Chronicle - *See* South Philadelphia Review-Chronicle
Philadelphia South Review-East - *See* South Philadelphia Review-Chronicle
Philadelphia South Review-West - *See* South Philadelphia Review-Chronicle
Philadelphia Southwest Globe Times - Philadelphia, PA - *BaconPubCkNews 84; NewsDir 84*
Philadelphia Spirit - Philadelphia, PA - *BaconPubCkNews 84; Ed&PubIntYB 82*
Philadelphia Supply Corp. - Fountain Valley, CA - *WhoWMicrocom 83*
Philadelphia Town & Country News [of Gouverneur Town & Country News of Jefferson County] - Gouverneur, NY *NewsDir 84*
Philadelphia Tribune - Philadelphia, PA - *BaconPubCkNews 84; NewsDir 84*
Philadelphia Welcomat Inc. - Philadelphia, PA - *NewsDir 84*
Philadelphia West Oak Lane Leader - *See* Intercounty Newspaper Group
Philam Books Inc. - Vancouver, BC, Canada - *BoPubDir 4, 5*
Philatelic Directory Publishing Co. - St. Augustine, FL - *BoPubDir 4, 5; LitMag&SmPr 83-84*
Philatelic Foundation - New York, NY - *BoPubDir 4, 5*
Philatelic Journalist [of Philatelic Directory Publishing Co.] - St. Augustine, FL - *LitMag&SmPr 83-84; MagDir 84; WritMar 84*
Philathea College - London, ON, Canada - *BoPubDir 4, 5*
Philco - *See* NAP Consumer Electronics
Philco Music - *See* Moody Music, Doug
Philella Music - *See* Pewter Pal Music
Philiba, Allan A. - Baldwin, NY - *LitMarPl 83, 84; MagIndMarPl 82-83*
Philip Pioneer-Review - Philip, SD - *BaconPubCkNews 84*
Philippi Barbour Democrat - Philippi, WV - *BaconPubCkNews 84; NewsDir 84*
Philippine Encoding Corp. - Pasig, Philippines - *ADAPSOMemDir 83-84*
Philips & King Advertising Co. Inc. - New York, NY - *StaDirAdAg 2-84*
Philips Business Systems Inc. - Woodbury, NY - *InfIndMarPl 83*
Philips Information Systems Inc. - Dallas, TX - *Datamation 6-83; DirInfWP 82; Top100Al 83*
Philips Offset Co. Inc. - Mamaroneck, NY - *LitMarPl 83, 84; MagIndMarPl 82-83*
Philips Television Systems Inc. - Mahwah, NJ - *AvMarPl 83*
Philipsburg Cable TV - Philipsburg, MT - *BrCabYB 84*
Philipsburg Daily Journal [of Moshannon Valley Publishing Co. Inc.] - Philipsburg, PA - *NewsDir 84*
Philipsburg Mail - Philipsburg, MT - *BaconPubCkNews 84; Ed&PubIntYB 82*
Philipson Agency, The - Boston, MA - *StaDirAdAg 2-84*
Phillips, A. J. - Vista, CA - *BoPubDir 4, 5*
Phillips Academy (Robert S. Peabody Foundation for Archaeology) - Andover, MA - *BoPubDir 4, 5*
Phillips Advertising Agency - Louisville, KY - *StaDirAdAg 2-84*
Phillips/Alogna Associates Inc. - Garden City, NY - *StaDirAdAg 2-84*
Phillips Bee - Phillips, WI - *BaconPubCkNews 84; NewsDir 84*
Phillips Brothers Printers - Springfield, IL - *LitMarPl 83, 84*
Phillips Collection - Washington, DC - *BoPubDir 5*
Phillips Communications Associates Inc., Jean - New York, NY - *DirPRFirms 83*

Phillips County News - Malta, MT - *AyerDirPub 83; Ed&PubIntYB 82*
Phillips County Review - Phillipsburg, KS - *AyerDirPub 83; Ed&PubIntYB 82*
Phillips County Telephone Co. - Holyoke, CO - *TelDir&BG 83-84*
Phillips/David Scott International Inc., Dan - Hollywood, CA - *BillIntBG 83-84*
Phillips, Douglas L. - *See* Flora Cable TV Co.
Phillips Editions, Michael Joseph - Bloomington, IN - *BoPubDir 4, 5*
Phillips, Euan - Stamford, CT - *LitMarPl 83, 84*
Phillips Inc., S. G. - Chatham, NY - *LitMarPl 83*
Phillips-Neuman Co. - Bethesda, MD - *BoPubDir 5*
Phillips, Odell - Frederick, MO - *Tel&CabFB 84C p.1697*
Phillips Organisation Ltd., The - San Diego, CA - *AdAge 3-28-84; StaDirAdAg 2-84*
Phillips Photo Illustrators - Colts Neck, NJ - *LitMarPl 84*
Phillips Photographic Lab - Denver, CO - *AvMarPl 83*
Phillips Publications - Williamstown, NJ - *BoPubDir 4, 5; LitMag&SmPr 83-84*
Phillips Publishing Inc. - Bethesda, MD - *EISS 5-84 Sup; InterCabHB 3*
Phillips-Ramsey Co. - San Diego, CA - *AdAge 3-28-84; StaDirAdAg 2-84*
Phillipsburg Cable TV - Phillipsburg, MT - *Tel&CabFB 84C*
Phillipsburg Free Press [of Phillipsburg Publishing Co.] - Phillipsburg, NJ - *BaconPubCkNews 84; NewsDir 84*
Phillipsburg Phillips County Review [of Boyd Printing Co. Inc.] - Phillipsburg, KS - *BaconPubCkNews 84; NewsDir 84*
Phillipsburg TV Cable Co. [of CATV Inc.] - Phillipsburg, KS - *BrCabYB 84*
Philly Sound Works Entertainment Corp. - Cherry Hill, NJ - *BillIntBG 83-84*
Philly World Records - Philadelphia, PA - *BillIntBG 83-84*
Philmer Enterprises - Spring House, PA - *BoPubDir 4, 5; LitMag&SmPr 83-84*
Philo Records Inc. - North Ferrisburg, VT - *BillIntBG 83-84*
Philomath Benton Bulletin - *See* Tri-County Publications Inc.
Philomel Books [Div. of The Putnam Publishing Group] - New York, NY - *WritMar 84*
Philomel Books - *See* Putnam Publishing Group
Philosopher's Index [of Bowling Green State University] - Bowling Green, OH - *CompReadDB 82; DataDirOnSer 84; DirOnDB Spring 84; OnBibDB 3*
Philosophical Library Inc. - New York, NY - *LitMarPl 83, 84*
Philosophical Research Society Inc. - Los Angeles, CA - *BoPubDir 4, 5*
Philosophical Review, The - Ithaca, NY - *MagIndMarPl 82-83*
Philosophical Speculations in Science Fiction & Fantasy [of Burning Bush Publications] - Norristown, PA - *LitMag&SmPr 83-84*
Philosophie 1 und 3 [of Universitaet Duesseldorf] - Duesseldorf, West Germany - *CompReadDB 82*
Philosophie 2 [of Universitaet Duesseldorf] - Duesseldorf, West Germany - *CompReadDB 82*
Philosophy [of Centre de Documentation Sciences Humaines] - Paris, France - *CompReadDB 82*
Philosophy & Public Affairs - Princeton, NJ - *MagIndMarPl 82-83*
Philosophy & the Arts - Bronx, NY - *BoPubDir 4, 5; LitMag&SmPr 83-84*
Philosophy & the Arts Press - Bronx, NY - *LitMag&SmPr 83-84*
Philosophy Documentation Center [of Bowling Green State University] - Bowling Green, OH - *CompReadDB 82; DataDirOnSer 84; EISS 83; InfIndMarPl 83; MagIndMarPl 82-83; MicroMarPl 82-83*
Philosophy Information Service [of University of Dusseldorf] - Dusseldorf, West Germany - *EISS 83*
Philosophy of Science Association - East Lansing, MI - *BoPubDir 4, 5*
Philprom Inc. - Manila, Philippines - *StaDirAdAg 2-84*
Philsom Network [of Washington University] - St. Louis, MO - *EISS 83; InfIndMarPl 83*
PHINet FedTax - New York, NY - *DirOnDB Spring 84*
Phipps & Co. Productions - Tulsa, OK - *AvMarPl 83*
Phipps Associates - Epsom, England - *MicrocomSwDir 1*
Phipps Publishing Co. [Aff. of New England Manufacturing Co.] - Norwell, MA - *BoPubDir 4, 5*
Phoebe [of George Mason University] - Fairfax, VA - *ArtMar 84; LitMag&SmPr 83-84; WritMar 84*
Phoebus Magazine - Hampton, VA - *LitMag&SmPr 83-84*
Phoenix [of San Francisco State University] - San Francisco, CA - *NewsDir 84*
Phoenix - Richmondville, NY - *AyerDirPub 83*
Phoenix - Bristol, RI - *AyerDirPub 83*
Phoenix [of University of New Brunswick Libraries] - Fredericton, NB, Canada - *EISS 7-83 Sup*
Phoenix & Times Democrat - Muskogee, OK - *AyerDirPub 83; Ed&PubIntYB 82*
Phoenix Arizona Informant - Phoenix, AZ - *BaconPubCkNews 84; NewsDir 84*
Phoenix Arizona Republic [of Phoenix Newspapers Inc.] - Phoenix, AZ - *NewsDir 84*
Phoenix Book Shop - New York, NY - *BoPubDir 4, 5*
Phoenix Books Publishers [Aff. of Lotus Press] - Phoenix, AZ - *BoPubDir 4, 5; LitMag&SmPr 83-84; LitMarPl 84*
Phoenix Broadsheets - Leicester, England - *LitMag&SmPr 83-84*
Phoenix Business Journal [of Cordovan Corp.] - Phoenix, AZ - *BaconPubCkMag 84; WritMar 84*
Phoenix Cable - Baie Verte, NF, Canada - *BrCabYB 84*
Phoenix Cable Communications Corp. - Eustace, TX - *BrCabYB 84*
Phoenix Cable Communications Corp. - Gun Barrel, TX - *BrCabYB 84*
Phoenix Cable Communications Corp. - Mabank, TX - *BrCabYB 84*
Phoenix Cable Communications Corp. - Trinidad, TX - *BrCabYB 84*
Phoenix Cable Communications Corp. - *See* Prime Cable Corp.
Phoenix Cable TV [of Prime Cable Corp.] - Gun Barrel City, TX - *Tel&CabFB 84C*
Phoenix Color Corp. - Long Island City, NY - *LitMarPl 83, 84*
Phoenix Communications Press Ltd. - Phoenix, AZ - *LitMag&SmPr 83-84*
Phoenix Computer Corp. - Culver City, CA - *ADAPSOMemDir 83-84; DataDirSup 7-83*
Phoenix Computer Systems Pty. Ltd. - Newcastle, Australia - *ADAPSOMemDir 83-84*
Phoenix Data Processing - Naperville, IL - *ADAPSOMemDir 83-84*
Phoenix Digital Corp. - Phoenix, AZ - *MicrocomMPl 83, 84*
Phoenix Features - Long Island City, NY - *Ed&PubIntYB 82*
Phoenix Fields Ltd. - New York, NY - *IntDirMarRes 83*
Phoenix Films - New York, NY - *ArtMar 84; Tel&CabFB 84C*
Phoenix Gazette [of Phoenix Newspapers Inc.] - Phoenix, AZ - *BaconPubCkNews 84; Ed&PubIntYB 82; LitMarPl 83, 84; NewsBur 6; NewsDir 84*
Phoenix Home/Garden [of Arizona Home Garden Inc.] - Phoenix, AZ - *ArtMar 84; BaconPubCkMag 84; WritMar 84*
Phoenix Jewish News - Phoenix, AZ - *WritMar 84*
Phoenix Literary Agency Inc. - New York, NY - *LitMarPl 83, 84*
Phoenix Living - Phoenix, AZ - *MagDir 84; WritMar 84*
Phoenix Living - Dallas, TX - *MagIndMarPl 82-83*
Phoenix Log - Seward, AK - *AyerDirPub 83*
Phoenix Magazine - Phoenix, AZ - *BaconPubCkMag 84; MagDir 84; WritMar 84*
Phoenix MDS Co. - Englewood, NJ - *Tel&CabFB 84C*
Phoenix Metropolitan Chamber of Commerce - Phoenix, AZ - *BoPubDir 4 Sup, 5*
Phoenix New Times Weekly - Phoenix, AZ - *NewsDir 84*
Phoenix Performance Systems Inc. - Stillwater, MN - *MicrocomMPl 84; WhoWMicrocom 83*
Phoenix Press - Sandpoint, ID - *BoPubDir 4, 5*
Phoenix Press Weekly, The - Phoenix, AZ - *Ed&PubIntYB 82*
Phoenix Publications Inc. - Niles, OH - *BaconPubCkNews 84*
Phoenix Publishing - Canaan, NH - *LitMag&SmPr 83-84; LitMarPl 83, 84*
Phoenix Publishing Co. - Custer, WA - *BoPubDir 4 Sup, 5; LitMag&SmPr 83-84*
Phoenix Quarterly - Washington, DC - *BaconPubCkMag 84*
Phoenix Register - Phoenix, NY - *Ed&PubIntYB 82; NewsDir 84*
Phoenix Register - *See* Oswego County Weeklies

Phoenix Research Services [Div. of E. Friedman Marketing Services Inc.] - Phoenix, AZ - *IntDirMarRes 83*
Phoenix Software Inc. - Lake Zurich, IL - *MicrocomMPl 83, 84; MicrocomSwDir 1; WritMar 84*
Phoenix Studios Inc. - New York, NY - *Tel&CabFB 84C*
Phoenix Systems Inc. - Sewickley, PA - *MicrocomMPl 84; MicrocomSwDir 1; WhoWMicrocom 83*
Phoenix, The - Haydenville, MA - *MagIndMarPl 82-83*
Phoenix-Times Newspapers - Bristol, RI - *BaconPubCkNews 84*
Phoenix Typography [Subs. of Boston Phoenix Inc.] - Boston, MA - *LitMarPl 83, 84*
Phoenixongs - Chicago, IL - *BillIntBG 83-84*
Phoenixongs - Northbrook, IL - *BoPubDir 4, 5*
Phoenixville Evening Phoenix - Phoenixville, PA - *BaconPubCkNews 84; NewsDir 84*
Pholiota Press Inc. - Garden Grove, CA - *BoPubDir 4 Sup, 5*
Phone-A-Poem - Cambridge, MA - *LitMag&SmPr 83-84*
Phone-a-Writer Inc. - Westport, CT - *LitMarPl 83, 84*
Phone America - Asheville, NC - *TeleSy&SerDir 2-84*
Phone 1 Inc. - Loves Park, IL - *InfIndMarPl 83*
Phone 1 Inc. - Rockford, IL - *DataDirSup 7-83; MicrocomMPl 84*
Phonetones - Salem, MA - *BillIntBG 83-84*
Phono Music - *See* Music Craftshop Inc.
Phonograph-Herald, The - St. Paul, NE - *Ed&PubIntYB 82*
Photo Acquistions Researchers - New York, NY - *LitMarPl 84*
Photo & Sound Co. - San Francisco, CA - *AvMarPl 83*
Photo-Art Inc. - Wilmington, DE - *AvMarPl 83*
Photo Associates News Service Inc. - Flushing, NY - *Ed&PubIntYB 82; LitMarPl 84*
Photo-Communication Enterprises - Belchertown, MA - *AvMarPl 83*
Photo Communication Services - Ada, MI - *AvMarPl 83*
Photo Communications Co. Inc. - New York, NY - *Ed&PubIntYB 82*
Photo Communications Corp. - Jenkintown, PA - *AvMarPl 83*
Photo Control Corp. - Minneapolis, MN - *AvMarPl 83*
Photo Data - Washington, DC - *DataDirOnSer 84; LitMarPl 83, 84; MagIndMarPl 82-83*
Photo Dynamics Color - Cranford, NJ - *AvMarPl 83*
Photo Editors Inc. [Subs. of Photo Researchers Inc.] - New York, NY - *LitMarPl 83, 84*
Photo File, The - San Francisco, CA - *AvMarPl 83; MagIndMarPl 82-83*
Photo Files - Brooklyn, NY - *MagIndMarPl 82-83*
Photo Graphics Inc. - Glen Burnie, MD - *MagIndMarPl 82-83*
Photo Impressions Inc. - Glenview, IL - *AvMarPl 83*
Photo Industry Newsletter - New York, NY - *BaconPubCkMag 84*
Photo Insight - Jamaica, NY - *ArtMar 84; WritMar 84*
Photo Lab Management - Santa Monica, CA - *BaconPubCkMag 84; WritMar 84*
Photo-Library Inc. - New York, NY - *MagIndMarPl 82-83*
Photo Life - Markham, ON, Canada - *BaconPubCkMag 84*
Photo Marketing - Jackson, MI - *ArtMar 84; BaconPubCkMag 84; MagDir 84; MagIndMarPl 82-83; WritMar 84*
Photo Marketing Association International - Jackson, MI - *BoPubDir 5*
Photo Media Ltd. - New York, NY - *MagIndMarPl 82-83*
Photo Network - Tustin, CA - *AvMarPl 83*
Photo News, The - West Palm Beach, FL - *Ed&PubIntYB 82*
Photo Plastic International - Santa Monica, CA - *AvMarPl 83*
Photo Press - Fairmont, MN - *AyerDirPub 83*
Photo-Pros Inc. - Charlotte, NC - *AvMarPl 83*
Photo Researchers Inc. - New York, NY - *LitMarPl 83, 84; MagIndMarPl 82-83*
Photo Screen [of Sterling's Magazines Inc.] - New York, NY - *MagDir 84; MagIndMarPl 82-83; WritMar 84*
Photo Star - Willshire, OH - *AyerDirPub 83; Ed&PubIntYB 82*
Photo-Synthesis Inc. - Dallas, TX - *ArtMar 84*
Photo Tech Inc. - St. Paul, MN - *AvMarPl 83*
Photo-Technics [Div. of Photec Inc.] - Ft. Collins, CO - *AvMarPl 83*
Photo-Therm - Trenton, NJ - *AvMarPl 83*
Photo Trends - Freeport, NY - *LitMarPl 83, 84*
Photo Trends - New York, NY - *AvMarPl 83; Ed&PubIntYB 82; MagIndMarPl 82-83*
Photo Weekly - New York, NY - *BaconPubCkMag 84; MagDir 84; MagIndMarPl 82-83; WritMar 84*
Photoart Visual Service Corp. - Milwaukee, WI - *AvMarPl 83*
Photocom Productions - Grover City, CA - *AvMarPl 83*
Photocom Productions - Pismo Beach, CA - *ArtMar 84; WritMar 84*
Photocraft Inc. - Birmingham, AL - *AvMarPl 83*
PhotoDataBank [of PhotoSearch International] - Osceola, WI - *MagIndMarPl 82-83*
Photofile International Ltd. - New York, NY - *LitMarPl 83, 84*
Photoflash - Colorado Springs, CO - *LitMag&SmPr 83-84; WritMar 84*
Photogrammetric Engineering & Remote Sensing - Falls Church, VA - *BaconPubCkMag 84; MagDir 84; MagIndMarPl 82-83*
Photograph Collector, The - New York, NY - *DirMarMP 83*
Photographers' Color Service - Worcester, MA - *ArtMar 84; AvMarPl 83*
Photographers' Formulary, The [SU Tamwest Inc.] - Missoula, MT - *AvMarPl 83*
Photographer's Forum - Santa Barbara, CA - *BaconPubCkMag 84; WritMar 84*
Photographer's Market - Cincinnati, OH - *MagDir 84*
Photographer's Market Newsletter - Cincinnati, OH - *WritMar 84*
Photographic Analysis Co. - Wayne, NJ - *AvMarPl 83*
Photographic Book Co. Inc. [Aff. of PBC International Inc.] - New York, NY - *BoPubDir 5; LitMarPl 83, 84*
Photographic Calendar [of Open Space Gallery] - Victoria, BC, Canada - *LitMag&SmPr 83-84*
Photographic Color Specialists Inc. - Long Island City, NY - *AvMarPl 83*
PhotoGraphic Display Systems Inc. - Savage, MD - *AvMarPl 83*
Photographic Processing - Hempstead, NY - *MagDir 84*
Photographic Processing - Woodbury, NY - *BaconPubCkMag 84*
Photographic Science & Engineering - Washington, DC - *MagDir 84*
Photographic Science & Engineering - Springfield, VA - *BaconPubCkMag 84*
Photographic Specialties - Studio City, CA - *AvMarPl 83*
Photographic Specialties - Harleysville, PA - *AvMarPl 83*
Photographic Trade News - Woodbury, NY - *BaconPubCkMag 84; MagDir 84*
Photographit - Uniontown, PA - *BoPubDir 4 Sup, 5*
Photography at Open-Space [Aff. of Open Space Gallery] - Victoria, BC, Canada - *BoPubDir 4 Sup, 5; LitMag&SmPr 83-84*
Photography Book Society [of Macmillan Book Clubs Inc.] - New York, NY - *LitMarPl 83*
Photography for Industry - New York, NY - *AvMarPl 83; LitMarPl 83, 84; MagIndMarPl 82-83*
Photogravure & Color Co. [Subs. of Watkins Brothers] - Moonachie, NJ - *LitMarPl 83, 84; MagIndMarPl 82-83*
Photojournal - Vermillion, OH - *AyerDirPub 83*
Photoletter [of NewsNet Inc.] - Bryn Mawr, PA - *DataDirOnSer 84*
Photoletter, The [of Photosearch International] - Osceola, WI - *DirMarMP 83; DirOnDB Spring 84; LitMag&SmPr 83-84; MagIndMarPl 82-83*
Photomethods [of Ziff-Davis Publishing Co.] - New York, NY - *BaconPubCkMag 84; MagDir 84; MagIndMarPl 82-83; WritMar 84*
Photometric Database - Denver, CO - *DirOnDB Spring 84*
Photomurals Inc. - Houston, TX - *AvMarPl 83*
Photon & Charged Particle Data Center [of National Bureau of Standards] - Washington, DC - *InfIndMarPl 83*
Photon Chroma Inc. - Westfield, MA - *AvMarPl 83*
Photon Software [Div. of Care Computer System] - Bellevue, WA - *MicrocomMPl 84*
Photonet - New York, NY - *DirOnDB Spring 84*
Photonics Spectra - Pittsfield, MA - *BaconPubCkMag 84; MagDir 84; MagIndMarPl 82-83; WritMar 84*
Photonuclear Data Center [of National Bureau of Standards] - Washington, DC - *InfIndMarPl 83*
Photophile - San Diego, CA - *AvMarPl 83; LitMarPl 83, 84; MagIndMarPl 82-83*
Photopia Press - Corvallis, OR - *BoPubDir 5*
Photoplatemakers Bulletin - South Holland, IL - *BaconPubCkMag 84; MagDir 84*

Photoplay - New York, NY - *MagDir 84*
Photoquip - Fernandina Beach, FL - *AvMarPl 83*
Photorama [Div. of Photo Replicas Corp.] - New York, NY - *AvMarPl 83*
Photoreporters Inc. - New York, NY - *MagIndMarPl 82-83*
Photos by Arthur Matula - San Diego, CA - *LitMarPl 84*
Photoscope - New York, NY - *AvMarPl 83; WritMar 84*
Photosearch International [Aff. of The Photoletter] - Osceola, WI - *BoPubDir 4 Sup, 5; DataDirOnSer 84; LitMag&SmPr 83-84*
PhotoSearch International - Star Prairie, WI - *MagIndMarPl 82-83*
Photosix Inc. - Carol Stream, IL - *AvMarPl 83*
Photosound of Orlando Inc. - Orlando, FL - *AvMarPl 83*
Phototypesetting Etc. - Oceanside, NY - *MagIndMarPl 82-83*
Photovoltaics: The Solar Electric Magazine - Tempe, AZ - *BaconPubCkMag 84*
Photoworks - Phoenix, AZ - *AvMarPl 83*
Photoworld Inc. [Div. of Freelance Photographers Guild] - New York, NY - *AvMarPl 83; MagIndMarPl 82-83*
Photri Photo Research - Alexandria, VA - *LitMarPl 83, 84; MagIndMarPl 82-83*
Photron - Ames, IA - *LitMag&SmPr 83-84*
Phunn Publishers, J. - Wild Rose, WI - *ArtMar 84; BoPubDir 4, 5*
Phycom Service [of Fisher-Stevens Inc.] - Totowa, NJ - *DirOnDB Spring 84; EISS 5-84 Sup*
Physcomp - Eggenstein-Leopoldshafen, West Germany - *DirOnDB Spring 84*
Physical Data Group [of University of California] - Livermore, CA - *EISS 83; InfIndMarPl 83*
Physical Property Data Service [of Institution of Chemical Engineers] - Rugby, England - *EISS 83; InfIndMarPl 83*
Physical Review Letters - Ridge, NY - *MagIndMarPl 82-83*
Physical Society of Japan - Tokyo, Japan - *MicroMarPl 82-83*
Physical Therapy - Alexandria, VA - *BaconPubCkMag 84; MagDir 84*
Physician & Sportsmedicine, The - Edina, MN - *BaconPubCkMag 84*
Physician & Sportsmedicine, The - Minneapolis, MN - *MagIndMarPl 82-83*
Physician & Sportsmedicine, The - Philadelphia, PA - *MagDir 84*
Physician Assistant & Health Practitioner - New York, NY - *BaconPubCkMag 84; MagDir 84*
Physician Communications [of GTE Telenet] - Vienna, VA - *DataDirOnSer 84*
Physician Computer Monthly [of American Health Consultants] - Atlanta, GA - *MicrocomMPl 84*
Physician's Drug Alert - Millburn, NJ - *BaconPubCkMag 84*
Physician's Management - New York, NY - *MagDir 84; MagIndMarPl 82-83*
Physician's Management - Cleveland, OH - *ArtMar 84; BaconPubCkMag 84; WritMar 84*
Physicians Practice Management Inc. - Indianapolis, IN - *MicrocomMPl 84; MicrocomSwDir 1*
Physicians Radio Network Inc. - New York, NY - *BrCabYB 84*
Physics Abstracts [of INSPEC, Institution of Electrical Engineers] - Hitchin, England - *OnBibDB 3*
Physics Briefs - Eggenstein-Leopoldshafen, West Germany - *DirOnDB Spring 84*
Physics Teacher, The - Stony Brook, NY - *BaconPubCkMag 84; MagIndMarPl 82-83*
Physics Teacher, The - Wantagh, NY - *MagDir 84*
Physics Today [of American Institute of Physics] - New York, NY - *ArtMar 84; BaconPubCkMag 84; LitMarPl 83, 84; MagDir 84; MagIndMarPl 82-83*
Physiological Chemistry & Physics [of Meridional Publications] - Wake Forest, NC - *LitMag&SmPr 83-84*
Physiological Reviews - Washington, DC - *MagDir 84*
Physiological Zoology - Chicago, IL - *MagDir 84*
Physiology & Behavior - Elmsford, NY - *MagIndMarPl 82-83*
Physique - Norfolk, VA - *WritMar 84*
Physsardt Publishers - Bloomington, IN - *BoPubDir 4, 5*
Phytopathology - St. Paul, MN - *MagIndMarPl 82-83*
PI Inc. - Marietta, GA - *StaDirAdAg 2-84*
P.I. Industries Publishing Co. - Loveland, CO - *BoPubDir 4, 5*
Pi Press Inc. - Honolulu, HI - *BoPubDir 4, 5*
Pi Yee Press - La Jolla, CA - *BoPubDir 4, 5*
Piano for Two Directory - Kingston, NJ - *BoPubDir 5*
Piano Quarterly - Wilmington, VT - *MagIndMarPl 82-83*
Piano Technicians Journal - Seattle, WA - *BaconPubCkMag 84; MagDir 84*
Piaser Co., The Mike - Garfield Heights, OH - *MicrocomSwDir 1*
Piatt County Journal-Republican - Monticello, IL - *AyerDirPub 83*
Pic-Mount - Long Island City, NY - *AvMarPl 83*
Pic Studio - Burbank, CA - *AvMarPl 83*
PICA - Croydon, England - *DirOnDB Spring 84*
Picayune Cablevision Inc. [of Wometco Cable TV Inc.] - Picayune, MS - *BrCabYB 84; Tel&CabFB 84C*
Picayune Item - Picayune, MS - *BaconPubCkNews 84; Ed&PubIntYB 82; NewsDir 84*
Picayune Press - New Orleans, LA - *BoPubDir 4 Sup, 5; LitMag&SmPr 83-84*
Piccadilly Software Inc. - Summit, NJ - *MicrocomMPl 83, 84*
Piccasso Publishing Co. - *See* Kenwon Music
Picchione, R. - Reno, NV - *BoPubDir 4, 5*
Picckens County Herald - Carrolton, AL - *Ed&PubIntYB 82*
Picher Tri-State Tribune - Picher, OK - *BaconPubCkNews 84*
Pick Publications Inc. - Detroit, MI - *BoPubDir 4, 5*
Pick Publishing Corp. - New York, NY - *BoPubDir 4, 5; MicroMarPl 82-83*
Pickard, Geoffrey C. - Britannia Beach, BC, Canada - *BrCabYB 84*
Pickens County Progress - Jasper, GA - *AyerDirPub 83; Ed&PubIntYB 82*
Pickens Sentinel [of Pickens County Publishing Inc.] - Pickens, SC - *BaconPubCkNews 84; Ed&PubIntYB 82; NewsDir 84*
Pickering Cable TV Ltd. - Pickering, ON, Canada - *BrCabYB 84*
Pickering Post - Pickering, ON, Canada - *Ed&PubIntYB 82*
Pickering's Bay News - Pickering, ON, Canada - *AyerDirPub 83; Ed&PubIntYB 82*
Pickerington Sun - Pickerington, OH - *AyerDirPub 83; BaconPubCkNews 84; Ed&PubIntYB 82*
Pickett & Co. Inc., Robert - New York, NY - *DirPRFirms 83*
Pickett County Press - Byrdstown, TN - *AyerDirPub 83; Ed&PubIntYB 82*
Pickin' Post Enterprises - Lebanon, TN - *BillIntBG 83-84*
Pickin' Post Publishing - Lebanon, TN - *BillIntBG 83-84*
Pickles & Trout - Goleta, CA - *MicrocomMPl 83*
Pickneyville Democrat - Pickneyville, IL - *BaconPubCkNews 84*
Picks & Strings Music - *See* Jacobson, Jeffrey E.
Pickup, Van & 4WD [of Petersen Publishing Co.] - Los Angeles, CA - *BaconPubCkMag 84; MagDir 84; MagIndMarPl 82-83; WritMar 84*
Pickwick, Maslansky, Koenigsberg, Public Relations - New York, NY - *DirPRFirms 83*
Pickwick Press, The [Subs. of Pickwick-Morcraft Inc.] - Pittsburgh, PA - *LitMarPl 83*
Pickwick Publications - Allison Park, PA - *WritMar 84*
Piclear Inc. - Mamaroneck, NY - *AvMarPl 83*
Pico/Beverlywood Post [of Los Angeles Post Newspaper Group] - Los Angeles, CA - *NewsDir 84*
Pico Post - Los Angeles, CA - *AyerDirPub 83; NewsDir 84*
Pico Products Inc. - Liverpool, NY - *CabTVFinDB 83*
Pico Rivera Advertiser - South Gate, CA - *AyerDirPub 83*
Pico Rivera News [of Southern California Publishing Co.] - Los Angeles, CA - *NewsDir 84*
Pico Rivera News - *See* Southern California Publishing Co.
Pico Rivera News/Santa Fe Springs News - Pico Rivera, CA - *AyerDirPub 83*
Pico Riviera Advertiser - *See* Hearst Community Newspapers
Picotrin Technology Inc. - Lantana, FL - *MicrocomMPl 83, 84*
Pictograph Corp. - New York, NY - *LitMarPl 83, 84; MagIndMarPl 82-83*
Pictorial Histories Publishing Co. - Missoula, MT - *BoPubDir 4, 5*
Pictorial Parade - Studio City, CA - *Ed&PubIntYB 82*
Pictorial Parade Inc. - New York, NY - *LitMarPl 83, 84; MagIndMarPl 82-83*
Pictorial Press & Star Citizen - Tahlequah, OK - *AyerDirPub 83*
Pictorial Press, The [of Tahlequah Risenhoover Printing Co. Inc.] - Tahlequah, OK - *NewsDir 84*
Pictorial Publishers Inc. - Indianapolis, IN - *DirMarMP 83*
Pictorial Review - Gulfport, MS - *AyerDirPub 83*

Pictorial, The - Old Saybrook, CT - *Ed&PubIntYB 82*
Pictorial, The - Duncan, BC, Canada - *Ed&PubIntYB 82*
Pictou Advocate, The - Pictou, NS, Canada - *Ed&PubIntYB 82*
Picture Data Inc. - Toronto, ON, Canada - *VideoDir 82-83*
Picture Group Inc. - Providence, RI - *LitMarPl 83, 84*
Picture Post, The [of Waupaca County Post] - Waupaca, WI - *NewsDir 84*
Picture Research - Washington, DC - *FBInfSer 80*
Picture Research - Bethesda, MD - *LitMarPl 83, 84*
Picturemakers Inc. - Succasunna, NJ - *LitMarPl 83, 84; MagIndMarPl 82-83*
Pictures Inc. - Anchorage, AK - *AvMarPl 83*
PIE - Lawrence, KS - *MicrocomMPl 84*
PIE - Portland, OR - *DirOnDB Spring 84*
Pie Music Co., S. - Evanston, IL - *BillIntBG 83-84*
Pieceful Pleasures - San Mateo, CA - *BoPubDir 4, 5*
Pied Piper Films Ltd. - Shelburne, ON, Canada - *Tel&CabFB 84C*
Pied Piper Productions - Glendale, CA - *AvMarPl 83*
Piedmont - Greenville, SC - *AyerDirPub 83*
Piedmont Advertising Agency Inc. - Salisbury, NC - *StaDirAdAg 2-84*
Piedmont Cablevision Inc. [of Helicon Corp.] - Gaffney, SC - *Tel&CabFB 84C*
Piedmont Cablevision Inc. [of Helicon Corp.] - Union, SC - *Tel&CabFB 84C*
Piedmont CATV Associates [of U.S. Cable Corp.] - Gaffney, SC - *BrCabYB 84*
Piedmont CATV Associates [of U.S. Cable Corp.] - Union, SC - *BrCabYB 84*
Piedmont City Press - *See* Press Publications
Piedmont Herald - Piedmont, WV - *BaconPubCkNews 84; Ed&PubIntYB 82; NewsDir 84*
Piedmont Journal - Piedmont, AL - *Ed&PubIntYB 82; NewsDir 84*
Piedmont Journal Independent - Piedmont, AL - *AyerDirPub 83; BaconPubCkNews 84*
Piedmont Literary Review [of Piedmont Literary Society] - Danville, VA - *LitMag&SmPr 83-84; WritMar 84*
Piedmont/Oakland Bulletin - Oakland, CA - *AyerDirPub 83*
Piedmont/Oakland Bulletin - *See* Snyder Publications
Piedmont Peddler, The - Monroe, GA - *AyerDirPub 83*
Piedmont Press [of Oakland Press Publications] - Oakland, CA - *NewsDir 84*
Piedmont Rural Telephone Cooperative Inc. - Laurens, SC - *TelDir&BG 83-84*
Piedmont Telephone Membership Corp. - Lexington, NC - *TelDir&BG 83-84*
Piedmont Wayne County Journal-Banner - Piedmont, MO - *BaconPubCkNews 84; NewsDir 84*
Piedmonter, The - Oakland, CA - *AyerDirPub 83*
Piedmonter, The - Piedmont, CA - *Ed&PubIntYB 82*
Pieper, Linda - New York, NY - *LitMarPl 83, 84*
Pierce & Strain Advertising Inc. - San Francisco, CA - *AdAge 3-28-84; StaDirAdAg 2-84*
Pierce, Bob - Long Beach, CA - *BoPubDir 4, 5*
Pierce Brown Associates Inc. - Rochester, NY - *StaDirAdAg 2-84*
Pierce, C. C. [Aff. of American Cryptogram Association] - Ventura, CA - *BoPubDir 4, 5*
Pierce City Leader-Journal - Pierce City, MO - *BaconPubCkNews 84*
Pierce, Claire M. - Arnot, PA - *Tel&CabFB 84C*
Pierce, Claire M. - Wellsboro, PA - *BrCabYB 84 p.D-305*
Pierce County Herald - Puyallup, WA - *AyerDirPub 83; Ed&PubIntYB 82*
Pierce County Herald - Ellsworth, WI - *AyerDirPub 83; Ed&PubIntYB 82*
Pierce County Leader - Pierce, NE - *AyerDirPub 83; BaconPubCkNews 84; Ed&PubIntYB 82*
Pierce County Tribune [of Prarie Publishing Inc.] - Rugby, ND - *AyerDirPub 83; Ed&PubIntYB 82; NewsDir 84*
Pierce-Davis & Associates - Arlington, TX - *StaDirAdAg 2-84*
Pierce Telephone Co. Inc. - Pierce, NE - *TelDir&BG 83-84*
Pierce TV Cable Service - Pierce, ID - *BrCabYB 84*
Piercell Merchandising Ltd. - Windsor, ON, Canada - *StaDirAdAg 2-84*
Pierce's TV Cable Systems - Arnot, PA - *BrCabYB 84*
Pierce's TV Cable Systems - Catlin Hollow, PA - *Tel&CabFB 84C*
Pierce's TV Cable Systems - Kenneyville, PA - *Tel&CabFB 84C*
Pierce's TV Cable Systems - Mainesburg, PA - *BrCabYB 84*
Pierce's TV Cable Systems - Mitchell Creek, PA - *Tel&CabFB 84C*
Pierce's TV Cable Systems - Wellsboro, PA - *Tel&CabFB 84C*
Pierian Press - Ann Arbor, MI - *LitMag&SmPr 83-84; LitMarPl 83, 84*
Pierian Spring [of Pierian Press] - Brandon, MB, Canada - *LitMag&SmPr 83-84*
Pierre Cable Television [of Midcontinent Cable Systems Co.] - Pierre, SD - *BrCabYB 84; Tel&CabFB 84C*
Pierre Cossette Co. - Los Angeles, CA - *WritMar 84*
Pierre Daily Capital Journal [of Hipple Printing] - Pierre, SD - *BaconPubCkNews 84; NewsDir 84*
Pierre Times - Pierre, SD - *BaconPubCkNews 84; Ed&PubIntYB 82*
Pierre Trader - Pierre, SD - *NewsDir 84*
PIERS - New York, NY - *DirOnDB Spring 84*
Pierson & Co. - Chicago, IL - *StaDirAdAg 2-84*
Pierson Press - Pierson, IA - *BaconPubCkNews 84; Ed&PubIntYB 82*
Pig American - Mt. Morris, IL - *BaconPubCkMag 84*
Pig in a Poke - Pittsburgh, PA - *LitMag&SmPr 83-84*
Pig in a Poke Press - Pittsburgh, PA - *LitMag&SmPr 83-84*
Pig International - Mt. Morris, IL - *MagDir 84*
Pig Iron [of Pig Iron Press] - Youngstown, OH - *ArtMar 84; LitMag&SmPr 83-84; WritMar 84*
Pig Iron Press - Youngstown, OH - *BoPubDir 4, 5; LitMag&SmPr 83-84*
Pigeon Progress-Advance - Pigeon, MI - *BaconPubCkNews 84*
Pigeon Roost Press - Nashville, TN - *BoPubDir 4, 5*
Pigeon Telephone Co. - Pigeon, MI - *TelDir&BG 83-84*
Pigfoot Music - Hollywood, CA - *BillIntBG 83-84*
Piggott Times - Piggott, AR - *BaconPubCkNews 84; Ed&PubIntYB 82; NewsDir 84*
Piggott Video Cable Inc. - Piggott, AR - *BrCabYB 84; Tel&CabFB 84C*
Pigman, Edgar J. - Hazard, KY - *Tel&CabFB 84C*
Pig's Whisker Music - Los Angeles, CA - *BoPubDir 4, 5; LitMag&SmPr 83-84*
Pihas, Schmidt, Westerdahl Co., The - Portland, OR - *StaDirAdAg 2-84*
Piik Design Inc., Peter - New York, NY - *DirPRFirms 83; LitMarPl 83, 84*
Pikadilly Press - London, ON, Canada - *BoPubDir 4, 5*
Pike & Fisher Inc. - Bethesda, MD - *BrCabYB 84*
Pike County Cable - Petersburg, IN - *BrCabYB 84*
Pike County Cablevision [of Welbac Cable TV Corp.] - Petersburg, IN - *Tel&CabFB 84C*
Pike County Dispatch - Milford, PA - *AyerDirPub 83; Ed&PubIntYB 82; NewsDir 84*
Pike County Journal & Reporter - Pike County, GA - *Ed&PubIntYB 82*
Pike County Journal & Reporter - Zebulon, GA - *AyerDirPub 83*
Pike County News - Barry, IL - *AyerDirPub 83; Ed&PubIntYB 82*
Pike Inc., James A. - Plymouth, CA - *LitMarPl 83, 84*
Pike Press - Pittsfield, IL - *AyerDirPub 83; Ed&PubIntYB 82*
Pike Register [of Pace Publishing Inc.] - Indianapolis, IN - *Ed&PubIntYB 82; NewsDir 84*
Pike Register - *See* Topic Newspapers Inc.
Pikes Peak Broadcasting Co. - Colorado Springs, CO - *BrCabYB 84; Tel&CabFB 84S*
Pike's Peak Cable Co. - Herndon, PA - *BrCabYB 84*
Pikes Peak Journal - Manitou Springs, CO - *Ed&PubIntYB 82*
Pike's Peak TV Association - Herndon, PA - *Tel&CabFB 84C*
Pikestaff Forum, The - Normal, IL - *LitMag&SmPr 83-84*
Pikestaff Press [Aff. of Pikestaff Publications Inc.] - Normal, IL - *BoPubDir 4, 5; LitMag&SmPr 83-84*
Pikestaff Review, The - Normal, IL - *LitMag&SmPr 83-84*
Pikeville Appalachian News-Express - Pikeville, KY - *BaconPubCkNews 84*

Pikeville Bledsonian Banner - Pikeville, TN - *BaconPubCkNews 84*
Pikeville College Press - Pikeville, KY - *BoPubDir 4, 5; LitMag&SmPr 83-84*
Pilara Data Systems Inc. - San Diego, CA - *DirInfWP 82*
Pile of Bones Publishing Co. - Regina, SK, Canada - *BoPubDir 4, 5*
Pilger Herald, The - Pilger, NE - *Ed&PubIntYB 82*
Pilger Herald, The - Wisner, NE - *BaconPubCkNews 84*
Pilgrim Books - Norman, OK - *BoPubDir 4, 5*
Pilgrim Electric Co. - Plainview, NY - *DirInfWP 82*
Pilgrim International Ltd. - *See* Jacobson, Jeffrey E.
Pilgrim Press - Princeton, NJ - *BoPubDir 4, 5*
Pilgrim Press, The [Div. of United Church Board for Homeland Ministries] - New York, NY - *LitMarPl 83, 84*
Pilgrim Publications [Aff. of Pilgrim Baptist Church] - Pasadena, TX - *BoPubDir 4, 5*
Pilgrim Publishing Co. - Chattanooga, TN - *BoPubDir 4, 5*
Pilgrim Society - Plymouth, MA - *BoPubDir 4 Sup, 5*
Pilgrimage Inc. - Jonesboro, TN - *BoPubDir 4, 5*
Pilgrim's Hibiscus Music - *See* Jacobson, Jeffrey E.
Pillow Talk - New York, NY - *ArtMar 84; WritMar 84*
Pillsbury Co., The - Minneapolis, MN - *MicrocomMPl 84*
Pilot - Crested Butte, CO - *AyerDirPub 83*
Pilot - Canton, KS - *AyerDirPub 83*
Pilot - Dixon, MO - *AyerDirPub 83*
Pilot - Southern Pines, NC - *AyerDirPub 83; Ed&PubIntYB 82*
Pilot - Rockport, TX - *AyerDirPub 83*
Pilot - Lewisporte, NF, Canada - *AyerDirPub 83; Ed&PubIntYB 82*
Pilot Books - Babylon, NY - *LitMarPl 84; WritMar 84*
Pilot Books - New York, NY - *LitMarPl 83*
Pilot-Independent, The - Walker, MN - *AyerDirPub 83; Ed&PubIntYB 82; NewsDir 84*
Pilot Light - Stone Mountain, GA - *BoPubDir 5*
Pilot News - Plymouth, IN - *AyerDirPub 83; Ed&PubIntYB 82; NewsDir 84*
Pilot Point Post-Signal - Pilot Point, TX - *BaconPubCkNews 84*
Pilot Press - Philadelphia, PA - *BoPubDir 4, 5*
Pilot Productions Inc. - Evanston, IL - *AvMarPl 83; Tel&CabFB 84C*
Pilot Publications [Aff. of Cady Development Co. Inc.] - Mobile, AL - *BoPubDir 4, 5*
Pilot Rock News - Pilot Rock, OR - *AyerDirPub 83; BaconPubCkNews 84; Ed&PubIntYB 82*
Pilot Rock Television [of Rogers UA Cablesystems Inc.] - Pilot Rock, OR - *BrCabYB 84*
Pilot-Tribune - Storm Lake, IA - *AyerDirPub 83*
Pilot-Tribune - Blair, NE - *AyerDirPub 83; Ed&PubIntYB 82*
Pilot-Tribune Printing Co. - Storm Lake, IA - *BaconPubCkNews 84*
PIMA Magazine - Arlington Heights, IL - *BaconPubCkMag 84; MagDir 84; MagIndMarPl 82-83*
PIMS Data Base - Washington, DC - *DirOnDB Spring 84*
Pin Prick Press - Shaker Heights, OH - *BoPubDir 4, 5; LitMag&SmPr 83-84*
Pinchgut Press - Sydney, Australia - *LitMag&SmPr 83-84*
Pinchpenny - Sacramento, CA - *LitMag&SmPr 83-84*
Pinckney Post [of Sliger/Livingston Publications] - Howell, MI - *AyerDirPub 83; NewsDir 84*
Pinckney Post - *See* Sliger Livingston Publications
Pinckney Post, The - Pinckney, MI - *Ed&PubIntYB 82*
Pinckneyville Democrat - Pinckneyville, IL - *Ed&PubIntYB 82*
Pinconning Journal - Pinconning, MI - *BaconPubCkNews 84; Ed&PubIntYB 82*
Pine & Associates, Charles W. - Phoenix, AZ - *DirPRFirms 83*
Pine Associates Inc., Arthur - New York, NY - *LitMarPl 83, 84*
Pine Belt Telephone Co. Inc. - Arlington, AL - *TelDir&BG 83-84*
Pine Bluff Cable Television Co. Inc. [of WEHCO Video Inc.] - Pine Bluff, AR - *BrCabYB 84; Tel&CabFB 84C*
Pine Bluff Commercial [of Commercial Printing Co.] - Pine Bluff, AR - *BaconPubCkNews 84; Ed&PubIntYB 82; NewsDir 84*
Pine Bluff News - Pine Bluff, AR - *BaconPubCkNews 84; Ed&PubIntYB 82; NewsDir 84*
Pine Bluffs Community Television System - Pine Bluffs, WY - *BrCabYB 84; Tel&CabFB 84C*
Pine Bluffs Post - Pine Bluffs, WY - *BaconPubCkNews 84; Ed&PubIntYB 82*
Pine City Pioneer - Pine City, MN - *BaconPubCkNews 84; Ed&PubIntYB 82*
Pine Cone - Carmel, CA - *AyerDirPub 83*
Pine Cone Publishers - Medford, OR - *BoPubDir 4, 5*
Pine County Courier - Sandstone, MN - *AyerDirPub 83; Ed&PubIntYB 82*
Pine Drive Telephone Co. - Beulah, CO - *TelDir&BG 83-84*
Pine Island Record - Pine Island, MN - *BaconPubCkNews 84; Ed&PubIntYB 82*
Pine Island Telephone Co. [Aff. of Communications Systems Inc.] - Pine Island, MN - *BrCabYB 84; TelDir&BG 83-84*
Pine Knot - Cloquet, MN - *AyerDirPub 83*
Pine Mountain Cablevision Inc. - New York, NY - *BrCabYB 84*
Pine Mountain Press Inc. - West Allis, WI - *LitMag&SmPr 83-84; WritMar 84*
Pine Mountain Press Inc. (Publishing Group) - West Allis, WI - *LitMarPl 83*
Pine Plains Register-Herald [of Taconic Press Inc.] - Millbrook, NY - *AyerDirPub 83; NewsDir 84*
Pine Plains Register Herald - Pine Plains, NY - *Ed&PubIntYB 82*
Pine Plains Register Herald - *See* Taconic Press Inc.
Pine Press - Landisburg, PA - *BoPubDir 4, 5*
Pine Ridge Clipper Ltd. - *See* Castalia Music
Pine River Journal - Pine River, MN - *BaconPubCkNews 84; Ed&PubIntYB 82*
Pine Street Communications - New York, NY - *DirPRFirms 83*
Pine Telephone Co. - Broken Bow, OK - *TelDir&BG 83-84*
Pine Telephone System Inc. - Halfway, OR - *TelDir&BG 83-84*
Pine Tree - Orange, CA - *BoPubDir 4, 5*
Pine Tree Cablevision [of Consolidated Communications Corp.] - Eastport, ME - *BrCabYB 84; Tel&CabFB 84C*
Pine Tree Cablevision [of Consolidated Communications Corp.] - Machias, ME - *BrCabYB 84*
Pine Tree Cablevision Inc. - Jonesport, ME - *BrCabYB 84*
Pine Tree Communications Inc. - Minocqua, WI - *BrCabYB 84; Tel&CabFB 84C*
Pine Tree Publishing - Phippsburg, ME - *LitMag&SmPr 83-84*
Pine Tree Telephone & Telegraph Co. - Gray, ME - *TelDir&BG 83-84*
Pineapple Press Inc. - Englewood, FL - *BoPubDir 5; LitMag&SmPr 83-84; LitMarPl 84*
Pinebelt Cablevision [of The Essex Group] - Atmore, AL - *BrCabYB 84*
Pinebelt Cablevision [of The Essex Group] - Brewton, AL - *BrCabYB 84*
Pinebelt Cablevision - Gulf Breeze, FL - *BrCabYB 84*
Pinecrest Fund Inc. - Kansas City, MO - *BoPubDir 4, 5*
Pinedale Roundup - Pinedale, WY - *BaconPubCkNews 84; Ed&PubIntYB 82*
Pinehill Publishing Co. - Lafayette, LA - *BoPubDir 4, 5*
Pinehurst Co-Op TV System - Pinehurst, ID - *BrCabYB 84; Tel&CabFB 84C*
Pinehurst Syndicate, The - Ft. Lauderdale, FL - *Ed&PubIntYB 82*
Pinehurst TV System Inc. - Pinehurst, ID - *BrCabYB 84; Tel&CabFB 84C*
Pineland Telephone Cooperative Inc. - Metter, GA - *TelDir&BG 83-84*
Pinellas Music - *See* Arpell/Pinellas Music Publishing Co.
Pinellas Publishers Inc. - Tarpon Springs, FL - *BaconPubCkNews 84*
Pinetop-Lakeside News [of White Mountain Publishing Co.] - Pinetop, AZ - *AyerDirPub 83; BaconPubCkNews 84; NewsDir 84*
Pineville Independent Herald - Pineville, WV - *BaconPubCkNews 84; Ed&PubIntYB 82*
Pineville McDonald County News-Gazette - Pineville, MO - *BaconPubCkNews 84*
Pineville Pioneer - Pineville, NC - *BaconPubCkNews 84*
Pineville Red River Journal - Pineville, LA - *NewsDir 84*
Pineville Sun-Cumberland Courier [of Associated Publications] - Pineville, KY - *BaconPubCkNews 84; Ed&PubIntYB 82; NewsDir 84*
Pineville Telephone Co. - Pineville, NC - *TelDir&BG 83-84*

Pinewood Press - Houston, TX - *BoPubDir 4 Sup, 5*
Piney Mountain Air Force - Charlottesville, VA - *BoPubDir 4, 5*
Pinion Corp. - Salem, AR - *Tel&CabFB 84C p.1697*
Pinion Corp. - Lakeland, FL - *BrCabYB 84 p.D-305*
Pink House Publishing Co. - Honolulu, HI - *BoPubDir 4, 5*
Pink Music - *See* Kenwon Music
Pink Pig Music - *See* Funky but Music Inc.
Pink Records - Chicago, IL - *BillIntBG 83-84*
Pink Triangle Press - Toronto, ON, Canada - *BoPubDir 4, 5; LitMag&SmPr 83-84*
Pinkerton Computer Consultants Inc. - Trevose, PA - *DataDirSup 7-83*
Pinkerton Marketing Inc. - Lake Bluff, IL - *BoPubDir 5*
Pinnacle Books [Aff. of Michigan General Corp.] - New York, NY - *LitMarPl 83, 84; WritMar 84*
Pinnacle Peak View/Rio Verde - Cave Creek, AZ - *AyerDirPub 83*
Pinnacles Telephone Co. - Paicines, CA - *TelDir&BG 83-84*
Pinne, Garvin, Herbers & Hock Inc. - San Francisco, CA - *DirPRFirms 83; StaDirAdAg 2-84*
Pinole West County Times - Pinole, CA - *BaconPubCkNews 84*
Pinpoint Federal Contract Awards - Arlington, VA - *DirOnDB Spring 84*
Pinpoint Marketing - New York, NY - *HBIndAd&MS 82-83*
Pinpoint Music Publishing - Nashville, IN - *BillIntBG 83-84*
Pinsker Associates, Essie [Div. of H. Richard Silver Inc.] - New York, NY - *StaDirAdAg 2-84*
Pinzke Design Inc., Herbert - Chicago, IL - *LitMarPl 83, 84; MagIndMarPl 82-83*
Pion Inc. - Watertown, MA - *MicrocomMPl 84*
Pioneer - Sanborn, IA - *AyerDirPub 83*
Pioneer - Johnson, KS - *AyerDirPub 83*
Pioneer - Big Rapids, MI - *AyerDirPub 83; Ed&PubIntYB 82*
Pioneer - Bemidji, MN - *AyerDirPub 83; Ed&PubIntYB 82*
Pioneer - Hendricks, MN - *AyerDirPub 83*
Pioneer - Mahnomen, MN - *AyerDirPub 83*
Pioneer - Pine City, MN - *AyerDirPub 83*
Pioneer - Warroad, MN - *AyerDirPub 83*
Pioneer - Ronan, MT - *AyerDirPub 83*
Pioneer - West Fargo, ND - *AyerDirPub 83*
Pioneer - Madras, OR - *AyerDirPub 83*
Pioneer - MoLalla, OR - *AyerDirPub 83*
Pioneer - Bowdle, SD - *AyerDirPub 83*
Pioneer - Ft. Stockton, TX - *AyerDirPub 83*
Pioneer - Hamilton, ON, Canada - *Ed&PubIntYB 82*
Pioneer Advertiser - Cascade, IA - *AyerDirPub 83*
Pioneer Advertiser, The - Shelley, ID - *AyerDirPub 83*
Pioneer Artists - Montvale, NJ - *BillIntBG 83-84*
Pioneer Book Publishers - Seagraves, TX - *BoPubDir 4, 5*
Pioneer Broadcasting Co. - Austin, TX - *Tel&CabFB 84C p.1697*
Pioneer Cable TV Inc. [of Service Electric Cable TV Inc.] - Gordon, PA - *BrCabYB 84*
Pioneer Cablevision Ltd. - Agassiz, BC, Canada - *BrCabYB 84*
Pioneer Communications of America - Columbus, OH - *CabTVFinDB 83; HomeVid&CabYB 82-83*
Pioneer Drama Service - Denver, CO - *BoPubDir 4, 5; WritMar 84*
Pioneer Electronic Corp. - Moonachie, NJ - *HomeVid&CabYB 82-83*
Pioneer Electronics (USA) Inc. - Long Beach, CA - *BillIntBG 83-84*
Pioneer-Gazette - Wibaux, MT - *AyerDirPub 83*
Pioneer Journal - Wadena, MN - *AyerDirPub 83*
Pioneer Marketing Corp. - Burbank, CA - *AvMarPl 83*
Pioneer-Moss Reproductions - New York, NY - *LitMarPl 83, 84*
Pioneer National Advertising Inc. - Salem, OR - *StaDirAdAg 2-84*
Pioneer-News - Shepherdsville, KY - *AyerDirPub 83; Ed&PubIntYB 82*
Pioneer Press - St. Paul, MN - *AyerDirPub 83*
Pioneer Press - Cut Bank, MT - *AyerDirPub 83*
Pioneer Press - Gackle, ND - *Ed&PubIntYB 82*
Pioneer Press - Mott, ND - *AyerDirPub 83*
Pioneer Press [Aff. of Dixie Gun Works Inc.] - Union City, TN - *BoPubDir 4, 5*
Pioneer Press Inc. - Wilmette, IL - *BaconPubCkNews 84*
Pioneer Press Service Inc. - Worthington, OH - *Ed&PubIntYB 82*
Pioneer Publishing Co. [Aff. of Book Publishers Inc.] - Fresno, CA - *BoPubDir 4 Sup, 5*
Pioneer Record Co. - Tyler, TX - *BillIntBG 83-84*
Pioneer Republican - Marengo, IA - *AyerDirPub 83*
Pioneer Review - Philip, SD - *AyerDirPub 83; Ed&PubIntYB 82*
Pioneer Software - Lauderhill, FL - *MicrocomMPl 84; MicrocomSwDir 1*
Pioneer Telephone Association Inc. - Ulysses, KS - *TelDir&BG 83-84*
Pioneer Telephone Co. - Lacrosse, WA - *TelDir&BG 83-84*
Pioneer Telephone Cooperative - Philomath, OR - *TelDir&BG 83-84*
Pioneer Telephone Cooperative Inc. - Kingfisher, OK - *TelDir&BG 83-84*
Pioneer Times - Houlton, ME - *AyerDirPub 83*
Pioneer Times - Vassar, MI - *AyerDirPub 83*
Pioneer Times - Deadwood, SD - *AyerDirPub 83*
Pioneer-Tribune - Manistique, MI - *AyerDirPub 83; Ed&PubIntYB 82*
Pioneer Valley Cablevision [of Times Mirror Inc.] - Amherst, MA - *BrCabYB 84; Tel&CabFB 84C*
Pioneer Valley Cablevision [of Times Mirror Inc.] - Greenfield, MA - *BrCabYB 84; Tel&CabFB 84C*
Pioneer Valley Cablevision [of Times Mirror Inc.] - Palmer, MA - *BrCabYB 84*
Pioneer Valley Cablevision [of Times Mirror Inc.] - Shelburne Falls, MA - *BrCabYB 84*
Pioneer Valley Cablevision [of Times Mirror Inc.] - Ware, MA - *BrCabYB 84; Tel&CabFB 84C*
Pioneer Woman - New York, NY - *WritMar 84*
PIP College Helps Newsletter [of Partners in Publishing] - Tulsa, OK - *LitMag&SmPr 83-84*
Pipe Dream - Storrs, CT - *LitMag&SmPr 83-84*
Pipe Dream - Binghamton, NY - *NewsDir 84*
Pipe Line Industry [of Gulf Publishing Co.] - Houston, TX - *BaconPubCkMag 84; MagDir 84*
Pipe Prefabrication - Downsview, ON, Canada - *MicrocomSwDir 1*
Pipe Smoker - Chattanooga, TN - *BaconPubCkMag 84*
Pipe Smoker's Ephemeris, The - College Point, NY - *LitMag&SmPr 83-84*
Pipeline [of Oildom Publishing Co.] - Houston, TX - *BaconPubCkMag 84; MagDir 84*
Pipeline & Gas Journal [of Harcourt Brace Jovanovich] - Dallas, TX - *BaconPubCkMag 84; MagDir 84; WritMar 84*
Pipeline & Underground Utilities Construction [of Oildom Publishing Co.] - Houston, TX - *BaconPubCkMag 84; MagDir 84; WritMar 84*
Pipeline Carrier Accident Report System [of U.S. Dept. of Transportation] - Washington, DC - *EISS 83*
Pipeline Digest - Houston, TX - *BaconPubCkMag 84; WritMar 84*
Pipelines [of Plumbers/Steamfitters UA Local 38] - San Francisco, CA - *NewsDir 84*
Piper City Cable TV Inc. [of Illinois Community Cablevision] - Piper City, IL - *BrCabYB 84*
Piper City Journal - Piper City, IL - *Ed&PubIntYB 82*
Piper City Journal - *See* Cornbelt Press Inc.
Piper Publishing Inc. - Minneapolis, MN - *LitMarPl 83*
Piper Publishing, Peter - *See* Lanis Music, Stuart
Pipestone Cable TV [of Metro Cable Inc.] - Pipestone, MN - *BrCabYB 84; Tel&CabFB 84C*
Pipestone County Star [of Pipestone Publishing Co.] - Pipestone, MN - *AyerDirPub 83; BaconPubCkNews 84; Ed&PubIntYB 82; NewsDir 84*
Pipino Associates, Nicholas P. - Columbia, MD - *AvMarPl 83*
Pipkin Advertising Agency Inc., Dan - Danville, IL - *StaDirAdAg 2-84*
Piqua Call - Piqua, OH - *BaconPubCkNews 84; Ed&PubIntYB 82; NewsDir 84*
Pira [of Pergamon International Information Corp.] - McLean, VA - *DataDirOnSer 84*
PIRA [of Paper & Board, Printing & Packaging Industries Research Association] - Leatherhead, England - *DBBus 82; DirOnDB Spring 84; InfIndMarPl 83*
PIRA [of Paper & Board, Printing & Packaging Industries Research Association] - Surrey, England - *CompReadDB 82*

PIRA Abstracts [of Paper & Board, Printing, & Packaging Industries Research Association] - Leatherhead, England - *OnBibDB 3*
Pirate Press - London, England - *LitMag&SmPr 83-84*
Pirnie, R. M. - Union Springs, AL - *Tel&CabFB 84C p.1697*
Pirozzolo Co., Richard D. - Boston, MA - *DirPRFirms 83*
Piscataquis Observer - Dover-Foxcroft, ME - *AyerDirPub 83*
Piscataquis, The - Dover-Foxcroft, ME - *Ed&PubIntYB 82*
Pisces' Eye - Seattle, WA - *BoPubDir 4, 5*
Pisces Printer - Irvine, CA - *BoPubDir 4, 5*
Pit & Quarry - Chicago, IL - *BaconPubCkMag 84; BoPubDir 5; MagDir 84; MagIndMarPl 82-83*
Pitcairn Municipal Community Antenna System - Pitcairn, PA - *BrCabYB 84; Tel&CabFB 84C*
Pitcher, Donald T. - North Haven, CT - *MagIndMarPl 82-83*
Pitjon Press/Backback Media - Bloomington, IN - *LitMag&SmPr 83-84*
Pitkin Agency Inc., The Walter - Weston, CT - *LitMarPl 83, 84*
Pitluk Group - San Antonio, TX - *AdAge 3-28-84; StaDirAdAg 2-84; TelAl 83, 84*
Pitman Learning Inc. [Subs. of Pitman Ltd.] - Belmont, CA - *LitMarPl 83, 84; WritMar 84*
Pitman Publishing Inc. [Subs. of Pitman Ltd.] - Marshfield, MA - *LitMarPl 83, 84*
Pitman Review - Blackwood, NJ - *NewsDir 84*
Pitman Review - *See* Cam-Glo Newspapers Inc.
Pitney Bowes - Stamford, CT - *DataDirSup 7-83; DirInfWP 82*
Pitou Publications - Watertown, MA - *LitMag&SmPr 83-84*
Pitt News [of University of Pittsburgh] - Pittsburgh, PA - *NewsDir 84*
Pittman, Dorothy - Ossining, NY - *LitMarPl 83, 84*
Pittore Euforico - New York, NY - *BoPubDir 4, 5; LitMag&SmPr 83-84*
Pittsboro Chatham Record - Pittsboro, NC - *BaconPubCkNews 84*
Pittsburg Cable TV [of United Artists Cablesystems Corp.] - Pittsburg, KS - *BrCabYB 84; Tel&CabFB 84C*
Pittsburg Gazette - Pittsburg, TX - *BaconPubCkNews 84; Ed&PubIntYB 82; NewsDir 84*
Pittsburg Morning Sun [of Stauffer Communications Inc.] - Pittsburg, KS - *BaconPubCkNews 84; NewsDir 84*
Pittsburg Post Dispatch [of Worrell Newspapers of California Inc.] - Pittsburg, CA - *BaconPubCkNews 84; Ed&PubIntYB 82; NewsDir 84*
Pittsburg Press - Pittsburg, CA - *NewsDir 84*
Pittsburgh Brookline Journal - Pittsburgh, PA - *BaconPubCkNews 84; NewsDir 84*
Pittsburgh Business Journal - Pittsburgh, PA - *BaconPubCkMag 84*
Pittsburgh Business Times - Pittsburgh, PA - *BaconPubCkMag 84*
Pittsburgh Catholic - Pittsburgh, PA - *NewsDir 84*
Pittsburgh Green Sheet - Pittsburgh, PA - *BaconPubCkNews 84*
Pittsburgh Green Tab - Pittsburgh, PA - *BaconPubCkNews 84*
Pittsburgh Herald, The - Pittsburgh, PA - *NewsDir 84*
Pittsburgh History & Landmarks Foundation - Pittsburgh, PA - *BoPubDir 4, 5*
Pittsburgh Homewood-Brushton News - Pittsburgh, PA - *NewsDir 84*
Pittsburgh Jewish Chronicle - Pittsburgh, PA - *NewsDir 84*
Pittsburgh Legal Journal [of Allegheny County Bar Association] - Pittsburgh, PA - *Ed&PubIntYB 82; NewsDir 84*
Pittsburgh Magazine [of Metropolitan Pittsburgh Public Broadcasting Inc.] - Pittsburgh, PA - *ArtMar 84; BaconPubCkMag 84; MagDir 84; WritMar 84*
Pittsburgh Mt. Washington News [of Southwest Journal Inc.] - Pittsburgh, PA - *NewsDir 84*
Pittsburgh Mt. Washington News - *See* News Publishing Co. Inc.
Pittsburgh New Courier - Pittsburgh, PA - *BaconPubCkNews 84*
Pittsburgh North Hills News Record - Pittsburgh, PA - *BaconPubCkNews 84; NewsDir 84*
Pittsburgh Oakland News - Pittsburgh, PA - *BaconPubCkNews 84; NewsDir 84*
Pittsburgh Post-Gazette [of P.B. Publishing Co.] - Pittsburgh, PA - *BaconPubCkNews 84; Ed&PubIntYB 82; LitMarPl 83, 84; NewsBur 6; NewsDir 84*
Pittsburgh Press [of Scripps-Howard Co.] - Pittsburgh, PA - *BaconPubCkNews 84; Ed&PubIntYB 82; LitMarPl 83, 84; NewsBur 6; NewsDir 84; WritMar 84*
Pittsburgh Regional Library Center - Pittsburgh, PA - *EISS 83; InfIndMarPl 83*
Pittsburgh South Hills Record [of Dardanell Publications Inc.] - Monroeville, PA - *NewsDir 84*
Pittsburgh South Hills Record - Pittsburgh, PA - *BaconPubCkNews 84*
Pittsburgh South Reporter - Pittsburgh, PA - *BaconPubCkNews 84*
Pittsburgh Southwest Journal - *See* News Publishing Co. Inc.
Pittsburgh Theological Seminary (Clifford E. Barbour Library) - Pittsburgh, PA - *BoPubDir 4, 5*
Pittsburgh Town & Boro News - *See* News Publishing Co. Inc.
Pittsburgh Unione - Pittsburgh, PA - *BaconPubCkNews 84; NewsDir 84*
Pittsburgher Magazine, The - Pittsburgh, PA - *MagDir 84*
Pittsfield Advertiser, The - Pittsfield, ME - *AyerDirPub 83*
Pittsfield Cablevision Co. Inc. - Pittsfield, NH - *Tel&CabFB 84C*
Pittsfield Pike Press - Pittsfield, IL - *BaconPubCkNews 84*
Pittsfield Valley Times [of Royal Printing Service] - Pittsfield, ME - *BaconPubCkNews 84; Ed&PubIntYB 82; NewsDir 84*
Pittsford Brighton-Pittsford Post - *See* Wolfe Publications Inc.
Pittston Dispatch - Pittston, PA - *BaconPubCkNews 84*
Pittston Sunday Dispatch - Pittston, PA - *NewsDir 84*
Pittsville Record - Pittsville, WI - *BaconPubCkNews 84; Ed&PubIntYB 82*
Pittway Corp. - Northbrook, IL - *AdAge 6-28-84; KnowInd 83*
Pivot - University Park, PA - *LitMag&SmPr 83-84*
Pix Productions Inc. - Santa Ana, CA - *AvMarPl 83*
Pixel Computer Inc. - Wilmington, MA - *MicrocomMPl 84*
Pixie Press - Phoenix, AZ - *BoPubDir 5*
Pixley Enterprise - Pixley, CA - *BaconPubCkNews 84; Ed&PubIntYB 82; NewsDir 84*
Pizza Maker, The - Raleigh, NC - *BaconPubCkMag 84*
Pizzazz Press Inc. - Lincoln, NE - *BoPubDir 4, 5*
Pizzuto Ltd./Blacksmith Books - San Gabriel, CA - *BoPubDir 4 Sup, 5*
P.J. Cable Co. Inc. - Clay, OH - *BrCabYB 84*
PJD Publications Ltd. - Westbury, NY - *LitMarPl 83, 84; MagIndMarPl 82-83*
PJS Publications - Peoria, IL - *MagIndMarPl 82-83*
PK Services Corp. - Carmel, CA - *CabTVFinDB 83*
PK Systems Inc. - Bloomington, IL - *MicrocomMPl 83; WhoWMicrocom 83*
PL & P Advertising Studio - Ft. Lauderdale, FL - *StaDirAdAg 2-84*
Place in the Woods - Golden Valley, MN - *BoPubDir 4 Sup, 5; LitMag&SmPr 83-84*
Place of Herons Press - Austin, TX - *BoPubDir 4 Sup, 5; LitMag&SmPr 83-84*
Place Stamp Here [of Press Me Close] - Farmingdale, NJ - *LitMag&SmPr 83-84*
Placebo Press - Pensacola, FL - *LitMag&SmPr 83-84*
Placentia News-Times - Placentia, CA - *NewsDir 84*
Placentia News-Times - *See* Placentia News-Times Publishers
Placentia News-Times Publishers - Placentia, CA - *BaconPubCkNews 84*
Placer Herald - Rocklin, CA - *AyerDirPub 83; Ed&PubIntYB 82*
Placerville Mountain Democrat - Placerville, CA - *BaconPubCkNews 84; NewsDir 84*
Placerville Sierra Breeze - Placerville, CA - *NewsDir 84*
Placerville Sierra Breeze - Shingle Springs, CA - *BaconPubCkNews 84*
Plagman, Clifford - Milford, IA - *Tel&CabFB 84C p.1697*
Plain City Advocate - London, OH - *BaconPubCkNews 84*
Plain City Advocate - Plain City, OH - *Ed&PubIntYB 82*
Plain Dealer - North Vernon, IN - *AyerDirPub 83*
Plain Dealer - Wabash, IN - *AyerDirPub 83*
Plain Dealer - Kearny, NJ - *AyerDirPub 83*
Plain Dealer - Williamstown, NJ - *AyerDirPub 83; Ed&PubIntYB 82*
Plain Dealer - Cleveland, OH - *AyerDirPub 83; Ed&PubIntYB 82; LitMarPl 84; NewsBur 6*
Plain Dealer & Sun Inc. - North Vernon, IN - *BaconPubCkNews 84*
Plain Dealer & West Hudson Record - *See* West Hudson Publishers
Plain Dealer Magazine - Cleveland, OH - *ArtMar 84*

Plain Dealing Telephone Co. [Aff. of Century Telephone Enterprises Inc.] - Plain Dealing, LA - *TelDir&BG 83-84*
Plain Talk - Vermillion, SD - *AyerDirPub 83; Ed&PubIntYB 82*
Plain Talk - New Tazewell, TN - *AyerDirPub 83*
Plain Truth - Pasadena, CA - *MagIndMarPl 82-83*
Plain View Press - Austin, TX - *BoPubDir 4 Sup, 5*
Plain Wrapper Press - Verona, Italy - *LitMag&SmPr 83-84*
Plaindealer - McHenry, IL - *AyerDirPub 83*
Plaindealer - Almena, KS - *AyerDirPub 83*
Plaines Cooperative Telephone Association Inc. - Joes, CO - *TelDir&BG 83-84*
Plainfield Cablevision Inc. [of Storer Cable Communications] - Plainfield, NJ - *BrCabYB 84; Tel&CabFB 84C*
Plainfield Enterprise - Plainfield, IL - *BaconPubCkNews 84; NewsDir 84*
Plainfield Messenger - Plainfield, IN - *BaconPubCkNews 84; NewsDir 84*
Plains Cablevision Systems - Plains, TX - *Tel&CabFB 84C p.1697*
Plains Cablevision Systems [of Cable Installation Contractors Seventy Eight Ltd.] - Sundown, TX - *BrCabYB 84*
Plains Cablevision Systems - Tatum, TX - *BrCabYB 84*
Plains Chess [of Kansas/Oklahoma Chess Associations] - Wichita, KS - *LitMag&SmPr 83-84*
Plains Community TV - Plains, KS - *Tel&CabFB 84C*
Plains Distribution Service Inc. - Fargo, ND - *BoPubDir 4 Sup, 5*
Plains Journal - *See* Meade Globe-Press
Plains Plainsman - Plains, MT - *BaconPubCkNews 84*
Plains Poetry Journal [of Stronghold Press] - Bismarck, ND - *LitMag&SmPr 83-84; WritMar 84*
Plains Television Partnership - Champaign, IL - *Tel&CabFB 84S*
Plainsman - Plains, MT - *Ed&PubIntYB 82*
Plainsman - Huron, SD - *AyerDirPub 83*
Plainsman - Rapid City, SD - *AyerDirPub 83*
Plainsman-Clarion - Richland, IA - *AyerDirPub 83*
Plainsman-Clarion, The - Packwood, IA - *Ed&PubIntYB 82*
Plainsman-Herald - Springfield, CO - *Ed&PubIntYB 82*
Plainsman-News, The - Zachary, LA - *Ed&PubIntYB 82*
Plainsman Publications Ltd. - Vancouver, BC, Canada - *BoPubDir 4 Sup, 5*
Plainsong - Bowling Green, KY - *LitMag&SmPr 83-84*
Plainswoman - Grand Forks, ND - *LitMag&SmPr 83-84*
Plainview Cable TV [of Teleservice Corp. of America] - Plainview, TX - *BrCabYB 84; Tel&CabFB 84C*
Plainview Herald - Hicksville, NY - *AyerDirPub 83*
Plainview Herald [of The Hearst Corp.] - Plainview, TX - *BaconPubCkNews 84; Ed&PubIntYB 82; NewsDir 84*
Plainview Herald - *See* Mid-Island Herald Publishers
Plainview News - Plainview, MN - *Ed&PubIntYB 82; NewsDir 84*
Plainview News - Plainview, NE - *BaconPubCkNews 84; Ed&PubIntYB 82*
Plainview News - *See* Mack Publishing Co.
Plainview Old Bethpage Herald - Plainview, NY - *Ed&PubIntYB 82*
Plainview Pennysaver - Plainview, NY - *AyerDirPub 83*
Plainview Telephone Co. Inc. - Plainview, NE - *TelDir&BG 83-84*
Plainville News - Plainville, CT - *Ed&PubIntYB 82*
Plainville Times - Plainville, KS - *BaconPubCkNews 84; Ed&PubIntYB 82*
Plainville TV Cable [of CATV Inc.] - Plainville, KS - *BrCabYB 84; Tel&CabFB 84C*
Plainwell-Otsego Union Enterprise - Plainwell, MI - *BaconPubCkNews 84*
Plaisted Communication Services, Madelon Timmons - Worthington, OH - *LitMarPl 83, 84; MagIndMarPl 82-83*
Plaistow News - *See* Exeter News-Letter Co.
Plan & Print [of International Reprographic Association] - Franklin Park, IL - *ArtMar 84; BaconPubCkMag 84; MagDir 84; WritMar 84*
Plan 4000 [of Nestar Systems Inc.] - Palo Alto, CA - *TeleSy&SerDir 7-83*
Planada Cable TV [of San-Val Cablevision Inc.] - Planada, CA - *Tel&CabFB 84C*
Planck-Institut fur Plasmaphysik, Max - Munich, West Germany - *CompReadDB 82; InfIndMarPl 83*
Plane & Pilot Magazine [of Werner & Werner Corp.] - Encino, CA - *WritMar 84*
Plane & Pilot Magazine [of Werner & Werner Corp.] - Van Nuys, CA - *BaconPubCkMag 84; MagDir 84; MagIndMarPl 82-83*
Planet - Martinsville, IL - *AyerDirPub 83*
Planet - Metropolis, IL - *AyerDirPub 83*
Planet Books [Div. of Once Upon a Planet Inc.] - Bayside, NY - *WritMar 84*
Planet Books - Fresh Meadows, NY - *BoPubDir 5*
Planet Detroit - Detroit, MI - *LitMag&SmPr 83-84*
Planet Detroit Poems - Detroit, MI - *LitMag&SmPr 83-84*
Planetary Music Publishing Corp. - *See* Big Seven Music Corp.
Planetary Research - Santa Monica, CA - *LitMag&SmPr 83-84*
Planetary Research Center [of Lowell Observatory] - Flagstaff, AZ - *EISS 83*
Planicom/PNMD Inc. - *See* Baker Lovick Ltd.
Plankinton, Bruce R. - *See* Texkan Communications Inc.
Plankinton South Dakota Mail - Plankinton, SD - *BaconPubCkNews 84*
Planned Parenthood Federation of America Inc. - New York, NY - *BoPubDir 4, 5*
Planned Television Arts Ltd. - New York, NY - *DirPRFirms 83; LitMarPl 83, 84; MagIndMarPl 82-83*
Planners Press [Aff. of American Planning Association] - Chicago, IL - *BoPubDir 4, 5*
Planning [of American Planning Association] - Chicago, IL - *ArtMar 84; BaconPubCkMag 84; MagDir 84; MagIndMarPl 82-83; WritMar 84*
Planning Dept. [of University of Oslo] - Oslo, Norway - *EISS 83*
Planning Economics Group, The - Woburn, MA - *EISS 83; IntDirMarRes 83*
Planning Research Corp. - McLean, VA - *DataDirOnSer 84; DataDirSup 7-83; Datamation 6-83; KnowInd 83; Top100Al 83*
Plano Star-Courier - Plano, TX - *BaconPubCkNews 84; Ed&PubIntYB 82; NewsDir 84*
Plansky Public Relations - Palo Alto, CA - *DirPRFirms 83*
Plant & Production Data [of Computer Sciences Corp.] - Falls Church, VA - *DataDirOnSer 84*
Plant Breeding Abstracts [of Commonwealth Bureau of Plant Breeding & Genetics] - Cambridge, England - *CompReadDB 82*
Plant City Courier - Plant City, FL - *NewsDir 84*
Plant City Courier - *See* Hillsborough Community Pub. Inc.
Plant City Shopper - Plant City, FL - *AyerDirPub 83*
Plant Energy Management - Willow Grove, PA - *MagIndMarPl 82-83*
Plant Engineering [of Technical Publishing] - Barrington, IL - *BaconPubCkMag 84; Folio 83; MagDir 84; MagIndMarPl 82-83*
Plant Engineering & Maintenance - Oakville, ON, Canada - *BaconPubCkMag 84*
Plant Engineering Products - Barrington, IL - *MagDir 84*
Plant Inc., Bud - Grass Valley, CA - *BoPubDir 4, 5*
Plant Information Network [of U.S. Fish & Wildlife Service] - Ft. Collins, CO - *EISS 83*
Plant Management & Engineering - Toronto, ON, Canada - *BaconPubCkMag 84; WritMar 84*
Plant Physiology - Rockville, MD - *MagIndMarPl 82-83*
Plant Press - Halifax, MA - *BoPubDir 4 Sup, 5*
Plant, Richard - New York, NY - *LitMarPl 83, 84; MagIndMarPl 82-83*
Plant Services - Chicago, IL - *BaconPubCkMag 84; MagIndMarPl 82-83*
Plant Telephone & Power Co. Inc. - Tifton, GA - *TelDir&BG 83-84*
Plantagenet House Inc. - Blackshear, GA - *BoPubDir 4, 5; LitMag&SmPr 83-84*
Plantagenet Productions - Newbury, England - *LitMag&SmPr 83-84*
Plantation Cablevision [Aff. of Mid America Media] - Hilton Head Island, SC - *BrCabYB 84; InterCabHB 3; Tel&CabFB 84C*
Plantation News - Ft. Lauderdale, FL - *AyerDirPub 83*
Planter Newspaper - Apopka, FL - *AyerDirPub 83; Ed&PubIntYB 82*
Planter, The - Apopka, FL - *Ed&PubIntYB 82*
Planters Rural Telephone Cooperative Inc. - Newington, GA - *TelDir&BG 83-84*
Plants Alive - Seattle, WA - *MagDir 84*

Plants Alive Books [Aff. of Plants Inc.] - Woodinville, WA - *BoPubDir 4, 5*
Plants & Gardens - Brooklyn, NY - *MagDir 84; MagIndMarPl 82-83*
Plants & Processes Information System for Iron & Steel [of German Iron & Steel Association] - Dusseldorf, West Germany - *EISS 83*
Plants, Sites, & Parks - Coral Springs, FL - *BaconPubCkMag 84*
Plants, Sites, & Parks - Pompano Beach, FL - *MagDir 34*
Plapler & Associates - New York, NY - *BrCabYB 84; StaDirAdAg 2-84*
Plaquemine Post-Iberville South - Plaquemine, LA - *AyerDirPub 83; NewsDir 84*
Plaquemine Post-Iberville South - *See* Plaquemine Publishing Inc.
Plaquemine Publishing Inc. - Plaquemine, LA - *BaconPubCkNews 84*
Plaquemine White Castle Times - *See* Plaquemine Publishing Inc.
Plaquemines Cablevision - Boothville, LA - *BrCabYB 84*
Plaquemines Cablevision Inc. - Empire, LA - *Tel&CabFB 84C*
Plaquemines Gazette - Belle Chasse, LA - *AyerDirPub 83; NewsDir 84*
Plaquemines Gazette, The - Plaquemines, LA - *Ed&PubIntYB 82*
Plaquemines Watchman, The - Belle Chasse, LA - *AyerDirPub 83*
Plasma Physics Index [of Max Planck Institut fur Plasmaphysik] - Munich, West Germany - *CompReadDB 82*
Plasma Physics Library & Information Service [of Atomic Energy Authority] - Abingdon, England - *EISS 83*
Plastercrafts - Glendale, CA - *BaconPubCkMag 84*
Plasterer & Cement Mason, The - Washington, DC - *NewsDir 84*
Plastic & Reconstructive Surgery - Baltimore, MD - *MagDir 84*
Plastic & Reconstructive Surgery - Brookline, MA - *BaconPubCkMag 84*
Plastic Chemicals [of Probe Economics Inc.] - Mt. Kisco, NY - *DataDirOnSer 84; DirOnDB Spring 84*
Plastic Chemicals Forecast Database [of Probe Economics Inc.] - Mt. Kisco, NY - *DataDirOnSer 84; DirOnDB Spring 84*
Plastic Records - Southfield, MI - *BillIntBG 83-84*
Plastic Reel Corp. of America - Elmwood Park, NJ - *AvMarPl 83*
Plastican Corp. - Butler, NJ - *AvMarPl 83*
Plastics Brief (Design & Materials Div.) - Toledo, OH - *BaconPubCkMag 84*
Plastics Brief (Extrusion & Blow Molding Edition) - Toledo, OH - *BaconPubCkMag 84*
Plastics Brief (Injection Molding Edition) - Toledo, OH - *BaconPubCkMag 84*
Plastics Business - Toronto, ON, Canada - *BaconPubCkMag 84*
Plastics Compounding - Denver, CO - *BaconPubCkMag 84; MagIndMarPl 82-83*
Plastics Design & Processing - Libertyville, IL - *BaconPubCkMag 84; MagDir 84; MagIndMarPl 82-83*
Plastics Design Forum - Denver, CO - *BaconPubCkMag 84; MagDir 84; MagIndMarPl 82-83*
Plastics Engineering - Brookfield Center, CT - *BaconPubCkMag 84; MagDir 84*
Plastics Focus - New York, NY - *BaconPubCkMag 84*
Plastics in Building Construction - Lancaster, PA - *BaconPubCkMag 84*
Plastics Industry News - Denver, CO - *BaconPubCkMag 84*
Plastics Machinery & Equipment - Denver, CO - *BaconPubCkMag 84; MagDir 84; MagIndMarPl 82-83*
Plastics Magazine - Santa Monica, CA - *BaconPubCkMag 84; MagDir 84*
Plastics Technical Evaluation Center [of U.S. Army Material Development & Readiness Command] - Dover, NJ - *EISS 83; InfIndMarPl 83*
Plastics Technology - New York, NY - *BaconPubCkMag 84; MagDir 84; MagIndMarPl 82-83*
Plastics West - San Francisco, CA - *BaconPubCkMag 84*
Plastics World - Boston, MA - *BaconPubCkMag 84; MagDir 84; MagIndMarPl 82-83*
Plate Collector, The - Kermit, TX - *MagIndMarPl 82-83*
Plate Collector, The - San Marcos, TX - *MagDir 84*
Plate World [of Plate World Ltd.] - Chicago, IL - *BaconPubCkMag 84; WritMar 84*
Plateau Records Inc. - New York, NY - *BillIntBG 83-84*
Plateville Journal - Plateville, WI - *Ed&PubIntYB 82*
Plating & Surface Finishing - Winter Park, FL - *BaconPubCkMag 84; MagDir 84; MagIndMarPl 82-83*
Platinum - Atlanta, GA - *BaconPubCkMag 84; WritMar 84*
Platt & Munk - *See* Putnam Publishing Group
Platt & Munk Publishers [Div. of Grosset & Dunlap] - New York, NY - *WritMar 84*
Platt County Journal-Republican - Monticello, IL - *Ed&PubIntYB 82*
Plattdeutsche Post - Staten Island, NY - *Ed&PubIntYB 82*
Platte City Landmark - Platte City, MO - *BaconPubCkNews 84*
Platte Communications Inc., Lou - Wood River, NE - *Tel&CabFB 84C p.1688*
Platte Community Cable TV - Platte, SD - *Tel&CabFB 84C*
Platte Community Cable TV - Redfield, SD - *BrCabYB 84*
Platte County Citizen, The - Edgerton, MO - *Ed&PubIntYB 82*
Platte County Communications Co. [of Communications Services Inc.] - Platte County, MO - *BrCabYB 84; Tel&CabFB 84C*
Platte County Communications Co. [of Communications Services Inc.] - Weston, MO - *Tel&CabFB 84C*
Platte County Gazette - Parkville, MO - *AyerDirPub 83; Ed&PubIntYB 82*
Platte County Record-Times - Wheatland, WY - *AyerDirPub 83; Ed&PubIntYB 82*
Platte Dispatch Tribune [of Townsend Communications Inc.] - Kansas City, MO - *AyerDirPub 83; Ed&PubIntYB 82; NewsDir 84*
Platte Dispatch Tribune - *See* Townsend Communications Inc.
Platte Enterprise - Platte, SD - *BaconPubCkNews 84; Ed&PubIntYB 82*
Platte Shopper News - Platte City, MO - *Ed&PubIntYB 82*
Platteville Cable TV Corp. - Dickeyville, WI - *BrCabYB 84*
Platteville Cable TV Corp. [of Platteville Telephone Co.] - Platteville, WI - *BrCabYB 84; Tel&CabFB 84C*
Platteville Herald - Platteville, CO - *BaconPubCkNews 84; Ed&PubIntYB 82*
Platteville Journal - Platteville, WI - *BaconPubCkNews 84; NewsDir 84*
Platteville Telephone Co. - Platteville, WI - *TelDir&BG 83-84*
Platt's Data Bank [of Data Resources Inc.] - Lexington, MA - *DataDirOnSer 84*
Platt's Data Bank [of McGraw-Hill Inc.] - New York, NY - *DBBus 82; DirOnDB Spring 84*
Platt's Oilgrams [of McGraw-Hill Publications Co.] - New York, NY - *EISS 83*
Platt's Petroleum Network [of McGraw-Hill Publications Co.] - New York, NY - *DataDirOnSer 84*
Plattsburg Leader - Plattsburg, MO - *AyerDirPub 83; BaconPubCkNews 84; Ed&PubIntYB 82*
Plattsburgh North Country Living - *See* Denton Publications Inc.
Plattsburgh Press-Republican - Plattsburgh, NY - *NewsDir 84*
Plattsmouth Journal - Plattsmouth, NE - *BaconPubCkNews 84; Ed&PubIntYB 82; NewsDir 84*
Play Meter [of Skybird Publishing Co. Inc.] - Metairie, LA - *BaconPubCkMag 84; MagDir 84*
Play Meter [of Skybird Publishing Co. Inc.] - New Orleans, LA - *ArtMar 84; WritMar 84*
Play Schools Association Inc. - New York, NY - *BoPubDir 5*
Playa del Rey Argonaut - Marina del Rey, CA - *BaconPubCkNews 84*
Playbill - New York, NY - *ArtMar 84; MagDir 84; MagIndMarPl 82-83; WritMar 84*
Playboy [of Playboy Enterprises Inc.] - Chicago, IL - *ArtMar 84; BaconPubCkMag 84; Folio 83; LitMarPl 83, 84; MagDir 84; MagIndMarPl 82-83; NewsBur 6; WritMar 84*
Playboy Cable Network - Los Angeles, CA - *LitMarPl 83*
Playboy Channel, The - Woodbury, NY - *BrCabYB 84; CabTVPrDB 83; Tel&CabFB 84C*
Playboy Enterprises Inc. - Chicago, IL - *AdAge 6-28-84; HomeVid&CabYB 82-83; KnowInd 83*
PlayCable - New York, NY - *BrCabYB 84; CabTVPrDB 83; VideoDir 82-83*
Players [of Players International Publications] - Los Angeles, CA - *BaconPubCkMag 84; Folio 83; MagDir 84; MagIndMarPl 82-83; WritMar 84*
Players Press - Studio City, CA - *LitMarPl 84; WritMar 84*
Playette Corp. - Great Neck, NY - *AvMarPl 83; BillIntBG 83-84; BoPubDir 4, 5*

Playgirl [of Ritter/Geller Communications Inc.] - Santa Monica, CA - *ArtMar 84; BaconPubCkMag 84; DirMarMP 83; Folio 83; LitMarPl 84; MagDir 84; MagIndMarPl 82-83; WritMar 84*
Playground Daily News - Ft. Walton Beach, FL - *AyerDirPub 83; Ed&PubIntYB 82*
Playground Music - *See* Pewter Pal Music
Playground Records - Ojai, CA - *BillIntBG 83-84*
Playhouse Pictures - Hollywood, CA - *Tel&CabFB 84C*
PlayLab Children Research [Div. of The Creative Group Inc.] - Southfield, MI - *IntDirMarRes 83*
Playmore Inc. [Aff. of Prestige Books Inc.] - New York, NY - *LitMarPl 83, 84*
Plays, The Drama Magazine for Young People - Boston, MA - *LitMarPl 83, 84; MagIndMarPl 82-83; WritMar 84*
Playspaces International [Aff. of Child's Play] - Waltham, MA - *BoPubDir 4, 5*
Playthings - New York, NY - *BaconPubCkMag 84; MagDir 84; MagIndMarPl 82-83*
Playwrights Canada - Toronto, ON, Canada - *BoPubDir 4, 5*
Playwrights' Platform Inc. - Boston, MA - *WritMar 84*
Playwrights Press - Toronto, ON, Canada - *LitMarPl 83, 84*
Plaza Research - Paramus, NJ - *IntDirMarRes 83*
Plaza Sweet Music Inc. - New York, NY - *BillIntBG 83-84*
Pleasant Grove Review - Pleasant Grove, UT - *AyerDirPub 83; Ed&PubIntYB 82*
Pleasant Grove Review - *See* Newtah News Group
Pleasant Hill Messenger - Pleasant Hill, IL - *BaconPubCkNews 84*
Pleasant Hill Post [of Oakland Neighborhood Journal] - Oakland, CA - *Ed&PubIntYB 82; NewsDir 84*
Pleasant Hill Press - Sebastopol, CA - *BoPubDir 4, 5*
Pleasant Hill Times - Pleasant Hill, MO - *BaconPubCkNews 84; Ed&PubIntYB 82*
Pleasant Plains Press - Pleasant Plains, IL - *Ed&PubIntYB 82*
Pleasant Plains Press - *See* Swettman Publications
Pleasant TV Co. - Saugerties, NY - *BrCabYB 84*
Pleasant TV Co. Inc. - Shandaken, NY - *BrCabYB 84*
Pleasant Valley Press - Eleva, WI - *LitMag&SmPr 83-84*
Pleasant Valley Voice - *See* Taconic Press Inc.
Pleasant View Music - *See* Chestnut Mound Music
Pleasantdale Citizen [of La Grange Suburban Life/Citizen] - La Grange, IL - *NewsDir 84*
Pleasanton Express [of Wilkerson Publishing Co.] - Pleasanton, TX - *BaconPubCkNews 84; Ed&PubIntYB 82; NewsDir 84*
Pleasanton Linn County News - Pleasanton, KS - *BaconPubCkNews 84*
PleasanTrees Programming - Tucson, AZ - *MicrocomMPl 84*
Pleasants County Leader - Pleasants County, WV - *Ed&PubIntYB 82*
Pleasants County Leader - St. Marys, WV - *AyerDirPub 83*
Pleasantville Journal - Pleasantville, NY - *Ed&PubIntYB 82*
Pleasantville Journal - *See* Pleasantville Journal Publishers
Pleasantville Journal Publishers - Pleasantville, NY - *BaconPubCkNews 84*
Pleasantville Mainland Journal - Pleasantville, NJ - *BaconPubCkNews 84; NewsDir 84*
Pleasantville Marion County News - Pleasantville, IA - *BaconPubCkNews 84*
Pleasantville Post - Armonk, NY - *AyerDirPub 83*
Pleason Records - Sacramento, CA - *BillIntBG 83-84*
Pleasure Boating [of Graphcom Publishing Inc.] - North Miami, FL - *BaconPubCkMag 84; WritMar 84*
Pleasure Channel, The - Los Angeles, CA - *CabTVPrDB 83; Tel&CabFB 84C*
Pleasure Trove Books - Jamaica, NY - *BoPubDir 4*
Pleasure Trove Books - Merrick, NY - *BoPubDir 5*
Pledger Advertising Co. - San Francisco, CA - *StaDirAdAg 2-84*
Plein Jour de Charlevoix - La Malbaie, PQ, Canada - *Ed&PubIntYB 82*
Plein Jour Saguenay - Forestville, PQ, Canada - *Ed&PubIntYB 82*
Plein Jour sur Manicouagan - Baie Comeau, PQ, Canada - *Ed&PubIntYB 82*
Pleion Corp. - Santa Ana, CA - *DirInfWP 82*
Plentywood Cable TV Co. - Plentywood, MT - *BrCabYB 84; Tel&CabFB 84C*
Plentywood Herald - Plentywood, MT - *BaconPubCkNews 84; Ed&PubIntYB 82*
Plenum Press [Subs. of Plenum Publishing Corp.] - New York, NY - *MagIndMarPl 82-83*
Plenum Publishing Corp. - New York, NY - *LitMarPl 83, 84; WritMar 84*
Plenum Publishing Corp. - *See* Canner & Co., J. S.
Plessas Inc., James - San Francisco, CA - *StaDirAdAg 2-84*
Plessey Communications - South Melville, NY - *DirInfWP 82*
Plessey Co. - Ilford, England - *ElecNews 7-25-83*
Plessey Peripheral Systems - Irvine, CA - *DataDirSup 7-83; DirInfWP 82; MicrocomMPl 84; WhoWMicrocom 83*
Plexus [of Feminist Publishing Alliance Inc.] - Oakland, CA - *LitMag&SmPr 83-84*
Plexus Publishing Inc. - Marlton, NJ - *BoPubDir 4*
Plexus Publishing Inc. - Medford, NJ - *BoPubDir 5; LitMag&SmPr 83-84*
Plexus Trading Corp. - White Plains, NY - *BillIntBG 83-84*
Plezia, Valerie - Cleveland, OH - *BoPubDir 5*
Plibby Music - *See* Four Moons Music Publishing Group
Pliskin, Berenice Chaplan - White Plains, NY - *LitMarPl 83, 84; MagIndMarPl 82-83*
Plog Research Inc. - Reseda, CA - *IntDirMarRes 83*
Ploss, Douglas A. - Lake Villa, IL - *BoPubDir 4, 5*
Plough Broadcasting Co. - Memphis, TN - *BrCabYB 84*
Plough Publishing House, The [Subs. of Hutterian Society of Brothers] - Rifton, NY - *LitMarPl 83, 84*
Ploughshares - Cambridge, MA - *LitMag&SmPr 83-84; WritMar 84*
Plourde, Philip G. - Caribou, ME - *Tel&CabFB 84C p.1697*
Plowshare Press - Little Current, ON, Canada - *BoPubDir 5*
Plowshare Press - Toronto, ON, Canada - *BoPubDir 4*
PLS Performance Texts [Aff. of Poculi Ludique Societas] - Toronto, ON, Canada - *BoPubDir 4, 5*
Plum Cable TV [of Eastern Telecom Corp.] - Plum, PA - *BrCabYB 84; Tel&CabFB 84C*
Plumb - Decatur, GA - *BaconPubCkMag 84*
Plumb & Associates, James W. - *See* Ruder Finn & Rotman Inc.
Plumbers Friend [of Utah Plumbing & Heating Contractors] - Salt Lake City, UT - *BaconPubCkMag 84; MagDir 84*
Plumbers Ink Books - Cerrillos, NM - *BoPubDir 4, 5; LitMag&SmPr 83-84*
Plumbing Engineer [of Miramar Publishing] - Los Angeles, CA - *MagDir 84*
Plumbing Engineer - Elmhurst, IL - *BaconPubCkMag 84*
Plunkett Family Trust - Rochester, MN - *Tel&CabFB 84C p.1697*
Pluribus Press [Aff. of Teach'em Inc.] - Chicago, IL - *BoPubDir 4 Sup, 5; LitMag&SmPr 83-84; LitMarPl 84; WritMar 84*
Plus Computer Technology Inc. - Chicago, IL - *MicrocomMPl 83*
Plus Three Music Inc. - *See* Pride Music Group
Pluto Press - New York, NY - *LitMarPl 83*
Pluto Research Group - Palo Alto, CA - *WhoWMicrocom 83*
Plycon Press - Redondo Beach, CA - *BoPubDir 4, 5*
Plymouth Advertiser - Plymouth, OH - *BaconPubCkNews 84; Ed&PubIntYB 82*
Plymouth-Canton Community Crier - Plymouth, MI - *BaconPubCkNews 84*
Plymouth Colony Research Group - Warwick, RI - *BoPubDir 4 Sup, 5*
Plymouth Music Co. Inc. - Ft. Lauderdale, FL - *ArtMar 84*
Plymouth Observer [of Livonia Suburban Communications Corp.] - Livonia, MI - *AyerDirPub 83; NewsDir 84*
Plymouth Observer - Plymouth, MI - *Ed&PubIntYB 82*
Plymouth Observer - *See* Observer & Eccentric Newspapers
Plymouth Old Colony Memorial - *See* MPG Communications
Plymouth Pilot-News - Plymouth, IN - *BaconPubCkNews 84*
Plymouth Press - Miami, FL - *BoPubDir 4, 5*
Plymouth Record-Citizen - Plymouth, NH - *BaconPubCkNews 84; NewsDir 84*
Plymouth Review - *See* Wisconsin Newspress Inc.
Plymouth Roanoke Beacon - Plymouth, NC - *BaconPubCkNews 84*
Plymouth Rock Foundation Inc. - Marlborough, NH - *BoPubDir 5*
Plymouth Tri-County Scribe - Plymouth, IL - *BaconPubCkNews 84*

Plywood & Panel Magazine - Indianapolis, IN - *MagDir 84*
Plywood & Panel World [of Hatton-Brown Publishers] - Montgomery, AL - *BaconPubCkMag 84; DirMarMP 83; MagIndMarPl 82-83*
PM Business Services - St. Paul, MN - *MicrocomMPl 84*
PM Group Ltd. - New York, NY - *ArtMar 84*
PM Media - Lake Hill, NY - *AvMarPl 83*
PM Records Inc. - Woodcliff Lake, NJ - *BillIntBG 83-84*
PM Video Corp. - Montclair, NJ - *Tel&CabFB 84C*
PMA Books - Agincourt, ON, Canada - *LitMarPl 83*
PMA Books [Aff. of Peter Martin Associates Ltd.] - Toronto, ON, Canada - *BoPubDir 4*
PMA Industries Inc. - West Babylon, NY - *LitMarPl 83, 84; MagIndMarPl 82-83*
PMB - Toronto, ON, Canada - *DirOnDB Spring 84; EISS 83*
PMC Software - Mountain View, CA - *MicrocomMPl 83, 84*
PMI Micro Wholesalers - Fairfield, NJ - *MicrocomMPl 84*
PMLA - New York, NY - *MagDir 84; MagIndMarPl 82-83*
PMS Systems Corp. - Santa Monica, CA - *DataDirOnSer 84*
PNG Communications Co. - Charlotte, NC - *Tel&CabFB 84C*
PNG Communications Co. [of Piedmont Natural Gas Co.] - River Hills Plantation, SC - *BrCabYB 84*
PNI - *See* Pharmaceutical News Index
PNPA Press - Harrisburg, PA - *BaconPubCkMag 84; MagDir 84*
P'Nye Press - Palo Alto, CA - *BoPubDir 4, 5*
Poage Publishing Co. - Brooksville, KY - *BaconPubCkNews 84*
P.O.B. [of P.O.B. Publishing Co.] - Wayne, MI - *BaconPubCkMag 84; WritMar 84*
Poca River Records - Fairmont, WV - *BillIntBG 83-84*
Pocahonkes County Advertiser - Laurens, IA - *AyerDirPub 83*
Pocahontas/Laurens Cable TV [of Cable Communications of Iowa] - Laurens, IA - *BrCabYB 84*
Pocahontas/Laurens Cable TV [of Cable Communications of Iowa] - Pocahontas, IA - *BrCabYB 84*
Pocahontas Record-Democrat - Pocahontas, IA - *BaconPubCkNews 84; Ed&PubIntYB 82*
Pocahontas Star Herald - Pocahontas, AR - *BaconPubCkNews 84; Ed&PubIntYB 82; NewsDir 84*
Pocahontas Times - Marlinton, WV - *AyerDirPub 83; NewsDir 84*
Pocahontas TV Cable [of TCA Cable TV Inc.] - Pocahontas, AR - *BrCabYB 84; Tel&CabFB 84C*
Pocatello Idaho State Journal - Pocatello, ID - *NewsDir 84*
Pocker, Beth Bird - New York, NY - *DirInfWP 82*
Pocket Books [Div. of Simon & Schuster] - New York, NY - *LitMarPl 83, 84; WritMar 84*
Pocket Books (Art Dept.) - New York, NY - *ArtMar 84*
Pocket Computer Newsletter - Seymour, CT - *BaconPubCkMag 84*
PocketInfo Corp. - Beaverton, OR - *MicrocomMPl 84*
Pockets - Nashville, TN - *WritMar 84*
Poco Loco Music Co. - *See* Faro Music Publishing
Pocomoke Worcester County Messenger - Pocomoke, MD - *BaconPubCkNews 84*
Pocono CATV Inc. - White Haven, PA - *BrCabYB 84*
Pocono Record - Stroudsburg, PA - *AyerDirPub 83; BaconPubCkNews 84; Ed&PubIntYB 82*
Pocono Shopper - Stroudsburg, PA - *NewsDir 84*
Pocumtuck Valley Memorial Association - Deerfield, MA - *BoPubDir 4, 5*
Podiatry - Orlando, FL - *MagDir 84*
Podiatry Management - Philadelphia, PA - *ArtMar 84; WritMar 84*
Poe & Associates, E. D. - Los Angeles, CA - *DirInfWP 82*
Poem [of Huntsville Literary Association] - Huntsville, AL - *LitMag&SmPr 83-84; WritMar 84*
Poes Camera Co. Inc. - Evanston, IL - *AvMarPl 83*
Poesis - Bryn Mawr, PA - *LitMag&SmPr 83-84*
Poet & Critic [of Iowa State University Press] - Ames, IA - *LitMag&SmPr 83-84*
Poet Gallery Press - New York, NY - *BoPubDir 4, 5; LitMag&SmPr 83-84; WritMar 84*
Poet Lore - Washington, DC - *LitMag&SmPr 83-84*
Poet News [of The Poet Tree Inc.] - Sacramento, CA - *LitMag&SmPr 83-84*
Poet Papers - Topanga, CA - *BoPubDir 4, 5; LitMag&SmPr 83-84*
Poet Tree Inc., The - Sacramento, CA - *LitMag&SmPr 83-84*
Poetalk Quarterly [of Owlseye Publications] - Hayward, CA - *LitMag&SmPr 83-84*
Poetic Justice - Los Angeles, CA - *LitMag&SmPr 83-84*
Poetics Journal - Berkeley, CA - *LitMag&SmPr 83-84*
Poetry [of The Modern Poetry Association] - Chicago, IL - *LitMag&SmPr 83-84; LitMarPl 83, 84; MagIndMarPl 82-83; WritMar 84*
Poetry Australia [of South Head Press] - Berrima, Australia - *LitMag&SmPr 83-84; WritMar 84*
Poetry Canada Poesie Review Inc. - Toronto, ON, Canada - *LitMag&SmPr 83-84*
Poetry Canada Review - Toronto, ON, Canada - *LitMag&SmPr 83-84; WritMar 84*
Poetry Durham - New Elvet, England - *LitMag&SmPr 83-84*
Poetry East - Earlysville, VA - *LitMag&SmPr 83-84*
Poetry Eastwest - Sumter, SC - *BoPubDir 4, 5*
Poetry Flash - Berkeley, CA - *LitMag&SmPr 83-84*
Poetry for the People - San Francisco, CA - *LitMag&SmPr 83-84*
Poetry in English Society, The - Haifa, Iceland - *LitMag&SmPr 83-84*
Poetry in Motion [of Nobodaddy Press] - Lansing, NY - *LitMag&SmPr 83-84*
Poetry/LA [of Peggor Press] - Los Angeles, CA - *LitMag&SmPr 83-84; WritMar 84*
Poetry Leeds Publications - Leeds, England - *LitMag&SmPr 83-84*
Poetry London/Apple Magazine - London, England - *LitMag&SmPr 83-84*
Poetry Magazine [of Spectrum Publishing] - Portland, OR - *WritMar 84*
Poetry Miscellany, The - Chattanooga, TN - *LitMag&SmPr 83-84*
Poetry 'n Prose [of Ahnene Publications] - Maxville, ON, Canada - *LitMag&SmPr 83-84*
Poetry Nation Review [of Carcanet New Press] - Manchester, England - *LitMag&SmPr 83-84*
Poetry Newsletter - Philadelphia, PA - *LitMag&SmPr 83-84*
Poetry Nippon - Nagoya, Japan - *LitMag&SmPr 83-84*
Poetry Nippon Press, The - Nagoya, Japan - *LitMag&SmPr 83-84*
Poetry North Review - Anchorage, AK - *LitMag&SmPr 83-84*
Poetry Northwest - Seattle, WA - *LitMag&SmPr 83-84*
Poetry Nottingham - Sheffield, England - *LitMag&SmPr 83-84*
Poetry Nottingham Society Publications - Sheffield, England - *LitMag&SmPr 83-84*
Poetry Now - Eureka, CA - *LitMag&SmPr 83-84*
Poetry Project Newsletter - New York, NY - *LitMag&SmPr 83-84*
Poetry Projects - Huron, OH - *LitMag&SmPr 83-84*
Poetry Quarterly [of The Curlew Press] - Harrogate, England - *LitMag&SmPr 83-84*
Poetry Resource Center of Michigan Newsletter & Calendar - Detroit, MI - *LitMag&SmPr 83-84*
Poetry Review - London, England - *LitMag&SmPr 83-84*
Poetry Society of America Bulletin, The - New York, NY - *LitMag&SmPr 83-84*
Poetry Society of Australia, The - Sydney, Australia - *LitMag&SmPr 83-84*
Poetry Today [of Spectrum Books] - Portland, OR - *LitMag&SmPr 83-84*
Poetry Toronto - Willowdale, ON, Canada - *LitMag&SmPr 83-84; WritMar 84*
Poetry Wales - Bridgend, Wales - *LitMag&SmPr 83-84*
Poetry Wales Press - Bridgend, Wales - *LitMag&SmPr 83-84*
Poets & Writers - New York, NY - *BoPubDir 4, 5; LitMag&SmPr 83-84; LitMarPl 83, 84*
Poets Audio Center [Subs. of The Watershed Foundation] - Washington, DC - *AvMarPl 83*
Poets' League of Greater Cleveland Newsletter [of League Books] - Cleveland, OH - *LitMag&SmPr 83-84*
Poets On - Chaplin, CT - *LitMag&SmPr 83-84*
Poet's Pride - Clifton, NJ - *WritMar 84*
Pofcher Co. - New York, NY - *InfIndMarPl 83; LitMarPl 83, 84*
Pohlman Film Productions Inc. - Milwaukee, WI - *TelAl 83, 84; Tel&CabFB 84C*
Point & Shoreland Journal [of Welch Publishing Co.] - Toledo, OH - *AyerDirPub 83; NewsDir 84*
Point Communications - Dallas, TX - *AdAge 3-28-84; StaDirAdAg 2-84*

Point Coupee Banner - New Roads, LA - *AyerDirPub 83*
Point de Repere [of Bibliotheque Nationale du Quebec] - Montreal, PQ, Canada - *DataDirOnSer 84; DirOnDB Spring 84*
Point Edward Gazette - Point Edward, ON, Canada - *Ed&PubIntYB 82*
Point Edward Gazette - Wyoming, ON, Canada - *Ed&PubIntYB 82*
Point Edward Gazette, The - Sarnia, ON, Canada - *AyerDirPub 83*
Point Foundation - Sausalito, CA - *BoPubDir 4, 5*
Point 4 Data Corp. - Irvine, CA - *DataDirSup 7-83; DirInfWP 82*
Point Lobos Productions - Woodland Hills, CA - *AvMarPl 83*
Point Loma Pennysaver - Mission Viejo, CA - *AyerDirPub 83*
Point Loma Publications Inc. - San Diego, CA - *BoPubDir 4, 5*
Point Marion News - Point Marion, PA - *BaconPubCkNews 84*
Point of View Productions - San Francisco, CA - *Tel&CabFB 84C*
Point Pleasant Beach Ocean County Leader [of Precision Publications Inc.] - Point Pleasant Beach, NJ - *BaconPubCkNews 84; NewsDir 84*
Point Pleasant Register [of Ohio Valley Publishing Co.] - Point Pleasant, WV - *BaconPubCkNews 84; Ed&PubIntYB 82; NewsDir 84*
Point Reyes Light - Point Reyes Station, CA - *AyerDirPub 83; BaconPubCkNews 84; Ed&PubIntYB 82*
Point Riders Press [Aff. of Cottonwood Arts Foundation] - Norman, OK - *BoPubDir 4, 5; LitMag&SmPr 83-84*
Pointe Coupee Banner - New Roads, LA - *NewsDir 84*
Pointe Coupee Banner - Pointe Coupee, LA - *Ed&PubIntYB 82*
Pointer-Economist Newspapers - Lansing, IL - *BaconPubCkNews 84*
Pointless Music - *See* JEDO Music
Points, M. J. - San Francisco, CA - *BoPubDir 4, 5*
Poirot & Co., H. M. - Amarillo, TX - *BoPubDir 4, 5*
Poisindex [of Micromedex Inc.] - Englewood, CO - *EISS 83*
Poison Pen Press [Aff. of Masiform D] - Brooklyn, NY - *BoPubDir 4 Sup, 5*
Poisoned Pen, The - Brooklyn, NY - *LitMag&SmPr 83-84*
Poka-Lambro Rural Telephone Cooperative Inc. - Tahoka, TX - *TelDir&BG 83-84*
Pol-Am Journal - Scranton, PA - *NewsDir 84*
Polak Amerikanski - Jamesburg, NJ - *Ed&PubIntYB 82*
Poland China World - Knoxville, IL - *BaconPubCkMag 84; MagDir 84*
Poland Clarion [of Phoenix Publications Inc.] - Niles, OH - *AyerDirPub 83; NewsDir 84*
Poland Clarion - Poland, OH - *Ed&PubIntYB 82*
Poland Clarion - *See* Phoenix Publications Inc.
Polar Communications Mutual Aid Corp. - Park River, ND - *Tel&CabFB 84C p.1697; TelDir&BG 83-84*
Polar Communications Mutual Aid Corp. - St. Thomas, ND - *Tel&CabFB 84C*
Polar Information Service [of U.S. National Science Foundation] - Washington, DC - *EISS 83*
Polar Palm Productions Inc. - Anchorage, AK - *BoPubDir 4, 5*
Polaris Enterprises - Culver City, CA - *MicrocomSwDir 1*
Polaris Inc. - Arlington, VA - *MicrocomMPl 84*
Polaris Press - Los Gatos, CA - *ArtMar 84; BoPubDir 4, 5; WritMar 84*
Polaris Research Associates Inc. - New York, NY - *IntDirMarRes 83*
Polaris Software - San Diego, CA - *MicrocomMPl 84*
Polestar Publications [Aff. of Polestar International] - Sioux Falls, SD - *BoPubDir 4 Sup, 5; LitMag&SmPr 83-84*
Policano Inc. - New York, NY - *DirPRFirms 83*
Police & Security Bulletin - Mt. Airy, MD - *BaconPubCkMag 84*
Police Chief, The - Gaithersburg, MD - *BaconPubCkMag 84; MagDir 84; MagIndMarPl 82-83*
Police Magazine - New York, NY - *MagDir 84; MagIndMarPl 82-83*
Police Product News - Carlsbad, CA - *BaconPubCkMag 84; MagDir 84; MagIndMarPl 82-83; WritMar 84*
Police Times/Command Magazine - North Miami, FL - *WritMar 84*
Policy - Versailles, OH - *AyerDirPub 83*
Policy Development Corp. - New York, NY - *MagIndMarPl 82-83*
Policy Options - Halifax, NS, Canada - *BaconPubCkMag 84*
Policy Review Associates Inc. - McLean, VA - *CompReadDB 82*
Policy Studies Associates [Aff. of Council on International & Public Affairs] - Croton-on-Hudson, NY - *BoPubDir 4, 5*
Policy Studies Div. [of Mathematics Policy Research Inc.] - Washington, DC - *EISS 83*
Policy Studies Organization - Urbana, IL - *BoPubDir 4, 5*
Polimetrics Laboratory [of Ohio State University] - Columbus, OH - *EISS 83*
POLIS - Kiln Farm, England - *OnBibDB 3*
POLIS - Milton, England - *DirOnDB Spring 84*
Polish American World - Baldwin, NY - *AyerDirPub 83; NewsDir 84*
Polish Canadian Courier - Toronto, ON, Canada - *Ed&PubIntYB 82*
Polish Daily Dziennik Zwiazkowy [of Alliance Printers & Publishers Inc.] - Chicago, IL - *NewsDir 84*
Polish Daily Zgoda - Chicago, IL - *Ed&PubIntYB 82*
Polish Institute of Arts & Sciences - New York, NY - *BoPubDir 4, 5*
Polish Press Agency - New York, NY - *Ed&PubIntYB 82*
Polish Record Center of America - Chicago, IL - *BillIntBG 83-84*
Polish Star - Philadelphia, PA - *NewsDir 84*
Polish Translating Service - Chicago, IL - *MagIndMarPl 82-83*
Politechnika Warszawska/Technical University of Warsaw (Central Library) - Warsaw, Poland - *InfIndMarPl 83*
Political Action Report - McLean, VA - *DirOnDB Spring 84*
Political Affairs - New York, NY - *MagIndMarPl 82-83*
Political & Current Events Information Bank - Paris, France - *EISS 83*
Political & Diplomatic History of the Arab World: 1900-1967 [of University of Wisconsin-Madison] - Madison, WI - *EISS 83*
Political Information Service [of Mead Data Central] - Dayton, OH - *DataDirOnSer 84*
Political Memo from Cope - Washington, DC - *NewsDir 84*
Political Profiles - Washington, DC - *WritMar 84*
Political Research Inc. - Dallas, TX - *BoPubDir 4, 5*
Political Science Data Archive [of Michigan State University] - East Lansing, MI - *EISS 83*
Political Science Micro Review - Raleigh, NC - *MicrocomMPl 84*
Political Science Quarterly - New York, NY - *MagIndMarPl 82-83*
Politics Online - Arlington, VA - *DirOnDB Spring 84*
Politz Media Studies, Alfred - New York, NY - *BrCabYB 84*
Politz Research Inc., Alfred [Subs. of Admar Research Co. Inc.] - New York, NY - *IntDirMarRes 83; Tel&CabFB 84C*
Polizos Associates Inc., Arthur - Norfolk, VA - *StaDirAdAg 2-84*
Polk & Co., R. L. - Norcross, GA - *LitMarPl 83, 84*
Polk & Co., R. L. (Motor Statistical Div.) - Detroit, MI - *BoPubDir 5*
Polk City Big Creek News - Polk City, IA - *BaconPubCkNews 84; Ed&PubIntYB 82*
Polk County Democrat [of Frisbie Publishing Co. Inc.] - Bartow, FL - *AyerDirPub 83; Ed&PubIntYB 82; NewsDir 84*
Polk County Democrat & The Ft. Meade Leader - Ft. Meade, FL - *Ed&PubIntYB 82*
Polk County Enterprise - Livingston, TX - *AyerDirPub 83; Ed&PubIntYB 82*
Polk County Itemizer-Observer - Dallas, OR - *AyerDirPub 83; Ed&PubIntYB 82*
Polk County Ledger - Balsam Lake, WI - *AyerDirPub 83*
Polk County Ledger, The - Polk, WI - *Ed&PubIntYB 82*
Polk County News - Benton, TN - *Ed&PubIntYB 82*
Polk County Publishing - Livingston, TX - *BaconPubCkNews 84*
Polk Progress - Polk, NE - *BaconPubCkNews 84; Ed&PubIntYB 82*
Polk Shopper Shopping News - Lakeland, FL - *AyerDirPub 83*
Polka Towne Music [Div. of Polka Music Corp.] - Westbury, NY - *BillIntBG 83-84*
Polled Hereford World - Kansas City, MO - *BaconPubCkMag 84; MagDir 84; WritMar 84*
Poller & Jordan Advertising Agency Inc. - Miami, FL - *StaDirAdAg 2-84*
Pollock Prairie Pioneer - Pollock, SD - *BaconPubCkNews 84*
Pollock/Uniphoto, Robert - Kansas City, MO - *AvMarPl 83*
Pollution Abstracts [of Cambridge Scientific Abstracts] - Washington, DC - *CompReadDB 82*

Pollution Abstracts [of Cambridge Scientific Abstracts] - Bethesda, MD - *BaconPubCkMag 84; DataDirOnSer 84; DBBus 82; DirOnDB Spring 84; EISS 83; OnBibDB 3*

Pollution Engineering - Northbrook, IL - *BaconPubCkMag 84; MagDir 84; MagIndMarPl 82-83*

Pollution Equipment News - Pittsburgh, PA - *BaconPubCkMag 84; MagDir 84; MagIndMarPl 82-83*

Pollution Incident Reporting System [of U.S. Coast Guard] - Washington, DC - *EISS 83*

Pollution Probe/Ecology House [Aff. of Pollution Probe Foundation] - Toronto, ON, Canada - *BoPubDir 5*

Pollyday Publishing Co. - *See* Su-Ma Publishing Co. Inc.

Polo - Gaithersburg, MD - *MagIndMarPl 82-83*

Polo Group Inc., The - Scottsdale, AZ - *IntDirMarRes 83*

Polo Tri-County Press - Polo, IL - *BaconPubCkNews 84*

Poloris Enterprises - Culver City, CO - *MicrocomMPl 84*

Polson, A. Irene - Chicago, IL - *BoPubDir 4, 5*

Polson Flathead Courier [of Western Publishing Co.] - Polson, MT - *BaconPubCkNews 84; NewsDir 84*

Polumat - Brest, France - *DirOnDB Spring 84*

Polumbaum Photography, Ted - Cambridge, MA - *LitMarPl 83, 84; MagIndMarPl 82-83*

Poly Com Group Inc., The - Chicago, IL - *ArtMar 84*

Poly Post [of California State Polytechnic University] - Pomona, CA - *NewsDir 84*

Poly Tone Press - Sepulveda, CA - *BoPubDir 4, 5*

Polyanthos Inc. - New Orleans, LA - *BoPubDir 4, 5*

PolyCom Corp. - Chicago, IL - *AvMarPl 83*

PolyCom Systems Ltd. - Don Mills, ON, Canada - *DataDirOnSer 84; DataDirSup 7-83*

Polyglot Press, The - New York, NY - *LitMarPl 83, 84*

Polygon Associates Inc. - St. Louis, MO - *MicrocomMPl 84*

Polygon Computer Systems Ltd. - London, England - *MicrocomSwDir 1*

Polygon Industries Inc. - Metairie, LA - *MicrocomMPl 84*

Polygonal Publishing House - Passaic, NJ - *BoPubDir 4, 5; LitMag&SmPr 83-84*

PolyGram Classics Inc. - New York, NY - *BillIntBG 83-84*

PolyGram Corp. - Culver City, CA - *BillIntBG 83-84*

PolyGram Direct Marketing Inc. - New York, NY - *BillIntBG 83-84*

PolyGram Records Inc. - Los Angeles, CA - *BillIntBG 83-84*

PolyGram Records Inc. - New York, NY - *BillIntBG 83-84*

Polygram TV - Culver City, CA - *Tel&CabFB 84C*

Polykoff Advertising Inc., Shirley - New York, NY - *HBIndAd&MS 82-83*

Polyline Corp. - Des Plaines, IL - *AvMarPl 83*

Polyline On-Line Bibliographic Search Service [of Liverpool Polytechnic] - Liverpool, England - *EISS 83*

Polymer Engineering & Science - Brookfield Center, CT - *BaconPubCkMag 84; MagDir 84*

Polymer Science & Technology [of Chemical Abstracts Service] - Columbus, OH - *CompReadDB 82*

Polymetric Services Inc. [Aff. of AMJ Publishing Co.] - Carmarillo, CA - *BoPubDir 4, 5*

Polymorph Films Inc. - Boston, MA - *AvMarPl 83*

PolyMorphic Systems - Santa Barbara, CA - *DataDirSup 7-83; WhoWMicrocom 83*

Polyphonic Publications - *See* Birch Tree Group Ltd.

Polyphony - Oklahoma City, OK - *BaconPubCkMag 84; WritMar 84*

Polyprobe - San Diego, CA - *DirOnDB Spring 84*

Polytechnic Engineer, The - Brooklyn, NY - *MagDir 84*

Pomegranate Art Books Inc. - Corte Madera, CA - *BoPubDir 4, 5*

Pomegranate Press - Cambridge, MA - *BoPubDir 4, 5*

Pomer Agency, Bella - Toronto, ON, Canada - *LitMarPl 83, 84*

Pomeroy Cablevision - Pomeroy, WA - *BrCabYB 84; Tel&CabFB 84C*

Pomeroy Daily Sentinel [of Multimedia Inc.] - Pomeroy, OH - *NewsDir 84*

Pomeroy East Washingtonian - Pomeroy, WA - *BaconPubCkNews 84*

Pomeroy Herald - Pomeroy, IA - *BaconPubCkNews 84; Ed&PubIntYB 82*

Pomfret Book Production, J. B. - Yonkers, NY - *LitMarPl 83*

Pommard - Nashville, TN - *BillIntBG 83-84*

Pomona Progress Bulletin - Pomona, CA - *BaconPubCkNews 84; LitMarPl 83; NewsDir 84*

Pompano Beach Sun-Sentinel [of Gore Newspapers Co.] - Pompano Beach, FL - *NewsDir 84*

Pompano Ledger, The - Pompano Beach, FL - *AyerDirPub 83*

Pompano Shopper - Pompano Beach, FL - *AyerDirPub 83*

Ponca City News - Ponca City, OK - *BaconPubCkNews 84; Ed&PubIntYB 82; NewsDir 84*

Ponca City Publishing Co. - Ponca City, OK - *BrCabYB 84*

Ponca Nebraska Journal-Leader - Ponca, NE - *BaconPubCkNews 84*

Ponce Broadcasting Corp. - Ponce, PR - *BrCabYB 84*

Poncelet Printers Inc. - Monterey, CA - *MagIndMarPl 82-83*

Ponchatoula Enterprise - Ponchatoula, LA - *BaconPubCkNews 84*

Ponchatoula News Herald [of Hammond Murray-Huber Publishing Inc.] - Hammond, LA - *NewsDir 84*

Ponchatoula Times, The - Ponchatoula, LA - *Ed&PubIntYB 82*

Pond Branch Telephone Co. - Gilbert, SC - *TelDir&BG 83-84*

Pond Creek Herald - Pond Creek, OK - *BaconPubCkNews 84; Ed&PubIntYB 82*

Pond, Samuel A. - Woodside, CA - *BoPubDir 4, 5*

Pond Woods Press - Stony Brook, NY - *BoPubDir 4, 5*

Ponderosa Cable Co. Inc. - Groveland, CA - *BrCabYB 84*

Ponderosa Publishers - St. Ignatius, MT - *BoPubDir 4, 5*

Ponderosa Telephone Co., The - O'Neals, CA - *TelDir&BG 83-84*

Ponoka Herald, The - Ponoka, AB, Canada - *Ed&PubIntYB 82*

Pont a Mousson Industrial Information Bank [of Pont a Mousson Research Center] - Pont a Mousson, France - *EISS 83*

Pontbriand, Benoit - Sillery, PQ, Canada - *BoPubDir 4, 5*

Ponteix TV Club - Ponteix, SK, Canada - *BrCabYB 84*

Pontiac Leader - Pontiac, IL - *BaconPubCkNews 84; NewsDir 84*

Pontiac-Oakland Club International Inc. - Salem, OR - *BoPubDir 5*

Pontiac Times - *See* Times Newspapers

Pontiac Wide Track News - *See* Monday Morning Newspapers

Pontifical Institute of Mediaeval Studies - Toronto, ON, Canada - *BoPubDir 4, 5*

Ponton Inc., W. S. - Pittsburgh, PA - *EISS 7-83 Sup*

Pontotoc Progress - Pontotoc, MS - *BaconPubCkNews 84; Ed&PubIntYB 82; NewsDir 84*

Pony Express Services [Subs. of Skill Services Inc.] - Coral Gables, FL - *MicrocomMPl 84; WhoWMicrocom 83*

Poodle Review - New York, NY - *MagDir 84*

Pool & Spa News - Los Angeles, CA - *BaconPubCkMag 84; MagDir 84; WritMar 84*

Pool Industry Canada - Don Mills, ON, Canada - *BaconPubCkMag 84*

Pool News - Los Angeles, CA - *MagDir 84*

Pool/Sarraille Advertising - Beverly Hills, CA - *AdAge 3-28-84; StaDirAdAg 2-84*

Poole Advertising Inc. - Houston, TX - *StaDirAdAg 2-84*

Poor Man's Press - Ottawa, ON, Canada - *LitMag&SmPr 83-84*

Poor Richard's Press [Aff. of Men's Rights Association] - Forest Lake, MN - *BoPubDir 4, 5; LitMag&SmPr 83-84*

Poor Souls Press/Scaramouche Books - Millbrae, CA - *BoPubDir 4, 5; LitMag&SmPr 83-84*

Poorman-Douglas Corp. - Portland, OR - *ADAPSOMemDir 83-84*

Pop-Facts [of National Decision Systems Inc.] - Encinitas, CA - *DataDirOnSer 84*

Pop Francais USA - Warrington, PA - *BillIntBG 83-84*

Pop Record Research - Pelham, NY - *BillIntBG 83-84*

Pop Shop Inc. - Tazewell, VA - *BrCabYB 84; Tel&CabFB 84C p.1697*

Pop Shop Three TV Cable Inc. [of Pop Shop Inc.] - Amonate, VA - *BrCabYB 84; Tel&CabFB 84C*

Pop Shop Three TV Cable Inc. [of Pop Shop Inc.] - Squire, VA - *Tel&CabFB 84C*

Popcorn Publications - Canaan, CT - *BoPubDir 4, 5*

Pope Advertising, Roy - Sherman Oaks, CA - *DirMarMP 83*

Pope County Tribune - Glenwood, MN - *AyerDirPub 83; Ed&PubIntYB 82*

Pope, D. H. - Paducah, TX - *Tel&CabFB 84C p.1697*

Pope International Publications - Abbotsford, BC, Canada - *BoPubDir 4, 5*

Popeil Records - Chicago, IL - *BillIntBG 83-84*

Popejoy & Fischel Advertising Agency Inc. - Dallas, TX - *StaDirAdAg 2-84*

Popejoy, Charles L. [Aff. of The Gregath Co.] - Juneau, AK - *BoPubDir 4, 5*
Popick Associates Inc., Bernard - Atlantic City, NJ - *StaDirAdAg 2-84*
Poplar Bluff Daily American Republic [of Poplar Bluff Printing Co. Inc.] - Poplar Bluff, MO - *NewsDir 84*
Poplar Bluff Journal - *See* Butler County Publishing
Poplar Bluff Ozark Beacon - *See* Butler County Publishing
Poplar Hill Ozark Beacon & Butler County News - Poplar Bluff, MO - *NewsDir 84*
Poplarville Democrat - Poplarville, MS - *BaconPubCkNews 84*
Popline [of Johns Hopkins University] - Baltimore, MD - *DirOnDB Spring 84; OnBibDB 3*
Popline [of U.S. National Library of Medicine] - Bethesda, MD - *EISS 83*
Popoff Studio, Christo - Edwardsville, IL - *MagIndMarPl 82-83*
Popofsky Advertising Inc. - New York, NY - *StaDirAdAg 2-84*
Popovich Ltd. - Willoughby, OH - *BillIntBG 83-84*
Poppa Willie Music - *See* Williams Music Group, Don
Poppe Tyson - New York, NY - *DirPRFirms 83; StaDirAdAg 2-84*
Pops - *See* Jacobson, Jeffrey E.
Popular Archaeology - Arlington, VA - *MagDir 84*
Popular Bridge - Encino, CA - *MagIndMarPl 82-83*
Popular Ceramics - Glendale, CA - *BaconPubCkMag 84; MagDir 84*
Popular Communications - Hicksville, NY - *BaconPubCkMag 84*
Popular Computing [of McGraw-Hill Publishing Inc.] - Hancock, NH - *ArtMar 84*
Popular Computing [of McGraw-Hill Publishing Inc.] - Peterborough, NH - *BaconPubCkMag 84; Folio 83; MagDir 84; WritMar 84*
Popular Culture in Britain - Brighton, England - *LitMag&SmPr 83-84*
Popular Electronics [of Ziff-Davis Publishing Co.] - New York, NY - *MagDir 84; MagIndMarPl 82-83*
Popular Hot Rodding [of Argus Publishers Corp.] - Los Angeles, CA - *BaconPubCkMag 84; Folio 83; MagDir 84; MagIndMarPl 82-83*
Popular Mechanics [of The Hearst Corp.] - New York, NY - *BaconPubCkMag 84; Folio 83; LitMarPl 83, 84; MagDir 84; MagIndMarPl 82-83; NewsBur 6; WritMar 84*
Popular Music Co. - New York, NY - *BillIntBG 83-84*
Popular Photography - New York, NY - *BaconPubCkMag 84; MagDir 84; MagIndMarPl 82-83; WritMar 84*
Popular Photography Book Club - *See* Watson-Guptill Book Clubs
Popular Photography's Color Photography - New York, NY - *MagDir 84*
Popular Photography's 35-mm Photography - New York, NY - *MagDir 84*
Popular Press, The - Bowling Green, OH - *LitMarPl 83, 84*
Popular Science [of Times Mirror Magazines Inc.] - New York, NY - *ArtMar 84; BaconPubCkMag 84; DirOnDB Spring 84; Folio 83; LitMarPl 84; MagIndMarPl 82-83*
Popular Science Book Club [of Times Mirror Magazines Inc.] - New York, NY - *LitMarPl 83, 84*
Popular Science Books [Subs. of Times Mirror Co.] - New York, NY - *WritMar 84*
Popular Science Monthly - New York, NY - *MagDir 84; WritMar 84*
Popular Subscription Service - Terre Haute, IN - *MagIndMarPl 82-83*
Population & Development Review - New York, NY - *MagIndMarPl 82-83*
Population Bibliography [of Carolina Population Center] - Chapel Hill, NC - *CompReadDB 82; DataDirOnSer 84; DBBus 82; DirOnDB Spring 84; OnBibDB 3*
Population Bulletin - Washington, DC - *MagIndMarPl 82-83*
Population Census [of Computer Sciences of Australia Pty. Ltd.] - St. Leonards, Australia - *DataDirOnSer 84*
Population Clearing-House & Information Section [of Economic & Social Commission for Asia & the Pacific] - Bangkok, Thailand - *EISS 83*
Population Council - New York, NY - *BoPubDir 4, 5*
Population Documentation Center [of Food & Agriculture Organization] - Rome, Italy - *EISS 83*
Population Index [of Princeton University] - Princeton, NJ - *EISS 83; MagIndMarPl 82-83*
Population Information Online [of Johns Hopkins University] - Baltimore, MD - *CompReadDB 82; DataDirOnSer 84*
Population Information Online [of U.S. National Library of Medicine] - Bethesda, MD - *DBBus 82*
Population Information Program [of Johns Hopkins University] - Baltimore, MD - *CompReadDB 82; DataDirOnSer 84; EISS 83; InfIndMarPl 83*
Population Reference Bureau - Washington, DC - *BoPubDir 4, 5; EISS 83*
Population Research Laboratory [of University of Alberta] - Edmonton, AB, Canada - *EISS 83*
Porch - Bisbee, AZ - *LitMag&SmPr 83-84*
Porch Publications - Bisbee, AZ - *LitMag&SmPr 83-84*
Porch Publications - Phoenix, AZ - *BoPubDir 4, 5*
Porcupine Press Inc. - Philadelphia, PA - *LitMarPl 83, 84*
Porcupine's Quill Inc. - Erin, ON, Canada - *BoPubDir 4, 5; LitMag&SmPr 83-84*
Pordes, H. - London, England - *MicroMarPl 82-83*
Porelon Inc. [Div. of Johnson Wax] - Cookeville, TN - *DirInfWP 82*
Poretz & Jaffe Inc. - *See* Jaffe Associates Inc.
Pork 83 - Shawnee Mission, KS - *BaconPubCkMag 84*
Pork Industry Outlook - Ames, IA - *BaconPubCkMag 84*
Porphyrion Press - Middle Grove, NY - *BoPubDir 4, 5*
Porro, Alfred A. Jr. - Lyndhurst, NJ - *LitMarPl 83, 84; MagIndMarPl 82-83*
Port-A-Soft - Coral Gables, FL - *MicrocomMPl 84*
Port Allegany Reporter-Argus - Port Allegany, PA - *BaconPubCkNews 84; Ed&PubIntYB 82*
Port Allen West Side Journal - Port Allen, LA - *BaconPubCkNews 84; Ed&PubIntYB 82; NewsDir 84*
Port Angeles Chronicle - Port Angeles, WA - *Ed&PubIntYB 82*
Port Angeles Daily News - Port Angeles, WA - *BaconPubCkNews 84; NewsDir 84*
Port Angeles Telecable Inc. - Port Angeles, WA - *BrCabYB 84; Tel&CabFB 84C*
Port Aransas South Jetty - Port Aransas, TX - *BaconPubCkNews 84; Ed&PubIntYB 82*
Port Arthur News [of Cox Enterprises] - Port Arthur, TX - *BaconPubCkNews 84; Ed&PubIntYB 82; NewsDir 84*
Port Authority of New York & New Jersey - New York, NY - *BoPubDir 5*
Port Byron Globe - *See* News Publishing Co.
Port Byron Telephone Co. [Aff. of Lakes Area Communications Inc.] - Port Byron, NY - *TelDir&BG 83-84*
Port Chester Guide News - Port Chester, NY - *BaconPubCkNews 84*
Port Chester Item [of Westchester Rockland Newspapers Inc.] - Port Chester, NY - *NewsDir 84*
Port Chester Item - White Plains, NY - *AyerDirPub 83; Ed&PubIntYB 82*
Port Chester Item - *See* Westchester-Rockland Newspapers
Port Chester Westmore News - Port Chester, NY - *BaconPubCkNews 84*
Port City Press Inc. [Subs. of Judd's Inc.] - Baltimore, MD - *LitMarPl 83, 84*
Port Claridge Music - Glendale, CA - *BillIntBG 83-84*
Port Clinton News-Herald - Port Clinton, OH - *BaconPubCkNews 84*
Port Clinton TV Cable Association - Port Clinton, PA - *BrCabYB 84; Tel&CabFB 84C*
Port Colborne News - Port Colborne, ON, Canada - *AyerDirPub 83; Ed&PubIntYB 82*
Port Gibson Reveille - Port Gibson, MS - *BaconPubCkNews 84; Ed&PubIntYB 82*
Port Hope Evening Guide - Port Hope, ON, Canada - *BaconPubCkNews 84*
Port Huron Paper Co. - Port Huron, MI - *LitMarPl 83, 84*
Port Huron Times Herald - Port Huron, MI - *BaconPubCkNews 84*
Port Isabel-South Padre Press - Port Isabel, TX - *AyerDirPub 83; BaconPubCkNews 84; Ed&PubIntYB 82; NewsDir 84*
Port Jefferson-North Shore Record - Port Jefferson, NY - *NewsDir 84*
Port Jefferson Record - Port Jefferson, NY - *Ed&PubIntYB 82*

Port Jefferson Record - *See* Port Jefferson Record Publishers
Port Jefferson Record Publishers - Port Jefferson, NY - *BaconPubCkNews 84*
Port Lavaca Wave - Port Lavaca, TX - *BaconPubCkNews 84; Ed&PubIntYB 82; NewsDir 84*
Port Lions General Store Inc. - Port Lions, AK - *BrCabYB 84*
Port Neches Chronicle - Port Neches, TX - *Ed&PubIntYB 82*
Port Neches Midcounty Chronicle - Port Neches, TX - *BaconPubCkNews 84*
Port Neches Midcounty Chronicle-Review [of The Enterprise Co.] - Port Neches, TX - *NewsDir 84*
Port of Baltimore - Baltimore, MD - *BaconPubCkMag 84*
Port of Catoosa Times-Herald - Catoosa, OK - *Ed&PubIntYB 82*
Port Orchard Independent - Port Orchard, WA - *BaconPubCkNews 84; Ed&PubIntYB 82; NewsDir 84*
Port Orford News - Port Orford, OR - *BaconPubCkNews 84*
Port Record - New Orleans, LA - *MagDir 84*
Port Reporter - Seattle, WA - *BaconPubCkMag 84*
Port Royal Times - Port Royal, PA - *BaconPubCkNews 84; NewsDir 84*
Port St. Joe Star - Port St. Joe, FL - *BaconPubCkNews 84*
Port St. Lucie Mirror, The - Port St. Lucie, FL - *Ed&PubIntYB 82*
Port Studios Inc. - Chicago, IL - *LitMarPl 83, 84; MagIndMarPl 82-83*
Port Townsend Leader [of Port Townsend Publishing Co. Inc.] - Port Townsend, WA - *BaconPubCkNews 84; Ed&PubIntYB 82; NewsDir 84*
Port TV Cable Co. - Port Allegany, PA - *BrCabYB 84*
Port Video Corp. - Deerpark, NY - *BrCabYB 84*
Port Video Corp. - Port Jervis, NY - *BrCabYB 84*
Port Washington Mail - Manhasset, NY - *AyerDirPub 83*
Port Washington Mail - *See* Carr Communications Inc.
Port Washington Mail & Reporter [of Manhasset Carr Communications Inc.] - Manhasset, NY - *NewsDir 84*
Port Washington-Manhasset Pennysaver - Great Neck, NY - *AyerDirPub 83*
Port Washington-Manhasset Shopping News - Jericho, NY - *AyerDirPub 83*
Port Washington News - Great Neck, NY - *Ed&PubIntYB 82*
Port Washington News [of Community Newspapers Inc.] - Port Washington, NY - *Ed&PubIntYB 82; NewsDir 84*
Port Washington News - *See* Community Newspapers Inc.
Port Washington News & Times Post - Glen Cove, NY - *AyerDirPub 83*
Port Washington Ozaukee Press [of Port Publications Inc.] - Port Washington, WI - *BaconPubCkNews 84; NewsDir 84*
Port Washington Pilot - Port Washington, WI - *Ed&PubIntYB 82*
Port Washington Port Mail-Reporter - Manhasset, NY - *Ed&PubIntYB 82*
Porta-Panel Displays - Winnetka, IL - *AvMarPl 83*
Porta-Pattern Inc. - Los Angeles, CA - *AvMarPl 83*
Portable Computer [of Miller Freeman Publications] - San Francisco, CA - *BaconPubCkMag 84; MagDir 84; MicrocomMPl 84; WritMar 84*
Portable Computer, The [of Osborne Computer Corp.] - Hayward, CA - *MicrocomMPl 84*
Portable Computing Magazine [of Falsoft Inc.] - Prospect, KY - *MicrocomMPl 84*
Portable Music Co. Inc. - *See* Notable Music Co. Inc.
Portable 100 [of Computer Publishing Co.] - Camden, ME - *MicrocomMPl 84*
Portable Software Inc. - Menlo Park, CA - *MicrocomMPl 83*
Portac Inc. - Goleta, CA - *AvMarPl 83*
Portafilms Inc. - Drayton Plains, MI - *AvMarPl 83*
Portage Cable TV [of Eastern Telecom Corp.] - Portage, PA - *BrCabYB 84; Tel&CabFB 84C*
Portage Daily Register - Portage, WI - *BaconPubCkNews 84; Ed&PubIntYB 82; NewsDir 84*
Portage Dispatch - Portage, PA - *Ed&PubIntYB 82; NewsDir 84*
Portage Dispatch - *See* Sedloff Publications Inc.
Portage Headliner - Portage, MI - *BaconPubCkNews 84*
Portage Leader/MacGregor Herald - Portage La Prairie, MB, Canada - *AyerDirPub 83; Ed&PubIntYB 82*
Portage Newspaper Supply [Subs. of Knight-Ridder Newspapers Inc.] - Akron, OH - *AvMarPl 83*
Portage Park Journal [of Portage Enterprises Inc.] - Chicago, IL - *NewsDir 84*
Portage Park Leader [of Chicago Leader Newspapers-Leader Papers Inc.] - Chicago, IL - *AyerDirPub 83; NewsDir 84*
Portage Park News - Chicago, IL - *AyerDirPub 83*
Portage Park News - Portage Park, IL - *Ed&PubIntYB 82*
Portage Park Passage [of Chicago Passage Publications] - Chicago, IL - *AyerDirPub 83; NewsDir 84*
Portage Park Times - Chicago, IL - *AyerDirPub 83*
Portage Park Times - Portage Park, IL - *Ed&PubIntYB 82*
Portage Press - Toronto, ON, Canada - *BoPubDir 4, 5*
Portage Publishing Co. - Rosemount, MN - *BillIntBG 83-84*
Portageville Missourian - Portageville, MO - *BaconPubCkNews 84; Ed&PubIntYB 82*
Portageville Review - Portageville, MO - *BaconPubCkNews 84; Ed&PubIntYB 82*
Portal Publications Ltd. - Corte Madera, CA - *WritMar 84*
Portales News Tribune - Portales, NM - *BaconPubCkNews 84; Ed&PubIntYB 82; NewsDir 84*
Portals Press - Tuscaloosa, AL - *BoPubDir 4, 5*
Portasound [Div. of Sound-Craft] - Morrilton, AR - *AvMarPl 83*
Porte Advertising Agency - Jersey City, NJ - *StaDirAdAg 2-84*
Porte Publishing Co. - Salt Lake City, UT - *DirMarMP 83*
Porter & Mills Advertising - Fairfield, CT - *StaDirAdAg 2-84*
Porter Books, Bern - Belfast, ME - *BoPubDir 4, 5; LitMag&SmPr 83-84; LitMarPl 83, 84; MagIndMarPl 82-83*
Porter Broadcasting Services - Bath, ME - *BrCabYB 84*
Porter County Cable Co. - Valparaiso, IN - *BrCabYB 84; Tel&CabFB 84C*
Porter County Herald - Hebron, IN - *AyerDirPub 83; Ed&PubIntYB 82*
Porter County Publishing Co. - Hebron, IN - *BaconPubCkNews 84*
Porter Data Systems Inc. - Colorado Springs, CO - *MicrocomMPl 84*
Porter, Dierks & Porter-Lent - Chicago, IL - *LitMarPl 83, 84*
Porter, Levay & Rose Inc. - New York, NY - *DirPRFirms 83*
Porter, Novelli & Associates [Div. of Needham, Harper & Steers Inc.] - Washington, DC - *DirPRFirms 83; IntDirMarRes 83*
Porter, Novelli & Associates - *See* Needhan, Harper & Steers Inc.
Porter Sargent Publishers Inc. - Boston, MA - *ArtMar 84; LitMag&SmPr 83-84; LitMarPl 83, 84; WritMar 84*
Porterville Recorder - Porterville, CA - *BaconPubCkNews 84; NewsDir 84*
Portfolio - New York, NY - *BaconPubCkMag 84; MagIndMarPl 82-83*
Porthole Press - Belmont, MA - *BoPubDir 4, 5*
Portland Bee - Portland, OR - *BaconPubCkNews 84*
Portland Cable TV [of Marsh Media Inc.] - Portland, TN - *BrCabYB 84; Tel&CabFB 84C*
Portland Cement Association - Skokie, IL - *BoPubDir 4, 5*
Portland Commercial Review [of The Graphic Printing Co. Inc.] - Portland, IN - *BaconPubCkNews 84; NewsDir 84*
Portland Daily Journal of Commerce - Portland, OR - *NewsDir 84*
Portland Evening Express - Portland, ME - *BaconPubCkNews 84*
Portland Independent Review & Observer - Portland, MI - *Ed&PubIntYB 82*
Portland Leader - Portland, TN - *AyerDirPub 83; BaconPubCkNews 84; Ed&PubIntYB 82*
Portland Magazine - Portland, OR - *BaconPubCkMag 84; MagDir 84*
Portland MDS Co. - Pasadena, MD - *Tel&CabFB 84C*
Portland Men's Resource Center - Portland, OR - *BoPubDir 4, 5*
Portland News - Portland, TX - *AyerDirPub 83; Ed&PubIntYB 82*
Portland News - *See* San Patricio Publishing Co.
Portland Observer [of Exie Publishing Co. Inc.] - Portland, OR - *BaconPubCkNews 84; Ed&PubIntYB 82; NewsDir 84*
Portland Oregon Journal [of Oregonian Publishing Co.] - Portland, OR - *NewsDir 84*
Portland Oregonian [of Newhouse Newspapers] - Portland, OR - *BaconPubCkNews 84; NewsDir 84*
Portland Press Herald [of Guy Gannett Publishing Co.] - Portland, ME - *BaconPubCkNews 84; Ed&PubIntYB 82; LitMarPl 83, 84; NewsBur 6; NewsDir 84*
Portland Review [of Portland State University] - Portland, OR - *ArtMar 84; LitMag&SmPr 83-84; WritMar 84*

Portland Review & Observer - Portland, MI - *Ed&PubIntYB 82*
Portland School of Languages - Portland, OR - *MagIndMarPl 82-83*
Portland Sellwood-Moreland Bee - Portland, OR - *BaconPubCkNews 84*
Portland Skanner News - Portland, OR - *BaconPubCkNews 84*
Portland Skanner, The - Portland, OR - *NewsDir 84*
Portland St. Johns Review - Portland, OR - *BaconPubCkNews 84; NewsDir 84*
Portland State University (Continuing Education Div.) - Portland, OR - *BoPubDir 4, 5*
Portland Symphony Orchestra (Women's Committee) - Portland, ME - *BoPubDir 4, 5*
Portland Willamette Week - Portland, OR - *BaconPubCkNews 84*
Portman Agency, Julian [Div. of Equitable International Funding] - Hollywood, CA - *LitMarPl 83*
Portnoff, Collice - Tempe, AZ - *LitMarPl 83, 84*
Portola Press - Santa Barbara, CA - *BoPubDir 4, 5*
Portola Reporter - Portola, CA - *Ed&PubIntYB 82*
Portola Reporter - *See* Feather Publishing Co. Inc.
Portolan Press - Brielle, NJ - *BoPubDir 4, 5*
Portrayal Press - Bloomfield, NJ - *BoPubDir 4, 5*
Portriga Publication - Los Angeles, CA - *BoPubDir 4 Sup, 5*
Ports Annual - Montreal, PQ, Canada - *BaconPubCkMag 84*
Ports O' Call - Santa Rosa, CA - *WritMar 84*
Portsmouth Herald - Portsmouth, NH - *AyerDirPub 83; BaconPubCkNews 84; Ed&PubIntYB 82; NewsDir 84*
Portsmouth: Sakonnet Times [of Bristol Phoenix-Times Publishing Co.] - Portsmouth, RI - *NewsDir 84*
Portsmouth Sakonnet Times - *See* Phoenix-Times Newspapers
Portsmouth Times - Portsmouth, OH - *BaconPubCkNews 84*
Portuguese Journal - San Pablo, CA - *Ed&PubIntYB 82*
Portuguese Tymnet/Telenet Node [of Companhia Portuguesa Radio Marconi] - Lisbon, Portugal - *InfIndMarPl 83*
Posan, Lynn & Co. - Ft. Lauderdale, FL - *StaDirAdAg 2-84*
Poseidon Press [Div. of Pocket Books] - New York, NY - *LitMarPl 83, 84*
Posey County News - Poseyville, IN - *AyerDirPub 83; Ed&PubIntYB 82*
Posey, Parry & Quest - Greenwich, CT - *AdAge 3-28-84; StaDirAdAg 2-84*
Posey Publications [Aff. of Posey Genealogical Enterprises] - Orem, UT - *BoPubDir 4 Sup, 5*
Poseyville Telephone Co. Inc. - Poseyville, IN - *TelDir&BG 83-84*
Posh Boy Records & Tapes - Los Angeles, CA - *BillIntBG 83-84*
Position - Baltimore, MD - *ArtMar 84*
Positive Productions - Highland Park, NJ - *BillIntBG 83-84*
Positive Thinkers Inc. - Ft. Lauderdale, FL - *LitMag&SmPr 83-84*
Positive Thinkers Newsletter - Ft. Lauderdale, FL - *LitMag&SmPr 83-84*
Posner & Associates Inc., Judith L. - Milwaukee, WI - *ArtMar 84*
Posner Associates, James - New York, NY - *IntDirMarRes 83*
Posner, Jack - New York, NY - *Ed&PubIntYB 82*
Posner Public Relations Inc. - New York, NY - *DirPRFirms 83*
Posse Records Inc. - New York, NY - *BillIntBG 83-84*
Post - Fullerton, CA - *AyerDirPub 83*
Post - Oakland, CA - *Ed&PubIntYB 82*
Post - Paradise, CA - *AyerDirPub 83*
Post - Pleasant Hill, CA - *AyerDirPub 83*
Post - San Mateo, CA - *AyerDirPub 83*
Post - Denver, CO - *AyerDirPub 83*
Post - Bridgeport, CT - *AyerDirPub 83*
Post - Pinellas Park, FL - *AyerDirPub 83; Ed&PubIntYB 82*
Post - West Palm Beach, FL - *AyerDirPub 83; Ed&PubIntYB 82*
Post - Galesburg, IL - *AyerDirPub 83*
Post - Pawnee, IL - *AyerDirPub 83*
Post - Rockford, IL - *AyerDirPub 83*
Post - Lynn, MA - *AyerDirPub 83*
Post - Vicksburg, MS - *AyerDirPub 83*
Post - Ridgewood, NJ - *AyerDirPub 83*
Post - Farmingdale, NY - *AyerDirPub 83*
Post - New York, NY - *AyerDirPub 83*
Post - Charlotte, NC - *AyerDirPub 83*
Post - Salisbury, NC - *AyerDirPub 83*
Post - Cincinnati, OH - *AyerDirPub 83*
Post - Sandy, OR - *AyerDirPub 83*
Post - Dallas, PA - *AyerDirPub 83*
Post - Parkesburg, PA - *AyerDirPub 83*
Post - Charleston, SC - *AyerDirPub 83*
Post - Belle Fourche, SD - *Ed&PubIntYB 82*
Post - Houston, TX - *AyerDirPub 83*
Post - Paducah, TX - *AyerDirPub 83*
Post - Big Stone Gap, VA - *AyerDirPub 83; Ed&PubIntYB 82; NewsDir 84*
Post - Evansville, WI - *AyerDirPub 83*
Post - New Glarus, WI - *AyerDirPub 83*
Post - Waterford, WI - *AyerDirPub 83*
Post - Fairview, AB, Canada - *AyerDirPub 83*
Post - Lac la Biche, AB, Canada - *AyerDirPub 83; Ed&PubIntYB 82*
Post - Oromocto, NB, Canada - *AyerDirPub 83*
Post - Burlington, ON, Canada - *Ed&PubIntYB 82*
Post - Hanover, ON, Canada - *AyerDirPub 83*
Post - Iroquois, ON, Canada - *AyerDirPub 83*
Post - Lindsay, ON, Canada - *Ed&PubIntYB 82*
Post - Buckingham, PQ, Canada - *AyerDirPub 83; Ed&PubIntYB 82*
Post/Ambassador - Blue Earth, MN - *AyerDirPub 83; Ed&PubIntYB 82*
Post & Advertiser - Wagner, SD - *Ed&PubIntYB 82*
Post & News - Leamington, ON, Canada - *AyerDirPub 83*
Post & News Chronicle - Benkelman, NE - *AyerDirPub 83*
Post & Wave - Seal Beach, CA - *AyerDirPub 83*
Post-Athenian - Athens, TN - *AyerDirPub 83; Ed&PubIntYB 82*
Post-Bulletin - Rochester, MN - *AyerDirPub 83; Ed&PubIntYB 82*
Post Communication Services, Ken - New York, NY - *AvMarPl 83*
Post Co., The - Idaho Falls, ID - *BrCabYB 84*
Post Corp. - Appleton, WI - *BrCabYB 84; Ed&PubIntYB 82; KnowInd 83; Tel&CabFB 84S*
Post Corp./Sun Newspapers - Euclid, OH - *BaconPubCkNews 84*
Post-Crescent, The - Appleton, WI - *AyerDirPub 83; Ed&PubIntYB 82; NewsDir 84*
Post-Dispatch - Dardanelle, AR - *AyerDirPub 83*
Post-Dispatch - Pittsburg, CA - *AyerDirPub 83*
Post-Dispatch - Center, CO - *AyerDirPub 83*
Post-Dispatch - Sykesville, PA - *AyerDirPub 83*
Post-Dispatch - Post, TX - *BaconPubCkNews 84; Ed&PubIntYB 82*
Post Eagle - Clifton, NJ - *AyerDirPub 83; NewsDir 84*
Post Eagle - Jersey City, NJ - *Ed&PubIntYB 82*
Post Enterprise, The - Lisbon Falls, ME - *Ed&PubIntYB 82*
Post Falls Tribune - Post Falls, ID - *BaconPubCkNews 84; Ed&PubIntYB 82*
Post-Gazette - Boston, MA - *AyerDirPub 83; NewsDir 84*
Post-Gazette - Pittsburgh, PA - *AyerDirPub 83*
Post Graphics Corp., J. M. - East Keansburg, NJ - *LitMarPl 83, 84; MagIndMarPl 82-83*
Post-Harvest Documentation Service [of Kansas State University] - Manhattan, KS - *EISS 83*
Post-Herald [of Birmingham Post Co.] - Birmingham, AL - *AyerDirPub 83; Ed&PubIntYB 82*
Post-Herald - Wyoming, IL - *AyerDirPub 83*
Post-Herald - Beckley, WV - *AyerDirPub 83*
Post-Herald-Register - Beckley, WV - *AyerDirPub 83*
Post-Intelligencer - Paris, TN - *AyerDirPub 83*
Post-Intelligencer - Seattle, WA - *AyerDirPub 83*
Post-Journal [of The Ogden Newspapers Inc.] - Jamestown, NY - *AyerDirPub 83; Ed&PubIntYB 82; NewsDir 84*
Post Mercury - Lindsay, ON, Canada - *Ed&PubIntYB 82*
Post Modernist Records - Nutley, NJ - *BillIntBG 83-84*
Post Newspaper Group - Los Angeles, CA - *BaconPubCkNews 84*
Post Newspaper Group [of Oakland Alameda Publishing Corp.] - Oakland, CA - *NewsDir 84*
Post-Newsweek Programs [Div. of Post-Newsweek Stations] - Washington, DC - *TelAl 83, 84*
Post-Newsweek Stations - Washington, DC - *BrCabYB 84; Tel&CabFB 84S*
Post-Newsweek Video [Div. of Washington Post Co.] - New York, NY - *Tel&CabFB 84C*
Post Poetry [of Realities] - San Jose, CA - *LitMag&SmPr 83-84*
Post Publications Inc. - Arcadia, CA - *BoPubDir 4, 5*

Post Publications Inc. - Minneapolis, MN - *BaconPubCkNews 84*
Post Publications Inc. - Camas, WA - *BaconPubCkNews 84*
Post-Record - San Jose, CA - *Ed&PubIntYB 82*
Post-Register - Idaho Falls, ID - *AyerDirPub 83; Ed&PubIntYB 82*
Post-Register - Lockhart, TX - *AyerDirPub 83*
Post Republican - Penfield, NY - *AyerDirPub 83*
Post-Review - North Branch, MN - *AyerDirPub 83*
Post-Review - Hudson Bay, SK, Canada - *AyerDirPub 83; Ed&PubIntYB 82*
Post-Searchlight, The - Bainbridge, GA - *Ed&PubIntYB 82*
Post Shopper - Camas, WA - *AyerDirPub 83*
Post Signal - Crowley, LA - *AyerDirPub 83*
Post Signal - Pilot Point, TX - *Ed&PubIntYB 82*
Post-Standard [of The Syracuse Newspapers Inc.] - Syracuse, NY - *AyerDirPub 83; Ed&PubIntYB 82; LitMarPl 84*
Post-Star, The - Glens Falls, NY - *AyerDirPub 83; Ed&PubIntYB 82*
Post-Telegraph - Princeton, MO - *AyerDirPub 83; Ed&PubIntYB 82*
Post, The - Loves Park, IL - *Ed&PubIntYB 82*
Post, The - Paramus, NJ - *Ed&PubIntYB 82*
Post, The [of Ohio University] - Athens, OH - *NewsDir 84*
Post, The - Middleburg, PA - *AyerDirPub 83*
Post-Times - West Palm Beach, FL - *Ed&PubIntYB 82*
Post-Transcript - Dresden, OH - *AyerDirPub 83*
Post-Tribune - Gary, IN - *AyerDirPub 83; BaconPubCkNews 84; Ed&PubIntYB 82; LitMarPl 84; NewsBur 6*
Post-Tribune - Bernie, MO - *AyerDirPub 83; Ed&PubIntYB 82*
Post-Tribune - Jefferson City, MO - *AyerDirPub 83; Ed&PubIntYB 82; NewsDir 84*
Post-Tribune - Dallas, TX - *Ed&PubIntYB 82*
Postal World - Silver Spring, MD - *BaconPubCkMag 84; MagIndMarPl 82-83*
Postcard Art/Postcard Fiction - Brooklyn, NY - *LitMag&SmPr 83-84*
Postgraduate International Inc. - Cherry Hill, NJ - *BoPubDir 4, 5*
Postgraduate Medicine - Minneapolis, MN - *BaconPubCkMag 84; MagDir 84; MagIndMarPl 82-83*
Posthorn Recordings - New York, NY - *AvMarPl 83*
Postillion Press - Boulder, CO - *BoPubDir 4, 5*
Posts' Information Service - Philadelphia, PA - *FBInfSer 80*
Postup - Winnipeg, MB, Canada - *Ed&PubIntYB 82*
Postville Herald - Postville, IA - *BaconPubCkNews 84; Ed&PubIntYB 82*
Postville Telephone Co. - Postville, IA - *TelDir&BG 83-84*
Posy Publications - Charlottesville, VA - *BoPubDir 4 Sup, 5*
Potash Advertising - Louisville, KY - *StaDirAdAg 2-84*
Potash & Co. - Oakland, CA - *DirPRFirms 83*
Potash & Phosphate Institute - Atlanta, GA - *BoPubDir 5*
Potashville-Miner Journal - Esterhazy, SK, Canada - *AyerDirPub 83; Ed&PubIntYB 82*
Potato Data Bank - Washington, DC - *DirOnDB Spring 84*
Potato Grower of Idaho - Idaho Falls, ID - *MagDir 84; MagIndMarPl 82-83; WritMar 84*
Poteau News & Sun [of Enterprise Group Inc.] - Poteau, OK - *BaconPubCkNews 84; Ed&PubIntYB 82; NewsDir 84*
Potentials Development for Health & Aging Services - Buffalo, NY - *BoPubDir 4, 5; LitMag&SmPr 83-84; WritMar 84*
Potentials in Marketing [of Lakewood Publications] - Minneapolis, MN - *BaconPubCkMag 84; MagDir 84; MagIndMarPl 82-83*
Potes & Poets Press - Elmwood, CT - *BoPubDir 5; LitMag&SmPr 83-84*
Potes & Poets Press - Hartford, CT - *BoPubDir 4*
Potlatch Publications - Stoney Creek, ON, Canada - *BoPubDir 4, 5*
Potlatch Publications Ltd. - Hamilton, ON, Canada - *LitMarPl 83*
Potlatch Telephone Co. Inc. - Kendrik, ID - *TelDir&BG 83-84*
Potluck Publications - Los Angeles, CA - *BoPubDir 4, 5*
Potomac Appalachian Trail Club - Washington, DC - *BoPubDir 4, 5*
Potomac Asia Communications - Alexandria, VA - *LitMag&SmPr 83-84*
Potomac Books Inc. - Washington, DC - *LitMarPl 83, 84*
Potomac Micro-Magic Inc. - Falls Church, VA - *MicrocomMPl 84; WhoWMicrocom 83*
Potomac Micro Resources Inc. - Riverdale, MO - *MicrocomMPl 84*
Potomac Middlefork Journal - Potomac, IL - *BaconPubCkNews 84*
Potomac News - Woodbridge, VA - *AyerDirPub 83; BaconPubCkNews 84; Ed&PubIntYB 82; NewsDir 84*
Potomac Press - McLean, VA - *ArtMar 84*
Potomac Valley Television Co. Inc. - Cumberland, MD - *BrCabYB 84; Tel&CabFB 84C p.1697*
Potomac Valley Television Co. Inc. - Paw Paw, WV - *BrCabYB 84*
Potomac Valley Television Co. Inc. - Romney, WV - *BrCabYB 84*
Potosi Independent-Journal - Potosi, MO - *BaconPubCkNews 84; NewsDir 84*
Potpourri International [Aff. of The Littlefield Group] - Exton, PA - *BoPubDir 5*
Potpourri International - Wyomissing, PA - *BoPubDir 4*
Potsdam Courier & Freeman - Potsdam, NY - *BaconPubCkNews 84; Ed&PubIntYB 82; NewsDir 84*
Potsdam NewChannels [of NewChannels Corp.] - Potsdam, NY - *BrCabYB 84; InterCabHB 3; Tel&CabFB 84C*
Pottawatomie Telephone Co. Inc., The - Earlsboro, OK - *TelDir&BG 83-84*
Potter Co., J. W. - Rock Island, IL - *BrCabYB 84*
Potter County News - Gettysburg, SD - *AyerDirPub 83; Ed&PubIntYB 82*
Potter Enterprise - Coudersport, PA - *AyerDirPub 83; Ed&PubIntYB 82; NewsDir 84*
Potter Hazlehurst Inc. - East Greenwich, RI - *DirPRFirms 83; StaDirAdAg 2-84*
Potter Inc., Clarkson N. [Div. of Crown Publishers Inc.] - New York, NY - *ArtMar 84; LitMarPl 83, 84; WritMar 84*
Potters Programs [Subs. of DeArper Inc.] - Roseville, MI - *WhoWMicrocom 83*
Pottersfield Press - Porters Lake, NS, Canada - *BoPubDir 4 Sup, 5*
Pottstown Mercury - Pottstown, PA - *BaconPubCkNews 84; Ed&PubIntYB 82; NewsDir 84*
Pottstown Motorist - Lansdale, PA - *MagDir 84*
Pottsville Republican [of J. H. Zerbey Newspapers Inc.] - Pottsville, PA - *BaconPubCkNews 84; Ed&PubIntYB 82; NewsDir 84*
POTV - Port Lions, AK - *Tel&CabFB 84C*
Poughkeepsie Cablevision Inc. [of Community Tele-Communications Inc.] - Poughkeepsie, NY - *BrCabYB 84; Tel&CabFB 84C*
Poughkeepsie Journal [of Gannett Co. Inc.] - Poughkeepsie, NY - *BaconPubCkNews 84; Ed&PubIntYB 82; NewsDir 84*
Poughkeepsie Spackenkill Sentinel - Poughkeepsie, NY - *Ed&PubIntYB 82*
Poulin, Clarence - Penacook, NH - *BoPubDir 4, 5*
Poulsbo Kitsap County Herald - Poulsbo, WA - *BaconPubCkNews 84; NewsDir 84*
Poultry - Truro, MA - *LitMag&SmPr 83-84*
Poultry & Egg Marketing - Gainsville, GA - *MagDir 84*
Poultry & Egg Marketing - Vineland, NJ - *BaconPubCkMag 84*
Poultry Digest - Cullman, AL - *BaconPubCkMag 84; MagDir 84*
Poultry International - Mt. Morris, IL - *BaconPubCkMag 84; MagDir 84*
Poultry Press - York, PA - *BaconPubCkMag 84; MagDir 84*
Poultry Science - Champaign, IL - *MagDir 84*
Poultry Times, The - Gainesville, GA - *BaconPubCkMag 84; MagDir 84*
Poultry Tribune - Mt. Morris, IL - *BaconPubCkMag 84; MagDir 84*
Poutray & Holyoke Associates Inc. - Norwalk, CT - *StaDirAdAg 2-84*
Poverty Bay Publishing Co. - Federal Way, WA - *BoPubDir 4, 5*
Poverty Hill Press - Reno, NV - *BoPubDir 5*
Poverty Records - San Diego, CA - *BillIntBG 83-84*
Powahatan Music Publishing - Salem, VA - *BillIntBG 83-84*
Powassam/Almaguin News - Burks Falls, ON, Canada - *Ed&PubIntYB 82*
Poway News-Chieftain - Poway, CA - *BaconPubCkNews 84; Ed&PubIntYB 82*
Poway Pennysaver - Mission Viejo, CA - *AyerDirPub 83*

Powder/Bulk Solids - Minneapolis, MN - *MagDir 84*
Powder Magazine - Dana Point, CA - *BaconPubCkMag 84; WritMar 84*
Powder River Cable TV Inc. - Edgerton, WY - *BrCabYB 84; Tel&CabFB 84C*
Powder River Examiner - Broadus, MT - *AyerDirPub 83; Ed&PubIntYB 82*
Powder Springs-Mableton-Austell Neighbor - Powder Springs, GA - *Ed&PubIntYB 82*
Powder Springs Neighbor [of Marietta Neighbor Newspapers Inc.] - Marietta, GA - *NewsDir 84*
Powell & Jones - Charlotte, NC - *AdAge 3-28-84; StaDirAdAg 2-84*
Powell Design, Dean - New York, NY - *DirMarMP 83; LitMarPl 83, 84*
Powell, James Wooldridge - Kansas City, MO - *BoPubDir 4, 5*
Powell Publishing Co., Samuel - Sacramento, CA - *BoPubDir 4, 5; LitMag&SmPr 83-84*
Powell River Cablenet Ltd. - Powell River, BC, Canada - *BrCabYB 84*
Powell Systems Inc. - Austin, TX - *MicrocomMPl 84*
Powell Telephone Co. [Aff. of Allied Telephone Co.] - Powell, TN - *TelDir&BG 83-84*
Powell Tribune - Powell, WY - *BaconPubCkNews 84; Ed&PubIntYB 82*
Powell Valley News - Pennington Gap, VA - *AyerDirPub 83; Ed&PubIntYB 82*
Power [of SDC Search Service] - Santa Monica, CA - *DataDirOnSer 84*
Power [of U.S. Dept. of Energy] - Washington, DC - *CompReadDB 82; DirOnDB Spring 84; OnBibDB 3*
Power [of McGraw-Hill Publishing Inc.] - New York, NY - *ArtMar 84; BaconPubCkMag 84; Folio 83; MagDir 84; MagIndMarPl 82-83*
Power & Condon - Chattanooga, TN - *StaDirAdAg 2-84*
Power Automotive Consumer Profile, J. D. - Westlake Village, CA - *DirOnDB Spring 84*
Power Conversion International - Oxnard, CA - *BaconPubCkMag 84*
Power County Press - American Falls, ID - *AyerDirPub 83; Ed&PubIntYB 82*
Power Data Base [of Utility Data Institute] - Washington, DC - *DataDirOnSer 84*
Power Engineering - Barrington, IL - *BaconPubCkMag 84; MagDir 84; MagIndMarPl 82-83*
Power Information Center [of Interagency Advanced Power Group] - Philadelphia, PA - *EISS 5-84 Sup*
Power/Play - Wayne, PA - *BaconPubCkMag 84*
Power/Play [of Commodore Business Machines] - West Chester, PA - *WritMar 84*
Power Play Music [Div. of Gusta Records Inc.] - Nashville, TN - *BillIntBG 83-84*
Power Press - Nevada City, CA - *BoPubDir 4, 5*
Power Publishers [Aff. of Ethical Hypnosis Training Center Inc.] - South Orange, NJ - *BoPubDir 4, 5*
Power Reactor Docket Information - Oak Ridge, TN - *DirOnDB Spring 84*
Power Transmission Design - Cleveland, OH - *ArtMar 84; BaconPubCkMag 84; MagDir 84; WritMar 84*
Powerboat Magazine [of Nordco Publishing Inc.] - Van Nuys, CA - *BaconPubCkMag 84; MagDir 84; MagIndMarPl 82-83; WritMar 84*
Powerbyte Software - West Berlin, NJ - *MicrocomMPl 84*
Powerline Systems - Lincroft, NJ - *MicrocomMPl 83*
Powers & Co. Publishers Inc., Nancy - New York, NY - *BoPubDir 5*
Powers Associates Inc. - Houston, TX - *DirPRFirms 83*
Powers, Bill - New York, NY - *MagIndMarPl 82-83*
Powers International Inc. - New York, NY - *Ed&PubIntYB 82*
Powers, Martha Ammidon - Berkeley, CA - *FBInfSer 80; InfIndMarPl 83*
Powers Process Controls - Skokie, IL - *AvMarPl 83*
PowerSoft - Dallas, TX - *MicrocomMPl 83, 84*
Powersoft Inc. - Pitman, NJ - *MicrocomMPl 83; MicrocomSwDir 1*
Powertec Inc. - Chatsworth, CA - *DirInfWP 82*
Powhatan Gazette - Powhatan, VA - *AyerDirPub 83*
Powhatan Point Cable Co. - Barton, OH - *BrCabYB 84; Tel&CabFB 84C*
Powley Stations, John R. - Altoona, PA - *BrCabYB 84*
Poynette Press - Poynette, WI - *BaconPubCkNews 84; Ed&PubIntYB 82*
Pozzi Public Relations, Bruce - Anchorage, AK - *DirPRFirms 83*
PPA Publications - Des Plaines, IL - *BoPubDir 4, 5*
PPDS - Rugby, England - *DirOnDB Spring 84*
PPI Press Inc. - Bronx, NY - *LitMarPl 83, 84*
PPIData - New York, NY - *DirOnDB Spring 84*
P.P.R.J. Enterprises - Buena Park, CA - *BoPubDir 4, 5*
PPX Publishers - New York, NY - *BillIntBG 83-84*
PR Aids - New York, NY - *LitMarPl 83, 84; MagIndMarPl 82-83*
PR Aid's Party Line - New York, NY - *MagIndMarPl 82-83*
PR Associates Inc. - Detroit, MI - *DirPRFirms 83*
PR Associates Inc. - Akron, OH - *StaDirAdAg 2-84*
PR Associates of New York Inc. [Subs. of Gaynor & Co.] - New York, NY - *DirPRFirms 83*
PR Data Systems Inc. - Wilton, CT - *EISS 7-83 Sup; ProGuPRSer 4*
PR Group, The - Chicago, IL - *DirPRFirms 83*
PR News Service - Chicago, IL - *ProGuPRSer 4*
PR Newswire [Subs. of United Newspapers] - New York, NY - *DataDirOnSer 84; DirOnDB Spring 84; Ed&PubIntYB 82; EISS 5-84 Sup; ProGuPRSer 4*
PR Professional Associates - Albuquerque, NM - *DirPRFirms 83*
PR Reporter - Exeter, NH - *BaconPubCkMag 84; MagDir 84; MagIndMarPl 82-83*
PR West - Los Angeles, CA - *DirPRFirms 83*
PRA Inc. - Omaha, NE - *DirPRFirms 83*
Praco Ltd. - Colorado Springs, CO - *StaDirAdAg 2-84*
PracTek Associates Inc. - Chicopee, MA - *AvMarPl 83*
Practical Accountant [of Institute for Continuing Professional Development] - New York, NY - *BaconPubCkMag 84; MagDir 84*
Practical Automation Inc. - Shelton, CT - *MicrocomMPl 84*
Practical Business Systems Inc. - Rolling Meadows, IL - *MicrocomMPl 83, 84*
Practical Cardiology - Morganville, NJ - *MagIndMarPl 82-83*
Practical Data Corp. - Pomona, NY - *MicrocomMPl 84*
Practical Gastroenterology - Long Island City, NY - *BaconPubCkMag 84; MagDir 84; MagIndMarPl 82-83*
Practical Gourmet, The - Middle Island, NY - *BaconPubCkMag 84*
Practical Horseman [of Gum Tree Store Press Inc.] - Unionville, PA - *BaconPubCkMag 84; MagDir 84; WritMar 84*
Practical Knowledge - Chicago, IL - *MagDir 84; WritMar 84*
Practical Lawyer, The - Philadelphia, PA - *MagDir 84; MagIndMarPl 82-83*
Practical Parenting Newsletter - Wayzata, MN - *LitMag&SmPr 83-84; MagDir 84*
Practical Peripherals Inc. - Westlake Village, CA - *MicrocomMPl 84; WhoWMicrocom 83*
Practical Programs - Toms River, NJ - *MicrocomMPl 83, 84; MicrocomSwDir 1; WritMar 84*
Practical Publications [Aff. of Practical Products] - Chicago, IL - *BoPubDir 4, 5*
Practical Publishers Co. - Ithaca, NY - *BoPubDir 4, 5*
Practical Publishing Co. Ltd. [Aff. of Men Can Enterprises Ltd.] - Toronto, ON, Canada - *BoPubDir 4 Sup, 5*
Practical Solutions - Cupertino, CA - *MicrocomSwDir 1*
Practices of the Wind - Kalamazoo, MI - *BoPubDir 4 Sup, 5; LitMag&SmPr 83-84*
Practicing Law Institute - New York, NY - *BoPubDir 4, 5*
Practicing Midwife Journal, The [of The Book Publishing Co.] - Summertown, TN - *LitMag&SmPr 83-84*
Practicing Planner [of American Institute of Planners] - Washington, DC - *MagDir 84*
Practorcare Inc. - San Diego, CA - *MicrocomMPl 84*
Praeger Publishers [of CBS Educational & Professional Publishing] - New York, NY - *LitMarPl 83, 84*
Praeske Productions Inc., Del - Milwaukee, WI - *ArtMar 84*
Praestant Press - Delaware, OH - *BoPubDir 4, 5*
Prager Associates, N. J. - New York, NY - *IntDirMarRes 83*
Pragma Applications - Broken Arrow, OK - *BoPubDir 5*
Pragmatic Publications - St. Paul, MN - *BoPubDir 4, 5*

Pragmatronics Inc. - Boulder, CO - *DataDirSup 7-83*
Prague Times-Herald - Prague, OK - *BaconPubCkNews 84*
Prairie City News - Prairie City, IA - *AyerDirPub 83; BaconPubCkNews 84; Ed&PubIntYB 82*
Prairie Co-Ax TV Ltd. - Moose Jaw, SK, Canada - *BrCabYB 84*
Prairie Drummer, The - Colby, KS - *AyerDirPub 83; Ed&PubIntYB 82*
Prairie Du Chien Courier-Press - Prairie Du Chien, WI - *BaconPubCkNews 84*
Prairie Dust Records - Nashville, TN - *BillIntBG 83-84*
Prairie Farmer - Hinsdale, IL - *BaconPubCkMag 84; MagDir 84; MagIndMarPl 82-83*
Prairie Fire [of MWN Publications] - Winnipeg, MB, Canada - *LitMag&SmPr 83-84*
Prairie Grove Enterprise - Prairie Grove, AR - *BaconPubCkNews 84; Ed&PubIntYB 82*
Prairie Grove Telephone Co. - Prairie Grove, AR - *TelDir&BG 83-84*
Prairie Hotelman - Winnipeg, MB, Canada - *BaconPubCkMag 84*
Prairie Messenger [of Benedictine Monks of St. Peter's Abbey] - Muenster, SK, Canada - *WritMar 84*
Prairie News - Lester, MN - *Ed&PubIntYB 82*
Prairie Pioneer - Pollock, SD - *AyerDirPub 83; Ed&PubIntYB 82*
Prairie Post - Maroa, IL - *AyerDirPub 83; Ed&PubIntYB 82*
Prairie Press [Aff. of Prairie Bible Institute] - Three Hills, AB, Canada - *BoPubDir 4, 5; LitMarPl 83, 84*
Prairie Profile - Brookings, SD - *AyerDirPub 83*
Prairie Publications - Dell Rapids, SD - *BaconPubCkNews 84*
Prairie Publishing Co. - Winnipeg, MB, Canada - *BoPubDir 4, 5; LitMag&SmPr 83-84*
Prairie Schooner - Lincoln, NE - *LitMag&SmPr 83-84; WritMar 84*
Prairie Sun [of Prairie Sun Communications Inc.] - Peoria, IL - *ArtMar 84; LitMag&SmPr 83-84; WritMar 84*
Prairie Sun Communications Inc. - Peoria, IL - *BoPubDir 4, 5; LitMag&SmPr 83-84*
Prairie Telephone Co. - Champaign, IL - *TelDir&BG 83-84*
Prairie Telephone Co. Inc. - Breda, IA - *TelDir&BG 83-84*
Prairie Times - Blooming, MN - *Ed&PubIntYB 82*
Prairie/Valley Shopping News - Lodi, WI - *AyerDirPub 83*
Prairie View Vernon Town Crier - *See* Frontier Publishing Corp.
Prairie Village Sun [of Overland Park Sun Newspapers] - Shawnee Mission, KS - *NewsDir 84*
Prairie Village Sun - *See* Sun Publications
Prairie Wind Music - Norfolk, NE - *BillIntBG 83-84*
Prairie Wind Records - Norfolk, NE - *BillIntBG 83-84*
Prairieburg Telephone Co. Inc. - Prairieburg, IA - *TelDir&BG 83-84*
Prairieland Broadcasting Inc. - Centralia, IL - *BrCabYB 84*
Prairieland Cable Corp. - Heyworth, IL - *Tel&CabFB 84C*
Prairieland Cable Corp. - Normal, IL - *Tel&CabFB 84C p.1697*
Prairieland Stations - Decatur, IL - *BrCabYB 84*
Praise - *See* Jacobson, Jeffrey E.
Praise Industries Corp. - Bellingham, WA - *BillIntBG 83-84*
Prakken Publications Inc. - Ann Arbor, MI - *AvMarPl 83; DirMarMP 83; LitMarPl 83, 84*
Pran Inc. - New Braunfels, TX - *AvMarPl 83*
Prasada Press Inc. - Cincinnati, OH - *ArtMar 84*
Prasek Computer Systems Inc. - Santa Clara, CA - *MicrocomMPl 84*
Pratt Cable TV [of Communications Services Inc.] - Pratt, KS - *BrCabYB 84; Tel&CabFB 84C*
Pratt Free Library, Enoch - Baltimore, MD - *BoPubDir 4, 5*
Pratt Paper Co. - Boston, MA - *LitMarPl 83, 84*
Pratt Tribune - Pratt, KS - *BaconPubCkNews 84; NewsDir 84*
Prattville Progress [of Multimedia Corp.] - Prattville, AL - *BaconPubCkNews 84; Ed&PubIntYB 82; NewsDir 84*
Praxis - New York, NY - *MicrocomMPl 83*
Praxis: A Journal of Cultural Criticism - Santa Monica, CA - *LitMag&SmPr 83-84*
Pray Curser Press - Dutton, VA - *BoPubDir 4, 5; LitMag&SmPr 83-84*
Prayer Book Press Inc. [Subs. of Media Judaica Inc.] - Bridgeport, CT - *LitMarPl 83, 84*
Pre-Empt Computer Distributors Inc. - Atlanta, GA - *MicrocomMPl 84*
Pre-History & Protohistory [of Centre de Documentation Sciences Humaines] - Paris, France - *CompReadDB 82*
Pre-Med [of Bibliographic Retrieval Services Inc.] - Latham, NY - *CompReadDB 82; DataDirOnSer 84; DBBus 82; DirOnDB Spring 84; OnBibDB 3*
Pre-Psych [of Bibliographic Retrieval Services Inc.] - Latham, NY - *DataDirOnSer 84*
Pre-Pub Book Club [of Waldenbooks] - Stamford, CT - *LitMarPl 84*
Pre-Pub Book Club [Subs. of Sky Books International Inc.] - New York, NY - *LitMarPl 83, 84*
Pre-Vue - Billings, MT - *WritMar 84*
Preble County News - Camden, OH - *AyerDirPub 83; Ed&PubIntYB 82*
Precedent Publishing Inc. - Chicago, IL - *MicroMarPl 82-83; WritMar 84*
Precedent Publishing Inc. - South Holland, IL - *BoPubDir 4, 5*
Precellent Record Corp. - Brooklyn, NY - *BillIntBG 83-84*
Precinct Reporter - San Bernardino, CA - *Ed&PubIntYB 82*
Precious Resources [Aff. of The National Foster Parents Association] - Union, KY - *BoPubDir 4, 5*
Precise Communications Inc. - Chicago, IL - *DirPRFirms 83*
Precisely [of RK Editions] - New York, NY - *LitMag&SmPr 83-84*
Precision [Subs. of J & R Film Co. Inc.] - Hollywood, CA - *AvMarPl 83*
Precision Computer Ribbon Co. - Berkeley Heights, NJ - *DataDirSup 7-83*
Precision Film Laboratories Inc. [Subs. of Precision Film & Video Corp.] - New York, NY - *AvMarPl 83*
Precision Graphics - Champaign, IL - *LitMarPl 83, 84*
Precision Interviewing Service - Niles, IL - *IntDirMarRes 83*
Precision Metal - Cleveland, OH - *BaconPubCkMag 84; MagDir 84*
Precision Models - Minneapolis, MN - *BoPubDir 5*
Precision Offset Printing Co. Inc. - Upper Darby, PA - *AvMarPl 83; LitMarPl 83, 84*
Precision People Inc. - Jacksonville, FL - *MicrocomMPl 83, 84*
Precision Photographics Inc. [Div. of Precision Graphics of Ann Arbor Inc.] - Ann Arbor, MI - *AvMarPl 83*
Precision Prototypes - Refugro, TX - *MicrocomMPl 83, 84*
Precision Publishing Co. - North Ft. Myers, FL - *BoPubDir 4, 5*
Precision Shooting - East Hartford, CT - *BaconPubCkMag 84*
Precision Shooting - Augusta, ME - *MagDir 84*
Precision Software Ltd. - Worcester Park, England - *MicrocomSwDir 1*
Precision Technology Documentation Center [of Technical Information Center] - Frankfurt, West Germany - *EISS 83*
Precision Technology Inc. - Salt Lake City, UT - *MicrocomMPl 84*
Precision Typographers Inc. - New Hyde Park, NY - *LitMarPl 83, 84*
Precision Visuals Inc. - Boulder, CO - *DataDirSup 7-83; MicrocomMPl 84*
Predator Literature Storage & Retrieval [of U.S. Fish & Wildlife Service] - Denver, CO - *EISS 83*
Predecessor & Defunct Cos. [of QL Systems Ltd.] - Ottawa, ON, Canada - *DataDirOnSer 84*
Predecessor & Defunct Cos. [of Financial Post] - Toronto, ON, Canada - *CompReadDB 82; DirOnDB Spring 84*
Predicasts Inc. [Aff. of Indian Head] - Cleveland, OH - *BoPubDir 4 Sup, 5; CompReadDB 82; DataDirOnSer 84; EISS 83; InfIndMarPl 83; InfoS 83-84*
Predicasts Indexes [of Predicasts Inc.] - Cleveland, OH - *CompReadDB 82*
Predicasts International Inc. - Orpington, England - *InfIndMarPl 83*
Predicasts Overview of Markets & Technology [of Predicasts Inc.] - Cleveland, OH - *CompReadDB 82*
Prediction Systems Inc. - Manasquan, NJ - *MicrocomMPl 84; MicrocomSwDir 1*
Preeceville Progress - Preeceville, SK, Canada - *AyerDirPub 83; Ed&PubIntYB 82*
Preema Publishing - Garden City, NY - *BillIntBG 83-84*
Preferred Choice Bookplan [Div. of Crown Publishers Inc.] - New York, NY - *LitMarPl 83, 84*
Preiss Inc., Alvin - New York, NY - *HBIndAd&MS 82-83*

Preiss Printing Co. Inc. - Melville, NY - *LitMarPl 83, 84; MagIndMarPl 82-83*
Prelude Records Inc. - New York, NY - *BillIntBG 83-84*
Premack Research Corp. - St. Petersburg, FL - *IntDirMarRes 83*
Premier [Div. of Martin Yale Industries Inc.] - Chicago, IL - *AvMarPl 83*
Premier Film & Recording - St. Louis, MO - *ArtMar 84; AvMarPl 83; TelAl 83, 84; Tel&CabFB 84C; WritMar 84*
Premier Press - Berkeley, CA - *BoPubDir 4, 5*
Premier Printing & Letter Service Inc. - Houston, TX - *LitMarPl 83, 84; MagIndMarPl 82-83*
Premier Printing Corp. - Fullerton, CA - *MagIndMarPl 82-83*
Premier Publishing - Winnipeg, MB, Canada - *BoPubDir 4 Sup, 5*
Premier Software - Rosehill, KS - *MicrocomMPl 84*
Premier Wholesale Book News - Ft. Worth, TX - *LitMag&SmPr 83-84*
Premiere Artists & Productions Agency - Los Angeles, CA - *Tel&CabFB 84C*
Premiere Performance Corp. - New York, NY - *AvMarPl 83*
Preminger Films, Otto - New York, NY - *LitMarPl 83*
Premium Channels Cable TV Inc. [of Millhaven Public Service Corp.] - *BrCabYB 84*
Premium/Incentive Business [of Gralla Publications] - New York, NY - *BaconPubCkMag 84; MagDir 84; MagIndMarPl 82-83*
Premium Products Sales - Greenwich, CT - *HBIndAd&MS 82-83; IntDirMarRes 83*
Prendergast & Associates Inc., James W. - New York, NY - *DirMarMP 83; MagIndMarPl 82-83*
Prendergast & Associates Inc., James W. - *See* Tatham-Laird & Kudner
Prensa Latina - New York, NY - *Ed&PubIntYB 82*
Prentice Corp. - Sunnyvale, CA - *DataDirSup 7-83; MicrocomMPl 84; WhoWMicrocom 83*
Prentice-Hall Canada Inc. - Scarborough, ON, Canada - *LitMarPl 83, 84*
Prentice-Hall Developmental Learning Centers [Subs. of Prentice-Hall Inc.] - West Paterson, NJ - *AvMarPl 83; LitMarPl 83, 84*
Prentice-Hall Inc. - Englewood Cliffs, NJ - *HomeVid&CabYB 82-83; InfoS 83-84; KnowInd 83; LitMarPl 83, 84; MicrocomMPl 83, 84*
Prentice-Hall Inc. (Children's Book Div.) - Englewood Cliffs, NJ - *WritMar 84*
Prentice-Hall Inc. (General Publishing Div.) - Englewood Cliffs, NJ - *WritMar 84*
Prentice-Hall International Inc. [Subs. of Prentice-Hall Inc.] - Englewood Cliffs, NJ - *LitMarPl 83, 84*
Prentice-Hall Media Inc. [Subs. of Prentice-Hall Inc.] - Tarrytown, NY - *AvMarPl 83; WritMar 84*
Prentice, Robert M. - Cos Cob, CT - *HBIndAd&MS 82-83*
Prentiss Headlight - Prentiss, MS - *AyerDirPub 83; BaconPubCkNews 84*
Prentiss Highlight - Prentiss, MS - *Ed&PubIntYB 82*
Pres-Kliping Novinska Dokumentacija - Belgrade, Yugoslavia - *ProGuPRSer 4*
Presbyterian & Reformed Publishing Co. - Phillipsburg, NJ - *BoPubDir 4, 5; LitMarPl 84*
Presbyterian Historical Society - Philadelphia, PA - *MicroMarPl 82-83*
Presbyterian Journal [of Southern Presbyterian Journal Co. Inc.] - Asheville, NC - *WritMar 84*
Presbyterian Outlook, The - Richmond, VA - *MagIndMarPl 82-83*
Presbyterian Record - Don Mills, ON, Canada - *ArtMar 84; WritMar 84*
Presbyterian Survey [of Presbyterian Publishing House] - Atlanta, GA - *ArtMar 84; BaconPubCkMag 84; MagDir 84; MagIndMarPl 82-83; WritMar 84*
Prescob Publishing Co. - Tulsa, OK - *BoPubDir 4, 5*
Prescott, Ball & Turben Inc. (Research Div.) - Cleveland, OH - *ADAPSOMemDir 83-84*
Prescott Co. Inc., Eileen - New York, NY - *DirPRFirms 83; LitMarPl 83, 84*
Prescott Courier - Prescott, AZ - *BaconPubCkNews 84*
Prescott Journal - Prescott, WI - *Ed&PubIntYB 82*
Prescott Journal - *See* Weekly Newspapers Inc.
Prescott Journal, The - Prescott, ON, Canada - *Ed&PubIntYB 82*
Prescott Nevada County Picayune - Prescott, AR - *BaconPubCkNews 84; NewsDir 84*
Prescott Street Press - Portland, OR - *BoPubDir 4, 5; LitMag&SmPr 83-84*
Prescott Telephone & Telegraph Co. - Roslyn, WA - *TelDir&BG 83-84*
Prescott Video Inc. [of WEHCO Video Inc.] - Prescott, AR - *BrCabYB 84; Tel&CabFB 84C*
Prescott's Weekly - Prescott, AZ - *Ed&PubIntYB 82*
Prescription Co. - Port Washington, NY - *BillIntBG 83-84*
Prescription Record Co. - Washington, DC - *BillIntBG 83-84*
Present Futures - Cambridge, MA - *FBInfSer 80*
Present Tense - New York, NY - *LitMarPl 83, 84; MagIndMarPl 82-83; WritMar 84*
Presentation Technical Aids Inc. - New York, NY - *AvMarPl 83*
Presentations Inc. - Phoenix, AZ - *AvMarPl 83*
Preservation Ink [Aff. of Steve Slaske Illustration Design] - Milwaukee, WI - *BoPubDir 5*
Preservation League of New York State - Albany, NY - *BoPubDir 5*
Preservation Press [Subs. of National Trust for Historic Preservation] - Washington, DC - *LitMarPl 83, 84; WritMar 84*
Preserve Data Base [of The Nature Conservatory] - Arlington, VA - *EISS 7-83 Sup*
Preserved Context Index System [of British Library] - London, England - *EISS 83*
Presho Lyman County Herald - Presho, SD - *BaconPubCkNews 84*
President Music Corp. - Great Neck, NY - *BillIntBG 83-84*
Presidial Press [Aff. of Military History Associates Inc.] - Austin, TX - *BoPubDir 4, 5*
Presidio Press - Novato, CA - *LitMag&SmPr 83-84; LitMarPl 83, 84; WritMar 84*
Presidio TV Cable - Presidio, TX - *BrCabYB 84; Tel&CabFB 84C*
Presque Isle County Advance - Rogers City, MI - *AyerDirPub 83*
Presque Isle Star-Herald - Presque Isle, ME - *BaconPubCkNews 84; Ed&PubIntYB 82; NewsDir 84*
Press - Centreville, AL - *AyerDirPub 83*
Press [of The Mobile Press Register Inc.] - Mobile, AL - *AyerDirPub 83; Ed&PubIntYB 82; NewsDir 84*
Press - Lynwood, CA - *AyerDirPub 83*
Press - McFarland, CA - *AyerDirPub 83*
Press - Oakland, CA - *AyerDirPub 83*
Press - Paso Robles, CA - *AyerDirPub 83*
Press - Shafter, CA - *AyerDirPub 83*
Press - South Gate, CA - *AyerDirPub 83*
Press - Tracy, CA - *AyerDirPub 83*
Press - Weed, CA - *AyerDirPub 83*
Press - Montrose, CO - *AyerDirPub 83*
Press - Enfield, CT - *AyerDirPub 83*
Press - Ridgefield, CT - *AyerDirPub 83*
Press - Mulberry, FL - *AyerDirPub 83*
Press - Savannah, GA - *AyerDirPub 83*
Press - Coeur d'Alene, ID - *AyerDirPub 83*
Press - Greenup, IL - *AyerDirPub 83*
Press - Pleasant Plains, IL - *AyerDirPub 83*
Press - Rantoul, IL - *AyerDirPub 83*
Press - Sumner, IL - *AyerDirPub 83*
Press - West Chicago, IL - *AyerDirPub 83*
Press - Evansville, IN - *AyerDirPub 83*
Press - Jamestown, IN - *AyerDirPub 83*
Press - Muncie, IN - *AyerDirPub 83*
Press - Doon, IA - *AyerDirPub 83*
Press - Guttenberg, IA - *AyerDirPub 83*
Press - Lost Nation, IA - *AyerDirPub 83*
Press - Manchester, IA - *AyerDirPub 83*
Press - Springfield, MA - *AyerDirPub 83*
Press - Watertown, MA - *AyerDirPub 83*
Press - Escanaba, MI - *AyerDirPub 83*
Press - Marion, MI - *AyerDirPub 83*
Press - Saginaw, MI - *AyerDirPub 83*
Press - Ypsilanti, MI - *AyerDirPub 83*
Press - Paynesville, MN - *AyerDirPub 83*
Press - Pelican Rapids, MN - *AyerDirPub 83*
Press - St. Charles, MN - *AyerDirPub 83*
Press - De Soto, MO - *AyerDirPub 83*

Press - Green City, MO - *AyerDirPub 83*
Press - Marceline, MO - *AyerDirPub 83*
Press - Bellevue, NE - *AyerDirPub 83*
Press [of South Jersey Publishing Co.] - Atlantic City, NJ - *AyerDirPub 83; Ed&PubIntYB 82; LitMarPl 83, 84*
Press - Blairstown, NJ - *AyerDirPub 83*
Press - Chatham, NJ - *AyerDirPub 83*
Press - Cranbury, NJ - *AyerDirPub 83*
Press - New Egypt, NJ - *AyerDirPub 83*
Press - Artesia, NM - *AyerDirPub 83*
Press - Eunice, NM - *AyerDirPub 83*
Press - Binghamton, NY - *AyerDirPub 83; Ed&PubIntYB 82; LitMarPl 84*
Press - Ellenville, NY - *AyerDirPub 83*
Press - Utica, NY - *AyerDirPub 83*
Press - Franklin, NC - *AyerDirPub 83*
Press - Carson, ND - *AyerDirPub 83*
Press - Cleveland, OH - *AyerDirPub 83*
Press - Germantown, OH - *AyerDirPub 83*
Press - Rockford, OH - *AyerDirPub 83*
Press - Frederick, OK - *AyerDirPub 83*
Press - Lawton, OK - *AyerDirPub 83*
Press - Woodward, OK - *AyerDirPub 83*
Press - Bloomsburg, PA - *AyerDirPub 83*
Press - Johnsonburg, PA - *AyerDirPub 83*
Press - Pittsburgh, PA - *AyerDirPub 83*
Press - Springfield, PA - *AyerDirPub 83*
Press - Kadoka, SD - *AyerDirPub 83*
Press - Miller, SD - *AyerDirPub 83*
Press - Redfield, SD - *AyerDirPub 83*
Press - Bremond, TX - *AyerDirPub 83*
Press - Buffalo, TX - *AyerDirPub 83*
Press - Cisco, TX - *AyerDirPub 83*
Press - Overton, TX - *AyerDirPub 83*
Press - Pharr, TX - *AyerDirPub 83*
Press - Rowena, TX - *AyerDirPub 83*
Press - Beaver, UT - *AyerDirPub 83*
Press - Floyd, VA - *AyerDirPub 83*
Press - Newport News, VA - *AyerDirPub 83*
Press - Sequim, WA - *AyerDirPub 83*
Press - Ashland, WI - *AyerDirPub 83; Ed&PubIntYB 82*
Press - Blair, WI - *AyerDirPub 83*
Press - Denmark, WI - *AyerDirPub 83*
Press - Poynette, WI - *AyerDirPub 83*
Press - Sheboygan, WI - *AyerDirPub 83*
Press - Verona, WI - *AyerDirPub 83*
Press - Sheridan, WY - *AyerDirPub 83; Ed&PubIntYB 82*
Press - Neepawa, MB, Canada - *AyerDirPub 83*
Press - Timmins, ON, Canada - *AyerDirPub 83*
Press - Winchester, ON, Canada - *AyerDirPub 83; Ed&PubIntYB 82*
Press - Eston, SK, Canada - *AyerDirPub 83*
Press - Wilkie, SK, Canada - *AyerDirPub 83; Ed&PubIntYB 82*
Press & Banner - Abbeville, SC - *AyerDirPub 83; Ed&PubIntYB 82*
Press & Dakotan - Yankton, SD - *AyerDirPub 83*
Press & Dietrich Special Gazette - Teutopolis, IL - *AyerDirPub 83*
Press & Guide - Dearborn, MI - *AyerDirPub 83*
Press & Independent - Silver City, NM - *AyerDirPub 83; Ed&PubIntYB 82*
Press & Journal - Chicago, IL - *Ed&PubIntYB 82*
Press & Journal - Middletown, PA - *AyerDirPub 83; Ed&PubIntYB 82*
Press & News Journal - Springhill, LA - *AyerDirPub 83*
Press & Standard - Walterboro, SC - *AyerDirPub 83; Ed&PubIntYB 82; NewsDir 84*
Press & Standard, The - Colleton, SC - *Ed&PubIntYB 82*
Press & Sun-Bulletin [of Gannett Co. Inc.] - Binghamton, NY - *NewsDir 84*
Press Argus - Van Buren, AR - *AyerDirPub 83; Ed&PubIntYB 82*
Press Associates Inc. - Washington, DC - *Ed&PubIntYB 82; LitMarPl 84*
Press Association [Subs. of Associated Press] - New York, NY - *BrCabYB 84*
Press at Vision Studios - LaGrange, IL - *BoPubDir 4, 5*
Press Box, The - Westfield, NJ - *AyerDirPub 83; Ed&PubIntYB 82; NewsDir 84*
Press Broadcasting Co. - Asbury Park, NJ - *BrCabYB 84*
Press-Chronicle - Johnson City, TN - *AyerDirPub 83*
Press-Citizen - Iowa City, IA - *AyerDirPub 83*
Press Clipping Services Pty. Ltd. - Sydney, Australia - *ProGuPRSer 4*
Press-Courier - Oxnard, CA - *AyerDirPub 83; Ed&PubIntYB 82*
Press-Democrat - Santa Rosa, CA - *AyerDirPub 83; Ed&PubIntYB 82; LitMarPl 84*
Press-Dispatch - Petersburg, IN - *AyerDirPub 83; Ed&PubIntYB 82*
Press-Dispatch [of Townsend Communications Inc.] - Kansas City, MO - *AyerDirPub 83; Ed&PubIntYB 82; NewsDir 84*
Press-Enterprise - Riverside, CA - *AyerDirPub 83; Ed&PubIntYB 82; NewsDir 84*
Press-Enterprise - Bloomsburg, PA - *BaconPubCkNews 84; Ed&PubIntYB 82*
Press Features International - New York, NY - *Ed&PubIntYB 82*
Press 451 - Arlington, VA - *BoPubDir 4, 5*
Press Galvin Advertising Inc. - Cincinnati, OH - *StaDirAdAg 2-84*
Press Gang Publishers - Vancouver, BC, Canada - *BoPubDir 4, 5; LitMag&SmPr 83-84*
Press-Gazette - Milton, FL - *AyerDirPub 83; Ed&PubIntYB 82*
Press-Gazette - Hillsboro, OH - *AyerDirPub 83; Ed&PubIntYB 82*
Press-Gazette - Green Bay, WI - *AyerDirPub 83*
Press-Gazette, The - Wheatland, IA - *AyerDirPub 83; Ed&PubIntYB 82*
Press-Herald - Torrance, CA - *AyerDirPub 83*
Press-Herald - Minden, LA - *AyerDirPub 83*
Press-Herald - Portland, ME - *AyerDirPub 83*
Press-Herald - Pine Grove, PA - *Ed&PubIntYB 82*
Press Herald - Ravine, PA - *AyerDirPub 83*
Press Inc. - Johnson City, TN - *BrCabYB 84*
Press Inc., The - Chanhassen, MN - *MagIndMarPl 82-83*
Press Intelligence Inc. - Washington, DC - *ProGuPRSer 4*
Press-Journal - Vero Beach, FL - *AyerDirPub 83*
Press-Journal - Strawberry Point, IA - *AyerDirPub 83*
Press-Journal [of St. Louis Suburban Newspapers Inc.] - Ballwin, MO - *NewsDir 84*
Press-Journal - Louisiana, MO - *AyerDirPub 83*
Press-Journal [of Holiday Communications Inc.] - Englewood, NJ - *AyerDirPub 83; Ed&PubIntYB 82; NewsDir 84*
Press Magazine, The - Westminster, CO - *BaconPubCkMag 84*
Press Me Close - Farmingdale, NJ - *LitMag&SmPr 83-84*
Press-Mentor - Newton, IL - *AyerDirPub 83; Ed&PubIntYB 82*
Press-Merit - Malden, MO - *AyerDirPub 83*
Press-News - East Canton, OH - *AyerDirPub 83; Ed&PubIntYB 82*
Press-News Journal - Canton, MO - *AyerDirPub 83*
Press News Ltd. - Toronto, ON, Canada - *CompReadDB 82; DataDirOnSer 84; Ed&PubIntYB 82*
Press Newspapers - Chicago, IL - *BaconPubCkNews 84*
Press of Arden Park - Sacramento, CA - *BoPubDir 4, 5; LitMag&SmPr 83-84*
Press of Circumstances - Redding, CA - *BoPubDir 4, 5*
Press of Inverness - Inverness, CA - *BoPubDir 4, 5*
Press of Paul Maravelas - Watertown, MN - *BoPubDir 5; LitMag&SmPr 83-84*
Press of the Golden Unicorn - Hayward, CA - *LitMag&SmPr 83-84*
Press of the Nightowl - Athens, GA - *BoPubDir 4, 5*
Press of the Nova Scotia College of Art & Design - Halifax, NS, Canada - *BoPubDir 4, 5*
Press of Ward Schori - Evanston, IL - *BoPubDir 4, 5; LitMag&SmPr 83-84*
Press Office, The - New York, NY - *DirPRFirms 83*
Press Pacifica [Div. of Pacific Trade Group] - Kailua, HI - *LitMag&SmPr 83-84; LitMarPl 83; WritMar 84*
Press Photo Service - Jamaica, NY - *Ed&PubIntYB 82*
Press Photos - New York, NY - *Ed&PubIntYB 82*
Press Porcepic Ltd. - Victoria, BC, Canada - *LitMag&SmPr 83-84; LitMarPl 83, 84*
Press Publications - Oakland, CA - *AyerDirPub 83; BaconPubCkNews 84*
Press Publications - Elmhurst, IL - *BaconPubCkNews 84*

Press Publications - White Bear Lake, MN - *BaconPubCkNews 84; NewsDir 84*
Press Publishing Co. - Drexel Hill, PA - *BaconPubCkNews 84*
Press-Radio Bible Service Inc. - Cincinnati, OH - *Ed&PubIntYB 82*
Press-Record - Granite City, IL - *AyerDirPub 83; Ed&PubIntYB 82*
Press Register [of The Mobile Press Register Inc.] - Mobile, AL - *AyerDirPub 83; Ed&PubIntYB 82; LitMarPl 84; NewsDir 84*
Press Register - Clarksdale, MS - *AyerDirPub 83; Ed&PubIntYB 82*
Press Relations Newswire - Southfield, MI - *Ed&PubIntYB 82; ProGuPRSer 4*
Press Relations Services - Greenwich, CT - *DirPRFirms 83*
Press Relations Wire - Washington, DC - *Ed&PubIntYB 82; ProGuPRSer 4*
Press-Reporter - Pukwana, SD - *AyerDirPub 83; Ed&PubIntYB 82*
Press-Reporter - Lamesa, TX - *AyerDirPub 83*
Press Republican - Plattsburgh, NY - *AyerDirPub 83; BaconPubCkNews 84; Ed&PubIntYB 82*
Press Research Bureau, The - Auckland, New Zealand - *ProGuPRSer 4*
Press-Scimitar - Memphis, TN - *AyerDirPub 83*
Press Sentinel - Jesup, GA - *AyerDirPub 83*
Press-Spectator - Salisbury, MO - *AyerDirPub 83*
Press-Star - New London, WI - *AyerDirPub 83; Ed&PubIntYB 82*
Press-Telegram [of Knight-Ridder Publications Inc.] - Long Beach, CA - *AyerDirPub 83; Ed&PubIntYB 82; LitMarPl 83, 84; NewsDir 84*
Press, The - North Oakland, CA - *Ed&PubIntYB 82*
Press, The - Bossier City, LA - *Ed&PubIntYB 82*
Press, The [of The Greater Buffalo Press Inc.] - Buffalo, NY - *WritMar 84*
Press, The - Towner, ND - *AyerDirPub 83*
Press, The - Oxford, OH - *AyerDirPub 83*
Press, The - Rittman, OH - *AyerDirPub 83; Ed&PubIntYB 82*
Press, The - St. Marys, PA - *AyerDirPub 83*
Press, The - Bryan, TX - *AyerDirPub 83*
Press, The - Gibsons, BC, Canada - *Ed&PubIntYB 82*
Press, The - Sechelt, BC, Canada - *AyerDirPub 83*
Press-Tribune - Roseville, CA - *AyerDirPub 83; BaconPubCkNews 84*
Press-Tribune - Auburn, NE - *AyerDirPub 83*
Press-Tribune - White Haven, PA - *Ed&PubIntYB 82*
Press-Tribune-Record - Balaton, MN - *Ed&PubIntYB 82*
Press West - Chico, CA - *BoPubDir 4, 5*
Press Wire Services - Flushing, NY - *Ed&PubIntYB 82; LitMarPl 83, 84; MagIndMarPl 82-83*
Pressclips Inc. - New Hyde Park, NY - *LitMarPl 83, 84; ProGuPRSer 4*
Presse-Archiv - Pfungstadt, West Germany - *ProGuPRSer 4*
Presse-Clearing - Paris, France - *ProGuPRSer 4*
Pressed Curtains - Kent, ME - *LitMag&SmPr 83-84*
Presser & Associates Inc., R. - New York, NY - *StaDirAdAg 2-84*
Presser & Co., E. J. - Charlotte, NC - *StaDirAdAg 2-84*
Presser Co., Theodore - Bryn Mawr, PA - *BillIntBG 83-84; BoPubDir 4, 5*
Presser, David - Beachwood, OH - *MagIndMarPl 82-83*
Presser, David - Shaker Heights, OH - *LitMarPl 83*
Presses Laurentiennes Inc. - Charlesbourg, PQ, Canada - *BoPubDir 5*
Presses Laurentiennes Inc. - Notre-Dame-des-Laurentides, PQ, Canada - *BoPubDir 4*
Pressman Liberty Printing & Litho Co., Pearl - Philadelphia, PA - *LitMarPl 83, 84*
Pressnet [of Teleconcepts in Communications Inc.] - New York, NY - *TeleSy&SerDir 2-84*
Pressure - St. Clair Shores, MI - *BaconPubCkMag 84*
Pressure Vessel Handbook Publishing Inc. - Tulsa, OK - *BoPubDir 4, 5*
Pressworks Publishing Inc. - Dallas, TX - *LitMag&SmPr 83-84; LitMarPl 83, 84; WritMar 84*
Prestel Program [of Council for Educational Technology] - London, England - *EISS 83*
Prestel System [of British Telecommunications] - London, England - *EISS 83; InfIndMarPl 83; VideoDir 82-83*
Prestel World Videotex Service [of Torch Computers Ltd.] - Woburn, MA - *DataDirOnSer 84*
Prestige Art Galleries Inc. - Skokie, IL - *ArtMar 84*
Prestige Cable TV Inc. - Spotsylvania, VA - *Tel&CabFB 84C p.1697*
Presto Books - Shoreham, NY - *BoPubDir 5; LitMag&SmPr 83-84*
Preston Advertising Inc. - St. Petersburg, FL - *StaDirAdAg 2-84*
Preston & Betts - Victoria, BC, Canada - *BoPubDir 4, 5*
Preston Area Cablevision - Preston, IA - *Tel&CabFB 84C*
Preston Cable TV [of Community Tele-Communications Inc.] - Preston, ID - *Tel&CabFB 84C*
Preston Cable TV Inc. - Preston, MN - *BrCabYB 84; Tel&CabFB 84C p.1697*
Preston Citizen - Preston, ID - *AyerDirPub 83; Ed&PubIntYB 82*
Preston Citizen - *See* Citizen Publishing Co. Inc.
Preston County Journal - Kingwood, WV - *Ed&PubIntYB 82*
Preston County News - Terra Alta, WV - *AyerDirPub 83; Ed&PubIntYB 82; NewsDir 84*
Preston Films, Howard - Santa Monica, CA - *AvMarPl 83*
Preston Group Inc., The - Lexington, KY - *DirPRFirms 83*
Preston-Hill Inc. - Chapel Hill, NC - *BoPubDir 4, 5*
Preston, Jane - Brooklyn, NY - *LitMarPl 83, 84*
Preston, John - Portland, ME - *MagIndMarPl 82-83*
Preston News & Farmer - Preston, MD - *BaconPubCkNews 84; NewsDir 84*
Preston Publications Inc. [Subs. of Preston Industries] - Niles, IL - *CompReadDB 82; DirMarMP 83; EISS 83; MicroMarPl 82-83*
Preston Publishing Co. - New York, NY - *BoPubDir 4, 5*
Preston Republican - Preston, MN - *BaconPubCkNews 84; Ed&PubIntYB 82*
Preston Telephone Co. - Preston, IA - *TelDir&BG 83-84*
Preston Telephone Co. [Aff. of Mid-Continent Telephone Corp.] - Masontown, WV - *TelDir&BG 83-84*
Preston Times - Preston, IA - *BaconPubCkNews 84; Ed&PubIntYB 82*
Prestonsburg Floyd County Times - Prestonsburg, KY - *NewsDir 84*
Prestressed Concrete Institute - Chicago, IL - *BoPubDir 4, 5*
Prestwick Publishing Co. - San Diego, CA - *BoPubDir 5*
Prestype - Carlstadt, NJ - *AvMarPl 83*
Pretoria State Library, The - Pretoria, South Africa - *MicroMarPl 82-83*
Pretty Prairie Ninnescah Valley News - Pretty Prairie, KS - *BaconPubCkNews 84*
Pretzelland Software - Ypsilanti, MI - *MicrocomMPl 83, 84*
Prevention [of Rodale Press Inc.] - Emmaus, PA - *BaconPubCkMag 84; Folio 83; MagDir 84; MagIndMarPl 82-83*
Prevention Book Club [Subs. of Rodale Press Inc.] - Emmaus, PA - *LitMarPl 83, 84*
Preventive Medicine - New York, NY - *BaconPubCkMag 84*
Preview [of Time Inc.] - New York, NY - *CabTVPrDB 83*
Preview Community Weekly - Traverse City, MI - *AyerDirPub 83*
Previews - New York, NY - *MagDir 84*
Prevton Offset Printing Inc. [Div. of Colt Graphics Inc.] - New York, NY - *LitMarPl 83, 84*
Priam Corp. - San Jose, CA - *DataDirSup 7-83; MicrocomMPl 84; WhoWMicrocom 83*
Price Advertising Inc., Phil - Lubbock, TX - *StaDirAdAg 2-84*
Price Broadcasting Co. - Salt Lake City, UT - *BrCabYB 84*
Price Communications Corp. Stations - New York, NY - *BrCabYB 84*
Price Co., H & J - Maplewood, NJ - *DataDirOnSer 84*
Price County Telephone Co. - Phillips, WI - *Tel&CabFB 84C; TelDir&BG 83-84*
Price Database [of Data Resources Inc.] - Lexington, MA - *DataDirOnSer 84*
Price Films Inc., John M. - Radnor, PA - *AvMarPl 83*
Price Inc., Daniel H. - New York, NY - *StaDirAdAg 2-84*
Price Index Numbers for Current Cost Accounting [of Dept. of Industry] - Newport, England - *EISS 83*
Price/McNabb Advertising Inc. - Asheville, NC - *StaDirAdAg 2-84*
Price Music, James - Lexington, KY - *BillIntBG 83-84*

Price-Pottenger Nutrition Foundation - La Mesa, CA - *BoPubDir 5*
Price-Pottenger Nutrition Foundation - San Diego, CA - *BoPubDir 4*
Price, Stephen - New York, NY - *ProGuPRSer 4*
Price/Stern/Sloan, Publishers Inc. - Los Angeles, CA - *LitMarPl 83, 84; WritMar 84*
Price Sun Advocate - *See* Sun Advocate Publishers Inc.
Pricedata - Rome, Italy - *DirOnDB Spring 84*
Pricketts Radio & TV - Wheeler, OR - *BrCabYB 84*
Pride, Barber & Pride Inc. - Edina, MN - *StaDirAdAg 2-84*
Pride in America Co. - Pittsburgh, PA - *BoPubDir 4 Sup, 5*
Pride Music Group - Nashville, TN - *BillIntBG 83-84*
Priest & Fine Inc. - Washington, DC - *DirPRFirms 83*
Priest Literary Agency Inc., The Aaron M. - New York, NY - *LitMarPl 83, 84*
Priest River Cablevision - Priest River, ID - *Tel&CabFB 84C*
Priest River Times - Priest River, ID - *BaconPubCkNews 84; Ed&PubIntYB 82*
Priest, The [of Our Sunday Visitor Inc.] - Huntington, IN - *BaconPubCkMag 84; MagDir 84; MagIndMarPl 82-83; WritMar 84*
Prima Agua Press - Las Cruces, NM - *LitMag&SmPr 83-84*
Prima Inc. - Lubbock, TX - *BrCabYB 84*
Primages Inc. - Bohemia, NY - *MicrocomMPl 84*
PrimaLux Video Inc. - New York, NY - *AvMarPl 83*
Primary Books - Harlingen, TX - *BoPubDir 4, 5*
Primary Cardiology - New York, NY - *MagIndMarPl 82-83*
Primary Color Laboratory Inc. - New Orleans, LA - *AvMarPl 83*
Primary Communications Research Centre [of University of Leicester] - Leicester, England - *EISS 5-84 Sup; LitMag&SmPr 83-84*
Primary Press - Parker Ford, PA - *BoPubDir 4, 5; LitMag&SmPr 83-84*
Primate Information Center [of University of Washington] - Seattle, WA - *EISS 83; InfIndMarPl 83*
Primaute Advertising Inc. - New York, NY - *StaDirAdAg 2-84*
Primavera [of University of Chicago] - Chicago, IL - *ArtMar 84; LitMag&SmPr 83-84; WritMar 84*
Primavera Public Relations - Yorktown Heights, NY - *DirPRFirms 83*
Prime Cable - Atlanta, GA - *Tel&CabFB 84C*
Prime Cable Corp. - Austin, TX - *BrCabYB 84 p.D-305; CabTVFinDB 83; LitMarPl 84; Tel&CabFB 84C p.1697*
Prime Cable of Marlboro - Marlboro, MA - *BrCabYB 84*
Prime Cable of Portland - Portland, TX - *BrCabYB 84; Tel&CabFB 84C*
Prime Computer Inc. - Natick, MA - *DataDirSup 7-83; Datamation 6-83; Top100Al 83*
Prime Computer Inc. - Wellesley, MA - *DirInfWP 82*
Prime Cuts Records - Lyndonville, VT - *BillIntBG 83-84*
Prime Factors - Oakland, CA - *MicrocomSwDir 1*
Prime National Publishing Corp. - Weston, MA - *BoPubDir 4, 5*
Prime Time Music - *See* Brown & Associates, J. Aaron
Prime Time Post - Los Angeles, CA - *AvMarPl 83*
Prime Time Records - Ferrum, VA - *BillIntBG 83-84*
Prime Time School Television - Chicago, IL - *Tel&CabFB 84C*
Prime Times - Brazil, IN - *AyerDirPub 83*
Prime Times [of Narcup Inc.] - Madison, WI - *WritMar 84*
Prime TV Films Inc. - New York, NY - *TelAl 83, 84; Tel&CabFB 84C*
Primedia Productions Ltd. - Toronto, ON, Canada - *Tel&CabFB 84C*
Primenet [of Prime Computer Inc.] - Natick, MA - *TeleSy&SerDir 7-83*
Primer Advertising Inc., Leonard - Chicago, IL - *StaDirAdAg 2-84*
Primer Press - Florence, AL - *LitMag&SmPr 83-84*
Primer Press - Stanford, CA - *BoPubDir 5*
Primer Publishers - Phoenix, AZ - *BoPubDir 4, 5; LitMag&SmPr 83-84*
Primero Records - San Antonio, TX - *BillIntBG 83-84*
Primesoft Corp. - Cabin John, MD - *MicrocomMPl 84*
Primetime Radio Classics - San Jose, CA - *DirOnDB Spring 84*
Primetime Television - New York, NY - *TelAl 84*
Primghar O'Brien County Bell - Primghar, IA - *BaconPubCkNews 84*
Primipara - Oconto, WI - *LitMag&SmPr 83-84*
Primrose Film Productions Ltd. - London, England - *Tel&CabFB 84C*
Primrose Press - Prescott, AZ - *BoPubDir 4, 5*
Prince Albert Daily Herald - Prince Albert, SK, Canada - *BaconPubCkNews 84; Ed&PubIntYB 82*
Prince Analysis Inc. - Washington, DC - *ADAPSOMemDir 83-84*
Prince Arthur Advertising - Toronto, ON, Canada - *StaDirAdAg 2-84*
Prince Associates Inc., Barbara - Colorado Springs, CO - *IntDirMarRes 83*
Prince County Cablevision Ltd. - Summerside, PE, Canada - *BrCabYB 84*
Prince Edward Island Heritage Foundation - Charlottetown, PE, Canada - *BoPubDir 4, 5*
Prince Frederick Calvert Independent - Prince Frederick, MD - *BaconPubCkNews 84*
Prince Frederick Recorder - Prince Frederick, MD - *NewsDir 84*
Prince Frederick Recorder - *See* Lexleon Inc.
Prince George Broadcasting Ltd. - Prince George, BC, Canada - *BrCabYB 84*
Prince George Telephone Co. - Disputanta, VA - *TelDir&BG 83-84*
Prince George's County Genealogical Society - Bowie, MD - *BoPubDir 4, 5*
Prince George's Journal - Washington, DC - *Ed&PubIntYB 82*
Prince George's Journal - College Park, MD - *AyerDirPub 83; NewsDir 84*
Prince George's Journal - Lanham, MD - *BaconPubCkNews 84*
Prince George's Post - Hyattsville, MD - *AyerDirPub 83; NewsDir 84*
Prince George's Sentinel - Hyattsville, MD - *AyerDirPub 83*
Prince George's Sentinel [of Rockville Sentinel Newspapers] - Rockville, MD - *NewsDir 84*
Prince Photography, Norman - San Francisco, CA - *AvMarPl 83; LitMarPl 83, 84*
Prince Video Enr. - Princeville, PQ, Canada - *BrCabYB 84*
Princess Anne Marylander & Herald - Princess Anne, MD - *BaconPubCkNews 84*
Princess Enterprises - Fredericton, NB, Canada - *BoPubDir 4, 5*
Princess Music Publishing Corp. - *See* Webman & Co., H. B.
Princess Productions Ltd. - Burbank, CA - *BillIntBG 83-84*
Princeton Advertising Co. - Princeton, NJ - *StaDirAdAg 2-84*
Princeton Alumni Weekly [of Princeton University Press] - Princeton, NJ - *WritMar 84*
Princeton Antiques Bookservice - Atlantic City, NJ - *ProGuPRSer 4*
Princeton Book Co. - Princeton, NJ - *LitMarPl 83, 84; WritMar 84*
Princeton Bureau County Republican - Princeton, IL - *BaconPubCkNews 84*
Princeton Cable TV - Princeton, IL - *BrCabYB 84; Tel&CabFB 84C*
Princeton Cablevision Inc. - Mercer, MO - *BrCabYB 84*
Princeton Cablevision Inc. - Princeton, MO - *BrCabYB 84*
Princeton Cablevision Inc. - Plainsboro, NJ - *BrCabYB 84*
Princeton Caldwell County Times - Princeton, KY - *BaconPubCkNews 84; NewsDir 84*
Princeton Clarion [of Princeton Newspapers Co. Inc.] - Princeton, IN - *BaconPubCkNews 84; Ed&PubIntYB 82; NewsDir 84*
Princeton Datafilm Inc. - Princeton Junction, NJ - *MagIndMarPl 82-83; MicroMarPl 82-83*
Princeton Electronic Products Inc. - North Brunswick, NJ - *DataDirSup 7-83*
Princeton Engineer [of Haskins Press Inc.] - Princeton, NJ - *BaconPubCkMag 84; MagDir 84*
Princeton Features - Princeton, NJ - *Ed&PubIntYB 82; LitMarPl 84*
Princeton Graphic Systems - Princeton, NJ - *MicrocomMPl 84*
Princeton Herald - Princeton, TX - *Ed&PubIntYB 82*
Princeton Language Group Inc., The - Kingston, NJ - *LitMarPl 83, 84*
Princeton Leader - Princeton, KY - *BaconPubCkNews 84; Ed&PubIntYB 82*
Princeton Love Romances - Morristown, NJ - *WritMar 84*
Princeton Microfilm Corp. - Princeton Junction, NJ - *LitMarPl 83, 84; MagIndMarPl 82-83; MicroMarPl 82-83*

Princeton Packet - Princeton, NJ - *BaconPubCkNews 84; Ed&PubIntYB 82; NewsDir 84*
Princeton Partners Inc. - Princeton, NJ - *DirMarMP 83*
Princeton Post-Telegraph - Princeton, MO - *BaconPubCkNews 84*
Princeton Publishing Co. [Aff. of Princeton Institute for Historic Research] - Princeton, NJ - *BoPubDir 4, 5*
Princeton Research Institute - Princeton, NJ - *BoPubDir 4, 5*
Princeton-Rutgers Census Data Project [of Princeton University] - Princeton, NJ - *EISS 83*
Princeton Similkameen Spotlight - Princeton, BC, Canada - *Ed&PubIntYB 82*
Princeton Spectrum [of Trenton Times] - Princeton, NJ - *AyerDirPub 83; NewsDir 84*
Princeton Telecable [of Telecable Corp.] - Princeton, WV - *BrCabYB 84; Tel&CabFB 84C*
Princeton Telephone Co. - Princeton, IN - *TelDir&BG 83-84*
Princeton Television Ltd. - Princeton, BC, Canada - *BrCabYB 84*
Princeton Times - Princeton, WV - *BaconPubCkNews 84; Ed&PubIntYB 82; NewsDir 84*
Princeton Times-Republic - Berlin, WI - *AyerDirPub 83*
Princeton Times-Republic - Princeton, WI - *Ed&PubIntYB 82*
Princeton Times-Republic - *See* Journal Co., The
Princeton Town Topics - Princeton, NJ - *BaconPubCkNews 84; Ed&PubIntYB 82; NewsDir 84*
Princeton Union-Eagle - Princeton, MN - *AyerDirPub 83; BaconPubCkNews 84; Ed&PubIntYB 82; NewsDir 84*
Princeton University (Art Museum) - Princeton, NJ - *BoPubDir 4, 5*
Princeton University (Center of International Studies) - Princeton, NJ - *BoPubDir 5*
Princeton University (Friends of the Library) - Princeton, NJ - *BoPubDir 4, 5*
Princeton University Press - Princeton, NJ - *LitMarPl 83, 84; WritMar 84*
Princeville Communications Co. [of Princeville Cablevision Inc.] - Hanalei, HI - *Tel&CabFB 84C*
Princeville Communications Co. - Princeville, HI - *BrCabYB 84*
Princeville Telephone - Princeville, IL - *AyerDirPub 83; Ed&PubIntYB 82*
Princeville Telephone - *See* News Publishing Co.
Principal - Arlington, VA - *MagIndMarPl 82-83*
Principal - Falls Church, VA - *MagDir 84*
Principal International Businesses [of Dun & Bradstreet International] - Parsippany, NJ - *DataDirOnSer 84*
Principal International Businesses [of Dun & Bradstreet International] - New York, NY - *EISS 7-83 Sup*
Principia Press - Chicago, IL - *BoPubDir 4, 5*
Principle Press [Aff. of T'ai] - Elmhurst, IL - *BoPubDir 4, 5*
Prineville Central Oregonian [of Eagle Newspapers Inc.] - Prineville, OR - *BaconPubCkNews 84; Ed&PubIntYB 82; NewsDir 84*
Pringle Dixon Pringle - Atlanta, GA - *AdAge 3-28-84; ArtMar 84; StaDirAdAg 2-84*
Pringle Dixon Pringle (Public Relations Div.) - Atlanta, GA - *DirPRFirms 83*
Pringle, Laurence - West Nyack, NY - *MagIndMarPl 82-83*
Pringle Music Publishers - Canoga Park, CA - *BillIntBG 83-84*
Prinit Press - Dublin, IN - *BoPubDir 4, 5*
Print - New York, NY - *BaconPubCkMag 84; LitMarPl 83, 84; MagDir 84*
Print & Press - Fredericton, NB, Canada - *BoPubDir 4 Sup, 5*
Print Animatic Tests - New York, NY - *IntDirMarRes 83*
Print-Equip News - Glendale, CA - *BaconPubCkMag 84; MagDir 84*
Print Measurement Bureau - Toronto, ON, Canada - *DataDirOnSer 84*
Print Media Services Ltd. - Elk Grove Village, IL - *BoPubDir 4, 5*
Print Music Co. Inc. - New York, NY - *BillIntBG 83-84*
Print-o-Stat Inc. - York, PA - *MagIndMarPl 82-83*
Printable Arts Society Inc., The - New York, NY - *LitMag&SmPr 83-84*
Printed Circuit Fabrication - Alpharetta, GA - *BaconPubCkMag 84*
Printed Editions - Barrytown, NY - *LitMag&SmPr 83-84; LitMarPl 83, 84*
Printed Horse - Ft. Collins, CO - *BoPubDir 4, 5*
Printed Matter [of Tokyo English Literature Society] - Tokyo, Japan - *LitMag&SmPr 83-84*
Printed Matter Inc. - New York, NY - *BoPubDir 4, 4 Sup, 5; LitMag&SmPr 83-84; LitMarPl 83, 84*
Printed Matter Publishing Co. Inc. - Arlington Heights, IL - *BoPubDir 5; LitMag&SmPr 83-84*
Printed Word Publishing - Houston, TX - *BoPubDir 5*
Printed Word Publishing - Tomball, TX - *BoPubDir 4*
Printek - Benton Harbor, MI - *DataDirSup 7-83; MicrocomMPl 84; WhoWMicrocom 83*
Printemps Books Inc. - Wilmette, IL - *WritMar 84*
Printer Products [Div. of Capitol Circuits Corp.] - Allston, MA - *MicrocomMPl 84*
Printer Terminal Communications Corp. - Ramona, CA - *DirInfWP 82; WhoWMicrocom 83*
Printer's Computer Services - Brea, CA - *MicrocomMPl 84*
Printers' Devil - Arlington, MA - *BoPubDir 4, 5*
Printer's Devil Press - Richmond Hill, ON, Canada - *BoPubDir 4, 5*
Printer's News - Lufkin, TX - *BaconPubCkMag 84; MagDir 84*
Printers Pie - Portree, Scotland - *LitMag&SmPr 83-84*
Printers Software Inc. - Pompton Plains, NJ - *WhoWMicrocom 83*
Printery - St. Louis, MO - *BoPubDir 4, 5*
Printing & Information Technology Div. [of Pira: Research Association for the Paper & Board, Printing & Packaging Industries] - Leatherhead, England - *EISS 7-83 Sup*
Printing & Publishing Book Club [Div. of North American Publishing] - Philadelphia, PA - *LitMarPl 83*
Printing by Yazge - Washington, DC - *MagIndMarPl 82-83*
Printing Impressions - Philadelphia, PA - *BaconPubCkMag 84; MagDir 84; MagIndMarPl 82-83*
Printing Journal - Mountain View, CA - *BaconPubCkMag 84; MagDir 84*
Printing News - New York, NY - *BaconPubCkMag 84; LitMarPl 84; MagDir 84; MagIndMarPl 82-83*
Printing Paper Quarterly - Westfield, MA - *MagIndMarPl 82-83*
Printing Views - Skokie, IL - *BaconPubCkMag 84; MagDir 84; WritMar 84*
Printmakers, The - Studio City, CA - *ArtMar 84*
Print'n Press Publications - St. Stephen, NB, Canada - *BoPubDir 4 Sup; LitMarPl 83*
PrintNet - Arlington, VA - *DirOnDB Spring 84*
Printout - Newtonville, MA - *BaconPubCkMag 84*
Printronix Inc. - Irvine, CA - *DataDirSup 7-83; Datamation 6-83; MicrocomMPl 84; Top100Al 83; WhoWMicrocom 83*
Printup & Associates/Marketing Inc. - Honolulu, HI - *StaDirAdAg 2-84*
Prion Instruments - Woodside, CA - *MicrocomMPl 84*
Prior Lake American - Prior Lake, MN - *AyerDirPub 83; BaconPubCkNews 84; Ed&PubIntYB 82*
Priority Music - Nashville, TN - *BillIntBG 83-84*
Priority 1 Electronics - Chatsworth, CA - *MicrocomMPl 84*
Priority Plus Corp. - Garden Grove, CA - *DataDirSup 7-83*
Priour TV Cable, J. W. Jr. - Ingram, TX - *BrCabYB 84 p.D-305; Tel&CabFB 84C p.1698*
Prise de Parole Inc. - Sudbury, ON, Canada - *BoPubDir 4, 5*
Prism - Ft. Lauderdale, FL - *BaconPubCkMag 84*
Prism - Bala Cynwyd, PA - *BrCabYB 84; CabTVPrDB 83; Tel&CabFB 84C*
Prism [of Spectator & Chroma Enterprises] - Philadelphia, PA - *HomeVid&CabYB 82-83; TelAl 83*
PRISM - *See* Doremus & Co.
Prism Books - Sydney, Australia - *LitMag&SmPr 83-84*
Prism Corp., The - Washington, DC - *IntDirMarRes 83*
Prism International - Vancouver, BC, Canada - *LitMag&SmPr 83-84; WritMar 84*
Prism Management Systems Inc. - Dallas, TX - *ADAPSOMemDir 83-84*
Prism Press - Houston, TX - *BoPubDir 4, 5; LitMag&SmPr 83-84*
Prism Productions - Dallas, TX - *AvMarPl 83*
Prism Records Inc. - New York, NY - *BillIntBG 83-84*
Prismatic Music Publishing - *See* Spier Inc., Larry
Prison Arts Project [Aff. of William James Association] - Santa Cruz, CA - *BoPubDir 4 Sup, 5*
Pritchett Publications - Palmdale, CA - *BillIntBG 83-84*
Pritzker, Deborah - Bronx, NY - *LitMarPl 83, 84*

Privacy Journal - Washington, DC - *BoPubDir 4, 5; LitMag&SmPr 83-84*
Private Cable - Littleton, CO - *BaconPubCkMag 84*
Private Carrier, The - Washington, DC - *BaconPubCkMag 84; MagDir 84*
Private Enterprise - Troy, MI - *BoPubDir 4, 5*
Private Islands Unltd. - Granada Hills, CA - *BoPubDir 4, 5*
Private Label - New York, NY - *BaconPubCkMag 84; WritMar 84*
Private Line Service [of ITT World Communications Inc.] - New York, NY - *TeleSy&SerDir 7-83*
Private Local Area Network [of Racal-Milgo Information Systems] - Plantation, FL - *TeleSy&SerDir 2-84*
Private Networks Inc. - Pasadena, MD - *Tel&CabFB 84C*
Private Pilot [of Macro/Comm Corp.] - San Clemente, CA - *ArtMar 84; BaconPubCkMag 84; MagDir 84; MagIndMarPl 82-83; WritMar 84*
Private Placements [of Securities Data Co.] - New York, NY - *DataDirOnSer 84; DBBus 82; DirOnDB Spring 84*
Private Practice - Oklahoma City, OK - *ArtMar 84; BaconPubCkMag 84; MagDir 84; MagIndMarPl 82-83; WritMar 84*
Private Press of Emily Woodward - San Anselmo, CA - *BoPubDir 4, 5*
Private Press of John Cumming - Mt. Pleasant, MI - *BoPubDir 4, 5*
Private Satellite Television Inc. - Charlotte, NC - *Tel&CabFB 84C*
Private Screenings [of Satori Productions Inc.] - New York, NY - *AvMarPl 83; BrCabYB 84; CabTVPrDB 83; HomeVid&CabYB 82-83; Tel&CabFB 84C*
Private System Services [of Overseas Telecommunications Commission] - Sydney, Australia - *TeleSy&SerDir 2-84*
Private Telecommunications Systems Service [of Radio-Suisse Ltd.] - Berne, Switzerland - *TeleSy&SerDir 7-83*
Privilege [of Associated BankCard Holders] - Cherry Hill, NJ - *BaconPubCkMag 84; WritMar 84*
Prizm - New York, NY - *HBIndAd&MS 82-83*
Prizm Computer Products Inc. - Northbrook, IL - *MicrocomMPl 84*
PRM/Communications - Studio City, CA - *DirMarMP 83; DirPRFirms 83*
Pro! - Los Angeles, CA - *BaconPubCkMag 84; MagDir 84*
Pro Bass [of National Reporter Publishing Co.] - Bixby, OK - *BaconPubCkMag 84; WritMar 84*
Pro Bike News - Washington, DC - *BaconPubCkMag 84*
Pro Clinica - New York, NY - *StaDirAdAg 2-84*
Pro Com Systems [Div. of Audio Innovators Inc.] - Pittsburgh, PA - *AvMarPl 83*
Pro/Comm - Austin, TX - *BaconPubCkMag 84; MagDir 84; WritMar 84*
Pro Data Systems Inc. - San Carlos, CA - *WhoWMicrocom 83*
Pro-Ed - Austin, TX - *BoPubDir 4; LitMarPl 83, 84*
Pro-80-Systems - Cedar Falls, IA - *MicrocomMPl 83, 84*
Pro-Files - Solana Beach, CA - *BaconPubCkMag 84*
Pro Football Weekly - Chicago, IL - *BaconPubCkMag 84; MagDir 84; MagIndMarPl 82-83*
Pro-Indie Records - Phoenix, AZ - *BillIntBG 83-84*
Pro Lab, The - Denver, CO - *AvMarPl 83*
Pro Libris Press [Aff. of Pro Libris Bookshop] - Bangor, ME - *BoPubDir 5*
Pro-Log Corp. - Monterey, CA - *DataDirSup 7-83*
Pro Media Inc. - Natick, MA - *StaDirAdAg 2-84*
Pro Micro Systems - Poway, CA - *MicrocomMPl 84*
PRO/PAC Inc. - Houston, TX - *MicrocomMPl 84; WhoWMicrocom 83*
Pro Photo Lab Inc. - Oklahoma City, OK - *AvMarPl 83*
Pro/Press Publishing Co. - San Jose, CA - *LitMag&SmPr 83-84*
PRO Sound News - Carle Place, NY - *WritMar 84*
Pro Sports Network - San Diego, CA - *BrCabYB 84*
Pro/Tem Software Inc. - Stanford, CA - *MicrocomMPl 84*
Pro-2 Records - Conshohocken, PA - *BillIntBG 83-84*
Pro Video - Salt Lake City, UT - *BrCabYB 84*
Pro Visual Research Corp. - Ocean, NJ - *AvMarPl 83*
Pro West - Paradise Valley, AZ - *BoPubDir 4, 5*
ProActive Press - Berkeley, CA - *BoPubDir 4, 5; LitMag&SmPr 83-84*
ProActive Systems - Palo Alto, CA - *MicrocomMPl 83, 84; MicrocomSwDir 1*
Probe [of Arthur D. Little Inc.] - Cambridge, MA - *EISS 83*
Probe [of Baptist Brotherhood Commission] - Memphis, TN - *ArtMar 84; WritMar 84*
PROBE - *See* ACCESS
Probe Economics Inc. - Mt. Kisco, NY - *DataDirOnSer 84*
Probe International Inc. - Stamford, CT - *BoPubDir 5*
Probe Research - Dallas, TX - *IntDirMarRes 83*
Probe Research Inc. - Morristown, NJ - *TeleSy&SerDir 2-84*
Probity - New Lenox, IL - *MicrocomMPl 84*
Problem Solvers - Burnsville, MN - *WhoWMicrocom 83*
Problems of Communism - Washington, DC - *WritMar 84*
Proceedings of the Entomological Society of Washington - Washington, DC - *MagDir 84*
Proceedings of the IEEE [of Institute of Electrical & Electronics Engineers] - New York, NY - *BaconPubCkMag 84; MagDir 84*
Proceedings of the Society for Experimental Biology - New York, NY - *MagDir 84*
Process Communications - Bridgehampton, NY - *AvMarPl 83*
Process Control Systems Inc. - Brookfield, WI - *WhoWMicrocom 83*
Process Control Technology - Stockton, CA - *MicrocomMPl 84*
Process Displays Inc. - New Berlin, WI - *LitMarPl 83, 84; MagIndMarPl 82-83*
Process Materials Corp. [Subs. of Lindenmeyr] - Rutherford, NJ - *LitMarPl 83, 84*
Process Music Publications - *See* Country Star Music
Processed Prepared Foods [of Gorman Publishing Co.] - Chicago, IL - *BaconPubCkMag 84; MagDir 84; MagIndMarPl 82-83*
Processing Supply Co. - Schaumburg, IL - *DirInfWP 82*
Processor, The [of Peed Publishing Inc.] - Webster City, IA - *MicrocomMPl 84*
Proclamation Productions Inc. - Port Jervis, NY - *BillIntBG 83-84*
Procom Systems Inc. [Subs. of Professional Geophysics Inc.] - Dallas, TX - *WhoWMicrocom 83*
Procreations Publishing Co. - New Orleans, LA - *ArtMar 84*
Proctor & Gardner Advertising Inc. - Chicago, IL - *StaDirAdAg 2-84*
Proctor Journal - Proctor, MN - *BaconPubCkNews 84; Ed&PubIntYB 82*
Proctorsville & Cavendish TV Cable - Proctorsville, VT - *BrCabYB 84*
Prodata Inc. - Boise, ID - *MicrocomMPl 84*
Prodata Inc. - Albuquerque, NM - *MicrocomMPl 83, 84; WhoWMicrocom 83*
Prodata Inc. - Hickory, NC - *MicrocomMPl 84*
Prodata Systems Inc. - Seattle, WA - *ADAPSOMemDir 83-84; DataDirOnSer 84*
Prodigy Systems - Iselin, NJ - *DataDirSup 7-83; MicrocomMPl 83, 84; WhoWMicrocom 83*
Produce Marketing Association - Newark, DE - *BoPubDir 5*
Produce News, The - Englewood Cliffs, NJ - *MagDir 84*
Produce News, The - Ft. Lee, NJ - *BaconPubCkMag 84; WritMar 84*
Produce Reporter Co. - Wheaton, IL - *BoPubDir 5*
Producer - Seminole, OK - *AyerDirPub 83*
Producer Price Index by Commodity [of Chase Econometrics/Interactive Data Corp.] - Waltham, MA - *DataDirOnSer 84*
Producer Price Index by Industry [of Chase Econometrics/Interactive Data Corp.] - Waltham, MA - *DataDirOnSer 84*
Producer Price Index Database [of Evans Economics Inc.] - Washington, DC - *DataDirOnSer 84; DirOnDB Spring 84*
Producer Price Indexes [of Wharton Econometric Forecasting Associates] - Philadelphia, PA - *DataDirOnSer 84*
Producer Services Group Inc. - Brookline, MA - *Tel&CabFB 84C*
Producers Color Service Inc. - Southfield, MI - *AvMarPl 83*
Producers Group Ltd. - Chicago, IL - *AvMarPl 83*
Producers Inc., The - Phoenix, AZ - *AvMarPl 83*
Producers Studio Inc. - Hollywood, CA - *Tel&CabFB 84C*
Product Acceptance & Research Inc. - Evansville, IN - *IntDirMarRes 83*
Product Alert [of Marketing Intelligence Service] - Naples, NY - *BaconPubCkMag 84; MagDir 84*
Product & Consumer Evaluations Inc. - Farmington Hills, MI - *IntDirMarRes 83*

Product Associates Inc. - Redwood City, CA - *WhoWMicrocom 83*
Product Design & Development [of Chilton Co.] - Radnor, PA - *BaconPubCkMag 84; Folio 83; MagIndMarPl 82-83*
Product Information Network [of McGraw-Hill Information Systems Co.] - New York, NY - *EISS 83*
Product Marketing/Cosmetic & Fragrance Retailing [of Charleson Publications] - New York, NY - *BaconPubCkMag 84; MagDir 84; MagIndMarPl 82-83*
Product Safety Letter - Washington, DC - *MagIndMarPl 82-83*
Production - Bloomfield Hills, MI - *BaconPubCkMag 84; MagDir 84; MagIndMarPl 82-83*
Production & Inventory Management Review - Hollywood, FL - *BaconPubCkMag 84*
Production & Programming Associates - Dallas, TX - *BrCabYB 84*
Production Data On-Line - Littleton, CO - *DirOnDB Spring 84*
Production Data Systems - Sacramento, CA - *MicrocomMPl 84*
Production Database [of Petroleum Information Corp.] - Denver, CO - *DataDirOnSer 84*
Production Engineering - Cleveland, OH - *BaconPubCkMag 84; MagDir 84; MagIndMarPl 82-83; WritMar 84*
Production House Corp. - San Diego, CA - *BoPubDir 4, 5*
Production House, The - Sarasota, FL - *Tel&CabFB 84C*
Production Publishing Co. - Nashville, TN - *BoPubDir 5*
Production Systems for Architects & Engineers [Subs. of The American Institute of Architects Services Corp.] - Washington, DC - *DataDirOnSer 84*
Productive Computer Systems - Chicago, IL - *MicrocomMPl 84; MicrocomSwDir 1; WhoWMicrocom 83*
Productivity Improvement Bulletin - Waterford, CT - *WritMar 84*
Productivity Specialists Inc. - Hoffman Estates, IL - *DataDirOnSer 84*
Products Finishing - Brooklyn, NY - *AvMarPl 83*
Products Finishing - Cincinnati, OH - *BaconPubCkMag 84; MagDir 84; WritMar 84*
Produits Pour l'Industrie Quebecoise - Pointe Claire, PQ, Canada - *BaconPubCkMag 84*
Professional Abstracts Registries [of Database Innovations Inc.] - Ossining, NY - *EISS 83*
Professional Agent - Alexandria, VA - *ArtMar 84; BaconPubCkMag 84; MagDir 84; MagIndMarPl 82-83; WritMar 84*
Professional Audio-Visual [Div. of PSI] - Merrifield, VA - *AvMarPl 83*
Professional Book Distributors Inc. - Columbus, OH - *LitMarPl 83, 84*
Professional Books [Aff. of Fairchild Publications] - Jackson, TN - *BoPubDir 4, 5*
Professional Books Service - Dayton, OH - *BoPubDir 4, 5*
Professional Broadcast Productions - Tampa, FL - *AvMarPl 83*
Professional Builder/Apartment Business - Chicago, IL - *MagIndMarPl 82-83*
Professional Builder/Apartment Business [of Cahners Publishing Co. Inc.] - Des Plaines, IL - *BaconPubCkMag 84; Folio 83; MagDir 84*
Professional Business Software - San Francisco, CA - *MicrocomMPl 83; WhoWMicrocom 83*
Professional Camera Repair Service - New York, NY - *AvMarPl 83*
Professional Chef Book Guild [of CBI Publishing Co. Inc.] - Boston, MA - *LitMarPl 83*
Professional Chef Book Guild [Div. of Van Nostrand Reinhold Co. Inc.] - New York, NY - *LitMarPl 84*
Professional Civil Engineering Book Club [of Macmillan Book Clubs Inc.] - New York, NY - *LitMarPl 83, 84*
Professional Color Service - Minneapolis, MN - *AvMarPl 83*
Professional Composition Inc. - East Lansing, MI - *LitMarPl 84*
Professional Computer Store - La Crescenta, CA - *WhoWMicrocom 83*
Professional Computer Systems - Bloomingdale, IL - *WhoWMicrocom 83*
Professional Data Corp. - Columbia, SC - *MicrocomMPl 84; MicrocomSwDir 1*
Professional Data Management - Scottsdale, AZ - *MicrocomMPl 84*
Professional Data Services Inc. - Barberton, OH - *ADAPSOMemDir 83-84*
Professional Development Press - San Diego, CA - *LitMag&SmPr 83-84*
Professional Drug Systems Inc. [Subs. of Medicare-Glaser Corp.] - St. Louis, MO - *DataDirOnSer 84*
Professional Editing & Typing Co. & Literary Agency - New York, NY - *LitMarPl 83, 84; MagIndMarPl 82-83*
Professional Editorial Services - Kent, OH - *LitMarPl 83, 84*
Professional Education Systems Inc. - Eau Claire, WI - *DirMarMP 83*
Professional Electronics [of National Electronic Service Dealers Association] - Ft. Worth, TX - *ArtMar 84; BaconPubCkMag 84; MagDir 84*
Professional Engineer [of National Society of Professional Engineers] - Washington, DC - *BaconPubCkMag 84; MagDir 84; MagIndMarPl 82-83*
Professional Engineer, The - Raleigh, NC - *BaconPubCkMag 84*
Professional Field Service - Levittown, NY - *IntDirMarRes 83*
Professional Floral Designer - Costa Mesa, CA - *BaconPubCkMag 84*
Professional Furniture Merchant [of Gralla Publications] - New York, NY - *MagDir 84; MagIndMarPl 82-83*
Professional Furniture Merchant Magazine - Coral Springs, FL - *WritMar 84*
Professional Geographer, The - Washington, DC - *MagDir 84*
Professional Golf Association [of CompuServe Inc.] - Columbus, OH - *DataDirOnSer 84*
Professional Graphics - Corte Madera, CA - *ArtMar 84*
Professional Hospital Services [Subs. of American Medical International] - Los Angeles, CA - *DataDirOnSer 84*
Professional Indexing [Div. of Southern Professional Group] - Cartersville, GA - *LitMarPl 83, 84*
Professional Insurance Agent - Glenmont, NY - *BaconPubCkMag 84*
Professional List Services - Cleveland, OH - *MagIndMarPl 82-83*
Professional Management Services - Palo Alto, CA - *MicrocomSwDir 1*
Professional Marketing & Advertising Services Inc. - Detroit, MI - *DirMarMP 83*
Professional Marketing Communications Inc. - Dayton, OH - *DirMarMP 83*
Professional Marketing Group - Los Angeles, CA - *AdAge 3-28-84; StaDirAdAg 2-84*
Professional Mechanical Engineering Book Club [of Macmillan Book Clubs Inc.] - New York, NY - *LitMarPl 83, 84*
Professional Media Services - Cupertino, CA - *LitMarPl 83, 84; MagIndMarPl 82-83*
Professional Medical Assistant, The - Chicago, IL - *BaconPubCkMag 84; MagDir 84; MagIndMarPl 82-83*
Professional Medical Software - La Canada, CA - *WhoWMicrocom 83*
Professional Medical Software - La Crescenta, CA - *MicrocomMPl 83; WhoWMicrocom 83*
Professional Microwave - Highland Park, IL - *MicrocomMPl 84*
Professional Music Productions Inc. - Tustin, CA - *BillIntBG 83-84*
Professional Office Data Management - Minneapolis, MN - *WhoWMicrocom 83*
Professional Photographer, The - Des Plaines, IL - *ArtMar 84; BaconPubCkMag 84; MagDir 84; MagIndMarPl 82-83*
Professional Photographic Products - Hammonton, NJ - *AvMarPl 83*
Professional Pilot - Washington, DC - *BaconPubCkMag 84; MagDir 84*
Professional Placement Center [Subs. of New York State Employment Service] - New York, NY - *InfIndMarPl 83; LitMarPl 83, 84*
Professional Press [Aff. of Fairchild Publications] - Chicago, IL - *BoPubDir 4, 5; MagIndMarPl 82-83*
Professional Publications Inc. - San Carlos, CA - *LitMarPl 83, 84; MicrocomMPl 84*
Professional Publishing - Chicago, IL - *BaconPubCkMag 84*
Professional Remodeling [of Harcourt Brace Jovanovich] - Cleveland, OH - *BaconPubCkMag 84; MagDir 84*
Professional Research Inc. - Evanston, IL - *AvMarPl 83*

Professional Research Organization Inc. - Little Rock, AR - *IntDirMarRes 83*
Professional Research Services Inc. - Tempe, AZ - *BrCabYB 84*
Professional Safety - Park Ridge, IL - *BaconPubCkMag 84; MagDir 84; MagIndMarPl 82-83*
Professional Sanitation Management - Largo, FL - *BaconPubCkMag 84; MagDir 84*
Professional Selling - Waterford, CT - *WritMar 84*
Professional Software Associates - Minneapolis, MN - *MicrocomMPl 84; MicrocomSwDir 1*
Professional Software Inc. - Needham, MA - *MicrocomMPl 83; WhoWMicrocom 83*
Professional Software Systems - Costa Mesa, CA - *MicrocomMPl 84*
Professional Surveyor - Washington, DC - *BaconPubCkMag 84*
Professional Systems Corp. - Torrance, CA - *MicrocomMPl 84; MicrocomSwDir 1; WhoWMicrocom 83*
Professional Systems Corp. - Montclair, NJ - *ADAPSOMemDir 83-84*
Professional Tape Co. - Burr Ridge, IL - *AvMarPl 83*
Professional Toolbox Inc. - Houston, TX - *MicrocomMPl 84*
Professional Translators - Portland, OR - *MagIndMarPl 82-83*
Professional True Color Photo - Brooklyn, NY - *AvMarPl 83*
Professional Typing Service - Evansville, IN - *LitMarPl 83, 84*
Professor, The - Swanton, VT - *MicrocomSwDir 1*
Proffitt & Associates Inc. - Orinda, CA - *MicrocomMPl 84*
Proficiency Examination Review - St. Louis, MO - *BoPubDir 5*
Profile - Chicago, IL - *LitMag&SmPr 83-84*
Profile Marketing Research - Palm Beach Gardens, FL - *IntDirMarRes 83*
Profile Press - New York, NY - *LitMarPl 83, 84*
Profile Records Inc. - New York, NY - *BillIntBG 83-84*
Profimatics Inc. - Thousand Oaks, CA - *ADAPSOMemDir 83-84*
Profit Ideas [Aff. of George Sterne Agency] - San Diego, CA - *BoPubDir 4 Sup, 5*
Profit Improvement Consultants Inc. - New York, NY - *StaDirAdAg 2-84*
Profit Index Systems Inc. - Los Angeles, CA - *HBIndAd&MS 82-83*
Profit Press Inc. - New York, NY - *BoPubDir 4, 5*
Profit Sharing Council of Canada - Rexdale, ON, Canada - *BoPubDir 4 Sup, 5*
Profit Sharing Research Foundation - Evanston, IL - *BoPubDir 4, 5*
Profit Systems Inc. - Berkley, MI - *MicrocomMPl 84*
Profitable Craft Merchandising - Peoria, IL - *ArtMar 84; BaconPubCkMag 84; MagDir 84; MagIndMarPl 82-83*
Profitool Inc. - Denver, CO - *DataDirOnSer 84; DataDirSup 7-83*
Profitunities/Better Buys - New York, NY - *BaconPubCkMag 84*
Proforma Software [Div. of LTS Corp.] - Costa Mesa, CA - *MicrocomMPl 84*
Progmatic Designs Inc. - Sunnyvale, CA - *WhoWMicrocom 83*
Prognos AG [of European Center for Applied Economic Research] - Basel, Switzerland - *DirOnDB Spring 84; IntDirMarRes 83*
Program Counsel - Chicago, IL - *BoPubDir 4*
Program Design Inc. - Greenwich, CT - *MicrocomMPl 83, 84; WhoWMicrocom 83*
Program for Cincinnati - Cincinnati, OH - *BoPubDir 5*
Program Guide - Toronto, ON, Canada - *BaconPubCkMag 84*
Program House Productions - Kinnelon, NJ - *AvMarPl 83*
Program Information System [of Informationszentrum Sozialwissenschaften] - Bonn, West Germany - *CompReadDB 82*
Program Innovations - Lumberton, NC - *MicrocomMPl 83, 84*
Program Management Systems - Washington, DC - *CabTVFinDB 83*
Program Store, The [Subs. of Computer Cablevision Inc.] - Washington, DC - *WhoWMicrocom 83*
Program Syndication Services Inc. - New York, NY - *TelAl 83, 84; Tel&CabFB 84C*
Programart Corp. - Cambridge, MA - *DataDirSup 7-83*
Programma International - Burbank, CA - *DirInfWP 82*
Programme de Recherche sur l'Amiante [of Universite de Sherbrooke] - Sherbrooke, PQ, Canada - *CompReadDB 82*
Programme on Exchange & Transfer of Information on Community Water Supply & .... [of World Health Organization] - Rijswijk, Netherlands - *EISS 83*
Programmed Press - Elmont, NY - *BoPubDir 4, 5; LitMag&SmPr 83-84; MicrocomMPl 84*
Programmer's Institute - Chapel Hill, NC - *MicrocomMPl 83, 84*
Programmer's Shop, The - Dedham, MA - *EISS 5-84 Sup*
Programmers Software - Cabot, AR - *MicrocomMPl 83, 84*
Programming & Systems Management Inc. - Dayton, OH - *MicrocomMPl 83, 84*
Programming Enterprises Inc. - Marina del Rey, CA - *ADAPSOMemDir 83-84*
Programming Services & Support Inc. - LaCrosse, WI - *ADAPSOMemDir 83-84*
Programming Shop, The - San Jose, CA - *MicrocomSwDir 1; WhoWMicrocom 83*
Programs & Analysis Inc. - Burlington, MA - *DataDirOnSer 84; DataDirSup 7-83*
Programs & Publications - Philadelphia, PA - *BoPubDir 4, 5*
Programs for Achievement in Reading - Providence, RI - *BoPubDir 4, 5*
Programs for Learning Inc. - New Milford, CT - *MicrocomMPl 83, 84; WhoWMicrocom 83*
Programs in Communication Press - Boulder, CO - *BoPubDir 4*
Programs in Communication Press - Monument, CO - *BoPubDir 5*
Programs on Change - New York, NY - *BoPubDir 4, 5*
Programs Software - Columbus, OH - *MicrocomMPl 84*
Programs Unltd. - Jericho, NY - *MicrocomMPl 83*
Progresiv Publishr - Chicago, IL - *BoPubDir 4, 5; LitMag&SmPr 83-84*
Progress - Ashland, AL - *AyerDirPub 83*
Progress - Prattville, AL - *AyerDirPub 83*
Progress - Scottsdale, AZ - *AyerDirPub 83*
Progress - Wynne, AR - *AyerDirPub 83*
Progress - Monterey Park, CA - *AyerDirPub 83*
Progress - Perris, CA - *AyerDirPub 83*
Progress - Sandersville, GA - *AyerDirPub 83*
Progress - O'Fallon, IL - *AyerDirPub 83*
Progress - Diagonal, IA - *AyerDirPub 83*
Progress - Dawson Springs, KY - *AyerDirPub 83*
Progress - Framingham, MA - *MagDir 84*
Progress - Wanamingo, MN - *AyerDirPub 83*
Progress - Leland, MS - *AyerDirPub 83*
Progress - Pontotoc, MS - *AyerDirPub 83*
Progress - Holden, MO - *AyerDirPub 83*
Progress - Polk, NE - *AyerDirPub 83*
Progress - Caldwell, NJ - *AyerDirPub 83; Ed&PubIntYB 82; NewsDir 84*
Progress - Paulding, OH - *AyerDirPub 83*
Progress - Claremore, OK - *AyerDirPub 83*
Progress - Clearfield, PA - *AyerDirPub 83; BaconPubCkNews 84; Ed&PubIntYB 82*
Progress - Horsham, PA - *AyerDirPub 83; Ed&PubIntYB 82*
Progress - Easley, SC - *AyerDirPub 83*
Progress - Lexington, TN - *AyerDirPub 83*
Progress - Aransas Pass, TX - *AyerDirPub 83*
Progress - Deer Park, TX - *AyerDirPub 83*
Progress - Gorman, TX - *AyerDirPub 83*
Progress - Jacksonville, TX - *AyerDirPub 83*
Progress - Mt. Enterprise, TX - *AyerDirPub 83*
Progress - Charlottesville, VA - *AyerDirPub 83*
Progress - Chilliwack, BC, Canada - *AyerDirPub 83*
Progress - Atikokan, ON, Canada - *AyerDirPub 83*
Progress - Meadow Lake, SK, Canada - *AyerDirPub 83*
Progress-Advance - Pigeon, MI - *AyerDirPub 83; Ed&PubIntYB 82*
Progress-Argus - Jackson, GA - *AyerDirPub 83*
Progress Bulletin [of Donrey Media Group] - Pomona, CA - *AyerDirPub 83; Ed&PubIntYB 82; LitMarPl 84*
Progress-Dimanche - Chicoutimi, PQ, Canada - *Ed&PubIntYB 82*
Progress-Enterprise - Lunenberg, NS, Canada - *Ed&PubIntYB 82*
Progress-Enterprise - Lunenburg, NS, Canada - *AyerDirPub 83*
Progress-Examiner - Orleans, IN - *AyerDirPub 83; Ed&PubIntYB 82*
Progress in Cardiovascular Diseases - New York, NY - *BaconPubCkMag 84; MagDir 84*
Progress-Index - Petersburg, VA - *AyerDirPub 83; Ed&PubIntYB 82*
Progress Industries Inc. - Huntington Beach, CA - *AvMarPl 83*
Progress-Item - Ellisville, MS - *AyerDirPub 83; Ed&PubIntYB 82*

Progress News - Emlenton, PA - *AyerDirPub 83*
Progress/News Advertiser - Rutland, BC, Canada - *Ed&PubIntYB 82*
Progress Newspapers Inc. - Horsham, PA - *BaconPubCkNews 84*
Progress Publications Inc. - Maple Shade, NJ - *BaconPubCkNews 84*
Progress-Reporter - Momence, IL - *AyerDirPub 83*
Progress Review - La Porte City, IA - *AyerDirPub 83; Ed&PubIntYB 82*
Progress, The - Christopher, IL - *AyerDirPub 83; Ed&PubIntYB 82*
Progress, The - Wells, NV - *AyerDirPub 83*
Progress, The [of Dardanell Publications Inc.] - Monroeville, PA - *AyerDirPub 83; NewsDir 84*
Progress, The - Pen Hills, PA - *Ed&PubIntYB 82*
Progress, The [of Liberty Newspapers Inc.] - Anahuac, TX - *AyerDirPub 83; NewsDir 84*
Progress, The - Three Rivers, TX - *AyerDirPub 83; Ed&PubIntYB 82*
Progressive Architecture [of Reinhold Publishing] - Stamford, CT - *BaconPubCkMag 84; Folio 83; MagDir 84; MagIndMarPl 82-83; WritMar 84*
Progressive Communications Inc. - Burdett, KS - *Tel&CabFB 84C p.1698*
Progressive Concepts Inc. - Chesapeake, VA - *BoPubDir 5*
Progressive Data Services - Winchester, IN - *MicrocomMPl 84*
Progressive Education - Nashville, TN - *BoPubDir 5; LitMag&SmPr 83-84*
Progressive Farmer - Birmingham, AL - *MagDir 84; MagIndMarPl 82-83*
Progressive Farmer - Dallas, TX - *MagDir 84*
Progressive Farmer (Delta Report) - Memphis, TN - *BaconPubCkMag 84*
Progressive Farmer (Kentucky-Tennessee Edition) - Memphis, TN - *BaconPubCkMag 84*
Progressive Farmer (Mid-South Edition) - Memphis, TN - *BaconPubCkMag 84*
Progressive Farmer (Southeast Edition) - Tifton, GA - *BaconPubCkMag 84*
Progressive Farmer (Southwest Edition) - Dallas, TX - *BaconPubCkMag 84*
Progressive Farmer (Upper South Edition) - Raleigh, NC - *BaconPubCkMag 84*
Progressive Foundation Inc. - Madison, WI - *BoPubDir 5*
Progressive Grocer - Stamford, CT - *BaconPubCkMag 84; BoPubDir 5; MagDir 84*
Progressive Grocer - New York, NY - *BoPubDir 4; Folio 83; MagIndMarPl 82-83; NewsBur 6*
Progressive Grocer Publishing Co. - New York, NY - *InfIndMarPl 83*
Progressive Mail Trade - Springfield, IL - *MagDir 84*
Progressive Management - St. Louis, MO - *BaconPubCkMag 84*
Progressive Management Services Inc. - Minneapolis, MN - *DataDirOnSer 84*
Progressive Periodical Directories - Nashville, TN - *BoPubDir 5*
Progressive Publishing Co. - Clearfield, PA - *BrCabYB 84*
Progressive Radio Network - New York, NY - *BrCabYB 84*
Progressive Railroading - Chicago, IL - *BaconPubCkMag 84; MagDir 84*
Progressive Records Inc. - Tifton, GA - *BillIntBG 83-84*
Progressive Rural Telephone Cooperative Inc. - Rentz, GA - *TelDir&BG 83-84*
Progressive Teacher, The - Augusta, GA - *MagDir 84*
Progressive Technologies Co. - Aspen, CO - *Tel&CabFB 84C*
Progressive, The - Madison, WI - *ArtMar 84; LitMarPl 83, 84; MagDir 84; MagIndMarPl 82-83; WritMar 84*
Progressive Typographers Inc. - Emigsville, PA - *LitMarPl 83, 84; MagIndMarPl 82-83*
Progressor Times, The - Carey, OH - *AyerDirPub 83; Ed&PubIntYB 82*
PROGRIS Projektgruppe Informationssystem GmbH - Berlin, West Germany - *InfIndMarPl 83*
Proini Greek-American Newspaper [of Petallides Publishing Co. Inc.] - New York, NY - *WritMar 84*
Project Bait Publishing - Detroit, MI - *BoPubDir 4, 5*
Project Communications Co. Inc. - Chicago, IL - *DirPRFirms 83*
Project Fair [of Medical Research Council] - Harrow, England - *EISS 83*
Project Films Inc. - Beverly Hills, CA - *AvMarPl 83*
Project for Integrated Catalogue Automation [of Consortium of Royal Library & University Libraries] - The Hauge, Netherlands - *EISS 83*
Project Green Thumb [of University of Kentucky] - Lexington, KY - *EISS 83*
Project Hermes [of Dept. of Trade & Industry] - London, England - *TeleSy&SerDir 2-84*
Project IDA [of Manitoba Telephone System] - Winnipeg, MB, Canada - *EISS 83*
Project Infoe [of University of Tennesee, Knoxville] - Knoxville, TN - *EISS 83*
Project IRIS [of Canadian Broadcasting Corp.] - Ottawa, ON, Canada - *EISS 5-84 Sup; TeleSy&SerDir 2-84*
Project Mutual Telephone Cooperative Association - Rupert, ID - *TelDir&BG 83-84*
Project Publishing & Design Inc. - Oakhurst, CA - *LitMarPl 83, 84*
Project Publishing & Design Inc. - Santa Monica, CA - *MagIndMarPl 82-83*
Project Share [of U.S. Dept. of Health & Human Services] - Rockville, MD - *EISS 83*
Project Smart [of Cornell University] - Ithaca, NY - *EISS 83*
Project Talent Data Bank [of American Institutes for Research] - Palo Alto, CA - *EISS 83; InfIndMarPl 83*
Project Telephone Co. Inc. - Worden, MT - *TelDir&BG 83-84*
Project 3 Records - New York, NY - *BillIntBG 83-84*
Project Videotex of Telesp [of Telecommunicacoes de Sao Paulo SA] - Sao Paulo, Brazil - *VideoDir 82-83*
Projected Learning Programs Inc. - Chico, CA - *AvMarPl 83*
Projection Optics Co. - Florham Park, NJ - *AvMarPl 83*
Projection Systems International - New York, NY - *AvMarPl 83*
Projections - Keene, NH - *IntDirMarRes 83*
Projector-Recorder Belt Corp. - Whitewater, WI - *AvMarPl 83*
Prolab Inc. - Seattle, WA - *AvMarPl 83*
Proletarian Publishers - Chicago, IL - *BoPubDir 4, 5*
Prolink Corp. - Boulder, CO - *DataDirSup 7-83; DirInfWP 82*
Prolog - Dallas, TX - *WritMar 84*
Prologue Publications - Menlo Park, CA - *BoPubDir 4, 5; LitMag&SmPr 83-84*
Proloop [of Prolink Corp.] - Boulder, CO - *TeleSy&SerDir 7-83*
Promax Photo Industries - Eden Prairie, MN - *AvMarPl 83*
Promedics Data Corp. - Palo Alto, CA - *MicrocomMPl 83, 84*
Promenade - New York, NY - *BaconPubCkMag 84; MagDir 84*
Prometheus Books - Buffalo, NY - *LitMarPl 83, 84; WritMar 84*
Prometheus Nemesis Book Co. - Del Mar, CA - *BoPubDir 4 Sup, 5*
Prometheus Products Inc. - Fremont, CA - *MicrocomMPl 84*
Promicro Inc. - Washington, DC - *MicrocomMPl 84*
Promin - Winnipeg, MB, Canada - *Ed&PubIntYB 82*
Promised Land Publications Inc. - Provo, UT - *BoPubDir 4, 5*
Promotion Development Corp. - Westport, CT - *StaDirAdAg 2-84*
Promotion Finders [Div. of Rosenberg International] - New York, NY - *HBIndAd&MS 82-83; LitMarPl 83, 84; MagIndMarPl 82-83*
Promotion House, The [Div. of Western International Premiums Corp.] - Los Angeles, CA - *StaDirAdAg 2-84*
Promotion Marketing Letter - Dallas, TX - *BaconPubCkMag 84*
Promotion Newsletter - Lighthouse Point, FL - *WritMar 84*
Promotional Consultants Inc. - New York, NY - *StaDirAdAg 2-84*
Promotional Services Group Inc. - *See* Tracy-Locke/BBDO
PromptDock Inc. - Colorado Springs, CO - *MicrocomMPl 84*
Pronet [of Proteon Associates Inc.] - Waltham, MA - *TeleSy&SerDir 7-83*
Pronto Home Information System [of Chemical Bank] - New York, NY - *EISS 83*
Proof Press - Berkeley, CA - *BoPubDir 4, 5; LitMag&SmPr 83-84*
Proof Rock - Halifax, VA - *LitMag&SmPr 83-84*
Proofs, The Magazine of Dental Sales & Marketing [of Penn Well Publishing Co.] - Tulsa, OK - *BaconPubCkMag 84; MagDir 84; WritMar 84*
Propane Canada - Calgary, AB, Canada - *BaconPubCkMag 84*
Proper Motion of Faint Stars Survey [of University of Minnesota] - Minneapolis, MN - *EISS 83*

Proper Tales Press - Toronto, ON, Canada - *BoPubDir 4, 5; LitMag&SmPr 83-84*
Properties - Cleveland, OH - *BaconPubCkMag 84; MagDir 84; WritMar 84*
Property Press [Aff. of Questor Associates] - San Francisco, CA - *BoPubDir 4, 5*
Prophecy Publishing Inc. - Austin, TX - *BillIntBG 83-84*
Prophet Music Inc. - *See* Bicycle Music Co., The
Prophet 21 Inc. - Hopewell, NJ - *DataDirSup 7-83*
Prophetic SDA Church/Health & Happiness House - Penngrove, CA - *BoPubDir 4*
Prophetic Voices - Novato, CA - *LitMag&SmPr 83-84*
Prophetstown Echo - Prophetstown, IL - *BaconPubCkNews 84; Ed&PubIntYB 82*
Proprietary Computer Systems - Van Nuys, CA - *DirInfWP 82; EISS 83; InfIndMarPl 83*
Proprietary Software Systems Inc. - Los Angeles, CA - *DataDirSup 7-83*
Props for Today - New York, NY - *AvMarPl 83*
Prorodeo Sports News - Colorado Springs, CO - *BaconPubCkMag 84; MagDir 84; WritMar 84*
Proscenium Press - Newark, DE - *BoPubDir 4, 5*
Prosoft - North Hollywood, CA - *MicrocomMPl 83, 84*
Prospect Books - Prospect, NY - *BoPubDir 4, 5*
Prospect Hill - Baltimore, MD - *BoPubDir 5*
Prospect-News - Prospect, KY - *AyerDirPub 83*
Prospect-News - Doniphan, MO - *AyerDirPub 83; Ed&PubIntYB 82*
Prospect Park Interboro News - Prospect Park, PA - *BaconPubCkNews 84; Ed&PubIntYB 82; NewsDir 84*
Prospect Southwest News - *See* Scripps-Howard Press
Prospector - Del Norte, CO - *AyerDirPub 83*
Prospector - Carson City, NV - *AyerDirPub 83*
Prospector Research Services Inc. - Waltham, MA - *DirMarMP 83*
Prospects [of The Futures Group] - Glastonbury, CT - *DBBus 82*
Prospice - Portree, England - *LitMag&SmPr 83-84*
Prosser-Grandview Publishers - Grandview, WA - *BaconPubCkNews 84*
Prosser Record-Bulletin - Prosser, WA - *Ed&PubIntYB 82*
Prosser Record-Bulletin - *See* Prosser-Grandview Publishers
Prosveta - Burr Ridge, IL - *Ed&PubIntYB 82*
Prosveta [of Slovene National Benefit Society] - Hinsdale, IL - *NewsDir 84*
Protano, Generosa Gina - Larchmont, NY - *LitMarPl 83, 84; MagIndMarPl 82-83*
Protean Publications - Edgbaston, England - *LitMag&SmPr 83-84*
Protech Audio - St. James, NY - *AvMarPl 83*
Protech Micros Ltd. - Manchester, England - *WhoWMicrocom 83*
Protection Marketing Letter - Madison, WI - *BaconPubCkMag 84*
Protection Post - Protection, KS - *BaconPubCkNews 84; Ed&PubIntYB 82*
Protein Data Bank [of Brookhaven National Laboratory] - Upton, NY - *CompReadDB 82; EISS 83*
Proteon Associates Inc. - Waltham, MA - *DataDirSup 7-83; DirInfWP 82*
PROTEUS - Redwood City, CA - *MicrocomMPl 83*
Proteus Press [Aff. of Proteus Design Inc.] - College Park, MD - *BoPubDir 4, 5*
Proteus Press - Arlington, VA - *BoPubDir 4, 5*
Proteus Publishing Co. Inc. [Subs. of Proteus Publishing Ltd.] - New York, NY - *LitMarPl 83, 84*
Proteus Systems Inc. - Chatsworth, CA - *ADAPSOMemDir 83-84*
Protex Industries Inc. (Starnet Div.) - Denver, CO - *DataDirSup 7-83*
Protex Reel Band Co. [Subs. of Anderson Industries Inc.] - Cleveland, OH - *AvMarPl 83*
Prothmann Associates Inc. - Baldwin, NY - *MagIndMarPl 82-83*
Proto Music - *See* Cotillion Music Inc.
Protocol Computers Inc. - Woodland Hills, CA - *DataDirSup 7-83*
Protocol Data Query [of National Library of Medicine] - Bethesda, MD - *DataDirOnSer 84*
Protone Music [Div. of Protone Records] - Los Angeles, CA - *BillIntBG 83-84*
Protone Records - Los Angeles, CA - *BillIntBG 83-84*
Protools [Subs. of Newberry Microsystems] - Los Altos, CA - *WhoWMicrocom 83*
Prototype - Toronto, ON, Canada - *LitMag&SmPr 83-84*
Prototype Machine Works - Canoga Park, CA - *MicrocomMPl 84*
Protozoological Abstracts [of Commonwealth Institute of Helminthology] - St. Albans, England - *CompReadDB 82*
Protter, Susan Ann - New York, NY - *LitMarPl 83, 84*
Protzman & Associates, Roy - Two Rivers, WI - *StaDirAdAg 2-84*
Provandie & Chirurg Inc. - Boston, MA - *CabTVFinDB 83; StaDirAdAg 2-84*
Providence - Innisfail, AB, Canada - *AyerDirPub 83*
Providence Bulletin - Providence, RI - *NewsDir 84*
Providence Eagle - Providence, RI - *AyerDirPub 83; Ed&PubIntYB 82*
Providence Evening Bulletin - Providence, RI - *BaconPubCkNews 84; NewsBur 6*
Providence Journal - Providence, RI - *AdAge 6-28-84; BaconPubCkNews 84; KnowInd 83; LitMarPl 83; NewsBur 6; NewsDir 84*
Providence Journal & Fairfax Herald - McLean, VA - *AyerDirPub 83*
Providence Journal-Bulletin - Providence, RI - *BrCabYB 84; NewsDir 84*
Providence Journal Co. - *See* Colony Communications Inc.
Providence Journal Enterprise - Providence, KY - *BaconPubCkNews 84; Ed&PubIntYB 82; NewsDir 84*
Providence Lithograph Co. [Div. of Federated Lithographers-Printers Inc.] - Providence, RI - *LitMarPl 83, 84*
Providence Visitor - Providence, RI - *NewsDir 84*
Provident Press - West Covina, CA - *BoPubDir 4, 5*
Province [of Vancouver Newspapers Ltd.] - Vancouver, BC, Canada - *AyerDirPub 83; Ed&PubIntYB 82; LitMarPl 84*
Province Publishing - San Diego, CA - *BoPubDir 4, 5*
Provincetown Advocate - Provincetown, MA - *NewsDir 84*
Provincetown-Wellfleet Advocate - Provincetown, MA - *BaconPubCkNews 84*
Provincial Archives of British Columbia [Aff. of Government of British Columbia] - Victoria, BC, Canada - *BoPubDir 4, 5*
Provinciano Productions - Winnipeg, MB, Canada - *BoPubDir 4, 5*
Provision House - Austin, TX - *BoPubDir 4, 5; LitMag&SmPr 83-84*
Proviso Star-Sentinel [of West Suburban Press Inc.] - Melrose Park, IL - *AyerDirPub 83; NewsDir 84*
Proviso Star-Sentinel - Proviso, IL - *Ed&PubIntYB 82*
Proviso Star Sentinel - *See* West Suburban Press Inc.
Proviso Times - Chicago, IL - *AyerDirPub 83*
Proviso Times - Proviso, IL - *Ed&PubIntYB 82*
Proviso Times - *See* Lerner Times Newspapers
Provo Daily Herald [of Scripps League Newspapers Inc.] - Provo, UT - *NewsDir 84*
Provost & Worth Blaney, C. Antonio - Mission Viejo, CA - *BoPubDir 5*
Provost News, The - Provost, AB, Canada - *Ed&PubIntYB 82*
Prow Books/Franciscan Marytown Press [Aff. of Franciscan Friars of Marytown Inc.] - Libertyville, IL - *BoPubDir 4, 5*
Proximity Devices Corp. - Ft. Lauderdale, FL - *MicrocomMPl 84*
PRS Corp. - New York, NY - *MicrocomMPl 83, 84; WhoWMicrocom 83*
Prudential-Bache Securities - New York, NY - *ADAPSOMemDir 83-84*
Prudential Publishing Co. - San Francisco, CA - *BoPubDir 4*
Prudential Publishing Co. - South Lake Tahoe, CA - *BoPubDir 5*
Pruett Music Inc., Jeanne - Nashville, TN - *BillIntBG 83-84*
Pruett Publishing Co. - Boulder, CO - *LitMag&SmPr 83-84; LitMarPl 83, 84; WritMar 84*
Pruitt Humphress Powers Advertising Agency Inc. - Tallahassee, FL - *ArtMar 84; StaDirAdAg 2-84*
Pryor Corp. - Chicago, IL - *ADAPSOMemDir 83-84; DataDirSup 7-83*
Pryor Jeffersonian - Pryor, OK - *BaconPubCkNews 84; Ed&PubIntYB 82; NewsDir 84*
Pryor Pettengill Publishers - Ann Arbor, MI - *BoPubDir 4 Sup, 5*
Pryor Times - Pryor, OK - *BaconPubCkNews 84; NewsDir 84*
Prytaneum Press - Amarillo, TX - *BoPubDir 4, 5*
PS Associates Inc. - Brookline, MA - *LitMarPl 84*
PS Associates Inc. - Sterling, MA - *LitMarPl 83*

P.S. Research - *See* Research Services of North Carolina
PSA - Minneapolis, MN - *MicrocomSwDir 1*
PSA Journal - Philadelphia, PA - *BaconPubCkMag 84; MagDir 84; MagIndMarPl 82-83*
PSA Magazine [of East-West Network Inc.] - Los Angeles, CA - *ArtMar 84; BaconPubCkMag 84; MagDir 84; MagIndMarPl 82-83; WritMar 84*
PSAE [Div. of AIA/SC] - Washington, DC - *MicrocomMPl 84*
Psalm 68:11 Editorial Services [Div. of Wordland] - Santa Ana, CA - *LitMarPl 83*
Psalms Continued - *See* Sure-Fire Music Co. Inc.
PSC Computer Systems Inc. - Montclair, NJ - *ADAPSOMemDir 83-84*
Pseudo Songs - *See* Kaye Publications, Richard
PSFQ [of Megatherium Press] - Cupertino, CA - *LitMag&SmPr 83-84*
PSG Advertising - Littleton, MA - *StaDirAdAg 2-84*
PSG/Wright Publishing Co. Inc. - Littleton, MA - *LitMarPl 84*
PSI Group Inc. - New York, NY - *DataDirSup 7-83*
PSI Mobile Products Inc. - Mt. Clemens, MI - *AvMarPl 83*
PSI/Professional Sound, Film & Video Inc. - Boston, MA - *AvMarPl 83*
P.S.I. Rhythms Inc. - Ormond Beach, FL - *BoPubDir 4, 5*
PSI/Systems - Andover, MA - *MicrocomMPl 84; MicrocomSwDir 1*
PsiTech - Tustin, CA - *DataDirSup 7-83*
PSJA Advance News - San Juan, TX - *AyerDirPub 83*
PSP Records & Tapes - Dallas, TX - *BillIntBG 83-84*
PSS Inc. [Div. of Dancer Fitzgerald Sample Inc.] - New York, NY - *StaDirAdAg 2-84*
Pssst! - London, England - *LitMag&SmPr 83-84*
PST Advertising Associates Inc. - Melville, NY - *StaDirAdAg 2-84*
PSTA - Munich, West Germany - *DirOnDB Spring 84*
Psycalert [of Psychological Abstracts Information Services] - Washington, DC - *DataDirOnSer 84*
Psycalert - Arlington, VA - *DirOnDB Spring 84*
Psych/Graphic Publishers - La Jolla, CA - *BoPubDir 4, 5*
Psychiatric Annals - Thorofare, NJ - *BaconPubCkMag 84; MagDir 84; MagIndMarPl 82-83*
Psychiatric News - Washington, DC - *MagDir 84*
Psychic Books - Oxnard, CA - *LitMag&SmPr 83-84*
Psychic Observer, The [of ESPress Inc.] - Washington, DC - *LitMag&SmPr 83-84; MagIndMarPl 82-83*
Psychoanalytic Quarterly - New York, NY - *BoPubDir 4, 5; MagDir 84; MagIndMarPl 82-83*
Psychographics Research Corp. Inc. - Bedford, NY - *IntDirMarRes 83*
Psychohistory Press - New York, NY - *BoPubDir 4, 5; LitMag&SmPr 83-84*
Psychological Abstracts Information Services [of American Psychological Association Inc.] - Washington, DC - *CompReadDB 82; DataDirOnSer 84; EISS 83; InfIndMarPl 83; OnBibDB 3*
Psychological Assessment Resources Inc. - Tampa, FL - *MicrocomMPl 84*
Psychological Bulletin - Washington, DC - *MagDir 84*
Psychological Dimensions Inc. - New York, NY - *LitMarPl 83, 84*
Psychological Motivations Inc. - Dobbs Ferry, NY - *IntDirMarRes 83*
Psychological Press - Seattle, WA - *BoPubDir 4, 5; LitMag&SmPr 83-84*
Psychological Product Profiles Inc. - Glendale, CA - *IntDirMarRes 83*
Psychological Reports & Perceptual & Motor Skills - Missoula, MT - *MicroMarPl 82-83*
Psychological Review - Ann Arbor, MI - *BaconPubCkMag 84; MagDir 84*
Psychology & Consulting Associates Press - La Jolla, CA - *BoPubDir 4, 5*
Psychology & Social Theory - Ithaca, NY - *LitMag&SmPr 83-84*
Psychology & Social Theory Press - Ithaca, NY - *LitMag&SmPr 83-84*
Psychology of Women Quarterly - New York, NY - *MagIndMarPl 82-83*
Psychology Today - Washington, DC - *BaconPubCkMag 84*
Psychology Today [of Ziff-Davis Publishing Co.] - New York, NY - *Folio 83; LitMarPl 83, 84; MagDir 84; MagIndMarPl 82-83; WritMar 84*
Psychometric Affiliates - Munster, IN - *BoPubDir 4, 5*
Psychonomic Society Inc. - Austin, TX - *MagIndMarPl 82-83*
Psychophysics Inc. - Atlantic City, NJ - *MicrocomMPl 84*
Psychosocial Nursing & Mental Health Services - Thorofare, NJ - *MagDir 84*
Psychosomatics - Greenwich, CT - *MagDir 84; MagIndMarPl 82-83*
Psychotechnics Inc. - Glenview, IL - *AvMarPl 83; MicrocomMPl 84; MicrocomSwDir 1*
Psychotherapy & Social Science Book Club [Div. of Jason Aronson Inc.] - New York, NY - *LitMarPl 83, 84*
Psychotherapy Digest - Del Mar, CA - *LitMag&SmPr 83-84*
Psychotherapy: Theory, Research & Practice [of American Psychological Association] - Los Angeles, CA - *MagIndMarPl 82-83*
Psycinfo - Arlington, VA - *DirOnDB Spring 84; InfoS 83-84*
Psyndex - Trier, West Germany - *DirOnDB Spring 84*
P.T. Boats Inc. - Memphis, TN - *BoPubDir 4, 5*
Ptarmigan Publishing - Orillia, ON, Canada - *BoPubDir 4 Sup, 5*
Pteranodon [of Lieb/Schott Publications] - Bourbonnais, IL - *LitMag&SmPr 83-84; WritMar 84*
Pterodactyl Press - Cumberland, IA - *BoPubDir 4, 5; LitMag&SmPr 83-84*
PTL Free Lance Translating Services - Miami, FL - *LitMarPl 84*
PTL Television Network [of Heritage Village Church & Missionary Fellowship Inc.] - Charlotte, NC - *BrCabYB 84; CabTVPrDB 83; Ed&PubIntYB 82; Tel&CabFB 84C*
PTM - Des Plaines, IL - *MagDir 84*
PTN Publishing Corp. - Woodbury, NY - *MagDir 84; MagIndMarPl 82-83*
Ptolemy/Browns Mills Review - Browns Mills, NJ - *LitMag&SmPr 83-84*
Ptolemy Press Ltd. - Grove City, PA - *BoPubDir 4, 5*
PTS Abstract Services [of Predicasts Inc.] - Cleveland, OH - *DataDirOnSer 84*
PTS Annual Reports Abstracts [of Predicasts Inc.] - Cleveland, OH - *DataDirOnSer 84; DirOnDB Spring 84*
PTS Defense Markets & Technology [of Predicasts Inc.] - Cleveland, OH - *DirOnDB Spring 84*
PTS Indexes [of Predicasts Inc.] - Cleveland, OH - *DataDirOnSer 84; DBBus 82; DirOnDB Spring 84*
PTS International Forecasts Abstracts [of Predicasts Inc.] - Cleveland, OH - *DBBus 82*
PTS International Forecasts Abstracts - *See* PTS U.S. Forecasts Abstracts
PTS International Time Series [of Predicasts Inc.] - Cleveland, OH - *DBBus 82*
PTS International Time Series - *See* PTS U.S. Time Series
PTS Literature [of Predicasts Inc.] - Cleveland, OH - *DataDirOnSer 84*
PTS PROMT [of Predicasts Inc.] - Cleveland, OH - *DBBus 82; DirOnDB Spring 84; OnBibDB 3*
PTS Statistical Services [of Predicasts Inc.] - Cleveland, OH - *DataDirOnSer 84*
PTS U.S. Forecasts Abstracts [of Predicasts Inc.] - Cleveland, OH - *DBBus 82; DirOnDB Spring 84*
PTS U.S. Time Series [of Predicasts Inc.] - Cleveland, OH - *DirOnDB Spring 84*
Pub [of Ansuda Publications] - Harris, IA - *LitMag&SmPr 83-84; WritMar 84*
Pub/Data Inc. - Cicero, IL - *MagIndMarPl 82-83*
Pub Set Inc. - Union, NJ - *MagIndMarPl 82-83*
Public Administration Review [of American Society for Public Administration] - Washington, DC - *MagDir 84; MagIndMarPl 82-83*
Public Affairs Analysts Inc. - New York, NY - *DirPRFirms 83*
Public Affairs Information - Sacramento, CA - *DirOnDB Spring 84; InfoS 83-84*
Public Affairs Information Service - New York, NY - *BoPubDir 4, 5; DataDirOnSer 84; EISS 83; InfIndMarPl 83*
Public Affairs Information Service (Bulletin) - New York, NY - *CompReadDB 82*
Public Affairs Information Service (Foreign Language Index) - New York, NY - *CompReadDB 82*

Public Affairs Lecture Bureau [Div. of Writers Alliance Ltd.] - New York, NY - *LitMarPl 83, 84*
Public Affairs Press - Washington, DC - *LitMarPl 83, 84*
Public Archives of Canada - *See* Archives Canada Microfiches (Picture Div.)
Public Attitude Surveys Research Ltd. - High Wycombe, England - *IntDirMarRes 83*
Public Broadcasting Report - Washington, DC - *BaconPubCkMag 84; DirOnDB Spring 84; MagDir 84*
Public Broadcasting Report [of NewsNet Inc.] - Bryn Mawr, PA - *DataDirOnSer 84*
Public Broadcasting Service - Washington, DC - *BrCabYB 84; TelAl 83, 84; Tel&CabFB 84C*
Public Cable Co. [of American TV & Communications Corp.] - Portland, ME - *BrCabYB 84; Tel&CabFB 84C*
Public Citizen - Washington, DC - *WritMar 84*
Public Communications Inc. - Chicago, IL - *DirPRFirms 83*
Public Computing Inc. - Lafayette, IN - *WhoWMicrocom 83*
Public Demographics Inc. - Cincinnati, OH - *EISS 83*
Public Domain Forest Inventory System [of U.S. Bureau of Land Management] - Denver, CO - *EISS 83*
Public Domain Inc. - West Milton, OH - *MicrocomMPl 84*
Public Employee Press [of District Council 37, AFSCME] - New York, NY - *NewsDir 84*
Public Employee, The [of AFSCME] - Washington, DC - *BaconPubCkMag 84; NewsDir 84*
Public Events Partnership, The - St. Louis, MO - *DirPRFirms 83*
Public Eye, The - Sayreville, NJ - *DirPRFirms 83*
Public Historian, The [of University of California Press] - Berkeley, CA - *LitMag&SmPr 83-84*
Public Information Press Inc. - Miami Beach, FL - *BoPubDir 4, 5*
Public Interest Economics Foundation & Center - Washington, DC - *BoPubDir 4, 5*
Public Interest Public Relations - New York, NY - *DirPRFirms 83*
Public Interest, The - New York, NY - *LitMarPl 83, 84; MagIndMarPl 82-83*
Public Interest Video - Washington, DC - *Tel&CabFB 84C*
Public Law Education Institute - Washington, DC - *BoPubDir 4, 5*
Public Ledger - Oxford, NC - *AyerDirPub 83*
Public Library Quarterly [of Haworth Press Journals] - New York, NY - *LitMarPl 83, 84*
Public Management - Washington, DC - *BaconPubCkMag 84; MagIndMarPl 82-83*
Public Management Institute - San Francisco, CA - *BoPubDir 4, 5*
Public Management/PM/ICMA [of International City Management Association] - Washington, DC - *MagDir 84*
Public Media Center - San Francisco, CA - *StaDirAdAg 2-84*
Public Mirror - Arapahoe, NE - *AyerDirPub 83*
Public Opinion [of American Enterprise Institute] - Washington, DC - *MagDir 84; WritMar 84*
Public Opinion - Decorah, IA - *AyerDirPub 83*
Public Opinion - Westerville, OH - *AyerDirPub 83; Ed&PubIntYB 82*
Public Opinion - Chambersburg, PA - *AyerDirPub 83; Ed&PubIntYB 82*
Public Opinion - Watertown, SD - *AyerDirPub 83*
Public Opinion Quarterly - New York, NY - *MagIndMarPl 82-83*
Public Personnel Management - Washington, DC - *MagIndMarPl 82-83*
Public Policy Group Inc. - Lafayette, NJ - *EISS 5-84 Sup*
Public Post, The - Raeford, NC - *AyerDirPub 83*
Public Power - Washington, DC - *BaconPubCkMag 84; MagDir 84; WritMar 84*
Public Press Newsletter, The - New York, NY - *LitMag&SmPr 83-84*
Public Press, The - New York, NY - *LitMag&SmPr 83-84*
Public Records Office [of U.S. Federal Election Commission] - Washington, DC - *EISS 83*
Public Relations Advisors Inc. [Div. of The Bloom Cos.] - Dallas, TX - *DirPRFirms 83*
Public Relations Advisors Inc. - *See* Bloom Cos. Inc., The
Public Relations Affiliates [Aff. of Electronics Information Bureau] - Highland Park, IL - *DirPRFirms 83*
Public Relations Aids Inc. - New York, NY - *EISS 83; LitMarPl 83, 84; MagIndMarPl 82-83*
Public Relations Analysts Inc. - New York, NY - *DirPRFirms 83*
Public Relations Associates - Helena, MT - *DirPRFirms 83*
Public Relations Bank, The - San Francisco, CA - *DirPRFirms 83*
Public Relations Board Inc., The - Chicago, IL - *DirPRFirms 83*
Public Relations/Chicago - Chicago, IL - *BaconPubCkMag 84*
Public Relations Counsel Inc. - *See* Read Associates
Public Relations Desk Inc., The - East Brunswick, NJ - *DirPRFirms 83*
Public Relations Institute Inc. [Aff. of Lawler Ballard Advertising] - Norfolk, VA - *DirPRFirms 83*
Public Relations International Inc. - Los Angeles, CA - *DirPRFirms 83*
Public Relations International Ltd. - Tulsa, OK - *DirPRFirms 83*
Public Relations Journal - New York, NY - *BaconPubCkMag 84; MagDir 84*
Public Relations News - New York, NY - *BaconPubCkMag 84; MagDir 84; MagIndMarPl 82-83*
Public Relations of Cape Cod Inc. - Centerville, MA - *LitMarPl 83, 84*
Public Relations of Cape Cod Inc. - Yarmouth Port, MA - *DirPRFirms 83; MagIndMarPl 82-83*
Public Relations Plus Inc. - Washington Depot, CT - *BoPubDir 4 Sup, 5*
Public Relations Programs - Green Brook, NJ - *DirPRFirms 83*
Public Relations Publishing Co. - New York, NY - *BoPubDir 4, 5*
Public Relations Quarterly, The - Rhinebeck, NY - *BaconPubCkMag 84; MagDir 84*
Public Response Associates Inc. - San Francisco, CA - *ProGuPRSer 4*
Public Securities Association - New York, NY - *BoPubDir 5*
Public Sentiment - Grass Lake, MI - *AyerDirPub 83*
Public Service Materials Center - Hartsdale, NY - *BoPubDir 4, 5*
Public Service Satellite Consortium - Washington, DC - *BrCabYB 84; CabTVFinDB 83; Tel&CabFB 84C; TeleSy&SerDir 7-83*
Public Service Telephone Co. Inc. - Reynolds, GA - *TelDir&BG 83-84*
Public Spirit - Ayer, MA - *AyerDirPub 83; Ed&PubIntYB 82; NewsDir 84*
Public Spirit Publishing Co. Inc. - Ayer, MA - *BaconPubCkNews 84*
Public Transit Report - Silver Spring, MD - *BaconPubCkMag 84*
Public Utilities Fortnightly - Arlington, VA - *BaconPubCkMag 84; MagDir 84*
Public Utilities Reports Inc. - Arlington, VA - *BoPubDir 5*
Public Welfare - Washington, DC - *MagIndMarPl 82-83*
Public Works Magazine [of Public Works Journal Corp.] - Ridgewood, NJ - *BaconPubCkMag 84; MagDir 84*
Publicaciones Portavoz Evangelico [Div. of Kregel Publications] - Grand Rapids, MI - *LitMarPl 84*
Publicacoes Tecnicas Internacionais Ltda. - Sao Paulo, Brazil - *InfoS 83-84*
Publication & Information Services [of SAE] - Warrendale, PA - *EISS 83*
Publication Arts - Hawthorne, NJ - *LitMarPl 83; MagIndMarPl 82-83*
Publication Arts - Ridgewood, NJ - *LitMarPl 83, 84*
Publication Associates - Mercer Island, WA - *LitMarPl 83*
Publication Management Group - Arlington Heights, IL - *MagIndMarPl 82-83*
Publication Press Inc. - Baltimore, MD - *LitMarPl 83*
Publication Services - Urbana, IL - *LitMarPl 84*
Publication Services Branch [of Alberta Government Services] - Edmonton, AB, Canada - *EISS 83*
Publications & Information Branch [of U.S. Public Health Service] - Hyattsville, MD - *EISS 83*
Publications & Information Services Div. [of Rutgers University] - New Brunswick, NJ - *EISS 83*
Publications Arts Inc. - Minnetonka, MN - *DirMarMP 83*
Publications Development Co. of Texas [of Texas Phinmarc Books] - Crockett, TX - *BoPubDir 4, 5*
Publications Div. [of Runzheimer & Co. Inc.] - Northbrook, IL - *EISS 5-84 Sup*
Publications for Living - St. Louis, MO - *BoPubDir 4, 5*

Publications, Illustrations & Presentations Inc. - Freeport, NY - *LitMarPl 83, 84*
Publications International Ltd. - *See* Consumer Guide/Publications International Ltd.
Publications Orientalistes de France - Paris, France - *MicroMarPl 82-83*
Publications West - North Hollywood, CA - *LitMarPl 83, 84*
Publicidad Causa - Lima, Peru - *StaDirAdAg 2-84*
Publicidad Siboney International - New York, NY - *StaDirAdAg 2-84*
Publicis-Intermarco-Farner - Paris, France - *AdAge 6-25-84*
Publicist - New York, NY - *MagDir 84; MagIndMarPl 82-83*
Publicitas/IMAA Inc. - Lima, Peru - *StaDirAdAg 2-84*
Publicite GRS Lte. - *See* Grey Ronalds Smith Ltd.
Publicity in Print - San Jose, CA - *BoPubDir 4, 5*
Publicom - Cleveland, OH - *DirPRFirms 83*
Publifoto - New York, NY - *Ed&PubIntYB 82*
Publim Inc. Communication Marcheage - Quebec City, PQ, Canada - *StaDirAdAg 2-84*
Publish or Perish Inc. - Wilmington, DE - *BoPubDir 4, 5*
Publishers - Las Vegas, NV - *BoPubDir 4, 5*
Publishers Advertising Associates - New York, NY - *StaDirAdAg 2-84*
Publishers Advertising Reports - New York, NY - *Tel&CabFB 84C*
Publishers Agency Inc., The [Subs. of Pubco Corp.] - Bensalem, PA - *LitMarPl 83, 84*
Publishers Aide - San Diego, CA - *MagIndMarPl 82-83*
Publishers' Auxiliary - Washington, DC - *BaconPubCkMag 84; MagDir 84*
Publishers' Book Bindery Inc. - Winchester, MA - *LitMarPl 83, 84*
Publishers Book Bindery Inc. - Long Island City, NY - *LitMarPl 83, 84; MagIndMarPl 82-83*
Publishers Choice Book Manufacturing Co. - Mars, PA - *LitMarPl 83, 84*
Publishers Clearance Corp. - Secaucus, NJ - *LitMarPl 83, 84*
Publishers Clearing House - Port Washington, NY - *MagIndMarPl 82-83*
Publishers Data Center Inc. - Brooklyn, NY - *LitMarPl 83, 84; MagIndMarPl 82-83*
Publishers Development Corp. - San Diego, CA - *DirMarMP 83; MagIndMarPl 82-83*
Publishers Development Corp. - Princeton, NJ - *LitMarPl 83, 84; MagIndMarPl 82-83*
Publishers Distribution Center - East Rutherford, NJ - *LitMarPl 83, 84*
Publishers, Distributors & Wholesalers [of R. R. Bowker Co.] - New York, NY - *DataDirOnSer 84*
Publishers Editorial Services Inc. - Katonah, NY - *LitMarPl 83, 84*
Publishers' Exposition Display [Div. of Turner Subscription Agency Inc.] - New York, NY - *MagIndMarPl 82-83*
Publisher's Financial Bureau - Wellesley Hills, MA - *BaconPubCkNews 84; Ed&PubIntYB 82*
Publisher's Graphics - Westport, CT - *LitMarPl 83, 84; MagIndMarPl 82-83*
Publishers Group West - Emeryville, CA - *BoPubDir 4 Sup, 5*
Publishers-Hall Syndicate - *See* Field Newspaper Syndicate
Publishers Information Bureau Inc. - New York, NY - *Tel&CabFB 84C*
Publishers' Licensing Corp. - Englewood, NJ - *BillIntBG 83-84*
Publishers Marketing Enterprises Inc. - New York, NY - *LitMarPl 83*
Publishers' Marketing Group [of Tom Brown Associates Communicative Arts Group] - Richardson, TX - *BoPubDir 4 Sup, 5; LitMarPl 83, 84*
Publishers Media - North Hollywood, CA - *BoPubDir 4 Sup, 5; LitMarPl 83, 84*
Publishers of Truth - Oreland, PA - *BoPubDir 4, 5*
Publishers' Press - Portland, OR - *BoPubDir 5*
Publishers Press Inc. [Subs. of Publishers Printing Co.] - Shepherdsville, KY - *MagIndMarPl 82-83*
Publishers Storage & Shipping Corp. - Ypsilanti, MI - *LitMarPl 83, 84*
Publishers Unltd. Inc. - Hot Springs, AR - *BoPubDir 4 Sup, 5*
Publishers Weekly [of R. R. Bowker Co.] - New York, NY - *BaconPubCkMag 84; Folio 83; LitMarPl 83, 84; MagDir 84; MagIndMarPl 82-83; WritMar 84*
Publishers Workshop Inc. - Brooklyn Heights, NY - *LitMarPl 83, 84; MagIndMarPl 82-83*
Publishers's Research Inc. - New York, NY - *LitMarPl 84*
Publishing Center for Cultural Resources - New York, NY - *BoPubDir 5; LitMarPl 83, 84; MagIndMarPl 82-83*
Publishing Committee of Byelorussian (Canadian Co-Ordinating Committee) - Barrie, ON, Canada - *BoPubDir 4, 5*
Publishing Concepts Inc. - Dallas, TX - *BoPubDir 5*
Publishing Corp. of America - Canton, OH - *DirMarMP 83*
Publishing Group, The - Rockville, MD - *HBIndAd&MS 82-83*
Publishing in the Output Mode [of Padre Productions] - San Luis Obispo, CA - *LitMag&SmPr 83-84*
Publishing Packagers Corp. - New York, NY - *MagIndMarPl 82-83*
Publishing Resources Inc. - San Juan, PR - *BoPubDir 4 Sup, 5; LitMarPl 83, 84*
Publishing Services Inc. - Oakland, CA - *BoPubDir 4*
Publishing Services Inc. - Sunnyvale, CA - *BoPubDir 5*
Publishing Synthesis Ltd. - New York, NY - *LitMarPl 83, 84; MagIndMarPl 82-83*
Publishing Trade - Des Plaines, IL - *BaconPubCkMag 84; WritMar 84*
Publishing Trade - Winnetka, IL - *MagDir 84*
Publishing Ventures Inc. - New York, NY - *BillIntBG 83-84*
Publishing Ward Inc., The - Ft. Collins, CO - *LitMag&SmPr 83-84; WritMar 84*
Publix Publications - McMurray, PA - *BaconPubCkNews 84*
Pubrelco - New York, NY - *DirPRFirms 83*
Puck-The Comic Weekly - New York, NY - *Ed&PubIntYB 82*
Puckerbrush Press - Orono, ME - *BoPubDir 4, 5; LitMag&SmPr 83-84; LitMarPl 84*
Puckerbrush Review, The [of Puckerbrush Press] - Orono, ME - *LitMag&SmPr 83-84*
Pudding Magazine [of Pudding Publications] - Columbus, OH - *LitMag&SmPr 83-84; WritMar 84*
Pudding Publications - Columbus, OH - *LitMag&SmPr 83-84*
Pueblo Catholic Crosswinds - Pueblo, CO - *NewsDir 84*
Pueblo Chieftain - Pueblo, CO - *BaconPubCkNews 84; NewsBur 6*
Pueblo Colorado Tribune - Pueblo, CO - *BaconPubCkNews 84*
Pueblo Poetry Project - Pueblo, CO - *BoPubDir 4, 5; LitMag&SmPr 83-84*
Pueblo Publishing Press - Yukon, OK - *LitMarPl 83, 84*
Pueblo Research - Tucson, AZ - *IntDirMarRes 83*
Pueblo Star-Journal - Pueblo, CO - *BaconPubCkNews 84; NewsBur 6; NewsDir 84*
Pueblo TV Power Inc. [of Community Tele-Communications Inc.] - Pueblo, CO - *BrCabYB 84; Tel&CabFB 84C*
Pueo Press - San Rafael, CA - *BoPubDir 4, 5; LitMag&SmPr 83-84*
Puerto Rico Almanacs Inc. - Santurce, PR - *BoPubDir 4, 5*
Puerto Rico Census Data Center [of Puerto Rico Planning Board] - San Juan, PR - *EISS 7-83 Sup*
Puget Sound Mail - La Conner, WA - *Ed&PubIntYB 82*
Pugh-Roberts Associates Inc. - Cambridge, MA - *MicrocomSwDir 1*
Pukwana Press-Reporter - Pukwana, SD - *BaconPubCkNews 84*
Pulaski Broadcasting Co. - Pulaski, TN - *BrCabYB 84*
Pulaski Cable TV [of Rogers Cablesystems Inc.] - Pulaski, TN - *BrCabYB 84; Tel&CabFB 84C*
Pulaski Citizen - Pulaski, TN - *BaconPubCkNews 84; Ed&PubIntYB 82*
Pulaski County Democrat, The - Waynesville, MO - *Ed&PubIntYB 82*
Pulaski County Independent, The - Winamac, IN - *AyerDirPub 83*
Pulaski County Journal - Winamac, IN - *AyerDirPub 83; Ed&PubIntYB 82*
Pulaski Democrat [of Town & Country News of Jefferson County] - Gouverneur, NY - *NewsDir 84*
Pulaski Democrat & Advertiser - Pulaski, NY - *BaconPubCkNews 84*
Pulaski Democrat & Town & Country News - Pulaski, NY - *Ed&PubIntYB 82*
Pulaski Enterprise - Mounds, IL - *AyerDirPub 83; Ed&PubIntYB 82*

Pulaski Giles Free Press - Pulaski, TN - *BaconPubCkNews 84; NewsDir 84*
Pulaski Salmon River News - *See* Oswego County Weeklies
Pulaski Southwest Times [of New River Newspapers] - Pulaski, VA - *BaconPubCkNews 84; NewsDir 84*
Pulaski-White Rural Telephone Cooperative Inc. - Star City, IN - *TelDir&BG 83-84*
Puleo Electronics Inc. - Lynbrook, NY - *DataDirSup 7-83*
Puli Club of America Inc. - Whitewater, WI - *BoPubDir 4, 5*
Pulin, Chuck - New York, NY - *MagIndMarPl 82-83*
Pulitzer Broadcast Stations, The - St. Louis, MO - *BrCabYB 84*
Pulitzer Publishing Co. - St. Louis, MO - *AdAge 6-28-84; BrCabYB 84; Ed&PubIntYB 82; KnowInd 83; Tel&CabFB 84S*
Pullin Productions - Calgary, AB, Canada - *ArtMar 84; AvMarPl 83*
Pullman - *See* Warner Bros. Music
Pullman Herald [of Whitman Publishing Co.] - Pullman, WA - *BaconPubCkNews 84; Ed&PubIntYB 82; NewsDir 84*
Pullman TV Cable Co. - Moscow, ID - *Tel&CabFB 84C p.1698*
Pullman TV Cable Co. - Pullman, WA - *BrCabYB 84; Tel&CabFB 84C*
Pulp [of Sage Press] - New York, NY - *BoPubDir 4, 5; LitMag&SmPr 83-84; WritMar 84*
Pulp & Paper - San Francisco, CA - *MagDir 84; MagIndMarPl 82-83*
Pulp & Paper - Atlanta, GA - *BaconPubCkMag 84*
Pulp & Paper Canada - Montreal, PQ, Canada - *WritMar 84*
Pulp & Paper Canada - Westmount, PQ, Canada - *BaconPubCkMag 84*
Pulp & Paper Data Bank - Washington, DC - *DirOnDB Spring 84*
Pulp & Paper Data Bank [of Data Resources Inc.] - Lexington, MA - *DataDirOnSer 84*
Pulp & Paper International - San Francisco, CA - *BaconPubCkMag 84*
Pulp & Paper Journal - Toronto, ON, Canada - *BaconPubCkMag 84*
Pulp & Paper Week - San Francisco, CA - *BaconPubCkMag 84*
Pulp Press [Div. of Arsenal Pulp Press Book Publishers Ltd.] - Vancouver, BC, Canada - *BoPubDir 4; LitMag&SmPr 83-84; LitMarPl 83, 84*
Pulpit Digest - Jackson, MS - *MagDir 84*
Pulpit Helps - Chattanooga, TN - *MagIndMarPl 82-83*
Pulpsmith - New York, NY - *LitMag&SmPr 83-84; WritMar 84*
Pulse - Pico Rivera, CA - *MagDir 84*
Pulse Analytics Inc. - Ridgewood, NJ - *IntDirMarRes 83*
Pulse-Finger Press - Yellow Springs, OH - *BoPubDir 4, 5*
Pulse-Journal, The [of Harte-Hanks Communications Inc.] - Mason, OH - *NewsDir 84*
Pulse Productions - Chicago, IL - *BillIntBG 83-84*
Pumpko Industries Ltd. - North Hollywood, CA - *BillIntBG 83-84*
Punch Films Inc. - New York, NY - *Tel&CabFB 84C*
Punch Publishing Inc. - Annandale, VA - *LitMag&SmPr 83-84*
Puncture - San Francisco, CA - *LitMag&SmPr 83-84*
Pundick, Douglas - San Francisco, CA - *LitMarPl 83*
Punta Gorda Herald News - Punta Gorda, FL - *NewsDir 84*
Punxsutawney Spirit - Punxsutawney, PA - *BaconPubCkNews 84; NewsDir 84*
Punxsutawney TV Cable Co. [of Adelphia Communications Corp.] - Punxsutawney, PA - *BrCabYB 84; Tel&CabFB 84C*
Puopolo Productions - New York, NY - *Tel&CabFB 84C*
Puppet Masters - Palo Alto, CA - *BoPubDir 4, 5*
Purcell Associates Ltd., Gerard W. - New York, NY - *BillIntBG 83-84*
Purcell/Lexington Cable TV [of Telecable System Corp.] - Purcell, OK - *BrCabYB 84*
Purcell Productions Inc. - New York, NY - *AvMarPl 83*
Purcell Register - Purcell, OK - *BaconPubCkNews 84; Ed&PubIntYB 82; NewsDir 84*
Purcells Inc. - Broken Bow, NE - *BoPubDir 4, 5*
Purchasing [of Reed Holdings Inc.] - Boston, MA - *BaconPubCkMag 84; MagDir 84; MagIndMarPl 82-83*
Purchasing Digest - Dover, NJ - *BaconPubCkMag 84; MagDir 84*
Purchasing Digest - Morristown, NJ - *MagIndMarPl 82-83*
Purchasing Executive's Bulletin - Waterford, CT - *WritMar 84*
Purchasing Management - Minneapolis, MN - *BaconPubCkMag 84; MagDir 84*
Purchasing Management Digest - Oakville, ON, Canada - *BaconPubCkMag 84*
Purchasing Professional, The - Buffalo, NY - *BaconPubCkMag 84; MagDir 84*
Purchasing World - Barrington, IL - *BaconPubCkMag 84; MagDir 84*
Purchasor-New York State - Buffalo, NY - *BaconPubCkMag 84; MagDir 84*
Purchasor-New York State [of Quorum Publications] - Rochester, NY - *WritMar 84*
Purdom & Co., Paul - Burlingame, CA - *DirPRFirms 83*
Purdue Alumnus, The - West Lafayette, IN - *WritMar 84*
Purdue Engineer - Lafayette, IN - *BaconPubCkMag 84; MagDir 84*
Purdue Exponent [of Purdue Student Publishing Foundation] - West Lafayette, IN - *NewsDir 84*
Purdue University (Engineering Experiment Station) - West Lafayette, IN - *BoPubDir 4, 5*
Purdue University Press - West Lafayette, IN - *LitMarPl 83, 84; WritMar 84*
Pure & Easy Records - North Chelmsford, MA - *BillIntBG 83-84*
Pure-Bred Dogs/American Kennel Gazette [of American Kennel Club] - New York, NY - *BaconPubCkMag 84; DirMarMP 83; MagDir 84; MagIndMarPl 82-83; WritMar 84*
Purgatory Pie Press - New York, NY - *BoPubDir 4 Sup, 5*
Purnell Co. Inc. - Boston, MA - *LitMarPl 83, 84*
Purolator Courier Corp. [Subs. of Purolator Inc.] - New Hyde Park, NY - *LitMarPl 83, 84; MagIndMarPl 82-83*
Purple Cow - Atlanta, GA - *WritMar 84*
Purple Mouth Press - Newport News, VA - *BoPubDir 4, 5*
Purple Pegasus - Port St. Joe, FL - *LitMag&SmPr 83-84*
Purpleville Publishing [Aff. of Pala Graphics Ltd.] - Mississauga, ON, Canada - *BoPubDir 4 Sup, 5*
Purpose - Scottdale, PA - *WritMar 84*
Purpose Products - Aurora, ON, Canada - *BoPubDir 4 Sup, 5*
Pursifull, Carmen M. - Champaign, IL - *BoPubDir 5*
Purvis & Co. - Brooklyn, NY - *BoPubDir 4, 5*
Purvis Lamar County News - Purvis, MS - *BaconPubCkNews 84*
Push Pin AV - New York, NY - *AvMarPl 83*
Pushcart Music - Brooklyn, NY - *BillIntBG 83-84*
Pushcart Press - Wainscott, NY - *LitMag&SmPr 83-84; LitMarPl 83, 84*
Pushkin Press - Washington, DC - *BoPubDir 5; LitMag&SmPr 83-84*
Pushpin, Lubalin, Peckolick - New York, NY - *LitMarPl 83, 84; MagIndMarPl 82-83*
Pussycat Press - Geneva, Switzerland - *LitMag&SmPr 83-84*
Putman Publishing Co. - Chicago, IL - *MagIndMarPl 82-83*
Putnam All-Channel Cable Vision Inc. [of Horizon Communications Corp.] - Greencastle, IN - *Tel&CabFB 84C*
Putnam City-Northwest News - Warr Acres, OK - *Ed&PubIntYB 82*
Putnam County Courier [of Carmel Publishing Co. Inc.] - Carmel, NY - *AyerDirPub 83; Ed&PubIntYB 82; NewsDir 84*
Putnam County Courier-Journal - Crescent City, FL - *AyerDirPub 83*
Putnam County News & Recorder - Cold Spring, NY - *Ed&PubIntYB 82*
Putnam County Record - Granville, IL - *Ed&PubIntYB 82*
Putnam County Sentinel - Ottawa, OH - *AyerDirPub 83; Ed&PubIntYB 82; NewsDir 84*
Putnam County Vidette - Columbus Grove, OH - *AyerDirPub 83; Ed&PubIntYB 82*
Putnam Democrat - Winfield, WV - *AyerDirPub 83; Ed&PubIntYB 82*
Putnam Observer-Patriot - Putnam, CT - *NewsDir 84*
Putnam Publishing Group [Subs. of MCA Inc.] - New York, NY - *DirMarMP 83; LitMarPl 83, 84*
Putnam TV Cable Inc. - Ottawa, OH - *BrCabYB 84; Tel&CabFB 84C*
Putnam, William L. - *See* Springfield Television Corp.
Putnam Windham County Observer-Patriot - Putnam, CT - *BaconPubCkNews 84*
Putnam's Sons, G. P. - New York, NY - *ArtMar 84*
Putnam's Sons, G. P. - *See* Putnam Publishing Group

Putnum Post - Culloden, WV - *AyerDirPub 83*
Putterman, Arlene - Elkins Park, PA - *LitMarPl 83, 84*
Puyallup Pierce County Herald - Puyallup, WA - *BaconPubCkNews 84; NewsDir 84*
Puzar, Vincent D. - St. Pete Beach, FL - *MicrocomMPl 83*
PWS Publishers [Div. of Wadsworth Inc.] - Boston, MA - *LitMarPl 83, 84*
Pyle Communications Inc. - Sherman, TX - *BrCabYB 84*
Pyle, Dolores - Merchantville, NJ - *Ed&PubIntYB 82*
Pyle, Robert N. - Washington, DC - *DirPRFirms 83*
Pym-Randall Press - Roslindale, MA - *LitMag&SmPr 83-84*
Pymatuning Area News [of Gazette Printing Co. Inc.] - Andover, OH - *Ed&PubIntYB 82*
Pymatuning Area News [of Gazette Printing Co. Inc.] - Jefferson, OH - *NewsDir 84*
Pymatuning Independent Telephone Co. - Greenville, PA - *TelDir&BG 83-84*
Pynwon Pty. Ltd. - Randwick, Australia - *MicrocomSwDir 1*
Pynyon Press Inc. - Atlanta, GA - *BoPubDir 4, 5*
Pyquag Books - Wethersfield, CT - *BoPubDir 4, 5*
Pyramid - Mt. Pleasant, UT - *AyerDirPub 83; Ed&PubIntYB 82*
Pyramid Film & Video - Santa Monica, CA - *AvMarPl 83; Tel&CabFB 84C*
Pyramid Records - Taylor, MI - *BillIntBG 83-84*
Pyramid Records - New York, NY - *BillIntBG 83-84*
Pyramid Records - Nashville, TN - *BillIntBG 83-84*
Pyramid, The - Springfield, IL - *WritMar 84*
Pyrofiche - London, England - *LitMag&SmPr 83-84*
Pythagorean Press - Maple, ON, Canada - *BoPubDir 4, 5*
Python Publishing Co. - Newark, NJ - *BoPubDir 4, 5*
Pyxel Applications - Richmond, VA - *MicrocomMPl 84; MicrocomSwDir 1*
Pyxidium Press - New York, NY - *BoPubDir 4, 5*

Q

Q/A Research Centers-Syracuse - Fayetteville, NY - *IntDirMarRes 83*
Q & A Research Inc. - Hicksville, NY - *IntDirMarRes 83*
Q & D Advertising - San Francisco, CA - *StaDirAdAg 2-84*
Q & M Publishing - Provo, UT - *MicrocomMPl 84*
Q & Q Research Inc. - *See* Brown, Koff & Fried Inc.
Q Broadcasting Ltd. - Vancouver, BC, Canada - *BrCabYB 84*
Q-Fax [of RCA Global Communications Inc.] - New York, NY - *TeleSy&SerDir 2-84*
Q1 Corp. - Hauppauge, NY - *DataDirSup 7-83; DirInfWP 82; WhoWMicrocom 83*
Q-Vo Magazine - Los Angeles, CA - *MagIndMarPl 82-83*
Qantel Corp. - Hayward, CA - *DirInfWP 82*
Qantex Div. [of North Atlantic Industries] - Hauppauge, NY - *DataDirSup 7-83; DirInfWP 82; WhoWMicrocom 83*
QCTV Ltd. - Bon Accord, AB, Canada - *BrCabYB 84*
QCTV Ltd. - Edmonton, AB, Canada - *BrCabYB 84*
QED Enterprises - Pittsburgh, PA - *Tel&CabFB 84C*
Q.E.D. Information Sciences Inc. - Wellesley, MA - *BoPubDir 4, 5; LitMarPl 83, 84; WritMar 84*
Q.E.D. Productions Inc. - New York, NY - *TelAl 83, 84; Tel&CabFB 84C*
QEI Inc. - Bedford, MA - *MicrocomMPl 84*
QL/Mail Directory [of QL Systems Ltd.] - Ottawa, ON, Canada - *DataDirOnSer 84*
QL Records - Coral Gables, FL - *BillIntBG 83-84*
QL Systems Ltd. - Kingston, ON, Canada - *DataDirOnSer 84; EISS 83; InfIndMarPl 83*
QL Systems Ltd. - Ottawa, ON, Canada - *DataDirOnSer 84; DirInfWP 82*
QM Productions - Hollywood, CA - *Tel&CabFB 84C*
QM Productions [Div. of Taft Entertainment Co.] - Los Angeles, CA - *TelAl 83, 84*
Qmetrics Inc. - New York, NY - *ADAPSOMemDir 83-84*
QML Communications [Div. of Q Marketing Ltd. Inc.] - Dedham, MA - *StaDirAdAg 2-84*
QSI Inc. - Reseda, CA - *MicrocomMPl 84*
QSR Service Corp. - Teaneck, NJ - *MicrocomMPl 84*
QST - Newington, CT - *BaconPubCkMag 84; MagDir 84*
QT Computer Systems Inc. - Lawndale, CA - *MicrocomMPl 83*
QTech Associates - Old Lyme, CT - *DataDirSup 7-83*
Quackenbush Music Ltd. - Los Angeles, CA - *BillIntBG 83-84*
Quad-City Herald - Brewster, WA - *AyerDirPub 83*
Quad City News - Margate, FL - *Ed&PubIntYB 82*
Quad-City News - Pompano Beach, FL - *AyerDirPub 83*
Quad-City Times - Davenport, IA - *AyerDirPub 83; BaconPubCkNews 84; Ed&PubIntYB 82*
Quad County Communications Co. - Cameron, MO - *BrCabYB 84*
Quad County Newspapers - Fremont, IA - *BaconPubCkNews 84*
Quad/Graphics Inc. - Pewaukee, WI - *MagIndMarPl 82-83*
Quadcom Inc. - Cos Cob, CT - *CabTVFinDB 83*
Quade Books, Vicki - Evanston, IL - *BoPubDir 4, 5*
Quadex Corp. - Cambridge, MA - *DirInfWP 82*
Quadram Corp. - Norcross, GA - *MicrocomMPl 84*
Quadrangle Management - Los Angeles, CA - *BillIntBG 83-84*
Quadrant Concepts - Miramar, FL - *BoPubDir 4, 5*
Quadrant Press Inc. - New York, NY - *BoPubDir 4, 5*
Quadraphonic Talent Inc. - Miami, FL - *BillIntBG 83-84*
Quadrature - Paris, France - *EISS 83*
Quadrum Corp. - Norcross, GA - *MicrocomMPl 83*
Quadstar Corp. - Dallas, TX - *DataDirSup 7-83*
Quail Ridge Press Inc. - Brandon, MS - *BoPubDir 4, 5*
Quail Run Publications Inc. - Phoenix, AZ - *BoPubDir 4, 5*
Quail Video - Pittsburgh, PA - *AvMarPl 83*
Quaker CATV [of Landmark Cablevision Associates] - Lisbon, OH - *BrCabYB 84; Tel&CabFB 84C*
Quaker CATV [of Landmark Cablevision Associates] - Salem, OH - *BrCabYB 84; Tel&CabFB 84C*
Quaker City Carrier [of National Association of Letter Carriers Branch 157] - Philadelphia, PA - *NewsDir 84*
Quaker Press - Washington, DC - *BoPubDir 4, 5*
Quaker State Telephone Co. [Aff. of Continental Telephone Corp.] - Hershey, PA - *TelDir&BG 83-84*
Quakertown Free Press - Quakertown, PA - *BaconPubCkNews 84; NewsDir 84*
Quakertown Free Press Journal - Quakertown, PA - *NewsDir 84*
Qualex Technology Inc. - Westlake Village, CA - *WhoWMicrocom 83*
Quali-Color Lab [Div. of Ed Stewart & Associates Inc.] - Houston, TX - *AvMarPl 83*
Qualified Lists Corp. [Div. of The Walter Karl Cos.] - Armonk, NY - *LitMarPl 83, 84; MagIndMarPl 82-83*
Qualified Remodeler - Chicago, IL - *BaconPubCkMag 84; MagDir 84*
Qualigraphics Inc. - Englewood, NJ - *LitMarPl 83, 84*
Qualitative Consultancy, The - London, England - *IntDirMarRes 83*
Qualitative Decisions Center Inc. - New York, NY - *IntDirMarRes 83*
Qualitative Insights - Milwaukee, WI - *IntDirMarRes 83*
Quality - Wheaton, IL - *BaconPubCkMag 84; MagIndMarPl 82-83*
Quality Books Inc. - Northbrook, IL - *LitMarPl 83, 84*
Quality Books of Kansas City, Missouri - Kansas City, MO - *BoPubDir 4, 5*
Quality Broadcasting - Mayaguez, PR - *BrCabYB 84*
Quality Cable Network Corp. - New York, NY - *Tel&CabFB 84C*
Quality Cablevision Co. - Elgin, WI - *BrCabYB 84*
Quality Cablevision Co. - Prairie du Chien, WI - *Tel&CabFB 84C p.1698*
Quality CATV Inc. - Sheridan, IN - *BrCabYB 84 p.D-305; Tel&CabFB 84C p.1698*
Quality Color Lab Inc. - New York, NY - *AvMarPl 83*
Quality Control Scanner, The - Livonia, NY - *BaconPubCkMag 84*
Quality Control Supervisor's Bulletin - Waterford, CT - *WritMar 84*
Quality Controlled Services - Fenton, MO - *IntDirMarRes 83*
Quality Education Data [Subs. of National Business Lists Inc.] - Denver, CO - *LitMarPl 83, 84*

Quality Educational Designs - Portland, OR - *MicrocomMPl 83, 84; MicrocomSwDir 1*
Quality Educators Ltd. - Ft. Lauderdale, FL - *BoPubDir 4, 5*
Quality Film Laboratories Inc. - Baltimore, MD - *AvMarPl 83*
Quality/For Better Product Assurance & Reliability - Wheaton, IL - *MagDir 84*
Quality Guide - Chautauyan County, NY - *Ed&PubIntYB 82*
Quality Guide - Westfield, NY - *AyerDirPub 83*
Quality House of Graphics - Long Island City, NY - *LitMarPl 84*
Quality-in-Field - Philadelphia, PA - *IntDirMarRes 83*
Quality Information Center Inc. - Staten Island, NY - *IntDirMarRes 83*
Quality Letter Service Inc. - New York, NY - *DirInfWP 82*
Quality Micro Systems Inc. - Mobile, AL - *DataDirSup 7-83*
Quality Newspapers/Suburban Publications - South Milwaukee, WI - *BaconPubCkNews 84*
Quality on Time Interviewing - Leawood, KS - *IntDirMarRes 83*
Quality Paperback Book Club - *See* Book-of-the-Month Club Inc.
Quality Photoengraving Corp. - Long Island City, NY - *LitMarPl 83, 84*
Quality Photoengraving Corp. - New York, NY - *LitMarPl 83*
Quality Productions - Oklahoma City, OK - *AvMarPl 83*
Quality Program Sales Inc. - Los Angeles, CA - *TelAl 83, 84*
Quality Progress - Milwaukee, WI - *BaconPubCkMag 84; MagDir 84; MagIndMarPl 82-83*
Quality Publications - Tigard, OR - *BoPubDir 4, 5*
Quality Publications Inc. [Aff. of S-W Enterprises] - Lakewood, OH - *BoPubDir 4, 5; LitMag&SmPr 83-84; WritMar 84*
Quality Records - New York, NY - *BillIntBG 83-84*
Quality Respondents - New York, NY - *IntDirMarRes 83*
Quality Review Bulletin: The Journal of Quality Assurance - Chicago, IL - *MagIndMarPl 82-83*
Quality Services Co. - Santa Barbara, CA - *BoPubDir 4 Sup, 5*
Quality Software - Reseda, CA - *MicrocomMPl 83; MicrocomSwDir 1; WhoWMicrocom 83*
Quality Systems Corp. - Chicago, IL - *WhoWMicrocom 83*
Quality Technology Information Service [of Atomic Energy Authority] - Didcot, England - *EISS 83*
Qually & Co. Inc. - Chicago, IL - *StaDirAdAg 2-84*
Quam Press, Martin - Cedar Falls, IA - *LitMag&SmPr 83-84*
Quam Press, Martin - Rio, WI - *BoPubDir 4, 5*
Quanah Cablevision Inc. [of Communications Systems Inc.] - Quanah, TX - *BrCabYB 84; Tel&CabFB 84C*
Quanah Tribune Chief - Quanah, TX - *BaconPubCkNews 84*
Quant Systems - Charleston, SC - *MicrocomMPl 83, 84; WhoWMicrocom 83*
Quanta Advertising - Syracuse, NY - *StaDirAdAg 2-84*
Quanta Corp. - New Orleans, LA - *ADAPSOMemDir 83-84*
Quanta Data Systems - New Orleans, LA - *DataDirOnSer 84*
Quantal Publishing - Goleta, CA - *BoPubDir 4, 5; LitMag&SmPr 83-84*
QuanTeckna Research Corp. - Mountlake Terrace, WA - *MicrocomSwDir 1; WhoWMicrocom 83*
Quantime Ltd. - London, England - *IntDirMarRes 83*
Quantiplex - New York, NY - *BrCabYB 84*
Quantitape - Chicago, IL - *AvMarPl 83*
Quantitative Medical Systems - Emeryville, CA - *DataDirOnSer 84*
Quantitative Software Management Inc. - McLean, VA - *DataDirOnSer 84; WhoWMicrocom 83*
Quantum Analysis Inc. - Buffalo, NY - *IntDirMarRes 83*
Quantum Corp. - Milpitas, CA - *DataDirSup 7-83; MicrocomMPl 84; WhoWMicrocom 83*
Quantum Data Inc. - Costa Mesa, CA - *WhoWMicrocom 83*
Quantum Information Resources Ltd. - Toronto, ON, Canada - *DataDirSup 7-83*
Quantum Instruments Inc. - Garden City, NY - *AvMarPl 83*
Quantum Productions Inc. - New York, NY - *AvMarPl 83*
Quantum Publishers Inc. - New York, NY - *BoPubDir 4, 5*
Quantum Science Corp. - New York, NY - *DirInfWP 82; InfIndMarPl 83*
Quantum Software System Inc. - San Jose, CA - *MicrocomSwDir 1*
Quantum Systems Inc. - Metairie, LA - *WhoWMicrocom 83*
Quantumn Information Systems - Seattle, WA - *MicrocomMPl 83, 84; WhoWMicrocom 83*
Quark Engineering - *See* Quark Inc.
Quark Inc. - Denver, CO - *MicrocomMPl 83, 84; MicrocomSwDir 1; WhoWMicrocom 83*
Quarry Magazine - Kingston, ON, Canada - *ArtMar 84; LitMag&SmPr 83-84; WritMar 84*
Quarry Press [Aff. of Quarry Magazine] - Kingston, ON, Canada - *BoPubDir 4 Sup, 5; LitMag&SmPr 83-84*
Quarryville Sun-Ledger - Quarryville, PA - *BaconPubCkNews 84*
Quarter Horse Journal, The - Amarillo, TX - *BaconPubCkMag 84; MagDir 84; MagIndMarPl 82-83; WritMar 84*
Quarter Horse Northwest - Yakima, WA - *BaconPubCkMag 84*
Quarter Horse of the Pacific Coast, The - Sacramento, CA - *ArtMar 84*
Quarter Horse Track - Ft. Worth, TX - *BaconPubCkMag 84; MagDir 84*
Quarter Moon [of C. Z. Calder] - Warwick, NY - *LitMag&SmPr 83-84; WritMar 84*
Quarter Racing Record - Ft. Worth, TX - *BaconPubCkMag 84; MagDir 84*
Quarterdeck Press - Pacific Palisades, CA - *BoPubDir 4, 5*
Quarterly [of B.W.M.T. Inc.] - San Francisco, CA - *WritMar 84*
Quarterly Committee [of Queen's University] - Kingston, ON, Canada - *LitMag&SmPr 83-84*
Quarterly Journal of Economics [of John Wiley & Sons Inc.] - Cambridge, MA - *MagDir 84*
Quarterly Journal of Economics - New York, NY - *MagIndMarPl 82-83*
Quarterly Journal of Speech - Amherst, MA - *MagIndMarPl 82-83*
Quarterly Journal of Speech - Annandale, VA - *MagDir 84*
Quarterly Oil Statistics [of I. P. Sharp Associates Ltd.] - Toronto, ON, Canada - *DataDirOnSer 84*
Quarterly Review of Literature - Princeton, NJ - *LitMag&SmPr 83-84*
Quarterly Statement - Chicago, IL - *BaconPubCkMag 84*
Quarterly West - Salt Lake City, UT - *LitMag&SmPr 83-84*
Quarterman Publications Inc. - Lawrence, MA - *LitMarPl 83, 84*
Quartet Books Inc. [Subs. of The Namara Group] - New York, NY - *LitMarPl 83, 84*
Quartet Films - Studio City, CA - *AvMarPl 83; Tel&CabFB 84C*
Quartet International Inc. - Pearl River, NY - *Tel&CabFB 84C*
Quarto - Morton Grove, IL - *LitMarPl 84*
Quarto Marketing Ltd. - New York, NY - *LitMarPl 83, 84*
Quarto Publishing - New York, NY - *LitMarPl 83, 84*
Quartuccio, Anthony - San Jose, CA - *BoPubDir 5*
Quartz Publications - Freehold, NJ - *LitMag&SmPr 83-84*
Quasar Co. [Div. of Matsushita Electric Corp. of America] - Franklin Park, IL - *BillIntBG 83-84; WhoWMicrocom 83*
Quasar Data Products Inc. - Brecksville, OH - *WhoWMicrocom 83*
Quasar Data Products Inc. - Cleveland, OH - *MicrocomMPl 84*
Quasar Graphics Inc. - Chicago, IL - *MagIndMarPl 82-83*
Quasitronics Inc. - Houston, PA - *MicrocomMPl 84; WhoWMicrocom 83*
Quay Corp. - Freehold, NJ - *WhoWMicrocom 83*
Quay County Sun - Tucumcari, NM - *AyerDirPub 83; Ed&PubIntYB 82*
Quazon Corp. - Carrollton, TX - *TeleSy&SerDir 2-84*
Qube Cable [of Warner Amex Cable Communications Inc.] - New York, NY - *CabTVPrDB 83*
Qube Cable/Houston Cable TV Inc. [of Warner Amex Cable Communications Inc.] - Houston, TX - *BrCabYB 84; Tel&CabFB 84C*
Qube Cable of Dallas [of Warner Amex Cable Communications Inc.] - Dallas, TX - *Tel&CabFB 84C*
QuCes Inc. - Metuchen, NJ - *MicrocomMPl 83, 84*
Que Corp. - Indianapolis, IN - *BoPubDir 5; WritMar 84*
Quebec-Actualite [of Microfor Inc.] - Quebec City, PQ, Canada - *CompReadDB 82*
Quebec/Amerique - Montreal, PQ, Canada - *BaconPubCkMag 84*
Quebec Association for Children & Adults with Learning Disabilities - Montreal, PQ, Canada - *BoPubDir 4, 5*
Quebec Ministere de l'Education (Centrale des Bibliotheques) - Montreal, PQ, Canada - *BoPubDir 4, 5*
Quebec Society for Legal Information - Montreal, PQ, Canada - *EISS 83*

Quebecor Inc. - Montreal, PQ, Canada - *Ed&PubIntYB 82*
Queen [of Montfort Missionaries] - Bay Shore, NY - *WritMar 84*
Queen Anne News - Seattle, WA - *AyerDirPub 83; Ed&PubIntYB 82*
Queen Anne News - *See* Murray Publishing Co.
Queen Anne's Record-Observer - Centreville, MD - *AyerDirPub 83*
Queen City Mail - Spearfish, SD - *AyerDirPub 83; Ed&PubIntYB 82*
Queen City Publishing Ltd. - Toronto, ON, Canada - *BoPubDir 4, 5*
Queen City Suburban Press Inc. - Cincinnati, OH - *BaconPubCkNews 84*
Queen City Telecommunications Inc. [of Belo Broadcasting Corp.] - Clarksville, TN - *BrCabYB 84; Tel&CabFB 84C*
Queen of Hearts Music - Shreveport, LA - *BillIntBG 83-84*
Queen, Robert I. - Flushing, NY - *LitMarPl 83, 84; MagIndMarPl 82-83*
Queens College (Council on Research in Bibliography Inc.) - Flushing, NY - *BoPubDir 4, 5*
Queens College Press - Flushing, NY - *BoPubDir 4, 5*
Queens House - Larchmont, NY - *BoPubDir 4, 5*
Queens Illustrated News [of New Hyde Park Nassau Illustrated News] - New Hyde Park, NY - *Ed&PubIntYB 82; NewsDir 84*
Queens Ledger - Flushing, NY - *AyerDirPub 83*
Queens Ledger - Queens, NY - *Ed&PubIntYB 82*
Queens-Long Island Evening News [of Interboro Associates] - Sunnyside, NY - *NewsDir 84*
Queen's Quarterly [of Queen's University] - Kingston, ON, Canada - *LitMag&SmPr 83-84; WritMar 84*
Queens Tribune - Flushing, NY - *AyerDirPub 83; Ed&PubIntYB 82*
Queen's University (Centre for Resource Studies) - Kingston, ON, Canada - *BoPubDir 4, 5*
Queen's University (Industrial Relations Centre) - Kingston, ON, Canada - *BoPubDir 4, 5*
Queen's University (Institute of Intergovernmental Relations) - Kingston, ON, Canada - *BoPubDir 4 Sup, 5*
Queen's University (Kingston Douglas Library) - Kingston, ON, Canada - *BoPubDir 4 Sup, 5*
Queens University, Belfast (Computer Centre) - Belfast, Nothern Ireland - *InfIndMarPl 83*
Queen's University Interrogation on Legal Literature [of Queen's University, Belfast] - Belfast, Nothern Ireland - *EISS 83*
Queens Village Pennysaver - Rockville Centre, NY - *AyerDirPub 83*
Queensland Online Users' Group [of University of Queensland] - Queensland, Australia - *InfIndMarPl 83*
Queenston House Publishing Co. Ltd. - Winnipeg, MB, Canada - *BoPubDir 4; LitMarPl 83*
Quelo - Seattle, WA - *MicrocomMPl 84*
Quentin Research Inc. - Chatsworth, CA - *MicrocomMPl 84*
Quercus [of The Poet Tree Inc.] - Sacramento, CA - *LitMag&SmPr 83-84*
Quesnel Cariboo Observer - Quesnel, BC, Canada - *Ed&PubIntYB 82*
Quest [of Human Kinetics Pub. Inc.] - Champaign, IL - *LitMag&SmPr 83-84*
Quest Educational Aids Inc. - Fairfield, CT - *AvMarPl 83*
Quest/80 - New York, NY - *MagDir 84*
Quest Magazine - Toronto, ON, Canada - *BaconPubCkMag 84*
Quest Publishing Co. - Brea, CA - *BoPubDir 4, 5*
Questa Cable TV Co. [of Mickelson Media Inc.] - Questa, NM - *Tel&CabFB 84C*
Questa6 & Questa7 [of Questel Inc.] - Washington, DC - *DataDirOnSer 84*
Questa6 & Questa7 - Paris, France - *DirOnDB Spring 84*
Questar - New Hope, PA - *AvMarPl 83*
Questar Controls Inc. - Chehalis, WA - *MicrocomMPl 84*
Questel [of Telesystemes Questel] - Paris, France - *EISS 83*
Questel Inc. [Subs. of Telesystemes Questel] - Washington, DC - *DataDirOnSer 84*
Question Shop Inc., The - Orange, CA - *IntDirMarRes 83*
Questionnaire Service Co. - Lansing, MI - *MicrocomMPl 84; MicrocomSwDir 1*
Questions & Answers Inc. - West Dundee, IL - *IntDirMarRes 83*
Questronics Inc. - Salt Lake City, UT - *DataDirSup 7-83*
Quetico Centre - Atikokan, ON, Canada - *BoPubDir 4 Sup, 5*
Quetletet library - Brussels, Belgium - *DirOnDB Spring 84*
Queue Inc. - Fairfield, CT - *MicrocomMPl 83*
Quick Books - Pueblo, CO - *BoPubDir 4, 5; LitMag&SmPr 83-84*
Quick Brown Fox - New York, NY - *MicrocomMPl 84*
Quick Cassette Corp. - New York, NY - *AvMarPl 83*
Quick Fox - *See* Putnam Publishing Group
Quick Frozen Foods - Cleveland, OH - *BaconPubCkMag 84; WritMar 84*
Quick Frozen Foods International [of Harcourt Brace Jovanovich Publications] - New York, NY - *BaconPubCkMag 84; MagDir 84; WritMar 84*
Quick-N-Easy Products - Langhorne, PA - *MicrocomMPl 84*
Quick Printing - Ft. Pierce, FL - *BaconPubCkMag 84; MagDir 84*
Quick Quote [of CompuServe Inc.] - Columbus, OH - *DBBus 82*
Quick Strokes - West Sacramento, CA - *MicrocomMPl 84*
Quick Tax Ltd. - Richmond, NY - *MicrocomSwDir 1*
Quick Tax Ltd. - Staten Island, NY - *MicrocomMPl 83, 84; WhoWMicrocom 83*
Quick Test - Cornwell Heights, PA - *IntDirMarRes 83*
Quickmix Music Inc. - *See* Jiru Music Inc.
Quicksilver Productions - Ashland, OR - *BoPubDir 4, 5; LitMag&SmPr 83-84; WritMar 84*
Quiet Designs Inc. - Sunnyvale, CA - *DirInfWP 82*
Quietprint Inc. - Windsor, CA - *DirInfWP 82*
Quigley Publishing Co. Inc. - New York, NY - *BoPubDir 4, 5*
Quik-Type Service - Greenwich, CT - *LitMarPl 84*
Quikdata Computer Service - Sheboygan, WI - *MicrocomMPl 83, 84*
Quill - Chicago, IL - *BaconPubCkMag 84; MagDir 84; MagIndMarPl 82-83*
Quill - West Plains, MO - *AyerDirPub 83*
Quill [Div. of William Morrow & Co. Inc.] - New York, NY - *LitMarPl 83*
Quill & Quire - Toronto, ON, Canada - *BaconPubCkMag 84; LitMag&SmPr 83-84; LitMarPl 83, 84*
Quill & Scroll - Coralville, IA - *MagDir 84*
Quill & Scroll - Iowa City, IA - *BaconPubCkMag 84; MagIndMarPl 82-83*
Quill & Scroll Society - Iowa City, IA - *BoPubDir 4, 5*
Quill Corp. - Northbrook, IL - *DirInfWP 82*
Quill Publications - Santa Barbara, CA - *BoPubDir 4, 5*
Quill Trade Paperbacks [Div. of William Morrow & Co. Inc.] - New York, NY - *LitMarPl 84*
Quillen Elsea & Associates Inc. - Wichita, KS - *StaDirAdAg 2-84*
Quillin & Associates Inc., L. - La Crosse, WI - *AdAge 3-28-84; StaDirAdAg 2-84*
Quilt - Berkeley, CA - *LitMag&SmPr 83-84*
Quilt World - Brooksville, FL - *ArtMar 84*
Quilter's Newsletter Magazine - Wheatridge, CO - *WritMar 84*
Quimper Press [Aff. of Port Townsend Publishing Co. Inc.] - Port Townsend, WA - *BoPubDir 4, 5*
Quin ABI Broadcasting Inc. - Tullahoma, TN - *BrCabYB 84*
Quincenario Hispano - Vancouver, BC, Canada - *Ed&PubIntYB 82*
Quincy Broadcasting Co. - Quincy, IL - *Tel&CabFB 84S*
Quincy Cable TV Inc. - Quincy, WA - *BrCabYB 84; Tel&CabFB 84C*
Quincy Cablesystems [of American Cablesystems Corp.] - Quincy, MA - *BrCabYB 84; Tel&CabFB 84C*
Quincy Community TV Association Inc. - Quincy, CA - *BrCabYB 84; Tel&CabFB 84C*
Quincy Feather River Bulletin - *See* Feather Publishing Co. Inc.
Quincy Gadsden County Times - Quincy, FL - *BaconPubCkNews 84; NewsDir 84*
Quincy Herald Whig - Quincy, IL - *BaconPubCkNews 84; Ed&PubIntYB 82; NewsDir 84*
Quincy Newspapers - Quincy, IL - *BrCabYB 84; Ed&PubIntYB 82*
Quincy Sun - Quincy, MA - *BaconPubCkNews 84; Ed&PubIntYB 82; NewsDir 84*
Quincy Telephone Co. [Aff. of Telephone & Data Systems Inc.] - Altamonte Springs, FL - *TelDir&BG 83-84*
Quincy Valley Post-Register - Quincy, WA - *AyerDirPub 83; BaconPubCkNews 84; Ed&PubIntYB 82*
Quindaro - Kansas City, KS - *LitMag&SmPr 83-84*

Quinebaug Valley Cablevision Inc. [of Greater Media Inc.] - Southbridge, MA - *BrCabYB 84; Tel&CabFB 84C*
Quinlan & Co. Ltd., Tom - New York, NY - *HBIndAd&MS 82-83*
Quinlan, Campbell Publishers - Medford, MA - *LitMarPl 84*
Quinlan Keene Peck & McShay - Indianapolis, IN - *AdAge 3-28-84; ArtMar 84; StaDirAdAg 2-84*
Quinlan Tawakoni News - Quinlan, TX - *BaconPubCkNews 84*
Quinn & Johnson/BBDO [Subs. of BBDO International Inc.] - Boston, MA - *AdAge 3-28-84; LitMarPl 83, 84; StaDirAdAg 2-84*
Quinn & Johnson Public Relations - *See* Doremus & Co. Public Relations
Quinn-Gallagher Press - Pittsburgh, PA - *BoPubDir 4, 5*
Quinn, Gerald H. - Marietta, GA - *WhoWMicrocom 83*
Quinn Woodbine Inc. - Woodbine, NJ - *LitMarPl 83, 84*
Quinones, Melvyn O. - San Francisco, CA - *LitMarPl 83, 84*
Quinones Music Co. - St. Louis, MO - *BillIntBG 83-84*
Quinsept - Lexington, MA - *MicrocomMPl 84*
Quinte Cablevision Ltd. - Picton, ON, Canada - *BrCabYB 84*
Quinte Scanner, The - Deseronto, ON, Canada - *Ed&PubIntYB 82*
Quinter Grove County Advocate - Quinter, KS - *BaconPubCkNews 84*
Quintessence International/Dental Digest [of Quintessence Publishing Co. Inc.] - Chicago, IL - *BaconPubCkMag 84; MagDir 84; MagIndMarPl 82-83*
Quintessence Publications [Subs. of Quintessence Press] - Amador City, CA - *ArtMar 84; BoPubDir 4, 5; LitMag&SmPr 83-84; LitMarPl 83, 84*
Quintessence Publishing Co. Inc. - Chicago, IL - *LitMarPl 83, 84; MagIndMarPl 82-83; WritMar 84*
Quinto Records - Toluca Lake, CA - *BillIntBG 83-84*
Quinton Cable TV Inc. - Quinton, OK - *BrCabYB 84; Tel&CabFB 84C*
QUIP-Arbuckle, Cohen & Trewhella Inc. - New York, NY - *IntDirMarRes 83*
Quitaque Valley Tribune - Quitaque, TX - *BaconPubCkNews 84*
Quitman Cable TV [of Texas Community Antennas Inc.] - Quitman, TX - *BrCabYB 84*
Quitman Clarke County Tribune - Quitman, MS - *BaconPubCkNews 84; NewsDir 84*
Quitman County Democrat - Marks, MS - *AyerDirPub 83; Ed&PubIntYB 82*
Quitman Free Press - Quitman, GA - *BaconPubCkNews 84; Ed&PubIntYB 82*
Quixote - Houston, TX - *LitMag&SmPr 83-84*
Quixote Press - Houston, TX - *LitMag&SmPr 83-84*
Quixote Publishing Co. Inc., Don - Amarillo, TX - *BoPubDir 4 Sup, 5*
Quixote, Quixotl - Houston, TX - *BoPubDir 4, 5*
Quixsilver Press - Baltimore, MD - *LitMag&SmPr 83-84*
Quiz - Ord, NE - *AyerDirPub 83*
Quiz Features - Washington, DC - *Ed&PubIntYB 82*
Qume Corp. [Subs. of International Telephone & Telegraph] - San Jose, CA - *DataDirSup 7-83; DirInfWP 82; MicrocomMPl 84; WhoWMicrocom 83*
Quo Vadis Inc. - Knoxville, IA - *Tel&CabFB 84C*
Quodata Corp. - Hartford, CT - *DataDirSup 7-83*
Quoddy Tides, The - Eastport, ME - *NewsDir 84*
Quorum Editions - Cranbury, NJ - *LitMag&SmPr 83-84*
Quotation Information Center KK [of Nihon Keizai Shimbun Inc.] - Tokyo, Japan - *EISS 5-84 Sup*
Quote - Atlanta, GA - *BaconPubCkMag 84*
Quote/Unquote - Princeton, NJ - *WritMar 84*
Quotel Insurance Services Ltd. - London, England - *EISS 83*
Quotron 800 [of Quotron Systems Inc.] - Los Angeles, CA - *DataDirOnSer 84; DBBus 82; DirOnDB Spring 84*
Quotron Symbol Guide - Los Angeles, CA - *DirOnDB Spring 84*
Quotron Systems Inc. - Los Angeles, CA - *DataDirOnSer 84; Datamation 6-83; EISS 83; InfIndMarPl 83; Top100Al 83*
Qwest Records - Los Angeles, CA - *BillIntBG 83-84*
Qwint Systems Inc. - Northbrook, IL - *DataDirSup 7-83; MicrocomMPl 84; WhoWMicrocom 83*

R

R & B Computer Systems Inc. [Subs. of Dimis Inc.] - Tempe, AZ - *MicrocomMPl 83, 84; WhoWMicrocom 83*
R & B Efx - Glendale, CA - *AvMarPl 83*
R & D Management Digest - Mt. Airy, MD - *MagIndMarPl 82-83*
R & D Services - Des Moines, IA - *BoPubDir 4, 5; DirMarMP 83; LitMag&SmPr 83-84*
R & E Cablevision Inc. [of Mercure Telecommunications Inc.] - Mayport Naval Station, FL - *Tel&CabFB 84C*
R & E Publishers [of R & E Research Associates] - Saratoga, CA - *LitMarPl 84*
R & E Research Associates Inc. - Palo Alto, CA - *LitMarPl 83*
R & E Research Association - Saratoga, CA - *WritMar 84*
R & K Interviewing Service - Philadelphia, PA - *IntDirMarRes 83*
R & L Data Centers Inc. - Bloomsbury, NJ - *ADAPSOMemDir 83-84*
R & M Associates - Sea Girt, NJ - *MicrocomSwDir 1*
R & M Communications Co. - Markesan, WI - *BrCabYB 84; Tel&CabFB 84C*
R & M Publishing Co. Inc. - Holly Hill, SC - *BoPubDir 5; LitMag&SmPr 83-84*
R & M Publishing Co. Inc. - Marion, SC - *BoPubDir 4*
R & R Cable Co. - Roslyn, WA - *BrCabYB 84; Tel&CabFB 84C*
R & R Entertainment Digest [of R & R Werbe GmbH] - Heidelberg, West Germany - *WritMar 84*
R & R Newkirk - Indianapolis, IN - *WritMar 84*
R & R Records Inc./Ren Rome - New York, NY - *BillIntBG 83-84*
R & R Technical Bookfinders - Littleton, CO - *BoPubDir 4 Sup, 5*
R & S Cable TV Inc. - Laurel County, KY - *BrCabYB 84*
R & W Computer Research Inc. - Vero Beach, FL - *DataDirOnSer 84*
R. & W. Distribution Inc. - Jersey City, NJ - *MagIndMarPl 82-83*
R/C Modeler - Sierra Madre, CA - *BaconPubCkMag 84; MagIndMarPl 82-83*
R/C Sportsman - Reno, NV - *MagDir 84*
R/J Associates - Livermore, CA - *BoPubDir 4, 5*
R/L Laboratories Inc. - Baltimore, MD - *AvMarPl 83*
R-S-2 Computer System [of Texas A & M University] - College Station, TX - *EISS 7-83 Sup*
R-12 - Lansdale, PA - *BaconPubCkMag 84*
R2E of America [Subs. of Cii-Honeywell Bull] - Roseville, MN - *WhoWMicrocom 83*
R-Way Furniture Co. - Sheboygan, WI - *DirInfWP 82*
Ra-Jo International - Bronx, NY - *BillIntBG 83-84*
Rabbit Creek Journal - Clipper Mills, CA - *AyerDirPub 83*
Rabco Enterprises - Harleysville, PA - *MicrocomMPl 84*
Rabin Associates Inc., Jules - Valley Stream, NY - *AdAge 3-28-84; StaDirAdAg 2-84*
Rabin Research Co. - Chicago, IL - *IntDirMarRes 83*
Rabinowitz Hebrew Book Store, Solomon - New York, NY - *BoPubDir 4, 5*
Rabun Cablevision [of Mountain View Enterprises Inc.] - Clayton, GA - *BrCabYB 84*
RAC Information Systems Inc. - Great Neck, NY - *EISS 83; IntDirMarRes 83*
Racal Data Communications Inc. - Miami, FL - *Datamation 6-83*
Racal Electronics - Bracknell, England - *ElecNews 7-25-83; Top100Al 83*
Racal-Milgo Inc. - Miami, FL - *DataDirSup 7-83; InfIndMarPl 83*
Racal Redac Inc. - Westford, MA - *DataDirSup 7-83*
Racal-Telesystems Network Inc. - Chicago, IL - *DirInfWP 82*
Racal-Vadic - Milpitas, CA - *MicrocomMPl 84*
Racal-Vadic - Sunnyvale, CA - *DataDirSup 7-83; WhoWMicrocom 83*
Raccoon [of St. Luke's Press] - Memphis, TN - *LitMag&SmPr 83-84*
Race & Associates, Robert W. - Chicago, IL - *StaDirAdAg 2-84*
Race & Rally - Alexandria, MN - *MagDir 84*
Race Today - London, England - *LitMag&SmPr 83-84*
Racecar [of Formula Enterprises Inc.] - Los Angeles, CA - *MagDir 84*
Racener Advertising Agency - Evansville, IN - *StaDirAdAg 2-84*
Racet Computes - Orange, CA - *MicrocomMPl 83, 84; WhoWMicrocom 83*
Rachel's Own Music - *See* Schroeder International Ltd., A.
Racine Courier - *See* Courier Communications Group
Racine Journal Times - Racine, WI - *NewsDir 84*
Racine Labor, The [of Union Labor Publishing Co. Inc.] - Racine, WI - *NewsDir 84*
Racine Shoreline Leader - Racine, WI - *BaconPubCkNews 84; NewsDir 84*
Racine TeleCable Corp. - Racine, WI - *BrCabYB 84; Tel&CabFB 84C*
Racing Digest - Dover, PA - *MagDir 84; WritMar 84*
Racing Pictorial - Indianapolis, IN - *MagIndMarPl 82-83*
Racing Pigeon Pictorial [of The Racing Pigeon Publishing Co. Ltd.] - London, England - *WritMar 84*
Racing Wheels - Vancouver, WA - *BaconPubCkMag 84; MagDir 84*
Rack Merchandisers of America - Durham, NC - *BillIntBG 83-84*
Racquet - New York, NY - *BaconPubCkMag 84*
Racquetball & Total Fitness Magazine - Bixby, OK - *MagDir 84*
Racquetball Illustrated - Hollywood, CA - *ArtMar 84; BaconPubCkMag 84; MagDir 84; NewsBur 6; WritMar 84*
Racquets Canada - Toronto, ON, Canada - *BaconPubCkMag 84; WritMar 84*
Racz Publishing Co. - Oxnard, CA - *BoPubDir 4, 5; LitMag&SmPr 83-84*
Rada Press - Champlin, MN - *BoPubDir 5*
Rada Press - Minneapolis, MN - *BoPubDir 4*
Rada Recruitment Communications [Div. of Grey Advertising Inc.] - Chicago, IL - *StaDirAdAg 2-84*
Radar - Cincinnati, OH - *ArtMar 84; WritMar 84*
Radar - *See* Point de Repere

Radar Entertainment Corp. - Elmhurst, NY - *BillIntBG 83-84*
Radaus-Data-Service [of Radio-Austria AG] - Vienna, Austria - *TeleSy&SerDir 2-84*
Radcliff Sentinel - Radcliff, KY - *BaconPubCkNews 84; NewsDir 84*
Radcliffe Telephone Co. Inc. - Radcliffe, IA - *TelDir&BG 83-84*
Radford Messenger, The - Radford, VA - *Ed&PubIntYB 82; NewsDir 84*
Radford News-Journal [of New River Newspapers] - Radford, VA - *BaconPubCkNews 84; NewsDir 84*
Radford, Ruth - Sooke, BC, Canada - *BoPubDir 4, 5*
Radian Corp. - Austin, TX - *DataDirSup 7-83; EISS 83*
Radiation Chemistry Data Center [of University of Notre Dame] - Notre Dame, IN - *CompReadDB 82; EISS 83; InfIndMarPl 83*
Radiation Shielding Computer Codes [of Oak Ridge National Laboratory] - Oak Ridge, TN - *DataDirOnSer 84; DirOnDB Spring 84*
Radiation Shielding Information Center [of Oak Ridge National Laboratory] - Oak Ridge, TN - *EISS 83*
Radiation Shielding Information Data Base [of Oak Ridge National Laboratory] - Oak Ridge, TN - *DataDirOnSer 84; DirOnDB Spring 84*
Radiation Systems Inc. - Sterling, VA - *HomeVid&CabYB 82-83*
Radiation Technology Programs Inc. - West Palm Beach, FL - *AvMarPl 83*
Radical America [of Alternative Education Project Inc.] - Somerville, MA - *BoPubDir 4, 5; LitMag&SmPr 83-84; WritMar 84*
Radical Reviewer, The - Vancouver, BC, Canada - *LitMag&SmPr 83-84*
Radim Films Inc. - Oak Park, IL - *TelAl 83, 84; Tel&CabFB 84C*
Radimer & Son Inc., C. - Pompton Lakes, NJ - *LitMarPl 83, 84*
Radio - Kelvington, SK, Canada - *AyerDirPub 83*
Radio Advertising Bureau Inc. - New York, NY - *BoPubDir 5*
Radio Americas Corp. - *See* La Gran Cadena Network
Radio & Records - Los Angeles, CA - *BaconPubCkMag 84*
Radio & Rewards - Los Angeles, CA - *MagDir 84*
Radio & Television Packagers Inc. - New York, NY - *TelAl 83, 84; Tel&CabFB 84C*
Radio & TV Distribution Ltd. - Parry Sound, ON, Canada - *BrCabYB 84*
Radio Broadcasting Co. - Philadelphia, PA - *HomeVid&CabYB 82-83*
Radio Campaigns [of National Research Bureau] - Burlington, IA - *MagDir 84*
Radio City Bookstore - New York, NY - *BoPubDir 4, 5*
Radio Cleveland Inc. - Cleveland, MS - *BrCabYB 84*
Radio Communications Report - Denver, CO - *BaconPubCkMag 84*
Radio Contacts - New York, NY - *MagDir 84*
Radio Cote-Nord Inc. - Hauterive, PQ, Canada - *BrCabYB 84*
Radio-Electronics [of Gernsback Publications Inc.] - New York, NY - *ArtMar 84; BaconPubCkMag 84; DirMarMP 83; LitMarPl 83, 84; MagDir 84; MagIndMarPl 82-83; WritMar 84*
Radio Information Center - New York, NY - *BrCabYB 84*
Radio-Matic of America Inc. - Maplewood, NJ - *AvMarPl 83*
Radio Megantic Ltee. - Thetford Mines, PQ, Canada - *BrCabYB 84*
Radio News - Bethesda, MD - *BaconPubCkMag 84*
Radio News Washington - Arlington, VA - *BrCabYB 84*
Radio-Nord Inc. - Noranda, PQ, Canada - *BrCabYB 84*
Radio Observatory [of Ohio State University] - Columbus, OH - *EISS 83*
Radio Post - Fredericksburg, TX - *AyerDirPub 83; BaconPubCkNews 84; Ed&PubIntYB 82*
Radio Publications Inc. - Wilton, CT - *BoPubDir 4, 5*
Radio Pulsebeat News [Div. of Pulsebeat News Inc.] - New York, NY - *BrCabYB 84*
Radio Quebec - Montreal, PQ, Canada - *BrCabYB 84*
Radio Recall Research Inc. - Holmdel, NJ - *IntDirMarRes 83*
Radio Rentals Contracts Ltd. - Feltham, England - *InfIndMarPl 83*
Radio Science - Washington, DC - *BaconPubCkMag 84; MagDir 84*
Radio Shack [Subs. of Tandy Corp.] - Ft. Worth, TX - *DirInfWP 82; LitMarPl 84; MicrocomMPl 83, 84; VideoDir 82-83; WhoWMicrocom 83*
Radio South Inc. - Jasper, AL - *BrCabYB 84*
Radio Station Playlists [of AYA Associates Inc.] - Paramus, NJ - *DataDirOnSer 84*
Radio Technical Commission for Maritime Services - Washington, DC - *TeleSy&SerDir 2-84*
Radio-Television Representatives Ltd. - Toronto, ON, Canada - *TelAl 83, 84*
Radio Times - Norman, OK - *MagIndMarPl 82-83*
Radio-TV Monitoring Service - Washington, DC - *ProGuPRSer 4*
Radio-TV News Monitoring Service Ltd. - Dorval, PQ, Canada - *ProGuPRSer 4*
Radio TV Reports Inc. - Chevy Chase, MD - *BrCabYB 84*
Radio-TV Reports Inc. - New York, NY - *ProGuPRSer 4; Tel&CabFB 84C*
Radio World - Falls Church, VA - *MagDir 84*
Radioassay News - Anaheim, CA - *BaconPubCkMag 84; MagDir 84*
Radiocall Corp. - Honolulu, HI - *Tel&CabFB 84C*
Radiodiffusion Mutuelle Ltee. - Montreal, PQ, Canada - *BrCabYB 84*
Radiofone - Metairie, LA - *Tel&CabFB 84C*
Radiographic Specialties - Freeport, NY - *AvMarPl 83*
Radiola Co., The - Sandy Hook, CT - *BillIntBG 83-84*
Radiologic Technology - Chicago, IL - *BaconPubCkMag 84*
Radiologic Technology - Detroit, MI - *MagDir 84*
Radiology - Hinsdale, IL - *MagDir 84*
Radiology - Southfield, MI - *MagIndMarPl 82-83*
Radiology - Easton, PA - *BaconPubCkMag 84*
Radiology Letter - Brea, CA - *BaconPubCkMag 84*
Radiology Management - Melrose, MA - *BaconPubCkMag 84*
Radiometric Age Data Bank [of U.S. Geological Survey] - Denver, CO - *EISS 83*
RadioNews [of NewsNet Inc.] - Bryn Mawr, PA - *DataDirOnSer 84*
Radiopharmaceutical Internal Dose Information Center [of Oak Ridge Associated Universities] - Oak Ridge, TN - *EISS 83*
Radiosource - *See* Primetime Radio Classics
Radix Books Inc. - Beaver Falls, PA - *BoPubDir 4, 5*
Radix Corp. - Salt Lake City, UT - *DataDirSup 7-83*
Radix Systems Corp. [Subs. of Mid-State Automotive Distributors Inc.] - Cambridge, MA - *WhoWMicrocom 83*
Radke, George - Havertown, PA - *BoPubDir 5*
Radler Associates Inc., Stan - Framingham, MA - *ArtMar 84; StaDirAdAg 2-84*
Radmar Inc. - Highland Park, IL - *AvMarPl 83*
Radmus Publishing Inc. - *See* Shayne Enterprises, Larry
Radofin Electronics Ltd. - Avenel, NJ - *VideoDir 82-83*
Rae Publishing Co. Inc. - Cedar Grove, NJ - *LitMarPl 83, 84*
Raeford News-Journal - Raeford, NC - *BaconPubCkNews 84; Ed&PubIntYB 82; NewsDir 84*
Raema Communications - Marengo, SK, Canada - *BoPubDir 4, 5*
Raemsch, D. C. - West Oneonta, NY - *BoPubDir 4, 5*
Raetz & Raetz - Culver City, CA - *StaDirAdAg 2-84*
Rafaj Marketing Services, Susan M. - New York, NY - *HBIndAd&MS 82-83*
Raffeen Press, The - Fowey, England - *LitMag&SmPr 83-84*
Rafshoon Shivers Vargas Tolpin - Atlanta, GA - *ArtMar 84; DirPRFirms 83*
Raft Theatre - New York, NY - *WritMar 84*
Rafu Shimpo - Los Angeles, CA - *AyerDirPub 83; Ed&PubIntYB 82; NewsDir 84*
Ragan Communications Inc., Lawrence - Chicago, IL - *BoPubDir 4, 5*
Ragan Report, The - Chicago, IL - *BaconPubCkMag 84; MagDir 84; MagIndMarPl 82-83*
Ragdoll Enterprises - Savannah, GA - *BillIntBG 83-84*
Ragged Island Music - Old Hickory, TN - *BillIntBG 83-84*
Ragland Telephone Co. Inc. - Ragland, AL - *TelDir&BG 83-84*
Rago, Christina - Chestnut Hills, MA - *LitMarPl 84*
Ragsdale Associates Inc., Carl - Houston, TX - *AvMarPl 83; TelAl 83, 84; Tel&CabFB 84C*
Ragusan Press - San Carlos, CA - *BoPubDir 4, 5*
Ragweed Press Inc. - Charlottetown, PE, Canada - *BoPubDir 4, 5*
Rahall Communications - *See* Gulf Broadcast Group

RAHM Advertising & Public Relations - Oakland, CA - *AdAge 3-28-84; StaDirAdAg 2-84*
Rahman, Habibur - Centralia, IL - *BoPubDir 4 Sup, 5*
Rahn, Joan Elma - Highland Park, IL - *LitMarPl 83*
Rahola Inc. - Santurce, PR - *AvMarPl 83*
Rahway News-Record [of Tabloid Lithographers Inc.] - Rahway, NJ - *Ed&PubIntYB 82; NewsDir 84*
Rahway News-Record - *See* Tabloid Lithographers Inc.
Railfan & Railroad - Newton, NJ - *BaconPubCkMag 84; MagDir 84; MagIndMarPl 82-83*
Railfare Enterprises Ltd. - West Hill, ON, Canada - *BoPubDir 4, 5; LitMarPl 83, 84*
Railroad Cable TV [of GS Communications Inc.] - Railroad, PA - *BrCabYB 84*
Railroad Model Craftsman - Fredon, NJ - *MagIndMarPl 82-83*
Railroad Model Craftsman - Newton, NJ - *ArtMar 84; BaconPubCkMag 84; MagDir 84; WritMar 84*
Railroad Research Information Service [of Transportation Research Board] - Washington, DC - *CompReadDB 82; EISS 83; InfIndMarPl 83*
Railsback Subscription Agency, Leigh M. - Pasadena, CA - *MagIndMarPl 82-83*
Railway Age - New York, NY - *BaconPubCkMag 84; MagDir 84; MagIndMarPl 82-83*
Railway Carmen's Journal - Kansas City, MO - *NewsDir 84*
Railway Milepost Books - North Vancouver, BC, Canada - *BoPubDir 4 Sup, 5*
Railway Track & Structures - Chicago, IL - *BaconPubCkMag 84; MagDir 84*
Raimi, Ralph A. - Rochester, NY - *BoPubDir 5*
Rain [of Rain Umbrella Inc.] - Portland, OR - *LitMag&SmPr 83-84*
Rain Barrel Music - Lawton, OK - *BillIntBG 83-84*
Rain Umbrella Inc. - Portland, OR - *BoPubDir 4, 5; LitMag&SmPr 83-84*
Raina Productions - Phoenix, AZ - *BillIntBG 83-84*
Rainbo Record Manufacturing Corp. - Santa Monica, CA - *BillIntBG 83-84*
Rainbolt & Brown Inc. - Minneapolis, MN - *DirPRFirms 83*
Rainbow Books/Betty Wright - Moore Haven, FL - *BoPubDir 4, 5; LitMarPl 84*
Rainbow Books Inc. - Carlstadt, NJ - *LitMarPl 83*
Rainbow Computing - Northridge, CA - *MicrocomMPl 83, 84; MicrocomSwDir 1; WhoWMicrocom 83; WritMar 84*
Rainbow Enterprises - West Friendship, MD - *BoPubDir 5*
Rainbow Kabl TV [of Heritage Communications Inc.] - Columbia, MS - *Tel&CabFB 84C*
Rainbow Magazine [of Falsoft Inc.] - Prospect, KY - *MicrocomMPl 84*
Rainbow Press - Huntington Beach, CA - *BoPubDir 4, 5; LitMag&SmPr 83-84*
Rainbow Productions - Chicago, IL - *AvMarPl 83*
Rainbow Programming Services - Denver, CO - *TelAl 83*
Rainbow Programming Services - Woodbury, NY - *BrCabYB 84; Tel&CabFB 84C*
Rainbow Publications - Seattle, WA - *BoPubDir 4, 5; LitMag&SmPr 83-84*
Rainbow Publishing Co. - Chesterland, OH - *BoPubDir 4, 5; LitMag&SmPr 83-84*
Rainbow Records & Tapes - Burbank, CA - *BillIntBG 83-84*
Rainbow Room - New York, NY - *BillIntBG 83-84*
Rainbow Satellite Inc. - Laguna Hills, CA - *Tel&CabFB 84C*
Rainbow Sound Inc. - Dallas, TX - *BillIntBG 83-84*
Rainbow Telephone Cooperative Association Inc., The - Everest, KS - *TelDir&BG 83-84*
Rainbow, The - Prospect, KY - *BaconPubCkMag 84*
Rainbow Vision Cable - Flanagan, IL - *BrCabYB 84; Tel&CabFB 84C*
Rainelle Meadow River Post - Rainelle, WV - *BaconPubCkNews 84*
Rainelle TV Corp. - Rainelle, WV - *BrCabYB 84; Tel&CabFB 84C*
Rainer Sales Associates Inc., Robert - Northfield, IL - *LitMarPl 83, 84*
Raines & Raines - New York, NY - *LitMarPl 83, 84*
Rainfeather Press - Mt. Rainier, MD - *LitMag&SmPr 83-84*
Rainfire Music Publishing - Sherman Oaks, CA - *BillIntBG 83-84*
Rainfire Records - Sherman Oaks, CA - *BillIntBG 83-84*
Rainier Community TV - Rainier, OR - *BrCabYB 84; Tel&CabFB 84C*
Rainmaker Press Ltd. - Richmond, VA - *BoPubDir 4, 5*
Rainoldi-Bowles - San Francisco, CA - *AdAge 3-28-84; StaDirAdAg 2-84*
Rains County Leader - Emory, TX - *AyerDirPub 83; Ed&PubIntYB 82*
Rainsville Sand Mountain News - Rainsville, AL - *BaconPubCkNews 84*
Raintree Inc., George Philip [Subs. of Raintree Publishers Inc.] - Milwaukee, WI - *LitMarPl 83, 84*
Raintree Music - *See* Budd Music Corp.
Raintree Press - Bloomington, IN - *BoPubDir 4, 5*
Raintree Publishers Group - Milwaukee, WI - *ArtMar 84; DirMarMP 83; LitMarPl 83, 84*
Raintree Publishers Inc. - Milwaukee, WI - *LitMarPl 83, 84*
Raintree Publishers International Ltd. [Subs. of Raintree Publishers Inc.] - Milwaukee, WI - *LitMarPl 83, 84*
Rainville Rose Publications - Thousand Oaks, CA - *BoPubDir 4, 5*
Rainy Day Books - Fairway, KS - *BoPubDir 4, 5*
Rainy Day Press - Sausalito, CA - *BoPubDir 4, 5*
Rainy Day Press - Eugene, OR - *BoPubDir 4, 5; LitMag&SmPr 83-84*
Rainy Lake Chronicle - Ranier, MN - *AyerDirPub 83*
Rainy Now Music - *See* Cherry Lane Music Publishing Co. Inc.
Rainy River Record - Rainy River, ON, Canada - *Ed&PubIntYB 82*
R.A.I.R. Inc. - Mountain View, CA - *DataDirOnSer 84*
Rair Microcomputer Corp. - Santa Clara, CA - *WhoWMicrocom 83*
Raitt, Mary H. - Washington, DC - *LitMarPl 83, 84; MagIndMarPl 82-83*
Raivaaja - Fitchburg, MA - *NewsDir 84*
Raizman Public Relations, Marc - Boulder, CO - *DirPRFirms 83*
Raja Press - Oakland, CA - *BoPubDir 4 Sup, 5*
Rajkay, Leslie - Baltimore, MD - *LitMarPl 83, 84; MagIndMarPl 82-83*
Rajneesh Foundation International - Antelope, OR - *BoPubDir 4, 5*
RAK Electronics - Orange Park, FL - *MicrocomMPl 83, 84; MicrocomSwDir 1*
Rake Register - Rake, IA - *AyerDirPub 83; BaconPubCkNews 84; Ed&PubIntYB 82*
Rakennustietosaatio/Building Information Institute - Helsinki, Finland - *InfIndMarPl 83*
Raker, C. Frederic - New York, NY - *LitMarPl 83, 84*
Raleigh Advertising - Los Angeles, CA - *StaDirAdAg 2-84*
Raleigh Carolinian - Raleigh, NC - *BaconPubCkNews 84; NewsDir 84*
Raleigh Group Ltd., The - New York, NY - *DirPRFirms 83; LitMarPl 83, 84*
Raleigh Microwave Communications - Sacramento, CA - *Tel&CabFB 84C*
Raleigh News & Observer - Raleigh, NC - *NewsDir 84*
Raleigh Register - Beckley, WV - *AyerDirPub 83; BaconPubCkNews 84; Ed&PubIntYB 82; NewsDir 84*
Raleigh Smith County Reformer - *See* Buckley Newspapers Inc.
Raleigh Times [of News & Observer Publishing Co.] - Raleigh, NC - *BaconPubCkNews 84; NewsDir 84*
Ralls Banner - Ralls, TX - *BaconPubCkNews 84; Ed&PubIntYB 82*
Ralls County Herald-Record - New London, MO - *AyerDirPub 83; Ed&PubIntYB 82*
Rally Music - *See* Ralph's Radio Music
Ralph Records [Div. of The Cryptic Corp.] - San Francisco, CA - *BillIntBG 83-84*
Ralph's Radio Music - Demorest, GA - *BillIntBG 83-84*
Ralston & Associates Inc., Joanne - Phoenix, AZ - *ArtMar 84; DirPRFirms 83*
Ralston-Clearwaters Electronics - Grants Pass, OR - *MicrocomMPl 84*
Ralston-Pilot Inc. - Cedar City, UT - *BoPubDir 4, 5*
Ralston Recorder - Ralston, NE - *BaconPubCkNews 84; Ed&PubIntYB 82*
Ram Associates Ltd. - Poquoson, VA - *BoPubDir 5*

Ram Publishing Co. - Dallas, TX - *BoPubDir 4, 5; LitMag&SmPr 83-84*
Ram Records - Old Hickory, TN - *BillIntBG 83-84*
Ram Rose Records - Wood-Ridge, NJ - *BillIntBG 83-84*
Ram, The [of Fordham University] - Bronx, NY - *NewsDir 84*
Ram-The Letter Box - Brooklyn, NY - *LitMag&SmPr 83-84*
RAMA - Paris, France - *DirOnDB Spring 84*
Ramage, David A. - Grand Forks, ND - *BrCabYB 84 p.D-305; Tel&CabFB 84C p.1698*
Ramage, William - Hallock, MN - *Tel&CabFB 84C p.1698*
Ramakrishna-Vivekananda Center of New York Inc. - New York, NY - *BoPubDir 4, 5*
Ramar Press - West End, NC - *BoPubDir 4, 5; LitMag&SmPr 83-84*
Rambed Music - *See* Hoffman, Ivan
Rambler Productions Inc. - Johnstown, CO - *BillIntBG 83-84*
Ramer Associates Inc., Joe - New York, NY - *LitMarPl 83, 84*
Ramex Records Inc. - Houston, TX - *BillIntBG 83-84*
Ramey Communications - Los Angeles, CA - *StaDirAdAg 2-84*
Ramico Publications - North Hollywood, CA - *BoPubDir 4 Sup, 5*
Ramm Advertising Inc. - Cranford, NJ - *StaDirAdAg 2-84*
Ramms Music [Div. of House of Falcon Inc.] - McAllen, TX - *BillIntBG 83-84*
Ramona Music Inc. - Lawrence, KS - *BillIntBG 83-84*
Ramona Pennysaver - Mission Viejo, CA - *AyerDirPub 83*
Ramona Sentinel - Ramona, CA - *Ed&PubIntYB 82*
Ramos Inc., Joseph - New York, NY - *IntDirMarRes 83*
Ramp - London, England - *LitMag&SmPr 83-84*
Rampant Lion Publishers Inc. - Las Vegas, NV - *BoPubDir 5*
Rampart Records [Div. of Gordo Enterprises] - Los Angeles, CA - *BillIntBG 83-84*
Ramparts Press - Palo Alto, CA - *LitMag&SmPr 83-84; LitMarPl 83, 84*
Ramparts Reprints & Permissions - San Rafael, CA - *MagIndMarPl 82-83*
Rams' Dell Press [Aff. of Arcana Workshops] - Manhattan Beach, CA - *BoPubDir 4 Sup, 5*
Ram's Horn Music - *See* Special Rider Music
Ramsay, Vera - Vancouver, BC, Canada - *BoPubDir 4, 5*
Ramsco Publishing Co. [Aff. of Ram Associates Ltd.] - Laurel, MD - *BoPubDir 4 Sup, 5*
Ramsey Advertising - Los Angeles, CA - *StaDirAdAg 2-84*
Ramsey Advertising Agency, L. W. - Davenport, IA - *BrCabYB 84; StaDirAdAg 2-84*
Ramsey & Associates - Vancouver, WA - *LitMarPl 84*
Ramsey Associates Inc., Bill - *See* Smith Associates Inc., J. Greg
Ramsey County Review - North St. Paul, MN - *AyerDirPub 83; Ed&PubIntYB 82*
Ramsey Home & Store News - Ramsey, NJ - *BaconPubCkNews 84; NewsDir 84*
Ramsey-Mahwah Reporter [of News Graphics Inc.] - Ramsey, NJ - *Ed&PubIntYB 82; NewsDir 84*
Ramsey News-Journal - Ramsey, IL - *BaconPubCkNews 84; Ed&PubIntYB 82*
Ramsey Reporter - *See* Bergen News Publishing Corp.
Ramsgate Films - Santa Monica, CA - *AvMarPl 83*
Ramsthal Advertising Agency - West Bend, WI - *StaDirAdAg 2-84*
Ramtek Corp. - Santa Clara, CA - *InfIndMarPl 83; WhoWMicrocom 83*
Rana Systems - Carson, CA - *MicrocomMPl 84*
Ranch House Press - Pagosa Springs, CO - *BoPubDir 4, 5*
Ranch Magazine, The - San Angelo, TX - *BaconPubCkMag 84; MagDir 84*
Ranch, The - Mission Viejo, CA - *AyerDirPub 83*
Ranchland Farm News - Simla, CO - *AyerDirPub 83; Ed&PubIntYB 82*
Rancho Bernardo Antenna System [of American TV & Communications Corp.] - Rancho Bernardo, CA - *Tel&CabFB 84C*
Rancho Bernardo Journal - Rancho Bernardo, CA - *Ed&PubIntYB 82*
Rancho Bernardo Journal [of Pomerado Publishing] - San Diego, CA - *AyerDirPub 83; NewsDir 84*
Rancho Bernardo/Stoneridge Pennysaver - Mission Viejo, CA - *AyerDirPub 83*
Rancho Cordovan [of Sacramento Suburban Newspapers Inc.] - Fair Oaks, CA - *NewsDir 84*
Rancho Cordovan, The - Rancho Cordova, CA - *Ed&PubIntYB 82*
Rancho-Cucamonga Times - Cucamonga, CA - *Ed&PubIntYB 82*
Rancho Cucamonga Times [of Ontario Bonita Publishing Co.] - Ontario, CA - *AyerDirPub 83; NewsDir 84*
Rancho Santa Fe Times [of North Coast Publishers Inc.] - Encinitas, CA - *NewsDir 84*
Rancho Santa Fe Times - Rancho Santa Fe, CA - *Ed&PubIntYB 82*
Rancho Santa Fe Times - *See* North Coast Publishers Inc.
Rancho Tierra Grande Associates Inc. - Rancho Tierra Grande, CA - *BrCabYB 84*
Rancho Transmission Co. [of Rancho San Diego Development Co.] - Spring Valley, CA - *Tel&CabFB 84C*
Rancourt & Co. Inc. - Orange City, FL - *AvMarPl 83*
Rand Corp. - Santa Monica, CA - *BoPubDir 4, 5*
Rand Editions/Tofua Press - Leucadia, CA - *BoPubDir 5; LitMag&SmPr 83-84*
Rand Editions/Tofua Press - San Diego, CA - *BoPubDir 4*
Rand Information Systems Inc. - San Francisco, CA - *ADAPSOMemDir 83-84; DataDirOnSer 84*
Rand McNally & Co. - Chicago, IL - *AvMarPl 83; KnowInd 83*
Rand McNally & Co. - Skokie, IL - *LitMarPl 83, 84*
Rand McNally & Co. (Book Manufacturing Div.) - Chicago, IL - *LitMarPl 83, 84*
Rand McNally & Co. (Publishing Group) - Chicago, IL - *WritMar 84*
Rand McNally Campground & Trailer Park Guide - Skokie, IL - *MagDir 84*
Rand Public Relations - New York, NY - *DirPRFirms 83*
Rand Youth Poll-Youth Research Institute - New York, NY - *IntDirMarRes 83*
Randall Communications, Jane - New York, NY - *DirPRFirms 83*
Randall House Publications [Aff. of Free Will Baptist Sunday School & Church Training Board] - Nashville, TN - *BoPubDir 4, 5*
Randall Inc., H. & G. - Milford, CT - *BillIntBG 83-84*
Randall Mailings Inc. - Farmingdale, NY - *MagIndMarPl 82-83*
Randall, Peter E. - Hampton, NH - *BoPubDir 4*
Randall, Peter E. - Portsmouth, NH - *BoPubDir 5*
Randall Records - Milford, CT - *BillIntBG 83-84*
Randata [of Rand McNally & Co.] - Chicago, IL - *EISS 83*
Randatamp Press - Dobbs Ferry, NY - *LitMag&SmPr 83-84*
Randazzo Music Inc., Teddy - *See* Razzle Dazzle Music Inc.
Randlett, Mary - Bainbridge Island, WA - *MagIndMarPl 82-83*
Randolph Advance - Randolph, WI - *BaconPubCkNews 84*
Randolph AFB Wingspread - Universal City, TX - *NewsDir 84*
Randolph & Son - Washington, DC - *BillIntBG 83-84*
Randolph Cablevision Inc. - Cuthbert, GA - *Tel&CabFB 84C*
Randolph County Herald Tribune - Chester, IL - *Ed&PubIntYB 82*
Randolph County Times-Herald - Huntsville, MO - *Ed&PubIntYB 82*
Randolph Enterprise-Review - Elkins, WV - *AyerDirPub 83; Ed&PubIntYB 82*
Randolph Guide - Asheboro, NC - *AyerDirPub 83; Ed&PubIntYB 82; NewsDir 84*
Randolph Herald - Randolph, MA - *Ed&PubIntYB 82*
Randolph Herald - *See* Bulletin Publishing Co.
Randolph Leader, The - Roanoke, AL - *NewsDir 84*
Randolph Press - Wedowee, AL - *Ed&PubIntYB 82*
Randolph Register - Randolph, NY - *BaconPubCkNews 84; Ed&PubIntYB 82*
Randolph Reporter - Mt. Freedom, NJ - *AyerDirPub 83*
Randolph Reporter - *See* Recorder Publishing Co.
Randolph Telephone Co. Inc. - Liberty, NC - *TelDir&BG 83-84*
Randolph Telephone Membership Corp. - Asheboro, NC - *TelDir&BG 83-84*
Randolph Times - Randolph, NE - *BaconPubCkNews 84; Ed&PubIntYB 82*
Randolph White River Valley Herald - Randolph, VT - *BaconPubCkNews 84; NewsDir 84*
Random Access International - Newark, CA - *BaconPubCkMag 84*
Random Enterprises - New York, NY - *BillIntBG 83-84*

Random House - New York, NY - *LitMarPl 83, 84; MicrocomMPl 84; WritMar 84*
Random House - Tulsa, OK - *MicrocomSwDir 1*
Random House (School Div.) - New York, NY - *ArtMar 84; BillIntBG 83-84; DirMarMP 83; MicrocomMPl 83; WritMar 84*
Random House/Miller-Brody, Newbery Productions Inc. - New York, NY - *AvMarPl 83*
Random House of Canada Ltd. - Mississauga, ON, Canada - *LitMarPl 83, 84*
Random Lake Sounder - Random Lake, WI - *BaconPubCkNews 84*
Random Lengths Data Bank - Washington, DC - *DirOnDB Spring 84*
Random Lengths Publications Inc. - Eugene, OR - *DataDirOnSer 84; EISS 5-84 Sup*
Random Lengths Wood Products Historical Price Data [of Random Lengths Publications Inc.] - Eugene, OR - *DataDirOnSer 84*
Randomex Data Maintenance Inc. - Signal Hill, CA - *DataDirSup 7-83*
Range - Raton, NM - *AyerDirPub 83*
Range Cable TV - Carriage Hills, CA - *BrCabYB 84*
Range Cable TV Co. Inc. - Hibbing, MN - *BrCabYB 84; Tel&CabFB 84C*
Range Facts - Aurora, MN - *AyerDirPub 83*
Range-Ledger - Cheyenne Wells, CO - *Ed&PubIntYB 82*
Range Management [of The Oryx Press] - Phoenix, AZ - *CompReadDB 82; DBBus 82*
Range Management [of SDC Search Service] - Santa Monica, CA - *DataDirOnSer 84*
Range Scene - Eveleth, MN - *Ed&PubIntYB 82*
Range Telephone Cooperative Inc. - Forsyth, MT - *TelDir&BG 83-84*
Rangefinder [of Rangefinder Publishing Co.] - Santa Monica, CA - *ArtMar 84; BaconPubCkMag 84; MagDir 84; MagIndMarPl 82-83; WritMar 84*
Rangely Times - Rangely, CO - *BaconPubCkNews 84; Ed&PubIntYB 82*
Ranger Associates Inc. - Manassas, VA - *BoPubDir 4, 5; WritMar 84*
Ranger-Review - Glendive, MT - *AyerDirPub 83*
Ranger-Review - Riverton, WY - *AyerDirPub 83*
Ranger Rick's Nature Magazine [of National Wildlife Federation] - Washington, DC - *ArtMar 84; MagIndMarPl 82-83; WritMar 84*
Ranger Times - Ranger, TX - *AyerDirPub 83; Ed&PubIntYB 82; NewsDir 84*
Ranger Times - *See* Eastland Country Newspapers
Rangertone Research Inc. - New York, NY - *AvMarPl 83*
Rankin/Bass Productions Inc. - New York, NY - *Tel&CabFB 84C*
Rankin Cable TV Service [of CMI Cable Communications Inc.] - McCamey, TX - *Tel&CabFB 84C*
Rankin Cable TV Service [of CMI Cable Communications Inc.] - Rankin, TX - *BrCabYB 84*
Rankin County Cablevision Co. Inc. - Brandon, MS - *BrCabYB 84*
Rankin County News [of RCN Corp.] - Brandon, MS - *AyerDirPub 83; NewsDir 84*
Rankin County News - Rankin County, MS - *Ed&PubIntYB 82*
Rankin Enterprises, Conrad Calvin - Burlingame, CA - *AvMarPl 83*
Rankin Independent - Rankin, IL - *Ed&PubIntYB 82*
Rankin Independent - *See* Baier Publishing Co.
Rankin News - Rankin, TX - *BaconPubCkNews 84; Ed&PubIntYB 82*
Ranlar Music - *See* Espy Music Group
Rannie, W. F. - Beamsville, ON, Canada - *BoPubDir 4, 5*
Ransom County Gazette & Enterprise - Lisbon, ND - *AyerDirPub 83*
Ransom County Gazette, The - Lisbon, ND - *Ed&PubIntYB 82*
Rantel Research - Laurel, MD - *BrCabYB 84*
Rantoul Chanute This Week - Rantoul, IL - *NewsDir 84*
Rantoul Press [of East Central Communications Inc.] - Rantoul, IL - *BaconPubCkNews 84; Ed&PubIntYB 82; NewsDir 84*
Ranwood Records - Santa Monica, CA - *BillIntBG 83-84*
Rap - New York, NY - *BoPubDir 4, 5*
RAP Communications - Los Angeles, CA - *DirPRFirms 83*
Rape Crisis Center - Washington, DC - *BoPubDir 4, 5*
Rape Prevention Books - San Francisco, CA - *BoPubDir 4, 5*
Raphael Books, Morris - New Iberia, LA - *BoPubDir 5*
Raphael Music Inc., Fred - Cathedral City, CA - *BillIntBG 83-84*
Rapicom Inc. - Fairfield, NJ - *DirInfWP 82*
Rapid Cable TV [of Community Tele-Communications Inc.] - Rapid City, SD - *BrCabYB 84; Tel&CabFB 84C*
Rapid Cablevision - Big Rapids, MI - *BrCabYB 84; Tel&CabFB 84C*
Rapid City Guide - Bethlehem, SD - *NewsDir 84*
Rapid City Guide - Rapid City, SD - *BaconPubCkNews 84*
Rapid City Journal [of Minneapolis Star & Tribune Co.] - Bethlehem, SD - *NewsDir 84*
Rapid City Journal [of Minneapolis Star & Tribune Co.] - Rapid City, SD - *BaconPubCkNews 84; Ed&PubIntYB 82*
Rapid Color Inc. - Glendale, CA - *AvMarPl 83*
Rapid Color West Texas - Lubbock, TX - *AvMarPl 83*
Rapid Data Inc. - Redlands, CA - *DataDirOnSer 84*
Rapid Film Technique Corp. - Long Island City, NY - *AvMarPl 83*
Rapid Patent Service [of Research Publications Inc.] - Arlington, VA - *EISS 5-84 Sup*
Rapidata Inc. [Subs. of National Data Corp.] - Fairfield, NJ - *DataDirOnSer 84; EISS 83; InfIndMarPl 83*
Rapides Symphony Guild - Alexandria, LA - *BoPubDir 4 Sup, 5*
Rapidforms Inc. - Bellmawr, NJ - *WhoWMicrocom 83*
Rapidly Solidified Materials Resource Centre [of Battelle Memorial Institute] - Columbus, OH - *EISS 83*
Rapidquote II [of Rapidata Inc.] - Fairfield, NJ - *DataDirOnSer 84*
Rapids Cable TV Inc. - Hector, MN - *Tel&CabFB 84C p.1698*
Rapids Cable TV Inc. - *See* North American Cable Systems
Rapidscan [of Polycom Systems Ltd.] - Don Mills, ON, Canada - *DataDirOnSer 84*
Rapoport Printing Corp. - New York, NY - *LitMarPl 84*
Rapp & Collins Inc. [of Doyle Dane Bernbach] - New York, NY - *BrCabYB 84; DirMarMP 83; HBIndAd&MS 82-83; StaDirAdAg 2-84*
Rappahannock News - Washington, VA - *AyerDirPub 83; Ed&PubIntYB 82*
Rappahannock Record - Kilmarnock, VA - *AyerDirPub 83; Ed&PubIntYB 82*
Rappahannock Times - Rappahannock, VA - *AyerDirPub 83; BaconPubCkNews 84; Ed&PubIntYB 82*
Rappaport Exhibits Inc. (Leasing Group) - Cleveland, OH - *AvMarPl 83*
Rapports de la Cour Supreme du Canada [of Federal Dept. of Justice] - Ottawa, ON, Canada - *CompReadDB 82*
Rapra [of Pergamon International Information Corp.] - McLean, VA - *DataDirOnSer 84*
RAPRA Abstracts [of Rubber & Plastics Research Association of Great Britain] - Shrewsbury, England - *CompReadDB 82; DBBus 82; DirOnDB Spring 84; OnBibDB 3*
RAPRA Information Centre [of Rubber & Plastics Research Association of Great Britain] - Shrewsbury, England - *EISS 83*
Rapscallion's Dream - Bronx, NY - *LitMag&SmPr 83-84*
Rara Avis [of Books of a Feather] - Los Angeles, CA - *LitMag&SmPr 83-84*
Rare Blue Music Inc. - *See* Chrysalis Music Group
Rare-Earth Information Center [of Energy & Mineral Resources Research Institute] - Ames, IA - *CompReadDB 82; EISS 83; FBInfSer 80; InfIndMarPl 83*
Rare Oriental Book Co. - Aptos, CA - *BoPubDir 4, 5*
Rare Reminder - Rocky Hill, CT - *AyerDirPub 83*
Raritan: A Quarterly Review - New Brunswick, NJ - *LitMag&SmPr 83-84*
Raritan Valley Cablevision Co. [of TKR Cable Co.] - Edison, NJ - *Tel&CabFB 84C*
Rarities - Encino, CA - *BaconPubCkMag 84; MagIndMarPl 82-83*
RAS Records - Washington, DC - *BillIntBG 83-84*
Rase Productions Inc., Bill - Sacramento, CA - *AvMarPl 83; BillIntBG 83-84; WritMar 84*
Rashid Sales Co. - Brooklyn, NY - *BillIntBG 83-84*
Rasky Productions Inc., Harry - Toronto, ON, Canada - *TelAl 83, 84*

Rasmussen Library Research Service - Los Angeles, CA - *EISS 83*
Rasnow MDS Co. - Manhattan Beach, CA - *Tel&CabFB 84C*
Raspberry Press - Puposky, MN - *LitMag&SmPr 83-84*
Raster Technologies Inc. - North Billerica, MA - *DataDirSup 7-83*
Rat & Mole Press - Amherst, MA - *LitMag&SmPr 83-84*
Rat Records - Boston, MA - *BillIntBG 83-84*
Ratcliffe Advertising Agency - Dallas, TX - *StaDirAdAg 2-84*
Ratcliffe, Alan - Steamboat Springs, CO - *Tel&CabFB 84C p.1698*
Rateavers - Pauma Valley, CA - *BoPubDir 4; LitMag&SmPr 83-84*
Rateavers - San Diego, CA - *BoPubDir 5*
RATES - New York, NY - *DirOnDB Spring 84*
Rath Organization, The - *See* Northrup & Teel Inc.
Rathdrum Cable TV [of Tele-Communications Inc.] - Rathdrum, ID - *Tel&CabFB 84C*
Rather Press - Oakland, CA - *BoPubDir 4, 5*
Rathke Blair Kerns & Frost - Rockford, IL - *AdAge 3-28-84; StaDirAdAg 2-84*
Rational Data Systems Inc. - New York, NY - *ADAPSOMemDir 83-84; MicrocomMPl 84*
Rational Island Publishers - Seattle, WA - *BoPubDir 4, 5*
Raton Range - Raton, NM - *BaconPubCkNews 84; Ed&PubIntYB 82; NewsDir 84*
Rattlesnake Cable Co. - Missoula, MT - *Tel&CabFB 84C*
Rattlesnake Cable Co. Inc. - Rattlesnake Valley, MT - *BrCabYB 84*
Raub Public Relations, Peggy - New York, NY - *LitMarPl 83, 84*
Rauch, Peter - New York, NY - *HBIndAd&MS 82-83*
Rauh, Good & Darlo Advertising Associates Inc. - Los Gatos, CA - *StaDirAdAg 2-84*
Rauland-Borg Corp. - Chicago, IL - *AvMarPl 83*
Raus, Bill - Big Cabin, OK - *Tel&CabFB 84C p.1698*
Ravaaja - Fitchburg, MA - *Ed&PubIntYB 82*
Ravagraph Co. - Salt Lake City, UT - *MicrocomMPl 84*
Ravalli Republic [of Southwest Montana Publishing Co.] - Hamilton, MT - *AyerDirPub 83; Ed&PubIntYB 82; NewsDir 84*
Rave Research - Decorah, IA - *MicrocomMPl 84*
Raven Music - Seattle, WA - *BillIntBG 83-84*
Raven Press - New York, NY - *LitMarPl 83, 84; MagIndMarPl 82-83*
Raven Publishers AKA Inc. - Grand Rapids, MI - *BoPubDir 4, 5*
Raven Rocks Press - Beallsville, OH - *LitMag&SmPr 83-84*
Raven Screen Corp. - New York, NY - *AvMarPl 83*
Ravena News-Herald - *See* Ravena News-Herald Publishers
Ravena News-Herald Publishers - Ravena, NY - *BaconPubCkNews 84*
Ravengate Press [Aff. of St. Benedict's Priory] - Cambridge, MA - *BoPubDir 4, 5*
Ravenna Cable Systems - Ravenna, NE - *Tel&CabFB 84C*
Ravenna News - Ravenna, NE - *BaconPubCkNews 84; Ed&PubIntYB 82*
Ravenna Record-Courier - Ravenna, OH - *BaconPubCkNews 84*
Ravenna Television Co-Op Inc. - Ravenna, KY - *BrCabYB 84; Tel&CabFB 84C*
Ravenous Duck Press - San Jose, CA - *BoPubDir 4, 5*
Ravenswood-Lincolnite [of Chicago Lerner Newspapers] - Chicago, IL - *AyerDirPub 83; NewsDir 84*
Ravenswood News - Chicago, IL - *AyerDirPub 83*
Ravenswood News - Ravenswood, WV - *BaconPubCkNews 84; Ed&PubIntYB 82*
Ravenswood Post [of Menlo Park Nowels Publishing] - Menlo Park, CA - *NewsDir 84*
Ravine Press-Herald [of The Call Papers] - Ravine, PA - *BaconPubCkNews 84; NewsDir 84*
Raw Dog Press - Doylestown, PA - *BoPubDir 4, 5; LitMag&SmPr 83-84*
Rawhide Music - *See* Merit Music Corp.
Rawlins Times - Rawlins, WY - *BaconPubCkNews 84; Ed&PubIntYB 82; NewsDir 84*
Rawls Bros. Productions - Mansfield, OH - *BillIntBG 83-84*
Rawson & Associates, Charles A. - Atlanta, GA - *StaDirAdAg 2-84*
Rawson Associates [Div. of The Scribner Book Cos. Inc.] - New York, NY - *LitMarPl 83, 84*
Rawson Associates Ltd. - Clemmons, NC - *IntDirMarRes 83*
Ray County Conservator - Richmond, MO - *AyerDirPub 83; Ed&PubIntYB 82*
Ray County Herald - Richmond, MO - *AyerDirPub 83; Ed&PubIntYB 82*
Ray, Edna O. - New York, NY - *LitMarPl 83, 84*
Ray-Pacific Co. - Los Angeles, CA - *StaDirAdAg 2-84*
Raybird Music - New York, NY - *BillIntBG 83-84*
Raycol Products - Tucson, AZ - *BoPubDir 4 Sup, 5*
Raydiola Music - Beverly Hills, CA - *BillIntBG 83-84*
Raylux Financial Advisory Service - Croton-on-Hudson, NY - *DirOnDB Spring 84*
Raymac Software Group - Tracey, CA - *MicrocomMPl 84*
Raymond & Associates Inc., Stan - Atlanta, GA - *CabTVFinDB 83*
Raymond & Co., Jack - New York, NY - *DirPRFirms 83*
Raymond Associates Inc., Miner - Cincinnati, OH - *HBIndAd&MS 82-83*
Raymond Herald - Raymond, WA - *Ed&PubIntYB 82*
Raymond Hinds County Gazette - Raymond, MS - *BaconPubCkNews 84*
Raymond International - Toronto, ON, Canada - *Tel&CabFB 84C*
Raymond News - Raymond, IL - *BaconPubCkNews 84; Ed&PubIntYB 82*
Raymond News - Raymond, MN - *BaconPubCkNews 84; Ed&PubIntYB 82*
Raymond Review - Raymond, AB, Canada - *AyerDirPub 83*
Raymond Times - *See* Exeter News-Letter Co.
Raymond's Quiet Press - Albuquerque, NM - *LitMag&SmPr 83-84*
Raymondville Chronicle & Willacy County News - Raymondville, TX - *AyerDirPub 83; BaconPubCkNews 84; Ed&PubIntYB 82*
Rayne Acadian Tribune [of Louisiana State Newspapers] - Rayne, LA - *BaconPubCkNews 84; NewsDir 84*
Rayne Cable TV [of TCA Cable TV Inc.] - Rayne, LA - *BrCabYB 84; Tel&CabFB 84C*
Rayne Church Point News [of Louisiana State Newspapers] - Rayne, LA - *BaconPubCkNews 84; NewsDir 84*
Rayne Independent - Rayne, LA - *BaconPubCkNews 84; Ed&PubIntYB 82; NewsDir 84*
Rayner Agency, The - Elgin, IL - *MagIndMarPl 82-83*
Rayner Div. [of Walter M. Carqueville Co.] - Elk Grove Village, IL - *LitMarPl 83*
Raynham Journal - *See* Bulletin Publishing Co.
Rays [of Free People Press] - Hazelton, BC, Canada - *LitMag&SmPr 83-84*
Raytheon Co. - Lexington, MA - *Datamation 6-83; ElecNews 7-25-83; KnowInd 83*
Raytheon Data Systems - Lexington, MA - *Top100Al 83*
Raytheon Data Systems [Subs. of Raytheon Co.] - Norwood, MA - *DataDirSup 7-83; DirInfWP 82; InfIndMarPl 83; WhoWMicrocom 83*
Raytheon Magazine [of Raytheon Co.] - Lexington, MA - *WritMar 84*
Raytown Dispatch Tribune [of Townsend Communications Inc.] - Kansas City, MO - *NewsDir 84*
Raytown Dispatch-Tribune - Raytown, MO - *AyerDirPub 83; Ed&PubIntYB 82*
Raytown Dispatch Tribune - *See* Townsend Communications Inc.
Raytown Post - Raytown, MO - *Ed&PubIntYB 82*
Raytown Post-Door Post - Raytown, MO - *BaconPubCkNews 84*
Rayville Richland Beacon-News - Rayville, LA - *Ed&PubIntYB 82; NewsDir 84*
Razor Records - Chicago, IL - *BillIntBG 83-84*
Razorback Cable Associates - Atkins, AR - *Tel&CabFB 84C*
Razorback Cable Associates - Blue Mountain, AR - *Tel&CabFB 84C*
Razorback Cable Associates - Dora, AR - *Tel&CabFB 84C*
Razzle Dazzle Music - New York, NY - *BillIntBG 83-84*
RB Robot Corp. - Golden, CO - *MicrocomMPl 84*
RBB Software Products - Anaheim, CA - *WhoWMicrocom 83*
R.B.H. Publishing Enterprises [Aff. of Advertising Unlimited Ltd.] - Las Vegas, NV - *BoPubDir 4 Sup, 5*
RBI Records Inc. - New York, NY - *BillIntBG 83-84*
RBOT [of Bibliographic Retrieval Services Inc.] - Latham, NY - *DataDirOnSer 84*
RC Data Inc. - San Jose, CA - *MicrocomMPl 84*
RC Electronics Inc. - Goleta, CA - *MicrocomMPl 83*

R.C. Electronics Inc. - Santa Barbara, CA - *MicrocomMPl 84*
R.C. Publications - Portland, OR - *BoPubDir 5*
RCA American Communications Inc. [Subs. of RCA Corp.] - Piscataway, NJ - *BrCabYB 84*
RCA American Communications Inc. [Subs. of RCA Corp.] - Princeton, NJ - *BrCabYB 84; HomeVid&CabYB 82-83; Tel&CabFB 84C; TeleSy&SerDir 2-84*
RCA Cablevision Systems - Van Nuys, CA - *CabTVFinDB 83; HomeVid&CabYB 82-83*
RCA/Columbia Pictures Home Video - Burbank, CA - *AvMarPl 83; BillIntBG 83-84*
RCA Commercial Communications Div. [of RCA Corp.] - Camden, NJ - *AvMarPl 83*
RCA Corp. - New York, NY - *AdAge 6-28-84; DataDirSup 7-83; ElecNews 7-25-83; HomeVid&CabYB 82-83; KnowInd 83; TelAl 83, 84; Tel&CabFB 84C*
RCA Corp. (Consumer Electronics Div.) - Indianapolis, IN - *BillIntBG 83-84*
RCA Cylix Communications Network [Subs. of RCA Corp.] - Memphis, TN - *DataDirSup 7-83; Tel&CabFB 84C; TeleSy&SerDir 2-84*
RCA Cylix Communications Network (Marketing Div.) - Memphis, TN - *ADAPSOMemDir 83-84*
RCA Distributing Corp. [Subs. of RCA Corp.] - Indianapolis, IN - *Tel&CabFB 84C*
RCA Distributor & Special Products Div. [of RCA Corp.] - Deptford, NJ - *Tel&CabFB 84C*
RCA Global Communications Inc. [Subs. of RCA Corp.] - New York, NY - *BrCabYB 84; Tel&CabFB 84C; TeleSy&SerDir 2-84*
RCA Microcomputer Products [of RCA Corp.] - Lancaster, PA - *MicrocomMPl 84; VideoDir 82-83*
RCA Newsletter [of RCA Corp.] - Somerville, NJ - *DirOnDB Spring 84*
RCA Picture Video Component & Display Div. [Div. of RCA Corp.] - Lancaster, PA - *Tel&CabFB 84C*
RCA Records - New York, NY - *BillIntBG 83-84*
RCA Research & Engineering [Subs. of RCA Corp.] - Princeton, NJ - *Tel&CabFB 84C*
RCA Review [of RCA Corp.] - Princeton, NJ - *MagDir 84; MagIndMarPl 82-83*
RCA Sales Corp. [Subs. of RCA Corp.] - Indianapolis, IN - *Tel&CabFB 84C*
RCA Service Co. [Div. of RCA Corp.] - Cherry Hill, NJ - *DataDirSup 7-83; DirInfWP 82; DirMarMP 83; Tel&CabFB 84C; WhoWMicrocom 83*
RCA VideoDiscs [Div. of RCA Corp.] - New York, NY - *AvMarPl 83; BillIntBG 83-84*
R.C.A.F. Association - Hamilton, ON, Canada - *BoPubDir 4*
R.C.A.F. Association (Book Committee) - Hamilton, ON, Canada - *BoPubDir 5*
RCC of Virginia Inc. - Harrisonburg, VA - *Tel&CabFB 84C*
RCDC Bibliographic Database [of Radiation Chemistry Data Center] - Notre Dame, IN - *CompReadDB 82*
RCH Cable Marketing - Riverside, NJ - *CabTVFinDB 83*
RCI Records Inc. - Elmsford, NY - *BillIntBG 83-84*
RCM Publications - San Diego, CA - *BoPubDir 4 Sup, 5*
RCP Publications Inc. [Aff. of Revolutionary Communist Party USA] - Chicago, IL - *BoPubDir 4, 5*
RCS Music Publishing Inc. - Baton Rouge, LA - *BillIntBG 83-84*
RCS Systems - Plano, TX - *WhoWMicrocom 83*
RD Software - Pacific Palisades, CA - *MicrocomMPl 83, 84; MicrocomSwDir 1*
RDA Historical Database [of Regional Data Associates] - New Brunswick, NJ - *DataDirOnSer 84*
RDA Sales & Marketing - East Brunswick, NJ - *LitMarPl 83, 84*
RDB Productions - Muncie, IN - *AvMarPl 83*
RDH - Waco, TX - *BaconPubCkMag 84*
R.D.H. Associates - Clarks Summit, PA - *StaDirAdAg 2-84*
R.D.J. Market Research Inc. - Armonk, NY - *IntDirMarRes 83*
RDR Associates Inc. - New York, NY - *StaDirAdAg 2-84*
Re-Geniusing Project - Berkeley, CA - *BoPubDir 5*
RE/International System - Los Angeles, CA - *MicrocomMPl 83*
Reachout International Records Inc./Roir Cassettes - New York, NY - *BillIntBG 83-84*
Reactive Systems Inc. - Englewood, NJ - *MicrocomMPl 84*
Reactor Plant Materials Crack Growth Database [of Battelle Columbus Laboratories] - Columbus, OH - *DataDirOnSer 84*
Read - Middletown, CT - *MagDir 84; MagIndMarPl 82-83; WritMar 84*
Read Associates - Clifton, NJ - *DirPRFirms 83*
Read-More Publications Inc. - New York, NY - *MagIndMarPl 82-83*
Read Paperback Book Club [of Xerox Education Publications] - Middletown, CT - *LitMarPl 83, 84*
Read/Philippa M. Lee & Associates Ltd., Michael Blake - Blackstock, ON, Canada - *BoPubDir 4 Sup, 5*
Read-Poland Associates Inc. - Austin, TX - *StaDirAdAg 2-84*
Read-Poland Associates Inc. - Dallas, TX - *ArtMar 84; DirPRFirms 83*
Read Publishing - Nepean, ON, Canada - *BoPubDir 4 Sup, 5*
Reader's Digest [of The Reader's Digest Association Inc.] - New York, NY - *ADAPSOMemDir 83-84; Folio 83*
Reader's Digest - Pleasantville, NY - *BaconPubCkMag 84; LitMarPl 83, 84; MagDir 84; MagIndMarPl 82-83; NewsBur 6; WritMar 84*
Reader's Digest Association - Pleasantville, NY - *AdAge 6-28-84; KnowInd 83; LitMarPl 83, 84*
Reader's Digest Association (Recorded Music Div.) - New York, NY - *BillIntBG 83-84*
Reader's Digest Association Ltd./Selection du Reader's Digest Ltee. - Westmount, PQ, Canada - *LitMarPl 83, 84*
Reader's Digest Condensed Books [Div. of Reader's Digest Association] - Pleasantville, NY - *LitMarPl 83, 84*
Reader's Digest Fund for the Blind Inc. [Div. of Reader's Digest Association] - Mt. Morris, IL - *BoPubDir 4, 5*
Reader's Digest General Books [Div. of Reader's Digest Association] - New York, NY - *LitMarPl 83, 84*
Reader's Digest Press [Div. of Reader's Digest Association] - New York, NY - *LitMarPl 83, 84*
Reader's Digest Services Inc. [Div. of Reader's Digest Association] - Pleasantville, NY - *LitMarPl 83, 84; MicrocomMPl 84*
Readers Nutshell [of Allied Publications] - Palm Beach, FL - *WritMar 84*
Readers Review [of The National Research Bureau Inc.] - Burlington, IA - *WritMar 84*
Reader's Subscription Book Club [Div. of New York Review of Books] - New York, NY - *LitMarPl 83, 84*
Readers's Choice - Toronto, ON, Canada - *WritMar 84*
Readex Inc. - St. Paul, MN - *MagIndMarPl 82-83*
Readex Microprint Corp. - New York, NY - *AvMarPl 83; LitMarPl 83, 84; MicroMarPl 82-83*
Reading-Berks Auto Club Magazine - Wyomissing, PA - *BaconPubCkMag 84*
Reading Berks County Record & Free Press - Reading, PA - *NewsDir 84*
Reading Chronicle [of Webner Daily Times Inc.] - Reading, MA - *Ed&PubIntYB 82; NewsDir 84*
Reading Eagle - Reading, PA - *BaconPubCkNews 84; Ed&PubIntYB 82; NewsDir 84*
Reading Enrichment Co. Inc. [Subs. of Prentice-Hall Inc.] - West Paterson, NJ - *LitMarPl 83, 84*
Reading House - Seal Beach, CA - *BoPubDir 4, 5*
Reading Improvement - Chula Vista, CA - *MagDir 84*
Reading Laboratory Inc. - Georgetown, CT - *AvMarPl 83; BoPubDir 4 Sup, 5*
Reading Material for the Blind & Physically Handicapped [of Library of Congress] - Washington, DC - *CompReadDB 82*
Reading Teacher, The - Newark, DE - *BaconPubCkMag 84; MagDir 84; MagIndMarPl 82-83*
Reading Times - Reading, PA - *BaconPubCkNews 84; Ed&PubIntYB 82; NewsDir 84*
Reading Times & Chronicle - Reading, MA - *BaconPubCkNews 84*
Reading Tutorium - Manassas, VA - *BoPubDir 5*
ReadiWare Systems Inc. - West Redding, CT - *MicrocomMPl 84*
Readlyn Telephone Co. - Readlyn, IA - *TelDir&BG 83-84*
Readon Publishing - Webster, TX - *BoPubDir 4, 5*
Readsboro Cable System [of Charlemont TV Inc.] - Readsboro, VT - *BrCabYB 84*
Ready Records & Filmworks Inc. - Ft. Wayne, IN - *BillIntBG 83-84*
Ready Reference Press - Santa Monica, CA - *BoPubDir 4, 5*
Ready to Rock Music - Hollywood, CA - *BillIntBG 83-84*

Ready to Rock Records - Hollywood, CA - *BillIntBG 83-84*
Reagan Fitzgerald Inc. - *See* Fitzgerald Gardner Advertising
Real Comet Press [Aff. of Such a Deal Corp.] - Seattle, WA - *BoPubDir 4, 5; LitMag&SmPr 83-84*
Real Computers & Intelligence - Santa Clara, CA - *BoPubDir 4, 5*
Real County American - Leakey, TX - *AyerDirPub 83; Ed&PubIntYB 82*
Real Decisions Corp. - Stamford, CT - *EISS 83*
Real-E-Data Inc. - Grand Prairie, TX - *MicrocomMPl 83, 84; MicrocomSwDir 1*
Real Equity Publishing Inc. - Denver, CO - *BoPubDir 4, 5*
Real Estate Board of Greater Vancouver - Vancouver, BC, Canada - *BoPubDir 4, 5*
Real Estate Books Institute [of Prentice-Hall Inc.] - Englewood, NJ - *LitMarPl 83, 84*
Real Estate Business - Chicago, IL - *BaconPubCkMag 84*
Real Estate Co-Op of America - Laguna Hills, CA - *DirMarMP 83*
Real Estate Data Inc. - Miami, FL - *EISS 83*
Real Estate Data Publishing - Framingham, MA - *BoPubDir 5*
Real Estate Education Co. [Div. of Development Systems Corp.] - Chicago, IL - *DirMarMP 83; LitMarPl 83, 84*
Real Estate Forum - New York, NY - *BaconPubCkMag 84; MagDir 84*
Real Estate House Calls - Rochester, NY - *Ed&PubIntYB 82*
Real Estate Information Services Group [of McGraw-Hill Information Systems Co.] - New York, NY - *EISS 83*
Real Estate Insider Newsletter - New York, NY - *BaconPubCkMag 84*
Real Estate Intelligence Reports [of NewsNet Inc.] - Bryn Mawr, PA - *DataDirOnSer 84*
Real Estate Investing Letter - New York, NY - *DirOnDB Spring 84*
Real Estate Investing Letter [of NewsNet Inc.] - Bryn Mawr, PA - *DataDirOnSer 84*
Real Estate Investor Information Center - Moraga, CA - *BoPubDir 4; LitMarPl 83*
Real Estate Listing Service [of MDR Telecom] - Marina del Rey, CA - *DataDirOnSer 84*
Real Estate News - Chicago, IL - *BaconPubCkMag 84; MagDir 84*
Real Estate Newsletter, The - Manhasset, NY - *BaconPubCkMag 84*
Real Estate Press - Willowdale, ON, Canada - *BoPubDir 4, 5*
Real Estate Publishing Co. - Sacramento, CA - *BoPubDir 4, 5*
Real Estate Record & Builder's Guide - New York, NY - *BaconPubCkMag 84*
Real Estate Review [of Warren, Gorham & Lamont Inc.] - Boston, MA - *MagDir 84*
Real Estate Review - Manhasset, NY - *BaconPubCkMag 84; MagIndMarPl 82-83*
Real Estate Today [of National Association of Realtors] - Chicago, IL - *BaconPubCkMag 84; Folio 83; MagIndMarPl 82-83*
Real Estate Weekly [of Hagedorn Publishing Co.] - New York, NY - *BaconPubCkMag 84; MagDir 84*
Real Estate West - Denver, CO - *BaconPubCkMag 84*
Real Fiction - San Francisco, CA - *LitMag&SmPr 83-84*
Real Life - Cresskill, NJ - *BaconPubCkMag 84*
Real People Press - Moab, UT - *BoPubDir 4, 5; LitMag&SmPr 83-84*
Real Records Inc. - Bogalusa, LA - *BillIntBG 83-84*
Real Soft Systems Inc. - Aspen, CO - *MicrocomMPl 83*
Real St. Laurent - Robertsonville, PQ, Canada - *Tel&CabFB 84C*
Real Time Devices - State College, PA - *MicrocomMPl 84*
Real-Time Engineering Systems Inc. - Oak Brook, IL - *DataDirSup 7-83*
Real-Time Weather Information System [of Weather Services International Corp.] - Bedford, MA - *DataDirOnSer 84; DirOnDB Spring 84*
Real-to-Reel Recording Inc. - New York, NY - *HBIndAd&MS 82-83*
Real to Reel Studio - Dallas, TX - *AvMarPl 83*
Real West - Derby, CT - *MagDir 84; MagIndMarPl 82-83*
Realcomp - Monterey, CA - *WhoWMicrocom 83*
Realist Inc. - Menononee Falls, WI - *AvMarPl 83*
Realities Library - San Jose, CA - *BoPubDir 4 Sup, 5; LitMag&SmPr 83-84*
Reality Productions - Buena Park, CA - *BoPubDir 5*
Reality Studios - London, England - *LitMag&SmPr 83-84*
Reality Studios Press - London, England - *LitMag&SmPr 83-84*
Realservice Advertising Agency Inc. - New York, NY - *StaDirAdAg 2-84*
RealTime Records [Div. of Miller & Kreisel Sound Corp.] - Culver City, CA - *BillIntBG 83-84*
Realtor [of Washington Board of Realtors] - Washington, DC - *MagDir 84*
Realtor News - Chicago, IL - *BaconPubCkMag 84*
Realtors National Marketing Institute [Aff. of National Association of Realtors] - Chicago, IL - *LitMarPl 83, 84; WritMar 84*
Realty [of Leader Observer Inc.] - Woodhaven, NY - *BaconPubCkMag 84; MagDir 84*
Realty & Building - Chicago, IL - *BaconPubCkMag 84; MagDir 84*
Realty Automation Inc. - La Habra, CA - *MicrocomMPl 83, 84; MicrocomSwDir 1*
Realty Round-Up - New York, NY - *BaconPubCkMag 84*
Realty Software Co. - Manhattan Beach, CA - *MicrocomMPl 83; MicrocomSwDir 1; WhoWMicrocom 83*
Realty Software Co. - Redondo Beach, CA - *MicrocomMPl 84*
Realval - Bloomington, IN - *MicrocomMPl 83, 84*
Ream Advertising Inc. - Wauwatosa, WI - *StaDirAdAg 2-84*
Reams Broadcasting - Toledo, OH - *BrCabYB 84*
REAP Inc. - Woburn, MA - *DataDirOnSer 84; DataDirSup 7-83*
Reaper - Richfield, UT - *AyerDirPub 83*
Reaper, The - Phoenix, AZ - *BaconPubCkMag 84*
Reaper, The - Evansville, IN - *LitMag&SmPr 83-84*
Reardon Inc., Paul M. - Marietta, GA - *DirMarMP 83*
Reark Research Pty. Ltd. - South Yarra, Australia - *IntDirMarRes 83*
Reason Foundation - Santa Barbara, CA - *BoPubDir 4, 5*
Reason Magazine - Santa Barbara, CA - *ArtMar 84; MagDir 84; MagIndMarPl 82-83; WritMar 84*
Reasonor Mutual Telephone Association - Reasonor, IA - *TelDir&BG 83-84*
Reast & Connolly Inc. - Bayville, NJ - *StaDirAdAg 2-84*
Reavis Communications Inc. - Cardiff by the Sea, CA - *StaDirAdAg 2-84*
Rebel Books - Edison, GA - *BoPubDir 4, 5*
Rebel Publishing Co. Inc. - Texarkana, TX - *BoPubDir 5*
Rebel Records of Virginia - Floyd, VA - *BillIntBG 83-84*
Rebello Associates - West Harwich, MA - *DataDirSup 7-83*
Rebirth Inc./Wenha Productions - Detroit, MI - *BillIntBG 83-84*
Rebirth of Artemis [of Astra Publications] - Methuen, MA - *LitMag&SmPr 83-84; WritMar 84*
Rebis Press - Berkeley, CA - *LitMag&SmPr 83-84*
REBK - Paris, France - *DirOnDB Spring 84*
Rebo Associates - New York, NY - *AvMarPl 83*
Reborn [of Fandom Unltd. Enterprises] - Sunnyvale, CA - *LitMag&SmPr 83-84*
Recipe Clinic - Manchester, CT - *Ed&PubIntYB 82*
Recipes Unltd. Inc. - Burnsville, MN - *BoPubDir 4, 5*
Reclamation Era - Denver, CO - *MagDir 84*
Recodex - Nykoping, Sweden - *DirOnDB Spring 84*
Recognition Business Systems Inc. - Elk Grove Village, IL - *InfIndMarPl 83*
Recognition Equipment - Dallas, TX - *DataDirSup 7-83; Top100Al 83*
Recognition Equipment Inc. - Irving, TX - *Datamation 6-83; DirInfWP 82*
Recommend-Florida - Hollywood, FL - *BaconPubCkMag 84; MagDir 84*
Recon - Philadelphia, PA - *LitMag&SmPr 83-84*
Recon Publications - Philadelphia, PA - *BoPubDir 4, 5; LitMag&SmPr 83-84*
Reconciliation Associates - Brookline, MA - *BoPubDir 4*
Reconciliation Associates - Newton, MA - *BoPubDir 5*
Reconstructionist - New York, NY - *MagIndMarPl 82-83*
Record - Dadeville, AL - *AyerDirPub 83*
Record - Batesville, AR - *AyerDirPub 83*
Record - Coalinga, CA - *AyerDirPub 83*
Record - Colfax, CA - *AyerDirPub 83*

Record - Delano, CA - *AyerDirPub 83*
Record - Lompoc, CA - *AyerDirPub 83*
Record - Mill Valley, CA - *AyerDirPub 83*
Record - Rialto, CA - *AyerDirPub 83*
Record - Stockton, CA - *AyerDirPub 83*
Record - Burlington, CO - *AyerDirPub 83*
Record - Canon City, CO - *AyerDirPub 83*
Record - St. Augustine, FL - *AyerDirPub 83*
Record - Lawrenceville, IL - *AyerDirPub 83*
Record - Paxton, IL - *AyerDirPub 83*
Record - Plano, IL - *AyerDirPub 83*
Record - St. Anne, IL - *AyerDirPub 83*
Record - Royal Center, IN - *AyerDirPub 83*
Record - Cedar Falls, IA - *AyerDirPub 83; Ed&PubIntYB 82*
Record - North English, IA - *AyerDirPub 83*
Record - Treynor, IA - *AyerDirPub 83*
Record - Victor, IA - *AyerDirPub 83*
Record - Erie, KS - *AyerDirPub 83*
Record - Hesston, KS - *AyerDirPub 83*
Record - Hutchinson, KS - *AyerDirPub 83*
Record - Miltonvale, KS - *AyerDirPub 83*
Record - Minneola, KS - *AyerDirPub 83*
Record - Russell, KS - *AyerDirPub 83*
Record - Bunkie, LA - *AyerDirPub 83*
Record - Havre de Grace, MD - *AyerDirPub 83; Ed&PubIntYB 82*
Record - Amherst, MA - *AyerDirPub 83*
Record - Chelsea, MA - *Ed&PubIntYB 82*
Record - West Springfield, MA - *AyerDirPub 83*
Record - Clarksville, MI - *AyerDirPub 83*
Record - Zeeland, MI - *AyerDirPub 83*
Record - East Grand Forks, MN - *AyerDirPub 83; Ed&PubIntYB 82*
Record - Red Lake Falls, MN - *AyerDirPub 83*
Record - Newton, MS - *AyerDirPub 83*
Record - Ocean Springs, MS - *AyerDirPub 83*
Record - Marthasville, MO - *AyerDirPub 83*
Record - New Madrid, MO - *AyerDirPub 83*
Record - Sarcoxie, MO - *AyerDirPub 83*
Record - Cairo, NE - *AyerDirPub 83*
Record - Osceola, NE - *AyerDirPub 83*
Record - Hackensack, NJ - *AyerDirPub 83; BaconPubCkNews 84; Ed&PubIntYB 82; NewsBur 6; NewsDir 84*
Record - Morristown, NJ - *AyerDirPub 83*
Record - Roswell, NM - *AyerDirPub 83*
Record - Amityville, NY - *AyerDirPub 83*
Record - Chateaugay, NY - *AyerDirPub 83*
Record - Middletown, NY - *AyerDirPub 83*
Record - Port Jefferson, NY - *AyerDirPub 83*
Record - Sodus, NY - *AyerDirPub 83; Ed&PubIntYB 82*
Record - Troy, NY - *AyerDirPub 83*
Record - Bessemer City, NC - *AyerDirPub 83*
Record - Denton, NC - *AyerDirPub 83*
Record - Greensboro, NC - *AyerDirPub 83*
Record - Hickory, NC - *AyerDirPub 83*
Record - Robbins, NC - *AyerDirPub 83*
Record - Grafton, ND - *AyerDirPub 83*
Record - Grove City, OH - *AyerDirPub 83; Ed&PubIntYB 82*
Record - New London, OH - *AyerDirPub 83*
Record - West Milton, OH - *AyerDirPub 83*
Record - Wooster, OH - *AyerDirPub 83*
Record - Covington, OK - *AyerDirPub 83*
Record - Gage, OK - *AyerDirPub 83*
Record - Hinton, OK - *AyerDirPub 83*
Record - Madill, OK - *AyerDirPub 83*
Record - Pendleton, OR - *AyerDirPub 83*
Record - Brockway, PA - *AyerDirPub 83*
Record [of Community Service Publishing Inc.] - Coatesville, PA - *AyerDirPub 83; Ed&PubIntYB 82; NewsDir 84*
Record - Duncannon, PA - *AyerDirPub 83*
Record - York, PA - *AyerDirPub 83*
Record - Columbia, SC - *AyerDirPub 83*
Record - Delmont, SD - *AyerDirPub 83*
Record - Marion, SD - *AyerDirPub 83*
Record - Mt. Pleasant, TN - *AyerDirPub 83*
Record - Canadian, TX - *AyerDirPub 83*
Record - Clifton, TX - *AyerDirPub 83*
Record - Colorado City, TX - *AyerDirPub 83*
Record - Lampasas, TX - *AyerDirPub 83*
Record - Robstown, TX - *AyerDirPub 83*
Record - Rowlett, TX - *AyerDirPub 83*
Record - San Marcos, TX - *AyerDirPub 83*
Record - Ellensburg, WA - *AyerDirPub 83*
Record - Odessa, WA - *AyerDirPub 83*
Record - Cashton, WI - *AyerDirPub 83; Ed&PubIntYB 82*
Record - Ellsworth, WI - *AyerDirPub 83*
Record - Mellen, WI - *AyerDirPub 83*
Record - Ft. Saskatchewan, AB, Canada - *AyerDirPub 83; Ed&PubIntYB 82*
Record - Rimbey, AB, Canada - *AyerDirPub 83; Ed&PubIntYB 82*
Record - Chesterville, ON, Canada - *Ed&PubIntYB 82*
Record - Rainy River, ON, Canada - *AyerDirPub 83*
Record [of Townships Communications Inc.] - Sherbrooke, PQ, Canada - *AyerDirPub 83; Ed&PubIntYB 82; LitMarPl 83, 84*
Record-Advertiser - North Tonawanda, NY - *AyerDirPub 83; NewsDir 84*
Record & Avenal Times, The - Avenal, CA - *Ed&PubIntYB 82*
Record & Landmark - Statesville, NC - *AyerDirPub 83*
Record & Mizpah Message - Northome, MN - *AyerDirPub 83*
Record & Music People Inc. - Birmingham, MI - *BillIntBG 83-84*
Record-Argus - Greenville, PA - *AyerDirPub 83*
Record-Breeze - Clementon, NJ - *Ed&PubIntYB 82*
Record-Breeze/Town Crier Herald - Clementon, NJ - *NewsDir 84*
Record-Bulletin - Prosser, WA - *AyerDirPub 83*
Record-Chronicle - Denton, TX - *AyerDirPub 83*
Record-Chronicle - Renton, WA - *AyerDirPub 83*
Record-Citizen - Plymouth, NH - *AyerDirPub 83; Ed&PubIntYB 82*
Record-Citizen - Bristow, OK - *AyerDirPub 83; Ed&PubIntYB 82*
Record Co. of the South - Baton Rouge, LA - *BillIntBG 83-84*
Record Co., The - Los Angeles, CA - *BillIntBG 83-84*
Record-Courier - Ravenna, OH - *AyerDirPub 83; Ed&PubIntYB 82*
Record-Courier & Carson City Sun - Gardnerville, NV - *AyerDirPub 83*
Record-Courier, The - Gardnerville, NV - *Ed&PubIntYB 82*
Record-Courier, The - Johnson City, TX - *Ed&PubIntYB 82*
Record-Cyrus Dispatch - Hancock, MN - *AyerDirPub 83*
Record Delta - Buckhannon, WV - *Ed&PubIntYB 82*
Record-Democrat - Pocahontas, IA - *AyerDirPub 83*
Record-Democrat - Wagoner, OK - *AyerDirPub 83*
Record-Eagle - Traverse City, MI - *AyerDirPub 83*
Record-Express - Lititz, PA - *AyerDirPub 83*
Record Game, The - *See* Monkey Music
Record-Gazette - Banning, CA - *AyerDirPub 83; Ed&PubIntYB 82*
Record-Gazette - Peace River, AB, Canada - *AyerDirPub 83; Ed&PubIntYB 82*
Record-Gazette Shopper - Banning, CA - *AyerDirPub 83*
Record Groove - Staunton, VA - *BoPubDir 4, 5*
Record Guild of America - Farmingdale, NY - *BillIntBG 83-84*
Record-Herald - Arcola, IL - *Ed&PubIntYB 82*
Record-Herald - Greensburg, KY - *AyerDirPub 83*
Record-Herald - Maysville, MO - *Ed&PubIntYB 82*
Record-Herald - Washington Court House, OH - *AyerDirPub 83; Ed&PubIntYB 82*
Record-Herald - Waynesboro, PA - *AyerDirPub 83; Ed&PubIntYB 82*
Record-Herald - Algoma, WI - *Ed&PubIntYB 82*
Record-Herald & Indianola Tribune - Indianola, IA - *AyerDirPub 83; Ed&PubIntYB 82*
Record-Journal - Meriden, CT - *AyerDirPub 83; Ed&PubIntYB 82; LitMarPl 83, 84; NewsDir 84*
Record Junkie - Los Angeles, CA - *BillIntBG 83-84*
Record Ledger [of Herald Community Newspapers] - Tujunga, CA - *AyerDirPub 83; Ed&PubIntYB 82; NewsDir 84*
Record-News - Mt. Ayr, IA - *AyerDirPub 83*
Record-News - Clearwater, NE - *AyerDirPub 83*
Record-News - Mantua, OH - *AyerDirPub 83*
Record-News [of Times Publishing Co.] - Wichita Falls, TX - *AyerDirPub 83; NewsDir 84*
Record-News, The - Smiths Falls, ON, Canada - *AyerDirPub 83*
Record of Greenburgh - Elmsford, NY - *Ed&PubIntYB 82*
Record of Greenburgh - New Rochelle, NY - *AyerDirPub 83*

Record of the Association of the Bar of the City of New York - New York, NY - *MagDir 84*
Record of Yonkers - Elmsford, NY - *Ed&PubIntYB 82*
Record of Yonkers - New Rochelle, NY - *AyerDirPub 83*
Record-Outlook, The - McDonald, PA - *AyerDirPub 83; Ed&PubIntYB 82; NewsDir 84*
Record Pilot - Glen Cove, NY - *AyerDirPub 83*
Record Printing Co. - Red Lake Falls, MN - *BaconPubCkNews 84*
Record Publishing Co. - Hollywood, CA - *BoPubDir 4, 5*
Record Publishing Co. - Linn, KS - *BaconPubCkNews 84*
Record Publishing Co. - Bedford, OH - *BaconPubCkNews 84*
Record Publishing Co. - Stow, OH - *BaconPubCkNews 84*
Record-Register - Coalgate, OK - *AyerDirPub 83*
Record Research Inc. - Menomonee Falls, WI - *BoPubDir 4, 5*
Record-Review - Barnesville, MN - *Ed&PubIntYB 82*
Record-Review - Edgar, WI - *AyerDirPub 83*
Record-Searchlight - Redding, CA - *AyerDirPub 83*
Record Shopping Guide - Napa, CA - *AyerDirPub 83*
Record Spirit [of Cam-Glo Newspapers Inc.] - Blackwood, NJ - *AyerDirPub 83; NewsDir 84*
Record Stockman - Denver, CO - *BaconPubCkMag 84; MagDir 84*
Record/Suburban West, The - Pittsburgh, PA - *AyerDirPub 83*
Record Sun, The [of Poet Papers] - Topanga, CA - *LitMag&SmPr 83-84*
Record, The - Hollywood, CA - *AyerDirPub 83*
Record, The - East Chicago, IN - *NewsDir 84*
Record, The - Northville, MI - *AyerDirPub 83*
Record, The - Detroit Lakes, MN - *Ed&PubIntYB 82*
Record, The - Middle River, MN - *Ed&PubIntYB 82*
Record, The [of Buffalo State College] - Buffalo, NY - *NewsDir 84*
Record, The - New York, NY - *BaconPubCkMag 84; NewsDir 84*
Record, The - Harrison, OH - *AyerDirPub 83; Ed&PubIntYB 82*
Record, The - Rossford, OH - *Ed&PubIntYB 82*
Record, The - Coraopolis, PA - *AyerDirPub 83; Ed&PubIntYB 82*
Record, The [of Gateway Publications Inc.] - Monroeville, PA - *NewsDir 84*
Record, The - Pittsburgh, PA - *AyerDirPub 83; Ed&PubIntYB 82*
Record, The - Renovo, PA - *AyerDirPub 83*
Record-Times - Gotebo, OK - *AyerDirPub 83*
Record Transcript - Milton, MA - *AyerDirPub 83*
Record-Tribune - Roundup, MT - *AyerDirPub 83*
Record World - New York, NY - *MagDir 84*
Recorded Anthology of American Music Inc. - New York, NY - *BillIntBG 83-84*
Recorded Books - Charlotte Hall, MD - *AvMarPl 83; WritMar 84*
Recorded Sound Ltd. - Pittsburgh, PA - *AvMarPl 83*
Recorded Sound Research - Peoria, IL - *BoPubDir 4, 5*
Recorded Treasures Inc. - North Hollywood, CA - *BillIntBG 83-84*
Recorder - Kingsburg, CA - *AyerDirPub 83*
Recorder - Porterville, CA - *AyerDirPub 83; Ed&PubIntYB 82*
Recorder - Wheat Ridge, CO - *BaconPubCkMag 84*
Recorder - Clinton, CT - *AyerDirPub 83*
Recorder - Virden, IL - *AyerDirPub 83*
Recorder - Indianapolis, IN - *AyerDirPub 83*
Recorder - Rising Sun, IN - *AyerDirPub 83*
Recorder - Greene, IA - *AyerDirPub 83*
Recorder - Holton, KS - *AyerDirPub 83*
Recorder - Westmoreland, KS - *AyerDirPub 83*
Recorder - Greenfield, MA - *AyerDirPub 83*
Recorder - Albion, MI - *AyerDirPub 83*
Recorder - Deckerville, MI - *AyerDirPub 83*
Recorder - East Brunswick, NJ - *AyerDirPub 83*
Recorder - Edison, NJ - *Ed&PubIntYB 82*
Recorder - Metuchen, NJ - *AyerDirPub 83*
Recorder [of Wm. J. Kline & Son] - Amsterdam, NY - *AyerDirPub 83; BaconPubCkNews 84; Ed&PubIntYB 82; NewsDir 84*
Recorder - Lima, NY - *AyerDirPub 83*
Recorder [of Philadelphia Inter County Publishing Co.] - Conshohocken, PA - *AyerDirPub 83; NewsDir 84*
Recorder - Fairfield, TX - *AyerDirPub 83*
Recorder - Monterey, VA - *AyerDirPub 83; Ed&PubIntYB 82; NewsDir 84*
Recorder - Boissevain, MB, Canada - *AyerDirPub 83; Ed&PubIntYB 82*
Recorder - Reston, MB, Canada - *AyerDirPub 83*
Recorder - Dundas, ON, Canada - *Ed&PubIntYB 82*
Recorder - Tisdale, SK, Canada - *AyerDirPub 83*
Recorder - Wakaw, SK, Canada - *AyerDirPub 83*
Recorder & Times - Brockville, ON, Canada - *AyerDirPub 83; BaconPubCkNews 84; Ed&PubIntYB 82; LitMarPl 84*
Recorder for the Laundry & Dry Cleaning Industry - Wheat Ridge, CO - *MagDir 84*
Recorder Herald - Salmon, ID - *AyerDirPub 83; Ed&PubIntYB 82*
Recorder Newspapers - Burlington, KY - *BaconPubCkNews 84*
Recorder Publishing Co. - Bernardsville, NJ - *BaconPubCkNews 84*
Recorder Sunset Press [Div. of Recorder Printing & Publishing Co.] - San Francisco, CA - *LitMarPl 83, 84*
Recorder, The - San Francisco, CA - *Ed&PubIntYB 82*
Recordex Corp. [Div. of WAPCO Inc.] - Marietta, GA - *AvMarPl 83*
Recording Engineer/Producer - Hollywood, CA - *BaconPubCkMag 84; MagDir 84; WritMar 84*
Recording for the Blind Inc. - Princeton, NJ - *AvMarPl 83*
Recordo Music Publishers - *See* Rene Publications, Leon
Recorte - Lisbon, Portugal - *ProGuPRSer 4*
Recortec Inc. - Mountain View, CA - *DataDirSup 7-83*
Recovery Engineering News - Philadelphia, PA - *BaconPubCkMag 84*
Recreation Sports & Leisure - Minneapolis, MN - *BaconPubCkMag 84*
Recruitment Advertising Inc. [Div. of Bell & Wilson Inc.] - Burlington, MA - *StaDirAdAg 2-84*
Recruitment Advertising Inc. - Nashville, TN - *StaDirAdAg 2-84*
Recruitment Advertising Network - *See* Sponza & Associates Inc., J.
Rector Clay County Democrat - Rector, AR - *BaconPubCkNews 84*
Rector Democrat - Rector, AR - *Ed&PubIntYB 82*
Rector-Duncan Associates Inc. - Austin, TX - *StaDirAdAg 2-84*
Recycling Today - New York, NY - *BaconPubCkMag 84; MagDir 84*
Red Admiral Music Inc. - *See* Chrysalis Music Group
Red Alder Books - Santa Cruz, CA - *BoPubDir 4, 5; LitMag&SmPr 83-84*
Red & Black, The - Athens, GA - *NewsDir 84*
Red Angel Press - New York, NY - *BoPubDir 5*
Red Barn Music Publishing Co. - Strausstown, PA - *BillIntBG 83-84*
Red Barron Inc. - Minnetonka, MN - *AdAge 3-28-84; StaDirAdAg 2-84*
Red Bay News [of Boone Newspaper Group] - Red Bay, AL - *AyerDirPub 83; BaconPubCkNews 84; Ed&PubIntYB 82; NewsDir 84*
Red Bay TV Cable [of Heritage Communications Inc.] - Red Bay, AL - *Tel&CabFB 84C*
Red Bird Records - Tamarac, FL - *BillIntBG 83-84*
Red Bluff News [of Donrey Media Group] - Red Bluff, CA - *BaconPubCkNews 84; NewsDir 84*
Red Bud North County News - Red Bud, IL - *BaconPubCkNews 84; NewsDir 84*
Red Candle Press - London, England - *LitMag&SmPr 83-84*
Red Carpet Cable Inc. - Crescent, KS - *BrCabYB 84*
Red Cedar Press - East Lansing, MI - *LitMag&SmPr 83-84*
Red Cedar Review - East Lansing, MI - *LitMag&SmPr 83-84*
Red Clay Books - Sullivans Island, SC - *LitMag&SmPr 83-84*
Red Clay Press - Sullivans Island, SC - *BoPubDir 4, 5*
Red Cloud Chief - Red Cloud, NE - *BaconPubCkNews 84; Ed&PubIntYB 82*
Red Creek Herald - Red Creek, NY - *Ed&PubIntYB 82; NewsDir 84*
Red Creek Herald - *See* Wayuga Community Newspapers Inc.
Red Deer Advocate, The - Red Deer, AB, Canada - *BaconPubCkNews 84*
Red Deer & District Museum Society - Red Deer, AB, Canada - *BoPubDir 4 Sup, 5*
Red Deer College Press - Red Deer, AB, Canada - *BoPubDir 4, 5*

Red Deer County News - Sylvan Lake, AB, Canada - *Ed&PubIntYB 82*
Red Deer Shopper - Red Deer, AB, Canada - *Ed&PubIntYB 82*
Red Desert Cable TV [of Sweetwater Cable TV Co.] - Wamsutter, WY - *BrCabYB 84*
Red Dust - New York, NY - *LitMag&SmPr 83-84; LitMarPl 83, 84*
Red Dwarf Music - North Hollywood, CA - *BillIntBG 83-84*
Red Earth Press - St. Louis, MO - *BoPubDir 5*
Red Earth Press - Corrales, NM - *BoPubDir 4*
Red Farm Studio - Pawtucket, RI - *WritMar 84*
Red Feather Publishing Co. - Lubbock, TX - *BoPubDir 4, 5*
Red Flag Publishing/The Forge Publications - Montreal, PQ, Canada - *BoPubDir 4, 5*
Red Herring Poets [Aff. of Channing-Murray Foundation] - Urbana, IL - *BoPubDir 4, 5*
Red Herring Press - Urbana, IL - *LitMag&SmPr 83-84*
Red Hill Press - San Francisco, CA - *LitMag&SmPr 83-84*
Red Hill Telecommunications Corp. - Olney, IL - *Tel&CabFB 84C*
Red Hook Telephone Co. [Aff. of Continental Telecom Inc.] - Johnstown, NY - *TelDir&BG 83-84*
Red Key Press - Port St. Joe, FL - *LitMag&SmPr 83-84*
Red Lake District News - Red Lake, ON, Canada - *Ed&PubIntYB 82*
Red Lake Falls Gazette - *See* Record Printing Co.
Red Lion Books - West Babylon, NY - *BoPubDir 4, 5*
Red Lodge Cable TV Co. - Red Lodge, MT - *BrCabYB 84*
Red Lodge Carbon County News - Red Lodge, MT - *BaconPubCkNews 84*
Red Lotus Press - Berkeley, CA - *LitMag&SmPr 83-84*
Red Lyon Publications - Corvallis, OR - *BoPubDir 4, 5*
Red Oak Express [of Landmark Community Newspapers Inc.] - Red Oak, IA - *AyerDirPub 83; BaconPubCkNews 84; Ed&PubIntYB 82; NewsDir 84*
Red Oak Publishers - Middleton, WI - *BoPubDir 4 Sup, 5*
Red Ochre Press - Takoma Park, MD - *BoPubDir 4, 5*
Red Onion Enterprises - Dayton, OH - *BillIntBG 83-84*
Red Onion Records - Dayton, OH - *BillIntBG 83-84*
Red Ozier Press, The - New York, NY - *LitMag&SmPr 83-84*
Red Poll News - Louisville, KY - *BaconPubCkMag 84; MagDir 84*
Red River Rural Telephone Association - Abercrombie, ND - *TelDir&BG 83-84*
Red River Shopper [of Halstad Valley Journal Inc.] - Crookston, MN - *NewsDir 84*
Red River Songs Inc. - Burbank, CA - *BillIntBG 83-84*
Red River Valley Echo - Altona, MB, Canada - *AyerDirPub 83; Ed&PubIntYB 82*
Red Robin Music Corp. - *See* Gallico Music Corp., Al
Red Rock Music Co. - Denver, CO - *BillIntBG 83-84*
Red Rock News - Sedona, AZ - *AyerDirPub 83; Ed&PubIntYB 82*
Red Rose Books - *See* Greenleaf Press/Red Rose Books
Red Rose Studio - Willow Street, PA - *BoPubDir 4, 5*
Red Springs Citizen - Red Springs, NC - *BaconPubCkNews 84; Ed&PubIntYB 82*
Red Stripe Music - *See* Williams Music Group, Don
Red Sun Press - Boston, MA - *BoPubDir 4, 5*
Red-Tape Publications - Ft. Collins, CO - *BoPubDir 5*
Red Tennies Music - Los Angeles, CA - *BillIntBG 83-84*
Red Weather Press - Eau Claire, WI - *BoPubDir 4, 5*
Red Wheelbarrow Press - San Francisco, CA - *LitMag&SmPr 83-84*
Red Wing Business Systems - Red Wing, MN - *MicrocomMPl 83, 84; MicrocomSwDir 1; WhoWMicrocom 83*
Red Wing Cablevision [of NorCom Video Inc.] - Red Wing, MN - *Tel&CabFB 84C*
Red Wing Publishing Co. - Red Wing, MN - *Ed&PubIntYB 82*
Red Wing Republican Eagle - Red Wing, MN - *BaconPubCkNews 84; NewsDir 84*
Redbird Press - Memphis, TN - *BoPubDir 4, 5*
Redbook [of The Hearst Corp.] - New York, NY - *BaconPubCkMag 84; Folio 83; LitMarPl 83, 84; MagDir 84; MagIndMarPl 82-83; WritMar 84*
Redbook's Be Beautiful - New York, NY - *MagDir 84*
Redbook's Young Mother - New York, NY - *MagDir 84*
Redbud Records [Div. of CAEinc.] - Bloomington, IN - *BillIntBG 83-84*
Redcomp Services - Castle Creek, NY - *MicrocomMPl 83, 84*
Redcor Book Publishing Co. - Phoenix, AZ - *BoPubDir 4, 5*
Redden Cable TV - Vici, OK - *BrCabYB 84 p.D-305*
Redden Enterprises - Comanche, OK - *BrCabYB 84; Tel&CabFB 84C*
Redden Enterprises - Waurika, OK - *BrCabYB 84*
Redden Enterprises Inc. - Meridian, OK - *Tel&CabFB 84C*
Redden Enterprises Inc. - Walters, OK - *Tel&CabFB 84C*
Redden, Jerry, Joe & Oran - Vici, OK - *Tel&CabFB 84C p.1698*
Reddens's Cable TV Ltd. - Campbellford, ON, Canada - *BrCabYB 84*
Reddick-Essex Courier - Reddick, IL - *AyerDirPub 83*
Redding Group Inc. - Ridgefield, CT - *MicrocomMPl 83, 84; MicrocomSwDir 1*
Redding Pilot - Georgetown, CT - *AyerDirPub 83*
Redding Pilot [of Acorn Press Inc.] - Ridgefield, CT - *NewsDir 84*
Redding Pilot - *See* Acorn Press Inc.
Redding Pilot, The - Redding, CT - *Ed&PubIntYB 82*
Redding Record Searchlight - Redding, CA - *BaconPubCkNews 84; Ed&PubIntYB 82; NewsDir 84*
Reddox Corp. - Pittsburgh, PA - *MicrocomMPl 83*
Reddy Communications Inc. - Greenwich, CT - *DirPRFirms 83*
Redeye Records - St. Joseph, MO - *BillIntBG 83-84*
Redfield Cable Television [of Midcontinent Cable Systems Co.] - Redfield, SD - *BrCabYB 84; Tel&CabFB 84C*
Redfield Dexfield Review Sentinel - Redfield, IA - *BaconPubCkNews 84*
Redfield Press - Redfield, SD - *BaconPubCkNews 84; Ed&PubIntYB 82; NewsDir 84*
Redfield Telephone Co. Inc. - Redfield, AR - *TelDir&BG 83-84*
Redford Observer [of Suburban Communications Corp.] - Livonia, MI - *AyerDirPub 83; NewsDir 84*
Redford Observer - Redford, MI - *Ed&PubIntYB 82*
Redford Observer - *See* Observer & Eccentric Newspapers
Redford Record - *See* Suburban Newspapers
Redford Township News - *See* Suburban Newspapers
Redgrave Publishing Co. [Div. of Docent Corp.] - South Salem, NY - *LitMarPl 83; MagIndMarPl 82-83*
Redi/Multi-List Database [of Redi/Multi-List Inc.] - Lakewood, CO - *DataDirOnSer 84*
Redi/Multi-List Inc. [Subs. of Colonial Penn Group Inc.] - Lakewood, CO - *DataDirOnSer 84*
Redick Music Publishing Co., Jack - Georgetown, SC - *BillIntBG 83-84*
Rediffusion Computer Ltd. - Crawley, England - *VideoDir 82-83*
Redington Inc. - Stamford, CT - *DirPRFirms 83*
Redlands Daily Facts [of Donrey Media Group] - Redlands, CA - *BaconPubCkNews 84; Ed&PubIntYB 82; NewsDir 84*
Redlin Productions Inc. - Reseda, CA - *TelAl 83, 84*
Redline Records & Videoworks - Yonkers, NY - *BillIntBG 83-84*
Redmond, Amundson & Rice Advertising Agency Inc. - Virginia Beach, VA - *AdAge 3-28-84; StaDirAdAg 2-84*
Redmond Sammamish Valley News - Redmond, WA - *BaconPubCkNews 84*
Redmond Spokesman [of Western Communications Inc.] - Redmond, OR - *BaconPubCkNews 84; Ed&PubIntYB 82; NewsDir 84*
Redondo Beach Record - Redondo Beach, CA - *AyerDirPub 83; Ed&PubIntYB 82*
Redondo Beach Record - *See* Argonaut Newspapers
Redondo Reflex - Redondo Beach, CA - *AyerDirPub 83; Ed&PubIntYB 82*
Redondo Reflex - *See* Breeze Newspapers
Redosi [of Questel Inc.] - Washington, DC - *DataDirOnSer 84*
Redosi - Marseilles, France - *DirOnDB Spring 84*
Redshaw Inc. - Pittsburgh, PA - *MicrocomSwDir 1*
Redstockings of the Women's Liberation Movement - New York, NY - *BoPubDir 4, 5*
Redstone Cable TV Co. [of Satellite Cable TV Corp.] - Redstone Arsenal, AL - *BrCabYB 84; Tel&CabFB 84C*
Redwood Cable TV [of Todd Communications Inc.] - Redwood Falls, MN - *Tel&CabFB 84C*
Redwood Cablevision [of Storer Cable Communications Inc.] - Fortuna, CA - *BrCabYB 84; Tel&CabFB 84C*

Redwood City Almanac - Redwood City, CA - *AyerDirPub 83; BaconPubCkNews 84*
Redwood County Telephone Co. - Redwood Falls, MN - *TelDir&BG 83-84*
Redwood Empire Cablevision Inc. - Gualala, CA - *BrCabYB 84*
Redwood Empire Cablevision Inc. [of Freedom Newspapers Inc.] - The Sea Ranch, CA - *BrCabYB 84; Tel&CabFB 84C*
Redwood Falls Gazette - Redwood Falls, MN - *AyerDirPub 83; BaconPubCkNews 84; Ed&PubIntYB 82; NewsDir 84*
Redwood Press [Aff. of Syntax Associates] - San Mateo, CA - *BoPubDir 5*
Redwood Publishers - Menlo Park, CA - *BoPubDir 4, 5*
Redwood Publishing Co. - San Luis Obispo, CA - *BoPubDir 4, 5*
Redwood Rancher - San Francisco, CA - *MagDir 84*
Redwood Record - Garberville, CA - *Ed&PubIntYB 82*
Redwood Records - Oakland, CA - *BillIntBG 83-84; BoPubDir 5*
Redwood Software Systems Ltd. - St. Albans, England - *MicrocomSwDir 1*
Ree Heights Review - Ree Heights, SD - *BaconPubCkNews 84; Ed&PubIntYB 82*
Reed & Associates Inc., Bill - Clearwater, FL - *StaDirAdAg 2-84*
Reed & Cannon Communications Co. - Berkeley, CA - *BoPubDir 4 Sup, 5*
Reed & Nottage Inc. - Clifton, NJ - *StaDirAdAg 2-84*
Reed Books, I. - Berkeley, CA - *LitMag&SmPr 83-84*
Reed City Osceola County Herald - Reed City, MI - *BaconPubCkNews 84; NewsDir 84*
Reed Kaina Schaller Advertising Inc. - Honolulu, HI - *StaDirAdAg 2-84*
Reed Ltd., A. H. & A. W. - Wellington, New Zealand - *WritMar 84*
Reed, Melnichek, Gentry & Associates - Dallas, TX - *StaDirAdAg 2-84*
Reed Publishers - Honolulu, HI - *BoPubDir 4, 5*
Reed Publishing Holdings Ltd. - Boston, MA - *KnowInd 83*
Reed Rock Bit Co. Rig Census - Houston, TX - *DirOnDB Spring 84*
Reed Springs Southwest Missourian - *See* Tri-Lakes Newspapers Inc.
Reed Starline Card Co. - Los Angeles, CA - *WritMar 84*
Reed TV Cable System, Leon - Wellsboro, PA - *BrCabYB 84; Tel&CabFB 84C*
Reeder Cable TV - Reeder, ND - *Tel&CabFB 84C*
Reeder Marketing/Research - Princeton, NJ - *IntDirMarRes 83*
Reedley Exponent - Reedley, CA - *BaconPubCkNews 84; Ed&PubIntYB 82; NewsDir 84*
Reedmor Magazine Co. Inc. - Philadelphia, PA - *MagIndMarPl 82-83*
Reeds, Farris, Lewis & Maisel - Los Angeles, CA - *AdAge 3-28-84; StaDirAdAg 2-84*
Reedsburg Times-Press - Reedsburg, WI - *BaconPubCkNews 84; NewsDir 84*
Reedsport Courier - Reedsport, OR - *BaconPubCkNews 84; Ed&PubIntYB 82*
Reef Dwellers Press - Bryn Athyn, PA - *BoPubDir 4, 5*
Reehl Litho [Div. of General Offset Co. Inc.] - New York, NY - *LitMarPl 83, 84*
Reel Research [Aff. of Foundation for Open Co. Inc.] - Albany, CA - *BoPubDir 4, 5*
Reelin & Rockin Records - Brooklyn, NY - *BillIntBG 83-84*
Reelsound Recording Co. - Manchaca, TX - *AvMarPl 83*
Reeltime Distributing Corp. - New York, NY - *Tel&CabFB 84C*
Reena Co. - Renton, WA - *MicrocomMPl 84*
Rees Literary Agency, Helen - Boston, MA - *LitMarPl 83, 84*
Reese Advertising Inc. - Great Neck, NY - *StaDirAdAg 2-84*
Reese & Associates Inc., Kay - New York, NY - *AvMarPl 83; LitMarPl 83, 84*
Reese Press Inc. - Baltimore, MD - *LitMarPl 83, 84; MagIndMarPl 82-83*
Reese Publishing Co. Inc. - New York, NY - *MagIndMarPl 82-83*
Reese River Reveille - Austin, NV - *AyerDirPub 83; Ed&PubIntYB 82*
Reeves Advertising Inc. - Cincinnati, OH - *StaDirAdAg 2-84*
Reeves & Associates, Henry - Framingham, MA - *DirPRFirms 83; HBIndAd&MS 82-83*
Reeves Audio Visual Systems Inc. [Subs. of Reeves Communications Corp.] - New York, NY - *AvMarPl 83*
Reeves Cable Productions [Div. of Reeves Communications Inc.] - New York, NY - *AvMarPl 83*
Reeves Communications Corp. - New York, NY - *HomeVid&CabYB 82-83; KnowInd 83*
Reeves Corporate Services [Div. of Reeves Communications Corp.] - New York, NY - *AvMarPl 83*
Reeves Enterprises Inc., Jim - Madison, TN - *BillIntBG 83-84*
Reeves Journal, Plumbing-Heating & Cooling [of Miramar Publishing Co.] - Canoga Park, CA - *BaconPubCkMag 84; MagDir 84*
Reeves, Pfeffer, Harrington & Co. Inc. - Cincinnati, OH - *ADAPSOMemDir 83-84*
Reeves Teletape Corp. - New York, NY - *Tel&CabFB 84C*
Referee [of Referee Enterprises Inc.] - Franksville, WI - *BaconPubCkMag 84; MagDir 84; WritMar 84*
Reference & Research Library Resources Systems [of New York State Library] - Albany, NY - *EISS 83*
Reference Desk, The - La Jolla, CA - *EISS 5-84 Sup*
Reference Librarian Enhancement System [of University of California, Los Angeles] - Los Angeles, CA - *EISS 7-83 Sup*
Reference Librarian, The [of Haworth Press Journals] - New York, NY - *LitMarPl 83, 84*
Reference Magazine [of Constant Communications Inc.] - Amherst, NH - *BaconPubCkMag 84; MicrocomMPl 84; WritMar 84*
Reference Publications Inc. - Algonac, MI - *LitMarPl 83, 84*
Reference Recordings - San Francisco, CA - *BillIntBG 83-84*
Reference Service Press - Santa Barbara, CA - *BoPubDir 4, 5*
Reference Services Review [of Pierian Press] - Ann Arbor, MI - *LitMag&SmPr 83-84*
Reference Systems Inc. - Carmel, NY - *ADAPSOMemDir 83-84*
Referral Service System [of United Nations University] - Tokyo, Japan - *EISS 83*
Reflect - Norfolk, VA - *LitMag&SmPr 83-84*
Reflection Films - Los Angeles, CA - *AvMarPl 83*
Reflection Sound Productions Inc. - Charlotte, NC - *BillIntBG 83-84*
Reflector - Greenville, NC - *AyerDirPub 83*
Reflector - Norwalk, OH - *AyerDirPub 83*
Reflector - Battle Ground, WA - *AyerDirPub 83; Ed&PubIntYB 82*
Reflector-Chronicle - Abilene, KS - *AyerDirPub 83*
Reflex & Advertiser [of Torrance Press-Herald] - Torrance, CA - *NewsDir 84*
Reflex Music - Nashville, TN - *BillIntBG 83-84*
Reform Judaism - New York, NY - *BaconPubCkMag 84; LitMarPl 83, 84; MagDir 84*
Reform West Alabama Advertiser - Reform, AL - *BaconPubCkNews 84*
Reformation Research Press Inc. - Philadelphia, PA - *BoPubDir 4, 5*
Reformed Church Press - New York, NY - *LitMarPl 83*
Reformer - Brattleboro, VT - *AyerDirPub 83*
Reformer - Simcoe, ON, Canada - *AyerDirPub 83*
Refrigerated Transporter [of Tunnell Publications Inc.] - Houston, TX - *BaconPubCkMag 84; MagDir 84; WritMar 84*
Refrigeration [of John W. Yopp Publications Inc.] - Atlanta, GA - *BaconPubCkMag 84; MagDir 84*
Refrigeration Service & Contracting - Des Plaines, IL - *BaconPubCkMag 84*
Refuge Music Inc. - *See* Elektra/Asylum Music Inc.
Refugio County Press - Refugio, TX - *AyerDirPub 83; BaconPubCkNews 84*
Refundle Bundle - Scarsdale, NY - *DirOnDB Spring 84*
Refware - Chappaqua, NY - *MicrocomMPl 83*
REG/CAN [of Chemical Abstracts Service] - Columbus, OH - *CompReadDB 82*
Reg-Ulate [of Legi-Slate Inc.] - Washington, DC - *EISS 83*
Regal Books [Div. of Gospel Light Publications] - Ventura, CA - *LitMarPl 83; WritMar 84*
Regal Music Publications [Div. of Century Records] - Pittsburgh, PA - *BillIntBG 83-84*
Regal Publishing Co. - Menlo Park, CA - *BaconPubCkNews 84*
Regal Tele-Com Inc. - Edgerton, WI - *BrCabYB 84*
Regal Tele-Com Inc. - Ft. Atkinson, WI - *BrCabYB 84*

Regardie's Magazine - Washington, DC - *BaconPubCkMag 84; MagDir 84; WritMar 84*
Regena - Cedar City, UT - *MicrocomMPl 84*
Regency Electronics Inc. - Indianapolis, IN - *CabTVFinDB 83*
Regency Network [of Hyatt Hotels Corp.] - Rosemont, IL - *TeleSy&SerDir 2-84*
Regency Productions Inc. - New York, NY - *TelAl 83, 84*
Regency Records Inc. - Los Angeles, CA - *BillIntBG 83-84*
Regency Systems - Champaign, IL - *AvMarPl 83*
Regenhardt Advertising Agency Inc. - St. Petersburg, FL - *StaDirAdAg 2-84*
Regensteiner Press [Div. of Regensteiner Publishing Enterprises Inc.] - Chicago, IL - *LitMarPl 83, 84; MagIndMarPl 82-83*
Regent Book Co. Inc. - Hillsdale, NJ - *LitMarPl 83*
Regent Book Co. Inc. - Saddlebrook, NJ - *LitMarPl 84*
Regent Books Co. Inc. - Hillsdale, NJ - *BoPubDir 4 Sup, 5*
Regent Cablevision - Regent, ND - *Tel&CabFB 84C*
Regent Graphic Services - Swissvale, PA - *BoPubDir 4, 5*
Regent House Publishers & Booksellers [Aff. of Zeppelin Publishing Co.] - Los Angeles, CA - *BoPubDir 4*
Regent House Publishers & Booksellers [Aff. of Zeppelin Publishing Co.] - Baton Rouge, LA - *BoPubDir 5*
Regent Music Corp. - *See* Goodman Group, The
Regents/ALA Co. - New York, NY - *MicrocomMPl 84*
Regents Publishing Co. [Subs. of Hachette SA] - New York, NY - *ArtMar 84; AvMarPl 83; LitMarPl 83, 84; WritMar 84*
Regester TV Cable Service - Richfield, PA - *BrCabYB 84; Tel&CabFB 84C*
Regie des Telegraphes et des Telephones [of Data Communication Dept.] - Brussels, Belgium - *InfIndMarPl 83*
Regina Books - Claremont, CA - *BoPubDir 5*
Regina Cablevision Co-operative Ltd. - Regina, SK, Canada - *BrCabYB 84*
Regina Leader Post - Regina, SK, Canada - *BaconPubCkNews 84*
Regina Press [Aff. of Malhame & Co.] - Hicksville, NY - *BoPubDir 4, 5*
Region - Baudette, MN - *AyerDirPub 83*
Region News - Mt. Zion, IL - *AyerDirPub 83*
Regional [of Chase Econometrics/Interactive Data Corp.] - Waltham, MA - *DBBus 82*
Regional & Urban Studies Information Center [of U.S. Dept. of Energy] - Oak Ridge, TN - *EISS 83*
Regional Broadcasters Group - Kingston, NY - *BrCabYB 84*
Regional Building Permits - *See* SMSA Building Permits
Regional Center for Educational Training - Hanover, NH - *BoPubDir 4*
Regional Center for Educational Training - Lebanon, NH - *BoPubDir 5*
Regional Construction Forecasts - Bala Cynwyd, PA - *DirOnDB Spring 84*
Regional Data Associates - New Brunswick, NJ - *DataDirOnSer 84; EISS 83*
Regional Data Associates - Princeton, NJ - *DBBus 82*
Regional Data Associates - Bala Cynwyd, PA - *DirOnDB Spring 84*
Regional Data Associates Forecasts - *See* Regional Construction Forecasts
Regional Documentation Center [of Asian Institute of Technology] - Bangkok, Thailand - *EISS 83*
Regional Economic Information System [of U.S. Dept. of Commerce] - Washington, DC - *EISS 5-84 Sup*
Regional Employment [of Chase Econometrics/Interactive Data Corp.] - Waltham, MA - *DBBus 82*
Regional Energy Information System [of Minnesota State Energy Agency] - St. Paul, MN - *EISS 83*
Regional Forecast [of Chase Econometrics/Interactive Data Corp.] - Waltham, MA - *DataDirOnSer 84; DBBus 82*
Regional Forecast - Bala Cynwyd, PA - *DirOnDB Spring 84*
Regional Forecasting Service [of Evans Economics Inc.] - Washington, DC - *DataDirOnSer 84*
Regional Foundation Center [Aff. of Free Library of Philadelphia] - Philadelphia, PA - *BoPubDir 5*
Regional Housing Data Base - Seattle, WA - *DirOnDB Spring 84*
Regional Industry [of Chase Econometrics/Interactive Data Corp.] - Waltham, MA - *DataDirOnSer 84; DBBus 82*
Regional Industry - *See* State Industry
Regional Industry Planning System - Bala Cynwyd, PA - *DirOnDB Spring 84*
Regional Information & Communication Exchange [of Rice University] - Houston, TX - *EISS 83; FBInfSer 80; InfIndMarPl 83*
Regional Information Service Data Bank - Washington, DC - *DirOnDB Spring 84*
Regional Insurance Data Bank - Washington, DC - *DirOnDB Spring 84*
Regional Insurance Data Bank [of Data Resources Inc.] - Lexington, MA - *DataDirOnSer 84*
Regional Market Patterns [of Data Resources Inc.] - Lexington, MA - *DataDirOnSer 84*
Regional Markets Service [of Charles River Associates Inc.] - Boston, MA - *EISS 83*
Regional News - Palos Heights, IL - *AyerDirPub 83; Ed&PubIntYB 82; NewsDir 84*
Regional News - La Crosse, IN - *AyerDirPub 83; Ed&PubIntYB 82; NewsDir 84*
Regional News - Whippany, NJ - *AyerDirPub 83*
Regional News - Lake Geneva, WI - *AyerDirPub 83; Ed&PubIntYB 82*
Regional News - Cayuga, ON, Canada - *Ed&PubIntYB 82*
Regional Planning Council - Baltimore, MD - *BoPubDir 5*
Regional SMSA Employment [of Chase Econometrics/Interactive Data Corp.] - Waltham, MA - *DataDirOnSer 84*
Regional SMSA Employment - *See* SMSA Employment
Regional SMSA Macro [of Chase Econometrics/Interactive Data Corp.] - Waltham, MA - *DataDirOnSer 84*
Regional SMSA Macro - *See* SMSA Macro
Regional State Employment [of Chase Econometrics/Interactive Data Corp.] - Waltham, MA - *DataDirOnSer 84*
Regional State Employment - *See* State Employment
Regional State Macro [of Chase Econometrics/Interactive Data Corp.] - Waltham, MA - *DataDirOnSer 84*
Regional State Macro - *See* State Macro
Regional Weekly News - East Hanover, NJ - *NewsDir 84*
Regional Weekly News - Whippany, NJ - *Ed&PubIntYB 82*
Regional Young Adult Project - San Francisco, CA - *BoPubDir 4 Sup, 5*
Register [of The Mobile Press Register Inc.] - Mobile, AL - *AyerDirPub 83; Ed&PubIntYB 82*
Register - Napa, CA - *AyerDirPub 83*
Register [of Freedom Newspapers Inc.] - Santa Ana, CA - *AyerDirPub 83; Ed&PubIntYB 82; LitMarPl 84*
Register - New Haven, CT - *AyerDirPub 83*
Register - Torrington, CT - *AyerDirPub 83; Ed&PubIntYB 82*
Register - East Dubuque, IL - *AyerDirPub 83*
Register - Harrisburg, IL - *AyerDirPub 83*
Register - Palestine, IL - *AyerDirPub 83*
Register - Crown Point, IN - *AyerDirPub 83*
Register - Des Moines, IA - *AyerDirPub 83*
Register - Oelwein, IA - *AyerDirPub 83; Ed&PubIntYB 82*
Register - Storm Lake, IA - *AyerDirPub 83*
Register - Iola, KS - *AyerDirPub 83*
Register - Richmond, KY - *AyerDirPub 83*
Register - Scotia, NE - *AyerDirPub 83*
Register - Stanton, NE - *AyerDirPub 83*
Register - Red Bank, NJ - *AyerDirPub 83*
Register - Fair Haven, NY - *AyerDirPub 83*
Register - Randolph, NY - *AyerDirPub 83*
Register - Sandusky, OH - *AyerDirPub 83*
Register - Purcell, OK - *AyerDirPub 83*
Register - Brookings, SD - *AyerDirPub 83*
Register - Chamberlain, SD - *AyerDirPub 83*
Register - Gainesville, TX - *AyerDirPub 83*
Register - Danville, VA - *AyerDirPub 83*
Register - Wilbur, WA - *AyerDirPub 83*
Register - Point Pleasant, WV - *AyerDirPub 83*
Register - Portage, WI - *AyerDirPub 83*
Register - Berwick, NS, Canada - *AyerDirPub 83; Ed&PubIntYB 82*
Register - Norwood, ON, Canada - *Ed&PubIntYB 82*
Register & Tribune Syndicate - Des Moines, IA - *BaconPubCkNews 84; Ed&PubIntYB 82; LitMarPl 83, 84; MagIndMarPl 82-83*
Register Broadcast Group - Des Moines, IA - *BrCabYB 84*

Register-Call - Central City, CO - *AyerDirPub 83*
Register for International Service in Education [of Institute of International Education] - New York, NY - *EISS 83*
Register-Guard - Eugene, OR - *AyerDirPub 83*
Register-Herald [of Brown Publishing Co.] - Eaton, OH - *Ed&PubIntYB 82; NewsDir 84*
Register-Mail [of Galesburg Printing & Publishing Co.] - Galesburg, IL - *AyerDirPub 83; BaconPubCkNews 84; Ed&PubIntYB 82; LitMarPl 83, 84; NewsDir 84*
Register-Mirror, The - Minneapolis, MN - *Ed&PubIntYB 82*
Register-News - Mt. Vernon, IL - *AyerDirPub 83; BaconPubCkNews 84; Ed&PubIntYB 82*
Register-News - Madrid, IA - *AyerDirPub 83*
Register-News - Bordentown, NJ - *AyerDirPub 83; Ed&PubIntYB 82*
Register of Exporters [of Finnish Foreign Trade Association] - Helsinki, Finland - *EISS 83*
Register-Pajaronian & Sun [of Watsonville Newspapers Inc.] - Watsonville, CA - *AyerDirPub 83; Ed&PubIntYB 82; LitMarPl 84*
Register Publications Inc. - Lawrenceburg, IN - *BaconPubCkNews 84*
Register-Republic [of Rockford Newspapers Inc.] - Rockford, IL - *NewsDir 84*
Register-Star [of Rockford Newspapers Inc.] - Rockford, IL - *AyerDirPub 83; NewsDir 84*
Register-Star - Hudson, NY - *AyerDirPub 83; Ed&PubIntYB 82*
Register, The - Sandoval, IL - *AyerDirPub 83; Ed&PubIntYB 82*
Register, The - Barnstable, MA - *Ed&PubIntYB 82*
Register, The - Yarmouth Port, MA - *AyerDirPub 83; NewsDir 84*
Register-Tribune - Union City, MI - *AyerDirPub 83; Ed&PubIntYB 82*
Registered Nurse Book Club [Div. of Jason Aronson] - New York, NY - *LitMarPl 83, 84*
Registered Representative, The [of Plaza Publishing Co. Inc.] - Newport Beach, CA - *MagDir 84*
Registry Nomenclature & Structure Service - Columbus, OH - *DirOnDB Spring 84*
Registry of Interpreters for the Deaf Inc. - Silver Spring, MD - *BoPubDir 4 Sup, 5*
Registry of Toxic Effects of Chemical Substances [of National Library of Medicine] - Bethesda, MD - *DataDirOnSer 84; EISS 83*
Registry of Toxic Effects of Chemical Substances [of National Institute for Occupational Safety & Health] - Cincinnati, OH - *CompReadDB 82*
Registry Publications Ltd. - Northbrook, IL - *BoPubDir 4, 5*
Reglement de la Chambre des Communes [of QL Systems Ltd.] - Ottawa, ON, Canada - *CompReadDB 82; DataDirOnSer 84; DirOnDB Spring 84*
Regnery/Gateway Inc. - Chicago, IL - *LitMarPl 83, 84; WritMar 84*
Rego Irish Records & Tapes Inc. - Garden City, NY - *BillIntBG 83-84*
Regu-late [of Legi-Slate] - Dallas, TX - *CompReadDB 82*
Regular Baptist Press [Aff. of General Association of Regular Baptist Churches] - Schaumburg, IL - *BoPubDir 4 Sup, 5*
Regular Common Carrier Conference [Aff. of American Trucking Associations Inc.] - Washington, DC - *BoPubDir 5*
Regulation - Washington, DC - *MagIndMarPl 82-83*
Regulatory Reporter [of QL Systems Ltd.] - Ottawa, ON, Canada - *DataDirOnSer 84*
Regulatory Watchdog Service - Washington, DC - *MagIndMarPl 82-83*
Rehab Council/Newsletter - New York, NY - *NewsDir 84*
Rehabdata [of National Rehabilitation Information Center] - Washington, DC - *DataDirOnSer 84*
Rehabilitation International USA - New York, NY - *BoPubDir 5*
Rehabilitation World - New York, NY - *BaconPubCkMag 84; MagDir 84*
Rehoboth Beach Delaware Coast Press - Rehoboth Beach, DE - *BaconPubCkNews 84*
Reich Group Inc., The - Philadelphia, PA - *ArtMar 84*
Reich Inc., Jay - Pittsburgh, PA - *AdAge 3-28-84; StaDirAdAg 2-84*
Reichert Digital Systems - Warren, NJ - *MicrocomMPl 83*
Reichert, Kenney & Scroggins Inc. - *See* Schmidt Co. Inc., Ken
Reid Advertising & Public Relations - Newport Beach, CA - *StaDirAdAg 2-84*
Reid, Chris - New York, NY - *LitMarPl 83, 84*
Reid Co. Inc., Russ - Pasadena, CA - *ArtMar 84; DirMarMP 83; StaDirAdAg 2-84*
Reid, David - Mill City, OR - *BoPubDir 4, 5*
Reid Walker Ltd. - London, England - *StaDirAdAg 2-84*
Reidel Publishing Co., D. [Subs. of Kluwer NV] - Hingham, MA - *LitMarPl 83, 84*
Reider Film & Television Inc. - Atlanta, GA - *AvMarPl 83*
Reidsville Review - Reidsville, NC - *BaconPubCkNews 84; Ed&PubIntYB 82; NewsDir 84*
Reidsville Tattnall Journal - Reidsville, GA - *BaconPubCkNews 84*
Reiff Press - Amelia, OH - *BoPubDir 4*
Reiff Press - Indiana, PA - *BoPubDir 5*
Reilly & Associates Inc., E. M. - St. Louis, MO - *StaDirAdAg 2-84*
Reilly & Maloney Music - Seattle, WA - *BillIntBG 83-84*
Reilly, F/S - San Francisco, CA - *StaDirAdAg 2-84*
Reilly Group Inc., The Gene - Darien, CT - *HBIndAd&MS 82-83; IntDirMarRes 83; Tel&CabFB 84C*
Reilly, William A. - Dover, MA - *LitMag&SmPr 83-84*
Reiman Publications Inc. - Milwaukee, WI - *LitMarPl 83, 84*
Reimei News, The - New York, NY - *Ed&PubIntYB 82*
Reimel Carter Advertising - Philadelphia, PA - *AdAge 3-28-84; LitMarPl 83, 84; StaDirAdAg 2-84*
Reimer Advertising Ltd., C. - Winnipeg, MB, Canada - *StaDirAdAg 2-84*
Reims, Gordon A. - Orrtanna, PA - *LitMarPl 83, 84; MagIndMarPl 82-83*
Reina's Secretarial Service - Whittier, CA - *LitMarPl 83, 84; MagIndMarPl 82-83*
Reinbeck Courier - Reinbeck, IA - *BaconPubCkNews 84; Ed&PubIntYB 82*
Reincarnation Report [of Sutphen Corp.] - Malibu, CA - *WritMar 84*
Reiner Contemporary Casting Ltd., Mark - New York, NY - *HBIndAd&MS 82-83*
Reiner, Marian - New Rochelle, NY - *LitMarPl 83, 84; MagIndMarPl 82-83*
Reinforcement Learning Inc. - Upper Saddle River, NJ - *AvMarPl 83*
Reinforcing Steel Institute of Ontario - Willowdale, ON, Canada - *BoPubDir 4 Sup, 5*
Reinhardt, Patricia - North Haledon, NJ - *LitMarPl 84*
Reinhardt, Patricia - New York, NY - *LitMarPl 83*
Reiser Williams Deyong/C & W - Irvine, CA - *StaDirAdAg 2-84*
Reisman & Associates, Emil - Beverly Hills, CA - *StaDirAdAg 2-84*
Reiss, Otto F. - Flushing, NY - *LitMag&SmPr 83-84*
Reisterstown & Owings Mills Edition [of Baltimore Star Publications] - Baltimore, MD - *NewsDir 84*
Reitt Editing Services Inc. - Atlanta, GA - *LitMarPl 83, 84*
Reitter, Wilkins & Associates Inc. - New York, NY - *IntDirMarRes 83*
Reizner & Reizner Film & Video - San Jose, CA - *AvMarPl 83*
Related Arts Counsellors - New York, NY - *DirPRFirms 83*
Relational Database Systems Inc. - Sunnyvale, CA - *MicrocomMPl 84; WhoWMicrocom 83*
Relational Solutions Inc. - Houston, TX - *MicrocomMPl 84*
Relational Systems International - Salem, OR - *WhoWMicrocom 83*
Relational Technology Inc. - Berkeley, CA - *ADAPSOMemDir 83-84; MicrocomMPl 84*
Relativity Records Inc. - Jamaica, NY - *BillIntBG 83-84*
Relay 53 [of Northeast Florida Letter Carriers Local Union 53] - Jacksonville, FL - *NewsDir 84*
Release I.O. - New York, NY - *BaconPubCkMag 84*
Release Press - Brooklyn, NY - *BoPubDir 4, 5; LitMag&SmPr 83-84*
Release Records - St. Louis, MO - *BillIntBG 83-84*
Relentless Music - New York, NY - *BillIntBG 83-84*
Relevant Publications Ltd. - Del Mar, CA - *BoPubDir 4, 5*
Reliability Analysis Center [of IIT Research Institute] - Franklin Springs, NY - *CompReadDB 82; EISS 83*
Reliance Audio Visual Corp. - New York, NY - *AvMarPl 83*

Reliance Distributors of British Columbia Ltd. - Squamish, BC, Canada - *BrCabYB 84*
Reliance Energy Services - New York, NY - *EISS 5-84 Sup*
Reliance Plastics & Packaging [Subs. of Reliance Folding Carton Corp.] - Bloomfield, NJ - *AvMarPl 83; LitMarPl 83, 84; WhoWMicrocom 83*
Religion & Ethics Institute - Evanston, IL - *BoPubDir 4, 5*
Religion Index [of American Theological Library Association] - Chicago, IL - *OnBibDB 3*
Religion Index One: Periodicals [of American Theological Library Association] - Chicago, IL - *CompReadDB 82*
Religion Index Two: Multi-Author Works [of American Theological Library Association] - Chicago, IL - *CompReadDB 82*
Religion Teacher's Journal [of Twenty-Third Publications] - Mystic, CT - *WritMar 84*
Religion Today - Washington, DC - *Ed&PubIntYB 82*
Religious Activities Press - Mt. Juliet, TN - *BoPubDir 4, 5*
Religious Book Club - Tarrytown, NY - *LitMarPl 83, 84*
Religious Drawings Inc. - Dallas, TX - *Ed&PubIntYB 82*
Religious Education - New Haven, CT - *MagIndMarPl 82-83*
Religious Education Press - Birmingham, AL - *BoPubDir 4, 5; LitMarPl 84*
Religious Lists [Div. of Martin Sass Inc.] - New City, NY - *LitMarPl 83, 84; MagIndMarPl 82-83*
Religious News Service - New York, NY - *AvMarPl 83; Ed&PubIntYB 82; LitMarPl 83, 84; MagIndMarPl 82-83*
Relix Magazine - Brooklyn, NY - *ArtMar 84; LitMag&SmPr 83-84; MagIndMarPl 82-83; WritMar 84*
Relix Records Inc. - Brooklyn, NY - *BillIntBG 83-84*
RELS - Marina del Ray, CA - *DirOnDB Spring 84*
REM Productions [Aff. of Radiation Technology Programs Inc.] - West Palm Beach, FL - *AvMarPl 83; BoPubDir 4 Sup, 5*
Remac Information Corp. - Gaithersburg, MD - *EISS 83*
Remanco Systems Inc. - Toronto, ON, Canada - *DataDirSup 7-83*
Remarc [of Dialog Information Services Inc.] - Palo Alto, CA - *DataDirOnSer 84*
REMARC [of Carrollton Press] - Arlington, VA - *CompReadDB 82; DBBus 82; DirOnDB Spring 84; EISS 83; OnBibDB 3*
REMark [of Health Users Group] - St. Joseph, MI - *MicrocomMPl 84*
Remark Datacom Inc. - Woodbury, NY - *DataDirSup 7-83*
Rembrandt Films - New York, NY - *Tel&CabFB 84C*
Rembrandt Graphics Div. [of Rembrandt's Mother Inc.] - New York, NY - *LitMarPl 83, 84*
Rembrandt's Mother Inc. - New York, NY - *MagIndMarPl 82-83*
Remco Advertising Agency - Houston, TX - *StaDirAdAg 2-84*
Remembrance Music - *See* Tiki Enterprises Inc.
Remer-Ribolow Employment Agency - New York, NY - *InfIndMarPl 83; LitMarPl 83, 84; MagIndMarPl 82-83*
Remex Div. [of Ex-Cell-O Corp.] - Irvine, CA - *DataDirSup 7-83; WhoWMicrocom 83*
Remi Books Inc. - New York, NY - *BoPubDir 4 Sup, 5*
Remick, Lloyd Zane - Philadelphia, PA - *BillIntBG 83-84*
Reminder - Rockville, CT - *AyerDirPub 83*
Reminder - Stafford Springs, CT - *AyerDirPub 83*
Reminder - Algona, IA - *AyerDirPub 83*
Reminder - Humboldt, IA - *AyerDirPub 83*
Reminder - Knoxville, IA - *AyerDirPub 83*
Reminder - Alma, MI - *AyerDirPub 83*
Reminder - Hastings, MI - *AyerDirPub 83*
Reminder - St. Johns, MI - *AyerDirPub 83*
Reminder - Coventry, RI - *AyerDirPub 83*
Reminder - Mobridge, SD - *AyerDirPub 83*
Reminder - Flin Flon, MB, Canada - *AyerDirPub 83; BaconPubCkNews 84; Ed&PubIntYB 82*
Reminder-Enterprise - Cudahy, WI - *Ed&PubIntYB 82*
Reminder, The - Wilbraham, MA - *AyerDirPub 83*
Reminder, The - Ortonville, MI - *AyerDirPub 83; Ed&PubIntYB 82*
Reminder, The - Pierre, SD - *AyerDirPub 83*
Reminder, The - New London, WI - *AyerDirPub 83*
Reminder, The [of Panopticum Press London] - Upminster, England - *LitMag&SmPr 83-84*
Remine, Shields - New York, NY - *LitMarPl 83, 84*
Remington Press - Remington, IN - *AyerDirPub 83; BaconPubCkNews 84; Ed&PubIntYB 82*
Remington Rand Corp. - Princeton, NJ - *DirInfWP 82*
Remlap Publishing Co. - Beverly Hills, CA - *BoPubDir 4 Sup, 5*
Remley & Co. - Albion, NY - *MagIndMarPl 82-83*
Remodeling Contractor [of Maclean-Hunter Publishing Co.] - Chicago, IL - *BaconPubCkMag 84; MagDir 84*
Remodeling World - Wheeling, IL - *BaconPubCkMag 84*
Remote Computing Corp. [Subs. of Hale Systems] - Palo Alto, CA - *ADAPSOMemDir 83-84; DataDirOnSer 84; DataDirSup 7-83*
Remote Computing Corp. [Div. of Hale Systems Inc.] - Roslyn, NY - *MicrocomMPl 84; MicrocomSwDir 1*
Remote Computing Supplies - Downers Grove, IL - *WhoWMicrocom 83*
Remote Sensing On-line Retrieval System [of Canada Centre for Remote Sensing] - Ottawa, ON, Canada - *DataDirOnSer 84; EISS 83*
Remsen Bell-Enterprise - Remsen, IA - *BaconPubCkNews 84; Ed&PubIntYB 82*
Remsoft Inc. - Euclid, OH - *MicrocomMPl 83, 84*
Ren-Maur Music Corp. - New York, NY - *BillIntBG 83-84*
Renaissance Books - Milwaukee, WI - *BoPubDir 4, 5*
Renaissance House - New York, NY - *BoPubDir 4, 5; LitMag&SmPr 83-84*
Renaissance Productions International - Tucson, AZ - *BoPubDir 4, 5*
Renaissance Publications - *See* El Renacimiento Inc./Renaissance Publications
Renaissance Publishers & Book Distributors - North Miami Beach, FL - *BoPubDir 4, 5*
Renaissance Publishing [Aff. of Pregnancy & Natural Childbirth Education Center] - Los Angeles, CA - *BoPubDir 4, 5*
Renaissance Systems Inc. - San Diego, CA - *WhoWMicrocom 83*
Renaud Enterprises - Long Valley, NJ - *BoPubDir 4, 5*
Renbourn's Mule - *See* Kicking Mule Music
Renda Music Inc. - Phoenix, AZ - *BillIntBG 83-84*
Renda Stations, Anthony F. - East McKeesport, PA - *BrCabYB 84*
Render - Riverside, CA - *BaconPubCkMag 84; MagDir 84*
Rendina, Dave - Newfield, NJ - *BoPubDir 4, 5*
Rene Publications, Leon - Los Angeles, CA - *BillIntBG 83-84*
Renewable Energy & Conservation Information Center - *See* Conservation & Energy Inquiry & Referral Service
Renewable Energy in Canada - Toronto, ON, Canada - *BoPubDir 4, 5*
Renewable Energy News - Washington, DC - *BaconPubCkMag 84*
Renewable Energy News [of Cren Publishing Ltd.] - Ottawa, ON, Canada - *LitMag&SmPr 83-84*
Renewable Energy News-Northeast - Ashfield, MA - *WritMar 84*
Renews - Deerfield, IL - *BaconPubCkMag 84; MagDir 84*
Renfield, Richard L. - Falls Church, VA - *LitMarPl 83, 84*
Renfrew Cablevision Ltd. [of Ottawa Cablevision Ltd.] - Renfrew, ON, Canada - *BrCabYB 84*
Renfrew Mercury, The - Renfrew, ON, Canada - *Ed&PubIntYB 82*
Renfro & Associates, C. G. - Bala Cynwyd, PA - *EISS 5-84 Sup*
Renfro Studios, Nancy - Austin, TX - *BoPubDir 4, 5*
Renner Burns Advertising Inc. - Minneapolis, MN - *StaDirAdAg 2-84*
Renner Co., Richard L. - North Wales, PA - *StaDirAdAg 2-84*
Rennert Bilingual Translations - New York, NY - *MagIndMarPl 82-83*
Reno Cable TV Co. - Reno, PA - *BrCabYB 84*
Reno Evening Gazette - Reno, NV - *BaconPubCkNews 84; Ed&PubIntYB 82; NewsBur 6; NewsDir 84*
Reno/Metz Music Inc. - Los Angeles, CA - *BillIntBG 83-84*
Reno Nevada State Journal - Reno, NV - *NewsDir 84*
Reno Observer, The - Reno, NV - *Ed&PubIntYB 82*
Renouf Publishing Co. Ltd. - Montreal, PQ, Canada - *LitMarPl 83, 84*
Renouf/USA Inc. - Brookfield, VT - *LitMarPl 83, 84*
Renovo Record - Renovo, PA - *BaconPubCkNews 84*
Rensselaer County Cablevision Corp. [of Adams-Russell Co. Inc.] - Rensselaer, NY - *BrCabYB 84; Tel&CabFB 84C*
Rensselaer Engineer [of Rensselaer Union] - Troy, NY - *MagDir 84*

Rensselaer Republican [of Hoosier Northwest Inc.] - Rensselaer, IN - *AyerDirPub 83; BaconPubCkNews 84; NewsDir 84*
Rent All - Duluth, MN - *MagDir 84*
Rental Age - Moline, IL - *BaconPubCkMag 84; MagDir 84*
Rental Equipment Register - Los Angeles, CA - *ArtMar 84; BaconPubCkMag 84; MagDir 84*
Rental Product News - Ft. Atkinson, WI - *BaconPubCkMag 84; MagDir 84; MagIndMarPl 82-83*
Rentavision of Brunswick Inc. [of Century Communications Corp.] - Brunswick, GA - *BrCabYB 84; Tel&CabFB 84C*
Rentsch Public Relations, Gail - New York, NY - *LitMarPl 83, 84*
Renville County Farmer - Mohall, ND - *AyerDirPub 83; Ed&PubIntYB 82*
Renville County Shopper [of Olivia Times-Journal Inc.] - Olivia, MN - *NewsDir 84*
Renville Star Farmer - Renville, MN - *BaconPubCkNews 84*
R.E.P. Publishers - Maryland Heights, MO - *BoPubDir 5*
Rep World - Sinking Spring, PA - *BaconPubCkMag 84*
Repdata - Lyme, CT - *WhoWMicrocom 83*
Repdata - Bedford, MA - *MicrocomMPl 84*
Repeat-O-Type Manufacturing Corp. - Wayne, NJ - *DirInfWP 82*
Repertoire Analytique d'Articles de Revues du Quebec [of Informatech] - Montreal, PQ, Canada - *CompReadDB 82; DataDirOnSer 84*
Repertory of Arts & Archaeology [of Centre de Documentation Sciences Humaines] - Paris, France - *CompReadDB 82*
Reply-O-Letter Co. Inc. [Subs. of Grow Group Inc.] - New York, NY - *LitMarPl 83, 84; MagIndMarPl 82-83*
Reply Systems Inc. - Chanhassen, NY - *MagIndMarPl 82-83*
Report - Ontario, CA - *AyerDirPub 83*
Report - Swan River, MB, Canada - *Ed&PubIntYB 82*
Report Collection Index [of Studsvik Energiteknik AB Studsvikbiblioteket] - Nykoping, Sweden - *CompReadDB 82; EISS 83*
Report Store, The [of Ergosyst Associates Inc.] - Lawrence, KS - *EISS 5-84 Sup*
Report, The - Santa Barbara, CA - *MicrocomMPl 84*
Reporter - Long Beach, CA - *AyerDirPub 83*
Reporter - Vacaville, CA - *AyerDirPub 83*
Reporter - Lake City, FL - *AyerDirPub 83*
Reporter - Casey, IL - *AyerDirPub 83*
Reporter - Chicago, IL - *AyerDirPub 83; Ed&PubIntYB 82*
Reporter - Downers Grove, IL - *AyerDirPub 83*
Reporter - Fisher, IL - *AyerDirPub 83*
Reporter - Greenfield, IN - *AyerDirPub 83*
Reporter - Lebanon, IN - *AyerDirPub 83*
Reporter - Martinsville, IN - *AyerDirPub 83; Ed&PubIntYB 82*
Reporter - Emmetsburg, IA - *AyerDirPub 83; Ed&PubIntYB 82*
Reporter - Nashua, IA - *AyerDirPub 83*
Reporter - Spencer, IA - *AyerDirPub 83*
Reporter - Ellsworth, KS - *AyerDirPub 83*
Reporter - Independence, KS - *AyerDirPub 83*
Reporter - Rose Hill, KS - *AyerDirPub 83*
Reporter - Foxboro, MA - *AyerDirPub 83*
Reporter - Marblehead, MA - *AyerDirPub 83*
Reporter - Coldwater, MI - *AyerDirPub 83*
Reporter - Saline, MI - *AyerDirPub 83*
Reporter [of Mankato State University] - Mankato, MN - *NewsDir 84*
Reporter - Gibbon, NE - *AyerDirPub 83*
Reporter - Newman Grove, NE - *AyerDirPub 83*
Reporter - Berlin, NH - *AyerDirPub 83*
Reporter [of Courier Printing Inc.] - North Conway, NH - *AyerDirPub 83; Ed&PubIntYB 82; NewsDir 84*
Reporter - Santa Fe, NM - *AyerDirPub 83*
Reporter - Shelter Island, NY - *AyerDirPub 83*
Reporter - Walton, NY - *AyerDirPub 83; NewsDir 84*
Reporter - Akron, OH - *Ed&PubIntYB 82*
Reporter - Republic, OH - *AyerDirPub 83*
Reporter - Reynoldsburg, OH - *AyerDirPub 83*
Reporter - Chelsea, OK - *AyerDirPub 83*
Reporter - Owasso, OK - *AyerDirPub 83*
Reporter - Lansdale, PA - *AyerDirPub 83; BaconPubCkNews 84; Ed&PubIntYB 82*
Reporter - Royersford, PA - *AyerDirPub 83*
Reporter - Glen Rose, TX - *AyerDirPub 83*
Reporter - Hillsboro, TX - *AyerDirPub 83; Ed&PubIntYB 82*
Reporter - Spearman, TX - *AyerDirPub 83*
Reporter - Sweetwater, TX - *AyerDirPub 83*
Reporter - Springville, UT - *AyerDirPub 83*
Reporter - Stowe, VT - *AyerDirPub 83*
Reporter - Mercer Island, WA - *AyerDirPub 83*
Reporter - Edgerton, WI - *AyerDirPub 83*
Reporter - Fond du Lac, WI - *AyerDirPub 83*
Reporter - Friendship, WI - *AyerDirPub 83*
Reporter - Horicon, WI - *AyerDirPub 83*
Reporter - New Holstein, WI - *AyerDirPub 83*
Reporter - Sharon, WI - *AyerDirPub 83*
Reporter - Stony Plain, AB, Canada - *AyerDirPub 83; Ed&PubIntYB 82*
Reporter - Cambridge, ON, Canada - *AyerDirPub 83*
Reporter - Gananoque, ON, Canada - *AyerDirPub 83; Ed&PubIntYB 82*
Reporter - Kingsville, ON, Canada - *AyerDirPub 83*
Reporter - Toronto, ON, Canada - *AyerDirPub 83; Ed&PubIntYB 82*
Reporter - West Hill, ON, Canada - *Ed&PubIntYB 82*
Reporter-Advertiser/North & South - Jefferson, WI - *AyerDirPub 83*
Reporter & Andrew County Democrat - Savannah, MO - *AyerDirPub 83*
Reporter & Farmer - Webster, SD - *AyerDirPub 83; Ed&PubIntYB 82*
Reporter & Messenger - Rockdale, TX - *AyerDirPub 83*
Reporter-Argus - Port Allegany, PA - *AyerDirPub 83*
Reporter Extra, The - Lansdale, PA - *AyerDirPub 83*
Reporter-Herald - Loveland, CO - *AyerDirPub 83*
Reporter-News - Abilene, TX - *AyerDirPub 83*
Reporter Newspapers - Toronto, ON, Canada - *Ed&PubIntYB 82*
Reporter of the Spring-Ford Area [of Ches-Mont Publications Inc.] - Royersford, PA - *Ed&PubIntYB 82; NewsDir 84*
Reporter Progress Newspapers - Downers Grove, IL - *BaconPubCkNews 84*
Reporter Publications - Chicago Ridge, IL - *BaconPubCkNews 84*
Reporter Publishing Co. - San Francisco, CA - *BaconPubCkNews 84*
Reporter Publishing Co. - Dundee, MI - *BaconPubCkNews 84*
Reporter-Telegram - Midland, TX - *AyerDirPub 83*
Reporter, The - Placerville, CA - *AyerDirPub 83*
Reporter, The - Tavernier, FL - *Ed&PubIntYB 82*
Reporter, The - East St. Louis, IL - *Ed&PubIntYB 82*
Reporter, The [of St. Matthews Jefferson Publishing Inc.] - Louisville, KY - *AyerDirPub 83; NewsDir 84*
Reporter, The - Monticello, KY - *Ed&PubIntYB 82*
Reporter, The - Ramsey, NJ - *AyerDirPub 83*
Reporter, The - South Plainfield, NJ - *AyerDirPub 83*
Reporter, The [of Baruch College] - New York, NY - *NewsDir 84*
Reporter, The - Huron, OH - *Ed&PubIntYB 82*
Reporter, The - Spring City, PA - *Ed&PubIntYB 82*
Reportero Industrial [of Keller Publishing Corp.] - Great Neck, NY - *BaconPubCkMag 84; MagDir 84*
Reports Publications [Subs. of Associates International Inc.] - Washington, DC - *DataDirOnSer 84; EISS 5-84 Sup*
Repository - Canton, OH - *AyerDirPub 83; Ed&PubIntYB 82*
Repository Press - Prince George, BC, Canada - *BoPubDir 4, 5*
Representations [of University of California Press] - Berkeley, CA - *LitMag&SmPr 83-84*
Representative - Leduc, AB, Canada - *AyerDirPub 83*
Re:Print [of The Printable Arts Society Inc.] - New York, NY - *LitMag&SmPr 83-84*
Reprint Co. - Spartanburg, SC - *LitMarPl 83, 84*
Reprint Distribution Service Inc. - Kent, CT - *BoPubDir 4 Sup, 5*
Repro Art Service - Dunmore, PA - *LitMarPl 83, 84; MagIndMarPl 82-83*
Reprographics - Northbrook, IL - *MagDir 84*
Reprographics - West New York, NJ - *MagIndMarPl 82-83*
Republic - Fairfield, CA - *AyerDirPub 83*
Republic - Geneseo, IL - *AyerDirPub 83*
Republic - Union, OR - *AyerDirPub 83*
Republic - Meyersdale, PA - *AyerDirPub 83; Ed&PubIntYB 82*
Republic - Beresford, SD - *AyerDirPub 83*
Republic - Mitchell, SD - *AyerDirPub 83; Ed&PubIntYB 82*

Republic-Appeal - Albert City, IA - *AyerDirPub 83*
Republic Community Tele-Communications Inc. [of Tele-Communications Inc.] - Republic, MO - *BrCabYB 84*
Republic Monitor - Republic, MO - *BaconPubCkNews 84; Ed&PubIntYB 82*
Republic Music Corp. - *See* World Music Inc.
Republic News-Miner - Republic, WA - *Ed&PubIntYB 82*
Republic News Services - Silver Spring, MD - *MagIndMarPl 82-83*
Republic Recording Corp. - Houston, TX - *BillIntBG 83-84*
Republic Reporter - Republic, OH - *Ed&PubIntYB 82*
Republic Reporter - *See* Seneca Publishing Inc.
Republic Scene [of East/West Network Inc.] - Los Angeles, CA - *ArtMar 84; BaconPubCkMag 84; MagDir 84; MagIndMarPl 82-83; WritMar 84*
Republic Service Bureau Inc. - Torrance, CA - *DataDirOnSer 84*
Republic, The - Columbus, IN - *AyerDirPub 83; Ed&PubIntYB 82*
Republic Times - Waterloo, IL - *AyerDirPub 83*
Republic-Times Shopper - Waterloo, IL - *AyerDirPub 83*
Republican - Bradford, IL - *AyerDirPub 83*
Republican - Geneva, IL - *AyerDirPub 83*
Republican - Marion, IL - *AyerDirPub 83*
Republican - Danville, IN - *AyerDirPub 83; Ed&PubIntYB 82*
Republican - Paoli, IN - *AyerDirPub 83*
Republican - Rensselaer, IN - *Ed&PubIntYB 82*
Republican - Rushville, IN - *AyerDirPub 83*
Republican - Versailles, IN - *AyerDirPub 83*
Republican - Humboldt, IA - *AyerDirPub 83*
Republican - Montezuma, IA - *AyerDirPub 83*
Republican - Wapello, IA - *AyerDirPub 83*
Republican - Burlington, KS - *AyerDirPub 83*
Republican - Council Grove, KS - *AyerDirPub 83; Ed&PubIntYB 82*
Republican - Jetmore, KS - *AyerDirPub 83*
Republican - Logan, KS - *AyerDirPub 83*
Republican - Springfield, MA - *AyerDirPub 83; Ed&PubIntYB 82; LitMarPl 83, 84; NewsDir 84*
Republican - Preston, MN - *AyerDirPub 83*
Republican - Woodville, MS - *AyerDirPub 83*
Republican - Unionville, MO - *AyerDirPub 83*
Republican - Imperial, NE - *AyerDirPub 83*
Republican - Wakefield, NE - *AyerDirPub 83; Ed&PubIntYB 82*
Republican - Weeping Water, NE - *AyerDirPub 83*
Republican - Cazenovia, NY - *AyerDirPub 83*
Republican - Cherokee, OK - *AyerDirPub 83*
Republican - Kane, PA - *AyerDirPub 83*
Republican - Pottsville, PA - *AyerDirPub 83*
Republican - Waynesburg, PA - *AyerDirPub 83*
Republican - Stanley, WI - *AyerDirPub 83*
Republican & American - Waterbury, CT - *AyerDirPub 83*
Republican & Bulletin - Anthony, KS - *AyerDirPub 83*
Republican & Flume - Fairplay, CO - *Ed&PubIntYB 82*
Republican-Clipper - Bethany, MO - *AyerDirPub 83*
Republican-Eagle - Red Wing, MN - *AyerDirPub 83; Ed&PubIntYB 82*
Republican-Journal - Belfast, ME - *AyerDirPub 83; Ed&PubIntYB 82*
Republican-Journal - Darlington, WI - *AyerDirPub 83; Ed&PubIntYB 82*
Republican-News - Marengo, IL - *AyerDirPub 83*
Republican Nonpareil - Central City, NE - *AyerDirPub 83*
Republican-Record - Carrollton, MO - *Ed&PubIntYB 82*
Republican-Register - Mt. Carmel, IL - *AyerDirPub 83*
Republican-Register - Moravia, NY - *AyerDirPub 83*
Republican-Reporter - Oregon, IL - *AyerDirPub 83; Ed&PubIntYB 82*
Republican Rustler - Basin, WY - *AyerDirPub 83; Ed&PubIntYB 82*
Republican-Standard - Waukon, IA - *AyerDirPub 83*
Republican, The - Oakland, MD - *AyerDirPub 83; Ed&PubIntYB 82; NewsDir 84*
Republican, The - Wauseon, OH - *Ed&PubIntYB 82*
Republican-Times - Trenton, MO - *AyerDirPub 83; Ed&PubIntYB 82*
Republican-Tribune - Sandusky, MI - *AyerDirPub 83; Ed&PubIntYB 82*
Request System [of System Automation Corp.] - Silver Spring, MD - *EISS 83*
RER Software - Appleton, WI - *WhoWMicrocom 83*
RES Consultants - Sugarland, TX - *MicrocomSwDir 1*
Resagri - *DirOnDB Spring 84*
Resco - Meriden, CT - *ArtMar 84; AvMarPl 83; WritMar 84*
Rescue Cable Co. - Weston, OH - *Tel&CabFB 84C p.1698*
Research - Minneapolis, MN - *MagIndMarPl 82-83*
Research Alliance, The - San Francisco, CA - *IntDirMarRes 83*
Research & Data Resources Co. Ltd. - Bangkok, Thailand - *IntDirMarRes 83*
Research & Development Dept. [of British Library] - London, England - *EISS 83*
Research & Development Laboratories [Div. of Calle & Co.] - Greenwich, CT - *IntDirMarRes 83*
Research & Development Program Planning [of Defense Technical Information Center] - Alexandria, VA - *DataDirOnSer 84*
Research & Education Association - New York, NY - *BoPubDir 4, 5*
Research & Engineering Information Services [of Exxon Research & Engineering Co.] - Linden, NJ - *EISS 83*
Research & Forecasts Inc. - New York, NY - *EISS 7-83 Sup; IntDirMarRes 83*
Research & Forecasts Inc. - *See* Ruder Finn & Rotman Inc.
Research & Information Services for Education [of Montgomery County Intermediate Unit] - King of Prussia, PA - *EISS 83*
Research & Information Systems Div. [of Montana State Dept. of Administration] - Helena, MT - *EISS 83*
Research & Service Institute - Nashville, TN - *BoPubDir 5*
Research & Special Projects Div. [of Bureau of National Affairs Inc.] - Washington, DC - *EISS 83*
Research & Technology Work Unit Information System [of Defense Technical Information Center] - Alexandria, VA - *DataDirOnSer 84; DirOnDB Spring 84*
Research Applications Group - Wilton, CT - *IntDirMarRes 83*
Research Associates Inc. - Indianapolis, IN - *EISS 83*
Research Associates International - New York, NY - *InfIndMarPl 83; LitMarPl 83*
Research Books Inc. - Guilford, CT - *BoPubDir 4 Sup, 5; LitMarPl 83, 84*
Research Center for Library & Information Science [of Indiana University] - Bloomington, IN - *EISS 83*
Research Center, The - Norwalk, CT - *IntDirMarRes 83*
Research Centers Directory [of Gale Research Co.] - Detroit, MI - *EISS 83*
Research Communications Ltd. - Chestnut Hill, MA - *IntDirMarRes 83*
Research Consultants Inc. - Norwalk, CT - *BrCabYB 84*
Research Coordinating Unit [of Oklahoma State Dept. of Vocational & Technical Education] - Stillwater, OK - *EISS 83*
Research Counsel Inc., The - New York, NY - *HBIndAd&MS 82-83*
Research Data Center [of Mid-America Regional Council] - Kansas City, MO - *EISS 5-84 Sup*
Research Data Inc. - Framingham, MA - *IntDirMarRes 83*
Research Dept. [of United Way of Greater Indianapolis] - Indianapolis, IN - *EISS 83*
Research Dept., The - New York, NY - *IntDirMarRes 83*
Research Designs for Marketing [Div. of Starch INRA Hooper Inc.] - Mamaroneck, NY - *IntDirMarRes 83*
Research Documentation Section [of U.S. Public Health Service] - Bethesda, MD - *EISS 83*
Research Engineers Inc. - Marlton, NJ - *MicrocomMPl 84*
Research Enterprise - Toronto, ON, Canada - *BoPubDir 4, 5*
Research Evaluation Service [of I. P. Sharp Associates Ltd.] - Toronto, ON, Canada - *DataDirOnSer 84*
Research for Advertising & Marketing - New York, NY - *IntDirMarRes 83*
Research for Policy Decisions - Hartford, CT - *IntDirMarRes 83*
Research Group Inc., The - Niles, IL - *IntDirMarRes 83*
Research Group, The - East Seattle, WA - *BrCabYB 84*
Research House Inc., The - Overland Park, KS - *IntDirMarRes 83*
Research in Marketing Inc. - Chicago, IL - *IntDirMarRes 83*
Research in Perspective Inc. - New York, NY - *IntDirMarRes 83*
Research in Progress - Oak Ridge, TN - *DirOnDB Spring 84*

Research Information Center Inc. [Subs. of The Greyhound Corp.] - Phoenix, AZ - *BrCabYB 84*
Research Information Service - Salem, OR - *LitMarPl 83, 84*
Research Information Services [of Rutgers University] - New Brunswick, NJ - *FBInfSer 80*
Research Information Services Inc. - Louisville, KY - *IntDirMarRes 83*
Research Institute for Information Science & Engineering Inc. - Pittsburgh, PA - *EISS 83*
Research Institute of America Inc., The [Subs. of Lawyers Cooperative Publishing Co.] - New York, NY - *DirMarMP 83*
Research Institute of Fundamental Information Science [of Kyushu University] - Fukuoka City, Japan - *EISS 5-84 Sup*
Research Institute of Telecommunications & Economics - Tokyo, Japan - *ADAPSOMemDir 83-84*
Research International - London, England - *IntDirMarRes 83*
Research Libraries Group Inc. - Stanford, CA - *DataDirOnSer 84; EISS 83; InfIndMarPl 83*
Research Libraries Information Network [of The Research Libraries Group Inc.] - Stanford, CA - *DataDirOnSer 84; EISS 83*
Research Management - New York, NY - *BaconPubCkMag 84; MagDir 84*
Research Media Inc. - Cambridge, MA - *BoPubDir 4, 5*
Research Medical Library [of University of Texas System Cancer Center] - Houston, TX - *EISS 83*
Research Monitor News - Washington, DC - *DirOnDB Spring 84*
Research Monitor News [of NewsNet Inc.] - Bryn Mawr, PA - *DataDirOnSer 84*
Research News - Ann Arbor, MI - *MagIndMarPl 82-83*
Research 100 - Princeton, NJ - *IntDirMarRes 83*
Research-One Inc. - Southfield, MI - *IntDirMarRes 83*
Research Press - Champaign, IL - *AvMarPl 83; LitMarPl 83, 84*
Research Projects Corp. - Hempstead, NY - *LitMarPl 83, 84; MagIndMarPl 82-83*
Research Publications - Saratoga, CA - *BoPubDir 4, 5*
Research Publications - Glen Rock, NJ - *BoPubDir 5*
Research Publications Inc. [Aff. of International Thomson Holdings Inc.] - Woodbridge, CT - *BoPubDir 5; InfoS 83-84; LitMarPl 83, 84; MagIndMarPl 82-83; MicroMarPl 82-83*
Research Publishers - Arlington Heights, IL - *BoPubDir 4, 5*
Research Referral Service [of International Federation for Documentation] - The Hague, Netherlands - *EISS 83*
Research Reports & Pictures - New York, NY - *FBInfSer 80; MagIndMarPl 82-83*
Research Resources - Atlanta, GA - *IntDirMarRes 83*
Research Service - New York, NY - *BoPubDir 4, 5*
Research Services Corp. - Ft. Worth, TX - *MagIndMarPl 82-83*
Research Services of North Carolina - Greensboro, NC - *IntDirMarRes 83*
Research Strategies Corp. - Princeton, NJ - *IntDirMarRes 83*
Research Systems Corp. - Evansville, IN - *BrCabYB 84; IntDirMarRes 83; Tel&CabFB 84C*
Research Tapings - Santa Monica, CA - *IntDirMarRes 83*
Research Technology International - Lincolnwood, IL - *AvMarPl 83*
Research Triangle Park Leader - Research Triangle Park, NC - *BaconPubCkNews 84*
Research Unltd. - Sacramento, CA - *IntDirMarRes 83*
Research Ventures - Berkeley, CA - *EISS 83; FBInfSer 80*
Researcher Publications Inc. - Lynnwood, WA - *BoPubDir 4 Sup, 5*
Reseau de Documentation en Economie Agricole [of Ministere de l'Agriculture] - Paris, France - *InfIndMarPl 83*
Reseau Urbamet [of Institut d'Amenagement et d'Urbanisme de la Region d'Ile-de-France] - Paris, France - *InfIndMarPl 83*
Reseda Times - Encino, CA - *AyerDirPub 83*
Reseda Times - *See* Associated Valley Publications
Reservation Telephone Cooperative - Parshall, ND - *BrCabYB 84; Tel&CabFB 84C; TelDir&BG 83-84*
Reserve Research Ltd. - New York, NY - *DirMarMP 83*
Reserve Telephone Co. Inc. - Reserve, LA - *TelDir&BG 83-84*
Reshus - *See* FRANCIS: Reshus
Resident & Staff Physician - Port Washington, NY - *ArtMar 84; BaconPubCkMag 84; MagDir 84; MagIndMarPl 82-83*
Residential Interiors - New York, NY - *MagDir 84*
Resilient Records - Paramus, NJ - *BillIntBG 83-84*
Resistance Welder Manufacturers Association - Philadelphia, PA - *BoPubDir 5*
Resnick, Robert Horn - New York, NY - *DirPRFirms 83*
Resnick, Sandi - Brooklyn, NY - *LitMarPl 83, 84*
RESORS - Ottawa, ON, Canada - *DirOnDB Spring 84*
Resort - Lake View, IA - *AyerDirPub 83*
Resort Cable TV [of Cox Cable Communications Inc.] - Saranac Lake, NY - *BrCabYB 84; Tel&CabFB 84C*
Resort Cable TV [of Cox Cable Communications Inc.] - Tupper Lake, NY - *Tel&CabFB 84C*
Resort Management [of Western Specialty Publications Inc.] - San Diego, CA - *MagDir 84*
Resort Management - Memphis, TN - *BaconPubCkMag 84*
Resort Management Systems Inc. - Denver, CO - *MicrocomMPl 84*
Resort Television Cable Co. Inc. [of WEHCO Video Inc.] - Hot Springs, AR - *BrCabYB 84; Tel&CabFB 84C*
Resort Timesharing Today - Los Altos, CA - *BaconPubCkMag 84*
Resorts Campgrounds & Attractions - Nashville, TN - *BaconPubCkMag 84*
Resource & Information Syndicate - Columbia, MD - *Ed&PubIntYB 82*
Resource Development - West Vancouver, BC, Canada - *WritMar 84*
Resource Inc. - Tampa, FL - *AvMarPl 83*
Resource Information Laboratory [of Cornell University] - Ithaca, NY - *EISS 83*
Resource Management Consultants - Derry, NH - *TeleSy&SerDir 2-84*
Resource Organizations & Meetings for Educators [of The National Center for Research in Vocational Education] - Columbus, OH - *DataDirOnSer 84; DirOnDB Spring 84*
Resource Publications Inc. - San Jose, CA - *ArtMar 84; BoPubDir 4, 5; LitMag&SmPr 83-84*
Resource Publications Inc. - Saratoga, CA - *WritMar 84*
Resource Recovery Report - Washington, DC - *BaconPubCkMag 84*
Resource Software International - Englewood Cliffs, NJ - *MicrocomMPl 83*
Resource Software International - Fords, NJ - *MicrocomMPl 84*
Resource Statistics Div. [of U.S. National Marine Fisheries Service] - Washington, DC - *EISS 83*
Resource Systems Institute [Aff. of East-West Center] - Honolulu, HI - *BoPubDir 4, 5*
Resourcebook - Great Neck, NY - *MagDir 84*
Resources - Cambridge, MA - *BoPubDir 4, 5*
Resources for Advanced Management Inc. - San Antonio, TX - *InfIndMarPl 83*
Resources for Children in Hospitals - Belmont, MA - *BoPubDir 5*
Resources for Communication - Windsor, CA - *EISS 5-84 Sup*
Resources for Feminist Research/Documentation sur la Recherche Feministe - Toronto, ON, Canada - *LitMag&SmPr 83-84*
Resources for the Future Inc. - Washington, DC - *BoPubDir 4 Sup, 5*
Resources for the Gifted - Phoenix, AZ - *DirMarMP 83*
Resources for Women - Boulder Creek, CA - *LitMag&SmPr 83-84*
Resources in Computer Education [of Northwest Regional Educational Laboratory] - Portland, OR - *DataDirOnSer 84; DirOnDB Spring 84; EISS 7-83 Sup*
Resources in Education [of Educational Resources Information Center] - Washington, DC - *CompReadDB 82*
Resources in Education [of ORI Inc.] - Bethesda, MD - *DataDirOnSer 84*
Resources in Vocational Education [of The National Center for Research in Vocational Education] - Columbus, OH - *CompReadDB 82; DataDirOnSer 84; DirOnDB Spring 84*
Resources Informatiques Quantum Ltd. - Montreal, PQ, Canada - *DirInfWP 82*
Resources Software International Inc. - Fords, NJ - *MicrocomSwDir 1*
Respect Music Co. - Los Angeles, CA - *BillIntBG 83-84*
Respiratory Care - Cheshire, CT - *BaconPubCkMag 84*
Respiratory Care - Philadelphia, PA - *MagDir 84*
Respiratory Therapy [of Brentwood Publishing Corp.] - Los Angeles, CA - *ArtMar 84; BaconPubCkMag 84; MagDir 84; MagIndMarPl 82-83*

Respond Records Inc. - Sunnyvale, CA - *BillIntBG 83-84*
Response! - Solana Beach, CA - *BaconPubCkMag 84*
Response - New York, NY - *MagIndMarPl 82-83*
Response Analysis Corp. - Princeton, NJ - *BrCabYB 84; IntDirMarRes 83*
Response Group Inc. - North Miami Beach, FL - *DirMarMP 83; LitMarPl 83, 84; MagIndMarPl 82-83; StaDirAdAg 2-84*
Response Imperatives Ltd. - Newburyport, MA - *DirMarMP 83; HBIndAd&MS 82-83*
Response Inc. - Vienna, VA - *DirMarMP 83*
Response Mailing Lists [Div. of Response Group] - Park Ridge, NJ - *LitMarPl 83, 84; MagIndMarPl 82-83*
Response Marketing Inc. - Eden Prairie, MN - *DirMarMP 83*
Response Research - Queens, NY - *IntDirMarRes 83*
Response Strategems Inc. [Div. of Sacks & Rosen Advertising] - New York, NY - *DirMarMP 83*
Response Systems Corp. - Edgemont, PA - *AvMarPl 83*
Response Technologies Advertising Inc. - Redondo Beach, CA - *DirMarMP 83*
Restaurant & Hotel Design [of Bill Communications] - New York, NY - *ArtMar 84; BaconPubCkMag 84; MagDir 84; WritMar 84*
Restaurant & Institution - Des Plaines, IL - *BaconPubCkMag 84*
Restaurant Assistance - Tampa, FL - *BaconPubCkMag 84*
Restaurant Business [of Bill Communications] - New York, NY - *ArtMar 84; BaconPubCkMag 84; Folio 83; MagDir 84; MagIndMarPl 82-83*
Restaurant Buyers Guide [of Urner Barry Publications Inc.] - Bayville, NJ - *NewsDir 84*
Restaurant Employee - New York, NY - *NewsDir 84*
Restaurant Exchange News - New City, NY - *BaconPubCkMag 84*
Restaurant Hospitality [of Penton/IPC] - Cleveland, OH - *ArtMar 84; BaconPubCkMag 84; Folio 83; MagDir 84; MagIndMarPl 82-83; WritMar 84*
Restaurant Merchandising News - Fairfield, CT - *BaconPubCkMag 84*
Restaurant News - Los Angeles, CA - *MagDir 84*
Restaurant News-Mobile & Industrial Catering - Los Angeles, CA - *BaconPubCkMag 84*
Restaurant South Magazine - Greensboro, NC - *MagDir 84*
Restaurants & Institutions [of Reed Publishing Corp.] - Chicago, IL - *MagDir 84; MagIndMarPl 82-83*
Restaurants & Institutions [of Cahners Publishing Co.] - Des Plaines, IL - *Folio 83*
Restaurateur - Chevy Chase, MD - *MagDir 84*
Reston Publishing Co. [Div. of Prentice-Hall Co.] - Reston, VA - *DirMarMP 83; LitMarPl 83, 84; MicrocomMPl 83, 84; WritMar 84*
Reston Recorder Ltd. - Reston, MB, Canada - *Ed&PubIntYB 82*
Reston Repertory Television Theatre - Reston, VA - *WritMar 84*
Reston Times [of Loudoun Times Publishing Co. Inc.] - Reston, VA - *AyerDirPub 83; Ed&PubIntYB 82; NewsDir 84*
Reston Times - *See* Loudoun Times Publishing Co. Inc.
Restoration Research - Bountiful, UT - *BoPubDir 5; LitMag&SmPr 83-84*
Result Radio Group, The - Winona, MN - *BrCabYB 84*
Results Inc. - Rutherford, NJ - *StaDirAdAg 2-84*
Retail Advertising Group - New York, NY - *StaDirAdAg 2-84*
Retail Advertising Group - *See* Keller Crescent Co.
Retail Broadcaster - New York, NY - *BaconPubCkMag 84*
Retail Clerks 698 Star - Akron, OH - *NewsDir 84*
Retail Concepts Inc. - Oakland, CA - *StaDirAdAg 2-84*
Retail Concepts Inc. - Frankenmuth, MI - *DataDirSup 7-83*
Retail Directions - New York, NY - *MagDir 84*
Retail Food Clerks Union, Local 1500 - Queens Village, NY - *NewsDir 84*
Retail Gasoline Dealers Association News - Rochester, NY - *MagDir 84*
Retail Journal, The - Milwaukee, WI - *MagDir 84*
Retail Lumberman - Kansas City, MO - *BaconPubCkMag 84; MagDir 84*
Retail Microsystems Inc. - Bernardsville, NJ - *MicrocomMPl 84*
Retail News Bureau - New York, NY - *Ed&PubIntYB 82*
Retail Price Survey [of Lundberg Survey Inc.] - North Hollywood, CA - *DataDirOnSer 84*
Retail Reporter [of Retail Publications Inc.] - Gastonia, NC - *BaconPubCkMag 84; MagDir 84*
Retail Reporting Bureau [Div. of Milton B. Conhaim Inc.] - New York, NY - *Ed&PubIntYB 82*
Retail Reporting Corp. [Subs. of Milton B. Conhaim Inc.] - New York, NY - *DirMarMP 83*
Retail Solutions Inc. - Sunnyvale, CA - *DataDirSup 7-83; MicrocomMPl 84*
Retail Technology - New York, NY - *BaconPubCkMag 84*
Retail Unionist [of Retail Clerks Union No. 648] - San Francisco, CA - *NewsDir 84*
Retail Week - New York, NY - *MagDir 84*
Retailer & Marketing News [of Ramnvest Inc.] - Dallas, TX - *BaconPubCkMag 84; MagDir 84; WritMar 84*
Retailer News [of Target Publishing Inc.] - Anaheim, CA - *BaconPubCkMag 84; MagDir 84*
Retcom Systems - Longwood, FL - *MicrocomMPl 84*
Retel TV Cable Co. - Canton, PA - *BrCabYB 84*
Retel TV Cable Co. - Cogan Station, PA - *Tel&CabFB 84C*
Retel TV Cable Co. - Williamsport, PA - *BrCabYB 84 p.D-306; Tel&CabFB 84C p.1698*
Retina - Philadelphia, PA - *MagIndMarPl 82-83*
Retired Officer, The - Alexandria, VA - *ArtMar 84; BaconPubCkMag 84; MagDir 84; MagIndMarPl 82-83; WritMar 84*
Retirement Life - Washington, DC - *BaconPubCkMag 84; MagDir 84; MagIndMarPl 82-83*
Retirement Research - Appleton, WI - *BoPubDir 4, 5*
Retlaw Broadcasting Co. - Fresno, CA - *BrCabYB 84*
Retlaw Enterprises Inc. - Fresno, CA - *Tel&CabFB 84S*
Retrieve [of Hoffmann-LaRoche Inc.] - Nutley, NJ - *EISS 83*
Retriever Books - New York, NY - *BoPubDir 4, 5*
Retrix Systems Inc. - Santa Ana, CA - *DirInfWP 82*
Retro Music - *See* Firelight Publishing
Retrospect, The [of Collingwood Publishing Co.] - Camden, NJ - *NewsDir 84*
Retrospect, The - Collingswood, NJ - *Ed&PubIntYB 82*
Reuben Records - Los Angeles, CA - *BillIntBG 83-84*
Reuland Advertising Agency - Aurora, IL - *StaDirAdAg 2-84*
Reuse/Recycle - Lancaster, PA - *BaconPubCkMag 84; MagDir 84*
Reuter Monitor, The - New York, NY - *DirOnDB Spring 84*
Reuters Ltd. - New York, NY - *BaconPubCkNews 84; BrCabYB 84; DataDirOnSer 84; Ed&PubIntYB 82; KnowInd 83; NewsBur 6; Tel&CabFB 84C; VideoDir 82-83*
Reuters Ltd. - London, England - *InfIndMarPl 83*
Reuters News-View [of Reuters Ltd.] - New York, NY - *BrCabYB 84; CabTVPrDB 83; HomeVid&CabYB 82-83; TelAl 83; Tel&CabFB 84C*
Revay & Associates Ltd. - Ottawa, ON, Canada - *BoPubDir 4, 5*
Revealer Cassettes - Kimpton, England - *LitMag&SmPr 83-84*
Reveille - Port Gibson, MS - *AyerDirPub 83*
Reveille [of Hub City Publishing Co. Inc.] - Camdenton, MO - *AyerDirPub 83; NewsDir 84*
Reveille-Enterprise - Vevay, IN - *AyerDirPub 83*
Revelation House Publishers Inc. - Metairie, LA - *BoPubDir 4 Sup, 5*
Revelation Music Publishing Corp. - *See* Valando Publishing Group Inc., Tommy
Revell Co., Fleming H. [Subs. of SFN Cos. Inc.] - Old Tappan, NJ - *LitMarPl 83, 84; WritMar 84*
Revelstoke Cable TV Ltd. - Revelstoke, BC, Canada - *BrCabYB 84*
Revelstoke Herald - Revelstoke, BC, Canada - *Ed&PubIntYB 82*
Revelstoke Review - Revelstoke, BC, Canada - *Ed&PubIntYB 82*
Revenue Canada (Customs & Excise) - Ottawa, ON, Canada - *CompReadDB 82*
Reverchon Press - Dallas, TX - *BoPubDir 4, 5*
Revere Associates - New York, NY - *DirPRFirms 83*
Revere Journal - Revere, MA - *BaconPubCkNews 84; Ed&PubIntYB 82; NewsDir 84*
Review - Burbank, CA - *AyerDirPub 83*
Review - Hayward, CA - *AyerDirPub 83*
Review - Lemon Grove, CA - *AyerDirPub 83*
Review - Darien, CT - *AyerDirPub 83*
Review - Parma, ID - *AyerDirPub 83*
Review - Hinckley, IL - *AyerDirPub 83*
Review - Roanoke, IL - *AyerDirPub 83*

Review - Tuscola, IL - *AyerDirPub 83*
Review - Westfield, IL - *AyerDirPub 83*
Review - Lapel, IN - *AyerDirPub 83*
Review - Dayton, IA - *AyerDirPub 83*
Review - Denison, IA - *AyerDirPub 83*
Review - Ellis, KS - *AyerDirPub 83*
Review - Garnett, KS - *AyerDirPub 83*
Review - Morgan City, LA - *AyerDirPub 83*
Review - Ft. Fairfield, ME - *AyerDirPub 83*
Review - Lake Orion, MI - *AyerDirPub 83*
Review - Richmond, MI - *AyerDirPub 83; Ed&PubIntYB 82*
Review - Battle Lake, MN - *AyerDirPub 83*
Review - Byron, MN - *AyerDirPub 83*
Review - Chikio, MN - *AyerDirPub 83*
Review - Herman, MN - *AyerDirPub 83*
Review - Portageville, MO - *AyerDirPub 83*
Review - Windsor, MO - *AyerDirPub 83*
Review - Elgin, NE - *AyerDirPub 83*
Review - Blackwood, NJ - *AyerDirPub 83*
Review - Interlaken, NY - *AyerDirPub 83*
Review - Liverpool, NY - *Ed&PubIntYB 82*
Review [of East-West Network Inc.] - New York, NY - *ArtMar 84; LitMag&SmPr 83-84*
Review - Ronkonkoma, NY - *AyerDirPub 83*
Review - Watkins Glen, NY - *AyerDirPub 83*
Review - Benson, NC - *AyerDirPub 83*
Review - St. Pauls, NC - *AyerDirPub 83*
Review - Alliance, OH - *AyerDirPub 83*
Review - East Liverpool, OH - *AyerDirPub 83*
Review - Fayette, OH - *AyerDirPub 83*
Review - Hydro, OK - *AyerDirPub 83*
Review - Shidler, OK - *AyerDirPub 83*
Review - Lake Oswego, OR - *AyerDirPub 83*
Review - Ephrata, PA - *AyerDirPub 83*
Review - Towanda, PA - *AyerDirPub 83*
Review - Rosholt, SD - *AyerDirPub 83*
Review - Rogersville, TN - *AyerDirPub 83*
Review - Athens, TX - *AyerDirPub 83*
Review - Crosbyton, TX - *AyerDirPub 83*
Review - Cross Plains, TX - *AyerDirPub 83*
Review - Clifton Forge, VA - *Ed&PubIntYB 82*
Review - Follansbee, WV - *AyerDirPub 83*
Review - Evansville, WI - *AyerDirPub 83*
Review - Plymouth, WI - *AyerDirPub 83; Ed&PubIntYB 82*
Review - Coronation, AB, Canada - *AyerDirPub 83; Ed&PubIntYB 82*
Review - Raymond, AB, Canada - *Ed&PubIntYB 82*
Review - Viking, AB, Canada - *AyerDirPub 83*
Review - Creston, BC, Canada - *AyerDirPub 83*
Review - Revelstoke, BC, Canada - *AyerDirPub 83*
Review - Richmond, BC, Canada - *Ed&PubIntYB 82*
Review - Sidney, BC, Canada - *AyerDirPub 83*
Review - Summerland, BC, Canada - *AyerDirPub 83*
Review - Rossburn, MB, Canada - *AyerDirPub 83*
Review - Harriston, ON, Canada - *AyerDirPub 83*
Review - Madoc, ON, Canada - *Ed&PubIntYB 82*
Review - Niagara Falls, ON, Canada - *AyerDirPub 83*
Review - Elrose, SK, Canada - *AyerDirPub 83; Ed&PubIntYB 82*
Review - Foam Lake, SK, Canada - *Ed&PubIntYB 82*
Review - Weyburn, SK, Canada - *AyerDirPub 83*
Review & Herald Publishing Association - Washington, DC - *LitMarPl 83; MagIndMarPl 82-83*
Review & Herald Publishing Association - Hagerstown, MD - *LitMarPl 84; WritMar 84*
Review-Appeal - Franklin, TN - *AyerDirPub 83; Ed&PubIntYB 82*
Review Atlas - Monmouth, IL - *AyerDirPub 83*
Review-Courier - Alva, OK - *Ed&PubIntYB 82*
Review for Religious - St. Louis, MO - *MagIndMarPl 82-83; WritMar 84*
Review Herald - Thornbury, ON, Canada - *AyerDirPub 83*
Review Herald/Collingwood Blue Mountain Group - Thornbury, ON, Canada - *Ed&PubIntYB 82*
Review-Journal - Las Vegas, NV - *AyerDirPub 83*
Review-Messenger - Sebeka, MN - *AyerDirPub 83; Ed&PubIntYB 82*
Review of Applied Entomology A [of Commonwealth Institute of Entomology] - London, England - *CompReadDB 82*
Review of Applied Entomology B [of Commonwealth Institute of Entomology] - London, England - *CompReadDB 82*
Review of Books & Religion, The - Lexington, KY - *WritMar 84*
Review of Books & Religion, The - Cincinnati, OH - *LitMag&SmPr 83-84*
Review of Contemporary Fiction, The - Elmwood Park, IL - *LitMag&SmPr 83-84*
Review of International Broadcasting - Knoxville, TN - *LitMag&SmPr 83-84*
Review of Medical & Veterinary Mycology [of Commonwealth Mycological Institute] - Richmond, England - *CompReadDB 82*
Review of Metaphysics - Washington, DC - *MagIndMarPl 82-83*
Review of Optometry - Radnor, PA - *BaconPubCkMag 84*
Review of Plant Pathology [of Commonwealth Mycological Institute] - Richmond, England - *CompReadDB 82*
Review of Politics, The - Notre Dame, IN - *MagDir 84*
Review of Psychoanalytic Books [of International Universities Press Inc.] - New York, NY - *LitMag&SmPr 83-84*
Review of Scientific Instruments - Argonne, IL - *BaconPubCkMag 84*
Review of Scientific Instruments - New York, NY - *MagDir 84*
Review of the Arts [of Newsbank Inc.] - New Canaan, CT - *CompReadDB 82*
Review of the Graphic Arts - Kissimmee, FL - *BaconPubCkMag 84; MagDir 84; MagIndMarPl 82-83*
Review of the Graphic Arts - Cincinnati, OH - *MagDir 84*
Review of the News - Belmont, MA - *ArtMar 84; BaconPubCkMag 84; WritMar 84*
Review-Republican - Williamsport, IN - *AyerDirPub 83; Ed&PubIntYB 82*
Review Shopper, The - Ronkonkoma, NY - *AyerDirPub 83*
Review Shoppers News [of Ronkonkoma Review] - Ronkonkoma, NY - *NewsDir 84*
Review, The - Ft. Collins, CO - *Ed&PubIntYB 82*
Review, The [of University of Delaware] - Newark, DE - *NewsDir 84*
Review, The [of Des Plaines Publishing Co.] - Chicago, IL - *NewsDir 84*
Review, The - Edison/Norwood, IL - *Ed&PubIntYB 82*
Review, The - Erie, IL - *Ed&PubIntYB 82*
Review, The [of Morrison Shawver Press] - Morrison, IL - *NewsDir 84*
Review, The - Ste. Genevieve, MO - *Ed&PubIntYB 82*
Review, The - Edison, NJ - *AyerDirPub 83*
Review, The - Pitman, NJ - *Ed&PubIntYB 82*
Review, The - Reidsville, NC - *AyerDirPub 83*
Review, The - Roxborough, PA - *Ed&PubIntYB 82*
Review, The - Vankleek Hill, ON, Canada - *Ed&PubIntYB 82*
Review-Times - Oxford, NY - *AyerDirPub 83*
Review-Times - Fostoria, OH - *AyerDirPub 83; Ed&PubIntYB 82*
Reviewer - Salt Lake City, UT - *BoPubDir 4, 5*
Reviewing Librarian [of Ontario Library Association] - Toronto, ON, Canada - *LitMag&SmPr 83-84*
Reviews of Geophysics & Space Physics - Washington, DC - *MagDir 84*
Reviews on File - Walton, NY - *LitMarPl 83, 84*
Revised Statutes of British Columbia [of Attorney General's Ministry] - Victoria, BC, Canada - *CompReadDB 82*
Revised Statutes of Canada [of Canada Federal Dept. of Justice] - Ottawa, ON, Canada - *CompReadDB 82; DataDirOnSer 84; DirOnDB Spring 84*
Revised Statutes of Ontario [of QL Systems Ltd.] - Ottawa, ON, Canada - *CompReadDB 82; DataDirOnSer 84*
ReVision Journal - Cambridge, MA - *LitMag&SmPr 83-84*
Revisionary Press [Aff. of Perspectives Press] - St. James, NY - *BoPubDir 4, 5*
Revista Aerea Latinoamericana [of Strato Publishing Co. Inc.] - New York, NY - *BaconPubCkMag 84; MagDir 84*
Revista Chicano-Riquena [of Arte Publico Press] - Houston, TX - *LitMag&SmPr 83-84*
Revista/Review Interamericana [of Inter American University Press] - San Juan, PR - *WritMar 84*
Revolutionary Publications - Santa Barbara, CA - *BoPubDir 5*
Revolver Music - St. Petersburg, FL - *BillIntBG 83-84*
Revolver Records - Los Angeles, CA - *BillIntBG 83-84*
Revolving Credit & Electronics Systems Letter - Westport, CT - *BaconPubCkMag 84*

Revonah Records - Ferndale, NY - *BillIntBG 83-84*
Revox Systems Inc. [Div. of Educational Technology Inc.] - Merrick, NY - *AvMarPl 83*
Revumer - Brest, France - *DirOnDB Spring 84*
Reward Record Inc. - Westville, NJ - *BillIntBG 83-84*
Rex Broadcasting Corp. - Tucson, AZ - *BrCabYB 84*
Rex Cable TV - Rexburg, ID - *Tel&CabFB 84C p.1698*
Rex Color Separations - Miami, FL - *MagIndMarPl 82-83*
REX TV Inc. - Rexburg, ID - *BrCabYB 84*
Rexburg Journal - Rexburg, ID - *Ed&PubIntYB 82*
Rexburg Journal - *See* Standard-Journal Inc.
Rexburg Publishing Co. Inc. - Rexburg, ID - *NewsDir 84*
Rexburg Standard - Rexburg, ID - *Ed&PubIntYB 82*
Rexburg Standard - *See* Standard-Journal Inc.
Rexnord Data Systems [Subs. of Rexnord Inc.] - Milwaukee, WI - *DataDirOnSer 84*
Rexon Business Machines Corp. - Culver City, CA - *WhoWMicrocom 83*
Rexroad, Ruth & Michael - Webster Springs, WV - *Tel&CabFB 84C p.1698*
Reymer & Gersin Associates Inc. - Southfield, MI - *BrCabYB 84; InterCabHB 3; Tel&CabFB 84C; TeleSy&SerDir 2-84*
Reymont Associates - Boca Raton, FL - *BoPubDir 5; WritMar 84*
Reymont Associates - Rye, NY - *BoPubDir 4*
Reynolds Advertising Agency - Tyler, TX - *StaDirAdAg 2-84*
Reynolds & Associates Inc., M. B. - New York, NY - *DirPRFirms 83*
Reynolds & Reynolds - Dayton, OH - *ADAPSOMemDir 83-84; DataDirOnSer 84; DataDirSup 7-83; Datamation 6-83; Top100Al 83*
Reynolds Association, Robert T. - West Hartford, CT - *StaDirAdAg 2-84*
Reynolds, Cheryl L. - Morristown, NJ - *ADAPSOMemDir 83-84*
Reynolds County Courier - Ellington, MO - *AyerDirPub 83; Ed&PubIntYB 82*
Reynolds, Dave - New Richmond, OH - *Tel&CabFB 84C p.1698*
Reynolds, Donald W. - *See* Donrey Media Group Inc.
Reynolds, George I. Jr. - Seymour, CT - *Tel&CabFB 84C p.1698*
Reynolds/Gould Inc. [Aff. of Robert T. Reynolds Associates] - West Hartford, CT - *DirPRFirms 83; StaDirAdAg 2-84*
Reynolds Inc., Paul R. - New York, NY - *LitMarPl 83, 84*
Reynolds, Jane - Dana Point, CA - *BoPubDir 4*
Reynolds, Jane - Del Mar, CA - *BoPubDir 5*
Reynolds/Leteron Co. - Torrance, CA - *AvMarPl 83*
Reynolds Lithographing Corp. - New York, NY - *LitMarPl 83*
Reynolds, Martha S. - White Plains, NY - *LitMarPl 83, 84*
Reynolds Photography - Homewood, IL - *LitMarPl 84*
Reynolds Productions Inc., Art - Beverly Hills, CA - *Tel&CabFB 84C*
Reynolds-Sullivan - Mobile, AL - *StaDirAdAg 2-84*
Reynolds Telephone Co. - Reynolds, IL - *TelDir&BG 83-84*
Reynolds TV Cable Service - Utica, PA - *BrCabYB 84; Tel&CabFB 84C*
Reynoldsburg Reporter - Reynoldsburg, OH - *BaconPubCkNews 84; Ed&PubIntYB 82*
Reynoldsville Star - Reynoldsville, PA - *BaconPubCkNews 84; Ed&PubIntYB 82*
Reynsong Music - *See* Wrensong Inc.
Rezey Music Co., William - Albany, NY - *BillIntBG 83-84*
RF Analysts Inc. - Fenton, MI - *InterCabHB 3*
R.F. Design [of Cardiff Publishing Co.] - Denver, CO - *MagDir 84*
R.F. Design [of Cardiff Publishing Co.] - Englewood, CO - *BaconPubCkMag 84*
RFA Records - Albuquerque, NM - *BillIntBG 83-84*
RFB Enterprises Inc. - Los Angeles, CA - *TelAl 83, 84*
RFC News Service - Windsor, CA - *DirOnDB Spring 84*
RFC News Service [of NewsNet Inc.] - Bryn Mawr, PA - *DataDirOnSer 84*
RFD - Bakersville, NC - *LitMag&SmPr 83-84*
RFD News - Bellevue, OH - *BaconPubCkMag 84*
RFM Associates Inc. - Trenton, NJ - *ArtMar 84*
RFP Inc. - Rockville, MD - *InfoS 83-84*
RFS Graphic Design Inc. - Great Neck, NY - *LitMarPl 83*
RGA Cable TV - Toledo, WA - *BrCabYB 84; Tel&CabFB 84C*
RGB Designs - Santa Clara, CA - *MicrocomMPl 84*
R.G.D.A. News - Rochester, NY - *BaconPubCkMag 84*
R.G.E. - Berkeley, CA - *LitMag&SmPr 83-84*
RGNNS Publishing [Aff. of Regina Group for a Non-Nuclear Society] - Regina, SK, Canada - *BoPubDir 4, 5*
RGT Advertising Agency - Los Altos, CA - *StaDirAdAg 2-84*
RH Electronics Inc. - Buellton, CA - *MicrocomMPl 83, 84*
Rhaco Advertising - York, PA - *StaDirAdAg 2-84*
Rhea & Kaiser Advertising Inc. - Oak Brook, IL - *AdAge 3-28-84; StaDirAdAg 2-84*
Rhein, Elizabeth - Chicago, IL - *LitMarPl 83*
Rheinisch-Westfalische Technische Hochschule - Aachen, West Germany - *InfIndMarPl 83*
Rheology - Berlin, West Germany - *DirOnDB Spring 84*
Rheology & Tribology Documentation Center [of Federal Institute for Materials Testing] - Berlin, West Germany - *EISS 83*
Rhiannon Press - Eau Claire, WI - *BoPubDir 4, 5; LitMag&SmPr 83-84*
Rhinebeck Gazette Advertiser - *See* Taconic Press Inc.
Rhinelander Daily News - Rhinelander, WI - *BaconPubCkNews 84; Ed&PubIntYB 82; NewsDir 84*
Rhinelander Music Inc. - *See* Marsaint Music Inc.
Rhinelander Telephone Co. - Rhinelander, WI - *TelDir&BG 83-84*
Rhinetek Inc. - Columbia, MD - *MicrocomMPl 84*
Rhino - Highland Park, IL - *LitMag&SmPr 83-84*
Rhino Press [Aff. of Photography at Open Space] - Victoria, BC, Canada - *BoPubDir 4, 5*
Rhino Records Inc. - Santa Monica, CA - *BillIntBG 83-84*
Rhinoceros Press - El Cerrito, CA - *BoPubDir 4, 5*
Rhino's Press - Laguna Hills, CA - *BoPubDir 4, 5*
RHM Press [Subs. of RHM Associates] - Glen Cove, NY - *LitMarPl 83, 84*
Rho Delta Press - Los Angeles, CA - *BoPubDir 4, 5*
Rhode Island Beverage Journal [of Beverage Publications Inc.] - Hamden, CT - *BaconPubCkMag 84; MagDir 84*
Rhode Island Bicentennial Foundation - Providence, RI - *BoPubDir 4*
Rhode Island CATV Corp. - Providence, RI - *BrCabYB 84; Tel&CabFB 84C*
Rhode Island Dept. of Economic Development - Providence, RI - *BoPubDir 5*
Rhode Island Dept. of Employment Security - Providence, RI - *BoPubDir 5*
Rhode Island Genealogical Society - Warwick, RI - *BoPubDir 4, 5*
Rhode Island Historical Society - Providence, RI - *BoPubDir 4, 5*
Rhode Island Medical Journal - Providence, RI - *BaconPubCkMag 84; MagDir 84*
Rhode Island Pendulum - East Greenwich, RI - *AyerDirPub 83; Ed&PubIntYB 82*
Rhode Island Publications Society - Providence, RI - *BoPubDir 5*
Rhode Island Review - Providence, RI - *LitMag&SmPr 83-84*
Rhode Island School of Design (Museum of Art) - Providence, RI - *BoPubDir 4, 5*
Rhodes Communications - Los Angeles, CA - *BillIntBG 83-84*
Rhodes Geographic Library Inc. - Naples, FL - *BoPubDir 4, 5*
Rhodes, George F. - *See* De-Cal Cable Inc.
Rhodes, George F. & Tom A. Garner Jr. - Port Lavaca, TX - *BrCabYB 84 p.D-306*
Rhodes Inc., Taylor - Beverly Hills, CA - *StaDirAdAg 2-84*
Rhodes Literary Agency Inc., Barbara - New York, NY - *LitMarPl 83, 84*
Rhodes, Marion A. - *See* De-Cal Cable Inc.
Rhodes Productions - Manhattan Beach, CA - *Tel&CabFB 84C*
Rhodes, Robert C. - Higginsville, MO - *BrCabYB 84 p.D-306; Tel&CabFB 84C p.1698*
Rhome Telephone Co. - Rhome, TX - *TelDir&BG 83-84*
RHR Filmedia Inc. - New York, NY - *ProGuPRSer 4*
RHTM - London, England - *DirOnDB Spring 84*
Rhyme Time Poetry Newsletter - Coeur d'Alene, ID - *LitMag&SmPr 83-84*
Rhythm & Blues Channel [of Satellite Cable Audio Networks] - Tulsa, OK - *CabTVPrDB 83*
Rhythm Valley Music - Graham, TX - *BillIntBG 83-84*
Rhythms Productions - Los Angeles, CA - *AvMarPl 83; BillIntBG 83-84; WritMar 84*
R.I. Review Inc. - Providence, RI - *LitMag&SmPr 83-84*

Riallus Advertising Inc. - Pittsburgh, PA - *StaDirAdAg 2-84*
Rialto Cable [of Acton CATV Inc.] - Rialto, CA - *BrCabYB 84*
Rialto Record - Rialto, CA - *BaconPubCkNews 84; Ed&PubIntYB 82; NewsDir 84*
Rib Lake Telephone Co. - Rib Lake, WI - *TelDir&BG 83-84*
Ribaudo & Schaefer Inc. - New York, NY - *StaDirAdAg 2-84*
Ribbit Records & Publishing Co. - Oklahoma City, OK - *BillIntBG 83-84*
Ribnick & Associates Inc. - Houston, TX - *StaDirAdAg 2-84*
Ric Rac Music - Nashville, IN - *BillIntBG 83-84*
Ric Rac Records - Nashville, IN - *BillIntBG 83-84*
Ricci Telephone Research Inc. - Broomall, PA - *IntDirMarRes 83*
Rice Advertising Agency Inc. - Oklahoma City, OK - *StaDirAdAg 2-84*
Rice, Allan Lake - Kimberton, PA - *LitMarPl 83, 84; MagIndMarPl 82-83*
Rice Associates Inc., Rose - Miami Beach, FL - *StaDirAdAg 2-84*
Rice Belt Telephone Co. - Weiner, AR - *TelDir&BG 83-84*
Rice County Monitor-Journal - Little River, KS - *Ed&PubIntYB 82*
Rice Farming - Tucson, AZ - *MagDir 84*
Rice Farming - Memphis, TN - *BaconPubCkMag 84*
Rice, Jim - Hico, TX - *LitMarPl 83, 84*
Rice Journal, The - McLean, VA - *MagDir 84*
Rice Lake Chronotype - Rice Lake, WI - *BaconPubCkNews 84; Ed&PubIntYB 82; NewsDir 84*
Rice Lake Television [of Midwest Communications Inc.] - Rice Lake, WI - *BrCabYB 84; Tel&CabFB 84C*
Rice Records Inc. - Nashville, TN - *BillIntBG 83-84*
Rice, Stanley - Monterey, CA - *LitMarPl 83, 84*
Rice, Stanley - Pacific Grove, CA - *MagIndMarPl 82-83*
Rice University (Institute for the Arts) - Houston, TX - *BoPubDir 4, 5*
Rice University Studies - Houston, TX - *BoPubDir 4, 5; LitMarPl 84*
Riceville Recorder - Riceville, IA - *BaconPubCkNews 84; Ed&PubIntYB 82*
Rich Advertising Agency, Stuart P. - Berwyn, PA - *StaDirAdAg 2-84*
Rich Concepts Enterprises - La Jolla, CA - *BoPubDir 5*
Rich Enterprises - Belmore, NY - *IntDirMarRes 83*
Rich-Errington Publisher - Bay City, MI - *BoPubDir 4, 5*
Rich Hill Cablevision Inc. [of Scorpio Enterprises] - Rich Hill, MO - *BrCabYB 84*
Rich Hill Mining Review - Rich Hill, MO - *BaconPubCkNews 84; Ed&PubIntYB 82*
Rich Inc., Dick - New York, NY - *HBIndAd&MS 82-83*
Rich Printing Co. Inc. - Nashville, TN - *LitMarPl 83, 84*
Rich Publishers - Clemson, SC - *BoPubDir 4, 5*
Rich Publishing Co. [Aff. of Dobson & Associates Inc.] - Houston, TX - *BoPubDir 5*
Rich Publishing Inc. - Temecula, CA - *MagIndMarPl 82-83*
Richard & Edwards - New York, NY - *AdAge 3-28-84; StaDirAdAg 2-84*
Richard-Lewis Corp. - Scarsdale, NY - *ArtMar 84; StaDirAdAg 2-84*
Richard Manufacturing Co. Inc. - Fernandina Beach, FL - *AvMarPl 83*
Richards Cable Inc. - Malaga Township, OH - *BrCabYB 84; Tel&CabFB 84C*
Richards Enterprises Inc. - Aransas Pass, TX - *BaconPubCkNews 84*
Richards Group - Dallas, TX - *AdAge 3-28-84; StaDirAdAg 2-84*
Richards Inc., Cecil L. - Falls Church, VA - *CabTVFinDB 83*
Richards, Paul E. - Jerusalem, OH - *Tel&CabFB 84C p.1698*
Richards Publishing Co. Inc. - Gonvick, MN - *BaconPubCkNews 84*
Richards Publishing Co. Inc., Frank E. - Phoenix, NY - *BoPubDir 4, 5*
Richards Telecable - Ulster, PA - *BrCabYB 84; Tel&CabFB 84C*
Richardson & McElveen Inc., Public Relations - Chicago, IL - *DirPRFirms 83*
Richardson & Snyder - New York, NY - *LitMarPl 84*
Richardson Associates Inc. - Portland, OR - *StaDirAdAg 2-84*
Richardson Associates Inc., William J. - Dix Hills, NY - *LitMarPl 83, 84; MagIndMarPl 82-83*
Richardson Daily News - Farmers Branch, TX - *Ed&PubIntYB 82*
Richardson Daily News [of News-Texan Inc.] - Richardson, TX - *BaconPubCkNews 84; NewsDir 84*
Richardson, Myers & Donofrio Advertising Agency - Baltimore, MD - *AdAge 3-28-84; ArtMar 84; StaDirAdAg 2-84*
Richardson, Myers & Donofrio Advertising Agency - *See* RM & D Associates
Richardson Records - Annapolis, MD - *BillIntBG 83-84*
Richardson, Thomas & Bushman Inc. - Ft. Washington, PA - *AdAge 3-28-84; StaDirAdAg 2-84*
Richboro Press - Richboro, PA - *LitMag&SmPr 83-84; LitMarPl 83, 84; WritMar 84*
Richcal Enterprises Ltd. Inc. - Placentia, CA - *MicrocomMPl 84*
Richcolor Systems Inc. - Wylie, TX - *AvMarPl 83*
Richcraft Engineering Ltd. - Chautauqua, NY - *MicrocomMPl 83, 84*
Richert, Barbara - New York, NY - *LitMarPl 83*
Richey-Bosch News/Feature Service - Beaumont, TX - *Ed&PubIntYB 82*
Richey Cable Inc. - Concho Valley, AZ - *BrCabYB 84*
Richey Cable Inc. - Eagar, AZ - *BrCabYB 84; Tel&CabFB 84C*
Richey Cable Inc. - Springerville, AZ - *BrCabYB 84*
Richey Cable Inc. - St. Johns, AZ - *BrCabYB 84; Tel&CabFB 84C*
Richey, Milford G. - St. Johns, AZ - *BrCabYB 84 p.D-306; Tel&CabFB 84C p.1698*
Richey Records - Ft. Worth, TX - *BillIntBG 83-84*
Richfield Reaper - Richfield, UT - *BaconPubCkNews 84; Ed&PubIntYB 82; NewsDir 84*
Richfield Sun - Edina, MN - *AyerDirPub 83*
Richfield Sun - Richfield, MN - *Ed&PubIntYB 82*
Richfield Sun - *See* Sun Newspapers
Richfield Sun & Free Section [of Minnesota Suburban Newspapers Inc.] - Minneapolis, MN - *NewsDir 84*
Richland Cable System - Richland Center, WI - *BrCabYB 84; Tel&CabFB 84C*
Richland Center Observer - Richland Center, WI - *AyerDirPub 83; BaconPubCkNews 84; Ed&PubIntYB 82; NewsDir 84*
Richland Grant Telephone Cooperative Inc. - Blue River, WI - *TelDir&BG 83-84*
Richland Journal - Galesburg, MI - *AyerDirPub 83*
Richland Journal - Richland, MI - *BaconPubCkNews 84; Ed&PubIntYB 82*
Richland Mirror - Richland, MO - *BaconPubCkNews 84; Ed&PubIntYB 82*
Richland Northeast Newsweekly - Columbia, SC - *AyerDirPub 83*
Richland Plainsman - Richland, IA - *Ed&PubIntYB 82*
Richland Press, The - Attica, IN - *AyerDirPub 83; Ed&PubIntYB 82*
Richland Publishing Co. - Hankinson, ND - *BaconPubCkNews 84*
Richland Review - Clarkston, WA - *AyerDirPub 83*
Richland Review - *See* Tribune Newspapers Inc.
Richland Stewart Webster Journal - Richland, GA - *Ed&PubIntYB 82*
Richland TV Cable [of Group W Cable] - Richland, WA - *BrCabYB 84*
Richlands-Beulaville Advertiser News - Richlands, NC - *Ed&PubIntYB 82*
Richlands News-Press [of Richlands Southwest Virginia Newspapers Inc.] - Richlands, VA - *BaconPubCkNews 84; Ed&PubIntYB 82; NewsDir 84*
Richman Associates, Phil - Chicago, IL - *DirPRFirms 83*
Richman Inc., Mel - Balå Cynwyd, PA - *AdAge 3-28-84; HBIndAd&MS 82-83; StaDirAdAg 2-84*
Richman Publishing [Aff. of Richman Communications] - Salt Lake City, UT - *BoPubDir 5*
Richmond Advertising/Reinhold Associates - New York, NY - *AdAge 3-28-84; StaDirAdAg 2-84*
Richmond Advertising/Reinhold Associates - *See* MacLaren Advertising

Richmond Afro-American [of Baltimore Afro-American Newspapers] - Baltimore, MD - *NewsDir 84*
Richmond Afro-American - Richmond, VA - *BaconPubCkNews 84; Ed&PubIntYB 82*
Richmond Afro-American & Planet - Richmond, VA - *AyerDirPub 83*
Richmond-Bridesburg Gazette [of Greater Philadelphia Group Inc.] - Philadelphia, PA - *NewsDir 84*
Richmond Cable TV [of Centel Cable Television Co.] - Richmond, KY - *BrCabYB 84*
Richmond Country Times - Augusta, GA - *Ed&PubIntYB 82*
Richmond County Historical Society - Augusta, GA - *BoPubDir 4, 5*
Richmond County Journal - Rockingham, NC - *AyerDirPub 83; BaconPubCkNews 84; Ed&PubIntYB 82*
Richmond Cream Off the Top, Norman - Toronto, ON, Canada - *Ed&PubIntYB 82*
Richmond Daily News - Richmond, MO - *BaconPubCkNews 84*
Richmond Gazette [of Free Press Inc.] - Richmond, IL - *Ed&PubIntYB 82; NewsDir 84*
Richmond Gazette - *See* Free Press Inc.
Richmond Graphic - Richmond, IN - *BaconPubCkNews 84; NewsDir 84*
Richmond Hill/Thornhill Liberal - Richmond Hill, ON, Canada - *AyerDirPub 83; Ed&PubIntYB 82*
Richmond House Publishing Ltd. - Toronto, ON, Canada - *BoPubDir 4, 5*
Richmond Inc., Thomas L. - New York, NY - *DirPRFirms 83*
Richmond Independent & Gazette [of Brown Newspaper Publishing Co. Inc.] - Richmond, CA - *NewsDir 84*
Richmond Madison County Newsweek - Richmond, KY - *NewsDir 84*
Richmond Madison County Post - Richmond, KY - *BaconPubCkNews 84*
Richmond Metro Reporter - *See* Reporter Publishing Co.
Richmond News Leader [of Richmond Newspapers Inc.] - Richmond, VA - *BaconPubCkNews 84; Ed&PubIntYB 82; LitMarPl 83, 84; NewsDir 84*
Richmond Palladium-Item [of Gannett Co. Inc.] - Richmond, IN - *BaconPubCkNews 84; NewsDir 84*
Richmond Post [of Alameda Publishing Corp.] - Oakland, CA - *AyerDirPub 83; NewsDir 84*
Richmond Post - *See* Alameda Publishing Corp.
Richmond Ray County Herald-Conservator - Richmond, MO - *NewsDir 84*
Richmond Register - Richmond, KY - *BaconPubCkNews 84; Ed&PubIntYB 82; NewsDir 84*
Richmond Review - Vancouver, BC, Canada - *AyerDirPub 83*
Richmond Review - *See* Sommerville Communications Corp.
Richmond Review Corp. [of Sommerville Communications Inc.] - Richmond, MI - *NewsDir 84*
Richmond Telephone Co. - Richmond, MA - *TelDir&BG 83-84*
Richmond Times-Dispatch [of Richmond Newspapers Inc.] - Richmond, VA - *BaconPubCkNews 84; Ed&PubIntYB 82; LitMarPl 83, 84; NewsBur 6; NewsDir 84*
Richmondville Phoenix - Richmondville, NY - *BaconPubCkNews 84; Ed&PubIntYB 82*
Richner Publications Inc. - Lawrence, NY - *BaconPubCkNews 84*
Richter Productions - New York, NY - *ArtMar 84; AvMarPl 83*
Richton Dispatch - Richton, MS - *AyerDirPub 83; BaconPubCkNews 84; Ed&PubIntYB 82*
Richtown/Gospel Truth Records & Tapes & Film Works Inc. - Richmond, VA - *BillIntBG 83-84*
Richwood Gazette - Richwood, OH - *AyerDirPub 83; BaconPubCkNews 84; Ed&PubIntYB 82*
Richwood Nicholas County News Leader - Richwood, WV - *BaconPubCkNews 84*
Rickard Studio, George - London, ON, Canada - *BoPubDir 4, 5*
Ricker, Dorothy - Tampa, FL - *Ed&PubIntYB 82*
Rico Records Distributor Inc. - New York, NY - *BillIntBG 83-84*
Rico Telephone Co. - Rico, CO - *TelDir&BG 83-84*
Ricochet Records - East Norwich, NY - *BillIntBG 83-84*
Ricoh of America Inc. - Fairfield, NJ - *DirInfWP 82; MicrocomMPl 84*
Ricsher Productions Ltd. - Bethesda, MD - *Tel&CabFB 84C*
Riddick Flynn & Associates Inc. - Louisville, KY - *IntDirMarRes 83*
Rider - Agoura, CA - *BaconPubCkMag 84; MagDir 84; MagIndMarPl 82-83; WritMar 84*
Ridge Citizen, The - Johnston, SC - *Ed&PubIntYB 82*
Ridge Review [of An Apple Press] - Mendocino, CA - *LitMag&SmPr 83-84*
Ridge Row Press - Montrose, PA - *LitMag&SmPr 83-84*
Ridge Row Press - Scranton, PA - *BoPubDir 4 Sup, 5*
Ridge Telephone Co. Inc. - Ridge Spring, SC - *TelDir&BG 83-84*
Ridge Type Service - Hawthorne, NJ - *LitMarPl 83, 84; MagIndMarPl 82-83*
Ridgecrest Independent [of Huggard Printing Inc.] - Ridgecrest, CA - *NewsDir 84*
Ridgefield Group Inc., The - Ridgefield, CT - *IntDirMarRes 83*
Ridgefield Pennysaver - Yorktown Heights, NY - *AyerDirPub 83*
Ridgefield Press - Ridgefield, CT - *Ed&PubIntYB 82; NewsDir 84*
Ridgefield Press - *See* Acorn Press Inc.
Ridgefield Publishing Co. - Tarzana, CA - *BoPubDir 4, 5*
Ridgeland Jasper County News - Ridgeland, SC - *BaconPubCkNews 84*
Ridgetop Records Inc. - Nashville, TN - *BillIntBG 83-84*
Ridgetown Dominion - Ridgetown, ON, Canada - *AyerDirPub 83; Ed&PubIntYB 82*
Ridgeview Publishing Co. - Atascadero, CA - *BoPubDir 4, 5*
Ridgeville Telephone Co. - Ridgeville, OH - *TelDir&BG 83-84*
Ridgeway Cablevision - Ridgeway, MO - *BrCabYB 84*
Ridgeway Inc., L. D. - Silver Spring, MD - *WhoWMicrocom 83*
Ridgeway News, The - Ridgeway, IL - *Ed&PubIntYB 82*
Ridgeway Press - Roseville, MI - *BoPubDir 4, 5*
Ridgeway Telephone Co. Inc. - Ridgeway, SC - *TelDir&BG 83-84*
Ridgewood News Publishers - Ridgewood, NJ - *BaconPubCkNews 84*
Ridgewood News, The - Ridgewood, NJ - *Ed&PubIntYB 82; NewsDir 84*
Ridgewood News, The - *See* Ridgewood News Publishers
Ridgewood Park Ridge Local Review - *See* Ridgewood News Publishers
Ridgewood Times - Brooklyn, NY - *AyerDirPub 83*
Ridgewood Times - Ridgewood, NY - *BaconPubCkNews 84*
Ridgway Record - Ridgway, PA - *AyerDirPub 83; BaconPubCkNews 84; Ed&PubIntYB 82; NewsDir 84*
Ridings Public Relations Inc., Paul - Ft. Worth, TX - *DirPRFirms 83*
Ridley, Charles P. - Palo Alto, CA - *LitMarPl 83, 84*
Ridley Press [of Drexel Hill Press Publishing Co.] - Drexel Hill, PA - *NewsDir 84*
Ridley Press - Folsom, PA - *AyerDirPub 83; Ed&PubIntYB 82*
Riechers, A. - Palo Alto, CA - *BoPubDir 4, 5*
Riesel Rustler - Riesel, TX - *BaconPubCkNews 84; Ed&PubIntYB 82*
Rievman Consulting Corp. - Westport, CT - *ADAPSOMemDir 83-84*
Rife Market Research Inc. - Miami, FL - *IntDirMarRes 83*
Riffkin & Associates Inc., Leslie A. - New York, NY - *IntDirMarRes 83*
Rifkin & Associates - Denver, CO - *BrCabYB 84 p.D-306; Tel&CabFB 84C p.1698*
Rifkind Pondel & Parson - Santa Monica, CA - *DirPRFirms 83*
Rifle Magazine, The - Prescott, AZ - *BaconPubCkMag 84; MagDir 84*
Rifle Telegram - Rifle, CO - *Ed&PubIntYB 82; NewsDir 84*
Rifle Telegram - *See* Mountain States Communications Inc.
Rigas, Constantine J. - Wellsville, NY - *BrCabYB 84 p.D-306*
Rigas, Constantine J. - *See* Adelphia Communications Corp.
Rigas, John J. - Coudersport, PA - *BrCabYB 84 p.D-306*
Rigas, John J. - *See* Adelphia Communications Corp.
Rigby Jefferson Star - Rigby, ID - *BaconPubCkNews 84*
Rigel Inc. - Newark, DE - *BoPubDir 4 Sup, 5*
Riger Advertising Agency Inc., Fred - Binghamton, NY - *StaDirAdAg 2-84*
Riggers Bible - Springfield, MO - *BoPubDir 4, 5*
Riggins TV Cable Inc. - Riggins, ID - *BrCabYB 84; Tel&CabFB 84C*
Riggs, Karl A. - Mississippi State, MS - *BoPubDir 4, 5*
Right Note Music - Memphis, TN - *BillIntBG 83-84*
Right Note Records - Memphis, TN - *BillIntBG 83-84*

Right of Way - Culver City, CA - *BaconPubCkMag 84*
Right On - Hollywood, CA - *MagIndMarPl 82-83*
Right On - Los Angeles, CA - *MagDir 84*
Right On! - Cresskill, NJ - *BaconPubCkMag 84*
Right On! Presents Class - Cresskill, NJ - *BaconPubCkMag 84*
Right on Programs [Div. of Computeam Inc.] - Greenlawn, NY - *MicrocomMPl 84*
Right On Programs [Div. of Computeam Inc.] - Huntington, NY - *MicrocomMPl 83; MicrocomSwDir 1*
Right On Records - New York, NY - *BillIntBG 83-84*
Rigley Book Co. - San Francisco, CA - *BoPubDir 4 Sup, 5*
Riina, John R. - Baltimore, MD - *LitMarPl 83, 84*
Rijks Universiteit Utrecht (Bibliotheek) - Utrecht, Netherlands - *InfIndMarPl 83*
RILA [of J. Paul Getty Museum] - Williamstown, MA - *DirOnDB Spring 84; EISS 83*
Riley Advertising Ltd. - *See* Stewart & Associates Ltd./IMAA Inc., Rex
Riley & Associates, Robert H. - Red Bank, NJ - *EISS 7-83 Sup; InfoS 83-84*
Riley Associates, Michael A. - Fullerton, CA - *StaDirAdAg 2-84*
Riley, Bill - Boston, MA - *LitMarPl 83, 84*
Riley Communications Services - Burlingame, CA - *DirPRFirms 83*
Riley Countian - Leonardville, KS - *Ed&PubIntYB 82*
Riley Countian - Riley, KS - *BaconPubCkNews 84*
Riley, Edward - Mountain Home, AR - *Tel&CabFB 84C p.1698*
Riley, Jocelyn - Madison, WI - *LitMarPl 84*
Riley Market Research Services - New Windsor, NY - *IntDirMarRes 83*
Riley, Maurice W. - Ypsilanti, MI - *BoPubDir 4, 5*
Riling Arms Books Co., Ray - Philadelphia, PA - *BoPubDir 4, 5*
RILM [of RILM Abstracts of Music Literature] - New York, NY - *DataDirOnSer 84*
RILM Abstracts of Music Literature [of Commission Internationale Mixte] - New York, NY - *CompReadDB 82; DataDirOnSer 84; DirOnDB Spring 84; InfIndMarPl 83; OnBibDB 3*
Rim Country News - Payson, AZ - *AyerDirPub 83; Ed&PubIntYB 82*
Rind Total Media Inc. - New York, NY - *HBIndAd&MS 82-83; StaDirAdAg 2-84*
Ring/Boxing Illustrated, The - New York, NY - *BaconPubCkMag 84; MagDir 84*
Ring Communications Inc. - Melville, NY - *DataDirSup 7-83*
Ring King Visibles Inc. - Muscatine, IA - *DirInfWP 82; WhoWMicrocom 83*
Ring, Leonard M. - *See* Combined Cable Corp.
Ring-Ting-A-Ling Productions - New York, NY - *TelAl 83, 84*
Ringa Press - Chicago, IL - *BoPubDir 5*
Ringdoc [of SDC Search Service] - Santa Monica, CA - *DataDirOnSer 84*
Ringdoc [of Derwent Publishing Ltd.] - London, England - *DirOnDB Spring 84; OnBibDB 3*
Ringenberg, J. A. - Hicksville, OH - *LitMag&SmPr 83-84*
Ringer Video Services - Burbank, CA - *AvMarPl 83*
Ringgold Catoosa County News - Ringgold, GA - *BaconPubCkNews 84*
Ringgold Management Systems - Beaverton, OR - *EISS 83; MicrocomMPl 84*
Ringgold Record - Ringgold, LA - *BaconPubCkNews 84; Ed&PubIntYB 82*
Ringgold Telephone Co. - Ringgold, GA - *TelDir&BG 83-84*
Ringgold Telephone Co. Inc. - Ringgold, LA - *TelDir&BG 83-84*
Ringier Documentation Center [of Ringier & Co.] - Zurich, Switzerland - *EISS 83*
Ringling Eagle - Ringling, OK - *BaconPubCkNews 84; Ed&PubIntYB 82*
Ringling Museums - Sarasota, FL - *BoPubDir 4, 5*
Ringsted Dispatch - Ringsted, IA - *BaconPubCkNews 84; Ed&PubIntYB 82*
Ringsted Telephone Co. - Ringsted, IA - *TelDir&BG 83-84*
Ringwood Bulletin Argus Today - *See* Today Newspapers
Rio Cablevision Inc. [of Masada Corp.] - Ft. Bliss, TX - *Tel&CabFB 84C*
Rio Grande City Herald - Rio Grande City, TX - *BaconPubCkNews 84; Ed&PubIntYB 82*
Rio Grande Press Inc., The - Glorieta, NM - *LitMarPl 83, 84*
Rio Grande Sun - Espanola, NM - *AyerDirPub 83; Ed&PubIntYB 82*
Rio Grande Valley Group - Harlingen, TX - *Ed&PubIntYB 82*
Rio Grande Writers Newsletter - Albuquerque, NM - *LitMag&SmPr 83-84*
Rio Linda World, The - Sacramento, CA - *NewsDir 84*
Rio Rancho Cable TV [of Capital Cities Communications Inc.] - Rio Rancho, NM - *Tel&CabFB 84C*
Rio Virgin Telephone Co. Inc. - Mesquite, NV - *TelDir&BG 83-84*
Rio Vista River News-Herald & Journal - Rio Vista, CA - *BaconPubCkNews 84*
Riondel Community Cable Video Society - Riondel, BC, Canada - *BrCabYB 84*
Rip Music - *See* Creative Music Group
Rip 'n' Read News Service - San Francisco, CA - *BrCabYB 84; MagIndMarPl 82-83*
Rip Off Press Inc. - San Francisco, CA - *BoPubDir 4, 5; LitMag&SmPr 83-84*
Rip-Shin TV Association Inc. - Philippi, WV - *BrCabYB 84; Tel&CabFB 84C*
Ripchord Records - New York, NY - *BillIntBG 83-84*
Ripcord Music - New York, NY - *BillIntBG 83-84*
Ripcord Recording Services - Vancouver, WA - *BillIntBG 83-84*
Ripley & Associates Inc., John M. - *See* Zylke Public Relations
Ripley Bee - Ripley, OH - *BaconPubCkNews 84; Ed&PubIntYB 82*
Ripley Jackson Herald [of Simmons Publishing Co.] - Ripley, WV - *BaconPubCkNews 84; NewsDir 84*
Ripley Lauderdale County Enterprise - *See* Lauderdale County Enterprise
Ripley Lauderdale Voice - Ripley, TN - *BaconPubCkNews 84*
Ripley Publishing Co. Inc. - Versailles, IN - *BaconPubCkNews 84*
Ripley Southern Sentinel - Ripley, MS - *BaconPubCkNews 84; Ed&PubIntYB 82; NewsDir 84*
Ripley Video Cable Co. - Ripley, MS - *BrCabYB 84; Tel&CabFB 84C*
Ripley-Woodbury Advertising Inc. - Cerritos, CA - *StaDirAdAg 2-84*
Ripon Cable Co. Inc. - Ripon, WI - *Tel&CabFB 84C*
Ripon Commonwealth-Press - Ripon, WI - *BaconPubCkNews 84; Ed&PubIntYB 82*
Ripon Record - Ripon, CA - *AyerDirPub 83; BaconPubCkNews 84; Ed&PubIntYB 82*
Ripples [of Shining Waters Press] - Ann Arbor, MI - *LitMag&SmPr 83-84*
Rippon Cable Co. Inc. - Ripon, WI - *BrCabYB 84*
Ripps, Susan Shapiro - New York, NY - *LitMarPl 83, 84*
Ripsaw Record Co. - Washington, DC - *BillIntBG 83-84*
R.I.S. Christie Ltd. - Toronto, ON, Canada - *IntDirMarRes 83*
Ris Paper Co. Inc. - Garden City, NY - *LitMarPl 83*
Ris Paper Co. Inc. - Long Island City, NY - *LitMarPl 84*
Ris Paper Co. Inc. - New York, NY - *DirInfWP 82*
Risdall & Associates, John - New Brighton, MN - *StaDirAdAg 2-84*
Riseman Inc., George J. M. - Newton, MA - *StaDirAdAg 2-84*
Riser Enterprises/Bertman Corp. - Hightstown, NJ - *InterCabHB 3*
Rising Paper Co. - Housatonic, MA - *LitMarPl 83, 84*
Rising Star - Moorestown, NJ - *WritMar 84*
Rising Star - *See* Eastland Country Newspapers
Rising Star, The - Rising Star, TX - *Ed&PubIntYB 82; NewsDir 84*
Rising Sun Christianity Publishers [Aff. of Hippocrates Health Institute] - Boston, MA - *BoPubDir 4, 5*
Rising Sun Press - Durango, CO - *LitMag&SmPr 83-84*
Rising Sun Recorder - Rising Sun, IN - *Ed&PubIntYB 82; NewsDir 84*
Risk Analysis & Research Corp. [Aff. of Design Professionals Financial Corp.] - San Francisco, CA - *BoPubDir 4, 5*
Risk Management - New York, NY - *ArtMar 84; BaconPubCkMag 84; MagDir 84*
Risk Management Ltd. - Hildenborough, England - *InfIndMarPl 83*

Risk Management Society Publishing Inc. [Aff. of Risk & Insurance Management Society Inc.] - New York, NY - *BoPubDir 4, 5*
Riso Library [of Riso National Laboratory] - Roskilde, Denmark - *EISS 83; InfIndMarPl 83*
Rison Cablevision [of Valley Communications Inc.] - Rison, AR - *Tel&CabFB 84C*
Rison Cleveland County Herald - Rison, AR - *BaconPubCkNews 84*
Risser Color Service Inc. - Milwaukee, WI - *AvMarPl 83*
RIST Computer Components - Brooklyn, NY - *MicrocomMPl 84*
Ritam Corp. - Fairfield, IA - *MicrocomMPl 83, 84; WhoWMicrocom 83*
Ritchie & Sattler Inc. - Cleveland, OH - *StaDirAdAg 2-84*
Ritchie Gazette - Harrisville, WV - *Ed&PubIntYB 82*
Ritchie Gazette & Cairo Standard - Harrisville, WV - *AyerDirPub 83*
Ritchie, George F. - San Francisco, CA - *BoPubDir 4, 5*
Ritchie Telephone Co., The [Aff. of Armstrong Utilities Inc.] - Harrisville, WV - *TelDir&BG 83-84*
Rite Music - Cincinnati, OH - *BillIntBG 83-84*
Rite Record Productions Inc. - Cincinnati, OH - *BillIntBG 83-84*
Riter, A. W. Jr. - Tyler, TX - *BrCabYB 84 p.D-306*
Ritmo Latino Inc. - Miami, FL - *BillIntBG 83-84*
Ritt, Dottie - Laguna Niguel, CA - *LitMarPl 83, 84*
Ritter Telephone Co., E. - Marked Tree, AR - *TelDir&BG 83-84*
Ritter-Waxberg & Associates - Chicago, IL - *AvMarPl 83*
Rittman Main Street Press - Rittman, OH - *BaconPubCkNews 84*
Rittners Publishing Co. - Boston, MA - *BoPubDir 4, 5*
Ritz & Associates - Los Angeles, CA - *StaDirAdAg 2-84*
Ritzville-Adams County Journal - Ritzville, WA - *AyerDirPub 83; BaconPubCkNews 84; Ed&PubIntYB 82*
Rival Publishers - Everett, WA - *BoPubDir 4, 5*
Rivelin Press - Bradford, England - *LitMag&SmPr 83-84*
Rivendell Marketing Co. - New York, NY - *LitMarPl 83, 84*
River & Hills Epitaph, The - La Farge, WI - *Ed&PubIntYB 82*
River Basin Publishing Co. - St. Paul, MN - *BoPubDir 4, 5*
River Bend Cablevision Inc. [of Wisconsin Cablevision & Radio Co. Inc.] - West Bend, WI - *Tel&CabFB 84C*
River City Press - Louisville, KY - *LitMag&SmPr 83-84*
River City Review - Louisville, KY - *LitMag&SmPr 83-84*
River City Shopper, The - Decatur, AL - *NewsDir 84*
River Country Cablevision [of Marcus Communications Inc.] - Black River Falls, WI - *BrCabYB 84*
River Falls Journal - River Falls, WI - *BaconPubCkNews 84; Ed&PubIntYB 82*
River Forest Forest Leaves - *See* Pioneer Press Inc.
River Graphics Inc., James [Subs. of James River Corp.] - South Hadley, MA - *LitMarPl 84*
River Grove Messenger [of Pioneer Press Inc.] - Oak Park, IL - *NewsDir 84*
River Grove Messenger - River Grove, IL - *Ed&PubIntYB 82*
River Grove Messenger - Wilmette, IL - *AyerDirPub 83*
River Grove Messenger - *See* Pioneer Press Inc.
River Grove Post [of Elmwood Park Post Newspapers-Meese Papers Inc.] - Chicago, IL - *NewsDir 84*
River Grove Post - Elmwood Park, IL - *AyerDirPub 83*
River Grove Post - *See* Meese' Newspaper Group
River Grove Times - Chicago, IL - *AyerDirPub 83*
River Grove Times - River Grove, IL - *Ed&PubIntYB 82*
River Grove Times - *See* Lerner Times Newspapers
River House Music - *See* Special Rider Music
River News Herald & Isleton Journal - Rio Vista, CA - *AyerDirPub 83; Ed&PubIntYB 82*
River Oaks News [of Suburban Newspapers Inc.] - Ft. Worth, TX - *AyerDirPub 83; NewsDir 84*
River Oaks News - *See* Suburban Newspapers Inc.
River Parishes Guide - Boutte, LA - *AyerDirPub 83*
River Press - Ft. Benton, MT - *AyerDirPub 83; Ed&PubIntYB 82*
River Ranch Resort [of All American Holding Corp.] - River Ranch Shores, FL - *Tel&CabFB 84C*
River Review - Winnipeg, MB, Canada - *Ed&PubIntYB 82*
River Rouge Herald - River Rouge, MI - *AyerDirPub 83; Ed&PubIntYB 82*
River Styx [of Big River Association] - St. Louis, MO - *LitMag&SmPr 83-84; WritMar 84*
River Utilities Inc. [of GAC Properties Inc.] - River Ranch Shores, FL - *BrCabYB 84*
River Valley Cable TV Inc. - Marathon, NY - *BrCabYB 84*
River Valley Cablevision Inc. [of Simmons Communications of New York] - Marathon, NY - *Tel&CabFB 84C*
River Valley Clarion - Cary, IL - *Ed&PubIntYB 82*
Riverbank News - Riverbank, CA - *BaconPubCkNews 84; Ed&PubIntYB 82*
Riverbank Software Inc. - Denton, MD - *MicrocomMPl 83; WhoWMicrocom 83*
Riverdale Clayton Sun - *See* Decatur News Publishing Co. Inc.
Riverdale Co. Inc., The - Riverdale, MD - *WritMar 84*
Riverdale Free Press - Coalinga, CA - *AyerDirPub 83*
Riverdale Free Press, The - Riverdale, CA - *Ed&PubIntYB 82*
Riverdale Pointer Economist [of Chicago Daily Southtown Economist Newspapers] - Chicago, IL - *NewsDir 84*
Riverdale Pointer Economist - Riverdale, IL - *Ed&PubIntYB 82*
Riverdale Pointer Economist - South Holland, IL - *AyerDirPub 83*
Riverdale Pointer-Economist - *See* Pointer-Economist Newspapers
Riverdale Press, The [of Dale Press Inc.] - Bronx, NY - *NewsDir 84*
Riverdale Press, The - New York, NY - *AyerDirPub 83*
Riverdale Press, The - Riverdale, NY - *Ed&PubIntYB 82*
Riveredge Cablevision Inc. - Riveredge, OH - *Tel&CabFB 84C*
Riverfront - Omaha, NE - *LitMag&SmPr 83-84*
Riverhead News-Review - Riverhead, NY - *BaconPubCkNews 84; NewsDir 84*
Riverlake Systems Inc. - Roswell, GA - *MicrocomMPl 84*
Riverland Review - Dunnellon, FL - *Ed&PubIntYB 82*
Riverlands Cablevision [of MetroVision Inc.] - La Place, LA - *BrCabYB 84; Tel&CabFB 84C*
Riverrun Press Inc. [Aff. of John Calder Publishers Ltd.] - New York, NY - *LitMarPl 83, 84*
Riverrun Publishing - Vancouver, BC, Canada - *BoPubDir 4, 5*
Riversedge - Edinburg, TX - *ArtMar 84; LitMag&SmPr 83-84*
Riversedge Press - Edinburg, TX - *BoPubDir 4, 5; LitMag&SmPr 83-84*
Riverside Book Bindery Inc. - Rochester, NY - *LitMarPl 83, 84*
Riverside Cable Co. Inc. - Muskingum Township, OH - *Tel&CabFB 84C*
Riverside Cable TV [of Acton CATV Inc.] - El Granada, CA - *BrCabYB 84*
Riverside Cable TV Inc. - Little Rock, AR - *BrCabYB 84; Tel&CabFB 84C*
Riverside Cablevision [of Daniels & Associates] - Hemet, CA - *BrCabYB 84; Tel&CabFB 84C*
Riverside Cablevision - Perris, CA - *BrCabYB 84*
Riverside Cablevision - Rubidoux, CA - *BrCabYB 84; Tel&CabFB 84C*
Riverside Citizen [of La Grange Suburban Life/Citizen] - La Grange, IL - *NewsDir 84*
Riverside County Record - Riverside, CA - *AyerDirPub 83*
Riverside County Record - Rubidoux, CA - *Ed&PubIntYB 82*
Riverside Current - Riverside, IA - *BaconPubCkNews 84*
Riverside March Air Force Base Beacon - Riverside, CA - *BaconPubCkNews 84*
Riverside MDS Co. - Pasadena, MD - *Tel&CabFB 84C*
Riverside Press Enterprise - Riverside, CA - *BaconPubCkNews 84; NewsBur 6*
Riverside Press, The - Riverside, CT - *LitMag&SmPr 83-84*
Riverside Publishing Co., The [Subs. of Houghton Mifflin Co.] - Chicago, IL - *LitMarPl 83, 84*
Riverside Quarterly - Hartsville, SC - *LitMag&SmPr 83-84*
Riverside Review [of Worral Publishing Inc.] - Buffalo, NY - *AyerDirPub 83; NewsDir 84*
Riverside Suburban Life Citizen - *See* Life Printing & Publishing Co.
Riverstone Press of the Foothills Art Center - Golden, CO - *BoPubDir 4, 5*
Riverton Cable TV [of Tele-Communications Inc.] - Riverton, WY - *BrCabYB 84; Tel&CabFB 84C*
Riverton Ranger - Riverton, WY - *BaconPubCkNews 84; Ed&PubIntYB 82; NewsDir 84*
Riverton Register - Riverton, IL - *Ed&PubIntYB 82*
Riverton Register - *See* Riverton Register Publishing
Riverton Register Publishing - Riverton, IL - *BaconPubCkNews 84*

Riverview News-Herald [of News-Herald Newspapers] - Wyandotte, MI - *AyerDirPub 83; NewsDir 84*
Riverview News Herald - *See* News-Herald Newspapers
Riverwood Publishers Ltd. - New York, NY - *BoPubDir 4, 5*
Rives Smith Baldwin & Carlberg [Subs. of Young & Rubicam Inc.] - Houston, TX - *BrCabYB 84; StaDirAdAg 2-84*
Riviera Productions - Hollywood, CA - *TelAl 83, 84; Tel&CabFB 84C*
Riviera Telephone Co. Inc. - Riviera, TX - *TelDir&BG 83-84*
Riviera Utilities Cable TV - Foley, AL - *BrCabYB 84; Tel&CabFB 84C*
Rixon Inc. [Subs. of Sangamo Weston] - Silver Spring, MD - *DataDirSup 7-83; MicrocomMPl 84; WhoWMicrocom 83*
Rizzo Data Systems Corp. - Bridgeton, NJ - *WhoWMicrocom 83*
Rizzo, Simons, Cohn - Boston, MA - *AdAge 3-28-84; StaDirAdAg 2-84*
Rizzoli International Publications [Subs. of Rizzoli SPA] - New York, NY - *DirMarMP 83; LitMarPl 83, 84*
Rizzuto Associates, Dennis - Flushing, NY - *AvMarPl 83; WritMar 84*
R.J.A. - Amsterdam, Netherlands - *StaDirAdAg 2-84*
RJE Data Processing Inc. - Chicago, IL - *ADAPSOMemDir 83-84*
RK Editions - New York, NY - *LitMag&SmPr 83-84*
RKO General Inc. [Subs. of General Tire & Rubber Co.] - New York, NY - *BrCabYB 84; KnowInd 83; TelAl 83, 84; Tel&CabFB 84S*
RKO General Inc. [Subs. of Gencorp] - Akron, OH - *AdAge 6-28-84*
RKO Tape Corp. [Subs. of RKO General Inc.] - West Caldwell, NJ - *AvMarPl 83*
RKO Videogroup [Div. of RKO Pictures Inc.] - New York, NY - *Tel&CabFB 84C*
RKS Industries Inc. - Scotts Valley, CA - *MicrocomMPl 84*
RLG - *See* RLIN
RLG Conspectus On-Line - Stanford, CA - *DirOnDB Spring 84*
RLG Corp. [Subs. of Computer Consoles Inc.] - Reston, VA - *DirInfWP 82; WhoWMicrocom 83*
RLIN - *DirOnDB Spring 84*
RLM Associates - Sunnyvale, CA - *MicrocomMPl 83*
RLR Associates Ltd. - New York, NY - *LitMarPl 83, 84*
RM & D Associates [Div. of Richardson, Myers & Donofrio Inc.] - Baltimore, MD - *DirPRFirms 83*
R.M. of the Gap No. 39 History Committee - Ceylon, SK, Canada - *BoPubDir 4 Sup, 5*
RMC International - Oakland, CA - *IntDirMarRes 83*
RMF Products Inc. - Batavia, IL - *AvMarPl 83*
RMH Research Inc. - Fair Lawn, NJ - *IntDirMarRes 83*
RMI Software - Glastonbury, CT - *MicrocomMPl 83*
RMP Financial Consultants - New Orleans, LA - *BoPubDir 4, 5*
RMS Electronics Inc. - Bronx, NY - *CabTVFinDB 83; HomeVid&CabYB 82-83*
RMS Inc. - Indianapolis, IN - *StaDirAdAg 2-84*
RMS Publishing Co. - *See* RMS Triad Productions
RMS Triad Productions - West Bloomfield, MI - *BillIntBG 83-84*
RN [of Medical Economics Co.] - Oradell, NJ - *ArtMar 84; BaconPubCkMag 84; Folio 83; MagDir 84; MagIndMarPl 82-83; WritMar 84*
RNF Media Corp. Inc. - Beverly Hills, CA - *StaDirAdAg 2-84*
RNM Images - Des Plaines, IL - *BaconPubCkMag 84*
RNM Images - Mt. Prospect, IL - *MagDir 84*
ROA Films [Div. of MJE Corp.] - Milwaukee, WI - *AvMarPl 83*
Road & Track [of CBS Publications] - Newport Beach, CA - *BaconPubCkMag 84; Folio 83; MagDir 84; MagIndMarPl 82-83; WritMar 84*
Road Data Bank [of National Swedish Road Administration] - Borlange, Sweden - *EISS 83*
Road Information Center [of Arab Contractors Co.] - Cairo, Egypt - *EISS 83*
Road King - Park Forest, IL - *MagDir 84*
Road King - Richton Park, IL - *ArtMar 84; BaconPubCkMag 84; MagIndMarPl 82-83; WritMar 84*
Road Research Documentation Center [of Federal Ministry of Buildings & Technology] - Vienna, Austria - *EISS 83*
Road Research Programme [of Organisation for Economic Cooperation & Development] - Paris, France - *CompReadDB 82*
Road Rider - Laguna Beach, CA - *BaconPubCkMag 84; MagDir 84*
Road Rider - South Laguna, CA - *ArtMar 84; WritMar 84*
Road Street Press - Washington, DC - *BoPubDir 5*
Road Test Magazine - Dallas, TX - *MagDir 84*
Roadie Products Inc. - Ronkonkoma, NY - *AvMarPl 83*
Roadrunner - Rio Rancho, NM - *AyerDirPub 83*
Roadrunner-Bio [of Rainfeather Press] - Mt. Rainier, MD - *LitMag&SmPr 83-84*
Roadshow Records Corp. - New York, NY - *BillIntBG 83-84*
Roadwerk [of On The Move Press] - San Francisco, CA - *LitMag&SmPr 83-84; WritMar 84*
Roadwise - Helena, MT - *BaconPubCkMag 84; MagDir 84*
Roanco Associates - Clearwater, FL - *WhoWMicrocom 83*
Roane County News - Kingston, TN - *AyerDirPub 83*
Roane County News, The - Roane County, TN - *Ed&PubIntYB 82*
Roane County Reporter - Spencer, WV - *AyerDirPub 83; Ed&PubIntYB 82*
Roanoke & Botetourt Telephone Co. - Daleville, VA - *TelDir&BG 83-84*
Roanoke Beacon - Plymouth, NC - *AyerDirPub 83; Ed&PubIntYB 82; NewsDir 84*
Roanoke Herald - Roanoke Rapids, NC - *BaconPubCkNews 84*
Roanoke Leader, The - Roanoke, AL - *Ed&PubIntYB 82*
Roanoke News - Weldon, NC - *Ed&PubIntYB 82*
Roanoke Randolph Leader - Roanoke, AL - *BaconPubCkNews 84*
Roanoke Rapids Daily Herald - Roanoke Rapids, NC - *NewsDir 84*
Roanoke Rapids TeleCable [of Telecable Corp.] - Roanoke Rapids, NC - *BrCabYB 84; Tel&CabFB 84C*
Roanoke Review - Roanoke, IL - *BaconPubCkNews 84; Ed&PubIntYB 82; NewsDir 84*
Roanoke Telephone Co. Inc. - Roanoke, AL - *TelDir&BG 83-84*
Roanoke Times & World-News [of Landmark Communication Inc.] - Roanoke, VA - *BaconPubCkNews 84; Ed&PubIntYB 82; LitMarPl 83, 84; NewsBur 6; NewsDir 84*
Roanoke Tribune - Roanoke, VA - *AyerDirPub 83; BaconPubCkNews 84; Ed&PubIntYB 82; NewsDir 84*
Roanoke Valley Cablevision - Roanoke, VA - *Tel&CabFB 84C*
Roanoker [of Leisure Publishing Co.] - Roanoke, VA - *BaconPubCkMag 84; WritMar 84*
Roar - Shorewood, WI - *LitMag&SmPr 83-84*
Roaring Fork Valley Journal - Carbondale, CO - *AyerDirPub 83; Ed&PubIntYB 82*
Roaring Springs Cable Television Co. - Roaring Springs, TX - *BrCabYB 84; Tel&CabFB 84C*
Rob-Lee Music - Merchantville, NJ - *BillIntBG 83-84*
Robadon Music - Sheffield Lake, OH - *BillIntBG 83-84*
Robb Report, The - Acton, MA - *BaconPubCkMag 84*
Robbins & Covey Associates - New York, NY - *LitMarPl 83, 84*
Robbins & Ries Inc. - New York, NY - *StaDirAdAg 2-84*
Robbins, Caroline - New York, NY - *LitMarPl 83, 84*
Robbins Enterprises, Marty - Nashville, TN - *BillIntBG 83-84*
Robbins Record - Robbins, NC - *BaconPubCkNews 84; Ed&PubIntYB 82*
Robbins Records - Leesville, LA - *BillIntBG 83-84*
Robbinsdale-Crystal North Hennepin Post - *See* Post Publications Inc.
Robbinsville Graham Star - Robbinsville, NC - *BaconPubCkNews 84*
Robersonville Weekly Herald - Robersonville, NC - *BaconPubCkNews 84; NewsDir 84*
Robert Broadcasting Co., F. W. - New Orleans, LA - *BrCabYB 84*
Robert County Telephone Cooperative Association - New Effington, SD - *TelDir&BG 83-84*
Robert Lee Observer - Robert Lee, TX - *Ed&PubIntYB 82*
Robert Lee Observer - *See* Bronte Enterprise Publishers
Roberta Georgia Post - Roberta, GA - *BaconPubCkNews 84*
Roberts Advertising, Van - Dallas, TX - *StaDirAdAg 2-84*
Roberts Broadcasting Inc. - Sarasota, FL - *BrCabYB 84*
Roberts, Carla Mintz - Redmond, WA - *IntDirMarRes 83*
Roberts Color Productions, Mike - Oakland, CA - *AvMarPl 83*
Roberts Co. Inc. - Framingham, MA - *BoPubDir 4 Sup, 5*
Roberts Enterprises, F. M. - Dana Point, CA - *BoPubDir 4, 5*
Roberts, Gilda M. - Brooklyn, NY - *LitMarPl 83, 84*
Roberts, Homer - State College, PA - *LitMarPl 83*
Roberts Inc., Flora - New York, NY - *LitMarPl 83, 84*

Roberts Inc., H. Armstrong - New York, NY - *Ed&PublntYB 82*
Roberts Inc., H. Armstrong - Philadelphia, PA - *AvMarPl 83; LitMarPl 83, 84; MagIndMarPl 82-83*
Roberts Inc., Ian - Toronto, ON, Canada - *StaDirAdAg 2-84*
Roberts Information Services - Fairfax, VA - *EISS 83; FBInfSer 80*
Roberts, June - Sea Cliff, NY - *LitMarPl 83, 84; MagIndMarPl 82-83*
Roberts Publishing Co., Ken - Fitzwilliam, NH - *BoPubDir 4, 5*
Roberts Publishing Corp. - New York, NY - *BoPubDir 4, 5*
Roberts-Rector Associates - State College, PA - *LitMarPl 84*
Roberts, Richard Owen - Wheaton, IL - *BoPubDir 4, 5*
Roberts, William M. - Mulberry, FL - *Tel&CabFB 84C p.1699*
Robertsdale Independent - Robertsdale, AL - *BaconPubCkNews 84*
Robertson Advertising Co. Ltd., John D. - Downsview, ON, Canada - *StaDirAdAg 2-84*
Robertson Advertising Inc. - Palo Alto, CA - *StaDirAdAg 2-84*
Robertson Advertising Ltd. - London, England - *StaDirAdAg 2-84*
Robertson & Associates Inc. - Bryn Mawr, PA - *IntDirMarRes 83*
Robertson County Cable TV Inc. [of Matrix Enterprises Inc.] - Springfield, TN - *BrCabYB 84; Tel&CabFB 84C*
Robertson County Review - Mt. Olivet, KY - *AyerDirPub 83*
Robertson County Times [of Berlin Clinard Inc.] - Springfield, TN - *AyerDirPub 83; Ed&PublntYB 82; NewsDir 84*
Robertson, James E. - Woodland Hills, CA - *BoPubDir 4, 5*
Robertson Music Corp., Don - Thousand Oaks, CA - *BillIntBG 83-84*
Robesonian - Lumberton, NC - *AyerDirPub 83; Ed&PublntYB 82*
Robin & Dackerman - Beverly Hills, CA - *TeleSy&SerDir 7-83, 2-84*
Robin & Russ Handweavers - McMinnville, OR - *BoPubDir 4, 5*
Robins Review - Warner Robins, GA - *AyerDirPub 83*
Robinson, Alma - Warrenton, VA - *BoPubDir 4, 5*
Robinson & Associates Inc., Gordon - Sioux City, IA - *StaDirAdAg 2-84*
Robinson Argus - Robinson, IL - *BaconPubCkNews 84; Ed&PublntYB 82*
Robinson Associates - Boston, MA - *AdAge 3-28-84; StaDirAdAg 2-84*
Robinson Books, Ruth E. - Morgantown, WV - *BoPubDir 4, 5*
Robinson Communications Co. - Federal Way, WA - *BaconPubCkNews 84*
Robinson Co., C. H. (Ross Div.) - Eden Prairie, MN - *MagIndMarPl 82-83*
Robinson Co., C. H. (T Systems) - Eden Prairie, MN - *ADAPSOMemDir 83-84*
Robinson Constitution - Robinson, IL - *BaconPubCkNews 84*
Robinson Consulting & Design - Syracuse, NY - *WhoWMicrocom 83*
Robinson Daily News - Robinson, IL - *BaconPubCkNews 84; Ed&PublntYB 82; NewsDir 84*
Robinson, Gilbert de Beauregard - Toronto, ON, Canada - *BoPubDir 4 Sup, 5*
Robinson Inc., Clark L. - Wilton, CT - *StaDirAdAg 2-84*
Robinson Inc., William A. - Northbrook, IL - *StaDirAdAg 2-84*
Robinson, John - Eastchester, NY - *MagIndMarPl 82-83*
Robinson, Nelson B. - Rockport, MA - *BoPubDir 4, 5*
Robinson Press Inc. - Ft. Collins, CO - *BoPubDir 4 Sup, 5*
Robinson, Wayne - Forest, MS - *Tel&CabFB 84C p.1699*
Robinson, Yesawich & Pepperdine - Orlando, FL - *AdAge 3-28-84*
Robinsons Inc. - Orlando, FL - *DirMarMP 83; IntDirMarRes 83; StaDirAdAg 2-84*
Robison Agency - Los Angeles, CA - *StaDirAdAg 2-84*
Robles Rodriguez Inc. - New York, NY - *StaDirAdAg 2-84*
Roblin News, The - Roblin, MB, Canada - *Ed&PublntYB 82*
Roblin Press [Div. of Roblin Publications] - Yonkers, NY - *DirMarMP 83; LitMag&SmPr 83-84*
Roblin Review Ltd. - Roblin, MB, Canada - *AyerDirPub 83; Ed&PublntYB 82*
Robocom Ltd. - London, England - *MicrocomSwDir 1*
Robomatix Information System [of EIC/Intelligence Inc.] - New York, NY - *EISS 5-84 Sup*
Robomatix Online [of EIC/Intelligence Inc.] - New York, NY - *DataDirOnSer 84*
Robomatix Reporter - New York, NY - *DirOnDB Spring 84*
Robot Insider - Chicago, IL - *BaconPubCkMag 84*
Robot/X News - Mansfield, MA - *BaconPubCkMag 84*
Robotics Age - Peterborough, NH - *BaconPubCkMag 84; MicrocomMPl 84*
Robotics Information [of Cincinnati Milacron Industries Inc.] - Cincinnati, OH - *DirOnDB Spring 84; EISS 5-84 Sup*
Robotics Report, The - Annandale, VA - *BaconPubCkMag 84*
Robotics Today - Dearborn, MI - *BaconPubCkMag 84*
Robotics World - Atlanta, GA - *BaconPubCkMag 84*
Robotronics Age [of NewsNet Inc.] - Bryn Mawr, PA - *DataDirOnSer 84*
Robotronics Age Newsletter - Vancouver, BC, Canada - *DirOnDB Spring 84*
Robson Valley Courier - McBride, BC, Canada - *AyerDirPub 83; Ed&PublntYB 82*
Robstown Cable TV [of Tele-Communications Inc.] - Robstown, TX - *Tel&CabFB 84C*
Robstown Record - Robstown, TX - *BaconPubCkNews 84; Ed&PublntYB 82; NewsDir 84*
Rocappi [of Lehigh Press Inc.] - Pennsauken, NJ - *EISS 83; LitMarPl 83; MagIndMarPl 82-83*
Rochelle Leader, The - Rochelle, IL - *Ed&PublntYB 82*
Rochelle Leader, The - *See* Rochelle Newspapers Inc.
Rochelle News - *See* Rochelle Newspapers Inc.
Rochelle News/Leader - Rochelle, IL - *NewsDir 84*
Rochelle News, The - Rochelle, IL - *Ed&PublntYB 82*
Rochelle Newspapers Inc. - Rochelle, IL - *BaconPubCkNews 84*
Rochester AFL-CIO Labor News - Rochester, NY - *NewsDir 84*
Rochester Clarion - Rochester, MI - *BaconPubCkNews 84; Ed&PublntYB 82; NewsDir 84*
Rochester Communicade - Rochester, NY - *BaconPubCkNews 84; NewsDir 84*
Rochester Courier - Rochester, NH - *AyerDirPub 83; Ed&PublntYB 82; NewsDir 84*
Rochester Courier - *See* Rochester Courier Publishers
Rochester Courier Journal - Rochester, NY - *NewsDir 84*
Rochester Courier Publishers - Rochester, NH - *BaconPubCkNews 84*
Rochester Democrat & Chronicle [of Gannett Co. Inc.] - Rochester, NY - *BaconPubCkNews 84; LitMarPl 83; NewsBur 6; NewsDir 84*
Rochester Eccentric - Livonia, MI - *AyerDirPub 83*
Rochester Eccentric [of Livonia Suburban Communications Corp.] - Rochester, MI - *Ed&PublntYB 82; NewsDir 84*
Rochester Eccentric - *See* Observer & Eccentric Newspapers
Rochester Folk Art Guild - Middlesex, NY - *BoPubDir 4, 5*
Rochester Gates-Chili News - Rochester, NY - *BaconPubCkNews 84; Ed&PublntYB 82; NewsDir 84*
Rochester Greece Post - *See* Wolfe Publications Inc.
Rochester Institute of Technology (Technical & Education Center of the Graphic Arts) - Rochester, NY - *BoPubDir 4, 5*
Rochester Irondequoit Press - Rochester, NY - *BaconPubCkNews 84*
Rochester Post-Bulletin - Rochester, MN - *BaconPubCkNews 84; NewsDir 84*
Rochester Regional Research Library Council - Rochester, NY - *EISS 83*
Rochester Routes/Creative Arts Projects - Rochester, NY - *LitMag&SmPr 83-84*
Rochester Sentinel - Rochester, IN - *BaconPubCkNews 84; Ed&PublntYB 82; NewsDir 84*
Rochester Telephone Co. Inc. - Rochester, IN - *TelDir&BG 83-84*
Rochester Telephone Corp. [Aff. of Sylvan Lake Telephone Co.] - Rochester, NY - *TelDir&BG 83-84*
Rochester Tenth Ward Courier & Vicinity Post - Spencerport, NY - *NewsDir 84*
Rochester Times-Union [of Gannett Co. Inc.] - Rochester, NY - *BaconPubCkNews 84; Ed&PublntYB 82; NewsBur 6; NewsDir 84*
Rochester Twin Cities News - Rochester, TX - *BaconPubCkNews 84*
Rochester Vicinity Post - Rochester, NY - *NewsDir 84*
Rochford Inc. - Hillsdale, NJ - *StaDirAdAg 2-84*
ROCI Inc. - Lakewood, CO - *DataDirOnSer 84*
Rocin Press - New York, NY - *BoPubDir 5*
Rock-A-Nash-Billy Records - Nashville, TN - *BillIntBG 83-84*
Rock Aerobics Channel [of Satellite Cable Audio Networks] - Tulsa, OK - *CabTVPrDB 83*

Rock Analysis Storage System [of U.S. Geological Survey] - Denver, CO - *EISS 83*
Rock Analysis Storage System - Norman, OK - *DirOnDB Spring 84*
Rock & Co., James A. - Bloomington, IN - *BoPubDir 4, 5*
Rock & Gem - Encino, CA - *MagDir 84; MagIndMarPl 82-83*
Rock & Soul Songs - Derby, CT - *BaconPubCkMag 84; MagIndMarPl 82-83*
Rock Associates Inc. - Kirkland, WA - *Tel&CabFB 84C p.1699*
Rock Cablevision [of Helicon Corp.] - Scarbro, WV - *Tel&CabFB 84C*
Rock Cablevision Co. - Beckwith, WV - *BrCabYB 84*
Rock Cablevision Inc. - Ansted, WV - *BrCabYB 84*
Rock County Leader - Bassett, NE - *AyerDirPub 83; Ed&PubIntYB 82*
Rock County Telephone Co. [Aff. of HunTel Systems Inc.] - Blair, NE - *TelDir&BG 83-84*
Rock Dell Telphone Co. [Aff. of Kasson & Mantorville Telephone Co.] - Kasson, MN - *TelDir&BG 83-84*
Rock Garden Music Inc. - Canyon Country, CA - *BillIntBG 83-84*
Rock, Gordon - Kirkland, WA - *BrCabYB 84 p.D-306; Tel&CabFB 84C p.1699*
Rock Hill Evening Herald - Rock Hill, SC - *BaconPubCkNews 84; NewsDir 84*
Rock Hill Telephone Co. - Rock Hill, SC - *TelDir&BG 83-84*
Rock Hills Black View - Columbia, SC - *AyerDirPub 83*
Rock Hills Black View - *See* Juju Publishing Co.
Rock Information System [of Carnegie Institution] - Washington, DC - *EISS 83*
Rock Island Argus [of J. W. Potter Co.] - Rock Island, IL - *BaconPubCkNews 84; NewsDir 84*
Rock Island News - Rock Island, IL - *Ed&PubIntYB 82*
Rock Magazine - Los Angeles, CA - *BaconPubCkMag 84*
Rock Mechanics Information Service [of Imperial College of Science & Technology] - London, England - *CompReadDB 82; DataDirOnSer 84; EISS 83; InfIndMarPl 83*
Rock/Pop Syndicate - Malibu, CA - *Ed&PubIntYB 82*
Rock Port Atchison County Mail - Rock Port, MO - *BaconPubCkNews 84*
Rock Port Telephone Co. - Rock Port, MO - *TelDir&BG 83-84*
Rock Products [of Maclean-Hunter Publishing Corp.] - Chicago, IL - *BaconPubCkMag 84; MagDir 84*
Rock Rapids Lyon County Reporter - Rock Rapids, IA - *BaconPubCkNews 84; NewsDir 84*
Rock River Cablevision Co. [of Rock Island Broadcasting Co.] - Sterling, IL - *BrCabYB 84; Tel&CabFB 84C*
Rock River Telephone Co. [Aff. of Telephone & Data Systems] - Johnson Creek, WI - *TelDir&BG 83-84*
Rock River Valley Advisor - Oregon, IL - *Ed&PubIntYB 82*
Rock Smooth Productions - Studio City, CA - *BillIntBG 83-84*
Rock Solid Productions - Burbank, CA - *Tel&CabFB 84C*
Rock Springs Rocket-Miner - Rock Springs, WY - *BaconPubCkNews 84; NewsDir 84*
Rock Valley Bee - Rock Valley, IA - *BaconPubCkNews 84; Ed&PubIntYB 82*
Rock Valley Cablevision [of Firstcable Communications Inc.] - Oregon, IL - *BrCabYB 84*
Rock Valley Cablevision Ltd. [of Firstcable Communications Inc.] - Byron, IL - *Tel&CabFB 84C*
Rock Valley Cablevision Ltd. [of Firstcable Communications Inc.] - Forreston, IL - *Tel&CabFB 84C*
Rock Valley Cablevision Ltd. [of Firstcable Communications Inc.] - Franklin Grove, IL - *Tel&CabFB 84C*
Rock Valley Cablevision Ltd. [of Firstcable Communications Inc.] - Polo, IL - *Tel&CabFB 84C*
Rock Valley Review - Rock Falls, IL - *AyerDirPub 83*
Rockaway Beach South Queens Forum - Rockaway Beach, NY - *BaconPubCkNews 84*
Rockaway Beach Wave - Far Rockaway, NY - *AyerDirPub 83*
Rockaway Beach Wave - Rockaway Beach, NY - *BaconPubCkNews 84*
Rockaway Journal - Far Rockaway, NY - *AyerDirPub 83*
Rockaway Journal [of Lawrence Bi-County Publishers Inc.] - Lawrence, NY - *NewsDir 84*
Rockaway Journal - Rockaway, NY - *Ed&PubIntYB 82*
Rockaway Journal - *See* Richner Publications Inc.
Rockaway Manufacturing Co. - Inwood, NY - *DirInfWP 82*
Rockaway Record - Rockaway Park, NY - *Ed&PubIntYB 82*
Rockbill [of Rave Communications] - New York, NY - *BaconPubCkMag 84; WritMar 84*
Rockbridge Weekly, The - Buena Vista, VA - *AyerDirPub 83*
Rockcliffe Productions - Halifax, NS, Canada - *BoPubDir 4, 5*
Rockdale Cable TV Co. [of Kraus Electronic Systems] - Rockdale, IL - *BrCabYB 84; Tel&CabFB 84C*
Rockdale Citizen - Conyers, GA - *AyerDirPub 83; BaconPubCkNews 84; Ed&PubIntYB 82*
Rockdale Neighbor - Marietta, GA - *AyerDirPub 83*
Rockdale Neighbor - Woodstock, GA - *Ed&PubIntYB 82*
Rockdale Reporter - Rockdale, TX - *NewsDir 84*
Rockdale Reporter & Messenger - Rockdale, TX - *BaconPubCkNews 84; Ed&PubIntYB 82*
Rockdale Ridge Press [Aff. of Rockdale Temple Sisterhood] - Cincinnati, OH - *BoPubDir 4, 5*
Rockefeller Center Inc. - New York, NY - *BrCabYB 84*
Rockefeller University Press - New York, NY - *BoPubDir 4, 5; LitMarPl 84; MagIndMarPl 82-83; MicroMarPl 82-83*
Rocken Music Corp. - Memphis, TN - *BillIntBG 83-84*
Rocket Courier, The - Wyalusing, PA - *AyerDirPub 83*
Rocket-Miner - Rock Springs, WY - *AyerDirPub 83*
Rocket/Penny Saver - Le Mars, IA - *AyerDirPub 83*
Rocket Publishing Co. - Normangee, TX - *BoPubDir 4, 5*
Rocketlab - Florence, OR - *BoPubDir 4, 5*
Rockets - Corona, CA - *BoPubDir 4, 5*
Rockey Co. Inc., The - Seattle, WA - *DirPRFirms 83*
Rockford Chronicle, The - Rockford, IL - *Ed&PubIntYB 82*
Rockford Communications Co. Inc. - Rockford, IL - *Tel&CabFB 84C*
Rockford Northland News - Cedar Springs, MI - *BaconPubCkNews 84*
Rockford Observer, The [of Catholic Diocese of Rockford] - Rockford, IL - *NewsDir 84*
Rockford/Park Cablevision Inc. [of R. R. Donnelley & Sons Communications Co.] - Rockford, IL - *BrCabYB 84; InterCabHB 3; Tel&CabFB 84C*
Rockford Press - Rockford, OH - *BaconPubCkNews 84; Ed&PubIntYB 82*
Rockford Register - Rockford, IA - *BaconPubCkNews 84; Ed&PubIntYB 82*
Rockford Register Star - Rockford, IL - *BaconPubCkNews 84; Ed&PubIntYB 82*
Rockford Register, The - Rockford, MI - *Ed&PubIntYB 82; NewsDir 84*
Rockford Review, The - Rockford, IL - *LitMag&SmPr 83-84*
Rocking Horse Press - Storrs, CT - *BoPubDir 4, 5; LitMag&SmPr 83-84*
Rockingham Cable TV Inc. [of Signet Cablevision Co.] - Eden, NC - *BrCabYB 84; Tel&CabFB 84C*
Rockingham Cable TV Inc. - Madison County, NC - *BrCabYB 84*
Rockingham County Gazette - Hampton, NH - *AyerDirPub 83*
Rockingham County Gazette-Exeter - Exeter, NH - *Ed&PubIntYB 82*
Rockingham Gazette - *See* Exeter News-Letter Co.
Rockingham-Hamlet Cablevision [of American TV & Communications Corp.] - Rockingham, NC - *BrCabYB 84; Tel&CabFB 84C*
Rockingham/Jutkins Marketing - El Segundo, CA - *DirMarMP 83*
Rockingham Richmond County Journal - Rockingham, NC - *NewsDir 84*
Rockin'horse Records - New York, NY - *BillIntBG 83-84*
Rockland Cablesystems [of American Cablesystems Corp.] - Rockland County, NY - *Tel&CabFB 84C*
Rockland Cablevision System [of Bushnell Communications Ltd.] - Rockland, ON, Canada - *BrCabYB 84*
Rockland Colloid - Piermont, NY - *AvMarPl 83*
Rockland County Times - Haverstraw, NY - *AyerDirPub 83; Ed&PubIntYB 82*
Rockland Courier-Gazette - Rockland, ME - *BaconPubCkNews 84; NewsDir 84*
Rockland Journal-News - White Plains, NY - *AyerDirPub 83; Ed&PubIntYB 82*
Rockland Review - Nanuet, NY - *AyerDirPub 83; Ed&PubIntYB 82*

Rockland South Shore News - *See* Franklin Publishing Co.
Rockland Standard - Rockland, MA - *Ed&PublntYB 82*
Rockland Standard - *See* Franklin Publishing Co.
Rockland Telephone Co. Inc. - Rockland, ID - *TelDir&BG 83-84*
Rockledge Breeze - *See* Intercounty Newspaper Group
Rockledge Breeze, The - Philadelphia, PA - *AyerDirPub 83*
Rockledge Reporter - Rockledge, FL - *BaconPubCkNews 84*
Rocklin & Associates, Irving - Chicago, IL - *TelAl 83*
Rocklin & Loomis Placer Herald [of Auburn Journal Inc.] - Auburn, CA - *BaconPubCkNews 84; NewsDir 84*
Rocklin, Irving & Associates - Chicago, IL - *TelAl 84*
Rockmart Journal - Rockmart, GA - *BaconPubCkNews 84; Ed&PublntYB 82*
Rockmasters Publishing - *See* Guida Productions Network
Rockmore Co., The - Greenwich, CT - *Ed&PublntYB 82*
Rockmore Music - Los Angeles, CA - *BillIntBG 83-84*
Rockola Enterprises - Toronto, ON, Canada - *BoPubDir 4, 5*
Rockport Cable TV Co. Inc. - Rockport, TX - *BrCabYB 84; Tel&CabFB 84C*
Rockport Cablevision [of Kentuckiana Cablevision Inc.] - Rockport, IN - *BrCabYB 84*
Rockport Democrat, The - Rockport, IN - *Ed&PublntYB 82; NewsDir 84*
Rockport Herald - Rockport, TX - *BaconPubCkNews 84*
Rockport Journal Democrat - Rockport, IN - *BaconPubCkNews 84*
Rockport Pilot - Rockport, TX - *BaconPubCkNews 84; Ed&PublntYB 82*
Rockport Toast of the Coast Herald - Rockport, TX - *BaconPubCkNews 84*
Rocksprings Canyon TV Co. - Rocksprings, TX - *BrCabYB 84; Tel&CabFB 84C*
Rocksprings Texas Mohair Weekly - Rocksprings, TX - *BaconPubCkNews 84*
Rockton Herald [of North Central Associated Publishers] - Durand, IL - *AyerDirPub 83; NewsDir 84*
Rockton Herald - Rockton, IL - *Ed&PublntYB 82*
Rockton Herald - *See* North Central Associated Publishers
Rockville Centre Long Island News & Owl - Rockville Centre, NY - *BaconPubCkNews 84; NewsDir 84*
Rockville Centre Pennysaver - Rockville Centre, NY - *AyerDirPub 83*
Rockville House Publishers Inc. [Div. of Sigma Marketing Systems] - Garden City, NY - *LitMarPl 83*
Rockville Montgomery Advertiser - *See* Morkap Publishing
Rockville Montgomery Journal - Rockville, MD - *BaconPubCkNews 84*
Rockville Montgomery Sentinel - *See* Morkap Publishing
Rockville Parke County Sentinel [of Torch Newspapers Inc.] - Rockville, IN - *BaconPubCkNews 84; NewsDir 84*
Rockville-Potomac Advertiser - Bethesda, MD - *AyerDirPub 83*
Rockville Tri-Town Reporter - Rockville, CT - *BaconPubCkNews 84*
Rockwall Success, The - Rockwall, TX - *AyerDirPub 83*
Rockwall Texas Success - Rockwall, TX - *BaconPubCkNews 84; Ed&PublntYB 82*
Rockware Data Corp. - Dallas, TX - *MicrocomMPl 84*
Rockwell & Newell Inc. - New York, NY - *LitMarPl 83, 84; MagIndMarPl 82-83*
Rockwell Audio Visual Inc. - East Hartford, CT - *AvMarPl 83*
Rockwell City Advocate - Rockwell City, IA - *BaconPubCkNews 84; Ed&PublntYB 82*
Rockwell Cooperative Telephone Association - Rockwell, IA - *TelDir&BG 83-84*
Rockwell International Corp. - Pittsburgh, PA - *DataDirSup 7-83; ElecNews 7-25-83*
Rockwell International Corp. (Graphic Systems Div.) - Chicago, IL - *LitMarPl 83, 84*
Rockwell International Corp. (Wescom Div.) - Oak Brook, IL - *DirInfWP 82*
Rockwell Museum Inc., The Norman - Northbrook, IL - *ArtMar 84*
Rockwood Cable TV Inc. - Rockwood, PA - *BrCabYB 84; Tel&CabFB 84C*
Rockwood Times - Rockwood, TN - *BaconPubCkNews 84; Ed&PublntYB 82; NewsDir 84*
Rockwood TV Cable Co. [of National Telecommunications] - Rockwood, TN - *BrCabYB 84; Tel&CabFB 84C*
Rocky Ford Cable TV - Rocky Ford, CO - *Tel&CabFB 84C*
Rocky Ford Gazette - Rocky Ford, CO - *BaconPubCkNews 84; Ed&PublntYB 82; NewsDir 84*
Rocky Fork Enterprise - Columbus, OH - *NewsDir 84*
Rocky Fork Enterprise - Gahanna, OH - *AyerDirPub 83; Ed&PublntYB 82*
Rocky Hill Post - Rocky Hill, CT - *AyerDirPub 83*
Rocky Mountain Arms & Antiques - Englewood, CO - *BoPubDir 4, 5*
Rocky Mountain Books - Calgary, AB, Canada - *BoPubDir 4, 5*
Rocky Mountain Business Journal [of Cordovan Corp.] - Denver, CO - *BaconPubCkMag 84; MagDir 84*
Rocky Mountain Cable TV - Avon, CO - *BrCabYB 84*
Rocky Mountain CATV Ltd. - Hinton, AB, Canada - *BrCabYB 84*
Rocky Mountain Construction [of Mountain Publishing Co. Inc.] - Denver, CO - *BaconPubCkMag 84; MagDir 84*
Rocky Mountain Data - Albuquerque, NM - *WhoWMicrocom 83*
Rocky Mountain Food Dealer [of Rocky Mountain Food Dealers Association] - Denver, CO - *MagDir 84*
Rocky Mountain Food Dealer - Lakewood, CO - *BaconPubCkMag 84*
Rocky Mountain Journal - Denver, CO - *Ed&PublntYB 82*
Rocky Mountain Magazine - Denver, CO - *MagIndMarPl 82-83*
Rocky Mountain Miniature Journal - Littleton, CO - *WritMar 84*
Rocky Mountain Motorist - Denver, CO - *BaconPubCkMag 84; MagDir 84*
Rocky Mountain News [of The Denver Publishing Co. Inc.] - Denver, CO - *AyerDirPub 83; BaconPubCkNews 84; Ed&PublntYB 82; LitMarPl 83, 84; NewsBur 6*
Rocky Mountain Press - Long Beach, CA - *BoPubDir 4, 5*
Rocky Mountain Software Systems - Walnut Creek, CA - *MicrocomMPl 83, 84; MicrocomSwDir 1; WhoWMicrocom 83*
Rocky Mountain Translators Inc. - Boulder, CO - *LitMarPl 84*
Rocky Mountain Writers Guild Inc. - Boulder, CO - *BoPubDir 5; LitMag&SmPr 83-84*
Rocky Mt. Cable TV Inc. [of Omni Cable TV Corp.] - Rocky Mt., VA - *Tel&CabFB 84C*
Rocky Mt. Cablevision - Rocky Mt., VA - *BrCabYB 84*
Rocky Mt. Evening Telegram [of Rocky Mt. Publishing Co. Inc.] - Rocky Mt., NC - *BaconPubCkNews 84; LitMarPl 83; NewsDir 84*
Rocky Mt. Franklin County Times, The - Rocky Mt., VA - *NewsDir 84*
Rocky Mt. Franklin News-Post - Rocky Mt., VA - *BaconPubCkNews 84; NewsDir 84*
Rocky Mt. Sunday Telegram, The - Rocky Mt., NC - *LitMarPl 83*
Rocky Point North Shore Record - *See* Port Jefferson Record Publishers
Rocky View News - Calgary, AB, Canada - *AyerDirPub 83*
Rocky View Times - Airdrie, AB, Canada - *AyerDirPub 83*
Rocky View Times & Airdrie Echo - Airdrie, AB, Canada - *Ed&PublntYB 82*
Rocky's Ragdoll Publishing Co. - Savannah, GA - *BillIntBG 83-84*
Rocshire Records - Anaheim, CA - *BillIntBG 83-84*
Rod Action - Canoga Park, CA - *BaconPubCkMag 84*
Rod & Reel - Camden, ME - *BaconPubCkMag 84*
Rod & Staff Publishers Inc. - Crockett, KY - *BoPubDir 4, 5*
Rod Serling's The Twilight Zone Magazine - New York, NY - *ArtMar 84; MagIndMarPl 82-83*
Roda Marketing Research Inc. - Wyncote, PA - *IntDirMarRes 83*
Rodale Press - Toronto, ON, Canada - *LitMarPl 83, 84*
Rodale Press Inc. - Emmaus, PA - *DirMarMP 83; KnowInd 83; LitMarPl 83, 84; MagIndMarPl 82-83*
Rodale's New Shelter - Emmaus, PA - *ArtMar 84; MagIndMarPl 82-83*
Roday Literary Agency - New York, NY - *LitMarPl 83, 84*
Rodeheaver Co. [Div. of Word Inc.] - Winona Lake, IN - *BillIntBG 83-84*
Rodel Audio Services - Washington, DC - *AvMarPl 83*
Rodell-Frances Collin Literary Agency, Marie - New York, NY - *LitMarPl 83, 84*
Roden Stations, E. O. - Jackson, MS - *BrCabYB 84*

Rodeo News - Pauls Valley, OK - *BaconPubCkMag 84; MagDir 84; MagIndMarPl 82-83; WritMar 84*
Rodeo Telephone Inc. - Burwell, NE - *TelDir&BG 83-84*
Rodes, Toby E. - Basel, Switzerland - *DirPRFirms 83*
Rodgers, Cauthen, Barton & Cureton Inc. - Columbia, SC - *StaDirAdAg 2-84*
Rodgers Public Relations - Glen Rock, NJ - *DirPRFirms 83*
Rodime Inc. - Mission Viejo, CA - *DataDirSup 7-83; MicrocomMPl 84*
Rodkin & Associates Inc. - Northfield, IL - *StaDirAdAg 2-84*
Rodney Mercury, The - Rodney, ON, Canada - *Ed&PubIntYB 82*
Rodsongs - *See* Rondor Music International Inc.
Roe Jan Independent - Copake, NY - *Ed&PubIntYB 82*
Roeland Park Sun [of Overland Park Sun Newspapers] - Shawnee Mission, KS - *NewsDir 84*
Roerich Museum, Nicholas - New York, NY - *BoPubDir 4, 5*
Roerick Music Co. - Sherman Oaks, CA - *BoPubDir 5*
Roesmer, Josef - Pittsburgh, PA - *LitMarPl 83, 84*
Roffman Associates, Richard H. [Subs. of Roffman Productions] - New York, NY - *ArtMar 84; DirPRFirms 83; LitMarPl 83, 84; MagIndMarPl 82-83; TelAl 83, 84; Tel&CabFB 84C*
Roger Music Inc. - Irvine, CA - *BillIntBG 83-84*
Roger Williams College (Ampersand Press) - Bristol, RI - *BoPubDir 4 Sup, 5*
Rogers & Associates Inc. - Los Angeles, CA - *DirPRFirms 83*
Rogers & Co. - Riverside, CT - *HBIndAd&MS 82-83*
Rogers & Co., E. H. - Los Angeles, CA - *AdAge 3-28-84; StaDirAdAg 2-84*
Rogers & Cowan Inc. - Beverly Hills, CA - *ArtMar 84; DirPRFirms 83*
Rogers Associates, Peter - New York, NY - *StaDirAdAg 2-84*
Rogers, Bill Arthur [of Intermedia Editorial Service] - Oak Park, IL - *MagIndMarPl 82-83*
Rogers Book Service - New York, NY - *BoPubDir 4, 5*
Rogers Cable TV-Brampton [of Rogers Cablesystems Inc.] - Brampton, ON, Canada - *BrCabYB 84*
Rogers Cable TV-Brantford [of Rogers Cablesystems Inc.] - Brantford, ON, Canada - *BrCabYB 84*
Rogers Cable TV-Kitchener [of Rogers Cablesystems Inc.] - Kitchener, ON, Canada - *BrCabYB 84*
Rogers Cable TV-Mississauga [of Rogers Cablesystems Inc.] - Mississauga, ON, Canada - *BrCabYB 84*
Rogers Cable TV-Newmarket [of Rogers Cablesystems Inc.] - Newmarket, ON, Canada - *BrCabYB 84*
Rogers Cable TV-Pine Ridge - Oshawa, ON, Canada - *BrCabYB 84*
Rogers Cable TV-Toronto [of Rogers Cablesystems Inc.] - Toronto, ON, Canada - *BrCabYB 84*
Rogers Cablesystems Inc. - Yuma, AZ - *Tel&CabFB 84C*
Rogers Cablesystems Inc. - El Centro, CA - *Tel&CabFB 84C*
Rogers Cablesystems Inc. - Minneapolis, MN - *BrCabYB 84*
Rogers Cablesystems Inc. - San Angelo, TX - *Tel&CabFB 84C*
Rogers Cablesystems Inc. - Toronto, ON, Canada - *AdAge 6-28-84; BrCabYB 84; CabTVFinDB 83; HomeVid&CabYB 82-83; Tel&CabFB 84C*
Rogers Cablesystems of Alamagordo Inc. - Alamogordo, NM - *Tel&CabFB 84C*
Rogers Cablesystems of East Texas Inc. - Mt. Pleasant, TX - *Tel&CabFB 84C*
Rogers Cablesystems of Laredo Inc. - Laredo, TX - *Tel&CabFB 84C*
Rogers Cablesystems of Texas Inc. - San Antonio, TX - *HomeVid&CabYB 82-83; Tel&CabFB 84C p.1699*
Rogers City Cablevision [of Paradigm Communications Inc.] - Rogers City, MI - *BrCabYB 84; Tel&CabFB 84C*
Rogers City Presque Isle County Advance - Rogers City, MI - *BaconPubCkNews 84; NewsDir 84*
Rogers Daily/Sunday News - Rogers, AR - *NewsDir 84*
Rogers, French & Co. - Irvine, CA - *DirPRFirms 83*
Rogers, Helga M. - New Port Richey, FL - *BoPubDir 4*
Rogers, Helga M. - St. Petersburg, FL - *BoPubDir 5*
Rogers House Museum Gallery - Ellsworth, KS - *BoPubDir 4, 5*
Rogers, Ken - Beverly Hills, CA - *MagIndMarPl 82-83*
Rogers Merchandising Inc. - Downers Grove, IL - *DirMarMP 83; StaDirAdAg 2-84*
Rogers Park/Edgewater News [of Chicago Lerner Newspapers] - Chicago, IL - *AyerDirPub 83; NewsDir 84*
Rogers Park Records - Chicago, IL - *BillIntBG 83-84*
Rogers Products Co. Inc. - Orange, CA - *DataDirSup 7-83*
Rogers, Roger M. - Tyler, TX - *BrCabYB 84 p.D-306*
Rogers Telecommunications Ltd. - *See* Rogers Cablesystems Inc.
Rogers TV Cable Inc. [of Donrey Media Group] - Rogers, AR - *Tel&CabFB 84C*
Rogers UA Cablesystems Inc. - Westport, CT - *BrCabYB 84 p.D-306; CabTVFinDB 83; TelAl 83, 84*
Rogers-UA Columbia Cablevision of New Jersey Inc. [of Rogers-UA Cablesystems Inc.] - Oakland, NJ - *HomeVid&CabYB 82-83*
Rogers UA Columbia Cablevision of New Jersey Inc. - Wayne, NJ - *BrCabYB 84*
Rogers/Uniphoto, Joel - Seattle, WA - *AvMarPl 83*
Rogers, Weiss/Cole & Weber Advertising - *See* Cole & Weber Inc.
Rogersound Records - Anderson, SC - *BillIntBG 83-84*
Rogersville East Lauderdale News - Rogersville, AL - *BaconPubCkNews 84; NewsDir 84*
Rogersville Review - Rogersville, TN - *BaconPubCkNews 84; Ed&PubIntYB 82; NewsDir 84*
Rogersville TV Cable - Rogersville, AL - *Tel&CabFB 84C*
Rogersville TV Cable [of Signet Cablevision Co.] - Rogersville, TN - *BrCabYB 84; Tel&CabFB 84C*
Roggen Telephone Cooperative Co. - Roggen, CO - *TelDir&BG 83-84*
Roggers, French & Co. - Irvine, CA - *AdAge 3-28-84; StaDirAdAg 2-84*
Roghaar Associates - Reston, VA - *LitMarPl 84*
Rogofsky, Howard - Flushing, NY - *ProGuPRSer 4*
Rogovin Public Relations Inc., Gerald A. - Newton, MA - *DirPRFirms 83*
Rogue Records - Woodland Hills, CA - *BillIntBG 83-84*
Rogue Valley Cablevision [of The Western Co.] - Rogue River, OR - *BrCabYB 84; Tel&CabFB 84C*
Rohde Associates Inc., Elliot - Atlanta, GA - *ADAPSOMemDir 83-84*
Rohde Literary Service - Los Angeles, CA - *LitMarPl 83; MagIndMarPl 82-83*
Roher Inc., Daniel S. - New York, NY - *DirPRFirms 83*
Rohlfing Publishing Co. - Tamarac, FL - *BillIntBG 83-84*
Rohn Staging & Visual Productions - New York, NY - *AvMarPl 83*
Rohner & Rohner Public Relations Consultants - Blonay, Switzerland - *DirPRFirms 83*
Rohnert Park Cotati Clarion [of Scripps-Sonoma Publishing] - Cotati, CA - *Ed&PubIntYB 82; NewsDir 84*
Rohnert Park Cotati Times - San Rafael, CA - *AyerDirPub 83*
Roklan Corp. - Arlington Heights, IL - *MicrocomMPl 84*
Rola Boza-God's Field - Scranton, PA - *Ed&PubIntYB 82; NewsDir 84*
Rolan, David E. - Scottsdale, AZ - *Tel&CabFB 84C p.1699*
Roles & Parker Ltd. - London, England - *StaDirAdAg 2-84*
Rolette Cable TV - Rolette, ND - *BrCabYB 84; Tel&CabFB 84C*
Rolf Slide Laboratories [Div. of Bob Wright Studio Inc.] - Pittsford, NY - *AvMarPl 83*
Rolfe Arrow - Rolfe, IA - *BaconPubCkNews 84; Ed&PubIntYB 82*
Roling, Rau & Davis Advertising Inc. - Williams Bay, WI - *StaDirAdAg 2-84*
Roll & Co. Inc., Win - *See* Jason Group Inc., The
Roll Call Report - Washington, DC - *Ed&PubIntYB 82; WritMar 84*
Roll Top Record Co. - Warren, OH - *BillIntBG 83-84*
Rolla Cable System Inc. [of Omega Communications Inc.] - Rolla, MO - *BrCabYB 84; Tel&CabFB 84C*
Rolla Cable TV Inc. - Grand Forks, ND - *Tel&CabFB 84C*
Rolla Cable TV Inc. - Rolla, ND - *BrCabYB 84*
Rolla News [of Sowers' Newspapers Inc.] - Rolla, MO - *BaconPubCkNews 84; Ed&PubIntYB 82; NewsDir 84*
Rolla Turtle Mountain Star - Rolla, ND - *BaconPubCkNews 84; NewsDir 84*
Rolle & Associates Inc., Bill - Washington, DC - *DirPRFirms 83*
Rollefstad, Floyd [Div. of Laser Graphics] - Redmond, WA - *LitMarPl 83*
Rollin' Rock Records - Van Nuys, CA - *BillIntBG 83-84*
Rolling Along - Bismarck, ND - *BaconPubCkMag 84*
Rolling Block Press - Buena Park, CA - *BoPubDir 5*

Rolling Fork Deer Creek Pilot - Rolling Fork, MS - *BaconPubCkNews 84*
Rolling Meadows Herald [of Paddock Publications] - Arlington Heights, IL - *NewsDir 84*
Rolling Meadows Herald - *See* Paddock Publications
Rolling Meadows Topics - *See* Journal & Topics Newspapers
Rolling Stock - Boulder, CO - *LitMag&SmPr 83-84*
Rolling Stone [of Straight Arrow Publishers] - New York, NY - *ArtMar 84; BaconPubCkMag 84; DirMarMP 83; Folio 83; LitMarPl 83, 84; MagDir 84; MagIndMarPl 82-83; NewsBur 6; WritMar 84*
Rolling Stone Press - New York, NY - *LitMarPl 83, 84*
Rolling Thunder - Berkeley, CA - *LitMag&SmPr 83-84*
Rollins Cable Vue Inc. [Div. of Rollins Inc.] - Atlanta, GA - *LitMarPl 84*
Rollins Cablevision [of Rollins Inc.] - Wilmington, DE - *BrCabYB 84; HomeVid&CabYB 82-83; Tel&CabFB 84C*
Rollins Cablevision of Connecticut [of Rollins Inc.] - Wallingford, CT - *BrCabYB 84; Tel&CabFB 84C*
Rollins Cablevision of Massachusetts [of Rollins Inc.] - Andover, MA - *BrCabYB 84*
Rollins Cablevision of Rhode Island - Lincoln, RI - *BrCabYB 84*
Rollins Cablevision of Rhode Island [of Rollins Inc.] - Narragansett, RI - *Tel&CabFB 84C*
Rollins CableVision of Rhode Island [of Rollins Inc.] - Providence County, RI - *Tel&CabFB 84C*
Rollins Inc. - Atlanta, GA - *AdAge 6-28-84; BrCabYB 84 p.D-306; CabTVFinDB 83; HomeVid&CabYB 82-83; KnowInd 83; Tel&CabFB 84C p.1699, 84S*
Rollins Press Inc. - Orlando, FL - *LitMarPl 83, 84*
Rolm Corp. - Santa Clara, CA - *Datamation 6-83*
Rolm Corp. (Mil-Spec Computer Div.) - Santa Clara, CA - *WhoWMicrocom 83*
Rolm Telecommunications - Santa Clara, CA - *DirInfWP 82*
Rolnik Productions Inc., Robert - New York, NY - *ProGuPRSer 4*
Rolnik Publishers - New York, NY - *BoPubDir 5*
Rolyn Optics - Covina, CA - *AvMarPl 83*
Romain Telephone Co. Inc. [Aff. of Great Southwest Telephone Corp.] - Plains, TX - *TelDir&BG 83-84*
Romaine Pierson Publishers Inc. - Port Washington, NY - *BoPubDir 4, 5; MagIndMarPl 82-83*
Roman Associates Inc., Edith - New York, NY - *MagIndMarPl 82-83*
Roman Enterprises, Angelo - Covina, CA - *BillIntBG 83-84*
Romance Book Club [of Waldenbooks] - Stamford, CT - *LitMarPl 84*
Romance Monographs Inc. - University, MS - *BoPubDir 4, 5*
Romance Records - New York, NY - *BillIntBG 83-84*
Romanian Review - Bucharest, Romania - *LitMag&SmPr 83-84*
Romann & Tannenholz Advertising Inc. - New York, NY - *StaDirAdAg 2-84*
Romano, George - Tucson, AZ - *CabTVFinDB 83*
Romantic Dining & Travel Letter [of James Dines & Co. Inc.] - Belvedere, CA - *WritMar 84*
Romantic Times - Brooklyn Heights, NY - *WritMar 84*
Romantist, The [of F. Marion Crawford Memorial Society] - Nashville, TN - *LitMag&SmPr 83-84; WritMar 84*
Rome Cable TV Co. [of TeleScripps Cable Co.] - Rome, GA - *BrCabYB 84; Tel&CabFB 84C*
Rome Daily Sentinel - Rome, NY - *NewsDir 84*
Rome-Dougherty Public Relations - Beverly Hills, CA - *LitMarPl 84*
Rome NewChannels [of NewChannels Corp.] - Rome, NY - *BrCabYB 84; Tel&CabFB 84C*
Rome News-Tribune - Rome, GA - *BaconPubCkNews 84; Ed&PubIntYB 82; NewsDir 84*
Rome Public Relations Inc., Edye - Beverly Hills, CA - *DirPRFirms 83; LitMarPl 83; MagIndMarPl 82-83*
Romeike & Curtice Ltd. - London, England - *ProGuPRSer 4*
Romeo Advisor - *See* Advisor Newspapers
Romeo Observer - Romeo, MI - *AyerDirPub 83; BaconPubCkNews 84; Ed&PubIntYB 82; NewsDir 84*
Romeo-Washington Advisor - Romeo, MI - *AyerDirPub 83; Ed&PubIntYB 82*
Romeoville Beacon - Romeoville, IL - *Ed&PubIntYB 82*
Romeoville Beacon - *See* Beacon Sun Newspapers
Rominger Advertising Agency Inc. - Dallas, TX - *StaDirAdAg 2-84*
Romney Hampshire Review - Romney, WV - *BaconPubCkNews 84*
Romney Press - Iowa City, IA - *BoPubDir 4 Sup, 5*
Romper Room Enterprises Inc. - Towson, MD - *Tel&CabFB 84C*
Romulus Roman - Wayne, MI - *AyerDirPub 83; NewsDir 84*
Romulus Roman - *See* Associated Newspapers Inc.
Romulus Roman, The - Romulus, MI - *Ed&PubIntYB 82*
Ron-Ken Music Inc. - *See* Jet-Eye Music Inc.
Ronalds Federated Ltd. [Subs. of Bell Canada Enterprises Inc.] - Montreal, PQ, Canada - *LitMarPl 83, 84*
Ronalds Printing Ltd. [Div. of Ronalds Federated Ltd.] - Willowdale, ON, Canada - *LitMarPl 83, 84*
Ronalds-Reynolds & Co. Ltd. - Toronto, ON, Canada - *StaDirAdAg 2-84*
Ronan Howard Associates Inc. - Spring Valley, NY - *ArtMar 84; LitMarPl 83, 84; MagIndMarPl 82-83; StaDirAdAg 2-84*
Ronan Pioneer [of Western Publishing Co.] - Ronan, MT - *BaconPubCkNews 84; NewsDir 84*
Ronan Telephone Co. - Ronan, MT - *TelDir&BG 83-84*
Ronarte Publications - *See* Sound Column Cos., The
Ronceverte Television Corp. - Ronceverte, WV - *BrCabYB 84*
Ronceverte TV Cable - Ronceverte, WV - *Tel&CabFB 84C*
Ronco Teleproducts - Elk Grove Village, IL - *BillIntBG 83-84*
Roncom Music Co. - Great Neck, NY - *BillIntBG 83-84*
Rondeau, Fernard - Berthier, PQ, Canada - *BrCabYB 84*
Rondor Music International Inc. - Hollywood, CA - *BillIntBG 83-84*
Roneo Alcatel Inc. - Little Ferry, NJ - *DirInfWP 82*
Rong Songs - Nashville, TN - *BillIntBG 83-84*
Rongwen Music - *See* Broude Bros. Ltd.
Ronin Music Records - Farmingdale, NY - *BillIntBG 83-84*
Ronkonkoma Review [of Review Graphics Inc.] - Ronkonkoma, NY - *Ed&PubIntYB 82; NewsDir 84*
Ronkonkoma Review - *See* Ronkonkoma Review Publishers
Ronkonkoma Review Publishers - Ronkonkoma, NY - *BaconPubCkNews 84*
Rontel Corp. - Vienna, VA - *DirInfWP 82*
Rontom Music Co. - Nashville, TN - *BillIntBG 83-84*
Roof Design - Middleburg Heights, OH - *BaconPubCkMag 84*
Roofer, The - Ft. Myers, FL - *BaconPubCkMag 84*
Roofers, Waterproofers & Allied Workers [of United Union of Roofers, Waterproofers, and Allied Workers] - Washington, DC - *BaconPubCkMag 84; MagDir 84*
Roofing, Siding, & Insulation [of Harcourt Brace Jovanovich Publications] - New York, NY - *MagDir 84*
Roofing Spec - Chicago, IL - *BaconPubCkMag 84*
Roofing Spec - Oak Park, IL - *MagDir 84*
Rooftop Records Inc. - Wilderville, OR - *BillIntBG 83-84*
Rook Press - Ruffsdale, PA - *BoPubDir 4, 5*
Rookfield Press [Aff. of Peacehaven Inc.] - Deer, AR - *BoPubDir 4, 5*
Rooks County Record - Stockton, KS - *AyerDirPub 83; Ed&PubIntYB 82*
Room-Co. Inc. - Bradford, RI - *BillIntBG 83-84*
Room Mate Magazine - Portland, OR - *BaconPubCkMag 84*
Room of One's Own [of Growing Room Collective] - Vancouver, BC, Canada - *ArtMar 84; LitMag&SmPr 83-84; WritMar 84*
Room of One's Own Press - Victoria, BC, Canada - *BoPubDir 4, 5*
Room 7 Music [Div. of Seven Arts Press] - Hollywood, CA - *BillIntBG 83-84*
Room 10 Recording Studios Inc. - Washington, DC - *BillIntBG 83-84*
Room Toons Music - Bradford, RI - *BillIntBG 83-84*
Roome Telecommunications Inc. - Halsey, OR - *TelDir&BG 83-84*
Roosevelt County Rural Telephone Cooperative Inc. - Portales, NM - *TelDir&BG 83-84*
Roosevelt Library, Franklin D. - Hyde Park, NY - *BoPubDir 4, 5; MicroMarPl 82-83*
Roosevelt Paper Co. - Philadelphia, PA - *LitMarPl 83, 84; MagIndMarPl 82-83*
Roosevelt Record - Clarkston, WA - *AyerDirPub 83*
Roosevelt Record - *See* Tribune Newspapers Inc.

Roosevelt Syndicate, Edith Kermit - Washington, DC - *Ed&PubIntYB 82*
Roosevelt Uintah Basin Standard - Roosevelt, UT - *BaconPubCkNews 84*
Rooster Blues Records - Chicago, IL - *BillIntBG 83-84*
Rooster Music [Div. of WW Associates Inc.] - Seattle, WA - *BillIntBG 83-84*
Rooster Records - Bethel, VT - *BillIntBG 83-84*
Rooster Valley Shopper - Richfield, UT - *AyerDirPub 83*
Root & Associates Inc. - Baton Rouge, LA - *StaDirAdAg 2-84*
Root & Branch - Somerville, MA - *BoPubDir 4, 5*
Root Co., A. I. - Medina, OH - *BoPubDir 4, 5*
Root Computers Ltd. - London, England - *MicrocomSwDir 1*
Root, Virginia - Webster Springs, WV - *Tel&CabFB 84C p.1699*
ROP Color Service for Newspapers - Chicago, IL - *Ed&PubIntYB 82*
Roper Center - Storrs, CT - *EISS 83*
Roper Organization Inc., The [Div. of Starch INRA Hooper Inc.] - New York, NY - *IntDirMarRes 83*
Roper Records Inc. - Long Island City, NY - *BillIntBG 83-84*
Roper Reports - New York, NY - *DirOnDB Spring 84*
Roperry Music - New York, NY - *BillIntBG 83-84*
Roperry Records - New York, NY - *BillIntBG 83-84*
Rorge Publishing Co. - Evergreen, CO - *BoPubDir 4, 5*
Rosado, A. J. - Janesville, WI - *Tel&CabFB 84C p.1699*
Rosallen Publications - North Hollywood, CA - *BoPubDir 5*
Roscoe & Gruber - New York, NY - *LitMarPl 84; StaDirAdAg 2-84*
Roscoe Cable TV Corp. [of The Vinegarroon Corp.] - Del Rio, TX - *BrCabYB 84*
Roscoe Community TV Corp. - Roscoe, NY - *BrCabYB 84*
Roscoe-Hosmer Independent - Roscoe, SD - *AyerDirPub 83; Ed&PubIntYB 82*
Roscoe-Hosmer Independent - *See* Ipswich Tribune
Roscoe Times - Roscoe, TX - *BaconPubCkNews 84; Ed&PubIntYB 82*
Roscommon Herald-News - Roscommon, MI - *BaconPubCkNews 84; Ed&PubIntYB 82; NewsDir 84*
ROSCOP - Brest, France - *DirOnDB Spring 84*
Roscor Inc. - Morton Grove, IL - *AvMarPl 83*
Rose & Brosse Advertising Inc. [Div. of Edwin Bird Wilson Inc.] - New York, NY - *StaDirAdAg 2-84*
Rose & Co. Inc., John M. - Knoxville, TN - *StaDirAdAg 2-84*
Rose Associates Inc. - Costa Mesa, CA - *StaDirAdAg 2-84*
Rose Bibliography [of George Washington University] - Washington, DC - *EISS 83*
Rose, Bill - New York, NY - *LitMarPl 83, 84*
Rose Bridge Music Inc. - *See* Barton Music Inc., Earl
Rose Canyon Music - *See* Kjos Music Co., Neil A.
Rose Hill Group Inc., The - Marcellus, NY - *BillIntBG 83-84*
Rose Hill Press - Waynesboro, PA - *BoPubDir 4, 5*
Rose Hill Reporter - Rose Hill, KS - *Ed&PubIntYB 82*
Rose Hill Reporter - *See* Times Publishing Co.
Rose Manufacturing Co. - Grand Rapids, MI - *DirInfWP 82*
Rose, Marilyn Gaddis - Binghamton, NY - *LitMarPl 83, 84*
Rose of Indiana, Edward - Speedway, IN - *Tel&CabFB 84C*
Rose Press - Berkeley, CA - *BoPubDir 5*
Rose Printing Co. Inc. - Tallahassee, FL - *LitMarPl 83, 84*
Rose Public Relations, Pat - Albany, CA - *LitMarPl 84*
Rose Publishing Co. - Little Rock, AR - *BoPubDir 4, 5; LitMag&SmPr 83-84; LitMarPl 84*
Rose Records Co. Inc. - Atlanta, GA - *BillIntBG 83-84*
Rose/Sound Inc., Jay - Boston, MA - *AvMarPl 83*
Rose Valley Telephone Co. [Aff. of Telephone Utilities Inc.] - Lebanon, OR - *TelDir&BG 83-84*
Rose, William A. - New York, NY - *MagIndMarPl 82-83*
Roseart/Rosenbaum Fine Art Inc. - Ft. Lauderdale, FL - *ArtMar 84*
Roseau Times-Region - Roseau, MN - *BaconPubCkNews 84; Ed&PubIntYB 82; NewsDir 84*
Rosebrier Publishing Co. - Blowing Rock, NC - *WritMar 84*
Rosebud News - Rosebud, TX - *BaconPubCkNews 84; Ed&PubIntYB 82*
Rosebud Records - Tyler, TX - *BillIntBG 83-84*
Roseburg News-Review - Roseburg, OR - *NewsDir 84*
Roseburg Woodsman [of Roseburg Lumber Co.] - Beaverton, OR - *WritMar 84*
Rosedale-Laurelton Pennysaver - Rockville Centre, NY - *AyerDirPub 83*
Rosegarden Press - Austin, TX - *BoPubDir 5*
Roseland Park Sun - *See* Sun Publications
Roselle Medinah Voice - *See* Voice Newspapers
Roselle North Suburban Press - *See* Press Publications
Roselle Record - Roselle, IL - *AyerDirPub 83; Ed&PubIntYB 82*
Roselle Record - *See* Copey Newspaper Group
Roselle Spectator - Union, NJ - *AyerDirPub 83*
Roselle Star - Roselle, IL - *Ed&PubIntYB 82*
Rosemarie's Baby [of Grace A. Dow Memorial Library] - Midland, MI - *EISS 83*
Rosemary Melody Line Recording Co. - Vineland, NJ - *BillIntBG 83-84*
Rosemead Independent - *See* Sun Independent Newspapers
Rosemont Journal - *See* Journal & Topics Newspapers
Rosemont Progress - Rosemont, IL - *Ed&PubIntYB 82*
Rosemont Progress - Wilmette, IL - *AyerDirPub 83*
Rosemont Suburban Progress - *See* Pioneer Press Inc.
Rosemont Suburban Times - Des Plaines, IL - *AyerDirPub 83*
Rosemont Suburban Times - Rosemont, IL - *Ed&PubIntYB 82*
Rosemont Times - *See* Des Plaines Publishing Co.
Rosemore Publications - Los Angeles, CA - *BoPubDir 5*
Rosemount Office Systems Inc. - Lakeville, MN - *DirInfWP 82*
Rosen Advertising Inc., John H. - Birmingham, MI - *StaDirAdAg 2-84*
Rosen Associates Inc., Fred - New York, NY - *DirPRFirms 83; LitMarPl 83, 84*
Rosen Grandon Associates - Tampa, FL - *MicrocomSwDir 1; WhoWMicrocom 83*
Rosen Inc., Alan R. - Buffalo, NY - *WhoWMicrocom 83*
Rosen Press Inc., Richards - New York, NY - *LitMarPl 83, 84*
Rosen Productions Inc., Peter - New York, NY - *AvMarPl 83*
Rosen Publishing Group, The - New York, NY - *WritMar 84*
Rosen Research - New York, NY - *ADAPSOMemDir 83-84*
Rosen Research - Cleveland, OH - *IntDirMarRes 83*
Rosenak, Robert - Eagle River, WI - *Tel&CabFB 84C p.1699*
Rosenbach Museum & Library - Philadelphia, PA - *BoPubDir 4, 5*
Rosenberg & Co. - Dallas, TX - *StaDirAdAg 2-84*
Rosenberg Associates, Anna M. - New York, NY - *DirPRFirms 83*
Rosenberg Associates Inc., Alan H. - New York, NY - *DirMarMP 83; LitMarPl 83, 84; MagIndMarPl 82-83; StaDirAdAg 2-84*
Rosenberg Herald-Coaster - Rosenberg, TX - *BaconPubCkNews 84; NewsDir 84*
Rosenberg Inc., Mary S. - New York, NY - *BoPubDir 4, 5*
Rosenberg Publications/Micronesian Seminar - Kealakekua, HI - *BoPubDir 5*
Rosenberg Video Services, Warren - New York, NY - *AvMarPl 83*
Rosenberg, Vivian Graff - Germantown, NY - *BoPubDir 4, 5*
Rosenblatt Advertising, Ned K. - Santa Fe Springs, CA - *StaDirAdAg 2-84*
Rosenblum, Sig - Southampton, NY - *LitMarPl 83, 84; MagIndMarPl 82-83*
Rosenfeld, Sirowitz & Lawson - New York, NY - *AdAge 3-28-84; Br 1-23-84; StaDirAdAg 2-84*
Rosenstein Associates Inc., Alvin J. - Roslyn, NY - *IntDirMarRes 83*
Rosenstein, Sylvia J. - Highland Park, IL - *LitMarPl 83, 84*
Rosenstiel, Leonie - New York, NY - *LitMarPl 83*
Rosenstone/Wender - New York, NY - *LitMarPl 83, 84*
Rosenthal & Co., Albert Jay - Chicago, IL - *AdAge 3-28-84; ArtMar 84; StaDirAdAg 2-84*
Rosenthal & Co., Albert Jay - New York, NY - *ArtMar 84*
Rosenthal & Co. Inc., S. - Cincinnati, OH - *LitMarPl 83, 84; MagIndMarPl 82-83*
Rosenthal Art Slides - Chicago, IL - *LitMarPl 83, 84*
Rosenthal Inc., Rolf Werner - New York, NY - *AdAge 3-28-84; StaDirAdAg 2-84*
Rosenwald/Batson Inc. - *See* Berneta Communications Inc.
Rose's Hope, The - Ardmore, PA - *WritMar 84*
RoseSoft Inc. - Seattle, WA - *MicrocomMPl 84*

Rosetown Eagle, The - Rosetown, SK, Canada - *Ed&PubIntYB 82*
Rosetta Stone Associates Inc. - Nashua, NH - *MagIndMarPl 82-83*
Rosetta Stone, The - Glastonbury, CT - *MicrocomMPl 83*
Roseville Cablevision [of Storer Cable Communications Inc.] - Roseville, CA - *BrCabYB 84; Tel&CabFB 84C*
Roseville Independent [of Roseville Carlberg Publishing Co.] - Roseville, IL - *Ed&PubIntYB 82; NewsDir 84*
Roseville Independent - *See* Acklin Newspaper Group
Roseville Press-Tribune - Roseville, CA - *NewsDir 84*
Roseville Review - *See* Lillie Suburban Newspapers
Roseville Sun - Edina, MN - *AyerDirPub 83*
Roseville Sun [of Minnesota Suburban Newspapers Inc.] - Minneapolis, MN - *NewsDir 84*
Roseville Sun - Roseville, MN - *Ed&PubIntYB 82*
Roseville Sun - *See* Sun Newspapers
Roseville Telephone Co. - Roseville, CA - *TelDir&BG 83-84*
Roseville World - Roseville, CA - *BaconPubCkNews 84*
Rosewood Records - Minneapolis, MN - *BillIntBG 83-84*
Rosholt Review - Rosholt, SD - *BaconPubCkNews 84; Ed&PubIntYB 82*
Rosicrucian Digest [of Rosicrucian Order] - San Jose, CA - *MagIndMarPl 82-83; WritMar 84*
Rosicrucian Fellowship - Oceanside, CA - *BoPubDir 4, 5*
Roskowski, John B. - Archbold, OH - *Tel&CabFB 84C p.1699*
Rosler, Martha - Brooklyn, NY - *BoPubDir 4, 5; LitMag&SmPr 83-84*
Roslindale Parkway Transcript - Roslindale, MA - *Ed&PubIntYB 82*
Roslyn-Albertson Pennysaver - Great Neck, NY - *AyerDirPub 83*
Roslyn News [of Community Newspapers Inc.] - Glen Cove, NY - *AyerDirPub 83; NewsDir 84*
Roslyn News - Roslyn, NY - *Ed&PubIntYB 82*
Roslyn News - *See* Community Newspapers Inc.
Roslyn Shopping News - Jericho, NY - *AyerDirPub 83*
Rosner-Lewis Advertising Agency - Bridgeport, CT - *StaDirAdAg 2-84*
Rosner Television Systems Inc. - New York, NY - *InterCabHB 3*
Ross Advertising - Peoria, IL - *AdAge 3-28-84; StaDirAdAg 2-84*
Ross & Associates Inc., Steven W. - *See* Wellington Communications Inc.
Ross & Associates Inc., T. J. - New York, NY - *DirPRFirms 83*
Ross & Casey Advertising - New York, NY - *LitMarPl 83, 84*
Ross & Co. - Rye, NY - *LitMarPl 83, 84*
Ross & Co. Inc., Robert H. - Denver, PA - *DataDirOnSer 84*
Ross & Haines Old Books Co. - St. Paul, MN - *BoPubDir 5*
Ross & Haines Old Books Co. - Wayzata, MN - *BoPubDir 4*
Ross Associates Inc., J. - Cranbury, NJ - *IntDirMarRes 83*
Ross Books - Berkeley, CA - *LitMag&SmPr 83-84; LitMarPl 83, 84; WritMar 84*
Ross-Carlson Associates - Boston, MA - *ArtMar 84; DirPRFirms 83*
Ross-Cooper Associates Inc. - New York, NY - *IntDirMarRes 83*
Ross County Cable TV Inc. - Adelphia, OH - *Tel&CabFB 84C*
Ross-Erikson Inc. - Santa Barbara, CA - *BoPubDir 4 Sup, 5; LitMag&SmPr 83-84; LitMarPl 83, 84; WritMar 84*
Ross-Gaffney Inc. - New York, NY - *AvMarPl 83*
Ross Inc., K. P. - New York, NY - *DirPRFirms 83*
Ross, James K. - New York, NY - *LitMarPl 84*
Ross Llewellyn Inc. - Chicago, IL - *StaDirAdAg 2-84*
Ross, Mary Jane - Tenafly, NJ - *LitMarPl 83, 84*
Ross Music, Brian - Los Angeles, CA - *BillIntBG 83-84*
Ross Music Corp., Jerry - Southampton, PA - *BillIntBG 83-84*
Ross Publications, Betsy - Bloomfield Hills, MI - *BoPubDir 4 Sup, 5*
Ross Research Center Inc. - New York, NY - *IntDirMarRes 83*
Ross, Shannon - Edmonton, AB, Canada - *BoPubDir 4, 5*
Ross Systems Inc. - Palo Alto, CA - *DataDirOnSer 84; DataDirSup 7-83; MicrocomMPl 83, 84*
Ross Valley Reporter [of Marin Suburban Newspapers] - San Anselmo, CA - *AyerDirPub 83; Ed&PubIntYB 82; NewsDir 84*
Rossburn Review, The - Rossburn, MB, Canada - *Ed&PubIntYB 82*
Rosscomp Corp. - Cerritos, CA - *MicrocomMPl 84*
Rossel Books [Div. of The Seymour Rossel Co. Inc.] - Chappaqua, NY - *BoPubDir 4; LitMarPl 83, 84; WritMar 84*
Rossford Record - *See* Welch Publishing Co.
Rossford Record-Journal [of Welch Publishing Co.] - Rossford, OH - *AyerDirPub 83; NewsDir 84*
Rossi Publications - Beverly Hills, CA - *BoPubDir 4, 5; LitMag&SmPr 83-84; WritMar 84*
Rosslyn Review - Arlington, VA - *BaconPubCkNews 84*
Rossmoor News [of Golden Rain Foundation] - Walnut Creek, CA - *AyerDirPub 83; Ed&PubIntYB 82; NewsDir 84*
Rosston, Kim - New York, NY - *LitMarPl 83*
Rosston, Kremer & Slawter Inc. - New York, NY - *StaDirAdAg 2-84*
Rossville Cable TV - Rossville, KS - *BrCabYB 84*
Roston & Co. - Great Neck, NY - *StaDirAdAg 2-84*
Roswell-Alpharetta Neighbor - Roswell, GA - *Ed&PubIntYB 82*
Roswell Associates - New York, NY - *Tel&CabFB 84C*
Roswell Daily Record - Roswell, NM - *BaconPubCkNews 84; Ed&PubIntYB 82; NewsDir 84*
Roswell Neighbor [of Marietta Neighbor Newspapers Inc.] - Marietta, GA - *NewsDir 84*
Roswell North Fulton Today [of Times-Journal Inc.] - Roswell, GA - *NewsDir 84*
Roszel, Eleanor Merryman - Baltimore, MD - *LitMarPl 83, 84*
Rotan Advance Star Record - Rotan, TX - *BaconPubCkNews 84*
Rotarian, The - Evanston, IL - *ArtMar 84; BaconPubCkMag 84; LitMarPl 83, 84; MagDir 84; MagIndMarPl 82-83; WritMar 84*
Rotary Rocket - Rolling Hills Estates, CA - *BaconPubCkMag 84*
RotaScan - Columbus, OH - *DirInfWP 82*
Rotelcom Data Inc. [Subs. of Rochester Telephone Corp.] - Fairport, NY - *DataDirOnSer 84; DataDirSup 7-83*
Roth Advertising - Orange, NJ - *StaDirAdAg 2-84*
Roth Advertising [Subs. of Charles A. Roth Inc.] - Roslyn Heights, NY - *LitMarPl 83, 84; MagIndMarPl 82-83*
Roth Associates Inc., Herrick S. - Denver, CO - *DirPRFirms 83*
Roth Broadcast Group - Lincoln, MA - *BrCabYB 84*
Roth, Chuck - Oakridge, OR - *Tel&CabFB 84C p.1699*
Roth Features, June - Teaneck, NJ - *Ed&PubIntYB 82*
Rothco Cartoons Inc. - Yonkers, NY - *Ed&PubIntYB 82*
Rothenberg Information Systems - Palo Alto, CA - *DirInfWP 82; WhoWMicrocom 83*
Rotheudt Advertising - Houston, TX - *StaDirAdAg 2-84*
Rothholz Associates Inc., Peter - New York, NY - *ArtMar 84*
Rothines Associates - Great Neck, NY - *EISS 83; InfIndMarPl 83*
Rothkopf, Carol Z. - Summit, NJ - *LitMarPl 83, 84*
Rothman & Co., Fred B. - Littleton, CO - *LitMarPl 83, 84; MagIndMarPl 82-83; MicroMarPl 82-83*
Rothman & Lowry Inc. - Little Rock, AR - *BrCabYB 84*
Rotholz Associates Inc., Peter - New York, NY - *DirPRFirms 83*
Rothsay Telephone Co. Inc. - Rothsay, MN - *TelDir&BG 83-84*
Rothschild Advertising, David E. - Florida, NY - *StaDirAdAg 2-84*
Rothstein Music Ltd. - Brooklyn, NY - *BillIntBG 83-84*
Rothstein-Tauber Inc. - Stamford, CT - *IntDirMarRes 83*
Rotman, Jeffrey L. - Somerville, MA - *LitMarPl 83, 84*
Rotor & Wing International [of PJS Publications Inc.] - Peoria, IL - *BaconPubCkMag 84; MagDir 84; MagIndMarPl 82-83; WritMar 84*
Rotrosen Agency, Jane - New York, NY - *LitMarPl 83, 84*
Rough Notes - Indianapolis, IN - *ArtMar 84; BaconPubCkMag 84; BoPubDir 5; MagDir 84*
Rough Rider Music - *See* Annextra Music
Rough Trade Inc. - San Francisco, CA - *BillIntBG 83-84*
Rouleau Community Club - Rouleau, SK, Canada - *BoPubDir 4, 5*
Roulette Records Inc. - New York, NY - *BillIntBG 83-84*
Round Lake News [of Lakeland Publishers Inc.] - Grayslake, IL - *NewsDir 84*
Round Lake News - Round Lake, IL - *AyerDirPub 83; Ed&PubIntYB 82*
Round Lake News - *See* Lakeland Publishers Inc.
Round Rock Leader - Round Rock, TX - *BaconPubCkNews 84; Ed&PubIntYB 82; NewsDir 84*
Round Sound Music - Dothan, AL - *BillIntBG 83-84*
Round Table - Millbrook, NY - *AyerDirPub 83*
Round Top Television Club Inc. - Livingston Manor, NY - *BrCabYB 84; Tel&CabFB 84C*
Round Up [of New Mexico State University] - Las Cruces, NM - *NewsDir 84*

Round-Up - Sundre, AB, Canada - *AyerDirPub 83*
Round Valley News - Covelo, CA - *AyerDirPub 83; Ed&PubIntYB 82*
Rounder Records Corp. - Cambridge, MA - *BillIntBG 83-84*
Roundtable Films Inc. - Beverly Hills, CA - *AvMarPl 83*
Roundtable Press [Aff. of Bolton Institute for Sustainable Future Inc.] - Wellesley, MA - *BoPubDir 4, 5*
Roundtable Press Inc. - New York, NY - *LitMarPl 83, 84*
Roundtop TV Association - Warren, PA - *BrCabYB 84; Tel&CabFB 84C*
Roundup - Payson, AZ - *AyerDirPub 83*
Roundup - Pinedale, WY - *AyerDirPub 83*
Roundup Cable Inc. - Roundup, MT - *Tel&CabFB 84C*
Roundup Record-Tribune - Roundup, MT - *Ed&PubIntYB 82*
Roundup Record-Tribune - *See* Roundup Record Tribune Publishers
Roundup Record Tribune Publishers - Roundup, MT - *BaconPubCkNews 84*
Rountree Report, The [of Rountree Publishing Co. Inc.] - Garden City, NY - *MagDir 84*
Rourke-Eno Paper Co., The [Div. of Unisource Corp.] - Hartford, CT - *LitMarPl 83, 84*
Rourke Productions, Jack - Burbank, CA - *AvMarPl 83; TelAl 83, 84; Tel&CabFB 84C*
Rouses Point North Countryman [of Denton Publications Inc.] - Elizabethtown, NY - *NewsDir 84*
Rouses Point North Countryman - Rouses Point, NY - *Ed&PubIntYB 82*
Rouses Point North Countryman - *See* Denton Publications Inc.
Rouseville TV Club Inc. - Rouseville, PA - *Tel&CabFB 84C*
Roush Books - North Hollywood, CA - *BoPubDir 4, 5; LitMag&SmPr 83-84*
Rouslin, Albert H. - New York, NY - *LitMarPl 83, 84; MagIndMarPl 82-83*
Rousseau, M. F. - Longueuil, PQ, Canada - *BoPubDir 4, 5*
Routes - London, England - *DirOnDB Spring 84*
Routledge & Kegan Paul of America Ltd. [Aff. of Routledge & Kegan Paul Ltd.] - Boston, MA - *LitMarPl 83, 84; WritMar 84*
Roux, Seguela, Cayzac & Goudard - Paris, France - *AdAge 6-25-84*
Rouyn-Noranda Press - Rouyn, PQ, Canada - *AyerDirPub 83*
Rouzer Studio, Danny - Hollywood, CA - *TelAl 83, 84; Tel&CabFB 84C*
Rovelstad & Associates - Racine, WI - *IntDirMarRes 83*
Rovern Press - Willimantic, CT - *ArtMar 84; BoPubDir 5*
Rowalba Music Publishing - New York, NY - *BillIntBG 83-84*
Rowan Tree Press - Boston, MA - *ArtMar 84; BoPubDir 4, 5*
Rowe & Associates, M. B. - Hickory, NC - *MicrocomMPl 83*
Rowe & Field Inc. - Evansville, IN - *StaDirAdAg 2-84*
Rowe International Inc. (Customusic Div.) - Whippany, NJ - *Tel&CabFB 84C*
Rowe Price Associates Inc., T. (Research Div.) - Baltimore, MD - *ADAPSOMemDir 83-84*
Rowe Publishing Corp. - Milwaukee, WI - *BoPubDir 4 Sup, 5; LitMag&SmPr 83-84; WritMar 84*
Rowell Printing Co. Inc., J. R. - Charleston, SC - *StaDirAdAg 2-84*
Rowen Booklet Service, Thomas J. - Santa Clara, CA - *BoPubDir 4, 5*
Rowena Press - Rowena, TX - *BaconPubCkNews 84; Ed&PubIntYB 82*
Rowland, C. - Berkeley Springs, WV - *BoPubDir 4 Sup, 5*
Rowland CATV Inc. - Rowland, PA - *Tel&CabFB 84C*
Rowland Co. Inc., The - New York, NY - *DirPRFirms 83*
Rowland Heights-Walnut Highlander - *See* Highlander Publications Inc.
Rowland Translating Co. - Fayetteville, NC - *LitMarPl 83*
Rowlette Enterprises Inc. (Modern Software Systems Div.) - Eldon, MI - *MicrocomMPl 84*
Rowley & Linder Inc. - Wichita, KS - *DirMarMP 83*
Rowley Northeast Ohio Group - Ashtabula, OH - *Ed&PubIntYB 82*
Rowman & Allanheld [Subs. of Littlefield, Adams & Co.] - Totowa, NJ - *LitMarPl 84; WritMar 84*
Rowman & Littlefield [Div. of Littlefield, Adams & Co.] - Totowa, NJ - *LitMarPl 83; MicroMarPl 82-83*
Rowman & Littlefield - *See* Rowman & Allanheld
Rowntree Advertising Ltd. - Vancouver, BC, Canada - *StaDirAdAg 2-84*
Roxboro Cablevision Inc. - Roxboro, NC - *BrCabYB 84; Tel&CabFB 84C*
Roxboro Courier-Times - Roxboro, NC - *BaconPubCkNews 84; NewsDir 84*
Roxborough Review [of Inter County Publishing Co.] - Philadelphia, PA - *AyerDirPub 83; NewsDir 84*
Roxbury Bay State Banner - Dorchester, MA - *BaconPubCkNews 84*
Roxbury Data Interface - Verdi, NV - *BoPubDir 5*
Roxbury Data Interface - Succasunna, NJ - *BoPubDir 4*
Roxbury Poetry Enterprises - Needham, MA - *BoPubDir 4, 5*
Roxy Recorders Inc. - New York, NY - *AvMarPl 83*
Roy Inc., Ross - Detroit, MI - *AdAge 3-28-84; Br 1-23-84; BrCabYB 84; DirMarMP 83; DirPRFirms 83; StaDirAdAg 2-84*
Roy Lakeside Review - Layton, UT - *BaconPubCkNews 84*
Royal Advertising International Co. - Montville, NJ - *DirPRFirms 83; StaDirAdAg 2-84*
Royal Business Machines Inc. - Hartford, CT - *DirInfWP 82*
Royal Canadian Regimental Headquarters - London, ON, Canada - *BoPubDir 4 Sup, 5*
Royal Center Record - Royal Center, IN - *BaconPubCkNews 84; Ed&PubIntYB 82*
Royal City Banner - Royal City, WA - *BaconPubCkNews 84*
Royal Composing Room Inc. - New York, NY - *LitMarPl 83, 84*
Royal Court Reports - Aberdeen, MS - *BoPubDir 4 Sup, 5*
Royal Flair Music Publishing - Council Bluffs, IA - *BillIntBG 83-84*
Royal Gazette - Hamilton, Bermuda - *AyerDirPub 83*
Royal House Publishing Co. Inc. [of Recipes-of-the-Month Club] - Beverly Hills, CA - *ArtMar 84*
Royal Institute of Technology Library (Information & Documentation Center) - Stockholm, Sweden - *CompReadDB 82; InfIndMarPl 83*
Royal Life Saving Society Canada - Toronto, ON, Canada - *BoPubDir 4, 5*
Royal Martian Music - Hollywood, CA - *BillIntBG 83-84*
Royal Neighbor, The - Rock Island, IL - *BaconPubCkMag 84; MagDir 84*
Royal Netherlands Academy of Arts & Sciences Library - Amsterdam, Netherlands - *EISS 83*
Royal Oak - *See* Tree International
Royal Oak Cablevision Ltd. [of Greenridge Enterprises Ltd.] - Saanich, BC, Canada - *BrCabYB 84*
Royal Ontario Museum Publication Services - Toronto, ON, Canada - *LitMarPl 83, 84*
Royal Palm Beach Town Crier - *See* Town Crier Newspapers
Royal Paper Corp. [Subs. of Walter, Wilcox, Furlong] - New York, NY - *LitMarPl 83, 84*
Royal Pioneer Industries - Philadelphia, PA - *AvMarPl 83; DirInfWP 82*
Royal Publishing Co. [Subs. of Recipes of the Month Club] - Beverly Hills, CA - *LitMarPl 83, 84; WritMar 84*
Royal Society of Canada - Ottawa, ON, Canada - *BoPubDir 4, 5*
Royal Society of Chemistry - London, England - *MicroMarPl 82-83*
Royal Society of Chemistry [of The University of Nottingham] - Nottingham, England - *InfIndMarPl 83*
Royal Society of Chemistry (Information Services) - Nottingham, England - *DataDirOnSer 84*
Royal Software - Howard Beach, NY - *MicrocomMPl 83*
Royal Software - Eugene, OR - *MicrocomSwDir 1*
Royal T Music - Ft. Worth, TX - *BillIntBG 83-84*
Royal Telephone Co. - Royal, IA - *Tel&CabFB 84C; TelDir&BG 83-84*
Royal Tropical Institute (Dept. of Agricultural Research) - Amsterdam, Netherlands - *CompReadDB 82; DataDirOnSer 84*
Royal Zenith Corp. [Div. of Dyson Kissner Moran Inc.] - Great Neck, NY - *LitMarPl 84*
Royal Zenith Corp. [Div. of Dyson Kissner Moran Inc.] - New Hyde Park, NY - *LitMarPl 83*
Royalhaven Music Inc. - *See* Pride Music Group
Royce & Rader Inc. - Farmingdale, NY - *StaDirAdAg 2-84*

Royds Advertising Group Ltd., The - London, England - *StaDirAdAg 2-84*
Royersford Reporter - Royersford, PA - *BaconPubCkNews 84*
Royle Publishing Co. Inc. - Sun Prairie, WI - *BaconPubCkNews 84*
Royle Systems Inc. - Bethel Park, PA - *MicrocomSwDir 1*
Royse City American - Rockwall, TX - *BaconPubCkNews 84*
Royse City American - Royse City, TX - *Ed&PubIntYB 82*
Royston News Leader - Royston, GA - *BaconPubCkNews 84*
Roznique Music Inc. - *See* Laurie Publishing Group
RPM Press Inc. - Verndale, MN - *WritMar 84*
R.P.W. Publishing Corp. - Lexington, SC - *BoPubDir 5*
RPW Systems & Services Inc. - Montreal, PQ, Canada - *WhoWMicrocom 83*
RQ - Chicago, IL - *MagDir 84; MagIndMarPl 82-83*
RR Art Resources International Ltd. - Pound Ridge, NY - *ArtMar 84*
R.R. Software - Madison, WI - *MicrocomMPl 83, 84; MicrocomSwDir 1; WhoWMicrocom 83*
RRAD - Chicago, IL - *Tel&CabFB 84C*
R.S. Means Co. Inc. - Kingston, MA - *WhoWMicrocom 83*
RSA Products [Div. of R. Shriver Associates] - Parsippany, NJ - *DataDirSup 7-83*
RSC Book & Music Publishers [Aff. of Research Services Corp.] - Ft. Worth, TX - *BoPubDir 4, 5*
RSC/Refrigeration Service & Contracting [of Nickerson & Collins Co.] - Des Plaines, IL - *MagDir 84; MagIndMarPl 82-83*
RSE Inc. - Cushing, OK - *MicrocomMPl 84*
RSG Publishing Inc. - Detroit, MI - *BoPubDir 4, 5*
R.S.I. - New York, NY - *BaconPubCkMag 84*
R.S.M. & K. - New York, NY - *AdAge 3-28-84; BrCabYB 84; DirPRFirms 83; StaDirAdAg 2-84*
RSO Records - New York, NY - *BillIntBG 83-84*
RSTS Professional [of M Systems Inc.] - Springhouse, PA - *MicrocomMPl 84*
RSV Publishing Inc. - Brooklyn, NY - *BoPubDir 4, 5*
RSVP/Interviewing Services - Philadelphia, PA - *IntDirMarRes 83*
RSVP Sports - New York, NY - *CabTVPrDB 83*
RSWB - Stuttgart, West Germany - *DirOnDB Spring 84*
RTECS - Cincinnati, OH - *DirOnDB Spring 84*
RTG Data Systems - Santa Monica, CA - *WhoWMicrocom 83*
R.T.N.D.A. Communicator - Washington, DC - *BaconPubCkMag 84*
RTR Software - El Paso, TX - *MicrocomMPl 83, 84; MicrocomSwDir 1; WhoWMicrocom 83*
RTS Systems Inc. [Subs. of Compact Video Inc.] - Burbank, CA - *AvMarPl 83*
RTW Ready to Wear [of Harcourt Brace Jovanovich Publications] - New York, NY - *MagDir 84*
Rub Group/Advertising Inc., The - Baton Rouge, LA - *ArtMar 84; StaDirAdAg 2-84*
Rubank Inc. - Miami, FL - *BillIntBG 83-84*
Rubber & Plastics News - Akron, OH - *BaconPubCkMag 84; MagDir 84*
Rubber & Plastics Research Association - Shrewsbury, England - *CompReadDB 82; InfIndMarPl 83*
Rubber Bros. Publishing Co. - *See* Video Dideo Publishing Co.
Rubber Records - Birmingham, AL - *BillIntBG 83-84*
Rubber World - Akron, OH - *BaconPubCkMag 84; MagDir 84*
Rubel, David - Woodsfield, OH - *Tel&CabFB 84C p.1699*
Ruben Publishing - Avon, CT - *BoPubDir 4, 5*
Rubenstein & Co. Inc., Wolfson - New York, NY - *DirPRFirms 83*
Rubenstein Associates Inc., Howard J. - New York, NY - *DirPRFirms 83*
Rubicom Associates Inc. - *See* Rubin-Van Slyke Inc.
Rubicon Corp. - Richardson, TX - *ADAPSOMemDir 83-84*
Rubicon Music - North Hollywood, CA - *BillIntBG 83-84*
Rubicon Press - Salem, OR - *BoPubDir 4, 5; LitMag&SmPr 83-84*
Rubin & Co., Jeff - El Sobrante, CA - *LitMarPl 83, 84*
Rubin Associates, Bruce - Miami, FL - *DirPRFirms 83*
Rubin, Ken - Ottawa, ON, Canada - *BoPubDir 4, 5*
Rubin, Leonard - New York, NY - *DirPRFirms 83*
Rubin Response Services Inc. - Rolling Meadows, IL - *StaDirAdAg 2-84*
Rubin-Van Slyke - Bannockburn, IL - *AdAge 3-28-84; StaDirAdAg 2-84*
Rubinson & Friends Inc., David - San Francisco, CA - *BillIntBG 83-84*
Ruborge Publishers - Pompano Beach, FL - *BoPubDir 4, 5*
Rubric Press, The - Yonkers, NY - *LitMag&SmPr 83-84*
Ruby-Spears Enterprises Inc. [Div. of The Taft Entertainment Co.] - Hollywood, CA - *TelAl 83, 84*
Ruby Valley Cable Co. Inc. - Sheridan, MT - *Tel&CabFB 84C*
Rucker Enterprises - Greensboro, NC - *BoPubDir 4, 5*
Rudd International Corp. - Washington, DC - *DirInfWP 82*
Rudder [of Petersen Publishing Co.] - Annapolis, MD - *ArtMar 84; BaconPubCkMag 84; MagIndMarPl 82-83; WritMar 84*
Ruddick Research International Inc. - Tulsa, OK - *IntDirMarRes 83*
Ruddy Duck Press - Seattle, WA - *LitMag&SmPr 83-84*
Rude [of Acme Print & Litho] - Stratford, ON, Canada - *LitMag&SmPr 83-84*
Ruder & Finn Inc. - New York, NY - *LitMarPl 83; TelAl 83, 84*
Ruder, Avima - Springfield, OR - *MagIndMarPl 82-83*
Ruder, Finn & Rotman Inc. - New York, NY - *DirPRFirms 83; LitMarPl 84; StaDirAdAg 2-84*
Rudnik, Maryka & Raphael - New York, NY - *LitMarPl 83, 84*
Rudnik, Raphael - New York, NY - *LitMarPl 83, 84*
Rudor Communications Inc. - New York, NY - *MicrocomMPl 84*
Ruegemer & Associates - Hopkins, MN - *IntDirMarRes 83*
Ruehl & Co. Inc. - Baltimore, MD - *StaDirAdAg 2-84*
Ruf Corp. - Olathe, KS - *MicrocomSwDir 1*
Ruff Associates, Carl - New York, NY - *DirPRFirms 83; LitMarPl 83, 84; MagIndMarPl 82-83*
Ruff Software Inc. - Plant City, FL - *MicrocomMPl 84*
Ruffled Feathers Publishing Co. - Boulder, CO - *BoPubDir 4 Sup, 5*
Ruff's Financial Survival Report, Howard - Pleasanton, CA - *DirOnDB Spring 84*
Rugby Associates Inc. - Knoxville, TN - *LitMarPl 83*
Rugby Cable TV [of NoDaKable Inc.] - Bottineau, ND - *BrCabYB 84*
Rugby Pierce County Tribune - Rugby, ND - *BaconPubCkNews 84*
Ruhl Information Management Inc. - Alexandria, VA - *EISS 83*
Ruhr Advertising, Chuck - Minneapolis, MN - *AdAge 3-28-84; ArtMar 84; StaDirAdAg 2-84*
Ruidoso News - Ruidoso, NM - *BaconPubCkNews 84; Ed&PubIntYB 82; NewsDir 84*
Ruiter Associates Inc. - Upper Montclair, NJ - *StaDirAdAg 2-84*
Ruiz, Victor Manuel - Oakland, CA - *LitMarPl 83, 84; MagIndMarPl 82-83*
Ruka Publications Inc. [Aff. of The Fmali Umbrella Herb Co.] - Santa Cruz, CA - *BoPubDir 4, 5*
Rules Service Co. - Bethesda, MD - *BrCabYB 84*
Rule's TV - Bay Center, WA - *Tel&CabFB 84C*
Rullman & Munger Advertising - Los Angeles, CA - *StaDirAdAg 2-84*
Rumble Records - Urbana, IL - *BillIntBG 83-84*
Rumbleseat Press Inc. - Greensboro, PA - *BoPubDir 4, 5*
Rumblin' Songs - Urbana, IL - *BillIntBG 83-84*
Rumford Falls Times - Rumford, ME - *AyerDirPub 83; BaconPubCkNews 84; NewsDir 84*
Rumford National Graphics Inc. - New York, NY - *MagIndMarPl 82-83*
Rumpelstiltsongs - *See* Wood'n Music Inc.
Rumrill-Hoyt Inc. [Subs. of Compton Advertising] - New York, NY - *AdAge 3-28-84; BrCabYB 84; StaDirAdAg 2-84*
Rumrill-Hoyt Inc. - Rochester, NY - *TelAl 83, 84*
Rumrill-Hoyt Inc. (Public Relations Div.) - New York, NY - *DirPRFirms 83*
RUN [of Wayne Green Inc.] - Peterborough, NH - *BaconPubCkMag 84; MicrocomMPl 84*
Runa Press - Dublin, Ireland - *LitMag&SmPr 83-84*
Runaway - Alta Loma, CA - *MagIndMarPl 82-83*
Rundell Advertising, E. Ralph - Chicago, IL - *StaDirAdAg 2-84*
Rundle Inc., J. B. - New York, NY - *StaDirAdAg 2-84*
Rundt World Risk Analysis Package, S. J. - New York, NY - *DirOnDB Spring 84*

Rundt World Risk Analysis Package, S. J. [of I. P. Sharp Associates Ltd.] - Toronto, ON, Canada - *DataDirOnSer 84*
Runestone [of Asatru Free Assembly] - Denair, CA - *ArtMar 84; WritMar 84*
Runestone Telephone Association - Hoffman, MN - *TelDir&BG 83-84*
Runkle Co., Lowe - Oklahoma City, OK - *BrCabYB 84; StaDirAdAg 2-84; TelAl 83, 84*
Runkle, John H. - Boise, ID - *CabTVFinDB 83*
Runnells, Clive - Houston, TX - *BrCabYB 84 p.D-306; Tel&CabFB 84C p.1699*
Runnels Publications, Tom - Marble Hill, MO - *BoPubDir 4, 5*
Runnemede Black Horse Suburban - *See* Suburban Newspapers
Runner, The - New York, NY - *BaconPubCkMag 84; MagDir 84; MagIndMarPl 82-83; WritMar 84*
Runner's World [of Runner's World Magazine Co.] - Mountain View, CA - *BaconPubCkMag 84; Folio 83; MagDir 84; MagIndMarPl 82-83; NewsBur 6*
Runner's World Magazine Co. - Mountain View, CA - *MagIndMarPl 82-83*
Running & Fitness [of American Running & Fitness Association] - Washington, DC - *ArtMar 84; MagIndMarPl 82-83*
Running Press - Philadelphia, PA - *LitMag&SmPr 83-84; LitMarPl 83, 84*
Running Times - Woodbridge, VA - *ArtMar 84; BaconPubCkMag 84; MagDir 84; MagIndMarPl 82-83; WritMar 84*
Running Wild - Lafayette, CA - *BoPubDir 4 Sup, 5*
Runzheimer & Co. Inc. - Rochester, WI - *BoPubDir 5*
Runzheimer Reports on Automotive Alternatives - Northbrook, IL - *DirOnDB Spring 84*
Runzheimer Reports on Automotive Alternatives [of NewsNet Inc.] - Bryn Mawr, PA - *DataDirOnSer 84*
Rupert Minidoka County News - Rupert, ID - *BaconPubCkNews 84*
Ruprecht & Associates Inc., Mary M. - Duluth, MN - *DirInfWP 82*
Rural American - Oakland, CA - *AyerDirPub 83*
Rural & Urban Roads - Des Plaines, IL - *BaconPubCkMag 84; MagDir 84*
Rural Antenna Systems [of Razorback Cable Associates] - Alma, AR - *BrCabYB 84*
Rural Antenna Systems Inc. - Blue Mountain, AR - *BrCabYB 84*
Rural Antenna Systems Inc. - Ft. Smith, AR - *BrCabYB 84; Tel&CabFB 84C p.1699*
Rural Arkansas - Little Rock, AR - *BaconPubCkMag 84; MagDir 84*
Rural Arts Services - Mendocino, CA - *LitMag&SmPr 83-84*
Rural Cablevision Inc. [of Cable Communications Inc.] - Springville, AL - *Tel&CabFB 84C*
Rural Development Abstracts [of Commonwealth Bureau of Agricultural Economics] - Oxford, England - *CompReadDB 82*
Rural Electric Missourian - Jefferson City, MO - *MagDir 84*
Rural Electric Nebraskan - Lincoln, NE - *BaconPubCkMag 84; MagDir 84*
Rural Electrification - Washington, DC - *BaconPubCkMag 84; MagDir 84*
Rural Extension, Education & Training Abstracts [of Commonwealth Bureau of Agricultural Economics] - Oxford, England - *CompReadDB 82*
Rural Georgia - Atlanta, GA - *BaconPubCkMag 84; MagDir 84*
Rural Kentuckian - Louisville, KY - *BaconPubCkMag 84; MagDir 84; WritMar 84*
Rural Living - Richmond, VA - *BaconPubCkMag 84*
Rural Louisiana - Baton Rouge, LA - *BaconPubCkMag 84; MagDir 84*
Rural Minnesota News - Alexandria, MN - *BaconPubCkMag 84; MagDir 84*
Rural Missouri - Jefferson City, MO - *BaconPubCkMag 84*
Rural Missouri Cable TV Inc. - Branson, MO - *BrCabYB 84; Tel&CabFB 84C*
Rural Montana - Great Falls, MT - *BaconPubCkMag 84; WritMar 84*
Rural News, The - Canton, NY - *AyerDirPub 83*
Rural Pennysaver - Conklin, NY - *AyerDirPub 83*
Rural Retreat Cable TV Inc. - Rural Retreat, VA - *BrCabYB 84; Tel&CabFB 84C*
Rural Route, The - Grande Prairie, AB, Canada - *Ed&PubIntYB 82*
Rural Satellite Program [of Agency for International Development] - Washington, DC - *TeleSy&SerDir 2-84*
Rural Sociology - Lexington, KY - *MagDir 84*
Rural Telephone Cooperative Inc. - Dalhart, TX - *TelDir&BG 83-84*
Rural Telephone Service Co. Inc. - Lenora, KS - *TelDir&BG 83-84*
Rural Television Cable - Greenwood, NY - *BrCabYB 84*
Rural-Urban Record - Columbia Station, OH - *AyerDirPub 83; Ed&PubIntYB 82*
Rural Video Corp. - Belfast, NY - *BrCabYB 84; Tel&CabFB 84C*
Rural Virginian - Charlottesville, VA - *AyerDirPub 83*
Ruralife - Mason City, IA - *BaconPubCkMag 84*
Ruralite - Forest Grove, OR - *BaconPubCkMag 84; MagDir 84; WritMar 84*
Rusco Electronic Systems - Glendale, CA - *DataDirSup 7-83*
Rush Associates Inc., James E. - Powell, OH - *EISS 83*
Rush Associates, James - New York, NY - *StaDirAdAg 2-84*
Rush City East Central Minnesota Post-Review - North Branch, MN - *BaconPubCkNews 84*
Rush County News - La Crosse, KS - *AyerDirPub 83; Ed&PubIntYB 82*
Rush Springs Cable Television Inc. - Rush Springs, OK - *BrCabYB 84; Tel&CabFB 84C*
Rush Springs Gazette - Rush Springs, OK - *BaconPubCkNews 84; Ed&PubIntYB 82*
Rush Street Records - Chicago, IL - *BillIntBG 83-84*
Rushford Tri-County Record - Rushford, MN - *BaconPubCkNews 84*
Rushlight Club - Talcottville, CT - *BoPubDir 4, 5*
Rushmore Micro Systems - Rapid City, SD - *MicrocomSwDir 1*
Rushville Cable TV [of Connersville Cable TV Inc.] - Rushville, IN - *BrCabYB 84*
Rushville Republican - Rushville, IN - *BaconPubCkNews 84; Ed&PubIntYB 82; NewsDir 84*
Rushville Sheridan County Star - Rushville, NE - *BaconPubCkNews 84*
Rushville Telegram - Rushville, IN - *BaconPubCkNews 84*
Rushville Times - Rushville, IL - *BaconPubCkNews 84; Ed&PubIntYB 82; NewsDir 84*
RUSI Journal [of Royal United Services Institute for Defence Studies] - Whitehall, England - *WritMar 84*
Rusk Cherokeean - Rusk, TX - *BaconPubCkNews 84; BrCabYB 84*
Ruskin Shopper & Observer News - Ruskin, FL - *NewsDir 84*
Russell Advertising Co., The - Huntington, NY - *StaDirAdAg 2-84*
Russell & Volkening Inc. - New York, NY - *LitMarPl 83, 84*
Russell Banner - Russell, MB, Canada - *Ed&PubIntYB 82*
Russell County News - Jamestown, KY - *AyerDirPub 83; Ed&PubIntYB 82*
Russell Daily News - Russell, KS - *BaconPubCkNews 84; Ed&PubIntYB 82; NewsDir 84*
Russell, E. T. - Saskatoon, SK, Canada - *BoPubDir 4 Sup, 5*
Russell-Manning Productions - Minneapolis, MN - *AvMarPl 83*
Russell Marketing Research Inc. - New York, NY - *IntDirMarRes 83; Tel&CabFB 84C*
Russell, Martin - Yonkers, NY - *LitMarPl 84*
Russell Press - Nottingham, England - *LitMag&SmPr 83-84*
Russell Publications - Peotone, IL - *BaconPubCkNews 84*
Russell Record - Russell, KS - *BaconPubCkNews 84; Ed&PubIntYB 82; NewsDir 84*
Russell Records Inc. - Ventura, CA - *BillIntBG 83-84*
Russell Sage Foundation - New York, NY - *LitMarPl 83, 84*
Russell Springs Times Journal - Russell Springs, KY - *BaconPubCkNews 84; NewsDir 84*
Russell Wilks Associates Ltd. - *See* Doremus & Co. Public Relations
Russells Guides Inc. - Cedar Rapids, IA - *BoPubDir 5*
Russells Point Cablevision Inc. [of Intertie Inc.] - Russells Point, OH - *BrCabYB 84*
Russellville Courier Democrat - Russellville, AR - *BaconPubCkNews 84*

Russellville Franklin County Times - Russellville, AL - *BaconPubCkNews 84*
Russellville Logan Leader - Russellville, KY - *NewsDir 84*
Russellville Logan Leader - *See* Smith Communications Inc., Al
Russellville News Democrat [of Russellville Logan Ink Inc.] - Russellville, KY - *Ed&PubIntYB 82; NewsDir 84*
Russellville News Democrat - *See* Smith Communications Inc., Al
Russian Hill House Books - San Francisco, CA - *BoPubDir 4 Sup, 5*
Russian House Translation Services - Monterey, CA - *LitMarPl 83, 84*
Russian Life - San Francisco, CA - *AyerDirPub 83; Ed&PubIntYB 82; NewsDir 84*
Russian Literature Triquarterly [of Ardis] - Ann Arbor, MI - *LitMag&SmPr 83-84*
Russian Review - Stanford, CA - *BoPubDir 4*
Russian Review - Cambridge, MA - *BoPubDir 5*
Russian River News - Guerneville, CA - *AyerDirPub 83; Ed&PubIntYB 82*
Russica Publishers [Aff. of Russica Book & Art Shop Inc.] - New York, NY - *BoPubDir 4, 5; WritMar 84*
Russky Golos - New York, NY - *Ed&PubIntYB 82; NewsDir 84*
Russo Photographic Services Corp. - New York, NY - *LitMarPl 83*
Russom & Leeper - San Francisco, CA - *DirPRFirms 83; StaDirAdAg 2-84*
Russoniello Advertising, L. L. - Scranton, PA - *StaDirAdAg 2-84*
Rust Communications Group - Leesburg, VA - *BrCabYB 84*
Rust Enterprises Inc. - *See* Laurie Publishing Group
Rusten, Shelly - New York, NY - *LitMarPl 83, 84; MagIndMarPl 82-83*
Rusting Associates Inc., Robert - Washington, DC - *DirPRFirms 83*
Rustler - King City, CA - *AyerDirPub 83; Ed&PubIntYB 82*
Rustler - Scribner, NE - *AyerDirPub 83*
Rustler - Riesel, TX - *AyerDirPub 83*
Ruston Leader - Ruston, LA - *BaconPubCkNews 84; NewsDir 84*
Ruston Seemore TV Inc. - Ruston, LA - *BrCabYB 84; Tel&CabFB 84C*
Rustron Music Productions - White Plains, NY - *BillIntBG 83-84*
Rutan Publishing & Research Inc. - Minneapolis, MN - *BoPubDir 4 Sup, 5*
Rutgers University (Center of Alcohol Studies) - New Brunswick, NJ - *BoPubDir 4, 5; CompReadDB 82*
Rutgers University (Graduate School of Social Work) - New Brunswick, NJ - *BoPubDir 4 Sup, 5*
Rutgers University (Institute of Management & Labor Relations) - New Brunswick, NJ - *BoPubDir 4, 5*
Rutgers University Press - New Brunswick, NJ - *LitMarPl 83, 84; WritMar 84*
Ruth Cablevision [of Helicon Corp.] - Brownsville, PA - *BrCabYB 84; Tel&CabFB 84C*
Ruth Cablevision [of Helicon Corp.] - Clarksville, PA - *BrCabYB 84*
Ruth Cablevision [of Helicon Corp.] - Dawson, PA - *Tel&CabFB 84C*
Ruth Cablevision [of Helicon Corp.] - Smithfield, PA - *BrCabYB 84*
Ruth Cablevision [of Helicon Corp.] - Uniontown, PA - *BrCabYB 84*
Ruther & Associates Inc., James E. - Chicago, IL - *StaDirAdAg 2-84*
Rutherford Cablevision [of Daniels & Associates Inc.] - Forest City, NC - *BrCabYB 84*
Rutherford County Cable TV Inc. [of Matrix Enterprises Inc.] - Smyrna, TN - *BrCabYB 84; Tel&CabFB 84C*
Rutherford County News & Enterprise [of Mid-South Management Co. Inc.] - Rutherfordton, NC - *AyerDirPub 83; Ed&PubIntYB 82; NewsDir 84*
Rutherford Courier - Smyrna, TN - *AyerDirPub 83; Ed&PubIntYB 82*
Rutherford News Leader - Lyndhurst, NJ - *AyerDirPub 83*
Rutherford News Leader - *See* Leader Newspapers Inc.
Rutherford South Bergenite - Rutherford, NJ - *BaconPubCkNews 84; NewsDir 84*
Rutherfordton Rutherford County News - Rutherfordton, NC - *BaconPubCkNews 84*
Ruthven Cable TV [of Terril Telephone Co.] - Ruthven, IA - *Tel&CabFB 84C*
Ruthven Telephone Exchange Co. - Ruthven, IA - *TelDir&BG 83-84*
Ruthven Zip Code - Ruthven, IA - *Ed&PubIntYB 82*
Ruthville Cable TV Inc. - Ruthville, ND - *BrCabYB 84; Tel&CabFB 84C*
Rutland Area Shopper - Rutland, VT - *AyerDirPub 83*
Rutland Herald - Rutland, VT - *BaconPubCkNews 84; Ed&PubIntYB 82; LitMarPl 83, 84; NewsDir 84*
Rutledge Co., The - Oshkosh, WI - *StaDirAdAg 2-84*
Rutledge Grainger County News - Rutledge, TN - *BaconPubCkNews 84; NewsDir 84*
Rutledge Press, The - New York, NY - *LitMarPl 83*
Ruttle, Shaw & Wetherill - Philadelphia, PA - *LitMarPl 83, 84*
Ruvane-Leverte [Subs. of Bozell & Jacobs Inc.] - New York, NY - *AdAge 3-28-84; StaDirAdAg 2-84*
Ruxton Associates - New Milford, CT - *TeleSy&SerDir 7-83*
Ruzicka-South Inc., Joseph - Greensboro, NC - *LitMarPl 83, 84*
Ruzicka, Thomas S. - Tinton Falls, NJ - *LitMarPl 83, 84*
RV Aftermarket - Chicago, IL - *MagDir 84*
RV Business - Agoura, CA - *BaconPubCkMag 84*
R.V. Cable TV Inc. - Rock Valley, IA - *BrCabYB 84; Tel&CabFB 84C*
R.V. Cable-Vision Inc. - Harrodsburg, KY - *BrCabYB 84; Tel&CabFB 84C p.1699*
R.V. Cable-Vision Inc. - Lawrenceburg, KY - *BrCabYB 84*
RV Dealer - Chicago, IL - *MagDir 84*
RV News - Agoura, CA - *MagDir 84*
RV Sales & Service News - Chicago, IL - *BaconPubCkMag 84*
RVB - Agoura, CA - *WritMar 84*
RVBusiness - Agoura, CA - *MagDir 84; WritMar 84*
R.V.K. Publishing Co. - Menomonee Falls, WI - *BoPubDir 4, 5*
RV'n On - North Hollywood, CA - *WritMar 84*
RVS Cablevision Corp. - Elm Grove, WI - *InterCabHB 3; Tel&CabFB 84C p.1699*
RVS Cablevision Corp. - Wauwatosa, WI - *BrCabYB 84*
RW Cablevision Inc. [of The Western Co. Inc.] - Ridgecrest, CA - *BrCabYB 84; Tel&CabFB 84C*
RW Records - Woodland Hills, CA - *BillIntBG 83-84*
RW Underground Parachuting Publications - Fullerton, CA - *LitMag&SmPr 83-84*
R.W. Underground Publishing Co. - Fullerton, CA - *BoPubDir 4, 5*
RWB Associates - Tustin, CA - *WhoWMicrocom 83*
RWK Ltd. - Rio de Janeiro, Brazil - *EISS 5-84 Sup*
RX Home Care [of Brentwood Publishing Corp.] - Los Angeles, CA - *ArtMar 84; BaconPubCkMag 84; MagDir 84; MagIndMarPl 82-83; WritMar 84*
Ryan Advertising & Public Relations - Albany, OR - *DirPRFirms 83*
Ryan & Adams Inc. - New York, NY - *StaDirAdAg 2-84*
Ryan & Boerner Associates Inc. - Mineola, NY - *StaDirAdAg 2-84*
Ryan Associates Inc., Charles - Charleston, WV - *DirPRFirms 83*
Ryan/Hutchins Advertising & Public Relations [Div. of Ryan Communications] - Albany, OR - *StaDirAdAg 2-84*
Ryan Inc., Philip G. - New York, NY - *DirPRFirms 83*
Ryan, Joseph A. - Hingham, MA - *CabTVFinDB 83*
Ryan Leader - Ryan, OK - *BaconPubCkNews 84; Ed&PubIntYB 82*
Ryan Market Research Inc. - Ridgefield, CT - *IntDirMarRes 83*
Ryan-McFarland Corp. - Aptos, CA - *MicrocomMPl 83; MicrocomSwDir 1*
Ryan-McFarland Corp. - Rolling Hills Estates, CA - *ADAPSOMemDir 83-84*
Ryan-McFarland Corp. - Round Rock, TX - *WhoWMicrocom 83*
Ryan-McFarland Corp. (Language Products) - Aptos, CA - *WhoWMicrocom 83*
Ryan-McFarland Corp. (Software Products) - Aptos, CA - *WhoWMicrocom 83*
Ryan Publishing Enterprises Inc., Regina - New York, NY - *LitMarPl 83, 84*
Ryan, Redden & McGrath Inc. - Scarsdale, NY - *IntDirMarRes 83*
Ryan/Uniphoto, David - San Francisco, CA - *AvMarPl 83*
Ryan-Williams Inc. - New York, NY - *StaDirAdAg 2-84*

Ryder & Schild Inc. - Miami, FL - *StaDirAdAg 2-84*
Ryder Enterprises Inc., Red - Tampa, FL - *Tel&CabFB 84C*
Ryder Press - Shaker Heights, OH - *BoPubDir 4, 5*
Ryder, Trey - Scottsdale, AZ - *LitMarPl 83, 84*
Rye Big Thicket Messenger - *See* Polk County Publishing
Rye Boy Music - *See* Beserkley
Rye Chronicle - Rye, NY - *BaconPubCkNews 84; Ed&PubIntYB 82; NewsDir 84*
Rye Chronicle & Sound View News - Rye, NY - *AyerDirPub 83*
Rye Greenhorn Valley-News - Rye, CO - *BaconPubCkNews 84*
Rye Telephone Co. Inc. - Colorado City, CO - *TelDir&BG 83-84*
Ryen Associates, Richard R. - Oradell, NJ - *LitMarPl 83, 84*
Ryerson Polytechnical Institute (Nutrition Information Service) - Toronto, ON, Canada - *BoPubDir 4 Sup, 5*
Ryffel Associates, David J. - Fairfield, CT - *StaDirAdAg 2-84*
Rymer Books - Tollhouse, CA - *BoPubDir 4, 5*
Rynders Publications, B. - New Brighton, MN - *BoPubDir 4, 5*
Rystl Electronics Corp. - North Miami Beach, FL - *AvMarPl 83*
Ryter Advertising - Minneapolis, MN - *DirMarMP 83*

S

S & A Publications - Champaign, IL - *BoPubDir 4, 5*
S. & A. Telephone Co. Inc. - Allen, KS - *TelDir&BG 83-84*
S & FA Reporting Services Inc. - Washington, DC - *EISS 7-83 Sup*
S & G Cablevision - Town Creek, AL - *Tel&CabFB 84C*
S & G Cablevision - Iuka, MS - *Tel&CabFB 84C p.1699*
S & H Consumer Group [Subs. of Sudley & Hennessey Inc.] - New York, NY - *BrCabYB 84*
S & H Software - Harrington Park, NJ - *MicrocomMPl 84; MicrocomSwDir 1*
S & H Software - Manvel, ND - *WhoWMicrocom 83*
S & J Music Publishing Corp. - *See* Laurie Publishing Group
S & K TV Systems [of Scott & Krenz TV Systems] - Stanley, WI - *Tel&CabFB 84C*
S & K Video - Los Angeles, CA - *Tel&CabFB 84C*
S & M Systems Inc. - Haverhill, MA - *MicrocomMPl 83; MicrocomSwDir 1; WhoWMicrocom 83*
S & O Consultants Inc. - San Francisco, CA - *HBIndAd&MS 82-83*
S & P MarketScope [of Standard & Poor's Corp.] - New York, NY - *DataDirOnSer 84; DirOnDB Spring 84*
S & R Music Publishing Co. - Rancho Mirage, CA - *BillIntBG 83-84*
S & S Cable TV - Covington, LA - *BrCabYB 84*
S & S Co., The - Addison, IL - *MicrocomMPl 84*
S & S Press - Austin, TX - *BoPubDir 4, 5; LitMag&SmPr 83-84*
S & S Public Relations Inc. - Chicago, IL - *DirPRFirms 83*
S & S Services Inc. - Arnett, WV - *BrCabYB 84; Tel&CabFB 84C*
S & T Associates - Los Angeles, CA - *MicrocomMPl 84*
S. & T. Telephone Cooperative Association, The - Brewster, KS - *TelDir&BG 83-84*
S-C Software Corp. - Dallas, TX - *MicrocomMPl 84; WhoWMicrocom 83*
S Gaugian - River Forest, IL - *BaconPubCkMag 84; MagDir 84*
S/T Videocassette Duplicating Corp. - Leonia, NJ - *AvMarPl 83*
S-Tab Inc. - New York, NY - *IntDirMarRes 83*
S3C - *See* Souham Group of Communications Cos., Gerard
S-W Enterprises - Lakewood, OH - *BoPubDir 4 Sup, 5; LitMag&SmPr 83-84*
SA Films Inc. - Spring Valley, NY - *AvMarPl 83*
S.A. Press Cutting Agency Pty. Ltd. - Durban, South Africa - *ProGuPRSer 4*
SAA Publishing - Ann Arbor, MI - *BoPubDir 4 Sup, 5*
Saab Club - Duluth, MN - *ArtMar 84*
Saanich Cablevision Ltd. - Sidney, BC, Canada - *BrCabYB 84*
SAAS Advertising Inc. - New York, NY - *StaDirAdAg 2-84*
Saatchi & Saatchi Compton Worldwide - New York, NY - *AdAge 3-28-84; StaDirAdAg 2-84*
Saatchi & Saatchi Compton Worldwide - London, England - *AdAge 6-25-84*
Sabadell Computing Center - Barcelona, Spain - *EISS 83*
Saber Communications International - Irvine, CA - *DirPRFirms 83*
Sabetha Cable TV Systems Inc. [of Texkan Communications Inc.] - Sabetha, KS - *Tel&CabFB 84C*
Sabetha Herald - Sabetha, KS - *BaconPubCkNews 84; Ed&PubIntYB 82*
Sabetha-Seneca Cable TV - Seneca, KS - *BrCabYB 84*
Sabinal Times - Sabinal, TX - *AyerDirPub 83; Ed&PubIntYB 82*
Sabinal Times - *See* Associated Texas Newspapers Inc.
Sabinal TV Cable Co. - Sabinal, TX - *BrCabYB 84; Tel&CabFB 84C*
Sabine Cable TV - Pineland, TX - *BrCabYB 84; Tel&CabFB 84C*
Sabine Cable TV Co. - Hemphill, TX - *BrCabYB 84; Tel&CabFB 84C*
Sabine County Reporter - Hemphill, TX - *AyerDirPub 83; Ed&PubIntYB 82*
Sabine Index - Many, LA - *AyerDirPub 83; Ed&PubIntYB 82; NewsDir 84*
Sabine News, The - Many, LA - *Ed&PubIntYB 82*
Sabteca Music Co. - Oakland, CA - *BillIntBG 83-84*
Sac City County Star - Sac City, IA - *BaconPubCkNews 84*
Sac City Sun - Sac City, IA - *BaconPubCkNews 84*
Sac County Mutual Telephone Co. - Odebolt, IA - *TelDir&BG 83-84*
Sac County Star - Sac City, IA - *AyerDirPub 83; Ed&PubIntYB 82*
Sac Sun - Sac City, IA - *AyerDirPub 83; Ed&PubIntYB 82*
Sacco Inc., Joe - New York, NY - *HBIndAd&MS 82-83*
Sachem Press - Old Chatham, NY - *BoPubDir 4 Sup, 5; LitMag&SmPr 83-84*
Sachem Publishing Associates Inc. - Guilford, CT - *LitMarPl 83, 84*
Sachs & Associates Inc., S. M. - New York, NY - *AdAge 3-28-84; StaDirAdAg 2-84*
Sack-Sons Carton Co. Inc. - Ridgewood, NY - *LitMarPl 83, 84*
Sackbut Press - Milwaukee, WI - *BoPubDir 5; LitMag&SmPr 83-84*
Sackett Publications - Grants Pass, OR - *BoPubDir 4, 5*
Sackett, Richard - New Orleans, LA - *StaDirAdAg 2-84*
Sacks & Rosen - New York, NY - *AdAge 3-28-84; StaDirAdAg 2-84*
Sackville Tribune Post, The - Sackville, NB, Canada - *Ed&PubIntYB 82*
Saco/Lowey Inc. - White Plains, NY - *AvMarPl 83*
Saco River Communications Corp. - Buxton, ME - *BrCabYB 84*
Saco River Telegraph & Telephone Co. - Bar Mills, ME - *TelDir&BG 83-84*
Sacramento Bee [of McClatchy Newspapers] - Sacramento, CA - *BaconPubCkNews 84; DirOnDB Spring 84; Ed&PubIntYB 82; LitMarPl 83, 84; NewsBur 6; NewsDir 84*
Sacramento Catholic Herald - Sacramento, CA - *NewsDir 84*
Sacramento Magazine - Sacramento, CA - *ArtMar 84; BaconPubCkMag 84; MagDir 84; MagIndMarPl 82-83; WritMar 84*
Sacramento Microband Inc. - Stockton, CA - *Tel&CabFB 84C*

Sacramento Observer - Sacramento, CA - *BaconPubCkNews 84; NewsDir 84*
Sacramento Suburban - Fair Oaks, CA - *NewsDir 84*
Sacramento Suburban, The - Sacramento, CA - *Ed&PubIntYB 82*
Sacramento/The Happening - Sacramento, CA - *BaconPubCkNews 84*
Sacramento Union [of Richard Scaife Co.] - Sacramento, CA - *AyerDirPub 83; BaconPubCkNews 84; Ed&PubIntYB 82; LitMarPl 83, 84; NewsBur 6; NewsDir 84*
Sacramento Valley Cable TV [of Mickelson Media Inc.] - Dixon, CA - *BrCabYB 84*
Sacramento Valley Union Labor Bulletin - Sacramento, CA - *NewsDir 84*
Sacred Heart News - Sacred Heart, MN - *BaconPubCkNews 84; Ed&PubIntYB 82*
Sacred Heart Program Inc. - St. Louis, MO - *Tel&CabFB 84C*
Sacred Heart Telephone - Sacred Heart, MN - *TelDir&BG 83-84*
Sacred Music Press - *See* Lorenz Creative Services
Sacred Selections Inc. - Kendallville, IN - *BoPubDir 4, 5*
Saddle & Bridle - St. Louis, MO - *BaconPubCkMag 84; MagDir 84; MagIndMarPl 82-83*
Saddle Horse Report - Shelbyville, TN - *BaconPubCkMag 84*
Saddleback Valley News [of Golden West Publishing Inc.] - Mission Viejo, CA - *NewsDir 84*
Saddleback Valley News - Saddleback Valley, CA - *Ed&PubIntYB 82*
Saddleback Valley News - San Juan Capistrano, CA - *AyerDirPub 83*
Saddleback Valley Vaguero - Tustin, CA - *AyerDirPub 83*
Saddlebrook Corp. - Cambridge, MA - *DataDirSup 7-83*
Saddler Engineers & Consultants - Altadena, CA - *MicrocomMPl 84*
Sader & Ackerman - New York, NY - *AdAge 3-28-84; DirMarMP 83; StaDirAdAg 2-84*
Sadler & Co., John M. - Massapequa, NY - *BoPubDir 4, 5*
Sadler Recording Studio Inc. - New York, NY - *AvMarPl 83*
Sadlier Inc., William H. - New York, NY - *ArtMar 84; LitMarPl 83, 84*
Sadlier-Oxford [Div. of William H. Sadlier Inc.] - New York, NY - *LitMarPl 83, 84*
Sadowsky & Associates, Horace - Long Island, NY - *ArtMar 84*
Sadowsky & Associates Inc., Horace - Hicksville, NY - *StaDirAdAg 2-84*
Sadtler Research Laboratories [Aff. of Bio-Rad Laboratories Inc.] - Philadelphia, PA - *BoPubDir 4, 5; InfIndMarPl 83*
Sadtler Standard & Commercial Spectra [of Sadtler Research Laboratories Inc.] - Philadelphia, PA - *EISS 83*
SAE - Warrendale, PA - *LitMarPl 84*
SAE Abstracts [of Society of Automotive Engineers Inc.] - Warrendale, PA - *DataDirOnSer 84; DirOnDB Spring 84; OnBibDB 3*
S.A.E. de Relaciones Publicas - Barcelona, Spain - *DirPRFirms 83*
Safari Magazine - Tucson, AZ - *BaconPubCkMag 84; MagDir 84*
Safe Access to Files of Estate [of Howrex Corp.] - Moorestown, NJ - *EISS 5-84 Sup*
Safe Computing Ltd. - Leicester, England - *MicrocomSwDir 1*
Safeguard Business Systems Inc. - Ft. Washington, PA - *ADAPSOMemDir 83-84*
Safelink [of Western Union Telegraph Co.] - McLean, VA - *TeleSy&SerDir 2-84*
Safety [of SDC Information Systems] - Santa Monica, CA - *DataDirOnSer 84*
Safety [of Cambridge Scientific Abstracts] - Bethesda, MD - *DBBus 82*
Safety Harbor Herald - Safety Harbor, FL - *AyerDirPub 83; Ed&PubIntYB 82*
Safety Harbor Herald [of The Tarpon Springs Herald Newspapers] - Tarpon Springs, FL - *NewsDir 84*
Safety Harbor Herald - *See* Pinellas Publishers Inc.
Safety Journal - Anderson, SC - *BaconPubCkMag 84; MagDir 84*
Safety Net - Ft. Lauderdale, FL - *BillIntBG 83-84*
Safety Now Co. Inc. [Aff. of Ft. Belknap Genealogical Association] - Jenkintown, PA - *BoPubDir 4, 5*
Safety Science Abstracts [of Cambridge Scientific Abstracts] - Bethesda, MD - *EISS 83*
Safety Science Abstracts Journal [of Cambridge Scientific Abstracts] - Bethesda, MD - *CompReadDB 82; OnBibDB 3*
Saffer, Cravit & Freedman Advertising Inc. - Toronto, ON, Canada - *StaDirAdAg 2-84*
Safford Eastern Arizona Courier - Safford, AZ - *BaconPubCkNews 84*
Safier Inc., Gloria - New York, NY - *LitMarPl 83, 84*
Safmar Publishing Co. - Mooresville, NC - *BillIntBG 83-84*
SAFT America - St. Paul, MN - *MicrocomMPl 84*
Sag Harbor Express - Sag Harbor, NY - *BaconPubCkNews 84; Ed&PubIntYB 82*
Saga - Paris, France - *DirOnDB Spring 84*
Saga Books [Aff. of Ft. Belknap Genealogical Association] - Graham, TX - *BoPubDir 4 Sup, 5*
Saga Magazine - New York, NY - *MagDir 84; MagIndMarPl 82-83*
Sagalyn Inc., Raphael - Washington, DC - *LitMarPl 83, 84*
Sagamore Hill Music Inc. - *See* Lipservices
Sagamore Press - Terre Haute, IN - *BoPubDir 4, 5*
Sage Advertising - Helena, MT - *StaDirAdAg 2-84*
Sage Advertising/Billings - Billings, MT - *ArtMar 84*
Sage Computer Technology - Reno, NV - *WhoWMicrocom 83*
Sage Press - New York, NY - *LitMag&SmPr 83-84*
Sage Publications Inc. - Beverly Hills, CA - *LitMarPl 83, 84; MagIndMarPl 82-83*
Sage Software - Berkeley, CA - *MicrocomMPl 84*
Sage Surveys Inc. - Port Washington, NY - *IntDirMarRes 83*
Sage Systems Software Products Inc. - Bethesda, MD - *ADAPSOMemDir 83-84*
Sagebrush [of Associated Students, University of Nevada] - Reno, NV - *NewsDir 84*
Sagebrush Press - Morongo Valley, CA - *BoPubDir 4 Sup, 5*
Sager Associates Inc. - Sarasota, FL - *ArtMar 84*
Sager Associates Inc., Arthur - Topsfield, MA - *ProGuPRSer 4*
Sagetrieb [of National Poetry Foundation] - Orono, ME - *LitMag&SmPr 83-84*
Saginaw Catholic Weekly, The - Saginaw, MI - *NewsDir 84*
Saginaw Courier - *See* Saginaw Valley News Inc.
Saginaw News [of Booth Newspapers Inc.] - Saginaw, MI - *BaconPubCkNews 84; Ed&PubIntYB 82; NewsDir 84*
Saginaw Northwest Sentinel - Saginaw, TX - *BaconPubCkNews 84*
Saginaw Press - Saginaw, MI - *BaconPubCkNews 84; Ed&PubIntYB 82*
Saginaw Township Times - Saginaw, MI - *BaconPubCkNews 84; NewsDir 84*
Saginaw Valley News - Chesaning, MI - *BaconPubCkNews 84; Ed&PubIntYB 82*
Saginaw Valley State College (Green River Press) - University Center, MI - *BoPubDir 4, 5*
Sagittar Records - Dallas, TX - *BillIntBG 83-84*
Sagittarius Publications - Oneroa, New Zealand - *LitMag&SmPr 83-84*
Sagittarius Rising - Arlington, MA - *LitMag&SmPr 83-84*
Sagittarius Rising Publishing Co. - Arlington, MA - *BoPubDir 4, 5*
Saguache Crescent - Saguache, CO - *BaconPubCkNews 84; Ed&PubIntYB 82*
Saguaro Cable Communications Inc. [of Jones Intercable Inc.] - Tucson, AZ - *Tel&CabFB 84C*
Saguaro Software - Tucson, AZ - *WhoWMicrocom 83*
Sahagian & Associates Inc. - Oak Park, IL - *StaDirAdAg 2-84*
SAI Group Inc. - Cherry Hill, NJ - *ArtMar 84*
Saifman, Richards & Associates - Beachwood, OH - *StaDirAdAg 2-84*
S.A.I.L. - Scottsdale, AZ - *MicrocomMPl 83*
Sail - Boston, MA - *ArtMar 84; BaconPubCkMag 84; MagDir 84; MagIndMarPl 82-83; WritMar 84*
Sail Books [Div. of Sail Publishers Inc.] - Boston, MA - *LitMarPl 83, 84; WritMar 84*
Sail Publications Inc. - Boston, MA - *MagIndMarPl 82-83*
S.A.I.L. Systems - Mesa, AZ - *MicrocomMPl 84*
Sailboard News [of Sports Ink Magazines Inc.] - Fair Haven, VT - *MagIndMarPl 82-83; WritMar 84*
Sailboat & Equipment Directory - Boston, MA - *MagDir 84*
Sailing - Port Washington, WI - *ArtMar 84; BaconPubCkMag 84; MagDir 84; MagIndMarPl 82-83; WritMar 84*

Sailors' Gazette [of Coastal Communicators of St. Petersburg Inc.] - St. Petersburg, FL - *BaconPubCkMag 84; MagDir 84; WritMar 84*
Saipan Cable TV System - Saipan, CM - *Tel&CabFB 84C*
Sakamoto Co., R. K. - Albertson, NY - *MagIndMarPl 82-83*
Sakonnet Times - Portsmouth, RI - *AyerDirPub 83; Ed&PubIntYB 82*
S.A.L. Cable Communications Inc. - Melville, NY - *CabTVFinDB 83*
Sal Magundi Enterprises - Portland, OR - *LitMag&SmPr 83-84*
Salamanca Cable Television Inc. - Highland Falls, NY - *BrCabYB 84*
Salamanca CATV Associates [of Simmons Communications Inc.] - Salamanca, NY - *Tel&CabFB 84C*
Salamanca Press - Salamanca, NY - *Ed&PubIntYB 82; NewsDir 84*
Salamanca Republican-Press - Salamanca, NY - *AyerDirPub 83; BaconPubCkNews 84*
Salant, Michael A. - Washington, DC - *BoPubDir 4 Sup, 5*
Salarcon Inc. - Ann Arbor, MI - *BoPubDir 4 Sup*
Salary Gross-Ups 1983-1984 - Greenwich, CT - *DirOnDB Spring 84*
Salay Productions, Richard E. - Southfield, MI - *Tel&CabFB 84C*
Sale Comunication Services, Lillian - Los Angeles, CA - *DirMarMP 83*
Salem Cable TV [of Booth American Co.] - Salem, VA - *BrCabYB 84; Tel&CabFB 84C*
Salem Cable TV Co. Inc. [of Flora Cable TV Co.] - Salem, IL - *BrCabYB 84; Tel&CabFB 84C*
Salem Cablevision Inc. [of Tele-Communications Inc.] - Salem, IN - *BrCabYB 84; Tel&CabFB 84C*
Salem Democrat [of Salem Leader Publishing Co.] - Salem, IN - *AyerDirPub 83; Ed&PubIntYB 82; NewsDir 84*
Salem Democrat - *See* Leader Publishing Co.
Salem Evening News - Salem, MA - *BaconPubCkNews 84; Ed&PubIntYB 82; LitMarPl 83, 84; NewsDir 84*
Salem Farm & Dairy - Salem, OH - *NewsDir 84*
Salem Headlight - Salem, AR - *Ed&PubIntYB 82; NewsDir 84*
Salem House - Salem, NH - *LitMarPl 84*
Salem Leader - Salem, IN - *AyerDirPub 83; Ed&PubIntYB 82; NewsDir 84*
Salem Leader - *See* Leader Publishing Co.
Salem News - Salem, AR - *BaconPubCkNews 84*
Salem News - Salem, MO - *BaconPubCkNews 84; Ed&PubIntYB 82; NewsDir 84*
Salem News [of Thomson Newspapers] - Salem, OH - *BaconPubCkNews 84; Ed&PubIntYB 82; NewsDir 84*
Salem Observer - Salem, NH - *BaconPubCkNews 84; Ed&PubIntYB 82; NewsDir 84*
Salem Oregon Statesman - Salem, OR - *NewsDir 84*
Salem Press Inc. - Englewood Cliffs, NJ - *LitMarPl 84*
Salem Press Inc. - Ft. Lee, NJ - *LitMarPl 83*
Salem Press, The - Salem, MO - *NewsDir 84*
Salem Services - Tornwood, NY - *IntDirMarRes 83*
Salem Special - Salem, SD - *BaconPubCkNews 84*
Salem Telephone Co. Inc. - Salem, KY - *TelDir&BG 83-84*
Salem Times Commoner - Salem, IL - *BaconPubCkNews 84; Ed&PubIntYB 82; NewsDir 84*
Salem Times-Register - Salem, VA - *AyerDirPub 83; BaconPubCkNews 84; Ed&PubIntYB 82; NewsDir 84*
Salem Today's Sunbeam - Salem, NJ - *NewsDir 84*
Salem Tri County Record - Salem, AR - *BaconPubCkNews 84*
Salemson, Harold J. - Glen Cove, NY - *LitMarPl 83, 84; MagIndMarPl 82-83*
Salenger Educational Media - Santa Monica, CA - *AvMarPl 83*
Salerno, Al - Ho-Ho-Kus, NJ - *LitMarPl 83, 84*
Sales & Marketing Briefs - Rockford, IL - *BaconPubCkMag 84*
Sales & Marketing Management [Aff. of Bill Communications] - New York, NY - *ArtMar 84; BaconPubCkMag 84; BoPubDir 4 Sup, 5; Folio 83; LitMarPl 83, 84; MagDir 84; MagIndMarPl 82-83*
Sales & Marketing Management in Canada [of Ingmar Communications Ltd.] - Toronto, ON, Canada - *BaconPubCkMag 84; WritMar 84*
Sales Book Club [of Prentice-Hall Inc.] - Englewood, NJ - *LitMarPl 83, 84*
Sales Builders Div. [of Sales & Marketing Management Magazine] - New York, NY - *DirMarMP 83*
Sales Catalog Index Project Input On-Line [of Art Institute of Chicago] - Chicago, IL - *EISS 83*
Sales Executive, The - New York, NY - *BaconPubCkMag 84; MagDir 84; MagIndMarPl 82-83*
Sales Letters Inc. [Subs. of ALCO Industries] - New York, NY - *LitMarPl 83, 84*
Sales Manager's Bulletin - Waterford, CT - *WritMar 84*
Salesman's Guide Inc., The - New York, NY - *DirMarMP 83; LitMarPl 83, 84*
Salesman's Opportunity - Chicago, IL - *ArtMar 84; DirMarMP 83; MagIndMarPl 82-83; WritMar 84*
Salesmanship & Foremanship [of Dartnell Corp.] - Chicago, IL - *ArtMar 84*
Salgo Research Inc., L. H. - Great Neck, NY - *IntDirMarRes 83*
Salida Cable TV [of Community Tele-Communications Inc.] - Salida, CO - *BrCabYB 84; Tel&CabFB 84C*
Salida Mountain Mail [of Arkansas Valley Publishing Co.] - Salida, CO - *NewsDir 84*
Salina Cable TV System Inc. [of Communications Services Inc.] - Kingman, KS - *BrCabYB 84; Tel&CabFB 84C*
Salina Cable TV System Inc. [of Communications Services Inc.] - Salina, KS - *BrCabYB 84; Tel&CabFB 84C*
Salina Journal - Salina, KS - *BaconPubCkNews 84; Ed&PubIntYB 82; NewsDir 84*
Salina-Spavinaw Telephone Co. Inc. - Salina, OK - *TelDir&BG 83-84*
Salina Sun - Salina, UT - *Ed&PubIntYB 82*
Salina Sun - *See* Richfield Reaper
Salinas Californian - Salinas, CA - *BaconPubCkNews 84; Ed&PubIntYB 82; NewsDir 84*
Salinas North County News - Salinas, CA - *NewsDir 84*
Saline County Cable TV Inc. [of Central Cable Services Inc.] - Slater, MO - *Tel&CabFB 84C*
Saline Reporter - Saline, MI - *BaconPubCkNews 84; Ed&PubIntYB 82; NewsDir 84*
Salisbury & Salisbury - New York, NY - *AvMarPl 83*
Salisbury Evening Post - Salisbury, NC - *Ed&PubIntYB 82; NewsDir 84*
Salisbury News & Advertiser [of Independent Newspapers Inc.] - Salisbury, MD - *BaconPubCkNews 84; Ed&PubIntYB 82; NewsDir 84*
Salisbury Post - Salisbury, NC - *BaconPubCkNews 84*
Salisbury Press-Spectator - Salisbury, MO - *BaconPubCkNews 84; Ed&PubIntYB 82*
Salisbury Sunday Post - Salisbury, NC - *Ed&PubIntYB 82*
Salisbury Times [of Thomson Newspapers Inc.] - Salisbury, MD - *BaconPubCkNews 84; NewsDir 84*
Salit & Associates Inc., Murray - New York, NY - *AdAge 3-28-84; StaDirAdAg 2-84*
Salle Productions Inc. - Beverly Hills, CA - *AvMarPl 83*
Sallisaw Sequoyah County Times [of Cookson Hills Publishers Inc.] - Sallisaw, OK - *BaconPubCkNews 84; NewsDir 84*
Sally Music Co. - *See* Langley Music Co.
Salmagundi - Saratoga Springs, NY - *MagIndMarPl 82-83*
Salmo Cabled Programmes Ltd. - Salmo, BC, Canada - *BrCabYB 84*
Salmon - Vallejo, CA - *Ed&PubIntYB 82*
Salmon Arm Observer - Salmon Arm, BC, Canada - *Ed&PubIntYB 82*
Salmon Cable TV Inc. - Salmon, ID - *BrCabYB 84; Tel&CabFB 84C*
Salmon Recorder Herald - Salmon, ID - *BaconPubCkNews 84; NewsDir 84*
Salmon River News [of Galamon River News] - Central Square, NY - *NewsDir 84*
Salmon Trout Steelheader - Portland, OR - *BaconPubCkMag 84*
Salome: A Literary Dance Magazine [of Ommation Press] - Chicago, IL - *LitMag&SmPr 83-84*
Salon Economist, The - Salon, IA - *AyerDirPub 83*
Salon, Marrow, Dyckman, Kellman & Trager - New York, NY - *ADAPSOMemDir 83-84*
Salon Publishing Co. - Norborne, MO - *BoPubDir 4, 5*

Salsbury Associates Inc. - New Bern, NC - *MicrocomMPl 84*
Salsoul Music Publishing Corp. - New York, NY - *BillIntBG 83-84*
Salsoul Record Corp. - New York, NY - *BillIntBG 83-84*
Salt Ash Images [of Salt Ash Inn Corp.] - Proctorsville, VT - *Tel&CabFB 84C*
Salt Ash Images - Cavendish, VT - *BrCabYB 84*
Salt Lake City Deseret News - Salt Lake City, UT - *LitMarPl 83; NewsDir 84*
Salt Lake City Sunset News - Bountiful, UT - *BaconPubCkNews 84*
Salt Lake City Tribune - Salt Lake City, UT - *BaconPubCkNews 84; Ed&PubIntYB 82; LitMarPl 83, 84; NewsBur 6; NewsDir 84*
Salt Lake Times - Salt Lake City, UT - *AyerDirPub 83; Ed&PubIntYB 82*
Salt Lick Press - Quincy, IL - *BoPubDir 4*
Salt Lick Press - Austin, TX - *ArtMar 84; BoPubDir 5; LitMag&SmPr 83-84; WritMar 84*
Salt Water Sportsman - Boston, MA - *ArtMar 84; BaconPubCkMag 84; MagDir 84; MagIndMarPl 82-83; WritMar 84*
Salt-Works Press - Vineyard Haven, MA - *BoPubDir 4*
Salt-Works Press - Grenada, MS - *BoPubDir 5; LitMag&SmPr 83-84*
Saltaire Publishing Ltd. - Sidney, BC, Canada - *BoPubDir 4*
Saltaire Publishing Ltd. - Victoria, BC, Canada - *BoPubDir 5*
Salter Research Services Inc. - Phoenix, AZ - *IntDirMarRes 83*
Salter Stations, Russ - Aurora, IL - *BrCabYB 84*
Saltese TV Cable Service - Saltese, MT - *BrCabYB 84; Tel&CabFB 84C*
Salthouse Mining Co. - Milwaukee, WI - *BoPubDir 5; LitMag&SmPr 83-84*
Saltillo-Guntown Cable TV [of Heritage Communications Inc.] - Saltillo, MS - *Tel&CabFB 84C*
Saltillo Telephone Co. [Aff. of United Telecommunications Inc.] - Orbisonia, PA - *TelDir&BG 83-84*
Saltman, David - Wantagh, NY - *MagIndMarPl 82-83*
Saltsburg Press - Saltsburg, PA - *AyerDirPub 83; BaconPubCkNews 84; Ed&PubIntYB 82*
Saltspring Cablevision Ltd. - Ganges, BC, Canada - *BrCabYB 84*
Saltville Cablesystems [of American Cablesystems Corp.] - Saltville, VA - *Tel&CabFB 84C*
Saltville News-Messenger - Saltville, VA - *BaconPubCkNews 84*
Saluda Mountain Telephone Co. - Saluda, NC - *TelDir&BG 83-84*
Saluda Standard Sentinel - Saluda, SC - *BaconPubCkNews 84; NewsDir 84*
Salvage Locator - Whiting, IA - *MagDir 84*
Salvation Army Archives & Research Center - New York, NY - *MicroMarPl 82-83*
Salvation Army Supplies [Aff. of The Salvation Army Southern Territory] - Atlanta, GA - *BoPubDir 4, 5*
Salvation Music - *See* Stanyan Music Co.
Salyer Publishing Co. - Oklahoma City, OK - *BoPubDir 4, 5*
Salyer Radio Co. - Whitesburg, KY - *BrCabYB 84; Tel&CabFB 84C*
Salyers TV Cable - Keyrock, WV - *BrCabYB 84*
Salyersville Independent [of Sandy Valley Press Inc.] - Paintsville, KY - *NewsDir 84*
Salyersville Independent - Salyersville, KY - *BaconPubCkNews 84; Ed&PubIntYB 82*
SAM [of SAM Publications Inc.] - Chicago, IL - *MagDir 84*
Sam Har Press [Aff. of Story House Corp.] - Charlotteville, NY - *BoPubDir 4, 5*
Sam Houston State University (National Employment Listing Service) - Huntsville, TX - *BoPubDir 4, 5*
Sam Record Inc. - Long Island City, NY - *BillIntBG 83-84*
Sam-Vox Music Inc. - *See* President Music Corp.
Samardge Inc., Nick - New York, NY - *LitMarPl 83, 84*
Same Old Music Publishing - Orangevale, CA - *BillIntBG 83-84*
Samfred Music Inc. - *See* Fox Publishing Co. Inc., Sam
SAMI [of Selling Areas-Marketing Inc.] - Chicago, IL - *DBBus 82*
SAMI - New York, NY - *DirOnDB Spring 84; IntDirMarRes 83*
SAMI [of Management Science Associates Inc.] - Pittsburgh, PA - *DataDirOnSer 84*
Samisdat - Richford, VT - *BoPubDir 4, 5; LitMag&SmPr 83-84*
Samisdat Associates - Richford, VT - *LitMag&SmPr 83-84*
Sammamish Data Systems Inc. - Bellevue, WA - *EISS 7-83 Sup*
Sammamish Valley News - Redmond, WA - *AyerDirPub 83; Ed&PubIntYB 82*
Sammis Publishing Corp. - New York, NY - *LitMarPl 84*
Sammons Cable of Ft. Worth [Aff. of Sammons Communications Inc.] - Ft. Worth, TX - *InterCabHB 3*
Sammons Communications Inc. - Moulton, AL - *BrCabYB 84*
Sammons Communications Inc. - Russellville, AL - *BrCabYB 84; Tel&CabFB 84C*
Sammons Communications Inc. - Ceres, CA - *BrCabYB 84; Tel&CabFB 84C*
Sammons Communications Inc. - Glendale, CA - *BrCabYB 84; Tel&CabFB 84C*
Sammons Communications Inc. - La Cresenta, CA - *BrCabYB 84*
Sammons Communications Inc. - Sylmar, CA - *BrCabYB 84*
Sammons Communications Inc. - Turlock, CA - *BrCabYB 84; Tel&CabFB 84C*
Sammons Communications Inc. - Whittier, CA - *BrCabYB 84; Tel&CabFB 84C*
Sammons Communications Inc. - Waterbury, CT - *BrCabYB 84*
Sammons Communications Inc. - Live Oak, FL - *BrCabYB 84; Tel&CabFB 84C*
Sammons Communications Inc. - West Point, GA - *BrCabYB 84*
Sammons Communications Inc. - Logansport, IN - *BrCabYB 84; Tel&CabFB 84C*
Sammons Communications Inc. - Estherville, IA - *Tel&CabFB 84C*
Sammons Communications Inc. - Graettinger, IA - *BrCabYB 84*
Sammons Communications Inc. - Middlesboro, KY - *BrCabYB 84; Tel&CabFB 84C*
Sammons Communications Inc. - Vidalla, LA - *BrCabYB 84*
Sammons Communications Inc. - Brookhaven, MS - *BrCabYB 84; Tel&CabFB 84C*
Sammons Communications Inc. - McComb, MS - *BrCabYB 84; Tel&CabFB 84C*
Sammons Communications Inc. - Natchez, MS - *BrCabYB 84; Tel&CabFB 84C*
Sammons Communications Inc. - Neosho, MO - *BrCabYB 84; Tel&CabFB 84C*
Sammons Communications Inc. - East Hampton, NY - *BrCabYB 84; Tel&CabFB 84C*
Sammons Communications Inc. - Black Mountain, NC - *BrCabYB 84; Tel&CabFB 84C*
Sammons Communications Inc. - Waynesville, NC - *BrCabYB 84; Tel&CabFB 84C*
Sammons Communications Inc. - Clinton, OK - *BrCabYB 84; Tel&CabFB 84C*
Sammons Communications Inc. - Elk City, OK - *BrCabYB 84; Tel&CabFB 84C*
Sammons Communications Inc. - Bristol, TN - *BrCabYB 84; Tel&CabFB 84C*
Sammons Communications Inc. - Elizabethton, TN - *BrCabYB 84*
Sammons Communications Inc. - Johnson City, TN - *Tel&CabFB 84C*
Sammons Communications Inc. - Morristown, TN - *BrCabYB 84; Tel&CabFB 84C*
Sammons Communications Inc. - Newport, TN - *BrCabYB 84; Tel&CabFB 84C*
Sammons Communications Inc. [of Sammons Enterprises Inc.] - Dallas, TX - *AdAge 6-28-84; BrCabYB 84 p.D-306; CabTVFinDB 83; HomeVid&CabYB 82-83; LitMarPl 84; TelAl 83, 84; Tel&CabFB 84C p.1700*
Sammons Communications Inc. - Dumas, TX - *Tel&CabFB 84C*
Sammons Communications of Illinois Inc. - Dwight, IL - *BrCabYB 84; Tel&CabFB 84C*
Sammons Communications of Illinois Inc. [Aff. of Sammons Communications Inc.] - Jacksonville, IL - *BrCabYB 84; InterCabHB 3; Tel&CabFB 84C*
Sammons Communications of Illinois Inc. - Ottawa, IL - *BrCabYB 84; Tel&CabFB 84C*
Sammons Communications of Illinois Inc. - Pontiac, IL - *BrCabYB 84; Tel&CabFB 84C*
Sammons Communications of Illinois Inc. - Streator, IL - *BrCabYB 84; Tel&CabFB 84C*
Sammons Communications of New Jersey Inc. - Dover, NJ - *BrCabYB 84; Tel&CabFB 84C*

Sammons Communications of New Jersey Inc. - Morristown, NJ - *BrCabYB 84*
Sammons Communications of New Jersey Inc. - Pleasantville, NJ - *BrCabYB 84; Tel&CabFB 84C*
Sammons Communications of New York Inc. - Cortland, NY - *BrCabYB 84; Tel&CabFB 84C*
Sammons Communications of New York Inc. - Gloversville, NY - *BrCabYB 84*
Sammons Communications of New York Inc. - Johnstown, NY - *InterCabHB 3*
Sammons Communications of New York Inc. - Penn Yan, NY - *BrCabYB 84; Tel&CabFB 84C*
Sammons Communications of New York Inc. - Wellsville, NY - *BrCabYB 84; Tel&CabFB 84C*
Sammons Communications of Pennsylvania Inc. - Easton, PA - *BrCabYB 84; Tel&CabFB 84C*
Sammons Communications of Pennsylvania Inc. - Emmaus, PA - *BrCabYB 84; Tel&CabFB 84C*
Sammons Communications of Pennsylvania Inc. - Fleetwood, PA - *Tel&CabFB 84C*
Sammons Communications of Pennsylvania Inc. - Harrisburg, PA - *BrCabYB 84; Tel&CabFB 84C*
Sammons Communications of Pennsylvania Inc. - Oil City, PA - *BrCabYB 84; Tel&CabFB 84C*
Sammons Communications of Texas Inc. - Borger, TX - *Tel&CabFB 84C*
Sammons Communications of Texas Inc. - Pampa, TX - *BrCabYB 84; Tel&CabFB 84C*
Sammons Communications of Virginia Inc. - Covington, VA - *BrCabYB 84; Tel&CabFB 84C*
Sammons Communications of Virginia Inc. - Petersburg, VA - *BrCabYB 84; Tel&CabFB 84C*
Sammons Communications of Washington Inc. - Ephrata, WA - *BrCabYB 84; Tel&CabFB 84C*
Sammons Communications of Washington Inc. - Moses Lake, WA - *BrCabYB 84; Tel&CabFB 84C*
Sammons Communications of Washington Inc. - Othello, WA - *BrCabYB 84; Tel&CabFB 84C*
Sammons Enterprises Inc. - Dallas, TX - *KnowInd 83*
Sammons of Benbrook [of Sammons Communications Inc.] - Benbrook, TX - *BrCabYB 84; Tel&CabFB 84C*
Sammons of Ft. Worth [of Sammons Communications Inc.] - Ft. Worth, TX - *BrCabYB 84; Tel&CabFB 84C*
Samostijna Ukraina - Chicago, IL - *Ed&PubIntYB 82; NewsDir 84*
SAMPE Journal - Azusa, CA - *BaconPubCkMag 84*
Sample Case, The [of The Order of United Commercial Travelers of America] - Columbus, OH - *BaconPubCkMag 84; MagIndMarPl 82-83; WritMar 84*
Sample, Joseph S. - *See* Montana Television Network
Sample Survey Centre [of University of Sydney] - Sydney, Australia - *EISS 83*
Sample Surveys Ltd. - London, England - *MicrocomSwDir 1*
Sampler - Dover, DE - *AyerDirPub 83*
Sampler, The - Salem, NJ - *Ed&PubIntYB 82*
Sampson Advertising Co. Inc. - New York, NY - *ArtMar 84; StaDirAdAg 2-84*
Sampson Independent - Clinton, NC - *AyerDirPub 83; BaconPubCkNews 84; Ed&PubIntYB 82*
SAMS - Augusta, GA - *BrCabYB 84*
Sams & Co. Inc., Howard W. [of ITT Publishing] - Indianapolis, IN - *DirOnDB Spring 84; InterCabHB 3; LitMarPl 83, 84; MicrocomMPl 84; WritMar 84*
Samsom Datanet [of Samsom Data Systems] - Alphen aan den Rijn, Netherlands - *EISS 83, 7-83 Sup; InfIndMarPl 83*
Samson Data Systemen BV [Subs. of Wolters Samson Group] - Alphen aan den Rijn, Netherlands - *DataDirOnSer 84*
Samson Graphics - New York, NY - *LitMarPl 83, 84*
Samson International Book Distributors Inc. - Huntington, NY - *LitMarPl 83, 84*
Samson Ledger - Samson, AL - *BaconPubCkNews 84; Ed&PubIntYB 82*
Samsonite Corp. (Contract Furniture Div.) - Denver, CO - *WhoWMicrocom 83*
Samuel Advertising, Douglas - West Caldwell, NJ - *AdAge 3-28-84; StaDirAdAg 2-84*
Samuel Public Relations, Jack - St. Louis, MO - *DirPRFirms 83*
Samuels Advertising Agency Inc., Milton - New York, NY - *StaDirAdAg 2-84*
Samuels Artists & Productions Ltd. - Los Angeles, CA - *AvMarPl 83*
San Andreas Calaveras Prospect - *See* Calaveras Publishing Co.
San Angelo Standard - San Angelo, TX - *BaconPubCkNews 84; LitMarPl 83*
San Angelo Standard Times - San Angelo, TX - *BaconPubCkNews 84; LitMarPl 83; NewsDir 84*
San Angelo Times - San Angelo, TX - *LitMarPl 83*
San Angelo West Texas Angelus - San Angelo, TX - *NewsDir 84*
San Anselmo Publishing Co. - Norman, OK - *BoPubDir 4 Sup, 5*
San Anselmo Ross Valley Reporter - *See* Marin Suburban Newspapers Inc.
San Antonio Area Online Users Group [of University of Texas Health Sciences Center] - San Antonio, TX - *InfIndMarPl 83*
San Antonio Express - San Antonio, TX - *BaconPubCkNews 84; Ed&PubIntYB 82; LitMarPl 84; NewsBur 6; NewsDir 84*
San Antonio Express & News - San Antonio, TX - *Ed&PubIntYB 82; LitMarPl 83, 84*
San Antonio Light [of The Hearst Corp.] - San Antonio, TX - *BaconPubCkNews 84; Ed&PubIntYB 82; LitMarPl 83, 84; NewsBur 6; NewsDir 84*
San Antonio Living - Dallas, TX - *MagIndMarPl 82-83*
San Antonio Living - San Antonio, TX - *MagDir 84*
San Antonio Magazine [of Greater San Antonio Chamber of Commerce] - San Antonio, TX - *ArtMar 84; BaconPubCkMag 84; MagDir 84; WritMar 84*
San Antonio Monthly [of San Antonio Publishing Corp.] - San Antonio, TX - *WritMar 84*
San Antonio News [of Express News Corp.] - San Antonio, TX - *BaconPubCkNews 84; Ed&PubIntYB 82; LitMarPl 84; NewsBur 6; NewsDir 84*
San Antonio North San Antonio Times [of Fisher Publications Inc.] - Alamo Heights, TX - *NewsDir 84*
San Antonio North San Antonio Times - San Antonio, TX - *BaconPubCkNews 84*
San Antonio Register - San Antonio, TX - *BaconPubCkNews 84; Ed&PubIntYB 82*
San Augustine Cable TV Inc. [of Center Broadcasting Co.] - San Augustine, TX - *BrCabYB 84; Tel&CabFB 84C*
San Augustine Rambler - San Augustine, TX - *AyerDirPub 83; BaconPubCkNews 84; Ed&PubIntYB 82; NewsDir 84*
San Augustine Tribune - San Augustine, TX - *BaconPubCkNews 84; Ed&PubIntYB 82; NewsDir 84*
San/Bar Corp. - Irvine, CA - *DataDirSup 7-83*
San Benito News [of News Publishing Co. Inc.] - San Benito, TX - *BaconPubCkNews 84; Ed&PubIntYB 82; NewsDir 84*
San Bernardino American - San Bernardino, CA - *BaconPubCkNews 84*
San Bernardino County Museum Association - Redlands, CA - *BoPubDir 4, 5*
San Bernardino Precinct Reporter - San Bernardino, CA - *BaconPubCkNews 84; NewsDir 84*
San Bernardino Sun - San Bernardino, CA - *BaconPubCkNews 84; NewsDir 84*
San Bernardino Valley Genealogical Society - San Bernardino, CA - *BoPubDir 4, 5*
San Bruno Enterprise-Journal [of Industrial City Publishing Co.] - South San Francisco, CA - *NewsDir 84*
San Bruno Herald - *See* San Mateo Times Group Newspapers
San Bruno Herald & Recorder Progress [of Amphlett Printing Co.] - San Bruno, CA - *NewsDir 84*
San Bruno Municipal Cable TV - San Bruno, CA - *BrCabYB 84*
San Bruno North County Post [of Amphlett Printing Co.] - San Bruno, CA - *NewsDir 84*
San Carlos Enquirer [of Nowels Publishing] - Menlo Park, CA - *NewsDir 84*
San Carlos Enquirer - San Carlos, CA - *Ed&PubIntYB 82*
San Carlos Enquirer - *See* Regal Publishing Co.
San Carlos/Lake Murray Pennysaver - Mission Viejo, CA - *AyerDirPub 83*
San Clemente Cablevision [of Times Mirror Cable TV] - San Clemente, CA - *Tel&CabFB 84C*

San Clemente Coastline Dispatch - San Clemente, CA - *BaconPubCkNews 84*
San Clemente Pennysaver/North & South - Mission Viejo, CA - *AyerDirPub 83*
San Clemente Sun-Post [of Coastline Publishers] - San Clemente, CA - *BaconPubCkNews 84; NewsDir 84*
San Diego Business Journal - San Diego, CA - *BaconPubCkMag 84*
San Diego County's Health & Resource Guide [of Community Resource Group] - San Diego, CA - *WritMar 84*
San Diego East/San Diego South Pennysaver - Mission Viejo, CA - *AyerDirPub 83*
San Diego Home/Garden [of Westward Press] - San Diego, CA - *BaconPubCkMag 84; WritMar 84*
San Diego Jewish Press-Heritage - San Diego, CA - *AyerDirPub 83*
San Diego Labor Leader, The [of SDICLC] - San Diego, CA - *NewsDir 84*
San Diego Magazine [of San Diego Magazine Publishing Co.] - San Diego, CA - *BaconPubCkMag 84; Folio 83; MagDir 84; WritMar 84*
San Diego MDS Co. - Pasadena, MD - *Tel&CabFB 84C*
San Diego Newsline Monthly Magazine - San Diego, CA - *WritMar 84*
San Diego Publishing Co. - San Diego, CA - *LitMag&SmPr 83-84; LitMarPl 84*
San Diego Rancho Bernardo Journal - San Diego, CA - *BaconPubCkNews 84*
San Diego Sentinel [of Harte-Hank Communications Inc.] - San Diego, CA - *BaconPubCkNews 84; NewsDir 84*
San Diego Sound Post - San Diego, CA - *NewsDir 84*
San Diego State University Press - San Diego, CA - *BoPubDir 5*
San Diego Surveys - San Diego, CA - *IntDirMarRes 83*
San Diego Transcript - San Diego, CA - *BaconPubCkMag 84; Ed&PubIntYB 82; NewsDir 84*
San Diego Tribune - San Diego, CA - *BaconPubCkNews 84*
San Diego Union [of Union-Tribune Publishing Co.] - San Diego, CA - *BaconPubCkNews 84; Ed&PubIntYB 82; LitMarPl 83, 84; NewsBur 6; NewsDir 84*
San Diego Voice News & Viewpoint - San Diego, CA - *BaconPubCkNews 84; NewsDir 84*
San Dimas Press [of Bonita Publishing Co.] - Ontario, CA - *AyerDirPub 83; NewsDir 84*
San Dimas Press - San Dimas, CA - *Ed&PubIntYB 82*
San Dimas Press - *See* Pomona Progress Bulletin
San Fernando Poetry Journal [of Kent Publications] - Northridge, CA - *LitMag&SmPr 83-84; WritMar 84*
San Fernando Valley Chronicle - Canoga Park, CA - *NewsDir 84*
San Fernando Valley Chronicle - West San Fernando Valley, CA - *Ed&PubIntYB 82*
San Fernando Valley Chronicle - Woodland Hills, CA - *AyerDirPub 83*
San Fernando Valley Sun - San Fernando, CA - *Ed&PubIntYB 82; NewsDir 84*
San Fernando Valley Sun - *See* San Fernando Valley Sun Publishers
San Fernando Valley Sun Publishers - San Fernando, CA - *BaconPubCkNews 84*
San Fernando Valley View - *See* San Fernando Valley Sun Publishers
San Francisco Arts & Letters/PAL - San Francisco, CA - *LitMag&SmPr 83-84*
San Francisco Ballet - San Francisco, CA - *MagDir 84*
San Francisco Banner - San Francisco, CA - *BaconPubCkNews 84; Ed&PubIntYB 82*
San Francisco Bay Area Online Users' Group - Palo Alto, CA - *InfIndMarPl 83*
San Francisco Bay Area People's Yellow Pages - San Francisco, CA - *BoPubDir 4, 5*
San Francisco Bay Guardian - San Francisco, CA - *ArtMar 84; AyerDirPub 83; LitMarPl 83, 84; NewsDir 84; WritMar 84*
San Francisco Business [of San Francisco Chamber of Commerce] - San Francisco, CA - *BaconPubCkMag 84; MagDir 84*
San Francisco Business Journal [of E. W. Scripps Co.] - San Francisco, CA - *BaconPubCkMag 84; MagDir 84*
San Francisco Chronicle - San Francisco, CA - *BaconPubCkNews 84; LitMarPl 83; NewsBur 6; NewsDir 84*
San Francisco Daily Commercial News - San Francisco, CA - *NewsDir 84*
San Francisco Examiner [of The Hearst Corp.] - San Francisco, CA - *BaconPubCkNews 84; LitMarPl 83; NewsBur 6; NewsDir 84*
San Francisco Focus - San Francisco, CA - *MagIndMarPl 82-83*
San Francisco Historic Records - Colma, CA - *BoPubDir 4, 5*
San Francisco Institute of Automotive Ecology - San Francisco, CA - *BoPubDir 4, 5*
San Francisco Jewish Bulletin - San Francisco, CA - *AyerDirPub 83*
San Francisco Lightworks Inc. - San Francisco, CA - *AvMarPl 83*
San Francisco Magazine - San Francisco, CA - *ArtMar 84; BaconPubCkMag 84; LitMarPl 83, 84; MagIndMarPl 82-83; WritMar 84*
San Francisco Market - San Francisco, CA - *DirOnDB Spring 84*
San Francisco Metro Reporter - San Francisco, CA - *Ed&PubIntYB 82*
San Francisco Metro Reporter - *See* Reporter Publishing Co.
San Francisco Mime Troupe - San Francisco, CA - *BoPubDir 4 Sup, 5*
San Francisco Museum of Modern Art - San Francisco, CA - *BoPubDir 4, 5*
San Francisco Observer/Oakland Bay Area, The - San Francisco, CA - *NewsDir 84*
San Francisco Post [of Alameda Publishing Corp.] - Oakland, CA - *AyerDirPub 83; NewsDir 84*
San Francisco Post - *See* Alameda Publishing Corp.
San Francisco Press Inc. - San Francisco, CA - *BoPubDir 4, 5; LitMarPl 84*
San Francisco Progress - San Francisco, CA - *AyerDirPub 83; BaconPubCkNews 84; Ed&PubIntYB 82; NewsDir 84*
San Francisco Review of Books - San Francisco, CA - *LitMag&SmPr 83-84; WritMar 84*
San Francisco State University (Audio Visual/ITV Center) - San Francisco, CA - *VideoDir 82-83*
San Francisco Study Center - San Francisco, CA - *BoPubDir 4, 5*
San Francisco Sun Reporter - San Francisco, CA - *NewsDir 84*
San Francisco Sunday Examiner & Chronicle - San Francisco, CA - *LitMarPl 83*
San Francisco Today [of Industrial City Publishing Co.] - South San Francisco, CA - *Ed&PubIntYB 82; NewsDir 84*
San Francisco Today - *See* San Mateo Times Group Newspapers
San Gabriel Progress [of Monterey Park Progress Newspapers] - Monterey Park, CA - *NewsDir 84*
San Gabriel Progress - *See* Southern California Publishing Co.
San Gabriel Sun - San Gabriel, CA - *Ed&PubIntYB 82*
San Gabriel Sun - *See* Sun Independent Newspapers
San Gabriel Sun Independent [of Media General Corp.] - San Gabriel, CA - *NewsDir 84*
San Gabriel Valley Independent - San Gabriel, CA - *AyerDirPub 83*
San Gabriel Valley Magazine, The - Alhambra, CA - *WritMar 84*
San Gabriel Valley Tribune - Covina, CA - *AyerDirPub 83; BaconPubCkNews 84; Ed&PubIntYB 82; LitMarPl 84*
San Gabriel Valley Tribune - West Covina, CA - *NewsDir 84*
San Jacinto Valley Register - San Jacinto, CA - *AyerDirPub 83; BaconPubCkNews 84; Ed&PubIntYB 82*
San Jancinto News-Times - Shepherd, TX - *Ed&PubIntYB 82*
San Joaq & Tranquility Advance - Kerman, CA - *Ed&PubIntYB 82*
San Joaquin Metro Reporter - San Francisco, CA - *NewsDir 84*
San Joaquin Metro Reporter - *See* Reporter Publishing Co.
San Joaquin TV Services Inc. - Fresno, CA - *Tel&CabFB 84C*
San Jose Associates - Chicago, IL - *StaDirAdAg 2-84*
San Jose Evening Mercury News - San Jose, CA - *BaconPubCkNews 84*
San Jose Mercury - San Jose, CA - *LitMarPl 83*
San Jose Mercury-News - San Jose, CA - *LitMarPl 83*
San Jose Metro Reporter - San Francisco, CA - *NewsDir 84*
San Jose Metro Reporter - *See* Reporter Publishing Co.
San Jose Morning Mercury News - San Jose, CA - *BaconPubCkNews 84*
San Jose News - San Jose, CA - *LitMarPl 83*

San Jose Studies [of San Jose State University] - San Jose, CA - *ArtMar 84; WritMar 84*
San Jose Sun - *See* Meredith Newspapers
San Juan Advance News - San Juan, TX - *BaconPubCkNews 84*
San Juan Airlines - Portland, OR - *BaconPubCkMag 84*
San Juan Avenue Music - Beverly Hills, CA - *BillIntBG 83-84*
San Juan Cable TV Inc. - Silverton, CO - *Tel&CabFB 84C*
San Juan Cable TV Inc. [of Group W Cable Corp.] - Aztec, NM - *BrCabYB 84*
San Juan Cable TV Inc. - Friday Harbor, WA - *BrCabYB 84*
San Juan Cable TV of Wyoming Inc. - Saratoga, WY - *BrCabYB 84; Tel&CabFB 84C*
San Juan Cablevision [of Rock Associates Inc.] - Friday Harbor, WA - *Tel&CabFB 84C*
San Juan Capistrano Coastline Dispatch - San Clemente, CA - *Ed&PubIntYB 82*
San Juan Capistrano News-Post [of Laguna Publishing Co.] - Laguna Hills, CA - *NewsDir 84*
San Juan Capistrano News-Post - San Juan Capistrano, CA - *Ed&PubIntYB 82*
San Juan Capistrano Pennysaver - Mission Viejo, CA - *AyerDirPub 83*
San Juan County Book Co. - Silverton, CO - *BoPubDir 5*
San Juan MDS Inc. - San Juan, PR - *Tel&CabFB 84C*
San Juan Music Group - Brooklyn, NY - *BillIntBG 83-84*
San Juan Record [of Sacramento Suburban Newspapers Inc.] - Fair Oaks, CA - *Ed&PubIntYB 82; NewsDir 84*
San Juan Record - Monticello, UT - *AyerDirPub 83; Ed&PubIntYB 82*
San Leandro American [of Oakland Neighborhood Journal] - Oakland, CA - *NewsDir 84*
San Leandro Cable Television Inc. [of United Cable Television Corp.] - San Leandro, CA - *BrCabYB 84*
San Leandro Observer - San Leandro, CA - *AyerDirPub 83*
San Lorenzo, Guy - Lancaster, NY - *Tel&CabFB 84C p.1700*
San Luis Costilla County Free Press - San Luis, CO - *BaconPubCkNews 84*
San Luis Obispo Central Coast Times [of Paso Robles Newspapers Inc.] - San Luis Obispo, CA - *NewsDir 84*
San Luis Obispo County Telegram-Tribune [of John P. Scripps Newspapers] - San Luis Obispo, CA - *BaconPubCkNews 84; Ed&PubIntYB 82; NewsDir 84*
San Luis Quest Press - San Luis Obispo, CA - *BoPubDir 4, 5; LitMag&SmPr 83-84*
San Luis Software Inc. - San Luis Obispo, CA - *WhoWMicrocom 83*
San-Lyn Group - Syracuse, NY - *BillIntBG 83-84*
San Manuel Miner - San Manuel, AZ - *BaconPubCkNews 84; Ed&PubIntYB 82*
San Marcos Cablevision [of Times Mirror Cable TV] - San Marcos, CA - *BrCabYB 84; Tel&CabFB 84C*
San Marcos Courier - San Marcos, CA - *Ed&PubIntYB 82*
San Marcos Courier - Vista, CA - *AyerDirPub 83*
San Marcos Daily Record - San Marcos, TX - *BaconPubCkNews 84; Ed&PubIntYB 82; NewsDir 84*
San Marcos Outlook - San Marcos, CA - *Ed&PubIntYB 82*
San Marcos Pennysaver - Mission Viejo, CA - *AyerDirPub 83*
San Marcos Telephone Co. Inc. - San Marcos, TX - *TelDir&BG 83-84*
San Marino Tribune - San Marino, CA - *BaconPubCkNews 84; Ed&PubIntYB 82; NewsDir 84*
San Mateo County Advocate - Redwood City, CA - *Ed&PubIntYB 82*
San Mateo Educational Resources Center [of San Mateo County Office of Education] - Redwood City, CA - *EISS 83*
San Mateo Post, The [of Amphlett Printing Co.] - San Mateo, CA - *NewsDir 84*
San Mateo Times [of Amphlett Printing Co.] - San Mateo, CA - *BaconPubCkNews 84; NewsDir 84*
San Mateo Times Group Newspapers - San Francisco, CA - *BaconPubCkNews 84*
San Miguel Basin Forum - Norwood, CO - *AyerDirPub 83*
San Miguel Basin Forum - Nucla, CO - *Ed&PubIntYB 82*
San Miguel Cable Systems Inc. - Montrose, CO - *Tel&CabFB 84C*
San Miguel Cable Systems Inc. - Nucla, CO - *BrCabYB 84*
San Patricio County Cable TV Inc. - Sinton, TX - *BrCabYB 84*
San Patricio County News - Sinton, TX - *AyerDirPub 83; Ed&PubIntYB 82*
San Patricio Publishing Co. - Sinton, TX - *BaconPubCkNews 84*
San Pedro News-Pilot [of Copley Newspapers] - San Pedro, CA - *NewsDir 84*
San Pedro Press - St. David, AZ - *LitMag&SmPr 83-84*
San Pedro Valley News-Sun - Benson, AZ - *AyerDirPub 83; Ed&PubIntYB 82*
San Rafael Independent-Journal - San Rafael, CA - *LitMarPl 83*
San Rafael News Pointer - *See* Marin Suburban Newspapers Inc.
San Rafael Terra Linda News - San Rafael, CA - *NewsDir 84*
San Ramon Valley Herald - Danville, CA - *BaconPubCkNews 84; NewsDir 84*
San Saba-Goldthwaite Cablevision Inc. - Goldthwaite, TX - *BrCabYB 84; Tel&CabFB 84C*
San Saba-Goldthwaite Cablevision Inc. - San Saba, TX - *BrCabYB 84; Tel&CabFB 84C p.1700*
San Saba News & Star - San Saba, TX - *BaconPubCkNews 84; Ed&PubIntYB 82*
San Val Inc. - Maryland Heights, MO - *LitMarPl 83, 84*
San Val Inc. - Steelville, MO - *MagIndMarPl 82-83*
Sanborn Pioneer - Sanborn, IA - *BaconPubCkNews 84; Ed&PubIntYB 82*
Sanborn Sentinel - Sanborn, MN - *Ed&PubIntYB 82*
Sanborn Telephone Cooperative - Woonsocket, SD - *Tel&CabFB 84C; TelDir&BG 83-84*
Sand & Co., M. R. - Sandusky, OH - *BillIntBG 83-84*
Sand Creek Telephone Co. - Sand Creek, MI - *TelDir&BG 83-84*
Sand Dollar - Albany, CA - *LitMag&SmPr 83-84*
Sand Hills Books Inc. - St. Jacobs, ON, Canada - *BoPubDir 4, 5*
Sand Mountain News - Rainsville, AL - *AyerDirPub 83; NewsDir 84*
Sand Mountain Reporter - Albertville, AL - *AyerDirPub 83; Ed&PubIntYB 82*
Sand Springs Leader - Sand Springs, OK - *BaconPubCkNews 84; Ed&PubIntYB 82*
Sand Springs Times [of Sand Springs Leader] - Sand Springs, OK - *NewsDir 84*
Sandage Advertising & Marketing Inc. - Burlington, VT - *StaDirAdAg 2-84*
Sandal Prints - Detroit, MI - *WritMar 84*
Sandara - Chicago, IL - *Ed&PubIntYB 82; NewsDir 84*
Sandbank Films Co. Inc. - New York, NY - *Tel&CabFB 84C*
Sandcastle Records - New York, NY - *BillIntBG 83-84*
Sanders Advertising & Public Relations Agency Inc., Rita - Tempe, AZ - *DirPRFirms 83*
Sanders Advertising Inc., Lew - Chicago, IL - *StaDirAdAg 2-84*
Sanders & Morton Advertising - El Paso, TX - *StaDirAdAg 2-84*
Sanders Associates - Nashua, NH - *DataDirSup 7-83; Datamation 6-83; Top100Al 83*
Sanders County Ledger - Thompson Falls, MT - *AyerDirPub 83; Ed&PubIntYB 82*
Sanders Publications - Geneseo, NY - *BaconPubCkNews 84*
Sanders Technology Systems Inc. - Nashua, NH - *DirInfWP 82; WhoWMicrocom 83*
Sanderson Organization, T. K. - Baltimore, MD - *BoPubDir 4, 5*
Sanderson Times - Sanderson, TX - *BaconPubCkNews 84; Ed&PubIntYB 82*
Sandersville Progress - Sandersville, GA - *BaconPubCkNews 84; Ed&PubIntYB 82; NewsDir 84*
Sandesa News Agency - Colombo, Sri Lanka - *Ed&PubIntYB 82*
Sandhaus Associates Inc., Paul - New York, NY - *StaDirAdAg 2-84*
Sandhill Citizen - Aberdeen, NC - *AyerDirPub 83; Ed&PubIntYB 82*
Sandhill Community Antenna Corp. [of American TV & Communications Corp.] - Southern Pines, NC - *BrCabYB 84; Tel&CabFB 84C*
Sandhill Foxfire - Minden, NC - *BillIntBG 83-84*
Sandhill Telephone Co. [Aff. of Mid-Continent Telephone Corp.] - Aberdeen, NC - *TelDir&BG 83-84*
Sandhill Telephone Cooperative Inc. - Jefferson, SC - *TelDir&BG 83-84*
Sandhills Press - Ord, NE - *LitMag&SmPr 83-84*
Sandhills, The - Ord, NE - *LitMag&SmPr 83-84*
Sandia Cablevision Inc. [of Warner Amex Cable Communications Inc.] - Immokalee, FL - *Tel&CabFB 84C*

Sandia Market Research - Albuquerque, NM - *IntDirMarRes 83*
Sandidge & Sandidge - West Dundee, IL - *AvMarPl 83*
Sandlapper Publishing Co. Inc. - Orangeburg, SC - *BoPubDir 4, 5*
Sandler & Associates, Gilbert - Baltimore, MD - *AdAge 3-28-84; ArtMar 84; StaDirAdAg 2-84*
Sandler Institutional Films Inc. - Hollywood, CA - *TelAl 83*
Sandlin Group, The - Amarillo, TX - *StaDirAdAg 2-84*
Sandoval County Cable TV [of Capital Cities Cable Inc.] - Rio Rancho, NM - *BrCabYB 84*
Sandoval County Times-Independent - Bernalillo, NM - *AyerDirPub 83; NewsDir 84*
Sandoval-Odin Cable TV Co. [of Flora Cable TV Co.] - Sandoval, IL - *BrCabYB 84*
Sandoval-Odin-Junction City Cable TV Co. [of Flora Cable TV Co.] - Sandoval, IL - *Tel&CabFB 84C*
Sandoval Register - Sandoval, IL - *NewsDir 84*
Sandpaper, The - Surf City, NJ - *WritMar 84*
Sandpiper Press - Solana Beach, CA - *BoPubDir 4 Sup, 5*
Sandpiper Press - Oviedo, FL - *BoPubDir 4, 5*
Sandpiper Press - Brookings, OR - *BoPubDir 4, 5*
Sandpoint Daily Bee [of Pend Oreille Printers Inc.] - Sandpoint, ID - *BaconPubCkNews 84; NewsDir 84*
Sandpoint News-Bulletin [of Pend Oreille Printers Inc.] - Sandpoint, ID - *NewsDir 84*
Sandrock & Foster Memorial Foundation [Aff. of Friends of Peaceful Alternatives Free Trade Exchange] - Winona, MN - *BoPubDir 4 Sup, 5*
Sands - Dallas, TX - *LitMag&SmPr 83-84*
Sands Productions, Alan - New York, NY - *AvMarPl 83*
Sandscript [of Cape Cod Writers Inc.] - Cummaquid, MA - *LitMag&SmPr 83-84*
Sandstone Pine County Courier - Sandstone, MN - *BaconPubCkNews 84*
Sandstone Press - New York, NY - *BoPubDir 4*
Sandstrom, Joanne - Oakland, CA - *LitMarPl 84*
Sandusky Newspapers Inc. - Los Angeles, CA - *BrCabYB 84*
Sandusky Newspapers Inc. - Santa Ynez, CA - *BrCabYB 84*
Sandusky-Norwalk Newspapers - Sandusky, OH - *Ed&PubIntYB 82*
Sandusky Register - Sandusky, OH - *BaconPubCkNews 84; Ed&PubIntYB 82; NewsDir 84*
Sandusky Republican Tribune Inc. - Sandusky, MI - *NewsDir 84*
Sandusky Sanilac County News - Sandusky, MI - *BaconPubCkNews 84*
Sandusky Sanilac County News-Advisor - Sandusky, MI - *NewsDir 84*
Sandusky Sunday Register - Sandusky, OH - *Ed&PubIntYB 82*
Sandusky Tribune - Sandusky, MI - *BaconPubCkNews 84*
Sandwich Tri-County Today - Sandwich, IL - *BaconPubCkNews 84; NewsDir 84*
Sandwich Village Broadsider - *See* MPG Communications
Sandy Cable TV [of Acton CATV Inc.] - Acton, MA - *BrCabYB 84*
Sandy Corp. - Southfield, MI - *AvMarPl 83*
Sandy Corp. - Troy, MI - *WritMar 84*
Sandy Creek News [of Town & Country News of Jefferson County] - Gouverneur, NY - *NewsDir 84*
Sandy Creek News - Pulaski, NY - *AyerDirPub 83; BaconPubCkNews 84*
Sandy Crossing Enterprises Inc. - Farson, WY - *Tel&CabFB 84C*
Sandy Hook Cable Co. - Sandy Hook, KY - *BrCabYB 84; Tel&CabFB 84C*
Sandy Hook Elliott County News - *See* Courier Publishing Co. Inc.
Sandy Post - Gresham, OR - *AyerDirPub 83*
Sandy Post - Sandy, OR - *Ed&PubIntYB 82; NewsDir 84*
Sandy Post - *See* Gresham Outlook Inc.
Sandy Springs Neighbor, The - Sandy Springs, GA - *Ed&PubIntYB 82*
Sanford Corp. - Bellwood, IL - *AvMarPl 83; LitMarPl 83*
Sanford Evening Herald - Sanford, FL - *BaconPubCkNews 84; NewsDir 84*
Sanford Herald - Sanford, NC - *BaconPubCkNews 84; Ed&PubIntYB 82; NewsDir 84*
Sanford Inc., H. H. - New York, NY - *StaDirAdAg 2-84*
Sanford Organization Inc., The - Rolling Meadows, IL - *StaDirAdAg 2-84*
Sanga Music Inc. - New York, NY - *BillIntBG 83-84*
Sangamon Cablevision [of Combined Cable Corp.] - Mt. Pulaski, IL - *BrCabYB 84; Tel&CabFB 84C p.1700*
Sangamon Cablevision South Inc. [of Combined Cable Corp.] - Breeze, IL - *BrCabYB 84*
Sangamon Greeting Card Co. - Taylorville, IL - *WritMar 84*
Sangamon State University (Sangamon Poets) - Springfield, IL - *BoPubDir 4, 5*
Sangamon Valley Cablevision - Breese, IL - *Tel&CabFB 84C*
Sanger Courier - Sanger, TX - *BaconPubCkNews 84; Ed&PubIntYB 82*
Sanger Herald - Sanger, CA - *BaconPubCkNews 84; Ed&PubIntYB 82*
Sangre Productions - Sacramento, CA - *BillIntBG 83-84*
Sanguinaria Publishing [Aff. of Bloodroot Ltd.] - Bridgeport, CT - *BoPubDir 4, 5; LitMag&SmPr 83-84*
Sanibel-Captiva Islander - Sanibel, FL - *BaconPubCkNews 84*
Sanilac County News - Sandusky, MI - *Ed&PubIntYB 82*
Sanilac County News-Advisor - Sandusky, MI - *AyerDirPub 83*
Sanilac Jeffersonian - Croswell, MI - *Ed&PubIntYB 82*
Sanitary Maintenance - Milwaukee, WI - *BaconPubCkMag 84; MagDir 84*
Sankey 2 Inc. - Birmingham, AL - *StaDirAdAg 2-84*
Sanlando Cablevision Inc. [of Storer Cable Communications] - Altamonte Springs, FL - *BrCabYB 84; Tel&CabFB 84C*
Sanoma-International - Helsinki, Finland - *InfoS 83-84*
Sanskrit Publishing Co. - Minneapolis, MN - *BillIntBG 83-84*
Sanskrit Records - Minneapolis, MN - *BillIntBG 83-84*
Sansom Park Cable Communications [of CBS Inc.] - Sansom Park Village, TX - *BrCabYB 84*
Sanson-Antobal Music Co. Inc. - *See* Ahlert Music Corp., Fred
SANSS - Bethesda, MD - *DirOnDB Spring 84*
Sansui Electronics Corp. - Lyndhurst, NJ - *BillIntBG 83-84*
Santa Ana Register [of Sunday Fine Arts Supplement of the Register] - Santa Ana, CA - *BaconPubCkNews 84; LitMarPl 83*
Santa Anna News - Santa Anna, TX - *BaconPubCkNews 84; Ed&PubIntYB 82*
Santa Barbara Botanic Garden - Santa Barbara, CA - *BoPubDir 4, 5*
Santa Barbara Magazine - Santa Barbara, CA - *BaconPubCkMag 84*
Santa Barbara Museum of Natural History - Santa Barbara, CA - *BoPubDir 4, 5*
Santa Barbara News & Review - Santa Barbara, CA - *AyerDirPub 83; Ed&PubIntYB 82; NewsDir 84*
Santa Barbara News-Press - Santa Barbara, CA - *AyerDirPub 83; BaconPubCkNews 84; LitMarPl 83, 84; NewsDir 84*
Santa Clara American - Santa Clara, CA - *Ed&PubIntYB 82*
Santa Clara County Business - San Jose, CA - *BaconPubCkMag 84*
Santa Clara Sun [of Meredith Corp.] - Cupertino, CA - *AyerDirPub 83; NewsDir 84*
Santa Clara Sun - Santa Clara, CA - *Ed&PubIntYB 82*
Santa Clara Sun - *See* Meredith Newspapers
Santa Clara Systems Inc. - Campbell, CA - *MicrocomMPl 84*
Santa Cruz Educational Software - Soquel, CA - *MicrocomMPl 83*
Santa Cruz Operation Inc., The - Santa Cruz, CA - *MicrocomSwDir 1*
Santa Cruz Sentinel - Santa Cruz, CA - *BaconPubCkNews 84; Ed&PubIntYB 82; LitMarPl 83, 84; NewsDir 84*
Santa Fe Cablevision - Santa Fe, NM - *BrCabYB 84*
Santa Fe Community School Publications - Santa Fe, NM - *BoPubDir 4, 5*
Santa Fe East Publishers [Aff. of Santa Fe East Gallery] - Santa Fe, NM - *BoPubDir 4 Sup, 5; LitMarPl 84*
Santa Fe New Mexican [of Gannett Co. Inc.] - Santa Fe, NM - *BaconPubCkNews 84; NewsDir 84*
Santa Fe/Poetry & the Arts - Santa Fe, NM - *LitMag&SmPr 83-84*
Santa Fe Publishing Co. - Santa Fe, NM - *LitMag&SmPr 83-84*
Santa Fe Springs News - *See* Southern California Publishing Co.
Santa Gertrudis Journal, The - Ft. Worth, TX - *MagDir 84*
Santa Maria Times [of Scripps League Newspapers] - Santa Maria, CA - *BaconPubCkNews 84; NewsDir 84*
Santa Maria Valley Historical Society - Santa Maria, CA - *BoPubDir 4, 5*

Santa Monica Advertiser - Santa Monica, CA - *AyerDirPub 83; Ed&PubIntYB 82*
Santa Monica Evening Outlook [of United Western Newspapers Inc.] - Santa Monica, CA - *BaconPubCkNews 84; NewsDir 84*
Santa Monica Independent - Santa Monica, CA - *Ed&PubIntYB 82; NewsDir 84*
Santa Monica Independent - *See* Independent-Journal Newspapers
Santa Monica Outlook Mail - *See* Copley Press Inc.
Santa Monica Southside Advertiser [of United Western Newspapers Inc.] - Santa Monica, CA - *NewsDir 84*
Santa Paula Chronicle [of Santa Clara Valley Publishing Co. Inc.] - Santa Paula, CA - *BaconPubCkNews 84; NewsDir 84*
Santa Rosa Cable TV - Santa Rosa, NM - *BrCabYB 84*
Santa Rosa Cablevision [of Clearview Management Corp.] - Milton, FL - *BrCabYB 84; Tel&CabFB 84C*
Santa Rosa Communicator - Santa Rosa, NM - *BaconPubCkNews 84*
Santa Rosa Computer Center - Santa Rosa, CA - *WhoWMicrocom 83*
Santa Rosa News - Santa Rosa, NM - *Ed&PubIntYB 82; NewsDir 84*
Santa Rosa News-Herald - Santa Rosa, CA - *Ed&PubIntYB 82; NewsDir 84*
Santa Rosa Press Democrat [of Press Democrat Publishing Co.] - Santa Rosa, CA - *BaconPubCkNews 84; LitMarPl 83; NewsDir 84*
Santa Rosa Telephone Cooperative Inc. - Vernon, TX - *TelDir&BG 83-84*
Santa Ynez Valley News - Solvang, CA - *AyerDirPub 83; Ed&PubIntYB 82*
Sant'Andrea East Inc., Jim - New York, NY - *ArtMar 84; AvMarPl 83*
Sant'Andrea Midwest Inc., Jim - Chicago, IL - *ArtMar 84; WritMar 84*
Sant'Andrea West Inc., Jim - Compton, CA - *ArtMar 84*
Santaquin Cable Television Corp. - Santaquin, UT - *BrCabYB 84; Tel&CabFB 84C*
Santec Corp. - Amherst, NH - *DataDirSup 7-83*
Santee Pennysaver - Mission Viejo, CA - *AyerDirPub 83*
Santel Communications - Islington, ON, Canada - *DirInfWP 82*
Santiam Cable Vision Inc. - Mill City, OR - *Tel&CabFB 84C*
Santiam Cable Vision Inc. - Stayton, OR - *BrCabYB 84 p.D-306; Tel&CabFB 84C p.1700*
Santillana Publishing Co. Inc. - Northvale, NJ - *LitMarPl 83, 84*
Santilli, Al Jr. - La Habra, CA - *BoPubDir 4, 5*
Santucci, Tedeschi & Scott Inc. - New York, NY - *DirPRFirms 83*
Santype-Byrd [Div. of The William Byrd Press] - Richmond, VA - *LitMarPl 83, 84*
Sanval Cablevision Inc. - Chowchilla, CA - *Tel&CabFB 84C p.1700*
Sanyo Business Systems Corp. - Moonachie, NJ - *DataDirSup 7-83; MicrocomMPl 84; WhoWMicrocom 83*
Sanyo Consumer Electronics - Compton, CA - *BillIntBG 83-84*
Sanyo Electric Co. Inc. - Compton, CA - *AvMarPl 83; BillIntBG 83-84*
Sanyo Marubeni Business Equipment Corp. - Moonachie, NJ - *DirInfWP 82*
SAP-Database [of University Library of Lund] - Lund, Sweden - *CompReadDB 82; DirOnDB Spring 84*
Sapana Micro Software - Pittsburg, KS - *MicrocomMPl 84; MicrocomSwDir 1*
Saphrograph Corp. - Brooklyn, NY - *BoPubDir 4, 5*
Sapien Books - Saskatoon, SK, Canada - *BoPubDir 4, 5*
Sapiens - Millburn, NJ - *LitMag&SmPr 83-84*
Sapiens Press - Millburn, NJ - *LitMag&SmPr 83-84*
Sapphire Systems - Ilford, England - *MicrocomSwDir 1*
Sapulpa Herald - Sapulpa, OK - *BaconPubCkNews 84; Ed&PubIntYB 82; NewsDir 84*
Sar-An Computer Products - Buffalo, NY - *MicrocomMPl 84*
SAR Magazine, The - Louisville, KY - *BaconPubCkMag 84*
Sara Lee Music Publishing Co. - *See* Chris Music Publishing Co.
Saralake Estates Mobile Home Park - Saralake Estates, FL - *BrCabYB 84; Tel&CabFB 84C*
Saraland News-Herald - Saraland, AL - *BaconPubCkNews 84*
Saran Music Co. - Dallas, TX - *BillIntBG 83-84*
Saranac Lake Adirondack Enterprise - Saranac Lake, NY - *NewsDir 84*
Sarasota Bulletin - Sarasota, FL - *BaconPubCkNews 84; NewsDir 84*
Sarasota Herald-Tribune [of New York Times Co.] - Sarasota, FL - *BaconPubCkNews 84; NewsDir 84*
Sarasota Pelican Press - Sarasota, FL - *BaconPubCkNews 84*
Saratoga Cable TV Co. Inc. - Saratoga Springs, NY - *BrCabYB 84*
Saratoga News [of Meredith Corp.] - Cupertino, CA - *NewsDir 84*
Saratoga News - Saratoga, CA - *AyerDirPub 83; Ed&PubIntYB 82*
Saratoga News - *See* Meredith Newspapers
Saratoga Springs Saratogian - Saratoga Springs, NY - *NewsDir 84*
Saratoga Sun - Saratoga, WY - *BaconPubCkNews 84; Ed&PubIntYB 82*
Saratogian & Tri-County News - Saratoga Springs, NY - *AyerDirPub 83; BaconPubCkNews 84; Ed&PubIntYB 82*
Sarcoxie Record - Sarcoxie, MO - *BaconPubCkNews 84; Ed&PubIntYB 82*
Sardinas-Wyssling, Karen - Hamilton Square, NJ - *LitMarPl 83, 84*
Sardis Southern Reporter - Sardis, MS - *BaconPubCkNews 84; Ed&PubIntYB 82*
Sarg Recording Co. - Luling, TX - *BillIntBG 83-84*
Sargent Leader - Sargent, NE - *BaconPubCkNews 84; Ed&PubIntYB 82*
Sarkett & Associates Inc. - Chicago, IL - *DirPRFirms 83*
Sarlat Public Relations Inc., Gladys - Tucson, AZ - *DirPRFirms 83*
Sarm, Macel Goff - Catonsville, MD - *BoPubDir 4, 5*
Sarnia Gazette - Sarnia, ON, Canada - *AyerDirPub 83; Ed&PubIntYB 82*
Sarnia Lambton County Gazette - Forest, ON, Canada - *Ed&PubIntYB 82*
Sarnia Observer, The - Sarnia, ON, Canada - *BaconPubCkNews 84*
Sarpy County Sun [of Omaha Sun Newspapers] - Omaha, NE - *NewsDir 84*
Sarra Associates Inc., Robert - New York, NY - *StaDirAdAg 2-84*
Sarris Bookmarketing Service - New York, NY - *LitMarPl 83, 84; MagIndMarPl 82-83*
Saru - Miyagiken, Japan - *LitMag&SmPr 83-84*
Sarver & Witzerman Advertising - Long Beach, CA - *StaDirAdAg 2-84*
SAS Arcade Supplies - Orlando, FL - *MicrocomMPl 84*
SAS Institute Inc. - Cary, NC - *BoPubDir 4, 5; DataDirSup 7-83; EISS 83*
Sas 'n Ras Music - Anderson, SC - *BillIntBG 83-84*
Sasco Associates - Southport, CT - *BoPubDir 4, 5*
SashaSongs Unltd. - *See* Grand Pasha Publisher, The
Sashay Music - *See* Morris Music Inc.
Saska-Music Publishing - Saskatoon, SK, Canada - *BoPubDir 4 Sup, 5*
Saskatchewan-Alberta Surveys & Market Research - Bruno, SK, Canada - *IntDirMarRes 83*
Saskatchewan Business - Winnipeg, MB, Canada - *BaconPubCkMag 84*
Saskatchewan Dept. of Industry & Commerce - Regina, SK, Canada - *BoPubDir 5*
Saskatchewan Federation of Agriculture - Regina, SK, Canada - *BoPubDir 4 Sup, 5*
Saskatchewan Genealogical Society - Regina, SK, Canada - *BoPubDir 4, 5*
Saskatchewan Museums Association - Regina, SK, Canada - *BoPubDir 5*
Saskatchewan Natural History Society - Regina, SK, Canada - *BoPubDir 4, 5*
Saskatchewan Telecommunications - Regina, SK, Canada - *VideoDir 82-83*
Saskatchewan Valley News - Rosthern, SK, Canada - *AyerDirPub 83; Ed&PubIntYB 82*
Saskatoon Commentator - Saskatoon, SK, Canada - *Ed&PubIntYB 82*
Saskatoon Shopper, The - Saskatoon, SK, Canada - *AyerDirPub 83*
Saskatoon Telecable Ltd. - Saskatoon, SK, Canada - *BrCabYB 84*

Sasquatch Publishing Co. Inc. - Seattle, WA - *BoPubDir 5*
Sassafras Press - Atlanta, GA - *BoPubDir 4, 5*
SAT Guide - Hailey, ID - *BaconPubCkMag 84; WritMar 84*
Sat Time - Aspen, CO - *TeleSy&SerDir 2-84*
Sat Trak International - Colorado Springs, CO - *MicrocomMPl 83; WhoWMicrocom 83*
Satanta Community TV - Satanta, KS - *BrCabYB 84*
Satcom Technologies Inc. [of Radiation Systems Inc.] - Norcross, GA - *CabTVFinDB 83*
Sateldata [of European Space Agency] - Paris, France - *DirOnDB Spring 84*
Sateldata [of European Space Agency] - Frascati, Italy - *DataDirOnSer 84*
Satellease - Northbrook, IL - *BrCabYB 84; TeleSy&SerDir 2-84*
Satellink Corp. - Englewood, CO - *Tel&CabFB 84C*
Satellite Age [of Martin Roberts & Associates Inc.] - Beverly Hills, CA - *TeleSy&SerDir 7-83*
Satellite & Production Services - Tallahassee, FL - *TeleSy&SerDir 2-84*
Satellite Business Systems - McLean, VA - *BrCabYB 84; DataDirSup 7-83; TeleSy&SerDir 7-83*
Satellite Cable Service of Arlington - Howard, SD - *BrCabYB 84*
Satellite Cable Service of Lake Preston - Lake Preston, SD - *BrCabYB 84*
Satellite Cable Service of Salem - Salem, SD - *BrCabYB 84*
Satellite Cable Service of Volga - De Smet, SD - *BrCabYB 84*
Satellite Cable Service of Wessington Springs - Wessington Springs, SD - *BrCabYB 84*
Satellite Cable Services Inc. - De Smet, SD - *Tel&CabFB 84C p.1700*
Satellite Cable Services Inc. - Flandreau, SD - *BrCabYB 84*
Satellite Cable Television Inc. - Mitchell, NE - *BrCabYB 84 p.D-306*
Satellite Cable Television Inc. - Oshkosh, NE - *BrCabYB 84*
Satellite Cable TV Corp. - Phoenix, AZ - *BrCabYB 84 p.D-306; Tel&CabFB 84C p.1700*
Satellite Cable TV Corp. - Richland, MO - *Tel&CabFB 84C*
Satellite Cablevision Inc. [of Capital Cities Cable Inc.] - Greenwood, IN - *BrCabYB 84; Tel&CabFB 84C*
Satellite Communications [of Cardiff Publishing Co.] - Englewood, CO - *BaconPubCkMag 84; MagDir 84; MagIndMarPl 82-83; TeleSy&SerDir 2-84; WritMar 84*
Satellite Communications Cable Television Inc. - Eaton, CO - *BrCabYB 84; Tel&CabFB 84C p.1700*
Satellite Communications Co. of Nebraska - Blair, NE - *Tel&CabFB 84C p.1700*
Satellite Communications Network Inc. - Glen Rock, NJ - *BrCabYB 84; TeleSy&SerDir 2-84*
Satellite Data Services Div. [of U.S. National Oceanic & Atmospheric Administration] - Washington, DC - *EISS 83*
Satellite Development Trust - New York, NY - *BrCabYB 84*
Satellite Music Network - Dallas, TX - *BrCabYB 84; LitMarPl 84*
Satellite Networking Associates Inc. - New York, NY - *Tel&CabFB 84C; TeleSy&SerDir 2-84*
Satellite Networks Inc. - New York, NY - *BrCabYB 84*
Satellite News - Bethesda, MD - *DirOnDB Spring 84*
Satellite News [of NewsNet Inc.] - Bryn Mawr, PA - *DataDirOnSer 84*
Satellite News Bulletin Service [of NewsNet Inc.] - Bryn Mawr, PA - *DataDirOnSer 84*
Satellite News Channels - Stamford, CT - *CabTVPrDB 83; HomeVid&CabYB 82-83*
Satellite Orbit [of CommTek Publishing Co.] - Hailey, ID - *BaconPubCkMag 84; WritMar 84*
Satellite Program Network [of Satellite Syndicated Systems] - Tulsa, OK - *BrCabYB 84; CabTVPrDB 83; HomeVid&CabYB 82-83; Tel&CabFB 84C*
Satellite Signals Inc. - Horsham, PA - *Tel&CabFB 84C*
Satellite Software International - Orem, UT - *DirInfWP 82; MicrocomMPl 84; MicrocomSwDir 1; WhoWMicrocom 83*
Satellite Syndicated Systems - Tulsa, OK - *BrCabYB 84; HomeVid&CabYB 82-83; Tel&CabFB 84C, 84S*
Satellite Systems Corp. - Virginia Beach, VA - *TeleSy&SerDir 2-84*
Satellite Systems Technology - Chicago, IL - *Tel&CabFB 84C*
Satellite Television [of Overseas Telecommunications Commission] - Sydney, Australia - *TeleSy&SerDir 2-84*
Satellite Television & Associated Resources - Santa Monica, CA - *HomeVid&CabYB 82-83*
Satellite Television Corp. [Subs. of ComSat] - Washington, DC - *BrCabYB 84; HomeVid&CabYB 82-83; TeleSy&SerDir 7-83*
Satellite Television of New York Associates - New York, NY - *Tel&CabFB 84C*
Satellite-TV Services Ltd. - Rockville, MD - *BrCabYB 84; Tel&CabFB 84C*
Satellite Vision Broadcasting Co. - Alexandria, LA - *Tel&CabFB 84C*
Satellite Week - Washington, DC - *BaconPubCkMag 84; DirOnDB Spring 84; MagDir 84*
Satellite Week [of NewsNet Inc.] - Bryn Mawr, PA - *DataDirOnSer 84*
Satellitevision Systems Partners - New York, NY - *Tel&CabFB 84C*
Sater's Antique & Auction News, Joel - Marietta, PA - *MagDir 84; WritMar 84*
Satori Entertainment Corp. - New York, NY - *Tel&CabFB 84C*
Satori Group, The - Atlanta, GA - *EISS 83*
Satori Productions - New York, NY - *AvMarPl 83; TelAl 83*
Satrycon Music - Los Angeles, CA - *BillIntBG 83-84*
SatServ - Washington, DC - *BrCabYB 84*
Sattler International - Bloomfield Hills, MI - *DirPRFirms 83*
Saturday Enquirer & Ledger [of The R. W. Page Corp.] - Columbus, GA - *Ed&PubIntYB 82; LitMarPl 83, 84*
Saturday Evening Post [of Saturday Evening Post Society] - Indianapolis, IN - *ArtMar 84; BaconPubCkMag 84; Folio 83; LitMarPl 83, 84; MagDir 84; MagIndMarPl 82-83; WritMar 84*
Saturday Evening Post (Book Div.) - Indianapolis, IN - *LitMarPl 83, 84*
Saturday Night - Toronto, ON, Canada - *BaconPubCkMag 84*
Saturday Press - Upper Montclair, NJ - *BoPubDir 4, 5; LitMag&SmPr 83-84*
Saturday Review [of Missouri Life Publishing Co.] - Columbia, MO - *BaconPubCkMag 84; LitMarPl 84; WritMar 84*
Saturday Review [of Macro Communications Corp.] - New York, NY - *DirMarMP 83; MagDir 84; MagIndMarPl 82-83; NewsBur 6*
Saturn Records Inc. - Atlanta, GA - *BillIntBG 83-84*
Saturn Systems - Minneapolis, MN - *DirInfWP 82*
Saturn Systems Inc. - Ann Arbor, MI - *MicrocomMPl 83, 84; WhoWMicrocom 83*
Saucer Eyes Music Co. - *See* Music Exchange, The
Saudi Marketing & Research Consultants - Jeddah, Saudi Arabia - *IntDirMarRes 83*
Saudi Oriented Guide Specifications [of Bowne Information Systems Inc.] - New York, NY - *DataDirOnSer 84*
Saugatuck Commercial Record - Saugatuck, MI - *BaconPubCkNews 84*
Saugatuck Group Inc., The - Westport, CT - *CabTVFinDB 83*
Saugeen Telecable Ltd. - Hanover, ON, Canada - *BrCabYB 84*
Saugerties Old Dutch Post-Star [of Lee Publications Inc.] - Saugerties, NY - *BaconPubCkNews 84; NewsDir 84*
Saugus Advertiser - Saugus, MA - *BaconPubCkNews 84; Ed&PubIntYB 82; NewsDir 84*
Sauk Centre Herald - Sauk Centre, MN - *BaconPubCkNews 84; Ed&PubIntYB 82; NewsDir 84*
Sauk City Prairie Star - *See* News Publishing Co. Inc.
Sauk County Media - Reedsburg, WI - *AyerDirPub 83*
Sauk Prairie Star - Sauk City, WI - *AyerDirPub 83; Ed&PubIntYB 82*
Sauk Rapids Herald - Sauk Rapids, MN - *BaconPubCkNews 84; Ed&PubIntYB 82*
Sauls Lithograph Co. Inc. - Washington, DC - *LitMarPl 83, 84*
Sault News Printing - Sault Ste. Marie, MI - *Ed&PubIntYB 82*
Sault Star, The - Sault Ste. Marie, ON, Canada - *AyerDirPub 83; Ed&PubIntYB 82*
Sault Ste. Marie Evening News - Sault Ste. Marie, MI - *NewsDir 84*
Saunders College - Philadelphia, PA - *LitMarPl 83, 84*
Saunders Co. Canada Ltd., W. B. - Toronto, ON, Canada - *LitMarPl 83, 84*

Saunders Co., W. B. [of CBS Educational & Professional Publishing] - Philadelphia, PA - *DirMarMP 83; LitMarPl 83, 84; MagIndMarPl 82-83*
Saunders, Dawn M. - Manhattan Beach, CA - *FBInfSer 80*
Saunders Group [Subs. of Saunders Photo/Graphic Inc.] - Rochester, NY - *AvMarPl 83*
Saunders, Lubinski & White Inc. - Dallas, TX - *StaDirAdAg 2-84*
Saunders Manufacturing Co. Inc. - Winthrop, ME - *DataDirSup 7-83*
Saunders of Toronto Ltd. - East Markham, ON, Canada - *LitMarPl 83*
Sauppe Media Inc. - North Hollywood, CA - *AvMarPl 83*
Saur Publishing Inc., K. G. - New York, NY - *LitMarPl 84*
Saur Verlag, K. G. - Munich, West Germany - *EISS 83; MicroMarPl 82-83*
Saura Computer Software & Consulting - Anchorage, AK - *MicrocomMPl 84*
Saurian Press - Socorro, NM - *LitMag&SmPr 83-84*
Savage, Candace - Saskatoon, SK, Canada - *BoPubDir 4, 5*
Savage Group, The - New York, NY - *LitMarPl 83, 84*
Savage Information Services - Rancho Palo Verdes, CA - *FBInfSer 80*
Savage Information Services - Rolling Hills Estates, CA - *DataDirOnSer 84; EISS 83; InfIndMarPl 83*
Savan Co., The - St. Louis, MO - *StaDirAdAg 2-84*
Savanna Northwestern Illinois Dispatch - Savanna, IL - *BaconPubCkNews 84*
Savanna Times Journal - Savanna, IL - *BaconPubCkNews 84; Ed&PubIntYB 82; NewsDir 84*
Savannah Cablevision [of News-Press & Gazette Co.] - Savannah, MO - *BrCabYB 84*
Savannah Cablevision [of Group W Cable Inc.] - Savannah, TN - *Tel&CabFB 84C*
Savannah Courier - Savannah, TN - *BaconPubCkNews 84; Ed&PubIntYB 82; NewsDir 84*
Savannah Evening Press - Savannah, GA - *Ed&PubIntYB 82; LitMarPl 84*
Savannah Herald - Savannah, GA - *BaconPubCkNews 84; Ed&PubIntYB 82*
Savannah Morning News [of Savannah News-Press] - Savannah, GA - *Ed&PubIntYB 82; LitMarPl 83, 84*
Savannah News - Savannah, GA - *BaconPubCkNews 84*
Savannah News-Press [of Southeastern Newspapers Corp.] - Savannah, GA - *NewsDir 84*
Savannah Press - Savannah, GA - *BaconPubCkNews 84*
Savannah Reporter & Andrew County Democrat - Savannah, MO - *BaconPubCkNews 84; Ed&PubIntYB 82; NewsDir 84*
Savannah Research Center - Savannah, GA - *IntDirMarRes 83*
Savannah Southern Cross - Savannah, GA - *NewsDir 84*
Savannah/Sumner - Savannah, GA - *DirMarMP 83*
Savannah Tribune - Savannah, GA - *BaconPubCkNews 84*
Savannah TV Cable [of American Television & Communications Corp.] - Savannah, GA - *BrCabYB 84; Tel&CabFB 84C*
Savant - Fullerton, CA - *AvMarPl 83*
Savant Corp. - Houston, TX - *MicrocomMPl 84*
Savant Enterprises - Carnforth, Englad - *MicrocomSwDir 1*
Savant Software Inc. - Houston, TX - *WritMar 84*
Save the Children - Westport, CT - *AvMarPl 83; WritMar 84*
Saver, The - Madison, WV - *Ed&PubIntYB 82*
Saverservice [of Telecom Systems Inc.] - Daleville, VA - *TeleSy&SerDir 2-84*
Savin Corp. - Valhalla, NY - *DirInfWP 82*
Savin Information Systems - Sunnyvale, CA - *DirInfWP 82*
Saving Energy - Bellevue, WA - *BaconPubCkMag 84; WritMar 84*
Savings & Loan [of Federal Home Loan Bank Board] - Washington, DC - *DBBus 82; DirOnDB Spring 84*
Savings & Loan [of ADP Network Services] - Ann Arbor, MI - *DataDirOnSer 84*
Savings & Loan News - Chicago, IL - *ArtMar 84; MagIndMarPl 82-83*
Savings Bank Journal [of Thrift Publishers Inc.] - New York, NY - *BaconPubCkMag 84; MagDir 84*
Savings Banker [of Savings Banks Association of Massachusetts] - Boston, MA - *BaconPubCkMag 84; MagDir 84*
Savings Institutions [of U.S. League of Savings Institutions] - Chicago, IL - *BaconPubCkMag 84; MagDir 84*
Savings Management Computer Corp. - Boston, MA - *DataDirSup 7-83*
Savitt Group Inc., The - New York, NY - *IntDirMarRes 83*
Savitz Research Center Inc. - Dallas, TX - *IntDirMarRes 83*
Savoy Records Inc. - Elizabeth, NJ - *BillIntBG 83-84*
Savvy - New York, NY - *ArtMar 84; BaconPubCkMag 84; Folio 83; LitMarPl 83, 84; MagDir 84; MagIndMarPl 82-83; WritMar 84*
Savvy Management Inc. - New York, NY - *LitMarPl 83, 84; MagIndMarPl 82-83*
Sawan Kirpal Publications [Aff. of Sawan Kirpal Rehani Mission Inc.] - Bowling Green, VA - *BoPubDir 4, 5*
Sawdon & Bess Advertising Inc. - New York, NY - *AdAge 3-28-84; BrCabYB 84; StaDirAdAg 2-84*
Sawgrass Music Publishers Inc. - Nashville, TN - *BillIntBG 83-84*
Sawyer Advertising - Gainesville, GA - *AdAge 3-28-84; StaDirAdAg 2-84*
Sawyer Camera & Instrument Co. - Los Angeles, CA - *AvMarPl 83*
Sawyer Co., The - Columbus, OH - *HBIndAd&MS 82-83*
Sawyer County Gazette - Winter, WI - *AyerDirPub 83; Ed&PubIntYB 82*
Sawyer County Record - Hayward, WI - *Ed&PubIntYB 82*
Sawyer County Record & Hayward Republican - Hayward, WI - *AyerDirPub 83*
Sawyer-Ferguson-Walker Co. Inc. - New York, NY - *LitMarPl 83, 84*
Sawyer Press - Los Angeles, CA - *BoPubDir 4, 5; Ed&PubIntYB 82; LitMarPl 83, 84; MagIndMarPl 82-83*
Sawyer Public Relations [Div. of Sawyer Advertising Inc.] - Gainesville, GA - *DirPRFirms 83*
Saxe Co. Inc., The - New York, NY - *StaDirAdAg 2-84*
Saxe Mitchell - Woodbury, NY - *AdAge 3-28-84; StaDirAdAg 2-84*
Saxon Associates Inc. - Los Angeles, CA - *StaDirAdAg 2-84*
Saxon Business Products - Miami Lakes, FL - *DirInfWP 82*
Saxon Paper-New York [Div. of Saxon Industries Inc.] - Long Island City, NY - *LitMarPl 83, 84; MagIndMarPl 82-83*
Saxon Personnel Agency - New York, NY - *LitMarPl 83, 84*
Saxton Broad Top Bulletin - Saxton, PA - *BaconPubCkNews 84*
Saxton Communications Group Ltd. - New York, NY - *ArtMar 84; AvMarPl 83; DirMarMP 83; DirPRFirms 83; IntDirMarRes 83; LitMarPl 83, 84; StaDirAdAg 2-84; WritMar 84*
Say-Soft Products - San Jose, CA - *MicrocomMPl 84*
Saybrook Gazette - Saybrook, IL - *BaconPubCkNews 84; Ed&PubIntYB 82*
Saybrook Press Inc., The - Old Saybrook, CT - *LitMarPl 83, 84*
Saylor Electronics International - Carson City, NV - *WhoWMicrocom 83*
Saylor Inc., Lee - Walnut Creek, CA - *BoPubDir 4, 5*
Sayre Journal - Sayre, OK - *BaconPubCkNews 84; NewsDir 84*
Sayre Sun - Sayre, OK - *AyerDirPub 83; Ed&PubIntYB 82*
Sayre TV Cable System [of Dorate Inc.] - Sayre, OK - *BrCabYB 84; Tel&CabFB 84C*
Sayville Suffolk County News - Sayville, NY - *BaconPubCkNews 84*
SAZTEC - Rolling Hills Estates, CA - *DataDirSup 7-83; EISS 7-83 Sup; LitMarPl 83, 84*
SB & W Associates - Boston, MA - *AdAge 3-28-84; StaDirAdAg 2-84*
SB-I [of Questel Inc.] - Washington, DC - *DataDirOnSer 84*
SB-I - Creteil, France - *DirOnDB Spring 84*
SBA Advertising - Canton, OH - *StaDirAdAg 2-84*
S.B.C. Cable [of Susquehanna Broadcasting Co.] - Benton, IL - *Tel&CabFB 84C*
SBC Small Business Computers Ltd. - Calgary, AB, Canada - *WhoWMicrocom 83*
SBC Today - Decatur, GA - *BaconPubCkMag 84*
SBCS - Lincoln, NE - *MicrocomMPl 83*
SBD Computer Services Corp. - Hyattsville, MD - *DataDirOnSer 84*
SBD Data Base [of Booksellers Association] - Paris, France - *EISS 83*
SBI Inc. - San Diego, CA - *BrCabYB 84*
SBI, Publishers in Sound - South Lee, MA - *DirMarMP 83*

SBN Public Relations [Div. of Spencer Bennett] - Seekonk, MA - *DirPRFirms 83*
SBS Publishing Inc. - Englewood, NJ - *LitMarPl 83, 84*
SBSG Inc. - Westford, MA - *MicrocomMPl 84*
S.C. Digital - Aurora, IL - *WhoWMicrocom 83*
SC Software Corp. - Dallas, TX - *MicrocomMPl 83*
Scafa-Tornabene Art Publishing Co. Inc. - West Nyack, NY - *ArtMar 84*
Scagnetti Talent Agency, Jack - North Hollywood, CA - *LitMarPl 83, 84*
Scaife Newspapers - Greensburg, PA - *Ed&PubIntYB 82*
Scala Fine Arts Publishers Inc. - New York, NY - *AvMarPl 83*
Scala Fine Arts Transparencies - New York, NY - *LitMarPl 83, 84*
Scalacs [of Southern California, American Chemical Society] - Los Angeles, CA - *BaconPubCkMag 84; MagDir 84*
Scales Associates Inc., Ray - Oklahoma City, OK - *DirPRFirms 83*
Scales of Justice Music Inc. - Lafayette, LA - *BillIntBG 83-84*
Scali, McCabe, Sloves [Subs. of Ogilvy & Mather International] - New York, NY - *AdAge 3-28-84, 6-25-84; Br 1-23-84; BrCabYB 84; StaDirAdAg 2-84*
Scan [of Remote Computing] - Palo Alto, CA - *DataDirOnSer 84*
SCAN - Washington, DC - *DirOnDB Spring 84*
Scan - Milton, England - *DirOnDB Spring 84*
Scan Corp. - Peoria, IL - *Ed&PubIntYB 82*
Scan-Data Corp. - Norristown, PA - *DataDirSup 7-83; DirInfWP 82; InfIndMarPl 83*
Scan-Optics Inc. - East Hartford, CT - *DataDirSup 7-83; DirInfWP 82*
Scan-Tron Corp. - Long Beach, CA - *DataDirSup 7-83*
Scan200 [of ADP Network Services] - Ann Arbor, MI - *DataDirOnSer 84; DirOnDB Spring 84*
Scandia Historical Committee - Scandia, AB, Canada - *BoPubDir 4 Sup, 5*
Scandia Journal - Scandia, KS - *BaconPubCkNews 84; Ed&PubIntYB 82*
Scandiline Industries Inc. - Compton, CA - *DirInfWP 82*
Scandinavia Telephone Co. [Aff. of Telephone & Data Systems] - Iola, WI - *TelDir&BG 83-84*
Scandinavian Business Librarians Group [of Helsinki School of Economics Library] - Helsinki, Finland - *CompReadDB 82*
Scandinavian Periodicals Index in Economics & Business [of Scandinavian Business Librarians Group] - Helsinki, Finland - *CompReadDB 82*
Scandinavian Review [of American-Scandinavian Foundation] - New York, NY - *LitMag&SmPr 83-84; MagDir 84; MagIndMarPl 82-83; WritMar 84*
Scandura Training Systems Inc. - Narberth, PA - *MicrocomSwDir 1*
Scanfax [of Institute of Electrical & Electronics Engineers] - Chicago, IL - *BaconPubCkMag 84; MagDir 84*
Scanlon, Skalsky & Menken Ltd. - New York, NY - *DirPRFirms 83*
Scannell Inc. - *See* Brady Co., The
Scanner & King County Labor News [of KCLC, AFL-CIO] - Seattle, WA - *NewsDir 84*
Scannet Foundation [of Nordic Cooperative Organization for Applied Research] - Gothenburg, Sweden - *EISS 83*
Scannet Foundation [of Nordic Cooperative Organization for Applied Research] - Stockholm, Sweden - *EISS 5-84 Sup; InfIndMarPl 83*
Scanning Electron Microscopy Inc. - Chicago, IL - *BoPubDir 4, 5*
Scanp - Aarhus, Denmark - *DirOnDB Spring 84*
Scantel-Sherman Group Ltd., The - *See* Sherman Group Inc., The
Scape - Seattle, WA - *LitMag&SmPr 83-84*
Scappoose Spotlight - Scappoose, OR - *AyerDirPub 83; BaconPubCkNews 84; Ed&PubIntYB 82*
Scarab Press - Orinda, CA - *BoPubDir 4, 5*
Scarab Publishing Corp. - *See* Famous Music Corp.
Scaramouche Books - *See* Poor Souls Press/Scaramouche Books
Scaramouche' Records - Warner Robins, GA - *BillIntBG 83-84*
Scarboro Cable Communications [of CUC Ltd.] - Scarborough, ON, Canada - *BrCabYB 84*
Scarborough Mirror - Scarborough, ON, Canada - *AyerDirPub 83; Ed&PubIntYB 82*
Scarborough Publishing Co. - Scarborough, ME - *BoPubDir 4 Sup, 5; LitMag&SmPr 83-84*
Scarborough Reports [of Interactive Market Systems] - New York, NY - *DataDirOnSer 84; DirOnDB Spring 84*
Scarborough Research Corp. - New York, NY - *IntDirMarRes 83; MagIndMarPl 82-83*
Scarecrow Press [Div. of Grolier Educational Corp.] - Metuchen, NJ - *LitMag&SmPr 83-84; LitMarPl 83, 84; WritMar 84*
Scarf Press - New York, NY - *BoPubDir 4, 5; LitMag&SmPr 83-84*
Scarlet Ibis Press - Bloomington, IL - *BoPubDir 4, 5*
Scarlett Letter [of Big Red Apple Club] - Norfolk, NE - *MicrocomMPl 84*
Scarlett Letters Inc. - New York, NY - *LitMarPl 84*
Scarpa, Frank S. - Vineland, NJ - *Tel&CabFB 84C p.1700*
Scarpa, John F. - Seaside Heights, NJ - *Tel&CabFB 84C p.1700*
Scarsdale Inquirer [of S.I. Communications Inc.] - Scarsdale, NY - *BaconPubCkNews 84; Ed&PubIntYB 82; NewsDir 84*
Scatcom Inc. [of Adams Electric Cooperative] - Adams County, PA - *Tel&CabFB 84C*
Scates & Blanton Publishing - *See* Axbar Productions
Scattawave Publishing - *See* Jacobson, Jeffrey E.
SCDC - Clovis, CA - *MicrocomMPl 83*
S.C.E. Editions l'Etincelle - Montreal, PQ, Canada - *WritMar 84*
Scene Magazine - San Francisco, CA - *WritMar 84*
Scene Magazine - Dallas, TX - *MagIndMarPl 82-83*
Scene Productions - Beckley, WV - *BillIntBG 83-84*
Scene, The - Solana Beach, CA - *BaconPubCkMag 84*
Scenic Range News - Bovey, MN - *AyerDirPub 83; Ed&PubIntYB 82*
Scenographic Media - Norwalk, CT - *BoPubDir 4, 5*
Scepter Publishers - New Rochelle, NY - *BoPubDir 4, 5*
SCG Advertising [Subs. of Synergistic Communications Group Inc.] - Overland Park, KS - *HBIndAd&MS 82-83; StaDirAdAg 2-84*
Schaaf, Miv - Pasadena, CA - *Ed&PubIntYB 82*
Schab Gallery Inc., William H. - New York, NY - *BoPubDir 4, 5*
Schabraf Music [Div. of Bee Jay Booking Agency & Recording Studios Inc.] - Orlando, FL - *BillIntBG 83-84*
Schachat Associates Construction Computing, Brett - Johannesburg, South Africa - *MicrocomSwDir 1*
Schacht Public Relations, Janis - New York, NY - *DirPRFirms 83*
Schachtman-Fagan Inc. - Stamford, CT - *IntDirMarRes 83*
Schade & Associates Inc., R. C. - New Paltz, NY - *AdAge 3-28-84; StaDirAdAg 2-84*
Schaechter Advertising Co., The - East Hartford, CT - *StaDirAdAg 2-84*
Schaefer Advertising - Valley Forge, PA - *AdAge 3-28-84; DirMarMP 83; StaDirAdAg 2-84*
Schaefer, Jack W. - Mitchell, SD - *Tel&CabFB 84C p.1700*
Schaefer/Karpf Productions - Hollywood, CA - *TelAl 83*
Schaefer/Karpf Productions - Studio City, CA - *TelAl 84; Tel&CabFB 84C*
Schafer Advertising - Tucson, AZ - *AdAge 3-28-84; StaDirAdAg 2-84*
Schafer Promotions, Don - Dallas, TX - *BillIntBG 83-84*
Schaffner Associates Inc., John - New York, NY - *LitMarPl 83, 84*
Schafler Enterprises - Mill Valley, CA - *BoPubDir 4, 5*
Schaghticoke Sun - Schaghticoke, NY - *Ed&PubIntYB 82*
Schalaco - Paradise Valley, AZ - *BoPubDir 5*
Schalit, Michael - Livermore, CA - *BoPubDir 4, 5*
Schalkenbach Foundation, Robert - New York, NY - *BoPubDir 4, 5*
Schaller Direct Mail Marketing, George - Vernon Hills, IL - *DirMarMP 83*
Schaller Herald - Schaller, IA - *BaconPubCkNews 84; Ed&PubIntYB 82*
Schaller Telephone Co. - Schaller, IA - *Tel&CabFB 84C p.1700*
Schank Associates, Bernard - New York, NY - *StaDirAdAg 2-84*
Scharer Associates - Great Neck, NY - *AdAge 3-28-84; StaDirAdAg 2-84*
Scharfberg & Associates - Jenkintown, PA - *AdAge 3-28-84; StaDirAdAg 2-84*

Scharff, Witchel & Co. - *See* Kanan, Corbin, Schupak & Aronow Inc.
Schaum Publications Inc. - Milwaukee, WI - *BillIntBG 83-84*
Schaumburg Record - Schaumburg, IL - *Ed&PubIntYB 82*
Schaumburg Voice - *See* Voice Newspapers
Schawkgraphics - Chicago, IL - *MagIndMarPl 82-83*
Schechter Group, The - New York, NY - *HBIndAd&MS 82-83*
Schecterson & Schecterson - New York, NY - *LitMarPl 83, 84; MagIndMarPl 82-83*
Schecterson Associates Inc., Jack - New York, NY - *LitMarPl 83, 84; MagIndMarPl 82-83; StaDirAdAg 2-84*
Schedule - Denver, CO - *DirOnDB Spring 84*
Scheduled Mailings [Div. of La Salle Industries] - New York, NY - *LitMarPl 83, 84*
Scheel, Ronald E. - Plano, TX - *LitMarPl 83, 84*
Scheer Advertising Agency, William N. - South Orange, NJ - *StaDirAdAg 2-84*
Scheer Associates, George - Chapel Hill, NC - *BoPubDir 4 Sup, 5; LitMarPl 83, 84*
Scheffel'sche Verlagsbuchhandlung - Langenfeld, West Germany - *MicroMarPl 82-83*
Scheib Associates, Ann - Dobbs Ferry, NY - *IntDirMarRes 83*
Scheid & Associates, Kenneth G. - Pittsburgh, PA - *LitMarPl 83*
Schein/Blattstein Advertising - New York, NY - *AdAge 3-28-84; DirMarMP 83; StaDirAdAg 2-84*
Schell Books - Stockton, CA - *BoPubDir 4, 5*
Schenectady Cablevision Inc. [of Athena Communications Corp.] - Schenectady, NY - *BrCabYB 84; Tel&CabFB 84C*
Schenectady Gazette - Schenectady, NY - *BaconPubCkNews 84; Ed&PubIntYB 82; NewsBur 6; NewsDir 84*
Schenevus TV Cable Service [of NewChannels Corp.] - Schenevus, NY - *BrCabYB 84*
Schenkein/Associates - Englewood, CO - *AdAge 3-28-84; StaDirAdAg 2-84*
Schenkman Publishing Co. Inc. - Cambridge, MA - *LitMarPl 83, 84; WritMar 84*
Scherer, J. L. - Minneapolis, MN - *BoPubDir 4, 5*
Schereville/St. John Town & Country - Hammond, IN - *AyerDirPub 83*
Scherick Associates, Edgar J. - New York, NY - *LitMarPl 83*
Schering-Oriented Literature Analysis & Retrieval [of Schering-Plough Corp.] - Bloomfield, NJ - *EISS 83*
Schettino Co., Elaine F. - White Plains, NY - *IntDirMarRes 83; LitMarPl 83, 84*
Schey Advertising - Houston, TX - *AdAge 3-28-84; StaDirAdAg 2-84*
Schick Information Systems Ltd. - Edmonton, AB, Canada - *EISS 83; FBInfSer 80; InfIndMarPl 83*
Schick Information Systems Ltd. - *See* Nichols Applied Management
Schiedt, Duncan P. - Pittsboro, IN - *BoPubDir 4, 5*
Schiff Inc., Ralph - Newton, MA - *StaDirAdAg 2-84*
Schiff-Jones Ltd. - New York, NY - *Tel&CabFB 84C*
Schiff Photo Mechanics - Santa Ana, CA - *AvMarPl 83*
Schiffer Publishing Ltd. - Exton, PA - *LitMarPl 83, 84; WritMar 84*
Schiffli Lace & Embroidery Manufacturers Association - Union City, NJ - *BoPubDir 5*
Schiffman, Keith - New York, NY - *LitMarPl 84*
Schiffmann Associates, R. F. - New York, NY - *HBIndAd&MS 82-83*
Schilder, Rosalind - Plymouth Meeting, PA - *BoPubDir 5*
Schiller & Co., W. - St. Louis, MO - *AvMarPl 83*
Schiller Co., J. - Edison, NJ - *DirInfWP 82*
Schiller Market Research Inc., Audrey - Levittown, NY - *IntDirMarRes 83*
Schiller Marketing Research & Consulting, Nathan - Stamford, CT - *IntDirMarRes 83*
Schiller Park Independent [of Franklin Park Publishing Co.] - Franklin Park, IL - *NewsDir 84*
Schiller Park Independent - Schiller Park, IL - *Ed&PubIntYB 82*
Schiller Park Independent - Wilmette, IL - *AyerDirPub 83*
Schiller Park Independent - *See* Pioneer Press Inc.
Schiller Park Post [of Elmwood Park Post Newspapers-Meese Papers Inc.] - Chicago, IL - *NewsDir 84*
Schiller Park Post - Elmwood Park, IL - *AyerDirPub 83*
Schiller Park Post - Schiller Park, IL - *Ed&PubIntYB 82*
Schiller Park Post - *See* Meese' Newspaper Group
Schiller Park Times - Schiller Park, IL - *Ed&PubIntYB 82*
Schiller Park Times - *See* Lerner Times Newspapers
Schimmelpfeng GmbH - Frankfurt, West Germany - *EISS 5-84 Sup*
Schimmelpfeng Information Broker Service [of Schimmelpfeng GmbH] - Frankfurt, West Germany - *EISS 5-84 Sup*
Schindler Broadcasting - Houston, TX - *BrCabYB 84*
Schine & Co. Inc., David - Los Angeles, CA - *BillIntBG 83-84*
Schipa, Mary - Watertown, MA - *LitMarPl 83, 84*
Schirmer Books [of Macmillan Publishing Co. Inc.] - New York, NY - *LitMarPl 83, 84; WritMar 84*
Schirmer Inc., G. - New York, NY - *BillIntBG 83-84*
Schirmer Inc., G. [Subs. of Macmilliam Inc.] - Woodside, NY - *LitMarPl 84*
Schirmer Music Co., E. C. - Boston, MA - *BillIntBG 83-84*
Schlackman Group Ltd. - London, England - *IntDirMarRes 83*
Schlaifer & Co. Inc., Charles - New York, NY - *BrCabYB 84; StaDirAdAg 2-84*
Schleier Reviews, Curt - River Vale, NJ - *LitMarPl 83, 84*
Schleier Syndicate, Curt - Riverdale, NJ - *Ed&PubIntYB 82*
Schleifer Co., Bernard - New York, NY - *LitMarPl 83, 84*
Schleiger, Arlene - Redlands, CA - *BoPubDir 4, 5*
Schlesinger Associates, Sarah B. - Woodbridge, NJ - *IntDirMarRes 83*
Schlessinger & Associates - San Francisco, CA - *StaDirAdAg 2-84*
Schleswig Leader - Schleswig, IA - *BaconPubCkNews 84; Ed&PubIntYB 82*
Schlumberger Ltd. - New York, NY - *Datamation 6-83; ElecNews 7-25-83; Top100Al 83*
Schmelzer & Associates, Jerome H. - Cleveland, OH - *AdAge 3-28-84; ArtMar 84; StaDirAdAg 2-84*
Schmidt & Associates Inc., Arthur - New York, NY - *DirPRFirms 83*
Schmidt Co., Arthur P. - *See* Birch Tree Group Ltd.
Schmidt Co. Inc., Ken - Milwaukee, WI - *AdAge 3-28-84; DirPRFirms 83; StaDirAdAg 2-84*
Schmidt, Robert E. - Hays, KS - *BrCabYB 84 p.D-306; Tel&CabFB 84C p.1700*
Schmidt, Terrie J. - Indialantic, FL - *LitMarPl 84*
Schmidt, Walter E. - New York, NY - *ADAPSOMemDir 83-84*
Schmitt & Associates, Gar - Cedar Grove, NJ - *DirPRFirms 83*
Schnapp Software Consulting, R. - San Diego, CA - *MicrocomSwDir 1*
Schnase, Annemarie (Reprint Dept.) - Scarsdale, NY - *BoPubDir 4, 5*
Schnase Microfilm Systems - Scarsdale, NY - *MicroMarPl 82-83*
Schnectady Reporter - Schnectady, NY - *Ed&PubIntYB 82*
Schneeberger & Associates, Tilly - Ojai, CA - *BoPubDir 4, 5*
Schneider & Associates Inc. - Brookline, MA - *DirPRFirms 83*
Schneider, Coleman - Tenafly, NJ - *BoPubDir 4, 5*
Schneider Corp. of America - Woodbury, NY - *AvMarPl 83*
Schneider, David L. - New York, NY - *IntDirMarRes 83*
Schneider Enterprises - Burlington, WI - *MicrocomMPl 83*
Schneider Enterprises Inc. - Salem, VA - *BoPubDir 4, 5*
Schneider Parker Jakuc Inc. - Boston, MA - *AdAge 3-28-84; DirPRFirms 83; StaDirAdAg 2-84*
Schneider Publishers, R. - Stevens Point, WI - *BoPubDir 4 Sup, 5*
Schnur Appel Television Corp. - Short Hills, NJ - *Tel&CabFB 84C*
Schocken Books Inc. - New York, NY - *ArtMar 84; LitMarPl 83, 84; WritMar 84*
Schoen Co., Michael W. - Scarsdale, NY - *StaDirAdAg 2-84*
Schoenback Advertising Inc. - Baltimore, MD - *StaDirAdAg 2-84*
Schoenbrod Inc., Robert D. - Chicago, IL - *StaDirAdAg 2-84*
Schoenfeld Inc., Gerald - New York, NY - *HBIndAd&MS 82-83*
Schoenfeld Straus - New York, NY - *AdAge 3-28-84; StaDirAdAg 2-84*
Schoenhof's Foreign Books [Subs. of Editions Gallimard] - Cambridge, MA - *LitMarPl 83, 84*
Schoenthal Inc., Harriet - New York, NY - *DirPRFirms 83*
Schoepfer, G. R. - Howell, NJ - *BoPubDir 5*
Schoepfer, G. R. - Floral Park, NY - *BoPubDir 4*
Schoharie County Cablevision [of Home Entertainment Co.] - Cobleskill, NY - *BrCabYB 84; Tel&CabFB 84C*
Scholarly Book Center - Waukegan, IL - *LitMarPl 84*

Scholarly Publishing, A Journal for Authors & Publishers [of University of Toronto Press] - Toronto, ON, Canada - *LitMarPl 83, 84*
Scholarly Resources Inc. - Wilmington, DE - *LitMarPl 83, 84; MagIndMarPl 82-83; MicroMarPl 82-83; WritMar 84*
Scholars Book Co. - Houston, TX - *BoPubDir 4, 5*
Scholars' Facsimiles & Reprints - Delmar, NY - *LitMarPl 83, 84; MicroMarPl 82-83*
Scholars Portable Publications - Evansville, IN - *BoPubDir 4, 5*
Scholars Press - Chico, CA - *LitMarPl 83, 84; MicroMarPl 82-83*
Scholarships, Fellowships, & Loans News Service - Arlington, MA - *MagDir 84*
Scholastic Coach - New York, NY - *BaconPubCkMag 84; MagDir 84*
Scholastic Editor - Minneapolis, MN - *BaconPubCkMag 84; MagDir 84*
Scholastic Inc. - New York, NY - *DirMarMP 83; KnowInd 83; LitMarPl 83, 84; MagIndMarPl 82-83; MicrocomMPl 84; WritMar 84*
Scholastic Inc. (Pretzel Books) - New York, NY - *WritMar 84*
Scholastic Magazines for Students in Elementary & Secondary Schools - New York, NY - *MagDir 84*
Scholastic Newstime - New York, NY - *MagDir 84*
Scholastic Scope [of Scholastic Magazines Inc.] - New York, NY - *MagDir 84; MagIndMarPl 82-83; WritMar 84*
Scholastic-Tab Publications [Subs. of Scholastic Inc.] - Richmond Hill, ON, Canada - *LitMarPl 83, 84; WritMar 84*
Scholastic Update - New York, NY - *BaconPubCkMag 84*
Scholia Satyrica - Tampa, FL - *LitMag&SmPr 83-84*
Scholium International Inc. - Great Neck, NY - *ArtMar 84; LitMarPl 83, 84; WritMar 84*
Scholl & Co. Inc., Len - Los Angeles, CA - *AdAge 3-28-84; StaDirAdAg 2-84*
Schon Ltd., Kurt E. - New Orleans, LA - *BoPubDir 4 Sup, 5*
Schonek & Rudolph, W. E. - *See* Green Group, Howard
School & Community - Columbia, MO - *BaconPubCkMag 84; MagDir 84*
School & Home CourseWare Inc. - Fresno, CA - *MicrocomMPl 84*
School Arts Magazine - Worcester, MA - *BaconPubCkMag 84; MagDir 84; MagIndMarPl 82-83; WritMar 84*
School Bus Fleet - Redondo Beach, CA - *BaconPubCkMag 84; MagDir 84*
School Business Affairs - Park Ridge, IL - *BaconPubCkMag 84; MagDir 84; MagIndMarPl 82-83*
School Food Service Journal - Denver, CO - *BaconPubCkMag 84; MagDir 84; MagIndMarPl 82-83*
School Library Journal [of R. R. Bowker Co.] - New York, NY - *BaconPubCkMag 84; LitMarPl 83, 84; MagDir 84; MagIndMarPl 82-83*
School Library Media Quarterly - Chicago, IL - *BaconPubCkMag 84; MagDir 84; MagIndMarPl 82-83*
School Lists Mailing Inc. - Tinton Falls, NJ - *LitMarPl 83, 84*
School Management Systems - Sweet Home, OR - *MicrocomMPl 84*
School Media Associates - Atlanta, GA - *AvMarPl 83; LitMarPl 83, 84*
School Microcomputing Bulletin [of Learning Publication Inc.] - Holmes Beach, FL - *MicrocomMPl 84*
School Musician, Director & Teacher, The - Chicago, IL - *BaconPubCkMag 84; MagDir 84; MagIndMarPl 82-83*
School of American Research Press - Santa Fe, NM - *BoPubDir 4, 5*
School of Economic Science [Aff. of Henry George School of Social Science] - Toronto, ON, Canada - *BoPubDir 4, 5*
School of Living, The - York, PA - *LitMag&SmPr 83-84*
School of Spiritual Psychology [Aff. of Morningstar Enterprises Inc.] - Milwaukee, WI - *BoPubDir 4 Sup, 5*
School Practices Information File [of Bibliographic Retrieval Services] - Latham, NY - *CompReadDB 82; DataDirOnSer 84; DirOnDB Spring 84*
School Practices Information Network [of Bibliographic Retrieval Services] - Latham, NY - *EISS 83*
School Product News - Cleveland, OH - *BaconPubCkMag 84; MagDir 84; MagIndMarPl 82-83*
School Projectionist Club of America - State College, PA - *BoPubDir 4, 5*
School Science & Mathematics - Tempe, AZ - *MagIndMarPl 82-83*
School Shop - Ann Arbor, MI - *ArtMar 84; BaconPubCkMag 84; MagDir 84; MagIndMarPl 82-83; WritMar 84*
School Specialty Supply Inc. - Salina, KS - *AvMarPl 83*
Schoolhouse Press - Pittsville, WI - *BoPubDir 5*
Schoolhouse Software - Elk Grove, IL - *MicrocomMPl 84*
Schoonover Advertising, Raymond - New York, NY - *StaDirAdAg 2-84*
Schor Associates Inc., Harold - New York, NY - *DirPRFirms 83*
Schorr & Howard Co. - New York, NY - *DirPRFirms 83*
Schott - *See* European American Music Corp.
Schott Inc., Marian G. - Mt. Kisco, NY - *IntDirMarRes 83*
Schpitfeir Enterprises - Richfield, MN - *BoPubDir 5*
Schrader, Michael - New York, NY - *LitMarPl 83*
Schrader Research & Rating Service - Cranbury, NJ - *IntDirMarRes 83*
Schram Advertising Co. - Chicago, IL - *ArtMar 84; DirMarMP 83; StaDirAdAg 2-84*
Schram Ltd., Abner [Div. of Allanheld & Schram] - Montclair, NJ - *LitMarPl 83, 84; WritMar 84*
Schramm, Gloria - North Bellmore, NY - *LitMarPl 83*
Schreiber Inc., Sydney - Philadelphia, PA - *AdAge 3-28-84; StaDirAdAg 2-84*
Schreier, Carl - Moose, WY - *LitMarPl 84*
Schreiner Associates - Boston, MA - *DirPRFirms 83*
Schroder Music Co. - Berkeley, CA - *BillIntBG 83-84; BoPubDir 4, 5*
Schroeder & Gunther - *See* Schirmer Inc., G.
Schroeder Eastwood Photography - Washington, DC - *LitMarPl 84*
Schroeder Editorial Services - Lombard, IL - *LitMarPl 83, 84; MagIndMarPl 82-83*
Schroeder International Ltd., A. - New York, NY - *BillIntBG 83-84*
Schroeder Paper Co. Inc., Arthur [Div. of The Hearst Corp.] - New York, NY - *LitMarPl 83, 84*
Schroeppel, Tom - Miami, FL - *BoPubDir 4 Sup, 5*
Schroer Advertising, Robert - Naples, FL - *StaDirAdAg 2-84*
Schroll Press Inc. - Merrick, NY - *BoPubDir 4 Sup*
Schubert, Bernard L. - New York, NY - *Tel&CabFB 84C*
Schuck, L. Pearl - Regina, SK, Canada - *BoPubDir 5*
Schuessler Case Co. Inc. - Chicago, IL - *AvMarPl 83*
Schulaner, Franklin L. - Kealakekua, HI - *LitMarPl 83, 84*
Schulberg Dorese Agency - New York, NY - *LitMarPl 83, 84*
Schuldt, Lesley M. - Newbury Park, CA - *LitMarPl 83*
Schuldt, Lesley M. - Portland, OR - *LitMarPl 84*
Schulenburg Sticker - Schulenburg, TX - *BaconPubCkNews 84; Ed&PubIntYB 82*
Schuller, Briggs & Mitchell Inc. - San Francisco, CA - *BrCabYB 84*
Schuller Ministries, Robert - Orange, CA - *Tel&CabFB 84C*
Schulman Co., Paul [Subs. of Advanswers Media/Programming Inc.] - New York, NY - *HBIndAd&MS 82-83*
Schulman Co., Paul - *See* Gardner Advertising Co. Inc.
Schulman Literary Agency, Susan - New York, NY - *LitMarPl 83, 84*
Schulman, Ronca & Bucuvalas Inc. - New York, NY - *IntDirMarRes 83*
Schulte Ross & Aguilar Inc. - Miami, FL - *DirPRFirms 83*
Schultz & Co., E. C. - Elk Grove Village, IL - *LitMarPl 83, 84*
Schultz, Bob - Forsyth, MT - *Tel&CabFB 84C p.1700*
Schultz Investment Co., J. M. - Fairfield, IL - *Tel&CabFB 84C p.1700*
Schulwolf, Frank - Coral Gables, FL - *HBIndAd&MS 82-83*
Schumacher Publications - Duluth, MN - *BoPubDir 4, 5*
Schuman, Jacqueline Wilsdon - New York, NY - *LitMarPl 83, 84*
Schur, Susan E. - Boston, MA - *StaDirAdAg 2-84*
Schurz Communications Inc. - South Bend, IN - *BrCabYB 84; Ed&PubIntYB 82; KnowInd 83; Tel&CabFB 84C p.1701, 84S*
Schutze, Frieda - Woodstock, NY - *LitMarPl 83, 84*
Schuyler Communications Inc. - Sacramento, CA - *BrCabYB 84*
Schuyler Sun - Schuyler, NE - *BaconPubCkNews 84; Ed&PubIntYB 82; NewsDir 84*
Schuyler Telephone Co., The - Rushville, IL - *TelDir&BG 83-84*
Schuylkill Haven Call - *See* West Schuylkill Herald Publishers
Schuylkill Haven Call, The - Schuylkill Haven, PA - *NewsDir 84*

Schuylkill Valley Trans Video Corp. - Brockton, PA - *BrCabYB 84; Tel&CabFB 84C*
Schwab Beatty [Div. of Marsteller Inc.] - New York, NY - *BrCabYB 84; DirMarMP 83; LitMarPl 83, 84*
Schwab Safe Co. Inc. - Lafayette, IN - *WhoWMicrocom 83*
Schwalb, Susan - Newton Centre, MA - *LitMarPl 83*
Schwalb, Susan - Watertown, MA - *LitMarPl 84*
Schwalf, Susan - New York, NY - *MagIndMarPl 82-83*
Schwalm Historical Association Inc., Johannes - Lyndhurst, OH - *BoPubDir 4, 5*
Schwan's Sales Enterprises (Syncom Div.) - Mitchell, SD - *DirInfWP 82*
Schwartz Agency, Gerald - Miami Beach, FL - *ArtMar 84*
Schwartz & Associates Inc., Harold S. - Chicago, IL - *StaDirAdAg 2-84*
Schwartz & Associates Inc., Howard M. - Philadelphia, PA - *StaDirAdAg 2-84*
Schwartz & Associates, Robert - New York, NY - *LitMarPl 83, 84; MagIndMarPl 82-83; StaDirAdAg 2-84*
Schwartz & Co. Inc., G. S. - New York, NY - *DirPRFirms 83*
Schwartz, Arthur P. - New York, NY - *LitMarPl 83, 84*
Schwartz Associates Inc., Richard A. - Dover, DE - *LitMarPl 83, 84*
Schwartz Brothers Inc. - Lanham, MD - *MicrocomMPl 84*
Schwartz Literary Agency, Frances - New York, NY - *LitMarPl 83, 84*
Schwartz Music Co. Inc. - *See* Laurie Publishing Group
Schwartz Public Relations Agency, Gerald - Miami Beach, FL - *DirPRFirms 83*
Schwartz Public Relations Associates Inc. - New York, NY - *DirPRFirms 83*
Schwarz Leather Corp. [Div. of Beatrice Foods Co.] - Edgewater, NJ - *LitMarPl 83, 84*
Schweizer-Journal - San Francisco, CA - *Ed&PubIntYB 82*
Schwenger, Jane - New York, NY - *LitMarPl 83, 84*
Schwenksville Item - Schwenksville, PA - *BaconPubCkNews 84; Ed&PubIntYB 82*
Schwilgin, F. A. - Ottawa, ON, Canada - *BoPubDir 4, 5*
Sci-Com Computer Systems - Bridgewater, NJ - *MicrocomMPl 84; WhoWMicrocom 83*
SCI Library Systems [of Systems Control Inc.] - Palo Alto, CA - *EISS 83*
Sci-Mate [of Institute for Scientific Information] - Philadelphia, PA - *EISS 5-84 Sup*
SCI Systems Inc. - Huntsville, AL - *DataDirSup 7-83; Datamation 6-83; DirInfWP 82; WhoWMicrocom 83*
Scicon Computer Services Ltd. - Milton Keynes, England - *EISS 83*
Scicon Computer Services Ltd. (Information Systems Div.) - Milton Keynes, England - *InfIndMarPl 83*
Scicon-Hansard - Milton Keynes, England - *DirOnDB Spring 84*
Science [of American Association for the Advancement of Science] - Washington, DC - *BaconPubCkMag 84; Folio 83; LitMarPl 83, 84; MagDir 84; MagIndMarPl 82-83*
Science Accessories Corp. - Southport, CT - *DataDirSup 7-83*
Science Activities - Washington, DC - *BaconPubCkMag 84; MagDir 84*
Science & Behavior Books - Palo Alto, CA - *LitMarPl 83, 84*
Science & Children [of National Science Teachers Association] - Washington, DC - *ArtMar 84; BaconPubCkMag 84; MagDir 84; MagIndMarPl 82-83*
Science & Electronics - New York, NY - *MagDir 84*
Science & Mankind Inc. - Mt. Kisco, NY - *AvMarPl 83*
Science & Mechanics [of Davis Publications] - New York, NY - *BaconPubCkMag 84; MagDir 84; MagIndMarPl 82-83; WritMar 84*
Science & Medicine Inc. - New York, NY - *DirPRFirms 83*
Science & Society - New York, NY - *BaconPubCkMag 84; MagIndMarPl 82-83*
Science & Technology Div. [of U.S. Library of Congress] - Washington, DC - *EISS 83*
Science & Technology Information Center [of National Science Council] - Taipei, China - *EISS 83*
Science & Technology Libraries [of Haworth Press Journals] - New York, NY - *LitMarPl 83, 84*
Science & Technology Policies Information Exchange System [of United Nations Educational, Scientific, & Cultural Organization] - Paris, France - *EISS 83*
Science Associates/International Inc. - New York, NY - *LitMarPl 83, 84*
Science Book & Serial Exchange - Ann Arbor, MI - *FBInfSer 80*
Science Books & Films - Washington, DC - *MagIndMarPl 82-83*
Science Books International [of The International Thomson Organisation Inc.] - Boston, MA - *LitMarPl 83, 84*
Science Challenge - Highland Park, IL - *MagIndMarPl 82-83*
Science Citation Index [of Institute for Scientific Information] - Philadelphia, PA - *CompReadDB 82*
Science Communication Div. [of George Washington University Medical Center] - Washington, DC - *EISS 83*
Science Data Base [of Ohio State University Libraries] - Columbus, OH - *CompReadDB 82*
Science Digest [of Hearst Corp.] - New York, NY - *BaconPubCkMag 84; Folio 83; LitMarPl 83; MagDir 84; MagIndMarPl 82-83; WritMar 84*
Science Dynamics Corp. - Torrance, CA - *DataDirOnSer 84*
Science Editors Inc. - Louisville, KY - *BoPubDir 4, 5*
Science 84 [of American Association for the Advancement of Science] - Washington, DC - *ArtMar 84; WritMar 84*
Science 83 [of The American Association for the Advancement of Science] - Washington, DC - *BaconPubCkMag 84; LitMarPl 84*
Science 82 [of American Association for the Advancement of Science] - Washington, DC - *Folio 83; MagIndMarPl 82-83*
Science Enterprises Inc. - Indianapolis, IN - *BoPubDir 4, 5*
Science Fantasy Associates - Hollywood, CA - *LitMarPl 83, 84*
Science Features Syndicate - Sherman Oaks, CA - *LitMarPl 83, 84*
Science Fiction Book Club [Subs. of Doubleday & Co. Inc.] - Garden City, NY - *LitMarPl 83*
Science Fiction Book Club - *See* Doubleday Book Clubs
Science Fiction Chronicle [of Algol Press] - New York, NY - *LitMag&SmPr 83-84; MagIndMarPl 82-83; WritMar 84*
Science Fiction Poetry Association - Los Angeles, CA - *LitMag&SmPr 83-84*
Science Fiction Services - Hollywood, CA - *LitMarPl 83, 84; MagIndMarPl 82-83*
Science Information Dept. [of Squibb Institute for Medical Research] - Princeton, NJ - *EISS 83*
Science Information Services [of Pharmaceutical Manufacturers Association] - Washington, DC - *FBInfSer 80*
Science Media [Subs. of J. Huley Associates Inc.] - Boca Raton, FL - *AvMarPl 83*
Science News [of Science Service] - Washington, DC - *BaconPubCkMag 84; Folio 83; LitMarPl 83, 84; MagDir 84; MagIndMarPl 82-83*
Science of Mind Publications - Los Angeles, CA - *BoPubDir 4, 5*
Science Photo Library International Inc. [Div. of Taurus Photos Inc.] - New York, NY - *LitMarPl 83, 84*
Science Press - Ephrata, PA - *EISS 83; LitMarPl 84; MagIndMarPl 82-83*
Science Reference Library [of The British Library] - London, England - *InfIndMarPl 83*
Science Research Abstracts [of Cambridge Scientific Abstracts] - Bethesda, MD - *EISS 83*
Science Research Associates Inc. [Subs. of IBM Corp.] - Chicago, IL - *AvMarPl 83; LitMarPl 83; MicrocomMPl 84; WhoWMicrocom 83*
Science Research Associates Ltd. [Div. of IBM Corp.] - Willowdale, ON, Canada - *LitMarPl 83, 84*
Science Service - Washington, DC - *BaconPubCkNews 84*
Science Software Systems Inc. - West Los Angeles, CA - *AvMarPl 83*
Science Teacher, The [of National Science Teacher Association] - Washington, DC - *ArtMar 84; BaconPubCkMag 84; LitMarPl 83, 84; MagDir 84; MagIndMarPl 82-83*
Science Trends - Washington, DC - *BaconPubCkMag 84; MagDir 84*
Science Typographers Inc. - Medford, NY - *LitMarPl 83, 84*
Science World - New York, NY - *BaconPubCkMag 84; MagDir 84; MagIndMarPl 82-83*
Scienceland - New York, NY - *MagIndMarPl 82-83*
Sciences, The [of New York Academy of Sciences] - New York, NY - *LitMarPl 83, 84; MagDir 84; MagIndMarPl 82-83*

Scientific Advertising Sales Inc. - Hartsdale, NY - *MagIndMarPl 82-83*
Scientific American - New York, NY - *BaconPubCkMag 84; Folio 83; KnowInd 83; LitMarPl 83, 84; MagDir 84; MagIndMarPl 82-83; WritMar 84*
Scientific American Books - New York, NY - *LitMarPl 84*
Scientific & Business Systems Inc. - New York, NY - *ADAPSOMemDir 83-84*
Scientific & Educational Software Inc. - Dayton, OH - *MicrocomMPl 84*
Scientific & Technical Aerospace Reports [of U.S. National Aeronautics & Space Administration] - Washington, DC - *CompReadDB 82*
Scientific & Technical Documentation [of National Institute for Scientific Investigation] - Lisbon, Portugal - *EISS 83*
Scientific & Technical Documentation Center [of National Center for Scientific Research] - Paris, France - *EISS 83*
Scientific & Technical Information Branch [of U.S. National Aeronautics & Space Administration] - Washington, DC - *EISS 83*
Scientific Atlanta - Atlanta, GA - *CabTVFinDB 83; HomeVid&CabYB 82-83*
Scientific Calculations Inc. - Fishers, NY - *DataDirSup 7-83*
Scientific Computer Applications Inc. - Tulsa, OK - *DataDirOnSer 84*
Scientific Computers Inc. - Minnetonka, MN - *ADAPSOMemDir 83-84; DataDirOnSer 84; DataDirSup 7-83*
Scientific Data Systems - Venice, CA - *DirInfWP 82; WhoWMicrocom 83*
Scientific Documentation Centre Ltd. - Dunfermline, Scotland - *EISS 83*
Scientific Event Alert Network [of Smithsonian Institution] - Washington, DC - *EISS 83*
Scientific Information Center [of Polish Academy of Sciences] - Warsaw, Poland - *EISS 83*
Scientific Information Notes - Washington, DC - *BaconPubCkMag 84; MagDir 84*
Scientific Information Retrieval Inc. - Evanston, IL - *EISS 83*
Scientific Information Systems Dept. [of Merrell Dow Pharmaceuticals Inc.] - Cincinnati, OH - *EISS 83*
Scientific Library & Documentation Div. [of National Science & Technology Authority] - Manila, Philippines - *EISS 83*
Scientific Marketing Inc. - Costa Mesa, CA - *MicrocomMPl 84*
Scientific Micro Systems Inc. - Mountain View, CA - *DataDirSup 7-83*
Scientific MicroPrograms - Raleigh, NC - *WhoWMicrocom 83*
Scientific Numeric Databases [of National Research Council of Canada] - Ottawa, ON, Canada - *EISS 83*
Scientific Parameters for Health & the Environment [of U.S. Environmental Protection Agency] - Washington, DC - *EISS 5-84 Sup*
Scientific Press, The - Palo Alto, CA - *LitMarPl 83, 84*
Scientific Process & Research Inc. - Somerset, NJ - *DataDirOnSer 84; DataDirSup 7-83; EISS 83*
Scientific Publications [Aff. of The American Heart Association] - Dallas, TX - *BoPubDir 4, 5*
Scientific Software Products Inc. - Indianapolis, IN - *MicrocomMPl 83*
Scientific Systems Services Inc. - Melbourne, FL - *ADAPSOMemDir 83-84*
Scientivic Software - Fairborn, OH - *MicrocomMPl 84*
Scillonian Magazine - Cornwall, England - *LitMag&SmPr 83-84*
SCIMP - London, England - *DirOnDB Spring 84*
Scio Mutual Telephone Association - Scio, OR - *TelDir&BG 83-84*
Scio Tribune - Scio, OR - *Ed&PubIntYB 82*
Scion Computer Services Ltd. (Information Systems) - Milton Keynes, England - *InfIndMarPl 83*
Scion Corp. - Reston, VA - *MicrocomMPl 84; WhoWMicrocom 83*
Scioto Voice, The - Wheelersburg, OH - *AyerDirPub 83; Ed&PubIntYB 82*
Scipio - Stanford, CA - *DirOnDB Spring 84*
Scisearch [of Institute for Scientific Information] - Philadelphia, PA - *DataDirOnSer 84; DirOnDB Spring 84; OnBibDB 3*
Scisoft - Eastwood, England - *MicrocomSwDir 1*
Scissortail Publications - Pensacola, FL - *BoPubDir 4, 5*
Scitec - Anchorage, AK - *MicrocomMPl 84*
Scitec Corp. - Middletown, RI - *DataDirSup 7-83*
Scitran - Santa Barbara, CA - *MagIndMarPl 82-83*
Scitronics Inc. - Bethlehem, PA - *MicrocomMPl 83, 84*
Scituate Cablesystems [of American Cablesystems Corp.] - Scituate, MA - *Tel&CabFB 84C*
Scituate Mirror - Scituate, MA - *AyerDirPub 83; Ed&PubIntYB 82*
Scobey Daniels County Leader - Scobey, MT - *BaconPubCkNews 84*
Scofield Broadcasting Co. - Williston, ND - *BrCabYB 84*
Scofield, Michael - Palo Alto, CA - *LitMarPl 83, 84*
Scolar Press - Berkeley, CA - *BoPubDir 5*
Scolar Press Ltd. - London, England - *MicroMarPl 82-83*
Sconnix Group Broadcasting Inc. - Laconia, NH - *BrCabYB 84*
SCOP Publications Inc. - College Park, MD - *BoPubDir 4, 5; LitMag&SmPr 83-84*
Scopcraeft Press Inc. - Stevens Point, WI - *BoPubDir 4, 5*
Scope - Minneapolis, MN - *WritMar 84*
Scope - Flushing, NY - *MicrocomMPl 84*
Scope Associates - New York, NY - *AvMarPl 83*
Scope Cable Television of Nebraska Co. - Elkhorn, NE - *BrCabYB 84*
Scope Cable Television of Nebraska Co. - Neligh, NE - *BrCabYB 84*
Scope Cable TV of Nebraska - Bloomfield, NE - *Tel&CabFB 84C*
Scope Communications Inc. - Westport, CT - *TelAl 83, 84*
Scope Newspaper - Slave Lake, AB, Canada - *AyerDirPub 83; Ed&PubIntYB 82*
Scope Productions Inc. - Ahwahnee, CA - *AvMarPl 83*
Scope Unltd. - Chicago, IL - *StaDirAdAg 2-84*
Score Productions Inc. - New York, NY - *AvMarPl 83*
Scorpion Systems Inc. - Frederick, MD - *MicrocomMPl 83, 84; MicrocomSwDir 1; WhoWMicrocom 83*
Scotch Plains Times [of Foster Publications] - Scotch Plains, NJ - *BaconPubCkNews 84; NewsDir 84*
Scotia Capital District Trader - *See* Journal Newspapers
Scotia-Glenville Journal [of Ballston Journal Newspapers] - Ballston Spa, NY - *NewsDir 84*
Scotia Register - Scotia, NE - *BaconPubCkNews 84; Ed&PubIntYB 82*
Scotia Sun, The - Port Hawkesbury, NS, Canada - *AyerDirPub 83; Ed&PubIntYB 82*
Scotland Journal - Scotland, SD - *BaconPubCkNews 84; Ed&PubIntYB 82*
Scotland Neck Halifax County This Week - Scotland Neck, NC - *BaconPubCkNews 84; NewsDir 84*
Scotsman - Cambridge, MN - *AyerDirPub 83*
Scott & Associates, M. L. - Ithaca, NY - *BoPubDir 4, 5*
Scott & Associates, Wilbur B. - Sycamore, IL - *BoPubDir 4, 5*
Scott & Daughters Publishing Inc. - Los Angeles, CA - *BoPubDir 5*
Scott & Krenz TV Systems - Ladysmith, WI - *Tel&CabFB 84C p.1701*
Scott & Scott Advertising - Evanston, IL - *AdAge 3-28-84; BrCabYB 84; StaDirAdAg 2-84*
Scott Associates - Champaign, IL - *StaDirAdAg 2-84*
Scott Associates, Arthur J. - New York, NY - *BoPubDir 4, 5*
Scott Associates Inc., Robert J. - Indianapolis, IN - *StaDirAdAg 2-84*
Scott Associates, Louis - New York, NY - *StaDirAdAg 2-84*
Scott-Atkinson, Only International Ltd. - Toronto, ON, Canada - *DirPRFirms 83*
Scott Cable Communications Inc. - Russels Point, OH - *Tel&CabFB 84C*
Scott Cable Communications Inc. - Irving, TX - *Tel&CabFB 84C p.1701*
Scott Cable TV Co. - Forest, MS - *BrCabYB 84*
Scott Cable TV Inc. - Morton, MS - *Tel&CabFB 84C*
Scott City News-Chronicle - Scott City, KS - *BaconPubCkNews 84; Ed&PubIntYB 82*
Scott Co., J. I. - Grand Rapids, MI - *AdAge 3-28-84; StaDirAdAg 2-84*
Scott County Cablevision Inc. - Weber City, VA - *BrCabYB 84; Tel&CabFB 84C*
Scott County Herald-Virginian - Gate City, VA - *Ed&PubIntYB 82*
Scott County Journal - Scottsburg, IN - *AyerDirPub 83*

Scott County Journal - *See* Journal & Chronicle Inc.
Scott County Journal & The Austin Chronicle - Scottsburg, IN - *Ed&PublntYB 82*
Scott County News - Oneida, TN - *Ed&PublntYB 82*
Scott County Telephone Cooperative Inc. - Gate City, VA - *TelDir&BG 83-84*
Scott County Times - Forest, MS - *AyerDirPub 83; Ed&PublntYB 82*
Scott, David H. - Blue Hill, ME - *LitMarPl 83, 84*
Scott Enterprises Inc., Raymond - Van Nuys, CA - *Tel&CabFB 84C*
Scott Enterprises, Liz - Pittsburgh, PA - *ArtMar 84*
Scott Fetzer Co., The - Lakewood, OH - *KnowInd 83*
Scott, Foresman & Co. [Subs. of SFN Cos. Inc.] - Glenview, IL - *ArtMar 84; LitMarPl 83, 84; MicrocomMPl 84*
Scott, Foresman & Co. (Electronic Publishing Div.) - Glenview, IL - *MicrocomMPl 83*
Scott Inc. of Milwaukee - Milwaukee, WI - *StaDirAdAg 2-84*
Scott Inc., Rita - New York, NY - *LitMarPl 83, 84*
Scott Instruments Corp. - Denton, TX - *MicrocomMPl 83, 84; WhoWMicrocom 83*
Scott Lancaster Jackman Mills Atha - Los Angeles, CA - *AdAge 3-28-84; ArtMar 84; StaDirAdAg 2-84*
Scott, Marshall, Sands & McGinley Inc. - Los Angeles, CA - *Ed&PublntYB 82*
Scott Music Publications - Hollywood, CA - *BillIntBG 83-84*
Scott Music Publishing Co., G. - *See* JTL Publications
Scott Publications - Livonia, MI - *BoPubDir 5*
Scott Publications - Victoria, BC, Canada - *BoPubDir 4, 5*
Scott Publishing Co. [Subs. of Scott Collectibles Ltd.] - New York, NY - *BoPubDir 4; LitMarPl 83, 84*
Scott Resources Inc. - Ft. Collins, CO - *WritMar 84*
Scott Rice Telephone Co. - Prior Lake, MN - *TelDir&BG 83-84*
Scott Stamp Monthly - New York, NY - *WritMar 84*
Scott-Textor Productions Inc. - New York, NY - *Tel&CabFB 84C*
Scottdale Independent Observer - Scottdale, PA - *BaconPubCkNews 84*
Scotti Bros. Music Publishing - Santa Monica, CA - *BillIntBG 83-84*
Scotti Bros. Records - Santa Monica, CA - *BillIntBG 83-84*
Scottish Libraries Co-Operative Automation Project [of National Library of Scotland] - Edinburgh, Scotland - *EISS 83; InfIndMarPl 83*
Scott's Industrial Directories - Oakville, ON, Canada - *BoPubDir 4, 5*
Scotts Valley Banner - Santa Cruz, CA - *AyerDirPub 83*
Scotts Valley Banner - Scotts Valley, CA - *Ed&PublntYB 82*
Scottsbluff County Community TV [of Tele-Communications Inc.] - Scottsbluff, NE - *BrCabYB 84; Tel&CabFB 84C*
Scottsbluff Star-Herald [of Western Publishing Co.] - Scottsbluff, NE - *BaconPubCkNews 84; NewsDir 84*
Scottsboro Sentinel [of Scottsboro Newspapers Inc.] - Scottsboro, AL - *BaconPubCkNews 84; NewsDir 84*
Scottsboro TV Cable Inc. - Cedar Bluff, AL - *Tel&CabFB 84C*
Scottsboro TV Cable Inc. - Cherokee, AL - *BrCabYB 84*
Scottsboro TV Cable Inc. - Courtland, AL - *Tel&CabFB 84C*
Scottsboro TV Cable Inc. - Rainsville, AL - *BrCabYB 84; Tel&CabFB 84C*
Scottsboro TV Cable Inc. - Scottsboro, AL - *BrCabYB 84*
Scottsboro TV Cable Inc. - Belmont, MS - *Tel&CabFB 84C*
Scottsboro TV Cable Inc. - Burnsville, MS - *BrCabYB 84*
Scottsboro TV Cable Inc. - Tishomingo, MS - *BrCabYB 84; Tel&CabFB 84C*
Scottsburg Chronicle - *See* Journal & Chronicle Inc.
Scottsdale-Ashburn Independent - Chicago, IL - *Ed&PublntYB 82*
Scottsdale-Ashburn Independent [of Midlothian Southwest Messenger Newspapers] - Midlothian, IL - *AyerDirPub 83; NewsDir 84*
Scottsdale-Ashburn Independent - *See* Southwest Messenger Newspapers
Scottsdale Daily Progress - Scottsdale, AZ - *BaconPubCkNews 84; Ed&PublntYB 82; NewsDir 84*
Scottsville Allen County News - Scottsville, KY - *BaconPubCkNews 84*
Scottsville Citizen-Times - Scottsville, KY - *BaconPubCkNews 84; NewsDir 84*
Scouting Magazine - Dallas, TX - *MagIndMarPl 82-83*
Scouting Magazine - Irving, TX - *BaconPubCkMag 84; MagDir 84*
Scoville Press Inc. - Minneapolis, MN - *MagIndMarPl 82-83*
SCP Records [Div. of Sound Column Cos.] - Salt Lake City, UT - *BillIntBG 83-84*
SCR Associati Relazioni Pubbliche - Milan, Italy - *DirPRFirms 83*
Scramb-L-Gram Inc. - Cuyahoga Falls, OH - *Ed&PublntYB 82*
Scramrock Music Co. - Springfield, OH - *BillIntBG 83-84*
Scranton Cablevision Co. - Scranton, ND - *Tel&CabFB 84C*
Scranton Catholic Light - Scranton, PA - *NewsDir 84*
Scranton Community Antenna Television - Scranton, IA - *Tel&CabFB 84C*
Scranton Journal - Scranton, IA - *BaconPubCkNews 84; Ed&PublntYB 82*
Scranton Lithographing Co. - Pittston, PA - *MagIndMarPl 82-83*
Scranton Telephone Co. - Scranton, IA - *TelDir&BG 83-84*
Scranton Times - Scranton, PA - *BaconPubCkNews 84; NewsDir 84*
Scranton Tribune - Scranton, PA - *LitMarPl 83*
Scrantonian [of Tribune Publishing] - Scranton, PA - *AyerDirPub 83; Ed&PublntYB 82; LitMarPl 83, 84; NewsDir 84*
Scrap Age [of Three Sons Publishing Co.] - Chicago, IL - *MagDir 84*
Scrap Age - Niles, IL - *BaconPubCkMag 84*
Scraper, The - Frankfort, KY - *BaconPubCkMag 84; MagDir 84*
Scratching River Post, The - Morris, MB, Canada - *AyerDirPub 83*
Scree [of Duck Down Press] - Fallon, NV - *LitMag&SmPr 83-84*
Screen - Chicago, IL - *BaconPubCkMag 84*
Screen Actor [of Screen Actors Guild] - Los Angeles, CA - *NewsDir 84*
Screen Actors Guild - New York, NY - *AvMarPl 83*
Screen Cartoonists - New York, NY - *AvMarPl 83*
Screen Education Enterprises Inc. - Bellevue, WA - *AvMarPl 83*
Screen Gems-EMI Music Inc. - Hollywood, CA - *BillIntBG 83-84*
Screen Printing - Cincinnati, OH - *ArtMar 84; BaconPubCkMag 84; MagDir 84; MagIndMarPl 82-83; WritMar 84*
Screen Sonics Inc. - Chesterfield, MO - *MicrocomMPl 84*
Screen Works, The - Chicago, IL - *AvMarPl 83*
Screenscope Inc. - Washington, DC - *AvMarPl 83; WritMar 84*
Screven County News - Sylvania, GA - *Ed&PublntYB 82*
Screw - New York, NY - *WritMar 84*
Scribe [of University of Bridgeport Student Center] - Bridgeport, CT - *NewsDir 84*
Scribe Data Systems Inc. - Boston, MA - *MagIndMarPl 82-83; MicrocomMPl 84*
Scribe Publications, B. C. - Berkeley, CA - *BoPubDir 4*
Scribe Publications, B. C. - Providence, RI - *BoPubDir 5*
Scribner Advertising, J. M. - Incline Village, NV - *StaDirAdAg 2-84*
Scribner Book Cos. Inc., The - New York, NY - *KnowInd 83; LitMarPl 83, 84*
Scribner Rustler - Scribner, NE - *BaconPubCkNews 84; Ed&PublntYB 82*
Scribner's Sons, Charles [Div. of The Scribner Book Cos. Inc.] - New York, NY - *ArtMar 84; LitMarPl 84; WritMar 84*
Scribner's Sons, Charles (Children's Books Dept.) - New York, NY - *WritMar 84*
Scripps Co., E. W. - Cincinnati, OH - *KnowInd 83*
Scripps Data Systems Inc. - San Diego, CA - *MicrocomSwDir 1*
Scripps-Howard Broadcasting Co. [Subs. of E. W. Scripps Co.] - Cincinnati, OH - *AdAge 6-28-84; BrCabYB 84; Ed&PublntYB 82; HomeVid&CabYB 82-83; KnowInd 83; LitMarPl 84; Tel&CabFB 84S*
Scripps-Howard Cable Services Co. [of Scripps-Howard Broadcasting Co.] - Cleveland, OH - *BrCabYB 84 p.D-306; CabTVFinDB 83; Tel&CabFB 84C p.1701*
Scripps-Howard Newspapers - New York, NY - *LitMarPl 83*
Scripps-Howard Press - St. Matthews, KY - *BaconPubCkNews 84*
Scripps-Ifft Newspapers - Seattle, WA - *Ed&PublntYB 82*
Scripps League Newspapers Inc. - Washington, DC - *Ed&PublntYB 82*
Scripps League Newspapers Inc. - Charlottesville, VA - *KnowInd 83*

Scripps Newspaper Group, John P. - Ventura, CA - *Ed&PubIntYB 82*
Scripps Newspapers, James G. - Seattle, WA - *Ed&PubIntYB 82*
Scripta Medica & Technica - South Orange, NJ - *LitMarPl 84*
Scripta Publishing Co. [Div. of Scripta Technica Inc.] - Silver Spring, MD - *LitMarPl 83, 84; MagIndMarPl 82-83*
Scriptural Living Ministries - St. Ann, MO - *BoPubDir 5*
Scripture Press Publications Inc. - Wheaton, IL - *LitMarPl 83, 84; MagIndMarPl 82-83*
Scripture Press Publications Ltd. - Whitby, ON, Canada - *LitMarPl 83*
Scriptwriters Market [of Joshua Publishing Co.] - Los Angeles, CA - *LitMag&SmPr 83-84*
Scrivener [of McGill University] - Montreal, PQ, Canada - *WritMar 84*
Scroggin & Fischer Advertising - San Francisco, CA - *AdAge 3-28-84; StaDirAdAg 2-84*
Scroll Press Inc. - Merrick, NY - *BoPubDir 5*
Scruggs Films, Roger - Cocoa Beach, FL - *AvMarPl 83*
SCTD-FM - Federalsburg, MD - *BrCabYB 84*
Scuba Times [of MWP Publishing Co.] - Pensacola, FL - *WritMar 84*
Scully Music/Orange Bear Music - Philadelphia, PA - *BillIntBG 83-84*
Sculpt Nouveau - San Rafael, CA - *BoPubDir 4, 5*
SCW Inc. - Chatsworth, CA - *Ed&PubIntYB 82*
SD Systems [Subs. of Michigan General] - Dallas, TX - *MicrocomMPl 84; WhoWMicrocom 83*
SDA Equipment Corp. - New York, NY - *DirInfWP 82*
S.D.A. Productions Ltee. - Montreal, PQ, Canada - *Tel&CabFB 84C*
SDA Products Inc. - New York, NY - *DataDirSup 7-83*
SDA Records & Tapes - Ames, IA - *BillIntBG 83-84*
SDC Information Services [Div. of System Development Corp.] - Santa Monica, CA - *DataDirOnSer 84; EISS 7-83 Sup; InfoS 83-84*
SDC Search Service [of System Development Corp.] - Santa Monica, CA - *EISS 83; InfIndMarPl 83*
SDD Inc. - Boulder, CO - *DataDirSup 7-83*
SDF - London, England - *DirOnDB Spring 84*
SDI - San Mateo, CA - *DataDirSup 7-83*
SDI/Laval & Telereference Service [of Laval University Library] - Quebec, PQ, Canada - *EISS 83*
SDILINE [of National Library of Medicine] - Bethesda, MD - *CompReadDB 82*
SDIM [of Bundesanstalt fur Materialprufung] - Berlin, West Germany - *OnBibDB 3*
SDIM1 - Berlin, West Germany - *DirOnDB Spring 84*
SDIM2 - Berlin, West Germany - *DirOnDB Spring 84*
SDK Medical Computer Services Corp. - Chestnut Hill, MA - *DataDirOnSer 84*
SDM - Des Plaines, IL - *BaconPubCkMag 84; MagDir 84*
SDNET [of Software Dynamics] - Anaheim, CA - *TeleSy&SerDir 7-83*
SDR - Washington, DC - *DirOnDB Spring 84*
SDR [of United Information Services] - Kansas City, MO - *DataDirOnSer 84*
SDR Public Relations - Westport, CT - *DirPRFirms 83*
SDS/Las Vegas Surveys Inc. - Las Vegas, NV - *IntDirMarRes 83*
SE Music Inc. - Worcester, MA - *BillIntBG 83-84*
SE Surveys Inc. - New York, NY - *IntDirMarRes 83*
Sea & Pacific Skipper [of Petersen Publishing Co.] - Newport Beach, CA - *ArtMar 84; BaconPubCkMag 84; MagDir 84; MagIndMarPl 82-83; WritMar 84*
Sea Book Club [Subs. of Sky Books International Inc.] - New York, NY - *LitMarPl 83, 84*
Sea Breeze Record Co. - Mentone, CA - *BillIntBG 83-84*
Sea Challengers - Los Osos, CA - *BoPubDir 4, 5; LitMag&SmPr 83-84*
Sea Coast Echo - Bay St. Louis, MS - *AyerDirPub 83; Ed&PubIntYB 82*
Sea Crest Publishing Co. Inc. - Cape Canaveral, FL - *LitMag&SmPr 83-84*
Sea Crest Publishing Co. Inc. - Cocoa Beach, FL - *BoPubDir 5*
Sea Cruise Music - *See* Briarmeade Music Unltd.
Sea Cruise Productions - Gretna, LA - *BillIntBG 83-84*
Sea Fog Press - San Francisco, CA - *LitMag&SmPr 83-84*
Sea Frontiers - Miami, FL - *BaconPubCkMag 84; MagDir 84; MagIndMarPl 82-83; WritMar 84*
Sea Grant Marine Information Service - College Station, TX - *BoPubDir 4, 5*
Sea History - Brooklyn, NY - *MagIndMarPl 82-83*
Sea Horse Press Ltd. - New York, NY - *BoPubDir 4, 5*
SEA Inc. - Carmel, IN - *WhoWMicrocom 83*
Sea Jay Publishing - Salt Lake City, UT - *BoPubDir 4, 5*
Sea Lion Publications - San Diego, CA - *BoPubDir 4, 5*
Sea of Storms Publishing - San Francisco, CA - *BoPubDir 4, 5*
Sea Pen Press & Paper Mill - Seattle, WA - *BoPubDir 4, 5*
Sea Power - Arlington, VA - *BaconPubCkMag 84; MagDir 84; WritMar 84*
Sea Technology - Arlington, VA - *BaconPubCkMag 84; MagDir 84; MagIndMarPl 82-83*
Sea Urchin Press - Oakland, CA - *BoPubDir 4 Sup, 5*
Sea Wind Press - Carmel, CA - *BoPubDir 5*
Seablom Design Books - Seattle, WA - *BoPubDir 4, 5*
Seaboard Lithograph Corp. - New York, NY - *LitMarPl 83, 84; MagIndMarPl 82-83*
Seaboard Paper Co. - San Francisco, CA - *LitMarPl 83, 84*
Seaboard Press - Drexel Hill, PA - *BoPubDir 4, 5*
Seaboard Subscription Agency - Allentown, PA - *MagIndMarPl 82-83*
Seabrook International Group Ltd. - Freeport, NY - *BillIntBG 83-84*
Seabury Press Inc., The - New York, NY - *LitMarPl 83, 84; WritMar 84*
Seacoast Flyer - Kennebunk, ME - *AyerDirPub 83*
Seafarer's Log [of SIU] - Camp Springs, MD - *NewsDir 84*
Seafirst Computer Services [Subs. of Seattle First National Bank] - Seattle, WA - *DataDirOnSer 84*
Seafood America - Camden, ME - *BaconPubCkMag 84*
Seafood Business Report [of Diversified Communications] - Seattle, WA - *BaconPubCkMag 84; MagDir 84*
Seafood Leader - Seattle, WA - *BaconPubCkMag 84*
Seafood Music - San Francisco, CA - *BillIntBG 83-84*
Seaford/Antagh Observer - Bellmore, NY - *AyerDirPub 83*
Seaford Leader-State Register [of Chesapeake Publishing Corp.] - Seaford, DE - *NewsDir 84*
Seaford-Wantagh Observer [of Bellmore-Merrick Observer] - Bellmore, NY - *NewsDir 84*
Seaford/Wantagh Observer - Seaford, NY - *Ed&PubIntYB 82*
Seaford-Wantagh Observer - *See* Observer Newspapers
Seaforth Publications - Bratenahl, OH - *BoPubDir 4, 5*
Seagate Technology - Scotts Valley, CA - *DataDirSup 7-83; MicrocomMPl 84*
Seagoville Suburbia News - Seagoville, TX - *BaconPubCkNews 84*
Seagrape Music - Los Angeles, CA - *BillIntBG 83-84*
Seagraves Gaines County News - Seagraves, TX - *BaconPubCkNews 84*
Seagulls Artistic Publications - Rowland Heights, CA - *BoPubDir 5; LitMag&SmPr 83-84*
Seagulls Artistic Publications - Roseburg, OR - *BoPubDir 4*
Seaholm Interstate Directories Inc. - New Paltz, NY - *BoPubDir 4, 5*
Seal Beach Journal - Seal Beach, CA - *AyerDirPub 83; Ed&PubIntYB 82*
Seal Beach Journal & Huntington Harbour Sun - Seal Beach, CA - *BaconPubCkNews 84; NewsDir 84*
Seal Beach Post & Wave - Seal Beach, CA - *Ed&PubIntYB 82*
Seal Press - Seal Beach, CA - *BoPubDir 4, 5*
Seal Press - Seattle, WA - *BoPubDir 4, 5; LitMag&SmPr 83-84; LitMarPl 84*
Seal Products Inc. [Subs. of Seal Inc.] - Naugatuck, CT - *AvMarPl 83*
Seals Camera & AV Center Inc. - Auburn, NY - *AvMarPl 83*
Seals, Howard E. - Chicago, IL - *BoPubDir 4, 5*
Sealy News - Sealy, TX - *BaconPubCkNews 84; Ed&PubIntYB 82; NewsDir 84*
Seaman-Patrick Paper Co. - Detroit, MI - *MagIndMarPl 82-83*
Seamark Inc. - Norfolk, VA - *StaDirAdAg 2-84*
Seaneen Music - *See* DeWhit Music
Seapen Books Inc. - New York, NY - *BoPubDir 4, 5*
Seaports & the Shipping World - Montreal, PQ, Canada - *BaconPubCkMag 84*
Sear Sound - New York, NY - *AvMarPl 83*

Search [of Computer Sciences Corp.] - El Segundo, CA - *DataDirOnSer 84*
Search - Washington, DC - *DirOnDB Spring 84*
Search [of Merging Media] - Westfield, NJ - *LitMag&SmPr 83-84*
Search - Amherst, WI - *MagIndMarPl 82-83*
Search Analysts' Interest Group of the Mississippi Library Association (Automation & Networking Round Table) - Mississippi State, MS - *InfIndMarPl 83*
Search & Rescue Magazine - Montrose, CA - *MagDir 84*
Search Check - Arlington, VA - *CompReadDB 82*
Search/J [of System Development Corp. of Japan Ltd.] - Tokyo, Japan - *EISS 83*
Search Program for Infrared Spectra [of Canada Institute for Scientific & Technical Information] - Ottawa, ON, Canada - *DataDirOnSer 84*
Searchable Physics Information Notices [of American Institute of Physics] - New York, NY - *CompReadDB 82; DataDirOnSer 84; DBBus 82*
Searchers Publications - Mercer Island, WA - *BoPubDir 4, 5*
Searchlight - Culbertson, MT - *AyerDirPub 83; Ed&PubIntYB 82*
Searchline - Lisle, IL - *EISS 83; FBInfSer 80; InfIndMarPl 83*
Searchline - Brookline, MA - *EISS 7-83 Sup*
Searchmart Corp. - North Palm Beach, FL - *DataDirOnSer 84*
Searcy Citizen - Searcy, AR - *BaconPubCkNews 84*
Sears Technical Public Relations, Warren - Cleveland, OH - *DirPRFirms 83*
Searsboro Telephone Co. - Searsboro, IA - *TelDir&BG 83-84*
SEASHA Community Cablevision Co. - *BrCabYB 84*
Seaside Cable TV Ltd. - Glace Bay, NS, Canada - *BrCabYB 84*
Seaside Heights Ocean County Review - Seaside Heights, NJ - *BaconPubCkNews 84; NewsDir 84*
Seaside Post [of Alameda Publishing Corp.] - Oakland, CA - *NewsDir 84*
Seaside Post News-Sentinel - Seaside, CA - *AyerDirPub 83; BaconPubCkNews 84; Ed&PubIntYB 82; NewsDir 84*
Seaside Signal - Seaside, OR - *BaconPubCkNews 84; Ed&PubIntYB 82; NewsDir 84*
Seasonal Thermal Energy Storage [of Battelle Memorial Institute] - Richland, WA - *CompReadDB 82*
Seasun Experience Music - Daytona Beach, FL - *BillIntBG 83-84*
Seaton Group - Coffeyville, KS - *Ed&PubIntYB 82*
Seaton Stations - Coffeyville, KS - *BrCabYB 84*
Seattle Argus - Seattle, WA - *Ed&PubIntYB 82; NewsDir 84*
Seattle Art Museum - Seattle, WA - *BoPubDir 4 Sup, 5*
Seattle Ballard News-Tribune - Seattle, WA - *BaconPubCkNews 84*
Seattle Beacon Hill News - Seattle, WA - *Ed&PubIntYB 82*
Seattle Beacon Hill News - *See* News-Journal Inc.
Seattle Business [of Vernon Publications Inc.] - Seattle, WA - *BaconPubCkMag 84; MagDir 84; WritMar 84*
Seattle Business Journal - Seattle, WA - *BaconPubCkMag 84*
Seattle Capitol Hill Times - Seattle, WA - *BaconPubCkNews 84; NewsDir 84*
Seattle Catholic Northwest Progress - Seattle, WA - *NewsDir 84*
Seattle Computer Products Inc. - Seattle, WA - *MicrocomMPl 83, 84; WhoWMicrocom 83*
Seattle Consumer Opinion Research Inc. [Subs. of E. Friedman Marketing Services Inc.] - Tukwila, WA - *IntDirMarRes 83*
Seattle Daily Journal of Commerce - Seattle, WA - *Ed&PubIntYB 82; NewsDir 84*
Seattle Facts - Seattle, WA - *BaconPubCkNews 84; NewsDir 84*
Seattle Magnolia News - *See* Murray Publishing Co.
Seattle Medium - Seattle, WA - *BaconPubCkNews 84*
Seattle Motion Picture Services/Aurora Films - Seattle, WA - *AvMarPl 83*
Seattle Northwest Facts, The - Seattle, WA - *NewsDir 84*
Seattle Post Intelligencer [of The Hearst Corp.] - Seattle, WA - *BaconPubCkNews 84; Ed&PubIntYB 82; LitMarPl 83, 84; NewsBur 6; NewsDir 84*
Seattle Repertory Theatre - Seattle, WA - *WritMar 84*
Seattle South District Journal - Seattle, WA - *Ed&PubIntYB 82*
Seattle Times - Seattle, WA - *AdAge 6-28-84; BaconPubCkNews 84; Ed&PubIntYB 82; KnowInd 83; LitMarPl 83, 84; NewsBur 6; NewsDir 84*
Seattle Weekly, The [of Sasquatch Publishing] - Seattle, WA - *NewsDir 84; WritMar 84*
Seattle-West Seattle Herald Inc. - Seattle, WA - *NewsDir 84*
Seattle White Center News - *See* Robinson Communications Co.
Seaver Books - New York, NY - *LitMarPl 83, 84*
Seaview/Putnam - *See* Putnam Publishing Group
Seaway Communications Inc. - Rhinelander, WI - *Tel&CabFB 84S*
Seaway Review - Elmira, MI - *MagDir 84*
Seaway Review - Maple City, MI - *BaconPubCkMag 84; MagIndMarPl 82-83; WritMar 84*
Seban System [of Technical University of Wroclaw] - Wroclaw, Poland - *CompReadDB 82*
Sebastian Music, John - *See* MizMo Enterprises
Sebastopol Times - Sebastopol, CA - *BaconPubCkNews 84; Ed&PubIntYB 82*
Sebastopol Times & Times Guide - Sebastopol, CA - *NewsDir 84*
Sebeka/Menahga Review Messenger - Sebeka, MN - *BaconPubCkNews 84; NewsDir 84*
Sebewaing Blade-Crescent - Sebewaing, MI - *BaconPubCkNews 84; NewsDir 84*
Sebewaing Blade, The - Sebewaing, MI - *Ed&PubIntYB 82*
Sebree Banner - Sebree, KY - *BaconPubCkNews 84; Ed&PubIntYB 82*
Sebring News [of New York Times Co.] - Sebring, FL - *BaconPubCkNews 84; Ed&PubIntYB 82; NewsDir 84*
Sebring Times - Sebring, OH - *BaconPubCkNews 84; Ed&PubIntYB 82*
Sebstad, Lutrey & Evenson - Chicago, IL - *StaDirAdAg 2-84*
Secaucus Home News - Secaucus, NJ - *BaconPubCkNews 84; NewsDir 84*
Secaucus Press [of West New Yorker Inc.] - Fairview, NJ - *NewsDir 84*
Secaucus Press - Secaucus, NJ - *Ed&PubIntYB 82*
Secaucus Press & Meadowlander - *See* West New Yorker Inc.
Secker & Warburg - North Pomfret, VT - *LitMarPl 83, 84*
Second Aeon Publications - Cardiff, Wales - *LitMag&SmPr 83-84*
Second Back Row Press - Leura, Australia - *LitMag&SmPr 83-84*
Second Chance at Love [Subs. of Berkley Publishing Group] - New York, NY - *WritMar 84*
Second Chance Press - Sag Harbor, NY - *LitMag&SmPr 83-84; LitMarPl 83, 84*
Second Coming - San Francisco, CA - *BoPubDir 4, 5; LitMag&SmPr 83-84; WritMar 84*
Second Coming Press - San Francisco, CA - *LitMag&SmPr 83-84*
Second Exodus Publications Society - Burnaby, BC, Canada - *BoPubDir 4 Sup, 5*
Second Growth: Appalachian Nature & Culture - Johnson City, TN - *LitMag&SmPr 83-84*
Second Hand - Plymouth, WI - *BoPubDir 4, 5; LitMag&SmPr 83-84*
Second Language Publications - Burnaby, BC, Canada - *BoPubDir 4, 5*
Second Market Information System [of Computer Equipment Information Bureau] - Boston, MA - *DataDirOnSer 84; DirOnDB Spring 84*
Second Sun Productions - Burton, WA - *BillIntBG 83-84*
Secretarial Service, The - Ontario, CA - *LitMarPl 83, 84; MagIndMarPl 82-83*
Secretarial Services of Sarasota - Sarasota, FL - *LitMarPl 83, 84*
Secretary - Kansas City, MO - *BaconPubCkMag 84; MagDir 84; MagIndMarPl 82-83*
Secretary Inc. - Stafford, TX - *DirInfWP 82*
Secretary's World - Concord, NH - *WritMar 84*
Secrets [of Macfadden Women's Group] - New York, NY - *MagDir 84; MagIndMarPl 82-83; WritMar 84*
Sector Systems Inc. - Anchorage, AK - *MicrocomMPl 84*
Secureware - Highland Park, IL - *BoPubDir 4 Sup, 5*
Securities [of Financial Post] - Toronto, ON, Canada - *DBBus 82*
Securities & Commodities Corp. - Northport, NY - *DataDirOnSer 84*
Securities Data Co. [Subs. of Capital Cities Communication] - New York, NY - *DataDirOnSer 84; EISS 83; InfIndMarPl 83; MicrocomMPl 84*
Securities Database [of Data Resources Inc.] - Lexington, MA - *DataDirOnSer 84*
Securities Database [of Capital Market Systems Inc.] - Waltham, MA - *DataDirOnSer 84; EISS 83*
Securities Industry Automation Corp. - New York, NY - *EISS 83*
Securities Industry Data Bank - *DirOnDB Spring 84*

Securities Law Advance [of The Bureau of National Affairs] - Washington, DC - *DataDirOnSer 84; DirOnDB Spring 84*
Securities Prices [of Interactive Data Services Inc.] - New York, NY - *DataDirOnSer 84*
Securities Week - New York, NY - *BaconPubCkMag 84*
Security Advertiser & Fountain Valley News - Fountain, CO - *AyerDirPub 83; Ed&PubIntYB 82*
Security Channel, The - Duarte, CA - *InterCabHB 3*
Security Dealer - Woodbury, NY - *BaconPubCkMag 84*
Security Letter - New York, NY - *BaconPubCkMag 84; MagIndMarPl 82-83*
Security Management - Washington, DC - *MagIndMarPl 82-83*
Security Management - Arlington, VA - *ArtMar 84; BaconPubCkMag 84; WritMar 84*
Security Management: Protecting Property, People & Assets - Waterford, CT - *WritMar 84*
Security Market Data [of Chase Econometrics/Interactive Data Corp.] - Waltham, MA - *DataDirOnSer 84*
Security Market Data - Bala Cynwyd, PA - *DirOnDB Spring 84*
Security Pacific National Bank [Subs. of Security Pacific Corp.] - Los Angeles, CA - *DataDirOnSer 84*
Security Systems Administration - Woodbury, NY - *BaconPubCkMag 84; MagDir 84*
Security World - Chicago, IL - *MagIndMarPl 82-83*
Security World - Des Plaines, IL - *BaconPubCkMag 84; MagDir 84*
Sedalia Capital - Sedalia, MO - *NewsDir 84*
Sedalia Democrat - Sedalia, MO - *BaconPubCkNews 84*
Sedalia Green Ridge Local News - Sedalia, MO - *BaconPubCkNews 84*
Sedan Times-Star - Sedan, KS - *Ed&PubIntYB 82*
Sedan Times-Star - *See* Star Publications
Sedgwick Pantagraph - Herington, KS - *AyerDirPub 83*
Sedgwick Pantagraph - Sedgwick, KS - *Ed&PubIntYB 82*
Sedgwick Printout Systems - Princeton, NJ - *EISS 83; LitMarPl 83, 84; MagIndMarPl 82-83*
Sedloff Publications Inc. - Portage, PA - *BaconPubCkNews 84*
Sedna Information Management System [of Sedna Corp.] - St. Paul, MN - *EISS 83*
Sedona Red Rock News - Sedona, AZ - *BaconPubCkNews 84; NewsDir 84*
Sedro Woolley Courier Times - Sedro Woolley, WA - *Ed&PubIntYB 82*
Sedro Woolley Outlook - Sedro Woolley, WA - *BaconPubCkNews 84*
See Daytona Beach - Sarasota, FL - *BaconPubCkMag 84*
See Hear Industries [Div. of RJA Inc.] - Carson, CA - *AvMarPl 83*
See Magazines - Sarasota, FL - *MagDir 84*
See Mor TV of Yoakum Inc. [of Communications Services Inc.] - Yoakum, TX - *BrCabYB 84; Tel&CabFB 84C*
See-More TV Corp. [of Omega Communications Inc.] - Westville, IL - *BrCabYB 84; Tel&CabFB 84C*
See No Evil Music - *See* Espy Music Group
See-Saw Book Club [of Scholastic Book Services] - New York, NY - *LitMarPl 83, 84*
See TV Co. [of Tele-Communications Inc.] - Mexico, MO - *BrCabYB 84; Tel&CabFB 84C*
Seeburg Music Library Inc. [of Capitol Broadcasting Co. Inc.] - Raleigh, NC - *CabTVPrDB 83; Tel&CabFB 84C*
Seed Center - Garberville, CA - *LitMag&SmPr 83-84*
Seed-In-Hand Poetry Series - Blackstock, SC - *BoPubDir 4, 5*
Seed Publications - Rail Road Flat, CA - *BoPubDir 4, 5*
Seed Savers Exchange - Princeton, MO - *LitMag&SmPr 83-84*
Seed Trade News - Eden Prairie, MN - *BaconPubCkMag 84*
Seed Trade News [of Dean Enterprises Inc.] - Minneapolis, MN - *MagDir 84*
Seed World [of Scranton Gillette Communications Inc.] - Des Plaines, IL - *BaconPubCkMag 84; MagDir 84*
Seedsmen's Digest [of The Webb Co.] - St. Louis, MO - *BaconPubCkMag 84; MagDir 84*
Seeger Studios Inc., Hal - New York, NY - *Tel&CabFB 84C*
Seehafer Broadcasting Corp. - Manitowoc, WI - *BrCabYB 84*
Seek [of Standard Publishing] - Cincinnati, OH - *ArtMar 84; WritMar 84*
Seek Information Service - San Dimas, CA - *DataDirOnSer 84; EISS 83; FBInfSer 80; InfIndMarPl 83*
Seek-It Publishing Co. - Birmingham, MI - *BoPubDir 4, 5*
Seeker Magazine, The [of LP Publications] - San Diego, CA - *LitMag&SmPr 83-84*
Seekonk Star [of East Providence Post] - East Providence, RI - *NewsDir 84*
Seelig & Co. - Sun City West, AZ - *StaDirAdAg 2-84*
Seemore TV Inc. - Philadelphia, MS - *BrCabYB 84; Tel&CabFB 84C*
Seems - Sheboygan, WI - *LitMag&SmPr 83-84*
Seen - Millburn, NJ - *AyerDirPub 83*
Seequa Computer Corp. - Annapolis, MD - *WhoWMicrocom 83*
Seesaw Music Corp. - New York, NY - *BillIntBG 83-84*
Sefel Records Ltd. - Park Ridge, NJ - *BillIntBG 83-84*
Sefton Associates Inc. - Grand Rapids, MI - *AvMarPl 83; StaDirAdAg 2-84*
Sega Enterprises - Los Angeles, CA - *MicrocomMPl 84*
Segal's Executive Computing - Boulder, CO - *BaconPubCkMag 84*
Segerdahl Corp., The - Wheeling, IL - *LitMarPl 83, 84; MagIndMarPl 82-83*
Segue Foundation - New York, NY - *BoPubDir 4, 5*
Seguin Cable Communications Systems Inc. [of Communications Services Inc.] - Seguin, TX - *BrCabYB 84; Tel&CabFB 84C*
Seguin Gazette-Enterprise [of Taylor Communications Inc.] - Seguin, TX - *BaconPubCkNews 84; NewsDir 84*
Segull Enterprises - Taunton, MA - *MicrocomMPl 84*
Seham Associates Inc., David E. - Metuchen, NJ - *LitMarPl 83, 84*
SEI Corp. - Wayne, PA - *DataDirOnSer 84*
Seide Advertising Inc., Allan - Hawthorne, NY - *StaDirAdAg 2-84*
Seidel, Alison P. - Lubbock, TX - *LitMarPl 83, 84*
Seiden, Arthur - Woodmere, NY - *LitMarPl 83, 84; MagIndMarPl 82-83*
Seiden Communications - New York, NY - *DirPRFirms 83*
Seidenberg Music Ltd., Sidney A. - New York, NY - *BillIntBG 83-84*
Seidman, Lenore - Elmont, NY - *LitMarPl 83, 84*
Seigel, Fran - New York, NY - *LitMarPl 83, 84*
Seigle Rolfs & Wood Advertising Inc. - Honolulu, HI - *DirPRFirms 83*
Seiling TV Cable Systems [of Redden Enterprises] - Seiling, OK - *BrCabYB 84; Tel&CabFB 84C*
Seismic Crew Count [of CISInetwork] - Van Nuys, CA - *DataDirOnSer 84*
Seismic Crew Count - Tulsa, OK - *DirOnDB Spring 84*
Seismic Music - Wilmington, MA - *BillIntBG 83-84*
Seismological Central Observatory GRF [of Federal Institute for Geosciences & Natural Resources] - Erlangen, West Germany - *EISS 7-83 Sup*
Seitz, Beatrice West - Janeville, WI - *BoPubDir 4, 5*
Seitz/Tarnoff Inc. - Los Angeles, CA - *StaDirAdAg 2-84*
Seix Co. Inc., James C. - New York, NY - *StaDirAdAg 2-84*
Seixas Music - Massapequa, NY - *BillIntBG 83-84*
Sekai Bunka Photo - New York, NY - *LitMarPl 83; MagIndMarPl 82-83*
Selah Valley Optimist - Selah, WA - *AyerDirPub 83; BaconPubCkNews 84; Ed&PubIntYB 82*
Selame Design - Newton Lower Falls, MA - *HBIndAd&MS 82-83*
Selbrook Cable [of ALSAT 11 Cable Div. Inc.] - Selbrook, AL - *BrCabYB 84*
Selbstverlag Press - Bloomington, IN - *BoPubDir 4, 5*
Selby Associates Inc. - New York, NY - *MagIndMarPl 82-83*
Selby Record - Selby, SD - *Ed&PubIntYB 82*
Selby Record - *See* Selby Record Publishers
Selby Record Publishers - Selby, SD - *BaconPubCkNews 84*
Select Books - Mountain View, MO - *BoPubDir 4, 5*
Select Homes Magazine - Vancouver, BC, Canada - *WritMar 84*
Select Information Exchange - New York, NY - *MagIndMarPl 82-83*
Select Information Systems - Kentfield, CA - *MicrocomMPl 84; WhoWMicrocom 83*
Select Magazines Inc. - New York, NY - *MagIndMarPl 82-83*
Select Reservations Inc. - New York, NY - *MagIndMarPl 82-83*
Selectavision of Cazenovia & Nelson Inc. - Cazenovia, NY - *Tel&CabFB 84C*
Selected Educational Aids Inc. - Evanston, IL - *AvMarPl 83*
Selected Reading [of The National Research Bureau Inc.] - Burlington, IA - *WritMar 84*

Selected Water Resources Abstracts [of Water Resources Scientific Information Center] - Washington, DC - *CompReadDB 82*
Selected Water Resources Abstracts [of Water Resources Scientific Information Center] - Reston, VA - *DataDirOnSer 84; DirOnDB Spring 84*
Selective Cooperative Indexing of Management Periodicals [of European Business School Librarians Group] - Helsinki, Finland - *CompReadDB 82*
Selective Dissemination of Information On-line [of National Library of Medicine] - Bethesda, MD - *DataDirOnSer 84*
Selective Publishers Inc. - Clearwater, FL - *BoPubDir 4, 5; LitMag&SmPr 83-84*
Selectone Corp. - Hayward, CA - *MicrocomMPl 84*
SelecTV of California Inc. [of Clarion Corp.] - Marina del Rey, CA - *BrCabYB 84; CabTVPrDB 83*
SelecTV Programming Inc. - Marina del Rey, CA - *HomeVid&CabYB 82-83; Tel&CabFB 84C*
Selecval - Paris, France - *DirOnDB Spring 84*
Self [of Conde Nast Publications] - New York, NY - *BaconPubCkMag 84; Folio 83; LitMarPl 84; MagIndMarPl 82-83; WritMar 84*
Self & Society - London, England - *LitMag&SmPr 83-84*
Self-Counsel Press Inc. [Aff. of International Self-Counsel Press Ltd.] - Seattle, WA - *BoPubDir 4, 5; LitMarPl 83, 84; WritMar 84*
Self-Defense Kaleidoscope Publications - Oakland, CA - *BoPubDir 5*
Self-Help Manual - Riverside, CA - *BoPubDir 5*
Self-Motivated Careers - Duluth, GA - *BoPubDir 4 Sup, 5*
Self-Programmed Control Press - Los Angeles, CA - *BoPubDir 4, 5*
Self-Realization Fellowship - Los Angeles, CA - *BoPubDir 4, 5*
Self-Sufficiency Book Club [Subs. of Rodale Press Inc.] - Emmaus, PA - *LitMarPl 83, 84*
Selgem System [of Smithsonian Institution] - Washington, DC - *EISS 83*
Seligmann Agency, James - New York, NY - *LitMarPl 83, 84*
Selinsgrove Times Tribune - Selinsgrove, PA - *BaconPubCkNews 84; Ed&PubIntYB 82*
Selkirk Communications Inc. - Ft. Lauderdale, FL - *BrCabYB 84; InterCabHB 3; Tel&CabFB 84C*
Selkirk Communications Inc. - Hallandale, FL - *Tel&CabFB 84C*
Selkirk Communications Ltd. - Toronto, ON, Canada - *BrCabYB 84; Tel&CabFB 84C p.1701*
Sell Communications - Chicago, IL - *StaDirAdAg 2-84*
Sell Publishing Co. - Forest Lake, MN - *BaconPubCkNews 84*
Sellens, Alvin - Augusta, KS - *BoPubDir 4, 5*
Sellers Inc., Don - *See* Birch Tree Group Ltd.
Sellers Photographic - Decatur, IL - *AvMarPl 83*
Selling Areas-Marketing Inc. [Subs. of Time Inc.] - New York, NY - *AdAge 5-17-84 p.17; EISS 83; InfIndMarPl 83*
Selling Christmas Decorations - New York, NY - *BaconPubCkMag 84*
Selling Direct - Atlanta, GA - *ArtMar 84; BaconPubCkMag 84; WritMar 84*
Selling Direct - Chicago, IL - *MagDir 84*
Selling Sporting Goods - Chicago, IL - *MagDir 84*
Sellwood-Moreland Bee - Portland, OR - *AyerDirPub 83*
Selma Enterprise - Selma, CA - *BaconPubCkNews 84; Ed&PubIntYB 82*
Selma Johnstonian-Sun - Selma, NC - *BaconPubCkNews 84; Ed&PubIntYB 82*
Selma TeleCable Corp. - Selma, AL - *BrCabYB 84; Tel&CabFB 84C*
Selma Times-Journal [of Selma Newspapers Inc.] - Selma, AL - *BaconPubCkNews 84; Ed&PubIntYB 82; NewsDir 84*
Selman, Edythea Ginis - New York, NY - *LitMarPl 83, 84*
Selman, Richard - New York, NY - *LitMarPl 83, 84*
Selmer Cable Ltd. [of Tribune Cable Communications Inc.] - Selmer, TN - *BrCabYB 84*
Selmer Independent Appeal [of McNairy County Publishing Co.] - Selmer, TN - *NewsDir 84*
Selmer Independent-Appeal - *See* McNairy County Publishing Co.
Seltel Inc. - New York, NY - *TelAl 83, 84*
Seltzer & Associates Inc., Nancy - New York, NY - *DirPRFirms 83*
Seltzer, Ralph L. - Selma, OR - *BillIntBG 83-84*
Seluzicki Fine Books, Charles - Salem, OR - *BoPubDir 4, 5*
Selva Systems Inc. - Wellesley, MA - *MicrocomMPl 84*
Selven Ltd. - Witham, England - *MicrocomSwDir 1*
Selwitz Associates, Robert - New York, NY - *DirPRFirms 83*
Selwyn Advertising Inc. - Cedarhurst, NY - *StaDirAdAg 2-84*
Selwyn Advertising Inc. (Public Relations Div.) - Cedarhurst, NY - *DirPRFirms 83*
Selwyn & Associates - West Hartford, CT - *AdAge 3-28-84; StaDirAdAg 2-84*
Selwyn-Simpson & Associates Inc. - Santa Rosa, CA - *StaDirAdAg 2-84*
Selz, Seabolt & Associates Inc. - Chicago, IL - *DirPRFirms 83*
Selzer Books [Aff. of Philemon Foundation] - Ukiah, CA - *BoPubDir 4, 5*
Selzer Productions Inc., Max - Philadelphia, PA - *AvMarPl 83*
SEM Communications Inc. - Clayton, MO - *StaDirAdAg 2-84*
Semantodontics - Phoenix, AZ - *DirMarMP 83; LitMarPl 83, 84*
Sembrich Advertising Inc., Alfred S. - Rowayton, CT - *StaDirAdAg 2-84*
Semel/Kaye & Co. - Northbrook, IL - *AdAge 3-28-84; StaDirAdAg 2-84*
Semenya Music Co. - *See* Gopam Enterprises Inc.
Semerak Publishing Co. - Chicago, IL - *BillIntBG 83-84*
Semi-Sentient Software - New York, NY - *WhoWMicrocom 83*
Semiconductor Industry & Business Survey - Sunnyvale, CA - *BaconPubCkMag 84*
Semiconductor International - Des Plaines, IL - *BaconPubCkMag 84; WritMar 84*
Semiconductor Trade Statistics Program - Washington, DC - *DirOnDB Spring 84*
Semidisk Systems - Beaverton, OR - *MicrocomMPl 83, 84*
Semier Research Services, Ethel - Ft. Lauderdale, FL - *IntDirMarRes 83*
Seminal Publishing House - Northampton, MA - *BoPubDir 4 Sup, 5*
Seminar Clearinghouse International Inc. - St. Paul, MN - *EISS 83*
Seminars in Perinatology - New York, NY - *MagDir 84*
Seminary Library System [of Progressive Management Services Inc.] - Minneapolis, MN - *DataDirOnSer 84*
Seminary Music Co. - *See* Clonetone Music Co.
Seminary Press - Enid, OK - *BoPubDir 4, 5*
Seminole Buyers Guide - Largo, FL - *AyerDirPub 83*
Seminole Producer - Seminole, OK - *BaconPubCkNews 84; Ed&PubIntYB 82; NewsDir 84*
Seminole Sentinel - Seminole, TX - *BaconPubCkNews 84; Ed&PubIntYB 82*
Semit Productions - St. Petersburg, FL - *Tel&CabFB 84C*
Semler Advertising Inc., Ron - New York, NY - *StaDirAdAg 2-84*
Semline Inc. - Braintree, MA - *LitMarPl 83, 84*
Semloh Inc. - Medford, OR - *StaDirAdAg 2-84*
Semo Communications Corp. - Ava, MO - *BrCabYB 84*
Semo Communications Inc. - Sikeston, MO - *Tel&CabFB 84C p.1701*
Semo News - Lilbourn, MO - *AyerDirPub 83; Ed&PubIntYB 82*
Semon, Thomas T. - Demarest, NJ - *IntDirMarRes 83*
S.E.M.P. - Paris, France - *MicroMarPl 82-83*
Sena - Siena, Italy - *DirOnDB Spring 84*
Senate Library - Washington, DC - *EISS 83*
Senath Dunklin County Press - Senath, MO - *BaconPubCkNews 84*
Senatobia Tate County Democrat - Senatobia, MS - *BaconPubCkNews 84; NewsDir 84*
Send-Art & Video Communications - San Francisco, CA - *BaconPubCkMag 84*
Senda Nueva de Ediciones Inc. - Montclair, NJ - *BoPubDir 4, 5*
Sendor Bindery Inc. - New York, NY - *LitMarPl 83, 84; MagIndMarPl 82-83*
Seneb Cable Services Inc. [of Central Cable Services Inc.] - De Witt, NE - *BrCabYB 84; Tel&CabFB 84C*
Seneb Cable Services Inc. - Plymouth, NE - *BrCabYB 84*
Seneb Cable Services Inc. [of Central Cable Services Inc.] - Syracuse, NE - *Tel&CabFB 84C*
Seneb Cable Services Inc. [of Central Cable Services Inc.] - Wilber, NE - *Tel&CabFB 84C*
Seneca Cable TV Co. - Seneca, IL - *Tel&CabFB 84C*

Seneca Cable TV Inc. - Baldwinsville, NY - *BrCabYB 84; Tel&CabFB 84C*
Seneca Cable TV System Inc. [of Texkan Communications Inc.] - Seneca, KS - *Tel&CabFB 84C*
Seneca Courier-Tribune - Seneca, KS - *BaconPubCkNews 84; Ed&PubIntYB 82*
Seneca Falls Pennysaver - Seneca Falls, NY - *AyerDirPub 83*
Seneca Falls-Waterloo Reveille [of Reveille Publishing Co. Inc.] - Seneca Falls, NY - *AyerDirPub 83; BaconPubCkNews 84; Ed&PubIntYB 82; NewsDir 84*
Seneca Gorham Telephone Cooperative - Holcomb, NY - *TelDir&BG 83-84*
Seneca Journal & Tugaloo Tribune - Seneca, SC - *BaconPubCkNews 84; Ed&PubIntYB 82; NewsDir 84*
Seneca News-Dispatch - Seneca, MO - *BaconPubCkNews 84*
Seneca Press - Springfield, VA - *BoPubDir 4, 5*
Seneca Publishing Inc. - Attica, OH - *BaconPubCkNews 84*
Seneca Review - Geneva, NY - *LitMag&SmPr 83-84*
Seneca Telephone Co. - Seneca, MO - *TelDir&BG 83-84*
Seneca Town & Country Newspaper, The - Seneca, IL - *Ed&PubIntYB 82*
Senegraphics Inc. - Poughkeepsie, NY - *LitMarPl 84*
Senft Research Associates, Henry - Port Washington, NY - *IntDirMarRes 83*
Senior American News - Weston, MA - *BaconPubCkMag 84; MagDir 84*
Senior Golf Journal - North Myrtle Beach, SC - *BaconPubCkMag 84*
Senior Golfer - Clearwater, FL - *MagDir 84*
Senior Life - Vista, CA - *BaconPubCkMag 84*
Senior Record, The - Dryden, NY - *AyerDirPub 83*
Senior Scholastic - New York, NY - *MagDir 84; MagIndMarPl 82-83*
Senior World - El Cajon, CA - *ArtMar 84; BaconPubCkMag 84; MagDir 84; WritMar 84*
Senior World - San Diego, CA - *NewsDir 84*
Seniority Magazine - Syracuse, NY - *BaconPubCkMag 84*
Senne Corp., Henry - Chicago, IL - *StaDirAdAg 2-84*
Sensible Software Inc. - West Bloomfield, MI - *MicrocomMPl 83, 84*
Sensible Solutions Inc. - New York, NY - *LitMarPl 83, 84*
Sensible Sound, The - Buffalo, NY - *MagDir 84*
$ensible Sound, The - Snyder, NY - *ArtMar 84; WritMar 84*
Sensitive Wildlife Information [of U.S. Army] - Vicksburg, MS - *EISS 83*
Sensor-Based Systems - Chatfield, MN - *MicrocomMPl 84; MicrocomSwDir 1*
Sensors - Peterborough, NH - *BaconPubCkMag 84*
Sensory Resources Inc. - Concord, MA - *IntDirMarRes 83*
Sentec Inc. - Santa Rosa, CA - *DataDirSup 7-83*
Sentient Software Inc. - Aspen, CO - *MicrocomMPl 83, 84; MicrocomSwDir 1; WhoWMicrocom 83*
Sentinel [of Scottsboro Newspapers Inc.] - Scottsboro, AL - *AyerDirPub 83; Ed&PubIntYB 82*
Sentinel [of Arrowhead Press] - Sitka, AK - *AyerDirPub 83; Ed&PubIntYB 82*
Sentinel - Hanford, CA - *AyerDirPub 83*
Sentinel - Los Angeles, CA - *AyerDirPub 83; Ed&PubIntYB 82*
Sentinel - Ramona, CA - *AyerDirPub 83*
Sentinel - Santa Cruz, CA - *AyerDirPub 83*
Sentinel - Cortez, CO - *AyerDirPub 83*
Sentinel - Grand Junction, CO - *AyerDirPub 83*
Sentinel - Westminster, CO - *AyerDirPub 83*
Sentinel - Ansonia, CT - *AyerDirPub 83; Ed&PubIntYB 82*
Sentinel - Gulf Breeze, FL - *AyerDirPub 83; Ed&PubIntYB 82*
Sentinel - Largo, FL - *AyerDirPub 83*
Sentinel - Centralia, IL - *AyerDirPub 83*
Sentinel - Illipolis, IL - *AyerDirPub 83*
Sentinel - Woodstock, IL - *AyerDirPub 83*
Sentinel - Rochester, IN - *AyerDirPub 83*
Sentinel - Aurelia, IA - *AyerDirPub 83*
Sentinel - Hartley, IA - *AyerDirPub 83*
Sentinel - Le Mars, IA - *AyerDirPub 83*
Sentinel - Marion, IA - *AyerDirPub 83*
Sentinel - Osceola, IA - *AyerDirPub 83*
Sentinel - Shenandoah, IA - *AyerDirPub 83; Ed&PubIntYB 82*
Sentinel - Cheney, KS - *AyerDirPub 83*
Sentinel - Hoxie, KS - *AyerDirPub 83*
Sentinel - McPherson, KS - *AyerDirPub 83*
Sentinel - Radcliff, KY - *AyerDirPub 83; Ed&PubIntYB 82*
Sentinel - Waterville, ME - *AyerDirPub 83*
Sentinel - Clare, MI - *AyerDirPub 83*
Sentinel - Holland, MI - *AyerDirPub 83*
Sentinel - L'Anse, MI - *AyerDirPub 83*
Sentinel - Dawson, MN - *AyerDirPub 83*
Sentinel - Fairmont, MN - *AyerDirPub 83; Ed&PubIntYB 82*
Sentinel - Edina, MO - *AyerDirPub 83*
Sentinel - Franklin, NE - *AyerDirPub 83*
Sentinel - Eureka, NV - *AyerDirPub 83*
Sentinel - East Brunswick, NJ - *AyerDirPub 83; Ed&PubIntYB 82*
Sentinel - Milltown, NJ - *AyerDirPub 83*
Sentinel - Granville, NY - *AyerDirPub 83*
Sentinel - Mayville, NY - *AyerDirPub 83*
Sentinel - Rome, NY - *AyerDirPub 83*
Sentinel - Ticonderoga, NY - *AyerDirPub 83*
Sentinel [of Piedmont Publishing Co. Inc.] - Winston-Salem, NC - *AyerDirPub 83; Ed&PubIntYB 82; LitMarPl 83, 84*
Sentinel - Ashtabula, OH - *Ed&PubIntYB 82*
Sentinel - Pomeroy, OH - *AyerDirPub 83; BaconPubCkNews 84*
Sentinel - South Charleston, OH - *AyerDirPub 83; Ed&PubIntYB 82*
Sentinel - Trotwood, OH - *AyerDirPub 83*
Sentinel - Woodsfield, OH - *AyerDirPub 83; Ed&PubIntYB 82*
Sentinel - Youngstown, OH - *AyerDirPub 83*
Sentinel - Cottage Grove, OR - *AyerDirPub 83*
Sentinel - Carlisle, PA - *AyerDirPub 83*
Sentinel - Lewistown, PA - *AyerDirPub 83; Ed&PubIntYB 82*
Sentinel - Masontown, PA - *AyerDirPub 83*
Sentinel - Loris, SC - *AyerDirPub 83*
Sentinel - Pickens, SC - *AyerDirPub 83*
Sentinel - Nacogdoches, TX - *AyerDirPub 83*
Sentinel - Seminole, TX - *AyerDirPub 83*
Sentinel - Goldendale, WA - *AyerDirPub 83*
Sentinel [of Ogden Newspapers Inc.] - Parkersburg, WV - *AyerDirPub 83; NewsDir 84*
Sentinel - Cadott, WI - *AyerDirPub 83*
Sentinel - Milwaukee, WI - *AyerDirPub 83*
Sentinel - Kamloops, BC, Canada - *AyerDirPub 83; Ed&PubIntYB 82*
Sentinel - Chapleau, ON, Canada - *AyerDirPub 83; Ed&PubIntYB 82*
Sentinel - Lucknow, ON, Canada - *AyerDirPub 83; Ed&PubIntYB 82*
Sentinel-Bulletin - Tampa, FL - *Ed&PubIntYB 82*
Sentinel Communications of Muncie [of Century Communications Corp.] - Muncie, IN - *BrCabYB 84; Tel&CabFB 84C*
Sentinel Computer Corp. - Cincinnati, OH - *DataDirSup 7-83; WhoWMicrocom 83*
Sentinel Courier, The - Pilot Mound, MB, Canada - *AyerDirPub 83*
Sentinel East, The [of Midvale Sentinel Inc.] - Midvale, UT - *NewsDir 84*
Sentinel-Echo - London, KY - *AyerDirPub 83; Ed&PubIntYB 82*
Sentinel-Laurel, The - Laurel, MD - *Ed&PubIntYB 82*
Sentinel-Leader - Warren, IL - *AyerDirPub 83; Ed&PubIntYB 82*
Sentinel Leader - Sentinel, OK - *BaconPubCkNews 84; Ed&PubIntYB 82*
Sentinel-Ledger - Ocean City, NJ - *AyerDirPub 83; Ed&PubIntYB 82; NewsDir 84*
Sentinel-Mist Chronicle - St. Helens, OR - *AyerDirPub 83*
Sentinel-News - Shelbyville, KY - *AyerDirPub 83*
Sentinel Newspapers - Denver, CO - *BaconPubCkNews 84; Ed&PubIntYB 82*
Sentinel Newspapers - East Brunswick, NJ - *BaconPubCkNews 84*
Sentinel-Prince George's, The - Hyattsville, MD - *Ed&PubIntYB 82*
Sentinel Record - Hot Springs, AR - *AyerDirPub 83; Ed&PubIntYB 82*
Sentinel-Republican - Lincoln, KS - *AyerDirPub 83*
Sentinel-Review - Woodstock, ON, Canada - *AyerDirPub 83*
Sentinel-Standard - Ionia, MI - *Ed&PubIntYB 82*
Sentinel Star - Orlando, FL - *Ed&PubIntYB 82*
Sentinel Televue - Sentinel, OK - *BrCabYB 84; Tel&CabFB 84C*

Sentinel, The - Clarendon, AR - *AyerDirPub 83; Ed&PubIntYB 82*
Sentinel, The - San Diego, CA - *AyerDirPub 83; Ed&PubIntYB 82*
Sentinel, The - Chicago, IL - *BaconPubCkMag 84; MagDir 84*
Sentinel, The - Rockville, MD - *Ed&PubIntYB 82*
Sentinel, The - Franklinville, NJ - *Ed&PubIntYB 82*
Sentinel, The - New Windsor, NY - *Ed&PubIntYB 82*
Sentinel, The - Channelview, TX - *Ed&PubIntYB 82*
Sentinel-Tribune - Bowling Green, OH - *AyerDirPub 83*
Sentinel West, The [of Midvale Sentinel Inc.] - Midvale, UT - *NewsDir 84*
Sentinela - Vancouver, BC, Canada - *Ed&PubIntYB 82*
Sentry - Wellston, OH - *AyerDirPub 83*
Sentry Broadcasting Inc. - Stevens Point, WI - *BrCabYB 84*
Sentry Database Publishing - Hudson, MA - *BoPubDir 5*
Sentry-Enterprise - Hillsboro, WI - *AyerDirPub 83; Ed&PubIntYB 82*
Sentry Group, Frank - Los Angeles, CA - *ProGuPRSer 4*
Sentry-News - Slidell, LA - *Ed&PubIntYB 82*
Separate Doors [of Jelm Mountain Publications] - Canyon, TX - *LitMag&SmPr 83-84*
Separations Science Database [of US Dept. of Energy] - Oak Ridge, TN - *DataDirOnSer 84; DirOnDB Spring 84*
Sepher Hermon Press Inc. - New York, NY - *LitMarPl 83, 84*
Sepia - Beverly Hills, CA - *WritMar 84*
Sepia - Los Angeles, CA - *MagDir 84*
Sepia - Dallas, TX - *BaconPubCkMag 84*
Sepia - Ft. Worth, TX - *MagIndMarPl 82-83*
Sepia - Cornwall, England - *LitMag&SmPr 83-84*
September Days [of Days Inns of America Inc.] - Atlanta, GA - *WritMar 84*
September Music Corp. - New York, NY - *BillIntBG 83-84*
September Productions - Boston, MA - *Tel&CabFB 84C*
Sequence A-V/Videotex [Div. of Sequence Media Services Ltd.] - Ottawa, ON, Canada - *AvMarPl 83*
Sequim Jimmy Come Lately Gazette - Sequim, WA - *BaconPubCkNews 84*
Sequim Press - Sequim, WA - *BaconPubCkNews 84; Ed&PubIntYB 82; NewsDir 84*
Sequoia - Stanford, CA - *LitMag&SmPr 83-84*
Sequoia Cablevision Inc. [of McClatchy Newspapers] - Tulare, CA - *Tel&CabFB 84C*
Sequoia Cablevision Inc. [of McClatchy Newspapers] - Visalia, CA - *BrCabYB 84*
Sequoyah County Times - Sallisaw, OK - *AyerDirPub 83; Ed&PubIntYB 82*
Seraphim Press - Buena Park, CA - *BoPubDir 4 Sup, 5; LitMag&SmPr 83-84; LitMarPl 83*
Serbin Co. Inc., Lew - San Francisco, CA - *AvMarPl 83*
Sercolab - Arlington, MA - *BoPubDir 4 Sup, 5*
Sercomp Corp. - Chatsworth, CA - *DirInfWP 82*
Sercon Corp. - Dallas, TX - *DataDirSup 7-83; WhoWMicrocom 83*
Serenade [of Sylvan Press Publishers] - Richmond, VA - *WritMar 84*
Serendipity Press - Wilmington, DE - *ArtMar 84*
Serendipity Systems Inc. - Ithaca, NY - *MicrocomMPl 83; WhoWMicrocom 83*
Serenity Weavers - Eugene, OR - *BoPubDir 4, 5*
Serenus Corp. - Dobbs Ferry, NY - *BillIntBG 83-84*
Sergeants [of Air Force Sergeants Association] - Washington, DC - *ArtMar 84*
Sergeants [of Air Force Sergeants Association] - Temple Hills, MD - *BaconPubCkMag 84; WritMar 84*
Serial Printers [of GML Corp.] - Lexington, MA - *CompReadDB 82*
Serial Sources for the BIOSIS Data Base [of BioSciences Information Service] - Philadelphia, PA - *MagDir 84*
Serial Title Automated Record [of U.S. Dept. of Agriculture] - Beltsville, MD - *CompReadDB 82*
Serials Data Management & Control System [of Ballen Booksellers International Inc.] - Commack, NY - *EISS 83*
Serials Librarian [of Haworth Press Journals] - New York, NY - *LitMarPl 83, 84; MagIndMarPl 82-83*
Serials On-line [of National Library of Medicine] - Bethesda, MD - *CompReadDB 82; DataDirOnSer 84*
Serials Review - Ann Arbor, MI - *MagIndMarPl 82-83*
Serina Press - Alexandria, VA - *BoPubDir 4, 5*
Serino, Coyne & Nappi - New York, NY - *AdAge 3-28-84; StaDirAdAg 2-84*
Serious Business Co. - Oakland, CA - *ArtMar 84*
Serious Music - *See* Wrensong Inc.
Seripress - Toronto, ON, Canada - *BoPubDir 4, 5*
SERIX - Solna, Sweden - *DirOnDB Spring 84*
Serline [of U.S. National Library of Medicine] - Bethesda, MD - *DirOnDB Spring 84; EISS 83*
Serpent & Eagle Press - Oneonta, NY - *BoPubDir 4 Sup, 5*
Serra Mesa Pennysaver - Mission Viejo, CA - *AyerDirPub 83*
Serre, Robert - Ottawa, ON, Canada - *BoPubDir 4, 5*
Serrell & Simons Publishers - Winnebago, WI - *BoPubDir 4 Sup, 5*
SERS - *See* Sorkin-Enenstein Research Service Inc.
Sertoman, The [of Sertoma International] - Kansas City, MO - *ArtMar 84; WritMar 84*
Servant Publications - Ann Arbor, MI - *ArtMar 84; LitMarPl 83, 84; WritMar 84*
Service & Smiles Distributors Ltd. - Toronto, ON, Canada - *BoPubDir 4, 5*
Service Bureau Co., The - *See* Control Data Corp. (Business Information Services)
Service Business [of Cleaning Consultant Service Inc.] - Seattle, WA - *ArtMar 84; MagDir 84*
Service Calvados [of American College in Paris] - Paris, France - *EISS 7-83 Sup*
Service Center for Aging Information [of U.S. Dept. of Health & Human Services] - Washington, DC - *EISS 83*
Service de Cablo Distrobution SFC Moisie - Moisie, PQ, Canada - *BrCabYB 84*
Service Difficulty Reporting System [of Federal Aviation Administration] - Washington, DC - *DBBus 82*
Service Electric Cable TV Inc. - Allentown, PA - *BrCabYB 84*
Service Electric Cable TV Inc. [of Roundtop TV Association] - Mahanoy City, PA - *BrCabYB 84 p.D-306; CabTVFinDB 83; KnowInd 83; LitMarPl 84; TelAl 83, 84; Tel&CabFB 84C p.1701*
Service Electric Cable TV Inc. - Sunbury, PA - *Tel&CabFB 84C*
Service Employee [of Service Employees International Union] - Washington, DC - *NewsDir 84*
Service Employees News - Detroit, MI - *NewsDir 84*
Service International de Microfilms - Paris, France - *MicroMarPl 82-83*
Service Messenger Co. Inc. - New York, NY - *MagIndMarPl 82-83*
Service Publications Inc. - New York, NY - *DirMarMP 83; MagIndMarPl 82-83*
Service Reporter [of Technical Reporting Corp.] - Wheeling, IL - *BaconPubCkMag 84; MagDir 84*
Service Software - Dallas, TX - *MicrocomMPl 84*
Service Station & Garage Management - Toronto, ON, Canada - *BaconPubCkMag 84; WritMar 84*
Service Station Dealers News [of Hunter Publishing Co.] - Southfield, MI - *BaconPubCkMag 84; MagDir 84*
Service Station Management - Des Plaines, IL - *BaconPubCkMag 84; MagDir 84*
Service Telephone Co. [Aff. of Telephone & Data Systems Inc.] - Fair Bluff, NC - *TelDir&BG 83-84*
Service to Publishers Inc. - Lewisburg, PA - *LitMarPl 83, 84*
Service Typesetters - Austin, TX - *LitMarPl 84*
Service Union Reporter [of SEIU] - Los Angeles, CA - *NewsDir 84*
Service Web Offset Corp. - Chicago, IL - *LitMarPl 83, 84; MagIndMarPl 82-83*
Services by Satellite Inc. - Washington, DC - *BrCabYB 84; CabTVFinDB 83; Tel&CabFB 84C*
Services Unique Inc. - Dayton, OH - *MicrocomSwDir 1; WhoWMicrocom 83*
Servicios Internacionales - La Marque, TX - *BoPubDir 4, 5*
Servico de Acesso a Bancos de Dados [of Portuguese Radio Marconi Co.] - Lisbon, Portugal - *TeleSy&SerDir 7-83*
Serving America - Long Beach, CA - *NewsDir 84*
Servisound Inc. - New York, NY - *AvMarPl 83*
Servoss-Barnhart Public Relations - Denver, CO - *DirPRFirms 83*
SES Associates - Cambridge, MA - *BoPubDir 4, 5*

SES Marketscan [of I. P. Sharp Associates Ltd.] - Toronto, ON, Canada - *DataDirOnSer 84*
Sesac Inc. - New York, NY - *Tel&CabFB 84C*
Sesame Press - Windsor, ON, Canada - *BoPubDir 4, 5; LitMag&SmPr 83-84*
Sesame Street [of Children's Television Workshop] - New York, NY - *ArtMar 84; Folio 83; MagIndMarPl 82-83*
Sesame Street Records [Div. of Distinguished Productions Inc.] - New York, NY - *BillIntBG 83-84*
Sesanet Corp. - Reston, VA - *ADAPSOMemDir 83-84*
Sesco Music - San Jose, CA - *BillIntBG 83-84*
Seslar-McAllister Inc. - Ft. Wayne, IN - *StaDirAdAg 2-84*
Sesser/Valier Cablevision Corp. [of Omni Cable TV Corp.] - Sesser, IL - *BrCabYB 84; Tel&CabFB 84C*
Sessions Records Inc. - Lisle, IL - *BillIntBG 83-84*
Setauket/Stony Brook Village Times, The - East Setauket, NY - *NewsDir 84*
Setcom Corp. - Mountain View, CA - *AvMarPl 83*
Sethco [Div. of Met Pro Corp.] - Hauppauge, NY - *AvMarPl 83*
Seton Hall University (Institute of Far Eastern Studies) - South Orange, NJ - *BoPubDir 4, 5*
Settel Associates Inc. - Jericho, NY - *LitMarPl 83, 84*
Setter & Associates Inc. - Wichita, KS - *StaDirAdAg 2-84*
Setterington & Co. Ontario Inc. - St. Catherines, ON, Canada - *ArtMar 84*
Settles Books - Aurora, IL - *BoPubDir 5*
Seven - Oklahoma City, OK - *WritMar 84*
Seven Arts Feature Syndicate - New York, NY - *Ed&PubIntYB 82*
Seven Arts Press Inc. - Hollywood, CA - *BoPubDir 4, 5*
Seven Buffaloes Press - Big Timber, MT - *BoPubDir 4, 5; LitMag&SmPr 83-84*
7 C's Press Inc. - Riverside, CT - *LitMarPl 83, 84*
Seven Cycles - New York, NY - *BoPubDir 4 Sup, 5*
Seven Days Magazine - New York, NY - *MagDir 84*
Seven Figure Music Corp. - *See* Gallico Music Corp., Al
7 Hills Books [Div. of Books for the Decorative Arts Inc.] - Cincinnati, OH - *LitMarPl 84*
Seven Hills Publishing & Recording Co. Inc. - Evansville, IN - *BillIntBG 83-84*
Seven Locks Press Inc. [Subs. of Calvin Kytle Associates] - Cabin John, MD - *LitMarPl 83, 84; WritMar 84*
Seven Mile Systems Inc. - The Dalles, OR - *MicrocomMPl 84*
Seven Network Australia - New York, NY - *Tel&CabFB 84C*
Seven Oaks - Savannah, GA - *BoPubDir 5*
Seven Oaks Press - St. Charles, IL - *BoPubDir 4, 5; LitMag&SmPr 83-84*
Seven of Us Music - Dover, NJ - *BillIntBG 83-84*
Seven Seas Press [Subs. of Davis Publications] - Newport, RI - *ArtMar 84; LitMarPl 83, 84; WritMar 84*
Seven Songs - *See* Schroeder International Ltd., A.
Seven Systems Inc. - Huntsville, AL - *InterCabHB 3*
Seven Woods Press - New York, NY - *BoPubDir 4, 5; LitMag&SmPr 83-84*
Seventeen [of Triangle Communications Inc.] - New York, NY - *BaconPubCkMag 84; Folio 83; LitMarPl 83, 84; MagDir 84; MagIndMarPl 82-83; NewsBur 6; WritMar 84*
1750 Arch Inc. - Berkeley, CA - *BillIntBG 83-84*
Seventel [of Brisbane TV Ltd.] - Brisbane, Australia - *VideoDir 82-83*
Seventh Son Music - *See* Campbell Music Inc., Glen
Seventh Son Press - Baltimore, MD - *LitMag&SmPr 83-84*
77 Publishing - Port Colborne, ON, Canada - *BoPubDir 4, 5*
Seventy Six Magazine - Los Angeles, CA - *WritMar 84*
'76 Press - Atlanta, GA - *BoPubDir 4, 5*
73 Magazine - Peterborough, NH - *ArtMar 84; BaconPubCkMag 84; MagDir 84; MagIndMarPl 82-83; WritMar 84*
Severance & Associates Inc. - Nashville, TN - *StaDirAdAg 2-84*
Severance Photo Inc. - Watertown, NY - *AvMarPl 83*
Severy Publishing, Frank - Alhambra, CA - *BoPubDir 4, 5*
Sevier County Cable Communications Co. [of Telephone & Data Systems Inc.] - Seymour, TN - *Tel&CabFB 84C*
Sevier County News Record - Pigeon Forge, TN - *AyerDirPub 83; BaconPubCkNews 84*
Sevier County News Record - Sevierville, TN - *Ed&PubIntYB 82; NewsDir 84*
Sevierville Cable Communications Co. Inc. [of Telephone & Data Systems Inc.] - Sevierville, TN - *Tel&CabFB 84C*
Seville Publishing - Van Nuys, CA - *BoPubDir 4 Sup, 5*
Sew Business - Ft. Lee, NJ - *BaconPubCkMag 84; WritMar 84*
Sew Business - New York, NY - *MagDir 84*
Sew/Fit Co. - Addison, IL - *BoPubDir 4*
Sew/Fit Co. - La Grange, IL - *BoPubDir 5*
Sew News - Seattle, WA - *WritMar 84*
Sewanee Review [of University of the South] - Sewanee, TN - *LitMag&SmPr 83-84; MagIndMarPl 82-83; WritMar 84*
Seward County Independent - Seward, NE - *AyerDirPub 83; BaconPubCkNews 84; Ed&PubIntYB 82; NewsDir 84*
Seward Phoenix Log - Seward, AK - *BaconPubCkNews 84; Ed&PubIntYB 82*
Sewickley Herald [of Gateway Publications] - Sewickley, PA - *AyerDirPub 83; Ed&PubIntYB 82; NewsDir 84*
Sewickley Herald - *See* Gateway Press Inc.
Sewickley Presbyterian Church (Women's Association) - Sewickley, PA - *BoPubDir 4, 5*
Sewing Knits Inc. - Arcadia, CA - *BoPubDir 4, 5*
Sex Behavior Case Histories [of Institute for Sex Research Inc.] - Bloomington, IN - *CompReadDB 82*
Sexology Today - New York, NY - *MagIndMarPl 82-83; WritMar 84*
Sextant [of Sextant Publishing Co.] - Washington, DC - *MicrocomMPl 84*
Sextant Inc. - New York, NY - *TelAl 83; Tel&CabFB 84C*
Sextet Music Co. - *See* Ahlert Music Corp., Fred
Sexton, Mark - Salem, MA - *LitMarPl 83, 84; MagIndMarPl 82-83*
Sexton Public Relations, Rose - New York, NY - *DirPRFirms 83*
Sexual Medicine Today - New York, NY - *MagIndMarPl 82-83*
Sexuality Today - New York, NY - *DirOnDB Spring 84*
Sexuality Today [of NewsNet Inc.] - Bryn Mawr, PA - *DataDirOnSer 84*
Sexually Transmitted Diseases - Philadelphia, PA - *MagDir 84*
Seyah Music - Atlanta, GA - *BillIntBG 83-84*
Seybold Consulting Group Inc. - Boston, MA - *DirInfWP 82*
Seybold Publications Inc. - Media, PA - *BoPubDir 4 Sup, 5; EISS 5-84 Sup*
Seybold Report on Office Systems - Boston, MA - *BaconPubCkMag 84*
Seybold Report on Office Systems [of NewsNet Inc.] - Bryn Mawr, PA - *DataDirOnSer 84*
Seybold Report on Office Systems - Media, PA - *DirOnDB Spring 84; MagIndMarPl 82-83*
Seybold Report on Professional Computing [of NewsNet Inc.] - Bryn Mawr, PA - *DataDirOnSer 84*
Seybold Report on Professional Computing - Media, PA - *BaconPubCkMag 84; DirOnDB Spring 84*
Seybold Report on Publishing Systems [of NewsNet Inc.] - Bryn Mawr, PA - *DataDirOnSer 84*
Seybold Report on Publishing Systems - Media, PA - *DirOnDB Spring 84; MagIndMarPl 82-83*
Seyer Catechism Workbooks, Herman D. - Visalia, CA - *BoPubDir 4, 5*
Seymour Add-Vertizer - Seymour, WI - *AyerDirPub 83*
Seymour Baylor County Banner - Seymour, TX - *BaconPubCkNews 84*
Seymour Cable TV Inc. - Seymour, TX - *BrCabYB 84*
Seymour Cablevision Ltd. - Seymour, WI - *BrCabYB 84; Tel&CabFB 84C*
Seymour Charles Advertising - Union, NJ - *StaDirAdAg 2-84*
Seymour, Dorothy Z. - Newton Centre, MA - *LitMarPl 83, 84*
Seymour Herald - Seymour, IA - *BaconPubCkNews 84; Ed&PubIntYB 82*
Seymour-Smith Publishers - San Jose, CA - *BoPubDir 4, 5*
Seymour Times Press - Seymour, WI - *BaconPubCkNews 84; NewsDir 84*
Seymour Tri-County News - Seymour, TN - *BaconPubCkNews 84; NewsDir 84*
Seymour Tribune - Seymour, IN - *BaconPubCkNews 84; Ed&PubIntYB 82; NewsDir 84*
Seymour Webster County Citizen - Seymour, MO - *BaconPubCkNews 84*
Sez [of Shadow Press U.S.A.] - Minneapolis, MN - *LitMag&SmPr 83-84*

SFBRI - Bryan, TX - *BoPubDir 4, 5*
SFM Media Service Corp. - New York, NY - *HBIndAd&MS 82-83; StaDirAdAg 2-84; TelAl 83, 84; Tel&CabFB 84C*
SFN Cos. Inc. - Glenview, IL - *KnowInd 83*
SFS Publishing Co. [Aff. of Sassafras Enterprises Inc.] - Chicago, IL - *BoPubDir 4 Sup, 5*
SFSU Videotex System [of San Francisco State University] - San Francisco, CA - *EISS 7-83 Sup*
SFW/PRI Inc. - New York, NY - *Ed&PubIntYB 82*
SGA Journal - New York, NY - *BaconPubCkMag 84*
SGB Data Base [of Societe Generale de Banque] - Brussels, Belgium - *CompReadDB 82; DirOnDB Spring 84; EISS 83*
SGL Homalite - Wilmington, DE - *DataDirSup 7-83*
SGL Waber Electric - Westville, NJ - *DataDirSup 7-83*
Shable, Sawyer & Pitluk [Aff. of The Pitluk Group] - Houston, TX - *AdAge 3-28-84; StaDirAdAg 2-84*
Shackelford Agency - Azusa, CA - *StaDirAdAg 2-84*
Shade Information Systems Inc. - Green Bay, WI - *DataDirSup 7-83*
Shade Tree Music Inc. - Redding, CA - *BillIntBG 83-84*
Shades Valley Sun [of Sun Newspapers South & West] - Birmingham, AL - *BaconPubCkNews 84; Ed&PubIntYB 82; NewsDir 84*
Shadix Radio & TV Inc. - Beverly, OH - *BrCabYB 84*
Shadix TV Cable Inc. - Beverly, OH - *Tel&CabFB 84C*
Shadow Press - Minneapolis, MN - *LitMag&SmPr 83-84*
Shadow Press [Aff. of House of Shadows Art Studio] - Gananoque, ON, Canada - *BoPubDir 4, 5*
Shadow Press U.S.A. - Minneapolis, MN - *BoPubDir 4, 5*
Shadow Records - Minneapolis, MN - *BillIntBG 83-84*
Shadow Voyages [of Golden Sails Press] - Birmingham, AL - *LitMag&SmPr 83-84*
Shadowfax Music - *See* OAS Music Group Inc.
Shadowgraph Press - Newburyport, MA - *BoPubDir 4, 5*
ShadowLight Music - Marina del Rey, CA - *BillIntBG 83-84*
Shadowlight Records - Marina del Rey, CA - *BillIntBG 83-84*
Shadowrock Music Inc. - *See* Barton Music Inc., Earl
Shadwold Press - Kennebunkport, ME - *BoPubDir 4, 5*
Shady Dell Music Inc. - *See* Barton Music Inc., Earl
Shafer Associates Inc. - Gaithersburg, MD - *CabTVFinDB 83*
Shaffer, Dale E. - Salem, OH - *AvMarPl 83; BoPubDir 4, 5*
Shaffer Enterprises - San Anselmo, CA - *StaDirAdAg 2-84*
Shaffer/MacGill & Associates - Chicago, IL - *AdAge 3-28-84; StaDirAdAg 2-84*
Shaffer Records - Sylmar, CA - *BillIntBG 83-84*
Shaffer Shaffer Shaffer Inc. - Cleveland, OH - *StaDirAdAg 2-84*
Shaffstall Corp. - Indianapolis, IN - *DirInfWP 82; LitMarPl 83, 84*
Shafter Press - Shafter, CA - *BaconPubCkNews 84; Ed&PubIntYB 82*
Shafter Shopper - Shafter, CA - *AyerDirPub 83*
Shah, Kirit N. - Piedmont, CA - *BoPubDir 4 Sup, 5; LitMag&SmPr 83-84*
Shailer Davidoff Rogers Inc. - Fairfield, CT - *StaDirAdAg 2-84*
Shaker Advertising Agency - Oak Park, IL - *AdAge 3-28-84; StaDirAdAg 2-84*
Shaker Computer & Management Services Inc. - Schenectady, NY - *DataDirOnSer 84*
Shaker Museum - Old Chatham, NY - *BoPubDir 4, 5*
Shaker Press [Aff. of United Society of Shakers] - Poland Spring, ME - *BoPubDir 4 Sup, 5*
Shakespeare Newsletter, The - Evanston, IL - *LitMag&SmPr 83-84*
Shakespeare Quarterly - Washington, DC - *MagIndMarPl 82-83*
Shakopee Valley News - Shakopee, MN - *BaconPubCkNews 84; Ed&PubIntYB 82; NewsDir 84*
Shakti Systems Inc. - Schaumburg, IL - *MicrocomMPl 83; WhoWMicrocom 83*
Shakti Systems Inc. - Indianapolis, IN - *MicrocomMPl 84*
Shaller Advertising Inc., Robert E. - New York, NY - *DirMarMP 83*
Shaller, Rubin & Winer - New York, NY - *AdAge 3-28-84; BrCabYB 84; StaDirAdAg 2-84*
Shalley, Doris P. - Washington Crossing, PA - *FBInfSer 80; LitMarPl 83, 84; MagIndMarPl 82-83*
Shallotte Brunswick Beacon - Shallotte, NC - *BaconPubCkNews 84*
Shallway Foundation - Connellsville, PA - *BoPubDir 4, 5*
Shamal Books Inc. - New York, NY - *BoPubDir 4, 5*
Shamba Publishing Co. - Los Angeles, CA - *BillIntBG 83-84*
Shambhala Publications Inc. - Boulder, CO - *LitMarPl 83, 84; WritMar 84*
Shameless Hussy Press - Berkeley, CA - *LitMag&SmPr 83-84; LitMarPl 83, 84*
Shamokin News-Item - Shamokin, PA - *BaconPubCkNews 84; NewsDir 84*
Shamrock Broadcasting Co. - Hollywood, CA - *BrCabYB 84*
Shamrock Broadcasting Co. - Los Angeles, CA - *Tel&CabFB 84S*
Shamrock Communications Inc. - Scranton, PA - *BrCabYB 84*
Shamrock Community TV System - Shamrock, TX - *BrCabYB 84; Tel&CabFB 84C*
Shamrock Publications - Fairborn, OH - *BoPubDir 4 Sup, 5*
Shamrock Texan - Shamrock, TX - *BaconPubCkNews 84; Ed&PubIntYB 82*
Shana Corp., The - Livonia, MI - *AvMarPl 83*
Shanachie Records Corp. - Ho Ho Kus, NJ - *BillIntBG 83-84*
Shanahan & Associates Inc., James A. - Chicago, IL - *DirPRFirms 83*
Shane Press - Portland, OR - *LitMag&SmPr 83-84*
Shaner-Grandelis Associates - Convent Station, NJ - *DirPRFirms 83*
Shank, Thomas D. - Somerset, KY - *Tel&CabFB 84C p.1701*
Shanken Communications Inc., M. - New York, NY - *BoPubDir 4, 5*
Shannon, Joseph - Port Hawkesbury, NS, Canada - *BrCabYB 84*
Shannon Publications - Englewood, CO - *BoPubDir 4 Sup, 5*
Shantih - Brooklyn, NY - *LitMag&SmPr 83-84*
Shape [of Weider Enterprises] - Woodland Hills, CA - *ArtMar 84; BaconPubCkMag 84; MagIndMarPl 82-83; WritMar 84*
Shape Inc. - Dallas, TX - *MicrocomMPl 84; MicrocomSwDir 1*
Shapian & Associates - Los Angeles, CA - *LitMarPl 83, 84; MagIndMarPl 82-83*
Shapiro Bernstein & Co. Inc. - New York, NY - *BillIntBG 83-84*
Shapiro Budrow & Associates Inc. - New York, NY - *StaDirAdAg 2-84*
Shapiro Public Relations, Selma - New York, NY - *LitMarPl 83, 84*
Shapiro Research Corp., S. A. - New York, NY - *IntDirMarRes 83*
Sharar, V. E. - Tucson, AZ - *Tel&CabFB 84C p.1701*
Share of Market [of I. P. Sharp Associates Ltd.] - Toronto, ON, Canada - *DataDirOnSer 84*
Shared Care - Phoenix, AZ - *BoPubDir 5*
Shared Commodity Database [of ContiCommodity Services Inc.] - Memphis, TN - *DataDirOnSer 84*
Shared Medical Systems Corp. - King of Prussia, PA - *Datamation 6-83*
Shared Medical Systems Corp. - Malvern, PA - *DataDirOnSer 84; Top100Al 83*
Shared Systems Technologies Inc. - Bennington, VT - *MicrocomMPl 84; MicrocomSwDir 1*
Shareholder Communications Corp. - New York, NY - *DirPRFirms 83; ProGuPRSer 4*
Sharfstein, Marvin B. - King of Prussia, PA - *Tel&CabFB 84C p.1701*
Shari Music Publishing Corp. - *See* Sanga Music Inc.
Sharing [of Western Sun Publications] - Yuma, AZ - *LitMag&SmPr 83-84*
Sharing Barbara's Mail - Springfield, MO - *LitMag&SmPr 83-84*
Sharkey Music Inc. - *See* Croma Music Co. Inc.
Sharnborg & Associates, Jon - Costa Mesa, CA - *DirPRFirms 83*
Sharon Advocate - Sharon, MA - *BaconPubCkNews 84; Ed&PubIntYB 82; NewsDir 84*
Sharon Herald - Sharon, PA - *BaconPubCkNews 84; NewsDir 84*
Sharon Publications Inc. - Closter, NJ - *BoPubDir 4*
Sharon Publications Inc. [Aff. of Magazines Inc.] - Cresskill, NJ - *BoPubDir 5; LitMarPl 84*
Sharon Reporter - Sharon, WI - *BaconPubCkNews 84; Ed&PubIntYB 82*
Sharon Sentinel - *See* Bulletin Publishing Co.
Sharon Springs Western Times - Sharon Springs, KS - *BaconPubCkNews 84; Ed&PubIntYB 82*

Sharon Telephone Co. - Hills, IA - *TelDir&BG 83-84*
Sharon Telephone Co. - Sharon, WI - *TelDir&BG 83-84*
Sharp Advertising Agency - Seattle, WA - *StaDirAdAg 2-84*
Sharp Advertising Inc. - Cleveland, OH - *StaDirAdAg 2-84*
Sharp APL Communications Network [of I. P. Sharp Associates Ltd.] - Toronto, ON, Canada - *TeleSy&SerDir 7-83*
Sharp Associates, I. P. - Toronto, ON, Canada - *CompReadDB 82; DataDirOnSer 84; DataDirSup 7-83; EISS 83; InfIndMarPl 83*
Sharp Electronics Corp. [Subs. of Sharp Corp.] - Paramus, NJ - *AvMarPl 83; BillIntBG 83-84; DataDirSup 7-83; DirInfWP 82; MicrocomMPl 84; WhoWMicrocom 83*
Sharp Hartwig Advertising Inc. - Seattle, WA - *AdAge 3-28-84; StaDirAdAg 2-84*
Sharp Publications [Aff. of Vintage House] - Scarborough, ON, Canada - *BoPubDir 4, 5*
Sharp Telecommunications Network, I. P. [of I. P. Sharp Associates Ltd.] - Toronto, ON, Canada - *TeleSy&SerDir 2-84*
Sharpburg Herald - *See* News-Record Div. [of News Printing Co.]
Sharpe & Associates, Irwin P. - West Orange, NJ - *IntDirMarRes 83*
Sharpe Inc., John K. - Wilmette, IL - *LitMarPl 83*
Sharpe Inc., M. E. - Armonk, NY - *LitMarPl 83, 84; MagIndMarPl 82-83*
Sharpsburg Cable TV Co. [of G.S. Communications Inc.] - Sharpsburg, MD - *Tel&CabFB 84C*
Shashinka Photo Inc. - New York, NY - *LitMarPl 84*
Shasta Abbey Press - Mt. Shasta, CA - *BoPubDir 4, 5*
Shasta General Systems - Sunnyvale, CA - *DataDirSup 7-83; DirInfWP 82; MicrocomSwDir 1; WhoWMicrocom 83*
Shattuck Northwest Oklahoman - Shattuck, OK - *Ed&PubIntYB 82*
Shattuck Northwest Oklahoman & News - Shattuck, OK - *BaconPubCkNews 84*
Shatzkin & Co. - Croton-on-Hudson, NY - *LitMarPl 83, 84; MagIndMarPl 82-83*
Shatzkin, Eleanor - New York, NY - *MagIndMarPl 82-83*
Shavian-Journal of Bernard Shaw [of High Orchard Press] - Dagenham, England - *LitMag&SmPr 83-84*
Shaw [of Pennsylvania State University Press] - University Park, PA - *LitMag&SmPr 83-84*
Shaw AFB Recon [of Carolina Printing Center] - Cayce, SC - *NewsDir 84*
Shaw & Koulermous - New York, NY - *HBIndAd&MS 82-83*
Shaw & Todd Inc. - New York, NY - *StaDirAdAg 2-84*
Shaw Associates Inc. - West Springfield, MA - *DirPRFirms 83*
Shaw Associates, Rik - New York, NY - *AvMarPl 83*
Shaw Cable TV Co. [of Satellite Cable TV Corp.] - Shaw Air Force Base, SC - *BrCabYB 84*
Shaw Cablesystems B.C. Ltd. - North Vancouver, BC, Canada - *Tel&CabFB 84C*
Shaw Cablesystems Ltd. - Edmonton, AB, Canada - *Tel&CabFB 84C*
Shaw Communications Consultants - Miami, FL - *TeleSy&SerDir 7-83*
Shaw Data Services Inc. - New York, NY - *EISS 5-84 Sup*
Shaw Festival - Niagara-on-the-Lake, ON, Canada - *WritMar 84*
Shaw, James R. - Edmonton, AB, Canada - *Tel&CabFB 84C*
Shaw Laboratories Ltd. - Hayword, CA - *MicrocomMPl 84*
Shaw, Leslie E. - Edmonton, AB, Canada - *Tel&CabFB 84C*
Shaw, Li Kung - San Francisco, CA - *BoPubDir 5*
Shaw Mountain Cable TV Inc. - Long Lake, NY - *BrCabYB 84; Tel&CabFB 84C*
Shaw Newsletter [of Shaw Society] - Dagenham, England - *LitMag&SmPr 83-84*
Shaw Newspapers, B. F. - Dixon, IL - *Ed&PubIntYB 82*
Shaw Productions - Fallbrook, CA - *Tel&CabFB 84C*
Shaw Publishers, Harold - Wheaton, IL - *ArtMar 84; LitMarPl 83, 84; WritMar 84*
Shaw Publishing, Rufus - Dallas, TX - *BoPubDir 5*
Shaw, Ray - New York, NY - *LitMarPl 83, 84; MagIndMarPl 82-83*
Shaw Society - Dagenham, England - *LitMag&SmPr 83-84*
Shaw, Steven E. - Tampa, FL - *WhoWMicrocom 83*
Shaw Systems Associates Inc. - Houston, TX - *DataDirSup 7-83; MicrocomMPl 84*
Shaw-Walker Co. - Muskegon, MI - *DirInfWP 82*
Shawano Evening Leader - Shawano, WI - *BaconPubCkNews 84; Ed&PubIntYB 82; NewsDir 84*
Shawmut Systems - Somerset, MA - *MicrocomMPl 84*
Shawnee American - Shawnee, OK - *BaconPubCkNews 84; Ed&PubIntYB 82*
Shawnee County Democrat - Shawnee, OK - *BaconPubCkNews 84*
Shawnee County Historical Society - Topeka, KS - *BoPubDir 4, 5*
Shawnee/Cridersville Press - Shawnee Township, OH - *Ed&PubIntYB 82*
Shawnee Cridersville Press - *See* Daily News Printing Co.
Shawnee Journal [of Prairie Publishing Co. Inc.] - Shawnee Mission, KS - *NewsDir 84*
Shawnee Journal Herald - Shawnee Mission, KS - *BaconPubCkNews 84*
Shawnee Mission Countryside Sun - *See* Sun Publications
Shawnee News-Star [of Stauffer Communications Inc.] - Shawnee, OK - *BaconPubCkNews 84; Ed&PubIntYB 82; NewsDir 84*
Shawnee Press Inc. [Aff. of Waring Enterprises Inc.] - Delaware Water Gap, PA - *BillIntBG 83-84; BoPubDir 4, 5*
Shawnee Sun [of Overland Park Sun Newspapers] - Shawnee Mission, KS - *NewsDir 84*
Shawnee Sun - *See* Sun Publications
Shawnee TV Cable Co. - Hunlock Creek Township, PA - *Tel&CabFB 84C*
Shawneetown Gallatin Democrat - Shawneetown, IL - *BaconPubCkNews 84*
Shawneetown Ridgway News - Shawneetown, IL - *BaconPubCkNews 84*
Shayna Ltd. - Newton, MA - *BoPubDir 4, 5*
Shayne Enterprises, Larry - Hollywood, CA - *BillIntBG 83-84*
Shea & Associates - Los Altos Hills, CA - *TeleSy&SerDir 7-83*
Shea, Ralph A. - Ridgefield, NJ - *BoPubDir 4, 5*
Sheaf - Warren, MN - *AyerDirPub 83*
Shearer & Co. - Jewel, IA - *LitMarPl 83, 84*
Shearer Publishing [of Shoal Creek Publishers Inc.] - Bryan, TX - *LitMarPl 84*
Shearman Newspapers - Lake Charles, LA - *Ed&PubIntYB 82*
Shearwater Press - Wellfleet, MA - *BoPubDir 4 Sup, 5; LitMag&SmPr 83-84*
Sheba Review Inc. - Jefferson City, MO - *LitMag&SmPr 83-84*
Sheboygan Falls News - Sheboygan Falls, WI - *AyerDirPub 83; Ed&PubIntYB 82*
Sheboygan Falls News - *See* Wisconsin Newspress Inc.
Sheboygan Press - Sheboygan, WI - *BaconPubCkNews 84; Ed&PubIntYB 82; NewsDir 84*
Shecter & Levin Advertising/Public Relations - Baltimore, MD - *ArtMar 84; StaDirAdAg 2-84*
Sheedy Literary Agency Inc., Charlotte - New York, NY - *LitMarPl 83, 84*
Sheehan Associates Europe SARL - Paris, France - *DirPRFirms 83*
Sheehy & Knopf - Louisville, KY - *AdAge 3-28-84; StaDirAdAg 2-84*
Sheep Breeder & Sheepman - Columbia, MO - *BaconPubCkMag 84; MagDir 84*
Sheep Magazine - Helenville, WI - *BaconPubCkMag 84; WritMar 84*
Sheep Meadow Press - New York, NY - *BoPubDir 4, 5; LitMag&SmPr 83-84; LitMarPl 84*
Sheep River Historical Society - Turner Valley, AB, Canada - *BoPubDir 4 Sup, 5*
Sheer Communications Inc. - Farmingdale, NY - *IntDirMarRes 83*
Sheer Press - Walnut Creek, CA - *BoPubDir 4, 5*
Sheet Metal & Air Conditioning Contractors' National Association Inc. - Vienna, VA - *BoPubDir 5*
Sheet Music Magazine - Katonah, NY - *MagDir 84; MagIndMarPl 82-83*
Sheets Productions, Don D. - Nashville, IN - *BillIntBG 83-84*
Sheffer & Peters Advertising Agency - South Bend, IN - *AdAge 3-28-84; StaDirAdAg 2-84*
Sheffield Bulletin - Sheffield, IL - *BaconPubCkNews 84; Ed&PubIntYB 82*
Sheffield Laboratory Inc. - Santa Barbara, CA - *BillIntBG 83-84*
Sheffield Lake Times - Lorain, OH - *NewsDir 84*
Sheffield Micro Information Systems Ltd. - Sheffield, England - *MicrocomSwDir 1*
Sheffield Press - Manhattan Beach, CA - *BoPubDir 4, 5*

Sheffield Press - Sheffield, IA - *BaconPubCkNews 84; Ed&PubIntYB 82*
Sheffield Standard & Times - Sheffield, AL - *BaconPubCkNews 84; Ed&PubIntYB 82*
Sheffield TV Cable - Sheffield, TX - *BrCabYB 84; Tel&CabFB 84C*
Sheffield West Side Association - Sheffield, PA - *BrCabYB 84*
Shefielder Times - *See* Gottschalk Publishing Co., E. J.
Shefrin Co., The - Los Angeles, CA - *DirPRFirms 83; StaDirAdAg 2-84*
Shefter Productions Inc., Bert - Los Angeles, CA - *AvMarPl 83*
Shekere Music - Richmond, VA - *BillIntBG 83-84*
SheLan Records - Rochester, MI - *BillIntBG 83-84*
Shelbina Democrat - Shelbina, MO - *BaconPubCkNews 84; Ed&PubIntYB 82*
Shelburn American - Shelburn, IN - *AyerDirPub 83; Ed&PubIntYB 82*
Shelburne Museum - Shelburne, VT - *BoPubDir 4, 5*
Shelby Cleveland Times - Shelby, NC - *BaconPubCkNews 84*
Shelby County Herald - Shelbyville, MO - *AyerDirPub 83*
Shelby County Historical & Genealogical Society - Shelbyville, IL - *BoPubDir 4, 5*
Shelby County News-Gazette - Windsor, IL - *Ed&PubIntYB 82*
Shelby County Record - Shelby County, MO - *Ed&PubIntYB 82*
Shelby County Reporter - Columbiana, AL - *AyerDirPub 83; Ed&PubIntYB 82*
Shelby Globe - Shelby, OH - *BaconPubCkNews 84; NewsDir 84*
Shelby Promoter - Shelby, MT - *AyerDirPub 83; BaconPubCkNews 84; Ed&PubIntYB 82*
Shelby Report of the Southeast, The [of Shelby Publishing Co. Inc.] - Atlanta, GA - *MagDir 84*
Shelby Report of the Southeast, The [0f Shelby Publishing Co. Inc.] - Gainesville, GA - *BaconPubCkMag 84*
Shelby Report of the Southwest, The [of Shelby Publishing Co. Inc.] - Garland, TX - *BaconPubCkMag 84*
Shelby Star [of Clay Communications Inc.] - Shelby, NC - *BaconPubCkNews 84; Ed&PubIntYB 82; NewsDir 84*
Shelby Sun - Shelby, NE - *BaconPubCkNews 84; Ed&PubIntYB 82*
Shelby Times - Shelby, MT - *Ed&PubIntYB 82*
Shelbyville Cable TV [of Fairfield Cable TV Inc.] - Shelbyville, IL - *BrCabYB 84; Tel&CabFB 84C*
Shelbyville News - Shelbyville, IN - *BaconPubCkNews 84; Ed&PubIntYB 82; NewsDir 84*
Shelbyville Sentinel-News [of Landmark] - Shelbyville, KY - *BaconPubCkNews 84; Ed&PubIntYB 82; NewsDir 84*
Shelbyville Shelby County Herald - Shelbyville, MO - *BaconPubCkNews 84*
Shelbyville Times-Gazette - Shelbyville, TN - *BaconPubCkNews 84; Ed&PubIntYB 82; NewsDir 84*
Shelbyville Union - Shelbyville, IL - *BaconPubCkNews 84; NewsDir 84*
Sheldon Communications Inc. - New York, NY - *DirMarMP 83*
Sheldon Electronics - San Jose, CA - *Tel&CabFB 84C p.1701*
Sheldon Fredericks Advertising Associates Inc. - New York, NY - *AdAge 3-28-84 p.112; BrCabYB 84; StaDirAdAg 2-84*
Sheldon Mail - Sheldon, IA - *Ed&PubIntYB 82*
Sheldon Mail - *See* Sheldon Publishing Co.
Sheldon Publishing Co. - Sheldon, IA - *BaconPubCkNews 84*
Sheldon Publishing, Marc - Azusa, CA - *BoPubDir 4, 5*
Sheldon Satin Associates Inc. - New York, NY - *CabTVFinDB 83*
Sheldon Sun [of Sheldon Mail] - Sheldon, IA - *Ed&PubIntYB 82; NewsDir 84*
Sheldon Sun - *See* Sheldon Publishing Co.
Shelfpower - Newcastle upon Tyne, England - *FBInfSer 80*
Shell Cabinet - Falls Church, VA - *BoPubDir 4, 5*
Shell Lake Telephone Co. Inc. - Shell Lake, WI - *TelDir&BG 83-84*
Shell Lake Washburn County Register - Shell Lake, WI - *BaconPubCkNews 84*
Shell Rock News - Shell Rock, IA - *BaconPubCkNews 84; Ed&PubIntYB 82*
Shell Rock Press - Glenville, MN - *Ed&PubIntYB 82*
Shell Rock Telephone Co. - Shell Rock, IA - *TelDir&BG 83-84*
Shell: Shellphoto, Bob - Radford, VA - *LitMarPl 83, 84*
Shellbird Cable Ltd. - Corner Brook, NF, Canada - *BrCabYB 84; Tel&CabFB 84C*
Shellbrook Chronicle - Shellbrook, SK, Canada - *Ed&PubIntYB 82*
Shelley Graphics Ltd. [Subs. of Interlyth Ltd.] - Edgewater, NJ - *LitMarPl 83*
Shelley Pioneer - Shelley, ID - *AyerDirPub 83; BaconPubCkNews 84; Ed&PubIntYB 82*
Shelter [of Associations Publications Inc.] - Germantown, TN - *BaconPubCkMag 84*
Shelter [of Associations Publications Inc.] - Memphis, TN - *MagDir 84*
Shelter Books Inc. - New York, NY - *BoPubDir 4, 5*
Shelter Island Reporter - Shelter Island, NY - *BaconPubCkNews 84; Ed&PubIntYB 82; NewsDir 84*
Shelter Publications Inc. - Bolinas, CA - *BoPubDir 4, 5*
Shelter Recording Co. - New York, NY - *BillIntBG 83-84*
Shelterforce - East Orange, NJ - *MagIndMarPl 82-83*
Shelton Clipper - Shelton, NE - *BaconPubCkNews 84; Ed&PubIntYB 82*
Shelton Huntington Herald - *See* Trumbull Times Publishers
Shelton Mason County Journal - Shelton, WA - *AyerDirPub 83; BaconPubCkNews 84; Ed&PubIntYB 82; NewsDir 84*
Shelton Publications - Sausalito, CA - *BoPubDir 4, 5*
Shelton Suburban News - Shelton, CT - *BaconPubCkNews 84; NewsDir 84*
Shelview Publications Co. - Chicago, IL - *BillIntBG 83-84*
Shen-Heights TV Associates Inc. - Shenandoah, PA - *BrCabYB 84; Tel&CabFB 84C*
Shenandoah - Lexington, VA - *LitMag&SmPr 83-84*
Shenandoah Cable Television Co. Inc. [of Shenandoah Telecommunications Inc.] - Edinburg, VA - *BrCabYB 84; Tel&CabFB 84C*
Shenandoah Evening Herald - Shenandoah, PA - *BaconPubCkNews 84; Ed&PubIntYB 82; NewsDir 84*
Shenandoah Herald - Woodstock, VA - *AyerDirPub 83*
Shenandoah Music - *See* Terrace Music Group Inc.
Shenandoah Sentinel - Shenandoah, IA - *BaconPubCkNews 84; NewsDir 84*
Shenandoah Telephone Co. [Aff. of Shenandoah Telecommunications Co.] - Edinburg, VA - *TelDir&BG 83-84*
Shenandoah Valley-Herald, The [of Page-Shenandoah Newspaper Corp.] - Woodstock, VA - *Ed&PubIntYB 82; NewsDir 84*
Shenandoah Valley Press Inc. - Strasburg, VA - *MagIndMarPl 82-83*
Shenandoah/Virginia Town & Country - Mint Springs, VA - *MagDir 84*
Shenandoah/Virginia Town & Country - Staunton, VA - *BaconPubCkMag 84*
Shenango Cable TV Inc. - Sharon, PA - *BrCabYB 84; Tel&CabFB 84C*
Shengold Publishers Inc. - New York, NY - *LitMarPl 83, 84*
Shenmac Trans-Video Corp. - Harpers Ferry, WV - *BrCabYB 84*
Shep, R. L. - Lopez, WA - *BoPubDir 4, 5*
Shepard, Alyce N. - El Cerrito, CA - *FBInfSer 80*
Shepard Publishing - Santa Maria, CA - *BoPubDir 4, 5*
Shepard's Citations [of Mead Data Central] - Dayton, OH - *DataDirOnSer 84*
Shepard's Citations Data Base [of Shepard's/McGraw-Hill] - Colorado Springs, CO - *DirOnDB Spring 84; EISS 83*
Shepard's/McGraw-Hill - Colorado Springs, CO - *LitMarPl 84*
Sheperd Records - Scranton, PA - *BillIntBG 83-84*
Shepherd & Sheep Raiser, The - Sheffield, MA - *MagDir 84*
Shepherd Argus - Shepherd, MI - *BaconPubCkNews 84; Ed&PubIntYB 82*
Shepherd Enterprises - Moberly, MO - *BrCabYB 84*
Shepherd Marketing Inc. - Bloomington, MN - *BoPubDir 4, 5*
Shepherd Press - Northvale, NJ - *LitMarPl 84*
Shepherd Press - South Hacksensack, NJ - *LitMarPl 83*
Shepherd Publishers [Aff. of Landell Corp.] - Williamsburg, VA - *BoPubDir 5; LitMag&SmPr 83-84*
Shepherd-San Jacinto News-Times - *See* Polk County Publishing
Shepherd, Tibball & Calog Associates - *See* STG Marketing Communications Inc.
Shepherdsville Pioneer-News - Shepherdsville, KY - *BaconPubCkNews 84; NewsDir 84*
Shepler, Ralph S. - Elkins, WV - *BrCabYB 84 p.D-306*

Shepler, Ralph S. - *See* Ohio Valley Cable Corp.
Sheppard Music Press, John - *See* European American Music Corp.
Sheppard Software Co. - Sunnyvale, CA - *WhoWMicrocom 83*
Sheppard, Walter Lee Jr. - Havertown, PA - *BoPubDir 4, 5*
Sheptow Publishing [Subs. of PMS Publishing Co. Inc.] - San Francisco, CA - *DirMarMP 83*
Sher, Jones, Shear & Associates Inc. - Kansas City, MO - *StaDirAdAg 2-84*
Sherbrooke Record, The - Sherbrooke, PQ, Canada - *BaconPubCkNews 84*
Sherburn Cable TV Co. [of North American Communications Corp.] - Rochester, MN - *BrCabYB 84*
Sherburn Cable TV Co. [of North American Communications Corp.] - Sherburn, MN - *Tel&CabFB 84C*
Sherburn West Martin Weekly News - Sherburn, MN - *BaconPubCkNews 84*
Sherburne County Rural Telephone Co. - Big Lake, MN - *TelDir&BG 83-84*
Sherburne County Star News - Elk River, MN - *Ed&PubIntYB 82*
Sherburne News - Sherburne, NY - *BaconPubCkNews 84; Ed&PubIntYB 82*
Shereff, Dorothy L. - New York, NY - *LitMarPl 83*
Sheriar Press - North Myrtle Beach, SC - *BoPubDir 4, 5; LitMag&SmPr 83-84*
Sheridan - New York, NY - *LitMag&SmPr 83-84*
Sheridan Broadcasting Corp. - Pittsburgh, PA - *BrCabYB 84*
Sheridan Broadcasting Network [Subs. of Sheridan Broadcasting Corp.] - Pittsburgh, PA - *BrCabYB 84; LitMarPl 83, 84*
Sheridan Broadcasting Network [Subs. of Sheridan Broadcasting Corp.] - Arlington, VA - *MagIndMarPl 82-83*
Sheridan Cablevision [of Quality CATV Inc.] - Sheridan, IN - *BrCabYB 84*
Sheridan Cablevision [of MetroVision Inc.] - Sheridan, WY - *BrCabYB 84; Tel&CabFB 84C*
Sheridan County Star - Rushville, NE - *AyerDirPub 83; Ed&PubIntYB 82*
Sheridan Headlight - Sheridan, AR - *BaconPubCkNews 84; Ed&PubIntYB 82; NewsDir 84*
Sheridan House Inc. - White Plains, NY - *LitMarPl 83, 84; WritMar 84*
Sheridan News [of Pace Publishing Inc.] - Sheridan, IN - *Ed&PubIntYB 82; NewsDir 84*
Sheridan News - *See* Topic Newspapers Inc.
Sheridan Press - Sheridan, WY - *BaconPubCkNews 84; NewsDir 84*
Sheridan Press, The - Hanover, PA - *LitMarPl 83, 84; MagIndMarPl 82-83*
Sheridan Publications Services - Nevada City, CA - *LitMarPl 83, 84*
Sheridan Square Publications Inc. - New York, NY - *BoPubDir 5*
Sheridan Sun - Sheridan, OR - *BaconPubCkNews 84; Ed&PubIntYB 82*
Sherlyn Publishing Co. - *See* Big Seven Music Corp.
Sherman & Associates Inc., Robert A. - Warren, OH - *StaDirAdAg 2-84*
Sherman & Brown Associates Inc. - Miami, FL - *CabTVFinDB 83*
Sherman & Morris Inc. - New York, NY - *HBIndAd&MS 82-83*
Sherman Associates, Eleanor - New York, NY - *MagIndMarPl 82-83*
Sherman, Bob - North Miami Beach, FL - *MagIndMarPl 82-83*
Sherman Chautauqua News - *See* Ogden Newspapers Inc.
Sherman County Herald - Goodland, KS - *AyerDirPub 83; Ed&PubIntYB 82*
Sherman County Journal - Moro, OR - *AyerDirPub 83*
Sherman County Journal - Sherman County, OR - *Ed&PubIntYB 82*
Sherman County Times - Loup City, NE - *AyerDirPub 83*
Sherman County Times - Sherman County, NE - *Ed&PubIntYB 82*
Sherman Democrat - Sherman, TX - *BaconPubCkNews 84; Ed&PubIntYB 82; NewsDir 84*
Sherman, Faith - Tygh Valley, OR - *BoPubDir 5*
Sherman Group Inc., The - Great Neck, NY - *HBIndAd&MS 82-83; IntDirMarRes 83*
Sherman Inc., Otto David - New York, NY - *AvMarPl 83*
Sherman, Jason - Long Beach, CA - *LitMarPl 84*
Sherman Oaks Sun [of Associated Valley Publications Inc.] - Encino, CA - *AyerDirPub 83; Ed&PubIntYB 82; NewsDir 84*
Sherman Oaks Sun - *See* Associated Valley Publications
Sherman Publishing Co., Edward A. - Newport, RI - *BaconPubCkNews 84*
Sherman Real Estate Books, Patricia J. - Los Angeles, CA - *BoPubDir 4, 5*
Sherman, Stanley S. - Greenville, MS - *Tel&CabFB 84C p.1701*
Sherr Engravers, H. - New York, NY - *LitMarPl 83, 84*
Sherrill Co., The - Dallas, TX - *BrCabYB 84; StaDirAdAg 2-84*
Sherrill, John - Austin, TX - *BoPubDir 4, 5*
Sherrod, Paul - Lubbock, TX - *BoPubDir 4, 5*
Sherry Associates Inc., Henry - Atlanta, GA - *IntDirMarRes 83*
Sherry Urie - West Glover, VT - *LitMag&SmPr 83-84*
Shersman Books - Plymouth, England - *LitMag&SmPr 83-84*
Sherwin Associates - Chicago, IL - *LitMarPl 84*
Sherwood Agency Inc., The - New York, NY - *StaDirAdAg 2-84*
Sherwood & Schneider Inc. [Subs. of Della Femina, Travisano & Partners Inc.] - New York, NY - *StaDirAdAg 2-84*
Sherwood Co. - Denver, CO - *BoPubDir 4, 5*
Sherwood Mutual Telephone Association Inc. - Sherwood, OH - *TelDir&BG 83-84*
Sherwood Park News - Sherwood Park, AB, Canada - *AyerDirPub 83; Ed&PubIntYB 82*
Sherwood Press - Chatsworth, CA - *LitMag&SmPr 83-84*
Sherwood Telephone Co. Inc. - Merigold, MS - *TelDir&BG 83-84*
Sherwood Video Production Co. - Chicago, IL - *BillIntBG 83-84*
Sherwood Voice - Sherwood, AR - *BaconPubCkNews 84*
Shetal Enterprises - Chicago, IL - *BoPubDir 4, 5*
Shetland Enterprises International - Nashville, TN - *BillIntBG 83-84*
Shevchenko Scientific Society Inc. - New York, NY - *BoPubDir 4, 5*
Sheyenne Cable TV - West Fargo, ND - *BrCabYB 84; Tel&CabFB 84C*
Shiawasee Telephone Co. - Perry, MI - *TelDir&BG 83-84*
Shiawassee County Journal [of J. R. Dunn Publishing Inc.] - Perry, MI - *AyerDirPub 83; Ed&PubIntYB 82; NewsDir 84*
Shickshinny TV Cable Co. Inc. - Millville, PA - *BrCabYB 84*
Shickshinny TV Cable Co. Inc. - Orangeville, PA - *BrCabYB 84*
Shickshinny TV Cable Co. Inc. - Shickshinny, PA - *BrCabYB 84; Tel&CabFB 84C*
Shidler Review - Shidler, OK - *BaconPubCkNews 84; Ed&PubIntYB 82*
Shidler Telephone Co. - Shidler, OK - *TelDir&BG 83-84*
Shiefman & Associates - Detroit, MI - *DirPRFirms 83*
Shield [of N.J. Shield Publishing Co.] - Englewood, NJ - *MagDir 84; NewsDir 84*
Shield Productions Inc. - Chicago, IL - *AvMarPl 83; Tel&CabFB 84C*
Shields Publications - Eagle River, WI - *BoPubDir 4, 5*
Shields Remine - New York, NY - *MagIndMarPl 82-83*
Shiffman/Ferguson/Stone Advertising Inc. - Ft. Lee, NJ - *AdAge 3-28-84; StaDirAdAg 2-84*
Shih Shih Wu Ai Records Inc. - Bloomington, MN - *BillIntBG 83-84*
Shiller Park Times - Chicago, IL - *AyerDirPub 83*
Shilling & Co. Inc., A. Gary - New York, NY - *EISS 5-84 Sup*
Shilling Economic Forecast, A. Gary [of General Electric Information Services Co.] - Rockville, MD - *DataDirOnSer 84*
Shilling Economic Forecast, A. Gary [of A. Gary Shilling & Co. Inc.] - New York, NY - *DirOnDB Spring 84*
Shilo Cablevision [of CFB Shilo Base Fund] - Shilo, MB, Canada - *BrCabYB 84*
Shiloh Research Associates Inc. - Dayton, OH - *IntDirMarRes 83*
Shiner Cablevision Inc. [of Cardiff Cablevision Inc.] - Shiner, TX - *Tel&CabFB 84C*
Shiner Cablevision Inc. - Yoakum, TX - *BrCabYB 84*
Shiner Gazette - Shiner, TX - *BaconPubCkNews 84; Ed&PubIntYB 82*
Shing Wah Daily News - Toronto, ON, Canada - *AyerDirPub 83; Ed&PubIntYB 82*
Shingle, The - Philadelphia, PA - *ArtMar 84*
Shining Waters Press - Ann Arbor, MI - *LitMag&SmPr 83-84*

Shinn Publications, Duane - Central Point, OR - *BoPubDir 4, 5; DirMarMP 83*
Shinnston News - Shinnston, WV - *BaconPubCkNews 84; Ed&PubIntYB 82*
Ship Abstracts [of Samson Data Systemen BV] - Alphen, Netherlands - *DataDirOnSer 84*
Ship Abstracts [of Norsk Skipsforskningsinstitutt] - Oslo, Norway - *CompReadDB 82; DBBus 82; DirOnDB Spring 84; EISS 83; OnBibDB 3*
Ship Alteration Management Information System [of U.S. Navy] - Washington, DC - *EISS 7-83 Sup*
Ship Bottom Beachcomber - Ship Bottom, NJ - *BaconPubCkNews 84*
Ship Casualty Library [of Maritime Data Network Ltd.] - Stamford, CT - *DataDirOnSer 84*
Ship Movement Library [of Maritime Data Network Ltd.] - Stamford, CT - *DataDirOnSer 84*
Shipdes [of Samson Data Systemen BV] - Alphen, Netherlands - *DataDirOnSer 84*
Shipdes - Rotterdam, Netherlands - *DirOnDB Spring 84*
Shipley Associates Inc. - Greenville, DE - *ArtMar 84*
Shipley Associates Inc. - Wilmington, DE - *AdAge 3-28-84; StaDirAdAg 2-84*
Shipmate - Annapolis, MD - *MagDir 84*
Shippen TV Cable Co. - Shippensburg, PA - *BrCabYB 84; Tel&CabFB 84C*
Shippensburg News-Chronicle - Shippensburg, PA - *NewsDir 84*
Shippensburg News Chronicle - *See* News Chronicle Co. Inc.
Shipping Digest [of Geyer-McAllister Publications Inc.] - New York, NY - *BaconPubCkMag 84; MagDir 84*
Shipping Information Services - London, England - *EISS 83; InfIndMarPl 83*
Ships Characteristics [of Maritime Data Network Ltd.] - Stamford, CT - *DataDirOnSer 84*
Ships on Order Library [of Maritime Data Network Ltd.] - Stamford, CT - *DataDirOnSer 84*
Shipstats - London, England - *EISS 7-83 Sup*
Shire Press - Santa Cruz, CA - *BoPubDir 4, 5; LitMag&SmPr 83-84*
Shirim - Los Angeles, CA - *LitMag&SmPr 83-84*
Shirley Basin Service Co. [of United Cable TV Corp.] - Shirley Basin, WY - *BrCabYB 84; Tel&CabFB 84C*
Shirley Institute - Manchester, England - *CompReadDB 82; InfIndMarPl 83*
Shirley Moriches Bay Tide - Shirley, NY - *BaconPubCkNews 84; NewsDir 84*
Shiroma & Meyers Inc. - Dallas, TX - *DirPRFirms 83*
Shivell-Hall Co., The [Div. of Management Methods Inc.] - Riverside, CT - *StaDirAdAg 2-84*
Shively Newsweek Inc. - Louisville, KY - *NewsDir 84*
Shively Newsweek Inc. - Shively, KY - *BaconPubCkNews 84*
Shively, Richard E. - North Platte, NE - *Tel&CabFB 84S*
Shivers Communications - Atlanta, GA - *StaDirAdAg 2-84*
Shkurkin, Vlad - San Pablo, CA - *BoPubDir 4, 5; MicroMarPl 82-83*
Shmate - Berkeley, CA - *LitMag&SmPr 83-84*
Shmate Press - Berkeley, CA - *LitMag&SmPr 83-84*
Shnavel Publishing - *See* Orb Music Co.
Shoaf, Mary Jo Davis - Lexington, NC - *BoPubDir 4, 5*
Shoal Creek Publishers Inc. - Bryan, TX - *LitMarPl 83*
Shoal Lake Star, The - Shoal Lake, MB, Canada - *Ed&PubIntYB 82*
Shoals News - Shoals, IN - *BaconPubCkNews 84; Ed&PubIntYB 82*
Shoals News-Leader - Florence, AL - *Ed&PubIntYB 82*
Shock & Vibration Information Center [of U.S. Navy] - Washington, DC - *EISS 83*
Shock Wave Data Center [of University of California] - Livermore, CA - *EISS 83; InfIndMarPl 83*
Shockley Research Inc. - Nashville, TN - *IntDirMarRes 83*
Shocks [of Momo's Press] - San Francisco, CA - *LitMag&SmPr 83-84*
Shoe Productions Inc. - Memphis, TN - *BillIntBG 83-84*
Shoe Service - Chicago, IL - *BaconPubCkMag 84; MagDir 84; WritMar 84*
Shoe String Press Inc., The - Hamden, CT - *LitMarPl 83, 84; WritMar 84*
Shoe Trades Publishing Co. - Cambridge, MA - *BoPubDir 4, 5*
Shoemaker Motion Picture Co. - Indianapolis, IN - *AvMarPl 83*
Shoemaker, Rhoda - Menlo Park, CA - *BoPubDir 4, 5*
Shoenfeld Associates - Blairstown, NJ - *BoPubDir 4 Sup, 5; LitMarPl 84*
Shoenfeld Associates - Huntington, NY - *LitMarPl 83*
Shoestring Records - Alton, IL - *BillIntBG 83-84*
Shoffman-Graves, Monica - Old Greenwich, CT - *LitMarPl 83; MagIndMarPl 82-83*
Shoffman-Graves, Monica - Key Largo, FL - *LitMarPl 84*
Shondo-Shando Press - Quincy, IL - *BoPubDir 4, 5*
Shooshan & Jackson Inc. - Washington, DC - *CabTVFinDB 83; VideoDir 82-83*
Shooting Commercials & Industrials - Los Angeles, CA - *MagDir 84*
Shooting Gallery, The - Chicago, IL - *AvMarPl 83*
Shooting Industry - San Diego, CA - *BaconPubCkMag 84; MagDir 84; MagIndMarPl 82-83; WritMar 84*
Shooting Sports Retailer - Montgomery, AL - *BaconPubCkMag 84*
Shooting Star Photo Agency Inc. - Hollywood, CA - *MagIndMarPl 82-83*
Shooting Times [of PJS Enterprises Inc.] - Peoria, IL - *BaconPubCkMag 84; Folio 83; MagDir 84; MagIndMarPl 82-83*
Shop - Don Mills, ON, Canada - *BaconPubCkMag 84*
Shop Talk - Chicago, IL - *BaconPubCkMag 84*
Shopper - Chula Vista, CA - *AyerDirPub 83*
Shopper - Lake Wales, FL - *AyerDirPub 83*
Shopper - La Grange, IL - *AyerDirPub 83*
Shopper - Lincoln, IL - *AyerDirPub 83*
Shopper - Sioux Center, IA - *AyerDirPub 83*
Shopper [of The West Columbia Journal] - West Columbia, SC - *NewsDir 84*
Shopper - Ellsworth, WI - *AyerDirPub 83*
Shopper-Advertiser - Delavan, WI - *AyerDirPub 83*
Shopper & News Note - Lindsay, OK - *AyerDirPub 83*
Shopper Guide - Three Rivers, MI - *AyerDirPub 83*
Shopper News - Paducah, KY - *AyerDirPub 83; Ed&PubIntYB 82; NewsDir 84*
Shopper News - Stoneham, MA - *AyerDirPub 83*
Shopper News - Keene, NH - *AyerDirPub 83*
Shopper Stopper - Merrimac, WI - *AyerDirPub 83*
Shopper, The - Lockport, IL - *AyerDirPub 83*
Shopper, The - Halstad, MN - *AyerDirPub 83*
Shopper, The - Lake City, MN - *AyerDirPub 83*
Shopper, The - Albion, NE - *AyerDirPub 83*
Shopper, The - Elmira, NY - *AyerDirPub 83*
Shoppers Fair - Cheboygen, MI - *AyerDirPub 83*
Shopper's Guide - Pompano Beach, FL - *AyerDirPub 83*
Shoppers' Guide - Caro, MI - *AyerDirPub 83*
Shoppers Guide - Hartford, MI - *AyerDirPub 83*
Shoppers Guide - Otsego, MI - *AyerDirPub 83*
Shoppers Guide - Cherry Hill, NJ - *AyerDirPub 83*
Shoppers Guide - Brevard, NC - *AyerDirPub 83*
Shoppers Guide - Hendersonville, NC - *AyerDirPub 83*
Shopper's Guide - Shawano, WI - *AyerDirPub 83*
Shoppers Guide, The - Paulding, OH - *AyerDirPub 83*
Shopper's Helper, The - Greenwich, OH - *AyerDirPub 83*
Shoppers News - Rensselaer, IN - *AyerDirPub 83*
Shoppers News Inc. - Little Rock, AR - *AyerDirPub 83*
Shoppers News, The - Alamogordo, NM - *AyerDirPub 83*
Shopper's Newsletter - Oxford, WI - *AyerDirPub 83*
Shopping Center Digest - Suffern, NY - *BaconPubCkMag 84*
Shopping Center Newsletter - Burlington, IA - *MagDir 84*
Shopping Center World - Atlanta, GA - *BaconPubCkMag 84; MagDir 84; MagIndMarPl 82-83*
Shopping Centers Today - New York, NY - *BaconPubCkMag 84*
Shopping Experience - Brooklyn, NY - *BoPubDir 4, 5*
Shopping Guide - Bradenton, FL - *AyerDirPub 83*
Shopping Guide - Sarasota, FL - *AyerDirPub 83*
Shopping Guide - Griffin, GA - *AyerDirPub 83*
Shopping Guide - Charlotte, MI - *AyerDirPub 83*
Shopping Guide - Port Byron, NY - *AyerDirPub 83*
Shopping News - Corona, CA - *AyerDirPub 83*
Shopping News - Oroville, CA - *AyerDirPub 83*
Shopping News - Dallas, TX - *AyerDirPub 83*
Shopping News - Beloit, WI - *AyerDirPub 83*

Shopping News - Berlin, WI - *AyerDirPub 83*
Shopping News - Platteville, WI - *AyerDirPub 83*
Shopping News - Richland Center, WI - *AyerDirPub 83*
Shopping News of Lancaster County - Ephrata, PA - *AyerDirPub 83; Ed&PubIntYB 82*
Shopping News, The - Fleming, KY - *Ed&PubIntYB 82*
Shopping Reminder - Columbus, WI - *AyerDirPub 83*
Shore Associates, Michael - Stamford, CT - *BoPubDir 4 Sup, 5*
Shore Line Times - Guilford, CT - *AyerDirPub 83; Ed&PubIntYB 82*
Shore, Michael - Milford, CT - *LitMarPl 84*
Shore, Michael - Stamford, CT - *LitMarPl 83; MagIndMarPl 82-83*
Shore Television Co. Inc. [of Storer Cable Communications] - Pocomoke City, MD - *BrCabYB 84; Tel&CabFB 84C*
Shoreham Telephone Co. Inc. - Shoreham, VT - *TelDir&BG 83-84*
Shoreland - Chicago, IL - *Ed&PubIntYB 82*
Shoreline Journal - Lake Forest Park, WA - *Ed&PubIntYB 82*
Shoreline Leader - Racine, WI - *AyerDirPub 83; Ed&PubIntYB 82*
Shoreview Bulletin - *See* Bulletin Newspapers
Shorewood Fine Art Books Inc. - New York, NY - *LitMarPl 83, 84*
Shorewood Fine Art Reproductions Inc. - New York, NY - *AvMarPl 83*
Shorewood Herald - Oak Creek, WI - *AyerDirPub 83*
Shorewood Herald - Shorewood, WI - *Ed&PubIntYB 82*
Shorewood Herald - *See* Community Newspapers Inc.
Shorey & Walter Inc. - Greenville, SC - *ArtMar 84; StaDirAdAg 2-84*
Short Circuit, The - Omaha, NE - *NewsDir 84*
Short Course Publications - Arcadia, CA - *BoPubDir 4 Sup, 5*
Short Hills-Millburn Independent - Millburn, NJ - *Ed&PubIntYB 82*
Short Hills-Millburn Independent [of New Providence Passaic Valley Independent Press] - New Providence, NJ - *NewsDir 84*
Short Hills-Millburn Independent - Summit, NJ - *AyerDirPub 83*
Short, Richard - Brandywine, WV - *Tel&CabFB 84C*
Short Rose Music - Nashville, TN - *BillIntBG 83-84*
Short Run Bindery Inc. - Medford, NJ - *LitMarPl 83, 84*
Short Shepler & Fogleman Advertising [Div. of Inform Inc.] - Hickory, NC - *AdAge 3-28-84; ArtMar 84; StaDirAdAg 2-84*
Short Story International - Great Neck, NY - *MagIndMarPl 82-83*
Short Term Projections & Long Term Projections [of ADP Network Services] - Ann Arbor, MI - *DataDirOnSer 84*
Short Term Projections & Long Term Projections [of Townsend-Greenspan & Co. Inc.] - New York, NY - *DBBus 82; DirOnDB Spring 84*
Short-Timer's Journal [of Winter Soldier Archive] - Berkeley, CA - *LitMag&SmPr 83-84*
Shortcuts - Toronto, ON, Canada - *BoPubDir 4, 5*
Shorthorn Country - Omaha, NE - *BaconPubCkMag 84; MagDir 84*
Shoshone Lincoln County Journal - Shoshone, ID - *BaconPubCkNews 84*
Shoshoni Pioneer - Shoshoni, WY - *BaconPubCkNews 84*
Shoss & Associates Inc. - St. louis, MO - *DirMarMP 83; StaDirAdAg 2-84*
Shostal Associates - New York, NY - *AvMarPl 83; LitMarPl 83, 84; MagIndMarPl 82-83*
Shosteck Associates, Herschel - Silver Spring, MD - *BrCabYB 84*
Shotgun Music Co. - Freeport, NY - *BillIntBG 83-84*
Shotgun Sports - Reno, NV - *BaconPubCkMag 84; WritMar 84*
Shotwell & Associates - San Francisco, CA - *EISS 83*
Shotwell & Partners Inc. - Boston, MA - *TelAl 84*
Shotwell & Partners Inc. - Charlotte, NC - *DirPRFirms 83; StaDirAdAg 2-84; TelAl 83*
Shourot/Undersea Systems Inc., Robert J. - Bay Shore, NY - *MagIndMarPl 82-83*
Show - New York, NY - *MagDir 84*
Show & Tell Audio-Visuals - Kalamazoo, MI - *AvMarPl 83*
Show Biz Inc. - Nashville, TN - *TelAl 83*
Show Biz, The - Warren, OH - *AvMarPl 83*
Show/Book Week of the Chicago Sun-Times - Chicago, IL - *MagIndMarPl 82-83*
Show Business [of Leo Shull Publications] - New York, NY - *BaconPubCkMag 84; MagDir 84; MagIndMarPl 82-83*
Show Low White Mountain Independent - Show Low, AZ - *BaconPubCkNews 84*
Show Management Advertising - Ft. Lauderdale, FL - *StaDirAdAg 2-84*
Show Reporter - Newton Center, MA - *MagDir 84*
Showbill - New York, NY - *MagDir 84*
Showboat - San Antonio, TX - *MagIndMarPl 82-83*
Showcase - New York, NY - *MagDir 84*
Showcase Cablevision Systems - Merkel, TX - *Tel&CabFB 84C*
Showcase Cablevision Systems - Roscoe, TX - *Tel&CabFB 84C*
Showcase Cablevision Systems - Tuscola, TX - *Tel&CabFB 84C p.1701*
Showcase Publications - Pasadena, CA - *BoPubDir 4, 5*
Showcase U.S.A. - Woodland Hills, CA - *BaconPubCkMag 84*
Showcorporation - Stamford, CT - *TelAl 83, 84*
Showman Inc. - Hollywood, CA - *Tel&CabFB 84C*
Showmedia - Beverly Hills, CA - *AvMarPl 83*
Shownote Music Co. - *See* Showpiece Productions
Showoff Publishing Co. - *See* Showpiece Productions
Showpiece Productions - Yonkers, NY - *AvMarPl 83; BillIntBG 83-84*
Showpros, The - Tustin, CA - *AvMarPl 83*
Showtime Entertainment Cable Information Service - New York, NY - *DirOnDB Spring 84*
Showtime Entertainment Cable Information Service [of CompuServe Inc.] - Columbus, OH - *DataDirOnSer 84*
Showtime Entertainment Inc. - Los Angeles, CA - *BrCabYB 84*
Showtime Entertainment Inc. [of Viacom International Inc.] - New York, NY - *BrCabYB 84; CabTVPrDB 83; HomeVid&CabYB 82-83; TelAl 83*
Showtime Magazine - Reno, NV - *BaconPubCkMag 84*
Showtime Publishing Co. - Washington, DC - *BillIntBG 83-84*
Showtime/The Movie Channel Inc. - New York, NY - *Tel&CabFB 84C*
Shredmaster Corp. [Div. of General Building Corp.] - Ft. Lauderdale, FL - *DirInfWP 82*
Shreveport [of Shreveport Chamber of Commerce] - Shreveport, LA - *BaconPubCkMag 84; MagDir 84; WritMar 84*
Shreveport Community Ebony Tribune - Shreveport, LA - *Ed&PubIntYB 82; NewsDir 84*
Shreveport Journal - Shreveport, LA - *BaconPubCkNews 84; Ed&PubIntYB 82; NewsDir 84*
Shreveport Sun - Shreveport, LA - *BaconPubCkNews 84; Ed&PubIntYB 82; NewsDir 84*
Shreveport Times, The - Shreveport, LA - *NewsBur 6*
Shrewsbury Cable TV [of GS Communications Inc.] - Frederick, MD - *BrCabYB 84*
Shrewsbury's Community Cablevision - Shrewsbury, MA - *Tel&CabFB 84C*
Shrine of the Eternal Breath of Tao [Aff. of College of Tao & Traditional Chinese Healing] - Los Angeles, CA - *BoPubDir 4, 5*
Shriver Associates, R. - Parsippany, NJ - *DataDirSup 7-83*
Shrum Secretarial/Literary Service, Carol - Concord, CA - *LitMarPl 83, 84*
Shryock Brothers - Downingtown, PA - *LitMarPl 83, 84*
Shugart Associates - Sunnyvale, CA - *MicrocomMPl 84; WhoWMicrocom 83*
Shugoll Inc., Joan - Chevy Chase, MD - *IntDirMarRes 83*
Shull Publications Co., Leo - New York, NY - *BoPubDir 4, 5*
Shulman, Lillian - New York, NY - *LitMarPl 84*
Shulsinger Sales Inc. - Brooklyn, NY - *BoPubDir 4, 5*
Shumway, George - York, PA - *BoPubDir 4, 5*
Shure Brothers Inc. - Evanston, IL - *AvMarPl 83*
Shurvell Publishing, H. F. - Kingston, ON, Canada - *BoPubDir 4 Sup, 5*
Shutterbug Ads [of Patch Publishing] - Titusville, FL - *ArtMar 84; DirMarMP 83*
Shuttle, Spindle, & Dyepot - West Hartford, CT - *ArtMar 84; MagDir 84; MagIndMarPl 82-83*
Shwerz, Harry E. - New York, NY - *LitMarPl 83, 84*
SI Artists [Subs. of Selecciones Illustradas] - New York, NY - *LitMarPl 83, 84*
SIA Computer Services - London, England - *EISS 83; InfIndMarPl 83*

Sialbach Press - Gardiner, NY - *BoPubDir 4 Sup, 5*
SIAM - Philadelphia, PA - *MicroMarPl 82-83*
SIANET [of SIA Computer Services] - London, England - *InfIndMarPl 83*
Sibley Gazette - Sibley, IA - *Ed&PubIntYB 82*
Sibley Music Library Microform Service [of Eastman School of Music] - Rochester, NY - *MagIndMarPl 82-83; MicroMarPl 82-83*
Sibley Osceola County Gazette Tribune - Sibley, IA - *BaconPubCkNews 84*
Sibley Tribune - Sibley, IA - *Ed&PubIntYB 82*
Siboney Advertising Corp. - *See* Publicidad Siboney International
Sibyl-Child Press - Hyattsville, MD - *BoPubDir 4 Sup, 5*
SIC - Paris, France - *DirOnDB Spring 84*
SIC & SIC72 - Washington, DC - *DirOnDB Spring 84*
SIC & SIC72 [of General Electric Information Services Co.] - Rockville, MD - *DataDirOnSer 84*
SIC Publishing Co. [Aff. of The Hereld Organization] - Lawrenceville, NJ - *BoPubDir 4 Sup, 5*
Sicilian Antigruppo/Cross-Cultural Communications - Trapani, Italy - *LitMag&SmPr 83-84*
Sick - New York, NY - *MagDir 84*
Sickinger Co., Hans - Pontiac, MI - *LitMarPl 83, 84*
Sickles Photo Reporting Service - Maplewood, NJ - *LitMarPl 83, 84*
Siddall, Matus & Coughter - Richmond, VA - *ArtMar 84; StaDirAdAg 2-84*
Sidelines - Oxford, England - *MicrocomSwDir 1*
Sidell Journal - Sidell, IL - *BaconPubCkNews 84*
Sidgwick & Jackson - Salem, NH - *LitMarPl 84*
Sidha Corp. International - Fairfield, IA - *DirMarMP 83*
Sidney Argus Herald - Sidney, IA - *BaconPubCkNews 84; Ed&PubIntYB 82*
Sidney Cable TV Co. [of Community Tele-Communications Inc.] - Sidney, NE - *BrCabYB 84; Tel&CabFB 84C*
Sidney Cablevision [of Montana Cablevision] - Sidney, MT - *BrCabYB 84; Tel&CabFB 84C*
Sidney Daily News [of Amos Press Inc.] - Dayton, OH - *NewsDir 84*
Sidney Daily News - Sidney, OH - *BaconPubCkNews 84; Ed&PubIntYB 82*
Sidney Herald - Sidney, MT - *AyerDirPub 83; BaconPubCkNews 84; Ed&PubIntYB 82; NewsDir 84*
Sidney NewChannels [of NewChannels Corp.] - Sidney, NY - *BrCabYB 84; Tel&CabFB 84C*
Sidney Newspapers Inc. [of Worrell Newspapers Inc.] - Sidney, NE - *NewsDir 84*
Sidney Review, The - Sidney, BC, Canada - *Ed&PubIntYB 82*
Sidney Telegraph - Sidney, NE - *BaconPubCkNews 84; Ed&PubIntYB 82*
Sidney Tri-Town News - Sidney, NY - *Ed&PubIntYB 82; NewsDir 84*
Sidney Tri-Town News - *See* Twin Valley Publishers Inc.
SIE Publishing - Westlake Village, CA - *BoPubDir 5*
Siebel/Mohr Inc. - New York, NY - *HBIndAd&MS 82-83; StaDirAdAg 2-84*
Sieber & McIntyre - Chicago, IL - *AdAge 3-28-84; ArtMar 84; StaDirAdAg 2-84*
Siebring Cable TV - George, IA - *Tel&CabFB 84C*
Siebring Electric Co. - George, IA - *BrCabYB 84*
Siecor Fiberlan - Research Triangle Park, NC - *DataDirSup 7-83; TeleSy&SerDir 2-84*
Siegel & Gale - New York, NY - *HBIndAd&MS 82-83; ProGuPRSer 4; StaDirAdAg 2-84*
Siegel, Bobbe - New York, NY - *LitMarPl 83, 84; MagIndMarPl 82-83*
Siegel Electronics - San Diego, CA - *AvMarPl 83*
Siegel, Leah - New York, NY - *LitMarPl 83, 84*
Siegel Publishing, Kenneth L. - Newport Beach, CA - *BoPubDir 4, 5*
Siegel, Rosalie - Pennington, NJ - *LitMarPl 83, 84*
Siemens - Munich, West Germany - *ElecNews 7-25-83*
Siemens Communication Systems Inc. - Iselin, NJ - *DataDirSup 7-83*
Siemens Corp. - Anaheim, CA - *MicrocomMPl 83*
Siemens Corp. - Iselin, NJ - *DirInfWP 82*
Siemens Electric Ltd. - Pointe Claire, PQ, Canada - *DataDirSup 7-83*
Sierra [of Sierra Club] - San Francisco, CA - *ArtMar 84; BaconPubCkMag 84; LitMarPl 83, 84; MagDir 84; MagIndMarPl 82-83; WritMar 84*
Sierra Breeze - Placerville, CA - *Ed&PubIntYB 82*
Sierra Breeze - Shingle Springs, CA - *AyerDirPub 83*
Sierra Club Books - San Francisco, CA - *ArtMar 84; LitMarPl 83, 84; WritMar 84*
Sierra Communication Systems Inc. - Lake Wildwood, CA - *BrCabYB 84*
Sierra Features - Roche Harbor, WA - *Ed&PubIntYB 82*
Sierra Home Advertiser - Oakhurst, CA - *AyerDirPub 83; Ed&PubIntYB 82*
Sierra Information Systems Corp. [Subs. of Sierra Research Corp.] - Buffalo, NY - *DataDirSup 7-83; WhoWMicrocom 83*
Sierra Madre News - Sierra Madre, CA - *BaconPubCkNews 84; Ed&PubIntYB 82; NewsDir 84*
Sierra On-Line Inc. - Coarsegold, CA - *MicrocomMPl 84; MicrocomSwDir 1; WhoWMicrocom 83*
Sierra On-Line Inc. (Corporate Div.) - Coarsegold, CA - *ADAPSOMemDir 83-84*
Sierra Publications - San Jose, CA - *BoPubDir 4, 5*
Sierra Records - Pasadena, CA - *BillIntBG 83-84*
Sierra Scientific Corp. [Subs. of Picker International Corp.] - Mountain View, CA - *AvMarPl 83*
Sierra Star - Oakhurst, CA - *AyerDirPub 83*
Sierra Sun - Truckee, CA - *AyerDirPub 83; Ed&PubIntYB 82; NewsDir 84*
Sierra Telephone Co. Inc. [Aff. of Mariposa County Telephone Co. Inc.] - Oakhurst, CA - *TelDir&BG 83-84*
Sierra Trading Post - San Francisco, CA - *BoPubDir 4 Sup, 5; LitMag&SmPr 83-84*
Sierra Vista Daily Herald Dispatch [of Wick Newspaper Group] - Sierra Vista, AZ - *NewsDir 84*
Siesel Co. Inc., The - New York, NY - *AdAge 3-28-84; BrCabYB 84; DirPRFirms 83; StaDirAdAg 2-84*
Sievers Research Co. - San Marino, CA - *IntDirMarRes 83*
Siftings Herald [of Arkadelphia Publishing Co.] - Arkadelphia, AR - *Ed&PubIntYB 82*
Sight & Sound Corp. - Greensburg, IN - *BrCabYB 84*
Sight & Sound Electronics - New York, NY - *BaconPubCkMag 84*
Sight & Sound Inc. - Omaha, NE - *AvMarPl 83*
Sight & Sound International Inc. - New Berlin, WI - *BillIntBG 83-84*
Sight & Sound Marketing - New York, NY - *BaconPubCkMag 84; MagDir 84; MagIndMarPl 82-83*
Sight Line Research Ltd. - Massapequa, NY - *IntDirMarRes 83*
Sightlines - New York, NY - *ArtMar 84; WritMar 84*
Sights & Sounds Cable Vision - Alma, WI - *BrCabYB 84; Tel&CabFB 84C*
Sightsaving - New York, NY - *MagDir 84*
Sightseer Publications - Miami, FL - *BoPubDir 4, 5*
Sigismund Advertising & Public Relations, Rita - Seattle, WA - *StaDirAdAg 2-84*
SIGLE - Rhode-St.-Agnese, Belgium - *DirOnDB Spring 84*
Sigler, Dexter W. - Hornbeck, LA - *BrCabYB 84*
Sigma Data Computing Corp. - Rockville, MD - *EISS 83*
Sigma Designs Inc. - Santa Clara, CA - *WhoWMicrocom 83*
Sigma Distributing [Subs. of Omega Northwest Inc.] - Bellevue, WA - *WhoWMicrocom 83*
Sigma Electronics Inc. - East Petersburg, PA - *AvMarPl 83*
Sigma Press Inc. - Brentwood, NY - *LitMarPl 83, 84*
Sigma Research Associates - San Diego, CA - *WhoWMicrocom 83*
Sigma Research Co. - Ft. Lee, NJ - *IntDirMarRes 83*
Sign - Union City, NJ - *MagDir 84; MagIndMarPl 82-83*
Sign of the Rain Music - *See* Delev Music Co.
Sign of the Times-A Chronicle of Decadence in the Atomic Age [of Studio 403 Corp.] - Portland, OR - *LitMag&SmPr 83-84*
Signal - Atwater, CA - *AyerDirPub 83*
Signal - Weiser, ID - *AyerDirPub 83*
Signal - Manly, IA - *AyerDirPub 83*
Signal - Springport, MI - *AyerDirPub 83*
Signal - Taylorsville, MS - *AyerDirPub 83*
Signal - Canal Fulton, OH - *AyerDirPub 83; Ed&PubIntYB 82*
Signal - Manchester, OH - *AyerDirPub 83*

Signal - Seaside, OR - *AyerDirPub 83*
Signal - Burke, VA - *BaconPubCkMag 84; MagDir 84*
Signal-American Printers Inc. - Weiser, ID - *BaconPubCkNews 84*
Signal Cable TV Inc. - Beach, ND - *BrCabYB 84; Tel&CabFB 84C*
Signal Citizen - Honey Grove, TX - *Ed&PubIntYB 82*
Signal Cos. Inc. - La Jolla, CA - *Datamation 6-83; HomeVid&CabYB 82-83*
Signal Design Ltd. - *See* Creswell, Munsell, Fultz & Zirbel Inc.
Signal-Enterprise - Alma, KS - *AyerDirPub 83; Ed&PubIntYB 82*
Signal-Gram - Washington, DC - *BaconPubCkMag 84; MagDir 84*
Signal Hill Star/Tribune - Signal Hill, CA - *BaconPubCkNews 84*
Signal Hill Tribune - Signal Hill, CA - *Ed&PubIntYB 82*
Signal Inc. - Mallard, IA - *BrCabYB 84*
Signal Inc. - Ringsted, IA - *BrCabYB 84*
Signal Inc. - Rolfe, IA - *BrCabYB 84*
Signal Inc. - West Bend, IA - *BrCabYB 84 p.D-306; Tel&CabFB 84C p.1701*
Signal Inc. - Whittemore, IA - *BrCabYB 84*
Signal-Item - Carnegie, PA - *AyerDirPub 83; Ed&PubIntYB 82*
Signal Master Inc. - Poway, CA - *BrCabYB 84; Tel&CabFB 84C*
Signal Media Corp. - Dallas, TX - *BrCabYB 84*
Signal/North Scott County News - Chaffee, MO - *AyerDirPub 83*
Signal Records - Beverly Hills, CA - *BillIntBG 83-84*
Signal-Star - Goderich, ON, Canada - *AyerDirPub 83*
Signal Technology Inc. - Goleta, CA - *MicrocomMPl 84*
Signalman's Journal, The - Mt. Prospect, IL - *BaconPubCkMag 84; MagDir 84*
Signature - Detroit, MI - *MagDir 84*
Signature [of Citicorp/Diners Club International] - New York, NY - *BaconPubCkMag 84; Folio 83; LitMarPl 83, 84; MagIndMarPl 82-83; WritMar 84*
Signature Systems Marketing Inc. - Alexandria, VA - *DirInfWP 82*
Signet - Elmira, ON, Canada - *AyerDirPub 83; Ed&PubIntYB 82*
Signet Cablevision Co. - Grosse Pointe Park, MI - *Tel&CabFB 84C p.1701*
Signet Cablevision Inc. - Rockdale, TX - *Tel&CabFB 84C*
Signet Research Inc. - Scarsdale, NY - *IntDirMarRes 83; MagIndMarPl 82-83*
Signmaker Press - Berkeley, CA - *BoPubDir 4*
Signmaker Press - Ashland, OR - *BoPubDir 5*
Signon - Balboa, CA - *EISS 5-84 Sup*
Signpost [of Weber State College] - Ogden, UT - *NewsDir 84*
Signpost [of Northwest Trails Association] - Lynnwood, WA - *LitMag&SmPr 83-84; WritMar 84*
Signpost - Dorchester, ON, Canada - *AyerDirPub 83; Ed&PubIntYB 82*
Signpost Books - Edmonds, WA - *LitMarPl 83, 84; WritMar 84*
Signpost Press - Bellingham, WA - *BoPubDir 4, 5; LitMag&SmPr 83-84*
Signs: Journal of Women in Culture & Society - Stanford, CA - *LitMag&SmPr 83-84; MagIndMarPl 82-83*
Signs of the Times [of ST Publications] - Cincinnati, OH - *BaconPubCkMag 84; MagDir 84; MagIndMarPl 82-83; WritMar 84*
Signs of the Times Publishing Co. - Cincinnati, OH - *BoPubDir 4, 5; LitMarPl 84*
Sigo Press - Santa Monica, CA - *LitMarPl 83*
Sigo Press - Boston, MA - *LitMarPl 84*
Sigourney News Review - Sigourney, IA - *BaconPubCkNews 84; NewsDir 84*
SIGSAC Review - New York, NY - *BaconPubCkMag 84*
Sikeston Standard [of Thomson Newspapers Inc.] - Sikeston, MO - *BaconPubCkNews 84; NewsDir 84*
Silangan - Winnipeg, MB, Canada - *Ed&PubIntYB 82*
Silberman, Michael - New York, NY - *LitMarPl 84*
Silberman Whitebrow Dolan - Philadelphia, PA - *AdAge 3-28-84; StaDirAdAg 2-84*
Silbert & Bress Publications - Mahopac, NY - *BoPubDir 4, 5*
Silbert, Layle - New York, NY - *LitMarPl 83, 84; MagIndMarPl 82-83*
Silent Network - Beverly Hills, CA - *CabTVPrDB 83; Tel&CabFB 84C*
Siler City Chatham News - Siler City, NC - *BaconPubCkNews 84; Ed&PubIntYB 82; NewsDir 84*
Siler's Library Distributors - New Orleans, LA - *BoPubDir 4 Sup, 5; LitMarPl 83, 84*
Silhouette Books [Subs. of Simon & Schuster] - New York, NY - *LitMarPl 83, 84; WritMar 84*
Silicon/Ferrosilicon Forecast [of Chase Econometrics/Interactive Data Corp.] - Waltham, MA - *DataDirOnSer 84*
Silicon/Ferrosilicon Forecast - Bala Cynwyd, PA - *DirOnDB Spring 84*
Silicon Gulch Gazette [of Initiative Inc.] - Woodside, CA - *BaconPubCkMag 84; MicrocomMPl 84*
Silicon Music Inc. - Garland, TX - *BillIntBG 83-84*
Silicon Valley Systems Inc. - Belmont, CA - *MicrocomMPl 84; MicrocomSwDir 1*
Silk Purse Music - Alameda, CA - *BillIntBG 83-84*
Silk Screen Industries Inc. - Chicago, IL - *LitMarPl 84*
Silkwood Music - Nashville, TN - *BillIntBG 83-84*
Sillcocks-Miller Co., The - Berkeley Heights, NJ - *DataDirSup 7-83*
Sillerman Morrow Broadcasting Group Inc. - Middletown, NY - *BrCabYB 84*
Siloam Springs Cable TV [of Texas Community Antennas Inc.] - Siloam Springs, AR - *BrCabYB 84*
Siloam Springs Herald & Democrat - Siloam Springs, AR - *BaconPubCkNews 84; NewsDir 84*
Siloam Springs Interstate News - Siloam Springs, AR - *BaconPubCkNews 84; NewsDir 84*
Silsbee Bee - Silsbee, TX - *BaconPubCkNews 84; Ed&PubIntYB 82; NewsDir 84*
Silsbee Cablevision Inc. - Silsbee, TX - *BrCabYB 84; Tel&CabFB 84C*
Silton/Turner Inc. - Boston, MA - *BrCabYB 84; TelAl 83, 84*
Siltran Digital - Atascadero, CA - *WhoWMicrocom 83*
Silver Advertising Ltd. - London, England - *StaDirAdAg 2-84*
Silver & Associates Inc., Al - Sherman Oaks, CA - *StaDirAdAg 2-84*
Silver Associates Inc., M. - New York, NY - *DirPRFirms 83*
Silver Associates Inc., R. L. - New York, NY - *LitMarPl 83, 84; StaDirAdAg 2-84*
Silver Associates, Robert [Subs. of Randall Book Co. Inc.] - New York, NY - *LitMarPl 83, 84*
Silver Associates, Robert I. - Wayne, NJ - *LitMarPl 83, 84*
Silver Blue Music Ltd. - Penthouse, NY - *BillIntBG 83-84*
Silver Blue Productions - New York, NY - *BillIntBG 83-84*
Silver Burdett Co. [Subs. of SFN Cos. Inc.] - Morristown, NJ - *ArtMar 84; AvMarPl 83; DirMarMP 83; LitMarPl 83, 84; WritMar 84*
Silver City Enterprise - Silver City, NM - *AyerDirPub 83; BaconPubCkNews 84; Ed&PubIntYB 82*
Silver City Press & Independent - Silver City, NM - *BaconPubCkNews 84; NewsDir 84*
Silver City Record - Kansas City, KS - *AyerDirPub 83*
Silver Cloud Productions - North Hollywood, CA - *AvMarPl 83*
Silver Crow Music - *See* Windham Hill Music
Silver Forecast [of Chase Econometrics/Interactive Data Corp.] - Waltham, MA - *DataDirOnSer 84*
Silver Forecast - Bala Cynwyd, PA - *DirOnDB Spring 84*
Silver Fox Connections Inc. - Federal Way, WA - *BoPubDir 4 Sup, 5*
Silver Heart Music - Hendersonville, TN - *BillIntBG 83-84*
Silver Inc., H. Richard - New York, NY - *DirPRFirms 83; StaDirAdAg 2-84*
Silver Institute - Washington, DC - *BoPubDir 5*
Silver Lake Leader - Silver Lake, MN - *BaconPubCkNews 84; Ed&PubIntYB 82*
Silver Lake News - Pembroke, MA - *Ed&PubIntYB 82*
Silver Lake News - Plymouth, MA - *AyerDirPub 83*
Silver Lining Records - North Hollywood, CA - *BillIntBG 83-84*
Silver Music - *See* Blanchris Music
Silver-Reed America Inc. - Culver City, CA - *DirInfWP 82; MicrocomMPl 84*
Silver Rose Recordings - Atlanta, GA - *BillIntBG 83-84*
Silver Saddle Records - Nashville, TN - *BillIntBG 83-84*
Silver Sage Cable TV [of Mickelson Media Inc.] - Mountain Home, ID - *BrCabYB 84; Tel&CabFB 84C*
Silver Spring Suburban Record - Silver Spring, MD - *BaconPubCkNews 84; Ed&PubIntYB 82; NewsDir 84*

Silver Spring-Wheaton Advertiser - Bethesda, MD - *AyerDirPub 83*
Silver Spring-Wheaton Advertiser [of Panax of Virginia Inc.] - Fairfax, VA - *NewsDir 84*
Silver Star Telephone Co. Inc. - Freedom, WY - *TelDir&BG 83-84*
Silver State Post - Deer Lodge, MT - *AyerDirPub 83; Ed&PubIntYB 82*
Silver Valley Cable TV - Kellogg, ID - *Tel&CabFB 84C*
Silver Ware - Santa Barbara, CA - *MicrocomMPl 84*
Silverado Publishing Co. - St. Helena, CA - *BoPubDir 5*
Silverado Publishing Co. - New York, NY - *BoPubDir 4 Sup*
Silverdale Kitsap Journal - Silverdale, WA - *NewsDir 84*
Silverfish Review - Eugene, OR - *LitMag&SmPr 83-84*
Silverhill Music - Los Angeles, CA - *BillIntBG 83-84*
Silveri Associates Inc., Peter - New York, NY - *DirPRFirms 83*
Silverline Music Inc. - Hendersonville, TN - *BillIntBG 83-84*
Silverman & Co., William - Cleveland, OH - *DirPRFirms 83*
Silverman Inc., Robert - Cleveland, OH - *DirMarMP 83; StaDirAdAg 2-84*
Silverman Mower - Syracuse, NY - *AdAge 3-28-84; ArtMar 84; DirMarMP 83; StaDirAdAg 2-84*
Silverman, Richard - Kew Gardens, NY - *LitMarPl 83, 84; MagIndMarPl 82-83*
Silverman/The Scientific Translation Co., Robert H. - Cambridge, MA - *LitMarPl 83; MagIndMarPl 82-83*
Silvermine Films Inc. - New York, NY - *AvMarPl 83*
Silverstate Publishing - *See* Vegas Star Music
Silverstein, Doris - New York, NY - *LitMarPl 83, 84*
Silverton Appeal Tribune/Mt. Angel News - Silverton, OR - *BaconPubCkNews 84; Ed&PubIntYB 82; NewsDir 84*
Silverton Briscoe County News - Silverton, TX - *BaconPubCkNews 84*
Silverton Cable TV - Olney, TX - *BrCabYB 84*
Silverton Cable TV - Silverton, TX - *Tel&CabFB 84C*
Silverton-Mt. Angel Cable TV - Silverton, OR - *BrCabYB 84; Tel&CabFB 84C*
Silverton Standard & The Miner - Silverton, CO - *BaconPubCkNews 84; Ed&PubIntYB 82*
Silvestri Studio Inc. - Los Angeles, CA - *AvMarPl 83*
Silwa Enterprises Inc. - Hampton, VA - *MicrocomMPl 83*
Sim Productions Inc. - Weston, CT - *Tel&CabFB 84C*
Simco Cable TV Co. Inc. - Magee, MS - *Tel&CabFB 84C*
Simco Co. Inc., The [Subs. of Ransburg Corp.] - Hatfield, PA - *AvMarPl 83*
Simcoe Reformer, The - Simcoe, ON, Canada - *BaconPubCkNews 84; Ed&PubIntYB 82; LitMarPl 83*
Simcom International - Beverly Hills, CA - *Tel&CabFB 84C*
Simcom Ltd. - Toronto, ON, Canada - *Tel&CabFB 84C*
Simcon Inc. - McLean, VA - *WhoWMicrocom 83*
Simcost II [of Arthur D. Little Inc.] - Cambridge, MA - *DataDirOnSer 84*
Simi Valley Enterprise [of Entsunews] - Simi Valley, CA - *AyerDirPub 83; NewsDir 84*
Similkameen Spotlight - Princeton, BC, Canada - *AyerDirPub 83*
Simla Ranchland News - Simla, CO - *BaconPubCkNews 84*
Simma Music Co. - *See* NRP Music Group
Simmental Shield - Lindsborg, KS - *MagDir 84; WritMar 84*
Simmons Advertising Inc. - Grand Forks, ND - *StaDirAdAg 2-84*
Simmons-Boardman Publishing Corp. - New York, NY - *BoPubDir 5; MagIndMarPl 82-83*
Simmons-Boardman Publishing Corp. (Book Div.) - Omaha, NE - *BoPubDir 4 Sup, 5*
Simmons Cable TV - Cambridge, MD - *Tel&CabFB 84C*
Simmons Cable TV - Leonardtown, MD - *Tel&CabFB 84C*
Simmons Cable TV of Walton - Walton, NY - *Tel&CabFB 84C*
Simmons Communications Inc. - Stamford, CT - *BrCabYB 84; Tel&CabFB 84C p.1702*
Simmons Communications Inc. - Harrington, DE - *Tel&CabFB 84C*
Simmons Custom Studies [Div. of Simmons Market Research Bureau Inc.] - New York, NY - *IntDirMarRes 83*
Simmons, Donald M. - *See* Green Group, Howard
Simmons Market Research Bureau [Subs. of JWT Group] - New York, NY - *AdAge 5-17-84 p.35; BoPubDir 5; BrCabYB 84; DataDirOnSer 84; DBBus 82; EISS 5-84 Sup; LitMarPl 83; MagIndMarPl 82-83; Tel&CabFB 84C*
Simmons Market Research Bureau - *See* JWT Group Inc.
Simmons Media Studies [Div. of Simmons Market Research Bureau Inc.] - New York, NY - *IntDirMarRes 83*
Simmons of Salamanca - Salamanca, NY - *BrCabYB 84*
Simmons Productions, Peter - Watertown, MA - *ArtMar 84; AvMarPl 83; WritMar 84*
Simmons Teen Age Research Study [of Simmons Market Research Bureau Inc.] - New York, NY - *DataDirOnSer 84*
Simms & McIvor - Bound Brook, NJ - *StaDirAdAg 2-84*
Simon & Pierre Publishing Co. Ltd. - Toronto, ON, Canada - *LitMag&SmPr 83-84; LitMarPl 83, 84*
Simon & Schuster Enterprises Inc. [Subs. of Simon & Schuster Inc.] - New York, NY - *DirMarMP 83*
Simon & Schuster Inc. - New York, NY - *LitMarPl 83, 84*
Simon & Schuster Inc. (Trade Books Div.) - New York, NY - *WritMar 84*
Simon Associates - Mill Valley, CA - *AvMarPl 83*
Simon Co. Inc., H. K. - Yonkers, NY - *StaDirAdAg 2-84*
Simon Fraser University - Burnaby, BC, Canada - *MicroMarPl 82-83*
Simon Inc., George - Palm Springs, CA - *BillIntBG 83-84*
Simon, Joseph - Malibu, CA - *BoPubDir 4, 5*
Simon, Paul - New York, NY - *BillIntBG 83-84*
Simon Productions Inc., Jamil - Cambridge, MA - *AvMarPl 83*
Simon/Public Relations Inc. - Los Angeles, CA - *DirPRFirms 83*
Simon Research Service Inc., Marion - Rochester, NY - *IntDirMarRes 83*
Simon Software - Redditch, England - *MicrocomSwDir 1*
Simon, William Jr. - Scarsdale, NY - *LitMarPl 83*
Simons Michelson Zieve - Troy, MI - *AdAge 3-28-84; BrCabYB 84; StaDirAdAg 2-84; TelAl 83, 84*
Simonton Music - *See* Hat Band Music
Simple Remedies & Preventive Medicine - Seale, AL - *Ed&PubIntYB 82*
Simple Soft Inc. - Elk Grove, IL - *MicrocomMPl 84; MicrocomSwDir 1*
Simplex Specialty Co. Inc. [Subs. of Carl Hostert GmbH] - Hackensack, NJ - *AvMarPl 83*
Simplex Systems Inc. - New York, NY - *DataDirOnSer 84*
Simplicity Today - New York, NY - *BaconPubCkMag 84*
Simplified Software Systems [Div. of M. B. Rowe & Associates] - Hickory, NC - *MicrocomMPl 83, 84; MicrocomSwDir 1*
Simply Elegant - Winnetka, IL - *BoPubDir 4, 5*
Simply Superb Publications [Aff. of Junior League of Elizabeth-Plainfield, NJ, Inc.] - Cranford, NJ - *BoPubDir 4, 5*
Simpson & Co., Martin - New York, NY - *ADAPSOMemDir 83-84*
Simpson County News - Mendenhall, MS - *AyerDirPub 83; Ed&PubIntYB 82*
Simpson Marketing Communications Agency - Columbus, OH - *DirMarMP 83; StaDirAdAg 2-84*
Simpson Paper Co. - San Francisco, CA - *LitMarPl 83, 84*
Simpson, Ruth M. Rasey - North Tonawanda, NY - *BoPubDir 4, 5*
Sims & Associates - San Diego, CA - *StaDirAdAg 2-84*
Simsbury Farmington Valley Herald [of Tunxis Publishing Co. Inc.] - Simsbury, CT - *BaconPubCkNews 84; NewsDir 84*
SimSoft Inc. - Port Huron, MI - *MicrocomMPl 84*
Simtek - Cambridge, MA - *BoPubDir 4, 5; EISS 7-83 Sup; MicrocomMPl 84; MicrocomSwDir 1; WhoWMicrocom 83*
Simulation - La Jolla, CA - *BaconPubCkMag 84*
Simulation Software - Sandy Hook, CT - *MicrocomMPl 84*
Simultaneous Wireless Interpretations - New York, NY - *MagIndMarPl 82-83*
Simulusion - Lemon Grove, CA - *MicrocomMPl 84; WritMar 84*
Simutek Computer Products - Tucson, AZ - *MicrocomSwDir 1; WhoWMicrocom 83*
SIN Inc. - New York, NY - *BrCabYB 84*
Sin Television Network - New York, NY - *BrCabYB 84; Tel&CabFB 84C*
Sinar Bron Inc. - Edison, NJ - *AvMarPl 83*
Sinauer Associates Inc. - Sunderland, MA - *LitMarPl 83, 84*
Sincerely Yours Services - Pasadena, CA - *DirMarMP 83*

Sinclair Broadcasting - Crawfordsville, IN - *BrCabYB 84*
Sinclair, John - Indianapolis, IN - *Tel&CabFB 84C p.1702*
Sinclair Optics Inc. - Pittsford, NY - *MicrocomSwDir 1*
Sinclair Place - Redmond, WA - *MicrocomMPl 84*
Sinclair Printing Co. - Los Angeles, CA - *MagIndMarPl 82-83*
Sinclair Research Ltd. - Nashua, NH - *WhoWMicrocom 83*
Sinclair Telecable Inc. - Hendricks County, IN - *BrCabYB 84; Tel&CabFB 84C*
Sindacato Ispettivo [of Centro per la Documentazione Automatica] - Rome, Italy - *CompReadDB 82*
Sindlinger & Co. Inc. - Media, PA - *BrCabYB 84; Tel&CabFB 84C*
Sine Qua Non Cassettes & Records - Providence, RI - *BillIntBG 83-84*
Sing Heavenly Muse! - Minneapolis, MN - *LitMag&SmPr 83-84*
Sing Out! - New York, NY - *MagIndMarPl 82-83*
Sing Out! - Easton, PA - *LitMag&SmPr 83-84; MagDir 84*
Sing Sweeter Music - *See* Sweet Singer Music
Singapore Corporate Statistics [of I. P. Sharp Associates Ltd.] - Toronto, ON, Canada - *DataDirOnSer 84*
Singapore Stock Exchange [of I. P. Sharp Associates Ltd.] - Toronto, ON, Canada - *DataDirOnSer 84; DirOnDB Spring 84*
Singapore Tymnet/Telenet Node [of Telecommunication Authority of Singapore] - Singapore, Singapore - *InfIndMarPl 83*
Singcorp - Kent Ridge, Singapore - *DirOnDB Spring 84*
Singer Agency Inc., Evelyn - White Plains, NY - *LitMarPl 83, 84*
Singer Communications Corp., Gary - Westport, CT - *StaDirAdAg 2-84*
Singer Communications Inc. - Anaheim, CA - *ArtMar 84; AvMarPl 83; Ed&PubIntYB 82; LitMarPl 83, 84; MagIndMarPl 82-83*
Singer Co. - Stamford, CT - *ElecNews 7-25-83*
Singer Data Products - Elk Grove Village, IL - *DataDirSup 7-83*
Singer, Donald E. - Hector, NY - *Tel&CabFB 84C*
Singer Inc., Niki - New York, NY - *DirPRFirms 83*
Singer Media Services - Boston, MA - *StaDirAdAg 2-84*
Singer Printing & Publishing Co. - Highland Park, IL - *BaconPubCkNews 84*
Singer Studio Film Design, Rebecca - New York, NY - *AvMarPl 83*
Singh Seven Seas! Publication - Lansing, MI - *BoPubDir 4, 5*
Singing Horse Press - Blue Bell, PA - *BoPubDir 4, 5; LitMag&SmPr 83-84*
Singing News, The - Pensacola, FL - *BaconPubCkMag 84; MagDir 84; MagIndMarPl 82-83*
Singing Wire Music - *See* Widget Publishing
Single Crystal Reduction & Search System [of Chemical Information Systems Inc.] - Baltimore, MD - *DataDirOnSer 84*
Single Impressions - Tucson, AZ - *BoPubDir 4, 5*
Single Parent, The [of Parents Without Partners Inc.] - Bethesda, MD - *ArtMar 84; MagIndMarPl 82-83; WritMar 84*
Singlejack Books - San Pedro, CA - *LitMag&SmPr 83-84*
Singlelife Magazine - Milwaukee, WI - *WritMar 84*
Singles Scene Magazine - Albuquerque, NM - *WritMar 84*
Singles World - Phoenix, AZ - *WritMar 84*
Singleton Corp., Shelby - Nashville, TN - *BillIntBG 83-84*
Singleton's Cablevision Systems Inc. - Montrose, IA - *Tel&CabFB 84C p.1702*
Singletree Music - *See* Hat Band Music
Singspiration Inc. - *See* Zondervan Corp., The
Singular Speech Press - Canton, CT - *BoPubDir 5; LitMag&SmPr 83-84*
Singular Speech Press - Collinsville, CT - *BoPubDir 4*
Sink Stations, J. Ardell - Burnsville, NC - *BrCabYB 84*
Sino Express - New York, NY - *AyerDirPub 83*
Sino Information Resources - Davenport, IA - *EISS 83*
Sinsemilla Tips - Corvallis, OR - *WritMar 84*
Sinta - Brighton, England - *MicrocomSwDir 1*
Sinton County News - *See* San Patricio Publishing Co.
Sioux Center News - Sioux Center, IA - *BaconPubCkNews 84; Ed&PubIntYB 82*
Sioux City Globe - Sioux City, IA - *NewsDir 84*
Sioux City Journal - Sioux City, IA - *BaconPubCkNews 84; Ed&PubIntYB 82; LitMarPl 83, 84; MagIndMarPl 82-83; NewsDir 84*
Sioux City MDS Co. - New York, NY - *Tel&CabFB 84C*
Sioux County Capital - Orange City, IA - *Ed&PubIntYB 82*
Sioux County Index-Reporter - Hull, IA - *AyerDirPub 83; Ed&PubIntYB 82*
Sioux Falls Argus-Leader - Sioux Falls, SD - *LitMarPl 83; NewsBur 6*
Sioux Falls Cable Television [Aff. of Tele-Communications Inc.] - Sioux Falls, SD - *BrCabYB 84; InterCabHB 3*
Sioux Falls Shopping News Informer - Sioux Falls, SD - *AyerDirPub 83*
Sioux Falls Tribune - Sioux Falls, SD - *AyerDirPub 83*
Sioux Rapids Bulletin-Press - Sioux Rapids, IA - *BaconPubCkNews 84; Ed&PubIntYB 82*
Sioux Rosenberg Co. - San Turcea, PR - *Ed&PubIntYB 82*
Sioux Valley News - Canton, SD - *Ed&PubIntYB 82*
Sioux Valley Telephone Co. [Aff. of Ollig Utilities Co.] - Dell Rapids, SD - *TelDir&BG 83-84*
SIPA News Syndicate [Subs. of Pan-American Information Service] - New York, NY - *Ed&PubIntYB 82; LitMarPl 83, 84; MagIndMarPl 82-83*
Sipapu [of Konocti Books] - Winters, CA - *LitMag&SmPr 83-84*
Sippican Sentinel (Marion Edition) - Marion, MA - *Ed&PubIntYB 82*
Sippican Sentinel (Mattapoisett Edition) - Mattapoisett, MA - *Ed&PubIntYB 82*
Sir-Tech Software Inc. - Ogdensburg, NY - *MicrocomMPl 83, 84; MicrocomSwDir 1; WhoWMicrocom 83*
Sirak-Paul Petrulakis, James - Lake Hiawatha, NJ - *BoPubDir 4 Sup, 5; LitMarPl 83, 84*
SIRC Sport Database [of Sport Information Resource Centre] - Ottawa, ON, Canada - *DataDirOnSer 84*
Sirco Enterprises Inc. - Troy, MI - *ADAPSOMemDir 83-84*
Sirco Records - Freeport, NY - *BillIntBG 83-84*
Sire Records Co. - New York, NY - *BillIntBG 83-84*
Sire Trini Music - *See* MizMo Enterprises
Siren Telephone Co. Inc. - Siren, WI - *TelDir&BG 83-84*
Sirius Books - Eureka, CA - *BoPubDir 4, 5*
Sirius Books - Freeport, ME - *BoPubDir 4, 5*
Sirius House - San Francisco, CA - *LitMarPl 83, 84*
Sirius League, The - Albuquerque, NM - *LitMag&SmPr 83-84*
Sirius Publications - Beverly Hills, CA - *BoPubDir 5; LitMag&SmPr 83-84*
Sirius Software Inc. - Sacramento, CA - *MicrocomMPl 83, 84; WhoWMicrocom 83; WritMar 84*
Sirius Systems Inc. - Thornton, NH - *Tel&CabFB 84C p.1702*
Siriusware - Lexington, MA - *MicrocomMPl 84*
SIRLS [of University of Waterloo] - Waterloo, ON, Canada - *CompReadDB 82*
Sirmans Corp. - Anaheim, CA - *MicrocomMPl 84*
Siroco Enterprises - Los Angeles, CA - *Tel&CabFB 84C*
Sirois Cable Engineering - Chandler, PQ, Canada - *BrCabYB 84*
Sirsi Corp. - Huntsville, AL - *EISS 83*
Sirtage Inc. - Raleigh, NC - *AvMarPl 83*
Sis Enterprises - Palo Alto, CA - *BoPubDir 4, 5*
SIS Sundata - Wayne, PA - *DataDirOnSer 84*
Sisdata [of ADP Network Services] - Ann Arbor, MI - *DataDirOnSer 84*
Sisdata - Rome, Italy - *DirOnDB Spring 84*
Sisk Group - *See* Air South Radio Inc.
Siskiyou Cablevision Inc. - Etna, CA - *BrCabYB 84*
Siskiyou Cablevision Inc. - Ft. Jones, CA - *BrCabYB 84; Tel&CabFB 84C*
Siskiyou News - Yreka, CA - *AyerDirPub 83; BaconPubCkNews 84; Ed&PubIntYB 82*
Siskiyou Telephone Co., The - Ft. Jones, CA - *TelDir&BG 83-84*
Sisseton Cablevision Inc. [of Tele-Communications Inc.] - Browns Valley, MN - *Tel&CabFB 84C*
Sisseton Cablevision Inc. [of Tele-Communications Inc.] - Sisseton, SD - *BrCabYB 84; Tel&CabFB 84C*
Sisseton Cablevision Inc. [of Tele-Communications Inc.] - Wilmot, SD - *Tel&CabFB 84C*
Sisseton Courier - Sisseton, SD - *BaconPubCkNews 84; Ed&PubIntYB 82; NewsDir 84*
Sisson, Foss & Co. - Charlottesville, VA - *LitMarPl 83, 84*
Sisson Genealogical Publications - Upper Kent, NB, Canada - *BoPubDir 4 Sup, 5*
Sisson Video Communications Inc. - Poplar Bluff, MO - *Tel&CabFB 84C p.1702*
Sisson's Community TV - Schreiber, ON, Canada - *BrCabYB 84*

Sister Kenny Institute [Aff. of Abbott-Northwestern Hospital] - Minneapolis, MN - *BoPubDir 5*
Sister Kenny Institute (Research & Education Div.) - Minneapolis, MN - *BoPubDir 4*
Sister Source - Chicago, IL - *LitMag&SmPr 83-84*
Sisters Cable Co. - Sisters, OR - *BrCabYB 84; Tel&CabFB 84C*
Sisters' Choice Press - Berkeley, CA - *BoPubDir 4, 5; LitMag&SmPr 83-84*
Sistersville Tyler Star-News - Sistersville, WV - *BaconPubCkNews 84; NewsDir 84*
Sistler & Associates, Byron - Nashville, TN - *BoPubDir 5*
Sita - Helsinki, Finland - *ProGuPRSer 4*
Sitare Inc. - Los Angeles, CA - *BoPubDir 4, 5*
Site-Potential [of CACI Inc.] - Arlington, VA - *DataDirOnSer 84; DBBus 82; DirOnDB Spring 84*
Site II [of Data Resources Inc.] - Lexington, MA - *DataDirOnSer 84*
Site II [of CACI Inc.] - Arlington, VA - *DBBus 82; DirOnDB Spring 84*
Siteman/Brodhead/Blarz Inc. - Beverly Hills, CA - *DirPRFirms 83*
Siteman/Uniphoto, Frank - Winchester, MA - *AvMarPl 83*
Sitenet - Atlanta, GA - *DirOnDB Spring 84*
Sites-Architectural Magazine - New York, NY - *LitMag&SmPr 83-84*
Sitka Telephone Co. [Aff. of Telphone Utilities Inc.] - Sitka, AK - *TelDir&BG 83-84*
Sitnalta Press - San Francisco, CA - *BoPubDir 4, 5; LitMag&SmPr 83-84*
Siuslaw News - Florence, OR - *AyerDirPub 83; Ed&PubIntYB 82*
Sivatt Music - Greenville, SC - *BillIntBG 83-84*
Sive Associates Inc. - Cincinnati, OH - *StaDirAdAg 2-84*
Six Mile Run TV Corp. - Six Mile Run, PA - *Tel&CabFB 84C*
6M's Burke Industries, The - Washington, DC - *MagIndMarPl 82-83*
605 Advertising Group - New York, NY - *StaDirAdAg 2-84*
Six Shooter Music - *See* Merit Music Corp.
16 Magazine - New York, NY - *BaconPubCkMag 84; MagIndMarPl 82-83*
'68 Micro Journal [of Computer Publishing Inc.] - Hixson, TN - *BaconPubCkMag 84; MicrocomMPl 84*
65 News [of Local 65, United Steel Workers of America] - Chicago, IL - *NewsDir 84*
6502 Program Exchange, The - Reno, NV - *MicrocomMPl 83, 84*
6502 Program Exchange, The - Dallas, TX - *WhoWMicrocom 83*
Sizzle Sheet, The - Framingham, MA - *BaconPubCkMag 84*
SJ & L Communications Inc. - Bossier City, LA - *Tel&CabFB 84C p.1702*
SJB Distributors - Dallas, TX - *MicrocomMPl 84*
SJL Inc. - Billings, MT - *BrCabYB 84*
SJM Cablevision Inc. - Macksville, KS - *BrCabYB 84*
SJM Cablevision Inc. - St. John, KS - *Tel&CabFB 84C*
Sjoberg's Cable TV Inc. - Karlstad, MN - *BrCabYB 84*
Sjoberg's Cable TV Inc. - Thief River Falls, MN - *Tel&CabFB 84C p.1702*
S.J.V. Leader Shopping News - Three Rivers, MI - *Ed&PubIntYB 82*
S.K. Concepts - Highland, NY - *WhoWMicrocom 83*
SK Publications - Northfield Center, OH - *BoPubDir 4, 5*
Skaar & Co., A. L. - Spokane, WA - *ArtMar 84; StaDirAdAg 2-84*
Skaggs Telecommunications Services - Salt Lake City, UT - *Tel&CabFB 84C*
Skagit Argus - Mt. Vernon, WA - *AyerDirPub 83*
Skagit Farmer [of Lewis Publishing Co. Inc.] - Lynden, WA - *NewsDir 84*
Skagit Valley Herald - Mt. Vernon, WA - *AyerDirPub 83; BaconPubCkNews 84; Ed&PubIntYB 82; NewsDir 84*
Skagway Cable TV [of E.D. & D. Inc.] - Skagway, AK - *Tel&CabFB 84C*
Skagway Network - Skagway, AK - *BrCabYB 84*
Skamania County Pioneer, The - Stevenson, WA - *Ed&PubIntYB 82*
SKAMP Computer Services Inc. - Minntonka, MN - *WhoWMicrocom 83*
Skaneateles-Marcellus Pennysaver - Skaneateles, NY - *AyerDirPub 83*
Skaneateles Press - Skaneateles, NY - *Ed&PubIntYB 82; LitMarPl 83, 84*
Skaneateles Press - *See* Wobo Corp.
Skaneateles Press & Marcellus Observer - Skaneateles, NY - *AyerDirPub 83; NewsDir 84*
Skanner - Minority, OK - *Ed&PubIntYB 82*
Skanner, The - Portland, OR - *AyerDirPub 83; Ed&PubIntYB 82*
Skarbek Computers Inc. - St. Louis, MO - *BoPubDir 5*
Skateboarder Magazine - Dana Point, CA - *MagDir 84*
Skating [of United States Figure Skating Association] - Colorado Springs, CO - *ArtMar 84; BaconPubCkMag 84; MagDir 84; MagIndMarPl 82-83; WritMar 84*
Skeena Broadcasters Ltd. - Kitimat, BC, Canada - *BrCabYB 84*
Skeena Broadcasters Ltd. - Prince Rupert, BC, Canada - *BrCabYB 84*
Skeena Broadcasters Ltd. - Terrace, BC, Canada - *BrCabYB 84; Tel&CabFB 84C*
Skeet Shooting Review, The - San Antonio, TX - *BaconPubCkMag 84; MagDir 84*
Skeptical Inquirer - Buffalo, NY - *MagIndMarPl 82-83*
Skerrett Communication - Halifax, NS, Canada - *AvMarPl 83*
Skerritt, Mabel L. - Huntsville, ON, Canada - *BoPubDir 4, 5*
Ski [of Times Mirror Magazines Inc.] - New York, NY - *ArtMar 84; BaconPubCkMag 84; Folio 83; MagDir 84; MagIndMarPl 82-83; WritMar 84*
Ski America - Pittsfield, MA - *BaconPubCkMag 84*
Ski Area Management - North Salem, NY - *MagDir 84; MagIndMarPl 82-83*
Ski Business - Darien, CT - *BaconPubCkMag 84; WritMar 84*
Ski Business - New York, NY - *MagDir 84; MagIndMarPl 82-83*
Ski Canada - Toronto, ON, Canada - *BaconPubCkMag 84*
Ski Coach [of Human Kinetics Pub. Inc.] - Champaign, IL - *LitMag&SmPr 83-84*
Ski Industry Bulletin - Montreal, PQ, Canada - *BaconPubCkMag 84*
Ski Racing - Fair Haven, VT - *BaconPubCkMag 84; MagIndMarPl 82-83; WritMar 84*
Ski Racing - Poultney, VT - *MagDir 84*
Ski X-C - New York, NY - *BaconPubCkMag 84*
Skiatook Cablevision [of Community Cablevision Co.] - Skiatook, OK - *BrCabYB 84; Tel&CabFB 84C*
Skiatook News, The - Skiatook, OK - *Ed&PubIntYB 82*
Skidaway Cable TV - Skidaway Island, GA - *BrCabYB 84; Tel&CabFB 84C*
Skier's World - Mountain View, CA - *MagIndMarPl 82-83*
Skiing [of Ziff-Davis Publishing Co.] - New York, NY - *ArtMar 84; BaconPubCkMag 84; Folio 83; MagDir 84; MagIndMarPl 82-83; WritMar 84*
Skiing Trade News - New York, NY - *ArtMar 84; BaconPubCkMag 84; MagDir 84; MagIndMarPl 82-83; WritMar 84*
Skillbook Co. - Springhouse, PA - *BoPubDir 4, 5*
Skillcorp Software Inc. - Irvine, CA - *MicrocomMPl 84*
Skillings Mining Review - Duluth, MN - *BaconPubCkMag 84; MagDir 84*
Skilset Typographers Inc. - New York, NY - *LitMarPl 83*
SkiMedia Network - San Francisco, CA - *BrCabYB 84*
Skin & Allergy News - Rockville, MD - *MagDir 84; MagIndMarPl 82-83*
Skin Diver [of Petersen Publishing Co.] - Los Angeles, CA - *BaconPubCkMag 84; Folio 83; MagDir 84; MagIndMarPl 82-83; WritMar 84*
Skinner Music Publishing, Jimmie - Cincinnati, OH - *BillIntBG 83-84*
Skinny Zach Music Inc. - Tarzana, CA - *BillIntBG 83-84*
Skip Jack Music - *See* Mimic Music
Skipworth Press Inc. - Richmond, VA - *BoPubDir 4, 5*
Skirboll & Garber Advertising Inc. - Pittsburgh, PA - *AdAge 3-28-84; StaDirAdAg 2-84*
Skirmisher, The - Baltimore, MD - *BaconPubCkMag 84*
Skisport - Antioch, IL - *MagDir 84*
SKK Inc. - Rosemont, IL - *ADAPSOMemDir 83-84*
Sklar, Idelson - Washington, DC - *DirPRFirms 83*
Sklar-Lenett Associates Inc. - Rye Brook, NY - *StaDirAdAg 2-84*
SKM Cable TV [of Polar Communications Mutual Aid Corp.] - Cavalier, ND - *BrCabYB 84*

SKM Cable TV [of Polar Communications Mutual Aid Corp.] - Park River, ND - *BrCabYB 84*
Skokie Life - Skokie, IL - *AyerDirPub 83; Ed&PubIntYB 82*
Skokie Life - *See* Myers Publishing Co.
Skokie Life Newspaper Group [of Lerner Newspapers] - Chicago, IL - *NewsDir 84*
Skokie-Lincolnwood Bugle - *See* Bugle Publications
Skokie Music - *See* Catalogue Music Inc.
Skokie-News - Skokie, IL - *BaconPubCkNews 84; NewsDir 84*
Skokie Review [of Pickwick Publishing Co.] - Park Ridge, IL - *NewsDir 84*
Skokie Review - Skokie, IL - *Ed&PubIntYB 82*
Skokie Review - Wilmette, IL - *AyerDirPub 83*
Skokie-Review - *See* Pioneer Press Inc.
Skowhegan Somerset Reporter - Skowhegan, ME - *BaconPubCkNews 84; NewsDir 84*
SKP Associates - New York, NY - *EISS 83; LitMarPl 83, 84*
Skreczko, Lynne - Brooklyn, NY - *LitMarPl 83, 84*
SKS Computers Inc. - Hilliard, OH - *MicrocomMPl 84*
SKS Productions Inc. - Santa Fe, NM - *Tel&CabFB 84C*
SKT Enterprises - Washington, DC - *MicrocomMPl 84*
SKU - Berkeley, CA - *MicrocomMPl 84*
Sky & Telescope - Boston, MA - *MagDir 84*
Sky & Telescope - Cambridge, MA - *ArtMar 84; BaconPubCkMag 84; MagIndMarPl 82-83*
Sky Book Club [Subs. of Sky Books International Inc.] - New York, NY - *LitMarPl 83, 84*
Sky Books International Inc. - New York, NY - *MagIndMarPl 82-83*
Sky Corp. - New York, NY - *BrCabYB 84*
Sky Harbor Music - *See* Seagrape Music
Sky-Hi News - Granby, CO - *AyerDirPub 83; Ed&PubIntYB 82*
Sky Meadow Bindery - Suffern, NY - *LitMarPl 83, 84*
Sky Publishing Corp. - Cambridge, MA - *BoPubDir 4, 5*
Sky Riders Music - Richmond, CA - *BillIntBG 83-84*
Sky Valley Cablevision [of Mountain View Enterprises Inc.] - Sky Valley, GA - *BrCabYB 84; Tel&CabFB 84C*
Skyband Inc. - New York, NY - *BrCabYB 84*
Skydiving [of Aerograpics Inc.] - Deltona, FL - *ArtMar 84; BaconPubCkMag 84; DirMarMP 83; LitMag&SmPr 83-84; WritMar 84*
Skydog Press [Aff. of NRG Magazine] - Portland, OR - *BoPubDir 4, 5; LitMag&SmPr 83-84*
SkyGuide [of American Express Europe Ltd.] - Brighton, England - *EISS 5-84 Sup*
Skyhill Publishing Co. Inc. - New York, NY - *BillIntBG 83-84*
Skyland Post - West Jefferson, NC - *AyerDirPub 83; Ed&PubIntYB 82*
Skyles Electric Works - Mountain View, CA - *MicrocomMPl 83, 84*
Skylight Press - Philadelphia, PA - *BoPubDir 4 Sup, 5*
Skyline - Chicago, IL - *AyerDirPub 83; Ed&PubIntYB 82*
Skyline Cable Inc. - Brookings, OR - *BrCabYB 84; Tel&CabFB 84C*
Skyline Cablevision Inc. - Aurora, CO - *Tel&CabFB 84C p.1702*
Skyline Cablevision Inc. - Berthoud, CO - *Tel&CabFB 84C*
Skyline Cablevision Inc. - Fairplay, CO - *BrCabYB 84*
Skyline Cablevision Ltd. - Ottawa, ON, Canada - *BrCabYB 84*
Skyline Communications Corp. [of Penn Communications Inc.] - Georgetown, IN - *BrCabYB 84; Tel&CabFB 84C*
Skyline/Encanto Pennysaver - Mission Viejo, CA - *AyerDirPub 83*
Skyline Telephone Membership Corp. - West Jefferson, NC - *TelDir&BG 83-84*
Skylines [of Building Owners & Managers Association International] - Washington, DC - *BaconPubCkMag 84; MagDir 84*
Skylink America Inc. - Fairhope, AL - *Tel&CabFB 84C*
Skylite [of Halsey Publishing Co.] - North Miami, FL - *BaconPubCkMag 84; MagIndMarPl 82-83; WritMar 84*
Skylite-Sing Inc. - Nashville, TN - *BillIntBG 83-84*
Skynet Satellite Services [of American Telephone & Telegraph Co.] - Bedminster, NJ - *TeleSy&SerDir 2-84*
Skyscraper Engineer - Pittsburgh, PA - *MagDir 84*
Skyview Music - *See* Neil Music Inc.
Skyview Publishing - Bellmore, NY - *BoPubDir 4, 5*
Skyviews Survey Inc. - Westbury, NY - *AvMarPl 83; MagIndMarPl 82-83*
Skyvision Corp. - Washington, DC - *Tel&CabFB 84C*
Skyway - Auckland, New Zealand - *ArtMar 84*
Skywrighter - Dayton, OH - *AyerDirPub 83*
Skywriting [of Blue Mountain Press] - South Haven, MI - *LitMag&SmPr 83-84*
Slack Inc., Charles B. - Thorofare, NJ - *LitMarPl 83, 84; MagIndMarPl 82-83*
Slackwater Review, The [of Confluence Press Inc.] - Lewiston, ID - *LitMag&SmPr 83-84*
Slade-Best Advertising - Rockford, IL - *StaDirAdAg 2-84*
Slade Record Co. - Crookston, MN - *BillIntBG 83-84*
Slade Research Associates Inc. - Rochester, NY - *IntDirMarRes 83*
Slamark International SpA - Rome, Italy - *EISS 83; InfIndMarPl 83*
Slap Shot Music - *See* Williams Music Group, Don
Slash Music - Los Angeles, CA - *BillIntBG 83-84*
Slash Records - Los Angeles, CA - *BillIntBG 83-84*
Slate Services - Westminster, CA - *BoPubDir 4, 5*
Slater, Carol - Ossining, NY - *LitMarPl 83, 84*
Slater Hanft Martin - New York, NY - *AdAge 3-28-84; StaDirAdAg 2-84*
Slater News-Rustler - Slater, MO - *BaconPubCkNews 84*
Slater Publishing - Garden Grove, CA - *BoPubDir 5*
Slater Tri-County Times - Slater, IA - *BaconPubCkNews 84; NewsDir 84*
Slatington News - Slatington, PA - *Ed&PubIntYB 82*
Slaton TV Cable Service [of Landmark Cablevision Associates] - Slaton, TX - *BrCabYB 84; Tel&CabFB 84C*
Slatonite - Slaton, TX - *AyerDirPub 83; BaconPubCkNews 84; Ed&PubIntYB 82*
Slatter/Banks Advertising Inc. - Branford, CT - *StaDirAdAg 2-84*
Slatton Stations, John - Haleyville, AL - *BrCabYB 84*
Slauf, Manley & Associates Inc. - Oak Brook, IL - *StaDirAdAg 2-84*
Slavia Library - State College, PA - *BoPubDir 4, 5*
Slavic Philology [of University of Alberta] - Edmonton, AB, Canada - *DataDirOnSer 84*
Slavica Publishers Inc. - Columbus, OH - *BoPubDir 4 Sup, 5; LitMarPl 83, 84; WritMar 84*
Slavin Design Consultants, Barry - Chicago, IL - *StaDirAdAg 2-84*
Slavuta Publishers - Edmonton, AB, Canada - *BoPubDir 4, 5*
Slaymaker & Associates - Indianapolis, IN - *DirPRFirms 83*
Slayton Murray County Herald - Slayton, MN - *BaconPubCkNews 84*
SLE Music - North Hollywood, CA - *BillIntBG 83-84*
Sled Software - Minneapolis, MN - *MicrocomMPl 83, 84*
Sledge Telephone Co. - Sunflower, MS - *TelDir&BG 83-84*
Sleeping Bear Software - Cincinnati, OH - *MicrocomSwDir 1; WhoWMicrocom 83*
Sleepy Deacon Ltd. - Los Angeles, CA - *BillIntBG 83-84*
Sleepy Eye CATV Inc. - Russell, MN - *BrCabYB 84*
Sleepy Eye CATV Inc. - Sleepy Eye, MN - *BrCabYB 84 p.D-307; Tel&CabFB 84C*
Sleepy Eye Herald-Dispatch - Sleepy Eye, MN - *BaconPubCkNews 84; Ed&PubIntYB 82*
Sleepy Eye Telephone Co. [Aff. of Ollig Utilities Co.] - Sleepy Eye, MN - *TelDir&BG 83-84*
Sleepy Hollow Press - Tarrytown, NY - *LitMag&SmPr 83-84; LitMarPl 83; WritMar 84*
Sleight of Word - Arleta, CA - *LitMarPl 83, 84*
Slesar & Manuela Inc. - New York, NY - *StaDirAdAg 2-84*
Slesinger Inc., Stephen - Tampa, FL - *TelAl 83, 84*
Slesinger, Yaranoff & Associates Advertising Inc. - Phoenix, AZ - *StaDirAdAg 2-84*
Slick - San Francisco, CA - *WritMar 84*
Slick, Myrna H. - Holsopple, PA - *BoPubDir 5*
Slick Press - Houston, TX - *LitMag&SmPr 83-84*
Slide Factor - West Roxbury, MA - *AvMarPl 83*
Slide Factory - San Francisco, CA - *AvMarPl 83*
Slide Strip Laboratory Inc. - New York, NY - *AvMarPl 83*
Slide Transfer Service Inc. - Atlantic Highlands, NJ - *AvMarPl 83*
Slidecraft Laboratories - South Bend, IN - *AvMarPl 83*

Slidell Daily Sentry-News - Slidell, LA - *BaconPubCkNews 84; NewsDir 84*
Slidell Daily Times [of Enterprise Group Inc.] - Slidell, LA - *BaconPubCkNews 84; NewsDir 84*
Slidemagic System Inc. - Wall, NJ - *AvMarPl 83*
Slidemakers Inc. - Los Angeles, CA - *AvMarPl 83*
Slidemakers Inc. - Springfield, NJ - *AvMarPl 83*
Slidemasters/Honolulu [Div. of Leo, Tanaka & Co.] - Honolulu, HI - *AvMarPl 83*
SlideScan [Div. of Windmill Productions] - Atlanta, GA - *AvMarPl 83*
Sliger Livingston Publications - Howell, MI - *BaconPubCkNews 84*
Sligos - Puteaux Cedex, France - *EISS 7-83 Sup*
Slimmer [of Playgirl Magazine] - Santa Monica, CA - *BaconPubCkMag 84; WritMar 84*
SLIMS Corp., The - Greensboro, NC - *DataDirSup 7-83*
Slingshot Music [Div. of TRC Corp.] - Indianapolis, IN - *BillIntBG 83-84*
Sliwa Enterprises Inc. - Hampton, VA - *MicrocomMPl 84; MicrocomSwDir 1*
Sloan Inc., Mike - Miami, FL - *AdAge 3-28-84; StaDirAdAg 2-84*
Sloan Management Review - Cambridge, MA - *MagIndMarPl 82-83*
Slohm Associates Inc., Natalie - Cambridge, NY - *BoPubDir 4, 5; LitMag&SmPr 83-84*
Slosson Educational Publications Inc. - East Aurora, NY - *MicrocomMPl 84*
Slough Press - Austin, TX - *LitMag&SmPr 83-84*
Slovak v Amerike - Middletown, PA - *Ed&PubIntYB 82; NewsDir 84*
Slovenska Drzava - Toronto, ON, Canada - *Ed&PubIntYB 82*
Slovensky Hlas - Windsor, ON, Canada - *Ed&PubIntYB 82*
Sloves Organization [Div. of The Franklin Mint] - New York, NY - *LitMarPl 83, 84*
Slow Baby Music - *See* Windham Hill Music
Slow Dancing Music Inc. - *See* Buttermilk Sky Music Publishing Corp.
Slow Loris Press - Pittsburgh, PA - *LitMag&SmPr 83-84*
Slow Loris Reader - Pittsburgh, PA - *LitMag&SmPr 83-84*
Slowpitch Tips - Lima, OH - *LitMag&SmPr 83-84*
SLR Productions - Hollywood, CA - *AvMarPl 83*
SLRS Communications Inc. - Athens, GA - *StaDirAdAg 2-84*
SLT Communications Inc. - Sugar Land, TX - *TelDir&BG 83-84*
Sludge [of NewsNet Inc.] - Bryn Mawr, PA - *DataDirOnSer 84*
Sludge Newsletter - Silver Spring, MD - *BaconPubCkMag 84; DirOnDB Spring 84*
Slurry Transport Association - Washington, DC - *BoPubDir 4, 5*
Slurzberg Research Inc., Lee - Ft. Lee, NJ - *BrCabYB 84; IntDirMarRes 83; Tel&CabFB 84C*
Slurzberg Research Inc., Lee - New York, NY - *MagIndMarPl 82-83*
SLUSA - Somerville, NJ - *BoPubDir 4, 5*
Sly-Fox Films Inc. - Minneapolis, MN - *AvMarPl 83*
SM/Strategic Marketing Facts for Decisions Inc. [Div. of BSI/Business Science International] - New York, NY - *IntDirMarRes 83*
Smackover Journal - Smackover, AR - *BaconPubCkNews 84; Ed&PubIntYB 82*
Small & Associates - Goodwood, ON, Canada - *BoPubDir 4, 5*
Small & Associates Inc., Peter - New York, NY - *DirPRFirms 83*
Small & Associates Ltd., Frank - Hong Kong - *IntDirMarRes 83*
Small Boat Journal, The - Bennington, VT - *BaconPubCkMag 84 p.D-307; MagDir 84*
Small Business Applications Inc. - Houston, TX - *WhoWMicrocom 83*
Small Business Book Service [of CBI Publishing Co. Inc.] - Boston, MA - *LitMarPl 83*
Small Business Book Service [Div. of Van Nostrand Reinhold Co. Inc.] - New York, NY - *LitMarPl 84*
Small Business Computer News [of Management Information Corp.] - Cherry Hill, NJ - *MicrocomMPl 84*
Small Business Computer Systems - Lincoln, NE - *MicrocomMPl 84; MicrocomSwDir 1; WhoWMicrocom 83*
Small Business Computers - Morris Plains, NJ - *MagIndMarPl 82-83*
Small Business Computers [of SBC Publishing Co.] - Upper Montclair, NJ - *BaconPubCkMag 84; MagDir 84*
Small Business Computers & Consulting - Santa Ana, CA - *MicrocomMPl 83*
Small Business Data Processing Corp. - Cincinnati, OH - *ADAPSOMemDir 83-84*
Small Business Database [of Control Data Corp.] - Minneapolis, MN - *CompReadDB 82*
Small Business Digest [of Costar Enterprises] - Pineville, WV - *MagDir 84*
Small Business Executive Report - Richboro, PA - *MagIndMarPl 82-83*
Small Business Publications Inc. - Hyannis, MA - *BoPubDir 4, 5*
Small Business Report - Monterey, CA - *BaconPubCkMag 84; DirMarMP 83*
Small Business Report - Hartford, CT - *BaconPubCkMag 84*
Small Business Reports - Chappaqua, NY - *DirOnDB Spring 84*
Small Business Reports [of CompuServe Inc.] - Columbus, OH - *DataDirOnSer 84*
Small Business Systems Group - Westford, MA - *WhoWMicrocom 83*
Small Business Systems Inc. - La Grange Park, IL - *MicrocomSwDir 1*
Small Business Tax Control - Arlington, VA - *MagIndMarPl 82-83*
Small Business Tax Review, The - Melville, NY - *DirOnDB Spring 84*
Small Business Technology Corp. - Sunnyvale, CA - *MicrocomMPl 84*
Small Businesswoman's Newsletter - Mt. Dora, FL - *LitMag&SmPr 83-84*
Small Cities Communications Inc. - Carrboro, NC - *Tel&CabFB 84C p.1702*
Small Computer Book Club [of Macmillan Book Clubs Inc.] - New York, NY - *LitMarPl 84*
Small Computer Co. Inc., The - New York, NY - *MicrocomSwDir 1*
Small Computer Program Index [of ALLM Books] - Watford, England - *EISS 83*
Small Computers in Libraries [of University of Arizona Graduate Library School] - Tucson, AZ - *EISS 7-83 Sup; MicrocomMPl 84*
Small Computers in the Arts News - Philadelphia, PA - *MicrocomMPl 84*
Small Farm Press - Dandridge, TN - *LitMag&SmPr 83-84*
Small Farm, The - Dandridge, TN - *LitMag&SmPr 83-84*
Small Newspapers - Kankakee, IL - *Ed&PubIntYB 82*
Small Pond Magazine of Literature, The - Stratford, CT - *ArtMar 84; LitMag&SmPr 83-84; WritMar 84*
Small Press Book Club, The [Subs. of Dust Books] - Paradise, CA - *LitMarPl 83, 84*
Small Press Distribution Inc. - Berkeley, CA - *BoPubDir 4 Sup, 5; LitMarPl 83, 84*
Small Press News [of Zahir] - New Sharon, ME - *LitMag&SmPr 83-84*
Small Press Review [of Dust Books] - Paradise, CA - *LitMag&SmPr 83-84; LitMarPl 83, 84; WritMar 84*
Small Press: The Magazine of Independent Book Publishing [of R. R. Bowker Co.] - New York, NY - *LitMarPl 84*
Small-Small Press - Rumford, ME - *LitMag&SmPr 83-84*
Small System Design - Hudson, NH - *MicrocomMPl 84*
Small System Design - Manchester, NH - *MicrocomMPl 83; MicrocomSwDir 1; WhoWMicrocom 83*
Small System Group - Santa Monica, CA - *DirInfWP 82*
Small System Services Inc. - Greensboro, NC - *WhoWMicrocom 83*
Small Systems World - Des Plaines, IL - *BaconPubCkMag 84; WritMar 84*
Small World [of Volkswagen of America] - Troy, MI - *ArtMar 84; WritMar 84*
Small World [of Earnshaw Publications Inc.] - New York, NY - *BaconPubCkMag 84; MagDir 84*
Small World Press Inc. - Northfield, MN - *BoPubDir 5*
Smallsystem Center, The - New Hartford, CT - *MicrocomMPl 83*
Smallwood & Co. - New York, NY - *LitMarPl 83*
Smallwood & Stewart - New York, NY - *LitMarPl 84*

Smart Communications Inc. - New York, NY - *DataDirOnSer 84; EISS 7-83 Sup; WhoWMicrocom 83*
Smart Data Processing [Div. of Smart Inc.] - Meriden, CT - *DataDirSup 7-83*
Smart Inc. - Meriden, CT - *DataDirSup 7-83*
Smart Inc. - Wilton, CT - *DataDirOnSer 84*
Smart Money - Old Tappan, NJ - *BaconPubCkMag 84*
Smart Shopper - Oak Brook, IL - *AyerDirPub 83*
Smart Systems Inc. - Frederick, MD - *MicrocomSwDir 1*
Smart Translators [of Smart Communications Inc.] - New York, NY - *DataDirOnSer 84; DirOnDB Spring 84*
Smartcopy Inc. - Milford, PA - *DataDirSup 7-83*
Smartware - Dayton, OH - *MicrocomMPl 83, 84; MicrocomSwDir 1; WhoWMicrocom 83*
Smason Public Relations, Edmund A. - Chicago, IL - *DirPRFirms 83*
SMC Software Systems Div. [of SMC Corp.] - Bridgewater, NJ - *DataDirSup 7-83; MicrocomMPl 84; MicrocomSwDir 1*
SMEAC [of SMEAC Information Reference Center] - Columbus, OH - *DataDirOnSer 84*
SMEAC Information Reference Center [of Ohio State University] - Columbus, OH - *DataDirOnSer 84*
Smee's Advertising Ltd. - London, England - *StaDirAdAg 2-84*
Smelkinson, Cerrati & Co. - Hilton Head Island, SC - *AdAge 3-28-84; DirPRFirms 83; StaDirAdAg 2-84*
Smeloff Teleproductions - Denver, CO - *Tel&CabFB 84C*
Smethport McKean County Miner - *See* McKean County Press Inc.
SMI Records Corp. - New York, NY - *BillIntBG 83-84*
Smiley/Hanchulak Inc. - Akron, OH - *StaDirAdAg 2-84*
Smillie/Concepts, Jeanne - Chicago, IL - *HBIndAd&MS 82-83*
Smirnoff Associates, Aaron - Ottawa, ON, Canada - *BoPubDir 4 Sup, 5*
Smith Advertising Agency, Allen R. - Woodsboro, MD - *StaDirAdAg 2-84*
Smith Advertising & Associates Inc. - Fayetteville, NC - *StaDirAdAg 2-84*
Smith Advertising Inc., C. W. - Tampa, FL - *StaDirAdAg 2-84*
Smith Advertising, Lee Robert - Atlanta, GA - *StaDirAdAg 2-84*
Smith & Associates - Charlotte, NC - *AdAge 3-28-84; StaDirAdAg 2-84*
Smith & Associates Inc., Greg - *See* Smith & Myers Inc.
Smith & Associates Inc., James G. - *See* Driscoll & Associates Inc., Mike
Smith & Associates Inc., M. F. - Bernardsville, NJ - *ADAPSOMemDir 83-84*
Smith & Associates, Kenneth C. - La Jolla, CA - *StaDirAdAg 2-84*
Smith & Co. - Somers Point, NJ - *StaDirAdAg 2-84*
Smith & Co. Inc., Jim R. - Sierra Vista, AZ - *BrCabYB 84 p.D-307; Tel&CabFB 84C p.1702*
Smith & Co. Inc., Kerry - White Plains, NY - *DirPRFirms 83*
Smith & Harroff Inc. - Washington, DC - *DirPRFirms 83*
Smith & Jennings Inc. - Little Rock, AR - *DirPRFirms 83; StaDirAdAg 2-84*
Smith & Myers Inc. - Santa Ana, CA - *DirPRFirms 83*
Smith & Sons, A. - Philadelphia, PA - *AvMarPl 83*
Smith & Yehle - Kansas City, MO - *AdAge 3-28-84; StaDirAdAg 2-84*
Smith Associates Inc., Donald S. - Anaheim, CA - *StaDirAdAg 2-84*
Smith Associates Inc., J. Greg - Lincoln, NE - *ArtMar 84; StaDirAdAg 2-84*
Smith Associates Ltd., Richard E. - New York, NY - *LitMarPl 83, 84*
Smith, Badofsky & Raffel - Chicago, IL - *AdAge 3-28-84; StaDirAdAg 2-84*
Smith/Bill Ramsey Associates Inc., J. Greg [Div. of J. Greg Smith Associates Inc.] - Omaha, NE - *StaDirAdAg 2-84*
Smith Books, Genny - Palo Alto, CA - *BoPubDir 4, 5; LitMag&SmPr 83-84*
Smith Broadcasting Inc. - Huntsville, AL - *BrCabYB 84*
Smith Burke & Azzam - Baltimore, MD - *AdAge 3-28-84; StaDirAdAg 2-84*
Smith Cable TV [of Marsh Media Inc.] - Smithville, TN - *Tel&CabFB 84C*
Smith Center Cable Television [of Great Plains Communications Systems Inc.] - Smith Center, KS - *BrCabYB 84; Tel&CabFB 84C*
Smith Center Smith County Pioneer - Smith Center, KS - *BaconPubCkNews 84; NewsDir 84*
Smith College (Museum of Art) - Northampton, MA - *BoPubDir 4, 5*
Smith Communications Inc., Al - Russellville, KY - *BaconPubCkNews 84*
Smith Communications Inc., T. D. - Omaha, NE - *WhoWMicrocom 83*
Smith Co., Donald L. - San Antonio, TX - *AvMarPl 83*
Smith Co. Inc., Marc - Severna Park, MD - *ArtMar 84; StaDirAdAg 2-84*
Smith Co. Inc., Wayne - Washington, DC - *DirPRFirms 83*
Smith Co., The Allen - Indianapolis, IN - *LitMarPl 83, 84; WritMar 84*
Smith Consultants Inc., Don - New York, NY - *DirPRFirms 83*
Smith-Corona [Subs. of SCM Corp.] - New Canaan, CT - *DirInfWP 82; MicrocomMPl 84; WhoWMicrocom 83*
Smith Corp., A. O. (Data Systems Div.) - Brown Deer, WI - *ADAPSOMemDir 83-84*
Smith, Cortland Gray - Plandome, NY - *BoPubDir 4, 5*
Smith County Pioneer - Smith Center, KS - *Ed&PubIntYB 82*
Smith County Reformer - Raleigh, MS - *AyerDirPub 83; Ed&PubIntYB 82*
Smith County Weekly - Tyler, TX - *AyerDirPub 83*
Smith Data Systems, A. O. [Div. of A. O. Smith Corp.] - Brown Deer, WI - *DataDirOnSer 84; DataDirSup 7-83*
Smith, Dean Lance - Houston, TX - *MicrocomSwDir 1*
Smith Design Inc., Edward - New York, NY - *LitMarPl 84*
Smith, Dorian & Burman Inc. - West Hartford, CT - *ArtMar 84; DirPRFirms 83; StaDirAdAg 2-84*
Smith, Doug - Corvallis, OR - *BoPubDir 4, 5*
Smith-Edwards-Dunlap Co. - Philadelphia, PA - *LitMarPl 83, 84*
Smith, Elliott Varner - Berkeley, CA - *LitMarPl 83, 84; MagIndMarPl 82-83*
Smith Enterprizes, Joan K. - Mt. Morris, MI - *BoPubDir 4, 5*
Smith Feature Service, Al - Bomoseen, VT - *Ed&PubIntYB 82*
Smith Fifth Avenue Agency Inc. - New York, NY - *IntDirMarRes 83*
Smith, Frank D. Jr. - Cartersville, GA - *BoPubDir 4, 5*
Smith, G. Lee & Donna - Ontario, OR - *BrCabYB 84 p.D-307*
Smith, George - Bright's Grove, ON, Canada - *BoPubDir 4, 5*
Smith/Greenland - New York, NY - *AdAge 3-28-84; BrCabYB 84; StaDirAdAg 2-84*
Smith Group, Ron - San Francisco, CA - *BoPubDir 4 Sup, 5*
Smith-Hemmings-Gosden - El Monte, CA - *AdAge 3-28-84; DirMarMP 83; StaDirAdAg 2-84*
Smith Interviewing Service Inc. - Oklahoma City, OK - *IntDirMarRes 83*
Smith, Kaplan, Allen & Reynolds Advertising Agency - Omaha, NE - *AdAge 3-28-84; ArtMar 84; DirMarMP 83; StaDirAdAg 2-84*
Smith Kaufman Public Relations - *See* Stockton West Burkhart Inc.
Smith Library of the Health Sciences, George F. [of College of Medicine & Dentistry of New Jersey] - Newark, NJ - *FBInfSer 80*
Smith Ltd., J. Richard - Old Bethpage, NY - *StaDirAdAg 2-84*
Smith Lithograph Corp. - Rockville, MD - *MagIndMarPl 82-83*
Smith Marketing Inc., Frederic - *See* Smithmark
Smith McNeal Advertising - Atlanta, GA - *StaDirAdAg 2-84*
Smith Micro Software - Sunset Beach, CA - *MicrocomMPl 84*
Smith Newspapers Inc. - Ft. Payne, AL - *Ed&PubIntYB 82*
Smith, Nicholas T. [Aff. of Walter W. Smith Inc.] - Bronxville, NY - *BoPubDir 4, 5*
Smith Office Machines Co. Inc. - Shreveport, LA - *WhoWMicrocom 83*
Smith Office Supply - Minneapolis, MN - *DirInfWP 82*
Smith, Patricia K. - Washington, DC - *FBInfSer 80*
Smith Personnel Service Inc. - New York, NY - *IntDirMarRes 83*
Smith, Phillips & Di Pietro - Yakima, WA - *StaDirAdAg 2-84*
Smith, Phoebe - Hapeville, GA - *BoPubDir 4, 5*
Smith Photography, Bradley [Div. of Gemini Smith Inc.] - La Jolla, CA - *AvMarPl 83; LitMarPl 83, 84; MagIndMarPl 82-83*

Smith Photography, Dick - North Conway, NH - *LitMarPl 83, 84; MagIndMarPl 82-83*
Smith Publisher Inc., Peter - Magnolia, MA - *LitMarPl 83, 84*
Smith Publishers Inc., W. H. [Subs. of W. H. Smith & Son Ltd.] - New York, NY - *LitMarPl 83, 84*
Smith Publishing Co., W. R. C. - Atlanta, GA - *MagIndMarPl 82-83*
Smith Publishing Corp., Patterson - Montclair, NJ - *LitMarPl 83, 84*
Smith Research Associates, Harry - New York, NY - *IntDirMarRes 83*
Smith, Roger W. - Jackson Heights, NY - *LitMarPl 84*
Smith, Ruth - New York, NY - *BoPubDir 4, 5*
Smith Secretarial Services - Denver, CO - *LitMarPl 84*
Smith, Smith & Smith Publishing Co. - Lake Oswego, OR - *BoPubDir 4, 5*
Smith, Stanley & Co. Inc. - Darien, CT - *IntDirMarRes 83*
Smith Stations, Bob - New Richmond, WI - *BrCabYB 84*
Smith Stations, Ted A. - Pendleton, OR - *BrCabYB 84*
Smith System Manufacturing Co. - St. Paul, MN - *AvMarPl 83*
Smith/Tarter & Co. - Amarillo, TX - *StaDirAdAg 2-84*
Smith, The [Subs. of The Generalist Association Inc.] - New York, NY - *LitMag&SmPr 83-84; LitMarPl 83, 84; WritMar 84*
Smith TV - Arcadia, LA - *Tel&CabFB 84C*
Smith Two-Way Radio - Fayetteville, AR - *Tel&CabFB 84C p.1702*
Smith Two Way Radio Inc. - Prairie Grove, AR - *BrCabYB 84*
Smith Two Way Radio Inc. - West Fork, AR - *BrCabYB 84*
Smith-Winchester Inc. - Southfield, MI - *StaDirAdAg 2-84*
Smith-Yehle - Kansas City, MO - *ArtMar 84*
Smithereens Press - Bolinas, CA - *LitMag&SmPr 83-84*
Smithereens Seasonal Sampler - Bolinas, CA - *LitMag&SmPr 83-84*
Smithers Community TV Line Inc. - Smithers, WV - *BrCabYB 84*
Smithfield Herald [of News & Observer Publishing Co.] - Smithfield, NC - *BaconPubCkNews 84; NewsDir 84*
Smithfield Herald, The - Johnson County, NC - *Ed&PubIntYB 82*
Smithfield Times - Smithfield, VA - *AyerDirPub 83; BaconPubCkNews 84; Ed&PubIntYB 82*
SmithKline Beckman - Fullerton, CA - *ElecNews 7-25-83*
Smithland Livingston Ledger - Smithland, KY - *BaconPubCkNews 84*
Smithmark - Birmingham, AL - *StaDirAdAg 2-84*
SmithRick Associates - Greer, SC - *MicrocomMPl 84*
Smiths Falls Cable Telecommunications Inc. - Smiths Falls, ON, Canada - *BrCabYB 84*
Smith's Fifth Avenue Agency - New York, NY - *InfIndMarPl 83; LitMarPl 83, 84; MagIndMarPl 82-83*
Smithsongs - Belleville, NJ - *BillIntBG 83-84*
Smithsonian [of Smithsonian Institution National Associates] - Washington, DC - *BaconPubCkMag 84; Folio 83; LitMarPl 83, 84; MagDir 84; MagIndMarPl 82-83; WritMar 84*
Smithsonian [of Smithsonian Institution] - New York, NY - *DirMarMP 83*
Smithsonian Books [Subs. of Smithsonian Institution Press] - Washington, DC - *DirMarMP 83*
Smithsonian Institution - Washington, DC - *AvMarPl 83*
Smithsonian Institution (Office of Museum Programs) - Washington, DC - *BoPubDir 5*
Smithsonian Institution (Performing Arts Div.) - Washington, DC - *BillIntBG 83-84*
Smithsonian Institution Press - Washington, DC - *LitMarPl 83, 84*
Smithsonian Science Information Exchange - Washington, DC - *BoPubDir 5; CompReadDB 82; DBBus 82*
Smithtown Messenger - Smithtown, NY - *BaconPubCkNews 84; Ed&PubIntYB 82; NewsDir 84*
Smithtown News - Smithtown, NY - *BaconPubCkNews 84; Ed&PubIntYB 82; NewsDir 84*
Smithtown-St. James Pennysaver - Huntington, NY - *AyerDirPub 83*
Smithville Bastrop County Times - Smithville, TX - *BaconPubCkNews 84*
Smithville Cable TV Inc. [of LBJ Co.] - Smithville, TX - *BrCabYB 84*
Smithville Democrat-Herald, The - Smithville, MO - *Ed&PubIntYB 82*
Smithville Lake Democrat-Herald - Smithville, MO - *AyerDirPub 83; BaconPubCkNews 84*
Smithville Review [of Morris Newspaper Corp.] - Smithville, TN - *AyerDirPub 83; BaconPubCkNews 84; Ed&PubIntYB 82; NewsDir 84*
Smithville Telephone Co. Inc. - Ellettsville, IN - *TelDir&BG 83-84*
Smithville Telephone Corp. - Smithville, MS - *TelDir&BG 83-84*
Smoke [of Windows Project] - Liverpool, England - *LitMag&SmPr 83-84*
Smoke Shop Press - Houston, TX - *LitMag&SmPr 83-84*
Smoke Signal Broadcasting - Westlake Village, CA - *MicrocomMPl 84; WhoWMicrocom 83*
Smoke Signals [of Black Market Press] - Brooklyn, NY - *LitMag&SmPr 83-84*
SmokeRoot - Missoula, MT - *LitMag&SmPr 83-84*
Smokeshop - New York, NY - *BaconPubCkMag 84; MagDir 84*
Smokestack Lightning Music - Hollywood, CA - *BillIntBG 83-84*
Smokestack Lightning Records - Hollywood, CA - *BillIntBG 83-84*
Smokey River Express - Falher, AB, Canada - *Ed&PubIntYB 82*
Smoky Lake Signal - Smoky Lake, AB, Canada - *AyerDirPub 83*
Smoky Mountain Times - Bryson City, NC - *Ed&PubIntYB 82*
Smoley & Sons Inc., C. K. - Grand Haven, MI - *BoPubDir 5; LitMag&SmPr 83-84*
Smoley & Sons Inc., C. K. - Chautauqua, NY - *BoPubDir 4*
Smoloskyp Inc. - Ellicott City, MD - *BoPubDir 4, 5*
Smootee Tunes Publishing - Brooklyn, NY - *BillIntBG 83-84*
Smooth Groove Music - Brooklyn, NY - *BillIntBG 83-84*
SMPTE Journal [of Society of Motion Picture & Television Engineers] - Scarsdale, NY - *BaconPubCkMag 84; MagDir 84; MagIndMarPl 82-83*
SMR Evaluations - Danvers, MA - *IntDirMarRes 83*
SMR News - Washington, DC - *DirOnDB Spring 84*
SMRB - New York, NY - *DirOnDB Spring 84*
SMS - Claremont, CA - *BoPubDir 4, 5*
SMS - Malvern, PA - *DataDirSup 7-83*
SMS Cable Co. - Carnegie, OK - *BrCabYB 84; Tel&CabFB 84C*
SMS Research Inc. - Honolulu, HI - *IntDirMarRes 83*
SMSA Building Permits - Bala Cynwyd, PA - *DirOnDB Spring 84*
SMSA Business Structures - Bala Cynwyd, PA - *DirOnDB Spring 84*
SMSA Employment - Bala Cynwyd, PA - *DirOnDB Spring 84*
SMSA Macro - Bala Cynwyd, PA - *DirOnDB Spring 84*
SMT Guild Inc. - Indianapolis, IN - *BoPubDir 4, 5*
SMU Press - Dallas, TX - *LitMag&SmPr 83-84*
Smuggler's Cove Publishing - Seattle, WA - *BoPubDir 4, 5*
Smullin, William B. - *See* California-Oregon Broadcasting Co.
SMY Inc. - Chicago, IL - *HBIndAd&MS 82-83; StaDirAdAg 2-84*
Smyrna Cable TV - Smyrna, GA - *BrCabYB 84; Tel&CabFB 84C*
Smyrna Neighbor - Marietta, GA - *AyerDirPub 83*
Smyrna Neighbor - Smyrna, GA - *Ed&PubIntYB 82*
Smyrna Neighbor, The - Stone Mountain, GA - *Ed&PubIntYB 82*
Smyrna Press - Brooklyn, NY - *BoPubDir 4, 5; LitMag&SmPr 83-84*
Smyrna Rutherford Courier - Smyrna, TN - *BaconPubCkNews 84; NewsDir 84*
Smyrna Times - Smyrna, DE - *BaconPubCkNews 84; Ed&PubIntYB 82*
Smyth Agency Inc. - Richmond, VA - *StaDirAdAg 2-84*
Smyth Business Systems Inc. - North Canton, OH - *DataDirSup 7-83*
Smyth Co. Inc., H. M. - St. Paul, MN - *LitMarPl 83, 84*
Smyth County News - Marion, VA - *AyerDirPub 83; Ed&PubIntYB 82*
Snack Food [of Harcourt Brace Jovanovich Publications] - Duluth, MN - *BaconPubCkMag 84; MagDir 84; WritMar 84*
Snail Records - Chicago, IL - *BillIntBG 83-84*
Snail's Pace: A Small Press - Garden Grove, CA - *BoPubDir 4 Sup, 5*
Snake Mountain Software - Raleigh, NC - *MicrocomMPl 84*
Snake Rattle & Roll - Austin, TX - *BoPubDir 4, 5*
Snake River Press - Craig, CO - *AyerDirPub 83; Ed&PubIntYB 82*
SNAP - Reseda, CA - *AvMarPl 83*
Snapdragon - Moscow, ID - *LitMag&SmPr 83-84*
Snapkat Productions Inc. - Azle, TX - *BillIntBG 83-84*

Snappware Inc. - Cincinnati, OH - *MicrocomMPl 84*
Snarf [of Kitchen Sink Press] - Princeton, WI - *LitMag&SmPr 83-84*
Snazelle Film Tape Inc. - San Francisco, CA - *AvMarPl 83*
Sneedville Cable TV Co. - Sneedville, TN - *BrCabYB 84; Tel&CabFB 84C*
Snell Associates Inc., George R. - Mountainside, NJ - *AvMarPl 83*
Snell Inc., H. Michael - Wayland, MA - *LitMarPl 83, 84*
Snelling & Snelling Inc. - New York, NY - *LitMarPl 83, 84; MagIndMarPl 82-83*
Snelson Advertising Inc. - Midland, TX - *StaDirAdAg 2-84*
Snips - Bellwood, IL - *BaconPubCkMag 84; MagDir 84; MagIndMarPl 82-83; WritMar 84*
Snohomish County Tribune - Snohomish, WA - *AyerDirPub 83; BaconPubCkNews 84; NewsDir 84*
Snoqualmie North Bend Valley Record - Snoqualmie, WA - *BaconPubCkNews 84; Ed&PubIntYB 82*
Snow & Depew Inc. - Amityville, NY - *StaDirAdAg 2-84*
Snow Bookmark Ltd. Press, Helen Foster [Aff. of Helen Foster Snow Literary Trust] - Madison, CT - *BoPubDir 4, 5*
Snow Goer [of The Webb Co.] - St. Paul, MN - *BaconPubCkMag 84; MagDir 84; MagIndMarPl 82-83; WritMar 84*
Snow Goer Trade - St. Paul, MN - *BaconPubCkMag 84*
Snow Hill Standard-Laconic - Snow Hill, NC - *BaconPubCkNews 84; Ed&PubIntYB 82*
Snow Man Press Ltd. - Victoria, BC, Canada - *BoPubDir 4, 5*
Snow Micro Systems Inc. - Fairfax, VA - *MicrocomMPl 84*
Snow Music - Los Angeles, CA - *BillIntBG 83-84*
Snow Press - Des Plaines, IL - *BoPubDir 4 Sup, 5; LitMag&SmPr 83-84*
Snow Productions Inc., Phoebe T. - New York, NY - *ArtMar 84; WritMar 84*
Snow Week - St. Paul, MN - *BaconPubCkMag 84*
Snowball Association of Canada - Lantzville, BC, Canada - *BoPubDir 4 Sup, 5*
Snowden Publishing Ltd., John & Diana - Hanover, ON, Canada - *BoPubDir 4 Sup, 5*
Snowfox Music - *See* Brown & Associates, J. Aaron
Snowmobile [of Winter Sports Publications Inc.] - Minneapolis, MN - *BaconPubCkMag 84; WritMar 84*
Snowmobile - Milwaukee, WI - *MagDir 84; MagIndMarPl 82-83*
Snowmobile Canada - Mississauga, ON, Canada - *BaconPubCkMag 84*
Snowmobile Canada [of CRV Publications Canada Ltd.] - Montreal, PQ, Canada - *WritMar 84*
Snowmobile Sports - Toronto, ON, Canada - *BaconPubCkMag 84*
Snowmobile West - Idaho Falls, ID - *BaconPubCkMag 84; MagDir 84; MagIndMarPl 82-83; WritMar 84*
Snowmobiler's Race & Rally - Alexandria, MN - *BaconPubCkMag 84*
Snowstorm Publications - Breckenridge, CO - *BoPubDir 4 Sup, 5*
Snowy Egret - Williamsburg, KY - *LitMag&SmPr 83-84; WritMar 84*
Snug Harbor Cultural Center Inc. - Staten Island, NY - *BoPubDir 4 Sup, 5*
Snugglebug Music Co. - *See* Snugglebush Music Co.
Snugglebush Music Co. - Beverly Hills, CA - *BillIntBG 83-84*
Snyder Advertising, Robert - Northfield, IL - *AdAge 3-28-84; StaDirAdAg 2-84*
Snyder & Co. Ltd., Joe - New York, NY - *ArtMar 84; DirPRFirms 83; WritMar 84*
Snyder Cablevision - Snyder, OK - *BrCabYB 84*
Snyder Community Antenna TV - Snyder, TX - *BrCabYB 84; Tel&CabFB 84C p.1702*
Snyder Enterprises, Ken - Santa Barbara, CA - *Tel&CabFB 84C*
Snyder Films Inc., Bill - Fargo, ND - *AvMarPl 83*
Snyder Institute of Research - Redondo Beach, CA - *BoPubDir 4, 5*
Snyder Kiowa County Democrat - Snyder, OK - *BaconPubCkNews 84*
Snyder, Mark - Brookville, NY - *StaDirAdAg 2-84*
Snyder News - Snyder, TX - *BaconPubCkNews 84; NewsDir 84*
Snyder Publications - Oakland, CA - *BaconPubCkNews 84*
Snyder Publishing - Ft. Myers, FL - *BoPubDir 4, 5*
Snyder Publishing Co. - Santa Rosa, CA - *BoPubDir 5*
Soabar [Div. of Avery International] - Philadelphia, PA - *DataDirSup 7-83*
Soap/Cosmetics/Chemical Specialties [of MacNair-Dorland Co.] - New York, NY - *BaconPubCkMag 84; MagDir 84; MagIndMarPl 82-83*
Soap Opera Digest [of Network Publishing Co.] - New York, NY - *Folio 83; MagDir 84; MagIndMarPl 82-83; WritMar 84*
Soap Opera World - New York, NY - *MagDir 84*
Soaring [of Soaring Society of America] - Los Angeles, CA - *ArtMar 84*
Soaring Society of America - Los Angeles, CA - *BoPubDir 5*
Soaring Symposia - Keyser, WV - *BoPubDir 4, 5*
Sobel Associates Inc., Nat - New York, NY - *LitMarPl 83, 84*
Sobel Knight Advertising Inc. [of Austin Knight Group] - San Rafael, CA - *StaDirAdAg 2-84*
Sobredo, Sergio - Miami, FL - *LitMarPl 83, 84*
Sobus & Partners Ltd., R. J. - Bethesda, MD - *IntDirMarRes 83*
Socadis Inc. - St. Laurent, PQ, Canada - *BoPubDir 4 Sup, 5*
Soccer America - Oakland, CA - *MagIndMarPl 82-83; WritMar 84*
Soccer Associates [Aff. of Australian Book Center & Sportshelf] - New Rochelle, NY - *LitMarPl 83, 84*
Soccer Corner - Burbank, CA - *MagDir 84*
Soccer Corner - Van Nuys, CA - *MagDir 84; MagIndMarPl 82-83*
Soccer Digest - Evanston, IL - *BaconPubCkMag 84; MagIndMarPl 82-83*
Soccer Magazine [of Holden-Lea Soccer Publications Ltd.] - Surrey, BC, Canada - *WritMar 84*
Sochurek Inc., Howard - New York, NY - *MagIndMarPl 82-83*
Sociaal-Wetenschappelijk Informatie-en Documentatiecentrum [of Koninklijke Nederlandse Akademie van Wetenschappen] - Amsterdam, Netherlands - *InfIndMarPl 83*
Social Analysis Laboratory [of State University of New York at Binghamton] - Binghamton, NY - *EISS 83*
Social Anarchism - Baltimore, MD - *LitMag&SmPr 83-84*
Social Area Research Inc. - Scarsdale, NY - *IntDirMarRes 83*
Social Casework: Journal of Contemporary Social Work - New York, NY - *MagIndMarPl 82-83*
Social Education - Washington, DC - *BaconPubCkMag 84; MagDir 84; MagIndMarPl 82-83*
Social Forces - Chapel Hill, NC - *MagIndMarPl 82-83*
Social Interest Press Inc., The - Wooster, OH - *LitMag&SmPr 83-84*
Social Justice Review - St. Louis, MO - *WritMar 84*
Social Policy - New York, NY - *ArtMar 84; LitMag&SmPr 83-84; MagIndMarPl 82-83*
Social Psychology Quarterly - Washington, DC - *MagDir 84*
Social Psychology Quarterly - Bloomington, IN - *MagIndMarPl 82-83*
Social Register Association - New York, NY - *BoPubDir 4, 5*
Social Research Inc. - Chicago, IL - *LitMarPl 83; Tel&CabFB 84C*
Social Science Computer Research Institute [of University of Pittsburgh] - Pittsburgh, PA - *EISS 83*
Social Science Consulting Service [of Dartmouth College] - Hanover, NH - *EISS 83*
Social Science Data Archive [of Yale University] - New Haven, CT - *EISS 83*
Social Science Data Archive [of University of Iowa] - Iowa City, IA - *EISS 83*
Social Science Data Archive [of University of Maine, Orono] - Orono, ME - *EISS 83*
Social Science Data Archives [of University of California, Los Angeles] - Los Angeles, CA - *EISS 83*
Social Science Data Archives [of Australian National University] - Canberra, Australia - *EISS 7-83 Sup*
Social Science Data Archives [of Carlton University] - Ottawa, ON, Canada - *EISS 83*
Social Science Data Base [of Ohio State University Libraries] - Columbus, OH - *CompReadDB 82*
Social Science Data Center [of University of Pennsylvania] - Philadelphia, PA - *EISS 83*
Social Science Data Center [of Brown University] - Providence, RI - *EISS 83*
Social Science Data Library [of University of North Carolina] - Chapel Hill, NC - *EISS 83*

Social Science Documentation Center [of United Nations Educational, Scientific, & Cultural Organization] - Paris, France - *EISS 83*
Social Science Documentation Centre [of Indian Council of Social Science Research] - New Delhi, India - *EISS 83*
Social Science Education Consortium Inc. - Boulder, CO - *BoPubDir 4, 5; WritMar 84*
Social Science Information & Documentation Center [of Royal Netherlands Academy of Arts & Sciences] - Amsterdam, Netherlands - *EISS 83*
Social Science Information System [of York University] - Downsview, ON, Canada - *CompReadDB 82*
Social Science Institute - Harborside, ME - *BoPubDir 4, 5*
Social Science User Services [of Princeton University] - Princeton, NJ - *EISS 83*
Social Sciences Citation Index [of Institute for Scientific Information] - Philadelphia, PA - *CompReadDB 82*
Social Sciences in Forestry [of Virginia Polytechnic Institute & State University] - Blacksburg, VA - *EISS 7-83 Sup*
Social Sciences Information Center [of Association of Social Sciences Institutes] - Bonn, West Germany - *EISS 83*
Social Scisearch [of Institute for Scientific Information] - Philadelphia, PA - *DataDirOnSer 84; DBBus 82; DirOnDB Spring 84; OnBibDB 3*
Social Studies School Service - Culver City, CA - *AvMarPl 83*
Social Work - New York, NY - *MagDir 84; MagIndMarPl 82-83*
Social Work Research & Abstracts [of National Association of Social Workers] - New York, NY - *EISS 83; MagIndMarPl 82-83*
Socialist Party of Canada - Victoria, BC, Canada - *BoPubDir 4, 5*
Sociedad International de Sonido - Coral Gables, FL - *BillIntBG 83-84*
Societe Canadienne du Microfilm Inc. - *See* Canadian Microfilming Co. Ltd.
Societe d'Editions Medico-Pharmaceutiques - *See* S.E.M.P.
Societe d'Etudes Marketing Marocaine - Casablanca, Morocco - *IntDirMarRes 83*
Societe Generale de Banque (Centre de Documentation) - Brussels, Belgium - *CompReadDB 82; InfIndMarPl 83*
Societe Generale de Services et de Gestion [of Centre d'Information Temps Reel Europe] - Paris, France - *InfIndMarPl 83*
Societe Historique de Quebec - Quebec, PQ, Canada - *BoPubDir 4, 5*
Society [of Rutgers University] - New Brunswick, NJ - *LitMarPl 83, 84; MagDir 84; MagIndMarPl 82-83*
Society for American Baseball Research Inc. - Cooperstown, NY - *BoPubDir 5*
Society for Animal Rights Inc. - Clarks Summit, PA - *BoPubDir 4, 5*
Society for Computer Applications in Engineering, Planning, & Architecture - Rockville, MD - *EISS 83*
Society for Industrial & Applied Mathematics - Philadelphia, PA - *BoPubDir 4, 5; MagIndMarPl 82-83*
Society for Industrial & Applied Mathematics - *See* SIAM
Society for Information & Documentation - Frankfurt, West Germany - *EISS 83*
Society for Management Information Systems - Chicago, IL - *EISS 83*
Society for Mathematics & Data Processing - Augustin, West Germany - *EISS 83*
Society for Neuroscience - Bethesda, MD - *BoPubDir 4, 5*
Society for New Language Study - Denver, CO - *BoPubDir 4, 5*
Society for Nutrition Education - Oakland, CA - *AvMarPl 83*
Society for Occupational & Environmental Health - Washington, DC - *BoPubDir 4, 5*
Society for Preserving & Encouraging the Arts & Knowledge of the Church Inc. - Eureka Springs, AR - *LitMarPl 84*
Society for Technical Communication - Washington, DC - *MicroMarPl 82-83*
Society for the Advancement of Material & Process Engineering - Azusa, CA - *BoPubDir 4, 5*
Society for the Promotion of Science & Scholarship Inc. - Palo Alto, CA - *BoPubDir 4, 5*
Society for the Protection of New Hampshire Forests - Concord, NH - *BoPubDir 4, 5*
Society for the Scientific Study of Religion Inc. - Storrs, CT - *BoPubDir 4, 5*
Society for the Study of Amphibians & Reptiles - Athens, OH - *BoPubDir 4 Sup, 5*
Society for the Study of Myth & Tradition, The - New York, NY - *LitMag&SmPr 83-84*
Society for Understanding Nature Inc. - Prescott, AZ - *BoPubDir 4, 5*
Society for Visual Education Inc. - Chicago, IL - *AvMarPl 83; MicrocomMPl 84*
Society for Worldwide Interbank Financial Telecommunication - Brussel, Belgium - *TeleSy&SerDir 7-83*
Society of Actuaries - Chicago, IL - *BoPubDir 4, 5*
Society of American Archivists - Chicago, IL - *BoPubDir 4, 5*
Society of Architectural Historians - Philadelphia, PA - *BoPubDir 4, 5*
Society of Authors - London, England - *LitMag&SmPr 83-84*
Society of Automotive Engineers Abstracts - Warrendale, PA - *CompReadDB 82; DBBus 82*
Society of Automotive Engineers Inc. - Warrendale, PA - *CompReadDB 82; DataDirOnSer 84; LitMarPl 83; MicroMarPl 82-83*
Society of Automotive Engineers Inc. (Publication & Information Services) - Warrendale, PA - *InfIndMarPl 83*
Society of Cable Television Engineers - Washington, DC - *BoPubDir 4*
Society of Cable Television Engineers - Alexandria, VA - *BoPubDir 5; InterCabHB 3*
Society of Exploration Geophysicists - Tulsa, OK - *BoPubDir 4 Sup, 5*
Society of Indexers - Cambridge, England - *InfIndMarPl 83*
Society of Industrial Realtors - Washington, DC - *BoPubDir 5*
Society of Management Accountants of Canada - Hamilton, ON, Canada - *BoPubDir 4, 5*
Society of Manufacturing Engineers - Dearborn, MI - *BoPubDir 4, 5; MicroMarPl 82-83*
Society of Mayflower Descendants in the State of RI & Providence Plantations - Warwick, RI - *BoPubDir 4, 5*
Society of Mining Engineers [of American Institute of Mining, Metallurgical, & Petroleum Engineers Inc.] - Littleton, CO - *BoPubDir 4, 5*
Society of Naval Architects & Marine Engineers - New York, NY - *BoPubDir 4, 5*
Society of Nuclear Medicine Inc. - New York, NY - *BoPubDir 4, 5*
Society of Petroleum Engineers Journal - Dallas, TX - *BaconPubCkMag 84; MagDir 84*
Society of Photo-Optical Instrumentation Engineers - Bellingham, WA - *BoPubDir 4, 5*
Society of Photographic Scientists & Engineers - Springfield, VA - *BoPubDir 4, 5*
Society of Pragmatic Mysticism - Pawlet, VT - *BoPubDir 4, 5*
Society of Real Estate Appraisers - Chicago, IL - *BoPubDir 4 Sup, 5*
Society of Satellite Professionals - Washington, DC - *TeleSy&SerDir 2-84*
Society of Spanish & Spanish-American Studies - Lincoln, NE - *BoPubDir 4, 5*
Society of Telecommunications Consultants - New York, NY - *TeleSy&SerDir 7-83*
Society of the Descendants of Washington's Army at Valley Forge - Valley Forge, PA - *BoPubDir 5*
Society of the Montreal Military & Maritime Museum - Montreal, PQ, Canada - *BoPubDir 4 Sup, 5*
Society of the Plastics Industry Inc. - New York, NY - *BoPubDir 4, 5*
Society Ordo Templi Orientis International - Nashville, TN - *LitMag&SmPr 83-84*
Socioeconomic Data Bank on the Mediterranean Countries [of International Center for Higher Studies in Mediterranean Agronomy] - Montpellier, France - *EISS 83*
Sociological Abstracts [of Dialog Information Services Inc.] - Palo Alto, CA - *DataDirOnSer 84*
Sociological Abstracts - San Diego, CA - *CompReadDB 82; DBBus 82; DirOnDB Spring 84; EISS 83; InfIndMarPl 83; OnBibDB 3*

Sociological Practice [of Progresiv Publishr] - Chicago, IL - *LitMag&SmPr 83-84*
Sociology [of Centre de Documentation Sciences Humaines] - Paris, France - *CompReadDB 82*
Sociology & Social Research - Los Angeles, CA - *MagDir 84*
Sociology of Education - Washington, DC - *MagDir 84*
Sociology Press - Mill Valley, CA - *BoPubDir 4, 5*
Socioscope Inc. - Ottawa, ON, Canada - *EISS 7-83 Sup; VideoDir 82-83*
Socorro Defensor-Chieftain - Socorro, NM - *BaconPubCkNews 84; Ed&PubIntYB 82*
Soda Springs Caribou County Sun - Soda Springs, ID - *BaconPubCkNews 84*
Soddy-Daisy Cable TV [of Athena Communications Corp.] - Soddy-Daisy, TN - *Tel&CabFB 84C*
Soderberg & Associates - Seattle, WA - *AdAge 3-28-84; StaDirAdAg 2-84*
Soderberg MacEwan Inc. - Seattle, WA - *ArtMar 84*
Sodsisky & Sons - Bethesda, MD - *LitMarPl 83, 84*
Sodtown Telephone Co. - Ravenna, NE - *TelDir&BG 83-84*
Sodus Record [of Empire State Weeklies] - Webster, NY - *NewsDir 84*
Sodus Record - *See* Empire State Weeklies
Sof/Sys Inc. - Minneapolis, MN - *MicrocomMPl 84; MicrocomSwDir 1*
Sofia Information - Sofia, Bulgaria - *ProGuPRSer 4*
Sofie - Meylan, France - *DirOnDB Spring 84*
Soflex Games - Lexington, MA - *MicrocomMPl 84*
Sofprotex - Belmont, CA - *MicrocomMPl 83, 84*
SOFRATEV - *See* Antiope
Sofsearch Software Locator Service [of CCS Inc.] - San Antonio, TX - *EISS 83*
Sofstar Inc. - Juno Beach, FL - *MicrocomMPl 83, 84; MicrocomSwDir 1*
Sofsys Inc. - Minneapolis, MN - *MicrocomMPl 83; WhoWMicrocom 83*
Soft Byte - Seattle, WA - *MicrocomSwDir 1*
Soft Energy Notes - San Francisco, CA - *BaconPubCkMag 84*
Soft Energy Wares - Point Arena, CA - *MicrocomMPl 84*
Soft Images - Mahwah, NJ - *MicrocomMPl 84; MicrocomSwDir 1*
Soft Kat Inc. - Van Nuys, CA - *MicrocomMPl 84*
Soft Lab - Sandy, UT - *MicrocomMPl 84; WhoWMicrocom 83*
Soft Need [of Expanded Media Editions] - Bonn, West Germany - *LitMag&SmPr 83-84*
Soft Point Co. - Carnegie, PA - *MicrocomMPl 84*
Soft Rent - Solana Beach, CA - *MicrocomMPl 84*
Soft Sector Marketing - Garden City, MI - *MicrocomMPl 83*
Soft Sectre - Plano, TX - *MicrocomSwDir 1*
Soft Spot Micro Systems - North Canton, CT - *MicrocomSwDir 1*
Soft Touch - Costa Mesa, CA - *MicrocomMPl 83, 84*
Soft Warehouse, The - Honolulu, HI - *MicrocomSwDir 1; WhoWMicrocom 83*
Soft-Way - San Diego, CA - *MicrocomMPl 84*
Softa Group Inc., The - Northfield, IL - *MicrocomMPl 84*
Softalk for the IBM Personal Computer [of Softalk Publishing Inc.] - North Hollywood, CA - *BaconPubCkMag 84; MicrocomMPl 84; WritMar 84*
Softape/Artsci Inc. - North Hollywood, CA - *MicrocomMPl 83; WhoWMicrocom 83*
Softball Illustrated - Lima, OH - *LitMag&SmPr 83-84*
Softbyte Computing - Wallingford, CT - *MicrocomMPl 83, 84*
Softcenter Industries - Pomona, CA - *MicrocomSwDir 1*
SoftCraft Inc. - Los Angeles, CA - *MicrocomMPl 84; MicrocomSwDir 1*
SoftCraft Inc. - Austin, TX - *MicrocomMPl 84; MicrocomSwDir 1; WhoWMicrocom 83*
Softech Inc. - Waltham, MA - *ADAPSOMemDir 83-84; DataDirSup 7-83; WhoWMicrocom 83*
Softech Microsystems Inc. [Subs. of Softech Inc.] - San Diego, CA - *MicrocomMPl 83, 84; MicrocomSwDir 1; WhoWMicrocom 83*
Softerware Inc. - Ft. Washington, PA - *MicrocomMPl 84*
Softhouse - Rochester, MN - *MicrocomMPl 83, 84*
Softline [of Softalk Publishing Inc.] - North Hollywood, CA - *BaconPubCkMag 84; MicrocomMPl 84*
Softlink Corp. - Santa Clara, CA - *ADAPSOMemDir 83-84; MicrocomMPl 84*
Softness Group Inc., The - New York, NY - *DirPRFirms 83*
Softool Systems - Denver, CO - *MicrocomMPl 84*
Softov Consultants - Toronto, ON, Canada - *MicrocomSwDir 1*
Softpak Associates - Marina Del Rey, CA - *MicrocomMPl 83*
Softquest Inc. - McLean, VA - *MicrocomMPl 84*
Softrend Inc. [Subs. of The Business Group Inc.] - Charlottesville, VA - *WhoWMicrocom 83*
Softron Inc. - New York, NY - *MicrocomMPl 84*
Softronics - Roosevelt, NJ - *MicrocomMPl 83, 84; WhoWMicrocom 83*
Softronics - Memphis, TN - *MicrocomSwDir 1*
Softronix - Charlotte, NC - *MicrocomMPl 83*
Softsel Computer Products Inc. - Inglewood, CA - *MicrocomMPl 83, 84; WhoWMicrocom 83*
Softshell - Baltimore, MD - *MicrocomMPl 84*
Softside - Milford, NH - *BaconPubCkMag 84; MicrocomMPl 83, 84; WritMar 84*
Softsmith Corp. - Union City, CA - *MicrocomMPl 84*
Softstalker - Steamboat Springs, CO - *MicrocomMPl 84*
Softsync - New York, NY - *MicrocomMPl 84; MicrocomSwDir 1; WhoWMicrocom 83*
Softwar III Co. - Sterling, IL - *MicrocomSwDir 1*
Software [of Fast Access] - Santa Monica, CA - *MicrocomMPl 84*
Software Access International Inc. - Mountain View, CA - *ADAPSOMemDir 83-84*
Software Affair - Sunnyvale, CA - *MicrocomMPl 84; WhoWMicrocom 83*
Software AG of North America Inc. - Reston, VA - *ADAPSOMemDir 83-84; DataDirSup 7-83; EISS 83*
Software Arts - Wellesley, MA - *MicrocomMPl 84; MicrocomSwDir 1*
Software Association, The - Houston, TX - *WhoWMicrocom 83*
Software Authority, The - Sunnyvale, CA - *ADAPSOMemDir 83-84*
Software Banc - Arlington, MA - *MicrocomMPl 83*
Software by H - Hillsboro Beach, FL - *MicrocomMPl 84*
Software Canada - Toronto, ON, Canada - *BaconPubCkMag 84*
Software Concepts - Dallas, TX - *MicrocomMPl 83, 84; WhoWMicrocom 83*
Software Connection, The - Silver Spring, MD - *MicrocomMPl 83, 84*
Software Connections - Santa Clara, CA - *MicrocomMPl 84; MicrocomSwDir 1*
Software Consultation, Design, & Production - Tujunga, CA - *WhoWMicrocom 83*
Software Consulting Services - Allentown, PA - *DirInfWP 82; WhoWMicrocom 83*
Software Consulting Services - Bethlehem, PA - *MicrocomMPl 84; MicrocomSwDir 1*
Software Consulting Services - Kennewick, WA - *MicrocomMPl 83, 84*
Software Corp. - Jackson, MI - *MicrocomMPl 84*
Software Data Systems - West Orange, NJ - *MicrocomMPl 83, 84*
Software Design Associates Inc. - New York, NY - *ADAPSOMemDir 83-84; DataDirSup 7-83*
Software Development & Training Inc. - Huntsville, AL - *WhoWMicrocom 83*
Software Development Association - Phoenix, AZ - *MicrocomMPl 84*
Software Development Corp. - Woodbridge, CT - *MicrocomMPl 84; MicrocomSwDir 1*
Software Digest - Annandale, VA - *BaconPubCkMag 84*
Software Dimensions Inc. - Citrus Heights, CA - *MicrocomMPl 83; MicrocomSwDir 1*
Software Dimensions Inc. - Folsom, CA - *MicrocomMPl 84*
Software Dimensions Inc. - San Jose, CA - *WhoWMicrocom 83*
Software Distribution Services - Buffalo, NY - *MicrocomMPl 84*
Software Distributors - Culver City, CA - *MicrocomMPl 83, 84*
Software Dynamics - Anaheim, CA - *DataDirSup 7-83; MicrocomMPl 83, 84; MicrocomSwDir 1; WhoWMicrocom 83*
Software Dynamics - Birmingham, MI - *ADAPSOMemDir 83-84*
Software Engineering Bibliographic Database [of Illinois Institute of Technology Research Institute] - Rome, NY - *CompReadDB 82*
Software Engineering Research Projects Database [of Data & Analysis Center for Software] - Franklin Springs, NY - *CompReadDB 82*

Software Engineering Systems Inc. - Lubbock, TX - *WhoWMicrocom 83*
Software Establishment, The - Newbury Park, CA - *MicrocomSwDir 1*
Software Establishment, The [Subs. of Infinet Inc.] - Westlake Village, CA - *MicrocomMPl 83; WhoWMicrocom 83*
Software Exchange, The - Milford, NH - *MicrocomMPl 83*
Software Federation Inc. - Arlington Heights, IL - *MicrocomMPl 83, 84*
Software Firm Inc. - Denver, CO - *MicrocomMPl 83*
Software Group - Anaheim, CA - *MicrocomMPl 83; WhoWMicrocom 83*
SoftWare House Inc. [Subs. of CDS Corp.] - Logan, UT - *WhoWMicrocom 83*
Software Hows [Subs. of MicroDaSys Inc.] - Los Angeles, CA - *MicrocomMPl 83; WhoWMicrocom 83*
Software Industries - Richardson, TX - *WhoWMicrocom 83*
Software Ireland - New York, NY - *MicrocomMPl 84*
Software Ireland Ltd. - Belfast, Ireland - *MicrocomSwDir 1*
Software Laboratories Inc. - San Bernardino, CA - *ADAPSOMemDir 83-84*
Software Laboratories Inc. - Dublin, OH - *MicrocomMPl 84; MicrocomSwDir 1*
Software Management Group Inc. - Miami, FL - *MicrocomMPl 84*
Software Masters - Houston, TX - *MicrocomMPl 84*
Software Merchandising [of Eastman Publishing] - Encino, CA - *BaconPubCkMag 84; MicrocomMPl 84*
Software Module Marketing - Sacramento, CA - *ADAPSOMemDir 83-84; DataDirSup 7-83; MicrocomSwDir 1*
Software News [of Technical Publishing Co.] - Hudson, MA - *BaconPubCkMag 84; MicrocomMPl 84*
Software Options Inc. - New York, NY - *MicrocomMPl 84*
Software Plantation - Tacoma, WA - *MicrocomMPl 83, 84*
Software Productions - Columbus, OH - *MicrocomMPl 84*
Software Products International - San Diego, CA - *MicrocomMPl 84*
Software Projections Inc. [Subs. of Polymer Projection Inc.] - Flourtown, PA - *MicrocomMPl 84*
Software Publishing Corp. - Mountain View, CA - *MicrocomMPl 83, 84; MicrocomSwDir 1*
Software Publishing Corp. - Palo Alto, CA - *WhoWMicrocom 83*
Software Publishing Report [of Knowledge Industries Publications Inc.] - White Plains, NY - *BaconPubCkMag 84; MicrocomMPl 84*
Software Pursuits Inc. - San Francisco, CA - *ADAPSOMemDir 83-84; DataDirSup 7-83*
Software Quality Associates - Palo Alto, CA - *MicrocomSwDir 1*
Software Research Co. - Irvine, CA - *MicrocomSwDir 1*
Software Resource - San Rafael, CA - *MicrocomMPl 84*
Software Resources Inc. - Cambridge, MA - *MicrocomMPl 84; MicrocomSwDir 1; WhoWMicrocom 83*
Software Retailing - Dover, NJ - *BaconPubCkMag 84*
Software Review [of Meckler Publishing] - Westport, CT - *MicrocomMPl 84*
Software Review Corp. - York, PA - *WhoWMicrocom 83*
Software Sciences Ltd. - Farnborough, England - *MicrocomSwDir 1*
Software Services of America Inc. - Lawrence, MA - *DataDirSup 7-83*
Software Solutions - Scotts Valley, CA - *WhoWMicrocom 83*
Software Solutions - Stratford, CT - *WhoWMicrocom 83*
Software Sorcery - McLean, VA - *MicrocomMPl 83, 84; MicrocomSwDir 1*
Software Store Ltd., The - Marquette, MI - *MicrocomMPl 83, 84; MicrocomSwDir 1; WhoWMicrocom 83*
Software Street - Chino, CA - *MicrocomMPl 83*
Software Supply Corp. - Tampa, FL - *MicrocomMPl 83*
Software Systems Ltd. - Portland, OR - *MicrocomMPl 84*
Software Technology for Computers - Belmont, MA - *MicrocomMPl 83, 84; WhoWMicrocom 83*
Software Technology Inc. - Lincoln, NE - *MicrocomMPl 84; WhoWMicrocom 83*
Software 1040 - New Hyde Park, NY - *MicrocomMPl 84; WhoWMicrocom 83*
Software III - Sterling, IL - *MicrocomMPl 84*
Software Toolworks - Sherman Oaks, CA - *MicrocomMPl 83, 84; MicrocomSwDir 1*
Software 2000 Inc. - Arroyo Grande, CA - *WhoWMicrocom 83*
Software Wholesalers Inc. - Avon, MA - *MicrocomMPl 84*
Software Wizardry Inc. - St. Charles, MO - *MicrocomMPl 83, 84*
Software Works Inc., The - Palo Alto, CA - *MicrocomMPl 83, 84*
Softwarehouse International - Clovis, CA - *MicrocomMPl 83*
Softworks Inc. - Scottsdale, AZ - *WhoWMicrocom 83*
Softworks Ltd. - Chicago, IL - *MicrocomMPl 83, 84; WhoWMicrocom 83*
Softworx Inc. - Seattle, WA - *WhoWMicrocom 83*
Soghigian & Macuga Advertising - Washington, DC - *AdAge 3-28-84; StaDirAdAg 2-84*
Sogides Ltee. - Montreal, PQ, Canada - *BoPubDir 4, 5*
Soho Bodhi - New York, NY - *BoPubDir 4, 5*
Soho Broadcasting - Los Angeles, CA - *BrCabYB 84*
Soho News - New York, NY - *Ed&PubIntYB 82*
Soho Repertory Theatre - New York, NY - *WritMar 84*
Soil Mechanics Information Analysis Center [of U.S. Army] - Vicksburg, MS - *EISS 83*
Soil Science [of Williams & Wilkins Co.] - New Brunswick, NJ - *BaconPubCkMag 84; MagDir 84*
Soil Science Society of America - Madison, WI - *BoPubDir 4, 5*
Soil Science Society of America Journal - Madison, WI - *BaconPubCkMag 84; MagDir 84*
Soil Staff [of U.S. Dept. of Agriculture] - Lanham, MD - *EISS 83*
Soil Studies Service [of National Institute of Agronomic Research] - Montpellier, France - *EISS 83*
Soils & Fertilizers [of Commonwealth Bureau of Soils] - Harpenden, England - *CompReadDB 82*
Sojourn - New York, NY - *BaconPubCkMag 84*
Sojourner - Cambridge, MA - *LitMag&SmPr 83-84*
Sojourners - Washington, DC - *LitMarPl 84*
Sokit Music - Dayton, OH - *BillIntBG 83-84*
Sokol Polski - Pittsburgh, PA - *NewsDir 84*
Sokol Times - Orange, NJ - *Ed&PubIntYB 82*
Sokolinsky, Martin - Brooklyn, NY - *LitMarPl 83, 84; MagIndMarPl 82-83*
Sol International Records/River Records - Orangevale, CA - *BillIntBG 83-84*
Sol Press - Madison, WI - *LitMag&SmPr 83-84*
Sola Electric [Subs. of General Signal] - Elk Grove Village, IL - *DirInfWP 82; WhoWMicrocom 83*
Sola Gratia - *See* Schabraf Music
Sola Scriptura Songs [Div. of Ark Records] - Tigard, OR - *BillIntBG 83-84*
Solana Beach Citizen - Solana Beach, CA - *BaconPubCkNews 84*
Solana Beach/Del Mar Pennysaver - Mission Viejo, CA - *AyerDirPub 83*
Solar Age [of SolarVision Inc.] - Harrisville, NH - *ArtMar 84; BaconPubCkMag 84; MagDir 84; MagIndMarPl 82-83; WritMar 84*
Solar Age Press - Indian Mills, WV - *BoPubDir 4, 5*
Solar & Wind Energy Research Program [of University of Alberta] - Edmonton, AB, Canada - *DataDirOnSer 84*
Solar & Wind Energy Research Program (Information Centre) - Edmonton, AB, Canada - *EISS 83*
Solar Data - Hampton, NH - *BoPubDir 4, 5*
Solar Energy - Cambridge, MA - *BaconPubCkMag 84*
Solar Energy Business & Marketing Report - New York, NY - *BaconPubCkMag 84*
Solar Energy in Architecture - Irvine, CA - *BoPubDir 4, 5*
Solar Energy Industries Association - Washington, DC - *BoPubDir 5*
Solar Energy Information Data Bank [of Solar Energy Research Institute] - Golden, CO - *DBBus 82*
Solar Energy Information Services - Sacramento, CA - *InfIndMarPl 83*
Solar Energy Information Services - San Mateo, CA - *FBInfSer 80*
Solar Energy Intelligence Report - Silver Spring, MD - *BaconPubCkMag 84; DirOnDB Spring 84*
Solar Energy Intelligence Report [of NewsNet Inc.] - Bryn Mawr, PA - *DataDirOnSer 84*

Solar Energy Research Institute [Subs. of Mid-West Research Institute] - Golden, CO - *CompReadDB 82; DataDirOnSer 84*
Solar Energy Research Institute (Technical Information Office) - Golden, CO - *CompReadDB 82*
Solar Engineering & Contracting - Troy, MI - *BaconPubCkMag 84*
Solar Flashes - Alamosa, CO - *LitMag&SmPr 83-84*
Solar Heating & Cooling [of Gordon Publications Inc.] - Morristown, NJ - *MagDir 84*
Solar Information Systems Program [of Solar Energy Research Institute] - Golden, CO - *EISS 83*
Solar Press Inc. - Naperville, IL - *MagIndMarPl 82-83*
Solar Products & Manufacturers Data Base [of Solar Energy Research Institute] - Golden, CO - *CompReadDB 82*
Solar Records - Los Angeles, CA - *BillIntBG 83-84*
Solar Satellite Communications Inc. - Denver, CO - *Tel&CabFB 84C*
Solar Systems Music - New York, NY - *BillIntBG 83-84*
Solarcon Inc. - Ann Arbor, MI - *BoPubDir 5*
Solaris Press - Rochester, MI - *LitMarPl 83, 84*
Solarsoft Inc. [Div. of Kinetic Software Inc.] - Snowmass, CO - *MicrocomMPl 84*
Solartek - Guilderland, NY - *WhoWMicrocom 83*
Solartek - West Hurley, NY - *MicrocomMPl 83, 84; MicrocomSwDir 1*
Solarz Co., The Sanford - Trenton, NJ - *StaDirAdAg 2-84*
Soldier Book Club [Subs. of Sky Books International Inc.] - New York, NY - *LitMarPl 83, 84*
Soldier Creek Press - Lake Crystal, MN - *BoPubDir 4, 5; LitMarPl 84*
Soldier of Fortune [of Omega Group Ltd.] - Boulder, CO - *MagIndMarPl 82-83; WritMar 84*
Soldiers Magazine - Alexandria, VA - *ArtMar 84; MagDir 84*
Soledad Bee - Soledad, CA - *Ed&PubIntYB 82*
Soledad Bee - *See* Casey Newspapers Inc.
Solem & Associates - San Francisco, CA - *StaDirAdAg 2-84*
Solemene & Associates - Dallas, TX - *StaDirAdAg 2-84*
Solia - Detroit, MI - *Ed&PubIntYB 82*
Solid Smoke Records - San Francisco, CA - *BillIntBG 83-84*
Solid Smoke Songs - San Francisco, CA - *BillIntBG 83-84*
Solid Software Inc. - Atlanta, GA - *MicrocomMPl 84; WhoWMicrocom 83*
Solid State Abstracts [of Cambridge Scientific Abstracts] - Bethesda, MD - *EISS 83*
Solid State Div. [of RCA Corp.] - Somerville, NJ - *Tel&CabFB 84C*
Solid State Systems Inc. - Marietta, GA - *DataDirSup 7-83; DirInfWP 82*
Solid State Technology [of Technical Publishing] - Port Washington, NY - *BaconPubCkMag 84; MagDir 84; MagIndMarPl 82-83*
Solid State Technology Inc. - Woburn, MA - *WhoWMicrocom 83*
Solid Waste Council of the Paper Industry - Washington, DC - *BoPubDir 5*
Solid Waste Management [of QL Systems Ltd.] - Ottawa, ON, Canada - *CompReadDB 82; DataDirOnSer 84; DirOnDB Spring 84*
Solid Waste Report - Silver Spring, MD - *BaconPubCkMag 84*
Solid Wastes Management - Atlanta, GA - *MagIndMarPl 82-83*
Solidarity - Carle Place, NY - *MagIndMarPl 82-83*
Solidarity Magazine [of United Auto Workers] - Detroit, MI - *ArtMar 84*
Solidarity Publications - San Francisco, CA - *BoPubDir 5; LitMag&SmPr 83-84; LitMarPl 84*
Solidstate Controls Inc. - Columbus, OH - *DataDirSup 7-83*
Solidus International Corp. - Bellingham, WA - *MicrocomMPl 84; MicrocomSwDir 1*
Solidus International Corp. - North Vancouver, BC, Canada - *WhoWMicrocom 83*
Solis - Bonn, West Germany - *DirOnDB Spring 84*
Solis-Navarro, Kelly - Menlo Park, CA - *LitMarPl 84*
Solk & Associates Inc., Bud - Chicago, IL - *StaDirAdAg 2-84*
Solo [of Solo Enterprises] - El Segundo, CA - *BaconPubCkMag 84*
Solo [of Solo Ministries Inc.] - Tulsa, OK - *BaconPubCkMag 84*
Solo [of Solo Ministries Inc.] - Sisters, OR - *WritMar 84*
Solo Music Inc. - Sherman Oaks, CA - *BillIntBG 83-84; BoPubDir 4, 5*
Solo News Network Inc. - Atlanta, GA - *Ed&PubIntYB 82*
Solo Press [Aff. of India Inc.] - Atascadero, CA - *BoPubDir 4, 5*
Solomen Agency, The - Studio City, CA - *DirPRFirms 83*
Solomon & Associates Advertising Inc., Robert - Bloomfield Hills, MI - *StaDirAdAg 2-84*
Solomon, Elisabeth F. S. - Greens Farms, CT - *Ed&PubIntYB 82*
Solomon Preview, The - Solomon, KS - *Ed&PubIntYB 82*
Solomon Valley Post - Beloit, KS - *AyerDirPub 83; Ed&PubIntYB 82*
Solon Consultants - London, England - *FBInfSer 80*
Solon Economist - Solon, IA - *BaconPubCkNews 84; Ed&PubIntYB 82*
Solon Springs Telephone Co. Inc. [Aff. of Universal Telephone Inc.] - Frederic, WI - *TelDir&BG 83-84*
Solon Times, The [of The Chagrin Valley Publishing Co.] - Chagrin Falls, OH - *NewsDir 84*
Solow Creative Service Inc., Martin - New York, NY - *HBIndAd&MS 82-83*
Solpub Co. [Aff. of Solar Church of Universal Life] - Bryan, TX - *BoPubDir 4*
Solpub Co. [Aff. of Solar Church of Universal Life] - Houston, TX - *BoPubDir 5*
Soltec Corp. - Sun Valley, CA - *MicrocomMPl 84; WhoWMicrocom 83*
Solters/Roskin/Friedman Inc. - New York, NY - *DirPRFirms 83*
Solumatics Inc. - White Plains, NY - *ADAPSOMemDir 83-84*
Solus Impress - Sirdar, BC, Canada - *BoPubDir 4, 5*
Solutek Corp. - Boston, MA - *AvMarPl 83*
Solution Software Systems - Mt. Prospect, IL - *MicrocomSwDir 1*
Solution Systems Inc. - Narberth, PA - *ADAPSOMemDir 83-84*
Solutions - Peoria, IL - *BaconPubCkMag 84; MagDir 84*
Solutions Inc. - Sea Cliff, NY - *IntDirMarRes 83*
Solutions Inc. - Montpelier, VT - *MicrocomMPl 84; MicrocomSwDir 1; WhoWMicrocom 83*
Solvang Santa Ynez Valley News - Solvang, CA - *NewsDir 84*
Solway-Camillus Pennysaver - Syracuse, NY - *AyerDirPub 83*
Soma Advertising Agency - Portland, OR - *StaDirAdAg 2-84*
Somat Publishing Ltd. - New York, NY - *Tel&CabFB 84C*
Some Other Magazine - Wayne, NJ - *LitMag&SmPr 83-84*
Somerset Cable TV Co. - Morganfield, KY - *BrCabYB 84*
Somerset Cable TV Co. - Somerset, KY - *BrCabYB 84*
Somerset Commonwealth-Journal - Somerset, KY - *BaconPubCkNews 84; NewsDir 84*
Somerset County Cable Associates [of Tele-Media Corp.] - Berlin, PA - *BrCabYB 84*
Somerset County Cable TV - Berlin, PA - *Tel&CabFB 84C*
Somerset County Shopper - Somerset, PA - *AyerDirPub 83*
Somerset Daily American - Somerset, PA - *NewsDir 84*
Somerset-Franklin News Record - *See* Princeton Packet Inc.
Somerset House - *See* Chadwyck-Healey Inc.
Somerset Messenger-Gazette - Somerville, NJ - *AyerDirPub 83; Ed&PubIntYB 82*
Somerset Observer - Somerset, KY - *BaconPubCkNews 84*
Somerset Press - Bound Brook, NJ - *BaconPubCkNews 84*
Somerset Press - *See* Hope Publishing Co.
Somerset Reporter, The - Skowhegan, ME - *Ed&PubIntYB 82*
Somerset Spectator - Fall River, MA - *NewsDir 84*
Somerset Spectator - Somerset, NJ - *BaconPubCkNews 84; Ed&PubIntYB 82; NewsDir 84*
Somerset Spectator - *See* Hathaway Publishing Corp.
Somerset Star - Prescott, WI - *AyerDirPub 83*
Somerset Star - Somerset, WI - *Ed&PubIntYB 82*
Somerset Star - *See* Weekly Newspapers Inc.
Somerset Telephone Co. [Aff. of Telephone & Data Systems Inc.] - North Anson, ME - *TelDir&BG 83-84*
Somerset Telephone Co. Inc. - Somerset, WI - *TelDir&BG 83-84*
Somersworth-Berwicks Free Press [of Rochester Courier Publishing Co.] - Rochester, NH - *NewsDir 84*
Somerville Fayette Falcon - Somerville, TN - *BaconPubCkNews 84*
Somerville Journal - West Somerville, MA - *Ed&PubIntYB 82; NewsDir 84*
Somerville Journal - *See* Dole Publishing Co. Inc.
Somerville Somerset Messenger Gazette [of Somerset Press Inc.] - Somerville, NJ - *BaconPubCkNews 84; NewsDir 84*
Somerville Tribune - Somerville, TX - *Ed&PubIntYB 82*

Somerville Tribune - *See* Burleson County Publishing Co. Inc.
Somesuch Press - Dallas, TX - *BoPubDir 4 Sup, 5; LitMag&SmPr 83-84*
Sommer Inc. - Englewood, NJ - *AdAge 3-28-84; StaDirAdAg 2-84*
Sommer Inc., Elyse - Woodmere, NY - *LitMarPl 83, 84*
Sommers, Henry J. - Silver Spring, MD - *BillIntBG 83-84*
Sommers/Rosen Inc. - Philadelphia, PA - *DirPRFirms 83*
Sommerville Communications Corp. - Richmond, MI - *BaconPubCkNews 84*
Somrie Press - Brooklyn, NY - *BoPubDir 4, 5; LitMag&SmPr 83-84*
Son-Deane Publishers - Hartsdale, NY - *BillIntBG 83-84*
Son-Ton Music Co. - Fostoria, OH - *BillIntBG 83-84*
Sonante Publications - Toronto, ON, Canada - *BoPubDir 4, 5*
Sonata Records - San Diego, CA - *BillIntBG 83-84*
Sonberg Book Services, Lynn - New York, NY - *LitMarPl 83, 84*
S'one Songs - Cockeysville, MD - *BillIntBG 83-84*
Song - Stevens Point, WI - *LitMag&SmPr 83-84*
Song Farm Music - Nashville, TN - *BillIntBG 83-84*
Song Hits - Derby, CT - *MagDir 84*
Song of Kong Music - *See* Publishing Ventures Inc.
Song of Songs Music - Langhorne, PA - *BillIntBG 83-84*
Song Press - Stevens Point, WI - *LitMag&SmPr 83-84*
Song Songs - Santa Monica, CA - *BillIntBG 83-84*
Song Tailors Music Co. - *See* I've Got the Music Co.
Song Yard Music - *See* Tree International
Songbird Agency, The - Kirtland, OH - *StaDirAdAg 2-84*
Songbud Music - *See* Budd Music Corp.
Songfest Music Corp. - *See* Gil Music Corp.
Songpainter Music - *See* Tree International
Songs for Real [Div. of Real Records Inc.] - Bogalusa, LA - *BillIntBG 83-84*
Songs for Today Inc. - New York, NY - *BillIntBG 83-84*
Songs from the Box - Memphis, TN - *BillIntBG 83-84*
Songs of a Servant - Jackson, MS - *WritMar 84*
Songs of Bandier-Koppelman - *See* Entertainment Co. Music Group, The
Songs of Manhattan Island Music Co. - *See* Entertainment Co. Music Group, The
Songs of the Southland - *See* Short Rose Music
Songsellers Co. [Div. of Aloft Music Enterprises Inc.] - New York, NY - *BillIntBG 83-84*
Songsmith Journal, The - Chicago, IL - *LitMag&SmPr 83-84*
Songsmith Society - Chicago, IL - *LitMag&SmPr 83-84*
Songwriters Records - Santa Cruz, CA - *BillIntBG 83-84*
Sonic Arts Corp. - San Francisco, CA - *AvMarPl 83; BillIntBG 83-84*
Sonic Cable TV - Arroyo Grande, CA - *Tel&CabFB 84C*
Sonic Cable TV - Capitola, CA - *BrCabYB 84*
Sonic Cable TV - Dixon, CA - *Tel&CabFB 84C*
Sonic Cable TV - Los Angeles, CA - *Tel&CabFB 84C p.1702*
Sonic Cable TV - Morro Bay, CA - *Tel&CabFB 84C*
Sonic Cable TV - Riverbank, CA - *Tel&CabFB 84C*
Sonic Cable TV - San Luis Obispo, CA - *BrCabYB 84 p.D-307*
Sonic Cable TV - Watsonville, CA - *BrCabYB 84; Tel&CabFB 84C*
Sonic Cable TV of Auburn - Auburn, CA - *Tel&CabFB 84C*
Sonic Cable TV of Woodland - Woodland, CA - *Tel&CabFB 84C*
Sonic Wave Records - Chicago, IL - *BillIntBG 83-84*
Sonica Press [Aff. of Haywater Concepts of California Inc.] - Los Angeles, CA - *BoPubDir 4, 5; LitMag&SmPr 83-84*
Sonics Super Channel [of Seattle SuperSonics] - Seattle, WA - *CabTVPrDB 83*
Sonlife Music Co. [Div. of Paul Johnson Music Productions Inc.] - Woodland Hills, CA - *BillIntBG 83-84*
Sonlight Christian Newspapers - Lake Worth, FL - *WritMar 84*
Sonnenreich, Joseph I. - New York, NY - *StaDirAdAg 2-84*
Sonney Amusement Enterprises Inc. - Los Angeles, CA - *TelAl 83, 84*
Sonntagpost - Chicago, IL - *AyerDirPub 83; NewsDir 84*
Sono Nis Press [Div. of Morriss Publishing Ltd.] - Victoria, BC, Canada - *BoPubDir 4; LitMarPl 83, 84*
Sono Publishers - Los Angeles, CA - *BoPubDir 4, 5*
Sonocraft Corp. - New York, NY - *AvMarPl 83*
Sonoma Classified Gazette - Santa Rosa, CA - *AyerDirPub 83*
Sonoma County Bike Trails - Penngrove, CA - *BoPubDir 4, 5*
Sonoma County Daily Herald-Recorder [of Herald Publishing Co.] - Santa Rosa, CA - *Ed&PubIntYB 82; NewsDir 84*
Sonoma Index Tribune - Sonoma, CA - *BaconPubCkNews 84; Ed&PubIntYB 82; NewsDir 84*
Sonoma Mandala - Rohnert Park, CA - *LitMag&SmPr 83-84*
Sonoma Valley Historical Society - Sonoma, CA - *BoPubDir 4, 5*
Sonoma Valley Shopping News & Penny Pincher - Sonoma, CA - *AyerDirPub 83*
SONOR Productions Inc. - Gretna, LA - *BillIntBG 83-84*
Sonora Devil's River News - Sonora, TX - *BaconPubCkNews 84*
Sonora Review - Tucson, AZ - *LitMag&SmPr 83-84*
Sonora Union Democrat - Sonora, CA - *BaconPubCkNews 84; NewsDir 84*
Sonrise Mercantile Corp. - Hollywood, CA - *BillIntBG 83-84*
Sons of Italy Times [of Grand Lodge of Pennsylvania Order Sons of Italy in America] - Philadelphia, PA - *Ed&PubIntYB 82; NewsDir 84*
Sons of Liberty Books [Aff. of New Christian Crusade Church] - Metairie, LA - *BoPubDir 4 Sup, 5*
Sonstein On Wines, Bill - Elkins Park, PA - *Ed&PubIntYB 82*
Sontheimer-Hazlett Ltd. - New York, NY - *DirPRFirms 83*
Sony Corp. of America - Park Ridge, NJ - *BillIntBG 83-84; HomeVid&CabYB 82-83; MicrocomMPl 84*
Sony Corp. of America - New York, NY - *InfoS 83-84; TelAl 83, 84; VideoDir 82-83*
Sony Corp. of America (Office Products Div.) - New York, NY - *DirInfWP 82*
Sony Ltd. (Communication Systems Div.) - Sunbury-on-Thames, England - *InfIndMarPl 83*
Sony Microcomputer Products [Subs. of Sony Corp. of America] - Park Ridge, NJ - *WhoWMicrocom 83*
Sony Video Communications [Div. of Sony Corp. of America] - Park Ridge, NJ - *AvMarPl 83*
Sonyatone Records - Santa Barbara, CA - *BillIntBG 83-84*
Soo Cable TV Co. [of Apollo Communications Inc.] - South Sioux City, NE - *BrCabYB 84; Tel&CabFB 84C*
Sooland Cablecom Corp. [of Capital Cities Communications Inc.] - Sioux City, IA - *BrCabYB 84; Tel&CabFB 84C*
Sooner Catholic, The [of Archdiocese of Oklahoma] - Oklahoma City, OK - *NewsDir 84*
Sooner CATV System Inc. - Lone Grove, OK - *Tel&CabFB 84C*
Sooner LPG Times [of Oklahoma Liquefied Petroleum Gas Association] - Oklahoma City, OK - *ArtMar 84; BaconPubCkMag 84; MagDir 84*
Sooner State Telephone Co. - Oklahoma City, OK - *TelDir&BG 83-84*
Soot Publications, Granny - Vancouver, BC, Canada - *BoPubDir 4 Sup, 5*
Soper Sound Music Library [Subs. of International Media Marketing Inc.] - Palo Alto, CA - *AvMarPl 83*
Soperton News - Soperton, GA - *BaconPubCkNews 84; Ed&PubIntYB 82*
Sophisticated Data Research Inc. - Atlanta, GA - *DataDirOnSer 84; EISS 83; IntDirMarRes 83*
Sophisticated Microsystems Inc. - Northfield, IL - *MicrocomMPl 83, 84*
Sophisticated Software - La Canada, CA - *MicrocomMPl 84*
Soque Publishers - Clarkesville, GA - *BoPubDir 5*
Sorbus Service Div. [of MAI International Corp.] - Frazer, PA - *DataDirSup 7-83*
Sorcim Corp. - San Jose, CA - *ADAPSOMemDir 83-84; MicrocomMPl 84; WhoWMicrocom 83*
Sorel-O-Vision Inc. - Sorel, PQ, Canada - *BrCabYB 84*
Sorell Inc., Carole - New York, NY - *DirPRFirms 83*
Sorensen, Chris - New York, NY - *LitMarPl 83, 84; MagIndMarPl 82-83*
Sorensen/Evans Advertising Inc. - Dallas, TX - *AdAge 3-28-84; StaDirAdAg 2-84*
Sorenson Broadcasting Corp. - Pierre, SD - *BrCabYB 84*
Sorento News - Sorento, IL - *BaconPubCkNews 84; Ed&PubIntYB 82; NewsDir 84*
Sorg Paper Co., The - Middletown, OH - *LitMarPl 83, 84; MagIndMarPl 82-83*
Sorgel-Lee Inc. - Milwaukee, WI - *ArtMar 84*
Sorites Group Inc., The - Springfield, VA - *MicrocomMPl 84*

Sorkin-Enenstein Research Service Inc. - Chicago, IL - *IntDirMarRes 83*
Soroc Technology Inc. - Anaheim, CA - *DataDirSup 7-83; InfIndMarPl 83; WhoWMicrocom 83*
Sorrento Valley Associates - San Diego, CA - *MicrocomMPl 83*
S.O.S. Books - Washington, DC - *LitMag&SmPr 83-84*
S.O.S. Directory Inc. - Jacksonville, FL - *BoPubDir 4, 5*
SOS Electronics - Cottonwood, ID - *BrCabYB 84; Tel&CabFB 84C*
SOS Productions Ltd. - New York, NY - *BillIntBG 83-84*
SOS Publications [Subs. of Bradley Products] - Los Angeles, CA - *WritMar 84*
So's Your Old Lady - Minneapolis, MN - *BoPubDir 4, 5*
Sosa & Associates - San Antonio, TX - *StaDirAdAg 2-84*
Soskin/Thompson Associates [Div. of J. Walter Thompson U.S.A. Inc.] - New York, NY - *DirMarMP 83; LitMarPl 83, 84*
Soskin/Thompson Associates - *See* Thompson U.S.A. Inc., J. Walter
SoSoft Ltd. - Poole, England - *MicrocomSwDir 1*
Sotera Inc., Frank P. - New York, NY - *StaDirAdAg 2-84*
Sotnick, Claire - New York, NY - *LitMarPl 83; MagIndMarPl 82-83*
Sotres Link Ltd. - New York, NY - *LitMarPl 83, 84*
Souderton Independent - Souderton, PA - *BaconPubCkNews 84; Ed&PubIntYB 82; NewsDir 84*
Souham Group of Communication Cos., Gerard - Paris, France - *DirPRFirms 83*
Souhegan Cablevision Corp. [of Americable Inc.] - Merrimack, NH - *BrCabYB 84; Tel&CabFB 84C*
Soul - Beverly Hills, CA - *MagIndMarPl 82-83*
Soul - Los Angeles, CA - *MagDir 84*
Soul Teen - Hollywood, CA - *MagIndMarPl 82-83*
Soules Book Publishers, Gordon - Vancouver, BC, Canada - *BoPubDir 4, 5*
Sound Advertising - Massapequa, NY - *StaDirAdAg 2-84*
Sound Advice Enterprises - Roslyn Heights, NY - *LitMag&SmPr 83-84*
Sound & Communications - New York, NY - *BaconPubCkMag 84; MagDir 84*
Sound & Vibration - Bay Village, OH - *BaconPubCkMag 84; MagIndMarPl 82-83*
Sound & Vibration [of Acoustical Publications Inc.] - Cleveland, OH - *MagDir 84*
Sound & Video Contractor - Overland Park, KS - *BaconPubCkMag 84*
Sound Approach - Huntington Station, NY - *BillIntBG 83-84*
Sound Arts Merchandising Journal - Carle Place, NY - *BaconPubCkMag 84*
Sound Canada - Markham, ON, Canada - *BaconPubCkMag 84*
Sound Column Cos., The - Salt Lake City, UT - *BillIntBG 83-84*
Sound-Craft Systems Inc. - Morrilton, AR - *AvMarPl 83*
Sound Electronics Inc. - Lafayette, LA - *Tel&CabFB 84C*
Sound Heights Recording Studios - Brooklyn, NY - *AvMarPl 83*
Sound Hound Inc. - New York, NY - *AvMarPl 83*
Sound Image Entertainment Inc. - North Hollywood, CA - *BillIntBG 83-84*
Sound Image Music - New Haven, MI - *BillIntBG 83-84*
Sound Image Publishing - *See* Sound Image Music
Sound Inc. Music - New Haven, MI - *BillIntBG 83-84*
Sound of New York Records - New York, NY - *BillIntBG 83-84*
Sound of Nolan Music - *See* Nolan Publishing Co., Kenny
Sound Patrol Ltd., The - New York, NY - *AvMarPl 83*
Sound Photo Film Laboratories Inc. - Lubbock, TX - *AvMarPl 83*
Sound Publishing Co. Inc. - New York, NY - *BoPubDir 4, 5*
Sound Records Inc. - New Haven, MI - *BillIntBG 83-84*
Sound Service, The - San Francisco, CA - *AvMarPl 83*
Sound South Records Inc. - Charleston, SC - *BillIntBG 83-84*
Sound Stage Studios Inc. - Nashville, TN - *BillIntBG 83-84*
Sound Syndicate - Los Angeles, CA - *BillIntBG 83-84*
Sound Technique Inc. - New York, NY - *AvMarPl 83*
Sound/Video Impressions Inc. - Des Plaines, IL - *AvMarPl 83*
Sounder, The - Random Lake, WI - *AyerDirPub 83; Ed&PubIntYB 82*
Soundings - Essex, CT - *BaconPubCkMag 84; MagDir 84; WritMar 84*
Soundings: An Interdisciplinary Journal - Nashville, TN - *MagIndMarPl 82-83*
Soundings/East - Salem, MA - *LitMag&SmPr 83-84*
Soundlab Inc. - Hialeah, FL - *AvMarPl 83*
Soundmark Ltd. - Denver, CO - *AvMarPl 83*
Sounds Ambient Music Inc. - Queens, NY - *BillIntBG 83-84*
Sounds of Memphis Inc. - Memphis, TN - *BillIntBG 83-84*
Sounds of Memphis Publishing - *See* Beckie Publishing Co.
Sounds of Winchester - Winchester, VA - *BillIntBG 83-84*
Soundwave International Inc. - Los Angeles, CA - *BillIntBG 83-84*
Soundwaves Records - Nashville, TN - *BillIntBG 83-84*
Soundwords Inc. - Bayside, NY - *AvMarPl 83*
Source - Boca Raton, FL - *DirOnDB Spring 84*
Source [of NewsNet Inc.] - Bryn Mawr, PA - *DataDirOnSer 84*
Source Books - San Diego, CA - *BoPubDir 4, 5*
Source Books Toronto - Toronto, ON, Canada - *BoPubDir 4, 5*
Source Communications - Grand Rapids, MI - *AvMarPl 83; Tel&CabFB 84C*
Source/Inc. - Chicago, IL - *DirPRFirms 83; HBIndAd&MS 82-83*
Source Records - Los Angeles, CA - *BillIntBG 83-84*
Source Records - Chicago, IL - *BillIntBG 83-84*
Source System Inc. - Addison, IL - *WhoWMicrocom 83*
Source Technologies - Mukilteo, WA - *AvMarPl 83*
Source Telecomputing Corp. [Subs. of The Reader's Digest Association Inc.] - McLean, VA - *DataDirOnSer 84; DataDirSup 7-83; HomeVid&CabYB 82-83; InfoS 83-84; InterCabHB 3; VideoDir 82-83*
Source, The [of Source Telecomputing Corp.] - McLean, VA - *DataDirOnSer 84; DBBus 82; EISS 83; MicrocomMPl 84; TeleSy&SerDir 2-84*
Source, The - Montreal, PQ, Canada - *Ed&PubIntYB 82*
Source, The - *See* Dimensions Unltd.
Source Unltd., The - New York, NY - *BillIntBG 83-84*
Sourcebook Project - Glen Arm, MD - *BoPubDir 4, 5*
Sourcebook Publications Inc. - Winter Park, FL - *BoPubDir 4, 5*
SourceNet - Santa Barbara, CA - *LitMag&SmPr 83-84*
Sources - Atlanta, GA - *LitMag&SmPr 83-84*
Sources - Hopewell, NJ - *BoPubDir 4, 5*
Sources Unltd. - Norman, OK - *EISS 5-84 Sup*
Souris Plaindealer - Souris, MB, Canada - *AyerDirPub 83; Ed&PubIntYB 82*
Souris River Telephone Mutual Aid Cooperative - Berthold, ND - *BrCabYB 84*
Souris River Telephone Mutual Aid Cooperative - Minot, ND - *Tel&CabFB 84C p.1702; TelDir&BG 83-84*
Souris River Telephone Mutual Aid Cooperative - Westhope, ND - *BrCabYB 84*
Souris Valley Cable TV - Minot, ND - *Tel&CabFB 84C*
Souris Valley Cable TV - Minot Air Force Base, ND - *BrCabYB 84*
South Advertiser [of Menomonee Falls Publishing Co.] - Menomonee Falls, WI - *NewsDir 84*
South Africa [of Chase Econometrics/Interactive Data Corp.] - Waltham, MA - *DataDirOnSer 84*
South African Advertising Research Foundation [of Interactive Market Systems] - New York, NY - *DataDirOnSer 84*
South African Advertising Research Foundation - Johannesburg, South Africa - *DirOnDB Spring 84*
South African Online User Group [of Centre for Scientific & Technical Information] - Pretoria, South Africa - *InfIndMarPl 83*
South African Water Information Centre - Pretoria, South Africa - *CompReadDB 82; InfIndMarPl 83*
South Alabamian, The - Jackson, AL - *AyerDirPub 83; Ed&PubIntYB 82; NewsDir 84*
South Amboy Citizen - South Amboy, NJ - *BaconPubCkNews 84; Ed&PubIntYB 82*
South American Advertising [Div. of Inter Media] - Coral Gables, FL - *Ed&PubIntYB 82*
South American Explorer - Denver, CO - *LitMag&SmPr 83-84*
South & West Telephone Co. Inc. - Sandborn, IN - *TelDir&BG 83-84*
South Antelope Valley Foothill News - Littlerock, CA - *AyerDirPub 83; Ed&PubIntYB 82*
South Arkansas Accent - Hampton, AR - *Ed&PubIntYB 82*
South Arkansas Telephone Co. Inc. - Hampton, AR - *TelDir&BG 83-84*
South Asia Books - Columbia, MO - *BoPubDir 4, 5*

South Atlantic Quarterly - Durham, NC - *MagDir 84*
South Bay Word Processing - San Diego, CA - *MicrocomMPl 84*
South Bay's Newspaper - Lindenhurst, NY - *AyerDirPub 83*
South Bay's Shopper [of South Bay's Newspapers] - Lindenhurst, NY - *NewsDir 84*
South Bay's Shopping Newspaper - Lindenhurst, NY - *AyerDirPub 83*
South Bend Journal & Harbor Pilot - South Bend, WA - *Ed&PubIntYB 82*
South Bend Tri-County News - South Bend, IN - *BaconPubCkNews 84; NewsDir 84*
South Bend Tribune [of Schurz Communications Inc.] - South Bend, IN - *BaconPubCkNews 84; Ed&PubIntYB 82; LitMarPl 83, 84; NewsDir 84*
South Benton Star-Press - Blairstown, IA - *Ed&PubIntYB 82*
South Bergenite - Rutherford, NJ - *AyerDirPub 83; Ed&PubIntYB 82*
South Boston Gazette Virginian - South Boston, VA - *BaconPubCkNews 84; Ed&PubIntYB 82; NewsDir 84*
South Boston News & Record - South Boston, VA - *BaconPubCkNews 84; NewsDir 84*
South Boston Tribune - South Boston, MA - *AyerDirPub 83; Ed&PubIntYB 82; NewsDir 84*
South Brunswick Central Post - *See* Princeton Packet Inc.
South Buffalo News - Buffalo, NY - *Ed&PubIntYB 82*
South Buffalo News [of Front Page Inc.] - Lackawanna, NY - *NewsDir 84*
South Buffalo Review - Buffalo, NY - *Ed&PubIntYB 82*
South Buffalo Review [of Leader Publishing Co.] - Lackawanna, NY - *AyerDirPub 83; NewsDir 84*
South Buffalo-West Seneca News - Buffalo, NY - *AyerDirPub 83*
South California E/C News [of Bender Publications Inc.] - Los Angeles, CA - *MagDir 84*
South Canaan Telephone Co., The - South Canaan, PA - *TelDir&BG 83-84*
South Carolina Dental Bulletin - Columbia, SC - *MagDir 84*
South Carolina Dept. of Archives & History - Columbia, SC - *MicroMarPl 82-83*
South Carolina Educational Television Network - Columbia, SC - *WritMar 84*
South Carolina Farmer - Columbia, SC - *BaconPubCkMag 84; MagDir 84*
South Carolina Food Journal - Columbia, SC - *BaconPubCkMag 84*
South Carolina Review - Clemson, SC - *LitMag&SmPr 83-84*
South Carolina Telephone Corp. [Aff. of Mid Continent Telephone Corp.] - Lexington, SC - *TelDir&BG 83-84*
South Carolina Wildlife - Columbia, SC - *ArtMar 84; WritMar 84*
South Carroll Herald - Sykesville, MD - *AyerDirPub 83*
South Cayuga Tribune-Union - King Ferry, NY - *Ed&PubIntYB 82*
South Central Bell Telephone Co. - Birmingham, AL - *TelDir&BG 83-84*
South Central Communications Corp. - Evansville, IN - *BrCabYB 84*
South Central Research Library Council - Ithaca, NY - *EISS 83*
South Central Rural Telephone Cooperative Corp. Inc. - Glasgow, KY - *TelDir&BG 83-84*
South Central Telephone Association Inc. - Medicine Lodge, KS - *TelDir&BG 83-84*
South Central Uthal Telephone Association Inc. - Escalante, TX - *TelDir&BG 83-84*
South Charleston Sentinel - London, OH - *BaconPubCkNews 84*
South Coast Week - Coos Bay, OR - *Ed&PubIntYB 82*
South Coaster - Largo, FL - *AyerDirPub 83*
South County Advertiser - Everman, TX - *AyerDirPub 83*
South County Cablevision - Hobe Sound, FL - *Tel&CabFB 84C*
South County Journal [of St. Louis Suburban Newspapers Inc.] - St. Louis, MO - *AyerDirPub 83; Ed&PubIntYB 82; NewsDir 84*
South County Publications - Auburn, IL - *BaconPubCkNews 84*
South Dade News [of South Miami Community Newspapers] - Miami, FL - *AyerDirPub 83; NewsDir 84*
South Dade News - *See* Community Newspapers of Florida Inc.
South Dade News Leader [of Homestead News Inc.] - Homestead, FL - *AyerDirPub 83; BaconPubCkNews 84; Ed&PubIntYB 82; NewsDir 84*
South Dakota Cable Inc. - Belle Fourche, SD - *BrCabYB 84*
South Dakota Cable Inc. - Central City, SD - *BrCabYB 84*
South Dakota Cable Inc. - Deadwood, SD - *Tel&CabFB 84C p.1702*
South Dakota Cable Inc. - Spearfish, SD - *BrCabYB 84*
South Dakota Independent Oil Jobber - Pierre, SD - *BaconPubCkMag 84*
South Dakota Journal of Medicine - Sioux Falls, SD - *BaconPubCkMag 84; MagDir 84*
South Dakota Mail - Plankinton, SD - *Ed&PubIntYB 82*
South Dakota Medical Information Exchange [of University of South Dakota] - Sioux Falls, SD - *TeleSy&SerDir 7-83*
South Dakota Motor Carrier - Sioux Falls, SD - *MagDir 84*
South Dakota Municipalities [of South Dakota Municipal League] - Pierre, SD - *BaconPubCkMag 84; MagDir 84*
South Dakota Review - Vermillion, SD - *LitMag&SmPr 83-84; WritMar 84*
South Dakota State University (South Dakota Memorial Art Center) - Brookings, SD - *BoPubDir 4, 5*
South Dakota Stock Grower - Rapid City, SD - *BaconPubCkMag 84; MagDir 84*
South Dakota Trucking News - Sioux Falls, SD - *BaconPubCkMag 84*
South Dekalb Neighbor - Clarkston, GA - *Ed&PubIntYB 82*
South Dekalb Neighbor - Marietta, GA - *AyerDirPub 83*
South District Journal - Seattle, WA - *AyerDirPub 83*
South District Journal - *See* News-Journal Inc.
South Dutchess Beacon Pennysaver - Yorktown Heights, NY - *AyerDirPub 83*
South East Lance - St.-Boniface, MB, Canada - *Ed&PubIntYB 82*
South East Metro Shopper [of Washington County Bulletin] - Cottage Grove, MN - *NewsDir 84*
South End News - Cleveland, OH - *AyerDirPub 83*
South End Press - Boston, MA - *LitMag&SmPr 83-84; LitMarPl 83, 84; WritMar 84*
South End, The [of Wayne State University] - Warren, MI - *NewsDir 84*
South Florida Cable Television - Bonita Springs, FL - *BrCabYB 84; Tel&CabFB 84C*
South Florida Communications Inc. - Bonita Springs, FL - *Tel&CabFB 84C*
South Florida Living [of Baker Publications Inc.] - Deerfield Beach, FL - *BaconPubCkMag 84; WritMar 84*
South Florida Living - Dallas, TX - *MagIndMarPl 82-83*
South Florida Online Searchers - Miami, FL - *InfIndMarPl 83*
South Fork Times - South Fork, CO - *BaconPubCkNews 84; Ed&PubIntYB 82*
South Fulton Argus, The - Astoria, IL - *Ed&PubIntYB 82*
South Fulton Neighbor, The - College Park, GA - *Ed&PubIntYB 82; NewsDir 84*
South Fulton Neighbor, The - Hapeville, GA - *Ed&PubIntYB 82*
South Fulton Neighbor, The - Marietta, GA - *AyerDirPub 83*
South Gate Press - South Gate, CA - *Ed&PubIntYB 82; NewsDir 84*
South Gate Press - *See* Hearst Community Newspapers
South Georgia Telephone Co. Inc. [Aff. of Continental Telephone Corp.] - Sylvania, GA - *TelDir&BG 83-84*
South Hamilton Publishing Inc. - Jewell, IA - *BoPubDir 4 Sup, 5*
South Hamilton Record News - Jewell, IA - *AyerDirPub 83*
South Hanover Cablevision Inc. - Hershey, PA - *BrCabYB 84*
South Hardin Signal-Review, The - Hubbard, IA - *Ed&PubIntYB 82*
South Haven New Era - Conway Springs, KS - *BaconPubCkNews 84*
South Haven New Era - South Haven, KS - *Ed&PubIntYB 82*
South Haven Tribune - South Haven, MI - *BaconPubCkNews 84; Ed&PubIntYB 82; NewsDir 84*
South Head Press - Berrima, Australia - *LitMag&SmPr 83-84*
South Hempstead Computer - South Hempstead, NY - *MicrocomMPl 84*
South Hill Enterprise - South Hill, VA - *BaconPubCkNews 84; NewsDir 84*
South Hills Computer Center Inc. - Pittsburgh, PA - *ADAPSOMemDir 83-84*
South Hills Record - Pittsburgh, PA - *AyerDirPub 83*
South Hills Record, The - South Hills, PA - *Ed&PubIntYB 82*
South Hills TV Cable Co. [of Adelphia Communications Corp.] - Peters Township, PA - *Tel&CabFB 84C*

South Holland Pointer [of Daily Southtown Economist Newspapers] - Chicago, IL - *NewsDir 84*
South Holland Pointer Economist - South Holland, IL - *AyerDirPub 83; Ed&PubIntYB 82*
South Holland Pointer-Economist - *See* Pointer-Economist Newspapers
South Holland Star/Tribune [of Oak Forest Star Herald Publications] - Chicago Heights, IL - *NewsDir 84*
South Holland Star-Tribune - South Holland, IL - *AyerDirPub 83*
South Holland Star/Tribune - *See* Star Publications
South Huntington Pennysaver - Huntington, NY - *AyerDirPub 83*
South Idaho Press - Burley, ID - *AyerDirPub 83; BaconPubCkNews 84; Ed&PubIntYB 82*
South Jefferson Sentinel - *See* Sentinel Newspapers
South Jersey Advisor (Atlantic City Edition) - Cologne, NJ - *AyerDirPub 83*
South Jersey Advisor (Mainland Edition) - Cologne, NJ - *AyerDirPub 83*
South Jersey Radio Inc. - Linwood, NJ - *BrCabYB 84; Tel&CabFB 84C*
South Jersey TV Cable Co. [of Cablentertainment Inc.] - Ocean City, NJ - *BrCabYB 84*
South Jersey TV Cable Co. [of Cablentertainment Inc.] - Ventnor, NJ - *BrCabYB 84*
South Jersey TV Cable Co. [of Group W Cable Corp.] - Wildwood, NJ - *BrCabYB 84*
South Jones Cable Co. Inc. [of Coosa Valley Cable Co.] - Ellisville, MS - *Tel&CabFB 84C*
South Laguna Niguel Pennysaver - Mission Viejo, CA - *AyerDirPub 83*
South Lake County Advertiser [of Lowell Pilcher Publishing Co.] - Lowell, IN - *AyerDirPub 83; NewsDir 84*
South Lake Press - Clermont, FL - *AyerDirPub 83; Ed&PubIntYB 82*
South Lake Tahoe Daily Tribune - South Lake Tahoe, CA - *NewsDir 84*
South Lake Tahoe News - South Lake Tahoe, CA - *BaconPubCkNews 84*
South Lyon Herald [of Sliger-Livingston Publications Inc.] - South Lyon, MI - *Ed&PubIntYB 82; NewsDir 84*
South Magazine, The [of Trend Publications Inc.] - Tampa, FL - *MagDir 84*
South Miami-Kendall News - *See* Community Newspapers of Florida Inc.
South Miami South West News - *See* Community Newspapers of Florida Inc.
South Milwaukee East Sider - *See* Quality Newspapers/Suburban Publications
South Milwaukee News Graphic - Oak Creek, WI - *AyerDirPub 83*
South Milwaukee News-Graphic - South Milwaukee, WI - *Ed&PubIntYB 82*
South Milwaukee News Graphic - *See* Community Newspapers Inc.
South Milwaukee Southtown Advisor - *See* Quality Newspapers/Suburban Publications
South Milwaukee Voice-Journal - South Milwaukee, WI - *Ed&PubIntYB 82*
South Milwaukee Voice-Journal - *See* Quality Newspapers/Suburban Publications
South Minneapolis Shopping Guide - Minneapolis, MN - *AyerDirPub 83*
South Minneapolis Sun - Edina, MN - *AyerDirPub 83*
South Minneapolis Sun - Minneapolis, MN - *Ed&PubIntYB 82*
South Minneapolis Sun - *See* Sun Newspapers
South Mississippi Sun - Biloxi, MS - *Ed&PubIntYB 82; NewsBur 6*
South Missourian-Democrat - Alton, MO - *AyerDirPub 83; Ed&PubIntYB 82*
South News - Aliquippa, PA - *Ed&PubIntYB 82*
South-North-DeKalb News/Sun - Decatur, GA - *Ed&PubIntYB 82*
South Omaha Sun - Omaha, NE - *Ed&PubIntYB 82*
South Omaha Sun - South Omaha, NE - *NewsDir 84*
South Omaha Sun/Sarpy County Sun - South Omaha, NE - *AyerDirPub 83*
South Ontario News - Chino, CA - *AyerDirPub 83*
South Ottawa Cablevision Inc. [of Cable Group Management Inc.] - Holland, MI - *BrCabYB 84; Tel&CabFB 84C*
South Padre Cable Inc. [of CATV Systems Inc.] - South Padre Island, TX - *BrCabYB 84*
South Pasadena Journal [of Northeast Los Angeles Publishing Co.] - Los Angeles, CA - *AyerDirPub 83; Ed&PubIntYB 82; NewsDir 84*
South Pasadena Journal - *See* Northeast Los Angeles Publishing Co.
South Pasadena Review - South Pasadena, CA - *BaconPubCkNews 84; Ed&PubIntYB 82; NewsDir 84*
South Pass Press - Amarillo, TX - *BoPubDir 4, 5*
South Peace News - High Prairie, AB, Canada - *Ed&PubIntYB 82*
South Philadelphia Chronicle - Philadelphia, PA - *Ed&PubIntYB 82; NewsDir 84*
South Philadelphia Review-Chronicle - Philadelphia, PA - *BaconPubCkNews 84; Ed&PubIntYB 82*
South Philadelphia Review, East - Philadelphia, PA - *Ed&PubIntYB 82; NewsDir 84*
South Philadelphia Review, West - Philadelphia, PA - *Ed&PubIntYB 82; NewsDir 84*
South Pierce County Buyer's Guide - Eatonville, WA - *AyerDirPub 83*
South Pittsburg Hustler - South Pittsburg, TN - *BaconPubCkNews 84; Ed&PubIntYB 82; NewsDir 84*
South Pittsburgh Reporter - Pittsburgh, PA - *AyerDirPub 83; NewsDir 84*
South Placer World - Roseville, CA - *AyerDirPub 83*
South Plains Telephone Cooperative - Lubbock, TX - *TelDir&BG 83-84*
South Reporter - Holly Springs, MS - *AyerDirPub 83; Ed&PubIntYB 82*
South River Suburban - *See* Sentinel Newspapers
South Rockwood News-Herald - Wyandotte, MI - *AyerDirPub 83*
South Rowan Times - China Grove, NC - *AyerDirPub 83; Ed&PubIntYB 82*
South Sacramento News [of Sacramento Suburban Newspapers Inc.] - Fair Oaks, CA - *NewsDir 84*
South Sacramento News, The - Sacramento, CA - *Ed&PubIntYB 82*
South Sacramento Reporter [of Sacramento Suburban Newspapers Inc.] - Fair Oaks, CA - *NewsDir 84*
South Sacramento Reporter, The - Sacramento, CA - *Ed&PubIntYB 82*
South San Francisco Enterprise-Journal - South San Francisco, CA - *Ed&PubIntYB 82; NewsDir 84*
South San Francisco Enterprise Journal - *See* San Mateo Times Group Newspapers
South San Gabriel-Rosemead Progress [of Progress Newspapers] - Monterey Park, CA - *NewsDir 84*
South San Gabriel-Rosemead Progress - *See* Southern California Publishing Co.
South San Jose Sun - San Jose, CA - *Ed&PubIntYB 82*
South Saskatchewan Star - Radville, SK, Canada - *AyerDirPub 83*
South Sausalito Cable TV [of Entertainment Financial Corp.] - Sausalito, CA - *BrCabYB 84; Tel&CabFB 84C*
South Sea Sales - Honolulu, HI - *BoPubDir 4, 5*
South Shore Gazette - South Shore, SD - *BaconPubCkNews 84; Ed&PubIntYB 82*
South Shore Mirror - Marshfield, MA - *Ed&PubIntYB 82*
South Shore News - Hanover, MA - *AyerDirPub 83*
South Shore News - Bridgewater, NS, Canada - *AyerDirPub 83*
South Shore Record - Hewlett, NY - *AyerDirPub 83; Ed&PubIntYB 82; NewsDir 84*
South Shore Reporter - Baldwin, NY - *AyerDirPub 83; Ed&PubIntYB 82*
South Shore Scene - Chicago, IL - *AyerDirPub 83*
South Side Cable Co. - Titusville, PA - *BrCabYB 84; Tel&CabFB 84C*
South Side Journal [of St. Louis Suburban Newspapers Inc.] - St. Louis, MO - *AyerDirPub 83; NewsDir 84*
South Side News - Syracuse, NY - *AyerDirPub 83*
South Side TV Association - Sheffield, PA - *BrCabYB 84; Tel&CabFB 84C*
South Sioux City Star - South Sioux City, NE - *BaconPubCkNews 84; Ed&PubIntYB 82; NewsDir 84*

South Slocan Television Co-operative Association - South Slocan, BC, Canada - *BrCabYB 84*
South Slope Cooperative Telephone Co. - Norway, IA - *TelDir&BG 83-84*
South St. Louis County News - Affton, MO - *AyerDirPub 83*
South St. Louis County News - St. Louis, MO - *Ed&PubIntYB 82*
South St. Paul Inver Grove Heights Sun - South St. Paul/Inver Grove Heights, MN - *Ed&PubIntYB 82*
South St. Paul Inver Grove Heights Sun - *See* Sun Newspapers
South St. Paul-Inver Grove Heights Sun & Free Section [of Minnesota Suburban Newspapers Inc.] - Minneapolis, MN - *NewsDir 84*
South St. Paul Sun & West St. Paul Sun - Edina, MN - *AyerDirPub 83*
South Suburban Shopping Guide - Minneapolis, MN - *AyerDirPub 83*
South Texas Agri-News - Mission, TX - *AyerDirPub 83*
South Texas Catholic - Corpus Christi, TX - *NewsDir 84*
South Texas Newspapers Inc. - Nixon, TX - *BaconPubCkNews 84*
South Texas Reporter - Roma, TX - *Ed&PubIntYB 82*
South Texas Retailer - Houston, TX - *BaconPubCkMag 84*
South Today [of Morton Tazewell Publishing Co.] - Morton, IL - *NewsDir 84*
South Town Advertiser News - South Milwaukee, WI - *NewsDir 84*
South Vancouver Revue - Vancouver, BC, Canada - *Ed&PubIntYB 82*
South West Cable Corp. [of Highland Cable Television Inc.] - West Union, OH - *BrCabYB 84*
South West City Republican - South West City, MO - *BaconPubCkNews 84; Ed&PubIntYB 82*
South West Lance - Winnipeg, MB, Canada - *Ed&PubIntYB 82*
South West News [of South Miami Community Newspapers] - Miami, FL - *AyerDirPub 83; NewsDir 84*
South-Western Cable TV Inc. [of First Carolina Communications Inc.] - Maryville, IL - *BrCabYB 84; Tel&CabFB 84C*
South-Western Cable TV Ltd. - Columbia, IL - *Tel&CabFB 84C*
South-Western Cable TV Ltd. - Waterloo, IL - *Tel&CabFB 84C*
South Western Ontario Poetry - London, ON, Canada - *BoPubDir 4 Sup, 5*
South-Western Publishing Co. [Subs. of SFN Cos. Inc.] - Cincinnati, OH - *AvMarPl 83; DirInfWP 82; DirMarMP 83; LitMarPl 83, 84; MicrocomMPl 84*
South Whitley Tribune-News - South Whitley, IN - *BaconPubCkNews 84*
Southam Building Guide - Toronto, ON, Canada - *BaconPubCkMag 84*
Southam Business Publications Ltd. - Don Mills, ON, Canada - *BoPubDir 5*
Southam Comic Group - Toronto, ON, Canada - *Ed&PubIntYB 82*
Southampton Press - Southampton, NY - *AyerDirPub 83; Ed&PubIntYB 82; NewsDir 84*
Southampton Press - *See* Southampton Press Publishing Co.
Southampton Press Publishing Co. - Southampton, NY - *BaconPubCkNews 84*
Southampton Spirit [of Montgomery Publishing Co.] - Hatboro, PA - *NewsDir 84*
Southampton Spirit - Southampton Township, PA - *Ed&PubIntYB 82*
Southampton Spirit - Warminster, PA - *AyerDirPub 83*
Southampton Spirit - *See* Montgomery Publishing Co.
Southbury Voices - Southbury, CT - *BaconPubCkNews 84; NewsDir 84*
Southcombe Advertising Agency Ltd., W. J. - *See* Royds Advertising Group Ltd., The
Southeast Acoustics Institute - Madison, GA - *BoPubDir 4, 5*
Southeast & Henrietta Weekly Journal - Rochester, NY - *AyerDirPub 83*
Southeast Asia Chronicle [of Southeast Asia Resource Center] - Berkeley, CA - *LitMag&SmPr 83-84*
Southeast Asia Resource Center - Berkeley, CA - *LitMag&SmPr 83-84*
Southeast Cable TV Inc. - Hankinson, ND - *BrCabYB 84; Tel&CabFB 84C*
Southeast Data Center - San Diego, CA - *DataDirOnSer 84*
Southeast Farm Press - Clarksdale, MS - *AyerDirPub 83; BaconPubCkMag 84; MagDir 84*
Southeast Food Service News - Atlanta, GA - *BaconPubCkMag 84; MagDir 84*
Southeast Georgian - Kingsland, GA - *AyerDirPub 83; Ed&PubIntYB 82*
Southeast Indiana Rural Telephone Co. [Aff. of Hoosier Communications] - Dillsboro, IN - *TelDir&BG 83-84*
Southeast Lincoln Sun - Lincoln, NE - *AyerDirPub 83; Ed&PubIntYB 82; NewsDir 84*
Southeast Media Research Inc. - St. Simons Island, GA - *BrCabYB 84*
Southeast Missourian - Cape Girardeau, MO - *AyerDirPub 83; BaconPubCkNews 84; Ed&PubIntYB 82*
Southeast Mobilphone Inc. - Knoxville, TN - *Tel&CabFB 84C*
Southeast Nebraska Telephone Co. - Falls City, NE - *TelDir&BG 83-84*
Southeast News - Matthews, NC - *Ed&PubIntYB 82*
Southeast News & Downey Champion - Downey, CA - *AyerDirPub 83*
Southeast Polk Shopping News - Monmouth, OR - *AyerDirPub 83*
Southeast Real Estate News [of Communications Channels Inc.] - Atlanta, GA - *BaconPubCkMag 84; MagDir 84*
Southeast Subscription Corp. - Richmond, VA - *MagIndMarPl 82-83*
Southeast Sun [of Cleveland Sun Newspapers] - Cleveland, OH - *AyerDirPub 83; NewsDir 84*
Southeast Telephone Co. - Waterford, WI - *TelDir&BG 83-84*
Southeast Tulsa News [of Tulsa Retherford Publications Inc.] - Tulsa, OK - *NewsDir 84*
Southeast Village Squire - Castle Rock, CO - *AyerDirPub 83*
Southeast Watertown Town & Country News [of Gouverneur Town & Country News of Jefferson County] - Gouverneur, NY - *NewsDir 84*
Southeast Wave-Star [of Central News-Wave Publications] - Los Angeles, CA - *AyerDirPub 83; NewsDir 84*
Southeastern Academy of Theatre & Music - Atlanta, GA - *WritMar 84*
Southeastern Cable TV Co. [of American Cablesystems Corp.] - Aston Township, PA - *Tel&CabFB 84C*
Southeastern Color Comic Sections - Atlanta, GA - *Ed&PubIntYB 82*
Southeastern Contractor - Darlington, SC - *BaconPubCkMag 84*
Southeastern Dairy Review - Orlando, FL - *BaconPubCkMag 84*
Southeastern Films Inc. - Atlanta, GA - *AvMarPl 83*
Southeastern Institute of Research Inc. - Richmond, VA - *IntDirMarRes 83*
Southeastern Library Network - Atlanta, GA - *EISS 83; InfIndMarPl 83*
Southeastern Magazine - New London, CT - *MagIndMarPl 82-83*
Southeastern New York Library Resources Council - Poughkeepsie, NY - *EISS 83*
Southeastern News - Cordele, GA - *Ed&PubIntYB 82*
Southeastern Newspapers Corp. - *See* Morris Communications Corp.
Southeastern Oil Review [of The Oil Review Publishing Co.] - Jackson, MS - *BaconPubCkMag 84; MagDir 84*
Southeastern Peanut Farmer - Tifton, GA - *BaconPubCkMag 84; MagDir 84*
Southeastern Press Relations Newswire - Atlanta, GA - *ProGuPRSer 4*
Southeastern Printing Co. [Subs. of Burnup & Sims] - Stuart, FL - *LitMarPl 83, 84*
Southeastern Software - New Orleans, LA - *MicrocomMPl 83, 84; WhoWMicrocom 83*
Southeastern University Press - Greenville, SC - *BoPubDir 4, 5*
Southern Accents [of W. R. C. Smith Publishing Co.] - Atlanta, GA - *BaconPubCkMag 84; MagIndMarPl 82-83; WritMar 84*
Southern Advertising/Markets [of Ernest H. Abernethy Publishing Co.] - Atlanta, GA - *MagDir 84*
Southern Agitator [of On Da Bayou Press & Publishing] - New Orleans, LA - *LitMag&SmPr 83-84*
Southern Angler's & Hunter's Guide - Hot Springs, AR - *ArtMar 84*
Southern Appalachian Resource Catalog - Warne, NC - *BoPubDir 4, 5*

Southern Asia Resource Center Inc. - Berkeley, CA - *BoPubDir 4, 5*
Southern Association on Children Under Six - Little Rock, AR - *BoPubDir 4, 5*
Southern Aviation [of Data Publications Inc.] - Brookfield, CT - *MagDir 84*
Southern Banker [of McFadden Business Publications] - Norcross, GA - *BaconPubCkMag 84; MagDir 84*
Southern Baptist Convention (Historical Commission) - Nashville, TN - *CompReadDB 82; MicroMarPl 82-83*
Southern Baptist Convention (Sunday School Board) - Nashville, TN - *MagIndMarPl 82-83*
Southern Baptists' Radio & Television Commission - Ft. Worth, TX - *Tel&CabFB 84C*
Southern Beacon - Statesboro, GA - *Ed&PubIntYB 82*
Southern Beef Producer - Franklin, TN - *BaconPubCkMag 84*
Southern Beef Producer - Nashville, TN - *MagDir 84*
Southern Bell Telephone & Telegraph Co. - Atlanta, GA - *TelDir&BG 83-84*
Southern Beverage Journal [of Associated Beverage Publications] - Miami, FL - *BaconPubCkMag 84; MagDir 84*
Southern Boating [of Southern Boating & Yatching Inc.] - Miami, FL - *BaconPubCkMag 84; MagDir 84; WritMar 84*
Southern Building Magazine [of Southern Building Code Congress International Inc.] - Birmingham, AL - *BaconPubCkMag 84; MagDir 84*
Southern Business Systems Inc. - Dothan, AL - *WhoWMicrocom 83*
Southern Cable Corp. [of High Industries Inc.] - Corbin, KY - *BrCabYB 84; Tel&CabFB 84C*
Southern Cable TV [of LBJ Co.] - Benevides, TX - *BrCabYB 84*
Southern Cable TV [of LBJ Co.] - Freer, TX - *BrCabYB 84*
Southern Cable TV [of LBJ Co.] - Hebbronville, TX - *BrCabYB 84*
Southern Cable TV [of LBJ Co.] - Zapata, TX - *BrCabYB 84*
Southern Cablecom [of Arkansas Cable TV Group] - Benton County, AR - *BrCabYB 84*
Southern Cablecom - Pea Ridge, AR - *BrCabYB 84*
Southern Cablevision Corp. - Bryan, TX - *Tel&CabFB 84C p.1702*
Southern Cablevision Inc. - Ft. Myers, FL - *BrCabYB 84; Tel&CabFB 84C*
Southern California Answering Network [of Los Angeles Public Library] - Los Angeles, CA - *EISS 83*
Southern California Business [of Los Angeles Area Chamber of Commerce] - Los Angeles, CA - *BaconPubCkMag 84; MagDir 84*
Southern California Coast - Los Angeles, CA - *BaconPubCkMag 84*
Southern California Guide - Los Angeles, CA - *MagDir 84*
Southern California Heavy Construction - Santa Fe Springs, CA - *MagDir 84*
Southern California Interviewing Service - Encino, CA - *IntDirMarRes 83*
Southern California Publishing Co. - Montebello, CA - *BaconPubCkNews 84*
Southern California Rancher - Lemon Grove, CA - *MagDir 84*
Southern Case Inc. - Raleigh, NC - *AvMarPl 83*
Southern Cayuga Tribune & Union Springs News - Kings Ferry, NY - *AyerDirPub 83*
Southern Cemetery - Atlanta, GA - *BaconPubCkMag 84; MagDir 84*
Southern Champaign County Today - Philo, IL - *Ed&PubIntYB 82*
Southern Champaign County Today - Sidney South, IL - *Ed&PubIntYB 82*
Southern Communications Inc. - Beckley, WV - *BrCabYB 84*
Southern Community Antenna TV Co. Inc. - Bradshaw, WV - *Tel&CabFB 84C*
Southern Community Antenna TV Co. Inc. - Iaeger, WV - *BrCabYB 84; Tel&CabFB 84C*
Southern Computer Systems Inc. - Birmingham, AL - *MicrocomMPl 83, 84; MicrocomSwDir 1; WhoWMicrocom 83*
Southern Connecticut Cablevision - Bridgeport, CT - *BrCabYB 84*
Southern Connection Inc., The - New York, NY - *ArtMar 84; DirPRFirms 83*
Southern County News - Thornton, IA - *AyerDirPub 83; Ed&PubIntYB 82*
Southern Crescent Publishing - Easton, PA - *BillIntBG 83-84*
Southern Cross [of Catholic Diocese of San Diego] - San Diego, CA - *NewsDir 84*
Southern Cross Records - Walnut Creek, CA - *BillIntBG 83-84*
Southern Delaware County [of Media Town Talk Newspapers] - Media, PA - *NewsDir 84*
Southern Democrat - Oneonta, AL - *AyerDirPub 83; Ed&PubIntYB 82; NewsDir 84*
Southern Digital Systems Inc. - Kinston, NC - *MicrocomMPl 83; MicrocomSwDir 1*
Southern Dutchess News - Wappingers Falls, NY - *AyerDirPub 83; Ed&PubIntYB 82*
Southern Economic Journal - Chapel Hill, NC - *MagIndMarPl 82-83*
Southern Educational Communications Association - Columbia, SC - *BrCabYB 84; Tel&CabFB 84C*
Southern Engineer - Raleigh, NC - *BaconPubCkMag 84; MagDir 84*
Southern Exposure [of Institute for Southern Studies] - Durham, NC - *LitMag&SmPr 83-84; MagDir 84; WritMar 84*
Southern Film Lab - Chamblee, GA - *AvMarPl 83*
Southern Florist & Nurseryman - Ft. Worth, TX - *BaconPubCkMag 84*
Southern Forestry Information Network [of U.S. Forest Service] - Athens, GA - *EISS 83*
Southern Funeral Director - Atlanta, GA - *BaconPubCkMag 84; MagDir 84*
Southern Gazette, The - Marystown, NF, Canada - *Ed&PubIntYB 82*
Southern Genealogist's Exchange Society Inc. - Jacksonville, FL - *BoPubDir 4, 5*
Southern Golf - Tampa, FL - *BaconPubCkMag 84*
Southern Golf Course Operations - Elm Grove, WI - *MagDir 84*
Southern Graphics - Kissimmee, FL - *ArtMar 84; BaconPubCkMag 84; MagDir 84*
Southern Hardware - Atlanta, GA - *MagIndMarPl 82-83; WritMar 84*
Southern Herald - Liberty, MS - *AyerDirPub 83; Ed&PubIntYB 82*
Southern Historical Press Inc. - Easley, SC - *BoPubDir 4, 5*
Southern Hog Producer - Nashville, TN - *MagDir 84*
Southern Hospitals [of Billian Publishing Co.] - Atlanta, GA - *BaconPubCkMag 84; MagDir 84*
Southern Humanities Review - Auburn, AL - *LitMag&SmPr 83-84*
Southern Illinois Cable TV Inc. [of Tele-Communications Inc.] - Harrisburg, IL - *BrCabYB 84; Tel&CabFB 84C*
Southern Illinois Cable TV Inc. [of Tele-Communications Inc.] - Herrin, IL - *BrCabYB 84; Tel&CabFB 84C*
Southern Illinois Cable TV Inc. [of Tele-Communications Inc.] - Murphysboro, IL - *BrCabYB 84; Tel&CabFB 84C*
Southern Illinois University, Carbondale (University Graphics Office) - Carbondale, IL - *BoPubDir 4, 5*
Southern Illinois University Press - Carbondale, IL - *LitMarPl 83, 84; MicroMarPl 82-83; WritMar 84*
Southern Illinoisan [of Lee Enterprises Inc.] - Carbondale, IL - *AyerDirPub 83; Ed&PubIntYB 82; NewsDir 84*
Southern Industrial Supplier [of Southern Trade Publications Co.] - Greensboro, NC - *BaconPubCkMag 84; MagDir 84*
Southern Insurance - New Orleans, LA - *BaconPubCkMag 84; MagDir 84*
Southern Israelite - Atlanta, GA - *AyerDirPub 83*
Southern Jeweler - Atlanta, GA - *BaconPubCkMag 84; MagDir 84*
Southern Jewish Weekly - Jacksonville, FL - *ArtMar 84; AyerDirPub 83; WritMar 84*
Southern Journal of Optometry - Atlanta, GA - *BaconPubCkMag 84*
Southern Journal of Optometry - Dunwoody, GA - *MagDir 84*
Southern Kansas Telephone Co. Inc. - Clearwater, KS - *TelDir&BG 83-84*
Southern Libertarian Messenger - Florence, SC - *LitMag&SmPr 83-84*
Southern Library of Recorded Music [Div. of Southern Music Publishing Co.] - New York, NY - *AvMarPl 83*
Southern-Lite Publishing Co. - Atlanta, GA - *BoPubDir 5*

Southern Living [of Southern Progress Corp.] - Birmingham, AL - *BaconPubCkMag 84; Folio 83; LitMarPl 84; MagDir 84; MagIndMarPl 82-83*
Southern Loggin' Times - Montgomery, AL - *BaconPubCkMag 84; MagDir 84*
Southern Lumberman - Nashville, TN - *BaconPubCkMag 84; MagDir 84*
Southern Manitoba Review - Cartwright, MB, Canada - *AyerDirPub 83; Ed&PubIntYB 82*
Southern Market Preview & Shopping Planner - High Point, NC - *BaconPubCkMag 84*
Southern Marketing Services Inc. - Hilton Head, SC - *DirMarMP 83*
Southern Mediator - Little Rock, AR - *AyerDirPub 83; Ed&PubIntYB 82; NewsDir 84*
Southern Medical Journal - Birmingham, AL - *BaconPubCkMag 84; MagDir 84*
Southern Melody Publishing Co. - Durham, NC - *BillIntBG 83-84*
Southern Methodist University Press - Dallas, TX - *LitMarPl 83, 84; WritMar 84*
Southern Micro Systems for Educators - Burlington, NC - *MicrocomMPl 84; MicrocomSwDir 1*
Southern Minnesota Broadcasting Co. - Rochester, MN - *BrCabYB 84*
Southern Minnesota Software - North Mankato, MN - *MicrocomSwDir 1*
Southern Montana Telephone Co. - Wisdom, MT - *TelDir&BG 83-84*
Southern Monterey County CATV [of Communications Systems Inc.] - Pine Canyon, CA - *Tel&CabFB 84C*
Southern Motor Cargo - Memphis, TN - *ArtMar 84; BaconPubCkMag 84; MagDir 84; WritMar 84*
Southern Motoracing - Winston-Salem, NC - *BaconPubCkMag 84; MagDir 84*
Southern Motorsports Journal - Opp, AL - *BaconPubCkMag 84; MagDir 84*
Southern Music Co. - San Antonio, TX - *BillIntBG 83-84*
Southern New England Telephone Co., The - New Haven, CT - *TelDir&BG 83-84*
Southern New England Typographic Service Inc. - Hamden, CT - *LitMarPl 83, 84*
Southern Newspapers Inc. - *See* Walls Newspapers
Southern Office [of Market/Show Publications Inc.] - Atlanta, GA - *MagDir 84*
Southern Office Dealer [of Abernethy Publishing Co. Inc.] - Atlanta, GA - *BaconPubCkMag 84*
Southern Oklahoma Cable Inc. [of Signet Cablevision Co.] - Healdton, OK - *BrCabYB 84; Tel&CabFB 84C*
Southern Oklahoma Cable Inc. - Ringling, OK - *BrCabYB 84*
Southern Oklahoma Cable Inc. [of Signet Cablevision Co.] - Waurika, OK - *BrCabYB 84; Tel&CabFB 84C*
Southern Oklahoma Cable Inc. - Wilson, OK - *BrCabYB 84*
Southern Outdoors [of B.A.S.S. Publications] - Montgomery, AL - *BaconPubCkMag 84; MagDir 84; MagIndMarPl 82-83; WritMar 84*
Southern Pacific Communications Co. - Burlingame, CA - *DataDirSup 7-83*
Southern Pacific Co. - San Francisco, CA - *HomeVid&CabYB 82-83*
Southern Pharmacy Journal - Atlanta, GA - *BaconPubCkMag 84; MagDir 84*
Southern Pines Moore County News - Southern Pines, NC - *BaconPubCkNews 84*
Southern Pines Pilot - Southern Pines, NC - *BaconPubCkNews 84; NewsDir 84*
Southern Plumbing, Heating, & Air Conditioning [of Southern Trade Publications Co.] - Greensboro, NC - *MagDir 84*
Southern Plumbing-Heating-Cooling - Greensboro, NC - *BaconPubCkMag 84*
Southern Poetry Review - Charlotte, NC - *LitMag&SmPr 83-84*
Southern Productions, Hal - Panorama City, CA - *BillIntBG 83-84*
Southern Progress Corp. - Birmingham, AL - *AdAge 6-28-84; KnowInd 83*
Southern Progressive Periodicals Update Directory [of Progressive Education] - Nashville, TN - *LitMag&SmPr 83-84*
Southern Pulp & Paper - Atlanta, GA - *BaconPubCkMag 84; MagDir 84*
Southern Purchasor - Greensboro, NC - *BaconPubCkMag 84; MagDir 84*
Southern Quarterly - Hattiesburg, MS - *LitMag&SmPr 83-84*
Southern Regional Education Board - Atlanta, GA - *BoPubDir 4, 5*
Southern Reporter - Sardis, MS - *AyerDirPub 83*
Southern Review, The - Baton Rouge, LA - *LitMag&SmPr 83-84; WritMar 84*
Southern Satellite Systems [Subs. of Satellite Syndicated Systems Inc.] - Tulsa, OK - *BrCabYB 84; Tel&CabFB 84C; VideoDir 82-83*
Southern School Supply - Bowling Green, KY - *AvMarPl 83*
Southern Sentinel - Ripley, MS - *AyerDirPub 83*
Southern Shopping - Oneonta, AL - *AyerDirPub 83*
Southern Siskiyou Newspapers Inc. - Mt. Shasta, CA - *BaconPubCkNews 84*
Southern Software - Eastleigh, England - *MicrocomSwDir 1*
Southern Software Systems - Merritt Island, FL - *MicrocomMPl 84*
Southern Software Systems - Germantown, TN - *MicrocomSwDir 1*
Southern Sound Productions - Tabor City, NC - *BillIntBG 83-84*
Southern Standard - Arkadelphia, AR - *AyerDirPub 83; Ed&PubIntYB 82*
Southern Standard - McMinnville, TN - *AyerDirPub 83; Ed&PubIntYB 82*
Southern Star Recording - Shreveport, LA - *BillIntBG 83-84*
Southern Star, The - Ozark, AL - *Ed&PubIntYB 82*
Southern Starr Broadcasting Group Inc. - Altamonte Springs, FL - *BrCabYB 84*
Southern Stationer & Office Outfitter - Atlanta, GA - *MagDir 84*
Southern Stock Photos - Sunrise, FL - *LitMarPl 83, 84; MagIndMarPl 82-83*
Southern Supermarketing [of The Progressive Farmer Co.] - Birmingham, AL - *BaconPubCkMag 84; MagDir 84*
Southern Systems Inc. - Ft. Lauderdale, FL - *DataDirSup 7-83; WhoWMicrocom 83*
Southern Telecom Inc. - Peachtree City, GA - *Tel&CabFB 84C p.1702*
Southern Telephone Co. [Aff. of C.C. & S. Systems Inc.] - Camden, MI - *TelDir&BG 83-84*
Southern Television Systems [of Tele-Communications Inc.] - Eastland, TX - *BrCabYB 84*
Southern Territory Associates - Arlington, TX - *BoPubDir 4 Sup, 5; LitMarPl 83, 84*
Southern Textile News - Charlotte, NC - *BaconPubCkMag 84; MagDir 84*
Southern Tier Publications Inc. - Vestal, NY - *BaconPubCkNews 84*
Southern Tobacco Journal - Greensboro, NC - *BaconPubCkMag 84; MagDir 84*
Southern Traveller, The - Peachtree City, GA - *LitMarPl 83, 84*
Southern TV Systems [of Tele-Communications Inc.] - Eastland, TX - *Tel&CabFB 84C*
Southern TV Systems [of Tele-Communications Inc.] - Ranger, TX - *Tel&CabFB 84C*
Southern Ulster Pioneer - Marlboro, NY - *AyerDirPub 83*
Southern University Press Marketing Group - Houston, TX - *LitMarPl 83, 84*
Southern Utah News - Kanab, UT - *AyerDirPub 83; Ed&PubIntYB 82*
Southern Vermont Telecable Corp. - Putney, VT - *BrCabYB 84*
Southern Vermont Telecable Corp. - Vernon, VT - *BrCabYB 84*
Southern Vermont Valley News - Wilmington, VT - *Ed&PubIntYB 82*
Southern Wisconsin Cable Inc. - Lake Geneva, WI - *BrCabYB 84; Tel&CabFB 84C*
Southern Writers Group - Nashville, TN - *BillIntBG 83-84*
Southerner - Tarboro, NC - *AyerDirPub 83; Ed&PubIntYB 82*
Southfield Eccentric [of Suburban Communications Corp.] - Livonia, MI - *AyerDirPub 83; NewsDir 84*
Southfield Eccentric - Southfield, MI - *Ed&PubIntYB 82*
Southfield Eccentric - *See* Observer & Eccentric Newspapers

Southfield Jewish News Publishing Co. - Southfield, MI - *NewsDir 84*
Southfield Sun - *See* Suburban Newspapers
Southgate News-Herald - Wyandotte, MI - *AyerDirPub 83*
Southgate Sentinel [of Mellus Newspapers Inc.] - Lincoln Park, MI - *AyerDirPub 83; NewsDir 84*
Southgate Sentinel - *See* Mellus Newspapers Inc.
Southgate Sentinel, The - Southgate, MI - *Ed&PubIntYB 82*
Southhold Long Island Traveler Watchman - Southold, NY - *BaconPubCkNews 84*
Southington Observer, The - Southington, CT - *NewsDir 84*
Southlake & Cedar Lake Register - Crown Point, IN - *AyerDirPub 83*
Southland Communications Inc. - Providence, RI - *BrCabYB 84 p.D-307*
Southland Records Inc. - Arlington, TX - *BillIntBG 83-84*
Southland Telephone Co. - Atmore, AL - *TelDir&BG 83-84*
Southmedia Co. - *See* Telescripps Cable Co.
Southmount Tel-e-vents Ltd. - Hamilton, ON, Canada - *BrCabYB 84*
Southport Cable TV Ltd. - Port Elgin, ON, Canada - *BrCabYB 84*
Southport Press - Kenosha, WI - *LitMag&SmPr 83-84*
Southport State Port Pilot - Southport, NC - *BaconPubCkNews 84*
Southside & Fayette Sun [of Decatur News Publishing Co. Inc.] - Atlanta, GA - *NewsDir 84*
Southside & Fayette Sun - East Point, GA - *AyerDirPub 83; Ed&PubIntYB 82*
Southside Journal [of Central News-Wave Publications] - Los Angeles, CA - *AyerDirPub 83; NewsDir 84*
Southside Sentinel - Urbanna, VA - *AyerDirPub 83; Ed&PubIntYB 82*
Southside Shopper's Guide - Petersburg, VA - *AyerDirPub 83*
Southside Sun - Emporia, VA - *AyerDirPub 83; Ed&PubIntYB 82*
Southside Times [of McWilliams Publications Inc.] - Broken Arrow, OK - *AyerDirPub 83; NewsDir 84*
Southside Times - Tulsa, OK - *Ed&PubIntYB 82*
Southtown Economist - Chicago, IL - *AyerDirPub 83; BaconPubCkNews 84; Ed&PubIntYB 82; NewsDir 84*
Southward & Associates Inc. - Chicago, IL - *StaDirAdAg 2-84*
Southwest Advertiser - Louisville, KY - *AyerDirPub 83*
Southwest Advertiser - Omaha, NE - *AyerDirPub 83*
Southwest Advertiser Advocate - Alief, TX - *AyerDirPub 83*
Southwest Airlines Magazine - San Antonio, TX - *BaconPubCkMag 84; MagDir 84*
Southwest & Texas Water Works Journal - Temple, TX - *BaconPubCkMag 84; MagDir 84*
Southwest Arkansas Telephone Cooperative Inc. - Texarkana, AR - *TelDir&BG 83-84*
Southwest Art - Houston, TX - *BaconPubCkMag 84; WritMar 84*
Southwest Bell Telephone Co. - St. Louis, MO - *TelDir&BG 83-84*
Southwest Booster, The - Swift Current, SK, Canada - *AyerDirPub 83; Ed&PubIntYB 82*
Southwest Builder News [of Leesville Leader Inc.] - Sulphur, LA - *AyerDirPub 83; Ed&PubIntYB 82; NewsDir 84*
Southwest Business [of Equity Media Inc.] - Dallas, TX - *MagDir 84*
Southwest Business Publications Co. - Houston, TX - *MagIndMarPl 82-83*
Southwest Cable Corp. - Espanola, NM - *BrCabYB 84; Tel&CabFB 84C*
Southwest Cablevision Inc. [of Jim R. Smith & Co. Inc.] - Douglas, AZ - *BrCabYB 84*
Southwest Cablevision Inc. [of Jim R. Smith & Co. Inc.] - Payson, AZ - *BrCabYB 84*
Southwest Cablevision Inc. - Williams, AZ - *BrCabYB 84*
Southwest Cablevision Inc. - Hondo, TX - *BrCabYB 84*
Southwest Communications Inc. - Bellevue, WA - *Tel&CabFB 84C*
Southwest Computer Center - Las Cruces, NM - *MicrocomMPl 83, 84*
Southwest Dailies Inc. - New York, NY - *LitMarPl 83, 84*
Southwest Data Systems Inc. - Burbank, CA - *DataDirSup 7-83*
SouthWest EdPsych Services Inc. - Phoenix, AZ - *MicrocomMPl 83, 84; MicrocomSwDir 1*
Southwest Electronic News [of Bender Publications Inc.] - Los Angeles, CA - *MagDir 84*
Southwest Farm Press - Clarksdale, MS - *AyerDirPub 83; BaconPubCkMag 84*
Southwest Film Laboratory Inc. - Dallas, TX - *AvMarPl 83; Tel&CabFB 84C*
Southwest Floor Covering - Dallas, TX - *BaconPubCkMag 84*
Southwest Floor Covering [of Target Publications] - Farmers Branch, TX - *MagDir 84*
Southwest Georgian - Albany, GA - *Ed&PubIntYB 82*
Southwest Globe Times - Philadelphia, PA - *AyerDirPub 83*
Southwest/International News Service - Austin, TX - *AvMarPl 83; BrCabYB 84*
Southwest Lincoln Sun - Lincoln, NE - *AyerDirPub 83; Ed&PubIntYB 82; NewsDir 84*
Southwest Messenger Newspapers - Midlothian, IL - *BaconPubCkNews 84*
Southwest Microwave Inc. - Ozona, TX - *BrCabYB 84*
Southwest Missouri Cable TV Inc. - Aurora, MO - *BrCabYB 84*
Southwest Missouri Cable TV Inc. - Lamar, MO - *BrCabYB 84*
Southwest Missouri Cable TV of Aurora - Aurora, MO - *BrCabYB 84; Tel&CabFB 84C*
Southwest Missouri Cable TV of Lamar - Lamar, MO - *Tel&CabFB 84C*
Southwest Missourian - Reeds Spring, MO - *Ed&PubIntYB 82*
Southwest Museum - Los Angeles, CA - *BoPubDir 4, 5*
Southwest News-Herald - Chicago, IL - *AyerDirPub 83; Ed&PubIntYB 82*
Southwest News Wave [of Central News-Wave Publications] - Los Angeles, CA - *AyerDirPub 83; NewsDir 84*
Southwest Offset - Dallas, TX - *MagIndMarPl 82-83*
Southwest Oklahoma Telephone Co. - Duke, OK - *TelDir&BG 83-84*
Southwest Parks & Monuments Association - Globe, AZ - *BoPubDir 4, 5*
Southwest Pennsylvania Cable TV Inc. [of Armstrong Utilities Inc.] - California, PA - *BrCabYB 84; Tel&CabFB 84C*
Southwest Press Relations Newswire Inc. - Dallas, TX - *ProGuPRSer 4*
Southwest Progress - St. Louis, MO - *NewsDir 84*
Southwest Purchasing - Dallas, TX - *BaconPubCkMag 84*
Southwest Real Estate News [of Communications Channels Inc.] - Mesquite, TX - *BaconPubCkMag 84; MagDir 84; WritMar 84*
Southwest Research & Information Center - Albuquerque, NM - *BoPubDir 4, 5; LitMag&SmPr 83-84*
Southwest Research Inc. - Dallas, TX - *BrCabYB 84; IntDirMarRes 83; Tel&CabFB 84C*
Southwest Research Institute - San Antonio, TX - *CompReadDB 82*
Southwest Review [of Southern Methodist University] - Dallas, TX - *LitMag&SmPr 83-84; WritMar 84*
Southwest Ribbon Co. - Austin, TX - *DirInfWP 82*
Southwest Scientific Publishing - Dalhart, TX - *BoPubDir 4, 5*
Southwest Suburban Publications - Verona, WI - *BaconPubCkNews 84*
Southwest Suburbia-Reporter - Houston, TX - *Ed&PubIntYB 82*
Southwest Systems - Chula Vista, CA - *MicrocomMPl 84*
Southwest Technical Products Corp. - San Antonio, TX - *WhoWMicrocom 83*
Southwest Telephone Exchange Inc. [Aff. of Interstate 35 Telephone Co.] - Emerson, IA - *TelDir&BG 83-84*
Southwest Teleproductions [Subs. of Northwest Teleproductions] - Dallas, TX - *AvMarPl 83*
Southwest Texas Telephone Co. - Rocksprings, TX - *TelDir&BG 83-84*
Southwest Times - Liberal, KS - *AyerDirPub 83; BaconPubCkNews 84; Ed&PubIntYB 82*
Southwest Times - Pulaski, VA - *AyerDirPub 83; Ed&PubIntYB 82*
Southwest Times Record - Ft. Smith, AR - *AyerDirPub 83; BaconPubCkNews 84; Ed&PubIntYB 82*
Southwest Topics News - Los Angeles, CA - *AyerDirPub 83*
Southwest Topics-Wave [of Central News-Wave Publications] - Los Angeles, CA - *NewsDir 84*
Southwest Video Corp. [of Group W Cable Inc.] - Baytown, TX - *BrCabYB 84; Tel&CabFB 84C*

Southwest Virginia Enterprise - Wytheville, VA - *AyerDirPub 83; Ed&PubIntYB 82*
Southwest Washington Cable TV [of Summit Communications Inc.] - Ridgefield, WA - *BrCabYB 84*
Southwest Watertown Town & Country News [of Town & Country News of Jefferson County] - Gouverneur, NY - *NewsDir 84*
Southwest Wave [of Central News-Wave Publications] - Los Angeles, CA - *AyerDirPub 83; NewsDir 84*
Southwest Words & Music [Div. of Suncountry Enterprises] - Tucson, AZ - *BillIntBG 83-84*
Southwestern Broadcasting Stations - McComb, MS - *BrCabYB 84*
Southwestern Cable TV [of American Television & Communications Corp.] - San Diego, CA - *BrCabYB 84; HomeVid&CabYB 82-83; Tel&CabFB 84C*
Southwestern CATV Inc. - Cement, OK - *BrCabYB 84*
Southwestern CATV Inc. - Grandfield, OK - *BrCabYB 84*
Southwestern CATV Inc. - Medicine Park, OK - *Tel&CabFB 84C p.1702*
Southwestern CATV Inc. - Sterling, OK - *BrCabYB 84*
Southwestern CATV Inc. - Tuttle, OK - *BrCabYB 84*
Southwestern Computing Service Inc. - Tulsa, OK - *ADAPSOMemDir 83-84*
Southwestern Data Systems - Santee, CA - *MicrocomMPl 83, 84; MicrocomSwDir 1; WhoWMicrocom 83; WritMar 84*
Southwestern Features - Phoenix, AZ - *Ed&PubIntYB 82*
Southwestern Historical Quarterly - Austin, TX - *MagDir 84*
Southwestern Lore - Denver, CO - *MagDir 84*
Southwestern Marketing Information Service - Oklahoma City, OK - *IntDirMarRes 83*
Southwestern Media Associates - Lubbock, TX - *CabTVFinDB 83*
Southwestern Musician-Texas Music Educator - Austin, TX - *MagDir 84*
Southwestern Newspapers Corp. - *See* Morris Communications Corp.
Southwestern Ohio Cablevision Inc. [of Warner Amex Cable Communications Inc.] - Clermont County, OH - *BrCabYB 84*
Southwestern Poultry Times - Nacogdoches, TX - *MagDir 84*
Southwestern Programming Service - Mesa, AZ - *WhoWMicrocom 83*
Southwestern Review, The - Lafayette, LA - *LitMag&SmPr 83-84*
Southwestern Sun - Los Angeles, CA - *AyerDirPub 83*
Southwestern Telepone Co., The - Salome, AZ - *TelDir&BG 83-84*
Southwestern Veterinarian, The - Brazos, TX - *MagDir 84*
Southworth, Miles F. - Livonia, NY - *LitMarPl 83, 84*
Southworth, Miles F. - Rochester, NY - *MagIndMarPl 82-83*
Souvenirs & Novelties [of Kane Communications Inc.] - Philadelphia, PA - *BaconPubCkMag 84; MagDir 84; MagIndMarPl 82-83*
Sou'Wester [of Southern Illinois University] - Edwardsville, IL - *LitMag&SmPr 83-84; WritMar 84*
Sovereign Press - Rochester, WA - *BoPubDir 4, 5; LitMag&SmPr 83-84; WritMar 84*
Sovereign Record Corp. [Div. of Aloft Music Enterprises Inc.] - New York, NY - *BillIntBG 83-84*
Sovfoto/Eastfoto Agency - New York, NY - *AvMarPl 83; Ed&PubIntYB 82; LitMarPl 83, 84; MagIndMarPl 82-83*
Soviet Aerospace [of Space Publications Inc.] - Washington, DC - *NewsDir 84*
Soviet & East European Data [of University of Alberta] - Edmonton, AB, Canada - *DataDirOnSer 84*
SOVIN-Online Training Centre - Amsterdam, Netherlands - *InfIndMarPl 83*
Sowa Books - San Antonio, TX - *BoPubDir 4 Sup, 5*
Sowd Typing Service, The [Subs. of The Sowd Newspaper Syndicate] - Canton, OH - *LitMarPl 83, 84*
Sowers Newspapers - Rolla, MO - *Ed&PubIntYB 82*
Sowers Printing Co. - Lebanon, PA - *MagIndMarPl 82-83*
Soybean Digest - St. Louis, MO - *ArtMar 84; BaconPubCkMag 84; MagDir 84; MagIndMarPl 82-83; WritMar 84*
Soybean Insect Research Information Center [of University of Illinois] - Champaign, IL - *EISS 83*
Soyfoods Center - Lafayette, CA - *BoPubDir 4; LitMag&SmPr 83-84; LitMarPl 83, 84*
Soziologisches Literatur-Informationssystem [of Informationszentrum Sozialwissenschaften] - Bonn, West Germany - *CompReadDB 82*
Sozo Music - Ft. Worth, TX - *BillIntBG 83-84*
SP Medical & Scientific Books [Div. of Spectrum Publications Inc.] - Jamaica, NY - *LitMarPl 83, 84*
Spa & Sauna - Santa Ana, CA - *BaconPubCkMag 84*
Space Age Computer Systems - Washington, DC - *ADAPSOMemDir 83-84*
Space Age Press Ltd. - Ft. Worth, TX - *BoPubDir 4, 5*
Space & Time - New York, NY - *WritMar 84*
Space & Time Inc. - Kansas City, MO - *StaDirAdAg 2-84*
Space Breaker - Green Bay, WI - *MicrocomMPl 84*
Space Business Week - Washington, DC - *NewsDir 84*
Space Cable of Strongsville Ltd. - Strongsville, OH - *Tel&CabFB 84C*
Space Components Databank [of European Space Agency] - Rome, Italy - *CompReadDB 82*
Space Environment Services Center [of U.S. National Oceanic & Atmospheric Administration] - Boulder, CO - *EISS 83*
Space for All People - San Francisco, CA - *LitMag&SmPr 83-84*
Space Productions - New York, NY - *ArtMar 84*
Space Publications Inc. - Washington, DC - *BoPubDir 4, 5*
Space Records - Albuquerque, NM - *BillIntBG 83-84*
Space Solar Power Review - Elmsford, NY - *BaconPubCkMag 84*
Space Time Associates - Manchester, NH - *MicrocomMPl 84; MicrocomSwDir 1*
Space World [of Palmer Publications Inc.] - Amherst, WI - *BaconPubCkMag 84; MagDir 84*
Spaceark Enterprises - Yermo, CA - *BillIntBG 83-84*
Spacecomps [of European Space Agency] - Frascati, Italy - *DataDirOnSer 84; DirOnDB Spring 84*
Spacelink Ltd. - Englewood, CO - *Tel&CabFB 84C p.1702*
Spacelink of Clear Creek Ltd. - Georgetown, CO - *Tel&CabFB 84C*
Spacelink of Clear Creek Ltd. - Idaho Springs, CO - *Tel&CabFB 84C*
Spacemaker MCB [Div. of Madera Industries Inc.] - North Miami, FL - *AvMarPl 83*
Spaceman Press - Monterey, CA - *BoPubDir 4, 5*
Spacesaver Corp. - Ft. Atkinson, WI - *DirInfWP 82*
Spacetext [of Equatorial Communications Co.] - Mountain View, CA - *EISS 5-84 Sup*
Spackenkill Sentinel [of Wappingers Falls Shopper Inc.] - Wappingers Falls, NY - *AyerDirPub 83; NewsDir 84*
Spain, Frank - *See* WTWV Inc.
Spalding Enterprise - Spalding, NE - *BaconPubCkNews 84; Ed&PubIntYB 82*
Spalla Video Productions, Rick [Subs. of Hollywood Newsreel Syndicate Inc.] - Hollywood, CA - *TelAl 83, 84; Tel&CabFB 84C*
Spalla Video Productions, Rick [Subs. of Hollywood Newsreel Syndicate Inc.] - New York, NY - *AvMarPl 83*
Spanalysis - New York, NY - *IntDirMarRes 83*
Spangler/Fischer Advertising Inc. - Minneapolis, MN - *StaDirAdAg 2-84*
Spanish Advertising & Marketing Inc. - New York, NY - *HBIndAd&MS 82-83*
Spanish Automated Science Information Network - Madrid, Spain - *EISS 83*
Spanish Fork Press - Spanish Fork, UT - *AyerDirPub 83; BaconPubCkNews 84; Ed&PubIntYB 82*
Spanish International Communications Corp. - New York, NY - *BrCabYB 84; Tel&CabFB 84S*
Spanish International Network [of Televisa SA] - New York, NY - *CabTVPrDB 83; HomeVid&CabYB 82-83; TelAl 83*
Spanish Language Center of New York, The - New York, NY - *MagIndMarPl 82-83*
Spanish Literature Publications Co. Inc. - York, SC - *BoPubDir 4, 5*
Spanish Music Center Inc. - New York, NY - *BillIntBG 83-84*
Spanish Pharmaceutical Specialities Data Bank [of Information Center on Medicaments] - Madrid, Spain - *EISS 83*
Spanish Publicity - Austin, TX - *BoPubDir 5*
Spanish Society for Documentation & Information Sciences - Madrid, Spain - *EISS 83*

Spanish Television Systems Inc. - Los Angeles, CA - *Tel&CabFB 84C*
Spanish Universal Network - Houston, TX - *BrCabYB 84; CabTVPrDB 83*
Spanishtech Inc. [Div. of Editor's Bureau Ltd.] - Westport, CT - *LitMarPl 84*
Spano Public Relations Inc., Wyman L. - Minneapolis, MN - *DirPRFirms 83*
SPAR - Elmsford, NY - *HBIndAd&MS 82-83; IntDirMarRes 83*
Spare Time - Milwaukee, WI - *MagDir 84; MagIndMarPl 82-83*
Sparhawk Books Inc. [Aff. of Pawprints Inc.] - Jaffrey, NH - *BoPubDir 4, 5*
Sparkal Records - Belmont Hills, PA - *BillIntBG 83-84*
Sparks Eagle, The - Sparks, GA - *Ed&PubIntYB 82*
Sparks Journal [of Society of Wireless Pioneers] - Santa Rosa, CA - *ArtMar 84*
Sparks Newspapers - Hayward, CA - *Ed&PubIntYB 82*
Sparks Press - Raleigh, NC - *BoPubDir 4, 5*
Sparks Tribune [of Kearns Tribune Corp.] - Sparks, NV - *BaconPubCkNews 84; NewsDir 84*
Sparrow Poverty Pamphlets [of Sparrow Press] - West Lafayette, IN - *WritMar 84*
Sparrow Press - West Lafayette, IN - *BoPubDir 4, 5*
Sparrow Records Inc. - Canoga Park, CA - *BillIntBG 83-84*
Sparta Alleghany News - Sparta, NC - *BaconPubCkNews 84*
Sparta Blue Ridge Sun - Sparta, NC - *BaconPubCkNews 84*
Sparta Cable TV Co. [of The Essex Group] - Sparta, NC - *Tel&CabFB 84C*
Sparta Cablevision [of Omni Cable TV Corp.] - Sparta, IL - *BrCabYB 84; Tel&CabFB 84C*
Sparta Doyle TV Cable Co. Inc. [of National Telecommunications] - Sparta, TN - *Tel&CabFB 84C*
Sparta Expositor - Sparta, TN - *BaconPubCkNews 84; Ed&PubIntYB 82; NewsDir 84*
Sparta Herald [of Monroe County Publishers Inc.] - Sparta, WI - *Ed&PubIntYB 82; NewsDir 84*
Sparta Herald - *See* Monroe County Publishers Inc.
Sparta Ishmaelite - Sparta, GA - *BaconPubCkNews 84; Ed&PubIntYB 82*
Sparta Monroe County Democrat - *See* Monroe County Publishers Inc.
Sparta News-Plaindealer - Sparta, IL - *BaconPubCkNews 84; Ed&PubIntYB 82; NewsDir 84*
Sparta North Kent Advance - Sparta, MI - *BaconPubCkNews 84*
Sparta TV Cable Co. [of National TV Cable Co.] - Sparta, TN - *BrCabYB 84*
Sparta White County Times - Sparta, TN - *BaconPubCkNews 84*
Spartacist Publishing Co. - New York, NY - *BoPubDir 4, 5*
Spartacus Computers Inc. - Bedford, MA - *ADAPSOMemDir 83-84; DataDirSup 7-83*
Spartan Daily [of San Francisco State University] - San Jose, CA - *NewsDir 84*
Spartanburg Herald - Spartanburg, SC - *Ed&PubIntYB 82; NewsDir 84*
Spartanburg Herald-Journal - Spartanburg, SC - *BaconPubCkNews 84; Ed&PubIntYB 82*
Spartanburg Journal - Spartanburg, SC - *Ed&PubIntYB 82; NewsDir 84*
Spaulding Co. Inc. - *See* Graphic Microfilm
SPB Advertising [Div. of Sotheby Parke Bernet] - New York, NY - *StaDirAdAg 2-84*
Speahrhead [of The Society for the Protection of East Asians' Human Rights] - New York, NY - *LitMag&SmPr 83-84*
Speakeasy Inc. - Atlanta, GA - *ProGuPRSer 4*
Speaker Builder - Peterborough, NH - *MagIndMarPl 82-83*
Speaker's & Toastmaster's Book Club [of Prentice-Hall Inc.] - Englewood, NJ - *LitMarPl 83, 84*
Speakers Rulings [of QL Systems Ltd.] - Ottawa, ON, Canada - *CompReadDB 82; DataDirOnSer 84; DirOnDB Spring 84*
Speaking Up - San Francisco, CA - *ProGuPRSer 4*
Spearfish Queen City Mail - Spearfish, SD - *BaconPubCkNews 84*
Spearhead Press - *See* Friends of Israel Gospel Ministry Inc./ Spearhead Press
Spearman Cable TV - Spearman, TX - *BrCabYB 84; Tel&CabFB 84C*
Spearman Hansferd Plainsman - *See* Spearman Reporter Publishers
Spearman Reporter - Spearman, TX - *Ed&PubIntYB 82*
Spearman Reporter - *See* Spearman Reporter Publishers
Spearman Reporter Publishers - Spearman, TX - *BaconPubCkNews 84*
Spears Consulting Group Ltd. - Tulsa, OK - *IntDirMarRes 83*
Spears, W. H. Jr. - Arlington Heights, IL - *BoPubDir 4, 5*
Spearville News - Spearville, KS - *BaconPubCkNews 84; Ed&PubIntYB 82*
SPEBSQSA - Kenosha, WI - *BillIntBG 83-84*
Spec Graph Corp. - Norristown, PA - *LitMarPl 83, 84*
Specht, Gilbert & Partners [of Jordan Case & McGrath] - New York, NY - *AdAge 3-28-84; StaDirAdAg 2-84*
Special Aviation Publications - China Spring, TX - *BoPubDir 4, 5*
Special Care in Dentistry - Chicago, IL - *BaconPubCkMag 84*
Special Child Publications - Seattle, WA - *BoPubDir 4, 5*
Special Collections [of Haworth Press Journals] - New York, NY - *LitMarPl 83, 84*
Special Education: Forward Trends - London, England - *WritMar 84*
Special Events Report - Chicago, IL - *BaconPubCkMag 84*
Special Features Workshop - Westport, CT - *BoPubDir 4, 5*
Special-Interest Autos - Bennington, VT - *BaconPubCkMag 84; MagDir 84; MagIndMarPl 82-83*
Special Learning Corp. - Guilford, CT - *LitMarPl 83, 84*
Special Learning ED Software - Minneapolis, MN - *MicrocomSwDir 1*
Special Libraries - New York, NY - *ArtMar 84; BaconPubCkMag 84; MagIndMarPl 82-83*
Special Libraries Association - New York, NY - *LitMarPl 83, 84; WritMar 84*
Special Libraries Association (Mailing List Service) - New York, NY - *LitMarPl 83, 84*
Special Press - Columbus, OH - *LitMarPl 83, 84*
Special Report to the Office Products Industry - Alexandria, VA - *BaconPubCkMag 84*
Special Rider Music - New York, NY - *BillIntBG 83-84*
Special, The - Salem, SC - *Ed&PubIntYB 82*
Specialist Publishing Co. - Burlingame, CA - *BoPubDir 4, 5*
Specialist Software Ltd. - London, England - *EISS 7-83 Sup*
Specialized Book Service Inc. - Essex Junction, VT - *LitMarPl 83, 84*
Specialized Computer Services Inc. - Lincoln, NE - *DataDirSup 7-83*
Specialized Computer Services Inc. - Portland, OR - *DataDirSup 7-83*
Specialized Media Services - Northfield, IL - *DirMarMP 83*
Specialized Media Services - Charlotte, NC - *StaDirAdAg 2-84*
Specialized Mobile Radio [of NewsNet Inc.] - Bryn Mawr, PA - *DataDirOnSer 84*
Specialized Textile Information [of Shirley Institute] - Manchester, England - *DBBus 82*
SpecialNet [Subs. of National Association of State Directors of Special Education] - Washington, DC - *DataDirOnSer 84*
Specialty Advertising Business - Irving, TX - *BaconPubCkMag 84*
Specialty & Custom Dealer [of Babcox Publishing] - Akron, OH - *BaconPubCkMag 84; MagDir 84; WritMar 84*
Specialty Bakers Voice - New York, NY - *BaconPubCkMag 84; MagDir 84*
Specialty Electronics - Milpitas, CA - *TeleSy&SerDir 2-84*
Specialty Features Syndicate - Detroit, MI - *Ed&PubIntYB 82*
Specialty Food Merchandising - Manhasset, NY - *BaconPubCkMag 84*
Specialty Press Inc. - Ocean, NJ - *BoPubDir 4, 5*
Specialty Press Publishers & Wholesalers Inc. - Osceola, WI - *BoPubDir 4, 5; LitMarPl 83, 84*
Specialty Promotions Co. Inc. - Chicago, IL - *LitMarPl 83, 84*
Specialty Publishing Co. - Onalaska, WI - *BoPubDir 4 Sup, 5*
Specialty Records Inc. - Los Angeles, CA - *BillIntBG 83-84*
Specialty Salesman Magazine [of Communications Channels Inc.] - Atlanta, GA - *DirMarMP 83*
Specialty Software - Capitola, CA - *MicrocomSwDir 1*
Specifying Engineer - Chicago, IL - *MagIndMarPl 82-83*
Specifying Engineer [of Cahners Publishing Co.] - Des Plaines, IL - *BaconPubCkMag 84; MagDir 84*
Speckter Associates Inc. - New York, NY - *StaDirAdAg 2-84*
Spectacular Diseases - London, England - *LitMag&SmPr 83-84*
Spectator - Somerset, MA - *AyerDirPub 83; Ed&PubIntYB 82*

Spectator - Palmyra, MO - *AyerDirPub 83*
Spectator - Roselle, NJ - *Ed&PubIntYB 82*
Spectator - Somerset, NJ - *AyerDirPub 83*
Spectator - Brooklyn, NY - *AyerDirPub 83*
Spectator - Hornell, NY - *AyerDirPub 83; Ed&PubIntYB 82*
Spectator Magazine - Raleigh, NC - *MagDir 84*
Spectator, The - Ozark, AR - *Ed&PubIntYB 82*
Spectator, The - Union, NJ - *NewsDir 84*
Spectator, The [of Seattle University] - Seattle, WA - *NewsDir 84*
Spectator, The - Annapolis Royal, NS, Canada - *Ed&PubIntYB 82*
Spectator, The [of Southam Inc.] - Hamilton, ON, Canada - *AyerDirPub 83; BaconPubCkNews 84; Ed&PubIntYB 82; LitMarPl 83, 84*
Spectext on Comspec [of Bowne Information Systems Inc.] - New York, NY - *DataDirOnSer 84*
Spector & Associates, J. J. - Ft. Lauderdale, FL - *ArtMar 84; DirMarMP 83; LitMarPl 83, 84; MagIndMarPl 82-83*
Spector International, Phil - Los Angeles, CA - *BillIntBG 83-84*
Spectra Films Inc. - New York, NY - *TelAl 83, 84*
Spectra/Soft Inc. - Chandler, AZ - *MicrocomMPl 84; MicrocomSwDir 1*
Spectra II Color Separations Inc. - New York, NY - *MagIndMarPl 82-83*
Spectra Video Inc. - New York, NY - *WhoWMicrocom 83*
Spectradyne - Richardson, TX - *CabTVPrDB 83; TelAl 83; Tel&CabFB 84C*
Spectragraphic Inc. - Commack, NY - *MagIndMarPl 82-83*
Spectragraphics - Ft. Lee, NJ - *LitMarPl 83, 84; MagIndMarPl 82-83*
Spectral Associates - Tacoma, WA - *MicrocomMPl 83, 84; WritMar 84*
Spectron Corp. - Tulsa, OK - *DataDirOnSer 84*
Spectron Div. [of Northern Telecom Ltd.] - Moorestown, NJ - *DataDirSup 7-83*
Spectron Instrument Corp. - Denver, CO - *AvMarPl 83*
Spectrum - Champaign, IL - *Ed&PubIntYB 82*
Spectrum [of Computer Direction Advisors Inc.] - Silver Spring, MD - *DBBus 82*
Spectrum [of The Institute of Electrical & Electronics Engineers Inc.] - New York, NY - *BaconPubCkMag 84; Folio 83*
Spectrum [of Headplay Press] - Arlington, TX - *WritMar 84*
Spectrum - St. George, UT - *NewsDir 84*
Spectrum Books - Portland, OR - *LitMag&SmPr 83-84*
Spectrum Communications Services Inc. - Dilworth, MN - *BrCabYB 84; Tel&CabFB 84C p.1703*
Spectrum Communications Services Inc. - Mahnomen, MN - *BrCabYB 84*
Spectrum Communications Services Inc. - Pelican Rapids, MN - *BrCabYB 84*
Spectrum Computers - Lathrup Village, MI - *MicrocomMPl 84*
Spectrum Computers - Southfield, MI - *MicrocomMPl 83*
Spectrum Enterprises - Morristown, NJ - *DirInfWP 82*
Spectrum Fidelity Magnetics - Lancaster, PA - *AvMarPl 83*
Spectrum Inc. - Denver, CO - *MagIndMarPl 82-83*
Spectrum Laboratories Inc. [Div. of Spectrum Industries] - Carol Stream, IL - *AvMarPl 83; Tel&CabFB 84C*
Spectrum Literary Agency - New York, NY - *LitMarPl 83, 84*
Spectrum Marketing Inc. - New York, NY - *StaDirAdAg 2-84*
Spectrum Ownership Profiles Online [of Computer Directions Advisors Inc.] - Silver Spring, MD - *DirOnDB Spring 84; EISS 83*
Spectrum Productions - Los Angeles, CA - *BoPubDir 4, 5; LitMag&SmPr 83-84*
Spectrum Productions (Audio/Visual Div.) - New York, NY - *StaDirAdAg 2-84*
Spectrum Publications - San Carlos, CA - *BillIntBG 83-84*
Spectrum Records - San Carlos, CA - *BillIntBG 83-84*
Spectrum Sight & Sound - Hollywood, CA - *AvMarPl 83*
Spectrum Software - Sunnyvale, CA - *MicrocomMPl 84; MicrocomSwDir 1*
Spectrum Software - Lincoln, MA - *MicrocomMPl 84*
Spectrum Sports - Minneapolis, MN - *CabTVPrDB 83*
Spectrum Systems Ltd. - London, England - *MicrocomSwDir 1*
Spectrum Teltronics Inc. - Jonesboro, AR - *Tel&CabFB 84C p.1703*
Spectrum, The [of Spectrum Student Periodical Inc.] - Buffalo, NY - *NewsDir 84*
Spectrum 3 & 4 Institutional Holdings Retrieval Service - Silver Spring, MD - *DirOnDB Spring 84*
Spectrum 3 & 4 Institutional Holdings Retrieval Service [of ADP Network Services Inc.] - Ann Arbor, MI - *DataDirOnSer 84*
Speculator Hamilton County News - *See* Denton Publications Inc.
Speculum - Cambridge, MA - *MagIndMarPl 82-83*
Spedea Press Inc. - Milford, NJ - *BoPubDir 4, 5*
Speech Dynamics Inc. - New York, NY - *ProGuPRSer 4*
Speech Foundation of America - Memphis, TN - *BoPubDir 4, 5*
Speechmakers - Montclair, NJ - *ProGuPRSer 4*
Speechworks - Stony Brook, NY - *ProGuPRSer 4*
Speed-O-Print Business Machines - Chicago, IL - *DirInfWP 82*
Speedhorse Inc. - Norman, OK - *BoPubDir 4, 5*
Speedi Telex International - Atlanta, GA - *TeleSy&SerDir 2-84*
Speedimpex - Long Island City, NY - *LitMarPl 84*
Speednews - Los Angeles, CA - *BaconPubCkMag 84*
Speedstat [of SoftCorp International Inc.] - Westerville, OH - *EISS 5-84 Sup*
Speedway-Northwest Suburban Press - Indianapolis, IN - *AyerDirPub 83; NewsDir 84*
Speedway West Side Messenger - *See* Mid State Newspapers Inc.
Speer Music, Ben - Nashville, TN - *BillIntBG 83-84*
Speer, Young & Hollander Inc. - Los Angeles, CA - *StaDirAdAg 2-84*
Spek - Madison, WI - *LitMag&SmPr 83-84*
Spelce Communications, Neal - Austin, TX - *AdAge 3-28-84; ArtMar 84; DirPRFirms 83; StaDirAdAg 2-84*
Spell-Right Corp. - Washington, DC - *DirInfWP 82*
Spellbinder Inc. - Concord, MA - *AvMarPl 83*
Speller & Sons Publishers Inc., Robert - New York, NY - *LitMarPl 83, 84*
Spelling-Goldberg Productions - Beverly Hills, CA - *TelAl 83, 84*
Spelling Productions Inc., Aaron - Beverly Hills, CA - *TelAl 83, 84*
Spelling Productions Inc., Aaron - Hollywood, CA - *Tel&CabFB 84C*
Spellman Co., I. Orrin - Philadelphia, PA - *DirPRFirms 83*
Spellman Inc., Cathy Cash - New York, NY - *HBIndAd&MS 82-83*
Spellman Inc., Douglas T. - Beverly Hills, CA - *StaDirAdAg 2-84*
Spelman Public Relations Inc. - Troy, MI - *DirPRFirms 83*
Spencer Advocate - Spencer, NE - *BaconPubCkNews 84; Ed&PubIntYB 82*
Spencer & Associates Inc., Dwight - Columbus, OH - *IntDirMarRes 83*
Spencer & Rubinow Ltd. - New York, NY - *DirPRFirms 83*
Spencer Bennett Nowak - Seekonk, MA - *AdAge 3-28-84; ArtMar 84; StaDirAdAg 2-84*
Spencer Community Antenna System Inc. - Spencer, IA - *BrCabYB 84; Tel&CabFB 84C*
Spencer Daily Reporter [of Mid America Publishing Corp.] - Spencer, IA - *BaconPubCkNews 84; NewsDir 84*
Spencer Daily Reporter Weekender - Spencer, IA - *NewsDir 84*
Spencer Evening World - Spencer, IN - *Ed&PubIntYB 82; NewsDir 84*
Spencer Magnet - Taylorsville, KY - *AyerDirPub 83*
Spencer Music Co. - New York, NY - *BillIntBG 83-84*
Spencer Needle - Spencer, NY - *BaconPubCkNews 84*
Spencer Needle/Town Crier - Spencer, NY - *Ed&PubIntYB 82*
Spencer Newspapers Inc. - Spencer, WV - *BaconPubCkNews 84*
Spencer Owen Leader - Spencer, IN - *BaconPubCkNews 84; Ed&PubIntYB 82*
Spencer Productions Inc. - New York, NY - *WritMar 84*
Spencer Research-SRO II Inc. - Daly City, CA - *IntDirMarRes 83*
Spencer Roane County Reporter - *See* Spencer Newspapers Inc.
Spencer Times-Record - South Charleston, WV - *NewsDir 84*
Spencer Times-Record - Spencer, WV - *Ed&PubIntYB 82*
Spencer Times Record - *See* Spencer Newspapers Inc.
Spencer-Wood Inc. - New York, NY - *DirPRFirms 83*
Spencer World - Spencer, IN - *BaconPubCkNews 84*
Spencerport Suburban News - Spencerport, NY - *Ed&PubIntYB 82; NewsDir 84*
Spencerville Journal News - Spencerville, OH - *BaconPubCkNews 84*

Sperber Communications - Santa Monica, CA - *CabTVFinDB 83*
Sperika Enterprises Ltd. - Canada - *BoPubDir 4, 5*
Sperry Corp. - New York, NY - *DataDirSup 7-83; Datamation 6-83; ElecNews 7-25-83*
Sperry Corp. - Blue Bell, PA - *ADAPSOMemDir 83-84*
Sperry Corp. (Sperry Univac Div.) - Blue Bell, PA - *DirInfWP 82*
Sperry Univac [Div. of Sperry Corp.] - Blue Bell, PA - *InfIndMarPl 83; Top100Al 83*
SPF Advertising Agency Inc. - San Diego, CA - *StaDirAdAg 2-84*
SPHERE - Washington, DC - *DirOnDB Spring 84*
Sphere [of Chemical Information Systems Inc.] - Baltimore, MD - *DataDirOnSer 84*
Sphinx - Paris, France - *DirOnDB Spring 84*
Sphinx Press Inc. [Aff. of International Universities Press Inc.] - New York, NY - *LitMarPl 83, 84*
Sphinx, The - Regina, SK, Canada - *LitMag&SmPr 83-84*
SPI [Aff. of Waterloo Self-Patenting Institute] - Buffalo, NY - *BoPubDir 5*
SPI/Sage Plastics Data Base - New York, NY - *DirOnDB Spring 84*
Spice West Publishing Co. - Pocatello, ID - *BoPubDir 4 Sup, 5*
SPIDEL [of Societe pour l'Informatique] - Clichy, France - *EISS 83; InfIndMarPl 83*
Spiegelberg, Harry - Beach, ND - *Tel&CabFB 84C p.1703*
Spiegler, Paul A. - Valley Cottage, NY - *LitMarPl 83, 84; MagIndMarPl 82-83*
Spier Inc., Franklin [Subs. of BBDO International] - New York, NY - *LitMarPl 83, 84; StaDirAdAg 2-84*
Spier Inc., Larry - New York, NY - *BillIntBG 83-84*
Spill Prevention Control & Countermeasure System [of U.S. Environmental Protection Agency] - Washington, DC - *EISS 83*
SPIN [of AmericanE Institute of Physics] - New York, NY - *DirOnDB Spring 84; OnBibDB 3*
Spin-A-Test Publishing Co. - Danville, CA - *BoPubDir 4, 5; MicrocomMPl 83, 84*
Spin-Off [of Interweave Press] - Loveland, CO - *WritMar 84*
Spin These Tunes - *See* Live Music Publishing Group
Spina Music - Hollywood, CA - *BillIntBG 83-84*
Spinal Column Newsweekly - Union Lake, MI - *AyerDirPub 83; BaconPubCkNews 84; Ed&PubIntYB 82*
Spindex Corp. - Great Neck, NY - *LitMarPl 84*
Spindex Corp. - Long Island City, NY - *LitMarPl 83*
Spindex Users' Network - Portland, OR - *EISS 83*
Spindler Productions [Subs. of Spindler Slides Inc.] - New York, NY - *AvMarPl 83*
Spine - Philadelphia, PA - *MagIndMarPl 82-83*
Spinelli Associates Inc., Martin - New York, NY - *AvMarPl 83*
Spinit/Eggplant Records - Los Angeles, CA - *BillIntBG 83-84*
Spinn Records - Stuart, VA - *BillIntBG 83-84*
Spinnaker Software - Cambridge, MA - *MicrocomMPl 84; MicrocomSwDir 1*
Spinning Inc., Rolfe C. - Birmingham, MI - *StaDirAdAg 2-84*
Spinning Wheel - Annapolis, MD - *BaconPubCkMag 84; MagDir 84; WritMar 84*
Spinosa, Frank - San Antonio, TX - *HBIndAd&MS 82-83*
Spinsters - Albion, CA - *BoPubDir 5; LitMag&SmPr 83-84*
Spinsters, Ink - Argyle, NY - *BoPubDir 4*
SPIR - Ottawa, ON, Canada - *DirOnDB Spring 84*
Spira, Robert - Iowa City, IA - *BoPubDir 4*
Spira, Robert - East Lansing, MI - *BoPubDir 5*
Spiral Enterprises - Willow Park, TX - *MicrocomMPl 84*
Spiral Record Corp. - New York, NY - *BillIntBG 83-84*
Spiral Records & Publishing - New York, NY - *BillIntBG 83-84*
Spiratone Inc. - Flushing, NY - *AvMarPl 83*
Spirit & Soul Publishing Co. - Tulsa, OK - *BillIntBG 83-84*
Spirit Lake Beacon [of Blue Water Publishing Co. Inc.] - Spirit Lake, IA - *BaconPubCkNews 84; Ed&PubIntYB 82; NewsDir 84*
Spirit Lake Cable TV - Spirit Lake, IA - *BrCabYB 84; Tel&CabFB 84C*
Spirit of Aloha - Honolulu, HI - *BaconPubCkMag 84*
Spirit of Democracy - Woodsfield, OH - *AyerDirPub 83; Ed&PubIntYB 82*
Spirit of Jefferson-Advocate [of Jefferson Publishing Co. Inc.] - Charles Town, WV - *AyerDirPub 83; Ed&PubIntYB 82; NewsDir 84*
Spirit Records - Lexington, MA - *BillIntBG 83-84*
Spirit Records - Charlotte, NC - *BillIntBG 83-84*
Spirit Shopping Guide - Kentland, IN - *AyerDirPub 83*
Spirit That Moves Us Inc., The - Iowa City, IA - *LitMag&SmPr 83-84; WritMar 84*
Spirit That Moves Us Press - Iowa City, IA - *BoPubDir 5*
Spirit, The - Punxsutawney, PA - *AyerDirPub 83; Ed&PubIntYB 82*
Spirit Today - East Peoria, IL - *Ed&PubIntYB 82*
Spirit Today - Morton, IL - *AyerDirPub 83*
Spiritual Advisory Press - Santa Barbara, CA - *BoPubDir 4, 5*
Spiritual Book Associates - Notre Dame, IN - *LitMarPl 83, 84*
Spiritual Community Inc. - Berkeley, CA - *BoPubDir 4, 5*
Spiritual Community Publications - San Rafael, CA - *LitMag&SmPr 83-84*
Spiritual Life - Washington, DC - *WritMar 84*
Spiritual Press - Toronto, ON, Canada - *BoPubDir 4; LitMarPl 83*
Spiritual Renaissance Press [Aff. of Family of God Foundation] - Berkeley, CA - *BoPubDir 4, 5*
Spirituality Today [of Aquinas Institute] - St. Louis, MO - *WritMar 84*
Spiritwarrior Publishing Co. - Waynoka, OK - *BoPubDir 4, 5*
Spiritwood Herald - Spiritwood, SK, Canada - *Ed&PubIntYB 82*
Spiro & Associates - Philadelphia, PA - *AdAge 3-28-84; DirPRFirms 83; StaDirAdAg 2-84; TelAl 83, 84*
Spiro Graphic - Spiro, OK - *BaconPubCkNews 84; Ed&PubIntYB 82*
Spit in the Ocean - Pleasant Hill, OR - *LitMag&SmPr 83-84*
Spitz Advertising Inc. - Syracuse, NY - *ArtMar 84; StaDirAdAg 2-84; TelAl 83, 84*
Spitz, Stuart - New York, NY - *Tel&CabFB 84C p.1703*
Spitzer Associates, Carl - *See* Manning, Selvage & Lee Inc.
Spitzer Literary Agency, Philip G. - Forest Hills, NY - *LitMarPl 83*
Spitzer Literary Agency, Philip G. - New York, NY - *LitMarPl 84*
Spizel Advertising Inc., Edgar S. - San Francisco, CA - *ArtMar 84; StaDirAdAg 2-84*
Spizzirri Publishing Co. Inc. - Medinah, IL - *BoPubDir 4, 5*
Splitrock Telephone Cooperative Inc. - Garretson, SD - *Tel&CabFB 84C; TelDir&BG 83-84*
SPNB California Databank [of Security Pacific National Bank] - Los Angeles, CA - *EISS 83; InfoS 83-84*
SPNB California Databank [of Chase Econometrics/Interactive Data Corp.] - Waltham, MA - *DataDirOnSer 84*
Spodheim Associates, Renee - New York, NY - *LitMarPl 83*
Spoglio Reviste [of Centro per la Documentazione Automatica] - Rome, Italy - *CompReadDB 82*
Spohler, Albert A. C. - Palos Verdes, CA - *BoPubDir 4, 5*
Spokane Area Economic Development Council - Spokane, WA - *BoPubDir 5*
Spokane Chronicle [of Cowles Publishing Co.] - Spokane, WA - *AyerDirPub 83; BaconPubCkNews 84; Ed&PubIntYB 82; NewsDir 84*
Spokane Community Press [of Community Publications Inc.] - Spokane, WA - *NewsDir 84*
Spokane Fairchild Times - Spokane, WA - *BaconPubCkNews 84*
Spokane Heritage Publishing Co. - Spokane, WA - *BoPubDir 4, 5*
Spokane Magazine - Spokane, WA - *MagDir 84*
Spokane Spokesman-Review [of Cowles Publishing Co.] - Spokane, WA - *NewsDir 84*
Spokane Valley Herald - Spokane, WA - *BaconPubCkNews 84; NewsDir 84*
Spoke Press - Kenora, ON, Canada - *BoPubDir 4, 5*
Spoken Arts Inc. - New Rochelle, NY - *AvMarPl 83; BillIntBG 83-84; LitMarPl 83, 84*
Spoken Language Services Inc. - Ithaca, NY - *AvMarPl 83; LitMarPl 83, 84*
Spokesman - Flint, MI - *Ed&PubIntYB 82*
Spokesman - Redmond, OR - *AyerDirPub 83*
Spokesman-Review - Spokane, WA - *AyerDirPub 83; BaconPubCkNews 84; Ed&PubIntYB 82*
Spokesman-Review/Spokane Chronicle [of Cowles Publishing Co.] - Spokane, WA - *LitMarPl 84*
Spokesman, The - Herrin, IL - *AyerDirPub 83*
Spokesman, The - Wood Dale, IL - *WritMar 84*

Spokesman, The [of Po Med. Inc.] - New Brunswick, NJ - *AyerDirPub 83; Ed&PubIntYB 82; NewsDir 84*
Sponza & Associates Inc., J. - Wilton, CT - *StaDirAdAg 2-84*
Spoolie Tunes - Detroit, MI - *BillIntBG 83-84*
Spoon River Poetry Press - Peoria, IL - *BoPubDir 4, 5*
Spoon River Press - Peoria, IL - *BoPubDir 4, 5*
Spooner Advocate - Spooner, WI - *BaconPubCkNews 84; Ed&PubIntYB 82*
Spooner & Co. - Verona, NJ - *ArtMar 84; StaDirAdAg 2-84*
Spoonwood Press Ltd. - Hartford, CT - *BoPubDir 4, 5*
Spoor - Aberdeen, WA - *LitMag&SmPr 83-84*
Sport [of Sports Media Corp.] - New York, NY - *BaconPubCkMag 84; Folio 83; LitMarPl 84; MagDir 84; MagIndMarPl 82-83; NewsBur 6; WritMar 84*
Sport [of Sport Information Resource Centre] - Ottawa, ON, Canada - *DataDirOnSer 84; DBBus 82; DirOnDB Spring 84*
Sport & Recreation Index [of Sport Information Resource Center] - Ottawa, ON, Canada - *CompReadDB 82; OnBibDB 3*
Sport & Sports-Scientific Information System [of Federal Institute for Sports Science] - Cologne, West Germany - *EISS 83*
Sport Aviation - Franklin, WI - *MagDir 84*
Sport Aviation - Hales Corners, WI - *BaconPubCkMag 84; MagIndMarPl 82-83*
Sport Books Publishers - Toronto, ON, Canada - *BoPubDir 4 Sup, 5*
Sport Fishing Institute - Washington, DC - *BoPubDir 4, 5*
Sport Information Resource Centre [of Coaching Association of Canada] - Ottawa, ON, Canada - *CompReadDB 82; DataDirOnSer 84; EISS 83; InfIndMarPl 83*
Sport Style - New York, NY - *BaconPubCkMag 84*
Sporthirado - Toronto, ON, Canada - *Ed&PubIntYB 82*
Sporting Book Center Inc. [Aff. of J. A. Allen Publishing Co.] - Barnstead, NH - *BoPubDir 4, 5*
Sporting Classics - Camden, SC - *BaconPubCkMag 84*
Sporting Goods Business - New York, NY - *BaconPubCkMag 84; MagDir 84; MagIndMarPl 82-83*
Sporting Goods Dealer, The - St. Louis, MO - *BaconPubCkMag 84; MagDir 84; MagIndMarPl 82-83; WritMar 84*
Sporting News [of Times-Mirror Co.] - St. Louis, MO - *BaconPubCkMag 84; Folio 83; MagDir 84; MagIndMarPl 82-83; WritMar 84*
Sporting News Publishing Co. [Aff. of Times-Mirror Co.] - St. Louis, MO - *BoPubDir 4, 5; LitMarPl 84*
Sporting Times, The [Subs. of Times-Mirror Co.] - St. Louis, MO - *LitMarPl 83*
Sportlite Films - Chicago, IL - *AvMarPl 83; TelAl 83, 84; Tel&CabFB 84C*
Sportplane Builder Publications - Austin, TX - *BoPubDir 4, 5*
Sports Afield [of The Hearst Corp.] - New York, NY - *BaconPubCkMag 84; Folio 83; LitMarPl 83, 84; MagDir 84; MagIndMarPl 82-83; NewsBur 6; WritMar 84*
Sports Afield Bass Fishing - New York, NY - *MagDir 84*
Sports Afield Deer Hunting - New York, NY - *MagDir 84*
Sports Afield Fishing Annual - New York, NY - *MagDir 84*
Sports Afield Hunting Annual - New York, NY - *MagDir 84*
Sports All Stars Baseball - New York, NY - *MagDir 84*
Sports & Athletes - Bellevue, WA - *MagDir 84; MagIndMarPl 82-83*
Sports & Recreation - Maple Grove, MN - *BaconPubCkMag 84*
Sports & Recreation - Osseo, MN - *MagDir 84*
Sports Car - Fountain Valley, CA - *BaconPubCkMag 84*
Sports Car - Nyack, NY - *MagDir 84*
Sports Channel, The - San Antonio, TX - *CabTVPrDB 83*
Sports Collectors Digest [of Krause Publications] - Iola, WI - *BaconPubCkMag 84; MagIndMarPl 82-83; WritMar 84*
Sports Exchange [of Total Entertainment Network] - Cleveland, OH - *CabTVPrDB 83*
Sports Features Syndicate Inc. - Maple Shade, NJ - *LitMarPl 84*
Sports Films & Talents Inc. [Subs. of Carlson Cos.] - Minneapolis, MN - *AvMarPl 83*
Sports Illustrated - Chicago, IL - *MagDir 84*
Sports Illustrated [of Time Inc.] - New York, NY - *BaconPubCkMag 84; Folio 83; LitMarPl 83, 84; MagIndMarPl 82-83; NewsBur 6; WritMar 84*
Sports Illustrated Pictures [Div. of Time Inc.] - New York, NY - *LitMarPl 83, 84*
Sports Information Center - North Quincy, MA - *EISS 83*
Sports Journal, The - Calgary, AB, Canada - *WritMar 84*
Sports Marketing Center - San Dimas, CA - *StaDirAdAg 2-84*
Sports Merchandiser - Atlanta, GA - *BaconPubCkMag 84; MagDir 84; MagIndMarPl 82-83; WritMar 84*
Sports 'n Spokes - Phoenix, AZ - *BaconPubCkMag 84*
Sports Network, The - Huntingdon Valley, PA - *BrCabYB 84*
Sports News Syndication - Mt. Vernon, NY - *BrCabYB 84*
Sports Parade [of Meridian Publishing Co. Inc.] - Ogden, UT - *ArtMar 84; WritMar 84*
Sports People - Toronto, ON, Canada - *BaconPubCkMag 84*
Sports Philatelists International [Aff. of American Philatelic Society] - Cleveland, OH - *BoPubDir 4, 5*
Sports Radio, Don - Claxton, GA - *BrCabYB 84*
Sports Report [of Dow Jones News/Retrieval Service] - Princeton, NJ - *DataDirOnSer 84*
Sports Report Service - New York, NY - *Ed&PubIntYB 82*
Sports Retailer - Mt. Prospect, IL - *ArtMar 84; BaconPubCkMag 84; WritMar 84*
Sports Time Cable Network - St. Louis, MO - *Tel&CabFB 84C*
Sports Trade Canada - Toronto, ON, Canada - *BaconPubCkMag 84; WritMar 84*
Sports View Inc. - Nashville, TN - *Tel&CabFB 84C*
Sportsbooks - Bolivar, NY - *BoPubDir 4, 5*
Sportscape - Brookline, MA - *WritMar 84*
Sportschannel New England - Woburn, MA - *CabTVPrDB 83*
Sportschannel New York - Woodbury, NY - *CabTVPrDB 83*
Sportsguide Inc. - Princeton, NJ - *BoPubDir 4, 5*
Sportshelf & Soccer Associates - New Rochelle, NY - *BoPubDir 4, 5*
SportsLine - Vienna, VA - *DirOnDB Spring 84*
Sportsman's Hunting [of Harris Publications Outdoor Group] - New York, NY - *WritMar 84*
Sportsman's Library - Palatine, IL - *LitMarPl 83, 84*
Sportsmedicine Digest - Van Nuys, CA - *BaconPubCkMag 84*
Sportsticker - Scarsdale, NY - *BrCabYB 84*
Sportstyle [of Fairchild Publications] - New York, NY - *BaconPubCkMag 84; Folio 83; MagIndMarPl 82-83*
SportStyle (Business Edition) - New York, NY - *Folio 83*
Sportsvision of Chicago - Chicago, IL - *CabTVPrDB 83; Tel&CabFB 84C*
Sportswear International - New York, NY - *BaconPubCkMag 84*
Sportswise: New York - New York, NY - *BaconPubCkMag 84*
Spot Records - New York, NY - *BillIntBG 83-84*
Spotlight - Santa Monica, CA - *BrCabYB 84; HomeVid&CabYB 82-83*
Spotlight - Indianapolis, IN - *AyerDirPub 83*
Spotlight [of Newsgraphics of Delmar Inc.] - Delmar, NY - *AyerDirPub 83; NewsDir 84*
Spotlight - Grand Beach, MB, Canada - *Ed&PubIntYB 82*
Spotlight International - New York, NY - *LitMarPl 84; MagIndMarPl 82-83*
Spotlight Presents Inc. - New York, NY - *AvMarPl 83; TeleSy&SerDir 7-83; WritMar 84*
Spotlight, The - Washington, DC - *MagDir 84; MagIndMarPl 82-83*
Spotlite News Inc. [Aff. of Allend'or Productions Inc.] - Sherman Oaks, CA - *TelAl 83, 84*
Spots Alive Consultants Inc. - New York, NY - *AvMarPl 83; HBIndAd&MS 82-83*
Spotsylvania County Cable TV [of Prestige Cable TV Inc.] - Spotsylvania, VA - *BrCabYB 84; Tel&CabFB 84C*
Spottswood Studios - Mobile, AL - *ArtMar 84*
SPQR Music - Clifton, NJ - *BillIntBG 83-84*
Sprague Advocate - Sprague, WA - *BaconPubCkNews 84; Ed&PubIntYB 82*
Spratt Woodwind Shop, Jack - Old Greenwich, CT - *BoPubDir 4, 5*
Spray, The - Valier, MT - *Ed&PubIntYB 82*
Spray's Water Ski Magazine - Winter Park, FL - *BaconPubCkMag 84; WritMar 84*
Sprayway - Addison, IL - *AvMarPl 83*
Spreadsheet [of Intercalc] - Scarsdale, NY - *MicrocomMPl 84*
SpreadSoft - Clinton, MD - *MicrocomMPl 84*
Spriggle Publishers, Howard [Aff. of EdiType Computerized Photocomposition] - Lewes, DE - *BoPubDir 4, 5*

Spring [of Rodale Press Inc.] - Emmaus, PA - *ArtMar 84; BaconPubCkMag 84; Folio 83; MagIndMarPl 82-83; WritMar 84*
Spring - Dallas, TX - *LitMag&SmPr 83-84*
Spring Arbor Distributors - Ann Arbor, MI - *BoPubDir 4 Sup, 5*
Spring Church Book Co. - Spring Church, PA - *LitMag&SmPr 83-84*
Spring City Cable TV Inc. - Spring City, TN - *Tel&CabFB 84C*
Spring Green Home News - Spring Green, WI - *BaconPubCkNews 84*
Spring Grove Cable TV [of GS Communications Inc.] - Frederick, MD - *BrCabYB 84*
Spring Grove Cooperative Telephone Co. - Spring Grove, MN - *TelDir&BG 83-84*
Spring Grove Herald - Spring Grove, MN - *BaconPubCkNews 84; Ed&PubIntYB 82*
Spring Hill Center - Wayzata, MN - *BoPubDir 4, 5*
Spring Hope Enterprise - Spring Hope, NC - *AyerDirPub 83; BaconPubCkNews 84; Ed&PubIntYB 82; NewsDir 84*
Spring North Harris County News - Spring, TX - *BaconPubCkNews 84; NewsDir 84*
Spring O'Brien & Co. Inc. - New York, NY - *StaDirAdAg 2-84*
Spring Publications - Dallas, TX - *BoPubDir 4; LitMag&SmPr 83-84; LitMarPl 83, 84; WritMar 84*
Spring Records Inc. - New York, NY - *BillIntBG 83-84*
Spring River Times - Hardy, AR - *Ed&PubIntYB 82*
Spring Valley Bulletin - Lemon Grove, CA - *AyerDirPub 83; NewsDir 84*
Spring Valley Bulletin - Spring Valley, CA - *Ed&PubIntYB 82*
Spring Valley Bulletin - *See* Homeland Publishing Co.
Spring Valley Cable TV [of Preston Cable TV Inc.] - Preston, MN - *BrCabYB 84*
Spring Valley Cable TV [of Preston Cable TV Inc.] - Spring Valley, MN - *Tel&CabFB 84C*
Spring Valley Gazette - Spring Valley, IL - *BaconPubCkNews 84; Ed&PubIntYB 82*
Spring Valley Lake Cable TV Inc. - Spring Valley Lake, CA - *BrCabYB 84*
Spring Valley Pennysaver - Mission Viejo, CA - *AyerDirPub 83*
Spring Valley Sun - Spring Valley, WI - *BaconPubCkNews 84*
Spring Valley Telephone Co. Inc. - Spring Valley, WI - *TelDir&BG 83-84*
Spring Valley Tribune [of Phillips Publishing Inc.] - Spring Valley, MN - *BaconPubCkNews 84; Ed&PubIntYB 82; NewsDir 84*
Springboro Star Free Press - Springboro, OH - *BaconPubCkNews 84*
Springbrook Publications Inc. - Fraser, MI - *BoPubDir 5*
Springdale American Sunbeam - Springdale, AR - *BaconPubCkNews 84*
Springdale Cable TV [of TCA Cable TV Inc.] - Springdale, AR - *BrCabYB 84; Tel&CabFB 84C*
Springdale News [of Donrey Media Group] - Springdale, AR - *BaconPubCkNews 84; Ed&PubIntYB 82; NewsDir 84*
Springdale Observer - West Chester, OH - *AyerDirPub 83*
Springer & Rosenblatt & Co. - New York, NY - *HBIndAd&MS 82-83*
Springer Associates Inc., John - New York, NY - *DirPRFirms 83*
Springer Foreign News Service - New York, NY - *Ed&PubIntYB 82*
Springer Publishing Co. Inc. - New York, NY - *LitMarPl 83, 84*
Springer-Verlag New York Inc. [Subs. of Springer-Verlag GmbH & Co. KG] - New York, NY - *LitMarPl 83, 84; MagIndMarPl 82-83; MicroMarPl 82-83*
Springfield Advance Press - Springfield, MN - *BaconPubCkNews 84; Ed&PubIntYB 82*
Springfield Cable TV [of Centel Cable Television Co.] - Springfield, KY - *BrCabYB 84*
Springfield Cable TV [of Rapids Cable TV Inc.] - Springfield, MN - *Tel&CabFB 84C*
Springfield Catholic Observer, The - Springfield, MA - *NewsDir 84*
Springfield Daily News - Springfield, MA - *BaconPubCkNews 84*
Springfield Daily News [of Springfield Newspapers Inc.] - Springfield, MO - *BaconPubCkNews 84; Ed&PubIntYB 82; LitMarPl 84; NewsDir 84*
Springfield Herald - Springfield, GA - *BaconPubCkNews 84; NewsDir 84*
Springfield Herald - Springfield, TN - *NewsDir 84*
Springfield Illinois State Journal-Register [of The Copley Press Inc.] - Springfield, IL - *NewsDir 84*
Springfield Illinois Times - Springfield, IL - *BaconPubCkNews 84*
Springfield Independent - Springfield, VA - *AyerDirPub 83; Ed&PubIntYB 82*
Springfield Independent/Fairfax Tribune - Springfield, VA - *BaconPubCkNews 84*
Springfield Labor Record - Springfield, MO - *NewsDir 84*
Springfield Leader - Springfield, NJ - *Ed&PubIntYB 82*
Springfield Leader [of Union Vailsburg Leader] - Union, NJ - *AyerDirPub 83; NewsDir 84*
Springfield Leader - Lac du Bonnet, MB, Canada - *Ed&PubIntYB 82*
Springfield Leader & Press [of Springfield Newspapers Inc.] - Springfield, MO - *BaconPubCkNews 84; Ed&PubIntYB 82; LitMarPl 84*
Springfield Monitor - Springfield, NE - *BaconPubCkNews 84; Ed&PubIntYB 82*
Springfield News [of Capital Cities Communications Inc.] - Springfield, OR - *BaconPubCkNews 84; Ed&PubIntYB 82; NewsDir 84*
Springfield News & Leader [of Springfield Newspapers Inc.] - Springfield, MO - *Ed&PubIntYB 82; LitMarPl 83, 84*
Springfield News-Sun - Springfield, OH - *BaconPubCkNews 84; Ed&PubIntYB 82*
Springfield Plainsman Herald - Springfield, CO - *BaconPubCkNews 84*
Springfield Press - Springfield, MA - *Ed&PubIntYB 82; NewsDir 84*
Springfield Press [of Crowe Printers & Publishers] - Springfield, PA - *BaconPubCkNews 84; Ed&PubIntYB 82; NewsDir 84*
Springfield Robertson County Times - Springfield, TN - *BaconPubCkNews 84*
Springfield Sun - Springfield, KY - *BaconPubCkNews 84; NewsDir 84*
Springfield Sun [of Montgomery Publishing Co.] - Ft. Washington, PA - *AyerDirPub 83; NewsDir 84*
Springfield Sun - Springfield Township, PA - *Ed&PubIntYB 82*
Springfield Sun, The - Washington County, KY - *Ed&PubIntYB 82*
Springfield Television Corp. - Springfield, MA - *Tel&CabFB 84S*
Springfield Time & Eternity [of Diocese of Springfield] - Springfield, IL - *NewsDir 84*
Springfield Times - Springfield, SD - *BaconPubCkNews 84; Ed&PubIntYB 82*
Springfield TV Cable System [of Dorate Interstate Inc.] - Springfield, CO - *BrCabYB 84; Tel&CabFB 84C*
Springfield Union [of Republican Publishing Co.] - Springfield, MA - *BaconPubCkNews 84; LitMarPl 83; NewsBur 6; NewsDir 84*
Springhill & Parrsboro Record - Springhill, NS, Canada - *AyerDirPub 83; Ed&PubIntYB 82*
Springhill Cable Co. - Springhill, LA - *BrCabYB 84*
Springhill Cable TV Ltd. - Springhill, NS, Canada - *BrCabYB 84*
Springhill Press - Silver Spring, MD - *BoPubDir 4 Sup, 5*
Springhill Press & News Journal - Springhill, LA - *BaconPubCkNews 84; Ed&PubIntYB 82; NewsDir 84*
Springport Signal - Springport, MI - *BaconPubCkNews 84; Ed&PubIntYB 82*
Springport Telephone Co. - Springport, MI - *TelDir&BG 83-84*
Springs - Wheeling, IL - *BaconPubCkMag 84*
Springs Valley Cablevision - French Lick, IN - *BrCabYB 84*
Springs Valley Herald - French Lick, IN - *AyerDirPub 83; Ed&PubIntYB 82*
Springtown Epigraph - Springtown, TX - *BaconPubCkNews 84; Ed&PubIntYB 82*
Springview Herald - Keya Paha County, NE - *Ed&PubIntYB 82*
Springview Herald - Springview, NE - *BaconPubCkNews 84*
Springville Cable Co. - Springville, IA - *Tel&CabFB 84C*
Springville Cable TV [of Acton CATV Inc.] - Acton, MA - *BrCabYB 84*
Springville Cooperative Telephone Association Inc. - Springville, IA - *TelDir&BG 83-84*
Springville Herald - Springville, UT - *Ed&PubIntYB 82*
Springville Herald - *See* Art City Publishing Co.

Springville Journal - Springville, NY - *BaconPubCkNews 84; Ed&PubIntYB 82; NewsDir 84*
Springville Penny Saver - Springville, NY - *AyerDirPub 83*
Sprint [of GTE Sprint Communications Corp.] - Burlingame, CA - *TeleSy&SerDir 2-84*
Sprint - Elgin, IL - *WritMar 84*
Sproing Books - Tampa, FL - *BoPubDir 4, 5; LitMag&SmPr 83-84*
Sprott, Professor J. C. - Madison, WI - *MicrocomSwDir 1*
Sprout Publications Inc. - Sarasota, FL - *BoPubDir 4, 5; LitMag&SmPr 83-84*
Sprouting Publications - Ashland, OR - *LitMag&SmPr 83-84*
Sproutletter, The [of Sprouting Publications] - Ashland, OR - *LitMag&SmPr 83-84; WritMar 84*
Spruce Pine Tri-County News - Spruce Pine, NC - *Ed&PubIntYB 82; NewsDir 84*
Spruce Pine Tri-County News-Journal - Spruce Pine, NC - *BaconPubCkNews 84*
Spruce Street Books - Vancouver, BC, Canada - *BoPubDir 4 Sup, 5*
SPSS Inc. - Chicago, IL - *DataDirSup 7-83; EISS 83; MicrocomMPl 84*
Spudman - Monterey, CA - *BaconPubCkMag 84*
Spungbuggy Works Inc. - Los Angeles, CA - *ArtMar 84; AvMarPl 83*
Spur - Middleburg, VA - *BaconPubCkMag 84; MagDir 84; WritMar 84*
Spur - London, England - *LitMag&SmPr 83-84*
Spur Products Corp. - Marina Del Rey, CA - *DataDirSup 7-83*
Spur Texas Spur - Spur, TX - *BaconPubCkNews 84*
Sputz, David - Brooklyn, NY - *BoPubDir 4, 5*
Spuyten Duyvil - New York, NY - *BoPubDir 5*
Spyglass Catalog Co. - Alameda, CA - *BoPubDir 4, 5*
Spyglass Productions - Monterey, CA - *AvMarPl 83*
Squadron/Signal Publications Inc. - Carrollton, TX - *BoPubDir 4 Sup, 5*
Squamish Citizen Shopper - Squamish, BC, Canada - *AyerDirPub 83*
Square Deals Press - Kansas City, MO - *BoPubDir 5*
Square One Management Ltd. - Ottawa, ON, Canada - *BoPubDir 4 Sup, 5*
Square-Rigger Press, The - Lexington, KY - *LitMag&SmPr 83-84*
Squarebooks Inc. - Mill Valley, CA - *BoPubDir 4, 5*
Squid Inc. - Willowdale, ON, Canada - *BoPubDir 5*
Squire Buresh Associates Inc. - Worcester, MA - *MicrocomMPl 84*
Squirrel Hill News - Homestead, PA - *AyerDirPub 83*
Squirrel Hill Times - Pittsburgh, PA - *AyerDirPub 83*
Squirrel Hill Times - *See* Gateway Press Inc.
SR Software Inc. - Atlanta, GA - *MicrocomMPl 84*
SRA [Subs. of IBM] - Chicago, IL - *LitMarPl 84*
SRDS Data Base Publishing Services - Delran, NJ - *InfoS 83-84*
SRDS Media Plan Management Services - New York, NY - *InfoS 83-84*
SREA Market Data Center Inc. - Arcadia, CA - *EISS 83*
SRG International Ltd. - New York, NY - *IntDirMarRes 83*
SRI International - Menlo Park, CA - *ADAPSOMemDir 83-84; DataDirOnSer 84; EISS 83*
SRI International (Business Intelligence Program Index) - Menlo Park, CA - *DirOnDB Spring 84*
SRI International (Marketing Service Group) - Menlo Park, CA - *BoPubDir 5*
Sri Rama Publishing [Aff. of Sri Rama Foundation Inc.] - Santa Cruz, CA - *BoPubDir 4, 5*
Sri Shirdi Sai Publications - Morgantown, WV - *BoPubDir 4 Sup, 5*
Sroda, George - Amherst Junction, WI - *BoPubDir 4, 5; LitMag&SmPr 83-84*
Sroge Publishing Inc., Maxwell - Colorado Springs, CO - *BoPubDir 4 Sup, 5; DirMarMP 83; HBIndAd&MS 82-83*
Sroge Publishing Inc., Maxwell - Chicago, IL - *LitMarPl 83; MagIndMarPl 82-83*
Sroge Publishing Inc., Maxwell - Schiller Park, IL - *HBIndAd&MS 82-83*
SRS Enterprises Inc. [Div. of Gambling Times Inc.] - Hollywood, CA - *WritMar 84*
SRS Microwave Inc. - Rotan, TX - *Tel&CabFB 84C*
SRS Programming Reserve Inc. - New York, NY - *ADAPSOMemDir 83-84*
SRT Corp. - Norcross, GA - *MicrocomMPl 84*
SS & S Publications - Willowdale, ON, Canada - *BoPubDir 4, 5*
SSC & B: Lintas Worldwide - New York, NY - *AdAge 3-28-84, 6-25-84; Br 1-23-84; BrCabYB 84*
SSC & B: Lintas Worldwide [Subs. of The Interpublic Group of Cos. Inc.] - London, England - *StaDirAdAg 2-84*
SSEA Publications - Mississauga, ON, Canada - *BoPubDir 4 Sup, 5*
SSIE Current Research [of Dialog Information Services Inc.] - Palo Alto, CA - *DataDirOnSer 84*
SSIE Current Research - Springfield, VA - *DirOnDB Spring 84*
SSK & F Inc. - New York, NY - *StaDirAdAg 2-84*
SSM Microcomputer Products - San Jose, CA - *MicrocomMPl 83, 84; WhoWMicrocom 83*
S.S.R. Corp. - Rochester, NY - *MicrocomMPl 84; MicrocomSwDir 1*
SSR Inc. - Washington, DC - *LitMarPl 83, 84*
SSVA - Murano, Italy - *DirOnDB Spring 84*
St. Agatha Cable TV Inc. - St. Agatha, ME - *BrCabYB 84*
St. Alban Press [Aff. of The Liberal Catholic Church] - Ojai, CA - *BoPubDir 4, 5*
St. Albans Advertiser - St. Albans, WV - *Ed&PubIntYB 82; NewsDir 84*
St. Albans Cablevision Inc. [of Tele-Communications Inc.] - St. Albans, VT - *BrCabYB 84; Tel&CabFB 84C*
St. Albans Episcopal Church - Chattanooga, TN - *BoPubDir 4*
St. Albans Episcopal Church - Hixson, TN - *BoPubDir 5*
St. Albans Messenger [of Vermont Publishing Co.] - St. Albans, VT - *BaconPubCkNews 84; Ed&PubIntYB 82; LitMarPl 83, 84; NewsDir 84*
St. Andrews Cable TV [of Wiggins Cable TV] - Jackson County, MS - *Tel&CabFB 84C*
St. Andrew's Press - Laurinburg, NC - *BoPubDir 4, 5; LitMag&SmPr 83-84*
St. Andrews Review - Laurinburg, NC - *LitMag&SmPr 83-84*
St. Anne Record - St. Anne, IL - *BaconPubCkNews 84*
St. Annes Point Press [Aff. of Arctician Books] - Fredericton, NB, Canada - *BoPubDir 4, 5*
St. Ansgar Enterprise - St. Ansgar, IA - *BaconPubCkNews 84; Ed&PubIntYB 82*
St. Anthony Bulletin - *See* Bulletin Newspapers
St. Anthony Cable TV Inc. - St. Anthony, ID - *BrCabYB 84*
St. Anthony Fremont County Chronicle-News - St. Anthony, ID - *BaconPubCkNews 84*
St. Anthony Messenger - Cincinnati, OH - *BaconPubCkMag 84; MagDir 84; MagIndMarPl 82-83; WritMar 84*
St. Anthony Messenger Press - Cincinnati, OH - *LitMarPl 83, 84; WritMar 84*
St. Augustine Record [of Florida Publishing Co.] - St. Augustine, FL - *BaconPubCkNews 84; Ed&PubIntYB 82; NewsDir 84*
St. Benedict's Farm - Waelder, TX - *MicrocomMPl 83, 84; MicrocomSwDir 1*
St. Bernard Guide [of Gretna Guide Newspaper Corp.] - Chalmette, LA - *NewsDir 84*
St. Bernard Voice - Arabi, LA - *AyerDirPub 83*
St. Boniface Journal - Winnipeg, MB, Canada - *Ed&PubIntYB 82*
St. Catharines Historical Museum - St. Catharines, ON, Canada - *BoPubDir 4 Sup, 5*
St. Catharines Standard, The - St. Catharines, ON, Canada - *BaconPubCkNews 84*
St. Charles Cable TV [of Preston Cable TV Inc.] - St. Charles, MN - *BrCabYB 84; Tel&CabFB 84C*
St. Charles CATV [of Interstate General Corp.] - St. Charles, MD - *BrCabYB 84*
St. Charles CATV Inc. - Waldorf, MD - *Tel&CabFB 84C*
St. Charles Chronicle - St. Charles, IL - *AyerDirPub 83; Ed&PubIntYB 82; NewsDir 84*
St. Charles Chronicle - *See* Chronicle Publishing Co.
St. Charles Herald - Norco, LA - *AyerDirPub 83*
St. Charles Journal [of Donnelly Publications] - St. Charles, MO - *AyerDirPub 83; Ed&PubIntYB 82; NewsDir 84*
St. Charles Press - St. Charles, MN - *Ed&PubIntYB 82*
St. Charles Press - *See* Mack Publishing Co.
St. Clair Cable Vision Corp. [of Omni Cable TV Corp.] - New Athens, IL - *Tel&CabFB 84C*

St. Clair Cablevision - Marrisa, IL - *BrCabYB 84*
St. Clair Chronicle - St. Clair, MO - *BaconPubCkNews 84; Ed&PubIntYB 82; NewsDir 84*
St. Clair County Courier - Osceola, MO - *AyerDirPub 83*
St. Clair County Courier - St. Clair County, MO - *Ed&PubIntYB 82*
St. Clair County Herald - Belleville, IL - *Ed&PubIntYB 82*
St. Clair County Herald - Mascoutah, IL - *AyerDirPub 83; NewsDir 84*
St. Clair Examiner, The - Toronto, ON, Canada - *Ed&PubIntYB 82*
St. Clair Gazette - Corunna, ON, Canada - *Ed&PubIntYB 82*
St. Clair Gazette - Sarnia, ON, Canada - *AyerDirPub 83*
St. Clair News-Aegis - Pell City, AL - *AyerDirPub 83; Ed&PubIntYB 82*
St. Clair Shores Herald [of Detroit Northeast Detroiter] - Detroit, MI - *AyerDirPub 83; NewsDir 84*
St. Clair Shores Herald - *See* Harper Woods Herald
St. Clair Shores/Roseville/East Detroit Community News [of Community News] - Mt. Clemens, MI - *NewsDir 84*
St. Clair Shores-Roseville-East Detroit Community News - St. Clair Shores, MI - *Ed&PubIntYB 82*
St. Clair Shores/Roseville News - *See* Community News
St. Clairsville Gazette-Chronicle - St. Clairsville, OH - *BaconPubCkNews 84; Ed&PubIntYB 82*
St. Cloud News - St. Cloud, FL - *BaconPubCkNews 84; Ed&PubIntYB 82; NewsDir 84*
St. Cloud News & Kissimmee Gazette - St. Cloud, FL - *AyerDirPub 83; BaconPubCkNews 84*
St. Cloud Shopping News - St. Cloud, MN - *AyerDirPub 83*
St. Cloud State University Chronicle - St. Cloud, MN - *NewsDir 84*
St. Cloud Times [of Gannett Co. Inc.] - St. Cloud, MN - *BaconPubCkNews 84; Ed&PubIntYB 82; NewsDir 84*
St. Cloud Visitor [of Diocese of St. Cloud] - St. Cloud, MN - *NewsDir 84*
St. Croix Avis - St. Croix, VI - *AyerDirPub 83*
St. Croix Cable TV - Calais, ME - *BrCabYB 84*
St. Croix Cable TV - St. Croix, VI - *BrCabYB 84; Tel&CabFB 84C*
St. Croix Courier - St. Stephen, NB, Canada - *AyerDirPub 83; Ed&PubIntYB 82*
St. Croix Falls Standard Press - St. Croix Falls, WI - *BaconPubCkNews 84; NewsDir 84*
St. Croix Mirror - St. Thomas, VI - *AyerDirPub 83*
St. Croix Press Inc. - New Richmond, WI - *MagIndMarPl 82-83*
St. Croix Review - Stillwater, MN - *LitMag&SmPr 83-84*
St. Croix Telephone Co. - New Richmond, WI - *TelDir&BG 83-84*
St. Croix TV Inc. - Calais, ME - *Tel&CabFB 84C*
St. Croix Valley Peach [of Sell Publishing Co.] - Forest Lake, MN - *AyerDirPub 83; NewsDir 84*
St. Croix Valley Peach - *See* Sell Publishing Co.
St. Croix Valley Press - Stillwater, MN - *Ed&PubIntYB 82*
St. Croix Valley Press - White Bear Lake, MN - *AyerDirPub 83; NewsDir 84*
St. Donat Telecable - St. Donat, PQ, Canada - *BrCabYB 84*
St. Edward Advance - St. Edward, NE - *BaconPubCkNews 84; Ed&PubIntYB 82*
St. Elmo Banner - St. Elmo, IL - *BaconPubCkNews 84; Ed&PubIntYB 82*
St. Francis Herald - St. Francis, KS - *BaconPubCkNews 84; Ed&PubIntYB 82*
St. Francis Music Co. - *See* Derry Music Co.
St. Francis Reminder-Enterprise - *See* Community Newspapers Inc.
St. Francisville Democrat - St. Francisville, LA - *AyerDirPub 83; Ed&PubIntYB 82*
St. Francisville Democrat - *See* Louisiana Suburban Press
St. Genevieve Cablevision Inc. - St. Genevieve, MO - *BrCabYB 84*
St. Genevieve Herald - St. Genevieve, MO - *BaconPubCkNews 84; NewsDir 84*
St. George Cablevision Inc. - St. George, SC - *Tel&CabFB 84C*
St. George Dorchester Eagle-Record - St. George, SC - *BaconPubCkNews 84*
St. George Publications [Aff. of St. George Book Service Inc.] - Spring Valley, NY - *BoPubDir 4, 5*
St. George Spectrum - St. George, UT - *Ed&PubIntYB 82*
St. George Washington County News - St. George, UT - *BaconPubCkNews 84; NewsDir 84*
St. Giles Press - Lafayette, CA - *BoPubDir 5*
St. Heironymous Press Inc. - Berkeley, CA - *BoPubDir 4, 5; LitMag&SmPr 83-84*
St. Helena Echo - Greensburg, LA - *AyerDirPub 83*
St. Helena Echo, The - St. Helena Parish, LA - *Ed&PubIntYB 82*
St. Helena Star - St. Helena, CA - *BaconPubCkNews 84; Ed&PubIntYB 82; NewsDir 84*
St. Helens Chronicle, The - St. Helens, OR - *NewsDir 84*
St. Helens Sentinel-Mist - St. Helens, OR - *BaconPubCkNews 84*
St. Henri la Voix Populaire - Montreal, PQ, Canada - *Ed&PubIntYB 82*
St. Ignace News - St. Ignace, MI - *BaconPubCkNews 84; Ed&PubIntYB 82; NewsDir 84*
St. Ignace News & Cedarville Wave Edition - St. Ignace, MI - *AyerDirPub 83*
St. James' Anglican Church - Flin Flon, MB, Canada - *BoPubDir 4 Sup, 5*
St. James Leader-Journal - St. James, MO - *BaconPubCkNews 84; Ed&PubIntYB 82; NewsDir 84*
St. James Metro One - Winnipeg, MB, Canada - *Ed&PubIntYB 82*
St. James Plaindealer - St. James, MN - *AyerDirPub 83; BaconPubCkNews 84; Ed&PubIntYB 82; NewsDir 84*
St. Jo Tribune - St. Jo, TX - *BaconPubCkNews 84; Ed&PubIntYB 82*
St. Joan's Press [Aff. of The New York Feminist Art Institute] - New York, NY - *BoPubDir 4 Sup, 5*
St. Joe News - St. Joe, IN - *BaconPubCkNews 84*
St. John Associates Inc. - Bronx, NY - *LitMarPl 83, 84*
St. John News - St. John, KS - *BaconPubCkNews 84; Ed&PubIntYB 82; NewsDir 84*
St. John Telegraph-Journal - St. John, NB, Canada - *LitMarPl 83*
St. John Telephone Co. - St. John, WA - *TelDir&BG 83-84*
St. John Times-Globe - St. John, NB, Canada - *LitMarPl 83*
St. John Valley Times - Madawaska, ME - *AyerDirPub 83; Ed&PubIntYB 82*
St. John's Clinton County News - St. John's, MI - *BaconPubCkNews 84; NewsDir 84*
St. John's Dewitt/Bath Review - St. John's, MI - *BaconPubCkNews 84*
St. John's Educational Thresholds Center - San Francisco, CA - *BoPubDir 4, 5*
St. Johns-Oklawaha Rivers Trading Co. - Deland, FL - *BoPubDir 5; LitMag&SmPr 83-84*
St. Johns Reminder - St. Johns, MI - *NewsDir 84*
St. Johns Review - North Portland, OR - *Ed&PubIntYB 82*
St. Johns Review - Portland, OR - *AyerDirPub 83*
St. Johnsbury Caledonian-Record - St. Johnsbury, VT - *BaconPubCkNews 84; NewsDir 84*
St. Johnsbury Community TV Corp. [of Simmons Communications Inc.] - St. Johnsbury, VT - *BrCabYB 84; Tel&CabFB 84C p.1699*
St. Joseph Cable Communications Inc. - St. Joseph, MO - *Tel&CabFB 84C p.1700*
St. Joseph Cablevision [of News-Press & Gazette Co.] - Country Club Village, MO - *Tel&CabFB 84C*
St. Joseph Cablevision [of News-Press & Gazette Co.] - Savannah, MO - *Tel&CabFB 84C*
St. Joseph Cablevision [of News-Press & Gazette Co.] - St. Joseph, MO - *BrCabYB 84; Tel&CabFB 84C*
St. Joseph County News - White Pigeon, MI - *Ed&PubIntYB 82*
St. Joseph Gazette - St. Joseph, MO - *BaconPubCkNews 84; NewsDir 84*
St. Joseph Journal of Livestock & Agriculture Inc. - St. Joseph, MO - *NewsDir 84*
St. Joseph News Press - St. Joseph, MO - *BaconPubCkNews 84; NewsDir 84*
St. Joseph Telephone & Telegraph Co. - Port St. Joe, FL - *TelDir&BG 83-84*
St. Joseph Tensas Gazette - St. Joseph, LA - *BaconPubCkNews 84; Ed&PubIntYB 82*

St. Joseph's Messenger & Advocate of the Blind [of Sisters of St. Joseph of Peace] - Jersey City, NJ - *WritMar 84*
St. Lambert Metro-Expansion - Longueuil, PQ, Canada - *AyerDirPub 83*
St. Landry Cable TV Inc. [of Wometco Cable TV Inc.] - Opelousas, LA - *BrCabYB 84; Tel&CabFB 84C*
St. Lawrence Plaindealer - Canton, NY - *AyerDirPub 83*
St. Lawrence Sun, The - Valleyfield, PQ, Canada - *Ed&PubIntYB 82*
St. Lazare Cable TV - St. Lazare, MB, Canada - *BrCabYB 84*
St. Louis - St. Louis, MO - *BaconPubCkMag 84; MagDir 84; WritMar 84*
St. Louis American - St. Louis, MO - *AyerDirPub 83; BaconPubCkNews 84; Ed&PubIntYB 82; NewsDir 84*
St. Louis Argus - St. Louis, MO - *BaconPubCkNews 84; Ed&PubIntYB 82*
St. Louis Art Museum - St. Louis, MO - *BoPubDir 4, 5*
St. Louis Bowling Review - Hazelwood, MO - *MagDir 84*
St. Louis Business Journal - St. Louis, MO - *BaconPubCkMag 84*
St. Louis Commerce [of St. Louis Regional Commerce & Growth Association] - St. Louis, MO - *MagDir 84*
St. Louis Construction News & Review [of Finan Publishing Co.] - St. Louis, MO - *BaconPubCkMag 84; MagDir 84; WritMar 84*
St. Louis Countian - Clayton, MO - *Ed&PubIntYB 82*
St. Louis Countian [of Daily Record Co.] - St. Louis, MO - *NewsDir 84*
St. Louis County Historical Society - Duluth, MN - *BoPubDir 4, 5*
St. Louis County Star - Bridgeton, MO - *AyerDirPub 83*
St. Louis County Star - Hazelwood, MO - *NewsDir 84*
St. Louis County Star - St. Louis, MO - *Ed&PubIntYB 82*
St. Louis Courier Journal - *See* St. Louis Suburban Newspapers Inc.
St. Louis Crusader - St. Louis, MO - *BaconPubCkNews 84; Ed&PubIntYB 82; NewsDir 84*
St. Louis Daily Record - St. Louis, MO - *Ed&PubIntYB 82; NewsDir 84*
St. Louis Evening Whirl - St. Louis, MO - *BaconPubCkNews 84; Ed&PubIntYB 82*
St. Louis Globe Democrat - St. Louis, MO - *BaconPubCkNews 84; Ed&PubIntYB 82; LitMarPl 83, 84; NewsBur 6; NewsDir 84*
St. Louis Information Systems [Subs. of S.I.S. Inc.] - St. Louis, MO - *WhoWMicrocom 83*
St. Louis Journalism Review [of Focus/Midwest Publishing Co. Inc.] - St. Louis, MO - *ArtMar 84; LitMag&SmPr 83-84; MagDir 84; MagIndMarPl 82-83; WritMar 84*
St. Louis Labor Tribune [of Labor Tribune Publishing Co.] - St. Louis, MO - *NewsDir 84*
St. Louis Metro-Sentinel - St. Louis, MO - *BaconPubCkNews 84*
St. Louis Metropolitan Medicine - St. Louis, MO - *BaconPubCkMag 84*
St. Louis Naborhood Link News - St. Louis, MO - *BaconPubCkNews 84; NewsDir 84*
St. Louis Neighborhood News - *See* St. Louis Suburban Newspapers Inc.
St. Louis North & Northwest County Journal - St. Louis, MO - *NewsDir 84*
St. Louis North Side Community News - Jennings, MO - *BaconPubCkNews 84*
St. Louis North Side Community News - St. Louis, MO - *NewsDir 84*
St. Louis Park Sun - Edina, MN - *AyerDirPub 83*
St. Louis Park Sun - St. Louis Park, MN - *Ed&PubIntYB 82*
St. Louis Park Sun - *See* Sun Newspapers
St. Louis Park Sun & Free Section [of Minnesota Suburban Newspapers Inc.] - Minneapolis, MN - *NewsDir 84*
St. Louis Post-Dispatch [of The Pulitzer Publishing Co.] - St. Louis, MO - *AyerDirPub 83; BaconPubCkNews 84; Ed&PubIntYB 82; LitMarPl 83, 84; NewsBur 6; NewsDir 84*
St. Louis Post Dispatch Classified Ads - St. Louis, MO - *DirOnDB Spring 84*
St. Louis Post Dispatch Classified Ads [of CompuServe Inc.] - Columbus, OH - *DataDirOnSer 84*
St. Louis Public Library - St. Louis, MO - *BoPubDir 4, 5*
St. Louis Purchaser - St. Louis, MO - *BaconPubCkMag 84; MagDir 84*
St. Louis Review [of Archdiocese of St. Louis] - St. Louis, MO - *NewsDir 84*
St. Louis Sentinel - St. Louis, MO - *Ed&PubIntYB 82; NewsDir 84*
St. Louis South County Journal - *See* St. Louis Suburban Newspapers Inc.
St. Louis South Side Journal - St. Louis, MO - *Ed&PubIntYB 82*
St. Louis South Side Journal - *See* St. Louis Suburban Newspapers Inc.
St. Louis South St. Louis County News - St. Louis, MO - *NewsDir 84*
St. Louis Suburban Newspapers Inc. - St. Louis, MO - *BaconPubCkNews 84; BrCabYB 84*
St. Louis Tri-County Journal - *See* St. Louis Suburban Newspapers Inc.
St. Louis University (Institute of Jesuit Sources) - St. Louis, MO - *BoPubDir 4, 5*
St. Louis University (Pius XII Memorial Library) - St. Louis, MO - *BoPubDir 4, 5*
St. Louis West County Journal - *See* St. Louis Suburban Newspapers Inc.
St. Luke's Press [Div. of Tickle Inc.] - Memphis, TN - *LitMag&SmPr 83-84; LitMarPl 83, 84; WritMar 84*
St. Luke's Publishing Co. [Aff. of St. Luke's Press/Fine Arts Productions] - South Bend, IN - *BoPubDir 4, 5; LitMag&SmPr 83-84*
St. Maries Gazette-Record - St. Maries, ID - *BaconPubCkNews 84; NewsDir 84*
St. Mark Coptic Orthodox Church - Troy, MI - *BoPubDir 5*
St. Martin Cable TV [of Telecable Associates Inc.] - St. Martinville, LA - *BrCabYB 84*
St. Martin's Press [Subs. of Macmillan Publishers Ltd.] - New York, NY - *LitMarPl 83, 84; WritMar 84*
St. Martinville Teche News [of St. Martin Publishing Co. Inc.] - St. Martinville, LA - *BaconPubCkNews 84; NewsDir 84*
St. Mary & Franklin Banner-Tribune - Franklin, LA - *Ed&PubIntYB 82*
St. Mary Journal [of Morgan City Newspapers Inc.] - Morgan City, LA - *AyerDirPub 83; NewsDir 84*
St. Mary's Beacon - Leonardtown, MD - *AyerDirPub 83; Ed&PubIntYB 82*
St. Mary's Camden County Tribune - St. Mary's, GA - *BaconPubCkNews 84*
St. Marys Daily Press - St. Marys, PA - *NewsDir 84*
St. Mary's Leader - St. Mary's, OH - *BaconPubCkNews 84; NewsDir 84*
St. Marys Oracle - Pleasants County, WV - *Ed&PubIntYB 82*
St. Marys Oracle - *See* St. Marys Oracle Publishers
St. Marys Oracle Publishers - St. Marys, WV - *BaconPubCkNews 84*
St. Marys Pleasant County Leader - *See* St. Marys Oracle Publishers
St. Mary's Press [of Christian Brothers Publications] - Winona, MN - *LitMarPl 83, 84*
St. Marys Star - St. Marys, KS - *BaconPubCkNews 84*
St. Marys Star & Valley Ho - St. Marys, KS - *Ed&PubIntYB 82*
St. Marys TV - St. Marys, PA - *BrCabYB 84; Tel&CabFB 84C*
St. Mary's University (Occasional Papers in Anthropology) - Halifax, NS, Canada - *BoPubDir 4, 5*
St. Matthews Calhoun Times - St. Matthews, SC - *BaconPubCkNews 84*
St. Matthews Telephone Co. Inc. - St. Matthews, SC - *TelDir&BG 83-84*
St. Mawr of Vermont - Randolph Center, VT - *BoPubDir 4, 5*
St. Nectarios Press - Seattle, WA - *BoPubDir 4, 5*
St. Nicholas Music Inc. - New York, NY - *BillIntBG 83-84*
St. Olaf College (Norwegian-American Historical Association) - Northfield, MN - *BoPubDir 4, 5*
St. Onge, Achille J. - Worcester, MA - *BoPubDir 4, 5*
St. Paul Advertising Co. - St. Paul, MN - *StaDirAdAg 2-84*
St. Paul Book & Stationery Co. - St. Paul, MN - *AvMarPl 83*
St. Paul Cablesystems [of American Cablesystems Corp.] - St. Paul, VA - *Tel&CabFB 84C*
St. Paul Catholic Bulletin, The - St. Paul, MN - *NewsDir 84*

St. Paul Clinch Valley Times - St. Paul, VA - *BaconPubCkNews 84*
St. Paul Cooperative Telephone Association - St. Paul, OR - *TelDir&BG 83-84*
St. Paul Dispatch [of Northwest Publications Inc.] - St. Paul, MN - *BaconPubCkNews 84; Ed&PubIntYB 82; LitMarPl 83, 84; NewsBur 6*
St. Paul Journal - St. Paul, AB, Canada - *Ed&PubIntYB 82*
St. Paul Legal Ledger - St. Paul, MN - *Ed&PubIntYB 82; NewsDir 84*
St. Paul Phonograph-Herald - St. Paul, NE - *BaconPubCkNews 84*
St. Paul Pioneer Press [of Northwest Publications Inc.] - St. Paul, MN - *BaconPubCkNews 84; Ed&PubIntYB 82; LitMarPl 83, 84; NewsBur 6; NewsDir 84; WritMar 84*
St. Paul Pioneer Press-Dispatch [of Northwest Publications Inc.] - St. Paul, MN - *Ed&PubIntYB 82; LitMarPl 83, 84*
St. Paul Recorder - Minneapolis, MN - *Ed&PubIntYB 82*
St. Paul Recorder - St. Paul, MN - *AyerDirPub 83; NewsDir 84*
St. Paul Recorder - *See* Minneapolis Spokesman
St. Paul South-West Review - *See* Lillie Suburban Newspapers
St. Pauls Review - St. Pauls, NC - *BaconPubCkNews 84; Ed&PubIntYB 82*
St. Peter Cablevision Inc. [of North American Communications] - St. Peter, MN - *BrCabYB 84*
St. Peter Herald - St. Peter, MN - *BaconPubCkNews 84; Ed&PubIntYB 82; NewsDir 84*
St. Peters Courier-Post - St. Peters, MO - *NewsDir 84*
St. Peter's Printing & Publishing Co. Ltd. - Mississauga, ON, Canada - *BoPubDir 4, 5*
St. Petersburg Buyers Guide - Largo, FL - *AyerDirPub 83*
St. Petersburg Independent [of Times Publishing Co.] - St. Petersburg, FL - *BaconPubCkNews 84; NewsDir 84*
St. Petersburg Pinellas County Review - St. Petersburg, FL - *BaconPubCkNews 84*
St. Petersburg Times [of Times Publishing Co.] - St. Petersburg, FL - *BaconPubCkNews 84; Ed&PubIntYB 82; LitMarPl 83, 84; NewsBur 6; NewsDir 84*
St. Raphael's Better Health - New Haven, CT - *BaconPubCkMag 84*
St. Regis Paper Co. - New York, NY - *LitMarPl 83, 84*
St. Scholastica Priory Press - Duluth, MA - *BoPubDir 4, 5*
St. Stephen Telephone Co. [Aff. of Telephone Data Systems] - St. Stephen, SC - *TelDir&BG 83-84*
St. Stephen's Episcopal Church - Indianola, MS - *BoPubDir 4, 5*
St. Tammany Cablevision Inc. [of Wometco Cable TV Inc.] - Slidell, LA - *BrCabYB 84; Tel&CabFB 84C*
St. Tammany Farmer - Covington, LA - *AyerDirPub 83*
St. Tammany Guide [of Gretna Guide Newspaper Corp.] - Gretna, LA - *NewsDir 84*
St. Tammany News-Banner - Covington, LA - *AyerDirPub 83*
St. Tammany News-Banner - Mandeville, LA - *Ed&PubIntYB 82*
St. Thomas Cable Corp. - St. Thomas Township, PA - *Tel&CabFB 84C*
St. Thomas Times-Journal - St. Thomas, ON, Canada - *BaconPubCkNews 84; Ed&PubIntYB 82; LitMarPl 83, 84*
St. Thomas University (Owl & the Pussycat Publications) - Fredericton, NB, Canada - *BoPubDir 4, 5*
St. Vincent, Milone & McConnells Advertising - New York, NY - *AdAge 3-28-84; StaDirAdAg 2-84*
St. Vital Lance - Winnipeg, MB, Canada - *Ed&PubIntYB 82*
St. Vital Leader - Winnipeg, MB, Canada - *Ed&PubIntYB 82*
St. Vladimir's Seminary Press [Aff. of St. Vladimir's Orthodox Theological Seminary] - Crestwood, NY - *BoPubDir 4, 5; LitMarPl 84*
Sta-Hi Color Service - *See* Sun Color Service
Staats-Zeitung und Herold - Long Island City, NY - *Ed&PubIntYB 82*
Stable Music Co. - Austin, TX - *BillIntBG 83-84*
Stabur Communications Inc. - Southfield, MI - *BillIntBG 83-84*
Stabur East Music - *See* Stabur Communications Inc.
Stack & Associates, Tom - Colorado Springs, CO - *AvMarPl 83; LitMarPl 83, 84; MagIndMarPl 82-83*
Stack Sampling News - Lancaster, PA - *BaconPubCkMag 84*
Stack the Deck Inc. - Chicago, IL - *BoPubDir 4*
Stack the Deck Inc. - Orland Park, IL - *BoPubDir 5*
Stackig, Sanderson & White Inc. - McLean, VA - *ArtMar 84; DirMarMP 83; StaDirAdAg 2-84*
Stackpole Books [of Commonwealth Communications Services] - Harrisburg, PA - *LitMarPl 83, 84; WritMar 84*
StackWorks, The - Bloomington, IN - *WhoWMicrocom 83*
StackWorks, The - New Bern, NC - *WhoWMicrocom 83*
Stacs Information Systems Ltd. - Calgary, AB, Canada - *EISS 7-83 Sup*
Stacy-Lee Label, The - Hackensack, NJ - *BillIntBG 83-84*
Stacyville Monitor Review - Stacyville, IA - *BaconPubCkNews 84*
Stadt-und Universitatbibliothek Frankfurt - Frankfurt, West Germany - *CompReadDB 82*
Staedtler Inc., J. S. - Chatsworth, CA - *AvMarPl 83*
Stafford Cable TV - Stafford, KS - *Tel&CabFB 84C*
Stafford Cable TV - Crawford, NE - *BrCabYB 84; Tel&CabFB 84C*
Stafford Cable TV - Stafford Country, VA - *Tel&CabFB 84C*
Stafford Cable TV - Stafford County, VA - *BrCabYB 84*
Stafford Courier - Stafford, KS - *BaconPubCkNews 84; Ed&PubIntYB 82*
Stafford Ft. Bend Mirror - Missouri City, TX - *BaconPubCkNews 84*
Stafford Ft. Bend Mirror - Stafford, TX - *NewsDir 84*
Stafford Press - Stafford Springs, CT - *AyerDirPub 83; BaconPubCkNews 84; NewsDir 84*
Stafford Sound - New York, NY - *AvMarPl 83*
Stag [of Swank Corp.] - New York, NY - *BaconPubCkMag 84; WritMar 84*
Stage Engineering & Supply Inc. - Colorado Springs, CO - *AvMarPl 83*
Stage Engineering International Ltd. - Colorado Springs, CO - *AvMarPl 83*
Stage, John Lewis - New Milford, NY - *MagIndMarPl 82-83*
Stage One Marketing Research - Cambridge, MA - *IntDirMarRes 83*
Stage One: The Louisville Children's Theatre - Louisville, KY - *WritMar 84*
Stage West Edmonton - Edmonton, AB, Canada - *WritMar 84*
Stagebill - New York, NY - *MagIndMarPl 82-83*
StageCoach Cable TV - Nederland, CO - *Tel&CabFB 84C*
Stagn System Services - Dearborn, MI - *MicrocomMPl 84*
Stahl Animated, Al - New York, NY - *AvMarPl 83; WritMar 84*
Stahl Associates Inc., The - Maumee, OH - *StaDirAdAg 2-84*
Stain Technology [of Williams & Wilkens] - Baltimore, MD - *MagDir 84*
Stained Glass [of Stained Glass Association of America] - Bronxville, NY - *MagDir 84*
Stainer & Bell - *See* Galaxy Music Corp.
Stair, Julia - Kingston, MA - *LitMarPl 83, 84*
Staley & Associates, W. C. - High Point, NC - *BillIntBG 83-84*
Stambaugh Cable Co. - Stambaugh, MI - *BrCabYB 84*
Stamford American - Stamford, TX - *BaconPubCkNews 84; Ed&PubIntYB 82*
Stamford Genealogical Society Inc. - Stamford, CT - *BoPubDir 4, 5*
Stamford Group Inc., The (PM & E Div.) - New Bedford, MA - *AvMarPl 83*
Stamford Marketing Field Research - Stamford, CT - *IntDirMarRes 83*
Stamford Mirror-Recorder [of Catskill Mountain Publishing Co.] - Stamford, NY - *Ed&PubIntYB 82; NewsDir 84*
Stamford Mirror Recorder - *See* Catskill Mountain Publishing Corp.
Stamford Weekly Mail - Stamford, CT - *BaconPubCkNews 84; NewsDir 84*
Stamp Art [Aff. of Abracadabra Stamp Co.] - San Francisco, CA - *BoPubDir 4, 5*
Stamp Collector Newspaper - Albany, OR - *MagDir 84*
Stamp Wholesaler, The - Albany, OR - *MagDir 84; WritMar 84*
Stamp World [of Amos Press Inc.] - Sidney, OH - *MagIndMarPl 82-83; WritMar 84*
Stamping Grounds - Long Beach, NY - *Ed&PubIntYB 82*
Stamps Cablevision - Stamps, AR - *BrCabYB 84*
Stan Educational Software - Akron, OH - *MicrocomMPl 84*
Stanart Studios - New York, NY - *AvMarPl 83*
Stanberry Headlight - Stanberry, MO - *BaconPubCkNews 84; Ed&PubIntYB 82*

Stand - Jaffrey, NH - *WritMar 84*
Stand [of Northern House] - Newcastle-on-Tyne, England - *LitMag&SmPr 83-84*
Stand By - Louisville, KY - *NewsDir 84*
Stand By [of New York Local AFTRA] - New York, NY - *NewsDir 84*
Stand-By Consultoria de Relacoes Publicas S/C Ltfa. - Sao Paulo, Brazil - *DirPRFirms 83*
Standard - Brewton, AL - *AyerDirPub 83*
Standard - Gustine, CA - *AyerDirPub 83*
Standard - Rexburg, ID - *AyerDirPub 83*
Standard - Boonville, IN - *AyerDirPub 83*
Standard - La Grange, IN - *AyerDirPub 83*
Standard - Quincy, MA - *BaconPubCkMag 84; MagDir 84*
Standard - Chelsea, MI - *AyerDirPub 83*
Standard - Fairfax, MN - *AyerDirPub 83*
Standard - Lakefield, MN - *AyerDirPub 83*
Standard - Excelsior Springs, MO - *AyerDirPub 83; Ed&PubIntYB 82*
Standard - Milan, MO - *AyerDirPub 83*
Standard - Sikeston, MO - *AyerDirPub 83*
Standard - Humboldt, NE - *AyerDirPub 83*
Standard - Oxford, NE - *AyerDirPub 83*
Standard - Brewster, NY - *AyerDirPub 83*
Standard - Cortland, NY - *AyerDirPub 83*
Standard - Windsor, NY - *AyerDirPub 83*
Standard - Westhope, ND - *AyerDirPub 83*
Standard - Celina, OH - *AyerDirPub 83*
Standard - Pataskala, OH - *AyerDirPub 83*
Standard - Milton, PA - *AyerDirPub 83*
Standard - Uniontown, PA - *NewsDir 84*
Standard - Aiken, SC - *AyerDirPub 83*
Standard - Fredericksburg, TX - *AyerDirPub 83*
Standard - San Angelo, TX - *Ed&PubIntYB 82*
Standard - Strathmore, AB, Canada - *AyerDirPub 83*
Standard - Vermilion, AB, Canada - *AyerDirPub 83*
Standard - Hope, BC, Canada - *AyerDirPub 83*
Standard - Benito, MB, Canada - *Ed&PubIntYB 82*
Standard - Elliot Lake, ON, Canada - *AyerDirPub 83; Ed&PubIntYB 82*
Standard - Espanola, ON, Canada *Ed&PubIntYB 82*
Standard - Forest, ON, Canada - *AyerDirPub 83*
Standard - Markdale, ON, Canada - *AyerDirPub 83*
Standard - St. Catharines, ON, Canada - *AyerDirPub 83; Ed&PubIntYB 82*
Standard - Shaunavon, SK, Canada - *Ed&PubIntYB 82*
Standard [of Norwegian Standards Association] - Oslo, Norway - *DirOnDB Spring 84; EISS 83*
Standard Abstract Corp. - New York, NY - *BoPubDir 4, 5*
Standard Advertising Inc. - Tokyo, Japan - *StaDirAdAg 2-84*
Standard Analytical Service Inc. - St. Louis, MO - *BoPubDir 5*
Standard & Heart O'Texas News - Brady, TX - *AyerDirPub 83*
Standard & Poor's Blue List - New York, NY - *DirOnDB Spring 84*
Standard & Poor's Compustat Services Inc. [Subs. of Standard & Poor's Corp.] - Englewood, CO - *DataDirOnSer 84; InfIndMarPl 83*
Standard & Poor's Corporate Descriptions [of Standard & Poor's Corp.] - New York, NY - *DirOnDB Spring 84; EISS 5-84 Sup*
Standard & Poors Corp. [Aff. of McGraw-Hill Inc.] - New York, NY - *BoPubDir 5; CompReadDB 82; DataDirOnSer 84; InfIndMarPl 83; InfoS 83-84; MicrocomMPl 83, 84; ProGuPRSer 4; WhoWMicrocom 83*
Standard & Poor's Daily Dividend Record - New York, NY - *Ed&PubIntYB 82*
Standard & Poor's General Information File - New York, NY - *DBBus 82; DirOnDB Spring 84*
Standard & Poor's Industry Financial Data Bank - Washington, DC - *DirOnDB Spring 84*
Standard & Poor's Industry Financial Data Bank [of Data Resources Inc.] - Lexington, MA - *DataDirOnSer 84; DBBus 82*
Standard & Poor's News Online [of Dialog Information Services Inc.] - Palo Alto, CA - *DataDirOnSer 84*
Standard & Poor's News Online [of Standard & Poor's Corp.] - New York, NY - *CompReadDB 82; DBBus 82; DirOnDB Spring 84; EISS 83*
Standard & Poor's Stock Guide Retrieval Service - New York, NY - *DBBus 82*
Standard & The Miner - Silverton, CO - *AyerDirPub 83*
Standard Arts Press - Butler, MD - *BoPubDir 4, 5*
Standard Banner - Jefferson City, TN - *AyerDirPub 83*
Standard Broadcast News - Toronto, ON, Canada - *BrCabYB 84*
Standard Broadcasting Corp. - Toronto, ON, Canada - *BrCabYB 84*
Standard Broadcasting Corp. Ltd. - *See* Bushnell Communications Ltd.
Standard Catalog of American Cars [of Krause Publications] - Iola, WI - *WritMar 84*
Standard Communications Inc. - Salt Lake City, UT - *BrCabYB 84*
Standard Corp., The - Salt Lake City, UT - *Tel&CabFB 84S*
Standard Corp., The - *See* Standard Communications Inc.
Standard Data - Ft. Lauderdale, FL - *MicrocomMPl 84*
Standard Data Corp. - New York, NY - *ADAPSOMemDir 83-84*
Standard Drug File [of SDC Information Services] - Santa Monica, CA - *DataDirOnSer 84*
Standard Duplicating Machines - Andover, MA - *DirInfWP 82*
Standard Editions - New York, NY - *BoPubDir 4, 5*
Standard Educational Corp. - Chicago, IL - *LitMarPl 83, 84*
Standard Engineering Corp. - Fremont, CA - *DataDirSup 7-83*
Standard-Examiner - Ogden, UT - *AyerDirPub 83*
Standard-Freeholder [of Canadian Newspapers Ltd.] - Cornwall, ON, Canada - *AyerDirPub 83; BaconPubCkNews 84; Ed&PubIntYB 82; LitMarPl 84*
Standard-Herald - Warrensburg, MO - *AyerDirPub 83; Ed&PubIntYB 82*
Standard Historical Book Society - Standard, AB, Canada - *BoPubDir 4 Sup, 5*
Standard-Journal Inc. - Rexburg, ID - *BaconPubCkNews 84*
Standard Logic Inc. - Santa Ana, CA - *DataDirSup 7-83*
Standard Manifold Co. - Chicago, IL - *DirInfWP 82*
Standard Microsystems Inc. - Langhorne, PA - *MicrocomMPl 83; WhoWMicrocom 83*
Standard News - Mountain View, MO - *AyerDirPub 83*
Standard-Observer - Irwin, PA - *AyerDirPub 83*
Standard Periodical Directory Data Bank [of Oxbridge Communications Inc.] - New York, NY - *EISS 83*
Standard Press - Bennington, VT - *AyerDirPub 83*
Standard Press - Burlington, WI - *AyerDirPub 83*
Standard-Press - St. Croix Falls, WI - *AyerDirPub 83; Ed&PubIntYB 82*
Standard Press, The - Hoosick Falls, NY - *Ed&PubIntYB 82*
Standard Printing Service - Chicago, IL - *LitMarPl 83, 84*
Standard Publishing [Div. of Standex International] - Cincinnati, OH - *ArtMar 84; DirMarMP 83; LitMarPl 83, 84; MagIndMarPl 82-83; WritMar 84*
Standard Rate & Data Service Inc. [Subs. of Macmillan Inc.] - Skokie, IL - *DirMarMP 83; EISS 83*
Standard-Register - Tekoa, WA - *AyerDirPub 83*
Standard Register Co. - Dayton, OH - *DataDirSup 7-83; DirInfWP 82*
Standard-Register, The - Rosalia, WA - *Ed&PubIntYB 82*
Standard Rex-Rotary - Englewood, NJ - *DirInfWP 82*
Standard-Sentinel - Saluda, SC - *AyerDirPub 83; Ed&PubIntYB 82*
Standard Software Corp. of America - Randolph, MA - *MicrocomMPl 83; MicrocomSwDir 1; WhoWMicrocom 83*
Standard-Speaker - Hazleton, PA - *AyerDirPub 83; Ed&PubIntYB 82*
Standard Tape Laboratory Inc. - Hayward, CA - *AvMarPl 83*
Standard Telephone Co. [Aff. of Teledata Corp.] - Cornelia, GA - *TelDir&BG 83-84*
Standard, The - Vermillion, AB, Canada - *Ed&PubIntYB 82*
Standard, The - Blyth, ON, Canada - *Ed&PubIntYB 82*
Standard Theatre Supply Co. - Greensboro, NC - *AvMarPl 83*
Standard-Times - New Bedford, MA - *AyerDirPub 83; BaconPubCkNews 84; Ed&PubIntYB 82; LitMarPl 84*
Standard Times - North Kingstown, RI - *AyerDirPub 83; Ed&PubIntYB 82*
Standard-Times - San Angelo, TX - *AyerDirPub 83; Ed&PubIntYB 82; LitMarPl 84*
Standard Tobacco Co. Inc. - Maysville, KY - *BrCabYB 84 p.D-307; Tel&CabFB 84C p.1703*

Standard-Tribune - Greybull, WY - *AyerDirPub 83; Ed&PubIntYB 82*
Standardization & Automation of Terminology [of French Association for Standardization] - Paris, France - *EISS 83*
Standards & Specifications [of Dialog Information Services Inc.] - Palo Alto, CA - *DataDirOnSer 84*
Standards & Specifications [of National Standards Association Inc.] - Washington, DC - *DBBus 82*
Standards & Specifications [of National Standards Association Inc.] - Bethesda, MD - *CompReadDB 82; DirOnDB Spring 84; EISS 83*
Standards Information Service [of U.S. National Bureau of Standards] - Washington, DC - *EISS 83*
Standards Information Service [of Standards Council of Canada] - Ottawa, ON, Canada - *EISS 83*
Standards Information Service - *See* National Center for Standards & Certification Information
Standardsville Greene County Record - *See* Green Publishers Inc.
Standing Orders of the House of Commons [of QL Systems Ltd.] - Ottawa, ON, Canada - *CompReadDB 82; DataDirOnSer 84; DirOnDB Spring 84*
Standish Arenac County Independent - Standish, MI - *BaconPubCkNews 84; NewsDir 84*
Standish Telephone Co. - Standish, ME - *TelDir&BG 83-84*
Standun Controls Inc. - Santa Ana, CA - *MicrocomMPl 84*
Standy Records Inc. - Utica, NY - *BillIntBG 83-84*
Stanfield Film Associates - Santa Monica, CA - *AvMarPl 83*
Stanfield House, The - Los Angeles, CA - *AvMarPl 83*
Stanfill & Associates Inc. - Englewood, CO - *DirPRFirms 83*
Stanford Daily, The - Stanford, CA - *NewsDir 84*
Stanford Interior Journal - Stanford, KY - *BaconPubCkNews 84*
Stanford Judith Basin Press - Stanford, MT - *BaconPubCkNews 84*
Stanford Paper Co. - Washington, DC - *LitMarPl 83, 84*
Stanford Public Information Retrieval System [of Stanford University] - Stanford, CA - *EISS 83*
Stanford University (Environmental Law Society) - Stanford, CA - *BoPubDir 4, 5*
Stanford University (School of Earth Sciences) - Stanford, CA - *BoPubDir 4, 5*
Stanford University Libraries, The - Stanford, CA - *MicroMarPl 82-83*
Stanford University Press - Stanford, CA - *LitMarPl 83, 84; WritMar 84*
Stangel & Associates, Harvey J. - Highland Park, NJ - *IntDirMarRes 83*
Stanger Report - Fair Haven, NJ - *DirOnDB Spring 84*
Stanger Report [of NewsNet Inc.] - Bryn Mawr, PA - *DataDirOnSer 84*
Stangl, Jean - Camarillo, CA - *BoPubDir 4 Sup, 5*
Stangland Co., Thomas C. - Portland, OR - *BillIntBG 83-84*
Stanhill Music - *See* Cornelius Music, Stan
Stanley & Associates, Jay S. - North Little Rock, AR - *AvMarPl 83*
Stanley Cablevision Inc. - Stanley, ND - *Tel&CabFB 84C*
Stanley Communications Co. [Subs. of Carlton Bates Co.] - Little Rock, AR - *AvMarPl 83*
Stanley Foundation - Muscatine, IA - *BoPubDir 4, 5*
Stanley Gazette - Stanley, KS - *BaconPubCkNews 84*
Stanley Mountrail County Promoter - Stanley, ND - *BaconPubCkNews 84*
Stanley Republican - Stanley, WI - *BaconPubCkNews 84; Ed&PubIntYB 82*
Stanley Sun - *See* Sun Publications
Stanley-Winthrops Inc. - Quincy, MA - *AvMarPl 83*
Stanley's Law International - Windsor, ON, Canada - *BoPubDir 4 Sup, 5*
Stanly News & Press - Albemarle, NC - *AyerDirPub 83; Ed&PubIntYB 82*
Stanstead Journal - Rock Island, PQ, Canada - *AyerDirPub 83*
Stanstead Journal, The - Stanstead County, PQ, Canada - *Ed&PubIntYB 82*
Stanton & Associates - Denver, CO - *DirPRFirms 83*
Stanton & Lee Publishers Inc. [Subs. of The Carley Capital Group] - Madison, WI - *LitMarPl 83, 84*
Stanton Associates Inc., Ivens - New York, NY - *DirPRFirms 83*
Stanton Cable TV Inc. - Stanton, KY - *BrCabYB 84; Tel&CabFB 84C*
Stanton Cable TV Inc. - Stanton, ND - *BrCabYB 84; Tel&CabFB 84C*
Stanton Films - Redondo Beach, CA - *AvMarPl 83*
Stanton Register - Stanton, NE - *BaconPubCkNews 84; Ed&PubIntYB 82*
Stanton Reporter - Stanton, TX - *AyerDirPub 83; BaconPubCkNews 84; Ed&PubIntYB 82*
Stanton Telephone Co. Inc. - Stanton, NE - *TelDir&BG 83-84*
Stanton TV Cable [of Landmark Cablevision Associates] - Stanton, TX - *Tel&CabFB 84C*
Stanwix House Inc. - Pittsburgh, PA - *LitMarPl 83*
Stanwood Cable TV - Stanwood, WA - *BrCabYB 84; Tel&CabFB 84C*
Stanwood/Camano News - Stanwood, WA - *AyerDirPub 83; BaconPubCkNews 84; Ed&PubIntYB 82*
Stanwood/Camano Shopping News - Stanwood, WA - *AyerDirPub 83*
Stanyan Books - *See* Cheval Books/Stanyon Books
Stanyan Music Co. - Hollywood, CA - *BillIntBG 83-84*
Stanyan Record Co. - Hollywood, CA - *BillIntBG 83-84*
Staples World - Staples, MN - *BaconPubCkNews 84; Ed&PubIntYB 82; NewsDir 84*
Stapleton Enterprise - Stapleton, NE - *BaconPubCkNews 84; Ed&PubIntYB 82*
Star - Anniston, AL - *AyerDirPub 83*
Star - Tucson, AZ - *AyerDirPub 83*
Star - Hope, AR - *AyerDirPub 83*
Star - Mena, AR - *AyerDirPub 83*
Star - Dos Palos, CA - *AyerDirPub 83*
Star - St. Helena, CA - *AyerDirPub 83*
Star - Golden, CO - *AyerDirPub 83*
Star - Port St. Joe, FL - *AyerDirPub 83; Ed&PubIntYB 82*
Star - Ocilla, GA - *AyerDirPub 83*
Star - Columbia, IL - *AyerDirPub 83*
Star - Gilman, IL - *AyerDirPub 83*
Star - Heyworth, IL - *AyerDirPub 83*
Star - Indianapolis, IN - *AyerDirPub 83*
Star - Muncie, IN - *AyerDirPub 83*
Star - Terre Haute, IN - *AyerDirPub 83; Ed&PubIntYB 82*
Star - Clarksville, IA - *AyerDirPub 83*
Star - New Sharon, IA - *AyerDirPub 83*
Star - Hammond, LA - *AyerDirPub 83*
Star - Braintree, MA - *AyerDirPub 83*
Star - Seekonk, MA - *AyerDirPub 83*
Star - Winchester, MA - *AyerDirPub 83*
Star - Niles, MI - *AyerDirPub 83*
Star - Cambridge, MN - *AyerDirPub 83*
Star - Stewartville, MN - *AyerDirPub 83*
Star - Meridian, MS - *AyerDirPub 83*
Star - Drexel, MO - *AyerDirPub 83*
Star - Gerald, MO - *AyerDirPub 83*
Star - Kansas City, MO - *AyerDirPub 83*
Star - La Belle, MO - *AyerDirPub 83*
Star - Miles City, MT - *AyerDirPub 83*
Star - Townsend, MT - *AyerDirPub 83*
Star - Lincoln, NE - *AyerDirPub 83*
Star - South Sioux City, NE - *AyerDirPub 83*
Star - East Hampton, NY - *AyerDirPub 83*
S.T.A.R. [of News Group Publications] - New York, NY - *BaconPubCkMag 84; DirOnDB Spring 84; Folio 83; MagDir 84; MagIndMarPl 82-83; NewsBur 6; WritMar 84*
Star - Oneonta, NY - *AyerDirPub 83*
Star - Peekskill, NY - *AyerDirPub 83*
Star - West Winfield, NY - *AyerDirPub 83*
Star - Shelby, NC - *AyerDirPub 83*
Star - Wilmington, NC - *AyerDirPub 83*
Star - Aneta, ND - *AyerDirPub 83*
Star - Wishek, ND - *AyerDirPub 83*
Star - Marion, OH - *AyerDirPub 83*
Star - Chickasha, OK - *AyerDirPub 83*
Star - Geary, OK - *AyerDirPub 83*
Star - Nowata, OK - *AyerDirPub 83*
Star - Barnesboro, PA - *AyerDirPub 83*
Star - Delta, PA - *AyerDirPub 83*
Star - Reynoldsville, PA - *AyerDirPub 83*

Star - San Juan, PR - *AyerDirPub 83*
Star - North Augusta, SC - *AyerDirPub 83; Ed&PubIntYB 82*
Star - Hot Springs, SD - *AyerDirPub 83*
Star - Elizabethton, TN - *AyerDirPub 83*
Star - Boerne, TX - *AyerDirPub 83*
Star - Burleson, TX - *AyerDirPub 83*
Star - Friona, TX - *AyerDirPub 83*
Star - Highlands, TX - *AyerDirPub 83*
Star - Stephenville, TX - *AyerDirPub 83*
Star - Stockdale, TX - *AyerDirPub 83; Ed&PubIntYB 82*
Star - Stratford, TX - *AyerDirPub 83*
Star - Kewaunee, WI - *AyerDirPub 83*
Star - Mauston, WI - *AyerDirPub 83*
Star - Milwaukee, WI - *Ed&PubIntYB 82*
Star - Green River, WY - *AyerDirPub 83*
Star - Bashaw, AB, Canada - *AyerDirPub 83*
Star - Whitecourt, AB, Canada - *AyerDirPub 83*
Star - Golden, BC, Canada - *AyerDirPub 83; Ed&PubIntYB 82*
Star - Cobourg, ON, Canada - *AyerDirPub 83*
Star - Creemore, ON, Canada - *AyerDirPub 83*
Star - Hastings, ON, Canada - *Ed&PubIntYB 82*
Star - Port Perry, ON, Canada - *AyerDirPub 83; Ed&PubIntYB 82*
Star - Sudbury, ON, Canada - *AyerDirPub 83*
Star - Toronto, ON, Canada - *AyerDirPub 83*
Star - Windsor, ON, Canada - *AyerDirPub 83*
Star - Val D'Or, PQ, Canada - *AyerDirPub 83; Ed&PubIntYB 82*
Star - Gravelbourg, SK, Canada - *Ed&PubIntYB 82*
Star - Radville, SK, Canada - *Ed&PubIntYB 82*
Star - Whitehorse, YT, Canada - *Ed&PubIntYB 82; LitMarPl 84*
Star Advertiser - Imperial Beach, CA - *AyerDirPub 83*
Star Advertising Agency - Houston, TX - *StaDirAdAg 2-84*
Star-Advocate - Titusville, FL - *AyerDirPub 83; Ed&PubIntYB 82*
Star & Argonia Argosy - Conway Springs, KS - *AyerDirPub 83*
Star & Herald - Dwight, IL - *AyerDirPub 83*
Star & Times - Swan River, MB, Canada - *AyerDirPub 83; Ed&PubIntYB 82*
Star & Tribune - Waverly, MN - *Ed&PubIntYB 82*
Star & Vidette - Grand Valley, ON, Canada - *AyerDirPub 83; Ed&PubIntYB 82*
Star & Wave - Cape May, NJ - *AyerDirPub 83*
Star Bar - Burleson, TX - *AyerDirPub 83*
Star-Beacon - Ashtabula, OH - *AyerDirPub 83; Ed&PubIntYB 82*
Star-Beacon - Geneva, OH - *AyerDirPub 83; Ed&PubIntYB 82*
Star Bible Publications Inc. - Ft. Worth, TX - *BoPubDir 4, 5*
Star Blazers Fan Club, The - Merrick, NY - *LitMag&SmPr 83-84*
Star Blazers Fandom Report, The [of The Star Blazers Fan Club] - Merrick, NY - *LitMag&SmPr 83-84*
Star Broadcasting Corp. - Fredericksburg, VA - *BrCabYB 84*
Star Bulletin - Honolulu, HI - *AyerDirPub 83*
Star Bulletin & Advertiser - Honolulu, HI - *AyerDirPub 83; NewsDir 84*
Star CATV Investment Corp. - Sibley, LA - *Tel&CabFB 84C*
Star CATV Investment Corp. - Aubrey, TX - *BrCabYB 84*
Star CATV Investment Corp. - Brookshire, TX - *Tel&CabFB 84C*
Star CATV Investment Corp. - Celina, TX - *BrCabYB 84*
Star CATV Investment Corp. - Charlotte, TX - *BrCabYB 84*
Star CATV Investment Corp. - Idalou, TX - *Tel&CabFB 84C*
Star CATV Investment Corp. - Keene, TX - *Tel&CabFB 84C*
Star CATV Investment Corp. - Poteet, TX - *BrCabYB 84; Tel&CabFB 84C*
Star CATV Investment Corp. - Waxahachie, TX - *Tel&CabFB 84C p.1703*
Star Channel Services Ltd., The - Halifax, NS, Canada - *BrCabYB 84*
Star Chronicle - Wainwright, AB, Canada - *Ed&PubIntYB 82*
Star City Cable TV - Velva, ND - *BrCabYB 84; Tel&CabFB 84C*
Star City Lincoln Ledger - Star City, AR - *BaconPubCkNews 84*
Star City Software - Lincoln, NE - *MicrocomMPl 83, 84; WhoWMicrocom 83*
Star-Clipper - Traer, IA - *AyerDirPub 83*
Star Computer Systems Inc. - Torrance, CA - *MicrocomMPl 83*
Star-Countryman [of Royle Publishing Inc.] - Sun Prairie, WI - *AyerDirPub 83; Ed&PubIntYB 82; NewsDir 84*
Star-Courier - Kewanee, IL - *AyerDirPub 83; Ed&PubIntYB 82*
Star-Courier - Plano, TX - *AyerDirPub 83*
Star-Democrat - Easton, MD - *AyerDirPub 83; Ed&PubIntYB 82*
Star-Echo - Owensville, IN - *AyerDirPub 83; Ed&PubIntYB 82*
Star-Enterprise - Afton, IA - *AyerDirPub 83*
Star-Exponent - Culpeper, VA - *AyerDirPub 83; Ed&PubIntYB 82*
Star-Farmer - Renville, MN - *AyerDirPub 83; Ed&PubIntYB 82*
Star Food - Jackson, WY - *BoPubDir 4, 5*
Star-Free Press - Ventura, CA - *Ed&PubIntYB 82*
Star-Free Press [of Brown Publishing Co.] - Springboro, OH - *Ed&PubIntYB 82; NewsDir 84*
Star Gazers Inc. - Flandreau, SD - *Tel&CabFB 84C p.1703*
Star Gazette - Blandinsville, IL - *Ed&PubIntYB 82*
Star Gazette - Hastings, MN - *AyerDirPub 83*
Star Gazette - Moose Lake, MN - *AyerDirPub 83; Ed&PubIntYB 82*
Star-Gazette - Elmira, NY - *AyerDirPub 83*
Star-Gazing - Council Bluffs, IA - *Ed&PubIntYB 82*
Star Graphics Agency - Dallas, TX - *StaDirAdAg 2-84*
Star-Herald - Cabot, AR - *AyerDirPub 83*
Star-Herald - Pocahontas, AR - *AyerDirPub 83*
Star-Herald - Presque Isle, ME - *AyerDirPub 83*
Star-Herald - Luverne, MN - *AyerDirPub 83; Ed&PubIntYB 82; NewsDir 84*
Star-Herald - Kosciusko, MS - *AyerDirPub 83; Ed&PubIntYB 82*
Star-Herald - Scottsbluff, NE - *AyerDirPub 83; Ed&PubIntYB 82*
Star-Independent, The - Lewisburg, WV - *Ed&PubIntYB 82*
Star Jazz Records Inc. - Ft. Lauderdale, FL - *BillIntBG 83-84*
Star-Journal - Pueblo, CO - *AyerDirPub 83; Ed&PubIntYB 82*
Star-Journal - Hope, IN - *AyerDirPub 83; Ed&PubIntYB 82*
Star-Journal - Hillsboro, KS - *AyerDirPub 83*
Star-Journal - Ainsworth, NE - *AyerDirPub 83*
Star-Journal & Chieftain - Pueblo, CO - *AyerDirPub 83*
Star-Journal & Sunday Chieftain - Pueblo, CO - *Ed&PubIntYB 82*
Star-Journal, The - Gulfport, MS - *Ed&PubIntYB 82*
Star-Journal, The - Warrensburg, MO - *AyerDirPub 83*
Star-Kits - Mt. Kisco, NY - *MicrocomMPl 83, 84*
Star-Leader - Humansville, MO - *AyerDirPub 83; Ed&PubIntYB 82*
Star Ledger - Newark, NJ - *AyerDirPub 83; Ed&PubIntYB 82; LitMarPl 84; NewsBur 6*
Star Line [of Science Fiction Poetry Association] - Los Angeles, CA - *LitMag&SmPr 83-84*
Star Line - Nantucket, MA - *WritMar 84*
Star-Mail - Madison, NE - *AyerDirPub 83*
Star-Mercury - Manchester, GA - *AyerDirPub 83*
Star Micronics Inc. [Subs. of Star Manufacturing Co. Ltd.] - New York, NY - *MicrocomMPl 83; WhoWMicrocom 83*
Star Micronics Inc. - Dallas, TX - *MicrocomMPl 84*
Star-News - Andalusia, AL - *AyerDirPub 83*
Star-News - Chula Vista, CA - *AyerDirPub 83*
Star-News - Imperial Beach, CA - *AyerDirPub 83*
Star-News [of Twin Coast Newspapers] - Pasadena, CA - *AyerDirPub 83; Ed&PubIntYB 82; LitMarPl 84*
Star-News - San Diego, CA - *AyerDirPub 83*
Star-News - North Syracuse, NY - *AyerDirPub 83; Ed&PubIntYB 82*
Star-News - Wilmington, NC - *AyerDirPub 83; NewsDir 84*
Star-News - Mangum, OK - *AyerDirPub 83*
Star-News - Coraopolis, PA - *Ed&PubIntYB 82*
Star-News - Hendersonville, TN - *AyerDirPub 83; Ed&PubIntYB 82*
Star-News - Sistersville, WV - *Ed&PubIntYB 82*
Star-News - Medford, WI - *AyerDirPub 83; Ed&PubIntYB 82*
Star-News Publishing Co. Inc. - Chula Vista, CA - *BaconPubCkNews 84*
Star-Observer - Hudson, WI - *AyerDirPub 83*
Star of Zion [of African Methodist Episcopal Zion Denomination] - Charlotte, NC - *Ed&PubIntYB 82; NewsDir 84*
Star Pennysaver - Glendale, CA - *AyerDirPub 83*
Star People Records - Casselberry, FL - *BillIntBG 83-84*
Star-Phoenix - Saskatoon, SK, Canada - *AyerDirPub 83; BaconPubCkNews 84; Ed&PubIntYB 82; LitMarPl 83, 84*
Star Press - Holyoke, MA - *MagIndMarPl 82-83*
Star Printing Co. - Miles City, MT - *BrCabYB 84*
Star-Progress - Berryville, AR - *AyerDirPub 83; Ed&PubIntYB 82*
Star-Progress - La Habra, CA - *AyerDirPub 83*
Star Publications - Chicago Heights, IL - *BaconPubCkNews 84*
Star Publications - Sedan, KS - *BaconPubCkNews 84*

Star Publications - Kansas City, MO - *BoPubDir 4, 5*
Star Publishing Co. [Subs. of Star Business Group Inc.] - Belmont, CA - *LitMarPl 84; WritMar 84*
Star Publishing Co. - Palo Alto, CA - *BoPubDir 4, 5*
Star Publishing Co. - Chickasha, OK - *BaconPubCkNews 84*
Star-Record - Dodge Center, MN - *AyerDirPub 83*
Star Record Co. - New York, NY - *BillIntBG 83-84*
Star-Reporter - Columbia, SC - *AyerDirPub 83*
Star-Republican, The - Blanchester, OH - *Ed&PubIntYB 82*
Star Rover House - Oakland, CA - *LitMag&SmPr 83-84*
Star Service Syndicate - Ft. Lauderdale, FL - *Ed&PubIntYB 82; LitMarPl 84; WritMar 84*
Star Services - Los Angeles, CA - *MagIndMarPl 82-83*
Star Shopper - Stoughton, WI - *AyerDirPub 83*
Star Shopper, The - Virginia, IL - *AyerDirPub 83*
Star Shopping Guide - Hammond, LA - *AyerDirPub 83*
Star Software Systems - Torrance, CA - *MicrocomMPl 84; MicrocomSwDir 1*
Star Song Records - Marietta, GA - *BillIntBG 83-84*
Star Song Records - Pasadena, TX - *BillIntBG 83-84*
Star Standard - Arcola, SK, Canada - *AyerDirPub 83; Ed&PubIntYB 82*
Star System Press - Seattle, WA - *BoPubDir 4, 5*
Star Tech Journal - Merchantville, NJ - *BaconPubCkMag 84*
Star Telephone Co. Inc. [Aff. of C.A.I.L. Enterprises] - Maringouin, LA - *TelDir&BG 83-84*
Star Telephone Membership Corp. - Clinton, NC - *TelDir&BG 83-84*
Star, The - El Dorado Springs, MO - *Ed&PubIntYB 82*
Star, The - Rising Star, TX - *AyerDirPub 83*
Star-Times - Staunton, IL - *AyerDirPub 83; Ed&PubIntYB 82*
Star Tree Press - Stratford, CT - *BoPubDir 4 Sup, 5*
Star-Tribune - Markham, IL - *Ed&PubIntYB 82*
Star-Tribune - South Holland, IL - *Ed&PubIntYB 82*
Star-Tribune - Hagerman, NM - *AyerDirPub 83; Ed&PubIntYB 82*
Star-Tribune - Chatham, VA - *AyerDirPub 83; Ed&PubIntYB 82; NewsDir 84*
Star-Tribune - Casper, WY - *AyerDirPub 83; Ed&PubIntYB 82*
Star-Tronic Service Group [Subs. of CAP-TECH] - Farmington, MI - *WhoWMicrocom 83*
Star Valley Independent - Afton, WY - *AyerDirPub 83; Ed&PubIntYB 82*
Star Value Software - Austin, TX - *MicrocomMPl 84*
Star Video Systems - New York, NY - *AvMarPl 83; Tel&CabFB 84C*
Star-Web Paper - La Mesilla, NM - *LitMag&SmPr 83-84*
Star West [Aff. of S-B Gazette] - Sausalito, CA - *BoPubDir 4, 5*
Star West Communications - Ogden, UT - *Tel&CabFB 84C p.1703*
Starborn Records - Los Angeles, CA - *BillIntBG 83-84*
Starborne Productions Corp. - Sherman Oaks, CA - *BillIntBG 83-84*
Starbound Software - Cocoa Beach, FL - *MicrocomMPl 83*
Starbright Books - Freeland, WA - *BoPubDir 4, 5*
Starbuck Star - Clarkston, WA - *AyerDirPub 83*
Starbuck Telephone Co. - Starbuck, MN - *TelDir&BG 83-84*
Starbuck Times - Starbuck, MN - *BaconPubCkNews 84; Ed&PubIntYB 82*
Starch INRA Hooper - Mamaroneck, NY - *AdAge 5-17-84 p.38; BrCabYB 84; IntDirMarRes 83; MagIndMarPl 82-83; Tel&CabFB 84C*
Starchand Press - Wainscott, NY - *BoPubDir 4 Sup, 5; LitMag&SmPr 83-84*
Starchild, Adam - New York, NY - *LitMarPl 83, 84; MagIndMarPl 82-83*
Starcom Advertising Inc. - *See* Media West Group Inc., The
Starcom Inc. - Phoenix, AZ - *Tel&CabFB 84C*
Starcom Inc. - Denver, CO - *Tel&CabFB 84C*
Starcom Telecomputing Co. [Subs. of Starcom Corp.] - Westminster, CA - *DataDirOnSer 84*
Starcomm Cable TV - Springfield, IL - *Tel&CabFB 84C p.1703*
Starcountry Music Co. - *See* Stargold Publications Inc.
Starcraft Music - Granada Hills, CA - *BillIntBG 83-84*
Stardancer [of Ampersand Press] - Colchester, England - *LitMag&SmPr 83-84*
Starex Inc. - Kearny, NJ - *AvMarPl 83*
Starfire Books - Santa Fe, NM - *BoPubDir 5*
Starfox Publishing - Atlanta, GA - *BillIntBG 83-84*
Stargem Records Inc. - Nashville, TN - *BillIntBG 83-84*
Stargold Publications Inc. - Nashville, TN - *BillIntBG 83-84*
Stark County News - Toulon, IL - *AyerDirPub 83; Ed&PubIntYB 82*
Stark, Edward W. - Barnesville, GA - *Tel&CabFB 84C p.1703*
Stark, Howard E. - New York, NY - *CabTVFinDB 83*
Stark, Pitt - *See* C-K Video Inc.
Stark Records & Tape Co. - Mt. Airy, NC - *BillIntBG 83-84*
Stark, Sylvia M. - New York, NY - *LitMarPl 83, 84*
Starke Bradford County Telegraph - Starke, FL - *BaconPubCkNews 84; NewsDir 84*
Starke-County Leader - Knox, IN - *AyerDirPub 83; Ed&PubIntYB 82*
Stark's A & M Advertising Inc., Al - Hoffman Estates, IL - *StaDirAdAg 2-84*
Starkville News [of Harris Newspapers Inc.] - Starkville, MS - *BaconPubCkNews 84; Ed&PubIntYB 82; NewsDir 84*
Starkville TV Cable Co. - Maben, MS - *BrCabYB 84*
Starkville TV Cable Co. - Starkville, MS - *BrCabYB 84; Tel&CabFB 84C p.1703*
Starland Music Inc. - Lisle, IL - *BillIntBG 83-84*
Starlight International - Brooklyn, NY - *MicrocomMPl 84*
Starlight Press - Long Island City, NY - *BoPubDir 4, 5*
Starlog Magazine - New York, NY - *LitMarPl 83, 84*
Starlog Publications [Div. of Starlog Press] - New York, NY - *LitMarPl 83, 84*
Starman Records & Productions - Sacramento, CA - *BillIntBG 83-84*
Starmark - Chicago, IL - *AdAge 3-28-84; StaDirAdAg 2-84*
Starmont House - Mercer Island, WA - *BoPubDir 4, 5*
Starnet Data Systems [Subs. of Protec Industries Inc.] - Denver, CO - *WhoWMicrocom 83*
Starnet II [of Protex Industries Inc.] - Denver, CO - *TeleSy&SerDir 7-83*
Starogubski Press - New York, NY - *BoPubDir 4, 5*
Starpath Inc. - Fisk, MO - *Tel&CabFB 84C*
Starr Advertising - Northville, MI - *AdAge 3-28-84; StaDirAdAg 2-84*
Starr Computer Systems Inc. - Omaha, NE - *WhoWMicrocom 83*
Starr Marketing Research - Burlington, VT - *IntDirMarRes 83*
Starr Photo Productions Inc. - Coral Gables, FL - *AvMarPl 83; WritMar 84*
Starr Record Co. - Florida, NY - *BillIntBG 83-84*
Starr-Rose Productions - Ashland City, TN - *BillIntBG 83-84*
Starr/Ross Photo Productions Inc. - Coral Gables, FL - *ArtMar 84*
Starr Seigle McCombs Inc. - Honolulu, HI - *StaDirAdAg 2-84*
Starrucca Valley Publications - Starrucca, PA - *BoPubDir 4, 5*
Stars & Bars Publishing - McLean, VA - *BillIntBG 83-84*
Stars & Stripes Music - *See* Americus Music
Stars & Stripes-The National Tribune - Washington, DC - *MagIndMarPl 82-83*
Starshine Cable TV Inc. - Belleview, FL - *Tel&CabFB 84C*
Starship: The Magazine about Science Fiction [of Algol Press] - New York, NY - *LitMag&SmPr 83-84; MagIndMarPl 82-83*
Starside Engineering - Rochester, NY - *MicrocomMPl 83, 84; MicrocomSwDir 1*
Starsoft - Los Altos, CA - *MicrocomMPl 84; MicrocomSwDir 1*
Starsound Music - Cincinnati, OH - *BillIntBG 83-84*
Starstream Records - Houston, TX - *BillIntBG 83-84*
Start - Stoke-on-Trent, England - *LitMag&SmPr 83-84*
Startext [of Ft. Worth Star-Telegram] - Ft. Worth, TX - *EISS 7-83 Sup; TeleSy&SerDir 7-83*
Startime Music - La Quinta, CA - *BillIntBG 83-84*
Starting Line - Reseda, CA - *WritMar 84*
Startling Detective [of Detective Files Group] - Montreal, PQ, Canada - *WritMar 84*
Starview [Subs. of Columbia Satellite Systems Inc.] - Houston, TX - *Tel&CabFB 84C*
Starview Systems Inc. - Pocahontas, AR - *Tel&CabFB 84C*
Starware - Washington, DC - *MicrocomMPl 84; MicrocomSwDir 1*
Starweek Magazine [of Toronto Star Newspapers Ltd.] - Toronto, ON, Canada - *WritMar 84*
Starwest Inc. - Atkins, IA - *Tel&CabFB 84C p.1703*
Starwest Music - Longview, WA - *BillIntBG 83-84*
Starwest Productions - Arvada, CO - *AvMarPl 83*

Starwest Records - Longview, WA - *BillIntBG 83-84*
Starworth, I. J. [Subs. of Struct-O-Globe Corp.] - Elmont, NY - *LitMarPl 83, 84*
Stash Records Inc. - Brooklyn, NY - *BillIntBG 83-84*
Stat [of American Publishing Exchange] - Peterborough, NH - *MicrocomMPl 84*
Stat-Scan - Bridgeport, CT - *DirOnDB Spring 84*
Statcom Corp. - Austin, TX - *MicrocomMPl 83, 84; WhoWMicrocom 83*
State - Raleigh, NC - *BaconPubCkMag 84; MagDir 84; WritMar 84*
State Acreage & Farm Income Forecast [of Chase Econometrics/Interactive Data Corp.] - Waltham, MA - *DataDirOnSer 84*
State Acreage & Farm Income Forecast - Bala Cynwyd, PA - *DirOnDB Spring 84*
State Advertising Agency Inc. - Chicago, IL - *StaDirAdAg 2-84*
State Advertising Service Inc. - Brooklyn, NY - *StaDirAdAg 2-84*
State Agriculture [of Chase Econometrics/Interactive Data Corp.] - Waltham, MA - *DataDirOnSer 84*
State Agriculture - Bala Cynwyd, PA - *DirOnDB Spring 84*
State Alcoholism Profile Information System [of U.S. Public Health Service] - Rockville, MD - *EISS 83*
State & Area Forecasting Service Data Bank [of Data Resources Inc.] - Lexington, MA - *DataDirOnSer 84*
State & Regional Indicators Archive [of University of New Hampshire] - Durham, NH - *EISS 83*
State Business Structures - Bala Cynwyd, PA - *DirOnDB Spring 84*
State Cable TV Corp. [of Whitney Communications Corp.] - Augusta, ME - *BrCabYB 84 p.D-307; Tel&CabFB 84C p.1703*
State Cable TV Corp. - Livermore Falls, ME - *BrCabYB 84*
State Cable TV Corp. - Norway, ME - *BrCabYB 84*
State Cable TV Corp. - Rumford, ME - *BrCabYB 84; Tel&CabFB 84C*
State Cable TV Corp. - Lincoln, NH - *BrCabYB 84*
State Cable TV Corp. - Lisbon, NH - *BrCabYB 84*
State Cable TV Corp. - Littleton, NH - *Tel&CabFB 84C*
State Cable TV Corp. - North Conway, NH - *BrCabYB 84*
State Center Enterprise - State Center, IA - *BaconPubCkNews 84; Ed&PubIntYB 82*
State College Centre Daily Times - State College, PA - *BaconPubCkNews 84*
State College TV Supply - State College, PA - *AvMarPl 83*
State Data Program [of University of California, Berkeley] - Berkeley, CA - *EISS 83*
State Employment - Bala Cynwyd, PA - *DirOnDB Spring 84*
State Energy Data System - Washington, DC - *DirOnDB Spring 84*
State Energy Data System [of I. P. Sharp Associates Ltd.] - Toronto, ON, Canada - *DataDirOnSer 84*
State Fertilizer [of Chase Econometrics/Interactive Data Corp.] - Waltham, MA - *DataDirOnSer 84*
State Fertilizer - Bala Cynwyd, PA - *DirOnDB Spring 84*
State Gazette [of New York Times] - Dyersburg, TN - *AyerDirPub 83; Ed&PubIntYB 82; NewsDir 84*
State Government News [of Council of State Governments] - Lexington, KY - *BaconPubCkMag 84; MagIndMarPl 82-83*
State Historical Society of Colorado - *See* Colorado Historical Society
State Historical Society of Wisconsin - Madison, WI - *LitMarPl 84; MicroMarPl 82-83; WritMar 84*
State Historical Society of Wisconsin (The Society Press) - Madison, WI - *LitMarPl 83*
State Hornet Newspaper - Sacramento, CA - *NewsDir 84*
State Industry - Bala Cynwyd, PA - *DirOnDB Spring 84*
State Information System [of Virginia Polytechnic Institute & State University] - Blacksburg, VA - *EISS 7-83 Sup*
State Journal - Frankfort, KY - *AyerDirPub 83; BaconPubCkNews 84; Ed&PubIntYB 82*
State Journal - Lansing, MI - *AyerDirPub 83*
State Journal-Register [of The Copley Press Inc.] - Springfield, IL - *ArtMar 84; AyerDirPub 83; BaconPubCkNews 84; Ed&PubIntYB 82; LitMarPl 84*
State Legislatures - Denver, CO - *WritMar 84*
State Line Cablevision [of Omni Cable TV Corp.] - Junction City, AR - *BrCabYB 84*
State Line News, The - Rindge-Jeffrey (NH), MA - *Ed&PubIntYB 82*
State Line Tribune - Farwell, TX - *AyerDirPub 83; Ed&PubIntYB 82*
State Long Distance Telephone Co. - Elkhorn, WI - *TelDir&BG 83-84*
State Macro - Bala Cynwyd, PA - *DirOnDB Spring 84*
State Mutual Book & Periodical Service Ltd. - New York, NY - *BoPubDir 4, 5; MagIndMarPl 82-83*
State News, The - East Lansing, MI - *NewsDir 84*
State of the Art Inc. - Costa Mesa, CA - *MicrocomMPl 84; MicrocomSwDir 1*
State of the Art Systems Inc. - Mountain View, CA - *MicrocomMPl 84*
State of the Union - Chicago, IL - *BaconPubCkMag 84*
State Photo Supply Corp. - Albany, NY - *AvMarPl 83*
State Port Pilot - Southport, NC - *AyerDirPub 83; Ed&PubIntYB 82; NewsDir 84*
State Press, The [of Students of Arizona State University] - Tempe, AZ - *NewsDir 84*
State Publications [of Bibliographic Retrieval Services Inc.] - Latham, NY - *DataDirOnSer 84*
State Publications Depository & Distribution Center [of Colorado State Library] - Denver, CO - *EISS 83*
State Publications Index [of Capitol Services International] - Washington, DC - *DBBus 82; EISS 83*
State Publications Index [of Information Technology Group] - Alexandria, VA - *CompReadDB 82*
State-Record Co. - Columbia, SC - *Ed&PubIntYB 82*
State Register - Laurel, DE - *AyerDirPub 83*
State Services Group [of the Martin-Haley Cos.] - Falls Church, VA - *EISS 83; InfIndMarPl 83*
State Street Bank & Trust Co. (Correspondent Services Div.) - Boston, MA - *DataDirOnSer 84*
State Street Banking Services Inc. [Subs. of State Street Bank & Trust Co.] - Hanover, NH - *DataDirOnSer 84*
State Street Press - Pittsford, NY - *LitMag&SmPr 83-84*
State Street Publications - San Diego, CA - *BoPubDir 4, 5*
State Telephone Co. - Coxsackie, NY - *TelDir&BG 83-84*
State, The [of Columbia Newspapers Inc.] - Columbia, SC - *AyerDirPub 83; Ed&PubIntYB 82; LitMarPl 84; NewsBur 6; NewsDir 84*
State Times [of Capital City Press] - Baton Rouge, LA - *AyerDirPub 83; Ed&PubIntYB 82; LitMarPl 84*
State TV Cable [of Western Communications Inc.] - Chico, CA - *BrCabYB 84; Tel&CabFB 84C*
State TV Cable [of Western Communications Inc.] - Corning, CA - *BrCabYB 84*
State TV Cable [of Western Communications Inc.] - Orland, CA - *BrCabYB 84*
State TV Cable [of Western Communications Inc.] - Willows, CA - *BrCabYB 84*
State University College (Project Child) - Geneseo, NY - *BoPubDir 4*
State University of New York, Binghamton (Publications in Geomorphology) - Binghamton, NY - *BoPubDir 4, 5*
State University of New York, Buffalo (Arethusa) - Buffalo, NY - *BoPubDir 4, 5*
State University of New York, Buffalo (Educational Communications Center, Media Library) - Buffalo, NY - *AvMarPl 83*
State University of New York Press - Albany, NY - *LitMarPl 83, 84*
State University of New York, Stony Brook (Foundation for the Quarterly Review of Biology) - Stony Brook, NY - *BoPubDir 4, 5*
State Video Cable Inc. - El Granada, CA - *BrCabYB 84 p.D-307*
State Video Cable Inc. - La Mesa Village, CA - *BrCabYB 84*
Staten Island [of Motivational Communications] - New York, NY - *WritMar 84*
Staten Island Advance - Staten Island, NY - *BaconPubCkNews 84; Ed&PubIntYB 82; LitMarPl 84; NewsDir 84*
Staten Island Register - Staten Island, NY - *AyerDirPub 83; BaconPubCkNews 84; Ed&PubIntYB 82; NewsDir 84*
Staten Islander Shopping Guide - Staten Island, NY - *AyerDirPub 83*

Statens Vag- och Trafikinstitut/National Road & Traffic Research Institute - Linkoping, Sweden - *InfIndMarPl 83*
Statens Vagverk/National Road Administration - Borlange, Sweden - *InfIndMarPl 83*
States-Graphic - Brownsville, TN - *AyerDirPub 83; Ed&PubIntYB 82*
States Information Center [of Council of State Governments] - Lexington, KY - *EISS 83*
States-Item [of Times-Picayune Publishing Corp.] - New Orleans, LA - *LitMarPl 83; NewsBur 6; NewsDir 84*
States News Service - Washington, DC - *BrCabYB 84; EISS 7-83 Sup; InfoS 83-84*
Statesboro CATV Inc. - Statesboro, GA - *BrCabYB 84; Tel&CabFB 84C*
Statesboro Herald - Statesboro, GA - *BaconPubCkNews 84; Ed&PubIntYB 82; NewsDir 84*
Statesboro Southern Beacon [of Morris Newspapers] - Statesboro, GA - *BaconPubCkNews 84; NewsDir 84*
Statesboro Telephone Co., The - Statesboro, GA - *TelDir&BG 83-84*
Statesman - Stony Brook, NY - *AyerDirPub 83; NewsDir 84*
Statesman - Gruver, TX - *AyerDirPub 83*
Statesman - Kewaskum, WI - *AyerDirPub 83*
Statesman-Examiner - Colville, WA - *AyerDirPub 83*
Statesman-Journal [of Gannett Co. Inc.] - Salem, OR - *AyerDirPub 83; BaconPubCkNews 84; Ed&PubIntYB 82; LitMarPl 83, 84; NewsDir 84*
Statesville Broadcasting Co. - Statesville, NC - *BrCabYB 84*
Statesville Record & Landmark [of Park Newspapers] - Statesville, NC - *BaconPubCkNews 84; Ed&PubIntYB 82; LitMarPl 83, 84; NewsDir 84*
Stateways [of Jobson Publishing Corp.] - New York, NY - *BaconPubCkMag 84; MagDir 84*
Statewide Broadcasting - Pompano Beach, FL - *BrCabYB 84*
Statewide Planning & Research Cooperative System [of New York State Dept. of Health] - Albany, NY - *EISS 83*
Statewide Telephone-Teletype Reference System [of Mississippi State Library Commission] - Jackson, MS - *EISS 83*
Statham Cable Co. Inc. - Statham, GA - *Tel&CabFB 84C*
Static Memory Systems Inc. - Freeport, IL - *MicrocomMPl 83*
Statigraphic Research Services Inc. - New York, NY - *EISS 83*
Station Hill Press [Aff. of The Other Publishers] - Barrytown, NY - *BoPubDir 4; LitMag&SmPr 83-84; LitMarPl 83, 84*
Stations [of Membrane Press] - Milwaukee, WI - *LitMag&SmPr 83-84*
Statistical Computing Consultants - Burke, VA - *MicrocomSwDir 1; WhoWMicrocom 83*
Statistical Graphics Corp. - Princeton, NJ - *MicrocomMPl 84; MicrocomSwDir 1*
Statistical Office [of United Nations] - New York, NY - *EISS 83*
Statistical Policy Branch [of U.S. Office of Management & Budget] - Washington, DC - *EISS 83*
Statistical Research Inc. - Westfield, NJ - *BrCabYB 84; IntDirMarRes 83; Tel&CabFB 84C*
Statistical Tabulating Corp. - Chicago, IL - *DataDirOnSer 84*
Statistics Canada (Cansim Div.) - Ottawa, ON, Canada - *DataDirOnSer 84*
Statistics Dept. [of American Petroleum Institute] - Washington, DC - *EISS 83*
Statistics of Income Div. [of U.S. Dept. of the Treasury] - Washington, DC - *EISS 7-83 Sup*
Statistics of Postal Services [of Universal Postal Union] - Berne, Switzerland - *EISS 83*
Statistics Section [of Farm & Industrial Equipment Institute] - Chicago, IL - *EISS 83*
Statistikon Corp., The - East Norwich, NY - *IntDirMarRes 83*
Statler Office Services - Cleveland, OH - *DirInfWP 82*
Statmark SA - Caracas, Venezuela - *IntDirMarRes 83*
STATSID [of General Electric Information Services Co.] - Rockville, MD - *DataDirOnSer 84*
STATSID [of National ELF Acquitaine Co.] - Paris, France - *DirOnDB Spring 84; EISS 83*
Statue of Life Inc. - Aldan, PA - *BoPubDir 4, 5*
Status [of Atomic Energy Authority] - Didcot, England - *EISS 83*
Status Users Group - Didcot, England - *EISS 5-84 Sup*
Statutes of Alberta - Edmonton, AB, Canada - *DirOnDB Spring 84*
Statutes of Alberta Citator [of University of Calgary Law Library] - Calgary, AB, Canada - *CompReadDB 82*
Statutes of Alberta Citator [of QL Systems Ltd.] - Ottawa, ON, Canada - *DataDirOnSer 84*
Statutes of British Columbia - Victoria, BC, Canada - *DirOnDB Spring 84*
Statutes of British Columbia [of QL Systems Ltd.] - Ottawa, ON, Canada - *DataDirOnSer 84*
Statutes of Manitoba - Winnipeg, MB, Canada - *DirOnDB Spring 84*
Statutes of Manitoba Citator - Winnipeg, MB, Canada - *DirOnDB Spring 84*
Statutes of Manitoba Citator [of Canadian Law Information Council] - Ottawa, ON, Canada - *CompReadDB 82; DataDirOnSer 84*
Statutes of New Brunswick [of Office of Attorney General] - Fredericton, NB, Canada - *CompReadDB 82; DataDirOnSer 84; DirOnDB Spring 84*
Statutes of Ontario [of QL Systems Ltd.] - Ottawa, ON, Canada - *DataDirOnSer 84; DirOnDB Spring 84*
Statutes of Saskatchewan - Regina, SK, Canada - *DirOnDB Spring 84*
Statutory Orders & Regulations of Canada [of QL Systems Ltd.] - Ottawa, ON, Canada - *CompReadDB 82; DataDirOnSer 84; DirOnDB Spring 84*
Statuts Revises du Canada [of Federal Dept. of Justice] - Ottawa, ON, Canada - *CompReadDB 82; DirOnDB Spring 84*
Staub, Charlotte - New York, NY - *LitMarPl 83, 84*
Stauch-Vetromile Inc. - East Providence, RI - *DirPRFirms 83; StaDirAdAg 2-84*
Stauffer Communications - Topeka, KS - *AdAge 6-28-84; BrCabYB 84; Ed&PubIntYB 82; KnowInd 83; TelAl 83, 84; Tel&CabFB 84S*
Stauffer Edition Binding Co. - Monterey Park, CA - *LitMarPl 83, 84*
Staunton Leader [of Multimedia Inc.] - Staunton, VA - *BaconPubCkNews 84; Ed&PubIntYB 82; NewsDir 84*
Staunton News-Leader, The - Staunton, VA - *Ed&PubIntYB 82*
Staunton Star Times - Staunton, IL - *BaconPubCkNews 84; NewsDir 84*
Staunton Video Corp. - Staunton, VA - *BrCabYB 84; Tel&CabFB 84C*
Stax Music - Berkley, CA - *BillIntBG 83-84*
Stay Away Joe Publishers - Great Falls, MT - *BoPubDir 4, 5*
Stayner Sun, The - Stayner, ON, Canada - *Ed&PubIntYB 82*
Stayton Cablevision-Sublimity Cablevision [of Stayton Cooperative Telephone Co.] - Aumsville, OR - *Tel&CabFB 84C*
Stayton Cooperative Telephone Co. - Stayton, OR - *TelDir&BG 83-84*
Stayton Mail - Stayton, OR - *BaconPubCkNews 84; Ed&PubIntYB 82; NewsDir 84*
Stazybo Music - *See* Mietus Copyright Management
STC Advertising Services [Div. of Storage Technology Corp.] - Louisville, CO - *StaDirAdAg 2-84*
STC Systems Inc. [Subs. of Storage Technology Inc.] - Waldwick, NJ - *DataDirSup 7-83; LitMarPl 83, 84; MagIndMarPl 82-83*
STC Systems Inc. - Wildwood, NJ - *LitMarPl 83*
Ste. Broadcasting Corp. - Modesto, CA - *BrCabYB 84*
Ste. Broadcasting Corp. - Salinas, CA - *Tel&CabFB 84S*
Ste. Genevieve Cablevision Inc. - Ste. Genevieve, MO - *Tel&CabFB 84C*
Ste. Genevieve Herald - Ste. Genevieve, MO - *Ed&PubIntYB 82*
Steam from the Boiler - Chicago, IL - *ArtMar 84*
Steam Press - Cambridge, MA - *LitMarPl 83, 84*
Steam Trains of the Soo - Fortuna, CA - *BoPubDir 4 Sup, 5*
Steamboat Cablevision - Steamboat Springs, CO - *BrCabYB 84; Tel&CabFB 84C*
Steamboat Pilot - Steamboat Springs, CO - *AyerDirPub 83; BaconPubCkNews 84; Ed&PubIntYB 82; NewsDir 84*
Steamship Historical Society of America Inc. - Staten Island, NY - *BoPubDir 5*
Steamship Historical Society of America Inc. - Providence, RI - *BoPubDir 4*
Stearns & Beale - New York, NY - *LitMarPl 83, 84*
Stearns-Morrison Enterprise - Albany, MN - *Ed&PubIntYB 82*

Stearns-Morrison Enterprise - Albert Lea, MN - *AyerDirPub 83*
Stebbins, John D. - Lake Forest, IL - *CabTVFinDB 83*
Steck-Vaughn Co. [Div. of National Education Corp.] - Austin, TX - *LitMarPl 83, 84*
Steckler, William - Glen Ullin, ND - *Tel&CabFB 84C p.1703*
Steddum, Wayne & Rita - Pampa, TX - *Tel&CabFB 84C p.1703*
Steeg Productions - New York, NY - *AvMarPl 83*
Steel Country Bee - Daingerfield, TX - *AyerDirPub 83; Ed&PubIntYB 82*
Steel Country News-Ledger - Lone Star, TX - *AyerDirPub 83*
Steel Data Banks - Washington, DC - *DirOnDB Spring 84*
Steel Data Banks [of Data Resources Inc.] - Lexington, MA - *DBBus 82*
Steel Data Base [of Data Resources Inc.] - Lexington, MA - *DataDirOnSer 84*
Steel '82 - Washington, DC - *MagDir 84*
Steel Founders' Society of America - Rocky River, OH - *BoPubDir 5*
Steel Industry Monitor Report - Washington, DC - *DirOnDB Spring 84*
Steel News - Pueblo, CO - *NewsDir 84*
Steel Products Databank - Sault Ste. Marie, ON, Canada - *DirOnDB Spring 84*
Steel Rail Educational Publishing - Ottawa, ON, Canada - *BoPubDir 4, 5*
Steel Yacht, The - Arcadia, CA - *ArtMar 84*
Steelabor [of United Steelworkers of America] - Pittsburgh, PA - *NewsDir 84*
Steelcase Inc. - Grand Rapids, MI - *DirInfWP 82*
Steele County Press - Finley, ND - *AyerDirPub 83*
Steele Enterprise - Steele, MO - *BaconPubCkNews 84; Ed&PubIntYB 82*
Steele Group Ltd., The - San Francisco, CA - *DirPRFirms 83*
Steele Ozone Press - Steele, ND - *AyerDirPub 83; BaconPubCkNews 84; Ed&PubIntYB 82*
Steele Video Cable - Steele, MO - *BrCabYB 84*
Steeleville Ledger - Steeleville, IL - *BaconPubCkNews 84; Ed&PubIntYB 82*
Steeleville Percy Cablevision - Steeleville, IL - *BrCabYB 84*
Steelstone Press - Valparaiso, IN - *BoPubDir 4, 5*
Steelville Crawford Mirror - Steelville, MO - *BaconPubCkNews 84*
Steelville Star - Steelville, MO - *AyerDirPub 83; BaconPubCkNews 84*
Steelville Telephone Exchange Inc. [Aff. of Viburnum Communications Inc.] - Steelville, MO - *TelDir&BG 83-84*
Steelville TV Cable [of Meramec Valley Communications Inc.] - Steelville, MO - *Tel&CabFB 84C*
Steen Advertising - Lynbrook, NY - *AdAge 3-28-84; MagIndMarPl 82-83; StaDirAdAg 2-84*
Steenbeck Inc. - Chatsworth, CA - *AvMarPl 83*
SteepleChase Productions Inc. - Chicago, IL - *BillIntBG 83-84*
Steering Wheel - Austin, TX - *BaconPubCkMag 84; MagDir 84*
Steffanides, George F. - Fitchburg, MS - *BoPubDir 4, 5*
Steffen Associates Inc., John F. - St. Louis, MO - *DataDirOnSer 84*
Steger News - Steger, IL - *Ed&PubIntYB 82*
Steger News - *See* Russell Publications
Stegman & Associates Productions Inc. - Tulsa, OK - *AvMarPl 83*
Stehle's Cable TV - Paint Township, PA - *Tel&CabFB 84C*
Stehles Trailer Sales - Knox, PA - *BrCabYB 84*
Stehles Trailer Sales - Paint Township, PA - *BrCabYB 84*
Stehsel, Donald L. - Arcadia, CA - *BoPubDir 4, 5*
Steiger Associates, Dale - New York, NY - *MagIndMarPl 82-83*
Stein & Day Publishers - Briarcliff Manor, NY - *ArtMar 84; LitMarPl 83, 84; WritMar 84*
Stein Co., W. L. - San Antonio, TX - *TeleSy&SerDir 7-83*
Stein, Fredric - Chicago, IL - *MagIndMarPl 82-83*
Stein, Judith - New York, NY - *MagIndMarPl 82-83*
Stein, Larry - New York, NY - *LitMarPl 83, 84*
Stein Public Relations, Julian - Washington, DC - *DirPRFirms 83*
Stein, Ruth - New York, NY - *LitMarPl 83*
Stein Studios, Mark - Richmond Hill, NY - *LitMarPl 83, 84; MagIndMarPl 82-83*
Steinberg Electronics Inc. - Philadelphia, PA - *AvMarPl 83*
Steinberg, Fern - Springfield, NJ - *LitMarPl 83; MagIndMarPl 82-83*
Steinberg, Sheila - Forest Hills, NY - *LitMarPl 83, 84; MagIndMarPl 82-83*
Steiner Associates Inc., William - New York, NY - *DirMarMP 83; LitMarPl 83, 84; MagIndMarPl 82-83; StaDirAdAg 2-84*
Steiner Book Centre - North Vancouver, BC, Canada - *BoPubDir 4, 5*
Steiner/Bressler Advertising - Birmingham, AL - *StaDirAdAg 2-84*
Steiner-Prag, Eleanor F. - New York, NY - *LitMarPl 83, 84*
Steinheimer Advertising, Leoda - St. Louis, MO - *ArtMar 84; StaDirAdAg 2-84*
Steinmetz Archives [of Royal Netherlands Academy of Arts & Sciences] - Amsterdam, Netherlands - *EISS 83*
Stein's Compass Productions, Hal - Chicago, IL - *Tel&CabFB 84C*
Stel-Mar Publishing - Lancaster, PA - *BoPubDir 4, 5*
Stellar Classification File [of Northwestern University] - Evanston, IL - *EISS 83*
Stellar Data Center [of Strasbourg Observatory] - Strasbourg, France - *EISS 83*
Stellar Vision Inc. - Corpus Christi, TX - *Tel&CabFB 84C p.1703*
Stellar Vision Inc. - Seadrift, TX - *BrCabYB 84*
Stellation Two - Santa Barbara, CA - *MicrocomMPl 83, 84; MicrocomSwDir 1; WhoWMicrocom 83*
StellaVision [of Ketner Electronics Inc.] - Stella, NE - *Tel&CabFB 84C*
Stelle Group - Stelle, IL - *BoPubDir 4, 5*
Stelzer Advertising & Public Relations Inc., Joan - Port Chester, NY - *DirPRFirms 83*
Stemmer House Publishers Inc. - Owings Mills, MD - *ArtMar 84; LitMag&SmPr 83-84; LitMarPl 83, 84*
Stemmos Ltd. - London, England - *MicrocomSwDir 1*
Stempien Publishing Co., G. - Joliet, IL - *BoPubDir 4, 5*
Stencil-Art Publishing Co. Inc. - Jacksonville, FL - *BoPubDir 4 Sup, 5*
Stenocord Dictating Systems - Los Angeles, CA - *DirInfWP 82*
Step Saver, The - Southington, CT - *AyerDirPub 83*
Stephan Advertising Agency Inc. - Wichita, KS - *StaDirAdAg 2-84*
Stephan & Brady - Madison, WI - *AdAge 3-28-84; DirMarMP 83; StaDirAdAg 2-84*
Stephen Argyle Messenger - Stephen, MN - *AyerDirPub 83*
Stephen Associates Inc. - New York, NY - *StaDirAdAg 2-84*
Stephen Cable TV Inc. - Stephen, MN - *Tel&CabFB 84C p.1703*
Stephen Messenger - Stephen, MN - *BaconPubCkNews 84*
Stephens Cablevision Corp. [of Omni Cable TV Corp.] - Stephens, AR - *BrCabYB 84*
Stephens College (Open Places Poets Series) - Columbia, MO - *BoPubDir 4, 5*
Stephens-Hutchinson Advertising Inc. - Kansas City, MO - *StaDirAdAg 2-84*
Stephens Star - Camden, AR - *AyerDirPub 83*
Stephens Star - Stephens, AR - *Ed&PubIntYB 82*
Stephenson Agency, The - Tulsa, OK - *StaDirAdAg 2-84*
Stephenson-Brothers Inc. - Philadelphia, PA - *LitMarPl 83, 84*
Stephenson County Scope [of Durand North Central Associated Publishers] - Durand, IL - *AyerDirPub 83; Ed&PubIntYB 82; NewsDir 84*
Stephenson Inc. - Alexandria, VA - *MagIndMarPl 82-83*
Stephenson Menominee County Journal - Stephenson, MI - *BaconPubCkNews 84*
Stephenson School Supply Co. - Lincoln, NE - *AvMarPl 83*
Stephenville Empire-Tribune [of Woodson Newspapers Inc.] - Stephenville, TX - *BaconPubCkNews 84; Ed&PubIntYB 82; NewsDir 84*
Stephenville Star - Stephenville, TX - *BaconPubCkNews 84*
Steppenwolf - Tucson, AZ - *LitMag&SmPr 83-84*
Stepping Stone Literary Agency Inc. - New York, NY - *LitMarPl 83, 84*
Stepping Stone Music - *See* Mimic Music
Steps Music Co. - *See* McHugh Music Inc., Jimmy
Stereo - Great Barrington, MA - *MagDir 84*
Stereo & Hi-Fi Times - New York, NY - *MagDir 84*
Stereo Guide [of Infracom Ltd.] - Brampton, ON, Canada - *BaconPubCkMag 84; WritMar 84*
Stereo Publications - Brooklyn, NY - *BoPubDir 4, 5*

Stereo Review [of Ziff-Davis Publishing Co.] - New York, NY - *ArtMar 84; BaconPubCkMag 84; LitMarPl 83, 84; MagDir 84; MagIndMarPl 82-83*
Stereo World - Columbus, OH - *LitMag&SmPr 83-84*
Stereotronics Television Co. [Subs. of 3D Pictures Corp.] - Van Nuys, CA - *AvMarPl 83*
Stereotypers & Electrotypers Union Journal - Cleveland, OH - *NewsDir 84*
Sterling Bulletin - Sterling, KS - *AyerDirPub 83; BaconPubCkNews 84; Ed&PubIntYB 82*
Sterling Cablevision Inc. - Sterling, KS - *BrCabYB 84; Tel&CabFB 84C*
Sterling City News-Record - Sterling City, TX - *BaconPubCkNews 84; Ed&PubIntYB 82*
Sterling Community TV [of Community Tele-Communications Inc.] - Sterling, CO - *BrCabYB 84; Tel&CabFB 84C*
Sterling Educational Films [Div. of Walter Reade Organization Inc.] - New York, NY - *AvMarPl 83*
Sterling Gazette - Sterling, IL - *BaconPubCkNews 84; NewsDir 84*
Sterling Heights Advisor - *See* Advisor Newspapers
Sterling Heights Community News [of Mt. Clemens Community News] - Mt. Clemens, MI - *NewsDir 84*
Sterling Heights-Shelby-Utica Advisor, The - Utica, MI - *Ed&PubIntYB 82*
Sterling Heights-Utica-Shelby Community News - *See* Community News
Sterling Heights-Utica-Shelby Township Community News - Sterling Heights, MI - *Ed&PubIntYB 82*
Sterling Johnson County Courier - *See* Maverick Media Inc.
Sterling Journal-Advocate - Sterling, CO - *BaconPubCkNews 84; Ed&PubIntYB 82; NewsDir 84*
Sterling Music Co. - *See* Ahlert Music Corp., Fred
Sterling Newspapers - Canada - *Ed&PubIntYB 82*
Sterling Photographer, Joseph - Chicago, IL - *MagIndMarPl 82-83*
Sterling Publishing - New York, NY - *LitMarPl 83, 84; WritMar 84*
Sterling Recreation Organization - Bellevue, WA - *BrCabYB 84*
Sterling Software Inc. - Dallas, TX - *ADAPSOMemDir 83-84*
Sterling Suburban [of Suburban Newspaper Group] - Cherry Hill, NJ - *AyerDirPub 83; NewsDir 84*
Sterling Suburban, The - Magnolia, NJ - *Ed&PubIntYB 82*
Sterling Swift Publishing Co. - Austin, TX - *MicrocomMPl 83, 84; MicrocomSwDir 1; WhoWMicrocom 83*
Sterling's Magazines Inc. - New York, NY - *MagIndMarPl 82-83*
Stern Advertising - Pepper Pike, OH - *AdAge 3-28-84; StaDirAdAg 2-84*
Stern Advertising Inc., H. - Boston, MA - *StaDirAdAg 2-84*
Stern Advertising Inc., Les - Miami Shores, FL - *StaDirAdAg 2-84*
Stern Agency Inc., Charles H. - Los Angeles, CA - *BoPubDir 5*
Stern & Ingalls Inc. - New York, NY - *StaDirAdAg 2-84*
Stern Associates, Charles M. - San Antonio, TX - *LitMarPl 83, 84*
Stern Associates Inc., Claire - New York, NY - *CabTVFinDB 83; InterCabHB 3*
Stern Associates, Lee Edward - New York, NY - *ArtMar 84; DirPRFirms 83*
Stern, Charles M. - New York, NY - *LitMarPl 83, 84; MagIndMarPl 82-83*
Stern Communications Inc., S. D. - New York, NY - *LitMarPl 83, 84; MagIndMarPl 82-83*
Stern, Edward L. - New York, NY - *LitMarPl 83, 84*
Stern/Frank Advertising Inc. - Boston, MA - *StaDirAdAg 2-84*
Stern Literary Agency, Gloria - New York, NY - *LitMarPl 83, 84*
Stern/Monroe Advertising - Dallas, TX - *AdAge 3-28-84; StaDirAdAg 2-84*
Stern Productions, Don - Van Nuys, CA - *AvMarPl 83; Tel&CabFB 84C*
Stern Telecommunications Corp. - New York, NY - *CabTVFinDB 83; InterCabHB 3*
Stern Walters/Earle Ludgin [Subs. of Ted Bates Co.] - Chicago, IL - *AdAge 3-28-84; BrCabYB 84; StaDirAdAg 2-84*
Sternberg, Martha - San Francisco, CA - *LitMarPl 83, 84*
Sterne Advertising & Public Relations, William P. - Tulsa, OK - *StaDirAdAg 2-84*
Sternig Literary Agency, Larry - San Francisco, CA - *LitMarPl 84*
Sternig Literary Agency, Larry - Milwaukee, WI - *LitMarPl 83*
Stettler Independent - Stettler, AB, Canada - *Ed&PubIntYB 82*
Steuben Community TV System - Steuben, WI - *BrCabYB 84; Tel&CabFB 84C*
Steuben Courier Advocate [of Greenhow Newspaper Inc.] - Bath, NY - *AyerDirPub 83; Ed&PubIntYB 82; NewsDir 84*
Steuben Glass [Aff. of Corning Glass Works] - New York, NY - *BoPubDir 4, 5*
Steubenville Herald Star - Steubenville, OH - *BaconPubCkNews 84; NewsDir 84*
Steubenville TV Cable Co. [of Tele-Communications Inc.] - Steubenville, OH - *BrCabYB 84*
Stevens & Shea Publishers - Stockton, CA - *BoPubDir 4, 5*
Stevens Associates, Gary - New York, NY - *Ed&PubIntYB 82*
Stevens Associates, Michael [Subs. of Bizcom Inc.] - Bethel, CT - *DirMarMP 83*
Stevens Features - Chappaqua, NY - *Ed&PubIntYB 82*
Stevens Inc. - Grand Rapids, MI - *StaDirAdAg 2-84*
Stevens Point Journal - Stevens Point, WI - *BaconPubCkNews 84; Ed&PubIntYB 82; NewsDir 84*
Stevens Point Shoppers Herald - Stevens Point, WI - *AyerDirPub 83*
Stevens Research Services Inc. - Louisville, KY - *IntDirMarRes 83*
Stevenson Inc., Robert L. - Pittsburgh, PA - *StaDirAdAg 2-84; TelAl 83, 84*
Stevenson International - Fullerton, CA - *BoPubDir 4, 5*
Stevenson Learning Skills Inc. - Attleboro, MA - *BoPubDir 5*
Stevenson North Jackson Progress - Stevenson, AL - *BaconPubCkNews 84*
Stevenson Press - Austin, TX - *BoPubDir 4, 5*
Stevenson Skamania County Pioneer - Stevenson, WA - *BaconPubCkNews 84*
Stevenson Strategies & Tactics - Dallas, TX - *HBIndAd&MS 82-83*
Steve's Electronics Inc. - Hollister, FL - *Tel&CabFB 84C p.1704*
Steward & Sons - Long Beach, CA - *BoPubDir 4, 5*
Stewardson Clipper - Stewardson, IL - *Ed&PubIntYB 82*
Stewart Advertising & Public Relations Inc., B. J. - Newport Beach, CA - *DirPRFirms 83*
Stewart Advertising Inc. - Oakdale, PA - *StaDirAdAg 2-84*
Stewart & Associates Ltd./IMAA Inc., Rex - London, England - *StaDirAdAg 2-84*
Stewart & Hudson Books - Swift Current, SK, Canada - *BoPubDir 4, 5*
Stewart, B. M. - Okemos, MI - *BoPubDir 4, 5*
Stewart Citizen - Newburgh, NY - *Ed&PubIntYB 82*
Stewart Citizen - Walden, NY - *AyerDirPub 83*
Stewart Color Laboratories Inc. - New York, NY - *AvMarPl 83*
Stewart Filmscreen Corp. - Torrance, CA - *AvMarPl 83*
Stewart, Hap - San Francisco, CA - *MagIndMarPl 82-83*
Stewart-Houston Times - Dover, TN - *AyerDirPub 83; Ed&PubIntYB 82*
Stewart Inc., E. J. - Primos, PA - *AvMarPl 83; WritMar 84*
Stewart, Jo - New York, NY - *LitMarPl 83, 84*
Stewart, Lucille - Encino, CA - *LitMarPl 83, 84*
Stewart Music - *See* Mustard Tree Music
Stewart Newspaper Clipping Service, John P. - La Salle, PQ, Canada - *LitMarPl 83, 84*
Stewart Surveys Inc. - Ridgewood, NJ - *IntDirMarRes 83*
Stewart, Tabori & Chang - New York, NY - *LitMarPl 83, 84*
Stewart-Taylor Co. - Duluth, MN - *StaDirAdAg 2-84*
Stewart Tribune - Stewart, MN - *AyerDirPub 83; BaconPubCkNews 84; Ed&PubIntYB 82*
Stewart University Press - Centre, AL - *BoPubDir 4 Sup, 5*
Stewart-Warner Datafax Corp. - Chicago, IL - *DirInfWP 82*
Stewart-Webster Journal - Richland, GA - *AyerDirPub 83*
Stewartstown Cable TV [of GS Communications Inc.] - Frederick, MD - *BrCabYB 84*
Stewartstown Cable TV [of G.S. Communications Inc.] - Stewartstown, MD - *Tel&CabFB 84C*
Stewartville Star - Stewartville, MN - *BaconPubCkNews 84; Ed&PubIntYB 82*
Steyn, Ruth - Hancock, ME - *LitMarPl 83, 84*

STG Marketing Communications Inc. - Fairfield, CT - *StaDirAdAg 2-84*
STG Marketing Communications Inc. (Public Relations Dept.) - Fairfield, CT - *DirPRFirms 83*
STI Cablevision - Peachtree City, GA - *Tel&CabFB 84C*
Sticht, Martin - Brooklyn, NY - *LitMarPl 83, 84; MagIndMarPl 82-83*
Stichting Nederlands Orgaan voor de Bevordering van de Informatieverzorging - The Hague, Netherlands - *InfIndMarPl 83*
Stichting Nederlandse Informatie Combinatie - *See* Nederlandse Informatie Combinatie
Stickel-McAllister Inc. - Los Angeles, CA - *AvMarPl 83*
Sticker - Schulenburg, TX - *AyerDirPub 83*
Stickley Co., George F. - Philadelphia, PA - *LitMarPl 83, 84*
Stickney Argus - Stickney, SD - *BaconPubCkNews 84; Ed&PubIntYB 82*
Stickney Life [of Life Printing & Publishing Co. Inc.] - Berwyn, IL - *NewsDir 84*
Stickney Life - *See* Life Printing & Publishing Co.
Stiefel/Raymond Public Relations - *See* HBM/Stiefel Public Relations
Stiegler & Wells - Allentown, PA - *AdAge 3-28-84; StaDirAdAg 2-84*
Stiftung Wissenschaft und Politik [of Forschungsinsitut fur Internationale Politik und Sicherheit] - Isar, West Germany - *CompReadDB 82; InfIndMarPl 83*
Stigler Cable TV [of Satellite Syndicated Systems Inc. of Tulsa] - Stigler, OK - *BrCabYB 84; Tel&CabFB 84C*
Stigler News-Sentinel - Stigler, OK - *BaconPubCkNews 84; Ed&PubIntYB 82; NewsDir 84*
Still Publishing - Port Ludlow, WA - *BoPubDir 5; LitMag&SmPr 83-84*
Stiller Advertising Inc. - Costa Mesa, CA - *StaDirAdAg 2-84*
Stillgate Publishers - Alstead, NH - *BoPubDir 4, 5*
Stillhouse Hollow Publishing Co. - Temple, TX - *BoPubDir 4, 5*
Stillman Advertising Inc. - Melville, NY - *StaDirAdAg 2-84*
Stills Music, Stephen - *See* Gold Hill Music Inc.
Stillwater Canyon Press - Flagstaff, AZ - *BoPubDir 4, 5*
Stillwater County Citizen, The - Columbus, MT - *Ed&PubIntYB 82*
Stillwater Gazette - Stillwater, MN - *BaconPubCkNews 84; Ed&PubIntYB 82; NewsDir 84*
Stillwater News-Press - Stillwater, OK - *BaconPubCkNews 84; NewsDir 84*
Stillwater Publishing Co. - Stillwater, OK - *BrCabYB 84*
Stillwater St. Croix Valley Press - *See* Press Publications
Stillwater Valley Advertiser [of Covington Arens Corp.] - Covington, OH - *AyerDirPub 83; Ed&PubIntYB 82; NewsDir 84*
Stillwater Weekly Gazette - Stillwater, MN - *BaconPubCkNews 84*
Stilwell Democrat-Journal - Stilwell, OK - *BaconPubCkNews 84; Ed&PubIntYB 82; NewsDir 84*
Stilwell Sun - *See* Sun Publications
Stilwill, Charles - Waterloo, IA - *WritMar 84*
Stimpson Associates Inc., The - Seattle, WA - *StaDirAdAg 2-84*
Stimson Financial Communications - New London, CT - *DirPRFirms 83*
Stimulus - Willowdale, ON, Canada - *BaconPubCkMag 84*
Stinehour Press, The [Div. of Meriden-Stinehour Inc.] - Lunenburg, VT - *LitMarPl 83, 84*
Stinger Music - *See* Firedrum Music Publishers
Stinson Records - Granada Hills, CA - *BillIntBG 83-84*
Stipes Publishing Co. - Champaign, IL - *BoPubDir 4, 5; WritMar 84*
Stirling Echoes-Sentinel [of Recorder Publishing Co.] - Stirling, NJ - *Ed&PubIntYB 82; NewsDir 84*
Stirling Echoes Sentinel - *See* Recorder Publishing Co.
Stirling News-Argus - Stirling, ON, Canada - *Ed&PubIntYB 82*
Stiskin, Oscar B. - Stamford, CT - *LitMarPl 83*
Stitch 'n Sew - Brooksville, FL - *ArtMar 84*
Stittsville News, The - Stittsville, ON, Canada - *AyerDirPub 83; Ed&PubIntYB 82*
Stittsville Women's Institute - Stittsville, ON, Canada - *BoPubDir 4 Sup, 5*
STM Electronics Corp. - Menlo Park, CA - *WhoWMicrocom 83*
Stock Advisors' Alert [of NewsNet Inc.] - Bryn Mawr, PA - *DataDirOnSer 84*
Stock Advisors' Alert - Yardley, PA - *DirOnDB Spring 84*
Stock, Boston Inc. - Boston, MA - *LitMarPl 83, 84; MagIndMarPl 82-83*
Stock Car Racing Magazine - Burlington, MA - *MagDir 84; MagIndMarPl 82-83*
Stock Car Racing Magazine - Ipswich, MA - *ArtMar 84; BaconPubCkMag 84; WritMar 84*
Stock Drive Products [Aff. of Designatronics Inc.] - New Hyde Park, NY - *BoPubDir 4, 5*
Stock Imagery - Denver, CO - *LitMarPl 84*
Stock Market Graphic Features - Ft. Worth, TX - *Ed&PubIntYB 82*
Stock Market Magazine, The [of Wall Street Publishing Institute] - Yonkers, NY - *BaconPubCkMag 84; MagDir 84; MagIndMarPl 82-83; WritMar 84*
Stock Market Photo Agency, The - New York, NY - *LitMarPl 84*
Stock Market Software Inc. - Ashland, MA - *MicrocomMPl 84*
Stock Research Corp. - New York, NY - *ProGuPRSer 4*
Stockbridge & Sherwood Telephone Co. [Aff. of Telephone & Data Systems Inc.] - Sherwood, WI - *TelDir&BG 83-84*
Stockbridge Town Crier - Stockbridge, MI - *BaconPubCkNews 84; NewsDir 84*
Stockbroker - Los Angeles, CA - *MagDir 84*
Stockbrokers Association Inc., The - Chicago, IL - *ProGuPRSer 4*
Stockbroker's Society - Los Angeles, CA - *ProGuPRSer 4*
Stockcheck - *DirOnDB Spring 84*
Stockdale Corp. - Salt Lake City, UT - *AvMarPl 83*
Stockdale Star - *See* South Texas Newspapers Inc.
Stockdata [of FRI Information Services Ltd.] - Montreal, PQ, Canada - *DataDirOnSer 84; DirOnDB Spring 84*
Stockholder Systems Inc. - Atlanta, GA - *DataDirSup 7-83*
Stockholm Computing Center - Stockholm, Sweden - *EISS 83*
Stockholm-Strandburg Telephone Co. - Stockholm, SD - *TelDir&BG 83-84*
Stockinger, Blair & Scott - St. Cloud, MN - *AdAge 3-28-84; StaDirAdAg 2-84*
StockLine - Vienna, VA - *DirOnDB Spring 84*
Stockman - Ozona, TX - *AyerDirPub 83*
Stockman/Andrews Inc. - East Providence, RI - *StaDirAdAg 2-84*
Stockman/Grass Farmer - Jackson, MS - *BaconPubCkMag 84*
Stockman, Russell M. - Brattleboro, VT - *LitMarPl 83, 84*
Stockphotos Inc. - New York, NY - *AvMarPl 83*
Stocks, Emma Jo - Calhoun, GA - *Tel&CabFB 84C p.1704*
Stockton Cedar County Republican - Stockton, MO - *NewsDir 84*
Stockton Cedar County Republican & Journal - Stockton, MO - *BaconPubCkNews 84*
Stockton Herald News - Stockton, IL - *BaconPubCkNews 84; Ed&PubIntYB 82*
Stockton News - Stockton, CA - *NewsDir 84*
Stockton, Ott & Bortner Inc. - New York, NY - *IntDirMarRes 83*
Stockton Record [of Gannett Newspapers Inc.] - Stockton, CA - *BaconPubCkNews 84; Ed&PubIntYB 82; NewsDir 84*
Stockton Rooks County Record - Stockton, KS - *BaconPubCkNews 84*
Stockton TV Cable [of CATV Inc.] - Stockton, KS - *BrCabYB 84; Tel&CabFB 84C*
Stockton West Burkhart Inc. - Cincinnati, OH - *StaDirAdAg 2-84*
Stoddard County News - Dexter, MO - *AyerDirPub 83; Ed&PubIntYB 82*
Stoddart Publishing [Div. of General Publishing Co. Ltd.] - Don Mills, ON, Canada - *LitMarPl 83, 84*
Stoeger Canada Ltd. - Markham, ON, Canada - *BoPubDir 4 Sup, 5*
Stoeger Publishing Co. [Subs. of Stoeger Industries] - South Hackensack, NJ - *BoPubDir 4, 5; LitMarPl 84*
Stogel Co. Inc., Philip - New York, NY - *AdAge 3-28-84; StaDirAdAg 2-84*
Stok Computer Interface - New York, NY - *MicrocomMPl 83, 84*
Stok Software Inc. - New York, NY - *MicrocomSwDir 1*
Stokes & Associates Inc., J. - Walnut Creek, CA - *StaDirAdAg 2-84*
Stokes Associates, Bill - Dallas, TX - *AvMarPl 83*
Stokes Cable Co. Inc. [of Daniels & Associates Inc.] - Round Rock, TX - *BrCabYB 84; Tel&CabFB 84C*
Stokes Communications, Jim - Minneapolis, MN - *AvMarPl 83*

Stokes Publishing Co. - Palo Alto, CA - *BoPubDir 4, 5*
Stokes Record & Danbury Reporter - Danbury, NC - *Ed&PubIntYB 82*
Stokes Record & Danbury Reporter - Walnut Cove, NC - *AyerDirPub 83*
Stokes, S. C. W. - Victoria, BC, Canada - *BoPubDir 4, 5*
Stokes Slide Services Inc. - Austin, TX - *AvMarPl 83*
Stokesville Publishing Co. - Atlanta, GA - *BoPubDir 4, 5*
Stokey Enterprises Inc., Mike - Sherman Oaks, CA - *Tel&CabFB 84C*
Stoll Associates Inc., Bernard - New York, NY - *StaDirAdAg 2-84*
Stoll Gasman Inc. - Chapel Hill, NC - *TeleSy&SerDir 2-84*
Stollberg Research Associates Inc. - Stony Brook, NY - *MicrocomMPl 84*
Stolz Advertising - St. Louis, MO - *AdAge 3-28-84; ArtMar 84; StaDirAdAg 2-84*
Stolzberg Research Associates Inc. - Stony Brook, NY - *MicrocomSwDir 1*
Stolzenberg Wertkin Inc. - Rye, NY - *IntDirMarRes 83*
Stone Advertising Inc., Sid - Milwaukee, WI - *StaDirAdAg 2-84*
Stone Agate Music - *See* Jobete Music Co. Inc.
Stone & Adler [Subs. of Young & Rubicam Inc.] - Chicago, IL - *AdAge 3-28-84; ArtMar 84; DirMarMP 83; StaDirAdAg 2-84; VideoDir 82-83*
Stone & Associates, Morton B. - Chicago, IL - *DirPRFirms 83*
Stone & Cox Ltd. - Toronto, ON, Canada - *BoPubDir 4, 5*
Stone & Manning Advertising Inc. - Boston, MA - *StaDirAdAg 2-84*
Stone & Simons Advertising - Southfield, MI - *AdAge 3-28-84; StaDirAdAg 2-84*
Stone, August & Co. - Birmingham, MI - *AdAge 3-28-84; StaDirAdAg 2-84*
Stone Bluff Music - *See* Lorenz Creative Services
Stone/Clark - New York, NY - *Tel&CabFB 84C*
Stone Country - Menemsha, MA - *ArtMar 84; LitMag&SmPr 83-84; WritMar 84*
Stone Country Press - Menemsha, MA - *BoPubDir 4, 5; LitMag&SmPr 83-84*
Stone County Enterprise - Wiggins, MS - *AyerDirPub 83; Ed&PubIntYB 82; NewsDir 84*
Stone County Leader - Mountain View, AR - *Ed&PubIntYB 82*
Stone County Republican - Crane, MO - *Ed&PubIntYB 82*
Stone, David M. - Needham Heights, MA - *LitMarPl 83, 84; MagIndMarPl 82-83*
Stone Diamond Music Corp. - *See* Jobete Music Co. Inc.
Stone, Erika - New York, NY - *LitMarPl 83, 84; MagIndMarPl 82-83*
Stone Group, The - New York, NY - *DirPRFirms 83*
Stone/Hallinan Public Relations Associates Inc. - Los Angeles, CA - *DirPRFirms 83*
Stone, Hand & Dewar Inc. - Toronto, ON, Canada - *StaDirAdAg 2-84*
Stone House Inc. - Tallahassee, FL - *BoPubDir 4, 5*
Stone House Press - Roslyn Harbor, NY - *BoPubDir 4 Sup, 5*
Stone in America [of American Monument Association] - Worthington, OH - *ArtMar 84; BaconPubCkMag 84; MagDir 84; WritMar 84*
Stone Mountain Neighbor - Marietta, GA - *AyerDirPub 83*
Stone Press - San Francisco, CA - *BoPubDir 4, 5*
Stone Press [Aff. of Happiness Holding Tank Magazine] - Okemos, MI - *BoPubDir 4, 5; LitMag&SmPr 83-84*
Stone Productions Inc., H. M. - New York, NY - *AvMarPl 83*
Stone Software Marketing Inc. - La Jolla, CA - *MicrocomMPl 84*
Stone Soup - Santa Cruz, CA - *LitMag&SmPr 83-84*
Stone Street Press - Staten Island, NY - *BoPubDir 4 Sup, 5*
Stone, The - Santa Cruz, CA - *LitMag&SmPr 83-84*
Stone Wall Press Inc. - Washington, DC - *ArtMar 84; LitMag&SmPr 83-84; LitMarPl 83, 84; WritMar 84*
Stonebass Music Co. - San Francisco, CA - *BillIntBG 83-84*
Stonebridge Music - *See* Bicycle Music Co., The
Stoneham Cooperative Telephone Corp. - Stoneham, CO - *TelDir&BG 83-84*
Stoneham Independent - Stoneham, MA - *BaconPubCkNews 84; Ed&PubIntYB 82*
Stoneham Shoppers News [of The Stoneham Independent] - Stoneham, MA - *NewsDir 84*
Stonehenge Press - San Diego, CA - *BoPubDir 4, 5*
Stonehouse Publications - Sweet, ID - *BoPubDir 4, 5; LitMag&SmPr 83-84*
Stonehouse Publications - St. Catharines, ON, Canada - *BoPubDir 4, 5*
Stoner Associates Inc. - Carlisle, PA - *ADAPSOMemDir 83-84*
Stoner Broadcasting System Inc. - Des Moines, IA - *BrCabYB 84*
Stoner Inc., Stan - Enid, OK - *StaDirAdAg 2-84*
Stone's Southern School Supply - Raleigh, NC - *AvMarPl 83*
Stonesong Press Inc., The - Bedford Hills, NY - *LitMarPl 83, 84*
Stoneware Inc. [Subs. of Marin Micro Information Systems Inc.] - San Rafael, CA - *MicrocomMPl 83, 84; MicrocomSwDir 1; WhoWMicrocom 83*
Stoney Creek News - Stoney Creek, ON, Canada - *Ed&PubIntYB 82*
Stoney Point Music - Charlotte, NC - *BillIntBG 83-84*
Stoneydale Press Publishing Co. - Stevensville, MT - *LitMag&SmPr 83-84; WritMar 84*
Stonington Island-Ad-Vantages - Stonington, ME - *BaconPubCkNews 84*
Stony Brook Three Village Herald - Stony Brook, NY - *BaconPubCkNews 84; NewsDir 84*
Stony Hills: News & Review of the Small Press - New Sharon, ME - *LitMag&SmPr 83-84*
Stony Thursday Book, The - Limerick, Iran - *LitMag&SmPr 83-84*
STOP - Montreal, PQ, Canada - *BoPubDir 4, 5*
Stor-Wel Systems - Burbank, CA - *DirInfWP 82*
Storage Technology Corp. - Louisville, CO - *DataDirSup 7-83; Datamation 6-83; ElecNews 7-25-83; Top100Al 83*
Storch & Associates Inc., D. J. - Summit, NJ - *DirPRFirms 83*
Storck Communications - Thief River Falls, MN - *BrCabYB 84*
Storden Times/Jeffers Review - Storden, MN - *Ed&PubIntYB 82*
Storden Times/Review Market - Storden, MN - *BaconPubCkNews 84*
Store Audits-Q.E.D. - Englewood Cliffs, NJ - *IntDirMarRes 83*
Store News - Dunellen, NJ - *AyerDirPub 83*
Storeel Corp. - Atlanta, GA - *AvMarPl 83*
Storer Broadcasting Co. - Miami Beach, FL - *HomeVid&CabYB 82-83*
Storer Cable Communications - Bay Minette, AL - *BrCabYB 84*
Storer Cable Communications - Elba, AL - *BrCabYB 84*
Storer Cable Communications - Fairhope, AL - *BrCabYB 84; Tel&CabFB 84C*
Storer Cable Communications - Florala, AL - *BrCabYB 84*
Storer Cable Communications - Geneva, AL - *BrCabYB 84*
Storer Cable Communications - Hartford, AL - *BrCabYB 84*
Storer Cable Communications - Montgomery, AL - *BrCabYB 84; Tel&CabFB 84C*
Storer Cable Communications - Prattville, AL - *BrCabYB 84; Tel&CabFB 84C*
Storer Cable Communications - Samson, AL - *BrCabYB 84*
Storer Cable Communications - Slocomb, AL - *BrCabYB 84*
Storer Cable Communications - Sylacauga, AL - *BrCabYB 84; Tel&CabFB 84C*
Storer Cable Communications - Troy, AL - *BrCabYB 84; Tel&CabFB 84C*
Storer Cable Communications - Phoenix, AZ - *BrCabYB 84*
Storer Cable Communications - Banning, CA - *Tel&CabFB 84C*
Storer Cable Communications - Fairfield, CA - *Tel&CabFB 84C*
Storer Cable Communications - Fillmore, CA - *Tel&CabFB 84C*
Storer Cable Communications - Frazier Park, CA - *Tel&CabFB 84C*
Storer Cable Communications - Hermosa Beach, CA - *Tel&CabFB 84C*
Storer Cable Communications - Laguna Niguel, CA - *Tel&CabFB 84C*
Storer Cable Communications - Ojai, CA - *Tel&CabFB 84C*
Storer Cable Communications - Rohnert Park, CA - *Tel&CabFB 84C*
Storer Cable Communications - Santa Paula, CA - *Tel&CabFB 84C*
Storer Cable Communications - Sonoma, CA - *Tel&CabFB 84C*
Storer Cable Communications - Thousand Oaks, CA - *TelAl 83, 84*
Storer Cable Communications - Westlake Village, CA - *Tel&CabFB 84C*

Storer Cable Communications - Clinton, CT - *BrCabYB 84*
Storer Cable Communications - Arcadia, FL - *BrCabYB 84*
Storer Cable Communications - Chipley, FL - *Tel&CabFB 84C*
Storer Cable Communications - De Funiak Springs, FL - *Tel&CabFB 84C*
Storer Cable Communications - Englewood, FL - *BrCabYB 84*
Storer Cable Communications [of Storer Broadcasting Co.] - Miami, FL - *BrCabYB 84 p.D-307; CabTVFinDB 83; HomeVid&CabYB 82-83; LitMarPl 84*
Storer Cable Communications - North Port, FL - *BrCabYB 84*
Storer Cable Communications - Port Charlotte, FL - *BrCabYB 84*
Storer Cable Communications - Albany, GA - *BrCabYB 84; Tel&CabFB 84C*
Storer Cable Communications - Americus, GA - *BrCabYB 84; Tel&CabFB 84C*
Storer Cable Communications - Bainbridge, GA - *BrCabYB 84; Tel&CabFB 84C*
Storer Cable Communications - Cordele, GA - *BrCabYB 84; Tel&CabFB 84C*
Storer Cable Communications - Moultrie, GA - *BrCabYB 84; Tel&CabFB 84C*
Storer Cable Communications - Nashville, GA - *BrCabYB 84; Tel&CabFB 84C*
Storer Cable Communications - Tifton, GA - *BrCabYB 84; Tel&CabFB 84C*
Storer Cable Communications - St. Cloud, MN - *BrCabYB 84*
Storer Cable Communications - Cinnaminson, NJ - *BrCabYB 84*
Storer Cable Communications - Eatontown, NJ - *BrCabYB 84*
Storer Cable Communications - Lambertville, NJ - *BrCabYB 84*
Storer Cable Communications - Port Murray, NJ - *BrCabYB 84*
Storer Cable Communications - Balch Springs, TX - *BrCabYB 84*
Storer Cable Communications - Burleson, TX - *BrCabYB 84*
Storer Cable Communications - Cedar Hill, TX - *BrCabYB 84*
Storer Cable Communications - Cleburne, TX - *BrCabYB 84*
Storer Cable Communications - Garland, TX - *BrCabYB 84*
Storer Cable Communications - Grand Prairie, TX - *BrCabYB 84*
Storer Cable Communications - Lancaster, TX - *BrCabYB 84*
Storer Cable Communications - Ft. Belvoir, VA - *BrCabYB 84; Tel&CabFB 84C*
Storer Cable Communications Inc. - Blountstown, FL - *BrCabYB 84*
Storer Cable Communications Inc. - Chattahoochee, FL - *BrCabYB 84*
Storer Cable Communications Inc. - Ashburn, GA - *BrCabYB 84*
Storer Cable Communications Inc. - Camilla, GA - *BrCabYB 84*
Storer Cable Communications Inc. - Donalsonville, GA - *BrCabYB 84*
Storer Cable Communications Inc. - Sylvester, GA - *BrCabYB 84*
Storer Cable of Bowling Green/Warren County Inc. [of Storer Cable Communications] - Bowling Green, KY - *BrCabYB 84; Tel&CabFB 84C*
Storer Cable of Carolina Inc. [of Storer Cable Communications] - Beaufort, SC - *Tel&CabFB 84C*
Storer Cable of Carolina Inc. [of Storer Cable Communications] - Charleston, SC - *BrCabYB 84; Tel&CabFB 84C*
Storer Cable of Carolina Inc. [of Storer Cable Communications] - Laurel Bay, SC - *BrCabYB 84*
Storer Cable of Carolina Inc. [of Storer Cable Communications] - Walterboro, SC - *BrCabYB 84; Tel&CabFB 84C*
Storer Cable of Leesburg Inc. [of Storer Cable Communications] - Leesburg, VA - *BrCabYB 84*
Storer Cable of Maryland Inc. [of Storer Cable Communications] - Prince George's County, MD - *BrCabYB 84*
Storer Cable of Prince Georges County Inc. [of Storer Cable Communications] - Bowie, MD - *Tel&CabFB 84C*
Storer Cable of Texas Inc. [of Storer Cable Communications] - De Soto, TX - *Tel&CabFB 84C*
Storer Cable of Texas Inc. [of Storer Cable Communications] - Ft. Worth, TX - *Tel&CabFB 84C*
Storer Cable of Texas Inc. [of Storer Cable Communications] - Terrell, TX - *BrCabYB 84*
Storer Cable of Texas Inc. [of Storer Cable Communications] - Tomball, TX - *Tel&CabFB 84C*
Storer Cable TV Inc. [of Storer Cable Communications] - Clanton, AL - *BrCabYB 84*
Storer Cable TV Inc. [of Storer Cable Communications] - Anaheim, CA - *BrCabYB 84; Tel&CabFB 84C*
Storer Cable TV Inc. [of Storer Cable Communications] - Banning, CA - *BrCabYB 84*
Storer Cable TV Inc. - Calistoga, CA - *BrCabYB 84*
Storer Cable TV Inc. [of Storer Cable Communications] - Fairfield, CA - *BrCabYB 84*
Storer Cable TV Inc. [of Storer Cable Communications] - Fillmore, CA - *BrCabYB 84*
Storer Cable TV Inc. [of Storer Cable Communications] - Frazier Park, CA - *BrCabYB 84*
Storer Cable TV Inc. [of Storer Cable Communications] - Hermosa Beach, CA - *BrCabYB 84*
Storer Cable TV Inc. [of Storer Cable Communications] - Laguna Beach, CA - *BrCabYB 84*
Storer Cable TV Inc. [of Storer Cable Communications] - Moorpark, CA - *BrCabYB 84; Tel&CabFB 84C*
Storer Cable TV Inc. [of Storer Cable Communications] - Ojai, CA - *BrCabYB 84*
Storer Cable TV Inc. - Rohnert Park, CA - *BrCabYB 84*
Storer Cable TV Inc. [of Storer Cable Communications] - Santa Paula, CA - *BrCabYB 84*
Storer Cable TV Inc. [of Storer Cable Communications] - Sebastopol, CA - *BrCabYB 84*
Storer Cable TV Inc. [of Storer Cable Communications] - Sonoma, CA - *BrCabYB 84*
Storer Cable TV Inc. [of Storer Cable Communications] - St. Helena, CA - *Tel&CabFB 84C*
Storer Cable TV Inc. [of Storer Cable Communications] - Thousand Oaks, CA - *BrCabYB 84*
Storer Cable TV Inc. [of Storer Cable Communications] - Union City, CA - *BrCabYB 84; Tel&CabFB 84C*
Storer Cable TV Inc. - Westlake Village, CA - *BrCabYB 84*
Storer Cable TV Inc. [of Storer Cable Communications] - Wikiup, CA - *Tel&CabFB 84C*
Storer Cable TV Inc. [of Storer Cable Communications] - Loveland, CO - *BrCabYB 84*
Storer Cable TV Inc. [of Storer Cable Communications] - Clackamas, OR - *BrCabYB 84; Tel&CabFB 84C*
Storer Cable TV of Connecticut Inc. [of Storer Cable Communications] - New Haven, CT - *BrCabYB 84; InterCabHB 3; Tel&CabFB 84C*
Storer Cable TV of Florida Inc. [of Storer Cable Communications] - Arcadia, FL - *Tel&CabFB 84C*
Storer Cable TV of Florida Inc. [of Storer Cable Communications] - Bartow, FL - *BrCabYB 84; Tel&CabFB 84C*
Storer Cable TV of Florida Inc. [of Storer Cable Communications] - Cape Haze, FL - *Tel&CabFB 84C*
Storer Cable TV of Florida Inc. - Dade County, FL - *BrCabYB 84*
Storer Cable TV of Florida Inc. [of Storer Cable Communications] - Ft. Meade, FL - *Tel&CabFB 84C*
Storer Cable TV of Florida Inc. [of Storer Cable Communications] - Lake Placid, FL - *Tel&CabFB 84C*
Storer Cable TV of Florida Inc. [of Storer Cable Communications] - Lake Wales, FL - *Tel&CabFB 84C*
Storer Cable TV of Florida Inc. - Miami, FL - *BrCabYB 84*
Storer Cable TV of Florida Inc. [of Storer Cable Communications] - North Miami, FL - *Tel&CabFB 84C*
Storer Cable TV of Florida Inc. [of Storer Cable Communications] - North Port, FL - *Tel&CabFB 84C*
Storer Cable TV of Florida Inc. [of Storer Cable Communications] - Port Charlotte, FL - *Tel&CabFB 84C*
Storer Cable TV of Florida Inc. [of Storer Cable Communications] - Sarasota, FL - *BrCabYB 84; Tel&CabFB 84C*
Storer Cable TV of Florida Inc. [of Storer Cable Communications] - Venice, FL - *BrCabYB 84; Tel&CabFB 84C*
Storer Cable TV of Florida Inc. [of Storer Cable Communications] - Wauchula, FL - *Tel&CabFB 84C*
Storer Cable TV of Radnor Inc. [of Storer Cable Communications] - Radnor, PA - *Tel&CabFB 84C*
Storer Cable TV of Radnor Inc. - Radnor Township, PA - *BrCabYB 84*
Storer Cable TV of Texas [of Storer Cable Communications] - Carrollton, TX - *BrCabYB 84; Tel&CabFB 84C*
Storer Cable TV of Texas Inc. - Balch Springs, TX - *Tel&CabFB 84C*

Storer Cable TV of Texas Inc. [of Storer Cable Communications] - Bedford, TX - *Tel&CabFB 84C*
Storer Cable TV of Texas Inc. - Burleson, TX - *Tel&CabFB 84C*
Storer Cable TV of Texas Inc. [of Storer Cable Communications] - Cleburne, TX - *Tel&CabFB 84C*
Storer Cable TV of Texas Inc. [of Storer Cable Communications] - Forest Hill, TX - *Tel&CabFB 84C*
Storer Cable TV of Texas Inc. - Garland, TX - *Tel&CabFB 84C*
Storer Cable TV of Texas Inc. - Grand Prairie, TX - *Tel&CabFB 84C*
Storer Cable TV of Texas Inc. [of Storer Cable Communications] - Harris County, TX - *BrCabYB 84; Tel&CabFB 84C*
Storer Cable TV of Texas Inc. [of Storer Cable Communications] - Lancaster, TX - *Tel&CabFB 84C*
Storer Cable TV of Texas Inc. - Richland Hills, TX - *BrCabYB 84*
Storer Cable TV of Texas Inc. [of Storer Cable Communications] - Rockwall, TX - *BrCabYB 84; Tel&CabFB 84C*
Storer Cable TV of Texas Inc. - Saginaw, TX - *Tel&CabFB 84C*
Storer Cable TV of Texas Inc. - Terrell, TX - *Tel&CabFB 84C*
Storer Cable TV of Texas Inc. [of Storer Cable Communications] - Weatherford, TX - *BrCabYB 84*
Storer Cable TV of Texas Inc. [of Storer Cable Communications] - White Settlement, TX - *BrCabYB 84; Tel&CabFB 84C*
Storer Communications Inc. - Miami, FL - *AdAge 6-28-84; BrCabYB 84; KnowInd 83; TelAl 83, 84; Tel&CabFB 84C p.1704, 84S*
Storer Communications of Clinton Inc. [of Storer Cable Communications] - Clinton, CT - *Tel&CabFB 84C*
Storer Communications of Gloucester County Inc. [of Storer Cable Communications] - Woodbury, NJ - *BrCabYB 84; Tel&CabFB 84C*
Storer Communications of Groton Inc. [of Storer Cable Communications] - Groton, CT - *BrCabYB 84; Tel&CabFB 84C*
Storer Communications of Jefferson County Inc. [of Storer Cable Communications] - Jefferson County, KY - *BrCabYB 84*
Storer Communications of Newport Inc. [of Storer Cable Communications] - Newport, KY - *BrCabYB 84; Tel&CabFB 84C*
Storer Communications of Northern Kentucky Inc. [of Storer Cable Communications] - Boone County, KY - *BrCabYB 84*
Storer Communications of Northern Kentucky Inc. - Campbell County, KY - *BrCabYB 84*
Storer Communications of Northern Kentucky Inc. - Covington, KY - *BrCabYB 84*
Storer Metro Communications Co. [of Storer Cable Communications] - Beaverton, OR - *BrCabYB 84; Tel&CabFB 84C*
Storer Television Sales Inc. - New York, NY - *TelAl 83, 84*
Stores - New York, NY - *BaconPubCkMag 84; MagDir 84; MagIndMarPl 82-83; WritMar 84*
Storey Berman & Freer - Chicago, IL - *AdAge 3-28-84; StaDirAdAg 2-84*
Stories - Boston, MA - *LitMag&SmPr 83-84; LitMarPl 83, 84*
Storm Antenna Service - Siletz, OR - *BrCabYB 84; Tel&CabFB 84C*
Storm Lake Cable TV [of Heritage Communications Inc.] - Storm Lake, IA - *Tel&CabFB 84C*
Storm Lake Pilot-Tribune - Storm Lake, IA - *Ed&PubIntYB 82; NewsDir 84*
Storm Lake Pilot-Tribune - *See* Pilot-Tribune Printing Co.
Storm Lake Register [of Pilot-Tribune Printing Co.] - Storm Lake, IA - *Ed&PubIntYB 82; NewsDir 84*
Storm Marketing Research Inc. - New York, NY - *IntDirMarRes 83*
Storm Opinion Center Ltd. - Howard Beach, NY - *IntDirMarRes 83*
Storm Printing Co. [Div. of American-Standard Inc.] - Dallas, TX - *MagIndMarPl 82-83*
Stormking Music Inc. - *See* Sanga Music Inc.
Story & Kelly-Smith Inc. - New York, NY - *LitMarPl 83, 84*
Story City Herald - Story City, IA - *AyerDirPub 83; BaconPubCkNews 84; Ed&PubIntYB 82; NewsDir 84*
Story Friends [of Mennonite Publishing House] - Scottdale, PA - *WritMar 84*
Story House Corp. - Charlotteville, NY - *LitMarPl 83, 84*
Story Press - Chicago, IL - *BoPubDir 4, 5; LitMag&SmPr 83-84*
Story Quarterly - Northbrook, IL - *LitMag&SmPr 83-84*
Story, The - Lexington, KY - *Tel&CabFB 84C*
Storyboard Inc. - *See* Hubley Studio Inc.
Storybooks of the Future - San Francisco, CA - *MicrocomMPl 83, 84*
Storybooks of the Future - Santa Clara, CA - *MicrocomSwDir 1*
Storyville Publishing Co. - *See* Berthelot & Associates, John
Storz Broadcasting Co. - Omaha, NE - *BrCabYB 84*
Stotz, Conrad - Grayson, KY - *Tel&CabFB 84C p.1704*
Stouffer Productions Ltd., Marty - Aspen, CO - *AvMarPl 83; Tel&CabFB 84C*
Stoughton Chronicle - Stoughton, MA - *Ed&PubIntYB 82; NewsDir 84*
Stoughton Chronicle - *See* Bulletin Publishing Co.
Stoughton Courier - Stoughton, WI - *Ed&PubIntYB 82*
Stoughton Courier-Hub - Stoughton, WI - *BaconPubCkNews 84*
Stoughton Hub - Stoughton, WI - *Ed&PubIntYB 82*
Stoughton U.S. Cable of Viking [of U.S. Cable Corp.] - Stoughton, WI - *BrCabYB 84*
Stout, John - Baker, OR - *BoPubDir 4, 5*
Stoutland Telephone Co., The - Columbia, MO - *TelDir&BG 83-84*
Stovepipe Press - Kalamazoo, MI - *BoPubDir 4, 5*
Stover Morgan County Press - Stover, MO - *BaconPubCkNews 84*
Stow Citizen - Stow, OH - *Ed&PubIntYB 82*
Stow/Davis Furniture Co. - Grand Rapids, MI - *DirInfWP 82*
Stow Sentry - Cuyahoga Falls, OH - *NewsDir 84*
Stow Sentry - Stow, OH - *Ed&PubIntYB 82*
Stow Sentry/Citizen - *See* Record Publishing Co.
Stowe & Bowden Ltd. - *See* Royds Advertising Group Ltd., The
Stowe-Day Foundation - Hartford, CT - *BoPubDir 4, 5*
Stowe Reporter [of The Reporter Press Inc.] - Stowe, VT - *BaconPubCkNews 84; Ed&PubIntYB 82; NewsDir 84*
STR Corp. - Norcross, GA - *MicrocomMPl 83; MicrocomSwDir 1*
Strafford Inc., T. S. - Strafford, PA - *StaDirAdAg 2-84*
Straight [of Standard Publishing Co.] - Cincinnati, OH - *WritMar 84*
Straight Furrow Productions Inc. - Birmingham, AL - *AvMarPl 83*
Straight Modi Press - Birmingham, MI - *BoPubDir 4, 5*
Straight Talk - Jupiter, FL - *AyerDirPub 83*
Straight Talk Distributing - Point Reyes Station, CA - *BoPubDir 4 Sup, 5*
Straitjacket/Chariscourt - *See* Rondor Music International Inc.
Straiton, Pearson & Martin Ltd. - Toronto, ON, Canada - *StaDirAdAg 2-84*
Straitsland Resorter - Indian River, MI - *AyerDirPub 83; Ed&PubIntYB 82*
Stral Advertising Co. Inc. - Chicago, IL - *StaDirAdAg 2-84*
Strand, Janann - Pasadena, CA - *BoPubDir 4, 5*
Strange Music - *See* Excellorec Music Co. Inc.
Strange, William - *See* Sammons Communications Inc.
Strasburg Eastern Colorado News - Strasburg, CO - *BaconPubCkNews 84*
Strasburg Telephone Co. - Strasburg, CO - *TelDir&BG 83-84*
Strasburg Weekly News - Strasburg, PA - *BaconPubCkNews 84; Ed&PubIntYB 82*
Strata-East Records Inc. - New York, NY - *BillIntBG 83-84*
Stratagem Cybernetics - Brooklyn, NY - *MicrocomMPl 83, 84; WhoWMicrocom 83*
Strategic Business Services - San Jose, CA - *BoPubDir 5*
Strategic Communications Inc. - Troy, MI - *StaDirAdAg 2-84*
Strategic Consulting Group Inc. - New York, NY - *IntDirMarRes 83*
Strategic Financial Systems Inc. - New York, NY - *DataDirSup 7-83*
Strategic Inc. - San Jose, CA - *EISS 83; InterCabHB 3*
Strategic Information Services Inc. - Columbus, OH - *IntDirMarRes 83*
Strategic Marketing Corp. - Merion Station, PA - *IntDirMarRes 83*
Strategic Materials Management - Washington, DC - *BaconPubCkMag 84*

Strategic Options Inc. - Ho-Ho-Kus, NJ - *IntDirMarRes 83*
Strategic Radio Research Inc. - Chicago, IL - *BrCabYB 84*
Strategic Research Center - Cleveland, OH - *HBIndAd&MS 82-83*
Strategic Simulations Inc. - Mountain View, CA - *MicrocomMPl 83, 84; WhoWMicrocom 83*
Strategic System Solutions Inc. - Troy, MI - *ADAPSOMemDir 83-84*
Strategy & Tactics [of Simulation Publications Inc.] - New York, NY - *WritMar 84*
Strategy Research Corp. - Miami, FL - *IntDirMarRes 83*
Strategy Workshop Inc., The - New York, NY - *HBIndAd&MS 82-83*
Stratford Bard - Stratford, CT - *Ed&PubIntYB 82; NewsDir 84*
Stratford Cablevision Inc. [of Communications Systems Inc.] - Stratford, TX - *BrCabYB 84; Tel&CabFB 84C*
Stratford Courier - Stratford, IA - *BaconPubCkNews 84*
Stratford Journal - Stratford, WI - *BaconPubCkNews 84; Ed&PubIntYB 82*
Stratford Mutual Telephone Co. - Stratford, IA - *TelDir&BG 83-84*
Stratford News - Stratford, CT - *NewsDir 84*
Stratford Press Inc. - Los Angeles, CA - *BoPubDir 4, 5*
Stratford Star - Stratford, OK - *Ed&PubIntYB 82*
Stratford Star - Stratford, TX - *BaconPubCkNews 84; Ed&PubIntYB 82*
Stratford Star - *See* Konawa Newspapers
Strathcona Publishing - Princeton, NJ - *BoPubDir 4, 5*
Strathmore - Geneva, IL - *MagIndMarPl 82-83*
Strathmore Paper Co. [Div. of Hammermill Paper Co.] - Westfield, MA - *LitMarPl 83, 84*
Strathmore Standard - Strathmore, AB, Canada - *Ed&PubIntYB 82*
Stratmar Research Corp. - New York, NY - *IntDirMarRes 83*
Stratmar Systems Inc. - New York, NY - *HBIndAd&MS 82-83*
Stratmar/TMG - Geneva, Switzerland - *IntDirMarRes 83*
Stratoroute 2000 [of Telecom Canada] - Ottawa, ON, Canada - *TeleSy&SerDir 2-84*
Stratta, M. Cecile - New York, NY - *LitMarPl 83, 84; MagIndMarPl 82-83*
Stratton Press - Stratton, CO - *BaconPubCkNews 84; Ed&PubIntYB 82*
Stratus Computer Inc. - Natick, MA - *DataDirSup 7-83*
Strauch, Ralph - New York, NY - *LitMarPl 83, 84*
Straus Associates Inc., Irving L. - *See* Financial Relations Board Inc., The
Strauss, Daniel - Bronx, NY - *BoPubDir 5*
Strauss Technical Services Inc. - Washington, DC - *AvMarPl 83*
Stravon Educational Press [Subs. of Stravon Publishers Inc.] - New York, NY - *LitMarPl 83, 84*
Strawberry Hill Music - *See* Barton Music Inc., Earl
Strawberry Hill Press - San Francisco, CA - *LitMarPl 83, 84; WritMar 84*
Strawberry Patch - Marietta, GA - *BillIntBG 83-84*
Strawberry Patchworks - Fayetteville, NC - *LitMag&SmPr 83-84*
Strawberry Point Clayton County Press - Strawberry Point, IA - *BaconPubCkNews 84*
Strawberry Point Press Journal - Strawberry Point, IA - *Ed&PubIntYB 82*
Strawberry Press - New York, NY - *BoPubDir 4, 5; LitMag&SmPr 83-84*
Strawberry Software Inc. - Vashon Island, WA - *WhoWMicrocom 83*
Strawberry Tree Computers - Sunnyvale, CA - *MicrocomMPl 83, 84; MicrocomSwDir 1*
Strawberry Valley Press - Idyllwild, CA - *BoPubDir 4, 5*
Strawn Cable Co. - Strawn, TX - *BrCabYB 84*
Strawn Studios Inc. - Des Moines, IA - *LitMag&SmPr 83-84*
Strawn TV Cable Inc. - Strawn, TX - *Tel&CabFB 84C*
Strayton Corp., The - Wellesley, MA - *DirPRFirms 83*
Straz - Scranton, PA - *Ed&PubIntYB 82; NewsDir 84*
Streamwood/Bartlett Voice - *See* Voice Newspapers
Streamwood Star - Streamwood, IL - *Ed&PubIntYB 82*
Streamwood Township Times - *See* Copley Newspaper Group
Streator Times-Press [of Small Newspapers] - Streator, IL - *BaconPubCkNews 84; Ed&PubIntYB 82; NewsDir 84*
Street Chopper - Anaheim, CA - *BaconPubCkMag 84; MagDir 84; MagIndMarPl 82-83*
Street Electronics Corp. - Anaheim, CA - *MicrocomMPl 83*
Street Electronics Corp. - Carpinteria, CA - *MicrocomMPl 84; WhoWMicrocom 83*
Street Fiction Inc. - Newport, RI - *BoPubDir 4, 5*
Street Magazine - Port Jefferson, NY - *LitMag&SmPr 83-84*
Street, Mary - Tahoe City, CA - *LitMarPl 83, 84*
Street Press - Port Jefferson, NY - *BoPubDir 4, 5; LitMag&SmPr 83-84*
Street Rodder [of TRM Publications Inc.] - Anaheim, CA - *BaconPubCkMag 84; MagIndMarPl 82-83; WritMar 84*
Streeterville Studios Inc. - Chicago, IL - *AvMarPl 83; Tel&CabFB 84C*
Streetlight Records - Beverly Hills, CA - *BillIntBG 83-84*
Streetsboro-Mantua Record-News - Kent, OH - *NewsDir 84*
Streetsboro Record-News - Streetsboro, OH - *BaconPubCkNews 84*
Streetsville Booster - Streetsville, ON, Canada - *AyerDirPub 83*
Streetwise Records - New York, NY - *BillIntBG 83-84*
Streicker & Co. Inc. - Providence, RI - *StaDirAdAg 2-84*
Stremecki, Edward - Grand Centre, AB, Canada - *BoPubDir 4, 5*
Strength & Health [of S & H Publishing Co. Inc.] - York, PA - *MagDir 84; MagIndMarPl 82-83; WritMar 84*
Streshinsky, Ted - Berkeley, CA - *MagIndMarPl 82-83*
Stress Analysis Associates Inc. - Pasadena, CA - *MicrocomMPl 84*
Strether & Swann Publishers - New Orleans, LA - *BoPubDir 4, 5*
Strick & Associates, Jack - Hollywood, FL - *MicrocomMPl 84*
Strickland & Associates - Palatine, IL - *DirPRFirms 83*
Strictly Administration Music - *See* Sweet Glenn Music
Strictly Color Software - West Point, PA - *MicrocomMPl 84*
Strictly Soft Ware - Granville, OH - *MicrocomMPl 84*
Strine Printing Co. Inc. - York, PA - *LitMarPl 83, 84*
String Bender Music - *See* Kentucky Colonel Music
Stripe [of Sentinel Newspapers] - Rockville, MD - *NewsDir 84*
Striper Magazine - Antioch, TN - *BaconPubCkMag 84*
Stripprinter Inc. [Subs. of OKC Graphics] - Oklahoma City, OK - *AvMarPl 83*
Strobe Inc. - Mountain View, CA - *MicrocomMPl 84; WhoWMicrocom 83*
Strode Publishers, The - Huntsville, AL - *LitMarPl 83, 84*
Strohl Systems - Plymouth Meeting, PA - *MicrocomMPl 84*
Stroke - Dallas, TX - *BaconPubCkMag 84*
Stroker - New York, NY - *LitMag&SmPr 83-84*
Stromberg-Carlson Corp. - Tampa, FL - *DirInfWP 82*
Stromberg-Carlson Corp. - Charlottesville, VA - *DataDirSup 7-83*
Stromquist, Marjorie - New York, NY - *LitMarPl 83, 84*
Stromsburg Headlight - Stromsburg, NE - *BaconPubCkNews 84*
Strong Associates, Marianne - New York, NY - *LitMarPl 83, 84*
Strong Electric Corp. [Subs. of Canrad Hanovia Inc.] - Toledo, OH - *AvMarPl 83*
Stronghold Press - Bismarck, ND - *LitMag&SmPr 83-84*
Stronghurst Henderson County Quill - Stronghurst, IL - *BaconPubCkNews 84*
Strongsville Sun Star - Cleveland, OH - *AyerDirPub 83*
Strongsville Sun Star - Strongsville, OH - *Ed&PubIntYB 82*
Strongsville Sun Star - *See* Sun Newspapers
Strongville-North Royalton Sun Star [of Sun Newspapers] - Cleveland, OH - *NewsDir 84*
Strother & Faltis - Dundee, IL - *AdAge 3-28-84; StaDirAdAg 2-84*
Stroud American - Stroud, OK - *BaconPubCkNews 84; Ed&PubIntYB 82*
Stroudsburg Pocono Record, The - Stroudsburg, PA - *NewsDir 84*
Strubblejumper Press - Saskatoon, SK, Canada - *BoPubDir 5*
Strube Coughlin Associates - New York, NY - *Ed&PubIntYB 82*
Structural Concepts Corp. - Spring Lake, MI - *DirInfWP 82*
Structural Members Users Group - Charlottesville, VA - *DataDirOnSer 84*
Structural Programming Inc. - Sudbury, MA - *MicrocomMPl 83, 84*
Structural Research & Analysis - Santa Monica, CA - *MicrocomMPl 84*
Structural Software Services - London, England - *MicrocomSwDir 1*
Structure & Nomenclature Search System [of Computer Sciences Corp.] - Falls Church, VA - *DataDirOnSer 84*
Structure Probe Inc. - West Chester, PA - *HBIndAd&MS 82-83*
Structured Analysis Systems - Reston, VA - *WhoWMicrocom 83*

Structured Language World [of Southwater Corp.] - Mt. Carmel, CT - *BaconPubCkMag 84; MicrocomMPl 84*
Structured Methods Inc. - New York, NY - *DirMarMP 83*
Structured MicroSyst - Columbia, SC - *MicrocomMPl 84*
Structured Systems Group - Oakland, CA - *MicrocomMPl 83, 84; WhoWMicrocom 83*
Structures Publishing Co. - Milwaukee, WI - *WritMar 84*
Struhl Co. Inc., Joseph - Garden City Park, NY - *AvMarPl 83*
Strunk Secretarial Service - Phoenix, AZ - *LitMarPl 84*
Struthers Journal - Struthers, OH - *BaconPubCkNews 84; NewsDir 84*
Struzick Music - *See* Espy Music Group
Stryker Advance - Stryker, OH - *Ed&PubIntYB 82*
Stryker Advance-Reporter - West Unity, OH - *BaconPubCkNews 84*
Stryker-Post Publications - Washington, DC - *BoPubDir 4, 5*
Stryker Weiner Associates Inc. - Honolulu, HI - *DirPRFirms 83*
Stryker, William N. - Alexandria, VA - *BoPubDir 4, 5*
STS Consultants Ltd. - Northbrook, IL - *DataDirOnSer 84*
STS Systems Ltd. - Dorval, CA - *DataDirSup 7-83*
STSC Inc. [of Contel] - Rockville, MD - *BoPubDir 4 Sup, 5; DataDirOnSer 84; DataDirSup 7-83; EISS 83; InfIndMarPl 83; MicrocomMPl 84; MicrocomSwDir 1*
Stuart Associates - Los Angeles, CA - *DirInfWP 82*
Stuart Associates, Errett - Valley Center, CA - *BoPubDir 4 Sup, 5; LitMarPl 83, 84*
Stuart Broadcasting Co. - Lincoln, NE - *BrCabYB 84*
Stuart Bull Mountain Bugle - Stuart, VA - *BaconPubCkNews 84*
Stuart Communications Inc., Martha - Hillsdale, NY - *Tel&CabFB 84C*
Stuart Enterprise - Stuart, VA - *BaconPubCkNews 84*
Stuart, Gordon - Pacific Palisades, CA - *BoPubDir 4, 5*
Stuart Herald - Stuart, IA - *BaconPubCkNews 84; Ed&PubIntYB 82*
Stuart Inc., Lyle - Secaucus, NJ - *LitMarPl 83, 84; WritMar 84*
Stuart, Kiel - Stony Brook, NY - *LitMarPl 83, 84*
Stuart News [of Scripps-Howard Newspapers] - Stuart, FL - *BaconPubCkNews 84; Ed&PubIntYB 82; NewsDir 84*
Stubblejumper Press - Saskatoon, SK, Canada - *BoPubDir 4*
Stubs Communications Co. - New York, NY - *StaDirAdAg 2-84*
Stubs Publications - New York, NY - *BoPubDir 4, 5*
Stuck Electric Inc. - Sheridan, OR - *BrCabYB 84; Tel&CabFB 84C*
Stuckey Publishing Co. - Brentwood, TN - *BillIntBG 83-84*
Student Activities Programming - Columbia, SC - *BaconPubCkMag 84*
Student Lawyer - Chicago, IL - *MagDir 84; MagIndMarPl 82-83; WritMar 84*
Student Printz, The [of The University of Southern Mississippi] - Hattiesburg, MS - *NewsDir 84*
Student Publications Board - Greeley, CO - *LitMag&SmPr 83-84*
Student Skier - Seekonk, MA - *BaconPubCkMag 84*
Student, The - Nashville, TN - *WritMar 84*
Studer Revox America - Nashville, TN - *AvMarPl 83*
Studia Celtica [of University of Wales Press] - Cardiff, Wales - *LitMag&SmPr 83-84*
Studia Hispanica Editors - Austin, TX - *BoPubDir 4, 5; LitMag&SmPr 83-84*
Studia Humanitatis [Aff. of Jose Porrua Turanzas SA] - Potomac, MD - *BoPubDir 4, 5*
Studia Mystica - Sacramento, CA - *LitMag&SmPr 83-84*
Studies in Design Education Craft & Technology - Keele, England - *LitMag&SmPr 83-84*
Studies in Family Planning - New York, NY - *MagIndMarPl 82-83*
Studio Center Corp. - Norfolk, VA - *AvMarPl 83*
Studio City Graphic - Encino, CA - *AyerDirPub 83*
Studio City Graphic - *See* Associated Valley Publications
Studio E. Martin - White Rock, BC, Canada - *BoPubDir 4, 5*
Studio 8 - Bellerose, NY - *AvMarPl 83*
Studio Esprit - Montreal, PQ, Canada - *VideoDir 82-83*
Studio Film & Tape Inc. - New York, NY - *Tel&CabFB 84C*
Studio 403 Corp. - Portland, OR - *LitMag&SmPr 83-84*
Studio G Recording - Clayton, MO - *AvMarPl 83*
Studio M Productions - Honolulu, HI - *BrCabYB 84*
Studio 932 Ltd. - Seattle, WA - *AvMarPl 83*
Studio Photography - Hempstead, NY - *MagDir 84*
Studio Photography - Woodbury, NY - *BaconPubCkMag 84*
Studio Press - Toronto, ON, Canada - *BoPubDir 4 Sup, 5*
Studio S - Morro Bay, CA - *BoPubDir 4, 5*
Studio Software - Wootton Wawen, England - *MicrocomSwDir 1*
Studio Sonscript - Montreal, PQ, Canada - *AvMarPl 83*
Studio II Inc. - Grand Rapids, MI - *StaDirAdAg 2-84*
Studio Typing - Brentwood, CA - *LitMarPl 83, 84*
Studio West - New York, NY - *AvMarPl 83*
Studioline Premium Stereo Network - Arlington, VA - *CabTVPrDB 83*
Studios Kaminski Photography Ltd. - Reno, NV - *ArtMar 84*
Studioworks - Charlotte, NC - *BillIntBG 83-84*
Studium Corp. - Jamaica, NY - *BoPubDir 4 Sup, 5*
Studley Press Inc., The - Dalton, MA - *LitMarPl 83, 84*
Studsvik Energiteknik AB [of Studsvikbiblioteket] - Nykoping, Sweden - *CompReadDB 82; InfIndMarPl 83*
Study of Major Market Newspapers - Larchmont, NY - *DirOnDB Spring 84*
Study of Media & Markets [of Simmons Market Research Bureau Inc.] - New York, NY - *DataDirOnSer 84*
Stuhlmann, Gunther - Becket, MA - *LitMarPl 83, 84*
Stull Financial News [of Stull & Co.] - New York, NY - *MagDir 84*
Stull Golden Rule Observer [of Stull & Co.] - Cleveland, OH - *MagDir 84*
Stumpf Advertising Agency, The - Akron, OH - *StaDirAdAg 2-84*
Sturgeon Bay Door County Advocate - Sturgeon Bay, WI - *BaconPubCkNews 84; NewsDir 84*
Sturgeon Falls Tribune - Sturgeon Falls, ON, Canada - *Ed&PubIntYB 82*
Sturgis Black Hills Press - *See* Allison Publishing
Sturgis Journal - Sturgis, MI - *BaconPubCkNews 84; Ed&PubIntYB 82; NewsDir 84*
Sturgis Meade County Times Tribune - *See* Allison Publishing
Sturgis News - Sturgis, KY - *BaconPubCkNews 84; Ed&PubIntYB 82; NewsDir 84*
Sturgis Tri-State Livestock News - Sturgis, SD - *NewsDir 84*
Sturm Research Inc. - New York, NY - *IntDirMarRes 83*
Sturman, Buckstein & Co. Ltd. - *See* Buckstein & Associates Inc., Murray E.
Stursberg & Hewitt Inc. - Los Angeles, CA - *DirPRFirms 83; StaDirAdAg 2-84*
Sturzebecker, Russell L. - West Chester, PA - *BoPubDir 4, 5*
Stutman Associates Inc. - New York, NY - *LitMarPl 83, 84*
Stuttgart Cablevision Inc. - Stuttgart, AR - *BrCabYB 84; Tel&CabFB 84C*
Stuttgart Daily Leader [of Harte-Hanks Communications] - Stuttgart, AR - *BaconPubCkNews 84; Ed&PubIntYB 82; NewsDir 84*
Stuttman Inc., H. S. - Westport, CT - *LitMarPl 83, 84*
Stygian Songs - *See* Rondor Music International Inc.
Style - Toronto, ON, Canada - *BaconPubCkMag 84*
Style & Affairs - Jackson, MS - *NewsDir 84*
Styling Magazine - Shreveport, LA - *WritMar 84*
Su-Ma Publishing Co. Inc. - Shreveport, LA - *BillIntBG 83-84*
Subject Access Project [of University of Lund Library] - Lund, Sweden - *EISS 83*
Subject Analysis Systems Collection [of University of Toronto] - Toronto, ON, Canada - *EISS 83*
Sublette Community TV - Sublette, KS - *BrCabYB 84; Tel&CabFB 84C*
Sublette Haskell County Monitor-Chief - Sublette, KS - *BaconPubCkNews 84*
Sublimity/Aumsville Cablevision [of Stayton Cooperative Telephone Co.] - Aumsville, OR - *BrCabYB 84*
Sublogic Communications Corp. - Champaign, IL - *MicrocomMPl 83, 84; MicrocomSwDir 1; WhoWMicrocom 83*
Subotnik, Chessler Inc. - Baltimore, MD - *StaDirAdAg 2-84*
Subscription Television of America - McLean, VA - *HomeVid&CabYB 82-83*
Subsoil Data Bank [of Bureau of Geological & Mining Research] - Orleans, France - *EISS 83*
Subsystem of Documentary Reference of Siplan [of Ministry of the Interior] - Brasilia, DF, Brazil - *EISS 83*
Subterranean Co. - Eugene, OR - *BoPubDir 4 Sup, 5; LitMarPl 83, 84*
Subterranean Records - San Francisco, CA - *BillIntBG 83-84*

Subtle Magic Music - Rochester, MI - *BillIntBG 83-84*
Subtractive Technology - Boston, MA - *AvMarPl 83*
Suburban - East Brunswick, NJ - *AyerDirPub 83*
Suburban - Old Bridge, NJ - *Ed&PubIntYB 82*
Suburban - South River, NJ - *AyerDirPub 83*
Suburban - Montreal, PQ, Canada - *AyerDirPub 83; Ed&PubIntYB 82*
Suburban Advertiser - Kansas City, KS - *AyerDirPub 83*
Suburban Advertiser - Paoli, PA - *AyerDirPub 83; Ed&PubIntYB 82*
Suburban & Wayne Times - Wayne, PA - *AyerDirPub 83; Ed&PubIntYB 82*
Suburban Associates - Ridgewood, NJ - *IntDirMarRes 83*
Suburban Bee - Amherst, NY - *Ed&PubIntYB 82*
Suburban Bee - Williamsville, NY - *AyerDirPub 83*
Suburban Cable TV [of Lenfest Communications Inc.] - Perkasie, PA - *BrCabYB 84*
Suburban Cable TV [Aff. of Lenfest Group] - Sellersville, PA - *InterCabHB 3; Tel&CabFB 84C*
Suburban Cable TV - *See* Lenfest Communications Inc.
Suburban Cablevision - Berkeley Heights, NJ - *BrCabYB 84*
Suburban Cablevision [of Maclean-Hunter Cable TV Ltd.] - East Orange, NJ - *BrCabYB 84; HomeVid&CabYB 82-83; LitMarPl 84; Tel&CabFB 84C p.1704*
Suburban Cablevision - Linden, NJ - *BrCabYB 84*
Suburban Cablevision - Secaucus, NJ - *BrCabYB 84*
Suburban Cablevision - Westfield, NJ - *BrCabYB 84*
Suburban Cablevision Inc. - Millburn, NJ - *BrCabYB 84*
Suburban Cablevision Inc. - Montclair, NJ - *BrCabYB 84*
Suburban Communications Inc. [of Lenfest Communications Inc.] - Phoenixville, PA - *BrCabYB 84; Tel&CabFB 84C*
Suburban Features - New York, NY - *Ed&PubIntYB 82*
Suburban Gazette - McKees Rocks, PA - *AyerDirPub 83; NewsDir 84*
Suburban Journal [of Journal-News Publications] - Des Plaines, IL - *NewsDir 84*
Suburban Journal - Dickinson, TX - *AyerDirPub 83; Ed&PubIntYB 82*
Suburban Leader [of Leader Newspapers-Leader Papers Inc.] - Chicago, IL - *AyerDirPub 83; NewsDir 84*
Suburban Life - Dewitt, NY - *Ed&PubIntYB 82*
Suburban Life Citizen - La Grange Park, IL - *AyerDirPub 83; Ed&PubIntYB 82*
Suburban Life Graphic - Downers Grove, IL - *AyerDirPub 83; Ed&PubIntYB 82; NewsDir 84*
Suburban News - Shelton, CT - *AyerDirPub 83; Ed&PubIntYB 82*
Suburban News - Westfield, NJ - *AyerDirPub 83; Ed&PubIntYB 82*
Suburban News - Spencerport, NY - *AyerDirPub 83*
Suburban News - Clarksville, TN - *AyerDirPub 83*
Suburban News [of News-Texan Inc.] - Farmers Branch, TX - *AyerDirPub 83; Ed&PubIntYB 82; NewsDir 84*
Suburban News Marketer - Oak Lawn, IL - *AyerDirPub 83*
Suburban News Publications - Columbus, OH - *BaconPubCkNews 84*
Suburban News South - Nashville, TN - *Ed&PubIntYB 82*
Suburban News, The - Flint, MI - *Ed&PubIntYB 82*
Suburban News, The [of The Charleston Journal] - Charleston, SC - *NewsDir 84*
Suburban News West, The - Nashville, TN - *Ed&PubIntYB 82*
Suburban Newspapers - Detroit, MI - *BaconPubCkNews 84*
Suburban Newspapers - Cherry Hill, NJ - *BaconPubCkNews 84*
Suburban Newspapers Inc. - Ft. Worth, TX - *BaconPubCkNews 84*
Suburban Pottstown Cable TV Co. [of Lenfest Communications Inc.] - Pottstown, PA - *BrCabYB 84; Tel&CabFB 84C*
Suburban Press - Orchard Park, NY - *AyerDirPub 83; Ed&PubIntYB 82*
Suburban Press - Genoa, OH - *AyerDirPub 83*
Suburban Press - Sharonville, OH - *AyerDirPub 83; Ed&PubIntYB 82*
Suburban Printing Corp. - Mt. Vernon, GA - *BaconPubCkNews 84*
Suburban Progress [of Franklin Park Publishing Co.] - Franklin Park, IL - *NewsDir 84*
Suburban Publications Inc. - Wayne, PA - *BaconPubCkNews 84*
Suburban Radio Group - Belmont, NC - *BrCabYB 84*
Suburban Record - Boston, MA - *AyerDirPub 83*
Suburban Software - Ridgewood, NJ - *IntDirMarRes 83*
Suburban South-West Pittsburgh Gazette - McKees Rocks, PA - *Ed&PubIntYB 82*
Suburban Systems Inc. - Houston, TX - *DirInfWP 82*
Suburban, The - Mt. Prospect, IL - *Ed&PubIntYB 82*
Suburban, The - Audubon, NJ - *Ed&PubIntYB 82*
Suburban, The - Cherry Hill, NJ - *AyerDirPub 83; NewsDir 84*
Suburban Times - Des Plaines, IL - *AyerDirPub 83*
Suburban Times - Tacoma, WA - *Ed&PubIntYB 82*
Suburban Today - Lubbock, TX - *Ed&PubIntYB 82*
Suburban Trends [of Butler Riverdale Publishing Inc.] - Butler, NJ - *AyerDirPub 83; Ed&PubIntYB 82; NewsDir 84*
Suburban Trib, The - Hinsdale, IL - *AyerDirPub 83*
Suburban Tribune - Dallas, TX - *AyerDirPub 83; Ed&PubIntYB 82*
Suburban West Business Magazine - Westtown, PA - *BaconPubCkMag 84*
Suburban World Inc. - Needham, MA - *BaconPubCkNews 84*
Suburbanaire - Union, NJ - *AyerDirPub 83*
Suburbanite Economist [of Chicago Daily Southtown Economist Newspapers] - Chicago, IL - *Ed&PubIntYB 82; NewsDir 84*
Suburbanite, The - Winston-Salem, NC - *AyerDirPub 83; Ed&PubIntYB 82*
Suburbanite, The [of South Milwaukee Voice-Journal] - South Milwaukee, WI - *NewsDir 84*
Suburbia News - Westerville, OH - *Ed&PubIntYB 82*
Suburbia News - Seagoville, TX - *Ed&PubIntYB 82*
Suburbia-Reporter - Houston, TX - *AyerDirPub 83*
Suburbia Today [of Gannett Newspapers] - White Plains, NY - *LitMarPl 84; WritMar 84*
Suburbia West Today [of Independent-Journal Newspapers] - Santa Monica, CA - *NewsDir 84*
Success - Denver, CO - *WritMar 84*
Success [of Success Unltd. Inc.] - Chicago, IL - *BaconPubCkMag 84; Folio 83; MagDir 84; MagIndMarPl 82-83; WritMar 84*
Success & Money! [of Beninda Books] - Canton, OH - *LitMag&SmPr 83-84*
Success Foundation Inc. - Louisville, KY - *BoPubDir 5*
Success Management Consultants - Pacific Palisades, CA - *MicrocomMPl 84*
Success Publications - Regina, SK, Canada - *LitMag&SmPr 83-84*
Success Records International Inc. - Miami, FL - *BillIntBG 83-84*
Success Systems - Watsonville, CA - *WhoWMicrocom 83*
Success Unltd. Inc. [Aff. of Success Magazine] - Chicago, IL - *BoPubDir 4, 5*
Success with Youth Publishers - La Jolla, CA - *LitMarPl 83*
Successful Dealer, The [of Kona-Cal Inc.] - Deerfield, IL - *BaconPubCkMag 84; WritMar 84*
Successful Farming [of Meredith Corp.] - Des Moines, IA - *BaconPubCkMag 84; LitMarPl 84; MagDir 84; MagIndMarPl 82-83; MicrocomMPl 84; WritMar 84*
Successful Meetings [of Bill Communications Inc.] - New York, NY - *BaconPubCkMag 84; MagDir 84*
Successful Meetings [of Bill Communications Inc.] - Philadelphia, PA - *EISS 83*
Successful Meetings - Phildelphia, PA - *MagIndMarPl 82-83*
Sucess Foundation Inc. - Louisville, KY - *BoPubDir 4*
Suckling, R. Paul - Toronto, ON, Canada - *InfIndMarPl 83*
Sudan Beacon News - Sudan, TX - *Ed&PubIntYB 82*
Sudan Beacon-News - *See* Sudan Beacon-News Publishers
Sudan Beacon-News Publishers - Sudan, TX - *BaconPubCkNews 84*
Sudbrink Broadcasting - Ft. Lauderdale, FL - *BrCabYB 84*
Sudbury Cable Services Ltd. [of Northern Cable Services Ltd.] - Sudbury, ON, Canada - *BrCabYB 84*
Sudbury Services Inc. - Blytheville, AR - *BrCabYB 84*
Sudbury Star, The - Sudbury, ON, Canada - *BaconPubCkNews 84; Ed&PubIntYB 82*
Sudbury Town Crier - *See* Town Crier Publications
Sudbury Town Crier & Fence Viewer - Sudbury, MA - *Ed&PubIntYB 82; NewsDir 84*
Sudden Infant Death Syndrome Clearinghouse [of U.S. Public Health Service] - Arlington, VA - *EISS 83*
Sudler & Hennessey [Subs. of Young & Rubicam] - New York, NY - *AdAge 3-28-84; BrCabYB 84; StaDirAdAg 2-84*

Sue Ann - North Haven, CT - *BoPubDir 4, 5*
Sueno Publishing Co. - Troutman, NC - *BillIntBG 83-84*
Sueno Records - Troutman, NC - *BillIntBG 83-84*
Suffolk County News - Sayville, NY - *AyerDirPub 83; NewsDir 84*
Suffolk County News & Islip Bulletin - Sayville, NY - *Ed&PubIntYB 82*
Suffolk Life - Long Island City, NY - *AyerDirPub 83*
Suffolk Life - Suffolk County, NY - *Ed&PubIntYB 82*
Suffolk Marketing - Smithtown, NY - *BillIntBG 83-84*
Suffolk-Nassau Online Retrievers [of Eaton Corp.] - Melville, NY - *InfIndMarPl 83*
Suffolk News-Herald - Suffolk, VA - *BaconPubCkNews 84; NewsDir 84*
Suffolk Times [of Four Twenty Nine Main St. Corp.] - Greenport, NY - *AyerDirPub 83; NewsDir 84*
Suffolk Times, The - Southold, NY - *Ed&PubIntYB 82*
Sufi Islamia/Prophecy Publications [Aff. of Sufi Islamia Ruhaniat Society] - San Francisco, CA - *BoPubDir 4, 5*
Sufi Order Publications/Omega Press [Aff. of The Sufi Order in the West] - Santa Fe, NM - *BoPubDir 4, 5; LitMag&SmPr 83-84*
Sufism Reoriented - Walnut Creek, CA - *BoPubDir 4, 5*
Sugar Azucar - Ft. Lee, NJ - *BaconPubCkMag 84*
Sugar Azucar - New York, NY - *MagDir 84*
Sugar Bulletin - New Orleans, LA - *BaconPubCkMag 84; MagDir 84*
Sugar Creek Co. - *See* Hot Bear Enterprises
Sugar Hill Records Inc. - Englewood, NJ - *BillIntBG 83-84*
Sugar Hill Records Inc. - Durham, NC - *BillIntBG 83-84*
Sugar Journal - New Orleans, LA - *BaconPubCkMag 84; MagDir 84*
Sugar Land Telephone Co. [Aff. of SLT Communications Corp.] - Sugar Land, TX - *TelDir&BG 83-84*
Sugar Producer, The - Idaho Falls, ID - *MagDir 84; MagIndMarPl 82-83; WritMar 84*
Sugar Software - Reynoldsburg, OH - *MicrocomMPl 84; WhoWMicrocom 83*
Sugar Valley Telephone Co. [Aff. of Telephone & Data Systems Inc.] - Loganton, PA - *TelDir&BG 83-84*
Sugarbeet Grower, The - Fargo, ND - *BaconPubCkMag 84; MagDir 84*
Sugarcreek Budget - Sugarcreek, OH - *BaconPubCkNews 84; NewsDir 84*
Sugarplum Music Co. - Nashville, TN - *BillIntBG 83-84*
Sugartree Records - St. Petersburg, FL - *BillIntBG 83-84*
Sugarvine Music - Davenport, IA - *BillIntBG 83-84*
Sugden & Co. - La Salle, IL - *LitMarPl 83, 84*
Sugden & Co., Sherwood - La Salle, IL - *LitMag&SmPr 83-84; LitMarPl 83, 84; WritMar 84*
Suggin Productions - Little Rock, AR - *BoPubDir 4, 5*
Suhrkamp/Insel Boston [Subs. of Suhrkamp Verlag & Insel Verlag] - Cambridge, MA - *LitMarPl 84*
Suits News Co. Inc. - Lansing, MI - *MagIndMarPl 82-83*
Suki Music - *See* JEDO Music
Sulligent Lamar County Leader - Sulligent, AL - *BaconPubCkNews 84*
Sullivan Advertising Inc., J. G. - South Bend, IN - *StaDirAdAg 2-84*
Sullivan & Brugnatelli Advertising Inc. - New York, NY - *AdAge 3-28-84; ArtMar 84; StaDirAdAg 2-84*
Sullivan Associates Stock Photo File - Austin, TX - *MagIndMarPl 82-83*
Sullivan Cable of Maryland - Cambridge, MD - *BrCabYB 84*
Sullivan Communications - Doylestown, PA - *AdAge 3-28-84*
Sullivan Co. Inc., Daniel F. - Boston, MA - *BrCabYB 84; StaDirAdAg 2-84*
Sullivan County Democrat - Callicoon, NY - *AyerDirPub 83*
Sullivan County Democrat - Sullivan County, NY - *Ed&PubIntYB 82*
Sullivan County News - Blountville, TN - *AyerDirPub 83; Ed&PubIntYB 82; NewsDir 84*
Sullivan, Higdon & Sink - Wichita, KS - *AdAge 3-28-84; DirPRFirms 83; StaDirAdAg 2-84*
Sullivan Independent News - Sullivan, MO - *BaconPubCkNews 84; Ed&PubIntYB 82; NewsDir 84*
Sullivan Letter, The - New York, NY - *BrCabYB 84*
Sullivan News-Progress [of Best Newspapers in Illinois Inc.] - Sullivan, IL - *NewsDir 84*
Sullivan News-Progress - *See* Best Newspapers in Illinois Inc.
Sullivan Productions Inc. - Los Angeles, CA - *Tel&CabFB 84C*
Sullivan Review - Dushore, PA - *AyerDirPub 83; NewsDir 84*
Sullivan Review, The - Sullivan County, PA - *Ed&PubIntYB 82*
Sullivan Sarria & Associates Inc. - New York, NY - *DirPRFirms 83*
Sullivan Telephone Co. - Sullivan, WI - *TelDir&BG 83-84*
Sullivan Times [of Pierce Oil Co. Inc.] - Sullivan, IN - *AyerDirPub 83; BaconPubCkNews 84; Ed&PubIntYB 82; NewsDir 84*
Sullivan Tri-County News [of Franklin Newspapers Inc.] - Sullivan, MO - *BaconPubCkNews 84; NewsDir 84*
Sullivan TV Cable Co. [of Horizon Communications Corp.] - Sullivan, IN - *Tel&CabFB 84C*
Sullivan Union - Sullivan, IN - *AyerDirPub 83; BaconPubCkNews 84; Ed&PubIntYB 82*
Sullwold Publishing Inc., William S. - Taunton, MA - *BoPubDir 4, 5*
Sully Buttes Telephone Cooperative - Highmore, SD - *Tel&CabFB 84C; TelDir&BG 83-84*
Sully Diamond Trail News - Sully, IA - *BaconPubCkNews 84*
Sully Telephone Association - Sully, IA - *TelDir&BG 83-84*
Sulpher Springs Telephone Co. Inc. - Sulpher Springs, IN - *TelDir&BG 83-84*
Sulphur Cable TV Fund VIII-C [of Jones Intercable Inc.] - Sulphur, LA - *BrCabYB 84*
Sulphur-Davis-Cable-Vision [of Harmon & Co.] - Sulphur, OK - *BrCabYB 84*
Sulphur River - Commerce, TX - *LitMag&SmPr 83-84*
Sulphur Southwest Builder News - Sulphur, LA - *BaconPubCkNews 84*
Sulphur Springs Cable TV [of Texas Community Antennas Inc.] - Sulphur Springs, TX - *BrCabYB 84*
Sulphur Springs News-Telegram [of Echo Publishing Co.] - Sulphur Springs, TX - *BaconPubCkNews 84; Ed&PubIntYB 82; NewsDir 84*
Sulphur Times-Democrat - Sulphur, OK - *BaconPubCkNews 84; Ed&PubIntYB 82*
Sultan Valley News - Sultan, WA - *BaconPubCkNews 84*
Sultana Press/Premier Printing Corp. - Fullerton, CA - *LitMarPl 83, 84*
Sulzer Music - Philadelphia, PA - *BillIntBG 83-84*
Suma Records - New York, NY - *BillIntBG 83-84*
Sumac Music Inc. - New York, NY - *BillIntBG 83-84*
Sumac Press - Fremont, MI - *BoPubDir 4, 5*
Sumac Press - La Crosse, WI - *BoPubDir 4, 5*
Sumet-Bernet Sound Studios Inc. - Dallas, TX - *AvMarPl 83*
Sumicom Inc. [Subs. of Sumitomo Corp.] - Tustin, CA - *WhoWMicrocom 83*
Sumiko Inc. - Berkeley, CA - *BillIntBG 83-84*
Sumiton Community News - Sumiton, AL - *BaconPubCkNews 84*
Summa Publications Inc. - Birmingham, AL - *LitMarPl 84*
Summagraphics Corp. - Fairfield, CT - *DataDirSup 7-83*
Summer, Anita - Westbury, NY - *Ed&PubIntYB 82*
Summer Institute of Linguistics - Dallas, TX - *BoPubDir 4, 5*
Summer News-Review & Lakes Observer - Summer, WA - *BaconPubCkNews 84*
Summer Stream Press - Santa Barbara, CA - *BoPubDir 4, 5; LitMag&SmPr 83-84*
Summerfield Sun - Frankfort, KS - *BaconPubCkNews 84*
Summerland Review - Summerland, BC, Canada - *Ed&PubIntYB 82*
Summersville Beacon - Houston, MO - *BaconPubCkNews 84*
Summersville Beacon - Summersville, MO - *Ed&PubIntYB 82*
Summersville Nicholas Chronicle - Summersville, WV - *BaconPubCkNews 84; NewsDir 84*
Summersville West Virginia Hillbilly - Summersville, WV - *BaconPubCkNews 84; NewsDir 84*
Summerthought Ltd. - Banff, AB, Canada - *BoPubDir 4, 5; LitMag&SmPr 83-84*
Summerville CATV Inc. - Holland, PA - *BrCabYB 84*
Summerville Enterprises - Aliceville, AL - *MicrocomMPl 84*
Summerville Enterprises (Computer Services Div.) - Aliceville, AL - *WhoWMicrocom 83*

Summerville Journal-Scene - Summerville, SC - *BaconPubCkNews 84; Ed&PubIntYB 82*
Summerville News - Summerville, GA - *BaconPubCkNews 84; Ed&PubIntYB 82; NewsDir 84*
Summet Advertising - Norfolk, VA - *StaDirAdAg 2-84*
Summit Books [Div. of Simon & Schuster] - New York, NY - *LitMarPl 83, 84; WritMar 84*
Summit Cable Services of Forsyth County Inc. [of Summit Communications Inc.] - Winston-Salem, NC - *Tel&CabFB 84C*
Summit Cable Services of Georgia Inc. [of Summit Communications Inc.] - Cobb County, GA - *BrCabYB 84*
Summit Cable Services of Georgia Inc. [of Summit Communications Inc.] - Woodstock, GA - *Tel&CabFB 84C*
Summit Cable Services of Iredell County Inc. [of Summit Communications Inc.] - Mocksville, NC - *BrCabYB 84*
Summit Cable Services of Iredell County Inc. - Statesville, NC - *BrCabYB 84*
Summit Cable Services of Statesville Inc. [of Summit Communications Inc.] - Statesville, NC - *Tel&CabFB 84C*
Summit Cable Services of Thom-A-Lex Inc. [of Summit Communications Inc.] - Lexington, NC - *BrCabYB 84*
Summit Cable Services of Winston-Salem Inc. [of Summit Communications Inc.] - Winston-Salem, NC - *BrCabYB 84*
Summit Communications Inc. - Winston-Salem, NC - *BrCabYB 84 p.D-307; Tel&CabFB 84C p.1704*
Summit Communications Inc. - Bellevue, WA - *Tel&CabFB 84C*
Summit Communications Inc. - Napavine, WA - *Tel&CabFB 84C*
Summit Communications Inc. - Port Townsend, WA - *BrCabYB 84; Tel&CabFB 84C*
Summit Communications Inc. - Ridgefield, WA - *Tel&CabFB 84C*
Summit County Bee - Coalville, UT - *AyerDirPub 83; Ed&PubIntYB 82*
Summit County Journal - Breckenridge, CO - *AyerDirPub 83; Ed&PubIntYB 82*
Summit County Sentinel - Dillon, CO - *AyerDirPub 83; Ed&PubIntYB 82*
Summit Films Inc. - Gypsum, CO - *AvMarPl 83*
Summit Group Inc., The - Coral Gables, FL - *StaDirAdAg 2-84*
Summit Herald - Summit, NJ - *BaconPubCkNews 84; Ed&PubIntYB 82*
Summit Independent [of Passaic Valley Independent Press] - New Providence, NJ - *NewsDir 84*
Summit Independent - Summit, NJ - *AyerDirPub 83; Ed&PubIntYB 82*
Summit Independent - *See* Passaic Valley Independent Press
Summit-Leoni Cable TV [of Booth American Co.] - Summit Township, MI - *BrCabYB 84*
Summit-Leoni Cable TV Co. [of Booth American Co.] - Summit-Leoni, MI - *Tel&CabFB 84C*
Summit Press Syndicate - Milwaukee, WI - *Ed&PubIntYB 82*
Summit Publications - Munroe Falls, OH - *BoPubDir 4, 5*
Summit Publishing Co. - Hudson, OH - *BoPubDir 5*
Summit Sun - Summit, MS - *BaconPubCkNews 84; Ed&PubIntYB 82*
Summit University Press - Malibu, CA - *BoPubDir 4, 5; LitMag&SmPr 83-84*
Summit Valley Times [of Lyons Enterprise Publishing Co.] - Lyons, IL - *NewsDir 84*
Summitville Sun - Summitville, IN - *BaconPubCkNews 84; Ed&PubIntYB 82*
Summy-Birchard Music - *See* Birch-Tree Group Ltd.
Sumner-Berry-Brown - Dallas, TX - *StaDirAdAg 2-84*
Sumner Cable TV Co. - Wellington, KS - *BrCabYB 84; Tel&CabFB 84C*
Sumner Gazette - Sumner, IA - *BaconPubCkNews 84; Ed&PubIntYB 82*
Sumner Press - Sumner, IL - *BaconPubCkNews 84; Ed&PubIntYB 82*
Sumner Press - Windsor, ON, Canada - *BoPubDir 4, 5*
Sumner Rider & Associates Inc. - New York, NY - *DirPRFirms 83*
Sumpter Valley Cable TV - Sumpter, OR - *Tel&CabFB 84C*
Sumrall Evangelistic Association Inc., Lester - South Bend, IN - *Tel&CabFB 84S*
Sumter Black Post - Columbia, SC - *AyerDirPub 83*
Sumter Black Post - *See* Juju Publishing Co.
Sumter County Journal - York, AL - *AyerDirPub 83; Ed&PubIntYB 82*
Sumter County Times - Bushnell, FL - *AyerDirPub 83*
Sumter County Times - Sumter County, FL - *Ed&PubIntYB 82*
Sumter Item [of Osteen Publishing Co.] - Sumter, SC - *BaconPubCkNews 84; Ed&PubIntYB 82; NewsDir 84*
Sun - Oxford, AL - *AyerDirPub 83*
Sun - Superior, AZ - *AyerDirPub 83*
Sun - Wickenburg, AZ - *AyerDirPub 83*
Sun - Yuma, AZ - *AyerDirPub 83*
Sun - Jonesboro, AR - *AyerDirPub 83*
Sun - Exeter, CA - *AyerDirPub 83*
Sun - Millbrae, CA - *AyerDirPub 83*
Sun - San Gabriel, CA - *AyerDirPub 83*
Sun - Aurora, CO - *AyerDirPub 83*
Sun - Colorado Springs, CO - *AyerDirPub 83*
Sun - Pagosa Springs, CO - *AyerDirPub 83*
Sun - Clearwater, FL - *AyerDirPub 83*
Sun - Gainesville, FL - *AyerDirPub 83*
Sun - Zephyrhills, FL - *AyerDirPub 83*
Sun - Hartwell, GA - *AyerDirPub 83*
Sun - Warner Robins, GA - *AyerDirPub 83*
Sun - Naperville, IL - *AyerDirPub 83*
Sun - Trenton, IL - *AyerDirPub 83*
Sun - North Vernon, IN - *AyerDirPub 83*
Sun - Laurens, IA - *AyerDirPub 83*
Sun - Sheldon, IA - *AyerDirPub 83*
Sun - Edna, KS - *AyerDirPub 83*
Sun - Glasco, KS - *AyerDirPub 83*
Sun - Parsons, KS - *AyerDirPub 83*
Sun - Pittsburg, KS - *AyerDirPub 83*
Sun - Wakefield, KS - *AyerDirPub 83*
Sun - Paducah, KY - *AyerDirPub 83*
Sun - Springfield, KY - *AyerDirPub 83*
Sun - Winchester, KY - *AyerDirPub 83*
Sun - Holbrook, MA - *AyerDirPub 83*
Sun - Lowell, MA - *AyerDirPub 83; Ed&PubIntYB 82*
Sun - Marlborough, MA - *AyerDirPub 83*
Sun - Quincy, MA - *AyerDirPub 83*
Sun - Mt. Pleasant, MI - *AyerDirPub 83*
Sun - Morris, MN - *AyerDirPub 83*
Sun - Summit, MS - *AyerDirPub 83*
Sun - Beatrice, NE - *AyerDirPub 83*
Sun - Schuyler, NE - *AyerDirPub 83*
Sun - Shelby, NE - *AyerDirPub 83*
Sun - Las Vegas, NV - *AyerDirPub 83; Ed&PubIntYB 82*
Sun - Nutley, NJ - *AyerDirPub 83*
Sun - Ft. Covington, NY - *AyerDirPub 83*
Sun - New York, NY - *BoPubDir 4, 5*
Sun - Norwich, NY - *AyerDirPub 83*
Sun - Durham, NC - *AyerDirPub 83*
Sun - Fairfield, OH - *AyerDirPub 83*
Sun - New Carlisle, OH - *AyerDirPub 83*
Sun [of Reynoldsburg Reporter] - Reynoldsburg, OH - *NewsDir 84*
Sun - Toledo, OH - *AyerDirPub 83; NewsDir 84*
Sun - Edmond, OK - *AyerDirPub 83*
Sun - Grove, OK - *AyerDirPub 83*
Sun - Sheridan, OR - *AyerDirPub 83*
Sun - Hanover, PA - *AyerDirPub 83*
Sun - Hummelstown, PA - *AyerDirPub 83*
Sun - Westerly, RI - *AyerDirPub 83*
Sun - Greeneville, TN - *AyerDirPub 83*
Sun - Jackson, TN - *AyerDirPub 83*
Sun - Corsicana, TX - *AyerDirPub 83*
Sun - El Paso, TX - *AyerDirPub 83*
Sun - Grand Saline, TX - *AyerDirPub 83*
Sun - Texas City, TX - *AyerDirPub 83*
Sun - Whitewright, TX - *AyerDirPub 83*
Sun - Bremerton, WA - *AyerDirPub 83*
Sun - Osceola, WI - *AyerDirPub 83*
Sun - Spring Valley, WI - *AyerDirPub 83; Ed&PubIntYB 82*
Sun - Union Grove, WI - *AyerDirPub 83*
Sun - Saratoga, WY - *AyerDirPub 83*
Sun - Edmonton, AB, Canada - *AyerDirPub 83*
Sun - Vancouver, BC, Canada - *AyerDirPub 83; BaconPubCkNews 84*

Sun - Brandon, MB, Canada - *AyerDirPub 83*
Sun - Cobden, ON, Canada - *AyerDirPub 83*
Sun - Milverton, ON, Canada - *Ed&PubIntYB 82*
Sun - Stayner, ON, Canada - *AyerDirPub 83*
Sun - Toronto, ON, Canada - *AyerDirPub 83*
Sun - West Lorne, ON, Canada - *AyerDirPub 83*
Sun - Grenfell, SK, Canada - *Ed&PubIntYB 82*
Sun - Swift Current, SK, Canada - *AyerDirPub 83*
Sun, A Magazine of Ideas - Chapel Hill, NC - *LitMag&SmPr 83-84*
Sun Advertiser - Toledo, OH - *AyerDirPub 83*
Sun Advocate - Price, UT - *AyerDirPub 83; Ed&PubIntYB 82; NewsDir 84*
Sun Advocate Publishers Inc. - Price, UT - *BaconPubCkNews 84*
Sun & Eric County Independent - Hamburg, NY - *AyerDirPub 83*
Sun & Moon: A Journal of Literature & Art - College Park, MD - *LitMag&SmPr 83-84*
Sun & Moon Press - College Park, MD - *BoPubDir 4, 5; LitMag&SmPr 83-84*
Sun & News Advertiser - Grapevine, TX - *AyerDirPub 83*
Sun & Sand - Largo, FL - *AyerDirPub 83*
Sun & Sentinel - Williamson, NY - *AyerDirPub 83*
Sun Belt Buildings Journal - Phoenix, AZ - *BaconPubCkMag 84*
Sun Belt Market Research - Tucson, AZ - *IntDirMarRes 83*
Sun-Bulletin - Morro Bay, CA - *AyerDirPub 83*
Sun-Bulletin - Ridgefield Park, NJ - *AyerDirPub 83; Ed&PubIntYB 82*
Sun-Bulletin [of Binghamton Press Co.] - Binghamton, NY - *AyerDirPub 83; Ed&PubIntYB 82; LitMarPl 84*
Sun Cable of Chelan - Chelan, WA - *Tel&CabFB 84C p.1704*
Sun Cable TV [of Mickelson Media Inc.] - Deming, NM - *BrCabYB 84; Tel&CabFB 84C*
Sun Cable TV [of Mickelson Media Inc.] - Hatch, NM - *Tel&CabFB 84C*
Sun Cablevision [of Mega Vision Inc.] - Durand, MI - *BrCabYB 84; Tel&CabFB 84C p.1704*
Sun Cablevision Co. [of TCI-Taft Cablevision Associates] - Cheboygan, MI - *BrCabYB 84*
Sun Cablevision Co. [of TCI-Taft Cablevision Associates] - Mackinaw City, MI - *BrCabYB 84*
Sun Cablevision Co. [of Jones Intercable Inc.] - Newberry, MI - *BrCabYB 84*
Sun Cablevision Co. [of TCI-Taft Cablevision Associates] - St. Ignace, MI - *BrCabYB 84*
Sun Cablevision of Hawaii [of Mega Vision Co.] - Kailua-Kona, HI - *BrCabYB 84*
Sun Cablevision of the South - South Pittsburg, TN - *BrCabYB 84; Tel&CabFB 84C*
Sun Cablevision of the South - Whitwell, TN - *Tel&CabFB 84C*
Sun Chronicle - Layton, UT - *AyerDirPub 83*
Sun Chronicle [of Roy Printing Co. Newspapers] - Roy, UT - *NewsDir 84*
Sun Chronicle, The - Attleboro, MA - *AyerDirPub 83; Ed&PubIntYB 82*
Sun City Citizen [of Independent Newspapers Inc.] - Sun City, AZ - *Ed&PubIntYB 82; NewsDir 84*
Sun City Independent - Sun City, AZ - *BaconPubCkNews 84*
Sun City News [of Press-Enterprise Co.] - Sun City, CA - *BaconPubCkNews 84; Ed&PubIntYB 82; NewsDir 84*
Sun City News-Sun - Sun City, AZ - *NewsDir 84*
Sun City Pennysaver - Mission Viejo, CA - *AyerDirPub 83*
Sun/Coast Architect-Builder [of McKellar Publications Inc.] - Los Angeles, CA - *BaconPubCkMag 84; MagDir 84*
Sun Coast Gondolier - Venice, FL - *AyerDirPub 83; Ed&PubIntYB 82*
Sun Coast Media Group Inc. - Venice, FL - *BaconPubCkNews 84*
Sun Coast Times [of Sun Coast Gondolier Inc.] - Venice, FL - *AyerDirPub 83; NewsDir 84*
Sun Color Service - Newport Beach, CA - *Ed&PubIntYB 82*
Sun-Commercial - Vincennes, IN - *AyerDirPub 83*
Sun Co. - *Top100Al 83*
Sun Country Publications - Page, AZ - *BoPubDir 4, 5*
Sun Courier - Brecksville, OH - *Ed&PubIntYB 82*
Sun Courier [of Sun Newspapers] - Cleveland, OH - *AyerDirPub 83; NewsDir 84*
Sun-Cumberland Courier - Pineville, KY - *AyerDirPub 83*
Sun/Daily Herald, The [of Gulf Publishing Co. Inc.] - Gulfport, MS - *NewsDir 84*
Sun Dance Books - Hollywood, CA - *BoPubDir 4, 5*
Sun-Diamond Grower - Stockton, CA - *BaconPubCkMag 84*
Sun Dog [of Florida State University] - Tallahassee, FL - *ArtMar 84; LitMag&SmPr 83-84*
Sun-Enterprise - Monmouth, OR - *Ed&PubIntYB 82*
Sun Features Inc. - Cardiff, CA - *BaconPubCkNews 84; BoPubDir 4 Sup, 5; Ed&PubIntYB 82; LitMag&SmPr 83-84*
Sun Features Inc. - Rockville, MD - *LitMarPl 84*
Sun-Gazette - Fulton, MO - *AyerDirPub 83*
Sun-Gazette - Williamsport, PA - *AyerDirPub 83*
Sun-Glo Records Inc. - Miami, FL - *BillIntBG 83-84*
Sun Group Inc. - Knoxville, TN - *BrCabYB 84*
Sun Group, The - New York, NY - *AvMarPl 83*
Sun-Herald - Colusa, CA - *AyerDirPub 83*
Sun-Herald - Winter Park, FL - *AyerDirPub 83; Ed&PubIntYB 82*
Sun Herald [of Gulf Publishing Co. Inc.] - Biloxi, MS - *AyerDirPub 83; Ed&PubIntYB 82; NewsDir 84*
Sun Herald [of Sun Newspapers] - Cleveland, OH - *AyerDirPub 83; NewsDir 84*
Sun-Herald, The - North Olmsted, OH - *Ed&PubIntYB 82*
Sun Independent Newspapers - San Gabriel, CA - *BaconPubCkNews 84*
Sun Information Services Co. [of SIS Corp.] - Radnor, PA - *ADAPSOMemDir 83-84; DataDirOnSer 84; DataDirSup 7-83*
Sun Island Music Publishing Co. - Bronx, NY - *BillIntBG 83-84*
Sun-Journal - Brooksville, FL - *AyerDirPub 83*
Sun-Journal - Lansing, IL - *AyerDirPub 83*
Sun-Journal - New Bern, NC - *AyerDirPub 83; Ed&PubIntYB 82*
Sun Leader Journal - Cleveland, OH - *AyerDirPub 83*
Sun Leader Journal - Wickliffe, OH - *Ed&PubIntYB 82*
Sun Ledger - Quarryville, PA - *AyerDirPub 83*
Sun-Ledger, The - Southern Lancaster County, PA - *Ed&PubIntYB 82*
Sun Life - Thaxton, VA - *BoPubDir 5*
Sun, Man, Moon Inc. - Huntington Beach, CA - *BoPubDir 4, 5; LitMag&SmPr 83-84*
Sun Messenger [of Sun Newspapers] - Cleveland, OH - *AyerDirPub 83; NewsDir 84*
Sun Messenger - Mayfield Heights, OH - *Ed&PubIntYB 82*
Sun-News - De Land, FL - *AyerDirPub 83*
Sun-News - Rockledge, FL - *AyerDirPub 83*
Sun-News - Lowden, IA - *AyerDirPub 83; Ed&PubIntYB 82*
Sun-News - Tupelo, MS - *Ed&PubIntYB 82*
Sun-News - Las Cruces, NM - *AyerDirPub 83*
Sun-News - Myrtle Beach, SC - *AyerDirPub 83; BaconPubCkNews 84; Ed&PubIntYB 82*
Sun Newspapers - Edina, MN - *BaconPubCkNews 84*
Sun Newspapers - Omaha, NE - *BaconPubCkNews 84*
Sun Newspapers - Cleveland, OH - *BaconPubCkNews 84*
Sun Newspapers of Lincoln Inc. - Lincoln, NE - *BaconPubCkNews 84*
Sun Photo - Ann Arbor, MI - *AvMarPl 83*
Sun-Post - San Clemente, CA - *AyerDirPub 83*
Sun Prairie Star Countryman - *See* Royle Publishing Co. Inc.
Sun Press - Cleveland, OH - *AyerDirPub 83*
Sun Press - Cleveland Heights, OH - *Ed&PubIntYB 82*
Sun Press [of McCarthy Publishing] - Yakima, WA - *NewsDir 84*
Sun Publications - Shawnee Mission, KS - *BaconPubCkNews 84*
Sun Publishing Co. - Albuquerque, NM - *LitMag&SmPr 83-84; LitMarPl 83, 84; WritMar 84*
Sun Publishing Corp., The - Canada - *Ed&PubIntYB 82*
Sun-Ray Records - Lexington, KY - *BillIntBG 83-84*
Sun-Register - Neodesha, KS - *AyerDirPub 83*
Sun Reporter - San Francisco, CA - *AyerDirPub 83; NewsDir 84*
Sun Reporter - South Gate, CA - *Ed&PubIntYB 82; NewsDir 84*
Sun Research Inc. [Subs. of Phase-R Corp.] - New Durham, NH - *MicrocomMPl 84; WhoWMicrocom 83*
Sun Ridge Press - Point Arena, CA - *BoPubDir 4 Sup, 5*
Sun Rise Fall Down Artpress - Madison, WI - *BoPubDir 4, 5*
Sun Rise House - Longwood, FL - *BoPubDir 4, 5*
Sun-Scape Publications - Tucson, AZ - *BoPubDir 4, 5*
Sun Scoop Journal - Cleveland, OH - *AyerDirPub 83*
Sun Scoop Journal - East Cleveland, OH - *Ed&PubIntYB 82*
Sun Sentinel - Ft. Lauderdale, FL - *AyerDirPub 83; BaconPubCkNews 84; Ed&PubIntYB 82; NewsDir 84*

Sun Sentinel - Charleston, MS - *AyerDirPub 83; Ed&PubIntYB 82*
Sun Shopper, The - Clarksville, VA - *AyerDirPub 83*
Sun-Standard - Blue Island, IL - *AyerDirPub 83*
Sun-Standard - Calumet Park, IL - *Ed&PubIntYB 82*
Sun-Star - Merced, CA - *AyerDirPub 83*
Sun-Stone - Surry, ME - *BoPubDir 4 Sup, 5*
Sun-Suwannee Valley News - Williston, FL - *Ed&PubIntYB 82*
Sun-Tattler - Hollywood, FL - *AyerDirPub 83*
Sun, The - San Bernardino, CA - *AyerDirPub 83; Ed&PubIntYB 82*
Sun, The - Mt. Vernon, IA - *AyerDirPub 83; Ed&PubIntYB 82*
Sun, The [of A. S. Abell Co.] - Baltimore, MD - *Ed&PubIntYB 82; LitMarPl 83, 84*
Sun, The - Biloxi, MS - *AyerDirPub 83; BaconPubCkNews 84*
Sun, The [of Eastern Suffolk Sun Corp.] - Sag Harbor, NY - *WritMar 84*
Sun, The - North Canton, OH - *Ed&PubIntYB 82*
Sun, The - Springfield, OH - *Ed&PubIntYB 82*
Sun, The - Hershey, PA - *Ed&PubIntYB 82*
Sun, The - Houston, TX - *Ed&PubIntYB 82*
Sun, The - Clarksville, VA - *AyerDirPub 83*
Sun-Times - Chicago, IL - *AyerDirPub 83; Ed&PubIntYB 82*
Sun-Times - Layton, UT - *AyerDirPub 83*
Sun-Times [of Roy Printing Co. Newspapers] - Roy, UT - *NewsDir 84*
Sun-Times [of Southam Inc.] - Owen Sound, ON, Canada - *AyerDirPub 83; BaconPubCkNews 84; Ed&PubIntYB 82*
Sun Tracks: An American Literary Series - Tucson, AZ - *LitMag&SmPr 83-84*
Sun-Tribune - Sutherlin, OR - *AyerDirPub 83; Ed&PubIntYB 82*
Sun Tronics Inc. - Sunriver, OR - *BrCabYB 84; Tel&CabFB 84C*
Sun-Up Energy News Digest - Yucca Valley, CA - *BaconPubCkMag 84*
Sun Valley Book - Sun Valley, ID - *BoPubDir 5*
Sun Valley Cable Vision [of TCA Cable TV Group] - Ketchum, ID - *BrCabYB 84; Tel&CabFB 84C*
Sun Valley Cable Vision Inc. - Hailey, ID - *BrCabYB 84*
Sun Valley News - McAllen, TX - *AyerDirPub 83*
Sun Valley Scene - Tujunga, CA - *AyerDirPub 83*
Sun Valley Systems - Phoenix, AZ - *WhoWMicrocom 83*
Sun Weekender, The - Edina, MN - *AyerDirPub 83*
Sun Weekender, The - Minneapolis/St. Paul, MN - *Ed&PubIntYB 82*
Sun Words Editorial Services Inc. - Hurley, NY - *LitMarPl 83, 84*
Sun World Satellite News - Washington, DC - *BrCabYB 84*
Sunbeam Advertising Agency - New York, NY - *StaDirAdAg 2-84*
Sunbeam Books - Monroe, WA - *LitMag&SmPr 83-84*
Sunbeam Records Inc. - Van Nuys, CA - *BillIntBG 83-84*
Sunbelt Cable Ltd. [of Jones Intercable Inc.] - Belle Glade, FL - *BrCabYB 84; Tel&CabFB 84C p.1704*
Sunbelt Cable Ltd. - Lake Worth, FL - *Tel&CabFB 84C*
Sunbelt Cable Ltd. [of Jones Intercable Inc.] - Pahokee, FL - *BrCabYB 84; Tel&CabFB 84C*
Sunbelt Cablevision of St. Charles Inc. - Destrehan, LA - *Tel&CabFB 84C*
Sunbelt Cablevision of St. Charles Inc. - St. Charles Parish, LA - *BrCabYB 84*
Sunbelt Communications Ltd. - Colorado Springs, CO - *BrCabYB 84*
Sunbelt Dairyman, The - Franklin, TN - *BaconPubCkMag 84*
Sunbelt Dairyman, The - Nashville, TN - *MagDir 84*
Sunbelt Data Resources Inc. - Atlanta, GA - *DataDirOnSer 84*
Sunbelt Executive - New Orleans, LA - *BaconPubCkMag 84*
Sunbelt Music Co. - *See* Music Craftshop Inc.
Sunbelt Publishing Co. - Naples, FL - *BaconPubCkNews 84*
Sunbelt Television Programs - Altamonte Springs, FL - *Tel&CabFB 84C*
Sunbonnet Records - Pensacola, FL - *BillIntBG 83-84*
Sunbox Press - Laguna Beach, CA - *BoPubDir 4, 5*
Sunburst Advertising Inc. - Port St. Lucie, FL - *StaDirAdAg 2-84*
Sunburst Communications - Pleasantville, NY - *AvMarPl 83; DirMarMP 83; MicrocomMPl 83, 84*
Sunburst Farms Publishing Co. [Aff. of Sunburst Communities Inc.] - Goleta, CA - *BoPubDir 4*
Sunburst Press - Portland, OR - *BoPubDir 4, 5*
Sunburst Software - Provo, UT - *MicrocomMPl 84*
Sunbury Daily Item [of Ottaway Newspapers Inc.] - Sunbury, PA - *NewsDir 84*
Sunbury Music Canada Ltd. - Scarborough, ON, Canada - *Tel&CabFB 84C*
Sunbury News - Sunbury, OH - *BaconPubCkNews 84; Ed&PubIntYB 82; NewsDir 84*
Sunbury Press - Bronx, NY - *LitMag&SmPr 83-84*
Sunbury Press - Raleigh, NC - *BoPubDir 4, 5*
Suncoast News - New Port Richey, FL - *AyerDirPub 83*
Suncoast Opinion Surveys - St. Petersburg, FL - *IntDirMarRes 83*
Suncoast Records - Clearwater, FL - *BillIntBG 83-84*
Suncoast Sentinel - Crystal River, FL - *Ed&PubIntYB 82*
Suncom Inc. - Northbrook, IL - *MicrocomMPl 84*
Suncountry Productions Inc. - Tucson, AZ - *BillIntBG 83-84*
Sundance [Div. of Hyletronics Corp.] - Littleton, MA - *LitMarPl 83, 84*
Sundance Broadcasting Inc. - Milwaukee, WI - *BrCabYB 84*
Sundance Cable TV - Sundance, WY - *BrCabYB 84; Tel&CabFB 84C*
Sundance Publications Ltd. - Silverton, CO - *BoPubDir 4, 5*
Sundance Times - Sundance, WY - *BaconPubCkNews 84*
Sunday Advocate [of Capital City Press] - Baton Rouge, LA - *NewsDir 84*
Sunday Bulletin - Philadelphia, PA - *NewsDir 84*
Sunday Call-Chronicle - Allentown, PA - *Ed&PubIntYB 82; LitMarPl 84*
Sunday Camera - Boulder, CO - *Ed&PubIntYB 82*
Sunday Constitution [of Lawton Publishing Co. Inc.] - Lawton, OK - *AyerDirPub 83; Ed&PubIntYB 82; NewsDir 84*
Sunday Courier & Press, The - Evansville, IN - *Ed&PubIntYB 82*
Sunday Courier Merchandiser - Cranbrook, BC, Canada - *Ed&PubIntYB 82*
Sunday Digest [of David C. Cook Publishing Co.] - Elgin, IL - *ArtMar 84; WritMar 84*
Sunday Dispatch - Pittston, PA - *Ed&PubIntYB 82*
Sunday Eagle-Tribune - Lawrence, MA - *Ed&PubIntYB 82*
Sunday Exponent-Telegram - Clarksburg, WV - *Ed&PubIntYB 82*
Sunday Fine Arts Supplement of the Register - Santa Ana, CA - *LitMarPl 84*
Sunday Gazette-Mail - Charleston, WV - *Ed&PubIntYB 82; LitMarPl 84*
Sunday Grit, The - Williamsport, PA - *Ed&PubIntYB 82*
Sunday Herald - Arlington Heights, IL - *Ed&PubIntYB 82*
Sunday Herald - Roanoke Rapids, NC - *Ed&PubIntYB 82*
Sunday Herald American - Syracuse, NY - *NewsDir 84*
Sunday Herald-Times - Bedford, IN - *Ed&PubIntYB 82*
Sunday Herald-Times - Bloomington, IN - *Ed&PubIntYB 82; LitMarPl 83, 84*
Sunday Independent [of Beacon Publishing Co. Inc.] - Acton, MA - *AyerDirPub 83; NewsDir 84*
Sunday Independent - Wilkes-Barre, PA - *AyerDirPub 83; Ed&PubIntYB 82*
Sunday Journal [of Idaho State Journal Inc.] - Pocatello, ID - *NewsDir 84*
Sunday Journal & Star - Lincoln, NE - *LitMarPl 83, 84*
Sunday Ledger-Enquirer, The - Columbus, GA - *Ed&PubIntYB 82*
Sunday Life - Chicago, IL - *AyerDirPub 83*
Sunday Life, The - Skokie, IL - *Ed&PubIntYB 82*
Sunday Mag/Net - New York, NY - *MagIndMarPl 82-83*
Sunday Magazine [of Gannett-Westchester Newspapers] - New Rochelle, NY - *LitMarPl 83, 84*
Sunday Magazine Network - *Folio 83*
Sunday Magazine, The - Providence, RI - *MagIndMarPl 82-83*
Sunday Messenger - Athens, OH - *NewsDir 84*
Sunday Mirror, The - Columbia, MS - *NewsDir 84*
Sunday News [of Lancaster Newspaper Inc.] - Lancaster, PA - *Ed&PubIntYB 82; NewsDir 84*
Sunday News - North Vancouver, BC, Canada - *Ed&PubIntYB 82*
Sunday News & Leader [of Springfield Newspapers Inc.] - Springfield, MO - *NewsDir 84*
Sunday News Journal - Wilmington, DE - *Ed&PubIntYB 82*
Sunday News, The - Jacksonville, AR - *Ed&PubIntYB 82*
Sunday News, The [of Ridgewood Newspapers] - Ridgewood, NJ - *Ed&PubIntYB 82; NewsDir 84*
Sunday News, The - Georgetown, TX - *Ed&PubIntYB 82*

Sunday Nonpareil, The - Council Bluffs, IA - *Ed&PubIntYB 82; LitMarPl 84*
Sunday Northwest - Chicago, IL - *Ed&PubIntYB 82*
Sunday Oklahoman [of The Oklahoma Publishing Co.] - Oklahoma City, OK - *Ed&PubIntYB 82; LitMarPl 83, 84; NewsDir 84*
Sunday Paper - Richmond, CA - *Ed&PubIntYB 82; LitMarPl 83*
Sunday Paper, The - Painesville, OH - *Ed&PubIntYB 82*
Sunday Patriot-News - Harrisburg, PA - *Ed&PubIntYB 82; LitMarPl 84; NewsBur 6; NewsDir 84*
Sunday Pennsylvanian - Lebanon, PA - *Ed&PubIntYB 82*
Sunday Plain Dealer Magazine - Cleveland, OH - *MagIndMarPl 82-83*
Sunday Post - Lynn, MA - *Ed&PubIntYB 82*
Sunday Post - Salisbury, NC - *NewsDir 84*
Sunday Post - Kingsport, TN - *AyerDirPub 83*
Sunday Post, The - Bridgeport, CT - *Ed&PubIntYB 82; LitMarPl 83, 84*
Sunday Post, The - Paramus, NJ - *Ed&PubIntYB 82*
Sunday Post, The [of RNI Publications Inc.] - Ridgewood, NJ - *NewsDir 84*
Sunday Record - Hackensack, NJ - *Ed&PubIntYB 82; NewsDir 84*
Sunday Record - Middletown, NY - *Ed&PubIntYB 82*
Sunday Record [of Troy Publishing Co. Inc.] - Troy, NY - *Ed&PubIntYB 82; NewsDir 84*
Sunday Republican - Waterbury, CT - *Ed&PubIntYB 82*
Sunday Republican - Springfield, MA - *NewsBur 6*
Sunday Roto - Pittsburgh, PA - *MagIndMarPl 82-83*
Sunday Sentinel - East Brunswick, NJ - *AyerDirPub 83*
Sunday Sentinel [of Herald Publishing Co. Inc.] - Nacogdoches, TX - *Ed&PubIntYB 82; NewsDir 84*
Sunday Spectator - Hornell, NY - *Ed&PubIntYB 82*
Sunday Standard-Times - New Bedford, MA - *Ed&PubIntYB 82; LitMarPl 84*
Sunday Star [of Chicago Lerner Newspapers] - Chicago, IL - *AyerDirPub 83; Ed&PubIntYB 82; NewsDir 84*
Sunday Star Bulletin & Advertiser - Honolulu, HI - *Ed&PubIntYB 82; LitMarPl 83, 84*
Sunday Star-News, The - Wilmington, NC - *Ed&PubIntYB 82*
Sunday Star, The - Peekskill, NY - *Ed&PubIntYB 82*
Sunday Sun - Georgetown, TX - *AyerDirPub 83; Ed&PubIntYB 82; NewsDir 84*
Sunday Sun - Edmonton, AB, Canada - *Ed&PubIntYB 82*
Sunday Sun, The - Warner Robins, GA - *Ed&PubIntYB 82*
Sunday Sun, The [of A. S. Abell Co.] - Baltimore, MD - *Ed&PubIntYB 82; LitMarPl 83, 84*
Sunday Sun, The - Lowell, MA - *Ed&PubIntYB 82*
Sunday Telegram - Worcester, MA - *Ed&PubIntYB 82; LitMarPl 83, 84*
Sunday Telegram [of Elmira Star-Gazette Inc.] - Elmira, NY - *Ed&PubIntYB 82; NewsDir 84*
Sunday Telegram [of Rocky Mt. Publishing Co. Inc.] - Rocky Mt., NC - *Ed&PubIntYB 82; LitMarPl 84; NewsDir 84*
Sunday Times - Cumberland, MD - *NewsDir 84*
Sunday Times [of Thomson Newspapers Inc.] - Salisbury, MD - *NewsDir 84*
Sunday Times - Scranton, PA - *NewsDir 84*
Sunday Times-Advertiser - Trenton, NJ - *Ed&PubIntYB 82; LitMarPl 84*
Sunday Times-Sentinel [of Ohio Valley Publishing Co.] - Gallipolis, OH - *Ed&PubIntYB 82; NewsDir 84*
Sunday Times-Sentinel, The - Pomeroy, OH - *Ed&PubIntYB 82*
Sunday Trader - Pierre, SD - *AyerDirPub 83*
Sunday Trentonian, The [of Capitol City Publishing Co. Inc.] - Trenton, NJ - *Ed&PubIntYB 82; LitMarPl 83, 84*
Sunday Tribune Eagle [of Cheyenne Newspapers Inc.] - Cheyenne, WY - *Ed&PubIntYB 82; LitMarPl 84; NewsDir 84*
Sunday Tribune, The - Warren, OH - *Ed&PubIntYB 82*
Sunday Woman [of The King Features Syndicate] - New York, NY - *WritMar 84*
Sundel, Alfred - Hartsdale, NY - *LitMarPl 83, 84; MagIndMarPl 82-83*
Sundheim Inc., Thomas R. - Jenkintown, PA - *AdAge 3-28-84; ArtMar 84; StaDirAdAg 2-84*
Sundowner Services - San Francisco, CA - *BoPubDir 4, 5*
Sundre Round-Up - Sundre, AB, Canada - *Ed&PubIntYB 82*
Sunfield Sentinel - Sunfield, MI - *BaconPubCkNews 84; Ed&PubIntYB 82*
Sunfire Publications Ltd. - Langley, BC, Canada - *BoPubDir 4; LitMarPl 83, 84*
Sunflower & Grain Marketing - Davenport, IA - *BaconPubCkMag 84*
Sunflower Books [Div. of W. H. Smith] - New York, NY - *LitMarPl 83*
Sunflower Cablevision [of The World Co.] - Lawrence, KS - *BrCabYB 84; Tel&CabFB 84C*
Sunflower Co. - Cincinnati, OH - *BillIntBG 83-84*
Sunflower County News - Drew, MS - *AyerDirPub 83; Ed&PubIntYB 82*
Sunflower Group, The [Div. of Dennis Garberg & Associates] - Lenexa, KS - *StaDirAdAg 2-84*
Sunflower Ink - Carmel, CA - *BoPubDir 4, 5*
Sunflower Music Corp. - *See* Goodman Group, The
Sunflower Press Music - Cincinnati, OH - *BillIntBG 83-84*
Sunflower Software Inc. - Shawnee, KS - *MicrocomMPl 83, 84*
Sunflower Telephone Co. Inc. - Dodge City, KS - *Tel&CabFB 84C p.1704; TelDir&BG 83-84*
Sunflower, The [of Wichita State University] - Wichita, KS - *NewsDir 84*
Sunflower, The - Fargo, ND - *BaconPubCkMag 84*
Sunflower University Press [Aff. of Journal of the West Inc.] - Manhattan, KS - *BoPubDir 4, 5; LitMag&SmPr 83-84*
Sunier Productions - Kentfield, CA - *AvMarPl 83*
Sunken Forum Press - Dewittvile, PQ, Canada - *LitMag&SmPr 83-84*
Sunlight Advertiser - Mt. Vernon, IA - *AyerDirPub 83*
Sunman Direct Inc. - Glenview, IL - *DirMarMP 83*
Sunman Telephone Co. Inc. - Sunman, IN - *TelDir&BG 83-84*
Sunny Day Productions - Portland, OR - *BillIntBG 83-84*
Sunny South News - Coaldale, AB, Canada - *AyerDirPub 83; Ed&PubIntYB 82*
Sunnyland-Taz-Wood North [of Tazewell Publishing Co.] - Morton, IL - *NewsDir 84*
Sunnymead Butterfield Express/Valley Times [of Lewis Publications] - Sunnymead, CA - *BaconPubCkNews 84; NewsDir 84*
Sunnyside Sun [of Sun-Shopper] - Sunnyside, WA - *BaconPubCkNews 84; Ed&PubIntYB 82; NewsDir 84*
Sunnyslope Music [Div. of Hal Bernard Enterprises] - Cincinnati, OH - *BillIntBG 83-84*
Sunnyvale Marketing - Rockford, IL - *LitMag&SmPr 83-84*
Sunnyvale Scribe [of Meredith Corp.] - Cupertino, CA - *AyerDirPub 83; NewsDir 84*
Sunnyvale Scribe - Sunnyvale, CA - *Ed&PubIntYB 82*
Sunnyvale Scribe - *See* Meredith Newspapers
Sunnyvale Valley Journal [of Peninsula Times Tribune] - Sunnyvale, CA - *AyerDirPub 83; BaconPubCkNews 84; Ed&PubIntYB 82; NewsDir 84*
Sunray Cablecomm [of Golden Southwest Inc.] - Johnson, KS - *Tel&CabFB 84C*
Sunrise - Bloomfield, NM - *LitMag&SmPr 83-84*
Sunrise Books [Aff. of One-Way Books Ltd.] - Eureka, CA - *BoPubDir 4, 5*
Sunrise Corp. - Providence, RI - *AdAge 3-28-84; StaDirAdAg 2-84*
Sunrise Enterprises - Garfield Heights, OH - *MicrocomMPl 83*
Sunrise Mirror - Sunrise, FL - *BaconPubCkNews 84*
Sunrise Press - Evanston, IL - *BoPubDir 4, 5; LitMag&SmPr 83-84*
Sunrise Publications Inc. - Bloomington, IN - *DirMarMP 83*
Sunrise Publishing - Eugene, OR - *BoPubDir 4*
Sunrise Publishing - Lincoln City, OR - *BoPubDir 5*
Sunrise Publishing Co. Inc. - Maryland Heights, MO - *BoPubDir 4 Sup, 5*
Sunrise Publishing House - Los Angeles, CA - *BoPubDir 5*
Sunrise-Tamarac News - Ft. Lauderdale, FL - *AyerDirPub 83*
Sunrise-Tamarac News - Sunrise, FL - *Ed&PubIntYB 82*
Sunset [of Lane Publishing Co.] - Menlo Park, CA - *BaconPubCkMag 84; DirMarMP 83; Folio 83; LitMarPl 84; MagDir 84; MagIndMarPl 82-83*
Sunset & Gower Studios - Hollywood, CA - *AvMarPl 83*
Sunset Cable Co. - Connell, WA - *BrCabYB 84*
Sunset Films [Subs. of Lane Publishing Co.] - San Francisco, CA - *AvMarPl 83*

Sunset News - Salt Lake City, UT - *Ed&PubIntYB 82*
Sunset Productions [Div. of A & G Productions] - San Diego, CA - *AvMarPl 83*
Sunset Records Inc. - Harvey, LA - *BillIntBG 83-84*
Sunshine - Austin, TX - *BoPubDir 4, 5*
Sunshine Artists USA - Winter Park, FL - *MagIndMarPl 82-83*
Sunshine Cable TV Co. - Cedar Key, FL - *BrCabYB 84*
Sunshine Coast News, The - Gibsons, BC, Canada - *Ed&PubIntYB 82*
Sunshine Computer Software Co. - Houston, TX - *MicrocomMPl 84; MicrocomSwDir 1*
Sunshine Country Enterprises Inc. - Dallas, TX - *BillIntBG 83-84*
Sunshine Country Records - Dallas, TX - *BillIntBG 83-84*
Sunshine Group Ltd., The - Philadelphia, PA - *BillIntBG 83-84*
Sunshine Magazine [of Henry F. Henrichs Publications] - Litchfield, IL - *MagIndMarPl 82-83; WritMar 84*
Sunshine Music Co. - *See* Gordon Music Co. Inc.
Sunshine National Record Distributors - New York, NY - *BillIntBG 83-84*
Sunshine News, The [of Canada Sunshine Publishing Ltd.] - Toronto, ON, Canada - *WritMar 84*
Sunshine Peripherals Inc. - Brooklyn, NY - *MicrocomMPl 84*
Sunshine Press [Div. of Henrichs Publications Inc.] - Litchfield, IL - *DirMarMP 83*
Sunshine Service News [of Florida Power & Light Co.] - Miami, FL - *WritMar 84*
Sunshine Wireless Co. - Hollywood, FL - *BrCabYB 84*
Sunstone Foundation - Salt Lake City, UT - *BoPubDir 4, 5*
Sunstone Press, The [Subs. of Sunstone Corp.] - Santa Fe, NM - *LitMag&SmPr 83-84; LitMarPl 83, 84; WritMar 84*
SunTran Publishing Co. - Mentor, OH - *BillIntBG 83-84*
Suntree Development Co. Inc. - Brevard County, FL - *BrCabYB 84*
Suntree Productions Ltd. - New York, NY - *AvMarPl 83*
Sunward Systems Inc. - Chicago, IL - *MicrocomMPl 84; MicrocomSwDir 1*
Sunwest Media - Albuquerque, NM - *CabTVFinDB 83*
Sunwest Publishing - Bodega Bay, CA - *BoPubDir 5; LitMag&SmPr 83-84*
SunWorld - Elmsford, NY - *MagIndMarPl 82-83*
SUNY/OCLC Library Network [of State University of New York] - Albany, NY - *EISS 83; InfIndMarPl 83*
Suomen Standardisoimisliitto ry/Finnish Standards Association - Helsinki, Finland - *InfIndMarPl 83*
Supa Press - San Francisco, CA - *BoPubDir 4, 5*
Supe'N Dupe [Div. of Icom Inc.] - Columbus, OH - *AvMarPl 83*
Super BMX - Canoga Park, CA - *BaconPubCkMag 84*
Super Business Machines Co. Inc. - New York, NY - *WhoWMicrocom 83*
Super Chevy [of Argus Publishing] - Los Angeles, CA - *BaconPubCkMag 84; MagDir 84; MagIndMarPl 82-83; WritMar 84*
Super Computer Inc. - Santa Ana, CA - *MicrocomMPl 84*
Super8 Sound - Cambridge, MA - *AvMarPl 83*
Super Office Store - Addison, TX - *DirInfWP 82*
Super Score - Saugus, CA - *MicrocomMPl 83*
Super Service Station [of Irving-Cloud Publishing Co.] - Chicago, IL - *MagDir 84*
Super Service Station - Lincolnwood, IL - *BaconPubCkMag 84; MagIndMarPl 82-83*
Super Shopper - Petoskey, MI - *AyerDirPub 83*
Super Shopper - Clarksville, VA - *AyerDirPub 83*
Super Songs - *See* Schroeder International Ltd., A.
Super Stock & Drag Illustrated [of Lopez Publications] - Alexandria, VA - *BaconPubCkMag 84; MagDir 84; MagIndMarPl 82-83; WritMar 84*
Super Teen - New York, NY - *MagIndMarPl 82-83*
Super-V Corp. - Philadelphia, PA - *AvMarPl 83*
Superchannel - Toronto, ON, Canada - *BrCabYB 84*
SuperCine Inc. - Burbank, CA - *AvMarPl 83*
Supercolossal Pictures Corp. - Los Angeles, CA - *AvMarPl 83*
Superhype Publishing INc. - *See* Cotillion Music Inc.
Superindex [of Superindex Inc.] - Boca Raton, FL - *DirOnDB Spring 84; EISS 83; OnBibDB 3*
Superindex [of Bibliographic Retrieval Services Inc.] - Latham, NY - *DataDirOnSer 84*
Superintendent's Profile & Pocket Equipment Directory - Dunkirk, NY - *WritMar 84*
Superior Cablevision [of Todd Communications Inc.] - Silver Bay, MN - *Tel&CabFB 84C*
Superior Cablevision Installers Inc. - Livingstone, NJ - *InterCabHB 3*
Superior Cablevision Systems - Goldsmith, TX - *Tel&CabFB 84C*
Superior Communication Systems Ltd. [of Northern Cablevision Ltd.] - Athabasca, AB, Canada - *BrCabYB 84*
Superior Electric Co., The - Bristol, CT - *MicrocomMPl 84*
Superior Evening Telegram - Superior, WI - *BaconPubCkNews 84; NewsDir 84*
Superior Express - Superior, NE - *BaconPubCkNews 84; Ed&PubIntYB 82*
Superior Graphics Software Products - Canton, NC - *MicrocomMPl 84*
Superior Mineral Independent - Superior, MT - *BaconPubCkNews 84*
Superior Publishing Co. - Seattle, WA - *LitMarPl 83, 84*
Superior Satellite Systems Co. of Michigan - Fairchild AFB, WA - *Tel&CabFB 84C*
Superior Screen Industries Inc. - Chicago, IL - *LitMarPl 83*
Superior Software - Kansas City, MO - *MicrocomMPl 83*
Superior Sound Studio - Hendersonville, TN - *BillIntBG 83-84*
Superior Sun - Superior, AZ - *BaconPubCkNews 84; Ed&PubIntYB 82*
Superior Surveys of St. Louis - St. Louis, MO - *IntDirMarRes 83*
Superior Telephone Cooperative - Superior, IA - *TelDir&BG 83-84*
Superior Television Cable System - Chapleau, ON, Canada - *BrCabYB 84*
Superior TV Cable - Superior, MT - *BrCabYB 84; Tel&CabFB 84C*
Superletter [of Abrams Creative Services] - Beverly Hills, CA - *MicrocomMPl 84*
Superlove - Lakewood, CA - *BoPubDir 4, 5*
Supermail [of Rieschling Network Ltd.] - Seattle, WA - *TeleSy&SerDir 2-84*
Supermarket Business [of Fieldmark Media Inc.] - New York, NY - *BaconPubCkMag 84; MagDir 84; MagIndMarPl 82-83*
Supermarket Engineering Magazine - Chicago, IL - *WritMar 84*
Supermarket Management [of Publishing Dynamics] - Stamford, CT - *MagDir 84*
Supermarket News [of Fairchild Publications] - New York, NY - *BaconPubCkMag 84; Folio 83; MagDir 84; MagIndMarPl 82-83*
Supermedia - New York, NY - *StaDirAdAg 2-84*
SuperPET Gazette [of International SuperPET User Group] - Hatteras, NC - *MicrocomMPl 84*
Supersat - Bedford, MA - *DirOnDB Spring 84*
Superset Inc. - San Diego, CA - *DataDirSup 7-83*
Supershift Composing Room Inc. - New York, NY - *MagIndMarPl 82-83*
Supersoft Associates - Champaign, IL - *WhoWMicrocom 83*
SuperSoft Inc. - Champaign, IL - *MicrocomMPl 83, 84; MicrocomSwDir 1; WritMar 84*
Superson, Edward T. - Panama City, FL - *BoPubDir 4, 5*
SuperSports - Bedford, MA - *DirOnDB Spring 84*
Superstat - Rome, Italy - *DirOnDB Spring 84*
Supervision [of National Research Bureau Inc.] - Burlington, IA - *BaconPubCkMag 84; MagDir 84; WritMar 84*
Supervisor Nurse - Cincinnati, OH - *MagDir 84*
Supervisor, The [of Kemper Group] - Long Grove, IL - *ArtMar 84*
Supervisory Management [of American Management Association] - New York, NY - *BaconPubCkMag 84; MagDir 84; MagIndMarPl 82-83*
Supervisory Sense [of American Management Association] - New York, NY - *MagIndMarPl 82-83*
Supplemental Press - Mt. Pleasant, SC - *BoPubDir 4, 5*
Supplier Identification System [of London Enterprise Agency] - London, England - *EISS 5-84 Sup*
Suppliers & Equipment Information Retrieval System [of International Civil Aviation Organization] - Montreal, PQ, Canada - *EISS 83*
Supply House Times [of Horton Publishing Co.] - Skokie, IL - *BaconPubCkMag 84; MagDir 84*
Support Systems International Corp. - Richmond, CA - *WhoWMicrocom 83*

Support Systems International Corp. (Cables & Accessories Div.) - Richmond, CA - *DataDirSup 7-83*
Supra Color Inc. - Minneapolis, MN - *AvMarPl 83*
Supreme Court Journal [of Gant Publishing Co.] - Lincoln, NE - *NewsDir 84*
Supreme Court Reports [of QL Systems Ltd.] - Ottawa, ON, Canada - *DataDirOnSer 84; DirOnDB Spring 84*
Supreme Magnetics Corp. - Los Angeles, CA - *DirInfWP 82*
Supreme Record Co. - Nashville, TN - *BillIntBG 83-84*
Sure-Fire Music Co. Inc. - Nashville, TN - *BillIntBG 83-84*
Sure Music & Record Co. Inc. - Broomall, PA - *BillIntBG 83-84*
Sureshot Records - Lomita, CA - *BillIntBG 83-84*
Surety Communications Inc. - Meridian, TX - *Tel&CabFB 84C p.1704*
Surety Communications Inc. - Valley Mills, TX - *Tel&CabFB 84C*
Surevelation Services - Concord, CA - *BoPubDir 4, 5*
Surface & Vacuum Physics Index [of Max Planck Institut fur Plasmaphysik] - Munich, West Germany - *CompReadDB 82*
Surface Checking Gage Co. - Prescott, AZ - *BoPubDir 4, 5*
Surface Coatings Abstracts [of Dialog Information Services Inc.] - Palo Alto, CA - *DataDirOnSer 84*
Surface Coatings Abstracts [of Paint Research Association] - Teddington, England - *CompReadDB 82; DBBus 82; OnBibDB 3*
Surface Coatings Abstracts - *See* World Surface Coatings Abstracts
Surface Mining & Environment Information System [of University of Arizona] - Tucson, AZ - *EISS 83*
Surfer - Dana Point, CA - *BaconPubCkMag 84; MagDir 84; WritMar 84*
Surfer - San Juan Capistrano, CA - *MagIndMarPl 82-83*
Surfing [of Western Empire] - San Clemente, CA - *BaconPubCkMag 84; MagDir 84; MagIndMarPl 82-83; WritMar 84*
Surfside Hawaii Inc. - Honolulu, HI - *BillIntBG 83-84*
Surgery - St. Louis, MO - *BaconPubCkMag 84; MagDir 84; MagIndMarPl 82-83*
Surgery, Gynecology & Obstetrics - Chicago, IL - *BaconPubCkMag 84; MagDir 84*
Surgical Business - Union City, NJ - *BoPubDir 5*
Surgical Neurology - New York, NY - *BaconPubCkMag 84*
Surgical Practice News - Georgetown, CT - *BaconPubCkMag 84; MagDir 84*
Surgical Products - Dover, NJ - *BaconPubCkMag 84*
Surgical Rounds - Port Washington, NY - *BaconPubCkMag 84; MagIndMarPl 82-83; WritMar 84*
Surgical Technologist - Littleton, CO - *BaconPubCkMag 84; MagDir 84; WritMar 84*
Suring Cablevision Inc. - Suring, WI - *Tel&CabFB 84C*
Surplus Record - Chicago, IL - *BaconPubCkMag 84; MagDir 84*
Surrey Broadcasting Co. - Denver, CO - *BrCabYB 84*
Surrey Cable TV Inc. - Surrey, ND - *BrCabYB 84; Tel&CabFB 84C*
Surrey Consulting & Research - Denver, CO - *BrCabYB 84*
Surrey-Delta Messenger - Surrey, BC, Canada - *Ed&PubIntYB 82*
Surrey Music Co. - *See* Pavanne Music Co.
Surrey/North Delta Today - Surrey, BC, Canada - *AyerDirPub 83*
Surrey/North Delta Today - Surrey/North Delta, BC, Canada - *Ed&PubIntYB 82*
Surrey Press - Warminster, PA - *LitMag&SmPr 83-84*
Surry Telephone Membership Corp. - Dobson, NC - *TelDir&BG 83-84*
Survey Analysis Inc. - Port Washington, NY - *IntDirMarRes 83*
Survey & Evaluation Services Ltd. - Stamford, CT - *LitMarPl 83*
Survey & Marketing Services Inc. - *See* SMS Research Inc.
Survey & Research Service Inc. - Cambridge, MA - *IntDirMarRes 83*
Survey Archive [of Social Science Research Council] - Colchester, England - *EISS 83*
Survey Centers Inc. - Cherry Hill, NJ - *IntDirMarRes 83*
Survey Data Research Inc. - Birmingham, MI - *IntDirMarRes 83*
Survey Force Ltd. - Sittingbourne, England - *EISS 7-83 Sup*
Survey of Adults & Markets of Affluence - New York, NY - *DirOnDB Spring 84*
Survey of Anesthesiology - Baltimore, MD - *MagDir 84*
Survey of Business Trends in the Electrical Manufacturing Industry [of National Electrical Manufacturers Association] - Washington, DC - *EISS 83*
Survey of Minority-Owned Business Enterprises [of U.S. Bureau of the Census] - Washington, DC - *EISS 7-83 Sup*
Survey of Ophthalmology - Boston, MA - *MagDir 84*
Survey of Ophthalmology - Brookline, MA - *BaconPubCkMag 84*
Survey of Wall Street Research - Rye, NY - *BaconPubCkMag 84*
Survey Publishing Co. - Kansas City, MO - *BoPubDir 4, 5; DirMarMP 83*
Survey Research Center [of Oregon State University] - Corvallis, OR - *EISS 83*
Survey Research Consultants International Inc. - Williamstown, MA - *EISS 83*
Survey Research Corp. - Washington, DC - *ProGuPRSer 4*
Survey Research Dynamics Inc. - New Monmouth, NJ - *IntDirMarRes 83*
Survey Research Group Ltd. - *See* SRG International Ltd.
Survey Research Laboratory [of University of Illinois] - Urbana, IL - *EISS 83*
Survey Research Unit [of Polytechnic of North London] - London, England - *EISS 83*
Survey Sampling Inc. - Westport, CT - *EISS 83; IntDirMarRes 83*
Survey Service of Western New York Inc. - Buffalo, NY - *IntDirMarRes 83*
Survey Tabulation Services Inc. - Cambridge, MA - *EISS 83; IntDirMarRes 83*
Surveying & Mapping [of The American Congress on Surveying] - Falls Church, VA - *BaconPubCkMag 84; MagDir 84*
Surveyor - New York, NY - *MagIndMarPl 82-83*
Surveyors Supply Co. - Apex, NC - *MicrocomMPl 83, 84*
Survival - Haddam, CT - *BoPubDir 4, 5*
Survival Anglia Ltd. - New York, NY - *TelAl 83, 84*
Survival Anglia Ltd. - *See* JWT Group Inc.
Survival Cards - Bloomington, IN - *BoPubDir 4, 5*
Survival Education Association - Tacoma, WA - *BoPubDir 4, 5*
Survival Guide [of McMullen Publishing Inc.] - Anaheim, CA - *WritMar 84*
Survival News Service - Los Angeles, CA - *LitMag&SmPr 83-84*
Survival Software - San Mateo, CA - *MicrocomMPl 83*
Survive [of Survive Publications Inc.] - Boulder, CO - *MagIndMarPl 82-83; WritMar 84*
Survivor Records Inc. - Venice, CA - *BillIntBG 83-84*
Survivors Magazine, The [of Le'Dor Inc.] - Springfield, IL - *WritMar 84*
Survivors' Manual Books [Aff. of Independent Learning] - Rockville Centre, NY - *BoPubDir 4, 5; LitMag&SmPr 83-84*
Susann Publications Inc. - Dallas, TX - *WritMar 84*
Susanville Cablevision [of CDA Cable Inc.] - Susanville, CA - *BrCabYB 84; Tel&CabFB 84C*
Susanville Lassen Advocate - Susanville, CA - *BaconPubCkNews 84; NewsDir 84*
Susanville Lassen County Times - *See* Feather Publishing Co. Inc.
Susie Software - Mt. Prospect, IL - *MicrocomMPl 84*
Susquehanna Broadcasting Co. - York, PA - *BrCabYB 84 p.D-307; Tel&CabFB 84C p.1704*
Susquehanna County Press [of Susquehanna Publishers Corp.] - Montrose, PA - *NewsDir 84*
Susquehanna County Press - Susquehanna, PA - *AyerDirPub 83; BaconPubCkNews 84; Ed&PubIntYB 82*
Susquehanna Monthly Magazine [of Susquehanna Times & Magazine Inc.] - Marietta, PA - *WritMar 84*
Susquehanna Transcript - Susquehanna, PA - *Ed&PubIntYB 82; NewsDir 84*
Susquehanna Transcript & Free Press - Susquehanna, PA - *BaconPubCkNews 84*
Sussex Countian - Georgetown, DE - *AyerDirPub 83; Ed&PubIntYB 82*
Sussex Spectator - Newton, NJ - *AyerDirPub 83; Ed&PubIntYB 82*
Sussex Sun [of Lake Country Reporter Publishers] - Hartland, WI - *NewsDir 84*
Sussex Sun - *See* Lake Country Reporter Publishers
Sussex-Surry Dispatch - Sussex-Surry Counties, VA - *Ed&PubIntYB 82*

Sussex-Surry Dispatch [of Roanoke Valley Publishing Co.] - Wakefield, VA - *AyerDirPub 83; NewsDir 84*
Susskind Associates, J. & L. - La Palma, CA - *ADAPSOMemDir 83-84*
Susskind Co., The - New York, NY - *Tel&CabFB 84C*
Sussman & Sugar Inc. [Subs. of Ogilvy & Mather Inc.] - New York, NY - *LitMarPl 83, 84; MagIndMarPl 82-83; StaDirAdAg 2-84*
Sutherland Courier - Sutherland, IA - *BaconPubCkNews 84; Ed&PubIntYB 82*
Sutherland Courier-Times - Sutherland, NE - *BaconPubCkNews 84*
Sutherland Group Inc., Dorothy B. - Chicago, IL - *LitMarPl 83, 84*
Sutherland Learning Associates - Northridge, CA - *AvMarPl 83; BoPubDir 5*
Sutherland Learning Associates Inc. - Van Nuys, CA - *BoPubDir 4*
Sutherland Publications - Berkeley, CA - *BoPubDir 4, 5*
Sutherlin Communications Inc. - Sutherlin, OR - *Tel&CabFB 84C*
Sutherlin Sun-Tribune - Sutherlin, OR - *BaconPubCkNews 84*
Sutphen Studio, Dick - Scottsdale, AZ - *BoPubDir 4, 5*
Sutter House - Lititz, PA - *LitMarPl 83, 84*
Sutter's Mill Ltd. - Los Angeles, CA - *StaDirAdAg 2-84*
Sutton Braxton Citizens News - Sutton, WV - *BaconPubCkNews 84*
Sutton Capital Associates Inc. - New York, NY - *BrCabYB 84 p.D-307; CabTVFinDB 83; Tel&CabFB 84C p.1704*
Sutton Clay County News - Sutton, NE - *BaconPubCkNews 84*
Sutton Communications - New York, NY - *AdAge 3-28-84; StaDirAdAg 2-84*
Suwannee Democrat - Live Oak, FL - *AyerDirPub 83; Ed&PubIntYB 82*
Suzuki Method International - *See* Birch Tree Group Ltd.
Sveinungsgard, Gunnar - Grande Prairie, AB, Canada - *BoPubDir 4, 5*
Svenska Amerikanaren Tribunen - Chicago, IL - *Ed&PubIntYB 82*
Svenson Co. Inc., Andrew - Sarasota, FL - *LitMarPl 83, 84; MagIndMarPl 82-83*
Sverge-Haus Publishers - Milton, MA - *BoPubDir 4, 5*
Sveriges Geologiska Undersokning/Geological Survey of Sweden - Uppsala, Sweden - *InfIndMarPl 83*
SVH Research Service - Fair Lawn, NJ - *IntDirMarRes 83*
Svitlo - Weston, ON, Canada - *Ed&PubIntYB 82*
Svoboda - Jersey City, NJ - *AyerDirPub 83; Ed&PubIntYB 82; NewsDir 84*
SVP Benelux - Brussels, Belgium - *EISS 83*
SVP Canada [of Micromedia Ltd.] - Toronto, ON, Canada - *EISS 83; InfIndMarPl 83*
SVP Conseil - Bale, Switzerland - *EISS 83*
SVP France - Paris, France - *EISS 83*
SVP Italia - Milan, Italy - *EISS 83*
SVP Korea - Seoul, South Korea - *EISS 83*
SVP South Africa Ltd. - Johannesburg, South Africa - *EISS 83*
SWA Productions Ltd. - New York, NY - *AvMarPl 83*
Swafford & Co. - Beverly Hills, CA - *StaDirAdAg 2-84*
Swaggart Ministries, Jimmy - Baton Rouge, LA - *BrCabYB 84*
Swain Productions, Hack - Sarasota, FL - *AvMarPl 83; Tel&CabFB 84C*
Swainsboro Blade - Swainsboro, GA - *BaconPubCkNews 84*
Swainsboro Forest-Blade - Swainsboro, GA - *NewsDir 84*
SWALCAP - Bristol, England - *InfIndMarPl 83*
Swallow Press, The - Athens, OH - *LitMag&SmPr 83-84*
Swallow's Tale Magazine - Tallahassee, FL - *LitMag&SmPr 83-84*
Swallowtail Records - Ithaca, NY - *BillIntBG 83-84*
Swamp Press - Amherst, MA - *BoPubDir 4, 5; LitMag&SmPr 83-84*
Swampscott Reporter - Ipswich, MA - *AyerDirPub 83; NewsDir 84*
Swampscott Reporter - Swampscott, MA - *AyerDirPub 83; Ed&PubIntYB 82*
Swampscott Reporter - *See* North Shore Weeklies Inc.
Swan Books - Fair Oaks, CA - *BoPubDir 4, 5*
Swan, Dave - Bend, OR - *MagIndMarPl 82-83*
Swan House Publishing Co. - Brooklyn, NY - *BoPubDir 4, 5*
Swan Software - Columbia, MD - *MicrocomMPl 84*
Swand Publications - Linthicum Heights, MD - *BoPubDir 4, 5; LitMag&SmPr 83-84*
Swani Publishing - Beloit, IL - *StaDirAdAg 2-84*
Swank [of Swank Magazine Corp.] - New York, NY - *BaconPubCkMag 84; Folio 83*
Swansboro Tideland News - Swansboro, NC - *BaconPubCkNews 84*
Swanson Broadcasting Inc. - Tulsa, OK - *BrCabYB 84*
Swanson, Evadene B. - Ft. Collins, CO - *BoPubDir 4, 5*
Swanson Inc., H. N. - Los Angeles, CA - *LitMarPl 83*
Swanson Publishing Co. - Moline, IL - *BoPubDir 4, 5*
Swanson, Rollheiser, Holland Inc. - Lincoln, NE - *StaDirAdAg 2-84*
Swanson Schmidt Productions - Milwaukee, WI - *AvMarPl 83*
Swanston & Associates Inc., David - Washington, DC - *DirPRFirms 83*
Swanton Courier - Swanton, VT - *Ed&PubIntYB 82*
Swanton Enterprise [of Bellevue Gazette Corp.] - Swanton, OH - *BaconPubCkNews 84; Ed&PubIntYB 82; NewsDir 84*
Swarthmore College Phoenix [of Press Publishing Co.] - Swarthmore, PA - *NewsDir 84*
Swarthmorean - Swarthmore, PA - *AyerDirPub 83; BaconPubCkNews 84; Ed&PubIntYB 82*
Swartz Creek Flint Township News - Fenton, MI - *NewsDir 84*
Swartz Creek/Flint Township News - Swartz Creek, MI - *Ed&PubIntYB 82*
Swartz, Fred - Los Angeles, CA - *LitMarPl 83, 84; MagIndMarPl 82-83*
Swayzee Telephone Co. Inc. - Swayzee, IN - *TelDir&BG 83-84*
SWCP Catalyst - Long Beach, CA - *ArtMar 84*
Swea City Cable TV [of D & V Inc.] - Swea City, IA - *BrCabYB 84; Tel&CabFB 84C*
Swea City Herald - Swea City, IA - *BaconPubCkNews 84; Ed&PubIntYB 82*
Swearingen & Conaway Communications Inc. - Memphis, TN - *StaDirAdAg 2-84*
Swearingen Software - Houston, TX - *MicrocomMPl 84*
Sweda International Inc. - Pine Brook, NJ - *DataDirSup 7-83*
Swedenborg Foundation - New York, NY - *LitMarPl 83, 84*
Swedish Behavioral Sciences Data Base [of National Library for Psychology & Education] - Stockholm, Sweden - *EISS 7-83 Sup*
Swedish Behavioural Sciences - Stockholm, Sweden - *DirOnDB Spring 84*
Swedish Books - Goteborg, Sweden - *LitMag&SmPr 83-84*
Swedish Building Centre - Stockholm, Sweden - *InfIndMarPl 83*
Swedish Council of Environmental Information (Ministry of Agriculture) - Stockholm, Sweden - *CompReadDB 82*
Swedish Delegation for Scientific & Technical Information - Stockholm, Sweden - *EISS 83*
Swedish Drug Information System [of National Board of Health & Welfare] - Uppsala, Sweden - *EISS 83*
Swedish Environmental Research Index [of National Swedish Environment Protection Board] - Solna, Sweden - *EISS 83*
Swedish Environmental Research Index [of Swedish Council of Environmental Information] - Stockholm, Sweden - *CompReadDB 82*
Swedish Information Service - New York, NY - *Ed&PubIntYB 82*
Swedish Institute of Building Documentation - Stockholm, Sweden - *CompReadDB 82; EISS 83*
Swedish Market Information Bank [of Pressurklipp] - Stockholm, Sweden - *EISS 83*
Swedish Online User Group [of Svalof AB] - Svalov, Sweden - *InfIndMarPl 83*
Sweeney & Associates, Charles - Los Angeles, CA - *StaDirAdAg 2-84*
Sweeney & James Co. - Lakewood, OH - *StaDirAdAg 2-84*
Sweeny-Old Ocean Telephone Co. [Aff. of Sugar Land Telephone Co.] - Sweeny, TX - *TelDir&BG 83-84*
Sweester Telephone Co. Inc. - Sweester, IN - *TelDir&BG 83-84*
Sweet Advertising Agency - Mt. Morris, IL - *StaDirAdAg 2-84*
Sweet & Co. - New York, NY - *DirPRFirms 83; StaDirAdAg 2-84*
Sweet & Co. Inc., G. F. - Glastonbury, CT - *StaDirAdAg 2-84*
Sweet Bernadette Music - *See* Mighty Matthew Music
Sweet Glenn Music - Santa Monica, CA - *BillIntBG 83-84*
Sweet Home New Era - Sweet Home, OR - *BaconPubCkNews 84; NewsDir 84*
Sweet Home TV Cable Co. - Sweet Home, OR - *BrCabYB 84*
Sweet Karol Music - *See* Sweet Glenn Music
Sweet Polly Music - Newberry, SC - *BillIntBG 83-84*

Sweet Printing Co. - Austin, TX - *LitMarPl 83, 84; MagIndMarPl 82-83*
Sweet Publishing Co. - Austin, TX - *LitMarPl 83*
Sweet Publishing Co. - Ft. Worth, TX - *LitMarPl 84*
Sweet Singer Music - Nashville, TN - *BillIntBG 83-84*
Sweet Sixteen Music - *See* Bicycle Music Co., The
Sweet Springs Cable TV [of Missouri Valley Communications Inc.] - Sweet Springs, MO - *BrCabYB 84*
Sweet Springs Herald - Sweet Springs, MO - *BaconPubCkNews 84; Ed&PubIntYB 82*
Sweet Swamp Music - Fleischmanns, NY - *BillIntBG 83-84*
Sweet Tooth Publishing - Irving, TX - *BillIntBG 83-84*
Sweetbrier Press - Palo Alto, CA - *BoPubDir 4 Sup, 5*
Sweeter than Honey - Tyler, TX - *BoPubDir 4, 5*
Sweetlight Books - Arcata, CA - *BoPubDir 4, 5*
Sweetman, Leonard - Coatesville, PA - *BoPubDir 4, 5*
Sweet's Div. [of McGraw-Hill Information Systems Co.] - New York, NY - *EISS 83*
Sweetser, Albert G. - Clifton Park, NY - *BoPubDir 4, 5*
Sweetsong Records - Parkersburg, WV - *BillIntBG 83-84*
Sweetwater Cable Television Co. - Rock Springs, WY - *BrCabYB 84 p.D-307; Tel&CabFB 84C p.1704*
Sweetwater Monroe County Advocate - Sweetwater, TN - *BaconPubCkNews 84*
Sweetwater Nolan County News - Sweetwater, TX - *BaconPubCkNews 84*
Sweetwater Reporter [of Donrey Media Group] - Sweetwater, TX - *BaconPubCkNews 84; Ed&PubIntYB 82; NewsDir 84*
Swell Pictures - Chicago, IL - *AvMarPl 83*
Swerdlow Interviewing Service, Estelle - Philadelphia, PA - *IntDirMarRes 83*
Swets & Zeitlinger BV - Lisse, Netherlands - *MicroMarPl 82-83*
Swets Subscription Service - Lisse, Netherlands - *EISS 83*
Swettman Publications - Pleasant Plains, IL - *BaconPubCkNews 84*
SWEZ - Ft. Myers Beach, FL - *BrCabYB 84*
Swift Adhesives & Coatings [Subs. of Eschem Inc.] - Chicago, IL - *LitMarPl 83, 84*
Swift-Chaplin Productions Inc. - Hollywood, CA - *Tel&CabFB 84C*
Swift Co. Inc., John S. - St. Louis, MO - *LitMarPl 83, 84; MagIndMarPl 82-83*
Swift County Monitor - Benson, MN - *Ed&PubIntYB 82*
Swift County Monitor & News - Benson, MN - *AyerDirPub 83; BaconPubCkNews 84*
Swift County News - Benson, MN - *Ed&PubIntYB 82*
Swift Current Cablevision Ltd. - Swift Current, SK, Canada - *BrCabYB 84*
Swift Current Sun - Swift Current, SK, Canada - *Ed&PubIntYB 82*
Swift, Elizabeth Pierce - Cushing, ME - *LitMarPl 83, 84*
Swift Inc., Allen - New York, NY - *TelAl 83, 84; Tel&CabFB 84C*
Swift Lizard Distributors - Socorro, NM - *BoPubDir 4 Sup, 5*
Swift Mail Service Inc. - Brentwood, MD - *MagIndMarPl 82-83*
Swift-Pioneer Newspapers - Carson City, NV - *Ed&PubIntYB 82*
Swift River [of Tree Toad Press] - Leverett, MA - *LitMag&SmPr 83-84*
Swiftware Corp. - Newton Centre, MA - *MicrocomMPl 84*
Swiftwater Books - Tampa, FL - *WritMar 84*
Swifty Software Inc. - Melville, NY - *MicrocomMPl 83*
Swimming Pool Age & Spa Merchandiser - Ft. Lauderdale, FL - *MagDir 84*
Swimming Pool Age & Spa Merchandiser - Atlanta, GA - *BaconPubCkMag 84; WritMar 84*
Swimming Technique - Inglewood, CA - *MagIndMarPl 82-83*
Swimming World & Junior Swimmer - Inglewood, CA - *MagDir 84; MagIndMarPl 82-83; WritMar 84*
Swimming World & Junior Swimmer - Los Angeles, CA - *BaconPubCkMag 84*
Swinburne, Irene & Laurence - East Norwich, NY - *LitMarPl 83, 84*
Swinehart Advertising, C. R. - Plainfield, IN - *StaDirAdAg 2-84*
Swink Advertising, Howard - Marion, OH - *AdAge 3-28-84; StaDirAdAg 2-84*
Swink Cable Vision - Swink, CO - *Tel&CabFB 84C*
Swiss American Review - New York, NY - *Ed&PubIntYB 82; NewsDir 84*
Swiss Association of Telecommunications Users - Zurich, Switzerland - *TeleSy&SerDir 2-84*
Swiss Center of Documentation in Microtechnology - Neuchatel, Switzerland - *EISS 83*
Swiss Coordination Center for Research in Education - Aarau, Switzerland - *EISS 83*
Swiss Institute for Technical Information - Berne, Switzerland - *EISS 83; InfIndMarPl 83*
Swiss Journal - San Francisco, CA - *AyerDirPub 83; NewsDir 84*
Swiss Viewdata Information Providers Association - Zurich, Switzerland - *EISS 7-83 Sup*
Swiss Wildlife Information Service - Zurich, Switzerland - *EISS 7-83 Sup*
Switzerland Democrat - Vevay, IN - *AyerDirPub 83; Ed&PubIntYB 82*
Swofford & Scharff Inc. - New York, NY - *DirPRFirms 83*
Swoger, Arthur - New York, NY - *LitMarPl 84*
Sword & Stone Press - Marina del Rey, CA - *BoPubDir 4*
Sword & Stone Press - Dallas, TX - *BoPubDir 5*
Sword of the Lord Publications - Murfreesboro, TN - *BoPubDir 4, 5*
Swordsman Press - Sherman Oaks, CA - *ArtMar 84; BoPubDir 4, 5*
SWP Microcomputer Products Inc. - Arlington, TX - *MicrocomMPl 84*
SWS Organization Inc. - New York, NY - *BillIntBG 83-84*
Sybex - Berkeley, CA - *AvMarPl 83; LitMag&SmPr 83-84; LitMarPl 83, 84; MicrocomMPl 84; WhoWMicrocom 83; WritMar 84*
Sycamore Messenger News - Cincinnati, OH - *NewsDir 84*
Sycamore Messenger News - Montgomery, OH - *AyerDirPub 83; Ed&PubIntYB 82*
Sycamore Mohawk Leader - Sycamore, OH - *BaconPubCkNews 84*
Sycamore News [of Free Press Newspaper Group] - Carpentersville, IL - *NewsDir 84*
Sycamore News - Sycamore, IL - *AyerDirPub 83; Ed&PubIntYB 82*
Sycamore News - *See* Free Press Inc.
Sycamore Press Inc. - Terre Haute, IN - *BoPubDir 4, 5*
Sycamore Telephone Co. - Sycamore, OH - *TelDir&BG 83-84*
Sycom - Madison, WI - *MicrocomMPl 83, 84; MicrocomSwDir 1; WhoWMicrocom 83*
Sycor Inc. - Ann Arbor, MI - *InfIndMarPl 83*
SYDA Foundation - South Fallsburg, NY - *BoPubDir 4, 5*
Sydney Box Associates Ltd. - London, England - *Tel&CabFB 84C*
Sydney Development Co. Ltd. - London, England - *MicrocomSwDir 1*
Sydney Morning Herald Ltd. - New York, NY - *Ed&PubIntYB 82*
Sydney Stock Exchange Share Prices - Sydney, Australia - *DirOnDB Spring 84*
Sydney Stock Exchange Share Prices [of I. P. Sharp Associates Ltd.] - Toronto, ON, Canada - *DataDirOnSer 84*
Sydney Stock Exchange Statex Service - Sydney, Australia - *DirOnDB Spring 84*
Sydney Stock Exchange Statex Service [of I. P. Sharp Associates Ltd.] - Toronto, ON, Canada - *DataDirOnSer 84*
Sydon Inc. - Stockton, CA - *BoPubDir 4, 5; LitMag&SmPr 83-84*
Sydoni [of Questel Inc.] - Washington, DC - *DataDirOnSer 84*
Sydoni Flash - Paris, France - *DirOnDB Spring 84*
Sydoni SA - Paris, France - *DirOnDB Spring 84; EISS 83; InfIndMarPl 83*
Syentek Inc. - San Francisco, CA - *BoPubDir 4, 5*
SYGMA - New York, NY - *LitMarPl 83, 84*
Sykam Systems Ltd. - Nepean, ON, Canada - *WhoWMicrocom 83*
Sykes Datatronics Inc. - Rochester, NY - *WhoWMicrocom 83*
Sykesville Post-Dispatch - Sykesville, PA - *BaconPubCkNews 84; Ed&PubIntYB 82*
Sylacauga Daily Advance - Sylacauga, AL - *NewsDir 84*
Sylva Herald & Ruralite - Sylva, NC - *BaconPubCkNews 84; Ed&PubIntYB 82; NewsDir 84*
Sylvan Book Shop - New York, NY - *MagIndMarPl 82-83*
Sylvan Institute - Vancouver, WA - *BoPubDir 4, 5*
Sylvan Lake News - Sylvan Lake, AB, Canada - *Ed&PubIntYB 82*

Sylvan Lake Telephone Co. Inc. [Aff. of Rochester Telephone Corp.] - Hopewell Junction, NY - *TelDir&BG 83-84*
Sylvan Press Publishers Ltd. - Richmond, VA - *BoPubDir 4, 5; WritMar 84*
Sylvan Publications - Northville, MI - *BoPubDir 5*
Sylvan Valley CATV Co. [of Citizens Telephone Co.] - Brevard, NC - *BrCabYB 84; Tel&CabFB 84C*
Sylvania - *See* NAP Consumer Electronics
Sylvania Herald - Sylvania, OH - *AyerDirPub 83; Ed&PubIntYB 82*
Sylvania Herald [of Toledo Herald Newspapers] - Toledo, OH - *BaconPubCkNews 84; NewsDir 84*
Sylvania Telephone - Sylvania, GA - *BaconPubCkNews 84; Ed&PubIntYB 82*
Sylvester Local - Sylvester, GA - *BaconPubCkNews 84; Ed&PubIntYB 82; NewsDir 84*
Sylvia Porter's Personal Finance Magazine [of Davis Publications Inc.] - New York, NY - *BaconPubCkMag 84; LitMarPl 84; WritMar 84*
Symbol Technologies Inc. - Hauppauge, NY - *DataDirSup 7-83*
Symbolic Systems Inc. - Summit, NJ - *MicrocomMPl 83, 84*
Symbolics Financial Systems Inc. - Richardson, TX - *DataDirSup 7-83; MicrocomMPl 84*
Symmes Systems - Atlanta, GA - *AvMarPl 83; BoPubDir 4, 5; WritMar 84*
Symon & Hilliard - New York, NY - *AdAge 3-28-84; StaDirAdAg 2-84*
Sympathetic Software - Huntington Beach, CA - *MicrocomMPl 84; MicrocomSwDir 1; WhoWMicrocom 83*
Symphony Magazine - Washington, DC - *BaconPubCkMag 84; WritMar 84*
Symposia - Wheat Ridge, CO - *MagDir 84*
Symposia Specialists Inc. - Miami, FL - *BoPubDir 4, 5*
Symposium [of Heldref Publications] - Washington, DC - *LitMarPl 83, 84*
Symposium Music Publishing Inc. - Minneapolis, MN - *BillIntBG 83-84*
Symposium Press - Los Angeles, CA - *BoPubDir 4, 5*
Symposium Records - Minneapolis, MN - *BillIntBG 83-84*
Synapse Inc. - Philadelphia, PA - *BoPubDir 4, 5*
Synapse Information Resources Inc. - Vestal, NY - *LitMarPl 83, 84*
Synapse Software - Kensington, CA - *MicrocomMPl 83*
Synapse Software - Richmond, CA - *MicrocomMPl 84; MicrocomSwDir 1*
Synaxis Press [Aff. of Sts. Kyril & Methody Orthodox Christian Educational Society] - Chilliwack, BC, Canada - *BoPubDir 4; LitMarPl 83, 84*
Sync [of AHL Computing] - Morris Plains, NJ - *BaconPubCkMag 84; MagIndMarPl 82-83; MicrocomMPl 83, 84; WritMar 84*
Sync Film Lab - Hollywood, CA - *AvMarPl 83*
Synchro Swim Canada - Ottawa, ON, Canada - *BoPubDir 4, 5*
Synchronous Media International - Lansing, MI - *AvMarPl 83*
Syncline - Chicago, IL - *LitMag&SmPr 83-84*
Syncline Press - Chicago, IL - *LitMag&SmPr 83-84*
Syncom [Subs. of Schwan's Sales Enterprises Inc.] - Mitchell, SD - *WhoWMicrocom 83*
Syncom International - Amherst, NY - *WhoWMicrocom 83*
Syncro Inc. - Westlake Village, CA - *MicrocomMPl 83*
Syncro-Sette [of S & S Co.] - Addison, IL - *MicrocomMPl 84*
Syncsort Inc. - Englewood Cliffs, NJ - *ADAPSOMemDir 83-84; DataDirSup 7-83*
Syndicable Inc. - Jericho, NY - *TelAl 83*
Syndicable Inc. - *See* Television Syndication Group Inc.
Syndicast Services Inc. - New York, NY - *TelAl 83, 84; Tel&CabFB 84C*
Syndicate Magazines Inc. - New York, NY - *MagIndMarPl 82-83*
Syndicated Ad Features Inc. - Chestnut Hill, MA - *Ed&PubIntYB 82*
Syndicated Newspaper Services Inc. - New York, NY - *Ed&PubIntYB 82*
Syndicated Sound [Subs. of Dougal Productions] - Weston, CT - *AvMarPl 83*
Syndicated Study of Major Market Newspaper Audiences [of Three Sigma Research Center Inc.] - Larchmont, NY - *EISS 83*
Syndicor Inc. - Bedford Hills, NY - *IntDirMarRes 83*
Syndicore Music [Div. of ESP-Disk Ltd.] - New York, NY - *BillIntBG 83-84*
Synercom Technology Inc. - Sugar Land, TX - *DataDirSup 7-83*
Synergistic Press - San Francisco, CA - *BoPubDir 4, 5; LitMag&SmPr 83-84*
Synergistic Software - Renton, WA - *MicrocomMPl 83, 84; MicrocomSwDir 1*
Synergistic Solar Inc. - Miami, FL - *MicrocomMPl 83*
Synergistics Inc. - Natick, MA - *DataDirSup 7-83*
Synergon - Houston, TX - *MicrocomMPl 83, 84*
Synergy House [Aff. of Charles D. Leviton & Associates] - Costa Mesa, CA - *BoPubDir 4, 5*
Synergy Records Inc. - New Haven, CT - *BillIntBG 83-84*
Synergy Systems Inc. - New York, NY - *ADAPSOMemDir 83-84*
Synerjy - New York, NY - *LitMag&SmPr 83-84*
Synertek Inc. - Santa Clara, CA - *DataDirSup 7-83*
Synfuels Week - Arlington, VA - *BaconPubCkMag 84*
Synnet [of Syntrex Inc.] - Eatontown, NJ - *TeleSy&SerDir 2-84*
Synsor Corp. - Woodinville, WA - *AvMarPl 83*
Syntactics Corp. - Santa Clara, CA - *MicrocomMPl 84*
Syntauri Corp. - Los Altos, CA - *MicrocomMPl 84*
Syntauri Corp. - Palo Alto, CA - *MicrocomMPl 83, 84; WhoWMicrocom 83*
Syntax [of Syntax ZX80 Inc.] - Harvard, MA - *MicrocomMPl 84; WritMar 84*
Syntax Advertising Agency - Cleveland, OH - *StaDirAdAg 2-84*
Syntax Corp. - Prairie Village, KS - *MicrocomMPl 83, 84; MicrocomSwDir 1; WhoWMicrocom 83*
Syntax International Pvt. Ltd. - York, PA - *LitMarPl 83, 84*
Syntax Publications - Boulder, CO - *BoPubDir 4 Sup, 5; LitMag&SmPr 83-84*
Syntax Quarterly [of Syntax ZX80 Inc.] - Harvard, MA - *MicrocomMPl 84*
Syntel - South Bend, IN - *MicrocomMPl 83*
Syntest Corp. - Marboro, MA - *DirInfWP 82*
Syntha Corp. - Greenwich, CT - *ADAPSOMemDir 83-84*
Synthegraphics Corp. - Chicago, IL - *LitMarPl 83, 84; MagIndMarPl 82-83*
Synthesis Publications - San Francisco, CA - *BoPubDir 4, 5; LitMag&SmPr 83-84; LitMarPl 84*
Syntonic Research Inc. - New York, NY - *BillIntBG 83-84*
Syntrex Inc. - Eatontown, NJ - *DataDirSup 7-83; DirInfWP 82*
Syosset Advance - Hicksville, NY - *AyerDirPub 83*
Syosset Advance - Syosset, NY - *Ed&PubIntYB 82*
Syosset Advance - *See* Litmore Publications
Syosset Pennysaver - Plainview, NY - *AyerDirPub 83*
Syosset Tribune - Syosset, NY - *Ed&PubIntYB 82; NewsDir 84*
Syosset Tribune - *See* Mid-Island Herald Publishers
Syracuse Cablesystems [of Rogers Cablesystems Inc.] - Syracuse, NY - *BrCabYB 84; InterCabHB 3; Tel&CabFB 84C*
Syracuse Chemist, The [of American Chemical Society, Syracuse Section] - Syracuse, NY - *BaconPubCkMag 84; MagDir 84*
Syracuse Data Base - Fayetteville, NY - *MicrocomMPl 84*
Syracuse Herald-American Post-Standard - Syracuse, NY - *LitMarPl 83*
Syracuse Herald Journal [of The Syracuse Newspapers Inc.] - Syracuse, NY - *BaconPubCkNews 84; Ed&PubIntYB 82; LitMarPl 83, 84; NewsDir 84*
Syracuse Impartial Citizen - Syracuse, NY - *BaconPubCkNews 84*
Syracuse Information Retrieval Software [of Syracuse University] - Syracuse, NY - *EISS 7-83 Sup*
Syracuse Journal - Syracuse, KS - *BaconPubCkNews 84; Ed&PubIntYB 82*
Syracuse Journal-Democrat [of Maverick Media Inc.] - Syracuse, NE - *Ed&PubIntYB 82; NewsDir 84*
Syracuse Journal-Democrat - *See* Maverick Media Inc.
Syracuse Magazine - Syracuse, NY - *WritMar 84*
Syracuse MDS Co. - New Rochelle, NY - *Tel&CabFB 84C*
Syracuse New Times [of Springfield Valley Advocate] - Springfield, MA - *NewsDir 84*
Syracuse New Times - Syracuse, NY - *AyerDirPub 83; Ed&PubIntYB 82; NewsDir 84*
Syracuse NewChannels [of NewChannels Corp.] - Dewitt, NY - *BrCabYB 84*
Syracuse NewChannels [of NewChannels Corp.] - North Syracuse, NY - *BrCabYB 84*

Syracuse NewChannels [Aff. of NewChannels Corp.] - Syracuse, NY - *InterCabHB 3; Tel&CabFB 84C*
Syracuse Onondaga Valley News - Syracuse, NY - *BaconPubCkNews 84*
Syracuse Peace Council - Syracuse, NY - *BoPubDir 4, 5; LitMag&SmPr 83-84*
Syracuse Post-Standard - Syracuse, NY - *BaconPubCkNews 84; LitMarPl 83; NewsDir 84*
Syracuse Research Corp. - Syracuse, NY - *DataDirOnSer 84*
Syracuse South Side News - Syracuse, NY - *Ed&PubIntYB 82*
Syracuse University (Film Center) - Syracuse, NY - *AvMarPl 83*
Syracuse University (Foreign & Comparative Studies Program) - Syracuse, NY - *BoPubDir 4, 5*
Syracuse University (Publications in Continuing Education) - Syracuse, NY - *BoPubDir 4, 5*
Syracuse University (Radio News Service) - Syracuse, NY - *BrCabYB 84*
Syracuse University Libraries (Information System) - Syracuse, NY - *EISS 83*
Syracuse University Press - Syracuse, NY - *BoPubDir 4 Sup, 5; LitMarPl 83, 84; WritMar 84*
Syringa Community Cable TV - Syringa, ID - *BrCabYB 84; Tel&CabFB 84C*
Syscom Inc. - Miami, FL - *WhoWMicrocom 83*
Syscon Corp. of America - San Diego, CA - *MicrocomSwDir 1; WhoWMicrocom 83*
Sysdes Inc. - Alexandria, VA - *InterCabHB 3*
Sysgen Inc. - Durham, NC - *ADAPSOMemDir 83-84*
Systech Inc. - Countryside, IL - *DataDirOnSer 84*
Systek Inc. - Mississippi State, MS - *MicrocomMPl 84*
Systel - Torino, Italy - *EISS 5-84 Sup*
System-Aid Computer Control Inc. - Flushing, NY - *MicrocomMPl 84*
System Development - Phoenix, AZ - *BaconPubCkMag 84*
System Development Corp. [Subs. of Burroughs Corp.] - Santa Monica, CA - *CompReadDB 82; DataDirOnSer 84; DataDirSup 7-83*
System for Documentation & Information in Metallurgy [of Federal Institute for Materials Testing] - Berlin, West Germany - *CompReadDB 82; EISS 83*
System for Information on Grey Literature in Europe [of Commission of the European Communities] - Kirchberg, Luxembourg - *EISS 83*
System Logistics Inc. - Honolulu, HI - *BoPubDir 4, 5*
System Network Inc. - Kalamazoo, MI - *MicrocomMPl 84*
System of Computerized Processing of Scientific Information [of Technical University of Wroclaw] - Wroclaw, Poland - *EISS 83*
System of Information Retrieval & Analysis Planning [of U.S. Army] - Ft. Belvoir, VA - *EISS 83*
System of Interactive Guidance & Information [of Educational Testing Service] - Princeton, NJ - *EISS 7-83 Sup*
System Purchasing Network [of Applied Computer Services Inc.] - Palos Heights, IL - *DataDirOnSer 84*
System Research Services - McLean, VA - *MicrocomMPl 84*
System Support Software Inc. - Dayton, OH - *DataDirSup 7-83*
System 1022 [of Software House] - Cambridge, MA - *EISS 83*
System/3 World [of Informatics Inc.] - Pound Ridge, NY - *MagDir 84*
System 2000 DBMS [of Intel Systems Corp.] - Austin, TX - *EISS 83*
Systematica - London, England - *MicrocomSwDir 1*
Systematics General Corp. - Sterling, VA - *InfIndMarPl 83*
Systematics Inc. - Little Rock, AR - *DataDirOnSer 84*
Systeme Corp. - Orlando, FL - *DataDirSup 7-83*
Systemed Corp. - Mountain City, TN - *MicrocomMPl 83*
Systemetric Software Inc. - San Bernardino, CA - *MicrocomMPl 84*
Systemetrics - Martinsville, NJ - *MagIndMarPl 82-83*
Systemhouse Inc. - Fairfax, VA - *ADAPSOMemDir 83-84*
Systemhouse Ltd. - Ottawa, ON, Canada - *VideoDir 82-83*
Systemics - West Bloomfield, MI - *MicrocomMPl 84; MicrocomSwDir 1*
Systemp - New York, NY - *DataDirSup 7-83*
Systems Analysis, Control, & Design Activity [of University of Western Ontario] - London, ON, Canada - *EISS 83*
Systems & Applied Sciences Corp. - Riverdale, MD - *EISS 7-83 Sup*
Systems & Data Processing Div. [of Florida State Legislature] - Tallahassee, FL - *EISS 83*
Systems & Methods [of GBC Press] - Las Vegas, NV - *LitMag&SmPr 83-84; WritMar 84*
Systems & Planning Unit [of University of Saskatchewan Library] - Saskatoon, SK, Canada - *EISS 83*
Systems & Programming International Inc. - Englewood, NJ - *ADAPSOMemDir 83-84*
Systems & Software - Downers Grove, IL - *MicrocomMPl 84; MicrocomSwDir 1*
Systems & Software - Rochelle Park, NJ - *MagDir 84*
Systems & Solutions Inc. - Roswell, NM - *MicrocomMPl 84; MicrocomSwDir 1*
Systems Communications - Lyndhurst, OH - *StaDirAdAg 2-84*
Systems Data Inc. - Akron, OH - *DataDirSup 7-83*
Systems Data Processing Corp. - Sacramento, CA - *ADAPSOMemDir 83-84; DataDirOnSer 84*
Systems Design [Div. of Synergistic Development Inc.] - Marina del Rey, CA - *AvMarPl 83*
Systems Design Associates Inc. - Charleston, WV - *MicrocomMPl 84; MicrocomSwDir 1*
Systems Design Lab - Redondo Beach, CA - *MicrocomMPl 83, 84; WhoWMicrocom 83*
Systems Development & Research Dept. [of Council of Better Business Bureaus] - Arlington, VA - *EISS 83*
Systems Development Dept. [of University of California, San Diego] - La Jolla, CA - *EISS 83*
Systems Engineering Services - Clifton, TX - *MicrocomSwDir 1*
Systems Formulate Corp. U.S.A. - Mountain View, CA - *MicrocomMPl 83*
Systems Furniture Co. - Torrance, CA - *WhoWMicrocom 83*
Systems Group - Orange, CA - *WhoWMicrocom 83*
Systems Industries - *Top100Al 83*
Systems Integration - New York, NY - *MicrocomMPl 83*
Systems Investments Ltd. - Calgary, AB, Canada - *BoPubDir 4, 5*
Systems Management Inc. - Rosemont, IL - *ADAPSOMemDir 83-84*
Systems Manufacturing Corp. - Binghamton, NY - *DataDirSup 7-83; DirInfWP 82*
Systems Network Inc. - Kalamazoo, MI - *MicrocomMPl 83*
Systems Planning Association Inc. [Aff. of New England Center for Continuing Education] - Keen, NH - *BoPubDir 5*
Systems Plus - Palo Alto, CA - *MicrocomMPl 84; MicrocomSwDir 1; WhoWMicrocom 83*
Systems Products International Inc. - Miami, FL - *ADAPSOMemDir 83-84*
Systems Shoppe, The [Subs. of TDL Electronics] - Greenwood, MO - *WhoWMicrocom 83*
Systems Technology Automated Resources Inc. - Bakersfield, CA - *WhoWMicrocom 83*
Systems Technology Forum - Burke, VA - *TeleSy&SerDir 7-83*
Systems Technology Inc. - New Haven, CT - *DirInfWP 82*
Systems Union Ltd. - London, England - *MicrocomSwDir 1*
Systems Unit [of Metropolitan Toronto Library Board] - Toronto, ON, Canada - *EISS 83*
Systems User - North Hollywood, CA - *BaconPubCkMag 84*
Systemshare - East Pilton, England - *MicrocomSwDir 1*
Systronics Business Systems [Subs. of Systronics Marketing Inc.] - Hasbrouck Heights, NJ - *WhoWMicrocom 83*
Systronics Inc. - New York, NY - *ADAPSOMemDir 83-84*
Systronics Inc. - Houston, TX - *WhoWMicrocom 83*
Sytek Inc. - Mountain View, CA - *DataDirSup 7-83; TeleSy&SerDir 7-83*
Sytek Inc. - Sunnyvale, CA - *DirInfWP 82*
Syzygy - Rush, NY - *BoPubDir 5; LitMag&SmPr 83-84*
SZ Software Systems - Altadena, CA - *WhoWMicrocom 83*
Szabadsag - Cleveland, OH - *Ed&PubIntYB 82*
Szell, Timea K. - Tenafly, NJ - *LitMarPl 83, 84*
SZF Inc. - New York, NY - *AdAge 3-28-84; StaDirAdAg 2-84*
Szoke Graphics Inc., John - New York, NY - *ArtMar 84*

T

T & ACS - London, England - *MicrocomSwDir 1*
T & E Associates Inc. - Millersville, MD - *MicrocomMPl 83, 84*
T & F Software Co. - North Hollywood, CA - *MicrocomSwDir 1*
T & J Advertising Agency - Chicago, IL - *StaDirAdAg 2-84*
T & M Computing - St. Louis, MO - *MicrocomMPl 84*
T. & R. Engraving - Denver, CO - *MagIndMarPl 82-83*
T & S Sales Co. - Mobile, AL - *AvMarPl 83*
T & T Cable Corp. - Hennessey, OK - *BrCabYB 84*
T & T Cable Corp. - Okeene, OK - *BrCabYB 84; Tel&CabFB 84C*
T & T Cable Corp. - Watonga, OK - *BrCabYB 84 p.D-307; Tel&CabFB 84C p.1705*
T & T Cable Hennessey [of T & T Cable Corp.] - Hennessey, OK - *Tel&CabFB 84C*
T & T Consulting Associates Inc. - Lindenhurst, NY - *EISS 5-84 Sup*
T & T Publishing Co. - Canada - *BoPubDir 4 Sup, 5*
T & W Cable TV [of Scripps-Howard Cable Co.] - De Bary, FL - *Tel&CabFB 84C*
T & W Systems Inc. - Fountain Valley, CA - *WhoWMicrocom 83*
T-Bar Inc. - Wilton, CT - *DataDirSup 7-83*
T-Boy Music Publishing - *See* Lipservices
T/C Publications [Aff. of Technology Conferences] - El Segundo, CA - *BoPubDir 5*
T J Records - Stanford, CA - *BillIntBG 83-84*
T/Maker Co. - Mountain View, CA - *MicrocomMPl 84*
T/Maker Co. - Palo Alto, CA - *MicrocomMPl 84; MicrocomSwDir 1*
T/Maker Co. - Falls Church, VA - *WhoWMicrocom 83*
T9 - Washington, DC - *DirOnDB Spring 84*
T-Shirt Retailer & Screen Printer - Long Valley, NJ - *BaconPubCkMag 84*
T6 - Washington, DC - *DirOnDB Spring 84*
T6 Air Charter [of I. P. Sharp Associates Ltd.] - Toronto, ON, Canada - *DataDirOnSer 84*
TA Press [Aff. of International Transactional Analysis Association] - San Francisco, CA - *BoPubDir 4, 5*
TAA Inc. - Cedar Knolls, NJ - *ArtMar 84; StaDirAdAg 2-84*
TAAD - Rolling Hills Estates, CA - *BaconPubCkMag 84*
Tab - Little Rock, AR - *BaconPubCkMag 84; MagDir 84*
TAB Books Inc. - East Norwalk, CT - *ArtMar 84*
TAB Books Inc. - Blue Ridge Summit, PA - *ArtMar 84; LitMarPl 83, 84; MicrocomMPl 84; WritMar 84*
TAB Inc. - Sparta Village, MI - *BrCabYB 84*
TAB Products Co. - Palo Alto, CA - *MicrocomMPl 84*
Tab Products Co. (Electronics Office Products Div.) - Palo Alto, CA - *DirInfWP 82; WhoWMicrocom 83*
Tab Products Co. (Office Filing Systems Div.) - Palo Alto, CA - *DirInfWP 82*
Taber Cable Television Ltd. - Taber, AB, Canada - *BrCabYB 84; Tel&CabFB 84C*
Tabernacle Publishing Co. - *See* Hope Publishing Co.
Table Rock Gazette - Reeds Spring, MO - *AyerDirPub 83*
Tablet, The - Brooklyn, NY - *BaconPubCkMag 84*
Tabletop Plus - Scarborough, ON, Canada - *BaconPubCkMag 84*
Tabloid Lithographers Inc. - Rahway, NJ - *BaconPubCkNews 84*
Tabor Beacon-Enterprise - Tabor, IA - *Ed&PubIntYB 82*
Tabor City CATV LP - Tabor City, NC - *Tel&CabFB 84C*
Tabor City Tribune - Tabor City, NC - *BaconPubCkNews 84; Ed&PubIntYB 82; NewsDir 84*
Tabor Corp. - Westford, MA - *MicrocomMPl 84*
Tabor Fremont-Mills Beacon Enterprise - Tabor, IA - *BaconPubCkNews 84*
TAC-CAN of Alabama Inc. - Calera, AL - *BrCabYB 84*
TAC-CAN of Alabama Inc. - Jameson, AL - *BrCabYB 84*
TAC-CAN of Alabama Inc. - Mobile County, AL - *BrCabYB 84*
TAC-CAN of Alabama Inc. [of Omni Cable TV Corp.] - Montevallo, AL - *Tel&CabFB 84C*
TAC-CAN of Alabama Inc. [of Omni Cable TV Corp.] - Shelby County, AL - *Tel&CabFB 84C*
Tac-G Gilts - Rickmansworth, England - *DirOnDB Spring 84*
Tack 'n Togs Merchandising - Minneapolis, MN - *BaconPubCkMag 84; MagDir 84; WritMar 84*
Taco Times - Perry, FL - *Ed&PubIntYB 82*
Tacoma Daily Index - Tacoma, WA - *Ed&PubIntYB 82; NewsDir 84*
Tacoma Facts [of Seattle Facts Newspapers] - Seattle, WA - *NewsDir 84*
Tacoma News-Tribune - Tacoma, WA - *AyerDirPub 83; BaconPubCkNews 84; BrCabYB 84; Ed&PubIntYB 82; NewsBur 6; NewsDir 84*
Tacoma Suburban Times - Lakewood Center, WA - *AyerDirPub 83*
Tacoma Suburban Times - Tacoma, WA - *BaconPubCkNews 84; NewsDir 84*
Tacoma True Citizen - Tacoma, WA - *BaconPubCkNews 84*
Tacomarc Project [of Tacoma Public Library] - Tacoma, WA - *EISS 83*
Taconic Press Inc. - Millbrook, NY - *BaconPubCkNews 84*
Taconic Telephone Corp. - Chatham, NY - *TelDir&BG 83-84*
Taconite Cable TV - Taconite, MN - *BrCabYB 84*
Tactical Design Technology Park - Norcross, GA - *MicrocomMPl 84*
Tactical Technology Center [of Battelle Memorial Institute] - Columbus, OH - *EISS 83*
Tactical Weapon Guidance & Control Information Analysis [of IIT Research Institute] - Chicago, IL - *EISS 83*
Tactype - New York, NY - *AvMarPl 83*
Tadder, Morton - Baltimore, MD - *MagIndMarPl 82-83*
Taemouth Sun - Orleans, MA - *AyerDirPub 83*
Taeper Music [Div. of Barcus-Berry Inc.] - Huntington Beach, CA - *BillIntBG 83-84*
Taffner/Ltd., D. L. - New York, NY - *TelAl 83, 84; Tel&CabFB 84C*
Tafnews Press - Los Altos, CA - *BoPubDir 4, 5*
Tafoya, Alfonso - New York, NY - *LitMarPl 83*
Taft Broadcasting - Cincinnati, OH - *AdAge 6-28-84; BrCabYB 84; HomeVid&CabYB 82-83; KnowInd 83; LitMarPl 84; TelAl 83, 84; Tel&CabFB 84S*
Taft Broadcasting - Houston, TX - *Tel&CabFB 84C*

Taft Corp. [Div. of The Taft Group] - Washington, DC - *LitMarPl 83, 84*
Taft Entertainment Co., The - Los Angeles, CA - *TelAl 83, 84*
Taft H-B International - New York, NY - *Tel&CabFB 84C*
Taft Midway Driller - Taft, CA - *BaconPubCkNews 84; NewsDir 84*
Taft Tribune - Taft, TX - *AyerDirPub 83; Ed&PubIntYB 82*
Taft Tribune - *See* San Patricio Publishing Co.
Taggie Music Co. - *See* Gopam Enterprises Inc.
Tagliarino Public Relations, Peggy - New York, NY - *LitMarPl 83, 84*
Tagumi Features Syndicate - El Cerrito, CA - *Ed&PubIntYB 82*
Tahlequah Cable Television Inc. [of WEHCO Video Inc.] - Tahlequah, OK - *BrCabYB 84; Tel&CabFB 84C*
Tahlequah Cherokee County Chronicle - Tahlequah, OK - *NewsDir 84*
Tahlequah Press - Tahlequah, OK - *BaconPubCkNews 84; Ed&PubIntYB 82*
Tahlequah Star Citizen [of Tahlequah Risenhoover Printing Co. Inc.] - Tahlequah, OK - *NewsDir 84*
Tahoe Systems [of Group W Cable] - Kings Beach, CA - *BrCabYB 84; Tel&CabFB 84C*
Tahoe Tribune - South Lake Tahoe, CA - *AyerDirPub 83; BaconPubCkNews 84; Ed&PubIntYB 82*
Tahoe TV Cable Inc. [of Community Tele-Communications Inc.] - South Lake Tahoe, CA - *Tel&CabFB 84C*
Tahoe World - North Lake Tahoe, CA - *Ed&PubIntYB 82*
Tahoe World - Tahoe City, CA - *AyerDirPub 83; BaconPubCkNews 84; NewsDir 84*
Tahoka Lynn County News - Tahoka, TX - *BaconPubCkNews 84*
Tai Chi [of Wayfarer Publications] - Los Angeles, CA - *LitMag&SmPr 83-84*
Taihan Corp. - Chatsworth, CA - *BillIntBG 83-84*
Tailwind, The - Fairfield, CA - *AyerDirPub 83*
Tait Appraisal Co. - Los Angeles, CA - *CabTVFinDB 83*
Taiwan [of Chase Econometrics/Interactive Data Corp.] - Waltham, MA - *DataDirOnSer 84*
Tajah Music - *See* Raybird Music
Take Home Tunes! Record Co. - Beverly Hills, CA - *BillIntBG 83-84*
Take Ten - Des Plaines, IL - *AvMarPl 83*
Takla Computer Services Ltd. - London, ON, Canada - *WhoWMicrocom 83*
Takoma Records Corp. - Los Angeles, CA - *BillIntBG 83-84*
TAL Aroyo - Tel Aviv, Israel - *StaDirAdAg 2-84*
TAL Inc. - Erie, PA - *StaDirAdAg 2-84*
Talarzyk, W. Wayne - Columbus, OH - *VideoDir 82-83*
Talas [Div. of Technical Library Service Inc.] - New York, NY - *LitMarPl 83, 84*
Talbot & Associates, Paul - Vancouver, BC, Canada - *DirInfWP 82*
Talbot Banner - Easton, MD - *AyerDirPub 83*
Talbot Microsystems - Redondo Beach, CA - *MicrocomMPl 84; MicrocomSwDir 1*
Talbot Microsystems - Riverside, CA - *WhoWMicrocom 83*
Talbot, Mrs. Toby - New York, NY - *LitMarPl 83, 84*
Talbot, Talbot, Hundemer & Williams - Baton Rouge, LA - *StaDirAdAg 2-84*
Talbotton New Era - Talbotton, GA - *Ed&PubIntYB 82*
Talbotton New Era - *See* Tri-County Newspapers Inc.
Talco Productions [Div. of Alan Lawrence Co.] - New York, NY - *ArtMar 84; AvMarPl 83; WritMar 84*
Talco Times - Talco, TX - *Ed&PubIntYB 82*
Talent & Residuals Inc. - Chicago, IL - *HBIndAd&MS 82-83*
Tales of the Mojave Road Publishing Co. - Norco, CA - *BoPubDir 4, 5*
Taliaferro & Associates Inc. - Tampa, FL - *DirPRFirms 83; StaDirAdAg 2-84*
Talihina American - Talihina, OK - *BaconPubCkNews 84; Ed&PubIntYB 82*
Talisman Literary Research Inc. - Georgetown, CA - *BoPubDir 4, 5*
Talisman Press - Georgetown, CA - *BoPubDir 4, 5*
Talk-A-Phone Co. - Chicago, IL - *AvMarPl 83*
Talk It Over-Focus Groups Unltd. - Atlanta, GA - *IntDirMarRes 83*
Talk Lab Workshop - New York, NY - *ProGuPRSer 4*
Talking Food Co. - Salem, MA - *BoPubDir 4, 5*
Talking Seal Press - Flint, MI - *BoPubDir 4, 5*
Tall City TV Cable [of Times Mirror Cable Television Inc.] - Midland, TX - *BrCabYB 84; Tel&CabFB 84C*
Tall Ships Art Productions Ltd. - Waverley, NS, Canada - *BoPubDir 4, 5*
Tall Tree Systems - Los Altos, CA - *MicrocomMPl 84; MicrocomSwDir 1; WhoWMicrocom 83*
Tallahassee Advertiser - Tallahassee, FL - *AyerDirPub 83*
Tallahassee Camera Center Inc. - Tallahassee, FL - *AvMarPl 83*
Tallahassee Capital Outlook - Tallahassee, FL - *BaconPubCkNews 84*
Tallahassee Democrat [of Knight-Ridder Newspapers Inc.] - Tallahassee, FL - *BaconPubCkNews 84; Ed&PubIntYB 82; NewsBur 6; NewsDir 84*
Tallahassee Magazine [of Homes & Land Publishing Corp.] - Tallahassee, FL - *WritMar 84*
Tallant/Yates Advertising Inc. - Englewood, CO - *DirPRFirms 83; StaDirAdAg 2-84*
Tallapoosa Journal-Beacon [of Carrollton Carroll Publishing Co.] - Carrollton, GA - *NewsDir 84*
Tallapoosa Journal-Beacon - Tallapoosa, GA - *BaconPubCkNews 84; Ed&PubIntYB 82*
Tallassee Tribune - Tallassee, AL - *BaconPubCkNews 84; Ed&PubIntYB 82; NewsDir 84*
Talley Radio Stations - Litchfield, IL - *BrCabYB 84*
Tallgrass Technologies Corp. - Overland Park, KS - *MicrocomMPl 84; WhoWMicrocom 83*
Tallmadge Express - Tallmadge, OH - *Ed&PubIntYB 82*
Tallmadge Express - *See* Record Publishing Co.
Tallulah Cablevision Corp. - Tallulah, LA - *BrCabYB 84; Tel&CabFB 84C*
Tallulah Madison Journal - Tallulah, LA - *BaconPubCkNews 84; NewsDir 84*
Tally Ho - Peoria, AZ - *AyerDirPub 83*
Tally Press - Lincolnton, NC - *BoPubDir 4, 5*
Tallyrand Music Inc. - *See* Bicycle Music Co., The
Talmadge & Associates, Hal - Scottsdale, AZ - *DataDirOnSer 84*
Talmadge Productions - *See* Catalogue Music Inc.
Talmage Associates [Aff. of Travel Agent Magazine] - Abington, PA - *BoPubDir 5*
Talmage Topics [of Syracuse Maverick Media Inc.] - Syracuse, NE - *NewsDir 84*
Talmis Industry Update [of Talmis Inc.] - Oak Park, IL - *MicrocomMPl 84*
Taloga Cable TV - Taloga, OK - *BrCabYB 84; Tel&CabFB 84C*
Taloga Times-Advocate - Taloga, OK - *BaconPubCkNews 84; Ed&PubIntYB 82*
Talon - Colorado Springs, CO - *BaconPubCkMag 84; MagDir 84*
Talon Books Ltd. - Vancouver, BC, Canada - *LitMag&SmPr 83-84; LitMarPl 83, 84*
Talos Systems Inc. [Subs. of Sanders Associates Inc.] - Scottsdale, AZ - *WhoWMicrocom 83*
Talponia Press - Alden, MI - *BoPubDir 5*
Talquin Corp. [Subs. of Florida Progress Corp.] - St. Petersburg, FL - *WhoWMicrocom 83*
Taltek Electronics Ltd. - Montreal, PQ, Canada - *DataDirSup 7-83*
Talton Broadcasting Co. - Selma, AL - *BrCabYB 84*
Tama News-Herald - Tama, IA - *BaconPubCkNews 84; Ed&PubIntYB 82; NewsDir 84*
Tamal Land Press - Fairfax, CA - *BoPubDir 4, 5*
Tamal Vista Publications - Larkspur, CA - *BoPubDir 4, 5; LitMag&SmPr 83-84*
Tamalpa Press - Larkspur, CA - *BoPubDir 4 Sup, 5*
Tamalpais Press - Santa Barbara, CA - *BoPubDir 4, 5*
Tamara Press - New York, NY - *LitMag&SmPr 83-84*
Tamarack Communications Inc. - Portland, OR - *BrCabYB 84*
Tamarack Editions - Syracuse, NY - *BoPubDir 4, 5; LitMag&SmPr 83-84*
Tamarack Press - Madison, WI - *LitMag&SmPr 83-84*
Tamarack Software - Darby, MT - *MicrocomMPl 84; MicrocomSwDir 1*
Tamarisk - Philadelphia, PA - *BoPubDir 4, 5; LitMag&SmPr 83-84*
Tambur - Cedarhurst, NY - *BillIntBG 83-84*
Tamburine, Jean - Meriden, CT - *LitMarPl 83, 84*

Tamburitza Press [Aff. of Duquesne University Tamburitzans Institute of Folk Arts] - Pittsburgh, PA - *BoPubDir 4, 5*
Tampa Bay Business - Tampa, FL - *BaconPubCkMag 84*
Tampa Bay Monthly [of Florida City Magazines Inc.] - Tampa, FL - *BaconPubCkMag 84; WritMar 84*
Tampa Bay Opinion Mart [Div. of Gulf Coast Research Corp.] - Tampa, FL - *IntDirMarRes 83*
Tampa Cable TV Inc. [of Tribune Cable Communications Inc.] - Tampa, FL - *Tel&CabFB 84C*
Tampa Free Press - Tampa, FL - *BaconPubCkNews 84*
Tampa MacDill Thunderbolt [of Tampa Suburban Newspapers] - Tampa, FL - *NewsDir 84*
Tampa Metro Neighbor - Tampa, FL - *BaconPubCkNews 84; Ed&PubIntYB 82*
Tampa News Reporter - Tampa, FL - *BaconPubCkNews 84; NewsDir 84*
Tampa Sentinel-Bulletin - Tampa, FL - *BaconPubCkNews 84; NewsDir 84*
Tampa Suburban Independent - Tampa, FL - *NewsDir 84*
Tampa Suburban Newspapers Inc. - Tampa, FL - *BaconPubCkNews 84*
Tampa Times - Tampa, FL - *Ed&PubIntYB 82; LitMarPl 83, 84*
Tampa Tribune - Tampa, FL - *BaconPubCkNews 84; Ed&PubIntYB 82; LitMarPl 83, 84; NewsBur 6; NewsDir 84*
Tampa Tribune & News, The - Tampa, FL - *LitMarPl 84*
Tampa Tribune & Times, The - Tampa, FL - *Ed&PubIntYB 82; LitMarPl 83*
Tamron Industries Inc. - Port Washington, NY - *AvMarPl 83*
Tams Books Inc. - Los Angeles, CA - *BoPubDir 4, 5*
Tanadgusix Corp. - St. Pasul Island, AK - *BoPubDir 4, 5*
Tanam Press - New York, NY - *BoPubDir 4, 5; LitMag&SmPr 83-84*
Tandberg Data A/S - Oslo, Norway - *DataDirSup 7-83*
Tandberg Data Inc. - Orange, CA - *MicrocomMPl 84*
Tandberg of America Inc. [Subs. of Tandberg Data A/S] - Armonk, NY - *AvMarPl 83*
Tandem Computers Inc. - Cupertino, CA - *Datamation 6-83; Top100Al 83*
Tandem Inc. - Pittsburgh, PA - *StaDirAdAg 2-84*
Tandem Press Inc. - Tannersville, PA - *LitMarPl 83, 84; WritMar 84*
Tandem Productions - Los Angeles, CA - *KnowInd 83; Tel&CabFB 84C*
Tandem Productions - *See* Communications Services Inc.
Tandem Productions - *See* Embassy Television
Tandem Records Inc. - Bristol, VA - *BillIntBG 83-84*
Tandon Corp. - Chatsworth, CA - *DataDirSup 7-83; Datamation 6-83; MicrocomMPl 84; Top100Al 83; WhoWMicrocom 83*
Tandy Corp. - Ft. Worth, TX - *DataDirSup 7-83; Datamation 6-83; ElecNews 7-25-83; HomeVid&CabYB 82-83; Top100Al 83; WhoWMicrocom 83*
Tandy Corp. - Walsall, England - *MicrocomSwDir 1*
Tandy Newsletter [of CompuServe Inc.] - Columbus, OH - *DataDirOnSer 84*
Tandy Newsletter - Ft. Worth, TX - *DirOnDB Spring 84*
Tanenbaum Services Ltd. - New York, NY - *LitMarPl 83, 84*
Taney County Republican - Branson, MO - *AyerDirPub 83*
Taney County Republican - Forsyth, MO - *Ed&PubIntYB 82*
Tangent Books - New Malden, England - *LitMag&SmPr 83-84*
Tangi-Talk - Amite, LA - *AyerDirPub 83*
Tangier Island Cablevision [of Tangier Island TV Corp.] - Tangier Island, VA - *BrCabYB 84*
Tanjung News Agency - New York, NY - *Ed&PubIntYB 82*
Tankard, Elaine F. - Austin, TX - *LitMarPl 83*
Tannahill, Cecil C. - White Rock, BC, Canada - *BoPubDir 4 Sup, 5*
Tannebring-Rose Associates Inc. - Dallas, TX - *AvMarPl 83; Tel&CabFB 84C; WritMar 84*
Tannen Music Inc. - Stamford, CT - *BillIntBG 83-84*
Tannenbaum, Allan - New York, NY - *MagIndMarPl 82-83*
Tanner Co. Inc., William B. - *See* General Broadcast Services Inc.
Tanner, R. T. - Singapore, Singapore - *InfIndMarPl 83*
Tano Corp. - New Orleans, LA - *InfIndMarPl 83; WhoWMicrocom 83*
Tansky Advertising Co., The Ron - Sherman Oaks, CA - *StaDirAdAg 2-84*
Tansoft Ltd. - Ely, England - *MicrocomSwDir 1*
Tantalus Inc. - Cleveland, OH - *EISS 83*
Tantalus Research Ltd. - Vancouver, BC, Canada - *BoPubDir 4, 5*
Tanzania National Documentation Centre [of National Central Library] - Dar es Salaam, Tanzania - *EISS 5-84 Sup*
Tao of Wing Chun Do Publishing - Kirkland, WA - *BoPubDir 5*
Tao of Wing Chun Do Publishing - Redmond, WA - *BoPubDir 4*
Tao Records - Bonita, CA - *BillIntBG 83-84*
Taoist Publishers - Waterford, MI - *BoPubDir 5*
Taos Cable TV Co. [of Mickelson Media Inc.] - Angel Fire, NM - *Tel&CabFB 84C*
Taos Cable TV Co. [of Mickelson Media Inc.] - Taos, NM - *BrCabYB 84; Tel&CabFB 84C*
Taos News - Taos, NM - *BaconPubCkNews 84; Ed&PubIntYB 82; NewsDir 84*
Tapadero Music - *See* Merit Music Corp.
Tape Cartridges [of GML Corp.] - Lexington, MA - *CompReadDB 82*
Tape-Film Industries - New York, NY - *TelAl 83, 84; Tel&CabFB 84C*
T.A.P.E. Ltd. - New York, NY - *BrCabYB 84*
Tape 'n Text Publishing Co. - Fredonia, NY - *MicrocomSwDir 1; WhoWMicrocom 83*
Tapley-Rutter Co. Inc. [Subs. of The Zondervan Corp.] - Moonachie, NJ - *LitMarPl 83, 84*
Taplinger Publishing Co. Inc. - New York, NY - *LitMarPl 83, 84; WritMar 84*
Tappahannock Cable TV Corp. [of Atlantic MetroVision Corp.] - Tappahannock, VA - *BrCabYB 84; Tel&CabFB 84C*
Tappan Group Inc., The - Englewood, NJ - *LitMarPl 84*
TAPPI - Atlanta, GA - *BaconPubCkMag 84; MagDir 84; MagIndMarPl 82-83*
TAPPI Press [Aff. of Technical Association of the Pulp & Paper Industry Inc.] - Atlanta, GA - *BoPubDir 4, 5*
Tapwe - Hay River, NT, Canada - *Ed&PubIntYB 82*
Tar Heel Software Systems Inc. - Burlington, NC - *MicrocomMPl 83, 84*
Tar River Cable TV Inc. - Nash County, NC - *BrCabYB 84*
Tar River Cable TV Inc. - Rocky Mt., NC - *BrCabYB 84*
Tar River Cable TV Inc. - Tarboro, NC - *BrCabYB 84*
Tar River Communications Inc. [of Multimedia Cablevision Inc.] - Rocky Mt., NC - *Tel&CabFB 84C p.1705*
Tar River Poetry [of East Carolina University] - Greenville, NC - *LitMag&SmPr 83-84; WritMar 84*
Tara Center - Burbank, CA - *BoPubDir 5*
Tara Center - North Hollywood, CA - *BoPubDir 4*
Tara Computer Products Inc. - Buffalo, NY - *MicrocomMPl 84*
Tara Leader - Tara, ON, Canada - *AyerDirPub 83*
TARA Ltd. - Selden, NY - *MicrocomMPl 84*
Tarakan Music Letter, The [of Sound Advice Enterprises] - Roslyn Heights, NY - *LitMag&SmPr 83-84*
Taranto & Associates Inc. - San Rafael, CA - *MicrocomMPl 83, 84; MicrocomSwDir 1; WhoWMicrocom 83*
Taraxacum - Washington, DC - *BoPubDir 4, 5*
Taray Publications - Scottsville, VA - *LitMag&SmPr 83-84*
Tarbell Electronics - Carson, CA - *MicrocomMPl 83, 84; WhoWMicrocom 83*
Tarboro Southerner - Tarboro, NC - *BaconPubCkNews 84; NewsDir 84*
Tarbox, Todd - Tulsa, OK - *LitMarPl 83; MagIndMarPl 82-83*
Tarbox, Todd - El Paso, TX - *LitMarPl 84*
Tarcher Inc., Jeremy P. [Subs. of Houghton Mifflin Co.] - Los Angeles, CA - *LitMarPl 83, 84; WritMar 84*
Tardy Phoenix Press - Austin, TX - *BoPubDir 4, 5*
Tarentum-New Kensington-Vandergrift-Valley News [of Gannett Co. Inc.] - Tarentum, PA - *NewsDir 84*
Tarentum Valley News Dispatch - Tarentum, PA - *AyerDirPub 83; Ed&PubIntYB 82*
Targ Literary Agency Inc., Roslyn - New York, NY - *LitMarPl 83, 84*
Target [of Target Publications] - Spencerville, OH - *MicrocomMPl 84*
Target Advertising & Research Inc. - Hauppauge, NY - *IntDirMarRes 83*
Target Communications Inc. - Boston, MA - *HBIndAd&MS 82-83*
Target Distribution - New York, NY - *ProGuPRSer 4*
Target Enterprises Ltd. - Hollywood, CA - *StaDirAdAg 2-84*

Target Group Inc., The - New York, NY - *StaDirAdAg 2-84*
Target Group Index [of Interactive Market Systems] - New York, NY - *DataDirOnSer 84; DBBus 82*
Target Group Index [of British Market Research Bureau Ltd.] - London, England - *DirOnDB Spring 84; EISS 83*
Target Group Index, Major Market Index & Target Teen Index [of Simmons Market Research Bureau Inc.] - New York, NY - *DataDirOnSer 84*
Target Mailing Lists Inc. - New York, NY - *MagIndMarPl 82-83*
Target Publishers - San Ramon, CA - *DirMarMP 83*
Target Records - Los Angeles, CA - *BillIntBG 83-84*
Target Research Group [Div. of Business Marketing Services] - Tuckahoe, NY - *IntDirMarRes 83*
Target Software Inc. - Atlanta, GA - *WhoWMicrocom 83*
Targets Advertising - *See* Burnett Co. Inc., Leo
Tarharka Publishing Co. - Annapolis, MD - *BoPubDir 4*
Tarheel Banker [of North Carolina Bankers Association] - Raleigh, NC - *BaconPubCkMag 84; MagDir 84*
Tarheel Cablevision Inc. - Mebane, NC - *Tel&CabFB 84C*
Tarheel Wheels - Raleigh, NC - *BaconPubCkMag 84; MagDir 84*
Tari Book Publishers - Eugene, OR - *BoPubDir 5*
Tari Book Publishers - Molalla, OR - *BoPubDir 4*
Tarka Press - Oakville, ON, Canada - *BoPubDir 4, 5*
Tarkenton Stations, Dallas - Athens, GA - *BrCabYB 84*
Tarkio Avalanche - Tarkio, MO - *BaconPubCkNews 84; Ed&PubIntYB 82; NewsDir 84*
Tarpon Beacon - Pass Christian, MS - *Ed&PubIntYB 82*
Tarpon Springs Herald - Tarpon Springs, FL - *AyerDirPub 83; Ed&PubIntYB 82*
Tarpon Springs Herald - *See* Pinellas Publishers Inc.
Tarpon Springs/Holiday Herald - Tarpon Springs, FL - *NewsDir 84*
Tarpon Springs/Holiday Herald - *See* Pinellas Publishers Inc.
Tarpon Springs/Holiday Leader - Tarpon Springs, FL - *NewsDir 84*
Tarpon Springs/Holiday Leader - *See* Leader Publishing
Tarpon Springs Leader - Tarpon Springs, FL - *Ed&PubIntYB 82*
Tarpon Springs Leader - *See* Leader Publishing
Tarragano Co., The - New York, NY - *ArtMar 84; DirPRFirms 83*
Tarrance & Associates, V. Lance - Houston, TX - *BrCabYB 84*
Tarrant Cable Communications [of Storer Cable Communications Inc.] - Bedford, TX - *BrCabYB 84*
Tarrant Cable Communications - Forest Hill, TX - *BrCabYB 84*
Tarrant Cable Communications [of Storer Cable Communications Inc.] - Saginaw, TX - *BrCabYB 84*
Tarrant Cable Communications - Watauga, TX - *BrCabYB 84*
Tarrant Cable Communications - *See* Storer Cable Communications Inc.
Tarrtec Enterprises - Commack, NY - *MicrocomSwDir 1*
Tarrytown News [of Westchester-Rockland Newspapers] - Tarrytown, NY - *NewsDir 84*
Tarrytown News - White Plains, NY - *AyerDirPub 83; Ed&PubIntYB 82*
Tarrytown News - *See* Westchester-Rockland Newspapers
Tarzana Music Press - *See* Bock Music Co., Fred
Tarzana Times - Encino, CA - *AyerDirPub 83*
Tarzana Times - *See* Associated Valley Publications
Tarzian Inc., Sarkes - Bloomington, IN - *BrCabYB 84; Tel&CabFB 84S*
Tashmoo Press - Vineyard Haven, MA - *BoPubDir 4, 5*
Taskforce on the Churches & Corporate Responsibility - Toronto, ON, Canada - *BoPubDir 4 Sup, 5*
Tass Agency - New York, NY - *Ed&PubIntYB 82*
Tassin, Doris - Shelton, CT - *LitMarPl 83, 84; MagIndMarPl 82-83*
T.A.T. Communications Co. - Los Angeles, CA - *TelAl 83*
T.A.T. Communications Co. - *See* Tandem Productions
Tat Journal - Bellaire, OH - *WritMar 84*
Tata Grande Publishing Co. - Houston, TX - *BillIntBG 83-84*
Tate County Democrat - Senatobia, MS - *AyerDirPub 83; Ed&PubIntYB 82*
Tatham-Laird & Kudner - Chicago, IL - *AdAge 3-28-84; Br 1-23-84; BrCabYB 84; TelAl 83, 84*
Tatlow House - North Vancouver, BC, Canada - *BoPubDir 4, 5*
Tat's Inc. - Costa Mesa, CA - *BoPubDir 4, 5*
Tatsch Associates - Sudbury, MA - *BoPubDir 4, 5*
Tattler, The - Little Chute, WI - *AyerDirPub 83*
Tattnall Electronics Co. Inc. - Glennville, GA - *BrCabYB 84; Tel&CabFB 84C*
Tattnall Journal - Reidsville, GA - *AyerDirPub 83; Ed&PubIntYB 82*
Tatum Labs - Hawleyville, CT - *MicrocomMPl 84; MicrocomSwDir 1*
Tatum Telephone Co. - Tatum, TX - *TelDir&BG 83-84*
Tatung Co. of America Inc. - Long Beach, CA - *DataDirSup 7-83; MicrocomMPl 84*
Tatung Co. of America Inc. (Marketing Div.) - Long Beach, CA - *BillIntBG 83-84*
Tau Mark Inc. - Middleton, WI - *WhoWMicrocom 83*
Tau-Tron - Chelmsford, MA - *DataDirSup 7-83*
Taube/Violante Inc. - Norwalk, CT - *StaDirAdAg 2-84*
Tauber's Bookbindery Inc. - Jersey City, NJ - *LitMarPl 83, 84; MagIndMarPl 82-83*
Taucher Group - Helsinki, Finland - *StaDirAdAg 2-84*
Taugus House Publishers Inc. - San Marcos, CA - *BoPubDir 4, 5*
Taumark Inc. - Middleton, WI - *InfIndMarPl 83*
Taunacious Music - Seattle, WA - *BillIntBG 83-84*
Taunton Daily Gazette [of Thomson Newspaper Publishing Co. Inc.] - Taunton, MA - *BaconPubCkNews 84; Ed&PubIntYB 82; NewsDir 84*
Taunton Press Inc. - Newtown, CT - *BoPubDir 4, 5; LitMarPl 83, 84*
Taurus - Gladstone, OR - *LitMag&SmPr 83-84; WritMar 84*
Taurus Computer Systems - West Newton, MA - *MicrocomMPl 84*
Taurus Marketing Inc. - Newburyport, MA - *DirMarMP 83; HBIndAd&MS 82-83*
Taurus Photos - New York, NY - *LitMarPl 83, 84; MagIndMarPl 82-83*
Taurus Press of Willow Dene - Heath, England - *LitMag&SmPr 83-84*
Taurus Software Corp. - Lafayette, CA - *MicrocomSwDir 1*
Tavarelli, Evelyn - New York, NY - *MagIndMarPl 82-83*
Tavares Citizen - Tavares, FL - *BaconPubCkNews 84*
Tawakoni Area Advertiser - Quinlan, TX - *AyerDirPub 83*
Tawakoni News - Quinlan, TX - *AyerDirPub 83*
Tawakoni News, The - Lake Tawakoni, TX - *Ed&PubIntYB 82*
Tawas Herald - Tawas City, MI - *AyerDirPub 83; Ed&PubIntYB 82; NewsDir 84*
Tax Advance Rulings [of QL Systems Ltd.] - Ottawa, ON, Canada - *CompReadDB 82; DataDirOnSer 84; DirOnDB Spring 84*
Tax Adviser, The - New York, NY - *MagIndMarPl 82-83*
Tax Analysts - Arlington, VA - *DataDirOnSer 84; EISS 5-84 Sup*
Tax CK/PRI - Statesville, NC - *MicrocomMPl 84; MicrocomSwDir 1*
Tax Facts for You [of Phoenix Communications Press Ltd.] - Phoenix, AZ - *LitMag&SmPr 83-84*
Tax Foundation Inc. - Washington, DC - *BoPubDir 4, 5*
Tax Notes Bulletin Service [of NewsNet Inc.] - Bryn Mawr, PA - *DataDirOnSer 84*
Tax Notes Bulletin Service - Arlington, VA - *DirOnDB Spring 84*
Tax Notes International [of NewsNet Inc.] - Bryn Mawr, PA - *DataDirOnSer 84*
Tax Notes International - Arlington, VA - *DirOnDB Spring 84*
Tax Notes Microfiche Data Base - Arlington, VA - *MicroMarPl 82-83*
Tax Notes Today [of NewsNet Inc.] - Bryn Mawr, PA - *DataDirOnSer 84*
Tax Notes Today - Arlington, VA - *DirOnDB Spring 84*
Tax Reform Research Group [Aff. of Ralph Nader's Public Citizen] - Washington, DC - *BoPubDir 4, 5*
Tax Research Institute of America Inc., The [Subs. of The Lawyers Co-Operative Publishing Co.] - New York, NY - *DirMarMP 83*
Tax Review - Washington, DC - *MagIndMarPl 82-83*
Tax Shelter Insider - Boca Raton, FL - *DirOnDB Spring 84*
Tax Shelter Insider - New York, NY - *BaconPubCkMag 84*
Tax Shelter Insider [of NewsNet Inc.] - Bryn Mawr, PA - *DataDirOnSer 84*
Tax Shelter Monitor - New York, NY - *MagIndMarPl 82-83*
Taxada Community TV Association - Vananda, BC, Canada - *BrCabYB 84*

Taxation Canada - Ottawa, ON, Canada - *CompReadDB 82*
Taxcalc Inc. - Ft. Worth, TX - *MicrocomMPl 84*
Taxes Interpreted [of NewsNet Inc.] - Bryn Mawr, PA - *DataDirOnSer 84*
Taxi Drivers Voice - New York, NY - *NewsDir 84*
Taxicab Management - Rockville, MD - *MagDir 84*
Taxicab Management - Asheville, NC - *BaconPubCkMag 84*
Taxx Inc. - Metairie, LA - *ADAPSOMemDir 83-84*
Taylor Advertising - Tucson, AZ - *AdAge 3-28-84; StaDirAdAg 2-84*
Taylor Advertising Agency - Amarillo, TX - *StaDirAdAg 2-84*
Taylor & Associates - San Francisco, CA - *FBInfSer 80*
Taylor & Associates Inc. - Tampa, FL - *DirPRFirms 83*
Taylor & Co. - Los Angeles, CA - *StaDirAdAg 2-84*
Taylor & Co., Jon - Bountiful, UT - *Ed&PubIntYB 82*
Taylor & Francis Inc. - New York, NY - *LitMarPl 84*
Taylor & Francis Ltd. - London, England - *MicroMarPl 82-83*
Taylor & Friends, Sally - San Francisco, CA - *BoPubDir 4 Sup, 5*
Taylor & Ng - Brisbane, CA - *LitMarPl 83*
Taylor & Ng [Subs. of Environmental Ceramics Inc.] - Fairfield, CA - *LitMarPl 84*
Taylor Audio-Visual Inc. - Huron, SD - *AvMarPl 83*
Taylor Brown & Barnhill Inc. - Houston, TX - *StaDirAdAg 2-84*
Taylor-Carlisle Book Co. - New York, NY - *LitMarPl 83, 84*
Taylor, Charles D. & Georgeanne L. - Manchester-by-the-Sea, MA - *LitMarPl 84*
Taylor Clarion - *See* Burwell Newspapers
Taylor Clarion, The - Taylor, NE - *Ed&PubIntYB 82*
Taylor Communications Inc. - Seguin, TX - *Ed&PubIntYB 82*
Taylor County Tribune, The - Butler, GA - *Ed&PubIntYB 82*
Taylor Inc., Creed - New York, NY - *BillIntBG 83-84*
Taylor Interviewing Service - Augusta, GA - *IntDirMarRes 83*
Taylor James Ltd. - La Crescenta, CA - *BoPubDir 4 Sup, 5*
Taylor-Jessop Advertising Co. Inc. - Akron, OH - *TelAl 83, 84*
Taylor, John M. - New York, NY - *LitMarPl 83, 84; MagIndMarPl 82-83*
Taylor, Lillian - New York, NY - *Ed&PubIntYB 82*
Taylor-Merchant Corp. - New York, NY - *AvMarPl 83; DirInfWP 82*
Taylor Newspapers Inc. - Taylor, TX - *BaconPubCkNews 84*
Taylor Press - Taylor, TX - *BaconPubCkNews 84; Ed&PubIntYB 82*
Taylor Public Relations Inc., Alan - New York, NY - *DirPRFirms 83*
Taylor Publishers, Alister - Martinborough, New Zealand - *WritMar 84*
Taylor Publishing - Anacortes, WA - *BoPubDir 5*
Taylor Publishing Co. - Camp Point, IL - *BaconPubCkNews 84*
Taylor Publishing Co. [Subs. of Insilco] - Dallas, TX - *LitMarPl 83; WritMar 84*
Taylor Street Press - Fairfax, CA - *LitMag&SmPr 83-84*
Taylor/Teevan Advertising Inc. - San Francisco, CA - *StaDirAdAg 2-84*
Taylor Telephone Cooperative Inc. - Merkel, TX - *TelDir&BG 83-84*
Taylor Tribune [of Mellus Newspapers Inc.] - Lincoln Park, MI - *AyerDirPub 83; NewsDir 84*
Taylor Tribune - *See* Mellus Newspapers Inc.
Taylor Tribune, The - Taylor, MI - *Ed&PubIntYB 82*
Taylor TV Cable Co. - Taylor, TX - *BrCabYB 84; Tel&CabFB 84C*
Taylor, W. Thomas - Austin, TX - *BoPubDir 4 Sup, 5*
Taylor, William M. - San Anselmo, CA - *BoPubDir 4, 5*
Taylor Wilson Systems Ltd. - Solihull, England - *MicrocomSwDir 1*
Tayloreel Corp. - Rochester, NY - *AvMarPl 83*
Taylormade Software - Lincoln, NE - *MicrocomMPl 84*
Taylorsville CATV - Taylorsville, MS - *Tel&CabFB 84C*
Taylorsville Signal - Taylorsville, MS - *Ed&PubIntYB 82; NewsDir 84*
Taylorsville Signal - *See* Buckley Newspapers Inc.
Taylorsville Spencer Magnet - Taylorsville, KY - *BaconPubCkNews 84; Ed&PubIntYB 82*
Taylorsville Times - Taylorsville, NC - *BaconPubCkNews 84; Ed&PubIntYB 82; NewsDir 84*
Taylorville Breeze-Courier - Taylorville, IL - *BaconPubCkNews 84; Ed&PubIntYB 82; NewsDir 84*
Tayson Information Technology Inc. - Calgary, AB, Canada - *EISS 7-83 Sup; VideoDir 82-83*
Tayu Press [Aff. of Tayu Order Inc.] - Santa Rosa, CA - *BoPubDir 4, 5*
Taz-Wood North Today - Washington, IL - *AyerDirPub 83; Ed&PubIntYB 82*
Tazewell Claiborne Progress - Tazewell, TN - *BaconPubCkNews 84*
Tazewell Clinch Valley News - Tazewell, VA - *BaconPubCkNews 84*
Tazewell News - Morton, IL - *AyerDirPub 83; Ed&PubIntYB 82*
Tazewell Publishing Co. - Morton, IL - *BaconPubCkNews 84*
Tazewell Reporter - Washington, IL - *AyerDirPub 83; Ed&PubIntYB 82*
Tazewell South Today - Morton, IL - *AyerDirPub 83*
Tazewell South Today - Southern Tazewell County, IL - *Ed&PubIntYB 82*
Tazmanian Music - *See* Hat Band Music
T.B.N. Enterprises - Alexandria, VA - *BoPubDir 4, 5*
TBS Computer Centers Corp. - New York, NY - *IntDirMarRes 83*
TBW Books - Woolwich, ME - *BoPubDir 4, 5; LitMag&SmPr 83-84*
TBWA Advertising - New York, NY - *AdAge 3-28-84, 6-25-84; StaDirAdAg 2-84*
TC Interface - Los Altos, CA - *BaconPubCkMag 84*
TCA Cable [of TCA Cable TV Inc.] - Norman, AR - *Tel&CabFB 84C*
TCA Cable TV Inc. - Mena, AR - *Tel&CabFB 84C*
TCA Cable TV Inc. - St. Martinville, LA - *Tel&CabFB 84C*
TCA Cable TV Inc. - Mineola, TX - *Tel&CabFB 84C*
TCA Cable TV Inc. - Sulphur Springs, TX - *Tel&CabFB 84C*
TCA Cable TV Inc. - Tyler, TX - *BrCabYB 84 p.D-308; CabTVFinDB 83; Tel&CabFB 84C p.1705*
TCA Group - Tyler, TX - *LitMarPl 84*
TCD Inc. - Bryan, TX - *MicrocomMPl 83, 84*
TCI Advertising - Stamford, CT - *AdAge 3-28-84*
TCI Cable TV [of Tele-Communications Inc.] - Burley, ID - *BrCabYB 84*
TCI Cable TV [of Tele-Communications Inc.] - Shawnee Mission, KS - *BrCabYB 84*
TCI Cable TV [of Tele-Communications Inc.] - Brighton, MI - *Tel&CabFB 84C*
TCI Cablevision Inc. [of Tele-Communications Inc.] - Titusville, FL - *BrCabYB 84; Tel&CabFB 84C*
TCI Cablevision Inc. [of Tele-Communications Inc.] - Huntsville, MO - *BrCabYB 84*
TCI Cablevision Inc. [of Tele-Communications Inc.] - Jefferson City, MO - *BrCabYB 84*
TCI Cablevision Inc. [of Tele-Communications Inc.] - Moberly, MO - *BrCabYB 84; Tel&CabFB 84C*
TCI Cablevision Inc. [of Tele-Communications Inc.] - Richland County, SC - *BrCabYB 84; Tel&CabFB 84C*
TCI Cablevision of Mt. Airy [of Tele-Communications Inc.] - Mt. Airy, NC - *Tel&CabFB 84C*
TCI-Development Inc. - Denver, CO - *Tel&CabFB 84C p.1705*
TCI Growth Inc. - De Soto, CO - *BrCabYB 84*
TCI-Growth Inc. - Denver, CO - *Tel&CabFB 84C p.1705*
TCI Growth Inc. [of Tele-Communications Inc.] - Alton, IL - *BrCabYB 84; Tel&CabFB 84C*
TCI Growth Inc. - Bonner Springs, KS - *BrCabYB 84*
TCI Growth Inc. - Gardner, KS - *BrCabYB 84*
TCI Growth Inc. - Kansas City, KS - *BrCabYB 84*
TCI Growth Inc. [of Tele-Communications Inc.] - Grandview, MO - *Tel&CabFB 84C*
TCI Growth Inc. [of Tele-Communications Inc.] - Gassaway, WV - *BrCabYB 84*
TCI Growth Inc. - Summersville, WV - *BrCabYB 84*
TCI Growth Inc. [of Tele-Commuications Inc.] - Weston, WV - *Tel&CabFB 84C*
TCI Growth Inc. - *See* Tele-Communications Inc.
T.C.I. Mt. Vernon Inc. [of Horizon Communications Corp.] - Mt. Vernon, IN - *Tel&CabFB 84C*
TCI Oceanside Cable TV [of Tele-Communications Inc.] - Oceanside, CA - *BrCabYB 84*

TCI of Maryland Inc. [of Tele-Communications Inc.] - Cumberland, MD - *Tel&CabFB 84C*
TCI of West Virginia Inc. [of Tele-Communications Inc.] - Parkersburg, WV - *Tel&CabFB 84C*
TCI Pacifica Corp. [of Tele-Communications Inc.] - Pacifica, CA - *BrCabYB 84*
TCI Pacifica Corp. - *See* Tele-Communications Inc.
TCI Pomona Cable TV [of TCI-Taft Cablevision Associates] - Pomona, CA - *BrCabYB 84; Tel&CabFB 84C*
TCI Software - Flourtown, PA - *MicrocomMPl 84; MicrocomSwDir 1*
TCI-Sunnyvale Cable TV [of Tele-Communications Inc.] - Sunnyvale, CA - *BrCabYB 84*
TCI-Taft Cablevision Associates - Denver, CO - *BrCabYB 84 p.D-308*
TCI-Taft Cablevision Associates - Barnstable, MA - *BrCabYB 84*
TCI-Taft Cablevision Associates - Brighton, MI - *BrCabYB 84*
TCI-Taft Cablevision Associates - Cheboygan, MI - *Tel&CabFB 84C*
TCI-Taft Cablevision Associates - Montrose, MI - *BrCabYB 84*
TCI-Taft Cablevision Associates - Muskegon, MI - *Tel&CabFB 84C p.1705*
TCI-Taft Cablevision Associates - Newberry, MI - *Tel&CabFB 84C*
TCI-Taft Cablevision Associates - Petoskey, MI - *Tel&CabFB 84C*
TCI-Taft Cablevision Associates - Ypsilanti, MI - *BrCabYB 84; Tel&CabFB 84C*
TCI-Taft Cablevision Associates Inc. - St. Joseph, MI - *BrCabYB 84*
TCIC of Texas Inc. - West, TX - *BrCabYB 84*
TCID of Texas Inc. [of Tele-Communications Inc.] - Clifton, TX - *BrCabYB 84*
TCP Business Systems [Subs. of Azcar Technologies Inc.] - Toronto, ON, Canada - *WhoWMicrocom 83*
TCR Service Inc. - Englewood Cliffs, NJ - *CompReadDB 82; EISS 83; FBInfSer 80; InfIndMarPl 83*
TCS Communications Consultants [of TCS Management Group Inc.] - Nashville, TN - *TeleSy&SerDir 7-83*
TCS Software - Houston, TX - *MicrocomMPl 83, 84; MicrocomSwDir 1; WhoWMicrocom 83*
TDC - Riverton, WY - *MicrocomMPl 83*
TDK Electronics - Port Washington, NY - *AvMarPl 83; HomeVid&CabYB 82-83*
TDM Advertising Inc. - Oak Brook, IL - *StaDirAdAg 2-84*
TDS Engineering Co. - Carthage, MO - *Tel&CabFB 84C*
Te-Cum-Tom Enterprises - Coos Bay, OR - *BoPubDir 4, 5*
TE Enterprises Inc. - Carlstadt, NJ - *LitMarPl 83, 84*
Tea & Coffee Trade Journal - Whitestone, NY - *BaconPubCkMag 84; MagDir 84*
Tea Garden Press [Aff. of Randolph & Claudia Laub Studio & Workshop] - Los Angeles, CA - *BoPubDir 4 Sup, 5*
Tea Jar Music - *See* Terrace Music Group Inc.
Tea Rose Press - East Lansing, MI - *BoPubDir 5*
TEAC Corp. of America - Montebello, CA - *MicrocomMPl 84; WhoWMicrocom 83*
Teach Yourself by Computer Software - Geneseo, NY - *MicrocomSwDir 1; WhoWMicrocom 83*
Teach Yourself by Computer Software - Pittsford, NY - *MicrocomMPl 84*
Teacher Advocate - Indianapolis, IN - *MagDir 84*
Teacher Book Club [of Macmillan Book Clubs Inc.] - New York, NY - *LitMarPl 83, 84*
Teacher Feature - Spring Valley, NY - *Ed&PubIntYB 82*
Teacher Magazine - Stamford, CT - *MagDir 84*
Teacher Support Software - Gainesville, FL - *MicrocomMPl 84*
Teacher Tested Materials - Putnam, IL - *BoPubDir 4 Sup, 5*
Teacher Update - Saddle River, NJ - *BoPubDir 4, 5; LitMag&SmPr 83-84; WritMar 84*
Teachers & Writers Collaborative - New York, NY - *BoPubDir 4, 5; LitMag&SmPr 83-84*
Teachers & Writers Magazine [of Teachers & Writers Collaborative] - New York, NY - *LitMag&SmPr 83-84*
Teachers College Press [of Columbia University] - New York, NY - *LitMarPl 83, 84; WritMar 84*
Teacher's Pet Software - Berkeley, CA - *MicrocomSwDir 1*
Teacher's Pet Software - Livermore, CA - *MicrocomMPl 84*
Teachers Tax Service - Newport Beach, CA - *BoPubDir 4, 5*
Teacher's Voice - East Lansing, MI - *BaconPubCkMag 84; MagDir 84*
Teaching Aids Inc. - Costa Mesa, CA - *AvMarPl 83*
Teaching & Computers - New York, NY - *BaconPubCkMag 84*
Teaching Assistant, The - Huntington Station, NY - *MicrocomMPl 83, 84; MicrocomSwDir 1; WhoWMicrocom 83*
Teaching Electronics & Computing - Toronto, ON, Canada - *WritMar 84*
Teaching Exceptional Children - Reston, VA - *MagDir 84*
Teaching Films Inc. - Dallas, TX - *AvMarPl 83*
Teaching, Learning, Computing - Placenta, CA - *BaconPubCkMag 84*
Teaching Resources Corp. [Aff. of The New York Times] - Hingham, MA - *LitMarPl 83, 84*
Teaching Systems Inc. - Dallas, TX - *AvMarPl 83*
Teaching Tools: Microcomputer Services - Palo Alto, CA - *MicrocomMPl 83, 84*
Teague Chronicle - Teague, TX - *BaconPubCkNews 84; Ed&PubIntYB 82*
Teal & Watt Literary Agency - Fullerton, CA - *LitMarPl 83, 84*
Tealtronic of America Inc. [Subs. of National Unltd. Business Systems Inc.] - New York, NY - *WhoWMicrocom 83*
Team Records [Div. of Team Entertainment Corp.] - Philadelphia, PA - *BillIntBG 83-84*
Teaman/Lehman Associates Inc. - Norwalk, CT - *IntDirMarRes 83*
Teaneck News - Teaneck, NJ - *AyerDirPub 83; Ed&PubIntYB 82*
Teaneck Suburbanite - Cresskill, NJ - *AyerDirPub 83*
Tear Drop Record Co. - San Antonio, TX - *BillIntBG 83-84*
Teardrop Music - Nashville, TN - *BillIntBG 83-84*
Tebo, Jay D. - Vestal, NY - *FBInfSer 80*
TEC America Inc. - Torrance, CA - *DataDirSup 7-83*
Tec Inc. - Tucson, AZ - *DataDirSup 7-83; InfIndMarPl 83; WhoWMicrocom 83*
T.E.C. Inc. - Fullerton, CA - *BoPubDir 4, 5*
TEC Measures Inc. - New York, NY - *HBIndAd&MS 82-83*
TEC/West - Los Angeles, CA - *AvMarPl 83*
Tecfilms Inc. - Dallas, TX - *AvMarPl 83*
Tech Briefs [of National Research Council Canada] - Ottawa, ON, Canada - *CompReadDB 82*
Tech Center News - Detroit, MI - *AyerDirPub 83*
Tech Center News [of Monday Morning Newspapers Inc.] - Warren, MI - *NewsDir 84*
Tech Designs Inc. - Ellicott City, MD - *MicrocomMPl 84*
Tech Extra [of Policy Studies Corp.] - Springfield, VA - *DataDirOnSer 84*
Tech-Net [of Information Handling Services] - Englewood, CO - *CompReadDB 82; DataDirOnSer 84; DBBus 82; EISS 83*
Tech/Ops Inc. - *See* McCormick Communications Inc.
Tech/Services Inc. - Oshkosh, WI - *AvMarPl 83*
Tech Street Journal - Chelmsford, MA - *BaconPubCkMag 84*
Tech, The - Cambridge, MA - *NewsDir 84*
Tech Weekly - Sharon, MA - *BaconPubCkMag 84*
Techcom Enterprises - Lawndale, CA - *MicrocomMPl 84*
Teche News - St. Martin Parish, LA - *Ed&PubIntYB 82*
Teche News - St. Martinville, LA - *AyerDirPub 83*
Techkits Inc. - Demarest, NJ - *BoPubDir 4, 5*
Techland Systems Inc. - New York, NY - *MicrocomMPl 84*
Techline - Arlington, TX - *DirOnDB Spring 84*
Techna Type Inc. - York, PA - *LitMarPl 84*
Technassociates Inc. - Rockville, MD - *DataDirOnSer 84*
Techne - Princeton, NJ - *AvMarPl 83*
Techne Software Corp. - Lafayette, CA - *MicrocomMPl 84; MicrocomSwDir 1*
Technell Inc. - Stamford, CT - *LitMarPl 83, 84*
Technet [of Association for Educational Communications & Technology] - Washington, DC - *TeleSy&SerDir 2-84*
Technical Advisors Inc. - Wayne, MI - *DataDirOnSer 84; DataDirSup 7-83*
Technical Analysis & Communications Inc. - Teaneck, NJ - *IntDirMarRes 83*
Technical Analysis Corp. - Atlanta, GA - *DataDirSup 7-83*
Technical Analysis Group, The - New Orleans, LA - *MicrocomMPl 83, 84*
Technical Analysis of Stocks & Commodities - Seattle, WA - *WritMar 84*

Technical Communication Journal [of The Society for Technical Communication] - Washington, DC - *BaconPubCkMag 84; MagDir 84*
Technical Communications Associates - Stevensville, MI - *LitMarPl 84*
Technical Communications Corp. - Concord, MA - *DataDirSup 7-83*
Technical Data - Boston, MA - *DirOnDB Spring 84; MicrocomSwDir 1*
Technical Data Center [of U.S. Dept. of Labor] - Washington, DC - *EISS 7-83 Sup*
Technical Data Management Center [of U.S. Dept. of Energy] - Oak Ridge, TN - *EISS 83*
Technical Database Corp. - Conroe, TX - *EISS 5-84 Sup*
Technical Directions Inc. - West Lafayette, IN - *BoPubDir 4, 5*
Technical Documentation Services - Santa Barbara, CA - *BoPubDir 4, 5*
Technical Economics Inc. - Berkeley, CA - *EISS 5-84 Sup*
Technical Education Press - Seal Beach, CA - *BoPubDir 4, 5*
Technical Educational Consultants - Plainview, NY - *AvMarPl 83*
Technical Help to Exporters [of British Standards Institution] - Hemel Hempstead, England - *EISS 83; InfIndMarPl 83*
Technical Impex Corp. - Lawrence, MA - *LitMarPl 83, 84*
Technical Indexes Ltd. - Bracknell, England - *EISS 83*
Technical Industries Inc. - Nashville, TN - *AvMarPl 83*
Technical Industries Inc. of Georgia - Atlanta, GA - *AvMarPl 83*
Technical Information & Library Services [of Depts. of the Environment & Transport] - Crowthorne, England - *EISS 83*
Technical Information Branch [of Atomic Energy of Canada Ltd.] - Chalk River, ON, Canada - *EISS 83*
Technical Information Center [of Union Oil Co. of California] - Brea, CA - *EISS 83*
Technical Information Center [of Lockheed Corp.] - Burbank, CA - *EISS 83*
Technical Information Center [of U.S. Public Health Service] - Rockville, MD - *EISS 83*
Technical Information Center [of U.S. Army] - Vicksburg, MS - *EISS 83*
Technical Information Center [of Xerox Corp.] - Webster, NY - *EISS 83*
Technical Information Center [of North Carolina State University Library] - Raleigh, NC - *EISS 83*
Technical Information Center [of University of Puerto Rico] - Mayaguez, PR - *EISS 83*
Technical Information Center [of U.S. Dept. of Energy] - Oak Ridge, TN - *EISS 83*
Technical Information Center - Frankfurt, West Germany - *EISS 83*
Technical Information Centre [of Bell-Northern Research] - Ottawa, ON, Canada - *EISS 83*
Technical Information Dept. [of Lockheed Corp.] - Marietta, GA - *EISS 83*
Technical Information Dept. [of Burroughs Wellcome Co.] - Research Triangle Park, NC - *EISS 83*
Technical Information Dept. Libraries [of University of California] - Livermore, CA - *EISS 83*
Technical Information Div. [of Romar Consultants Inc.] - Philadelphia, PA - *EISS 83*
Technical Information Div. [of National Atomic Energy Commission] - Buenos Aires, Argentina - *EISS 83*
Technical Information Div. [of Japan Atomic Energy Research Institute] - Tokyo, Japan - *EISS 83*
Technical Information-Documentation Consultants Ltd. - Montreal, PQ, Canada - *EISS 83*
Technical Information Processing System [of Rockwell International Corp.] - Downey, CA - *EISS 83*
Technical Information Project Inc. - Washington, DC - *BoPubDir 4, 5*
Technical Information Section [of Pulp & Paper Research Institute of Canada] - Pointe Claire, PQ, Canada - *EISS 83*
Technical Information Service [of American Institute of Aeronautics & Astronautics] - New York, NY - *EISS 83*
Technical Information Service [of Organisation for Economic Co-Operation & Development] - London, England - *EISS 83*
Technical Information Service [of Technical Research Centre of Finland] - Espoo, Finland - *EISS 83*
Technical Information Service [of Finnish Pulp & Paper Research Institute] - Helsinki, Finland - *EISS 83*
Technical Information Service [of Caribbean Industrial Research Institute] - Trinidad - *EISS 83*
Technical Information Services [of Acurex Corp.] - Mountain View, CA - *EISS 83*
Technical Information Services [of Institute of Gas Technology] - Chicago, IL - *EISS 83*
Technical Information Services [of Electromagnetic Compatibility Analysis Center] - Annapolis, MD - *EISS 83*
Technical Information Services [of Atomic Energy of Canada Ltd.] - Pinawa, MB, Canada - *EISS 83*
Technical Libraries [of Boeing Inc.] - Seattle, WA - *EISS 83*
Technical Library Div. [of U.S. Navy] - Dahlgren, VA - *EISS 83*
Technical Library Service - New York, NY - *EISS 83; FBInfSer 80; InfIndMarPl 83; ProGuPRSer 4*
Technical Marketing Associates Inc. - Sudbury, MA - *IntDirMarRes 83*
Technical Marketing Services Inc. - New York, NY - *WhoWMicrocom 83*
Technical Photography - Hempstead, NY - *MagDir 84*
Technical Photography - Woodbury, NY - *BaconPubCkMag 84; MagIndMarPl 82-83; WritMar 84*
Technical Products Co. - Boone, NC - *MicrocomMPl 83*
Technical Publishing [Div. of Dun & Bradstreet Corp.] - New York, NY - *LitMarPl 83, 84; MagIndMarPl 82-83*
Technical Publishing Co. [Div. of Dun & Bradstreet Corp.] - Barrington, IL - *DirMarMP 83*
Technical Reference Branch [of U.S. Dept. of Transportation] - Washington, DC - *EISS 83*
Technical Reports [of Defense Technical Information Center] - Alexandria, VA - *DataDirOnSer 84*
Technical Reports Database - Alexandria, VA - *DirOnDB Spring 84*
Technical Research Services Inc. - Tulsa, OK - *MicrocomMPl 84*
Technical Services [of Baker & Taylor Co.] - Somerville, NJ - *EISS 83*
Technical Services - New York, NY - *LitMarPl 83, 84; MagIndMarPl 82-83*
Technical Services Div. [of Blackwell North America Inc.] - Lake Oswego, OR - *EISS 83*
Technical Software Centre [Subs. of Bhra Fluid Engineering] - Cranfield, England - *WhoWMicrocom 83*
Technical Software Inc. - Metairie, LA - *MicrocomSwDir 1; WhoWMicrocom 83*
Technical Software Systems - Freehold, NJ - *MicrocomMPl 84*
Technical Software Systems - Shrewsbury, NJ - *MicrocomMPl 83*
Technical Systems Consultants Inc. - West Lafayette, IN - *WhoWMicrocom 83*
Technical University of Nova Scotia (Tech-Press) - Halifax, NS, Canada - *BoPubDir 4 Sup, 5*
Technical University of Wroclaw (Biblioteka Glowna) - Wroclaw, Poland - *CompReadDB 82*
Technician [of North Carolina State University] - Raleigh, NC - *NewsDir 84*
Technico Inc. - Columbia, MD - *WhoWMicrocom 83*
Technicolor Audio Visual [Div. of Technicolor Inc.] - Costa Mesa, CA - *AvMarPl 83*
Technicolor Inc. - Los Angeles, CA - *HomeVid&CabYB 82-83*
Technicolor-Vidtronics Div. [of Technicolor Inc.] - Hollywood, CA - *AvMarPl 83*
Technicraft Inc. [Div. of Jackson Industries Inc.] - Columbia, SC - *AvMarPl 83*
Technics - Secaucus, NJ - *BillIntBG 83-84*
Technimetrics Inc. - New York, NY - *ProGuPRSer 4*
Technique - Port Angeles, WA - *MicrocomMPl 83*
Technique for Report & Index Management [of University of California, Riverside] - Riverside, CA - *EISS 83*
Technique Learning Corp. - Dobbs Ferry, NY - *ADAPSOMemDir 83-84*
Technique Learning Corp. - Freeport, NY - *BoPubDir 4, 5*
Techniques in Wood - Rochester, NY - *DirInfWP 82*
Technisonic Studios Inc. - St. Louis, MO - *AvMarPl 83; Tel&CabFB 84C*
Technivisuals Group Inc., The - Douglaston, NY - *ArtMar 84*
Techno-Search - Tokyo, Japan - *DirOnDB Spring 84*

Technobank Program [of Technology Resource Center] - Manila, Philippines - *EISS 5-84 Sup*
Technocracy Inc. - Savannah, OH - *BoPubDir 4, 5*
Technological Developments Section [of Techical Information Service, National Research Council Canada] - Ottawa, ON, Canada - *CompReadDB 82*
Technology & Business Communications Inc. - Sudbury, MA - *EISS 7-83 Sup*
Technology & Conservation of Art, Architecture & Antiquities [of The Technology Organization Inc.] - Boston, MA - *BaconPubCkMag 84; MagDir 84; MagIndMarPl 82-83*
Technology & Information Transfer [of U.S. Dept. of the Interior] - Washington, DC - *InfIndMarPl 83*
Technology Application Center [of University of New Mexico] - Albuquerque, NM - *EISS 83; InfIndMarPl 83*
Technology Assessment & Forecast Reports Data Base [of U.S. Patent & Trademark Office] - Washington, DC - *EISS 83*
Technology Catalysts Inc. - Arlington, VA - *EISS 7-83 Sup*
Technology Catalysts Inc. - Falls Church, VA - *DataDirOnSer 84*
Technology Communications Group, The - Montclair, NJ - *DirPRFirms 83*
Technology Concepts Inc. - Sudbury, MA - *TeleSy&SerDir 2-84*
Technology Consulting Corp. - Hartford, CT - *WhoWMicrocom 83*
Technology Database [of Policy Studies Corp.] - Springfield, VA - *DataDirOnSer 84*
Technology Forecasts - Beverly Hills, CA - *BaconPubCkMag 84*
Technology Group - Pasadena, CA - *BoPubDir 4, 5*
Technology Group Inc. - Lincoln, NE - *ADAPSOMemDir 83-84*
Technology Illustrated [of Goldhirsh Group Inc.] - Boston, MA - *BaconPubCkMag 84; Folio 83; WritMar 84*
Technology Index for Plasma Physics Research & Fusion [of Max Planck Institut fur Plasmaphysik] - Munich, West Germany - *CompReadDB 82*
Technology Information Div. [of Canada Centre for Mineral & Energy Technology] - Ottawa, ON, Canada - *EISS 83*
Technology Information System [of University of California] - Livermore, CA - *EISS 83*
Technology International Corp. - Orlando, FL - *DirInfWP 82; MicrocomMPl 84*
Technology Management Inc. - Chestnut Hill, MA - *BoPubDir 4, 5*
Technology Marketing Group Ltd. - Des Plaines, IL - *BoPubDir 5; IntDirMarRes 83*
Technology New York - Troy, NY - *BaconPubCkMag 84; MagDir 84*
Technology News of America - New York, NY - *BaconPubCkMag 84*
Technology Press Inc. - Fairfax Station, VA - *BoPubDir 4, 5*
Technology Reports Centre (Dialtech Unit) - *See* IRS Dialtech
Technology Review [of M.I.T. Alumni Association] - Cambridge, MA - *ArtMar 84; BaconPubCkMag 84; DirMarMP 83; MagDir 84; MagIndMarPl 82-83; WritMar 84*
Technology Service Corp. (Commercial Services Div.) - Santa Monica, CA - *Tel&CabFB 84C*
Technology Solutions Corp. - Malibu, CA - *MicrocomMPl 84*
Technology Systems Inc. - Bethel, CT - *MicrocomMPl 84; WhoWMicrocom 83*
Technology Teacher, The - Reston, VA - *BaconPubCkMag 84*
Technology Transfer Data Bank [of California State University] - Sacramento, CA - *EISS 83*
Technology Transfer Div. [of Waste Management Branch, Environmental Protection Service] - Ottawa, ON, Canada - *CompReadDB 82*
Technology Transfer Institute - Santa Monica, CA - *TeleSy&SerDir 7-83*
Technology Transfer News - Washington, DC - *BaconPubCkMag 84*
Technology Trends Newsletter - Scottsdale, AZ - *BaconPubCkMag 84*
Technology Update [of Predicasts Information Corp.] - Cleveland, OH - *BaconPubCkMag 84; MagDir 84*
Technology Watch [of Policy Studies Corp.] - Springfield, VA - *BaconPubCkMag 84; DataDirOnSer 84*
Technomic Consultants - Chicago, IL - *IntDirMarRes 83*
Technomic Publishing Co. Inc. - Westport, CT - *LitMarPl 83; MagIndMarPl 82-83*
Technomic Publishing Co. Inc. - Lancaster, PA - *LitMarPl 84*
Technotec [of Control Data Corp.] - Minneapolis, MN - *CompReadDB 82; DataDirOnSer 84; DBBus 82; DirOnDB Spring 84; EISS 83*
Technovations - Portland, OR - *AvMarPl 83*
Techscience Inc. - Hawthorne, CA - *BoPubDir 4, 5*
TechSearch - Arvada, CO - *EISS 5-84 Sup; InfIndMarPl 83*
TechSearch - Lakewood, CO - *FBInfSer 80*
Techtran Industries Inc. - Rochester, NY - *WhoWMicrocom 83*
TechType Graphics [Div. of HRM Enterprises Inc.] - Moorestown, NJ - *LitMarPl 83, 84; MagIndMarPl 82-83*
Techware - Eugene, OR - *MicrocomMPl 84; MicrocomSwDir 1*
Teck Associates - White Bear Lake, MN - *MicrocomMPl 83, 84; MicrocomSwDir 1; WhoWMicrocom 83*
Teck Color Lab - Boston, MA - *AvMarPl 83*
Tecmar Inc. - Cleveland, OH - *MicrocomMPl 84; WhoWMicrocom 83*
Tecnomedia - Udine, Italy - *EISS 83*
Tecolote Press Inc. - Glenwood, NM - *BoPubDir 4, 5*
Tecsi Software - Paris, France - *ADAPSOMemDir 83-84*
Tecstor Inc. - Huntington Beach, CA - *DataDirSup 7-83*
Tectonics Productions - Edmonds, WA - *EISS 5-84 Sup*
Tecumseh Chieftain - Tecumseh, NE - *BaconPubCkNews 84; Ed&PubIntYB 82*
Tecumseh County-Wide News - Tecumseh, OK - *BaconPubCkNews 84; Ed&PubIntYB 82*
Tecumseh Herald - Tecumseh, MI - *BaconPubCkNews 84; Ed&PubIntYB 82; NewsDir 84*
Tecumseh Press Ltd. - Ottawa, ON, Canada - *BoPubDir 4 Sup, 5*
TED - Luxembourg - *DirOnDB Spring 84*
T.E.D. Associates - Needham Heights, MA - *BoPubDir 4, 5*
Teddy Jack Music - Hendersonville, TN - *BillIntBG 83-84*
Tedesco Music, Dale - Northridge, CA - *BillIntBG 83-84*
Tedesco Tunes - *See* Tedesco Music, Dale
Tee Girl Music Publishing - *See* Lipservices
Teen [of Petersen Publishing Co.] - Los Angeles, CA - *ArtMar 84; BaconPubCkMag 84; Folio 83; LitMarPl 84; MagDir 84; MagIndMarPl 82-83; NewsBur 6*
Teen Age Book Club [of Scholastic Book Services] - New York, NY - *LitMarPl 83, 84*
Teen-age Research Unltd. - Lake Forest, IL - *BrCabYB 84*
Teen Beat - New York, NY - *BaconPubCkMag 84; MagDir 84; MagIndMarPl 82-83*
Teen Generation - Toronto, ON, Canada - *BaconPubCkMag 84*
Teen Magazine - Hollywood, CA - *WritMar 84*
Teen Power [of SP Ministries] - Glen Ellyn, IL - *WritMar 84*
Teen Times - Washington, DC - *MagIndMarPl 82-83*
Teenage - Lowell, MA - *MagDir 84*
Teenage Corner Inc. - Rancho Mirage, CA - *Ed&PubIntYB 82*
Teens & Boys [of Larkin Publications] - New York, NY - *BaconPubCkMag 84; MagDir 84; MagIndMarPl 82-83; WritMar 84*
Teens Today [of Church of the Nazarene] - Kansas City, MO - *ArtMar 84; WritMar 84*
Teepee Creek Stampede Historical Society - Sexsmith, AB, Canada - *BoPubDir 4 Sup, 5*
Teeswater News - Teeswater, ON, Canada - *Ed&PubIntYB 82*
Tehachapi News - Tehachapi, CA - *BaconPubCkNews 84; Ed&PubIntYB 82; NewsDir 84*
Tehachapi TV Cable [of American TV & Communications Corp.] - Arvin, CA - *BrCabYB 84; Tel&CabFB 84C*
Tehachapi TV Cable [of American Television & Communications Corp.] - Tehachapi, CA - *BrCabYB 84*
Teikoku Data Bank Ltd. - Tokyo, Japan - *EISS 5-84 Sup*
Tejas Art Press - San Antonio, TX - *BoPubDir 4, 5; LitMag&SmPr 83-84*
Tek-Com Inc. - San Jose, CA - *DataDirSup 7-83*
Tek Translation & International Print Inc. - New York, NY - *LitMarPl 84*
Tek Translation & International Print Inc. - Houston, TX - *LitMarPl 83; MagIndMarPl 82-83*
Tekamah Burt County Plaindealer - Tekamah, NE - *BaconPubCkNews 84*
Tekelec Inc. - Santa Monica, CA - *DataDirSup 7-83*
Tekkom Inc. - San Diego, CA - *Tel&CabFB 84C*
Teknifilm Inc. - Portland, OR - *AvMarPl 83*
Tekoa Standard Register - Tekoa, WA - *BaconPubCkNews 84*

Tekst-TV [of Danmarks Radio] - Soborg, Denmark - *VideoDir 82-83*
Tektronix Inc. - Beaverton, OR - *DataDirSup 7-83; Datamation 6-83; ElecNews 7-25-83; HomeVid&CabYB 82-83; Top100Al 83*
Tektronix Inc. - Wilsonville, OR - *MicrocomSwDir 1*
Tektronix Inc. (Information Display Div.) - Beaverton, OR - *InfIndMarPl 83; WhoWMicrocom 83*
Tektronix Inc. (Information Display Div.) - Wilsonville, OR - *WhoWMicrocom 83*
Tel-A-Cast Inc. - Aiken, SC - *Tel&CabFB 84C*
Tel-A-Data Inc. - Miami, FL - *DataDirOnSer 84; DataDirSup 7-83*
Tel-A-Train Inc. - Chattanooga, TN - *AvMarPl 83*
Tel-Air Interests Inc. - Miami, FL - *AvMarPl 83; WritMar 84*
Tel-Aire Publications Inc. - Dallas, TX - *Ed&PubIntYB 82*
Tel-Car Corp. - Englewood, NJ - *Tel&CabFB 84C*
Tel Com Highlights - Midland Park, NJ - *BaconPubCkMag 84*
Tel-Com Inc. - Harold, KY - *BrCabYB 84; Tel&CabFB 84C*
Tel-Com Inc. - Little Robinson, KY - *BrCabYB 84*
Tel-Com Inc. - Long Fork, KY - *BrCabYB 84*
Tel-Com Inc. - Blackberry City, WV - *BrCabYB 84*
Tel-Econ Consultants Inc. - Greenlawn, NY - *TeleSy&SerDir 7-83*
Tel Master - Deming, NM - *Tel&CabFB 84C*
Tel-Radio Communications Properties Inc. - Madison, WI - *Tel&CabFB 84C*
Tel-Share Telecommunications Inc. - Omaha, NE - *TeleSy&SerDir 2-84*
Tel-Star Cable Systems Inc. - Glen Ullin, ND - *Tel&CabFB 84C*
Tel-Star Cable Systems Inc. - Hebron, ND - *Tel&CabFB 84C*
Tel-Tech Cable TV Inc. - Ashland, ME - *BrCabYB 84*
Tel-Tech Cable TV Inc. - Mapleton, ME - *BrCabYB 84*
Telaco Inc. [of Mid-Atlantic Network Inc.] - Front Royal, VA - *Tel&CabFB 84C*
Telaktiv Ltd. - New York, NY - *VideoDir 82-83*
Telamarketing Communications Inc. - Tampa, FL - *TeleSy&SerDir 2-84*
Telamon - San Francisco, CA - *BoPubDir 5*
Telarc Records - Cleveland, OH - *BillIntBG 83-84*
Telautaograph Corp. - Los Angeles, CA - *DirInfWP 82*
Telcab Communications Inc. - Reno, NV - *BrCabYB 84*
Telco Cablevision Inc. [of UltraCom Inc.] - Asbury Park, NJ - *BrCabYB 84*
Telco Cablevision Inc. - Ocean, NJ - *BrCabYB 84; Tel&CabFB 84C*
Telco Research Corp. - Nashville, TN - *TeleSy&SerDir 7-83*
Telco Strategies Inc. - New York, NY - *TeleSy&SerDir 7-83*
Telcom Engineering Inc. - Chesterfield, MO - *Tel&CabFB 84C p.1705*
Telcom Research [of Burke Marketing Services Inc.] - Teaneck, NJ - *HBIndAd&MS 82-83; IntDirMarRes 83*
Telcom Services Inc. - El Cajon, CA - *Tel&CabFB 84C p.1705*
Telcon Associates Inc. - Overland Park, KS - *TeleSy&SerDir 2-84*
Telcon Associates Inc. - Shawnee Mission, KS - *TeleSy&SerDir 7-83*
Telcon Industries Inc. - Ft. Lauderdale, FL - *WhoWMicrocom 83*
Tele-Cable Charlevoix Inc. - La Malbaie, PQ, Canada - *BrCabYB 84*
Tele Cable Enrg. - Ste. Marie, PQ, Canada - *BrCabYB 84; Tel&CabFB 84C*
Tele Cable Inc. - Leslie, MI - *BrCabYB 84*
Tele-Cable Inc. of Huntsville [of Community Tele-Communications Inc.] - Huntsville, TX - *BrCabYB 84; Tel&CabFB 84C*
Tele-Cable Sales Inc. - North Syracuse, NY - *CabTVPrDB 83*
Tele-Cable Service Corp. - Borrego Springs, CA - *BrCabYB 84; Tel&CabFB 84C*
Tele Cable St. Gregoire - Cap de la Madeliene, PQ, Canada - *BrCabYB 84*
Tele-Cable St. Hyacinthe Ltee. - St. Hyacinthe, PQ, Canada - *BrCabYB 84*
Tele-Cable St. Methode Engr. - St. Methode, PQ, Canada - *BrCabYB 84*
Tele-Capital Ltd. - Ste.-Foy, PQ, Canada - *BrCabYB 84*
Tele-Ception of Winchester Inc. [of Cable Information Systems Inc.] - Winchester, KY - *Tel&CabFB 84C*
Tele-Color Productions Inc. - Alexandria, VA - *AvMarPl 83; Tel&CabFB 84C*
Tele-Com Music - *See* Kenwon Music
Tele-Communications Inc. - Denver, CO - *AdAge 6-28-84; BrCabYB 84 p.D-308; CabTVFinDB 83; HomeVid&CabYB 82-83; KnowInd 83; LitMarPl 84; TelAl 83, 84; Tel&CabFB 84C p.1705*
Tele-Communications Inc. - Andover, KS - *BrCabYB 84*
Tele-Communications Inc. - Hesston, KS - *BrCabYB 84*
Tele-Communications Inc. - Hazelwood, MO - *BrCabYB 84*
Tele-Communications Inc. - Republic, MO - *Tel&CabFB 84C*
Tele-Communications Inc. - Bishop, TX - *Tel&CabFB 84C*
Tele-Communications Inc. - Cheyenne, WY - *Tel&CabFB 84C*
Tele-Communications of Key West - Key West, FL - *Tel&CabFB 84C*
Tele-Communications of Key West Inc. - Key Largo, FL - *BrCabYB 84*
Tele-Communications of South Suburbia Inc. - Chicago Heights, IL - *Tel&CabFB 84C*
Tele-Direct Ltd. - Toronto, ON, Canada - *EISS 83*
Tele-Direct Ltd. (Videotex Services Dept.) - Don Mills, ON, Canada - *VideoDir 82-83*
Tele-Edit Inc. - Minneapolis, MN - *AvMarPl 83*
Tele-Engineering Corp. - Framingham, MA - *TeleSy&SerDir 7-83*
Tele-Equip - Ft. Dodge, IA - *DirOnDB Spring 84*
Tele-Gestion - Loretteville, PQ, Canada - *TeleSy&SerDir 2-84*
Tele Graphics - Baldwin City, KS - *AyerDirPub 83*
Tele-Log - Atlanta, GA - *Ed&PubIntYB 82*
Tele-Measurements Inc. - Clifton, NJ - *AvMarPl 83*
Tele-Media Cable Co. [of Tele-Media Corp.] - Madison, FL - *Tel&CabFB 84C*
Tele-Media Cable of Greenup County [of Tele-Media ADDIL] - Boyd County, KY - *BrCabYB 84*
Tele-Media Co. of Addil - Calcutta, OH - *BrCabYB 84*
Tele-Media Co. of Addil - Columbiana, OH - *BrCabYB 84; Tel&CabFB 84C*
Tele-Media Co. of Addil - East Palestine, OH - *Tel&CabFB 84C*
Tele-Media Co. of Addil - Senecaville, OH - *BrCabYB 84; Tel&CabFB 84C*
Tele-Media Co. of Addil - Gallitzin, PA - *BrCabYB 84*
Tele-Media Co. of Addil - Pleasantville, PA - *BrCabYB 84*
Tele-Media Co. of Addil - Tionesta, PA - *BrCabYB 84; Tel&CabFB 84C*
Tele-Media Co. of Addil - Bethany, WV - *BrCabYB 84*
Tele-Media Co. of Addil Inc. - Adena, OH - *BrCabYB 84*
Tele-Media Co. of Addil Inc. - Island Creek Township, OH - *BrCabYB 84*
Tele-Media Co. of Addil Inc. - Maynard, OH - *BrCabYB 84*
Tele-Media Co. of Addil Inc. - Piney Fork, OH - *BrCabYB 84*
Tele-Media Co. of Addil Inc. - Emienton, PA - *BrCabYB 84*
Tele-Media Co. of Andover - Andover, OH - *BrCabYB 84*
Tele-Media Co. of Andover - Blooming Valley, PA - *BrCabYB 84*
Tele-Media Co. of Andover - Guys Mills, PA - *BrCabYB 84*
Tele-Media Co. of Cambria County - Carrolltown, PA - *Tel&CabFB 84C*
Tele-Media Co. of Central Pennsylvania - Central City, PA - *BrCabYB 84*
Tele-Media Co. of Darke County - New Madison, OH - *Tel&CabFB 84C*
Tele-Media Co. of Elberton [of Tele-Media Corp.] - Elberton, GA - *Tel&CabFB 84C*
Tele-Media Co. of Georgia - Elberton, GA - *BrCabYB 84*
Tele-Media Co. of Georgia - Homerville, GA - *BrCabYB 84*
Tele-Media Co. of Georgia - Jesup, GA - *BrCabYB 84; Tel&CabFB 84C*
Tele-Media Co. of Georgia - Sylvania, GA - *BrCabYB 84*
Tele-Media Co. of Georgia Ltd. - Washington, GA - *BrCabYB 84*
Tele-Media Co. of Homerville - Homerville, GA - *Tel&CabFB 84C*
Tele-Media Co. of Kent-Ravenna - Ravenna, OH - *BrCabYB 84; Tel&CabFB 84C*
Tele-Media Co. of Key West - Key West, FL - *Tel&CabFB 84C*
Tele-Media Co. of Kiski Valley - Saltsburg, PA - *BrCabYB 84*
Tele-Media Co. of Lake County - Concord Township, OH - *BrCabYB 84; Tel&CabFB 84C*
Tele-Media Co. of Lake Erie - Conneaut, OH - *BrCabYB 84; Tel&CabFB 84C*
Tele-Media Co. of Lake Erie - Geneva, OH - *BrCabYB 84; Tel&CabFB 84C*

Tele-Media Co. of Moshannon Valley - Philipsburg, PA - *Tel&CabFB 84C*
Tele-Media Co. of Paulding County - Dallas, GA - *BrCabYB 84; Tel&CabFB 84C*
Tele-Media Co. of Pennsylvania - Carrollton, PA - *Tel&CabFB 84C*
Tele-Media Co. of Pennsylvania - Dayton, PA - *BrCabYB 84*
Tele-Media Co. of Pennsylvania - Rural Valley, PA - *BrCabYB 84*
Tele-Media Co. of Port Clinton [of Tele-Media Co. of Ottawa County] - Port Clinton, OH - *BrCabYB 84; Tel&CabFB 84C*
Tele-Media Co. of Quitman - Quitman, GA - *Tel&CabFB 84C*
Tele-Media Co. of Ridgway - Brockport, PA - *BrCabYB 84*
Tele-Media Co. of Ridgway - Ridgway, PA - *BrCabYB 84; Tel&CabFB 84C*
Tele-Media Co. of Somerset County - Somerset, PA - *Tel&CabFB 84C*
Tele-Media Co. of Waynesboro - Waynesboro, GA - *Tel&CabFB 84C*
Tele-Media Co. of Waynesburg - Waynesburg, PA - *Tel&CabFB 84C*
Tele-Media Co. of West Virginia - Blacksville, WV - *BrCabYB 84*
Tele-Media Co. of West Virginia - Daybrook, WV - *BrCabYB 84*
Tele-Media Co. of West Virginia - Hundred, WV - *BrCabYB 84*
Tele-Media Co. of West Virginia - Littleton, WV - *BrCabYB 84*
Tele-Media Co. of West Virginia - Pentress, WV - *BrCabYB 84*
Tele-Media Co. of Western Ohio - Greenville, OH - *BrCabYB 84; Tel&CabFB 84C*
Tele-Media Corp. - Blue Ridge, GA - *Tel&CabFB 84C*
Tele-Media Corp. - Freeport, OH - *BrCabYB 84*
Tele-Media Corp. - Minerva, OH - *Tel&CabFB 84C*
Tele-Media Corp. - Millcreek Township, PA - *BrCabYB 84*
Tele-Media Corp. - Shippingport, PA - *BrCabYB 84*
Tele-Media Corp. - State College, PA - *BrCabYB 84 p.D-308; CabTVFinDB 83; LitMarPl 84; Tel&CabFB 84C p.1706*
Tele-Media Corp. - Newberry, SC - *Tel&CabFB 84C*
Tele-Media Corp. of Georgia - Hartwell, GA - *BrCabYB 84*
Tele-Media Corp. of Lake Erie - Ashtabula, OH - *BrCabYB 84; Tel&CabFB 84C*
Tele-Media Corp. of Lake Erie - East Palestine, OH - *BrCabYB 84*
Tele-Media Corp. of Ohio - Negley, OH - *BrCabYB 84*
Tele-Media Corp. of Ohio - New Waterford, OH - *BrCabYB 84*
Tele Media of Andover - Ashtabula, OH - *BrCabYB 84*
Tele Media of Andover - Linesville, PA - *BrCabYB 84*
Tele-Media of Mt. Union - Mt. Union, PA - *BrCabYB 84; Tel&CabFB 84C*
Tele-Media of Rittman - Rittman, OH - *Tel&CabFB 84C*
Tele-Missions International (Focus-on-Faith Series) - Nyack, NY - *Tel&CabFB 84C*
Tele-News - Baldwin City, KS - *AyerDirPub 83*
Tele-Press Associates - New York, NY - *DirPRFirms 83*
Tele-Quest WATS Marketing Services - Long Beach, NY - *IntDirMarRes 83*
Tele-Remote Systems - Lamesa, CA - *WhoWMicrocom 83*
Tele Research Inc. - Los Angeles, CA - *HBIndAd&MS 82-83*
Tele-Research Inc. - Westport, CT - *IntDirMarRes 83*
Tele/Resources - Armonk, NY - *DirInfWP 82*
Tele/Resources [Div. of Acton Corp.] - Ballston Lake, NY - *DataDirSup 7-83*
Tele-Sav Communications - Springfield, IL - *TeleSy&SerDir 2-84*
Tele Sciences Inc. - Marlton, NJ - *DirInfWP 82*
Tele/Scope [of EIC/Intelligence Inc.] - New York, NY - *DataDirOnSer 84; DirOnDB Spring 84*
Tele-Tenna Corp. [of Midwest Video Corp.] - Victoria, TX - *BrCabYB 84; Tel&CabFB 84C*
Tele-Trex Software Systems - Littleton, CO - *MicrocomMPl 84*
Tele Vend Inc. - Baltimore, MD - *MicrocomMPl 84; MicrocomSwDir 1; WhoWMicrocom 83*
Tele-Video [of Pinion Corp.] - St. Robert, MO - *Tel&CabFB 84C*
Tele-Video Corp. of Creswell - Creswell, OR - *BrCabYB 84; Tel&CabFB 84C*
Tele-View Inc. - Roma, TX - *BrCabYB 84; Tel&CabFB 84C*
Tele-Vu Inc. - Grants, NM - *BrCabYB 84*
Tele-Vu Inc. - Socorro, NM - *Tel&CabFB 84C*
Tele-Vu Inc. - Thoreau, NM - *Tel&CabFB 84C*
Tele-Vue Cable TV - Ord, NE - *Tel&CabFB 84C*
Tele-Vue of Clarksville Inc. - Clarksville, TX - *BrCabYB 84; Tel&CabFB 84C*
Tele Vue Optics Inc. - Spring Valley, NY - *AvMarPl 83*
Tele-Vue Systems Inc. [of Viacom International Inc.] - Pittsburg, CA - *Tel&CabFB 84C*
Tele-Vue Systems Inc. [of Viacom International Inc.] - Sonoma County, CA - *Tel&CabFB 84C*
Tele-Vue Systems Inc. - *See* Viacom International Inc.
Telecable Associates Inc. [of TCA Cable TV Inc.] - Tyler, TX - *BrCabYB 84*
Telecable Black Lake-Robertsonville Inc. - Black Lake, PQ, Canada - *BrCabYB 84*
Telecable Black Lake-Robertsonville Inc. - Robertsonville, PQ, Canada - *BrCabYB 84*
Telecable Blouin Engrg. - Lac Des Ecores, PQ, Canada - *BrCabYB 84*
Telecable Blouin Engrg. - Notre Dame du Laus, PQ, Canada - *BrCabYB 84*
Telecable Broadcasting of America Inc. - East Cleveland, OH - *Tel&CabFB 84C p.1705*
Telecable Communications Corp. - Frederica, DE - *BrCabYB 84*
Telecable Communications Corp. - Baltimore, MD - *BrCabYB 84 p.D-308*
Telecable Communications Corp. - Federalsburg, MD - *BrCabYB 84*
Telecable Communications Corp. - Trappe, MD - *BrCabYB 84*
Telecable Corp. [of Landmark Communications Inc.] - Norfolk, VA - *BrCabYB 84 p.D-308; CabTVFinDB 83; HomeVid&CabYB 82-83; LitMarPl 84; TelAl 83, 84; Tel&CabFB 84C p.1705*
Telecable de la Rive Sud [of Telecable Videotron Ltee.] - St. Hubert, PQ, Canada - *BrCabYB 84*
Telecable de l'Annonciation Enrg. - L'Annonciation, PQ, Canada - *BrCabYB 84*
Telecable des Mille-Iles Inc. - Terrebonne, PQ, Canada - *BrCabYB 84*
Telecable Inc. - Jonesboro, LA - *BrCabYB 84*
Telecable Inc. - Lake Odessa, MI - *BrCabYB 84*
Telecable Lac Carre Enrg. - Lac Carre, PQ, Canada - *BrCabYB 84*
Telecable Laurentation Inc. [of Bushnell Communications Ltd.] - Hull, PQ, Canada - *BrCabYB 84*
TeleCable of Bloomington-Normal - Bloomington, IL - *BrCabYB 84*
TeleCable of Broward County - Broward County, FL - *Tel&CabFB 84C*
TeleCable of Broward County - Margate, FL - *BrCabYB 84*
TeleCable of Broward County - North Lauderdale, FL - *Tel&CabFB 84C*
TeleCable of Cleveland [of TeleCable Corp.] - Cleveland, TN - *BrCabYB 84; Tel&CabFB 84C*
TeleCable of Columbus - Columbus, GA - *BrCabYB 84; Tel&CabFB 84C*
TeleCable of Greenville Inc. - Greenville, SC - *BrCabYB 84; Tel&CabFB 84C*
Telecable of Kokomo [of Telecable Corp.] - Kokomo, IN - *BrCabYB 84; Tel&CabFB 84C*
TeleCable of Lexington - Lexington, KY - *BrCabYB 84; Tel&CabFB 84C*
Telecable of Montgomery County - Philadelphia, PA - *BrCabYB 84*
TeleCable of Overland Park [of TeleCable Corp.] - Overland Park, KS - *BrCabYB 84; InterCabHB 3; Tel&CabFB 84C*
TeleCable of Radcliff - Radcliff, KY - *BrCabYB 84; Tel&CabFB 84C*
TeleCable of Richardson - Richardson, TX - *BrCabYB 84*
TeleCable of Spartanburg - Spartanburg, SC - *BrCabYB 84; Tel&CabFB 84C*
TeleCable of Springfield - Springfield, MO - *BrCabYB 84; Tel&CabFB 84C*
Telecable of Springfield [of Adelphia Communications Corp.] - Springfield Township, PA - *Tel&CabFB 84C*
Telecable Signals Inc. - Viroqua, WI - *BrCabYB 84; Tel&CabFB 84C*
TeleCable St. Victor Enrg. - St. Evariste, PQ, Canada - *BrCabYB 84*

Telecable Ste.-Marie Inc. - Ste. Marie, PQ, Canada - *BrCabYB 84*
Telecable Videotron Ltee. - St. Hubert, PQ, Canada - *BrCabYB 84; Tel&CabFB 84C*
Telecast International - Burbank, CA - *Tel&CabFB 84C*
Teleception of Winchester Inc. [of Cable Information Systems Inc.] - Winchester, KY - *BrCabYB 84*
Telecine Film Studios Inc. - Park Ridge, IL - *AvMarPl 83; TelAl 83, 84; Tel&CabFB 84C*
Telecki Publishing Services - Malverne, NY - *MagIndMarPl 82-83*
Telecom [of Samson Data Systemen BV] - Alphen, Netherlands - *DataDirOnSer 84; DirOnDB Spring 84*
Telecom Analysis Inc. - Independence, OH - *TeleSy&SerDir 2-84*
Telecom Associates Inc. - Pierrefonds, PQ, Canada - *TeleSy&SerDir 2-84*
Telecom Engineering Inc. - Ft. Madison, IA - *Tel&CabFB 84C*
Telecom Entertainment Inc. - *See* Benton & Bowles Inc.
Telecom Library Inc. - New York, NY - *BoPubDir 4, 5; TeleSy&SerDir 7-83*
Telecom Market Survey [of Dawson-Butwick Publishers] - Washington, DC - *TeleSy&SerDir 2-84*
Telecom Planning - Melbourne Beach, FL - *TeleSy&SerDir 7-83*
Telecom Productions Inc. - Des Plaines, IL - *Tel&CabFB 84C*
Telecom Services International - Juneau, AK - *TeleSy&SerDir 2-84*
Telecomm-Automation Corp. - Southbury, CT - *DataDirSup 7-83*
Telecommunication Center [of St. Vincent Hospital & Health Center] - Billings, MT - *TeleSy&SerDir 2-84*
Telecommunication Products & Technology - Littleton, MA - *BaconPubCkMag 84*
Telecommunication Services International - Burnaby, BC, Canada - *TeleSy&SerDir 2-84*
Telecommunications [of Horizon House-Microwave Inc.] - Dedham, MA - *BaconPubCkMag 84; MagDir 84; MagIndMarPl 82-83; TeleSy&SerDir 7-83; WritMar 84*
Telecommunications & Computing Program [of Institute for the Future] - Menlo Park, CA - *TeleSy&SerDir 7-83*
Telecommunications & Reservations Systems Consulting - Huntington, NY - *TeleSy&SerDir 2-84*
Telecommunications Compustat II [of Standard & Poor's Compustat Services Inc.] - Englewood, CO - *DataDirOnSer 84*
Telecommunications Cooperative Network - New York, NY - *TeleSy&SerDir 2-84*
Telecommunications Counselor - New York, NY - *DirOnDB Spring 84*
Telecommunications Counselor [of NewsNet Inc.] - Bryn Mawr, PA - *DataDirOnSer 84*
Telecommunications Dept. [of Richard A. Eisner & Co.] - New York, NY - *TeleSy&SerDir 2-84*
Telecommunications Dept. [of Radio-Suisse Ltd.] - Berne, Switzerland - *TeleSy&SerDir 7-83*
Telecommunications Div. [of Denmark General Directorate of Posts & Telegraphs] - Copenhagen, Denmark - *TeleSy&SerDir 7-83*
Telecommunications Engineering Inc. - Dallas, TX - *TeleSy&SerDir 7-83*
Telecommunications for the Deaf Inc. - Silver Spring, MD - *TeleSy&SerDir 7-83*
Telecommunications Information Center [of George Washington University] - Washington, DC - *EISS 5-84 Sup*
Telecommunications Management Corp. - Los Angeles, CA - *CabTVFinDB 83*
Telecommunications Management Corp. - Wellesley Hills, MA - *TeleSy&SerDir 7-83*
Telecommunications Reports - Washington, DC - *BaconPubCkMag 84*
Telecommunications Research & Action Center - Washington, DC - *BoPubDir 5*
Telecommunications Research Group [of University of Southern California] - Los Angeles, CA - *TeleSy&SerDir 2-84*
Telecommunications Research Program [of Charles River Associates Inc.] - Boston, MA - *TeleSy&SerDir 2-84*
Telecommunications Retailer - New York, NY - *BaconPubCkMag 84*
Telecommunications Software Inc. - Westbury, NY - *DataDirSup 7-83*
Telecommunications Systems Inc. - Pasadena, MD - *Tel&CabFB 84C*
Telecompute Integrated Systems Inc. - Toronto, ON, Canada - *WhoWMicrocom 83*
Telecomputer Research Inc. - Bala Cynwyd, PA - *DataDirOnSer 84; TeleSy&SerDir 2-84*
Telecomputer Systems Inc. - Bakersfield, CA - *ADAPSOMemDir 83-84*
Telecon Systems - San Jose, CA - *MicrocomMPl 84*
Teleconcepts in Communications Inc. - New York, NY - *ArtMar 84; AvMarPl 83; DataDirSup 7-83; TeleSy&SerDir 7-83*
Teleconference - San Ramon, CA - *BaconPubCkMag 84*
Teleconference Design Group [of South Carolina Educational Television] - Columbia, SC - *TeleSy&SerDir 2-84*
Teleconference Network of Texas [of University of Texas] - San Antonio, TX - *TeleSy&SerDir 7-83*
Teleconference System [of Memorial University of Newfoundland] - St. John's, NF, Canada - *TeleSy&SerDir 7-83*
Teleconferencing Service [of KVCT-TV/FM] - San Bernardino, CA - *TeleSy&SerDir 2-84*
Teleconferencing Service [of Louisiana Educational TV Authority] - Baton Rouge, LA - *TeleSy&SerDir 7-83*
Teleconferencing Service [of Teleglobe Canada] - Montreal, PQ, Canada - *TeleSy&SerDir 7-83*
Teleconnect Co. Inc. - Cedar Rapids, IA - *TeleSy&SerDir 2-84*
Teleconsult Inc. - Washington, DC - *TeleSy&SerDir 7-83*
Telecourier Magazine - Palm City, FL - *BaconPubCkMag 84*
Telecrafter Communications Corp. - Billings, MT - *Tel&CabFB 84C*
Telecrest Corp. [of Crestwood Village Inc.] - Crestwood Village, NJ - *Tel&CabFB 84C*
Telectro Systems Corp. - Corona, NY - *AvMarPl 83*
Telectronics [of Data Processing & Printing] - Houston, TX - *MagDir 84*
TeleCulture Inc. - New York, NY - *AvMarPl 83*
Teledata [of Danish Telecommunications Administrations] - Copenhagen, Denmark - *InfIndMarPl 83; VideoDir 82-83*
Telediffusion Ste. Adele Inc. - Ste. Adele, PQ, Canada - *BrCabYB 84*
Teledira/Telephone Directory Advertising Services [Div. of Griswold Inc.] - Cleveland, OH - *StaDirAdAg 2-84*
Teledistribution - Amos, PQ, Canada - *BrCabYB 84*
Teledistribution Cablouis Inc. - Cabano, PQ, Canada - *BrCabYB 84*
Teledoc [of Questel Inc.] - Washington, DC - *DataDirOnSer 84*
Teledoc [of National Center for the Study of Telecommunications] - Issy les Moulineaux, France - *CompReadDB 82; DirOnDB Spring 84; EISS 83*
Teledyne Amco [Div. of Teledyne Inc.] - Reading, PA - *AvMarPl 83*
Teledyne Inc. - Los Angeles, CA - *ElecNews 7-25-83*
Teledyne Inet - Torrance, CA - *DirInfWP 82*
Teledyne Systems Co. - Northridge, CA - *DirInfWP 82*
Telefile Computer Products Inc. - Irvine, CA - *DataDirSup 7-83*
Telefirm - Paris, France - *DirOnDB Spring 84*
Telefirst - New York, NY - *Tel&CabFB 84C*
Telefood Magazine [of Davies Publishing Co.] - Hinsdale, IL - *BaconPubCkMag 84; MagDir 84*
TeleFrance USA [of Gaumont Films] - New York, NY - *CabTVPrDB 83; HomeVid&CabYB 82-83*
Telegen Information System [of Environment Information Center Inc.] - New York, NY - *DirOnDB Spring 84; EISS 83*
Telegenix Inc. - Cherry Hill, NJ - *DataDirSup 7-83*
Telegenline [of EIC/Intelligence Inc.] - New York, NY - *DataDirOnSer 84; OnBibDB 3*
Telegiornali e Trasmissioni TV - Rome, Italy - *DirOnDB Spring 84*
Teleglobe Canada - Montreal, PQ, Canada - *TeleSy&SerDir 7-83*
Teleglobe Canada (NOVATEX Group) - Montreal, PQ, Canada - *VideoDir 82-83*
Telegram [of Post Publishing Co.] - Bridgeport, CT - *AyerDirPub 83; Ed&PubIntYB 82; LitMarPl 83, 84*
Telegram - Garden City, KS - *AyerDirPub 83*
Telegram - Norton, KS - *AyerDirPub 83; Ed&PubIntYB 82*
Telegram - Worcester, MA - *AyerDirPub 83*
Telegram - Ecorse, MI - *AyerDirPub 83*
Telegram - Columbus, NE - *AyerDirPub 83*

Telegram - Elmira, NY - *AyerDirPub 83*
Telegram - Herkimer, NY - *AyerDirPub 83*
Telegram - Malone, NY - *AyerDirPub 83*
Telegram - Rocky Mt., NC - *AyerDirPub 83*
Telegram - Eastland, TX - *AyerDirPub 83*
Telegram - Temple, TX - *AyerDirPub 83; BaconPubCkNews 84*
Telegram - Clarksburg, WV - *AyerDirPub 83; BaconPubCkNews 84*
Telegram - Superior, WI - *AyerDirPub 83*
Telegram - Torrington, WY - *AyerDirPub 83*
Telegram - St. John's, NF, Canada - *AyerDirPub 83*
Telegram, The - Mechanicsburg, OH - *Ed&PubIntYB 82*
Telegram-Tribune - San Luis Obispo, CA - *AyerDirPub 83*
Telegraph - Folsom, CA - *AyerDirPub 83*
Telegraph - Macon, GA - *AyerDirPub 83*
Telegraph - Alton, IL - *AyerDirPub 83*
Telegraph - Dixon, IL - *AyerDirPub 83*
Telegraph - Waterville, KS - *AyerDirPub 83*
Telegraph - North Platte, NE - *AyerDirPub 83*
Telegraph - Sidney, NE - *AyerDirPub 83*
Telegraph - Nashua, NH - *AyerDirPub 83*
Telegraph - Painesville, OH - *AyerDirPub 83; BaconPubCkNews 84; Ed&PubIntYB 82*
Telegraph [of Brownsville Publishing Corp.] - Brownsville, PA - *AyerDirPub 83; Ed&PubIntYB 82; NewsDir 84*
Telegraph - Mifflinburg, PA - *AyerDirPub 83*
Telegraph - Tyler, TX - *AyerDirPub 83*
Telegraph - Bluefield, WV - *AyerDirPub 83*
Telegraph Agency of the USSR - New York, NY - *Ed&PubIntYB 82*
Telegraph & News - Macon, GA - *AyerDirPub 83; NewsDir 84*
Telegraph-Forum - Bucyrus, OH - *AyerDirPub 83; Ed&PubIntYB 82*
Telegraph Herald - Dubuque, IA - *AyerDirPub 83; BaconPubCkNews 84; Ed&PubIntYB 82*
Telegraph Journal [of New Brunswick Publishing Co. Ltd.] - St. John, NB, Canada - *AyerDirPub 83; BaconPubCkNews 84; Ed&PubIntYB 82; LitMarPl 84*
Telegraph Press [Subs. of Commmonwealth Communications Services] - Harrisburg, PA - *LitMarPl 83, 84; MagIndMarPl 82-83*
Telegraph Workers Journal [of UTW, AFL-CIO] - Rockville, MD - *NewsDir 84*
Telegraphic Cable & Radio Registrations Inc. - Mamaroneck, NY - *BoPubDir 4, 5*
TeleGraphics Inc. - Baldwin City, KS - *NewsDir 84*
Telehop Inc. - Fresno, CA - *TeleSy&SerDir 2-84*
Teleketics - Los Angeles, CA - *AvMarPl 83*
Telekurs AG - Zurich, Switzerland - *InfIndMarPl 83*
Telelogic Inc. - Cambridge, MA - *DataDirSup 7-83*
Telemail [of GTE Telenet Communications Corp.] - Vienna, VA - *TeleSy&SerDir 7-83*
Telemark Dance Records - McLean, VA - *AvMarPl 83; BillIntBG 83-84*
Telemark/Telephone Directory Advertising - *See* Cabell Eanes Inc.
Telemarketing - Norwalk, CT - *BaconPubCkMag 84*
Telemated Motion Pictures - New York, NY - *ArtMar 84; AvMarPl 83; TelAl 83, 84; Tel&CabFB 84C*
Telematica SpA [of Compagnie Financiere Conseil SpA] - Milan, Italy - *EISS 7-83 Sup; InfIndMarPl 83*
Telemation Productions/Denver [Div. of Telemation Inc.] - Denver, CO - *AvMarPl 83*
Telemation Productions Inc. - Glenview, IL - *AvMarPl 83*
Telemation Productions Inc. - Seattle, WA - *ArtMar 84*
Telemation Program Services Inc. - New York, NY - *TelAl 83*
Telemax Inc. - Warrington, PA - *MicrocomMPl 84*
Telemedia Communications Ltee. - Montreal, PQ, Canada - *BrCabYB 84*
Telemedia International Inc. - Denver, CO - *Tel&CabFB 84C; TeleSy&SerDir 2-84*
Telemedia of Central Pennsylvania Co. - Houtzdale, PA - *BrCabYB 84*
Telemedia of Waynesboro - Waynesboro, GA - *BrCabYB 84*
TeleMine Co. Inc. - New York, NY - *AvMarPl 83*
Telemount Pictures Inc. - Santa Monica, CA - *TelAl 83, 84; Tel&CabFB 84C*
TeleNational Communications Inc. - Harpersville, AL - *BrCabYB 84*
TeleNational Communications Inc. - Pensacola, FL - *BrCabYB 84 p.D-308*
Telenational Communications Inc. - Omaha, NE - *Tel&CabFB 84C p.1706*
Telenet [of GTE Telenet Communications Corp.] - Vienna, VA - *InfIndMarPl 83*
TeleNews - Baldwin City, KS - *Ed&PubIntYB 82*
Telepak [of Central Administration of Telecommunications] - Farsta, Sweden - *InfIndMarPl 83*
Telepak [of National Swedish Telecommunications Administration] - Stockholm, Sweden - *EISS 83*
Telephone [of Telephone Books] - Guilford, CT - *LitMag&SmPr 83-84*
Telephone - Sylvania, GA - *AyerDirPub 83*
Telephone & Data Systems Inc. - Chicago, IL - *TelDir&BG 83-84*
Telephone & Data Systems Inc. - Madison, WI - *Tel&CabFB 84C p.1706*
Telephone Angles [of Telephone Angles Newsletter] - West Hartford, CT - *BaconPubCkMag 84; DataDirOnSer 84; DirOnDB Spring 84; TeleSy&SerDir 7-83; WritMar 84*
Telephone Books - Guilford, CT - *LitMag&SmPr 83-84*
Telephone Books Press - Guilford, CT - *BoPubDir 4, 5*
Telephone Bypass News [of NewsNet Inc.] - Bryn Mawr, PA - *DataDirOnSer 84*
Telephone Bypass News - McLean, VA - *DirOnDB Spring 84*
Telephone Conference Network [of University of Nebraska Medical Center] - Omaha, NE - *TeleSy&SerDir 7-83*
Telephone Consultants of America - Bergenfield, NJ - *TeleSy&SerDir 7-83*
Telephone Corp. - Ponce, PR - *BrCabYB 84*
Telephone Engineer & Management [of Harcourt Brace Jovanovich Publications Inc.] - Geneva, IL - *BaconPubCkMag 84; MagDir 84; TeleSy&SerDir 2-84*
Telephone Engineering Co. - Simpson, PA - *DataDirSup 7-83*
Telephone Line - Lawrence, IN - *NewsDir 84*
Telephone Management Systems - Waltham, MA - *DataDirSup 7-83*
Telephone Marketing Programs Inc. - New York, NY - *StaDirAdAg 2-84*
Telephone Marketing Report - Lake Forest, IL - *MagIndMarPl 82-83*
Telephone News - Bethesda, MD - *BaconPubCkMag 84; DirOnDB Spring 84*
Telephone News [of NewsNet Inc.] - Bryn Mawr, PA - *DataDirOnSer 84*
Telephone Service Co., The - Wapakoneta, OH - *TelDir&BG 83-84*
Telephone Software Connection - Torrance, CA - *MicrocomMPl 84; MicrocomSwDir 1; WhoWMicrocom 83*
Telephone Utilities of Alaska Inc. [Aff. of Telephone Utilities Inc.] - Ft. Wainwright, AK - *TelDir&BG 83-84*
Telephone Utilities of Eastern Oregon Inc. [Aff. of Telephone Utilities Inc.] - Lebanon, OR - *TelDir&BG 83-84*
Telephone Utilities of Washington Inc. [Aff. of Telephone Utilities Inc.] - Cheney, WA - *TelDir&BG 83-84*
Telephone Utilities of Washington Inc. [Aff. of Telephone Utilities Inc.] - Gig Harbor, WA - *TelDir&BG 83-84*
Telephone Utilities of West Virginia Inc. [Aff. of Mid-Continent Telephone Corp.] - Webster Springs, WV - *TelDir&BG 83-84*
Telephone Video System [of NEC America Inc.] - Elk Grove Village, IL - *TeleSy&SerDir 7-83*
Telephony [of Telephony Publishing Corp.] - Chicago, IL - *BaconPubCkMag 84; MagDir 84; TeleSy&SerDir 7-83*
Telephony Publishing Corp. - Chicago, IL - *BoPubDir 5*
Telepictures Corp. - Beverly Hills, CA - *AvMarPl 83*
Telepictures Corp. - New York, NY - *TelAl 83, 84; Tel&CabFB 84C*
Telepoints [of Telecomputer Research Inc.] - Bala Cynwyd, PA - *DataDirOnSer 84; DirOnDB Spring 84*
Teleport Chicago [Div. of Midwestern Relay Co.] - Milwaukee, WI - *BrCabYB 84*
Telepost Systems Ltd. - Gerrards Cross, England - *MicrocomSwDir 1*
Teleprinter Terminals [of GML Corp.] - Lexington, MA - *CompReadDB 82*
Teleprocessing Products Inc. - Simi Valley, CA - *DataDirSup 7-83*
Teleprocessors Inc., The - Houston, TX - *ADAPSOMemDir 83-84*

Teleproduct News - New York, NY - *BaconPubCkMag 84*
Teleprompter Cable Television [Aff. of Group W Cable] - Chalmette, LA - *InterCabHB 3*
Teleprompter Corp. - New York, NY - *LitMarPl 84; TelAl 83, 84*
Teleprompter of Newark Inc. [of Group W Cable] - Newark, CA - *BrCabYB 84*
Teleprompter of Worcester Inc. [of Group W Cable] - Worcester, MA - *InterCabHB 3*
Telequote III [of Bunker Ramo Information Systems] - Trumbull, CT - *DBBus 82; DirOnDB Spring 84*
Telequote III [of Canadian Law Information Council] - Ottawa, ON, Canada - *DataDirOnSer 84*
Teleram Communications Corp. - White Plains, NY - *DataDirSup 7-83; InfIndMarPl 83; MicrocomMPl 84; WhoWMicrocom 83*
Telerate Financial Information Network [of Telerate Systems Inc.] - New York, NY - *DataDirOnSer 84; DirOnDB Spring 84*
Telerate Historical Databases [of Telerate Systems Inc.] - New York, NY - *DBBus 82*
Telerate Systems Inc. - New York, NY - *DataDirOnSer 84; EISS 83*
Telerate II Historical Database [of Telerate Systems Inc.] - New York, NY - *DirOnDB Spring 84*
Telerate II Historical Domestic & International Database [of Telerate Systems Inc.] - New York, NY - *DataDirOnSer 84*
Teleray [Div. of Research Inc.] - Minneapolis, MN - *InfIndMarPl 83; MicrocomMPl 84; WhoWMicrocom 83*
Telerep Inc. - New York, NY - *TelAl 83, 84*
Telesag Inc. - Chicoutimi, PQ, Canada - *BrCabYB 84*
Telesat Cablevision - Pompano Beach, FL - *Tel&CabFB 84C*
Telesat Canada - Ottawa, ON, Canada - *BrCabYB 84; Tel&CabFB 84C*
Telescan - Washington, DC - *BaconPubCkMag 84*
Telescene Inc. - Salt Lake City, UT - *AvMarPl 83; Tel&CabFB 84C*
Telescope - Belleville, KS - *AyerDirPub 83*
Telescope [of The Galileo Press] - Baltimore, MD - *LitMag&SmPr 83-84; WritMar 84*
TeleScope [of Arthur D. Little Inc.] - Cambridge, MA - *DataDirOnSer 84; DirOnDB Spring 84*
Telescope Making - Milwaukee, WI - *MagDir 84*
TeleScripps Cable Co. [of E. W. Scripps Co.] - Elizabethtown, KY - *Tel&CabFB 84C*
TeleScripps Cable Co. [of E. W. Scripps Co.] - Cincinnati, OH - *BrCabYB 84 p.D-308*
Telescripps Cable Co. [of E. W. Scripps Co.] - Knoxville, TN - *Tel&CabFB 84C p.1706*
Telescript Inc. - Demarest, NJ - *AvMarPl 83*
TeleService Co. of Wyoming Valley [of Service Electric Cable TV Inc.] - Wilkes-Barre, PA - *BrCabYB 84; Tel&CabFB 84C*
Teleservice Corp. of America [of TCA Cable TV Inc.] - Tyler, TX - *BrCabYB 84 p.D-308*
Teleservice Research - Wynnewood, PA - *IntDirMarRes 83*
Teleservices Report - Bethesda, MD - *BaconPubCkMag 84*
TeleSession Corp. - New York, NY - *IntDirMarRes 83*
Telesis Development Co. Ltd. - Gold River, BC, Canada - *BrCabYB 84*
Telesis Group - Minneapolis, MN - *HBIndAd&MS 82-83*
Telesis Laboratory - Chillicothe, OH - *WhoWMicrocom 83*
TeleSoft - San Diego, CA - *MicrocomSwDir 1; WhoWMicrocom 83*
Teleson-America - Somerville, MA - *BillIntBG 83-84*
Telesound San Francisco - San Francisco, CA - *Tel&CabFB 84C*
Telespan - Altadena, CA - *TeleSy&SerDir 2-84*
Telespond Inc. - Colorado Springs, CO - *HBIndAd&MS 82-83*
Telestrategies Inc. - McLean, VA - *TeleSy&SerDir 7-83*
Telesystemes-Eurodial - Boulogne, France - *InfIndMarPl 83*
Telesystemes-Questel - Paris, France - *InfIndMarPl 83*
TeleSystems Cable Corp. [of Times Mirror Cable TV] - Philadelphia, PA - *Tel&CabFB 84C*
Telesystems Journal - Ft. Lee, NJ - *WritMar 84*
TeleSystems of Connecticut Inc. [of Times Mirror Cable TV] - Meriden, CT - *BrCabYB 84; Tel&CabFB 84C*
Teletax [of H.W. Systems Inc.] - Van Nuys, CA - *DataDirOnSer 84; DirOnDB Spring 84*
Teleteach Expanded Delivery System [of U.S. Air Force] - Dayton, OH - *TeleSy&SerDir 7-83*
Teletek Enterprises Inc. - Sacramento, CA - *WhoWMicrocom 83*
Teletekst [of Belgische Radio en Televisie] - Brussels, Belgium - *VideoDir 82-83*
Teletekst [of Nederlandse Omroep Stichting] - Hilversum, Netherlands - *VideoDir 82-83*
Teletel [of Intelmatique] - Paris, France - *InfIndMarPl 83*
Teletel 3-V [of French PTT] - Paris, France - *VideoDir 82-83*
Teletex [of Telecom Canada] - Ottawa, ON, Canada - *TeleSy&SerDir 2-84*
Teletex [of Swiss Broadcasting Corp.] - Bern, Switzerland - *VideoDir 82-83*
Teletex Service [of Transcanada Telephone System] - Ottawa, ON, Canada - *TeleSy&SerDir 7-83*
Teletext [of Oesterreichischer Rundfunk] - Vienna, Austria - *VideoDir 82-83*
Teletext [of Oy Yleisradio] - Helsinki, Finland - *VideoDir 82-83*
Teletext [of Norsk Rikskringkasting] - Oslo, Norway - *VideoDir 82-83*
Teletext & Videotex - Budapest, Hungary - *VideoDir 82-83*
Teletext Service on Public Television Project [of New York University] - New York, NY - *EISS 83*
Teletext Services [of KCET/Los Angeles] - Los Angeles, CA - *EISS 5-84 Sup*
Teletitle [of H.W. Systems Inc.] - Van Nuys, CA - *DataDirOnSer 84; DirOnDB Spring 84*
Teletouch Exhibition Services - Newtonville, MA - *InfoS 83-84*
Teletron - Skokie, IL - *BrCabYB 84*
Teletronics Cable TV - Howard, KS - *BrCabYB 84; Tel&CabFB 84C*
Teletype Corp. [Subs. of Western Electric Co.] - Skokie, IL - *DataDirSup 7-83; Datamation 6-83; InfIndMarPl 83; Top100Al 83; WhoWMicrocom 83*
TeleTypesetting Co. - Ann Arbor, MI - *MicrocomSwDir 1*
Televal Inc. - Girardville, PQ, Canada - *BrCabYB 84*
Televal Inc. - Normandin, PQ, Canada - *BrCabYB 84*
Televal Inc. - Roberval, PQ, Canada - *Tel&CabFB 84C*
Televector Inc. - New York, NY - *IntDirMarRes 83*
Televents Inc. - Walnut Creek, CA - *BrCabYB 84 p.D-308; CabTVFinDB 83; Tel&CabFB 84C p.1706*
Televents Inc. - Wright, WY - *Tel&CabFB 84C*
Televents of Camarillo Inc. [of Televents Group Inc.] - Camarillo, CA - *BrCabYB 84; Tel&CabFB 84C*
Televents of Colorado Inc. - Craig, CO - *BrCabYB 84; Tel&CabFB 84C*
Televents of Colorado Inc. - Meeker, CO - *BrCabYB 84*
Televents of Colorado Inc. - Rangley, CO - *Tel&CabFB 84C*
Televents of Contra Costa County Inc. [of Televents Group Inc.] - Martinez, CA - *Tel&CabFB 84C*
Televents of Coronado Inc. - Coronado, CA - *BrCabYB 84*
Televents of East County Inc. - Brentwood, CA - *Tel&CabFB 84C*
Televents of El Cerrito Inc. [of Televents Group Inc.] - El Cerrito, CA - *Tel&CabFB 84C*
Televents of Florida Inc. [of Televents Group Inc.] - Citrus County, FL - *Tel&CabFB 84C*
Televents of Florida Inc. - Crystal River, FL - *BrCabYB 84*
Televents of Jeffco Inc. - Jefferson County, CO - *Tel&CabFB 84C*
Televents of Powder River Inc. [of Televents of California] - Buffalo, WY - *BrCabYB 84*
Televents of San Joaquin Inc. [of Televents Group Inc.] - Los Banos, CA - *BrCabYB 84; Tel&CabFB 84C*
Televents of San Joaquin Inc. - Oristimba, CA - *BrCabYB 84*
Televents of San Joaquin Valley Inc. - Gustine, CA - *BrCabYB 84*
Televents of San Joaquin Valley Inc. - Mendota, CA - *BrCabYB 84*
Televents of San Joaquin Valley Inc. - Newman, CA - *BrCabYB 84*
Televents of San Joaquin Valley Inc. - Walnut Creek, CA - *BrCabYB 84*
Televideo Cable TV - St. Robert, MO - *BrCabYB 84*
Televideo Consultants Inc. - Evanston, IL - *TeleSy&SerDir 2-84*
Televideo Productions Inc. - New York, NY - *Tel&CabFB 84C*
TeleVideo Systems Inc. - Sunnyvale, CA - *Datamation 6-83; MicrocomMPl 83, 84; Top100Al 83; WhoWMicrocom 83*
Teleview [of Min-G Inc.] - Urbana, IL - *EISS 7-83 Sup*

Teleview Cable Inc. - Holdenville, OK - *BrCabYB 84*
Teleview Cable Service [of TeleNational Communications Inc.] - Ft. Eustis, VA - *Tel&CabFB 84C*
Teleview Cablevision Inc. [of Greer Associates Corp.] - Simpsonville, SC - *BrCabYB 84*
Teleview Systems Corp. - Decorah, IA - *BrCabYB 84; Tel&CabFB 84C*
Television Access Inc. - San Antonio, TX - *Tel&CabFB 84C p.1706*
Television Advertising Representatives Inc. - New York, NY - *TelAl 83, 84*
Television Antenna Cable Co. [of Mid Atlantic Network] - Front Royal, VA - *BrCabYB 84*
Television Associates Inc. - Mountain View, CA - *AvMarPl 83*
Television Association of Coulee Dam - Coulee Dam, WA - *BrCabYB 84; Tel&CabFB 84C*
Television Association of Republic - Republic, WA - *BrCabYB 84; Tel&CabFB 84C*
Television Audience Estimates/Radio Audience Estimates [of BBM Bureau of Measurement] - Don Mills, ON, Canada - *DataDirOnSer 84*
Television Broadcasting Service Inc. - Forest Hills, NY - *Tel&CabFB 84C*
Television Business Inc. - Chicago, IL - *Tel&CabFB 84C*
Television, Cable, & Radio Action Updates - Washington, DC - *MagDir 84*
Television Cable Communications - DeLand, FL - *CabTVFinDB 83*
Television Cable Service Co. - New Holland, PA - *BrCabYB 84; Tel&CabFB 84C*
Television Cable Service Inc. [of Times Mirror Cable Television Inc.] - Empire, OH - *BrCabYB 84*
Television Cable Service Inc. [of United Cable Television Corp.] - Abilene, TX - *BrCabYB 84*
Television Cable Service Inc. [of United Cable Television Corp.] - Jacksonville, TX - *BrCabYB 84*
Television Cable Service Inc. [of United Cable Television Corp.] - Perryton, TX - *BrCabYB 84*
Television Cable Service Inc. [of United Cable Television Corp.] - Sweetwater, TX - *BrCabYB 84*
Television Center Inc. - Phoenicia, NY - *Tel&CabFB 84C*
Television Contacts - New York, NY - *MagDir 84*
Television Corp. Stations, The - Norfolk, VA - *Tel&CabFB 84S*
Television Corp. Stations, The - Virginia Beach, VA - *BrCabYB 84*
Television Digest - Washington, DC - *BaconPubCkMag 84; BoPubDir 4, 5; DirMarMP 83; DirOnDB Spring 84; MagDir 84*
Television Digest [of NewsNet Inc.] - Bryn Mawr, PA - *DataDirOnSer 84*
Television Engineering Corp. - Chesterfield, MO - *AvMarPl 83*
Television Equipment Associates - South Salem, NY - *AvMarPl 83*
Television Exploitation - New York, NY - *TelAl 83*
Television Hornepayne Ltd. - Hornepayne, ON, Canada - *BrCabYB 84*
Television Interamericana SA - Coral Gables, FL - *Tel&CabFB 84C*
Television International Magazine - Hollywood, CA - *WritMar 84*
Television International Magazine - Los Angeles, CA - *MagDir 84*
Television Latina Inc. - Miami, FL - *Tel&CabFB 84C*
Television Production Services Corp. - Edison, NJ - *AvMarPl 83; WritMar 84*
Television Quarterly [of The National Academy of Television Arts & Sciences] - New York, NY - *LitMarPl 83, 84*
Television/Radio Age [of Television Editorial Corp.] - New York, NY - *BaconPubCkMag 84; MagDir 84; NewsBur 6*
Television Signal Service [of Texas Community Antennas Inc.] - Glenwood, AR - *BrCabYB 84*
Television Signal Service - Mena, AR - *BrCabYB 84*
Television Signal Service - Mountain Harbour Resort, AR - *BrCabYB 84*
Television Signal Service [of Texas Community Antennas Inc.] - Norman, AR - *BrCabYB 84*
Television Station Partners - New York, NY - *BrCabYB 84; Tel&CabFB 84S*
Television Syndication Center [Div. of Group W Productions] - Universal City, CA - *AvMarPl 83*
Television Syndication Group Inc. - Jericho, NY - *TelAl 83; Tel&CabFB 84C*
Television Syndications - Houston, TX - *Tel&CabFB 84C*
TeleVisual Productions [Div. of Beatty TeleVisual Inc.] - Springfield, IL - *AvMarPl 83*
Televox Music - Malibu, CA - *BillIntBG 83-84*
Telewhich? [of Consumers' Association] - London, England - *EISS 83*
Telewide Systems Inc. - New York, NY - *Tel&CabFB 84C*
Telewoman - Pleasant Hill, CA - *LitMag&SmPr 83-84; WritMar 84*
Telewords - Santa Monica, CA - *TeleSy&SerDir 2-84*
Teleworld Inc. - New York, NY - *TelAl 83, 84; Tel&CabFB 84C*
Telex Communications Inc. - Minneapolis, MN - *AvMarPl 83*
Telex Computer Products Inc. - Tulsa, OK - *DataDirSup 7-83; InfIndMarPl 83*
Telex Corp. - Tulsa, OK - *Datamation 6-83; Top100Al 83*
Telex 476L Library Terminal [of Telex Computer Products Inc.] - Tulsa, OK - *EISS 7-83 Sup*
Telex Service [of Western Union Telegraph Co.] - Upper Saddle River, NJ - *TeleSy&SerDir 7-83*
Telex Service [of RCA Global Communications Inc.] - New York, NY - *TeleSy&SerDir 7-83, 2-84*
Telex Service [of MCI International Inc.] - Rye Brook, NY - *TeleSy&SerDir 2-84*
Telexport - Paris, France - *DirOnDB Spring 84*
Telexpress Inc. - Willingboro, NJ - *MicrocomMPl 84*
Telextra [of RCA Global Communications Inc.] - New York, NY - *TeleSy&SerDir 2-84*
Telfair Enterprise - McRae, GA - *AyerDirPub 83; Ed&PubIntYB 82*
Telford Indian Valley Echo - Quakertown, PA - *NewsDir 84*
Telford Indian Valley Echo - Telford, PA - *BaconPubCkNews 84*
Telic - New York, NY - *TelAl 83, 84; Tel&CabFB 84C*
Telidon [of Dept. of Communications] - Ottawa, ON, Canada - *EISS 83*
Telidon Marketing Secretariat - Ottawa, ON, Canada - *VideoDir 82-83*
Telidon Technology Development Center [of Polytechnical School of Montreal] - Montreal, PQ, Canada - *EISS 7-83 Sup*
Telidon-Venezuela [of Presidential Central Office of Statistics & Information] - Caracas, Venezuela - *VideoDir 82-83*
Telios Systems Co. - Portland, OR - *MicrocomSwDir 1*
Tell City-Cannelton Cable TV System [of Tennessee-Kentucky Cable TV Co.] - Tell City, IN - *Tel&CabFB 84C*
Tell City News - Tell City, IN - *BaconPubCkNews 84; NewsDir 84*
Tellem Public Relations - *See* Grody/Tellem Communications Inc.
Teller - Milnor, ND - *AyerDirPub 83; Ed&PubIntYB 82*
Teller Enterprises - Waltham, MA - *WhoWMicrocom 83*
Teller, Joan W. - Tacoma, WA - *LitMarPl 83, 84; MagIndMarPl 82-83*
Tellico Telephone Co. Inc. - Tellico Plains, TN - *TelDir&BG 83-84*
Telluride Cablevision [of Wilco Enterprises Inc.] - Telluride, CO - *BrCabYB 84; Tel&CabFB 84C*
Telluride Times - Telluride, CO - *BaconPubCkNews 84; Ed&PubIntYB 82*
Telmar Business Systems Inc. - New York, NY - *HBIndAd&MS 82-83*
Telmar Educational Services Inc. - New York, NY - *HBIndAd&MS 82-83*
Telmar Group Inc. - New York, NY - *HBIndAd&MS 82-83; IntDirMarRes 83; MagIndMarPl 82-83*
Telmar Media Systems - New York, NY - *DataDirOnSer 84; EISS 83; HBIndAd&MS 82-83*
Telocator - Washington, DC - *BaconPubCkMag 84; MagDir 84*
Telos - St. Louis, MO - *LitMag&SmPr 83-84*
Telos Computing Inc. - Santa Monica, CA - *DataDirSup 7-83; WhoWMicrocom 83*
Telos Press - St. Louis, MO - *BoPubDir 4, 5; LitMag&SmPr 83-84*
Telos Software Products - Santa Monica, CA - *MicrocomSwDir 1*
Telpar Inc. - Addison, TX - *DataDirSup 7-83*
Telplan System [of Michigan State University] - East Lansing, MI - *EISS 83*
Telser Inc., Gene - Evanston, IL - *HBIndAd&MS 82-83*

Telset [of Helsingin Telset Oy] - Helsinki, Finland - *EISS 83; InfIndMarPl 83; VideoDir 82-83*
TELSET (Data Products Div.) - New York, NY - *DirInfWP 82*
Telstar Cable TV [of Omni Cable TV Corp.] - Whitesboro, TX - *BrCabYB 84; Tel&CabFB 84C*
Telstar Inc. - St. Paul, MN - *WritMar 84*
Telstar TV Inc. [of Omni Cable TV Corp.] - Marietta, OK - *Tel&CabFB 84C*
Telstar Video - St. Paul, MN - *AvMarPl 83*
Telstat Systems Inc. - New York, NY - *DataDirSup 7-83; DirOnDB Spring 84; EISS 83*
Telsys Consultants Group Inc. - Washington, DC - *TeleSy&SerDir 7-83*
Telsys Consultants Group Inc. - Boston, MA - *TeleSy&SerDir 2-84*
Teltone Corp. - Kirkland, WA - *WhoWMicrocom 83*
Teltran Inc. - Tecumseh, OK - *Tel&CabFB 84C p.1706*
Teltrend Inc. - West Chicago, IL - *DataDirSup 7-83*
Teltrix Inc. - Toronto, ON, Canada - *VideoDir 82-83*
Teltron - Douglassville, PA - *AvMarPl 83*
Teltron Cable TV [of The Journal Co.] - Stevens Point, WI - *BrCabYB 84; Tel&CabFB 84C*
Teltron Cable TV [of The Journal Co.] - Wausau, WI - *BrCabYB 84 p.D-308; Tel&CabFB 84C*
Teltron Cable TV [of The Journal Co.] - Wisconsin Rapids, WI - *BrCabYB 84; Tel&CabFB 84C*
Teltron Inc. - Milwaukee, WI - *Tel&CabFB 84C p.1706*
Teltron Inc. - *See* Teltron Cable TV
Telview Antenna System - Osburn, ID - *BrCabYB 84; Tel&CabFB 84C*
Telvue Cable Alabama [of Liberty Communications Inc.] - Jefferson County, AL - *BrCabYB 84; Tel&CabFB 84C*
Telxon Corp. - Akron, OH - *DataDirSup 7-83; WhoWMicrocom 83*
Telxon Ltd. - Poole, England - *MicrocomSwDir 1*
Temar Music - Riverside, IL - *BillIntBG 83-84*
Temas, U.S. Edition - New York, NY - *MagDir 84*
Temiskaming Speaker - New Liskeard, ON, Canada - *AyerDirPub 83; Ed&PubIntYB 82*
Tempe Daily News - Mesa, AZ - *AyerDirPub 83*
Tempe News [of Cox Newspapers] - Tempe, AZ - *BaconPubCkNews 84; NewsDir 84*
Tempe Publishers Inc. - Tempe, AZ - *BoPubDir 4, 5*
Temperance Bedford Courier - Temperance, MI - *NewsDir 84*
Tempest: Avant-Garde Poetry [of Earthwise Publications] - Miami, FL - *LitMag&SmPr 83-84*
Temple Associates, G. - Southfield, MI - *AdAge 3-28-84; StaDirAdAg 2-84*
Temple, Barker & Sloane Inc. - Lexington, MA - *CabTVFinDB 83*
Temple Cable TV - Temple, OK - *BrCabYB 84; Tel&CabFB 84C*
Temple Cablevision [of MetroVision Inc.] - Temple, TX - *BrCabYB 84; Tel&CabFB 84C*
Temple City Arcadia Pacesetter - *See* Highlander Publications Inc.
Temple City Pacesetter - San Gabriel, CA - *Ed&PubIntYB 82*
Temple City Pacesetter - *See* Sun Independent Newspapers
Temple City Times [of Foothill Inter-City Newspapers] - Arcadia, CA - *AyerDirPub 83; NewsDir 84*
Temple City Times - Temple City, CA - *Ed&PubIntYB 82*
Temple City Times - *See* Foothill Inter-City Newspapers
Temple Daily Telegram [of Frank Mayborn Enterprises Inc.] - Stephenville, TX - *NewsDir 84*
Temple Daily Telegram - Temple, TX - *Ed&PubIntYB 82*
Temple, Ellen C. - Austin, TX - *BoPubDir 4, 5*
Temple Ft. Hood Sentinel - Temple, TX - *BaconPubCkNews 84*
Temple Terrace Beacon [of Tampa Suburban Newspapers Inc.] - Tampa, FL - *NewsDir 84*
Temple Terrace Beacon - *See* Tampa Suburban Newspapers Inc.
Temple University (Dept. of English) - Philadelphia, PA - *MagIndMarPl 82-83*
Temple University News - Philadelphia, PA - *NewsDir 84*
Temple University Press - Philadelphia, PA - *LitMarPl 83, 84; WritMar 84*
Templegate Publishers - Springfield, IL - *LitMarPl 83, 84*
Templeman, Eleanor Lee - Arlington, VA - *BoPubDir 4 Sup, 5*
Templeton Publishing Co. Inc. - *See* Shawnee Press Inc.
Templeton Telephone Co. - Templeton, IA - *TelDir&BG 83-84*
Tempo - Byron, IL - *Ed&PubIntYB 82*
Tempo - Scranton, PA - *LitMag&SmPr 83-84*
Tempo Advertising Inc. - New York, NY - *StaDirAdAg 2-84*
Tempo Books [Div. of The Berkley Publishing Group] - New York, NY - *WritMar 84*
Tempo Music Publications - *See* Alexandria House Inc.
Tempo of the Towns - Endicott, NY - *Ed&PubIntYB 82*
Tempo of the Towns [of Southern Tier Publications Inc.] - Vestal, NY - *AyerDirPub 83; NewsDir 84*
Temporarily Yours Personnel Service Inc. - New York, NY - *LitMarPl 83, 84; MagIndMarPl 82-83*
Temporary Services Inc. - New York, NY - *DirInfWP 82*
Tempro Inc. - Moundridge, KS - *BaconPubCkNews 84*
Ten Mile River Press - Ft. Bragg, CA - *BoPubDir 4, 5*
Ten Mile River Press - Petaluma, CA - *LitMag&SmPr 83-84*
Ten-O-Nine Records - Cincinnati, OH - *BillIntBG 83-84*
Ten Penny Players Inc. - New York, NY - *BoPubDir 4, 5; LitMag&SmPr 83-84*
1060 News - South Orange, NJ - *NewsDir 84*
Ten Speed Press - Berkeley, CA - *ArtMar 84; LitMag&SmPr 83-84; LitMarPl 83, 84; WritMar 84*
Ten Talents Cookbook - Chisholm, MN - *BoPubDir 4, 5*
1033 News & Views - Chicago, IL - *NewsDir 84*
Tenant Resource Center - Madison, WI - *BoPubDir 4, 5*
Tenba - New York, NY - *AvMarPl 83*
Tenderheart Records - Canoga Park, CA - *BillIntBG 83-84*
Tendril - Green Harbor, MA - *LitMag&SmPr 83-84; WritMar 84*
Tengerdy, Robert P. - Ft. Collins, CO - *LitMarPl 83, 84*
Tenino Independent & South County Sun - Tenino, WA - *BaconPubCkNews 84; NewsDir 84*
Tenino Independent, The - Tenino, WA - *Ed&PubIntYB 82*
Tenino Telephone Co. - Tenino, WA - *TelDir&BG 83-84*
Tenn-Tex Music Co. Inc. - *See* Sure-Fire Music Co.
Tennant Co., Don - Chicago, IL - *AdAge 3-28-84; ArtMar 84; HBIndAd&MS 82-83; StaDirAdAg 2-84*
Tennant Publishing House - Halifax, NS, Canada - *BoPubDir 4 Sup, 5*
Tennessean, The [of Gannett Co. Inc.] - Nashville, TN - *AyerDirPub 83; BaconPubCkNews 84; Ed&PubIntYB 82; LitMarPl 83, 84; NewsBur 6; NewsDir 84*
Tennessee Banker [of Tennessee Bankers Association] - Nashville, TN - *BaconPubCkMag 84; MagDir 84*
Tennessee Business - Nashville, TN - *BaconPubCkMag 84*
Tennessee Cablevision Inc. - Oak Ridge, TN - *BrCabYB 84; Tel&CabFB 84C*
Tennessee Chapter [of American Society of Interior Designers] - Nashville, TN - *BoPubDir 4 Sup, 5*
Tennessee Dept. of Employment Security - Nashville, TN - *BoPubDir 5*
Tennessee Engineer [of The University of Tennessee] - Knoxville, TN - *MagDir 84*
Tennessee Farm Bureau News - Columbia, TN - *BaconPubCkMag 84; MagDir 84*
Tennessee Farmer - Nashville, TN - *BaconPubCkMag 84; MagDir 84*
Tennessee Folklore Society - Murfreesboro, TN - *BillIntBG 83-84*
Tennessee Genealogical Society - Memphis, TN - *BoPubDir 4, 5*
Tennessee-Kentucky Cable TV Co. - Somerset, KY - *Tel&CabFB 84C p.1706*
Tennessee-Kentucky Cable TV Co. - Jamestown, TN - *Tel&CabFB 84C*
Tennessee-Kentucky Cable TV Co. [of Athena Communications Corp.] - Lake City, TN - *Tel&CabFB 84C*
Tennessee Livestock - Symrna, TN - *MagDir 84*
Tennessee Magazine - Nashville, TN - *BaconPubCkMag 84; MagDir 84; MagIndMarPl 82-83*
Tennessee Press Association - Knoxville, TN - *ProGuPRSer 4*
Tennessee Realtor - Nashville, TN - *BaconPubCkMag 84; MagDir 84*
Tennessee Republican - Huntingdon, TN - *AyerDirPub 83; Ed&PubIntYB 82*
Tennessee Sportsman - Marietta, GA - *BaconPubCkMag 84*
Tennessee State Data Center [of Tennessee State Planning Office] - Nashville, TN - *EISS 7-83 Sup*
Tennessee Teacher - Nashville, TN - *BaconPubCkMag 84; MagDir 84*

Tennessee Telephone Co. [Aff. of Telephone & Data Systems] - Knoxville, TN - *TelDir&BG 83-84*
Tennessee Town & City - Nashville, TN - *MagDir 84*
Tennessee Valley CableCom Inc. - Hohenwald, TN - *BrCabYB 84; Tel&CabFB 84C*
Tennessee Valley Cablecom Inc. - Mt. Pleasant, TN - *Tel&CabFB 84C p.1706*
Tennessee Valley Cablevision Corp. - Westmoreland, TN - *BrCabYB 84*
Tennessee Valley Music - *See* Woodrich Publishing Co.
Tennessee Valley Video Inc. - Clifton, TN - *BrCabYB 84*
Tennessee Valley Video Inc. - Collinwood, TN - *Tel&CabFB 84C p.1707*
Tennessee Valley Video Inc. - Iron City, TN - *BrCabYB 84*
Tennessee Valley Video Inc. - Linden, TN - *BrCabYB 84*
Tennessee Valley Video Inc. - Loretto, TN - *Tel&CabFB 84C*
Tenney Telephone Co. - Alma, WI - *TelDir&BG 83-84*
Tennis [of Golf Digest/Tennis Inc.] - Norwalk, CT - *ArtMar 84; BaconPubCkMag 84; Folio 83; LitMarPl 83, 84; MagDir 84; MagIndMarPl 82-83; WritMar 84*
Tennis Everyone - Chicago, IL - *BaconPubCkMag 84; MagDir 84; WritMar 84*
Tennis for Travelers - Cincinnati, OH - *BoPubDir 4, 5*
Tennis Inc. - *See* Golf Digest/Tennis Inc.
Tennis Industry - North Miami, FL - *BaconPubCkMag 84; MagDir 84; WritMar 84*
Tennis Talk & Sport Review - Wood Land Hills, CA - *BaconPubCkMag 84*
Tennis USA [of CBS Consumer Publishing] - New York, NY - *MagIndMarPl 82-83; WritMar 84*
Tennis USA - Radnor, PA - *MagDir 84*
Tennis Week - New York, NY - *BaconPubCkMag 84; WritMar 84*
Tennsco Corp. - Dickson, TN - *DirInfWP 82*
Tennyson & Associates Inc., Jon - Lake Forest, IL - *StaDirAdAg 2-84*
Tennyson & Wheeler Inc. - Long Grove, IL - *DirPRFirms 83*
Tenpenny Music - *See* Music Craftshop Inc.
Tensegrity Inc. - Chicago, IL - *MicrocomMPl 84*
Tension-in-Repose - New York, NY - *BoPubDir 4*
Tension-in-Repose - Cincinnati, OH - *BoPubDir 5*
Tensleep Publications - Aberdeen, SD - *BoPubDir 5; LitMag&SmPr 83-84*
Tensor Technology Inc. - Laguna Hills, CA - *MicrocomMPl 83*
Tentel - Campbell, CA - *AvMarPl 83*
Tenth House Enterprises Inc. - New York, NY - *BoPubDir 4, 5; LitMag&SmPr 83-84*
Tenth Muse - Pacifica, CA - *BoPubDir 4, 5*
TEP (Publishing Div.) - Boston, MA - *LitMag&SmPr 83-84*
Tepe Hensler & Westerkamp - Cincinnati, OH - *AdAge 3-28-84; StaDirAdAg 2-84*
Terado Corp. - St. Paul, MN - *DataDirSup 7-83; MicrocomMPl 84*
Terak Corp. - Scottsdale, AZ - *DataDirSup 7-83; MicrocomSwDir 1; WhoWMicrocom 83*
Teratology Lookout [of Karolinska Institutet] - Stockholm, Sweden - *CompReadDB 82*
Teresa Gramophone Co. Ltd. - New York, NY - *BillIntBG 83-84*
Term [of Bibliographic Retrieval Services] - Latham, NY - *DataDirOnSer 84; EISS 7-83 Sup*
Term-Comm Corp. - Terre Haute, IN - *Tel&CabFB 84C*
Terman Public Relations, Diane - New York, NY - *DirPRFirms 83*
Termdok - Stockholm, Sweden - *DirOnDB Spring 84*
Termiflex Corp. - Nashua, NH - *DataDirSup 7-83; InfIndMarPl 83; WhoWMicrocom 83*
Terminal Data Corp. - Woodland Hills, CA - *EISS 83*
Terminal Data Corp. of Maryland - Rockville, MD - *DataDirSup 7-83; DirInfWP 82; InfIndMarPl 83; WhoWMicrocom 83*
Terminal Photo Offset Co. [Div. of Olympic Press] - New York, NY - *LitMarPl 83, 84; MagIndMarPl 82-83*
Terminal Rentals Inc. - Orange, CA - *WhoWMicrocom 83*
Terminals Guide - Ispra, Italy - *DirOnDB Spring 84*
Terminology & Documentation Section [of Ministry of Foreign Affairs] - The Hague, Netherlands - *EISS 83*
Terminology Bank of Quebec [of French Language Board] - Quebec, PQ, Canada - *EISS 83*
Terminology Evaluation & Acquisition Method [of Siemens AG] - Munich, West Germany - *EISS 83*
TermTronics Inc. - San Diego, CA - *DataDirSup 7-83*
Termyra Music Publishing Co. - Toledo, OH - *BillIntBG 83-84*
Tern Press, Eddie - Seattle, WA - *BoPubDir 4 Sup, 5*
Terr Productions, Michael R. - Hollywood, CA - *TelAl 83, 84*
Terra Alta Preston County News - Terra Alta, WV - *BaconPubCkNews 84*
Terra Bella News - Terra Bella, CA - *BaconPubCkNews 84; Ed&PubIntYB 82*
Terra Cable Ltd. - St. Stephen, NB, Canada - *BrCabYB 84*
Terra Linda News - San Rafael, CA - *Ed&PubIntYB 82*
Terra Publishing - Jeffersontown, KY - *BoPubDir 4, 5*
Terrace Bay Schreiber News - Terrace Bay, ON, Canada - *Ed&PubIntYB 82*
Terrace-Kitimat Daily Herald - Terrace, BC, Canada - *AyerDirPub 83; Ed&PubIntYB 82*
Terrace Music - *See* Terrace Music Group Inc.
Terrace Music Group Inc. - Nashville, TN - *BillIntBG 83-84*
Terral Telephone Co. - Terral, OK - *TelDir&BG 83-84*
Terrapin Inc. - Cambridge, MA - *MicrocomMPl 83, 84; WhoWMicrocom 83*
Terrapin Music - *See* Folklore Music
Terraspace Inc. - Rockville, MD - *BoPubDir 4, 5*
Terre Haute Macksville Gazette - Terre Haute, IN - *BaconPubCkNews 84*
Terre Haute Tribune Star - Terre Haute, IN - *BaconPubCkNews 84*
Terrell, Bob - Asheville, NV - *BoPubDir 4, 5*
Terrell Publishing Co. - Atlanta, GA - *BoPubDir 4, 5*
Terrell Tribune - Terrell, TX - *BaconPubCkNews 84; Ed&PubIntYB 82; NewsDir 84*
Terrible Tunes - *See* Kenwon Music
Terril Telephone Co. - Terril, IA - *Tel&CabFB 84C p.1707; TelDir&BG 83-84*
Territorial Publishers Inc. - Tucson, AZ - *BaconPubCkNews 84*
Territory of Oklahoma: Literature & the Arts - Norman, OK - *LitMag&SmPr 83-84*
Terrorism Data Base [of Risks International Inc.] - Alexandria, VA - *EISS 83*
Terry & Joseph P. Rawley, Randall B. Jr. - High Point, NC - *Ed&PubIntYB 82*
Terry, Ben - Henderson, NC - *Tel&CabFB 84C p.1707*
Terry Headlight - Terry, MS - *BaconPubCkNews 84; Ed&PubIntYB 82*
Terry Robie Industrial Advertising Inc. - *See* TRIAD
Terry Tribune - Terry, MT - *BaconPubCkNews 84; Ed&PubIntYB 82*
Tersch Products Inc. - Rogers, MN - *AvMarPl 83*
Tertium Quid Ltd. - Cardiff, CA - *IntDirMarRes 83*
Terzian Associates, Carl - Los Angeles, CA - *DirPRFirms 83*
Tesco TV/FM Cable Systems [of Telesystems Co.] - Topanga, CA - *BrCabYB 84*
Tesdata Systems Corp. - McLean, VA - *DataDirSup 7-83*
Tessalou Music - Nashville, TN - *BillIntBG 83-84*
Tesseract Corp. - San Francisco, CA - *DataDirOnSer 84*
Test - Oakhurst, NJ - *BaconPubCkMag 84; MagDir 84*
Test & Measurement World - Allston, MA - *MagDir 84*
Test & Measurement World - Boston, MA - *BaconPubCkMag 84*
Test Patterns - New York, NY - *Tel&CabFB 84C*
Tested Recipe Publishers Inc. [Aff. of John Blair & Co.] - Chicago, IL - *BoPubDir 4, 5*
Testing 1-2-3 [Div. of Harry Heller Research Corp.] - New York, NY - *IntDirMarRes 83*
Testologen AB - Sollentuna, Sweden - *IntDirMarRes 83*
Testrite Instrument Co. Inc. - Newark, NJ - *AvMarPl 83*
Teton Bookshop Publishing Co. - Jackson, WY - *BoPubDir 4, 5*
Teton Magazine - Jackson, WY - *BaconPubCkMag 84; MagDir 84*
Teton Valley News - Driggs, ID - *AyerDirPub 83; Ed&PubIntYB 82*
Tetrac - Santa Clara, CA - *EISS 7-83 Sup*
Tetragrammaton Press [Aff. of AMNET] - Los Angeles, CA - *BoPubDir 4, 5*

Teutopolis Press-Dieterich Special Gazette - Teutopolis, IL - *BaconPubCkNews 84; Ed&PubIntYB 82*
Tevis Music, Peter - Burbank, CA - *BillIntBG 83-84*
Teviskes Ziburiai - Mississauga, ON, Canada - *Ed&PubIntYB 82*
Tevyne - New York, NY - *Ed&PubIntYB 82*
Tewksbury Merrimack Valley Advertiser - Tewksbury, MA - *NewsDir 84*
Tewksbury Merrimack Valley Advertiser - *See* Dole Publishing Co. Inc.
Tex-Co TV Cable System Inc. - Houston, MO - *BrCabYB 84*
Tex-La Cable TV Inc. - Ft. Polk, LA - *BrCabYB 84*
Tex-Mex Books - San Juan, TX - *BoPubDir 4, 5*
Texan - Dalhart, TX - *AyerDirPub 83*
Texan - Shamrock, TX - *AyerDirPub 83*
Texarkana Courier - Texarkana, TX - *Ed&PubIntYB 82*
Texarkana Gazette - Texarkana, TX - *BaconPubCkNews 84; Ed&PubIntYB 82; NewsDir 84*
Texarkana TV Cable Co. Inc. [of Times Mirror Cable TV] - Texarkana, TX - *Tel&CabFB 84C*
Texas - Houston, TX - *MagIndMarPl 82-83*
Texas A & M University (Thermodynamics Research Center) - College Station, TX - *BoPubDir 4 Sup, 5*
Texas A & M University Press - College Station, TX - *LitMarPl 83, 84; WritMar 84*
Texas AFL-CIO News - Austin, TX - *NewsDir 84*
Texas Agriculture - Waco, TX - *BaconPubCkMag 84; MagDir 84*
Texas American Microfilm Inc. [Subs. of West Canadian Graphic Industries Ltd.] - Dallas, TX - *LitMarPl 84*
Texas & Southwest Hotel-Motel Review - Alamo Heights, TX - *MagDir 84*
Texas & Southwest Hotel-Motel Review - San Antonio, TX - *BaconPubCkMag 84*
Texas Architect [of Texas Society of Architects] - Austin, TX - *BaconPubCkMag 84; MagDir 84*
Texas Bankers Record - Austin, TX - *BaconPubCkMag 84*
Texas Bar Journal - Austin, TX - *BaconPubCkMag 84*
Texas Beverage News - Ft. Worth, TX - *BaconPubCkMag 84; MagDir 84*
Texas Business [of Commerce Publishing Corp.] - Dallas, TX - *BaconPubCkMag 84*
Texas Business [of Commerce Publishing Corp.] - Farmers Branch, TX - *MagDir 84*
Texas Cablevision [of Rogers UA Cablesystems Inc.] - Miles, TX - *BrCabYB 84*
Texas Cablevision [of Rogers UA Cablesystems Inc.] - San Angelo, TX - *BrCabYB 84*
Texas Cablevision Co. - Hooks, TX - *BrCabYB 84*
Texas Cablevision Co. - Kaufman, TX - *BrCabYB 84; Tel&CabFB 84C*
Texas Cablevision Co. [of Warner Amex Cable Communications Inc.] - New Boston, TX - *BrCabYB 84; Tel&CabFB 84C p.1707*
Texas Christian University Press - Ft. Worth, TX - *LitMag&SmPr 83-84; LitMarPl 83, 84; WritMar 84*
Texas City Sun - Texas City, TX - *BaconPubCkNews 84; Ed&PubIntYB 82; NewsDir 84*
Texas Civil Engineer [of American Society of Civil Engineers] - San Antonio, TX - *BaconPubCkMag 84; MagDir 84*
Texas Co-Op Power - Austin, TX - *BaconPubCkMag 84; MagDir 84*
Texas Coach - Austin, TX - *MagDir 84*
Texas Color Printers Inc. [Subs. of Providence Gravure Inc.] - Dallas, TX - *MagIndMarPl 82-83*
Texas Commission on Alcoholism - Austin, TX - *BoPubDir 5*
Texas Community Antennas Group - Tyler, TX - *BrCabYB 84 p.D-309; TelAl 83, 84*
Texas Computer Systems - Brady, TX - *MicrocomMPl 83, 84*
Texas Contractor - Dallas, TX - *BaconPubCkMag 84*
Texas Contractor [of Peters Publishing Co. of Texas] - Garland, TX - *MagDir 84*
Texas CPA News [of Texas Society of CPA's] - Dallas, TX - *MagDir 84*
Texas Daily Press League Inc. - New York, NY - *LitMarPl 83, 84*
Texas Educational Aids - Houston, TX - *AvMarPl 83*
Texas Farm & Ranch News - San Antonio, TX - *AyerDirPub 83; BaconPubCkMag 84; MagDir 84*
Texas Field Service - Austin, TX - *IntDirMarRes 83*
Texas Fisherman, The [of Cordovan Corp.] - Houston, TX - *MagDir 84; WritMar 84*
Texas Flyer, The - Los Angeles, CA - *MagDir 84*
Texas Food & Service News - Austin, TX - *ArtMar 84; BaconPubCkMag 84; MagDir 84; WritMar 84*
Texas Food Merchant [of Texas Retail Grocers Association] - Austin, TX - *BaconPubCkMag 84; MagDir 84*
Texas Foundation for Women's Resources - Austin, TX - *BoPubDir 4 Sup, 5*
Texas Future Farmer - Austin, TX - *BaconPubCkMag 84; MagDir 84*
Texas Gardener [of Suntex Communications Inc.] - Waco, TX - *BaconPubCkMag 84; WritMar 84*
Texas Gas Data Base - Houston, TX - *DirOnDB Spring 84*
Texas Highways - Austin, TX - *BaconPubCkMag 84; MagDir 84*
Texas Historian - Austin, TX - *MagDir 84*
Texas Historical Commission - Austin, TX - *BoPubDir 5*
Texas Homes - Dallas, TX - *BaconPubCkMag 84; MagDir 84*
Texas Hospitals [of Texas Hospital Association] - Austin, TX - *BaconPubCkMag 84; MagDir 84*
Texas Instruments Inc. - Austin, TX - *WhoWMicrocom 83*
Texas Instruments Inc. - Dallas, TX - *DataDirSup 7-83; Datamation 6-83; DirInfWP 82; ElecNews 7-25-83; HomeVid&CabYB 82-83; InfIndMarPl 83; MicrocomMPl 83, 84; Top100Al 83; WhoWMicrocom 83*
Texas Instruments Inc. - Houston, TX - *InfoS 83-84*
Texas Instruments Learning Center [Subs. of Texas Instruments Inc.] - Dallas, TX - *BoPubDir 4, 5; WritMar 84*
Texas Insuror, The - Austin, TX - *BaconPubCkMag 84*
Texas Journal of Plumbing, Heating & Cooling Contractors - Austin, TX - *BaconPubCkMag 84; MagDir 84*
Texas Lakes Cablevision Inc. - Irving, TX - *BrCabYB 84*
Texas Law Review - Austin, TX - *MagDir 84*
Texas League Savings Account [of S & L Communications Inc.] - Austin, TX - *BaconPubCkMag 84; MagDir 84*
Texas Library Book Sales - Austin, TX - *LitMarPl 83, 84*
Texas LP-Gas News [of Texas LP-Gas Association] - Austin, TX - *BaconPubCkMag 84; MagDir 84*
Texas Medicine - Austin, TX - *BaconPubCkMag 84; MagDir 84*
Texas-Midland Telephone Co. [Aff. of Great Southwest Telephone Corp.] - Grandview, TX - *TelDir&BG 83-84*
Texas Mohair Weekly - Rocksprings, TX - *AyerDirPub 83*
Texas Monthly [of Mediatex Communications Corp.] - Austin, TX - *BaconPubCkMag 84; DirMarMP 83; Folio 83; MagIndMarPl 82-83*
Texas Monthly Press [Subs. of Mediatex Communications Corp.] - Austin, TX - *LitMarPl 83, 84; WritMar 84*
Texas Natural Resources Information System - Austin, TX - *EISS 83*
Texas Observer - Austin, TX - *NewsDir 84; WritMar 84*
Texas Oil Marketer [of The Texas Oil Marketers Association] - Austin, TX - *BaconPubCkMag 84; MagDir 84*
Texas Optometry - Austin, TX - *BaconPubCkMag 84; MagDir 84*
Texas Outdoor Guide - Houston, TX - *MagDir 84*
Texas Outlook - Austin, TX - *BaconPubCkMag 84; MagDir 84*
Texas Pacific Film Video Inc. - Austin, TX - *AvMarPl 83*
Texas Parks & Wildlife - Austin, TX - *MagDir 84*
Texas Pharmacy [of Texas Pharmaceutical Association] - Austin, TX - *BaconPubCkMag 84; MagDir 84*
Texas Posten - Austin, TX - *Ed&PubIntYB 82*
Texas Press Association - Austin, TX - *ProGuPRSer 4*
Texas Press Clipping Bureau - Dallas, TX - *ProGuPRSer 4*
Texas Press Messenger - Austin, TX - *MagDir 84*
Texas Professional Engineer [of Texas Society of Professional Engineers] - Austin, TX - *BaconPubCkMag 84; MagDir 84*
Texas Public Employee [of Texas Public Employees Association] - Austin, TX - *MagDir 84*
Texas Realtor - Austin, TX - *BaconPubCkMag 84*
Texas Review, The - Huntsville, TX - *LitMag&SmPr 83-84*
Texas Sportsman - Marietta, GA - *BaconPubCkMag 84; WritMar 84*
Texas Sportsman - San Antonio, TX - *MagDir 84*
Texas Spur - Spur, TX - *AyerDirPub 83; Ed&PubIntYB 82*
Texas Starway Song Publishers - Ft. Worth, TX - *BillIntBG 83-84*
Texas State Bar (Professional Development Program) - Austin, TX - *BoPubDir 4 Sup, 5*

Texas State Dept. of Water Resources Library - Austin, TX - *EISS 83*
Texas State Genealogical Society - Dallas, TX - *BoPubDir 4, 5*
Texas State Historical Association - Austin, TX - *BoPubDir 4, 5*
Texas Sunday Comic Section Inc. - Dallas, TX - *Ed&PubIntYB 82*
Texas Systems Computer Services Inc. - Waco, TX - *WhoWMicrocom 83*
Texas Tech Press - Lubbock, TX - *LitMarPl 84*
Texas Tech University (Institute for Communications Research) - Lubbock, TX - *InterCabHB 3*
Texas Tech University (Institute for Studies in Pragmaticism) - Lubbock, TX - *BoPubDir 4 Sup, 5*
Texas Tech University (Texas Tech Press) - Lubbock, TX - *BoPubDir 4, 5*
Texas Telecable Inc. [of TCA Cable TV Group] - Conroe, TX - *BrCabYB 84; Tel&CabFB 84C*
Texas Town & City [of Texas Municipal League] - Austin, TX - *BaconPubCkMag 84; MagDir 84*
Texas Tribune, The - Houston, TX - *Ed&PubIntYB 82*
Texas Weekly Magazine - Pasadena, TX - *WritMar 84*
Texas Western Press [of The University of Texas at El Paso] - El Paso, TX - *LitMarPl 83, 84; WritMar 84*
Texas Woman's University Press - Denton, TX - *BoPubDir 5*
Texasoft Inc. - Dallas, TX - *MicrocomSwDir 1*
Texcom Inc. [of Tele-Communications Inc.] - Refugio, TX - *Tel&CabFB 84C*
Texcom Inc. - Refugio County, TX - *BrCabYB 84*
Texcom Inc. [of Community Tele-Communications Inc.] - Woodsboro, TX - *Tel&CabFB 84C*
Texhoma Times - Texhoma, OK - *BaconPubCkNews 84; Ed&PubIntYB 82*
Texian Press - Waco, TX - *BoPubDir 4, 5*
Texkan Communications Inc. - Junction City, KS - *Tel&CabFB 84C p.1707*
Texoma Cable TV Co. - Kingston, OK - *BrCabYB 84*
Texoman, The - Kingston, OK - *AyerDirPub 83*
Texprint Inc. - Burlington, MA - *DataDirSup 7-83*
Texscan Corp. - Phoenix, AZ - *CabTVFinDB 83*
Texscan Corp. - Indianapolis, IN - *HomeVid&CabYB 82-83*
Text-Fiche Press - Glencoe, IL - *BoPubDir 4, 5*
Text Information Processing Services [of University of Florida Libraries] - Gainesville, FL - *FBInfSer 80*
Text Processing/Retrieval Programs [of International Business Machines Corp.] - White Plains, NY - *EISS 83*
Text-TV [of Sveriges Television] - Stockholm, Sweden - *VideoDir 82-83*
Textile & Clothing Information Centre - Brussels, Belgium - *EISS 5-84 Sup*
Textile Artists' Newsletter - Berkeley, CA - *LitMag&SmPr 83-84*
Textile Book Service Inc. - Broadway, NJ - *BoPubDir 4, 5*
Textile Booklist, The - Lopez Island, WA - *LitMag&SmPr 83-84*
Textile Bridge Press [Aff. of Moody Street Irregulars Inc.] - Clarence Center, NY - *BoPubDir 4 Sup, 5; LitMag&SmPr 83-84*
Textile Chemist & Colorist - Durham, NC - *MagDir 84*
Textile Chemist & Colorist - Research Triangle Park, NC - *BaconPubCkMag 84*
Textile Economics Bureau Inc. - Roseland, NJ - *BoPubDir 5*
Textile Executive Forum - Charlotte, NC - *BaconPubCkMag 84*
Textile Industries - Atlanta, GA - *BaconPubCkMag 84; MagDir 84*
Textile Industries - Greenville, SC - *MagIndMarPl 82-83*
Textile Information Services [of Institute of Textile Technology] - Charlottesville, VA - *EISS 83*
Textile Information Services [of Shirley Institute] - Manchester, England - *EISS 83*
Textile Information Treatment Users' Service [of Institut Textile de France] - Boulogne, France - *CompReadDB 82; DBBus 82; EISS 83; OnBibDB 3*
Textile Maintenance Reporter - Austin, TX - *BaconPubCkMag 84; MagDir 84*
Textile Museum - Washington, DC - *BoPubDir 4, 5*
Textile Products & Processes - Atlanta, GA - *MagDir 84; MagIndMarPl 82-83*
Textile Rental - Hallandale, FL - *BaconPubCkMag 84; MagDir 84*
Textile Research Journal - Princeton, NJ - *BaconPubCkMag 84; MagDir 84*
Textile Technology Digest [of Institute of Textile Technology] - Charlottesville, VA - *CompReadDB 82; DataDirOnSer 84; DirOnDB Spring 84*
Textile Technology Digest (Keyterm Index) - Charlottesville, VA - *CompReadDB 82*
Textile World - Atlanta, GA - *BaconPubCkMag 84; MagDir 84; MagIndMarPl 82-83; WritMar 84*
Textiles Panamericanos - Atlanta, GA - *BaconPubCkMag 84; MagDir 84*
Textline [of Finsbury Data Services] - London, England - *CompReadDB 82; DataDirOnSer 84; DirOnDB Spring 84; EISS 83; OnBibDB 3*
Textstyle - Cambridge, MA - *LitMarPl 83, 84*
Texturefects - Magalia, CA - *AvMarPl 83*
Textype - Palo Alto, CA - *LitMarPl 83, 84; MagIndMarPl 82-83*
Texwipe Co., The - Upper Saddle River, NJ - *WhoWMicrocom 83*
Texwood Furniture Corp. - Austin, TX - *AvMarPl 83*
TFB Public Relations [Div. of Tycer-Fultz-Bellack Ltd.] - Palo Alto, CA - *DirPRFirms 83*
T.F.H. Publications Inc. - Neptune City, NJ - *LitMarPl 83, 84; WritMar 84*
TFR Marketing Research Inc. - Dallas, TX - *IntDirMarRes 83*
TG Products - Plano, TX - *MicrocomMPl 83, 84; WhoWMicrocom 83*
TGI Graphics Inc. - Deer Park, NY - *LitMarPl 84*
TH Record & Tapes Inc. - Hialeah Gardens, FL - *BillIntBG 83-84*
Thacker Cable - South Pikeville, KY - *BrCabYB 84*
Thacker-Grigsby Telephone Co. Inc. - Hindman, KY - *TelDir&BG 83-84*
Thalia - Ottawa, ON, Canada - *LitMag&SmPr 83-84*
Thalner Electronic Laboratories - Ann Arbor, MI - *AvMarPl 83*
Thames & Hudson Inc. - New York, NY - *LitMarPl 83, 84*
Thames Book Co. - New London, CT - *LitMarPl 83, 84*
Thanatos - Tallahassee, FL - *MagDir 84*
Tharpe Photo Library, Max [Subs. of Photoscope] - Ft. Lauderdale, FL - *LitMarPl 83, 84; MagIndMarPl 82-83*
That New Publishing Co. - Fairbanks, AK - *BoPubDir 4, 5*
Thatcher Co., T. L. - Bountiful, UT - *LitMarPl 84*
Thayer Advertising Co. [Div. of Thayer Publishing Corp.] - Westville, NJ - *DirMarMP 83*
Thayer-Jacoby - Brooklyn, NY - *BoPubDir 4, 5*
Thayer News - Thayer, MO - *BaconPubCkNews 84; Ed&PubIntYB 82*
T.H.E. Journal [of Information Synergy Inc.] - Irvine, CA - *BaconPubCkMag 84; MicrocomMPl 84*
T.H.E. Journal - Santa Ana, CA - *MagDir 84*
Thea Music - *See* Ferry Boat Music
Theater - New Haven, CT - *LitMag&SmPr 83-84*
Theater of the Open Eye - New York, NY - *WritMar 84*
Theaterwork Magazine [of Cherry Creek Inc.] - Mankato, MN - *LitMag&SmPr 83-84*
Theatre Arts Books - New York, NY - *LitMarPl 83, 84*
Theatre Communications Center of the Bay Area - San Francisco, CA - *BoPubDir 4, 5*
Theatre Communications Group - New York, NY - *BoPubDir 4; LitMarPl 83, 84*
Theatre Crafts [of Theatre Crafts Associates] - New York, NY - *BaconPubCkMag 84; MagDir 84; MagIndMarPl 82-83; WritMar 84*
Theatre Design & Technology [of U.S. Institute for Theatre Technology Inc.] - New York, NY - *BaconPubCkMag 84; MagDir 84*
Theatre Design & Technology [of U.S. Institute for Theatre Technology Inc.] - Charlottesville, VA - *LitMag&SmPr 83-84*
Theatre Journal [of American Theatre Association] - Washington, DC - *MagDir 84*
Theatre L.A. - San Francisco, CA - *MagDir 84*
Theatre Library Association - New York, NY - *BoPubDir 4, 5*
Theatre News - Washington, DC - *MagIndMarPl 82-83*
Theatre Notebook - London, England - *LitMag&SmPr 83-84*
Theatre Service & Supply - Baltimore, MD - *AvMarPl 83*
Theatrebooks Ltd. - Toronto, ON, Canada - *BoPubDir 4 Sup, 5*
Thelema Publications - Kings Beach, CA - *BoPubDir 4, 5*
Thelphini Press - New Haven, CT - *BoPubDir 4, 5*
Thematic Advertising Productions Inc. - Saddle Brook, NJ - *StaDirAdAg 2-84*

Theobald & Co., Paul - Chicago, IL - *BoPubDir 4, 5*
Theologia 21 [of Dominion Press] - San Marcos, CA - *LitMag&SmPr 83-84*
Theological Studies - Washington, DC - *MagIndMarPl 82-83*
Theology Digest - St. Louis, MO - *MagIndMarPl 82-83*
Theology Today - Princeton, NJ - *MagIndMarPl 82-83*
Theory into Practice - Columbus, OH - *MagIndMarPl 82-83*
Theoscience Foundation Publishers - Burlingame, CA - *BoPubDir 4, 5*
Theosophical Book Association for the Blind Inc. - Ojai, CA - *LitMarPl 83, 84*
Theosophical Publishing House [Div. of The Theosophical Society in America] - Wheaton, IL - *LitMarPl 83, 84; WritMar 84*
Theosophical University Press [Aff. of The Theosophical Society] - Pasadena, CA - *BoPubDir 4, 5*
Theotes-Logos Research Inc. - Minneapolis, MN - *BoPubDir 4, 5*
Therafields Books - Toronto, ON, Canada - *BoPubDir 4, 5*
Theresa Records - Albany, CA - *BillIntBG 83-84*
Thermal Belt News Journal, The - Columbus, NC - *Ed&PubIntYB 82*
Thermo - Washington, DC - *DirOnDB Spring 84*
Thermo [of Chemical Information Systems Inc.] - Baltimore, MD - *DataDirOnSer 84*
Thermodata - St. Martin d'Heres, France - *DirOnDB Spring 84*
Thermodata-Thermodoc Data Bank [of Thermodata Association] - St. Martin d'Heres, France - *EISS 83*
Thermodoc - St. Martin d'Heres, France - *DirOnDB Spring 84*
Thermodynamics Research Center [of Texas A & M University] - College Station, TX - *EISS 83; InfIndMarPl 83*
Thermophysical & Electronic Properties Information Analysis Center [of Purdue University] - West Lafayette, IN - *CompReadDB 82; InfIndMarPl 83*
Thermophysical Properties Data Center [of Academy of Sciences of the USSR] - Moscow, USSR - *EISS 83*
Thermophysical Properties Research Center [of Thermophysical & Electronic Properties Information Analysis Center] - West Lafayette, IN - *CompReadDB 82*
Thermopolis Independent Record - Thermopolis, WY - *BaconPubCkNews 84; Ed&PubIntYB 82*
These Times [of Review & Herald Publishing Association] - Washington, DC - *ArtMar 84; MagIndMarPl 82-83; WritMar 84*
Theses in Education [of University of Alberta] - Edmonton, AB, Canada - *DataDirOnSer 84*
T.H.E.S.I.S. - Garden City, MI - *MicrocomMPl 83, 84; MicrocomSwDir 1; WhoWMicrocom 83*
Theta Business Systems - Glendale, CA - *MicrocomMPl 83, 84; MicrocomSwDir 1; WhoWMicrocom 83*
Theta Labs Inc. - Dallas, TX - *MicrocomMPl 83*
Thetford Video Inc. - Thetford Mines, PQ, Canada - *BrCabYB 84; Tel&CabFB 84C*
Thevenin, Tine - Minneapolis, MN - *BoPubDir 5*
Theytus Books Ltd. - Nanaimo, BC, Canada - *BoPubDir 4 Sup, 5*
Thibodaux Comet - Thibodaux, LA - *BaconPubCkNews 84; NewsDir 84*
Thibodeau, A. - New York, NY - *LitMarPl 84*
Thief River Falls Times - Thief River Falls, MN - *BaconPubCkNews 84; Ed&PubIntYB 82; NewsDir 84*
Thielen & Associates - Fresno, CA - *StaDirAdAg 2-84*
Thieme-Stratton Inc. [Subs. of Georg Thieme Verlag] - New York, NY - *LitMarPl 83, 84*
Thien/Uniphoto, Alex - Milwaukee, WI - *AvMarPl 83*
Thiessen, Richard L. - *See* Community Antenna Systems Inc.
Thieves Guild [of Gamelords Ltd.] - Gaithersburg, MD - *WritMar 84*
Things Antique - New York, NY - *AvMarPl 83*
Think Ink [Aff. of Resources for the Gifted Inc.] - Phoenix, AZ - *BoPubDir 4 Sup, 5*
Thinkers' Press - Davenport, IA - *BoPubDir 5*
Thinker's Soft Inc. - Garden City, NY - *MicrocomMPl 84*
Third Coast Archives - Shorewood, WI - *LitMag&SmPr 83-84*
Third Eye - Buffalo, NY - *LitMag&SmPr 83-84*
Third Eye Publications Inc. - London, ON, Canada - *BoPubDir 4, 5*
Third Party Publishing Co. [Aff. of Third Party Associates Inc.] - Oakland, CA - *BoPubDir 5*
Third Sector Press - Cleveland, OH - *BoPubDir 4 Sup, 5*
Third Story Records - Philadelphia, PA - *BillIntBG 83-84*
Third Stream Music Inc. - *See* MJQ Music Inc.
Third Street Jazz & Rock Records - Philadelphia, PA - *BillIntBG 83-84*
Third Way - London, England - *LitMag&SmPr 83-84*
Third Wind, The - South Hamilton, MA - *LitMag&SmPr 83-84*
Third World Books & Crafts - Toronto, ON, Canada - *BoPubDir 4, 5*
Third World Press [Aff. of Institute of Positive Education] - Chicago, IL - *BoPubDir 4, 5; LitMag&SmPr 83-84*
Third World Publications Ltd. - Birmingham, England - *LitMag&SmPr 83-84*
Thirteen - Portlandville, NY - *LitMag&SmPr 83-84*
Thirteen Towns - Fosston, MN - *AyerDirPub 83; Ed&PubIntYB 82*
13th Moon - New York, NY - *BoPubDir 4, 5; LitMag&SmPr 83-84; WritMar 84*
39th Street Neighborhood News [of St. Louis Suburban Newspapers Inc.] - St. Louis, MO - *NewsDir 84*
Thirty Press Ltd. - London, England - *LitMag&SmPr 83-84*
33 Metal Producing - New York, NY - *MagDir 84; MagIndMarPl 82-83; WritMar 84*
32-B - New York, NY - *NewsDir 84*
32-Events - New York, NY - *NewsDir 84*
This - Oakland, CA - *LitMag&SmPr 83-84*
This Is Important - Santa Cruz, CA - *LitMag&SmPr 83-84*
This Magazine - Toronto, ON, Canada - *LitMag&SmPr 83-84*
This People - Salt Lake City, UT - *BaconPubCkMag 84*
This Press - Berkeley, CA - *LitMag&SmPr 83-84*
This Press - Oakland, CA - *BoPubDir 4, 5*
This Week - Kissimmee, FL - *AyerDirPub 83*
This Week - Lumberton, NC - *AyerDirPub 83*
This Week [of Journal Publishing Co.] - Oklahoma City, OK - *NewsDir 84*
This Week [of R.F.D. Publications Inc.] - Portland, OR - *Ed&PubIntYB 82; NewsDir 84; WritMar 84*
This Week - Kingston, ON, Canada - *AyerDirPub 83*
This Week - Yorkton, SK, Canada - *AyerDirPub 83*
This Week in Peachtree City [of Fayette Newspapers Inc.] - Peachtree City, GA - *AyerDirPub 83; Ed&PubIntYB 82; NewsDir 84*
This Week in Rockdale - Conyers, GA - *AyerDirPub 83*
This Week Marketplace - Yorkton, SK, Canada - *AyerDirPub 83*
This Week Newspaper - Osceola County, FL - *Ed&PubIntYB 82*
This Week on Martha's Vineyard - Vineyard Haven, MA - *AyerDirPub 83*
This Week Shopper - Yorkton, SK, Canada - *AyerDirPub 83*
This World [of San Francisco Chronicle] - San Francisco, CA - *LitMarPl 84*
This'n That Press - Pine Grove, CA - *BoPubDir 5*
Thistledown Press Ltd. - Saskatoon, SK, Canada - *BoPubDir 4; LitMag&SmPr 83-84; LitMarPl 83, 84*
Thistlerose Publications - White Bear Lake, MN - *BoPubDir 4, 5*
Thode & Associates, I. L. - Greenwich, CT - *ADAPSOMemDir 83-84*
Thomas Advertising Co. - Studio City, CA - *StaDirAdAg 2-84*
Thomas & Associates Inc., Bob - Redondo Beach, CA - *DirPRFirms 83*
Thomas & Associates, Robert B. - Los Angeles, CA - *StaDirAdAg 2-84*
Thomas Associates Inc., Ira - Youngstown, OH - *AdAge 3-28-84; StaDirAdAg 2-84*
Thomas Associates Inc., Ted - Philadelphia, PA - *AdAge 3-28-84; StaDirAdAg 2-84*
Thomas, Charles C. - Springfield, IL - *LitMarPl 83, 84*
Thomas-CSF - Paris, France - *ElecNews 7-25-83*
Thomas Engineering Co. - Concord, MA - *DataDirSup 7-83*
Thomas Hardy Yearbook [of Toucan] - Guernsey, England - *LitMag&SmPr 83-84*
Thomas Law Book Co. - St. Louis, MO - *BoPubDir 4, 5; LitMarPl 83, 84*
Thomas, Marita - New York, NY - *LitMarPl 83; MagIndMarPl 82-83*
Thomas Marketing Information Center [of Thomas Publishing Co.] - New York, NY - *EISS 5-84 Sup; IntDirMarRes 83*
Thomas Music Co., Harold - Charleston, SC - *BillIntBG 83-84*

Thomas National Group Inc. - New York, NY - *EISS 83*
Thomas National Inc. [Subs. of Thomas National Group Inc.] - New York, NY - *LitMarPl 83, 84*
Thomas Press Inc. - Ann Arbor, MI - *BoPubDir 4, 5*
Thomas Printing & Publishing Co. - Kaukauna, WI - *BoPubDir 4, 5*
Thomas Productions, Bob - Wayne, NJ - *WritMar 84*
Thomas Productions, Bob - New York, NY - *TelAl 83, 84*
Thomas Publishing Co. - New York, NY - *BoPubDir 5; InfoS 83-84*
Thomas Regional Directory Co. [Aff. of Thomas Publishing Co.] - New York, NY - *BoPubDir 4 Sup, 5*
Thomas Research Inc. - Houston, TX - *IntDirMarRes 83*
Thomas Tape Co., The - Springfield, OH - *LitMarPl 83, 84*
Thomas, Terry - Redfield, SD - *Tel&CabFB 84C p.1707*
Thomas Tribune - Thomas, OK - *BaconPubCkNews 84; Ed&PubIntYB 82*
Thomas TV Cable Co. [of Redden Cable TV] - Thomas, OK - *BrCabYB 84; Tel&CabFB 84C*
Thomas Video Cassette Duplicating Co. [Div. of Bob Thomas Productions] - Wayne, NJ - *AvMarPl 83*
Thomason Press Inc. - Moorestown, NJ - *MagIndMarPl 82-83*
Thomasson-Grant Inc. - Charlottesville, VA - *BoPubDir 5*
Thomaston Cable Television Co. - Thomaston, GA - *BrCabYB 84; Tel&CabFB 84C*
Thomaston Express - Thomaston, CT - *BaconPubCkNews 84*
Thomaston Times & Free Press - Thomaston, GA - *BaconPubCkNews 84*
Thomaston Times, The - Thomaston, GA - *Ed&PubIntYB 82; NewsDir 84*
Thomasville Courier - Thomasville, GA - *Ed&PubIntYB 82*
Thomasville Times - Thomasville, AL - *BaconPubCkNews 84; Ed&PubIntYB 82*
Thomasville Times [of High Point Enterprise Inc.] - Thomasville, NC - *BaconPubCkNews 84; NewsDir 84*
Thomasville Times-Enterprise [of Thomson Newspapers Inc.] - Thomasville, GA - *BaconPubCkNews 84; Ed&PubIntYB 82; NewsDir 84*
Thompson Advertising Agency Inc., Michael H. - Memphis, TN - *StaDirAdAg 2-84*
Thompson Advertising, C. Franklin - Windsor, CT - *StaDirAdAg 2-84*
Thompson Advertising Inc., B. J. - Mishawaka, IN - *StaDirAdAg 2-84*
Thompson Advertising Inc., George E. S. - Oakland, CA - *StaDirAdAg 2-84*
Thompson Advertising Productions Inc. - Farmington Hills, MI - *StaDirAdAg 2-84*
Thompson & Associates Inc. - Springfield, VA - *DirMarMP 83*
Thompson & Associates Inc., Ray - Hunt Valley, MD - *StaDirAdAg 2-84*
Thompson Associates - Warwick, RI - *StaDirAdAg 2-84*
Thompson Cablevision Co. Inc. [of TV Antenna Service Inc.] - War, WV - *BrCabYB 84*
Thompson Citizen - Thompson, MB, Canada - *BaconPubCkNews 84*
Thompson Communications Cos. Inc. - New York, NY - *StaDirAdAg 2-84*
Thompson Community TV - Thompson, PA - *BrCabYB 84*
Thompson Co. Inc., John S. - Los Altos, CA - *IntDirMarRes 83*
Thompson Co., J. Walter - Atlanta, GA - *ArtMar 84*
Thompson Co., J. Walter - Detroit, MI - *ArtMar 84*
Thompson Co., J. Walter - New York, NY - *AdAge 3-28-84, 6-25-84; Br 1-23-84; BrCabYB 84; HomeVid&CabYB 82-83; StaDirAdAg 2-84; TelAl 83, 84*
Thompson Co., Pat - Aurora, CO - *CabTVFinDB 83*
Thompson Courier - Thompson, IA - *BaconPubCkNews 84; Ed&PubIntYB 82*
Thompson, Dean - *See* Badger Mountain Cable TV
Thompson Falls Sanders County Ledger - Thompson Falls, MT - *BaconPubCkNews 84*
Thompson/Grande Advertising Inc. - Minneapolis, MN - *StaDirAdAg 2-84*
Thompson Inc., Jules E. - Burlingame, CA - *MagIndMarPl 82-83*
Thompson, John W. - Waitsburg, WA - *Tel&CabFB 84C p.1707*
Thompson-Koch Co. Inc., The - New York, NY - *StaDirAdAg 2-84*
Thompson Ltd., Henry - Sunningdale, England - *InfIndMarPl 83*
Thompson, Matelan & Hawbaker Inc. - Pittsburgh, PA - *StaDirAdAg 2-84*
Thompson, Paul J. - Cleveland, OH - *BoPubDir 4, 5*
Thompson, Pierce & Associates Inc. - Excelsior, MN - *DirPRFirms 83*
Thompson Publishing Group - Washington, DC - *DirMarMP 83*
Thompson Recruitment Advertising Inc. [Subs. of J. Walter Thompson Co.] - Los Angeles, CA - *StaDirAdAg 2-84*
Thompson-Rosenbaum Publishing - Minneapolis, MN - *LitMarPl 84*
Thompson, Torchia & Dymond Inc. - Charlotte, NC - *ArtMar 84; StaDirAdAg 2-84*
Thompson/Uniphoto, Dale - Chicago, IL - *AvMarPl 83*
Thompson Worldwide Recruitment - Los Angeles, CA - *HBIndAd&MS 82-83*
Thomsic, Michael F. III - Scottsbluff, NE - *Tel&CabFB 84C p.1707*
Thomson & Thomson [Subs. of International Thomson Information Inc.] - Boston, MA - *DataDirOnSer 84; InfoS 83-84*
Thomson Carroll County Review - Thomson, IL - *BaconPubCkNews 84*
Thomson Comics Group - Toronto, ON, Canada - *Ed&PubIntYB 82*
Thomson-Leeds Co. Inc. - New York, NY - *HBIndAd&MS 82-83*
Thomson McDuffie Progress - Thomson, GA - *BaconPubCkNews 84; NewsDir 84*
Thomson Newspapers - Canada - *Ed&PubIntYB 82*
Thomson Newspapers - Toronto, ON, Canada - *Ed&PubIntYB 82*
Thomson Newspapers Inc. - New York, NY - *LitMarPl 83, 84*
Thomson Newspapers Inc. (Comic Group) - New York, NY - *Ed&PubIntYB 82*
Thomson Newspapers Ltd. - Des Plaines, IL - *KnowInd 83*
Thomson, Phillip - Williamston, MI - *BoPubDir 4, 5*
Thomson Publications - Fresno, CA - *BoPubDir 4, 5*
Thomson-Shore Inc. - Dexter, MI - *LitMarPl 83, 84*
Thor Data Inc. - New York, NY - *IntDirMarRes 83*
Thor Publishing Co. - Ventura, CA - *LitMarPl 83, 84*
Thoreau Journal Quarterly - Minneapolis, MN - *LitMag&SmPr 83-84*
Thorn EMI - London, England - *ElecNews 7-25-83*
Thorn EMI plc - New York, NY - *KnowInd 83*
Thorn-EMI Video - New York, NY - *BillIntBG 83-84*
Thorn Press - Don Mills, ON, Canada - *LitMarPl 83, 84*
Thorndale Champion - Thorndale, TX - *Ed&PubIntYB 82*
Thorndale Champion - *See* Taylor Newspapers Inc.
Thorndike Press - Thorndike, ME - *LitMag&SmPr 83-84; LitMarPl 83, 84; WritMar 84*
Thorne & Co. - Cary, NC - *StaDirAdAg 2-84*
Thorne Bay Community TV Inc. - Thorne Bay, AK - *BrCabYB 84; Tel&CabFB 84C*
Thorne Creative Research Services - Brooklyn, NY - *IntDirMarRes 83*
Thornhill Month Magazine [of Thornhill Publications Ltd.] - Thornhill, ON, Canada - *WritMar 84*
Thornhill Publishing Enr'g. - Pointe Claire, PQ, Canada - *BoPubDir 4, 5*
Thorniley, Chris W. - Marietta, OH - *BrCabYB 84*
Thorniley, Chris W. - *See* Ohio Valley Cable Corp.
Thornton Features, Robert - Portland, OR - *Ed&PubIntYB 82*
Thornton Southern County News - Thornton, IA - *BaconPubCkNews 84*
Thornton, Susan Hallelujah - Columbus, OH - *LitMarPl 83, 84*
Thorntown Hoosier Graphic - Thorntown, IN - *NewsDir 84*
Thorntown Telephone Co. - Thorntown, IN - *Tel&CabFB 84C; TelDir&BG 83-84*
Thornwood Book Publishers - Florence, AL - *BoPubDir 5; LitMag&SmPr 83-84*
Thorold News, The - Thorold, ON, Canada - *Ed&PubIntYB 82*
Thoroughbred of California - Arcadia, CA - *BaconPubCkMag 84; MagDir 84*
Thoroughbred Press Co. Inc. - Lexington, KY - *MagIndMarPl 82-83*
Thoroughbred Record [of Thoroughbred Publishers Inc.] - Lexington, KY - *BaconPubCkMag 84; MagDir 84; WritMar 84*
Thoroughbred Records - Austin, TX - *BillIntBG 83-84*

Thorp Cablevision Inc. [of Thorp Telephone Co.] - Thorp, WI - *Tel&CabFB 84C*
Thorp Courier - Thorp, WI - *BaconPubCkNews 84; Ed&PubIntYB 82; NewsDir 84*
Thorp Springs Press - Austin, TX - *LitMag&SmPr 83-84*
Thorp Telephone Co. - Thorp, WI - *TelDir&BG 83-84*
Thorpe Pty. Ltd., D. W. - Melbourne, Australia - *MicroMarPl 82-83*
Thorpe Public Relations, Lawrence - Arlington Heights, IL - *DirPRFirms 83*
Thorsons Publishers Inc. [Subs. of Thorsons Publishing Group] - New York, NY - *LitMarPl 84*
Thorsons Publishers Ltd. - Wellingborough, England - *WritMar 84*
Thorwald & Associates Advertising Inc. - Eugene, OR - *StaDirAdAg 2-84*
Thought Works Inc. - Phoenix, AZ - *MicrocomMPl 84*
Thoughts for All Seasons [of Valley Press] - Geneseo, NY - *LitMag&SmPr 83-84*
Thoughtware Inc. - Tucson, AZ - *MicrocomMPl 84*
Thoughtware Publishing Co. - Grants Pass, OR - *MicrocomMPl 84; MicrocomSwDir 1*
Thousand Islands Cable TV Inc. - Clayton, NY - *BrCabYB 84; Tel&CabFB 84C*
Thousand Islands Sun - Alexandria Bay, NY - *AyerDirPub 83; Ed&PubIntYB 82; NewsDir 84*
Thousand Islands Sun Vacationer - Alexandria Bay, NY - *NewsDir 84*
1000 Islands Town & Country News [of Gouverneur Town & Country News of Jefferson County] - Gouverneur, NY - *NewsDir 84*
Thousand Oaks MDS Co. - Pasadena, MD - *Tel&CabFB 84C*
Thousand Oaks News-Chronicle [of John P. Scripps Newspapers] - Thousand Oaks, CA - *BaconPubCkNews 84; NewsDir 84*
Thousandsticks-News, The - Hyden, KY - *Ed&PubIntYB 82*
Thrasher Publications - Homestead, FL - *BoPubDir 4, 5*
Threadgill, Jack M. - Hearne, TX - *Tel&CabFB 84C p.1707*
Three Arts Inc. - Cedar Rapids, IA - *StaDirAdAg 2-84*
Three Bamboo Studio - Durham, NC - *LitMarPl 83, 84*
3Com Corp. - Mountain View, CA - *DataDirSup 7-83*
Three Continents Press - Washington, DC - *LitMag&SmPr 83-84; LitMarPl 83, 84; WritMar 84*
3-D Publishers - Edgerton, OH - *BoPubDir 4, 5*
3D Video Corp. - North Hollywood, CA - *AvMarPl 83*
3-Deal Music - Chicago, IL - *BillIntBG 83-84*
Three Forks Herald & Manhattan Intermountain Press - Three Forks, MT - *BaconPubCkNews 84; Ed&PubIntYB 82*
340 Leader, The - New York, NY - *NewsDir 84*
3G Co. Inc. - Gaston, OR - *MicrocomMPl 84; WhoWMicrocom 83*
3 G's Industries Inc. - Kansas City, MO - *BillIntBG 83-84*
Three Herons Press - Rochester, NY - *BoPubDir 4, 5*
Three Hills Capital, The - Three Hills, AB, Canada - *Ed&PubIntYB 82*
3-J Records [Div. of Mende Music] - West Plains, MO - *BillIntBG 83-84*
Three Lakes News - Eagle River, WI - *BaconPubCkNews 84*
Three Lions Inc. - New York, NY - *AvMarPl 83*
3M Co. - St. Paul, MN - *BoPubDir 4; DataDirSup 7-83; Datamation 6-83; Top100Al 83*
3M Co. (Audio Visual Div.) - St. Paul, MN - *AvMarPl 83*
3M Co. (Copying Products Div.) - St. Paul, MN - *DirInfWP 82*
3M Co. (Data Recording Products Div.) - St. Paul, MN - *DirInfWP 82*
3M Co. (Interactive Systems) - Ann Arbor, MI - *DirInfWP 82*
3M Co. (Micrographics Products Div.) - St. Paul, MN - *DirInfWP 82*
3M New Zealand Ltd. - Aukland, New Zealand - *MicroMarPl 82-83*
3M Publishing [of 3M Co.] - St. Paul, MN - *LitMarPl 83, 84*
Three Mountain Press - New York, NY - *LitMag&SmPr 83-84*
Three Oaks Galien River Gazette - Three Oaks, MI - *BaconPubCkNews 84*
Three PM Inc. - Livonia, MI - *DataDirOnSer 84*
Three Point Landing - St. Paul, MN - *AvMarPl 83*
3R Software - Jamaica, NY - *MicrocomMPl 83; MicrocomSwDir 1; WhoWMicrocom 83*
3RIP [of Paralog] - Stockholm, Sweden - *EISS 83*
Three River Telco - Lynch, NE - *TelDir&BG 83-84*
Three Rivers Commercial - Three Rivers, MI - *BaconPubCkNews 84; Ed&PubIntYB 82; NewsDir 84*
Three Rivers Computer Corp. - Pittsburgh, PA - *DataDirSup 7-83; WhoWMicrocom 83*
Three Rivers Progress - Three Rivers, TX - *BaconPubCkNews 84*
Three Rivers St. Joseph Valley Leader - Three Rivers, MI - *NewsDir 84*
3 Rivers Telephone Cooperative Inc. - Fairfield, MT - *TelDir&BG 83-84*
Three S Publishers [Aff. of Three S Fitness Group Ltd.] - Ganges, BC, Canada - *BoPubDir 4 Sup, 5*
3 Score - Atlanta, GA - *DirMarMP 83*
Three Sigma Major Market Newspaper Audiences-1980 [of Interactive Market Systems] - New York, NY - *DataDirOnSer 84*
Three Sigma Research Center - Larchmont, NY - *MagIndMarPl 82-83*
III Systems Inc. - Cambridge, MA - *EISS 83*
338 News - New York, NY - *NewsDir 84*
Three Tree - Lansing, MI - *LitMag&SmPr 83-84*
Three Trees Press - Toronto, ON, Canada - *LitMarPl 83, 84*
328 News Digest - Providence, RI - *NewsDir 84*
3-2-1 Contact [of Children's Television Workshop] - New York, NY - *MagIndMarPl 82-83; WritMar 84*
Three Village Herald - Stony Brook, NY - *AyerDirPub 83; Ed&PubIntYB 82*
3 Wheeling - Costa Mesa, CA - *BaconPubCkMag 84*
Three Willows Music - Chicago, IL - *BillIntBG 83-84*
Threepenny Review, The - Berkeley, CA - *LitMag&SmPr 83-84*
Thresh Publications - Bethel Island, CA - *BoPubDir 4, 5*
Threshman, Clara I. - Milford, CT - *LitMarPl 83, 84; MagIndMarPl 82-83*
Threshold Books - Putney, VT - *BoPubDir 4, 5; LitMag&SmPr 83-84*
Threshold of Fantasy [of Fandom Unltd. Enterprises] - Sunnyvale, CA - *LitMag&SmPr 83-84*
Threshold Software Inc. - Sacramento, CA - *MicrocomMPl 84*
Threshold Technology Inc. - Delran, NJ - *DataDirSup 7-83*
Thrice Music Inc. - *See* Kaplan Productions Inc., A.
Thrif-t-Nickel Weekly [of F. W. Gray & Associates Ltd.] - Ottawa, IL - *AyerDirPub 83; NewsDir 84*
Thrift Publishers Inc. [Aff. of National Association of Mutual Savings Banks] - New York, NY - *BoPubDir 5*
Thrifticall [of NCR Telecommunication Services Inc.] - Dayton, OH - *TeleSy&SerDir 2-84*
Thrifty Neighbor [of Oklahoma City Capitol Hill Beacon] - Oklahoma City, OK - *NewsDir 84*
Thrifty Reporter - Enfield, CT - *AyerDirPub 83*
Throckmorton Associates Inc. - New York, NY - *DirMarMP 83*
Throckmorton Cablevision - Throckmorton, TX - *Tel&CabFB 84C*
Throckmorton Tribune - Throckmorton, TX - *BaconPubCkNews 84; Ed&PubIntYB 82*
Through the Looking Glass - Seattle, WA - *LitMag&SmPr 83-84*
Throwkoff Press, G. - Lawrenceville, NJ - *BoPubDir 5*
Thrushwood Records - Pomfret, CT - *BillIntBG 83-84*
Thrust - Gaithersburg, MD - *LitMag&SmPr 83-84*
Thrust; For Educational Leadership - Burlingame, CA - *MagIndMarPl 82-83*
T.H.T. Productions Inc. - New York, NY - *Tel&CabFB 84C*
Thueson, James D. - Minneapolis, MN - *BoPubDir 5*
Thumb Music, Tom [Div. of Rhythms Productions] - Los Angeles, CA - *BillIntBG 83-84*
Thumbprint Press - Tucson, AZ - *BoPubDir 4, 5*
Thunder City Press - Birmingham, AL - *BoPubDir 4, 5; LitMag&SmPr 83-84*
Thunder Mountain Review [of Thunder City Press] - Birmingham, AL - *LitMag&SmPr 83-84*
Thunderbird Automation Group Inc. [Subs. of Thunderbird Financial Corp.] - Tulsa, OK - *WhoWMicrocom 83*
Thunderchief Corp. - Portland, OR - *BoPubDir 4, 5*
Thunder's Mouth Press - Oak Park, IL - *BoPubDir 4*
Thunder's Mouth Press - New York, NY - *ArtMar 84; BoPubDir 5; LitMag&SmPr 83-84; LitMarPl 84; WritMar 84*
Thunderthrust Music - *See* Var Music Publishing Co.

Thurber Inc., John T. - Grafton, VT - *BrCabYB 84*
Thurber Inc., John T. - Springfield, VT - *Tel&CabFB 84C p.1707*
Thurber Inc., John T. - Weston, VT - *BrCabYB 84*
Thurds: From the Art of Rosalea's Hotel - Harper, KS - *LitMag&SmPr 83-84*
Thure Video Productions, T. - Tucson, AZ - *AvMarPl 83*
Thurm Associates Inc., Andrew - New York, NY - *IntDirMarRes 83*
Thurmont Catoctin Enterprise - *See* Valley Register Inc.
Thursday - Cambridge, MA - *AyerDirPub 83*
Thursday Music Corp. - *See* Ahlert Music Corp., Fred
Thursday Post, The - Lindsay, ON, Canada - *AyerDirPub 83*
Thursday Publishers - Stevens Point, WI - *BoPubDir 4, 5*
Thyssen-Bornemisza nv - New York, NY - *KnowInd 83*
Ti-Mix News - Austin, TX - *BaconPubCkMag 84*
TI Technical Indexes Ltd. - Bracknell, England - *InfIndMarPl 83*
Tianabhiag - Portree, Scotland - *LitMag&SmPr 83-84*
TIB Publications [Aff. of The Bureau Inc.] - Ft. Lauderdale, FL - *BoPubDir 4; DirMarMP 83*
TIB Publications - Margate, FL - *BoPubDir 5; LitMag&SmPr 83-84*
Tiber Reference Press Ltd. - Bethesda, MD - *BoPubDir 5*
Tiburon & Belvedere Ark - Belvedere, CA - *NewsDir 84*
TIC [of Ticonium Co.] - North Chatham, NY - *ArtMar 84; MagDir 84; WritMar 84*
TIC Serial Titles [of US Dept. of Energy] - Oak Ridge, TN - *DataDirOnSer 84; DirOnDB Spring 84*
Tice Lee County Reporter - Tice, FL - *BaconPubCkNews 84*
Tichenor Media System Inc. - Harlingen, TX - *BrCabYB 84*
TICK [of National Computer Network of Chicago] - Chicago, IL - *DataDirOnSer 84*
Tick - New York, NY - *DirOnDB Spring 84*
Ticknor & Fields [Subs. of Houghton Mifflin Co.] - New Haven, CT - *LitMarPl 83*
Ticknor & Fields [Subs. of Houghton Mifflin Co.] - New York, NY - *LitMarPl 84*
Ticonderoga Sentinel - Ticonderoga, NY - *Ed&PubIntYB 82; NewsDir 84*
Ticonderoga Times of Ti [of Denton Publications Inc.] - Ticonderoga, NY - *NewsDir 84*
TIDA Network [of Compania Telefonica Nacional de Espana] - Madrid, Spain - *InfIndMarPl 83*
Tidal Press - Cranberry Isles, ME - *BoPubDir 4, 5*
Tidbits for the TI-99/2 [of Regena] - Cedar City, UT - *MicrocomMPl 84*
Tide Book Publishing Co. [Aff. of Tide Media Enterprises] - Bethlehem, CT - *BoPubDir 4*
Tide Book Publishing Co. [Aff. of Tide Media Enterprises] - Manchester, MA - *BoPubDir 5; LitMag&SmPr 83-84*
Tidel Communications Inc. - Crescent City, CA - *Tel&CabFB 84C p.1707*
Tideland News - Swansboro, NC - *Ed&PubIntYB 82*
Tideline Press - Tannersville, NY - *BoPubDir 4, 5; LitMag&SmPr 83-84*
Tidewater Audio-Visual Center - Norfolk, VA - *AvMarPl 83*
Tidewater Motorist - Norfolk, VA - *BaconPubCkMag 84*
Tidewater Music Co. - Huntsville, AL - *BillIntBG 83-84*
Tidewater News - Franklin, VA - *AyerDirPub 83; Ed&PubIntYB 82*
Tidewater Publishers [Div. of Cornell Maritime Press Inc.] - Centreville, MD - *LitMarPl 83, 84*
Tidewater Review [of Atlantic Publications Inc.] - West Point, VA - *AyerDirPub 83; Ed&PubIntYB 82; NewsDir 84*
Tidewater Virginian - Norfolk, VA - *WritMar 84*
Tidings - Los Angeles, CA - *BaconPubCkMag 84*
Tidle Communications - Oakridge, OR - *BrCabYB 84*
Tidle Communications - Sutherlin, OR - *BrCabYB 84*
Tidmore Group, The - Pottsville, PA - *BrCabYB 84*
TIE/Communications Inc. - Shelton, CT - *DataDirSup 7-83*
Tie-Line [of Georgia State Office of Consumer Affairs] - Atlanta, GA - *EISS 83*
Tie-Line [of South Dakota State Office of the Tie-Line] - Pierre, SD - *EISS 83*
Tienet [of Pragmatronics Inc.] - Boulder, CO - *TeleSy&SerDir 7-83*
Tierra Grande [of Texas Real Estate Research Center] - College Station, TX - *ArtMar 84*
Tierrasanta Pennysaver - Mission Viejo, CA - *AyerDirPub 83*
Ties - Roseville, MN - *MicrocomMPl 84*
Tiffany Press - Newton, MA - *BoPubDir 4, 5*
Tiffany Stand & Furniture Co. - St. Louis, MO - *WhoWMicrocom 83*
Tiffen Manufacturing Corp. (AV Div.) - Hauppauge, NY - *AvMarPl 83*
Tiffin Advertiser Tribune - Tiffin, OH - *BaconPubCkNews 84; NewsDir 84*
Tifton Gazette [of Thomson Newspapers Inc.] - Tifton, GA - *BaconPubCkNews 84; Ed&PubIntYB 82; NewsDir 84*
Tifton Gazette, The - Thomson, GA - *AyerDirPub 83*
Tigard Times - Tigard, OR - *Ed&PubIntYB 82*
Tigard Times - *See* Times Publishing Co.
Tiger Beat - Hollywood, CA - *MagIndMarPl 82-83*
Tiger Beat - Los Angeles, CA - *MagDir 84*
Tiger Beat Magazine [of W.P. Magazines Inc.] - Cresskill, NJ - *WritMar 84*
Tiger Beat Star [of W.P. Magazines Inc.] - Cresskill, NJ - *BaconPubCkMag 84; WritMar 84*
Tiger Lil Music - *See* Mighty Matthew Music
Tigerton Chronicle - Tigerton, WI - *Ed&PubIntYB 82*
Tigervision - Baton Rouge, LA - *CabTVPrDB 83*
Tightrope [of Swamp Press] - Amherst, MA - *LitMag&SmPr 83-84; WritMar 84*
Tii Industries Inc. - Copiague, NY - *DataDirSup 7-83; WhoWMicrocom 83*
TIJL Datapress BV - Zwolle, Netherlands - *EISS 83; InfoS 83-84*
Tiki Enterprises Inc. - San Jose, CA - *BillIntBG 83-84*
Tilbury Cable Co. - Plymouth Township, PA - *BrCabYB 84; Tel&CabFB 84C*
Tilbury Times, The - Tilbury, ON, Canada - *Ed&PubIntYB 82*
Tilden Citizen - Tilden, NE - *BaconPubCkNews 84; Ed&PubIntYB 82*
Tilden Press - Washington, DC - *BoPubDir 4, 5; LitMarPl 84*
Tile & Decorative Surfaces [of Decorative Surfaces Publishing Co.] - Encino, CA - *BaconPubCkMag 84; MagDir 84*
Till-Cable TV Ltd. - Tillsonburg, ON, Canada - *BrCabYB 84*
Tillamook Headlight-Herald - Tillamook, OR - *BaconPubCkNews 84; NewsDir 84*
Tillamook Television Inc. - Tillamook, OR - *BrCabYB 84; Tel&CabFB 84C*
Tiller & Toiler - Larned, KS - *AyerDirPub 83; Ed&PubIntYB 82*
Tilley Marlieb Advertising Inc. - New York, NY - *StaDirAdAg 2-84*
Tillis Music, Mel - Nashville, TN - *BillIntBG 83-84*
Tillman Music Co., Floyd - Houston, TX - *BillIntBG 83-84*
Tillotson Publications - *See* Boone Newspaper Group
Tillsonburg News, The - Tillsonburg, ON, Canada - *Ed&PubIntYB 82*
Tilton Films Inc., Roger - San Diego, CA - *ArtMar 84; AvMarPl 83; WritMar 84*
TIM - New York, NY - *BillIntBG 83-84*
TIM-Formation Inc. - Albany, NY - *DataDirOnSer 84; DataDirSup 7-83*
Timber Cutter - Chehalis, WA - *BaconPubCkMag 84; MagDir 84*
Timber Harvesting - Montgomery, AL - *BaconPubCkMag 84; MagDir 84*
Timber Information Keyword Retrieval [of Timber Research & Development Association] - High Wycombe, England - *EISS 83*
Timber Lake Topic - Timber Lake, SD - *BaconPubCkNews 84; Ed&PubIntYB 82*
Timber Mart South Data Bank - Washington, DC - *DirOnDB Spring 84*
Timber Mart South Data Bank [of Data Resources Inc.] - Lexington, MA - *DataDirOnSer 84*
Timber Mart South Inc. - Highlands, NC - *EISS 7-83 Sup*
Timber Press - Beaverton, OR - *LitMag&SmPr 83-84; LitMarPl 83, 84; WritMar 84*
Timber Processing Industry - Montgomery, AL - *BaconPubCkMag 84; MagDir 84*
Timber Producers Bulletin - Tomahawk, WI - *BaconPubCkMag 84; MagDir 84*
Timber Publishing Co. Inc. - *See* Tree International
Timber River Associates [Subs. of ITT Financial Corp.] - Minneapolis, MN - *StaDirAdAg 2-84*
Timber/West - Edmonds, WA - *BaconPubCkMag 84*

Timberjack Music - *See* Tyner International Inc., Harrison
Timberland Publishing Co. - Forest City, IA - *BillIntBG 83-84*
Timberline Books Ltd. - Kersey, CO - *BoPubDir 4, 5*
Timberline Journal - Lake Arrowhead, CA - *AyerDirPub 83*
Timberline Press - Fulton, MO - *BoPubDir 4, 5; LitMag&SmPr 83-84*
Timberline Systems - Portland, OR - *DataDirSup 7-83; MicrocomMPl 84*
Timbertree Publishing - Kingsport, TN - *BillIntBG 83-84*
Timberwolf Music Inc. - *See* Mystery Music Inc.
Timbes & Yeager Inc. - Mobile, AL - *StaDirAdAg 2-84*
Time - New York, NY - *AdAge 6-28-84; BaconPubCkMag 84; Folio 83; HomeVid&CabYB 82-83; KnowInd 83; LitMarPl 83, 84; MagDir 84; MagIndMarPl 82-83; NewsBur 6; WritMar 84*
Time & Space Advertising Inc. - Riverdale, NY - *StaDirAdAg 2-84*
Time & Space Processing - Santa Clara, CA - *DataDirSup 7-83*
Time Break [of AMF Geo Space Corp.] - Houston, TX - *WritMar 84*
Time Capsule - New York, NY - *LitMag&SmPr 83-84*
Time Computer Corp. - Indianapolis, IN - *MicrocomMPl 84; MicrocomSwDir 1; WhoWMicrocom 83*
Time Distribution Services Inc. - New York, NY - *MagIndMarPl 82-83*
T.I.M.E. East Inc. - St. Clairsville, OH - *IntDirMarRes 83*
T.I.M.E. Inc. - Columbus, OH - *IntDirMarRes 83*
Time Inc. - *See* American TV & Communications Corp.
Time Inc. (Direct Mail & Fulfillment Services) - Chicago, IL - *MagIndMarPl 82-83*
Time-Lee Publications - Melbourne, FL - *BoPubDir 4, 5*
Time-Life Books Inc. [Subs. of Time Inc.] - Alexandria, VA - *ArtMar 84; LitMarPl 83, 84; WritMar 84*
Time-Life Video [Subs. of Time Inc.] - New York, NY - *AvMarPl 83*
Time Music - *See* Rondor Music International
Time N Talent Inc. - Highland Park, IL - *IntDirMarRes 83*
T.I.M.E. North - Erie, PA - *IntDirMarRes 83*
Time Pix Syndication [Div. of Time Magazine] - New York, NY - *LitMarPl 83, 84*
Time Sharing Industry Review - South Miami, FL - *WritMar 84*
Time Sharing Resources Inc. - Great Neck, NY - *EISS 83*
Time-Sharing Services [of National Data Corp.] - Boston, MA - *EISS 83*
Time-Sharing Systems Inc. [Subs. of Computer Services Inc.] - Milwaukee, WI - *DataDirOnSer 84*
Time Signatures - Austin, TX - *BillIntBG 83-84*
Time Step Music - *See* MizMo Enterprises
Time Teletext Service [of Time Inc.] - New York, NY - *CabTVPrDB 83*
Time Video Information Services [Subs. of Time Inc.] - New York, NY - *BrCabYB 84; EISS 83; InfoS 83-84; VideoDir 82-83*
Time-Wise Publications - Yucca Valley, CA - *BoPubDir 4 Sup, 5*
Timebuying Services Inc. [Div. of RDR Associates] - New York, NY - *StaDirAdAg 2-84*
Timeless Books [Aff. of Association for the Development of Human Potential] - Porthill, ID - *BoPubDir 4, 5; LitMag&SmPr 83-84*
Timeless Entertainment Corp. - New York, NY - *BillIntBG 83-84*
Timely Books - New Milford, CT - *LitMag&SmPr 83-84; LitMarPl 83*
Timely Tips - Paulding, OH - *MagDir 84*
Timeplex Inc. - Woodcliffe Lake, NJ - *DataDirSup 7-83*
Times - Birmingham, AL - *Ed&PubIntYB 82*
Times - Cullman, AL - *AyerDirPub 83*
Times - Gadsden, AL - *AyerDirPub 83*
Times - Huntsville, AL - *AyerDirPub 83*
Times - Thomasville, AL - *AyerDirPub 83*
Times - Anchorage, AK - *AyerDirPub 83*
Times - Gurdon, AR - *AyerDirPub 83*
Times - Osceola, AR - *AyerDirPub 83*
Times - Piggott, AR - *AyerDirPub 83*
Times - West Memphis, AR - *AyerDirPub 83*
Times - Escalon, CA - *AyerDirPub 83*
Times - Hilmar, CA - *AyerDirPub 83*
Times - Los Angeles, CA - *AyerDirPub 83*
Times - Santa Maria, CA - *AyerDirPub 83; Ed&PubIntYB 82*
Times - Sebastopol, CA - *AyerDirPub 83*
Times - Aspen, CO - *AyerDirPub 83*
Times - Ft. Morgan, CO - *AyerDirPub 83*
Times - Louisville, CO - *AyerDirPub 83*
Times - Rangely, CO - *AyerDirPub 83*
Times - Telluride, CO - *AyerDirPub 83*
Times - Greenwich, CT - *AyerDirPub 83*
Times - New Milford, CT - *AyerDirPub 83*
Times - Trumbull, CT - *AyerDirPub 83*
Times - Apalachicola, FL - *AyerDirPub 83*
Times - Daytona Beach, FL - *Ed&PubIntYB 82*
Times - Miami, FL - *AyerDirPub 83*
Times - Orlando, FL - *AyerDirPub 83; Ed&PubIntYB 82*
Times - St. Petersburg, FL - *AyerDirPub 83*
Times - Tampa, FL - *AyerDirPub 83*
Times - West Palm Beach, FL - *AyerDirPub 83*
Times - Winter Garden, FL - *AyerDirPub 83*
Times - Albany, GA - *AyerDirPub 83*
Times - Alma, GA - *AyerDirPub 83*
Times - Blackshear, GA - *AyerDirPub 83*
Times - Chatsworth, GA - *AyerDirPub 83*
Times - Columbus, GA - *Ed&PubIntYB 82*
Times - Gainesville, GA - *AyerDirPub 83; BaconPubCkNews 84; Ed&PubIntYB 82*
Times - Macon, GA - *AyerDirPub 83*
Times - Valdosta, GA - *AyerDirPub 83*
Times - Aberdeen, ID - *AyerDirPub 83*
Times - Priest River, ID - *AyerDirPub 83*
Times - Carmi, IL - *Ed&PubIntYB 82*
Times - Delavan, IL - *AyerDirPub 83*
Times - Franklin, IL - *AyerDirPub 83*
Times - Grayslake, IL - *AyerDirPub 83*
Times - London Mills, IL - *AyerDirPub 83*
Times - Morrisonville, IL - *AyerDirPub 83*
Times - Odell, IL - *AyerDirPub 83*
Times - Okawville, IL - *AyerDirPub 83*
Times - Orion, IL - *AyerDirPub 83*
Times - Ottawa, IL - *AyerDirPub 83*
Times - Pekin, IL - *AyerDirPub 83*
Times - Rushville, IL - *AyerDirPub 83*
Times - Vienna, IL - *AyerDirPub 83*
Times - Winchester, IL - *AyerDirPub 83*
Times - Brazil, IN - *AyerDirPub 83*
Times - Frankfort, IN - *AyerDirPub 83; Ed&PubIntYB 82*
Times - Ft. Branch, IN - *AyerDirPub 83*
Times - Kouts, IN - *AyerDirPub 83*
Times - Mooresville, IN - *AyerDirPub 83; Ed&PubIntYB 82*
Times - New Harmony, IN - *AyerDirPub 83*
Times - Worthington, IN - *AyerDirPub 83*
Times - Zionsville, IN - *AyerDirPub 83*
Times - Battle Creek, IA - *AyerDirPub 83*
Times - Cherokee, IA - *AyerDirPub 83*
Times - Fonda, IA - *AyerDirPub 83*
Times - Paulina, IA - *AyerDirPub 83*
Times - Preston, IA - *AyerDirPub 83*
Times - West Branch, IA - *AyerDirPub 83*
Times - Clearwater, KS - *AyerDirPub 83*
Times - El Dorado, KS - *AyerDirPub 83*
Times - Herington, KS - *AyerDirPub 83*
Times - Hill City, KS - *AyerDirPub 83*
Times - Leavenworth, KS - *AyerDirPub 83*
Times - Lebanon, KS - *AyerDirPub 83*
Times - Ottawa, KS - *AyerDirPub 83*
Times - Plainville, KS - *AyerDirPub 83*
Times - St. Francis, KS - *AyerDirPub 83*
Times - Wamego, KS - *AyerDirPub 83*
Times - Wathena, KS - *AyerDirPub 83*
Times - Glasgow, KY - *AyerDirPub 83; Ed&PubIntYB 82*
Times - Jackson, KY - *AyerDirPub 83*
Times - Louisville, KY - *NewsDir 84*
Times - Natchitoches, LA - *AyerDirPub 83*
Times [of Gannett Co. Inc.] - Shreveport, LA - *AyerDirPub 83; BaconPubCkNews 84; Ed&PubIntYB 82; NewsDir 84*
Times - Slidell, LA - *AyerDirPub 83*
Times - Rumford, ME - *Ed&PubIntYB 82*
Times - Crisfield, MD - *AyerDirPub 83*
Times - Cumberland, MD - *AyerDirPub 83; Ed&PubIntYB 82*

Times - Beverly, MA - *AyerDirPub 83*
Times - Gloucester, MA - *AyerDirPub 83*
Times - Lynn, MA - *AyerDirPub 83*
Times - Needham, MA - *AyerDirPub 83*
Times - Peabody, MA - *AyerDirPub 83*
Times - Webster, MA - *AyerDirPub 83*
Times - Armada, MI - *AyerDirPub 83*
Times - Bay City, MI - *AyerDirPub 83*
Times - Edmore, MI - *AyerDirPub 83*
Times - Harbor Beach, MI - *AyerDirPub 83*
Times - New Buffalo, MI - *AyerDirPub 83*
Times - Trenton, MI - *AyerDirPub 83*
Times - Cass Lake, MN - *AyerDirPub 83*
Times - Forest Lake, MN - *AyerDirPub 83*
Times - Ivanhoe, MN - *AyerDirPub 83*
Times - Monticello, MN - *AyerDirPub 83*
Times - Norwood, MN - *AyerDirPub 83*
Times - Starbuck, MN - *AyerDirPub 83*
Times - Thief River Falls, MN - *AyerDirPub 83*
Times - Twin Valley, MN - *AyerDirPub 83*
Times - Tylertown, MS - *AyerDirPub 83*
Times - Winona, MS - *AyerDirPub 83*
Times - Bowling Green, MO - *AyerDirPub 83*
Times - Kansas City, MO - *AyerDirPub 83*
Times - Monett, MO - *AyerDirPub 83*
Times - Pleasant Hill, MO - *AyerDirPub 83*
Times - Tipton, MO - *AyerDirPub 83*
Times - Fairfield, MT - *AyerDirPub 83*
Times - Roundup, MT - *AyerDirPub 83*
Times - Shelby, MT - *AyerDirPub 83*
Times - Gothenburg, NE - *AyerDirPub 83*
Times - Milford, NE - *AyerDirPub 83*
Times - Papillion, NE - *AyerDirPub 83*
Times - Pender, NE - *AyerDirPub 83*
Times - Ely, NV - *AyerDirPub 83*
Times - Hillside, NJ - *AyerDirPub 83*
Times - Montclair, NJ - *AyerDirPub 83*
Times - Trenton, NJ - *AyerDirPub 83*
Times - Cheektowaga, NY - *AyerDirPub 83*
Times - Little Falls, NY - *AyerDirPub 83*
Times - Livonia, NY - *AyerDirPub 83*
Times - Malverne, NY - *AyerDirPub 83*
Times - New York, NY - *AyerDirPub 83*
Times - Waterville, NY - *AyerDirPub 83*
Times - White Plains, NY - *AyerDirPub 83*
Times - Whitehall, NY - *AyerDirPub 83*
Times - Asheville, NC - *AyerDirPub 83; Ed&PubIntYB 82; LitMarPl 84*
Times - Fayetteville, NC - *AyerDirPub 83*
Times - Mt. Airy, NC - *AyerDirPub 83*
Times [of News & Observer Publishing Co.] - Raleigh, NC - *AyerDirPub 83; Ed&PubIntYB 82; LitMarPl 84*
Times - Taylorsville, NC - *AyerDirPub 83*
Times - Thomasville, NC - *AyerDirPub 83; Ed&PubIntYB 82*
Times - Wilson, NC - *AyerDirPub 83*
Times - Bryan, OH - *AyerDirPub 83*
Times - Greenfield, OH - *AyerDirPub 83*
Times - Kenton, OH - *AyerDirPub 83; Ed&PubIntYB 82*
Times - Loudonville, OH - *AyerDirPub 83*
Times - Marietta, OH - *AyerDirPub 83*
Times - Niles, OH - *AyerDirPub 83*
Times - Pandora, OH - *AyerDirPub 83*
Times - Portsmouth, OH - *AyerDirPub 83*
Times - Sebring, OH - *AyerDirPub 83*
Times [of The Bellevue Gazette Corp.] - Willard, OH - *AyerDirPub 83; NewsDir 84*
Times - Altus, OK - *AyerDirPub 83*
Times - Duke, OK - *AyerDirPub 83*
Times - Kingfisher, OK - *AyerDirPub 83*
Times - Oklahoma City, OK - *AyerDirPub 83*
Times - Okmulgee, OK - *AyerDirPub 83; Ed&PubIntYB 82*
Times - Pryor, OK - *AyerDirPub 83*
Times - Tuttle, OK - *AyerDirPub 83*
Times - Junction City, OR - *AyerDirPub 83*
Times - Erie, PA - *AyerDirPub 83*
Times - Gettysburg, PA - *AyerDirPub 83*
Times - Reading, PA - *AyerDirPub 83*
Times - Sayre, PA - *AyerDirPub 83*
Times - Scranton, PA - *AyerDirPub 83; Ed&PubIntYB 82*
Times - Yeadon, PA - *AyerDirPub 83*
Times - Barrington, RI - *AyerDirPub 83*
Times - Pawtucket, RI - *AyerDirPub 83*
Times - Ft. Mill, SC - *AyerDirPub 83*
Times - Georgetown, SC - *AyerDirPub 83*
Times - Inman, SC - *AyerDirPub 83*
Times - Manning, SC - *AyerDirPub 83*
Times - North Myrtle Beach, SC - *AyerDirPub 83*
Times - Union, SC - *AyerDirPub 83*
Times - Lake Preston, SD - *AyerDirPub 83*
Times - Springfield, SD - *AyerDirPub 83*
Times - Chattanooga, TN - *AyerDirPub 83*
Times - Manchester, TN - *AyerDirPub 83*
Times - Maryville, TN - *AyerDirPub 83; BaconPubCkNews 84*
Times - Rockwood, TN - *AyerDirPub 83*
Times - Angleton, TX - *AyerDirPub 83*
Times - Bellville, TX - *AyerDirPub 83*
Times - Clarksville, TX - *AyerDirPub 83*
Times - Corpus Christi, TX - *AyerDirPub 83; NewsDir 84*
Times - Corrigan, TX - *AyerDirPub 83*
Times - Deport, TX - *AyerDirPub 83*
Times - El Paso, TX - *AyerDirPub 83*
Times - Everman, TX - *AyerDirPub 83*
Times - Ft. Worth, TX - *Ed&PubIntYB 82*
Times - Kerrville, TX - *AyerDirPub 83*
Times - La Marque, TX - *AyerDirPub 83*
Times - Laredo, TX - *AyerDirPub 83*
Times - San Angelo, TX - *Ed&PubIntYB 82*
Times - Sanderson, TX - *AyerDirPub 83*
Times - Talco, TX - *AyerDirPub 83*
Times - Wichita Falls, TX - *NewsDir 84*
Times - Seattle, WA - *AyerDirPub 83*
Times - Waitsburg, WA - *AyerDirPub 83*
Times - Princeton, WV - *AyerDirPub 83*
Times - Weirton, WV - *AyerDirPub 83*
Times - Fennimore, WI - *AyerDirPub 83*
Times - Kaukauna, WI - *AyerDirPub 83*
Times - Monroe, WI - *AyerDirPub 83*
Times - Mosinee, WI - *AyerDirPub 83*
Times - Peshtigo, WI - *AyerDirPub 83*
Times - Turtle Lake, WI - *AyerDirPub 83*
Times - Walworth, WI - *AyerDirPub 83; Ed&PubIntYB 82; NewsDir 84*
Times - Washburn, WI - *AyerDirPub 83*
Times - Watertown, WI - *AyerDirPub 83*
Times - Whitehall, WI - *AyerDirPub 83*
Times - Rawlins, WY - *AyerDirPub 83*
Times - Sundance, WY - *AyerDirPub 83*
Times - Bassano, AB, Canada - *Ed&PubIntYB 82*
Times - High River, AB, Canada - *AyerDirPub 83; Ed&PubIntYB 82*
Times - Taber, AB, Canada - *AyerDirPub 83; Ed&PubIntYB 82*
Times - Wetaskiwin, AB, Canada - *AyerDirPub 83; Ed&PubIntYB 82*
Times - Clearwater, BC, Canada - *AyerDirPub 83; Ed&PubIntYB 82*
Times - Nanaimo, BC, Canada - *Ed&PubIntYB 82*
Times - Osoyoos, BC, Canada - *AyerDirPub 83; Ed&PubIntYB 82*
Times - Squamish, BC, Canada - *AyerDirPub 83; Ed&PubIntYB 82*
Times - Trail, BC, Canada - *AyerDirPub 83*
Times - Treherne, MB, Canada - *AyerDirPub 83; Ed&PubIntYB 82*
Times - Woodworth, MB, Canada - *Ed&PubIntYB 82*
Times - Moncton, NB, Canada - *AyerDirPub 83; Ed&PubIntYB 82*
Times - Collingwood, ON, Canada - *AyerDirPub 83*
Times - Midland, ON, Canada - *Ed&PubIntYB 82*
Times - Oshawa, ON, Canada - *AyerDirPub 83*
Times - Tilbury, ON, Canada - *AyerDirPub 83*
Times - Assiniboia, SK, Canada - *AyerDirPub 83*
Times - Ft. Qu'Appelle, SK, Canada - *AyerDirPub 83; Ed&PubIntYB 82*
Times - Lloydminster, SK, Canada - *AyerDirPub 83*
Times - Nikomis, SK, Canada - *AyerDirPub 83*

Times - Stoughton, SK, Canada - *Ed&PubIntYB 82*
Times - Zamboanga, Philippines - *AyerDirPub 83*
Times-Advertiser - Pemberton, NJ - *Ed&PubIntYB 82*
Times-Advertiser - Trenton, NJ - *AyerDirPub 83*
Times-Advertiser, The - Fredericktown, OH - *AyerDirPub 83*
Times-Advocate - Escondido, CA - *AyerDirPub 83; Ed&PubIntYB 82*
Times-Advocate - Gregory, SD - *Ed&PubIntYB 82*
Times-Advocate - Exeter, ON, Canada - *AyerDirPub 83; Ed&PubIntYB 82*
Times & Chronicle - Reading, MA - *AyerDirPub 83*
Times & Chronicle - Woburn, MA - *AyerDirPub 83*
Times & Democrat - Orangeburg, SC - *AyerDirPub 83; Ed&PubIntYB 82*
Times & News - Giddings, TX - *AyerDirPub 83; Ed&PubIntYB 82*
Times & News Leader - San Mateo, CA - *AyerDirPub 83; Ed&PubIntYB 82*
Times & News Publishing Co. - Gettysburg, PA - *BrCabYB 84*
Times & Rainy Lake Herald - Ft. Frances, ON, Canada - *AyerDirPub 83*
Times & San Martin News - Morgan Hill, CA - *AyerDirPub 83*
Times & Star - Deloraine, MB, Canada - *AyerDirPub 83*
Times & World News - Roanoke, VA - *AyerDirPub 83*
Times-Argus - Central City, KY - *AyerDirPub 83; Ed&PubIntYB 82*
Times-Argus - Barre, VT - *BaconPubCkNews 84; Ed&PubIntYB 82*
Times-Argus - New Lisbon, WI - *Ed&PubIntYB 82*
Times-Beacon - Tampa, FL - *Ed&PubIntYB 82*
Times Bonanza & Goldfield News - Tonopah, NV - *AyerDirPub 83; Ed&PubIntYB 82*
Times Books [of The New York Times Book Co. Inc.] - New York, NY - *LitMarPl 83, 84; WritMar 84*
Times-Bulletin - Van Wert, OH - *AyerDirPub 83; Ed&PubIntYB 82*
Times-Call - Longmont, CO - *AyerDirPub 83*
Times-Canogan [of Encino Associated Valley Publications Inc.] - Encino, CA - *AyerDirPub 83; Ed&PubIntYB 82; NewsDir 84*
Times Change Press - San Rafael, CA - *BoPubDir 4, 5; LitMag&SmPr 83-84*
Times Chronicle [of Montgomery Publishing Co.] - Jenkintown, PA - *AyerDirPub 83; Ed&PubIntYB 82; NewsDir 84*
Times Chronicle Newspapers - Carrollton, TX - *Ed&PubIntYB 82*
Times-Clarion - Harlowton, MT - *AyerDirPub 83; Ed&PubIntYB 82*
Times Colonist [of Canadian Newspapers Ltd.] - Victoria, BC, Canada - *AyerDirPub 83; BaconPubCkNews 84; Ed&PubIntYB 82; LitMarPl 83, 84*
Times-Commoner - Salem, IL - *AyerDirPub 83*
Times-Courier - Ellijay, GA - *AyerDirPub 83*
Times-Courier - Charleston, IL - *AyerDirPub 83*
Times-Crescent, The - La Plata, MD - *AyerDirPub 83; Ed&PubIntYB 82*
Times-Delta - Visalia, CA - *AyerDirPub 83*
Times-Democrat - Flemingsburg, KY - *AyerDirPub 83*
Times-Democrat - Sulphur, OK - *AyerDirPub 83*
Times-Dispatch - Walnut Ridge, AR - *AyerDirPub 83; Ed&PubIntYB 82*
Times-Dispatch - Richmond, VA - *AyerDirPub 83*
Times-Enterprise - Thomasville, GA - *AyerDirPub 83*
Times-Enterprise - Wessington, SD - *Ed&PubIntYB 82*
Times-Express, The [of Dardanell Publications Inc.] - Monroeville, PA - *NewsDir 84*
Times Fiber Communications Inc. - Wallingford, CT - *CabTVFinDB 83; HomeVid&CabYB 82-83*
Times-Free Press - East Pepperell, MA - *AyerDirPub 83*
Times Free Press - Pepperell, MA - *Ed&PubIntYB 82*
Times-Gazette - Ashland, OH - *AyerDirPub 83*
Times-Gazette - Warren, RI - *AyerDirPub 83*
Times-Gazette - Shelbyville, TN - *AyerDirPub 83*
Times-Georgian - Carrollton, GA - *AyerDirPub 83; BaconPubCkNews 84; Ed&PubIntYB 82*
Times-Globe [of New Brunswick Publishing Co. Ltd.] - St. John, NB, Canada - *AyerDirPub 83; Ed&PubIntYB 82; LitMarPl 84*
Times Guardian - Canyon Lake, TX - *Ed&PubIntYB 82*
Times Guardian - New Braunfels, TX - *AyerDirPub 83*
Times Guide Shopper - Sebastopol, CA - *AyerDirPub 83*
Times Guthrian Publishing Co. Inc. - Guthrie Center, IA - *BaconPubCkNews 84*
Times-Herald - Forrest City, AR - *Ed&PubIntYB 82*
Times-Herald - Vallejo, CA - *AyerDirPub 83*
Times-Herald - Newnan, GA - *AyerDirPub 83*
Times-Herald - Washington, IN - *AyerDirPub 83*
Times-Herald - Carroll, IA - *AyerDirPub 83*
Times-Herald - Dearborn, MI - *AyerDirPub 83*
Times Herald [of Gannett Co. Inc.] - Port Huron, MI - *AyerDirPub 83; Ed&PubIntYB 82; LitMarPl 83, 84; NewsDir 84*
Times-Herald - Alliance, NE - *AyerDirPub 83*
Times-Herald - Olean, NY - *AyerDirPub 83; Ed&PubIntYB 82*
Times-Herald - Prague, OK - *AyerDirPub 83; Ed&PubIntYB 82*
Times-Herald - Norristown, PA - *AyerDirPub 83; Ed&PubIntYB 82*
Times-Herald - Dallas, TX - *AyerDirPub 83*
Times-Herald [of Daily Press Inc.] - Newport News, VA - *AyerDirPub 83; BaconPubCkNews 84; Ed&PubIntYB 82; LitMarPl 84*
Times-Herald - Moose Jaw, SK, Canada - *AyerDirPub 83; Ed&PubIntYB 82*
Times-Herald-Record [of Ottaway Newspapers Inc.] - Middletown, NY - *AyerDirPub 83; Ed&PubIntYB 82; NewsDir 84*
Times-Independent - Moab, UT - *Ed&PubIntYB 82*
Times-Indicator - Fremont, MI - *AyerDirPub 83*
Times Information & Marketing Intelligence Unit, The - London, England - *InfIndMarPl 83*
Times-Journal [of Ft. Payne Newspapers Inc.] - Ft. Payne, AL - *AyerDirPub 83; BaconPubCkNews 84; Ed&PubIntYB 82*
Times-Journal - Selma, AL - *AyerDirPub 83*
Times-Journal - Albany, CA - *Ed&PubIntYB 82*
Times Journal - Richmond, CA - *AyerDirPub 83*
Times-Journal - Savanna, IL - *AyerDirPub 83*
Times-Journal - Mound Valley, KS - *AyerDirPub 83*
Times-Journal - Russell Springs, KY - *AyerDirPub 83; Ed&PubIntYB 82*
Times-Journal - Olivia, MN - *AyerDirPub 83*
Times-Journal - Vineland, NJ - *AyerDirPub 83*
Times-Journal - Cobleskill, NY - *AyerDirPub 83; Ed&PubIntYB 82*
Times-Journal - Condon, OR - *Ed&PubIntYB 82*
Times-Journal - Chilton, WI - *AyerDirPub 83*
Times-Journal - St. Thomas, ON, Canada - *AyerDirPub 83*
Times-Journal - Uxbridge, ON, Canada - *AyerDirPub 83; Ed&PubIntYB 82*
Times Journal Co. - Springfield, VA - *AdAge 6-28-84*
Times Journal-Spotlight - Eastman, GA - *Ed&PubIntYB 82*
Times Large Type Weekly - New York, NY - *AyerDirPub 83*
Times-Leader - Chardon, OH - *Ed&PubIntYB 82*
Times-Leader - Martins Ferry, OH - *AyerDirPub 83; BaconPubCkNews 84; Ed&PubIntYB 82*
Times-Leader [of Brown-Thompson Newspapers] - Union City, PA - *AyerDirPub 83; Ed&PubIntYB 82; NewsDir 84*
Times-Leader - Wilkes-Barre, PA - *AyerDirPub 83*
Times Magazine, The [of Army Times Publishing Co.] - Washington, DC - *MagIndMarPl 82-83; WritMar 84*
Times-Mail, The - Bedford, IN - *AyerDirPub 83; Ed&PubIntYB 82*
Times Management Corp. - Virginia Beach, VA - *BillIntBG 83-84*
Times Marketing & Business Information Service - London, England - *FBInfSer 80*
Times-Messenger - Madelia, MN - *AyerDirPub 83; Ed&PubIntYB 82*
Times-Messenger - Fairmont, NC - *AyerDirPub 83; Ed&PubIntYB 82*
Times Military Group - *Folio 83*
Times Minden, The - Minden, ON, Canada - *Ed&PubIntYB 82*
Times-Mirror - Hollywood, CA - *TelAl 83*
Times Mirror Broadcasting - Greenwich, CT - *BrCabYB 84*
Times Mirror Cable of Riverside County Inc. - Thousand Palms, CA - *BrCabYB 84*
Times Mirror Cable Television Inc. [of The Times Mirror Co.] - Irvine, CA - *BrCabYB 84 p.D-309; CabTVFinDB 83; HomeVid&CabYB 82-83; LitMarPl 84; Tel&CabFB 84C p.1707*
Times Mirror Cable Television Inc. - Longmeadow, MA - *Tel&CabFB 84C*

Times Mirror Cable Television Inc. - Philadelphia, PA - *BrCabYB 84*
Times Mirror Cable Television of Beaver County Inc. - Beaver Falls, PA - *BrCabYB 84*
Times Mirror Cable Television of Brookline Inc. - Brookline, MA - *BrCabYB 84*
Times Mirror Cable Television of Cambridge Inc. - Cambridge, OH - *BrCabYB 84*
Times Mirror Cable Television of Defiance Inc. - Defiance, OH - *Tel&CabFB 84C*
Times Mirror Cable Television of Haverhill Inc. - Haverhill, MA - *BrCabYB 84*
Times Mirror Cable Television of Kerrville Inc. - Kerrville, TX - *Tel&CabFB 84C*
Times Mirror Cable Television of Licking County Inc. - Newark, OH - *BrCabYB 84*
Times Mirror Cable Television of Louisville Inc. - Louisville, KY - *BrCabYB 84; Tel&CabFB 84C*
Times Mirror Cable Television of Marlin Inc. - Marlin, TX - *Tel&CabFB 84C*
Times Mirror Cable Television of Ohio Inc. - Greenfield, OH - *BrCabYB 84; Tel&CabFB 84C*
Times Mirror Cable Television of Ohio Inc. - New Philadelphia, OH - *BrCabYB 84*
Times Mirror Cable Television of Ohio Inc. - Newcomerstown, OH - *BrCabYB 84*
Times Mirror Cable Television of Ohio Inc. - Waverly, OH - *BrCabYB 84*
Times Mirror Cable Television of Ohio Valley Inc. - Toronto, OH - *BrCabYB 84*
Times Mirror Cable Television of Ohio Valley Inc. - Weirton, WV - *BrCabYB 84*
Times Mirror Cable Television of Orange County Inc. - Modjeska Canyon, CA - *BrCabYB 84*
Times Mirror Cable Television of Rhode Island Inc. - Warwick, RI - *BrCabYB 84*
Times Mirror Cable Television of Riverside County Inc. - Murrieta Hot Springs, CA - *BrCabYB 84*
Times Mirror Cable Television of Springfield Inc. - Springfield, IL - *Tel&CabFB 84C*
Times Mirror Cable Television of Texarkana Inc. - Texarkana, TX - *BrCabYB 84*
Times Mirror Cable Television of Uvalde Inc. - Uvalde, TX - *Tel&CabFB 84C*
Times Mirror Cable Television of Washington Inc. - Washington, PA - *BrCabYB 84*
Times Mirror Cablevision - Irvine, CA - *TelAl 84*
Times Mirror Cablevision [Subs. of Times Mirror Co.] - Los Angeles, CA - *TelAl 83*
Times Mirror Co. - Irvine, CA - *BrCabYB 84*
Times Mirror Co. - Los Angeles, CA - *AdAge 6-28-84; BrCabYB 84; Ed&PubIntYB 82; HomeVid&CabYB 82-83; KnowInd 83; Tel&CabFB 84S*
Times Mirror Co., The - Oceanside, CA - *BrCabYB 84*
Times Mirror Magazines - New York, NY - *MagIndMarPl 82-83*
Times Mirror Magazines (Book Div.) - New York, NY - *LitMarPl 83, 84*
Times Mirror Press - Los Angeles, CA - *BoPubDir 4 Sup, 5*
Times Mirror Videotex Services [Subs. of Times Mirror Co.] - Costa Mesa, CA - *EISS 83; InfoS 83-84; VideoDir 82-83*
Times-News - McGehee, AR - *AyerDirPub 83*
Times-News - Twin Falls, ID - *AyerDirPub 83; Ed&PubIntYB 82*
Times-News - Mt. Pulaski, IL - *AyerDirPub 83; Ed&PubIntYB 82*
Times-News - De Witt, NE - *Ed&PubIntYB 82*
Times-News - Burlington, NC - *AyerDirPub 83*
Times-News - Hendersonville, NC - *AyerDirPub 83; BaconPubCkNews 84; Ed&PubIntYB 82*
Times-News - Erie, PA - *AyerDirPub 83; Ed&PubIntYB 82; LitMarPl 83, 84; NewsDir 84*
Times-News - Lehighton, PA - *AyerDirPub 83; Ed&PubIntYB 82*
Times-News - Kingsport, TN - *AyerDirPub 83*
Times-News - Nephi, UT - *AyerDirPub 83; Ed&PubIntYB 82*
Times-News - Thunder Bay, ON, Canada - *AyerDirPub 83; Ed&PubIntYB 82*
Times-News/Chronicle-Journal - Thunder Bay, ON, Canada - *BaconPubCkNews 84*
Times/News Record - Cuthbert, GA - *AyerDirPub 83*
Times Newspapers - Pontiac, MI - *BaconPubCkNews 84*
Times Newspapers - Scranton, PA - *Ed&PubIntYB 82*
Times Newspapers of Great Britain - New York, NY - *Ed&PubIntYB 82*
Times-Observer - Los Gatos, CA - *AyerDirPub 83*
Times-Observer - Oregon, MO - *AyerDirPub 83; Ed&PubIntYB 82*
Times-Observer - Warren, PA - *AyerDirPub 83*
Times of Boyertown Area, The - Boyertown, PA - *Ed&PubIntYB 82*
Times of Fountain Hills, The - Fountain Hills, AZ - *AyerDirPub 83; Ed&PubIntYB 82*
Times of Pea Ridge Country, The - Pea Ridge, AR - *AyerDirPub 83*
Times of Ti, The - Ticonderoga, NY - *Ed&PubIntYB 82*
Times of Ticonderoga - *See* Denton Publications Inc.
Times-Picayune [of Newhouse Newspapers] - New Orleans, LA - *Ed&PubIntYB 82; LitMarPl 83, 84; NewsBur 6; NewsDir 84*
Times-Picayune/States-Item - New Orleans, LA - *AyerDirPub 83; BaconPubCkNews 84; Ed&PubIntYB 82; LitMarPl 84*
Times-Plain Dealer - Cresco, IA - *AyerDirPub 83; Ed&PubIntYB 82*
Times Post - Houston, MS - *AyerDirPub 83; Ed&PubIntYB 82*
Times-Press - Streator, IL - *AyerDirPub 83*
Times-Press - Bedford, IA - *AyerDirPub 83*
Times-Press - Hartford, WI - *Ed&PubIntYB 82*
Times-Press - Reedsburg, WI - *Ed&PubIntYB 82*
Times-Press - Seymour, WI - *AyerDirPub 83; Ed&PubIntYB 82*
Times Publishing Co. - St. Petersburg, FL - *AdAge 6-28-84; KnowInd 83*
Times Publishing Co. - El Dorado, KS - *BaconPubCkNews 84*
Times Publishing Co. - Beaverton, OR - *BaconPubCkNews 84*
Times Publishing Co. - Edinboro, PA - *Tel&CabFB 84C p.1707*
Times-Record - Aledo, IL - *AyerDirPub 83; Ed&PubIntYB 82*
Times-Record [of Brunswick Publishing Co.] - Brunswick, ME - *AyerDirPub 83; BaconPubCkNews 84; Ed&PubIntYB 82; NewsDir 84*
Times-Record - Troy, NY - *AyerDirPub 83; BaconPubCkNews 84; Ed&PubIntYB 82*
Times-Record - Valley City, ND - *AyerDirPub 83*
Times-Record - Blackwell, OK - *AyerDirPub 83*
Times-Record - Doland, SD - *Ed&PubIntYB 82*
Times-Record - Spencer, WV - *AyerDirPub 83*
Times-Recorder - Americus, GA - *AyerDirPub 83*
Times-Recorder - Zanesville, OH - *AyerDirPub 83; Ed&PubIntYB 82*
Times-Recorder Midweek - Zanesville, OH - *AyerDirPub 83*
Times-Region - Roseau, MN - *AyerDirPub 83*
Times-Register - Bedford, OH - *AyerDirPub 83*
Times-Reporter - New Philadelphia, OH - *AyerDirPub 83; Ed&PubIntYB 82*
Times-Republic - Watseka, IL - *AyerDirPub 83*
Times-Republic Shopping Guide - Watseka, IL - *Ed&PubIntYB 82*
Times-Republican - Corydon, IA - *AyerDirPub 83*
Times-Republican - Marshalltown, IA - *AyerDirPub 83; Ed&PubIntYB 82*
Times-Republican - Hayes Center, NE - *AyerDirPub 83*
Times-Review - Storden, MN - *AyerDirPub 83*
Times-Review - Cleburne, TX - *AyerDirPub 83*
Times-Review - Ft. Erie, ON, Canada - *AyerDirPub 83; Ed&PubIntYB 82*
Times-Review - Weston/Rexdale/Downsview, ON, Canada - *Ed&PubIntYB 82*
Times-Sentinel - Gallipolis, OH - *AyerDirPub 83*
Times-Sentinel - Pomeroy, OH - *NewsDir 84*
Times-Signal - Jena, LA - *AyerDirPub 83*
Times-Standard - Eureka, CA - *AyerDirPub 83; BaconPubCkNews 84; Ed&PubIntYB 82*
Times-Star - Alameda, CA - *AyerDirPub 83*
Times-Star - Middletown, CA - *AyerDirPub 83; Ed&PubIntYB 82*
Times-Star - Sedan, KS - *AyerDirPub 83*
Times-Star - Geraldton, ON, Canada - *AyerDirPub 83*
Times-Sun [of The Laurel Group Press] - West Newton, PA - *AyerDirPub 83; Ed&PubIntYB 82; NewsDir 84*
Times, The - North Little Rock, AR - *Ed&PubIntYB 82*

Times, The - Melbourne, FL - *Ed&PubIntYB 82*
Times, The - Brookfield, IL - *Ed&PubIntYB 82*
Times, The [of Howard Publications Inc.] - Hammond, IN - *AyerDirPub 83; Ed&PubIntYB 82; NewsDir 84*
Times, The - Noblesville, IN - *AyerDirPub 83*
Times, The - Augusta, KY - *AyerDirPub 83*
Times, The [of The Shield Press] - Baltimore, MD - *Ed&PubIntYB 82; NewsDir 84*
Times, The - Scotch Plains, NJ - *AyerDirPub 83; Ed&PubIntYB 82*
Times, The - Canal Winchester, OH - *AyerDirPub 83; Ed&PubIntYB 82*
Times, The - Lorain, OH - *Ed&PubIntYB 82*
Times, The - Central Linn County, OR - *Ed&PubIntYB 82*
Times, The - Port Royal, PA - *Ed&PubIntYB 82*
Times, The - Pierre, SD - *AyerDirPub 83*
Times, The - Atlanta, TX - *AyerDirPub 83*
Times, The - Mackenzie, BC, Canada - *Ed&PubIntYB 82*
Times, The - Minden, ON, Canada - *AyerDirPub 83*
Times, The - Windsor, ON, Canada - *Ed&PubIntYB 82*
Times Today - Vancouver, BC, Canada - *AyerDirPub 83*
Times-Tri-Cities Daily - Florence, AL - *AyerDirPub 83*
Times-Tribune - Mancos, CO - *AyerDirPub 83*
Times-Tribune - Alexandria, IN - *AyerDirPub 83*
Times-Tribune - Corbin, KY - *AyerDirPub 83; Ed&PubIntYB 82*
Times-Tribune - Grant City, MO - *AyerDirPub 83; Ed&PubIntYB 82*
Times-Tribune - Beaver City, NE - *AyerDirPub 83; Ed&PubIntYB 82*
Times-Tribune - Selinsgrove, PA - *AyerDirPub 83*
Times-Tribune - De Forest, WI - *AyerDirPub 83*
Times Tribune - Middleton, WI - *AyerDirPub 83*
Times-Union - Warsaw, IN - *AyerDirPub 83; Ed&PubIntYB 82*
Times-Union [of Capitol Newspapers] - Albany, NY - *AyerDirPub 83; Ed&PubIntYB 82; LitMarPl 84; NewsBur 6*
Times-Union [of Gannett Co. Inc.] - Rochester, NY - *AyerDirPub 83; LitMarPl 83, 84*
Times-Virginian - Appomattox, VA - *AyerDirPub 83; Ed&PubIntYB 82*
Times-West Virginian [of Thomson Newspapers] - Fairmont, WV - *AyerDirPub 83; Ed&PubIntYB 82; NewsDir 84*
Timesaver - Palmyra, NY - *AyerDirPub 83*
Timeshared Business Systems - Palo Alto, CA - *DataDirOnSer 84*
Timesharing Consultants Inc. [Subs. of Horizon Corp.] - Tucson, AZ - *DataDirOnSer 84; DataDirSup 7-83*
Timesharing Consultants Inc. - Irvine, CA - *DataDirOnSer 84*
Timesharing Management Inc. - Cambridge, MA - *DataDirOnSer 84*
Timesharing Services Inc. - Jacksonville, FL - *ADAPSOMemDir 83-84*
Timesharing Unltd. Inc. - Nashville, TN - *DataDirOnSer 84*
Timespann Music - *See* Lorenz Creative Services
Timestream Video - Whittier, CA - *AvMarPl 83*
Timetran [of ITT World Communications Inc.] - New York, NY - *TeleSy&SerDir 7-83*
Timeware Corp. - Palo Alto, CA - *ADAPSOMemDir 83-84*
Timewell Telephone Exchange - Timewell, IL - *TelDir&BG 83-84*
Timeworks Inc. - Deerfield, IL - *MicrocomMPl 84*
Timex Computer Corp. - Waterbury, CT - *WhoWMicrocom 83*
Timex Sinclair User - Buffalo, NY - *BaconPubCkMag 84*
Timin Engineering Co., Mitchell E. - San Diego, CA - *MicrocomMPl 83; WhoWMicrocom 83*
Timmins Cable Services Ltd. [of Northern Cable Services Ltd.] - Timmins, ON, Canada - *BrCabYB 84*
Timms Press Information Ltd. - London, England - *ProGuPRSer 4*
Tin Forecasts [of Chase Econometrics/Interactive Data Corp.] - Waltham, MA - *DataDirOnSer 84*
Tin Forecasts - Bala Cynwyd, PA - *DirOnDB Spring 84*
Tina Marie Music - *See* Tessalou Music
Tine Thevenin - Minneapolis, MN - *BoPubDir 4*
Tingle Music - *See* Goosebump Music
Tinker Take-Off, The - Oklahoma City, OK - *AyerDirPub 83*
Tinkers Dam Press - Jackson, MI - *BoPubDir 4 Sup, 5; LitMag&SmPr 83-84*
Tinley Park Southtown Economist - Chicago, IL - *AyerDirPub 83; NewsDir 84*
Tinley Park Southtown Economist - *See* Southtown Economist Inc.
Tinley Park Star Herald - Chicago Heights, IL - *NewsDir 84*
Tinley Park Star Herald - Tinley Park, IL - *AyerDirPub 83; Ed&PubIntYB 82*
Tinley Park Star Herald - *See* Star Publications
Tinnitus Music - Sherman Oaks, CA - *BillIntBG 83-84*
Tino Publications Inc. - Phoenix, AZ - *BoPubDir 4, 5*
Tinory Productions, Rik - Cohasset, MA - *BillIntBG 83-84*
Tinsley Advertising, Sandy - Miami, FL - *StaDirAdAg 2-84*
Tiny C Associates - Holmdel, NJ - *MicrocomMPl 83, 84; WhoWMicrocom 83*
Tiny Systems Inc. - Richardson, TX - *MicrocomMPl 84; MicrocomSwDir 1; WhoWMicrocom 83*
Tiny Tek Inc. - Dallas, TX - *MicrocomMPl 84*
Tio, Boyler & Folkersma Corp., The - West Palm Beach, FL - *StaDirAdAg 2-84*
Tioch Productions Inc. - New York, NY - *BillIntBG 83-84*
Tioga Cablevision Inc. - Tioga, ND - *BrCabYB 84; Tel&CabFB 84C p.1707*
Tioga Cablevision of Wisconsin - Clintonville, WI - *Tel&CabFB 84C p.1707*
Tioga News [of Greater Philadelphia Group Inc.] - Philadelphia, PA - *NewsDir 84*
Tioga Publishing Co. - Palo Alto, CA - *BoPubDir 4, 5*
Tioga Tribune - Tioga, ND - *BaconPubCkNews 84; Ed&PubIntYB 82*
Tionesta Forest Press - Tionesta, PA - *BaconPubCkNews 84*
Tiotis Poetry News [of M.O.P. Press] - Ft. Myers, FL - *LitMag&SmPr 83-84*
TIP - New York, NY - *BoPubDir 5*
Tip Top Cable TV Co. - Rollingstone, MN - *Tel&CabFB 84C*
TIPCO - Plymouth, MI - *WhoWMicrocom 83*
Tipp City Herald [of Bowling-Moorman Publications] - Tipp City, OH - *Ed&PubIntYB 82; NewsDir 84*
Tipp City Herald - *See* Bowling-Moorman Publications
Tippett Advertising Inc., Barry W. - Westlake Village, CA - *StaDirAdAg 2-84*
T.I.P.R.O. Reporter, The [of Texas Independent Producers & Royalty Owners Association] - Austin, TX - *BaconPubCkMag 84; MagDir 84*
Tipton Cable TV [of San-Val Cablevision Inc.] - Tipton, CA - *Tel&CabFB 84C*
Tipton Conservative & Advertiser - Tipton, IA - *BaconPubCkNews 84; Ed&PubIntYB 82; NewsDir 84*
Tipton News Leader - Frederick, OK - *BaconPubCkNews 84*
Tipton Telephone Co. Inc. - Tipton, IN - *TelDir&BG 83-84*
Tipton Times - Tipton, MO - *BaconPubCkNews 84; Ed&PubIntYB 82*
Tipton Tribune [of Elwood Publishing Co.] - Tipton, IN - *BaconPubCkNews 84; NewsDir 84*
Tiptonville Lake County Banner - Tiptonville, TN - *BaconPubCkNews 84*
Tire Business - Akron, OH - *BaconPubCkMag 84*
Tire Review [of Babcox Automotive Publications] - Akron, OH - *BaconPubCkMag 84; MagDir 84*
Tiresias Press Inc. - New York, NY - *BoPubDir 4, 5*
Tisbury Grapevine - Tisbury, MA - *BaconPubCkNews 84*
Tischer Corp. - Columbia, MD - *AvMarPl 83*
Tischler, Gail - San Angelo, TX - *LitMarPl 84*
Tischler/Levy Inc. [Aff. of Retail Advertising Group Inc.] - New York, NY - *StaDirAdAg 2-84*
Tisdale Recorder, The - Tisdale, SK, Canada - *Ed&PubIntYB 82*
Tisdall Clark & Partners Ltd. - Toronto, ON, Canada - *DirPRFirms 83*
Tisdata [of Dutch State Mines] - Geleen, Netherlands - *EISS 7-83 Sup*
Tishomingo County News - Iuka, MS - *AyerDirPub 83; Ed&PubIntYB 82*
Tishomingo Johnston County Capital Democrat - Tishomingo, OK - *BaconPubCkNews 84; NewsDir 84*
Tiskilwa Bureau Valley Chief - Tiskilwa, IL - *BaconPubCkNews 84*
Titan Publishing Co. Inc. - Mesilla, NM - *BoPubDir 4, 5*
Titania Publications - Eugene, OR - *LitMag&SmPr 83-84*
Titanic Books - Washington, DC - *LitMag&SmPr 83-84*
Tithonus Music Ltd. - *See* Memnon Ltd.

TITIS-F - Boulogne, France - *DirOnDB Spring 84*
Title-Search - Tokyo, Japan - *DirOnDB Spring 84*
TITN - Morangis, France - *InfIndMarPl 83*
Titonka Telephone Co. - Titonka, IA - *TelDir&BG 83-84*
Titonka Topic - Titonka, IA - *BaconPubCkNews 84; Ed&PubIntYB 82*
Titra Sound Corp. - New York, NY - *Tel&CabFB 84C*
Titton Advertising Inc., Mark - New York, NY - *StaDirAdAg 2-84*
TITUS-E [of Questel Inc.] - Washington, DC - *DataDirOnSer 84*
TITUS-E - Boulogne, France - *DirOnDB Spring 84*
Titus Productions Inc. - New York, NY - *TelAl 83, 84; Tel&CabFB 84C*
Titusville Cable TV Inc. - Titusville, PA - *BrCabYB 84; Tel&CabFB 84C*
Titusville Herald - Titusville, PA - *BaconPubCkNews 84; Ed&PubIntYB 82; NewsDir 84*
Titusville North Brevard Shopping News - Melbourne, FL - *AyerDirPub 83*
Titusville Star-Advocate [of Cape Publications Inc.] - Titusville, FL - *BaconPubCkNews 84; NewsDir 84*
TJH Associates Inc. - Westport, CT - *StaDirAdAg 2-84*
TJL Media - Englewood Cliffs, NJ - *StaDirAdAg 2-84*
TJ's Community Bulletin - Cornell, WI - *AyerDirPub 83*
TK - Baltimore, MD - *MagDir 84*
TKL Research Inc. - New York, NY - *IntDirMarRes 83*
TKR Cable Co. - Denver, CO - *Tel&CabFB 84C p.1707*
TKR Cable Co. - Bound Brook, NJ - *BrCabYB 84*
TKR Cable Co. - Edison, NJ - *BrCabYB 84*
TKR Cable Co. - Parlin, NJ - *Tel&CabFB 84C*
TKR Cable Co. - Warren, NJ - *Tel&CabFB 84C*
TL Enterprises Inc. - Agoura, CA - *MagIndMarPl 82-83*
TL Enterprises Inc. (Book Div.) - Agoura, CA - *LitMarPl 83, 84; WritMar 84*
TL Industries - Toledo, OH - *DataDirSup 7-83*
TLB Associates Inc. - Findlay, OH - *MicrocomMPl 83, 84; WhoWMicrocom 83*
TLC Press & the Library Club [Aff. of The Association of Private Libraries] - New York, NY - *BoPubDir 4, 5*
TLK - Chicago, IL - *StaDirAdAg 2-84*
TLK Direct Marketing - New York, NY - *DirMarMP 83*
TM Cablevision [of Times Mirror Cable TV] - Palos Verdes, CA - *BrCabYB 84*
TM Cablevision [of Times Mirror Cable TV] - San Juan Capistrano, CA - *Tel&CabFB 84C*
TM Cablevision of Riverside County [of Times Mirror Cable TV] - Murrieta Hot Springs, CA - *Tel&CabFB 84C*
TM Cablevision of Riverside County [of Times Mirror Cable TV] - Perris, CA - *Tel&CabFB 84C*
TM Cablevision of Riverside County [of Times Mirror Cable TV] - Thousand Palms, CA - *Tel&CabFB 84C*
TM Cablevision of Riverside County [of Times Mirror Cable TV] - Tustin, CA - *Tel&CabFB 84C*
TM Cablevision of San Diego County [of Times Mirror Cable TV] - Escondido, CA - *Tel&CabFB 84C*
TM Cablevision of Victor Valley [of Times Mirror Cable TV] - Victorville, CA - *BrCabYB 84*
TM Creative [Div. of James Peter Associates Inc.] - Westwood, NJ - *LitMarPl 83*
TM International Records - Indianapolis, IN - *BillIntBG 83-84*
TM of Longmeadow [of Times Mirror Cable Television Inc.] - Longmeadow, MA - *BrCabYB 84*
TM Productions - Wilmette, IL - *BoPubDir 4, 5*
TM Productions - Dallas, TX - *Tel&CabFB 84C*
TM Visual Industries Inc. [Div. of The Taylor-Merchant Corp.] - New York, NY - *AvMarPl 83*
TMC - Chandler, AZ - *AyerDirPub 83*
TMC Ltd. [of Philips Business Systems] - Malmesbury, England - *InfIndMarPl 83*
TMC Press [Aff. of Liberty Bookstores] - Sunnyvale, CA - *BoPubDir 4, 5*
TMC Productions - San Antonio, TX - *BillIntBG 83-84*
TMC Publishing - Oakville, ON, Canada - *BoPubDir 4 Sup, 5*
TMCTMT-Adirondacks Inc. [of Tele-Media Corp.] - Adams, NY - *BrCabYB 84; Tel&CabFB 84C*
TMCTMT-Adirondacks Inc. [of Tele-Media Corp.] - Boonville, NY - *BrCabYB 84; Tel&CabFB 84C*
TMCTMT-Adirondacks Inc. [of Tele-Media Corp.] - Lowville, NY - *BrCabYB 84; Tel&CabFB 84C*
TMI Systems Corp. - Lexington, MA - *DataDirSup 7-83*
TMQ Software Inc. - Buffalo Grove, IL - *MicrocomMPl 84; MicrocomSwDir 1; WhoWMicrocom 83*
TMQ Software Inc. - Des Plaines, IL - *MicrocomMPl 83*
TMS Production - San Antonio, TX - *AvMarPl 83*
TMV Enterprises - New York, NY - *BillIntBG 83-84*
TNW Corp. - San Diego, CA - *MicrocomMPl 83, 84; WhoWMicrocom 83*
Toast of the Coast Herald, The - Rockport, TX - *AyerDirPub 83; Ed&PubIntYB 82*
Toastmaster, The - Santa Ana, CA - *BaconPubCkMag 84; MagDir 84; MagIndMarPl 82-83; WritMar 84*
Toastmasters International - Santa Ana, CA - *BoPubDir 4, 5; ProGuPRSer 4*
Tobacco Import-Export Database [of Tobacco Merchants Association of the United States] - New York, NY - *EISS 5-84 Sup*
Tobacco/International - New York, NY - *BaconPubCkMag 84; MagDir 84*
Tobacco Reporter - Raleigh, NC - *BaconPubCkMag 84; MagDir 84; WritMar 84*
Tobacco Valley News - Eureka, MT - *AyerDirPub 83; Ed&PubIntYB 82*
Tobacco Works International - Washington, DC - *NewsDir 84*
Tobias & Associates Inc., Herb - Los Angeles, CA - *TelAl 83, 84*
Tobias Associates Inc. - New York, NY - *StaDirAdAg 2-84*
Tobias Associates Inc. - Ivyland, PA - *AvMarPl 83*
Tobias, Meyer & Nebenzahl, Advertising [Div. of Retail Reporting Bureau] - New York, NY - *Ed&PubIntYB 82*
Toby's Tunes Inc. - Minneapolis, MN - *AvMarPl 83*
Toccoa Record - Toccoa, GA - *AyerDirPub 83; BaconPubCkNews 84; Ed&PubIntYB 82; NewsDir 84*
TOCOM Inc. - Dallas, TX - *CabTVFinDB 83; VideoDir 82-83*
TOCOM Inc. - Irving, TX - *HomeVid&CabYB 82-83*
Today [of Cape Publications] - Cocoa, FL - *AyerDirPub 83; BaconPubCkNews 84; Ed&PubIntYB 82; NewsDir 84*
Today - Wayne, NJ - *AyerDirPub 83*
Today - White Plains, NY - *AyerDirPub 83; Ed&PubIntYB 82*
Today [of CompuServe Inc.] - Columbus, OH - *MicrocomMPl 84*
Today [of Mead Data Central] - Dayton, OH - *DataDirOnSer 84*
Today - Allentown, PA - *BaconPubCkMag 84*
Today [of Thirty Press Ltd.] - London, England - *LitMag&SmPr 83-84*
Today News Service Inc. - Washington, DC - *BoPubDir 4, 5; Ed&PubIntYB 82*
Today Newspapers - Wayne, NJ - *BaconPubCkNews 84*
Today/Sun News - Phoenix, AZ - *Ed&PubIntYB 82*
Today's Animal News - Santa Rosa, CA - *BaconPubCkMag 84; MagDir 84; MagIndMarPl 82-83*
Today's Art & Graphics - New York, NY - *MagDir 84; MagIndMarPl 82-83*
Today's Bride - Don Mills, ON, Canada - *BaconPubCkMag 84*
Today's Catholic Teacher - Ormond Beach, FL - *WritMar 84*
Today's Catholic Teacher - Dayton, OH - *BaconPubCkMag 84; MagDir 84; MagIndMarPl 82-83*
Today's Chef - Cape Coral, FL - *MagDir 84*
Today's Chicago Woman - Chicago, IL - *BaconPubCkMag 84*
Today's Chiropractic [of Life Chiropractic College] - Marietta, GA - *MagDir 84*
Today's Christian Parent - Cincinnati, OH - *ArtMar 84; WritMar 84*
Today's Christian Women [of Fleming H. Revell Co.] - Old Tappan, NJ - *DirMarMP 83*
Today's Clinician - New York, NY - *MagDir 84*
Today's Education - Washington, DC - *BaconPubCkMag 84; MagDir 84; MagIndMarPl 82-83; WritMar 84*
Today's Farmer - Columbia, MO - *BaconPubCkMag 84; MagDir 84*
Today's Hunters' Gun - New York, NY - *MagDir 84*
Today's Living - New York, NY - *MagDir 84; MagIndMarPl 82-83*
Today's Mail - Monongahela, PA - *AyerDirPub 83*

Today's Marketing [of Roberts Publishing Co.] - Schaumburg, IL - *MagDir 84*
Today's Nursing Home - Northfield, IL - *BaconPubCkMag 84*
Today's Office - Garden City, NY - *BaconPubCkMag 84; MagDir 84*
Today's OR Nurse - Thorofare, NJ - *BaconPubCkMag 84; MagIndMarPl 82-83; WritMar 84*
Today's Policeman - Kansas City, MO - *ArtMar 84*
Today's Post - King of Prussia, PA - *AyerDirPub 83*
Today's Post [of Montgomery Publishing Co.] - Norristown, PA - *NewsDir 84*
Today's Professionals [of Widmaier & Goss] - Los Angeles, CA - *MagDir 84*
Today's Spirit - Hatboro, PA - *AyerDirPub 83; BaconPubCkNews 84; Ed&PubIntYB 82*
Today's Sunbeam - Salem, NJ - *AyerDirPub 83; BaconPubCkNews 84; Ed&PubIntYB 82*
Today's Transport International - Westport, CT - *BaconPubCkMag 84; MagDir 84; MagIndMarPl 82-83*
Todd & Associates Inc., Jerre R. - Ft. Worth, TX - *AdAge 3-28-84; DirPRFirms 83; StaDirAdAg 2-84*
Todd & Honeywell Inc. - Great Neck, NY - *BoPubDir 4, 5*
Todd Communications Inc. - Minneapolis, MN - *Tel&CabFB 84C p.1708*
Todd County Standard - Elkton, KY - *AyerDirPub 83; Ed&PubIntYB 82; NewsDir 84*
Todd County Tribune - Mission, SD - *AyerDirPub 83; Ed&PubIntYB 82*
Todd Sales - Couina, CA - *MicrocomMPl 84*
Todd Tarbox Books - El Paso, TX - *LitMag&SmPr 83-84*
Toews, Milton & Margaret - Neilburg, SK, Canada - *BoPubDir 4 Sup, 5*
Tofield Mercury - Tofield, AB, Canada - *Ed&PubIntYB 82*
Toft, Dickman & Associates Inc. - New York, NY - *HBIndAd&MS 82-83*
Tofua Press - *See* Rand Editions/Tofua Press
Togetherness Productions/Poets Pay Rent Too - Los Angeles, CA - *BoPubDir 4, 5*
TOGG Films Inc. - New York, NY - *ArtMar 84; AvMarPl 83*
Token & Medal Society Inc. - El Cajon, CA - *BoPubDir 4, 5*
Token/Net [of Concord Data Systems] - Waltham, MA - *TeleSy&SerDir 2-84*
Tokyo English Literature Society - Tokyo, Japan - *LitMag&SmPr 83-84*
TOLA Specialties - Chicago, IL - *DataDirSup 7-83*
Toledo Anthony Wayne Herald - Toledo, OH - *BaconPubCkNews 84*
Toledo Blade Co. - Toledo, OH - *BaconPubCkNews 84; BrCabYB 84; KnowInd 83; LitMarPl 83; NewsDir 84; Tel&CabFB 84S*
Toledo Blade Co. - *See* Buckeye Cablevision Inc.
Toledo Catholic Chronicle - Toledo, OH - *NewsDir 84*
Toledo Chronicle - Toledo, IA - *AyerDirPub 83; BaconPubCkNews 84; Ed&PubIntYB 82*
Toledo Democrat - Toledo, IL - *BaconPubCkNews 84; Ed&PubIntYB 82*
Toledo Journal - Toledo, OH - *BaconPubCkNews 84; Ed&PubIntYB 82*
Toledo Lincoln County Leader - *See* Newport News-Times Publishers
Toledo Magazine - Toledo, OH - *MagIndMarPl 82-83*
Toledo Point-Shoreland Journal - *See* Welch Publishing Co.
Toledo Scale - Worthington, OH - *DataDirSup 7-83*
Toledo Sun - Toledo, OH - *BaconPubCkNews 84*
Toledo Telephone Co. Inc. - Toledo, WA - *TelDir&BG 83-84*
Toledo Theatre Supply Co. [Div. of Concession Supply Co.] - Toledo, OH - *AvMarPl 83*
Toledo West Toledo Herald - Toledo, OH - *BaconPubCkNews 84*
Toledot: The Journal of Jewish Genealogy - New York, NY - *LitMag&SmPr 83-84*
TOLFF Publishers [Aff. of The Trinity of Light Fellowship Foundation] - Carpinteria, CA - *BoPubDir 4, 5*
Toll Marketing Trends Inc. - New York, NY - *IntDirMarRes 83*
Toll Reporter [of ORTT, IBEW Local Union 1011] - San Francisco, CA - *NewsDir 84*
Toll, Wilbur - Scarsdale, NY - *LitMarPl 83, 84*
Tolmach, Ned - Miami, FL - *HBIndAd&MS 82-83*
Tolono County Star - Tolono, IL - *BaconPubCkNews 84*
Tolson & Co. Advertising Inc. - New York, NY - *StaDirAdAg 2-84*
Toluca Lake Graphic - Encino, CA - *AyerDirPub 83*
Toluca Lake Graphic - *See* Associated Valley Publications
Toluca Lake Tolucan & Canyon Crier - Toluca Lake, CA - *BaconPubCkNews 84*
Tolucan & Magnolian, The - North Hollywood, CA - *AyerDirPub 83*
Tolucan & Magnolian, The - Toluca Lake, CA - *Ed&PubIntYB 82*
Tolucan, The [of Tujunga American Publishing Co.] - Tujunga, CA - *NewsDir 84*
Tolvan Co. - Appleton, WI - *BoPubDir 4, 5*
Tom Advertising Inc. - Oak Brook, IL - *DirMarMP 83*
TOM Inc. - Seattle, WA - *ADAPSOMemDir 83-84*
Tomah Journal - Tomah, WI - *Ed&PubIntYB 82; NewsDir 84*
Tomah Journal & Monitor-Herald - Tomah, WI - *BaconPubCkNews 84*
Tomah Monitor-Herald [of Tomah Journal Printing Co. Inc.] - Tomah, WI - *Ed&PubIntYB 82; NewsDir 84*
Tomahawk Leader - Tomahawk, WI - *BaconPubCkNews 84; Ed&PubIntYB 82*
Tomahawk, The - Mountain City, TN - *Ed&PubIntYB 82*
Tomake Music Co. Inc. - *See* Drake Music Group
Tomalin, Norman Owen - New York, NY - *MagIndMarPl 82-83*
Tomark-Cyber Associates Inc. - Roslyn, NY - *WhoWMicrocom 83*
Tomaselli, Mary F. - Whitestone, NY - *LitMarPl 83, 84*
Tomash Publishers - Los Angeles, CA - *BoPubDir 4, 5; LitMag&SmPr 83-84*
Tomball Sun - *See* Houston Community Newspapers
Tomberlin-Princeton Cable TV - Princeton, KY - *Tel&CabFB 84C*
Tomberlin, William F. - Hendersonville, TN - *Tel&CabFB 84C p.1708*
Tombouctou Books - Bolinas, CA - *BoPubDir 4, 5; LitMag&SmPr 83-84*
Tombras Advertising Inc., Charles - Knoxville, TN - *StaDirAdAg 2-84*
Tombstone Epitaph - Tombstone, AZ - *NewsDir 84*
Tominy Inc. - Cincinnati, OH - *ADAPSOMemDir 83-84; WhoWMicrocom 83*
Tomkins & Son Inc., J. E. - Farmingdale, NY - *LitMarPl 83, 84*
Tomkins & Son Inc., J. E. - New York, NY - *MagIndMarPl 82-83*
Tomkinsville News - Tomkinsville, KY - *AyerDirPub 83*
Tomlew Publishing - Cleveland, OH - *BillIntBG 83-84*
Tomlin Film Productions Inc. - Sloatsburg, NY - *Tel&CabFB 84C*
Tommaney Marketing Services - New York, NY - *IntDirMarRes 83*
Tommy Boy Music Inc. - New York, NY - *BillIntBG 83-84*
Tomoka Cable TV Inc. - Volusia County, FL - *Tel&CabFB 84C*
Tomorrow Entertainment Inc. - *See* Dancer Fitzgerald Sample Inc.
Tomorrow River Records - Madison, WI - *BillIntBG 83-84*
Tomorrow's Office Products Inc. - Chicago, IL - *DirInfWP 82*
Tompalland Music - Nashville, TN - *BillIntBG 83-84*
Tompaul Music Co. - Mt. Airy, NC - *BillIntBG 83-84*
Tompkins County Rural News - Dryden, NY - *AyerDirPub 83*
Tompkinsville Cable TV Inc. [of Centel Communications Co.] - Tompkinsville, KY - *Tel&CabFB 84C*
Tompkinsville News - Tompkinsville, KY - *BaconPubCkNews 84; Ed&PubIntYB 82; NewsDir 84*
Tompson & Rutter Inc. - Grantham, NH - *BoPubDir 4; LitMag&SmPr 83-84; LitMarPl 83, 84; WritMar 84*
Toms River Ocean County Reporter - Toms River, NJ - *BaconPubCkNews 84*
Tonapah TV Inc. - Tonapah, NV - *BrCabYB 84*
Tonatiuh-Quinto Sol International Inc. - Berkeley, CA - *BoPubDir 4, 5*
Tonawanda News - North Tonawanda, NY - *AyerDirPub 83; Ed&PubIntYB 82; NewsDir 84*
Tone Commander Systems Inc. - Richmond, WA - *DataDirSup 7-83*
Tone Craft Music - *See* Sure Music & Record Co.
Tone Software Corp. - Anaheim, CA - *DataDirSup 7-83*
Toney Fork TV Line Service [of Bahakel Communications] - Toney Fork Junction, WV - *BrCabYB 84*

Tonganoxie Mirror - Tonganoxie, KS - *BaconPubCkNews 84; Ed&PubIntYB 82*
Tongue Press - Great River, NY - *LitMag&SmPr 83-84*
Tongue River Cable TV - Story, WY - *BrCabYB 84; Tel&CabFB 84C*
Tongue River Cable TV Inc. - Ranchester, WY - *BrCabYB 84; Tel&CabFB 84C*
Tonica News - Tonica, IL - *BaconPubCkNews 84; Ed&PubIntYB 82*
Tonica Telephone Co. Inc. - Tonica, IL - *TelDir&BG 83-84*
Tonkawa Maverick - Tonkawa, OK - *BaconPubCkNews 84*
Tonkawa News - Tonkawa, OK - *BaconPubCkNews 84; Ed&PubIntYB 82*
Tonopah Times-Bonanza & Goldfield News - *See* Central Nevada Newspapers Inc.
Tonopah TV Inc. - Tonopah, NV - *Tel&CabFB 84C*
Tony B. Enterprises - *See* Tony Press/Tony B. Enterprises
Tony Press/Tony B. Enterprises - San Francisco, CA - *BoPubDir 4, 5*
Tooele Bulletin - Tooele, UT - *Ed&PubIntYB 82; NewsDir 84*
Tooele Bulletin - *See* Transcript Bulletin Publishing Co.
Tooele Transcript - Tooele, UT - *Ed&PubIntYB 82; NewsDir 84*
Tooele Transcript - *See* Transcript Bulletin Publishing Co.
Tool, Dennis C. - Laramie, WY - *LitMarPl 84*
Toole Inc., Philip B. - Providence, RI - *StaDirAdAg 2-84*
Tooling & Production - Cleveland, OH - *MagDir 84*
Tooling & Production [of Huebner Publications Inc.] - Solon, OH - *BaconPubCkMag 84; Folio 83; MagIndMarPl 82-83*
Toolsmith, The - Davis, CA - *MicrocomMPl 83, 84; MicrocomSwDir 1*
Toor Furniture Corp. - Los Angeles, CA - *MicrocomMPl 83*
Tooter Scooter Music - *See* Tiki Enterprises Inc.
Tooth of Time Books - Santa Fe, NM - *BoPubDir 4, 5; LitMag&SmPr 83-84*
Toothpaste Press - West Branch, IA - *BoPubDir 4; LitMag&SmPr 83-84; LitMarPl 83, 84*
Tootikian & Associates Inc., Lawrence - Chicago, IL - *IntDirMarRes 83; MagIndMarPl 82-83*
Top Business Systems Ltd. - Nottingham, England - *MicrocomSwDir 1*
Top Drawer Music - Mobile, AL - *BillIntBG 83-84*
Top-Ecol Press - La Crescenta, CA - *BoPubDir 4, 5*
Top Notch Typesetting Inc. - Oaklyn, NJ - *LitMarPl 83*
Top Notch Typesetting Inc. - Sicklerville, NJ - *LitMarPl 84*
Top of the News - Chicago, IL - *BaconPubCkMag 84; MagDir 84; MagIndMarPl 82-83*
Top of the Town Music Co. - *See* Entertainment Co. Music Group, The
Topaz - San Diego, CA - *DataDirSup 7-83; DirInfWP 82; MicrocomMPl 84; WhoWMicrocom 83*
Topaz Systems Inc. - Ridgefield, CT - *MicrocomMPl 84*
Topeka Capital-Journal [of Stauffer Communications Inc.] - Topeka, KS - *BaconPubCkNews 84; Ed&PubIntYB 82; LitMarPl 83, 84; NewsBur 6*
Topeka Daily Legal News [of Kansas Secured Title Co.] - Topeka, KS - *Ed&PubIntYB 82; NewsDir 84*
Topeka Genealogical Society - Topeka, KS - *BoPubDir 4, 5*
Topflight Records - New York, NY - *BillIntBG 83-84*
Topgallant Publishing Co. Inc. - Honolulu, HI - *BoPubDir 4, 5*
Topic - Mt. Dora, FL - *AyerDirPub 83*
Topic - Titonka, IA - *AyerDirPub 83*
Topic - Timber Lake, SD - *AyerDirPub 83*
TOPIC [of The Stock Exchange] - London, England - *EISS 83*
Topic Newsmagazine - York, ON, Canada - *Ed&PubIntYB 82*
Topic Newspapers Inc. - Indianapolis, IN - *BaconPubCkNews 84*
Topical Review Book Co. - Auburn, NY - *BoPubDir 4, 5*
Topical Time - Milwaukee, WI - *MagDir 84*
Topicator - Denver, CO - *MagDir 84*
Topics Newspapers - Indianapolis, IN - *AyerDirPub 83*
Topitzes & Associates Inc. - Madison, WI - *StaDirAdAg 2-84*
Topline Research Corp. - New York, NY - *IntDirMarRes 83*
Topologic Inc. - Burlington, IA - *MicrocomMPl 84*
Toponymic Branch [of U.S. Dept. of Defense] - Washington, DC - *EISS 83*
Toppan Printing Co. Inc. - New York, NY - *LitMarPl 83, 84*
Toppenish Review - Toppenish, WA - *BaconPubCkNews 84; Ed&PubIntYB 82*
Toppenish Review-Mirror - Toppenish, WA - *NewsDir 84*
Topper - Clinton, WI - *AyerDirPub 83*
Topping Paper Corp. - Port Washington, NY - *LitMarPl 83, 84; MagIndMarPl 82-83*
Toppino Agency Inc., The - Albuquerque, NM - *StaDirAdAg 2-84*
Tops News - Milwaukee, WI - *BaconPubCkMag 84*
Tops Programming Enterprises - Portland, OR - *MicrocomMPl 84*
Topsfield Tri-Town Transcript - Ipswich, MA - *AyerDirPub 83; NewsDir 84*
Topsfield Tri-Town Transcript - *See* North Shore Weeklies Inc.
Topsham Telephone Co. Inc. - East Corinth, VT - *TelDir&BG 83-84*
Topsy Turvy-Patas Arribas - Tucson, AZ - *LitMag&SmPr 83-84*
Tor Books [Subs. of Tom Doherty Associates] - New York, NY - *LitMarPl 83, 84; WritMar 84*
Tor Music Co. - *See* Gordon Music Co. Inc.
Torah Resources - Brooklyn, NY - *BoPubDir 4, 5*
Torah Umesorah Publications - New York, NY - *BoPubDir 4, 5*
Torbert, Harold - Irving, TX - *LitMarPl 83, 84*
Torc Publishers - Whitehorse, YT, Canada - *BoPubDir 4, 5*
Torch Computers Ltd. - Boston, MA - *WhoWMicrocom 83*
Torch Computers Ltd. - Woburn, MA - *DataDirOnSer 84*
Torch Computers Ltd. - Cambridge, England - *MicrocomSwDir 1*
Torch, The - Central Lake, MI - *AyerDirPub 83; Ed&PubIntYB 82*
Tornberg & Co. Inc., Edwin - Washington, DC - *CabTVFinDB 83*
Tornquist, David - Newport, RI - *LitMarPl 83, 84; MagIndMarPl 82-83*
Torobin Advertising Ltd. - Don Mills, ON, Canada - *StaDirAdAg 2-84*
Toronto Board of Education (Research Dept.) - Toronto, ON, Canada - *BoPubDir 4, 5*
Toronto Business Executives & Careers Study [of Interactive Market Systems] - New York, NY - *DataDirOnSer 84*
Toronto Haiku Workshop - Toronto, ON, Canada - *LitMag&SmPr 83-84*
Toronto Herald - Toronto, SD - *Ed&PubIntYB 82*
Toronto Herald - *See* Lundgren Publishing Co.
Toronto Jewish Press - Downsview, ON, Canada - *Ed&PubIntYB 82*
Toronto Life - Toronto, ON, Canada - *BaconPubCkMag 84; WritMar 84*
Toronto Metropolitan Paper Co. Ltd. - Toronto, ON, Canada - *LitMarPl 83, 84*
Toronto Public Library - Toronto, ON, Canada - *BoPubDir 4, 5*
Toronto Section [of the Alpine Club of Canada] - Toronto, ON, Canada - *BoPubDir 4, 5*
Toronto Star - Toronto, ON, Canada - *BaconPubCkNews 84; Ed&PubIntYB 82; LitMarPl 83, 84*
Toronto Star Syndicate [Div. of Toronto Star Newspapers Ltd.] - Toronto, ON, Canada - *BaconPubCkNews 84; Ed&PubIntYB 82; LitMarPl 84*
Toronto Stock Exchange 300 Composite Index [of I. P. Sharp Associates] - Toronto, ON, Canada - *DBBus 82; DirOnDB Spring 84*
Toronto Stock Exchange 300 Index & Stock Statistics [of I. P. Sharp Associates Ltd.] - Toronto, ON, Canada - *DataDirOnSer 84*
Toronto Sun Publishing Corp. - Toronto, ON, Canada - *BoPubDir 4 Sup, 5*
Toronto Sun, The [of Maclean-Hunter Ltd.] - Toronto, ON, Canada - *BaconPubCkNews 84; Ed&PubIntYB 82; LitMarPl 84*
Toronto Tribune - Toronto, OH - *AyerDirPub 83; BaconPubCkNews 84; Ed&PubIntYB 82*
Toronto Wages for Housework Committee - Toronto, ON, Canada - *BoPubDir 4, 5*
Toronto Word Processing Centre - Toronto, ON, Canada - *DirInfWP 82*
Torrance County Citizen - Estancia, NM - *AyerDirPub 83; Ed&PubIntYB 82*
Torrance Daily Breeze [of The Copley Press Inc.] - Torrance, CA - *NewsDir 84*
Torrance News [of Culver City Coast Media Newspapers] - Culver City, CA - *NewsDir 84*
Torrance Press-Herald - Torrance, CA - *Ed&PubIntYB 82*
Torrance Press-Herald - *See* Breeze Newspapers
Torrance Tribune - Culver City, CA - *AyerDirPub 83*

Torrence, Allan - Centreville, MS - *Tel&CabFB 84C p.1708*
Torrence Broadcasting Co. - Centreville, MS - *Tel&CabFB 84C*
Torrence Cablevision - Pearl, MS - *Tel&CabFB 84C*
Torrey Ltd. - Grosse Pointe, MI - *InfIndMarPl 83*
Torrey Research Group - Grosse Pointe, MI - *TeleSy&SerDir 2-84*
Torrington Register - Torrington, CT - *BaconPubCkNews 84; NewsDir 84*
Torrington Telegram - Torrington, WY - *Ed&PubIntYB 82*
Torrington Telegram - *See* Lindsey Publishing
Torskript Publishers - San Francisco, CA - *BoPubDir 4, 5*
Torstar Corp. - Tarrytown, NY - *KnowInd 83*
Tortoise Music - *See* Folklore Music
Tortoise Press - Palos Verdes Estates, CA - *BoPubDir 4, 5; LitMag&SmPr 83-84*
Tosack Songs - *See* Music Exchange, The
Tosaw Publishing Co. Inc. - Ceres, CA - *BoPubDir 5*
TOSC International Inc. - Houston, TX - *ADAPSOMemDir 83-84; DataDirSup 7-83*
Toshiba America Inc. - Tustin, CA - *MicrocomMPl 84; WhoWMicrocom 83*
Toshiba America Inc. - Wayne, NJ - *BillIntBG 83-84*
Toshiba America Inc. (Information Processing Div.) - Tustin, CA - *DirInfWP 82*
Totah Telephone Co. Inc., The - Ochelata, OK - *TelDir&BG 83-84*
Total Abandon - Portland, OR - *LitMag&SmPr 83-84*
Total Access - Richardson, TX - *MicrocomMPl 83, 84*
Total Audio Visual Service - New York, NY - *AvMarPl 83*
Total Audio Visual Services Inc. - Atlanta, GA - *AvMarPl 83*
Total Cable TV of Delphi Inc. [of Tele-Communications Inc.] - Delphi, IN - *BrCabYB 84; Tel&CabFB 84C*
Total Cable TV of Fowler Inc. [of Tele-Communications Inc.] - Fowler, IN - *BrCabYB 84; Tel&CabFB 84C*
Total CATV Inc. [of Daniels & Associates] - Baton Rouge, LA - *BrCabYB 84; HomeVid&CabYB 82-83*
Total Comfort Dealer [of Eneguess Publishing Co.] - Peterborough, NH - *BaconPubCkMag 84; MagDir 84*
Total Communication Systems - New Kensington, PA - *BrCabYB 84; Tel&CabFB 84C*
Total Communications - St. Louis, MO - *AdAge 3-28-84; StaDirAdAg 2-84*
Total Communications Cable Co. [of Tele-Communications Inc.] - Monticello, IN - *BrCabYB 84; Tel&CabFB 84C*
Total Data Base Management System [of Cincom Systems Inc.] - Cincinnati, OH - *EISS 83*
Total Environmental System - East Lansing, MI - *DataDirOnSer 84*
Total Fitness [of National Reporter Publications Inc.] - Bixby, OK - *BaconPubCkMag 84; WritMar 84*
Total Health [of Trio Publications] - Los Angeles, CA - *MagDir 84; WritMar 84*
Total Involvement Inc. - New York, NY - *AvMarPl 83*
Total Living Institute - New York, NY - *BoPubDir 4, 5*
Total Research Corp. - Princeton, NJ - *IntDirMarRes 83*
Total Systems Inc. - Indianapolis, IN - *WhoWMicrocom 83*
Total Technical Services Inc. - North Royalton, OH - *DataDirSup 7-83*
Total TV - Delavan, WI - *BrCabYB 84*
Total TV - Janesville, WI - *BrCabYB 84 p.D-309; Tel&CabFB 84C p.1708*
Total TV Central Region - Hustisford, WI - *Tel&CabFB 84C*
Total TV of Amarillo - Amarillo, TX - *BrCabYB 84; Tel&CabFB 84C*
Total TV of Brown County - Ashwaubenon, WI - *Tel&CabFB 84C*
Total TV of Brown County - Chilton, WI - *Tel&CabFB 84C*
Total TV of Brown County - Green Bay, WI - *Tel&CabFB 84C*
Total TV of Brown County - Oconto, WI - *Tel&CabFB 84C*
Total TV of Burlington - Burlington, WI - *BrCabYB 84; Tel&CabFB 84C*
Total TV of Chilton - Chilton, WI - *BrCabYB 84*
Total TV of Dodge County - Beaver Dam, WI - *BrCabYB 84*
Total TV of Dodge-Point - Janesville, WI - *Tel&CabFB 84C*
Total TV of Grant & Lafayette Counties - Mineral Point, WI - *BrCabYB 84*
Total TV of Manitowoc - Manitowoc, WI - *BrCabYB 84; Tel&CabFB 84C*
Total TV of New London - New London, WI - *BrCabYB 84*
Total TV of Ozaukee County - Cedarburg, WI - *BrCabYB 84; Tel&CabFB 84C*
Total TV of Santa Rosa [of Capital Cities Cable Inc.] - Santa Rosa, CA - *BrCabYB 84; Tel&CabFB 84C*
Total TV of Shawano - Shawano, WI - *BrCabYB 84; Tel&CabFB 84C*
Total TV of Washington County - Hartford, WI - *BrCabYB 84*
Total TV of Waupaca - Waupaca, WI - *BrCabYB 84; Tel&CabFB 84C*
Total Typography Inc. - Chicago, IL - *LitMarPl 83, 84*
Total Universe Book Co. [Aff. of International Mena Consulting Co.] - Dearborn, MI - *BoPubDir 4, 5*
Totalgraphics Inc. - Silver Spring, MD - *MagIndMarPl 82-83*
Totalistics Advertising - Port Chester, NY - *AdAge 3-28-84; StaDirAdAg 2-84*
Totally Housewares - New York, NY - *BaconPubCkMag 84*
Totec, USA - Northridge, CA - *DirInfWP 82*
Totl Software Inc. - Walnut Creek, CA - *MicrocomMPl 84*
Tottenham News, The - Tottenham, ON, Canada - *Ed&PubIntYB 82*
Tottenham Times - Beeton, ON, Canada - *AyerDirPub 83*
Toucan - St. Peter Port, England - *LitMag&SmPr 83-84*
Toucan Software - Fair Oaks, CA - *MicrocomMPl 84*
Touch - Grand Rapids, MI - *WritMar 84*
Touch Stone Software Corp. - Seal Beach, CA - *MicrocomMPl 84*
Touchable-Lovespun Music - *See* Funky but Music Inc.
Touchdown Illustrated - San Francisco, CA - *MagDir 84; MagIndMarPl 82-83*
Touche Records - El Cerrito, CA - *BillIntBG 83-84*
Touchet & Associates - Houston, TX - *MagIndMarPl 82-83*
Touchet Valley Television Inc. - Dayton, WA - *BrCabYB 84; Tel&CabFB 84C*
Touchette Corp. - East Syracuse, NY - *DataDirOnSer 84*
Touchstone [of Houston Writer's Guild] - Houston, TX - *LitMag&SmPr 83-84; WritMar 84*
Touchstone Center Publications [Aff. of Touchstone Center for Children Inc.] - New York, NY - *BoPubDir 4 Sup, 5*
Touchstone Press, The - Beaverton, OR - *LitMarPl 83, 84; WritMar 84*
Touchstones Enterprises Inc. - Fargo, ND - *BoPubDir 4, 5*
Toulon Stark County News - Toulon, IL - *BaconPubCkNews 84*
Toulouse Music Publications - El Cerrito, CA - *BillIntBG 83-84*
Touring Bike [of Touring Bike Publishing Co. Inc.] - Anaheim, CA - *BaconPubCkMag 84; MagDir 84; MagIndMarPl 82-83; WritMar 84*
Touring Times [of RFD Inc.] - Kansas City, MO - *WritMar 84*
Tourism Newfoundland [of Newfoundland Telephone] - St. Johns, NF, Canada - *EISS 5-84 Sup*
Tourism Reference & Data Centre [of Dept. of Industry, Trade, & Commerce] - Ottawa, ON, Canada - *EISS 83*
Tourist Attractions & Parks - Philadelphia, PA - *ArtMar 84; BaconPubCkMag 84; MagDir 84*
Tournament Times, The [of Western Tennis Publications] - Santa Fe, NM - *WritMar 84*
Tourtel [of English Tourist Board] - London, England - *EISS 83*
Tout de Suite a la Microwave Inc. - Lafayette, LA - *BoPubDir 4, 5*
T.O.V. Publishers - San Jose, CA - *BoPubDir 4, 5*
Tow-Age [of Info-Quest Inc.] - Franklin, MA - *ArtMar 84; MagDir 84; WritMar 84*
Towa Corp. of America - Morrisville, PA - *DataDirSup 7-83*
Towanda Daily Review - Towanda, PA - *NewsDir 84*
Towards - Fair Oaks, CA - *LitMag&SmPr 83-84*
Towell Inc. - Madison, WI - *StaDirAdAg 2-84*
Tower Cable Co. - Tower, MN - *Tel&CabFB 84C*
Tower Cable Inc. [of Times Mirror Cable TV] - Newark, OH - *Tel&CabFB 84C*
Tower Cable Systems Corp. [of Times Mirror Cable TV] - Beaver Falls, PA - *Tel&CabFB 84C*
Tower Cablevision Inc. [of Times Mirror Cable TV] - Ashland, KY - *BrCabYB 84; Tel&CabFB 84C*
Tower CATV - Tower, MN - *BrCabYB 84*
Tower City West Schuylkill Herald - *See* West Schuylkill Herald Publishers
Tower Communications Inc. [of Times Mirror Cable TV] - Caldwell, OH - *BrCabYB 84; Tel&CabFB 84C*

Tower Communications Inc. [of Times Mirror Cable TV] - Coshocton, OH - *BrCabYB 84; Tel&CabFB 84C*
Tower Communications Inc. [of Times Mirror Cable TV] - Fresno, OH - *Tel&CabFB 84C*
Tower Communications Inc. [of Times Mirror Cable TV] - Ironton, OH - *BrCabYB 84; Tel&CabFB 84C*
Tower Communications Inc. [of Times Mirror Cable TV] - New Philadelphia, OH - *Tel&CabFB 84C*
Tower Communications Inc. [of Times Mirror Cable TV] - Sugarcreek, OH - *BrCabYB 84*
Tower Communications Inc. [of Times Mirror Cable TV] - Uhrichsville, OH - *BrCabYB 84; Tel&CabFB 84C*
Tower Communications Inc. [of Times Mirror Cable TV Inc.] - Warsaw, OH - *Tel&CabFB 84C*
Tower Communications Inc. [of Times Mirror Cable TV] - Waverly, OH - *Tel&CabFB 84C*
Tower Hill Press [Aff. of Eastern Data Graphics] - Doylestown, PA - *BoPubDir 4, 5*
Tower News - Tower, MN - *BaconPubCkNews 84; Ed&PubIntYB 82*
Tower Press Inc. - Seabrook, NH - *MagIndMarPl 82-83*
Tower Productions - North Hollywood, CA - *TelAl 83, 84*
Tower Publishing Co. - Portland, ME - *BoPubDir 4, 5*
Tower Records' Pulse! [of MTS Inc.] - Sacramento, CA - *WritMar 84*
Tower Systems - Irvine, CA - *DataDirSup 7-83*
Towerhill Records [Div. of Towerhill Corp.] - Hollywood, CA - *BillIntBG 83-84*
Towers Advertising Inc., Robert - New York, NY - *StaDirAdAg 2-84*
Towers & Co., Frederic C. - Bethesda, MD - *DataDirOnSer 84; InfIndMarPl 83*
Towers Club Press [Aff. of Jerry Buchanan Advertising Agency] - Vancouver, WA - *BoPubDir 4, 5*
Towers Club, USA [of Towers Club Press] - Vancouver, WA - *ArtMar 84; DirMarMP 83; MagIndMarPl 82-83; WritMar 84*
Towers, Perrin, Forster & Crosby Inc. - New York, NY - *DirPRFirms 83*
Towertronics Inc. - Ft. Worth, TX - *AvMarPl 83*
Town Advertising Associates - *See* Lewis Advertising Agency
Town & Country - Seneca, IL - *AyerDirPub 83*
Town & Country [of The Hearst Corp.] - New York, NY - *ArtMar 84; BaconPubCkMag 84; Folio 83; LitMarPl 83, 84; MagDir 84; MagIndMarPl 82-83; WritMar 84*
Town & Country - Pennsburg, PA - *AyerDirPub 83; Ed&PubIntYB 82*
Town & Country - Union City, PA - *AyerDirPub 83; Ed&PubIntYB 82*
Town & Country - Waupaca, WI - *AyerDirPub 83*
Town & Country - Ft. St. John, BC, Canada - *AyerDirPub 83; Ed&PubIntYB 82*
Town & Country Crier - Mildmay, ON, Canada - *Ed&PubIntYB 82*
Town & Country East & Central [of Brown-Thompson Newspapers] - Union City, PA - *NewsDir 84*
Town & Country Leader - Excelsior Springs, MO - *AyerDirPub 83*
Town & Country News - Gouverneur, NY - *Ed&PubIntYB 82*
Town & Country News - Everman, TX - *AyerDirPub 83*
Town & Country Shopper - Gainesville, FL - *AyerDirPub 83*
Town & Country Shopper - Princeton, MN - *AyerDirPub 83*
Town & Country Shopper - Oak Grove, MO - *AyerDirPub 83*
Town & Country Shopper - Brookings, SD - *AyerDirPub 83*
Town & Country Shopper - Tomah, WI - *AyerDirPub 83*
Town & Country Trader 1 - Chagrin Falls, OH - *AyerDirPub 83*
Town & Country Trader 2 - Chagrin Falls, OH - *AyerDirPub 83*
Town & Country Trader 4 - Chagrin Falls, OH - *AyerDirPub 83*
Town & Country Trader 5 - Chagrin Falls, OH - *AyerDirPub 83*
Town & Country Travel Directions - New York, NY - *BaconPubCkMag 84*
Town & Country-West [of Brown-Thompson Newspapers] - Girard, PA - *NewsDir 84*
Town & Village - New York, NY - *AyerDirPub 83; Ed&PubIntYB 82*
Town Crier - Idyllwild, CA - *AyerDirPub 83*
Town Crier - La Porte, IN - *AyerDirPub 83*
Town Crier - Anamosa, IA - *AyerDirPub 83*
Town Crier - Greenfield, MA - *AyerDirPub 83*
Town Crier - Wilmington, MA - *AyerDirPub 83; Ed&PubIntYB 82*
Town Crier - Brattleboro, VT - *AyerDirPub 83*
Town Crier - Powell River, BC, Canada - *AyerDirPub 83; Ed&PubIntYB 82*
Town Crier Agency - Council Bluffs, IA - *StaDirAdAg 2-84*
Town Crier-France Viewer - Sudbury, MA - *AyerDirPub 83*
Town Crier-Herald - Haddonfield, NJ - *Ed&PubIntYB 82*
Town Crier Newspapers - West Palm Beach, FL - *BaconPubCkNews 84*
Town Crier Publications [Div. of Henrich Publications Inc.] - Litchfield, IL - *DirMarMP 83*
Town Crier Publications - Sudbury, MA - *BaconPubCkNews 84*
Town Crier Shopper, The - Stockbridge, MI - *AyerDirPub 83*
Town Crier, The - Newington, CT - *AyerDirPub 83*
Town Crier, The - Stockbridge, MI - *AyerDirPub 83; Ed&PubIntYB 82*
Town Crier, The - Lake City, TN - *Ed&PubIntYB 82*
Town House Press Inc., The - Spring Valley, NY - *LitMarPl 83, 84*
Town 'n Country Video Inc. [of East Otter Tail Telephone Co.] - New York Mills, MN - *BrCabYB 84; Tel&CabFB 84C*
Town 'n Country Video Inc. [of East Otter Tail Telephone Co.] - Walker, MN - *Tel&CabFB 84C*
Town News/North - Paramus, NJ - *AyerDirPub 83*
Town of Mt. Royal Weekly Post - Montreal, PQ, Canada - *AyerDirPub 83*
Town Publishing Associates Inc., Joshua - Lyme, CT - *LitMarPl 83*
Town Talk - Clinton, IA - *AyerDirPub 83*
Town Talk - Alexandria, LA - *AyerDirPub 83*
Town Talk - Media, PA - *AyerDirPub 83*
Town Talk (Aston-Brookhaven Edition) - Media, PA - *NewsDir 84*
Town Talk Newspapers [of Wing Publications] - Folsom, PA - *NewsDir 84*
Town Times - Oakville, CT - *AyerDirPub 83*
Town Topics - Princeton, NJ - *AyerDirPub 83*
Towne Advertising, W. L. - Stamford, CT - *StaDirAdAg 2-84*
Towne & Countre Shopper - Lockport, IL - *AyerDirPub 83*
Towne Courier [of Ingham Newspaper Co.] - East Lansing, MI - *AyerDirPub 83; BaconPubCkNews 84; Ed&PubIntYB 82; NewsDir 84*
Towne, Silverstein, Rotter - New York, NY - *AdAge 3-28-84; StaDirAdAg 2-84*
Towner Cable TV Inc. - Towner, ND - *BrCabYB 84; Tel&CabFB 84C*
Towner County Record Herald - Cando, ND - *AyerDirPub 83; Ed&PubIntYB 82*
Towner Mouse River Farmers Press - Towner, ND - *BaconPubCkNews 84*
TownHall Records - Santa Barbara, CA - *BillIntBG 83-84*
Towns County Herald - Hiawassee, GA - *AyerDirPub 83; Ed&PubIntYB 82*
Towns-Union CATV Inc. [of US Cable Corp.] - Hiawassee, GA - *Tel&CabFB 84C*
Townsend & Associates Inc., R. S. - Shawnee Mission, KS - *StaDirAdAg 2-84*
Townsend Cable TV - Townsend, MT - *Tel&CabFB 84C*
Townsend Communications Inc. - Kansas City, MO - *BaconPubCkNews 84*
Townsend-Greenspan & Co. Inc. - New York, NY - *EISS 83*
Townsend Press [Aff. of Sunday School Publishing Board] - Nashville, TN - *BoPubDir 4, 5*
Townsend Star - Townsend, MT - *BaconPubCkNews 84; Ed&PubIntYB 82*
Townsfolk - Chicago, IL - *BaconPubCkMag 84*
Township of Ennismore - Ennismore, ON, Canada - *BoPubDir 4 Sup, 5*
Township Telephone Co. - Chaumont, NY - *TelDir&BG 83-84*
Township Times [of Copley Press Inc.] - Wheaton, IL - *NewsDir 84*
Township Times - Saginaw, MI - *AyerDirPub 83; Ed&PubIntYB 82*
Townshops Sun, The - Lennoxville, PQ, Canada - *LitMag&SmPr 83-84*

Townsman - Wellesley, MA - *AyerDirPub 83*
Townsman - Cranbrook, BC, Canada - *AyerDirPub 83*
Towpaths - Cleveland, OH - *LitMag&SmPr 83-84*
Towson Jeffersonian - Baltimore, MD - *NewsDir 84*
Towson Jeffersonian - Towson, MD - *BaconPubCkNews 84*
Toxen Computer Systems, Bob - San Jose, CA - *WhoWMicrocom 83*
Toxic Materials News - Silver Spring, MD - *BaconPubCkMag 84; DirOnDB Spring 84*
Toxic Materials News [of NewsNet Inc.] - Bryn Mawr, PA - *DataDirOnSer 84*
Toxic Materials Transport - Silver Spring, MD - *BaconPubCkMag 84*
Toxic Substances Control Act Chemical Substances Inventory [of U.S. Environmental Protection Agency] - Washington, DC - *EISS 83*
Toxic Substances Control Act Initial Inventory [of U.S. Environmental Protection Agency] - Washington, DC - *CompReadDB 82*
Toxicology Abstracts [of Information Retrieval Ltd.] - London, England - *CompReadDB 82*
Toxicology Data Bank [of National Library of Medicine] - Bethesda, MD - *CompReadDB 82; DataDirOnSer 84; DBBus 82; DirOnDB Spring 84; EISS 83*
Toxicology Information On-Line [of National Library of Medicine] - Bethesda, MD - *CompReadDB 82; DataDirOnSer 84*
Toxicology Information Program [of U.S. National Library of Medicine] - Bethesda, MD - *EISS 83; InfIndMarPl 83*
Toxicology Information Response Center [of U.S. Dept. of Energy] - Oak Ridge, TN - *EISS 83; InfIndMarPl 83*
TOXLINE [of U.S. National Library of Medicine] - Bethesda, MD - *DBBus 82; DirOnDB Spring 84; EISS 83; OnBibDB 3*
Toy & Hobby World - New York, NY - *BaconPubCkMag 84; MagDir 84*
Toy Car Press - San Jose, CA - *LitMag&SmPr 83-84*
Toy Records - New York, NY - *BillIntBG 83-84*
Toye Corp. - Chatsworth, CA - *DirInfWP 82*
Toys & Games - Downsview, ON, Canada - *BaconPubCkMag 84*
Toys, Hobbies & Crafts - New York, NY - *BaconPubCkMag 84; MagDir 84*
Toys 'n Things Press [Aff. of Resources for Child Caring Inc.] - St. Paul, MN - *BoPubDir 4, 5*
Toys Trade News - New York, NY - *MagDir 84*
TP Printing Co. - Abbotsford, WI - *BaconPubCkNews 84*
TPA Publishing Ltd. [Aff. of Tax Practitioners Association] - Los Angeles, CA - *BoPubDir 5*
TPC Communications Inc. - Pittsburgh, PA - *ArtMar 84*
TPC Communications Inc. - Sewickely, PA - *Tel&CabFB 84C*
TPC Communications Inc. - Sewickley, PA - *AvMarPl 83*
TPG Enterprises Inc. - Fredericktown, MO - *BrCabYB 84*
TPS Electronics - Palo Alto, CA - *EISS 83*
TR Productions - Boston, MA - *AvMarPl 83*
Tra-Flix Inc. - New York, NY - *HBIndAd&MS 82-83*
TRAC Line Computer Corp. - Freeport, NY - *MicrocomMPl 83*
TRAC Line Software Inc. - Hicksville, NY - *ADAPSOMemDir 83-84; MicrocomMPl 84; MicrocomSwDir 1*
Trace Systems Inc. - Mountain View, CA - *MicrocomMPl 83*
Track & Field News - Los Altos, CA - *BaconPubCkMag 84; MagDir 84; MagIndMarPl 82-83*
Track-Man Systems Inc. - New York, NY - *MicrocomMPl 84*
Trackaday - New Market, VA - *BoPubDir 4, 5*
Traco Advertising Inc. - Tulsa, OK - *StaDirAdAg 2-84; Tel&CabFB 84C*
Tracor Inc. - Austin, TX - *DataDirSup 7-83*
Tracor Jitco Inc. - Rockville, MD - *FBInfSer 80*
Tracor Publications [Subs. of Tracor Inc.] - Austin, TX - *LitMarPl 83, 84; MagIndMarPl 82-83*
Traction - Upper Darby, PA - *BaconPubCkMag 84*
Tracy City Grundy County Herald [of Lakeway Publishings Inc.] - Tracy City, TN - *BaconPubCkNews 84; NewsDir 84*
Tracy Clinic, John - Los Angeles, CA - *BoPubDir 4, 5*
Tracy Headlight Herald - Tracy, MN - *BaconPubCkNews 84; Ed&PubIntYB 82; NewsDir 84*
Tracy-Locke Advertising Inc. - Dallas, TX - *BrCabYB 84; TelAl 83, 84*
Tracy-Locke/BBDO - Englewood, CO - *DirMarMP 83*
Tracy-Locke/BBDO - Dallas, TX - *AdAge 3-28-84; Br 1-23-84; StaDirAdAg 2-84*
Tracy-Locke/BBDO - *See* Doremus & Co. Public Relations
Tracy Press - Tracy, CA - *BaconPubCkNews 84; Ed&PubIntYB 82*
Tracy Publishing - Osprey, FL - *BoPubDir 4, 5*
Tracy Research - New York, NY - *IntDirMarRes 83*
Tradd Street Press - Charleston, SC - *BoPubDir 4; LitMarPl 83, 84*
Trade Access Group [of Progressive Grocer Co.] - New York, NY - *EISS 83*
Trade & Commerce - Winnipeg, MB, Canada - *BaconPubCkMag 84*
Trade & Industry ASAP [of Information Access Co.] - Belmont, CA - *DataDirOnSer 84; DirOnDB Spring 84*
Trade & Industry Index [of Information Access Co.] - Belmont, CA - *DataDirOnSer 84*
Trade & Industry Index [of Information Access Corp.] - Menlo Park, CA - *CompReadDB 82; DBBus 82; DirOnDB Spring 84; EISS 83; OnBibDB 3*
Trade Information Service [of Journal of Commerce] - New York, NY - *EISS 83*
Trade Media International Corp. - New York, NY - *StaDirAdAg 2-84*
Trade Media News - New York, NY - *MagIndMarPl 82-83*
Trade News Service - Wilton, CT - *Ed&PubIntYB 82*
Trade Opportunities [of Dialog Information Services Inc.] - Palo Alto, CA - *DataDirOnSer 84*
Trade Opportunities Program [of U.S. Dept. of Commerce] - Washington, DC - *CompReadDB 82; DirOnDB Spring 84; EISS 83*
Trade Opportunities Weekly [of Dialog Information Services Inc.] - Palo Alto, CA - *DataDirOnSer 84*
Trade Opportunities Weekly [of U.S. Dept. of Commerce] - Washington, DC - *DBBus 82*
Trade Opportunity Referral Service [of U.S. Dept. of Agriculture] - Washington, DC - *EISS 83*
Trade Statistics-EPCA Database [of Unilever Computer Services Ltd.] - Watford, England - *DataDirOnSer 84*
Trade Union Research Bureau - Vancouver, BC, Canada - *BoPubDir 4, 5*
Tradelook - Rego Park, NY - *MagIndMarPl 82-83*
TradeMarc Music - Los Angeles, CA - *BillIntBG 83-84*
Trademark Communications Inc. - Minnetonka, MN - *StaDirAdAg 2-84*
Trademark Data Base [of TCR Service Inc.] - Englewood Cliffs, NJ - *CompReadDB 82*
Trademark Register - Washington, DC - *BoPubDir 4, 5*
Trademark Reporter - New York, NY - *MagDir 84*
Trademarkscan [of Thomson & Thomson Inc.] - Boston, MA - *DataDirOnSer 84; DirOnDB Spring 84; EISS 5-84 Sup*
Tradenet Dimensions [of Barter Worldwide Inc.] - Culver City, CA - *DataDirOnSer 84; DBBus 82; DirOnDB Spring 84*
Traders [of Control Data Corp.] - Minneapolis, MN - *DBBus 82*
Traders Press Inc. - Greenville, SC - *BoPubDir 4, 5*
Trader's Shoppers Guide of Laramie - Cheyenne, WY - *AyerDirPub 83*
Trader's The Shopper's Guide - Cheyenne, WY - *AyerDirPub 83*
Trades & Labor News - Nashville, TN - *NewsDir 84*
Tradeshow/Convention Guide Data Bank [of Budd Publications Inc.] - New York, NY - *EISS 83*
Tradeshow Week - Los Angeles, CA - *BaconPubCkMag 84; MagIndMarPl 82-83*
Tradex Publications - Houston, TX - *BoPubDir 4*
Trading Post - Cheyenne, WY - *AyerDirPub 83*
Tradition - Council Bluffs, IA - *WritMar 84*
Tradition Music Co. - El Cerrito, CA - *BillIntBG 83-84*
Traditional Studies Press - Toronto, ON, Canada - *BoPubDir 4, 5*
Trado-Medic Books [Div. of Conch Magazine Ltd.] - Buffalo, NY - *ArtMar 84; LitMag&SmPr 83-84; LitMarPl 83, 84; WritMar 84*
Traer Star-Clipper - Traer, IA - *BaconPubCkNews 84; Ed&PubIntYB 82; NewsDir 84*
Trafalgar House Publishing Inc. - New York, NY - *LitMarPl 84*
Trafco Inc. - *See* United Methodist Communications
Traffic Management [of Cahners Publishing Co.] - Boston, MA - *MagDir 84; MagIndMarPl 82-83*

Traffic Management - New York, NY - *BaconPubCkMag 84; NewsBur 6*
Traffic Manager [of Who's Who Publications Inc.] - Portland, OR - *MagDir 84*
Traffic Safety - Chicago, IL - *BaconPubCkMag 84; MagDir 84; MagIndMarPl 82-83*
Traffic Service Corp. - Washington, DC - *BoPubDir 4 Sup, 5; DirMarMP 83*
Traffic World [of Traffic Service Corp.] - Washington, DC - *BaconPubCkMag 84; MagDir 84; MagIndMarPl 82-83*
Traficante Music Publishing House - *See* Birch Tree Group Ltd.
Tragon Corp. - Palo Alto, CA - *IntDirMarRes 83*
Tragos, Bonnange, Wiesendanger, Ajroldi - *See* TBWA Advertising Inc.
Trahan, Burden & Charles - Baltimore, MD - *AdAge 3-28-84; StaDirAdAg 2-84*
Trail Blazer Systems - Palo Alto, CA - *DataDirOnSer 84*
Trail Blazer's Almanac & Pioneer Guide Book - Kewanee, IL - *MagDir 84*
Trail City Archives - Trail, BC, Canada - *BoPubDir 4 Sup, 5*
Trail Daily Times - Trail, BC, Canada - *BaconPubCkNews 84; Ed&PubIntYB 82*
Trail Gazette - Estes Park, CO - *AyerDirPub 83*
Trail Records [Div. of 2006 Multimedia Production Group] - Kingsport, TN - *BillIntBG 83-84*
Trailblazer - Seattle, WA - *BaconPubCkMag 84*
Trailer Boats [of Poole Publications Inc.] - Gardena, CA - *BaconPubCkMag 84; MagDir 84; MagIndMarPl 82-83; WritMar 84*
Trailer-Body Builders - Houston, TX - *BaconPubCkMag 84; MagDir 84*
Trailer Life [of TL Enterprises Inc.] - Agoura, CA - *BaconPubCkMag 84; MagDir 84; MagIndMarPl 82-83; WritMar 84*
Trailer Life Book Div. [of Trailer Life Publishing Co. Inc.] - Agoura, CA - *BoPubDir 4, 5*
Traill County Tribune - Mayville, ND - *AyerDirPub 83; Ed&PubIntYB 82*
Trails [of Pioneer Ministries Inc.] - Wheaton, IL - *WritMar 84*
Trails-A-Way [of TAW Publishing Co.] - Greenville, MI - *BaconPubCkMag 84; MagDir 84; MagIndMarPl 82-83; WritMar 84*
Train Dispatcher, The - Berwyn, IL - *NewsDir 84*
Traina, Robert A. - Wilmore, KY - *BoPubDir 4, 5*
Training - Minneapolis, MN - *ArtMar 84; BaconPubCkMag 84; MagDir 84; WritMar 84*
Training & Development Journal - Washington, DC - *BaconPubCkMag 84; MagDir 84*
Training Associates Ltd. - Vancouver, BC, Canada - *BoPubDir 4, 5*
Training News - Boston, MA - *BaconPubCkMag 84*
Training Resource Associates - Harrisburg, PA - *AvMarPl 83*
Training Service Inc. - Wilmington, DE - *AvMarPl 83*
Trainor/Salic & Associates Inc. - Menomonee Falls, WI - *DirInfWP 82*
Trains - Milwaukee, WI - *BaconPubCkMag 84; MagDir 84; MagIndMarPl 82-83*
TRAK Microcomputer Corp. - Downers Grove, IL - *MicrocomMPl 84; WhoWMicrocom 83*
Tranet - Rangeley, ME - *LitMag&SmPr 83-84*
Trans-Am Communications Co. - Ada, OK - *BrCabYB 84; Tel&CabFB 84C*
Trans-American Video Inc. - Hollywood, CA - *Tel&CabFB 84C*
Trans/Audio Inc. - New York, NY - *AvMarPl 83*
Trans-Canada Group - Canada - *Ed&PubIntYB 82*
Trans-Canada Press [Div. of The Cardamon Corp.] - Toronto, ON, Canada - *BoPubDir 4; LitMarPl 83, 84*
Trans-International Films - Key Biscayne, FL - *Tel&CabFB 84C*
Trans-Lux Corp. - Norwalk, CT - *DataDirSup 7-83*
Trans-Lux Multimedia Corp. [Subs. of Trans-Lux Corp.] - New York, NY - *AvMarPl 83*
Trans-Media Div. [of Charles H. Bohn & Co. Inc.] - Dobbs Ferry, NY - *MagIndMarPl 82-83*
Trans-Media/The Oceana Group [Div. of Glanville Information Services Inc.] - Dobbs Ferry, NY - *LitMarPl 83, 84; MicroMarPl 82-83*
Trans Micro Systems - San Jose, CA - *MicrocomMPl 84*
Trans-Oceanic Trouser Press Inc. - New York, NY - *LitMag&SmPr 83-84*
Trans Spectrum Services Ltd. - Lower Sackville, NS, Canada - *Tel&CabFB 84C*
Trans Tech Management Press - Sacramento, CA - *BoPubDir 4, 5; LitMag&SmPr 83-84*
Trans Tech Publications - Rockport, MA - *BoPubDir 4, 5*
Trans Tek - Bloomingdale, IL - *MicrocomMPl 84*
Trans-Video Inc. - Northfield, VT - *BrCabYB 84; Tel&CabFB 84C*
Trans-Vision de Danville Inc. - Danville, PQ, Canada - *BrCabYB 84*
Trans World Communications Inc. - New York, NY - *BrCabYB 84*
Trans World Design - Camarillo, CA - *MagIndMarPl 82-83*
Trans-World Films Inc. - Chicago, IL - *AvMarPl 83*
Trans World International Inc. - Los Angeles, CA - *Tel&CabFB 84C*
Trans-World Productions - Las Vegas, NV - *Tel&CabFB 84C*
Transaction Books [of Rutgers University] - New Brunswick, NJ - *LitMarPl 83, 84; WritMar 84*
Transaction Data Systems Inc. - Orlando, FL - *MicrocomSwDir 1*
Transaction Management Inc. - Montgomeryville, PA - *DataDirSup 7-83*
Transaction Music Ltd. - New York, NY - *BillIntBG 83-84*
Transaction Periodicals Consortium [of Rutgers University] - New Brunswick, NJ - *MagIndMarPl 82-83*
Transaction Security Products Inc. - Newtown Square, PA - *DataDirSup 7-83*
Transaction/Society [of Rutgers University] - New Brunswick, NJ - *WritMar 84*
Transactions of the American Mathematical Society - Providence, RI - *MagDir 84*
TransAmerican Airports Inc. - Leesburg, VA - *BrCabYB 84*
Transatlantic Arts Inc. - Albuquerque, NM - *LitMarPl 83, 84*
Transatlantic Video - New York, NY - *Tel&CabFB 84C*
Transbooks Inc. - New York, NY - *BoPubDir 4 Sup, 5*
TransCanada Telephone System (Computer Communications Group) - Ottawa, ON, Canada - *VideoDir 82-83*
Transcendental Books - Hartford, CT - *BoPubDir 4, 5*
Transcity Records - Birmingham, MI - *BillIntBG 83-84*
Transcolog Ltd. - Ottawa, ON, Canada - *DirInfWP 82*
Transcomm Data Systems Inc. - Pittsburgh, PA - *DataDirSup 7-83*
Transcommunications Corp. - Greenwich, CT - *Tel&CabFB 84C*
Transcona News - Winnipeg, MB, Canada - *Ed&PubIntYB 82*
Transcriber Corp. - Houston, TX - *DirInfWP 82*
Transcript - Concord, CA - *AyerDirPub 83*
Transcript - San Diego, CA - *AyerDirPub 83*
Transcript - Golden, CO - *AyerDirPub 83*
Transcript - Dedham, MA - *AyerDirPub 83*
Transcript [of Ingersoll Publications Co.] - North Adams, MA - *AyerDirPub 83; BaconPubCkNews 84; Ed&PubIntYB 82; NewsDir 84*
Transcript - North Reading, MA - *AyerDirPub 83*
Transcript - Little Falls, MN - *AyerDirPub 83*
Transcript - Peterborough, NH - *AyerDirPub 83*
Transcript - Orange, NJ - *AyerDirPub 83*
Transcript - New Rockford, ND - *AyerDirPub 83*
Transcript - Norman, OK - *AyerDirPub 83*
Transcript - Susquehanna, PA - *AyerDirPub 83*
Transcript - Tooele, UT - *AyerDirPub 83*
Transcript - Moncton, NB, Canada - *AyerDirPub 83; Ed&PubIntYB 82*
Transcript & Free Press - Glencoe, ON, Canada - *Ed&PubIntYB 82*
Transcript Bulletin Publishing Co. - Tooele, UT - *BaconPubCkNews 84*
Transcript Newspapers Inc. - Dedham, MA - *BaconPubCkNews 84*
Transcript-Telegram [of Newspapers of New England] - Holyoke, MA - *AyerDirPub 83; BaconPubCkNews 84; Ed&PubIntYB 82; LitMarPl 83, 84; NewsDir 84*
Transcript, The - Morrisville, VT - *AyerDirPub 83*
Transcultural Communications Center - Los Angeles, CA - *BoPubDir 4, 5*
Transdata Ltd. (Sales & Marketing Div.) - London, England - *InfIndMarPl 83*

TRANSDOC [of European Conference of Ministers of Transport] - Paris, France - *CompReadDB 82; DirOnDB Spring 84*
Transearch [of Reebie Associates] - Greenwich, CT - *EISS 83*
Transemantics Inc. - Washington, DC - *LitMarPl 83, 84; MagIndMarPl 82-83*
Transemantics Publications - *See* Gemini Books/Transemantics Publications
Transformaction - Sidmouth, England - *LitMag&SmPr 83-84*
Transformation Technologies - Bloomingdale, IL - *MicrocomMPl 83, 84*
Transformations Press - Berkeley, CA - *BoPubDir 4, 5*
Transformer Maintenance Institute [Aff. of S. D. Myers Inc.] - Cuyahoga Falls, OH - *BoPubDir 4, 5*
Transfusion - Philadelphia, PA - *MagDir 84; MagIndMarPl 82-83*
Transglobal Advertising - Pico Rivera, CA - *StaDirAdAg 2-84*
Transientpress, The - Albuquerque, NM - *LitMag&SmPr 83-84*
Transilwrap Co. Inc. - Chicago, IL - *AvMarPl 83*
Transimpex Translation Service - Belton, MO - *LitMarPl 83, 84; MagIndMarPl 82-83*
Transin [of Questel Inc.] - Washington, DC - *DataDirOnSer 84*
Transin - Paris, France - *DirOnDB Spring 84*
Transinove [of Transinove International] - Paris, France - *CompReadDB 82*
Transinove International - Paris, France - *CompReadDB 82; EISS 83; InfIndMarPl 83*
Transit Journal - Washington, DC - *MagDir 84*
Transitions - Amherst, MA - *ArtMar 84; LitMag&SmPr 83-84; WritMar 84*
Translating Associates - New York, NY - *LitMarPl 83; MagIndMarPl 82-83*
Translation [Aff. of The Translation Center] - New York, NY - *BoPubDir 4, 5; LitMag&SmPr 83-84*
Translation Center, The [of Columbia University] - New York, NY - *LitMarPl 83, 84; MagIndMarPl 82-83*
Translation/Computer Branch Reform Div. [of Office of Attorney General] - Fredericton, NB, Canada - *DataDirOnSer 84*
Translation Referral Service [of State University of New York] - Binghamton, NY - *MagIndMarPl 82-83*
Translation Research Institute - Philadelphia, PA - *BoPubDir 4, 5; LitMarPl 83*
Translation Review - Richardson, TX - *LitMag&SmPr 83-84*
Translations Press - Ann Arbor, MI - *BoPubDir 4, 5*
Translator Co., The - Las Vegas, NV - *Tel&CabFB 84C*
Translight Media Associates Inc. - Wheaton, IL - *AvMarPl 83*
Translog - Washington, DC - *BaconPubCkMag 84; MagDir 84*
Transmedia - La Mesa, CA - *BoPubDir 4, 5*
Transmission & Distribution - Cos Cob, CT - *BaconPubCkMag 84; MagDir 84; MagIndMarPl 82-83*
Transmission Digest - Springfield, MO - *BaconPubCkMag 84*
Transmission Micrographics Co. Ltd. - Taipei, Taiwan - *MicroMarPl 82-83*
Transnational Data Reporting Service Inc. - Washington, DC - *EISS 83*
Transnational Investments Ltd. - Washington, DC - *BoPubDir 4, 5*
Transnational Publishers Inc. - Dobbs Ferry, NY - *BoPubDir 4 Sup, 5; LitMarPl 84*
TransNet Corp. - Union, NJ - *DataDirSup 7-83; WhoWMicrocom 83*
Transociates - London, England - *FBInfSer 80*
TRANSPAC [of Direction Commerciale] - Paris, France - *EISS 83; InfIndMarPl 83*
Transplantation Proceedings - New York, NY - *MagDir 84*
Transponder Access Services [of Satellite Business Systems] - McLean, VA - *TeleSy&SerDir 7-83*
Transport Canada - Ottawa, ON, Canada - *InfIndMarPl 83*
Transport Canada Library & Information Centre [of Dept of Transport] - Ottawa, ON, Canada - *CompReadDB 82; DataDirOnSer 84*
Transport Deregulation Report - New York, NY - *BaconPubCkMag 84*
Transport Environment Inc. - Kitty Hawk, NC - *BoPubDir 5*
Transport Fleet News - Chicago, IL - *BaconPubCkMag 84*
Transport History Press - Park Forest, IL - *BoPubDir 4, 5; LitMag&SmPr 83-84*
Transport News of Tennessee - Nashville, TN - *BaconPubCkMag 84; MagDir 84*
Transport Routier du Quebec - Montreal, PQ, Canada - *BaconPubCkMag 84*
Transport Topics - Washington, DC - *BaconPubCkMag 84; MagDir 84; MagIndMarPl 82-83*
Transport 2000 - Novato, CA - *BaconPubCkMag 84; MagDir 84*
Transportation Association of America - Washington, DC - *BoPubDir 5*
Transportation Cost Service [of A. T. Kearney Inc.] - Chicago, IL - *DBBus 82; DirOnDB Spring 84*
Transportation Cost Service [of Data Resources Inc.] - Lexington, MA - *DataDirOnSer 84*
Transportation Data Bank - Washington, DC - *DirOnDB Spring 84*
Transportation Data Base [of Data Resources Inc.] - Lexington, MA - *DataDirOnSer 84; DBBus 82*
Transportation Engineer - Newport Beach, CA - *MagDir 84*
Transportation Engineer - Dearborn, MI - *BaconPubCkMag 84*
Transportation Journal - University Park, PA - *MagIndMarPl 82-83*
Transportation Management Systems Inc. - Hunt Valley, MD - *ADAPSOMemDir 83-84*
Transportation News Ticker Inc. - New York, NY - *Ed&PubIntYB 82*
Transportation Quarterly - Westport, CT - *MagIndMarPl 82-83*
Transportation Research Board [of National Academy of Sciences] - Washington, DC - *CompReadDB 82; DataDirOnSer 84*
Transportation Research Information Services [of National Academy of Sciences] - Washington, DC - *DataDirOnSer 84; OnBibDB 3*
Transporte Moderno [of Intercontinental Publications Inc.] - Westport, CT - *BaconPubCkMag 84; MagDir 84*
Transswitch Associates - Los Altos, CA - *TeleSy&SerDir 2-84*
Transtar - Bellevue, WA - *MicrocomMPl 84*
Transtar Radio Network - Colorado Springs, CO - *BrCabYB 84*
Transtector Systems - Post Falls, ID - *MicrocomMPl 84*
Transvision Cookshire Inc. - Cookshire, PQ, Canada - *BrCabYB 84*
Transvision Cowansville Inc. [of Video St. Laurent Inc.] - Cowansville, PQ, Canada - *BrCabYB 84*
Transvision Disraeli Inc. - Disraeli, PQ, Canada - *BrCabYB 84; Tel&CabFB 84C*
Transvision East-Angus Inc. [of Transvision Lennoxville Inc.] - Lennoxville, PQ, Canada - *BrCabYB 84*
Transvision Granby Inc. [of Video St. Laurent Inc.] - Granby, PQ, Canada - *BrCabYB 84*
Transvision Inc. - Coaticook, PQ, Canada - *BrCabYB 84*
Transvision Magog Inc. - Magog, PQ, Canada - *BrCabYB 84; Tel&CabFB 84C*
Transvision Pare Inc. - Ascot Corner, PQ, Canada - *BrCabYB 84*
Transvision Rive Sud - Boucherville, PQ, Canada - *BrCabYB 84*
Transvision Sawyerville Inc. - Sherbrooke, PQ, Canada - *BrCabYB 84*
Transvision Weedon Enrg. - Weedon, PQ, Canada - *BrCabYB 84*
Transvue Pictures Corp. - Sherman Oaks, CA - *Tel&CabFB 84C*
Transvue TV International Co. [Div. of Transvue Pictures Corp.] - Sherman Oaks, CA - *TelAl 83, 84*
Transwestern Video Inc. - Barling, AR - *Tel&CabFB 84C*
Transwestern Video Inc. - Mountainburg, AR - *BrCabYB 84*
Transwestern Video Inc. - Poteau, OK - *BrCabYB 84 p.D-309; Tel&CabFB 84C p.1708*
Transworld Advertising/Marketing Inc. - Dallas, TX - *StaDirAdAg 2-84*
Transworld Art Inc. - New York, NY - *ArtMar 84*
Transworld Distribution Services Inc. - Edison, NJ - *LitMarPl 83; MagIndMarPl 82-83*
Transworld Feature Syndicate Inc. [Subs. of NZS Photography] - New York, NY - *Ed&PubIntYB 82; LitMarPl 83, 84; MagIndMarPl 82-83*
Transylvania Times - Brevard, NC - *AyerDirPub 83; Ed&PubIntYB 82*
Tranter & Co., Charles R. - Warren, PA - *DirPRFirms 83*
Trantor Systems Ltd. - Fremont, CA - *MicrocomMPl 84*
Tranz Productions - Brooklyn, NY - *BillIntBG 83-84*

Trap & Field - Indianapolis, IN - *BaconPubCkMag 84; MagDir 84*
Trapper, The - Sutton, NE - *BaconPubCkMag 84*
Traq Records - Syosset, NY - *BillIntBG 83-84*
Trask House Books Inc. - Portland, OR - *LitMag&SmPr 83-84*
Tratec/McGraw-Hill - Los Angeles, CA - *LitMarPl 84*
Trauma Works - Royal Oak, MI - *BoPubDir 4, 5*
Traumwald Press - Chicago, IL - *BoPubDir 4, 5; LitMag&SmPr 83-84*
TRAV - Atlanta, GA - *Tel&CabFB 84C*
Travel Advisor, The - Bronxville, NY - *MagDir 84; WritMar 84*
Travel Agent - New York, NY - *BaconPubCkMag 84; MagDir 84; WritMar 84*
Travel & Leisure [of American Express Co.] - New York, NY - *ArtMar 84; BaconPubCkMag 84; Folio 83; LitMarPl 83, 84; MagDir 84; MagIndMarPl 82-83; NewsBur 6; WritMar 84*
Travel & Leisure Features [Subs. of Jaffee-Gun Publications] - Newton, MA - *LitMarPl 84*
Travel & Tourism Press [Aff. of Tourism Information Systems Inc.] - Santa Cruz, CA - *BoPubDir 4, 5*
Travel & Tourism Research Association - Salt Lake City, UT - *BoPubDir 4, 5*
Travel Destination Canada - Toronto, ON, Canada - *BaconPubCkMag 84*
Travel Digest - New York, NY - *BaconPubCkMag 84; MagDir 84; MagIndMarPl 82-83*
Travel Digests [Aff. of Paul Richmond & Co.] - Palm Desert, CA - *BoPubDir 4, 5*
Travel Facts - New York, NY - *Ed&PubIntYB 82*
Travel Fax - Great Neck, NY - *DirOnDB Spring 84*
Travel Food & Duty Free International - Miami Springs, FL - *BaconPubCkMag 84*
Travel/Holiday - Floral Park, NY - *BaconPubCkMag 84; Folio 83; MagDir 84; MagIndMarPl 82-83; WritMar 84*
Travel Information Bureau - Farmingdale, NY - *BoPubDir 4, 5*
Travel Interludes - Carmel, CA - *BoPubDir 5*
Travel Management Daily - New York, NY - *BaconPubCkMag 84; NewsBur 6*
Travel Management Newsletter - New York, NY - *BaconPubCkMag 84; NewsBur 6*
Travel Press - San Mateo, CA - *BoPubDir 4, 5*
Travel Publications Inc. - Miami, FL - *BoPubDir 4, 5*
Travel Smart [of Communications House Inc.] - Dobbs Ferry, NY - *BaconPubCkMag 84; MagDir 84; WritMar 84*
Travel Smart for Business [of Communications House] - Dobbs Ferry, NY - *WritMar 84*
Travel Trade - New York, NY - *BaconPubCkMag 84; MagDir 84; NewsBur 6*
Travel Utah - Salt Lake City, UT - *BaconPubCkMag 84*
Travel Weekly - New York, NY - *BaconPubCkMag 84; MagDir 84; NewsBur 6*
Travelage East - New York, NY - *BaconPubCkMag 84; MagDir 84; NewsBur 6*
Travelage MidAmerica - Chicago, IL - *BaconPubCkMag 84; MagDir 84; NewsBur 6; WritMar 84*
Travelage Southeast - Miami, FL - *NewsBur 6*
Travelage Southeast - New York, NY - *BaconPubCkMag 84; MagDir 84; NewsBur 6*
Travelage West - San Francisco, CA - *BaconPubCkMag 84; MagDir 84; NewsBur 6; WritMar 84*
Traveler - Arkansas City, KS - *AyerDirPub 83*
Traveler's Directory - Philadelphia, PA - *BoPubDir 4, 5*
Traveler's Report - Kissimmee, FL - *BaconPubCkMag 84*
Travelers Rest Cablevision - Travelers Rest, SC - *BrCabYB 84; Tel&CabFB 84C*
Traveler's World Syndicate, The - East Hills, NY - *Ed&PubIntYB 82*
Travelfare Publishers - Escondido, CA - *BoPubDir 4, 5*
Travelhost - Dallas, TX - *BaconPubCkMag 84; Folio 83; MagDir 84; MagIndMarPl 82-83*
Traveller's World Communications Inc. - Greenwich, CT - *Tel&CabFB 84C*
Travelling Image Co. - Portland, OR - *AvMarPl 83*
Travelog - Houston, TX - *MagDir 84*
Travelore Report - Philadelphia, PA - *BaconPubCkMag 84; MagDir 84; WritMar 84*
Travelpic Publications - Niagara Falls, ON, Canada - *BoPubDir 4, 5*
Travelscene - New York, NY - *MagDir 84; NewsBur 6*
TravelVision - Convent Station, NJ - *DirOnDB Spring 84*
Travelwriter Marketletter - New York, NY - *BaconPubCkMag 84; DirOnDB Spring 84; MagIndMarPl 82-83*
Travelwriter Marketletter [of NewsNet Inc.] - Bryn Mawr, PA - *DataDirOnSer 84*
Traverse City Record-Eagle [of Ottaway Newspapers Inc.] - Traverse City, MI - *BaconPubCkNews 84; Ed&PubIntYB 82; NewsDir 84*
Travis County Cablevision Inc. - River Oaks, TX - *BrCabYB 84*
Travis County Cablevision Inc. [of Communications Systems Inc.] - Travis County, TX - *Tel&CabFB 84C*
Travis Piano Service - Takoma Park, MD - *BoPubDir 4 Sup, 5*
Travis/Walz & Associates - Shawnee Mission, KS - *ArtMar 84; StaDirAdAg 2-84*
Travltips - Flushing, NY - *BaconPubCkMag 84*
TRC Corp. - Indianapolis, IN - *BillIntBG 83-84*
TRC Data Surveys - Princeton, NJ - *IntDirMarRes 83*
Treacle Press - New Paltz, NY - *LitMarPl 83*
Treasure [of Jess Publishing] - Van Nuys, CA - *WritMar 84*
Treasure Chest Publications - Tucson, AZ - *BoPubDir 4, 5*
Treasure Valley Reminder - Ontario, OR - *AyerDirPub 83*
Treasure Valley Tele-Cable - Ontario, OR - *BrCabYB 84; Tel&CabFB 84C p.1708*
Treasure Valley Tele-Cable Inc. - Sumpter, OR - *BrCabYB 84*
Treasured Publications Inc. - Encino, CA - *DirMarMP 83*
Treats for My Sweets - Bay Minette, AL - *BoPubDir 4 Sup, 5*
Treaty Research Center [of University of Washington] - Seattle, WA - *CompReadDB 82; EISS 83; InfIndMarPl 83*
Trebron Music Inc. - Franklin, TN - *BillIntBG 83-84*
Tree by the River Publishing - Riverside, CA - *BoPubDir 4; LitMag&SmPr 83-84; LitMarPl 83, 84; WritMar 84*
Tree Communications Inc. - New York, NY - *LitMarPl 83, 84*
Tree Frog Press Ltd. - Edmonton, AB, Canada - *BoPubDir 4, 5; LitMag&SmPr 83-84; LitMarPl 84*
Tree International - Nashville, TN - *BillIntBG 83-84*
Tree Marketing Co. [Div. of Beatrice Foods Co.] - Ferdinand, IN - *StaDirAdAg 2-84*
Tree Publishing Co. Inc. - *See* Tree International
Tree Shrew Press - Holliston, MA - *BoPubDir 4, 5; LitMag&SmPr 83-84*
Tree Toad Press - Leverett, MA - *LitMag&SmPr 83-84*
Treece Community Antenna System - Marshall, AR - *Tel&CabFB 84C*
Treece, Jack - Heber Springs, AR - *Tel&CabFB 84C p.1708*
Treece TV Cable Service - Marshall, AR - *BrCabYB 84*
Trees [of Acorn] - Weston, MA - *LitMag&SmPr 83-84*
Trefethen Photography Inc., Jim - Charlestown, MA - *MagIndMarPl 82-83*
Treibick, Richard - Greenwich, CT - *BrCabYB 84 p.D-309*
Treibick, Richard - New York, NY - *Tel&CabFB 84C p.1708*
Treise Engineering - San Fernando, CA - *AvMarPl 83*
Tremco Computer Consultants (Information Systems Div.) - Orem, UT - *ADAPSOMemDir 83-84*
Tremont Press - Silver Spring, MD - *BoPubDir 4 Sup, 5*
Tremonton Leader-Garland Times - Tremonton, UT - *BaconPubCkNews 84*
Trempealeau Press - Santa Fe, NM - *BoPubDir 4, 5*
Trend House - St. Petersburg, FL - *BoPubDir 5; WritMar 84*
Trend Record Corp. - Los Angeles, CA - *BillIntBG 83-84*
Trend Records - Smyrna, GA - *BillIntBG 83-84*
Trendata Corp. - Santa Ana, CA - *DataDirSup 7-83; WhoWMicrocom 83*
Trendex Inc. [Div. of IMS International Inc.] - Westport, CT - *BrCabYB 84; IntDirMarRes 83; Tel&CabFB 84C*
TrendFacts Research/Field Services [Div. of The Creative Group Inc.] - Southfield, MI - *IntDirMarRes 83*
Trends & Events Inc. - Fayette, IA - *BoPubDir 5*
Trends in Biochemical Sciences - New York, NY - *BaconPubCkMag 84*
Trends in Neurosciences - New York, NY - *BaconPubCkMag 84*
Trends Publishing Co. [Aff. of Bell & Hansen Inc.] - Southfield, MI - *BoPubDir 4, 5*
Trendsetters Magazine - West Palm Beach, FL - *WritMar 84*

Trent University - Peterborough, ON, Canada - *LitMag&SmPr 83-84*
Trent University (Dept. of Geography) - Peterborough, ON, Canada - *BoPubDir 4, 5*
Trenton Cable TV Co. [of Capital Cities Cable Inc.] - Trenton, MO - *BrCabYB 84; Tel&CabFB 84C*
Trenton Clearview Cable [of Florida Clearview Inc.] - Trenton, FL - *Tel&CabFB 84C*
Trenton Dade County Sentinel - Trenton, GA - *BaconPubCkNews 84*
Trenton Evening Times - Trenton, NJ - *BaconPubCkNews 84; NewsDir 84*
Trenton Gilchrist County Journal - Trenton, FL - *BaconPubCkNews 84*
Trenton Herald-Gazette - Trenton, TN - *BaconPubCkNews 84; NewsDir 84*
Trenton Hitchcock County News - Trenton, NE - *BaconPubCkNews 84*
Trenton Mercer County Messenger - Trenton, NJ - *BaconPubCkNews 84*
Trenton News-Herald [of News-Herald Newspapers] - Wyandotte, MI - *AyerDirPub 83; NewsDir 84*
Trenton News-Herald - *See* News-Herald Newspapers
Trenton Republican Times - Trenton, MO - *BaconPubCkNews 84*
Trenton Sun - Trenton, IL - *BaconPubCkNews 84; Ed&PubIntYB 82*
Trenton Sunday Times-Advertiser - Trenton, NJ - *LitMarPl 83*
Trenton Telephone Co. - Trenton, GA - *TelDir&BG 83-84*
Trenton Times - Trenton, MI - *BaconPubCkNews 84; Ed&PubIntYB 82; NewsDir 84*
Trenton Times - Trenton, NJ - *Ed&PubIntYB 82; LitMarPl 83, 84; NewsBur 6*
Trenton Trentonian [of Capitol City Publishing Co. Inc.] - Trenton, NJ - *NewsDir 84*
Trenton Tribune - Trenton, TX - *BaconPubCkNews 84; Ed&PubIntYB 82*
Trenton TV Cable Co. - Trenton, TN - *BrCabYB 84; Tel&CabFB 84C*
Trentonian & Tri-County News - Trenton, ON, Canada - *AyerDirPub 83; Ed&PubIntYB 82*
Trentonian, The [of Capitol City Publishing Co. Inc.] - Trenton, NJ - *AyerDirPub 83; BaconPubCkNews 84; Ed&PubIntYB 82; LitMarPl 83, 84; NewsBur 6*
Tretbar Public Relations - Highland Park, IL - *DirPRFirms 83*
Tretter-Gorman Inc. - St. Louis, MO - *DirPRFirms 83*
Trewhella, Cohen & Arbuckle Inc. - New York, NY - *IntDirMarRes 83*
Treynor Record - Treynor, IA - *BaconPubCkNews 84; Ed&PubIntYB 82*
TRF Music Inc. - New York, NY - *AvMarPl 83*
TRF Music Inc. - *See* Alpha Music Inc.
TRG Communications Inc. - New York, NY - *StaDirAdAg 2-84*
TRI - Cary, IL - *WhoWMicrocom 83*
Tri-Ad Advertising Inc. - Rapid City, SD - *StaDirAdAg 2-84*
Tri-B Publications - Edina, MN - *BoPubDir 4 Sup, 5*
Tri-Boro Cablevision - Susquehanna, PA - *BrCabYB 84; Tel&CabFB 84C*
Tri-Cities Advance - Jenison, MI - *AyerDirPub 83*
Tri-Cities Broadcasting - Amory, MS - *Tel&CabFB 84C p.1708*
Tri-Cities Cable Vision - Edgerton, KS - *BrCabYB 84*
Tri-City Cable TV Co. [of Nichols Investment Corp.] - Allegan, MI - *BrCabYB 84; Tel&CabFB 84C*
Tri-City Cablevision - Blue Ridge, GA - *BrCabYB 84*
Tri-City Cablevision Inc. - Appleton City, MO - *BrCabYB 84*
Tri-City Cablevision Inc. - Higginsville, MO - *Tel&CabFB 84C p.1708*
Tri-City Cablevision Inc. - King City, MO - *BrCabYB 84*
Tri-City Cablevision Inc. - Stanberry, MO - *BrCabYB 84*
Tri-City Herald - Pasco, WA - *AyerDirPub 83; BaconPubCkNews 84; Ed&PubIntYB 82*
Tri-City Journal - Chicago Heights, IL - *Ed&PubIntYB 82*
Tri-City Labor Review - Rock Island, IL - *NewsDir 84*
Tri-City Ledger, The - Flomaton, AL - *Ed&PubIntYB 82*
Tri-City Media Inc. - Mauldin, SC - *BrCabYB 84*
Tri-City News - Cumberland, KY - *AyerDirPub 83; Ed&PubIntYB 82*
Tri-City Register - Buffalo, IL - *Ed&PubIntYB 82*
Tri-City Reporter - Dyer, TN - *AyerDirPub 83; Ed&PubIntYB 82*
Tri-City Times - Almont, MI - *BaconPubCkNews 84*
Tri-City Times - Imlay City, MI - *AyerDirPub 83; Ed&PubIntYB 82*
Tri-City Tribune - Cozad, NE - *AyerDirPub 83; Ed&PubIntYB 82; NewsDir 84*
Tri-College University Libraries Consortium - Moorhead, MN - *EISS 83*
Tri-Color Photo Inc. - Royal Oak, MI - *AvMarPl 83*
Tri-Comm Audio Visuals [Subs. of Modern Mass Media Inc.] - Savannah, GA - *AvMarPl 83*
Tri-Comm Audio Visuals [Subs. of Modern Mass Media Inc.] - Hilton Head Island, SC - *AvMarPl 83*
Tri-Comm Productions Inc. - Hilton Head Island, SC - *AvMarPl 83*
Tri-Communications Industries - East Norwalk, CT - *DataDirSup 7-83*
Tri-County Advertiser - Clarkesville, GA - *AyerDirPub 83; Ed&PubIntYB 82*
Tri-County Advertiser - Milford, MA - *Ed&PubIntYB 82*
Tri-County Advertiser - Brockport, NY - *AyerDirPub 83*
Tri-County Advertiser - Syracuse, NY - *AyerDirPub 83*
Tri-County Advertiser - Frederic, WI - *AyerDirPub 83*
Tri-County Banner [of Knightstown Mayhill Publications Inc.] - Knightstown, IN - *AyerDirPub 83; Ed&PubIntYB 82; NewsDir 84*
Tri-County Broadcasting - Elkin, NC - *BrCabYB 84*
Tri-County Broadcasting - Colville, WA - *BrCabYB 84*
Tri-County Buyers' Guide - Sault Ste. Marie, MI - *AyerDirPub 83*
Tri-County Cable TV [of Connersville Cable TV Inc.] - North Vernon, IN - *BrCabYB 84; Tel&CabFB 84C*
Tri-County Cable TV Co. [of American TV & Communications Corp.] - Salem, NJ - *BrCabYB 84; Tel&CabFB 84C*
Tri-County Cable TV Inc. [of Cardinal Communications Inc.] - Seymour, IN - *BrCabYB 84; Tel&CabFB 84C*
Tri-County Cable TV Inc. [of Cardinal Communications Inc.] - Westport, IN - *Tel&CabFB 84C*
Tri-County Cablevision Inc. - Lakeland, GA - *Tel&CabFB 84C p.1708*
Tri-County Cablevision Inc. - Pearson, GA - *Tel&CabFB 84C*
Tri-County Cablevision Inc. [of Cablevision Industries Inc.] - Albion, NY - *Tel&CabFB 84C*
Tri-County Independent - Florence, WI - *AyerDirPub 83; Ed&PubIntYB 82*
Tri-County Independent - *See* Florence Mining News Publishers
Tri-County Journal [of St. Louis Suburban Newspapers Inc.] - St. Louis, MO - *AyerDirPub 83; Ed&PubIntYB 82; NewsDir 84*
Tri County Mini Trib - Clintonville, WI - *AyerDirPub 83*
Tri-County Mutual Telephone Co. - Emery, SD - *TelDir&BG 83-84*
Tri-County News - South Bend, IN - *AyerDirPub 83; Ed&PubIntYB 82*
Tri-County News - Zearing, IA - *AyerDirPub 83; Ed&PubIntYB 82*
Tri-County News - Fenton, MI - *AyerDirPub 83*
Tri-County News - Kimball, MN - *AyerDirPub 83; Ed&PubIntYB 82*
Tri-County News - King City, MO - *AyerDirPub 83; Ed&PubIntYB 82*
Tri-County News - Sullivan, MO - *AyerDirPub 83*
Tri-County News - Lockport, NY - *AyerDirPub 83*
Tri-County News - Steubenville, OH - *AyerDirPub 83*
Tri-County News - Junction City, OR - *AyerDirPub 83; Ed&PubIntYB 82*
Tri-County News - Irene, SD - *Ed&PubIntYB 82*
Tri-County News - Friendship, TN - *AyerDirPub 83; Ed&PubIntYB 82*
Tri-County News - Seymour, TN - *AyerDirPub 83*
Tri-County News - Osseo, WI - *AyerDirPub 83; Ed&PubIntYB 82*
Tri-County News-Journal - Spruce Pine, NC - *AyerDirPub 83*
Tri-County Newspapers Inc. - Manchester, GA - *BaconPubCkNews 84*
Tri County Observer - Madisonville, TN - *AyerDirPub 83*
Tri-County Observer - Monroe, TN - *Ed&PubIntYB 82*
Tri-County Penny Saver - Hinesville, GA - *AyerDirPub 83*
Tri-County Press - Polo, IL - *AyerDirPub 83; Ed&PubIntYB 82*

Tri-County Press - Emerson, NE - *AyerDirPub 83; Ed&PubIntYB 82*
Tri-County Press - Cuba City, WI - *AyerDirPub 83; Ed&PubIntYB 82*
Tri-County Publications Inc. - Veneta, OR - *BaconPubCkNews 84*
Tri-County Publishing Inc. - Churubusco, IN - *BaconPubCkNews 84*
Tri-County Record - Dongola, IL - *AyerDirPub 83; Ed&PubIntYB 82*
Tri-County Record - Rushford, MN - *AyerDirPub 83; Ed&PubIntYB 82*
Tri-County Record - Kiel, WI - *AyerDirPub 83; Ed&PubIntYB 82*
Tri-County Research - New City, NY - *IntDirMarRes 83*
Tri-County Scribe - Plymouth, IL - *Ed&PubIntYB 82*
Tri-County Shopper [of Marten Publications Inc.] - De Soto, MO - *AyerDirPub 83; NewsDir 84*
Tri-County Shopper - Veneta, OR - *AyerDirPub 83*
Tri-County Shoppers Guide - Big Rapids, MI - *AyerDirPub 83*
Tri-County Shoppers Guide - Rushford, MN - *AyerDirPub 83*
Tri-County Special - Auburn, IA - *AyerDirPub 83*
Tri-County Sun - Fordville, ND - *AyerDirPub 83*
Tri-County Telephone Association Inc. - Council Grove, KS - *TelDir&BG 83-84*
Tri-County Telephone Association Inc. - Basin, WY - *TelDir&BG 83-84*
Tri-County Telephone Co. - Everton, AR - *TelDir&BG 83-84*
Tri-County Telephone Co. Inc. - New Richmond, IN - *Tel&CabFB 84C p.1708; TelDir&BG 83-84*
Tri-County Telephone Co. Inc. - Garrison, TX - *TelDir&BG 83-84*
Tri-County Telephone Cooperative Inc. - Strum, WI - *TelDir&BG 83-84*
Tri-County Telephone Membership Corp. - Belhaven, NC - *TelDir&BG 83-84*
Tri-County Times - Slater, IA - *AyerDirPub 83; Ed&PubIntYB 82*
Tri-County Today - Sandwich, IL - *AyerDirPub 83; Ed&PubIntYB 82*
Tri-County Tribune - Deer Trail, CO - *AyerDirPub 83; Ed&PubIntYB 82*
Tri-County Tribune - Deer Park, WA - *AyerDirPub 83*
Tri-County Truth - Churubusco, IN - *AyerDirPub 83; Ed&PubIntYB 82*
Tri-County Video Service - Washington, MO - *Tel&CabFB 84C*
Tri-County Weekly - Jamesport, MO - *AyerDirPub 83; Ed&PubIntYB 82*
Tri-Data - Mountain View, CA - *DataDirSup 7-83; DirInfWP 82; WhoWMicrocom 83*
Tri-Lakes Newspapers Inc. - Branson, MO - *BaconPubCkNews 84*
Tri-Med Press - Montclair, NJ - *BoPubDir 4, 5; LitMag&SmPr 83-84*
Tri-Palm Estates [of Great Western Properties Inc.] - Tri-Palm Estates, CA - *Tel&CabFB 84C*
Tri-Quarterly - Evanston, IL - *WritMar 84*
Tri-River Cable - Delphos, CO - *BrCabYB 84*
Tri-River Cable [of Cardiff Cablevision Inc.] - Bennington, KS - *BrCabYB 84; Tel&CabFB 84C*
Tri-River Cable [of Cardiff Cablevision Inc.] - Chapman, KS - *BrCabYB 84*
Tri-River Cable [of Cardiff Cablevision Inc.] - Clifton, KS - *BrCabYB 84*
Tri-River Cable [of Cardiff Cablevision Inc.] - Enterprise, KS - *BrCabYB 84*
Tri-River Cable [of Cardiff Cablevision Inc.] - Glasco, KS - *BrCabYB 84*
Tri-River Cable [of Cardiff Cablevision Inc.] - Milford, KS - *BrCabYB 84*
Tri-River Cable [of Cardiff Cablevision Inc.] - Miltonvale, KS - *BrCabYB 84*
Tri-River Cable Inc. - Minneapolis, KS - *BrCabYB 84*
Tri-River Cable Inc. - Riley, KS - *BrCabYB 84*
Tri-S Associates Inc. - Ruston, LA - *EISS 5-84 Sup*
Tri-Science Publishers - Los Angeles, CA - *BoPubDir 4*
Tri-Science Publishers - Pico Rivera, CA - *BoPubDir 5*
Tri-Star Cablevision Inc. - Greenup, IL - *Tel&CabFB 84C p.1708*
Tri-Star Productions Inc. - New York, NY - *AvMarPl 83*
Tri-State Advertising - Warsaw, IN - *AdAge 3-28-84; StaDirAdAg 2-84*
Tri-State Cable Systems - Ewing, VA - *BrCabYB 84; Tel&CabFB 84C*
Tri-State Cable TV Inc. - Boonsboro, MD - *BrCabYB 84*
Tri-State Cable TV Inc. - Hancock, MD - *BrCabYB 84 p.D-309; Tel&CabFB 84C p.1708*
Tri-State Cable TV Inc. - McConnellsburg, PA - *BrCabYB 84*
Tri-State Cablevision Inc. - Gosnell, AR - *BrCabYB 84; Tel&CabFB 84C*
Tri-State Cablevision Inc. [of Combined Cable Corp.] - Cuba City, WI - *BrCabYB 84; Tel&CabFB 84C*
Tri-State College Library Cooperative - Rosemont, PA - *EISS 5-84 Sup*
Tri-State Daily News, The - Lamar, CO - *Ed&PubIntYB 82*
Tri-State Defender - Memphis, TN - *Ed&PubIntYB 82*
Tri-State Digest [of Tri-State Publishing Co.] - Steubenville, OH - *NewsDir 84*
Tri-State Food News [of Gateway Press Inc.] - Monroeville, PA - *BaconPubCkMag 84; MagDir 84*
Tri-State Gazette [of Ottaway Newspapers Inc.] - Port Jervis, NY - *BaconPubCkNews 84; NewsDir 84*
Tri-State Livestock News - Sturgis, SD - *BaconPubCkMag 84; Ed&PubIntYB 82*
Tri-State Promotions - Amarillo, TX - *BoPubDir 5*
Tri-State Railway Historical Society Inc. - Clifton, NJ - *BoPubDir 5*
Tri-State Real Estate Journal [of East Coast Publications Inc.] - Accord, MA - *MagDir 84*
Tri-State Research - Ringgold, GA - *IntDirMarRes 83*
Tri-State Trader [of Mayhill Publishing] - Knightstown, IN - *BaconPubCkMag 84; Ed&PubIntYB 82; NewsDir 84; WritMar 84*
Tri-State Tribune - Picher, OK - *AyerDirPub 83; Ed&PubIntYB 82*
Tri-Town Cable TV Ltd. - Lunenberg County, NS, Canada - *BrCabYB 84*
Tri-Town Cablevision - Frederick, CO - *BrCabYB 84; Tel&CabFB 84C*
Tri-Town News - Sidney, NY - *AyerDirPub 83*
Tri-Town Reporter - Rockville, CT - *AyerDirPub 83; Ed&PubIntYB 82; NewsDir 84*
Tri-Town Transcript - Topsfield, MA - *Ed&PubIntYB 82*
Tri-Unity Press - East Wenatchee, WA - *BoPubDir 4 Sup, 5*
Tri-Valley Herald - Livermore, CA - *AyerDirPub 83; BaconPubCkNews 84; Ed&PubIntYB 82*
Tri-Video [of Pinion Corp.] - Salem, AR - *BrCabYB 84*
Tri-Village News - Columbus, OH - *AyerDirPub 83; NewsDir 84*
Tri-Village News - Grandview Heights, OH - *Ed&PubIntYB 82*
Tri-Village Pennysaver - Interlaken, NY - *AyerDirPub 83*
TRIAD - Toledo, OH - *AdAge 3-28-84*
Triad Cablevision Inc. [of Triad Stations Inc.] - Albany, IN - *Tel&CabFB 84C*
Triad Cablevision Inc. [of Triad Stations Inc.] - Berne, IN - *Tel&CabFB 84C*
Triad CATV Inc. [of Penn Communications Inc.] - Willards, MD - *Tel&CabFB 84C*
Triad CATV Inc. - Charlotte, MI - *BrCabYB 84; Tel&CabFB 84C*
Triad CATV Inc. - Hastings, MI - *BrCabYB 84; Tel&CabFB 84C*
Triad CATV of Indiana Inc. [of Triad Stations Inc.] - Portland, IN - *BrCabYB 84; Tel&CabFB 84C*
Triad Press [Aff. of Triad Interests Inc.] - Houston, TX - *BoPubDir 4, 5; LitMag&SmPr 83-84*
Triad Publishing Co. - Fairfield, CT - *BoPubDir 4, 5*
Triad Publishing Co. Inc. - Gainesville, FL - *LitMag&SmPr 83-84; LitMarPl 83, 84*
Triad Stations Inc. - Albion, MI - *BrCabYB 84*
Triad Stations Inc. - Marshall, MI - *BrCabYB 84 p.D-309; Tel&CabFB 84C p.1708*
Triad Systems Corp. - Sunnyvale, CA - *Top100Al 83*
TRIAD-Terry Robie Industrial Advertising Inc. - Toledo, OH - *StaDirAdAg 2-84*
Triadoption Publications [Aff. of Triadoption Library] - Westminster, CA - *BoPubDir 5*
Trial - Washington, DC - *BaconPubCkMag 84; MagDir 84; MagIndMarPl 82-83*
Triangle Cable TV Inc. [of Prime Cable Corp.] - Quantico, VA - *BrCabYB 84; Tel&CabFB 84C*

Triangle Cable TV of Oakdale [of Capital Cities Communications Inc.] - Oakdale, CA - *BrCabYB 84; Tel&CabFB 84C*
Triangle Electronics Co. Inc. - Pittsburgh, PA - *MicrocomMPl 84*
Triangle Press - Kemp, TX - *BoPubDir 4, 5*
Triangle Publications - Radnor, PA - *AdAge 6-28-84; KnowInd 83; MagIndMarPl 82-83*
Triangle Telephone Cooperative Association Inc. - Havre, MT - *TelDir&BG 83-84*
Triangle, The - Glenmont, NY - *MagDir 84*
Triangle Universities Computation Center - Research Triangle Park, NC - *DataDirOnSer 84*
Trianon Publications - Detroit, MI - *BillIntBG 83-84*
Tribal Jargon/Skids Records - Newton, MA - *BillIntBG 83-84*
Tribeca Communications Inc. - New York, NY - *LitMarPl 83, 84*
Tribology Index - Berlin, West Germany - *DirOnDB Spring 84*
Triboro Banner - Old Forge, PA - *Ed&PubIntYB 82*
Tribune - Arab, AL - *AyerDirPub 83*
Tribune - Cullman, AL - *AyerDirPub 83*
Tribune - Eufaula, AL - *AyerDirPub 83*
Tribune - Lineville, AL - *AyerDirPub 83*
Tribune - Tallassee, AL - *AyerDirPub 83*
Tribune - Mesa, AZ - *AyerDirPub 83; Ed&PubIntYB 82*
Tribune - Dixon, CA - *AyerDirPub 83*
Tribune - Gonzales, CA - *AyerDirPub 83*
Tribune - Holtville, CA - *AyerDirPub 83*
Tribune - Madera, CA - *AyerDirPub 83*
Tribune - Oakland, CA - *AyerDirPub 83*
Tribune - Pacifica, CA - *AyerDirPub 83*
Tribune [of Union-Tribune Publishing Co.] - San Diego, CA - *AyerDirPub 83; Ed&PubIntYB 82; LitMarPl 84; NewsDir 84*
Tribune - San Marino, CA - *AyerDirPub 83*
Tribune - Fowler, CO - *AyerDirPub 83*
Tribune - Greeley, CO - *AyerDirPub 83*
Tribune - Ft. Lauderdale, FL - *NewsDir 84*
Tribune - Tampa, FL - *AyerDirPub 83*
Tribune - Clayton, GA - *AyerDirPub 83*
Tribune - Savannah, GA - *Ed&PubIntYB 82*
Tribune - Lewiston, ID - *AyerDirPub 83; Ed&PubIntYB 82; LitMarPl 84*
Tribune - Post Falls, ID - *AyerDirPub 83*
Tribune - Chicago, IL - *AdAge 6-28-84; AyerDirPub 83; Ed&PubIntYB 82; HomeVid&CabYB 82-83; KnowInd 83*
Tribune - Freeburg, IL - *AyerDirPub 83*
Tribune - Chesterton, IN - *Ed&PubIntYB 82*
Tribune - Francesville, IN - *AyerDirPub 83*
Tribune - Kokomo, IN - *AyerDirPub 83*
Tribune - Mitchell, IN - *AyerDirPub 83*
Tribune - New Albany, IN - *AyerDirPub 83; Ed&PubIntYB 82*
Tribune - Peru, IN - *AyerDirPub 83*
Tribune - Seymour, IN - *AyerDirPub 83*
Tribune - South Bend, IN - *AyerDirPub 83*
Tribune - Terre Haute, IN - *AyerDirPub 83; Ed&PubIntYB 82*
Tribune - Tipton, IN - *AyerDirPub 83; Ed&PubIntYB 82*
Tribune - Warren, IN - *AyerDirPub 83*
Tribune - Ames, IA - *AyerDirPub 83*
Tribune - Anita, IA - *AyerDirPub 83*
Tribune - Buffalo Center, IA - *AyerDirPub 83*
Tribune - Des Moines, IA - *AyerDirPub 83*
Tribune - Harlan, IA - *AyerDirPub 83*
Tribune - New Hampton, IA - *AyerDirPub 83*
Tribune - Osceola, IA - *AyerDirPub 83*
Tribune - Chanute, KS - *AyerDirPub 83; Ed&PubIntYB 82*
Tribune - Douglas, KS - *AyerDirPub 83*
Tribune - Great Bend, KS - *AyerDirPub 83*
Tribune - Pratt, KS - *AyerDirPub 83; Ed&PubIntYB 82*
Tribune - Cheboygan, MI - *AyerDirPub 83*
Tribune - Coleman, MI - *AyerDirPub 83*
Tribune - Grand Haven, MI - *AyerDirPub 83*
Tribune - Royal Oak, MI - *AyerDirPub 83*
Tribune - Albert Lea, MN - *AyerDirPub 83; Ed&PubIntYB 82*
Tribune - Detroit Lakes, MN - *AyerDirPub 83; Ed&PubIntYB 82*
Tribune - Granite Falls, MN - *AyerDirPub 83*
Tribune - Hibbing, MN - *AyerDirPub 83*
Tribune - Lake Crystal, MN - *AyerDirPub 83*
Tribune - Minnesota Lake, MN - *AyerDirPub 83*
Tribune - Morris, MN - *AyerDirPub 83*
Tribune - Spring Valley, MN - *AyerDirPub 83*
Tribune - Columbia, MO - *AyerDirPub 83*
Tribune - Great Falls, MT - *AyerDirPub 83*
Tribune - Miles City, MT - *AyerDirPub 83*
Tribune - Terry, MT - *AyerDirPub 83*
Tribune - Burwell, NE - *AyerDirPub 83*
Tribune - Fremont, NE - *AyerDirPub 83*
Tribune - Hastings, NE - *AyerDirPub 83*
Tribune - Sparks, NV - *AyerDirPub 83; Ed&PubIntYB 82*
Tribune - Albuquerque, NM - *AyerDirPub 83*
Tribune - Hicksville, NY - *AyerDirPub 83*
Tribune - Hornell, NY - *AyerDirPub 83; Ed&PubIntYB 82*
Tribune - Levittown, NY - *AyerDirPub 83*
Tribune - Concord, NC - *AyerDirPub 83*
Tribune - Elkin, NC - *AyerDirPub 83; Ed&PubIntYB 82*
Tribune - Mooresville, NC - *AyerDirPub 83*
Tribune - Mt. Olive, NC - *AyerDirPub 83*
Tribune - Tabor City, NC - *AyerDirPub 83*
Tribune - Berthold, ND - *AyerDirPub 83*
Tribune - Bismarck, ND - *AyerDirPub 83*
Tribune - Coshocton, OH - *AyerDirPub 83*
Tribune - Gallipolis, OH - *AyerDirPub 83*
Tribune - Mt. Sterling, OH - *AyerDirPub 83*
Tribune - El Reno, OK - *AyerDirPub 83*
Tribune - Thomas, OK - *AyerDirPub 83*
Tribune - Tulsa, OK - *AyerDirPub 83*
Tribune - Wagoner, OK - *AyerDirPub 83*
Tribune - Dayton, OR - *AyerDirPub 83*
Tribune - Scio, OR - *AyerDirPub 83*
Tribune - Meadville, PA - *AyerDirPub 83*
Tribune - Monroeville, PA - *Ed&PubIntYB 82*
Tribune - Philadelphia, PA - *AyerDirPub 83; Ed&PubIntYB 82*
Tribune - Scranton, PA - *AyerDirPub 83; BaconPubCkNews 84; Ed&PubIntYB 82; LitMarPl 84; NewsDir 84*
Tribune - Dell Rapids, SD - *AyerDirPub 83*
Tribune - Ipswich, SD - *AyerDirPub 83*
Tribune - Mobridge, SD - *AyerDirPub 83*
Tribune - Volga, SD - *AyerDirPub 83*
Tribune - Dunlap, TN - *AyerDirPub 83*
Tribune - Lewisburg, TN - *AyerDirPub 83*
Tribune - Bay City, TX - *AyerDirPub 83*
Tribune - East Bernard, TX - *AyerDirPub 83*
Tribune - Ganado, TX - *AyerDirPub 83*
Tribune - Grandview, TX - *AyerDirPub 83*
Tribune - Kerens, TX - *AyerDirPub 83*
Tribune - Meridian, TX - *AyerDirPub 83*
Tribune - Morton, TX - *AyerDirPub 83*
Tribune - Mt. Pleasant, TX - *AyerDirPub 83*
Tribune - San Augustine, TX - *AyerDirPub 83*
Tribune - St. Jo, TX - *AyerDirPub 83*
Tribune - Terrell, TX - *AyerDirPub 83*
Tribune - Throckmorton, TX - *AyerDirPub 83*
Tribune - Salt Lake City, UT - *AyerDirPub 83*
Tribune - Glenwood City, WI - *AyerDirPub 83*
Tribune - La Crosse, WI - *AyerDirPub 83*
Tribune - Waunakee, WI - *AyerDirPub 83*
Tribune - Wisconsin Rapids, WI - *AyerDirPub 83*
Tribune - Powell, WY - *AyerDirPub 83*
Tribune - Trochu, AB, Canada - *Ed&PubIntYB 82*
Tribune - Williams Lake, BC, Canada - *AyerDirPub 83; Ed&PubIntYB 82*
Tribune - Minnedosa, MB, Canada - *AyerDirPub 83*
Tribune - Campbellton, NB, Canada - *AyerDirPub 83; Ed&PubIntYB 82*
Tribune - Stouffville, ON, Canada - *AyerDirPub 83; Ed&PubIntYB 82*
Tribune - Sturgeon Falls, ON, Canada - *AyerDirPub 83*
Tribune - Toronto/Leaside, ON, Canada - *Ed&PubIntYB 82*
Tribune Advertiser, The - Elkin, NC - *AyerDirPub 83*
Tribune & Register - Tyndall, SD - *Ed&PubIntYB 82*
Tribune & Star - Terre Haute, IN - *AyerDirPub 83*
Tribune Broadcasting Co. - Chicago, IL - *BrCabYB 84; Tel&CabFB 84S*
Tribune Cable Communications Inc. - Lancaster, CA - *Tel&CabFB 84C*
Tribune Cable Communications Inc. - Mahwah, NJ - *BrCabYB 84 p.D-309; CabTVFinDB 83*

Tribune Cable Communications Inc. - Fredonia, NY - *BrCabYB 84*
Tribune Cable Communications Inc. - Glens Falls, NY - *Tel&CabFB 84C*
Tribune Cable Communications Inc. - Jackson, TN - *BrCabYB 84*
Tribune Cable Co. of California [of Tribune Cable Communications Inc.] - Lakewood, CA - *Tel&CabFB 84C*
Tribune Cable of Alexandria Inc. [of Tribune Cable Communications Inc.] - Alexandria, VA - *BrCabYB 84; Tel&CabFB 84C*
Tribune Cablevision Co. - Houghton, MI - *BrCabYB 84*
Tribune-Chief - Quanah, TX - *AyerDirPub 83; Ed&PubIntYB 82*
Tribune Chronicle, The - Warren, OH - *AyerDirPub 83; Ed&PubIntYB 82*
Tribune Co. Cable Inc. - Houghton, MI - *Tel&CabFB 84C*
Tribune Co. Cable Inc. - Mahwah, NJ - *LitMarPl 84*
Tribune Co. Syndicate Inc. [Subs. of Tribune Co.] - New York, NY - *BaconPubCkNews 84; Ed&PubIntYB 82; LitMarPl 83, 84*
Tribune-Courier - Benton, KY - *AyerDirPub 83*
Tribune-Courier - Ontario, OH - *AyerDirPub 83; Ed&PubIntYB 82*
Tribune-Democrat - La Junta, CO - *AyerDirPub 83; Ed&PubIntYB 82*
Tribune-Democrat - Johnstown, PA - *AyerDirPub 83; Ed&PubIntYB 82*
Tribune Echo - Deer Park, WA - *AyerDirPub 83*
Tribune, Enterprise & Scimitar - Healdsburg, CA - *AyerDirPub 83*
Tribune-Examiner - Dillon, MT - *AyerDirPub 83*
Tribune Films Inc. - New York, NY - *Tel&CabFB 84C*
Tribune-Gazette - Clintonville, WI - *AyerDirPub 83; Ed&PubIntYB 82*
Tribune Greeley County Republican - Tribune, KS - *BaconPubCkNews 84*
Tribune-Herald - Hallettsville, TX - *AyerDirPub 83*
Tribune-Herald - Waco, TX - *AyerDirPub 83*
Tribune-Keystone - Elroy, WI - *AyerDirPub 83; Ed&PubIntYB 82*
Tribune-News - Holbrook, AZ - *AyerDirPub 83*
Tribune-News - Cartersville, GA - *AyerDirPub 83*
Tribune-News - South Whitley, IN - *AyerDirPub 83; Ed&PubIntYB 82*
Tribune News Wave [of Central News Wave Publications] - Los Angeles, CA - *AyerDirPub 83; NewsDir 84*
Tribune Newspapers Inc. - Clarkston, WA - *BaconPubCkNews 84*
Tribune-Phonograph - Abbotsford, WI - *AyerDirPub 83; Ed&PubIntYB 82*
Tribune-Post - Sackville, NB, Canada - *AyerDirPub 83*
Tribune-Press - Chisholm, MN - *AyerDirPub 83*
Tribune-Press - Gouverneur, NY - *AyerDirPub 83; Ed&PubIntYB 82*
Tribune Productions Inc. - Chicago, IL - *Tel&CabFB 84C*
Tribune Publishing Co. - Boston, MA - *BaconPubCkNews 84*
Tribune Publishing Co. - Livingston, NJ - *BoPubDir 4, 5; LitMag&SmPr 83-84*
Tribune Publishing Co. - Tacoma, WA - *BrCabYB 84 p.D-309; Tel&CabFB 84C p.1708*
Tribune-Record-Gleaner - Loyal, WI - *AyerDirPub 83; Ed&PubIntYB 82*
Tribune-Review - Bethany, OK - *AyerDirPub 83; Ed&PubIntYB 82*
Tribune-Review - Greensburg, PA - *AyerDirPub 83; BaconPubCkNews 84; Ed&PubIntYB 82*
Tribune-Sentinel - Grant, NE - *AyerDirPub 83*
Tribune Shopping News - New Lexington, OH - *AyerDirPub 83; NewsDir 84*
Tribune-Star - Terre Haute, IN - *Ed&PubIntYB 82; NewsDir 84*
Tribune, The - Monument, CO - *AyerDirPub 83; Ed&PubIntYB 82*
Tribune, The - Cocoa, FL - *Ed&PubIntYB 82*
Tribune, The - Fairview Heights, IL - *AyerDirPub 83; Ed&PubIntYB 82*
Tribune, The - Homestead, PA - *AyerDirPub 83*
Tribune, The - Austin, TX - *AyerDirPub 83*
Tribune, The - Bathurst, NB, Canada - *Ed&PubIntYB 82*
Tribune-Times - Fountain Inn, SC - *NewsDir 84*
Tribune-Times - Mauldin, SC - *AyerDirPub 83; Ed&PubIntYB 82*
Tribune-United of Montgomery County - Montgomery County, MD - *BrCabYB 84*
Tributaries [of Iroquois House Publishers] - Mountain Park, NM - *LitMag&SmPr 83-84*
Tribute - Tyler, MN - *AyerDirPub 83*
Tribute Publishing Inc. - *See* PPX Publishing
Trichter, Nancy J. - New York, NY - *LitMarPl 83, 84*
TriCities CableVision [of Cable TV of Willsville & Edgerton Inc.] - Wellsville, KS - *BrCabYB 84*
TriCities CableVision Inc. [of W.W. Communications] - Baldwin City, KS - *Tel&CabFB 84C*
Trico-Telecom Inc. - Media, PA - *Tel&CabFB 84C p.1708*
Tricoder Cambridge - Cambridge, England - *MicrocomSwDir 1*
Tricolor Inc. - Wilmington, DE - *AvMarPl 83*
Tricomi & Daughter, Ernest - Cherry Hill, NJ - *StaDirAdAg 2-84*
Tricor Inc. - Ambler, PA - *BoPubDir 5*
Tricor Industries Inc. - New York, NY - *DirInfWP 82*
Trident America Programs Inc. - New York, NY - *TelAl 83, 84*
Trident Communications [Div. of International Audio Visual Designers Inc.] - New York, NY - *AvMarPl 83*
Trident Television Associates Inc. - New York, NY - *TelAl 83, 84*
Tridex Music Co. - Burbank, CA - *BillIntBG 83-84*
Triformation Systems Inc. - Stuart, FL - *DataDirSup 7-83*
Trig Graphics - Dobbs Ferry, NY - *ArtMar 84*
Triggs Color Printing Corp. [Div. of Wisdom Press] - New York, NY - *LitMarPl 83, 84*
Trigild Ltd. - Rexdald, ON, Canada - *DirInfWP 82*
Trigon Press - Beckenham, England - *LitMag&SmPr 83-84; MicroMarPl 82-83*
Trigon Video Services - *See* Videoworks
Trigram Systems - Pittsburgh, PA - *MicrocomMPl 84; MicrocomSwDir 1*
Trike - San Francisco, CA - *BoPubDir 4, 5*
TriKraft Inc. - Williamston, MI - *MagIndMarPl 82-83*
Trillium Books (Fonthill Studio) - Fonthill, ON, Canada - *BoPubDir 4, 5*
Trillium Books/Les Livres Trillium - Montreal, PQ, Canada - *BoPubDir 4 Sup, 5*
Trillium Press - New York, NY - *BoPubDir 4; LitMarPl 83, 84*
Trilobite Press Inc. - Denton, TX - *BoPubDir 4, 5*
Trilog Inc. - Irvine, CA - *WhoWMicrocom 83*
Trilogy Publishers/Ardis Publishing Co. - Ann Arbor, MI - *BoPubDir 4, 5*
Trim-A-Tree Merchandising - New York, NY - *BaconPubCkMag 84*
Trimble Banner Democrat, The - Bedford, KY - *Ed&PubIntYB 82*
Trimm Enclosure Products [Subs. of Trimm Industries] - North Hollywood, CA - *WhoWMicrocom 83*
Trimont Progress-Ceylon Herald - Trimont, MN - *Ed&PubIntYB 82*
Trimont West Martin Weekly News - Trimont, MN - *BaconPubCkNews 84*
Trina Jill Music Corp. - New York, NY - *BillIntBG 83-84*
Trinc Transportation Consultants [Aff. of Dun & Bradstreet Inc.] - Washington, DC - *BoPubDir 5*
Trine Books - Wallingford, CT - *LitMag&SmPr 83-84*
Trinidad Chronicle News [of Lake Charles American Press] - Trinidad, CO - *BaconPubCkNews 84; NewsDir 84*
Trinity Associates - San Jose, CA - *MicrocomMPl 84*
Trinity Books - East Hartford, CT - *BoPubDir 4, 5*
Trinity Broadcasting Network - Santa Ana, CA - *BrCabYB 84; CabTVPrDB 83; HomeVid&CabYB 82-83; Tel&CabFB 84S*
Trinity Broadcasting Network - Tustin, CA - *Tel&CabFB 84C*
Trinity Cable TV Co. Inc. [of Dickinson Communications Ltd.] - Trinity County, CA - *Tel&CabFB 84C*
Trinity Cable TV Inc. [of Dickinson Communications Ltd.] - Weaverville, CA - *BrCabYB 84*
Trinity Computing Systems - Houston, TX - *MicrocomMPl 84*
Trinity Journal - Weaverville, CA - *AyerDirPub 83; Ed&PubIntYB 82*
Trinity Press - San Francisco, CA - *BoPubDir 4, 5*
Trinity Press - Burlington, ON, Canada - *LitMarPl 83*
Trinity Standard - Trinity, TX - *Ed&PubIntYB 82*
Trinity Standard - *See* Polk County Publishing
Trinity University Press - San Antonio, TX - *BoPubDir 4; LitMarPl 83, 84*
Trinity Valley Telephone Co. [Aff. of Great Southwest Telephone Corp.] - Winnie, TX - *TelDir&BG 83-84*

Trinon Bureau, The - Richmond, VA - *BillIntBG 83-84*
Trio Music Co. Inc. - New York, NY - *BillIntBG 83-84*
Trionics - Baltimore, MD - *MicrocomMPl 84; WhoWMicrocom 83*
Triple P Publications International [Aff. of De Mesne Ltd.] - Boston, MA - *BoPubDir 4, 5*
Triple T Enterprises Inc. - Iowa City, IA - *AvMarPl 83*
Triplett Broadcasting Co. - Bellefontaine, OH - *BrCabYB 84*
Triplex Marketing Inc. - Huntington, IN - *StaDirAdAg 2-84*
Tripoli Leader - Tripoli, IA - *BaconPubCkNews 84; Ed&PubIntYB 82*
Tripoli Music [Div. of Elite Entertainment Enterprises] - Chicago, IL - *BillIntBG 83-84*
Tripp Communications Inc., Marian - Chicago, IL - *DirPRFirms 83*
Tripp County Journal - Winner, SD - *AyerDirPub 83*
Tripp Ledger, The - Tripp, SD - *Ed&PubIntYB 82*
Tripp Lite [Div. of Tripple Manufacturing] - Chicago, IL - *MicrocomMPl 84*
Tripp Star Ledger - Scotland, SD - *BaconPubCkNews 84*
Trippensee Publishing [Aff. of Trippensee Corp.] - Saginaw, MI - *BoPubDir 5*
TriQuarterly [of Northwestern University] - Evanston, IL - *ArtMar 84; LitMag&SmPr 83-84; LitMarPl 83, 84*
TRIS-On-Line [of Transportation Research Board] - Washington, DC - *CompReadDB 82; DBBus 82; DirOnDB Spring 84; EISS 83*
Triskell Press - Ottawa, ON, Canada - *BoPubDir 4 Sup, 5*
TriSoft - Austin, TX - *MicrocomMPl 84*
Tristar Data Systems - Cherry Hill, NJ - *DataDirOnSer 84; DataDirSup 7-83; MicrocomMPl 84; MicrocomSwDir 1*
TriStar Graphics [Div. of Cowles Media Co.] - Minneapolis, MN - *LitMarPl 83, 84; MagIndMarPl 82-83*
Triton Books - Los Angeles, CA - *BoPubDir 4 Sup, 5; LitMag&SmPr 83-84*
Triton Press - New York, NY - *ArtMar 84*
Tritone Music - Montclair, NJ - *BoPubDir 4 Sup, 5*
Triumph-Adler Inc. - *Top100Al 83*
Triumph Publishing Co. - Altadena, CA - *BoPubDir 4, 5; WritMar 84*
Triune Music Inc. - *See* Lorenz Creative Services
Triver Music - Pittsburgh, PA - *BillIntBG 83-84*
Trivium - Lampeter, Wales - *LitMag&SmPr 83-84*
Trix Records Inc. - Rosendale, NY - *BillIntBG 83-84*
TRL Productions - Cleveland, OH - *StaDirAdAg 2-84*
Trnka Group Inc. - Aurora, IL - *DirMarMP 83; StaDirAdAg 2-84*
TRO - New York, NY - *BillIntBG 83-84*
Trod Nossel Artists - Wallingford, CT - *BillIntBG 83-84*
Trojan Books - Wyomissing, PA - *LitMag&SmPr 83-84*
Troll Associates - Mahwah, NJ - *ArtMar 84; AvMarPl 83; LitMarPl 83, 84; WritMar 84*
Troll Associates (Book Div.) - Mahwah, NJ - *ArtMar 84*
Trolley Inc. - Nashville, TN - *LitMag&SmPr 83-84*
Trolley Talk [Aff. of Wagner Car Co.] - Cincinnati, OH - *BoPubDir 4, 5*
Tromba Publications - *See* Brass Press
Trombley, Irvine & Brinks Advertising - Fountain Valley, CA - *StaDirAdAg 2-84*
Tromson Monroe Advertising Inc. - New York, NY - *StaDirAdAg 2-84*
Tromson Monroe Production Co. [of Tromson Monroe Advertising Inc.] - New York, NY - *StaDirAdAg 2-84*
Tromson Monroe Public Relations [Subs. of Tromson Monroe Advertising Inc.] - New York, NY - *DirPRFirms 83*
Trona Argonaut - Trona, CA - *AyerDirPub 83; BaconPubCkNews 84; Ed&PubIntYB 82*
Trondequoit Press - Rochester, NY - *NewsDir 84*
Trone, Donohoe & Johnson Inc. - Greensboro, NC - *StaDirAdAg 2-84*
Trooper, The - Falmouth, MA - *WritMar 84*
TROPAG [of Koninklijk Instituut voor den Tropen] - Amsterdam, Netherlands - *DirOnDB Spring 84; OnBibDB 3*
Tropic [of Knight Ridder] - Miami, FL - *ArtMar 84; MagIndMarPl 82-83; WritMar 84*
Tropic Sound Inc. - Tamarac, FL - *BillIntBG 83-84*
Tropic Sound International Inc. - Miami Beach, FL - *BillIntBG 83-84*
Tropical Agriculture [of Royal Tropical Institute] - Amsterdam, Netherlands - *DBBus 82*
Tropical & Geographical Medicine [of Foris Publications USA-Bird-Sci Books] - Cinnaminson, NJ - *LitMag&SmPr 83-84*
Tropical Fish Hobbyist - Neptune City, NJ - *MagDir 84; MagIndMarPl 82-83*
Tropicana Records [Div. of Audio International Inc.] - Beverly Hills, CA - *BillIntBG 83-84*
Tropo Music - *See* Windham Hill Music
Trost Associates Inc. - Norwalk, CT - *IntDirMarRes 83*
Trot - Toronto, ON, Canada - *WritMar 84*
Trotevale Inc. - Lander, WY - *LitMag&SmPr 83-84*
Trotta Associates Inc. - Marina del Rey, CA - *IntDirMarRes 83*
Trotwood Argus-Sentinel - Dayton, OH - *Ed&PubIntYB 82; NewsDir 84*
Trotwood Argus-Sentinel - *See* Argus-Sentinel Inc.
Troubador Press [Div. of Price/Stern/Sloan Publishers Inc.] - San Francisco, CA - *ArtMar 84; LitMarPl 83, 84; WritMar 84*
Trouble Boys Music - Chicago, IL - *BillIntBG 83-84*
Troup-Overton Cablevision [of Omni Cable TV Corp.] - Arp, TX - *BrCabYB 84*
Troup-Overton Cablevision [of Omni Cable TV Corp.] - Overton, TX - *BrCabYB 84*
Troup-Overton Cablevision - Van, TX - *BrCabYB 84*
Troup Times-Banner - Troup, TX - *BaconPubCkNews 84*
Trouser Press [of Trans-Oceanic Trouser Press Inc.] - New York, NY - *BaconPubCkMag 84; LitMag&SmPr 83-84; MagIndMarPl 82-83; WritMar 84*
Trout - Washington, DC - *MagDir 84*
Trout - Taunton, MA - *BaconPubCkMag 84*
Trout & Ries Advertising - New York, NY - *DirPRFirms 83; StaDirAdAg 2-84*
Trout Creek Press - Parkdale, OR - *LitMag&SmPr 83-84*
Trowel - Washington, DC - *BaconPubCkMag 84*
Troxell & Associates Inc. - Houston, TX - *DirPRFirms 83; StaDirAdAg 2-84*
Troy Area Communications - Columbia Township, PA - *Tel&CabFB 84C*
Troy Cable Communications Inc. - Troy, PA - *Tel&CabFB 84C*
Troy Camera Shop Inc. [Div. of Berns Camera Stores] - Troy, NY - *AvMarPl 83*
Troy Daily News - Troy, OH - *BaconPubCkNews 84; Ed&PubIntYB 82; NewsDir 84*
Troy Eccentric [of Livonia Suburban Communications Corp.] - Livonia, MI - *AyerDirPub 83; NewsDir 84*
Troy Eccentric - *See* Observer & Eccentric Newspapers
Troy-Folan Productions Inc. - Wayne, NJ - *WhoWMicrocom 83*
Troy Free Press - Troy, MO - *BaconPubCkNews 84; Ed&PubIntYB 82*
Troy Free Press & Silex Index - Troy, MO - *NewsDir 84*
Troy Gazette Register - Troy, PA - *BaconPubCkNews 84; Ed&PubIntYB 82*
Troy Historical Society Inc. - Troy, OH - *BoPubDir 4, 5*
Troy Kansas Chief - Troy, KS - *BaconPubCkNews 84*
Troy Messenger [of Tillotson Publications] - Troy, AL - *BaconPubCkNews 84; Ed&PubIntYB 82; NewsDir 84*
Troy Montgomery Herald - Troy, NC - *BaconPubCkNews 84*
Troy NewChannels [of NewChannels Corp.] - Troy, NY - *BrCabYB 84; Tel&CabFB 84C*
Troy-Somerset Gazette - Troy, MI - *NewsDir 84*
Troy State University (TSU Press) - Troy, AL - *BoPubDir 4, 5*
Troy Telephone Co. Inc. [Aff. of Telephone & Data Systems Inc.] - Troy, ID - *TelDir&BG 83-84*
Troy Times Record - Troy, NY - *NewsDir 84*
Troy Tribune - Troy, IL - *BaconPubCkNews 84; Ed&PubIntYB 82*
Troy TV Cable Co. Inc. - Troy, ID - *BrCabYB 84; Tel&CabFB 84C*
Troy TV Cable Inc. - Troy, PA - *BrCabYB 84*
TRT Data Products - East Norwalk, CT - *DataDirSup 7-83*
Tru-Check Computer Systems Inc. - Rye, NY - *ADAPSOMemDir 83-84; DataDirOnSer 84*
Tru-Faith Publishing Co. - Gainesville, GA - *BoPubDir 4 Sup, 5*
Truart & Struppman Engraving - New York, NY - *LitMarPl 83, 84*
Truck & Equipment Salesman - Radnor, PA - *MagIndMarPl 82-83*
Truck Canada - Montreal, PQ, Canada - *BaconPubCkMag 84*

Truck Insider Newsletter - New York, NY - *BaconPubCkMag 84*
Truck Stop Management - Asheville, NC - *MagDir 84*
Truck Tracks - Lake Oswego, OR - *MagDir 84; MagIndMarPl 82-83*
Truck Trends - Chicago, IL - *MagDir 84*
Truckee River Cable TV [of Westar Communications I] - Truckee, CA - *BrCabYB 84; Tel&CabFB 84C*
Truckee Sierra Sun - Truckee, CA - *BaconPubCkNews 84*
Truckin' - Anaheim, CA - *BaconPubCkMag 84; MagDir 84; MagIndMarPl 82-83*
Trucking Today - Austin, TX - *MagDir 84*
True Blue Music Publishing Co. - Sepulveda, CA - *BillIntBG 83-84*
True Citizen, The - Waynesboro, GA - *AyerDirPub 83; Ed&PubIntYB 82*
True Confessions [of Macfadden Women's Group] - New York, NY - *ArtMar 84; BaconPubCkMag 84; MagDir 84; MagIndMarPl 82-83; WritMar 84*
True Data Corp. - Irvine, CA - *DataDirSup 7-83*
True Detective [of R.G.H. Publishing Corp.] - New York, NY - *MagDir 84; MagIndMarPl 82-83; WritMar 84*
True Experience [of Macfadden Women's Group] - New York, NY - *BaconPubCkMag 84; MagDir 84; MagIndMarPl 82-83; WritMar 84*
True Love [of Macfadden Women's Group] - New York, NY - *BaconPubCkMag 84; MagDir 84; MagIndMarPl 82-83; WritMar 84*
True Police Cases [of Detective Files Group] - Montreal, PQ, Canada - *WritMar 84*
True Romance [of Macfadden Women's Group] - New York, NY - *BaconPubCkMag 84; MagDir 84; MagIndMarPl 82-83; WritMar 84*
True Story [of Macfadden Women's Group] - New York, NY - *BaconPubCkMag 84; Folio 83; LitMarPl 84; MagDir 84; MagIndMarPl 82-83; WritMar 84*
True Vine Music - *See* Mustard Tree Music
True West [of Western Publications] - Iola, WI - *ArtMar 84; MagDir 84; MagIndMarPl 82-83; WritMar 84*
Truly Fine Press, A Review - Bemidji, MN - *LitMag&SmPr 83-84*
Truman Tribune, The - Truman, MN - *Ed&PubIntYB 82*
Trumann Cable TV - Trumann, AR - *BrCabYB 84*
Trumann Democrat - Trumann, AR - *BaconPubCkNews 84; NewsDir 84*
Trumansburg Free Press - Trumansburg, NY - *Ed&PubIntYB 82*
Trumansburg Free Press - *See* Odyssey Publications
Trumansburg Home Telephone Co. [Aff. of Ontario Telephone Co. Inc.] - Phelps, NY - *TelDir&BG 83-84*
Trumble & Associates Inc. - Minneapolis, MN - *DirPRFirms 83*
Trumble Co. Inc. - Jacksonville Beach, FL - *AvMarPl 83*
Trumbull Times - Trumbull, CT - *Ed&PubIntYB 82; NewsDir 84*
Trumbull Times - *See* Trumbull Times Publishers
Trumbull Times Publishers - Trumbull, CT - *BaconPubCkNews 84*
Trumpeter - Franklin, NH - *Ed&PubIntYB 82*
Trumpeter - London, ON, Canada - *Ed&PubIntYB 82*
Trunk Press - Hancock, MD - *BoPubDir 4, 5*
Truro Daily News, The - Truro, NS, Canada - *BaconPubCkNews 84*
Trust Music Management Inc. - Los Angeles, CA - *BillIntBG 83-84*
Trustcompare - New York, NY - *DirOnDB Spring 84*
Trustee [of American Hospital Association] - Chicago, IL - *BaconPubCkMag 84; MagDir 84; MagIndMarPl 82-83*
Trusts & Estates [of Communication Channels Inc.] - Atlanta, GA - *BaconPubCkMag 84; MagDir 84*
Trusty Publications - Nebo, KY - *BillIntBG 83-84*
Truth - Elkhart, IN - *AyerDirPub 83*
Truth - Philadelphia, PA - *Ed&PubIntYB 82*
Truth Center - Los Angeles, CA - *LitMag&SmPr 83-84*
Truth Consciousness - Boulder, CO - *BoPubDir 4, 5*
Truth in Money Inc. - Chagrin Falls, OH - *BoPubDir 4 Sup, 5*
Truth on Fire [of The Bible Holiness Movement] - Vancouver, BC, Canada - *WritMar 84*
Truth or Consequences Herald - Truth or Consequences, NM - *BaconPubCkNews 84*
Truth or Consequences Sierra County Sentinel - Truth or Consequences, NM - *NewsDir 84*
Truth Publishers - La Jolla, CA - *BoPubDir 4, 5*
Truth Publishing Co. - *See* Federated Media
Truth Seeker Co. Inc. - San Diego, CA - *BoPubDir 4, 5*
Truth Semi-Weekly - San Francisco, CA - *NewsDir 84*
Truth, The - Pottstown, PA - *NewsDir 84*
Trutone Records - Haworth, NJ - *BillIntBG 83-84*
Trux - Atlanta, GA - *BaconPubCkMag 84; MagDir 84*
TRW Business Credit Services [of TRW Information Services] - Orange, CA - *DataDirOnSer 84; InfIndMarPl 83*
TRW Corp. - Cleveland, OH - *Datamation 6-83; ElecNews 7-25-83; KnowInd 83; Top100Al 83*
TRW Credit Data [of TRW Information Services] - Orange, CA - *DataDirOnSer 84*
TRW/Customer Service [Subs. of TRW Inc.] - Fairfield, NJ - *WhoWMicrocom 83*
TRW Information Services [of TRW Inc.] - Orange, CA - *DataDirOnSer 84; InfIndMarPl 83; InfoS 83-84*
TRW Semiconductors - Lawndale, CA - *CabTVFinDB 83*
Tryon Daily Bulletin - Tryon, NC - *AyerDirPub 83; BaconPubCkNews 84; Ed&PubIntYB 82; NewsDir 84*
Tryon Graphic - Tryon, NE - *BaconPubCkNews 84; Ed&PubIntYB 82*
Tsai & Co. Inc., G. - New York, NY - *ProGuPRSer 4*
TSC [Aff. of Houghton Mifflin Co.] - Hanover, NH - *BoPubDir 4, 5; DataDirOnSer 84; MicrocomMPl 84; MicroMarPl 82-83*
TSCA Chemical Substances Inventory [of U.S. Environmental Protection Agency] - Washington, DC - *DBBus 82*
TSCA Initial Inventory [of Dialog Information Services Inc.] - Palo Alto, CA - *DataDirOnSer 84*
TSCA Initial Inventory - Washington, DC - *DirOnDB Spring 84*
TSCA Plant & Production [of Chemical Information Systems Inc.] - Baltimore, MD - *DataDirOnSer 84*
TSCAPP - Washington, DC - *DirOnDB Spring 84*
TSD Display Products Inc. - Bohemia, NY - *DataDirSup 7-83*
TSE/Hardside [Subs. of Robitaille & Sons] - Milford, NH - *WhoWMicrocom 83*
TSI International Ltd. - Norwalk, CT - *ADAPSOMemDir 83-84*
TSI Syndicate Features - Washington, DC - *LitMarPl 84*
TSK Electronics - City of Industry, CA - *MicrocomMPl 84*
TSL Press [Aff. of Time & Space Ltd.] - New York, NY - *BoPubDir 4, 5*
TSM Productions Inc. - Syosset, NY - *BoPubDir 4 Sup, 5*
TSOM Music - *See* De Walden Music
TSR-Bigs - Tokyo, Japan - *DirOnDB Spring 84*
TSR-Fins - Tokyo, Japan - *DirOnDB Spring 84*
TSR Inc. - Great Neck, NY - *DataDirOnSer 84*
TSR Records - Los Angeles, CA - *BillIntBG 83-84*
TSTA Advocate - Austin, TX - *BaconPubCkMag 84*
TSU Press - Troy, AL - *LitMarPl 84*
Tsukuba Integrated Campus Information Processing & Sharing System [of University of Tsukuba] - Ibaraki-ken, Japan - *EISS 83*
TT Kalendern - Stockholm, Sweden - *DirOnDB Spring 84*
TT Newsbank - Stockholm, Sweden - *EISS 83*
TT Nyhetsbanken - Stockholm, Sweden - *DirOnDB Spring 84*
Tua, Lynda M. - Clifton, NJ - *LitMarPl 83, 84; MagIndMarPl 82-83*
Tubb Music Inc., Ernest - *See* Drake Music Group
Tubs Software Ltd. - Leicester, England - *MicrocomSwDir 1*
Tuck, Donald S. - Summit, NJ - *MagIndMarPl 82-83*
Tuck Electronics - New Cumberland, PA - *DataDirSup 7-83; MicrocomMPl 84*
Tuckahoe Eastchester Record - Tuckahoe, NY - *BaconPubCkNews 84*
Tucker Anthony & R. L. Day Inc. - Stamford, CT - *ADAPSOMemDir 83-84*
Tucker, Bernard - Bellerose, NY - *MagIndMarPl 82-83*
Tucker County TV Cable System [of Ohio Valley Cable Corp.] - Davis, WV - *BrCabYB 84; Tel&CabFB 84C*
Tucker County TV Cable System [of Ohio Valley Cable Corp.] - Parsons, WV - *BrCabYB 84; Tel&CabFB 84C*
Tucker County TV Cable System [of Ohio Valley Cable Corp.] - Thomas, WV - *BrCabYB 84*
Tucker Wayne & Co. - Atlanta, GA - *AdAge 3-28-84; ArtMar 84; BrCabYB 84; StaDirAdAg 2-84*

Tuckerman Record - Tuckerman, AR - *BaconPubCkNews 84; Ed&PubIntYB 82*
Tuckerman TV Cable Inc. [of TCA Cable TV Inc.] - Tuckerman, AR - *Tel&CabFB 84C*
Tuckerton Times-Beacon - Manahawakin, NJ - *BaconPubCkNews 84*
Tucson Arizona Daily Star - Tucson, AZ - *NewsDir 84*
Tucson Arizona Territorial - *See* Territorial Publishers Inc.
Tucson Citizen [of Gannett Co. Inc.] - Tucson, AZ - *BaconPubCkNews 84; Ed&PubIntYB 82; NewsDir 84*
Tucson Daily Territorial - Tucson, AZ - *BaconPubCkNews 84*
Tucson Desert Airman - *See* Territorial Publishers Inc.
Tucson Estates Cable TV System [of Mobilife Corp.] - Tucson Estates, AZ - *Tel&CabFB 84C*
Tucson Estates Inc. - Tucson Estates, AZ - *BrCabYB 84*
Tucson Magazine - Tucson, AZ - *MagDir 84*
Tucson Newspapers Inc. - Tucson, AZ - *Ed&PubIntYB 82*
Tucumcari Quay County Sun - Tucumcari, NM - *BaconPubCkNews 84*
Tudor, Dean [of Ryerson Polytechnical Institution] - Toronto, ON, Canada - *FBInfSer 80*
Tuff Turkey Toons Inc. - Encino, CA - *BillIntBG 83-84*
Tuffy Books Inc. - New York, NY - *LitMarPl 83, 84*
Tujunga Record-Ledger - Tujunga, CA - *BaconPubCkNews 84*
Tulane University (Center for Business History Studies) - New Orleans, LA - *BoPubDir 4, 5*
Tulane University (Louisiana Conference on Hispanic Languages & Literatures) - New Orleans, LA - *BoPubDir 5*
Tulane University (Middle American Research Institute) - New Orleans, LA - *BoPubDir 4, 5*
Tulane University (Tulane Studies in Political Science) - New Orleans, LA - *BoPubDir 4, 5*
Tulare Advance-Register - Tulare, CA - *NewsDir 84*
Tulare Advance-Register & Times - Tulare, CA - *BaconPubCkNews 84*
Tulare & Kings County Times Weekly - Visalia, CA - *AyerDirPub 83*
Tulare Communications Corp. - Exeter, CA - *Tel&CabFB 84C*
Tulatin Times - *See* Times Publishing Co.
Tulchin Studios - New York, NY - *AvMarPl 83*
Tulelake Reporter - Tulelake, CA - *BaconPubCkNews 84; Ed&PubIntYB 82*
Tulia Cable Television - Tulia, TX - *BrCabYB 84; Tel&CabFB 84C*
Tulia Herald - Tulia, TX - *AyerDirPub 83; BaconPubCkNews 84; Ed&PubIntYB 82*
Tulip Press - Truckee, CA - *BoPubDir 5*
Tull Tracing/By the Mill Born - Cockeysville, MD - *LitMag&SmPr 83-84*
Tullahoma News - Tullahoma, TN - *BaconPubCkNews 84; Ed&PubIntYB 82*
Tully Independent - Tully, NY - *Ed&PubIntYB 82*
Tully-Menard Inc. - Tampa, FL - *StaDirAdAg 2-84*
Tulsa [of University of Tulsa] - Tulsa, OK - *ArtMar 84; BaconPubCkMag 84; DataDirOnSer 84; DirOnDB Spring 84; WritMar 84*
Tulsa Business Chronicle - Tulsa, OK - *BaconPubCkMag 84*
Tulsa Cable Television Inc. [of United Cable Television Corp.] - Tulsa, OK - *BrCabYB 84; HomeVid&CabYB 82-83; Tel&CabFB 84C*
Tulsa City-County Library (INFO 11) - Tulsa, OK - *DataDirOnSer 84*
Tulsa County News [of Tulsa Retherford Publications Inc.] - Tulsa, OK - *AyerDirPub 83; BaconPubCkNews 84; Ed&PubIntYB 82; NewsDir 84*
Tulsa Daily Legal News - Tulsa, OK - *Ed&PubIntYB 82*
Tulsa Fact - Tulsa, OK - *NewsDir 84*
Tulsa Genealogical Society - Tulsa, OK - *BoPubDir 4, 5*
Tulsa Oklahoma Eagle - Tulsa, OK - *BaconPubCkNews 84; NewsDir 84*
Tulsa Paper [Div. of The Mead Corp.] - Tulsa, OK - *MagIndMarPl 82-83*
Tulsa Southside Times - Tulsa, OK - *NewsDir 84*
Tulsa Star - Tulsa, OK - *NewsDir 84*
Tulsa Studies in Women's Literature - Tulsa, OK - *LitMag&SmPr 83-84*
Tulsa Surveys - Tulsa, OK - *IntDirMarRes 83*
Tulsa Tribune - Tulsa, OK - *BaconPubCkNews 84; Ed&PubIntYB 82; NewsDir 84*
Tulsa World [of World Publishing Co.] - Tulsa, OK - *BaconPubCkNews 84; Ed&PubIntYB 82; LitMarPl 83, 84; NewsBur 6; NewsDir 84; WritMar 84*
Tumbleweed Press Ltd. 1979 - Calgary, AB, Canada - *BoPubDir 4, 5*
Tundra Books of Montreal/Les Livres Toundra - Montreal, PQ, Canada - *LitMarPl 83, 84*
Tundra Books of Northern New York - Plattsburgh, NY - *BoPubDir 5; LitMarPl 83, 84*
Tundra Drums - Bethel, AK - *Ed&PubIntYB 82*
Tundra Telecommunications Systems Inc. - College, AK - *Tel&CabFB 84C*
Tundra Times [of Eskimo, Indian, Aleut Publishing Co.] - Anchorage, AK - *AyerDirPub 83; Ed&PubIntYB 82; NewsDir 84*
Tundra Times - Bush, AK - *Ed&PubIntYB 82*
Tune Room Inc., The - New York, NY - *BillIntBG 83-84*
Tune Wizard Records Inc. - Brooklyn, NY - *BillIntBG 83-84*
Tuned-In Magazine [of Jetpro Inc.] - San Diego, CA - *WritMar 84*
Tuneworks Records Co. - Encino, CA - *BillIntBG 83-84*
Tungsten Forecast - Bala Cynwyd, PA - *DirOnDB Spring 84*
Tunica Times Democrat - Tunica, MS - *BaconPubCkNews 84; Ed&PubIntYB 82*
Tunkhannock New Age-Examiner [of Scranton Times] - Tunkhannock, PA - *BaconPubCkNews 84; NewsDir 84*
Tunks Communications Group - Minneapolis, MN - *StaDirAdAg 2-84*
Tuolumne Cable Vision Inc. [of Viacom International Inc.] - Sonora, CA - *Tel&CabFB 84C*
Tuolumne Telephone Co. [Subs. of CP National Corp.] - Tuolumne, CA - *TelDir&BG 83-84*
Tupelo Community Antenna System [of Comcast Corp.] - Tupelo, MS - *BrCabYB 84; Tel&CabFB 84C*
Tupelo Daily Journal - Tupelo, MS - *NewsDir 84*
Tupper Lake Free Press & Herald [of Tri-Lake Three Press Corp.] - Tupper Lake, NY - *BaconPubCkNews 84; Ed&PubIntYB 82; NewsDir 84*
Turbine Music - *See* Gopam Enterprises Inc.
Turbomachinery International - Norwalk, CT - *BaconPubCkMag 84; MagDir 84*
Turbomachinery International (Publications) - Norwalk, CT - *BoPubDir 4, 5*
Turbomachinery Maintenance Newsletter - Norwalk, CT - *BaconPubCkMag 84*
Turchanik, Ann - Plymouth, PA - *Tel&CabFB 84C p.1709*
Turf & Sport Digest - Baltimore, MD - *ArtMar 84; BaconPubCkMag 84; MagDir 84; MagIndMarPl 82-83*
Turf & Sport International Ltd. - Baltimore, MD - *BoPubDir 4, 5*
Turf-Grass Times - Elm Grove, WI - *MagDir 84*
Turghee Software Labs - Sandy, UT - *MicrocomMPl 83*
Turk Communications Inc. - Alhambra, CA - *DirPRFirms 83*
Turkey Call - Edgefield, SC - *WritMar 84*
Turkey Creek Cable TV [of American Communications & Television Inc.] - Alachua County, FL - *BrCabYB 84*
Turkey Hill Press - Westport, CT - *BoPubDir 5*
Turkey Press - Isla Vista, CA - *BoPubDir 4, 5; LitMag&SmPr 83-84*
Turkey World - Mt. Morris, IL - *BaconPubCkMag 84; MagDir 84*
Turkish Scientific & Technical Documentation Center [of Scientific & Technical Research Council of Turkey] - Ankara, Turkey - *EISS 83*
Turlock Journal - Turlock, CA - *BaconPubCkNews 84; Ed&PubIntYB 82; NewsDir 84*
Turn of the Century Fights Inc. - New York, NY - *TelAl 83, 84*
Turnbull, Elsie G. - Victoria, BC, Canada - *BoPubDir 4 Sup, 5*
Turner & Associates Inc., Harry - Topeka, KS - *StaDirAdAg 2-84*
Turner & Winston - Washington, DC - *LitMarPl 83, 84*
Turner Broadcasting System - Atlanta, GA - *AdAge 6-28-84; BrCabYB 84; HomeVid&CabYB 82-83; KnowInd 83*
Turner Communications Associates Inc. - New York, NY - *DirPRFirms 83*
Turner Inc., Douglas - Newark, NJ - *AdAge 3-28-84; ArtMar 84; DirMarMP 83; StaDirAdAg 2-84*
Turner, Jack P. - Dalton, GA - *Tel&CabFB 84C p.1709*

Turner Publishing Inc. - Washington, DC - *BoPubDir 4, 5*
Turner, Robert E. - Windom, MN - *Tel&CabFB 84C p.1709*
Turner Subscription Agency Inc., The - New York, NY - *MagIndMarPl 82-83*
Turner Warwick Printers Inc. - North Battleford, SK, Canada - *BoPubDir 4, 5*
Turner, William - Welch, WV - *Tel&CabFB 84C p.1709*
TurneRound Productions - Grandville, MI - *BillIntBG 83-84*
Turning Wheel Press - New York, NY - *BoPubDir 4, 5*
Turnkey Interactive Management Systems Inc. - Rutherford, NJ - *ADAPSOMemDir 83-84*
Turnkey Systems Inc. - San Antonio, TX - *WhoWMicrocom 83*
Turnstone Books - Wellingborough, England - *WritMar 84*
Turnstone Press - Winnipeg, MB, Canada - *BoPubDir 4, 5; LitMag&SmPr 83-84*
Turquoise Books - Colorado Springs, CO - *BoPubDir 4, 5*
Turret Publishing - Flushing, NY - *ArtMar 84*
Turtle Bay Institute Inc. - New York, NY - *HBIndAd&MS 82-83; IntDirMarRes 83*
Turtle Island Foundation [Aff. of Netzahaulcoyotl Historical Society] - Berkeley, CA - *BoPubDir 4, 5*
Turtle Island Press - Philadelphia, PA - *BoPubDir 4, 5*
Turtle Lake Cable TV Inc. - Turtle Lake, ND - *BrCabYB 84; Tel&CabFB 84C*
Turtle Lake McLean County Journal - Turtle Lake, ND - *BaconPubCkNews 84*
Turtle Lake Telephone Co. Inc. - Turtle Lake, WI - *TelDir&BG 83-84*
Turtle Lake Times - Turtle Lake, WI - *BaconPubCkNews 84; Ed&PubIntYB 82*
Turtle Lodge Press - Scottsdale, AZ - *BoPubDir 4, 5*
Turtle Magazine for Preschool Kids [of Children's Better Health Institute] - Indianapolis, IN - *ArtMar 84; MagIndMarPl 82-83; WritMar 84*
Turtle Mountain Star - Rolla, ND - *AyerDirPub 83; Ed&PubIntYB 82*
Turtle News [of Young Peoples' Logo Association] - Richardson, TX - *MicrocomMPl 84*
Turtle Press Inc. - New York, NY - *BoPubDir 4, 5*
Turtledove Clemens Inc. - Portland, OR - *StaDirAdAg 2-84*
Turtle's Quill Scriptorium - Mendocino, CA - *BoPubDir 4, 5*
Tusa-McCelloster Publishing Co. - New Orleans, LA - *BoPubDir 5*
Tusan, Stan - Walnut Creek, CA - *LitMarPl 83, 84; MagIndMarPl 82-83*
Tusayan Gospel Ministries Inc. - Phoenix, AZ - *BoPubDir 4, 5*
Tuscaloosa Graphic - Tuscaloosa, AL - *BaconPubCkNews 84*
Tuscaloosa News - Tuscaloosa, AL - *BaconPubCkNews 84; Ed&PubIntYB 82; NewsDir 84*
Tuscola County Advertiser - Caro, MI - *AyerDirPub 83; Ed&PubIntYB 82*
Tuscola Journal - Tuscola, IL - *Ed&PubIntYB 82; NewsDir 84*
Tuscola Review - Tuscola, IL - *BaconPubCkNews 84; Ed&PubIntYB 82; NewsDir 84*
Tuscumbia Autogram Sentinel - Tuscumbia, MO - *BaconPubCkNews 84*
Tuscumbia Colbert County Reporter - Tuscumbia, AL - *BaconPubCkNews 84; NewsDir 84*
Tuskegee Cablevision Co. [of BECE Cable Inc.] - Tuskegee, AL - *BrCabYB 84*
Tuskegee Institute Tuskegeean - Tuskegee, AL - *NewsDir 84*
Tuskegee News - Tuskegee, AL - *BaconPubCkNews 84; Ed&PubIntYB 82; NewsDir 84*
Tustin News - Tustin, CA - *AyerDirPub 83; BaconPubCkNews 84; Ed&PubIntYB 82; NewsDir 84*
Tutch Music Co. - West Redding, CT - *BillIntBG 83-84*
Tutch Music Publishers/Red Kastle Productions - West Redding, CT - *BillIntBG 83-84*
Tuthill's Audio Visual Center [Subs. of Tuthill's Photo Center Inc.] - Binghamton, NY - *AvMarPl 83*
Tutor/Tape - Toms River, NJ - *WritMar 84*
Tutt Music, Scott - Nashville, TN - *BillIntBG 83-84*
Tuttle Co. Inc., Charles E. - Rutland, VT - *BoPubDir 4 Sup, 5; LitMarPl 83, 84*
Tuttle Co. Inc., Charles E. - Tokyo, Japan - *WritMar 84*
Tuttle Crystal Vision, Tom - Santa Barbara, CA - *LitMarPl 84*
Tuttle Times - Tuttle, OK - *Ed&PubIntYB 82*
Tuttle Times - *See* Star Publishing Co.
Tuumba Press - Berkeley, CA - *BoPubDir 4, 5; LitMag&SmPr 83-84*
TV-Airs - Washington, DC - *BrCabYB 84*
TV & Movie Screen - New York, NY - *BaconPubCkMag 84; MagDir 84; MagIndMarPl 82-83*
TV Antenna Service Inc. - Clay, WV - *Tel&CabFB 84C*
TV Antenna Service Inc. - War, WV - *BrCabYB 84 p.D-309*
TV Cable Co. - De Queen, AR - *BrCabYB 84*
TV Cable Co. - Bellevue, IA - *BrCabYB 84*
TV Cable Co. - Burlington, KS - *BrCabYB 84*
TV Cable Co. - Buffalo, OK - *BrCabYB 84*
TV Cable Co. - Cordell, OK - *BrCabYB 84 p.D-309; Tel&CabFB 84C p.1706*
TV Cable Co. - Shattuck, OK - *BrCabYB 84; Tel&CabFB 84C*
TV Cable Co. - Wright City, OK - *BrCabYB 84*
TV Cable Co. - Giddings, TX - *BrCabYB 84*
TV Cable Co. Inc. - Yellville, AR - *BrCabYB 84*
TV Cable Co. Ltd. - Yankeetown, FL - *Tel&CabFB 84C*
TV Cable Co. of Andalusia Inc. - Andalusia, AL - *BrCabYB 84; Tel&CabFB 84C*
TV Cable Co. of Brackettville Inc. - Brackettville, TX - *Tel&CabFB 84C*
TV Cable Co. of Guntersville Inc. [of McDonald Group Inc.] - Guntersville, AL - *BrCabYB 84; Tel&CabFB 84C*
TV Cable Co. of Rensselaer Inc. - Rensselaer, IN - *BrCabYB 84; Tel&CabFB 84C*
TV Cable Corp. - Van Buren, AR - *BrCabYB 84; Tel&CabFB 84C*
TV Cable Corp. - Paintsville, KY - *BrCabYB 84*
TV Cable Corp. - Caledonia, MS - *BrCabYB 84*
TV Cable Inc. - Waynesboro, MS - *BrCabYB 84*
TV Cable Inc. - Maud, TX - *Tel&CabFB 84C*
TV Cable of Baldwin-Jeanerette Inc. - Jeanerette, LA - *BrCabYB 84*
TV Cable of Bellefontaine [of Communications Systems Inc.] - Bellefontaine, OH - *Tel&CabFB 84C*
TV Cable of Bowie Inc. - Bowie, TX - *BrCabYB 84; Tel&CabFB 84C*
TV Cable of Brenham [of Tom S. Whitehead Inc.] - Brenham, TX - *BrCabYB 84; Tel&CabFB 84C*
TV Cable of Bridgeport - Bridgeport, TX - *Tel&CabFB 84C*
TV Cable of Burkburnett [of CATV Systems Inc.] - Burkburnett, TX - *BrCabYB 84; Tel&CabFB 84C*
TV Cable of Carlisle - Carlisle, PA - *BrCabYB 84; Tel&CabFB 84C*
TV Cable of Clyde [of Brownwood TV Cable Service Inc.] - Clyde, TX - *Tel&CabFB 84C*
TV Cable of Clyde - Clyde/Baird, TX - *BrCabYB 84*
TV Cable of Corrigan [of CATV Systems Inc.] - Corrigan, TX - *BrCabYB 84*
TV Cable of Decatur - Decatur, TX - *Tel&CabFB 84C*
TV Cable of Diboll [of Capital Cities Communications Inc.] - Diboll, TX - *BrCabYB 84; Tel&CabFB 84C*
TV Cable of Electra [of Tele-Communications Inc.] - Electra, TX - *Tel&CabFB 84C*
TV Cable of Frisco Inc. [of CATV Systems Inc.] - Frisco, TX - *BrCabYB 84*
TV Cable of Henrietta [of Tele-Communications Inc.] - Henrietta, TX - *Tel&CabFB 84C*
TV Cable of Henryetta Inc. [of Cardiff Cablevision Inc.] - Henryetta, OK - *Tel&CabFB 84C*
TV Cable of Highland Village Inc. [of CATV Systems Inc.] - Highland Village, TX - *BrCabYB 84*
TV Cable of Iowa Park [of Tele-Communications Inc.] - Iowa Park, TX - *BrCabYB 84; Tel&CabFB 84C*
TV Cable of Livingston [of CATV Systems Inc.] - Livingston, TX - *BrCabYB 84; Tel&CabFB 84C*
TV Cable of Quitman Inc. - Quitman, MS - *BrCabYB 84*
TV Cable of Sanger - Sanger, TX - *BrCabYB 84*
TV Cable of Seymour Inc. [of Tele-Communications Inc.] - Seymour, TX - *Tel&CabFB 84C*
TV Cable of Soda Springs - Soda Springs, ID - *BrCabYB 84; Tel&CabFB 84C*
TV Cable of Space City [Aff. of Rogers-UA Cablesystems Inc.] - Alamogordo, NM - *BrCabYB 84; InterCabHB 3*

TV Cable of Tennessee Inc. [of Tele-Communications Inc.] - Manchester, TN - *BrCabYB 84*
TV Cable of The Colony Inc. - The Colony, TX - *BrCabYB 84*
TV Cable of Trinity Inc. - Trinity, TX - *BrCabYB 84; Tel&CabFB 84C*
TV Cable of Vernon [of TCI-Growth Inc.] - Vernon, TX - *BrCabYB 84; Tel&CabFB 84C*
TV Cable of Waynesboro - Waynesboro, PA - *BrCabYB 84; Tel&CabFB 84C*
TV Cable of Winamac Inc. - Winamac, IN - *BrCabYB 84*
TV Cable Service [of Century Communications Corp.] - Ft. Payne, AL - *Tel&CabFB 84C*
TV Cable Service [of Times Mirror Cable TV] - Toronto, OH - *Tel&CabFB 84C*
TV Cable Service - Rauchtown, PA - *BrCabYB 84; Tel&CabFB 84C*
TV Cable Service - Comanche, TX - *BrCabYB 84; Tel&CabFB 84C*
TV Cable Service [of Times Mirror Cable TV] - Weirton, WV - *Tel&CabFB 84C*
TV Cable System Inc. [of Times Mirror Cable TV] - Cambridge, OH - *Tel&CabFB 84C*
TV Cable Week - Chicago, IL - *BaconPubCkMag 84*
TV Cinema Sales Corp. - Beverly Hills, CA - *Tel&CabFB 84C*
TV Compulog Services Inc. - Farmingdale, NY - *Ed&PubIntYB 82*
TV Data Inc. - Glens Falls, NY - *Ed&PubIntYB 82*
TV Enterprises Inc. - Brady, TX - *BrCabYB 84 p.D-308; Tel&CabFB 84C p.1706*
TV Enterprises Inc. - Eden, TX - *BrCabYB 84; Tel&CabFB 84C*
TV Enterprises Inc. - Eldorado, TX - *BrCabYB 84*
TV Enterprises Inc. - Junction, TX - *Tel&CabFB 84C*
TV Enterprises Inc. - Menard, TX - *BrCabYB 84*
TV Enterprises Inc. - Sonora, TX - *BrCabYB 84; Tel&CabFB 84C*
TV Extension Corp. [of Service Electric Cable TV Inc.] - Coal Township, PA - *BrCabYB 84; Tel&CabFB 84C*
TV Gems Inc. - Hollywood, CA - *Tel&CabFB 84C*
TV Guide [of Triangle Publications Inc.] - Radnor, PA - *ArtMar 84; BaconPubCkMag 84; Folio 83; LitMarPl 83, 84; MagIndMarPl 82-83; MicroMarPl 82-83; NewsBur 6; WritMar 84*
TV Guide - Toronto, ON, Canada - *WritMar 84*
TV Horizons Inc. [of Peoples Consolidated Communications Services Inc.] - Cambria, WI - *Tel&CabFB 84C*
TV Horizons Inc. [of Peoples Consolidated Communications Services Inc.] - Randolph, WI - *Tel&CabFB 84C*
TV Horizons Inc. [of Peoples Consolidated Communications Services Inc.] - Rio, WI - *Tel&CabFB 84C*
TV News - Los Angeles, CA - *Ed&PubIntYB 82*
TV Picture Life - New York, NY - *MagDir 84; WritMar 84*
TV Pix Inc. [of Tele-Communications Inc.] - South Lake Tahoe, CA - *BrCabYB 84*
TV Pix Inc. [of Community Tele-Communications Inc.] - Elko, NV - *BrCabYB 84; Tel&CabFB 84C*
TV Power of North County Inc. [of Community Tele-Communications Inc.] - Oceanside, CA - *Tel&CabFB 84C*
TV-R Inc. - New York, NY - *AvMarPl 83*
TV Reception Specialists - Houston, TX - *TeleSy&SerDir 2-84*
TV Selection System Inc. [of Comcast Corp.] - Meridian, MS - *BrCabYB 84; Tel&CabFB 84C*
TV Service Cable Inc. - Hindman, KY - *BrCabYB 84*
TV Service Cable Inc. - Wayland, KY - *Tel&CabFB 84C*
TV Service Co. [of Service Electric Cable TV Inc.] - Birdsboro, PA - *BrCabYB 84*
TV Service Co. [of Service Electric Cable TV Inc.] - Reading, PA - *BrCabYB 84*
TV Service Inc. - Wayland, KY - *BrCabYB 84*
TV Signal Service - Paducah, TX - *BrCabYB 84; Tel&CabFB 84C*
TV Signal Service Co. - Charlotte, NC - *Tel&CabFB 84C*
TV Signal Service Co. - Crowell, TX - *BrCabYB 84; Tel&CabFB 84C*
TV Sports Scene Inc. - Minneapolis, MN - *BrCabYB 84; Tel&CabFB 84C*
TV Systems Inc. - Honolulu, HI - *Tel&CabFB 84C*
TV Systems Inc. - Honolulu County, HI - *BrCabYB 84*
TV Time & Channel [of Cable Communications Media Inc.] - Lehigh Valley, PA - *WritMar 84*
TV Transmission Inc. [of MetroVision Inc.] - Crete, NE - *BrCabYB 84; Tel&CabFB 84C*
TV Transmission Inc. [of MetroVision Inc.] - David City, NE - *BrCabYB 84; Tel&CabFB 84C*
TV Transmission Inc. [of Metrovision Inc.] - Fairbury, NE - *BrCabYB 84*
TV Transmission Inc. [of MetroVision Inc.] - Lincoln, NE - *BrCabYB 84*
TV Transmission Inc. [of Metrovision Inc.] - Nebraska City, NE - *BrCabYB 84*
TV Transmission Inc. [of Metrovision Inc.] - Pawnee City, NE - *BrCabYB 84*
TV Transmission Inc. [of MetroVision Inc.] - Seward, NE - *BrCabYB 84; Tel&CabFB 84C*
TV2S - Friday Harbor, WA - *Tel&CabFB 84C*
TV Watch Inc. - Atlanta, GA - *Ed&PubIntYB 82*
TVA - Montreal, PQ, Canada - *BrCabYB 84*
TVC Video [Div. of TVC Image Technology Inc.] - New York, NY - *AvMarPl 83*
TVEC - Montreal, PQ, Canada - *BrCabYB 84*
TVIQ Inc. - Eagle Grove, IA - *BrCabYB 84; Tel&CabFB 84C*
TVOntario - Toronto, ON, Canada - *VideoDir 82-83*
TVQ [of Marketing Evaluations Inc.] - Port Washington, NY - *BrCabYB 84*
TVQ Ratings Services - Port Washington, NY - *Tel&CabFB 84C*
T.V.R.C. Corp. - New York, NY - *StaDirAdAg 2-84*
TVRT Press - New York, NY - *BoPubDir 4, 5*
TVS Television Network - New York, NY - *BrCabYB 84; TelAl 83, 84; Tel&CabFB 84C*
TW Communications Corp. - Great Neck, NY - *DataDirSup 7-83*
TWA Air Freight - Jamaica, NY - *MagIndMarPl 82-83*
TWA Ambassador [of The Webb Co.] - St. Paul, MN - *BaconPubCkMag 84; Folio 83; MagDir 84; MagIndMarPl 82-83*
Twain Rural Telephone Co., Mark - Hurland, MO - *TelDir&BG 83-84*
Twainland Enterprise - Perry, MO - *AyerDirPub 83*
Twayne Publishers [Div. of G. K. Hall & Co.] - Boston, MA - *LitMarPl 83, 84; WritMar 84*
TWC Entertainment Corp. - New York, NY - *BillIntBG 83-84*
Tweed News - Tweed, ON, Canada - *Ed&PubIntYB 82*
1245 News, The - Little Falls, NJ - *NewsDir 84*
12 Seconds of Laughter - Indianapolis, IN - *LitMag&SmPr 83-84; WritMar 84*
1262 Banner - Clifton, NJ - *NewsDir 84*
Twelvetrees Press - Pasadena, CA - *BoPubDir 4, 5*
Tweney, George H. - Seattle, WA - *LitMarPl 83, 84*
Twentieth Century Books [Aff. of Automated Reproductions Inc.] - New York, NY - *BoPubDir 4, 5*
Twentieth Century-Fox Film Corp. - Los Angeles, CA - *KnowInd 83*
Twentieth Century-Fox Film Corp. - New York, NY - *LitMarPl 83*
Twentieth Century-Fox Telecommunications - Beverly Hills, CA - *TelAl 83; Tel&CabFB 84C*
Twentieth Century-Fox Television [Div. of Twentieth Century-Fox Film Corp.] - Beverly Hills, CA - *TelAl 83, 84; Tel&CabFB 84C*
Twentieth Century-Fox Television Inc. [Div. of Twentieth Century-Fox Film Corp.] - Los Angeles, CA - *TelAl 83, 84*
Twentieth Century-Fox Television International Inc. - Beverly Hills, CA - *Tel&CabFB 84C*
Twentieth Century Labour Publications - Oakville, ON, Canada - *BoPubDir 4 Sup, 5*
Twenty CATV Inc. [of Tele-Communications Inc.] - Carrollton, GA - *BrCabYB 84; Tel&CabFB 84C*
25th Street Theatre - Saskatoon, SK, Canada - *WritMar 84*
Twenty Fifty Consultants Ltd. - Watlington, England - *MicrocomSwDir 1*
Twenty-First Century Publications - Fairfield, IA - *BoPubDir 4 Sup, 5; LitMag&SmPr 83-84*
2588 Newport Corp. - Los Angeles, CA - *BrCabYB 84*
2500 A.D. Software Inc. - Aurora, CO - *MicrocomMPl 83*
21 North Advertising - Phoenix, AZ - *StaDirAdAg 2-84*
21 Records Inc. - New York, NY - *BillIntBG 83-84*

Twenty-Third Publications - Mystic, CT - *BoPubDir 4; LitMarPl 83, 84; WritMar 84*
23 Club Series [of Intrepid Press] - Buffalo, NY - *LitMag&SmPr 83-84*
20/20 - New York, NY - *BaconPubCkMag 84; MagDir 84*
20/20 Services Inc. - New York, NY - *MagIndMarPl 82-83*
22 Press - Wilmington, DE - *LitMag&SmPr 83-84*
2227 News [of Pilgrim Press] - West Mifflin, PA - *NewsDir 84*
Twenty Year Forecast Project [of University of Southern California] - Los Angeles, CA - *EISS 83*
Twentynine Palms Desert Trail [of Hi Desert Publishing Co.] - Twentynine Palms, CA - *BaconPubCkNews 84*
Twesten, Gary - Millstadt, IL - *BoPubDir 4, 5*
Twickenham Press - New York, NY - *BoPubDir 4, 5; LitMag&SmPr 83-84*
Twiddy Advertising Inc., R. & J. - Riverside, CT - *StaDirAdAg 2-84*
Twiford Music - Phoenix, AZ - *BillIntBG 83-84*
Twiggs County New Era - Jeffersonville, GA - *AyerDirPub 83; Ed&PubIntYB 82*
Twilight City Music Publishers - *See* Songsellers Co.
Twin-Boro News - Bergenfield, NJ - *AyerDirPub 83; Ed&PubIntYB 82*
Twin Circle - Los Angeles, CA - *BaconPubCkMag 84; MagDir 84; WritMar 84*
Twin Cities - Minneapolis, MN - *BaconPubCkMag 84*
Twin Cities Cable - Batesburg, SC - *Tel&CabFB 84C*
Twin Cities Cable TV Co. [of Horizon Communications Corp.] - Henderson, KY - *Tel&CabFB 84C*
Twin Cities Courier - Minneapolis, MN - *AyerDirPub 83; Ed&PubIntYB 82*
Twin Cities News - Rochester, TX - *Ed&PubIntYB 82*
Twin Cities Reader - Minneapolis, MN - *AyerDirPub 83*
Twin Cities Times - Corte Madera, CA - *AyerDirPub 83; Ed&PubIntYB 82*
Twin City Cable TV Inc. [of TCA Cable TV Inc.] - Helena, AR - *Tel&CabFB 84C*
Twin City Cable TV Inc. - Marble Hill, MO - *BrCabYB 84; Tel&CabFB 84C*
Twin City Journal-Reporter - Gas City, IN - *AyerDirPub 83; Ed&PubIntYB 82*
Twin City News - Chattahoochee, FL - *AyerDirPub 83; Ed&PubIntYB 82*
Twin City-News, The - Batesburg, SC - *AyerDirPub 83; Ed&PubIntYB 82*
Twin City Post - Clarks, NE - *Ed&PubIntYB 82*
Twin City Post - Palmer, NE - *AyerDirPub 83*
Twin City Trade Lines - Eau Claire, MI - *AyerDirPub 83*
Twin City Tribune - West Helena, AR - *Ed&PubIntYB 82*
Twin County Cablevision - Quitman, MS - *Tel&CabFB 84C*
Twin County Cablevision - Waynesboro, MS - *Tel&CabFB 84C*
Twin County Trans-Video Inc. - Northampton, PA - *BrCabYB 84; Tel&CabFB 84C*
Twin Falls Times-News [of Howard Publications Inc.] - Twin Falls, ID - *BaconPubCkNews 84; NewsDir 84*
Twin Lakes Cable TV - Sweetwater, TN - *Tel&CabFB 84C p.1709*
Twin Lakes Shopper - Mountain Home, AR - *AyerDirPub 83*
Twin Lakes Telephone Cooperative - Gainesboro, TN - *TelDir&BG 83-84*
Twin Lakes Television Corp. - Berryville, AR - *BrCabYB 84; Tel&CabFB 84C*
Twin Lakes Television Corp. - Diamond City, AR - *BrCabYB 84*
Twin Lakes Television Corp. - Harrison, AR - *BrCabYB 84 p.D-309; Tel&CabFB 84C p.1709*
Twin Lakes Westosha Report - Twin Lakes, WI - *NewsDir 84*
Twin Lakes Westosha Report - *See* Zimmermann & Sons Inc.
Twin State Cable TV Inc. [of TCI-Taft Cablevision Associates] - Lebanon, NH - *BrCabYB 84; Tel&CabFB 84C*
Twin Tier Data Services Inc. - Big Flats, NY - *WhoWMicrocom 83*
Twin Valley Cable TV - Newport, NH - *Tel&CabFB 84C*
Twin Valley Cablevision Inc. - Germantown, OH - *BrCabYB 84; Tel&CabFB 84C*
Twin Valley CATV Inc. [of Comcast Corp.] - Hillsdale, MI - *BrCabYB 84; Tel&CabFB 84C*
Twin Valley News - West Alexandria, OH - *Ed&PubIntYB 82*
Twin Valley Publishers Inc. - Greene, NY - *BaconPubCkNews 84*
Twin Valley Telephone Inc. - Miltonvale, KS - *TelDir&BG 83-84*
Twin Valley Times & Gary Graphic - Twin Valley, MN - *BaconPubCkNews 84*
Twin Valley Times, The - Twin Valley, MN - *Ed&PubIntYB 82*
Twin Valley TV Inc. - Newport, NH - *BrCabYB 84*
Twin Valley TV Inc. - Sunapee, NH - *BrCabYB 84*
Twin Valley-Ulen Telephone Co. [Aff. of Herold Investment Inc.] - Twin Valley, MN - *TelDir&BG 83-84*
Twin Village Cable Co. Inc. [of Basil Cable Systems Inc.] - Milton-Freewater, OR - *BrCabYB 84; Tel&CabFB 84C*
Twin W Communications Co. - Detroit, MI - *BrCabYB 84*
Twining Telephone Co. - Twining, MI - *TelDir&BG 83-84*
Twinsburg Bulletin - Twinsburg, OH - *BaconPubCkNews 84*
Twisp Methow Valley News - Twisp, WA - *BaconPubCkNews 84*
Twitty Bird Music Publishing Co. - Nashville, TN - *BillIntBG 83-84*
Two Acre Publications - Lower West Pubnico, NS, Canada - *BoPubDir 4 Sup, 5*
2-Bit Software - Del Mar, CA - *MicrocomMPl 84*
2D Publications - Leicester, England - *LitMag&SmPr 83-84*
Two-Eighteen Press - New York, NY - *BoPubDir 4, 5; LitMag&SmPr 83-84*
Two Fifty Nine Music - Richmond, VA - *BillIntBG 83-84*
Two Harbors Lake County News-Chronicle - Two Harbors, MN - *BaconPubCkNews 84*
Two Horses Press - Tucson, AZ - *BoPubDir 4, 5*
2M - New York, NY - *LitMarPl 84*
Two M Cablevision Inc. - Bainbridge, OH - *BrCabYB 84; Tel&CabFB 84C*
2-Mac Records - Tucker, GA - *BillIntBG 83-84*
Two Magpie Press - Kendrick, ID - *LitMag&SmPr 83-84*
Two Minute Mystery Series - South Miami, FL - *Ed&PubIntYB 82*
Two Riders Press - Chestnut Hill, MA - *BoPubDir 4, 5*
Two Rivers Lakeshore Chronicle - Two Rivers, WI - *BaconPubCkNews 84*
Two Rivers Press - Aurora, OR - *BoPubDir 4, 5*
Two Sisters Music - *See* Mighty Matthew Music
Two/Sixteen [of NewsNet Inc.] - Bryn Mawr, PA - *DataDirOnSer 84*
Two/Sixteen - Lancaster, PA - *MicrocomMPl 84*
Two/Sixteen - *See* Advanced Computing
Two Star Record - Roselle, IL - *AyerDirPub 83*
2001 Colorcepts Inc. - New York, NY - *LitMarPl 84*
2001 Page Creation Corp. - Willowdale, ON, Canada - *VideoDir 82-83*
212 Music Co. - *See* Entertainment Co. Music Group, The
2 UT Music - *See* Iguana Music Inc.
Two-Way Radio Dealer - Denver, CO - *BaconPubCkMag 84; WritMar 84*
Two-Way Radio of Carolina Inc. - Charlotte, NC - *Tel&CabFB 84C*
Two Zee's Enterprises Inc. - Ft. Lee, NJ - *BoPubDir 4 Sup, 5*
TWS Inc. - Houston, TX - *DataDirOnSer 84*
TWU Express [of TWUA, AFL-CIO] - New York, NY - *NewsDir 84*
Twyman Films Inc. - Dayton, OH - *AvMarPl 83; TelAl 83, 84*
Tybee Cable TV Inc. [of US Cable Corp.] - Tybee Island, GA - *BrCabYB 84; Tel&CabFB 84C*
TYC Software - Geneseo, NY - *MicrocomMPl 83*
Tycer-Fultz-Bellack - Palo Alto, CA - *AdAge 3-28-84; StaDirAdAg 2-84*
TYCOM Associates - Pittsfield, MA - *MicrocomMPl 83, 84; MicrocomSwDir 1*
Tygart Valley Cable Corp. - Elkins, WV - *BrCabYB 84; Tel&CabFB 84C*
Tygart Valley Telephone Co. [Aff. of Mid-Continent Telephone Corp.] - Mill Creek, WV - *TelDir&BG 83-84*
Tyler, Bill - Olney, TX - *Tel&CabFB 84C p.1709*
Tyler Business Systems - Largo, FL - *MicrocomSwDir 1*
Tyler County Booster - Woodville, TX - *Ed&PubIntYB 82*
Tyler County Journal - Sistersville, WV - *AyerDirPub 83; Ed&PubIntYB 82*
Tyler Courier-Times [of T. B. Butler Publishing Co.] - Tyler, TX - *BaconPubCkNews 84; Ed&PubIntYB 82; LitMarPl 83, 84*

Tyler Courier-Times-Telegraph [of T. B. Butler Publishing Co.] - Tyler, TX - *Ed&PubIntYB 82; LitMarPl 83, 84*
Tyler Morning Telegraph [of T. B. Butler Publishing Co. Inc.] - Tyler, TX - *BaconPubCkNews 84; Ed&PubIntYB 82; LitMarPl 83, 84; NewsDir 84*
Tyler Publishing Co. - Tyler, TX - *BillIntBG 83-84*
Tyler, R. H. - Olney, TX - *Tel&CabFB 84C p.1709*
Tyler Research/Supervision - Forest Hills, NY - *IntDirMarRes 83*
Tyler Star-News - Sistersville, WV - *AyerDirPub 83*
Tyler Tribute - Tyler, MN - *BaconPubCkNews 84; Ed&PubIntYB 82*
Tylertown Cable TV Co. - Tylertown, MS - *BrCabYB 84; Tel&CabFB 84C*
Tylertown Times - Tylertown, MS - *BaconPubCkNews 84; Ed&PubIntYB 82; NewsDir 84*
Tylog Systems Inc. - Miami, FL - *MicrocomMPl 84*
Tymena Music - Pittsburgh, PA - *BillIntBG 83-84*
Tymer Music - Carlsbad, CA - *BillIntBG 83-84*
Tymnet [of Tymshare Inc.] - Cupertino, CA - *InfIndMarPl 83*
Tymnet Inc. [of Tymshare Inc.] - San Jose, CA - *DataDirOnSer 84; DataDirSup 7-83; TeleSy&SerDir 7-83, 2-84*
Tymquote Securities Database [of Tymshare Inc.] - Cupertino, CA - *DataDirOnSer 84*
Tymshare Inc. - Cupertino, CA - *ADAPSOMemDir 83-84; DataDirOnSer 84; DataDirSup 7-83; Datamation 6-83; EISS 83; HomeVid&CabYB 82-83; InfIndMarPl 83; Top100Al 83; VideoDir 82-83*
Tymshare Inc. - *See* Microband Corp. of America
Tyndale House Publishers - Wheaton, IL - *ArtMar 84; LitMarPl 83, 84; WritMar 84*
Tyndall Cablevision [of Southern Communications & Service Co. Inc.] - Tyndall Air Force Base, FL - *Tel&CabFB 84C*
Tyndall Tribune & Register - Tyndall, SD - *BaconPubCkNews 84*
Tyner International Inc., Harrison - Nashville, TN - *BillIntBG 83-84*
Tyner Music - *See* Tyner International Inc., Harrison
Tyomies-Eteenpain - Superior, WI - *Ed&PubIntYB 82*
Tyoweronh Arts & Publishing Ltd. - Paris, ON, Canada - *BoPubDir 4 Sup, 5*
Type Aids Co., The - San Rafael, CA - *LitMarPl 83*
Type & Press [of Press of the Golden Unicorn] - Hayward, CA - *LitMag&SmPr 83-84*
Type-O-Graphics - Springfield, MO - *MagIndMarPl 82-83*
Type-Share Inc. - Downey, CA - *MicrocomMPl 83, 84*
Type Yourself - Toronto, ON, Canada - *BoPubDir 4 Sup, 5*
TypeWorld Exhibits - Wilmington, MA - *BaconPubCkMag 84; MagDir 84; MagIndMarPl 82-83*
Typewriter [of Bird in the Bush] - Iowa City, IA - *LitMag&SmPr 83-84*
Typing by Nan - Southfield, MI - *LitMarPl 83, 84*
Typing Unltd. - New York, NY - *LitMarPl 83, 84; MagIndMarPl 82-83*
Typo Graphic Innovations Inc. - New York, NY - *MagIndMarPl 82-83*
Typofax - Norfolk, VA - *NewsDir 84*
Typographer, The - Washington, DC - *BaconPubCkMag 84; WritMar 84*
Typographeum Bookshop - Francestown, NH - *BoPubDir 4, 5*
Typographic Designers Inc. - New York, NY - *LitMarPl 83, 84*
Typographic Innovations Inc. - New York, NY - *LitMarPl 83, 84*
Typographic Sales Inc. - St. Louis, MO - *LitMarPl 83, 84; MagIndMarPl 82-83*
Typographic Services Inc. - Effingham, IL - *MagIndMarPl 82-83*
Typographica - Brea, CA - *LitMarPl 83, 84*
Typographical Journal - Colorado Springs, CO - *BaconPubCkMag 84; MagDir 84; NewsDir 84*
Typographical Union No. 6 Bulletin [of New York Typographical Union No. 6] - New York, NY - *NewsDir 84*
Typographics Communications Inc. - New York, NY - *LitMarPl 83, 84*
Typography Systems International Inc. - Dallas, TX - *DirInfWP 82*
Typoservice Corp. - Indianapolis, IN - *LitMarPl 83, 84*
Tyree & Gardner Inc. - New York, NY - *StaDirAdAg 2-84*
Tyrone Herald - Tyrone, PA - *AyerDirPub 83; BaconPubCkNews 84; Ed&PubIntYB 82; NewsDir 84*
Tyscot Music - *See* Clark Publishing
Tyscot Records Inc. - Indianapolis, IN - *BillIntBG 83-84*
Tyson Associates Inc. - Stamford, CT - *StaDirAdAg 2-84*

U

U & LC [of International Typeface Corp.] - New York, NY - *BaconPubCkMag 84; LitMarPl 83, 84; MagDir 84; MagIndMarPl 82-83*
U-B Newspaper Syndicate - Van Nuys, CA - *Ed&PubIntYB 82*
UA Cablesystems Corp. - *See* United Artists Cablesystems Corp.
UA-Columbia Cablevision - Westport, CT - *KnowInd 83; LitMarPl 84*
UA-Columbia Cablevision of Massachusetts [of Rogers UA Cablesystems Inc.] - North Attleboro, MA - *BrCabYB 84*
UA-Columbia Cablevision of Massachusetts [of Rogers UA Cablesystems Inc.] - Taunton, MA - *BrCabYB 84; Tel&CabFB 84C*
UA-Columbia Cablevision of Texas Inc. [of Rogers UA Cablesystems Inc.] - San Antonio, TX - *BrCabYB 84; InterCabHB 3*
UA-Columbia Cablevision of Westchester Inc. [of Rogers UA Cablesystems Corp.] - New Rochelle, NY - *BrCabYB 84; Tel&CabFB 84C*
U.A. Journal - Washington, DC - *BaconPubCkMag 84; NewsDir 84*
UARCO Computer Supplies - De Kalb, IL - *DirInfWP 82*
UARCO Inc. [Subs. of City Investing Co.] - Barrington, IL - *DataDirSup 7-83; DirInfWP 82; WhoWMicrocom 83*
UARCO Inc. - De Kalb, IL - *MicrocomMPl 83*
UC Color Lab Inc. - Chicago, IL - *AvMarPl 83*
UCA Telecable Inc. - Portland, MI - *BrCabYB 84*
Uchill, Ida Libert - Denver, CO - *BoPubDir 4, 5*
U.C.I. - Berwyn, PA - *DataDirSup 7-83*
UCLA - San Francisco, CA - *MagDir 84*
UCLA Business Forcasting Project [of University of California, Los Angeles] - Los Angeles, CA - *EISS 83*
UCLA Daily Bruin [of Associated Students UCLA-Communications Board] - Los Angeles, CA - *NewsDir 84*
Ucluelet Video Services Ltd. - Port Alberni, BC, Canada - *BrCabYB 84*
UCSB Daily Nexus [of University of California] - Santa Barbara, CA - *NewsDir 84*
UCSD Guardian, The - Warner Spring, CA - *NewsDir 84*
UEA Action - Salt Lake City, UT - *MagDir 84*
UFCW Action [of United Food & Commercial Workers Union] - Washington, DC - *BaconPubCkMag 84; MagDir 84; NewsDir 84*
UFCW Reporter [of UFCW Local 27] - Baltimore, MD - *NewsDir 84*
UFO Information Retrieval Center Inc. - Riderwood, MD - *EISS 83*
UFO Review [of Global Communications] - New York, NY - *WritMar 84*
UHDE Thermophysical Properties Program Package [of UHDE GmbH] - Dortmund, West Germany - *EISS 83*
Uhlenkott, Abe - Cottonwood, ID - *Tel&CabFB 84C p.1709*
Uhler Cine Machine Co. - Detroit, MI - *AvMarPl 83*
Uhl's Publishing Co. - Spencer, NY - *BoPubDir 5*
Uhrichsville-Dennison Chronicle [of Twin City Publishing Co.] - Uhrichsville, OH - *NewsDir 84*
Uinta Cable [of Cable West Corp.] - Lyman, WY - *Tel&CabFB 84C*
Uinta County Herald - Evanston, WY - *AyerDirPub 83; Ed&PubIntYB 82*
Uintah Basin Standard - Roosevelt, UT - *AyerDirPub 83; Ed&PubIntYB 82; NewsDir 84*
Uintah Basin Telephone Association Inc. - Roosevelt, UT - *TelDir&BG 83-84*
UIU Journal [of Upholsterers' International Union of N.A.] - Philadelphia, PA - *NewsDir 84*
UK Online User Group [of Institute of Information Scientists] - Reading, England - *InfIndMarPl 83*
UK Records Inc. - New York, NY - *BillIntBG 83-84*
UK Treasury - London, England - *DirOnDB Spring 84*
UK Treasury Macroeconomic Forecasting Model & Databank - London, England - *EISS 83*
Ukiah Daily Journal [of Mendocino Publishing Co.] - Ukiah, CA - *BaconPubCkNews 84; Ed&PubIntYB 82; NewsDir 84*
UKMARC [of British Library] - London, England - *CompReadDB 82; DirOnDB Spring 84; OnBibDB 3*
Ukrainian Museum of Canada [Aff. of Ukrainian Women's Association of Canada] - Saskatoon, SK, Canada - *BoPubDir 4, 5*
Ukrainian Women's Association of Canada [Aff. of Ukrainian Self-Reliance League] - Edmonton, AB, Canada - *BoPubDir 4 Sup, 5*
Ukrainske Narodne Slovo - Pittsburgh, PA - *Ed&PubIntYB 82*
Ukrainske Zhittia - Chicago, IL - *Ed&PubIntYB 82*
Ukrainski Visti - Edmonton, AB, Canada - *Ed&PubIntYB 82*
Ukrainsky Holos - Winnipeg, MB, Canada - *Ed&PubIntYB 82*
Ule & Co. Inc., Max - New York, NY - *MicrocomMPl 83, 84; WhoWMicrocom 83*
Ulen Union - Ulen, MN - *BaconPubCkNews 84; Ed&PubIntYB 82*
ULI/Urban Land Institute - Washington, DC - *BoPubDir 5; DirMarMP 83*
Ullman Organization, The - Philadelphia, PA - *StaDirAdAg 2-84*
Ulrich Consulting, Walter E. - Houston, TX - *ADAPSOMemDir 83-84*
Ulrich's Books Inc. - Ann Arbor, MI - *BoPubDir 4, 5*
Ulrich's International Periodicals Directory [of R. R. Bowker Co.] - Latham, NY - *DataDirOnSer 84*
Ulrich's International Periodicals Directory [of R. R. Bowker Co.] - New York, NY - *DBBus 82; DirOnDB Spring 84; OnBibDB 3*
Ulrich's International Periodicals Directory Data Base [of R. R. Bowker Co.] - New York, NY - *EISS 83*
Ulster County Townsman - Woodstock, NY - *AyerDirPub 83; Ed&PubIntYB 82*
Ulster Offset Corp. - New Paltz, NY - *BaconPubCkNews 84*
Ultima Corp. of West Palm Beach - West Palm Beach, FL - *BoPubDir 5*
Ultima Thule Music Publishing Co. - Sacramento, CA - *BillIntBG 83-84*
Ultimate Computer Systems Inc. - Hastings, MI - *MicrocomMPl 84*

Ultimate Records Music Publishing - San Jose, CA - *BillIntBG 83-84*
Ultimate Support Systems - Ft. Collins, CO - *AvMarPl 83*
Ultimedia Television - Fair Lawn, NJ - *HomeVid&CabYB 82-83*
Ultra [of Farb Publications Inc.] - Houston, TX - *BaconPubCkMag 84; WritMar 84*
Ultra Com of Gatlinburg Inc. - Gatlinburg, TN - *BrCabYB 84*
Ultra Com of Marple Inc. - Marple Township, PA - *BrCabYB 84*
Ultra-Vision Tele-Cable Engineering - Anse St. Jean, PQ, Canada - *BrCabYB 84*
Ultra-Vision Tele-Cable Engineering [of J. H. Duchesne Ltee.] - Petit Sagvenay, PQ, Canada - *BrCabYB 84*
Ultracom Inc. - Lansdale, PA - *BrCabYB 84 p.D-309; Tel&CabFB 84C p.1709*
Ultracom of Blanchester - Blanchester, OH - *BrCabYB 84; Tel&CabFB 84C*
Ultracom of Dade County Inc. - Miami Beach, FL - *BrCabYB 84*
Ultracom of Gatlinburg Inc. - Gatlinburg, TN - *Tel&CabFB 84C*
Ultracom of Haverford Inc. - Haverford, PA - *BrCabYB 84*
Ultracom of Lansdale Inc. - Lansdale, PA - *BrCabYB 84; Tel&CabFB 84C*
Ultracom of Montgomery County Inc. - North Wales, PA - *BrCabYB 84*
Ultracom of Pigeon Forge Inc. - Pigeon Forge, TN - *BrCabYB 84*
Ultracom of Rockmart Inc. - Rockmart, GA - *BrCabYB 84; Tel&CabFB 84C*
Ultracom of Sweetwater Inc. - Sweetwater, TN - *BrCabYB 84; Tel&CabFB 84C*
Ultradata Corp. - Hayward, CA - *ADAPSOMemDir 83-84; DataDirSup 7-83*
Ultragraphics Inc. - Atlanta, GA - *AvMarPl 83*
Ultralight Aircraft [of Werner & Werner Corp.] - Encino, CA - *WritMar 84*
Ultralight Aircraft - Los Angeles, CA - *ArtMar 84*
Ultralight Aircraft - Van Nuys, CA - *BaconPubCkMag 84*
Ultralight Flyer - Tacoma, WA - *BaconPubCkMag 84; MagDir 84; WritMar 84*
Ultralight Pilot [of Aircraft Owners & Pilots Association] - Frederick, MD - *MagDir 84; WritMar 84*
Ultralight Publications - Hummelstown, PA - *BoPubDir 4, 5; LitMag&SmPr 83-84; WritMar 84*
Ultramarine Publishing Co. Inc. - Hastings-on-Hudson, NY - *BoPubDir 4, 5; LitMag&SmPr 83-84*
Ultrasoft Inc. - Bellevue, WA - *MicrocomMPl 84*
Ululatus - Ft. Smith, AR - *LitMag&SmPr 83-84*
Ulysse - Paris, France - *DirOnDB Spring 84*
Ulysses News - Ulysses, KS - *BaconPubCkNews 84; Ed&PubIntYB 82*
Umatilla Cable TV [of Badger Mountain Cable TV] - Umatilla, OR - *Tel&CabFB 84C*
Umbrella - Glendale, CA - *LitMag&SmPr 83-84*
Umbrella Associates - Glendale, CA - *FBInfSer 80; LitMag&SmPr 83-84*
UMI Inc. - Pomona, CA - *MicrocomMPl 83*
UMI Research Press [Div. of University Microfilms International] - Ann Arbor, MI - *LitMarPl 83, 84*
UMLER - Washington, DC - *DirOnDB Spring 84*
UMOJA SASA News Journal [of Pre-Professional Publications] - Ithaca, NY - *ArtMar 84; WritMar 84*
Umphenour & Martin - Tucker, GA - *AdAge 3-28-84*
Umpoqua Valley Independent Shopper - Sutherlin, OR - *AyerDirPub 83*
Umweltbundesamt - *See* Informations- und Dokumentationssystems Umwelt
U.N. Demographics - New York, NY - *DirOnDB Spring 84*
U.N. National Income Accounts [of Chase Econometrics/ Interactive Data Corp.] - Waltham, MA - *DataDirOnSer 84*
U.N. National Income Accounts [of Chase Econometric/Interactive Data Corp.] - Bala Cynwyd, PA - *DirOnDB Spring 84*
UN Plaza - New York, NY - *MagIndMarPl 82-83*
Unabashed Librarian - New York, NY - *BoPubDir 4, 5; LitMag&SmPr 83-84*
Unarius Educational Foundation - El Cajon, CA - *BoPubDir 4, 5*
Uncle - Springfield, MO - *LitMag&SmPr 83-84*
Undena Publications - Malibu, CA - *BoPubDir 4, 5; LitMag&SmPr 83-84*
Undercover Graphics - San Francisco, CA - *ArtMar 84*
Undercurrent - Sausalito, CA - *WritMar 84*
Underground Camera Inc. (Audio Visual Div.) - Norwood, MA - *AvMarPl 83*
Underground Rag Mag - Rochester, MN - *LitMag&SmPr 83-84*
Underground Space [of Pergamon Press Inc.] - Elmsford, NY - *MagDir 84*
Underhill Cable TV Inc. - Nehalem, OR - *Tel&CabFB 84C*
Underhill, Charles S. - East Aurora, NY - *BoPubDir 4, 5*
Underhill TV Service - Nehalem, OR - *BrCabYB 84*
Undersea Systems Inc. - Bay Shore, NY - *MagIndMarPl 82-83*
Underwater Naturalist - Highlands, NJ - *MagIndMarPl 82-83*
Underwood Cable TV - Underwood, ND - *Tel&CabFB 84C*
Underwood Jordan Associates - *See* Ogilvy & Mather Public Relations
Underwood/Miller - Columbia, PA - *BoPubDir 4; LitMag&SmPr 83-84; LitMarPl 83, 84; WritMar 84*
Underwood News - Underwood, ND - *Ed&PubIntYB 82*
Underwood News - *See* Borlaug Publishing Co.
Underwriters Laboratories Inc. - Melville, NY - *BoPubDir 5*
Underwriters' Report - San Francisco, CA - *BaconPubCkMag 84; MagDir 84*
Underwriters Review - Topeka, KS - *MagDir 84*
Undinal Songs - Oakdale, NY - *ArtMar 84; LitMag&SmPr 83-84; WritMar 84*
UNESCAP/Statistics Information System [of Economic & Social Commission for Asia & the Pacific] - Bangkok, Thailand - *EISS 83*
Unfinished Furniture Industry - Northfield, IL - *BaconPubCkMag 84*
Unfinished Furniture Magazine - Northfield, IL - *WritMar 84*
Unfinished Monument Press - Toronto, ON, Canada - *BoPubDir 4, 5*
Ungar Publishing Co. Inc., Frederick - New York, NY - *LitMarPl 83, 84*
Unger Associates Inc. - Atlanta, GA - *StaDirAdAg 2-84*
Ungermann-Bass Inc. - Santa Clara, CA - *DataDirSup 7-83; DirInfWP 82; WhoWMicrocom 83*
Unhinged Voice Press, The - Portsmouth, NH - *LitMag&SmPr 83-84*
Uni-Coll Corp. [Subs. of CISInetwork Corp.] - Philadelphia, PA - *DataDirOnSer 84*
Uni-Com Foundation - Arcata, CA - *BoPubDir 5*
Uni-Com Foundation - Palo Alto, CA - *BoPubDir 4*
Uni-Linx Telephone Conferencing System [of Small World Exchange Inc.] - Milford, NH - *TeleSy&SerDir 7-83*
Uni Media Inc. - Canada - *Ed&PubIntYB 82*
Uni-Set - Rochester, NY - *AvMarPl 83*
Unica Inc. - Plainfield, IL - *BoPubDir 4, 5*
UNICO Inc. - Franksville, WI - *WhoWMicrocom 83*
Unicom [Div. of United Camera Inc.] - Providence, RI - *AvMarPl 83; MicrocomMPl 84; MicrocomSwDir 1*
Unicomm Inc. - Santa Monica, CA - *MicrocomMPl 83*
Unicorn/Fitzgerald - Fredericksburg, VA - *BoPubDir 4, 5*
Unicorn Press - Greensboro, NC - *LitMag&SmPr 83-84; LitMarPl 83, 84*
Unicorn Promotion - New York, NY - *LitMarPl 83, 84*
Unicorn Publishing House Inc., The - Verona, NJ - *LitMarPl 84*
Unicorn Records - Santa Monica, CA - *BillIntBG 83-84*
Unicorn Rising - Sheridan, OR - *LitMag&SmPr 83-84*
Unicorn Secretarial Copy Center, The - Great Barrington, MA - *LitMarPl 83, 84*
Unicorn Systems Co. - Los Angeles, CA - *MicrocomSwDir 1*
Unidata Inc. - Katy, TX - *MicrocomMPl 83*
Unidek [Subs. of CJM Industries] - Sterling, VA - *AvMarPl 83*
Unified Data Products Corp. - Fair Lawn, NJ - *DataDirSup 7-83*
Unified Software Systems - New Carrollton, MD - *MicrocomMPl 84*
Unifilm - New York, NY - *AvMarPl 83*
UNIFO Publishers Ltd. - Pleasantville, NY - *LitMarPl 83, 84; MicroMarPl 82-83*
Uniform Parole Reports Project [of National Council on Crime & Delinquency] - San Francisco, CA - *EISS 83*
Uniforms & Accessories Review [of AFG Enterprises Inc.] - New York, NY - *BaconPubCkMag 84; MagDir 84*
Unijax [Div. of IU Products Distribution Inc.] - Memphis, TN - *AvMarPl 83*

Unijax Inc. - Jacksonville, FL - *DirInfWP 82*
Unilever Computer Services Ltd. [Subs. of Unilever PLC] - Watford, England - *DataDirOnSer 84; EISS 83; InfIndMarPl 83*
Uniline Publishing [Div. of John Klein & Associates Inc.] - Cleveland, OH - *BoPubDir 4, 5*
Unimel Inc. - Burlington, IA - *Tel&CabFB 84C*
Uninet Inc. [Subs. of United Telecommunications] - Kansas City, MO - *DataDirOnSer 84*
Uninett - Trondheim, Norway - *EISS 83*
Union - Arcata, CA - *AyerDirPub 83; Ed&PubIntYB 82*
Union - San Diego, CA - *AyerDirPub 83*
Union - Shelbyville, IL - *AyerDirPub 83*
Union - Humboldt, KS - *AyerDirPub 83*
Union - Junction City, KS - *AyerDirPub 83*
Union [of The Republican Co.] - Springfield, MA - *AyerDirPub 83; Ed&PubIntYB 82; LitMarPl 84*
Union - Bird Island, MN - *AyerDirPub 83*
Union - Ulen, MN - *AyerDirPub 83*
Union - Hampton, NH - *AyerDirPub 83*
Union - Bradford, PA - *NewsDir 84*
Union - Alcester, SD - *AyerDirPub 83*
Union - Ottawa, ON, Canada - *DirOnDB Spring 84*
Union Advertising Inc. - New York, NY - *StaDirAdAg 2-84*
Union Advocate - St. Paul, MN - *NewsDir 84*
Union Appeal - Union, MS - *BaconPubCkNews 84; Ed&PubIntYB 82*
Union Banner - Carlyle, IL - *AyerDirPub 83; Ed&PubIntYB 82*
Union Bookbinding Co. Inc. - Boston, MA - *LitMarPl 83, 84*
Union Bulletin - Walla Walla, WA - *AyerDirPub 83*
Union Campus News - Chicago, IL - *NewsDir 84*
Union Catalog of Medical Monographs & Multimedia [of Medical Library Center of New York] - New York, NY - *CompReadDB 82*
Union Catalog of Medical Periodicals [of Medical Library Center of New York] - New York, NY - *CompReadDB 82*
Union CATV Inc. - Sturgis, KY - *BrCabYB 84; Tel&CabFB 84C*
Union City Daily Messenger - Union City, TN - *Ed&PubIntYB 82; NewsDir 84*
Union City Dispatch - Union City, NJ - *BaconPubCkNews 84*
Union City Hudson Dispatch - Union City, NJ - *NewsDir 84*
Union City Messenger - Union City, TN - *BaconPubCkNews 84*
Union City Microvision - Union City, TN - *Tel&CabFB 84C*
Union City Register-Tribune - Union City, MI - *BaconPubCkNews 84*
Union City Times Leader - *See* Brown Thompson Newspapers
Union College Character Research Project (Character Research Press) - Schenectady, NY - *BoPubDir 4, 5*
Union College Press - Syracuse, NY - *BoPubDir 4, 5*
Union County Advocate - Morganfield, KY - *AyerDirPub 83; Ed&PubIntYB 82*
Union County Cable Ltd. [of Tennessee-Kentucky Cable TV Co.] - Morganfield, KY - *Tel&CabFB 84C*
Union County Cable TV - Shawneetown, IL - *Tel&CabFB 84C*
Union County Journal - Lewisburg, PA - *AyerDirPub 83; Ed&PubIntYB 82*
Union County Leader - Clayton, NM - *AyerDirPub 83; Ed&PubIntYB 82*
Union County Times - Lake Butler, FL - *Ed&PubIntYB 82*
Union Daily Times [of Mid-South Management] - Union, SC - *BaconPubCkNews 84; Ed&PubIntYB 82; NewsDir 84*
Union Democrat - Sonora, CA - *AyerDirPub 83; Ed&PubIntYB 82*
Union Electric News - St. Louis, MO - *ArtMar 84*
Union Enterprise - Plainwell, MI - *AyerDirPub 83; Ed&PubIntYB 82; NewsDir 84*
Union Franklin Tribune - Union, MO - *BaconPubCkNews 84; NewsDir 84*
Union Gazette - Port Jervis, NY - *AyerDirPub 83; Ed&PubIntYB 82*
Union Grove Sun - Union Grove, WI - *Ed&PubIntYB 82*
Union Grove Westine Report - *See* Zimmermann & Sons Inc.
Union Irvington Herald - Union, NJ - *NewsDir 84*
Union Label & Service Trades News & Union Cons - New York, NY - *NewsDir 84*
Union Labor News - Santa Barbara, CA - *NewsDir 84*
Union Labor News - Madison, WI - *NewsDir 84*
Union Leader - Manchester, NH - *AyerDirPub 83; BaconPubCkNews 84; LitMarPl 83, 84*
Union Leader - Union, NJ - *AyerDirPub 83; Ed&PubIntYB 82*
Union Linden Leader Spectator - Union, NJ - *BaconPubCkNews 84*
Union List of Higher Degree Theses in Australian Libraries [of University of Tasmania Library] - Hobart, Australia - *EISS 83*
Union List of Higher Degree Theses in Australian Universities - Hobart, Australia - *DirOnDB Spring 84*
Union List of Scientific Serials in Canadian Libraries [of Canada Institute for Scientific & Technical Information] - Ottawa, ON, Canada - *CompReadDB 82; DataDirOnSer 84*
Union List of Selected Serials of Michigan [of Wayne State University Libraries] - Detroit, MI - *EISS 83*
Union Monroe Watchman - Union, WV - *BaconPubCkNews 84*
Union News - Detroit, MI - *NewsDir 84*
Union News & Home - Marshville, NC - *AyerDirPub 83; Ed&PubIntYB 82*
Union News Leader - Maynardville, TN - *Ed&PubIntYB 82*
Union Observer, The - St. Joseph, MO - *NewsDir 84*
Union of American Hebrew Congregations - New York, NY - *ArtMar 84; LitMarPl 83, 84*
Union Park Press - Boston, MA - *BoPubDir 4, 5; LitMag&SmPr 83-84*
Union Press - Berkeley, CA - *BoPubDir 4, 5*
Union Press-Courier - Patton, PA - *AyerDirPub 83; NewsDir 84*
Union-Recorder, The [of Macon Telegraph Publishing Co.] - Milledgeville, GA - *AyerDirPub 83; Ed&PubIntYB 82; NewsDir 84*
Union Register LPIW-UBC & J [of Western Council of Lumber, Production, & Industrial Workers Union] - Portland, OR - *NewsDir 84*
Union Republican - Albia, IA - *AyerDirPub 83*
Union River Telephone Co. - Aurora, ME - *TelDir&BG 83-84*
Union Springs Herald - Union Springs, AL - *BaconPubCkNews 84; Ed&PubIntYB 82*
Union Springs Telephone Co. [Aff. of Ropir Industries Inc.] - Union Springs, AL - *Tel&CabFB 84C; TelDir&BG 83-84*
Union Star - Brookneal, VA - *AyerDirPub 83; Ed&PubIntYB 82*
Union Station Records & Tapes - Nashville, TN - *BillIntBG 83-84*
Union-Sun & Journal - Lockport, NY - *AyerDirPub 83; Ed&PubIntYB 82*
Union Tabloid - Washington, DC - *MagDir 84*
Union Telephone Co. [Aff. of Century Telephone Enterprises Inc.] - Plain Dealing, LA - *TelDir&BG 83-84*
Union Telephone Co. [Aff. of Unitel of Nebraska] - Blair, NE - *TelDir&BG 83-84*
Union Telephone Co. - Farmington, NH - *TelDir&BG 83-84*
Union Telephone Co. - Hartford, SD - *TelDir&BG 83-84*
Union Telephone Co. - Plainfield, WI - *TelDir&BG 83-84*
Union Telephone Co. - Mt. View, WY - *TelDir&BG 83-84*
Union, The - Grass Valley, CA - *AyerDirPub 83; BaconPubCkNews 84; Ed&PubIntYB 82*
Union Times - West Chester, OH - *AyerDirPub 83*
Union Topics - Baltimore, MD - *NewsDir 84*
Uniondale Beacon [of Hempstead Nassau County Publications] - Hempstead, NY - *NewsDir 84*
Uniondale Beacon - *See* Nassau County Publication
Uniondale Long Island Courier - Uniondale, NY - *BaconPubCkNews 84; NewsDir 84*
Uniondale Long Island Globe - Uniondale, NY - *NewsDir 84*
Uniondale Pennysaver - Geneseo, NY - *AyerDirPub 83*
Unioneer, The - Dallas, TX - *NewsDir 84*
Unionist, The - Omaha, NE - *NewsDir 84*
Uniontown Herald-Standard - Uniontown, PA - *NewsDir 84*
Uniontown News-Letter - *See* Tribune Newspapers Inc.
Uniontown Telephone Co. Inc. - Uniontown, KY - *TelDir&BG 83-84*
Unionville Missouri CATV Authority - Unionville, MO - *Tel&CabFB 84C*
Unionville Republican - Unionville, MO - *BaconPubCkNews 84; Ed&PubIntYB 82; NewsDir 84*
Uniphot-Levit - Woodside, NY - *AvMarPl 83*
UNIPHOTO Picture Agency - Washington, DC - *AvMarPl 83; LitMarPl 83, 84; MagIndMarPl 82-83*
Unipub [of Xerox Corp.] - New York, NY - *DirMarMP 83; EISS 83; InfoS 83-84; LitMarPl 83, 84; MagIndMarPl 82-83; MicroMarPl 82-83*

Uniq Computer Corp. - Batavia, IL - *MicrocomMPl 83, 84*
Unique [of Infopro Systems] - East Hanover, NJ - *DirOnDB Spring 84; MicrocomMPl 84*
Unique [of NewsNet Inc.] - Bryn Mawr, PA - *DataDirOnSer 84*
Unique Automation Products - Irvine, CA - *MicrocomMPl 83*
Unique Automation Products - Tustin, CA - *MicrocomMPl 84*
Unique Color Corp. - Chicago, IL - *LitMarPl 83; MagIndMarPl 82-83*
Unique Graphics - Oakland, CA - *BoPubDir 4, 5; LitMag&SmPr 83-84*
Unique Information Systems - Chicago, IL - *MicrocomMPl 83, 84; MicrocomSwDir 1*
Unique Multiplex Systems Inc. - Chicago, IL - *DirInfWP 82*
Unique Publications - Hollywood, CA - *BoPubDir 4, 5*
Unisearch Inc. - Berkeley, CA - *IntDirMarRes 83*
Unisist International Center for Bibliographic Descriptions [of United Nations Educational, Scientific, & Cultural Organization] - London, England - *EISS 83*
UniSoft Systems Corp. - Berkeley, CA - *MicrocomMPl 84*
Unisource [Div. of Alco Standard] - Wayne, PA - *LitMarPl 83, 84*
Unisphere Pictures International Inc. - New York, NY - *AvMarPl 83*
Unistox - New York, NY - *DirOnDB Spring 84*
Unit - Ormond Beach, FL - *MagDir 84*
Unit Core - *See* Mayflower Music Corp.
Unit-Register - Orland, CA - *AyerDirPub 83*
Unitarian Universalist World - Boston, MA - *LitMarPl 83, 84; NewsDir 84*
Unite! Publications [Aff. of Communist Party U.S.A.] - Chicago, IL - *BoPubDir 4, 5*
United [of East/West Network Inc.] - New York, NY - *Folio 83; MagDir 84*
United Advertising Cos. Inc. - Downers Grove, IL - *StaDirAdAg 2-84*
United Artists - New York, NY - *LitMag&SmPr 83-84; LitMarPl 83*
United Artists Books - New York, NY - *BoPubDir 4, 5*
United Artists Cablesystems Corp. - Westport, CT - *Tel&CabFB 84C p.1709*
United Artists Music - Los Angeles, CA - *BillIntBG 83-84*
United Artists Television Inc. - New York, NY - *Tel&CabFB 84C*
United Audio-Visual Resources - Ottawa, ON, Canada - *VideoDir 82-83*
United Brethren, The - Huntington, IN - *WritMar 84*
United Broadcasting Co. - Bethesda, MD - *BrCabYB 84 p.D-309*
United Broadcasting Co. - Manchester, NH - *Tel&CabFB 84C p.1709*
United Business Equipment Corp. - Buffalo, NY - *DirInfWP 82*
United Business Publications Inc. - New York, NY - *MagIndMarPl 82-83*
United Business Service Co. - Boston, MA - *DirMarMP 83*
United Cable Co. - Craigsville, WV - *BrCabYB 84; Tel&CabFB 84C*
United Cable Co. Inc. - Hawkinsville, GA - *Tel&CabFB 84C p.1709*
United Cable Co. of New Hampshire Inc. [of United Broadcasting Co.] - Bedford, NH - *BrCabYB 84; Tel&CabFB 84C*
United Cable Co. of New Hampshire Inc. [of United Broadcasting Co.] - Manchester, NH - *BrCabYB 84; Tel&CabFB 84C*
United Cable of Colorado - Englewood, CO - *BrCabYB 84*
United Cable of Mid-Michigan - East Lansing, MI - *Tel&CabFB 84C*
United Cable of Santa Fe - Santa Fe, NM - *Tel&CabFB 84C*
United Cable Systems Inc. - Cowan, KY - *BrCabYB 84*
United Cable Systems Inc. [of TV Service Inc.] - Haymond, KY - *BrCabYB 84; Tel&CabFB 84C*
United Cable Systems Inc. - Hindman, KY - *BrCabYB 84*
United Cable Systems Inc. - Mayking, KY - *Tel&CabFB 84C*
United Cable Systems Inc. [of TV Service Inc.] - Pine Mountain, KY - *Tel&CabFB 84C*
United Cable Systems Inc. - *See* TV Service Inc.
United Cable Television Corp. - Scottsdale, AZ - *BrCabYB 84*
United Cable Television Corp. - Denver, CO - *AdAge 6-28-84; BrCabYB 84; CabTVFinDB 83; HomeVid&CabYB 82-83; KnowInd 83; LitMarPl 84; Tel&CabFB 84C p.1709*
United Cable Television Corp. - Woodhaven, MI - *BrCabYB 84*
United Cable Television of Bossier City Inc. - Bossier City, LA - *BrCabYB 84*
United Cable Television of Cupertino Inc. - Cupertino, CA - *BrCabYB 84; Tel&CabFB 84C*
United Cable Television of Eastern Shore - Ocean City, MD - *BrCabYB 84*
United Cable Television of Illinois Valley Inc. - Peru, IL - *BrCabYB 84; Tel&CabFB 84C*
United Cable Television of Mid-Michigan - East Lansing, MI - *BrCabYB 84*
United Cable Television of Northern Illinois Inc. [Aff. of United Cable Television Corp.] - Carpentersville, IL - *BrCabYB 84; InterCabHB 3; Tel&CabFB 84C*
United Cable Television of Northern Indiana Inc. - Hammond, IN - *BrCabYB 84; Tel&CabFB 84C*
United Cable Television of Sarpy County - Bellevue, NE - *BrCabYB 84; Tel&CabFB 84C*
United Cable Television of Southern Illinois Inc. - Effingham, IL - *BrCabYB 84; Tel&CabFB 84C*
United Cable Television of Southern Illinois Inc. - Mendota, IL - *BrCabYB 84*
United Cable Television of Treasure Valley - Boise, ID - *BrCabYB 84; Tel&CabFB 84C*
United Cable Television of Tyler - Tyler, TX - *BrCabYB 84; Tel&CabFB 84C*
United Cable TV [Aff. of United Cable Television Corp.] - Englewood, CO - *InterCabHB 3*
United Cable TV - Moab, UT - *Tel&CabFB 84C*
United Cable TV Corp. of Connecticut - New Britain, CT - *BrCabYB 84*
United Cable TV Corp. of Connecticut - Plainville, CT - *Tel&CabFB 84C*
United Cable TV Corp. of Eastern Connecticut - Vernon, CT - *Tel&CabFB 84C*
United Cable TV Corp. of Michigan - Woodhaven, MI - *Tel&CabFB 84C*
United Cable TV Corp. of Western Colorado - Grand Junction, CO - *BrCabYB 84; Tel&CabFB 84C*
United Cable TV Group - Forestville, CT - *TelAl 83*
United Cable TV Inc. [of TCA Cable TV Inc.] - Grubbs, AR - *Tel&CabFB 84C*
United Cable TV of Abilene - Abilene, TX - *Tel&CabFB 84C*
United Cable TV of Alameda Inc. - Alameda, CA - *BrCabYB 84*
United Cable TV of Bay Area - Hayward, CA - *Tel&CabFB 84C*
United Cable TV of Bay Area - San Leandro, CA - *Tel&CabFB 84C*
United Cable TV of Bay Area - San Lorenzo, CA - *Tel&CabFB 84C*
United Cable TV of Gallup - Gallup, NM - *Tel&CabFB 84C*
United Cable TV of Hamlin - Hamlin, TX - *Tel&CabFB 84C*
United Cable TV of Jacksonville - Jacksonville, TX - *Tel&CabFB 84C*
United Cable TV of Perryton - Perryton, TX - *Tel&CabFB 84C*
United Cable TV of Sweetwater - Sweetwater, TX - *Tel&CabFB 84C*
United Cable TV of Wyoming [Aff. of United Cable Television Corp.] - Casper, WY - *InterCabHB 3; Tel&CabFB 84C*
United Cablevision Funding - Greenwich, CT - *Tel&CabFB 84C p.1709*
United Cablevision of Mid-Michigan [Aff. of United Cable Television Corp.] - East Lansing, MI - *InterCabHB 3*
United Cargo Corp. [Subs. of Intercontinental Trailsea Corp.] - New York, NY - *LitMarPl 83, 84; MagIndMarPl 82-83*
United Cartoonist Syndicate [Subs. of Visions for Children] - Corpus Christi, TX - *Ed&PubIntYB 82; LitMarPl 84*
United Chinese Press - Honolulu, HI - *Ed&PubIntYB 82*
United Church Observer [Aff. of The United Church of Canada] - Toronto, ON, Canada - *BoPubDir 4, 5; WritMar 84*
United Church Renewal Fellowship - Barrie, ON, Canada - *BoPubDir 4, 5*
United Color Press - Dayton, OH - *LitMarPl 83, 84; MagIndMarPl 82-83*
United Communications Corp. - Wilmington, DE - *BrCabYB 84; Ed&PubIntYB 82*
United Communications Corp. - Kenosha, WI - *BrCabYB 84; Tel&CabFB 84S*

United Computers International - Kent, OH - *WhoWMicrocom 83*
United Controls Corp. - Huntsville, AL - *MicrocomMPl 83, 84*
United Daily News - Manila, Philippines - *AyerDirPub 83*
United Educators Inc. - Lake Bluff, IL - *LitMarPl 83, 84*
United Evangelical Action - Wheaton, IL - *WritMar 84*
United Farmers Telephone Co. - Everly, IA - *TelDir&BG 83-84*
United Feature Syndicate [Div. of United Media Enterprises] - New York, NY - *BaconPubCkNews 84; Ed&PubIntYB 82; LitMarPl 83, 84; MagIndMarPl 82-83; NewsBur 6*
United Film Enterprises Inc. - New York, NY - *Tel&CabFB 84C*
United Fresh Fruit & Vegetable Association - Alexandria, VA - *BoPubDir 5*
United Information Services Inc. [Div. of Control Data Corp.] - Overland Park, KS - *DataDirOnSer 84*
United Information Services Inc. [of Control Data Corp.] - Kansas City, MO - *ADAPSOMemDir 83-84; DataDirOnSer 84; EISS 83*
United Information Services Inc. - Pittsburgh, PA - *DataDirSup 7-83; DirInfWP 82*
United Information Systems Inc. - San Diego, CA - *ADAPSOMemDir 83-84*
United Inter-Mountain Telephone Co. [Aff. of United Telecommunications Inc.] - Bristol, TN - *TelDir&BG 83-84*
United International Copyright Representatives - New York, NY - *BillIntBG 83-84*
United Jewish Appeal - New York, NY - *WritMar 84*
United Journal - New York, NY - *AyerDirPub 83; Ed&PubIntYB 82; NewsDir 84*
United Kingdom Central Statistics Office [of I. P. Sharp Associates Ltd.] - Toronto, ON, Canada - *DataDirOnSer 84*
United Kingdom Online User Group - Reading, England - *EISS 83*
United Learning - Niles, IL - *AvMarPl 83*
United Magazine [of East-West Network Inc.] - New York, NY - *ArtMar 84; BaconPubCkMag 84*
United Mainliner - Los Angeles, CA - *MagIndMarPl 82-83*
United Media Enterprises Inc. - New York, NY - *Ed&PubIntYB 82*
United Methodist Board of Discipleship (Discipleship Resources) - Nashville, TN - *BoPubDir 4, 5*
United Methodist Church (Commission on Archives & History) - Madison, NJ - *BoPubDir 5*
United Methodist Church (Commission on Archives & History) - Lake Junaluska, NC - *BoPubDir 4*
United Methodist Communications [Div. of Public Media] - New York, NY - *Tel&CabFB 84C*
United Methodist Communications - Nashville, TN - *AvMarPl 83*
United Methodist Information [of NewsNet Inc.] - Bryn Mawr, PA - *DataDirOnSer 84*
United Methodist Information - Nashville, TN - *DirOnDB Spring 84*
United Methodist Publishing House - Nashville, TN - *MagIndMarPl 82-83*
United Methodist Reporter/National Christian Reporter - Dallas, TX - *WritMar 84*
United Microware Industries Inc. - Pomona, CA - *MicrocomMPl 83, 84*
United Midwest - New York, NY - *Tel&CabFB 84C*
United Mine Workers Journal - Washington, DC - *BaconPubCkMag 84; MagDir 84*
United Nations - New York, NY - *AvMarPl 83*
United Nations (Dept. of Public Information) - New York, NY - *Tel&CabFB 84C*
United Nations (Sales Section, Microfiche) - New York, NY - *MicroMarPl 82-83*
United Nations (Sales Section, Publishing Service) - New York, NY - *LitMarPl 83, 84*
United Nations Bibliographic Information System - New York, NY - *EISS 83*
United Nations Commodity Trade Statistics [of I. P. Sharp Associates Ltd.] - Toronto, ON, Canada - *DataDirOnSer 84; DirOnDB Spring 84*
United Nations Headquarters (Non-Governmental Organizations Youth Caucus) - New York, NY - *BoPubDir 4, 5*
United Nations Industrial Development Organization (Industrial Information Section) - Vienna, Austria - *CompReadDB 82*
United Nations Inter-Organization Board for Information Systems - Geneva, Switzerland - *EISS 83*
United Nations Latin American Demographic Center - Santiago, Chile - *CompReadDB 82*
United Parcel Service - New York, NY - *MagIndMarPl 82-83*
United Performers Inc. - New York, NY - *BillIntBG 83-84*
United Press - Cleveland, OH - *NewsBur 6*
United Press Canada - Toronto, ON, Canada - *BrCabYB 84; Tel&CabFB 84C*
United Press International [Subs. of Media News Inc.] - New York, NY - *BrCabYB 84; CabTVPrDB 83; DataDirOnSer 84; Ed&PubIntYB 82; LitMarPl 83, 84; MagIndMarPl 82-83; NewsBur 6; TelAl 83, 84; Tel&CabFB 84C*
United Press International [of NewsNet Inc.] - Bryn Mawr, PA - *DataDirOnSer 84*
United Press International (International Features Div.) - New York, NY - *Ed&PubIntYB 82*
United Press International Newspictures - New York, NY - *Ed&PubIntYB 82; LitMarPl 84; Tel&CabFB 84C*
United Printing Services Inc. - New Haven, CT - *LitMarPl 83*
United Production Services Inc. [Subs. of Unitel Video Inc.] - New York, NY - *AvMarPl 83*
United Productions Ltd. - Sherman Oaks, CA - *WritMar 84*
United Projector & Film Corp. - Buffalo, NY - *AvMarPl 83*
United Public Relations Inc. - New York, NY - *DirPRFirms 83*
United Publishing Co. Inc. - Ennis, TX - *BaconPubCkNews 84*
United Resin Adhesives Inc. - Lyons, IL - *LitMarPl 83, 84*
United Resin Adhesives of California Inc. - Vernon, CA - *LitMarPl 83, 84*
United Resin Adhesives of Georgia Inc. - Atlanta, GA - *LitMarPl 84*
United Resin Adhesives of Texas Inc. - Lewisville, TX - *LitMarPl 83, 84*
United Resin Products Inc. - Brooklyn, NY - *LitMarPl 83, 84*
United Rubber Worker - Akron, OH - *NewsDir 84*
United Satellite Communications - New York, NY - *BrCabYB 84; CabTVPrDB 83*
United Satellites Ltd. - London, England - *TeleSy&SerDir 2-84*
United Scottsdale Cablevision [of United Cable TV Corp.] - Scottsdale, AZ - *Tel&CabFB 84C*
United Service Efforts - Grand Rapids, MI - *Tel&CabFB 84C*
United Software Associates Inc. - Oakland, NJ - *MicrocomMPl 84*
United Software of America [Subs. of The Computer Factory] - New York, NY - *MicrocomMPl 83; WhoWMicrocom 83*
United Software Systems & Services Corp. - Los Angeles, CA - *ADAPSOMemDir 83-84*
United Sports Syndicate - Scotts Valley, CA - *Ed&PubIntYB 82*
United States Banker [of Cleworth Publishing Co. Inc.] - Cos Cob, CT - *BaconPubCkMag 84; MagDir 84; MagIndMarPl 82-83; NewsBur 6*
United States Bonds [of I. P. Sharp Associates Ltd.] - Toronto, ON, Canada - *DataDirOnSer 84*
United States Cancellation Club - Bonsall, CA - *BoPubDir 4, 5*
United States Catholic Conference - New York, NY - *BrCabYB 84*
United States Committee for Refugees [Aff. of American Council for Nationalities Service] - New York, NY - *BoPubDir 4*
United States Data Systems [Subs. of United States Instrument Rentals Inc.] - San Mateo, CA - *WhoWMicrocom 83*
United States Dept. of Energy - Washington, DC - *DirOnDB Spring 84*
United States Dept. of Energy [of I. P. Sharp Associates Ltd.] - Toronto, ON, Canada - *DataDirOnSer 84*
United States Dressage Federation Inc. - Lincoln, NE - *BoPubDir 5*
United States Flow of Funds, Quarterly [of I. P. Sharp Associates Ltd.] - Toronto, ON, Canada - *DataDirOnSer 84*
United States Gemological Services Inc. - Santa Ana, CA - *BoPubDir 4, 5*
United States Government Printing Office - Washington, DC - *MicroMarPl 82-83; ProGuPRSer 4*
United States Historicl Documents Institute Inc. - Arlington, VA - *LitMarPl 83*
United States Naval Institute - Annapolis, MD - *LitMarPl 83, 84; MagIndMarPl 82-83*
United States Naval Institute Proceedings - Annapolis, MD - *BaconPubCkMag 84; MagIndMarPl 82-83*

United States Newspaper Program [of U.S. National Foundation on the Arts & the Humanities] - Washington, DC - *EISS 5-84 Sup*
United States Petroleum Imports [of I. P. Sharp Associates Ltd.] - Toronto, ON, Canada - *DataDirOnSer 84*
United States Political Science Documents [of University of Pittsburgh] - Pittsburgh, PA - *DataDirOnSer 84; DBBus 82; EISS 83; OnBibDB 3*
United States Productions Inc. - New York, NY - *TelAl 83, 84*
United States Publishers Association [Div. of EME Corp.] - New Rochelle, NY - *AvMarPl 83*
United States Satellite Broadcasting Co. Inc. - St. Paul, MN - *BrCabYB 84*
United States Satellite Systems Inc. - New York, NY - *BrCabYB 84; Tel&CabFB 84C; TeleSy&SerDir 2-84*
United States Ski News - Los Angeles, CA - *BaconPubCkMag 84*
United States Ski News - Park City, UT - *MagIndMarPl 82-83*
United States Specialist, The - Norristown, PA - *MagDir 84*
United States Stock Market Database [of I. P. Sharp Associates Ltd.] - Toronto, ON, Canada - *DataDirOnSer 84*
United States Stock Market Database - London, England - *DirOnDB Spring 84*
United States Stock Options [of I. P. Sharp Associates Ltd.] - Toronto, ON, Canada - *DataDirOnSer 84*
United States Student Association - Washington, DC - *BoPubDir 4, 5*
United States Telecommunications Suppliers Association - Chicago, IL - *TeleSy&SerDir 2-84*
United States Tennis Association (Publications) - Princeton, NJ - *BoPubDir 4, 5*
United States Testing Co. - Wheeling, IL - *IntDirMarRes 83*
United States Tobacco Journal - New York, NY - *BaconPubCkMag 84; NewsBur 6*
United States Trademark Association - New York, NY - *BoPubDir 4, 5*
United States Transmission Inc. - Secaucus, NJ - *DataDirSup 7-83*
United States Travel Data Center - Washington, DC - *EISS 83*
United Suburban News - Franklin Lakes, NJ - *AyerDirPub 83; Ed&PubIntYB 82*
United Synagogue Book Service [Div. of United Synagogues of America] - New York, NY - *LitMarPl 83, 84*
United Synagogue Review - New York, NY - *MagDir 84; MagIndMarPl 82-83*
United Systems Corp. - Dayton, OH - *DirInfWP 82*
United Technical Products Inc. - Westwood, MA - *WhoWMicrocom 83*
United Technical Publications Inc. - *See* The Hearst Corp.
United Technical Publishing Co. [Aff. of Cox Broadcasting Corp.] - Garden City, NY - *BoPubDir 4, 5*
United Technologies Communications Co. - St. Louis, MO - *DataDirSup 7-83*
United Technologies Communications Development - Sarasota, FL - *DataDirSup 7-83*
United Technologies-Lexor Corp. - Los Angeles, CA - *DirInfWP 82*
United Technologies Telecom MIS - Upper Darby, PA - *DataDirSup 7-83*
United Tele-Communications Inc. - Westwood, KS - *Datamation 6-83*
United Telecom Computer Group/SEED Software - Philadelphia, PA - *DataDirSup 7-83*
United Telecommunications Inc. - Shawnee Mission, KS - *TelDir&BG 83-84*
United Telecommunications Inc. - Kansas City, MO - *Top100Al 83*
United Telephone Association Inc. - Dodge City, KS - *TelDir&BG 83-84*
United Telephone Co. [Aff. of Central Telephone Co. of Texas] - Killeen, TX - *TelDir&BG 83-84*
United Telephone Co. Inc. - Chapel Hill, TN - *TelDir&BG 83-84*
United Telephone Co. of Arkansas [Aff. of United Telecommunications Inc.] - Jefferson City, MO - *TelDir&BG 83-84*
United Telephone Co. of Florida [Aff. of United Telecommunications Inc.] - Altamonte Springs, FL - *TelDir&BG 83-84*
United Telephone Co. of Indiana Inc. [Aff. of United Telecommunications Inc.] - Warsaw, IN - *TelDir&BG 83-84*
United Telephone Co. of Iowa [Aff. of United Telecommunications Inc.] - Newton, IA - *TelDir&BG 83-84*
United Telephone Co. of Kansas [Aff. of United Telecommunications Inc.] - Junction City, KS - *TelDir&BG 83-84*
United Telephone Co. of Louisiana Inc. [Aff. of Century Telephone Enterprises Inc.] - Plain Dealing, LA - *TelDir&BG 83-84*
United Telephone Co. of Minneapolis [Aff. of United Telecommunications Inc.] - Chaska, MN - *TelDir&BG 83-84*
United Telephone Co. of Missouri [Aff. of United Telecommunications Inc.] - Jefferson City, MO - *TelDir&BG 83-84*
United Telephone Co. of New Jersey [Aff. of United Telecommunications Inc.] - Newton, NJ - *TelDir&BG 83-84*
United Telephone Co. of Ohio [Aff. of United Telecommunications Inc.] - Mansfield, OH - *TelDir&BG 83-84*
United Telephone Co. of Pennsylvania [Aff. of United Telecommunications Inc.] - Carlisle, PA - *TelDir&BG 83-84*
United Telephone Co. of Texas Inc. [Aff. of United Telephone Systems Inc.] - Tyler, TX - *TelDir&BG 83-84*
United Telephone Co. of the Carolinas [Aff. of United Telecommunications Inc.] - Bristol, TN - *TelDir&BG 83-84*
United Telephone Co. of the Northwest [Aff. of United Telecommunications Inc.] - Hood River, OR - *TelDir&BG 83-84*
United Telephone Co. of the West [Aff. of United Telecommunications Inc.] - Scottsbluff, NE - *TelDir&BG 83-84*
United Telephone Mutual Aid Corp. - Langdon, ND - *TelDir&BG 83-84*
United Telequipment Corp. - Monroe, WI - *TelDir&BG 83-84*
United Television Inc. - Minneapolis, MN - *BrCabYB 84; Tel&CabFB 84S*
United Transparencies Inc. - Binghamton, NY - *AvMarPl 83*
United Ventures Inc. (Tandom Div.) - Richmond, IL - *AvMarPl 83*
United Video Cablevision Inc. - Greenwich, CT - *Tel&CabFB 84C p.1710*
United Video Cablevision Inc. - Delhi, OH - *BrCabYB 84*
United Video Cablevision Inc. - Delhi Township, OH - *Tel&CabFB 84C*
United Video Electronic Program Guide Corp. - Tulsa, OK - *BrCabYB 84; Tel&CabFB 84C*
United Video Inc. - Tulsa, OK - *BrCabYB 84; Tel&CabFB 84C*
United Video Management Inc. - *See* Flinn, Lawrence Jr.
Unitel Video Services Inc. - New York, NY - *TeleSy&SerDir 2-84*
Unitrade Press - Toronto, ON, Canada - *BoPubDir 4 Sup, 5; LitMag&SmPr 83-84*
Unitron Graphics - New York, NY - *LitMarPl 83, 84; MagIndMarPl 82-83*
Unitros Bolivia [of the Univas Network] - Cochabamga, Bolivia - *StaDirAdAg 2-84*
Unitros Chile [of the Univas Network] - Santiago, Chile - *StaDirAdAg 2-84*
Unitros Dominicana y Extensa Publicidad SA [of the Univas Network] - Santo Domingo, Dominican Republic - *StaDirAdAg 2-84*
Unitros Group [of the Univas Network] - Madrid, Spain - *StaDirAdAg 2-84*
Unitros Portugal [of the Univas Network] - Lisbon, Portugal - *StaDirAdAg 2-84*
Unity Book Club [of Unity School of Christianity] - Unity Village, MO - *LitMarPl 83*
Unity Broadcasting Network - *See* National Black Network
Unity Magazine - Unity Village, MO - *MagIndMarPl 82-83; WritMar 84*
Unity Telephone Co. - Unity, ME - *TelDir&BG 83-84*
Univair Inc. - St. Louis, MO - *WhoWMicrocom 83*
Univair International - St. Louis, MO - *MicrocomMPl 83*
UnivAmp Inc. - Jefferson City, TN - *BrCabYB 84; Tel&CabFB 84C*
Univas Italia - Milan, Italy - *StaDirAdAg 2-84*
Univas Network - Neuilly sur Seine, France - *StaDirAdAg 2-84*
Univelt Inc. [Aff. of American Astronautical Society] - San Diego, CA - *ArtMar 84; BoPubDir 4, 4 Sup, 5; LitMarPl 83, 84; MagIndMarPl 82-83; MicroMarPl 82-83; WritMar 84*

Universal Artist Records/Delta Records - Madison, TN - *BillIntBG 83-84*
Universal-Athena Records - Peoria, IL - *BillIntBG 83-84*
Universal Black Writer, The - New York, NY - *LitMag&SmPr 83-84*
Universal Broadcasting Corp. - Mineola, NY - *BrCabYB 84*
Universal Christian Movement - Glencoe, IL - *BoPubDir 4 Sup, 5*
Universal City Herald-News - Universal City, TX - *BaconPubCkNews 84*
Universal City Randolph Air Force Base Wingspread - Universal City, TX - *BaconPubCkNews 84*
Universal Communications Corp. - *See* Evening News Association
Universal Custom Products Inc. [Subs. of Insilco Corp.] - San Antonio, TX - *LitMarPl 83, 84*
Universal Data Research Inc. - Buffalo, NY - *MicrocomMPl 84; MicrocomSwDir 1*
Universal Data Systems [Subs. of Motorola] - Huntsville, AL - *MicrocomMPl 84; WhoWMicrocom 83*
Universal Data Systems (Motorola-Information Systems Group) - Huntsville, AL - *DataDirSup 7-83*
Universal Data Transfer Service [of ITT World Communications Inc.] - New York, NY - *TeleSy&SerDir 7-83*
Universal Data Transfer Service [of Globe-Mackay Cable & Radio Corp.] - Manila, Philippines - *InfIndMarPl 83*
Universal Developments Publishing - Costa Mesa, CA - *BoPubDir 4, 5*
Universal Distributors Co. - New York, NY - *LitMarPl 83*
Universal Edition - *See* European American Music Corp.
Universal Information Services Inc. - Cincinnati, OH - *ADAPSOMemDir 83-84*
Universal Library Systems Ltd. - West Vancouver, BC, Canada - *EISS 83*
Universal Life Bookshelf - Anaheim, CA - *BoPubDir 4, 5*
Universal Life Church Inc. - Los Angeles, CA - *BoPubDir 4, 5*
Universal Lithographers - Cockeysville, MD - *LitMarPl 83*
Universal Machine Language Equipment Register [of Association of American Railroads] - Washington, DC - *EISS 5-84 Sup*
Universal Micro Systems - San Rafael, CA - *MicrocomMPl 84*
Universal News Services - London, England - *ProGuPRSer 4*
Universal Pay TV [Subs. of Universal City Studios] - Universal City, CA - *AvMarPl 83*
Universal Pictures [Div. of Universal City Studios Inc.] - New York, NY - *LitMarPl 83*
Universal Press Syndicate - Fairway, KS - *BaconPubCkNews 84; Ed&PubIntYB 82; LitMarPl 83, 84; MagIndMarPl 82-83*
Universal Printers Ltd. - Winnipeg, MB, Canada - *LitMarPl 83, 84*
Universal Printing Co. - St. Louis, MO - *LitMarPl 83, 84; MagIndMarPl 82-83*
Universal Public Relations Inc. - New York, NY - *DirPRFirms 83; StaDirAdAg 2-84*
Universal Rehearsal & Recording - New York, NY - *AvMarPl 83*
Universal Serials & Book Exchange - Washington, DC - *CompReadDB 82; DataDirOnSer 84; DBBus 82; DirOnDB Spring 84; EISS 83; MicroMarPl 82-83*
Universal Software - Ft. Collins, CO - *MicrocomMPl 84*
Universal Software Inc. - Brookfield, CT - *DataDirSup 7-83*
Universal Software Studios - Gallatin, TN - *MicrocomMPl 83*
Universal Sound Records - Mt. Juliet, TN - *BillIntBG 83-84*
Universal Stars Music Inc. - Leesville, LA - *BillIntBG 83-84*
Universal Systems for Education Inc. - Aurora, CO - *MicrocomMPl 84*
Universal Systems for Education Inc. - Colorado Springs, CO - *MicrocomMPl 83; MicrocomSwDir 1; WhoWMicrocom 83*
Universal Technology Corp. - Dayton, OH - *BoPubDir 4, 5*
Universal Telephone Co. of Colorado [Aff. of Universal Telephone Inc.] - Pagosa Springs, CO - *TelDir&BG 83-84*
Universal Telephone Co. of Northern Wisconsin Inc. [Aff. of Universal Telephone Inc.] - Manitowish Waters, WI - *TelDir&BG 83-84*
Universal Telephone Co. of Southwest [Aff. of Universal Telephone Inc.] - Keams Canyon, AZ - *TelDir&BG 83-84*
Universal Telephone Co. of Southwest (Pecos District) - Pecos, NM - *TelDir&BG 83-84*
Universal Telephone Co. of Southwest (Zuni District) - Zuni, NM - *TelDir&BG 83-84*
Universal Telephone Inc. - Milwaukee, WI - *TelDir&BG 83-84*
Universal Television [Div. of Universal City Studios Inc.] - Universal City, CA - *TelAl 83, 84; Tel&CabFB 84C*
Universal Training Systems Co. - Northbrook, IL - *AvMarPl 83*
Universal Video - Lubbock, TX - *Tel&CabFB 84C*
Universal Video Communications Inc. [of W.W. Communications] - Springhill, LA - *Tel&CabFB 84C*
Universal Video Communications Inc. - Carrollton, MO - *BrCabYB 84*
Universal Video Communications Inc. [of W.W. Communications] - Richmond, MO - *Tel&CabFB 84C*
Universe Books [Div. of South Park Press] - New York, NY - *LitMarPl 83, 84; WritMar 84*
Universe Communications - Los Angeles, CA - *BillIntBG 83-84*
Universe Kogaku America Inc. [Subs. of Universe Optical Industries Co. Ltd.] - Hicksville, NY - *AvMarPl 83*
Universe Technical Translation - Houston, TX - *LitMarPl 84*
Universitaet Duesseldorf (Forschungsabteilung fur Philosophische Information und Dokumentation) - Duesseldorf, West Germany - *CompReadDB 82*
Universitatsbibliothek Informationsstelle - Graz, Austria - *InfIndMarPl 83*
Universite de Moncton (Centre d'Etudes Acadiennes) - Moncton, NB, Canada - *BoPubDir 4 Sup, 5*
Universite de Montreal (L'Institut d'Etudes Medievales) - Montreal, PQ, Canada - *BoPubDir 5*
Universite de Sherbrooke (Editions Revue de Droit) - Sherbrooke, PQ, Canada - *BoPubDir 4, 5*
Universities Field Staff International Inc. - Hanover, NH - *BoPubDir 5; MicroMarPl 82-83*
University & College Placement Association - Toronto, ON, Canada - *BoPubDir 4, 5*
University Associates Inc. - San Diego, CA - *LitMarPl 83, 84; WritMar 84*
University Book Service - Worthington, OH - *BoPubDir 4 Sup, 5; LitMarPl 83, 84*
University Books Inc. [Div. of Lyle Stuart Inc.] - Secaucus, NJ - *LitMarPl 83, 84*
University City Pennysaver - Mission Viejo, CA - *AyerDirPub 83*
University College Tutors Inc. - Brooklyn, NY - *LitMarPl 83, 84*
University Community Video - Minneapolis, MN - *Tel&CabFB 84C*
University Computing Co. [Subs. of Wyly Corp.] - Dallas, TX - *ADAPSOMemDir 83-84; DataDirOnSer 84; DataDirSup 7-83*
University Consultants - Ft. Lauderdale, FL - *MicrocomMPl 83*
University Consultants - Euless, TX - *MicrocomMPl 84*
University Daily Kansan, The - Lawrence, KS - *NewsDir 84*
University Daily, The [of Texas Tech University] - Lubbock, TX - *NewsDir 84*
University Graphics - Atlantic Highlands, NJ - *LitMarPl 83, 84*
University Heights TV - Moscow, ID - *BrCabYB 84*
University Herald - Seattle, WA - *Ed&PubIntYB 82*
University Journal - Chico, CA - *LitMag&SmPr 83-84*
University Library [of University of Trondheim] - Trondheim, Norway - *EISS 83*
University Library of Lund - Lund, Sweden - *CompReadDB 82*
University Marketing Group - Hamden, CT - *LitMarPl 83, 84*
University Media [Div. of The Media Guild] - San Diego, CA - *AvMarPl 83*
University Microfilms International [Subs. of Xerox Corp.] - Ann Arbor, MI - *AvMarPl 83; CompReadDB 82; DataDirOnSer 84; InfIndMarPl 83; InfoS 83-84; LitMarPl 83, 84; MagIndMarPl 82-83; MicroMarPl 82-83*
University Music Editions [Div. of High Density Systems Inc.] - New York, NY - *LitMarPl 83, 84; MagIndMarPl 82-83; MicroMarPl 82-83*
University News Service - New York, NY - *Ed&PubIntYB 82*
University of Alabama (Center for Business & Economic Research) - University, AL - *BoPubDir 4, 5*
University of Alabama (Gorgas Oak Press) - University, AL - *BoPubDir 5*
University of Alabama (Parallel Editions) - University, AL - *BoPubDir 5*
University of Alabama, Huntsville (UAH Press) - Huntsville, AL - *BoPubDir 4, 5*

University of Alabama Press - University, AL - *LitMarPl 83, 84; MicroMarPl 82-83; WritMar 84*
University of Alaska (Geophysical Institute) - Fairbanks, AK - *BoPubDir 4 Sup, 5*
University of Alaska (Institute of Marine Science) - Fairbanks, AK - *BoPubDir 4, 5*
University of Alaska (Institute of Social & Economic Research) - Anchorage, AK - *BoPubDir 4 Sup, 5*
University of Alaska (Sea Grant Program) - Fairbanks, AK - *BoPubDir 5*
University of Alaska Press - Fairbanks, AK - *BoPubDir 4, 5; LitMarPl 84*
University of Alberta (Boreal Institute for Northern Studies) - Edmonton, AB, Canada - *BoPubDir 4, 5; DataDirOnSer 84*
University of Alberta (Canadian Institute of Ukrainian Studies) - Edmonton, AB, Canada - *BoPubDir 4, 5*
University of Alberta (Centre for Mental Retardation) - Edmonton, AB, Canada - *BoPubDir 4, 5*
University of Alberta (Computing Services) - Edmonton, AB, Canada - *DataDirOnSer 84*
University of Alberta (Dept. of Geography) - Edmonton, AB, Canada - *BoPubDir 4, 5*
University of Alberta (Legal Resource Centre) - Edmonton, AB, Canada - *BoPubDir 4, 5*
University of Alberta Press - Edmonton, AB, Canada - *BoPubDir 4, 5; LitMarPl 84*
University of Arizona - Tucson, AZ - *AvMarPl 83*
University of Arizona (Arizona Educational Materials Center) - Tucson, AZ - *BoPubDir 5*
University of Arizona (Economic & Business Research Div.) - Tucson, AZ - *InfIndMarPl 83*
University of Arizona Press - Speedway, AZ - *WritMar 84*
University of Arizona Press - Tucson, AZ - *LitMarPl 83, 84*
University of Arkansas Press - Fayetteville, AR - *LitMarPl 83, 84; WritMar 84*
University of Bristol - *See* SWALCAP
University of British Columbia (Centre for Continuing Education) - Vancouver, BC, Canada - *BoPubDir 4, 5*
University of British Columbia (Centre for Transportation Studies) - Vancouver, BC, Canada - *BoPubDir 4, 5*
University of British Columbia (Urban Land Economics Div.) - Vancouver, BC, Canada - *BoPubDir 4, 5*
University of British Columbia (Westwater Research Centre) - Vancouver, BC, Canada - *BoPubDir 4, 5*
University of British Columbia Press - Vancouver, BC, Canada - *LitMarPl 83, 84*
University of Calgary (Archaeological Association) - Calgary, AB, Canada - *BoPubDir 4, 5*
University of Calgary (Dept. of Archaeology) - Calgary, AB, Canada - *BoPubDir 4, 5*
University of Calgary (Foothills Educational Press) - Calgary, AB, Canada - *BoPubDir 4, 5*
University of Calgary (Law Library) - Calgary, AB, Canada - *CompReadDB 82*
University of Calgary (University Libraries Special Collections Div.) - Calgary, AB, Canada - *BoPubDir 4, 5*
University of California (Berkeley Papers in History of Science) - Berkeley, CA - *BoPubDir 4*
University of California (Extension Media Center) - Berkeley, CA - *AvMarPl 83*
University of California (Extension Publications) - Berkeley, CA - *BoPubDir 4, 5*
University of California (Institute of Business & Economic Research) - Berkeley, CA - *BoPubDir 4, 5*
University of California (Institute of East Asian Studies) - Berkeley, CA - *BoPubDir 4, 5*
University of California (Institute of Governmental Studies) - Berkeley, CA - *BoPubDir 4, 5*
University of California (Institute of International Studies) - Berkeley, CA - *BoPubDir 4, 5*
University of California (Jepson Herbarium) - Berkeley, CA - *BoPubDir 4, 5*
University of California (Lawrence Berkeley Laboratory) - Berkeley, CA - *CompReadDB 82*
University of California (Library Automation Div.) - Berkeley, CA - *BoPubDir 4 Sup, 5*
University of California (Office for History of Science & Technology) - Berkeley, CA - *BoPubDir 4 Sup, 5*
University of California, Davis (Institute of Governmental Affairs) - Davis, CA - *BoPubDir 4 Sup, 5*
University of California, Davis (Putah Creek Press) - Davis, CA - *BoPubDir 4, 5*
University of California, Irvine (Institute of Transportation Studies) - Irvine, CA - *BoPubDir 5*
University of California, Los Angeles (American Indian Studies Center) - Los Angeles, CA - *BoPubDir 4 Sup, 5*
University of California, Los Angeles (Asian American Studies Center) - Los Angeles, CA - *BoPubDir 4, 5*
University of California, Los Angeles (Center for Afro-American Studies) - Los Angeles, CA - *BoPubDir 4 Sup, 5*
University of California, Los Angeles (Chicano Studies Research Center Publications) - Los Angeles, CA - *BoPubDir 4, 5*
University of California, Los Angeles (Graduate School of Management) - Los Angeles, CA - *BoPubDir 4, 5*
University of California, Los Angeles (Housing, Real Estate, & Urban Land Studies Program) - Los Angeles, CA - *BoPubDir 4, 5*
University of California, Los Angeles (Institute of Archaeology) - Los Angeles, CA - *BoPubDir 4, 5*
University of California, Los Angeles (Institute of Industrial Relations) - Los Angeles, CA - *BoPubDir 4, 5*
University of California, Los Angeles (Latin American Center) - Los Angeles, CA - *BoPubDir 4, 5*
University of California, Los Angeles (Program in Ethnomusicology) - Los Angeles, CA - *BoPubDir 4, 5*
University of California, Los Angeles (Tissue Typing Laboratory) - Los Angeles, CA - *BoPubDir 4 Sup, 5*
University of California Press - Berkeley, CA - *LitMag&SmPr 83-84; LitMarPl 83, 84; MagIndMarPl 82-83; WritMar 84*
University of California, Richmond (Agricultural Sciences Publications) - Richmond, CA - *BoPubDir 4, 5*
University of California, Riverside (Deep Canyon Publications) - Riverside, CA - *BoPubDir 4, 5*
University of California, Santa Barbara (Art Museum) - Santa Barbara, CA - *BoPubDir 4, 5*
University of California, Santa Cruz (Mary Porter Sesnon Art Gallery) - Santa Cruz, CA - *BoPubDir 4, 5*
University of Charleston (Mountain State Press) - Charleston, WV - *BoPubDir 4, 5*
University of Chicago (Center for Health Administration Studies) - Chicago, IL - *BoPubDir 4, 5*
University of Chicago (Community & Family Study Center) - Chicago, IL - *BoPubDir 4, 5*
University of Chicago (Computation Center) - Chicago, IL - *DataDirOnSer 84*
University of Chicago (Dept. of Geography) - Chicago, IL - *BoPubDir 4, 5*
University of Chicago (Inter-University Seminar) - Chicago, IL - *BoPubDir 4, 5*
University of Chicago (Mesa Press) - Chicago, IL - *BoPubDir 4, 5*
University of Chicago (Midwest Administration Center) - Chicago, IL - *BoPubDir 4 Sup, 5*
University of Chicago (National Opinion Research Center) - Chicago, IL - *BoPubDir 4, 5*
University of Chicago (Oriental Institute) - Chicago, IL - *BoPubDir 4, 5*
University of Chicago Press - Chicago, IL - *LitMarPl 83, 84; MagIndMarPl 82-83; MicroMarPl 82-83*
University of Chicago Press (Chicago Visual Library, Text/Fiche Program) - Chicago, IL - *LitMarPl 84*
University of Colorado - Boulder, CO - *AvMarPl 83*
University of Colorado, Boulder (Business Research Div.) - Boulder, CO - *BoPubDir 4, 5*
University of Colorado, Boulder (Natural Hazards Research & Applications Information Center) - Boulder, CO - *BoPubDir 4 Sup, 5*
University of Connecticut (Center for Real Estate & Urban Economic Studies) - Storrs, CT - *BoPubDir 4 Sup, 5*
University of Connecticut (I. N. Thut World Education Center) - Storrs, CT - *BoPubDir 4, 5*

University of Connecticut (William Benton Museum of Art) - Storrs, CT - *BoPubDir 4, 5*
University of Dallas (UD Press) - Irving, TX - *BoPubDir 4 Sup, 5*
University of Delaware Press - Newark, DE - *LitMarPl 83, 84*
University of Denver (Monograph Series in World Affairs) - Denver, CO - *BoPubDir 4, 5*
University of Detroit (Computerized Folklore Archive) - Detroit, MI - *CompReadDB 82*
University of Detroit Press - Detroit, MI - *BoPubDir 4, 5*
University of Florida Libraries - Gainesville, FL - *LitMarPl 83, 84*
University of Florida Microphotography Library - Gainesville, FL - *MicroMarPl 82-83*
University of Georgia (Carl Vinson Institute of Government) - Athens, GA - *BoPubDir 5*
University of Georgia (Institute of Ecology) - Athens, GA - *BoPubDir 4 Sup, 5*
University of Georgia (Institute of Government) - Athens, GA - *BoPubDir 4*
University of Georgia (Office of Instructional Development) - Athens, GA - *CompReadDB 82*
University of Georgia Press - Athens, GA - *LitMarPl 83, 84*
University of Guelph - Guelph, ON, Canada - *CompReadDB 82*
University of Guelph Library - Guelph, ON, Canada - *CompReadDB 82*
University of Hawaii (Center for Korean Studies) - Honolulu, HI - *BoPubDir 4, 5*
University of Hawaii Press - Honolulu, HI - *LitMarPl 83, 84*
University of Healing Press [Aff. of God Unltd.] - Campo, CA - *BoPubDir 4, 5*
University of Houston (Latin American Studies Committee) - Houston, TX - *BoPubDir 4, 5*
University of Houston (Revista Chicano-Riquena/Arte Publico Press) - Houston, TX - *BoPubDir 4, 5*
University of Idaho (Center for Business Development & Research) - Moscow, ID - *BoPubDir 4, 5*
University of Idaho (Physical Plant Div.) - Moscow, ID - *BrCabYB 84*
University of Illinois - Champaign, IL - *AvMarPl 83*
University of Illinois (Bureau of Urban & Regional Planning Research) - Urbana, IL - *BoPubDir 4, 5*
University of Illinois (College of Agriculture) - Urbana, IL - *BoPubDir 4, 5*
University of Illinois (Graduate School of Library & Information Science) - Champaign, IL - *BoPubDir 4, 5*
University of Illinois (Institute for Tuberculosis Research) - Chicago, IL - *BoPubDir 4, 5*
University of Illinois (Policy Studies Organization) - Urbana, IL - *BoPubDir 4, 5*
University of Illinois (School of Music) - Urbana, IL - *BoPubDir 5*
University of Illinois Press - Champaign, IL - *LitMarPl 83, 84*
University of Iowa (Audiovisual Center) - Iowa City, IA - *AvMarPl 83*
University of Iowa (Institute of Hydraulic Research) - Iowa City, IA - *BoPubDir 4, 5*
University of Iowa (School of Social Work) - Iowa City, IA - *BoPubDir 4, 5*
University of Iowa Libraries - Iowa City, IA - *MicroMarPl 82-83*
University of Iowa Press - Iowa City, IA - *ArtMar 84; LitMarPl 83, 84; WritMar 84*
University of Kansas (Center for Public Affairs) - Lawrence, KS - *BoPubDir 4, 5*
University of Kansas (Cottonwood Magazine & Press) - Lawrence, KS - *BoPubDir 5*
University of Kansas (Cottonwood Review Press) - Lawrence, KS - *BoPubDir 4*
University of Kansas (Film Services) - Lawrence, KS - *AvMarPl 83*
University of Kansas (Museum of Natural History) - Lawrence, KS - *BoPubDir 4, 5*
University of Kentucky (OES Publications) - Lexington, KY - *BoPubDir 4, 5*
University of Kentucky (OIR-Audio Visual Services) - Lexington, KY - *AvMarPl 83*
University of Kentucky (Program for Cultural Resource Assessment) - Lexington, KY - *BoPubDir 4 Sup, 5*
University of King's College (Alumni Association of King's College) - Halifax, NS, Canada - *BoPubDir 4, 5*
University of Ljubljana (Medicinska Fakulteta) - Ljubljana, Yugoslavia - *CompReadDB 82*
University of London (Central Information Service) - London, England - *InfIndMarPl 83*
University of London (Institute of United States Studies) - London, England - *MicroMarPl 82-83*
University of Maine (Film Rental Library) - Orono, ME - *AvMarPl 83*
University of Maine at Augusta - Augusta, ME - *AvMarPl 83*
University of Maine, Orono (National Poetry Foundation Inc.) - Orono, ME - *BoPubDir 4, 5*
University of Manitoba (Centre for Transportation Studies) - Winnipeg, MB, Canada - *BoPubDir 4, 5*
University of Manitoba (Faculty of Agriculture) - Winnipeg, MB, Canada - *BoPubDir 4, 5*
University of Manitoba (Four Humours Press) - Winnipeg, MB, Canada - *BoPubDir 4, 5*
University of Manitoba (Legal Research Institute) - Winnipeg, MB, Canada - *BoPubDir 4, 5*
University of Manitoba (Monographs in Education) - Winnipeg, MB, Canada - *BoPubDir 4 Sup, 5*
University of Manitoba Press - Winnipeg, MB, Canada - *BoPubDir 4, 5; LitMarPl 84*
University of Maryland (College of Library & Information Services) - College Park, MD - *BoPubDir 4, 5*
University of Maryland (School of Law) - Baltimore, MD - *BoPubDir 5*
University of Massachusetts (Center for International Education) - Amherst, MA - *BoPubDir 4, 5*
University of Massachusetts (Citizen Involvement Training Program) - Amherst, MA - *BoPubDir 4, 5*
University of Massachusetts (Integrated Education Associates) - Amherst, MA - *BoPubDir 4, 5*
University of Massachusetts (University Gallery) - Amherst, MA - *BoPubDir 4, 5*
University of Massachusetts Press - Amherst, MA - *LitMarPl 83, 84; WritMar 84*
University of Miami (Comparative Sedimentology Laboratory) - Miami Beach, FL - *BoPubDir 4, 5*
University of Miami (Rosenstiel School of Marine & Atmospheric Science) - Miami, FL - *BoPubDir 4, 5*
University of Miami Music Publications - *See* Fox Publishing Co. Inc., Sam
University of Michigan (Center for Chinese Studies) - Ann Arbor, MI - *BoPubDir 4, 5*
University of Michigan (Center for Japanese Studies) - Ann Arbor, MI - *BoPubDir 4, 5*
University of Michigan (Center for Near Eastern & North African Studies) - Ann Arbor, MI - *BoPubDir 4, 5*
University of Michigan (Center for Research on Economic Development) - Ann Arbor, MI - *BoPubDir 4 Sup, 5*
University of Michigan (Center for South & Southeast Asian Studies) - Ann Arbor, MI - *BoPubDir 4, 5*
University of Michigan (Graduate School of Business) - Ann Arbor, MI - *BoPubDir 4*
University of Michigan (Graduate School of Business Administration Research Div.) - Ann Arbor, MI - *BoPubDir 5*
University of Michigan (Industrial Development Div.) - Ann Arbor, MI - *BoPubDir 4, 5*
University of Michigan (Institute for Social Research) - Ann Arbor, MI - *BoPubDir 4, 5*
University of Michigan (Institute of Gerontology) - Ann Arbor, MI - *BoPubDir 4, 5*
University of Michigan (Inter-University Consortium for Political & Social Research) - Ann Arbor, MI - *BoPubDir 4, 5*
University of Michigan (Media Resources Center) - Ann Arbor, MI - *Tel&CabFB 84C*
University of Michigan (Museum of Anthropology Publications) - Ann Arbor, MI - *BoPubDir 4, 5*
University of Michigan Library - Ann Arbor, MI - *BoPubDir 4, 5*
University of Michigan Press - Ann Arbor, MI - *LitMarPl 83, 84; WritMar 84*

University of Michigan/Wayne State University (Institute of Labor & Industrial Relations) - Ann Arbor, MI - *BoPubDir 4, 5*
University of Minnesota (Associates of the James Ford Bell Library) - Minneapolis, MN - *BoPubDir 4, 5*
University of Minnesota (Audio Visual Library Service) - Minneapolis, MN - *AvMarPl 83*
University of Minnesota (E. T. Bell Institute of Pathology) - Minneapolis, MN - *BoPubDir 4, 5*
University of Minnesota (Immigration History Research Center) - St. Paul, MN - *BoPubDir 4, 5*
University of Minnesota (Mineral Resources Research Center) - Minneapolis, MN - *BoPubDir 5*
University of Minnesota (Minnesota Geological Survey) - St. Paul, MN - *BoPubDir 4, 5*
University of Minnesota Press - Minneapolis, MN - *LitMarPl 83, 84*
University of Mississippi (Bureau of Business & Economic Research) - University, MS - *BoPubDir 4, 5*
University of Missouri (Museum of Anthropology) - Columbia, MO - *BoPubDir 4, 5*
University of Missouri-Columbia - Columbia, MO - *AvMarPl 83*
University of Missouri, Kansas City (New Letters) - Kansas City, MO - *BoPubDir 5*
University of Missouri Press - Columbia, MO - *LitMarPl 83, 84; WritMar 84*
University of Montana (Bureau of Business & Economic Research) - Missoula, MT - *BoPubDir 4, 5*
University of Montana (Cutbank) - Missoula, MT - *BoPubDir 4, 5*
University of Montana (Publications in History) - Missoula, MT - *BoPubDir 4, 5*
University of Nebraska, Lincoln (Bureau of Business Research) - Lincoln, NE - *BoPubDir 4, 5*
University of Nebraska Medical Center (Biomedical Communications) - Omaha, NE - *AvMarPl 83*
University of Nebraska, Omaha (Abattoir Editions) - Omaha, NE - *BoPubDir 4, 5*
University of Nebraska Press - Lincoln, NE - *ArtMar 84; LitMarPl 83, 84; WritMar 84*
University of Nevada Press - Reno, NV - *LitMarPl 83, 84; WritMar 84*
University of New Hampshire (Dept. of Media Services) - Durham, NH - *AvMarPl 83*
University of New Mexico (Bureau of Business & Economic Research) - Albuquerque, NM - *BoPubDir 5*
University of New Mexico (Institute for Native American Development) - Albuquerque, NM - *BoPubDir 4, 5*
University of New Mexico (University Art Museum) - Albuquerque, NM - *BoPubDir 4 Sup, 5*
University of New Mexico Press - Albuquerque, NM - *LitMarPl 83, 84; WritMar 84*
University of New Orleans (International Marketing Institute) - New Orleans, LA - *BoPubDir 4, 5*
University of New Orleans (School of Urban & Regional Studies) - New Orleans, LA - *BoPubDir 4, 5*
University of New South Wales Library - Kensington, Australia - *MicroMarPl 82-83*
University of North Carolina (Carolina Population Center) - Chapel Hill, NC - *BoPubDir 4, 5*
University of North Carolina (Institute for Research in Social Science) - Chapel Hill, NC - *BoPubDir 4, 5*
University of North Carolina (International Program of Laboratories for Population Statistics) - Chapel Hill, NC - *BoPubDir 5*
University of North Carolina (Water Resources Research Institute) - Raleigh, NC - *BoPubDir 4, 5*
University of North Carolina, Chapel Hill (International Program of Laboratories for Population Statistics) - Chapel Hill, NC - *BoPubDir 4*
University of North Carolina, Greensboro (Center for Applied Research/School of Business & Economics) - Greensboro, NC - *BoPubDir 5*
University of North Carolina Press - Chapel Hill, NC - *LitMarPl 83, 84; WritMar 84*
University of Northern Colorado (Michener Library) - Greeley, CO - *MicroMarPl 82-83*
University of Northern Iowa (Educational Media Center) - Cedar Falls, IA - *AvMarPl 83*
University of Northern Iowa (North American Review) - Cedar Falls, IA - *BoPubDir 4, 5*
University of Notre Dame Press - Notre Dame, IN - *LitMarPl 83, 84; WritMar 84*
University of Oklahoma (Bureau of Government Research) - Norman, OK - *BoPubDir 4, 5*
University of Oklahoma (Ceter for Economic & Management Research) - Norman, OK - *BoPubDir 4, 5*
University of Oklahoma (Information Systems Programs) - Norman, OK - *DataDirOnSer 84*
University of Oklahoma (Law Center) - Norman, OK - *BoPubDir 4, 5*
University of Oklahoma (Oklahoma Geological Survey) - Norman, OK - *BoPubDir 4, 5*
University of Oklahoma (Stovall Museum of Science & History) - Norman, OK - *BoPubDir 4, 5*
University of Oklahoma Press - Norman, OK - *LitMarPl 83, 84; WritMar 84*
University of Oregon (Bureau of Governmental Research & Service) - Eugene, OR - *BoPubDir 4, 5*
University of Oregon (Center for Educational Policy & Management) - Eugene, OR - *BoPubDir 4, 5*
University of Oregon (Center of Leisure Studies) - Eugene, OR - *BoPubDir 4, 5*
University of Oregon (College of Health, Physical Education, & Recreation-Microform Publications) - Eugene, OR - *MicroMarPl 82-83*
University of Oregon (Northwest Review) - Eugene, OR - *BoPubDir 4, 5*
University of Oregon Books - Eugene, OR - *BoPubDir 4, 5*
University of Ottawa Press/Editions de l'Universite d'Ottawa - Ottawa, ON, Canada - *LitMarPl 83, 84*
University of Pennsylvania (Human Resources Center) - Philadelphia, PA - *BoPubDir 4, 5*
University of Pennsylvania (Institute of Contemporary Art) - Philadelphia, PA - *BoPubDir 4, 5*
University of Pennsylvania (University Museum) - Philadelphia, PA - *BoPubDir 4, 5*
University of Pennsylvania Press - Philadelphia, PA - *ArtMar 84; LitMarPl 83, 84; WritMar 84*
University of Pittsburgh (Center for International Studies) - Pittsburgh, PA - *BoPubDir 4, 5; CompReadDB 82*
University of Pittsburgh Press - Pittsburgh, PA - *LitMarPl 83, 84; WritMar 84*
University of Puerto Rico (Center for Caribbean Studies) - Rio Piedras, PR - *BoPubDir 4, 5*
University of Puerto Rico Press - Rio Piedras, PR - *LitMarPl 83, 84*
University of Queensland Press - New York, NY - *LitMarPl 84*
University of Queensland Press (Microform Div.) - St. Lucia, Australia - *MicroMarPl 82-83*
University of Regina (Canadian Plains Research Center) - Regina, SK, Canada - *BoPubDir 4, 5*
University of Regina (Dept. of Geography) - Regina, SK, Canada - *BoPubDir 4, 5*
University of Regina (Norman Mackenzie Art Gallery) - Regina, SK, Canada - *BoPubDir 4, 5*
University of Rhode Island (Marine Advisory Service-Sea Grant) - Narragansett, RI - *BoPubDir 4, 5*
University of Rochester (Center for Research in Government Policy & Business) - Rochester, NY - *BoPubDir 4, 5*
University of Saskatchewan (Native Law Centre) - Saskatoon, SK, Canada - *BoPubDir 4, 5*
University of Saskatchewan Libraries (Machine-Assisted Reference Teleservices) - Saskatoon, SK, Canada - *EISS 83*
University of South Carolina (American Academy of Advertising) - Columbia, SC - *BoPubDir 4, 5*
University of South Carolina (Names in South Carolina) - Columbia, SC - *BoPubDir 4, 5*
University of South Carolina (Research Div., College of Business Administration) - Columbia, SC - *BoPubDir 4, 5*
University of South Carolina Press - Columbia, SC - *LitMarPl 83, 84*
University of South Dakota (Business Research Bureau) - Vermillion, SD - *BoPubDir 5*

University of South Dakota (Dakota Press) - Vermillion, SD - *BoPubDir 4, 5*
University of South Dakota (Governmental Research Bureau) - Vermillion, SD - *BoPubDir 4, 5*
University of South Florida (Film Library) - Tampa, FL - *AvMarPl 83*
University of Southern California - Los Angeles, CA - *Tel&CabFB 84C*
University of Southern California (Annenberg School of Communications) - Los Angeles, CA - *InterCabHB 3*
University of Southern California (Cinema-Television, Film Distribution Center) - Los Angeles, CA - *AvMarPl 83*
University of Southern California (Engineering Computer Laboratory) - Los Angeles, CA - *DataDirOnSer 84*
University of Southern California (National Information Center for Education Media) - Los Angeles, CA - *BoPubDir 4, 5*
University of Tennessee Press - Knoxville, TN - *LitMarPl 83, 84; WritMar 84*
University of Texas (Bureau of Business Research) - Austin, TX - *BoPubDir 4, 5*
University of Texas (Bureau of Economic Geology) - Austin, TX - *BoPubDir 4, 5*
University of Texas (Center for Mexican American Studies) - Austin, TX - *BoPubDir 4, 5*
University of Texas (Center for Occupational Curriculum Development) - Austin, TX - *BoPubDir 4, 5*
University of Texas (Center of Research in Water Resources) - Austin, TX - *BoPubDir 4 Sup, 5*
University of Texas (Film Library) - Austin, TX - *BoPubDir 5*
University of Texas (General Libraries/Film Library) - Austin, TX - *BoPubDir 4*
University of Texas (Humanities Research Center) - Austin, TX - *BoPubDir 4, 5*
University of Texas (Institute for Constructive Capitalism) - Austin, TX - *BoPubDir 4, 5*
University of Texas (Lyndon B. Johnson School of Public Affairs) - Austin, TX - *BoPubDir 4, 5*
University of Texas (Petroleum Extension Service) - Austin, TX - *AvMarPl 83; BoPubDir 4, 5*
University of Texas (Texas Law Review) - Austin, TX - *BoPubDir 4, 5*
University of Texas (Texas Memorial Museum) - Austin, TX - *BoPubDir 4, 5*
University of Texas, Arlington (UTA Press) - Arlington, TX - *BoPubDir 4, 5*
University of Texas, Dallas (Mundus Artium Press) - Richardson, TX - *BoPubDir 4, 5*
University of Texas, El Paso (Texas Western Press) - El Paso, TX - *BoPubDir 4, 5*
University of Texas Institute of Texan Cultures at San Antonio, The - *See* Institute of Texan Cultures, The
University of Texas Press - Austin, TX - *LitMarPl 83, 84; WritMar 84*
University of Texas, San Antonio (Center for Archaeological Research) - San Antonio, TX - *BoPubDir 4 Sup, 5*
University of Texas, San Antonio (Institute of Texas Cultures) - San Antonio, TX - *BoPubDir 4, 5*
University of the Pacific (Holt-Atherton Pacific Center for Western Studies) - Stockton, CA - *BoPubDir 4, 5*
University of the Trees Press - Boulder Creek, CA - *LitMarPl 83, 84*
University of Tokyo On-Line Information Retrieval System - Tokyo, Japan - *EISS 83*
University of Toronto (Centre for Industrial Relations) - Toronto, ON, Canada - *BoPubDir 4, 5*
University of Toronto (Centre for International Studies) - Toronto, ON, Canada - *BoPubDir 4 Sup, 5*
University of Toronto (Centre of Criminology) - Toronto, ON, Canada - *BoPubDir 4, 5*
University of Toronto (Faculty of Nursing) - Toronto, ON, Canada - *BoPubDir 4 Sup, 5*
University of Toronto (Guidance Centre) - Toronto, ON, Canada - *BoPubDir 4, 5*
University of Toronto (Institute for Aerospace Studies) - Toronto, ON, Canada - *BoPubDir 4, 5*
University of Toronto (Library Automation Systems Div.) - Toronto, ON, Canada - *BoPubDir 4 Sup*
University of Toronto (Microscopical Society of Canada) - Toronto, ON, Canada - *BoPubDir 4*
University of Toronto (New Hogtown Press) - Toronto, ON, Canada - *BoPubDir 4, 5*
University of Toronto (School of Physical & Health Education) - Toronto, ON, Canada - *BoPubDir 4 Sup, 5*
University of Toronto (UTLAS Inc.) - Toronto, ON, Canada - *BoPubDir 5*
University of Toronto Library Automation Systems - Toronto, ON, Canada - *EISS 83*
University of Toronto Press - Toronto, ON, Canada - *LitMarPl 83, 84; MicroMarPl 82-83*
University of Tulsa (Information Services Div.) - Tulsa, OK - *CompReadDB 82; DataDirOnSer 84*
University of Utah - Salt Lake City, UT - *AvMarPl 83*
University of Utah (Annie Clark Tanner Trust Fund) - Salt Lake City, UT - *BoPubDir 5*
University of Utah (Bureau of Economic & Business Research) - Salt Lake City, UT - *BoPubDir 5*
University of Utah (State Arboretum of Utah) - Salt Lake City, UT - *BoPubDir 5*
University of Utah Press - Salt Lake City, UT - *LitMarPl 83, 84; WritMar 84*
University of Victoria (English Literary Studies Monograph Series) - Victoria, BC, Canada - *BoPubDir 4, 5*
University of Victoria (Western Geographical Series) - Victoria, BC, Canada - *BoPubDir 4, 5*
University of Virginia (Institute of Government) - Charlottesville, VA - *BoPubDir 4, 5*
University of Virginia (Mid-Atlantic Center for Community Education) - Charlottesville, VA - *BoPubDir 4, 5*
University of Virginia (Tayloe Murphy Institute) - Charlottesville, VA - *BoPubDir 4 Sup, 5*
University of Virginia (Thomas Jefferson Center for Political Economy) - Charlottesville, VA - *BoPubDir 4, 5*
University of Virginia Library - Charlottesville, VA - *MicroMarPl 82-83*
University of Wales Press - Cardiff, Wales - *LitMag&SmPr 83-84*
University of Washington (Asian Music Publications) - Seattle, WA - *BoPubDir 4, 5*
University of Washington (Graduate School of Business Administration) - Seattle, WA - *BoPubDir 4, 5*
University of Washington (Henry Art Gallery) - Seattle, WA - *BoPubDir 5*
University of Washington Daily - Seattle, WA - *NewsDir 84*
University of Washington Press - Seattle, WA - *AvMarPl 83; LitMarPl 83, 84; MicroMarPl 82-83*
University of Waterloo (Historical Reflections Press) - Waterloo, ON, Canada - *BoPubDir 4 Sup, 5*
University of Waterloo (Solid Mechanics Publications) - Waterloo, ON, Canada - *BoPubDir 4 Sup, 5*
University of Western Ontario (Faculty of Education) - London, ON, Canada - *BoPubDir 4 Sup, 5*
University of Western Ontario (Research & Publication Div., School of Business Administration) - London, ON, Canada - *BoPubDir 4, 5*
University of Windsor (Dept. of Economics) - Windsor, ON, Canada - *BoPubDir 4, 5*
University of Windsor (Sesame Press) - Windsor, ON, Canada - *BoPubDir 4, 5*
University of Windsor Review - Windsor, ON, Canada - *LitMag&SmPr 83-84; WritMar 84*
University of Wisconsin (Bureau of Business Research) - Madison, WI - *BoPubDir 4, 5*
University of Wisconsin (Continuing Legal Education for Wisconsin) - Madison, WI - *BoPubDir 5*
University of Wisconsin (Dept. of South Asian Studies) - Madison, WI - *BoPubDir 4, 5*
University of Wisconsin (Institute for Research on Poverty) - Madison, WI - *BoPubDir 4, 5*
University of Wisconsin (Land Tenure Center) - Madison, WI - *BoPubDir 4, 5*
University of Wisconsin (Library School) - Madison, WI - *BoPubDir 4, 5*
University of Wisconsin (Stout Teleproduction Center) - Menomonie, WI - *WritMar 84*

University of Wisconsin, Extension (Continuing Legal Education for Wisconsin) - Madison, WI - *BoPubDir 4*
University of Wisconsin, La Crosse (Center for Contemporary Poetry) - La Crosse, WI - *BoPubDir 4, 5*
University of Wisconsin, La Crosse (Film Library) - La Crosse, WI - *AvMarPl 83*
University of Wisconsin, Milwaukee (Center for Architecture & Urban Planning Research) - Milwaukee, WI - *BoPubDir 4, 5*
University of Wisconsin, Milwaukee (Center for Latin America) - Milwaukee, WI - *BoPubDir 4, 5*
University of Wisconsin Press - Madison, WI - *ArtMar 84; LitMarPl 83, 84; WritMar 84*
University of Wisconsin Press (Journal Div.) - Madison, WI - *MagIndMarPl 82-83*
University of Wisconsin, River Falls (River Falls Press) - River Falls, WI - *BoPubDir 4, 5*
University of Wyoming (U.W. Publications) - Laramie, WY - *BoPubDir 4, 5*
University Park Press [of SFN Cos. Inc.] - Baltimore, MD - *DirMarMP 83; LitMarPl 83, 84*
University Place Book Shop - New York, NY - *BoPubDir 4, 5*
University Press - Greendale, MA - *LitMarPl 83*
University Press [Div. of Publishers Book Bindery Inc.] - Winchester, MA - *LitMarPl 84*
University Press Book Service [Subs. of UPBS Inc.] - New York, NY - *LitMarPl 83, 84*
University Press of America - Lanham, MD - *LitMarPl 84; WritMar 84*
University Press of America Inc. - Washington, DC - *LitMarPl 83*
University Press of Idaho [Aff. of Idaho Research Foundation Inc.] - Moscow, ID - *BoPubDir 4, 5; LitMarPl 84*
University Press of Kansas - Lawrence, KS - *LitMarPl 83, 84; WritMar 84*
University Press of Kentucky - Lexington, KY - *LitMarPl 83, 84; WritMar 84*
University Press of Mississippi - Jackson, MS - *LitMarPl 83, 84; WritMar 84*
University Press of New England - Hanover, NH - *LitMarPl 83, 84; WritMar 84*
University Press of the Pacific Inc. [Subs. of Athena Publishing Group BV] - Seattle, WA - *LitMarPl 83, 84; WritMar 84*
University Press of Virginia - Charlottesville, VA - *LitMarPl 83, 84; WritMar 84*
University Press of Washington, DC, The - Riverton, VA - *LitMarPl 83, 84*
University Presses of Florida, The - Gainesville, FL - *LitMarPl 83, 84*
University Prints - Winchester, MA - *AvMarPl 83*
University Publications of America Inc. - Frederick, MD - *LitMarPl 83, 84; MicroMarPl 82-83*
University Publishing - Berkeley, CA - *LitMag&SmPr 83-84*
University Research - Cedar City, UT - *AvMarPl 83*
University Science Books [Div. of University Books Inc.] - Mill Valley, CA - *BoPubDir 4, 5; LitMarPl 84*
University Software - Fitchville, CT - *MicrocomMPl 84*
University Times [of California State University Los Angeles] - Los Angeles, CA - *NewsDir 84*
Univerza Edvarda Kardelja v Ljubljani (Centralna Tehniska Knjiznica) - Ljubljana, Yugoslavia - *InfIndMarPl 83*
Univerza v Ljubljani (Narodna in Univerzitetna Knjiznica) - Ljubljana, Yugoslavia - *InfIndMarPl 83*
Univision Cable Systems Inc. - Richlands, NC - *BrCabYB 84; Tel&CabFB 84C p.1710*
Uniworld Group Inc. - New York, NY - *DirPRFirms 83; StaDirAdAg 2-84*
Uniworld Hispanic - New York, NY - *StaDirAdAg 2-84*
Uniworld Languages - Haddonfield, NJ - *MagIndMarPl 82-83*
Unix/World - Los Altos, CA - *BaconPubCkMag 84*
Unknowns - Atlanta, GA - *LitMag&SmPr 83-84*
Unlimited Service [of Communications Group Inc.] - Concord, MA - *TeleSy&SerDir 2-84*
Unlimited Solutions AV Inc. - New Berlin, WI - *AvMarPl 83*
Unlisted Drugs/Pharmaco-Medical Documentation Inc. - Chatham, NJ - *FBInfSer 80*
UNM Alumnus - Albuquerque, NM - *WritMar 84*
Unmuzzled Ox - New York, NY - *ArtMar 84; LitMag&SmPr 83-84; WritMar 84*
Unmuzzled Ox Books & Magazines [Aff. of Unmuzzled Ox Foundation Ltd.] - New York, NY - *BoPubDir 4, 5*
Uno Melodic Records - New York, NY - *BillIntBG 83-84*
Unregulated Record Co. Inc. - College, AK - *BillIntBG 83-84*
Unspeakable Visions of the Individual - California, PA - *ArtMar 84; BoPubDir 4, 5; LitMag&SmPr 83-84*
Unterrified Democrat - Linn, MO - *AyerDirPub 83; Ed&PubIntYB 82*
Unusual Films [of Bob Jones University] - Greenville, SC - *AvMarPl 83; Tel&CabFB 84C*
UOI Co. - Sherman Oaks, CA - *MicrocomMPl 84*
UOP Inc. - Des Plaines, IL - *DirInfWP 82*
Up Against the Wall Mother [of Miriam Press Inc.] - Alexandria, VA - *ArtMar 84; LitMag&SmPr 83-84; WritMar 84*
Up Beat Magazine - Chicago, IL - *WritMar 84*
Up Press - East Palo Alto, CA - *LitMag&SmPr 83-84*
Up With People - Tucson, AZ - *BillIntBG 83-84*
UPA Pictures Inc. - Burbank, CA - *TelAl 83, 84*
UPA Pictures Inc. - Los Angeles, CA - *Tel&CabFB 84C*
UPA Productions of America - Burbank, CA - *TelAl 83, 84*
UPA Productions of America - Los Angeles, CA - *Tel&CabFB 84C*
Upam Music Co. - *See* Gopam Enterprises Inc.
Updata Publications Inc. - Los Angeles, CA - *EISS 83; LitMarPl 83, 84; MagIndMarPl 82-83; MicroMarPl 82-83*
Update - Palo Alto, CA - *BaconPubCkMag 84*
Update - Tulare, CA - *AyerDirPub 83*
Update - Aarhus, Denmark - *LitMag&SmPr 83-84*
Update AB - Gothenburg, Sweden - *EISS 5-84 Sup*
Update Publicare Co. - Houston, TX - *LitMag&SmPr 83-84*
Update/The American States [Subs. of Tower Consultants International] - Lake Worth, FL - *DataDirOnSer 84; DirOnDB Spring 84; EISS 7-83 Sup*
Upgrade Data System [of Council on Environmental Quality] - Washington, DC - *EISS 83*
Upholstering Industry [of HDC Publications] - New York, NY - *MagDir 84*
Upholstering Today - High Point, NC - *BaconPubCkMag 84*
UPI (Broadcast Div.) - Chicago, IL - *BrCabYB 84*
UPI Audio Network - Washington, DC - *BrCabYB 84*
UPI Cable News - New York, NY - *BrCabYB 84*
UPI Datacable - Dallas, TX - *Tel&CabFB 84C*
UPI News - New York, NY - *DirOnDB Spring 84*
UPI News Database [of Source Telecomputing Corp.] - McLean, VA - *DataDirOnSer 84*
UPI Newsfeatures - New York, NY - *BaconPubCkNews 84*
UPI Newswire [of Scripps-Howard] - New York, NY - *HomeVid&CabYB 82-83*
UPI Photos - New York, NY - *MagIndMarPl 82-83*
UPITN [of United Press International & Independent Television News Ltd.] - New York, NY - *TelAl 83, 84; Tel&CabFB 84C*
Upjohn Institute for Employment Research, W. E. - Kalamazoo, MI - *BoPubDir 4, 5*
Upland Courier [of Claremont Courier Graphics Corp.] - Claremont, CA - *NewsDir 84*
Upland Courier - *See* Claremont Courier Graphics Corp.
Upland News [of Ontario Bonita Publishing Co.] - Ontario, CA - *NewsDir 84*
Upland News - Upland, CA - *AyerDirPub 83; Ed&PubIntYB 82*
Upland News - *See* Ontario Daily Report
Upland Press - Chicago, IL - *BoPubDir 4, 5*
Uplift Books [Aff. of Tanner Literary Associates] - Brea, CA - *BoPubDir 4 Sup, 5*
Upper Arlington News - Columbus, OH - *AyerDirPub 83*
Upper Arlington News - *See* Suburban News Publications
Upper Country News-Reporter - Cambridge, ID - *AyerDirPub 83; Ed&PubIntYB 82*
Upper Country People Probe - Hartsville, TN - *BoPubDir 5*
Upper Darby Delaware County Times - Upper Darby, PA - *Ed&PubIntYB 82*
Upper Darby News of Delaware County [of Acme Newspapers Inc.] - Upper Darby, PA - *NewsDir 84*
Upper Darby News of Delaware County - *See* Acme Newspapers Inc.

Upper Darby Press [of Press Publishing Co.] - Drexel Hill, PA - *AyerDirPub 83; NewsDir 84*
Upper Darby Press - Upper Darby, PA - *Ed&PubIntYB 82*
Upper Darby Press - *See* Press Publishing Co.
Upper Dauphin Sentinel [of Kocher Enterprises Inc.] - Millersburg, PA - *AyerDirPub 83; Ed&PubIntYB 82; NewsDir 84*
Upper Deck--The Affluent Population - New York, NY - *DirOnDB Spring 84*
Upper Des Moines - Algona, IA - *AyerDirPub 83*
Upper Islander - Campbell River, BC, Canada - *AyerDirPub 83*
Upper Marlboro Enquirer-Gazette - Upper Marlboro, MD - *BaconPubCkNews 84; NewsDir 84*
Upper Peninsula Telephone Co. - Carney, MI - *TelDir&BG 83-84*
Upper Room, The - Nashville, TN - *LitMarPl 83, 84; MagIndMarPl 82-83; WritMar 84*
Upper Sandusky Chief-Union [of Hardin County Publishing Co. Inc.] - Upper Sandusky, OH - *BaconPubCkNews 84; NewsDir 84*
Upper St. Clair Cable TV [of Adelphia Communications Corp.] - Upper St. Clair Township, PA - *Tel&CabFB 84C*
Upper Valley Cable Corp. [of St. Johnsbury Community TV Corp.] - Woodsville, NH - *BrCabYB 84; Tel&CabFB 84C*
Upper Valley Cable Corp. [of Simmons Communications Inc.] - Newbury, VT - *BrCabYB 84*
Upper Valley Cable Corp. [of St. Johnsbury Community TV Corp.] - Wells River, VT - *Tel&CabFB 84C*
Upper Valley Progress - Mission, TX - *AyerDirPub 83*
Upper Valley Telecable Co. Inc. - Idaho Falls, ID - *BrCabYB 84; Tel&CabFB 84C*
Upsala Cooperative Telephone Association - Upsala, MN - *TelDir&BG 83-84*
Upside Image Inc. - Miami, FL - *StaDirAdAg 2-84*
Upstairs Gallery - Willowdale, ON, Canada - *BoPubDir 4, 5*
Upstart Information Co. - Los Angeles, CA - *BoPubDir 4, 5*
Upstart Music Cos. - Arlington, TX - *BillIntBG 83-84*
Upstart Records - Santa Monica, CA - *BillIntBG 83-84*
Upstat Publishing Co. - Washington, DC - *BoPubDir 4, 5*
Upstate Labs - Rochester, NY - *MicrocomMPl 84*
Upstate Magazine - Rochester, NY - *WritMar 84*
Upstate NewChannels [Aff. of NewChannels Corp.] - North Syracuse, NY - *InterCabHB 3; Tel&CabFB 84C*
Upswing Artist Management Ltd. - New York, NY - *BillIntBG 83-84*
Upton Weston County Gazette - Upton, WY - *BaconPubCkNews 84*
Uptown Books - Glendale, CA - *BoPubDir 5*
Uptown News [of Chicago Lerner Newspapers] - Chicago, IL - *AyerDirPub 83; Ed&PubIntYB 82; NewsDir 84*
Upward Bound Music Co. Inc. - Miami, FL - *BillIntBG 83-84*
Urantia Foundation - Chicago, IL - *BoPubDir 4, 5*
Uranus - Beloit, WI - *LitMag&SmPr 83-84*
Uranus Publishing Co. - Woodland Hills, CA - *BoPubDir 4, 5*
Urbamet [of Questel Inc.] - Washington, DC - *DataDirOnSer 84*
Urbamet Network - Paris, France - *DirOnDB Spring 84; EISS 83*
Urban & Regional Information Systems Association - Washington, DC - *EISS 83*
Urban & Regional Information Systems Association - Bethesda, MD - *InterCabHB 3*
Urban & Schwarzenberg Inc. - Baltimore, MD - *LitMarPl 83, 84*
Urban & Social Change Review - Chestnut Hill, MA - *LitMag&SmPr 83-84*
Urban Cablevision Ltd. [of Capital Cable TV Ltd.] - Langford, BC, Canada - *BrCabYB 84*
Urban Data Bank of Paris & the Paris Region [of Paris Office of Urbanization] - Paris, France - *EISS 83*
Urban Data Processing Inc. - Burlington, MA - *DataDirSup 7-83; EISS 83*
Urban Decision Systems Inc. - Los Angeles, CA - *DataDirOnSer 84; EISS 83; InfIndMarPl 83; IntDirMarRes 83*
Urban Design Centre Society - Vancouver, BC, Canada - *BoPubDir 4, 5*
Urban Design Newsletter [of R.C. Publications] - New York, NY - *MagDir 84*
Urban Georgia [of Georgia Municipal Association] - Atlanta, GA - *BaconPubCkMag 84; MagDir 84*
Urban Information Center [of Milwaukee Urban Conservatory] - Milwaukee, WI - *EISS 83*
Urban Institute Press - Washington, DC - *LitMarPl 83, 84*
Urban Land - Washington, DC - *MagIndMarPl 82-83*
Urban Land Institute - Washington, DC - *BoPubDir 4*
Urban Mass Transportation Research Information Service [of National Academy of Sciences] - Washington, DC - *EISS 83*
Urban Outlook - Silver Spring, MD - *BaconPubCkMag 84*
Urban Public Relations Inc. - New York, NY - *DirPRFirms 83*
Urban Research Institute Inc. - Chicago, IL - *BoPubDir 5*
Urban Response Inc. - Canton, OH - *StaDirAdAg 2-84*
Urban Software Corp. - New York, NY - *MicrocomMPl 83, 84*
Urban Telephone Corp. - Clintonville, WI - *TelDir&BG 83-84*
Urban Transport News - Washington, DC - *BaconPubCkMag 84*
Urban Transportation Abroad - Washington, DC - *BaconPubCkMag 84*
Urban TV Cable Systems Inc. - Cumberland, OH - *BrCabYB 84; Tel&CabFB 84C*
Urban TV Cable Systems Inc. - Macksburg, OH - *BrCabYB 84*
Urban TV Cable Systems Inc. - Marietta, OH - *Tel&CabFB 84C p.1710*
Urbana Advertising & Marketing Inc. - East Orange, NJ - *StaDirAdAg 2-84*
Urbana Daily Citizen [of Brown Publishing Co.] - Urbana, OH - *BaconPubCkNews 84; Ed&PubIntYB 82; NewsDir 84*
Urbandale News - Des Moines, IA - *NewsDir 84*
Urbandale News - Urbandale, IA - *AyerDirPub 83; BaconPubCkNews 84; Ed&PubIntYB 82*
Urbanek, Mae - Lusk, WY - *BoPubDir 4 Sup, 5*
Urbanisme Amenagement Environnement Transports [of Institut d'Amenagement et d'Urbanisme de la Region d'Ille de France] - Paris, France - *CompReadDB 82*
Urbanite - Arlington, TX - *AyerDirPub 83*
Urbanna Southside Sentinel - Urbanna, VA - *BaconPubCkNews 84; NewsDir 84*
Urdang Inc., Laurence - Essex, CT - *EISS 83; LitMarPl 83, 84*
Ure Co., Jim - Salt Lake City, UT - *StaDirAdAg 2-84*
Urethane Abstracts [of Technomic Publishing Co. Inc.] - Westport, CT - *MagDir 84*
Urethane Foam Insulation - Dayton, OH - *BaconPubCkMag 84*
Urethane Plastics & Products [of Technomic Publishing Co. Inc.] - Lancaster, PA - *BaconPubCkMag 84; MagDir 84*
Urie, Sherry - West Glover, VT - *BoPubDir 4, 5*
Urion Press - San Jose, CA - *BoPubDir 5; LitMag&SmPr 83-84*
Urion Press - Eugene, OR - *BoPubDir 4*
Urner Barry's Price-Current - Bayville, NJ - *NewsDir 84*
Urner Barry's Price-Current - Toms River, NJ - *Ed&PubIntYB 82*
Urness, Reginald - Grand Forks Air Force, ND - *Tel&CabFB 84C p.1710*
U.R.O.B.A. Messenger - Pittsburgh, PA - *NewsDir 84*
Uroboros [of Allegany Mountain Press] - Olean, NY - *LitMag&SmPr 83-84*
Urology - Ridgewood, NJ - *MagDir 84*
Urology Times - Miami, FL - *MagDir 84*
Urology Times - New York, NY - *BaconPubCkMag 84*
Urquhart, O. - Toronto, ON, Canada - *BoPubDir 4, 5*
Urstadt Inc., Susan P. - New York, NY - *LitMarPl 83, 84*
Ury Associates Inc., Bernard E. - Chicago, IL - *DirPRFirms 83*
Us [of Concentric Enterprises Inc.] - New York, NY - *BaconPubCkMag 84; DirMarMP 83; Folio 83; LitMarPl 84; MagDir 84; MagIndMarPl 82-83; NewsBur 6; WritMar 84*
U.S. Advisory Council on Historic Preservation - Washington, DC - *BoPubDir 5*
U.S. Agriculture - Bala Cynwyd, PA - *DirOnDB Spring 84*
U.S. Agriculture Dept. (Radio & Television Center) - Washington, DC - *Tel&CabFB 84C*
US Air Magaine - New York, NY - *BaconPubCkMag 84*
U.S. Army (Cold Regions Research & Engineering Laboratory) - Hanover, NH - *CompReadDB 82*
U.S. Army (Construction Engineering Research Laboratory) - Champaign, IL - *BoPubDir 5*
U.S. Army Dept. - Washington, DC - *Tel&CabFB 84C*
U.S.-Asiatic Co. Ltd. - Tokyo, Japan - *EISS 83; InfIndMarPl 83; InfoS 83-84*
U.S. Association for the Club of Rome - Washington, DC - *BoPubDir 5*
US-AV Network Inc. - Ft. Lauderdale, FL - *AvMarPl 83*

U.S. Banks [of I. P. Sharp Associates Ltd.] - Toronto, ON, Canada - *DataDirOnSer 84*
U.S. Board on Geographic Names - Washington, DC - *EISS 83*
US Book Overseas Service - Great Neck, NY - *LitMarPl 83, 84*
U.S. Briefs Inc. [Subs. of Hughes Communications Inc.] - Rockford, IL - *DirMarMP 83*
U.S. Bureau of Labor Statistics [Aff. of U.S. Dept. of Labor] - Washington, DC - *BoPubDir 4*
US Bureau of the Census [of U.S. Dept. of Commerce] - Washington, DC - *DataDirOnSer 84*
U.S. Bureau of the Census (Foreign Trade Div.) - Washington, DC - *CompReadDB 82*
US Cable Corp. - Hackensack, NJ - *BrCabYB 84 p.D-309; Tel&CabFB 84C p.1710*
US Cable of Blue Ridge Associates [of US Cable Corp.] - Inman, SC - *BrCabYB 84; Tel&CabFB 84C*
US Cable of Lake County - Waukegan, IL - *BrCabYB 84; Tel&CabFB 84C*
US Cable of North Gibson [of US Cable Corp.] - Dyer, TN - *Tel&CabFB 84C*
US Cable of Northern Indiana - Griffith, IN - *Tel&CabFB 84C*
US Cable of Tri-County - Arcade, NY - *Tel&CabFB 84C*
US Cable of Tri-County Ltd. - Ellicottville, NY - *BrCabYB 84*
U.S. Cable of West Texas [of US Cable Corp.] - Denver City, TX - *BrCabYB 84; Tel&CabFB 84C*
U.S. Cable of West Texas [of West Texas CATV Associates] - Ft. Stockton, TX - *BrCabYB 84*
U.S. Cable of West Texas - Seagraves, TX - *BrCabYB 84*
U.S. Cable of West Texas - Seminole, TX - *BrCabYB 84*
U.S. Cablevision Corp. [of Colony Communications Inc.] - Beacon, NY - *BrCabYB 84; InterCabHB 3; Tel&CabFB 84C*
U.S. Cablevision Corp. [of Colony Communications Inc.] - Hyde Park, NY - *Tel&CabFB 84C*
U.S. Cablevision Corp. [of Colony Communications Inc.] - Lloyd, NY - *BrCabYB 84; Tel&CabFB 84C*
U.S. Cablevision Corp. [of Colony Communications Inc.] - Monroe, NY - *BrCabYB 84; Tel&CabFB 84C*
U.S. Cablevision Corp. [of Colony Communications Inc.] - Wappinger, NY - *Tel&CabFB 84C*
U.S. Cablevision Corp. [of Colony Communications Inc.] - Wappingers Falls, NY - *BrCabYB 84*
U.S.-Canadian Range Management Bibliography [of Oryx Press] - Phoenix, AZ - *EISS 83*
U.S. Capitol Historical Society - Washington, DC - *BoPubDir 4, 5*
U.S. Catholic [of Claretian Fathers] - Chicago, IL - *BaconPubCkMag 84; LitMarPl 83, 84; MagIndMarPl 82-83*
U.S. Catholic Conference (Dept. of Communication) - New York, NY - *Tel&CabFB 84C*
U.S. Catholic Historical Society - Yonkers, NY - *BoPubDir 4, 5*
U.S. Census 1980 [of Data Resources Inc.] - Lexington, MA - *DataDirOnSer 84*
U.S. Census 1980 Data Base - Washington, DC - *DirOnDB Spring 84*
U.S. Census of Agriculture [of On-Line Research Inc.] - Greenwich, CT - *DataDirOnSer 84*
U.S. Census of Agriculture - Washington, DC - *DBBus 82; DirOnDB Spring 84*
U.S. Census of Retail Trade [of On-Line Research Inc.] - Greenwich, CT - *DataDirOnSer 84*
U.S. Census of Retail Trade - Washington, DC - *DBBus 82*
U.S. Census Report - Silver Spring, MD - *DirOnDB Spring 84*
U.S. Census Report [of NewsNet Inc.] - Bryn Mawr, PA - *DataDirOnSer 84*
U.S. Central Data Bank - Washington, DC - *DirOnDB Spring 84*
U.S. Central Data Bank [of Data Resources Inc.] - Lexington, MA - *DataDirOnSer 84; DBBus 82*
U.S. Classifications [of Derwent Publications Ltd.] - London, England - *CompReadDB 82*
U.S. Committee for Refugees [Aff. of American Council for Nationalities Service] - New York, NY - *BoPubDir 5*
U.S. Committee for UNICEF - New York, NY - *BoPubDir 4, 5*
U.S. Congress (Congressional Budget Office) - Washington, DC - *BoPubDir 5*
U.S. Consumer Price Index [of I. P. Sharp Associates Ltd.] - Toronto, ON, Canada - *DataDirOnSer 84*
U.S. Contract Awards [of Washington Representative Services] - Arlington, VA - *CompReadDB 82*
U.S. County Data Bank - Washington, DC - *DirOnDB Spring 84*
U.S. County Data Bank [of Data Resources Inc.] - Lexington, MA - *DataDirOnSer 84; DBBus 82*
U.S. Dept. of Agriculture (Agricultural Stabilization & Conservation Service) - Washington, DC - *BoPubDir 5*
U.S. Dept. of Agriculture (Food Safety & Quality Service) - Washington, DC - *BoPubDir 5*
U.S. Dept. of Agriculture (Foreign Agricultural Service) - Washington, DC - *BoPubDir 5*
U.S. Dept. of Agriculture (Forest Service Pacific Northwest & Range Experiment Stations) - Portland, OR - *BoPubDir 5*
U.S. Dept. of Agriculture (Forest Service Pacific Southwest Experiment Station) - Berkeley, CA - *BoPubDir 5*
U.S. Dept. of Agriculture (National Veterinary Services Laboratories) - Ames, IA - *BoPubDir 5*
U.S. Dept. of Agriculture (Science & Education Administration Technical Information Systems) - Beltsville, MD - *CompReadDB 82*
U.S. Dept. of Commerce - Washington, DC - *BoPubDir 5; CompReadDB 82*
U.S. Dept. of Commerce (Bureau of Economic Analysis) - Washington, DC - *BoPubDir 5*
U.S. Dept. of Commerce (Bureau of Industrial Economics) - Washington, DC - *BoPubDir 5*
U.S. Dept. of Commerce (International Trade Commission) - Washington, DC - *BoPubDir 5*
U.S. Dept. of Commerce (National Bureau of Standards) - Washington, DC - *BoPubDir 5*
U.S. Dept. of Commerce (Trade Facilitation Information & Services Div.) - Washington, DC - *CompReadDB 82*
U.S. Dept. of Defense (Directorate for Information Operations & Reports) - Washington, DC - *BoPubDir 5*
U.S. Dept. of Education (National Center for Education Statistics) - Washington, DC - *BoPubDir 5; CompReadDB 82*
U.S. Dept. of Energy - Oak Ridge, TN - *BoPubDir 4*
U.S. Dept. of Energy (National Energy Software Center) - Argonne, IL - *InfIndMarPl 83*
U.S. Dept. of Energy (Technical Information Center) - Oak Ridge, TN - *BoPubDir 5; CompReadDB 82; DataDirOnSer 84*
U.S. Dept. of Energy Library - Washington, DC - *CompReadDB 82*
U.S. Dept. of Health & Human Services (National Center for Health Statistics) - Bethesda, MD - *BoPubDir 5*
U.S. Dept. of Health & Human Services (National Institutes of Health Research Resources) - Bethesda, MD - *BoPubDir 5*
U.S. Dept. of Health & Human Services (Office on Smoking & Health) - Rockville, MD - *BoPubDir 5*
U.S. Dept. of Interior (Oil & Gas Resources Branch of Geological Survey) - Reston, VA - *BoPubDir 5*
US Dept. of Justice (Information Systems Staff) - Washington, DC - *DataDirOnSer 84*
U.S. Dept. of Labor (Bureau of Labor Statistics) - Washington, DC - *BoPubDir 5; CompReadDB 82*
U.S. Dept. of Labor (Employment Standards Administration) - Washington, DC - *BoPubDir 4 Sup, 5*
U.S. Dept. of State (Bureau of Public Affairs) - Washington, DC - *BoPubDir 4, 5*
U.S. Dept. of the Interior - Washington, DC - *BoPubDir 5*
U.S. Dept. of the Interior (Bureau of Mines) - Washington, DC - *BoPubDir 5*
U.S. Dept. of the Interior (Office of Water Research & Technology) - Washington, DC - *CompReadDB 82*
U.S. Dept. of Transportation (Federal Aviation Administration) - Washington, DC - *BoPubDir 5*
U.S. Dept. of Transportation (Maritime Administration) - Washington, DC - *BoPubDir 5*
U.S. Dept. of Transportation (Maritime Administration) - New York, NY - *BoPubDir 5*
U.S. Dept. of Transportation (Materials Transportation Bureau) - Washington, DC - *BoPubDir 5*
U.S. Dept. of Transportation (National Highway Traffic Safety Administration) - Washington, DC - *BoPubDir 5*
U.S. Dept. of Treasury (Office of the Comptroller of the Currency) - Washington, DC - *BoPubDir 5*
U.S. Design Corp. - Lanham, MD - *DataDirSup 7-83*

US Directory Services - Miami, FL - *LitMarPl 83, 84*
U.S. Econ - Ann Arbor, MI - *DirOnDB Spring 84*
U.S. Economic [of ADP Network Services] - Ann Arbor, MI - *DataDirOnSer 84; DBBus 82*
U.S. Economic/CE [of Chase Econometrics/Interactive Data Corp.] - Waltham, MA - *DBBus 82*
U.S. Economic Data Base - Princeton, NJ - *DirOnDB Spring 84*
U.S. Economic Forecast Data Base - Mt. Kisco, NY - *DirOnDB Spring 84*
U.S. Electronic Industry Econometric Forecasts [of Data Resources Inc.] - Lexington, MA - *DataDirOnSer 84*
U.S. Electronics Industry Econometric Service - San Mateo, CA - *DirOnDB Spring 84*
U.S. Energy Data Bank - Washington, DC - *DirOnDB Spring 84*
U.S. Energy Forecast - Bala Cynwyd, PA - *DirOnDB Spring 84*
U.S. Environmental Protection Agency - Washington, DC - *CompReadDB 82; DataDirOnSer 84*
U.S. Environmental Protection Agency (Air Pollution Technical Information Center) - Research Triangle Park, NC - *CompReadDB 82*
U.S. Environmental Protection Agency (Information Dissemination Project) - Columbus, OH - *CompReadDB 82*
U.S. Environmental Protection Agency (Office of Pesticides & Toxic Substances) - Washington, DC - *CompReadDB 82*
U.S. Environmental Protection Agency (Office of Toxic Substances) - Washington, DC - *CompReadDB 82*
U.S. Environmental Protection Agency (Oil & Special Materials Control Div.) - Washington, DC - *CompReadDB 82*
U.S. Exports [of Dialog Information Services Inc.] - Palo Alto, CA - *DataDirOnSer 84; DirOnDB Spring 84*
U.S. Exports [of U.S. Census Bureau] - Washington, DC - *CompReadDB 82; DBBus 82*
U.S. Federal Communications Commission - Washington, DC - *TeleSy&SerDir 7-83, 2-84*
U.S. Fertilizer - Bala Cynwyd, PA - *DirOnDB Spring 84*
U.S. Fertilizer Forecast - Bala Cynwyd, PA - *DirOnDB Spring 84*
U.S. Financial [of ADP Network Services] - Ann Arbor, MI - *DataDirOnSer 84; DBBus 82*
U.S. Fish & Wildlife Service (Pacific Islands Study Group) - Portland, OR - *CompReadDB 82*
U.S. Flow of Funds Accounts [of U.S. Federal Reserve System] - Washington, DC - *EISS 83*
U.S. Foamed Plastics Markets & Directory - Westport, CT - *MagDir 84*
U.S. Food & Agriculture Forecast - Bala Cynwyd, PA - *DirOnDB Spring 84*
U.S. Forecasts Abstracts [of Predicasts Inc.] - Cleveland, OH - *CompReadDB 82*
U.S. Games Systems Inc. - New York, NY - *DirMarMP 83; LitMarPl 83, 84; WritMar 84*
U.S. Geological Survey [Aff. of U.S. Dept. of the Interior] - Reston, VA - *BoPubDir 4, 5*
U.S. Glass, Metal, & Glazing [of U.S. Glass Publications Inc.] - Memphis, TN - *BaconPubCkMag 84; MagDir 84*
U.S. Golf Association - Far Hills, NJ - *BoPubDir 4, 5*
U.S. Government Advertiser [of Ardole Publishing Co. Inc.] - New York, NY - *MagDir 84*
U.S. Government Contract Awards - Arlington, VA - *DBBus 82*
U.S. Historical Documents Institute - Arlington, VA - *LitMarPl 83, 84; MagIndMarPl 82-83; MicroMarPl 82-83*
U.S. Imports of Iron & Steel [of Chase Econometrics/Interactive Data Corp.] - Waltham, MA - *DataDirOnSer 84*
U.S. Information Moscow - Mountain View, CA - *LitMag&SmPr 83-84*
U.S. Institute for Theatre Technology Inc. - Charlottesville, VA - *LitMag&SmPr 83-84*
U.S. Insurance Data Bank - Washington, DC - *DirOnDB Spring 84*
U.S. Insurance Data Bank [of Data Resources Inc.] - Lexington, MA - *DataDirOnSer 84*
U.S. International Air Travel Statistics - Washington, DC - *DirOnDB Spring 84*
U.S. International Air Travel Statistics [of U.S. Dept. of Transportation] - Cambridge, MA - *EISS 83*
U.S. International Air Travel Statistics [of I. P. Sharp Associates Ltd.] - Toronto, ON, Canada - *DataDirOnSer 84*
U.S. International Marketing Co. Inc. - Bellflower, CA - *DirMarMP 83*
U.S. Iron & Steel Imports [of Chase Econometrics/Interactive Data Corp.] - Waltham, MA - *DBBus 82*
U.S. League of Savings Associations - Chicago, IL - *BoPubDir 5*
US Lithograph Inc. - New York, NY - *LitMarPl 83, 84; MagIndMarPl 82-83*
U.S. Macroeconomic [of Chase Econometrics/Interactive Data Corp.] - Waltham, MA - *DataDirOnSer 84*
U.S. Macroeconomic - Bala Cynwyd, PA - *DirOnDB Spring 84*
U.S. Macroeconomic Forecast - Bala Cynwyd, PA - *DirOnDB Spring 84*
U.S. Media Corp. - Walnut Creek, CA - *StaDirAdAg 2-84*
U.S. Medicine - Washington, DC - *BaconPubCkMag 84; MagDir 84*
U.S. Model Data Bank - Washington, DC - *DirOnDB Spring 84*
U.S. Model Data Bank [of Data Resources Inc.] - Lexington, MA - *DataDirOnSer 84; DBBus 82*
U.S. National Aeronautics & Space Administration (Scientific & Technical Information Branch) - Washington, DC - *CompReadDB 82*
U.S. National Aeronautics & Space Administration (Standard/Available Flight Qualified Equipment Project) - Washington, DC - *CompReadDB 82*
U.S. National Archives & Records Service (Publications Sales Branch) - Washington, DC - *MicroMarPl 82-83*
U.S. National Commission on Libraries & Information Science - Washington, DC - *EISS 83*
U.S. National Income & Product Accounts - Bala Cynwyd, PA - *DirOnDB Spring 84*
U.S. National Library of Medicine - Bethesda, MD - *EISS 83*
U.S. National Technical Information Service - Springfield, VA - *EISS 83*
U.S. Naval Institute Proceedings - Annapolis, MD - *MagDir 84; WritMar 84*
U.S. Naval Observatory Automated Data Service - Washington, DC - *DirOnDB Spring 84*
U.S. News & World Report - Washington, DC - *AdAge 6-28-84; BaconPubCkMag 84; DirMarMP 83; Folio 83; KnowInd 83; LitMarPl 83, 84; MagDir 84; MagIndMarPl 82-83; NewsBur 6; WritMar 84*
U.S. News Washington Letter - Washington, DC - *DirOnDB Spring 84*
U.S. Office of Management & Budget [of Executive Office of the President] - Washington, DC - *CompReadDB 82*
U.S. Oil Week - Arlington, VA - *BaconPubCkMag 84*
US1 Poets' Cooperative - Roosevelt, NJ - *BoPubDir 4 Sup, 5; LitMag&SmPr 83-84*
US1 Worksheets [of US1 Poets' Cooperative] - Roosevelt, NJ - *LitMag&SmPr 83-84*
U.S. Passenger Car & Light Truck Forecast - Bala Cynwyd, PA - *DirOnDB Spring 84*
U.S. Patent Classification System [of U.S. Patent & Trademark Office] - Washington, DC - *EISS 83*
U.S. Patent Information Service [of Japan Patent Information Center] - Tokyo, Japan - *CompReadDB 82*
U.S. Patent Office Files [of SDC Information Systems] - Santa Monica, CA - *DataDirOnSer 84*
U.S. Patents [of Derwent Publications Ltd.] - London, England - *CompReadDB 82*
U.S. Patents Files [of Derwent Inc.] - McLean, VA - *EISS 5-84 Sup*
U.S. Pharmacist [of Jobson Publishing Corp.] - New York, NY - *ArtMar 84; BaconPubCkMag 84; MagDir 84; MagIndMarPl 82-83*
US Pioneer Electronics Corp. - Moonachie, NJ - *BillIntBG 83-84*
U.S. Political Science Documents [of University of Pittsburgh] - Pittsburgh, PA - *CompReadDB 82; DirOnDB Spring 84*
U.S. Prices Data Bank - Washington, DC - *DirOnDB Spring 84*
U.S. Prices Data Bank [of Data Resources Inc.] - Lexington, MA - *DataDirOnSer 84; DBBus 82*
U.S. Professional Development Institute Inc. - Silver Spring, MD - *BoPubDir 5; InfoS 83-84*
U.S. Progressive Periodicals Directory Update [of Progressive Education] - Nashville, TN - *LitMag&SmPr 83-84*
U.S. Public School Directory [of Dialog Information Services Inc.] - Palo Alto, CA - *DataDirOnSer 84*

U.S. Public School Directory - Washington, DC - *CompReadDB 82; DBBus 82*
U.S. Quarterly Financial Report [of I. P. Sharp Associates Ltd.] - Toronto, ON, Canada - *DataDirOnSer 84*
U.S. Regional [of Data Resources Inc.] - Lexington, MA - *DBBus 82*
U.S. Regional Data Bank - Washington, DC - *DirOnDB Spring 84*
U.S. Regional Data Bank [of Data Resources Inc.] - Lexington, MA - *DataDirOnSer 84*
U.S. Regional Data Bank/Week - Washington, DC - *DirOnDB Spring 84*
U.S. Requests for Proposals [of Washington Representative Services Inc.] - Arlington, VA - *DBBus 82*
U.S. Requests for Proposals 1 (Announcements File) - Arlington, VA - *CompReadDB 82*
U.S. Requests for Proposals 2 (Summaries File) - Arlington, VA - *CompReadDB 82*
U.S. Requests for Proposals 3 (Amendments File) - Arlington, VA - *CompReadDB 82*
US Robotics - Chicago, IL - *DataDirSup 7-83; MicrocomMPl 84*
U.S. Satellite Broadcasting Co. [Subs. of Hubbard Broadcasting Inc.] - St. Paul, MN - *HomeVid&CabYB 82-83*
U.S. Securities & Exchange Commission - Washington, DC - *BoPubDir 5*
U.S. Small Business Administration - Washington, DC - *BoPubDir 5*
U.S. Software Inc. - Dallas, TX - *MicrocomMPl 84*
U.S. Steel Corp. (Audiovisual Services) - Pittsburgh, PA - *AvMarPl 83*
U.S. Stock Options - New York, NY - *DirOnDB Spring 84*
U.S. Stock Options Data Base [of Interactive Data Services Inc.] - New York, NY - *DBBus 82*
U.S. Suburban Press Inc. - Schaumburg, IL - *NewsDir 84*
U.S. Systems Corp. - Arlington, VA - *ADAPSOMemDir 83-84*
U.S. Time Series [of Predicasts Inc.] - Cleveland, OH - *CompReadDB 82*
U.S. Tobacco Journal - New York, NY - *MagDir 84*
U.S. Travel Data Center - Washington, DC - *BoPubDir 4 Sup, 5*
USA Cable Network - Glen Rock, NJ - *BrCabYB 84; CabTVPrDB 83*
USA Database [of Evans Economics Inc.] - Washington, DC - *DataDirOnSer 84*
USA Home Video - *See* Family Home Entertainment
USA Network - Glen Rock, NJ - *BrCabYB 84; HomeVid&CabYB 82-83; TelAl 83; Tel&CabFB 84C*
USA Publishing Co. - Emeryville, CA - *DirMarMP 83; LitMarPl 83, 84*
U.S.A. Syndicate - New York, NY - *Ed&PubIntYB 82*
USA Today [of Gannett Co. Inc.] - Washington, DC - *BaconPubCkNews 84; LitMarPl 84*
USA Today [of The Society for the Advancement of Education Inc.] - New York, NY - *ArtMar 84; BaconPubCkMag 84; LitMarPl 83, 84; MagDir 84; MagIndMarPl 82-83*
USAir Magazine [of East/West Network Inc.] - New York, NY - *MagDir 84; WritMar 84*
USBond - Toronto, ON, Canada - *DirOnDB Spring 84*
Usborne Hayes Books - Tulsa, OK - *BoPubDir 4, 5*
USC Broadcast Production/Media Services - Los Angeles, CA - *AvMarPl 83*
USC Engineer [of Josten's Publications] - Los Angeles, CA - *MagDir 84*
USC Engineer - Villanova, PA - *BaconPubCkMag 84*
USClass [of SDC Information Systems] - Santa Monica, CA - *DataDirOnSer 84*
USClass [of Derwent Inc.] - McLean, VA - *DirOnDB Spring 84; EISS 5-84 Sup*
USClass [of Derwent Publications Ltd.] - London, England - *DBBus 82*
USDA SEA Technical Information Systems - Beltsville, MD - *CompReadDB 82*
USData Corp. - Dallas, TX - *WhoWMicrocom 83*
USData Corp. - Richardson, TX - *WhoWMicrocom 83*
Use Electronics - Midland Park, NJ - *MicrocomMPl 84*
Used Computers Inc. - Berwyn, PA - *DataDirSup 7-83*
Used Equipment Directory - Jersey City, NJ - *MagIndMarPl 82-83*
User Education Resources Data Base [of Caufield Institute of Technology Library] - Caufield East, Austria - *EISS 83*
User-Friendly Software Inc. - Hollywood, FL - *MicrocomSwDir 1*
User-Friendly Software Inc. - Melville, NY - *MicrocomMPl 84; MicrocomSwDir 1*
User Friendly Systems Inc. - Fairfield, OH - *MicrocomSwDir 1*
User Group Inc., The - St. Louis, MO - *InfIndMarPl 83*
User Technology Services Inc. - Valley Cottage, NY - *ADAPSOMemDir 83-84*
Userkit [of Williams & Nevin] - Stockport, England - *EISS 83*
User's Guide to CP/M Systems & Software - Stanford, CA - *BaconPubCkMag 84*
Users Inc. - Valley Forge, PA - *ADAPSOMemDir 83-84; DataDirOnSer 84*
Userware International - Escondido, CA - *MicrocomSwDir 1*
USFL Kickoff Magazine - San Francisco, CA - *MagDir 84*
USGCA - Washington, DC - *DirOnDB Spring 84*
USGF Gymnastics - Indianapolis, IN - *BaconPubCkMag 84*
Ushio America Inc. [Subs. of Ushio Inc.] - Torrance, CA - *AvMarPl 83*
USI Computer Products - Brisbane, CA - *WhoWMicrocom 83*
USI International - Brisbane, CA - *MicrocomMPl 84*
Uslander, Arlene S. - Skokie, IL - *LitMarPl 84*
USP Needham Australia Party Ltd. - *See* Needham, Harper & Steers Inc.
USPatents - McLean, VA - *DirOnDB Spring 84*
USPO/USPA [of Derwent Publications Ltd.] - London, England - *DBBus 82*
USS Engineers & Consultants Inc. - Pittsburgh, PA - *DataDirSup 7-83*
USS Enterprises - San Jose, CA - *MicrocomSwDir 1*
USTV - Burlingame, CA - *TelAl 83*
U.T. Daily Beacon [of University of Tennessee] - Knoxville, TN - *NewsDir 84*
Utah Beverage Analyst [of Bevan Inc.] - Denver, CO - *BaconPubCkMag 84; MagDir 84*
Utah Cattleman, The - Salt Lake City, UT - *MagDir 84*
Utah Computer Retrieval Information Service [of Utah State Office of Education] - Salt Lake City, UT - *EISS 83*
Utah Div. of State History [of Utah State Historical Society] - Salt Lake City, UT - *BoPubDir 4, 5*
Utah Farmer-Stockman - Salt Lake City, UT - *MagDir 84*
Utah Farmer-Stockman - Spokane, WA - *BaconPubCkMag 84*
Utah Holiday - Salt Lake City, UT - *BaconPubCkMag 84; MagDir 84; WritMar 84*
Utah League of Cities & Towns - Salt Lake City, UT - *BoPubDir 5*
Utah Online Users Group [of Whitmore Branch Library] - Salt Lake City, UT - *InfIndMarPl 83*
Utah Press Association - Salt Lake City, UT - *ProGuPRSer 4*
Utah Satellite Co. - Nephi, UT - *BrCabYB 84*
Utah Satellite Co. Inc. - Price, MT - *Tel&CabFB 84C*
Utah Satellite Co. Inc. [of Western Satellite Inc.] - Roosevelt, UT - *Tel&CabFB 84C*
Utah Science - Logan, UT - *MagDir 84*
Utah State University Press - Logan, UT - *LitMarPl 83, 84; WritMar 84*
Utah Statesman, The [of Associated Students of Utah State University] - Logan, UT - *NewsDir 84*
Utah-Wyoming Telecom - Kamas, UT - *TelDir&BG 83-84*
Ute Independent - Ute, IA - *Ed&PubIntYB 82*
Ute Pass Courier - Woodland Park, CO - *AyerDirPub 83; Ed&PubIntYB 82*
Utelwico Inc., The [Aff. of Public Service Telephone Co.] - Reynolds, GA - *TelDir&BG 83-84*
UTI Inc. - Maple Plain, MN - *MicrocomMPl 84*
Utica Advisor Newspaper [of SEM Newspapers] - Utica, MI - *BaconPubCkNews 84; NewsDir 84*
Utica Daily Press [of The Observer Dispatch Inc.] - Utica, NY - *BaconPubCkNews 84; NewsDir 84*
Utica Herald - Utica, OH - *BaconPubCkNews 84; Ed&PubIntYB 82*
Utica Observer-Dispatch [of Gannett Co. Inc.] - Utica, NY - *BaconPubCkNews 84; NewsDir 84*
Utilities Engineering - Brigantine, NJ - *MicrocomMPl 84; MicrocomSwDir 1*

Utilities Management Group Ltd. - Islington, ON, Canada - *Tel&CabFB 84C*
Utility Co., The - Los Angeles, CA - *MicrocomSwDir 1*
Utility Compustat II [of Standard & Poor's Compustat Services Inc.] - Englewood, CO - *DataDirOnSer 84*
Utility Data Institute [Div. of Management Analysis Co.] - Washington, DC - *DataDirOnSer 84; EISS 83; InfIndMarPl 83*
Utility Devices Inc. - Salt Lake City, UT - *DataDirSup 7-83*
Utility Purchasing & Stores - Durham, NH - *BaconPubCkMag 84; MagDir 84*
Utility Reporter [of IBEW Members] - Walnut Creek, CA - *NewsDir 84*
Utility Spotlight - New York, NY - *BaconPubCkMag 84*
Utility Supervision & Safety Letter - Waterford, CT - *ArtMar 84; WritMar 84*
Utopia [of Bancroft-Parkman Inc.] - New York, NY - *CompReadDB 82*
Utopia Software Inc. - Morganville, NJ - *MicrocomMPl 84*
Utopian Records - Macon, GA - *BillIntBG 83-84*
Utopian Universe Publishing Co. - East Elmhurst, NY - *BoPubDir 4, 5*
Utopic Furnace Press - Canada - *BoPubDir 4, 5*
UTU News [of United Transportation Union] - Cleveland, OH - *BaconPubCkMag 84; MagDir 84; WritMar 84*
UTV Cable Network - Fairlawn, NJ - *BrCabYB 84; CabTVPrDB 83*
Uvalde Leader-News - Uvalde, TX - *BaconPubCkNews 84; Ed&PubIntYB 82; NewsDir 84*
Uvalde TV Cable Corp. [of Times Mirror Cable Television Inc.] - Uvalde, TX - *BrCabYB 84*
Uveon Computer Systems Inc. - Denver, CO - *MicrocomMPl 83, 84; MicrocomSwDir 1; WhoWMicrocom 83*
UWM Post, The - Milwaukee, WI - *NewsDir 84*
Uzzano Press - Menomonie, WI - *BoPubDir 4, 5*

V

V & G Electric Co. - Wheeling, WV - *BrCabYB 84*
V & R Advertising Inc. - New York, NY - *BrCabYB 84; StaDirAdAg 2-84*
V-R Corp. - Vandalia, IL - *BrCabYB 84 p.D-310; Tel&CabFB 84C p.1711*
VA Graphics Corp. [Div. of The Adams Group] - New York, NY - *LitMarPl 83, 84*
Va-Nytt [of K-Konsult] - Stockholm, Sweden - *EISS 83*
Vaam Music - Los Angeles, CA - *BillIntBG 83-84*
Vaba Eesti Sona [of The Nordic Press Inc.] - New York, NY - *Ed&PubIntYB 82; NewsDir 84*
Vaba Eestlane - Toronto, ON, Canada - *Ed&PubIntYB 82*
Vacation Exchange Club Inc. - Youngstown, AZ - *BoPubDir 5*
Vacation Exchange Club Inc. - New York, NY - *BoPubDir 4*
Vacationland - Anaheim, CA - *BaconPubCkMag 84*
Vacaville Reporter - Vacaville, CA - *BaconPubCkNews 84; Ed&PubIntYB 82; NewsDir 84*
Vado Music Co. - Brooklyn, NY - *BillIntBG 83-84*
Vagabond Creations Inc. - Dayton, OH - *WritMar 84*
Vagabond Press - Ellensburg, WA - *BoPubDir 4, 5; LitMag&SmPr 83-84*
Vail Cable Communications Inc. [of Heritage Communications Inc.] - Vail, CO - *Tel&CabFB 84C*
Vail Cable TV [of Heritage Communications Inc.] - Vail, CO - *BrCabYB 84*
Vail Inc., Phyllis - Atlanta, GA - *IntDirMarRes 83*
Vail Observer - Vail, IA - *BaconPubCkNews 84*
Vail, Richard - Salt Lake City, UT - *Tel&CabFB 84C*
Vail Trail - Vail, CO - *BaconPubCkNews 84; Ed&PubIntYB 82; NewsDir 84*
Vailsburg Leader - Union, NJ - *AyerDirPub 83*
Vailsburg Leader - Vailsburg, NJ - *Ed&PubIntYB 82*
Vajra Bodhi Sea [of Buddhist Text Translation Society] - San Fransicco, CA - *LitMag&SmPr 83-84*
Valando Publishing Group Inc., Tommy - New York, NY - *BillIntBG 83-84*
VALCOM Inc. - Roanoke, VA - *DataDirSup 7-83*
Valders Journal - Valders, WI - *BaconPubCkNews 84; Ed&PubIntYB 82*
Valders Telephone Co. [Aff. of Telephone & Data Systems Inc.] - Valders, WI - *TelDir&BG 83-84*
Valdes Research Co. - Bronx, NY - *IntDirMarRes 83*
Valdese News - Valdese, NC - *BaconPubCkNews 84; Ed&PubIntYB 82*
Valdez Cablevision [of Alaska Cablevision Inc.] - Valdez, AK - *BrCabYB 84; Tel&CabFB 84C*
Valdez Music, Rocky - Hawthorne, CA - *BillIntBG 83-84*
Valdez Vanguard - Valdez, AK - *AyerDirPub 83; BaconPubCkNews 84; Ed&PubIntYB 82*
Valdosta Daily Times - Valdosta, GA - *BaconPubCkNews 84; Ed&PubIntYB 82; NewsDir 84*
Vale Associates, Sheldon - Wilkes-Barre, PA - *StaDirAdAg 2-84*
Vale Malheur Enterprise - Vale, OR - *BaconPubCkNews 84*
Valencia County News-Bulletin - Belen, NM - *AyerDirPub 83; Ed&PubIntYB 82*
Valenti, Don & Pat - Highland Park, IL - *LitMarPl 84*
Valentine Cable Television Service [of Midcontinent Cable Systems Co.] - Valentine, NE - *BrCabYB 84; Tel&CabFB 84C*
Valentine Newspaper - Valentine, NE - *AyerDirPub 83; BaconPubCkNews 84; Ed&PubIntYB 82; NewsDir 84*
Valentine Publishing & Drama Co. - Rhinebeck, NY - *BoPubDir 4 Sup, 5; LitMag&SmPr 83-84*
Valentine-Radford - Kansas City, MO - *AdAge 3-28-84; StaDirAdAg 2-84*
Valentine TV Cable - Valentine, TX - *Tel&CabFB 84C*
Valentino Inc., Thomas J. - New York, NY - *AvMarPl 83; BillIntBG 83-84; Tel&CabFB 84C*
Valhalla [of Merging Media] - Westfield, NJ - *LitMag&SmPr 83-84*
Valhalla Press [Aff. of Leaf Ericson Society] - Chicago, IL - *BoPubDir 5*
Valhalla Press - St. John's, NF, Canada - *BoPubDir 4, 5*
Valhalla Publishers - Washington, DC - *BoPubDir 4 Sup, 5*
Valhalla Recording Corp. - New York, NY - *BillIntBG 83-84*
Valhalla Voice - *See* Pleasantville Journal Publishers
Valhalla Voice, The - Valhalla, NY - *Ed&PubIntYB 82*
Valiant Challenger - Valiant, OK - *Ed&PubIntYB 82*
Valiant International Multi-Media Corp. [Subs. of Weldotron Corp.] - Hackensack, NJ - *AvMarPl 83*
Valiant International Pictures - Hollywood, CA - *TelAl 83, 84*
Valiant Universal Microcomputer Supply - Hackensack, NJ - *MicrocomMPl 84*
Valid Data Inc. - Plainview, NY - *WhoWMicrocom 83*
Vallejo, Andrew - Sumner, WA - *Tel&CabFB 84C p.1710*
Vallejo Independent Press - Vallejo, CA - *AyerDirPub 83*
Vallejo Metro Reporter - San Francisco, CA - *NewsDir 84*
Vallejo Suisun Fairfield Metro Reporter - *See* Reporter Publishing Co.
Vallejo Times Herald [of Donrey Media Group] - Vallejo, CA - *BaconPubCkNews 84; Ed&PubIntYB 82; NewsDir 84*
Valley Advance - Vincennes, IN - *AyerDirPub 83; Ed&PubIntYB 82*
Valley Advance - Creston, BC, Canada - *AyerDirPub 83*
Valley Advertiser - Victorville, CA - *AyerDirPub 83*
Valley Advocate - Amherst, MA - *Ed&PubIntYB 82*
Valley Advocate - Hatfield, MA - *AyerDirPub 83*
Valley & Foothills News - Yuma, AZ - *AyerDirPub 83*
Valley & Foothills News, The - East Yuma, AZ - *Ed&PubIntYB 82*
Valley Antenna Systems Inc. - Piqua, OH - *BrCabYB 84; Tel&CabFB 84C p.1710*
Valley Bank of Nevada (Business Services Div.) - Las Vegas, NV - *DataDirSup 7-83*
Valley Banner - Elkton, VA - *AyerDirPub 83; NewsDir 84*
Valley Cable Corp. - Brownsville, MN - *Tel&CabFB 84C*
Valley Cable Corp. [of Marcus Communications Inc.] - Coon Valley, WI - *BrCabYB 84; Tel&CabFB 84C*
Valley Cable TV - Los Angeles, CA - *BrCabYB 84; Tel&CabFB 84C*

Valley Cable TV Co. [of New Hope Telephone Cooperative] - New Hope, AL - *BrCabYB 84; Tel&CabFB 84C*
Valley Cable TV Inc. - Ft. Valley, GA - *BrCabYB 84; Tel&CabFB 84C*
Valley Cable Vision Inc. - Ansonia, CT - *BrCabYB 84*
Valley Cable Vision Inc. - Seymour, CT - *Tel&CabFB 84C*
Valley Cable Vision Inc. - Canajoharie, NY - *BrCabYB 84; Tel&CabFB 84C*
Valley Cable Vision Ltd. - Morden, MB, Canada - *BrCabYB 84*
Valley Cablevision [of Cablevision Management Corp.] - Sayre, PA - *BrCabYB 84*
Valley Cablevision Co. - Pauls Valley, OK - *BrCabYB 84; Tel&CabFB 84C*
Valley Cablevision Inc. - Pikeville, KY - *BrCabYB 84; Tel&CabFB 84C*
Valley Cablevision Inc. [of Helicon Corp.] - Burnsville, WV - *BrCabYB 84; Tel&CabFB 84C*
Valley Cablevision Inc. [of Helicon Corp.] - Clendenin, WV - *Tel&CabFB 84C*
Valley Cablevision Inc. [of Helicon Corp.] - Elkview, WV - *BrCabYB 84; Tel&CabFB 84C*
Valley Cablevision Inc. [of Helicon Corp.] - Glenville, WV - *Tel&CabFB 84C*
Valley Cablevision Inc. [of Helicon Corp.] - Spencer, WV - *BrCabYB 84; Tel&CabFB 84C*
Valley Cablevision of South Dakota Inc. [of Ollig Utilities] - Dell Rapids, SD - *BrCabYB 84; Tel&CabFB 84C*
Valley CATV [of Tele-Communications Inc.] - Browns Valley, MN - *BrCabYB 84*
Valley Center Ark Valley News - Valley Center, KS - *BaconPubCkNews 84*
Valley Cinema/Sound Corp. - Chicopee, MA - *AvMarPl 83*
Valley City Times-Record [of Mid-America Publishing Corp.] - Valley City, ND - *BaconPubCkNews 84; Ed&PubIntYB 82; NewsDir 84*
Valley Communications Inc. - Rison, AR - *Tel&CabFB 84C p.1710*
Valley Communications Inc. - Twin Valley, MN - *Tel&CabFB 84C*
Valley Cottage Graphics - Valley Cottage, NY - *ArtMar 84*
Valley County Cable Television Inc. [of King Videocable Co.] - Newhall, CA - *BrCabYB 84*
Valley County Cable Television Inc. [of Group W Cable Corp.] - Simi, CA - *BrCabYB 84*
Valley Courier - Alamosa, CO - *BaconPubCkNews 84; Ed&PubIntYB 82; NewsDir 84*
Valley Courier - Thornbury, ON, Canada - *AyerDirPub 83; Ed&PubIntYB 82*
Valley Dispatch - Warwick, NY - *AyerDirPub 83*
Valley Echo - Invermere, BC, Canada - *Ed&PubIntYB 82*
Valley Falls Vindicator - Valley Falls, KS - *Ed&PubIntYB 82*
Valley Falls Vindicator - *See* Wilson-Davis Publications Inc.
Valley Farmer, The - Bay City, MI - *Ed&PubIntYB 82*
Valley Forge Associates - Valley Forge, PA - *StaDirAdAg 2-84*
Valley Forge Information Service - King of Prussia, PA - *IntDirMarRes 83*
Valley Forge Sentinel - Conshohocken, PA - *AyerDirPub 83*
Valley Gateway Graphic - Studio City, CA - *Ed&PubIntYB 82*
Valley Gazette, The - Lansford, PA - *NewsDir 84*
Valley Herald - Yuba City, CA - *AyerDirPub 83; Ed&PubIntYB 82*
Valley Herald - Milton-Freewater, OR - *AyerDirPub 83*
Valley Independent - Monesse, PA - *AyerDirPub 83; BaconPubCkNews 84; Ed&PubIntYB 82*
Valley Independent - Fabens, TX - *AyerDirPub 83; Ed&PubIntYB 82*
Valley Irrigator - Newell, SD - *AyerDirPub 83; Ed&PubIntYB 82*
Valley Journal - Halstad, MN - *AyerDirPub 83; Ed&PubIntYB 82*
Valley Leader, The - Carman, MB, Canada - *Ed&PubIntYB 82*
Valley Lights Publications [Aff. of Valley Light Center] - Oak View, CA - *BoPubDir 4, 5; LitMag&SmPr 83-84*
Valley Mills Tribune - Valley Mills, TX - *AyerDirPub 83; BaconPubCkNews 84; Ed&PubIntYB 82*
Valley Monthly Magazine - Middletown, PA - *MagDir 84*
Valley Morning Star - Harlingen, TX - *Ed&PubIntYB 82*
Valley Motorist, The - Wilkes Barre, PA - *BaconPubCkMag 84; MagDir 84*
Valley Music Center, The - Hillsdale, NJ - *AvMarPl 83*
Valley National Bank of Arizona (Economic Research Dept.) - Phoenix, AZ - *BoPubDir 5*
Valley News - Livermore, CA - *AyerDirPub 83*
Valley News - Van Nuys, CA - *NewsBur 6*
Valley News - Meridian, ID - *AyerDirPub 83; Ed&PubIntYB 82*
Valley News - Browns Valley, MN - *Ed&PubIntYB 82*
Valley News - Le Sueur, MN - *AyerDirPub 83*
Valley News - Shakopee, MN - *AyerDirPub 83*
Valley News - Hopewell, NJ - *Ed&PubIntYB 82*
Valley News - Elizabethtown, NY - *AyerDirPub 83*
Valley News - Fulton, NY - *NewsDir 84*
Valley News [of Gazette Printing Co. Inc.] - Orwell, OH - *Ed&PubIntYB 82; NewsDir 84*
Valley News - Chillicothe, TX - *Ed&PubIntYB 82*
Valley News - Schertz, TX - *AyerDirPub 83*
Valley News - White River Junction, VT - *AyerDirPub 83; BaconPubCkNews 84; Ed&PubIntYB 82*
Valley News - Sultan, WA - *AyerDirPub 83; Ed&PubIntYB 82*
Valley News Dispatch - Tarentum, PA - *BaconPubCkNews 84*
Valley News, The - Apple Valley, CA - *AyerDirPub 83*
Valley North Press - Cincinnati, OH - *Ed&PubIntYB 82*
Valley Observer - Lake Oswego, OR - *AyerDirPub 83*
Valley of the Sun Publishing Co. - Malibu, CA - *BoPubDir 4, 5*
Valley Pioneer - Danville, CA - *AyerDirPub 83; Ed&PubIntYB 82*
Valley Post [of Anderson Lyro Publications] - Anderson, CA - *AyerDirPub 83; Ed&PubIntYB 82; NewsDir 84*
Valley Press - Felton, CA - *AyerDirPub 83; Ed&PubIntYB 82*
Valley Press - Hayden, CO - *AyerDirPub 83*
Valley Publications - Huntington, WV - *BoPubDir 4, 5*
Valley Publishers - Fresno, CA - *BoPubDir 4, 5*
Valley Records - Patton, CA - *BillIntBG 83-84*
Valley Register - Middletown, MD - *AyerDirPub 83; BaconPubCkNews 84; Ed&PubIntYB 82*
Valley Reporter - Waitsfield, VT - *AyerDirPub 83*
Valley Reporter, The - Mad River Valley, VT - *Ed&PubIntYB 82*
Valley Rural Telephone Cooperative Association - Glasgow, MT - *TelDir&BG 83-84*
Valley Scene - North Hollywood, CA - *AyerDirPub 83; Ed&PubIntYB 82*
Valley Scene [of Tujunga American Publishing Co.] - Tujunga, CA - *NewsDir 84*
Valley Shopper - Yuba City, CA - *AyerDirPub 83*
Valley Shopper - West Des Moines, IA - *AyerDirPub 83*
Valley Shopper - Beloit, KS - *AyerDirPub 83*
Valley Shopper - Newberg, OR - *AyerDirPub 83*
Valley Spirit - Davis, CA - *LitMag&SmPr 83-84*
Valley Star [of Holiday Communications Inc.] - Englewood, NJ - *AyerDirPub 83; NewsDir 84*
Valley Star, The - Northern Valley, NJ - *Ed&PubIntYB 82*
Valley Stream Courier [of Courier/Kernel Inc.] - Freeport, NY - *NewsDir 84*
Valley Stream Maileader [of Maileader] - Valley Stream, NY - *BaconPubCkNews 84; Ed&PubIntYB 82; NewsDir 84*
Valley Stream Pennysaver - Rockville Centre, NY - *AyerDirPub 83*
Valley Sun - Encino, CA - *AyerDirPub 83*
Valley Sun - La Canada, CA - *AyerDirPub 83*
Valley Sun - San Fernando, CA - *AyerDirPub 83*
Valley Sun - Van Nuys, CA - *Ed&PubIntYB 82*
Valley Sun, The - Wasilla, AK - *Ed&PubIntYB 82*
Valley Telecasting Co. [of Rogers UA Cablesystems Inc.] - Yuma, AZ - *BrCabYB 84*
Valley Telecommunications Cooperative Association - Herreid, SD - *TelDir&BG 83-84*
Valley Telegram - San Bernardino, CA - *AyerDirPub 83*
Valley Telephone Co. - Browns Valley, MN - *TelDir&BG 83-84*
Valley Telephone Co. [Aff. of Dubois Telephone Exchange Inc.] - Baggs, WY - *TelDir&BG 83-84*
Valley Telephone Co. Inc. - West Point, GA - *TelDir&BG 83-84*
Valley Telephone Cooperative Inc. - Willcox, AZ - *TelDir&BG 83-84*
Valley Telephone Cooperative Inc. - Raymondville, TX - *TelDir&BG 83-84*
Valley Times - Central Valley, CA - *AyerDirPub 83; Ed&PubIntYB 82*

Valley Times - Pleasanton, CA - *AyerDirPub 83; Ed&PubIntYB 82*
Valley Times - North Las Vegas, NV - *AyerDirPub 83; Ed&PubIntYB 82*
Valley Times - Beaverton, OR - *Ed&PubIntYB 82*
Valley Times [of Tigard Times] - Portland, OR - *NewsDir 84*
Valley Times-News [of Valley Newspapers Inc.] - Lanett, AL - *AyerDirPub 83; Ed&PubIntYB 82*
Valley Times-News - Missouri Valley, IA - *AyerDirPub 83; Ed&PubIntYB 82*
Valley Times-Star - Newville, PA - *AyerDirPub 83; Ed&PubIntYB 82*
Valley Today, The - Stockton, CA - *AyerDirPub 83*
Valley Town Crier - McAllen, TX - *AyerDirPub 83; Ed&PubIntYB 82*
Valley Tribune - Quitaque, TX - *AyerDirPub 83; Ed&PubIntYB 82*
Valley Video [Div. of Simonton Prosperity Enterprises Inc.] - Burbank, CA - *AvMarPl 83*
Valley Video Cable Co. of Hershey - Devvy Township, PA - *BrCabYB 84*
Valley Video Cable Co. of Hershey [of Cable Management Associates Inc.] - Hershey, PA - *Tel&CabFB 84C*
Valley Video Cable TV Inc. - Larksville, PA - *BrCabYB 84; Tel&CabFB 84C*
Valley Video Inc. [of Century Communications Corp.] - Norwich, NY - *BrCabYB 84; Tel&CabFB 84C*
Valley Video Service Co. - Laurelton, PA - *BrCabYB 84*
Valley Video Service Co. - New Berlin, PA - *BrCabYB 84*
Valley Video Systems Inc. [of Cencom Inc.] - Brownsville, MN - *BrCabYB 84*
Valley Video Systems Inc. [of Cencom Inc.] - Houston, MN - *BrCabYB 84; Tel&CabFB 84C*
Valley Video Systems Inc. [of Cencom Inc.] - Lanesboro, MN - *Tel&CabFB 84C*
Valley Video Systems Inc. [of Cencom Inc.] - Lanesbow, MN - *BrCabYB 84*
Valley Video Systems Inc. [of Cencom Inc.] - New Lisbon, MN - *BrCabYB 84*
Valley Video Systems Inc. [of Cencom Inc.] - Peterson, MN - *BrCabYB 84; Tel&CabFB 84C*
Valley Video Systems Inc. [of Cencom Inc.] - Rushford, MN - *BrCabYB 84 p.D-310*
Valley Video Systems Inc. [of Cencom Inc.] - Camp Douglas, WI - *BrCabYB 84; Tel&CabFB 84C*
Valley Video Systems Inc. [of Cencom Inc.] - Cumberland, WI - *Tel&CabFB 84C*
Valley Video Systems Inc. [of Cencom Inc.] - New Lisbon, WI - *Tel&CabFB 84C*
Valley View - Granada Hills, CA - *Ed&PubIntYB 82*
Valley View - San Fernando, CA - *AyerDirPub 83*
Valley View Blueberry Press - Vancouver, WA - *BoPubDir 5*
Valley View Cable Inc. - Jordan, MN - *BrCabYB 84; Tel&CabFB 84C*
Valley View Cable Inc. [of Cable Services Inc.] - Slater, MO - *BrCabYB 84*
Valley View Citizen-Standard - Valley View, PA - *BaconPubCkNews 84*
Valley View Sun Courier - *See* Sun Newspapers
Valley View Sun Herald - *See* Sun Newspapers
Valley View Sun Messenger - *See* Sun Newspapers
Valley View Sun Press - *See* Sun Newspapers
Valley View Telephone Co. [Aff. of Muenster Telephone Corp. of Texas] - Muenster, TX - *TelDir&BG 83-84*
Valley View West Side Sun News - *See* Sun Newspapers
Valley Views - Valleyview, AB, Canada - *AyerDirPub 83; Ed&PubIntYB 82*
Valley Voice - Middlebury, VT - *AyerDirPub 83; Ed&PubIntYB 82*
Valley Wide Resorter - Hesperia, CA - *AyerDirPub 83*
Valley Wide Resorter - Victor Valley, CA - *Ed&PubIntYB 82*
Valleyfield Transvision Inc. - Valleyfield, PQ, Canada - *BrCabYB 84*
Valliant Telephone Co. - Valliant, OK - *TelDir&BG 83-84*
Valpar International Corp. - Tucson, AZ - *MicrocomMPl 84; MicrocomSwDir 1*
Valparaiso Bayou Times - Valparaiso, FL - *NewsDir 84*
Valparaiso Communication Systems - Valparaiso, FL - *BrCabYB 84; InterCabHB 3; Tel&CabFB 84C*
Valparaiso Vidette-Messenger - Valparaiso, IN - *BaconPubCkNews 84; NewsDir 84*
Valport System [of Frederic C. Towers & Co.] - Bethesda, MD - *DataDirOnSer 84; DirOnDB Spring 84; EISS 83*
Valtec - West Boylston, MA - *DataDirSup 7-83*
Valtion Teknillinen Tutkimuskeskus/Technical Research Center of Finland (Technical Information Service) - Espoo, Finland - *InfIndMarPl 83*
Valuation Press Inc. - Marina del Rey, CA - *BoPubDir 4, 5*
Valuation Systems Co. - Tulsa, OK - *MicrocomMPl 84*
Value [of CompuServe Inc.] - Columbus, OH - *DataDirOnSer 84*
Value Circulation Services - New York, NY - *MagIndMarPl 82-83*
Value Communications Inc. [Subs. of Oak Tree Publications Inc.] - San Diego, CA - *LitMarPl 83, 84*
Value Computing Inc. - Cherry Hill, NJ - *DataDirSup 7-83*
Value Line [of Value Line Data Service] - New York, NY - *DataDirOnSer 84*
Value Line Convertible Database [of Value Line Data Service] - New York, NY - *DataDirOnSer 84*
Value Line Data Base-II [of Arnold Bernhard & Co.] - New York, NY - *DBBus 82; DirOnDB Spring 84*
Value Line Data Services [Subs. of Value Line Inc.] - New York, NY - *DataDirOnSer 84; EISS 83; InfIndMarPl 83*
Value Shopper - Torrance, CA - *AyerDirPub 83*
Values & Lifestyles Program [of SRI International] - Menlo Park, CA - *DataDirOnSer 84*
Valve Magazine - Washington, DC - *BaconPubCkMag 84*
Vample Publishing Co., Jerry - Kansas City, MO - *BillIntBG 83-84*
Vample Records Inc. - Kansas City, MO - *BillIntBG 83-84*
Van Alstyne Leader - Van Alstyne, TX - *BaconPubCkNews 84; Ed&PubIntYB 82*
Van Bernard Productions - Rancho Mirage, CA - *Tel&CabFB 84C*
Van Brunt & Co. Advertising-Marketing Inc. - New York, NY - *AdAge 3-28-84; ArtMar 84; BrCabYB 84; StaDirAdAg 2-84; TelAl 83, 84*
Van Brunt/Schaeffer Public Relations [Div. of Van Brunt & Co.] - New York, NY - *DirPRFirms 83*
Van Buren County Advertiser - Bloomingdale, MI - *AyerDirPub 83*
Van Buren County Cablevision - Paw Paw, MI - *BrCabYB 84*
Van Buren County Democrat - Clinton, AR - *AyerDirPub 83; Ed&PubIntYB 82*
Van Buren County Register - Keosauqua, IA - *AyerDirPub 83; Ed&PubIntYB 82*
Van Buren Current Local - Van Buren, MO - *BaconPubCkNews 84*
Van Buren Press-Argus - Van Buren, AR - *BaconPubCkNews 84; NewsDir 84*
Van Buren Telephone Co. Inc. - Keosauqua, IA - *TelDir&BG 83-84*
Van Buren TV Cable Co. - Van Buren, ME - *BrCabYB 84*
Van Dahl Publications [Subs. of Capital Cities Communications Inc.] - Albany, OR - *DirMarMP 83*
Van de Car, De Porte & Johnson Inc. - Albany, NY - *StaDirAdAg 2-84*
Van Dean Educators Inc. - Malvern, PA - *BoPubDir 5*
Van der Linde Co. Inc., Victor - Westwood, NJ - *StaDirAdAg 2-84; TelAl 83*
Van Der Linde Co. Inc., Victor - New York, NY - *TelAl 84*
Van Dine Horton McNamara Manges - Pittsburgh, PA - *StaDirAdAg 2-84*
Van Dyk Publications - Butte, MT - *BoPubDir 4, 5*
Van Dyk Research - Whippany, NJ - *DirInfWP 82*
Van Dyke McCarthy Co. - Seattle, WA - *HBIndAd&MS 82-83*
Van Halm Associates, Johan - Amersfoort, Netherlands - *EISS 83; InfIndMarPl 83*
Van Handel Co. Inc. - Milwaukee, WI - *StaDirAdAg 2-84*
Van Hecker-Haring Inc. - Lincolnwood, IL - *StaDirAdAg 2-84*
Van Horn Advocate - Van Horn, TX - *BaconPubCkNews 84; Ed&PubIntYB 82*
Van Horn Cable TV Inc. [of U.S. Cable Corp.] - Van Horn, TX - *BrCabYB 84*

Van Horne Cooperative Telephone Co. - Van Horne, IA - *TelDir&BG 83-84*
Van Houten Associates - Petaluma, CA - *EISS 83*
Van Kleek, Edith - Stettler, AB, Canada - *BoPubDir 4 Sup, 5*
Van Meter, R. D. - Williamson, WV - *BrCabYB 84 p.D-310*
Van Nostrand Reinhold Co. [Div. of International Thomson Educational Publishing Inc.] - New York, NY - *AvMarPl 83; DirMarMP 83; LitMarPl 83, 84*
Van Nuys Sun Mailer - Encino, CA - *AyerDirPub 83*
Van Nuys Sun Mailer - *See* Associated Valley Publications
Van Nuys Valley Sun - *See* Associated Valley Publications
Van, Pickup, & Off-Road Industry News [of Bagnall Bros. Publishing Co.] - Newport Beach, CA - *MagDir 84*
Van Pragg Productions Inc. - New York, NY - *TelAl 83, 84*
Van Press, The - London, ON, Canada - *LitMag&SmPr 83-84*
Van Progress - Van, TX - *BaconPubCkNews 84; Ed&PubIntYB 82*
Van San Corp. - City of Industry, CA - *AvMarPl 83; DirInfWP 82*
Van Sant, Dugdale & Co. Inc. - Baltimore, MD - *ArtMar 84*
Van Vactor & Goodheart Inc. - Cambridge, MA - *BoPubDir 4 Sup, 5*
Van Vechten & Associates - New York, NY - *ArtMar 84; DirPRFirms 83*
Van Voorhis, Eugene - Port Clinton, OH - *BoPubDir 4, 5*
Van Wert Times-Bulletin - Van Wert, OH - *BaconPubCkNews 84; NewsDir 84*
Van World Magazine - Van Nuys, CA - *MagDir 84*
Vance Bibliographies - Monticello, IL - *BoPubDir 4, 5; WritMar 84*
Vance, John F. - Cos Cob, CT - *LitMarPl 84*
Vance-Mathews Inc. - Beaumont, TX - *StaDirAdAg 2-84*
Vance Publishing Co., Paul - New York, NY - *BillIntBG 83-84*
Vance Publishing Corp. - Chicago, IL - *MagIndMarPl 82-83*
Vance Publishing Corp. - New York, NY - *BoPubDir 4, 5*
Vance, W. Addington - Crawfordsville, IN - *Tel&CabFB 84C p.1710*
Vanceburg Lewis County Herald - Vanceburg, KY - *BaconPubCkNews 84*
Vancouver Art Gallery (Gallery Shop) - Vancouver, BC, Canada - *BoPubDir 4, 5*
Vancouver Cablevision [of Rogers Cablesystems Inc.] - Vancouver, BC, Canada - *BrCabYB 84*
Vancouver Columbian - Vancouver, WA - *BaconPubCkNews 84; NewsDir 84*
Vancouver Evergreen Post - *See* Post Publications Inc.
Vancouver Hazel Dell Post - Vancouver, WA - *Ed&PubIntYB 82*
Vancouver Herald - Vancouver, BC, Canada - *Ed&PubIntYB 82*
Vancouver North County News [of Vancouver East County News] - Vancouver, WA - *NewsDir 84*
Vancouver Province - Vancouver, BC, Canada - *LitMarPl 83*
Vancouver Sun - Vancouver, BC, Canada - *Ed&PubIntYB 82; LitMarPl 83*
Vancouver Weekly [of Vancouver East County News] - Vancouver, WA - *Ed&PubIntYB 82; NewsDir 84*
Vancouver Western News, The - Vancouver, BC, Canada - *Ed&PubIntYB 82*
Vandalia Butler Tribune - Vandalia, OH - *BaconPubCkNews 84; Ed&PubIntYB 82*
Vandalia Cable TV Co. Inc. - Vandalia, IL - *BrCabYB 84*
Vandalia Chronicle - Vandalia, OH - *NewsDir 84*
Vandalia Drummer News - Vandalia, OH - *BaconPubCkNews 84*
Vandalia Historical Society - Vandalia, IL - *BoPubDir 4, 5*
Vandalia Leader Press - Vandalia, MO - *BaconPubCkNews 84; Ed&PubIntYB 82*
Vandalia Leader-Union - Vandalia, IL - *BaconPubCkNews 84; Ed&PubIntYB 82; NewsDir 84*
Vandalia Records - Vandalia, MI - *BillIntBG 83-84*
Vandata - Seattle, WA - *MicrocomMPl 83, 84; MicrocomSwDir 1; WhoWMicrocom 83*
Vanderbilt Hustler, The [of Vanderbilt Student Communications Inc.] - Nashville, TN - *NewsDir 84*
Vanderbilt Review [of Vanderbilt Street Press] - Stephenville, TX - *LitMag&SmPr 83-84*
Vanderbilt Street Press - Stephenville, TX - *BoPubDir 4 Sup, 5; LitMag&SmPr 83-84*
Vanderbilt University Press - Nashville, TN - *LitMarPl 83, 84*
Vandergrift News-Citizen - Vandergrift, PA - *BaconPubCkNews 84; NewsDir 84*
Vanderhoof Express - Vanderhoof, BC, Canada - *AyerDirPub 83*
Vanderveer & Associates Inc., R. B. - Lansdale, PA - *IntDirMarRes 83*
Vanderwicken & Co. - Princeton, NJ - *DirPRFirms 83*
Vane Advertising, Peter [Div. of Marcon Dynamics Ltd.] - New York, NY - *DirMarMP 83; LitMarPl 83, 84; StaDirAdAg 2-84*
Vanguard - Yarmouth, NS, Canada - *AyerDirPub 83; Ed&PubIntYB 82*
Vanguard Advertising Agency Inc. - Minneapolis, MN - *StaDirAdAg 2-84*
Vanguard Associates Inc. - Minneapolis, MN - *ArtMar 84*
Vanguard Books - Chicago, IL - *BoPubDir 4, 5; LitMag&SmPr 83-84*
Vanguard Communications Inc. - *See* Gardner Advertising Co. Inc.
Vanguard Music Corp. - New York, NY - *BillIntBG 83-84*
Vanguard News - Brattleboro, VT - *BrCabYB 84*
Vanguard Press Inc. - New York, NY - *LitMarPl 83, 84; WritMar 84*
Vanguard Productions Inc. - Columbus, OH - *AvMarPl 83*
Vanguard Publications - Montreal, PQ, Canada - *BoPubDir 4, 5*
Vanguard Recording Society Inc. - New York, NY - *BillIntBG 83-84*
Vanguard Software - Pittsburgh, PA - *MicrocomMPl 83*
Vanguard Systems Corp. - San Antonio, TX - *WhoWMicrocom 83*
Vanishing Cab - San Francisco, CA - *LitMag&SmPr 83-84*
Vanity Fair [of Conde Nast Publications] - New York, NY - *BaconPubCkMag 84; Folio 83; LitMarPl 84*
Vanity Press - New York, NY - *LitMag&SmPr 83-84*
Vanlue Telephone Co. - Vanlue, OH - *TelDir&BG 83-84*
Vanmeer Publications Inc. - Clearwater, FL - *BoPubDir 4, 5*
Vanni, S. F. - New York, NY - *BoPubDir 4, 5*
Vanous Co., Arthur - River Edge, NJ - *LitMarPl 83, 84*
Vanpraag Productions Inc. - New York, NY - *Tel&CabFB 84C*
VanSant, Dugdale & Co. - Baltimore, MD - *AdAge 3-28-84; BrCabYB 84; DirMarMP 83; StaDirAdAg 2-84*
Vantage Advertising & Marketing Associates - San Leandro, CA - *AdAge 3-28-84; StaDirAdAg 2-84*
Vantage Art Inc. - Massapequa, NY - *LitMarPl 83, 84*
Vantage Communications Inc. - Nyack, NY - *AvMarPl 83*
Vantage Communicators Inc. - Pittsburgh, PA - *DirPRFirms 83*
Vantage Recording Co. - Pottstown, PA - *BillIntBG 83-84*
Vantage Sales & Marketing - Hazlet, NJ - *LitMarPl 83, 84*
Vanytt - Stockholm, Sweden - *DirOnDB Spring 84*
Vapaa Sana - Toronto, ON, Canada - *Ed&PubIntYB 82*
Var Music Publishing Co. - Woburn, MA - *BillIntBG 83-84*
Varchetta & Associates, Phil - Chicago, IL - *StaDirAdAg 2-84*
Vardaman Press - Tacoma, WA - *BoPubDir 5*
Varden Publications, Dolly - Carlsbad, CA - *BoPubDir 4, 5*
Varden Publications, Dolly - Rio Rancho, NM - *LitMag&SmPr 83-84*
Vardey Literary Agency, Lucinda - Toronto, ON, Canada - *LitMarPl 83, 84*
Varese Media - West Hollywood, CA - *AvMarPl 83*
Varese Sarabande Records Inc. - North Hollywood, CA - *BillIntBG 83-84*
Vargas, Glenn - Thermal, CA - *BoPubDir 4, 5*
Varhaug Cable Co. - Jefferson County, AR - *Tel&CabFB 84C*
Varhung, Ed & Irene - Clatskanie, OR - *Tel&CabFB 84C p.1710*
Variable Speech Control - San Francisco, CA - *AvMarPl 83*
Varian Associates - Palo Alto, CA - *ElecNews 7-25-83*
Varicom Inc. - *See* Campbell-Ewald Co.
Variety - New York, NY - *BaconPubCkMag 84; MagDir 84; MagIndMarPl 82-83; NewsBur 6; WritMar 84*
Variety Cable TV Inc. - Farrell, PA - *BrCabYB 84*
Variety Scenic Studios - Long Island City, NY - *AvMarPl 83*
Variety Sound Corp. - New York, NY - *AvMarPl 83*
Varigraph Inc. - Madison, WI - *AvMarPl 83*
Varisystems Corp. - Plainview, NY - *DirInfWP 82*
Varner, Nick - Owensboro, KY - *BoPubDir 5*
Varnes Publishers [Aff. of HomeHarvest Co.] - Escondido, CA - *BoPubDir 4 Sup, 5*
Varon Advertising Inc. - Southfield, MI - *StaDirAdAg 2-84*
Varsity, The [of University of Toronto] - Allentown, PA - *NewsDir 84*

Varulven Records & Distribution - Woburn, MA - *BillIntBG 83-84*
Vascular Diagnosis & Therapy [of Brentwood Publishing Corp.] - Los Angeles, CA - *ArtMar 84; BaconPubCkMag 84; MagIndMarPl 82-83*
Vaseco Inc. - Oklahoma City, OK - *AvMarPl 83*
Vashon-Maury Island Beachcomber - Vashon, WA - *AyerDirPub 83; BaconPubCkNews 84; Ed&PubIntYB 82*
Vashti Educational Center - Thomasville, GA - *BoPubDir 4 Sup, 5*
Vasilakes Industries Publicity - Lakewood, OH - *DirPRFirms 83*
Vassar Pioneer-Times [of Hearst Corp.] - Vassar, MI - *BaconPubCkNews 84; Ed&PubIntYB 82; NewsDir 84*
Vassilion, Harry J. - Raleigh, NC - *BoPubDir 4, 5*
Vaudell Music Publications - Cupertino, CA - *BillIntBG 83-84*
Vaughan, Thain & Spencer Inc. - Hinsdale, IL - *StaDirAdAg 2-84*
Vaughan Township Historical Society [Aff. of The Ontario Historical Society Inc.] - Maple, ON, Canada - *BoPubDir 4, 5*
Vaughn & Associates, Edward - Detroit, MI - *BoPubDir 4, 5*
Vaughn Associates - New York, NY - *DirPRFirms 83*
Vaughnsville Telephone Co. Inc. - Vaughnsville, OH - *TelDir&BG 83-84*
Vavin Inc. - New York, NY - *TelAl 83*
VAX/RSTS Professional - Washington, PA - *BaconPubCkMag 84*
Vaz Dias International - New York, NY - *Ed&PubIntYB 82; ProGuPRSer 4*
VBBL-FM - London, ON, Canada - *BrCabYB 84*
VCA Duplication Corp. [Div. of Video Corp. of America] - Edison, NJ - *AvMarPl 83*
VCA Fairview [of VCA Telecable Inc.] - Fairview, TN - *Tel&CabFB 84C*
VCA-Northborough Inc. - Harris County, TX - *BrCabYB 84*
VCA-Parkway South Ltd. - Harris County, TX - *BrCabYB 84*
VCA Telecable Inc. - Jackson, MI - *Tel&CabFB 84C p.1710*
VCA Teletronics [Div. of Video Corp. of America] - New York, NY - *AvMarPl 83*
VDI-Datenbank - Dusseldorf, West Germany - *DirOnDB Spring 84*
VDTA News - Des Moines, IA - *BaconPubCkMag 84*
Veach Development Co. [Div. of Veach Corp.] - Van Nuys, CA - *AvMarPl 83*
Veatch, Rich & Nadler - Northbrook, IL - *WhoWMicrocom 83*
Vebo Production Inc. - Chicago, IL - *Tel&CabFB 84C*
Vec Advertising - Springfield, NJ - *StaDirAdAg 2-84*
Vector [of British Science Fiction Association Ltd.] - Reading, England - *LitMag&SmPr 83-84*
Vector Associates - Bellevue, WA - *BoPubDir 4, 5*
Vector Automation Inc. - Baltimore, MD - *DataDirSup 7-83*
Vector Enterprises Inc. - Santa Monica, CA - *Tel&CabFB 84C*
Vector General Inc. - Woodland Hills, CA - *DataDirSup 7-83; WhoWMicrocom 83*
Vector Graphic Inc. - Thousand Oaks, CA - *MicrocomMPl 84; MicrocomSwDir 1; WhoWMicrocom 83*
Vector Graphic Inc. - Westlake Village, CA - *DirInfWP 82*
Vector Letter [of DeRusha & Associates] - Del Mar, CA - *MicrocomMPl 84*
Vector Linc [of Vector Graphic Inc.] - Thousand Oaks, CA - *TeleSy&SerDir 2-84*
Vector Mailinc [of Vector Graphic Inc.] - Thousand Oaks, CA - *TeleSy&SerDir 2-84*
Vector Music Corp. - *See* Drake Music Group
Vector Press - Santa Barbara, CA - *BoPubDir 4, 5*
Vectrix Corp. - Greensboro, NC - *MicrocomMPl 84*
Vectur Marketing Associates - Albany, CA - *StaDirAdAg 2-84*
Vedanta Centre Publishers - Cohasset, MA - *BoPubDir 4, 5*
Vedanta Press [Aff. of Vedanta Society of Southern California] - Hollywood, CA - *BoPubDir 4, 5*
Vedanta Society of St. Louis - St. Louis, MO - *BoPubDir 4, 5*
Vedette & Advocate - Greenfield, MO - *Ed&PubIntYB 82*
Vedo Films - Port Washington, NY - *AvMarPl 83*
Vee Jay International Music - Burbank, CA - *BillIntBG 83-84*
Vee Two Music - *See* Kaye Publications, Richard
Vee Ve Music Corp. - *See* Mietus Copyright Management
Veevo Record Co. - New York, NY - *BillIntBG 83-84*
Vega - Bloomfield, NJ - *LitMag&SmPr 83-84*
Vega Associates Inc. - New York, NY - *AvMarPl 83*
Vega Enterprise - Vega, TX - *BaconPubCkNews 84; Ed&PubIntYB 82*
Vega Press - Bloomfield, NJ - *LitMag&SmPr 83-84*
Vegas Records - Ft. Worth, TX - *BillIntBG 83-84*
Vegas Star Music - Las Vegas, NV - *BillIntBG 83-84*
Vegas Voice - Las Vegas, NV - *Ed&PubIntYB 82*
Vegetarian Times - Oak Park, IL - *ArtMar 84; MagDir 84; MagIndMarPl 82-83; WritMar 84*
Vegetarian Times [of Vegetarian Life & Times Inc.] - New York, NY - *BaconPubCkMag 84; DirMarMP 83*
Vegh, Steven Jr. - Bronx, NY - *LitMarPl 83, 84; MagIndMarPl 82-83*
Vegreville Observer - Vegreville, AB, Canada - *Ed&PubIntYB 82*
Vehicle Editions Inc. - New York, NY - *LitMag&SmPr 83-84*
Vehicule Press - Montreal, PQ, Canada - *BoPubDir 4, 5*
Velo-News [of Whetstone Publishing] - Brattleboro, VT - *ArtMar 84; BaconPubCkMag 84; BoPubDir 4, 5; LitMag&SmPr 83-84; MagDir 84; MagIndMarPl 82-83; WritMar 84*
Velocities - Berkeley, CA - *LitMag&SmPr 83-84*
Velva Cable TV Inc. - Velva, ND - *Tel&CabFB 84C*
Velva McHenry County Journal Register - Velva, ND - *BaconPubCkNews 84*
Velvet [of Eton Publishing Co. Inc.] - Los Angeles, CA - *Folio 83*
Velvet Apple Music - *See* Tree Publishing Co. Inc.
Velvet de Puerto Rico Inc. - Santurce, PR - *BillIntBG 83-84*
Ven-Tel Inc. - Santa Clara, CA - *MicrocomMPl 84; WhoWMicrocom 83*
Ven-TI Inc. - Santa Clara, CA - *DataDirSup 7-83*
Venant Deshaies - Ste.-Angele-de-Laval, PQ, Canada - *BrCabYB 84*
Venard Films Ltd. - East Peoria, IL - *AvMarPl 83; Tel&CabFB 84C*
Vending Times - New York, NY - *BaconPubCkMag 84; MagDir 84; WritMar 84*
Vendor Information File [of Information Handling Services] - Englewood, CO - *DataDirOnSer 84*
Vendor Information File - Virginia Beach, VA - *DirOnDB Spring 84*
Venet Advertising - New York, NY - *AdAge 3-28-84; StaDirAdAg 2-84*
Veneta West Lane News - *See* Tri-County Publications Inc.
Venezian Inc., Angelo R. - Long Island City, NY - *MagIndMarPl 82-83*
Venice Gondolier - *See* Sun Coast Media Group Inc.
Venice Gondolier Sun Coast Times - *See* Sun Coast Media Group Inc.
Venice Marina News - *See* Copley Press Inc.
Venice-Marina News & Vanguard [of United Western Newspapers Inc.] - Santa Monica, CA - *AyerDirPub 83; NewsDir 84*
Venice-Marina News & Vanguard - Venice, CA - *Ed&PubIntYB 82*
Venice Shopping Guide - Venice, FL - *AyerDirPub 83*
Venice West Publishers - Granada Hills, CA - *BoPubDir 5*
Venice West Publishers - Santa Barbara, CA - *BoPubDir 4*
Vensure Team Inc. - New York, NY - *HBIndAd&MS 82-83; IntDirMarRes 83*
Ventnor Publishers - Ventnor, NJ - *BoPubDir 4, 5*
Ventura Associates - New York, NY - *DirMarMP 83; StaDirAdAg 2-84*
Ventura County & Coast Reporter [of VCR Inc.] - Oxnard, CA - *WritMar 84*
Ventura County Star-Free Press [of John P. Scripps Newspapers Inc.] - Ventura, CA - *AyerDirPub 83; BaconPubCkNews 84; NewsDir 84*
Ventura Press - Guerneville, CA - *BoPubDir 4, 5*
Ventura Telephone Co. Inc. - Ventura, IA - *TelDir&BG 83-84*
VenturCom Inc. - Cambridge, MA - *MicrocomMPl 84*
Venture - San Diego, CA - *StaDirAdAg 2-84*
Venture - Wheaton, IL - *ArtMar 84; MagIndMarPl 82-83; WritMar 84*
Venture [of Venpub Inc.] - New York, NY - *BaconPubCkMag 84; DirMarMP 83; Folio 83; MagDir 84; WritMar 84*
Venture Computing Co. - Houston, TX - *DataDirOnSer 84*
Venture Development Corp. - Wellesley, MA - *BoPubDir 4 Sup, 5; IntDirMarRes 83; TeleSy&SerDir 2-84*

Venture Press - Toronto, ON, Canada - *BoPubDir 4 Sup, 5*
Venture Publishing Co. [Aff. of Center for Nonprofit Organization] - New York, NY - *BoPubDir 4, 5*
Venture Record Inc. - Greenbelt, MD - *BillIntBG 83-84*
Venture Records - Somerville, NJ - *BillIntBG 83-84*
Venture Software Inc. - Nashua, NH - *MicrocomMPl 84*
Venturecasts [of Venture Development Corp.] - Wellesley, MA - *EISS 83*
Venturecraft Kits Co. - New York, NY - *BoPubDir 5*
Venus Books - Dallas, TX - *BoPubDir 4 Sup, 5*
Venus Telephone Corp. - Venus, PA - *TelDir&BG 83-84*
Verbatim - Sunnyvale, CA - *Datamation 6-83; DirInfWP 82; Top100Al 83; WhoWMicrocom 83*
Verbatim Book Club [Subs. of Verbatim, The Language Quarterly] - Essex, CT - *LitMarPl 83, 84*
Verbatim Books [Aff. of Laurence Urdang Inc.] - Essex, CT - *LitMarPl 83, 84*
Verbatim, The Language Quarterly - Essex, CT - *LitMarPl 84; MagIndMarPl 82-83*
Verbit & Co., Consultants to Management - Bala Cynwyd, PA - *TeleSy&SerDir 7-83*
Vercom Cable Services Ltd. - Vernon, BC, Canada - *BrCabYB 84*
Verde Independent, The - Cottonwood, AZ - *AyerDirPub 83*
Verde View - Cottonwood, AZ - *Ed&PubIntYB 82*
Verde Vista Music - San Francisco, CA - *BillIntBG 83-84*
Verdigre Eagle - Verdigre, NE - *BaconPubCkNews 84; Ed&PubIntYB 82*
Verdun Messenger - Montreal, PQ, Canada - *AyerDirPub 83*
Verein Deutscher Eisenhuttenleute [of Betriebsforschungsinstitut] - Dusseldorf, West Germany - *InfIndMarPl 83*
Verfahrenstechnische Berichte-Tape Service [of Bayer AG] - Leverkusen, West Germany - *CompReadDB 82*
Vergennes Citizen - Vergennes, VT - *BaconPubCkNews 84*
Veridian - Bloomington, IN - *LitMag&SmPr 83-84*
Verilux - Greenwich, CT - *AvMarPl 83*
Veritas - Providence, RI - *LitMarPl 83, 84*
Veritas Book Club, The [Subs. of Devin Adair Publishing Co.] - Old Greenwich, CT - *LitMarPl 83, 84*
Veritas Communications - Tucson, AZ - *AvMarPl 83*
Veritas Productions Inc. - Englewood Cliffs, NJ - *TelAl 83, 84*
Veritas Publications - Arlington, VA - *BoPubDir 4 Sup, 5*
Veritechnology Electronics Corp. - St. Joseph, MI - *MicrocomMPl 84*
Veritie Press Inc. - Novelty, OH - *BoPubDir 4, 5*
Verlag Chemie International Inc. - Deerfield Beach, FL - *LitMarPl 83, 84; MicroMarPl 82-83*
Vermeer Arts Ltd. - Durango, CO - *BoPubDir 4, 5*
Vermilion Cable Communications - Vermilion, OH - *BrCabYB 84*
Vermilion Photojournal - Vermilion, OH - *Ed&PubIntYB 82; NewsDir 84*
Vermillion - *See* Dawn Productions Ltd.
Vermillion Cable Communications [of Adelphia Communications Corp.] - Vermillion, OH - *Tel&CabFB 84C*
Vermillion Cable TV Ltd. [of Zylstra Communications Corp.] - Vermillion, SD - *BrCabYB 84; Tel&CabFB 84C*
Vermillion Plain Talk - Vermillion, SD - *BaconPubCkNews 84; NewsDir 84*
Vermont Books: Publishers - Middlebury, VT - *BoPubDir 4, 5*
Vermont Catholic Tribune, The - Burlington, VT - *NewsDir 84*
Vermont Historical Society Inc. - Montpelier, VT - *BoPubDir 4, 5*
Vermont Information Processes Inc. - Palo Alto, CA - *EISS 83*
Vermont Information Processes Inc. - Rutland, VT - *FBInfSer 80*
Vermont Journal, The - Essex Junction, VT - *Ed&PubIntYB 82*
Vermont Life - Montpelier, VT - *LitMarPl 83, 84; MagDir 84; MagIndMarPl 82-83; WritMar 84*
Vermont News Guide - Manchester Center, VT - *AyerDirPub 83; Ed&PubIntYB 82*
Vermont Research Corp. - North Springfield, VT - *DataDirSup 7-83; WhoWMicrocom 83*
Vermont Standard - Woodstock, VT - *AyerDirPub 83; Ed&PubIntYB 82*
Vermont State Data Center [of University of Vermont] - Burlington, VT - *EISS 7-83 Sup*
Vermont Television Corp. - Barre, VT - *BrCabYB 84; Tel&CabFB 84C*
Vermont Vanguard Press - Burlington, VT - *AyerDirPub 83*
Vern Street Products - Sapulpa, OK - *MicrocomMPl 83, 84*
Vern-Wray - *See* Dawn Productions Ltd.
Vernal [of Rising Sun Press] - Durango, CO - *LitMag&SmPr 83-84*
Vernal Cable TV [of Acton Corp.] - Vernal, UT - *Tel&CabFB 84C*
Vernal Express - Vernal, UT - *BaconPubCkNews 84; Ed&PubIntYB 82; NewsDir 84*
Verndale Sun, The - Verndale, MN - *Ed&PubIntYB 82*
Vernier Software - Portland, OR - *MicrocomMPl 84*
Vernon Advertiser - Vernon, BC, Canada - *AyerDirPub 83*
Vernon Center News - Amboy, MN - *AyerDirPub 83*
Vernon Center News - Vernon Center, MN - *Ed&PubIntYB 82*
Vernon County Broadcaster Censor - Viroqua, WI - *AyerDirPub 83; Ed&PubIntYB 82*
Vernon Daily News - Vernon, BC, Canada - *BaconPubCkNews 84; Ed&PubIntYB 82*
Vernon Daily Record - Vernon, TX - *Ed&PubIntYB 82; NewsDir 84*
Vernon Hills Herald - Vernon Hills, IL - *Ed&PubIntYB 82*
Vernon Hills Herald - *See* Paddock Publications
Vernon Lamar Democrat - Vernon, AL - *BaconPubCkNews 84; NewsDir 84*
Vernon Publications Inc. - Seattle, WA - *MagIndMarPl 82-83*
Vernon Record - Vernon, TX - *BaconPubCkNews 84*
Vernon Review [of Pioneer Press Inc.] - Mundelein, IL - *NewsDir 84*
Vernon Review - Vernon Township, IL - *Ed&PubIntYB 82*
Vernon Review - Wilmette, IL - *AyerDirPub 83*
Vernon Review - *See* Pioneer Press Inc.
Vernon-Sulligent Cablevision Inc. [of Communications Systems Inc.] - Sulligent, AL - *BrCabYB 84; Tel&CabFB 84C*
Vernon-Sulligent Cablevision Inc. - Vernon, AL - *BrCabYB 84*
Vernon Tech Corp. - Springtown, PA - *WhoWMicrocom 83*
Vernon Telephone Co. Inc. - Vernon, NY - *TelDir&BG 83-84*
Vernon Telephone Cooperative - Westby, WI - *TelDir&BG 83-84*
Vernon This Week - Vernon, BC, Canada - *Ed&PubIntYB 82*
Vernon Town Crier [of Lake Zurich Frontier Enterprise] - Lake Zurich, IL - *NewsDir 84*
Vernon Town Crier - Long Grove, IL - *Ed&PubIntYB 82*
Vernon Town Crier - Prairie View, IL - *AyerDirPub 83*
Vernon Township News Advertiser - Highland Park, IL - *AyerDirPub 83*
Vernon Township News Advertiser - *See* Singer Printing & Publishing Co.
Vernonia CATV Inc. - Vernonia, OR - *BrCabYB 84; Tel&CabFB 84C*
Vernons & Sons Ltd., C. - London, England - *StaDirAdAg 2-84*
Vern's TV & Radio - Limon, CO - *Tel&CabFB 84C*
Vero Beach Advertiser - Melbourne, FL - *AyerDirPub 83*
Vero Beach Press Journal - Vero Beach, FL - *BaconPubCkNews 84; Ed&PubIntYB 82; NewsDir 84*
Verona Cablevision - Verona, WI - *Tel&CabFB 84C*
Verona-Cedar Grove Times - Verona, NJ - *AyerDirPub 83; BaconPubCkNews 84; Ed&PubIntYB 82; NewsDir 84*
Verona Fitchburg Star - *See* Southwest Suburban Publications
Verona Press - *See* Southwest Suburban Publications
Verona Press, The - Verona, WI - *Ed&PubIntYB 82*
Veronis, Suhler & Associates - New York, NY - *EISS 7-83 Sup; InfoS 83-84; LitMarPl 83; VideoDir 82-83*
Versa Computing Inc. - Newbury Park, CA - *MicrocomMPl 84*
Versailles Cable TV [of Centel Cable Television Co.] - Versailles, KY - *BrCabYB 84*
Versailles, Elizabeth Starr [Aff. of Hathaway Family Association] - Williamsburg, MA - *BoPubDir 4, 5*
Versailles Leader-Statesman - Versailles, MO - *BaconPubCkNews 84; Ed&PubIntYB 82; NewsDir 84*
Versailles Policy - Versailles, OH - *BaconPubCkNews 84; Ed&PubIntYB 82*
Versailles Republican - Versailles, IN - *Ed&PubIntYB 82; NewsDir 84*
Versailles Republican - *See* Ripley Publishing Co. Inc.
Versailles Totalvision Inc. [of Cardiff Cities Cable Inc.] - Versailles, MO - *BrCabYB 84*
Versailles Woodford Sun - Versailles, KY - *BaconPubCkNews 84; NewsDir 84*

Versatec Inc. [Subs. of Xerox Corp.] - Santa Clara, CA - *WhoWMicrocom 83*
Versaterm Systems Ltd. - Ottawa, ON, Canada - *MicrocomSwDir 1; WhoWMicrocom 83*
Versatile Records Ltd. - New York, NY - *BillIntBG 83-84*
Versatile Television Productions Inc. - Cape Girardeau, MO - *TelAl 83, 84*
Versitron Inc. - Washington, DC - *DataDirSup 7-83*
VerStandig Broadcasting - Washington, DC - *BrCabYB 84*
Vertec - Kings Beach, CA - *MicrocomMPl 84*
Vertex Peripherals - San Jose, CA - *MicrocomMPl 84*
Vertex Systems Inc. - Wayne, PA - *DataDirOnSer 84; DataDirSup 7-83; EISS 7-83 Sup*
Vertical Software Group - Long Beach, CA - *MicrocomMPl 84*
Vertical Software Marketing - Brea, CA - *MicrocomMPl 83*
Vertiflite [of American Helicopter Society] - Alexandria, VA - *BaconPubCkMag 84; MagDir 84*
Verto Cable TV - Scranton, PA - *BrCabYB 84; Tel&CabFB 84C*
Very Own Music Co. - *See* Schroeder International Ltd., A.
Verygraphics - Albany, CA - *LitMag&SmPr 83-84*
Vesely Production Services, Joseph - Jackson Heights, NY - *LitMarPl 83, 84*
Veson Inc. - New York, NY - *ADAPSOMemDir 83-84*
Vespa Computer Outlet - Detroit, MI - *MicrocomMPl 84*
Vesta Publications Ltd. - Cornwall, ON, Canada - *BoPubDir 4, 5; LitMag&SmPr 83-84; LitMarPl 84; WritMar 84*
Vestal News [of Southern Tier Publications Inc.] - Vestal, NY - *Ed&PubIntYB 82; NewsDir 84*
Vestal News - *See* Southern Tier Publications Inc.
Vestal Press Ltd. - Vestal, NY - *BoPubDir 4, 5*
Vestavia Sun [of Sun Newspapers South & West] - Birmingham, AL - *NewsDir 84*
Vestkusten - San Francisco, CA - *Ed&PubIntYB 82*
Vestnik - West, TX - *Ed&PubIntYB 82*
Vestron Video - Stamford, CT - *BillIntBG 83-84*
Veszpremi Vegyipari Egyetem Veszprem/University of Chemical Engineering (Central Library) - Veszprem, Hungary - *InfIndMarPl 83*
Vetco Records - Cincinnati, OH - *BillIntBG 83-84*
VETDOC [of SDC Information Services] - Santa Monica, CA - *DataDirOnSer 84*
VETDOC - McLean, VA - *DirOnDB Spring 84*
VETDOC [of Derwent Publishing Ltd.] - London, England - *OnBibDB 3*
Veteran Historical Society - Veteran, AB, Canada - *BoPubDir 4 Sup, 5*
Veterans Administration Library Network - Washington, DC - *EISS 83*
Veterans Information Service - East Moline, IL - *BoPubDir 4, 5*
Veterinarians Forum - Matarie, LA - *DirOnDB Spring 84*
Veterinary Bulletin [of Commonwealth Bureau of Animal Health] - Weybridge, England - *CompReadDB 82*
Veterinary Economics - Edwardsville, KS - *BaconPubCkMag 84; MagIndMarPl 82-83; WritMar 84*
Veterinary Economics - Kansas City, KS - *MagDir 84*
Veterinary Literature Documentation [of Derwent Publications Ltd.] - London, England - *CompReadDB 82; DBBus 82; EISS 83*
Veterinary Medical Data Program [of Association of Veterinary Medical Data Program Participants] - Ithaca, NY - *EISS 83*
Veterinary Medicine Publishing Co. - Edwardsville, KS - *BoPubDir 4, 5*
Veterinary Medicine/Small Animal Clinician - Bonner Springs, KS - *WritMar 84*
Veterinary Medicine/Small Animal Clinician - Edwardsville, KS - *BaconPubCkMag 84; MagIndMarPl 82-83*
Veterinary Medicine/Small Animal Clinician - Kansas City, KS - *MagDir 84*
Veterinary Practice Publishing Co. - Santa Barbara, CA - *BoPubDir 4, 5*
Veterinary Textbooks - Ithaca, NY - *BoPubDir 4 Sup, 5*
Vette - New York, NY - *BaconPubCkMag 84*
Vette Records - Hollywood, CA - *BillIntBG 83-84*
Vevay Cable TV [of OVC Telecommunications] - Vevay, IN - *BrCabYB 84*
Vevay Newspapers Inc. - Vevay, IN - *BaconPubCkNews 84*
Vevay Reveille-Enterprise - Vevay, IN - *Ed&PubIntYB 82*
Vevay Reveille Enterprise - *See* Vevay Newspapers Inc.
Vevay Reveille-Enterprise Switzerland Democrat [of Vevay Newspapers Inc.] - Vevay, IN - *NewsDir 84*
Vevay Switzerland Democrat - *See* Vevay Newspapers Inc.
VFW Auxiliary - Kansas City, MO - *MagDir 84*
VFW Magazine - Kansas City, MO - *BaconPubCkMag 84; MagDir 84; MagIndMarPl 82-83*
VG Electronics Ltd. - Sussex, England - *VideoDir 82-83*
VGM Career Horizons [Div. of of National Textbook Co.] - Lincolnwood, IL - *LitMarPl 84; WritMar 84*
VGM Career Horizons [Div. of National Textbook Co.] - Skokie, IL - *LitMarPl 83*
Vi-Tech Corp. - Camden, NJ - *AvMarPl 83*
Vi-Tel Inc. [Subs. of Central Oklahoma Telephone Co.] - Beggs, OK - *BrCabYB 84; Tel&CabFB 84C*
Vi-Tel Inc. [of Central Oklahoma Telephone Co.] - Davenport, OK - *BrCabYB 84; Tel&CabFB 84C*
Vi-Tel Inc. - *See* Central Oklahoma Telephone Co.
Via Cable Inc. - Ingram, TX - *Tel&CabFB 84C*
Via Cable Inc. - Walden, TX - *BrCabYB 84*
Via Satellite Corp. - Ventura, CA - *BrCabYB 84*
Via Satellite Inc. - Empire, CA - *BrCabYB 84 p.D-310; Tel&CabFB 84C p.1710*
Via Satellite Ltd. - Livingston, CA - *BrCabYB 84*
Via Video Inc. - Santa Clara, CA - *AvMarPl 83*
Viacom Broadcast Group - New York, NY - *BrCabYB 84*
Viacom Broadcasting Inc. - New York, NY - *Tel&CabFB 84S*
Viacom Cable [of Viacom Corp.] - New York, NY - *CabTVFinDB 83*
Viacom Cable East Bay [of Viacom International Inc.] - Dublin, CA - *BrCabYB 84*
Viacom Cable Long Island [of Viacom International Inc.] - Islip, NY - *BrCabYB 84*
Viacom Cable Marin [of Viacom International Inc.] - San Rafael, CA - *BrCabYB 84*
Viacom Cable Mountain View [of Viacom International Inc.] - Mountain View, CA - *BrCabYB 84*
Viacom Cable Napa/Pinole [of Viacom International Inc.] - Pinole, CA - *BrCabYB 84*
Viacom Cable North Shore [of Viacom International Inc.] - Glendale, WI - *BrCabYB 84*
Viacom Cable Pittsburg [of Viacom International Inc.] - Pittsburg, CA - *BrCabYB 84*
Viacom Cable Snohomish [of Viacom International Inc.] - Brier, WA - *BrCabYB 84*
Viacom Cable Snohomish [of Viacom International Inc.] - Granite Falls, WA - *BrCabYB 84*
Viacom Cable Snohomish [of Viacom International Inc.] - Lake Stevens, WA - *BrCabYB 84*
Viacom Cable South Suburban [of Viacom International Inc.] - Greenfield, WI - *BrCabYB 84*
Viacom Cable South Suburban [of Viacom International Inc.] - South Milwaukee, WI - *BrCabYB 84*
Viacom Cablevision - Colusa, CA - *BrCabYB 84*
Viacom Cablevision [of Viacom International Inc.] - Crockett, CA - *BrCabYB 84*
Viacom Cablevision - Dublin, CA - *LitMarPl 84*
Viacom Cablevision [of Viacom International Inc.] - East Bay, CA - *Tel&CabFB 84C*
Viacom Cablevision [of Viacom International Inc.] - Finer Living, CA - *Tel&CabFB 84C*
Viacom Cablevision - Gridley, CA - *BrCabYB 84*
Viacom Cablevision [of Viacom International Inc.] - Healdsburg, CA - *BrCabYB 84*
Viacom Cablevision - Oroville, CA - *BrCabYB 84*
Viacom Cablevision [of Viacom International Inc.] - Paradise, CA - *BrCabYB 84*
Viacom Cablevision [of Viacom International Inc.] - Petaluma, CA - *BrCabYB 84*
Viacom Cablevision [Div. of Viacom International Inc.] - Pleasanton, CA - *BrCabYB 84 p.D-310; HomeVid&CabYB 82-83*
Viacom Cablevision [of Viacom International Inc.] - Sonora, CA - *BrCabYB 84*
Viacom Cablevision [of Viacom International Inc.] - Salem, OR - *BrCabYB 84; Tel&CabFB 84C*
Viacom Cablevision [of Viacom International Inc.] - Nashville, TN - *BrCabYB 84; Tel&CabFB 84C*

Viacom Cablevision [of Viacom International Inc.] - Seattle, WA - *BrCabYB 84; Tel&CabFB 84C*
Viacom Cablevision [of Viacom International Inc.] - Snohomish County, WA - *Tel&CabFB 84C*
Viacom Cablevision Inc. [of Viacom International Inc.] - Biggs, CA - *BrCabYB 84*
Viacom Cablevision of Cleveland [of Viacom International Inc.] - Cleveland Heights, OH - *InterCabHB 3; Tel&CabFB 84C*
Viacom Cablevision of Cleveland [of Viacom International Inc.] - Shaker Heights, OH - *BrCabYB 84*
Viacom Cablevision of Dayton [of Viacom International Inc.] - Dayton, OH - *BrCabYB 84; InterCabHB 3; Tel&CabFB 84C*
Viacom Cablevision of Long Island [of Viacom International Inc.] - Central Islip, NY - *BrCabYB 84*
Viacom Cablevision of Long Island [of Viacom International Inc.] - Ronkonkoma, NY - *HomeVid&CabYB 82-83*
Viacom Cablevision of Mountain View [of Viacom International Inc.] - Mountain View, CA - *Tel&CabFB 84C*
Viacom Cablevision of San Francisco [of Viacom International Inc.] - San Francisco, CA - *BrCabYB 84; HomeVid&CabYB 82-83; InterCabHB 3; Tel&CabFB 84C*
Viacom Cablevision of Wisconsin [of Viacom International Inc.] - Glendale, WI - *Tel&CabFB 84C*
Viacom Cablevision of Wisconsin [of Viacom International Inc.] - Greenfield, WI - *Tel&CabFB 84C*
Viacom Communications - New York, NY - *TelAl 83, 84*
Viacom Enterprises - New York, NY - *TelAl 83, 84*
Viacom International [of Tele-Vue Systems Inc.] - Red Bluff, CA - *BrCabYB 84*
Viacom International - New York, NY - *AdAge 6-28-84; BrCabYB 84; HomeVid&CabYB 82-83; KnowInd 83; Tel&CabFB 84C p.1710; VideoDir 82-83*
Vibar Music - *See* Laurie Publishing Group
Viborg Enterprise - Viborg, SD - *BaconPubCkNews 84; Ed&PubIntYB 82*
Viburnum Communications Inc. [of Steelville Telephone Exchange Inc.] - Viburnum, MO - *Tel&CabFB 84C*
Vic-Nic-News [of The Byte House] - Salem, NH - *MicrocomMPl 84*
VICA - Leesburg, VA - *MagDir 84*
Vichitra Press - Los Angeles, CA - *BoPubDir 5*
Vici Beacon - Vici, OK - *BaconPubCkNews 84*
Vici Beacon-News - Vici, OK - *Ed&PubIntYB 82*
Vici Cable TV - Vici, OK - *BrCabYB 84*
Vicinanza, Ralph M. - New York, NY - *LitMarPl 84*
Vicinity Post & Tenth Ware Courier - Rochester, NY - *AyerDirPub 83*
Vickers & Benson Cos. Ltd. - Toronto, ON, Canada - *StaDirAdAg 2-84*
Vickers Associates Inc., Michael - Boulder, CO - *DirPRFirms 83*
Vickers Communications - San Diego, CA - *StaDirAdAg 2-84*
Vickers Institutional Stock System - New York, NY - *DirOnDB Spring 84*
Vicks Lithograph & Printing Corp. - Yorkville, NY - *LitMarPl 83, 84*
Vicksburg Commercial-Express - Vicksburg, MI - *BaconPubCkNews 84; Ed&PubIntYB 82*
Vicksburg Evening Post - Vicksburg, MS - *BaconPubCkNews 84; Ed&PubIntYB 82; NewsDir 84*
Vicksburg Video Inc. [of WEHCO Video Inc.] - Vicksburg, MS - *BrCabYB 84; Tel&CabFB 84C*
Vicom Associates - San Francisco, CA - *AdAge 3-28-84; StaDirAdAg 2-84*
Vicom Information Service - Chillicothe, OH - *VideoDir 82-83*
Victimology: An International Journal - Washington, DC - *ArtMar 84; LitMag&SmPr 83-84; WritMar 84*
Victor Books [Div. of Scripture Press Publications Inc.] - Wheaton, IL - *LitMarPl 83, 84; WritMar 84*
Victor Herald - Victor, NY - *AyerDirPub 83; Ed&PubIntYB 82*
Victor Herald [of Empire State Weeklies] - Webster, NY - *NewsDir 84*
Victor Herald - *See* Empire State Weeklies
Victor Record - Victor, IA - *BaconPubCkNews 84; Ed&PubIntYB 82*
Victor Systems & Equipment - Marietta, OH - *DirInfWP 82*
Victor Technologies [Subs. of Sirius Systems Technology Inc.] - Scotts Valley, CA - *DataDirSup 7-83; MicrocomMPl 84; WhoWMicrocom 83*
Victor Valley Daily Press - Victorville, CA - *AyerDirPub 83; BaconPubCkNews 84; Ed&PubIntYB 82*
Victorex Inc. - Walnut Creek, CA - *WhoWMicrocom 83*
Victoria Advocate - Victoria, TX - *BaconPubCkNews 84; Ed&PubIntYB 82; NewsDir 84*
Victoria Cablevision Ltd. [of Premier Cablesystems Ltd.] - Victoria, BC, Canada - *BrCabYB 84*
Victoria County Record - Perth-Andover, NB, Canada - *AyerDirPub 83; Ed&PubIntYB 82*
Victoria Group Inc. - Natick, MA - *BrCabYB 84*
Victoria Kenbridge-Victoria Dispatch - Victoria, VA - *BaconPubCkNews 84; NewsDir 84*
Victoria Sportcaster, The - Victoria, BC, Canada - *Ed&PubIntYB 82*
Victorian Homes [of The Renovator's Supply Inc.] - Millers Falls, MA - *DirMarMP 83*
Victorian Homes - Brooklyn, NY - *BaconPubCkMag 84*
Victorian Motor Vehicles Registrations Data Base - St. Leonards, Australia - *DirOnDB Spring 84*
Victorian Video Ltd. - New York, NY - *Tel&CabFB 84C*
Victorious Ministry Through Christ Inc. - Winter Park, FL - *BoPubDir 4 Sup, 5*
Victorville Daily Press [of Victory Valley Publishing Co. Inc.] - Victorville, CA - *NewsDir 84*
Victory Computer Systems Inc. - San Jose, CA - *WhoWMicrocom 83*
Victory Garden - Ithaca, NY - *DirOnDB Spring 84*
Victory Garden Data Base - Phoenixville, PA - *EISS 5-84 Sup*
Victory Garden, The [of Edward J. Batutis] - Cary, NC - *DataDirOnSer 84*
Victory Library - New Orleans, LA - *BoPubDir 4, 5*
Victory Software - Paoli, PA - *MicrocomMPl 84*
Victory Television - New York, NY - *TelAl 83; Tel&CabFB 84C*
Victory, The - St. Eustache, PQ, Canada - *Ed&PubIntYB 82*
VIDAC - Concord, CA - *DataDirSup 7-83*
Vidacable CATV Systems - Rosendale, NY - *BrCabYB 84*
Vidalia Advance - Vidalia, GA - *BaconPubCkNews 84; Ed&PubIntYB 82*
Vidalia Communications Corp. - Vidalia, GA - *BrCabYB 84*
Vidcom Telecommunication Services - Westlake Village, CA - *AvMarPl 83*
Videa Ltd. - Cedar Rapids, IA - *AvMarPl 83*
Videart Opticals - New York, NY - *AvMarPl 83*
Video [of Reese Publishing Co. Inc.] - New York, NY - *BaconPubCkMag 84; WritMar 84*
Video Aids of Colorado - Boulder, CO - *AvMarPl 83*
Video-Audio Electronics Inc. - Williamsport, PA - *BillIntBG 83-84*
Video Automation Systems Inc. - Pound Ridge, NY - *AvMarPl 83*
Video Base Inc., The - Merrimack, NH - *AvMarPl 83*
Video Business - New York, NY - *BaconPubCkMag 84; WritMar 84*
Video Cable [of Treeford Ltd.] - Fabreville, PQ, Canada - *BrCabYB 84*
Video Cable Systems Inc. - Ellington, MO - *BrCabYB 84*
Video Cable Systems Inc. - Craigsville, VA - *BrCabYB 84*
Video Cable Systems Inc. - Pembroke, VA - *BrCabYB 84; Tel&CabFB 84C*
Video Cable TV - Fredericktown, MO - *Tel&CabFB 84C*
Video-Centre - Gentilly, PQ, Canada - *BrCabYB 84*
Video-Cinema Films Inc. - New York, NY - *Tel&CabFB 84C*
Video Communications - New York, NY - *AvMarPl 83*
Video Communications Inc. [of Allegheny Valley Cable Co.] - Desert Hot Springs, CA - *BrCabYB 84*
Video Communications Systems - Ft. Myers, FL - *Tel&CabFB 84C*
Video Components Inc. - Spring Valley, NY - *AvMarPl 83*
Video/Computer Connections - Downsview, ON, Canada - *BaconPubCkMag 84*
Video Concepts - Woodstock, NY - *AvMarPl 83*
Video Concert Hall [of Henderson-Crowe Productions Inc.] - Atlanta, GA - *BrCabYB 84*
Video Corp. of America - Edison, NJ - *AvMarPl 83*
Video Corp. of America - New York, NY - *HomeVid&CabYB 82-83*

Video Corp. of America (S/T Videocassette Duplicating) - Leonia, NJ - *ADAPSOMemDir 83-84*
Video Craftsmen Inc. - Hollywood, CA - *AvMarPl 83*
Video Data Bank - Chicago, IL - *LitMag&SmPr 83-84*
Video Data Systems - Hauppauge, NY - *DataDirSup 7-83*
Video Dery Ltee. - St. Raymond, PQ, Canada - *BrCabYB 84; Tel&CabFB 84C*
Video Dery Ltee. - Ville de la Baie, PQ, Canada - *BrCabYB 84*
Video Dideo Publishing Co. - Birmingham, AL - *BillIntBG 83-84*
Video Dimensions - New York, NY - *BillIntBG 83-84*
Video Dub Inc. - New York, NY - *AvMarPl 83*
Video 80 Magazine - San Francisco, CA - *LitMag&SmPr 83-84*
Video Engineering - Hamilton Air Force Base, CA - *BrCabYB 84*
Video Engineering - Hercules, CA - *BrCabYB 84*
Video Engineering - La Mesa Village, CA - *Tel&CabFB 84C*
Video Engineering [of Tele-Communications Inc.] - Saratoga, CA - *BrCabYB 84; Tel&CabFB 84C*
Video Game All-Stars [of Video Newsletter Associates] - Garden City, NY - *MicrocomMPl 84*
Video Game Update & Computer Entertainer - North Hollywood, CA - *MicrocomMPl 84*
Video Games Magazine [of Pumpkin Press] - New York, NY - *WritMar 84*
Video Games Player [of Carnegie Publications] - New York, NY - *WritMar 84*
Video Genesis - Beachwood, OH - *AvMarPl 83*
Video/Hi Fi Buyer's Review - New York, NY - *BaconPubCkMag 84*
Video Horizons Inc. - Columbus, WI - *Tel&CabFB 84C*
Video in Phoenix - Phoenix, AZ - *AvMarPl 83*
Video-Info Publications - Santa Fe, NM - *BoPubDir 4, 5*
Video Information [of Winslow Associates] - Washington, DC - *DataDirOnSer 84; DirOnDB Spring 84; EISS 5-84 Sup*
Video International Productions Inc. - Dallas, TX - *BrCabYB 84*
Video International Publishers - Great Falls, MT - *AvMarPl 83*
Video-It Inc. - Hollywood, CA - *AvMarPl 83*
Video Link Inc. [of Helicon Corp.] - Bentleyville, PA - *BrCabYB 84; Tel&CabFB 84C*
Video Link Inc. [of Helicon Corp.] - Bobtown, PA - *Tel&CabFB 84C*
Video Link Inc. [of Helicon Corp.] - New Salem, PA - *Tel&CabFB 84C*
Video Link Inc. [of Helicon Corp.] - Point Marion, PA - *BrCabYB 84; Tel&CabFB 84C*
Video Link Ltd. - Marianna, PA - *BrCabYB 84*
Video Link Ltd. - Masontown, PA - *BrCabYB 84; Tel&CabFB 84C p.1710*
Video Link Ltd. - Perry Township, PA - *BrCabYB 84*
Video Marketing Game Letter - Hollywood, CA - *MicrocomMPl 84*
Video Marketing Game Letter - New York, NY - *BaconPubCkMag 84*
Video Marketing Newsletter - Hollywood, CA - *MicrocomMPl 84*
Video Marketing Newsletter - New York, NY - *BaconPubCkMag 84*
Video Monitor - Baltimore, MD - *BaconPubCkMag 84*
Video Movies - Skokie, IL - *BaconPubCkMag 84*
Video Patsearch [of Pergamon International Information Corp.] - McLean, VA - *EISS 83*
Video Play Report, The - Washington, DC - *BaconPubCkMag 84*
Video Pro - New York, NY - *BaconPubCkMag 84*
Video Probe Index - Bayside, NY - *CabTVFinDB 83; IntDirMarRes 83*
Video Probe Index Inc. - Weaverville, NC - *BrCabYB 84; Tel&CabFB 84C*
Video Product News - Palm Springs, CA - *BaconPubCkMag 84*
Video Production Services [Div. of Kayvid Inc.] - Stamford, CT - *AvMarPl 83; Tel&CabFB 84C*
Video Programs International - New Rochelle, NY - *TelAl 83, 84; Tel&CabFB 84C*
Video Properties Ltd. - Forest City, NC - *Tel&CabFB 84C*
Video Properties Ltd. [of Daniels & Associates Inc.] - Pickens, SC - *Tel&CabFB 84C*
Video Properties Ltd. [of Daniels & Associates Inc.] - Seneca, SC - *Tel&CabFB 84C*
Video Properties Ltd. [of Daniels & Associates Inc.] - Walhalla, SC - *Tel&CabFB 84C*
Video Properties Ltd. [of Daniels & Associates Inc.] - Williamston, SC - *Tel&CabFB 84C*
Video Quebec Inc. - Beauce, PQ, Canada - *BrCabYB 84*
Video Rentals [Subs. of Video Services Corp.] - Northvale, NJ - *AvMarPl 83*
Video Retailer, The - Syosset, NY - *MagIndMarPl 82-83*
Video Review - New York, NY - *ArtMar 84; BaconPubCkMag 84; MagIndMarPl 82-83*
Video Satellite Systems - Southfield, MI - *BrCabYB 84; HomeVid&CabYB 82-83*
Video Specialist, The - Fullerton, CA - *BaconPubCkMag 84*
Video Specialties [Div. of The Engineering Lab Inc.] - Solana Beach, CA - *AvMarPl 83*
Video St. Laurent Inc. - Shawinigan, PQ, Canada - *Tel&CabFB 84C*
Video Star Communications Inc. - Atlanta, GA - *DataDirSup 7-83*
Video Station Inc., The - Los Angeles, CA - *HomeVid&CabYB 82-83*
Video Store Magazine - Irvine, CA - *BaconPubCkMag 84*
Video Storyboard Tests - New York, NY - *HBIndAd&MS 82-83; IntDirMarRes 83*
Video Storyboards - New York, NY - *AvMarPl 83*
Video Studios of America Inc. - Little Neck, NY - *AvMarPl 83*
Video Swapper [of Arena Magazine Co.] - Annandale, MN - *WritMar 84*
Video Systems - Overland Park, KS - *BaconPubCkMag 84; MagIndMarPl 82-83; WritMar 84*
Video Systems - Shawnee Mission, KS - *MagDir 84*
Video Systems Div. [of Peirce-Phelps Inc.] - Philadelphia, PA - *TeleSy&SerDir 7-83*
Video Systems Inc. - Houston, TX - *AvMarPl 83*
Video Systems Network Inc. - Los Angeles, CA - *AvMarPl 83*
Video Tape Network Inc. - New York, NY - *AvMarPl 83*
Video Technical Institute - Dallas, TX - *AvMarPl 83*
Video Technology - Elk Grove Village, IL - *MicrocomMPl 84*
Video To Go International [Div. of Sinco Corp.] - Miami, FL - *AvMarPl 83*
Video Today & Tomorrow [of ABC Leisure Magazines Inc.] - New York, NY - *WritMar 84*
Video Trade News - Danbury, CT - *BaconPubCkMag 84; MagDir 84*
Video Transitions - Los Angeles, CA - *AvMarPl 83*
Video Transmission Control Group Inc. - Pasadena, MD - *Tel&CabFB 84C*
Video User - White Plains, NY - *BaconPubCkMag 84*
Video View - Hollywood, CA - *Tel&CabFB 84C*
Video Vision - Lancaster, SC - *BrCabYB 84; Tel&CabFB 84C*
Video Vision - Whitewright, TX - *BrCabYB 84; Tel&CabFB 84C*
Video Week - Washington, DC - *DirOnDB Spring 84; MagDir 84*
Video Week [of NewsNet Inc.] - Bryn Mawr, PA - *DataDirOnSer 84*
Video West [Div. of Bonneville Productions] - Salt Lake City, UT - *AvMarPl 83; Tel&CabFB 84C*
Video Wizard's Inc. - San Jose, CA - *MicrocomMPl 84*
Video Workshop - Portland, ME - *AvMarPl 83*
Video Yesteryear/Video Images - Sandy Hook, CT - *BillIntBG 83-84*
Videoaccess - London, ON, Canada - *EISS 5-84 Sup*
Videocom Inc. - Quaker Hill, CT - *AvMarPl 83*
Videocom Inc. - Dedham, MA - *ArtMar 84; WritMar 84*
Videocom of Saugerties Inc. - Saugerties, NY - *BrCabYB 84*
Videocom of Saugerties Inc. - Seneca Falls, NY - *BrCabYB 84*
Videocomp - Olympic Valley, CA - *VideoDir 82-83*
Videodata LAN/1 [of Interactive Systems/3M] - St. Paul, MN - *TeleSy&SerDir 2-84*
Videodex Inc. - New York, NY - *BrCabYB 84; Tel&CabFB 84C*
Videodial Inc. - New York, NY - *EISS 7-83 Sup; TeleSy&SerDir 7-83, 2-84; VideoDir 82-83*
Videodisc News - Arlington, VA - *BaconPubCkMag 84*
Videodisc/Videotex - Westport, CT - *BaconPubCkMag 84*
Videographic Systems of America Inc. - New York, NY - *EISS 5-84 Sup; LitMarPl 83, 84; TeleSy&SerDir 2-84*
Videography - New York, NY - *ArtMar 84; BaconPubCkMag 84; MagDir 84; MagIndMarPl 82-83; WritMar 84*
VideOhio Inc. - Columbus, OH - *Tel&CabFB 84C*
Videolearning Systems Inc. - Conshohocken, PA - *AvMarPl 83*
Videolog - Wilton, CT - *DirOnDB Spring 84*

Videomeetings - Dallas, TX - *AvMarPl 83*
Videonet [of Oak Industries] - Glendale, CA - *TeleSy&SerDir 7-83*
Videonet [Subs. of Myer Communications] - Melbourne, Australia - *VideoDir 82-83*
Videonews - Bethesda, MD - *BaconPubCkMag 84; DirOnDB Spring 84*
Videonews [of NewsNet Inc.] - Bryn Mawr, PA - *DataDirOnSer 84*
Videoplay Magazine - Danbury, CT - *BaconPubCkMag 84; MagIndMarPl 82-83*
Videopress - London, ON, Canada - *VideoDir 82-83*
VideoPrint [of International Resource Development Inc.] - Norwalk, CT - *BaconPubCkMag 84; MagIndMarPl 82-83; MicrocomMPl 84*
Videoproofs Inc. - West Palm Beach, FL - *AvMarPl 83*
Videostar Connections Inc. - Atlanta, GA - *Tel&CabFB 84C*
Videotape Works - Worcester, MA - *Tel&CabFB 84C*
Videotek Inc. - Pottstown, PA - *AvMarPl 83*
Videotel [of SIP Italian Telephone Operating Co.] - Rome, Italy - *EISS 7-83 Sup; TeleSy&SerDir 7-83; VideoDir 82-83*
Videotex [of Computer Power] - Sydney, Australia - *VideoDir 82-83*
Videotex [of Belgium PTT] - Brussels, Belgium - *VideoDir 82-83*
Videotex - Wellington, New Zealand - *VideoDir 82-83*
Videotex - Zurich, Switzerland - *VideoDir 82-83*
Videotex/America - *See* Times Mirror
Videotex Canada - Toronto, ON, Canada - *BaconPubCkMag 84*
Videotex Consulting Services - Regina, SK, Canada - *VideoDir 82-83*
Videotex Industry Association - Washington, DC - *EISS 83; InterCabHB 3; TeleSy&SerDir 7-83*
Videotex Industry Association - Rosslyn, VA - *TeleSy&SerDir 2-84*
Videotex Information Service Providers Association of Canada - Ottawa, ON, Canada - *EISS 83*
Videotex Pilot Trial [of ITT Austria] - Scheydgasse, Austria - *VideoDir 82-83*
Videotex Products - Boston, MA - *BaconPubCkMag 84; DirOnDB Spring 84*
Videotex Systems & Services Group [of Systemhouse Inc.] - Arlington, VA - *EISS 5-84 Sup*
Videotron Communications - Montreal, PQ, Canada - *VideoDir 82-83*
Videotron Ltee. - Gatineau, PQ, Canada - *BrCabYB 84*
Videotron Ltee. - Mont Laurier, PQ, Canada - *BrCabYB 84*
Videotron Ltee. - St. Hubert, PQ, Canada - *BrCabYB 84*
Videotron Ltee. - St. Jerome, PQ, Canada - *BrCabYB 84*
Videotron Ltee. - *See* Telecable Videotron Ltee.
VideoVision Inc. - Ridgefield, NJ - *HomeVid&CabYB 82-83*
Videoworks - New York, NY - *AvMarPl 83; Tel&CabFB 84C*
Viders Co. Inc., Arthur J. - Tampa, FL - *LitMarPl 83, 84*
Vidette - Highland, KS - *AyerDirPub 83*
Vidette - Hartsville, TN - *AyerDirPub 83*
Vidette - Montesano, WA - *AyerDirPub 83*
Vidette-Messenger - Valparaiso, IN - *AyerDirPub 83; Ed&PubIntYB 82*
Videx Inc. - Corvallis, OR - *MicrocomMPl 83, 84*
Vidicom [Div. of L. D. Bevan Co. Inc.] - Westlake Village, CA - *AvMarPl 83; TeleSy&SerDir 7-83*
Vidicom Inc. - Prince Frederick, MD - *Tel&CabFB 84C*
Vidicopy Corp. - Sunnyvale, CA - *AvMarPl 83*
Vidicue [Div. of Cue Recording Studios Inc.] - New York, NY - *AvMarPl 83*
Vidistrib Inc. - Studio City, CA - *TelAl 83, 84; Tel&CabFB 84C*
Viditel [of Netherlands PTT] - The Hague, Netherlands - *EISS 7-83 Sup; InfIndMarPl 83; TeleSy&SerDir 7-83; VideoDir 82-83*
Vidlo Corp., Videotape Productions - New York, NY - *AvMarPl 83*
Vidor Cablevision Inc. - Vidor, TX - *BrCabYB 84*
Vidorian - Vidor, TX - *AyerDirPub 83; BaconPubCkNews 84; Ed&PubIntYB 82*
Vidorian Shopper - Vidor, TX - *AyerDirPub 83*
Vidtronics - Hollywood, CA - *Tel&CabFB 84C*
Viehmann Corp. - Andover, MA - *MicrocomMPl 84; MicrocomSwDir 1*
Vienna International Centre Library [of International Atomic Energy Agency] - Vienna, Austria - *EISS 83*
Vienna Maries County Gazette-Advisor - *See* Lewis Publishing Co. Inc.
Vienna News-Observer - Vienna, GA - *BaconPubCkNews 84; Ed&PubIntYB 82*
Vienna Times - Vienna, IL - *BaconPubCkNews 84; Ed&PubIntYB 82; NewsDir 84*
Vienybe - Brooklyn, NY - *Ed&PubIntYB 82*
Vietnam Veterans Memorial Chapel - Springer, NM - *BoPubDir 4, 5*
Vietnam War Newsletter - Collinsville, CT - *LitMag&SmPr 83-84*
View - New York, NY - *BaconPubCkMag 84; WritMar 84*
View-All Cable TV - Whitley County, KY - *BrCabYB 84*
View Cable TV - Westworth Village, TX - *BrCabYB 84*
View Cable TV Inc. - Carswell Air Force Base, TX - *BrCabYB 84*
Viewdata Corp. of America [Subs. of Knight-Ridder Newspapers] - Miami Beach, FL - *VideoDir 82-83*
Viewdata Services [of Guinness Superlatives Ltd.] - Enfield, England - *EISS 83*
Viewdata Services [of Croner Publications Ltd.] - New Malden, England - *EISS 83*
Viewdata Services [of Link House Communications Ltd.] - Poole, England - *EISS 83*
Viewdata/Videotex Report - New York, NY - *BaconPubCkMag 84; DirOnDB Spring 84*
Viewdata/Videotex Report [of NewsNet Inc.] - Bryn Mawr, PA - *DataDirOnSer 84*
Viewfinder Qualitative Research - Stamford, CT - *IntDirMarRes 83*
Viewfinders Inc. - Evanston, IL - *AvMarPl 83*
Viewpoint Aquarius - Surrey, England - *ArtMar 84*
Viewpoint Publications Inc. - Montgomery, AL - *BoPubDir 4, 5*
Views of the Personal Computer Industry - Richardson, TX - *BaconPubCkMag 84*
Viewtel 202 [of Viewtel Services Ltd.] - Birmingham, England - *EISS 83*
Viewtext - Bethesda, MD - *BaconPubCkMag 84*
Viewtext - Boston, MA - *DirOnDB Spring 84*
ViewText [of NewsNet Inc.] - Bryn Mawr, PA - *DataDirOnSer 84*
Viewtron [of Viewdata Corp. of America Inc.] - Miami Beach, FL - *CabTVPrDB 83; EISS 83; TeleSy&SerDir 2-84*
Viewtron/New England [of Affiliated Publications Inc.] - Newton, MA - *EISS 5-84 Sup*
Vigilant - Cassopolis, MI - *AyerDirPub 83*
Vigilante Satellite Services - Chinook, MT - *BrCabYB 84; Tel&CabFB 84C*
Vigilante Satellite Services - Conrad, MT - *BrCabYB 84*
Vigilante Satellite Services - Ft. Benton, MT - *BrCabYB 84*
Vigilante Satellite Services - Malta, MT - *BrCabYB 84*
Vigilante Satellite Services - Townsend, MT - *BrCabYB 84*
Viguerie Co., The - Falls Church, VA - *DirMarMP 83*
Vik Video [of Programmer's Institute] - Chapel Hill, NC - *MicrocomMPl 84*
Vikatis Consultants, J. - Thomaston, CT - *MicrocomMPl 84*
Viking Acoustical Corp. - Lakeville, MN - *DirInfWP 82; WhoWMicrocom 83*
Viking Audio Visual - Hopkins, MN - *AvMarPl 83*
Viking Cable TV Ltd. - Yarmouth, NS, Canada - *BrCabYB 84*
Viking Cases [Div. of The Stemler Corp.] - St. Petersburg, FL - *AvMarPl 83*
Viking CATV Associates [of US Cable Corp.] - Monona, WI - *Tel&CabFB 84C*
Viking CATV Associates [of Complete Channel TV Co.] - Oregon, WI - *Tel&CabFB 84C*
Viking CATV Associates [of US Cable Corp.] - Sauk City, WI - *Tel&CabFB 84C*
Viking Communications - Providence, RI - *Tel&CabFB 84C*
Viking Films - New York, NY - *AvMarPl 83; TelAl 83, 84; Tel&CabFB 84C*
Viking Microband - New York, NY - *Tel&CabFB 84C*
Viking Penguin Inc. - New York, NY - *DirMarMP 83; WritMar 84*
Viking Press, The [Div. of Viking Penguin Inc.] - New York, NY - *LitMarPl 83, 84*

Viking Software Services Inc. - Tulsa, OK - *MicrocomMPl 84*
Vila Music - *See* Funky but Music Inc.
Viladas Co., J. M. - Greenwich, CT - *IntDirMarRes 83*
Vilas Advertising Inc. - Oakland, CA - *StaDirAdAg 2-84*
Vilas Cable Inc. - Eagle River, WI - *BrCabYB 84; Tel&CabFB 84C*
Vilas County News Review & Three Lakes News - Eagle River, WI - *AyerDirPub 83; Ed&PubIntYB 82; NewsDir 84*
Vile [of Banana Productions] - Vancouver, BC, Canada - *LitMag&SmPr 83-84*
Vilkaitis Consultants, J. - Thomaston, CT - *MicrocomMPl 83; MicrocomSwDir 1; WhoWMicrocom 83*
Villa Grove News - Villa Grove, IL - *BaconPubCkNews 84; Ed&PubIntYB 82*
Villa Park Argus [of Press Publications] - Elmhurst, IL - *AyerDirPub 83; NewsDir 84*
Villa Park Argus - *See* Press Publications
Villa Park Argus, The - Villa Park, IL - *Ed&PubIntYB 82*
Villa Park Review - Lombard, IL - *AyerDirPub 83*
Villa Park Review - Villa Park, IL - *Ed&PubIntYB 82*
Villa Park Review - *See* MacKay Enterprises Inc., E. A.
Villa Rican - Villa Rica, GA - *BaconPubCkNews 84; Ed&PubIntYB 82; NewsDir 84*
Village Advocate - Chapel Hill, NC - *AyerDirPub 83*
Village Book Store Press - Toronto, ON, Canada - *BoPubDir 4, 5*
Village Cable Co. - Oriole Beach, FL - *BrCabYB 84*
Village Cable Co. [of Oriole Homes Corp.] - West Delray Beach, FL - *Tel&CabFB 84C*
Village Cable Corp. [of Helicon Corp.] - Uniontown, PA - *Tel&CabFB 84C*
Village Cable Corp. [of Helicon Corp.] - Elizabeth, WV - *BrCabYB 84; Tel&CabFB 84C*
Village Cable Corp. [of Helicon Corp.] - Ellenboro, WV - *BrCabYB 84*
Village Cable Corp. [of Helicon Corp.] - Grantsville, WV - *BrCabYB 84; Tel&CabFB 84C*
Village Cable Corp. [of Helicon Corp.] - Harrisville, WV - *BrCabYB 84; Tel&CabFB 84C*
Village Cable Inc. - Chapel Hill, NC - *BrCabYB 84; Tel&CabFB 84C*
Village CATV Inc. - Bella Vista, AR - *BrCabYB 84; Tel&CabFB 84C p.1710*
Village CATV Inc. [of Cooper Communities Inc.] - Hot Springs Village, AR - *BrCabYB 84; Tel&CabFB 84C*
Village Cos., The - Chapel Hill, NC - *BrCabYB 84*
Village Gazette - Greenwich, CT - *AyerDirPub 83; Ed&PubIntYB 82*
Village Journal, The - Pleasantville, NY - *AyerDirPub 83*
Village Life - Greendale, WI - *Ed&PubIntYB 82*
Village News - Oxford, PA - *AyerDirPub 83*
Village Newspaper, The - New York, NY - *NewsDir 84*
Village of Boaz - Boaz, WI - *Tel&CabFB 84C*
Village of Point Edward - Point Edward, ON, Canada - *BoPubDir 4, 5*
Village Press - Kensington, MD - *BoPubDir 4, 5*
Village Press Inc., The - Concord, NH - *MagIndMarPl 82-83*
Village Software Inc. - Buffalo, NY - *WhoWMicrocom 83*
Village Times, The - East Setauket, NY - *AyerDirPub 83; Ed&PubIntYB 82*
Village Typing & Stenographic Service - New York, NY - *LitMarPl 83, 84*
Village Voice - Severna Park, MD - *Ed&PubIntYB 82*
Village Voice [of New Group Publications Inc.] - New York, NY - *Ed&PubIntYB 82; LitMarPl 83, 84; MagIndMarPl 82-83; NewsDir 84*
Village Weekly - Granbury, TX - *Ed&PubIntYB 82*
Villager - Bronxville, NY - *MagDir 84; WritMar 84*
Villager [of Serif Press Inc.] - New York, NY - *AyerDirPub 83; LitMarPl 83, 84*
Villager - Cedar Grove, WI - *AyerDirPub 83; Ed&PubIntYB 82*
Villager, The - Greenwich Village, NY - *Ed&PubIntYB 82*
Villager, The - Moscow, PA - *Ed&PubIntYB 82*
Villanova Engineer - Villanova, PA - *BaconPubCkMag 84*
Villard Books - *See* Random House Inc.
Ville Platte Gazette - Ville Platte, LA - *BaconPubCkNews 84; Ed&PubIntYB 82; NewsDir 84*
Villeneuve Publications - Montreal, PQ, Canada - *LitMag&SmPr 83-84*
Villisca Farmers Telephone Co. - Villisca, IA - *TelDir&BG 83-84*
Villisca Review & Stanton Viking - Villisca, IA - *BaconPubCkNews 84; Ed&PubIntYB 82*
Vilne Solvo - Toronto, ON, Canada - *Ed&PubIntYB 82*
Vilnis - Chicago, IL - *AyerDirPub 83; Ed&PubIntYB 82; NewsDir 84*
Vincennes Sun Commercial [of Central Newspapers Inc.] - Vincennes, IN - *BaconPubCkNews 84; Ed&PubIntYB 82; NewsDir 84*
Vincennes University - Vincennes, IN - *BrCabYB 84 p.D-310*
Vincennes Valley Advance [of Vincennes University] - Vincennes, IN - *BaconPubCkNews 84; NewsDir 84*
Vincent Associates, A. W. - Rochester, NY - *AvMarPl 83*
Vincent Publishing, Norm - Jacksonville, FL - *BillIntBG 83-84*
Vinco Press - Detroit, MI - *BoPubDir 4, 5*
Vindicator - Valley Falls, KS - *AyerDirPub 83*
Vindicator - Hammond, LA - *AyerDirPub 83*
Vindicator - Bloomfield, MO - *AyerDirPub 83*
Vindicator - Youngstown, OH - *AyerDirPub 83; Ed&PubIntYB 82; LitMarPl 84*
Vindicator - Liberty, TX - *AyerDirPub 83*
Vindicator Printing Co., The - Youngstown, OH - *BrCabYB 84*
Vineland Down Jersey Newspaper - Vineland, NJ - *NewsDir 84*
Vineland Times Journal [of Times Graphics Inc.] - Vineland, NJ - *BaconPubCkNews 84; Ed&PubIntYB 82; NewsDir 84*
Viner-Bell Consultant, Jeanne - Washington, DC - *DirPRFirms 83*
Vineyard Gazette - Edgartown, MA - *NewsDir 84*
Vineyard Gazette - Martha's Vineyard, MA - *Ed&PubIntYB 82*
Ving - Kent, ME - *LitMag&SmPr 83-84*
Vininfo - Bordeaux, France - *DirOnDB Spring 84*
Vinings-Northside-Sandy Springs Neighbor - Vinings, GA - *Ed&PubIntYB 82*
Vinita Cable TV [of Investment Enterprizes Inc.] - Vinita, OK - *BrCabYB 84*
Vinita Journal - Vinita, OK - *BaconPubCkNews 84; Ed&PubIntYB 82; NewsDir 84*
Vinnik, Ellen - New York, NY - *LitMarPl 83; MagIndMarPl 82-83*
Vintage - New York, NY - *BaconPubCkMag 84; MagDir 84; MagIndMarPl 82-83*
Vintage America Publishing Co. - Washington, DC - *BoPubDir 4, 5*
Vintage Image - St. Helena, CA - *BoPubDir 5*
Vinton Cablevision [of McDonald Group] - Vinton, IA - *Tel&CabFB 84C*
Vinton Cablevision Inc. - Birmingham, AL - *BrCabYB 84*
Vinton Cedar Valley Daily Times [of Mid America Publishing Corp.] - Vinton, IA - *NewsDir 84*
Vinton County Courier - *See* Jackson Publishing Co.
Vinton County Courier, The - McArthur, OH - *Ed&PubIntYB 82*
Vinton Messenger [of Herald Publishing Corp.] - Vinton, VA - *AyerDirPub 83; Ed&PubIntYB 82; NewsDir 84*
Vinton Messenger - *See* Herald Publishing Corp.
Vinton News - Vinton, LA - *BaconPubCkNews 84; Ed&PubIntYB 82*
Vinton Productions, Will - Portland, OR - *ArtMar 84*
Vinyard & Lee & Partners - St. Louis, MO - *AdAge 3-28-84; StaDirAdAg 2-84*
Vinzant & Associates - Hobart, IN - *MicrocomMPl 84*
Viola Advertising, Harry - New York, NY - *AdAge 3-28-84; StaDirAdAg 2-84*
Viola Home Telephone Co. - Viola, IL - *TelDir&BG 83-84*
Viola News - Viola, WI - *Ed&PubIntYB 82*
Violet Press - New York, NY - *BoPubDir 4, 5*
VIP Medical Grapevine - Round Lake, IL - *Ed&PubIntYB 82*
VIP Systems Corp. - Washington, DC - *ADAPSOMemDir 83-84*
VIP Systems International - New York, NY - *LitMarPl 83, 84*
Vipro Program Services Inc. - Chicago, IL - *Tel&CabFB 84C*
Vira Books - Ottawa, ON, Canada - *BoPubDir 4, 5*
Virag Productions, Norm - Lansing, MI - *AvMarPl 83*
Virago Press - Salem, NH - *LitMarPl 83, 84*
Virden Recorder - Virden, IL - *BaconPubCkNews 84; Ed&PubIntYB 82*
Virgin Boy Records - Dallas, TX - *BillIntBG 83-84*
Virgin Ear Music - *See* Kaye Publications, Richard

Virgin Islands Post Advertiser - Charlotte Amalie, VI - *AyerDirPub 83*
Virginia Arts Publishing Co. - Louisa, VA - *BillIntBG 83-84*
Virginia Beach Beacon - Virginia Beach, VA - *NewsDir 84*
Virginia Beach Sun [of Byerly Publications Inc.] - Virginia Beach, VA - *AyerDirPub 83; BaconPubCkNews 84; Ed&PubIntYB 82; NewsDir 84*
Virginia Beach Weekly - Virginia Beach, VA - *AyerDirPub 83*
Virginia Book Co. - Berryville, VA - *BoPubDir 4, 5*
Virginia Cavalcade [of Virginia State Library] - Richmond, VA - *MagIndMarPl 82-83; WritMar 84*
Virginia Citizen - Beardstown, IL - *Ed&PubIntYB 82*
Virginia Citizen - Virginia, IL - *AyerDirPub 83*
Virginia City Madisonian - Virginia City, MT - *BaconPubCkNews 84*
Virginia City Territorial Enterprise - Virginia City, NV - *BaconPubCkNews 84*
Virginia Contractor - Virginia Beach, VA - *BaconPubCkMag 84*
Virginia Data Center - Norfolk, VA - *DataDirOnSer 84*
Virginia Farm Bureau News - Richmond, VA - *BaconPubCkMag 84; MagDir 84*
Virginia Forests - Richmond, VA - *BaconPubCkMag 84*
Virginia Gazette - Williamsburg, VA - *AyerDirPub 83; Ed&PubIntYB 82; NewsDir 84*
Virginia Gazette-Times - Virginia, IL - *BaconPubCkNews 84*
Virginia Hot Springs Telephone Co. - Hot Springs, VA - *TelDir&BG 83-84*
Virginia Journal of Education - Richmond, VA - *BaconPubCkMag 84; MagDir 84*
Virginia Law Review - Charlottesville, VA - *MagDir 84*
Virginia Magazine of History & Biography - Richmond, VA - *MagIndMarPl 82-83*
Virginia Medical - Richmond, VA - *BaconPubCkMag 84*
Virginia Mesabi News - Virginia, MN - *NewsDir 84*
Virginia Micro Systems - Woodbridge, VA - *MicrocomMPl 83, 84*
Virginia Mountaineer, The - Grundy, VA - *Ed&PubIntYB 82*
Virginia Municipal Review [of Review Publishing Co. Inc.] - Richmond, VA - *MagDir 84*
Virginia Museum [Aff. of The Commonwealth of Virginia] - Richmond, VA - *BoPubDir 4, 5*
Virginia Music Co. - Ft. Lee, NJ - *BillIntBG 83-84*
Virginia Natural Diversity Information Program - Blacksburg, VA - *EISS 5-84 Sup*
Virginia P-H-C Image [of Virginia Association of Plumbing-Heating-Cooling Contractors] - Richmond, VA - *BaconPubCkMag 84; MagDir 84*
Virginia Pharmacist [of Virginia Pharmaceutical Association] - Richmond, VA - *BaconPubCkMag 84; MagDir 84*
Virginia Poultryman - Harrisonburg, VA - *BaconPubCkMag 84; MagDir 84*
Virginia Press Association Inc. - Richmond, VA - *ProGuPRSer 4*
Virginia Quarterly Review, The - Charlottesville, VA - *WritMar 84*
Virginia Record - Richmond, VA - *BaconPubCkMag 84; MagDir 84*
Virginia Recording Co. - Ft. Lee, NJ - *BillIntBG 83-84*
Virginia Review - Chester, VA - *BaconPubCkMag 84*
Virginia Road Builder - Richmond, VA - *MagDir 84*
Virginia State Chamber of Commerce Publications - Richmond, VA - *BoPubDir 4, 5*
Virginia State Data Center [of Virginia State Dept. of Planning & Budget] - Richmond, VA - *EISS 5-84 Sup*
Virginia State Div. of Legislative Automated Systems - Richmond, VA - *EISS 83*
Virginia Tech Library System [of Virginia Polytechnic Institute & State University Libraries] - Blacksburg, VA - *EISS 83*
Virginia-Tennessean - Bristol, VA - *AyerDirPub 83; Ed&PubIntYB 82*
Virginia Town & City [of Virginia Municipal League] - Richmond, VA - *BaconPubCkMag 84; MagDir 84*
Virginia Trucker - Richmond, VA - *MagDir 84*
Virginia Wildlife - Richmond, VA - *WritMar 84*
Virginian-Leader - Pearisburg, VA - *AyerDirPub 83; Ed&PubIntYB 82; NewsDir 84*
Virginian Pilot [of Landmark Communications Inc.] - Norfolk, VA - *AyerDirPub 83; BaconPubCkNews 84; Ed&PubIntYB 82; LitMarPl 83, 84; NewsBur 6; NewsDir 84*
Virginian-Pilot/Ledger-Star, The [of Landmark Communications Inc.] - Norfolk, VA - *LitMarPl 84*
Virginia's Press - Richmond, VA - *BaconPubCkMag 84; MagDir 84*
Virgins MDS Co. - Pasadena, MD - *Tel&CabFB 84C*
Virgo Press - Miami Beach, FL - *BoPubDir 4 Sup, 5*
Virology - San Diego, CA - *BaconPubCkMag 84*
Virology Abstracts [of Information Retrieval Ltd.] - London, England - *CompReadDB 82*
Viroqua Telephone Co. - Viroqua, WI - *TelDir&BG 83-84*
Viroqua Vernon County Broadcaster Censor - Viroqua, WI - *BaconPubCkNews 84; NewsDir 84*
Virtual City Associates Ltd. - London, England - *EISS 5-84 Sup; TeleSy&SerDir 2-84*
Virtual Combinatics - Rockport, MA - *MicrocomMPl 84*
Virtual Microsystems - Berkeley, CA - *MicrocomMPl 84*
Virtual Systems Inc. - Walnut Creek, CA - *WhoWMicrocom 83*
Virtue - Sisters, OR - *ArtMar 84; BaconPubCkMag 84; WritMar 84*
Virtue Notagraph Editions - La Mesa, CA - *BoPubDir 4, 5*
Visa Books - Glen Iris, Australia - *LitMag&SmPr 83-84*
Visa Music - *See* Jolly Cheeks Music
Visage Press Inc. - Arlington, VA - *BoPubDir 4, 5*
Visalia MDS Co. - Pasadena, MD - *Tel&CabFB 84C*
Visalia Times-Delta [of Gannett Co. Inc.] - Visalia, CA - *BaconPubCkNews 84; Ed&PubIntYB 82; NewsDir 84*
Viscerally Press - Kent, OH - *LitMag&SmPr 83-84*
Viscom Inc. - Baltimore, MD - *AvMarPl 83*
Viscom International Ltd. - New York, NY - *AvMarPl 83*
Visdata [of Heinze GmbH] - Celle, East Germany - *EISS 7-83 Sup*
Visibility Enterprises - New York, NY - *BoPubDir 4, 5*
Visible Computer Supply Corp. [Subs. of Wallace Computer Services Inc.] - St. Charles, IL - *DirInfWP 82; MicrocomMPl 83; WhoWMicrocom 83*
Visible Language - Cleveland, OH - *BaconPubCkMag 84*
VisiCorp - San Jose, CA - *ADAPSOMemDir 83-84; DataDirSup 7-83; MicrocomMPl 83, 84; MicrocomSwDir 1; WhoWMicrocom 83*
Vision Associates Ltd. - Weybridge, England - *MicrocomSwDir 1*
Vision Cable - Houma, LA - *BrCabYB 84*
Vision Cable Communications [of Newhouse Group Inc.] - New York, NY - *BrCabYB 84 p.D-310; CabTVFinDB 83; LitMarPl 84; TelAl 83, 84; Tel&CabFB 84C p.1710*
Vision Cable Communications Inc. - Albemarle, NY - *BrCabYB 84*
Vision Cable of Albemarle [of Vision Cable Communications Inc.] - Albemarle, NC - *Tel&CabFB 84C*
Vision Cable of Metrolina [of Vision Cable Communications Inc.] - Concord, NC - *BrCabYB 84; Tel&CabFB 84C*
Vision Cable of Morehead City [of Vision Cable Communications Inc.] - Morehead City, NC - *BrCabYB 84; Tel&CabFB 84C*
Vision Cable of North Carolina [of Vision Cable Communications Inc.] - Mecklenburg County, NC - *BrCabYB 84*
Vision Cable of Pinellas [of Vision Cable Communications Inc.] - Clearwater, FL - *BrCabYB 84; InterCabHB 3; Tel&CabFB 84C*
Vision Cable of Pinellas Inc. [of Vision Cable Communications Inc.] - Pinellas Park, FL - *BrCabYB 84*
Vision Cable of Salisbury [of Vision Cable Communications Inc.] - Salisbury, NC - *BrCabYB 84; Tel&CabFB 84C*
Vision Cable of Shelby [of Vision Cable Communications Inc.] - Shelby, NC - *BrCabYB 84; Tel&CabFB 84C*
Vision Cable of South Carolina [of Vision Cable Communications Inc.] - Florence, SC - *BrCabYB 84; Tel&CabFB 84C*
Vision Cable of South Carolina Inc. - Darlington, SC - *BrCabYB 84*
Vision Cable of Sumter [of Vision Cable Communications Inc.] - Sumter, SC - *BrCabYB 84; Tel&CabFB 84C*
Vision Cable of Wilmington - Southport, NC - *BrCabYB 84*
Vision Cable of Wilmington [of Vision Cable Communications Inc.] - Wilmington, NC - *BrCabYB 84; Tel&CabFB 84C*
Vision Cable Television Co. - Fort Lee, NJ - *BrCabYB 84*
Vision Cable Television Co. [Aff. of Vision Cable Communications Inc.] - Palisades Park, NJ - *InterCabHB 3*
Vision Communications [of WTVS Channel 56] - Detroit, MI - *TeleSy&SerDir 2-84*

Vision Computer Systems - Fullerton, CA - *ADAPSOMemDir 83-84*
Vision House Publishers Inc. - Santa Ana, CA - *BoPubDir 4, 5*
Vision House Publishers Inc. [Div. of G/L Publications] - Ventura, CA - *LitMarPl 83, 84; WritMar 84*
Vision Press Inc. - Huntington Beach, CA - *MicroMarPl 82-83*
Visionary Electronics Inc. - San Francisco, CA - *DataDirSup 7-83*
Visionary Radio Euphonics Inc. - Santa Rosa, CA - *BrCabYB 84*
Visions [of Black Buzzard Press] - Arlington, VA - *LitMag&SmPr 83-84; WritMar 84*
Visions Unltd. - Fairfield, IA - *AvMarPl 83*
Visitor - Jet, OK - *AyerDirPub 83*
Vismar Publishing Co. - Parma, OH - *BoPubDir 4, 5*
Visnews Ltd. - New York, NY - *BrCabYB 84*
Visotec Inc. - Tustin, CA - *AvMarPl 83*
Visschers & Associates, Robert - Chicago, IL - *StaDirAdAg 2-84*
Vista [of Wesleyan Publishing House] - Marion, IN - *WritMar 84*
Vista Cable Co. - Stevenson, WA - *BrCabYB 84; Tel&CabFB 84C*
Vista Cable Inc. - Brookston, IN - *BrCabYB 84*
Vista Cable Inc. - Monon, IN - *BrCabYB 84*
Vista Cable Inc. - Remington, IN - *BrCabYB 84*
Vista Cable Inc. - Reynolds, IN - *BrCabYB 84 p.D-310; Tel&CabFB 84C p.1710*
Vista Cable Inc. - Wolcott, IN - *BrCabYB 84*
Vista Cablevision Inc. [of Times Mirror Cable TV] - Vista, CA - *BrCabYB 84; Tel&CabFB 84C*
Vista Cablevision Inc. - Wichita Falls, TX - *BrCabYB 84*
Vista Cablevision Inc. [of Mid-Atlantic Network Inc,] - Buena Vista, VA - *BrCabYB 84; Tel&CabFB 84C*
Vista Com Inc. - Cuthbert, GA - *Tel&CabFB 84C p.1711*
Vista Computer - Santa Ana, CA - *MicrocomMPl 83, 84*
Vista Computer Inc. - Elmsford, NY - *DataDirOnSer 84*
Vista Data Systems Inc. - North Royalton, OH - *ADAPSOMemDir 83-84*
Vista East Pennysaver - Mission Viejo, CA - *AyerDirPub 83*
Vista Grande Cablevision Inc. [of Community Tele-Communications Inc.] - Daly City, CA - *BrCabYB 84; Tel&CabFB 84C*
Vista Morning Press - Vista, CA - *BaconPubCkNews 84*
Vista News, The - Vista, CA - *NewsDir 84*
Vista Press - Vista, CA - *AyerDirPub 83; Ed&PubIntYB 82*
Vista Publications - Santa Monica, CA - *BoPubDir 4, 5; LitMag&SmPr 83-84*
Vista San Marcos Courier - San Marcos, CA - *BaconPubCkNews 84*
Vista-United Telecommunications - Lake Buena Vista, FL - *TelDir&BG 83-84*
Vista/USA - Convent Station, NJ - *BaconPubCkMag 84; MagIndMarPl 82-83; WritMar 84*
Vista West Pennysaver - Mission Viejo, CA - *AyerDirPub 83*
Vistec Inc. - Morristown, NJ - *Tel&CabFB 84C*
Vistone - Hollywood, CA - *BillIntBG 83-84*
Visu-Flex Co. - Pico Rivera, CA - *DirInfWP 82*
Visual Aid Centers Inc. - Englewood, CO - *AvMarPl 83*
Visual Aid Equipment Corp. - Syracuse, NY - *AvMarPl 83*
Visual Aids Electronics Corp. - Washington, DC - *AvMarPl 83*
Visual Arts Associates Inc. - Schaumburg, IL - *AvMarPl 83*
Visual Arts Ontario - Toronto, ON, Canada - *BoPubDir 4, 5*
Visual Data Corp. - St. Louis, MO - *AvMarPl 83*
Visual Education Association [Div. of Graphic Paper Products] - Springfield, OH - *AvMarPl 83*
Visual Education Corp. - Princeton, NJ - *AvMarPl 83; LitMarPl 83, 84; WritMar 84*
Visual Evangels Publishing Co. - Michigan City, IN - *BoPubDir 4, 5*
Visual Graphics Corp. - Tamarac, FL - *AvMarPl 83*
Visual Horizons [Div. of Tatham Laird & Kudner Advertising] - New York, NY - *DirMarMP 83*
Visual Horizons - Rochester, NY - *AvMarPl 83; WritMar 84*
Visual Horizons - *See* Tatham-Laird & Kudner
Visual House International - New York, NY - *AvMarPl 83*
Visual Impact - Miami, FL - *MagIndMarPl 82-83*
Visual Information Systems - New York, NY - *AvMarPl 83*
Visual Instruction Productions [of Kayvid Inc.] - Stamford, CT - *AvMarPl 83*
Visual Instrumentation Corp. - Burbank, CA - *AvMarPl 83*
Visual Materials Inc. - Gurnee, IL - *AvMarPl 83*
Visual Merchandising - Baileys Harbor, WI - *MagDir 84*
Visual Merchandising & Store Design [of ST Publications] - Cincinnati, OH - *BaconPubCkMag 84; MagIndMarPl 82-83; WritMar 84*
Visual Methods - Westwood, NJ - *AvMarPl 83*
Visual Productions TV Ltd. - Toronto, ON, Canada - *Tel&CabFB 84C*
Visual Projects Ltd. - Roslyn Heights, NY - *AvMarPl 83*
Visual Promotions Inc. - New York, NY - *LitMarPl 83; MagIndMarPl 82-83*
Visual Purple - Berkeley, CA - *BoPubDir 4, 5*
Visual Resources - Santa Monica, CA - *BaconPubCkMag 84*
Visual Resources Group - Kansas City, MO - *BoPubDir 4 Sup, 5*
Visual Services - Briarcliff Manor, NY - *LitMarPl 83, 84*
Visual Songs - *See* Creative Corps.
Visual Sound Co. [Div. of The Camera Shop Inc.] - Broomall, PA - *AvMarPl 83*
Visual Studies Workshop Press - Rochester, NY - *AvMarPl 83; BoPubDir 4, 5; LitMag&SmPr 83-84*
Visual Systems Inc. - Milwaukee, WI - *AvMarPl 83*
Visual Technology Inc. - Tewksbury, MA - *DataDirSup 7-83; MicrocomMPl 83; WhoWMicrocom 83*
Visuality/Jean Callan King - New York, NY - *LitMarPl 83*
Visually Handicapped Inspirational Library - Penngrove, CA - *BoPubDir 5*
Visuals - Miami, FL - *MagIndMarPl 82-83*
Visualworld [Div. of American Phoenix Corp.] - Oak Park, IL - *LitMarPl 83, 84; MagIndMarPl 82-83*
Visucom Video Arts [Div. of Visucom Productions Inc.] - Redwood City, CA - *AvMarPl 83*
Vita Italiana - Toronto, ON, Canada - *Ed&PubIntYB 82*
Vita Music Publishing Co. - *See* Var Music Publishing Co.
Vita Press - Memphis, TN - *BoPubDir 4, 5*
Vitachart Inc. - Riverdale, NY - *ArtMar 84*
Vitak-Elsnic Co. - Downers Grove, IL - *BillIntBG 83-84*
Vital - Elk Grove, IL - *MagDir 84*
Vital - Evanston, IL - *MagIndMarPl 82-83*
Vital Christianity [of Warner Press Inc.] - Anderson, IN - *WritMar 84*
Vital Communications - Syracuse, NY - *AvMarPl 83*
Vital Information Inc. - Overland Park, KS - *MicrocomMPl 83, 84*
Vital Speeches of the Day - Southold, NY - *BaconPubCkMag 84; MagDir 84*
Vital Statistics Inc. - New York, NY - *IntDirMarRes 83*
Vitality Associates - Saratoga, CA - *LitMag&SmPr 83-84*
Vitek - San Marcos, CA - *MicrocomMPl 84*
Vitis - Siebeldingen, West Germany - *DirOnDB Spring 84*
Vitt Media International - New York, NY - *HBIndAd&MS 82-83; StaDirAdAg 2-84; Tel&CabFB 84C*
Viv-Val Publishing Co. - Van Nuys, CA - *BillIntBG 83-84*
Viva Records - Los Angeles, CA - *BillIntBG 83-84*
Viva-Tech - Rochester, NY - *AvMarPl 83*
Vivian Cable TV [of W.W. Communications] - Vivian, LA - *Tel&CabFB 84C*
Vivian Cable TV [of Universal Video Communications Inc.] - Excelsior Springs, MO - *BrCabYB 84*
Vivian Caddo Citizen [of T & T Enterprises] - Vivian, LA - *BaconPubCkNews 84; NewsDir 84*
Vivian Telephone Co. - Vivian, SD - *TelDir&BG 83-84*
Vivitar Corp. - Santa Monica, CA - *AvMarPl 83*
Viza Software - Gillingham, England - *MicrocomSwDir 1*
VJ Electronics Inc. - Torrance, CA - *AvMarPl 83*
VKM Publishing Co. - Rayville, MO - *BoPubDir 4, 5*
Vlasto & Co. Inc. - New York, NY - *DirPRFirms 83*
Vlcek, Douglas - Wilson, KS - *Tel&CabFB 84C p.1711*
VLSI Applications Inc. - Irvine, CA - *MicrocomMPl 84*
VLSI Design - Palo Alto, CA - *BaconPubCkMag 84*
VM/B Inc. [Subs. of Ogilvy & Mather Inc.] - Houston, TX - *DirMarMP 83*
VM Communications Inc. - New York, NY - *DirPRFirms 83*
VM Software Inc. - Falls Church, VA - *ADAPSOMemDir 83-84*
VMC Inc. - Miami, FL - *BillIntBG 83-84*
VMX Inc. - Richardson, TX - *DataDirSup 7-83*
VNU Amvest Inc. - Washington, DC - *InfoS 83-84*

VNU Business Press Group BV - Amsterdam, Netherlands - *InfoS 83-84*
VNU Data Publishing International BV - Amsterdam, Netherlands - *InflndMarPl 83*
VOAR - St. John's, NF, Canada - *BrCabYB 84*
Voc Ed - Arlington, VA - *BaconPubCkMag 84; MagDir 84; MagIndMarPl 82-83*
Vocab Inc. - Chicago, IL - *BillIntBG 83-84*
Vocational & Adult Education Unit [of Auburn University] - Auburn, AL - *EISS 83*
Vocational & Career Assessment - Lakeside, CA - *BoPubDir 4 Sup, 5*
Vocational Biographies Inc. - Sauk Centre, MN - *DirMarMP 83*
Vocational Education Curriculum Materials [of The National Center for Research in Vocational Education] - Columbus, OH - *DataDirOnSer 84; DirOnDB Spring 84*
Vocational Education Information Network [of Millersville State College] - Millersville, PA - *EISS 83*
Vocational Education Productions [Div. of California Polytechnic State University Foundation] - San Luis Obispo, CA - *AvMarPl 83; WritMar 84*
Vocational Films [Div. of Telecine Film Studios] - Park Ridge, IL - *AvMarPl 83*
Vocational Information Through Computer Systems [of Philadelphia School District] - Philadelphia, PA - *EISS 5-84 Sup*
VOCM - St. John's, NF, Canada - *BrCabYB 84*
VOE - Chadbourn, NC - *TV&RadDir 84*
Vogel, Leo F. - Connell, WA - *BoPubDir 4, 5*
Vogel Music Co. Inc., Jerry - New York, NY - *BillIntBG 83-84*
Vogel-Peterson - Elmhurst, IL - *DirInfWP 82*
Vogelback Computing Center [of Northwestern University] - Evanston, IL - *EISS 83*
Vogelsang Press - Yosemite, CA - *BoPubDir 4, 5*
Vogue [of Conde Nast Publications] - New York, NY - *ArtMar 84; BaconPubCkMag 84; Folio 83; LitMarPl 83, 84; MagDir 84; MagIndMarPl 82-83; NewsBur 6; WritMar 84*
Vogue Patterns - New York, NY - *MagIndMarPl 82-83*
Voice [of Scripps-Howard Newspapers] - Louisville, KY - *AyerDirPub 83; NewsDir 84*
Voice - Valhalla, NY - *AyerDirPub 83*
Voice - Harrisburg, PA - *BaconPubCkMag 84*
Voice - Arlington, VA - *BaconPubCkMag 84; MagDir 84*
Voice & Data Resources Inc. - New York, NY - *TeleSy&SerDir 2-84*
Voice & Jeffersonian, The - Louisville, KY - *Ed&PubIntYB 82*
Voice & Viewpoint News - San Diego, CA - *Ed&PubIntYB 82*
Voice & Vision of Vermont Inc. [of John T. Thurber Inc.] - Saxton's River, VT - *BrCabYB 84; Tel&CabFB 84C*
Voice Box Records - Memphis, TN - *BillIntBG 83-84*
Voice Express [of MCI International Inc.] - Rye Brook, NY - *TeleSy&SerDir 2-84*
Voice Journal - South Milwaukee, WI - *AyerDirPub 83; NewsDir 84*
Voice Message Exchange [of VMX Inc.] - Richardson, TX - *TeleSy&SerDir 2-84*
Voice News & View Point - San Diego, CA - *AyerDirPub 83*
Voice Newspapers - Schaumburg, IL - *BaconPubCkNews 84*
Voice Newspapers, The - Louisville, KY - *Ed&PubIntYB 82*
Voice of Addison - Addison, IL - *Ed&PubIntYB 82*
Voice of Addison - Roselle, IL - *AyerDirPub 83*
Voice of Bartlett/Streamwood - Roselle, IL - *AyerDirPub 83*
Voice of Bensenville/Wood Dale - Bensenville, IL - *Ed&PubIntYB 82*
Voice of Bensenville/Wood Dale - Roselle, IL - *AyerDirPub 83*
Voice of Bloomingdale - Bloomingdale, IL - *Ed&PubIntYB 82*
Voice of Bloomingdale - Roselle, IL - *AyerDirPub 83*
Voice of Carol Stream - Carol Stream, IL - *Ed&PubIntYB 82*
Voice of Carol Stream - Roselle, IL - *AyerDirPub 83*
Voice of 1865, The - Ashland, KY - *NewsDir 84*
Voice of Elk Grove Village - Elk Grove Village, IL - *Ed&PubIntYB 82*
Voice of Elk Grove Village - Roselle, IL - *AyerDirPub 83*
Voice of Glendale Heights - Glendale Heights, IL - *Ed&PubIntYB 82*
Voice of Glendale Heights - Roselle, IL - *AyerDirPub 83*
Voice of Hanover Park - Hanover Park, IL - *Ed&PubIntYB 82*
Voice of Hanover Park - Roselle, IL - *AyerDirPub 83*
Voice of Hoffman Estates - Hoffman Estates, IL - *Ed&PubIntYB 82*
Voice of Hoffman Estates - Roselle, IL - *AyerDirPub 83*
Voice of Itasca - Itasca, IL - *Ed&PubIntYB 82*
Voice of Itasca - Roselle, IL - *AyerDirPub 83*
Voice of Liberty Publications - Pearl River, NY - *LitMag&SmPr 83-84*
Voice of Local One [of United Food & Commercial Workers District Union Local 1] - Utica, NY - *NewsDir 84*
Voice of Paradise - *See* Songs from the Box
Voice of Roselle/Medinah - Roselle, IL - *AyerDirPub 83; Ed&PubIntYB 82*
Voice of Schaumburg - Roselle, IL - *AyerDirPub 83*
Voice of Schaumburg - Schaumburg, IL - *Ed&PubIntYB 82*
Voice of 770 [of Retail Clerks Union Local 770] - Los Angeles, CA - *NewsDir 84*
Voice of South Marion - Belleview, FL - *AyerDirPub 83; Ed&PubIntYB 82*
Voice of the Black Community - Decatur, IL - *AyerDirPub 83*
Voice of the Cement, Lime, Gypsum, & Allied Workers [of United Cement, Lime, Gypsum, & Allied Workers International] - Elk Grove Village, IL - *NewsDir 84*
Voice of 1319, The - Wilkes Barre, PA - *NewsDir 84*
Voice Publications - Goreville, IL - *DirMarMP 83*
Voice Retrieval System [of BBL Industries Inc.] - Atlanta, GA - *TeleSy&SerDir 2-84*
Voice, The - Sherwood, AR - *Ed&PubIntYB 82*
Voice, The - Miami, FL - *Ed&PubIntYB 82*
Voice, The [of Photojournals Inc.] - Huron, OH - *NewsDir 84*
Voice, The - Norwalk, OH - *Ed&PubIntYB 82*
Voice, The - Ripley, TN - *Ed&PubIntYB 82*
Voicemail International Inc. - Santa Clara, CA - *TeleSy&SerDir 2-84*
VoiceNews [of Stoneridge Technical Services] - Rockville, MD - *MicrocomMPl 84*
Voices - Southbury, CT - *AyerDirPub 83; Ed&PubIntYB 82*
Voices International - Little Rock, AR - *WritMar 84*
Voices-Israel - Haifa, Israel - *LitMag&SmPr 83-84*
Voicestor M [of Voicetek Corp.] - Newton, MA - *TeleSy&SerDir 2-84*
Voicetek - Goleta, CA - *MicrocomMPl 84*
Vokes Music Publishing Co. - New Kensington, PA - *BillIntBG 83-84*
Vokes Record Co. - New Kensington, PA - *BillIntBG 83-84*
Vol. No. Magazine [of Los Angeles Poets Press] - Newhall, CA - *WritMar 84*
Volan, Leon - San Francisco, CA - *BoPubDir 4, 5*
Volaphon Book & Printing Co. - Warwick, RI - *BoPubDir 5*
Volare Records Inc. - Englewood, NJ - *BillIntBG 83-84*
Volcano Communications Co. [of Volcano Telephone Co.] - Pine Grove, CA - *Tel&CabFB 84C*
Volcano Press Inc. - San Francisco, CA - *LitMag&SmPr 83-84; LitMarPl 83, 84; WritMar 84*
Volcano Review, The [of Peninhand Press] - Volcano, CA - *LitMag&SmPr 83-84*
Volcano Telephone Co. - Pine Grove, CA - *TelDir&BG 83-84*
Volga Tribune - Volga, SD - *BaconPubCkNews 84; Ed&PubIntYB 82*
Volin, Stan - Plainview, NY - *BoPubDir 4, 5*
Volition Systems - Del Mar, CA - *MicrocomMPl 84; WhoWMicrocom 83*
Volk Co., The John - Chicago, IL - *AdAge 3-28-84; DirPRFirms 83; StaDirAdAg 2-84*
Volkmuth Printers - St. Cloud, MN - *MagIndMarPl 82-83*
Volks Micro Computer Systems Inc. - Williamsburg, VA - *MicrocomMPl 84; MicrocomSwDir 1*
Volkswagenwerk - Wolfsburg, West Germany - *DirOnDB Spring 84*
Volkszeitung-Tribune - Omaha, NE - *Ed&PubIntYB 82*
Volkwein Bros. Inc. - Pittsburgh, PA - *BoPubDir 4, 5*
Vollmer/Public Relations, Helen - Houston, TX - *DirPRFirms 83*
Volt Information Sciences Inc. - New York, NY - *DataDirOnSer 84*
Volt Information Sciences Inc. - Syosset, NY - *LitMarPl 83, 84; MagIndMarPl 82-83; VideoDir 82-83*
Volt Temporary Services - Dallas, TX - *DirInfWP 82*

Volta Review - Washington, DC - *BaconPubCkMag 84; MagDir 84*
Voltaire Foundation - Oxford, England - *MicroMarPl 82-83*
Voltaire Press - Mississauga, ON, Canada - *BoPubDir 4 Sup, 5*
Volume Retail Merchandising - Toronto, ON, Canada - *BaconPubCkMag 84*
Voluntad Publishers Inc. [Subs. of National Textbook Co.] - Lincolnwood, IL - *LitMarPl 84*
Voluntad Publishers Inc. [Subs. of National Textbook Co.] - Skokie, IL - *LitMarPl 83*
Voluntary Standards Information Network [of Information Handling Services] - Englewood, CO - *DataDirOnSer 84; DirOnDB Spring 84*
Volunteer & Information Center of Greater Birmingham - Birmingham, AL - *EISS 83*
Volunteer Cable TV [of Marsh Media Inc.] - Gallatin, TN - *Tel&CabFB 84C*
Volunteer Fireman, The - Charlotte, NC - *WritMar 84*
Volunteer Leader, The [of American Hospital Publishing Inc.] - Chicago, IL - *MagDir 84*
Volunteer Services for the Blind Inc. - Philadelphia, PA - *LitMarPl 83, 84*
Volunteers in Technical Assistance - Mt. Rainier, MD - *FBInfSer 80*
Vomm, Ants - Toronto, ON, Canada - *BoPubDir 4, 5*
Von Gehr Press - Menlo Park, CA - *BoPubDir 4, 5*
Von Hoffmann Press Inc. - St. Louis, MO - *LitMarPl 83, 84*
Von Zerneck/Greenwald Music - *See* Fricon Entertainment Co. Inc., The
Vondrak Publications Inc. - Chicago, IL - *BaconPubCkNews 84*
Vongrutnorv Og Press - Troy, ID - *BoPubDir 4, 5*
Vorkapich/Lipson Inc. - New York, NY - *Tel&CabFB 84C*
VORT Corp. - Palo Alto, CA - *LitMarPl 83, 84*
Vortex Editions - San Francisco, CA - *BoPubDir 4, 5; LitMag&SmPr 83-84*
Vortex Records - San Francisco, CA - *BillIntBG 83-84*
Vortex, The [of Axios Newletter Inc.] - Los Angeles, CA - *LitMag&SmPr 83-84*
Vos Co. Inc., The Frank - New York, NY - *AdAge 3-28-84; DirMarMP 83; HBIndAd&MS 82-83; LitMarPl 83, 84; MagIndMarPl 82-83; StaDirAdAg 2-84*
Vos-Powers Group Inc. - New York, NY - *HBIndAd&MS 82-83*
Votan - Fremont, CA - *DataDirSup 7-83; MicrocomMPl 84*
Votes [of Canada Systems Group] - Mississauga, ON, Canada - *DataDirOnSer 84*
Votes Data Base [of Policy Review Associates Inc.] - Bethesda, MD - *DBBus 82*
Votes Data Base [of Policy Review Associates Inc.] - McLean, VA - *CompReadDB 82; EISS 83*
Votrax Div. [of Federal Screw Works] - Troy, MI - *DataDirSup 7-83; MicrocomMPl 84*
VOWR - St. John's, NF, Canada - *BrCabYB 84*
Voxcom [Div. of Tapecon Inc.] - Peachtree City, GA - *AvMarPl 83*
Voyager Recordings - Seattle, WA - *BillIntBG 83-84*
Voyager Software - Burlingame, CA - *MicrocomMPl 84*
Voyageur Art - Minneapolis, MN - *ArtMar 84*
Voyageur Books - Toronto, ON, Canada - *BoPubDir 4, 5*
Voz de Portugal - Hayward, CA - *Ed&PubIntYB 82*
Voz de Portugal - Montreal, PQ, Canada - *Ed&PubIntYB 82*
VP Records - Jamaica, NY - *BillIntBG 83-84*
VPC Press/Maltese Books - Redondo Beach, CA - *BoPubDir 4, 5*
VR Data Corp. - Folcroft, PA - *MicrocomMPl 84; WhoWMicrocom 83*
VR Information Systems Inc. [Aff. of Tektronix Inc.] - Austin, TX - *BoPubDir 4, 5*
VSA/Visual Sales Aids - Woodside, NY - *AvMarPl 83*
VSC Corp. [Subs. of Variable Speech Control Co.] - San Francisco, CA - *AvMarPl 83*
VSCOM - Ann Arbor, MI - *DirOnDB Spring 84*
VSN Satellite Communication Services - San Ramon, CA - *DirInfWP 82*
VTR Publishing Co. - Syosset, NY - *BoPubDir 4, 5*
VU/Quote - Leawood, KS - *DirOnDB Spring 84*
VU/Records - Chicago, IL - *BillIntBG 83-84*
VU/Text Information Services [Subs. of Knight-Ridder Newspapers Inc.] - Philadelphia, PA - *DataDirOnSer 84; EISS 7-83 Sup*
VU-TV - Phoenix, AZ - *TelAl 83*
VU-TV - Edison, NJ - *CabTVPrDB 83; Tel&CabFB 84C*
Vubis [of Free University of Brussels] - Brussels, Belgium - *EISS 7-83 Sup*
Vucor Inc. [of TeleNational Communications Inc.] - Ft. Riley, KS - *BrCabYB 84; Tel&CabFB 84C*
Vue-Fax Inc. - West Babylon, NY - *DirInfWP 82*
Vuecom Inc. - Grand Forks, ND - *BrCabYB 84; Tel&CabFB 84C*
Vuecom Inc. - Minto, ND - *Tel&CabFB 84C*
Vumore Co. of Laredo [of Rogers UA Cablesystems Inc.] - Laredo, TX - *BrCabYB 84*
Vumore TV Corp. [of Total TV Inc.] - Lancaster, WI - *BrCabYB 84; Tel&CabFB 84C*
Vurite Inc. [of Meyerhoff Cable Systems Inc.] - Pinecrest, CA - *BrCabYB 84; Tel&CabFB 84C*
VW & Porsche [of Argus Publishing] - Los Angeles, CA - *MagDir 84; WritMar 84*
VWR Scientific Inc. [Subs. of Univar] - San Francisco, CA - *AvMarPl 83*
Vycor Corp. - Washington, DC - *DataDirSup 7-83*
Vynet Corp. - Los Gatos, CA - *MicrocomMPl 84*

W

W [of Fairchild Publications] - New York, NY - *BaconPubCkMag 84; Folio 83; MagDir 84; MagIndMarPl 82-83*
W & W Films Inc. - New York, NY - *Tel&CabFB 84C*
W-C Communications Inc. - Bowerston, OH - *BrCabYB 84*
W-Hollow Books - Detroit, MI - *BoPubDir 4, 5*
WA Book Service Inc. - Hauppauge, NY - *LitMarPl 83, 84*
WA Graphic Concepts Group - *See* Weekley & Associates Inc.
WAAA - Winston-Salem, NC - *BrCabYB 84; NatRadPubDir Summer 83, Spring 84; TV&RadDir 84*
WAAC - Terre Haute, IN - *NatRadPubDir Summer 83; TV&RadDir 84*
WAAF-FM - Worcester, MA - *BrCabYB 84; NatRadPubDir Summer 83, Spring 84; TV&RadDir 84*
WAAG-FM - Galesburg, IL - *BrCabYB 84; NatRadPubDir Spring 84; TV&RadDir 84*
WAAK - Dallas, NC - *BrCabYB 84; TV&RadDir 84*
WAAL-FM - Binghamton, NY - *BrCabYB 84; NatRadPubDir Summer 83, Spring 84; TV&RadDir 84*
WAAM - Ann Arbor, MI - *BrCabYB 84; NatRadPubDir Summer 83, Spring 84; TV&RadDir 84*
WAAO - Andalusia, AL - *BrCabYB 84; TV&RadDir 84*
WAAQ - Big Rapids, MI - *BrCabYB 84*
WAAS - Thompson Station, TN - *BrCabYB 84*
WAAT-TV - Avalon, NJ - *TV&RadDir 84*
WAAT-TV - Linwood, NJ - *LitMarPl 84*
WAAT-TV - Wildwood, NJ - *BrCabYB 84; DirUSTelSta 83; TelAl 83, 84; Tel&CabFB 84S*
WAAV - Wilmington, NC - *TV&RadDir 84*
WAAV-FM - Wilmington, NC - *BrCabYB 84; TV&RadDir 84*
WAAW-FM - Murray, KY - *BrCabYB 84; TV&RadDir 84*
WAAX - Gadsden, AL - *BrCabYB 84; NatRadPubDir Summer 83, Spring 84; TV&RadDir 84*
WAAY-TV - Huntsville, AL - *BrCabYB 84; DirUSTelSta 83; TelAl 83, 84; Tel&CabFB 84S; TV&RadDir 84*
WAAZ-FM - Crestview, FL - *BrCabYB 84; TV&RadDir 84*
WABA - Aguadilla, PR - *BrCabYB 84*
Wabash Cablevision of Hendricks County Ltd. - Brownsburg, IN - *BrCabYB 84; Tel&CabFB 84C*
Wabash Cablevision of Hendricks County Ltd. - Darville, IN - *BrCabYB 84*
Wabash Cablevision of Hendricks County Ltd. - Indianapolis, IN - *Tel&CabFB 84C p.1711*
Wabash Cablevision of Hendricks County Ltd. - Mooresville, IN - *BrCabYB 84*
Wabash Cablevision of Hendricks County Ltd. - Plainfield, IN - *BrCabYB 84*
Wabash DataTech Inc. [Subs. of Kearney-National Inc.] - Rolling Meadows, IL - *DataDirSup 7-83; MicrocomMPl 83; WhoWMicrocom 83*
Wabash Mutual Telephone Co. - Celina, OH - *TelDir&BG 83-84*
Wabash Plain Dealer - Wabash, IN - *BaconPubCkNews 84; Ed&PubIntYB 82; NewsDir 84*
Wabash Tape Corp. - Rolling Meadows, IL - *DirInfWP 82*
Wabash Telephone Cooperative Inc. - Louisville, IL - *TelDir&BG 83-84*
Wabash Valley Broadcasting Corp. - Terre Haute, IN - *Tel&CabFB 84S*
Wabasha County Herald - Wabasha, MN - *BaconPubCkNews 84; Ed&PubIntYB 82*
Wabasso Standard - Wabasso, MN - *BaconPubCkNews 84; Ed&PubIntYB 82*
WABB - Mobile, AL - *BrCabYB 84; NatRadPubDir Summer 83, Spring 84; TV&RadDir 84*
WABB-FM - Mobile, AL - *BrCabYB 84; NatRadPubDir Summer 83, Spring 84; TV&RadDir 84*
WABC - New York, NY - *BrCabYB 84; LitMarPl 83, 84; NatRadPubDir Summer 83, Spring 84; TV&RadDir 84*
WABC-TV - New York, NY - *BrCabYB 84; DirUSTelSta 83; LitMarPl 83, 84; TelAl 83, 84; Tel&CabFB 84S; TV&RadDir 84*
WABD - Ft. Campbell, KY - *BrCabYB 84; TV&RadDir 84*
WABD-FM - Ft. Campbell, KY - *BrCabYB 84; TV&RadDir 84*
WABE-FM - Atlanta, GA - *BrCabYB 84; TV&RadDir 84*
WABF - Fairhope, AL - *BrCabYB 84; TV&RadDir 84*
WABG - Greenwood, MS - *BrCabYB 84; TV&RadDir 84*
WABG-TV - Greenwood, MS - *BrCabYB 84; DirUSTelSta 83; TelAl 83, 84; Tel&CabFB 84S; TV&RadDir 84*
WABI - Bangor, ME - *BrCabYB 84; NatRadPubDir Summer 83, Spring 84; TV&RadDir 84*
WABI-TV - Bangor, ME - *BrCabYB 84; DirUSTelSta 83; TelAl 83, 84; Tel&CabFB 84S; TV&RadDir 84*
WABJ - Adrian, MI - *BrCabYB 84; TV&RadDir 84*
WABK - Gardiner, ME - *BrCabYB 84; TV&RadDir 84*
WABK-FM - Gardiner, ME - *BrCabYB 84; TV&RadDir 84*
WABL - Amite, LA - *BrCabYB 84; TV&RadDir 84*
WABM-FM - Muskegon, MI - *NatRadPubDir Summer 83, Spring 84; TV&RadDir 84*
WABM-FM - Muskegon Heights, MI - *BrCabYB 84*
WABN-FM - Abingdon, VA - *BrCabYB 84; TV&RadDir 84*
WABO - Waynesboro, MS - *BrCabYB 84; TV&RadDir 84*
WABO-FM - Waynesboro, MS - *BrCabYB 84; TV&RadDir 84*
WABQ - Cleveland, OH - *BrCabYB 84; NatRadPubDir Summer 83, Spring 84; TV&RadDir 84*
WABR-FM - Tifton, GA - *BrCabYB 84; TV&RadDir 84*
WABS - Washington, DC - *NatRadPubDir Summer 83 p.53, Spring 84 p.53*
WABS - Arlington, VA - *BrCabYB 84; TV&RadDir 84*
WABT - Madison, AL - *BrCabYB 84*
WABT - Montgomery, AL - *TV&RadDir 84*
WABV - Abbeville, SC - *BrCabYB 84; TV&RadDir 84*
WABW-TV - Meigs, GA - *TV&RadDir 84*
WABW-TV - Pelham, GA - *BrCabYB 84; Tel&CabFB 84S*
WABX-FM - Detroit, MI - *BrCabYB 84; NatRadPubDir Summer 83, Spring 84*
WABX-FM - Oak Park, MI - *TV&RadDir 84*
WABY - Albany, NY - *BrCabYB 84; NatRadPubDir Summer 83, Spring 84; TV&RadDir 84*
Waby, Marian - Scotts Valley, CA - *BoPubDir 4, 5*
WABZ-FM - Albemarle, NC - *BrCabYB 84; TV&RadDir 84*
WACB - Kittanning, PA - *BrCabYB 84; TV&RadDir 84*

WACC-FM - Arnold, MD - *BrCabYB 84; NatRadPubDir Summer 83, Spring 84; TV&RadDir 84*
Wacco Inc. - Wayne, WV - *BrCabYB 84; Tel&CabFB 84C*
WACD - Alexander City, AL - *BrCabYB 84; TV&RadDir 84*
WACE - Springfield, MA - *BrCabYB 84; NatRadPubDir Summer 83, Spring 84 p.122; TV&RadDir 84*
WACF-FM - Paris, IL - *BrCabYB 84; TV&RadDir 84*
WACG-FM - Augusta, GA - *BrCabYB 84; NatRadPubDir Summer 83, Spring 84; TV&RadDir 84*
Wachs & Associates Inc., Mark - New York, NY - *DirPRFirms 83*
Wachsman Associates Inc., David S. - New York, NY - *DirPRFirms 83*
Wachusett Cablevision Inc. [of Coaxial Analysts Inc.] - Clinton, MA - *Tel&CabFB 84C*
WACK - Newark, NY - *BrCabYB 84; TV&RadDir 84*
WACL - Waycross, GA - *BrCabYB 84; TV&RadDir 84*
WACL-FM - Waycross, GA - *BrCabYB 84; TV&RadDir 84*
WACM - West Springfield, MA - *BrCabYB 84*
WACO - Waco, TX - *BrCabYB 84; NatRadPubDir Summer 83, Spring 84; TV&RadDir 84*
Waco Cablevision [of MetroVision Inc.] - Waco, TX - *BrCabYB 84; Tel&CabFB 84C*
Waco Citizen - Waco, TX - *BaconPubCkNews 84; Ed&PubIntYB 82; NewsDir 84*
Waco Messenger - Waco, TX - *BaconPubCkNews 84; Ed&PubIntYB 82*
Waco Texas Catholic Herald - Waco, TX - *NewsDir 84*
Waco Tribune-Herald [of Cox Enterprises Inc.] - Waco, TX - *BaconPubCkNews 84; Ed&PubIntYB 82; NewsDir 84*
Waconia Patriot - Waconia, MN - *BaconPubCkNews 84; Ed&PubIntYB 82; NewsDir 84*
WACQ - Tallassee, AL - *BrCabYB 84; TV&RadDir 84*
WACR - Columbus, MS - *BrCabYB 84; NatRadPubDir Summer 83, Spring 84*
WACR-FM - Columbus, MS - *BrCabYB 84; NatRadPubDir Summer 83, Spring 84; TV&RadDir 84*
WACS-TV - Dawson, GA - *BrCabYB 84; Tel&CabFB 84S*
WACT - Tuscaloosa, AL - *BrCabYB 84; NatRadPubDir Summer 83, Spring 84; TV&RadDir 84*
WACT-FM - Tuscaloosa, AL - *BrCabYB 84; NatRadPubDir Summer 83, Spring 84; TV&RadDir 84*
WACX - Austell, GA - *TV&RadDir 84*
WACZ - Bangor, ME - *BrCabYB 84; NatRadPubDir Summer 83; TV&RadDir 84*
WADA - Ft. Lauderdale/Hollywood, FL - *NatRadPubDir Summer 83*
WADA - Shelby, NC - *BrCabYB 84; TV&RadDir 84*
WADB-FM - Belmar, NJ - *TV&RadDir 84*
WADB-FM - Point Pleasant, NJ - *BrCabYB 84*
WADB-FM - South Belmar, NJ - *NatRadPubDir Summer 83, Spring 84*
WADC - Parkersburg, WV - *BrCabYB 84; NatRadPubDir Summer 83, Spring 84; TV&RadDir 84*
Waddington Advertising Agency Inc. - Lubbock, TX - *AdAge 3-28-84; StaDirAdAg 2-84*
WADE - Wadesboro, NC - *BrCabYB 84; TV&RadDir 84*
Wade Books - Kentfield, CA - *BoPubDir 5*
Wade Press - Edinburg, TX - *LitMag&SmPr 83-84*
Wade Productions Inc., Roger - New York, NY - *AvMarPl 83; TelAl 83, 84; Tel&CabFB 84C*
Wade West/Disco - Larchmont, NY - *IntDirMarRes 83*
Wade West Inc. - Van Nuys, CA - *IntDirMarRes 83*
Wadena News, The - Wadena, SK, Canada - *Ed&PubIntYB 82*
Wadena Pioneer Journal - Wadena, MN - *BaconPubCkNews 84; Ed&PubIntYB 82; NewsDir 84*
Wadesboro Anson Record - Wadesboro, NC - *BaconPubCkNews 84*
Wadesboro Messenger & Intelligencer - Wadesboro, NC - *NewsDir 84*
Wadesville Telephone Co. Inc. - Wadesville, IN - *TelDir&BG 83-84*
WADI-FM - Corinth, MS - *BrCabYB 84; TV&RadDir 84*
WADJ - Somerset, PA - *BrCabYB 84*
WADK - Newport, RI - *BrCabYB 84; NatRadPubDir Summer 83, Spring 84; TV&RadDir 84*
WADM - Decatur, IN - *BrCabYB 84; TV&RadDir 84*
WADM-FM - Decatur, IN - *BrCabYB 84; TV&RadDir 84*
WADO - New York, NY - *BrCabYB 84; LitMarPl 83, 84; NatRadPubDir Summer 83, Spring 84; TV&RadDir 84*
Wadowski-Bak, Alice [Subs. of Echota Folk Art Center] - Niagara Falls, NY - *LitMarPl 83, 84; MagIndMarPl 82-83*
WADR - Remsen, NY - *BrCabYB 84; TV&RadDir 84*
WADS - Ansonia, CT - *BrCabYB 84; NatRadPubDir Summer 83, Spring 84; TV&RadDir 84*
Wadsworth Atheneum - Hartford, CT - *BoPubDir 4, 5*
Wadsworth Electronic Publishing Co. - Belmont, CA - *MicrocomMPl 84*
Wadsworth Inc. [Subs. of International Thomson Organisation Inc.] - Belmont, CA - *LitMarPl 83, 84*
Wadsworth News Banner - Wadsworth, OH - *BaconPubCkNews 84; NewsDir 84*
Wadsworth Productions, Bill - Austin, TX - *AvMarPl 83*
Wadsworth Publishers of Canada Ltd. [Aff. of Wadsworth Inc.] - Markham, ON, Canada - *BoPubDir 5*
Wadsworth Publishing Co. [Div. of Wadsworth Inc.] - Belmont, CA - *LitMarPl 83, 84*
Wadsworth Publishing of Canada Ltd. [Aff. of Wadsworth Inc.] - Markham, ON, Canada - *BoPubDir 4*
WADX - Trenton, GA - *BrCabYB 84*
WADZ-FM - Americus, GA - *BrCabYB 84; TV&RadDir 84*
WAEB - Allentown, PA - *BrCabYB 84; NatRadPubDir Summer 83 p.209, Spring 84 p.209*
WAEB - Lehigh Valley, PA - *TV&RadDir 84*
WAEC - Atlanta, GA - *BrCabYB 84; TV&RadDir 84*
WAEC-FM - Atlanta, GA - *NatRadPubDir Summer 83, Spring 84*
Waechter und Anzeiger - Cleveland, OH - *Ed&PubIntYB 82*
WAED - Huntsville, AL - *BrCabYB 84*
WAEL - Mayaguez, PR - *BrCabYB 84*
WAEL-FM - Maricao, PR - *BrCabYB 84*
WAEM - Shallotte, NC - *BrCabYB 84*
WAEO-TV - Rhinelander, WI - *BrCabYB 84; DirUSTelSta 83; TelAl 83, 84; Tel&CabFB 84S; TV&RadDir 84*
WAER-FM - Syracuse, NY - *BrCabYB 84; NatRadPubDir Summer 83, Spring 84; TV&RadDir 84*
WAES - Remsen, NY - *BrCabYB 84*
WAEV-FM - Savannah, GA - *BrCabYB 84; NatRadPubDir Summer 83, Spring 84; TV&RadDir 84*
WAEW - Crossville, TN - *BrCabYB 84; TV&RadDir 84*
WAEY - Princeton, WV - *BrCabYB 84; TV&RadDir 84*
WAEY-FM - Princeton, WV - *BrCabYB 84; TV&RadDir 84*
WAEZ-FM - Akron, OH - *BrCabYB 84; NatRadPubDir Summer 83, Spring 84; TV&RadDir 84*
WAFB-FM - Baton Rouge, LA - *BrCabYB 84; NatRadPubDir Summer 83, Spring 84; TV&RadDir 84*
WAFB-TV - Baton Rouge, LA - *BrCabYB 84; DirUSTelSta 83; TelAl 83, 84; Tel&CabFB 84S; TV&RadDir 84*
WAFC - Clewiston, FL - *BrCabYB 84*
WAFF - Huntsville, AL - *BrCabYB 84; DirUSTelSta 83; Tel&CabFB 84S*
WAFF-TV - Huntsville, AL - *TelAl 83, 84; TV&RadDir 84*
WAFG-FM - Ft. Lauderdale, FL - *BrCabYB 84; TV&RadDir 84*
WAFL-FM - Milford, DE - *BrCabYB 84; TV&RadDir 84*
WAFM-FM - Amory, MS - *BrCabYB 84; TV&RadDir 84*
WAFR - Durham, NC - *BrCabYB 84*
WAFT-FM - Valdosta, GA - *BrCabYB 84; TV&RadDir 84*
WAFX - Ft. Wayne, IN - *BrCabYB 84; NatRadPubDir Summer 83, Spring 84; TV&RadDir 84*
WAGA-TV - Atlanta, GA - *BrCabYB 84; DirUSTelSta 83; LitMarPl 83, 84; TelAl 83, 84; Tel&CabFB 84S; TV&RadDir 84*
WAGC - Centre, AL - *BrCabYB 84; TV&RadDir 84*
WAGE - Leesburg, VA - *BrCabYB 84; TV&RadDir 84*
Wage Rounds Data Bank [of University of Aberdeen] - Aberdeen, Scotland - *EISS 83*
Wageman Advertising, Muriel - Chicago, IL - *StaDirAdAg 2-84*
Wagenvoord Studio Inc., James [Aff. of Oak Alley Inc.] - New York, NY - *BoPubDir 4, 5*
Wages for Students - Branford, CT - *BoPubDir 4, 5*
WAGF - Dothan, AL - *TV&RadDir 84*
WAGG - Birmingham, AL - *BrCabYB 84; NatRadPubDir Summer 83, Spring 84*
WAGI-FM - Gaffney, SC - *BrCabYB 84; TV&RadDir 84*
WAGL - Lancaster, SC - *BrCabYB 84; TV&RadDir 84*

WAGM-TV - Presque Isle, ME - *BrCabYB 84; DirUSTelSta 83; TelAl 83, 84; Tel&CabFB 84S; TV&RadDir 84*
WAGN - Menominee, MI - *BrCabYB 84; TV&RadDir 84*
Wagner & Baroody Inc. - Washington, DC - *DirPRFirms 83; StaDirAdAg 2-84*
Wagner Corp. - Simsbury, CT - *StaDirAdAg 2-84*
Wagner International/American Audio Visual Inc. - New York, NY - *MagIndMarPl 82-83*
Wagner International Photos Inc. - New York, NY - *Ed&PubIntYB 82*
Wagner Photoprint Co. Inc. - New York, NY - *LitMarPl 83*
Wagner Post & Advertiser - Wagner, SD - *BaconPubCkNews 84*
Wagner Production Inc., Alan - New York, NY - *AvMarPl 83*
WAGO - Oshkosh, WI - *TV&RadDir 84*
Wagon & Star - Inglewood, CA - *BoPubDir 4, 5*
Wagon Wheel Records - Georgetown, SC - *BillIntBG 83-84*
Wagoner Newspapers Inc. - Wagoner, OK - *BaconPubCkNews 84*
Wagoner Record-Democrat [of Wagoner Newspapers Inc.] - Wagoner, OK - *Ed&PubIntYB 82; NewsDir 84*
Wagoner Record Democrat - *See* Wagoner Newspapers Inc.
Wagoner Tribune [of Wagoner Newspapers Inc.] - Wagoner, OK - *Ed&PubIntYB 82; NewsDir 84*
Wagoner Tribune - *See* Wagoner Newspapers Inc.
WAGQ-FM - Athens, GA - *BrCabYB 84; NatRadPubDir Summer 83, Spring 84; TV&RadDir 84*
WAGR - Lumberton, NC - *BrCabYB 84; TV&RadDir 84*
WAGS - Bishopville, SC - *BrCabYB 84; TV&RadDir 84*
WAGT - Augusta, GA - *TV&RadDir 84*
WAGT-TV - Augusta, GA - *BrCabYB 84; DirUSTelSta 83; TelAl 84; Tel&CabFB 84S*
WAGY - Forest City, NC - *BrCabYB 84; TV&RadDir 84*
WAHC-FM - Appleton/Oshkosh, WI - *NatRadPubDir Summer 83, Spring 84 p.267*
WAHC-FM - Neenah, WI - *TV&RadDir 84*
WAHC-FM - Oshkosh, WI - *BrCabYB 84*
Wahkiakum County Eagle - Cathlamet, WA - *AyerDirPub 83; Ed&PubIntYB 82*
Wahl Agency Ltd., Austin - Chicago, IL - *LitMarPl 83, 84*
Wahlstrom & Co. Inc. [Subs. of Foote, Cone & Belding Communications Inc.] - Stamford, CT - *StaDirAdAg 2-84*
Wahoo Newspaper - Wahoo, NE - *AyerDirPub 83; BaconPubCkNews 84; Ed&PubIntYB 82; NewsDir 84*
Wahpeton-Breckenridge Daily News [of Tri-State Daily News Inc.] - Wahpeton, ND - *NewsDir 84*
Wahpeton Daily News - Wahpeton, ND - *BaconPubCkNews 84*
WAHR-FM - Huntsville, AL - *BrCabYB 84; NatRadPubDir Summer 83, Spring 84; TV&RadDir 84*
Wahr Publishing Co., George - Ann Arbor, MI - *BoPubDir 4, 5*
WAHS-FM - Auburn Heights, MI - *BrCabYB 84*
WAHS-FM - Pontiac, MI - *TV&RadDir 84*
WAHT - Annville-Cleona, PA - *BrCabYB 84*
WAHT - Lebanon, PA - *TV&RadDir 84*
WAIA-FM - Miami, FL - *BrCabYB 84; NatRadPubDir Summer 83, Spring 84; TV&RadDir 84*
Waianae Sun Times - Kaneohe, HI - *AyerDirPub 83*
WAIC-FM - Springfield, MA - *BrCabYB 84; NatRadPubDir Summer 83, Spring 84; TV&RadDir 84*
WAID-FM - Clarksdale, MS - *BrCabYB 84; TV&RadDir 84*
WAIF-FM - Cincinnati, OH - *BrCabYB 84; TV&RadDir 84*
WAIK - Galesburg, IL - *BrCabYB 84; NatRadPubDir Summer 83, Spring 84; TV&RadDir 84*
Waikel, Richard C. - Ft. Wayne, IN - *MicrocomSwDir 1*
Waikiki Beach Press [of Scripps League Newspapers Inc.] - Honolulu, HI - *NewsDir 84*
WAIL-FM - New Orleans, LA - *NatRadPubDir Spring 84*
WAIL-FM - Slidell, LA - *BrCabYB 84*
Wailuku Maui News - Wailuku, HI - *BaconPubCkNews 84*
WAIM - Anderson, SC - *BrCabYB 84; TV&RadDir 84*
WAIM-FM - Anderson, SC - *BrCabYB 84; TV&RadDir 84*
WAIM-TV - Anderson, SC - *LitMarPl 83; TelAl 83, 84; TV&RadDir 84*
WAIN - Columbia, KY - *BrCabYB 84; TV&RadDir 84*
WAIN-FM - Columbia, KY - *BrCabYB 84; TV&RadDir 84*
Waipahu Sun News - Kaneohe, HI - *AyerDirPub 83*
Waipahu Sun Press - Waipahu, HI - *Ed&PubIntYB 82*
WAIQ - Montgomery, AL - *BrCabYB 84; Tel&CabFB 84S*
WAIR - Winston-Salem, NC - *BrCabYB 84; NatRadPubDir Summer 83, Spring 84; TV&RadDir 84*
WAIT - Chicago, IL - *BrCabYB 84; NatRadPubDir Summer 83, Spring 84; TV&RadDir 84*
WAIT Index to Newspapers [of Western Australian Institute of Technology] - Bentley, Australia - *DirOnDB Spring 84; EISS 5-84 Sup*
Waite Photographer & Publisher Co. Ltd., Donald E. - Maple Ridge, BC, Canada - *BoPubDir 4, 5*
Waite Press Ltd., Benjamin & Martha - Chicago, IL - *BoPubDir 4, 5*
Waits: Books - Valparaiso, IN - *BoPubDir 4, 5*
Waitsburg TV Cable System - Starbuck, WA - *BrCabYB 84*
Waitsburg TV Cable System - Waitsburg, WA - *BrCabYB 84; Tel&CabFB 84C*
Waitsburg TV Cable System - Washtucna, WA - *Tel&CabFB 84C*
Waitsburg Walla Walla County Times - Waitsburg, WA - *BaconPubCkNews 84*
Waitsfield Cable Co. [of Waitsfield-Fayston Telephone Co.] - Waitsfield, VT - *Tel&CabFB 84C*
Waitsfield-Fayston Telephone Co. - Waitsfield, VT - *TelDir&BG 83-84*
Waitsfield Valley Reporter - Waitsfield, VT - *BaconPubCkNews 84*
WAIV-FM - Jacksonville, FL - *BrCabYB 84; NatRadPubDir Summer 83, Spring 84; TV&RadDir 84*
WAJC-FM - Indianapolis, IN - *BrCabYB 84; NatRadPubDir Summer 83, Spring 84; TV&RadDir 84*
WAJE - Ebensburg, PA - *BrCabYB 84; TV&RadDir 84*
WAJF - Decatur, AL - *BrCabYB 84; TV&RadDir 84*
WAJK-FM - La Salle, IL - *BrCabYB 84; TV&RadDir 84*
WAJL - Orlando, FL - *TV&RadDir 84*
WAJL - Winter Park, FL - *BrCabYB 84*
WAJN - Ashland City, TN - *BrCabYB 84*
WAJO - Marion, AL - *BrCabYB 84*
WAJP-FM - Joliet, IL - *BrCabYB 84; TV&RadDir 84*
WAJR - Morgantown, WV - *BrCabYB 84; NatRadPubDir Summer 83, Spring 84; TV&RadDir 84*
WAJX-FM - Titusville, FL - *BrCabYB 84; TV&RadDir 84*
WAJY-FM - New Orleans, LA - *BrCabYB 84; NatRadPubDir Spring 84; TV&RadDir 84*
Wakarusa Tribune - Wakarusa, IN - *BaconPubCkNews 84; Ed&PubIntYB 82*
Wakaw Recorder, The - Wakaw, SK, Canada - *Ed&PubIntYB 82*
WAKE - Valparaiso, IN - *BrCabYB 84; TV&RadDir 84*
Wake Brook House - Ft. Lauderdale, FL - *LitMarPl 83, 84*
Wake Forest University Press - Winston-Salem, NC - *BoPubDir 4, 5; LitMarPl 84*
Wake Forest Wake Weekly - Wake Forest, NC - *BaconPubCkNews 84; NewsDir 84*
Wake, H. S. - San Diego, CA - *BoPubDir 4, 5*
Wake Newslitter, A - Colchester, England - *LitMag&SmPr 83-84*
Wake Newslitter Press, A - Colchester, England - *LitMag&SmPr 83-84*
Wake Weekly - Wake Forest, NC - *AyerDirPub 83*
Wake Weekly, The - North Wake, NC - *Ed&PubIntYB 82*
Wakeeney Cable TV Co. [of KAYS Inc.] - Wakeeney, KS - *BrCabYB 84; Tel&CabFB 84C*
Wakeeney Western Kansas World - Wakeeney, KS - *BaconPubCkNews 84*
Wakefield Item - Wakefield, MA - *BaconPubCkNews 84; NewsDir 84*
Wakefield Narragansett Times - *See* Wilson Publishing Co.
Wakefield News - Wakefield, MI - *BaconPubCkNews 84; Ed&PubIntYB 82*
Wakefield Republican - Wakefield, NE - *BaconPubCkNews 84*
Wakefield Sussex-Surry Dispatch - Wakefield, VA - *BaconPubCkNews 84*
Wakeford & Associates, Kent - Los Angeles, CA - *Tel&CabFB 84C*
WAKG-FM - Danville, VA - *BrCabYB 84; TV&RadDir 84*
WAKH - McComb, MS - *BrCabYB 84*
WAKI - McMinnville, TN - *BrCabYB 84; TV&RadDir 84*
Wakita Herald - Wakita, OK - *BaconPubCkNews 84; Ed&PubIntYB 82*
WAKK - McComb, MS - *BrCabYB 84; TV&RadDir 84*
WAKM - Franklin, TN - *BrCabYB 84*
WAKN - Aiken, SC - *BrCabYB 84; TV&RadDir 84*

WAKO - Lawrenceville, IL - *BrCabYB 84; TV&RadDir 84*
WAKO-FM - Lawrenceville, IL - *BrCabYB 84; TV&RadDir 84*
Wakonda Times - Wakonda, SD - *Ed&PubIntYB 82*
WAKQ-FM - Russellville, KY - *BrCabYB 84; TV&RadDir 84*
WAKR - Akron, OH - *BrCabYB 84; NatRadPubDir Summer 83, Spring 84; TV&RadDir 84*
WAKR-TV - Akron, OH - *BrCabYB 84; DirUSTelSta 83; LitMarPl 83, 84; TelAl 83, 84; Tel&CabFB 84S; TV&RadDir 84*
WAKS - Fuquay Varina, NC - *BrCabYB 84; TV&RadDir 84*
WAKS-FM - Fuquay Varina, NC - *BrCabYB 84; TV&RadDir 84*
Wakulla News - Crawfordville, FL - *AyerDirPub 83; NewsDir 84*
Wakulla News, The - Wakulla County, FL - *Ed&PubIntYB 82*
WAKW-FM - Cincinnati, OH - *BrCabYB 84; NatRadPubDir Summer 83, Spring 84; TV&RadDir 84*
WAKX-FM - Duluth, MN - *BrCabYB 84; NatRadPubDir Summer 83, Spring 84; TV&RadDir 84*
WAKY - Louisville, KY - *BrCabYB 84; NatRadPubDir Summer 83, Spring 84; TV&RadDir 84*
WALA-TV - Mobile, AL - *BrCabYB 84; DirUSTelSta 83; TelAl 83, 84; Tel&CabFB 84S; TV&RadDir 84*
WALB-TV - Albany, GA - *BrCabYB 84; DirUSTelSta 83; TelAl 83, 84; Tel&CabFB 84S; TV&RadDir 84*
Walch, J. Weston - Portland, ME - *LitMarPl 83, 84; MicrocomMPl 84; WritMar 84*
Walck & Rikhoff - Silver Spring, MD - *LitMarPl 84*
Walck & Rikhoff - Ithaca, NY - *LitMarPl 83*
WALCO Inc. - Bruce, MS - *BrCabYB 84; Tel&CabFB 84C*
Walco Promotions Inc. - Palm Springs, CA - *StaDirAdAg 2-84*
WALD - Walterboro, SC - *BrCabYB 84; TV&RadDir 84*
WALD-FM - Walterboro, SC - *BrCabYB 84; TV&RadDir 84*
Waldbillig & Besteman - Madison, WI - *AdAge 3-28-84; StaDirAdAg 2-84*
Waldeck Publications - Pismo Beach, CA - *BoPubDir 4 Sup, 5*
Walden Cable TV - Walden, CO - *BrCabYB 84; Tel&CabFB 84C*
Walden Citizen Herald [of Ulster Offset Inc.] - Walden, NY - *NewsDir 84*
Walden Music Inc. - *See* Cotillion Music Inc.
Walden Public Relations Ltd. - Vancouver, BC, Canada - *DirPRFirms 83*
Walden Video Corp. - Gardiner, NY - *BrCabYB 84*
Walden Video Corp. [of Cablevision Industries Inc.] - Walden, NY - *BrCabYB 84; Tel&CabFB 84C*
Walden's Paper Report - Oradell, NJ - *BaconPubCkMag 84*
Waldman & Wroobel - Encino, CA - *StaDirAdAg 2-84*
Waldman/George Associates Ltd. - New York, NY - *StaDirAdAg 2-84*
Waldon Press Inc. - New York, NY - *LitMarPl 83, 84*
Waldorf Maryland Independent - Waldorf, MD - *BaconPubCkNews 84; NewsDir 84*
Waldron Enterprises - Haddonfield, NJ - *BoPubDir 4, 5*
Waldron News - Waldron, AR - *BaconPubCkNews 84; Ed&PubIntYB 82*
Waldron Telephone Co. - Waldron, MI - *TelDir&BG 83-84*
Waldron TV Cable Co. - Waldron, AR - *BrCabYB 84; Tel&CabFB 84C*
Waldrop Publications - Mt. Baldy, CA - *BoPubDir 4, 5*
WALE - Fall River, MA - *BrCabYB 84; NatRadPubDir Summer 83, Spring 84; TV&RadDir 84*
Wales & Co., Michael C. - South Bend, IN - *LitMarPl 83, 84; MagIndMarPl 82-83*
WALF-FM - Alfred, NY - *BrCabYB 84; NatRadPubDir Summer 83, Spring 84; TV&RadDir 84*
WALG - Albany, GA - *BrCabYB 84; NatRadPubDir Summer 83, Spring 84; TV&RadDir 84*
Walhalla Cable TV - Walhalla, ND - *BrCabYB 84; Tel&CabFB 84C*
Walhalla Keowee Courier - Walhalla, SC - *BaconPubCkNews 84*
Walhalla Mountaineer - Walhalla, ND - *Ed&PubIntYB 82*
WALI - Cumberland, MD - *BrCabYB 84; NatRadPubDir Spring 84; TV&RadDir 84*
WALJ-FM - Buffalo, NY - *NatRadPubDir Summer 83*
WALK - Patchogue, NY - *BrCabYB 84; TV&RadDir 84*
WALK - Suffolk County, Long Island, NY - *NatRadPubDir Summer 83 p.177, Spring 84 p.175*
WALK-FM - Patchogue, NY - *BrCabYB 84; TV&RadDir 84*
WALK-FM - Suffolk County, Long Island, NY - *NatRadPubDir Summer 83 p.177, Spring 84 p.175*
Walker & Associates Inc. - Memphis, TN - *DirPRFirms 83; StaDirAdAg 2-84*
Walker & Associates Inc., Bill - Nashville, TN - *StaDirAdAg 2-84*
Walker & Associates Inc., Steve - Ft. Lauderdale, FL - *StaDirAdAg 2-84*
Walker & Co. [Div. of Walker Publishing Co. Inc.] - New York, NY - *ArtMar 84; LitMarPl 83, 84; WritMar 84*
Walker Communications Inc. - Richardson, TX - *StaDirAdAg 2-84*
Walker Co., Frank R. - Chicago, IL - *BoPubDir 4, 5*
Walker County Cable Inc. [of TeleScripps Cable Co.] - Lafayette, GA - *BrCabYB 84; Tel&CabFB 84C*
Walker County Messenger - Lafayette, GA - *AyerDirPub 83; Ed&PubIntYB 82*
Walker County Telephone Co. - Lafayette, GA - *TelDir&BG 83-84*
Walker Educational Book Corp. [Subs. of Walker & Co.] - New York, NY - *LitMarPl 83*
Walker Interactive Products - San Francisco, CA - *ADAPSOMemDir 83-84*
Walker, Ken - Pocatello, ID - *Tel&CabFB 84C p.1711*
Walker Media & Management Inc. - Arlington, VA - *CabTVFinDB 83*
Walker Pilot-Independent - Walker, MN - *BaconPubCkNews 84*
Walker Press - Wolfe Island, ON, Canada - *BoPubDir 4, 5*
Walker Prismatic Engraving - New York, NY - *LitMarPl 83, 84*
Walker Research - Indianapolis, IN - *AdAge 5-17-84 p.32; IntDirMarRes 83; Tel&CabFB 84C*
Walker Systems Inc. - Duluth, MN - *AvMarPl 83*
Walker/Westside Advance - Jenison, MI - *AyerDirPub 83*
Walker-Westside Advance - Walker, MI - *Ed&PubIntYB 82*
Walker's Estimating & Construction Journal - Chicago, IL - *BaconPubCkMag 84*
Walker's Manual Inc. - Garden Grove, CA - *BoPubDir 5*
Walker's Manual Inc. - Long Beach, CA - *BoPubDir 4*
Walkerton Independent News - Walkerton, IN - *BaconPubCkNews 84*
Walking Horse Report - Shelbyville, TN - *BaconPubCkMag 84*
Walking News Inc. - New York, NY - *BoPubDir 5*
Walking Tours of San Juan [of Caribbean World Communications Inc.] - Santurce, PR - *WritMar 84*
WALL - Middletown, NY - *BrCabYB 84; NatRadPubDir Summer 83, Spring 84; TV&RadDir 84*
Wall & Associates Inc., Robert - Lawrenceville, GA - *Tel&CabFB 84C p.1711*
Wall & Sons, R. J. - Mahwah, NJ - *TeleSy&SerDir 2-84*
Wall & Walker Newsletter, Horan - Sydney, Australia - *LitMag&SmPr 83-84*
Wall Lake Blade - Wall Lake, IA - *BaconPubCkNews 84; Ed&PubIntYB 82*
Wall Paper, The - New York, NY - *BaconPubCkMag 84*
Wall Pennington County Courant - Wall, SD - *BaconPubCkNews 84*
Wall Street Computer Review - New York, NY - *BaconPubCkMag 84*
Wall Street Graphics Inc. - New York, NY - *MicrocomMPl 84*
Wall Street Group Inc., The - New York, NY - *DirPRFirms 83*
Wall Street Journal - Palo Alto, CA - *Ed&PubIntYB 82*
Wall Street Journal - Chicago, IL - *Ed&PubIntYB 82*
Wall Street Journal [of Dow Jones & Co. Inc.] - New York, NY - *AyerDirPub 83; Ed&PubIntYB 82; LitMarPl 83, 84; NewsBur 6*
Wall Street Journal - Cleveland, OH - *NewsBur 6*
Wall Street Journal - Dallas, TX - *Ed&PubIntYB 82*
Wall Street Journal (Eastern Edition) - New York, NY - *BaconPubCkMag 84; NewsDir 84*
Wall Street Journal (Highlights Online) - Princeton, NJ - *DBBus 82; DirOnDB Spring 84*
Wall Street Journal (Midwest Edition) - Chicago, IL - *BaconPubCkMag 84; NewsDir 84*
Wall Street Journal (Midwest Edition) - Naperville, IL - *AyerDirPub 83*
Wall Street Journal (Pacific Coast Edition) - San Francisco, CA - *NewsDir 84*
Wall Street Journal (Southwest Edition) - Dallas, TX - *BaconPubCkMag 84; NewsDir 84*

Wall Street Journal (Western Edition) - Los Angeles, CA - *AyerDirPub 83*
Wall Street Journal (Western Edition) - San Francisco, CA - *BaconPubCkMag 84*
Wall Street Journal Business Report, The - Princeton, NJ - *BrCabYB 84*
Wall Street Journal Online [of Dow Jones News/Retrieval Service] - Princeton, NJ - *DataDirOnSer 84*
Wall Street Monitor [of NewsNet Inc.] - Port Washington, NY - *DirOnDB Spring 84*
Wall Street Monitor [of NewsNet Inc.] - Bryn Mawr, PA - *DataDirOnSer 84*
Wall Street Reports - New York, NY - *BaconPubCkMag 84*
Wall Street Software - Eugene, OR - *MicrocomMPl 83*
Wall Street Transcript - New York, NY - *BaconPubCkMag 84; MagDir 84; NewsDir 84*
Wall Street Transcript [of VU/Text Information Services] - Philadelphia, PA - *DataDirOnSer 84*
Wall Street Transcript Online Service - New York, NY - *DirOnDB Spring 84; EISS 7-83 Sup*
Wall $treet Week [of Dow Jones & Co. Inc.] - Princeton, NJ - *DBBus 82*
Wall $treet Week Online - Baltimore, MD - *DirOnDB Spring 84*
Wall $treet Week Online [of Dow Jones News/Retrieval Service] - Princeton, NJ - *DataDirOnSer 84*
Wall Street Wizard - Roslyn, NY - *DirOnDB Spring 84*
Walla Walla County Times - Waitsburg, WA - *Ed&PubIntYB 82*
Walla Walla Union-Bulletin - Walla Walla, WA - *BaconPubCkNews 84; Ed&PubIntYB 82; LitMarPl 83, 84*
Wallace Advertising Inc. - Dallas, TX - *StaDirAdAg 2-84*
Wallace & Associates Advertising Inc. - Phoenix, AZ - *StaDirAdAg 2-84*
Wallace & Associates Inc., Roy - Minneapolis, MN - *ArtMar 84; DirPRFirms 83*
Wallace & Sheil Agency Inc. [Aff. of Anthony Sheil Associates] - New York, NY - *LitMarPl 83, 84*
Wallace Communications Consultants - Tampa, FL - *TeleSy&SerDir 7-83*
Wallace Enterprise - Wallace, NC - *BaconPubCkNews 84; Ed&PubIntYB 82; NewsDir 84*
Wallace-Homestead Book Co. [Div. of Farm Progress Publications] - Des Moines, IA - *LitMarPl 83, 84; MagIndMarPl 82-83; WritMar 84*
Wallace Micro-Mart - Peoria, IL - *WhoWMicrocom 83*
Wallace Miner - Wallace, ID - *BaconPubCkNews 84; Ed&PubIntYB 82*
Wallace North Idaho Press - Wallace, ID - *NewsDir 84*
Wallace Pencil Co. [Subs. of The Joseph Dixon Crucible Co.] - St. Louis, MO - *AvMarPl 83*
Wallace Press [Div. of Wallace Computer Services Inc.] - Hillside, IL - *LitMarPl 83, 84*
Wallaceburg News - Wallaceburg, ON, Canada - *AyerDirPub 83*
Wallaceburg News/Weekender - Wallaceburg, ON, Canada - *Ed&PubIntYB 82*
Wallaces Farmer - Des Moines, IA - *BaconPubCkMag 84; MagDir 84; MagIndMarPl 82-83*
Wallach & Associates Inc. - Cleveland, OH - *AvMarPl 83*
Wallach Associates Inc. - New York, NY - *DirPRFirms 83*
Wallcoverings - Stamford, CT - *BaconPubCkMag 84; MagDir 84; WritMar 84*
Wallcoverings Letter, The - Stamford, CT - *BaconPubCkMag 84*
Wallcur Inc. - Seal Beach, CA - *BoPubDir 4 Sup, 5*
Waller County News-Citizen - Hempstead, TX - *AyerDirPub 83*
Wallhalla Mountaineer - Wallhalla, ND - *BaconPubCkNews 84*
Wallingford Cable TV - Wallingford, IA - *BrCabYB 84; Tel&CabFB 84C*
Wallingford/North Haven Post - Wallingford, CT - *BaconPubCkNews 84*
Wallingford Post - Wallingford, CT - *AyerDirPub 83; Ed&PubIntYB 82*
Wallingford Telephone Cooperative - Wallingford, IA - *TelDir&BG 83-84*
Wallington Leader - *See* Leader Newspapers Inc.
Wallins TV Cable Co. - Wallins Creek, KY - *BrCabYB 84*
Wallis News-Review - *See* New Ulm Enterprise Publishers
Wallkill Valley World - Wallkill, NY - *Ed&PubIntYB 82*
Wallowa County Chieftain - Enterprise, OR - *AyerDirPub 83; Ed&PubIntYB 82*
Walls & Ceilings - Sherman Oaks, CA - *BaconPubCkMag 84; WritMar 84*
Walls & Ceilings - Van Nuys, CA - *MagDir 84*
Walls Newspapers - *Ed&PubIntYB 82*
Wallwork & Associates, Les - Los Angeles, CA - *Tel&CabFB 84C*
Walnut Bureau - Walnut, IA - *BaconPubCkNews 84; Ed&PubIntYB 82*
Walnut Cove Stokes Record - *See* Pepper Publishing Co.
Walnut Creek Contra Costa Times [of Lesher Communications Inc.] - Walnut Creek, CA - *NewsDir 84*
Walnut Creek Kernel [of Oakland Neighborhood Journal] - Oakland, CA - *NewsDir 84*
Walnut Creek Rossmoor News - Walnut Creek, CA - *BaconPubCkNews 84*
Walnut Creek Walnut Kernel - Oakland, CA - *Ed&PubIntYB 82*
Walnut Grove Associates - Watkins Glen, NY - *LitMarPl 83; MagIndMarPl 82-83*
Walnut Grove Associates - Mossistown, PA - *LitMarPl 84*
Walnut Grove Cable TV - Walnut Grove, MN - *BrCabYB 84*
Walnut Grove Tribune - Walnut Grove, MN - *BaconPubCkNews 84; Ed&PubIntYB 82*
Walnut Hill Telephone Co. - Lewisville, AR - *TelDir&BG 83-84*
Walnut Kernel - Oakland, CA - *AyerDirPub 83*
Walnut Leader - Walnut, IL - *BaconPubCkNews 84; Ed&PubIntYB 82*
Walnut Press - Fountain Hills, AZ - *BoPubDir 4*
Walnut Press - Phoenix, AZ - *BoPubDir 5; LitMag&SmPr 83-84*
Walnut Ridge Times Dispatch - Walnut Ridge, AR - *BaconPubCkNews 84; NewsDir 84*
Walnut Telephone Co. - Walnut, IA - *TelDir&BG 83-84*
Walnut Valley Special Fund [of Jones Intercable Inc.] - Walnut, CA - *BrCabYB 84; Tel&CabFB 84C*
WALO - Humacao, PR - *BrCabYB 84*
Walonick Associates - Minneapolis, MN - *MicrocomMPl 83, 84; MicrocomSwDir 1*
WALP - Corinth, MS - *BrCabYB 84*
Walpole Cable Co. [of Livengood Cable Co.] - Acworth, NH - *Tel&CabFB 84C*
Walpole Cable Co. [of Livengood Cable Co.] - Walpole, NH - *Tel&CabFB 84C*
Walpole Times - Walpole, MA - *BaconPubCkNews 84; Ed&PubIntYB 82; NewsDir 84*
WALR-FM - Union City, TN - *BrCabYB 84; TV&RadDir 84*
Walrath Advertising, Howard - Phoenix, AZ - *StaDirAdAg 2-84*
Walrus Said - St. Louis, MO - *BoPubDir 4, 5*
Walsenburg Huerfano World - Walsenburg, CO - *BaconPubCkNews 84*
Walser Design AG, Ludwig - *See* Wirz Inc., Adolf
Walsh & Associates Inc., Richard M. - Scranton, PA - *ADAPSOMemDir 83-84; DataDirOnSer 84*
Walsh Associates Inc., John R. - New York, NY - *DirPRFirms 83*
Walsh County Press - Park River, ND - *AyerDirPub 83; Ed&PubIntYB 82*
Walsh, D. G. - Janesville, WI - *Tel&CabFB 84C p.1711*
Walsh Inc., John P. - Dayton, OH - *LitMarPl 84*
Walsh Inc., John P. - Milwaukee, WI - *LitMarPl 83*
Walsh Messenger Service - Garden City Park, NY - *MagIndMarPl 82-83*
Walsh Press, Patrick - Tempe, AZ - *LitMag&SmPr 83-84*
Walsh, Rinehart, Puccio Inc. - New York, NY - *StaDirAdAg 2-84*
Walson Cable TV Inc. [of Service Electric Cable TV] - Mt. Carmel, PA - *BrCabYB 84*
Walsonavich, Esther & Margaret - Danville, PA - *BrCabYB 84 p.D-310; Tel&CabFB 84C p.1711*
Walsworth Publishing Co. Inc. - Marceline, MO - *LitMarPl 83, 84*
WALT - Meridian, MS - *BrCabYB 84; TV&RadDir 84*
Walter MFW Communications, Mary F. - Doylestown, PA - *DirPRFirms 83*
Walter Papers, Jim [Subs. of Jim Walter Corp.] - Jacksonville, FL - *LitMarPl 83, 84*
Walter Pepers-Nackie, Jim - Milwaukee, WI - *MagIndMarPl 82-83*

Walterboro Press & Standard - Walterboro, SC - *BaconPubCkNews 84*
Walters - Berkeley, CA - *ArtMar 84*
Walters & Co. - La Jolla, CA - *AdAge 3-28-84; StaDirAdAg 2-84*
Walters Art Gallery - Baltimore, MD - *BoPubDir 4, 5*
Walters Cable TV - Walters, OK - *BrCabYB 84*
Walters Herald - Cotton County, OK - *Ed&PubIntYB 82*
Walters Herald - Walters, OK - *BaconPubCkNews 84*
Walters Photography, Tom - Charlotte, NC - *MagIndMarPl 82-83*
Walters, Richard F. - Davis, CA - *MicrocomSwDir 1*
Walthall & Associates Inc. - Staples, MN - *StaDirAdAg 2-84*
Waltham News-Tribune - Waltham, MA - *BaconPubCkNews 84; NewsDir 84*
Walther Advertising Inc., M. G. - Oak Brook, IL - *StaDirAdAg 2-84*
Walthill Citizen - Walthill, NE - *BaconPubCkNews 84*
Waltner Enterprises - Tustin, CA - *BillIntBG 83-84*
Walton Associates, Albie - Newton Highlands, MA - *LitMarPl 83, 84; MagIndMarPl 82-83*
Walton Associates, John - Omaha, NE - *DirPRFirms 83; StaDirAdAg 2-84*
Walton Cablevision Inc. - Loganville, GA - *BrCabYB 84*
Walton Cablevision Inc. [of Omni Cable TV Corp.] - Walton County, GA - *Tel&CabFB 84C*
Walton Reporter - Walton, NY - *BaconPubCkNews 84; Ed&PubIntYB 82*
Walton Stations, John - Pebble Beach, CA - *BrCabYB 84*
Walton Tribune - Monroe, GA - *AyerDirPub 83; Ed&PubIntYB 82*
Walton TV Cable Co. Inc. - Walton County, FL - *Tel&CabFB 84C*
Walt's TV Sales & Service [of Cablevision Industries Inc.] - Callicoon, NY - *BrCabYB 84*
Waltz Audio Visual - Canton, OH - *AvMarPl 83*
WALV - Cleveland, TN - *BrCabYB 84*
Walworth Times - Walworth, WI - *BaconPubCkNews 84*
WALX-FM - Selma, AL - *BrCabYB 84; TV&RadDir 84*
WALZ - Machias, ME - *BrCabYB 84; TV&RadDir 84*
Walz, Barbra - New York, NY - *MagIndMarPl 82-83*
Walz Inc., Carl [Subs. of Book Bindery] - St. Louis, MO - *LitMarPl 83, 84*
Walz, Lawrence R. - *See* National Cable Systems Inc.
WAMA - Clearwater, FL - *BrCabYB 84*
WAMB - Donelson, TN - *BrCabYB 84*
WAMB - Nashville, TN - *NatRadPubDir Summer 83, Spring 84; TV&RadDir 84*
WAMC-FM - Albany, NY - *BrCabYB 84*
WAMC-FM - Schenectady, NY - *TV&RadDir 84*
WAMD - Aberdeen, MD - *BrCabYB 84; TV&RadDir 84*
WAME - Charlotte, NC - *BrCabYB 84; NatRadPubDir Summer 83, Spring 84; TV&RadDir 84*
Wamego Community Antenna System Inc. - Wamego, KS - *BrCabYB 84; Tel&CabFB 84C*
Wamego Smoke-Signal - Wamego, KS - *AyerDirPub 83*
Wamego Smoke-Signal - *See* Montgomery Publications Inc.
Wamego Telephone Co. Inc. - Wamego, KS - *TelDir&BG 83-84*
Wamego Times - Wamego, KS - *BaconPubCkNews 84; Ed&PubIntYB 82*
WAMF-FM - Tallahassee, FL - *BrCabYB 84; TV&RadDir 84*
WAMG - Gallatin, TN - *BrCabYB 84; TV&RadDir 84*
WAMH-FM - Amherst, MA - *BrCabYB 84; TV&RadDir 84*
WAMH-FM - Medford, MA - *NatRadPubDir Summer 83 p.290, Spring 84 p.292*
WAMI - Opp, AL - *BrCabYB 84; TV&RadDir 84*
WAMI-FM - Opp, AL - *BrCabYB 84; TV&RadDir 84*
WAMJ - Mishawaka, IN - *TV&RadDir 84*
WAMJ - South Bend, IN - *BrCabYB 84*
WAMK - Brockton, MA - *BrCabYB 84; TV&RadDir 84*
WAML - Laurel, MS - *BrCabYB 84; TV&RadDir 84*
WAMM - Woodstock, VA - *BrCabYB 84*
WAMO - Pittsburgh, PA - *BrCabYB 84; NatRadPubDir Summer 83, Spring 84; TV&RadDir 84*
WAMO-FM - Pittsburgh, PA - *BrCabYB 84; NatRadPubDir Summer 83, Spring 84; TV&RadDir 84*
WAMP-FM - Toledo, OH - *BrCabYB 84; NatRadPubDir Summer 83, Spring 84; TV&RadDir 84*
Wampeter Press - Green Harbor, MA - *BoPubDir 4, 5; LitMag&SmPr 83-84*
Wampler, Joseph - Berkeley, CA - *BoPubDir 4, 5*
Wampum Saver & Independent Shopper [of White Mountain Publishing Co.] - Show Low, AZ - *NewsDir 84*
WAMQ - Loretto, PA - *BrCabYB 84; TV&RadDir 84*
WAMR - Venice, FL - *BrCabYB 84; TV&RadDir 84*
WAMR-FM - Venice, FL - *BrCabYB 84; TV&RadDir 84*
WAMS - Wilmington, DE - *BrCabYB 84; NatRadPubDir Summer 83, Spring 84; TV&RadDir 84*
WAMT - Titusville, FL - *BrCabYB 84; TV&RadDir 84*
WAMU-FM [of The American University] - Washington, DC - *BrCabYB 84; LitMarPl 83, 84; NatRadPubDir Summer 83, Spring 84; TV&RadDir 84*
WAMV - Amherst, VA - *BrCabYB 84*
WAMW - Washington, IN - *BrCabYB 84; TV&RadDir 84*
WAMX-FM - Ashland, KY - *BrCabYB 84; TV&RadDir 84*
WAMX-FM - Huntington, WV - *NatRadPubDir Summer 83, Spring 84*
WAMY - Amory, MS - *BrCabYB 84; TV&RadDir 84*
WAMZ-FM - Louisville, KY - *BrCabYB 84; NatRadPubDir Summer 83, Spring 84; TV&RadDir 84*
WANA - Anniston, AL - *BrCabYB 84; TV&RadDir 84*
Wanamingo Progress - Wanamingo, MN - *BaconPubCkNews 84; Ed&PubIntYB 82*
WANB - Waynesburg, PA - *BrCabYB 84; TV&RadDir 84*
WANB-FM - Waynesburg, PA - *BrCabYB 84; TV&RadDir 84*
WANC - Aberdeen, NC - *BrCabYB 84*
WAND [Subs. of Lin Broadcasting Co. Inc.] - Decatur, IL - *BrCabYB 84; TelAl 83, 84; Tel&CabFB 84S*
WAND - Springfield, IL - *DirUSTelSta 83*
WAND-TV - Decatur, IL - *TV&RadDir 84*
Wanderer Books [Div. of Simon & Schuster] - New York, NY - *LitMarPl 83, 84; WritMar 84*
Wanderer Press - St. Paul, MN - *BoPubDir 5*
Wandon Music Co. - New York, NY - *BillIntBG 83-84*
WANE-TV - Ft. Wayne, IN - *BrCabYB 84; DirUSTelSta 83; TelAl 83, 84; Tel&CabFB 84S; TV&RadDir 84*
Wang Electronic Publishing [Subs. of Wang Laboratories] - Tijeras, NM - *MicrocomMPl 84*
Wang Laboratories - Lowell, MA - *ADAPSOMemDir 83-84; DataDirSup 7-83; Datamation 6-83; DirInfWP 82; ElecNews 7-25-83; InfIndMarPl 83; Top100Al 83; WhoWMicrocom 83*
WANH-FM - Manchester, NH - *BrCabYB 84*
WANJ-FM - Wheeling, WV - *BrCabYB 84; NatRadPubDir Summer 83, Spring 84; TV&RadDir 84*
Wank, Williams & Neylan - Menlo Park, CA - *AdAge 3-28-84; ArtMar 84; StaDirAdAg 2-84*
WANL - Lineville, AL - *TV&RadDir 84*
WANM - Tallahassee, FL - *BrCabYB 84; NatRadPubDir Summer 83, Spring 84; TV&RadDir 84*
WANN - Annapolis, MD - *BrCabYB 84; TV&RadDir 84*
Wannemacher, Mike L. - Indianapolis, IN - *LitMarPl 83, 84; MagIndMarPl 82-83*
Wannemacher, Sandra M. - Indianapolis, IN - *LitMarPl 83, 84; MagIndMarPl 82-83*
WANO - Pineville, KY - *BrCabYB 84; TV&RadDir 84*
WANR - Wheeling, WV - *BrCabYB 84; NatRadPubDir Summer 83, Spring 84*
WANS - Anderson, SC - *BrCabYB 84; TV&RadDir 84*
WANS-FM - Anderson, SC - *BrCabYB 84; TV&RadDir 84*
WANT - Richmond, VA - *BrCabYB 84; NatRadPubDir Summer 83, Spring 84; TV&RadDir 84*
Want Publishing Co. - Washington, DC - *BoPubDir 4, 5*
Wantagh-Seaford Citizen - Wantagh, NY - *AyerDirPub 83; BaconPubCkNews 84; Ed&PubIntYB 82; NewsDir 84*
Wantagh-Seaford Pennysaver - Levittown, NY - *AyerDirPub 83*
Wantahala Cablevision - Robbinsville, NC - *BrCabYB 84*
WANV - Waynesboro, VA - *BrCabYB 84; TV&RadDir 84*
WANX-TV - Atlanta, GA - *BrCabYB 84; DirUSTelSta 83; TelAl 83, 84; Tel&CabFB 84S; TV&RadDir 84*
WANY - Albany, KY - *BrCabYB 84; TV&RadDir 84*
WANY-FM - Albany, KY - *BrCabYB 84; TV&RadDir 84*
WAOA - Opelika, AL - *BrCabYB 84; TV&RadDir 84*
WAOB - Winamac, IN - *BrCabYB 84*
WAOC - St. Augustine, FL - *BrCabYB 84; TV&RadDir 84*

WAOK - Atlanta, GA - *BrCabYB 84; NatRadPubDir Summer 83, Spring 84; TV&RadDir 84*
WAOP - Otsego, MI - *BrCabYB 84*
WAOR-FM - Niles, MI - *BrCabYB 84; TV&RadDir 84*
WAOV - Vincennes, IN - *BrCabYB 84; TV&RadDir 84*
WAOW-TV - Wausau, WI - *BrCabYB 84; DirUSTelSta 83; TelAl 83, 84; Tel&CabFB 84S; TV&RadDir 84*
WAPA - San Juan, PR - *BrCabYB 84*
WAPA-TV - San Juan, PR - *BrCabYB 84; Tel&CabFB 84S*
Wapakoneta Daily News - Wapakoneta, OH - *BaconPubCkNews 84; Ed&PubIntYB 82; NewsDir 84*
Wapato Independent - Wapato, WA - *BaconPubCkNews 84; Ed&PubIntYB 82*
WAPB-TV - Annapolis, MD - *BrCabYB 84; Tel&CabFB 84S*
WAPB-TV - Owings Mills, MD - *TV&RadDir 84*
WAPE - Jacksonville, FL - *BrCabYB 84; NatRadPubDir Summer 83 p.59, Spring 84 p.58*
WAPE - Orange Park, FL - *TV&RadDir 84*
Wapello Republican - Wapello, IA - *BaconPubCkNews 84; Ed&PubIntYB 82*
WAPF - McComb, MS - *BrCabYB 84; TV&RadDir 84*
WAPG - Arcadia, FL - *BrCabYB 84; TV&RadDir 84*
WAPI - Birmingham, AL - *BrCabYB 84; NatRadPubDir Summer 83, Spring 84; TV&RadDir 84*
WAPI-FM - Birmingham, AL - *BrCabYB 84; NatRadPubDir Summer 83, Spring 84; TV&RadDir 84*
WAPL-FM - Appleton, WI - *BrCabYB 84; NatRadPubDir Summer 83, Spring 84; TV&RadDir 84*
WAPP-FM - Fresh Meadows, NY - *TV&RadDir 84*
WAPP-FM - New York, NY - *BrCabYB 84; NatRadPubDir Summer 83 p.172, Spring 84 p.170*
WAPR - Avon Park, FL - *BrCabYB 84; TV&RadDir 84*
WAPS-FM - Akron, OH - *BrCabYB 84; NatRadPubDir Summer 83, Spring 84; TV&RadDir 84*
WAPT-TV - Jackson, MI - *BrCabYB 84*
WAPT-TV - Jackson, MN - *DirUSTelSta 83*
WAPT-TV - Jackson, MS - *TelAl 83, 84; Tel&CabFB 84S; TV&RadDir 84*
WAQE - Rice Lake, WI - *BrCabYB 84; TV&RadDir 84*
WAQE-FM - Rice Lake, WI - *BrCabYB 84; TV&RadDir 84*
WAQI - Ashtabula, OH - *BrCabYB 84; TV&RadDir 84*
WAQP - Saginaw, MI - *BrCabYB 84; Tel&CabFB 84S*
WAQT-FM - Carrollton, AL - *BrCabYB 84; TV&RadDir 84*
WAQX-FM - Manlius, NY - *BrCabYB 84*
WAQX-FM - Syracuse, NY - *TV&RadDir 84*
WAQY-FM - East Longmeadow, MA - *TV&RadDir 84*
WAQY-FM - Springfield, MA - *BrCabYB 84*
War Cry [of The Salvation Army] - Verona, NJ - *WritMar 84*
War Cycles Institute - Kalispell, MT - *BoPubDir 4, 5*
War Resisters League - New York, NY - *BoPubDir 4, 5*
War Telephone Co. - War, WV - *TelDir&BG 83-84*
WARA - Attleboro, MA - *BrCabYB 84; TV&RadDir 84*
WARB - Covington, LA - *BrCabYB 84; TV&RadDir 84*
WARC-FM - Meadville, PA - *BrCabYB 84; NatRadPubDir Summer 83, Spring 84; TV&RadDir 84*
WARD - Pittston, PA - *BrCabYB 84; TV&RadDir 84*
Ward & Associates, Joseph B. - Seattle, WA - *Tel&CabFB 84C*
Ward & Sons Inc. - Spartanburg, SC - *Ed&PubIntYB 82*
Ward Communications - Pine Township, PA - *Tel&CabFB 84C*
Ward, Granberry H. III - Meridian, MS - *Tel&CabFB 84C p.1711*
Ward, H. C. - Deland, FL - *MicrocomSwDir 1*
Ward Inc., J. A. - Princeton, NJ - *IntDirMarRes 83*
Ward Institute, Lee - Piggott, AR - *BoPubDir 4, 5*
Ward Productions Inc. - Hollywood, CA - *Tel&CabFB 84C*
Ward Publications, Baldwin H. - Petaluma, CA - *BoPubDir 4, 5*
Warden Register - Warden, WA - *BaconPubCkNews 84; Ed&PubIntYB 82*
Wardley, Reginald R. - Ridgewood, NJ - *MagIndMarPl 82-83*
Wardrop, Murtaugh, Temple & Frank - Chicago, IL - *AdAge 3-28-84; StaDirAdAg 2-84*
Ward's Auto World [of International Thomson Business Press Inc.] - Detroit, MI - *BaconPubCkMag 84; MagDir 84; MagIndMarPl 82-83; WritMar 84*
Wards Autoinfobank [of Chase Econometrics/Interactive Data Corp.] - Waltham, MA - *DataDirOnSer 84*
Ward's Autoinfobank [of Ward's Communications Inc.] - Detroit, MI - *DirOnDB Spring 84; EISS 83*
Ward's Communications Inc. [Aff. of International Thomson Business Press] - Detroit, MI - *BoPubDir 4, 5*
Ward's Natural Science Establishment Inc. - Rochester, NY - *AvMarPl 83*
WARE - Ware, MA - *BrCabYB 84; TV&RadDir 84*
Ware & Associates, Peggy - Cos Cob, CT - *DirPRFirms 83*
Ware, Fletcher & Freidenrich - Palo Alto, CA - *ADAPSOMemDir 83-84*
Ware Literary Agency, John A. - New York, NY - *LitMarPl 83, 84*
Ware River News - Ware, MA - *AyerDirPub 83; BaconPubCkNews 84; Ed&PubIntYB 82; NewsDir 84*
Ware Shoals Cablevision [of Fender & Latham Inc.] - Ware Shoals, SC - *Tel&CabFB 84C*
Wareham Courier - Wareham, MA - *Ed&PubIntYB 82*
Wareham Courier - *See* MPG Communications
Warehouse Distribution - Chicago, IL - *MagDir 84*
Warehouse Distributor News [of Babcox Automotive Publications] - Akron, OH - *BaconPubCkMag 84; MagDir 84; WritMar 84*
Warehouse Recording Studio, The - New York, NY - *Tel&CabFB 84C*
Warehousing Supervisor's Bulletin - Waterford, CT - *ArtMar 84; WritMar 84*
WARF-FM - Jasper, AL - *BrCabYB 84; TV&RadDir 84*
WARG-FM - Argo, IL - *TV&RadDir 84*
WARG-FM - Summit, IL - *BrCabYB 84*
WARI - Abbeville, AL - *BrCabYB 84; TV&RadDir 84*
Waring & LaRosa - New York, NY - *AdAge 3-28-84; Br 1-23-84; BrCabYB 84; StaDirAdAg 2-84*
WARK - Hagerstown, MD - *BrCabYB 84; NatRadPubDir Summer 83, Spring 84*
Warkworth Journal - Warkworth, ON, Canada - *Ed&PubIntYB 82*
Warlick & Associates Inc. - Houston, TX - *IntDirMarRes 83*
Warlock Software [Div. of Tylos Inc.] - Atlanta, GA - *MicrocomMPl 84*
Warlock Warehouse - Pontiac, MI - *MicrocomMPl 83*
WARM - Pittston, PA - *TV&RadDir 84*
WARM - Scranton, PA - *BrCabYB 84; NatRadPubDir Summer 83, Spring 84 p.216*
Warm Fuzzy Newsletter [of Jalmar Press] - Rolling Hills Estates, CA - *LitMag&SmPr 83-84*
Warm Springs Cable System - Warm Springs, OR - *BrCabYB 84; Tel&CabFB 84C*
Warman Publishing Co. Inc. - Elkins Park, PA - *BoPubDir 4 Sup, 5; LitMag&SmPr 83-84*
Warmath Communications Inc. - Humboldt, TN - *BrCabYB 84; Tel&CabFB 84C*
Warmflash & Associates Inc., Herbert S. - East Orange, NJ - *StaDirAdAg 2-84*
Warminster Spirit [of Montgomery Publishing Co.] - Hatboro, PA - *NewsDir 84*
Warminster Spirit - Warminster, PA - *AyerDirPub 83; Ed&PubIntYB 82*
Warminster Spirit - *See* Montgomery Publishing Co.
Warn Electronics Ltd. - Knightdale, NC - *MicrocomMPl 83, 84*
Warne & Associates Inc., Keith K. - Toronto, ON, Canada - *ArtMar 84; StaDirAdAg 2-84*
Warne & Co. Inc., Frederick [Subs. of Frederick Warne Publishers Ltd.] - New York, NY - *LitMarPl 83, 84; WritMar 84*
Warne/McKenna Advertising [Div. of Robert Warne Advertising Inc.] - Syracuse, NY - *StaDirAdAg 2-84*
Warner Advertising Inc., Harold - Buffalo, NY - *StaDirAdAg 2-84*
Warner Amex Cable Communications - New York, NY - *BrCabYB 84 p.D-310; CabTVFinDB 83; HomeVid&CabYB 82-83; LitMarPl 84; TelAl 83, 84; VideoDir 82-83*
Warner Amex Cable Communications [Aff. of Warner Amex Cable Communications Inc.] - Cincinnati, OH - *HomeVid&CabYB 82-83; InterCabHB 3*
Warner Amex Cable Communications Co. - Kingman, AZ - *BrCabYB 84; Tel&CabFB 84C*
Warner Amex Cable Communications Inc. - Flagstaff, AZ - *BrCabYB 84; Tel&CabFB 84C*

Warner Amex Cable Communications Inc. - Russellville, AR - *Tel&CabFB 84C*
Warner Amex Cable Communications Inc. - Taft, CA - *Tel&CabFB 84C*
Warner Amex Cable Communications Inc. - Wrightwood, CA - *BrCabYB 84*
Warner Amex Cable Communications Inc. - Crestview, FL - *BrCabYB 84*
Warner Amex Cable Communications Inc. - Ft. Walton Beach, FL - *BrCabYB 84*
Warner Amex Cable Communications Inc. - Immokalee, FL - *BrCabYB 84*
Warner Amex Cable Communications Inc. - La Belle, FL - *Tel&CabFB 84C*
Warner Amex Cable Communications Inc. - Labelle, FL - *BrCabYB 84*
Warner Amex Cable Communications Inc. - Lake City, FL - *BrCabYB 84*
Warner Amex Cable Communications Inc. - Niceville, FL - *BrCabYB 84*
Warner Amex Cable Communications Inc. - Winter Haven, FL - *BrCabYB 84*
Warner Amex Cable Communications Inc. - Cedartown, GA - *BrCabYB 84; Tel&CabFB 84C*
Warner Amex Cable Communications Inc. - Altamont, IL - *BrCabYB 84*
Warner Amex Cable Communications Inc. - Danville, IL - *BrCabYB 84*
Warner Amex Cable Communications Inc. - De Kalb, IL - *BrCabYB 84*
Warner Amex Cable Communications Inc. - Rochelle, IL - *BrCabYB 84*
Warner Amex Cable Communications Inc. - Rolling Meadows, IL - *Tel&CabFB 84C*
Warner Amex Cable Communications Inc. - Hiawatha, KS - *BrCabYB 84*
Warner Amex Cable Communications Inc. - Island Falls, ME - *BrCabYB 84*
Warner Amex Cable Communications Inc. - Athol, MA - *BrCabYB 84*
Warner Amex Cable Communications Inc. - Lynn, MA - *BrCabYB 84*
Warner Amex Cable Communications Inc. - Medford, MA - *BrCabYB 84*
Warner Amex Cable Communications Inc. - Pittsfield, MA - *BrCabYB 84*
Warner Amex Cable Communications Inc. - Wakefield, MA - *Tel&CabFB 84C*
Warner Amex Cable Communications Inc. - Batesville, MS - *BrCabYB 84; Tel&CabFB 84C*
Warner Amex Cable Communications Inc. - Cleveland, MS - *BrCabYB 84; Tel&CabFB 84C*
Warner Amex Cable Communications Inc. - Lambert/Marks, MS - *BrCabYB 84*
Warner Amex Cable Communications Inc. - Yazoo City, MS - *BrCabYB 84; Tel&CabFB 84C*
Warner Amex Cable Communications Inc. - El Dorado Springs, MO - *BrCabYB 84*
Warner Amex Cable Communications Inc. - St. Louis County, MO - *BrCabYB 84*
Warner Amex Cable Communications Inc. - Warsaw, MO - *BrCabYB 84*
Warner Amex Cable Communications Inc. - Waynesville, MO - *BrCabYB 84*
Warner Amex Cable Communications Inc. - Olean, NY - *BrCabYB 84*
Warner Amex Cable Communications Inc. - Akron, OH - *BrCabYB 84; Tel&CabFB 84C*
Warner Amex Cable Communications Inc. - Canton, OH - *BrCabYB 84*
Warner Amex Cable Communications Inc. - Columbus, OH - *BrCabYB 84; HomeVid&CabYB 82-83*
Warner Amex Cable Communications Inc. - Delphos, OH - *BrCabYB 84*
Warner Amex Cable Communications Inc. - Ft. Shawnee, OH - *BrCabYB 84*
Warner Amex Cable Communications Inc. - Kenton, OH - *BrCabYB 84*
Warner Amex Cable Communications Inc. - Meyers Lake, OH - *BrCabYB 84*
Warner Amex Cable Communications Inc. - Norwood, OH - *Tel&CabFB 84C*
Warner Amex Cable Communications Inc. - Sidney, OH - *BrCabYB 84; Tel&CabFB 84C*
Warner Amex Cable Communications Inc. - St. Marys, OH - *BrCabYB 84*
Warner Amex Cable Communications Inc. - Youngstown, OH - *BrCabYB 84; Tel&CabFB 84C*
Warner Amex Cable Communications Inc. - Coos Bay, OR - *BrCabYB 84; Tel&CabFB 84C*
Warner Amex Cable Communications Inc. - Hood River, OR - *BrCabYB 84*
Warner Amex Cable Communications Inc. - Myrtle Point, OR - *BrCabYB 84*
Warner Amex Cable Communications Inc. - Powers, OR - *BrCabYB 84*
Warner Amex Cable Communications Inc. - Sandy, OR - *BrCabYB 84; Tel&CabFB 84C*
Warner Amex Cable Communications Inc. - Wemme, OR - *BrCabYB 84*
Warner Amex Cable Communications Inc. - Bradford, PA - *BrCabYB 84; Tel&CabFB 84C*
Warner Amex Cable Communications Inc. - Chambersburg, PA - *BrCabYB 84*
Warner Amex Cable Communications Inc. - Clearfield, PA - *BrCabYB 84*
Warner Amex Cable Communications Inc. - Morrison Cove, PA - *BrCabYB 84*
Warner Amex Cable Communications Inc. - Pittsburgh, PA - *HomeVid&CabYB 82-83*
Warner Amex Cable Communications Inc. - Pottsville, PA - *BrCabYB 84*
Warner Amex Cable Communications Inc. - Roaring Springs, PA - *BrCabYB 84*
Warner Amex Cable Communications Inc. - Erwin, TN - *BrCabYB 84*
Warner Amex Cable Communications Inc. - Greeneville, TN - *BrCabYB 84*
Warner Amex Cable Communications Inc. - Kingsport, TN - *BrCabYB 84; Tel&CabFB 84C*
Warner Amex Cable Communications Inc. - Burnet, TX - *BrCabYB 84*
Warner Amex Cable Communications Inc. - Crockett, TX - *BrCabYB 84*
Warner Amex Cable Communications Inc. - Dallas, TX - *BrCabYB 84; InterCabHB 3*
Warner Amex Cable Communications Inc. - Dumas, TX - *BrCabYB 84*
Warner Amex Cable Communications Inc. - Fairfield, TX - *BrCabYB 84*
Warner Amex Cable Communications Inc. - Farmers Branch, TX - *BrCabYB 84*
Warner Amex Cable Communications Inc. - Hico, TX - *BrCabYB 84*
Warner Amex Cable Communications Inc. - Mexia, TX - *BrCabYB 84*
Warner Amex Cable Communications Inc. - Navasota, TX - *BrCabYB 84*
Warner Amex Cable Communications Inc. - Rosebud, TX - *BrCabYB 84*
Warner Amex Cable Communications Inc. - Stephenville, TX - *BrCabYB 84*
Warner Amex Cable Communications Inc. - Harrisonburg, VA - *BrCabYB 84; Tel&CabFB 84C*
Warner Amex Cable Communications Inc. of Altamont - Altamont, IL - *Tel&CabFB 84C*
Warner Amex Cable Communications Inc. of Altoona - Altoona, PA - *BrCabYB 84; Tel&CabFB 84C*
Warner Amex Cable Communications Inc. of Avalon - Avalon, NJ - *Tel&CabFB 84C*
Warner Amex Cable Communications Inc. of Avenal - Avenal, CA - *BrCabYB 84; Tel&CabFB 84C*

Warner Amex Cable Communications Inc. of Barstow - Barstow, CA - *BrCabYB 84; Tel&CabFB 84C*
Warner Amex Cable Communications Inc. of Bellows Falls - Bellows Falls, VT - *BrCabYB 84*
Warner Amex Cable Communications Inc. of Berlin - Berlin, NH - *BrCabYB 84*
Warner Amex Cable Communications Inc. of Big Bear Lake - Big Bear Lake, CA - *BrCabYB 84; Tel&CabFB 84C*
Warner Amex Cable Communications Inc. of Blythe - Blythe, CA - *BrCabYB 84; Tel&CabFB 84C*
Warner Amex Cable Communications Inc. of Booneville - Booneville, AR - *BrCabYB 84*
Warner Amex Cable Communications Inc. of Brattleboro - Brattleboro, VT - *BrCabYB 84*
Warner Amex Cable Communications Inc. of Bristol - Bristol, VT - *BrCabYB 84*
Warner Amex Cable Communications Inc. of Claremont - Claremont, NH - *BrCabYB 84; Tel&CabFB 84C*
Warner Amex Cable Communications Inc. of Clarksville - Clarksville, AR - *BrCabYB 84*
Warner Amex Cable Communications Inc. of Clearfield [of Warner Amex Cable Communications Inc.] - Clearfield, PA - *Tel&CabFB 84C*
Warner Amex Cable Communications Inc. of Danville - Danville, IL - *Tel&CabFB 84C*
Warner Amex Cable Communications Inc. of DeKalb - DeKalb, IL - *Tel&CabFB 84C*
Warner Amex Cable Communications Inc. of Delphos [of Warner Amex Cable Communications Inc.] - Delphos, OH - *Tel&CabFB 84C*
Warner Amex Cable Communications Inc. of El Dorado Springs - Warrensburg, MO - *Tel&CabFB 84C*
Warner Amex Cable Communications Inc. of Ely - Ely, MN - *Tel&CabFB 84C*
Warner Amex Cable Communications Inc. of Fayetteville - Fayetteville, AR - *BrCabYB 84; Tel&CabFB 84C*
Warner Amex Cable Communications Inc. of Fergus Falls - Fergus Falls, MN - *Tel&CabFB 84C*
Warner Amex Cable Communications Inc. of Fox River Valley - Neenah, WI - *BrCabYB 84*
Warner Amex Cable Communications Inc. of Fox River Valley - Oshkosh, WI - *BrCabYB 84; Tel&CabFB 84C*
Warner Amex Cable Communications Inc. of Greater Cincinnati - Blue Ash, OH - *BrCabYB 84*
Warner Amex Cable Communications Inc. of Hampton - Hampton, VA - *Tel&CabFB 84C*
Warner Amex Cable Communications Inc. of Harrisonburg - New York, NY - *BrCabYB 84*
Warner Amex Cable Communications Inc. of Kern County - Bakersfield, CA - *BrCabYB 84*
Warner Amex Cable Communications Inc. of Lake Arrowhead - Lake Arrowhead, CA - *BrCabYB 84*
Warner Amex Cable Communications Inc. of Little Falls - Little Falls, MN - *Tel&CabFB 84C*
Warner Amex Cable Communications Inc. of Malibu - Malibu, CA - *BrCabYB 84; Tel&CabFB 84C*
Warner Amex Cable Communications Inc. of Marietta - Marietta, PA - *BrCabYB 84; Tel&CabFB 84C*
Warner Amex Cable Communications Inc. of Marinette - Marinette, WI - *Tel&CabFB 84C*
Warner Amex Cable Communications Inc. of Marinette-Menominee - Marinette, WI - *BrCabYB 84*
Warner Amex Cable Communications Inc. of Marshfield - Marshfield, WI - *BrCabYB 84*
Warner Amex Cable Communications Inc. of Martinsburg - Martinsburg, WV - *BrCabYB 84; Tel&CabFB 84C*
Warner Amex Cable Communications Inc. of Merrill - Merrill, WI - *BrCabYB 84*
Warner Amex Cable Communications Inc. of Nashua - Nashua, NH - *BrCabYB 84*
Warner Amex Cable Communications Inc. of New Jersey - Avalon, NJ - *BrCabYB 84*
Warner Amex Cable Communications Inc. of Olean - New York, NY - *Tel&CabFB 84C p.1711*
Warner Amex Cable Communications Inc. of Olean - Olean, NY - *Tel&CabFB 84C*
Warner Amex Cable Communications Inc. of Palm Springs - Palm Springs, CA - *BrCabYB 84; Tel&CabFB 84C*
Warner Amex Cable Communications Inc. of Paris - Paris, AR - *BrCabYB 84*
Warner Amex Cable Communications Inc. of Pecos - Pecos, TX - *BrCabYB 84; Tel&CabFB 84C*
Warner Amex Cable Communications Inc. of Reedsville - Newport, PA - *BrCabYB 84*
Warner Amex Cable Communications Inc. of Reedsville - Reedsville, PA - *BrCabYB 84; Tel&CabFB 84C*
Warner Amex Cable Communications Inc. of Reston - Reston, VA - *BrCabYB 84; Tel&CabFB 84C*
Warner Amex Cable Communications Inc. of Russell - Russell, KS - *BrCabYB 84; Tel&CabFB 84C*
Warner Amex Cable Communications Inc. of Russellville - Russellville, AR - *BrCabYB 84*
Warner Amex Cable Communications Inc. of Sedona - Sedona, AZ - *BrCabYB 84; Tel&CabFB 84C*
Warner Amex Cable Communications Inc. of Taft - Kern, CA - *BrCabYB 84*
Warner Amex Cable Communications Inc. of Union City - Union City, IN - *BrCabYB 84; Tel&CabFB 84C*
Warner Amex Cable Communications Inc. of Wapakoneta - Wapakoneta, OH - *BrCabYB 84; Tel&CabFB 84C*
Warner Amex Cable Communications Inc. of Warren - Warren, PA - *BrCabYB 84; Tel&CabFB 84C*
Warner Amex Cable Communications Inc. of Warrensburg - Harrisonville, MO - *BrCabYB 84*
Warner Amex Cable Communications Inc. of Warrensburg - Warrensburg, MO - *BrCabYB 84; Tel&CabFB 84C*
Warner Amex Cable Communications Inc. of Warrensburg - Windsor, MO - *BrCabYB 84*
Warner Amex Cable Communications Inc. of Warsaw - Warsaw, IN - *BrCabYB 84; Tel&CabFB 84C*
Warner Amex Cable Communications Inc. of Williamsburg - Hampton, VA - *BrCabYB 84*
Warner Amex Cable Communications of Harris County Inc. - New York, NY - *BrCabYB 84*
Warner Amex QUBE [Aff. of Warner Amex Cable Communications Inc.] - Columbus, OH - *InterCabHB 3; VideoDir 82-83*
Warner Amex Satellite Entertainment Co. - New York, NY - *BrCabYB 84; TelAl 83*
Warner Associates Inc., Paul A. - Teaneck, NJ - *IntDirMarRes 83*
Warner, Bicking & Fenwick - New York, NY - *AdAge 3-28-84; StaDirAdAg 2-84*
Warner Books [Subs. of Warner Communications] - New York, NY - *ArtMar 84; DirMarMP 83; LitMarPl 83, 84*
Warner Brothers Distributing Canada Ltd. - Toronto, ON, Canada - *Tel&CabFB 84C*
Warner Brothers Inc. - New York, NY - *LitMarPl 83*
Warner Brothers Music [Div. of Warner Bros. Inc.] - Los Angeles, CA - *BillIntBG 83-84*
Warner Brothers Records Inc. - Burbank, CA - *BillIntBG 83-84*
Warner Brothers Television - Burbank, CA - *TelAl 83, 84*
Warner Brothers Television Distribution - Burbank, CA - *Tel&CabFB 84C*
Warner Cable Corp. of Pittsburgh [Aff. of Warner Amex Cable Communications Inc.] - Pittsburgh, PA - *BrCabYB 84; InterCabHB 3; Tel&CabFB 84C*
Warner Cable of Athol - Athol, MA - *Tel&CabFB 84C*
Warner Cable of Berlin - Berlin, NH - *Tel&CabFB 84C*
Warner Cable of Brattleboro Inc. [of Warner Amex Cable Communications Inc.] - Brattleboro, VT - *Tel&CabFB 84C*
Warner Cable of Bristol [of Warner Amex Cable Communications Inc.] - Bristol, VT - *Tel&CabFB 84C*
Warner Cable of Canton [of Warner Amex Cable Communications Inc.] - Canton, OH - *Tel&CabFB 84C*
Warner Cable of Chambersburg [of Warner Amex Cable Communications Inc.] - Chambersburg, PA - *Tel&CabFB 84C*
Warner Cable of Columbus Inc. [of Warner Amex Cable Communications Inc.] - Columbus, OH - *Tel&CabFB 84C*
Warner Cable of Ft. Shawnee/Cridersville [of Warner Amex Cable Communications Inc.] - Ft. Shawnee, OH - *Tel&CabFB 84C*

Warner Cable of Ft. Walton Beach [of Warner Amex Cable Communications Inc.] - Crestview, FL - *Tel&CabFB 84C*
Warner Cable of Ft. Walton Beach [of Warner Amex Cable Communications] - Ft. Walton Beach, FL - *Tel&CabFB 84C*
Warner Cable of Ft. Walton Beach [of Warner Amex Cable Communications] - Niceville, FL - *Tel&CabFB 84C*
Warner Cable of Hood River [of Warner Amex Cable Communications Inc.] - Hood River, OR - *Tel&CabFB 84C*
Warner Cable of Kenton [of Warner Amex Cable Communications Inc.] - Kenton, OH - *Tel&CabFB 84C*
Warner Cable of Lake City Inc. [of Warner Amex Cable Communications Inc.] - Lake City, FL - *Tel&CabFB 84C*
Warner Cable of Marshfield [of Warner Amex Cable Communications Inc.] - Marshfield, WI - *Tel&CabFB 84C*
Warner Cable of Merrill [of Warner Amex Cable Communications Inc.] - Merrill, WI - *Tel&CabFB 84C*
Warner Cable of Nashua - Nashua, NH - *Tel&CabFB 84C*
Warner Cable of Patten/Island Falls - Patten/Island Falls, ME - *Tel&CabFB 84C*
Warner Cable of Pottsville - Pottsville, PA - *Tel&CabFB 84C*
Warner Cable of St. Marys [of Warner Amex Cable Communications Inc.] - St. Marys, OH - *Tel&CabFB 84C*
Warner Cable of Victorville [of Times Mirror Cable TV] - Victorville, CA - *Tel&CabFB 84C*
Warner Cable of Wrightwood [of Warner Amex Cable Communications Inc.] - Wrightwood, CA - *Tel&CabFB 84C*
Warner Communications - New York, NY - *AdAge 6-28-84; HomeVid&CabYB 82-83; KnowInd 83; Top100Al 83*
Warner Communications Inc. - *See* Warner Amex Cable Communications Inc.
Warner Communications Records Group [of Warner/Elektra/Atlantic Corp.] - Burbank, CA - *BillIntBG 83-84*
Warner Computer Systems Inc. - Teaneck, NJ - *DataDirOnSer 84*
Warner Computer Systems Inc. - New York, NY - *ADAPSOMemDir 83-84*
Warner-Eddison Associates Inc. - Cambridge, MA - *EISS 83; FBInfSer 80; InfIndMarPl 83; InfoS 83-84; WhoWMicrocom 83*
Warner Educational Productions - Fountain Valley, CA - *AvMarPl 83*
Warner Home Video - Burbank, CA - *AvMarPl 83; BillIntBG 83-84*
Warner, Howard W. - Ottawa, ON, Canada - *BoPubDir 4 Sup, 5*
Warner/Levinson Corp. - New York, NY - *BillIntBG 83-84; Tel&CabFB 84C*
Warner Press Inc. - Anderson, IN - *LitMarPl 83, 84*
Warner Productions, Robert - New York, NY - *AvMarPl 83*
Warner Publisher Services [Subs. of Warner Communications Inc.] - New York, NY - *MagIndMarPl 82-83*
Warner Robins Rev-Up, The - Warner Robins, GA - *AyerDirPub 83*
Warner Robins Sun [of Park Newspapers of GA Inc.] - Warner Robins, GA - *BaconPubCkNews 84; NewsDir 84*
Warner Stations - Lincoln, NE - *BrCabYB 84*
Warner Way, The - Paw Paw, MI - *BaconPubCkMag 84*
Warning Records - Orrville, OH - *BillIntBG 83-84*
WARO - Canonsburg, PA - *BrCabYB 84; TV&RadDir 84*
WARP-FM - Due West, SC - *BrCabYB 84; TV&RadDir 84*
Warp Publishing Co. - Minden, NE - *BoPubDir 4, 5*
WARR - Warrenton, NC - *TV&RadDir 84*
Warr Acres Putnam City Northwest Quill - Warr Acres, OK - *BaconPubCkNews 84*
Warr, Foote & Rose - Los Altos, CA - *AdAge 3-28-84; StaDirAdAg 2-84*
Warren & Epstein - New York, NY - *AdAge 3-28-84; StaDirAdAg 2-84*
Warren Anderson Advertising - Davenport, IA - *StaDirAdAg 2-84*
Warren, Andrea - Lawrence, KS - *LitMarPl 83, 84*
Warren-Bardeen Inc. - Seattle, WA - *HBIndAd&MS 82-83*
Warren Cable TV Inc. - Warren, MN - *Tel&CabFB 84C*
Warren Cablevision - Warrenton, GA - *BrCabYB 84*
Warren Cablevision Co. [of Community Communications Co.] - Monticello, AR - *BrCabYB 84*
Warren Cablevision Co. Inc. [of Community Communications Co.] - Warren, AR - *Tel&CabFB 84C*
Warren Centerline Community News [of Community News] - Mt. Clemens, MI - *NewsDir 84*
Warren CenterLine Community News - Warren, MI - *Ed&PubIntYB 82*
Warren Centerline Community News - *See* Community News
Warren Co., S. D. [Div. of Scott Paper Co.] - Boston, MA - *LitMarPl 83, 84*
Warren County Guide - Youngsville, PA - *AyerDirPub 83*
Warren County News - McMinnville, TN - *Ed&PubIntYB 82*
Warren Eagle Democrat - Warren, AR - *BaconPubCkNews 84; Ed&PubIntYB 82*
Warren Electronics - Redondo Beach, CA - *Tel&CabFB 84C*
Warren, Gorham & Lamont Inc. - Boston, MA - *DirMarMP 83; MagIndMarPl 82-83*
Warren, Gorham & Lamont Inc. [Subs. of International Thomson Organisation Ltd.] - New York, NY - *LitMarPl 83, 84*
Warren-Hilton Associates - North Hollywood, CA - *LitMarPl 83, 84*
Warren Inc., L. M. - Vancouver, BC, Canada - *EISS 83*
Warren/Kremer Advertising - New York, NY - *AdAge 3-28-84; StaDirAdAg 2-84*
Warren, McVeigh & Griffin Inc. - Newport Beach, CA - *BoPubDir 5*
Warren Miller's Ski World - Hermosa, CA - *MagDir 84*
Warren, Muller, Dolobowsky Inc. - New York, NY - *BrCabYB 84; StaDirAdAg 2-84*
Warren-Newport Press [of Lakeland Publishers Inc.] - Grayslake, IL - *NewsDir 84*
Warren-Newport Press - Gurnee, IL - *AyerDirPub 83*
Warren-Newport Press - *See* Lakeland Publishers Inc.
Warren Publishing Co. - Indianapolis, IN - *BoPubDir 4, 5*
Warren Publishing Co. - New York, NY - *MagIndMarPl 82-83*
Warren Record - Warrenton, NC - *AyerDirPub 83; Ed&PubIntYB 82*
Warren Sentinel - Front Royal, VA - *Ed&PubIntYB 82*
Warren Sentinel-Leader - Warren, IL - *BaconPubCkNews 84*
Warren Sheaf - Warren, MN - *BaconPubCkNews 84; Ed&PubIntYB 82; NewsDir 84*
Warren Tech Center News - *See* Monday Morning Newspapers
Warren Telephone Co. [Aff. of Telephone & Data Systems Inc.] - Warren, ME - *TelDir&BG 83-84*
Warren Telephone Co. - Warren, TX - *TelDir&BG 83-84*
Warren Times Gazette [of Phoenix-Times Newspapers] - Bristol, RI - *NewsDir 84*
Warren Times Gazette - Warren, RI - *Ed&PubIntYB 82*
Warren Times Gazette - *See* Phoenix-Times Newspapers
Warren Times Observer [of Central Publishing Co.] - Warren, PA - *BaconPubCkNews 84; Ed&PubIntYB 82; NewsDir 84*
Warren Tribune - Warren, IN - *BaconPubCkNews 84; Ed&PubIntYB 82*
Warren Tribune Chronicle - Warren, OH - *BaconPubCkNews 84; NewsDir 84*
Warren's Books [Aff. of Warren Sales Co.] - Richfield, NC - *BoPubDir 4, 5*
Warrensburg-Lake George News [of Elizabethtown Denton Publications Inc.] - Elizabethtown, NY - *NewsDir 84*
Warrensburg-Lake George News - Warrensburg, NY - *AyerDirPub 83; Ed&PubIntYB 82*
Warrensburg-Lake George News - *See* Denton Publications Inc.
Warrensburg Standard-Herald - Warrensburg, MO - *BaconPubCkNews 84*
Warrensburg Star-Journal - Warrensburg, MO - *Ed&PubIntYB 82; NewsDir 84*
Warrenton Banner [of St. Charles Journal] - Warrenton, MO - *BaconPubCkNews 84; Ed&PubIntYB 82; NewsDir 84*
Warrenton Cablevision Co. - Warrenton, AL - *BrCabYB 84; Tel&CabFB 84C*
Warrenton Clipper, The - Warrenton, GA - *Ed&PubIntYB 82*
Warrenton Columbia Press - Warrenton, OR - *BaconPubCkNews 84*
Warrenton Fauquier Democrat - Warrenton, VA - *BaconPubCkNews 84*
Warrenton News [of Warrenton Banner Inc.] - Warrenton, MO - *BaconPubCkNews 84; Ed&PubIntYB 82; NewsDir 84*
Warrenton Warren Record - Warrenton, NC - *BaconPubCkNews 84; NewsDir 84*
Warrick Cablevision Inc. [of Century Communications Corp.] - Newburgh, IN - *BrCabYB 84; Tel&CabFB 84C*

Warrick Enquirer - Boonville, IN - *AyerDirPub 83; Ed&PubIntYB 82*
Warrin Graphics - Dunmore, PA - *LitMarPl 83, 84; MagIndMarPl 82-83*
Warrington Associates - Hopkins, MN - *DataDirOnSer 84; DataDirSup 7-83*
Warrior, Betsy - Cambridge, MA - *BoPubDir 4, 5*
Warrior CATV Inc. - Warrior, AL - *BrCabYB 84*
Warroad Municipal Cable TV [of Sjoberg's Cable TV Inc.] - Warroad, MN - *Tel&CabFB 84C*
Warroad Pioneer - Warroad, MN - *BaconPubCkNews 84; Ed&PubIntYB 82*
Warsaw Benton County Enterprise - Warsaw, MO - *BaconPubCkNews 84; NewsDir 84*
Warsaw Cable Television Corp. - Warsaw, NY - *BrCabYB 84*
Warsaw Cable TV [of Centel Cable Television Co.] - Warsaw, KY - *BrCabYB 84*
Warsaw-Faison News - Warsaw, NC - *AyerDirPub 83; BaconPubCkNews 84; Ed&PubIntYB 82*
Warsaw Gallatin County News - Warsaw, KY - *BaconPubCkNews 84*
Warsaw Northern Neck News - Warsaw, VA - *BaconPubCkNews 84*
Warsaw Times-Union [of Reub Williams & Sons Inc.] - Warsaw, IN - *BaconPubCkNews 84; NewsDir 84*
Warsaw TV Cable Corp. - Warsaw, NY - *Tel&CabFB 84C*
Warsaw Western New Yorker - Warsaw, NY - *Ed&PubIntYB 82*
Warsaw Western New Yorker - *See* Sanders Publications
WART - Naranjito, PR - *BrCabYB 84; Tel&CabFB 84S*
Wartburg Morgan County News - Wartburg, TN - *BaconPubCkNews 84*
Warthog Press - West Orange, NJ - *BoPubDir 4, 5; LitMag&SmPr 83-84*
WARU - Peru, IN - *BrCabYB 84; TV&RadDir 84*
WARU-FM - Peru, IN - *BrCabYB 84; TV&RadDir 84*
Warus Music - Chicago, IL - *BillIntBG 83-84*
WARV - Providence/Pawtucket, RI - *NatRadPubDir Summer 83 p.219, Spring 84 p.219*
WARV - Warwick, RI - *BrCabYB 84; TV&RadDir 84*
Warwick Advertiser-Photo News [of Tunnell Publishing Co. Inc.] - Warwick, NY - *Ed&PubIntYB 82; NewsDir 84*
Warwick Advertiser-Photo News - *See* Advertiser Photo News Group
Warwick Advertising - New York, NY - *AdAge 3-28-84; Br 1-23-84; BrCabYB 84; StaDirAdAg 2-84*
Warwick & Associates Inc., Ken - New York, NY - *IntDirMarRes 83*
Warwick Beacon [of Southern R.I. Publications] - Warwick, RI - *BaconPubCkNews 84; Ed&PubIntYB 82; NewsDir 84*
Warwick Cable TV Corp. [of Group W Cable Inc.] - Warwick, NY - *BrCabYB 84; Tel&CabFB 84C*
Warwick Copy Products Inc. - Warwick, NY - *DirInfWP 82*
Warwick Publishers - Oklahoma City, OK - *BoPubDir 4, 5*
Warwick Statistics Service [of University of Warwick Library] - Coventry, England - *EISS 83; FBInfSer 80*
Warwick Valley Dispatch - Warwick, NY - *BaconPubCkNews 84; Ed&PubIntYB 82; NewsDir 84*
Warwick Valley Telephone Co. - Warwick, NY - *TelDir&BG 83-84*
Warwick, Welsh & Miller Inc. - New York, NY - *TelAl 83, 84*
WARY-FM - Valhalla, NY - *BrCabYB 84; NatRadPubDir Summer 83, Spring 84; TV&RadDir 84*
WASA - Havre de Grace, MD - *BrCabYB 84*
Wasatch CATV Associates [of Misco Cable TV Co.] - Heber City, UT - *Tel&CabFB 84C*
Wasatch Community Cable TV [of Tele-Communications Inc.] - Davis County, UT - *BrCabYB 84*
Wasatch Community TV Inc. [of Tele-Communications Inc.] - Farmington, UT - *Tel&CabFB 84C*
Wasatch Publishers Inc. - Salt Lake City, UT - *BoPubDir 4, 5*
Wasatch Wave - Heber City, UT - *AyerDirPub 83; Ed&PubIntYB 82*
WASC - Spartanburg, SC - *BrCabYB 84; NatRadPubDir Summer 83, Spring 84; TV&RadDir 84*
Wascana Review [of University of Regina] - Regina, SK, Canada - *WritMar 84*
Wascana Witness - Regina, SK, Canada - *Ed&PubIntYB 82*
Wasco News - Wasco, CA - *BaconPubCkNews 84; Ed&PubIntYB 82*
Wasco Shopping Spree - Shafter, CA - *AyerDirPub 83*
WASD - Exeter, PA - *BrCabYB 84*
Waseca Cable TV [of E. F. Johnson Co.] - Waseca, MN - *BrCabYB 84*
Waseca Daily Journal - Waseca, MN - *Ed&PubIntYB 82; NewsDir 84*
Wasey Inc., Erwin [Subs. of Interpublic Group of Cos. Inc.] - Los Angeles, CA - *BrCabYB 84*
WASG - Atmore, AL - *BrCabYB 84*
WASH-FM - Washington, DC - *BrCabYB 84; NatRadPubDir Summer 83, Spring 84; TV&RadDir 84*
Wash 'n Press - Seattle, WA - *LitMag&SmPr 83-84*
Washburn Cable Communications Inc. - Washburn, WI - *BrCabYB 84*
Washburn Cable TV Inc. - Washburn, ND - *BrCabYB 84; Tel&CabFB 84C*
Washburn Cablecom Inc. - Washburn, WI - *Tel&CabFB 84C*
Washburn Center Republican - *See* Borlaug Publishing Co.
Washburn County Register - Shell Lake, WI - *AyerDirPub 83; Ed&PubIntYB 82*
Washburn Leader [of Woodford Publishing Co.] - Metamora, IL - *NewsDir 84*
Washburn Leader - Washburn, ND - *Ed&PubIntYB 82*
Washburn Leader - *See* Borlaug Publishing Co.
Washburn Leader - *See* Woodford Publishing Co.
Washburn Leader, The - Washburn, IL - *Ed&PubIntYB 82*
Washburn Marketing Inc., Heidi - New York, NY - *IntDirMarRes 83*
Washburn Times - Washburn, WI - *BaconPubCkNews 84; Ed&PubIntYB 82*
Washington Actions on Health - Arlington, VA - *BaconPubCkMag 84*
Washington Afro-American - Washington, DC - *BaconPubCkNews 84*
Washington Afro-American Newspaper [of Baltimore Afro-American Newspapers] - Washington, DC - *NewsDir 84*
Washington Agency, The - Arlington, VA - *DirPRFirms 83*
Washington Alert Service [of Congressional Quarterly Inc.] - Washington, DC - *EISS 5-84 Sup*
Washington Architect - Madison, WI - *BaconPubCkMag 84*
Washington Beverage Analyst [of Bevan Inc.] - Denver, CO - *BaconPubCkMag 84; MagDir 84*
Washington Blade, The - Washington, DC - *WritMar 84*
Washington Business Information Inc. - Washington, DC - *BoPubDir 4, 5; EISS 7-83 Sup*
Washington Business Journal - McLean, VA - *BaconPubCkMag 84; MagDir 84*
Washington Cable Co. [of Tele-Media Corp.] - Washington, GA - *Tel&CabFB 84C*
Washington Cable TV - Washington, KS - *BrCabYB 84; Tel&CabFB 84C*
Washington Cablevision Inc. [of McDonald Group Inc.] - Washington, IA - *BrCabYB 84; Tel&CabFB 84C*
Washington Cablevision Inc. [of McDonald Group] - Bogalusa, LA - *BrCabYB 84*
Washington Cablevision Inc. [of McDonald Group] - Franklinton, LA - *BrCabYB 84; Tel&CabFB 84C*
Washington Capital Spotlight Newspaper - Washington, DC - *BaconPubCkNews 84*
Washington Cattleman - Ellensburg, WA - *MagDir 84*
Washington Channels Inc. [of Times Mirror Cable TV] - Washington, PA - *Tel&CabFB 84C*
Washington Citizen - Washington, MO - *Ed&PubIntYB 82*
Washington Citizen - *See* Missourian Publishing Co.
Washington Clubwoman - Battle Ground, WA - *MagDir 84*
Washington Communications Group Inc. - Washington, DC - *ProGuPRSer 4*
Washington Computer Services - New York, NY - *MicrocomMPl 83*
Washington Computer Services - Bellingham, WA - *MicrocomMPl 83, 84*
Washington Consulting Group - Alexandria, VA - *EISS 5-84 Sup*
Washington County Bulletin - Cottage Grove, MN - *AyerDirPub 83; Ed&PubIntYB 82*

Washington County News - Chipley, FL - *AyerDirPub 83; Ed&PubIntYB 82*
Washington County News - Washington, KS - *AyerDirPub 83; BaconPubCkNews 84; Ed&PubIntYB 82; NewsDir 84*
Washington County News - St. George, UT - *AyerDirPub 83; Ed&PubIntYB 82*
Washington County News - Abingdon, VA - *AyerDirPub 83; Ed&PubIntYB 82*
Washington County News-Times [of Tigard Times] - Portland, OR - *NewsDir 84*
Washington County News-Times, The - Forest Grove, OR - *Ed&PubIntYB 82*
Washington County Observer - West Fork, AR - *AyerDirPub 83; Ed&PubIntYB 82*
Washington County Post - Cambridge, NY - *AyerDirPub 83; Ed&PubIntYB 82*
Washington County Review - *See* Lillie Suburban Newspapers
Washington County Rural Telephone Cooperative - Pekin, IN - *TelDir&BG 83-84*
Washington Courier - Washington, IL - *BaconPubCkNews 84; NewsDir 84*
Washington Court House Record Herald - Washington Court House, OH - *BaconPubCkNews 84; NewsDir 84*
Washington Credit Letter - Silver Spring, MD - *DirOnDB Spring 84*
Washington Credit Letter [of NewsNet Inc.] - Bryn Mawr, PA - *DataDirOnSer 84*
Washington Daily News - Washington, NC - *Ed&PubIntYB 82; NewsDir 84*
Washington Document Service - Washington, DC - *EISS 83*
Washington Dolls' House & Toy Museum - Washington, DC - *BoPubDir 4 Sup, 5*
Washington Dossier, The [of Adler International Ltd.] - Washington, DC - *BaconPubCkMag 84; MagDir 84; WritMar 84*
Washington, Eliza - Waterloo, IA - *BoPubDir 5*
Washington Evening Journal [of Elder, Shannon & Co. Inc.] - Washington, IA - *Ed&PubIntYB 82; NewsDir 84*
Washington Farmer-Stockman - Spokane, WA - *BaconPubCkMag 84; MagDir 84*
Washington Farmletter [of NewsNet Inc.] - Bryn Mawr, PA - *DataDirOnSer 84*
Washington Fishing Holes [of Osprey Press Inc.] - Black Diamond, WA - *WritMar 84*
Washington Food Dealer - Seattle, WA - *BaconPubCkMag 84; MagDir 84*
Washington History Committee - Washington, NH - *BoPubDir 4, 5*
Washington Informer - Washington, DC - *BaconPubCkNews 84; NewsDir 84*
Washington Insurance Commissioner - Olympia, WA - *BoPubDir 5*
Washington International Arts Letter [Aff. of Allied Business Consultants Inc.] - Washington, DC - *BoPubDir 4, 5; LitMag&SmPr 83-84; MagDir 84; MagIndMarPl 82-83*
Washington International Report - Falls Church, VA - *BrCabYB 84*
Washington Journal - Washington, DC - *Ed&PubIntYB 82*
Washington Journal - Washington, IA - *BaconPubCkNews 84*
Washington Journalism Review - Washington, DC - *BaconPubCkMag 84; MagIndMarPl 82-83*
Washington Library Network [of Washington State Library] - Olympia, WA - *DataDirOnSer 84; EISS 83; InfIndMarPl 83*
Washington Missourian [of Washington Citizen] - Washington, MO - *Ed&PubIntYB 82; NewsDir 84*
Washington Missourian - *See* Missourian Publishing Co.
Washington Monitor Inc. - Washington, DC - *BoPubDir 4, 5; EISS 83; ProGuPRSer 4*
Washington Monthly - Washington, DC - *ArtMar 84; BaconPubCkMag 84; DirMarMP 83; LitMarPl 83, 84; MagIndMarPl 82-83; WritMar 84*
Washington Motorist, The - Seattle, WA - *BaconPubCkMag 84; MagDir 84*
Washington Natural Heritage Program [of Washington State Dept. of Natural Resources] - Olympia, WA - *EISS 5-84 Sup*
Washington New Observer - Washington, DC - *BaconPubCkNews 84; NewsDir 84*
Washington News - Washington, NC - *BaconPubCkNews 84*
Washington News Report - Grenloch, NJ - *Ed&PubIntYB 82*
Washington News-Reporter - Washington, GA - *BaconPubCkNews 84; Ed&PubIntYB 82; NewsDir 84*
Washington Newsletter - Los Angeles, CA - *MagIndMarPl 82-83*
Washington Observer-Reporter - Washington, DC - *BaconPubCkNews 84*
Washington Park Press - Albany, NY - *BoPubDir 4 Sup, 5*
Washington Patriot [of Pace Publishing Inc.] - Indianapolis, IN - *Ed&PubIntYB 82; NewsDir 84*
Washington Patriot - *See* Topic Newspapers Inc.
Washington Pharmacist - Renton, WA - *BaconPubCkMag 84*
Washington Post - Washington, DC - *AdAge 6-28-84; AyerDirPub 83; BaconPubCkNews 84; DataDirOnSer 84; DirMarMP 83; DirOnDB Spring 84; Ed&PubIntYB 82; HomeVid&CabYB 82-83; InfoS 83-84; KnowInd 83; LitMarPl 83, 84; NewsBur 6; NewsDir 84; WritMar 84*
Washington Post Co. - *See* Post-Newsweek Stations
Washington Post Index [of Dialog Information Services Inc.] - Palo Alto, CA - *DataDirOnSer 84*
Washington Post Index - Woodbridge, CT - *DirOnDB Spring 84*
Washington Post Index Data Base [of Research Publications Inc.] - Woodbridge, CT - *EISS 5-84 Sup*
Washington Post Magazine, The - Washington, DC - *MagIndMarPl 82-83; WritMar 84*
Washington Post Writers Group [Div. of The Washington Post] - Washington, DC - *BaconPubCkNews 84; Ed&PubIntYB 82; LitMarPl 84*
Washington Press - Florham Park, NJ - *BoPubDir 4, 5*
Washington Purchaser - Seattle, WA - *BaconPubCkMag 84; MagDir 84*
Washington Rappahannock News - Washington, VA - *BaconPubCkNews 84*
Washington Report [of US Chamber of Commerce] - Washington, DC - *BaconPubCkMag 84; Ed&PubIntYB 82; WritMar 84*
Washington Report - St. Petersburg, FL - *LitMag&SmPr 83-84*
Washington Reporter [of Morton Tazewell Publishing Co.] - Morton, IL - *AyerDirPub 83; NewsDir 84*
Washington Representative Services - Arlington, VA - *CompReadDB 82; FBInfSer 80*
Washington Representative Services - Falls Church, VA - *DataDirOnSer 84; EISS 83; InfIndMarPl 83*
Washington Researchers - Washington, DC - *BoPubDir 4, 5; EISS 83; FBInfSer 80; HBIndAd&MS 82-83; InfIndMarPl 83; LitMarPl 83, 84; ProGuPRSer 4*
Washington Review - Washington, DC - *LitMag&SmPr 83-84*
Washington Sea Grant Program - Seattle, WA - *BoPubDir 4, 5*
Washington Service Bureau Inc. - Washington, DC - *EISS 83; MicroMarPl 82-83*
Washington Square News - New York, NY - *NewsDir 84*
Washington Star, The - Washington, DC - *NewsBur 6*
Washington State Historical Society - Tacoma, WA - *BoPubDir 4, 5*
Washington State University Press - Pullman, WA - *BoPubDir 4, 5*
Washington Tariff & Trade Letter - Washington, DC - *BaconPubCkMag 84*
Washington Tazewell Reporter - *See* Tazewell Publishing Co.
Washington Times - Washington, DC - *BaconPubCkNews 84*
Washington Times-Herald - Washington, DC - *BaconPubCkNews 84*
Washington Times-Herald [of Donrey Inc.] - Washington, IN - *Ed&PubIntYB 82; NewsDir 84*
Washington University Press - St. Louis, MO - *BoPubDir 4, 5*
Washington Writer's Publishing House - Washington, DC - *BoPubDir 4, 5; LitMag&SmPr 83-84*
Washington Writers Syndicate - Washington, DC - *Ed&PubIntYB 82*
Washingtonian [of Washington Magazine Inc.] - Washington, DC - *ArtMar 84; BaconPubCkMag 84; DirMarMP 83; Folio 83; LitMarPl 83, 84; MagDir 84; MagIndMarPl 82-83; WritMar 84*
Washingtonian Books - Washington, DC - *BoPubDir 4, 5*
Washingtonville Orange County Post - Washingtonville, NY - *BaconPubCkNews 84*
Washinwear Music - *See* Songsellers Co.
Washita County Enterprise - Corn, OK - *AyerDirPub 83; Ed&PubIntYB 82*
Washline, The - Jersey City, NJ - *NewsDir 84*

Washout Publishing Co. - Schenectady, NY - *BoPubDir 4, 5*
Washtucna Cable System - Washtucna, WA - *BrCabYB 84*
Washtucna World - Clarkston, WA - *AyerDirPub 83*
Washtucna World - *See* Tribune Newspapers Inc.
Wasington Business Journal [of Cordovan Corp.] - McLean, VA - *WritMar 84*
WASK - Kokomo, IN - *TV&RadDir 84*
WASK - Lafayette, IN - *BrCabYB 84; TV&RadDir 84*
WASK-FM - Lafayette, IN - *BrCabYB 84; TV&RadDir 84*
Waskom Weekly Review - Waskom, TX - *AyerDirPub 83; BaconPubCkNews 84; Ed&PubIntYB 82*
WASL-FM - Dyersburg, TN - *BrCabYB 84; TV&RadDir 84*
WASM-FM - Saratoga Springs, NY - *BrCabYB 84; TV&RadDir 84*
WASP - Brownsville, PA - *BrCabYB 84; TV&RadDir 84*
WASR - Wolfeboro, NH - *BrCabYB 84; TV&RadDir 84*
Wasserman Literary Agency Inc., Harriet - New York, NY - *LitMarPl 83, 84*
WAST - Albany, NY - *TelAl 83, 84*
WAST-TV - Mednands, NY - *LitMarPl 83*
Waste Age - Washington, DC - *BaconPubCkMag 84; MagDir 84; MagIndMarPl 82-83*
Waste Management & Resources Recovery - Eagan, MN - *DirOnDB Spring 84*
Waste Management & Resources Recovery Information Database [of International Research & Evaluation] - Eagan, MN - *CompReadDB 82; DataDirOnSer 84*
Waste Management Information Bureau [of Atomic Energy Authority] - Didcot, England - *EISS 83*
Wastex Cable Corp. [of Times Mirror Cable Television Inc.] - Del Rio, TX - *BrCabYB 84*
WASU-FM - Boone, NC - *BrCabYB 84; NatRadPubDir Summer 83, Spring 84; TV&RadDir 84*
WASY - Gorham, ME - *BrCabYB 84; TV&RadDir 84*
WASZ - Ashland, AL - *BrCabYB 84*
WATA - Boone, NC - *BrCabYB 84; TV&RadDir 84*
Watauga Democrat - Boone, NC - *AyerDirPub 83; Ed&PubIntYB 82*
WATC - Gaylord, MI - *TV&RadDir 84*
Watch & Clock Review - Denver, CO - *BaconPubCkMag 84; MagDir 84; WritMar 84*
Watchman - Greensboro, AL - *AyerDirPub 83*
Watchman - Onida, SD - *AyerDirPub 83*
Watchman - Lachute, PQ, Canada - *AyerDirPub 83; Ed&PubIntYB 82*
Watchman, The - Clinton, LA - *Ed&PubIntYB 82*
Watchtower Bible & Tract Society of New York Inc. - Brooklyn, NY - *BoPubDir 4, 5*
Watchwords - London, ON, Canada - *LitMag&SmPr 83-84*
Watchwords Publications - London, ON, Canada - *LitMag&SmPr 83-84*
WATD-FM - Marshfield, MA - *BrCabYB 84; TV&RadDir 84*
WATDOC [of Environment Canada, Inland Water Directorate] - Ottawa, ON, Canada - *CompReadDB 82; DataDirOnSer 84; EISS 83; InfIndMarPl 83*
WATE-TV - Knoxville, TN - *BrCabYB 84; DirUSTelSta 83; LitMarPl 83, 84; TelAl 83, 84; Tel&CabFB 84S; TV&RadDir 84*
Water & Pollution Control - Don Mills, ON, Canada - *BaconPubCkMag 84*
Water & Wastes Digest - Des Plaines, IL - *BaconPubCkMag 84; MagDir 84*
Water Conditioning & Purification - Tucson, AZ - *BaconPubCkMag 84; MagDir 84*
Water Data Laboratory [of U.S. Dept. of Agriculture] - Beltsville, MD - *EISS 83*
Water Engineering & Management - Des Plaines, IL - *BaconPubCkMag 84; MagDir 84*
Water Equipment News - Urbana, IL - *BaconPubCkMag 84; MagDir 84*
Water Foundation [Aff. of Palisades Communications] - Santa Barbara, CA - *BoPubDir 4, 5*
Water Mark Press - Huntington Bay, NY - *BoPubDir 4, 5; LitMag&SmPr 83-84*
Water Newsletter & Research & Development News - Syosset, NY - *BaconPubCkMag 84*
Water Oak Shoppers Guide - Oakville, CT - *AyerDirPub 83*
Water Press - *See* Multi-Medea Enterprises/Water Press
Water Quality Association - Lombard, IL - *BoPubDir 5*
Water Research Centre - Stevenage, England - *InfIndMarPl 83*
Water Research Centre (Information Service on Toxicity & Biodegradability) - Stevenage, England - *InfIndMarPl 83*
Water Research Centre (Medmenham Laboratory) - Marlow, England - *CompReadDB 82*
Water Resources Abstracts [of Water Resources Scientific Information Center] - Washington, DC - *OnBibDB 3*
Water Resources Information Program [of University of Wisconsin-Madison] - Madison, WI - *EISS 83*
Water Resources Publications - Littleton, CO - *BoPubDir 4, 5*
Water Resources Research [of U.S. Dept. of the Interior] - Washington, DC - *BaconPubCkMag 84; CompReadDB 82; DirOnDB Spring 84; MagDir 84*
Water Resources Scientific Information Center [of Office of Water Research & Technology, U.S. Dept. of the Interior] - Washington, DC - *CompReadDB 82; EISS 83*
Water Resources Scientific Information Center - Reston, VA - *DataDirOnSer 84*
Water Skier, The - Winter Haven, FL - *ArtMar 84; MagDir 84; MagIndMarPl 82-83; WritMar 84*
Water Supply Improvement Association Journal - Topsfield, MA - *MagDir 84*
Water Survey of Canada [of Environment Canada] - Ottawa, ON, Canada - *EISS 83*
Water Technology - Latham, NY - *BaconPubCkMag 84*
Water Use Information System [of Westinghouse Hanford Co.] - Richland, WA - *EISS 83*
Water Valley North Mississippi Herald - Water Valley, MS - *BaconPubCkNews 84*
Water Well Journal - Worthington, OH - *BaconPubCkMag 84; MagDir 84*
Waterbed - Redondo Beach, CA - *BaconPubCkMag 84*
Waterbury American - Waterbury, CT - *BaconPubCkNews 84; Ed&PubIntYB 82*
Waterbury Community Antenna Inc. [of Sammons Communications Inc.] - Waterbury, CT - *Tel&CabFB 84C*
Waterbury Republican [of American-Republican Inc.] - Waterbury, CT - *BaconPubCkNews 84; Ed&PubIntYB 82; NewsDir 84*
Waterfall Press - El Cerrito, CA - *BoPubDir 4, 5; LitMag&SmPr 83-84*
Waterflower's World - Germantown, TN - *BaconPubCkMag 84*
Waterford Cablevision - Waterford Township, MI - *BrCabYB 84*
Waterford News - Waterford, CA - *Ed&PubIntYB 82*
Waterford News - *See* Waterford News Publishers
Waterford News Publishers - Waterford, CA - *BaconPubCkNews 84*
Waterford Post - Waterford, WI - *BaconPubCkNews 84; Ed&PubIntYB 82*
Waterford Spinal Column Newsweekly - *See* Spinal Column Newsweekly
Waterford Times - *See* Times Newspapers
Waterfowler's World [of Waterfowl Publications Ltd.] - Germantown, TN - *WritMar 84*
Waterfront - Costa Mesa, CA - *BaconPubCkMag 84*
Waterfront, The - Lake City, MI - *Ed&PubIntYB 82*
Waterfront World - Washington, DC - *BaconPubCkMag 84*
Waterhouse Music - Minneapolis, MN - *BillIntBG 83-84*
Waterhouse, Nicoll & Associates - New York, NY - *StaDirAdAg 2-84*
Waterhouse Records - Minneapolis, MN - *BillIntBG 83-84*
Watering Inc. - Bennington, VT - *DirMarMP 83*
Waterline - Worthington, OH - *DirOnDB Spring 84*
WaterLit [of SDC Information Services] - Santa Monica, CA - *DataDirOnSer 84*
Waterlit [of South African Water Information Centre] - Pretoria, South Africa - *CompReadDB 82; DirOnDB Spring 84; OnBibDB 3*
Waterloo Cablevision Inc. [of McDonald Group Inc.] - Waterloo, IA - *BrCabYB 84; Tel&CabFB 84C*
Waterloo Chronicle - Waterloo, ON, Canada - *Ed&PubIntYB 82*
Waterloo Computing Systems Ltd. - Waterloo, ON, Canada - *WhoWMicrocom 83*
Waterloo Courier [of W. H. Hartman Co.] - Waterloo, IA - *Ed&PubIntYB 82; NewsDir 84*
Waterloo Courier [of Royle Publishing Co. Inc.] - Waterloo, WI - *Ed&PubIntYB 82; NewsDir 84*

Waterloo Courier - *See* Royle Publishing Co. Inc.
Waterloo Daily Courier - Waterloo, IA - *BaconPubCkNews 84*
Waterloo Douglas County Gazette [of Record Enterprises Ltd.] - Waterloo, NE - *BaconPubCkNews 84; NewsDir 84*
Waterloo Music Co. Ltd. - Waterloo, ON, Canada - *BoPubDir 4, 5; LitMarPl 84*
Waterloo Public Interest Research Group - Waterloo, ON, Canada - *BoPubDir 5*
Waterloo Republic-Times [of Voris Printing Co. Inc.] - Waterloo, IL - *BaconPubCkNews 84; Ed&PubIntYB 82; NewsDir 84*
Waterloo Systems Specialists Ltd. (Fraser Research Div.) - Waterloo, ON, Canada - *VideoDir 82-83*
Waterloo Systems Specialists Ltd. (Fraser Videotex Services Div.) - Waterloo, ON, Canada - *VideoDir 82-83*
Waterloo Times - Waterloo, IL - *Ed&PubIntYB 82*
Waterloo TV Cable - Waterloo, PQ, Canada - *BrCabYB 84*
Waterman, Harriette - New York, NY - *LitMarPl 83, 84*
Watermill Publishers - Albertson, NY - *BoPubDir 4, 5*
Waternet [of Dialog Information Services Inc.] - Palo Alto, CA - *DataDirOnSer 84*
Waternet [of American Water Works Association] - Denver, CO - *DirOnDB Spring 84; EISS 7-83 Sup*
Waters & Associates Inc., Norman D. - Mamaroneck, NY - *StaDirAdAg 2-84*
Waters Newspapers - Columbia, MO - *Ed&PubIntYB 82*
Waters Syndicate - Sacramento, CA - *Ed&PubIntYB 82*
Waters/Uniphoto, Bruce - Nashville, TN - *AvMarPl 83*
Watershed Intermedia - Washington, DC - *LitMag&SmPr 83-84*
Watershed Tapes - Washington, DC - *LitMag&SmPr 83-84*
Waterside Press - New York, NY - *BoPubDir 4, 5*
Waterton Town Times & Water-Oak Shoppers Guide - Waterton, CT - *Ed&PubIntYB 82*
Watertown Cable TV [of Booth American Co.] - Watertown, SD - *BrCabYB 84; Tel&CabFB 84C*
Watertown Carver County News - Watertown, MN - *BaconPubCkNews 84*
Watertown Daily Times [of Johnson Newspaper Corp.] - Watertown, NY - *AyerDirPub 83; BaconPubCkNews 84; Ed&PubIntYB 82; LitMarPl 83, 84; NewsDir 84*
Watertown Daily Times - Watertown, WI - *Ed&PubIntYB 82; NewsDir 84*
Watertown Herald [of Belmont Offset Printing & Publishing Co. Inc.] - Belmont, MA - *NewsDir 84*
Watertown Press [of Dole Publishing Co. Inc.] - Somerville, MA - *NewsDir 84*
Watertown Press - Watertown, MA - *Ed&PubIntYB 82*
Watertown Press - *See* Dole Publishing Co. Inc.
Watertown Public Opinion - Watertown, SD - *BaconPubCkNews 84; Ed&PubIntYB 82; NewsDir 84*
Watertown Sun [of Belmont Offset Printing & Publishing Co. Inc.] - Belmont, MA - *AyerDirPub 83; Ed&PubIntYB 82; NewsDir 84*
Watertown Sun - *See* Herald Publishing Co.
Watertown Times - Watertown, WI - *BaconPubCkNews 84*
Watertown Town Times - Watertown, CT - *BaconPubCkNews 84*
Waterville Central Maine Morning Sentinel [of Guy Gannett Publishing Co.] - Waterville, ME - *NewsDir 84*
Waterville Empire-Press - Waterville, WA - *BaconPubCkNews 84; Ed&PubIntYB 82*
Waterville Lake Region Life - Waterville, MN - *BaconPubCkNews 84*
Waterville Telegraph - Waterville, KS - *BaconPubCkNews 84; Ed&PubIntYB 82*
Waterville Times - Waterville, NY - *BaconPubCkNews 84; Ed&PubIntYB 82*
Waterville TV Inc. - Waterville, WA - *BrCabYB 84; Tel&CabFB 84C*
Watervliet Record - Watervliet, MI - *BaconPubCkNews 84; Ed&PubIntYB 82*
Waterway Guide - Annapolis, MD - *BoPubDir 4, 5; WritMar 84*
Waterways [of Ten Penny Players Inc.] - New York, NY - *LitMag&SmPr 83-84*
Waterways Journal - St. Louis, MO - *BaconPubCkMag 84; MagDir 84*
Watford City Cablevision [of Tioga Cablevision Inc.] - Watford City, ND - *BrCabYB 84; Tel&CabFB 84C*
Watford City McKenzie County Farmer - Watford City, ND - *BaconPubCkNews 84*
WATH - Athens, OH - *BrCabYB 84; TV&RadDir 84*
Wathen Associates Inc. - Falls Church, VA - *DirPRFirms 83*
Wathena Times - Wathena, KS - *BaconPubCkNews 84; Ed&PubIntYB 82*
Wathill Citizen, The - Wathill, NE - *Ed&PubIntYB 82*
WATI - Indianapolis, IN - *BrCabYB 84; TV&RadDir 84*
WATK - Antigo, WI - *BrCabYB 84; TV&RadDir 84*
Watkins/Cassil & Associates - Little Rock, AR - *StaDirAdAg 2-84*
Watkins Express - Watkins Glen, NY - *Ed&PubIntYB 82*
Watkins Glen Express - *See* Watkins Glen Review Publishers
Watkins Glen Master TV Corp. - Watkins Glen, NY - *BrCabYB 84; Tel&CabFB 84C*
Watkins Glen Review - Watkins Glen, NY - *Ed&PubIntYB 82*
Watkins Glen Review - *See* Watkins Glen Review Publishers
Watkins Glen Review Publishers - Watkins Glen, NY - *BaconPubCkNews 84*
Watkins Inc., A. - New York, NY - *LitMarPl 83*
Watkins, Loomis Agency Inc. - New York, NY - *LitMarPl 84*
Watkins Patriot - Watkins, MN - *BaconPubCkNews 84; Ed&PubIntYB 82*
Watkinsville Oconee Enterprise - Watkinsville, GA - *BaconPubCkNews 84*
WATL-TV - Atlanta, GA - *BrCabYB 84; DirUSTelSta 83; TelAl 83, 84; Tel&CabFB 84S; TV&RadDir 84*
Watland Inc. - Blue Island, IL - *AvMarPl 83*
WATM - Atmore, AL - *BrCabYB 84; TV&RadDir 84*
WATN - Watertown, NY - *BrCabYB 84; TV&RadDir 84*
Watner, Carl - Baltimore, MD - *MicroMarPl 82-83*
WATO - Oak Ridge, TN - *BrCabYB 84; NatRadPubDir Summer 83, Spring 84; TV&RadDir 84*
Watonga Republican - Watonga, OK - *BaconPubCkNews 84; Ed&PubIntYB 82; NewsDir 84*
Watonwan County Shoppers Guide - St. James, MN - *AyerDirPub 83*
WATP - Marion, SC - *BrCabYB 84; TV&RadDir 84*
WATP-FM - Marion, SC - *BrCabYB 84; TV&RadDir 84*
WATR - Waterbury, CT - *BrCabYB 84; NatRadPubDir Summer 83, Spring 84; TV&RadDir 84*
WATR-TV - Waterbury, CT - *LitMarPl 83; TelAl 83; TV&RadDir 84*
Watrous Manitou, The - Watrous, SK, Canada - *Ed&PubIntYB 82*
WATS - Sayre, PA - *BrCabYB 84; TV&RadDir 84*
WATS Room, The - Englewood Cliffs, NJ - *IntDirMarRes 83*
Watseka Iroquois County Daily Times Republic [of Twin States Publishing Inc.] - Watseka, IL - *NewsDir 84*
Watson Academic Publications Inc., Neale - New York, NY - *LitMarPl 83*
Watson Advertising Inc., Harry - Portland, OR - *StaDirAdAg 2-84*
Watson, Aldren A. - Brattleboro, VT - *LitMarPl 83, 84; MagIndMarPl 82-83*
Watson & Dwyer Publishing Ltd. - Winnipeg, MB, Canada - *BoPubDir 4, 5*
Watson & Staff, W. R. - Berkeley, CA - *MagIndMarPl 82-83*
Watson Communications Co. - Lake Wildwood, GA - *BrCabYB 84; Tel&CabFB 84C*
Watson-Guptill Book Clubs [Div. of Billboard Publications Inc.] - New York, NY - *LitMarPl 83, 84*
Watson-Guptill Publications [Div. of Billboard Publications Inc.] - New York, NY - *LitMarPl 83, 84; WritMar 84*
Watson-Manning Inc. - Stratford, CT - *StaDirAdAg 2-84*
Watson Publishing, Ashley - *See* Starfox Publishing
Watson Publishing International - Canton, MA - *LitMarPl 84*
Watson, Robert - Centerville, GA - *Tel&CabFB 84C p.1711*
Watson/Whitlock - Denver, CO - *LitMag&SmPr 83-84*
Watson Witness, The - Watson, SK, Canada - *AyerDirPub 83; Ed&PubIntYB 82*
Watsontown CATV - Watsontown, PA - *BrCabYB 84; Tel&CabFB 84C*
Watsonville Register-Pajaronian [of Watsonville Newspapers Inc.] - Watsonville, CA - *BaconPubCkNews 84; NewsDir 84*
Watsonville Register-Pajaronian & Sun - Watsonville, CA - *LitMarPl 83*

WATT - Cadillac, MI - *BrCabYB 84; TV&RadDir 84*
Watt Advertising Inc. - Bettendorf, IA - *StaDirAdAg 2-84*
Watt International KK - Tokyo, Japan - *IntDirMarRes 83*
Watt Publishing Co. - Mt. Morris, IL - *MagIndMarPl 82-83*
WATT Works Inc. - Willow, NY - *BillIntBG 83-84*
Wattenmaker Advertising - Cleveland, OH - *DirMarMP 83; StaDirAdAg 2-84*
Watters/Rick Wilson Photography, Gary A. - Houston, TX - *MagIndMarPl 82-83*
Wattles Publications, Gordon - Orange, CA - *BoPubDir 4 Sup, 5*
Watts & Associates Ltd., R. J. - West Vancouver, BC, Canada - *BoPubDir 4, 5*
Watts Enterprises - Albuquerque, NM - *BoPubDir 4, 5*
Watts Inc., Franklin [Subs. of Grolier Inc.] - New York, NY - *DirMarMP 83; LitMarPl 83, 84*
Watts, Lamb, Kenyon & Herrick Inc. [Div. of PR Associates Inc.] - Cleveland, OH - *DirPRFirms 83; StaDirAdAg 2-84*
Watts Music, Wayne - Baltimore, MD - *BillIntBG 83-84*
Watts-Silverstein - Seattle, WA - *ArtMar 84; AvMarPl 83*
Watts Star Review - Los Angeles, CA - *AyerDirPub 83; Ed&PubIntYB 82*
Watts Times - Los Angeles, CA - *Ed&PubIntYB 82*
WATU-TV - Augusta, GA - *TelAl 83*
WATV - Birmingham, AL - *BrCabYB 84; NatRadPubDir Summer 83, Spring 84; TV&RadDir 84*
WATW - Ashland, WI - *BrCabYB 84; TV&RadDir 84*
WATW-FM - Ashland, WI - *BrCabYB 84; TV&RadDir 84*
WATX-TV - Arecibo, PR - *BrCabYB 84; Tel&CabFB 84S*
WATZ - Alpena, MI - *BrCabYB 84; TV&RadDir 84*
WATZ-FM - Alpena, MI - *BrCabYB 84; TV&RadDir 84*
WAUB - Auburn, NY - *BrCabYB 84; TV&RadDir 84*
Waubay Clipper - Waubay, SD - *Ed&PubIntYB 82*
WAUC - Wauchula, FL - *BrCabYB 84; TV&RadDir 84*
Wauchula Herald-Advocate - Wauchula, FL - *BaconPubCkNews 84; NewsDir 84*
Wauconda Herald - Arlington Heights, IL - *Ed&PubIntYB 82*
Wauconda Herald [of Paddock Publications] - Mundelein, IL - *NewsDir 84*
Wauconda Herald - *See* Paddock Publications
Wauconda Leader [of Lakeland Publishers Inc.] - Grayslake, IL - *NewsDir 84*
Wauconda Leader - Wauconda, IL - *AyerDirPub 83*
Wauconda Leader - *See* Lakeland Publishers Inc.
Wauconda Leader, The - Wauconda Lake, IL - *Ed&PubIntYB 82*
WAUD - Auburn, AL - *BrCabYB 84; NatRadPubDir Summer 83, Spring 84; TV&RadDir 84*
WAUG - Louisville, KY - *TV&RadDir 84*
WAUK - Milwaukee, WI - *NatRadPubDir Summer 83 p.267, Spring 84 p.269*
WAUK - Waukesha, WI - *BrCabYB 84; TV&RadDir 84*
Waukegan Herald [of Mundelein Paddock Circle Newspapers Inc.] - Mundelein, IL - *NewsDir 84*
Waukegan MDS - New York, NY - *Tel&CabFB 84C*
Waukesha Freeman [of The Des Moines Register & Tribune Co.] - Waukesha, WI - *BaconPubCkNews 84; Ed&PubIntYB 82; NewsDir 84*
Waukesha Post [of West Allis Suburban Milwaukee Post Newspapers] - Milwaukee, WI - *NewsDir 84*
Waukomis Oklahoma Hornet - Waukomis, OK - *BaconPubCkNews 84; Ed&PubIntYB 82*
Waukon & Mississippi Press - Des Moines, IA - *BoPubDir 5*
Waukon Cablevision - Waukon, IA - *BrCabYB 84; Tel&CabFB 84C*
Waukon Democrat - Waukon, IA - *Ed&PubIntYB 82; NewsDir 84*
Waukon Democrat - *See* Waukon Newspapers Inc.
Waukon Newspapers Inc. - Waukon, IA - *BaconPubCkNews 84*
Waukon Republican-Standard - Waukon, IA - *Ed&PubIntYB 82*
Waukon Republican-Standard - *See* Waukon Newspapers Inc.
Waumbek Books - Ashland, NH - *BoPubDir 4, 5*
WAUN - Kewaunee, WI - *BrCabYB 84*
WAUN-FM - Kewaunee, WI - *TV&RadDir 84*
Waunakee Telephone Co. [Aff. of Telephone & Data Systems Inc.] - Waunakee, WI - *TelDir&BG 83-84*
Waunakee Tribune - Waunakee, WI - *BaconPubCkNews 84; Ed&PubIntYB 82*
Wauneta Breeze - Wauneta, NE - *BaconPubCkNews 84; Ed&PubIntYB 82*
Wauneta Telephone Co. [Aff. of Benkelman Telephone Co. Inc.] - Benkelman, NE - *TelDir&BG 83-84*
WAUP-FM - Akron, OH - *BrCabYB 84; NatRadPubDir Summer 83, Spring 84; TV&RadDir 84*
Waupaca County Post - Waupaca, WI - *AyerDirPub 83; BaconPubCkNews 84; Ed&PubIntYB 82*
Waupaca Wisconsin State Farmer - Waupaca, WI - *BaconPubCkNews 84*
Waupun Leader-News - Waupun, WI - *BaconPubCkNews 84; NewsDir 84*
WAUR-FM - Aurora, IL - *BrCabYB 84; NatRadPubDir Summer 83, Spring 84; TV&RadDir 84*
Waurika News-Democrat - Waurika, OK - *BaconPubCkNews 84; Ed&PubIntYB 82*
WAUS-FM - South Bend, IN - *BrCabYB 84*
WAUS-FM - Andrews, MI - *TV&RadDir 84*
WAUS-FM - Berrien Springs, MI - *NatRadPubDir Summer 83, Spring 84*
Wausa Gazette - Wausa, NE - *BaconPubCkNews 84; Ed&PubIntYB 82*
Wausau Daily Herald - Wausau, WI - *BaconPubCkNews 84; NewsDir 84*
Wausau Paper Mills Co. - Brokaw, WI - *LitMarPl 83, 84*
Wausau Valley View - Waupaca, WI - *AyerDirPub 83*
Wausaukee Cablevision Inc. - Wausaukee, WI - *Tel&CabFB 84C*
Wauseon Republican [of Wauseon Chief Publishing Co.] - Wauseon, OH - *NewsDir 84*
Waushara Argus - Wautoma, WI - *AyerDirPub 83; Ed&PubIntYB 82*
Wautoma Waushara Argus - Wautoma, WI - *BaconPubCkNews 84; NewsDir 84*
Wauwatosa News-Times - Wauwatosa, WI - *AyerDirPub 83; Ed&PubIntYB 82*
Wauwatosa News-Times - *See* Community Newspapers Inc.
Wauwatosa Post [of West Allis Suburban Milwaukee Post Newspapers] - Milwaukee, WI - *NewsDir 84*
WAV Publications - Magill, Australia - *LitMag&SmPr 83-84*
WAVA-FM - Washington, DC - *NatRadPubDir Summer 83 p.53, Spring 84 p.53*
WAVA-FM - Arlington, VA - *BrCabYB 84; TV&RadDir 84*
WAVC - Duluth, MN - *BrCabYB 84*
Wave - Port Lavaca, TX - *AyerDirPub 83*
Wave Maker Music Inc. - *See* Lipservices
Wave Newspapers [of Central News-Wave Publications] - Los Angeles, CA - *NewsDir 84*
Wave of Long Island, The - Rockaway Beach, NY - *Ed&PubIntYB 82*
Wave Publishing Co. - Heber City, UT - *BaconPubCkNews 84*
Wave Records Inc. - New York, NY - *BillIntBG 83-84*
WAVE-TV - Louisville, KY - *BrCabYB 84; DirUSTelSta 83; LitMarPl 83, 84; TelAl 83, 84; Tel&CabFB 84S; TV&RadDir 84*
Waveland Press Inc. - Prospect Heights, IL - *LitMarPl 83, 84*
Waverly Bremer County Independent [of Woodward Communications Inc.] - Waverly, IA - *NewsDir 84*
Waverly Bremer County Independent - *See* Bremer County Independent Publishers
Waverly Cable Television Inc. - Waverly, TN - *BrCabYB 84; Tel&CabFB 84C*
Waverly Democrat [of Woodward Communications Inc.] - Waverly, IA - *Ed&PubIntYB 82; NewsDir 84*
Waverly Democrat - *See* Bremer County Independent Publishers
Waverly Gazette - Waverly, KS - *Ed&PubIntYB 82*
Waverly Hall Telephone Co. Inc. - Waverly Hall, GA - *TelDir&BG 83-84*
Waverly Journal - Waverly, IL - *BaconPubCkNews 84; Ed&PubIntYB 82*
Waverly News - Waverly, NE - *BaconPubCkNews 84*
Waverly News-Democrat - Waverly, TN - *BaconPubCkNews 84*
Waverly News-Watchman - Waverly, OH - *Ed&PubIntYB 82*
Waverly News Watchman - *See* Jackson Publishing Co.
Waverly Press Inc. - Baltimore, MD - *LitMarPl 83, 84; MagIndMarPl 82-83*
Waverly Times - Waverly, MO - *BaconPubCkNews 84; Ed&PubIntYB 82*
Waves - Thornhill, ON, Canada - *LitMag&SmPr 83-84; WritMar 84*
Waves Press - Richmond, VA - *BoPubDir 4, 5*

Wavetek - San Diego, CA - *HomeVid&CabYB 82-83*
Wavetek Indiana Inc. - Beech Grove, IN - *CabTVFinDB 83*
WAVG - Louisville, KY - *BrCabYB 84; NatRadPubDir Summer 83, Spring 84*
WAVI - Dayton, OH - *BrCabYB 84; NatRadPubDir Summer 83, Spring 84; TV&RadDir 84*
WAVL - Apollo, PA - *BrCabYB 84; TV&RadDir 84*
WAVM-FM - Maynard, MA - *BrCabYB 84; NatRadPubDir Summer 83, Spring 84; TV&RadDir 84*
WAVO - Decatur, GA - *BrCabYB 84; TV&RadDir 84*
WAVR-FM - Waverly, NY - *BrCabYB 84*
WAVR-FM - Sayre, PA - *TV&RadDir 84*
WAVS - Davie, FL - *BrCabYB 84*
WAVS - Ft. Lauderdale, FL - *NatRadPubDir Summer 83; TV&RadDir 84*
WAVT-FM - Pottsville, PA - *BrCabYB 84; TV&RadDir 84*
WAVU - Albertville, AL - *BrCabYB 84; TV&RadDir 84*
WAVV-FM - Vevay, IN - *BrCabYB 84; TV&RadDir 84*
WAVW-FM - Ft. Pierce, FL - *TV&RadDir 84*
WAVW-FM - Vero Beach, FL - *BrCabYB 84*
WAVY-TV - Portsmouth, VA - *BrCabYB 84; DirUSTelSta 83; LitMarPl 83, 84; TelAl 83, 84; Tel&CabFB 84S; TV&RadDir 84*
WAVZ - New Haven, CT - *BrCabYB 84; NatRadPubDir Summer 83 p.47, Spring 84 p.47; TV&RadDir 84*
WAWA - Milwaukee, WI - *NatRadPubDir Summer 83 p.267, Spring 84 p.269*
WAWA - West Allis, WI - *BrCabYB 84*
WAWK - Kendallville, IN - *BrCabYB 84; TV&RadDir 84*
WAWK-FM - Kendallville, IN - *BrCabYB 84; TV&RadDir 84*
WAWS-TV - Jacksonville, FL - *BrCabYB 84; DirUSTelSta 83; TelAl 83, 84; Tel&CabFB 84S*
WAWZ - Zarephath, NJ - *BrCabYB 84; TV&RadDir 84*
WAWZ-FM - Zarephath, NJ - *BrCabYB 84; TV&RadDir 84*
Wax & Associates Inc., Morton Dennis - New York, NY - *ArtMar 84; DirPRFirms 83; LitMarPl 83, 84; MagIndMarPl 82-83; TelAl 83, 84*
WAXA - Anderson, SC - *BrCabYB 84; Tel&CabFB 84S*
Waxahachie Daily Light [of Woodson Newspapers Inc.] - Waxahachie, TX - *BaconPubCkNews 84; Ed&PubIntYB 82; NewsDir 84*
WAXC - Wapakoneta, OH - *BrCabYB 84*
WAXE - Vero Beach, FL - *BrCabYB 84; TV&RadDir 84*
WAXI-FM - Rockville, IN - *BrCabYB 84; TV&RadDir 84*
WAXL - Lancaster, WI - *BrCabYB 84*
WAXO - Lewisburg, TN - *BrCabYB 84; TV&RadDir 84*
WAXT-FM - Alexandria, IN - *BrCabYB 84; TV&RadDir 84*
WAXU - Lexington, KY - *NatRadPubDir Summer 83, Spring 84*
WAXU-FM - Georgetown, KY - *BrCabYB 84*
WAXU-FM - Lexington, KY - *NatRadPubDir Summer 83, Spring 84; TV&RadDir 84*
Waxwing Productions - Toronto, ON, Canada - *BoPubDir 4, 5*
WAXX-FM - Eau Claire, WI - *BrCabYB 84; TV&RadDir 84*
WAXY-FM - Ft. Lauderdale, FL - *BrCabYB 84; TV&RadDir 84*
WAXY-FM - Miami/Miami Beach, FL - *NatRadPubDir Summer 83 p.60, Spring 84 p.60*
Way & Co., Robert L. - New York, NY - *DirPRFirms 83*
Way with Words - Terre Haute, IN - *LitMarPl 83; MagIndMarPl 82-83*
WAYB - Waynesboro, VA - *BrCabYB 84; TV&RadDir 84*
WAYC - Bedford, PA - *BrCabYB 84; TV&RadDir 84*
Waycross Cable Co. - Waycross, GA - *BrCabYB 84; Tel&CabFB 84C*
Waycross Journal-Herald - Waycross, GA - *BaconPubCkNews 84; Ed&PubIntYB 82; NewsDir 84*
WAYD - Ozark, AL - *BrCabYB 84; TV&RadDir 84*
WAYE - Baltimore, MD - *BrCabYB 84; NatRadPubDir Summer 83, Spring 84; TV&RadDir 84*
Wayfarer Publications - Los Angeles, CA - *LitMag&SmPr 83-84*
WAYL-FM - Minneapolis, MN - *BrCabYB 84; NatRadPubDir Summer 83 p.135, Spring 84 p.134*
Wayland Globe - Wayland, MI - *BaconPubCkNews 84; Ed&PubIntYB 82*
Wayland News - Wayland, IA - *BaconPubCkNews 84*
Wayland-Weston Town Crier - Sudbury, MA - *NewsDir 84*
Wayland-Weston Town Crier - Wayland, MA - *AyerDirPub 83; Ed&PubIntYB 82*
Wayland-Weston Town Crier - *See* Town Crier Publications
WAYN - Rockingham, NC - *BrCabYB 84; TV&RadDir 84*
Wayne, Allen - New York, NY - *LitMarPl 83*
Wayne Cable Vision Inc. [of Maclean Hunter Cable TV Ltd.] - Allen Park, MI - *Tel&CabFB 84C*
Wayne Cablevision - Taylor, MI - *BrCabYB 84; LitMarPl 84*
Wayne Cablevision [of Apollo Communications Inc.] - Wayne, NE - *BrCabYB 84; Tel&CabFB 84C*
Wayne City Cablevision [of Omni Cable TV Corp.] - Wayne City, IL - *BrCabYB 84; Tel&CabFB 84C*
Wayne Computer Resources - Goldsboro, NC - *ADAPSOMemDir 83-84*
Wayne County Cablevision Inc. [of Cablevision Industries Inc.] - Newark, NY - *BrCabYB 84*
Wayne County Journal-Banner - Piedmont, MO - *AyerDirPub 83*
Wayne County Journal-Banner - Wayne County, MO - *Ed&PubIntYB 82*
Wayne County Mail - Ontario, NY - *AyerDirPub 83*
Wayne County Mail [of Empire State Weeklies] - Webster, NY - *NewsDir 84*
Wayne County News - Waynesboro, MS - *AyerDirPub 83; Ed&PubIntYB 82; NewsDir 84*
Wayne County News - Waynesboro, TN - *AyerDirPub 83; Ed&PubIntYB 82*
Wayne County News - Wayne, WV - *BaconPubCkNews 84; Ed&PubIntYB 82; NewsDir 84*
Wayne County Outlook - Monticello, KY - *AyerDirPub 83; Ed&PubIntYB 82*
Wayne County Press - Fairfield, IL - *AyerDirPub 83; Ed&PubIntYB 82*
Wayne County Star - Lyons, NY - *AyerDirPub 83; Ed&PubIntYB 82*
Wayne Eagle - Wayne, MI - *AyerDirPub 83; Ed&PubIntYB 82; NewsDir 84*
Wayne Eagle - *See* Associated Newspapers Inc.
Wayne Engineer - Detroit, MI - *BaconPubCkMag 84; MagDir 84*
Wayne Exton Suburban Advertiser - *See* Suburban Publications Inc.
Wayne Herald - Wayne, NE - *AyerDirPub 83; BaconPubCkNews 84; Ed&PubIntYB 82; NewsDir 84*
Wayne Independent - Honesdale, PA - *AyerDirPub 83; NewsDir 84*
Wayne Independent, The - Wayne County, PA - *Ed&PubIntYB 82*
Wayne State University (Center for Black Studies) - Detroit, MI - *BoPubDir 4 Sup, 5*
Wayne State University (Center for Instructional Technology) - Detroit, MI - *AvMarPl 83*
Wayne State University (Computing Services Center) - Detroit, MI - *DataDirOnSer 84*
Wayne State University Press - Detroit, MI - *LitMarPl 83, 84; WritMar 84*
Wayne Suburban & Wayne Times - Wayne, PA - *NewsDir 84*
Wayne Suburban Times - *See* Suburban Publications Inc.
Wayne Today - *See* Today Newspapers
Wayne Tri-State Shoppers Guide News - Wayne, WV - *NewsDir 84*
Waynesboro Cable TV [of The Essex Group] - Waynesboro, TN - *Tel&CabFB 84C*
Waynesboro News-Virginian - Waynesboro, VA - *BaconPubCkNews 84; NewsDir 84*
Waynesboro Record-Herald - Waynesboro, PA - *BaconPubCkNews 84; NewsDir 84*
Waynesboro True Citizen - Waynesboro, GA - *BaconPubCkNews 84; NewsDir 84*
Waynesboro Wayne County News - Waynesboro, MS - *BaconPubCkNews 84*
Waynesboro Wayne County News - Waynesboro, TN - *BaconPubCkNews 84; NewsDir 84*
Waynesburg Democrat Messenger - Waynesburg, PA - *BaconPubCkNews 84*
Waynesburg Republican - Waynesburg, PA - *BaconPubCkNews 84; Ed&PubIntYB 82*
Waynesfield Journal - Waynesfield, OH - *Ed&PubIntYB 82*
Waynesfield Journal - *See* Daily News Printing Co.
Waynesville Ft. Gateway Guide [of Sowers Publications] - Waynesville, MO - *NewsDir 84*

Waynesville Mountaineer - Waynesville, NC - *BaconPubCkNews 84*
Waynesville Pulaski County Democrat - Waynesville, MO - *NewsDir 84*
Waynetown Cablevision [of Quality CATV Inc.] - Sheridan, IN - *BrCabYB 84*
Waynoka Community TV - Waynoka, OK - *BrCabYB 84; Tel&CabFB 84C*
Waynoka Woods County Enterprise & News - Waynoka, OK - *BaconPubCkNews 84*
WAYR - Orange Park, FL - *BrCabYB 84; TV&RadDir 84*
WAYS - Charlotte, NC - *BrCabYB 84; NatRadPubDir Summer 83, Spring 84; TV&RadDir 84*
Ways & Means Ltd. - Toronto, ON, Canada - *BoPubDir 4 Sup, 5*
Wayside Press- Progressive Graphics Co. - Mendota, IL - *MagIndMarPl 82-83*
Wayside Telephone Co., The - Greenleaf, WI - *TelDir&BG 83-84*
WAYT - Wabash, IN - *BrCabYB 84; TV&RadDir 84*
WAYU-FM - Lewiston, ME - *BrCabYB 84; TV&RadDir 84*
WAYU-FM - Portland, ME - *NatRadPubDir Summer 83 p.113, Spring 84 p.113*
Wayuga Community Newspapers Inc. - Red Creek, NY - *BaconPubCkNews 84*
WAYV - Atlantic City, NJ - *BrCabYB 84; NatRadPubDir Summer 83*
WAYV-FM - Atlantic City, NJ - *NatRadPubDir Spring 84; TV&RadDir 84*
WAYW - Worcester, MA - *BrCabYB 84*
Wayward Wind - Boulder, CO - *LitMag&SmPr 83-84*
WAYX - Waycross, GA - *BrCabYB 84; TV&RadDir 84*
WAYY - Chippewa Falls, WI - *BrCabYB 84*
WAYY - Eau Claire, WI - *TV&RadDir 84*
WAYZ - Waynesboro, PA - *BrCabYB 84; TV&RadDir 84*
WAYZ-FM - Waynesboro, PA - *BrCabYB 84; TV&RadDir 84*
WAZA - Bainbridge, GA - *BrCabYB 84; TV&RadDir 84*
WAZE - Dawson, GA - *BrCabYB 84*
WAZF - Yazoo City, MS - *BrCabYB 84; TV&RadDir 84*
WAZI-FM - Morristown, TN - *BrCabYB 84; TV&RadDir 84*
WAZL - Hazleton, PA - *BrCabYB 84; TV&RadDir 84*
WAZL - Scranton, PA - *NatRadPubDir Summer 83, Spring 84 p.216*
WAZS - Summerville, SC - *BrCabYB 84; TV&RadDir 84*
WAZU-FM - Springfield, OH - *BrCabYB 84; TV&RadDir 84*
WAZX-FM - Georgetown, SC - *BrCabYB 84; TV&RadDir 84*
WAZY-FM - Lafayette, IN - *BrCabYB 84; NatRadPubDir Summer 83, Spring 84; TV&RadDir 84*
WAZZ-FM - New Bern, NC - *BrCabYB 84; TV&RadDir 84*
WB Design & Development Inc. - St. Louis, MO - *LitMarPl 83, 84*
WB Systems - Westerly, RI - *MicrocomMPl 84; MicrocomSwDir 1*
WBAA - West Lafayette, IN - *BrCabYB 84; NatRadPubDir Summer 83, Spring 84; TV&RadDir 84*
WBAB-FM - Babylon, NY - *BrCabYB 84; TV&RadDir 84*
WBAB-FM - Suffolk County, Long Island, NY - *NatRadPubDir Summer 83 p.177, Spring 84 p.175*
WBAC - Cleveland, TN - *BrCabYB 84; TV&RadDir 84*
WBAD-FM - Greenville, MS - *TV&RadDir 84*
WBAD-FM - Leland, MS - *BrCabYB 84*
WBAF - Barnesville, GA - *BrCabYB 84; TV&RadDir 84*
WBAG-FM - Burlington, NC - *BrCabYB 84; TV&RadDir 84*
WBAI-FM - New York, NY - *BrCabYB 84; LitMarPl 83, 84; NatRadPubDir Summer 83, Spring 84; TV&RadDir 84*
WBAK-TV - Terre Haute, IN - *BrCabYB 84; DirUSTelSta 83; TelAl 83, 84; Tel&CabFB 84S; TV&RadDir 84*
WBAL - Baltimore, MD - *BrCabYB 84; NatRadPubDir Summer 83, Spring 84; TV&RadDir 84*
WBAL-TV - Baltimore, MD - *BrCabYB 84; DirUSTelSta 83; LitMarPl 83, 84; TelAl 83, 84; Tel&CabFB 84S; TV&RadDir 84*
WBAM - Montgomery, AL - *BrCabYB 84; NatRadPubDir Summer 83, Spring 84; TV&RadDir 84*
WBAM-FM - Montgomery, AL - *BrCabYB 84; NatRadPubDir Summer 83, Spring 84; TV&RadDir 84*
WBAP - Dallas/Ft. Worth, TX - *NatRadPubDir Summer 83, Spring 84 p.239*
WBAP - Ft. Worth, TX - *BrCabYB 84; TV&RadDir 84*
WBAQ-FM - Greenville, MS - *BrCabYB 84; NatRadPubDir Summer 83, Spring 84; TV&RadDir 84*
WBAR - Bartow, FL - *BrCabYB 84; TV&RadDir 84*
WBAS - Crescent City, FL - *BrCabYB 84*
WBAT - Marion, IN - *BrCabYB 84; NatRadPubDir Summer 83, Spring 84; TV&RadDir 84*
WBAU-FM - Garden City, NY - *BrCabYB 84; TV&RadDir 84*
WBAU-FM - New York, NY - *NatRadPubDir Summer 83 p.302, Spring 84 p.303*
WBAW - Barnwell, SC - *BrCabYB 84; TV&RadDir 84*
WBAW-FM - Barnwell, SC - *BrCabYB 84; TV&RadDir 84*
WBAX - Scranton/Wilkes-Barre/Hazelton/Avoca, PA - *NatRadPubDir Summer 83, Spring 84 p.216*
WBAX - Wilkes-Barre, PA - *BrCabYB 84; TV&RadDir 84*
WBAY-TV - Green Bay, WI - *BrCabYB 84; DirUSTelSta 83; TelAl 83, 84; Tel&CabFB 84S; TV&RadDir 84*
WBAZ - Southhold, NY - *BrCabYB 84*
WBBA - Pittsfield, IL - *BrCabYB 84; TV&RadDir 84*
WBBA-FM - Pittsfield, IL - *BrCabYB 84; TV&RadDir 84*
WBBB - Burlington, NC - *BrCabYB 84; TV&RadDir 84*
WBBC-FM - Blackstone, VA - *BrCabYB 84; TV&RadDir 84*
WBBE - Georgetown, KY - *BrCabYB 84*
WBBE - Lexington, KY - *TV&RadDir 84*
WBBF - Rochester, NY - *BrCabYB 84; NatRadPubDir Summer 83, Spring 84; TV&RadDir 84*
WBBG - Cleveland, OH - *BrCabYB 84; NatRadPubDir Summer 83, Spring 84; TV&RadDir 84*
WBBH-TV - Ft. Myers, FL - *BrCabYB 84; DirUSTelSta 83; TelAl 83, 84; Tel&CabFB 84S; TV&RadDir 84*
WBBI - Abingdon, VA - *BrCabYB 84; TV&RadDir 84*
WBBJ-TV - Jackson, TN - *DirUSTelSta 83; TelAl 83, 84; Tel&CabFB 84S; TV&RadDir 84*
WBBK - Blakely, GA - *BrCabYB 84; TV&RadDir 84*
WBBL - Richmond, VA - *BrCabYB 84; NatRadPubDir Summer 83, Spring 84; TV&RadDir 84*
WBBM - Chicago, IL - *BrCabYB 84; NatRadPubDir Summer 83, Spring 84; TV&RadDir 84*
WBBM-FM - Chicago, IL - *BrCabYB 84; NatRadPubDir Summer 83, Spring 84; TV&RadDir 84*
WBBM-TV - Chicago, IL - *BrCabYB 84; DirUSTelSta 83; LitMarPl 83, 84; TelAl 83, 84; Tel&CabFB 84S; TV&RadDir 84*
WBBO - Forest City, NC - *BrCabYB 84; TV&RadDir 84*
WBBO-FM - Forest City, NC - *BrCabYB 84*
WBBQ - Augusta, GA - *BrCabYB 84; NatRadPubDir Summer 83, Spring 84; TV&RadDir 84*
WBBQ-FM - Augusta, GA - *BrCabYB 84; NatRadPubDir Summer 83, Spring 84; TV&RadDir 84*
WBBR - Travelers Rest, SC - *BrCabYB 84; TV&RadDir 84*
WBBS-TV - Chicago, IL - *DirUSTelSta 83; TV&RadDir 84*
WBBS-TV - West Chicago, IL - *BrCabYB 84; Tel&CabFB 84S*
WBBT - Lyons, GA - *BrCabYB 84; TV&RadDir 84*
WBBW - Youngstown, OH - *BrCabYB 84; NatRadPubDir Summer 83, Spring 84; TV&RadDir 84*
WBBX - Portsmouth, NH - *NatRadPubDir Summer 83, Spring 84; TV&RadDir 84*
WBBX - Portsmouth, NM - *BrCabYB 84*
WBBY-FM - Sunbury, OH - *TV&RadDir 84*
WBBY-FM - Westerville, OH - *BrCabYB 84*
WBBZ - Ponca City, OK - *BrCabYB 84; TV&RadDir 84*
WBCA - Bay Minette, AL - *BrCabYB 84; TV&RadDir 84*
WBCB - Levittown, PA - *BrCabYB 84; NatRadPubDir Summer 83, Spring 84; TV&RadDir 84*
WBCE - Wicklife, KY - *BrCabYB 84*
WBCF - Florence, AL - *BrCabYB 84; TV&RadDir 84*
WBCG - Murfreesboro, NC - *BrCabYB 84*
WBCH - Hastings, MI - *BrCabYB 84; TV&RadDir 84*
WBCH-FM - Hastings, MI - *BrCabYB 84; TV&RadDir 84*
WBCK - Battle Creek, MI - *BrCabYB 84; NatRadPubDir Summer 83, Spring 84; TV&RadDir 84*
WBCL-FM - Ft. Wayne, IN - *BrCabYB 84; TV&RadDir 84*
WBCM - Bay City, MI - *BrCabYB 84; TV&RadDir 84*
WBCN-FM - Boston, MA - *BrCabYB 84; LitMarPl 83, 84; NatRadPubDir Summer 83, Spring 84; TV&RadDir 84*
WBCO - Bucyrus, OH - *BrCabYB 84; TV&RadDir 84*
WBCO-FM - Bucyrus, OH - *BrCabYB 84*
WBCQ-FM - Bucyrus, OH - *TV&RadDir 84*

WBCR-FM - Beloit, WI - *BrCabYB 84; NatRadPubDir Summer 83, Spring 84; TV&RadDir 84*
WBCS - Milwaukee, WI - *BrCabYB 84; NatRadPubDir Summer 83; TV&RadDir 84*
WBCS-FM - Milwaukee, WI - *NatRadPubDir Summer 83, Spring 84; TV&RadDir 84*
WBCT-FM - Columbia, SC - *NatRadPubDir Summer 83, Spring 84*
WBCT-TV - Bridgeport, CT - *BrCabYB 84; Tel&CabFB 84S*
WBCU - Union, SC - *BrCabYB 84; TV&RadDir 84*
WBCV - Bristol, TN - *BrCabYB 84; TV&RadDir 84*
WBCW - Jeannette, PA - *BrCabYB 84; TV&RadDir 84*
WBCY-FM - Charlotte, NC - *BrCabYB 84; NatRadPubDir Summer 83, Spring 84; TV&RadDir 84*
WBDC-FM - Huntingburg, IN - *BrCabYB 84; TV&RadDir 84*
WBDG-FM - Indianapolis, IN - *BrCabYB 84; TV&RadDir 84*
WBDJ-FM - Brazil, IN - *BrCabYB 84; TV&RadDir 84*
WBDN - Escanaba, MI - *BrCabYB 84; TV&RadDir 84*
WBDX - White Bluff, TN - *BrCabYB 84*
WBDY - Bluefield, VA - *BrCabYB 84; TV&RadDir 84*
WBDY-FM - Bluefield, VA - *BrCabYB 84; TV&RadDir 84*
WBEA-FM - Elyria, OH - *BrCabYB 84*
WBEC - Pittsfield, MA - *BrCabYB 84; NatRadPubDir Summer 83, Spring 84; TV&RadDir 84*
WBEC-FM - Pittsfield, MA - *BrCabYB 84; NatRadPubDir Summer 83, Spring 84; TV&RadDir 84*
WBEE - Chicago, IL - *NatRadPubDir Summer 83, Spring 84; TV&RadDir 84*
WBEE - Harvey, IL - *BrCabYB 84*
WBEJ - Elizabethton, TN - *BrCabYB 84; TV&RadDir 84*
WBEK-FM - Cherry Hill, NJ - *BrCabYB 84; TV&RadDir 84*
WBEL - Beloit, WI - *BrCabYB 84; TV&RadDir 84*
WBEN - Buffalo, NY - *BrCabYB 84; NatRadPubDir Summer 83, Spring 84; TV&RadDir 84*
WBEN-FM - Buffalo, NY - *BrCabYB 84; NatRadPubDir Summer 83, Spring 84; TV&RadDir 84*
WBER - Moncks Corner, SC - *BrCabYB 84; TV&RadDir 84*
WBES-FM - Charleston, WV - *BrCabYB 84; NatRadPubDir Summer 83, Spring 84; TV&RadDir 84*
WBET - Brockton, MA - *BrCabYB 84; TV&RadDir 84*
WBEU - Beaufort, SC - *BrCabYB 84; TV&RadDir 84*
WBEV - Beaver Dam, WI - *BrCabYB 84; TV&RadDir 84*
WBEX - Chillicothe, OH - *BrCabYB 84; TV&RadDir 84*
WBEX-FM - Chillicothe, OH - *TV&RadDir 84*
WBEY - Grasonville, MD - *BrCabYB 84*
WBEZ-FM - Chicago, IL - *BrCabYB 84; LitMarPl 83, 84; TV&RadDir 84*
WBFC - Stanton, KY - *BrCabYB 84; TV&RadDir 84*
WBFD - Bedford, PA - *BrCabYB 84; TV&RadDir 84*
WBFF-TV - Baltimore, MD - *BrCabYB 84; DirUSTelSta 83; TelAl 83, 84; Tel&CabFB 84S; TV&RadDir 84*
WBFG - Effingham, IL - *BrCabYB 84*
WBFH-FM - Bloomfield Hills, MI - *BrCabYB 84; NatRadPubDir Summer 83, Spring 84; TV&RadDir 84*
WBFJ - Winston-Salem, NC - *BrCabYB 84; NatRadPubDir Summer 83, Spring 84; TV&RadDir 84*
WBFL - Bellows Falls, VT - *BrCabYB 84*
WBFM-FM - Seneca, SC - *BrCabYB 84; TV&RadDir 84*
WBFN - Quitman, MS - *BrCabYB 84; TV&RadDir 84*
WBFO-FM - Buffalo, NY - *BrCabYB 84; NatRadPubDir Summer 83, Spring 84; TV&RadDir 84*
WBFS-TV - Miami, FL - *BrCabYB 84; Tel&CabFB 84S*
WBG Inc. - McLean, VA - *ADAPSOMemDir 83-84*
WBGA - Brunswick, GA - *BrCabYB 84; NatRadPubDir Spring 84*
WBGB - Mt. Dorn, FL - *BrCabYB 84*
WBGC - Chipley, FL - *BrCabYB 84; TV&RadDir 84*
WBGD - Bricktown, NJ - *BrCabYB 84; TV&RadDir 84*
WBGD-FM - Bricktown, NJ - *NatRadPubDir Summer 83, Spring 84*
WBGH-TV - Allston, MA - *TV&RadDir 84*
WBGL - Champaign, IL - *BrCabYB 84*
WBGM-FM - Tallahassee, FL - *BrCabYB 84; NatRadPubDir Summer 83, Spring 84; TV&RadDir 84*
WBGN - Bowling Green, KY - *BrCabYB 84; NatRadPubDir Summer 83, Spring 84; TV&RadDir 84*
WBGO-FM - Newark, NJ - *BrCabYB 84; NatRadPubDir Summer 83, Spring 84; TV&RadDir 84*
WBGU-FM - Bowling Green, OH - *BrCabYB 84; NatRadPubDir Summer 83, Spring 84; TV&RadDir 84*
WBGU-TV - Bowling Green, OH - *Tel&CabFB 84S; TV&RadDir 84*
WBGU-TV - Lima, OH - *BrCabYB 84*
WBGW-FM - Bangor, ME - *BrCabYB 84; TV&RadDir 84*
WBGY - Tullahoma, TN - *BrCabYB 84; TV&RadDir 84*
WBGY-FM - Tullahoma, TN - *BrCabYB 84; TV&RadDir 84*
WBGY-TV - Tullahoma, TN - *BrCabYB 84; Tel&CabFB 84S*
WBHB - Fitzgerald, GA - *BrCabYB 84; TV&RadDir 84*
WBHC - Hampton, SC - *BrCabYB 84; TV&RadDir 84*
WBHF - Cartersville, GA - *BrCabYB 84; TV&RadDir 84*
WBHI-FM - Chicago, IL - *BrCabYB 84; TV&RadDir 84*
WBHM-FM - Birmingham, AL - *BrCabYB 84; NatRadPubDir Summer 83, Spring 84; TV&RadDir 84*
WBHN - Bryson City, NC - *BrCabYB 84; TV&RadDir 84*
WBHP - Huntsville, AL - *BrCabYB 84; NatRadPubDir Summer 83, Spring 84; TV&RadDir 84*
WBHR-FM - Bellaire, OH - *BrCabYB 84; NatRadPubDir Summer 83, Spring 84; TV&RadDir 84*
WBHS - Brunswick, ME - *BrCabYB 84*
WBHT - Brownsville, TN - *BrCabYB 84; TV&RadDir 84*
WBIA - Augusta, GA - *NatRadPubDir Summer 83, Spring 84; TV&RadDir 84*
WBIB - Centreville, AL - *BrCabYB 84; TV&RadDir 84*
WBIC - New Bern, NC - *TV&RadDir 84*
WBIF-FM - Bedford, IN - *BrCabYB 84; TV&RadDir 84*
WBIG - Greensboro, NC - *BrCabYB 84; NatRadPubDir Summer 83, Spring 84; TV&RadDir 84*
WBIL - Tuskegee, AL - *BrCabYB 84; TV&RadDir 84*
WBIL-FM - Tuskegee, AL - *BrCabYB 84; TV&RadDir 84*
WBIM-FM - Bridgewater, MA - *BrCabYB 84; NatRadPubDir Summer 83, Spring 84; TV&RadDir 84*
WBIN - Benton, TN - *BrCabYB 84; TV&RadDir 84*
WBIP - Booneville, MS - *BrCabYB 84; TV&RadDir 84*
WBIP-FM - Booneville, MS - *BrCabYB 84; TV&RadDir 84*
WBIQ - Birmingham, AL - *BrCabYB 84; Tel&CabFB 84S; TV&RadDir 84*
WBIQ-TV - Birmingham, AL - *TV&RadDir 84*
WBIR-TV - Knoxville, TN - *BrCabYB 84; DirUSTelSta 83; LitMarPl 83, 84; TelAl 83, 84; Tel&CabFB 84S; TV&RadDir 84*
WBIS - Bristol, CT - *BrCabYB 84; TV&RadDir 84*
WBIS - Hartford/New Britain, CT - *NatRadPubDir Summer 83 p.46, Spring 84 p.46*
WBIT - Adel, GA - *BrCabYB 84; TV&RadDir 84*
WBIW - Bedford, IN - *BrCabYB 84; TV&RadDir 84*
WBIX - Jacksonville, FL - *BrCabYB 84; NatRadPubDir Summer 83, Spring 84; TV&RadDir 84*
WBIZ-FM - Eau Claire, WI - *BrCabYB 84; NatRadPubDir Summer 83, Spring 84; TV&RadDir 84*
WBJA - Guayama, PR - *BrCabYB 84*
WBJB-FM - Lincroft, NJ - *BrCabYB 84; NatRadPubDir Summer 83, Spring 84; TV&RadDir 84*
WBJC-FM - Baltimore, MD - *BrCabYB 84; NatRadPubDir Summer 83, Spring 84; TV&RadDir 84*
WBJW-FM - Orlando, FL - *BrCabYB 84; NatRadPubDir Summer 83, Spring 84 p.63; TV&RadDir 84*
WBJX - Goose Creek, SC - *BrCabYB 84*
WBJZ-FM - Olean, NY - *BrCabYB 84; TV&RadDir 84*
WBKB-TV - Alpena, MI - *BrCabYB 84; DirUSTelSta 83; TelAl 83, 84; Tel&CabFB 84S; TV&RadDir 84*
WBKC - Chardon, OH - *BrCabYB 84; TV&RadDir 84*
WBKE - North Manchester, IN - *TV&RadDir 84*
WBKE-FM - North Manchester, IN - *BrCabYB 84; TV&RadDir 84*
WBKF - MacLenny, FL - *BrCabYB 84*
WBKH - Hattiesburg, MS - *BrCabYB 84; NatRadPubDir Summer 83, Spring 84; TV&RadDir 84*
WBKM-FM - Lewiston, ME - *TV&RadDir 84*
WBKO-TV - Bowling Green, KY - *BrCabYB 84; DirUSTelSta 83; TelAl 83, 84; Tel&CabFB 84S; TV&RadDir 84*
WBKR-FM - Owensboro, KY - *BrCabYB 84; TV&RadDir 84*
WBKT-FM - Brockport, NY - *BrCabYB 84; TV&RadDir 84*
WBKV - West Bend, WI - *BrCabYB 84; TV&RadDir 84*
WBKV-FM - West Bend, WI - *BrCabYB 84; TV&RadDir 84*

WBKW-FM - Beckley, WV - *BrCabYB 84; TV&RadDir 84*
WBKY-FM - Lexington, KY - *BrCabYB 84; NatRadPubDir Summer 83, Spring 84; TV&RadDir 84*
WBKZ-FM - Baltimore, MD - *TV&RadDir 84*
WBLA - Elizabethtown, NC - *BrCabYB 84; TV&RadDir 84*
WBLB - Pulaski, VA - *BrCabYB 84; TV&RadDir 84*
WBLC - Lenoir City, TN - *BrCabYB 84; TV&RadDir 84*
WBLD-FM - Orchard Lake, MI - *BrCabYB 84*
WBLD-FM - West Bloomfield, MI - *NatRadPubDir Summer 83, Spring 84*
WBLE - Batesville, MS - *BrCabYB 84*
WBLF - Bellefonte, PA - *BrCabYB 84; TV&RadDir 84*
WBLI-FM - Patchogue, NY - *BrCabYB 84; TV&RadDir 84*
WBLI-FM - Suffolk County, Long Island, NY - *NatRadPubDir Summer 83 p.177, Spring 84 p.175*
WBLJ - Dalton, GA - *BrCabYB 84; TV&RadDir 84*
WBLK-FM - Buffalo, NY - *NatRadPubDir Summer 83, Spring 84; TV&RadDir 84*
WBLK-FM - Depew, NY - *BrCabYB 84*
WBLM-FM - Lewiston, ME - *BrCabYB 84*
WBLM-FM - Portland, ME - *NatRadPubDir Summer 83 p.113, Spring 84 p.113*
WBLN - Bloomington, IL - *BrCabYB 84; TelAl 84; Tel&CabFB 84S*
WBLP - Fairview, TN - *BrCabYB 84*
WBLR - Batesburg, SC - *BrCabYB 84; TV&RadDir 84*
WBLS-FM - New York, NY - *BrCabYB 84; LitMarPl 84; NatRadPubDir Summer 83, Spring 84; TV&RadDir 84*
WBLT - Bedford, VA - *BrCabYB 84; TV&RadDir 84*
WBLV - Twin Lake, MI - *BrCabYB 84*
WBLW - Royston, GA - *BrCabYB 84; TV&RadDir 84*
WBLX-FM - Mobile, AL - *BrCabYB 84; NatRadPubDir Summer 83, Spring 84; TV&RadDir 84*
WBLY - Springfield, OH - *BrCabYB 84; TV&RadDir 84*
WBLZ-FM - Hamilton, OH - *BrCabYB 84; TV&RadDir 84*
WBMA - Beaufort, NC - *TV&RadDir 84*
WBMA-TV - Kansas City, MO - *TelAl 83*
WBMB - West Branch, MI - *BrCabYB 84; TV&RadDir 84*
WBMC - McMinnville, TN - *BrCabYB 84; TV&RadDir 84*
WBMC-FM - McMinnville, TN - *BrCabYB 84; TV&RadDir 84*
WBMD - Baltimore, MD - *BrCabYB 84; NatRadPubDir Summer 83, Spring 84; TV&RadDir 84*
WBME - Belfast, ME - *BrCabYB 84; TV&RadDir 84*
WBMG-TV - Birmingham, AL - *BrCabYB 84; DirUSTelSta 83; LitMarPl 83, 84; TelAl 83, 84; Tel&CabFB 84S; TV&RadDir 84*
WBMI-FM - West Branch, MI - *BrCabYB 84; TV&RadDir 84*
WBMJ - San Juan, PR - *BrCabYB 84*
WBMK - Knoxville, TN - *BrCabYB 84; TV&RadDir 84*
WBML - Macon, GA - *BrCabYB 84; NatRadPubDir Summer 83, Spring 84; TV&RadDir 84*
WBMP-FM - Elwood, IN - *BrCabYB 84; TV&RadDir 84*
WBMR-FM - Telford, PA - *BrCabYB 84; TV&RadDir 84*
WBMT - Boxford, MA - *BrCabYB 84*
WBMT - Topsfield, MA - *TV&RadDir 84*
WBMU-FM - Asheville, NC - *BrCabYB 84; NatRadPubDir Summer 83, Spring 84; TV&RadDir 84*
WBMX-FM - Chicago, IL - *NatRadPubDir Summer 83 p.80, Spring 84 p.80*
WBMX-FM - Oak Park, IL - *BrCabYB 84; TV&RadDir 84*
WBN-TV - Chicago, IL - *BrCabYB 84*
WBNB-TV - Charlotte Amalie, VI - *BrCabYB 84; Tel&CabFB 84S*
WBNC - Conway, NH - *BrCabYB 84; TV&RadDir 84*
WBND - Biloxi, MS - *NatRadPubDir Spring 84; TV&RadDir 84*
WBNG-TV - Binghamton, NY - *BrCabYB 84; DirUSTelSta 83; TelAl 83, 84; Tel&CabFB 84S; TV&RadDir 84*
WBNI - Ft. Wayne, IN - *BrCabYB 84*
WBNL - Boonville, IN - *BrCabYB 84; TV&RadDir 84*
WBNL-FM - Boonville, IN - *BrCabYB 84; TV&RadDir 84*
WBNO - Bryan, OH - *BrCabYB 84; TV&RadDir 84*
WBNO-FM - Bryan, OH - *BrCabYB 84; TV&RadDir 84*
WBNQ-FM - Bloomington, IL - *BrCabYB 84; TV&RadDir 84*
WBNR - Beacon, NY - *BrCabYB 84; NatRadPubDir Summer 83, Spring 84; TV&RadDir 84*
WBNS - Columbus, OH - *BrCabYB 84; NatRadPubDir Summer 83, Spring 84; TV&RadDir 84*
WBNS-FM - Columbus, OH - *BrCabYB 84; NatRadPubDir Summer 83, Spring 84; TV&RadDir 84*
WBNS-TV - Columbus, OH - *BrCabYB 84; DirUSTelSta 83; LitMarPl 83, 84; TelAl 83, 84; Tel&CabFB 84S; TV&RadDir 84*
WBNT - Oneida, TN - *BrCabYB 84; TV&RadDir 84*
WBNT-FM - Oneida, TN - *BrCabYB 84; TV&RadDir 84*
WBNX - Rutherford, NJ - *TV&RadDir 84*
WBNX - New York, NY - *BrCabYB 84; NatRadPubDir Summer 83 p.172, Spring 84 p.170*
WBNY-FM - Buffalo, NY - *BrCabYB 84; NatRadPubDir Summer 83*
WBNZ-FM - Benzonia, MI - *TV&RadDir 84*
WBNZ-FM - Frankfort, MI - *BrCabYB 84*
WBOB - Galax, VA - *BrCabYB 84; TV&RadDir 84*
WBOB-FM - Galax, VA - *BrCabYB 84; TV&RadDir 84*
WBOC-TV - Salisbury, MD - *BrCabYB 84; DirUSTelSta 83; TelAl 83, 84; Tel&CabFB 84S; TV&RadDir 84*
WBOD - Canton, IL - *BrCabYB 84*
WBOE-FM - Cleveland, OH - *TV&RadDir 84*
WBOK - New Orleans, LA - *BrCabYB 84; NatRadPubDir Summer 83, Spring 84; TV&RadDir 84*
WBOL - Bolivar, TN - *BrCabYB 84; TV&RadDir 84*
WBOP - Pensacola, FL - *BrCabYB 84; NatRadPubDir Summer 83, Spring 84; TV&RadDir 84*
WBOQ-FM - Terre Haute, IN - *NatRadPubDir Summer 83; TV&RadDir 84*
WBOR-FM - Brunswick, ME - *BrCabYB 84; NatRadPubDir Summer 83, Spring 84; TV&RadDir 84*
WBOS-FM - Boston, MA - *NatRadPubDir Summer 83, Spring 84; TV&RadDir 84*
WBOS-FM - Brookline, MA - *BrCabYB 84*
WBOW - Terre Haute, IN - *BrCabYB 84; NatRadPubDir Summer 83, Spring 84; TV&RadDir 84*
WBOX - Bogalusa, LA - *BrCabYB 84; TV&RadDir 84*
WBOY-TV - Clarksburg, WV - *BrCabYB 84; DirUSTelSta 83; TelAl 83, 84; Tel&CabFB 84S; TV&RadDir 84*
WBOZ - San German, PR - *BrCabYB 84*
WBPA - Elkhorn City, KY - *BrCabYB 84; TV&RadDir 84*
WBPM-FM - Kingston, NY - *BrCabYB 84; LitMarPl 84; NatRadPubDir Summer 83, Spring 84; TV&RadDir 84*
WBPR-FM - Barrington, IL - *TV&RadDir 84*
WBPV-FM - Charlton, MA - *BrCabYB 84; TV&RadDir 84*
WBPZ - Lock Haven, PA - *BrCabYB 84; TV&RadDir 84*
WBPZ-FM - Lock Haven, PA - *TV&RadDir 84*
WBQM-FM - Decatur, AL - *BrCabYB 84; TV&RadDir 84*
WBQW - Scranton, PA - *BrCabYB 84; NatRadPubDir Summer 83, Spring 84; TV&RadDir 84*
WBRA-TV - Roanoke, VA - *BrCabYB 84; Tel&CabFB 84S; TV&RadDir 84*
WBRC-TV - Birmingham, AL - *BrCabYB 84; DirUSTelSta 83; LitMarPl 83, 84; TelAl 83, 84; Tel&CabFB 84S; TV&RadDir 84*
WBRD - Bradenton, FL - *BrCabYB 84; TV&RadDir 84*
WBRE - Wilkes-Barre, PA - *NatRadPubDir Summer 83; Tel&CabFB 84S*
WBRE-FM - Wilkes-Barre, PA - *NatRadPubDir Summer 83*
WBRE-TV - Scranton, PA - *DirUSTelSta 83*
WBRE-TV - Wilkes Barre, PA - *BrCabYB 84; LitMarPl 83, 84; TelAl 83, 84; TV&RadDir 84*
WBRG - Lynchburg, VA - *BrCabYB 84; TV&RadDir 84*
WBRH-FM - Baton Rouge, LA - *BrCabYB 84; TV&RadDir 84*
WBRI - Indianapolis, IN - *BrCabYB 84; NatRadPubDir Summer 83, Spring 84; TV&RadDir 84*
WBRJ - Marietta, OH - *BrCabYB 84; TV&RadDir 84*
WBRK - Pittsfield, MA - *BrCabYB 84; NatRadPubDir Summer 83, Spring 84; TV&RadDir 84*
WBRL - Berlin, NH - *BrCabYB 84; TV&RadDir 84*
WBRM - Marion, NC - *BrCabYB 84; TV&RadDir 84*
WBRN - Big Rapids, MI - *BrCabYB 84; TV&RadDir 84*
WBRN-FM - Big Rapids, MI - *BrCabYB 84; TV&RadDir 84*
WBRO - Waynesboro, GA - *BrCabYB 84; TV&RadDir 84*
WBRQ - Cidra, PR - *BrCabYB 84*
WBRS-FM - Boston, MA - *TV&RadDir 84*
WBRS-FM - Waltham, MA - *BrCabYB 84; NatRadPubDir Summer 83, Spring 84*
WBRT - Bardstown, KY - *BrCabYB 84; TV&RadDir 84*
WBRU - Providence, RI - *BrCabYB 84; NatRadPubDir Summer 83, Spring 84*

WBRU-FM - Providence, RI - *NatRadPubDir Summer 83, Spring 84; TV&RadDir 84*
WBRV - Boonville, NY - *BrCabYB 84; TV&RadDir 84*
WBRW - Somerville, NJ - *BrCabYB 84; NatRadPubDir Summer 83, Spring 84; TV&RadDir 84*
WBRX - Berwick, PA - *BrCabYB 84*
WBRX - Martins Creek, PA - *TV&RadDir 84*
WBRY - Woodbury, TN - *BrCabYB 84; TV&RadDir 84*
WBRZ-TV - Baton Rouge, LA - *BrCabYB 84; DirUSTelSta 83; TelAl 83, 84; Tel&CabFB 84S; TV&RadDir 84*
WBSA - Boaz, AL - *BrCabYB 84; TV&RadDir 84*
WBSB-FM - Baltimore, MD - *BrCabYB 84; NatRadPubDir Summer 83, Spring 84; TV&RadDir 84*
WBSC - Bennettsville, SC - *BrCabYB 84; TV&RadDir 84*
WBSD-FM - Burlington, WI - *BrCabYB 84; NatRadPubDir Summer 83, Spring 84; TV&RadDir 84*
WBSF - Biddeford, ME - *BrCabYB 84*
WBSG - Blackshear, GA - *TV&RadDir 84*
WBSJ-FM - Ellisville, MS - *BrCabYB 84; TV&RadDir 84*
WBSL-FM - Sheffield, MA - *BrCabYB 84; NatRadPubDir Summer 83, Spring 84; TV&RadDir 84*
WBSM - New Bedford, MA - *BrCabYB 84; TV&RadDir 84*
WBSN-FM - New Orleans, LA - *BrCabYB 84; TV&RadDir 84*
WBSP - Ocala, FL - *BrCabYB 84; Tel&CabFB 84S*
WBSR - Pensacola, FL - *BrCabYB 84; NatRadPubDir Summer 83, Spring 84; TV&RadDir 84*
WBSS - Ft. Lauderdale/Hollywood, FL - *NatRadPubDir Spring 84 p.57*
WBSS - Pompano Beach, FL - *BrCabYB 84; TV&RadDir 84*
WBST-FM - Muncie, IN - *BrCabYB 84; NatRadPubDir Summer 83, Spring 84; TV&RadDir 84*
WBSU-FM - Brockport, NY - *BrCabYB 84; TV&RadDir 84*
WBT - Charlotte, NC - *BrCabYB 84; NatRadPubDir Summer 83, Spring 84; TV&RadDir 84*
WBTA - Batavia, NY - *BrCabYB 84; NatRadPubDir Summer 83, Spring 84; TV&RadDir 84*
WBTB - Beaufort, NC - *BrCabYB 84*
WBTC - Uhrichsville, OH - *BrCabYB 84; TV&RadDir 84*
WBTE - Windsor, NC - *BrCabYB 84; TV&RadDir 84*
WBTF-FM - Attica, NY - *BrCabYB 84; NatRadPubDir Summer 83, Spring 84; TV&RadDir 84*
WBTG-FM - Sheffield, AL - *BrCabYB 84*
WBTG-FM - Tuscumbia, AL - *TV&RadDir 84*
WBTH - Williamson, WV - *BrCabYB 84; TV&RadDir 84*
WBTI-TV - Cincinnati, OH - *BrCabYB 84; DirUSTelSta 83; TelAl 83, 84; Tel&CabFB 84S; TV&RadDir 84*
WBTM - Danville, VA - *BrCabYB 84; NatRadPubDir Summer 83, Spring 84; TV&RadDir 84*
WBTN - Bennington, VT - *BrCabYB 84; TV&RadDir 84*
WBTO - Linton, IN - *BrCabYB 84; TV&RadDir 84*
WBTR-FM - Carrollton, GA - *BrCabYB 84; TV&RadDir 84*
WBTS - Bridgeport, AL - *BrCabYB 84; TV&RadDir 84*
WBTV - Charlotte, NC - *BrCabYB 84; LitMarPl 83, 84; TelAl 84*
WBTV-TV - Charlotte, NC - *DirUSTelSta 83; TelAl 83; Tel&CabFB 84S; TV&RadDir 84*
WBTW-TV - Florence, SC - *BrCabYB 84; DirUSTelSta 83; TelAl 83, 84; Tel&CabFB 84S; TV&RadDir 84*
WBTX - Broadway, VA - *BrCabYB 84; TV&RadDir 84*
WBTY-FM - Homerville, GA - *BrCabYB 84; TV&RadDir 84*
WBTZ - Oliver Springs, TN - *BrCabYB 84*
WBUC - Buckhannon, WV - *BrCabYB 84; TV&RadDir 84*
WBUD - Trenton, NJ - *BrCabYB 84; NatRadPubDir Spring 84*
WBUF-FM - Buffalo, NY - *BrCabYB 84; NatRadPubDir Summer 83, Spring 84; TV&RadDir 84*
WBUK - Kalamazoo, MI - *NatRadPubDir Summer 83, Spring 84; TV&RadDir 84*
WBUK - Portage, MI - *BrCabYB 84*
WBUL - Birmingham, AL - *NatRadPubDir Summer 83; TV&RadDir 84*
WBUO - Appleton, WI - *Tel&CabFB 84S*
WBUR-FM - Boston, MA - *BrCabYB 84; LitMarPl 83, 84; NatRadPubDir Summer 83, Spring 84; TV&RadDir 84*
WBUT - Butler, PA - *BrCabYB 84; TV&RadDir 84*
WBUX - Doylestown, PA - *BrCabYB 84; TV&RadDir 84*
WBUY - Lexington, NC - *BrCabYB 84; NatRadPubDir Summer 83, Spring 84; TV&RadDir 84*
WBUZ - Fredonia, NY - *BrCabYB 84; TV&RadDir 84*
WBVD - Beverly, MA - *BrCabYB 84; TV&RadDir 84*
WBVP - Beaver Falls, PA - *BrCabYB 84; TV&RadDir 84*
WBWA - Washburn, WI - *BrCabYB 84*
WBWB-FM - Bloomington, IN - *BrCabYB 84; TV&RadDir 84*
WBWC-FM - Berea, OH - *BrCabYB 84; TV&RadDir 84*
WBWC-FM - Cleveland, OH - *NatRadPubDir Summer 83 p.307, Spring 84 p.309*
WBXB-FM - Edenton, NC - *BrCabYB 84; TV&RadDir 84*
WBXL-FM - Baldwinsville, NY - *BrCabYB 84; NatRadPubDir Summer 83, Spring 84; TV&RadDir 84*
WBXQ - Cresson, PA - *BrCabYB 84*
WBYC-FM - Biddeford, ME - *BrCabYB 84; TV&RadDir 84*
WBYE - Calera, AL - *BrCabYB 84; TV&RadDir 84*
WBYG-FM - Kankakee, IL - *BrCabYB 84; TV&RadDir 84*
WBYO-FM - Boyertown, PA - *BrCabYB 84; TV&RadDir 84*
WBYQ - Baltimore, MD - *BrCabYB 84*
WBYS - Canton, IL - *BrCabYB 84; TV&RadDir 84*
WBYS-FM - Canton, IL - *BrCabYB 84; TV&RadDir 84*
WBYU-FM - New Orleans, LA - *BrCabYB 84; NatRadPubDir Summer 83, Spring 84; TV&RadDir 84*
WBYZ - Baxley, GA - *BrCabYB 84*
WBZ - Allston, MA - *TV&RadDir 84*
WBZ - Boston, MA - *BrCabYB 84; LitMarPl 83, 84; NatRadPubDir Summer 83, Spring 84*
WBZ-FM - Boston, MA - *LitMarPl 83*
WBZ-TV - Allston, MA - *TV&RadDir 84*
WBZ-TV - Boston, MA - *BrCabYB 84; DirUSTelSta 83; LitMarPl 83, 84; TelAl 83, 84; Tel&CabFB 84S*
WBZA - Glens Falls, NY - *BrCabYB 84; TV&RadDir 84*
WBZB - Selma, NC - *BrCabYB 84; TV&RadDir 84*
WBZI-FM - Xenia, OH - *BrCabYB 84; TV&RadDir 84*
WBZK - York, SC - *BrCabYB 84; TV&RadDir 84*
WBZQ - Greenville, NC - *BrCabYB 84; TV&RadDir 84*
WBZT - Waynesboro, PA - *BrCabYB 84; TV&RadDir 84*
WBZY - New Castle, PA - *BrCabYB 84; TV&RadDir 84*
WBZZ-FM - Pittsburgh, PA - *BrCabYB 84; NatRadPubDir Summer 83, Spring 84; TV&RadDir 84*
W.C. Communications Inc. - Dellroy, OH - *BrCabYB 84*
WCAB - Rutherfordton, NC - *BrCabYB 84; TV&RadDir 84*
WCAD - San Juan, PR - *BrCabYB 84*
WCAE-TV - St. John, IN - *BrCabYB 84; Tel&CabFB 84S; TV&RadDir 84*
WCAI - Ft. Myers, FL - *BrCabYB 84; NatRadPubDir Summer 83, Spring 84; TV&RadDir 84*
WCAJ - Birmingham, AL - *BrCabYB 84*
WCAK-FM - Catlettsburg, KY - *BrCabYB 84; TV&RadDir 84*
WCAL - Northfield, MN - *BrCabYB 84; NatRadPubDir Summer 83, Spring 84; TV&RadDir 84*
WCAL-FM - Northfield, MN - *BrCabYB 84; NatRadPubDir Summer 83, Spring 84; TV&RadDir 84*
WCAM - Camden, SC - *BrCabYB 84; TV&RadDir 84*
WCAO - Baltimore, MD - *BrCabYB 84; NatRadPubDir Summer 83, Spring 84; TV&RadDir 84*
WCAP - Lowell, MA - *BrCabYB 84; NatRadPubDir Summer 83, Spring 84; TV&RadDir 84*
WCAR - Garden City, MI - *TV&RadDir 84*
WCAR - Livonia, MI - *BrCabYB 84*
WCAS - Boston, MA - *NatRadPubDir Summer 83 p.119, Spring 84 p.119*
WCAS - Cambridge, MA - *BrCabYB 84; TV&RadDir 84*
WCAT - Orange, MA - *BrCabYB 84; TV&RadDir 84*
WCAU - Philadelphia, PA - *BrCabYB 84; LitMarPl 83, 84; NatRadPubDir Summer 83, Spring 84; TV&RadDir 84*
WCAU-FM - Philadelphia, PA - *BrCabYB 84; LitMarPl 83; NatRadPubDir Summer 83, Spring 84; TV&RadDir 84*
WCAU-TV - Philadelphia, PA - *BrCabYB 84; DirUSTelSta 83; LitMarPl 83, 84; TelAl 83, 84; Tel&CabFB 84S; TV&RadDir 84*
WCAV-FM - Brockton, MA - *BrCabYB 84; TV&RadDir 84*
WCAW - Charleston, WV - *BrCabYB 84; NatRadPubDir Summer 83, Spring 84; TV&RadDir 84*
WCAX-TV - Burlington, VT - *BrCabYB 84; DirUSTelSta 83; TelAl 83, 84; Tel&CabFB 84S; TV&RadDir 84*
WCAY - Columbia, SC - *NatRadPubDir Summer 83*
WCAY-TV - Nashville, TN - *BrCabYB 84; Tel&CabFB 84S*
WCAZ - Carthage, IL - *BrCabYB 84; TV&RadDir 84*
WCAZ-FM - Carthage, IL - *BrCabYB 84; TV&RadDir 84*

WCB-TV - Columbus, MI - *BrCabYB 84*
WCBA - Corning, NY - *BrCabYB 84; NatRadPubDir Summer 83, Spring 84; TV&RadDir 84*
WCBB - Augusta, ME - *BrCabYB 84; Tel&CabFB 84S*
WCBB-TV - Lewiston, ME - *TV&RadDir 84*
WCBC - Cumberland, MD - *BrCabYB 84; NatRadPubDir Summer 83, Spring 84; TV&RadDir 84*
WCBD-TV - Charleston, SC - *BrCabYB 84; DirUSTelSta 83; TelAl 83, 84; Tel&CabFB 84S*
WCBD-TV - Mt. Pleasant, SC - *TV&RadDir 84*
WCBE-FM - Columbus, OH - *BrCabYB 84; NatRadPubDir Summer 83, Spring 84; TV&RadDir 84*
WCBF - Seffner, FL - *TV&RadDir 84*
WCBF - Tampa, FL - *BrCabYB 84; NatRadPubDir Spring 84 p.65*
WCBG - Chambersburg, PA - *BrCabYB 84; TV&RadDir 84*
WCBI - Columbus, MS - *BrCabYB 84; NatRadPubDir Summer 83, Spring 84; TV&RadDir 84*
WCBI-TV - Columbus, MS - *DirUSTelSta 83; TelAl 83, 84; Tel&CabFB 84S; TV&RadDir 84*
WCBK-FM - Martinsville, IN - *BrCabYB 84; TV&RadDir 84*
WCBL - Benton, KY - *BrCabYB 84; TV&RadDir 84*
WCBL-FM - Benton, KY - *BrCabYB 84; TV&RadDir 84*
WCBM - Baltimore, MD - *BrCabYB 84; NatRadPubDir Summer 83 p.115, Spring 84 p.115*
WCBN-FM - Ann Arbor, MI - *BrCabYB 84; NatRadPubDir Summer 83, Spring 84; TV&RadDir 84*
WCBQ - Oxford, NC - *BrCabYB 84; TV&RadDir 84*
WCBR - Richmond, KY - *BrCabYB 84; TV&RadDir 84*
WCBR-FM - Richmond, KY - *BrCabYB 84; TV&RadDir 84*
WCBS - New York, NY - *BrCabYB 84; LitMarPl 83, 84; NatRadPubDir Summer 83, Spring 84; TV&RadDir 84*
WCBS-FM - New York, NY - *BrCabYB 84; LitMarPl 83; NatRadPubDir Summer 83, Spring 84; TV&RadDir 84*
WCBS-TV [Div. of Columbia Broadcasting System Inc.] - New York, NY - *BrCabYB 84; DirUSTelSta 83; LitMarPl 83, 84; TelAl 83, 84; Tel&CabFB 84S; TV&RadDir 84*
WCBT - Roanoke Rapids, NC - *BrCabYB 84; TV&RadDir 84*
WCBU-FM - Peoria, IL - *BrCabYB 84; NatRadPubDir Summer 83, Spring 84; TV&RadDir 84*
WCBW-FM - Columbia, IL - *BrCabYB 84; TV&RadDir 84*
WCBX - Eden, NC - *BrCabYB 84; TV&RadDir 84*
WCBY - Cheboygan, MI - *BrCabYB 84; TV&RadDir 84*
W.C.C. Directories Inc. [Aff. of Whitney Communications Corp.] - New York, NY - *BoPubDir 4, 5*
WCCA-FM - McComb, MS - *BrCabYB 84; TV&RadDir 84*
WCCB-TV - Charlotte, NC - *BrCabYB 84; DirUSTelSta 83; TelAl 83, 84; Tel&CabFB 84S; TV&RadDir 84*
WCCC - Hartford, CT - *BrCabYB 84; NatRadPubDir Summer 83, Spring 84; TV&RadDir 84*
WCCC-FM - Hartford, CT - *BrCabYB 84; NatRadPubDir Summer 83, Spring 84; TV&RadDir 84*
WCCD - Athens, GA - *BrCabYB 84*
WCCE-FM - Buies Creek, NC - *BrCabYB 84; TV&RadDir 84*
WCCF - Punta Gorda, FL - *BrCabYB 84; TV&RadDir 84*
WCCG - Camden, SC - *TV&RadDir 84*
WCCH-FM - Holyoke, MA - *BrCabYB 84; NatRadPubDir Summer 83, Spring 84; TV&RadDir 84*
WCCI-FM - Savanna, IL - *BrCabYB 84; TV&RadDir 84*
WCCK-FM - Erie, PA - *BrCabYB 84; NatRadPubDir Summer 83, Spring 84; TV&RadDir 84*
WCCL - Greenville, MS - *NatRadPubDir Summer 83 p.138, Spring 84*
WCCL - Jackson, MS - *BrCabYB 84; TV&RadDir 84*
WCCM - Rock Island, IL - *NatRadPubDir Summer 83, Spring 84*
WCCM - Lawrence, MA - *BrCabYB 84; NatRadPubDir Summer 83, Spring 84; TV&RadDir 84*
WCCN - Neillsville, WI - *BrCabYB 84; TV&RadDir 84*
WCCN-FM - Neillsville, WI - *BrCabYB 84; TV&RadDir 84*
WCCO - Minneapolis, MN - *BrCabYB 84; LitMarPl 83, 84; NatRadPubDir Summer 83, Spring 84; TV&RadDir 84*
WCCO-FM - Minneapolis, MN - *BrCabYB 84; NatRadPubDir Summer 83; TV&RadDir 84*
WCCO-TV - Minneapolis, MN - *BrCabYB 84; DirUSTelSta 83; LitMarPl 83, 84; TelAl 83, 84; Tel&CabFB 84S; TV&RadDir 84*
WCCP - Clemson, SC - *BrCabYB 84; TV&RadDir 84*
WCCQ - Cresthill, IL - *BrCabYB 84*
WCCR - Champaign, IL - *NatRadPubDir Summer 83, Spring 84; TV&RadDir 84*
WCCR - Urbana, IL - *BrCabYB 84*
WCCT-TV - Columbia, SC - *BrCabYB 84; DirUSTelSta 83; Tel&CabFB 84S*
WCCV - Cartersville, GA - *BrCabYB 84*
WCCW - Traverse City, MI - *BrCabYB 84; TV&RadDir 84*
WCCX-FM - Waukesha, WI - *BrCabYB 84; NatRadPubDir Spring 84; TV&RadDir 84*
WCCY - Houghton, MI - *BrCabYB 84; TV&RadDir 84*
WCCZ - New Smyrna Beach, FL - *BrCabYB 84; TV&RadDir 84*
WCDB-FM - Albany, NY - *BrCabYB 84; NatRadPubDir Summer 83, Spring 84; TV&RadDir 84*
WCDB-FM - Cedarville, OH - *NatRadPubDir Summer 83*
WCDC-TV - Adams, MA - *BrCabYB 84; TelAl 83, 84; Tel&CabFB 84S*
WCDC-TV - Albany, NY - *TV&RadDir 84*
WCDE-FM - Elkins, WV - *BrCabYB 84; TV&RadDir 84*
WCDJ - Edenton, NC - *TV&RadDir 84*
WCDL - Carbondale, PA - *BrCabYB 84; TV&RadDir 84*
WCDO - Sidney, NY - *BrCabYB 84*
WCDR-FM - Cedarville, OH - *BrCabYB 84; NatRadPubDir Spring 84; TV&RadDir 84*
WCDS - Glasgow, KY - *BrCabYB 84; TV&RadDir 84*
WCDT - Winchester, TN - *BrCabYB 84; TV&RadDir 84*
WCEA - New Bedford, MA - *BrCabYB 84*
WCEC - Rocky Mt., NC - *BrCabYB 84; NatRadPubDir Summer 83, Spring 84; TV&RadDir 84*
WCED - Du Bois, PA - *BrCabYB 84; TV&RadDir 84*
WCEE - Mt. Vernon, IL - *BrCabYB 84; TelAl 84; Tel&CabFB 84S*
WCEF - Ripley, WV - *BrCabYB 84*
WCEG - Middleborough, MA - *BrCabYB 84*
WCEH - Hawkinsville, GA - *BrCabYB 84; TV&RadDir 84*
WCEH-FM - Hawkinsville, GA - *BrCabYB 84; TV&RadDir 84*
WCEI - Easton, MD - *BrCabYB 84; TV&RadDir 84*
WCEI-FM - Easton, MD - *BrCabYB 84; TV&RadDir 84*
WCEL - Southern Pines, NC - *BrCabYB 84; TV&RadDir 84*
WCEM - Cambridge, MD - *BrCabYB 84; TV&RadDir 84*
WCEN - Mt. Pleasant, MI - *BrCabYB 84; TV&RadDir 84*
WCEN-FM - Mt. Pleasant, MI - *BrCabYB 84; TV&RadDir 84*
WCES-TV - Wrens, GA - *BrCabYB 84; Tel&CabFB 84S*
WCET-TV - Cincinnati, OH - *BrCabYB 84; Tel&CabFB 84S; TV&RadDir 84*
WCEV - Chicago, IL - *TV&RadDir 84*
WCEV - Cicero, IL - *BrCabYB 84*
WCEW-FM - Charleston, SC - *TV&RadDir 84*
WCEZ-FM - Jupiter, FL - *BrCabYB 84; TV&RadDir 84*
WCFB - Tupelo, MS - *BrCabYB 84; NatRadPubDir Summer 83, Spring 84*
WCFC-TV - Chicago, IL - *BrCabYB 84; DirUSTelSta 83; TelAl 83, 84; Tel&CabFB 84S*
WCFE-TV - Plattsburgh, NY - *BrCabYB 84; Tel&CabFB 84S; TV&RadDir 84*
WCFL - Chicago, IL - *BrCabYB 84; LitMarPl 83, 84; NatRadPubDir Summer 83, Spring 84; TV&RadDir 84*
WCFM-FM - Williamstown, MA - *BrCabYB 84; TV&RadDir 84*
WCFR - Springfield, VT - *BrCabYB 84; TV&RadDir 84*
WCFR-FM - Springfield, VT - *BrCabYB 84; TV&RadDir 84*
WCFT-TV - Tuscaloosa, AL - *BrCabYB 84; DirUSTelSta 83; TelAl 83, 84; Tel&CabFB 84S; TV&RadDir 84*
WCFW-FM - Chippewa Falls, WI - *BrCabYB 84; TV&RadDir 84*
WCFX-FM - Clare, MI - *TV&RadDir 84*
WCGA - Conyers, GA - *BrCabYB 84; TV&RadDir 84*
WCGB - Juana Diaz, PR - *BrCabYB 84*
WCGC - Belmont, NC - *BrCabYB 84; TV&RadDir 84*
WCGL - Jacksonville, FL - *BrCabYB 84; NatRadPubDir Summer 83, Spring 84; TV&RadDir 84*
WCGO - Chicago Heights, IL - *BrCabYB 84; NatRadPubDir Summer 83, Spring 84; TV&RadDir 84*
WCGQ-FM - Columbus, GA - *BrCabYB 84; NatRadPubDir Summer 83, Spring 84; TV&RadDir 84*
WCGR - Canandaigua, NY - *BrCabYB 84; TV&RadDir 84*
WCGV-TV - Milwaukee, WI - *BrCabYB 84; DirUSTelSta 83; TelAl 83, 84; Tel&CabFB 84S; TV&RadDir 84*

WCGY-FM - Lawrence, MA - *BrCabYB 84; NatRadPubDir Summer 83, Spring 84; TV&RadDir 84*
WCHA - Chambersburg, PA - *BrCabYB 84; TV&RadDir 84*
WCHB - Detroit, MI - *NatRadPubDir Summer 83 p.126, Spring 84 p.126*
WCHB - Inkster, MI - *BrCabYB 84; TV&RadDir 84*
WCHC-FM - Worcester, MA - *BrCabYB 84; TV&RadDir 84*
WCHE - West Chester, PA - *BrCabYB 84; TV&RadDir 84*
WCHI - Chillicothe, OH - *BrCabYB 84; TV&RadDir 84*
WCHJ - Brookhaven, MS - *BrCabYB 84; TV&RadDir 84*
WCHK - Canton, GA - *BrCabYB 84; TV&RadDir 84*
WCHK-FM - Canton, GA - *BrCabYB 84; TV&RadDir 84*
WCHL - Chapel Hill, NC - *BrCabYB 84; TV&RadDir 84*
WCHN - Norwich, NY - *BrCabYB 84; TV&RadDir 84*
WCHN-FM - Norwich, NY - *TV&RadDir 84*
WCHO-FM - Washington Court House, OH - *BrCabYB 84; TV&RadDir 84*
WCHQ-FM - Camuy, PR - *BrCabYB 84*
WCHR-FM - Trenton, NJ - *BrCabYB 84*
WCHR-FM - Morrisville, PA - *TV&RadDir 84*
WCHR-FM - Yardley, PA - *NatRadPubDir Summer 83, Spring 84*
WCHS - Charleston, WV - *BrCabYB 84; NatRadPubDir Summer 83, Spring 84; TV&RadDir 84*
WCHS-TV - Charleston, WV - *BrCabYB 84; DirUSTelSta 83; LitMarPl 83, 84; TelAl 83, 84; Tel&CabFB 84S; TV&RadDir 84*
WCHU-FM - Soddy-Daisy, TN - *BrCabYB 84*
WCHV - Charlottesville, VA - *BrCabYB 84; TV&RadDir 84*
WCHW-FM - Bay City, MI - *BrCabYB 84; NatRadPubDir Summer 83, Spring 84; TV&RadDir 84*
WCHY-FM - Savannah, GA - *BrCabYB 84; NatRadPubDir Summer 83, Spring 84; TV&RadDir 84*
WCIA-TV - Champaign, IL - *BrCabYB 84; TelAl 83, 84; Tel&CabFB 84S; TV&RadDir 84*
WCIA-TV - Springfield, IL - *DirUSTelSta 83*
WCIB-FM - Falmouth, MA - *BrCabYB 84; TV&RadDir 84*
WCIC - Pekin, IL - *BrCabYB 84*
WCIE-FM - Lakeland, FL - *BrCabYB 84; TV&RadDir 84*
WCIF-FM - Melbourne, FL - *BrCabYB 84; TV&RadDir 84*
WCIG-FM - Mullins, SC - *BrCabYB 84; TV&RadDir 84*
WCII - Louisville, KY - *BrCabYB 84; NatRadPubDir Summer 83, Spring 84; TV&RadDir 84*
WCIK - Bath, NY - *BrCabYB 84*
WCIL - Carbondale, IL - *BrCabYB 84; TV&RadDir 84*
WCIL-FM - Carbondale, IL - *BrCabYB 84; TV&RadDir 84*
WCIN - Cincinnati, OH - *BrCabYB 84; NatRadPubDir Summer 83, Spring 84; TV&RadDir 84*
WCIQ-TV - Birmingham, AL - *TV&RadDir 84*
WCIQ-TV - Mt. Cheaha State Park, AL - *BrCabYB 84; Tel&CabFB 84S*
WCIR-FM - Beckley, WV - *BrCabYB 84; TV&RadDir 84*
WCIT - Lima, OH - *BrCabYB 84; NatRadPubDir Summer 83, Spring 84; TV&RadDir 84*
WCIU-TV - Chicago, IL - *BrCabYB 84; DirUSTelSta 83; TelAl 83, 84; Tel&CabFB 84S; TV&RadDir 84*
WCIV-TV - Charleston, SC - *BrCabYB 84; DirUSTelSta 83; TelAl 83, 84; Tel&CabFB 84S; TV&RadDir 84*
WCIV-TV - Mt. Pleasant, SC - *TV&RadDir 84*
WCIX-TV - Miami, FL - *DirUSTelSta 83; TelAl 83, 84; Tel&CabFB 84S; TV&RadDir 84*
WCJB-TV - Gainesville, FL - *BrCabYB 84; DirUSTelSta 83; TelAl 83, 84; Tel&CabFB 84S; TV&RadDir 84*
WCJC-FM - Madison, IN - *BrCabYB 84; TV&RadDir 84*
WCJL - Marinette, WI - *BrCabYB 84; TV&RadDir 84*
WCJM-FM - West Point, GA - *BrCabYB 84; TV&RadDir 84*
WCJO-FM - Jackson, OH - *BrCabYB 84; TV&RadDir 84*
WCJU - Columbia, MS - *BrCabYB 84; TV&RadDir 84*
WCJW - Warsaw, NY - *BrCabYB 84; TV&RadDir 84*
WCKB - Dunn, NC - *BrCabYB 84; TV&RadDir 84*
WCKC - Milton, FL - *BrCabYB 84; TV&RadDir 84*
WCKG - Braddock, PA - *LitMarPl 83*
WCKI - Greer, SC - *BrCabYB 84; TV&RadDir 84*
WCKJ - Augusta, GA - *BrCabYB 84*
WCKK - Appleton/Oshkosh, WI - *NatRadPubDir Summer 83, Spring 84 p.267*
WCKK - Oshkosh, WI - *BrCabYB 84*
WCKL - Catskill, NY - *BrCabYB 84; TV&RadDir 84*
WCKM - Winnsboro, SC - *BrCabYB 84; TV&RadDir 84*
WCKO-FM - Ft. Lauderdale, FL - *NatRadPubDir Summer 83, Spring 84; TV&RadDir 84*
WCKO-FM - Pompano Beach, FL - *BrCabYB 84*
WCKQ-FM - Campbellsville, KY - *BrCabYB 84; TV&RadDir 84*
WCKR - Hornell, NY - *BrCabYB 84; TV&RadDir 84*
WCKS-FM - Cocoa Beach, FL - *BrCabYB 84; TV&RadDir 84*
WCKT-TV - Causeway, FL - *LitMarPl 83*
WCKT-TV - Miami, FL - *DirUSTelSta 83; TelAl 83; TV&RadDir 84*
WCKV - Ceredo, WV - *BrCabYB 84*
WCKW-FM - La Place, LA - *BrCabYB 84; TV&RadDir 84*
WCKX - Clearwater, FL - *BrCabYB 84*
WCKY - Cincinnati, OH - *BrCabYB 84; NatRadPubDir Summer 83, Spring 84; TV&RadDir 84*
WCKZ - Austell, GA - *BrCabYB 84*
WCLA - Claxton, GA - *BrCabYB 84; TV&RadDir 84*
WCLA-FM - Claxton, GA - *BrCabYB 84; TV&RadDir 84*
WCLB - Camilla, GA - *BrCabYB 84; TV&RadDir 84*
WCLC - Jamestown, TN - *BrCabYB 84; TV&RadDir 84*
WCLC-FM - Mansfield, OH - *TV&RadDir 84*
WCLD - Cleveland, MS - *BrCabYB 84; TV&RadDir 84*
WCLD-FM - Cleveland, MS - *BrCabYB 84; TV&RadDir 84*
WCLE - Cleveland, TN - *BrCabYB 84; TV&RadDir 84*
WCLF-TV - Clearwater, FL - *BrCabYB 84; DirUSTelSta 83; TelAl 83, 84; Tel&CabFB 84S*
WCLF-TV - Largo, FL - *TV&RadDir 84*
WCLG - Morgantown, WV - *BrCabYB 84; TV&RadDir 84*
WCLG-FM - Morgantown, WV - *TV&RadDir 84*
WCLH-FM - Shavertown, PA - *TV&RadDir 84*
WCLH-FM - Wilkes-Barre, PA - *BrCabYB 84; NatRadPubDir Summer 83, Spring 84*
WCLI - Corning, NY - *BrCabYB 84; TV&RadDir 84*
WCLK-FM - Atlanta, GA - *BrCabYB 84; TV&RadDir 84*
WCLL-FM - Wesson, MS - *BrCabYB 84*
WCLN - Clinton, NC - *BrCabYB 84; TV&RadDir 84*
WCLO - Janesville, WI - *BrCabYB 84; NatRadPubDir Summer 83, Spring 84; TV&RadDir 84*
WCLP-TV - Chatsworth, GA - *BrCabYB 84; Tel&CabFB 84S; TV&RadDir 84*
WCLQ-TV - Cleveland, OH - *BrCabYB 84; DirUSTelSta 83; TelAl 83, 84; Tel&CabFB 84S*
WCLR-FM - Chicago, IL - *NatRadPubDir Summer 83 p.80, Spring 84 p.80*
WCLR-FM - Skokie, IL - *BrCabYB 84; TV&RadDir 84*
WCLS - Phenix City, AL - *TV&RadDir 84*
WCLS - Columbus, GA - *BrCabYB 84; TV&RadDir 84*
WCLT - Newark, OH - *BrCabYB 84; NatRadPubDir Summer 83, Spring 84; TV&RadDir 84*
WCLT-FM - Newark, OH - *BrCabYB 84; NatRadPubDir Summer 83, Spring 84; TV&RadDir 84*
WCLU - Covington, KY - *BrCabYB 84; TV&RadDir 84*
WCLU - Cincinnati, OH - *NatRadPubDir Summer 83, Spring 84*
WCLV-FM - Cleveland, OH - *BrCabYB 84; NatRadPubDir Summer 83, Spring 84; TV&RadDir 84*
WCLW - Mansfield, OH - *BrCabYB 84; TV&RadDir 84*
WCLW-FM - Mansfield, OH - *BrCabYB 84*
WCLX-FM - Boyne City, MI - *BrCabYB 84; TV&RadDir 84*
WCLZ - Brunswick, ME - *BrCabYB 84*
WCMA - Corinth, MS - *BrCabYB 84; TV&RadDir 84*
WCMB - Camp Hill, PA - *TV&RadDir 84*
WCMB - Harrisburg, PA - *BrCabYB 84; NatRadPubDir Summer 83, Spring 84*
WCMC - Wildwood, NJ - *BrCabYB 84; TV&RadDir 84*
WCMC-TV - Wildwood, NJ - *LitMarPl 83*
WCMF-FM - Rochester, NY - *BrCabYB 84; NatRadPubDir Summer 83, Spring 84; TV&RadDir 84*
WCMF-TV - Montgomery, AL - *Tel&CabFB 84S*
WCMG - Lawrenceburg, TN - *BrCabYB 84*
WCMH-TV - Columbus, OH - *BrCabYB 84; DirUSTelSta 83; LitMarPl 83, 84; TelAl 83, 84; Tel&CabFB 84S; TV&RadDir 84*
WCMI - Ashland, KY - *BrCabYB 84; TV&RadDir 84*
WCMI - Huntington, WV - *NatRadPubDir Summer 83, Spring 84 p.265*
WCML-FM - Alpena, MI - *BrCabYB 84*
WCML-FM - Mt. Pleasant, MI - *TV&RadDir 84*

WCML-TV - Alpena, MI - *BrCabYB 84; Tel&CabFB 84S*
WCML-TV - Mt. Pleasant, MI - *TV&RadDir 84*
WCMN-FM - Arecibo, PR - *BrCabYB 84*
WCMO-FM - Marietta, OH - *BrCabYB 84; NatRadPubDir Summer 83, Spring 84; TV&RadDir 84*
WCMP - Pine City, MN - *BrCabYB 84; TV&RadDir 84*
WCMP-FM - Pine City, MN - *BrCabYB 84; TV&RadDir 84*
WCMQ - Miami, FL - *BrCabYB 84; NatRadPubDir Summer 83, Spring 84; TV&RadDir 84*
WCMQ-FM - Clearwater, FL - *TV&RadDir 84*
WCMQ-FM - Hialeah, FL - *BrCabYB 84*
WCMQ-FM - Miami, FL - *NatRadPubDir Summer 83, Spring 84; TV&RadDir 84*
WCMR - Elkhart, IN - *BrCabYB 84; TV&RadDir 84*
WCMS - Norfolk, VA - *BrCabYB 84; NatRadPubDir Summer 83 p.253, Spring 84 p.255*
WCMS - Virginia Beach, VA - *TV&RadDir 84*
WCMS-FM - Norfolk, VA - *BrCabYB 84; NatRadPubDir Summer 83 p.253, Spring 84 p.256*
WCMS-FM - Virginia Beach, VA - *TV&RadDir 84*
WCMT - Martin, TN - *BrCabYB 84; TV&RadDir 84*
WCMT-FM - Martin, TN - *BrCabYB 84; TV&RadDir 84*
WCMU-FM - Mt. Pleasant, MI - *BrCabYB 84; NatRadPubDir Summer 83, Spring 84; TV&RadDir 84*
WCMU-TV - Mt. Pleasant, MI - *BrCabYB 84; Tel&CabFB 84S; TV&RadDir 84*
WCMV - Cadillac, MI - *BrCabYB 84*
WCMW - Manistee, MI - *BrCabYB 84*
WCMX - Leominster, MA - *BrCabYB 84; TV&RadDir 84*
WCMY - Ottawa, IL - *BrCabYB 84; TV&RadDir 84*
WCMZ-FM - Crozet, VA - *TV&RadDir 84*
WCNB-FM - Connersville, IN - *BrCabYB 84; TV&RadDir 84*
WCNC - Elizabeth City, NC - *BrCabYB 84; TV&RadDir 84*
WCND - Louisville, KY - *NatRadPubDir Summer 83 p.104, Spring 84 p.104*
WCND - Shelbyville, KY - *BrCabYB 84; TV&RadDir 84*
WCNE-FM - Batavia, OH - *BrCabYB 84; TV&RadDir 84*
WCNE-FM - Owensville, OH - *NatRadPubDir Summer 83 p.309, Spring 84 p.311*
WCNF - Whitehall, MI - *BrCabYB 84*
WCNH - Quincy, FL - *BrCabYB 84; TV&RadDir 84*
WCNH-FM - Quincy, FL - *TV&RadDir 84*
WCNI-FM - New London, CT - *BrCabYB 84; TV&RadDir 84*
WCNL - Newport, NH - *BrCabYB 84; TV&RadDir 84*
WCNL-FM - Newport, NH - *BrCabYB 84; TV&RadDir 84*
WCNM - Lock Haven, PA - *BrCabYB 84*
WCNN - Atlanta, GA - *BrCabYB 84; LitMarPl 83, 84; NatRadPubDir Summer 83 p.69, Spring 84; TV&RadDir 84*
WCNR - Bloomsburg, PA - *BrCabYB 84; TV&RadDir 84*
WCNS - Latrobe, PA - *BrCabYB 84; TV&RadDir 84*
WCNT - Cidra, PR - *BrCabYB 84; Tel&CabFB 84S*
WCNU - Crestview, FL - *BrCabYB 84; TV&RadDir 84*
WCNV-FM - Amherst, VA - *BrCabYB 84; TV&RadDir 84*
WCNW - Fairfield, OH - *BrCabYB 84*
WCNW - Hamilton, OH - *TV&RadDir 84*
WCNX - Middletown, CT - *BrCabYB 84; NatRadPubDir Summer 83, Spring 84; TV&RadDir 84*
WCNY-FM - Liverpool, NY - *TV&RadDir 84*
WCNY-FM - Syracuse, NY - *BrCabYB 84; NatRadPubDir Summer 83 p.304, Spring 84 p.306*
WCNY-TV - Liverpool, NY - *TV&RadDir 84*
WCNY-TV - Syracuse, NY - *BrCabYB 84; Tel&CabFB 84S*
WCOA - Pensacola, FL - *BrCabYB 84; NatRadPubDir Summer 83, Spring 84; TV&RadDir 84*
WCOD-FM - Hyannis, MA - *BrCabYB 84; TV&RadDir 84*
WCOE-FM - La Porte, IN - *BrCabYB 84; NatRadPubDir Summer 83, Spring 84; TV&RadDir 84*
WCOG - Greensboro, NC - *BrCabYB 84; NatRadPubDir Summer 83, Spring 84; TV&RadDir 84*
WCOH - Newnan, GA - *BrCabYB 84; TV&RadDir 84*
WCOJ - Coatesville, PA - *BrCabYB 84; TV&RadDir 84*
WCOK - Sparta, NC - *BrCabYB 84; TV&RadDir 84*
WCOL - Columbus, OH - *BrCabYB 84; NatRadPubDir Summer 83, Spring 84; TV&RadDir 84*
WCOM-FM - Urbana, OH - *BrCabYB 84; TV&RadDir 84*
WCON - Cornelia, GA - *BrCabYB 84; TV&RadDir 84*
WCON-FM - Cornelia, GA - *BrCabYB 84; TV&RadDir 84*
WCOP - Warner Robins, GA - *BrCabYB 84; TV&RadDir 84*
WCOR - Lebanon, TN - *BrCabYB 84; TV&RadDir 84*
WCOS - Columbia, SC - *BrCabYB 84; NatRadPubDir Summer 83, Spring 84; TV&RadDir 84*
WCOS-FM - Columbia, SC - *BrCabYB 84; NatRadPubDir Summer 83, Spring 84; TV&RadDir 84*
WCOT - Orlando, FL - *BrCabYB 84; NatRadPubDir Spring 84 p.63*
WCOU - Lewiston, ME - *BrCabYB 84; TV&RadDir 84*
WCOU - Portland, ME - *NatRadPubDir Summer 83 p.113, Spring 84 p.113*
WCOV - Montgomery, AL - *BrCabYB 84; NatRadPubDir Summer 83, Spring 84; TV&RadDir 84*
WCOV-TV - Montgomery, AL - *BrCabYB 84; DirUSTelSta 83; TelAl 83, 84; Tel&CabFB 84S; TV&RadDir 84*
WCOW - Sparta, WI - *BrCabYB 84; TV&RadDir 84*
WCOW-FM - Sparta, WI - *BrCabYB 84; TV&RadDir 84*
WCOX - Camden, AL - *BrCabYB 84; TV&RadDir 84*
WCOZ-FM - Boston, MA - *BrCabYB 84; LitMarPl 84; NatRadPubDir Summer 83, Spring 84; TV&RadDir 84*
WCPA - Clearfield, PA - *BrCabYB 84; TV&RadDir 84*
WCPB - Salisbury, MD - *BrCabYB 84; Tel&CabFB 84S*
WCPC - Houston, MS - *BrCabYB 84; TV&RadDir 84*
WCPC-FM - Houston, MS - *BrCabYB 84; TV&RadDir 84*
WCPE-FM - Raleigh, NC - *BrCabYB 84; NatRadPubDir Summer 83, Spring 84; TV&RadDir 84*
WCPH - Etowah, TN - *BrCabYB 84; TV&RadDir 84*
WCPI-FM - Wheeling, WV - *BrCabYB 84; LitMarPl 84; NatRadPubDir Summer 83, Spring 84; TV&RadDir 84*
WCPK - Chesapeake, VA - *BrCabYB 84; TV&RadDir 84*
WCPK - Norfolk, VA - *NatRadPubDir Summer 83 p.254, Spring 84 p.256*
WCPL - Pageland, SC - *BrCabYB 84; TV&RadDir 84*
WCPL-FM - Pageland, SC - *BrCabYB 84; TV&RadDir 84*
WCPM - Cumberland, KY - *BrCabYB 84; TV&RadDir 84*
WCPN - Cleveland, OH - *BrCabYB 84*
WCPO-TV - Cincinnati, OH - *BrCabYB 84; DirUSTelSta 83; LitMarPl 83, 84; TelAl 83, 84; Tel&CabFB 84S; TV&RadDir 84*
WCPQ - Havelock, NC - *BrCabYB 84; TV&RadDir 84*
WCPR - Coamo, PR - *BrCabYB 84*
WCPS - Tabor City, NC - *TV&RadDir 84*
WCPS - Tarboro, NC - *BrCabYB 84; TV&RadDir 84*
WCPT-TV - Crossville, TN - *TelAl 83*
WCPX-TV - Orlando, FL - *BrCabYB 84; DirUSTelSta 83; LitMarPl 84; TelAl 84; Tel&CabFB 84S*
WCPZ - Sandusky, OH - *BrCabYB 84; TV&RadDir 84*
WCPZ-FM - Sandusky, OH - *NatRadPubDir Summer 83, Spring 84*
WCQL - Pewaukee, WI - *TV&RadDir 84*
WCQO - Blairsville, PA - *BrCabYB 84*
WCQR - Washington, DC - *BrCabYB 84; DirUSTelSta 83; TelAl 84; Tel&CabFB 84S*
WCRA - Effingham, IL - *BrCabYB 84; TV&RadDir 84*
WCRB-FM - Boston, MA - *NatRadPubDir Summer 83 p.119, Spring 84 p.119*
WCRB-FM - Waltham, MA - *BrCabYB 84; TV&RadDir 84*
WCRC-FM - Effingham, IL - *BrCabYB 84; TV&RadDir 84*
WCRD-FM - Bluffton, IN - *BrCabYB 84; TV&RadDir 84*
WCRE - Cheraw, SC - *BrCabYB 84; TV&RadDir 84*
WCRF-FM - Cleveland, OH - *BrCabYB 84; NatRadPubDir Summer 83, Spring 84; TV&RadDir 84*
WCRH-FM - Williamsport, MD - *BrCabYB 84; TV&RadDir 84*
WCRJ - Jacksonville, FL - *BrCabYB 84; TV&RadDir 84*
WCRJ-FM - Jacksonville, FL - *BrCabYB 84*
WCRK - Morristown, TN - *BrCabYB 84; TV&RadDir 84*
WCRL - Oneonta, AL - *BrCabYB 84; TV&RadDir 84*
WCRM-FM - Dundee, IL - *BrCabYB 84; TV&RadDir 84*
WCRO - Johnstown, PA - *BrCabYB 84; NatRadPubDir Summer 83, Spring 84; TV&RadDir 84*
WCRP - Guayama, PR - *BrCabYB 84*
WCRQ-FM - Arab, AL - *BrCabYB 84; TV&RadDir 84*
WCRR - Cornwall-on-the-Hudson, NY - *BrCabYB 84; TV&RadDir 84*
WCRS - Greenwood, SC - *BrCabYB 84; TV&RadDir 84*
WCRT - Birmingham, AL - *BrCabYB 84; NatRadPubDir Summer 83, Spring 84; TV&RadDir 84*

WCRV - Washington, NJ - *BrCabYB 84; TV&RadDir 84*
WCRW - Chicago, IL - *BrCabYB 84; NatRadPubDir Summer 83, Spring 84; TV&RadDir 84*
WCRX-FM - Chicago, IL - *BrCabYB 84; TV&RadDir 84*
WCSA - Ripley, MS - *TV&RadDir 84*
WCSB-FM - Cleveland, OH - *BrCabYB 84; NatRadPubDir Summer 83, Spring 84; TV&RadDir 84*
WCSC - Charleston, SC - *BrCabYB 84; NatRadPubDir Summer 83, Spring 84; TV&RadDir 84*
WCSC-TV - Charleston, SC - *BrCabYB 84; DirUSTelSta 83; TelAl 83, 84; Tel&CabFB 84S; TV&RadDir 84*
WCSD-FM - Warminster, PA - *BrCabYB 84; NatRadPubDir Summer 83, Spring 84; TV&RadDir 84*
WCSE-FM - Asheboro, NC - *BrCabYB 84; NatRadPubDir Summer 83, Spring 84; TV&RadDir 84*
WCSF - Clifton Park, NY - *BrCabYB 84*
WCSG-FM - Grand Rapids, MI - *BrCabYB 84; NatRadPubDir Summer 83, Spring 84; TV&RadDir 84*
WCSH-TV - Portland, ME - *BrCabYB 84; DirUSTelSta 83; LitMarPl 83, 84; TelAl 83, 84; Tel&CabFB 84S; TV&RadDir 84*
WCSI - Columbus, IN - *BrCabYB 84; TV&RadDir 84*
WCSI-FM - Columbus, IN - *BrCabYB 84; TV&RadDir 84*
WCSJ - Morris, IL - *BrCabYB 84; TV&RadDir 84*
WCSJ-FM - Morris, IL - *BrCabYB 84; TV&RadDir 84*
WCSK - Kingsport, TN - *BrCabYB 84*
WCSL - Cherryville, NC - *BrCabYB 84; TV&RadDir 84*
WCSM - Celina, OH - *BrCabYB 84; TV&RadDir 84*
WCSM-FM - Celina, OH - *BrCabYB 84; TV&RadDir 84*
WCSN - Tallahassee, FL - *BrCabYB 84; NatRadPubDir Summer 83, Spring 84*
WCSO-FM - Chattanooga, TN - *TV&RadDir 84*
WCSO-FM - Signal Mountain, TN - *BrCabYB 84*
WCSP - Crystal Springs, MS - *BrCabYB 84; TV&RadDir 84*
WCSQ-FM - Central Square, NY - *BrCabYB 84; TV&RadDir 84*
WCSR - Hillsdale, MI - *BrCabYB 84; TV&RadDir 84*
WCSR-FM - Hillsdale, MI - *BrCabYB 84; TV&RadDir 84*
WCSS - Amsterdam, NY - *BrCabYB 84; TV&RadDir 84*
WCST - Berkeley Springs, WV - *BrCabYB 84; TV&RadDir 84*
WCST-FM - Berkeley Springs, WV - *BrCabYB 84; TV&RadDir 84*
WCSU-FM - Wilberforce, OH - *BrCabYB 84; NatRadPubDir Summer 83, Spring 84; TV&RadDir 84*
WCSV - Crossville, TN - *BrCabYB 84; TV&RadDir 84*
WCSW - Shell Lake, WI - *BrCabYB 84; TV&RadDir 84*
WCSY - South Haven, MI - *BrCabYB 84*
WCTA - Alamo, TN - *BrCabYB 84*
WCTC - New Brunswick, NJ - *BrCabYB 84; NatRadPubDir Summer 83, Spring 84*
WCTC - Somerset, NJ - *TV&RadDir 84*
WCTE - Cookeville, TN - *BrCabYB 84; Tel&CabFB 84S*
WCTI-TV - Greenville, NC - *DirUSTelSta 83*
WCTI-TV - New Bern, NC - *BrCabYB 84; TelAl 83, 84; Tel&CabFB 84S; TV&RadDir 84*
WCTL-FM - Union City, PA - *BrCabYB 84; TV&RadDir 84*
WCTM - Eaton, OH - *BrCabYB 84*
WCTM - West Alexandria, OH - *TV&RadDir 84*
WCTN - Washington, DC - *NatRadPubDir Summer 83 p.53, Spring 84 p.53*
WCTN - Potomac-Cabin John, MD - *BrCabYB 84*
WCTO-FM - Huntington Station, NY - *TV&RadDir 84*
WCTO-FM - Smithtown, NY - *BrCabYB 84*
WCTO-FM - Suffolk County, Long Island, NY - *NatRadPubDir Summer 83 p.177, Spring 84 p.175*
WCTR - Chestertown, MD - *BrCabYB 84; TV&RadDir 84*
WCTS-FM - Minneapolis, MN - *BrCabYB 84; NatRadPubDir Summer 83, Spring 84; TV&RadDir 84*
WCTT - Corbin, KY - *BrCabYB 84; TV&RadDir 84*
WCTT-FM - Corbin, KY - *BrCabYB 84; TV&RadDir 84*
WCTV-TV - Tallahassee, FL - *DirUSTelSta 83; Tel&CabFB 84S; TV&RadDir 84*
WCTV-TV - Thomasville, FL - *TelAl 83, 84*
WCTV-TV - Thomasville, GA - *BrCabYB 84*
WCTW - New Castle, IN - *BrCabYB 84; TV&RadDir 84*
WCTX-FM - Palmyra, PA - *BrCabYB 84; TV&RadDir 84*
WCTY-FM - Norwich, CT - *BrCabYB 84; NatRadPubDir Summer 83, Spring 84; TV&RadDir 84*
WCUB - Manitowoc, WI - *BrCabYB 84*
WCUC - Clarion, PA - *TV&RadDir 84*
WCUC-FM - Clarion, PA - *BrCabYB 84*
WCUE - Akron, OH - *NatRadPubDir Summer 83, Spring 84*
WCUE - Cuyahoga Falls, OH - *BrCabYB 84; TV&RadDir 84*
WCUG - Cuthbert, GA - *BrCabYB 84; TV&RadDir 84*
WCUL-FM - Culpeper, VA - *BrCabYB 84; TV&RadDir 84*
WCUP-FM - Tifton, GA - *BrCabYB 84; TV&RadDir 84*
WCUR-FM - Randolph, VT - *TV&RadDir 84*
WCUW-FM - Worcester, MA - *BrCabYB 84; NatRadPubDir Summer 83, Spring 84; TV&RadDir 84*
WCUZ - Grand Rapids, MI - *BrCabYB 84; NatRadPubDir Summer 83, Spring 84; TV&RadDir 84*
WCUZ-FM - Grand Rapids, MI - *BrCabYB 84; NatRadPubDir Summer 83, Spring 84; TV&RadDir 84*
WCVA - Culpeper, VA - *BrCabYB 84; TV&RadDir 84*
WCVB-TV - Boston, MA - *BrCabYB 84; DirUSTelSta 83; LitMarPl 83, 84; TelAl 83, 84; Tel&CabFB 84S*
WCVB-TV - Needham, MA - *TV&RadDir 84*
WCVC - Tallahassee, FL - *BrCabYB 84; TV&RadDir 84*
WCVE-TV - Richmond, VA - *BrCabYB 84; Tel&CabFB 84S; TV&RadDir 84*
WCVF - Fredonia, NY - *NatRadPubDir Summer 83, Spring 84*
WCVF-FM - Fredonia, NY - *BrCabYB 84; NatRadPubDir Summer 83, Spring 84; TV&RadDir 84*
WCVH-FM - Flemington, NJ - *BrCabYB 84; NatRadPubDir Summer 83, Spring 84; TV&RadDir 84*
WCVI - Connellsville, PA - *BrCabYB 84; TV&RadDir 84*
WCVJ-FM - Jefferson, OH - *BrCabYB 84; TV&RadDir 84*
WCVL - Crawfordsville, IN - *BrCabYB 84; TV&RadDir 84*
WCVM-FM - Middlebury, VT - *BrCabYB 84; TV&RadDir 84*
WCVN-TV - Covington, KY - *BrCabYB 84; Tel&CabFB 84S*
WCVN-TV - Lexington, KY - *TV&RadDir 84*
WCVO-FM - Gahanna, OH - *BrCabYB 84*
WCVO-FM - New Albany, OH - *TV&RadDir 84*
WCVP - Murphy, NC - *BrCabYB 84; TV&RadDir 84*
WCVR - Randolph, VT - *BrCabYB 84; TV&RadDir 84*
WCVR-FM - Randolph, VT - *BrCabYB 84*
WCVS - Springfield, IL - *BrCabYB 84; NatRadPubDir Summer 83, Spring 84; TV&RadDir 84*
WCVT-FM - Baltimore, MD - *TV&RadDir 84*
WCVT-FM - Towson, MD - *BrCabYB 84; NatRadPubDir Summer 83, Spring 84*
WCVU-FM - Naples, FL - *BrCabYB 84; TV&RadDir 84*
WCVW-TV - Richmond, VA - *BrCabYB 84; Tel&CabFB 84S; TV&RadDir 84*
WCVY-FM - Coventry, RI - *BrCabYB 84; TV&RadDir 84*
WCVZ - Zanesville, OH - *BrCabYB 84*
WCWA - Toledo, OH - *BrCabYB 84; NatRadPubDir Summer 83, Spring 84; TV&RadDir 84*
WCWB-TV - Macon, GA - *DirUSTelSta 83; TelAl 83, 84; Tel&CabFB 84S; TV&RadDir 84*
WCWC - Ripon, WI - *BrCabYB 84; TV&RadDir 84*
WCWL-FM - Lenox, MA - *TV&RadDir 84*
WCWL-FM - Stockbridge, MA - *BrCabYB 84; NatRadPubDir Summer 83 p.291, Spring 84 p.293*
WCWM-FM - Williamsburg, VA - *BrCabYB 84; NatRadPubDir Summer 83, Spring 84; TV&RadDir 84*
WCWP-FM - Brookville, NY - *BrCabYB 84*
WCWP-FM - Greenvale, NY - *NatRadPubDir Summer 83, Spring 84; TV&RadDir 84*
WCWR - Cocoa, FL - *TV&RadDir 84*
WCWS-FM - Wooster, OH - *BrCabYB 84; NatRadPubDir Summer 83, Spring 84; TV&RadDir 84*
WCWT-FM - Centerville, OH - *BrCabYB 84; TV&RadDir 84*
WCWV - Summersville, WV - *BrCabYB 84*
WCXI - Detroit, MI - *BrCabYB 84; NatRadPubDir Summer 83, Spring 84; TV&RadDir 84*
WCXI-FM - Detroit, MI - *BrCabYB 84; NatRadPubDir Summer 83, Spring 84; TV&RadDir 84*
WCXL-FM - Kettering, OH - *BrCabYB 84; TV&RadDir 84*
WCXQ - Moca, PR - *BrCabYB 84*
WCXT - Hart, MI - *BrCabYB 84*
WCYB-TV - Johnson City, TN - *DirUSTelSta 83*
WCYB-TV - Bristol, VA - *BrCabYB 84; TelAl 83, 84; Tel&CabFB 84S; TV&RadDir 84*
WCYC-FM - Chicago, IL - *BrCabYB 84; TV&RadDir 84*

WCYJ-FM - Waynesburg, PA - *BrCabYB 84; NatRadPubDir Summer 83, Spring 84; TV&RadDir 84*
WCYN - Cynthiana, KY - *BrCabYB 84; TV&RadDir 84*
WCYN-FM - Cynthiana, KY - *BrCabYB 84; TV&RadDir 84*
WCZY-FM - Detroit, MI - *BrCabYB 84; NatRadPubDir Summer 83, Spring 84*
WCZY-FM - Oak Park, MI - *TV&RadDir 84*
WDAC-FM - Lancaster, PA - *BrCabYB 84; NatRadPubDir Summer 83, Spring 84; TV&RadDir 84*
WDAD - Indiana, PA - *BrCabYB 84; TV&RadDir 84*
WDAE - Tampa, FL - *BrCabYB 84; NatRadPubDir Summer 83, Spring 84; TV&RadDir 84*
WDAF - Kansas City, MO - *BrCabYB 84; NatRadPubDir Summer 83, Spring 84; TV&RadDir 84*
WDAF-TV - Kansas City, MO - *BrCabYB 84; DirUSTelSta 83; TelAl 83, 84; Tel&CabFB 84S; TV&RadDir 84*
WDAF-TV - Signal Hill, MO - *LitMarPl 83, 84*
WDAI - Gary, IN - *Tel&CabFB 84S*
WDAK - Columbus, GA - *BrCabYB 84; NatRadPubDir Summer 83, Spring 84; TV&RadDir 84*
WDAM-TV - Hattiesburg, MS - *DirUSTelSta 83; TV&RadDir 84*
WDAM-TV - Laurel, MS - *BrCabYB 84; TelAl 83, 84*
WDAN - Champaign/Urbana/Danville, IL - *NatRadPubDir Summer 83, Spring 84 p.79*
WDAN - Danville, IL - *BrCabYB 84; TV&RadDir 84*
WDAO-FM - Dayton, OH - *BrCabYB 84; NatRadPubDir Summer 83, Spring 84; TV&RadDir 84*
WDAQ-FM - Danbury, CT - *NatRadPubDir Summer 83, Spring 84; TV&RadDir 84*
WDAR-FM - Darlington, SC - *BrCabYB 84; TV&RadDir 84*
WDAS - Philadelphia, PA - *BrCabYB 84; NatRadPubDir Summer 83, Spring 84; TV&RadDir 84*
WDAS-FM - Philadelphia, PA - *BrCabYB 84; NatRadPubDir Summer 83, Spring 84; TV&RadDir 84*
WDAT - Daytona Beach, FL - *BrCabYB 84; NatRadPubDir Summer 83 p.57, Spring 84 p.57*
WDAT - Ormond Beach, FL - *TV&RadDir 84*
WDAU-TV - Scranton, PA - *BrCabYB 84; DirUSTelSta 83; LitMarPl 83, 84; TelAl 83, 84; Tel&CabFB 84S; TV&RadDir 84*
WDAV-FM - Davidson, NC - *BrCabYB 84; NatRadPubDir Summer 83, Spring 84; TV&RadDir 84*
WDAX - McRae, GA - *BrCabYB 84; TV&RadDir 84*
WDAX-FM - McRae, GA - *BrCabYB 84; TV&RadDir 84*
WDAY - Fargo, NV - *TV&RadDir 84*
WDAY - Fargo, ND - *BrCabYB 84; NatRadPubDir Summer 83, Spring 84*
WDAY-FM - Fargo, NV - *TV&RadDir 84*
WDAY-FM - Fargo, ND - *BrCabYB 84; NatRadPubDir Summer 83, Spring 84*
WDAY-TV - Fargo, NV - *TV&RadDir 84*
WDAY-TV - Fargo, ND - *BrCabYB 84; DirUSTelSta 83; TelAl 83, 84; Tel&CabFB 84S; TV&RadDir 84*
WDAZ-TV - Devils Lake, ND - *BrCabYB 84; TelAl 83, 84; Tel&CabFB 84S*
WDAZ-TV - Grand Forks, ND - *TV&RadDir 84*
WDBA-FM - Du Bois, PA - *BrCabYB 84; TV&RadDir 84*
WDBC - Escanaba, MI - *BrCabYB 84; TV&RadDir 84*
WDBD - Jackson, MS - *BrCabYB 84; Tel&CabFB 84S*
WDBF - Delray Beach, FL - *BrCabYB 84; TV&RadDir 84*
WDBF - West Palm Beach, FL - *NatRadPubDir Summer 83 p.66, Spring 84 p.66*
WDBI-FM - Tawas City, MI - *BrCabYB 84; TV&RadDir 84*
WDBJ-TV - Roanoke, VA - *BrCabYB 84; DirUSTelSta 83; TelAl 83, 84; Tel&CabFB 84S; TV&RadDir 84*
WDBK-FM - Blackwood, NJ - *BrCabYB 84; TV&RadDir 84*
WDBL-FM - Springfield, TN - *BrCabYB 84; TV&RadDir 84*
WDBM - Dothan, AL - *BrCabYB 84*
WDBN-FM - Akron, OH - *NatRadPubDir Summer 83 p.191, Spring 84 p.189*
WDBN-FM - Medina, OH - *BrCabYB 84; TV&RadDir 84*
WDBO - Orlando, FL - *BrCabYB 84; NatRadPubDir Summer 83, Spring 84; TV&RadDir 84*
WDBO-FM - Orlando, FL - *NatRadPubDir Summer 83, Spring 84; TV&RadDir 84*
WDBO-TV - Orlando, FL - *LitMarPl 83; TelAl 83; TV&RadDir 84*
WDBQ - Dubuque, IA - *BrCabYB 84; TV&RadDir 84*
WDBR-FM - Springfield, IL - *BrCabYB 84; NatRadPubDir Summer 83, Spring 84; TV&RadDir 84*
WDBS-FM - Durham, NC - *BrCabYB 84; TV&RadDir 84*
WDBS-FM - Raleigh/Durham, NC - *NatRadPubDir Summer 83, Spring 84 p.183*
WDBY - Duxbury, MA - *BrCabYB 84*
WDCA-TV [Div. of Taft Broadcasting] - Washington, DC - *AvMarPl 83; BrCabYB 84; DirUSTelSta 83; TelAl 83, 84; Tel&CabFB 84S; TV&RadDir 84*
WDCB-FM - Glen Ellyn, IL - *BrCabYB 84*
WDCB-FM - Glendale Hights, IL - *TV&RadDir 84*
WDCC-FM - Sanford, NC - *BrCabYB 84; NatRadPubDir Summer 83, Spring 84; TV&RadDir 84*
WDCE-FM - Richmond, VA - *BrCabYB 84*
WDCF - Dade City, FL - *BrCabYB 84; TV&RadDir 84*
WDCG-FM - Durham, NC - *BrCabYB 84; TV&RadDir 84*
WDCG-FM - Raleigh/Durham, NC - *NatRadPubDir Summer 83, Spring 84 p.183*
WDCJ - Lorton, VA - *BrCabYB 84*
WDCL - Somerset, KY - *BrCabYB 84*
WDCN-TV - Nashville, TN - *BrCabYB 84; Tel&CabFB 84S; TV&RadDir 84*
WDCO-FM - Cochran, GA - *BrCabYB 84*
WDCO-TV - Cochran, GA - *BrCabYB 84; Tel&CabFB 84S; TV&RadDir 84*
WDCR - Hanover, NH - *BrCabYB 84; NatRadPubDir Summer 83, Spring 84; TV&RadDir 84*
WDCS-FM - Portland, ME - *NatRadPubDir Summer 83 p.113, Spring 84 p.113; TV&RadDir 84*
WDCS-FM - Scarborough, ME - *BrCabYB 84*
WDCU - Washington, DC - *BrCabYB 84*
WDCV-FM - Carlisle, PA - *BrCabYB 84; NatRadPubDir Summer 83, Spring 84; TV&RadDir 84*
WDCX-FM - Buffalo, NY - *BrCabYB 84; NatRadPubDir Summer 83, Spring 84; TV&RadDir 84*
WDDC-FM - Portage, WI - *BrCabYB 84; TV&RadDir 84*
WDDD-FM - Marion, IL - *BrCabYB 84; TV&RadDir 84*
WDDD-TV - Marion, IL - *BrCabYB 84; TelAl 84; Tel&CabFB 84S; TV&RadDir 84*
WDDD-TV - Paducah, KY - *DirUSTelSta 83*
WDDJ-FM - Paducah, KY - *BrCabYB 84; TV&RadDir 84*
WDDO - Macon, GA - *BrCabYB 84; NatRadPubDir Summer 83, Spring 84; TV&RadDir 84*
WDDQ-FM - Adel, GA - *BrCabYB 84; TV&RadDir 84*
WDDT - Greenville, MS - *BrCabYB 84; NatRadPubDir Summer 83, Spring 84; TV&RadDir 84*
WDDW - Johnston City, IL - *BrCabYB 84*
WDDY - Gloucester, VA - *BrCabYB 84; TV&RadDir 84*
WDEA - Ellsworth, ME - *BrCabYB 84; TV&RadDir 84*
WDEA-FM - Ellsworth, ME - *TV&RadDir 84*
WDEB - Jamestown, TN - *BrCabYB 84; TV&RadDir 84*
WDEB-FM - Jamestown, TN - *BrCabYB 84; TV&RadDir 84*
WDEC - Americus, GA - *BrCabYB 84; TV&RadDir 84*
WDEE - Reed City, MI - *BrCabYB 84*
WDEF - Chattanooga, TN - *BrCabYB 84; NatRadPubDir Summer 83, Spring 84; TV&RadDir 84*
WDEF-FM - Chattanooga, TN - *BrCabYB 84; NatRadPubDir Summer 83, Spring 84; TV&RadDir 84*
WDEF-TV - Chattanooga, TN - *BrCabYB 84; DirUSTelSta 83; TelAl 83, 84; Tel&CabFB 84S; TV&RadDir 84*
WDEH - Sweetwater, TN - *BrCabYB 84; TV&RadDir 84*
WDEH-FM - Sweetwater, TN - *BrCabYB 84; TV&RadDir 84*
WDEK-FM - De Kalb, IL - *BrCabYB 84; NatRadPubDir Summer 83, Spring 84; TV&RadDir 84*
WDEL - Wilmington, DE - *BrCabYB 84; NatRadPubDir Summer 83, Spring 84; TV&RadDir 84*
WDEN-FM - Macon, GA - *BrCabYB 84; NatRadPubDir Summer 83, Spring 84; TV&RadDir 84*
WDEQ-FM - De Graff, OH - *BrCabYB 84; NatRadPubDir Summer 83, Spring 84; TV&RadDir 84*
WDER - Derry, NH - *BrCabYB 84*
WDET-FM - Detroit, MI - *BrCabYB 84; NatRadPubDir Summer 83, Spring 84; TV&RadDir 84*
WDEV - Waterbury, VT - *BrCabYB 84; TV&RadDir 84*
WDEX - Monroe, NC - *BrCabYB 84*

WDEY - Lapeer, MI - *BrCabYB 84; TV&RadDir 84*
WDEY-FM - Lapeer, MI - *BrCabYB 84*
WDEZ-FM - Wausau, WI - *BrCabYB 84; TV&RadDir 84*
WDFB - Junction City, KY - *BrCabYB 84*
WDFM-FM - State College, PA - *BrCabYB 84; NatRadPubDir Summer 83 p.314, Spring 84*
WDFM-FM - University Park, PA - *TV&RadDir 84*
WDFP-FM - Battle Creek, MI - *BrCabYB 84; TV&RadDir 84*
WDGC-FM - Downers Grove, IL - *BrCabYB 84; TV&RadDir 84*
WDGL - Douglasville, GA - *BrCabYB 84; TV&RadDir 84*
WDGR - Dahlonega, GA - *TV&RadDir 84*
WDGS - Jeffersonville, IN - *TV&RadDir 84*
WDGS - New Albany, IN - *BrCabYB 84*
WDGY - Bloomington, MN - *LitMarPl 83, 84*
WDGY - Minneapolis, MN - *BrCabYB 84; TV&RadDir 84*
WDGY - Minneapolis/St. Paul, MN - *NatRadPubDir Summer 83 p.135, Spring 84 p.135*
WDHA-FM - Dover, NJ - *BrCabYB 84; NatRadPubDir Summer 83, Spring 84; TV&RadDir 84*
WDHN-TV - Dothan, AL - *BrCabYB 84; DirUSTelSta 83; TelAl 83, 84; Tel&CabFB 84S; TV&RadDir 84*
WDHO-TV - Toledo, OH - *BrCabYB 84; DirUSTelSta 83; LitMarPl 83, 84; TelAl 84; Tel&CabFB 84S; TV&RadDir 84*
WDHP-FM - Presque Isle, ME - *BrCabYB 84; TV&RadDir 84*
WDHR-FM - Pikeville, KY - *BrCabYB 84; TV&RadDir 84*
WDHS - Gaston, IN - *BrCabYB 84*
WDIA - Memphis, TN - *BrCabYB 84; NatRadPubDir Summer 83, Spring 84; TV&RadDir 84*
WDIC - Clinchco, VA - *BrCabYB 84*
WDIC - Clintwood, VA - *TV&RadDir 84*
WDIF-FM - Marion, OH - *BrCabYB 84; TV&RadDir 84*
WDIG - Dothan, AL - *BrCabYB 84*
WDIO-TV - Duluth, MN - *BrCabYB 84; DirUSTelSta 83; LitMarPl 83, 84; TelAl 83, 84; Tel&CabFB 84S; TV&RadDir 84*
WDIQ - Dozier, AL - *BrCabYB 84; Tel&CabFB 84S*
WDIV-TV - Detroit, MI - *BrCabYB 84; DirUSTelSta 83; LitMarPl 83, 84; TelAl 83, 84; Tel&CabFB 84S; TV&RadDir 84*
WDIX-AM - Orangeburg, SC - *BrCabYB 84*
WDIX-FM - Huntington Station, NY - *TV&RadDir 84*
WDIZ-FM - Orlando, FL - *BrCabYB 84; NatRadPubDir Summer 83 p.62, Spring 84 p.63*
WDIZ-FM - Winter Park, FL - *TV&RadDir 84*
WDJB-FM - Windsor, NC - *TV&RadDir 84*
WDJC-FM - Birmingham, AL - *BrCabYB 84; NatRadPubDir Summer 83, Spring 84; TV&RadDir 84*
WDJD - Jackson, MI - *BrCabYB 84; TV&RadDir 84*
WDJF-FM - Westport, CT - *BrCabYB 84; NatRadPubDir Summer 83, Spring 84; TV&RadDir 84*
WDJM-FM - Framingham, MA - *BrCabYB 84; TV&RadDir 84*
WDJQ - Alliance, OH - *BrCabYB 84; TV&RadDir 84*
WDJS - Mt. Olive, NC - *BrCabYB 84; TV&RadDir 84*
WDJW-FM - Somers, CT - *BrCabYB 84; TV&RadDir 84*
WDJX-FM - Xenia, OH - *TV&RadDir 84*
WDJZ - Bridgeport, CT - *BrCabYB 84*
WDKA - Cross City, FL - *BrCabYB 84*
WDKD - Kingstree, SC - *BrCabYB 84; TV&RadDir 84*
WDKN - Dickson, TN - *BrCabYB 84; TV&RadDir 84*
WDKX-FM - Rochester, NY - *BrCabYB 84; NatRadPubDir Summer 83, Spring 84; TV&RadDir 84*
WDKY-TV - Danville, KY - *BrCabYB 84; Tel&CabFB 84S*
WDLA - Walton, NY - *BrCabYB 84; TV&RadDir 84*
WDLA-FM - Walton, NY - *BrCabYB 84; TV&RadDir 84*
WDLB - Marshfield, WI - *BrCabYB 84; TV&RadDir 84*
WDLC - Port Jervis, NY - *BrCabYB 84; NatRadPubDir Summer 83, Spring 84; TV&RadDir 84*
WDLC-FM - Port Jervis, NY - *BrCabYB 84; NatRadPubDir Summer 83, Spring 84; TV&RadDir 84*
WDLF - DeLand, FL - *BrCabYB 84; TV&RadDir 84*
WDLI - Canton, OH - *BrCabYB 84; Tel&CabFB 84S*
WDLK - Dadeville, AL - *BrCabYB 84; TV&RadDir 84*
WDLM-FM - East Moline, IL - *BrCabYB 84; TV&RadDir 84*
WDLP - Panama City, FL - *BrCabYB 84; TV&RadDir 84*
WDLR - Delaware, OH - *BrCabYB 84; TV&RadDir 84*
WDLV - Pinehurst, NC - *BrCabYB 84*
WDLV - Southern Pines, NC - *TV&RadDir 84*
WDLW - Boston, MA - *NatRadPubDir Summer 83 p.119, Spring 84 p.119*
WDLW - Waltham, MA - *BrCabYB 84; TV&RadDir 84*
WDMA-TV - Toledo, OH - *BrCabYB 84; Tel&CabFB 84S*
WDME - Dover Foxcroft, ME - *BrCabYB 84; TV&RadDir 84*
WDME-FM - Dover Foxcroft, ME - *BrCabYB 84; TV&RadDir 84*
WDMG - Douglas, GA - *BrCabYB 84; TV&RadDir 84*
WDMG-FM - Douglas, GA - *BrCabYB 84; TV&RadDir 84*
WDMJ - Marquette, MI - *BrCabYB 84; TV&RadDir 84*
WDMP-FM - Dodgeville, WI - *BrCabYB 84; TV&RadDir 84*
WDMS-FM - Greenville, MS - *BrCabYB 84; NatRadPubDir Summer 83, Spring 84; TV&RadDir 84*
WDMT-FM - Cleveland, OH - *BrCabYB 84; NatRadPubDir Summer 83 p.193, Spring 84*
WDMT-FM - Newbury, OH - *TV&RadDir 84*
WDMV - Pocomoke City, MD - *BrCabYB 84*
WDNA-FM - Miami, FL - *BrCabYB 84; TV&RadDir 84*
WDNC - Durham, NC - *BrCabYB 84; TV&RadDir 84*
WDNC - Raleigh/Durham, NC - *NatRadPubDir Summer 83, Spring 84 p.183*
WDND-FM - Wilmington, IL - *BrCabYB 84; TV&RadDir 84*
WDNE - Elkins, WV - *BrCabYB 84; TV&RadDir 84*
WDNE-FM - Elkins, WV - *BrCabYB 84*
WDNG - Anniston, AL - *BrCabYB 84; TV&RadDir 84*
WDNH - Honesdale, PA - *BrCabYB 84; TV&RadDir 84*
WDNH-FM - Honesdale, PA - *BrCabYB 84; TV&RadDir 84*
WDNL-FM - Danville, IL - *BrCabYB 84; TV&RadDir 84*
WDNR-FM - Chester, PA - *BrCabYB 84; TV&RadDir 84*
WDNS-FM - Bowling Green, KY - *BrCabYB 84; NatRadPubDir Summer 83, Spring 84; TV&RadDir 84*
WDNT - Dayton, TN - *BrCabYB 84; TV&RadDir 84*
WDNX-FM - Olive Hill, TN - *BrCabYB 84*
WDNX-FM - Savannah, TN - *NatRadPubDir Summer 83, Spring 84; TV&RadDir 84*
WDNY - Dansville, NY - *BrCabYB 84; TV&RadDir 84*
WDOC - Prestonsburg, KY - *BrCabYB 84; TV&RadDir 84*
WDOD - Chattanooga, TN - *BrCabYB 84; NatRadPubDir Summer 83, Spring 84; TV&RadDir 84*
WDOD-FM - Chattanooga, TN - *BrCabYB 84; NatRadPubDir Summer 83, Spring 84; TV&RadDir 84*
WDOE - Dunkirk, NY - *BrCabYB 84; TV&RadDir 84*
WDOG - Allendale, SC - *BrCabYB 84; TV&RadDir 84*
WDOH-FM - Delphos, OH - *BrCabYB 84; TV&RadDir 84*
WDOK-FM - Cleveland, OH - *BrCabYB 84; NatRadPubDir Summer 83, Spring 84; TV&RadDir 84*
WDOM-FM - Providence, RI - *BrCabYB 84; NatRadPubDir Summer 83, Spring 84; TV&RadDir 84*
WDOQ - Daytona Beach, FL - *BrCabYB 84*
WDOR - Sturgeon Bay, WI - *BrCabYB 84; TV&RadDir 84*
WDOR-FM - Sturgeon Bay, WI - *BrCabYB 84; TV&RadDir 84*
WDOS - Oneonta, NY - *BrCabYB 84; TV&RadDir 84*
WDOT - Burlington, VT - *BrCabYB 84; NatRadPubDir Summer 83, Spring 84; TV&RadDir 84*
WDOV - Dover, DE - *BrCabYB 84; NatRadPubDir Summer 83, Spring 84; TV&RadDir 84*
WDOW - Dowagiac, MI - *BrCabYB 84; TV&RadDir 84*
WDOW-FM - Dowagiac, MI - *BrCabYB 84; TV&RadDir 84*
WDOY - Fajardo, PR - *BrCabYB 84*
WDPB - Seaford, DE - *BrCabYB 84; Tel&CabFB 84S*
WDPN - Columbia, SC - *BrCabYB 84*
WDPS-FM - Dayton, OH - *BrCabYB 84; TV&RadDir 84*
WDQN - Duquoin, IL - *BrCabYB 84; TV&RadDir 84*
WDQN-FM - Duquoin, IL - *BrCabYB 84; TV&RadDir 84*
WDRB-TV - Louisville, KY - *BrCabYB 84; DirUSTelSta 83; TelAl 83, 84; Tel&CabFB 84S; TV&RadDir 84*
WDRC - Bloomfield, CT - *TV&RadDir 84*
WDRC - Hartford, CT - *BrCabYB 84; NatRadPubDir Summer 83 p.46, Spring 84 p.46*
WDRC-FM - Bloomfield, CT - *TV&RadDir 84*
WDRC-FM - Hartford, CT - *BrCabYB 84; NatRadPubDir Summer 83 p.46, Spring 84 p.46*
WDRE-FM - Ellenville, NY - *BrCabYB 84; TV&RadDir 84*
WDRG - Dahlonega, GA - *BrCabYB 84*
WDRK-FM - Greenville, OH - *BrCabYB 84; TV&RadDir 84*
WDRM-FM - Decatur, AL - *BrCabYB 84; TV&RadDir 84*
WDRQ-FM - Detroit, MI - *BrCabYB 84; NatRadPubDir Summer 83 p.126, Spring 84 p.126*
WDRQ-FM - Southfield, MI - *TV&RadDir 84*

WDRV - Statesville, NC - *BrCabYB 84; LitMarPl 83, 84; TV&RadDir 84*
WDS Forum [of Writer's Digest School] - Cincinnati, OH - *ArtMar 84; WritMar 84*
WDSC - Dillon, SC - *BrCabYB 84; TV&RadDir 84*
WDSC-FM - Dillon, SC - *BrCabYB 84; TV&RadDir 84*
WDSD-FM - Dover, DE - *BrCabYB 84; NatRadPubDir Summer 83, Spring 84; TV&RadDir 84*
WDSE-TV - Duluth, MN - *BrCabYB 84; Tel&CabFB 84S; TV&RadDir 84*
WDSG - Dyersburg, TN - *BrCabYB 84; TV&RadDir 84*
WDSI-TV - Chattanooga, TN - *BrCabYB 84; Tel&CabFB 84S*
WDSL - Mocksville, NC - *BrCabYB 84; TV&RadDir 84*
WDSM - Duluth, MN - *NatRadPubDir Summer 83, Spring 84; TV&RadDir 84*
WDSM - Superior, WI - *BrCabYB 84*
WDSO-FM - Chesterton, IN - *BrCabYB 84; TV&RadDir 84*
WDSR - Lake City, FL - *BrCabYB 84; TV&RadDir 84*
WDST-FM - Woodstock, NY - *BrCabYB 84; TV&RadDir 84*
WDSU-TV - New Orleans, LA - *BrCabYB 84; DirUSTelSta 83; LitMarPl 83, 84; TelAl 83, 84; Tel&CabFB 84S; TV&RadDir 84*
WDSY-FM - Pittsburgh, PA - *BrCabYB 84; NatRadPubDir Summer 83, Spring 84; TV&RadDir 84*
WDTB - Dimondale, MI - *BrCabYB 84*
WDTH-FM - Duluth, MN - *NatRadPubDir Summer 83, Spring 84*
WDTM - Selmer, TN - *BrCabYB 84; TV&RadDir 84*
WDTN-TV - Dayton, OH - *BrCabYB 84; DirUSTelSta 83; LitMarPl 83, 84; TelAl 83, 84; Tel&CabFB 84S; TV&RadDir 84*
WDTR-FM - Detroit, MI - *BrCabYB 84; LitMarPl 83, 84*
WDTV-TV - Bridgeport, WV - *TV&RadDir 84*
WDTV-TV - Charleston, WV - *DirUSTelSta 83*
WDTV-TV - Weston, WV - *BrCabYB 84; TelAl 83, 84; Tel&CabFB 84S*
WDUB-FM - Granville, OH - *BrCabYB 84; NatRadPubDir Summer 83, Spring 84; TV&RadDir 84*
WDUK - Havana, IL - *BrCabYB 84*
WDUK - Durham, NC - *NatRadPubDir Summer 83, Spring 84*
WDUK-FM - Havana, IL - *TV&RadDir 84*
WDUN - Gainesville, GA - *BrCabYB 84; TV&RadDir 84*
WDUQ-FM - Pittsburgh, PA - *BrCabYB 84; NatRadPubDir Summer 83, Spring 84; TV&RadDir 84*
WDUR - Durham, NC - *BrCabYB 84; TV&RadDir 84*
WDUR - Raleigh/Durham, NC - *NatRadPubDir Summer 83, Spring 84 p.183*
WDUV-FM - Bradenton, FL - *BrCabYB 84; TV&RadDir 84*
WDUX - Waupaca, WI - *BrCabYB 84; TV&RadDir 84*
WDUX-FM - Waupaca, WI - *BrCabYB 84; TV&RadDir 84*
WDUZ - Green Bay, WI - *BrCabYB 84; NatRadPubDir Summer 83, Spring 84; TV&RadDir 84*
WDUZ-FM - Green Bay, WI - *BrCabYB 84; NatRadPubDir Summer 83, Spring 84; TV&RadDir 84*
WDVA - Danville, VA - *BrCabYB 84; TV&RadDir 84*
WDVE-FM - Pittsburgh, PA - *BrCabYB 84; NatRadPubDir Summer 83, Spring 84; TV&RadDir 84*
WDVH - Gainesville, FL - *BrCabYB 84; NatRadPubDir Summer 83, Spring 84; TV&RadDir 84*
WDVI - Wilmington, DE - *BrCabYB 84; Tel&CabFB 84S*
WDVL - Vineland, NJ - *BrCabYB 84; TV&RadDir 84*
WDVM-TV [Div. of Evening News Association Inc.] - Washington, DC - *BrCabYB 84; DirUSTelSta 83; LitMarPl 83, 84; TelAl 83, 84; Tel&CabFB 84S; TV&RadDir 84*
WDVR - Ocean City, NJ - *BrCabYB 84*
WDW Publications Inc. - Baltimore, MD - *BoPubDir 4*
WDWD - Dawson, GA - *TV&RadDir 84*
WDWN-FM - Auburn, NY - *BrCabYB 84; NatRadPubDir Summer 83, Spring 84; TV&RadDir 84*
WDWQ-FM - St. George, SC - *BrCabYB 84; TV&RadDir 84*
WDWS - Champaign, IL - *BrCabYB 84; NatRadPubDir Summer 83, Spring 84; TV&RadDir 84*
WDWS-FM - Champaign, IL - *BrCabYB 84; NatRadPubDir Summer 83, Spring 84; TV&RadDir 84*
WDXB - Chattanooga, TN - *BrCabYB 84; NatRadPubDir Summer 83, Spring 84; TV&RadDir 84*
WDXE - Lawrenceburg, TN - *BrCabYB 84; TV&RadDir 84*
WDXE-FM - Lawrenceburg, TN - *BrCabYB 84; TV&RadDir 84*
WDXI - Jackson, TN - *BrCabYB 84; TV&RadDir 84*
WDXL - Lexington, TN - *BrCabYB 84; TV&RadDir 84*
WDXN - Clarksville, TN - *BrCabYB 84; NatRadPubDir Summer 83, Spring 84; TV&RadDir 84*
WDXR - Paducah, KY - *BrCabYB 84; TV&RadDir 84*
WDXY - Sumter, SC - *BrCabYB 84; TV&RadDir 84*
WDYL-FM - Chester, VA - *BrCabYB 84*
WDYL-FM - Richmond, VA - *NatRadPubDir Summer 83, Spring 84; TV&RadDir 84*
WDYN-FM - Chattanooga, TN - *BrCabYB 84; NatRadPubDir Summer 83, Spring 84; TV&RadDir 84*
WDYX - Buford, GA - *BrCabYB 84; TV&RadDir 84*
WDZ - Decatur, IL - *BrCabYB 84; NatRadPubDir Summer 83, Spring 84; TV&RadDir 84*
WDZD-FM - Shallotte, NC - *BrCabYB 84; TV&RadDir 84*
WDZK-FM - Chester, SC - *BrCabYB 84; TV&RadDir 84*
WDZL-TV - Miami, FL - *BrCabYB 84; DirUSTelSta 83; Tel&CabFB 84S*
WDZQ-FM - Decatur, IL - *BrCabYB 84; NatRadPubDir Summer 83, Spring 84; TV&RadDir 84*
WDZZ-FM - Flint, MI - *BrCabYB 84; TV&RadDir 84*
We the People of North Carolina [of North Carolina Citizens Association Inc.] - Raleigh, NC - *MagDir 84*
We Three Music Inc. - *See* Webman & Co., H. B.
WEA Action - Auburn, WA - *MagDir 84*
WEA International Inc. - New York, NY - *BillIntBG 83-84*
WEA News - Cheyene, WY - *BaconPubCkMag 84*
WEAA-FM - Balitmore, MD - *BrCabYB 84*
WEAA-FM - Baltimore, MD - *TV&RadDir 84*
WEAB - Greer, SC - *BrCabYB 84; TV&RadDir 84*
WEAC - Gaffney, SC - *BrCabYB 84; TV&RadDir 84*
WEAG - Alcoa, TN - *BrCabYB 84*
WEAG - Maryville, TN - *NatRadPubDir Summer 83 p.229, Spring 84 p.229; TV&RadDir 84*
WEAI-FM - Jacksonville, IL - *BrCabYB 84; TV&RadDir 84*
WEAK - Eddysville, KY - *BrCabYB 84*
Weakley County Press - Martin, TN - *Ed&PubIntYB 82*
WEAL - Greensboro, NC - *BrCabYB 84; NatRadPubDir Summer 83, Spring 84; TV&RadDir 84*
Wealthbuilding - Dallas, TX - *BaconPubCkMag 84*
WEAM - Washington, DC - *NatRadPubDir Summer 83 p.53, Spring 84 p.53*
WEAM - Arlington, VA - *BrCabYB 84*
WEAM - Falls Church, VA - *TV&RadDir 84*
WEAN - Providence, RI - *BrCabYB 84; NatRadPubDir Summer 83, Spring 84; TV&RadDir 84*
WEAO-TV - Akron, OH - *BrCabYB 84; Tel&CabFB 84S*
WEAO-TV - Kent, OH - *TV&RadDir 84*
WEAQ - Eau Claire, WI - *BrCabYB 84; NatRadPubDir Summer 83, Spring 84; TV&RadDir 84*
Wear [of Crow Publications Inc.] - Denver, CO - *WritMar 84*
WEAR-TV - Pensacola, FL - *BrCabYB 84; DirUSTelSta 83; TelAl 83, 84; Tel&CabFB 84S; TV&RadDir 84*
Weare, John H. - Burns, OR - *Tel&CabFB 84C p.1711*
Weare News Co. - Bradford, NH - *BoPubDir 4 Sup, 5*
Weary, F. G. III - Bethany, MO - *Tel&CabFB 84C p.1711*
Weary, Robert K. Jr. - Belleville, KS - *BrCabYB 84 p.D-310; Tel&CabFB 84C p.1712*
Weary, Robert K. Sr. - Bethany, MO - *BrCabYB 84 p.D-310*
Weary, Robert K. Sr. - *See* Community Antenna Systems Inc.
Weary, Rodney A. - Bethany, MO - *Tel&CabFB 84C p.1712*
WEAS - Savannah, GA - *BrCabYB 84; NatRadPubDir Summer 83, Spring 84; TV&RadDir 84*
WEAS-FM - Savannah, GA - *BrCabYB 84; NatRadPubDir Summer 83, Spring 84; TV&RadDir 84*
WEAT - West Palm Beach, FL - *BrCabYB 84; NatRadPubDir Summer 83, Spring 84; TV&RadDir 84*
WEAT-FM - West Palm Beach, FL - *BrCabYB 84; NatRadPubDir Summer 83, Spring 84; TV&RadDir 84*
Weather & Climate Report - Washington, DC - *BaconPubCkMag 84*
Weather Channel, The [of Landmark Communications] - Atlanta, GA - *BrCabYB 84; CabTVPrDB 83; Tel&CabFB 84C*
Weather Channel, The [of Landmark Communications] - New York, NY - *HomeVid&CabYB 82-83*

Weather Report [of Dow Jones News/Retrieval Service] - Princeton, NJ - *DataDirOnSer 84*
Weather Report Music - *See* MizMo Enterprises
Weather Services International Corp. - Bedford, MA - *EISS 83*
Weather Workbook Co. - Corvallis, OR - *BoPubDir 4, 5*
Weatherby, Thomas - Sharon, MA - *BoPubDir 4, 5*
Weatherdata Inc. - Wichita, KS - *BrCabYB 84*
Weatherford Daily News - Weatherford, OK - *BaconPubCkNews 84; Ed&PubIntYB 82; NewsDir 84*
Weatherford Democrat - Weatherford, TX - *AyerDirPub 83; BaconPubCkNews 84; Ed&PubIntYB 82; NewsDir 84*
Weatherhill Inc., John - New York, NY - *LitMarPl 83, 84*
Weatherly Herald, The - Weatherly, PA - *Ed&PubIntYB 82*
Weathermean - Boulder, CO - *BrCabYB 84*
Weatherscan Data Base [of Weatherscan International] - Oklahoma City, OK - *DataDirOnSer 84; DirOnDB Spring 84; MicrocomMPl 84*
Weatherscan International - Oklahoma City, OK - *DataDirOnSer 84*
Weathersfield Weekly - Weathersfield, VT - *AyerDirPub 83; Ed&PubIntYB 82*
Weathervane Books - Walnut Creek, CA - *BoPubDir 5*
Weatherwise [of Helen Dwight Reid Educational Foundation] - Washington, DC - *BaconPubCkMag 84; MagIndMarPl 82-83*
WEAU-TV - Eau Claire, WI - *BrCabYB 84; TelAl 83, 84; Tel&CabFB 84S; TV&RadDir 84*
WEAU-TV - La Crosse, WI - *DirUSTelSta 83*
WEAV - Plattsburgh, NY - *BrCabYB 84; TV&RadDir 84*
Weaver Communications Inc. - Englewood Cliffs, NJ - *DirPRFirms 83*
Weaver Composition Inc., Vance - New York, NY - *LitMarPl 83, 84; MagIndMarPl 82-83*
Weaver-Sutton Inc. - Cincinnati, OH - *StaDirAdAg 2-84*
Weaver's Journal Publications - Boulder, CO - *BoPubDir 5*
Weaver's Journal, The [of Colorado Fiber Center Inc.] - Boulder, CO - *LitMag&SmPr 83-84*
Weaverville Trinity Journal - Weaverville, CA - *BaconPubCkNews 84; NewsDir 84*
WEAW - Evanston, IL - *BrCabYB 84; TV&RadDir 84*
WEAX-FM - Angola, IN - *BrCabYB 84*
WEAZ-FM - Bala-Cynwyd, PA - *TV&RadDir 84*
WEAZ-FM - Philadelphia, PA - *BrCabYB 84; NatRadPubDir Summer 83 p.212, Spring 84 p.212*
Web IV Music Publishing - Atlanta, GA - *BillIntBG 83-84*
Web Graphics Inc. - Glen Falls, NY - *DataDirSup 7-83; DirInfWP 82*
WEBA-TV - Allendale, SC - *BrCabYB 84; Tel&CabFB 84S*
WEBA-TV - Barnwell, SC - *TV&RadDir 84*
WEBB - Baltimore, MD - *BrCabYB 84; NatRadPubDir Summer 83, Spring 84; TV&RadDir 84*
Webb Advertising Inc. - Tulsa, OK - *DirPRFirms 83; StaDirAdAg 2-84*
Webb & Associates - Lafayette, CA - *AdAge 3-28-84; StaDirAdAg 2-84*
Webb & Athey Inc. - Richmond, VA - *ArtMar 84; StaDirAdAg 2-84*
Webb & Co. Inc. - Cherry Hill, NJ - *AvMarPl 83*
Webb & Sons Inc. - New York, NY - *LitMarPl 83, 84*
Webb Audio Visual Specialists [Subs. of George Webb Sales Co. Inc.] - Salt Lake City, UT - *AvMarPl 83*
Webb City Sentinel - Webb City, MO - *AyerDirPub 83; BaconPubCkNews 84; Ed&PubIntYB 82*
Webb Co. - St. Paul, MN - *ArtMar 84; KnowInd 83; LitMarPl 83, 84; MagIndMarPl 82-83*
Webb, Damon L. [Aff. of Southern Book Travellers] - Dallas, TX - *LitMarPl 83, 84*
Webb-Dickens Telephone Corp. - Webb, IA - *TelDir&BG 83-84*
Webb-Newcomb Co. Inc. - Wilson, NC - *BoPubDir 4, 5; LitMag&SmPr 83-84*
Webb, Shawncey - Montpelier, IN - *LitMarPl 83, 84*
Webber Software - Southeastern, PA - *MicrocomSwDir 1*
Webbs Cable TV Inc. [of Tele-Media Corp.] - Calhoun, GA - *BrCabYB 84; Tel&CabFB 84C*
WEBC - Duluth, MN - *BrCabYB 84; NatRadPubDir Summer 83, Spring 84; TV&RadDir 84*
Webco Publishing Inc. - Stillwater, MN - *BoPubDir 5*
WEBCO Records - Gaithersburg, MD - *BillIntBG 83-84*
Webcom Ltd. - Scarborough, ON, Canada - *LitMarPl 84*
Webcrafters Inc. - Madison, WI - *LitMarPl 83, 84*
Weber & Associates, Gene - Forest Hills, NY - *DirPRFirms 83*
Weber & Sorensen, Reklamebureau A/S - Arhus, Denmark - *StaDirAdAg 2-84*
Weber & Stevens Inc. - Melville, NY - *MagIndMarPl 82-83*
Weber Audio Visual Inc. - Farmingdale, NY - *AvMarPl 83*
Weber Cohn & Riley Inc. - Chicago, IL - *StaDirAdAg 2-84*
Weber Co., Martin F. - Philadelphia, PA - *LitMarPl 83*
Weber Costello [Subs. of Harcourt Brace Jovanovich Inc.] - Jackson, TN - *AvMarPl 83; LitMarPl 83*
Weber, Eldon D. - Kitchener, ON, Canada - *BoPubDir 4, 5*
Weber, Geiger & Kalat Inc. - Dayton, OH - *StaDirAdAg 2-84*
Weber Hembrough Sonnenberg & Minkus Inc. - Ho Ho Kus, NJ - *StaDirAdAg 2-84*
Weber, Nathan - New York, NY - *MagIndMarPl 82-83*
Weber Systems Inc. - Chesterland, OH - *LitMarPl 83, 84*
WEBF-FM - Olean, NY - *BrCabYB 84; TV&RadDir 84*
WEBI - Sanford, ME - *BrCabYB 84*
WEBJ - Brewton, AL - *BrCabYB 84; TV&RadDir 84*
WEBL - Springfield, TN - *BrCabYB 84*
Webman & Co., H. B. - New York, NY - *BillIntBG 83-84*
WEBN-FM - Cincinnati, OH - *BrCabYB 84; NatRadPubDir Summer 83, Spring 84; TV&RadDir 84*
WEBO - Oswego, NY - *BrCabYB 84; TV&RadDir 84*
WEBQ - Harrisburg, IL - *BrCabYB 84; TV&RadDir 84*
WEBQ-FM - Harrisburg, IL - *BrCabYB 84; TV&RadDir 84*
WEBR - Buffalo, NY - *BrCabYB 84; NatRadPubDir Summer 83, Spring 84; TV&RadDir 84*
WEBS - Calhoun, GA - *BrCabYB 84; TV&RadDir 84*
Webster & Harris Advertising Agency - Lubbock, TX - *ArtMar 84; StaDirAdAg 2-84; TelAl 83, 84*
Webster Cable TV [of Midcontinent Cable Inc.] - Webster, SD - *BrCabYB 84; Tel&CabFB 84C*
Webster Calhoun Cooperative Telephone Association - Gowrie, IA - *TelDir&BG 83-84*
Webster City Freeman-Journal - Webster City, IA - *BaconPubCkNews 84*
Webster County Citizen - Seymour, MO - *AyerDirPub 83; Ed&PubIntYB 82*
Webster County Telephone Co. - Marshfield, MO - *TelDir&BG 83-84*
Webster Div. [of McGraw-Hill Book Co.] - New York, NY - *WritMar 84*
Webster Echo - Webster Springs, WV - *AyerDirPub 83; Ed&PubIntYB 82*
Webster Herald [of Empire State Weeklies] - Webster, NY - *AyerDirPub 83; Ed&PubIntYB 82; NewsDir 84*
Webster Herald Main - *See* Empire State Weeklies
Webster, Neil A. - Guttenberg, IA - *Tel&CabFB 84C p.1712*
Webster Pennysaver - Webster, NY - *AyerDirPub 83*
Webster Post - *See* Wolfe Publications Inc.
Webster Progress-Times - Eupora, MS - *AyerDirPub 83; Ed&PubIntYB 82*
Webster Reporter & Farmer - Webster, SD - *BaconPubCkNews 84; NewsDir 84*
Webster Republican - Webster Springs, WV - *AyerDirPub 83; Ed&PubIntYB 82*
Webster Review [of Webster College] - Webster Groves, MO - *LitMag&SmPr 83-84; WritMar 84*
Webster Springs Echo - Webster Springs, WV - *BaconPubCkNews 84*
Webster Springs Republican - Webster Springs, WV - *BaconPubCkNews 84*
Webster Times - Webster, MA - *BaconPubCkNews 84; Ed&PubIntYB 82; NewsDir 84*
Webster TV Cable Corp. - Cower, WV - *BrCabYB 84*
Webster TV Cable Corp. - Webster Springs, WV - *BrCabYB 84; Tel&CabFB 84C*
Webster, Walter L. - Guttenberg, IA - *Tel&CabFB 84C p.1712*
WECA-TV - Tallahassee, FL - *BrCabYB 84; DirUSTelSta 83; TelAl 83, 84; Tel&CabFB 84S; TV&RadDir 84*
WECB - Boston, MA - *NatRadPubDir Summer 83, Spring 84*
WECC-FM - Elkins, WV - *NatRadPubDir Summer 83, Spring 84*
WECI-FM - Richmond, IN - *BrCabYB 84; NatRadPubDir Summer 83, Spring 84; TV&RadDir 84*

WECK - Cheektowaga, NY - *BrCabYB 84; TV&RadDir 84*
Wecksler-Incomco - New York, NY - *LitMarPl 83, 84*
Wecksler, Sally - New York, NY - *LitMarPl 83, 84*
Weckstein, Joyce R. - Southfield, MI - *BoPubDir 4, 5*
WECL-FM - Elkhorn City, KY - *BrCabYB 84; TV&RadDir 84*
WECM-FM - Claremont, NH - *BrCabYB 84; TV&RadDir 84*
WECO - Wartburg, TN - *BrCabYB 84; TV&RadDir 84*
WECP - Carthage, MS - *BrCabYB 84; TV&RadDir 84*
WECQ-FM - Geneva, NY - *BrCabYB 84; TV&RadDir 84*
WECS - Willimantic, CT - *BrCabYB 84*
WECT-TV - Wilmington, NC - *BrCabYB 84; DirUSTelSta 83; TelAl 83, 84; Tel&CabFB 84S; TV&RadDir 84*
WECW - Charleston, SC - *BrCabYB 84*
WECW-FM - Elmira, NY - *BrCabYB 84; TV&RadDir 84*
WEDA-FM - Grove City, PA - *BrCabYB 84; TV&RadDir 84*
WEDB-TV - Berlin, NH - *Tel&CabFB 84S*
WEDC - Chicago, IL - *BrCabYB 84; LitMarPl 83, 84; NatRadPubDir Summer 83, Spring 84; TV&RadDir 84*
WEDG - Soddy-Daisy, TN - *TV&RadDir 84*
Wedge - New York, NY - *LitMag&SmPr 83-84*
Wedge, Dan - Sussex, NJ - *LitMarPl 84*
Wedge Music Inc. - *See* Skinny Zach Music Inc.
Wedge Publishing Foundation [Aff. of Radix Books Inc.] - Richmond, CA - *BoPubDir 5*
Wedge Publishing Foundation [Aff. of Radix Books Inc.] - Beaver Falls, PA - *BoPubDir 4*
WEDH-TV - Hartford, CT - *BrCabYB 84; Tel&CabFB 84S; TV&RadDir 84*
WEDM-FM - Cumberland, IN - *TV&RadDir 84*
WEDM-FM - Indianapolis, IN - *BrCabYB 84; NatRadPubDir Summer 83, Spring 84*
WEDN - Norwich, CT - *BrCabYB 84; Tel&CabFB 84S*
Wednesday Clay News - Gladstone, MO - *Ed&PubIntYB 82*
Wednesday Magazine, The - Kansas City, MO - *AyerDirPub 83; NewsDir 84*
Wednesday Nighter - Orillia, ON, Canada - *Ed&PubIntYB 82*
WEDO - McKeesport, PA - *BrCabYB 84; TV&RadDir 84*
WEDR-FM - Miami, FL - *BrCabYB 84; NatRadPubDir Summer 83, Spring 84; TV&RadDir 84*
WEDU-TV - Tampa, FL - *BrCabYB 84; Tel&CabFB 84S; TV&RadDir 84*
WEDW-TV - Bridgeport, CT - *BrCabYB 84; Tel&CabFB 84S*
WEDW-TV - Fairfield, CT - *TV&RadDir 84*
WEDY - New Haven, CT - *BrCabYB 84; Tel&CabFB 84S*
Wee-B Music Publishing Inc. - *See* World Wide Music Inc.
Wee Smile Books - Sparks, NV - *BoPubDir 4, 5*
Wee Wisdom - Unity Village, MO - *MagIndMarPl 82-83; WritMar 84*
WEEC-FM - Springfield, OH - *BrCabYB 84; TV&RadDir 84*
WEED - Rocky Mt., NC - *BrCabYB 84; TV&RadDir 84*
Weed Abstracts [of Weed Research Organization] - Oxford, England - *CompReadDB 82*
Weed Advertising - Lombard, IL - *StaDirAdAg 2-84*
Weed Control Manual - Willoughby, OH - *MagDir 84*
Weed Press - Weed, CA - *Ed&PubIntYB 82; NewsDir 84*
Weed Press, The - *See* Southern Siskiyou Newspapers Inc.
Weeds Today - Davis, CA - *BaconPubCkMag 84*
Weeds Today [of Weed Science Society of America] - Urbana, IL - *MagDir 84*
Weeds Trees & Turf - New York, NY - *MagIndMarPl 82-83*
Weeds, Trees & Turf [of The Harvest Publishing Co.] - Cleveland, OH - *ArtMar 84; BaconPubCkMag 84; MagDir 84*
Weedsport Cayuga Chief-Chronicle - *See* Wayuga Community Newspapers Inc.
Weedsport Cayuga Chief-Port Byron Chronicle - Weedsport, NY - *AyerDirPub 83*
Weedville Bennett's Valley News - Weedville, PA - *BaconPubCkNews 84*
WEEE-FM - Taylorville, IL - *BrCabYB 84; TV&RadDir 84*
WEEF - Highland Park, IL - *BrCabYB 84*
Weegar Pride Book Co. - North Bridgton, ME - *LitMarPl 83*
WEEI - Boston, MA - *BrCabYB 84; LitMarPl 83, 84; NatRadPubDir Summer 83, Spring 84; TV&RadDir 84*
WEEI-FM - Boston, MA - *TV&RadDir 84*
WEEJ - Port Charlotte, FL - *BrCabYB 84; TV&RadDir 84*
Week End - Lakewood Center, WA - *AyerDirPub 83*
WEEK-TV - Peoria, IL - *BrCabYB 84; DirUSTelSta 83; TelAl 83, 84; Tel&CabFB 84S; TV&RadDir 84*
Weekday [of Enterprise Publications] - Chicago, IL - *WritMar 84*
Weekend Booster [of Chicago Lerner Newspapers] - Chicago, IL - *AyerDirPub 83; Ed&PubIntYB 82; NewsDir 84*
Weekend News Advertiser - Merritt, BC, Canada - *Ed&PubIntYB 82*
Weekend Shopper - Yorkville, IL - *AyerDirPub 83*
Weekend World [of Wilmette Pioneer Press Inc.] - Oak Park, IL - *Ed&PubIntYB 82; NewsDir 84*
Weekender [of Somerville Dole Publishing Co. Inc.] - Somerville, MA - *AyerDirPub 83; NewsDir 84*
Weekender - Bronx, NY - *Ed&PubIntYB 82; NewsDir 84*
Weekender [of Times Publishing Co.] - Erie, PA - *Ed&PubIntYB 82; LitMarPl 83, 84*
Weekender, The - Cambridge, MA - *Ed&PubIntYB 82*
Weekender, The [of Kalispell Livestock News] - Kalispell, MT - *NewsDir 84*
Weeki Wachee West Hernando News - Spring Hill, FL - *BaconPubCkNews 84*
Weekley & Associates Inc. - Ft. Worth, TX - *StaDirAdAg 2-84*
Weekley & Penny - Houston, TX - *AdAge 3-28-84; ArtMar 84; StaDirAdAg 2-84*
Weekly Advance, The - Kemptville, ON, Canada - *Ed&PubIntYB 82*
Weekly Bond Buyer, The - New York, NY - *BaconPubCkMag 84*
Weekly Breeze [of Torrance Press-Herald] - Torrance, CA - *NewsDir 84*
Weekly Breeze, The - Westchester, CA - *Ed&PubIntYB 82*
Weekly Bulletin - Sarasota, FL - *Ed&PubIntYB 82*
Weekly Bulletin of Leather & Shoe News - Boston, MA - *BaconPubCkMag 84; MagDir 84*
Weekly Bulletin, Port of New Orleans - New Orleans, LA - *BaconPubCkMag 84; MagDir 84*
Weekly Bulletin, The - Dillsburg, PA - *Ed&PubIntYB 82*
Weekly Calistogan, The - Calistoga, CA - *Ed&PubIntYB 82*
Weekly Capital Journal - Pierre, SD - *Ed&PubIntYB 82*
Weekly Challenger - St. Petersburg, FL - *Ed&PubIntYB 82*
Weekly Chronicle - Keene, TX - *Ed&PubIntYB 82*
Weekly Congressional Monitor, The - Washington, DC - *MagIndMarPl 82-83*
Weekly Criminal Bulletin [of Canada Law Book Ltd.] - Aurora, ON, Canada - *CompReadDB 82; DirOnDB Spring 84*
Weekly Criminal Bulletin [of QL Systems Ltd.] - Ottawa, ON, Canada - *DataDirOnSer 84*
Weekly Democrat - Poplarville, MS - *Ed&PubIntYB 82*
Weekly Economic Survey [of Money Market Services Inc.] - Belmont, CA - *DBBus 82; DirOnDB Spring 84*
Weekly Economic Update [of Dow Jones & Co. Inc.] - Princeton, NJ - *DBBus 82; DirOnDB Spring 84*
Weekly Extra - Ada, OK - *Ed&PubIntYB 82*
Weekly Gazette - La Grange, NC - *Ed&PubIntYB 82*
Weekly Herald, The - Robersonville, NC - *Ed&PubIntYB 82*
Weekly Home News, The - Spring Green, WI - *Ed&PubIntYB 82*
Weekly in Mid Missouri, The - Jefferson City, MO - *AyerDirPub 83*
Weekly in Terre Haute, The - Terre Haute, IN - *AyerDirPub 83*
Weekly Insiders Dairy & Egg Letter [of Urner Barry Publications Inc.] - Bayville, NJ - *NewsDir 84*
Weekly Insiders Poultry Report [of Urner Barry Publications Inc.] - Bayville, NJ - *NewsDir 84*
Weekly Insiders Turkey Letter [of Urner Barry Publications Inc.] - Bayville, NJ - *NewsDir 84*
Weekly Journal/Tempo - Whittier, CA - *AyerDirPub 83*
Weekly Journal, The - Brewer, ME - *AyerDirPub 83; NewsDir 84*
Weekly Livestock Reporter - Ft. Worth, TX - *BaconPubCkMag 84; MagDir 84*
Weekly Mail - Stamford, CT - *Ed&PubIntYB 82*
Weekly Malton Messenger, The - Malton, ON, Canada - *Ed&PubIntYB 82*
Weekly Messenger, The - Pleasant Hill, IL - *Ed&PubIntYB 82*
Weekly Moultrie Observer - Moultrie, GA - *Ed&PubIntYB 82*
Weekly News - Lodi, NJ - *Ed&PubIntYB 82*
Weekly News - Craik, SK, Canada - *Ed&PubIntYB 82*
Weekly News - Lampman, SK, Canada - *Ed&PubIntYB 82*
Weekly News - Uranium City, SK, Canada - *Ed&PubIntYB 82*
Weekly News Letter - Chicago, IL - *NewsDir 84*

Weekly News, The - Lyndonville, VT - *Ed&PubIntYB 82*
Weekly Newspaper, The - Aspen, CO - *Ed&PubIntYB 82*
Weekly Newspaper, The [of Western Editorial Services Inc.] - Glenwood Spring, CO - *NewsDir 84*
Weekly Newspaper, The - Glenwood Springs, CO - *AyerDirPub 83*
Weekly Newspapers Inc. - Prescott, WI - *BaconPubCkNews 84*
Weekly Observer - Hemingway, SC - *Ed&PubIntYB 82; NewsDir 84*
Weekly of Business Aviation, The [of Ziff-Davis Publishing Co.] - Washington, DC - *BaconPubCkMag 84; MagDir 84*
Weekly Packet, The - Blue Hill, ME - *AyerDirPub 83; Ed&PubIntYB 82*
Weekly Pharmacy Reports - Chevy Chase, MD - *BaconPubCkMag 84*
Weekly Post - Newark, DE - *AyerDirPub 83*
Weekly Post - Montreal/Mt. Royal, PQ, Canada - *Ed&PubIntYB 82*
Weekly Press - Puxico, MO - *Ed&PubIntYB 82*
Weekly Pride - Akron, OH - *AyerDirPub 83; Ed&PubIntYB 82*
Weekly Reader Children's Book Clubs [of Xerox Education Publications] - Middletown, CT - *LitMarPl 83, 84*
Weekly Reader Mailing Lists - Middletown, CT - *LitMarPl 84*
Weekly Record - Mellen, WI - *Ed&PubIntYB 82*
Weekly Record, The - Truto, NS, Canada - *AyerDirPub 83*
Weekly Recorder - Claysville, PA - *AyerDirPub 83; Ed&PubIntYB 82*
Weekly Reflex - Kaysville, UT - *Ed&PubIntYB 82*
Weekly Register-Call - Central City, CO - *Ed&PubIntYB 82*
Weekly Regulatory Monitor [of NewsNet Inc.] - Bryn Mawr, PA - *DataDirOnSer 84*
Weekly Republic - Junction City, KS - *AyerDirPub 83; Ed&PubIntYB 82*
Weekly Review - Athens, TX - *AyerDirPub 83*
Weekly Sentinel, The - Erie, PA - *Ed&PubIntYB 82*
Weekly Shopper, The - Downey, CA - *AyerDirPub 83*
Weekly Shopper, The - Raytown, MO - *AyerDirPub 83*
Weekly Southtown Economist - Chicago, IL - *Ed&PubIntYB 82*
Weekly Statistical Bulletin - Washington, DC - *DirOnDB Spring 84*
Weekly Statistical Bulletin [of I. P. Sharp Associates Ltd.] - Toronto, ON, Canada - *DataDirOnSer 84*
Weekly Syndicate, The - Lakewood, CO - *Ed&PubIntYB 82; LitMarPl 84*
Weekly Temperatures [of I. P. Sharp Associates Ltd.] - Toronto, ON, Canada - *DataDirOnSer 84*
Weekly Territorial, The - Tucson, AZ - *NewsDir 84*
Weekly, The - Seattle, WA - *BaconPubCkMag 84*
Weekly Transcript - Golden, CO - *AyerDirPub 83*
Weekly Underwriter - Englewood, NJ - *MagDir 84*
Weekly Vista, The - Bella Vista, AR - *Ed&PubIntYB 82*
Weekly Wave - Cedarville, MI - *Ed&PubIntYB 82*
Weekly Western Livestock Journal (Central Edition) - Denver, CO - *BaconPubCkMag 84*
Weekly Western Livestock Journal (Western Edition) - Denver, CO - *BaconPubCkMag 84*
WEEL - Washington, DC - *NatRadPubDir Summer 83 p.53, Spring 84 p.53*
WEEL - Fairfax, VA - *BrCabYB 84; TV&RadDir 84*
WEEM-FM - Pendleton, IN - *BrCabYB 84; TV&RadDir 84*
Weems, Willie - Forest, MS - *Tel&CabFB 84C p.1712*
WEEN - Lafayette, TN - *BrCabYB 84; TV&RadDir 84*
WEEP - Pittsburgh, PA - *BrCabYB 84; NatRadPubDir Summer 83, Spring 84; TV&RadDir 84*
Weeping Water Republican - Weeping Water, NE - *BaconPubCkNews 84; Ed&PubIntYB 82*
WEET - Richmond, VA - *BrCabYB 84; NatRadPubDir Summer 83, Spring 84; TV&RadDir 84*
WEEU - Reading, PA - *BrCabYB 84; NatRadPubDir Summer 83, Spring 84; TV&RadDir 84*
WEEU Broadcasting Co. - Reading, PA - *BrCabYB 84*
WEEW - Washington, NC - *TV&RadDir 84*
WEEX - Allentown/Bethlehem/Easton, PA - *NatRadPubDir Summer 83, Spring 84 p.209*
WEEX - Easton, PA - *BrCabYB 84; TV&RadDir 84*
WEEZ-FM - Heidleburg, MS - *BrCabYB 84*
WEEZ-FM - Laurel, MS - *TV&RadDir 84*
WEFC - Roanoke, VA - *BrCabYB 84; Tel&CabFB 84S*
WEFM-FM - Michigan City, IN - *BrCabYB 84; TV&RadDir 84*
WEFT - Champaign, IL - *BrCabYB 84*
WEGA - Vega Baja, PR - *BrCabYB 84*
Wegener Communications Inc. - Norcross, GA - *VideoDir 82-83*
WEGG - Rose Hill, NC - *BrCabYB 84; TV&RadDir 84*
Wegge, Wallace - New York, NY - *HBIndAd&MS 82-83; IntDirMarRes 83*
WEGL-FM - Auburn, AL - *BrCabYB 84; NatRadPubDir Summer 83, Spring 84; TV&RadDir 84*
WEGN - Evergreen, AL - *BrCabYB 84; TV&RadDir 84*
WEGN-FM - Evergreen, AL - *BrCabYB 84*
WEGO - Concord, NC - *BrCabYB 84; TV&RadDir 84*
WEGP - Presque Isle, ME - *BrCabYB 84; TV&RadDir 84*
WEHB-FM - Grand Rapids, MI - *BrCabYB 84; TV&RadDir 84*
WEHCO Media Inc. - Camden, AR - *BrCabYB 84*
WEHCO Video Inc. - Little Rock, AR - *BrCabYB 84 p.D-310; Tel&CabFB 84C p.1712*
WEHH - Elmira Heights, NY - *BrCabYB 84*
WEHH - Horseheads, NY - *TV&RadDir 84*
WEHT-TV - Evansville, IN - *BrCabYB 84; DirUSTelSta 83; TelAl 83, 84; Tel&CabFB 84S; TV&RadDir 84*
Wei & Associates Ltd., Norman S. - Pickering, ON, Canada - *BoPubDir 4, 5*
WEIC - Charleston, IL - *BrCabYB 84; TV&RadDir 84*
WEIC-FM - Charleston, IL - *BrCabYB 84; TV&RadDir 84*
Weichselbaum, Lehman - New York, NY - *LitMarPl 83, 84; MagIndMarPl 82-83*
Weidenhammer Systems Corp. - Wyomissing, PA - *ADAPSOMemDir 83-84*
Weidner & Son Printers Inc., Fred - New York, NY - *LitMarPl 83, 84; MagIndMarPl 82-83*
Weidner Associates Inc. [Div. of Foris Publications-USA] - Cinnaminson, NJ - *LitMarPl 83, 84; MagIndMarPl 82-83*
Weidner Communications Corp. - Northbrook, IL - *MicrocomSwDir 1*
WEIF - Moundsville, WV - *BrCabYB 84; TV&RadDir 84*
Weighing & Measurement - Rockford, IL - *BaconPubCkMag 84; MagDir 84; MagIndMarPl 82-83; WritMar 84*
Weight Control Institute - Salt Lake City, UT - *BoPubDir 5*
Weight Watchers Magazine [of American/Harlequin Inc.] - New York, NY - *ArtMar 84; BaconPubCkMag 84; Folio 83; LitMarPl 83, 84; MagDir 84; MagIndMarPl 82-83; WritMar 84*
Weightman Inc. - Philadelphia, PA - *AdAge 3-28-84; BrCabYB 84; StaDirAdAg 2-84*
Weigl Educational Associates, L. A. - Regina, SK, Canada - *BoPubDir 4 Sup, 5*
Weil Inc., Ben H. - Warren, NJ - *EISS 5-84 Sup*
Weil, Warren/Communications Counselors - New York, NY - *DirPRFirms 83*
Weiler, Joseph Flack - Watertown, MA - *LitMarPl 83, 84*
WEIM - Fitchburg, MA - *BrCabYB 84; NatRadPubDir Summer 83, Spring 84; TV&RadDir 84*
Weimar Mercury - Weimar, TX - *BaconPubCkNews 84; NewsDir 84*
Weimaraner Club of America - Toledo, OH - *MagDir 84*
Weimer Mercury, The - Weimer, TX - *Ed&PubIntYB 82*
Weinberg, Alyce T. - Braddock Heights, MD - *BoPubDir 4 Sup, 5*
Weinberg, Michael Aron - Los Angeles, CA - *BoPubDir 4, 5*
Weinberg Productions Inc., Fred - Stamford, CT - *AvMarPl 83; BillIntBG 83-84*
Weinberg Publications, Robert - Oak Forest, IL - *BoPubDir 4, 5*
Weinberg, Thomas - Hanalei, HI - *BoPubDir 4 Sup, 5*
Weinberger Advertising Inc., Steve - Marlboro, NJ - *StaDirAdAg 2-84*
Weiner Associates Inc. - *See* Stryker Weiner Associates Inc.
Weiner Cable TV Inc. [of TCA Cable TV Inc.] - Weiner, AR - *Tel&CabFB 84C*
Weiner Inc., Richard - New York, NY - *DirPRFirms 83; LitMarPl 83, 84*
Weiner Literary Agency, Cherry - Rahway, NJ - *LitMarPl 83, 84*
Weinschenk-Tabernero, Pablo - Hartsdale, NY - *LitMarPl 83, 84*
Weinstein Associates Inc., S. J. - White Plains, NY - *StaDirAdAg 2-84*
Weinstein Associates, Lois - Palm Beach Gardens, FL - *IntDirMarRes 83*

Weinstock & Associates, H. F. - El Segundo, CA - *DirPRFirms 83*
Weintraub & Fitzsimons Inc. - New York, NY - *DirPRFirms 83*
Weintz Co., The - Stamford, CT - *DirMarMP 83*
WEIQ-TV - Birmingham, AL - *TV&RadDir 84*
WEIQ-TV - Mobile, AL - *BrCabYB 84; Tel&CabFB 84S*
WEIR - Steubenville, OH - *NatRadPubDir Summer 83, Spring 84 p.196*
WEIR - Weirton, WV - *BrCabYB 84; TV&RadDir 84*
Weir Media Service, Lou - Long Beach, CA - *StaDirAdAg 2-84*
Weir, Ralph L. Jr. - *See* Community Antenna Systems Inc.
Weirdbook Press - Buffalo, NY - *BoPubDir 4, 5; WritMar 84*
Weirton Daily Times [of Thomson Newspapers Inc.] - Weirton, WV - *BaconPubCkNews 84; Ed&PubIntYB 82; NewsDir 84*
WEIS - Centre, AL - *BrCabYB 84; TV&RadDir 84*
Weisberg, Harold - Frederick, MD - *BoPubDir 4, 5*
Weisbrot Associates - Long Island City, NY - *StaDirAdAg 2-84*
Weiser American - Weiser, ID - *Ed&PubIntYB 82*
Weiser American - *See* Signal-American Printers Inc.
Weiser & Associates, Michael - Chicago, IL - *DirPRFirms 83*
Weiser Inc., Samuel - York Beach, ME - *ArtMar 84; BoPubDir 4 Sup, 5; LitMarPl 83, 84*
Weiser Inc., Samuel - New York, NY - *BoPubDir 4*
Weiser Publishing, Ron - Van Nuys, CA - *BillIntBG 83-84*
Weiser/Rebodyne Corp. - Silver Spring, MD - *AvMarPl 83*
Weiser Signal - Weiser, ID - *Ed&PubIntYB 82*
Weiser Signal - *See* Signal-American Printers Inc.
Weisfeld, Glenn E. [of Wayne State University] - Detroit, MI - *LitMarPl 83, 84; MagIndMarPl 82-83*
Weiss Advertising Inc., Michael B. - New York, NY - *StaDirAdAg 2-84*
Weiss & Associates, Bernard - Stamford, CT - *ArtMar 84*
Weiss & Daughters, Mark - Miami Beach, FL - *BoPubDir 4, 5*
Weiss & Geller Inc. - New York, NY - *BrCabYB 84; StaDirAdAg 2-84; TelAl 83, 84*
Weiss Associates, Robert - Boston, MA - *DirPRFirms 83*
Weiss, Dale - Bethlehem, PA - *LitMarPl 83*
Weiss Global Enterprises - Oxnard, CA - *TelAl 83, 84; Tel&CabFB 84C*
Weiss Lithograph Co. Inc., A. D. - Hollywood, FL - *MagIndMarPl 82-83*
Weiss Philatelic-Numismatic Features - Cleveland, OH - *Ed&PubIntYB 82*
Weiss, Sigmund - Stony Brook, NY - *BoPubDir 4, 5*
Weiss, Stevens H. - New York, NY - *BillIntBG 83-84*
Weissberg Associates Inc. - New York, NY - *StaDirAdAg 2-84*
Weissman, Mottke & Mara - Vineyard Haven, MA - *MagIndMarPl 82-83*
Weitzell Inc. - West Des Moines, IA - *StaDirAdAg 2-84*
Weitzman, Dym & Associates - Washington, DC - *AdAge 3-28-84; DirPRFirms 83; StaDirAdAg 2-84*
Weitzman Inc., Natalie G. - North Miami, FL - *IntDirMarRes 83*
Weitzman Research Inc. - Los Angeles, CA - *IntDirMarRes 83*
WEIV-FM - Ithaca, NY - *BrCabYB 84; NatRadPubDir Summer 83 p.170*
WEIZ-FM - Phoenix City, AL - *BrCabYB 84*
WEIZ-FM - Columbus, GA - *TV&RadDir 84*
WEJC - Lexington, NC - *Tel&CabFB 84S*
WEJL - Scranton, PA - *BrCabYB 84; NatRadPubDir Summer 83, Spring 84; TV&RadDir 84*
WEJY - Monroe, MI - *BrCabYB 84*
WEKC - Williamsburg, KY - *BrCabYB 84*
WEKG - Jackson, KY - *BrCabYB 84; TV&RadDir 84*
WEKO - Cabo Rojo, PR - *BrCabYB 84*
WEKR - Fayetteville, TN - *BrCabYB 84; TV&RadDir 84*
WEKU-FM - Richmond, KY - *BrCabYB 84; NatRadPubDir Summer 83, Spring 84; TV&RadDir 84*
WEKW-TV - Keene, NH - *BrCabYB 84; Tel&CabFB 84S*
WEKY - Richmond, KY - *BrCabYB 84; TV&RadDir 84*
WEKZ - Monroe, WI - *BrCabYB 84; TV&RadDir 84*
WEKZ-FM - Monroe, WI - *BrCabYB 84; TV&RadDir 84*
WELA-FM - East Liverpool, OH - *BrCabYB 84; TV&RadDir 84*
WELB - Elba, AL - *BrCabYB 84; TV&RadDir 84*
Welbac Cable TV Corp. - Norwalk, CT - *BrCabYB 84 p.D-310; Tel&CabFB 84C p.1712*
Welbac Cable TV Corp. - Sylva, NC - *Tel&CabFB 84C*
Welbeck International Public Relations - *See* Byoir & Associates Inc., Carl
Welbeck Public Relations Ltd. - *See* Byoir & Associates Inc., Carl
Welborn Advertising Inc. - Springfield, NJ - *StaDirAdAg 2-84*
WELC - Welch, WV - *BrCabYB 84; TV&RadDir 84*
Welch Antenna Co. - Welch, WV - *BrCabYB 84; Tel&CabFB 84C*
Welch Antenna Co. Inc. - Gary, WV - *Tel&CabFB 84C*
Welch Associates - Ridgefield, CT - *DirPRFirms 83*
Welch Co. Ltd., G. R. - Burlington, ON, Canada - *LitMarPl 83*
Welch, Currier, Smith - Boston, MA - *HBIndAd&MS 82-83*
Welch News - Welch, WV - *AyerDirPub 83; BaconPubCkNews 84; Ed&PubIntYB 82; NewsDir 84*
Welch Publishing Co. - Perrysburg, OH - *BaconPubCkNews 84*
Welch Publishing House, Wendell R. - Nashville, TN - *BoPubDir 4, 5*
Welchy Grape Publishing Co. - West Barnstable, MA - *BillIntBG 83-84*
Welchy Grape Record Co. - West Barnstable, MA - *BillIntBG 83-84*
Welcomat - Philadelphia, PA - *AyerDirPub 83; Ed&PubIntYB 82*
Welcome to Miami & the Beach - Miami, FL - *MagDir 84*
WELD - Fisher, WV - *BrCabYB 84; TV&RadDir 84*
Weldasearch [of Dialog Information Services Inc.] - Palo Alto, CA - *DataDirOnSer 84*
Weldasearch [of The Welding Institute] - Abington, England - *DirOnDB Spring 84; OnBibDB 3*
Weldasearch [of The Welding Institute] - Cambridge, England - *CompReadDB 82; DBBus 82*
Welding Design & Fabrication - Cleveland, OH - *BaconPubCkMag 84; MagDir 84*
Welding Distributor, The - Cleveland, OH - *BaconPubCkMag 84; MagDir 84*
Welding Documentation [of Federal Institute for Materials Testing] - Berlin, West Germany - *EISS 83*
Welding Institute, The - Cambridge, England - *CompReadDB 82; InfIndMarPl 83*
Welding Journal - Miami, FL - *BaconPubCkMag 84; MagDir 84*
Weldon Roanoke News - Weldon, NC - *BaconPubCkNews 84*
WELE-FM - Deland, FL - *BrCabYB 84; TV&RadDir 84*
Weleetka Weleetkan - Weleetka, OK - *BaconPubCkNews 84*
WELI - New Haven, CT - *BrCabYB 84; NatRadPubDir Summer 83, Spring 84; TV&RadDir 84*
WELK - Elkins, WV - *BrCabYB 84*
Welk Music Group - Santa Monica, CA - *BillIntBG 83-84*
WELL - Albion, MI - *BrCabYB 84; TV&RadDir 84*
WELL - Marshall, MI - *TV&RadDir 84*
WELL-FM - Marshall, MI - *BrCabYB 84*
Well History Control System [of Petroleum Information Corp.] - Denver, CO - *EISS 83*
Well Information Network [of Hotline Energy Reports Inc.] - Denver, CO - *DataDirOnSer 84*
Well Received Music - *See* Beserkley
Well Servicing - Dallas, TX - *BaconPubCkMag 84*
Welland-Port Colborne Tribune - Welland, ON, Canada - *AyerDirPub 83*
Welland Regional Shopping News - Welland, ON, Canada - *AyerDirPub 83*
Wellauer, Maralyn A. - Milwaukee, WI - *BoPubDir 4, 5*
Wellbeing Books [Div. of Open Marketing Group] - Boston, MA - *LitMarPl 83, 84*
Weller & Associates - Monticello, AZ - *MicrocomMPl 83; WhoWMicrocom 83*
Wellesley & Gardens - Toronto, ON, Canada - *BoPubDir 4 Sup, 5*
Wellesley Press Inc. - Framingham, MA - *MagIndMarPl 82-83*
Wellesley Townsman - Wellesley, MA - *BaconPubCkNews 84; Ed&PubIntYB 82; NewsDir 84*
Wellesville Optic-News - Wellesville, MO - *Ed&PubIntYB 82*
Wellesville Pennysaver - Wellesville, NY - *AyerDirPub 83*
Welling, Minton & Vanderslice Inc. - Tulsa, OK - *IntDirMarRes 83; Tel&CabFB 84C*
Welling Motion Pictures - Elmont, NY - *AvMarPl 83*
Wellington Advertiser, The - Fergus, ON, Canada - *Ed&PubIntYB 82*
Wellington Communications Inc. - New York, NY - *StaDirAdAg 2-84*

Wellington Daily News - Wellington, KS - *BaconPubCkNews 84; Ed&PubIntYB 82*
Wellington Daily News Evening Paper - Wellington, KS - *NewsDir 84*
Wellington Enterprise - Wellington, OH - *BaconPubCkNews 84; Ed&PubIntYB 82*
Wellington Leader - Wellington, TX - *BaconPubCkNews 84; Ed&PubIntYB 82*
Wellington Letter Alert, The - Honolulu, HI - *DirOnDB Spring 84*
Wellington Letter, The - Honolulu, HI - *DirOnDB Spring 84*
Wellington Press [Aff. of Co-Operative Enterprises Inc.] - Tallahassee, FL - *BoPubDir 5*
Wellington Systems - Stamford, CT - *MicrocomMPl 84*
Wellman Advance - Wellman, IA - *BaconPubCkNews 84; Ed&PubIntYB 82*
Wellman & Co. - Los Angeles, CA - *StaDirAdAg 2-84*
Wellman Cooperative Telephone Association - Wellman, IA - *TelDir&BG 83-84*
Wellman Press Inc. - Lansing, MI - *MagIndMarPl 82-83*
Wellness Newsletter, The - Upper Nyack, NY - *BaconPubCkMag 84*
Wells & Co., J. N. - Oak Brook, IL - *CabTVFinDB 83*
Wells, Bob - Steamboat Springs, CO - *Tel&CabFB 84C p.1712*
Wells Cable TV Inc. - Wells, MN - *Tel&CabFB 84C*
Wells CATV - Wells, MN - *BrCabYB 84*
Wells County Free Press - Fessenden, ND - *AyerDirPub 83; Ed&PubIntYB 82*
Wells Drive Music - *See* Budd Music Corp.
Wells Fargo Bank - San Francisco, CA - *ADAPSOMemDir 83-84*
Wells Mirror - Wells, MN - *AyerDirPub 83; BaconPubCkNews 84; Ed&PubIntYB 82*
Wells Progress - Wells, NV - *BaconPubCkNews 84; Ed&PubIntYB 82*
Wells, Rich, Greene - New York, NY - *AdAge 3-28-84; ArtMar 84; Br 1-23-84; BrCabYB 84; StaDirAdAg 2-84*
Wells TV Inc. - Wells, NV - *BrCabYB 84; Tel&CabFB 84C*
Wellsboro Gazette [of Tioga Printing Corp.] - Wellsboro, PA - *BaconPubCkNews 84; Ed&PubIntYB 82; NewsDir 84*
Wellsburg Brooke News - Wellsburg, WV - *BaconPubCkNews 84*
Wellsburg Cable Co. Inc. [of Tele-Communications Inc.] - Wellsburg, WV - *Tel&CabFB 84C*
Wellsiana [of High Orchard Press] - Dagenham, England - *LitMag&SmPr 83-84*
Wellspring - Menlo Park, CA - *WritMar 84*
Wellston News - Wellston, OK - *BaconPubCkNews 84; Ed&PubIntYB 82*
Wellston Sentry [of Mid South Management] - Wellston, OH - *Ed&PubIntYB 82; NewsDir 84*
Wellston Sentry - *See* Jackson Publishing Co.
Wellston Telegram - Wellston, OH - *AyerDirPub 83; BaconPubCkNews 84; Ed&PubIntYB 82*
Wellsville Daily Reporter - Hornell, NY - *Ed&PubIntYB 82*
Wellsville Daily Reporter [of Greenbow Newspapers] - Wellsville, NY - *NewsDir 84*
Wellsville Daily Reporter/Sunday Spectator - Wellsville, NY - *AyerDirPub 83*
Wellsville Optic-News - Wellsville, MO - *BaconPubCkNews 84*
Wellsville Reporter-Spectator - Wellsville, NY - *BaconPubCkNews 84*
WELM - Elmira, NY - *BrCabYB 84; TV&RadDir 84*
WELO - Tupelo, MS - *BrCabYB 84; NatRadPubDir Summer 83, Spring 84; TV&RadDir 84*
WELP - Easley, SC - *BrCabYB 84; TV&RadDir 84*
WELP-FM - Easley, SC - *BrCabYB 84; TV&RadDir 84*
WELR - Roanoke, AL - *BrCabYB 84; TV&RadDir 84*
WELR-FM - Roanoke, AL - *BrCabYB 84; TV&RadDir 84*
WELS - Kinston, NC - *BrCabYB 84; TV&RadDir 84*
Welsch, Currier, Smith Inc. - Boston, MA - *StaDirAdAg 2-84*
Welsch, Mirabile & Co. Inc. - Baltimore, MD - *StaDirAdAg 2-84*
Welsh, Carson, Anderson & Stowe - New York, NY - *ADAPSOMemDir 83-84*
Welsh Citizen - Welsh, LA - *BaconPubCkNews 84; Ed&PubIntYB 82*
Welsh History Review [of University of Wales Press] - Cathays, Wales - *LitMag&SmPr 83-84*
Welton Music - *See* Protone Music
WELV - Ellenville, NY - *BrCabYB 84; TV&RadDir 84*
WELW - Cleveland, OH - *NatRadPubDir Summer 83 p.194, Spring 84 p.191*
WELW - Willoughby, OH - *BrCabYB 84; TV&RadDir 84*
WELX - Xenia, OH - *BrCabYB 84; TV&RadDir 84*
WELY - Ely, MN - *BrCabYB 84; TV&RadDir 84*
WELZ - Belzoni, MS - *BrCabYB 84; TV&RadDir 84*
WEMB - Erwin, TN - *BrCabYB 84; TV&RadDir 84*
WEMC-FM - Harrisonburg, VA - *BrCabYB 84; NatRadPubDir Summer 83, Spring 84; TV&RadDir 84*
WEMI-FM - Neenah-Menasha, WI - *BrCabYB 84; TV&RadDir 84*
WEMJ - Laconia, NH - *BrCabYB 84; TV&RadDir 84*
WEMM-FM - Huntington, WV - *BrCabYB 84; NatRadPubDir Summer 83, Spring 84; TV&RadDir 84*
Wemmers Communications Inc. [of The Barnum Group] - Atlanta, GA - *StaDirAdAg 2-84*
WEMP - Hales Corners, WI - *TV&RadDir 84*
WEMP - Milwaukee, WI - *BrCabYB 84; NatRadPubDir Summer 83 p.267, Spring 84 p.269*
Wemple Advertising Inc. - Green Bay, WI - *LitMarPl 83, 84; StaDirAdAg 2-84*
WEMU-FM - Ypsilanti, MI - *BrCabYB 84; NatRadPubDir Summer 83, Spring 84; TV&RadDir 84*
WENA - Penuelas, PR - *BrCabYB 84*
Wenatchee World - Wenatchee, WA - *BaconPubCkNews 84; Ed&PubIntYB 82; NewsDir 84*
WENC - Whiteville, NC - *BrCabYB 84; TV&RadDir 84*
WEND - Chattahoochee, FL - *TV&RadDir 84*
Wendell Gold Leaf Farmer - Wendell, NC - *BaconPubCkNews 84*
Wendover Associates Financial/Public Relations Inc. - Greensboro, NC - *DirPRFirms 83*
Wendover Press - *See* Biobehavioral Press/Wendover Press
Wendt Advertising Agency Inc. - Great Falls, MT - *AdAge 3-28-84; StaDirAdAg 2-84*
Wendt Engineering Library (Computerized Bibliographic Services) - Madison, WI - *InfIndMarPl 83*
Wendt Engineering Library (Information Services Div.) - Madison, WI - *InfIndMarPl 83*
Wendt Engineering Library (Water Resources Information Program) - Madison, WI - *InfIndMarPl 83*
Wendt Rotsinger Kuehnle Inc. - Toledo, OH - *StaDirAdAg 2-84*
WENE - Endicott, NY - *BrCabYB 84; TV&RadDir 84*
WENG - Englewood, FL - *BrCabYB 84; TV&RadDir 84*
Wenger Associates - San Francisco, CA - *StaDirAdAg 2-84*
WENH-TV - Durham, NH - *BrCabYB 84; Tel&CabFB 84S; TV&RadDir 84*
WENK - Union City, TN - *BrCabYB 84; TV&RadDir 84*
WENN - Birmingham, AL - *TV&RadDir 84*
WENN - Hudson Falls, NY - *BrCabYB 84*
WENN-FM - Birmingham, AL - *BrCabYB 84; NatRadPubDir Summer 83, Spring 84; TV&RadDir 84*
WENO - Chattahoochee, FL - *BrCabYB 84*
Wenona Index - Henry, IL - *AyerDirPub 83*
Wenona Index - Wenona, IL - *Ed&PubIntYB 82*
WENR - Athens, TN - *TV&RadDir 84*
WENR - Englewood, TN - *BrCabYB 84*
WENS - Shelbyville, IN - *BrCabYB 84*
WENS-FM - Indianapolis, IN - *TV&RadDir 84*
WENS-FM - Shelbyville, IN - *BrCabYB 84*
WENT - Gloversville, NY - *BrCabYB 84; TV&RadDir 84*
Wentronics Inc. [of United Cable Television Inc.] - Gallup, NM - *BrCabYB 84*
Wentronics Inc. [of United Cable Television Corp.] - Casper, WY - *BrCabYB 84*
Wentrontics Inc. [of United Cable] - Moab, UT - *BrCabYB 84*
Wentzell & Associates-Gorilla Graphics - San Francisco, CA - *MagIndMarPl 82-83*
Wentzville Messenger [of St. Charles Community News Inc.] - Wentzville, MO - *NewsDir 84*
Wentzville Union - Wentzville, MO - *BaconPubCkNews 84*
Wentzville Union & St. Charles County Record - Wentzville, MO - *AyerDirPub 83; Ed&PubIntYB 82*
WENU - Hudson Falls, NY - *BrCabYB 84*
WENY - Elmira, NY - *BrCabYB 84; NatRadPubDir Summer 83, Spring 84; TV&RadDir 84*

WENY-TV - Elmira, NY - *BrCabYB 84; DirUSTelSta 83; TelAl 83, 84; Tel&CabFB 84S; TV&RadDir 84*
WENZ - Richmond, VA - *TV&RadDir 84*
Wenz-Neely Co., The - Louisville, KY - *DirPRFirms 83*
Wenzel & Co. Inc. - Pennington, NJ - *StaDirAdAg 2-84*
WEOK - Poughkeepsie, NY - *BrCabYB 84; TV&RadDir 84*
WEOL - Elyria, OH - *BrCabYB 84*
WEOS-FM - Geneva, NY - *BrCabYB 84; NatRadPubDir Summer 83, Spring 84; TV&RadDir 84*
WEOZ-FM - Saegertown, PA - *BrCabYB 84; TV&RadDir 84*
WEPA - Eupora, MS - *BrCabYB 84; TV&RadDir 84*
WEPG - South Pittsburg, TN - *BrCabYB 84; TV&RadDir 84*
WEPM - Martinsburg, WV - *BrCabYB 84; TV&RadDir 84*
WEPR-FM - Clemson, SC - *TV&RadDir 84*
WEPR-FM - Greenville, SC - *BrCabYB 84*
WEPS-FM - Elgin, IL - *BrCabYB 84; NatRadPubDir Summer 83, Spring 84; TV&RadDir 84*
WEQO - Whitley City, KY - *BrCabYB 84; TV&RadDir 84*
WEQR-FM - Goldsboro, NC - *BrCabYB 84; TV&RadDir 84*
WERA - Plainfield, NJ - *BrCabYB 84; NatRadPubDir Summer 83, Spring 84; TV&RadDir 84*
WERB - Berlin, CT - *BrCabYB 84*
Werbel Publishing Co. Inc. - Smithtown, NY - *BoPubDir 4, 5*
Werbin & Morrill Inc. - New York, NY - *HBIndAd&MS 82-83*
WERC - Birmingham, AL - *BrCabYB 84; NatRadPubDir Summer 83, Spring 84; TV&RadDir 84*
WERD - Jacksonville, FL - *BrCabYB 84; NatRadPubDir Summer 83, Spring 84; TV&RadDir 84*
Werden, Frieda - New York, NY - *BoPubDir 4, 5*
WERE - Cleveland, OH - *BrCabYB 84; NatRadPubDir Summer 83, Spring 84; TV&RadDir 84*
WERF - Hazleton, PA - *BrCabYB 84; Tel&CabFB 84S*
WERG-FM - Erie, PA - *BrCabYB 84; NatRadPubDir Summer 83, Spring 84; TV&RadDir 84*
WERH - Hamilton, AL - *BrCabYB 84; TV&RadDir 84*
WERH-FM - Hamilton, AL - *BrCabYB 84; TV&RadDir 84*
WERI - Westerly, RI - *BrCabYB 84; TV&RadDir 84*
WERI-FM - Westerly, RI - *BrCabYB 84; TV&RadDir 84*
WERK - Muncie, IN - *BrCabYB 84*
WERL - Eagle River, WI - *BrCabYB 84; TV&RadDir 84*
WERL-FM - Eagle River, WI - *BrCabYB 84; TV&RadDir 84*
WERN-FM - Madison, WI - *BrCabYB 84; NatRadPubDir Summer 83, Spring 84*
Werner Data Processing, Jan - New York, NY - *IntDirMarRes 83*
Werner Frank Computer Group - Calabasas, CA - *ADAPSOMemDir 83-84*
Werner Graphics - New York, NY - *LitMarPl 83, 84*
Werner, John P. - North Philadelphia, PA - *BoPubDir 4, 5*
WERR - Utuado, PR - *BrCabYB 84*
WERS-FM - Boston, MA - *BrCabYB 84; NatRadPubDir Summer 83, Spring 84; TV&RadDir 84*
WERT - Van Wert, OH - *BrCabYB 84; TV&RadDir 84*
WERT-FM - Van Wert, OH - *BrCabYB 84; TV&RadDir 84*
Werth Associates Inc., Paul [Aff. of Hill & Knowlton Inc.] - Columbus, OH - *DirPRFirms 83*
Wertheim & Associates - New York, NY - *DirPRFirms 83*
Wertheim, Toby - New York, NY - *LitMarPl 83, 84; MagIndMarPl 82-83*
Wertz Publications - Niagara Falls, NY - *BoPubDir 5*
WERU - Sun Prairie, WI - *BrCabYB 84; TV&RadDir 84*
WERZ-FM - Exeter, NH - *BrCabYB 84; TV&RadDir 84*
WESA - Charleroi, PA - *BrCabYB 84; TV&RadDir 84*
WESA-FM - Charleroi, PA - *BrCabYB 84; TV&RadDir 84*
WESB - Bradford, PA - *BrCabYB 84; TV&RadDir 84*
WESC - Greenville, SC - *BrCabYB 84; NatRadPubDir Summer 83, Spring 84; TV&RadDir 84*
WESC-FM - Greenville, SC - *BrCabYB 84; NatRadPubDir Summer 83, Spring 84; TV&RadDir 84*
Wescom Associates Inc. - San Jose, CA - *DirPRFirms 83*
Wescom Productions - Los Angeles, CA - *Tel&CabFB 84C*
Wescott Cove Publishing Co. - Stamford, CT - *BoPubDir 4, 5*
WESD-FM - Schofield, WI - *BrCabYB 84; TV&RadDir 84*
WESE - Baldwyn, MS - *BrCabYB 84*
WESH-TV - Daytona Beach, FL - *BrCabYB 84; LitMarPl 83, 84; TelAl 83, 84; Tel&CabFB 84S; TV&RadDir 84*
WESH-TV - Orlando, FL - *DirUSTelSta 83*
Wesis Publications - Cedar Grove, NJ - *BoPubDir 4, 5*
Wesjac Music - Lake City, SC - *BillIntBG 83-84*
WESL - East St. Louis, IL - *BrCabYB 84; NatRadPubDir Summer 83, Spring 84; TV&RadDir 84*
Weslaco Mid-Valley News [of Central Valley Media Inc.] - Weslaco, TX - *BaconPubCkNews 84; Ed&PubIntYB 82; NewsDir 84*
Wesley Co., The Walt - Sierra Madre, CA - *IntDirMarRes 83*
Wesleyan Advocate, The [of The Wesleyan Church Corp.] - Marion, IN - *WritMar 84*
Wesleyan University Press - Middletown, CT - *LitMarPl 83, 84; WritMar 84*
Wesman Public Relations, Jane - New York, NY - *LitMarPl 83, 84*
WESN-FM - Bloomington, IL - *BrCabYB 84; NatRadPubDir Summer 83, Spring 84; TV&RadDir 84*
WESO - Southbridge, MA - *BrCabYB 84; TV&RadDir 84*
WESP - Cambridge, MD - *TV&RadDir 84*
WESP-FM - Cambridge, MD - *BrCabYB 84; TV&RadDir 84*
Wespel Cable TV Inc. - West Pelzer, SC - *BrCabYB 84*
Wespen Audio Visual Corp. - Hawthorn, PA - *AvMarPl 83*
Wesper Corp. - Tustin, CA - *DataDirSup 7-83*
Wesper Microsystems - Costa Mesa, CA - *MicrocomMPl 84*
WESR - Olney-Onancock, VA - *BrCabYB 84*
WESR - Tasley, VA - *TV&RadDir 84*
WESR-FM - Onley-Onancock, VA - *BrCabYB 84*
WESR-FM - Tasley, VA - *TV&RadDir 84*
WESS-FM - East Stroudsburg, PA - *BrCabYB 84; NatRadPubDir Summer 83, Spring 84; TV&RadDir 84*
Wess Plastic - Farmingdale, NY - *AvMarPl 83*
Wesselhoeft Associates Inc. - Oscoda, MI - *BoPubDir 5*
Wessington Springs Independent - *See* Wessington Springs Publishers
Wessington Springs Publishers - Wessington Springs, SD - *BaconPubCkNews 84*
Wessington Springs True Dakotan - Wessington Springs, SD - *BaconPubCkNews 84*
Wessington Times Enterprise - Wessington, SD - *BaconPubCkNews 84*
WEST - Allentown/Bethlehem/Easton, PA - *NatRadPubDir Summer 83, Spring 84 p.209*
WEST - Easton, PA - *BrCabYB 84; TV&RadDir 84*
West Alabama TV Cable Co. [of Communications Services Inc.] - Fayette, AL - *BrCabYB 84 p.D-310; Tel&CabFB 84C p.1712*
West Alabama TV Cable Co. - Hamilton, AL - *BrCabYB 84; Tel&CabFB 84C*
West Alabama TV Cable Co. Inc. - Winfield, AL - *Tel&CabFB 84C*
West Alexandria Twin Valley News - West Alexandria, OH - *BaconPubCkNews 84*
West Allis Advertiser [of Menomonee Falls Publishing Co.] - Menomonee Falls, WI - *NewsDir 84*
West Allis Cablevision [Aff. of American Television & Communications Corp.] - West Allis, WI - *InterCabHB 3; Tel&CabFB 84C*
West Allis Observer - *See* Community Newspapers Inc.
West Allis Star - West Allis, WI - *BaconPubCkNews 84; Ed&PubIntYB 82*
West & Associates, Cecil - Jacksonville, FL - *StaDirAdAg 2-84*
West & Brady - Bethesda, MD - *AdAge 3-28-84; StaDirAdAg 2-84*
West & Zajac Advertising Inc. - Olympia Fields, IL - *StaDirAdAg 2-84*
West Associates - Van Nuys, CA - *StaDirAdAg 2-84*
West Bank Guide [of Guide Newspaper Corp.] - Gretna, LA - *Ed&PubIntYB 82; NewsDir 84*
West Beach Cable TV Ltd. - South Beach, OR - *BrCabYB 84*
West Belmont Leader [of Chicago Leader Newspapers-Leader Papers Inc.] - Chicago, IL - *AyerDirPub 83; NewsDir 84*
West Bend Journal - West Bend, IA - *BaconPubCkNews 84; Ed&PubIntYB 82*
West Bend News [of Post Corp.] - West Bend, WI - *BaconPubCkNews 84; Ed&PubIntYB 82; NewsDir 84*
West, Bill - Glendora, CA - *BoPubDir 4, 5*
West Bloomfield Eccentric - Birmingham, MI - *Ed&PubIntYB 82*
West Bloomfield Eccentric [of Suburban Communications Corp.] - Livonia, MI - *AyerDirPub 83; NewsDir 84*

West Bloomfield Eccentric - *See* Observer & Eccentric Newspapers
West Bloomfield Spinal Column [of Union Lake Spinal Column] - Union Lake, MI - *NewsDir 84*
West Bloomfield Spinal Column Newsweekly - *See* Spinal Column Newsweekly
West Boca Cablevision Inc. [of Paducah Newspapers Inc.] - Boca Raton, FL - *BrCabYB 84*
West Boca Cablevision Inc. [of Narragansett Capital Corp.] - Palm Beach County, FL - *BrCabYB 84; Tel&CabFB 84C*
West Branch - Lewisburg, PA - *LitMag&SmPr 83-84*
West Branch Ogemaw County Herald - West Branch, MI - *BaconPubCkNews 84; NewsDir 84*
West Branch Telephone Co. - West Branch, IA - *TelDir&BG 83-84*
West Branch Times - West Branch, IA - *BaconPubCkNews 84; Ed&PubIntYB 82*
West Broward Jewish Chronicle - Sunrise, FL - *Ed&PubIntYB 82*
West Burlington Des Moines County News - West Burlington, IA - *BaconPubCkNews 84*
West Carolina Rural Telephone Cooperative Inc. - Abbeville, SC - *TelDir&BG 83-84*
West Carroll Gazette - Oak Grove, LA - *AyerDirPub 83; Ed&PubIntYB 82*
West-Central Kentucky Family Research Association - Owensboro, KY - *BoPubDir 4, 5*
West Central Missouri Genealogical Society - Warrensburg, MO - *BoPubDir 4, 5*
West Central Telephone Association - Sebeka, MN - *TelDir&BG 83-84*
West Central Tribune - Willmar, MN - *AyerDirPub 83; BaconPubCkNews 84; Ed&PubIntYB 82; NewsDir 84*
West Chatham Cablevision - Chatham County, GA - *Tel&CabFB 84C*
West Chatham Cablevision Inc. - Pooler, GA - *BrCabYB 84*
West Chester Citizen [of Downingtown East Branch Citizen] - Downingtown, PA - *NewsDir 84*
West Chester Citizen - West Chester, PA - *AyerDirPub 83; Ed&PubIntYB 82*
West Chester Daily Local News - West Chester, PA - *BaconPubCkNews 84; NewsDir 84*
West Chester Union Times - West Chester, OH - *BaconPubCkNews 84*
West Chicago Press - West Chicago, IL - *BaconPubCkNews 84; Ed&PubIntYB 82; NewsDir 84*
West Chicago Township Examiner - *See* Examiner Newspapers
West Clay Weekly News - Everly, IA - *Ed&PubIntYB 82*
West Coast Advertising - Westlake Village, CA - *ArtMar 84*
West Coast Business Products Inc. - Van Nuys, CA - *DirInfWP 82*
West Coast Cable TV Ltd. - Depoe Bay, OR - *BrCabYB 84; Tel&CabFB 84C*
West Coast Cable TV Ltd. - South Blend, OR - *Tel&CabFB 84C*
West Coast Cablevision Co. - Mexico Beach, FL - *Tel&CabFB 84C*
West Coast Cablevision Ltd. - Burnaby, BC, Canada - *BrCabYB 84*
West Coast Consultants - Tracy, CA - *MicrocomMPl 83, 84; WhoWMicrocom 83*
West Coast Environmental Law Research Foundation - Vancouver, BC, Canada - *BoPubDir 4 Sup, 5*
West Coast Marketing - Tarzana, CA - *IntDirMarRes 83*
West Coast Paper Co. - Seattle, WA - *LitMarPl 83, 84*
West Coast Plays [Aff. of California Theater Council] - Berkeley, CA - *BoPubDir 4 Sup, 5*
West Coast Poetry Review Press - Reno, NV - *LitMag&SmPr 83-84*
West Coast Print Center - Santa Cruz, CA - *LitMag&SmPr 83-84*
West Coast Review of Books [of Rapport Publishing Co. Inc.] - Hollywood, CA - *BaconPubCkMag 84; LitMarPl 84; MagIndMarPl 82-83; WritMar 84*
West Coast Syndicate - Mill Valley, CA - *Ed&PubIntYB 82; LitMarPl 84*
West Columbia Brazoria County News - West Columbia, TX - *NewsDir 84*
West Columbia Brazoria County News - *See* Brazoria County News Publishers
West Columbia Journal - West Columbia, SC - *BaconPubCkNews 84*
West Concord Enterprise - West Concord, MN - *BaconPubCkNews 84; Ed&PubIntYB 82*
West Cook County Press [of Press Publications] - Elmhurst, IL - *AyerDirPub 83; NewsDir 84*
West Cook County Press - Hillside, IL - *Ed&PubIntYB 82*
West Cook County Press - *See* Press Publications
West County Citizen - Clayton, MO - *Ed&PubIntYB 82*
West County Citizen - Creve Coeur, MO - *AyerDirPub 83*
West County Citizen - St. Louis, MO - *NewsDir 84*
West County Journal - St. Louis, MO - *AyerDirPub 83; Ed&PubIntYB 82; NewsDir 84*
West County Times - Pinole, CA - *AyerDirPub 83; Ed&PubIntYB 82; NewsDir 84*
West Des Moines Express - West Des Moines, IA - *BaconPubCkNews 84; Ed&PubIntYB 82; NewsDir 84*
West Des Moines New Iowa Bystander, The - West Des Moines, IA - *NewsDir 84*
West End Journal - Brooklyn, NY - *AyerDirPub 83*
West End Magazine - Montclair, NJ - *LitMag&SmPr 83-84*
West End Music Industries Inc. - New York, NY - *BillIntBG 83-84*
West End Press - Minneapolis, MN - *BoPubDir 4, 5; LitMag&SmPr 83-84*
West Essex Today [of Today Newspapers] - Wayne, NJ - *NewsDir 84*
West Essex Today - *See* Today Newspapers
West Essex Tribune - Livingston, NJ - *AyerDirPub 83; Ed&PubIntYB 82*
West Family Publishers - Beaverton, OR - *BoPubDir 4 Sup, 5; LitMag&SmPr 83-84*
West Fargo Pioneer - West Fargo, ND - *BaconPubCkNews 84; Ed&PubIntYB 82*
West Field Research Inc., M. R. - Tucson, AZ - *IntDirMarRes 83*
West Fork Washington County Observer - West Fork, AR - *BaconPubCkNews 84*
West Frankfort American - West Frankfort, IL - *BaconPubCkNews 84; NewsDir 84*
West Ft. Bend Suburbia Reporter - West Ft. Bend County, TX - *Ed&PubIntYB 82*
West, Gentry & Morris - Rockford, IL - *AdAge 3-28-84; StaDirAdAg 2-84*
West Georgia Cable Co. [of Southern TeleCom Inc.] - Villa Rica, GA - *Tel&CabFB 84C*
West German Statistical Data [of I. P. Sharp Associates Ltd.] - Toronto, ON, Canada - *DataDirOnSer 84*
West Glen Communications - New York, NY - *Tel&CabFB 84C*
West Hartford Newington Town Crier - West Hartford, CT - *BaconPubCkNews 84*
West Hartford News - Hartford, CT - *Ed&PubIntYB 82*
West Hartford News - West Hartford, CT - *AyerDirPub 83; BaconPubCkNews 84; NewsDir 84*
West Haven News - West Haven, CT - *AyerDirPub 83; Ed&PubIntYB 82; NewsDir 84*
West Hawaii Cable Vision Ltd. [of Mega Vision Co.] - Kailua-Kona, HI - *Tel&CabFB 84C*
West Hawaii Today - Kailua-Kona, HI - *BaconPubCkNews 84; Ed&PubIntYB 82*
West Helena Twin City Tribune - West Helena, AR - *BaconPubCkNews 84*
West Hempstead Beacon [of Nassau County Publications] - Hempstead, NY - *NewsDir 84*
West Hempstead Beacon - West Hempstead, NY - *Ed&PubIntYB 82*
West Hempstead Beacon - *See* Nassau County Publication
West Hempstead Pennysaver - Geneseo, NY - *AyerDirPub 83*
West Hernando Green Sheet - New Port Richey, FL - *AyerDirPub 83*
West Hickory Television Co. - West Hickory, PA - *BrCabYB 84; Tel&CabFB 84C*
West Hills Review: A Walt Whitman Journal - Huntington Station, NY - *LitMag&SmPr 83-84*
West Hollywood Post [of Post Newspaper Group] - Los Angeles, CA - *NewsDir 84*
West Hollywood Post - *See* Post Newspaper Group

West Hollywood Sun Living - Los Angeles, CA - *AyerDirPub 83*
West Hollywood Sun Living - West Hollywood, CA - *Ed&PubIntYB 82*
West Hollywood Sun Living - *See* Meredith Newspapers
West Hudson Publishers - Kearny, NJ - *BaconPubCkNews 84*
West Indian Group Inc. - Portland, OR - *Tel&CabFB 84C*
West Indies Advertising Co. Inc. - San Juan, Puerto Rico - *InfoS 83-84; StaDirAdAg 2-84*
West Iowa Telephone Co. - Remsen, IA - *TelDir&BG 83-84*
West Jefferson Skyland Post - West Jefferson, NC - *BaconPubCkNews 84; NewsDir 84*
West Jefferson Times - West Jefferson, NC - *BaconPubCkNews 84*
West Jersey Telephone Co. [Aff. of United Telecommunications Inc.] - Belvidere, NJ - *TelDir&BG 83-84*
West Jordan Cable - West Jordan, VT - *BrCabYB 84*
West Kentucky Rural Telephone Cooperative Corp. Inc. - Mayfield, KY - *TelDir&BG 83-84*
West Kootenay Today - Nelson, BC, Canada - *Ed&PubIntYB 82*
West Lafayette TV Cable Inc. - West Lafayette, OH - *BrCabYB 84; Tel&CabFB 84C*
West Lane News - Vaneta, OR - *AyerDirPub 83; Ed&PubIntYB 82*
West Lane Shopper - Vaneta, OR - *AyerDirPub 83*
West Lebanon Valley News - West Lebanon, NH - *NewsDir 84*
West Liberty Enterprise - West Liberty, IA - *BaconPubCkNews 84*
West Liberty Index - West Liberty, IA - *BaconPubCkNews 84; Ed&PubIntYB 82*
West Liberty Licking Valley Courier - West Liberty, KY - *NewsDir 84*
West Liberty Licking Valley Courier - *See* Courier Publishing Co. Inc.
West Liberty Telephone Co. - West Liberty, IA - *TelDir&BG 83-84*
West Life [of Photojournals Inc.] - Cleveland, OH - *NewsDir 84*
West Life - Westlake, OH - *AyerDirPub 83; Ed&PubIntYB 82*
West Lincoln Review - Smithville, ON, Canada - *AyerDirPub 83; Ed&PubIntYB 82*
West Linn Tidings - Lake Oswego, OR - *AyerDirPub 83*
West Lorne Sun, The - West Lorne, ON, Canada - *Ed&PubIntYB 82*
West Los Angeles Independent [of United Western Newspapers Inc.] - Santa Monica, CA - *AyerDirPub 83; NewsDir 84*
West Los Angeles Independent - West Los Angeles, CA - *Ed&PubIntYB 82*
West Los Angeles Independent - *See* Copley Press Inc.
West Los Angeles Pico Post - *See* Post Newspaper Group
West Louisiana Star - Many, LA - *AyerDirPub 83*
West Lyon Herald - Inwood, IA - *AyerDirPub 83; Ed&PubIntYB 82*
West Marketing Research - New York, NY - *IntDirMarRes 83*
West Martin Weekly News - Sherburn, MN - *AyerDirPub 83; Ed&PubIntYB 82*
West Memphis Evening Times - West Memphis, AR - *NewsDir 84*
West Michigan Magazine [of West Michigan Telecommunications Foundation] - Grand Rapids, MI - *BaconPubCkMag 84; WritMar 84*
West Mifflin Record - *See* Gateway Press Inc.
West Milford Argus Today - West Milford, NJ - *AyerDirPub 83*
West Milford Argus Today - *See* Today Newspapers
West Milton Record - West Milton, OH - *Ed&PubIntYB 82*
West Milton Record - *See* Bowling-Moorman Publications
West Minneapolis Shopping Guide - Minneapolis, MN - *AyerDirPub 83*
West Monroe Citizen - West Monroe, LA - *BaconPubCkNews 84*
West Morris Star Journal - Ledgewood, NJ - *AyerDirPub 83*
West Morris Star Journal - Roxbury, NJ - *Ed&PubIntYB 82*
West New Yorker Inc. - Fairview, NJ - *BaconPubCkNews 84*
West News [of Cechoslovak Publishing Co. Inc.] - West, TX - *BaconPubCkNews 84; Ed&PubIntYB 82; NewsDir 84*
West Newton Cable TV [of Adelphia Communications Corp.] - West Newton, PA - *Tel&CabFB 84C*
West Newton Times-Sun - West Newton, PA - *BaconPubCkNews 84*
West Newton TV Cable Inc. [of Adelphia Communications Corp.] - West Newton, PA - *BrCabYB 84*
West Oak Lane Leader, The [of Inter County Publishing Co.] - Philadelphia, PA - *NewsDir 84*
West Omaha Sun - Omaha, NE - *NewsDir 84*
West Omaha Sun/Dundee Sun - Omaha, NE - *AyerDirPub 83*
West Orange Chronicle [of Worrall Publications] - West Orange, NJ - *AyerDirPub 83; Ed&PubIntYB 82; NewsDir 84*
West Orange Chronicle - *See* Worrall Publications
West Orange Publishing Co. - Garden Grove, CA - *BaconPubCkNews 84*
West Palm Beach Florida Photo News - West Palm Beach, FL - *BaconPubCkNews 84*
West Palm Beach Town-Crier - West Palm Beach, FL - *BaconPubCkNews 84*
West Pasco Green Sheet - New Port Richey, FL - *AyerDirPub 83*
West Pasco Press - New Port Richey, FL - *AyerDirPub 83; Ed&PubIntYB 82*
West Penobscot Telephone & Telegraph Co. [Aff. of Telephone & Data Systems Inc.] - Corinna, ME - *TelDir&BG 83-84*
West Pike News - Barry, IL - *Ed&PubIntYB 82*
West Plains Daily Quill - West Plains, MO - *BaconPubCkNews 84; Ed&PubIntYB 82; NewsDir 84*
West Plains Gazette - West Plains, MO - *LitMag&SmPr 83-84*
West Point Bee - West Point, IA - *BaconPubCkNews 84; Ed&PubIntYB 82*
West Point Cablevision [of First Commonwealth Communications Inc.] - West Point, VA - *Tel&CabFB 84C*
West Point Community Antenna [of Comcast Corp.] - West Point, MS - *Tel&CabFB 84C*
West Point Community Antenna System [of American Cable Systems Inc.] - West Point, MS - *BrCabYB 84*
West Point Daily Times Leader [of Harris Newspapers Inc.] - West Point, MS - *BaconPubCkNews 84; NewsDir 84*
West Point News - West Point, NE - *BaconPubCkNews 84; Ed&PubIntYB 82; NewsDir 84*
West Point Telephone Co. Inc. - West Point, IN - *TelDir&BG 83-84*
West Point Tidewater Review - *See* Atlantic Publications
West Prince Graphic - Alberton, PE, Canada - *Ed&PubIntYB 82*
West Prince Graphic - Montague, PE, Canada - *AyerDirPub 83*
West Proviso Herald - Bellwood, IL - *Ed&PubIntYB 82*
West Proviso Herald [of Pioneer Press Inc.] - Melrose Park, IL - *NewsDir 84*
West Proviso Herald - Wilmette, IL - *AyerDirPub 83*
West Proviso Herald - *See* Pioneer Press Inc.
West Publishing Co. - St. Paul, MN - *CompReadDB 82; DataDirOnSer 84; InfIndMarPl 83; KnowInd 83; LitMarPl 83, 84; MicroMarPl 82-83*
West Records - Universal City, CA - *BillIntBG 83-84*
West Richland Richlander - *See* Tribune Newspapers Inc.
West Richlander - Clarkston, WA - *AyerDirPub 83*
West River Catholic [of Diocese of Rapid City] - Rapid City, SD - *NewsDir 84*
West River CATV [of West River Cooperative Telephone Co.] - Bison, SD - *Tel&CabFB 84C*
West River Cooperative Telephone Co. - Bison, SD - *TelDir&BG 83-84*
West River Progress - Dupree, SD - *AyerDirPub 83; Ed&PubIntYB 82*
West River Telephone Corp. - Hazen, ND - *TelDir&BG 83-84*
West Roxbury Transcript - Dedham, MA - *AyerDirPub 83; NewsDir 84*
West Roxbury Transcript - West Roxbury, MA - *Ed&PubIntYB 82*
West Roxbury Transcript - *See* Transcript Newspapers Inc.
West Sacramento News-Ledger - West Sacramento, CA - *BaconPubCkNews 84; NewsDir 84*
West Salem Advocate - West Salem, IL - *BaconPubCkNews 84; Ed&PubIntYB 82*
West Salem La Crosse County Countryman - West Salem, WI - *BaconPubCkNews 84*
West Schuylkill Herald - Tower City, PA - *AyerDirPub 83; Ed&PubIntYB 82*
West Schuylkill Herald Publishers - Tower City, PA - *BaconPubCkNews 84*

West Seattle Herald [of Robinson Newspapers] - Seattle, WA - *NewsDir 84*
West Seattle Herald - West Seattle, WA - *Ed&PubIntYB 82*
West Seattle Herald - *See* Robinson Communications Co.
West Seattle Herald/White Center News - Seattle, WA - *AyerDirPub 83*
West Sedgwick County News-Sentinel - Cheney, KS - *AyerDirPub 83*
West Sedgwick County News-Sentinel - Goddard, KS - *Ed&PubIntYB 82*
West Seneca Bee - West Seneca, NY - *Ed&PubIntYB 82*
West Seneca Bee - Williamsville, NY - *AyerDirPub 83*
West Seneca Bee - *See* Bee Publications Inc.
West Seneca News [of Front Page Inc.] - Lackawanna, NY - *NewsDir 84*
West Seneca News - West Seneca, NY - *Ed&PubIntYB 82*
West Seneca News - *See* Front Page Inc.
West Seneca Observer - Buffalo, NY - *AyerDirPub 83*
West Seneca Observer [of Leader Publishing Co.] - Lackawanna, NY - *NewsDir 84*
West Seneca Observer - West Seneca, NY - *Ed&PubIntYB 82*
West Seneca Pennysaver - Orchard Park, NY - *AyerDirPub 83*
West Sherturne Tribune - Big Lake, MN - *AyerDirPub 83*
West Shore Cable TV - North Olmsted, OH - *BrCabYB 84; Tel&CabFB 84C*
West Shore Shopper - Camp Hill, PA - *AyerDirPub 83*
West Shore Times [of Pallas Publishing Co.] - Mechanicsburg, PA - *AyerDirPub 83; Ed&PubIntYB 82; NewsDir 84*
West Shore TV Cable Co. [of Community Tele-Communications Inc.] - Mechanicsburg, PA - *BrCabYB 84; Tel&CabFB 84C*
West Side Advance - Kerman, CA - *AyerDirPub 83*
West Side Cable Service Inc. - Harrisburg, AR - *BrCabYB 84*
West Side Electronics Inc. - Chatsworth, CA - *MicrocomMPl 83, 84*
West Side Index - Newman, CA - *AyerDirPub 83; Ed&PubIntYB 82*
West Side Journal - Port Allen, LA - *AyerDirPub 83*
West Side Messenger [of Brownsburg Mid-State Newspapers Inc.] - Brownsburg, IN - *AyerDirPub 83; NewsDir 84*
West Side Messenger, The - Speedway, IN - *Ed&PubIntYB 82*
West Side Story - Knoxville, TN - *Ed&PubIntYB 82*
West Side Sun - Largo, FL - *AyerDirPub 83*
West Side Sun News [of Cleveland Sun Newspapers] - Cleveland, OH - *AyerDirPub 83; NewsDir 84*
West Side Sun News - West Cleveland, OH - *Ed&PubIntYB 82*
West Side Telephone Co. - Morgantown, WV - *TelDir&BG 83-84*
West Side Television Corp. - Warren, PA - *BrCabYB 84*
West Side Times - Chicago, IL - *AyerDirPub 83*
West Side Times - Buffalo, NY - *AyerDirPub 83*
West Side TV Association Inc. - Hood River, OR - *BrCabYB 84*
West Side TV Cable Co-Op - Oak Grove, OR - *BrCabYB 84; Tel&CabFB 84C*
West Side TV Corp. - Sheffield, PA - *Tel&CabFB 84C*
West Side TV Corp. - Warren, PA - *Tel&CabFB 84C*
West Southwest Book Publishing Co. - Redding, CA - *BoPubDir 4 Sup, 5; LitMag&SmPr 83-84*
West Springfield Record - West Springfield, MA - *BaconPubCkNews 84; Ed&PubIntYB 82; NewsDir 84*
West St. Paul Mendota Heights Sun - West St. Paul/Mendota Heights, MN - *Ed&PubIntYB 82*
West St. Paul Mendota Heights Sun - *See* Sun Newspapers
West Suburban Graphic, The - Maywood, IL - *Ed&PubIntYB 82*
West Suburban Press Inc. - Melrose Park, IL - *BaconPubCkNews 84*
West Suburban Times - Chicago, IL - *AyerDirPub 83; Ed&PubIntYB 82*
West Summit Press - Chagrin Falls, OH - *BoPubDir 4, 5*
West Tennessee Telephone Co. - Bradford, TN - *TelDir&BG 83-84*
West Texas Rural Telephone Cooperative Inc. - Hereford, TX - *TelDir&BG 83-84*
West Texas Times - Lubbock, TX - *Ed&PubIntYB 82*
West Tisbury Martha's Vineyard Grapevine - West Tisbury, MA - *NewsDir 84*
West Toledo Herald - Toledo, OH - *AyerDirPub 83; Ed&PubIntYB 82; NewsDir 84*
West Town Herald - Chicago, IL - *AyerDirPub 83*
West Town Publications - Chicago, IL - *BaconPubCkNews 84*
West Union Adams County News - *See* Defender Publishing Co.
West Union Fayette County Union - West Union, IA - *BaconPubCkNews 84*
West Union Herald Record - West Union, WV - *BaconPubCkNews 84; NewsDir 84*
West Union People's Defender - West Union, OH - *Ed&PubIntYB 82*
West Union People's Defender - *See* Defender Publishing Co.
West Union Union - West Union, IA - *NewsDir 84*
West Unity Advance Reporter - West Unity, OH - *BaconPubCkNews 84*
West Valley Courier - Hillsboro, OR - *AyerDirPub 83*
West Valley Courier - *See* Hillsboro Argus Inc.
West Valley View - Murray, UT - *AyerDirPub 83*
West Valley View - West Valley, UT - *AyerDirPub 83*
West Valley View - West Valley City, UT - *Ed&PubIntYB 82*
West Valley View - *See* Murray Printing Co. Inc.
West View Allegheny Journal - West View, PA - *Ed&PubIntYB 82*
West Village Publishing Co. - Orange, CA - *BoPubDir 4, 5*
West Virgina Comic Group - Parkersburg, WV - *Ed&PubIntYB 82*
West Virginia AFL-CIO Observer [of West Virginia Labor Federation AFL-CIO] - Charleston, WV - *NewsDir 84*
West Virginia Construction News [of Contractors Association of West Virginia] - Charleston, WV - *BaconPubCkMag 84; MagDir 84*
West Virginia Dental Journal [of Jarrett Printing Co.] - Charleston, WV - *BaconPubCkMag 84; MagDir 84*
West Virginia Dept. of Mines - Charleston, WV - *BoPubDir 5*
West Virginia Engineer, The - Charleston, WV - *BaconPubCkMag 84*
West Virginia Herald - Clendenin, WV - *AyerDirPub 83; Ed&PubIntYB 82*
West Virginia Hillbilly [Aff. of Cogar Center] - Richwood, WV - *BoPubDir 4, 5*
West Virginia Hillbilly - Statewide, WV - *Ed&PubIntYB 82*
West Virginia Library Network [of West Virginia State Library Commission] - Charleston, WV - *EISS 5-84 Sup*
West Virginia Medical Journal - Charleston, WV - *BaconPubCkMag 84; MagDir 84*
West Virginia News - Lewisburg, WV - *AyerDirPub 83; BaconPubCkNews 84*
West Virginia Press Services Inc. - Charleston, WV - *ProGuPRSer 4*
West Virginia School Journal - Charleston, WV - *BaconPubCkMag 84; MagDir 84*
West Virginia Telephone Co. [Aff. of Continental Telephone Corp.] - St. Marys, WV - *TelDir&BG 83-84*
West Virginia Transporter - Charleston, WV - *BaconPubCkMag 84*
West Virginia University (Bureau of Business Research) - Morgantown, WV - *BoPubDir 4, 5*
West Virginia University (Bureau of Government Research) - Morgantown, WV - *BoPubDir 4, 5*
West Virginia University (Perley Isaac Reed School of Journalism) - Morgantown, WV - *BoPubDir 4, 5*
West Virginia University Press - Morgantown, WV - *BoPubDir 4 Sup, 5*
West Volusia Blanket Shopper - Delray Beach, FL - *AyerDirPub 83*
West Warwick Pawtuxet Valley Daily Times - West Warwick, RI - *NewsDir 84*
West Whittier Independent - Pico Rivera, CA - *AyerDirPub 83*
West Wind Productions Inc. - Boulder, CO - *AvMarPl 83*
West Windsor-Plainsboro Chronicle - Princeton Junction, NJ - *AyerDirPub 83*
West Windsor-Plainsboro Chronicle - West Windsor, NJ - *Ed&PubIntYB 82*
West Winfield Star-Courier - West Winfield, NY - *BaconPubCkNews 84*
West Winfield Star, The - West Winfield, NY - *Ed&PubIntYB 82*
West Wisconsin Telephone Cooperative - Downsville, WI - *TelDir&BG 83-84*
Westag Werbeagentur Prigge, Hawel GmbH & Co. Kg - Cologne, West Germany - *StaDirAdAg 2-84*

WestArt - Auburn, CA - *ArtMar 84; LitMag&SmPr 83-84; WritMar 84*
Westat - Rockville, MD - *AdAge 5-17-84 p.31; EISS 83; IntDirMarRes 83*
Westbank Peachland News Advertiser - Kelowna, BC, Canada - *AyerDirPub 83*
Westbound Records Inc. - Southfield, MI - *BillIntBG 83-84*
Westbrook American Journal - Westbrook, ME - *BaconPubCkNews 84*
Westbrook Cable TV [of DeSutter Cable Inc.] - Westbrook, MN - *BrCabYB 84*
Westbrook Cablevision [of New England Cablevision Inc.] - Westbrook, ME - *BrCabYB 84; Tel&CabFB 84C*
Westbrook Sentinel - Westbrook, MN - *BaconPubCkNews 84; Ed&PubIntYB 82*
Westburg Associates - Fennimore, WI - *LitMag&SmPr 83-84*
Westburg, John - Fennimore, WI - *BoPubDir 4, 5*
Westbury Graphics Inc. - Smithtown, NY - *LitMarPl 83, 84*
Westbury Pennysaver - Levittown, NY - *AyerDirPub 83*
Westbury Times [of Community Newspapers Inc.] - Glen Cove, NY - *NewsDir 84*
Westbury Times - Westbury, NY - *Ed&PubIntYB 82; NewsDir 84*
Westbury Times - *See* Community Newspapers Inc.
Westbury Times & Long Island Forum - Glen Cove, NY - *AyerDirPub 83*
Westby Times - Westby, WI - *BaconPubCkNews 84; Ed&PubIntYB 82*
Westchase Advertising - Houston, TX - *StaDirAdAg 2-84*
Westchester Applied Business Systems - Briarcliff Manor, NY - *MicrocomMPl 84*
Westchester Book Composition - Yorktown Heights, NY - *LitMarPl 83, 84*
Westchester-Broadview Suburban Life - *See* Life Printing & Publishing Co.
Westchester Business Journal [of West/Conn Business Journals Inc.] - Harrison, NY - *BaconPubCkMag 84; NewsDir 84*
Westchester Cable TV [of Adams-Russell Telecommunications] - Port Chester, NY - *BrCabYB 84*
Westchester Cable TV [of Adams-Russell Telecommunications] - Yorktown Heights, NY - *BrCabYB 84; InterCabHB 3; Tel&CabFB 84C*
Westchester Cable TV Inc. [of Adams-Russell Telecommunications] - Mt. Kisco, NY - *Tel&CabFB 84C*
Westchester Cable TV Inc. [of Adams-Russell Co. Inc.] - Putnam Valley, NY - *Tel&CabFB 84C*
Westchester Citizen - Downington, PA - *Ed&PubIntYB 82*
Westchester Communications Inc. - Armont, NY - *StaDirAdAg 2-84*
Westchester County - Mt. Kisco, NY - *NatRadPubDir Summer 83 p.180*
Westchester County Community Services Information System [of Westchester Library System] - Elmsford, NY - *EISS 5-84 Sup*
Westchester County Press [of Negro Publishers of Westchester Inc.] - Hastings-on-Hudson, NY - *Ed&PubIntYB 82; NewsDir 84*
Westchester County Press - Yonkers, NY - *AyerDirPub 83*
Westchester Illustrated - Yonkers, NY - *MagDir 84*
Westchester Ladera Observer - *See* Copley Press Inc.
Westchester Ladera Observer & News Advertiser Press [of United Western Newspapers Inc.] - Santa Monica, CA - *AyerDirPub 83; NewsDir 84*
Westchester-Ladera Observer & News Advertiser-Press - Westchester, CA - *Ed&PubIntYB 82*
Westchester Law Journal - White Plains, NY - *BaconPubCkMag 84; MagDir 84; NewsDir 84*
Westchester Magazine - Mamaroneck, NY - *ArtMar 84; MagDir 84*
Westchester News - Culver City, CA - *AyerDirPub 83*
Westchester News - Westchester, CA - *Ed&PubIntYB 82*
Westchester News - Westchester, IL - *Ed&PubIntYB 82*
Westchester News - *See* Coast Media Newspapers
Westchester News Press [of Coast Media Newspapers] - Culver City, CA - *NewsDir 84*
Westchester-Rockland Newspapers - White Plains, NY - *BaconPubCkNews 84*
Westchester Wave - *See* Central News-Wave Publications
Westchester Weekly Breeze - *See* Breeze Newspapers
Westcliff Publications - Newport Beach, CA - *BoPubDir 4, 5*
Westcliffe Wet Mountain Tribune - Westcliffe, CO - *BaconPubCkNews 84*
Westcoast Films - San Francisco, CA - *AvMarPl 83*
Westcoaster, The - Ucluelet, BC, Canada - *AyerDirPub 83; Ed&PubIntYB 82*
Westech Corp. - Sparta, NJ - *WhoWMicrocom 83*
Westel Inc. - Rapid City, SD - *Tel&CabFB 84C p.1712*
Westend Cable TV - Tinsley, KY - *Tel&CabFB 84C p.1712*
Wester Graphtec Inc. - Irvine, CA - *MicrocomMPl 84*
Westerfield's Review [of Ashford Press] - Clinton, CT - *LitMag&SmPr 83-84*
Westerly Cable Television Inc. [of Colony Communications Inc.] - Westerly, RI - *BrCabYB 84; Tel&CabFB 84C*
Westerly Sun - Westerly, RI - *BaconPubCkNews 84; Ed&PubIntYB 82; NewsDir 84*
Western - Springfield, IL - *MagDir 84*
Western Advertiser - Beaver Falls, PA - *AyerDirPub 83*
Western Agricultural Publishing Co. Inc. - Fresno, CA - *MagIndMarPl 82-83*
Western America Films Inc. - Bozeman, MT - *AvMarPl 83*
Western American Literature - Logan, UT - *LitMag&SmPr 83-84*
Western & Eastern Treasures [of People's Publishing Inc.] - Arcata, CA - *WritMar 84*
Western & Eastern Treasures - Compton, CA - *MagDir 84*
Western Arizona CATV [of Warner Amex Cable Communications Inc.] - Parker, AZ - *BrCabYB 84; Tel&CabFB 84C*
Western Arizona Radio Corp. - San Antonio, TX - *Tel&CabFB 84C*
Western Association Newsletter - Los Angeles, CA - *BaconPubCkMag 84*
Western Association of Map Libraries - Santa Cruz, CA - *BoPubDir 4 Sup, 5*
Western Australian Institute of Technology - Bentley, Australia - *InfIndMarPl 83*
Western Banker - San Francisco, CA - *BaconPubCkMag 84; MagDir 84*
Western Bass Magazine - Santa Ana, CA - *BaconPubCkMag 84*
Western Boatman, The - Gardena, CA - *BaconPubCkMag 84*
Western Book Distributors - Berkeley, CA - *BoPubDir 4 Sup, 5*
Western Breeze - Cut Bank, MT - *Ed&PubIntYB 82*
Western Broadcasting Co. - Reno, NV - *Tel&CabFB 84S*
Western Builder - Milwaukee, WI - *BaconPubCkMag 84; MagDir 84*
Western Building Design/Sun Coast Architect-Builder [of McKellar Publications] - Los Angeles, CA - *MagDir 84*
Western Business - Billings, MT - *BaconPubCkMag 84*
Western Butler County Times, The - Towanda, KS - *Ed&PubIntYB 82*
Western Cable Inc. - Calvert, TX - *BrCabYB 84*
Western Cable Inc. - Cameron, TX - *Tel&CabFB 84C*
Western Cable Inc. - Franklin, TX - *BrCabYB 84*
Western Cable TV Ltd. [of CATV Ltd.] - Woodstock, ON, Canada - *BrCabYB 84*
Western Cablevision - Surrey, BC, Canada - *BrCabYB 84; Tel&CabFB 84C*
Western Cablevision Services Inc. [of Masada Corp.] - Phoenix, AZ - *Tel&CabFB 84C*
Western Canada Outdoors - North Battleford, SK, Canada - *ArtMar 84*
Western Canadian - Manitou, MB, Canada - *AyerDirPub 83; Ed&PubIntYB 82*
Western Carolinian [of Western Carolina University] - Cullowhee, NC - *NewsDir 84*
Western CATV [of American Television & Communications Corp.] - Canyon Country, CA - *BrCabYB 84; Tel&CabFB 84C*
Western Centre of Communication Research Inc. - Winnipeg, MB, Canada - *EISS 83*
Western Cities Broadcasting - Las Vegas, NV - *BrCabYB 84*
Western City [of League of California Cities] - Sacramento, CA - *BaconPubCkMag 84; MagDir 84*
Western Cleaner & Launderer - Glendale, CA - *BaconPubCkMag 84; MagDir 84*
Western Co-Axial Ltd. [of Trillium Cable Communications Ltd.] - Hamilton, ON, Canada - *BrCabYB 84*
Western Commerce & Industry - Winnipeg, MB, Canada - *BaconPubCkMag 84*

Western Communications Inc. [of Chronicle Publishing Co.] - Walnut Creek, CA - *BrCabYB 84 p.D-310; CabTVFinDB 83; LitMarPl 84; TelAl 83, 84; Tel&CabFB 84C*
Western Communications Inc. - Bend, OR - *Ed&PubIntYB 82*
Western Community TV Service - Big Lake, TX - *BrCabYB 84; Tel&CabFB 84C*
Western Co. Inc., The - Ridgecrest, CA - *Tel&CabFB 84C p.1712*
Western Computer Supply Co. - La Mirada, CA - *WhoWMicrocom 83*
Western Consultants - Bountiful, UT - *FBInfSer 80*
Western Counties Telephone Co. [Aff. of Continental Telecom Inc.] - Johnstown, NY - *TelDir&BG 83-84*
Western Dailies - New York, NY - *LitMarPl 83*
Western Digital Corp. - Irvine, CA - *MicrocomMPl 83, 84; WhoWMicrocom 83*
Western Dynex Corp. - Phoenix, AZ - *WhoWMicrocom 83*
Western Economic Research Co. - Sherman Oaks, CA - *IntDirMarRes 83*
Western Electric - New York, NY - *DirInfWP 82; ElecNews 7-25-83; TelDir&BG 83-84*
Western Electronics - Arcadia, CA - *BaconPubCkMag 84*
Western Epics Publishing Inc. [Aff. of Sam Weller's Zion Book Store Inc.] - Salt Lake City, UT - *BoPubDir 4, 5*
Western Extension College Educational Publishers - Saskatoon, SK, Canada - *BoPubDir 4, 5*
Western Farmer - Seattle, WA - *MagDir 84*
Western Film & Video - Westlake Village, CA - *AvMarPl 83*
Western Fire Journal [of Fire Publications Inc.] - Bellflower, CA - *BaconPubCkMag 84; MagDir 84; WritMar 84*
Western Fisheries - Vancouver, BC, Canada - *BaconPubCkMag 84*
Western Floors [of Specialist Publications Inc.] - Encino, CA - *BaconPubCkMag 84; MagDir 84*
Western Flyer [of Northwest Flyer Inc.] - Tacoma, WA - *BaconPubCkMag 84; MagDir 84; NewsDir 84; WritMar 84*
Western Foodservice - Los Angeles, CA - *BaconPubCkMag 84; MagDir 84*
Western Forestry Information Network [of U.S. Forest Service] - Berkeley, CA - *EISS 83*
Western Fruit Grower - San Rafael, CA - *MagDir 84*
Western Fruit Grower - Sausalito, CA - *MagDir 84*
Western Fruit Grower - Willoughby, OH - *BaconPubCkMag 84*
Western Grocer Magazine - Winnipeg, MB, Canada - *BaconPubCkMag 84*
Western Grocery News - Menlo Park, CA - *BaconPubCkMag 84*
Western Grower & Shipper - Irvine, CA - *MagDir 84*
Western Grower & Shipper - Newport Beach, CA - *BaconPubCkMag 84*
Western Guard - Madison, MN - *AyerDirPub 83; Ed&PubIntYB 82*
Western Hemisphere Music Co. - New Hyde Park, NY - *BillIntBG 83-84*
Western Hemisphere Publishers Representatives Inc. - Glendale, NY - *LitMarPl 83, 84; MagIndMarPl 82-83*
Western Herald [of Western Michigan University] - Kalamazoo, MI - *NewsDir 84*
Western Hills Press - Cincinnati, OH - *Ed&PubIntYB 82*
Western Hills Press - *See* Queen City Suburban Press Inc.
Western Hills Press/Family Shopping Guide - Cincinnati, OH - *AyerDirPub 83*
Western Horseman - Colorado Springs, CO - *BaconPubCkMag 84; MagDir 84; MagIndMarPl 82-83; WritMar 84*
Western Humanities Review [of University of Utah] - Salt Lake City, UT - *ArtMar 84; LitMag&SmPr 83-84; WritMar 84*
Western HVACR News [of Building News Inc.] - Los Angeles, CA - *BaconPubCkMag 84; MagDir 84*
Western Illinois Cablevision Inc. - Abingdon, IL - *BrCabYB 84; Tel&CabFB 84C p.1712*
Western Illinois Cablevision Inc. - Bushnell, IL - *BrCabYB 84*
Western Illinois Cablevision Inc. - Cambridge, IL - *BrCabYB 84*
Western Illinois Cablevision Inc. - Farmington, IL - *BrCabYB 84*
Western Illinois Cablevision Inc. - Galva, IL - *BrCabYB 84*
Western Illinois University (Essays in Literature Book Series) - Macomb, IL - *BoPubDir 4, 5*
Western Imprints [of the Oregon Historical Society] - Portland, OR - *LitMarPl 83, 84*
Western Information Network - New Westminster, BC, Canada - *BrCabYB 84*
Western Instructional Television Inc. - Los Angeles, CA - *AvMarPl 83; Tel&CabFB 84C*
Western International Marketing Consultants - Los Angeles, CA - *HBIndAd&MS 82-83*
Western International Media Corp. - Los Angeles, CA - *StaDirAdAg 2-84*
Western Investor [of Willamette Management Associates] - Portland, OR - *BaconPubCkMag 84; WritMar 84*
Western Iowa Telephone Association - Lawton, IA - *TelDir&BG 83-84*
Western Islands - Belmont, MA - *BoPubDir 4, 5; WritMar 84*
Western Itasca Review - Deer River, MN - *AyerDirPub 83; Ed&PubIntYB 82*
Western Jewish News - Winnipeg, MB, Canada - *Ed&PubIntYB 82*
Western Journal of Medicine - San Francisco, CA - *BaconPubCkMag 84; MagDir 84; MagIndMarPl 82-83*
Western Kansas World - Wa Keeney, KS - *AyerDirPub 83; Ed&PubIntYB 82*
Western Kentucky Cable Co. - Morgantown, KY - *BrCabYB 84*
Western Kentucky University (Kentucky Folklore Society) - Bowling Green, KY - *BoPubDir 4, 5*
Western Landscaping News - Irvine, CA - *BaconPubCkMag 84; WritMar 84*
Western Landscaping News [of Hester Communications Inc.] - Santa Ana, CA - *MagDir 84*
Western Legal Publications Ltd. - Vancouver, BC, Canada - *EISS 5-84 Sup*
Western Library Service - Los Angeles, CA - *LitMarPl 83*
Western Livestock Journal - Clovis, CA - *MagDir 84*
Western Livestock Journal - Denver, CO - *MagIndMarPl 82-83*
Western Livestock Reporter - Billings, MT - *BaconPubCkMag 84; MagDir 84*
Western Living [of Comac Communications Ltd.] - Vancouver, BC, Canada - *WritMar 84*
Western Louisiana Video Co. - Fisher, LA - *BrCabYB 84*
Western Louisiana Video Co. Inc. - Aimwell, LA - *BrCabYB 84*
Western Louisiana Video Co. Inc. - Many, LA - *BrCabYB 84 p.D-310; Tel&CabFB 84C*
Western Louisiana Video Co. Inc. - Zwolle, LA - *BrCabYB 84; Tel&CabFB 84C*
Western Machining & Metalworking - San Francisco, CA - *BaconPubCkMag 84; MagDir 84*
Western Manufacturing Co. - Aurora, IL - *DirInfWP 82*
Western Marine Enterprises Inc. - Ventura, CA - *BoPubDir 4, 5; LitMarPl 84*
Western Massachusetts Interviewing Service Inc. - Longmeadow, MA - *IntDirMarRes 83*
Western Material Handling/Packaging/Shipping [of Baymer Publications Inc.] - Los Angeles, CA - *MagDir 84*
Western Merchandiser [of Western Merchandise Mart] - San Francisco, CA - *BaconPubCkMag 84; MagDir 84*
Western Michigan Catholic, The [of Catholic Publishing Co. Inc.] - Grand Rapids, MI - *NewsDir 84*
Western Michigan Research - Grand Rapids, MI - *IntDirMarRes 83*
Western Michigan University (Computer Center) - Kalamazoo, MI - *DataDirOnSer 84*
Western Michigan University (New Issues Press) - Kalamazoo, MI - *BoPubDir 4, 5*
Western Micro Distributors Inc. - San Jose, CA - *MicrocomMPl 84*
Western Micro Systems Inc. - Aurora, CO - *MicrocomMPl 84*
Western Miner - Vancouver, BC, Canada - *BaconPubCkMag 84*
Western Mining Letter - Bisbee, AZ - *BaconPubCkMag 84*
Western Mobile News - Culver City, CA - *MagDir 84*
Western Monetary Report, The - Ft. Collins, CO - *BaconPubCkMag 84*
Western Motor Fleet - Winnipeg, MB, Canada - *BaconPubCkMag 84*
Western Municipal Product News - Calgary, AB, Canada - *BaconPubCkMag 84*
Western Nebraska Observer - Kimball, NE - *AyerDirPub 83; Ed&PubIntYB 82*
Western New Mexico Telephone Co. Inc. - Silver City, NM - *TelDir&BG 83-84*

Western New York [of Buffalo Area Chamber of Commerce] - Buffalo, NY - *BaconPubCkMag 84; MagDir 84; WritMar 84*
Western New York Computing Systems - Penfield, NY - *DataDirOnSer 84; DataDirSup 7-83*
Western New York Federation of Labor News [of Buffalo AFL-CIO Council] - Buffalo, NY - *NewsDir 84*
Western New York Library Resources Council - Buffalo, NY - *EISS 83*
Western New York Motorist, The - Williamsville, NY - *MagDir 84*
Western New York Offset Press Inc. - Lancaster, NY - *MagIndMarPl 82-83*
Western New Yorker/Warsaw - Geneseo, NY - *AyerDirPub 83*
Western News [of Cabinet Publishing Co.] - Libby, MT - *AyerDirPub 83; Ed&PubIntYB 82; NewsDir 84*
Western News - Vancouver, BC, Canada - *AyerDirPub 83*
Western News Advertiser - Penticton, BC, Canada - *AyerDirPub 83; Ed&PubIntYB 82*
Western News Records - Vacaville, CA - *BillIntBG 83-84*
Western News, The - Plantation, FL - *Ed&PubIntYB 82*
Western Newspapers Inc. - Yuma, AZ - *Ed&PubIntYB 82*
Western North Carolina Press Inc. - Dillsboro, NC - *BoPubDir 4, 5*
Western Observer - Anson, TX - *Ed&PubIntYB 82*
Western Office Dealer - San Francisco, CA - *BaconPubCkMag 84; MagDir 84; WritMar 84*
Western Ohio Cablevision [of Gilmore Broadcasting Corp.] - Bryan, OH - *BrCabYB 84; Tel&CabFB 84C*
Western Ohio Cablevision [of Gilmore Broadcasting Corp.] - Celina, OH - *BrCabYB 84; Tel&CabFB 84C*
Western Ohio Cablevision [of Gilmore Broadcasting Corp.] - Van Wert, OH - *BrCabYB 84; Tel&CabFB 84C*
Western Ohio Cablevision Inc. [of Gilmore Broadcasting Corp.] - Paulding, OH - *Tel&CabFB 84C*
Western Ohio Farm Exchange - Arcanum, OH - *NewsDir 84*
Western Oil Reporter [of Hart Publications Inc.] - Denver, CO - *BaconPubCkMag 84; MagDir 84*
Western Ontario Business - London, ON, Canada - *BaconPubCkMag 84*
Western Operations - Portland, OR - *MicrocomMPl 84*
Western Outdoor News - Costa Mesa, CA - *MagIndMarPl 82-83*
Western Outdoor News - Newport Beach, CA - *BaconPubCkMag 84; MagDir 84*
Western Outdoors - Costa Mesa, CA - *MagIndMarPl 82-83; WritMar 84*
Western Outdoors - Newport Beach, CA - *BaconPubCkMag 84; MagDir 84*
Western Outfitter [of The E. W. Scripps Co.] - Houston, TX - *BaconPubCkMag 84; MagDir 84; WritMar 84*
Western Packing News - San Francisco, CA - *BaconPubCkMag 84*
Western Paint & Decorating - Canoga Park, CA - *BaconPubCkMag 84*
Western Paint Industry - Los Angeles, CA - *MagDir 84*
Western Pennsylvania Cable Club - Harrisburg, PA - *CabTVPrDB 83*
Western Pennsylvania Motorist - Pittsburgh, PA - *BaconPubCkMag 84; MagDir 84*
Western People [of Western Producer Publications] - Saskatoon, SK, Canada - *WritMar 84*
Western Poconos Press-Tribune [of Dallas Pennaprint Inc.] - Dallas, PA - *NewsDir 84*
Western Press Clipping Bureau - Berthoud, CO - *ProGuPRSer 4*
Western Press Clipping Bureau - Vancouver, BC, Canada - *ProGuPRSer 4*
Western Press Clipping Services - Minneapolis, MN - *ProGuPRSer 4*
Western Producer Prairie Books - Saskatoon, SK, Canada - *LitMarPl 83, 84; WritMar 84*
Western Producer, The - Saskatoon, SK, Canada - *ArtMar 84; BaconPubCkMag 84; WritMar 84*
Western Psychological Services [Div. of Manson Western Group] - Los Angeles, CA - *DirMarMP 83; LitMarPl 83, 84*
Western Publications - Iola, WI - *MagIndMarPl 82-83*
Western Publisher - San Francisco, CA - *LitMag&SmPr 83-84*
Western Publishers - Lake Worth, FL - *BoPubDir 5*
Western Publishers - Jamestown, OH - *BoPubDir 4*
Western Publishers - Calgary, AB, Canada - *BoPubDir 4, 5*
Western Publishing Co. - Lincoln, NE - *Ed&PubIntYB 82*
Western Publishing Co. Inc. [Subs. of Mattel Inc.] - Racine, WI - *LitMarPl 83, 84*
Western Real Estate News - San Francisco, CA - *BaconPubCkMag 84*
Western Regional Information Service Center [of University of California] - Berkeley, CA - *EISS 83; InfIndMarPl 83*
Western Reserve Cablevision Inc. [of Adelphia Communications Corp.] - Macedonia, OH - *Tel&CabFB 84C*
Western Reserve Democrat - Niles, OH - *AyerDirPub 83*
Western Reserve Democrat - Warren, OH - *Ed&PubIntYB 82*
Western Reserve Historical Society - Cleveland, OH - *BoPubDir 4, 5*
Western Reserve Historical Society (Publications Dept.) - Cleveland, OH - *MicroMarPl 82-83*
Western Reserve Press Inc. - Ashtabula, OH - *BoPubDir 4, 5*
Western Reserve Publishing Services - Kent, OH - *LitMarPl 84*
Western Reserve Telephone Co., The [Aff. of Mid-Continent Telephone Corp.] - Hudson, OH - *TelDir&BG 83-84*
Western Review - Drayton Valley, AB, Canada - *AyerDirPub 83; Ed&PubIntYB 82*
Western Saltwater Fisherman [of Dyna Graphics Inc.] - Carlsbad, CA - *BaconPubCkMag 84; MagIndMarPl 82-83; WritMar 84*
Western Satellite Cablevision - Denver, CO - *Tel&CabFB 84C*
Western Satellite Inc. - Denver, CO - *Tel&CabFB 84C p.1712; TeleSy&SerDir 2-84*
Western Satellite Inc. - Englewood, CO - *Tel&CabFB 84C*
Western Satellite Inc. - Yale, OK - *BrCabYB 84; Tel&CabFB 84C*
Western Satellite Inc. - Kanab, UT - *BrCabYB 84; Tel&CabFB 84C*
Western Satellite Inc. - Milford, UT - *Tel&CabFB 84C*
Western Satellite Inc. - Nespelem, WA - *BrCabYB 84*
Western Scientific Marketing Inc. - San Diego, CA - *DataDirSup 7-83*
Western Sierra Music - *See* Sangre Productions Inc.
Western Software Development - Woodland Park, CO - *MicrocomSwDir 1; WhoWMicrocom 83*
Western Spirit - Paola, KS - *AyerDirPub 83; Ed&PubIntYB 82*
Western Sports Guides - *See* Craftsman Publications Inc./Western Sports Guides
Western Sportsman [of Nimrod Publications Ltd.] - Regina, SK, Canada - *ArtMar 84; BaconPubCkMag 84; WritMar 84*
Western Springs Citizen [of La Grange Suburban Life/Citizen] - La Grange, IL - *NewsDir 84*
Western Springs Suburban Life Citizen - *See* Life Printing & Publishing Co.
Western Springs Sun - La Grange, IL - *AyerDirPub 83*
Western Stabur Music - *See* Stabur Communications Inc.
Western Star - Coldwater, KS - *AyerDirPub 83; Ed&PubIntYB 82*
Western Star [of Brown Publishing Co.] - Lebanon, OH - *AyerDirPub 83; Ed&PubIntYB 82; NewsDir 84*
Western Star - Corner Brook, NF, Canada - *AyerDirPub 83; BaconPubCkNews 84; Ed&PubIntYB 82*
Western Star Marketing & Sales - San Mateo, CA - *LitMarPl 84*
Western Sun Publications [Aff. of Western Sun Associates Inc.] - Yuma, AZ - *BoPubDir 5; LitMag&SmPr 83-84*
Western Tanager Press - Santa Cruz, CA - *LitMarPl 83, 84; WritMar 84*
Western Telecommunications Inc. - Denver, CO - *DataDirSup 7-83; TeleSy&SerDir 2-84*
Western Telematic Inc. - Santa Ana, CA - *DataDirSup 7-83; MicrocomMPl 84; WhoWMicrocom 83*
Western Telephone Co. - Springfield, MN - *TelDir&BG 83-84*
Western Telephone Co. - Faulkton, SD - *TelDir&BG 83-84*
Western Telephone Equipment Co. - Palo Alto, CA - *DataDirSup 7-83*
Western Times - Sharon Springs, KS - *AyerDirPub 83*
Western TV Cable [of Western Communications Inc.] - San Mateo County, CA - *BrCabYB 84; Tel&CabFB 84C*
Western TV Cable [of Western Communications Inc.] - South San Francisco, CA - *BrCabYB 84; Tel&CabFB 84C*
Western TV Inc. - Evanston, WY - *BrCabYB 84*
Western Typesetting - Kansas City, MO - *LitMarPl 83, 84; MagIndMarPl 82-83*

Western Underwriter, Property-Casualty-Life & Health - San Rafael, CA - *MagDir 84*
Western Union Broadcast Services - Upper Saddle River, NJ - *BrCabYB 84*
Western Union Corp. - Upper Saddle River, NJ - *DataDirSup 7-83; HomeVid&CabYB 82-83*
Western Union Data Services Co. - Mahwah, NJ - *InfIndMarPl 83*
Western Union Telegraph Co. [Subs. of Western Union Corp.] - Upper Saddle River, NJ - *BrCabYB 84; HomeVid&CabYB 82-83; Tel&CabFB 84C; WhoWMicrocom 83*
Western Union Video Services [of Western Union Telegraph Co.] - Upper Saddle River, NJ - *TeleSy&SerDir 2-84*
Western Union VideoConferencing Inc. - Upper Saddle River, NJ - *BrCabYB 84; TeleSy&SerDir 7-83*
Western Union Voicemail Service [of Western Union Telegraph Co.] - Upper Saddle River, NJ - *TeleSy&SerDir 2-84*
Western Video Systems - San Diego, CA - *AvMarPl 83; Tel&CabFB 84C*
Western Videotape Productions - San Francisco, CA - *TeleSy&SerDir 2-84*
Western Viking - Seattle, WA - *AyerDirPub 83; Ed&PubIntYB 82; NewsDir 84*
Western Wahkiakum County Telephone Co. - Grays River, WA - *TelDir&BG 83-84*
Western Wake Herald - Apex, NC - *Ed&PubIntYB 82*
Western Wares - Norwood, CO - *MicrocomMPl 83, 84*
Western Washington University - Bellingham, WA - *LitMag&SmPr 83-84*
Western Washington University (Center for East Asian Studies) - Bellingham, WA - *BoPubDir 4, 5*
Western Washington University (Center for Pacific Northwest Studies) - Bellingham, WA - *BoPubDir 4, 5*
Western Wear & Equipment Magazine [of Bell Publications] - Denver, CO - *BaconPubCkMag 84; MagDir 84; WritMar 84*
Western Weekly Reports [of Carswell Co. Ltd.] - Agincourt, ON, Canada - *CompReadDB 82; DirOnDB Spring 84*
Western Weekly Reports [of Canadian Law Information Council] - Ottawa, ON, Canada - *DataDirOnSer 84*
Western Wheel - Calgary, AB, Canada - *AyerDirPub 83*
Western Wheel - Okotoks, AB, Canada - *Ed&PubIntYB 82*
Western Wisconsin Communications Cooperative - Independence, WI - *BrCabYB 84; Tel&CabFB 84C p.1712; TeleSy&SerDir 7-83*
Western Word Processing Inc. - Portland, OR - *DirInfWP 82*
Western World - San Francisco, CA - *BoPubDir 4, 5*
Western World Press - Sun City, CA - *BoPubDir 4, 5*
Western World Review - Sun City, CA - *LitMag&SmPr 83-84*
Westernlore Press - Tucson, AZ - *LitMarPl 83, 84; WritMar 84*
Westernlore Typographics Inc. - Tucson, AZ - *LitMarPl 83, 84*
Western's World - Beverly Hills, CA - *MagIndMarPl 82-83*
Western's World - Los Angeles, CA - *BaconPubCkMag 84; MagDir 84*
Westerville Public Opinion - Westerville, OH - *BaconPubCkNews 84; NewsDir 84*
Westerville Suburbia News - *See* Suburban News Publications
Westfield Community Antenna Association - Westfield, PA - *BrCabYB 84; Tel&CabFB 84C*
Westfield Enterprise [of Pace Publishing Inc.] - Indianapolis, IN - *Ed&PubIntYB 82; NewsDir 84*
Westfield Enterprise - *See* Topic Newspapers Inc.
Westfield Evening News - Westfield, MA - *AyerDirPub 83; BaconPubCkNews 84; Ed&PubIntYB 82; NewsDir 84*
Westfield Free Press-Courier [of Wellsboro Tioga Printing Corp.] - Westfield, PA - *BaconPubCkNews 84; Ed&PubIntYB 82; NewsDir 84*
Westfield Leader - Westfield, NJ - *BaconPubCkNews 84; Ed&PubIntYB 82; NewsDir 84*
Westfield Republican - Westfield, NY - *AyerDirPub 83; BaconPubCkNews 84; Ed&PubIntYB 82; NewsDir 84*
Westfield Review, The - Westfield, IL - *Ed&PubIntYB 82*
Westford Eagle - Westford, MA - *Ed&PubIntYB 82*
Westford Eagle - *See* Minute-Man Publications Inc.
Westford Eagle, The [of Beacon-Minute Man Corp.] - Acton, MA - *AyerDirPub 83; NewsDir 84*
Westford Independent Telephone Co. - Jamestown, PA - *TelDir&BG 83-84*
Westgard, Gilbert K. II - Des Plaines, IL - *BoPubDir 5*
Westgate Graphic Design Inc. - Oak Park, IL - *DirMarMP 83*
Westgate House - San Francisco, CA - *BoPubDir 5*
Westgate Research Inc. - St. Louis, MO - *IntDirMarRes 83*
Westgate Research Inc. - *See* Gardner Advertising Co. Inc.
Westhead Co. Inc., David J. - Pittsburgh, PA - *DirPRFirms 83*
Westhope Standard - Westhope, ND - *BaconPubCkNews 84; Ed&PubIntYB 82*
Westico - Norwalk, CT - *MicrocomMPl 83, 84; WhoWMicrocom 83*
Westin & Associates - Brick Town, NJ - *ArtMar 84; StaDirAdAg 2-84*
Westin Communications - Woodland Hills, CA - *BoPubDir 5; LitMarPl 84; WritMar 84*
Westine Report [of Zimmermann & Sons Inc.] - Union Grove, WI - *AyerDirPub 83; Ed&PubIntYB 82; NewsDir 84*
Westinghouse (Architectural Systems Div.) - Grand Rapids, MI - *DirInfWP 82*
Westinghouse Broadcasting & Cable Inc. - New York, NY - *BrCabYB 84*
Westinghouse Broadcasting & Cable Inc. - *See* Group W Cable
Westinghouse Broadcasting & Cable Inc. - *See* Group W Newsfeed
Westinghouse Broadcasting Co. [Subs. of Westinghouse Electric Corp.] - New York, NY - *TelAl 83, 84*
Westinghouse Broadcasting Co. Inc. - *See* Group W Cable Inc.
Westinghouse Canada Inc. [of Westinghouse Electric Corp.] - Burlington, ON, Canada - *DataDirSup 7-83; InfIndMarPl 83*
Westinghouse Electric Corp. - Pittsburgh, PA - *AdAge 6-28-84; DataDirSup 7-83; ElecNews 7-25-83; HomeVid&CabYB 82-83; KnowInd 83*
Westinghouse Electric Corp. (Industry Automation Div.) - Pittsburgh, PA - *DataDirOnSer 84; DirInfWP 82*
Westinghouse Information Services [Subs. of Westinghouse Electric Corp.] - Iowa City, IA - *DataDirOnSer 84; DirInfWP 82*
Westinghouse Information Services - Rochester, NY - *DataDirSup 7-83*
Westlake-Moss Bluff News - Westlake, LA - *AyerDirPub 83; BaconPubCkNews 84; Ed&PubIntYB 82*
Westlake-Moss Bluff News Buyer's Guide - Westlake, LA - *AyerDirPub 83*
Westlake Picayune - Austin, TX - *Ed&PubIntYB 82*
Westlake Post [of Meredith Newspapers] - Los Angeles, CA - *AyerDirPub 83; Ed&PubIntYB 82; NewsDir 84*
Westlake Times - *See* Associated Valley Publications
Westlake West Life - Westlake, OH - *BaconPubCkNews 84*
Westlake Westlaker Times - *See* Gottschalk Publishing Co., E. J.
Westland Eagle - Wayne, MI - *AyerDirPub 83; Ed&PubIntYB 82; NewsDir 84*
Westland Eagle - *See* Associated Newspapers Inc.
Westland Observer [of Suburban Communications Corp.] - Livonia, MI - *AyerDirPub 83; NewsDir 84*
Westland Observer - Westland, MI - *Ed&PubIntYB 82*
Westland Observer - *See* Observer & Eccentric Newspapers
Westland Publications - McNeal, AZ - *BoPubDir 4, 5*
Westland Times - *See* Suburban Newspapers
Westlaw [of Westlaw Publishing Co.] - St. Paul, MN - *CompReadDB 82; DataDirOnSer 84; DirOnDB Spring 84; EISS 83; MicrocomMPl 84*
Westman Media Cooperative Ltd. - Brandon, MB, Canada - *BrCabYB 84; Tel&CabFB 84C*
Westminister News, The - Westminister, SC - *Ed&PubIntYB 82*
Westminister Press, The - Philadelphia, PA - *WritMar 84*
Westminster Communications & Publications [Aff. of Seven Seas Publishers Inc.] - Washington, DC - *BoPubDir 4 Sup, 5*
Westminster Herald - Westminster, CA - *BaconPubCkNews 84; Ed&PubIntYB 82*
Westminster Journal-Sentinel [of Denver Community Publications Co.] - Denver, CO - *NewsDir 84*
Westminster News - Westminster, SC - *BaconPubCkNews 84*
Westminster Press, The [of The United Presbyterian Church in the USA] - Philadelphia, PA - *LitMarPl 83, 84*
Westminster Sentinel - *See* Sentinel Newspapers
Westminster Window - Westminster, CO - *AyerDirPub 83*
Westmont/Darien Du Page Progress, The - Westmont, IL - *Ed&PubIntYB 82*
Westmont Du Page Progress - *See* Reporter Progress Newspapers

Westmont Suburban Life Graphic - *See* Life Printing & Publishing Co.
Westmont Word - Helena, MT - *NewsDir 84*
Westmore News - Port Chester, NY - *AyerDirPub 83; Ed&PubIntYB 82*
Westmoreland Audience - Latrobe, PA - *Ed&PubIntYB 82*
Westmoreland Cable Co. [of Comcast Corp.] - East Deer Township, PA - *Tel&CabFB 84C*
Westmoreland Cable Co. [of Comcast Corp.] - New Kensington, PA - *BrCabYB 84*
Westmoreland Cable Co. [of Comcast Corp.] - West Deer Township, PA - *Tel&CabFB 84C*
Westmoreland, Larson & Hill Inc. - Duluth, MN - *StaDirAdAg 2-84*
Westmoreland News [of Eastern Shore News Inc.] - Accomac, VA - *NewsDir 84*
Westmoreland News - Montross, VA - *AyerDirPub 83; Ed&PubIntYB 82*
Westmoreland Recorder - Westmoreland, KS - *BaconPubCkNews 84; Ed&PubIntYB 82*
Westmoreland Star - Montrose, PA - *AyerDirPub 83*
Westmoreland Star - Murrysville, PA - *Ed&PubIntYB 82*
Westmoreland Star, The [of Dardanell Publications Inc.] - Monroeville, PA - *NewsDir 84*
Westmoreland World - Westmoreland, TN - *BaconPubCkNews 84; Ed&PubIntYB 82*
Westmount Examiner, The - Westmount, PQ, Canada - *Ed&PubIntYB 82*
Weston & Athena Community Television System - Athena, OR - *BrCabYB 84; Tel&CabFB 84C*
Weston Chronicle - Weston, MO - *AyerDirPub 83; BaconPubCkNews 84; Ed&PubIntYB 82*
Weston County Gazette - Upton, WY - *AyerDirPub 83; Ed&PubIntYB 82*
Weston Democrat - Weston, WV - *BaconPubCkNews 84; Ed&PubIntYB 82*
Weston Graphics - Cambridge, MA - *LitMag&SmPr 83-84*
Weston Group Inc. - Westport, CT - *HBIndAd&MS 82-83; StaDirAdAg 2-84*
Weston Independent - Weston, WV - *Ed&PubIntYB 82*
Weston, Jeremy - Watford, England - *FBInfSer 80*
Weston Television Cable Corp. - Weston, WV - *BrCabYB 84*
Weston Woods Studios Inc. - Weston, CT - *AvMarPl 83; Tel&CabFB 84C*
Westosha Report - Twin Lakes, WI - *AyerDirPub 83; Ed&PubIntYB 82*
Westover TV Cable Co. - Grafton, WV - *BrCabYB 84; Tel&CabFB 84C p.1712*
Westover TV Cable Co. - Meadowdale, WV - *BrCabYB 84; Tel&CabFB 84C*
Westover TV Cable Co. Inc. - Brookhaven, WV - *BrCabYB 84*
Westover TV Cable Co. Inc. - Westover, WV - *BrCabYB 84*
Westphalia Telephone Co. - Westphalia, MI - *TelDir&BG 83-84*
Westport & Rideau Valley Mirror - Westport, ON, Canada - *Ed&PubIntYB 82*
Westport Communications Group Inc., The - Westport, CT - *ArtMar 84; AvMarPl 83*
Westport News - Westport, CT - *Ed&PubIntYB 82*
Westport News - *See* Brooks Community Newspapers
Westport Video Inc. - Westport, CT - *AvMarPl 83*
Westrail Publications - Glendora, CA - *BoPubDir 4 Sup, 5*
Westrex OEM Products - Fall River, MA - *MicrocomMPl 84*
Westridge Press Ltd. - Salem, OR - *BoPubDir 4, 5*
Westroots - La Jolla, CA - *ArtMar 84*
Westside Gazette - Ft. Lauderdale, FL - *AyerDirPub 83*
Westside Independent Telephone Co. - Westside, IA - *TelDir&BG 83-84*
Westside News - Culver City, CA - *AyerDirPub 83*
Westside News - Hawthorne, CA - *Ed&PubIntYB 82*
Westside Record-Journal [of Ferndale Record Inc.] - Ferndale, WA - *AyerDirPub 83; Ed&PubIntYB 82; NewsDir 84*
Westside Shopper - New Haven, CT - *AyerDirPub 83*
Westside Shopper - West Des Moines, IA - *AyerDirPub 83*
Westside Shopping News - Taft, CA - *AyerDirPub 83*
Westside Suburbia-Reporter - Houston, TX - *Ed&PubIntYB 82*
Westside Sun - San Antonio, TX - *AyerDirPub 83*
Westsider - Avondale, AZ - *AyerDirPub 83*
Westsider, The - Goodyear, AZ - *NewsDir 84*
Westsider, The - Litchfield Park, AZ - *Ed&PubIntYB 82*
Westsider, The - New York, NY - *AyerDirPub 83; Ed&PubIntYB 82; NewsDir 84*
Westvaco Corp. - New York, NY - *MagIndMarPl 82-83*
Westvaco Corp. (Fine Papers Div.) - New York, NY - *LitMarPl 83, 84*
Westview - Nashville, TN - *AyerDirPub 83*
Westview Press - Boulder, CO - *LitMarPl 83, 84; WritMar 84*
Westville Cable TV - Westville, OK - *Tel&CabFB 84C*
Westville Indicator - Westville, IN - *BaconPubCkNews 84; Ed&PubIntYB 82; NewsDir 84*
Westville Reporter - Westville, OK - *AyerDirPub 83; BaconPubCkNews 84; Ed&PubIntYB 82*
Westward - Dallas, TX - *WritMar 84*
Westware Inc. - Ontario, OR - *MicrocomMPl 83; WhoWMicrocom 83*
Westwater Books [Aff. of Belknap Photographic Services Inc.] - Boulder City, NV - *BoPubDir 4, 5*
Westways - Los Angeles, CA - *ArtMar 84; BaconPubCkMag 84; MagDir 84; MagIndMarPl 82-83; WritMar 84*
Westwind Press - Farmington, WV - *BoPubDir 4, 5; LitMag&SmPr 83-84*
Westwood News [of Pascack Valley Community Life] - Westwood, NJ - *NewsDir 84*
Westwood Pasack Valley News - Westwood, NJ - *BaconPubCkNews 84*
Westwood Pine Press - Westwood, CA - *Ed&PubIntYB 82*
Westwood Pine Press - *See* Feather Publishing Co. Inc.
Westwood Publishing Co. - Glendale, CA - *BoPubDir 4, 5; DirMarMP 83*
Westwood Sun [of Overland Park Sun Newspapers] - Shawnee Mission, KS - *NewsDir 84*
Westwood Sun - *See* Sun Publications
WESU-FM - Middletown, CT - *BrCabYB 84; NatRadPubDir Summer 83, Spring 84; TV&RadDir 84*
WESX - Salem, MA - *BrCabYB 84; TV&RadDir 84*
WESY - Greenville, MS - *NatRadPubDir Summer 83, Spring 84; TV&RadDir 84*
WESY - Leland, MS - *BrCabYB 84*
Wet Mountain Tribune - Westcliffe, CO - *AyerDirPub 83; Ed&PubIntYB 82*
WETA-FM - Washington, DC - *BrCabYB 84; TV&RadDir 84*
WETA-TV - Washington, DC - *BrCabYB 84; Tel&CabFB 84S; TV&RadDir 84*
WETA-TV - Arlington, VA - *TV&RadDir 84*
Wetacom - Washington, DC - *TeleSy&SerDir 2-84*
Wetaskiwin News-Advertiser - Wetaskiwin, AB, Canada - *Ed&PubIntYB 82*
WETB - Johnson City, TN - *BrCabYB 84*
WETC - Wendell, NC - *BrCabYB 84; TV&RadDir 84*
WETD-FM - Alfred, NY - *BrCabYB 84; NatRadPubDir Summer 83, Spring 84; TV&RadDir 84*
WETG - Hartford, CT - *BrCabYB 84*
Wetherall Publishing Co. - Minneapolis, MN - *LitMarPl 84; WritMar 84*
Wetherell, Ron - Cleghorn, IA - *Tel&CabFB 84C p.1712*
Wethersfield Post [of West Hartford Imprint Newspapers] - West Hartford, CT - *NewsDir 84*
Wethersfield Post - Wethersfield, CT - *AyerDirPub 83; BaconPubCkNews 84*
WETK-TV - Burlington, VT - *BrCabYB 84; Tel&CabFB 84S*
WETK-TV - Winooski, VT - *TV&RadDir 84*
WETL-FM - South Bend, IN - *BrCabYB 84; TV&RadDir 84*
WETM-TV - Elmira, NY - *BrCabYB 84; TelAl 83, 84; Tel&CabFB 84S; TV&RadDir 84*
WETN-FM - Wheaton, IL - *BrCabYB 84; TV&RadDir 84*
WETQ-FM - Oak Ridge, TN - *NatRadPubDir Summer 83, Spring 84; TV&RadDir 84*
WETS-FM - Johnson City, TN - *BrCabYB 84; NatRadPubDir Summer 83, Spring 84; TV&RadDir 84*
WETT - Ocean City, MD - *BrCabYB 84*
Wetter & Co. Inc., Edward - Havre de Grace, MD - *CabTVFinDB 83*
Wettstein Advertising & Public Relations Inc. - Tucson, AZ - *StaDirAdAg 2-84*
WETU - Wetumpka, AL - *BrCabYB 84; TV&RadDir 84*

Wetumka Hughes County Times - *See* Hughes County Publishing Co.
Wetumpka Herald - Wetumpka, AL - *BaconPubCkNews 84; Ed&PubIntYB 82; NewsDir 84*
WETV-TV - Atlanta, GA - *BrCabYB 84; Tel&CabFB 84S; TV&RadDir 84*
WETZ - New Martinsville, WV - *BrCabYB 84; TV&RadDir 84*
Wetzel Chronicle [of New Martinsville Wetzel Chronicle Co. Inc.] - New Martinsville, WV - *AyerDirPub 83; Ed&PubIntYB 82; NewsDir 84*
Wetzel-Tyler County Green Tab - Moundsville, WV - *AyerDirPub 83*
WEUC-FM - Ponce, PR - *BrCabYB 84*
WEUP - Huntsville, AL - *BrCabYB 84; NatRadPubDir Summer 83, Spring 84; TV&RadDir 84*
WEUS - Eustis, FL - *BrCabYB 84; TV&RadDir 84*
WEVA - Emporia, VA - *BrCabYB 84; TV&RadDir 84*
WEVD-FM - New York, NY - *BrCabYB 84; LitMarPl 83, 84; NatRadPubDir Summer 83, Spring 84; TV&RadDir 84*
WEVE - Eveleth, MN - *BrCabYB 84; TV&RadDir 84*
WEVE-FM - Eveleth, MN - *BrCabYB 84; TV&RadDir 84*
WEVL-FM - Memphis, TN - *BrCabYB 84; TV&RadDir 84*
WEVO - Concord, NH - *BrCabYB 84*
WEVR - River Falls, WI - *BrCabYB 84; TV&RadDir 84*
WEVR-FM - River Falls, WI - *BrCabYB 84; TV&RadDir 84*
WEVU-TV - Ft. Myers, FL - *DirUSTelSta 83; TelAl 83, 84; TV&RadDir 84*
WEVU-TV - Naples, FL - *BrCabYB 84; Tel&CabFB 84S*
WEVV - Evansville, IN - *BrCabYB 84; Tel&CabFB 84S*
WEVZ - Cadillac, MI - *BrCabYB 84*
WEW - St. Louis, MO - *BrCabYB 84; NatRadPubDir Summer 83, Spring 84; TV&RadDir 84*
Wewahitchka Gulf County Breeze - Wewahitchka, FL - *BaconPubCkNews 84*
WEWO - Laurinburg, NC - *BrCabYB 84; TV&RadDir 84*
Wewoka Times [of Donrey Media Group] - Wewoka, OK - *BaconPubCkNews 84; Ed&PubIntYB 82; NewsDir 84*
WEWS-TV - Cleveland, OH - *BrCabYB 84; DirUSTelSta 83; LitMarPl 83, 84; TelAl 83, 84; Tel&CabFB 84S; TV&RadDir 84*
WEXA - Eupora, MS - *BrCabYB 84*
Wexford Press - Needham Heights, MA - *BoPubDir 4, 5*
WEXI - Jacksonville, FL - *BrCabYB 84; NatRadPubDir Summer 83, Spring 84; TV&RadDir 84*
WEXL - Royal Oak, MI - *BrCabYB 84; TV&RadDir 84*
Wexler, McCarron & Roth Advertising - Pompano Beach, FL - *HBIndAd&MS 82-83; StaDirAdAg 2-84*
Wexler Nature Photographer, Jerome - Madison, CT - *LitMarPl 84*
WEXM - Jamesville, VA - *BrCabYB 84*
WEXM - Onley, VA - *TV&RadDir 84*
WEXM-FM - Exmore, VA - *BrCabYB 84; TV&RadDir 84*
WEXP-FM - Gadsden, AL - *BrCabYB 84; TV&RadDir 84*
WEXY - Ft. Lauderdale, FL - *NatRadPubDir Summer 83, Spring 84; TV&RadDir 84*
WEXY - Oakland Park, FL - *BrCabYB 84*
Weyandt Publishing Co. - Solon Springs, WI - *BoPubDir 4, 5*
Weyauwega Chronicle - Weyauwega, WI - *BaconPubCkNews 84; Ed&PubIntYB 82*
Weyauwega Telephone Co. - Weyauwega, WI - *TelDir&BG 83-84*
Weybridge Publishing Co. - Dallas, TX - *BoPubDir 4, 5*
Weyburn Review - Weyburn, SK, Canada - *Ed&PubIntYB 82*
WEYE - Thomasville, NC - *BrCabYB 84*
Weyerhaeuser Co. (Paper Div.) - Plymouth Meeting, PA - *LitMarPl 83, 84*
Weyfarers [of Guildford Poets Press] - Woking, England - *LitMag&SmPr 83-84*
WEYI-TV - Flint, MI - *DirUSTelSta 83*
WEYI-TV - Saginaw, MI - *BrCabYB 84; LitMarPl 83; TelAl 83, 84; Tel&CabFB 84S; TV&RadDir 84*
Weylock Associates Inc. - New York, NY - *IntDirMarRes 83*
Weyman Music - *See* Amestoy Music
Weymouth News & Gazette [of Weymouth Publications Inc.] - Weymouth, MA - *BaconPubCkNews 84; Ed&PubIntYB 82; NewsDir 84*
WEYQ - Marietta, OH - *BrCabYB 84*
WEYY - Talladega, AL - *BrCabYB 84; TV&RadDir 84*
WEYZ - Erie, PA - *BrCabYB 84; NatRadPubDir Summer 83, Spring 84; TV&RadDir 84*
WEZB-FM - New Orleans, LA - *BrCabYB 84; NatRadPubDir Summer 83, Spring 84; TV&RadDir 84*
WEZC-FM - Charlotte, NC - *BrCabYB 84; NatRadPubDir Summer 83, Spring 84; TV&RadDir 84*
WEZE - Boston, MA - *BrCabYB 84; NatRadPubDir Summer 83 p.119, Spring 84 p.119*
WEZF-FM - Burlington, VT - *BrCabYB 84; NatRadPubDir Summer 83; TV&RadDir 84*
WEZF-TV - Burlington, VT - *TelAl 83; TV&RadDir 84*
WEZG - North Syracuse, NY - *BrCabYB 84; TV&RadDir 84*
WEZG-FM - North Syracuse, NY - *TV&RadDir 84*
WEZI-FM - Miami/Miami Beach, FL - *NatRadPubDir Summer 83, Spring 84 p.61*
WEZI-FM - Memphis, TN - *TV&RadDir 84*
WEZJ - Williamsburg, KY - *BrCabYB 84; TV&RadDir 84*
WEZK-FM - Knoxville, TN - *BrCabYB 84; NatRadPubDir Summer 83, Spring 84; TV&RadDir 84*
WEZL-FM - Bridgeport, CT - *BrCabYB 84*
WEZL-FM - Charleston, SC - *NatRadPubDir Summer 83, Spring 84; TV&RadDir 84*
WEZN-FM - Bridgeport, CT - *BrCabYB 84; NatRadPubDir Summer 83, Spring 84; TV&RadDir 84*
WEZO-FM - Rochester, NY - *BrCabYB 84; NatRadPubDir Summer 83, Spring 84; TV&RadDir 84*
WEZQ - Winfield, AL - *BrCabYB 84; TV&RadDir 84*
WEZR-FM - Washington, DC - *NatRadPubDir Summer 83 p.53, Spring 84 p.53*
WEZR-FM - Fairfax, VA - *TV&RadDir 84*
WEZR-FM - Manassas, VA - *BrCabYB 84*
WEZS-FM - Richmond, VA - *BrCabYB 84; NatRadPubDir Summer 83, Spring 84; TV&RadDir 84*
WEZV-FM - Ft. Wayne, IN - *BrCabYB 84; NatRadPubDir Summer 83, Spring 84; TV&RadDir 84*
WEZW-FM - Milwaukee, WI - *NatRadPubDir Summer 83, Spring 84; TV&RadDir 84*
WEZW-FM - Wauwatosa, WI - *BrCabYB 84*
WEZX-FM - Scranton, PA - *BrCabYB 84; NatRadPubDir Summer 83, Spring 84; TV&RadDir 84*
WEZY - Cocoa, FL - *BrCabYB 84; TV&RadDir 84*
WEZZ-FM - Clanton, AL - *BrCabYB 84; TV&RadDir 84*
WFAA - Dallas, TX - *LitMarPl 83, 84; NatRadPubDir Summer 83; TV&RadDir 84*
WFAA-TV - Dallas, TX - *BrCabYB 84; DirUSTelSta 83; LitMarPl 83, 84; TelAl 83, 84; Tel&CabFB 84S; TV&RadDir 84*
WFAB - Juncos, PR - *BrCabYB 84*
WFAD - Middlebury, VT - *BrCabYB 84; TV&RadDir 84*
WFAE-FM - Charlotte, NC - *BrCabYB 84; NatRadPubDir Summer 83, Spring 84; TV&RadDir 84*
WFAH - Alliance, OH - *BrCabYB 84; TV&RadDir 84*
WFAI - Fayetteville, NC - *BrCabYB 84; NatRadPubDir Summer 83, Spring 84; TV&RadDir 84*
WFAM-FM - Jacksonville, FL - *BrCabYB 84; TV&RadDir 84*
WFAN - Stonington, CT - *BrCabYB 84*
WFAR - Danbury, CT - *BrCabYB 84*
WFAS - Westchester County, NY - *NatRadPubDir Summer 83 p.179, Spring 84 p.177*
WFAS - White Plains, NY - *BrCabYB 84; TV&RadDir 84*
WFAS-FM - Westchester County, NY - *NatRadPubDir Spring 84 p.178*
WFAS-FM - White Plains, NY - *BrCabYB 84; TV&RadDir 84*
WFAT-TV - Johnstown, PA - *BrCabYB 84; TelAl 84; Tel&CabFB 84S*
WFAU - Augusta, ME - *BrCabYB 84; NatRadPubDir Summer 83, Spring 84; TV&RadDir 84*
WFAV-FM - Cordele, GA - *BrCabYB 84; TV&RadDir 84*
WFAW - Ft. Atkinson, WI - *BrCabYB 84; TV&RadDir 84*
WFAX - Washington, DC - *NatRadPubDir Summer 83 p.53, Spring 84 p.53*
WFAX - Falls Church, VA - *BrCabYB 84; TV&RadDir 84*
WFBC - Greenville, SC - *BrCabYB 84; NatRadPubDir Summer 83, Spring 84; TV&RadDir 84*
WFBC-FM - Greenville, SC - *BrCabYB 84; NatRadPubDir Summer 83, Spring 84; TV&RadDir 84*
WFBC-TV - Greenville, SC - *DirUSTelSta 83; LitMarPl 83; TelAl 83; TV&RadDir 84*

WFBE-FM - Flint, MI - *BrCabYB 84; NatRadPubDir Summer 83, Spring 84; TV&RadDir 84*
WFBG - Altoona, PA - *BrCabYB 84; NatRadPubDir Summer 83, Spring 84; TV&RadDir 84*
WFBG-FM - Altoona, PA - *BrCabYB 84; NatRadPubDir Summer 83, Spring 84; TV&RadDir 84*
WFBL - Syracuse, NY - *BrCabYB 84; NatRadPubDir Summer 83, Spring 84; TV&RadDir 84*
WFBM - Noblesville, IN - *BrCabYB 84; TV&RadDir 84*
WFBN-TV - Joliet, IL - *BrCabYB 84; TelAl 84; Tel&CabFB 84S; TV&RadDir 84*
WFBQ-FM - Indianapolis, IN - *BrCabYB 84; LitMarPl 84; NatRadPubDir Summer 83, Spring 84; TV&RadDir 84*
WFBR - Baltimore, MD - *BrCabYB 84; LitMarPl 83, 84; NatRadPubDir Summer 83, Spring 84; TV&RadDir 84*
WFBS - Spring Lake, NC - *TV&RadDir 84*
WFBS-FM - Freeport, IL - *TV&RadDir 84*
WFBT-TV - Minneapolis, MN - *BrCabYB 84; DirUSTelSta 83; TelAl 84; Tel&CabFB 84S*
WFBZ - Minocqua, WI - *BrCabYB 84; TV&RadDir 84*
WFC Advertising - Phoenix, AZ - *AdAge 3-28-84*
WFC Advertising - *See* Winters, Franceschi & Callahan
WFC/Howard Inc. - San Diego, CA - *DirPRFirms 83*
WFCB - Chillicothe, OH - *BrCabYB 84*
WFCG - Franklinton, LA - *BrCabYB 84; TV&RadDir 84*
WFCI-FM - Franklin, IN - *BrCabYB 84; NatRadPubDir Summer 83, Spring 84; TV&RadDir 84*
WFCJ-FM - Dayton, OH - *TV&RadDir 84*
WFCJ-FM - Miamisburg, OH - *BrCabYB 84; NatRadPubDir Summer 83, Spring 84*
WFCL-FM - Clintonville, WI - *BrCabYB 84*
WFCM-FM - Orangeburg, SC - *BrCabYB 84*
WFCR-FM - Amherst, MA - *BrCabYB 84; NatRadPubDir Summer 83, Spring 84; TV&RadDir 84*
WFCS-FM - New Britain, CT - *BrCabYB 84; TV&RadDir 84*
WFCT - Fayetteville, NC - *BrCabYB 84; Tel&CabFB 84S*
WFCV - Ft. Wayne, IN - *BrCabYB 84; TV&RadDir 84*
WFDD-FM - Winston Salem, NC - *BrCabYB 84; NatRadPubDir Summer 83, Spring 84; TV&RadDir 84*
WFDF - Flint, MI - *BrCabYB 84; NatRadPubDir Summer 83, Spring 84; TV&RadDir 84*
WFDG - New Bedford, MA - *BrCabYB 84; Tel&CabFB 84S*
WFDR - Manchester, GA - *TV&RadDir 84*
WFDU-FM - Teaneck, NJ - *BrCabYB 84; NatRadPubDir Summer 83, Spring 84; TV&RadDir 84*
WFEA - Manchester, NH - *BrCabYB 84; NatRadPubDir Summer 83, Spring 84*
WFEA - Merrimack, NH - *TV&RadDir 84*
WFEB - Sylacauga, AL - *BrCabYB 84; TV&RadDir 84*
WFEC - Harrisburg, PA - *BrCabYB 84; NatRadPubDir Summer 83, Spring 84; TV&RadDir 84*
WFEM-FM - Ellwood City, PA - *BrCabYB 84; TV&RadDir 84*
WFEZ - Meridian, MS - *BrCabYB 84; TV&RadDir 84*
WFFF - Columbia, MS - *BrCabYB 84; TV&RadDir 84*
WFFF-FM - Columbia, MS - *BrCabYB 84; TV&RadDir 84*
WFFG - Marathon, FL - *BrCabYB 84; TV&RadDir 84*
Wff'n Proof Learning Games Associates - Ann Arbor, MI - *AvMarPl 83; BoPubDir 4, 5*
WFFT-TV - Ft. Wayne, IN - *BrCabYB 84; DirUSTelSta 83; TelAl 83, 84; Tel&CabFB 84S; TV&RadDir 84*
WFFV-FM - Front Royal, VA - *BrCabYB 84*
WFFV-FM - Middletown, VA - *TV&RadDir 84*
WFGB - Kingston, NY - *BrCabYB 84*
WFGC - Palm Beach, FL - *BrCabYB 84; Tel&CabFB 84S*
WFGH-FM - Ft. Gay, WV - *BrCabYB 84; NatRadPubDir Summer 83, Spring 84; TV&RadDir 84*
WFGL - Fitchburg, MA - *BrCabYB 84; NatRadPubDir Summer 83, Spring 84; TV&RadDir 84*
WFGM-FM - Fairmont, WV - *BrCabYB 84; TV&RadDir 84*
WFGN - Gaffney, SC - *BrCabYB 84; TV&RadDir 84*
WFGW - Black Mountain, NC - *BrCabYB 84; TV&RadDir 84*
WFHC-FM - Henderson, TN - *BrCabYB 84; NatRadPubDir Summer 83, Spring 84; TV&RadDir 84*
WFHG - Bristol, VA - *BrCabYB 84*
WFHK - Pell City, AL - *BrCabYB 84; TV&RadDir 84*
WFHR - Wisconsin Rapids, WI - *BrCabYB 84; TV&RadDir 84*
WFI Publishing Co. [Aff. of WFI Corp.] - Los Angeles, CA - *BoPubDir 4, 5*
WFIA - Louisville, KY - *BrCabYB 84; NatRadPubDir Summer 83, Spring 84; TV&RadDir 84*
WFIB - Cincinnati, OH - *NatRadPubDir Summer 83, Spring 84*
WFIC - Collinsville, VA - *BrCabYB 84; TV&RadDir 84*
WFID - Rio Piedras, PR - *BrCabYB 84*
WFIE-TV - Evansville, IN - *BrCabYB 84; DirUSTelSta 83; TelAl 83, 84; Tel&CabFB 84S; TV&RadDir 84*
WFIF - Milford, CT - *BrCabYB 84; TV&RadDir 84*
WFIF - New Haven, CT - *NatRadPubDir Summer 83 p.47, Spring 84*
WFIG - Sumter, SC - *BrCabYB 84; TV&RadDir 84*
WFIL - Philadelphia, PA - *BrCabYB 84; LitMarPl 83, 84; NatRadPubDir Summer 83, Spring 84; TV&RadDir 84*
WFIN - Findlay, OH - *BrCabYB 84; NatRadPubDir Summer 83, Spring 84*
WFIN - Nowata, OK - *TV&RadDir 84*
WFIN-FM - Findlay, OH - *TV&RadDir 84*
WFIQ-TV - Florence, AL - *BrCabYB 84; Tel&CabFB 84S*
WFIQ-TV - Russellville, AL - *TV&RadDir 84*
WFIR - Roanoke, VA - *BrCabYB 84; NatRadPubDir Summer 83, Spring 84; TV&RadDir 84*
WFIS - Fountain Inn, SC - *BrCabYB 84; TV&RadDir 84*
WFIT-FM - Melbourne, FL - *BrCabYB 84; NatRadPubDir Summer 83, Spring 84; TV&RadDir 84*
WFIU-FM - Bloomington, IN - *BrCabYB 84; NatRadPubDir Summer 83, Spring 84; TV&RadDir 84*
WFIV - Kissimmee, FL - *BrCabYB 84*
WFIV - Orlando, FL - *NatRadPubDir Summer 83, Spring 84; TV&RadDir 84*
WFIW - Fairfield, IL - *BrCabYB 84; TV&RadDir 84*
WFIW-FM - Fairfield, IL - *BrCabYB 84; TV&RadDir 84*
WFIX - Huntsville, AL - *BrCabYB 84; NatRadPubDir Summer 83, Spring 84; TV&RadDir 84*
WFIZ - Fond du Lac, WI - *TV&RadDir 84*
WFJA-FM - Sanford, NC - *BrCabYB 84; TV&RadDir 84*
WFJT - Inez, KY - *BrCabYB 84; TV&RadDir 84*
WFKN - Franklin, KY - *TV&RadDir 84*
WFKX - Henderson, TN - *BrCabYB 84*
WFKY - Frankfort, KY - *BrCabYB 84; NatRadPubDir Summer 83, Spring 84; TV&RadDir 84*
WFLA - Tampa, FL - *BrCabYB 84; NatRadPubDir Summer 83, Spring 84; TV&RadDir 84*
WFLA-FM - Tampa, FL - *BrCabYB 84; NatRadPubDir Summer 83; TV&RadDir 84*
WFLA-TV - Tampa, FL - *DirUSTelSta 83; LitMarPl 83; TelAl 83; TV&RadDir 84*
WFLB - Fayetteville, NC - *BrCabYB 84*
WFLC-FM - Canandaigua, NY - *BrCabYB 84; TV&RadDir 84*
WFLD-TV - Chicago, IL - *BrCabYB 84; DirUSTelSta 83; TelAl 83, 84; Tel&CabFB 84S; TV&RadDir 84*
WFLE - Flemingsburg, KY - *BrCabYB 84*
WFLI - Chattanooga, TN - *NatRadPubDir Summer 83, Spring 84; TV&RadDir 84*
WFLI - Lookout Mountain, TN - *BrCabYB 84*
WFLN - Philadelphia, PA - *BrCabYB 84; NatRadPubDir Summer 83, Spring 84; TV&RadDir 84*
WFLN-FM - Philadelphia, PA - *BrCabYB 84; NatRadPubDir Summer 83, Spring 84; TV&RadDir 84*
WFLO - Farmville, VA - *BrCabYB 84; TV&RadDir 84*
WFLO-FM - Farmville, VA - *BrCabYB 84; TV&RadDir 84*
WFLQ - French Lick, IN - *BrCabYB 84*
WFLR - Dundee, NY - *BrCabYB 84; TV&RadDir 84*
WFLR-FM - Dundee, NY - *BrCabYB 84; TV&RadDir 84*
WFLS - Fredericksburg, VA - *BrCabYB 84; TV&RadDir 84*
WFLS-FM - Fredericksburg, VA - *BrCabYB 84; TV&RadDir 84*
WFLT - Flint, MI - *BrCabYB 84; NatRadPubDir Summer 83, Spring 84*
WFLW - Monticello, KY - *BrCabYB 84; TV&RadDir 84*
WFLX-TV - West Palm Beach, FL - *BrCabYB 84; DirUSTelSta 83; TelAl 84; Tel&CabFB 84S*
WFLY-FM - Albany, NY - *NatRadPubDir Summer 83, Spring 84; TV&RadDir 84*
WFLY-FM - Troy, NY - *BrCabYB 84*

WFMA-FM - Rocky Mt., NC - *BrCabYB 84; NatRadPubDir Summer 83, Spring 84; TV&RadDir 84*
WFMB-FM - Springfield, IL - *BrCabYB 84; NatRadPubDir Summer 83, Spring 84; TV&RadDir 84*
WFMC - Goldsboro, NC - *BrCabYB 84; TV&RadDir 84*
WFMD - Frederick, MD - *BrCabYB 84*
WFME-FM - Newark, NJ - *BrCabYB 84*
WFME-FM - West Orange, NJ - *LitMarPl 83, 84; TV&RadDir 84*
WFMF-FM - Baton Rouge, LA - *BrCabYB 84; NatRadPubDir Summer 83, Spring 84; TV&RadDir 84*
WFMG-FM - Grand Haven, MI - *BrCabYB 84; TV&RadDir 84*
WFMH - Cullman, AL - *BrCabYB 84; TV&RadDir 84*
WFMH Cable TV - Cullman, AL - *BrCabYB 84*
WFMH-FM - Cullman, AL - *BrCabYB 84; TV&RadDir 84*
WFMI-FM - Winchester, KY - *BrCabYB 84; TV&RadDir 84*
WFMJ - Daytona Beach, FL - *TV&RadDir 84*
WFMJ - Youngstown, OH - *BrCabYB 84; NatRadPubDir Summer 83, Spring 84; TV&RadDir 84*
WFMJ-TV - Youngstown, OH - *BrCabYB 84; DirUSTelSta 83; TelAl 83, 84; Tel&CabFB 84S; TV&RadDir 84*
WFMK-FM - East Lansing, MI - *BrCabYB 84; NatRadPubDir Summer 83, Spring 84; TV&RadDir 84*
WFML-FM - Washington, IN - *BrCabYB 84; TV&RadDir 84*
WFMM - North Muskegon, MI - *BrCabYB 84*
WFMN-FM - Newburgh, NY - *BrCabYB 84; NatRadPubDir Summer 83 p.176, Spring 84 p.174; TV&RadDir 84*
WFMO - Fairmont, NC - *BrCabYB 84; TV&RadDir 84*
WFMP - Fitchburg, MA - *BrCabYB 84; NatRadPubDir Summer 83, Spring 84*
WFMP-FM - Fitchburg, MA - *TV&RadDir 84*
WFMQ-FM - Lebanon, TN - *BrCabYB 84; NatRadPubDir Summer 83, Spring 84; TV&RadDir 84*
WFMR-FM - Milwaukee, WI - *BrCabYB 84; TV&RadDir 84*
WFMS-FM - Indianapolis, IN - *BrCabYB 84; NatRadPubDir Summer 83, Spring 84; TV&RadDir 84*
WFMT - Chicago, IL - *BrCabYB 84; CabTVPrDB 83*
WFMT [of United Video] - Tulsa, OK - *BrCabYB 84*
WFMT-FM - Chicago, IL - *LitMarPl 83, 84; NatRadPubDir Summer 83, Spring 84; TV&RadDir 84*
WFMT-FM [of United Video Inc.] - Tulsa, OK - *BrCabYB 84*
WFMU-FM - East Orange, NJ - *BrCabYB 84; NatRadPubDir Summer 83, Spring 84; TV&RadDir 84*
WFMV-FM - Blairstown, NJ - *BrCabYB 84; TV&RadDir 84*
WFMW - Madisonville, KY - *BrCabYB 84; TV&RadDir 84*
WFMX-FM - Statesville, NC - *BrCabYB 84; NatRadPubDir Summer 83, Spring 84; TV&RadDir 84*
WFMY-TV - Greensboro, NC - *BrCabYB 84; DirUSTelSta 83; LitMarPl 83, 84; TelAl 83, 84; Tel&CabFB 84S; TV&RadDir 84*
WFMZ-FM - Allentown, PA - *BrCabYB 84; NatRadPubDir Summer 83, Spring 84 p.209; TV&RadDir 84*
WFMZ-TV - Allentown, PA - *BrCabYB 84; DirUSTelSta 83; TelAl 83, 84; Tel&CabFB 84S; TV&RadDir 84*
WFNC - Fayetteville, NC - *BrCabYB 84; NatRadPubDir Summer 83, Spring 84; TV&RadDir 84*
WFNE-FM - Forsyth, GA - *BrCabYB 84; TV&RadDir 84*
WFNM-FM - Lancaster, PA - *BrCabYB 84; NatRadPubDir Summer 83, Spring 84; TV&RadDir 84*
WFNN - Clearwater, FL - *TV&RadDir 84*
WFNN-FM - Escanaba, MI - *BrCabYB 84; TV&RadDir 84*
WFNX - Lynn, MA - *BrCabYB 84*
WFNY-FM - Racine, WI - *BrCabYB 84; NatRadPubDir Summer 83, Spring 84; TV&RadDir 84*
WFOB - Fostoria, OH - *BrCabYB 84; TV&RadDir 84*
WFOB-FM - Fostoria, OH - *BrCabYB 84; TV&RadDir 84*
WFOG-FM - Norfolk, VA - *NatRadPubDir Spring 84; TV&RadDir 84*
WFOG-FM - Suffolk, VA - *BrCabYB 84; NatRadPubDir Summer 83*
WFOM - Atlanta, GA - *NatRadPubDir Summer 83, Spring 84 p.69*
WFOM - Marietta, GA - *BrCabYB 84; TV&RadDir 84*
WFON-FM - Fond du Lac, WI - *BrCabYB 84; NatRadPubDir Summer 83, Spring 84; TV&RadDir 84*
WFOR - Hattiesburg, MS - *BrCabYB 84; NatRadPubDir Summer 83, Spring 84; TV&RadDir 84*
WFOS-FM - Chesapeake, VA - *BrCabYB 84; TV&RadDir 84*
WFOX-FM - Gainesville, GA - *BrCabYB 84; TV&RadDir 84*
WFOY - St. Augustine, FL - *BrCabYB 84; TV&RadDir 84*
WFOY-FM - St. Augustine, FL - *BrCabYB 84; TV&RadDir 84*
WFPA - Ft. Payne, AL - *BrCabYB 84; TV&RadDir 84*
WFPG-FM - Atlantic City, NJ - *BrCabYB 84; NatRadPubDir Summer 83, Spring 84; TV&RadDir 84*
WFPK-FM - Louisville, KY - *BrCabYB 84; NatRadPubDir Summer 83, Spring 84; TV&RadDir 84*
WFPL-FM - Louisville, KY - *BrCabYB 84; NatRadPubDir Summer 83, Spring 84*
WFPR - Hammond, LA - *BrCabYB 84; TV&RadDir 84*
WFPS - Freeport, IL - *BrCabYB 84*
WFRA - Franklin, PA - *BrCabYB 84; TV&RadDir 84*
WFRB-FM - Frostburg, MD - *BrCabYB 84*
WFRD - Columbus, OH - *TV&RadDir 84*
WFRD-FM - Hanover, NH - *BrCabYB 84; NatRadPubDir Summer 83, Spring 84; TV&RadDir 84*
WFRE - Frederick, MD - *BrCabYB 84*
WFRI-FM - Auburn, AL - *BrCabYB 84*
WFRI-FM - Opelika, AL - *TV&RadDir 84*
WFRL - Freeport, IL - *BrCabYB 84; NatRadPubDir Summer 83, Spring 84; TV&RadDir 84*
WFRM - Coudersport, PA - *BrCabYB 84; TV&RadDir 84*
WFRN-FM - Elkhart, IN - *BrCabYB 84; TV&RadDir 84*
WFRO - Fremont, OH - *BrCabYB 84; TV&RadDir 84*
WFRO-FM - Fremont, OH - *BrCabYB 84; TV&RadDir 84*
WFRV-TV - Green Bay, WI - *BrCabYB 84; DirUSTelSta 83; TelAl 83, 84; Tel&CabFB 84S; TV&RadDir 84*
WFRX - West Frankfort, IL - *BrCabYB 84; TV&RadDir 84*
WFRX-FM - West Frankfort, IL - *BrCabYB 84; TV&RadDir 84*
WFSB-TV - Hartford, CT - *BrCabYB 84; DirUSTelSta 83; LitMarPl 83, 84; TelAl 83, 84; Tel&CabFB 84S; TV&RadDir 84*
WFSC - Franklin, NC - *BrCabYB 84; TV&RadDir 84*
WFSE - Edinboro, PA - *BrCabYB 84*
WFSH - Niceville, FL - *TV&RadDir 84*
WFSH - Valparaiso, FL - *BrCabYB 84*
WFSI-FM - Annapolis, MD - *BrCabYB 84; TV&RadDir 84*
WFSL-TV - Lansing, MI - *BrCabYB 84; DirUSTelSta 83; TelAl 84; Tel&CabFB 84S*
WFSP - Kingwood, WV - *BrCabYB 84; TV&RadDir 84*
WFSR - Harlan, KY - *BrCabYB 84; TV&RadDir 84*
WFSS-FM - Fayetteville, NC - *BrCabYB 84; TV&RadDir 84*
WFST - Caribou, ME - *BrCabYB 84; TV&RadDir 84*
WFSU-FM - Tallahassee, FL - *BrCabYB 84; NatRadPubDir Summer 83, Spring 84; TV&RadDir 84*
WFSU-TV [of Florida State University] - Tallahassee, FL - *BrCabYB 84; Tel&CabFB 84S; TeleSy&SerDir 2-84; TV&RadDir 84*
WFTA - Fulton, MS - *BrCabYB 84*
WFTC - Kinston, NC - *BrCabYB 84; TV&RadDir 84*
WFTE - Lafayette, IN - *BrCabYB 84; NatRadPubDir Summer 83, Spring 84; TV&RadDir 84*
WFTG - London, KY - *BrCabYB 84; TV&RadDir 84*
WFTH - Richmond, VA - *BrCabYB 84; NatRadPubDir Summer 83, Spring 84*
WFTL - Ft. Lauderdale, FL - *BrCabYB 84; NatRadPubDir Summer 83, Spring 84; TV&RadDir 84*
WFTM - Maysville, KY - *BrCabYB 84; TV&RadDir 84*
WFTM-FM - Maysville, KY - *BrCabYB 84; TV&RadDir 84*
WFTN - Franklin, NH - *BrCabYB 84; TV&RadDir 84*
WFTO - Fulton, MS - *BrCabYB 84; TV&RadDir 84*
WFTP - Ft. Pierce, FL - *BrCabYB 84; TV&RadDir 84*
WFTQ - Worcester, MA - *BrCabYB 84; NatRadPubDir Summer 83, Spring 84; TV&RadDir 84*
WFTR - Front Royal, VA - *BrCabYB 84; TV&RadDir 84*
WFTS-TV - Tampa, FL - *DirUSTelSta 83; Tel&CabFB 84S*
WFTV - Orlando, FL - *BrCabYB 84; DirUSTelSta 83; LitMarPl 83, 84; TelAl 83, 84; Tel&CabFB 84S; TV&RadDir 84*
WFTW - Ft. Walton Beach, FL - *BrCabYB 84*
WFTW - Pensacola, FL - *TV&RadDir 84*
WFTW-FM - Ft. Walton Beach, FL - *BrCabYB 84; TV&RadDir 84*
WFUL - Fulton, KY - *BrCabYB 84; TV&RadDir 84*

WFUM-TV - Flint, MI - *BrCabYB 84; Tel&CabFB 84S; TV&RadDir 84*
WFUN - Ashtabula, OH - *BrCabYB 84; TV&RadDir 84*
WFUR - Chicago, IL - *BrCabYB 84*
WFUR - Grand Rapids, MI - *BrCabYB 84; NatRadPubDir Summer 83, Spring 84; TV&RadDir 84*
WFUR-FM - Grand Rapids, MI - *BrCabYB 84; NatRadPubDir Summer 83, Spring 84; TV&RadDir 84*
WFUV-FM - Bronx, NY - *LitMarPl 83, 84; TV&RadDir 84*
WFUV-FM - New York, NY - *BrCabYB 84; NatRadPubDir Summer 83 p.302, Spring 84 p.303*
WFUZ-FM - Ocala, FL - *BrCabYB 84; TV&RadDir 84*
WFVA - Fredericksburg, VA - *BrCabYB 84; TV&RadDir 84*
WFVA-FM - Fredericksburg, VA - *BrCabYB 84; TV&RadDir 84*
WFVR - Aurora, IL - *BrCabYB 84; TV&RadDir 84*
WFWL - Camden, TN - *BrCabYB 84; TV&RadDir 84*
WFWQ-FM - Ft. Wayne, IN - *BrCabYB 84; NatRadPubDir Summer 83, Spring 84; TV&RadDir 84*
WFWY - Syracuse, NY - *BrCabYB 84; Tel&CabFB 84S*
WFXE-FM - Columbus, GA - *BrCabYB 84; NatRadPubDir Summer 83, Spring 84; TV&RadDir 84*
WFXI - Haines City, FL - *BrCabYB 84; TV&RadDir 84*
WFXL-TV - Tampa, FL - *TelAl 84*
WFXW - Geneva, IL - *BrCabYB 84*
WFXW - St. Charles, IL - *TV&RadDir 84*
WFXX - South Williamsport, PA - *BrCabYB 84; NatRadPubDir Spring 84*
WFXX-FM - South Williamsport, PA - *BrCabYB 84; NatRadPubDir Spring 84*
WFXY - Middlesboro, KY - *BrCabYB 84; TV&RadDir 84*
WFXZ - Pinconning, MI - *BrCabYB 84*
WFYC - Alma, MI - *BrCabYB 84; TV&RadDir 84*
WFYC-FM - Alma, MI - *BrCabYB 84; TV&RadDir 84*
WFYI-TV - Indianapolis, IN - *BrCabYB 84; Tel&CabFB 84S; TV&RadDir 84*
WFYN-FM - Key West, FL - *BrCabYB 84; TV&RadDir 84*
WFYR-FM - Chicago, IL - *NatRadPubDir Summer 83, Spring 84; TV&RadDir 84*
WFYV-FM - Atlantic Beach, FL - *BrCabYB 84*
WFYV-FM - Jacksonville, FL - *TV&RadDir 84*
WFYZ - Murfreesboro, TN - *BrCabYB 84; Tel&CabFB 84S*
WG & L Real Estate Outlook - Boston, MA - *BaconPubCkMag 84*
WGAA - Cedartown, GA - *BrCabYB 84; TV&RadDir 84*
WGAC - Augusta, GA - *BrCabYB 84; NatRadPubDir Summer 83, Spring 84; TV&RadDir 84*
WGAD - Gadsden, AL - *BrCabYB 84; NatRadPubDir Summer 83, Spring 84; TV&RadDir 84*
WGAE - Girard, PA - *BrCabYB 84*
WGAF - Valdosta, GA - *BrCabYB 84; TV&RadDir 84*
WGAG-FM - Orlando, FL - *BrCabYB 84; TV&RadDir 84*
WGAI - Elizabeth City, NC - *BrCabYB 84; TV&RadDir 84*
WGAJ - Deerfield, MA - *BrCabYB 84*
WGAL-TV - Harrisburg, PA - *DirUSTelSta 83*
WGAL-TV - Lancaster, PA - *BrCabYB 84; LitMarPl 83, 84; TelAl 83, 84; Tel&CabFB 84S; TV&RadDir 84*
WGAM - Dunnellon, FL - *TV&RadDir 84*
WGAN [Div. of Guy Gannett Broadcasting Services] - Portland, ME - *AvMarPl 83; BrCabYB 84; NatRadPubDir Summer 83, Spring 84; TV&RadDir 84*
WGAN-FM - Portland, ME - *BrCabYB 84; NatRadPubDir Summer 83, Spring 84; TV&RadDir 84*
WGAN-TV - Portland, ME - *DirUSTelSta 83; TelAl 83, 84; Tel&CabFB 84S; TV&RadDir 84*
WGAO-FM - Franklin, MA - *BrCabYB 84; TV&RadDir 84*
WGAP - Maryville, TN - *BrCabYB 84; NatRadPubDir Summer 83, Spring 84; TV&RadDir 84*
WGAQ - Franklin, IN - *BrCabYB 84*
WGAR - Cleveland, OH - *BrCabYB 84; LitMarPl 83, 84; NatRadPubDir Summer 83, Spring 84; TV&RadDir 84*
WGAS - Gastonia, NC - *BrCabYB 84; NatRadPubDir Summer 83, Spring 84; TV&RadDir 84*
WGAT - Gate City, VA - *BrCabYB 84; TV&RadDir 84*
WGAU - Athens, GA - *BrCabYB 84; NatRadPubDir Summer 83, Spring 84; TV&RadDir 84*
WGAW - Gardner, MA - *BrCabYB 84; TV&RadDir 84*
WGAY - Washington, DC - *NatRadPubDir Summer 83 p.53, Spring 84 p.53*
WGAY - Silver Spring, MD - *BrCabYB 84; TV&RadDir 84*
WGAY-FM - Washington, DC - *BrCabYB 84; NatRadPubDir Summer 83 p.53, Spring 84 p.53*
WGAY-FM - Silver Spring, MD - *TV&RadDir 84*
WGBB - Freeport, NY - *BrCabYB 84*
WGBB - Merrick, NY - *TV&RadDir 84*
WGBB - Nassau County, Long Island, NY - *NatRadPubDir Summer 83 p.171, Spring 84 p.169*
WGBF - Evansville, IN - *BrCabYB 84; NatRadPubDir Summer 83, Spring 84; TV&RadDir 84*
WGBH - Boston, MA - *BrCabYB 84; VideoDir 82-83*
WGBH-FM - Allston, MA - *TV&RadDir 84*
WGBH-FM - Boston, MA - *LitMarPl 83, 84; NatRadPubDir Summer 83, Spring 84*
WGBH-TV - Boston, MA - *BrCabYB 84; LitMarPl 83, 84; Tel&CabFB 84S*
WGBI - Scranton, PA - *BrCabYB 84; NatRadPubDir Summer 83, Spring 84; TV&RadDir 84*
WGBI-FM - Scranton, PA - *BrCabYB 84; NatRadPubDir Summer 83, Spring 84; TV&RadDir 84*
WGBM-FM - Viroqua, WI - *BrCabYB 84; TV&RadDir 84*
WGBP-FM - Green Bay, WI - *BrCabYB 84; NatRadPubDir Summer 83, Spring 84; TV&RadDir 84*
WGBQ-FM - Galesburg, IL - *BrCabYB 84; TV&RadDir 84*
WGBR - Goldsboro, NC - *BrCabYB 84; TV&RadDir 84*
WGBS - Miami, FL - *BrCabYB 84; LitMarPl 83, 84; NatRadPubDir Summer 83, Spring 84; TV&RadDir 84*
WGBU - Farrell, PA - *TV&RadDir 84*
WGBW-FM - Green Bay, WI - *BrCabYB 84; NatRadPubDir Summer 83, Spring 84; TV&RadDir 84*
WGBX-TV - Allston, MA - *TV&RadDir 84*
WGBX-TV - Boston, MA - *BrCabYB 84; Tel&CabFB 84S*
WGBY-TV - Springfield, MA - *BrCabYB 84; Tel&CabFB 84S; TV&RadDir 84*
WGCA - Charleston, SC - *BrCabYB 84; NatRadPubDir Summer 83, Spring 84; TV&RadDir 84*
WGCB - Red Lion, PA - *BrCabYB 84; TV&RadDir 84*
WGCB-FM - Red Lion, PA - *BrCabYB 84; TV&RadDir 84*
WGCB-TV - Harrisburg, PA - *DirUSTelSta 83*
WGCB-TV - Red Lion, PA - *BrCabYB 84; TelAl 83, 84; Tel&CabFB 84S; TV&RadDir 84*
WGCD - Chester, SC - *BrCabYB 84; TV&RadDir 84*
WGCG-TV - Greenwood, SC - *BrCabYB 84; Tel&CabFB 84S*
WGCH - Greenwich, CT - *BrCabYB 84; NatRadPubDir Summer 83, Spring 84; TV&RadDir 84*
WGCI - Chicago, IL - *BrCabYB 84*
WGCI-FM - Chicago, IL - *NatRadPubDir Summer 83, Spring 84; TV&RadDir 84*
WGCL-FM - Cleveland, OH - *BrCabYB 84; NatRadPubDir Summer 83, Spring 84; TV&RadDir 84*
WGCM-FM - Biloxi/Gulfport, MS - *NatRadPubDir Summer 83, Spring 84 p.137*
WGCM-FM - Gulfport, MS - *BrCabYB 84; TV&RadDir 84*
WGCO-FM - Buford, GA - *BrCabYB 84; TV&RadDir 84*
WGCR-FM - Mansfield, PA - *TV&RadDir 84*
WGCS-FM - Goshen, IN - *BrCabYB 84; TV&RadDir 84*
WGCT-TV - Greenwood, SC - *TelAl 84*
WGCV-FM - Port St. Joe, FL - *TV&RadDir 84*
WGDL - Lares, PR - *BrCabYB 84*
WGDR-FM - Plainfield, VT - *BrCabYB 84; NatRadPubDir Summer 83, Spring 84; TV&RadDir 84*
WGEA - Geneva, AL - *BrCabYB 84; TV&RadDir 84*
WGEA-FM - Geneva, AL - *BrCabYB 84; TV&RadDir 84*
WGEC-FM - Springfield, GA - *BrCabYB 84; TV&RadDir 84*
WGEE - Green Bay, WI - *BrCabYB 84; NatRadPubDir Summer 83, Spring 84; TV&RadDir 84*
WGEM - Quincy, IL - *BrCabYB 84; TV&RadDir 84*
WGEM-FM - Quincy, IL - *BrCabYB 84; TV&RadDir 84*
WGEM-TV - Quincy, IL - *BrCabYB 84; DirUSTelSta 83; TelAl 83, 84; Tel&CabFB 84S; TV&RadDir 84*
WGEN - Geneseo, IL - *BrCabYB 84; TV&RadDir 84*
WGEN-FM - Geneseo, IL - *BrCabYB 84; TV&RadDir 84*
WGEO-FM - Beaverton, MI - *BrCabYB 84*
WGER-FM - Bay City, MI - *BrCabYB 84; TV&RadDir 84*

WGER-FM - Saginaw/Bay City, MI - *NatRadPubDir Summer 83, Spring 84 p.131*
WGET - Gettysburg, PA - *BrCabYB 84; TV&RadDir 84*
WGET-FM - Gettysburg, PA - *BrCabYB 84*
WGEV-FM - Beaver Falls, PA - *BrCabYB 84; NatRadPubDir Summer 83, Spring 84; TV&RadDir 84*
WGEZ - Beloit, WI - *BrCabYB 84; TV&RadDir 84*
WGFA - Watseka, IL - *BrCabYB 84; TV&RadDir 84*
WGFA-FM - Watseka, IL - *BrCabYB 84; TV&RadDir 84*
WGFB-FM - Plattsburgh, NY - *BrCabYB 84; TV&RadDir 84*
WGFG-FM - Lake City, SC - *BrCabYB 84; TV&RadDir 84*
WGFM-FM - Albany/Schenectady/Troy, NY - *NatRadPubDir Summer 83, Spring 84 p.165*
WGFM-FM - Schenectady, NY - *BrCabYB 84*
WGFP - Webster, MA - *BrCabYB 84; TV&RadDir 84*
WGFR-FM - Glens Falls, NY - *BrCabYB 84; TV&RadDir 84*
WGFS - Covington, GA - *BrCabYB 84; TV&RadDir 84*
WGFT - Youngstown, OH - *BrCabYB 84; NatRadPubDir Summer 83, Spring 84; TV&RadDir 84*
WGFW - Morovis, PR - *BrCabYB 84*
WGGA - Gainesville, GA - *BrCabYB 84; TV&RadDir 84*
WGGB-TV - Springfield, MA - *BrCabYB 84; DirUSTelSta 83; TelAl 83, 84; Tel&CabFB 84S; TV&RadDir 84*
WGGC-FM - Glasgow, KY - *BrCabYB 84; TV&RadDir 84*
WGGF - Lebanon, PA - *BrCabYB 84; Tel&CabFB 84S*
WGGG - Gainesville, FL - *BrCabYB 84; NatRadPubDir Summer 83, Spring 84; TV&RadDir 84*
WGGH - Marion, IL - *BrCabYB 84; TV&RadDir 84*
WGGI - Owingsville, KY - *BrCabYB 84*
WGGL-FM - Houghton, MI - *BrCabYB 84; TV&RadDir 84*
WGGM - Chester, VA - *BrCabYB 84*
WGGM - Richmond, VA - *NatRadPubDir Summer 83, Spring 84; TV&RadDir 84*
WGGN - Castalia, OH - *BrCabYB 84*
WGGN-TV - Sandusky, OH - *BrCabYB 84; DirUSTelSta 83; Tel&CabFB 84S*
WGGO - Salamanca, NY - *BrCabYB 84; TV&RadDir 84*
WGGR-FM - Duluth, MN - *NatRadPubDir Summer 83; TV&RadDir 84*
WGGS-TV - Greenville, SC - *BrCabYB 84; DirUSTelSta 83; Tel&CabFB 84S*
WGGS-TV - Taylors, SC - *TV&RadDir 84*
WGGT-TV - Greensboro, NC - *BrCabYB 84; DirUSTelSta 83; TelAl 84; Tel&CabFB 84S*
WGGW-FM - Castalia, OH - *TV&RadDir 84*
WGH - Hampton, VA - *NatRadPubDir Summer 83; TV&RadDir 84*
WGHB - Farmville, NC - *BrCabYB 84; TV&RadDir 84*
WGHC - Clayton, GA - *BrCabYB 84; TV&RadDir 84*
WGHN - Grand Haven, MI - *BrCabYB 84; TV&RadDir 84*
WGHN-FM - Grand Haven, MI - *BrCabYB 84*
WGHP-TV - Greensboro, NC - *DirUSTelSta 83*
WGHP-TV - High Point, NC - *BrCabYB 84; LitMarPl 83, 84; TelAl 83, 84; Tel&CabFB 84S; TV&RadDir 84*
WGHQ - Hempstead, NY - *LitMarPl 83*
WGHQ - Kingston, NY - *BrCabYB 84; LitMarPl 84; NatRadPubDir Summer 83, Spring 84; TV&RadDir 84*
WGHR-FM - Marietta, GA - *BrCabYB 84; TV&RadDir 84*
WGHS-FM - Glen Ellyn, IL - *BrCabYB 84; TV&RadDir 84*
WGIB - Birmingham, AL - *BrCabYB 84*
WGIC - Xenia, OH - *BrCabYB 84; TV&RadDir 84*
WGIG - Brunswick, GA - *NatRadPubDir Summer 83; TV&RadDir 84*
WGIG-FM - Brunswick, GA - *BrCabYB 84; NatRadPubDir Spring 84*
WGIL - Galesburg, IL - *BrCabYB 84; NatRadPubDir Summer 83, Spring 84; TV&RadDir 84*
WGIQ - Louisville, AL - *BrCabYB 84; Tel&CabFB 84S*
WGIR - Manchester, NH - *BrCabYB 84; NatRadPubDir Summer 83, Spring 84; TV&RadDir 84*
WGIR-FM - Manchester, NH - *BrCabYB 84; NatRadPubDir Summer 83, Spring 84; TV&RadDir 84*
WGIT - Hormigueros, PR - *BrCabYB 84*
WGIV - Charlotte, NC - *BrCabYB 84; NatRadPubDir Summer 83, Spring 84; TV&RadDir 84*
WGKA - Atlanta, GA - *BrCabYB 84; NatRadPubDir Summer 83, Spring 84; TV&RadDir 84*
WGKR - Perry, FL - *BrCabYB 84; TV&RadDir 84*
WGKV - St. Albans, WV - *BrCabYB 84*
WGKX - Memphis, TN - *BrCabYB 84*
WGKY-FM - Greenville, KY - *BrCabYB 84*
WGL - Ft. Wayne, IN - *BrCabYB 84; NatRadPubDir Summer 83, Spring 84; TV&RadDir 84*
WGLB - Port Washington, WI - *BrCabYB 84; TV&RadDir 84*
WGLB-FM - Port Washington, WI - *BrCabYB 84; TV&RadDir 84*
WGLC - Mendota, IL - *BrCabYB 84; TV&RadDir 84*
WGLC-FM - Mendota, IL - *BrCabYB 84; TV&RadDir 84*
WGLD-FM - High Point, NC - *BrCabYB 84; TV&RadDir 84*
WGLE - Lima, OH - *BrCabYB 84*
WGLF-FM - Tallahassee, FL - *BrCabYB 84; NatRadPubDir Summer 83, Spring 84; TV&RadDir 84*
WGLI - Babylon, NY - *BrCabYB 84; TV&RadDir 84*
WGLI - Suffolk County, Long Island, NY - *NatRadPubDir Summer 83 p.178, Spring 84 p.175*
WGLO-FM - Pekin, IL - *BrCabYB 84; TV&RadDir 84*
WGLQ-FM - Escanaba, MI - *BrCabYB 84; TV&RadDir 84*
WGLR - Lancaster, WI - *BrCabYB 84; TV&RadDir 84*
WGLS-FM - Glassboro, NJ - *BrCabYB 84; NatRadPubDir Summer 83, Spring 84; TV&RadDir 84*
WGLT-FM - Normal, IL - *BrCabYB 84; NatRadPubDir Summer 83, Spring 84; TV&RadDir 84*
WGLU-FM - Johnstown, PA - *BrCabYB 84; TV&RadDir 84*
WGLX - Galion, OH - *BrCabYB 84; TV&RadDir 84*
WGLY-FM - Goulds, FL - *BrCabYB 84*
WGLY-FM - Miami, FL - *TV&RadDir 84*
WGMA - Spindale, NC - *BrCabYB 84*
WGMB-FM - Georgetown, SC - *BrCabYB 84; TV&RadDir 84*
WGMC-FM - North Greece, NY - *BrCabYB 84; TV&RadDir 84*
WGMD-FM - Lewes, DE - *TV&RadDir 84*
WGMD-FM - Rehoboth Beach, DE - *BrCabYB 84*
WGME-TV - Portland, ME - *BrCabYB 84*
WGMF - Watkins Glen, NY - *BrCabYB 84; TV&RadDir 84*
WGMK-FM - Donalsonville, GA - *BrCabYB 84; TV&RadDir 84*
WGML - Hinesville, GA - *BrCabYB 84; TV&RadDir 84*
WGMM-FM - Gladwin, MI - *BrCabYB 84; TV&RadDir 84*
WGMO-FM - Shell Lake, WI - *BrCabYB 84; TV&RadDir 84*
WGMR-FM - State College, PA - *TV&RadDir 84*
WGMR-FM - Tyrone, PA - *BrCabYB 84*
WGMS - Washington, DC - *NatRadPubDir Summer 83 p.53, Spring 84 p.54*
WGMS - Bethesda, MD - *BrCabYB 84*
WGMS-FM - Washington, DC - *BrCabYB 84; NatRadPubDir Summer 83 p.54, Spring 84 p.54*
WGMX-FM - Dayton, OH - *TV&RadDir 84*
WGMZ-FM - Flint, MI - *BrCabYB 84; NatRadPubDir Summer 83, Spring 84; TV&RadDir 84*
WGN [of Tribune Co.] - Chicago, IL - *BrCabYB 84; HomeVid&CabYB 82-83; LitMarPl 83, 84; NatRadPubDir Summer 83, Spring 84; TV&RadDir 84*
WGN-TV [of Tribune Co.] - Chicago, IL - *CabTVPrDB 83; DirUSTelSta 83; LitMarPl 83, 84; TelAl 83, 84; Tel&CabFB 84S; TV&RadDir 84*
WGN-TV [of United Video Inc.] - Tulsa, OK - *BrCabYB 84; Tel&CabFB 84C*
WGNA-FM - Albany, NY - *BrCabYB 84; NatRadPubDir Summer 83, Spring 84 p.165; TV&RadDir 84*
WGNB - Seminole, FL - *BrCabYB 84*
WGNB - St. Petersburg, FL - *TV&RadDir 84*
WGNC - Gastonia, NC - *BrCabYB 84; TV&RadDir 84*
WGNE-FM - Panama City, FL - *BrCabYB 84; TV&RadDir 84*
WGNG - Pawtucket, RI - *BrCabYB 84; TV&RadDir 84*
WGNG - Providence/Pawtucket, RI - *NatRadPubDir Summer 83 p.219, Spring 84 p.219*
WGNI - Wilmington, NC - *BrCabYB 84*
WGNO-TV - New Orleans, LA - *BrCabYB 84; DirUSTelSta 83; TelAl 83, 84; Tel&CabFB 84S; TV&RadDir 84*
WGNR-FM - Grand Rapids, MI - *BrCabYB 84; TV&RadDir 84*
WGNS - Murfreesboro, TN - *BrCabYB 84; NatRadPubDir Summer 83, Spring 84; TV&RadDir 84*
WGNT - Huntington, WV - *BrCabYB 84; NatRadPubDir Summer 83, Spring 84; TV&RadDir 84*
WGNU - Granite City, IL - *BrCabYB 84; TV&RadDir 84*

WGNU - St. Louis, MO - *NatRadPubDir Summer 83, Spring 84; TV&RadDir 84*
WGNW - Pewaukee, WI - *BrCabYB 84*
WGNY - Newburgh, NY - *BrCabYB 84; NatRadPubDir Summer 83, Spring 84; TV&RadDir 84*
WGOC - Kingsport, TN - *BrCabYB 84; NatRadPubDir Summer 83, Spring 84; TV&RadDir 84*
WGOE - Richmond, VA - *TV&RadDir 84*
WGOG - Walhalla, SC - *BrCabYB 84; TV&RadDir 84*
WGOH - Grayson, KY - *BrCabYB 84; TV&RadDir 84*
WGOJ-FM - Conneaut, OH - *BrCabYB 84; TV&RadDir 84*
WGOK - Mobile, AL - *BrCabYB 84; NatRadPubDir Summer 83, Spring 84; TV&RadDir 84*
WGOL-FM - Lynchburg, VA - *BrCabYB 84; TV&RadDir 84*
WGOM - Marion, IN - *BrCabYB 84; NatRadPubDir Summer 83, Spring 84; TV&RadDir 84*
WGOS - High Point, NC - *BrCabYB 84; NatRadPubDir Summer 83, Spring 84*
WGOS-FM - High Point, NC - *TV&RadDir 84*
WGOT - Manchester, NH - *BrCabYB 84*
WGOV - Valdosta, GA - *BrCabYB 84; TV&RadDir 84*
WGOV-FM - Valdosta, GA - *BrCabYB 84*
WGOW - Chattanooga, TN - *BrCabYB 84; NatRadPubDir Summer 83, Spring 84; TV&RadDir 84*
WGPA - Allentown/Bethlehem/Easton, PA - *NatRadPubDir Summer 83, Spring 84 p.209*
WGPA - Bethlehem, PA - *BrCabYB 84; TV&RadDir 84*
WGPC - Albany, GA - *BrCabYB 84; NatRadPubDir Summer 83, Spring 84; TV&RadDir 84*
WGPC-FM - Albany, GA - *BrCabYB 84; NatRadPubDir Summer 83, Spring 84; TV&RadDir 84*
WGPR-FM - Detroit, MI - *BrCabYB 84; NatRadPubDir Summer 83, Spring 84; TV&RadDir 84*
WGPR-TV - Detroit, MI - *BrCabYB 84; DirUSTelSta 83; TelAl 83, 84; Tel&CabFB 84S; TV&RadDir 84*
WGR - Buffalo, NY - *BrCabYB 84; NatRadPubDir Summer 83, Spring 84; TV&RadDir 84*
WGR-TV - Buffalo, NY - *DirUSTelSta 83; LitMarPl 83; TelAl 83, 84; TV&RadDir 84*
WGRA - Cairo, GA - *BrCabYB 84; TV&RadDir 84*
WGRB - Campbellsville, KY - *BrCabYB 84; Tel&CabFB 84S*
WGRC - Spring Valley, NY - *BrCabYB 84; TV&RadDir 84*
WGRD-FM - Grand Rapids, MI - *BrCabYB 84; NatRadPubDir Summer 83, Spring 84; TV&RadDir 84*
WGRE-FM - Greencastle, IN - *BrCabYB 84; NatRadPubDir Summer 83, Spring 84; TV&RadDir 84*
WGRF-FM - Atlantic City, NJ - *NatRadPubDir Summer 83; TV&RadDir 84*
WGRG-FM - Greensboro, GA - *BrCabYB 84; TV&RadDir 84*
WGRI - Greenville, GA - *TV&RadDir 84*
WGRI - Griffin, GA - *BrCabYB 84*
WGRK - Greensburg, KY - *BrCabYB 84; TV&RadDir 84*
WGRK-FM - Greensburg, KY - *BrCabYB 84; TV&RadDir 84*
WGRM - Greenwood, MS - *BrCabYB 84; TV&RadDir 84*
WGRN-FM - Greenville, IL - *BrCabYB 84; TV&RadDir 84*
WGRO - Lake City, FL - *BrCabYB 84; TV&RadDir 84*
WGRP-FM - Greenville, PA - *BrCabYB 84; TV&RadDir 84*
WGRQ-FM - Buffalo, NY - *BrCabYB 84; NatRadPubDir Summer 83, Spring 84; TV&RadDir 84*
WGRR - Prichard, AL - *BrCabYB 84*
WGRT-FM - Danville, IN - *BrCabYB 84; TV&RadDir 84*
WGRV - Greeneville, TN - *BrCabYB 84; TV&RadDir 84*
WGRY - Grayling, MI - *BrCabYB 84; TV&RadDir 84*
WGRZ-TV - Buffalo, NY - *BrCabYB 84; LitMarPl 84; Tel&CabFB 84S*
WGSA - Ephrata, PA - *BrCabYB 84; TV&RadDir 84*
WGSE - Myrtle Beach, SC - *BrCabYB 84; Tel&CabFB 84S*
WGSF - Arlington, TN - *BrCabYB 84*
WGSM - Huntington Station, NY - *BrCabYB 84; TV&RadDir 84*
WGSM - Suffolk County, Long Island, NY - *NatRadPubDir Summer 83 p.178, Spring 84 p.176*
WGSN - North Myrtle Beach, SC - *BrCabYB 84*
WGSO - New Orleans, LA - *NatRadPubDir Summer 83; TV&RadDir 84*
WGSQ-FM - Cookeville, TN - *BrCabYB 84; TV&RadDir 84*
WGSR - Millen, GA - *BrCabYB 84; TV&RadDir 84*
WGSS-FM - Lumberton, NC - *BrCabYB 84; TV&RadDir 84*
WGST - Atlanta, GA - *BrCabYB 84; NatRadPubDir Summer 83, Spring 84; TV&RadDir 84*
WGSU-FM - Geneseo, NY - *BrCabYB 84; TV&RadDir 84*
WGSV - Guntersville, AL - *BrCabYB 84; TV&RadDir 84*
WGSW - Greenwood, SC - *BrCabYB 84; TV&RadDir 84*
WGSX - Bayamon, PR - *BrCabYB 84*
WGTA - Summerville, GA - *BrCabYB 84; TV&RadDir 84*
WGTC-FM - Bloomington, IN - *BrCabYB 84; NatRadPubDir Summer 83, Spring 84*
WGTD-FM - Kenosha, WI - *BrCabYB 84; NatRadPubDir Summer 83, Spring 84; TV&RadDir 84*
WGTE-FM - Toledo, OH - *BrCabYB 84; NatRadPubDir Summer 83, Spring 84; TV&RadDir 84*
WGTE-TV - Toledo, OH - *BrCabYB 84; Tel&CabFB 84S; TV&RadDir 84*
WGTF-FM - Nantucket, MA - *BrCabYB 84*
WGTH - Richlands, VA - *BrCabYB 84*
WGTL - Kannapolis, NC - *BrCabYB 84; TV&RadDir 84*
WGTM - Wilson, NC - *BrCabYB 84; NatRadPubDir Summer 83, Spring 84; TV&RadDir 84*
WGTN - Georgetown, SC - *BrCabYB 84; TV&RadDir 84*
WGTO - Cypress Gardens, FL - *BrCabYB 84*
WGTO - Lakeland/Winter Haven, FL - *NatRadPubDir Summer 83 p.60, Spring 84 p.60*
WGTO - Winter Haven, FL - *TV&RadDir 84*
WGTQ-TV - Goetzville, MI - *TV&RadDir 84*
WGTQ-TV - Sault Ste. Marie, MI - *BrCabYB 84; TelAl 83, 84; Tel&CabFB 84S*
WGTQ-TV - Traverse City, MI - *TV&RadDir 84*
WGTR - Natick, MA - *TV&RadDir 84*
WGTR-TV - Marlborough, MA - *BrCabYB 84; TelAl 84; Tel&CabFB 84S*
WGTS-FM - Takoma Park, MD - *BrCabYB 84; NatRadPubDir Summer 83, Spring 84*
WGTU-TV - Traverse City, MI - *BrCabYB 84; DirUSTelSta 83; TelAl 83, 84; Tel&CabFB 84S; TV&RadDir 84*
WGTV - Athens, GA - *BrCabYB 84; Tel&CabFB 84S*
WGTX - De Funiak Springs, FL - *BrCabYB 84; TV&RadDir 84*
WGTY-FM - Gettysburg, PA - *TV&RadDir 84*
WGUC-FM - Cincinnati, OH - *BrCabYB 84; NatRadPubDir Summer 83, Spring 84; TV&RadDir 84*
WGUD-FM - Pascagoula, MS - *BrCabYB 84; TV&RadDir 84*
WGUF - Biloxi/Gulfport, MS - *NatRadPubDir Summer 83, Spring 84 p.137*
WGUF - Gulfport, MS - *BrCabYB 84; TV&RadDir 84*
WGUF-FM - Biloxi/Gulfport, MS - *NatRadPubDir Spring 84 p.137*
WGUF-FM - Gulfport, MS - *BrCabYB 84; TV&RadDir 84*
WGUL - New Port Richey, FL - *BrCabYB 84; TV&RadDir 84*
WGUN - Atlanta, GA - *BrCabYB 84*
WGUN - Decatur, GA - *TV&RadDir 84*
WGUS - Augusta, GA - *BrCabYB 84; NatRadPubDir Summer 83, Spring 84; TV&RadDir 84*
WGUS-FM - Augusta, GA - *BrCabYB 84; TV&RadDir 84*
WGUY-FM - Bangor, ME - *TV&RadDir 84*
WGUY-FM - Brewer, ME - *BrCabYB 84*
WGVA - Geneva, NY - *BrCabYB 84; TV&RadDir 84*
WGVC - Allendale, MI - *TV&RadDir 84*
WGVC - Grand Rapids, MI - *BrCabYB 84*
WGVC-FM - Allendale, MI - *BrCabYB 84*
WGVC-TV - Grand Rapids, MI - *Tel&CabFB 84S*
WGVE-FM - Gary, IN - *BrCabYB 84; NatRadPubDir Summer 83, Spring 84; TV&RadDir 84*
WGVL - Greenville, SC - *BrCabYB 84; NatRadPubDir Summer 83, Spring 84; TV&RadDir 84*
WGVM - Greenville, MS - *BrCabYB 84; NatRadPubDir Summer 83, Spring 84; TV&RadDir 84*
WGVO-FM - Greenville, OH - *BrCabYB 84; NatRadPubDir Summer 83, Spring 84; TV&RadDir 84*
WGVU - Dubuque, IA - *NatRadPubDir Summer 83, Spring 84*
WGWG - Birmingham, AL - *NatRadPubDir Spring 84*
WGWG - Boiling Springs, NC - *BrCabYB 84*
WGWG-FM - Boiling Springs, NC - *NatRadPubDir Summer 83, Spring 84; TV&RadDir 84*
WGWR - Asheboro, NC - *BrCabYB 84; NatRadPubDir Summer 83, Spring 84; TV&RadDir 84*
WGWY - Charlotte, MI - *BrCabYB 84; TV&RadDir 84*

WGXA-TV - Macon, GA - *BrCabYB 84; DirUSTelSta 83; Tel&CabFB 84S*
WGXM-FM - Dayton, OH - *BrCabYB 84; NatRadPubDir Summer 83, Spring 84*
WGY - Albany/Schenectady/Troy, NY - *NatRadPubDir Summer 83, Spring 84 p.165*
WGY - Schenectady, NY - *BrCabYB 84; TV&RadDir 84*
WGYL-FM - Vero Beach, FL - *BrCabYB 84; TV&RadDir 84*
WGYV - Greenville, AL - *BrCabYB 84; TV&RadDir 84*
WGZS - Waupun, WI - *BrCabYB 84; TV&RadDir 84*
WHA - Madison, WI - *BrCabYB 84; NatRadPubDir Summer 83, Spring 84; TV&RadDir 84*
WHA-TV - Madison, WI - *BrCabYB 84; LitMarPl 83, 84; Tel&CabFB 84S; TV&RadDir 84*
WHAB-FM - Acton, MA - *BrCabYB 84; TV&RadDir 84*
WHAD-FM - Delafield, WI - *BrCabYB 84; NatRadPubDir Summer 83 p.325, Spring 84 p.327*
WHAG - Hagerstown, MD - *NatRadPubDir Summer 83, Spring 84*
WHAG - Halfway, MD - *BrCabYB 84*
WHAG-TV - Hagerstown, MD - *BrCabYB 84; DirUSTelSta 83; LitMarPl 83, 84; TelAl 83, 84; Tel&CabFB 84S; TV&RadDir 84*
WHAH-TV - Portsmouth, VA - *TelAl 83*
WHAI - Greenfield, MA - *BrCabYB 84; TV&RadDir 84*
WHAI-FM - Greenfield, MA - *BrCabYB 84; TV&RadDir 84*
WHAJ-FM - Bluefield, WV - *BrCabYB 84; TV&RadDir 84*
WHAK - Rogers City, MI - *BrCabYB 84; TV&RadDir 84*
WHAL - Shelbyville, TN - *BrCabYB 84; TV&RadDir 84*
Whale & Eagle Publishing Co. - Costa Mesa, CA - *BoPubDir 4, 5*
Whale, The - Lewes, DE - *Ed&PubIntYB 82*
Whalen Computer Services Inc. - Millbrook, NY - *ADAPSOMemDir 83-84*
Whaling City Cable TV Inc. - New Bedford, MA - *BrCabYB 84*
WHAM - Rochester, NY - *BrCabYB 84; NatRadPubDir Summer 83, Spring 84; TV&RadDir 84*
Wham Bam Records - Ardmore, PA - *BillIntBG 83-84*
WHAP - Hopewell, VA - *BrCabYB 84; TV&RadDir 84*
WHAR - Clarksburg, WV - *BrCabYB 84; TV&RadDir 84*
Wharton Brazil Model [of Wharton Econometric Forecasting Associates] - Philadelphia, PA - *DataDirOnSer 84*
Wharton Econometric Forecasting Associates [Subs. of Ziff-Davis Publishing Co.] - Philadelphia, PA - *DataDirOnSer 84; EISS 83*
Wharton Econometric Forecasting Data Bases - Philadelphia, PA - *DBBus 82*
Wharton Econometric Foreign Exchange Service Forecast Data Base - Philadelphia, PA - *DirOnDB Spring 84*
Wharton Econometric International Agricultural Service Forecast Data Base - Philadelphia, PA - *DirOnDB Spring 84*
Wharton Econometric International Agricultural Service Historical Data Base - Philadelphia, PA - *DirOnDB Spring 84*
Wharton Econometric Latin American Service Forecast Data Base - Philadelphia, PA - *DirOnDB Spring 84*
Wharton Econometric Latin American Service Historical Data Base - Philadelphia, PA - *DirOnDB Spring 84*
Wharton Econometric Long-Term Service Forecast Data Base - Philadelphia, PA - *DirOnDB Spring 84*
Wharton Econometric Middle East Service Forecast Data Base - Philadelphia, PA - *DirOnDB Spring 84*
Wharton Econometric Middle East Service Historical Data Base - Philadelphia, PA - *DirOnDB Spring 84*
Wharton Econometric New York Service Forecast Data Base - Philadelphia, PA - *DirOnDB Spring 84*
Wharton Econometric New York Service Historical Data Base - Philadelphia, PA - *DirOnDB Spring 84*
Wharton Econometric Pacific Basin Service Forecast Data Base - Philadelphia, PA - *DirOnDB Spring 84*
Wharton Econometric Pacific Basin Service Historical Data Base - Philadelphia, PA - *DirOnDB Spring 84*
Wharton Econometric Regional Service Historical Data Base - Philadelphia, PA - *DirOnDB Spring 84*
Wharton Econometric U.S. Census Region Service Historical Data Base - Philadelphia, PA - *DirOnDB Spring 84*
Wharton Econometric U.S. Core Data Base - Philadelphia, PA - *DirOnDB Spring 84*
Wharton Econometric U.S. Industry Service Forecast Data Base - Philadelphia, PA - *DirOnDB Spring 84*
Wharton Econometric U.S. Industry Service Historical Data Base - Philadelphia, PA - *DirOnDB Spring 84*
Wharton Econometric U.S. Long-Term Service Historical Data Base - Philadelphia, PA - *DirOnDB Spring 84*
Wharton Econometric U.S. Quarterly Service Forecast Data Base - Philadelphia, PA - *DirOnDB Spring 84*
Wharton Econometric U.S. Quarterly Service Historical Data Base - Philadelphia, PA - *DirOnDB Spring 84*
Wharton Econometric World Service Forecast Data Base - Philadelphia, PA - *DirOnDB Spring 84*
Wharton Econometric World Service Historical Data Base - Philadelphia, PA - *DirOnDB Spring 84*
Wharton EFA Agricultural Model Database [of Wharton Econometric Forecasting Associates] - Philadelphia, PA - *DataDirOnSer 84*
Wharton EFA Annual Database [of Wharton Econometric Forecasting Associates] - Philadelphia, PA - *DataDirOnSer 84*
Wharton EFA Annual Model Database [of Wharton Econometric Forecasting Associates] - Philadelphia, PA - *DataDirOnSer 84*
Wharton EFA Monthly Database [of Wharton Econometric Forecasting Associates] - Philadelphia, PA - *DataDirOnSer 84*
Wharton EFA Quarterly Database [of Wharton Econometric Forecasting Associates] - Philadelphia, PA - *DataDirOnSer 84*
Wharton EFA Quarterly Model Database [of Wharton Econometric Forecasting Associates] - Philadelphia, PA - *DataDirOnSer 84*
Wharton EFA Regional Database [of Wharton Econometric Forecasting Associates] - Philadelphia, PA - *DataDirOnSer 84*
Wharton EFA World Economic Database [of Wharton Econometric Forecasting Associates] - Philadelphia, PA - *DataDirOnSer 84*
Wharton Journal-Spectator - Wharton, TX - *BaconPubCkNews 84; Ed&PubIntYB 82; NewsDir 84*
Wharton Magazine, The [of Trustees of the University of Pennsylvania] - Philadelphia, PA - *MagDir 84; MagIndMarPl 82-83*
Wharton Mexico Model [of Wharton Econometric Forecasting Associates] - Philadelphia, PA - *DataDirOnSer 84*
Wharton New York Regional Model Variables [of Wharton Econometric Forecasting Associates] - Philadelphia, PA - *DataDirOnSer 84*
Wharton Philadelphia Regional Model Variables [of Wharton Econometric Forecasting Associates] - Philadelphia, PA - *DataDirOnSer 84*
Wharton Regional Time Series, New York [of Wharton Econometric Forecasting Associates] - Philadelphia, PA - *DataDirOnSer 84*
Wharton Regional Time Series, Philadelphia [of Wharton Econometric Forecasting Associates] - Philadelphia, PA - *DataDirOnSer 84*
WHAS - Louisville, KY - *BrCabYB 84; NatRadPubDir Summer 83, Spring 84; TV&RadDir 84*
WHAS-TV - Louisville, KY - *BrCabYB 84; DirUSTelSta 83; LitMarPl 83, 84; TelAl 83, 84; Tel&CabFB 84S; TV&RadDir 84*
WHAT - Philadelphia, PA - *BrCabYB 84; NatRadPubDir Summer 83, Spring 84; TV&RadDir 84*
What Cheer Patriot-Chronicle - What Cheer, IA - *BaconPubCkNews 84; Ed&PubIntYB 82*
What Makes People Successful [of The National Research Bureau Inc.] - Burlington, IA - *WritMar 84*
Whatcom County Shopping News [of Lewis Publishing Co. Inc.] - Lynden, WA - *NewsDir 84*
Whatever Publishing Inc. - Mill Valley, CA - *LitMag&SmPr 83-84; LitMarPl 83, 84*
What's New in Home Economics - Washington, DC - *BaconPubCkMag 84; MagDir 84*
What's New in Medicine - Kensington, CT - *Ed&PubIntYB 82*
WHAV - Haverhill, MA - *BrCabYB 84; TV&RadDir 84*
WHAV-FM - Haverhill, MA - *TV&RadDir 84*
WHAW - Weston, WV - *BrCabYB 84; TV&RadDir 84*
WHAY-FM - Aberdeen, MS - *BrCabYB 84; TV&RadDir 84*
WHAZ - Albany/Schenectady/Troy, NY - *NatRadPubDir Summer 83, Spring 84 p.165*
WHAZ - Troy, NY - *BrCabYB 84; TV&RadDir 84*
WHB - Kansas City, MO - *BrCabYB 84; NatRadPubDir Summer 83, Spring 84; TV&RadDir 84*

WHB Consulting Service - Los Altos Hills, CA - *WhoWMicrocom 83*
WHBB - Selma, AL - *BrCabYB 84; NatRadPubDir Summer 83, Spring 84; TV&RadDir 84*
WHBC - Canton, OH - *BrCabYB 84; NatRadPubDir Summer 83, Spring 84; TV&RadDir 84*
WHBC-FM - Canton, OH - *BrCabYB 84; TV&RadDir 84*
WHBF - Rock Island, IL - *BrCabYB 84; TV&RadDir 84*
WHBF - Davenport, IA - *NatRadPubDir Summer 83 p.96*
WHBF-FM - Rock Island, IL - *BrCabYB 84; TV&RadDir 84*
WHBF-FM - Davenport, IA - *NatRadPubDir Summer 83 p.96*
WHBF-TV - Rock Island, IL - *BrCabYB 84; TelAl 83, 84; Tel&CabFB 84S; TV&RadDir 84*
WHBF-TV - Davenport, IA - *DirUSTelSta 83*
WHBG - Harrisonburg, VA - *BrCabYB 84; TV&RadDir 84*
WHBI-FM - Newark, NJ - *BrCabYB 84*
WHBI-FM - New York, NY - *NatRadPubDir Summer 83, Spring 84; TV&RadDir 84*
WHBL - Sheboygan, WI - *BrCabYB 84; TV&RadDir 84*
WHBN - Harrodsburg, KY - *BrCabYB 84; TV&RadDir 84*
WHBN-FM - Harrodsburg, KY - *BrCabYB 84; TV&RadDir 84*
WHBO - Tampa, FL - *BrCabYB 84; NatRadPubDir Summer 83, Spring 84; TV&RadDir 84*
WHBQ - Memphis, TN - *BrCabYB 84; NatRadPubDir Summer 83, Spring 84; TV&RadDir 84*
WHBQ-TV - Memphis, TN - *BrCabYB 84; DirUSTelSta 83; LitMarPl 83, 84; TelAl 83, 84; Tel&CabFB 84S; TV&RadDir 84*
WHBS-FM - Port Richey, FL - *TV&RadDir 84*
WHBT - Harriman, TN - *BrCabYB 84; TV&RadDir 84*
WHBU - Anderson, IN - *BrCabYB 84; NatRadPubDir Summer 83, Spring 84; TV&RadDir 84*
WHBY - Appleton, WI - *BrCabYB 84; NatRadPubDir Summer 83, Spring 84; TV&RadDir 84*
WHCB - Bristol, TN - *BrCabYB 84*
WHCC - Waynesville, NC - *BrCabYB 84; TV&RadDir 84*
WHCE-FM - Highland Springs, VA - *BrCabYB 84; TV&RadDir 84*
WHCF - Bangor, ME - *BrCabYB 84*
WHCG-FM - Metter, GA - *BrCabYB 84; TV&RadDir 84*
WHCJ-FM - Savannah, GA - *BrCabYB 84; TV&RadDir 84*
WHCL-FM - Clinton, NY - *BrCabYB 84; NatRadPubDir Summer 83, Spring 84; TV&RadDir 84*
WHCN-FM - Hartford, CT - *BrCabYB 84; NatRadPubDir Summer 83, Spring 84; TV&RadDir 84*
WHCO - Sparta, IL - *BrCabYB 84; TV&RadDir 84*
WHCR-FM - New York, NY - *BrCabYB 84*
WHCT-TV [Div. of Faith Center Inc.] - Hartford, CT - *BrCabYB 84; TelAl 83, 84; Tel&CabFB 84S*
WHCU - Ithaca, NY - *BrCabYB 84; TV&RadDir 84*
WHCU-FM - Ithaca, NY - *BrCabYB 84; TV&RadDir 84*
WHDG - Havre de Grace, MD - *BrCabYB 84*
WHDH - Boston, MA - *BrCabYB 84; LitMarPl 83, 84; NatRadPubDir Summer 83, Spring 84; TV&RadDir 84*
WHDL - Olean, NY - *BrCabYB 84; TV&RadDir 84*
WHDM - McKenzie, TN - *BrCabYB 84; TV&RadDir 84*
Wheat Center News - Fairfield, MT - *AyerDirPub 83*
Wheat Fordes - Washington, DC - *LitMag&SmPr 83-84*
Wheat Grower, The - Washington, DC - *BaconPubCkMag 84*
Wheat Life - Ritzville, WA - *BaconPubCkMag 84; MagDir 84*
Wheat Ridge Sentinel - *See* Sentinel Newspapers
Wheat Scoop, The [of Montana Grain Growers Association] - Great Falls, MT - *BaconPubCkMag 84; MagDir 84; NewsDir 84*
Wheat State Telecable Inc. - Oxford, KS - *BrCabYB 84*
Wheat State Telecable Inc. - Udall, KS - *Tel&CabFB 84C p.1712*
Wheat State Telephone Co. Inc., The - Udall, KS - *TelDir&BG 83-84*
Wheatfield Press - Winnipeg, MB, Canada - *BoPubDir 4, 5*
Wheatland Cablevision Inc. - Douglass, KS - *Tel&CabFB 84C p.1712*
Wheatland Platte County Record Times - *See* Lindsey Publishing
Wheatland Press-Gazette - Wheatland, IA - *BaconPubCkNews 84*
Wheatley Journal - Wheatley, ON, Canada - *AyerDirPub 83; Ed&PubIntYB 82*
Wheaton Daily Journal [of Copley Newspapers] - Wheaton, IL - *BaconPubCkNews 84; NewsDir 84*
Wheaton Du Page County Star & Press Lounge - Wheaton, IL - *NewsDir 84*
Wheaton Gazette - Wheaton, MN - *BaconPubCkNews 84; Ed&PubIntYB 82*
Wheaton Journal - Wheaton, MO - *BaconPubCkNews 84; Ed&PubIntYB 82*
Wheaton Leader [of Glen News Printing Co.] - Glen Ellyn, IL - *NewsDir 84*
Wheaton Leader - *See* Glen News Printing Co.
Wheaton Leader, The - Wheaton, IL - *Ed&PubIntYB 82*
Wheaton News - Silver Spring, MD - *NewsDir 84*
Wheaton-Silver Spring Montgomery Advertiser - *See* Morkap Publishing
Wheaton Times-Press [of Press Publications] - Elmhurst, IL - *AyerDirPub 83; NewsDir 84*
Wheaton Times-Press - Wheaton, IL - *Ed&PubIntYB 82*
Wheaton Times-Press - *See* Press Publishing
Wheatridge & Arvada East Jefferson Star [of Golden Jeffco Publications Inc.] - Golden, CO - *NewsDir 84*
WHEB - Portsmouth, NH - *BrCabYB 84; NatRadPubDir Summer 83, Spring 84; TV&RadDir 84*
WHEB-FM - Portsmouth, NH - *BrCabYB 84; NatRadPubDir Summer 83, Spring 84; TV&RadDir 84*
WHEC-TV - Rochester, NY - *BrCabYB 84; DirUSTelSta 83; TelAl 83, 84; Tel&CabFB 84S; TV&RadDir 84*
WHED-TV - Durham, NH - *TV&RadDir 84*
WHED-TV - Hanover, NH - *Tel&CabFB 84S*
WHEE - Martinsville, VA - *BrCabYB 84; TV&RadDir 84*
Wheel Advertiser - Slayton, MN - *AyerDirPub 83*
Wheel, The - Pleasanton, CA - *BaconPubCkMag 84*
Wheelchair Traveler - Milford, NH - *BoPubDir 4, 5*
Wheeldex [Div. of Lefebure] - Cedar Rapids, IA - *DirInfWP 82*
Wheeler Agency Inc., The - Oklahoma City, OK - *StaDirAdAg 2-84*
Wheeler County Eagle - Alamo, GA - *AyerDirPub 83*
Wheeler County Eagle - Wheeler County, GA - *Ed&PubIntYB 82*
Wheeler County Independent - Burwell, NE - *AyerDirPub 83; Ed&PubIntYB 82*
Wheeler Fishrapper - Wheeler, OR - *BaconPubCkNews 84*
Wheeler Inc., Mel - Denton, TX - *BrCabYB 84*
Wheeler-Kight & Gainey Inc. - Columbus, OH - *StaDirAdAg 2-84*
Wheeler Times - Wheeler, TX - *BaconPubCkNews 84; Ed&PubIntYB 82*
Wheeler TV System - Wheeler, TX - *BrCabYB 84; Tel&CabFB 84C*
Wheelers RV Resort & Campground Guide - Elk Grove Village, IL - *MagDir 84*
Wheelersburg Scioto Voice - Wheelersburg, OH - *BaconPubCkNews 84; NewsDir 84*
Wheeling Antenna Co. [of Tele-Communications Inc.] - Wheeling, WV - *BrCabYB 84; Tel&CabFB 84C*
Wheeling Herald [of Paddock Publications] - Arlington Heights, IL - *NewsDir 84*
Wheeling Herald - *See* Paddock Publications
Wheeling Intelligencer - Wheeling, WV - *NewsBur 6*
Wheeling Life - Deerfield, IL - *AyerDirPub 83*
Wheeling Life - Wheeling, IL - *Ed&PubIntYB 82*
Wheeling Life - *See* Lerner Life Newspapers
Wheeling News-Register - Wheeling, WV - *BaconPubCkNews 84*
Wheeling Telephone Co. - Wheeling, MO - *TelDir&BG 83-84*
Wheeling Topics - *See* Journal & Topics Newspapers
Wheelock Educational Resources [Subs. of Whitman Press] - Hanover, NH - *AvMarPl 83*
Wheels Book Club [Subs. of Sky Books International Inc.] - New York, NY - *LitMarPl 83, 84*
Wheelspin News - Mississauga, ON, Canada - *BaconPubCkMag 84*
Wheelwright Press Ltd. - Salt Lake City, UT - *BoPubDir 4, 5*
WHEI-FM - Tiffin, OH - *BrCabYB 84; NatRadPubDir Summer 83, Spring 84; TV&RadDir 84*
WHEN - Syracuse, NY - *BrCabYB 84; NatRadPubDir Summer 83, Spring 84; TV&RadDir 84*
WHEO - Stuart, VA - *BrCabYB 84; TV&RadDir 84*
WHEP - Foley, AL - *BrCabYB 84; TV&RadDir 84*
WHER-FM - Hattiesburg, MS - *BrCabYB 84; TV&RadDir 84*
Where Magazine - New York, NY - *BaconPubCkMag 84; MagDir 84*
Whetstone [of San Pedro Press] - St. David, AZ - *LitMag&SmPr 83-84*
Whetstone Publishing - Brattleboro, VT - *LitMag&SmPr 83-84*

Whetstone/San Pedro Press - St. David, AZ - *BoPubDir 4, 5*
WHEW-FM - Ft. Myers, FL - *BrCabYB 84; NatRadPubDir Spring 84; TV&RadDir 84*
WHEZ - Huntington, WV - *NatRadPubDir Spring 84 p.265*
WHEZ - Kenova, WV - *BrCabYB 84*
WHEZ-FM - Huntington, WV - *NatRadPubDir Summer 83; TV&RadDir 84*
WHFB - Benton Harbor, MI - *BrCabYB 84; TV&RadDir 84*
WHFB-FM - Benton Harbor, MI - *BrCabYB 84; TV&RadDir 84*
WHFC-FM - Bel Air, MD - *BrCabYB 84; TV&RadDir 84*
WHFD-FM - Archbold, OH - *BrCabYB 84; TV&RadDir 84*
WHFH-FM - Flossmoor, IL - *BrCabYB 84; TV&RadDir 84*
WHFL - Havana, FL - *BrCabYB 84*
WHFM-FM - Rochester, NY - *BrCabYB 84; NatRadPubDir Summer 83, Spring 84; TV&RadDir 84*
WHFR - Dearborn, MI - *BrCabYB 84*
WHFS-FM - Washington, DC - *NatRadPubDir Summer 83 p.54; TV&RadDir 84*
WHFS-FM - Annapolis, MD - *BrCabYB 84*
WHFT-TV - Miami, FL - *BrCabYB 84; DirUSTelSta 83; TelAl 83, 84; Tel&CabFB 84S; TV&RadDir 84*
WHGC-FM - Bennington, VT - *BrCabYB 84; TV&RadDir 84*
WHGI - Augusta, GA - *BrCabYB 84; NatRadPubDir Summer 83, Spring 84; TV&RadDir 84*
WHGM-FM - Altoona, PA - *NatRadPubDir Summer 83, Spring 84; TV&RadDir 84*
WHGM-FM - Bellwood, PA - *BrCabYB 84*
WHGR - Houghton Lake, MI - *BrCabYB 84; TV&RadDir 84*
WHHB - Holliston, MA - *BrCabYB 84*
WHHI-FM - Highland, WI - *BrCabYB 84; NatRadPubDir Summer 83 p.326, Spring 84 p.328*
WHHI-FM - Madison, WI - *TV&RadDir 84*
WHHJ-FM - Huntington Station, NY - *TV&RadDir 84*
WHHM - Henderson, TN - *TV&RadDir 84*
WHHO - Hornell, NY - *BrCabYB 84; NatRadPubDir Summer 83, Spring 84; TV&RadDir 84*
WHHO-FM - Hornell, NY - *NatRadPubDir Summer 83; TV&RadDir 84*
WHHQ - Hilton Head Island, SC - *BrCabYB 84*
WHHR-FM - Hilton Head Island, SC - *BrCabYB 84; TV&RadDir 84*
WHHS-FM - Havertown, PA - *BrCabYB 84; NatRadPubDir Summer 83, Spring 84; TV&RadDir 84*
WHHV - Hillsville, VA - *BrCabYB 84; TV&RadDir 84*
WHHY - Montgomery, AL - *BrCabYB 84; NatRadPubDir Summer 83, Spring 84; TV&RadDir 84*
WHHY-FM - Montgomery, AL - *BrCabYB 84; NatRadPubDir Summer 83, Spring 84; TV&RadDir 84*
WHIA-FM - Dawson, GA - *BrCabYB 84; TV&RadDir 84*
WHIC - Hardinsburg, KY - *BrCabYB 84; TV&RadDir 84*
WHIC-FM - Hardinsburg, KY - *BrCabYB 84; TV&RadDir 84*
Whidbey Island Record - Langley, WA - *AyerDirPub 83; Ed&PubIntYB 82*
Whidbey News Times - Oak Harbor, WA - *AyerDirPub 83*
Whidbey News TImes - Whidby, WA - *Ed&PubIntYB 82*
Whidbey Telephone Co. - Langley, WA - *TelDir&BG 83-84*
WHIE - Griffin, GA - *BrCabYB 84; TV&RadDir 84*
WHIF-TV - Boynton Beach, FL - *TV&RadDir 84*
Whig-Standard - Kingston, ON, Canada - *AyerDirPub 83; Ed&PubIntYB 82; LitMarPl 84*
WHII - Bay Springs, MS - *BrCabYB 84; TV&RadDir 84*
WHIJ - Washburn, WI - *BrCabYB 84*
WHIL-FM - Mobile, AL - *BrCabYB 84; TV&RadDir 84*
WHIM - East Providence, RI - *BrCabYB 84; NatRadPubDir Summer 83, Spring 84; TV&RadDir 84*
Whimsy Press - Arnold, MO - *BoPubDir 4, 5*
WHIN - Gallatin, TN - *BrCabYB 84; TV&RadDir 84*
WHIO - Dayton, OH - *BrCabYB 84; NatRadPubDir Summer 83, Spring 84; TV&RadDir 84*
WHIO-FM - Dayton, OH - *BrCabYB 84; NatRadPubDir Summer 83, Spring 84; TV&RadDir 84*
WHIO-TV - Dayton, OH - *BrCabYB 84; DirUSTelSta 83; LitMarPl 83, 84; TelAl 83, 84; Tel&CabFB 84S; TV&RadDir 84*
WHIP - Mooresville, NC - *BrCabYB 84; TV&RadDir 84*
Whippany Regional Weekly News - Whippany, NJ - *BaconPubCkNews 84*
Whippoorwill Press - Frankfort, KY - *BoPubDir 4, 5*
WHIQ - Huntsville, AL - *BrCabYB 84; Tel&CabFB 84S*
WHIQ-TV - Huntsville, AL - *TV&RadDir 84*
WHIR - Danville, KY - *BrCabYB 84; TV&RadDir 84*
WHIS - Bluefield, WV - *BrCabYB 84; TV&RadDir 84*
Whiskey Island Magazine [of Cleveland State University] - Cleveland, OH - *ArtMar 84; WritMar 84*
Whispering Wind Magazine - New Orleans, LA - *LitMag&SmPr 83-84*
Whispers - Binghamton, NY - *ArtMar 84*
Whispers Press - Staten Island, NY - *BoPubDir 4, 5*
Whistler Question, The - Vancouver, BC, Canada - *AyerDirPub 83*
WHIT - Madison, WI - *BrCabYB 84; NatRadPubDir Summer 83, Spring 84; TV&RadDir 84*
Whitaker & Baker International - San Francisco, CA - *DirPRFirms 83*
Whitaker & Sons Ltd., J. - London, England - *MicroMarPl 82-83*
Whitaker Associates Inc., William J. - Gaithersburg, MD - *LitMarPl 83, 84*
Whitaker, George - Ozark, AR - *Tel&CabFB 84C p.1713*
Whitaker House - Springdale, PA - *LitMarPl 83, 84; WritMar 84*
Whitby Free Press - Whitby, ON, Canada - *Ed&PubIntYB 82*
Whitby/Pickering News Advertiser - Whitby, ON, Canada - *Ed&PubIntYB 82*
Whitchappel's Herbal - Peterborough, NH - *ArtMar 84; WritMar 84*
Whitcomb Publications - Stillwater, OK - *BoPubDir 4*
White, Ab - Greenville, SC - *HBIndAd&MS 82-83*
White & Co. Inc., W. Herbert - Winnetka, IL - *MicrocomMPl 84*
White & Co., James T. - Clifton, NJ - *LitMarPl 83; MicroMarPl 82-83*
White & Co., Robert F. - Chicago, IL - *ADAPSOMemDir 83-84*
White Associates Inc., Oliver - Atlanta, GA - *HBIndAd&MS 82-83; StaDirAdAg 2-84*
White Bear Area Free Press - White Bear Lake, MN - *AyerDirPub 83; Ed&PubIntYB 82; NewsDir 84*
White Bear Lake Press - *See* Press Publications
White Bear Press - White Bear Lake, MN - *AyerDirPub 83; Ed&PubIntYB 82*
White Bluff Chronicle - Demopolis, AL - *AyerDirPub 83; Ed&PubIntYB 82*
White Castle Times - White Castle, LA - *AyerDirPub 83; Ed&PubIntYB 82*
White Castle Times, The - Plaquemine, LA - *NewsDir 84*
White Cat Music - Shawnee, KS - *BillIntBG 83-84*
White Center News [of Robinson Communications] - Seattle, WA - *NewsDir 84*
White Center News - White Center, WA - *Ed&PubIntYB 82*
White Co., Hooper - Barrington, IL - *HBIndAd&MS 82-83*
White Computing & Software Inc., Bob - Oak Brook, IL - *DataDirOnSer 84; DataDirSup 7-83*
White County Citizen - Searcy, AR - *AyerDirPub 83*
White County News - Cleveland, GA - *AyerDirPub 83; Ed&PubIntYB 82*
White County Press - Carmi, IL - *Ed&PubIntYB 82*
White County Record - Judsonia, AR - *Ed&PubIntYB 82*
White County Video [of WEHCO Video Inc.] - Searcy, AR - *BrCabYB 84; Tel&CabFB 84C*
White Crane Publications - Eugene, OR - *BoPubDir 5*
White Crescent Press - Luton, England - *LitMag&SmPr 83-84*
White Cross Press - Granger, TX - *BoPubDir 4, 5; LitMag&SmPr 83-84*
White Deer News - White Deer, TX - *BaconPubCkNews 84; Ed&PubIntYB 82*
White Dot Press - Baltimore, MD - *BoPubDir 4, 5; LitMag&SmPr 83-84*
White Dwarf Music - New York, NY - *BillIntBG 83-84*
White Eagle Publisher - Lowell, MA - *ArtMar 84; BoPubDir 5*
White Editions, Stephen - Los Angeles, CA - *BoPubDir 4 Sup, 5*
White, Eugene V. - Berryville, VA - *BoPubDir 4, 5*
White Ewe Press - Adelphi, MD - *BoPubDir 4, 5; LitMag&SmPr 83-84*
White Films, Ruth - Los Angeles, CA - *ArtMar 84; AvMarPl 83*
White, Good & Co. - Mt. Gretna, PA - *AdAge 3-28-84; StaDirAdAg 2-84*

White Hall North Greene News - White Hall, IL - *BaconPubCkNews 84*
White House Cablevision [of Durborow Communications] - White House, TN - *Tel&CabFB 84C*
White House Historical Association - Washington, DC - *BoPubDir 4, 5*
White Inc., David - Port Washington, NY - *LitMarPl 83, 84*
White Instruments Inc. - Austin, TX - *AvMarPl 83*
White, Jan V. - Westport, CT - *MagIndMarPl 82-83*
White, John A. - Millbrae, CA - *BoPubDir 4, 5*
White, John C. - Upper McVeigh, KY - *BrCabYB 84*
White Lake Aurora County Standard - White Lake, SD - *BaconPubCkNews 84*
White Lake Spinal Column Newsweekly - *See* Spinal Column Newsweekly
White Laker Observer - Montague, MI - *AyerDirPub 83; Ed&PubIntYB 82*
White Leader - White, SD - *Ed&PubIntYB 82*
White Mountain Independent [of White Mountain Publishing Co.] - Show Low, AZ - *NewsDir 84*
White Mountain Independent - St. Johns, AZ - *Ed&PubIntYB 82*
White Mountain Independent Navajo & Apache Counties - Show Low, AZ - *AyerDirPub 83*
White Mountain Publishing Co. - Phoenix, AZ - *LitMag&SmPr 83-84*
White Pine Journal - Buffalo, NY - *LitMag&SmPr 83-84*
White Pine Press - Buffalo, NY - *BoPubDir 4, 5; LitMag&SmPr 83-84*
White Plains Reporter-Dispatch [of Westchester Rockland Newspapers Inc.] - White Plains, NY - *AyerDirPub 83; BaconPubCkNews 84; Ed&PubIntYB 82; NewsDir 84*
White Productions, Leo - Westwood, MA - *Ed&PubIntYB 82*
White Productions, Ted - Richmond, VA - *LitMarPl 83*
White Publishing, Don - Philadelphia, PA - *BillIntBG 83-84*
White River Journal - Des Arc, AR - *AyerDirPub 83; Ed&PubIntYB 82*
White River Mellette County News - White River, SD - *BaconPubCkNews 84*
White River News - Hazelton, IN - *AyerDirPub 83*
White River Valley Herald - Randolph, VT - *AyerDirPub 83; Ed&PubIntYB 82*
White Rock & Surrey Sun - White Rock, BC, Canada - *Ed&PubIntYB 82*
White Rock Cablevision Ltd. - Surrey, BC, Canada - *BrCabYB 84*
White Rock Records Inc. - Scranton, PA - *BillIntBG 83-84*
White Rocker News - Dallas, TX - *AyerDirPub 83*
White Rocker, The - Dallas, TX - *Ed&PubIntYB 82*
White Rose AAA Traveler - York, PA - *BaconPubCkMag 84*
White Salmon Enterprise - White Salmon, WA - *BaconPubCkNews 84; Ed&PubIntYB 82*
White Sands Cable Co. - White Sands, NM - *BrCabYB 84; Tel&CabFB 84C*
White Sands Missile Ranger - Las Cruces, NM - *AyerDirPub 83*
White Settlement Bomber News [of Suburban Newspapers Inc.] - Ft. Worth, TX - *AyerDirPub 83; NewsDir 84*
White Settlement Bomber News, The - White Settlement, TX - *Ed&PubIntYB 82*
White Settlement News - *See* Suburban Newspapers Inc.
White Star Professional Film Services Inc. - Lansing, MI - *AvMarPl 83*
White Stetson Music - *See* Americus Music
White Sulphur Springs Meagher County News - White Sulphur Springs, MT - *BaconPubCkNews 84*
White Sulphur Springs Star - White Sulphur Springs, WV - *Ed&PubIntYB 82*
White Tower Inc. Press [Aff. of White Tower Inc.] - Los Angeles, CA - *BoPubDir 4, 5; LitMag&SmPr 83-84*
White Urp Press - Columbia, MD - *LitMag&SmPr 83-84*
White Walls - Chicago, IL - *LitMag&SmPr 83-84*
Whitebrook Books - Easthampton, MA - *BoPubDir 4, 5*
Whitecap Books Ltd. - North Vancouver, BC, Canada - *BoPubDir 4, 5*
Whitecourt Star, The - Whitecourt, AB, Canada - *Ed&PubIntYB 82*
Whitefish Bay Herald - Oak Creek, WI - *AyerDirPub 83*
Whitefish Bay Herald - *See* Community Newspapers Inc.
Whitefish Pilot - Whitefish, MT - *AyerDirPub 83; BaconPubCkNews 84; Ed&PubIntYB 82*
Whiteford International Enterprise [Aff. of Foreign Services Research Institute/Wheat Forder's Press] - Washington, DC - *BoPubDir 4*
Whitehall Co. - Wheeling, IL - *LitMarPl 83*
Whitehall Composition Inc. - Whitehall, PA - *LitMarPl 83, 84*
Whitehall Times - Whitehall, NY - *BaconPubCkNews 84; Ed&PubIntYB 82; NewsDir 84*
Whitehall Times - Whitehall, WI - *BaconPubCkNews 84; Ed&PubIntYB 82*
Whitehall Tribune [of Reynoldsburg Reporter] - Reynoldsburg, OH - *NewsDir 84*
Whitehaven Press - Memphis, TN - *AyerDirPub 83*
Whitehead Cinek Corp. - Long Island City, NY - *AvMarPl 83*
Whitehead, Kenneth D. - New Rochelle, NY - *LitMarPl 83, 84*
Whitehead, Titherington & Bowyer Ltd. - *See* W.T. & B. Advertising Ltd.
Whitehill Inc., Robert - New York, NY - *StaDirAdAg 2-84*
Whitehouse & Associates, Alton - Jacksonville, FL - *Tel&CabFB 84C*
Whitehouse Station Hunterdon Review [of Recorder Publishing Co.] - Whitehouse Station, NJ - *NewsDir 84*
Whitehouse Station Hunterdon Review - *See* Recorder Publishing Co.
Whiteley, Albert S. - Ottawa, ON, Canada - *BoPubDir 4, 5*
Whitemyer Advertising Inc. - Zoar, OH - *StaDirAdAg 2-84*
White's Advertising Agency - Sweet Home, OR - *StaDirAdAg 2-84*
White's TV Cable - McVeigh, KY - *Tel&CabFB 84C*
Whitesboro News-Record - Whitesboro, TX - *BaconPubCkNews 84*
Whitesburg Mountain Eagle - Whitesburg, KY - *BaconPubCkNews 84; Ed&PubIntYB 82; NewsDir 84*
Whiteside Associates Inc. - Decatur, GA - *ADAPSOMemDir 83-84*
Whiteside News Sentinel - Morrison, IL - *AyerDirPub 83; Ed&PubIntYB 82*
Whiteside Shopper [of Fulton Press Inc.] - Fulton, IL - *AyerDirPub 83; NewsDir 84*
Whitesmiths Ltd. - Concord, MA - *MicrocomMPl 84*
Whitesmiths Ltd. - Iselin, NJ - *MicrocomMPl 83*
Whitestone Ad World - Great Neck, NY - *AyerDirPub 83*
Whitestone Pennysaver - Jericho, NY - *AyerDirPub 83*
Whitestown Cablevision [of Quality CATV Inc.] - Whitestown, IN - *BrCabYB 84*
Whiteville News Reporter - Whiteville, NC - *BaconPubCkNews 84; NewsDir 84*
Whitewater Publications Inc. - Brookville, IN - *BaconPubCkNews 84*
Whitewater Register - Whitewater, WI - *BaconPubCkNews 84; Ed&PubIntYB 82*
Whitewing Music - *See* Jamil Music
Whitewood Centennial - Whitewood, SD - *AyerDirPub 83; Ed&PubIntYB 82*
Whitewood Centennial - *See* Allison Publishing
Whitewright Sun - Whitewright, TX - *BaconPubCkNews 84; Ed&PubIntYB 82*
Whitfield Books - Pleasant Hill, CA - *BoPubDir 4, 5*
Whitford Inc., K. Grant - Staten Island, NY - *DirPRFirms 83*
Whiting Inc., Donald E. - Deerfield, IL - *StaDirAdAg 2-84*
Whiting Paper Co., George A. - Menasha, WI - *LitMarPl 83, 84*
Whitinsville Blackstone Valley Tribune - Whitinsville, MA - *BaconPubCkNews 84*
Whitley City McCreary County Record - Whitley City, KY - *BaconPubCkNews 84*
Whitley Republican - Williamsburg, KY - *AyerDirPub 83*
Whitley Republican, The - Whitley, KY - *Ed&PubIntYB 82*
Whitman & Co., Albert - Niles, IL - *ArtMar 84; LitMarPl 83, 84*
Whitman Association, Walt - Camden, NJ - *BoPubDir 4*
Whitman Association, Walt - Haddonfield, NJ - *BoPubDir 5*
Whitman Bagged Comics - New York, NY - *MagIndMarPl 82-83*
Whitman Bowen Keller & Greco - Monterey, CA - *StaDirAdAg 2-84*
Whitman Golden Ltd. [Subs. of Western Publishing Inc.] - Cambridge, ON, Canada - *LitMarPl 84*
Whitman Golden Ltd. [Subs. of Wester Publishing Inc.] - Galt, ON, Canada - *LitMarPl 83*

Whitman-Latah Record - Palouse, WA - *AyerDirPub 83; Ed&PubIntYB 82*
Whitman Products Ltd. [Subs. of Preco Corp.] - West Warwick, RI - *LitMarPl 83, 84*
Whitman Times [of Hanover Franklin Publishing Co.] - Hanover, MA - *NewsDir 84*
Whitman Times - Whitman, MA - *Ed&PubIntYB 82*
Whitman Times - *See* Bulletin Publishing Co.
Whitman TV Cable Inc. - Albany, OH - *BrCabYB 84*
Whitmark Associates - Dallas, TX - *BoPubDir 5*
Whitmire News - Whitmire, SC - *BaconPubCkNews 84; Ed&PubIntYB 82*
Whitmore Publishing Co. - Ardmore, PA - *BoPubDir 4, 5; LitMag&SmPr 83-84*
Whitmore, Richard L. - Athens, OH - *Tel&CabFB 84C p.1713*
Whitmore TV Cable - Amesville, OH - *BrCabYB 84*
Whitmore TV Cable - *See* Whitmore, Richard L.
Whitmore TV Cable Inc. - Albany, OH - *Tel&CabFB 84C*
Whitney & Associates Cablevision, R. - Lucasville, OH - *BrCabYB 84*
Whitney & Associates Cablevision, R. - Piketon, OH - *BrCabYB 84*
Whitney & Whitney Inc. - Irvington, NY - *LitMarPl 83, 84; StaDirAdAg 2-84*
Whitney Cable TV - Piketon, OH - *Tel&CabFB 84C*
Whitney Cablevision of Indiana Inc. - Santa Claus, IN - *Tel&CabFB 84C*
Whitney Cablevision of Indiana Inc. - *See* Whitney, Richard L.
Whitney Cablevision of Michigan - West Branch, MI - *BrCabYB 84*
Whitney Cablevision of Michigan - *See* Whitney, Richard L.
Whitney Communications Corp. - New York, NY - *KnowInd 83; MagIndMarPl 82-83*
Whitney Communications Corp. (Magazine Div.) - New York, NY - *DirMarMP 83*
Whitney Eckstein Kiel Inc. - New York, NY - *LitMarPl 83, 84*
Whitney Library of Design, The [of Watson-Guptill Publications] - New York, NY - *LitMarPl 83, 84*
Whitney Messenger - Whitney, TX - *BaconPubCkNews 84; Ed&PubIntYB 82*
Whitney Museum of American Art - New York, NY - *BoPubDir 4, 5*
Whitney, Richard L. - Piketon, OH - *Tel&CabFB 84C p.1713*
Whitney Star - Clifton, TX - *BaconPubCkNews 84*
Whitney Star - Whitney, TX - *Ed&PubIntYB 82*
Whitston Publishing Co. - Troy, NY - *LitMarPl 83, 84; WritMar 84*
Whittell Memorial Press, George [Aff. of Animal Charity of Ohio] - Youngstown, OH - *BoPubDir 5; LitMag&SmPr 83-84*
Whittemore Champion - Whittemore, IA - *BaconPubCkNews 84; Ed&PubIntYB 82*
Whitten Broadcasting Co. - Navasota, TX - *BrCabYB 84*
Whittet & Shepperson - Richmond, VA - *LitMarPl 83, 84*
Whittier Daily News [of San Gabriel Valley Tribune Inc.] - Whittier, CA - *BaconPubCkNews 84; NewsDir 84*
Whittier East Whittier Review - Whittier, CA - *NewsDir 84*
Whittier Telephone Co. - Anchorage, AK - *TelDir&BG 83-84*
Whittier Weekly Journal - Whittier, CA - *Ed&PubIntYB 82*
Whittier West Independent - *See* Southern California Publishing Co.
Whittier West Pico Rivera Highlander - *See* Highlander Publications Inc.
Whittle Business Brokerage - Raleigh, NC - *CabTVFinDB 83*
Whittlesey & Associates - West Chester, PA - *IntDirMarRes 83*
WHIY - Moulton, AL - *BrCabYB 84; TV&RadDir 84*
WHIZ - Zanesville, OH - *BrCabYB 84; NatRadPubDir Summer 83, Spring 84; TV&RadDir 84*
WHIZ-FM - Zanesville, OH - *BrCabYB 84; NatRadPubDir Summer 83, Spring 84; TV&RadDir 84*
WHIZ-TV - Zanesville, OH - *BrCabYB 84; DirUSTelSta 83; TelAl 83, 84; Tel&CabFB 84S; TV&RadDir 84*
Whizeagle Records - Portland, OR - *BillIntBG 83-84*
WHJB - Greensburg, PA - *BrCabYB 84; TV&RadDir 84*
WHJC - Matewan, WV - *BrCabYB 84; TV&RadDir 84*
WHJE-FM - Carmel, IN - *BrCabYB 84; TV&RadDir 84*
WHJJ - East Providence, RI - *BrCabYB 84; NatRadPubDir Summer 83, Spring 84*
WHJJ-FM - East Providence, RI - *TV&RadDir 84*
WHJT-FM - Clinton, MS - *BrCabYB 84; NatRadPubDir Summer 83, Spring 84*
WHJT-FM - Conehatta, MS - *TV&RadDir 84*
WHJY-FM - East Providence, RI - *BrCabYB 84; NatRadPubDir Summer 83, Spring 84; TV&RadDir 84*
WHK - Cleveland, OH - *BrCabYB 84; LitMarPl 83, 84; NatRadPubDir Summer 83, Spring 84; TV&RadDir 84*
WHKC-FM - Henderson, KY - *BrCabYB 84; TV&RadDir 84*
WHKK-FM - Erlanger, KY - *BrCabYB 84; TV&RadDir 84*
WHKP - Hendersonville, NC - *BrCabYB 84; TV&RadDir 84*
WHKW-FM - Fayette, AL - *BrCabYB 84; TV&RadDir 84*
WHKY - Hickory, NC - *BrCabYB 84; TV&RadDir 84*
WHKY-FM - Hickory, NC - *BrCabYB 84; TV&RadDir 84*
WHKY-TV - Hickory, NC - *BrCabYB 84; DirUSTelSta 83; TelAl 83, 84; Tel&CabFB 84S; TV&RadDir 84*
WHLA-FM - La Crosse, WI - *BrCabYB 84; NatRadPubDir Summer 83 p.326, Spring 84 p.328*
WHLA-TV - La Crosse, WI - *BrCabYB 84; Tel&CabFB 84S*
WHLA-TV - Menomonie, WI - *TV&RadDir 84*
WHLB-FM - Virginia, MN - *BrCabYB 84*
WHLD - Grand Island, NY - *TV&RadDir 84*
WHLD - Niagara Falls, NY - *BrCabYB 84*
WHLF - South Boston, VA - *BrCabYB 84; TV&RadDir 84*
WHLG-FM - Jensen Beach, FL - *BrCabYB 84*
WHLG-FM - Stuart, FL - *TV&RadDir 84*
WHLI - Hempstead, NY - *BrCabYB 84; LitMarPl 83, 84; TV&RadDir 84*
WHLI - Nassau County, Long Island, NY - *NatRadPubDir Summer 83 p.171, Spring 84 p.169*
WHLM - Bloomsburg, PA - *BrCabYB 84; TV&RadDir 84*
WHLM-FM - Bloomsburg, PA - *BrCabYB 84; TV&RadDir 84*
WHLN - Harlan, KY - *BrCabYB 84; TV&RadDir 84*
WHLO - Akron, OH - *BrCabYB 84; LitMarPl 83, 84; NatRadPubDir Summer 83, Spring 84; TV&RadDir 84*
WHLP - Centerville, TN - *BrCabYB 84; TV&RadDir 84*
WHLP-FM - Centerville, TN - *BrCabYB 84; TV&RadDir 84*
WHLS - Port Huron, MI - *BrCabYB 84; TV&RadDir 84*
WHLT - Huntington, IN - *BrCabYB 84; TV&RadDir 84*
WHLT-FM - Huntington, IN - *TV&RadDir 84*
WHLX - Bethlehem, WV - *BrCabYB 84*
WHLY-FM - Leesburg, FL - *BrCabYB 84*
WHLY-FM - Orlando, FL - *TV&RadDir 84*
WHMA - Anniston, AL - *BrCabYB 84; NatRadPubDir Summer 83, Spring 84; TV&RadDir 84*
WHMA-FM - Anniston, AL - *BrCabYB 84; NatRadPubDir Summer 83, Spring 84; TV&RadDir 84*
WHMA-TV - Anniston, AL - *BrCabYB 84; DirUSTelSta 83; TelAl 83, 84; Tel&CabFB 84S; TV&RadDir 84*
WHMB-TV - Indianapolis, IN - *BrCabYB 84; DirUSTelSta 83; TelAl 83, 84; Tel&CabFB 84S; TV&RadDir 84*
WHMC - Conway, SC - *BrCabYB 84; Tel&CabFB 84S*
WHMD-FM - Hammond, LA - *BrCabYB 84; TV&RadDir 84*
WHME-FM - South Bend, IN - *BrCabYB 84; NatRadPubDir Summer 83, Spring 84; TV&RadDir 84*
WHME-TV - South Bend, IN - *BrCabYB 84; DirUSTelSta 83; TelAl 83, 84; Tel&CabFB 84S; TV&RadDir 84*
WHMH-FM - Sauk Rapids, MN - *BrCabYB 84*
WHMI - Howell, MI - *BrCabYB 84; TV&RadDir 84*
WHMI-FM - Howell, MI - *BrCabYB 84; TV&RadDir 84*
WHMM-TV - Washington, DC - *BrCabYB 84; Tel&CabFB 84S; TV&RadDir 84*
WHMP - Northampton, MA - *BrCabYB 84; TV&RadDir 84*
WHMP-FM - Northampton, MA - *BrCabYB 84; TV&RadDir 84*
WHMQ-FM - Findlay, OH - *BrCabYB 84; NatRadPubDir Summer 83, Spring 84; TV&RadDir 84*
WHMT - Humboldt, TN - *BrCabYB 84; TV&RadDir 84*
WHN - New York, NY - *BrCabYB 84; LitMarPl 83, 84; NatRadPubDir Summer 83, Spring 84; TV&RadDir 84*
WHNC - Henderson, NC - *BrCabYB 84; TV&RadDir 84*
WHND - Birmingham, MI - *TV&RadDir 84*
WHND - Detroit, MI - *NatRadPubDir Summer 83, Spring 84*
WHND - Monroe, MI - *BrCabYB 84; NatRadPubDir Summer 83, Spring 84*
WHNE - Cumming, GA - *BrCabYB 84; TV&RadDir 84*
WHNI - Mebane, NC - *BrCabYB 84; TV&RadDir 84*
WHNN-FM - Bay City, MI - *BrCabYB 84*

WHNN-FM - Saginaw, MI - *NatRadPubDir Summer 83, Spring 84; TV&RadDir 84*
WHNS-TV - Asheville, NC - *BrCabYB 84; TelAl 83, 84; Tel&CabFB 84S*
WHNT-TV - Huntsville, AL - *BrCabYB 84; DirUSTelSta 83; TelAl 83, 84; Tel&CabFB 84S; TV&RadDir 84*
WHNY - McComb, MS - *BrCabYB 84; TV&RadDir 84*
WHO - Des Moines, IA - *BrCabYB 84; NatRadPubDir Summer 83, Spring 84; TV&RadDir 84*
WHO Collaborating Center for International Drug Monitoring [of World Health Organization] - Uppsala, Sweden - *EISS 83*
Who Houston Inc. [Aff. of Who Publishing Co.] - Houston, TX - *BoPubDir 4*
Who Publishing Co. Inc. - Houston, TX - *BoPubDir 5*
WHO-TV - Des Moines, IA - *BrCabYB 84; DirUSTelSta 83; TelAl 83, 84; Tel&CabFB 84S; TV&RadDir 84*
WHOA - San Juan, PR - *BrCabYB 84*
WHOC - Philadelphia, MS - *BrCabYB 84; TV&RadDir 84*
WHOD - Jackson, AL - *BrCabYB 84; TV&RadDir 84*
WHOD-FM - Jackson, AL - *BrCabYB 84; TV&RadDir 84*
WHOG - Fernandina Beach, FL - *BrCabYB 84; TV&RadDir 84*
WHOK-FM - Lancaster, OH - *BrCabYB 84; TV&RadDir 84*
WHOL - Allentown, PA - *BrCabYB 84; NatRadPubDir Summer 83, Spring 84; TV&RadDir 84*
Whole Again Resource Guide [of SourceNet] - Santa Barbara, CA - *LitMag&SmPr 83-84*
Whole Foods - Santa Ana, CA - *BaconPubCkMag 84; WritMar 84*
Whole Person Associates Inc. - Duluth, MN - *BoPubDir 4, 5*
Whole World Publishing Inc. - Deerfield, IL - *BoPubDir 4 Sup, 5*
Wholesale Drugs - Indianapolis, IN - *BaconPubCkMag 84; MagDir 84; WritMar 84*
Wholesale Educational Suppliers Co. - Mt. Vernon, NY - *AvMarPl 83*
Wholesaler, The [of Scott Periodicals Corp.] - Elmhurst, IL - *BaconPubCkMag 84; MagDir 84*
Wholesome Film Center Inc. - Boston, MA - *AvMarPl 83*
Wholesome Press - Calgary, AB, Canada - *BoPubDir 4, 5*
WHOM-FM - Portland, ME - *NatRadPubDir Summer 83, Spring 84; TV&RadDir 84*
WHOM-FM - Mt. Washington, NH - *BrCabYB 84*
WHON - Centerville, IN - *BrCabYB 84*
WHON - Richmond, IN - *TV&RadDir 84*
WHOO - Orlando, FL - *BrCabYB 84; NatRadPubDir Summer 83, Spring 84; TV&RadDir 84*
WHOO-FM - Orlando, FL - *BrCabYB 84; NatRadPubDir Summer 83, Spring 84; TV&RadDir 84*
WHOP - Hopkinsville, KY - *BrCabYB 84; TV&RadDir 84*
WHOP-FM - Hopkinsville, KY - *BrCabYB 84; TV&RadDir 84*
WHOS - Decatur, AL - *BrCabYB 84; TV&RadDir 84*
Who's Who Historical Society - San Clemente, CA - *BoPubDir 4, 5*
Who's Who in Black Corporate America - Washington, DC - *BoPubDir 4 Sup, 5*
Who's Who in Electronics [of Harris Publishing Co.] - Twinsburg, OH - *MagDir 84*
WHOT - Campbell, OH - *BrCabYB 84*
WHOT - Youngstown, OH - *TV&RadDir 84*
WHOU - Houlton, ME - *BrCabYB 84; TV&RadDir 84*
WHOU-FM - Houlton, ME - *BrCabYB 84; TV&RadDir 84*
WHOV-FM - Hampton, VA - *BrCabYB 84; NatRadPubDir Summer 83, Spring 84; TV&RadDir 84*
WHOW - Clinton, IL - *BrCabYB 84; TV&RadDir 84*
WHOW-FM - Clinton, IL - *BrCabYB 84; TV&RadDir 84*
WHOY - Salinas, PR - *BrCabYB 84*
WHP - Harrisburg, PA - *BrCabYB 84; NatRadPubDir Summer 83, Spring 84; TV&RadDir 84*
WHP-FM - Harrisburg, PA - *BrCabYB 84; NatRadPubDir Summer 83, Spring 84; TV&RadDir 84*
WHP-TV - Harrisburg, PA - *BrCabYB 84; DirUSTelSta 83; LitMarPl 83, 84; TelAl 83, 84; Tel&CabFB 84S; TV&RadDir 84*
WHPA-FM - Hollidaysburg, PA - *BrCabYB 84; TV&RadDir 84*
WHPB - Belton, SC - *BrCabYB 84; TV&RadDir 84*
WHPC-FM - Garden City, NY - *BrCabYB 84; TV&RadDir 84*
WHPE-FM - High Point, NC - *BrCabYB 84; NatRadPubDir Summer 83, Spring 84; TV&RadDir 84*
WHPH-FM - Hanover, NJ - *BrCabYB 84; NatRadPubDir Summer 83, Spring 84; TV&RadDir 84*
WHPH-FM - Charleston, WV - *NatRadPubDir Summer 83, Spring 84*
WHPI - Herrin, IL - *BrCabYB 84; TV&RadDir 84*
WHPK-FM - Chicago, IL - *BrCabYB 84; NatRadPubDir Summer 83, Spring 84; TV&RadDir 84*
WHPO-FM - Hooperston, IL - *BrCabYB 84*
WHPR-FM - Highland Park, MI - *BrCabYB 84; NatRadPubDir Summer 83, Spring 84; TV&RadDir 84*
WHPW-FM - Charleston, WV - *TV&RadDir 84*
WHPW-FM - Huntington, WV - *BrCabYB 84*
WHPY - Clayton, NC - *BrCabYB 84; TV&RadDir 84*
WHRB-FM - Cambridge, MA - *BrCabYB 84; NatRadPubDir Summer 83, Spring 84; TV&RadDir 84*
WHRC - Haverford, PA - *NatRadPubDir Summer 83, Spring 84*
WHRC-FM - Port Henry, NY - *BrCabYB 84*
WHRF - Bel Air, MD - *BrCabYB 84*
WHRK - Memphis, TN - *BrCabYB 84*
WHRK-FM - Memphis, TN - *NatRadPubDir Summer 83, Spring 84; TV&RadDir 84*
WHRL-FM - Albany, NY - *BrCabYB 84; NatRadPubDir Summer 83, Spring 84; TV&RadDir 84*
WHRM-FM - Wausau, WI - *BrCabYB 84; NatRadPubDir Spring 84 p.329*
WHRM-TV - Green Bay, WI - *TV&RadDir 84*
WHRM-TV - Wausau, WI - *BrCabYB 84; Tel&CabFB 84S*
WHRO-FM - Norfolk, VA - *BrCabYB 84; NatRadPubDir Summer 83, Spring 84; TV&RadDir 84*
WHRO-TV - Hampton, VA - *BrCabYB 84; Tel&CabFB 84S*
WHRO-TV - Norfolk, VA - *TV&RadDir 84*
WHRS-FM - Boynton Beach, FL - *BrCabYB 84; TV&RadDir 84*
WHRS-TV - West Palm Beach, FL - *BrCabYB 84; Tel&CabFB 84S*
WHRT - Hartselle, AL - *BrCabYB 84; TV&RadDir 84*
WHRW-FM - Binghamton, NY - *BrCabYB 84; NatRadPubDir Summer 83, Spring 84; TV&RadDir 84*
WHRZ-FM - Providence, KY - *BrCabYB 84; TV&RadDir 84*
WHSA-FM - Brule, WI - *BrCabYB 84; NatRadPubDir Summer 83 p.325, Spring 84 p.327*
WHSB-FM - Alpena, MI - *BrCabYB 84; TV&RadDir 84*
WHSC - Hartsville, SC - *BrCabYB 84; TV&RadDir 84*
WHSD-FM - Hinsdale, IL - *BrCabYB 84; TV&RadDir 84*
WHSI - Portland, ME - *BrCabYB 84; Tel&CabFB 84S*
WHSK - Kokomo, IN - *BrCabYB 84*
WHSL-FM - Wilmington, NC - *BrCabYB 84; NatRadPubDir Summer 83; TV&RadDir 84*
WHSM - Hayward, WI - *BrCabYB 84; TV&RadDir 84*
WHSN-FM - Bangor, ME - *BrCabYB 84; NatRadPubDir Summer 83, Spring 84; TV&RadDir 84*
WHSP-FM - Fairhope, AL - *TV&RadDir 84*
WHSR-FM - Winchester, MA - *BrCabYB 84; TV&RadDir 84*
WHSS-FM - Hamilton, OH - *BrCabYB 84; NatRadPubDir Summer 83, Spring 84; TV&RadDir 84*
WHSV-TV - Harrisonburg, VA - *BrCabYB 84; DirUSTelSta 83; TelAl 83, 84; Tel&CabFB 84S; TV&RadDir 84*
WHSY - Hattiesburg, MS - *BrCabYB 84; NatRadPubDir Summer 83, Spring 84; TV&RadDir 84*
WHSY-FM - Hattiesburg, MS - *BrCabYB 84; NatRadPubDir Summer 83, Spring 84; TV&RadDir 84*
WHTB-FM - Talladega, AL - *BrCabYB 84; TV&RadDir 84*
WHTC - Holland, MI - *BrCabYB 84; NatRadPubDir Summer 83, Spring 84; TV&RadDir 84*
WHTC-FM - Holland, MI - *BrCabYB 84; TV&RadDir 84*
WHTF-FM - Starview, PA - *BrCabYB 84*
WHTF-FM - York, PA - *NatRadPubDir Spring 84*
WHTG - Asbury Park, NJ - *TV&RadDir 84*
WHTG - Eatontown, NJ - *BrCabYB 84*
WHTG-FM - Asbury Park, NJ - *TV&RadDir 84*
WHTG-FM - Eatontown, NJ - *BrCabYB 84*
WHTH - Heath, OH - *BrCabYB 84*
WHTH - Newark, OH - *TV&RadDir 84*
WHTI - Rocky Mount, VA - *BrCabYB 84*
WHTL-FM - Whitehall, WI - *BrCabYB 84*
WHTM-TV - Harrisburg, PA - *BrCabYB 84; DirUSTelSta 83; LitMarPl 83, 84; Tel&CabFB 84S; TV&RadDir 84*

WHTN - Huntington, WV - *NatRadPubDir Summer 83; TV&RadDir 84*
WHTT - Miami, FL - *TV&RadDir 84*
WHTT-FM - Boston, MA - *BrCabYB 84; NatRadPubDir Summer 83, Spring 84*
WHTV-TV - Laurel, MS - *TelAl 83, 84*
WHTV-TV - Meridian, MS - *BrCabYB 84; DirUSTelSta 83; Tel&CabFB 84S; TV&RadDir 84*
WHTX-FM - Pittsburgh, PA - *BrCabYB 84; NatRadPubDir Summer 83, Spring 84*
WHTZ - Mt. Dora, FL - *TV&RadDir 84*
WHTZ-FM - Newark, NJ - *BrCabYB 84*
WHUB - Cookeville, TN - *BrCabYB 84; TV&RadDir 84*
WHUB-FM - Cookeville, TN - *BrCabYB 84; TV&RadDir 84*
WHUC - Hudson, NY - *BrCabYB 84; TV&RadDir 84*
WHUD-FM - Peekskill, NY - *BrCabYB 84; TV&RadDir 84*
WHUD-FM - Westchester County, NY - *NatRadPubDir Summer 83 p.180, Spring 84 p.178*
WHUE - Boston, MA - *BrCabYB 84; NatRadPubDir Summer 83, Spring 84; TV&RadDir 84*
WHUE-FM - Boston, MA - *BrCabYB 84; NatRadPubDir Summer 83, Spring 84; TV&RadDir 84*
WHUF - Rochester, NY - *TelAl 84*
WHUG-FM - Jamestown, NY - *BrCabYB 84; TV&RadDir 84*
WHUH-FM - Houghton, MI - *BrCabYB 84; TV&RadDir 84*
WHUM - Reading, PA - *BrCabYB 84; NatRadPubDir Summer 83, Spring 84; TV&RadDir 84*
WHUN - Huntingdon, PA - *BrCabYB 84; TV&RadDir 84*
WHUR-FM - Washington, DC - *BrCabYB 84; NatRadPubDir Summer 83, Spring 84; TV&RadDir 84*
WHUS-FM - Storrs, CT - *BrCabYB 84; NatRadPubDir Summer 83, Spring 84; TV&RadDir 84*
WHUT - Anderson, IN - *BrCabYB 84; NatRadPubDir Summer 83, Spring 84; TV&RadDir 84*
WHUZ - Huntington, IN - *BrCabYB 84*
WHVL - Hendersonville, NC - *BrCabYB 84; TV&RadDir 84*
WHVN - Charlotte, NC - *BrCabYB 84; NatRadPubDir Summer 83, Spring 84*
WHVN - Derita, NC - *TV&RadDir 84*
WHVR - Hanover, PA - *BrCabYB 84; TV&RadDir 84*
WHVW - Hyde Park, NY - *BrCabYB 84*
WHVW - Poughkeepsie, NY - *TV&RadDir 84*
WHWB - Rutland, VT - *BrCabYB 84; NatRadPubDir Summer 83, Spring 84; TV&RadDir 84*
WHWB-FM - Rutland, VT - *BrCabYB 84; NatRadPubDir Summer 83, Spring 84*
WHWC-TV - Menomonie, WI - *BrCabYB 84; Tel&CabFB 84S*
WHWE-FM - Howe, IN - *BrCabYB 84; NatRadPubDir Summer 83, Spring 84; TV&RadDir 84*
WHWH - Princeton, NJ - *BrCabYB 84; NatRadPubDir Summer 83, Spring 84; TV&RadDir 84*
WHWL - Marquette, MI - *BrCabYB 84*
WHYD - Columbus, GA - *BrCabYB 84; NatRadPubDir Summer 83, Spring 84; TV&RadDir 84*
WHYH-FM - Braddock, PA - *BrCabYB 84*
WHYI-FM - Ft. Lauderdale, FL - *BrCabYB 84; NatRadPubDir Summer 83, Spring 84 p.57*
WHYI-FM - Hollywood, FL - *TV&RadDir 84*
WHYL - Carlisle, PA - *BrCabYB 84; NatRadPubDir Summer 83, Spring 84; TV&RadDir 84*
WHYL-FM - Carlisle, PA - *BrCabYB 84; NatRadPubDir Spring 84; TV&RadDir 84*
WHYM - Pensacola, FL - *BrCabYB 84; TV&RadDir 84*
WHYN - Springfield, MA - *BrCabYB 84; NatRadPubDir Summer 83, Spring 84; TV&RadDir 84*
WHYN-FM - Springfield, MA - *BrCabYB 84; NatRadPubDir Summer 83, Spring 84; TV&RadDir 84*
WHYP - North East, PA - *BrCabYB 84; TV&RadDir 84*
WHYP-FM - North East, PA - *BrCabYB 84; TV&RadDir 84*
WHYT-FM - Detroit, MI - *BrCabYB 84; LitMarPl 84; TV&RadDir 84*
WHYW - Braddock, PA - *LitMarPl 83, 84; TV&RadDir 84*
WHYW-FM - Braddock, PA - *LitMarPl 83; TV&RadDir 84*
WHYY-FM - Philadelphia, PA - *BrCabYB 84*
WHYY-TV - Wilmington, DE - *BrCabYB 84; Tel&CabFB 84S; TV&RadDir 84*
WHYY-TV - Philadelphia, PA - *DirUSTelSta 83; TV&RadDir 84*
WHYZ - Greenville, SC - *BrCabYB 84; NatRadPubDir Summer 83, Spring 84; TV&RadDir 84*
WIAA-FM - Interlochen, MI - *BrCabYB 84; NatRadPubDir Summer 83, Spring 84*
WIAC-FM - San Juan, PR - *BrCabYB 84*
WIAF - Clarkesville, GA - *BrCabYB 84; TV&RadDir 84*
WIAI-FM - Danville, IL - *BrCabYB 84; TV&RadDir 84*
WIAL-FM - Eau Claire, WI - *BrCabYB 84; NatRadPubDir Summer 83, Spring 84; TV&RadDir 84*
WIAM - Williamston, NC - *BrCabYB 84; TV&RadDir 84*
WIAN-FM - Indianapolis, IN - *BrCabYB 84; NatRadPubDir Summer 83, Spring 84; TV&RadDir 84*
Wiarton Echo, The - Wiarton, ON, Canada - *Ed&PubIntYB 82*
WIBA - Madison, WI - *BrCabYB 84; NatRadPubDir Summer 83, Spring 84; TV&RadDir 84*
WIBA-FM - Madison, WI - *BrCabYB 84; NatRadPubDir Summer 83, Spring 84; TV&RadDir 84*
Wibaux Cable TV - Wibaux, MT - *BrCabYB 84*
Wibaux Pioneer Gazette - Wibaux, MT - *BaconPubCkNews 84; Ed&PubIntYB 82*
WIBB - Macon, GA - *BrCabYB 84; NatRadPubDir Summer 83, Spring 84; TV&RadDir 84*
WIBC - Indianapolis, IN - *BrCabYB 84; NatRadPubDir Summer 83, Spring 84; TV&RadDir 84*
WIBF-FM - Jenkintown, PA - *BrCabYB 84; TV&RadDir 84*
WIBG - Ocean City, NJ - *BrCabYB 84; TV&RadDir 84*
WIBI-FM - Carlinville, IL - *BrCabYB 84; TV&RadDir 84*
WIBM-FM - Jackson, MI - *BrCabYB 84; NatRadPubDir Summer 83, Spring 84; TV&RadDir 84*
WIBN - Worcester, MA - *BrCabYB 84*
WIBQ-FM - Utica, NY - *BrCabYB 84; NatRadPubDir Summer 83, Spring 84; TV&RadDir 84*
WIBR - Baton Rouge, LA - *BrCabYB 84; NatRadPubDir Summer 83, Spring 84; TV&RadDir 84*
WIBS - Charlotte Amalie, VI - *BrCabYB 84*
WIBU - Madison, WI - *TV&RadDir 84*
WIBU - Poynette, WI - *BrCabYB 84*
WIBV - Belleville, IL - *BrCabYB 84; NatRadPubDir Summer 83, Spring 84; TV&RadDir 84*
WIBW - Topeka, KS - *BrCabYB 84; NatRadPubDir Summer 83, Spring 84; TV&RadDir 84*
WIBW-FM - Topeka, KS - *BrCabYB 84; NatRadPubDir Summer 83, Spring 84; TV&RadDir 84*
WIBW-TV - Topeka, KS - *BrCabYB 84; DirUSTelSta 83; TelAl 83, 84; Tel&CabFB 84S; TV&RadDir 84*
WIBX - Utica, NY - *BrCabYB 84; NatRadPubDir Summer 83, Spring 84; TV&RadDir 84*
WIBZ-FM - Parkersburg, WV - *BrCabYB 84; TV&RadDir 84*
WICAT Systems Inc. - Orem, UT - *WhoWMicrocom 83*
WICB-FM - Ithaca, NY - *BrCabYB 84; NatRadPubDir Summer 83, Spring 84; TV&RadDir 84*
WICC - Bridgeport, CT - *BrCabYB 84; NatRadPubDir Summer 83, Spring 84; TV&RadDir 84*
WICD-TV - Champaign, IL - *BrCabYB 84; TelAl 83, 84; Tel&CabFB 84S; TV&RadDir 84*
WICD-TV - Springfield, IL - *DirUSTelSta 83*
WICE - Providence, RI - *NatRadPubDir Summer 83; TV&RadDir 84*
WICH - Norwich, CT - *BrCabYB 84; NatRadPubDir Summer 83, Spring 84; TV&RadDir 84*
Wichita Business [of Wichita Area Chamber of Commerce] - Wichita, KS - *MagDir 84*
Wichita Catholic Advance, The - Wichita, KS - *NewsDir 84*
Wichita Eagle-Beacon [of Knight-Ridder Newspapers Inc.] - Wichita, KS - *BaconPubCkNews 84; Ed&PubIntYB 82; LitMarPl 83, 84; NewsBur 6; NewsDir 84*
Wichita Falls Record-News [of Times Publishing Co.] - Wichita Falls, TX - *BaconPubCkNews 84; Ed&PubIntYB 82; LitMarPl 84*
Wichita Falls Times - Wichita Falls, TX - *BaconPubCkNews 84; Ed&PubIntYB 82; LitMarPl 83, 84*
Wichita Great Empire Broadcasting Inc. - Wichita, KS - *BrCabYB 84*
Wichita Journal [of Harper Publishers] - Wichita, KS - *BaconPubCkNews 84; Ed&PubIntYB 82; NewsDir 84*

Wichita Kansas Black Journal - Wichita, KS - *BaconPubCkNews 84*
Wichita Software Corp. - Wichita, KS - *WhoWMicrocom 83*
Wichita Times - Wichita Falls, TX - *AyerDirPub 83*
Wichitan [of Wichita Publishing Co.] - Wichita, KS - *BaconPubCkMag 84; WritMar 84*
Wicht, Jim - *See* Cable TV of Georgia Inc.
WICK - Scranton, PA - *BrCabYB 84; NatRadPubDir Summer 83, Spring 84; TV&RadDir 84*
Wick Newspapers - Sierra Vista, AZ - *Ed&PubIntYB 82*
Wickenburg Star, The - Wickenburg, AZ - *Ed&PubIntYB 82*
Wickenburg Sun [of Sunland Publications Inc.] - Wickenburg, AZ - *BaconPubCkNews 84; NewsDir 84*
Wickersham Printing Co. Inc. - Lancaster, PA - *LitMarPl 83, 84*
Wickliffe Advance Yeoman - Wickliffe, KY - *BaconPubCkNews 84; Ed&PubIntYB 82; NewsDir 84*
Wickstrom Publishers - Miami, FL - *BoPubDir 4, 5*
WICN-FM - Worcester, MA - *BrCabYB 84; NatRadPubDir Summer 83, Spring 84; TV&RadDir 84*
WICO - Salisbury, MD - *BrCabYB 84; TV&RadDir 84*
Wico Corp. - Niles, IL - *MicrocomMPl 84*
WICO-FM - Salisbury, MD - *BrCabYB 84; TV&RadDir 84*
WICR-FM - Indianapolis, IN - *BrCabYB 84; NatRadPubDir Summer 83, Spring 84; TV&RadDir 84*
WICS-TV - Springfield, IL - *BrCabYB 84; DirUSTelSta 83; TelAl 83, 84; Tel&CabFB 84S*
WICU-TV - Erie, PA - *BrCabYB 84; DirUSTelSta 83; TelAl 83, 84; Tel&CabFB 84S; TV&RadDir 84*
WICY - Malone, NY - *BrCabYB 84; TV&RadDir 84*
WICZ-TV - Binghamton, NY - *BrCabYB 84; DirUSTelSta 83; TelAl 83, 84; Tel&CabFB 84S; TV&RadDir 84*
WIDA-FM - Carolina, PR - *BrCabYB 84*
Wida Software - London, England - *MicrocomSwDir 1*
WIDD - Elizabethton, TN - *BrCabYB 84; TV&RadDir 84*
WIDD-FM - Elizabethton, TN - *BrCabYB 84; TV&RadDir 84*
Widdoes, Eleanor B. - New York, NY - *LitMarPl 83, 84*
WIDE - Biddeford, ME - *BrCabYB 84; TV&RadDir 84*
Wide Skies Press - Polk, NE - *BoPubDir 4, 5*
Wide Track News [of Monday Morning Newspapers Inc.] - Detroit, MI - *NewsDir 84*
Wide World Photos [Subs. of The Associated Press] - New York, NY - *AvMarPl 83; Ed&PubIntYB 82; LitMarPl 83, 84; MagIndMarPl 82-83*
Wide World Publishing/Tetra House - San Carlos, CA - *LitMag&SmPr 83-84; LitMarPl 83, 84*
Wider Opportunities for Women - Washington, DC - *BoPubDir 4, 5*
Wideview - *See* Putnam Publishing Group
Wideworld News Service - St. Louis, MO - *Ed&PubIntYB 82*
Widget Publishing - Muscle Shoals, AL - *BillIntBG 83-84*
Widl Video - Chicago, IL - *WhoWMicrocom 83*
WIDO - Dunn, NC - *BrCabYB 84*
WIDR-FM - Kalamazoo, MI - *BrCabYB 84; NatRadPubDir Summer 83, Spring 84*
WIDS - Russell Springs, KY - *BrCabYB 84*
WIDU - Fayetteville, NC - *BrCabYB 84; TV&RadDir 84*
WIEL - Elizabethtown, KY - *BrCabYB 84; TV&RadDir 84*
Wien Air Alaska Flight Time Magazine - Portland, OR - *BaconPubCkMag 84*
Wiener Co., Bernard - New York, NY - *StaDirAdAg 2-84*
Wiener Publishing Inc., Markus - New York, NY - *LitMarPl 83, 84*
Wiese Film Productions, Michael - Westport, CT - *BoPubDir 5*
Wieser & Wieser Inc. - Chappaqua, NY - *LitMarPl 84*
Wieser & Wieser Inc. - Millwood, NY - *LitMarPl 83, 84*
Wieser & Wieser Inc. - New York, NY - *LitMarPl 84*
WIEZ - Blackshear, GA - *BrCabYB 84*
WIEZ-FM - Oneonta, NY - *TV&RadDir 84*
WIFC-FM - Wausau, WI - *BrCabYB 84; TV&RadDir 84*
WIFE - Indianapolis, IN - *NatRadPubDir Summer 83; TV&RadDir 84*
WIFF - Auburn, IN - *BrCabYB 84; TV&RadDir 84*
WIFF-FM - Auburn, IN - *BrCabYB 84; TV&RadDir 84*
WIFI-FM - Bala-Cynwyd, PA - *TV&RadDir 84*
WIFI-FM - Philadelphia, PA - *NatRadPubDir Summer 83 p.213*
WIFM - Poughkeepsie, NY - *TV&RadDir 84*
WIFM - Elkin, NC - *TV&RadDir 84*
WIFM-FM - Elkin, NC - *BrCabYB 84; TV&RadDir 84*
WIFN-FM - Franklin, IN - *TV&RadDir 84*
WIFO-FM - Jesup, GA - *BrCabYB 84; TV&RadDir 84*
WIFR-TV - Freeport, IL - *BrCabYB 84; Tel&CabFB 84S*
WIFR-TV - Rockford, IL - *DirUSTelSta 83; TelAl 83, 84; TV&RadDir 84*
WIFX - Jenkins, KY - *BrCabYB 84; TV&RadDir 84*
WIFX-FM - Jenkins, KY - *BrCabYB 84; TV&RadDir 84*
Wigan Pier Press - San Francisco, CA - *BoPubDir 4, 5*
WIGC - Troy, AL - *BrCabYB 84*
WIGC-FM - Troy, AL - *TV&RadDir 84*
WIGG - Wiggins, MS - *BrCabYB 84; TV&RadDir 84*
Wiggins Cable TV - Wiggins, MS - *Tel&CabFB 84C p.1713*
Wiggins Stone County Enterprise - Wiggins, MS - *BaconPubCkNews 84*
Wiggins Telephone Association - Wiggins, CO - *TelDir&BG 83-84*
WIGL-FM - Columbia, SC - *TV&RadDir 84*
WIGL-FM - Orangeburg, SC - *BrCabYB 84*
WIGM - Manitowoc, WI - *TV&RadDir 84*
WIGM - Medford, WI - *BrCabYB 84; TV&RadDir 84*
WIGM-FM - Medford, WI - *BrCabYB 84; TV&RadDir 84*
WIGO - Atlanta, GA - *BrCabYB 84; TV&RadDir 84*
WIGS - Gouverneur, NY - *BrCabYB 84; TV&RadDir 84*
WIGS-FM - Gouverneur, NY - *BrCabYB 84; TV&RadDir 84*
Wigs, Hats, & Accessories - Long Island, NY - *MagDir 84*
WIGY-FM - Bath, ME - *BrCabYB 84; TV&RadDir 84*
WIHN-FM - Bloomington, IL - *TV&RadDir 84*
WIHN-FM - Normal, IL - *BrCabYB 84*
WIHS-FM - Middletown, CT - *BrCabYB 84; TV&RadDir 84*
WIHT-TV - Ann Arbor, MI - *BrCabYB 84; DirUSTelSta 83; TelAl 83, 84; Tel&CabFB 84S*
WIIC-TV - Pittsburgh, PA - *LitMarPl 83*
WIIM-TV - Iron Mountain, MI - *BrCabYB 84; Tel&CabFB 84S*
WIIN - Atlantic City, NJ - *BrCabYB 84; NatRadPubDir Summer 83, Spring 84; TV&RadDir 84*
WIIQ-TV - Birmingham, AL - *TV&RadDir 84*
WIIQ-TV - Demopolis, AL - *BrCabYB 84; Tel&CabFB 84S*
WIIS-FM - Key West, FL - *BrCabYB 84; TV&RadDir 84*
WIIZ - Jacksonville, NC - *BrCabYB 84; TV&RadDir 84*
WIKB-FM - Iron River, MI - *BrCabYB 84*
WIKC - Bogalusa, LA - *BrCabYB 84; TV&RadDir 84*
WIKE - Newport, VT - *BrCabYB 84; TV&RadDir 84*
WIKI-FM - Carrollton, KY - *BrCabYB 84; TV&RadDir 84*
Wikman & Associates Inc., Michael R. - Minneapolis, MN - *DirMarMP 83*
WIKQ-FM - Greeneville, TN - *BrCabYB 84; TV&RadDir 84*
WIKS - Parkersburg, WV - *BrCabYB 84*
WIKS-FM - Greenfield, IN - *NatRadPubDir Summer 83; TV&RadDir 84*
Wikstrom Telephone Co. Inc. - Karlstad, MN - *TelDir&BG 83-84*
WIKU - Pikesville, TN - *BrCabYB 84*
WIKX - Immokalee, FL - *BrCabYB 84*
WIKY-FM - Evansville, IN - *BrCabYB 84; NatRadPubDir Summer 83, Spring 84; TV&RadDir 84*
WIKZ-FM - Chambersburg, PA - *BrCabYB 84; TV&RadDir 84*
WIL - St. Louis, MO - *BrCabYB 84; NatRadPubDir Summer 83, Spring 84; TV&RadDir 84*
WIL-FM - St. Louis, MO - *BrCabYB 84; NatRadPubDir Summer 83, Spring 84; TV&RadDir 84*
Wil-Kin Inc. - Atlanta, GA - *AvMarPl 83*
WILA - Danville, VA - *BrCabYB 84; TV&RadDir 84*
Wilber Co., The N. F. - New Berlin, NY - *AvMarPl 83*
Wilber, David F. III - Catskill, NY - *Tel&CabFB 84C p.1713*
Wilber Republican - Wilber, NE - *BaconPubCkNews 84; Ed&PubIntYB 82*
Wilbur Cable TV Inc. [of Western Satellite Inc.] - Wilbur, WA - *BrCabYB 84; Tel&CabFB 84C*
Wilbur Register - Wilbur, WA - *BaconPubCkNews 84; Ed&PubIntYB 82*
Wilburton Latimer County News-Tribune - Wilburton, OK - *BaconPubCkNews 84*
Wilburton Latimer County Today - Wilburton, OK - *BaconPubCkNews 84*
Wilcher Associates - Berkeley, CA - *LitMarPl 83, 84*
Wilco Vision - Joliet, IL - *Tel&CabFB 84C*
Wilcom Inc. - South Holland, IL - *AvMarPl 83*
Wilcop Cable TV - Brodhead, KY - *BrCabYB 84; Tel&CabFB 84C*

Wilcop Cable TV - Crab Orchard, KY - *Tel&CabFB 84C*
Wilcox Inc., Howard S. - Indianapolis, IN - *DirPRFirms 83*
Wilcox, Philip G. - Junction City, KS - *BrCabYB 84 p.D-310*
Wilcox, Philip G. - *See* Texkan Communications Inc.
Wilcox Progressive Era - Camden, AL - *AyerDirPub 83; Ed&PubIntYB 82*
Wilcox Walter Furlong Paper Co. - Philadelphia, PA - *MagIndMarPl 82-83*
WILD - Boston, MA - *BrCabYB 84; NatRadPubDir Summer 83, Spring 84; TV&RadDir 84*
Wild & Woolley - Glebe, Australia - *LitMag&SmPr 83-84*
Wild Card Records Inc. - New York, NY - *BillIntBG 83-84*
Wild Goose Inc. - Swannanoa, NC - *BoPubDir 4, 5*
Wild Hare Computer Systems Inc. - Boulder, CO - *DataDirSup 7-83*
Wild Heather Music - Nashville, TN - *BillIntBG 83-84*
Wild Horses Potted Plant - Palo Alto, CA - *LitMag&SmPr 83-84*
Wild Horses Publishing Co. - Palo Alto, CA - *BoPubDir 4, 5*
Wild Rivers Advertiser/North - Frederic, WI - *AyerDirPub 83*
Wild Rivers Advertiser/South - Frederic, WI - *AyerDirPub 83*
Wild West Publishing House - San Francisco, CA - *BoPubDir 4, 5*
Wild Wings - Lake City, MN - *DirMarMP 83*
Wildcat - Big Lake, TX - *AyerDirPub 83*
Wildcat Canyon Books - Richmond, CA - *BoPubDir 4, 5*
Wildebeest Records - Wexford, PA - *BillIntBG 83-84*
Wilder Music, Shane - Hollywood, CA - *BillIntBG 83-84*
Wilderness Cable Co. - Eleanor, WV - *BrCabYB 84*
Wilderness Cable Co. [of Century Communications Corp.] - Winfield, WV - *Tel&CabFB 84C*
Wilderness House - Cave Junction, OR - *BoPubDir 4, 5*
Wilderness Press - Berkeley, CA - *LitMarPl 83, 84; WritMar 84*
Wilderscenes - Palomar Mountain, CA - *LitMarPl 84*
Wildfire Publishing Co. - Carpinteria, CA - *BoPubDir 4*
Wildfire Publishing Co. - Goleta, CA - *BoPubDir 5*
Wilding Div. [of Bell & Howell Co.] - Southfield, MI - *Tel&CabFB 84C*
Wildlife Crusader - Winnipeg, MB, Canada - *BaconPubCkMag 84*
Wildlife Disease Association - Ames, IA - *MicroMarPl 82-83*
Wildlife Education Ltd. - San Diego, CA - *BoPubDir 4, 5*
Wildlife Harvest Magazine - Goose Lake, IA - *WritMar 84*
Wildlife Management Institute - Washington, DC - *BoPubDir 4, 5*
Wildlife Society Inc. - Bethesda, MD - *BoPubDir 4, 5*
Wildrick Advertising Agency - Whittier, CA - *StaDirAdAg 2-84*
Wildrick & Miller Inc. - New York, NY - *StaDirAdAg 2-84*
Wilds Associates Inc., Thomas - New York, NY - *DirInfWP 82*
Wildwater Designs Ltd. - Penllyn, PA - *BoPubDir 4, 5*
Wildwood Associates Ltd. - Lake Panasoffkee, FL - *BrCabYB 84*
Wildwood Cable TV Management Co. - Wildwood, FL - *BrCabYB 84*
Wildwood Entertainment Inc. - Berlin, NY - *BillIntBG 83-84*
Wildwood Gazette-Leader - Wildwood, NJ - *BaconPubCkNews 84*
Wildwood Publications - Traverse City, MI - *BoPubDir 4, 5*
WILE - Cambridge, OH - *BrCabYB 84; TV&RadDir 84*
WILE-FM - Cambridge, OH - *BrCabYB 84; TV&RadDir 84*
Wiley & Sons Canada Ltd., John [Subs. of John Wiley & Sons Inc.] - Rexdale, ON, Canada - *LitMarPl 83, 84*
Wiley & Sons Inc., John - New York, NY - *DirMarMP 83; InfoS 83-84; KnowInd 83; LitMarPl 83, 84; MicrocomMPl 83; WritMar 84*
Wiley Book News - New York, NY - *DirOnDB Spring 84*
Wiley Book News [of NewsNet Inc.] - Bryn Mawr, PA - *DataDirOnSer 84*
Wiley Catalog/Online [of John Wiley & Sons Inc.] - New York, NY - *DirOnDB Spring 84; EISS 5-84 Sup*
Wiley Interscience [of John Wiley & Sons Inc.] - New York, NY - *MagIndMarPl 82-83; MicroMarPl 82-83*
Wilfrid Laurier University Press - Waterloo, ON, Canada - *BoPubDir 4, 5; LitMarPl 84*
WILI - Willimantic, CT - *BrCabYB 84; NatRadPubDir Summer 83, Spring 84; TV&RadDir 84*
WILK - Lazerne, PA - *TV&RadDir 84*
WILK - Scranton/Wilkes-Barre/Hazelton/Avoca, PA - *NatRadPubDir Summer 83, Spring 84 p.216*
WILK - Wilkes-Barre, PA - *BrCabYB 84*
Wilk-Amite Record - Gloster, MS - *AyerDirPub 83; Ed&PubIntYB 82*
Wilk & Brichta Advertising - Chicago, IL - *ArtMar 84; StaDirAdAg 2-84*
Wilke Inc., Hubert - New York, NY - *TeleSy&SerDir 7-83*
Wilkens Group [of the Univas Network] - Hamburg, West Germany - *StaDirAdAg 2-84*
Wilker Inc. - Dublin, CA - *WhoWMicrocom 83*
Wilkerson & Associates - Louisville, KY - *IntDirMarRes 83*
Wilkerson National Surveys Inc. - Philadelphia, PA - *IntDirMarRes 83*
Wilkerson Stations, Arthur - Lenoir City, TN - *BrCabYB 84*
Wilkes-Barre Citizen's Voice - Wilkes-Barre, PA - *BaconPubCkNews 84*
Wilkes-Barre Sunday Independent - Wilkes-Barre, PA - *BaconPubCkNews 84; NewsDir 84*
Wilkes Barre Times-Leader [of Capital Cities Communications Inc.] - Wilkes Barre, PA - *BaconPubCkNews 84; Ed&PubIntYB 82; NewsDir 84*
Wilkes Ltd., Bert H. - Toronto, ON, Canada - *DirPRFirms 83*
Wilkes Telephone & Electric Co. - Washington, GA - *TelDir&BG 83-84*
Wilkes Telephone Membership Corp. - Wilkesboro, NC - *TelDir&BG 83-84*
Wilkie Marketing - Redondo Beach, CA - *BoPubDir 4 Sup, 5; LitMarPl 83, 84*
Wilkin Consulting Services - San Juan Capistrano, CA - *CabTVFinDB 83*
Wilkins, Devon - Orangeville, ON, Canada - *BoPubDir 4, 5*
Wilkins Research Services - Chattanooga, TN - *IntDirMarRes 83*
Wilkinsburg Gazette [of Dardanell Publications Inc.] - Monroeville, PA - *NewsDir 84*
Wilkinsburg Gazette - *See* Gateway Press Inc.
Wilkinson County Cablevision Inc. - Gordon, GA - *Tel&CabFB 84C*
Wilkinson County News - Irwinton, GA - *AyerDirPub 83; Ed&PubIntYB 82*
Wilkinson County Telephone Co. Inc. - Irwinton, GA - *TelDir&BG 83-84*
Wilkinson Inc., P. B. - Paoli, PA - *StaDirAdAg 2-84*
Wilkinson Public Relations Ltd., J. B. - Regina, SK, Canada - *DirPRFirms 83*
Wilks, Harry - New York, NY - *LitMarPl 83*
Wilks/Schwartz Broadcasting - East Longmeadow, MA - *BrCabYB 84*
WILL - Urbana, IL - *BrCabYB 84; NatRadPubDir Summer 83, Spring 84; TV&RadDir 84*
Will-Du Music Publishing Co. - Los Angeles, CA - *BillIntBG 83-84*
WILL-FM - Urbana, IL - *BrCabYB 84; TV&RadDir 84*
WILL-TV - Champaign, IL - *Tel&CabFB 84S*
WILL-TV - Urbana, IL - *BrCabYB 84; TV&RadDir 84*
Willamette Valley Observer - Eugene, OR - *Ed&PubIntYB 82*
Willamette Week [of Guard Publishing Co.] - Portland, OR - *AyerDirPub 83; Ed&PubIntYB 82; NewsDir 84*
Willapa Harbor Herald - *See* Community Media Corp.
Willapa Harbor Herald, The - Raymond, WA - *AyerDirPub 83; NewsDir 84*
Willard & Co. Inc. - Jackson, MS - *StaDirAdAg 2-84*
Willard Telephone Co. - Merino, CO - *TelDir&BG 83-84*
Willard/Thomas Inc. - Troy, MI - *DirPRFirms 83*
Willard Times - Willard, OH - *BaconPubCkNews 84; Ed&PubIntYB 82*
Willcox Arizona Range News - *See* Arizona Range News Inc.
Willcox, P. J. - Huntington, IN - *BoPubDir 5*
Willert, James - La Mirada, CA - *BoPubDir 4, 5*
Willett Associates Inc., Roslyn - New York, NY - *DirPRFirms 83; HBIndAd&MS 82-83*
William & Richards - San Francisco, CA - *BoPubDir 4, 5*
Williams Advertising, Charles E. - Milton, PA - *StaDirAdAg 2-84*
Williams & Associates - San Luis Obispo, CA - *DataDirOnSer 84*
Williams & Co., Thomas A. - Davidson, NC - *BoPubDir 4, 5*
Williams & Meyer Co. - Chicago, IL - *Tel&CabFB 84C*
Williams & Nevin - Stockport, England - *InfIndMarPl 83*
Williams & Wilkins [Div. of Waverly Press Inc.] - Baltimore, MD - *LitMarPl 83, 84; MagIndMarPl 82-83; MicroMarPl 82-83*

Williams Associates Inc., Stuart - Stamford, CT - *AdAge 3-28-84; StaDirAdAg 2-84*
Williams Associates, Tom - St. George, SC - *LitMarPl 83, 84*
Williams' Brick Music - *See* Jacobson, Jeffrey E.
Williams, Brown & Earle - Philadelphia, PA - *AvMarPl 83*
Williams, Carl M. - Denver, CO - *BrCabYB 84 p.D-311; Tel&CabFB 84C p.1713*
Williams Colusa County Farmer - Williams, CA - *BaconPubCkNews 84*
Williams Communications Co. - Goodman, MO - *Tel&CabFB 84C*
Williams Co., Mark - Chicago, IL - *ADAPSOMemDir 83-84; MicrocomMPl 83, 84; MicrocomSwDir 1; WhoWMicrocom 83*
Williams Co., The - Providence, RI - *StaDirAdAg 2-84*
Williams County Broadcasting System Inc. - Bryan, OH - *BrCabYB 84*
Williams, Frank O. - Chicago, IL - *LitMarPl 84*
Williams Group Advertising & Public Relations - Dallas, TX - *DirPRFirms 83*
Williams Group, The Fraser - Paramus, NJ - *InfIndMarPl 83*
Williams Group, The Fraser [of Fraser Williams Scientific Systems Ltd.] - Poynton, England - *InfIndMarPl 83*
Williams Group, The Fraser (Computer Services) - Liverpool, England - *InfIndMarPl 83*
Williams, Jonathan - Ottawa, ON, Canada - *LitMarPl 83, 84*
Williams, L. Allen - Scottsboro, AL - *Tel&CabFB 84C p.1713*
Williams, London, Marchin, Weltman & Associates - West Orange, NJ - *StaDirAdAg 2-84*
Williams Music Clearance, Mary - Hollywood, CA - *BillIntBG 83-84*
Williams Music Group, Don - Los Angeles, CA - *BillIntBG 83-84*
Williams News - Williams, AZ - *BaconPubCkNews 84; Ed&PubIntYB 82*
Williams Newspaper Feature Syndicate Inc. - Charlottesville, VA - *Ed&PubIntYB 82*
Williams Northern Light - Williams, MN - *AyerDirPub 83; BaconPubCkNews 84; Ed&PubIntYB 82*
Williams Printing Co. - Nashville, TN - *MagIndMarPl 82-83*
Williams Public Relations, Judy - Altadena, CA - *DirPRFirms 83*
Williams Publications, Dootsie - Los Angeles, CA - *BillIntBG 83-84*
Williams Publications, Ken J. - New York, NY - *BoPubDir 4, 5*
Williams Publishing Co. - Jamaica, NY - *BoPubDir 4, 5*
Williams Radio/TV Inc. (Computer Div.) - Jacksonville, FL - *WhoWMicrocom 83*
Williams Record, The - Williamstown, MA - *NewsDir 84*
Williams, Ripple & Associates Advertising Agency Inc. - Chattanooga, TN - *StaDirAdAg 2-84*
Williams Sound Corp. - Eden Prairie, MN - *AvMarPl 83*
Williams Systems Services - Tulsa, OK - *MicrocomSwDir 1*
Williams Technical & Economic Services Inc., Roger - Princeton, NJ - *BoPubDir 5*
Williams, W. G. - Washington, DC - *AvMarPl 83*
Williams-Wallace Productions International Inc. - Toronto, ON, Canada - *BoPubDir 4, 5; LitMarPl 84*
Williams, Whittle & Associates Inc. - Alexandria, VA - *StaDirAdAg 2-84*
Williams, Young & Associates - Madison, WI - *WhoWMicrocom 83*
Williamsburg Antenna Co. - Williamsburg, PA - *BrCabYB 84; Tel&CabFB 84C*
Williamsburg Cable TV [of Wometco Cable TV Inc.] - Johnsonville, SC - *BrCabYB 84; Tel&CabFB 84C*
Williamsburg Cablevision - Kingstree, SC - *BrCabYB 84; Tel&CabFB 84C*
Williamsburg Journal Tribune - Williamsburg, IA - *AyerDirPub 83; Ed&PubIntYB 82*
Williamsburg Journal Tribune - *See* Newspapers of Iowa County
Williamsburg Virginia Gazette - Williamsburg, VA - *BaconPubCkNews 84*
Williamsburg Whitley Republican - Williamsburg, KY - *BaconPubCkNews 84; NewsDir 84*
Williamsfield Times - Elmwood, IL - *AyerDirPub 83*
Williamsfield Times - Williamsfield, IL - *Ed&PubIntYB 82*
Williamson & Reinhard/Cline Inc. - Boise, ID - *StaDirAdAg 2-84*
Williamson, C. E. - St. Catharines, ON, Canada - *BoPubDir 4, 5*
Williamson County Cable TV [of Matrix Enterprises Inc.] - Williamson, TN - *Tel&CabFB 84C*
Williamson County Cable TV Inc. [of Matrix Enterprises Inc.] - Franklin, TN - *BrCabYB 84*
Williamson County Cablevision Co. Inc. - Georgetown, TX - *BrCabYB 84; Tel&CabFB 84C*
Williamson County Observer - Herrin, IL - *Ed&PubIntYB 82*
Williamson County Sun - Georgetown, TX - *AyerDirPub 83; BaconPubCkNews 84; Ed&PubIntYB 82*
Williamson Leader - Franklin, TN - *AyerDirPub 83; Ed&PubIntYB 82; NewsDir 84*
Williamson News - Williamson, WV - *BaconPubCkNews 84; NewsDir 84*
Williamson Road TV Co. Inc. - Blossburg, PA - *BrCabYB 84; Tel&CabFB 84C*
Williamson School of Horsemanship - Hamilton, MT - *BoPubDir 4 Sup, 5*
Williamson Sun & Sentinel - Williamson, NY - *BaconPubCkNews 84*
Williamson Sun, The - Williamson, NY - *Ed&PubIntYB 82*
Williamson Television Co. - Nolan, WV - *BrCabYB 84*
Williamson Television Co. - Williamson, WV - *BrCabYB 84; Tel&CabFB 84C p.1713*
Williamsport Grit - Williamsport, PA - *NewsDir 84*
Williamsport Review-Republican - Williamsport, IN - *BaconPubCkNews 84*
Williamsport Sun Gazette - Williamsport, PA - *BaconPubCkNews 84; Ed&PubIntYB 82; NewsDir 84*
Williamston Enterprise [of Ingham Newspaper Co.] - East Lansing, MI - *NewsDir 84*
Williamston Enterprise - Williamston, MI - *AyerDirPub 83; Ed&PubIntYB 82*
Williamston Enterprise - Williamston, NC - *BaconPubCkNews 84; NewsDir 84*
Williamston Enterprise - *See* Towne Courier Inc.
Williamston Journal - Williamston, SC - *BaconPubCkNews 84; NewsDir 84*
Williamstown Grant County News - Williamstown, KY - *BaconPubCkNews 84*
Williamstown Plain Dealer - Blackwood, NJ - *BaconPubCkNews 84*
Williamstown Plain Dealer [of Cam-Glo Newspapers Inc.] - Williamstown, NJ - *NewsDir 84*
Williamsville Sun - Williamsville, IL - *Ed&PubIntYB 82*
Williamsville Sun - *See* Riverton Register Publishing
Willie, B. V. - Eagle Grove, IA - *Tel&CabFB 84C p.1713*
Willie, Ralph G. - Federal Way, WA - *BoPubDir 4, 5*
Willimantic Chronicle - Willimantic, CT - *BaconPubCkNews 84; NewsDir 84*
Willingboro Tri-County News - Willingboro, NJ - *Ed&PubIntYB 82*
Willis Advertising Ltd. - Toronto, ON, Canada - *StaDirAdAg 2-84*
Willis Broadcasting Corp. - Norfolk, VA - *BrCabYB 84*
Willis/Case/Harwood Inc. - Dayton, OH - *StaDirAdAg 2-84; TelAl 83, 84*
Willis, Ellen L. & Sara Jane - Granite, OK - *Tel&CabFB 84C p.1713*
Willis, J. R. - Granite, OK - *Tel&CabFB 84C p.1713*
Willis, J. V. - Hammond, IN - *BoPubDir 4, 5*
Willis Music Co. - Florence, KY - *BillIntBG 83-84; DirMarMP 83*
Willis, William R. - Granite, OK - *Tel&CabFB 84C p.1713*
Williston Herald - Williston, ND - *BaconPubCkNews 84; Ed&PubIntYB 82; NewsDir 84*
Williston Plains Reporter - Williston, ND - *AyerDirPub 83; BaconPubCkNews 84; Ed&PubIntYB 82; NewsDir 84*
Williston Sun-Suwannee Valley News - Williston, FL - *AyerDirPub 83; BaconPubCkNews 84*
Williston Telephone Co. [Aff. of Telephone & Data Systems Inc.] - Williston, SC - *TelDir&BG 83-84*
Williston Times - Williston Park, NY - *AyerDirPub 83; Ed&PubIntYB 82*
Williston Times - *See* Litmore Publications
Williston Way - Williston, SC - *AyerDirPub 83; BaconPubCkNews 84; Ed&PubIntYB 82*
Willits News - Willits, CA - *BaconPubCkNews 84; Ed&PubIntYB 82*
Willmann Paper Co. Inc. - New York, NY - *LitMarPl 83, 84*

Willmar Video Inc. [of Heritage Communications Inc.] - Willmar, MN - *Tel&CabFB 84C*
Willmark Research Corp. - New York, NY - *IntDirMarRes 83*
Willoughby Lake County News-Herald [of The Lorain Journal Co.] - Willoughby, OH - *NewsDir 84*
Willow City Cable TV [of NoDaKable Inc.] - Willow City, ND - *BrCabYB 84; Tel&CabFB 84C*
Willow Creek Klamlty Kourier - Klamath/Trinity Valley, CA - *Ed&PubIntYB 82*
Willow Creek Klamlty Kourier - Willow Creek, CA - *BaconPubCkNews 84*
Willow Creek Press [Aff. of Wisconsin Sportsman Inc.] - Oshkosh, WI - *BoPubDir 4, 5*
Willow Grove Guide [of Montgomery Publishing Co.] - Willow Grove, PA - *Ed&PubIntYB 82; NewsDir 84*
Willow Grove Guide - *See* Montgomery Publishing Co.
Willow River Press Ltd. - Chicago, IL - *BoPubDir 4, 5*
Willow Springs - Cheney, WA - *LitMag&SmPr 83-84*
Willow Springs News - Willow Springs, MO - *BaconPubCkNews 84*
Willow TV Cable Co. - Willow Springs, MO - *BrCabYB 84; Tel&CabFB 84C*
Willowbrook Doings - Willowbrook, IL - *Ed&PubIntYB 82*
Willowbrook Doings - *See* Doings Newspapers, The
Willowbrook Suburban Life Graphic - *See* Life Printing & Publishing Co.
Willowdowns Cable-Vision Ltd. - Downsview, ON, Canada - *BrCabYB 84*
Willowood Press - Lexington, KY - *BoPubDir 4, 5; LitMag&SmPr 83-84*
Willows Journal [of Glenn-Colusa Newspapers Inc.] - Willows, CA - *BaconPubCkNews 84; Ed&PubIntYB 82; NewsDir 84*
Wills & Associates - Baltimore, MD - *DirPRFirms 83*
Wills Point Chronicle - Wills Point, TX - *BaconPubCkNews 84; Ed&PubIntYB 82*
Willshire Photo Star - Willshire, OH - *BaconPubCkNews 84; NewsDir 84*
Willson Broadcast Consultants, Gary - San Rafael, CA - *CabTVFinDB 83*
Willyshe Publishing Co. Inc. - Linthicum Heights, MD - *BoPubDir 4, 5*
WILM - Wilmington, DE - *BrCabYB 84; NatRadPubDir Summer 83, Spring 84; TV&RadDir 84*
Wilmar Publishers - Sherman Oaks, CA - *BoPubDir 4, 5*
Wilmarth, Christopher - New York, NY - *BoPubDir 5*
Wilmarth's TV - Hallstead, PA - *BrCabYB 84*
Wilmarth's TV - New Milford, PA - *BrCabYB 84; Tel&CabFB 84C p.1713*
Wilmette Life [of Wilmette Pioneer Press Inc.] - Wilmette, IL - *AyerDirPub 83; Ed&PubIntYB 82; NewsDir 84*
Wilmette Life - *See* Pioneer Press Inc.
Wilmette News Advertiser - Highland Park, IL - *AyerDirPub 83*
Wilmette News Advertiser - Wilmette, IL - *Ed&PubIntYB 82*
Wilmette News Advertiser - *See* Singer Printing & Publishing Co.
Wilmington Advocate - Wilmington, IL - *Ed&PubIntYB 82*
Wilmington Advocate - *See* Bailey Printing & Publishing Inc.
Wilmington Defender - Wilmington, DE - *NewsDir 84*
Wilmington Dialog - Wilmington, DE - *BaconPubCkNews 84; NewsDir 84*
Wilmington Evening Journal - Wilmington, DE - *NewsBur 6*
Wilmington Express - Wilmington, IL - *AyerDirPub 83*
Wilmington Express - *See* G.W. Communications
Wilmington Free Press - Wilmington, IL - *AyerDirPub 83; Ed&PubIntYB 82*
Wilmington Free Press - *See* G.W. Communications
Wilmington Journal - Wilmington, NC - *BaconPubCkNews 84; Ed&PubIntYB 82; NewsDir 84*
Wilmington Morning News - Wilmington, DE - *NewsBur 6*
Wilmington Morning Star - Wilmington, NC - *Ed&PubIntYB 82; NewsDir 84*
Wilmington News-Journal - Wilmington, OH - *BaconPubCkNews 84; Ed&PubIntYB 82; NewsDir 84*
Wilmington Press-Journal - Wilmington, CA - *Ed&PubIntYB 82*
Wilmington Star - Wilmington, NC - *BaconPubCkNews 84*
Wilmington/Tewksbury Town Crier - Wilmington, MA - *BaconPubCkNews 84; NewsDir 84*
Wilmor Warehouse & Shipping Co. Inc. [Div. of William Morrow Co. Inc.] - West Caldwell, NJ - *LitMarPl 83, 84*
Wilmore Cable TV [of Centel Cable Television Co.] - Nicholasville, KY - *BrCabYB 84*
Wilmore Electronics Co. Inc. - Hillsborough, NC - *MicrocomMPl 84*
Wilmot Enterprise - Wilmot, SD - *BaconPubCkNews 84; Ed&PubIntYB 82*
Wilmot Systems Inc. - New York, NY - *MicrocomMPl 84*
WILO - Frankfort, IN - *BrCabYB 84; TV&RadDir 84*
WILP - Paris, KY - *BrCabYB 84; TV&RadDir 84*
WILQ-FM - Williamsport, PA - *BrCabYB 84; NatRadPubDir Summer 83, Spring 84; TV&RadDir 84*
WILS - Lansing, MI - *BrCabYB 84; NatRadPubDir Summer 83, Spring 84; TV&RadDir 84*
WILS-FM - Lansing, MI - *BrCabYB 84; NatRadPubDir Summer 83, Spring 84; TV&RadDir 84*
Wilshire Book Co. - North Hollywood, CA - *ArtMar 84; DirMarMP 83; LitMarPl 83, 84; WritMar 84*
Wilshire Business [of Glendale Rotary Press] - Los Angeles, CA - *BaconPubCkMag 84; MagDir 84*
Wilshire Center's Larchmont Chronicle - Los Angeles, CA - *Ed&PubIntYB 82*
Wilshire Independent [of Los Angeles Meredith Newspapers] - Los Angeles, CA - *AyerDirPub 83; Ed&PubIntYB 82; NewsDir 84*
Wilshire Press [of Los Angeles Meredith Newspapers] - Los Angeles, CA - *AyerDirPub 83; NewsDir 84*
Wilshorn Music - *See* Hope Publishing Co.
WilSing Music Publisher - Stuart, VA - *BillIntBG 83-84*
Wilson, Adrian - San Francisco, CA - *LitMarPl 83, 84*
Wilson Advertising - *See* RMS Inc.
Wilson Advertising Agency, Thomas C. - Reno, NV - *ArtMar 84; StaDirAdAg 2-84*
Wilson Advertising Associates Inc. - Glendale, CA - *StaDirAdAg 2-84*
Wilson Advertising-Marketing Service - Libertyville, IL - *StaDirAdAg 2-84*
Wilson & Associates, Earl I. - Woodland Hills, CA - *IntDirMarRes 83*
Wilson & Associates Inc., J. W. - Washington, DC - *TeleSy&SerDir 7-83*
Wilson Associates Inc., Louis D. - Elkins Park, PA - *WhoWMicrocom 83*
Wilson Bros. Music - *See* Funky but Music Inc.
Wilson Brothers Publications - Yakima, WA - *LitMag&SmPr 83-84*
Wilson Co., H. - South Holland, IL - *ArtMar 84; AvMarPl 83*
Wilson Co., The H. W. - Bronx, NY - *LitMarPl 83, 84*
Wilson Composition Co. - Albuquerque, NM - *LitMarPl 84*
Wilson County Citizen - Fredonia, KS - *AyerDirPub 83; Ed&PubIntYB 82*
Wilson-Davis Publications Inc. - Valley Falls, KS - *BaconPubCkNews 84*
Wilson, Doug - Kirkland, WA - *MagIndMarPl 82-83*
Wilson Electronics - Las Vegas, NV - *ArtMar 84*
Wilson, Frank & Associates - San Diego, CA - *AdAge 3-28-84; StaDirAdAg 2-84*
Wilson, Horne, McClelland & Gray Inc. - Atlanta, GA - *StaDirAdAg 2-84*
Wilson Inc., Edwin Bird - New York, NY - *AdAge 3-28-84; StaDirAdAg 2-84*
Wilson Inc., H. Donald - White Plains, NY - *EISS 5-84 Sup; InfoS 83-84*
Wilson Inc., Jim - Indianapolis, IN - *AvMarPl 83*
Wilson Industries, Ralph C. Jr. - San Jose, CA - *Tel&CabFB 84S*
Wilson, John - Willowdale, ON, Canada - *BoPubDir 4 Sup, 5*
Wilson Jones Co. [Subs. of American Brands Inc.] - Chicago, IL - *DirInfWP 82; WhoWMicrocom 83*
Wilson Library Bulletin - Bronx, NY - *ArtMar 84; BaconPubCkMag 84; MagDir 84; MagIndMarPl 82-83; WritMar 84*
Wilson Post-Democrat - Wilson, OK - *BaconPubCkNews 84; Ed&PubIntYB 82*
Wilson Press Inc., J. B. - Fresno, CA - *BoPubDir 4, 5*
Wilson Productions Inc., Marty - New York, NY - *BillIntBG 83-84*
Wilson Publishing Co. - Wakefield, RI - *BaconPubCkNews 84*

Wilson Publishing Co. - Gilmer, TX - *BoPubDir 4, 5*
Wilson Publishing, John - Chattanooga, TN - *BoPubDir 5*
Wilson Quarterly, The [of Woodrow Wilson International Center for Scholars] - Washington, DC - *LitMarPl 83, 84; MagDir 84; MagIndMarPl 82-83*
Wilson Quarterly, The [of Smithsonian Institution] - New York, NY - *DirMarMP 83*
Wilson, Stephen - Cambridge, MA - *LitMarPl 83, 84*
Wilson Studio, Mike - New York, NY - *LitMarPl 83, 84*
Wilson Telephone Co. Inc. - Wilson, KS - *TelDir&BG 83-84*
Wilson Times - Wilson, NC - *BaconPubCkNews 84; Ed&PubIntYB 82; NewsDir 84*
Wilson World - Wilson, KS - *Ed&PubIntYB 82*
Wilson World - *See* Ellsworth Reporter
Wilson/Zario - *See* Sulzer Music
Wilsonville Times [of Tigard Times] - Portland, OR - *NewsDir 84*
Wilsonville Times - Wilsonville, OR - *AyerDirPub 83*
Wilsonville Times - *See* Times Publishing Co.
Wiltek Inc. - Norwalk, CT - *DataDirSup 7-83*
Wilton Bulletin [of Acorn Press Inc.] - Ridgefield, CT - *NewsDir 84*
Wilton Bulletin - *See* Acorn Press Inc.
Wilton Bulletin, The - Wilton, CT - *Ed&PubIntYB 82*
Wilton, Coombs & Colnett - San Francisco, CA - *AdAge 3-28-84; ArtMar 84; StaDirAdAg 2-84*
Wilton-Durant Advocate News - Wilton, IA - *BaconPubCkNews 84*
Wilton Enterprises Inc. (Book Div.) - Woodridge, IL - *BoPubDir 4, 5*
Wilton News [of Washburn Borlaug Publishing Co.] - Washburn, ND - *NewsDir 84*
Wilton News - Wilton, ND - *AyerDirPub 83; Ed&PubIntYB 82*
Wilton News - *See* Borlaug Publishing Co.
Wilton Telephone Co. - Wilton, IA - *TelDir&BG 83-84*
Wilton Telephone Co. - Wilton, NH - *TelDir&BG 83-84*
Wilwin Records - Carlsbad, CA - *BillIntBG 83-84*
WILX-TV - Lansing, MI - *DirUSTelSta 83; TelAl 83, 84; Tel&CabFB 84S; TV&RadDir 84*
WILX-TV - Onondaga, MI - *BrCabYB 84*
WILY - Centralia, IL - *BrCabYB 84; TV&RadDir 84*
WIM - Oakland, CA - *BoPubDir 4, 5*
W.I.M. Publications - College Corner, OH - *BoPubDir 4, 5; LitMag&SmPr 83-84*
WIMA - Lima, OH - *BrCabYB 84; NatRadPubDir Summer 83, Spring 84; TV&RadDir 84*
WIMA-FM - Lima, OH - *NatRadPubDir Summer 83, Spring 84*
Wimac Recorders [Subs. of Playette Corp.] - Great Neck, NY - *AvMarPl 83*
Wimberley View - Wimberley, TX - *AyerDirPub 83; BaconPubCkNews 84; Ed&PubIntYB 82*
Wimbledon Music Inc. - Los Angeles, CA - *BoPubDir 4 Sup, 5*
WIMC-FM - Orangeburg, SC - *BrCabYB 84*
WIMG - Princeton, NJ - *TV&RadDir 84*
WIMG - Trenton, NJ - *BrCabYB 84*
WIMI - Ironwood, MI - *BrCabYB 84*
WIMK-FM - Iron Mountain, MI - *BrCabYB 84*
Wimmer Brothers Books - Memphis, TN - *BoPubDir 4, 5; LitMag&SmPr 83-84; MagIndMarPl 82-83; WritMar 84*
Wimmershoff & Associates - Westwood, NJ - *AdAge 3-28-84; StaDirAdAg 2-84*
WIMO - Winder, GA - *BrCabYB 84; TV&RadDir 84*
WIMS - Michigan City, IN - *BrCabYB 84; NatRadPubDir Summer 83, Spring 84; TV&RadDir 84*
Wims Computer Consulting - Tulsa, OK - *MicrocomSwDir 1*
WIMT-FM - Lima, OH - *BrCabYB 84; TV&RadDir 84*
WIMZ - Knoxville, TN - *BrCabYB 84; NatRadPubDir Summer 83, Spring 84; TV&RadDir 84*
WIMZ-FM - Knoxville, TN - *BrCabYB 84; NatRadPubDir Summer 83, Spring 84; TV&RadDir 84*
WIN - Denver, CO - *DirOnDB Spring 84*
Win Magazine - Brooklyn, NY - *ArtMar 84; LitMag&SmPr 83-84; MagIndMarPl 82-83*
Win News - Lexington, MA - *LitMag&SmPr 83-84*
WINA - Charlottesville, VA - *BrCabYB 84; NatRadPubDir Summer 83, Spring 84; TV&RadDir 84*
Winamac Pulaski County Journal - Winamac, IN - *BaconPubCkNews 84; NewsDir 84*
Winard Advertising Agency Inc. - Pittsfield, MA - *ArtMar 84; StaDirAdAg 2-84*
WINC - Winchester, VA - *BrCabYB 84; TV&RadDir 84*
WINC-FM - Winchester, VA - *BrCabYB 84; TV&RadDir 84*
Winch & Associates, B. L. - Rolling Hills Estates, CA - *AvMarPl 83; LitMag&SmPr 83-84; WritMar 84*
Winchell Marketing Communications [Div. of The Winchell Co.] - Philadelphia, PA - *AdAge 3-28-84; DirPRFirms 83; StaDirAdAg 2-84*
Winchendon Courier - *See* Winchendon Courier-News Corp.
Winchendon Courier-News Corp. - Winchendon, MA - *BaconPubCkNews 84*
Winchendon Courier, The - Winchendon, MA - *Ed&PubIntYB 82*
Winchendon Group Inc., The - Alexandria, VA - *MicrocomMPl 83, 84; MicrocomSwDir 1; WhoWMicrocom 83*
Winchendon State Line News - *See* Winchendon Courier-News Corp.
Winchester Computer Corp. - New York, NY - *ADAPSOMemDir 83-84*
Winchester Herald Chronicle - Winchester, TN - *BaconPubCkNews 84; NewsDir 84*
Winchester Press [Subs. of New Century Publishers] - Piscataway, NJ - *LitMarPl 84; WritMar 84*
Winchester Star - Winchester, MA - *Ed&PubIntYB 82; NewsDir 84*
Winchester Star - Winchester, VA - *AyerDirPub 83; BaconPubCkNews 84; Ed&PubIntYB 82; NewsDir 84*
Winchester Star - *See* Century Newspapers Inc.
Winchester Sun - Winchester, KY - *BaconPubCkNews 84; Ed&PubIntYB 82; NewsDir 84*
Winchester Times - Winchester, IL - *BaconPubCkNews 84; Ed&PubIntYB 82*
Winchester TV Cable Co. [of Mid Atlantic Network] - Winchester, VA - *BrCabYB 84; Tel&CabFB 84C*
WIND - Chicago, IL - *BrCabYB 84; NatRadPubDir Summer 83, Spring 84; TV&RadDir 84*
Wind Chimes - Glen Burnie, MD - *LitMag&SmPr 83-84*
Wind Chimes Press - Glen Burnie, MD - *LitMag&SmPr 83-84*
Wind in the Trees Music - Los Angeles, CA - *BillIntBG 83-84*
Wind/Literary Journal - Pikeville, KY - *BoPubDir 4, 5; LitMag&SmPr 83-84; WritMar 84*
Wind Power Digest - Bascom, OH - *LitMag&SmPr 83-84*
Wind Power Publishing - Bascom, OH - *LitMag&SmPr 83-84*
Wind River Scribes - Auburn, WA - *BoPubDir 5*
Wind Surf - Dana Point, CA - *BaconPubCkMag 84*
Windber Cable TV [of Eastern Telecom Corp.] - Windber, PA - *BrCabYB 84; Tel&CabFB 84C*
Winder News - Winder, GA - *AyerDirPub 83; BaconPubCkNews 84; Ed&PubIntYB 82; NewsDir 84*
Windflower Press - Lincoln, NE - *BoPubDir 4, 5; LitMag&SmPr 83-84*
Windham Bay Press - Juneau, AK - *BoPubDir 4 Sup, 5*
Windham Hill Music - Stanford, CA - *BillIntBG 83-84*
Windham Hill Productions Inc. - Palo Alto, CA - *BillIntBG 83-84*
Windham Journal - *See* Catskill Mountain Publishing Corp.
Windham Newsletter [of Windham Software Inc.] - Williamantic, CT - *MicrocomMPl 84*
Windham Software Inc. - Willimantic, CT - *MicrocomMPl 83, 84*
Windless Orchard [of Indiana-Purdue University] - Ft. Wayne, IN - *BoPubDir 4, 5; LitMag&SmPr 83-84; WritMar 84*
Windmill Books Inc. - New York, NY - *LitMarPl 83*
Windmill Herald, The - New Westminster, BC, Canada - *Ed&PubIntYB 82*
Windmill Productions Inc. - Atlanta, GA - *AvMarPl 83*
Windmill Publishing Co. - El Cajon, CA - *BoPubDir 4, 5*
Windom Cottonwood County Citizen - Windom, MN - *BaconPubCkNews 84; NewsDir 84*
Window - Westminster, CO - *Ed&PubIntYB 82*
Window - Watertown, MA - *MicrocomMPl 84; MicrocomSwDir 1*
Window Energy Systems - St. Paul, MN - *BaconPubCkMag 84*
Window Music Publishing Co. Inc. - *See* Drake Music Group
Window Research - Woodinville, WA - *MicrocomMPl 84*
Windows Project - Liverpool, England - *LitMag&SmPr 83-84*
Windrush Micro Systems Ltd. - North Walsham, England - *MicrocomSwDir 1*

Windsong Books International - Huntington Beach, CA - *LitMag&SmPr 83-84*
Windsong Press - Denver, CO - *BoPubDir 4, 5*
Windsor Beacon - Windsor, CO - *BaconPubCkNews 84; Ed&PubIntYB 82*
Windsor Books [Div. of Windsor Marketing Corp.] - Brightwaters, NY - *LitMarPl 83, 84*
Windsor Cable Co. Inc. - Colesville, NY - *BrCabYB 84*
Windsor Cable Co. Inc. - Windsor, NY - *BrCabYB 84; Tel&CabFB 84C*
Windsor Cable TV Ltd. - Windsor, NS, Canada - *BrCabYB 84*
Windsor Cablevision Inc. - Plymouth, NC - *BrCabYB 84*
Windsor Cablevision Inc. - Williamston, NC - *Tel&CabFB 84C*
Windsor Cablevision Inc. - Windsor, NC - *BrCabYB 84 p.D-311*
Windsor Chronicle - Windsor, VT - *Ed&PubIntYB 82*
Windsor-Hights Herald [of Princeton Packet Inc.] - Hightstown, NJ - *AyerDirPub 83; Ed&PubIntYB 82; NewsDir 84*
Windsor House - San Diego, CA - *BoPubDir 4 Sup, 5*
Windsor Journal [of Imprint Newspapers] - Windsor, CT - *Ed&PubIntYB 82; NewsDir 84*
Windsor Locks Journal - Windsor, CT - *Ed&PubIntYB 82*
Windsor Pertie Ledger-Advance - Windsor, NC - *BaconPubCkNews 84*
Windsor Publications - Woodland Hills, CA - *LitMarPl 83, 84; WritMar 84*
Windsor Review - Windsor, MO - *BaconPubCkNews 84; Ed&PubIntYB 82; NewsDir 84*
Windsor Shelby County News-Gazette - Windsor, IL - *BaconPubCkNews 84*
Windsor Standard, The - Windsor, NY - *Ed&PubIntYB 82*
Windsor Star - Windsor, ON, Canada - *BaconPubCkNews 84; Ed&PubIntYB 82; LitMarPl 83, 84*
Windsor Systems Development Inc. - New York, NY - *DataDirOnSer 84; EISS 7-83 Sup*
Windsor This Month Magazine - Windsor, ON, Canada - *ArtMar 84; WritMar 84*
Windsor Total Video - New York, NY - *AvMarPl 83; Tel&CabFB 84C*
Windt, Bob - Brooklyn, NY - *DirPRFirms 83*
Windward Communications Inc. - Brunswick, ME - *BrCabYB 84*
Windward Publishing Inc. - Miami, FL - *BoPubDir 4, 5*
Windward Sun-Press - Kaneohe, HI - *AyerDirPub 83*
Windward Sun Press - Windward, HI - *Ed&PubIntYB 82*
Windy Row Press - Peterborough, NH - *BoPubDir 4, 5*
WINE - Brookfield, CT - *BrCabYB 84*
WINE - Danbury, CT - *NatRadPubDir Summer 83, Spring 84; TV&RadDir 84*
Wine & Dine - Nuns' Island, PQ, Canada - *BaconPubCkMag 84*
Wine Appreciation Guild Ltd. - San Francisco, CA - *BoPubDir 4, 5*
Wine Books - San Marcos, CA - *BoPubDir 4, 5*
Wine Consultants of California - San Francisco, CA - *BoPubDir 4, 5*
Wine Country - Benica, CA - *BaconPubCkMag 84*
Wine Country Records - San Jose, CA - *BillIntBG 83-84*
Wine, J. Floyd - Winchester, VA - *BoPubDir 4, 5*
Wine Library - Silver Spring, MD - *DirOnDB Spring 84*
Wine Library [of Source Telecomputing Corp.] - McLean, VA - *DataDirOnSer 84*
Wine Museum of San Francisco, The - San Francisco, CA - *MagIndMarPl 82-83*
Wine on the Table - Morris, CT - *Ed&PubIntYB 82*
Wine Press, The - Chicago, IL - *LitMag&SmPr 83-84*
Wine Publications - Berkeley, CA - *BoPubDir 4, 5*
Wine Spectator [of M. Shanken Communications Inc.] - San Francisco, CA - *BaconPubCkMag 84; WritMar 84*
Wine Tidings [of Kylix International Ltd.] - Montreal, PQ, Canada - *ArtMar 84; WritMar 84*
Wine West - Geyserville, CA - *BaconPubCkMag 84; WritMar 84*
Wine World - Van Nuys, CA - *BaconPubCkMag 84; MagDir 84; WritMar 84*
Winegard Co. - Burlington, IA - *Tel&CabFB 84C*
Wines & Vines [of Hiaring Co.] - San Rafael, CA - *ArtMar 84; BaconPubCkMag 84; MagDir 84; MagIndMarPl 82-83; WritMar 84*
Winetaster's Choice - Forest Hills, NY - *Ed&PubIntYB 82*
Winewood Journal - Black Hawk, CO - *LitMag&SmPr 83-84*
Winewood Publishing - Black Hawk, CO - *LitMag&SmPr 83-84*
WINF - Hartford/New Britain, CT - *NatRadPubDir Summer 83 p.46, Spring 84 p.46*
WINF - Manchester, CT - *BrCabYB 84; TV&RadDir 84*
Winfas Inc. - Jacksonville, NC - *BrCabYB 84*
Winfield Advertising Agency Inc. - St. Louis, MO - *StaDirAdAg 2-84*
Winfield Beacon & Wayland News - Winfield, IA - *BaconPubCkNews 84*
Winfield Beacon, The - Winfield, IA - *Ed&PubIntYB 82*
Winfield Courier - Winfield, KS - *BaconPubCkNews 84; Ed&PubIntYB 82; NewsDir 84*
Winfield Examiner - *See* Examiner Newspapers
Winfield Journal Record - Winfield, AL - *BaconPubCkNews 84*
Winfield Putnam Democrat - *See* P.C. Publishing Co.
WING - Princeton, NJ - *NatRadPubDir Summer 83*
WING - Trenton, NJ - *NatRadPubDir Spring 84*
WING - Dayton, OH - *BrCabYB 84; NatRadPubDir Summer 83, Spring 84*
WING - Kettering, OH - *TV&RadDir 84*
Wing Lynch Inc. - Beaverton, OR - *AvMarPl 83*
Wing Music Publishing, Mike - Bellevue, WA - *BillIntBG 83-84*
Wing Spread - Mountain Home, ID - *AyerDirPub 83*
Wingate & Associates Inc. - Tampa, FL - *MicrocomMPl 84*
Wingbow Press [Subs. of Bookpeople] - Berkeley, CA - *LitMag&SmPr 83-84; LitMarPl 83, 84; WritMar 84*
Winged Foot - New York, NY - *BaconPubCkMag 84; MagDir 84*
Winged Lion Publishing Ltd. - Los Angeles, CA - *BoPubDir 4, 5*
Wings [of Corvus Publishing Group Ltd.] - Calgary, AB, Canada - *BaconPubCkMag 84; WritMar 84*
Wings of Gold - Roseland, VA - *BaconPubCkMag 84*
Wings Press - Belfast, ME - *BoPubDir 5; LitMag&SmPr 83-84; LitMarPl 84*
Wings Press - Houston, TX - *BoPubDir 4, 5*
Wingstar Film Productions Inc. - New York, NY - *AvMarPl 83*
WINH - Georgetown, SC - *BrCabYB 84; TV&RadDir 84*
Winhill Corp. - Shoshoni, WY - *Tel&CabFB 84C*
WINI - Murphysboro, IL - *BrCabYB 84; TV&RadDir 84*
Winius-Brandon Advertising - Bellaire, TX - *AdAge 3-28-84; ArtMar 84; StaDirAdAg 2-84*
Winius-Brandon Advertising - Houston, TX - *DirPRFirms 83*
WINK - Ft. Myers, FL - *BrCabYB 84; NatRadPubDir Summer 83, Spring 84; TV&RadDir 84*
Wink Bulletin - Wink, TX - *BaconPubCkNews 84; Ed&PubIntYB 82*
WINK-FM - Ft. Myers, FL - *BrCabYB 84; NatRadPubDir Summer 83, Spring 84; TV&RadDir 84*
WINK-TV - Ft. Myers, FL - *BrCabYB 84; DirUSTelSta 83; TelAl 83, 84; Tel&CabFB 84S; TV&RadDir 84*
Winkler County News - Kermit, TX - *AyerDirPub 83; Ed&PubIntYB 82*
Winlock Lewis County News - Winlock, WA - *BaconPubCkNews 84*
Winmark Press - Stratford, CT - *BoPubDir 5*
WINN - Louisville, KY - *BrCabYB 84; NatRadPubDir Summer 83, Spring 84; TV&RadDir 84*
Winn Cable TV [of TCA Cable TV Inc.] - Winnfield, LA - *Tel&CabFB 84C*
Winn Parish Enterprise - Winn Parish, LA - *Ed&PubIntYB 82*
Winn Parish Enterprise - Winnfield, LA - *AyerDirPub 83*
Winn Telephone Co. - Winn, MI - *TelDir&BG 83-84*
Winnebago Cable TV Corp. - Winnebago, MN - *BrCabYB 84; Tel&CabFB 84C*
Winnebago Cablevision [of Winnebago Cooperative Telephone Association Corp.] - Lake Mills, IA - *BrCabYB 84*
Winnebago Cooperative Telephone Association - Lake Mills, IA - *Tel&CabFB 84C; TelDir&BG 83-84*
Winnebago News [of Durand North Central Associated Publishers] - Durand, IL - *AyerDirPub 83; NewsDir 84*
Winnebago News - Winnebago, IL - *Ed&PubIntYB 82*
Winnebago News - *See* North Central Associated Publishers
Winnebago Soft Ware Co. - La Crosse, WI - *MicrocomMPl 84*
Winneconne News - Winneconne, WI - *BaconPubCkNews 84; Ed&PubIntYB 82*
Winnemucca Humboldt Sun - Winnemucca, NV - *BaconPubCkNews 84*

Winner Advocate - Winner, SD - *AyerDirPub 83; BaconPubCkNews 84*
Winner Advocate & Journal - Winner, SD - *NewsDir 84*
Winner Cable Television [of Midcontinent Cable Systems Co.] - Winner, SD - *BrCabYB 84; Tel&CabFB 84C*
Winner Cline & Associates - Tampa, FL - *DirPRFirms 83*
Winner Communications Inc. - New York, NY - *StaDirAdAg 2-84*
Winner Music - Chicago, IL - *BillIntBG 83-84*
Winnetka News Advertiser - Highland Park, IL - *AyerDirPub 83*
Winnetka News-Advertiser - Winnetka, IL - *Ed&PubIntYB 82*
Winnetka News Advertiser - *See* Singer Printing & Publishing Co.
Winnetka Talk [of Wilmette Pioneer Press Inc.] - Wilmette, IL - *AyerDirPub 83; NewsDir 84*
Winnetka Talk - Winnetka, IL - *Ed&PubIntYB 82*
Winnetka Talk - *See* Pioneer Press Inc.
Winnett Times - Winnett, MT - *Ed&PubIntYB 82*
Winnett Times - *See* Roundup Record Tribune Publishers
Winnfield Cable TV [of Teleservice Corp. of America Inc.] - Winnfield, LA - *BrCabYB 84*
Winnfield Winn Parish Enterprise - Winnfield, LA - *BaconPubCkNews 84; NewsDir 84*
Winning [of National Reporter Publications Inc.] - Bixby, OK - *ArtMar 84; WritMar 84*
Winnipeg - Winnipeg, MB, Canada - *BaconPubCkMag 84*
Winnipeg Art Gallery - Winnipeg, MB, Canada - *BoPubDir 4, 5*
Winnipeg Free Press - Winnipeg, MB, Canada - *BaconPubCkNews 84; Ed&PubIntYB 82*
Winnipeg Sun - Winnipeg, MB, Canada - *AyerDirPub 83; BaconPubCkNews 84; Ed&PubIntYB 82*
Winnipeg Videon Inc. [of Moffat Communications Ltd.] - Winnipeg, MB, Canada - *BrCabYB 84; Tel&CabFB 84C*
Winnsboro Cable TV [of Texas Community Antennas Inc.] - Winnsboro, TX - *BrCabYB 84*
Winnsboro Cablevision Inc. - Winnsboro, SC - *BrCabYB 84; Tel&CabFB 84C*
Winnsboro Franklin Sun - Winnsboro, LA - *BaconPubCkNews 84; NewsDir 84*
Winnsboro Herald Independent - Winnsboro, SC - *BaconPubCkNews 84*
Winnsboro News - Winnsboro, TX - *BaconPubCkNews 84; Ed&PubIntYB 82; NewsDir 84*
Winona Cable Inc. - Winona, MS - *BrCabYB 84; Tel&CabFB 84C*
Winona Courier, The [of Diocese of Winona] - Winona, MN - *NewsDir 84*
Winona Daily News [of Republican & Herald Publishing Co.] - Winona, MN - *BaconPubCkNews 84; Ed&PubIntYB 82; NewsDir 84*
Winona Leader - Winona, KS - *BaconPubCkNews 84; Ed&PubIntYB 82*
Winona Research - Minneapolis, MN - *AdAge 5-17-84 p.34; BrCabYB 84; IntDirMarRes 83*
Winona Times - *See* Mid-State Publishing Co. Inc.
Winona Times, The - Winona, MS - *Ed&PubIntYB 82*
WINQ - Tampa/St. Petersburg, FL - *NatRadPubDir Summer 83 p.65*
WINQ-FM - Winchedon, MA - *BrCabYB 84*
WINR - Binghamton, NY - *BrCabYB 84; NatRadPubDir Summer 83, Spring 84; TV&RadDir 84*
WINS - New York, NY - *BrCabYB 84; LitMarPl 83, 84; NatRadPubDir Summer 83, Spring 84; TV&RadDir 84*
Winslow & De Young - Beaumont, TX - *DirPRFirms 83*
Winslow Associates - Washington, DC - *DataDirOnSer 84*
Winslow, Hope Emerson - Oakland, CA - *MagIndMarPl 82-83*
Winslow, John G. - New York, NY - *DirPRFirms 83*
Winslow Mail - Winslow, AZ - *BaconPubCkNews 84; Ed&PubIntYB 82; NewsDir 84*
Winsor Newspapers - Canton, IL - *Ed&PubIntYB 82*
Winsted Citizen - Winsted, CT - *BaconPubCkNews 84; NewsDir 84*
Winsted Corp. - Minneapolis, MN - *AvMarPl 83*
Winsted Evening Citizen - Winsted, CT - *Ed&PubIntYB 82*
Winsted Journal - Winsted, MN - *BaconPubCkNews 84; Ed&PubIntYB 82*
Winsted Telephone Co. - Winsted, MN - *TelDir&BG 83-84*
Winston & Sons, V. H. [Div. of Scripta Technica Inc.] - Silver Spring, MD - *LitMarPl 83, 84*
Winston, Clara - Brattleboro, VT - *MagIndMarPl 82-83*
Winston County Journal - Louisville, MS - *AyerDirPub 83; Ed&PubIntYB 82*
Winston-Derek Publishers - Nashville, TN - *BoPubDir 4; LitMag&SmPr 83-84; LitMarPl 83, 84; WritMar 84*
Winston, Krishna & Clara - Middletown, CT - *LitMarPl 84*
Winston, Krishna & Clara - Brattleboro, VT - *LitMarPl 83*
Winston Personnel Inc. - New York, NY - *IntDirMarRes 83; LitMarPl 84; MagIndMarPl 82-83*
Winston Press [of CBS Educational Publishing] - Minneapolis, MN - *ArtMar 84; LitMarPl 83, 84; WritMar 84*
Winston-Salem Chronicle - Winston-Salem, NC - *BaconPubCkNews 84; NewsDir 84*
Winston-Salem Journal [of Piedmont Publishing Co. Inc.] - Winston-Salem, NC - *BaconPubCkNews 84; Ed&PubIntYB 82; LitMarPl 83, 84; NewsBur 6; NewsDir 84*
Winston-Salem Sentinel [of Piedmont Publishing Co. Inc.] - Winston-Salem, NC - *BaconPubCkNews 84; NewsDir 84*
Winston-Salem Suburbanite [of Lindsay Publishing Co.] - Winston-Salem, NC - *BaconPubCkNews 84; NewsDir 84*
WINT-TV - Crossville, TN - *BrCabYB 84; TelAl 84; Tel&CabFB 84S; TV&RadDir 84*
Wintek Corp. - Lafayette, IN - *DataDirSup 7-83; WhoWMicrocom 83*
Winter Brook Publishing Co. - Covina, CA - *BoPubDir 4, 5*
Winter Communications, Foster - Traverse City, MI - *CabTVFinDB 83; Tel&CabFB 84C*
Winter Garden Cable TV [of LBJ Co.] - Crystal City, TX - *BrCabYB 84*
Winter Garden Times - Winter Garden, FL - *BaconPubCkNews 84; Ed&PubIntYB 82; NewsDir 84*
Winter Haven Herald - Winter Haven, FL - *NewsDir 84*
Winter Haven News-Chief - Winter Haven, FL - *BaconPubCkNews 84; Ed&PubIntYB 82; NewsDir 84*
Winter Park Manifest - Winter Park, CO - *AyerDirPub 83; BaconPubCkNews 84*
Winter Park Outlook - Winter Park, FL - *BaconPubCkNews 84*
Winter Park Sun Herald - Winter Park, FL - *BaconPubCkNews 84*
Winter Sawyer County Gazette - Winter, WI - *BaconPubCkNews 84*
Winter Soldier Archive - Berkeley, CA - *BoPubDir 4, 5; LitMag&SmPr 83-84*
Winter Sports - Delmar, NY - *BaconPubCkMag 84; MagDir 84*
Winter Sports Publishing Inc. - Milwaukee, WI - *MagIndMarPl 82-83*
Winterbrook Communications Inc. - Central Point, OR - *Tel&CabFB 84C*
Winterburn Women's Institute - Winterburn, AB, Canada - *BoPubDir 4, 5*
Wintergreen & Advance - Pacific Palisades, CA - *BoPubDir 4, 5*
Winterhalter & Associates Inc. - Ann Arbor, MI - *MicrocomSwDir 1; WhoWMicrocom 83*
Winterhalter Inc. - Ann Arbor, MI - *MicrocomMPl 84*
Winterkorn Lillis - Rochester, NY - *AdAge 3-28-84; ArtMar 84; StaDirAdAg 2-84*
Winters, Bayla - Burbank, CA - *LitMarPl 83, 84; MagIndMarPl 82-83*
Winters Enterprise - Winters, TX - *BaconPubCkNews 84; Ed&PubIntYB 82*
Winters Express - Winters, CA - *BaconPubCkNews 84; Ed&PubIntYB 82*
Winters, Franceschi & Callahan - Phoenix, AZ - *ArtMar 84; StaDirAdAg 2-84*
Winterset Madisonian - Winterset, IA - *BaconPubCkNews 84; Ed&PubIntYB 82; NewsDir 84*
Wintersville Citizen - Steubenville, OH - *NewsDir 84*
Wintersville Tri County News - Steubenville, OH - *BaconPubCkNews 84*
Winterthur Museum - Winterthur, DE - *BoPubDir 4, 5*
Winthrop Advertiser - Gardiner, ME - *Ed&PubIntYB 82*
Winthrop Advertiser - Winthrop, ME - *NewsDir 84*
Winthrop News - Winthrop, IA - *BaconPubCkNews 84; Ed&PubIntYB 82*
Winthrop News - Winthrop, MN - *AyerDirPub 83; BaconPubCkNews 84; Ed&PubIntYB 82*

Winthrop Sun-Transcript - Winthrop, MA - *BaconPubCkNews 84; Ed&PubIntYB 82*
Winthrop Telephone Co. [Aff. of Larson Utilities Inc.] - Winthrop, MN - *TelDir&BG 83-84*
Winton Times - Winton, CA - *Ed&PubIntYB 82*
Winton Times - *See* Waterford News Publishers
WINU - Highland, IL - *BrCabYB 84; TV&RadDir 84*
WINW - Canton, OH - *BrCabYB 84; TV&RadDir 84*
WINX - Rockville, MD - *BrCabYB 84; TV&RadDir 84*
WINY - Putnam, CT - *BrCabYB 84; NatRadPubDir Summer 83; TV&RadDir 84*
WINZ - Miami, FL - *BrCabYB 84; LitMarPl 83, 84; NatRadPubDir Summer 83, Spring 84*
WINZ - Opa Locka, FL - *TV&RadDir 84*
WINZ-FM - Miami, FL - *BrCabYB 84; LitMarPl 83; NatRadPubDir Summer 83, Spring 84*
WINZ-FM - Opa Locka, FL - *TV&RadDir 84*
WIOA - Mayaguez, PR - *BrCabYB 84*
WIOB-FM - San Juan, PR - *BrCabYB 84*
WIOC - Ponce, PR - *BrCabYB 84*
WIOD - Miami, FL - *BrCabYB 84; NatRadPubDir Summer 83, Spring 84; TV&RadDir 84*
WIOF-FM - Waterbury, CT - *BrCabYB 84; NatRadPubDir Summer 83, Spring 84; TV&RadDir 84*
WIOG-FM - Saginaw, MI - *BrCabYB 84; NatRadPubDir Summer 83, Spring 84*
WIOI - New Boston, OH - *BrCabYB 84*
WIOI - Portsmouth, OH - *TV&RadDir 84*
WIOK-FM - Falmouth, KY - *BrCabYB 84; TV&RadDir 84*
WION - Ionia, MI - *BrCabYB 84; TV&RadDir 84*
WIOO - Carlisle, PA - *BrCabYB 84; NatRadPubDir Summer 83, Spring 84; TV&RadDir 84*
WIOQ-FM - Bala-Cynwyd, PA - *TV&RadDir 84*
WIOQ-FM - Philadelphia, PA - *BrCabYB 84; NatRadPubDir Summer 83 p.213, Spring 84 p.213*
WIOS - Tawas City, MI - *BrCabYB 84; TV&RadDir 84*
WIOT-FM - Toledo, OH - *BrCabYB 84; NatRadPubDir Summer 83, Spring 84; TV&RadDir 84*
WIOU - Kokomo, IN - *BrCabYB 84; TV&RadDir 84*
WIOV-FM - Ephrata, PA - *BrCabYB 84; TV&RadDir 84*
WIOZ-FM - Southern Pines, NC - *BrCabYB 84; TV&RadDir 84*
WIP - Philadelphia, PA - *BrCabYB 84; LitMarPl 83, 84; NatRadPubDir Summer 83, Spring 84; TV&RadDir 84*
WIPB-TV - Muncie, IN - *BrCabYB 84; Tel&CabFB 84S; TV&RadDir 84*
WIPC - Lake Wales, FL - *BrCabYB 84; TV&RadDir 84*
WIPL-FM - Tupper Lake, NY - *TV&RadDir 84*
WIPM-TV - Mayaguez, PR - *BrCabYB 84; Tel&CabFB 84S*
WIPR - San Juan, PR - *BrCabYB 84*
WIPR-FM - San Juan, PR - *BrCabYB 84*
WIPR-TV - San Juan, PR - *BrCabYB 84; Tel&CabFB 84S*
WIPS - Ticonderoga, NY - *BrCabYB 84; TV&RadDir 84*
WIQB-FM - Ann Arbor, MI - *BrCabYB 84; NatRadPubDir Summer 83, Spring 84; TV&RadDir 84*
WIQH-FM - Concord, MA - *BrCabYB 84; NatRadPubDir Summer 83, Spring 84; TV&RadDir 84*
WIQI - Tampa, FL - *BrCabYB 84*
WIQI-FM - Tampa, FL - *NatRadPubDir Summer 83, Spring 84; TV&RadDir 84*
WIQO-FM - Covington, VA - *BrCabYB 84; TV&RadDir 84*
WIQR - Prattville, AL - *BrCabYB 84; TV&RadDir 84*
WIQT - Horseheads, NY - *BrCabYB 84; TV&RadDir 84*
WIQX - Millersville, PA - *BrCabYB 84*
WIRA - Ft. Pierce, FL - *BrCabYB 84; TV&RadDir 84*
WIRB - Enterprise, AL - *BrCabYB 84; TV&RadDir 84*
WIRC - Hickory, NC - *BrCabYB 84; TV&RadDir 84*
WIRD - Lake Placid, NY - *BrCabYB 84; TV&RadDir 84*
WIRE - Indianapolis, IN - *BrCabYB 84; NatRadPubDir Summer 83, Spring 84; TV&RadDir 84*
Wire Association International Inc. - Guilford, CT - *BoPubDir 4 Sup, 5*
Wire Business - Ridgefield, CT - *BaconPubCkMag 84; WritMar 84*
Wire Graphics Inc. - Farmingdale, NY - *DataDirSup 7-83*
Wire Industry News - Ridgefield, CT - *BaconPubCkMag 84*
Wire Journal International - Guilford, CT - *ArtMar 84; BaconPubCkMag 84; MagDir 84*
Wire Press - San Francisco, CA - *BoPubDir 4, 5*
Wire Rope News & Sling Technology - Clark, NJ - *BaconPubCkMag 84*
Wire Technology - Cleveland, OH - *MagDir 84*
Wire Technology - Solon, OH - *BaconPubCkMag 84; MagIndMarPl 82-83*
Wire Tele-View Corp. - Pottsville, PA - *BrCabYB 84; Tel&CabFB 84C p.1713*
Wire Tele-view Corp. - Tremont, PA - *BrCabYB 84*
Wiregrass Farmer & Stockman - Ashburn, GA - *AyerDirPub 83*
Wiresat Corp. - Ocala, FL - *Tel&CabFB 84C*
Wireworks - Hillside, NJ - *AvMarPl 83*
WIRJ - Humboldt, TN - *BrCabYB 84; TV&RadDir 84*
WIRK - West Palm Beach, FL - *NatRadPubDir Summer 83; TV&RadDir 84*
WIRK-FM - West Palm Beach, FL - *BrCabYB 84; NatRadPubDir Summer 83, Spring 84; TV&RadDir 84*
WIRL - Peoria, IL - *BrCabYB 84; NatRadPubDir Summer 83, Spring 84; TV&RadDir 84*
WIRO - Ironton, OH - *BrCabYB 84; TV&RadDir 84*
WIRQ-FM - Rochester, NY - *BrCabYB 84; NatRadPubDir Summer 83, Spring 84; TV&RadDir 84*
Wirt County Journal - Elizabeth, WV - *Ed&PubIntYB 82*
WIRT-TV - Duluth, MN - *LitMarPl 84; TV&RadDir 84*
WIRT-TV - Hibbing, MN - *BrCabYB 84; TelAl 83, 84; Tel&CabFB 84S*
Wirth, Diane E. - Danville, CA - *BoPubDir 4*
Wirth, Diane E. - Aurora, CO - *BoPubDir 5*
WIRV - Irvine, KY - *BrCabYB 84; TV&RadDir 84*
WIRX-FM - St. Joseph, MI - *BrCabYB 84; TV&RadDir 84*
WIRY - Plattsburgh, NY - *BrCabYB 84; TV&RadDir 84*
Wirz Inc., Adolf - Zurich, Switzerland - *StaDirAdAg 2-84*
WIS - Columbia, SC - *BrCabYB 84; NatRadPubDir Summer 83, Spring 84; TV&RadDir 84*
WIS-TV - Columbia, SC - *BrCabYB 84; DirUSTelSta 83; LitMarPl 83, 84; TelAl 83, 84; Tel&CabFB 84S; TV&RadDir 84*
WISA - Isabela, PR - *BrCabYB 84*
WISC-TV - Madison, WI - *BrCabYB 84; DirUSTelSta 83; TelAl 83, 84; Tel&CabFB 84S; TV&RadDir 84*
Wiscasset Newspaper, The - Wiscasset, ME - *Ed&PubIntYB 82*
Wisco Computer Consultants Inc. - Fullerton, CA - *WhoWMicrocom 83*
Wisconsin Academy Review - Madison, WI - *LitMag&SmPr 83-84*
Wisconsin Agriculturist - Madison, WI - *BaconPubCkMag 84; MagDir 84*
Wisconsin All-Sports Network - Milwaukee, WI - *CabTVPrDB 83*
Wisconsin Athlete - Madison, WI - *BaconPubCkMag 84*
Wisconsin Beverage Journal [of Zien Enterprises Inc.] - Milwaukee, WI - *BaconPubCkMag 84; MagDir 84*
Wisconsin Books - Madison, WI - *BoPubDir 4, 5*
Wisconsin Business Journal - Brookfield, WI - *BaconPubCkMag 84*
Wisconsin Cablevision & Radio Co. Inc. - Fond du Lac, WI - *Tel&CabFB 84C p.1713*
Wisconsin Career Information System [of Wisconsin Vocational Studies Center] - Madison, WI - *EISS 83*
Wisconsin CATV [of American TV & Communications Corp.] - Eau Claire, WI - *BrCabYB 84; Tel&CabFB 84C*
Wisconsin Clearinghouse [Aff. of University of Wisconsin Hospital & Clinics] - Madison, WI - *BoPubDir 4, 5*
Wisconsin Counties - Madison, WI - *BaconPubCkMag 84*
Wisconsin Cuneo Press Inc. - Milwaukee, WI - *MagIndMarPl 82-83*
Wisconsin Dells Events - Wisconsin Dells, WI - *BaconPubCkNews 84*
Wisconsin Dissemination Project [of Wisconsin State Dept. of Public Instruction] - Madison, WI - *EISS 83*
Wisconsin Education Fund - Port Washington, WI - *BoPubDir 4, 5*
Wisconsin Educational Television Network - Madison, WI - *BrCabYB 84*
Wisconsin Engineer [of Wisconsin Engineering Journal Association] - Madison, WI - *BaconPubCkMag 84; MagDir 84*
Wisconsin Food Dealer, The - Madison, WI - *BaconPubCkMag 84*
Wisconsin Food Service Review - Hartland, WI - *MagDir 84*
Wisconsin Industrial Product News [of S.I.C. Publishing Corp. Inc.] - Elm Grove, WI - *BaconPubCkMag 84; MagDir 84*

Wisconsin InterLibrary Services - Madison, WI - *InfIndMarPl 83*
Wisconsin Law Review - Madison, WI - *MagDir 84*
Wisconsin Magazine of History - Madison, WI - *MagIndMarPl 82-83*
Wisconsin Manufacturers & Commerce - Milwaukee, WI - *BoPubDir 4, 5*
Wisconsin Master Plumber - Grafton, WI - *MagIndMarPl 82-83*
Wisconsin Master Plumber - Mequon, WI - *BaconPubCkMag 84*
Wisconsin Medical Journal - Madison, WI - *BaconPubCkMag 84; MagDir 84*
Wisconsin Microware - Madison, WI - *MicrocomMPl 84; MicrocomSwDir 1*
Wisconsin Motor Carrier [of Wisconsin Motor Carriers Association] - Madison, WI - *MagDir 84; WritMar 84*
Wisconsin Newspaper Association - Madison, WI - *ProGuPRSer 4*
Wisconsin Newspress Inc. - Plymouth, WI - *BaconPubCkNews 84*
Wisconsin Pharmacist [of Wisconsin Pharmaceutical Association] - Madison, WI - *BaconPubCkMag 84; MagDir 84*
Wisconsin Professional Engineer - Madison, WI - *BaconPubCkMag 84*
Wisconsin Rapids Advertiser - Waupaca, WI - *AyerDirPub 83*
Wisconsin Rapids Advertiser - Wisconsin Rapids, WI - *BaconPubCkNews 84*
Wisconsin Rapids Tribune - Wisconsin Rapids, WI - *BaconPubCkNews 84; NewsDir 84*
Wisconsin Rec News - Madison, WI - *BaconPubCkMag 84; MagDir 84*
Wisconsin Research - Green Bay, WI - *IntDirMarRes 83*
Wisconsin Restaurateur - Madison, WI - *ArtMar 84; BaconPubCkMag 84; MagDir 84; WritMar 84*
Wisconsin Retailer - Hartland, WI - *BaconPubCkMag 84; MagDir 84*
Wisconsin Review - Oshkosh, WI - *ArtMar 84; LitMag&SmPr 83-84; WritMar 84*
Wisconsin Sheriff & Deputy - Chippewa Falls, WI - *ArtMar 84; WritMar 84*
Wisconsin Sportsman - Oshkosh, WI - *BaconPubCkMag 84; MagDir 84; WritMar 84*
Wisconsin State Data Center [of Wisconsin State Dept. of Administration] - Madison, WI - *EISS 83*
Wisconsin State Farmer [of Waupaca Publishing Co.] - Waupaca, WI - *AyerDirPub 83; BaconPubCkMag 84; Ed&PubIntYB 82; NewsDir 84*
Wisconsin State Genealogical Society Inc. - Madison, WI - *BoPubDir 4, 5*
Wisconsin State Journal [of Madison Newspapers Inc.] - Madison, WI - *AyerDirPub 83; BaconPubCkNews 84; Ed&PubIntYB 82; LitMarPl 83, 84; NewsBur 6*
Wisconsin Tales & Trails Inc. - Madison, WI - *ArtMar 84*
Wisconsin Telephone Co. - Milwaukee, WI - *TelDir&BG 83-84*
Wisconsin Trails [of Tamarack Press] - Madison, WI - *ArtMar 84; LitMag&SmPr 83-84; WritMar 84*
Wisconsin Vocational Studies Center [of University of Wisconsin-Madison] - Madison, WI - *InfIndMarPl 83*
Wisdom-Triggs Color Printing Corp. - New York, NY - *LitMarPl 84*
Wisdoms Child New York Guide - New York, NY - *NewsDir 84*
WISE - Asheville, NC - *BrCabYB 84; NatRadPubDir Summer 83, Spring 84; TV&RadDir 84*
Wise & Co., Don - New York, NY - *AdAge 3-28-84; StaDirAdAg 2-84*
Wise County Messenger - Decatur, TX - *AyerDirPub 83; Ed&PubIntYB 82*
Wise County Telephone Co. [Aff. of Central Telephone Co. of Texas] - Decatur, TX - *TelDir&BG 83-84*
Wise Owl Press - Southold, NY - *BoPubDir 4 Sup, 5*
Wise Owl Workshop - Livermore, CA - *MicrocomMPl 83, 84; WhoWMicrocom 83*
Wise Publishing Co. - Woodland Hills, CA - *BoPubDir 4, 5*
Wise Times, The - Decatur, TX - *Ed&PubIntYB 82*
Wiseman Computer Group - Bensenville, IL - *ADAPSOMemDir 83-84*
WISER - Toronto, ON, Canada - *DirOnDB Spring 84*
Wish Booklets - Reston, VA - *BoPubDir 4, 5*
W.I.S.H. Publications [Aff. of World Institute for Scientific Humanism] - New York, NY - *BoPubDir 4, 5*
WISH-TV - Indianapolis, IN - *BrCabYB 84; DirUSTelSta 83; LitMarPl 83, 84; TelAl 83, 84; Tel&CabFB 84S; TV&RadDir 84*
Wishbone Music - *See* Williams Music Group, Don
Wishek Star - Wishek, ND - *BaconPubCkNews 84; Ed&PubIntYB 82*
Wishing Well, The - Novato, CA - *LitMag&SmPr 83-84*
Wishner Communications Ltd. - New York, NY - *DirPRFirms 83*
Wishner Communications Ltd. - *See* Media West Group Inc.
WISK - Americus, GA - *BrCabYB 84; TV&RadDir 84*
WISL - Shamokin, PA - *BrCabYB 84; TV&RadDir 84*
WISM - Madison, WI - *BrCabYB 84; NatRadPubDir Summer 83, Spring 84; TV&RadDir 84*
WISM-FM - Madison, WI - *BrCabYB 84; NatRadPubDir Summer 83, Spring 84; TV&RadDir 84*
Wismer Associates Inc. - Canoga Park, CA - *DataDirOnSer 84*
WISN - Milwaukee, WI - *BrCabYB 84; NatRadPubDir Summer 83, Spring 84; TV&RadDir 84*
WISN-TV - Milwaukee, WI - *BrCabYB 84; DirUSTelSta 83; LitMarPl 83, 84; TelAl 83, 84; Tel&CabFB 84S; TV&RadDir 84*
Wisner News-Chronicle - Wisner, NE - *AyerDirPub 83; BaconPubCkNews 84; Ed&PubIntYB 82*
WISO - Ponce, PR - *BrCabYB 84*
WISP - Kinston, NC - *BrCabYB 84; TV&RadDir 84*
WISQ - West Salem, WI - *BrCabYB 84*
WISR - Butler, PA - *BrCabYB 84; TV&RadDir 84*
WISS - Berlin, WI - *BrCabYB 84; TV&RadDir 84*
WISS-FM - Berlin, WI - *BrCabYB 84; TV&RadDir 84*
WISSCO [Div. of Wanlass Industries Inc.] - Costa Mesa, CA - *AvMarPl 83*
Wissota Cable TV [of Scott & Krenz TV Systems] - Lafayette, WI - *BrCabYB 84; Tel&CabFB 84C*
WIST - Charlotte, NC - *NatRadPubDir Summer 83; TV&RadDir 84*
WIST - Lobelville, TN - *BrCabYB 84*
WISU-FM - Terre Haute, IN - *BrCabYB 84; TV&RadDir 84*
WISU-TV - Terre Haute, IN - *Tel&CabFB 84S*
WISV - Viroqua, WI - *BrCabYB 84; TV&RadDir 84*
WITA - Knoxville, TN - *BrCabYB 84; TV&RadDir 84*
WITB-FM - Salem, WV - *BrCabYB 84; NatRadPubDir Summer 83, Spring 84; TV&RadDir 84*
WITC-FM - Cazenovia, NY - *BrCabYB 84; TV&RadDir 84*
Witchcraft Digest Magazine [of Hero Press] - New York, NY - *LitMag&SmPr 83-84*
Witcher, Scott A. Jr. - Lampasas, TX - *Tel&CabFB 84C p.1713*
Witcom Group Inc. - San Juan, PR - *BoPubDir 4, 5*
WITF-FM - Harrisburg, PA - *LitMarPl 83, 84; NatRadPubDir Summer 83, Spring 84*
WITF-FM - Hershey, PA - *BrCabYB 84; TV&RadDir 84*
WITF-TV - Harrisburg, PA - *BrCabYB 84; TV&RadDir 84*
WITF-TV - Hershey, PA - *Tel&CabFB 84S*
WITH - Baltimore, MD - *BrCabYB 84; NatRadPubDir Summer 83, Spring 84; TV&RadDir 84*
WITH-FM - Baltimore, MD - *BrCabYB 84*
Withers Broadcasting Co. - Mt. Vernon, IL - *BrCabYB 84*
Witherspoon & Associates - Ft. Worth, TX - *AdAge 3-28-84; StaDirAdAg 2-84*
Withrow, James R. - Vanceburg, KY - *Tel&CabFB 84C p.1713*
WITI-TV - Milwaukee, WI - *BrCabYB 84; DirUSTelSta 83; LitMarPl 83, 84; TelAl 83, 84; Tel&CabFB 84S*
WITI-TV - Whitefish Bay, WI - *TV&RadDir 84*
WITL - Lansing, MI - *BrCabYB 84; NatRadPubDir Summer 83, Spring 84; TV&RadDir 84*
WITL-FM - Lansing, MI - *BrCabYB 84; NatRadPubDir Summer 83, Spring 84; TV&RadDir 84*
WITN - Washington, NC - *BrCabYB 84; TV&RadDir 84*
WITN-FM - Washington, NC - *BrCabYB 84; TV&RadDir 84*
WITN-FM - Greenville, NC - *DirUSTelSta 83*
WITN-TV - Washington, NC - *BrCabYB 84; TelAl 83, 84; Tel&CabFB 84S; TV&RadDir 84*
Witness, The - Dubuque, IA - *NewsDir 84*
Witness, The - Bradford, ON, Canada - *Ed&PubIntYB 82*
WITO-FM - Ironton, OH - *BrCabYB 84; TV&RadDir 84*
WITR-FM - Henrietta, NY - *BrCabYB 84*
WITR-FM - Rochester, NY - *NatRadPubDir Summer 83, Spring 84; TV&RadDir 84*

WITT-FM - Tuscola, IL - *BrCabYB 84; TV&RadDir 84*
Witt, Scott - Congers, NY - *MicrocomMPl 83*
Wittenberg Associates Inc., Ernest - Washington, DC - *DirPRFirms 83*
Wittenberg Cable TV Co. - Wittenberg, WI - *BrCabYB 84; Tel&CabFB 84C*
Wittenberg Door, The - El Cajon, CA - *ArtMar 84; WritMar 84*
Wittenberg Enterprise News - Wittenberg, WI - *BaconPubCkNews 84*
Wittenberg Northerner - Waupaca, WI - *AyerDirPub 83*
Wittenberg Telephone Co. - Wittenberg, WI - *TelDir&BG 83-84*
Wittenborn Art Books Inc. - New York, NY - *LitMarPl 83, 84*
Wittey, Merry F. - Dover, NJ - *LitMarPl 83, 84*
Wittman Publications Inc. - Baltimore, MD - *BoPubDir 5*
Witty, Helen - East Hampton, NY - *LitMarPl 83, 84*
WITV-TV - Charleston, SC - *BrCabYB 84; Tel&CabFB 84S*
WITV-TV - Mt. Pleasant, SC - *TV&RadDir 84*
WITW - Cadillac, MI - *NatRadPubDir Summer 83*
WITW-FM - Cadillac, MI - *NatRadPubDir Spring 84; TV&RadDir 84*
Witwatersrand University Press - Johannesburg, South Africa - *LitMag&SmPr 83-84*
Witwer Newspapers - Kendallville, IN - *Ed&PublIntYB 82*
WITY - Champaign/Urbana/Danville, IL - *NatRadPubDir Summer 83, Spring 84 p.80*
WITY - Danville, IL - *BrCabYB 84; TV&RadDir 84*
WITZ - Jasper, IN - *BrCabYB 84; TV&RadDir 84*
WITZ-FM - Jasper, IN - *BrCabYB 84; TV&RadDir 84*
WIUJ - St. Thomas, VI - *BrCabYB 84*
WIUM-FM - Macomb, IL - *BrCabYB 84; TV&RadDir 84*
WIUP-FM - Indiana, PA - *BrCabYB 84; NatRadPubDir Summer 83, Spring 84; TV&RadDir 84*
WIUS - Macomb, IL - *BrCabYB 84*
WIUS - Bloomington, IN - *TV&RadDir 84*
WIUS-FM - Bloomington, IN - *TV&RadDir 84*
WIUV-FM - Castleton, VT - *BrCabYB 84; NatRadPubDir Summer 83, Spring 84; TV&RadDir 84*
WIUW - High Point, NC - *BrCabYB 84; Tel&CabFB 84S*
WIVA-FM - Aguadilla, PR - *BrCabYB 84*
WIVB-TV - Buffalo, NY - *BrCabYB 84; DirUSTelSta 83; LitMarPl 83, 84; TelAl 83, 84; Tel&CabFB 84S; TV&RadDir 84*
WIVE - Ashland, VA - *BrCabYB 84; TV&RadDir 84*
WIVI-FM - Christiansted, VI - *BrCabYB 84*
WIVK - Knoxville, TN - *BrCabYB 84; NatRadPubDir Summer 83, Spring 84; TV&RadDir 84*
WIVK-FM - Knoxville, TN - *BrCabYB 84; NatRadPubDir Summer 83, Spring 84; TV&RadDir 84*
WIVQ-FM - Peru, IL - *BrCabYB 84; TV&RadDir 84*
WIVS - Crystal Lake, IL - *BrCabYB 84; TV&RadDir 84*
WIVV - Vieques, PR - *BrCabYB 84*
WIVY-FM - Jacksonville, FL - *BrCabYB 84; NatRadPubDir Summer 83, Spring 84; TV&RadDir 84*
WIXC - Fayetteville, TN - *BrCabYB 84; TV&RadDir 84*
WIXE - Monroe, NC - *BrCabYB 84; TV&RadDir 84*
WIXI - Lancaster, KY - *BrCabYB 84; TV&RadDir 84*
WIXK - New Richmond, WI - *BrCabYB 84; TV&RadDir 84*
WIXK-FM - New Richmond, WI - *BrCabYB 84; TV&RadDir 84*
WIXL-FM - Newton, NJ - *BrCabYB 84; TV&RadDir 84*
WIXN - Dixon, IL - *BrCabYB 84; TV&RadDir 84*
WIXN-FM - Dixon, IL - *BrCabYB 84; TV&RadDir 84*
WIXO - Mobile, AL - *TV&RadDir 84*
WIXR - Mt. Pleasant, SC - *BrCabYB 84*
WIXT-TV - Syracuse, NY - *BrCabYB 84; DirUSTelSta 83; TelAl 83, 84; Tel&CabFB 84S*
WIXV-FM - Savannah, GA - *NatRadPubDir Spring 84*
WIXV-FM - Front Royal, VA - *BrCabYB 84; TV&RadDir 84*
WIXX-FM - Holland, MI - *NatRadPubDir Spring 84*
WIXX-FM - Green Bay, WI - *BrCabYB 84; NatRadPubDir Summer 83, Spring 84; TV&RadDir 84*
WIXY - East Longmeadow, MA - *BrCabYB 84; TV&RadDir 84*
WIXZ - East McKeesport, PA - *BrCabYB 84; TV&RadDir 84*
WIYD - Palatka, FL - *BrCabYB 84; TV&RadDir 84*
WIYE - Leesburg, FL - *BrCabYB 84; DirUSTelSta 83; TelAl 84; Tel&CabFB 84S*
WIYN - Rome, GA - *BrCabYB 84; TV&RadDir 84*
WIYO-FM - Johnstown, PA - *TV&RadDir 84*
WIYQ - Ebensburg, PA - *BrCabYB 84*
WIYY-FM - Baltimore, MD - *BrCabYB 84; NatRadPubDir Summer 83, Spring 84; TV&RadDir 84*
Wizard Productions Inc. - Hollywood, FL - *BillIntBG 83-84*
Wizard Video Inc. - Los Angeles, CA - *BillIntBG 83-84*
Wizards Bookshelf - San Diego, CA - *BoPubDir 4, 5; LitMarPl 84*
WIZD-FM - Ft. Pierce, FL - *BrCabYB 84; TV&RadDir 84*
WIZE - Springfield, OH - *BrCabYB 84; TV&RadDir 84*
WIZM - La Crosse, WI - *BrCabYB 84; NatRadPubDir Summer 83, Spring 84; TV&RadDir 84*
WIZM-FM - La Crosse, WI - *BrCabYB 84; TV&RadDir 84*
WIZN - Vergennes, WI - *BrCabYB 84*
WIZO - Franklin, TN - *BrCabYB 84; TV&RadDir 84*
WIZR-FM - Johnstown, NY - *BrCabYB 84; TV&RadDir 84*
WIZS - Henderson, NC - *BrCabYB 84; TV&RadDir 84*
WIZY - Gordon, GA - *BrCabYB 84; TV&RadDir 84*
WIZY-FM - Gordon, GA - *TV&RadDir 84*
WIZZ - Streator, IL - *BrCabYB 84; TV&RadDir 84*
WJAC - Johnstown, PA - *BrCabYB 84; NatRadPubDir Summer 83, Spring 84; TV&RadDir 84*
WJAC-FM - Johnstown, PA - *BrCabYB 84; NatRadPubDir Summer 83; TV&RadDir 84*
WJAC-TV - Johnstown, PA - *BrCabYB 84; DirUSTelSta 83; TelAl 83, 84; Tel&CabFB 84S; TV&RadDir 84*
WJAD-FM - Bainbridge, GA - *BrCabYB 84; TV&RadDir 84*
WJAG - Norfolk, NE - *BrCabYB 84; TV&RadDir 84*
WJAI-FM - Eaton, OH - *BrCabYB 84; TV&RadDir 84*
WJAK - Jackson, TN - *BrCabYB 84; TV&RadDir 84*
WJAM - Marion, AL - *TV&RadDir 84*
WJAM-FM - Marion, AL - *BrCabYB 84*
WJAN-TV - Canton, OH - *DirUSTelSta 83; TelAl 83, 84*
WJAN-TV - Louisville, OH - *TV&RadDir 84*
WJAQ-FM - Marianna, FL - *BrCabYB 84; TV&RadDir 84*
WJAR-TV - Providence, RI - *BrCabYB 84; DirUSTelSta 83; LitMarPl 83, 84; TelAl 83, 84; Tel&CabFB 84S; TV&RadDir 84*
WJAS - Pittsburgh, PA - *BrCabYB 84; NatRadPubDir Summer 83, Spring 84; TV&RadDir 84*
WJAT - Swainsboro, GA - *BrCabYB 84; TV&RadDir 84*
WJAT-FM - Swainsboro, GA - *BrCabYB 84; TV&RadDir 84*
WJAX - Jacksonville, FL - *BrCabYB 84; NatRadPubDir Summer 83, Spring 84; TV&RadDir 84*
WJAX-FM - Jacksonville, FL - *BrCabYB 84; NatRadPubDir Summer 83, Spring 84; TV&RadDir 84*
WJAY - Mullins, SC - *BrCabYB 84; TV&RadDir 84*
WJAZ - Albany, GA - *BrCabYB 84; NatRadPubDir Summer 83, Spring 84; TV&RadDir 84*
WJBB - Haleyville, AL - *BrCabYB 84; TV&RadDir 84*
WJBB-FM - Haleyville, AL - *BrCabYB 84; TV&RadDir 84*
WJBC - Bloomington, IL - *BrCabYB 84; NatRadPubDir Summer 83, Spring 84; TV&RadDir 84*
WJBD - Salem, IL - *BrCabYB 84; TV&RadDir 84*
WJBD-FM - Salem, IL - *BrCabYB 84; TV&RadDir 84*
WJBE - Knoxville, TN - *NatRadPubDir Summer 83*
WJBF-TV - Augusta, GA - *BrCabYB 84; DirUSTelSta 83; TelAl 83, 84; Tel&CabFB 84S; TV&RadDir 84*
WJBI-FM - Clarksdale, MS - *BrCabYB 84; NatRadPubDir Summer 83, Spring 84; TV&RadDir 84*
WJBK-TV - Detroit, MI - *BrCabYB 84; DirUSTelSta 83; TelAl 83, 84; Tel&CabFB 84S*
WJBK-TV - Southfield, MI - *LitMarPl 83, 84; TV&RadDir 84*
WJBL-FM - Holland, MI - *BrCabYB 84; TV&RadDir 84*
WJBM - Jerseyville, IL - *BrCabYB 84; TV&RadDir 84*
WJBM-FM - Jerseyville, IL - *BrCabYB 84; TV&RadDir 84*
WJBO - Baton Rouge, LA - *BrCabYB 84; NatRadPubDir Summer 83, Spring 84; TV&RadDir 84*
WJBQ-FM - Portland, ME - *BrCabYB 84; NatRadPubDir Summer 83, Spring 84; TV&RadDir 84*
WJBR - Wilmington, DE - *BrCabYB 84; NatRadPubDir Summer 83, Spring 84; TV&RadDir 84*
WJBR-FM - Wilmington, DE - *BrCabYB 84; NatRadPubDir Summer 83, Spring 84; TV&RadDir 84*
WJBT - Brockport, NY - *BrCabYB 84; TV&RadDir 84*
WJBU - Port St. Joe, FL - *BrCabYB 84*
WJBW-FM - Hampton, SC - *BrCabYB 84; TV&RadDir 84*
WJCC - Norfolk, MA - *BrCabYB 84*
WJCD - Seymour, IN - *BrCabYB 84; TV&RadDir 84*

WJCD-FM - Seymour, IN - *BrCabYB 84; TV&RadDir 84*
WJCF - Westover, WV - *BrCabYB 84*
WJCK-FM - Rensselaer, IN - *TV&RadDir 84*
WJCL-FM - Savannah, GA - *BrCabYB 84; NatRadPubDir Summer 83, Spring 84; TV&RadDir 84*
WJCL-TV - Savannah, GA - *BrCabYB 84; DirUSTelSta 83; TelAl 83, 84; Tel&CabFB 84S; TV&RadDir 84*
WJCM - Sebring, FL - *BrCabYB 84; TV&RadDir 84*
WJCR-FM - Washington, PA - *BrCabYB 84; NatRadPubDir Summer 83, Spring 84; TV&RadDir 84*
WJCT-FM - Jacksonville, FL - *BrCabYB 84; TV&RadDir 84*
WJCT-TV - Jacksonville, FL - *BrCabYB 84; Tel&CabFB 84S; TV&RadDir 84*
WJCW - Johnson City, TN - *BrCabYB 84; NatRadPubDir Summer 83, Spring 84; TV&RadDir 84*
WJDA - Quincy, MA - *BrCabYB 84; TV&RadDir 84*
WJDB - Thomasville, AL - *BrCabYB 84; TV&RadDir 84*
WJDB-FM - Thomasville, AL - *BrCabYB 84; TV&RadDir 84*
WJDM - Elizabeth, NJ - *BrCabYB 84; TV&RadDir 84*
WJDQ - Meridian, MS - *BrCabYB 84; NatRadPubDir Summer 83, Spring 84; TV&RadDir 84*
WJDQ-FM - Meridian, MS - *NatRadPubDir Summer 83, Spring 84; TV&RadDir 84*
WJDR - Prentiss, MS - *BrCabYB 84*
WJDW - Corydon, IN - *BrCabYB 84; TV&RadDir 84*
WJDX - Jackson, MS - *BrCabYB 84; NatRadPubDir Summer 83, Spring 84; TV&RadDir 84*
WJDY - Salisbury, MD - *BrCabYB 84; TV&RadDir 84*
WJDZ - Levittown, PR - *BrCabYB 84*
WJEB - Gladwin, MI - *BrCabYB 84; TV&RadDir 84*
WJED - Somerville, TN - *BrCabYB 84*
WJEE-FM - Jacksonville, FL - *NatRadPubDir Summer 83*
WJEF-FM - Lafayette, IN - *BrCabYB 84; TV&RadDir 84*
WJEH - Gallipolis, OH - *BrCabYB 84; TV&RadDir 84*
WJEJ - Hagerstown, MD - *BrCabYB 84; NatRadPubDir Summer 83, Spring 84*
WJEL-FM - Indianapolis, IN - *BrCabYB 84; TV&RadDir 84*
WJEM - Valdosta, GA - *BrCabYB 84; TV&RadDir 84*
WJEQ - Macomb, IL - *BrCabYB 84*
WJER - Dover, OH - *BrCabYB 84; TV&RadDir 84*
WJER-FM - Dover, OH - *BrCabYB 84; TV&RadDir 84*
WJES - Johnston, SC - *BrCabYB 84; TV&RadDir 84*
WJET - Erie, PA - *BrCabYB 84; NatRadPubDir Summer 83, Spring 84; TV&RadDir 84*
WJET-TV - Albany, GA - *BrCabYB 84*
WJET-TV - Erie, PA - *BrCabYB 84; DirUSTelSta 83; TelAl 83, 84; Tel&CabFB 84S; TV&RadDir 84*
WJEZ-FM - Chicago, IL - *BrCabYB 84; NatRadPubDir Summer 83, Spring 84; TV&RadDir 84*
WJFC - Jefferson City, TN - *BrCabYB 84; TV&RadDir 84*
WJFD-FM - New Bedford, MA - *BrCabYB 84; TV&RadDir 84*
WJFL - Vicksburg, MS - *BrCabYB 84; NatRadPubDir Summer 83, Spring 84; TV&RadDir 84*
WJFM-FM - Grand Rapids, MI - *BrCabYB 84; NatRadPubDir Summer 83, Spring 84; TV&RadDir 84*
WJFR-TV - Schaumburg, IL - *TV&RadDir 84*
WJFT-TV - Albany, GA - *Tel&CabFB 84S*
WJGA-FM - Jackson, GA - *BrCabYB 84; TV&RadDir 84*
WJGF-FM - Romney, WV - *BrCabYB 84; NatRadPubDir Summer 83, Spring 84; TV&RadDir 84*
WJGS-FM - Houghton Lake, MI - *BrCabYB 84; TV&RadDir 84*
WJHD-FM - Portsmouth, RI - *BrCabYB 84; NatRadPubDir Summer 83, Spring 84; TV&RadDir 84*
WJHG-TV - Panama City, FL - *BrCabYB 84; DirUSTelSta 83; TelAl 83, 84; Tel&CabFB 84S; TV&RadDir 84*
WJHL-TV - Johnson City, TN - *BrCabYB 84; DirUSTelSta 83; TelAl 83, 84; Tel&CabFB 84S; TV&RadDir 84*
WJHO - Opelika, AL - *BrCabYB 84; TV&RadDir 84*
WJHR-FM - Jackson, TN - *BrCabYB 84; TV&RadDir 84*
WJHU-FM - Baltimore, MD - *BrCabYB 84; NatRadPubDir Summer 83, Spring 84*
WJIB-FM - Boston, MA - *BrCabYB 84; NatRadPubDir Summer 83, Spring 84; TV&RadDir 84*
WJIC - Salem, NJ - *BrCabYB 84; TV&RadDir 84*
WJIK - Camp LeJeune, NC - *BrCabYB 84*
WJIK - Jacksonville, NC - *TV&RadDir 84*
WJIL - Jacksonville, IL - *BrCabYB 84; TV&RadDir 84*
WJIM - Lansing, MI - *BrCabYB 84; NatRadPubDir Summer 83, Spring 84; TV&RadDir 84*
WJIM-FM - Lansing, MI - *BrCabYB 84; NatRadPubDir Summer 83, Spring 84; TV&RadDir 84*
WJIM-TV - Lansing, MI - *BrCabYB 84; DirUSTelSta 83; TelAl 83, 84; Tel&CabFB 84S; TV&RadDir 84*
WJIT - New York, NY - *BrCabYB 84; NatRadPubDir Summer 83, Spring 84; TV&RadDir 84*
WJIV-FM - Cherry Valley, NY - *BrCabYB 84; TV&RadDir 84*
WJIZ-FM - Albany, GA - *BrCabYB 84; TV&RadDir 84*
WJJA - Racine, WI - *BrCabYB 84; Tel&CabFB 84S*
WJJB-FM - Hyde Park, NY - *BrCabYB 84; TV&RadDir 84*
WJJC - Commerce, GA - *BrCabYB 84; TV&RadDir 84*
WJJD - Chicago, IL - *BrCabYB 84; NatRadPubDir Summer 83, Spring 84; TV&RadDir 84*
WJJJ - Christiansburg, VA - *BrCabYB 84; TV&RadDir 84*
WJJK - Eau Claire, WI - *BrCabYB 84; NatRadPubDir Summer 83, Spring 84; TV&RadDir 84*
WJJL - Buffalo, NY - *NatRadPubDir Summer 83 p.169, Spring 84 p.167*
WJJL - Niagara Falls, NY - *BrCabYB 84; TV&RadDir 84*
WJJM - Lewisburg, TN - *BrCabYB 84; TV&RadDir 84*
WJJM-FM - Lewisburg, TN - *BrCabYB 84; TV&RadDir 84*
WJJN - Newburgh, IN - *BrCabYB 84*
WJJQ - Tomahawk, WI - *BrCabYB 84; TV&RadDir 84*
WJJS-FM - Lynchburg, VA - *BrCabYB 84; TV&RadDir 84*
WJJT - Jellico, TN - *BrCabYB 84; TV&RadDir 84*
WJJW-FM - North Adams, MA - *BrCabYB 84; NatRadPubDir Summer 83, Spring 84; TV&RadDir 84*
WJJY-FM - Brainerd, MN - *BrCabYB 84; TV&RadDir 84*
WJJZ - Mt. Holly, NJ - *TV&RadDir 84*
WJKA - Wilmington, NC - *BrCabYB 84; Tel&CabFB 84S*
WJKC - Christiansted, VI - *BrCabYB 84*
WJKK - Beckley, WV - *BrCabYB 84; TV&RadDir 84*
WJKL-FM - Elgin, IL - *BrCabYB 84; TV&RadDir 84*
WJKM - Hartsville, TN - *BrCabYB 84; TV&RadDir 84*
WJKR - Muncy, PA - *BrCabYB 84*
WJKS-TV - Jacksonville, FL - *BrCabYB 84; DirUSTelSta 83; TelAl 83, 84; Tel&CabFB 84S; TV&RadDir 84*
WJKW-TV - Cleveland, OH - *BrCabYB 84; DirUSTelSta 83; LitMarPl 83, 84; TelAl 83, 84; Tel&CabFB 84S; TV&RadDir 84*
WJKX - Pascagoula, MS - *BrCabYB 84; TV&RadDir 84*
WJKY - Jamestown, KY - *BrCabYB 84; TV&RadDir 84*
WJKY-FM - Hempstead, NY - *LitMarPl 84*
WJKZ-FM - Franklin, TN - *BrCabYB 84*
WJKZ-FM - Nashville, TN - *NatRadPubDir Summer 83, Spring 84; TV&RadDir 84*
WJLA-TV - Washington, DC - *BrCabYB 84; DirUSTelSta 83; LitMarPl 83, 84; TelAl 83, 84; Tel&CabFB 84S; TV&RadDir 84*
WJLB - Detroit, MI - *BrCabYB 84; NatRadPubDir Summer 83*
WJLB-FM - Detroit, MI - *NatRadPubDir Summer 83, Spring 84; TV&RadDir 84*
WJLC-FM - South Boston, VA - *BrCabYB 84; TV&RadDir 84*
WJLD - Birmingham, AL - *NatRadPubDir Summer 83, Spring 84; TV&RadDir 84*
WJLD - Fairfield, AL - *BrCabYB 84*
WJLE - Smithville, TN - *BrCabYB 84; TV&RadDir 84*
WJLE-FM - Smithville, TN - *BrCabYB 84; TV&RadDir 84*
WJLK - Asbury Park, NJ - *BrCabYB 84; NatRadPubDir Summer 83, Spring 84; TV&RadDir 84*
WJLK-FM - Asbury Park, NJ - *BrCabYB 84; NatRadPubDir Summer 83, Spring 84; TV&RadDir 84*
WJLM-FM - Roanoke, VA - *NatRadPubDir Summer 83 p.256, Spring 84 p.258; TV&RadDir 84*
WJLM-FM - Salem, VA - *BrCabYB 84*
WJLQ-FM - Pensacola, FL - *BrCabYB 84; NatRadPubDir Summer 83, Spring 84; TV&RadDir 84*
WJLS - Beckley, WV - *BrCabYB 84; TV&RadDir 84*
WJLW - De Pere, WI - *BrCabYB 84*
WJLY - Braddock, PA - *BrCabYB 84*
WJMA - Orange, VA - *BrCabYB 84; TV&RadDir 84*
WJMA-FM - Orange, VA - *BrCabYB 84; TV&RadDir 84*
WJMB - Brookhaven, MS - *BrCabYB 84; TV&RadDir 84*
WJMC - Rice Lake, WI - *BrCabYB 84; TV&RadDir 84*
WJMC-FM - Rice Lake, WI - *BrCabYB 84; TV&RadDir 84*

WJMF-FM - Smithfield, PA - *BrCabYB 84; NatRadPubDir Summer 83, Spring 84*
WJMF-FM - Esmond, RI - *TV&RadDir 84*
WJMG - Hattiesburg, MS - *BrCabYB 84*
WJMI-FM - Jackson, MS - *BrCabYB 84; NatRadPubDir Summer 83, Spring 84; TV&RadDir 84*
WJMJ-FM - Hartford, CT - *BrCabYB 84; TV&RadDir 84*
WJML - Petoskey, MI - *BrCabYB 84; TV&RadDir 84*
WJML-FM - Petoskey, MI - *BrCabYB 84; TV&RadDir 84*
WJMM-FM - Lexington, KY - *TV&RadDir 84*
WJMM-FM - Versailles, KY - *BrCabYB 84*
WJMN-TV - Escanaba, MI - *BrCabYB 84; TelAl 83, 84; Tel&CabFB 84S; TV&RadDir 84*
WJMO - Cleveland, OH - *BrCabYB 84; NatRadPubDir Summer 83, Spring 84; TV&RadDir 84*
WJMR - Ridgeland, SC - *BrCabYB 84; TV&RadDir 84*
WJMS - Ironwood, MI - *BrCabYB 84*
WJMT - Merrill, WI - *BrCabYB 84; TV&RadDir 84*
WJMT-FM - Merrill, WI - *BrCabYB 84; TV&RadDir 84*
WJMU-FM - Decatur, IL - *BrCabYB 84; NatRadPubDir Summer 83, Spring 84; TV&RadDir 84*
WJMW - Athens, AL - *BrCabYB 84; TV&RadDir 84*
WJMX - Florence, SC - *BrCabYB 84; TV&RadDir 84*
WJNC - Jacksonville, NC - *BrCabYB 84; TV&RadDir 84*
WJNJ - Atlantic Beach, FL - *BrCabYB 84; TV&RadDir 84*
WJNJ - Jacksonville, FL - *NatRadPubDir Summer 83, Spring 84 p.59*
WJNL - Johnstown, PA - *BrCabYB 84; NatRadPubDir Summer 83, Spring 84; TV&RadDir 84*
WJNL-FM - Johnstown, PA - *BrCabYB 84; NatRadPubDir Summer 83, Spring 84; TV&RadDir 84*
WJNL-TV - Johnstown, PA - *TelAl 83; TV&RadDir 84*
WJNO - West Palm Beach, FL - *BrCabYB 84; NatRadPubDir Summer 83, Spring 84; TV&RadDir 84*
WJNR-FM - Iron Mountain, MI - *BrCabYB 84; TV&RadDir 84*
WJNS-FM - Yazoo City, MS - *BrCabYB 84; TV&RadDir 84*
WJNZ-FM - Greencastle, IN - *BrCabYB 84; TV&RadDir 84*
WJOB - Hammond, IN - *BrCabYB 84; TV&RadDir 84*
WJOE - Port St. Joe, FL - *TV&RadDir 84*
WJOI-FM - Detroit, MI - *BrCabYB 84; NatRadPubDir Summer 83, Spring 84 p.126*
WJOJ-FM - Picayune, MS - *BrCabYB 84; TV&RadDir 84*
WJOK - Gaithersburg, MO - *BrCabYB 84*
WJOL - Joliet, IL - *BrCabYB 84; NatRadPubDir Summer 83, Spring 84; TV&RadDir 84*
WJOL-FM - Detroit, MI - *TV&RadDir 84*
WJON - St. Cloud, MN - *BrCabYB 84; NatRadPubDir Summer 83, Spring 84; TV&RadDir 84*
WJOS - Elkin, NC - *BrCabYB 84*
WJOT - Lake City, SC - *BrCabYB 84; TV&RadDir 84*
WJOY - Burlington, VT - *BrCabYB 84; NatRadPubDir Summer 83, Spring 84; TV&RadDir 84*
WJOZ - Troy, PA - *BrCabYB 84*
WJPA - Washington, PA - *BrCabYB 84; TV&RadDir 84*
WJPC - Chicago, IL - *BrCabYB 84; LitMarPl 83, 84; NatRadPubDir Summer 83, Spring 84; TV&RadDir 84*
WJPD-FM - Ishpeming, MI - *BrCabYB 84*
WJPJ - Huntingdon, TN - *BrCabYB 84; TV&RadDir 84*
WJPM-TV - Florence, SC - *BrCabYB 84; Tel&CabFB 84S; TV&RadDir 84*
WJPR - Lynchburg, VA - *BrCabYB 84; Tel&CabFB 84S*
WJPT - Jacksonville, IL - *BrCabYB 84; Tel&CabFB 84S*
WJPW - Rockford, MI - *BrCabYB 84; TV&RadDir 84*
WJQI - New Bern, NC - *BrCabYB 84*
WJQS - Jackson, MS - *BrCabYB 84; NatRadPubDir Summer 83, Spring 84; TV&RadDir 84*
WJQY - Chickasaw, AL - *BrCabYB 84*
WJR - Detroit, MI - *BrCabYB 84; LitMarPl 83, 84; NatRadPubDir Summer 83, Spring 84; TV&RadDir 84*
WJRB - Madison, TN - *BrCabYB 84*
WJRB - Nashville, TN - *NatRadPubDir Spring 84; TV&RadDir 84*
WJRC - Joliet, IL - *BrCabYB 84; NatRadPubDir Summer 83, Spring 84; TV&RadDir 84*
WJRD - Tuscaloosa, AL - *BrCabYB 84; NatRadPubDir Summer 83, Spring 84; TV&RadDir 84*
WJRE - Kewanee, IL - *BrCabYB 84*
WJRH-FM - Easton, PA - *BrCabYB 84; NatRadPubDir Summer 83, Spring 84; TV&RadDir 84*
WJRI - Lenoir, NC - *BrCabYB 84; TV&RadDir 84*
WJRL - Calhoun City, MS - *BrCabYB 84; TV&RadDir 84*
WJRM - Troy, NC - *BrCabYB 84; TV&RadDir 84*
WJRN - Midland, MI - *NatRadPubDir Summer 83, Spring 84*
WJRO - Glen Burnie, MD - *BrCabYB 84*
WJRQ - Williston, FL - *BrCabYB 84*
WJRQ-FM - Gainesville, FL - *BrCabYB 84*
WJRS-FM - Jamestown, KY - *BrCabYB 84; TV&RadDir 84*
WJRT-TV - Flint, MI - *BrCabYB 84; DirUSTelSta 83; LitMarPl 83; TelAl 83, 84; Tel&CabFB 84S; TV&RadDir 84*
WJRZ-FM - Manahawkin, NJ - *BrCabYB 84; TV&RadDir 84*
WJSA - Jersey Shore, PA - *BrCabYB 84; TV&RadDir 84*
WJSB - Crestview, FL - *BrCabYB 84; TV&RadDir 84*
WJSC-FM - Johnson, VT - *BrCabYB 84; NatRadPubDir Summer 83, Spring 84; TV&RadDir 84*
WJSE-FM - Cumberland, MD - *TV&RadDir 84*
WJSK-FM - Lumberton, NC - *BrCabYB 84; TV&RadDir 84*
WJSL-FM - Houghton, NY - *BrCabYB 84; NatRadPubDir Summer 83, Spring 84; TV&RadDir 84*
WJSM - Martinsburg, PA - *BrCabYB 84; TV&RadDir 84*
WJSM-FM - Martinsburg, PA - *BrCabYB 84; TV&RadDir 84*
WJSN-FM - Jackson, KY - *BrCabYB 84; TV&RadDir 84*
WJSO - Johnson City, TN - *TV&RadDir 84*
WJSO - Jonesboro, TN - *BrCabYB 84*
WJSP-FM - Warm Springs, GA - *BrCabYB 84*
WJSP-TV - Columbus, GA - *BrCabYB 84; Tel&CabFB 84S*
WJSQ-FM - Athens, TN - *BrCabYB 84; TV&RadDir 84*
WJSR - Birmingham, AL - *BrCabYB 84*
WJST - Port St. Joe, FL - *BrCabYB 84*
WJSU-FM - Jackson, MS - *BrCabYB 84; TV&RadDir 84*
WJSV-FM - Morristown, NJ - *BrCabYB 84; NatRadPubDir Summer 83, Spring 84; TV&RadDir 84*
WJSY-FM - Harrisonburg, VA - *BrCabYB 84; TV&RadDir 84*
WJTB - Newark, NJ - *NatRadPubDir Summer 83, Spring 84*
WJTH - Calhoun, GA - *BrCabYB 84; TV&RadDir 84*
WJTM-TV - Greensboro, NC - *DirUSTelSta 83*
WJTM-TV - Winston-Salem, NC - *BrCabYB 84; Tel&CabFB 84S*
WJTN - Jamestown, NY - *BrCabYB 84; NatRadPubDir Summer 83, Spring 84; TV&RadDir 84*
WJTO - Bath, ME - *BrCabYB 84; TV&RadDir 84*
WJTP - Newland, NC - *BrCabYB 84; TV&RadDir 84*
WJTT-FM - Chattanooga, TN - *TV&RadDir 84*
WJTV-TV - Jackson, MI - *BrCabYB 84; Tel&CabFB 84S*
WJTV-TV - Jackson, MS - *DirUSTelSta 83; TelAl 83, 84; TV&RadDir 84*
WJTY - Lancaster, WI - *BrCabYB 84*
WJUL-FM - Lowell, MA - *BrCabYB 84; NatRadPubDir Summer 83, Spring 84; TV&RadDir 84*
WJUN - Mexico, PA - *BrCabYB 84; TV&RadDir 84*
WJVL-FM - Janesville, WI - *BrCabYB 84; NatRadPubDir Summer 83, Spring 84; TV&RadDir 84*
WJVM-FM - Sterling, IL - *BrCabYB 84; TV&RadDir 84*
WJVS-FM - Cincinnati, OH - *BrCabYB 84; TV&RadDir 84*
WJW - Cleveland, OH - *BrCabYB 84; NatRadPubDir Summer 83, Spring 84; TV&RadDir 84*
WJWF - Columbus, MS - *BrCabYB 84*
WJWJ-FM - Beaufort, SC - *BrCabYB 84*
WJWJ-TV - Beaufort, SC - *BrCabYB 84; Tel&CabFB 84S*
WJWK - Jamestown, NY - *BrCabYB 84*
WJWL - Georgetown, DE - *BrCabYB 84; TV&RadDir 84*
WJWS - South Hill, VA - *BrCabYB 84; TV&RadDir 84*
WJXL - Jackson, AL - *BrCabYB 84*
WJXN - Jackson, MS - *BrCabYB 84; NatRadPubDir Summer 83, Spring 84; TV&RadDir 84*
WJXQ - Jackson, MI - *BrCabYB 84*
WJXT-TV - Jacksonville, FL - *BrCabYB 84; DirUSTelSta 83; TelAl 83, 84; Tel&CabFB 84S; TV&RadDir 84*
WJXY - Conway, SC - *BrCabYB 84; TV&RadDir 84*
WJYA - Marietta, GA - *BrCabYB 84*
WJYE-FM - Buffalo, NY - *BrCabYB 84; NatRadPubDir Summer 83, Spring 84; TV&RadDir 84*
WJYF - La Grange, GA - *BrCabYB 84*
WJYI - Marietta, GA - *TV&RadDir 84*
WJYJ - Fredricksburg, VA - *BrCabYB 84*

WJYM - Bowling Green, OH - *BrCabYB 84; TV&RadDir 84*
WJYM - Perrysburg, OH - *NatRadPubDir Summer 83 p.191, Spring 84 p.189*
WJYN-FM - Nashville, TN - *TV&RadDir 84*
WJYO-FM - Mt. Dora, FL - *BrCabYB 84*
WJYO-FM - Orlando, FL - *NatRadPubDir Spring 84; TV&RadDir 84*
WJYR-FM - Myrtle Beach, FL - *BrCabYB 84*
WJYR-FM - Myrtle Beach, SC - *TV&RadDir 84*
WJYT - Quebradillas, PR - *BrCabYB 84*
WJYV - Forest, MS - *BrCabYB 84*
WJYW - Tampa, FL - *BrCabYB 84*
WJYY - Concord, NH - *BrCabYB 84*
WJZ-TV - Baltimore, MD - *BrCabYB 84; DirUSTelSta 83; LitMarPl 83, 84; TelAl 83, 84; Tel&CabFB 84S; TV&RadDir 84*
WJZM - Clarksville, TN - *BrCabYB 84; NatRadPubDir Summer 83, Spring 84; TV&RadDir 84*
WJZQ - Kenosha, WI - *BrCabYB 84*
WJZQ-FM - Kenosha, WI - *TV&RadDir 84*
WJZR-FM - Kannapolis, NC - *BrCabYB 84; TV&RadDir 84*
WJZZ-FM - Detroit, MI - *BrCabYB 84; NatRadPubDir Summer 83, Spring 84; TV&RadDir 84*
WKAA - Ocilla, GA - *BrCabYB 84*
WKAB-TV - Montgomery, AL - *BrCabYB 84; DirUSTelSta 83; TelAl 83, 84; Tel&CabFB 84S; TV&RadDir 84*
WKAC - Athens, AL - *BrCabYB 84; TV&RadDir 84*
WKAD-FM - Canton, PA - *BrCabYB 84; TV&RadDir 84*
WKAE - High Springs, FL - *BrCabYB 84*
WKAF - Syracuse, NY - *BrCabYB 84; Tel&CabFB 84S*
WKAI - Macomb, IL - *BrCabYB 84; TV&RadDir 84*
WKAI-FM - Macomb, IL - *BrCabYB 84; TV&RadDir 84*
WKAJ - Saratoga Springs, NY - *BrCabYB 84; TV&RadDir 84*
WKAK-FM - Albany, GA - *BrCabYB 84; NatRadPubDir Summer 83, Spring 84; TV&RadDir 84*
WKAL - Rome, NY - *BrCabYB 84; TV&RadDir 84*
WKAL-FM - Rome, NY - *BrCabYB 84; TV&RadDir 84*
WKAM - Goshen, IN - *BrCabYB 84; TV&RadDir 84*
WKAN - Kankakee, IL - *BrCabYB 84; NatRadPubDir Summer 83, Spring 84; TV&RadDir 84*
WKAO - Boynton Beach, FL - *BrCabYB 84; TV&RadDir 84*
WKAP - Allentown, PA - *BrCabYB 84; NatRadPubDir Summer 83 p.209, Spring 84 p.209*
WKAP - Whitehall, PA - *TV&RadDir 84*
WKAQ-FM - San Juan, PR - *BrCabYB 84*
WKAQ-TV - San Juan, PR - *BrCabYB 84; Tel&CabFB 84S*
WKAR - East Lansing, MI - *BrCabYB 84; NatRadPubDir Summer 83, Spring 84; TV&RadDir 84*
WKAR-FM - East Lansing, MI - *BrCabYB 84; TV&RadDir 84*
WKAR-TV - East Lansing, MI - *BrCabYB 84; Tel&CabFB 84S; TV&RadDir 84*
WKAS-TV - Ashland, KY - *BrCabYB 84; Tel&CabFB 84S*
WKAS-TV - Lexington, KY - *TV&RadDir 84*
WKAT - Miami Beach, FL - *BrCabYB 84; LitMarPl 83, 84; NatRadPubDir Summer 83, Spring 84; TV&RadDir 84*
WKAU - Kaukauna, WI - *BrCabYB 84; TV&RadDir 84*
WKAU-FM - Kaukauna, WI - *BrCabYB 84; TV&RadDir 84*
WKAX - Russellville, AL - *BrCabYB 84; TV&RadDir 84*
WKAY - Glasgow, KY - *BrCabYB 84; TV&RadDir 84*
WKAZ - Charleston, WV - *NatRadPubDir Summer 83; TV&RadDir 84*
WKBA - Roanoke, VA - *NatRadPubDir Summer 83, Spring 84; TV&RadDir 84*
WKBA - Vinton, VA - *BrCabYB 84*
WKBB-FM - West Point, MS - *BrCabYB 84; TV&RadDir 84*
WKBC - North Wilkesboro, NC - *BrCabYB 84; TV&RadDir 84*
WKBC-FM - North Wilkesboro, NC - *BrCabYB 84; TV&RadDir 84*
WKBD-TV - Detroit, MI - *BrCabYB 84; DirUSTelSta 83; TelAl 83, 84; Tel&CabFB 84S*
WKBD-TV - Southfield, MI - *TV&RadDir 84*
WKBI - St. Marys, PA - *BrCabYB 84; TV&RadDir 84*
WKBI-FM - Ridgway, PA - *TV&RadDir 84*
WKBJ - Milan, TN - *BrCabYB 84; TV&RadDir 84*
WKBJ-FM - Milan, TN - *BrCabYB 84; TV&RadDir 84*
WKBK - Keene, NH - *BrCabYB 84; NatRadPubDir Summer 83, Spring 84; TV&RadDir 84*
WKBL - Covington, TN - *BrCabYB 84; TV&RadDir 84*
WKBL-FM - Covington, TN - *BrCabYB 84; TV&RadDir 84*
WKBM-TV - Caguas, PR - *BrCabYB 84; Tel&CabFB 84S*
WKBN - Youngstown, OH - *BrCabYB 84; NatRadPubDir Summer 83, Spring 84; TV&RadDir 84*
WKBN Broadcasting Corp. - Youngstown, OH - *BrCabYB 84*
WKBN-FM - Youngstown, OH - *BrCabYB 84; NatRadPubDir Summer 83, Spring 84; TV&RadDir 84*
WKBN-TV - Youngstown, OH - *BrCabYB 84; DirUSTelSta 83; TelAl 83, 84; Tel&CabFB 84S; TV&RadDir 84*
WKBO - Harrisburg, PA - *BrCabYB 84; NatRadPubDir Summer 83, Spring 84; TV&RadDir 84*
WKBQ - Garner, NC - *BrCabYB 84*
WKBQ - Raleigh, NC - *NatRadPubDir Summer 83, Spring 84; TV&RadDir 84*
WKBR - Manchester, NH - *BrCabYB 84; NatRadPubDir Summer 83, Spring 84; TV&RadDir 84*
WKBS-TV - Philadelphia, PA - *DirUSTelSta 83; TelAl 83, 84; TV&RadDir 84*
WKBT-TV - La Crosse, WI - *BrCabYB 84; DirUSTelSta 83; TelAl 83, 84; Tel&CabFB 84S; TV&RadDir 84*
WKBV - Richmond, IN - *BrCabYB 84; TV&RadDir 84*
WKBW - Buffalo, NY - *BrCabYB 84; NatRadPubDir Summer 83, Spring 84; TV&RadDir 84*
WKBW-TV - Buffalo, NY - *BrCabYB 84; DirUSTelSta 83; LitMarPl 83, 84; TelAl 83, 84; Tel&CabFB 84S; TV&RadDir 84*
WKBX - Savannah, GA - *BrCabYB 84; NatRadPubDir Summer 83, Spring 84; TV&RadDir 84*
WKBY - Chatham, VA - *BrCabYB 84; TV&RadDir 84*
WKBZ - Muskegon, MI - *BrCabYB 84; NatRadPubDir Summer 83, Spring 84; TV&RadDir 84*
WKCB - Hindman, KY - *BrCabYB 84; TV&RadDir 84*
WKCB-FM - Hindman, KY - *BrCabYB 84; TV&RadDir 84*
WKCC-FM - Grayson, KY - *BrCabYB 84; NatRadPubDir Summer 83, Spring 84; TV&RadDir 84*
WKCD-FM - Mechanicsburg, PA - *BrCabYB 84; TV&RadDir 84*
WKCE - Harriman, TN - *BrCabYB 84*
WKCG-FM - Augusta, ME - *BrCabYB 84; NatRadPubDir Summer 83, Spring 84; TV&RadDir 84*
WKCH-TV - Knoxville, TN - *BrCabYB 84; Tel&CabFB 84S*
WKCI-FM - Hamden, CT - *BrCabYB 84; TV&RadDir 84*
WKCI-FM - New Haven, CT - *NatRadPubDir Summer 83 p.47, Spring 84 p.48*
WKCJ - Lewisburg, WV - *BrCabYB 84*
WKCK - Oracovis, PR - *BrCabYB 84*
WKCL - Ladson, SC - *BrCabYB 84*
WKCM - Hawesville, KY - *BrCabYB 84; TV&RadDir 84*
WKCN - North Charleston, SC - *BrCabYB 84; NatRadPubDir Summer 83, Spring 84; TV&RadDir 84*
WKCO-FM - Gambier, OH - *BrCabYB 84; TV&RadDir 84*
WKCQ-FM - Saginaw, MI - *BrCabYB 84; NatRadPubDir Summer 83, Spring 84; TV&RadDir 84*
WKCR-FM - New York, NY - *BrCabYB 84; NatRadPubDir Summer 83, Spring 84; TV&RadDir 84*
WKCS-FM - Knoxville, TN - *BrCabYB 84; NatRadPubDir Summer 83, Spring 84; TV&RadDir 84*
WKCT - Bowling Green, KY - *BrCabYB 84; NatRadPubDir Summer 83, Spring 84; TV&RadDir 84*
WKCU - Corinth, MS - *BrCabYB 84; TV&RadDir 84*
WKCU-FM - Corinth, MS - *BrCabYB 84; TV&RadDir 84*
WKCW - Warrenton, VA - *BrCabYB 84; TV&RadDir 84*
WKCX-FM - Rome, GA - *BrCabYB 84; NatRadPubDir Summer 83, Spring 84; TV&RadDir 84*
WKCY - Harrisonburg, VA - *BrCabYB 84; TV&RadDir 84*
WKCZ - Kalamazoo, MI - *NatRadPubDir Spring 84*
WKDA - Nashville, TN - *BrCabYB 84; NatRadPubDir Summer 83, Spring 84; TV&RadDir 84*
WKDC - Elmhurst, IL - *BrCabYB 84; TV&RadDir 84*
WKDD-FM - Akron, OH - *BrCabYB 84; NatRadPubDir Summer 83, Spring 84; TV&RadDir 84*
WKDE - Altavista, VA - *BrCabYB 84; TV&RadDir 84*
WKDE-FM - Altavista, VA - *BrCabYB 84; TV&RadDir 84*
WKDF-FM - Nashville, TN - *BrCabYB 84; NatRadPubDir Summer 83, Spring 84; TV&RadDir 84*
WKDJ - Memphis, TN - *BrCabYB 84; NatRadPubDir Summer 83, Spring 84*
WKDK - Newberry, SC - *BrCabYB 84; TV&RadDir 84*
WKDN-FM - Camden, NJ - *BrCabYB 84; TV&RadDir 84*

WKDO - Liberty, KY - *BrCabYB 84; TV&RadDir 84*
WKDO-FM - Liberty, KY - *BrCabYB 84; TV&RadDir 84*
WKDQ-FM - Henderson, KY - *BrCabYB 84; TV&RadDir 84*
WKDR - Plattsburgh, NY - *BrCabYB 84; TV&RadDir 84*
WKDS - Kalamazoo, MI - *BrCabYB 84*
WKDU-FM - Philadelphia, PA - *BrCabYB 84; NatRadPubDir Summer 83, Spring 84; TV&RadDir 84*
WKDW - Staunton, VA - *BrCabYB 84; TV&RadDir 84*
WKDX - Hamlet, NC - *BrCabYB 84; TV&RadDir 84*
WKDY - Spartanburg, SC - *BrCabYB 84; NatRadPubDir Summer 83, Spring 84; TV&RadDir 84*
WKDZ - Cadiz, KY - *BrCabYB 84; TV&RadDir 84*
WKDZ-FM - Cadiz, KY - *BrCabYB 84; TV&RadDir 84*
WKEA - Scottsboro, AL - *BrCabYB 84; TV&RadDir 84*
WKEA-FM - Scottsboro, AL - *BrCabYB 84; TV&RadDir 84*
WKED - Frankfort, KY - *BrCabYB 84; TV&RadDir 84*
WKEE - Huntington, WV - *BrCabYB 84; NatRadPubDir Spring 84*
WKEE-FM - Huntington, WV - *BrCabYB 84; NatRadPubDir Summer 83, Spring 84; TV&RadDir 84*
WKEF-TV - Dayton, OH - *BrCabYB 84; DirUSTelSta 83; LitMarPl 83, 84; TelAl 83, 84; Tel&CabFB 84S; TV&RadDir 84*
WKEG - Washington, PA - *BrCabYB 84; TV&RadDir 84*
WKEI - Kewanee, IL - *BrCabYB 84; TV&RadDir 84*
WKEM - Immokalee, FL - *BrCabYB 84; TV&RadDir 84*
WKEN - Dover, DE - *BrCabYB 84; TV&RadDir 84*
WKEQ - Burnside, KY - *BrCabYB 84*
WKER - Pompton Lakes, NJ - *BrCabYB 84; NatRadPubDir Summer 83, Spring 84; TV&RadDir 84*
WKES-FM - St. Petersburg, FL - *BrCabYB 84; TV&RadDir 84*
WKET-FM - Kettering, OH - *BrCabYB 84; NatRadPubDir Summer 83, Spring 84; TV&RadDir 84*
WKEU - Greenville, GA - *TV&RadDir 84*
WKEU - Griffin, GA - *BrCabYB 84*
WKEU-FM - Greenville, GA - *TV&RadDir 84*
WKEU-FM - Griffin, GA - *BrCabYB 84*
WKEW - Greensboro, NC - *BrCabYB 84; NatRadPubDir Summer 83, Spring 84; TV&RadDir 84*
WKEX - Blacksburg, VA - *BrCabYB 84; TV&RadDir 84*
WKEY - Covington, VA - *BrCabYB 84; TV&RadDir 84*
WKEZ-FM - Norfolk, VA - *TV&RadDir 84*
WKEZ-FM - Yorktown, VA - *TV&RadDir 84*
WKFE - Yauco, PR - *BrCabYB 84*
WKFI - Wilmington, OH - *BrCabYB 84; TV&RadDir 84*
WKFM-FM - Fulton, NY - *BrCabYB 84*
WKFM-FM - Oswego, NY - *TV&RadDir 84*
WKFN - Franklin, KY - *BrCabYB 84*
WKFR-FM - Battle Creek, MI - *BrCabYB 84; NatRadPubDir Summer 83, Spring 84; TV&RadDir 84*
WKFT-TV - Fayetteville, NC - *BrCabYB 84; DirUSTelSta 83; TelAl 83, 84; Tel&CabFB 84S*
WKFX - Gadsen, AL - *TV&RadDir 84*
WKFX - Rainbow City, AL - *BrCabYB 84*
WKGA - Grafton, WV - *BrCabYB 84; TV&RadDir 84*
WKGB-TV - Bowling Green, KY - *BrCabYB 84; Tel&CabFB 84S*
WKGB-TV - Lexington, KY - *TV&RadDir 84*
WKGC-FM - Panama City, FL - *BrCabYB 84; TV&RadDir 84*
WKGE - Darlington, SC - *BrCabYB 84; TV&RadDir 84*
WKGI-FM - New Martinsville, WV - *BrCabYB 84; TV&RadDir 84*
WKGK - Saltville, VA - *BrCabYB 84*
WKGL-FM - Middletown, NY - *BrCabYB 84; NatRadPubDir Summer 83, Spring 84; TV&RadDir 84*
WKGM - Smithfield, VA - *BrCabYB 84; NatRadPubDir Summer 83, Spring 84; TV&RadDir 84*
WKGN - Knoxville, TN - *BrCabYB 84; NatRadPubDir Summer 83, Spring 84; TV&RadDir 84*
WKGO-FM - Cumberland, MD - *BrCabYB 84; NatRadPubDir Summer 83, Spring 84; TV&RadDir 84*
WKGQ - Macon, GA - *NatRadPubDir Spring 84 p.72*
WKGQ - Milledgeville, GA - *BrCabYB 84*
WKGR - Gainesville, FL - *BrCabYB 84*
WKGW-FM - Oriskany, NY - *TV&RadDir 84*
WKGW-FM - Utica, NY - *BrCabYB 84*
WKGX - Lenoir, NC - *BrCabYB 84; TV&RadDir 84*
WKHA-TV - Hazard, KY - *BrCabYB 84; Tel&CabFB 84S*
WKHA-TV - Lexington, KY - *TV&RadDir 84*
WKHG - Leitchfield, KY - *BrCabYB 84*
WKHI - Ocean City, MD - *BrCabYB 84*
WKHJ - Holly Hill, SC - *BrCabYB 84; TV&RadDir 84*
WKHK-FM - New York, NY - *BrCabYB 84; LitMarPl 83, 84; NatRadPubDir Summer 83, Spring 84; TV&RadDir 84*
WKHM - Jackson, MI - *BrCabYB 84*
WKHO-TV - Toledo, OH - *TelAl 83*
WKHQ-FM - Charlevoix, MI - *BrCabYB 84; TV&RadDir 84*
WKHR-FM - Bainbridge, OH - *BrCabYB 84*
WKHR-FM - Chagrin Falls, OH - *TV&RadDir 84*
WKHS-FM - Worton, MD - *BrCabYB 84; TV&RadDir 84*
WKHX-FM - Marietta, GA - *BrCabYB 84; TV&RadDir 84*
WKIC - Hazard, KY - *BrCabYB 84; TV&RadDir 84*
WKID-TV - Ft. Lauderdale, FL - *BrCabYB 84; TelAl 83, 84; Tel&CabFB 84S*
WKID-TV - Hollywood, FL - *TV&RadDir 84*
WKID-TV - Miami, FL - *DirUSTelSta 83*
WKIE - Richmond, VA - *BrCabYB 84; NatRadPubDir Summer 83, Spring 84; TV&RadDir 84*
WKIG - Glennville, GA - *BrCabYB 84; TV&RadDir 84*
WKIG-FM - Glennville, GA - *BrCabYB 84; TV&RadDir 84*
WKIK - Leonardtown, MD - *BrCabYB 84*
WKIN - Kingsport, TN - *BrCabYB 84; NatRadPubDir Summer 83, Spring 84; TV&RadDir 84*
WKIO-FM - Champaign, IL - *TV&RadDir 84*
WKIO-FM - Urbana, IL - *BrCabYB 84*
WKIP - Poughkeepsie, NY - *BrCabYB 84; TV&RadDir 84*
WKIQ-FM - Bowling Green, OH - *TV&RadDir 84*
WKIR-FM - Jackson, TN - *BrCabYB 84; TV&RadDir 84*
WKIS - Orlando, FL - *BrCabYB 84; LitMarPl 83, 84; NatRadPubDir Summer 83, Spring 84; TV&RadDir 84*
WKIT-FM - Hendersonville, NC - *BrCabYB 84; TV&RadDir 84*
WKIX - Raleigh, NC - *BrCabYB 84; NatRadPubDir Summer 83, Spring 84; TV&RadDir 84*
WKIZ - Key West, FL - *TV&RadDir 84*
WKJA - Belhaven, NC - *BrCabYB 84*
WKJB-FM - Mayaguez, PR - *BrCabYB 84*
WKJC - Tawas City, MI - *BrCabYB 84*
WKJF - Cadillac, MI - *BrCabYB 84; NatRadPubDir Summer 83, Spring 84; TV&RadDir 84*
WKJF-FM - Cadillac, MI - *NatRadPubDir Summer 83, Spring 84; TV&RadDir 84*
WKJG-TV - Ft. Wayne, IN - *BrCabYB 84; DirUSTelSta 83; TelAl 83, 84; Tel&CabFB 84S; TV&RadDir 84*
WKJJ-FM - Louisville, KY - *BrCabYB 84; NatRadPubDir Summer 83, Spring 84; TV&RadDir 84*
WKJK - Granite Falls, NC - *BrCabYB 84; TV&RadDir 84*
WKJL-TV - Baltimore, MD - *BrCabYB 84; Tel&CabFB 84S*
WKJQ - Jefferson City, IN - *BrCabYB 84*
WKJR - Muskegon, MI - *BrCabYB 84; NatRadPubDir Summer 83, Spring 84; TV&RadDir 84*
WKJS-FM - Harriman, TN - *BrCabYB 84; TV&RadDir 84*
WKJY-FM - Hempstead, NY - *TV&RadDir 84*
WKJY-FM - Nassau County, Long Island, NY - *NatRadPubDir Summer 83 p.171, Spring 84 p.169*
WKKA - Cornwall, CT - *BrCabYB 84*
WKKB-FM - Manitowoc, WI - *BrCabYB 84; TV&RadDir 84*
WKKC-FM - Chicago, IL - *BrCabYB 84; TV&RadDir 84*
WKKD-FM - Aurora, IL - *BrCabYB 84; NatRadPubDir Summer 83, Spring 84; TV&RadDir 84*
WKKE - Jackson, MS - *TV&RadDir 84*
WKKE - Pearl, MS - *BrCabYB 84*
WKKI-FM - Celina, OH - *BrCabYB 84; TV&RadDir 84*
WKKJ - Chillicothe, OH - *BrCabYB 84*
WKKL-FM - West Barnstable, MA - *BrCabYB 84; NatRadPubDir Summer 83, Spring 84 p.293; TV&RadDir 84*
WKKM-FM - Harrison, MI - *BrCabYB 84; TV&RadDir 84*
WKKN - Rockford, IL - *BrCabYB 84; NatRadPubDir Summer 83, Spring 84; TV&RadDir 84*
WKKO - Cocoa, FL - *BrCabYB 84; TV&RadDir 84*
WKKQ - Hibbing, MN - *BrCabYB 84; TV&RadDir 84*
WKKQ-FM - Hibbing, MN - *TV&RadDir 84*
WKKR - Evansville, IN - *NatRadPubDir Summer 83; TV&RadDir 84*
WKKS - Vanceburg, KY - *BrCabYB 84; TV&RadDir 84*
WKKS-FM - Vanceburg, KY - *BrCabYB 84*
WKKW-FM - Clarksburg, WV - *BrCabYB 84; TV&RadDir 84*

WKKX - Paoli, IN - *BrCabYB 84; TV&RadDir 84*
WKKY-FM - Pascagoula, MS - *BrCabYB 84; TV&RadDir 84*
WKKZ-FM - Dublin, GA - *BrCabYB 84; TV&RadDir 84*
WKLA-FM - Ludington, MI - *BrCabYB 84*
WKLB - Manchester, KY - *BrCabYB 84*
WKLC-FM - St. Albans, WV - *BrCabYB 84; TV&RadDir 84*
WKLD-FM - Oneonta, AL - *BrCabYB 84; TV&RadDir 84*
WKLE-TV - Lexington, KY - *BrCabYB 84; Tel&CabFB 84S; TV&RadDir 84*
WKLF - Clanton, AL - *BrCabYB 84; TV&RadDir 84*
WKLH - St. John's, MI - *BrCabYB 84*
WKLK - Cloquet, MN - *BrCabYB 84; TV&RadDir 84*
WKLK-FM - Cloquet, MN - *BrCabYB 84; TV&RadDir 84*
WKLM - Wilmington, NC - *BrCabYB 84; NatRadPubDir Summer 83, Spring 84; TV&RadDir 84*
WKLN-FM - Cullman, AL - *BrCabYB 84; TV&RadDir 84*
WKLO - Caneyville, KY - *TV&RadDir 84*
WKLO - Danville, KY - *BrCabYB 84*
WKLP - Keyser, WV - *BrCabYB 84; TV&RadDir 84*
WKLR-FM - Toledo, OH - *BrCabYB 84; NatRadPubDir Summer 83, Spring 84; TV&RadDir 84*
WKLS - Atlanta, GA - *BrCabYB 84; NatRadPubDir Summer 83, Spring 84; TV&RadDir 84*
WKLS-FM - Atlanta, GA - *BrCabYB 84; NatRadPubDir Summer 83, Spring 84; TV&RadDir 84*
WKLT - Kalkaska, MI - *BrCabYB 84*
WKLV - Blackstone, VA - *BrCabYB 84; TV&RadDir 84*
WKLX-FM - Plymouth, NC - *BrCabYB 84*
WKLY - Hartwell, GA - *BrCabYB 84; TV&RadDir 84*
WKLZ - Kalamazoo, MI - *BrCabYB 84; TV&RadDir 84*
WKMA-TV - Lexington, KY - *TV&RadDir 84*
WKMA-TV - Madisonville, KY - *BrCabYB 84; Tel&CabFB 84S*
WKMB - Stirling, NJ - *BrCabYB 84; TV&RadDir 84*
WKMC - Roaring Spring, PA - *BrCabYB 84; TV&RadDir 84*
WKMC-FM - St. Ignace, MI - *TV&RadDir 84*
WKME-TV - Seaford, DE - *Tel&CabFB 84S*
WKMF - Flint, MI - *BrCabYB 84; NatRadPubDir Summer 83, Spring 84; TV&RadDir 84*
WKMG - Newberry, SC - *BrCabYB 84; TV&RadDir 84*
WKMI - Kalamazoo, MI - *BrCabYB 84; NatRadPubDir Summer 83, Spring 84; TV&RadDir 84*
WKMJ-TV - Lexington, KY - *TV&RadDir 84*
WKMJ-TV - Louisville, KY - *BrCabYB 84; Tel&CabFB 84S*
WKMK - Blountstown, FL - *BrCabYB 84; TV&RadDir 84*
WKMO - Hodgenville, KY - *BrCabYB 84; TV&RadDir 84*
WKMO-FM - Elizabethtown, KY - *TV&RadDir 84*
WKMR-TV - Lexington, KY - *TV&RadDir 84*
WKMR-TV - Morehead, KY - *BrCabYB 84; Tel&CabFB 84S*
WKMS-FM - Murray, KY - *BrCabYB 84; NatRadPubDir Summer 83, Spring 84; TV&RadDir 84*
WKMT - Kings Mountain, NC - *BrCabYB 84; TV&RadDir 84*
WKMU - Murray, KY - *BrCabYB 84; Tel&CabFB 84S*
WKMX-FM - Enterprise, AL - *BrCabYB 84; TV&RadDir 84*
WKMY - Princeton, WV - *BrCabYB 84*
WKMZ-FM - Martinsburg, WV - *BrCabYB 84; TV&RadDir 84*
WKNC-FM - Raleigh, NC - *BrCabYB 84; NatRadPubDir Summer 83, Spring 84; TV&RadDir 84*
WKND - Hartford/New Britain, CT - *NatRadPubDir Summer 83 p.46, Spring 84 p.46*
WKND - Windsor, CT - *BrCabYB 84; TV&RadDir 84*
WKNE - Keene, NH - *BrCabYB 84; NatRadPubDir Summer 83, Spring 84; TV&RadDir 84*
WKNG - Tallapoosa, GA - *BrCabYB 84; TV&RadDir 84*
WKNH - Keene, NH - *BrCabYB 84; NatRadPubDir Summer 83, Spring 84*
WKNH-FM - Keene, NH - *NatRadPubDir Spring 84; TV&RadDir 84*
WKNJ - Union Township, NJ - *BrCabYB 84; TV&RadDir 84*
WKNO-FM - Memphis, TN - *BrCabYB 84; NatRadPubDir Summer 83, Spring 84; TV&RadDir 84*
WKNO-TV - Memphis, TN - *BrCabYB 84; Tel&CabFB 84S; TV&RadDir 84*
WKNR - Battle Creek, MI - *BrCabYB 84; NatRadPubDir Summer 83, Spring 84; TV&RadDir 84*
WKNS-FM - Kinston, NC - *BrCabYB 84; TV&RadDir 84*
WKNT - Kent, OH - *BrCabYB 84; TV&RadDir 84*
WKNU-FM - Brewton, AL - *BrCabYB 84; TV&RadDir 84*
WKNX - Saginaw, MI - *BrCabYB 84; NatRadPubDir Summer 83, Spring 84; TV&RadDir 84*
WKNY - Kingston, NY - *BrCabYB 84; TV&RadDir 84*
WKNZ-FM - Collins, MS - *BrCabYB 84; TV&RadDir 84*
WKOA - Hopkinsville, KY - *BrCabYB 84; TV&RadDir 84*
WKOA-FM - Hopkinsville, KY - *BrCabYB 84; TV&RadDir 84*
WKOC-FM - Kankakee, IL - *BrCabYB 84; TV&RadDir 84*
WKOE - Dayton, TN - *BrCabYB 84; TV&RadDir 84*
WKOH - Owensboro, KY - *BrCabYB 84; Tel&CabFB 84S*
WKOI - Richmond, IN - *BrCabYB 84; TelAl 84; Tel&CabFB 84S*
WKOK - Sunbury, PA - *BrCabYB 84; TV&RadDir 84*
WKOL - Amsterdam, NY - *BrCabYB 84; TV&RadDir 84*
WKOM-FM - Columbia, TN - *BrCabYB 84; TV&RadDir 84*
WKON-TV - Lexington, KY - *TV&RadDir 84*
WKON-TV - Owenton, KY - *BrCabYB 84; Tel&CabFB 84S*
WKOP - Binghamton, NY - *BrCabYB 84; NatRadPubDir Summer 83, Spring 84; TV&RadDir 84*
WKOR - Starkville, MS - *BrCabYB 84; TV&RadDir 84*
WKOR-FM - Starkville, MS - *BrCabYB 84; TV&RadDir 84*
WKOS-FM - Murfreesboro, TN - *BrCabYB 84; TV&RadDir 84*
WKOS-FM - Nashville, TN - *NatRadPubDir Summer 83, Spring 84 p.231*
WKOV - Wellston, OH - *BrCabYB 84; TV&RadDir 84*
WKOV-FM - Wellston, OH - *BrCabYB 84; TV&RadDir 84*
WKOW-TV - Madison, WI - *BrCabYB 84; DirUSTelSta 83; TelAl 83, 84; Tel&CabFB 84S; TV&RadDir 84*
WKOX - Boston, MA - *NatRadPubDir Summer 83 p.120, Spring 84 p.120*
WKOX - Framingham, MA - *BrCabYB 84; TV&RadDir 84*
WKOY - Bluefield, WV - *BrCabYB 84; TV&RadDir 84*
WKOZ - Kosciusko, MS - *BrCabYB 84; TV&RadDir 84*
WKOZ-FM - Kosciusko, MS - *BrCabYB 84; TV&RadDir 84*
WKPA - New Kensington, PA - *BrCabYB 84; TV&RadDir 84*
WKPA - Pittsburgh, PA - *NatRadPubDir Summer 83 p.214, Spring 84 p.214*
WKPC-TV - Louisville, KY - *BrCabYB 84; Tel&CabFB 84S; TV&RadDir 84*
WKPD-TV - Paducah, KY - *BrCabYB 84; Tel&CabFB 84S*
WKPE - Orleans, MA - *BrCabYB 84*
WKPG - Port Gibson, MS - *BrCabYB 84; TV&RadDir 84*
WKPI-TV - Lexington, KY - *TV&RadDir 84*
WKPI-TV - Pikeville, KY - *BrCabYB 84; Tel&CabFB 84S*
WKPL - Platteville, WI - *BrCabYB 84*
WKPO - Prentiss, MS - *BrCabYB 84; TV&RadDir 84*
WKPQ-FM - Hornell, NY - *BrCabYB 84; NatRadPubDir Spring 84*
WKPR - Kalamazoo, MI - *BrCabYB 84; NatRadPubDir Summer 83, Spring 84; TV&RadDir 84*
WKPS-FM - New Wilmington, PA - *BrCabYB 84; NatRadPubDir Summer 83, Spring 84*
WKPT - Kingsport, TN - *BrCabYB 84; NatRadPubDir Summer 83, Spring 84; TV&RadDir 84*
WKPT-FM - Kingsport, TN - *NatRadPubDir Summer 83*
WKPT-TV - Kingsport, TN - *BrCabYB 84; DirUSTelSta 83; TelAl 83, 84; Tel&CabFB 84S; TV&RadDir 84*
WKPX - Sunrise, FL - *BrCabYB 84*
WKQA-FM - Pekin, IL - *BrCabYB 84*
WKQA-FM - Peoria, IL - *TV&RadDir 84*
WKQE - Tallahassee, FL - *BrCabYB 84; NatRadPubDir Summer 83, Spring 84; TV&RadDir 84*
WKQK - Eufaula, AL - *BrCabYB 84*
WKQQ-FM - Lexington, KY - *BrCabYB 84; TV&RadDir 84*
WKQS-FM - Boca Raton, FL - *BrCabYB 84; TV&RadDir 84*
WKQT - Garyville, LA - *BrCabYB 84; TV&RadDir 84*
WKQV-FM - Vineland, NJ - *BrCabYB 84; TV&RadDir 84*
WKQW - Oil City, PA - *BrCabYB 84*
WKQX-FM - Chicago, IL - *BrCabYB 84; NatRadPubDir Summer 83, Spring 84; TV&RadDir 84*
WKRA - Holly Springs, MS - *BrCabYB 84; TV&RadDir 84*
WKRA-FM - Holly Springs, MS - *BrCabYB 84; TV&RadDir 84*
WKRB-FM - Brooklyn, NY - *TV&RadDir 84*
WKRB-FM - New York, NY - *BrCabYB 84; NatRadPubDir Summer 83 p.302, Spring 84 p.304*
WKRC [of Taft Broadcasting] - Cincinnati, OH - *BrCabYB 84; NatRadPubDir Summer 83, Spring 84; TV&RadDir 84; VideoDir 82-83*

WKRC-TV - Cincinnati, OH - *BrCabYB 84; DirUSTelSta 83; LitMarPl 83, 84; TelAl 83, 84; Tel&CabFB 84S; TV&RadDir 84*
WKRG - Mobile, AL - *BrCabYB 84; NatRadPubDir Summer 83, Spring 84*
WKRG-FM - Mobile, AL - *BrCabYB 84; NatRadPubDir Summer 83, Spring 84; TV&RadDir 84*
WKRG-TV - Mobile, AL - *BrCabYB 84; DirUSTelSta 83; TelAl 83, 84; Tel&CabFB 84S; TV&RadDir 84*
WKRI - West Warwick, RI - *BrCabYB 84; TV&RadDir 84*
WKRK - Murphy, NC - *BrCabYB 84; TV&RadDir 84*
WKRM - Columbia, TN - *BrCabYB 84; TV&RadDir 84*
WKRN-TV - Nashville, TN - *BrCabYB 84*
WKRO - Cairo, IL - *BrCabYB 84; TV&RadDir 84*
WKRP - Dallas, GA - *BrCabYB 84; TV&RadDir 84*
WKRQ-FM - Cincinnati, OH - *BrCabYB 84; NatRadPubDir Summer 83, Spring 84; TV&RadDir 84*
WKRS - Waukegan, IL - *BrCabYB 84; NatRadPubDir Summer 83, Spring 84; TV&RadDir 84*
WKRT - Cortland, NY - *BrCabYB 84; TV&RadDir 84*
WKRV - Vandalia, IL - *BrCabYB 84*
WKRX-FM - Roxboro, NC - *BrCabYB 84; TV&RadDir 84*
WKRZ - Wilkes Barre, PA - *BrCabYB 84; TV&RadDir 84*
WKRZ-FM - Wilkes Barre, PA - *BrCabYB 84; TV&RadDir 84*
WKSA-FM - Isabela, PR - *BrCabYB 84*
WKSB-FM - Williamsport, PA - *BrCabYB 84; TV&RadDir 84*
WKSC - Kershaw, SC - *BrCabYB 84; TV&RadDir 84*
WKSC-FM - Kutztown, PA - *NatRadPubDir Summer 83, Spring 84*
WKSI-FM - Eldorado, IL - *BrCabYB 84; TV&RadDir 84*
WKSJ - Mobile, AL - *BrCabYB 84; TV&RadDir 84*
WKSJ - Prichard, AL - *BrCabYB 84*
WKSJ-FM - Mobile, AL - *NatRadPubDir Summer 83, Spring 84; TV&RadDir 84*
WKSK - West Jefferson, NC - *BrCabYB 84; TV&RadDir 84*
WKSL-FM - Greencastle, PA - *BrCabYB 84; TV&RadDir 84*
WKSM-FM - Tabor City, NC - *BrCabYB 84; TV&RadDir 84*
WKSN - Jamestown, NY - *BrCabYB 84; TV&RadDir 84*
WKSO-TV - Lexington, KY - *TV&RadDir 84*
WKSO-TV - Somerset, KY - *BrCabYB 84; Tel&CabFB 84S*
WKSP - Kingstree, SC - *BrCabYB 84; TV&RadDir 84*
WKSR - Pulaski, TN - *BrCabYB 84; TV&RadDir 84*
WKSS-FM - Hartford, CT - *BrCabYB 84; NatRadPubDir Summer 83, Spring 84; TV&RadDir 84*
WKST - New Castle, PA - *BrCabYB 84; TV&RadDir 84*
WKSU-FM - Kent, OH - *BrCabYB 84; NatRadPubDir Summer 83, Spring 84; TV&RadDir 84*
WKSW-FM - Cleveland, OH - *BrCabYB 84; NatRadPubDir Summer 83, Spring 84; TV&RadDir 84*
WKSY-FM - Columbia City, IN - *BrCabYB 84; TV&RadDir 84*
WKSZ - Media, PA - *BrCabYB 84*
WKTA-FM - McKenzie, TN - *BrCabYB 84; TV&RadDir 84*
WKTC-FM - Tarboro, NC - *BrCabYB 84; TV&RadDir 84*
WKTE - King, NC - *BrCabYB 84; TV&RadDir 84*
WKTG-FM - Madisonville, KY - *BrCabYB 84; TV&RadDir 84*
WKTI-FM - Milwaukee, WI - *BrCabYB 84; NatRadPubDir Summer 83, Spring 84; TV&RadDir 84*
WKTJ - Farmington, ME - *BrCabYB 84; TV&RadDir 84*
WKTJ-FM - Farmington, ME - *BrCabYB 84; TV&RadDir 84*
WKTK-FM - Baltimore, MD - *TV&RadDir 84*
WKTL-FM - Struthers, OH - *BrCabYB 84; NatRadPubDir Summer 83, Spring 84; TV&RadDir 84*
WKTM-FM - Charleston, SC - *BrCabYB 84; NatRadPubDir Summer 83, Spring 84; TV&RadDir 84*
WKTN-FM - Kenton, OH - *BrCabYB 84; TV&RadDir 84*
WKTQ-FM - Pittsfield, MA - *BrCabYB 84; NatRadPubDir Spring 84*
WKTR-FM - Millinocket, ME - *BrCabYB 84; TV&RadDir 84*
WKTS - Sheboygan, WI - *BrCabYB 84; TV&RadDir 84*
WKTU-FM - New York, NY - *BrCabYB 84; NatRadPubDir Summer 83, Spring 84; TV&RadDir 84*
WKTV-TV - Utica, NY - *BrCabYB 84; DirUSTelSta 83; TelAl 83, 84; Tel&CabFB 84S; TV&RadDir 84*
WKTY - La Crosse, WI - *BrCabYB 84; TV&RadDir 84*
WKTZ - Jacksonville, FL - *BrCabYB 84; NatRadPubDir Summer 83, Spring 84*
WKTZ-FM - Jacksonville, FL - *BrCabYB 84; NatRadPubDir Summer 83, Spring 84*
WKUB-FM - Blackshear, GA - *BrCabYB 84; TV&RadDir 84*
WKUN - Monroe, GA - *BrCabYB 84; TV&RadDir 84*
WKUZ-FM - Wabash, IN - *BrCabYB 84; TV&RadDir 84*
WKVA - Lewistown, PA - *BrCabYB 84; TV&RadDir 84*
WKVE - Cave City, KY - *BrCabYB 84; TV&RadDir 84*
WKVI-FM - Knox, IN - *BrCabYB 84; TV&RadDir 84*
WKVL - Clarksville, TN - *TV&RadDir 84*
WKVM - San Juan, PR - *BrCabYB 84*
WKVR-FM - Huntingdon, PA - *BrCabYB 84; TV&RadDir 84*
WKVT - Brattleboro, VT - *BrCabYB 84; NatRadPubDir Summer 83, Spring 84; TV&RadDir 84*
WKVT-FM - Brattleboro, VT - *NatRadPubDir Spring 84; TV&RadDir 84*
WKVU - Villanova, PA - *NatRadPubDir Summer 83, Spring 84*
WKWF - Key West, FL - *BrCabYB 84; TV&RadDir 84*
WKWI-FM - Kilmarnock, VA - *BrCabYB 84; TV&RadDir 84*
WKWK - Wheeling, WV - *BrCabYB 84; NatRadPubDir Summer 83, Spring 84; TV&RadDir 84*
WKWK-FM - Wheeling, WV - *BrCabYB 84; NatRadPubDir Summer 83, Spring 84; TV&RadDir 84*
WKWL - Florala, AL - *BrCabYB 84; TV&RadDir 84*
WKWM - Kentwood, MI - *BrCabYB 84*
WKWQ-FM - Batesburg, SC - *BrCabYB 84; TV&RadDir 84*
WKWR-TV - Cookeville, TN - *BrCabYB 84; Tel&CabFB 84S*
WKWX-FM - Savannah, TN - *BrCabYB 84; TV&RadDir 84*
WKWZ-FM - Syosset, NY - *BrCabYB 84; NatRadPubDir Summer 83, Spring 84; TV&RadDir 84*
WKXA - Bangor, ME - *NatRadPubDir Summer 83 p.113, Spring 84 p.113*
WKXA - Brunswick, ME - *BrCabYB 84; TV&RadDir 84*
WKXA-FM - Bangor, ME - *NatRadPubDir Summer 83 p.113, Spring 84 p.113*
WKXA-FM - Brunswick, ME - *TV&RadDir 84*
WKXC - New Albany, MS - *BrCabYB 84*
WKXF-FM - Cincinnati, OH - *NatRadPubDir Spring 84*
WKXI - Jackson, MS - *NatRadPubDir Summer 83, Spring 84; TV&RadDir 84*
WKXJ - Campbellsville, KY - *BrCabYB 84; TV&RadDir 84*
WKXK-FM - Pana, IL - *BrCabYB 84; TV&RadDir 84*
WKXL - Concord, NH - *BrCabYB 84; NatRadPubDir Summer 83, Spring 84; TV&RadDir 84*
WKXL-FM - Concord, NH - *BrCabYB 84; NatRadPubDir Summer 83, Spring 84; TV&RadDir 84*
WKXN-FM - Greenville, AL - *BrCabYB 84; TV&RadDir 84*
WKXO - Berea, KY - *BrCabYB 84; TV&RadDir 84*
WKXV - Knoxville, TN - *BrCabYB 84; NatRadPubDir Summer 83, Spring 84; TV&RadDir 84*
WKXW - Trenton, NJ - *NatRadPubDir Summer 83; TV&RadDir 84*
WKXW-FM - Trenton, NJ - *BrCabYB 84; NatRadPubDir Summer 83, Spring 84; TV&RadDir 84*
WKXX-FM - Birmingham, AL - *BrCabYB 84; NatRadPubDir Summer 83, Spring 84; TV&RadDir 84*
WKXY - Sarasota, FL - *BrCabYB 84; NatRadPubDir Summer 83, Spring 84; TV&RadDir 84*
WKXZ - Norwich, NY - *BrCabYB 84*
WKY - Oklahoma City, OK - *BrCabYB 84; NatRadPubDir Summer 83, Spring 84; TV&RadDir 84*
WKYA-FM - Central City, KY - *BrCabYB 84; TV&RadDir 84*
WKYB - Hemingway, SC - *BrCabYB 84; TV&RadDir 84*
WKYC-TV - Cleveland, OH - *BrCabYB 84; DirUSTelSta 83; LitMarPl 83, 84; TelAl 83, 84; Tel&CabFB 84S; TV&RadDir 84*
WKYD - Andalusia, AL - *BrCabYB 84; NatRadPubDir Summer 83, Spring 84; TV&RadDir 84*
WKYD-FM - Andalusia, AL - *BrCabYB 84; NatRadPubDir Summer 83, Spring 84; TV&RadDir 84*
WKYE-FM - Johnstown, PA - *BrCabYB 84; NatRadPubDir Spring 84*
WKYG - Parkersburg, WV - *BrCabYB 84; NatRadPubDir Summer 83, Spring 84; TV&RadDir 84*
WKYH-TV - Hazard, KY - *BrCabYB 84; DirUSTelSta 83; TelAl 83, 84; Tel&CabFB 84S; TV&RadDir 84*
WKYK - Burnsville, NC - *BrCabYB 84; TV&RadDir 84*
WKYM-FM - Monticello, KY - *BrCabYB 84; TV&RadDir 84*
WKYO - Caro, MI - *BrCabYB 84; TV&RadDir 84*
WKYO-FM - Caro, MI - *BrCabYB 84; TV&RadDir 84*
WKYQ-FM - Paducah, KY - *BrCabYB 84; TV&RadDir 84*

WKYR - Burkesville, KY - *BrCabYB 84; TV&RadDir 84*
WKYS-FM - Washington, DC - *BrCabYB 84; LitMarPl 84; NatRadPubDir Summer 83, Spring 84; TV&RadDir 84*
WKYT-TV - Lexington, KY - *BrCabYB 84; DirUSTelSta 83; TelAl 83, 84; Tel&CabFB 84S; TV&RadDir 84*
WKYU-FM - Bowling Green, KY - *BrCabYB 84*
WKYV-FM - Vicksburg, MS - *BrCabYB 84; TV&RadDir 84*
WKYW-FM - Frankfort, KY - *BrCabYB 84; NatRadPubDir Summer 83, Spring 84; TV&RadDir 84*
WKYX - Paducah, KY - *BrCabYB 84; TV&RadDir 84*
WKYZ - Salisbury, MD - *BrCabYB 84*
WKZA - Kane, PA - *BrCabYB 84; TV&RadDir 84*
WKZB-FM - Drew, MS - *BrCabYB 84; TV&RadDir 84*
WKZC - Scottville, MI - *BrCabYB 84*
WKZE-FM - Orleans, MA - *TV&RadDir 84*
WKZI - Casey, IL - *BrCabYB 84; TV&RadDir 84*
WKZK - Augusta, GA - *BrCabYB 84; NatRadPubDir Summer 83, Spring 84; TV&RadDir 84*
WKZL-FM - Winston Salem, NC - *BrCabYB 84; NatRadPubDir Summer 83, Spring 84; TV&RadDir 84*
WKZM - Sarasota, FL - *BrCabYB 84*
WKZN-FM - Zion, IL - *TV&RadDir 84*
WKZO - Kalamazoo, MI - *BrCabYB 84; NatRadPubDir Summer 83, Spring 84; TV&RadDir 84*
WKZO-TV - Kalamazoo, MI - *BrCabYB 84; DirUSTelSta 83; LitMarPl 83, 84; TelAl 83, 84; Tel&CabFB 84S; TV&RadDir 84*
WKZQ-FM - Myrtle Beach, SC - *BrCabYB 84; TV&RadDir 84*
WKZR-FM - Milledgeville, GA - *BrCabYB 84; TV&RadDir 84*
WKZS - Auburn, ME - *BrCabYB 84*
WKZT-TV - Elizabethtown, KY - *BrCabYB 84; Tel&CabFB 84S*
WKZT-TV - Lexington, KY - *TV&RadDir 84*
WKZU - Lanconia, NH - *BrCabYB 84*
WKZW-FM - Peoria, IL - *BrCabYB 84; NatRadPubDir Summer 83, Spring 84; TV&RadDir 84*
WKZX - Presque Isle, ME - *TV&RadDir 84*
WKZY - North Ft. Myers, FL - *BrCabYB 84*
WKZY - St. Johns, MI - *TV&RadDir 84*
WKZZ-FM - Lynchburg, VA - *BrCabYB 84; NatRadPubDir Summer 83, Spring 84; TV&RadDir 84*
WLAC - Nashville, TN - *BrCabYB 84; NatRadPubDir Summer 83, Spring 84; TV&RadDir 84*
WLAC-FM - Nashville, TN - *BrCabYB 84*
WLAD - Danbury, CT - *BrCabYB 84; NatRadPubDir Summer 83, Spring 84; TV&RadDir 84*
WLAD-FM - Danbury, CT - *BrCabYB 84*
WLAE-TV - New Orleans, LA - *BrCabYB 84; Tel&CabFB 84S*
WLAF - La Follette, TN - *BrCabYB 84; TV&RadDir 84*
WLAG - La Grange, GA - *BrCabYB 84; TV&RadDir 84*
WLAJ-TV - Lansing, MI - *BrCabYB 84; Tel&CabFB 84S*
WLAK-FM - Chicago, IL - *BrCabYB 84; NatRadPubDir Summer 83, Spring 84; TV&RadDir 84*
WLAM - Lewiston, ME - *BrCabYB 84; TV&RadDir 84*
WLAN - Lancaster, PA - *BrCabYB 84; NatRadPubDir Summer 83, Spring 84; TV&RadDir 84*
WLAN-FM - Lancaster, PA - *BrCabYB 84; NatRadPubDir Summer 83, Spring 84; TV&RadDir 84*
WLAP - Lexington, KY - *BrCabYB 84; NatRadPubDir Summer 83, Spring 84; TV&RadDir 84*
WLAP-FM - Lexington, KY - *BrCabYB 84; NatRadPubDir Summer 83, Spring 84; TV&RadDir 84*
WLAQ - Rome, GA - *BrCabYB 84; NatRadPubDir Summer 83, Spring 84; TV&RadDir 84*
WLAR - Athens, TN - *BrCabYB 84; TV&RadDir 84*
WLAS - Jacksonville, NC - *BrCabYB 84; TV&RadDir 84*
WLAT - Conway, SC - *BrCabYB 84; TV&RadDir 84*
WLAT-FM - Conway, SC - *BrCabYB 84*
WLAU - Laurel, MS - *TV&RadDir 84*
WLAV-FM - Grand Rapids, MI - *BrCabYB 84; TV&RadDir 84*
WLAW - Lawrenceville, GA - *BrCabYB 84; TV&RadDir 84*
WLAX-FM - Streator, IL - *BrCabYB 84; TV&RadDir 84*
WLAY - Muscle Shoals, AL - *BrCabYB 84*
WLAY - Sheffield, AL - *TV&RadDir 84*
WLAY-FM - Muscle Shoals, AL - *BrCabYB 84*
WLAY-FM - Sheffield, AL - *TV&RadDir 84*
WLBA - Gainesville, GA - *BrCabYB 84; TV&RadDir 84*
WLBB - Carrollton, GA - *BrCabYB 84; TV&RadDir 84*
WLBC - Muncie, IN - *BrCabYB 84; TV&RadDir 84*
WLBC-FM - Muncie, IN - *BrCabYB 84; TV&RadDir 84*
WLBE - Leesburg, FL - *TV&RadDir 84*
WLBG - Laurens, SC - *TV&RadDir 84*
WLBH - Mattoon, IL - *BrCabYB 84; TV&RadDir 84*
WLBH-FM - Mattoon, IL - *BrCabYB 84; TV&RadDir 84*
WLBI - Denham Springs, LA - *BrCabYB 84; TV&RadDir 84*
WLBJ - Bowling Green, KY - *BrCabYB 84; TV&RadDir 84*
WLBJ-FM - Bowling Green, KY - *BrCabYB 84; TV&RadDir 84*
WLBK - De Kalb, IL - *BrCabYB 84; NatRadPubDir Summer 83, Spring 84; TV&RadDir 84*
WLBL - Auburndale, WI - *BrCabYB 84; NatRadPubDir Summer 83 p.325, Spring 84 p.327*
WLBM-TV - Meridian, MI - *BrCabYB 84; Tel&CabFB 84S*
WLBN - Lebanon, KY - *BrCabYB 84; NatRadPubDir Summer 83, Spring 84; TV&RadDir 84*
WLBQ - Morgantown, KY - *BrCabYB 84; TV&RadDir 84*
WLBR - Lebanon, PA - *BrCabYB 84; TV&RadDir 84*
WLBS - New Brunswick, NJ - *NatRadPubDir Summer 83, Spring 84*
WLBS-FM - Mt. Clemens, MI - *BrCabYB 84*
WLBT-TV - Jackson, MS - *BrCabYB 84; DirUSTelSta 83; TelAl 83, 84; Tel&CabFB 84S; TV&RadDir 84*
WLBZ-TV - Bangor, ME - *BrCabYB 84; DirUSTelSta 83; LitMarPl 83, 84; TelAl 83, 84; Tel&CabFB 84S; TV&RadDir 84*
WLCA-FM - Godfrey, IL - *BrCabYB 84; TV&RadDir 84*
WLCB - Buffalo, KY - *BrCabYB 84*
WLCC - Luray, VA - *BrCabYB 84*
WLCF-FM - Southport, NC - *TV&RadDir 84*
WLCH - Lebanon, TN - *BrCabYB 84*
WLCK - Scottsville, KY - *BrCabYB 84; TV&RadDir 84*
WLCK-FM - Scottsville, KY - *BrCabYB 84; TV&RadDir 84*
WLCM - Lancaster, SC - *BrCabYB 84; TV&RadDir 84*
WLCN - Madisonville, KY - *BrCabYB 84; Tel&CabFB 84S*
WLCR-FM - Lawrence Township, NJ - *BrCabYB 84*
WLCR-FM - Trenton, NJ - *TV&RadDir 84*
WLCS - Baton Rouge, LA - *BrCabYB 84; NatRadPubDir Summer 83, Spring 84; TV&RadDir 84*
WLCT - New London, CT - *BrCabYB 84; Tel&CabFB 84S*
WLCX - La Crosse, WI - *TV&RadDir 84*
WLCX-FM - Dayton, TN - *BrCabYB 84*
WLCY - St. Petersburg, FL - *LitMarPl 83*
WLCY-FM - Dayton, TN - *TV&RadDir 84*
WLDC - New Orleans, LA - *NatRadPubDir Summer 83, Spring 84*
WLDM - Westfield, MA - *BrCabYB 84; TV&RadDir 84*
WLDR-FM - Traverse City, MI - *BrCabYB 84; TV&RadDir 84*
WLDS - Jacksonville, IL - *BrCabYB 84; TV&RadDir 84*
WLDY - Ladysmith, WI - *BrCabYB 84; TV&RadDir 84*
WLDY-FM - Ladysmith, WI - *BrCabYB 84*
WLEA - Hornell, NY - *BrCabYB 84; TV&RadDir 84*
WLEC - Sandusky, OH - *BrCabYB 84; NatRadPubDir Summer 83, Spring 84; TV&RadDir 84*
WLED-TV - Littleton, NH - *BrCabYB 84; Tel&CabFB 84S; TV&RadDir 84*
WLEE - Richmond, VA - *BrCabYB 84; NatRadPubDir Summer 83, Spring 84; TV&RadDir 84*
WLEF-TV - Park Falls, WI - *BrCabYB 84; Tel&CabFB 84S*
WLEJ - Ellijay, GA - *BrCabYB 84; TV&RadDir 84*
WLEM - Emporium, PA - *BrCabYB 84; TV&RadDir 84*
WLEN-FM - Adrian, MI - *BrCabYB 84; TV&RadDir 84*
WLEO - Ponce, PR - *BrCabYB 84*
WLEQ-FM - Bonita Springs, FL - *BrCabYB 84*
WLEQ-FM - Ft. Myers, FL - *TV&RadDir 84*
WLER-FM - Butler, PA - *BrCabYB 84; TV&RadDir 84*
WLES - Lawrenceville, VA - *BrCabYB 84; TV&RadDir 84*
WLET - Toccoa, GA - *BrCabYB 84; TV&RadDir 84*
WLET-FM - Toccoa, GA - *BrCabYB 84; TV&RadDir 84*
WLEV-FM - Allentown/Bethlehem/Easton, PA - *NatRadPubDir Summer 83, Spring 84 p.209*
WLEV-FM - Easton, PA - *BrCabYB 84; TV&RadDir 84*
WLEW - Bad Axe, MI - *BrCabYB 84; TV&RadDir 84*
WLEW-FM - Bad Axe, MI - *BrCabYB 84; TV&RadDir 84*
WLEX-TV - Lexington, KY - *BrCabYB 84; DirUSTelSta 83; TelAl 83, 84; Tel&CabFB 84S; TV&RadDir 84*
WLEY - Cayey, PR - *BrCabYB 84*

WLEZ-FM - Elmira, NY - *BrCabYB 84; NatRadPubDir Summer 83, Spring 84; TV&RadDir 84*
WLFA - La Fayette, GA - *BrCabYB 84; TV&RadDir 84*
WLFC-FM - Findlay, OH - *BrCabYB 84; NatRadPubDir Summer 83, Spring 84; TV&RadDir 84*
WLFE-FM - St. Albans, VT - *BrCabYB 84; NatRadPubDir Summer 83, Spring 84; TV&RadDir 84*
WLFF - Cayce, SC - *BrCabYB 84; TV&RadDir 84*
WLFF - Columbia, SC - *NatRadPubDir Spring 84*
WLFH - Little Falls, NY - *BrCabYB 84; TV&RadDir 84*
WLFI-TV - Lafayette, IN - *BrCabYB 84; DirUSTelSta 83; TelAl 83, 84; Tel&CabFB 84S; TV&RadDir 84*
WLFJ - Greenville, SC - *BrCabYB 84*
WLFL-TV - Durham, NC - *TelAl 84*
WLFL-TV - Raleigh, NC - *BrCabYB 84; DirUSTelSta 83; Tel&CabFB 84S*
WLFM-FM - Appleton, WI - *BrCabYB 84; NatRadPubDir Summer 83, Spring 84; TV&RadDir 84*
WLFQ-FM - Crawfordsville, IN - *BrCabYB 84; TV&RadDir 84*
WLFT - Flint, MI - *TV&RadDir 84*
WLFW - St. Petersburg, FL - *BrCabYB 84; TV&RadDir 84*
WLFW - Tampa/St. Petersburg, FL - *NatRadPubDir Spring 84 p.65*
WLGA-FM - Valdosta, GA - *BrCabYB 84; TV&RadDir 84*
WLGC - Greenup, KY - *BrCabYB 84*
WLGI - Hemingway, SC - *BrCabYB 84*
WLGM - Lynchburg, VA - *BrCabYB 84; TV&RadDir 84*
WLGN - Logan, OH - *BrCabYB 84; TV&RadDir 84*
WLGN-FM - Logan, OH - *BrCabYB 84; TV&RadDir 84*
WLHI-FM - Ft. Wayne, IN - *BrCabYB 84; TV&RadDir 84*
WLHN-FM - Anderson, IN - *BrCabYB 84; NatRadPubDir Summer 83, Spring 84; TV&RadDir 84*
WLHQ-FM - Enterprise, AL - *BrCabYB 84; TV&RadDir 84*
WLHS-FM - West Chester, OH - *BrCabYB 84; TV&RadDir 84*
WLHT - Hattiesburg, MI - *BrCabYB 84; Tel&CabFB 84S*
WLI Associates Advertising - Lowell, MA - *StaDirAdAg 2-84*
WLIB - New York, NY - *BrCabYB 84; LitMarPl 83, 84; NatRadPubDir Summer 83, Spring 84; TV&RadDir 84*
WLIC - Adamsville, TN - *TV&RadDir 84*
WLID - Vieques, PR - *BrCabYB 84*
WLIF-FM - Baltimore, MD - *BrCabYB 84; NatRadPubDir Summer 83 p.116, Spring 84 p.116; TV&RadDir 84*
WLIG - Riverhead, NY - *BrCabYB 84; Tel&CabFB 84S*
WLIJ - Shelbyville, TN - *BrCabYB 84; TV&RadDir 84*
WLIK - Newport, TN - *BrCabYB 84; TV&RadDir 84*
WLIL - Lenoir City, TN - *BrCabYB 84; TV&RadDir 84*
WLIL-FM - Lenoir City, TN - *BrCabYB 84; TV&RadDir 84*
WLIM - Patchogue, NY - *BrCabYB 84; TV&RadDir 84*
WLIN-FM - Jackson, MS - *BrCabYB 84; NatRadPubDir Summer 83, Spring 84; TV&RadDir 84*
WLIO-TV - Lima, OH - *BrCabYB 84; DirUSTelSta 83; TelAl 83, 84; Tel&CabFB 84S; TV&RadDir 84*
WLIP - Kenosha, WI - *BrCabYB 84; TV&RadDir 84*
WLIR-FM - Garden City, NY - *BrCabYB 84*
WLIR-FM - Hempstead, NY - *TV&RadDir 84*
WLIR-FM - Nassau County, Long Island, NY - *NatRadPubDir Summer 83 p.171, Spring 84 p.169*
WLIS - Old Saybrook, CT - *BrCabYB 84; TV&RadDir 84*
WLIT - Steubenville, OH - *BrCabYB 84; NatRadPubDir Summer 83, Spring 84; TV&RadDir 84*
WLIU-FM - Lincoln University, PA - *BrCabYB 84; TV&RadDir 84*
WLIV - Livingston, TN - *BrCabYB 84; TV&RadDir 84*
WLIW-TV - Garden City, NY - *BrCabYB 84; Tel&CabFB 84S*
WLIW-TV - Plainview, NY - *TV&RadDir 84*
WLIX - Bay Shore, NY - *TV&RadDir 84*
WLIX - Islip, NY - *BrCabYB 84*
WLIX - Suffolk County, Long Island, NY - *NatRadPubDir Summer 83 p.178, Spring 84 p.176*
WLIZ - Lake Worth, FL - *BrCabYB 84; TV&RadDir 84*
WLJC-FM - Beattyville, KY - *BrCabYB 84; TV&RadDir 84*
WLJC-TV - Beattyville, KY - *BrCabYB 84; TelAl 84; Tel&CabFB 84S*
WLJE-FM - Valparaiso, IN - *BrCabYB 84; TV&RadDir 84*
WLJN - Elmwood Township, MI - *BrCabYB 84*
WLJS-FM - Jacksonville, AL - *BrCabYB 84; TV&RadDir 84*
WLJT-TV - Jackson, TN - *TV&RadDir 84*
WLJT-TV - Lexington, TN - *BrCabYB 84; Tel&CabFB 84S*
WLJY-FM - Marshfield, WI - *BrCabYB 84; TV&RadDir 84*
WLK Cos. Inc. - Buffalo, NY - *StaDirAdAg 2-84*
WLKC - St. Mary's, GA - *BrCabYB 84*
WLKE-FM - Waupun, WI - *BrCabYB 84; TV&RadDir 84*
WLKF - Lakeland, FL - *BrCabYB 84; NatRadPubDir Spring 84*
WLKI-FM - Angola, IN - *BrCabYB 84; TV&RadDir 84*
WLKK - Erie, PA - *BrCabYB 84; NatRadPubDir Summer 83, Spring 84; TV&RadDir 84*
WLKL-FM - Mattoon, IL - *BrCabYB 84; TV&RadDir 84*
WLKM - Three Rivers, MI - *BrCabYB 84; TV&RadDir 84*
WLKM-FM - Three Rivers, MI - *BrCabYB 84; TV&RadDir 84*
WLKN - Lincoln, ME - *BrCabYB 84; TV&RadDir 84*
WLKN-FM - Lincoln, ME - *BrCabYB 84; TV&RadDir 84*
WLKR - Norwalk, OH - *BrCabYB 84; TV&RadDir 84*
WLKR-FM - Norwalk, OH - *BrCabYB 84; TV&RadDir 84*
WLKS - West Liberty, KY - *BrCabYB 84; TV&RadDir 84*
WLKW - Providence, RI - *BrCabYB 84; NatRadPubDir Summer 83, Spring 84; TV&RadDir 84*
WLKW-FM - Providence, RI - *BrCabYB 84; NatRadPubDir Summer 83, Spring 84; TV&RadDir 84*
WLKX-FM - Forest Lake, MN - *BrCabYB 84; TV&RadDir 84*
WLKY-TV - Louisville, KY - *BrCabYB 84; DirUSTelSta 83; LitMarPl 83, 84; TelAl 83, 84; Tel&CabFB 84S; TV&RadDir 84*
WLKZ - Wolfeboro, NH - *BrCabYB 84*
WLLA - Kalamazoo, MI - *BrCabYB 84; Tel&CabFB 84S*
WLLE - Raleigh, NC - *BrCabYB 84; NatRadPubDir Summer 83, Spring 84; TV&RadDir 84*
WLLH - Lowell, MA - *BrCabYB 84; NatRadPubDir Summer 83, Spring 84; TV&RadDir 84*
WLLI-FM - Joliet, IL - *BrCabYB 84; NatRadPubDir Spring 84; TV&RadDir 84*
WLLL - Lynchburg, VA - *BrCabYB 84; TV&RadDir 84*
WLLN - Lillington, NC - *BrCabYB 84; TV&RadDir 84*
WLLS - Hartford, KY - *BrCabYB 84; TV&RadDir 84*
WLLS-FM - Hartford, KY - *BrCabYB 84; TV&RadDir 84*
WLLT - Fairfield, OH - *BrCabYB 84*
WLLV-FM - Melbourne, FL - *BrCabYB 84; TV&RadDir 84*
WLLX - Minor Hill, TN - *BrCabYB 84*
WLLY - Wilson, NC - *BrCabYB 84*
WLLZ-FM - Detroit, MI - *NatRadPubDir Summer 83, Spring 84*
WLLZ-FM - Farmington, MI - *TV&RadDir 84*
WLMB - Jefferson Township, OH - *BrCabYB 84*
WLMC-FM - Okeechobee, FL - *BrCabYB 84; TV&RadDir 84*
WLMD - Laurel, MD - *BrCabYB 84*
WLMH-FM - Morrow, OH - *BrCabYB 84; TV&RadDir 84*
WLMJ - Jackson, OH - *BrCabYB 84; TV&RadDir 84*
WLN Database [of Washington Library Network] - Olympia, WA - *DataDirOnSer 84; DirOnDB Spring 84*
WLNA - Peekskill, NY - *BrCabYB 84; TV&RadDir 84*
WLNA - Westchester County, NY - *NatRadPubDir Summer 83 p.180, Spring 84 p.178*
WLNC - Laurinburg, NC - *BrCabYB 84; TV&RadDir 84*
WLNE-TV - New Bedford, MA - *BrCabYB 84; LitMarPl 83, 84; TV&RadDir 84*
WLNE-TV - Providence, RI - *DirUSTelSta 83; TelAl 83, 84; Tel&CabFB 84S*
WLNG - Sag Harbor, NY - *BrCabYB 84; TV&RadDir 84*
WLNG - Suffolk County, Long Island, NY - *NatRadPubDir Summer 83 p.178, Spring 84 p.176*
WLNG-FM - Sag Harbor, NY - *TV&RadDir 84*
WLNG-FM - Suffolk County, Long Island, NY - *BrCabYB 84; NatRadPubDir Summer 83 p.178, Spring 84 p.176*
WLNH-FM - Laconia, NH - *BrCabYB 84; TV&RadDir 84*
WLNK - Columbus, MS - *BrCabYB 84*
WLNR-FM - Chicago, IL - *NatRadPubDir Summer 83 p.82, Spring 84 p.82*
WLNR-FM - Lansing, IL - *BrCabYB 84; TV&RadDir 84*
WLNT - Loudon, TN - *BrCabYB 84*
WLNV - Derby, CT - *BrCabYB 84*
WLNX-FM - Lincoln, IL - *BrCabYB 84; NatRadPubDir Summer 83, Spring 84; TV&RadDir 84*
WLOB - Portland, ME - *BrCabYB 84; NatRadPubDir Summer 83, Spring 84; TV&RadDir 84*
WLOC - Munfordville, KY - *BrCabYB 84; TV&RadDir 84*
WLOC-FM - Munfordville, KY - *BrCabYB 84; TV&RadDir 84*

WLOE - Eden, NC - *BrCabYB 84; TV&RadDir 84*
WLOF - Orlando, FL - *NatRadPubDir Summer 83; TV&RadDir 84*
WLOG - Logan, WV - *BrCabYB 84; TV&RadDir 84*
WLOH - Lancaster, OH - *BrCabYB 84; TV&RadDir 84*
WLOI - La Porte, IN - *BrCabYB 84; NatRadPubDir Spring 84; TV&RadDir 84*
WLOI-FM - La Porte, IN - *NatRadPubDir Summer 83*
WLOK - Memphis, TN - *BrCabYB 84; NatRadPubDir Summer 83, Spring 84; TV&RadDir 84*
WLOL-FM - Minneapolis, MN - *BrCabYB 84*
WLOL-FM - Minneapolis/St. Paul, MN - *NatRadPubDir Summer 83, Spring 84 p.135*
WLOM-FM - Annapolis, MD - *NatRadPubDir Summer 83, Spring 84*
WLON - Lincolnton, NC - *BrCabYB 84; TV&RadDir 84*
WLOO-FM - Chicago, IL - *BrCabYB 84; NatRadPubDir Summer 83, Spring 84; TV&RadDir 84*
WLOP - Jesup, GA - *BrCabYB 84; TV&RadDir 84*
WLOQ-FM - Orlando, FL - *NatRadPubDir Summer 83 p.63, Spring 84 p.63; TV&RadDir 84*
WLOQ-FM - Winter Park, FL - *BrCabYB 84*
WLOR - Thomasville, GA - *BrCabYB 84; TV&RadDir 84*
WLOS-FM - Asheville, NC - *BrCabYB 84; NatRadPubDir Summer 83, Spring 84; TV&RadDir 84*
WLOS-TV - Asheville, NC - *BrCabYB 84; LitMarPl 83, 84; Tel&CabFB 84S; TV&RadDir 84*
WLOS-TV - Greenville, SC - *DirUSTelSta 83; TelAl 83, 84*
WLOT - Trenton, TN - *BrCabYB 84*
WLOU - Louisville, KY - *BrCabYB 84; NatRadPubDir Summer 83, Spring 84; TV&RadDir 84*
WLOV - Washington, GA - *BrCabYB 84; TV&RadDir 84*
WLOV-FM - Washington, GA - *BrCabYB 84; TV&RadDir 84*
WLOW-FM - Aiken, SC - *TV&RadDir 84*
WLOX - Biloxi, MS - *BrCabYB 84; NatRadPubDir Summer 83; TV&RadDir 84*
WLOX Broadcasting Co. - Biloxi, MS - *BrCabYB 84*
WLOX-TV - Biloxi, MS - *BrCabYB 84; DirUSTelSta 83; TelAl 83, 84; Tel&CabFB 84S; TV&RadDir 84*
WLOZ-FM - Wilmington, NC - *BrCabYB 84; NatRadPubDir Summer 83, Spring 84*
WLPA - Lancaster, PA - *BrCabYB 84; NatRadPubDir Summer 83, Spring 84; TV&RadDir 84*
WLPB-TV - Baton Rouge, LA - *BrCabYB 84; Tel&CabFB 84S; TV&RadDir 84*
WLPD - Mishawaka, IN - *BrCabYB 84*
WLPH - Birmingham, AL - *NatRadPubDir Summer 83, Spring 84; TV&RadDir 84*
WLPH - Irondale, AL - *BrCabYB 84*
WLPM - Norfolk, VA - *NatRadPubDir Summer 83, Spring 84*
WLPM - Suffolk, VA - *BrCabYB 84; TV&RadDir 84*
WLPO - La Salle, IL - *BrCabYB 84; TV&RadDir 84*
WLPQ - Pittsburg, KY - *BrCabYB 84*
WLPR-FM - Mobile, AL - *BrCabYB 84; NatRadPubDir Summer 83, Spring 84; TV&RadDir 84*
WLPW-FM - Lake Placid, NY - *BrCabYB 84; TV&RadDir 84*
WLPX-FM - Milwaukee, WI - *BrCabYB 84; NatRadPubDir Summer 83, Spring 84; TV&RadDir 84*
WLQB - Flint, MI - *NatRadPubDir Summer 83*
WLQE-FM - Atlantic City, NJ - *NatRadPubDir Spring 84*
WLQE-FM - Pleasantville, NJ - *BrCabYB 84*
WLQH - Chiefland, FL - *BrCabYB 84; TV&RadDir 84*
WLQI - Rensselaer, IN - *BrCabYB 84*
WLQR-FM - Toledo, OH - *BrCabYB 84; NatRadPubDir Summer 83, Spring 84; TV&RadDir 84*
WLQV - Detroit, MI - *BrCabYB 84; NatRadPubDir Summer 83, Spring 84*
WLQV - Southfield, MI - *TV&RadDir 84*
WLQY - Hollywood, FL - *BrCabYB 84; TV&RadDir 84*
WLRA-FM - Lockport, IL - *BrCabYB 84; NatRadPubDir Summer 83, Spring 84; TV&RadDir 84*
WLRC - Walnut, MS - *BrCabYB 84*
WLRE-TV - Green Bay, WI - *BrCabYB 84; DirUSTelSta 83; TelAl 83, 84; Tel&CabFB 84S; TV&RadDir 84*
WLRG-FM - Roanoke, VA - *NatRadPubDir Summer 83*
WLRH-FM - Huntsville, AL - *BrCabYB 84; TV&RadDir 84*
WLRN-FM - Miami, FL - *BrCabYB 84; TV&RadDir 84*
WLRN-TV - Miami, FL - *BrCabYB 84; Tel&CabFB 84S*
WLRO - Lorain, OH - *BrCabYB 84; TV&RadDir 84*
WLRP - San Sebastian, PR - *BrCabYB 84*
WLRS-FM - Louisville, KY - *BrCabYB 84; NatRadPubDir Summer 83, Spring 84; TV&RadDir 84*
WLRV - Lebanon, VA - *BrCabYB 84; TV&RadDir 84*
WLRW-FM - Champaign, IL - *BrCabYB 84; NatRadPubDir Summer 83, Spring 84; TV&RadDir 84*
WLRX-FM - Lincoln, IL - *BrCabYB 84; TV&RadDir 84*
WLS - Chicago, IL - *BrCabYB 84; LitMarPl 83, 84; NatRadPubDir Summer 83, Spring 84; TV&RadDir 84*
WLS-FM - Chicago, IL - *BrCabYB 84; LitMarPl 83; NatRadPubDir Summer 83, Spring 84; TV&RadDir 84*
WLS-TV - Chicago, IL - *BrCabYB 84; DirUSTelSta 83; LitMarPl 83, 84; TelAl 83, 84; Tel&CabFB 84C, 84S; TV&RadDir 84*
WLSA-FM - Louisa, VA - *BrCabYB 84; TV&RadDir 84*
WLSB - Copperhill, TN - *BrCabYB 84; TV&RadDir 84*
WLSC - Loris, SC - *BrCabYB 84; TV&RadDir 84*
WLSD - Big Stone Gap, VA - *BrCabYB 84; TV&RadDir 84*
WLSD-FM - Big Stone Gap, VA - *BrCabYB 84; TV&RadDir 84*
WLSE - Wallace, NC - *BrCabYB 84; TV&RadDir 84*
WLSH - Lansford, PA - *BrCabYB 84; TV&RadDir 84*
WLSI - Pikeville, KY - *BrCabYB 84; TV&RadDir 84*
WLSK-FM - Lebanon, KY - *BrCabYB 84; NatRadPubDir Summer 83, Spring 84; TV&RadDir 84*
WLSM - Louisville, MS - *BrCabYB 84; TV&RadDir 84*
WLSM-FM - Louisville, MS - *BrCabYB 84; TV&RadDir 84*
WLSN - Greenville, OH - *BrCabYB 84*
WLSO - Spencer, IN - *BrCabYB 84*
WLSP-FM - Carbondale, PA - *BrCabYB 84; TV&RadDir 84*
WLSQ - Montgomery, AL - *BrCabYB 84; NatRadPubDir Summer 83, Spring 84; TV&RadDir 84*
WLSR-FM - Lima, OH - *BrCabYB 84; NatRadPubDir Summer 83, Spring 84; TV&RadDir 84*
WLST-FM - Marinette, WI - *BrCabYB 84; TV&RadDir 84*
WLSU-FM - La Crosse, WI - *BrCabYB 84; NatRadPubDir Summer 83, Spring 84; TV&RadDir 84*
WLSV - Wellsville, NY - *BrCabYB 84; TV&RadDir 84*
WLSW-FM - Connellsville, PA - *TV&RadDir 84*
WLSW-FM - Scottdale, PA - *BrCabYB 84*
WLTA-FM - Atlanta, GA - *TV&RadDir 84*
WLTC - Gastonia, NC - *BrCabYB 84; NatRadPubDir Summer 83, Spring 84; TV&RadDir 84*
WLTD-FM - Lexington, MS - *BrCabYB 84; TV&RadDir 84*
WLTE-FM - Waycross, GA - *TV&RadDir 84*
WLTE-FM - Minneapolis, MN - *NatRadPubDir Spring 84*
WLTH - Gary, IN - *BrCabYB 84; NatRadPubDir Summer 83, Spring 84; TV&RadDir 84*
WLTL-FM - La Grange, IL - *BrCabYB 84; TV&RadDir 84*
WLTM - Franklin, NC - *BrCabYB 84; TV&RadDir 84*
WLTN - Littleton, NH - *BrCabYB 84; TV&RadDir 84*
WLTR-FM - Columbia, SC - *BrCabYB 84; NatRadPubDir Summer 83, Spring 84; TV&RadDir 84*
WLTT-FM - Washington, DC - *NatRadPubDir Summer 83 p.54, Spring 84 p.54*
WLTT-FM - Bethesda, MD - *BrCabYB 84*
WLTT-FM - Rockville, MD - *TV&RadDir 84*
WLTV-TV - Miami, FL - *BrCabYB 84; DirUSTelSta 83; TelAl 83, 84; Tel&CabFB 84S; TV&RadDir 84*
WLTX-TV - Columbia, SC - *BrCabYB 84; DirUSTelSta 83; TelAl 83, 84; Tel&CabFB 84S; TV&RadDir 84*
WLTY-FM - Norfolk, VA - *BrCabYB 84; NatRadPubDir Summer 83, Spring 84*
WLTZ-TV - Columbus, GA - *BrCabYB 84; DirUSTelSta 83; Tel&CabFB 84S; TV&RadDir 84*
WLUC-TV - Marquette, MI - *BrCabYB 84; DirUSTelSta 83; TelAl 83, 84; Tel&CabFB 84S; TV&RadDir 84*
WLUK-TV - Green Bay, WI - *BrCabYB 84; DirUSTelSta 83; TelAl 83, 84; Tel&CabFB 84S; TV&RadDir 84*
WLUM-FM - Elm Grove, WI - *TV&RadDir 84*
WLUM-FM - Milwaukee, WI - *BrCabYB 84; NatRadPubDir Summer 83 p.267, Spring 84 p.269*
WLUN - Lumberton, MS - *BrCabYB 84*
WLUP-FM - Chicago, IL - *BrCabYB 84; NatRadPubDir Summer 83, Spring 84*

WLUR-FM - Lexington, VA - *BrCabYB 84; NatRadPubDir Summer 83, Spring 84; TV&RadDir 84*
WLUV - Loves Park, IL - *BrCabYB 84*
WLUV - Rockford, IL - *TV&RadDir 84*
WLUV-FM - Loves Park, IL - *BrCabYB 84*
WLUV-FM - Rockford, IL - *TV&RadDir 84*
WLUW-FM - Chicago, IL - *BrCabYB 84; TV&RadDir 84*
WLUX - Baton Rouge, LA - *BrCabYB 84; NatRadPubDir Summer 83, Spring 84; TV&RadDir 84*
WLUY - Nashville, TN - *NatRadPubDir Spring 84; TV&RadDir 84*
WLUZ - Bayamon, PR - *BrCabYB 84*
WLUZ-TV - Ponce, PR - *BrCabYB 84; Tel&CabFB 84S*
WLV-TV Inc. - Nucla, CO - *Tel&CabFB 84C*
WLVA - Lynchburg, VA - *BrCabYB 84; NatRadPubDir Summer 83, Spring 84; TV&RadDir 84*
WLVC - Ft. Kent, ME - *BrCabYB 84*
WLVC - Madawaska, ME - *TV&RadDir 84*
WLVE-FM - Baraboo, WI - *BrCabYB 84*
WLVE-FM - Madison, WI - *NatRadPubDir Summer 83, Spring 84; TV&RadDir 84*
WLVH-FM - Hartford, CT - *BrCabYB 84; NatRadPubDir Summer 83, Spring 84; TV&RadDir 84*
WLVI-TV - Ayer, MA - *TV&RadDir 84*
WLVI-TV - Boston, MA - *DirUSTelSta 83; TelAl 83, 84*
WLVI-TV - Cambridge, MA - *BrCabYB 84; Tel&CabFB 84S*
WLVL - Lockport, NY - *BrCabYB 84; NatRadPubDir Summer 83, Spring 84; TV&RadDir 84*
WLVM - St. Ignace, MI - *BrCabYB 84; TV&RadDir 84*
WLVN - Luverne, AL - *BrCabYB 84; TV&RadDir 84*
WLVO - Mt. Zion, IL - *BrCabYB 84*
WLVQ-FM - Columbus, OH - *BrCabYB 84; LitMarPl 84; NatRadPubDir Summer 83, Spring 84; TV&RadDir 84*
WLVR-FM - Bethlehem, PA - *BrCabYB 84; NatRadPubDir Summer 83, Spring 84; TV&RadDir 84*
WLVS-FM - Germantown, TN - *BrCabYB 84*
WLVS-FM - Memphis, TN - *NatRadPubDir Summer 83, Spring 84; TV&RadDir 84*
WLVT-TV - Allentown, PA - *BrCabYB 84; Tel&CabFB 84S*
WLVT-TV - Bethlehem, PA - *TV&RadDir 84*
WLVU-FM - Erie, PA - *BrCabYB 84; NatRadPubDir Summer 83, Spring 84; TV&RadDir 84*
WLVV-FM - Statesville, NC - *BrCabYB 84; LitMarPl 84; TV&RadDir 84*
WLVW-FM - Tallahassee, FL - *TV&RadDir 84*
WLVW-FM - Moncks Corner, SC - *BrCabYB 84*
WLVY-FM - Elmira, NY - *BrCabYB 84; TV&RadDir 84*
WLW - Cincinnati, OH - *BrCabYB 84; NatRadPubDir Summer 83, Spring 84; TV&RadDir 84*
WLW Journal - Berkeley, CA - *LitMag&SmPr 83-84*
WLWI-FM - Montgomery, AL - *BrCabYB 84; NatRadPubDir Summer 83, Spring 84; TV&RadDir 84*
WLWL - Rockingham, NC - *BrCabYB 84; TV&RadDir 84*
WLWT-TV - Cincinnati, OH - *BrCabYB 84; DirUSTelSta 83; LitMarPl 83, 84; TelAl 83, 84; Tel&CabFB 84S; TV&RadDir 84*
WLXI-TV - Greensboro, NC - *BrCabYB 84; TelAl 84; Tel&CabFB 84S*
WLXN-FM - Lexington, NC - *BrCabYB 84; TV&RadDir 84*
WLXR-FM - La Crosse, WI - *BrCabYB 84; TV&RadDir 84*
WLXX-FM - Sault Ste. Marie, MI - *BrCabYB 84; TV&RadDir 84*
WLYC - Williamsport, PA - *BrCabYB 84; NatRadPubDir Summer 83, Spring 84; TV&RadDir 84*
WLYF-FM - Miami, FL - *BrCabYB 84; LitMarPl 84; NatRadPubDir Summer 83, Spring 84; TV&RadDir 84*
WLYH-TV - Harrisburg, PA - *DirUSTelSta 83*
WLYH-TV - Lancaster, PA - *BrCabYB 84; LitMarPl 83, 84; TelAl 83, 84; TV&RadDir 84*
WLYH-TV - Lebanon, PA - *Tel&CabFB 84S*
WLYJ - Clarksburg, WV - *BrCabYB 84; DirUSTelSta 83; Tel&CabFB 84S*
WLYK-FM - Cincinnati/Hamilton/Middletown, OH - *NatRadPubDir Summer 83 p.192, Spring 84 p.190*
WLYK-FM - Milford, OH - *BrCabYB 84; TV&RadDir 84*
WLYN - Lynn, MA - *BrCabYB 84; TV&RadDir 84*
WLYN-FM - Lynn, MA - *TV&RadDir 84*
WLYQ-FM - Norwalk, CT - *BrCabYB 84; NatRadPubDir Summer 83, Spring 84; TV&RadDir 84*
WLYT - Haverhill, MA - *BrCabYB 84*
WLYX-FM - Memphis, TN - *BrCabYB 84; NatRadPubDir Summer 83, Spring 84; TV&RadDir 84*
WLZM-FM - Hazleton, PA - *TV&RadDir 84*
WLZZ - Milwaukee, WI - *BrCabYB 84; NatRadPubDir Summer 83, Spring 84*
WLZZ-FM - Milwaukee, WI - *NatRadPubDir Summer 83*
WMAA-FM - Jackson, MS - *BrCabYB 84*
WMAA-TV - Jackson, MS - *BrCabYB 84; Tel&CabFB 84S; TV&RadDir 84*
WMAB-FM - Mississippi State, MS - *BrCabYB 84*
WMAB-TV - Mississippi State, MS - *BrCabYB 84; Tel&CabFB 84S*
WMAC - Metter, GA - *BrCabYB 84; TV&RadDir 84*
WMAD-FM - Madison, WI - *TV&RadDir 84*
WMAD-FM - Sun Prairie, WI - *BrCabYB 84*
WMAE-FM - Booneville, MS - *BrCabYB 84*
WMAE-TV - Booneville, MS - *Tel&CabFB 84S*
WMAF - Madison, FL - *BrCabYB 84; TV&RadDir 84*
WMAG - Forest, MS - *TV&RadDir 84*
WMAG-FM - Greensboro/High Point, NC - *NatRadPubDir Spring 84 p.183*
WMAG-FM - High Point, NC - *TV&RadDir 84*
WMAH-FM - Biloxi, MS - *BrCabYB 84*
WMAH-TV - Biloxi, MS - *BrCabYB 84; Tel&CabFB 84S*
WMAJ - State College, PA - *BrCabYB 84; TV&RadDir 84*
WMAK - Nashville, TN - *BrCabYB 84; TV&RadDir 84*
WMAK-FM - Hendersonville, TN - *BrCabYB 84*
WMAK-FM - Nashville, TN - *NatRadPubDir Summer 83, Spring 84; TV&RadDir 84*
WMAL - Washington, DC - *BrCabYB 84; LitMarPl 83, 84; NatRadPubDir Summer 83, Spring 84; TV&RadDir 84*
WMAM - Marinette, WI - *BrCabYB 84; TV&RadDir 84*
WMAN - Mansfield, OH - *BrCabYB 84; NatRadPubDir Summer 83, Spring 84*
WMAN-FM - Mansfield, OH - *TV&RadDir 84*
WMAO-FM - Greenwood, MS - *BrCabYB 84*
WMAO-TV - Greenwood, MS - *BrCabYB 84; Tel&CabFB 84S*
WMAP - Monroe, NC - *BrCabYB 84; TV&RadDir 84*
WMAQ - Chicago, IL - *BrCabYB 84; LitMarPl 83, 84; NatRadPubDir Summer 83, Spring 84; TV&RadDir 84*
WMAQ-TV - Chicago, IL - *BrCabYB 84; DirUSTelSta 83; LitMarPl 83, 84; TelAl 83, 84; Tel&CabFB 84C, 84S; TV&RadDir 84*
WMAR-FM - Baltimore, MD - *BrCabYB 84; LitMarPl 84; NatRadPubDir Spring 84*
WMAR Inc. [Subs. of WMAR-TV & WRLX-FM] - Baltimore, MD - *AvMarPl 83*
WMAR-TV - Baltimore, MD - *BrCabYB 84; DirUSTelSta 83; LitMarPl 84; TelAl 83, 84; Tel&CabFB 84S; TV&RadDir 84*
WMAS - Springfield, MA - *BrCabYB 84; NatRadPubDir Summer 83, Spring 84; TV&RadDir 84*
WMAS-FM - Springfield, MA - *BrCabYB 84; NatRadPubDir Summer 83, Spring 84; TV&RadDir 84*
WMAU-FM - Bude, MS - *BrCabYB 84*
WMAU-TV - Bude, MS - *BrCabYB 84; Tel&CabFB 84S*
WMAV-FM - Oxford, MS - *BrCabYB 84*
WMAV-TV - Oxford, MS - *BrCabYB 84; Tel&CabFB 84S*
WMAV-TV - Taylor, MS - *TV&RadDir 84*
WMAW-FM - Meridian, MS - *BrCabYB 84*
WMAW-TV - Meridian, MS - *BrCabYB 84; Tel&CabFB 84S*
WMAX - Grand Rapids, MI - *BrCabYB 84; NatRadPubDir Summer 83, Spring 84; TV&RadDir 84*
WMAY - Springfield, IL - *BrCabYB 84; NatRadPubDir Summer 83, Spring 84; TV&RadDir 84*
WMAZ - Macon, GA - *BrCabYB 84; NatRadPubDir Summer 83, Spring 84; TV&RadDir 84*
WMAZ-FM - Macon, GA - *BrCabYB 84; NatRadPubDir Summer 83, Spring 84; TV&RadDir 84*
WMAZ-TV - Macon, GA - *BrCabYB 84; DirUSTelSta 83; TelAl 83, 84; Tel&CabFB 84S; TV&RadDir 84*
WMBA - Ambridge, PA - *BrCabYB 84; TV&RadDir 84*
WMBB-TV - Panama City, FL - *BrCabYB 84; DirUSTelSta 83; TelAl 83, 84; Tel&CabFB 84S; TV&RadDir 84*
WMBC - Columbus, MS - *BrCabYB 84; NatRadPubDir Summer 83, Spring 84; TV&RadDir 84*

WMBD - Peoria, IL - *BrCabYB 84; NatRadPubDir Summer 83, Spring 84; TV&RadDir 84*
WMBD-TV - Peoria, IL - *BrCabYB 84; DirUSTelSta 83; TelAl 83, 84; Tel&CabFB 84S; TV&RadDir 84*
WMBE - Chilton, WI - *BrCabYB 84*
WMBG - Williamsburg, VA - *BrCabYB 84; TV&RadDir 84*
WMBH - Joplin, MO - *BrCabYB 84; TV&RadDir 84*
WMBI - Chicago, IL - *BrCabYB 84; NatRadPubDir Summer 83, Spring 84; TV&RadDir 84*
WMBI-FM - Chicago, IL - *BrCabYB 84; NatRadPubDir Summer 83, Spring 84; TV&RadDir 84*
WMBJ-FM - Morehead City, NC - *BrCabYB 84; TV&RadDir 84*
WMBL - Morehead City, NC - *BrCabYB 84; TV&RadDir 84*
WMBM - Miami Beach, FL - *BrCabYB 84; NatRadPubDir Summer 83, Spring 84; TV&RadDir 84*
WMBN-FM - Petoskey, MI - *BrCabYB 84; TV&RadDir 84*
WMBO - Auburn, NY - *BrCabYB 84; TV&RadDir 84*
WMBR-FM - Cambridge, MA - *BrCabYB 84; NatRadPubDir Summer 83, Spring 84; TV&RadDir 84*
WMBS - Uniontown, PA - *BrCabYB 84; TV&RadDir 84*
WMBT - Shenandoah, PA - *BrCabYB 84; TV&RadDir 84*
WMBW-FM - Chattanooga, TN - *BrCabYB 84; NatRadPubDir Summer 83, Spring 84; TV&RadDir 84*
WMC - Memphis, TN - *BrCabYB 84; NatRadPubDir Summer 83, Spring 84; TV&RadDir 84*
WMC-FM - Memphis, TN - *BrCabYB 84; NatRadPubDir Summer 83, Spring 84; TV&RadDir 84*
WMC-TV - Memphis, TN - *BrCabYB 84; DirUSTelSta 83; LitMarPl 83, 84; TelAl 83, 84; Tel&CabFB 84S; TV&RadDir 84*
WMCA - New York, NY - *BrCabYB 84; LitMarPl 83, 84; NatRadPubDir Summer 83, Spring 84; TV&RadDir 84*
WMCB - Martinsville, IN - *BrCabYB 84*
WMCC-FM - Etowah, TN - *BrCabYB 84; TV&RadDir 84*
WMCD-FM - Statesboro, GA - *BrCabYB 84; TV&RadDir 84*
WMCF-TV - Montgomery, AL - *BrCabYB 84; Tel&CabFB 84S*
WMCG - Milan, GA - *BrCabYB 84*
WMCH - Church Hill, TN - *BrCabYB 84; TV&RadDir 84*
WMCI - Brockton, MA - *BrCabYB 84*
WMCL - McLeansboro, IL - *BrCabYB 84; TV&RadDir 84*
WMCM-FM - Rockland, ME - *BrCabYB 84; TV&RadDir 84*
WMCN-FM - St. Paul, MN - *BrCabYB 84; TV&RadDir 84*
WMCO-FM - New Concord, OH - *BrCabYB 84; TV&RadDir 84*
WMCP - Columbia, TN - *BrCabYB 84; TV&RadDir 84*
WMCR-FM - Oneida, NY - *BrCabYB 84; TV&RadDir 84*
WMCS - Machias, ME - *BrCabYB 84; TV&RadDir 84*
WMCT - Mountain City, TN - *BrCabYB 84; TV&RadDir 84*
WMCU-FM - Miami, FL - *BrCabYB 84; NatRadPubDir Summer 83, Spring 84; TV&RadDir 84*
WMCW - Harvard, IL - *BrCabYB 84; TV&RadDir 84*
WMCX - West Long Branch, NJ - *BrCabYB 84; TV&RadDir 84*
WMCX-FM - West Long Branch, NJ - *NatRadPubDir Summer 83, Spring 84; TV&RadDir 84*
WMDB - Nashville, TN - *BrCabYB 84*
WMDC - Hazlehurst, MS - *BrCabYB 84; TV&RadDir 84*
WMDC-FM - Hazlehurst, MS - *BrCabYB 84; TV&RadDir 84*
WMDD - Fajardo, PR - *BrCabYB 84*
WMDF-FM - Milton, WI - *NatRadPubDir Spring 84*
WMDH-FM - New Castle, IN - *BrCabYB 84; TV&RadDir 84*
WMDI-FM - Erie, PA - *TV&RadDir 84*
WMDJ - Martin, KY - *BrCabYB 84*
WMDK-FM - Peterborough, NH - *BrCabYB 84; TV&RadDir 84*
WMDM-FM - Lexington Park, MD - *BrCabYB 84*
WMDO - Silver Spring, MD - *TV&RadDir 84*
WMDO - Wheaton, MD - *BrCabYB 84*
WMDT - Salisbury, MD - *BrCabYB 84; DirUSTelSta 83; TelAl 83, 84; Tel&CabFB 84S*
WMEA-FM - Old Town, ME - *TV&RadDir 84*
WMEA-FM - Portland, ME - *BrCabYB 84; TV&RadDir 84*
WMEB-FM - Old Town, ME - *TV&RadDir 84*
WMEB-FM - Orono, ME - *BrCabYB 84; NatRadPubDir Summer 83, Spring 84*
WMEB-TV - Orono, ME - *BrCabYB 84; Tel&CabFB 84S; TV&RadDir 84*
WMED-TV - Calais, ME - *BrCabYB 84; Tel&CabFB 84S*
WMED-TV - Old Town, ME - *TV&RadDir 84*
WMEE-FM - Ft. Wayne, IN - *BrCabYB 84; NatRadPubDir Summer 83, Spring 84; TV&RadDir 84*
WMEG-TV - Biddeford, ME - *BrCabYB 84; Tel&CabFB 84S*
WMEG-TV - Old Town, ME - *TV&RadDir 84*
WMEH-FM - Bangor, ME - *BrCabYB 84*
WMEH-FM - Old Town, ME - *TV&RadDir 84*
WMEH-FM - Orono, ME - *NatRadPubDir Summer 83, Spring 84*
WMEK - Chase City, VA - *BrCabYB 84; TV&RadDir 84*
WMEL - Melbourne, FL - *BrCabYB 84; TV&RadDir 84*
WMEM-FM - Old Town, ME - *TV&RadDir 84*
WMEM-FM - Presque Isle, ME - *BrCabYB 84*
WMEM-TV - Old Town, ME - *TV&RadDir 84*
WMEM-TV - Presque Isle, ME - *BrCabYB 84; Tel&CabFB 84S*
WMEQ-FM - Menomonie, WI - *BrCabYB 84*
WMER - Portland, ME - *NatRadPubDir Summer 83, Spring 84; TV&RadDir 84*
WMER - Westbrook, ME - *BrCabYB 84*
WMES - Ashburn, GA - *BrCabYB 84; TV&RadDir 84*
WMET-FM - Chicago, IL - *BrCabYB 84; NatRadPubDir Summer 83, Spring 84; TV&RadDir 84*
WMEV - Marion, VA - *BrCabYB 84; TV&RadDir 84*
WMEV-FM - Marion, VA - *BrCabYB 84; TV&RadDir 84*
WMEW - Waterville, ME - *BrCabYB 84*
WMEX - Clyde, OH - *BrCabYB 84*
WMEZ-FM - Pensacola, FL - *BrCabYB 84; NatRadPubDir Summer 83, Spring 84; TV&RadDir 84*
WMFC - Monroeville, AL - *BrCabYB 84; TV&RadDir 84*
WMFC-FM - Monroeville, AL - *BrCabYB 84; TV&RadDir 84*
WMFD - Wilmington, NC - *BrCabYB 84; NatRadPubDir Summer 83, Spring 84; TV&RadDir 84*
WMFE-FM - Orlando, FL - *BrCabYB 84; TV&RadDir 84*
WMFE-TV - Orlando, FL - *BrCabYB 84; Tel&CabFB 84S; TV&RadDir 84*
WMFG - Hibbing, MN - *BrCabYB 84; TV&RadDir 84*
WMFG-FM - Hibbing, MN - *BrCabYB 84; TV&RadDir 84*
WMFJ - Daytona Beach, FL - *BrCabYB 84; NatRadPubDir Summer 83, Spring 84*
WMFL - Monticello, FL - *BrCabYB 84; TV&RadDir 84*
WMFM-FM - Gainesville, FL - *BrCabYB 84*
WMFM-FM - Menomonie, WI - *TV&RadDir 84*
WMFO-FM - Medford, MA - *BrCabYB 84; NatRadPubDir Summer 83, Spring 84; TV&RadDir 84*
WMFQ-FM - Ocala, FL - *BrCabYB 84; TV&RadDir 84*
WMFR - Greensboro/High Point, NC - *NatRadPubDir Summer 83, Spring 84 p.183*
WMFR - High Point, NC - *BrCabYB 84; TV&RadDir 84*
WMFR-FM - Greensboro/High Point, NC - *NatRadPubDir Summer 83*
WMFR-FM - High Point, NC - *BrCabYB 84*
WMGA - Moultrie, GA - *BrCabYB 84; TV&RadDir 84*
WMGC-TV - Binghamton, NY - *BrCabYB 84; DirUSTelSta 83; TelAl 83, 84; Tel&CabFB 84S; TV&RadDir 84*
WMGE-FM - Danville, KY - *BrCabYB 84; TV&RadDir 84*
WMGF-FM - Milwaukee, WI - *BrCabYB 84; NatRadPubDir Summer 83, Spring 84*
WMGG-FM - Clearwater, FL - *BrCabYB 84*
WMGG-FM - Tampa/St. Petersburg, FL - *NatRadPubDir Summer 83 p.65, Spring 84 p.65*
WMGG-FM - Clearwater, SC - *TV&RadDir 84*
WMGI - Gainesville, FL - *BrCabYB 84; NatRadPubDir Summer 83, Spring 84*
WMGI-FM - Gainesville, FL - *TV&RadDir 84*
WMGK-FM - Bala Cynwyd, PA - *LitMarPl 84; TV&RadDir 84*
WMGK-FM - Philadelphia, PA - *BrCabYB 84; NatRadPubDir Summer 83 p.213, Spring 84 p.213*
WMGL-FM - Pulaski, TN - *BrCabYB 84; TV&RadDir 84*
WMGM-FM - Atlantic City, NJ - *BrCabYB 84*
WMGM-FM - Linwood, NJ - *NatRadPubDir Summer 83, Spring 84*
WMGM-FM - Pleasantville, NJ - *TV&RadDir 84*
WMGO - Canton, MS - *BrCabYB 84; TV&RadDir 84*
WMGQ-FM - New Brunswick, NJ - *BrCabYB 84; NatRadPubDir Summer 83, Spring 84*
WMGQ-FM - Somerset, NJ - *TV&RadDir 84*
WMGR - Bainbridge, GA - *BrCabYB 84; TV&RadDir 84*
WMGT - Macon, GA - *BrCabYB 84*
WMGW - Meadville, PA - *BrCabYB 84; TV&RadDir 84*
WMGX-FM - Portland, ME - *BrCabYB 84; TV&RadDir 84*
WMGY - Montgomery, AL - *BrCabYB 84; TV&RadDir 84*

WMGZ - Farrell, PA - *BrCabYB 84*
WMGZ - Sharpsburg, PA - *BrCabYB 84*
WMHB-FM - Waterville, ME - *BrCabYB 84; NatRadPubDir Summer 83, Spring 84; TV&RadDir 84*
WMHC-FM - South Hadley, MA - *BrCabYB 84; TV&RadDir 84*
WMHD - Terre Haute, IN - *BrCabYB 84*
WMHE-FM - Toledo, OH - *BrCabYB 84; NatRadPubDir Summer 83, Spring 84; TV&RadDir 84*
WMHK-FM - Columbia, SC - *BrCabYB 84; NatRadPubDir Summer 83, Spring 84*
WMHR-FM - Syracuse, NY - *BrCabYB 84; NatRadPubDir Summer 83, Spring 84; TV&RadDir 84*
WMHT - Schenectady, NY - *BrCabYB 84; Tel&CabFB 84S*
WMHT-FM - Schenectady, NY - *BrCabYB 84; NatRadPubDir Summer 83, Spring 84; TV&RadDir 84*
WMHW-FM - Mt. Pleasant, MI - *BrCabYB 84; NatRadPubDir Summer 83, Spring 84; TV&RadDir 84*
WMHY-TV - Schenectady, NY - *TV&RadDir 84*
WMIA - Arecibo, PR - *BrCabYB 84*
WMIB - Marco Island, FL - *BrCabYB 84*
WMIB - Naples, FL - *TV&RadDir 84*
WMIC - Sandusky, MI - *BrCabYB 84; TV&RadDir 84*
WMIC-FM - Sandusky, MI - *TV&RadDir 84*
WMID - Atlantic City, NJ - *BrCabYB 84; NatRadPubDir Summer 83, Spring 84; TV&RadDir 84*
WMIE - Cocoa, FL - *BrCabYB 84*
WMIK - Middlesboro, KY - *BrCabYB 84; TV&RadDir 84*
WMIK-FM - Middlesboro, KY - *BrCabYB 84; TV&RadDir 84*
WMIL-FM - Milwaukee, WI - *NatRadPubDir Spring 84*
WMIL-FM - Waukesha, WI - *BrCabYB 84; TV&RadDir 84*
WMIM - Mt. Carmel, PA - *BrCabYB 84; TV&RadDir 84*
WMIN - Maplewood, MN - *BrCabYB 84*
WMIQ - Iron Mountain, MI - *BrCabYB 84*
WMIR - Lake Geneva, WI - *BrCabYB 84; TV&RadDir 84*
WMIS - Natchez, MS - *BrCabYB 84; TV&RadDir 84*
WMIT-FM - Black Mountain, NC - *BrCabYB 84; TV&RadDir 84*
WMIX - Mt. Vernon, IL - *BrCabYB 84; TV&RadDir 84*
WMIX-FM - Mt. Vernon, IL - *BrCabYB 84; TV&RadDir 84*
WMJA - Panama City, FL - *BrCabYB 84; Tel&CabFB 84S*
WMJC-FM - Birmingham, MI - *BrCabYB 84; TV&RadDir 84*
WMJC-FM - Detroit, MI - *NatRadPubDir Summer 83, Spring 84*
WMJD-FM - Grundy, VA - *BrCabYB 84; TV&RadDir 84*
WMJI-FM - Cleveland, OH - *BrCabYB 84; NatRadPubDir Summer 83, Spring 84; TV&RadDir 84*
WMJJ-FM - Birmingham, AL - *BrCabYB 84; NatRadPubDir Spring 84*
WMJK - Kissimmee, FL - *BrCabYB 84; TV&RadDir 84*
WMJL - Marion, KY - *BrCabYB 84*
WMJM - Cordele, GA - *BrCabYB 84; TV&RadDir 84*
WMJQ-FM - Rochester, NY - *BrCabYB 84; NatRadPubDir Spring 84; TV&RadDir 84*
WMJS - Prince Frederick, MD - *BrCabYB 84*
WMJT - Mt. Juliet, TN - *BrCabYB 84*
WMJW - Nanticoke, PA - *BrCabYB 84*
WMJW-FM - Nanticoke, PA - *TV&RadDir 84*
WMJX-FM - Miami, FL - *TV&RadDir 84*
WMJX-FM - Allston, MA - *TV&RadDir 84*
WMJX-FM - Boston, MA - *BrCabYB 84*
WMJY-FM - Long Branch, NJ - *BrCabYB 84; NatRadPubDir Spring 84; TV&RadDir 84*
WMKC - St. Ignace, MI - *BrCabYB 84*
WMKE - Milwaukee, WI - *BrCabYB 84*
WMKI - Milwaukee, WI - *NatRadPubDir Spring 84*
WMKM - St. Augustine, FL - *BrCabYB 84*
WMKR - Millinocket, ME - *BrCabYB 84; TV&RadDir 84*
WMKT - Muskegon, MI - *BrCabYB 84; Tel&CabFB 84S*
WMKW-TV - Memphis, TN - *BrCabYB 84; Tel&CabFB 84S*
WMKX - Brookville, PA - *BrCabYB 84*
WMKY-FM - Morehead, KY - *BrCabYB 84; NatRadPubDir Summer 83, Spring 84; TV&RadDir 84*
WMLA-FM - Bloomington, IL - *TV&RadDir 84*
WMLA-FM - LeRoy, IL - *BrCabYB 84*
WMLB - Elmwood, CT - *TV&RadDir 84*
WMLB - Hartford/New Britain, CT - *NatRadPubDir Summer 83, Spring 84*
WMLB - West Hartford, CT - *BrCabYB 84*
WMLC - Monticello, MS - *BrCabYB 84; TV&RadDir 84*
WMLF - Indianapolis, IN - *BrCabYB 84*
WMLI - Bangor, ME - *BrCabYB 84; TV&RadDir 84*
WMLM - St. Louis, MI - *BrCabYB 84*
WMLN-FM - Milton, MA - *BrCabYB 84; NatRadPubDir Summer 83, Spring 84; TV&RadDir 84*
WMLO-FM - Sarasota, FL - *BrCabYB 84; TV&RadDir 84*
WMLP - Milton, PA - *BrCabYB 84; TV&RadDir 84*
WMLR - Hohenwald, TN - *BrCabYB 84; TV&RadDir 84*
WMLS - Indianapolis, IN - *NatRadPubDir Spring 84*
WMLS-FM - Sylacauga, AL - *BrCabYB 84; TV&RadDir 84*
WMLT - Dublin, GA - *BrCabYB 84; TV&RadDir 84*
WMLW-FM - Watertown, WI - *BrCabYB 84; TV&RadDir 84*
WMLX - Cincinnati, OH - *BrCabYB 84; NatRadPubDir Summer 83, Spring 84*
WMMB - Melbourne, FL - *BrCabYB 84; TV&RadDir 84*
WMMC-FM - North Andover, MA - *BrCabYB 84; NatRadPubDir Summer 83, Spring 84*
WMMG-FM - Brandenburg, KY - *BrCabYB 84; TV&RadDir 84*
WMMH - Marshall, NC - *BrCabYB 84; TV&RadDir 84*
WMMJ-FM - Brattleboro, VT - *BrCabYB 84; NatRadPubDir Summer 83, Spring 84; TV&RadDir 84*
WMMK - Destin, FL - *BrCabYB 84*
WMMM - Westport, CT - *BrCabYB 84; NatRadPubDir Summer 83, Spring 84; TV&RadDir 84*
WMMN - Fairmont, WV - *BrCabYB 84; TV&RadDir 84*
WMMQ-FM - Charlotte, MI - *BrCabYB 84*
WMMQ-FM - Lansing, MI - *TV&RadDir 84*
WMMR-FM - Philadelphia, PA - *BrCabYB 84; LitMarPl 83, 84; NatRadPubDir Summer 83, Spring 84; TV&RadDir 84*
WMMS-FM - Cleveland, OH - *BrCabYB 84; LitMarPl 83, 84; NatRadPubDir Summer 83, Spring 84; TV&RadDir 84*
WMMW - Hartford/New Britain, CT - *NatRadPubDir Summer 83 p.46, Spring 84 p.47*
WMMW - Meriden, CT - *BrCabYB 84; TV&RadDir 84*
WMNA - Gretna, VA - *BrCabYB 84; TV&RadDir 84*
WMNA-FM - Gretna, VA - *BrCabYB 84; TV&RadDir 84*
WMNB - North Adams, MA - *BrCabYB 84; NatRadPubDir Summer 83, Spring 84; TV&RadDir 84*
WMNB-FM - North Adams, MA - *BrCabYB 84; NatRadPubDir Summer 83, Spring 84; TV&RadDir 84*
WMNC - Morganton, NC - *BrCabYB 84; TV&RadDir 84*
WMNE - Menomonie, WI - *BrCabYB 84; TV&RadDir 84*
WMNF - Tampa, FL - *BrCabYB 84; TV&RadDir 84*
WMNF-FM - Seffner, FL - *TV&RadDir 84*
WMNI - Columbus, OH - *BrCabYB 84; NatRadPubDir Summer 83, Spring 84; TV&RadDir 84*
WMNJ - Madison, NJ - *BrCabYB 84*
WMNR-FM - Monroe, CT - *BrCabYB 84; TV&RadDir 84*
WMNS - Olean, NY - *BrCabYB 84; TV&RadDir 84*
WMNT - Manati, PR - *BrCabYB 84*
WMNX-FM - Tallahassee, FL - *BrCabYB 84*
WMNZ - Montezuma, GA - *BrCabYB 84; TV&RadDir 84*
WMOA - Marietta, OH - *BrCabYB 84; TV&RadDir 84*
WMOA-FM - Marietta, OH - *TV&RadDir 84*
WMOB - Mobile, AL - *BrCabYB 84*
WMOC - Chattanooga, TN - *NatRadPubDir Summer 83, Spring 84; TV&RadDir 84*
WMOD - Melbourne, FL - *BrCabYB 84; DirUSTelSta 83; TelAl 84; Tel&CabFB 84S*
WMOE - Alpharetta, GA - *BrCabYB 84*
WMOG - Brunswick, GA - *BrCabYB 84; NatRadPubDir Summer 83, Spring 84; TV&RadDir 84*
WMOH - Cincinnati/Hamilton/Middletown, OH - *NatRadPubDir Summer 83 p.192, Spring 84 p.191*
WMOH - Hamilton, OH - *BrCabYB 84; TV&RadDir 84*
WMOI-FM - Monmouth, IL - *BrCabYB 84; TV&RadDir 84*
WMOK - Metropolis, IL - *BrCabYB 84; TV&RadDir 84*
WMON - Montgomery, WV - *BrCabYB 84; TV&RadDir 84*
WMOO - Mobile, AL - *BrCabYB 84; NatRadPubDir Summer 83, Spring 84; TV&RadDir 84*
WMOP - Ocala, FL - *BrCabYB 84; TV&RadDir 84*
WMOR - Morehead, KY - *BrCabYB 84; TV&RadDir 84*
WMOR-FM - Morehead, KY - *BrCabYB 84; TV&RadDir 84*
WMOS - Bath, ME - *BrCabYB 84*
WMOT-FM - Murfreesboro, TN - *BrCabYB 84; NatRadPubDir Summer 83, Spring 84; TV&RadDir 84*
WMOU - Berlin, NH - *BrCabYB 84; TV&RadDir 84*

WMOV - Ravenswood, WV - *BrCabYB 84; TV&RadDir 84*
WMOX - Meridian, MS - *BrCabYB 84; NatRadPubDir Summer 83, Spring 84; TV&RadDir 84*
WMPA - Aberdeen, MS - *BrCabYB 84; TV&RadDir 84*
WMPB - Baltimore, MD - *BrCabYB 84; Tel&CabFB 84S*
WMPB-TV - Owings Mills, MD - *TV&RadDir 84*
WMPC - Lapeer, MI - *BrCabYB 84; TV&RadDir 84*
WMPG-FM - Gorham, ME - *BrCabYB 84; TV&RadDir 84*
WMPH-FM - Wilmington, DE - *BrCabYB 84; TV&RadDir 84*
WMPI-FM - Scottsburg, IN - *BrCabYB 84; TV&RadDir 84*
WMPL - Hancock, MI - *BrCabYB 84; TV&RadDir 84*
WMPM - Smithfield, NC - *BrCabYB 84; TV&RadDir 84*
WMPO - Middleport, OH - *TV&RadDir 84*
WMPO-FM - Middleport, OH - *BrCabYB 84; TV&RadDir 84*
WMPP - Chicago Heights, IL - *BrCabYB 84; TV&RadDir 84*
WMPR - Jackson, MS - *BrCabYB 84*
WMPS - Memphis, TN - *BrCabYB 84; TV&RadDir 84*
WMPT - Williamsport, PA - *NatRadPubDir Summer 83; TV&RadDir 84*
WMPT-FM - Williamsport, PA - *NatRadPubDir Summer 83; TV&RadDir 84*
WMPT-TV - Salisbury, MD - *TV&RadDir 84*
WMPV-TV - Mobile, AL - *Tel&CabFB 84S*
WMPX - Midland, MI - *BrCabYB 84; NatRadPubDir Summer 83, Spring 84; TV&RadDir 84*
WMPZ - Soperton, GA - *BrCabYB 84; TV&RadDir 84*
WMPZ-FM - Soperton, GA - *BrCabYB 84*
WMQM - Memphis, TN - *BrCabYB 84; NatRadPubDir Summer 83, Spring 84; TV&RadDir 84*
WMQT-FM - Ishpeming, MI - *BrCabYB 84; TV&RadDir 84*
WMRA-FM - Harrisonburg, VA - *BrCabYB 84; NatRadPubDir Summer 83, Spring 84; TV&RadDir 84*
WMRB - Greenville, SC - *BrCabYB 84; NatRadPubDir Summer 83, Spring 84; TV&RadDir 84*
WMRC - Milford, MA - *BrCabYB 84; TV&RadDir 84*
WMRE - Boston, MA - *BrCabYB 84; NatRadPubDir Summer 83, Spring 84; TV&RadDir 84*
WMRF - Lewistown, PA - *BrCabYB 84; TV&RadDir 84*
WMRF-FM - Lewistown, PA - *BrCabYB 84; TV&RadDir 84*
WMRI-FM - Marion, IN - *BrCabYB 84; NatRadPubDir Summer 83, Spring 84; TV&RadDir 84*
WMRK - Selma, AL - *BrCabYB 84*
WMRL - Portland, TN - *BrCabYB 84; TV&RadDir 84*
WMRN - Marion, OH - *BrCabYB 84; TV&RadDir 84*
WMRN-FM - Marion, OH - *BrCabYB 84; TV&RadDir 84*
WMRO - Aurora, IL - *BrCabYB 84; NatRadPubDir Summer 83, Spring 84; TV&RadDir 84*
WMRQ-FM - Brookhaven, MS - *BrCabYB 84; TV&RadDir 84*
WMRT-FM - Marietta, OH - *BrCabYB 84; NatRadPubDir Summer 83, Spring 84; TV&RadDir 84*
WMRV-FM - Endicott, NY - *BrCabYB 84; TV&RadDir 84*
WMRY-FM - Belleville, IL - *NatRadPubDir Summer 83, Spring 84; TV&RadDir 84*
WMRY-FM - East St. Louis, IL - *BrCabYB 84*
WMRZ - Moline, IL - *NatRadPubDir Spring 84*
WMSA - Massena, NY - *BrCabYB 84; TV&RadDir 84*
WMSB-FM - Mississippi State, MS - *BrCabYB 84; NatRadPubDir Summer 83, Spring 84; TV&RadDir 84*
WMSC-FM - Upper Montclair, NJ - *BrCabYB 84; NatRadPubDir Summer 83, Spring 84; TV&RadDir 84*
WMSE-FM - Milwaukee, WI - *BrCabYB 84; TV&RadDir 84*
WMSG - Oakland, MD - *BrCabYB 84*
WMSG [of Madison Square Garden Network] - New York, NY - *CabTVPrDB 83*
WMSI-FM - Jackson, MS - *BrCabYB 84; NatRadPubDir Summer 83, Spring 84; TV&RadDir 84*
WMSK - Morganfield, KY - *BrCabYB 84; TV&RadDir 84*
WMSK-FM - Morganfield, KY - *BrCabYB 84; TV&RadDir 84*
WMSL - Decatur, AL - *BrCabYB 84; TV&RadDir 84*
WMSO - Collierville, TN - *BrCabYB 84; TV&RadDir 84*
WMSP-FM - Harrisburg, PA - *BrCabYB 84; NatRadPubDir Summer 83, Spring 84; TV&RadDir 84*
WMSQ-FM - Havelock, NC - *BrCabYB 84; TV&RadDir 84*
WMSR - Manchester, TN - *BrCabYB 84; TV&RadDir 84*
WMSR-FM - Manchester, TN - *BrCabYB 84; TV&RadDir 84*
WMSS - Middletown, PA - *BrCabYB 84*
WMST - Mt. Sterling, KY - *BrCabYB 84; TV&RadDir 84*
WMST-FM - Mt. Sterling, KY - *BrCabYB 84; TV&RadDir 84*
WMSU-FM - Hattiesburg, MS - *BrCabYB 84; NatRadPubDir Summer 83, Spring 84*
WMSW - Hatillo, PR - *BrCabYB 84*
WMSY-TV - Marion, VA - *BrCabYB 84; Tel&CabFB 84S*
WMT - Cedar Rapids, IA - *BrCabYB 84; NatRadPubDir Summer 83, Spring 84; TelAl 83; TV&RadDir 84*
WMT-FM - Cedar Rapids, IA - *BrCabYB 84; NatRadPubDir Summer 83, Spring 84; TV&RadDir 84*
WMTA - Central City, KY - *BrCabYB 84; TV&RadDir 84*
WMTB-FM - Emmitsburg, MD - *BrCabYB 84*
WMTC - Vancleve, KY - *BrCabYB 84; TV&RadDir 84*
WMTD - Hinton, WV - *BrCabYB 84; TV&RadDir 84*
WMTD-FM - Hinton, WV - *BrCabYB 84*
WMTE - Manistee, MI - *BrCabYB 84; TV&RadDir 84*
WMTF - Stowe, VT - *BrCabYB 84*
WMTH-FM - Park Ridge, IL - *BrCabYB 84; TV&RadDir 84*
WMTJ - Fajardo, PR - *BrCabYB 84; Tel&CabFB 84S*
WMTL - Leitchfield, KY - *BrCabYB 84*
WMTM - Moultrie, GA - *BrCabYB 84; TV&RadDir 84*
WMTM-FM - Moultrie, GA - *BrCabYB 84; TV&RadDir 84*
WMTN - Morristown, TN - *BrCabYB 84; TV&RadDir 84*
WMTR - Morristown, NJ - *BrCabYB 84; NatRadPubDir Summer 83, Spring 84; TV&RadDir 84*
WMTS - Murfreesboro, TN - *BrCabYB 84; NatRadPubDir Summer 83, Spring 84; TV&RadDir 84*
WMTV-TV - Madison, WI - *BrCabYB 84; DirUSTelSta 83; TelAl 83, 84; Tel&CabFB 84S; TV&RadDir 84*
WMTW-TV - Poland Spring, ME - *BrCabYB 84; TelAl 83, 84; Tel&CabFB 84S; TV&RadDir 84*
WMTW-TV - Portland, ME - *DirUSTelSta 83*
WMTY - Greenwood, SC - *BrCabYB 84; TV&RadDir 84*
WMTZ - Martinez, GA - *BrCabYB 84*
WMUA-FM - Amherst, MA - *BrCabYB 84; NatRadPubDir Summer 83, Spring 84; TV&RadDir 84*
WMUB-FM - Oxford, OH - *BrCabYB 84; NatRadPubDir Summer 83, Spring 84; TV&RadDir 84*
WMUC-FM - College Park, MD - *BrCabYB 84; TV&RadDir 84*
WMUF - Paris, TN - *BrCabYB 84; TV&RadDir 84*
WMUH-FM - Allentown, PA - *BrCabYB 84; NatRadPubDir Summer 83, Spring 84; TV&RadDir 84*
WMUK-FM - Kalamazoo, MI - *BrCabYB 84; NatRadPubDir Summer 83, Spring 84; TV&RadDir 84*
WMUL-FM - Huntington, WV - *BrCabYB 84; NatRadPubDir Summer 83, Spring 84; TV&RadDir 84*
WMUM-FM - Marathon, FL - *BrCabYB 84; TV&RadDir 84*
WMUR-TV - Manchester, NH - *BrCabYB 84; DirUSTelSta 83; LitMarPl 83, 84; TelAl 83, 84; Tel&CabFB 84S; TV&RadDir 84*
WMUS - Muskegon, MI - *BrCabYB 84; NatRadPubDir Summer 83, Spring 84; TV&RadDir 84*
WMUS-FM - Muskegon, MI - *BrCabYB 84; NatRadPubDir Summer 83, Spring 84; TV&RadDir 84*
WMUU - Greenville, SC - *BrCabYB 84; TV&RadDir 84*
WMUU-FM - Greenville, SC - *BrCabYB 84; TV&RadDir 84*
WMUW - Columbus, MS - *BrCabYB 84*
WMUZ-FM - Detroit, MI - *BrCabYB 84; NatRadPubDir Summer 83, Spring 84; TV&RadDir 84*
WMVA - Martinsville, VA - *BrCabYB 84; TV&RadDir 84*
WMVA-FM - Martinsville, VA - *BrCabYB 84; TV&RadDir 84*
WMVB-FM - Millville, NJ - *BrCabYB 84*
WMVB-FM - Vineland, NJ - *TV&RadDir 84*
WMVG - Milledgeville, GA - *BrCabYB 84; TV&RadDir 84*
WMVI - Mechanicville, NY - *BrCabYB 84*
WMVN - Ishpeming, MI - *BrCabYB 84; TV&RadDir 84*
WMVO - Mt. Vernon, OH - *BrCabYB 84; TV&RadDir 84*
WMVO-FM - Mt. Vernon, OH - *BrCabYB 84; TV&RadDir 84*
WMVQ-FM - Amsterdam, NY - *BrCabYB 84; TV&RadDir 84*
WMVR - Sidney, OH - *BrCabYB 84; TV&RadDir 84*
WMVR-FM - Sidney, OH - *BrCabYB 84; TV&RadDir 84*
WMVS - Milwaukee, WI - *BrCabYB 84; TV&RadDir 84*
WMVS-TV - Milwaukee, WI - *LitMarPl 83, 84; Tel&CabFB 84S*
WMVT-TV - Milwaukee, WI - *BrCabYB 84; LitMarPl 84; Tel&CabFB 84S; TV&RadDir 84*
WMVV - McDonough, GA - *BrCabYB 84*
WMVY - Tisburg, MA - *BrCabYB 84*
WMWA - Glenview, IL - *BrCabYB 84*
WMWC - Gardner, MA - *BrCabYB 84*

WMWM-FM - Salem, MA - *BrCabYB 84; TV&RadDir 84*
WMWV-FM - Conway, NH - *BrCabYB 84; TV&RadDir 84*
WMXM-FM - Lake Forest, IL - *BrCabYB 84; TV&RadDir 84*
WMXR - Lexington, MS - *BrCabYB 84*
WMYD - North Kingstown, RI - *TV&RadDir 84*
WMYD - Wickford, RI - *BrCabYB 84*
WMYF - Exeter, NH - *BrCabYB 84; TV&RadDir 84*
WMYK - Elizabeth City, NC - *BrCabYB 84*
WMYK - Norfolk, NC - *NatRadPubDir Summer 83 p.254*
WMYK-FM - Moyock, NC - *TV&RadDir 84*
WMYK-FM - Norfolk, VA - *NatRadPubDir Spring 84*
WMYL - Johnstown, NY - *BrCabYB 84; TV&RadDir 84*
WMYN - Madison, NC - *TV&RadDir 84*
WMYN - Mayodan, NC - *BrCabYB 84*
WMYQ - Newton, MS - *BrCabYB 84; TV&RadDir 84*
WMYQ-FM - Newton, MS - *BrCabYB 84; TV&RadDir 84*
WMYR - Ft. Myers, FL - *BrCabYB 84; NatRadPubDir Summer 83, Spring 84; TV&RadDir 84*
WMYS-FM - New Bedford, MA - *BrCabYB 84; TV&RadDir 84*
WMYU-FM - Sevierville, TN - *BrCabYB 84; TV&RadDir 84*
WMYX-FM - Hales Corners, WI - *TV&RadDir 84*
WMYX-FM - Milwaukee, WI - *BrCabYB 84; NatRadPubDir Summer 83 p.268, Spring 84 p.270*
WMZK - Traverse City, MI - *BrCabYB 84*
WMZK-FM - Detroit, MI - *TV&RadDir 84*
WMZK-FM - Traverse City, MI - *TV&RadDir 84*
WMZQ-FM - Washington, DC - *BrCabYB 84; NatRadPubDir Summer 83, Spring 84; TV&RadDir 84*
WNAA-FM - Greensboro, NC - *BrCabYB 84; NatRadPubDir Summer 83, Spring 84; TV&RadDir 84*
WNAB - Bridgeport, CT - *BrCabYB 84; NatRadPubDir Summer 83, Spring 84; TV&RadDir 84*
WNAC-TV - Boston, MA - *TelAl 83, 84*
WNAD - Norman, OK - *BrCabYB 84*
WNAE - Warren, PA - *BrCabYB 84; TV&RadDir 84*
WNAH - Nashville, TN - *BrCabYB 84; NatRadPubDir Summer 83, Spring 84; TV&RadDir 84*
WNAK - Nanticoke, PA - *BrCabYB 84; TV&RadDir 84*
WNAL - Gasden, AL - *Tel&CabFB 84S*
WNAM - Neenah, WI - *BrCabYB 84; TV&RadDir 84*
WNAN-FM - Demopolis, AL - *BrCabYB 84; TV&RadDir 84*
WNAP-FM - Indianapolis, IN - *BrCabYB 84; NatRadPubDir Summer 83, Spring 84; TV&RadDir 84*
WNAR - Norristown, PA - *BrCabYB 84; TV&RadDir 84*
WNAS - New Albany, IN - *BrCabYB 84*
WNAT - Natchez, MS - *BrCabYB 84; TV&RadDir 84*
WNAU - New Albany, MS - *TV&RadDir 84*
WNAV - Annapolis, MD - *BrCabYB 84; NatRadPubDir Summer 83, Spring 84; TV&RadDir 84*
WNAV-FM - Annapolis, MD - *TV&RadDir 84*
WNAX - Yankton, SD - *BrCabYB 84; NatRadPubDir Summer 83, Spring 84; TV&RadDir 84*
WNAZ-FM - Nashville, TN - *BrCabYB 84; NatRadPubDir Summer 83, Spring 84; TV&RadDir 84*
WNBC - New York, NY - *BrCabYB 84; LitMarPl 83, 84; NatRadPubDir Summer 83, Spring 84; TV&RadDir 84*
WNBC-TV - New York, NY - *BrCabYB 84; DirUSTelSta 83; LitMarPl 83, 84; TelAl 83, 84; Tel&CabFB 84S; TV&RadDir 84*
WNBF - Binghamton, NY - *BrCabYB 84; NatRadPubDir Summer 83, Spring 84; TV&RadDir 84*
WNBG - Waynesboro, TN - *BrCabYB 84; TV&RadDir 84*
WNBH - New Bedford, MA - *TV&RadDir 84*
WNBI - Park Falls, WI - *BrCabYB 84; TV&RadDir 84*
WNBI-FM - Park Falls, WI - *BrCabYB 84; TV&RadDir 84*
WNBK-FM - New London, WI - *BrCabYB 84; TV&RadDir 84*
WNBP - Newburyport, MA - *BrCabYB 84; TV&RadDir 84*
WNBR-FM - Wildwood, NJ - *BrCabYB 84; TV&RadDir 84*
WNBS - Murray, KY - *BrCabYB 84; TV&RadDir 84*
WNBT - Wellsboro, PA - *TV&RadDir 84*
WNBT-FM - Wellsboro, PA - *BrCabYB 84*
WNBX-FM - Keene, NH - *BrCabYB 84; TV&RadDir 84*
WNBY - Newberry, MI - *BrCabYB 84*
WNBY-FM - Newberry, MI - *BrCabYB 84*
WNBZ - Saranac Lake, NY - *BrCabYB 84; TV&RadDir 84*
WNCA - Siler City, NC - *BrCabYB 84; TV&RadDir 84*
WNCB - Duluth, MN - *BrCabYB 84*
WNCC - Barnesboro, PA - *BrCabYB 84; TV&RadDir 84*
WNCC - Johnstown, PA - *NatRadPubDir Summer 83 p.211, Spring 84 p.211*
WNCE-FM - Lancaster, PA - *BrCabYB 84; NatRadPubDir Summer 83, Spring 84; TV&RadDir 84*
WNCI-FM - Columbus, OH - *BrCabYB 84; NatRadPubDir Summer 83, Spring 84; TV&RadDir 84*
WNCN-FM - New York, NY - *BrCabYB 84; NatRadPubDir Summer 83, Spring 84; TV&RadDir 84*
WNCO - Ashland, OH - *BrCabYB 84; TV&RadDir 84*
WNCO-FM - Ashland, OH - *BrCabYB 84; TV&RadDir 84*
WNCQ-FM - Watertown, NY - *BrCabYB 84; NatRadPubDir Summer 83, Spring 84; TV&RadDir 84*
WNCR - St. Pauls, NC - *BrCabYB 84; TV&RadDir 84*
WNCS-FM - Montpelier, VT - *TV&RadDir 84*
WNCT - Greenville, NC - *BrCabYB 84; TV&RadDir 84*
WNCT-FM - Greenville, NC - *BrCabYB 84; TV&RadDir 84*
WNCT-TV - Greenville, NC - *BrCabYB 84; DirUSTelSta 83; TelAl 83, 84; Tel&CabFB 84S; TV&RadDir 84*
WNCW-FM - Paris, KY - *BrCabYB 84; TV&RadDir 84*
WNCY-FM - Springvale, ME - *BrCabYB 84; NatRadPubDir Summer 83, Spring 84*
WNDA-FM - Huntsville, AL - *BrCabYB 84; NatRadPubDir Summer 83, Spring 84; TV&RadDir 84*
WNDB - Daytona Beach, FL - *BrCabYB 84; NatRadPubDir Summer 83, Spring 84; TV&RadDir 84*
WNDE - Indianapolis, IN - *BrCabYB 84; LitMarPl 83, 84; NatRadPubDir Summer 83, Spring 84; TV&RadDir 84*
WNDH-FM - Napoleon, OH - *BrCabYB 84; TV&RadDir 84*
WNDI - Sullivan, IN - *BrCabYB 84; TV&RadDir 84*
WNDN-FM - Salisbury, NC - *BrCabYB 84; TV&RadDir 84*
WNDR - Syracuse, NY - *BrCabYB 84; NatRadPubDir Summer 83, Spring 84; TV&RadDir 84*
WNDS - Derry, NH - *BrCabYB 84; Tel&CabFB 84S*
WNDU - South Bend, IN - *BrCabYB 84; NatRadPubDir Summer 83, Spring 84; TV&RadDir 84*
WNDU-FM - South Bend, IN - *BrCabYB 84; NatRadPubDir Summer 83, Spring 84; TV&RadDir 84*
WNDU-TV - South Bend, IN - *BrCabYB 84; DirUSTelSta 83; TelAl 83, 84; Tel&CabFB 84S; TV&RadDir 84*
WNDY-FM - Crawfordsville, IN - *BrCabYB 84; TV&RadDir 84*
WNEA - Newnan, GA - *BrCabYB 84; TV&RadDir 84*
WNEB - Worcester, MA - *BrCabYB 84; NatRadPubDir Summer 83, Spring 84; TV&RadDir 84*
WNEC-FM - Henniker, NH - *BrCabYB 84; NatRadPubDir Summer 83, Spring 84; TV&RadDir 84*
WNED-FM - Buffalo, NY - *BrCabYB 84; NatRadPubDir Summer 83, Spring 84; TV&RadDir 84*
WNED-TV - Buffalo, NY - *BrCabYB 84; Tel&CabFB 84S; TV&RadDir 84*
WNEG - Toccoa, GA - *BrCabYB 84; TV&RadDir 84*
WNEG-TV - Toccoa, GA - *BrCabYB 84; Tel&CabFB 84S*
WNEH - Greenwood, SC - *BrCabYB 84; Tel&CabFB 84S*
WNEK-FM - Springfield, MA - *BrCabYB 84; NatRadPubDir Summer 83, Spring 84*
WNEL - Caguas, PR - *BrCabYB 84*
WNEM-TV - Bay City, MI - *BrCabYB 84; TelAl 83, 84; Tel&CabFB 84S*
WNEM-TV - Flint, MI - *DirUSTelSta 83*
WNEM-TV - Saginaw, MI - *LitMarPl 83, 84; TV&RadDir 84*
WNEO-TV - Alliance, OH - *BrCabYB 84; Tel&CabFB 84S; TV&RadDir 84*
WNEP-TV - Avoca, PA - *LitMarPl 83, 84*
WNEP-TV - Pittston, PA - *TV&RadDir 84*
WNEP-TV - Scranton, PA - *BrCabYB 84; DirUSTelSta 83; TelAl 83, 84; Tel&CabFB 84S*
WNER - Live Oak, FL - *BrCabYB 84; TV&RadDir 84*
WNES - Central City, KY - *BrCabYB 84; TV&RadDir 84*
WNET - Newark, NJ - *BrCabYB 84*
WNET - New York, NY - *Tel&CabFB 84C*
WNET-TV - Newark, NJ - *TV&RadDir 84*
WNET-TV - New York, NY - *LitMarPl 83, 84; TV&RadDir 84*
WNEU - Wheeling, WV - *TV&RadDir 84*
WNEV-TV - Boston, MA - *BrCabYB 84; Tel&CabFB 84S; TV&RadDir 84*
WNEW - New York, NY - *BrCabYB 84; LitMarPl 83, 84; NatRadPubDir Summer 83, Spring 84; TV&RadDir 84*

WNEW-FM - New York, NY - *BrCabYB 84; LitMarPl 83; NatRadPubDir Summer 83, Spring 84; TV&RadDir 84*
WNEW-TV [Div. of Metromedia Inc.] - New York, NY - *BrCabYB 84; DirUSTelSta 83; LitMarPl 83, 84; TelAl 83, 84; Tel&CabFB 84S; TV&RadDir 84*
WNEX - Macon, GA - *BrCabYB 84; NatRadPubDir Summer 83, Spring 84; TV&RadDir 84*
WNEZ-FM - Aiken, SC - *BrCabYB 84; TV&RadDir 84*
WNFL - Green Bay, WI - *BrCabYB 84; NatRadPubDir Summer 83, Spring 84; TV&RadDir 84*
WNFQ-FM - Lake City, FL - *TV&RadDir 84*
WNFT - Jacksonville, FL - *BrCabYB 84; Tel&CabFB 84S*
WNFY-FM - Ormond Beach, FL - *TV&RadDir 84*
WNFY-FM - Palatka, FL - *BrCabYB 84*
WNGA - Nashville, GA - *BrCabYB 84; TV&RadDir 84*
WNGC-FM - Athens, GA - *BrCabYB 84; NatRadPubDir Summer 83, Spring 84; TV&RadDir 84*
WNGE-TV - Nashville, TN - *DirUSTelSta 83; LitMarPl 83, 84; TelAl 83, 84; Tel&CabFB 84S; TV&RadDir 84*
WNGO - Mayfield, KY - *BrCabYB 84; TV&RadDir 84*
WNGS-FM - West Palm Beach, FL - *BrCabYB 84; NatRadPubDir Summer 83, Spring 84; TV&RadDir 84*
WNGZ - Montour Falls, NY - *BrCabYB 84*
WNHC - New Haven, CT - *BrCabYB 84; NatRadPubDir Summer 83, Spring 84; TV&RadDir 84*
WNHS-FM - Portsmouth, VA - *BrCabYB 84; NatRadPubDir Summer 83, Spring 84; TV&RadDir 84*
WNHT - Concord, NH - *BrCabYB 84; Tel&CabFB 84S*
WNHU-FM - New Haven, CT - *NatRadPubDir Summer 83 p.280, Spring 84*
WNHU-FM - West Haven, CT - *BrCabYB 84; TV&RadDir 84*
WNHV - White River Junction, VT - *BrCabYB 84; NatRadPubDir Summer 83, Spring 84; TV&RadDir 84*
WNHV-FM - White River Junction, VT - *BrCabYB 84; NatRadPubDir Summer 83, Spring 84; TV&RadDir 84*
WNIB-FM - Chicago, IL - *BrCabYB 84; NatRadPubDir Summer 83, Spring 84; TV&RadDir 84*
WNIC - Dearborn, MI - *BrCabYB 84; TV&RadDir 84*
WNIC - Detroit, MI - *NatRadPubDir Summer 83 p.127, Spring 84 p.127*
WNIC-FM - Dearborn, MI - *BrCabYB 84; TV&RadDir 84*
WNIC-FM - Detroit, MI - *NatRadPubDir Summer 83 p.127, Spring 84 p.127*
WNIK-FM - Arecibo, PR - *BrCabYB 84*
WNIL - Niles, MI - *BrCabYB 84; TV&RadDir 84*
WNIN-FM - Evansville, IN - *BrCabYB 84; TV&RadDir 84*
WNIN-TV - Evansville, IN - *Tel&CabFB 84S; TV&RadDir 84*
WNIO - Niles, OH - *BrCabYB 84; TV&RadDir 84*
WNIQ-FM - Glen Falls, NY - *BrCabYB 84*
WNIQ-FM - Hudson Falls, NY - *TV&RadDir 84*
WNIR-FM - Kent, OH - *BrCabYB 84; TV&RadDir 84*
WNIS - Norfolk, VA - *NatRadPubDir Summer 83, Spring 84; TV&RadDir 84*
WNIS - Portsmouth, VA - *BrCabYB 84*
WNIT-TV - Mishawaka, IN - *TV&RadDir 84*
WNIT-TV - South Bend, IN - *BrCabYB 84; Tel&CabFB 84S*
WNIU-FM - De Kalb, IL - *BrCabYB 84; NatRadPubDir Summer 83, Spring 84; TV&RadDir 84*
WNIX - Greenville, MS - *BrCabYB 84; TV&RadDir 84*
WNIZ - Zion, IL - *BrCabYB 84*
WNJB-TV - New Brunswick, NJ - *BrCabYB 84; Tel&CabFB 84S*
WNJB-TV - Trenton, NJ - *TV&RadDir 84*
WNJC-FM - Senatobia, MS - *BrCabYB 84; NatRadPubDir Summer 83, Spring 84; TV&RadDir 84*
WNJM - Montclair, NJ - *BrCabYB 84; Tel&CabFB 84S*
WNJN-TV - Trenton, NJ - *TV&RadDir 84*
WNJR - Newark, NJ - *BrCabYB 84; NatRadPubDir Summer 83 p.158, Spring 84 p.158*
WNJR - Union, NJ - *LitMarPl 83, 84; TV&RadDir 84*
WNJS-TV - Camden, NJ - *BrCabYB 84; Tel&CabFB 84S*
WNJS-TV - Trenton, NJ - *TV&RadDir 84*
WNJT-TV - Trenton, NJ - *BrCabYB 84; Tel&CabFB 84S; TV&RadDir 84*
WNJU-TV - Linden, NJ - *BrCabYB 84*
WNJU-TV - Newark, NJ - *DirUSTelSta 83; TV&RadDir 84*
WNJU-TV - New York, NY - *TelAl 83, 84; Tel&CabFB 84S*
WNJX-TV - Mayaguez, PR - *BrCabYB 84*
WNJY-FM - Riviera Beach, FL - *BrCabYB 84; TV&RadDir 84*
WNJY-FM - West Palm Beach, FL - *NatRadPubDir Summer 83 p.66, Spring 84 p.67*
WNKJ-TV - Hopkinsville, KY - *BrCabYB 84; Tel&CabFB 84S*
WNKO-FM - Newark, OH - *BrCabYB 84; TV&RadDir 84*
WNKX - Clinton, TN - *BrCabYB 84*
WNKY - Neon, KY - *BrCabYB 84; TV&RadDir 84*
WNKZ - Nashville, TN - *NatRadPubDir Summer 83*
WNLA - Indianola, MS - *BrCabYB 84; TV&RadDir 84*
WNLA-FM - Indianola, MS - *BrCabYB 84; TV&RadDir 84*
WNLB - Rocky Mt., VA - *BrCabYB 84; TV&RadDir 84*
WNLC - New London, CT - *BrCabYB 84; NatRadPubDir Summer 83, Spring 84*
WNLC - Waterford, CT - *TV&RadDir 84*
WNLK - Norwalk, CT - *BrCabYB 84; NatRadPubDir Summer 83, Spring 84; TV&RadDir 84*
WNLR - Churchville, VA - *BrCabYB 84; TV&RadDir 84*
WNLT - Duluth, MN - *BrCabYB 84; TV&RadDir 84*
WNLV - Nicholasville, KY - *TV&RadDir 84*
WNMB-FM - North Myrtle Beach, SC - *BrCabYB 84; TV&RadDir 84*
WNMC-FM - Traverse City, MI - *BrCabYB 84*
WNMH - Northfield, MA - *BrCabYB 84*
WNMJ-TV - Marquette, MI - *Tel&CabFB 84S*
WNMT - Garden City, GA - *BrCabYB 84*
WNMT - Savannah, GA - *TV&RadDir 84*
WNMU-FM - Marquette, MI - *BrCabYB 84; TV&RadDir 84*
WNMU-TV - Marquette, MI - *BrCabYB 84; TV&RadDir 84*
WNNC - Newton, NC - *BrCabYB 84; TV&RadDir 84*
WNNE-TV - Burlington, VT - *DirUSTelSta 83*
WNNE-TV - Hartford, VT - *BrCabYB 84; TelAl 83, 84; Tel&CabFB 84S*
WNNE-TV - White River Junction, VT - *TV&RadDir 84*
WNNJ - Newton, NJ - *BrCabYB 84; TV&RadDir 84*
WNNN-FM - Canton, NJ - *BrCabYB 84*
WNNN-FM - Salem, NJ - *TV&RadDir 84*
WNNO - Wisconsin Dells, WI - *BrCabYB 84; TV&RadDir 84*
WNNO-FM - Wisconsin Dells, WI - *BrCabYB 84; TV&RadDir 84*
WNNR - New Orleans, LA - *BrCabYB 84; NatRadPubDir Summer 83; TV&RadDir 84*
WNNS-FM - Springfield, IL - *BrCabYB 84; TV&RadDir 84*
WNNT - Warsaw, VA - *BrCabYB 84; TV&RadDir 84*
WNNT-FM - Warsaw, VA - *BrCabYB 84; TV&RadDir 84*
WNOE - New Orleans, LA - *BrCabYB 84; NatRadPubDir Summer 83, Spring 84; TV&RadDir 84*
WNOE-FM - New Orleans, LA - *BrCabYB 84; NatRadPubDir Summer 83, Spring 84; TV&RadDir 84*
WNOG - Naples, FL - *BrCabYB 84; TV&RadDir 84*
WNOI-FM - Flora, IL - *BrCabYB 84; TV&RadDir 84*
WNOK - Columbia, SC - *BrCabYB 84; NatRadPubDir Summer 83, Spring 84; TV&RadDir 84*
WNOK-FM - Columbia, SC - *BrCabYB 84; NatRadPubDir Summer 83, Spring 84; TV&RadDir 84*
WNOL-TV - New Orleans, LA - *BrCabYB 84; Tel&CabFB 84S*
WNON-FM - Lebanon, IN - *BrCabYB 84; TV&RadDir 84*
WNOO - Chattanooga, TN - *BrCabYB 84; NatRadPubDir Summer 83, Spring 84; TV&RadDir 84*
WNOP - Newport, KY - *BrCabYB 84; TV&RadDir 84*
WNOR - Norfolk, VA - *BrCabYB 84; NatRadPubDir Summer 83, Spring 84; TV&RadDir 84*
WNOR-FM - Norfolk, VA - *BrCabYB 84; NatRadPubDir Summer 83, Spring 84; TV&RadDir 84*
WNOU-FM - Willimantic, CT - *BrCabYB 84; TV&RadDir 84*
WNOV - Milwaukee, WI - *BrCabYB 84; NatRadPubDir Summer 83, Spring 84; TV&RadDir 84*
WNOW - York, PA - *BrCabYB 84; NatRadPubDir Summer 83, Spring 84; TV&RadDir 84*
WNOX - Knoxville, TN - *BrCabYB 84; NatRadPubDir Summer 83, Spring 84; TV&RadDir 84*
WNPA Press-Clipping Service - Seattle, WA - *ProGuPRSer 4*
WNPB-TV - Morgantown, WV - *BrCabYB 84; Tel&CabFB 84S*
WNPC - Newport, TN - *BrCabYB 84*
WNPE-TV - Watertown, NY - *BrCabYB 84; Tel&CabFB 84S; TV&RadDir 84*
WNPI-TV - Norwood, NY - *BrCabYB 84; Tel&CabFB 84S*

WNPQ-FM - New Philadelphia, OH - *BrCabYB 84; TV&RadDir 84*
WNPQ-FM - Uhrichsville, OH - *TV&RadDir 84*
WNPR - Norwich, CT - *BrCabYB 84*
WNPT - Tuscaloosa, AL - *BrCabYB 84; NatRadPubDir Summer 83, Spring 84; TV&RadDir 84*
WNPV - Lansdale, PA - *BrCabYB 84; TV&RadDir 84*
WNRC-FM - Dudley, MA - *BrCabYB 84*
WNRC-FM - Webster, MA - *TV&RadDir 84*
WNRE - Circleville, OH - *BrCabYB 84; TV&RadDir 84*
WNRE-FM - Circleville, OH - *BrCabYB 84; TV&RadDir 84*
WNRG - Grundy, VA - *BrCabYB 84; TV&RadDir 84*
WNRI - Woonsocket, RI - *BrCabYB 84; NatRadPubDir Summer 83, Spring 84; TV&RadDir 84*
WNRK - Newark, DE - *BrCabYB 84; NatRadPubDir Summer 83, Spring 84*
WNRN - Virginia Beach, VA - *BrCabYB 84*
WNRP - Ponce, PR - *BrCabYB 84; Tel&CabFB 84S*
WNRR-FM - Bellevue, OH - *BrCabYB 84; TV&RadDir 84*
WNRS - Ann Arbor, MI - *TV&RadDir 84*
WNRS - Saline, MI - *BrCabYB 84*
WNRV - Narrows, VA - *BrCabYB 84; TV&RadDir 84*
WNSB - Norfolk, VA - *BrCabYB 84*
WNSC-FM - Rock Hill, SC - *BrCabYB 84; TV&RadDir 84*
WNSC-TV - Rock Hill, SC - *BrCabYB 84; Tel&CabFB 84S; TV&RadDir 84*
WNSI - St. Petersburg, FL - *NatRadPubDir Summer 83*
WNSL-FM - Laurel, MS - *BrCabYB 84; TV&RadDir 84*
WNST - Milton, WV - *BrCabYB 84; TV&RadDir 84*
WNST-FM - Milton, WV - *TV&RadDir 84*
WNSY - Norfolk, VA - *NatRadPubDir Spring 84 p.256*
WNSY-FM - Newport News, VA - *BrCabYB 84*
WNTB - Wellsboro, PA - *BrCabYB 84*
WNTC-FM - Potsdam, NY - *NatRadPubDir Summer 83, Spring 84*
WNTE-FM - Mansfield, PA - *BrCabYB 84; NatRadPubDir Summer 83, Spring 84; TV&RadDir 84*
WNTH-FM - Winnetka, IL - *BrCabYB 84; NatRadPubDir Summer 83, Spring 84; TV&RadDir 84*
WNTI-FM - Hackettstown, NJ - *BrCabYB 84; NatRadPubDir Summer 83, Spring 84; TV&RadDir 84*
WNTN - Auburndale, MA - *TV&RadDir 84*
WNTN - Boston, MA - *NatRadPubDir Summer 83 p.120, Spring 84 p.120*
WNTN - Newton, MA - *BrCabYB 84*
WNTQ-FM - Syracuse, NY - *BrCabYB 84; NatRadPubDir Summer 83 p.178, Spring 84; TV&RadDir 84*
WNTS - Indianapolis, IN - *BrCabYB 84; NatRadPubDir Summer 83, Spring 84; TV&RadDir 84*
WNTT - Tazewell, TN - *BrCabYB 84; TV&RadDir 84*
WNTV - Greenville, SC - *BrCabYB 84; Tel&CabFB 84S*
WNTY - Southington, CT - *BrCabYB 84; TV&RadDir 84*
WNUB-FM - Northfield, VT - *BrCabYB 84; TV&RadDir 84*
WNUE - Ft. Walton Beach, FL - *BrCabYB 84; TV&RadDir 84*
WNUF-FM - New Kensington, PA - *BrCabYB 84*
WNUF-FM - Pittsburgh, PA - *NatRadPubDir Summer 83 p.214, Spring 84 p.215; TV&RadDir 84*
WNUR-FM - Evanston, IL - *BrCabYB 84; NatRadPubDir Summer 83, Spring 84; TV&RadDir 84*
WNUS - Belpre, OH - *BrCabYB 84*
WNUV-TV - Baltimore, MD - *BrCabYB 84; DirUSTelSta 83; TelAl 84; Tel&CabFB 84S*
WNUZ - Talladega, AL - *BrCabYB 84; TV&RadDir 84*
WNVA - Norton, VA - *BrCabYB 84; TV&RadDir 84*
WNVA-FM - Norton, VA - *BrCabYB 84; TV&RadDir 84*
WNVC - Fairfax, VA - *BrCabYB 84; Tel&CabFB 84S*
WNVI-FM - North Vernon, IN - *BrCabYB 84*
WNVL - Nicholasville, KY - *BrCabYB 84*
WNVR - Naugatuck, CT - *BrCabYB 84*
WNVR - Waterbury, CT - *NatRadPubDir Summer 83, Spring 84; TV&RadDir 84*
WNVT - Goldvein, VA - *BrCabYB 84; Tel&CabFB 84S*
WNVY - Pensacola, FL - *BrCabYB 84; NatRadPubDir Summer 83, Spring 84; TV&RadDir 84*
WNVZ-FM - Norfolk, VA - *BrCabYB 84; NatRadPubDir Summer 83 p.254, Spring 84 p.256*
WNWC-FM - Madison, WI - *BrCabYB 84; NatRadPubDir Spring 84; TV&RadDir 84*
WNWI - Valparaiso, IN - *BrCabYB 84; TV&RadDir 84*
WNWN-FM - Coldwater, MI - *BrCabYB 84; TV&RadDir 84*
WNWR-FM - Canal Fulton, OH - *NatRadPubDir Summer 83 p.307,p.308, Spring 84 p.309*
WNWS - Miami, FL - *BrCabYB 84; NatRadPubDir Summer 83, Spring 84; TV&RadDir 84*
WNWZ - Highland Springs, VA - *BrCabYB 84*
WNWZ - Richmond, VA - *NatRadPubDir Summer 83, Spring 84*
WNXT - Portsmouth, OH - *BrCabYB 84; TV&RadDir 84*
WNXT-FM - Portsmouth, OH - *BrCabYB 84; TV&RadDir 84*
WNYC - New York, NY - *BrCabYB 84; LitMarPl 83, 84; NatRadPubDir Summer 83, Spring 84; TV&RadDir 84*
WNYC-FM - New York, NY - *BrCabYB 84; LitMarPl 83; NatRadPubDir Summer 83, Spring 84; TV&RadDir 84*
WNYC-TV - New York, NY - *BrCabYB 84; LitMarPl 83, 84; Tel&CabFB 84S; TV&RadDir 84*
WNYE-FM - Brooklyn, NY - *TV&RadDir 84*
WNYE-FM - New York, NY - *BrCabYB 84; NatRadPubDir Summer 83 p.302, Spring 84 p.304*
WNYE-TV - Brooklyn, NY - *TV&RadDir 84*
WNYE-TV - New York, NY - *BrCabYB 84; Tel&CabFB 84S*
WNYG - Babylon, NY - *BrCabYB 84; TV&RadDir 84*
WNYK - Nyack, NY - *BrCabYB 84*
WNYM - New York, NY - *BrCabYB 84; NatRadPubDir Summer 83 p.174, Spring 84 p.172; TV&RadDir 84*
WNYN - Canton, OH - *BrCabYB 84; NatRadPubDir Summer 83, Spring 84; TV&RadDir 84*
WNYR - Rochester, NY - *BrCabYB 84; NatRadPubDir Summer 83, Spring 84; TV&RadDir 84*
WNYS - Buffalo, NY - *BrCabYB 84; NatRadPubDir Spring 84*
WNYS-FM - Buffalo, NY - *BrCabYB 84; NatRadPubDir Spring 84; TV&RadDir 84*
WNYT-TV - Albany, NY - *BrCabYB 84; DirUSTelSta 83; Tel&CabFB 84S*
WNYT-TV - Menands, NY - *LitMarPl 84; TV&RadDir 84*
WNYU-FM - New York, NY - *BrCabYB 84; NatRadPubDir Summer 83, Spring 84; TV&RadDir 84*
WNYZ - Portland, ME - *BrCabYB 84*
WNZE-FM - Plymouth, IN - *BrCabYB 84; TV&RadDir 84*
WOAB - Ozark, AL - *BrCabYB 84; TV&RadDir 84*
WOAB-FM - Ozark, AL - *TV&RadDir 84*
WOAC - Canton, OH - *BrCabYB 84; DirUSTelSta 83; Tel&CabFB 84S*
WOAI - San Antonio, TX - *BrCabYB 84; NatRadPubDir Summer 83, Spring 84; TV&RadDir 84*
WOAI-FM - San Antonio, TX - *NatRadPubDir Summer 83*
WOAK - La Grange, GA - *BrCabYB 84*
WOAM - Otsego, MI - *BrCabYB 84; TV&RadDir 84*
WOAP - Owosso, MI - *BrCabYB 84; TV&RadDir 84*
WOAP-FM - Owosso, MI - *BrCabYB 84; TV&RadDir 84*
WOAS - Ontonagon, MI - *BrCabYB 84*
WOAY - Oak Hill, WV - *BrCabYB 84; TV&RadDir 84*
WOAY-FM - Oak Hill, WV - *BrCabYB 84; TV&RadDir 84*
WOAY-TV - Oak Hill, WV - *BrCabYB 84; DirUSTelSta 83; TelAl 83, 84; Tel&CabFB 84S; TV&RadDir 84*
WOBC-FM - Oberlin, OH - *BrCabYB 84; TV&RadDir 84*
WOBL - Oberlin, OH - *BrCabYB 84; TV&RadDir 84*
WOBM - Lakewood, NJ - *BrCabYB 84*
WOBM - Toms River, NJ - *BrCabYB 84; NatRadPubDir Summer 83, Spring 84; TV&RadDir 84*
WOBM-FM - Toms River, NJ - *NatRadPubDir Summer 83, Spring 84*
WOBN-FM - Westerville, OH - *BrCabYB 84; TV&RadDir 84*
Wobo Corp. - Skaneateles, NY - *BaconPubCkNews 84*
WOBR - Wanchese, NC - *BrCabYB 84; TV&RadDir 84*
WOBR-FM - Wanchese, NC - *BrCabYB 84; TV&RadDir 84*
WOBS - New Albany, IN - *BrCabYB 84; TV&RadDir 84*
WOBT - Rhinelander, WI - *BrCabYB 84; TV&RadDir 84*
Woburn Daily Times & Chronicle - Woburn, MA - *BaconPubCkNews 84*
WOC - Davenport, IA - *BrCabYB 84; NatRadPubDir Summer 83, Spring 84; TV&RadDir 84*
WOC-TV - Davenport, IA - *BrCabYB 84; DirUSTelSta 83; TelAl 83, 84; Tel&CabFB 84S; TV&RadDir 84*

WOCB - West Yarmouth, MA - *BrCabYB 84; TV&RadDir 84*
WOCG - Huntsville, AL - *BrCabYB 84; TV&RadDir 84*
WOCH - North Vernon, IN - *TV&RadDir 84*
WOCH-FM - North Vernon, IN - *TV&RadDir 84*
WOCN - Miami, FL - *BrCabYB 84; NatRadPubDir Summer 83, Spring 84; TV&RadDir 84*
WOCO - Oconto, WI - *BrCabYB 84; TV&RadDir 84*
WOCO-FM - Oconto, WI - *BrCabYB 84; TV&RadDir 84*
WOCQ - Berlin, MD - *BrCabYB 84*
WOCR-FM - Olivet, MI - *BrCabYB 84; TV&RadDir 84*
WODB - Camden, AL - *BrCabYB 84*
Wodell Associates, Jack - San Francisco, CA - *AdAge 3-28-84; StaDirAdAg 2-84*
WODI - Brookneal, VA - *BrCabYB 84; TV&RadDir 84*
WODU - Norfolk, VA - *NatRadPubDir Summer 83, Spring 84*
WODY - Bassett, VA - *BrCabYB 84; TV&RadDir 84*
WOEA - Rogers City, MI - *BrCabYB 84*
WOEL-FM - Elkton, MD - *BrCabYB 84; TV&RadDir 84*
Woerner, David R. - Salina, KS - *LitMarPl 84*
WOES-FM - Elsie, MI - *TV&RadDir 84*
WOES-FM - Ovid-Elsie, MI - *BrCabYB 84*
WOEZ-FM - Milton, PA - *BrCabYB 84; TV&RadDir 84*
WOFE - Rockwood, TN - *BrCabYB 84; TV&RadDir 84*
WOFF-FM - Camilla, GA - *BrCabYB 84; TV&RadDir 84*
Wofford College (Wofford Library Press) - Spartanburg, SC - *BoPubDir 5*
WOFL - Orlando, FL - *BrCabYB 84; DirUSTelSta 83; TelAl 83, 84; Tel&CabFB 84S*
WOFL-FM - Rockford, IL - *TV&RadDir 84*
WOFL-TV - Orlando, FL - *TV&RadDir 84*
WOFM - Moycock, NC - *BrCabYB 84*
WOFN - Bradenton, FL - *BrCabYB 84; TV&RadDir 84*
WOFR - Washington Court House, OH - *TV&RadDir 84*
Wofsy Fine Arts, Alan - San Francisco, CA - *LitMarPl 83, 84; WritMar 84*
WOGO - Cornell, WI - *BrCabYB 84*
WOHI - Alledonia, OH - *TV&RadDir 84*
WOHI - East Liverpool, OH - *BrCabYB 84*
Wohl Literary Agency, Gary S. - New York, NY - *LitMarPl 83*
WOHO - Toledo, OH - *BrCabYB 84; NatRadPubDir Summer 83, Spring 84; TV&RadDir 84*
WOHP - Bellefontaine, OH - *BrCabYB 84*
WOHS - Shelby, NC - *BrCabYB 84; TV&RadDir 84*
WOI - Ames, IA - *BrCabYB 84; LitMarPl 83, 84; TV&RadDir 84*
WOI-FM - Ames, IA - *BrCabYB 84; LitMarPl 83; TV&RadDir 84*
WOI-TV - Ames, IA - *BrCabYB 84; LitMarPl 83, 84; TelAl 83, 84; Tel&CabFB 84S; TV&RadDir 84*
WOI-TV - Des Moines, IA - *DirUSTelSta 83*
WOIC - Columbia, SC - *BrCabYB 84; NatRadPubDir Summer 83, Spring 84; TV&RadDir 84*
WOIO - Shaker Heights, OH - *BrCabYB 84; Tel&CabFB 84S*
WOIV-FM - Deruyter Township, NY - *BrCabYB 84*
WOIV-FM - Oneida, NY - *TV&RadDir 84*
WOIX - Blowing Rock, NC - *BrCabYB 84*
WOJB - Reserve, WI - *BrCabYB 84*
WOJC-FM - Tampa, FL - *NatRadPubDir Spring 84*
WOJO-FM - Chicago, IL - *NatRadPubDir Summer 83 p.83, Spring 84 p.83*
WOJO-FM - Evanston, IL - *BrCabYB 84; TV&RadDir 84*
WOKA - Douglas, GA - *BrCabYB 84; TV&RadDir 84*
WOKA-FM - Douglas, GA - *BrCabYB 84; TV&RadDir 84*
WOKB - Orlando, FL - *TV&RadDir 84*
WOKB - Winter Garden, FL - *BrCabYB 84*
WOKC - Okeechobee, FL - *BrCabYB 84; TV&RadDir 84*
WOKD-FM - Arcadia, FL - *BrCabYB 84; TV&RadDir 84*
WOKE - Charleston, SC - *BrCabYB 84; NatRadPubDir Summer 83, Spring 84; TV&RadDir 84*
WOKG - Warren, OH - *TV&RadDir 84*
WOKG - Youngstown, OH - *NatRadPubDir Summer 83 p.199, Spring 84 p.198*
WOKH-FM - Bardstown, KY - *BrCabYB 84; TV&RadDir 84*
WOKI-FM - Oak Ridge, TN - *BrCabYB 84; NatRadPubDir Summer 83, Spring 84; TV&RadDir 84*
WOKJ - Jackson, MS - *BrCabYB 84; NatRadPubDir Summer 83, Spring 84; TV&RadDir 84*
WOKK - Oak Ridge, TN - *BrCabYB 84*
WOKK-FM - Meridian, MS - *TV&RadDir 84*
WOKL - Eau Claire, WI - *BrCabYB 84; TV&RadDir 84*
WOKM-FM - New Albany, MS - *BrCabYB 84; TV&RadDir 84*
WOKN-FM - Goldsboro, NC - *BrCabYB 84; TV&RadDir 84*
WOKO - Albany, NY - *NatRadPubDir Summer 83; TV&RadDir 84*
WOKQ-FM - Dover, NH - *BrCabYB 84; TV&RadDir 84*
WOKR-TV - Rochester, NY - *BrCabYB 84; DirUSTelSta 83; TelAl 83, 84; Tel&CabFB 84S; TV&RadDir 84*
WOKS - Columbus, GA - *BrCabYB 84; NatRadPubDir Summer 83, Spring 84; TV&RadDir 84*
WOKU-FM - Greensburg, PA - *BrCabYB 84; TV&RadDir 84*
WOKV - Jacksonville, FL - *BrCabYB 84; NatRadPubDir Summer 83, Spring 84; TV&RadDir 84*
WOKW-FM - Cortland, NY - *BrCabYB 84; TV&RadDir 84*
WOKX - High Point, NC - *BrCabYB 84; TV&RadDir 84*
WOKY - Milwaukee, WI - *BrCabYB 84; NatRadPubDir Summer 83, Spring 84; TV&RadDir 84*
WOKZ - Alton, IL - *BrCabYB 84; TV&RadDir 84*
WOL - Washington, DC - *BrCabYB 84; NatRadPubDir Summer 83, Spring 84; TV&RadDir 84*
Wol Advertising Associates [Subs. of National Education Corp.] - Newport Beach, CA - *DirMarMP 83*
WOLA - Barranquitas, PR - *BrCabYB 84*
Wolbach Messenger - Wolbach, NE - *BaconPubCkNews 84; Ed&PubIntYB 82*
WOLC - Princess Anne, MD - *BrCabYB 84*
Wolcott Inc., Robert B. Jr. - Glendale, CA - *DirPRFirms 83*
Wolcott-Red Creek Pennysaver - Wolcott, NY - *AyerDirPub 83*
Wolcotts Inc. - Paramount, CA - *LitMag&SmPr 83-84*
WOLD - Marion, VA - *BrCabYB 84; TV&RadDir 84*
Wold Communications [Subs. of Robert Wold Co. Inc.] - Los Angeles, CA - *BrCabYB 84; Tel&CabFB 84C*
Wold Co. Inc., Robert - Los Angeles, CA - *BrCabYB 84*
WOLD-FM - Marion, VA - *BrCabYB 84; TV&RadDir 84*
WOLE-TV - Aguadilla, PR - *BrCabYB 84; Tel&CabFB 84S*
WOLF - Syracuse, NY - *BrCabYB 84; NatRadPubDir Summer 83, Spring 84; TV&RadDir 84*
Wolf Advertising Inc., Lawrence - *See* Goodis-Wolf Inc.
Wolf Advertising Ltd. - *See* Goodis-Wolf Inc.
Wolf & Associates Inc., E. J. - New York, NY - *IntDirMarRes 83*
Wolf & Co. Inc., Gene - New York, NY - *StaDirAdAg 2-84*
Wolf, Audrey Adler - Washington, DC - *LitMarPl 83, 84*
Wolf Blumberg Krody Inc. - Cincinnati, OH - *StaDirAdAg 2-84*
Wolf House Books - Cedar Springs, MI - *BoPubDir 4*
Wolf House Books - Grand Rapids, MI - *BoPubDir 5; WritMar 84*
Wolf Point Cablevision [of Daniels & Associates] - Sidney, MT - *BrCabYB 84*
Wolf Point Herald-News - *See* Herald-News Publishers Inc.
Wolf Publications, Ernest - Los Angeles, CA - *BoPubDir 4*
Wolf-Rottkay, Ursula - Camarillo, CA - *LitMarPl 83, 84*
Wolf Run - Minneapolis, MN - *BoPubDir 4, 5*
Wolfdata - Ithaca, NY - *VideoDir 82-83*
Wolfdata Inc. - Chelmsford, MA - *MicrocomMPl 84*
Wolfe & Co., Gene - New York, NY - *AdAge 3-28-84*
Wolfe & Co. Inc., Gordon H. - New York, NY - *DirPRFirms 83*
Wolfe Associates Inc., Al - Miami, FL - *DirPRFirms 83*
Wolfe Books, M. - Newark, DE - *BoPubDir 4, 5*
Wolfe City Mirror - Wolfe City, TX - *BaconPubCkNews 84*
Wolfe Computer Aptitude Testing Ltd. - Oradel, NJ - *DataDirSup 7-83*
Wolfe County News - Campton, KY - *AyerDirPub 83; Ed&PubIntYB 82*
Wolfe Group Inc., The - Winston-Salem, NC - *DirPRFirms 83*
Wolfe, Howard H. - Ft. Myers, FL - *BoPubDir 4, 5*
Wolfe Music, Lanny - *See* Paragon/Benson Publishing Group
Wolfe Publications, Ernest - Los Angeles, CA - *BoPubDir 5*
Wolfe Publications Inc. - Pittsford, NY - *BaconPubCkNews 84*
Wolfeboro Granite State News - Wolfeboro, NH - *BaconPubCkNews 84*
Wolff Associates Inc. - Rochester, NY - *StaDirAdAg 2-84*
Wolff Co., The - Baltimore, MD - *ArtMar 84; StaDirAdAg 2-84*

Wolff, Michael Field - New York, NY - *LitMarPl 83; MagIndMarPl 82-83*
Wolff Whitehill Inc./Wolff Whitehill & Thomas Inc. - New York, NY - *StaDirAdAg 2-84*
Wolfson & Co. - Atlanta, GA - *StaDirAdAg 2-84*
Wolfson Publishing Co. Inc. - Pittsburgh, PA - *BoPubDir 4, 5*
Wolfsong Publications - Sturtevant, WI - *BoPubDir 4, 5*
Wolhandler Associates, Joe - New York, NY - *DirPRFirms 83*
Wolkcas Advertising Inc. - Latham, NY - *ArtMar 84; StaDirAdAg 2-84*
Wollack & Associates, Fran - *See* Rosenthal & Co., Albert Jay
Wolnak & Associates, Bernard - Chicago, IL - *InfIndMarPl 83*
WOLO-TV - Columbia, SC - *BrCabYB 84; DirUSTelSta 83; TelAl 83, 84; Tel&CabFB 84S; TV&RadDir 84*
Wolodkowicz, Andrzej - Ottawa, ON, Canada - *BoPubDir 4, 5*
Woloshin Inc., Sid - New York, NY - *Tel&CabFB 84C*
Wolper Sales Agency - New York, NY - *MagIndMarPl 82-83*
WOLS - Florence, SC - *BrCabYB 84; TV&RadDir 84*
Wolsey News - Wessington, SD - *BaconPubCkNews 84*
Wolsey News - Wolsey, SD - *Ed&PubIntYB 82*
Wolsten's Projector House Inc. - East Orange, NJ - *AvMarPl 83*
WOLT - Florence, AL - *TV&RadDir 84*
Wolters-Samson (Aspen Systems Corp.) - Rockville, MD - *KnowInd 83*
Wolverine Cablevision Inc. [of TCI-Taft Cablevision Associates] - Battle Creek, MI - *BrCabYB 84; Tel&CabFB 84C*
Wolverine Telephone Co. - Millington, MI - *TelDir&BG 83-84*
Wolverton Telephone Co. - Wolverton, MN - *TelDir&BG 83-84*
Womach Products [Div. of National Music Service] - Spokane, WA - *AvMarPl 83*
Womack/Claypoole/Griffin - Dallas, TX - *AdAge 3-28-84; ArtMar 84; StaDirAdAg 2-84*
Womack Educational Publications [Aff. of Womack Machine Supply Co.] - Dallas, TX - *BoPubDir 4, 5*
Woman [of Harris Publishing] - New York, NY - *BaconPubCkMag 84; WritMar 84*
Woman Activist Fund Inc. - Falls Church, VA - *BoPubDir 4 Sup, 5*
Woman Beautiful - Palm Beach, FL - *ArtMar 84; WritMar 84*
Woman Bowler, The - Greendale, WI - *BaconPubCkMag 84; MagDir 84; MagIndMarPl 82-83; WritMar 84*
Woman CPA, The - Cincinnati, OH - *BaconPubCkMag 84*
Woman Engineer & The Minority Engineer - Greenlawn, NY - *WritMar 84*
Woman Matters Press - Cabin John, MD - *BoPubDir 4, 5*
Woman Poet [of Women-in-Literature Inc.] - Reno, NV - *LitMag&SmPr 83-84*
Woman Works Press - St. Paul, MN - *BoPubDir 4, 5; LitMag&SmPr 83-84*
Womanchild Press - Ware, MA - *BoPubDir 4, 5*
Womankind - Indianapolis, IN - *LitMag&SmPr 83-84*
Womankind Publications - Indianapolis, IN - *LitMag&SmPr 83-84*
Womanpress - Chicago, IL - *BoPubDir 4, 5*
Woman's Board [of Rush-Presbyterian-St. Luke's Medical Center] - Chicago, IL - *BoPubDir 4, 5*
Woman's Day [of CBS Publications] - New York, NY - *BaconPubCkMag 84; Folio 83; LitMarPl 83, 84; MagDir 84; MagIndMarPl 82-83; WritMar 84*
Woman's Day Best Ideas for Christmas - New York, NY - *BaconPubCkMag 84; MagDir 84*
Woman's Day Decorating Guide - New York, NY - *MagDir 84*
Woman's Day Granny Squares & Needlework - New York, NY - *BaconPubCkMag 84; MagDir 84*
Woman's Day Home Decorating Ideas - New York, NY - *BaconPubCkMag 84; MagDir 84*
Woman's Day 101 Gardening & Outdoor Ideas - New York, NY - *MagDir 84*
Woman's Day 101 Needlework & Sweater Ideas - New York, NY - *MagDir 84*
Woman's Day 101 Sweaters You Can Knit & Crochet - New York, NY - *MagDir 84*
Woman's Healthletter, The - Chicago, IL - *BaconPubCkMag 84*
Woman's Newspaper of Princeton Inc., The - Princeton, NJ - *LitMag&SmPr 83-84*
Woman's World [of Heinrich Bauer North American Inc.] - Englewood, NJ - *BaconPubCkMag 84; MagIndMarPl 82-83; WritMar 84*
Womanshare Books - Grants Pass, OR - *BoPubDir 4, 5*
Womanspirit - Wolf Creek, OR - *LitMag&SmPr 83-84*
Wombat Enterprises Unltd. - Latham, NY - *BoPubDir 5*
Wombat Press - Wolfville, NS, Canada - *BoPubDir 4, 5*
Wombat Productions Inc. - Ossining, NY - *AvMarPl 83*
WOMC-FM - Detroit, MI - *BrCabYB 84; NatRadPubDir Summer 83, Spring 84*
WOMC-FM - Ferndale, MI - *TV&RadDir 84*
Women: A Journal of Liberation - Baltimore, MD - *LitMag&SmPr 83-84*
Women & Literature Collective - Cambridge, MA - *BoPubDir 4, 5*
Women & Their Work Inc. - Austin, TX - *BoPubDir 4, 5*
Women Artists News [of Midmarch Associates] - New York, NY - *LitMag&SmPr 83-84; WritMar 84*
Women for Sobriety Inc. - Quakertown, PA - *BoPubDir 4 Sup, 5*
Women in Business [of The ABWA Co. Inc.] - Kansas City, MO - *ArtMar 84; BaconPubCkMag 84; MagDir 84; MagIndMarPl 82-83; WritMar 84*
Women in Communications Inc. - Austin, TX - *BoPubDir 5*
Women in Data-Processing Inc. - New York, NY - *ADAPSOMemDir 83-84*
Women-in-Literature Inc. - Reno, NV - *BoPubDir 4, 5; LitMag&SmPr 83-84*
Women in Sports [of University of Alberta] - Edmonton, AB, Canada - *DataDirOnSer 84*
Women in the Arts Bulletin/Newsletter - New York, NY - *LitMag&SmPr 83-84*
Women in the Arts Foundation - New York, NY - *BoPubDir 4, 5; LitMag&SmPr 83-84*
Women Library Workers - Berkeley, CA - *LitMag&SmPr 83-84*
Women on Words & Images - Princeton, NJ - *BoPubDir 4, 5*
Women Talking, Women Listening - Dublin, CA - *BoPubDir 4, 5*
Women Writing Press - Newfield, NY - *BoPubDir 4, 5*
Women's Action Alliance Inc. - New York, NY - *BoPubDir 4, 5*
Women's Aglow Fellowship - Lynnwood, WA - *LitMarPl 83, 84*
Women's Channel, The - Tulsa, OK - *BrCabYB 84*
Women's Circle - Seabrook, NH - *BaconPubCkMag 84; MagDir 84; WritMar 84*
Women's Circle Home Cooking - Brooksville, FL - *ArtMar 84; WritMar 84*
Women's Crisis Center - Ann Arbor, MI - *BoPubDir 4, 5*
Women's Educational Equity Communications Network [of Far West Laboratory for Educational Research & Development] - San Francisco, CA - *FBInfSer 80*
Women's Educational Press - Toronto, ON, Canada - *BoPubDir 4; LitMag&SmPr 83-84; LitMarPl 84*
Women's Equity Action League - Washington, DC - *BoPubDir 4, 5*
Women's History Research Center [Aff. of National Clearinghouse on Marital Rape] - Berkeley, CA - *BoPubDir 4, 5; FBInfSer 80; MicroMarPl 82-83*
Women's Information Exchange - San Francisco, CA - *EISS 83*
Women's Institute for Freedom of the Press - Washington, DC - *BoPubDir 4, 5; LitMag&SmPr 83-84*
Women's Institutes of Lanark County - Almonte, ON, Canada - *BoPubDir 4 Sup, 5*
Women's Institutes of Nova Scotia - Truro, NS, Canada - *BoPubDir 4, 5*
Women's Interart Center, The - New York, NY - *AvMarPl 83*
Women's International League for Peace & Freedom (U.S. Section) - Philadelphia, PA - *BoPubDir 4 Sup, 5*
Women's League Outlook - New York, NY - *MagDir 84; MagIndMarPl 82-83*
Women's Occupational Health Resource Center [of Columbia University] - New York, NY - *EISS 83*
Women's Press - Toronto, ON, Canada - *LitMag&SmPr 83-84*
Women's Research Action Project - Roslindale, MA - *BoPubDir 4, 5*
Women's Resources Distribution Co. - Philadelphia, PA - *LitMarPl 84*
Women's Resources Inc. - Philadelphia, PA - *BoPubDir 4, 5*
Women's Rights Law Reporter - Newark, NJ - *LitMag&SmPr 83-84; WritMar 84*
Women's Sports Magazine - Palo Alto, CA - *BaconPubCkMag 84; MagDir 84; MagIndMarPl 82-83; WritMar 84*

Women's Studies Quarterly [of The Feminist Press] - Old Westbury, NY - *LitMag&SmPr 83-84*
Women's Studio Workshop Print Center - Rosendale, NY - *LitMag&SmPr 83-84*
Women's Symphony League Publications [Aff. of Women's Symphony League of Austin] - Austin, TX - *BoPubDir 4, 5*
Women's Wear Daily [of Fairchild Publications] - New York, NY - *BaconPubCkMag 84; Ed&PubIntYB 82; Folio 83; WritMar 84*
Women's Works in Review - New York, NY - *LitMag&SmPr 83-84*
Women's World [of B'nai B'rith Women Inc.] - Washington, DC - *WritMar 84*
Womensports - New York, NY - *MagDir 84*
Wometco Cable TV Inc. - Miami, FL - *BrCabYB 84 p.D-310; CabTVFinDB 83; LitMarPl 84; Tel&CabFB 84C p.1713*
Wometco Cable TV of Alabama Inc. - Daleville, AL - *Tel&CabFB 84C*
Wometco Cable TV of Clayton County Inc. - Clayton County, GA - *BrCabYB 84*
Wometco Cable TV of Cobb County Inc. - Marietta, GA - *BrCabYB 84; Tel&CabFB 84C*
Wometco Cable TV of Fayette County - Fayette County, GA - *BrCabYB 84*
Wometco Cable TV of Fulton County Inc. - Hapeville, GA - *BrCabYB 84; Tel&CabFB 84C*
Wometco Cable TV of Georgia Inc. - Douglas County, GA - *BrCabYB 84*
Wometco Cable TV of Georgia Inc. - Douglasville, GA - *Tel&CabFB 84C*
Wometco Cable TV of Georgia Inc. - Gwinnett County, GA - *Tel&CabFB 84C*
Wometco Cable TV of Georgia Inc. - Kennesaw, GA - *BrCabYB 84*
Wometco Cable TV of Rockdale County Inc. - Conyers, GA - *BrCabYB 84; Tel&CabFB 84C*
Wometco Enterprises - Miami, FL - *AdAge 6-28-84; BrCabYB 84; HomeVid&CabYB 82-83; KnowInd 83; Tel&CabFB 84S*
Wometco Enterprises Inc. - Fairfield, NJ - *HomeVid&CabYB 82-83*
Wometco Film Laboratories - Miami, FL - *Tel&CabFB 84C*
Wometco Home Theatre [of Wometco Enterprises] - Fairfield, NJ - *CabTVPrDB 83; TelAl 83; Tel&CabFB 84C*
WOMI - Owensboro, KY - *BrCabYB 84; TV&RadDir 84*
WOMP - Bellaire, OH - *BrCabYB 84; TV&RadDir 84*
WOMP-FM - Bellaire, OH - *BrCabYB 84; TV&RadDir 84*
WOMR - Provincetown, MA - *BrCabYB 84*
WOMT - Manitowoc, WI - *BrCabYB 84; TV&RadDir 84*
WONA - Winona, MS - *BrCabYB 84; TV&RadDir 84*
WONA-FM - Winona, MS - *BrCabYB 84; TV&RadDir 84*
WONC-FM - Naperville, IL - *BrCabYB 84; TV&RadDir 84*
WOND - Atlantic City, NJ - *NatRadPubDir Summer 83 p.157, Spring 84*
WOND - Pleasantville, NJ - *BrCabYB 84; TV&RadDir 84*
Wonder Time - Kansas City, MO - *WritMar 84*
Wonderland Music Co. Inc. - *See* Disney Music Co., Walt
Wondirection Records - Burbank, CA - *BillIntBG 83-84*
WONE - Dayton, OH - *BrCabYB 84; NatRadPubDir Summer 83, Spring 84; TV&RadDir 84*
Wonewoc Reporter - Wonewoc, WI - *BaconPubCkNews 84; Ed&PubIntYB 82*
Wong, Jeanyee - New York, NY - *LitMarPl 83, 84; MagIndMarPl 82-83*
WONN - Lakeland, FL - *BrCabYB 84; NatRadPubDir Summer 83, Spring 84; TV&RadDir 84*
WONO - Black Mountain, NC - *BrCabYB 84; TV&RadDir 84*
WONO-FM - Syracuse, NY - *NatRadPubDir Summer 83*
WONT - Ontanagon, MI - *BrCabYB 84*
WONW - Defiance, OH - *BrCabYB 84; TV&RadDir 84*
WONX - Evanston, IL - *BrCabYB 84; TV&RadDir 84*
WONY-FM - Oneonta, NY - *BrCabYB 84; NatRadPubDir Summer 83, Spring 84; TV&RadDir 84*
WOOD - Grand Rapids, MI - *BrCabYB 84; NatRadPubDir Summer 83, Spring 84; TV&RadDir 84*
WOOD [of Royal Institute of Technology Library] - Stockholm, Sweden - *CompReadDB 82*
Wood & Associates, Ben - Wheaton, IL - *DirMarMP 83; LitMarPl 83, 84*
Wood & Clay - San Jose, CA - *MicrocomMPl 84*
Wood & Cohen Inc. - Tampa, FL - *StaDirAdAg 2-84*
Wood & Fiber Science - Washington, DC - *BaconPubCkMag 84*
Wood & Mitchell Advertising Ltd. - Wellington, New Zealand - *StaDirAdAg 2-84*
Wood & Wood Products - Chicago, IL - *MagDir 84; WritMar 84*
Wood & Wood Products - Lincolnshire, IL - *BaconPubCkMag 84*
Wood Books, Kerry - Red Deer, AB, Canada - *BoPubDir 4, 5*
WOOD Broadcasting Inc. - Grand Rapids, MI - *BrCabYB 84*
Wood County Democrat - Quitman, TX - *AyerDirPub 83; Ed&PubIntYB 82*
Wood County Telephone Co. - Wisconsin Rapids, WI - *TelDir&BG 83-84*
Wood Dale Chronicle, The - Wood Dale, IL - *Ed&PubIntYB 82*
WOOD-FM - Grand Rapids, MI - *BrCabYB 84; NatRadPubDir Summer 83, Spring 84; TV&RadDir 84*
Wood Ibis [of Place of Herons Press] - Austin, TX - *LitMag&SmPr 83-84*
Wood Inc., Cranford - New York, NY - *MagIndMarPl 82-83*
Wood Institute for the History of Medicine, Francis Clark [Aff. of College of Physicians of Philadelphia] - Philadelphia, PA - *BoPubDir 5*
Wood Lake Books Inc. - Winfield, BC, Canada - *BoPubDir 5*
Wood Lake News - Wood Lake, MN - *BaconPubCkNews 84; Ed&PubIntYB 82*
Wood Moulding & Millwork Producers Inc. - Portland, OR - *BoPubDir 5*
Wood Music, Curtis - Nashville, TN - *BillIntBG 83-84*
Wood 'n Energy - Concord, NH - *BaconPubCkMag 84*
Wood 'n Music Inc. - New York, NY - *BillIntBG 83-84*
Wood/Nature Alaska Photographic, Dick - Fairbanks, AK - *MagIndMarPl 82-83*
Wood Press Inc. - Paterson, NJ - *MagIndMarPl 82-83*
Wood, Richard D. - Kingston, RI - *BoPubDir 4, 5*
Wood Ridge Independent - Wood Ridge, NJ - *BaconPubCkNews 84; Ed&PubIntYB 82*
Wood River Journal - Hailey, ID - *AyerDirPub 83; Ed&PubIntYB 82*
Wood River Journal - Alton, IL - *AyerDirPub 83*
Wood River Journal - *See* Alton Citizen Inc.
Wood River Sunbeam - Wood River, NE - *BaconPubCkNews 84; Ed&PubIntYB 82*
Wood Television Corp. - Bowling Green, OH - *BrCabYB 84*
Wood TV Corp. - Bowling Green, OH - *Tel&CabFB 84C p.1714*
Woodall, Dr. Stella - Junction, TX - *LitMag&SmPr 83-84*
Woodall Publishing Co. - Highland Park, IL - *BoPubDir 4, 5; DirMarMP 83*
Woodall Stations, W. C. Jr. - Blakely, GA - *BrCabYB 84*
Woodall's Campground Management - Highland Park, IL - *BaconPubCkMag 84; MagDir 84*
Woodard Associates Inc. - Hartford, CT - *StaDirAdAg 2-84*
Woodard Associates Inc., Charles - Hastings-on-Hudson, NY - *CabTVFinDB 83*
Woodard, Eggers & Schaffer Inc. - East Hartford, CT - *DirMarMP 83*
Woodbine Twiner - Woodbine, IA - *AyerDirPub 83; BaconPubCkNews 84; Ed&PubIntYB 82*
Woodbridge Advertising - New Windsor, NY - *StaDirAdAg 2-84*
Woodbridge & Vaughan News - Woodbridge, ON, Canada - *Ed&PubIntYB 82*
Woodbridge Associates - Nanuet, NY - *LitMarPl 84*
Woodbridge Press Publishing Co. - Santa Barbara, CA - *LitMarPl 83, 84; WritMar 84*
Woodburn Cable TV Associates [of Northland Communications Corp.] - Woodburn, OR - *Tel&CabFB 84C*
Woodburn Independent - Woodburn, OR - *BaconPubCkNews 84; Ed&PubIntYB 82*
Woodbury Business Forms Inc. - La Grange, GA - *DataDirSup 7-83*
Woodbury Cannon Courier - Woodbury, TN - *BaconPubCkNews 84*
Woodbury-Deptford Spirit - Woodbury, NJ - *Ed&PubIntYB 82*

Woodbury Gloucester County Times - Woodbury, NJ - *NewsDir 84*
Woodbury, H. L. - Frisco, TX - *Tel&CabFB 84C*
Woodbury Press - Litchfield, ME - *BoPubDir 5*
Woodbury Record Spirit - *See* Cam-Glo Newspapers Inc.
Woodbury Review - *See* Lillie Suburban Newspapers
Woodbury Telephone Co., The - Woodbury, CT - *TelDir&BG 83-84*
Woodcock Press - Santa Rosa, CA - *BoPubDir 5; LitMag&SmPr 83-84*
Woodcock Publications - Pacific Grove, CA - *BoPubDir 4, 5*
Wooden Bear Music - *See* Big Heart Music Inc.
Wooden Boat - Brooklin, ME - *BaconPubCkMag 84*
Wooden Nickel Music Inc. - Beverly Hills, CA - *BillIntBG 83-84*
Wooden Nickel Records - Beverly Hills, CA - *BillIntBG 83-84*
Wooden Nutmeg Press - Bridgeport, CT - *BoPubDir 4, 5*
Woodenboat - Brooklin, ME - *ArtMar 84; MagIndMarPl 82-83; WritMar 84*
Woodford County Journal - Eureka, IL - *AyerDirPub 83; Ed&PubIntYB 82*
Woodford Memorial Editions Inc. - Seattle, WA - *BoPubDir 4, 5*
Woodford Music, Terry - *See* I've Got the Music Co.
Woodford Publishing Co. - Metamora, IL - *BaconPubCkNews 84*
Woodford Sun - Versailles, KY - *AyerDirPub 83; Ed&PubIntYB 82*
Woodglen Publications - Houston, TX - *BillIntBG 83-84*
Woodhaven Leader-Observer - Woodhaven, NY - *BaconPubCkNews 84*
Woodhaven News-Herald - Wyandotte, MI - *AyerDirPub 83*
Woodhaven News-Herald - *See* News-Herald Newspapers
Woodhull Community Telephone Co. - Woodhull, IL - *TelDir&BG 83-84*
Woodhull TV - Woodhull, NY - *BrCabYB 84*
Wooding & Housley - Providence, RI - *AdAge 3-28-84; DirPRFirms 83; StaDirAdAg 2-84*
Woodinville Citizen - Woodinville, WA - *BaconPubCkNews 84*
Woodinville Weekly & Northlake News - Woodinville, WA - *BaconPubCkNews 84*
Woodlake Echo - Woodlake, CA - *AyerDirPub 83; Ed&PubIntYB 82*
Woodlake Echo - *See* Mineral King Publishing
Woodland California Farm Observer, The - Woodland, CA - *NewsDir 84*
Woodland Farm Observer - Woodland, CA - *Ed&PubIntYB 82*
Woodland Hills Music Press - *See* Bock Music Co., Fred
Woodland Hills Times - Encino, CA - *AyerDirPub 83*
Woodland Hills Times - *See* Associated Valley Publications
Woodland Lewis River News - Woodland, WA - *BaconPubCkNews 84*
Woodland Park Ute Pass Courier - Woodland Park, CO - *BaconPubCkNews 84*
Woodland Publishing - Peterborough, ON, Canada - *BoPubDir 4 Sup, 5*
Woodland Publishing Co. Inc. - Wayzata, MN - *BoPubDir 4, 5*
Woodland Sun - *See* Houston Community Newspapers
Woodlands CATV [of Woodlands Venture Corp.] - The Woodlands, TX - *BrCabYB 84; Tel&CabFB 84C*
Woodlands Communication Network, The [Aff. of Mitchell Energy & Development Corp.] - The Woodlands, TX - *InterCabHB 3*
Woodlands Sun, The - Woodlands, TX - *Ed&PubIntYB 82*
Woodley Co. Inc., The Albert - New York, NY - *StaDirAdAg 2-84*
Woodman, Arthur W. - Canaan, NH - *LitMarPl 83, 84*
Woodman TV Cable System - Woodman, WI - *BrCabYB 84; Tel&CabFB 84C*
Woodmen of the World Magazine - Omaha, NE - *ArtMar 84; BaconPubCkMag 84; MagDir 84; MagIndMarPl 82-83; WritMar 84*
Woodmont Press - Green Village, NJ - *BoPubDir 4 Sup, 5*
Wood'n Music Inc. - New York, NY - *BillIntBG 83-84*
Woodrich Publishing Co. - Lexington, AL - *BillIntBG 83-84*
Woodridge Progress - Downers Grove, IL - *AyerDirPub 83; NewsDir 84*
Woodridge Progress - Woodridge, IL - *Ed&PubIntYB 82*
Woodridge Progress - *See* Reporter Progress Newspapers
Woodridge Suburban Life Graphic - *See* Life Printing & Publishing Co.
Woodridge Wire TV Co. [of Simmons Communications Inc.] - Woodridge, NY - *BrCabYB 84*
Woodrose - Waupaca, WI - *LitMag&SmPr 83-84*
Woodrose Editions - Waupaca, WI - *LitMag&SmPr 83-84*
Woodrose Fine Arts - Arcata, CA - *ArtMar 84*
Woodrow Evangelistic Association Inc., Ralph - Riverside, CA - *BoPubDir 4, 5*
Woodruff Cablevision - Washington, DC - *BrCabYB 84*
Woodruff News - Woodruff, SC - *BaconPubCkNews 84; Ed&PubIntYB 82*
Woodrum & Staff Ltd. - Honolulu, HI - *StaDirAdAg 2-84*
Woods Advertising Inc. - Jericho, NY - *StaDirAdAg 2-84*
Woods Books - Los Angeles, CA - *BoPubDir 4*
Woods Brothers Agency, The - Little Rock, AR - *StaDirAdAg 2-84*
Woods, Charles - *See* WTVY
Woods County Enterprise - Waynoka, OK - *Ed&PubIntYB 82*
Woods County Enterprise & Waynoka News - Waynoka, OK - *AyerDirPub 83*
Woods County News - Alva, OK - *Ed&PubIntYB 82*
Woods County News - Anadarko, OK - *AyerDirPub 83*
Woods Hole Data Base Inc. - Woods Hole, MA - *EISS 5-84 Sup*
Woods Hole Press - Woods Hole, MA - *BoPubDir 4, 5; LitMag&SmPr 83-84*
Woods Library Publishing Co. - Evergreen Park, IL - *BoPubDir 4, 5*
Woods, Miriam - New York, NY - *LitMarPl 83, 84; MagIndMarPl 82-83*
Woods Music & Books Publishing - Los Angeles, CA - *BoPubDir 5*
Woods Publications - Austin, TX - *BoPubDir 5*
Woods Publishing Co., Curtis L. - North Wilkesboro, NC - *BillIntBG 83-84*
Woodsfield Cable Co. - Woodsfield, OH - *BrCabYB 84; Tel&CabFB 84C*
Woodsfield Cable Co. Inc. - Sarahsville, OH - *Tel&CabFB 84C*
Woodsfield Monroe County Beacon - Woodsfield, OH - *BaconPubCkNews 84; NewsDir 84*
Woodsfield Spirit of Democracy - Woodsfield, OH - *BaconPubCkNews 84*
Woodside Herald - Long Island City, NY - *AyerDirPub 83; Ed&PubIntYB 82*
Woodside Herald - Sunnyside, NY - *NewsDir 84*
Woodside Publishing - *See* Miles Publishing Co., Earl
Woodsmoke [of Highland Publishing Co.] - Centerville, UT - *WritMar 84*
Woodsocket News - Woodsocket, SD - *BaconPubCkNews 84*
Woodson Newspapers Inc. - Brownwood, TX - *Ed&PubIntYB 82*
Woodsong Graphics - New Hope, PA - *WritMar 84*
Woodstock Community TV Ltd. - Woodstock, NB, Canada - *BrCabYB 84*
Woodstock News-Leader [of Free Press Inc.] - Woodstock, IL - *NewsDir 84*
Woodstock News Leader - *See* Free Press Inc.
Woodstock Shenandoah Valley Herald - Woodstock, VA - *BaconPubCkNews 84*
Woodstock Telephone Co. - Ruthton, MN - *TelDir&BG 83-84*
Woodstock Ulster County Townsman - Woodstock, NY - *BaconPubCkNews 84; NewsDir 84*
Woodstock Vermont Standard - Woodstock, VT - *BaconPubCkNews 84*
Woodstone Books - Albuquerque, NM - *BoPubDir 4, 5*
Woodville Leader - Woodville, WI - *BaconPubCkNews 84; Ed&PubIntYB 82*
Woodville Leon County News - *See* News Publishing
Woodville Republican - Woodville, MS - *BaconPubCkNews 84; Ed&PubIntYB 82*
Woodville TV Cable Co. - Woodville, AL - *Tel&CabFB 84C*
Woodville Tyler County Booster - Woodville, TX - *BaconPubCkNews 84; NewsDir 84*
Woodville Woodsman - Woodville, TX - *BaconPubCkNews 84*
Woodward & Schaefer Inc. [Subs. of Schaefer Advertising] - Valley Forge, PA - *DirPRFirms 83*
Woodward Books - Corte Madera, CA - *BoPubDir 4, 5*
Woodward Cable TV [of American Television & Communications Corp.] - Woodward, OK - *BrCabYB 84; Tel&CabFB 84C*
Woodward, Claire - Sun City, AZ - *BoPubDir 5*

Woodward Communications Inc. - Dubuque, IA - *BrCabYB 84*
Woodward Daily Press [of Oklahoma Press Service] - Woodward, OK - *BaconPubCkNews 84; Ed&PubIntYB 82; NewsDir 84*
Woodward Enterprise - *See* Northeast Dallas County Record
Woodward Journal - Woodward, OK - *Ed&PubIntYB 82; NewsDir 84*
Woodward Mutual Telephone Co. - Woodward, IA - *TelDir&BG 83-84*
Woodward Northeast Dallas County Record - Woodward, IA - *BaconPubCkNews 84*
Woodward Northwest Sun-Journal - Woodward, OK - *BaconPubCkNews 84*
Woodward, Ryan, Sharp & Davis - New York, NY - *DataDirOnSer 84*
Woodwind-Brass & Percussion - Deposit, NY - *MagIndMarPl 82-83*
Woodwork Corp. of America - Chicago, IL - *DirInfWP 82*
Woodworker's Journal, The [of Madrigal Publishing Co. Inc.] - New Milford, CT - *WritMar 84*
Woodworking & Furniture Digest - Wheaton, IL - *MagDir 84*
Woodworking Machinery Manufacturers of America - Philadelphia, PA - *BoPubDir 5*
Woody, W. Jasper - Benton, TN - *BrCabYB 84*
WOOF - Dothan, AL - *BrCabYB 84; TV&RadDir 84*
WOOF-FM - Dothan, AL - *BrCabYB 84; TV&RadDir 84*
WOOJ-FM - Lehigh Acres, FL - *BrCabYB 84*
WOOK-FM - Washington, DC - *BrCabYB 84; NatRadPubDir Summer 83, Spring 84; TV&RadDir 84*
Wool Sack, The - Brookings, SD - *BaconPubCkMag 84; MagDir 84*
Woolf Advertising Inc. - Los Angeles, CA - *ArtMar 84; StaDirAdAg 2-84*
Woolf List Co., Fred - Hartsdale, NY - *LitMarPl 83, 84; MagIndMarPl 82-83*
Woolf Quarterly Press, Virginia - San Isidro, CA - *BoPubDir 4, 5*
Woolf-Reitman Associates Inc. - Chicago, IL - *StaDirAdAg 2-84*
Woolf Software Systems - Canoga Park, CA - *MicrocomMPl 84; MicrocomSwDir 1*
Woollard Advertising - Boston, MA - *DirMarMP 83*
Woolley & Co. Inc., Frank - Reading, PA - *AvMarPl 83*
Woolmer/Brotherson Ltd. - Revere, PA - *BoPubDir 4, 5*
Woolstock Mutual Telephone Association - Woolstock, IA - *TelDir&BG 83-84*
Woonsocket Artesian Commonwealth - Woonsocket, SD - *BaconPubCkNews 84*
Woonsocket Call - Woonsocket, RI - *BaconPubCkNews 84; BrCabYB 84; NewsDir 84*
Woonsocket Call & Evening Reporter - Woonsocket, RI - *Ed&PubIntYB 82*
Woonsocket News - Woonsocket, SD - *Ed&PubIntYB 82*
WOOR-FM - Oxford, MS - *BrCabYB 84; TV&RadDir 84*
WOOS-FM - Canton, OH - *BrCabYB 84; TV&RadDir 84*
Wooster Daily Record - Wooster, OH - *NewsDir 84*
Wooster Mid Ohio Farmer - Wooster, OH - *BaconPubCkNews 84*
Wooton, Roger - Paducah, TX - *Tel&CabFB 84C p.1714*
Wootton Jeffreys & Partners - Woking, England - *MicrocomSwDir 1*
WOOW - Greenville, NC - *BrCabYB 84; TV&RadDir 84*
WOPA - Chicago, IL - *NatRadPubDir Summer 83 p.83, Spring 84 p.83*
WOPA - Oak Park, IL - *BrCabYB 84; TV&RadDir 84*
WOPC - Altoona, PA - *BrCabYB 84; TelAl 84; Tel&CabFB 84S*
WOPC - Dysart, PA - *TelAl 83*
WOPC - Johnstown, PA - *DirUSTelSta 83*
WOPC-TV - Altoona, PA - *TV&RadDir 84*
WOPI - Bristol, TN - *BrCabYB 84; NatRadPubDir Summer 83, Spring 84; TV&RadDir 84*
WOPP - Opp, AL - *BrCabYB 84; TV&RadDir 84*
WOPR-FM - Oak Park, MI - *BrCabYB 84; NatRadPubDir Summer 83, Spring 84*
WOQI - Ponce, PR - *BrCabYB 84*
WOQP - Greenville, TN - *BrCabYB 84*
WOR [of RKO General] - New York, NY - *BrCabYB 84; HomeVid&CabYB 82-83; LitMarPl 83, 84; NatRadPubDir Summer 83, Spring 84; TV&RadDir 84*
WOR-TV - Seacaucus, NJ - *BrCabYB 84*
WOR-TV - New York, NY - *DirUSTelSta 83; LitMarPl 83, 84; TelAl 83, 84; Tel&CabFB 84S; TV&RadDir 84*
WOR-TV - Syracuse, NY - *BrCabYB 84; CabTVPrDB 83; Tel&CabFB 84C*
WORA-TV - Mayaguez, PR - *BrCabYB 84; Tel&CabFB 84S*
WORB - Farmington Hills, MI - *BrCabYB 84*
WORC - Worcester, MA - *BrCabYB 84; NatRadPubDir Summer 83, Spring 84; TV&RadDir 84*
Worcester Area Cooperating Libraries - Worcester, MA - *EISS 83*
Worcester Art Museum - Worcester, MA - *BoPubDir 4, 5*
Worcester Catholic Free Press, The - Worcester, MA - *NewsDir 84*
Worcester County East - Shrewsbury, MA - *Ed&PubIntYB 82*
Worcester County Messenger [of Atlantic Publications Inc.] - Pocomoke City, MD - *AyerDirPub 83; Ed&PubIntYB 82; NewsDir 84*
Worcester County North - Boylston, MA - *Ed&PubIntYB 82*
Worcester Evening Gazette - Worcester, MA - *BaconPubCkNews 84*
Worcester Magazine - Worcester, MA - *ArtMar 84; WritMar 84*
Worcester Manufacturing Co. - Timonium, MD - *DirInfWP 82*
Worcester News Recorder/Suburban Review - Worcester, MA - *NewsDir 84*
Worcester Southbridge-Webster Hometown - Southbridge/Webster, MA - *Ed&PubIntYB 82*
Worcester Telegram - Worcester, ME - *NewsDir 84*
Worcester Telegram - Worcester, MA - *BaconPubCkNews 84; Ed&PubIntYB 82; LitMarPl 83, 84; NewsBur 6*
Worcester Telegram & Gazette Inc. - Worcester, MA - *BrCabYB 84; Ed&PubIntYB 82*
Worcester Times & Schenevus Monitor, The - Worcester, NY - *Ed&PubIntYB 82*
Worcester Video Inc. - Worcester, NY - *Tel&CabFB 84C*
WORD - Spartanburg, SC - *BrCabYB 84; NatRadPubDir Summer 83, Spring 84; TV&RadDir 84*
Word Algebra Inc. - Chicago, IL - *DirInfWP 82*
Word Associates - San Francisco, CA - *MicrocomMPl 84*
Word Beat - Tallahassee, FL - *LitMag&SmPr 83-84*
Word Beat Press - Tallahassee, FL - *BoPubDir 4 Sup, 5; LitMag&SmPr 83-84*
Word Book Club [Subs. of ABC Publishing Inc.] - Waco, TX - *LitMarPl 83, 84*
Word Craft Publishing Co. Inc. - Birmingham, AL - *BoPubDir 4, 5*
Word Direct Marketing Services Inc. [Subs. of Word Inc.] - Waco, TX - *DirMarMP 83*
Word Directions Ltd. - Ottawa, ON, Canada - *DirInfWP 82*
Word Factory - San Diego, CA - *BoPubDir 4 Sup, 5*
Word Foundation Inc. - Dallas, TX - *BoPubDir 4, 5*
Word/Fraction Math Aid Co. - Woodland Hills, CA - *BoPubDir 4, 5*
Word Inc. [Subs. of American Broadcasting Co.] - Waco, TX - *BillIntBG 83-84; LitMarPl 83, 84*
Word Loom - Winnipeg, MB, Canada - *LitMag&SmPr 83-84*
Word Movers Inc. - Elmhurst, NY - *DirInfWP 82*
Word Mover...s Inc., The - Mississauga, ON, Canada - *DirInfWP 82*
Word Music - Waco, TX - *BillIntBG 83-84*
Word of Mouth Enterprises - Burbank, CA - *LitMag&SmPr 83-84*
Word of Mouth Press - Takoma Park, MD - *BoPubDir 5*
Word Power Inc. - Seattle, WA - *BoPubDir 4, 5; LitMag&SmPr 83-84*
Word Pro Services Ltd. - Winnipeg, MB, Canada - *DirInfWP 82*
Word Processing Bureau Inc. - Boston, MA - *DirInfWP 82*
Word Processing Group - Metairie, LA - *DirInfWP 82*
Word Processing International Ltd. - Ottawa, ON, Canada - *DirInfWP 82*
Word Processing News [of Word of Mouth Enterprises] - Burbank, CA - *LitMag&SmPr 83-84; MicrocomMPl 84; WritMar 84*
Word Processing/Office Systems - Fairport, NY - *DirInfWP 82*
Word Processing Personnel Consultants Ltd. - Toronto, ON, Canada - *DirInfWP 82*
Word Processing Service of Florida Inc. - Ft. Lauderdale, FL - *DirInfWP 82*
Word Processing Society Inc. - Milwaukee, WI - *EISS 83*

Word Processing Specialists Inc. - Hawthorne, NY - *DirInfWP 82*
Word Processing Technology Inc. - New York, NY - *DirInfWP 82*
Word Processors Inc. - Washington, DC - *DirInfWP 82*
Word Pros Inc. - Willow Grove, PA - *DirInfWP 82*
Word-Set Systems Ltd. - South Harrow, England - *MicrocomSwDir 1*
Word Shop Publications - San Diego, CA - *BoPubDir 4, 5*
Word, The - Milwaukee, WI - *BaconPubCkMag 84*
Word Weavers - Madison, WI - *LitMarPl 83, 84*
Word Weavers Manuscript Service - Madison, WI - *LitMarPl 83*
Word-Wise Advertising - New York, NY - *LitMarPl 83, 84; MagIndMarPl 82-83*
Word Works Inc. - Washington, DC - *BoPubDir 4, 5; LitMag&SmPr 83-84*
Wordcom - Harrisburg, PA - *DirInfWP 82*
Wordcom Centres Ltd. - Toronto, ON, Canada - *DirInfWP 82*
Wordex Corp. - San Leandro, CA - *DirInfWP 82*
Wordex Inc. - Willowdale, ON, Canada - *DirInfWP 82*
Wordflow Systems [Div. of DAK Supply Corp.] - Cleveland, OH - *DirInfWP 82*
Wordland - Santa Ana, CA - *LitMag&SmPr 83-84*
Wordoctor Publications - North Hollywood, CA - *BoPubDir 4, 5; LitMag&SmPr 83-84*
Wordplex - Westlake Village, CA - *DirInfWP 82*
WordPro - New City, NY - *DirInfWP 82*
WordPro Center - Plainview, NY - *DirInfWP 82*
WORDS [of Houghton Mifflin Co.] - Boston, MA - *EISS 83*
Words - Willow Grove, PA - *ArtMar 84; BaconPubCkMag 84*
Words & Photographs by Stephen Trimble - Flagstaff, AZ - *LitMarPl 84*
Words & Visions/WAV Magazine [of WAV Publications] - Magill, Australia - *LitMag&SmPr 83-84*
Words Associated - Wakefield, PQ, Canada - *BoPubDir 4 Sup, 5*
Words Ink - Flossmoor, IL - *DirInfWP 82*
Words of Wall Street - Princeton, NJ - *DirOnDB Spring 84*
Words of Wisdom Enterprises & Records - Indianapolis, IN - *BillIntBG 83-84*
Words/Pictures Corp. Ltd. - Calgary, AB, Canada - *BoPubDir 4, 5*
WordService - Toronto, ON, Canada - *DirInfWP 82*
Wordshare Inc. - Dallas, TX - *DirInfWP 82*
Wordsmith, The - Montclair, NJ - *LitMarPl 83, 84*
Wordstream Inc. - *See* Management Assistance Inc.
Wordsworks Inc., The - New York, NY - *StaDirAdAg 2-84*
Wordtree - Shawnee Mission, KS - *BoPubDir 4, 5; LitMag&SmPr 83-84*
Wordtronix Inc. - Minneapolis, MN - *DirInfWP 82; MicrocomMPl 84*
Wordworks - Richmond, CA - *BoPubDir 4; LitMarPl 83, 84*
Wordworks - Houston, TX - *BoPubDir 4, 5*
Wordworks West - San Francisco, CA - *DirPRFirms 83*
Wordworth Associates - Wellesley, MA - *LitMarPl 84*
Wordworth Associates (Editorial Services) - Wellesley, MA - *LitMarPl 83; MagIndMarPl 82-83*
Wordwrights - Honolulu, HI - *LitMarPl 83*
WORG - Orangeburg, SC - *TV&RadDir 84*
WORG-FM - Orangeburg, SC - *BrCabYB 84; TV&RadDir 84*
WORI - Oak Ridge, TN - *BrCabYB 84; NatRadPubDir Summer 83, Spring 84; TV&RadDir 84*
WORJ-FM - Mt. Dora, FL - *BrCabYB 84*
WORJ-FM - Orlando, FL - *NatRadPubDir Summer 83*
WORK - Barre, VT - *BrCabYB 84*
Work Boat, The - Covington, LA - *ArtMar 84; BaconPubCkMag 84; MagIndMarPl 82-83; WritMar 84*
Work Boat, The - Mandeville, LA - *MagDir 84*
WORK-FM - Barre, VT - *TV&RadDir 84*
Work in America Institute Inc. - Scarsdale, NY - *BoPubDir 4, 5*
Workbasket [of Modern Hand Craft Inc.] - Kansas City, MO - *BaconPubCkMag 84; Folio 83; MagDir 84; MagIndMarPl 82-83; WritMar 84*
Workbench [of Modern Handcraft Inc.] - Kansas City, MO - *ArtMar 84; BaconPubCkMag 84; LitMarPl 83, 84; MagDir 84; MagIndMarPl 82-83; WritMar 84*
Workbook, The [of Southwest Research & Information Center] - Albuquerque, NM - *LitMag&SmPr 83-84*
Worker's Union Music - *See* Shayne Enterprises, Larry
Working Classics [of Red Wheelbarrow Press] - San Francisco, CA - *LitMag&SmPr 83-84*
Working for Boys - Danvers, MA - *WritMar 84*
Working Medium, The - Evanston, IL - *AvMarPl 83*
Working Mother [of McCall Publishing Co.] - New York, NY - *ArtMar 84; BaconPubCkMag 84; Folio 83; MagIndMarPl 82-83; WritMar 84*
Working Papers Magazine - Cambridge, MA - *MagIndMarPl 82-83*
Working Press - Livermore, CA - *BoPubDir 4, 5; LitMag&SmPr 83-84*
Working Week Press - Norman, OK - *BoPubDir 4, 5*
Working Woman [of Hal Publications Inc.] - New York, NY - *BaconPubCkMag 84; DirMarMP 83; Folio 83; LitMarPl 83, 84; MagDir 84; MagIndMarPl 82-83; WritMar 84*
Workingman's Press - Seattle, WA - *BoPubDir 4, 5*
Workman Publishing Co. Inc. - New York, NY - *LitMarPl 83, 84*
Workmen's Circle (Book Dept.) - New York, NY - *BoPubDir 4, 5*
Works - Singapore, Singapore - *DirOnDB Spring 84*
Workshop Records - Austin, TX - *BillIntBG 83-84*
Workshop West - Beverly Hills, CA - *HBIndAd&MS 82-83; StaDirAdAg 2-84*
Workstation Alert - Boston, MA - *BaconPubCkMag 84*
Workstation/Saver News [of Architecture Technology Corp.] - Minneapolis, MN - *MicrocomMPl 84*
WORL - Orlando, FL - *BrCabYB 84; NatRadPubDir Summer 83, Spring 84*
Worland Cable TV [of Community Tele-Communications Inc.] - Worland, WY - *Tel&CabFB 84C*
Worland Northern Wyoming Daily News [of Big Horn Basin Newspapers Inc.] - Worland, WY - *NewsDir 84*
World - Birmingham, AL - *Ed&PubIntYB 82*
World - Helena, AR - *AyerDirPub 83*
World - Spencer, IN - *AyerDirPub 83*
World - Everest, KS - *AyerDirPub 83*
World - Hiawatha, KS - *AyerDirPub 83*
World - Wilson, KS - *AyerDirPub 83*
World - Opelousas, LA - *AyerDirPub 83*
World - Staples, MN - *AyerDirPub 83*
World - Leigh, NE - *AyerDirPub 83*
World [of Multinational Computer Models Inc.] - Montclair, NJ - *DataDirOnSer 84; DirOnDB Spring 84*
World - Devils Lake, ND - *AyerDirPub 83*
World - Tulsa, OK - *AyerDirPub 83*
World - Yukon, OK - *AyerDirPub 83*
World - Aberdeen, WA - *AyerDirPub 83*
World - Wenatchee, WA - *AyerDirPub 83*
World Affairs Report [of Dialog Information Services Inc.] - Palo Alto, CA - *DataDirOnSer 84*
World Affairs Report [of California Institute of International Studies] - Stanford, CA - *DirOnDB Spring 84; EISS 83*
World Agricultural Economics & Rural Sociology Abstracts [of Commonwealth Bureau of Agricultural Economics] - Oxford, England - *CompReadDB 82*
World Agriculture Supply & Disposition [of Chase Econometrics/Interactive Data Corp.] - Waltham, MA - *DataDirOnSer 84; DBBus 82*
World Agriculture Supply & Disposition - Bala Cynwyd, PA - *DirOnDB Spring 84*
World Almanac Education Div., The [of United Media Enterprises] - Cleveland, OH - *DirMarMP 83*
World Almanac Publications [Div. of Newspaper Enterprise Association] - New York, NY - *LitMarPl 84; WritMar 84*
World Almanac, The [Div. of Newspaper Enterprise Association] - New York, NY - *LitMarPl 83*
World Aluminum Abstracts [of Aluminum Association] - Washington, DC - *EISS 83*
World Aluminum Abstracts [of American Society for Metals] - Metals Park, OH - *CompReadDB 82; DBBus 82; DirOnDB Spring 84; OnBibDB 3*
World Aluminum Abstracts [of QL Systems Ltd.] - Ottawa, ON, Canada - *DataDirOnSer 84*
World Artist Music Co. Inc. - *See* Cherry Lane Music Publishing Co. Inc.

World Aviation Directory [of Business Publications] - Washington, DC - *MagDir 84*
World Bank - Washington, DC - *BoPubDir 4, 5*
World Bank Debt Tables - Bala Cynwyd, PA - *DirOnDB Spring 84*
World Bank Debt Tables [of I. P. Sharp Associates Ltd.] - Toronto, ON, Canada - *DataDirOnSer 84; DBBus 82*
World Bank of Licensable Technology [of Dr. Dvorkovitz & Associates] - Ormond Beach, FL - *CompReadDB 82; DataDirOnSer 84*
World Bible Publishers Inc. [Subs. of Riverside Book & Bible House] - Iowa Falls, IA - *LitMarPl 83, 84*
World Book [Subs. of The Scott & Fetzer Co.] - Chicago, IL - *LitMarPl 83, 84*
World Book Encyclopedia Inc. [Subs. of World Book-Childcraft International Inc.] - Chicago, IL - *DirMarMP 83*
World Books - Albuquerque, NM - *BoPubDir 4, 5*
World Business Digest - New York, NY - *MagIndMarPl 82-83*
World Cablevision [of Omni Cable TV Corp.] - Centralia, IL - *BrCabYB 84*
World Cablevision [of Omni Cable TV Corp.] - Mt. Vernon, IL - *BrCabYB 84*
World Clippings Div. [of Microfacts] - Detroit, MI - *ProGuPRSer 4*
World Coal - San Francisco, CA - *BaconPubCkMag 84; MagDir 84*
World Coal Resources & Reserves Data Bank [of Organisation for Economic Co-Operation & Development] - London, England - *EISS 83*
World Coffee & Tea [of McKeand Publications Inc.] - West Haven, CT - *BaconPubCkMag 84; MagDir 84*
World Coin News [of Krause Publications] - Iola, WI - *MagDir 84; MagIndMarPl 82-83; WritMar 84*
World Color Press [Subs. of City Investing Co.] - New York, NY - *MagIndMarPl 82-83*
World Communications Syndicate - Buffalo, NY - *Ed&PubIntYB 82*
World Co. - Lawrence, KS - *Tel&CabFB 84C p.1714*
World Composition Services Inc. - New York, NY - *MagIndMarPl 82-83*
World Conference on Religion & Peace - New York, NY - *BoPubDir 4, 5*
World Construction [of Dun & Bradstreet Corp.] - New York, NY - *BaconPubCkMag 84; MagDir 84; MagIndMarPl 82-83; WritMar 84*
World Convention Dates [of Hendrickson Publishing Co. Inc.] - Hempstead, NY - *BaconPubCkMag 84; MagDir 84*
World Data Center A - Washington, DC - *EISS 83*
World Data Center A - Glaciology - Boulder, CO - *EISS 83*
World Data Center A - Glaciology (Cooperative Institute for Research in Environmental Sciences) - Boulder, CO - *CompReadDB 82*
World Data Center A - Marine Geology & Geophysics - Boulder, CO - *EISS 83*
World Data Center A - Meteorology & Nuclear Radiation - Asheville, NC - *EISS 83*
World Data Center A - Oceanography - Washington, DC - *EISS 83*
World Data Center A - Rockets & Satellites - Greenbelt, MD - *EISS 83*
World Data Center A - Rotation of the Earth - Washington, DC - *EISS 83*
World Data Center A - Solar-Terrestrial Physics - Boulder, CO - *EISS 83*
World Data Center A - Solid Earth Geophysics - Boulder, CO - *EISS 83*
World Debt Tables [of Chase Econometrics/Interactive Data Corp.] - Waltham, MA - *DataDirOnSer 84*
World Dredging & Marine Construction - Irvine, CA - *BaconPubCkMag 84; MagDir 84*
World Electronic Developments - Scotia, NY - *BaconPubCkMag 84*
World Encounter - Philadelphia, PA - *WritMar 84*
World Energy Data System [of U.S. Dept. of Energy] - Argonne, IL - *EISS 83*
World Energy Industry [of Business Information Display Inc.] - San Diego, CA - *DataDirOnSer 84; DBBus 82; DirOnDB Spring 84*
World Energy Industry Information Services - San Diego, CA - *EISS 83*
World Enterprises - New York, NY - *BillIntBG 83-84*
World Environment Report [of Alexander Research & Communications Inc.] - New York, NY - *BaconPubCkMag 84; DataDirOnSer 84; DirOnDB Spring 84*
World Farming - Overland Park, KS - *BaconPubCkMag 84*
World Farming - Shawnee Mission, KS - *MagDir 84*
World Food Press - Jamaica Plain, MA - *BoPubDir 4, 5*
World Future Society - Bethesda, MD - *AvMarPl 83; BoPubDir 4, 5*
World Gift Review Newsletter - Union City, NJ - *BaconPubCkMag 84; MagDir 84*
World Health Information Services Inc. - New York, NY - *DirPRFirms 83*
World Health Information Services Inc. - *See* Rosenthal Inc., Rolf Werner
World Health Organization - Geneva, Switzerland - *InfIndMarPl 83*
World Health Statistics Data Base [of World Health Organization] - Geneva, Switzerland - *EISS 83*
World Hunger Education Service - Washington, DC - *BoPubDir 5*
World in Color - Elmira, NY - *AvMarPl 83*
World Industrial Reporter [of Keller International Publishing Corp.] - Great Neck, NY - *BaconPubCkMag 84; MagDir 84; MagIndMarPl 82-83*
World Information & Trade System - *See* Automated Information Transfer System
World Journal - Ackley, IA - *AyerDirPub 83*
World Journal - Flushing, NY - *Ed&PubIntYB 82*
World Journal of Surgery - New York, NY - *MagIndMarPl 82-83*
World Literature Today - Chickasha, OK - *MagDir 84*
World Mariculture Society - Baton Rouge, LA - *BoPubDir 4, 5*
World Marketing - Jersey City, NJ - *MagIndMarPl 82-83*
World Marketing [of D & B International] - New York, NY - *MagDir 84*
World Marketing Systems & Publishing Co. Inc. [Aff. of World Publishing Systems] - Beverly Hills, CA - *BoPubDir 4, 5*
World Medical Journal - Chicago, IL - *BaconPubCkMag 84*
World Medical Journal - New York, NY - *MagDir 84*
World Merchandise-Import Center - Brookings, OR - *BoPubDir 4, 5*
World Metal Index [of Sheffield City Libraries] - Sheffield, England - *EISS 83*
World Microfilms Publications Ltd. - London, England - *MicroMarPl 82-83*
World Mining - San Francisco, CA - *BaconPubCkMag 84; MagDir 84; MagIndMarPl 82-83*
World Music Inc. - New York, NY - *BillIntBG 83-84*
World Muslim News - Chicago, IL - *Ed&PubIntYB 82*
World Natural History Publications [Aff. of Plexus Publishing Inc.] - Marlton, NJ - *BoPubDir 4*
World Natural History Publications [Aff. of Plexus Publishing Inc.] - Medford, NJ - *BoPubDir 5; WritMar 84*
World News Syndicate Ltd. - Hollywood, CA - *Ed&PubIntYB 82; LitMarPl 83, 84; MagIndMarPl 82-83*
World Nuclear Power Plant [of French Atomic Energy Commission] - Paris, France - *DBBus 82*
World of Art - Kings Point, NY - *DirOnDB Spring 84*
World of Banking, The - Rolling Meadows, IL - *BaconPubCkMag 84*
World of Darts Studio Publishers - Ashley, PA - *BoPubDir 4, 5*
World of Peripole Inc. - Browns Mills, NJ - *BoPubDir 4, 5*
World of Poetry - Sacramento, CA - *LitMag&SmPr 83-84*
World of Rodeo & Western Heritage, The [of Rodeo Construction Agency] - Billings, MT - *ArtMar 84; BaconPubCkMag 84; WritMar 84*
World Oil [of Gulf Publishing Co.] - Houston, TX - *BaconPubCkMag 84; Folio 83; MagDir 84*
World Oil Project [of Massachusetts Institute of Technology] - Cambridge, MA - *EISS 83*
World Order - New Haven, CT - *MagIndMarPl 82-83*
World Over - New York, NY - *MagDir 84; MagIndMarPl 82-83*

World Patents Index [of Derwent Publications Ltd.] - London, England - *CompReadDB 82; DBBus 82*
World Patents Index/World Patents Index Latest [of SDC Information Services] - Santa Monica, CA - *DataDirOnSer 84*
World Petrochemicals Program [of SRI International] - Menlo Park, CA - *DataDirOnSer 84*
World Policy Institute - New York, NY - *LitMarPl 84*
World Press Review [of Stanley Foundation] - New York, NY - *DirMarMP 83; Ed&PubIntYB 82; MagDir 84; MagIndMarPl 82-83*
World Press Watch - Palm Beach, FL - *LitMag&SmPr 83-84*
World Press Watch Press - Palm Beach, FL - *LitMag&SmPr 83-84*
World Print Council - San Francisco, CA - *BoPubDir 5*
World Priorities Inc. - Washington, DC - *BoPubDir 4 Sup, 5*
World Progress [of Standard Educational Corp.] - Chicago, IL - *LitMarPl 83, 84; MagDir 84; MagIndMarPl 82-83*
World Report [of Dow Jones News/Retrieval Service] - Princeton, NJ - *DataDirOnSer 84*
World Reporter [of Datasolve Ltd.] - London, England - *DirOnDB Spring 84; EISS 7-83 Sup*
World Research Inc. - San Diego, CA - *BoPubDir 4, 5*
World Research Systems Ltd. - Palatine, IL - *IntDirMarRes 83*
World Risk Analysis Package [of S. J. Rundt & Associates] - New York, NY - *EISS 7-83 Sup*
World Sound Recording Inc. - Livonia, MI - *BillIntBG 83-84*
World-Spectator - Moosomin, SK, Canada - *AyerDirPub 83; Ed&PubIntYB 82*
World Steel Forecast - Bala Cynwyd, PA - *DirOnDB Spring 84*
World Surface Coatings Abstracts [of Paint Research Association] - Teddington, England - *DirOnDB Spring 84; EISS 83*
World Tennis [of CBS Publications] - New York, NY - *BaconPubCkMag 84; Folio 83; MagDir 84; MagIndMarPl 82-83; WritMar 84*
World Textile Abstracts [of Shirley Institute] - Manchester, England - *OnBibDB 3*
World Textile Abstracts Database [of Shirley Institute] - Manchester, England - *CompReadDB 82*
World Textiles [of Dialog Information Services Inc.] - Palo Alto, CA - *DataDirOnSer 84*
World Textiles - Manchester, England - *DirOnDB Spring 84*
World, The - Rio Linda, CA - *Ed&PubIntYB 82*
World, The - Roseville, CA - *Ed&PubIntYB 82; NewsDir 84*
World, The - Sacramento, CA - *AyerDirPub 83*
World, The - New York, NY - *LitMag&SmPr 83-84*
World, The - Coos Bay, OR - *Ed&PubIntYB 82*
World Trade Academy Press - New York, NY - *BoPubDir 4, 5*
World Trade Business Information Center [of Golden Gate University] - San Francisco, CA - *FBInfSer 80*
World Trade Information Center - New York, NY - *FBInfSer 80; InfIndMarPl 83*
World Transindex [of International Translations Centre] - Delft, Netherlands - *CompReadDB 82; DirOnDB Spring 84; OnBibDB 3*
World Traveling [of Midwest News Service Inc.] - Farmington Hills, MI - *BaconPubCkMag 84; MagDir 84; WritMar 84*
World Union for Progressive Judaism Ltd. - New York, NY - *BoPubDir 4, 5*
World Union Press - New York, NY - *Ed&PubIntYB 82*
World University Press - Stamford, CT - *LitMag&SmPr 83-84*
World University Service of Canada - Ottawa, ON, Canada - *BoPubDir 4, 5*
World UNIX & C [of Southwater Corp.] - Mt. Carmel, CT - *MicrocomMPl 84*
World Video Inc. - Boyertown, PA - *AvMarPl 83*
World View Television Ltd. - Vancouver, BC, Canada - *BrCabYB 84*
World War IV [of BBPP Press Books] - Missoula, MT - *LitMag&SmPr 83-84*
World War II Publications [Aff. of Planes of Fame Publications] - Corona del Mar, CA - *BoPubDir 4, 5*
World Wastes - Atlanta, GA - *BaconPubCkMag 84*
World Wastes Equipment Catalog - Atlanta, GA - *MagDir 84*
World Water Skiing [of World Publications] - Winter Park, FL - *ArtMar 84; BaconPubCkMag 84; WritMar 84*
World Weather Watch [of World Meteorological Organization] - Geneva, Switzerland - *EISS 83*
World Wide Bingo, Radio & Television Bingo - Littleton, CO - *Tel&CabFB 84C*
World-Wide Book Service - New York, NY - *LitMarPl 83*
World Wide Data Systems Ltd. - Houston, TX - *MicrocomMPl 84*
World Wide Information Services Inc. - New York, NY - *BrCabYB 84; Ed&PubIntYB 82; FBInfSer 80; HBIndAd&MS 82-83; InfIndMarPl 83; ProGuPRSer 4; Tel&CabFB 84C*
World-Wide Institute of Valuation - Berkeley, CA - *WhoWMicrocom 83*
World Wide Music Inc. - Central City, KY - *BillIntBG 83-84*
World Wide Pictures - Burbank, CA - *WritMar 84*
World Wide Pictures Inc. [Subs. of Billy Graham Evangelistic Association] - Minneapolis, MN - *AvMarPl 83*
World-Wide Printer - Philadelphia, PA - *BaconPubCkMag 84; MagDir 84; MagIndMarPl 82-83; WritMar 84*
World Wide Products - San Francisco, CA - *BoPubDir 4, 5*
World Wide Publications [Aff. of Billy Graham Evangelistic Association] - Minneapolis, MN - *BoPubDir 4, 5*
World Wide Publishing Corp. - Ashland, OR - *BoPubDir 4, 5*
World Wide Trade Service - Medina, WA - *BoPubDir 4, 5*
World Without War Publications - Chicago, IL - *BoPubDir 4, 5*
World Wood - San Francisco, CA - *BaconPubCkMag 84; MagDir 84*
World Zionist Organization - New York, NY - *AvMarPl 83*
World Zionist Organization-American Section Inc. (Publications Dept.) - New York, NY - *LitMarPl 83, 84*
Worldfax [of ITT World Communications Inc.] - New York, NY - *TeleSy&SerDir 7-83*
Worldnet Telecommunications Co. - Cary, IL - *TeleSy&SerDir 7-83*
Worldradio - Sacramento, CA - *BaconPubCkMag 84*
World's Fair Collector's Society Inc. - Garden City, NY - *BoPubDir 4, 5*
World's Finest Music - Indianapolis, IN - *BillIntBG 83-84*
Worldscan Commercial Inc. - Wabash, IN - *Tel&CabFB 84C*
Worldstar Records - Lafayette, LA - *BillIntBG 83-84*
Worldtone Music Inc. - New York, NY - *BillIntBG 83-84*
Worldview - New York, NY - *LitMarPl 83, 84; MagIndMarPl 82-83*
Worldvision Enterprises Inc. - New York, NY - *TelAl 83, 84; Tel&CabFB 84C*
Worldvision Enterprises Inc. - Tokyo, Japan - *TelAl 84*
Worldvision Enterprises Inc. - Mexico City, Mexico - *TelAl 84*
Worldvision Enterprises of Australia Pty. Ltd. - Sydney, Australia - *TelAl 84*
Worldvision Enterprises of Canada - Toronto, ON, Canada - *TelAl 84*
Worldvision Enterprises U.K. Ltd. - London, England - *TelAl 84*
Worldvision Filmes do Brasil Ltd. - Rio de Janeiro, Brazil - *TelAl 84*
Worldvision GmbH - Munich, West Germany - *TelAl 84*
Worldvision International - Paris, France - *TelAl 84*
Worldvision International - Rome, Italy - *TelAl 84*
Worldwatch Institute - Washington, DC - *BoPubDir 4, 5; LitMag&SmPr 83-84; LitMarPl 84*
Worldwatch Papers - Washington, DC - *LitMag&SmPr 83-84*
Worldwide Chain Store Systems - Chicago, IL - *ADAPSOMemDir 83-84*
Worldwide Challenge - San Bernardino, CA - *MagIndMarPl 82-83*
Worldwide Convention Management Co. [Aff. of Lake Publishing Corp.] - Libertyville, IL - *BoPubDir 5*
Worldwide Entertainment Corp. - Malibu, CA - *Tel&CabFB 84C*
Worldwide Exchange - San Leandro, CA - *DirOnDB Spring 84*
Worldwide Films - Edison, NJ - *Tel&CabFB 84C*
Worldwide Integrated Communications [of Mohawk Data Sciences Corp.] - Parsippany, NJ - *TeleSy&SerDir 7-83*
Worldwide Media Service Inc. - New York, NY - *LitMarPl 83, 84*
Worldwide Music Publishers & Distributors - New York, NY - *BillIntBG 83-84*
Worldwide Projects [of Intercontinental Publications Inc.] - Westport, CT - *BaconPubCkMag 84; MagDir 84*

Worldwide Videotex Update - Boston, MA - *BaconPubCkMag 84; DirOnDB Spring 84; EISS 83*
Worldwide Videotex Update [of NewsNet Inc.] - Bryn Mawr, PA - *DataDirOnSer 84*
WORM - Savannah, TN - *BrCabYB 84; TV&RadDir 84*
WORM-FM - Savannah, TN - *BrCabYB 84; TV&RadDir 84*
Worman, Bob - Barrow, WI - *Tel&CabFB 84C p.1714*
Wormhoudt, Arthur - Oskaloosa, IA - *BoPubDir 4, 5*
Wormwood Review Press - Stockton, CA - *BoPubDir 4, 5; LitMag&SmPr 83-84*
Wormwood Review, The - Stockton, CA - *LitMag&SmPr 83-84; WritMar 84*
WORO - Corozal, PR - *BrCabYB 84*
Worobec, R. B. - Alexandria, VA - *LitMarPl 83*
Worrall Publications - Orange, NJ - *BaconPubCkNews 84*
Worrell & Associates, Chuck - Ft. Worth, TX - *StaDirAdAg 2-84*
Worrell Broadcasting Inc. - Charlottesville, VA - *BrCabYB 84; Tel&CabFB 84S*
Worrell Newspapers Inc. - Charlottesville, VA - *BrCabYB 84; Ed&PubIntYB 82; KnowInd 83*
WORT-FM - Madison, WI - *BrCabYB 84; NatRadPubDir Spring 84; TV&RadDir 84*
Worth Citizen [of Southwest Messenger Newspapers] - Midlothian, IL - *AyerDirPub 83; NewsDir 84*
Worth Citizen - Worth, IL - *Ed&PubIntYB 82*
Worth Citizen - *See* Southwest Messenger Newspapers
Worth-Palos Reporter - Worth, IL - *AyerDirPub 83; Ed&PubIntYB 82*
Worth-Palos Reporter - *See* Reporter Publications
Worth Publishers Inc. - New York, NY - *BoPubDir 4, 5; LitMarPl 84*
Worth Township Times [of Regional Publishing Corp.] - Palos Heights, IL - *Ed&PubIntYB 82; NewsDir 84*
Worthies Library [Aff. of F. Marion Crawford Memorial Society] - Nashville, TN - *BoPubDir 4, 5*
Worthington Cable TV [of Zylstra Communications Corp.] - Worthington, MN - *BrCabYB 84; Tel&CabFB 84C*
Worthington Community TV Association Inc. - Worthington, WV - *BrCabYB 84*
Worthington Daily Globe - Worthington, MN - *Ed&PubIntYB 82; NewsDir 84*
Worthington Globe - Worthington, MN - *AyerDirPub 83; BaconPubCkNews 84*
Worthington News - Worthington, OH - *AyerDirPub 83; BaconPubCkNews 84; Ed&PubIntYB 82; NewsDir 84*
Worthington Suburbia News - *See* Suburban News Publications
Worthington Times - Worthington, IN - *BaconPubCkNews 84; Ed&PubIntYB 82*
Worthless Music - *See* JEDO Music
Worthy Labor Press - Richmond, CA - *BoPubDir 4, 5*
WORV - Hattiesburg, MS - *BrCabYB 84; NatRadPubDir Summer 83, Spring 84; TV&RadDir 84*
WORW-FM - Port Huron, MI - *BrCabYB 84; NatRadPubDir Summer 83, Spring 84; TV&RadDir 84*
WORX - Madison, IN - *BrCabYB 84; TV&RadDir 84*
Worzalla Publishing Co. - Stevens Point, WI - *LitMarPl 83, 84*
WOSC - Fulton, NY - *BrCabYB 84*
WOSC - Oswego, NY - *TV&RadDir 84*
WOSE-FM - Port Clinton, OH - *BrCabYB 84; TV&RadDir 84*
WOSH-FM - Appleton/Oshkosh, WI - *NatRadPubDir Summer 83, Spring 84 p.267*
WOSH-FM - Oshkosh, WI - *BrCabYB 84; TV&RadDir 84*
WOSM-FM - Ocean Springs, MS - *BrCabYB 84; TV&RadDir 84*
WOSO - San Juan, PR - *BrCabYB 84*
WOSS-FM - Ossining, NY - *BrCabYB 84; TV&RadDir 84*
WOSS Publishing Co. [Aff. of Wells of Salvation Inc.] - Huntsville, OH - *BoPubDir 4, 5*
WOSU - Columbus, OH - *BrCabYB 84; NatRadPubDir Summer 83, Spring 84; TV&RadDir 84*
WOSU-FM - Columbus, OH - *BrCabYB 84; NatRadPubDir Summer 83, Spring 84; TV&RadDir 84*
WOSU-TV - Columbus, OH - *BrCabYB 84; Tel&CabFB 84S; TV&RadDir 84*
Wot - Sidney, BC, Canada - *LitMag&SmPr 83-84*
WOTB-FM - Middletown, RI - *BrCabYB 84; NatRadPubDir Summer 83, Spring 84*
WOTB-FM - Newport, RI - *TV&RadDir 84*
WOTR-FM - Detroit, MI - *TV&RadDir 84*
Wotring/Kowalski & Co. - Chicago, IL - *Tel&CabFB 84C*
WOTT - Watertown, NY - *BrCabYB 84; NatRadPubDir Summer 83, Spring 84; TV&RadDir 84*
WOTV-TV - Grand Rapids, MI - *BrCabYB 84; DirUSTelSta 83; LitMarPl 83, 84; TelAl 83, 84; Tel&CabFB 84S; TV&RadDir 84*
WOTW - Nashua, NH - *BrCabYB 84; NatRadPubDir Summer 83, Spring 84; TV&RadDir 84*
WOTW-FM - Nashua, NH - *NatRadPubDir Summer 83, Spring 84; TV&RadDir 84*
WOUB - Athens, OH - *BrCabYB 84; NatRadPubDir Summer 83, Spring 84; TV&RadDir 84*
WOUB-FM - Athens, OH - *BrCabYB 84; NatRadPubDir Summer 83, Spring 84; TV&RadDir 84*
WOUB-TV - Athens, OH - *BrCabYB 84; Tel&CabFB 84S; TV&RadDir 84*
WOUC-TV - Cambridge, OH - *BrCabYB 84; Tel&CabFB 84S*
WOUI-FM - Chicago, IL - *BrCabYB 84; TV&RadDir 84*
WOUR-FM - Utica, NY - *BrCabYB 84; NatRadPubDir Summer 83, Spring 84; TV&RadDir 84*
WOVI - Novi, MI - *BrCabYB 84*
WOVO-FM - Glasgow, KY - *BrCabYB 84; TV&RadDir 84*
WOVR-FM - Versailles, IN - *BrCabYB 84*
WOVV-FM - Ft. Pierce, FL - *BrCabYB 84; TV&RadDir 84*
WOW - Omaha, NE - *BrCabYB 84; NatRadPubDir Summer 83, Spring 84; TV&RadDir 84*
WOW - New York, NY - *MagDir 84*
WOW-FM - Omaha, NE - *BrCabYB 84*
WOWD - Tallahassee, FL - *BrCabYB 84; TV&RadDir 84*
WOWD-FM - Tallahassee, FL - *NatRadPubDir Summer 83, Spring 84*
WOWE-FM - Rossville, GA - *BrCabYB 84; TV&RadDir 84*
WOWE-FM - Chattanooga, TN - *NatRadPubDir Summer 83 p.227, Spring 84*
WOWE-FM - Johnson City, TN - *TV&RadDir 84*
WOWI-FM - Norfolk, VA - *BrCabYB 84; NatRadPubDir Summer 83, Spring 84; TV&RadDir 84*
WOWK-TV - Charleston, WV - *DirUSTelSta 83*
WOWK-TV - Huntington, WV - *BrCabYB 84; LitMarPl 83, 84; TelAl 83, 84; Tel&CabFB 84S; TV&RadDir 84*
WOWL-TV - Florence, AL - *BrCabYB 84; DirUSTelSta 83; TelAl 83, 84; Tel&CabFB 84S; TV&RadDir 84*
WOWN-FM - Shawano, WI - *BrCabYB 84; TV&RadDir 84*
WOWO - Ft. Wayne, IN - *BrCabYB 84; NatRadPubDir Summer 83, Spring 84; TV&RadDir 84*
WOWQ-FM - Du Bois, PA - *BrCabYB 84; TV&RadDir 84*
WOWT-TV - Omaha, NE - *BrCabYB 84; DirUSTelSta 83; TelAl 83, 84; Tel&CabFB 84S; TV&RadDir 84*
WOWW-FM - Gulf Breeze, FL - *TV&RadDir 84*
WOWW-FM - Pensacola, FL - *BrCabYB 84; NatRadPubDir Summer 83, Spring 84*
WOXO - Norway, ME - *BrCabYB 84; TV&RadDir 84*
WOXO - South Paris, ME - *BrCabYB 84*
WOXO-FM - Norway, ME - *TV&RadDir 84*
WOXY-FM - Oxford, OH - *BrCabYB 84; TV&RadDir 84*
WOYE-FM - Mayaguez, PR - *BrCabYB 84*
WOYK - York, PA - *NatRadPubDir Summer 83, Spring 84; TV&RadDir 84*
WOYL - Oil City, PA - *BrCabYB 84; TV&RadDir 84*
WOZ - New Orleans, LA - *BrCabYB 84*
WOZI-FM - Presque Isle, ME - *TV&RadDir 84*
WOZK - Ozark, AL - *BrCabYB 84; TV&RadDir 84*
WOZN - Jacksonville, FL - *BrCabYB 84; TV&RadDir 84*
Wozniak TV - Valdez, CO - *BrCabYB 84*
WOZO - Penn Yan, NY - *BrCabYB 84; TV&RadDir 84*
WOZQ - Northampton, MA - *BrCabYB 84*
WOZW - Monticello, ME - *BrCabYB 84*
WP Data - Menlo Park, CA - *DirOnDB Spring 84*
W.P. Magazines - Hollywood, CA - *DirMarMP 83*
WP News - Burbank, CA - *BaconPubCkMag 84*
WPAA-FM - Andover, MA - *BrCabYB 84; NatRadPubDir Summer 83, Spring 84; TV&RadDir 84*
WPAB - Ponce, PR - *BrCabYB 84*
WPAC - Ogdensburg, NY - *BrCabYB 84*
WPAD - Paducah, KY - *BrCabYB 84; TV&RadDir 84*
WPAG - Ann Arbor, MI - *BrCabYB 84; NatRadPubDir Summer 83, Spring 84; TV&RadDir 84*

WPAG-FM - Ann Arbor, MI - *BrCabYB 84; NatRadPubDir Summer 83, Spring 84; TV&RadDir 84*
WPAJ-FM - Lancaster, SC - *BrCabYB 84; TV&RadDir 84*
WPAK - Farmville, VA - *BrCabYB 84; TV&RadDir 84*
WPAL - Charleston, SC - *BrCabYB 84; NatRadPubDir Summer 83, Spring 84; TV&RadDir 84*
WPAM - Pottsville, PA - *BrCabYB 84; TV&RadDir 84*
WPAN - Ft. Walton Beach, FL - *BrCabYB 84; Tel&CabFB 84S*
WPAP-FM - Panama City, FL - *BrCabYB 84; TV&RadDir 84*
WPAQ - Mt. Airy, NC - *BrCabYB 84; TV&RadDir 84*
WPAR - Parkersburg, WV - *TV&RadDir 84*
WPAS - Zephyrhills, FL - *BrCabYB 84; TV&RadDir 84*
WPAT - Clifton, NJ - *LitMarPl 83, 84; TV&RadDir 84*
WPAT - Paterson, NJ - *BrCabYB 84; NatRadPubDir Summer 83 p.159, Spring 84 p.159*
WPAT-FM - Clifton, NJ - *LitMarPl 83; TV&RadDir 84*
WPAT-FM - Paterson, NJ - *BrCabYB 84; NatRadPubDir Summer 83 p.159, Spring 84 p.159*
WPAX - Thomasville, GA - *BrCabYB 84; TV&RadDir 84*
WPAY - Portsmouth, OH - *BrCabYB 84; TV&RadDir 84*
WPAY-FM - Portsmouth, OH - *BrCabYB 84; TV&RadDir 84*
WPAZ - Pottstown, PA - *BrCabYB 84; TV&RadDir 84*
WPBC - Bangor, ME - *BrCabYB 84*
WPBE-FM - Huntingdon, TN - *BrCabYB 84; TV&RadDir 84*
WPBF-FM - Cincinnati/Hamilton/Middletown, OH - *NatRadPubDir Summer 83 p.193*
WPBF-FM - Middletown, OH - *BrCabYB 84; TV&RadDir 84*
WPBH - Middlefield, CT - *BrCabYB 84*
WPBK - Whitehall, MI - *BrCabYB 84; TV&RadDir 84*
WPBM - Aiken, SC - *BrCabYB 84; TV&RadDir 84*
WPBM-FM - Aiken, SC - *BrCabYB 84; TV&RadDir 84*
WPBN-TV - Traverse City, MI - *BrCabYB 84; DirUSTelSta 83; TelAl 83, 84; Tel&CabFB 84S; TV&RadDir 84*
WPBO-TV - Portsmouth, OH - *BrCabYB 84; Tel&CabFB 84S*
WPBR - Palm Beach, FL - *BrCabYB 84; NatRadPubDir Summer 83, Spring 84 p.67; TV&RadDir 84*
WPBR-FM - Barrington, IL - *BrCabYB 84*
WPBT-TV - Miami, FL - *BrCabYB 84; Tel&CabFB 84S; TV&RadDir 84*
WPBX - Southampton, NY - *BrCabYB 84*
WPBY-TV - Huntington, WV - *BrCabYB 84; Tel&CabFB 84S; TV&RadDir 84*
WPCB-TV - Greensburg, PA - *BrCabYB 84; Tel&CabFB 84S*
WPCB-TV - Wall, PA - *DirUSTelSta 83*
WPCC - Clinton, SC - *BrCabYB 84; TV&RadDir 84*
WPCD-FM - Champaign, IL - *BrCabYB 84; TV&RadDir 84*
WPCE - Norfolk, VA - *NatRadPubDir Summer 83, Spring 84; TV&RadDir 84*
WPCE - Portsmouth, VA - *BrCabYB 84*
WPCF - Panama City Beach, FL - *BrCabYB 84; TV&RadDir 84*
WPCH-FM - Atlanta, GA - *BrCabYB 84; TV&RadDir 84*
WPCK - West Palm Beach, FL - *BrCabYB 84; NatRadPubDir Spring 84*
WPCM-FM - Burlington, NC - *BrCabYB 84; TV&RadDir 84*
WPCN - Mt. Pocono, PA - *BrCabYB 84*
WPCO - Mt. Vernon, IN - *BrCabYB 84; TV&RadDir 84*
WPCQ-TV - Charlotte, NC - *BrCabYB 84; DirUSTelSta 83; LitMarPl 83, 84; TelAl 83, 84; Tel&CabFB 84S; TV&RadDir 84*
WPCR-FM - Plymouth, NH - *BrCabYB 84; NatRadPubDir Summer 83, Spring 84*
WPCS-FM - Pensacola, FL - *BrCabYB 84; TV&RadDir 84*
WPCT-FM - Lobelville, TN - *TV&RadDir 84*
WPCV-FM - Lakeland/Winter Haven, FL - *NatRadPubDir Summer 83, Spring 84 p.60*
WPCV-FM - Winter Haven, FL - *BrCabYB 84; TV&RadDir 84*
WPCX-FM - Auburn, NY - *BrCabYB 84; TV&RadDir 84*
WPDC - Elizabethtown, PA - *BrCabYB 84; TV&RadDir 84*
WPDE-TV - Florence, SC - *BrCabYB 84; DirUSTelSta 83; TelAl 83, 84; Tel&CabFB 84S; TV&RadDir 84*
WPDH-FM - Poughkeepsie, NY - *BrCabYB 84; TV&RadDir 84*
WPDM - Potsdam, NY - *BrCabYB 84; TV&RadDir 84*
WPDQ - Jacksonville, FL - *BrCabYB 84; NatRadPubDir Summer 83, Spring 84; TV&RadDir 84*
WPDR - Portage, WI - *BrCabYB 84; TV&RadDir 84*
WPDS-TV - Indianapolis, IN - *BrCabYB 84; Tel&CabFB 84S*
WPDX - Clarksburg, WV - *BrCabYB 84; TV&RadDir 84*
WPDX-FM - Clarksburg, WV - *BrCabYB 84; TV&RadDir 84*
WPDZ-FM - Cheraw, SC - *BrCabYB 84; TV&RadDir 84*
WPEA-FM - Exeter, NH - *BrCabYB 84; NatRadPubDir Summer 83, Spring 84; TV&RadDir 84*
WPEB - Philadelphia, PA - *BrCabYB 84*
WPEC - West Palm Beach, FL - *BrCabYB 84; DirUSTelSta 83; Tel&CabFB 84S*
WPEC-TV - West Palm Beach, FL - *TelAl 83, 84; TV&RadDir 84*
WPED - Crozet, VA - *BrCabYB 84; TV&RadDir 84*
WPED-FM - Crozet, VA - *BrCabYB 84*
WPEG-FM - Concord, NC - *BrCabYB 84; TV&RadDir 84*
WPEH - Louisville, GA - *BrCabYB 84; TV&RadDir 84*
WPEH-FM - Louisville, GA - *BrCabYB 84; TV&RadDir 84*
WPEL - Montrose, PA - *BrCabYB 84; NatRadPubDir Summer 83, Spring 84; TV&RadDir 84*
WPEL-FM - Montrose, PA - *BrCabYB 84; NatRadPubDir Summer 83, Spring 84; TV&RadDir 84*
WPEN - Bala Cynwyd, PA - *LitMarPl 83, 84; TV&RadDir 84*
WPEN - Philadelphia, PA - *BrCabYB 84; NatRadPubDir Summer 83 p.213, Spring 84 p.213*
WPEO - Peoria, IL - *BrCabYB 84; NatRadPubDir Summer 83, Spring 84; TV&RadDir 84*
WPEP - Taunton, MA - *BrCabYB 84; NatRadPubDir Summer 83, Spring 84; TV&RadDir 84*
WPET - Greensboro, NC - *BrCabYB 84; NatRadPubDir Summer 83, Spring 84; TV&RadDir 84*
WPEX - Hampton, VA - *BrCabYB 84; TV&RadDir 84*
WPEZ-FM - Macon, GA - *BrCabYB 84; NatRadPubDir Summer 83, Spring 84; TV&RadDir 84*
WPFA - Pensacola, FL - *BrCabYB 84; NatRadPubDir Summer 83, Spring 84; TV&RadDir 84*
WPFB - Cincinnati/Hamilton/Middletown, OH - *NatRadPubDir Summer 83 p.193, Spring 84 p.191*
WPFB - Middletown, OH - *BrCabYB 84; TV&RadDir 84*
WPFB-FM - Cincinnati/Hamilton/Middletown, OH - *NatRadPubDir Spring 84 p.191*
WPFL-FM - Winter Park, FL - *BrCabYB 84; TV&RadDir 84*
WPFM-FM - Panama City, FL - *BrCabYB 84; TV&RadDir 84*
WPFR - Terre Haute, IN - *BrCabYB 84*
WPFR-FM - Terre Haute, IN - *NatRadPubDir Summer 83, Spring 84; TV&RadDir 84*
WPFW-FM - Washington, DC - *BrCabYB 84; TV&RadDir 84*
WPGA - Perry, GA - *BrCabYB 84; TV&RadDir 84*
WPGA-FM - Perry, GA - *BrCabYB 84; TV&RadDir 84*
WPGC - Washington, DC - *NatRadPubDir Summer 83, Spring 84; TV&RadDir 84*
WPGC - Morningside, MD - *BrCabYB 84*
WPGC-FM - Washington, DC - *NatRadPubDir Summer 83, Spring 84; TV&RadDir 84*
WPGC-FM - Morningside, MD - *BrCabYB 84*
WPGH-TV - Pittsburgh, PA - *BrCabYB 84; DirUSTelSta 83; TelAl 83, 84; Tel&CabFB 84S; TV&RadDir 84*
WPGM - Danville, PA - *BrCabYB 84; NatRadPubDir Summer 83, Spring 84*
WPGM-FM - Danville, PA - *BrCabYB 84; NatRadPubDir Summer 83, Spring 84; TV&RadDir 84*
WPGT-FM - Roanoke Rapids, NC - *BrCabYB 84; NatRadPubDir Summer 83, Spring 84; TV&RadDir 84*
WPGU-FM - Champaign, IL - *NatRadPubDir Summer 83, Spring 84; TV&RadDir 84*
WPGU-FM - Urbana, IL - *BrCabYB 84*
WPGW - Portland, IN - *BrCabYB 84; TV&RadDir 84*
WPGW-FM - Portland, IN - *BrCabYB 84; TV&RadDir 84*
WPHB - Philipsburg, PA - *BrCabYB 84; TV&RadDir 84*
WPHC - Waverly, TN - *BrCabYB 84; TV&RadDir 84*
WPHD-FM - Buffalo, NY - *BrCabYB 84; NatRadPubDir Summer 83, Spring 84; TV&RadDir 84*
WPHL Productions [Div. of WPHL-TV] - Philadelphia, PA - *AvMarPl 83*
WPHL-TV - Philadelphia, PA - *BrCabYB 84; DirUSTelSta 83; TelAl 83, 84; Tel&CabFB 84C, 84S; TV&RadDir 84*
WPHM - Port Huron, MI - *BrCabYB 84; TV&RadDir 84*
WPHP-FM - Wheeling, WV - *BrCabYB 84; TV&RadDir 84*
WPHS-FM - Warren, MI - *BrCabYB 84; TV&RadDir 84*
WPI - London, England - *DirOnDB Spring 84*

WPIC - Sharon, PA - *BrCabYB 84; TV&RadDir 84*
WPID - Piedmont, AL - *BrCabYB 84; TV&RadDir 84*
WPIG - Saco, ME - *BrCabYB 84*
WPIK - Flomaton, AL - *BrCabYB 84; TV&RadDir 84*
WPIO-FM - Titusville, FL - *BrCabYB 84; TV&RadDir 84*
WPIP - Ft. Lauderdale/Hollywood, FL - *NatRadPubDir Summer 83 p.57*
WPIQ-FM - Brunswick, GA - *BrCabYB 84; TV&RadDir 84*
WPIT - Pittsburgh, PA - *BrCabYB 84; NatRadPubDir Summer 83, Spring 84; TV&RadDir 84*
WPIT-FM - Pittsburgh, PA - *BrCabYB 84; NatRadPubDir Summer 83, Spring 84; TV&RadDir 84*
WPIX - New York, NY - *BrCabYB 84; DirUSTelSta 83; TelAl 83, 84; Tel&CabFB 84S*
WPIX-FM - New York, NY - *BrCabYB 84; LitMarPl 84; NatRadPubDir Summer 83, Spring 84; TV&RadDir 84*
WPIX-TV - New York, NY - *LitMarPl 83, 84; TV&RadDir 84*
WPJB-FM - Providence, RI - *BrCabYB 84; NatRadPubDir Summer 83, Spring 84; TV&RadDir 84*
WPJJ - Yazoo City, MS - *BrCabYB 84*
WPJL - Raleigh, NC - *BrCabYB 84; NatRadPubDir Summer 83, Spring 84; TV&RadDir 84*
WPJM - Adamsville, TN - *BrCabYB 84*
WPJS - Orangeburg, SC - *BrCabYB 84*
WPKE - Pikeville, KY - *BrCabYB 84; TV&RadDir 84*
WPKK-FM - Woodbridge, VA - *BrCabYB 84*
WPKN - Bridgeport, CT - *BrCabYB 84; NatRadPubDir Summer 83, Spring 84*
WPKN-FM - Bridgeport, CT - *NatRadPubDir Summer 83, Spring 84; TV&RadDir 84*
WPKX - Washington, DC - *NatRadPubDir Summer 83 p.54, Spring 84 p.55*
WPKX-FM - Washington, DC - *NatRadPubDir Summer 83 p.55, Spring 84 p.55*
WPKX-FM - Alexandria, VA - *TV&RadDir 84*
WPKY - Princeton, KY - *BrCabYB 84; TV&RadDir 84*
WPKY-FM - Princeton, KY - *BrCabYB 84; TV&RadDir 84*
WPKZ - Pickens, SC - *BrCabYB 84*
WPL Associates - Silver Spring, MD - *MicrocomMPl 84; WhoWMicrocom 83*
WPLA - Plant City, FL - *BrCabYB 84; TV&RadDir 84*
WPLB - Greenville, MI - *BrCabYB 84; TV&RadDir 84*
WPLB-FM - Greenville, MI - *BrCabYB 84; TV&RadDir 84*
WPLG - Miami, FL - *BrCabYB 84; DirUSTelSta 83; TelAl 83, 84; Tel&CabFB 84S*
WPLG-TV - Miami, FL - *LitMarPl 83, 84; TV&RadDir 84*
WPLJ-FM - New York, NY - *BrCabYB 84; LitMarPl 83, 84; NatRadPubDir Summer 83, Spring 84; TV&RadDir 84*
WPLK - Rockmart, GA - *BrCabYB 84; TV&RadDir 84*
WPLM - Plymouth, MA - *BrCabYB 84; TV&RadDir 84*
WPLM-FM - Plymouth, MA - *BrCabYB 84; TV&RadDir 84*
WPLN-FM - Nashville, TN - *BrCabYB 84; NatRadPubDir Summer 83, Spring 84; TV&RadDir 84*
WPLO - Atlanta, GA - *BrCabYB 84; NatRadPubDir Summer 83, Spring 84; TV&RadDir 84*
WPLP - Largo, FL - *TV&RadDir 84*
WPLP - Pinellas Park, FL - *BrCabYB 84*
WPLP - Tampa/St. Petersburg, FL - *NatRadPubDir Summer 83 p.65, Spring 84 p.65*
WPLR-FM - New Haven, CT - *BrCabYB 84; NatRadPubDir Summer 83, Spring 84; TV&RadDir 84*
WPLS-FM - Greenville, VT - *BrCabYB 84*
WPLT-FM - Plattsburgh, NY - *BrCabYB 84; NatRadPubDir Summer 83, Spring 84; TV&RadDir 84*
WPLW - Carnegie, PA - *BrCabYB 84*
WPLW - Pittsburgh, PA - *NatRadPubDir Summer 83, Spring 84; TV&RadDir 84*
WPLY - Plymouth, WI - *BrCabYB 84; TV&RadDir 84*
WPLZ-FM - Petersburg, VA - *BrCabYB 84; TV&RadDir 84*
WPMB - Vandalia, IL - *BrCabYB 84; TV&RadDir 84*
WPMH - Chesapeake, VA - *TV&RadDir 84*
WPMH - Norfolk, VA - *NatRadPubDir Summer 83, Spring 84 p.256*
WPMH - Portsmouth, VA - *BrCabYB 84; TV&RadDir 84*
WPMI-TV - Mobile, AL - *BrCabYB 84; DirUSTelSta 83; TelAl 84; Tel&CabFB 84S*
WPMJ - Owensboro, KY - *BrCabYB 84; Tel&CabFB 84S*
WPMO-FM - Pascagoula, MS - *BrCabYB 84; TV&RadDir 84*
WPMP - Pascagoula, MS - *BrCabYB 84; TV&RadDir 84*
WPMT - York, PA - *BrCabYB 84; Tel&CabFB 84S*
WPMW - Mullens, WV - *BrCabYB 84*
WPN Music Co. Inc. - *See* Print Music Co. Inc.
WPNC - Plymouth, NC - *BrCabYB 84; TV&RadDir 84*
WPNE - Green Bay, WI - *BrCabYB 84; Tel&CabFB 84S*
WPNE-FM - Green Bay, WI - *BrCabYB 84*
WPNE-TV - Green Bay, WI - *TV&RadDir 84*
WPNF - Brevard, NC - *BrCabYB 84; TV&RadDir 84*
WPNH - Plymouth, NH - *BrCabYB 84; TV&RadDir 84*
WPNH-FM - Plymouth, NH - *BrCabYB 84; TV&RadDir 84*
WPNM - Ottawa, OH - *BrCabYB 84; TV&RadDir 84*
WPNM-FM - Ottawa, OH - *TV&RadDir 84*
WPNR-FM - Utica, NY - *BrCabYB 84; TV&RadDir 84*
WPNT-FM - Pittsburgh, PA - *BrCabYB 84; NatRadPubDir Spring 84; TV&RadDir 84*
WPNX - Phenix City, AL - *BrCabYB 84*
WPNX - Columbus, GA - *NatRadPubDir Summer 83, Spring 84; TV&RadDir 84*
WPOB-FM - Plainview, NY - *BrCabYB 84; NatRadPubDir Summer 83, Spring 84; TV&RadDir 84*
WPOC-FM - Baltimore, MD - *BrCabYB 84; NatRadPubDir Summer 83, Spring 84; TV&RadDir 84*
WPOE - Greenfield, MA - *BrCabYB 84; TV&RadDir 84*
WPOK - Pontiac, IL - *BrCabYB 84; TV&RadDir 84*
WPOK-FM - Pontiac, IL - *BrCabYB 84; TV&RadDir 84*
WPOL - Gaylord, MI - *BrCabYB 84*
WPOM - Riviera Beach, FL - *BrCabYB 84*
WPOM - West Palm Beach, FL - *NatRadPubDir Summer 83, Spring 84; TV&RadDir 84*
WPON - Bloomfield Hills, MI - *TV&RadDir 84*
WPON - Pontiac, MI - *BrCabYB 84*
WPOP - Hartford, CT - *BrCabYB 84; NatRadPubDir Summer 83 p.46, Spring 84*
WPOP - Newington, CT - *TV&RadDir 84*
WPOR - Portland, ME - *BrCabYB 84; NatRadPubDir Summer 83, Spring 84; TV&RadDir 84*
WPOR-FM - Portland, ME - *BrCabYB 84; NatRadPubDir Summer 83, Spring 84; TV&RadDir 84*
WPOS-FM - Holland, OH - *BrCabYB 84; TV&RadDir 84*
WPOW - New York, NY - *BrCabYB 84; NatRadPubDir Summer 83, Spring 84 p.173; TV&RadDir 84*
WPPA - Pottsville, PA - *BrCabYB 84; TV&RadDir 84*
WPPC - Penuelas, PR - *BrCabYB 84*
WPPI - Carrollton, GA - *BrCabYB 84; TV&RadDir 84*
WPPL-FM - Blue Ridge, GA - *BrCabYB 84; TV&RadDir 84*
WPQR-FM - Uniontown, PA - *BrCabYB 84; TV&RadDir 84*
WPQZ - Clarksburg, WV - *BrCabYB 84; TV&RadDir 84*
WPRA - Mayaguez, PR - *BrCabYB 84*
WPRB-FM - Princeton, NJ - *BrCabYB 84; NatRadPubDir Summer 83, Spring 84; TV&RadDir 84*
WPRC - Lincoln, IL - *BrCabYB 84; TV&RadDir 84*
WPRE - Prairie du Chien, WI - *BrCabYB 84; TV&RadDir 84*
WPRE-FM - Prairie du Chien, WI - *BrCabYB 84; TV&RadDir 84*
WPRG-FM - Baton Rouge, LA - *TV&RadDir 84*
WPRI-TV - East Providence, RI - *LitMarPl 83, 84; TelAl 83; TV&RadDir 84*
WPRI-TV - Providence, RI - *BrCabYB 84; DirUSTelSta 83; TelAl 84; Tel&CabFB 84S*
WPRK-FM - Winter Park, FL - *BrCabYB 84; TV&RadDir 84*
WPRM-FM - San Juan, PR - *BrCabYB 84*
WPRN - Butler, AL - *BrCabYB 84; TV&RadDir 84*
WPRN-FM - Ripon, WI - *TV&RadDir 84*
WPRO - East Providence, RI - *BrCabYB 84; NatRadPubDir Summer 83, Spring 84; TV&RadDir 84*
WPRO-FM - East Providence, RI - *BrCabYB 84; NatRadPubDir Spring 84; TV&RadDir 84*
WPRP - Ponce, PR - *BrCabYB 84*
WPRR-FM - Altoona, PA - *BrCabYB 84; NatRadPubDir Summer 83, Spring 84; TV&RadDir 84*
WPRS - Paris, IL - *BrCabYB 84; TV&RadDir 84*
WPRT - Prestonsburg, KY - *BrCabYB 84; TV&RadDir 84*
WPRT-FM - Prestonsburg, KY - *BrCabYB 84; TV&RadDir 84*
WPRW - Manassas, VA - *BrCabYB 84; TV&RadDir 84*
WPRX - Sabana Grande, PR - *BrCabYB 84*

WPRY - Perry, FL - *BrCabYB 84; TV&RadDir 84*
WPRZ - Warrenton, VA - *BrCabYB 84; TV&RadDir 84*
WPSA-FM - Paul Smith's, NY - *BrCabYB 84; NatRadPubDir Summer 83, Spring 84*
WPSC - Wayne, NJ - *NatRadPubDir Summer 83, Spring 84*
WPSD-TV - Paducah, KY - *BrCabYB 84; DirUSTelSta 83; TelAl 83, 84; Tel&CabFB 84S; TV&RadDir 84*
WPSK-FM - Pulaski, VA - *BrCabYB 84; TV&RadDir 84*
WPSO-FM - New Port Richy, FL - *TV&RadDir 84*
WPSR - Evansville, IN - *BrCabYB 84*
WPSR - Terre Haute, IN - *NatRadPubDir Spring 84*
WPSR-FM - Evansville, IN - *NatRadPubDir Summer 83, Spring 84; TV&RadDir 84*
WPST-FM - Trenton, NJ - *BrCabYB 84; NatRadPubDir Summer 83, Spring 84; TV&RadDir 84*
WPSU-FM - Wilkes-Barre, PA - *NatRadPubDir Summer 83, Spring 84*
WPSX-TV - Clearfield, PA - *BrCabYB 84; Tel&CabFB 84S*
WPSX-TV - University Park, PA - *TV&RadDir 84*
WPT-TV - York, PA - *LitMarPl 84*
WPTA-TV - Ft. Wayne, IN - *BrCabYB 84; DirUSTelSta 83; TelAl 83, 84; Tel&CabFB 84S; TV&RadDir 84*
WPTB - Statesboro, GA - *BrCabYB 84; TV&RadDir 84*
WPTC - Macon, GA - *BrCabYB 84; NatRadPubDir Summer 83, Spring 84; TV&RadDir 84*
WPTD - Dayton, OH - *TV&RadDir 84*
WPTD - Kettering, OH - *BrCabYB 84; Tel&CabFB 84S*
WPTF - Raleigh, NC - *BrCabYB 84; NatRadPubDir Summer 83, Spring 84; TV&RadDir 84*
WPTF-TV - Durham, NC - *BrCabYB 84; TelAl 83, 84; Tel&CabFB 84S*
WPTF-TV - Raleigh, NC - *DirUSTelSta 83; LitMarPl 83, 84; TV&RadDir 84*
WPTG - Lancaster, PA - *BrCabYB 84*
WPTL - Canton, NC - *BrCabYB 84; TV&RadDir 84*
WPTM-FM - Roanoke Rapids, NC - *BrCabYB 84; TV&RadDir 84*
WPTN - Cookeville, TN - *BrCabYB 84; TV&RadDir 84*
WPTO - Dayton, OH - *TV&RadDir 84*
WPTO - Oxford, OH - *BrCabYB 84; Tel&CabFB 84S*
WPTR - Albany, NY - *BrCabYB 84; NatRadPubDir Summer 83, Spring 84; TV&RadDir 84*
WPTT-TV - Pittsburgh, PA - *BrCabYB 84; DirUSTelSta 83; TelAl 83, 84; Tel&CabFB 84S; TV&RadDir 84*
WPTV-TV - Palm Beach, FL - *BrCabYB 84; DirUSTelSta 83; TelAl 83, 84; Tel&CabFB 84S; TV&RadDir 84*
WPTW - Piqua, OH - *BrCabYB 84; TV&RadDir 84*
WPTW-FM - Piqua, OH - *BrCabYB 84; TV&RadDir 84*
WPTX - Lexington Park, MD - *BrCabYB 84*
WPTY-TV - Memphis, TN - *BrCabYB 84; DirUSTelSta 83; TelAl 83, 84; Tel&CabFB 84S; TV&RadDir 84*
WPTZ-TV - North Pole, NY - *BrCabYB 84*
WPTZ-TV - Plattsburgh, NY - *TelAl 83; Tel&CabFB 84S; TV&RadDir 84*
WPTZ-TV - Burlington, VT - *DirUSTelSta 83*
WPTZ-TV - Plattsburgh, VT - *TelAl 84*
WPUB-FM - Camden, SC - *BrCabYB 84; TV&RadDir 84*
WPUL - Bartow, FL - *BrCabYB 84; TV&RadDir 84*
WPUM-FM - Rensselaer, IN - *BrCabYB 84; TV&RadDir 84*
WPUR-FM - Americus, GA - *BrCabYB 84; TV&RadDir 84*
WPUT - Brewster, NY - *BrCabYB 84; NatRadPubDir Summer 83 p.180; TV&RadDir 84*
WPUT - Westchester County, NY - *NatRadPubDir Spring 84 p.178*
WPUV - Pulaski, VA - *BrCabYB 84; TV&RadDir 84*
WPVA - Petersburg, VA - *TV&RadDir 84*
WPVA-FM - Petersburg, VA - *BrCabYB 84; TV&RadDir 84*
WPVI-TV - Philadelphia, PA - *BrCabYB 84; DirUSTelSta 83; LitMarPl 83, 84; TelAl 83, 84; Tel&CabFB 84S; TV&RadDir 84*
WPVL - Painesville, OH - *BrCabYB 84; TV&RadDir 84*
WPVR-FM - Roanoke, VA - *BrCabYB 84; NatRadPubDir Summer 83, Spring 84; TV&RadDir 84*
WPWC - Dumfries, VA - *TV&RadDir 84*
WPWC - Quantico, VA - *BrCabYB 84*
WPWR-TV - Aurora, IL - *BrCabYB 84; Tel&CabFB 84S*
WPWR-TV - Chicago, IL - *DirUSTelSta 83*
WPWT-FM - Philadelphia, PA - *BrCabYB 84; NatRadPubDir Summer 83, Spring 84; TV&RadDir 84*
WPXE - Starke, FL - *BrCabYB 84; TV&RadDir 84*
WPXE-FM - Starke, FL - *BrCabYB 84; TV&RadDir 84*
WPXI-TV - Pittsburgh, PA - *BrCabYB 84; DirUSTelSta 83; TelAl 83, 84; Tel&CabFB 84S; TV&RadDir 84*
WPXN - Rochester, NY - *BrCabYB 84; NatRadPubDir Summer 83; TV&RadDir 84*
WPXY - Rochester, NY - *BrCabYB 84; NatRadPubDir Spring 84*
WPXY-FM - Rochester, NY - *NatRadPubDir Summer 83, Spring 84; TV&RadDir 84*
WPXZ - Punxsutawney, PA - *BrCabYB 84; TV&RadDir 84*
WPXZ-FM - Punxsutawney, PA - *BrCabYB 84; TV&RadDir 84*
WPYB - Benson, NC - *BrCabYB 84; TV&RadDir 84*
WPYK - Dora, AL - *BrCabYB 84*
WPYX-FM - Albany, NY - *BrCabYB 84; NatRadPubDir Summer 83, Spring 84 p.165*
WPYX-FM - Latham, NY - *TV&RadDir 84*
WPZK - Pickens, SC - *TV&RadDir 84*
WQAA - Luray, VA - *BrCabYB 84*
WQAB-FM - Philippi, WV - *BrCabYB 84; NatRadPubDir Summer 83, Spring 84; TV&RadDir 84*
WQAD-TV - Moline, IL - *BrCabYB 84; LitMarPl 83, 84; TelAl 83, 84; Tel&CabFB 84S; TV&RadDir 84*
WQAD-TV - Davenport, IA - *DirUSTelSta 83*
WQAL-FM - Cleveland, OH - *BrCabYB 84; NatRadPubDir Summer 83, Spring 84; TV&RadDir 84*
WQAM - Miami, FL - *BrCabYB 84; NatRadPubDir Summer 83, Spring 84; TV&RadDir 84*
WQAQ - Hamden, CT - *BrCabYB 84*
WQAW-FM - Parkersburg, WV - *BrCabYB 84; NatRadPubDir Summer 83, Spring 84; TV&RadDir 84*
WQAZ-FM - Cleveland, MS - *BrCabYB 84; TV&RadDir 84*
WQBA - Miami, FL - *BrCabYB 84; NatRadPubDir Summer 83, Spring 84; TV&RadDir 84*
WQBA-FM - Miami, FL - *BrCabYB 84; NatRadPubDir Summer 83, Spring 84*
WQBC - Vicksburg, MS - *BrCabYB 84; NatRadPubDir Summer 83, Spring 84; TV&RadDir 84*
WQBE - Charleston, WV - *BrCabYB 84; NatRadPubDir Spring 84*
WQBE-FM - Charleston, WV - *NatRadPubDir Summer 83, Spring 84; TV&RadDir 84*
WQBH - Detroit, MI - *BrCabYB 84; NatRadPubDir Summer 83, Spring 84*
WQBK - Albany, NY - *NatRadPubDir Summer 83, Spring 84*
WQBK - Glenmont, NY - *TV&RadDir 84*
WQBK - Rensselaer, NY - *BrCabYB 84*
WQBK-FM - Albany, NY - *NatRadPubDir Summer 83, Spring 84*
WQBK-FM - Glenmont, NY - *TV&RadDir 84*
WQBK-FM - Rennselaer, NY - *BrCabYB 84*
WQBN-FM - Groton, CT - *BrCabYB 84*
WQBQ - Selinsgrove, PA - *BrCabYB 84; TV&RadDir 84*
WQBS - San Juan, PR - *BrCabYB 84*
WQBX - Blacksburg, VA - *BrCabYB 84*
WQBX - Christiansburg, VA - *TV&RadDir 84*
WQBZ - Ft. Valley, GA - *BrCabYB 84*
WQCC - Charlotte, NC - *BrCabYB 84; TV&RadDir 84*
WQCC-FM - Charlotte, NC - *NatRadPubDir Summer 83, Spring 84*
WQCK-FM - Manchester, GA - *TV&RadDir 84*
WQCK-FM - Clinton, LA - *BrCabYB 84*
WQCM-FM - Hagerstown, MD - *NatRadPubDir Summer 83, Spring 84*
WQCM-FM - Halfway, MD - *BrCabYB 84*
WQCN - Savannah, GA - *BrCabYB 84; NatRadPubDir Spring 84; TV&RadDir 84*
WQCR-FM - Burlington, VT - *BrCabYB 84; NatRadPubDir Summer 83, Spring 84; TV&RadDir 84*
WQCS - Ft. Pierce, FL - *BrCabYB 84*
WQCW - Waycross, GA - *BrCabYB 84*
WQCY-FM - Quincy, IL - *BrCabYB 84; TV&RadDir 84*
WQDE - Albany, GA - *BrCabYB 84; NatRadPubDir Summer 83, Spring 84; TV&RadDir 84*
WQDI - Homestead, FL - *BrCabYB 84; TV&RadDir 84*

WQDI - Miami/Miami Beach, FL - *NatRadPubDir Summer 83 p.62, Spring 84 p.62*
WQDK-FM - Ahoskie, NC - *BrCabYB 84; TV&RadDir 84*
WQDQ - Lebanon, TN - *BrCabYB 84*
WQDR-FM - Raleigh, NC - *BrCabYB 84; NatRadPubDir Summer 83, Spring 84; TV&RadDir 84*
WQDW-FM - Kinston, NC - *BrCabYB 84; TV&RadDir 84*
WQDY - Calais, ME - *BrCabYB 84; TV&RadDir 84*
WQDY-FM - Calais, ME - *BrCabYB 84; TV&RadDir 84*
WQED-FM - Pittsburgh, PA - *BrCabYB 84; NatRadPubDir Summer 83, Spring 84; TV&RadDir 84*
WQED-TV - Pittsburgh, PA - *Tel&CabFB 84S; TV&RadDir 84*
WQEN-FM - Gadsden, AL - *BrCabYB 84; NatRadPubDir Summer 83, Spring 84; TV&RadDir 84*
WQEQ-FM - Freeland, PA - *BrCabYB 84*
WQEQ-FM - Hazleton, PA - *TV&RadDir 84*
WQEX-TV - Pittsburgh, PA - *BrCabYB 84; Tel&CabFB 84S; TV&RadDir 84*
WQEZ-FM - Birmingham, AL - *NatRadPubDir Summer 83; TV&RadDir 84*
WQFL - Rockford, IL - *BrCabYB 84*
WQFM-FM - Milwaukee, WI - *BrCabYB 84; NatRadPubDir Summer 83, Spring 84; TV&RadDir 84*
WQFS-FM - Greensboro, NC - *BrCabYB 84; NatRadPubDir Summer 83, Spring 84; TV&RadDir 84*
WQGL-FM - Butler, AL - *BrCabYB 84; TV&RadDir 84*
WQGN-FM - Groton, CT - *TV&RadDir 84*
WQGN-FM - New London, CT - *NatRadPubDir Summer 83 p.47, Spring 84 p.48*
WQHJ - Key West, FL - *BrCabYB 84*
WQHK - Ft. Wayne, IN - *BrCabYB 84; NatRadPubDir Summer 83, Spring 84; TV&RadDir 84*
WQHL-FM - Live Oak, FL - *BrCabYB 84; TV&RadDir 84*
WQHQ-FM - Salisbury, MD - *BrCabYB 84; NatRadPubDir Summer 83, Spring 84; TV&RadDir 84*
WQHY-FM - Prestonsburg, KY - *BrCabYB 84; TV&RadDir 84*
WQIC - Meridian, MS - *BrCabYB 84; NatRadPubDir Summer 83, Spring 84; TV&RadDir 84*
WQID-FM - Biloxi, MS - *BrCabYB 84; NatRadPubDir Summer 83, Spring 84; TV&RadDir 84*
WQII - San Juan, PR - *BrCabYB 84*
WQIK - Jacksonville, FL - *BrCabYB 84; NatRadPubDir Spring 84*
WQIK-FM - Jacksonville, FL - *BrCabYB 84; NatRadPubDir Summer 83, Spring 84; TV&RadDir 84*
WQIM-FM - Prattville, AL - *BrCabYB 84; TV&RadDir 84*
WQIN - Lykens, PA - *BrCabYB 84; TV&RadDir 84*
WQIO - Canton, OH - *TV&RadDir 84*
WQIQ - Aston, PA - *TV&RadDir 84*
WQIQ - Chester, PA - *BrCabYB 84*
WQIS - Laurel, MS - *BrCabYB 84; TV&RadDir 84*
WQIX-FM - Horseheads, NY - *BrCabYB 84; TV&RadDir 84*
WQIZ - St. George, SC - *BrCabYB 84; TV&RadDir 84*
WQKI - St. Matthews, SC - *BrCabYB 84; TV&RadDir 84*
WQKS-FM - Williamsburg, VA - *BrCabYB 84; TV&RadDir 84*
WQKT - Wooster, OH - *BrCabYB 84*
WQKX-FM - Sunbury, PA - *BrCabYB 84; TV&RadDir 84*
WQKY - Emporium, PA - *BrCabYB 84*
WQLA - Lafollette, TN - *BrCabYB 84*
WQLK-FM - Richmond, IN - *BrCabYB 84; TV&RadDir 84*
WQLM-FM - Punta Gorda, FL - *BrCabYB 84; TV&RadDir 84*
WQLN - Erie, PA - *BrCabYB 84; Tel&CabFB 84S; TV&RadDir 84*
WQLN-FM - Erie, PA - *BrCabYB 84; NatRadPubDir Summer 83, Spring 84; TV&RadDir 84*
WQLO-FM - Beaufort, SC - *BrCabYB 84; TV&RadDir 84*
WQLR-FM - Kalamazoo, MI - *NatRadPubDir Summer 83, Spring 84; TV&RadDir 84*
WQLS - Cleveland, TN - *BrCabYB 84*
WQLT - Florence, AL - *BrCabYB 84*
WQLX-FM - Galion, OH - *BrCabYB 84; TV&RadDir 84*
WQLZ-FM - Cheboygan, MI - *BrCabYB 84; TV&RadDir 84*
WQMA - Marks, MS - *BrCabYB 84; TV&RadDir 84*
WQMC-FM - Charlottesville, VA - *BrCabYB 84; NatRadPubDir Summer 83, Spring 84; TV&RadDir 84*
WQMF-FM - Jeffersonville, IN - *BrCabYB 84; NatRadPubDir Summer 83, Spring 84; TV&RadDir 84*
WQMG-FM - Greensboro, NC - *BrCabYB 84; NatRadPubDir Summer 83, Spring 84; TV&RadDir 84*
WQMR - Skowhegan, ME - *BrCabYB 84; TV&RadDir 84*
WQMS - Alabaster, AL - *BrCabYB 84*
WQMT-FM - Chatsworth, GA - *BrCabYB 84; TV&RadDir 84*
WQMU-FM - Indiana, PA - *BrCabYB 84; TV&RadDir 84*
WQMV-FM - Vicksburg, MS - *BrCabYB 84; NatRadPubDir Summer 83, Spring 84; TV&RadDir 84*
WQNA-FM - Springfield, IL - *BrCabYB 84; TV&RadDir 84*
WQNE-FM - Cleveland, TN - *BrCabYB 84; TV&RadDir 84*
WQNS-FM - Waynesville, NC - *BrCabYB 84; TV&RadDir 84*
WQNY-FM - Ithaca, NY - *NatRadPubDir Spring 84*
WQNY-FM - Newfield, NY - *TV&RadDir 84*
WQNZ-FM - Natchez, MS - *BrCabYB 84; TV&RadDir 84*
WQOD-FM - Youngstown, OH - *BrCabYB 84; NatRadPubDir Summer 83, Spring 84; TV&RadDir 84*
WQOK - Greenville, SC - *TV&RadDir 84*
WQOK - Myrtle Beach, SC - *BrCabYB 84; TV&RadDir 84*
WQON-FM - Grayling, MI - *BrCabYB 84; TV&RadDir 84*
WQOW-TV - Eau Claire, WI - *TelAl 83, 84; Tel&CabFB 84S; TV&RadDir 84*
WQOX-FM - Memphis, TN - *BrCabYB 84; NatRadPubDir Summer 83, Spring 84; TV&RadDir 84*
WQPD - Lake City, FL - *BrCabYB 84*
WQPD - Lakeland, FL - *NatRadPubDir Summer 83; TV&RadDir 84*
WQPM - Princeton, MN - *BrCabYB 84; TV&RadDir 84*
WQPM-FM - Princeton, MN - *BrCabYB 84; TV&RadDir 84*
WQPO-FM - Harrisonburg, VA - *BrCabYB 84; NatRadPubDir Summer 83, Spring 84; TV&RadDir 84*
WQPT-TV - Moline, IL - *BrCabYB 84; Tel&CabFB 84S*
WQQB - Bowling Green, KY - *BrCabYB 84*
WQQQ-FM - Easton, PA - *BrCabYB 84; NatRadPubDir Summer 83, Spring 84 p.209; TV&RadDir 84*
WQQT - Savannah, GA - *NatRadPubDir Summer 83*
WQQW - Waterbury, CT - *BrCabYB 84; NatRadPubDir Summer 83, Spring 84; TV&RadDir 84*
WQQW-TV - Eau Claire, WI - *BrCabYB 84*
WQRA - Warrenton, VA - *BrCabYB 84; TV&RadDir 84*
WQRB - Burlington, NC - *BrCabYB 84; TV&RadDir 84*
WQRC-FM - Barnstable, MA - *BrCabYB 84*
WQRC-FM - Hyannis, MA - *TV&RadDir 84*
WQRD - Mayaquez, PR - *Tel&CabFB 84S*
WQRF-TV - Rockford, IL - *BrCabYB 84; DirUSTelSta 83; TelAl 83, 84; Tel&CabFB 84S*
WQRK-FM - Virginia Beach, VA - *TV&RadDir 84*
WQRL-FM - Benton, IL - *BrCabYB 84; TV&RadDir 84*
WQRO - Huntingdon, PA - *BrCabYB 84; TV&RadDir 84*
WQRP-FM - Dayton, OH - *TV&RadDir 84*
WQRP-FM - West Carollton, OH - *BrCabYB 84*
WQRS-FM - Detroit, MI - *BrCabYB 84; NatRadPubDir Summer 83, Spring 84; TV&RadDir 84*
WQSA - Sarasota, FL - *BrCabYB 84; NatRadPubDir Summer 83, Spring 84; TV&RadDir 84*
WQSB-FM - Albertville, AL - *BrCabYB 84; TV&RadDir 84*
WQSM-FM - Fayetteville, NC - *BrCabYB 84; TV&RadDir 84*
WQSR-FM - Baltimore, MD - *NatRadPubDir Summer 83, Spring 84*
WQSR-FM - Catonsville, MD - *BrCabYB 84*
WQST-FM - Forest, MS - *BrCabYB 84; TV&RadDir 84*
WQSU-FM - Selinsgrove, PA - *BrCabYB 84; NatRadPubDir Summer 83, Spring 84; TV&RadDir 84*
WQTC-FM - Two Rivers, WI - *BrCabYB 84; TV&RadDir 84*
WQTE-FM - Adrian, MI - *BrCabYB 84; TV&RadDir 84*
WQTI-FM - Dunn, NC - *TV&RadDir 84*
WQTK-FM - St. Johns, MI - *BrCabYB 84; TV&RadDir 84*
WQTQ - Hartford, CT - *BrCabYB 84*
WQTR-FM - Whiteville, NC - *BrCabYB 84; TV&RadDir 84*
WQTU-FM - Rome, GA - *BrCabYB 84; TV&RadDir 84*
WQTV-TV - Boston, MA - *BrCabYB 84; DirUSTelSta 83; TelAl 83, 84; Tel&CabFB 84S*
WQTV-TV - Brookline, MA - *TV&RadDir 84*
WQTW - Latrobe, PA - *BrCabYB 84; NatRadPubDir Summer 83; TV&RadDir 84*
WQTY-FM - Linton, IN - *BrCabYB 84; TV&RadDir 84*
WQUA - Moline, IL - *TV&RadDir 84*
WQUA - Davenport, IA - *NatRadPubDir Summer 83 p.96*

WQUE - New Orleans, LA - *BrCabYB 84; NatRadPubDir Spring 84*
WQUE-FM - New Orleans, LA - *NatRadPubDir Summer 83, Spring 84; TV&RadDir 84*
WQUH-FM - De Funiak Springs, FL - *BrCabYB 84; TV&RadDir 84*
WQUT-FM - Johnson City, TN - *BrCabYB 84; NatRadPubDir Summer 83, Spring 84; TV&RadDir 84*
WQVR-FM - Southbridge, MA - *BrCabYB 84; TV&RadDir 84*
WQWK-FM - State College, PA - *BrCabYB 84; TV&RadDir 84*
WQWQ-FM - Muskegon, MI - *BrCabYB 84; NatRadPubDir Summer 83, Spring 84; TV&RadDir 84*
WQXA-FM - York, PA - *BrCabYB 84; NatRadPubDir Summer 83, Spring 84; TV&RadDir 84*
WQXA-TV - Macon, GA - *TelAl 84*
WQXB-FM - Grenada, MS - *BrCabYB 84; TV&RadDir 84*
WQXE-FM - Elizabethtown, KY - *BrCabYB 84; TV&RadDir 84*
WQXI - Atlanta, GA - *BrCabYB 84; NatRadPubDir Summer 83, Spring 84; TV&RadDir 84*
WQXI-FM - Atlanta, GA - *NatRadPubDir Summer 83, Spring 84; TV&RadDir 84*
WQXI-FM - Smyrna, GA - *BrCabYB 84*
WQXK-FM - Salem, OH - *BrCabYB 84; TV&RadDir 84*
WQXL - Columbia, SC - *BrCabYB 84; NatRadPubDir Summer 83, Spring 84; TV&RadDir 84*
WQXM-FM - Clearwater, FL - *BrCabYB 84*
WQXM-FM - Largo, FL - *TV&RadDir 84*
WQXM-FM - Tampa/St. Petersburg, FL - *NatRadPubDir Summer 83 p.65*
WQXO - Munising, MI - *BrCabYB 84; TV&RadDir 84*
WQXO-FM - Munising, MI - *BrCabYB 84; TV&RadDir 84*
WQXQ - West Springfield, MA - *TV&RadDir 84*
WQXR - New York, NY - *BrCabYB 84; LitMarPl 83, 84; NatRadPubDir Summer 83, Spring 84; TV&RadDir 84*
WQXR-FM - New York, NY - *BrCabYB 84; LitMarPl 83; NatRadPubDir Summer 83, Spring 84; TV&RadDir 84*
WQXX-FM - Morganton, NC - *BrCabYB 84; TV&RadDir 84*
WQXY-FM - Baton Rouge, LA - *BrCabYB 84; NatRadPubDir Summer 83, Spring 84; TV&RadDir 84*
WQXZ - Taylorsville, NC - *BrCabYB 84; TV&RadDir 84*
WQYK-FM - St. Petersburg, FL - *BrCabYB 84; TV&RadDir 84*
WQYK-FM - Tampa/St. Petersburg, FL - *NatRadPubDir Summer 83, Spring 84 p.66*
WQYT-FM - Binghamton, NY - *BrCabYB 84; NatRadPubDir Summer 83, Spring 84; TV&RadDir 84*
WQYX-FM - Clearfield, PA - *BrCabYB 84; TV&RadDir 84*
WQZK-FM - Keyser, WV - *BrCabYB 84; TV&RadDir 84*
WQZQ-FM - Chesapeake, VA - *TV&RadDir 84*
WQZY-FM - Dublin, GA - *BrCabYB 84; TV&RadDir 84*
WRAA - Luray, VA - *BrCabYB 84; TV&RadDir 84*
WRAB - Arab, AL - *BrCabYB 84; TV&RadDir 84*
WRAC - West Union, OH - *BrCabYB 84*
WRAD - Radford, VA - *BrCabYB 84; TV&RadDir 84*
WRAD-FM - Radford, VA - *TV&RadDir 84*
WRAF - Toccoa Falls, GA - *BrCabYB 84*
WRAG - Carrollton, AL - *BrCabYB 84; TV&RadDir 84*
WRAI - San Juan, PR - *BrCabYB 84*
WRAJ - Anna, IL - *BrCabYB 84; TV&RadDir 84*
WRAJ-FM - Anna, IL - *BrCabYB 84; TV&RadDir 84*
WRAK - Williamsport, PA - *BrCabYB 84; NatRadPubDir Summer 83, Spring 84; TV&RadDir 84*
WRAL-FM - Raleigh, NC - *BrCabYB 84; NatRadPubDir Summer 83, Spring 84; TV&RadDir 84*
WRAL-TV - Raleigh, NC - *BrCabYB 84; DirUSTelSta 83; LitMarPl 83, 84; TelAl 83, 84; Tel&CabFB 84S; TV&RadDir 84*
WRAM - Monmouth, IL - *BrCabYB 84; TV&RadDir 84*
WRAN - Dover, NJ - *BrCabYB 84; TV&RadDir 84*
Wrangell Cablevision [of Alaska Cablevision Inc.] - Wrangell, AK - *BrCabYB 84; Tel&CabFB 84C*
Wrangell Sentinel - Wrangell, AK - *AyerDirPub 83; BaconPubCkNews 84; Ed&PubIntYB 82*
WRAP - Norfolk, VA - *BrCabYB 84; NatRadPubDir Summer 83, Spring 84; TV&RadDir 84*
Wrap-Ups [Div. of Calle & Co.] - Greenwich, CT - *IntDirMarRes 83*
WRAQ - Asheville, NC - *BrCabYB 84; NatRadPubDir Summer 83, Spring 84; TV&RadDir 84*
WRAR - Tappahannock, VA - *BrCabYB 84; TV&RadDir 84*
WRAR-FM - Tappahannock, VA - *BrCabYB 84; TV&RadDir 84*
WRAS-FM - Atlanta, GA - *BrCabYB 84; NatRadPubDir Summer 83, Spring 84; TV&RadDir 84*
Wrather Corp. - Beverly Hills, CA - *HomeVid&CabYB 82-83; TelAl 83, 84; Tel&CabFB 84C*
WRAU-TV - Peoria, IL - *BrCabYB 84; DirUSTelSta 83; TelAl 83, 84; Tel&CabFB 84S; TV&RadDir 84*
WRAW - Reading, PA - *BrCabYB 84; NatRadPubDir Spring 84; TV&RadDir 84*
WRAX - Bedford, PA - *BrCabYB 84; TV&RadDir 84*
WRAY - Princeton, IN - *BrCabYB 84; TV&RadDir 84*
Wray Cablevision Inc. - Wray, CO - *BrCabYB 84; Tel&CabFB 84C*
WRAY-FM - Princeton, IN - *BrCabYB 84; TV&RadDir 84*
Wray Gazette - Wray, CO - *BaconPubCkNews 84; Ed&PubIntYB 82; NewsDir 84*
Wray/Ward Advertising - Charlotte, NC - *AdAge 3-28-84; StaDirAdAg 2-84*
WRBA - Normal, IL - *BrCabYB 84; TV&RadDir 84*
WRBB-FM - Boston, MA - *BrCabYB 84; NatRadPubDir Summer 83, Spring 84*
WRBC-FM - Lewiston, ME - *BrCabYB 84; TV&RadDir 84*
WRBD - Ft. Lauderdale, FL - *NatRadPubDir Summer 83, Spring 84; TV&RadDir 84*
WRBD - Pompano Beach, FL - *BrCabYB 84*
WRBE - Lucedale, MS - *BrCabYB 84; TV&RadDir 84*
WRBH - New Orleans, LA - *BrCabYB 84*
WRBI-FM - Batesville, IN - *BrCabYB 84; TV&RadDir 84*
WRBL-TV - Columbus, GA - *BrCabYB 84; DirUSTelSta 83; TelAl 83, 84; Tel&CabFB 84S; TV&RadDir 84*
WRBN - Warner Robins, GA - *BrCabYB 84; TV&RadDir 84*
WRBN-FM - Warner Robins, GA - *BrCabYB 84; TV&RadDir 84*
WRBO - Tampa, FL - *LitMarPl 84*
WRBQ - St. Petersburg, FL - *BrCabYB 84*
WRBQ - Tampa, FL - *NatRadPubDir Spring 84*
WRBQ-FM - Tampa, FL - *BrCabYB 84; NatRadPubDir Summer 83, Spring 84; TV&RadDir 84*
WRBR-FM - South Bend, IN - *NatRadPubDir Summer 83 p.92*
WRBS-FM - Baltimore, MD - *BrCabYB 84; NatRadPubDir Summer 83, Spring 84; TV&RadDir 84*
WRBT-TV - Baton Rouge, LA - *BrCabYB 84; DirUSTelSta 83; TelAl 83, 84; Tel&CabFB 84S; TV&RadDir 84*
WRBV-TV - Vineland, NJ - *BrCabYB 84; Tel&CabFB 84S*
WRBV-TV - Philadelphia, PA - *DirUSTelSta 83*
WRBX - Chapel Hill, NC - *BrCabYB 84*
WRBX - Durham, NC - *TV&RadDir 84*
WRC - Washington, DC - *BrCabYB 84; LitMarPl 83, 84; NatRadPubDir Summer 83, Spring 84; TV&RadDir 84*
WRC Publishing - Silver Spring, MD - *BoPubDir 5*
WRC-TV - Washington, DC - *BrCabYB 84; DirUSTelSta 83; LitMarPl 83, 84; TelAl 83, 84; Tel&CabFB 84S; TV&RadDir 84*
WRCB-TV - Chattanooga, TN - *BrCabYB 84; DirUSTelSta 83; TelAl 83, 84; Tel&CabFB 84S; TV&RadDir 84*
WRCBase - Marlow, England - *DirOnDB Spring 84*
WRCC-FM - Cape Coral, FL - *BrCabYB 84; TV&RadDir 84*
WRCD - Dalton, GA - *BrCabYB 84; TV&RadDir 84*
WRCG - Columbus, GA - *BrCabYB 84; NatRadPubDir Summer 83, Spring 84; TV&RadDir 84*
WRCH-FM - Farmington, CT - *TV&RadDir 84*
WRCH-FM - Hartford/New Britain, CT - *NatRadPubDir Summer 83 p.46, Spring 84 p.47*
WRCH-FM - New Britain, CT - *BrCabYB 84*
WRCI - Midland, MI - *BrCabYB 84*
WRCJ-FM - Cincinnati, OH - *TV&RadDir 84*
WRCJ-FM - Reading, OH - *BrCabYB 84; NatRadPubDir Summer 83, Spring 84*
WRCK-FM - Utica, NY - *BrCabYB 84; NatRadPubDir Summer 83, Spring 84; TV&RadDir 84*
WRCM-FM - Jacksonville, NC - *BrCabYB 84; TV&RadDir 84*
WRCN - Riverhead, NY - *TV&RadDir 84*
WRCN - Suffolk County, Long Island, NY - *NatRadPubDir Summer 83 p.178*
WRCN-FM - Riverhead, NY - *BrCabYB 84; TV&RadDir 84*
WRCN-FM - Suffolk County, Long Island, NY - *NatRadPubDir Summer 83 p.178, Spring 84 p.176*
WRCO - Richland Center, WI - *BrCabYB 84; TV&RadDir 84*

WRCO-FM - Richland Center, WI - *BrCabYB 84; TV&RadDir 84*
WRCP - Philadelphia, PA - *BrCabYB 84; TV&RadDir 84*
WRCP - North Providence, RI - *NatRadPubDir Spring 84*
WRCQ - Farmington, CT - *TV&RadDir 84*
WRCQ - Hartford/New Britain, CT - *NatRadPubDir Summer 83 p.46, Spring 84 p.47*
WRCQ - New Britain, CT - *BrCabYB 84*
WRCR-FM - Rushville, IN - *BrCabYB 84; TV&RadDir 84*
WRCS - Ahoskie, NC - *BrCabYB 84; TV&RadDir 84*
WRCT-FM - Pittsburgh, PA - *BrCabYB 84; NatRadPubDir Summer 83, Spring 84; TV&RadDir 84*
WRCU-FM - Hamilton, NY - *BrCabYB 84; NatRadPubDir Summer 83, Spring 84; TV&RadDir 84*
WRCV-FM - Mercersburg, PA - *BrCabYB 84; TV&RadDir 84*
WRCW - Canton, OH - *BrCabYB 84; NatRadPubDir Summer 83, Spring 84*
WRDB - Reedsburg, WI - *BrCabYB 84; TV&RadDir 84*
WRDB-FM - Reedsburg, WI - *BrCabYB 84; TV&RadDir 84*
WRDC - Cleveland, MS - *BrCabYB 84; TV&RadDir 84*
WRDG - Burlington, NC - *BrCabYB 84; Tel&CabFB 84S*
WRDJ - Samson, AL - *BrCabYB 84*
WRDL-FM - Ashland, OH - *BrCabYB 84; NatRadPubDir Summer 83, Spring 84; TV&RadDir 84*
WRDN - Durand, WI - *BrCabYB 84; TV&RadDir 84*
WRDN-FM - Durand, WI - *BrCabYB 84; TV&RadDir 84*
WRDO - Augusta, ME - *BrCabYB 84; TV&RadDir 84*
WRDR-FM - Egg Harbor, NJ - *BrCabYB 84*
WRDR-FM - Hammonton, NJ - *TV&RadDir 84*
WRDS - Sardis, MS - *BrCabYB 84*
WRDW - Augusta, GA - *BrCabYB 84; NatRadPubDir Summer 83, Spring 84; TV&RadDir 84*
WRDW-TV - Augusta, GA - *BrCabYB 84; DirUSTelSta 83; TelAl 83, 84; Tel&CabFB 84S; TV&RadDir 84*
WRDX-FM - Salisbury, NC - *BrCabYB 84; NatRadPubDir Summer 83, Spring 84; TV&RadDir 84*
WREB - Holyoke, MA - *BrCabYB 84; TV&RadDir 84*
WREB - Springfield/Holyoke/Chicopee, MA - *NatRadPubDir Summer 83, Spring 84 p.123*
WREC - Memphis, TN - *BrCabYB 84; NatRadPubDir Summer 83, Spring 84; TV&RadDir 84*
Wrecking & Salvage Journal - Braintree, MA - *BaconPubCkMag 84; MagDir 84*
WRED - Monroe, GA - *BrCabYB 84*
WRED - Johnson City, TN - *TV&RadDir 84*
Wreden, William P. - Palo Alto, CA - *BoPubDir 4, 5*
WREE - College Park, GA - *BrCabYB 84*
WREE - New York, NY - *BoPubDir 4, 5*
Wree-View - New York, NY - *LitMag&SmPr 83-84*
WREG-TV - Memphis, TN - *BrCabYB 84; DirUSTelSta 83; LitMarPl 83, 84; TelAl 83, 84; Tel&CabFB 84S; TV&RadDir 84*
WREI - Quebradillas, PR - *BrCabYB 84*
WREK-FM - Atlanta, GA - *BrCabYB 84; NatRadPubDir Summer 83, Spring 84; TV&RadDir 84*
WREL - Lexington, VA - *BrCabYB 84; TV&RadDir 84*
WREM - Orlando, FL - *TV&RadDir 84*
WREM - Pine Castle, FL - *BrCabYB 84*
WREN - Topeka, KS - *BrCabYB 84; NatRadPubDir Summer 83, Spring 84; TV&RadDir 84*
Wren Advertising Inc., Ronald R. - San Francisco, CA - *StaDirAdAg 2-84*
Wren Associates Inc. - Princeton, NJ - *AvMarPl 83*
Wren Co. - Cincinnati, OH - *DataDirSup 7-83*
Wren International [Subs. of Wren Associates Inc.] - Princeton, NJ - *AvMarPl 83*
Wrens Jefferson Reporter - Wrens, GA - *BaconPubCkNews 84*
Wrensong Inc. - St. Paul, MN - *BillIntBG 83-84*
Wrensong Music - *See* Wrensong Inc.
WREO-FM - Ashtabula, OH - *BrCabYB 84; TV&RadDir 84*
Wreschner, Ruth - New York, NY - *LitMarPl 83, 84*
WRET-TV - Spartanburg, SC - *BrCabYB 84; Tel&CabFB 84S*
WREV - Reidsville, NC - *BrCabYB 84; TV&RadDir 84*
WREX-TV - Rockford, IL - *BrCabYB 84; DirUSTelSta 83; TelAl 83, 84; Tel&CabFB 84S; TV&RadDir 84*
WREY - Millville, NJ - *BrCabYB 84*
WREY - Vineland, NJ - *TV&RadDir 84*
WREZ-FM - Montgomery, AL - *BrCabYB 84; NatRadPubDir Summer 83, Spring 84; TV&RadDir 84*
WRFB-FM - Stowe, VT - *BrCabYB 84; TV&RadDir 84*
WRFC - Athens, GA - *BrCabYB 84; NatRadPubDir Summer 83, Spring 84; TV&RadDir 84*
WRFD - Columbus, OH - *BrCabYB 84; NatRadPubDir Summer 83, Spring 84*
WRFE - Aguada, PR - *BrCabYB 84*
WRFG-FM - Atlanta, GA - *BrCabYB 84; TV&RadDir 84*
WRFK-FM - Richmond, VA - *BrCabYB 84; TV&RadDir 84*
WRFM-FM - New York, NY - *BrCabYB 84; NatRadPubDir Summer 83, Spring 84; TV&RadDir 84*
WRFN-FM - Nashville, TN - *BrCabYB 84; NatRadPubDir Summer 83, Spring 84; TV&RadDir 84*
WRFR-FM - Franklin, NC - *BrCabYB 84; TV&RadDir 84*
WRFS - Alexander City, AL - *BrCabYB 84; TV&RadDir 84*
WRFS-FM - Alexander City, AL - *BrCabYB 84*
WRFT-FM - Acton, IN - *TV&RadDir 84*
WRFT-FM - Indianapolis, IN - *BrCabYB 84*
WRFW-FM - River Falls, WI - *BrCabYB 84; NatRadPubDir Spring 84; TV&RadDir 84*
WRFY-FM - Reading, PA - *BrCabYB 84; NatRadPubDir Summer 83, Spring 84; TV&RadDir 84*
WRGA - Rome, GA - *BrCabYB 84; TV&RadDir 84*
WRGB-TV - Albany, NY - *DirUSTelSta 83; TelAl 83, 84*
WRGB-TV - Schenectady, NY - *BrCabYB 84; LitMarPl 83, 84; Tel&CabFB 84S; TV&RadDir 84*
WRGC - Sylva, NC - *BrCabYB 84; TV&RadDir 84*
WRGI-FM - Naples, FL - *BrCabYB 84; TV&RadDir 84*
WRGS - Rogersville, TN - *BrCabYB 84; TV&RadDir 84*
WRHC - Coral Gables, FL - *BrCabYB 84*
WRHC - Miami, FL - *NatRadPubDir Summer 83, Spring 84; TV&RadDir 84*
WRHD - Riverhead, NY - *BrCabYB 84*
WRHD - Suffolk County, Long Island, NY - *NatRadPubDir Spring 84 p.176*
WRHI - Rock Hill, SC - *BrCabYB 84; NatRadPubDir Summer 83, Spring 84; TV&RadDir 84*
WRHL - Rochelle, IL - *BrCabYB 84; TV&RadDir 84*
WRHL-FM - Rochelle, IL - *BrCabYB 84; TV&RadDir 84*
WRHN-FM - Rhinelander, WI - *BrCabYB 84; TV&RadDir 84*
WRHO-FM - Oneonta, NY - *BrCabYB 84; NatRadPubDir Summer 83, Spring 84; TV&RadDir 84*
WRHR - Henrietta, NY - *BrCabYB 84*
WRHS-FM - Park Forest, IL - *BrCabYB 84; TV&RadDir 84*
WRHU - Hempstead, NY - *BrCabYB 84*
WRHY-FM - York, PA - *NatRadPubDir Summer 83; TV&RadDir 84*
WRIA-FM - Richmond, IN - *BrCabYB 84; TV&RadDir 84*
WRIB - Providence, RI - *BrCabYB 84; NatRadPubDir Summer 83, Spring 84; TV&RadDir 84*
WRIC - Richlands, VA - *BrCabYB 84; TV&RadDir 84*
WRID - Homer City, PA - *BrCabYB 84*
WRIE - Erie, PA - *BrCabYB 84; NatRadPubDir Summer 83, Spring 84; TV&RadDir 84*
WRIF-FM - Detroit, MI - *BrCabYB 84; NatRadPubDir Summer 83 p.127, Spring 84 p.127*
WRIF-FM - Southfield, MI - *TV&RadDir 84*
WRIG - Wausau, WI - *BrCabYB 84; TV&RadDir 84*
Wright, Alvin - Valdese, NC - *Tel&CabFB 84C p.1714*
Wright & Manning Inc. - *See* Edelman Inc., Daniel J.
Wright Cablevision - Cathlamet, WA - *BrCabYB 84 p.D-311; Tel&CabFB 84C p.1714*
Wright Communications [Aff. of Ontario Film Association] - Mississauga, ON, Canada - *BoPubDir 5*
Wright Co. Inc., The [Subs. of Wright Offset Plate Co.] - Cambridge, MA - *LitMarPl 83, 84; MagIndMarPl 82-83*
Wright County Journal-Press - Buffalo, MN - *AyerDirPub 83; Ed&PubIntYB 82*
Wright County Monitor - Clarion, IA - *AyerDirPub 83*
Wright, Don E. - Skamokawa, WA - *BrCabYB 84*
Wright Enterprises, Carter - Hollywood, CA - *TelAl 83, 84; Tel&CabFB 84C*
Wright, Esther Clark - Wolfville, NS, Canada - *BoPubDir 4, 5*
Wright Line Inc. - Worcester, MA - *DataDirSup 7-83*
Wright, Martin & Associates Inc. - Guilford, CT - *DirPRFirms 83*

Wright, Mildred S. - Beaumont, TX - *BoPubDir 4, 5*
Wright Music Co., Johnny - *See* Dan the Man Music Publishing Co.
Wright Press, Stephen - New York, NY - *BoPubDir 4, 5*
Wright Printing & Publishing Co. - Des Moines, IA - *MagIndMarPl 82-83*
Wright/PSG Inc., John [Subs. of John Wright & Sons Ltd.] - Littleton, MA - *LitMarPl 83; WritMar 84*
Wright Studio Inc., Bob - Rochester, NY - *AvMarPl 83*
Wrightson Typographers - Newton, MA - *LitMarPl 83, 84; WhoWMicrocom 83*
Wrightstown Leader [of Lorraine Publishing Inc.] - Bordentown, NJ - *NewsDir 84*
Wrightstown Leader - *See* Lorraine Publishing Inc.
Wrightsville Headlight - Wrightsville, GA - *BaconPubCkNews 84; Ed&PubIntYB 82*
Wrightwood Entertainment Ltd. - Los Angeles, CA - *AvMarPl 83; TelAl 84*
Wrightwood Mountaineer Progress - Wrightwood, CA - *BaconPubCkNews 84*
WRIK - Metropolis, IL - *BrCabYB 84*
WRIN - Rensselaer, IN - *BrCabYB 84; TV&RadDir 84*
WRIO-FM - Rio Grande, NJ - *TV&RadDir 84*
WRIP - Rossville, GA - *BrCabYB 84; TV&RadDir 84*
WRIP-TV - Chattanooga, TN - *DirUSTelSta 83; TelAl 83, 84; TV&RadDir 84*
WRIQ - Radford, VA - *BrCabYB 84*
WRIS - Roanoke, VA - *BrCabYB 84; NatRadPubDir Summer 83, Spring 84; TV&RadDir 84*
WRIT - Stuart, FL - *BrCabYB 84*
Writ - Toronto, ON, Canada - *LitMag&SmPr 83-84; WritMar 84*
WRIT-FM - Stuart, FL - *TV&RadDir 84*
Writ, The - New Orleans, LA - *LitMag&SmPr 83-84*
W.R.I.T.E. - Los Altos, CA - *BoPubDir 4, 5*
Write-A-Book [Aff. of Prime Ltd.] - Las Vegas, NV - *BoPubDir 5*
Write Place - Evanston, IL - *AvMarPl 83*
Write to Sell - Carpinteria, CA - *BoPubDir 4, 5; LitMarPl 83*
Write Way, The - Plattsburgh, NY - *LitMarPl 83, 84*
Writer Inc., The - Boston, MA - *BaconPubCkMag 84; LitMarPl 83, 84; MagDir 84; MagIndMarPl 82-83; WritMar 84*
Writer Unltd. Agency Inc. - Rocky Point, NY - *LitMag&SmPr 83-84*
Writers Alliance Ltd. - New York, NY - *LitMarPl 83, 84; MagIndMarPl 82-83*
Writers & Artists Agency [Div. of Joan Scott Inc.] - New York, NY - *LitMarPl 83, 84*
Writers & Books - Rochester, NY - *BoPubDir 4 Sup, 5*
Writers' Center Press - Indianapolis, IN - *LitMag&SmPr 83-84*
Writers' Center Press - Bethesda, MD - *LitMag&SmPr 83-84*
Writer's Clearinghouse - Fabyan, CT - *Ed&PubIntYB 82*
Writers' Development Trust - Toronto, ON, Canada - *BoPubDir 4, 5*
Writer's Digest [Subs. of F & W Publishing] - Cincinnati, OH - *ArtMar 84; BaconPubCkMag 84; DirMarMP 83; LitMarPl 83, 84; MagDir 84; MagIndMarPl 82-83; WritMar 84*
Writer's Digest Book Club [Div. of F & W Publishing Corp.] - Cincinnati, OH - *LitMarPl 83, 84*
Writer's Digest Books [Subs. of F & W Publishing Corp.] - Cincinnati, OH - *LitMarPl 83, 84; WritMar 84*
Writer's Digest Books/North Light - Cincinnati, OH - *ArtMar 84*
Writer's Digest Criticism Service - Cincinnati, OH - *MagIndMarPl 82-83*
Writers Forum [of University of Colorado] - Colorado Springs, CO - *LitMag&SmPr 83-84; WritMar 84*
Writer's Forum - Murfreesboro, NC - *MagIndMarPl 82-83*
Writers Forum - London, England - *LitMag&SmPr 83-84*
Writers: Free-Lance Inc. - Ambler, PA - *DirMarMP 83; LitMarPl 83, 84; MagIndMarPl 82-83*
Writers Guild of America - Los Angeles, CA - *AvMarPl 83*
Writers Guild West - Los Angeles, CA - *BoPubDir 5*
Writer's Helpers, The - Tacoma, WA - *LitMarPl 83, 84*
Writers House Inc. - New York, NY - *LitMarPl 83, 84*
Writer's House Music Inc. - *See* Montgomery Music Inc., Bob
Writers Ink [of Writer Unltd. Agency Inc.] - Rocky Point, NY - *LitMag&SmPr 83-84*
Writer's Lifeline - Cornwall, ON, Canada - *LitMag&SmPr 83-84; WritMar 84*
Writers Pen [Div. of American Phoenix Corp.] - Oak Park, IL - *MagIndMarPl 82-83*
Writers Publishing Co. - New York, NY - *BoPubDir 4 Sup, 5*
Writer's Publishing Service Co. [Aff. of Cleaning Consultant Services Inc.] - Seattle, WA - *BoPubDir 4, 5; LitMarPl 84*
Writers' Service - Summerland, CA - *LitMarPl 83, 84*
Writer's Service Inc. - Miami Springs, FL - *LitMag&SmPr 83-84*
Writers' Union of Canada - Toronto, ON, Canada - *BoPubDir 4, 5*
Writers West [of Kriss Enterprises] - San Diego, CA - *LitMarPl 84*
Writers West Books - Colorado Springs, CO - *BoPubDir 4, 5*
Writer's Yearbook - Cincinnati, OH - *ArtMar 84; MagDir 84; WritMar 84*
Writing - Highland Park, IL - *BaconPubCkMag 84; MagIndMarPl 82-83; WritMar 84*
Writing [of The Raffeen Press] - Forwey, England - *LitMag&SmPr 83-84*
Writing Co., The - Culver City, CA - *AvMarPl 83*
Writing Service, The - Lenox, MA - *LitMarPl 83*
Writing Service, The - New York, NY - *LitMarPl 84*
Writing Works [Aff. of Morse Press Inc.] - Seattle, WA - *BoPubDir 4; LitMarPl 83, 84; WritMar 84*
WRIU - Kingston, RI - *BrCabYB 84*
WRIU - Wakefield, RI - *TV&RadDir 84*
WRIU-FM - Kingston, RI - *NatRadPubDir Summer 83, Spring 84*
WRIU-FM - Wakefield, RI - *TV&RadDir 84*
WRIV - Riverhead, NY - *BrCabYB 84; TV&RadDir 84*
WRIV - Suffolk County, Long Island, NY - *NatRadPubDir Summer 83 p.178, Spring 84 p.176*
WRIX-FM - Honea Path, SC - *BrCabYB 84; TV&RadDir 84*
WRJA-FM - Sumter, SC - *BrCabYB 84; NatRadPubDir Summer 83, Spring 84 p.318; TV&RadDir 84*
WRJA-TV - Sumter, SC - *BrCabYB 84; Tel&CabFB 84S; TV&RadDir 84*
WRJB-FM - Camden, TN - *BrCabYB 84; TV&RadDir 84*
WRJC - Mauston, WI - *BrCabYB 84; TV&RadDir 84*
WRJC-FM - Mauston, WI - *BrCabYB 84; TV&RadDir 84*
WRJH-FM - Brandon, MS - *BrCabYB 84; TV&RadDir 84*
WRJK-TV - Bluefield, VA - *BrCabYB 84; Tel&CabFB 84S*
WRJN - Racine, WI - *BrCabYB 84; TV&RadDir 84*
WRJQ - Tomahawk, WI - *BrCabYB 84*
WRJS-FM - Oil City, PA - *BrCabYB 84; TV&RadDir 84*
WRJW - Picayune, MS - *BrCabYB 84; TV&RadDir 84*
WRJZ - Knoxville, TN - *BrCabYB 84; NatRadPubDir Summer 83, Spring 84; TV&RadDir 84*
WRKA-FM - Louisville, KY - *TV&RadDir 84*
WRKA-FM - St. Mathews, KY - *BrCabYB 84*
WRKB - Kannapolis, NC - *BrCabYB 84; TV&RadDir 84*
WRKC - Wilkes-Barre, PA - *BrCabYB 84*
WRKC-FM - Lazerne, PA - *TV&RadDir 84*
WRKC-FM - Wilkes-Barre, PA - *NatRadPubDir Summer 83, Spring 84*
WRKD - Rockland, ME - *BrCabYB 84; TV&RadDir 84*
WRKF - Baton Rouge, LA - *BrCabYB 84*
WRKI-FM - Brookfield, CT - *BrCabYB 84*
WRKI-FM - Danbury, CT - *NatRadPubDir Summer 83, Spring 84; TV&RadDir 84*
WRKK-FM - Birmingham, AL - *BrCabYB 84; NatRadPubDir Summer 83, Spring 84; TV&RadDir 84*
WRKL - New City, NY - *BrCabYB 84*
WRKL - Pomona, NY - *TV&RadDir 84*
WRKL - Rockland County, NY - *NatRadPubDir Summer 83, Spring 84 p.175*
WRKM - Carthage, TN - *BrCabYB 84; TV&RadDir 84*
WRKM-FM - Carthage, TN - *BrCabYB 84; TV&RadDir 84*
WRKN - Brandon, MS - *BrCabYB 84; TV&RadDir 84*
WRKO - Boston, MA - *BrCabYB 84; LitMarPl 83, 84; NatRadPubDir Summer 83, Spring 84; TV&RadDir 84*
WRKQ - Madisonville, TN - *BrCabYB 84; TV&RadDir 84*
WRKR-FM - Racine, WI - *BrCabYB 84; TV&RadDir 84*
WRKS-FM - New York, NY - *BrCabYB 84; LitMarPl 84; NatRadPubDir Summer 83, Spring 84; TV&RadDir 84*
WRKT - Cocoa, FL - *BrCabYB 84; TV&RadDir 84*

WRKT-FM - Cocoa, FL - *BrCabYB 84; TV&RadDir 84*
WRKX - Big Rapids, MI - *NatRadPubDir Summer 83, Spring 84*
WRKX-FM - Ottawa, IL - *TV&RadDir 84*
WRKY-FM - Steubenville, OH - *BrCabYB 84; NatRadPubDir Summer 83, Spring 84; TV&RadDir 84*
WRKZ-FM - Elizabethtown, PA - *BrCabYB 84; TV&RadDir 84*
WRLC-FM - Williamsport, PA - *BrCabYB 84; NatRadPubDir Summer 83, Spring 84; TV&RadDir 84*
WRLD - Lanett, AL - *BrCabYB 84; TV&RadDir 84*
WRLH-TV - Richmond, VA - *BrCabYB 84; DirUSTelSta 83; Tel&CabFB 84S*
WRLK-TV - Columbia, SC - *BrCabYB 84; Tel&CabFB 84S; TV&RadDir 84*
WRLO-FM - Antigo, WI - *BrCabYB 84; TV&RadDir 84*
WRLP-TV - Springfield, MA - *TelAl 83*
WRLR-FM - Huntingdon, PA - *BrCabYB 84; TV&RadDir 84*
WRLS-FM - Hayward, WI - *BrCabYB 84; TV&RadDir 84*
WRLV - Salyersville, KY - *BrCabYB 84; TV&RadDir 84*
WRLX-FM - Baltimore, MD - *LitMarPl 83; NatRadPubDir Summer 83; TV&RadDir 84*
WRMB - Boynton Beach, FL - *BrCabYB 84; TV&RadDir 84*
WRMC-FM - Middlebury, VT - *BrCabYB 84; NatRadPubDir Summer 83, Spring 84; TV&RadDir 84*
WRMF-FM - West Palm Beach, FL - *BrCabYB 84; NatRadPubDir Summer 83, Spring 84; TV&RadDir 84*
WRMG - Red Bay, AL - *BrCabYB 84; TV&RadDir 84*
WRMJ-FM - Aledo, IL - *BrCabYB 84; TV&RadDir 84*
WRML - Portage, PA - *BrCabYB 84; TV&RadDir 84*
WRMN - Elgin, IL - *BrCabYB 84; TV&RadDir 84*
WRMR - Alexandria, VA - *BrCabYB 84; TV&RadDir 84*
WRMS - Beardstown, IL - *BrCabYB 84; TV&RadDir 84*
WRMS-FM - Beardstown, IL - *BrCabYB 84; TV&RadDir 84*
WRMT - Rocky Mt., NC - *BrCabYB 84; TV&RadDir 84*
WRMU-FM - Alliance, OH - *BrCabYB 84; NatRadPubDir Summer 83, Spring 84; TV&RadDir 84*
WRMV - Herkimer, NY - *BrCabYB 84; TV&RadDir 84*
WRMZ-FM - Columbus, OH - *BrCabYB 84; NatRadPubDir Summer 83, Spring 84; TV&RadDir 84*
WRNA - China Grove, NC - *BrCabYB 84; TV&RadDir 84*
WRNB - New Bern, NC - *BrCabYB 84; TV&RadDir 84*
WRNC - Reidsville, NC - *BrCabYB 84; TV&RadDir 84*
WRNE-FM - Houlton, ME - *BrCabYB 84; TV&RadDir 84*
WRNG-FM - Newnan, GA - *BrCabYB 84; TV&RadDir 84*
WRNJ - Hackettstown, NJ - *BrCabYB 84; TV&RadDir 84*
WRNL - Richmond, VA - *BrCabYB 84; NatRadPubDir Summer 83, Spring 84; TV&RadDir 84*
WRNN-FM - Clare, MI - *BrCabYB 84*
WRNO-FM - Metairie, LA - *TV&RadDir 84*
WRNO-FM - New Orleans, LA - *BrCabYB 84; NatRadPubDir Summer 83 p.108, Spring 84 p.109*
WRNP - New Paltz, NY - *NatRadPubDir Summer 83, Spring 84*
WRNP-FM - New Paltz, NY - *NatRadPubDir Summer 83, Spring 84*
WRNR - Martinsburg, WV - *BrCabYB 84; TV&RadDir 84*
WRNS-FM - Kinston, NC - *BrCabYB 84; TV&RadDir 84*
WRNV-FM - Annapolis, MD - *NatRadPubDir Summer 83, Spring 84*
WRNW-FM - Briarcliff Manor, NY - *TV&RadDir 84*
WRNY - Rome, NY - *BrCabYB 84; TV&RadDir 84*
WRNZ-FM - Wrens, GA - *BrCabYB 84; TV&RadDir 84*
WROA - Biloxi/Gulfport, MS - *NatRadPubDir Summer 83, Spring 84 p.137*
WROA - Gulfport, MS - *BrCabYB 84; TV&RadDir 84*
WROA-FM - Gulfport, MS - *BrCabYB 84*
WROB - West Point, MS - *BrCabYB 84; TV&RadDir 84*
WROC-TV - New York, NY - *TelAl 83*
WROC-TV - Rochester, NY - *BrCabYB 84; DirUSTelSta 83; TelAl 84; Tel&CabFB 84S; TV&RadDir 84*
WROD - Daytona Beach, FL - *BrCabYB 84; NatRadPubDir Summer 83, Spring 84; TV&RadDir 84*
WROE-FM - Neenah, WI - *BrCabYB 84; NatRadPubDir Summer 83, Spring 84; TV&RadDir 84*
WROG-FM - Cumberland, MD - *BrCabYB 84; NatRadPubDir Summer 83, Spring 84*
WROI-FM - Rochester, IN - *BrCabYB 84; TV&RadDir 84*
WROK - Rockford, IL - *BrCabYB 84; NatRadPubDir Summer 83, Spring 84; TV&RadDir 84*
WROL - Boston, MA - *BrCabYB 84; NatRadPubDir Summer 83, Spring 84; TV&RadDir 84*
WROM - Rome, GA - *BrCabYB 84; NatRadPubDir Summer 83, Spring 84; TV&RadDir 84*
WRON - Ronceverte, WV - *BrCabYB 84; TV&RadDir 84*
Wronker, Lili Cassel - Jamaica, NY - *LitMarPl 83, 84; MagIndMarPl 82-83*
WROQ-FM - Charlotte, NC - *BrCabYB 84; NatRadPubDir Summer 83, Spring 84; TV&RadDir 84*
WROR-FM - Boston, MA - *BrCabYB 84; LitMarPl 84; NatRadPubDir Summer 83, Spring 84; TV&RadDir 84*
WROS - Jacksonville, FL - *BrCabYB 84*
WROV - Roanoke, VA - *BrCabYB 84; NatRadPubDir Summer 83, Spring 84; TV&RadDir 84*
WROVA Reporter - Oneida, IL - *AyerDirPub 83; Ed&PubIntYB 82*
WROW - Albany, NY - *BrCabYB 84; NatRadPubDir Summer 83, Spring 84*
WROW - Menands, NY - *TV&RadDir 84*
WROW-FM - Albany, NY - *BrCabYB 84; NatRadPubDir Summer 83, Spring 84*
WROW-FM - Menands, NY - *TV&RadDir 84*
WROX - Clarksdale, MS - *BrCabYB 84; TV&RadDir 84*
WROY - Carmi, IL - *BrCabYB 84; TV&RadDir 84*
WROZ - Evansville, IN - *BrCabYB 84; NatRadPubDir Summer 83, Spring 84; TV&RadDir 84*
WRPC - San German, PR - *BrCabYB 84*
WRPI - Troy, NY - *BrCabYB 84; TV&RadDir 84*
WRPI-FM - Troy, NY - *NatRadPubDir Summer 83, Spring 84; TV&RadDir 84*
WRPM - Poplarville, MS - *BrCabYB 84; TV&RadDir 84*
WRPM-FM - Poplarville, MS - *BrCabYB 84; TV&RadDir 84*
WRPN-FM - Ripon, WI - *BrCabYB 84; NatRadPubDir Spring 84*
WRPQ - Baraboo, WI - *BrCabYB 84; TV&RadDir 84*
WRPR - Mahwah, NJ - *BrCabYB 84*
WRPS-FM - Rockland, MA - *BrCabYB 84; TV&RadDir 84*
WRPT - Peterborough, NH - *BrCabYB 84; TV&RadDir 84*
WRQC-FM - Cleveland Heights, OH - *BrCabYB 84; NatRadPubDir Summer 83, Spring 84; TV&RadDir 84*
WRQK-FM - Greensboro, NC - *BrCabYB 84; NatRadPubDir Summer 83, Spring 84; TV&RadDir 84*
WRQN - Bowling Green, OH - *BrCabYB 84*
WRQR-FM - Farmville, NC - *BrCabYB 84; TV&RadDir 84*
WRQX-FM - Washington, DC - *BrCabYB 84; LitMarPl 84; NatRadPubDir Summer 83, Spring 84; TV&RadDir 84*
WRR-FM - Dallas, TX - *BrCabYB 84; LitMarPl 83, 84; NatRadPubDir Summer 83, Spring 84; TV&RadDir 84*
WRRA - Frederikstead, VI - *BrCabYB 84*
WRRB-FM - Syracuse, NY - *BrCabYB 84; NatRadPubDir Spring 84; TV&RadDir 84*
WRRG-FM - River Grove, IL - *BrCabYB 84; TV&RadDir 84*
WRRH-FM - Franklin Lakes, NJ - *BrCabYB 84; NatRadPubDir Spring 84; TV&RadDir 84*
WRRK-FM - Manistee, MI - *BrCabYB 84; TV&RadDir 84*
WRRL - Rainelle, WV - *BrCabYB 84; TV&RadDir 84*
WRRL-FM - Rainelle, WV - *BrCabYB 84; TV&RadDir 84*
WRRM-FM - Cincinnati, OH - *BrCabYB 84; NatRadPubDir Summer 83, Spring 84; TV&RadDir 84*
WRRN-FM - Warren, PA - *BrCabYB 84; TV&RadDir 84*
WRRO - Warren, OH - *TV&RadDir 84*
WRRO - Youngstown, OH - *NatRadPubDir Summer 83 p.200, Spring 84 p.198*
WRRR-FM - St. Mary's, WV - *BrCabYB 84*
WRRZ - Clinton, NC - *BrCabYB 84; TV&RadDir 84*
WRRZ-FM - Clinton, NC - *BrCabYB 84; TV&RadDir 84*
WRS Motion Picture & Video Laboratory - Pittsburgh, PA - *AvMarPl 83; Tel&CabFB 84C*
WRSA-FM - Decatur, AL - *BrCabYB 84*
WRSA-FM - Huntsville/Decatur, AL - *NatRadPubDir Summer 83 p.3, Spring 84*
WRSB-FM - Weston, MA - *BrCabYB 84; NatRadPubDir Summer 83, Spring 84; TV&RadDir 84*
WRSC - State College, PA - *BrCabYB 84; TV&RadDir 84*
WRSD - Folsom, PA - *BrCabYB 84*

WRSE-FM - Elmhurst, IL - *BrCabYB 84; TV&RadDir 84*
WRSF-FM - Miamisburg, OH - *BrCabYB 84; TV&RadDir 84*
WRSG - Sylvester, GA - *BrCabYB 84; TV&RadDir 84*
WRSH-FM - Rockingham, NC - *BrCabYB 84; TV&RadDir 84*
WRSI - Greenfield, MA - *BrCabYB 84*
WRSJ - Bayamon, PR - *BrCabYB 84*
WRSL - Stanford, KY - *BrCabYB 84; TV&RadDir 84*
WRSL-FM - Stanford, KY - *BrCabYB 84; TV&RadDir 84*
WRSM - Sumiton, AL - *BrCabYB 84; TV&RadDir 84*
WRSP-TV - Springfield, IL - *BrCabYB 84; Tel&CabFB 84S*
WRST-FM - Oshkosh, WI - *BrCabYB 84; NatRadPubDir Spring 84; TV&RadDir 84*
WRSU-FM - New Brunswick, NJ - *BrCabYB 84; TV&RadDir 84*
WRSV-FM - Rocky Mt., NC - *BrCabYB 84; TV&RadDir 84*
WRSW - Warsaw, IN - *BrCabYB 84; TV&RadDir 84*
WRSW-FM - Warsaw, IN - *BrCabYB 84; TV&RadDir 84*
WRTA - Altoona, PA - *BrCabYB 84; NatRadPubDir Summer 83, Spring 84; TV&RadDir 84*
WRTB-FM - Vincennes, IN - *BrCabYB 84; TV&RadDir 84*
WRTC-FM - Hartford, CT - *BrCabYB 84; NatRadPubDir Summer 83, Spring 84; TV&RadDir 84*
WRTE-FM - Cahokia, IL - *BrCabYB 84*
WRTE-FM - East St. Louis, IL - *TV&RadDir 84*
WRTH - Wood River, IL - *BrCabYB 84*
WRTH - St. Louis, MO - *NatRadPubDir Summer 83, Spring 84; TV&RadDir 84*
WRTI-FM - Easton, PA - *NatRadPubDir Spring 84 p.315*
WRTI-FM - Philadelphia, PA - *BrCabYB 84; NatRadPubDir Summer 83; TV&RadDir 84*
WRTK - Rochester, NY - *BrCabYB 84; NatRadPubDir Spring 84; TV&RadDir 84*
WRTL - Rantoul, IL - *BrCabYB 84; TV&RadDir 84*
WRTL-FM - Rantoul, IL - *BrCabYB 84; TV&RadDir 84*
WRTM - Blountstown, FL - *BrCabYB 84*
WRTN-FM - New Rochelle, NY - *LitMarPl 84; TV&RadDir 84*
WRTN-FM - Westchester County, NY - *NatRadPubDir Summer 83 p.180, Spring 84 p.178*
WRTR - Two Rivers, WI - *BrCabYB 84; TV&RadDir 84*
WRTT - Vernon, CT - *BrCabYB 84*
WRTU - San Juan, PR - *BrCabYB 84*
WRTV-TV - Indianapolis, IN - *BrCabYB 84; DirUSTelSta 83; LitMarPl 83, 84; TelAl 83, 84; Tel&CabFB 84S; TV&RadDir 84*
WRUA - Monroeville, PA - *BrCabYB 84; TV&RadDir 84*
WRUC-FM - Schenectady, NY - *BrCabYB 84; NatRadPubDir Summer 83, Spring 84; TV&RadDir 84*
WRUF - Gainesville, FL - *BrCabYB 84; NatRadPubDir Summer 83, Spring 84; TV&RadDir 84*
WRUF-FM - Gainesville, FL - *BrCabYB 84; NatRadPubDir Summer 83, Spring 84; TV&RadDir 84*
WRUL-FM - Carmi, IL - *BrCabYB 84; TV&RadDir 84*
WRUM - Rumford, ME - *BrCabYB 84; TV&RadDir 84*
WRUN - Oriskany, NY - *TV&RadDir 84*
WRUN - Untica, NY - *BrCabYB 84*
WRUR - Rochester, NY - *NatRadPubDir Summer 83, Spring 84*
WRUR-FM - Rochester, NY - *BrCabYB 84; NatRadPubDir Summer 83, Spring 84; TV&RadDir 84*
WRUS - Russellville, KY - *BrCabYB 84; TV&RadDir 84*
WRUT-FM - Rutland, VT - *BrCabYB 84; TV&RadDir 84*
WRUV-FM - Burlington, VT - *BrCabYB 84; NatRadPubDir Summer 83, Spring 84; TV&RadDir 84*
WRUW-FM - Cleveland, OH - *BrCabYB 84; NatRadPubDir Summer 83, Spring 84; TV&RadDir 84*
WRVA - Richmond, VA - *BrCabYB 84; NatRadPubDir Summer 83, Spring 84; TV&RadDir 84*
WRVG-FM - Georgetown, KY - *BrCabYB 84; NatRadPubDir Summer 83, Spring 84; TV&RadDir 84*
WRVH-FM - Patterson, NY - *BrCabYB 84*
WRVH-FM - Westchester County, NY - *NatRadPubDir Spring 84 p.178*
WRVH-TV - Syracuse, NY - *TV&RadDir 84*
WRVI - Virden, IL - *BrCabYB 84*
WRVK - Mt. Vernon, KY - *BrCabYB 84*
WRVK - Renfro Valley, KY - *TV&RadDir 84*
WRVL - Lynchburg, VA - *BrCabYB 84*
WRVM-FM - Suring, WI - *BrCabYB 84; TV&RadDir 84*
WRVO-FM - Oswego, NY - *BrCabYB 84; NatRadPubDir Summer 83, Spring 84; TV&RadDir 84*
WRVQ-FM - Richmond, VA - *BrCabYB 84; NatRadPubDir Summer 83, Spring 84; TV&RadDir 84*
WRVR-FM - Memphis, TN - *BrCabYB 84; NatRadPubDir Summer 83, Spring 84; TV&RadDir 84*
WRVU-FM - Nashville, TN - *BrCabYB 84; NatRadPubDir Summer 83, Spring 84; TV&RadDir 84*
WRVW-FM - Hudson, NY - *BrCabYB 84; TV&RadDir 84*
WRWC-FM - Rockton, IL - *BrCabYB 84; TV&RadDir 84*
WRWH - Cleveland, GA - *BrCabYB 84; TV&RadDir 84*
WRWR-TV - San Juan, PR - *BrCabYB 84; Tel&CabFB 84S*
WRXB - St. Petersburg, FL - *TV&RadDir 84*
WRXB - St. Petersburg Beach, FL - *BrCabYB 84*
WRXB - Tampa/St. Petersburg, FL - *NatRadPubDir Summer 83, Spring 84 p.66*
WRXL - Richmond, VA - *BrCabYB 84; NatRadPubDir Summer 83*
WRXL-FM - Richmond, VA - *NatRadPubDir Spring 84*
WRXO - Roxboro, NC - *BrCabYB 84; TV&RadDir 84*
WRXV - Auburn, ME - *BrCabYB 84; TV&RadDir 84*
WRXX-FM - Centralia, IL - *BrCabYB 84; TV&RadDir 84*
WRXZ - Kane, PA - *BrCabYB 84*
Wry-Bred Press - New York, NY - *BoPubDir 4 Sup, 5*
WRYM - Hartford/New Britain, CT - *NatRadPubDir Summer 83 p.47, Spring 84 p.47*
WRYM - New Britain, CT - *BrCabYB 84*
WRYM - Newington, CT - *TV&RadDir 84*
WRYO-FM - Crystal River, FL - *BrCabYB 84; TV&RadDir 84*
WRZK - Spring Lake, NC - *BrCabYB 84*
WRZR - Raleigh, NC - *TV&RadDir 84*
W.S. Productions - Delta, BC, Canada - *BoPubDir 4, 5*
WSAC - Ft. Knox, KY - *BrCabYB 84; TV&RadDir 84*
WSAE-FM - Spring Arbor, MI - *BrCabYB 84; NatRadPubDir Summer 83, Spring 84; TV&RadDir 84*
WSAI - Cincinnati, OH - *BrCabYB 84; NatRadPubDir Summer 83, Spring 84; TV&RadDir 84*
WSAI-FM - Cincinnati, OH - *BrCabYB 84; NatRadPubDir Summer 83; TV&RadDir 84*
WSAJ - Grove City, PA - *BrCabYB 84; NatRadPubDir Summer 83, Spring 84; TV&RadDir 84*
WSAJ-FM - Grove City, PA - *BrCabYB 84; NatRadPubDir Summer 83, Spring 84; TV&RadDir 84*
WSAK-FM - Sullivan, IL - *BrCabYB 84; TV&RadDir 84*
WSAL - Logansport, IN - *BrCabYB 84; TV&RadDir 84*
WSAL-FM - Logansport, IN - *BrCabYB 84; TV&RadDir 84*
WSAM - Saginaw, MI - *BrCabYB 84; NatRadPubDir Summer 83, Spring 84; TV&RadDir 84*
WSAN - Allentown, PA - *BrCabYB 84; NatRadPubDir Summer 83 p.209, Spring 84 p.209; TV&RadDir 84*
WSAO - Senatobia, MS - *BrCabYB 84; TV&RadDir 84*
WSAP-FM - Laurinburg, NC - *NatRadPubDir Summer 83, Spring 84*
WSAQ-FM - Port Huron, MI - *BrCabYB 84; TV&RadDir 84*
WSAR - Fall River, MA - *BrCabYB 84; NatRadPubDir Summer 83, Spring 84; TV&RadDir 84*
WSAT - Salisbury, NC - *BrCabYB 84; TV&RadDir 84*
WSAU - Wausau, WI - *BrCabYB 84; TV&RadDir 84*
WSAU-TV - Wausau, WI - *TelAl 83*
WSAV-TV - Savannah, GA - *BrCabYB 84; DirUSTelSta 83; TelAl 83, 84; Tel&CabFB 84S; TV&RadDir 84*
WSAW-TV - Wausau, WI - *BrCabYB 84; DirUSTelSta 83; TelAl 84; Tel&CabFB 84S; TV&RadDir 84*
WSAY - Rochester, NY - *NatRadPubDir Summer 83*
WSAZ-TV - Charleston, WV - *DirUSTelSta 83*
WSAZ-TV - Huntington, WV - *BrCabYB 84; LitMarPl 83, 84; TelAl 83, 84; Tel&CabFB 84S; TV&RadDir 84*
WSB - Atlanta, GA - *BrCabYB 84; LitMarPl 83, 84; NatRadPubDir Summer 83, Spring 84; TV&RadDir 84*
WSB - Johnson City, TN - *TV&RadDir 84*
WSB-FM - Atlanta, GA - *BrCabYB 84; NatRadPubDir Summer 83, Spring 84; TV&RadDir 84*
WSB-TV - Atlanta, GA - *BrCabYB 84; DirUSTelSta 83; TelAl 83, 84; Tel&CabFB 84S; TV&RadDir 84*
WSBA - York, PA - *BrCabYB 84; NatRadPubDir Summer 83, Spring 84; TV&RadDir 84*
WSBA-FM - York, PA - *BrCabYB 84; NatRadPubDir Summer 83, Spring 84; TV&RadDir 84*

WSBA-TV - Harrisburg, PA - *DirUSTelSta 83*
WSBA-TV - York, PA - *DirUSTelSta 83; LitMarPl 83; TelAl 83, 84; TV&RadDir 84*
WSBB - Daytona Beach, FL - *NatRadPubDir Summer 83 p.57, Spring 84 p.57*
WSBB - New Smyrna Beach, FL - *BrCabYB 84; TV&RadDir 84*
WSBC - Chicago, IL - *BrCabYB 84; LitMarPl 83, 84; NatRadPubDir Summer 83, Spring 84; TV&RadDir 84*
WSBE-TV - Providence, RI - *BrCabYB 84; Tel&CabFB 84S; TV&RadDir 84*
WSBF-FM - Clemson, SC - *BrCabYB 84; NatRadPubDir Summer 83, Spring 84; TV&RadDir 84*
WSBH - Southampton, NY - *BrCabYB 84; TV&RadDir 84*
WSBH-FM - Suffolk County, Long Island, NY - *NatRadPubDir Summer 83 p.178, Spring 84 p.176*
WSBI-FM - Brunswick, GA - *NatRadPubDir Summer 83; TV&RadDir 84*
WSBK-TV - Boston, MA - *BrCabYB 84; DirUSTelSta 83; TelAl 83, 84; Tel&CabFB 84S*
WSBK-TV - Brighton, MA - *TV&RadDir 84*
WSBL - Sanford, NC - *BrCabYB 84; TV&RadDir 84*
WSBN-FM - Jefferson City, TN - *TV&RadDir 84*
WSBN-TV - Norton, VA - *BrCabYB 84; Tel&CabFB 84S; TV&RadDir 84*
WSBR - Boca Raton, FL - *BrCabYB 84; TV&RadDir 84*
WSBS - Great Barrington, MA - *BrCabYB 84; TV&RadDir 84*
WSBT - South Bend, IN - *BrCabYB 84; NatRadPubDir Summer 83, Spring 84; TV&RadDir 84*
WSBT-TV - South Bend, IN - *BrCabYB 84; DirUSTelSta 83; TelAl 83, 84; Tel&CabFB 84S; TV&RadDir 84*
WSBU-FM - St. Bonaventure, NY - *BrCabYB 84; NatRadPubDir Summer 83, Spring 84*
WSBV - South Boston, VA - *BrCabYB 84; TV&RadDir 84*
WSBW - Sturgeon Bay, WI - *BrCabYB 84*
WSBY - Salisbury, MD - *BrCabYB 84; NatRadPubDir Summer 83, Spring 84; TV&RadDir 84*
WSCA-FM - Union Springs, AL - *BrCabYB 84; TV&RadDir 84*
WSCB-FM - Springfield, MA - *BrCabYB 84; NatRadPubDir Summer 83, Spring 84; TV&RadDir 84*
WSCC-FM - Somerset, KY - *BrCabYB 84; NatRadPubDir Summer 83, Spring 84; TV&RadDir 84*
WSCD-FM - Duluth, MN - *BrCabYB 84; NatRadPubDir Summer 83, Spring 84; TV&RadDir 84*
WSCG-FM - Corinth, NY - *BrCabYB 84; TV&RadDir 84*
WSCH-FM - Aurora, IN - *BrCabYB 84; TV&RadDir 84*
WSCI-FM - Charleston, SC - *BrCabYB 84*
WSCI-FM - Columbia, SC - *NatRadPubDir Summer 83 p.316, Spring 84 p.318*
WSCI-FM - Mt. Pleasant, SC - *TV&RadDir 84*
WSCL-FM - Augusta, ME - *BrCabYB 84; TV&RadDir 84*
WSCM - Cobleskill, NY - *BrCabYB 84*
WSCO - Suring, WI - *BrCabYB 84; Tel&CabFB 84S*
WSCP - Pulaski, NY - *TV&RadDir 84*
WSCP - Sandy Creek, NY - *BrCabYB 84*
WSCQ-FM - West Columbia, SC - *BrCabYB 84; NatRadPubDir Summer 83, Spring 84; TV&RadDir 84*
WSCR - Hamden, CT - *BrCabYB 84*
WSCR - New Haven, CT - *NatRadPubDir Summer 83 p.47, Spring 84 p.48; TV&RadDir 84*
WSCS-FM - Sodus, NY - *BrCabYB 84; TV&RadDir 84*
WSCT - Melbourne, FL - *BrCabYB 84; Tel&CabFB 84S*
WSCW - South Charleston, WV - *BrCabYB 84; TV&RadDir 84*
WSCY - North Syracuse, NY - *BrCabYB 84*
WSCZ-FM - Greenwood, SC - *BrCabYB 84; TV&RadDir 84*
WSDC - Hartsville, SC - *BrCabYB 84; TV&RadDir 84*
WSDH-FM - East Sandwich, MA - *BrCabYB 84; TV&RadDir 84*
WSDL - New Orleans, LA - *NatRadPubDir Summer 83 p.108, Spring 84 p.109*
WSDL - Slidell, LA - *BrCabYB 84; TV&RadDir 84*
WSDM - Clare, MI - *BrCabYB 84*
WSDM - Mt. Pleasant, MI - *TV&RadDir 84*
WSDP-FM - Plymouth, MI - *BrCabYB 84; NatRadPubDir Summer 83, Spring 84; TV&RadDir 84*
WSDR - Dixon, IL - *TV&RadDir 84*
WSDR - Sterling, IL - *BrCabYB 84; TV&RadDir 84*
WSDS - Ypsilanti, MI - *BrCabYB 84; NatRadPubDir Summer 83, Spring 84; TV&RadDir 84*
WSDT - Soddy-Daisy, TN - *BrCabYB 84*
WSEA-FM - Georgetown, DE - *BrCabYB 84; TV&RadDir 84*
WSEB - Sebring, FL - *BrCabYB 84; TV&RadDir 84*
WSEC-FM - Williamston, NC - *BrCabYB 84; TV&RadDir 84*
WSEE-TV - Erie, PA - *BrCabYB 84; DirUSTelSta 83; TelAl 83, 84; Tel&CabFB 84S; TV&RadDir 84*
WSEG-FM - Erie, PA - *TV&RadDir 84*
WSEG-FM - Mckean, PA - *BrCabYB 84*
WSEI-FM - Olney, IL - *BrCabYB 84; TV&RadDir 84*
WSEK-FM - Somerset, KY - *BrCabYB 84; TV&RadDir 84*
WSEL - Pontotoc, MS - *BrCabYB 84; TV&RadDir 84*
WSEL-FM - Pontotoc, MS - *BrCabYB 84; TV&RadDir 84*
WSEM - Donalsonville, GA - *BrCabYB 84; TV&RadDir 84*
WSEN - Baldwinsville, NY - *BrCabYB 84; TV&RadDir 84*
WSEN-FM - Baldwinsville, NY - *BrCabYB 84; TV&RadDir 84*
WSEP-TV - Ft. Myers, FL - *BrCabYB 84*
WSER - Elkton, MD - *BrCabYB 84; TV&RadDir 84*
WSES - Raleigh, NC - *BrCabYB 84; NatRadPubDir Summer 83, Spring 84*
WSET-TV - Lynchburg, VA - *BrCabYB 84; TelAl 83, 84; Tel&CabFB 84S; TV&RadDir 84*
WSET-TV - Roanoke, VA - *DirUSTelSta 83*
WSEV - Sevierville, TN - *BrCabYB 84; TV&RadDir 84*
WSEX - Arlington Heights, IL - *BrCabYB 84*
WSEY - Sauk City, WI - *BrCabYB 84*
WSEZ-FM - Winston Salem, NC - *BrCabYB 84; NatRadPubDir Summer 83, Spring 84; TV&RadDir 84*
WSFA-TV - Montgomery, AL - *BrCabYB 84; DirUSTelSta 83; TelAl 83, 84; Tel&CabFB 84S; TV&RadDir 84*
WSFB - Quitman, GA - *BrCabYB 84; TV&RadDir 84*
WSFC - Somerset, KY - *BrCabYB 84; TV&RadDir 84*
WSFD - Seaford, DE - *TV&RadDir 84*
WSFJ-TV - Columbus, OH - *DirUSTelSta 83*
WSFJ-TV - Newark, OH - *BrCabYB 84; DirUSTelSta 83; TelAl 83, 84; Tel&CabFB 84S*
WSFJ-TV - Thornville, OH - *TV&RadDir 84*
WSFL-FM - Bridgeton, NC - *BrCabYB 84*
WSFL-FM - New Bern, NC - *TV&RadDir 84*
WSFM-FM - Harrisburg, PA - *BrCabYB 84; NatRadPubDir Summer 83, Spring 84; TV&RadDir 84*
WSFP-FM - Ft. Myers, FL - *BrCabYB 84*
WSFP-TV - Ft. Myers, FL - *Tel&CabFB 84S*
WSFT - Thomaston, GA - *BrCabYB 84; TV&RadDir 84*
WSFW - Seneca Falls, NY - *BrCabYB 84; TV&RadDir 84*
WSFW-FM - Seneca Falls, NY - *BrCabYB 84; TV&RadDir 84*
WSGA - Savannah, GA - *BrCabYB 84; NatRadPubDir Summer 83, Spring 84; TV&RadDir 84*
WSGB - Sutton, WV - *BrCabYB 84; TV&RadDir 84*
WSGC - Elberton, GA - *BrCabYB 84; TV&RadDir 84*
WSGE-FM - Dallas, NC - *BrCabYB 84; TV&RadDir 84*
WSGF-FM - Savannah, GA - *NatRadPubDir Summer 83; TV&RadDir 84*
WSGI - Springfield, TN - *BrCabYB 84*
WSGL-FM - Naples, FL - *BrCabYB 84; TV&RadDir 84*
WSGM-FM - Staunton, VA - *BrCabYB 84; TV&RadDir 84*
WSGN - Birmingham, AL - *BrCabYB 84; NatRadPubDir Summer 83, Spring 84; TV&RadDir 84*
WSGO - Oswego, NY - *BrCabYB 84; TV&RadDir 84*
WSGO-FM - Oswego, NY - *BrCabYB 84; TV&RadDir 84*
WSGR-FM - Port Huron, MI - *BrCabYB 84; NatRadPubDir Summer 83, Spring 84*
WSGS-FM - Hazard, KY - *BrCabYB 84; TV&RadDir 84*
WSGW - Saginaw, MI - *BrCabYB 84; NatRadPubDir Summer 83, Spring 84; TV&RadDir 84*
WSHA-FM - Raleigh, NC - *BrCabYB 84; NatRadPubDir Summer 83, Spring 84; TV&RadDir 84*
WSHB - Raeford, NC - *TV&RadDir 84*
WSHB-TV - Kansas City, MO - *TelAl 84*
WSHC-FM - Shepherdstown, WV - *BrCabYB 84; NatRadPubDir Summer 83, Spring 84; TV&RadDir 84*
WSHE-FM - Ft. Lauderdale, FL - *BrCabYB 84; NatRadPubDir Summer 83, Spring 84; TV&RadDir 84*
WSHF - Sheffield, AL - *BrCabYB 84; TV&RadDir 84*
WSHH-FM - Pittsburgh, PA - *BrCabYB 84; NatRadPubDir Summer 83; TV&RadDir 84*
WSHJ-FM - Southfield, MI - *BrCabYB 84; NatRadPubDir Summer 83, Spring 84; TV&RadDir 84*

WSHL-FM - Concord, MA - *NatRadPubDir Summer 83, Spring 84 p.292*
WSHL-FM - Easton, MA - *BrCabYB 84*
WSHL-FM - North Easton, MA - *TV&RadDir 84*
WSHN - Fremont, MI - *BrCabYB 84; TV&RadDir 84*
WSHN-FM - Fremont, MI - *BrCabYB 84; TV&RadDir 84*
WSHO - New Orleans, LA - *BrCabYB 84; NatRadPubDir Summer 83, Spring 84; TV&RadDir 84*
WSHP - Shippensburg, PA - *BrCabYB 84; TV&RadDir 84*
WSHR-FM - Lake Ronkonkoma, NY - *BrCabYB 84; TV&RadDir 84*
WSHS-FM - Sheboygan, WI - *BrCabYB 84; NatRadPubDir Spring 84; TV&RadDir 84*
WSHU-FM - Bridgeport, CT - *TV&RadDir 84*
WSHU-FM - Fairfield, CT - *BrCabYB 84; NatRadPubDir Summer 83, Spring 84*
WSHV-FM - South Hill, VA - *BrCabYB 84; TV&RadDir 84*
WSHW-FM - Frankfort, IN - *BrCabYB 84; TV&RadDir 84*
WSHY - Shelbyville, IL - *BrCabYB 84; TV&RadDir 84*
WSHY-FM - Shelbyville, IL - *BrCabYB 84; TV&RadDir 84*
WSI Corp. - Bedford, MA - *DataDirOnSer 84*
WSI Supersports - Bedford, MA - *BrCabYB 84*
WSIA - New York, NY - *BrCabYB 84*
W.S.I.A. Journal - Topsfield, MA - *BaconPubCkMag 84*
W.S.I.A. Newsletter - Topsfield, MA - *BaconPubCkMag 84*
WSIC - Statesville, NC - *BrCabYB 84; NatRadPubDir Summer 83, Spring 84; TV&RadDir 84*
WSID - Baltimore, MD - *TV&RadDir 84*
WSID-FM - Sidney, NY - *BrCabYB 84*
WSIE-FM - Edwardsville, IL - *BrCabYB 84; NatRadPubDir Summer 83, Spring 84; TV&RadDir 84*
WSIF-FM - Wilkesboro, NC - *BrCabYB 84; TV&RadDir 84*
WSIG - Mt. Jackson, VA - *BrCabYB 84; TV&RadDir 84*
WSIL-TV - Harrisburg, IL - *BrCabYB 84; TelAl 83, 84; Tel&CabFB 84S; TV&RadDir 84*
WSIL-TV - Paducah, KY - *DirUSTelSta 83*
WSIM - Red Bank, TN - *BrCabYB 84*
WSIP - Paintsville, KY - *BrCabYB 84; TV&RadDir 84*
WSIP-FM - Paintsville, KY - *BrCabYB 84; TV&RadDir 84*
WSIR - Lakeland/Winter Haven, FL - *NatRadPubDir Summer 83, Spring 84 p.60*
WSIR - Winter Haven, FL - *BrCabYB 84; TV&RadDir 84*
WSIU-FM - Carbondale, IL - *BrCabYB 84; NatRadPubDir Summer 83, Spring 84; TV&RadDir 84*
WSIU-TV - Carbondale, IL - *BrCabYB 84; Tel&CabFB 84S; TV&RadDir 84*
WSIV - East Syracuse, NY - *BrCabYB 84; TV&RadDir 84*
WSIX - Nashville, TN - *BrCabYB 84; NatRadPubDir Summer 83, Spring 84; TV&RadDir 84*
WSIX-FM - Nashville, TN - *BrCabYB 84; NatRadPubDir Summer 83, Spring 84; TV&RadDir 84*
WSIZ - Ocilla, GA - *BrCabYB 84; TV&RadDir 84*
WSJC - Magee, MS - *BrCabYB 84; TV&RadDir 84*
WSJC-FM - Magee, MS - *BrCabYB 84; TV&RadDir 84*
WSJK-TV - Knoxville, TN - *TV&RadDir 84*
WSJK-TV - Sneedville, TN - *BrCabYB 84; Tel&CabFB 84S*
WSJL - Cape May, NJ - *BrCabYB 84*
WSJM - St. Joseph, MI - *BrCabYB 84; TV&RadDir 84*
WSJN-TV - San Juan, PR - *BrCabYB 84; Tel&CabFB 84S*
WSJP - Murray, KY - *BrCabYB 84; TV&RadDir 84*
WSJR - Madawaska, ME - *BrCabYB 84; TV&RadDir 84*
WSJS - Winston Salem, NC - *BrCabYB 84; NatRadPubDir Summer 83, Spring 84; TV&RadDir 84*
WSJU - San Juan, PR - *BrCabYB 84; Tel&CabFB 84S*
WSJV [Subs. of Quincy Newspapers Inc.] - Elkhart, IN - *BrCabYB 84; TelAl 83, 84; Tel&CabFB 84S*
WSJV-TV - Elkhart, IN - *TV&RadDir 84*
WSJV-TV - South Bend, IN - *DirUSTelSta 83*
WSJW - Woodruff, SC - *BrCabYB 84; TV&RadDir 84*
WSJY-FM - Ft. Atkinson, WI - *BrCabYB 84; TV&RadDir 84*
WSKB-FM - Westfield, MA - *BrCabYB 84; TV&RadDir 84*
WSKE - Everett, PA - *BrCabYB 84; TV&RadDir 84*
WSKG-FM - Binghamton, NY - *BrCabYB 84*
WSKG-FM - Conklin, NY - *TV&RadDir 84*
WSKG-FM - Endicott, NY - *TV&RadDir 84*
WSKG-TV - Binghamton, NY - *BrCabYB 84; Tel&CabFB 84S*
WSKG-TV - Conklin, NY - *TV&RadDir 84*
WSKI - Montpelier, VT - *BrCabYB 84; TV&RadDir 84*
WSKP-FM - Sebring, FL - *BrCabYB 84; TV&RadDir 84*
WSKQ - Newark, NJ - *BrCabYB 84; NatRadPubDir Spring 84 p.158*
WSKR-FM - Atmore, AL - *BrCabYB 84; TV&RadDir 84*
WSKS-FM - Cincinnati/Hamilton/Middletown, OH - *NatRadPubDir Summer 83 p.193, Spring 84 p.191*
WSKS-FM - Hamilton, OH - *BrCabYB 84; TV&RadDir 84*
WSKT - Knoxville, TN - *BrCabYB 84; NatRadPubDir Summer 83, Spring 84; TV&RadDir 84*
WSKV-FM - Stanton, KY - *BrCabYB 84; TV&RadDir 84*
WSKY - Asheville, NC - *BrCabYB 84; NatRadPubDir Summer 83, Spring 84; TV&RadDir 84*
WSKZ-FM - Chattanooga, TN - *BrCabYB 84; NatRadPubDir Summer 83, Spring 84; TV&RadDir 84*
WSLA-TV - Montgomery, AL - *DirUSTelSta 83*
WSLA-TV - Selma, AL - *BrCabYB 84; TelAl 83, 84; Tel&CabFB 84S; TV&RadDir 84*
WSLB - Ogdensburg, NY - *BrCabYB 84; TV&RadDir 84*
WSLC - Roanoke, VA - *BrCabYB 84; NatRadPubDir Summer 83, Spring 84; TV&RadDir 84*
WSLE - Bremen, GA - *BrCabYB 84; TV&RadDir 84*
WSLG - Gonzales, LA - *BrCabYB 84; TV&RadDir 84*
WSLI - Jackson, MS - *BrCabYB 84; NatRadPubDir Summer 83, Spring 84; TV&RadDir 84*
WSLK - Hyden, KY - *BrCabYB 84; TV&RadDir 84*
WSLL - Centerville, MS - *BrCabYB 84*
WSLM - Salem, IN - *BrCabYB 84; TV&RadDir 84*
WSLM-FM - Salem, IN - *BrCabYB 84; TV&RadDir 84*
WSLN-FM - Delaware, OH - *BrCabYB 84; TV&RadDir 84*
WSLQ-FM - Roanoke, VA - *BrCabYB 84; NatRadPubDir Summer 83, Spring 84; TV&RadDir 84*
WSLR - Akron, OH - *BrCabYB 84; NatRadPubDir Summer 83, Spring 84; TV&RadDir 84*
WSLS-TV - Roanoke, VA - *BrCabYB 84; DirUSTelSta 83; TelAl 83, 84; Tel&CabFB 84S; TV&RadDir 84*
WSLT-FM - Ocean City, NJ - *BrCabYB 84; TV&RadDir 84*
WSLU-FM - Canton, NY - *BrCabYB 84; NatRadPubDir Summer 83, Spring 84; TV&RadDir 84*
WSLV - Ardmore, TN - *BrCabYB 84; TV&RadDir 84*
WSLW - White Sulphur Springs, WV - *BrCabYB 84; TV&RadDir 84*
WSLX-FM - New Canaan, CT - *BrCabYB 84; TV&RadDir 84*
WSLY-FM - York, AL - *BrCabYB 84; TV&RadDir 84*
WSM - Nashville, TN - *BrCabYB 84; NatRadPubDir Summer 83, Spring 84; TV&RadDir 84*
WSM-FM - Nashville, TN - *BrCabYB 84; NatRadPubDir Summer 83, Spring 84; TV&RadDir 84*
WSM-TV - Nashville, TN - *LitMarPl 83; TelAl 83, 84*
WSMA - Marine City, MI - *BrCabYB 84*
WSMB - New Orleans, LA - *BrCabYB 84; NatRadPubDir Summer 83, Spring 84; TV&RadDir 84*
WSMC-FM - Collegedale, TN - *BrCabYB 84; NatRadPubDir Summer 83, Spring 84; TV&RadDir 84*
WSME - Sanford, ME - *BrCabYB 84; TV&RadDir 84*
WSME-FM - Sanford, ME - *TV&RadDir 84*
WSMF - Florence, SC - *BrCabYB 84; Tel&CabFB 84S*
WSMG - Greeneville, TN - *BrCabYB 84; TV&RadDir 84*
WSMI - Litchfield, IL - *BrCabYB 84; TV&RadDir 84*
WSMI-FM - Litchfield, IL - *BrCabYB 84; TV&RadDir 84*
WSML - Graham, NC - *BrCabYB 84; TV&RadDir 84*
WSMN - Nashua, NH - *BrCabYB 84; NatRadPubDir Summer 83, Spring 84; TV&RadDir 84*
WSMQ - Bessemer, AL - *BrCabYB 84; TV&RadDir 84*
WSMQ - Birmingham, AL - *NatRadPubDir Summer 83 p.2, Spring 84*
WSMR - Raeford, NC - *BrCabYB 84*
WSMR-FM - Dayton, OH - *BrCabYB 84*
WSMS-FM - Memphis, TN - *BrCabYB 84; TV&RadDir 84*
WSMT - Sparta, TN - *BrCabYB 84; TV&RadDir 84*
WSMT-FM - Sparta, TN - *BrCabYB 84; TV&RadDir 84*
WSMU-FM - Starkville, MS - *BrCabYB 84; TV&RadDir 84*
WSMV-TV - Nashville, TN - *BrCabYB 84; DirUSTelSta 83; LitMarPl 84; Tel&CabFB 84S; TV&RadDir 84*
WSMW-TV - Boston, MA - *DirUSTelSta 83*
WSMW-TV - Worcester, MA - *BrCabYB 84; TelAl 83, 84; Tel&CabFB 84S; TV&RadDir 84*

WSMX - Winston Salem, NC - *BrCabYB 84; NatRadPubDir Summer 83, Spring 84; TV&RadDir 84*
WSMY - Roanoke Rapids, NC - *TV&RadDir 84*
WSMY - Weldon, NC - *BrCabYB 84*
WSNC - Winston-Salem, NC - *BrCabYB 84*
WSND-FM - Notre Dame, IN - *BrCabYB 84; NatRadPubDir Summer 83, Spring 84; TV&RadDir 84*
WSNE-FM - Taunton, MA - *BrCabYB 84; TV&RadDir 84*
WSNE-FM - Providence, RI - *NatRadPubDir Summer 83, Spring 84; TV&RadDir 84*
WSNG - Torrington, CT - *BrCabYB 84; TV&RadDir 84*
WSNI - Philadelphia, PA - *BrCabYB 84; NatRadPubDir Summer 83 p.213, Spring 84 p.213*
WSNI-FM - Philadelphia, PA - *NatRadPubDir Summer 83, Spring 84; TV&RadDir 84*
WSNJ - Bridgeton, NJ - *BrCabYB 84; TV&RadDir 84*
WSNJ-FM - Bridgeton, NJ - *BrCabYB 84; TV&RadDir 84*
WSNL-TV - De Witt, NY - *TV&RadDir 84*
WSNL-TV - Smithtown, NY - *BrCabYB 84; Tel&CabFB 84S*
WSNN-FM - Potsdam, NY - *BrCabYB 84; TV&RadDir 84*
WSNO - Barre, VT - *BrCabYB 84; TV&RadDir 84*
WSNS-TV - Chicago, IL - *BrCabYB 84; DirUSTelSta 83; TelAl 83, 84; Tel&CabFB 84S; TV&RadDir 84*
WSNT - Sandersville, GA - *BrCabYB 84; TV&RadDir 84*
WSNT-FM - Sandersville, GA - *BrCabYB 84; TV&RadDir 84*
WSNW - Seneca, SC - *BrCabYB 84; TV&RadDir 84*
WSNY-FM - Columbus, OH - *BrCabYB 84; NatRadPubDir Summer 83, Spring 84; TV&RadDir 84*
WSOC - Charlotte, NC - *BrCabYB 84; NatRadPubDir Summer 83, Spring 84; TV&RadDir 84*
WSOC-FM - Charlotte, NC - *BrCabYB 84; NatRadPubDir Summer 83, Spring 84; TV&RadDir 84*
WSOC-TV - Charlotte, NC - *BrCabYB 84; DirUSTelSta 83; LitMarPl 83, 84; TelAl 83, 84; Tel&CabFB 84S; TV&RadDir 84*
WSOE-FM - Elon College, NC - *BrCabYB 84; TV&RadDir 84*
WSOF-FM - Madisonville, KY - *BrCabYB 84; TV&RadDir 84*
WSOJ-FM - Jesup, GA - *BrCabYB 84; TV&RadDir 84*
WSOK - Savannah, GA - *BrCabYB 84; NatRadPubDir Summer 83, Spring 84; TV&RadDir 84*
WSOL - Elloree-Santee, SC - *BrCabYB 84*
WSOM - Salem, OH - *BrCabYB 84; TV&RadDir 84*
WSON - Henderson, KY - *BrCabYB 84; TV&RadDir 84*
WSOO - Sault Ste. Marie, MI - *BrCabYB 84*
WSOR-FM - Ft. Myers, FL - *BrCabYB 84; TV&RadDir 84*
WSOU-FM - South Orange, NJ - *BrCabYB 84; NatRadPubDir Summer 83, Spring 84; TV&RadDir 84*
WSOX - Newark, DE - *TV&RadDir 84*
WSOX-FM - West Yarmouth, MA - *BrCabYB 84; TV&RadDir 84*
WSOY - Decatur, IL - *BrCabYB 84; NatRadPubDir Summer 83, Spring 84; TV&RadDir 84*
WSOY-FM - Decatur, IL - *BrCabYB 84; NatRadPubDir Summer 83, Spring 84*
WSPA - Spartanburg, SC - *BrCabYB 84; NatRadPubDir Summer 83, Spring 84; TV&RadDir 84*
WSPA-FM - Spartanburg, SC - *BrCabYB 84; NatRadPubDir Summer 83, Spring 84; TV&RadDir 84*
WSPA-TV - Spartanburg, SC - *BrCabYB 84; DirUSTelSta 83; LitMarPl 83, 84; TelAl 83, 84; Tel&CabFB 84S; TV&RadDir 84*
WSPB - Sarasota, FL - *BrCabYB 84; NatRadPubDir Summer 83, Spring 84; TV&RadDir 84*
WSPB-FM - Sarasota, FL - *NatRadPubDir Summer 83, Spring 84*
WSPC - St. Paul, VA - *BrCabYB 84*
WSPD - Toledo, OH - *BrCabYB 84; NatRadPubDir Summer 83, Spring 84; TV&RadDir 84*
WSPF - Hickory, NC - *BrCabYB 84; TV&RadDir 84*
WSPH-FM - Baltimore, MD - *NatRadPubDir Summer 83, Spring 84; TV&RadDir 84*
WSPI-FM - Shamokin, PA - *BrCabYB 84; TV&RadDir 84*
WSPK - Poughkeepsie, NY - *BrCabYB 84*
WSPL-FM - La Crosse, WI - *BrCabYB 84; TV&RadDir 84*
WSPN-FM - Saratoga Springs, NY - *BrCabYB 84; TV&RadDir 84*
WSPR - Springfield, MA - *BrCabYB 84; NatRadPubDir Summer 83, Spring 84; TV&RadDir 84*
WSPS-FM - Concord, NH - *BrCabYB 84; NatRadPubDir Summer 83, Spring 84; TV&RadDir 84*
WSPT-FM - Stevens Point, WI - *BrCabYB 84; TV&RadDir 84*
WSPY-FM - Plano, IL - *BrCabYB 84; TV&RadDir 84*
WSQR - Sycamore, IL - *BrCabYB 84*
WSQV-FM - Jersey Shore, PA - *BrCabYB 84; TV&RadDir 84*
WSQY-TV - Forest City, NC - *BrCabYB 84; Tel&CabFB 84S*
WSRA - Guayama, PR - *BrCabYB 84*
WSRB-FM - Walpole, MA - *BrCabYB 84; NatRadPubDir Summer 83, Spring 84; TV&RadDir 84*
WSRC - Durham, NC - *BrCabYB 84; TV&RadDir 84*
WSRC - Raleigh/Durham, NC - *NatRadPubDir Summer 83, Spring 84 p.184*
WSRD-FM - Youngstown, OH - *BrCabYB 84; TV&RadDir 84*
WSRE-TV - Pensacola, FL - *BrCabYB 84; Tel&CabFB 84S; TV&RadDir 84*
WSRF - Ft. Lauderdale, FL - *BrCabYB 84; NatRadPubDir Summer 83, Spring 84; TV&RadDir 84*
WSRG - Elkton, KY - *BrCabYB 84; TV&RadDir 84*
WSRK-FM - Oneonta, NY - *BrCabYB 84; TV&RadDir 84*
WSRN-FM - Swarthmore, PA - *BrCabYB 84; TV&RadDir 84*
WSRO - Marlborough, MA - *BrCabYB 84; TV&RadDir 84*
WSRQ-FM - Eden, NC - *BrCabYB 84; TV&RadDir 84*
WSRS-FM - Worcester, MA - *BrCabYB 84; NatRadPubDir Summer 83, Spring 84; TV&RadDir 84*
WSRU - Slippery Rock, PA - *BrCabYB 84*
WSRW - Hillsboro, OH - *BrCabYB 84; TV&RadDir 84*
WSRW-FM - Hillsboro, OH - *BrCabYB 84; TV&RadDir 84*
WSRX-FM - Allendale, MI - *NatRadPubDir Summer 83, Spring 84; TV&RadDir 84*
WSRZ-FM - Sarasota, FL - *BrCabYB 84; NatRadPubDir Summer 83, Spring 84; TV&RadDir 84*
WSS Cable TV Inc. - White Sulphur Springs, MT - *BrCabYB 84*
WSSA - Morrow, GA - *BrCabYB 84; TV&RadDir 84*
WSSC - Sumter, SC - *BrCabYB 84; TV&RadDir 84*
WSSD-FM - Chicago, IL - *BrCabYB 84; TV&RadDir 84*
WSSG - Goldsboro, NC - *BrCabYB 84; TV&RadDir 84*
WSSH-FM - Lowell, MA - *BrCabYB 84; TV&RadDir 84*
WSSJ - Camden, NJ - *BrCabYB 84; NatRadPubDir Summer 83, Spring 84; TV&RadDir 84*
WSSL - Gray Court, SC - *BrCabYB 84*
WSSN-FM - Weston, WV - *BrCabYB 84; TV&RadDir 84*
WSSO - Starkville, MS - *BrCabYB 84; TV&RadDir 84*
WSSR-FM - Springfield, IL - *BrCabYB 84; TV&RadDir 84*
WSST - Largo, FL - *BrCabYB 84; TV&RadDir 84*
WSSU-FM - Superior, WI - *BrCabYB 84; NatRadPubDir Spring 84; TV&RadDir 84*
WSSV - Petersburg, VA - *BrCabYB 84; NatRadPubDir Summer 83, Spring 84; TV&RadDir 84*
WSSX-FM - Charleston, SC - *BrCabYB 84; NatRadPubDir Summer 83, Spring 84; TV&RadDir 84*
WSTA - Charlotte Amalie, VI - *BrCabYB 84*
WSTB-FM - Kent, OH - *TV&RadDir 84*
WSTB-FM - Streetsboro, OH - *BrCabYB 84; NatRadPubDir Summer 83, Spring 84*
WSTC - Stamford, CT - *BrCabYB 84; NatRadPubDir Summer 83, Spring 84; TV&RadDir 84*
WSTD - Milton, MA - *TV&RadDir 84*
WSTE - Fajardo, PR - *BrCabYB 84; Tel&CabFB 84S*
WSTG - Providence, RI - *BrCabYB 84; DirUSTelSta 83; TelAl 84; Tel&CabFB 84S*
WSTJ - St. Johnsbury, VT - *BrCabYB 84; TV&RadDir 84*
WSTL - Eminence, KY - *BrCabYB 84; TV&RadDir 84*
WSTM-TV - Syracuse, NY - *BrCabYB 84; DirUSTelSta 83; TelAl 83, 84; Tel&CabFB 84S; TV&RadDir 84*
WSTN-FM - Florence, SC - *BrCabYB 84; TV&RadDir 84*
WSTO-FM - Owensboro, KY - *BrCabYB 84; TV&RadDir 84*
WSTP - Salisbury, NC - *BrCabYB 84; NatRadPubDir Summer 83, Spring 84; TV&RadDir 84*
WSTR - Sturgis, MI - *BrCabYB 84; TV&RadDir 84*
WSTR-FM - Sturgis, MI - *BrCabYB 84; TV&RadDir 84*
WSTS-FM - Laurinburg, NC - *BrCabYB 84; TV&RadDir 84*
WSTT - Charlotte Amalie, VI - *BrCabYB 84*
WSTU - Stuart, FL - *BrCabYB 84; TV&RadDir 84*
WSTV - Steubenville, OH - *BrCabYB 84; NatRadPubDir Summer 83, Spring 84; TV&RadDir 84*

WSTW-FM - Wilmington, DE - *BrCabYB 84; NatRadPubDir Summer 83, Spring 84; TV&RadDir 84*
WSTX - Christiansted, VI - *BrCabYB 84*
WSUA - Miami, FL - *BrCabYB 84*
WSUB - Groton, CT - *BrCabYB 84; TV&RadDir 84*
WSUB - New London, CT - *NatRadPubDir Summer 83 p.48, Spring 84 p.48*
WSUC-FM - Albany, NY - *NatRadPubDir Summer 83, Spring 84*
WSUC-FM - Cortland, NY - *BrCabYB 84; TV&RadDir 84*
WSUE - Sault Ste. Marie, MI - *BrCabYB 84*
WSUH - Oxford, MS - *BrCabYB 84; TV&RadDir 84*
WSUI - Coralville, IA - *TV&RadDir 84*
WSUI - Iowa City, IA - *BrCabYB 84*
WSUL-FM - Monticello, NY - *BrCabYB 84; TV&RadDir 84*
WSUM - Cleveland, OH - *NatRadPubDir Summer 83 p.195, Spring 84 p.193; TV&RadDir 84*
WSUM - Parma, OH - *BrCabYB 84*
WSUN - St. Petersburg, FL - *BrCabYB 84; TV&RadDir 84*
WSUN - Tampa/St. Petersburg, FL - *NatRadPubDir Summer 83, Spring 84 p.66*
WSUP-FM - Platteville, WI - *BrCabYB 84; NatRadPubDir Spring 84; TV&RadDir 84*
WSUR-TV - Ponce, PR - *BrCabYB 84; Tel&CabFB 84S*
WSUS-FM - Franklin, NJ - *BrCabYB 84; TV&RadDir 84*
WSUW-FM - Whitewater, WI - *BrCabYB 84; NatRadPubDir Spring 84; TV&RadDir 84*
WSUX-FM - Seaford, DE - *BrCabYB 84; TV&RadDir 84*
WSUZ - Palatka, FL - *BrCabYB 84; TV&RadDir 84*
WSVA - Harrisonburg, VA - *BrCabYB 84; NatRadPubDir Summer 83, Spring 84; TV&RadDir 84*
WSVC - Dunlap, TN - *BrCabYB 84; TV&RadDir 84*
WSVE - Green Cove Springs, FL - *BrCabYB 84*
WSVH-FM - Savannah, GA - *BrCabYB 84; TV&RadDir 84*
WSVI - Christiansted, VI - *BrCabYB 84; Tel&CabFB 84S*
WSVL - Shelbyville, IN - *BrCabYB 84; TV&RadDir 84*
WSVM - Valdese, NC - *BrCabYB 84; TV&RadDir 84*
WSVN-TV - Causeway, FL - *LitMarPl 84*
WSVN-TV - Miami, FL - *BrCabYB 84; TelAl 84; Tel&CabFB 84S*
WSVQ - Harrogate, TN - *BrCabYB 84; TV&RadDir 84*
WSVS - Crewe, VA - *BrCabYB 84; TV&RadDir 84*
WSVS-FM - Crewe, VA - *BrCabYB 84; TV&RadDir 84*
WSVT - Smyrna, TN - *BrCabYB 84*
WSWB - Scranton, PA - *BrCabYB 84; Tel&CabFB 84S*
WSWF - Lehigh Acres, FL - *BrCabYB 84; TV&RadDir 84*
WSWF-FM - Lehigh Acres, FL - *TV&RadDir 84*
WSWG - Greenwood, MS - *BrCabYB 84; TV&RadDir 84*
WSWG-FM - Greenwood, MS - *BrCabYB 84; TV&RadDir 84*
WSWI - Evansville, IN - *BrCabYB 84; TV&RadDir 84*
WSWL - Milton, FL - *BrCabYB 84*
WSWN - Belle Glade, FL - *BrCabYB 84; TV&RadDir 84*
WSWN-FM - Belle Glade, FL - *BrCabYB 84; TV&RadDir 84*
WSWO-FM - Wilmington, OH - *BrCabYB 84; TV&RadDir 84*
WSWP-TV - Beckley, WV - *TV&RadDir 84*
WSWP-TV - Grandview, WV - *BrCabYB 84; Tel&CabFB 84S*
WSWR - Shelby, OH - *BrCabYB 84*
WSWS - Opelika, AL - *BrCabYB 84; DirUSTelSta 83; Tel&CabFB 84S*
WSWT-FM - Peoria, IL - *BrCabYB 84; NatRadPubDir Summer 83, Spring 84; TV&RadDir 84*
WSWV - Pennington Gap, VA - *BrCabYB 84; TV&RadDir 84*
WSWV-FM - Pennington Gap, VA - *BrCabYB 84; TV&RadDir 84*
WSWW - Platteville, WI - *TV&RadDir 84*
WSWW-FM - Platteville, WI - *TV&RadDir 84*
WSYB - Rutland, VT - *BrCabYB 84; TV&RadDir 84*
WSYC-FM - Shippensburg, PA - *BrCabYB 84; NatRadPubDir Summer 83, Spring 84; TV&RadDir 84*
WSYD - Mt. Airy, NC - *BrCabYB 84; TV&RadDir 84*
WSYL - Sylvania, GA - *BrCabYB 84; TV&RadDir 84*
WSYR - Syracuse, NY - *BrCabYB 84; NatRadPubDir Summer 83, Spring 84; TV&RadDir 84*
WSYR-FM - Syracuse, NY - *NatRadPubDir Summer 83; TV&RadDir 84*
WSYX-FM - London, OH - *TV&RadDir 84*
W.T. & B. Advertising Ltd. - Toronto, ON, Canada - *StaDirAdAg 2-84*
WTAB - Tabor City, NC - *BrCabYB 84; TV&RadDir 84*
WTAC - Flint, MI - *BrCabYB 84; NatRadPubDir Summer 83, Spring 84*
WTAD - Quincy, IL - *BrCabYB 84; TV&RadDir 84*
WTAE - Pittsburgh, PA - *BrCabYB 84; NatRadPubDir Summer 83, Spring 84; TV&RadDir 84*
WTAE-TV - Pittsburgh, PA - *BrCabYB 84; DirUSTelSta 83; LitMarPl 83, 84; TelAl 83, 84; Tel&CabFB 84S; TV&RadDir 84*
WTAF-TV - Philadelphia, PA - *BrCabYB 84; DirUSTelSta 83; TelAl 83, 84; Tel&CabFB 84S; TV&RadDir 84*
WTAG - Worcester, MA - *BrCabYB 84; NatRadPubDir Summer 83, Spring 84; TV&RadDir 84*
WTAI - Melbourne, FL - *BrCabYB 84; TV&RadDir 84*
WTAJ-TV - Altoona, PA - *BrCabYB 84; TelAl 83, 84; Tel&CabFB 84S; TV&RadDir 84*
WTAJ-TV - Johnstown, PA - *DirUSTelSta 83*
WTAK - Huntsville, AL - *BrCabYB 84; TV&RadDir 84*
WTAL - Tallahassee, FL - *BrCabYB 84; TV&RadDir 84*
WTAM - Biloxi/Gulfport, MS - *NatRadPubDir Summer 83, Spring 84 p.137*
WTAM - Gulfport, MS - *BrCabYB 84; TV&RadDir 84*
WTAN - Clearwater, FL - *BrCabYB 84; TV&RadDir 84*
WTAN - Tampa/St. Petersburg, FL - *NatRadPubDir Summer 83 p.65, Spring 84 p.66*
WTAO-FM - Murphysboro, IL - *BrCabYB 84; TV&RadDir 84*
WTAP-TV - Parkersburg, WV - *BrCabYB 84; DirUSTelSta 83; TelAl 83, 84; Tel&CabFB 84S; TV&RadDir 84*
WTAQ - La Grange, IL - *BrCabYB 84; TV&RadDir 84*
WTAR - Norfolk, VA - *BrCabYB 84; NatRadPubDir Summer 83, Spring 84; TV&RadDir 84*
WTAR-TV - Norfolk, VA - *LitMarPl 83, 84*
WTAS-FM - Chicago Heights, IL - *NatRadPubDir Summer 83, Spring 84; TV&RadDir 84*
WTAS-FM - Crete, IL - *BrCabYB 84*
WTAW - Bryan, TX - *TV&RadDir 84*
WTAW - College Station, TX - *BrCabYB 84*
WTAW-FM - Bryan, TX - *TV&RadDir 84*
WTAX - Springfield, IL - *BrCabYB 84; NatRadPubDir Summer 83, Spring 84; TV&RadDir 84*
WTAY - Robinson, IL - *BrCabYB 84; TV&RadDir 84*
WTAY-FM - Robinson, IL - *BrCabYB 84; TV&RadDir 84*
WTAZ-FM - Morton, IL - *BrCabYB 84; TV&RadDir 84*
WTBB - Bonifay, FL - *BrCabYB 84*
WTBC - Tuscaloosa, AL - *BrCabYB 84; NatRadPubDir Summer 83, Spring 84; TV&RadDir 84*
WTBF - Troy, AL - *BrCabYB 84; TV&RadDir 84*
WTBG-FM - Brownsville, TN - *BrCabYB 84; TV&RadDir 84*
WTBN - Brentwood, TN - *BrCabYB 84*
WTBO - Cumberland, MD - *BrCabYB 84; NatRadPubDir Summer 83, Spring 84; TV&RadDir 84*
WTBP - Parsons, TN - *BrCabYB 84; TV&RadDir 84*
WTBQ - Warwick, NY - *BrCabYB 84; NatRadPubDir Summer 83, Spring 84; TV&RadDir 84*
WTBR-FM - Pittsfield, MA - *BrCabYB 84*
WTBR-FM - Pittsfield, PA - *TV&RadDir 84*
WTBS-TV [of Turner Broadcasting System] - Atlanta, GA - *BrCabYB 84; CabTVPrDB 83; DirUSTelSta 83; HomeVid&CabYB 82-83; TelAl 83, 84; Tel&CabFB 84C, 84S; TV&RadDir 84*
WTBU - Boston, MA - *NatRadPubDir Summer 83, Spring 84*
WTBX - Hibbing, MN - *BrCabYB 84*
WTBY-TV - New York, NY - *DirUSTelSta 83*
WTBY-TV - Poughkeepsie, NY - *BrCabYB 84; TelAl 84; Tel&CabFB 84S*
WTBZ-FM - Grafton, WV - *BrCabYB 84; TV&RadDir 84*
WTCA - Plymouth, IN - *BrCabYB 84; TV&RadDir 84*
WTCC-FM - Springfield, MA - *BrCabYB 84; NatRadPubDir Summer 83, Spring 84; TV&RadDir 84*
WTCG - Andalusia, AL - *BrCabYB 84*
WTCH - Shawano, WI - *BrCabYB 84; TV&RadDir 84*
WTCI-TV - Chattanooga, TN - *BrCabYB 84; Tel&CabFB 84S; TV&RadDir 84*
WTCJ - Tell City, IN - *BrCabYB 84; TV&RadDir 84*
WTCL - Warren, OH - *BrCabYB 84*
WTCM - Traverse City, MI - *BrCabYB 84; TV&RadDir 84*

WTCM-FM - Traverse City, MI - *BrCabYB 84; TV&RadDir 84*
WTCN-TV - Minneapolis, MN - *BrCabYB 84; DirUSTelSta 83; LitMarPl 83, 84; TelAl 83, 84; Tel&CabFB 84S; TV&RadDir 84*
WTCO-FM - Arlington Heights, IL - *TV&RadDir 84*
WTCQ-FM - Vidalia, GA - *BrCabYB 84; TV&RadDir 84*
WTCR - Catlettsburg, KY - *TV&RadDir 84*
WTCR - Huntington, WV - *BrCabYB 84; NatRadPubDir Summer 83 p.263*
WTCR-FM - Huntington, WV - *NatRadPubDir Spring 84*
WTCS - Fairmont, WV - *BrCabYB 84; TV&RadDir 84*
WTCW - Whitesburg, KY - *BrCabYB 84; TV&RadDir 84*
WTCX - Saginaw, MI - *NatRadPubDir Spring 84 p.132*
WTEB - New Bern, NC - *BrCabYB 84*
WTEL - Philadelphia, PA - *BrCabYB 84; NatRadPubDir Summer 83, Spring 84; TV&RadDir 84*
WTEN-TV - Albany, NY - *BrCabYB 84; DirUSTelSta 83; LitMarPl 83, 84; TelAl 83, 84; Tel&CabFB 84S; TV&RadDir 84*
WTFM-FM - Kingsport, TN - *BrCabYB 84; NatRadPubDir Spring 84; TV&RadDir 84*
WTGA - Thomaston, GA - *BrCabYB 84; TV&RadDir 84*
WTGC - Lewisburg, PA - *BrCabYB 84; TV&RadDir 84*
WTGE - Kalkaska, MI - *BrCabYB 84*
WTGI-FM - Hammond, LA - *BrCabYB 84; TV&RadDir 84*
WTGL-TV - Cocoa, FL - *BrCabYB 84; DirUSTelSta 83; TelAl 84; Tel&CabFB 84S*
WTGN-FM - Lima, OH - *BrCabYB 84; TV&RadDir 84*
WTGP-FM - Greenville, PA - *BrCabYB 84; TV&RadDir 84*
WTGQ - Cairo, GA - *BrCabYB 84*
WTGR - Myrtle Beach, SC - *BrCabYB 84; TV&RadDir 84*
WTGS - Hardeeville, SC - *BrCabYB 84; Tel&CabFB 84S*
WTGV-FM - Sandusky, MI - *BrCabYB 84*
WTHB - Augusta, GA - *BrCabYB 84; NatRadPubDir Summer 83, Spring 84; TV&RadDir 84*
WTHE - Mineola, NY - *BrCabYB 84; TV&RadDir 84*
WTHE - Nassau County, Long Island, NY - *NatRadPubDir Summer 83 p.171, Spring 84 p.169*
WTHI - Terre Haute, IN - *BrCabYB 84; NatRadPubDir Summer 83, Spring 84; TV&RadDir 84*
WTHI-FM - Terre Haute, IN - *BrCabYB 84; NatRadPubDir Summer 83, Spring 84; TV&RadDir 84*
WTHI-TV - Terre Haute, IN - *BrCabYB 84; DirUSTelSta 83; TelAl 83, 84; Tel&CabFB 84S; TV&RadDir 84*
WTHO-FM - Thomson, GA - *BrCabYB 84; TV&RadDir 84*
WTHQ-FM - South Bend, IN - *BrCabYB 84; NatRadPubDir Spring 84; TV&RadDir 84*
WTHR [of Berkeley Solar Group] - Berkeley, CA - *DataDirOnSer 84*
WTHR-TV - Indianapolis, IN - *BrCabYB 84; DirUSTelSta 83; LitMarPl 83, 84; TelAl 83, 84; Tel&CabFB 84S; TV&RadDir 84*
WTHS-TV - Miami, FL - *Tel&CabFB 84S; TV&RadDir 84*
WTHU - Thurmont, MD - *BrCabYB 84; TV&RadDir 84*
WTI - Laguna Hills, CA - *AvMarPl 83*
WTIB-FM - Iuka, MS - *BrCabYB 84; TV&RadDir 84*
WTIC - Hartford, CT - *BrCabYB 84; NatRadPubDir Summer 83, Spring 84; TV&RadDir 84*
WTIC-FM - Hartford, CT - *BrCabYB 84; NatRadPubDir Summer 83, Spring 84; TV&RadDir 84*
WTIF - Tifton, GA - *BrCabYB 84; TV&RadDir 84*
WTIG - Massillon, OH - *BrCabYB 84; NatRadPubDir Summer 83, Spring 84; TV&RadDir 84*
WTIK - Durham, NC - *BrCabYB 84; TV&RadDir 84*
WTIK - Raleigh/Durham, NC - *NatRadPubDir Summer 83, Spring 84 p.184*
WTIL - Mayaguez, PR - *BrCabYB 84*
WTIM - Taylorville, IL - *BrCabYB 84; TV&RadDir 84*
WTIN - Ponce, PR - *BrCabYB 84; Tel&CabFB 84S*
WTIP - Charleston, WV - *BrCabYB 84; NatRadPubDir Summer 83, Spring 84; TV&RadDir 84*
WTIQ - Manistique, MI - *BrCabYB 84; TV&RadDir 84*
WTIS - St. Petersburg, FL - *TV&RadDir 84*
WTIS - Tampa, FL - *BrCabYB 84; NatRadPubDir Summer 83, Spring 84 p.66*
WTIU-TV - Bloomington, IN - *BrCabYB 84; Tel&CabFB 84S; TV&RadDir 84*
WTIV - Titusville, PA - *BrCabYB 84; TV&RadDir 84*
WTIX - New Orleans, LA - *BrCabYB 84; NatRadPubDir Summer 83, Spring 84; TV&RadDir 84*
WTJC-TV - Springfield, OH - *BrCabYB 84; DirUSTelSta 83; TelAl 83, 84; Tel&CabFB 84S; TV&RadDir 84*
WTJH - Atlanta, GA - *NatRadPubDir Summer 83 p.70, Spring 84 p.70; TV&RadDir 84*
WTJH - East Point, GA - *BrCabYB 84*
WTJM-FM - Pineville, KY - *BrCabYB 84; TV&RadDir 84*
WTJP - Gadsden, AL - *BrCabYB 84; Tel&CabFB 84S*
WTJR - Quincy, IL - *BrCabYB 84; Tel&CabFB 84S*
WTJS - Jackson, TN - *BrCabYB 84; TV&RadDir 84*
WTJT - Franklin, TN - *TV&RadDir 84*
WTJU-FM - Charlottesville, VA - *BrCabYB 84; NatRadPubDir Summer 83, Spring 84; TV&RadDir 84*
WTJX-TV - Charlotte Amalie, VI - *BrCabYB 84; Tel&CabFB 84S*
WTJY - Taylorville, IL - *BrCabYB 84*
WTJZ - Hampton, VA - *TV&RadDir 84*
WTJZ - Newport News, VA - *BrCabYB 84*
WTJZ - Norfolk, VA - *NatRadPubDir Summer 83, Spring 84 p.257*
WTKC - Lexington, KY - *BrCabYB 84; NatRadPubDir Summer 83, Spring 84; TV&RadDir 84*
WTKK-TV - Manassas, VA - *BrCabYB 84; DirUSTelSta 83; TelAl 83, 84; Tel&CabFB 84S; TV&RadDir 84*
WTKL - Baton Rouge, LA - *BrCabYB 84; NatRadPubDir Summer 83, Spring 84; TV&RadDir 84*
WTKM - Hartford, WI - *BrCabYB 84; TV&RadDir 84*
WTKM-FM - Hartford, WI - *BrCabYB 84; TV&RadDir 84*
WTKN - Pittsburgh, PA - *BrCabYB 84; NatRadPubDir Summer 83, Spring 84*
WTKO - Ithaca, NY - *BrCabYB 84; NatRadPubDir Summer 83, Spring 84; TV&RadDir 84*
WTKR-TV - Norfolk, VA - *BrCabYB 84; DirUSTelSta 83; LitMarPl 83, 84; TelAl 83, 84; Tel&CabFB 84S; TV&RadDir 84*
WTKS-FM - Washington, DC - *NatRadPubDir Spring 84*
WTKS-FM - Bethesda, MD - *BrCabYB 84*
WTKW - Key West, FL - *BrCabYB 84; Tel&CabFB 84S*
WTKX-FM - Pensacola, FL - *BrCabYB 84; NatRadPubDir Summer 83, Spring 84; TV&RadDir 84*
WTKY - Tompkinsville, KY - *BrCabYB 84; TV&RadDir 84*
WTKY-FM - Tompkinsville, KY - *BrCabYB 84; TV&RadDir 84*
WTLB - Utica, NY - *BrCabYB 84; NatRadPubDir Summer 83, Spring 84; TV&RadDir 84*
WTLC-FM - Indianapolis, IN - *BrCabYB 84; NatRadPubDir Summer 83, Spring 84; TV&RadDir 84*
WTLK - Taylorsville, NC - *BrCabYB 84; TV&RadDir 84*
WTLL - Richmond, VA - *BrCabYB 84; Tel&CabFB 84S*
WTLN - Apopka, FL - *BrCabYB 84*
WTLN - Orlando, FL - *NatRadPubDir Summer 83, Spring 84; TV&RadDir 84*
WTLN-FM - Apopka, FL - *BrCabYB 84*
WTLN-FM - Orlando, FL - *NatRadPubDir Summer 83, Spring 84; TV&RadDir 84*
WTLO - Somerset, KY - *BrCabYB 84; TV&RadDir 84*
WTLQ - Pittston, PA - *BrCabYB 84*
WTLR-FM - State College, PA - *BrCabYB 84; TV&RadDir 84*
WTLS - Tallassee, AL - *BrCabYB 84; TV&RadDir 84*
WTLV-TV - Jacksonville, FL - *BrCabYB 84; DirUSTelSta 83; TelAl 83, 84; Tel&CabFB 84S; TV&RadDir 84*
WTLW - Lima, OH - *BrCabYB 84; DirUSTelSta 83; Tel&CabFB 84S*
WTMA - Charleston, SC - *BrCabYB 84; NatRadPubDir Summer 83, Spring 84; TV&RadDir 84*
WTMB - Tomah, WI - *BrCabYB 84; TV&RadDir 84*
WTMB-FM - Tomah, WI - *BrCabYB 84; TV&RadDir 84*
WTMB-TV - Tomah, WI - *BrCabYB 84; Tel&CabFB 84S*
WTMC - Ocala, FL - *BrCabYB 84; TV&RadDir 84*
WTMI-FM - Miami, FL - *BrCabYB 84; NatRadPubDir Summer 83, Spring 84; TV&RadDir 84*
WTMJ - Milwaukee, WI - *BrCabYB 84; NatRadPubDir Summer 83, Spring 84; TV&RadDir 84*
WTMJ Inc. - *See* Teltron Inc.
WTMJ-TV - Milwaukee, WI - *BrCabYB 84; DirUSTelSta 83; LitMarPl 83, 84; TelAl 83, 84; Tel&CabFB 84S; TV&RadDir 84*
WTMP - Tampa, FL - *BrCabYB 84; NatRadPubDir Summer 83, Spring 84; TV&RadDir 84*
WTMR - Camden, NJ - *BrCabYB 84; NatRadPubDir Summer 83, Spring 84*
WTMS-FM - Presque Isle, ME - *BrCabYB 84; TV&RadDir 84*

WTMT - Louisville, KY - *BrCabYB 84; NatRadPubDir Summer 83, Spring 84; TV&RadDir 84*
WTMX - Ridgway, PA - *BrCabYB 84*
WTNC - Thomasville, NC - *BrCabYB 84; TV&RadDir 84*
WTND - Orangeburg, SC - *BrCabYB 84; TV&RadDir 84*
WTNE - Trenton, TN - *BrCabYB 84; TV&RadDir 84*
WTNE-FM - Trenton, TN - *TV&RadDir 84*
WTNH-TV - New Haven, CT - *BrCabYB 84; DirUSTelSta 83; LitMarPl 83, 84; TelAl 83, 84; Tel&CabFB 84S; TV&RadDir 84*
WTNJ-FM - Beckley, WV - *TV&RadDir 84*
WTNJ-FM - Mt. Hope, WV - *BrCabYB 84*
WTNL - Reidsville, GA - *BrCabYB 84; TV&RadDir 84*
WTNN - Millington, TN - *TV&RadDir 84*
WTNQ-FM - Dickson, TN - *BrCabYB 84; TV&RadDir 84*
WTNR - Kinston, TN - *BrCabYB 84*
WTNS - Coshocton, OH - *BrCabYB 84; TV&RadDir 84*
WTNS-FM - Coshocton, OH - *BrCabYB 84; TV&RadDir 84*
WTNT - Tallahassee, FL - *BrCabYB 84; NatRadPubDir Summer 83, Spring 84; TV&RadDir 84*
WTNX - Lynchburg, TN - *BrCabYB 84*
WTNY - Watertown, NY - *BrCabYB 84; NatRadPubDir Summer 83, Spring 84; TV&RadDir 84*
WTOB - Winston Salem, NC - *BrCabYB 84; NatRadPubDir Summer 83, Spring 84; TV&RadDir 84*
WTOC-TV - Savannah, GA - *BrCabYB 84; DirUSTelSta 83; TelAl 83, 84; Tel&CabFB 84S; TV&RadDir 84*
WTOD - Toledo, OH - *BrCabYB 84; NatRadPubDir Summer 83, Spring 84; TV&RadDir 84*
WTOE - Spruce Pine, NC - *BrCabYB 84; TV&RadDir 84*
WTOF-FM - Canton, OH - *BrCabYB 84; NatRadPubDir Summer 83, Spring 84; TV&RadDir 84*
WTOG-TV - St. Petersburg, FL - *BrCabYB 84; TelAl 83, 84; Tel&CabFB 84S; TV&RadDir 84*
WTOG-TV - Tampa, FL - *DirUSTelSta 83*
WTOH-FM - Mobile, AL - *BrCabYB 84; TV&RadDir 84*
WTOJ - Carthage, NY - *BrCabYB 84*
WTOK-TV - Laurel, MS - *TelAl 83, 84*
WTOK-TV - Meridian, MS - *BrCabYB 84; DirUSTelSta 83; Tel&CabFB 84S; TV&RadDir 84*
WTOL-TV - Toledo, OH - *BrCabYB 84; DirUSTelSta 83; LitMarPl 83, 84; TelAl 83, 84; Tel&CabFB 84S; TV&RadDir 84*
WTOM-TV - Cheboygan, MI - *BrCabYB 84; TelAl 83, 84; Tel&CabFB 84S*
WTOM-TV - Traverse City, MI - *TV&RadDir 84*
WTON - Staunton, VA - *BrCabYB 84; TV&RadDir 84*
WTOO-FM - Bellefontaine, OH - *BrCabYB 84; TV&RadDir 84*
WTOP - Washington, DC - *BrCabYB 84; NatRadPubDir Summer 83, Spring 84; TV&RadDir 84*
WTOQ - Platteville, WI - *BrCabYB 84*
WTOS-FM - Skowhegan, ME - *BrCabYB 84; TV&RadDir 84*
WTOT - Marianna, FL - *BrCabYB 84; TV&RadDir 84*
WTOV-TV - Steubenville, OH - *BrCabYB 84; DirUSTelSta 83; TelAl 83, 84; Tel&CabFB 84S; TV&RadDir 84*
WTOW - Baltimore, MD - *NatRadPubDir Summer 83 p.116, Spring 84 p.116*
WTOW - Towson, MD - *BrCabYB 84*
WTOY - Roanoke, VA - *BrCabYB 84; NatRadPubDir Summer 83, Spring 84; TV&RadDir 84*
WTPA - Harrisburg, PA - *TelAl 83, 84*
WTPA-FM - Harrisburg, PA - *BrCabYB 84; NatRadPubDir Summer 83, Spring 84; TV&RadDir 84*
WTPC-FM - Elsah, IL - *BrCabYB 84; TV&RadDir 84*
WTPL - Greeneville, TN - *NatRadPubDir Summer 83, Spring 84*
WTPL-FM - Tupper Lake, NY - *BrCabYB 84*
WTPM - Aguadilla, PR - *BrCabYB 84*
WTPR - Paris, TN - *BrCabYB 84; NatRadPubDir Summer 83, Spring 84; TV&RadDir 84*
WTPR-FM - Paris, TN - *BrCabYB 84; NatRadPubDir Summer 83, Spring 84; TV&RadDir 84*
WTQR-FM - Winston Salem, NC - *BrCabYB 84; NatRadPubDir Summer 83, Spring 84; TV&RadDir 84*
WTQX - Selma, AL - *BrCabYB 84; NatRadPubDir Summer 83, Spring 84; TV&RadDir 84*
WTRA - Mayaguez, PR - *BrCabYB 84; Tel&CabFB 84S*
WTRB - Ripley, TN - *BrCabYB 84; TV&RadDir 84*
WTRC - Elkhart, IN - *BrCabYB 84; TV&RadDir 84*
WTRE - Greensburg, IN - *BrCabYB 84; TV&RadDir 84*
WTRE-FM - Greensburg, IN - *BrCabYB 84; TV&RadDir 84*
WTRF-TV - Wheeling, WV - *BrCabYB 84; DirUSTelSta 83; TelAl 83, 84; Tel&CabFB 84S; TV&RadDir 84*
WTRI - Brunswick, MD - *BrCabYB 84; TV&RadDir 84*
WTRJ - Troy, OH - *BrCabYB 84*
WTRN - Tyrone, PA - *BrCabYB 84; TV&RadDir 84*
WTRO - Dyersburg, TN - *BrCabYB 84; TV&RadDir 84*
WTRP - La Grange, GA - *BrCabYB 84; TV&RadDir 84*
WTRQ - Warsaw, NC - *BrCabYB 84; TV&RadDir 84*
WTRR - Sanford, FL - *TV&RadDir 84*
WTRS - Dunnellon, FL - *BrCabYB 84*
WTRS - Ocala, FL - *BrCabYB 84*
WTRS-FM - Dunnellon, FL - *TV&RadDir 84*
WTRU - Muskegon, MI - *BrCabYB 84; NatRadPubDir Summer 83, Spring 84*
WTRX - Flint, MI - *BrCabYB 84; NatRadPubDir Summer 83, Spring 84; TV&RadDir 84*
WTRY - Albany/Schenectady/Troy, NY - *NatRadPubDir Summer 83 p.168, Spring 84 p.166*
WTRY - Latham, NY - *TV&RadDir 84*
WTRY - Troy, NY - *BrCabYB 84*
WTSA - Brattleboro, VT - *BrCabYB 84; NatRadPubDir Summer 83, Spring 84; TV&RadDir 84*
WTSB - Lumberton, NC - *BrCabYB 84; TV&RadDir 84*
WTSC-FM - Potsdam, NY - *BrCabYB 84; TV&RadDir 84*
WTSD - Drayton Plains, MI - *BrCabYB 84*
WTSF - Ashland, KY - *BrCabYB 84; Tel&CabFB 84S*
WTSG - Albany, GA - *BrCabYB 84; DirUSTelSta 83; TelAl 84; Tel&CabFB 84S*
WTSJ - Cincinnati, OH - *BrCabYB 84; NatRadPubDir Summer 83, Spring 84; TV&RadDir 84*
WTSK - Tuscaloosa, AL - *BrCabYB 84; TV&RadDir 84*
WTSL - Hanover, NH - *BrCabYB 84*
WTSL - Lebanon, NH - *TV&RadDir 84*
WTSN - Dover, NH - *BrCabYB 84; NatRadPubDir Summer 83, Spring 84; TV&RadDir 84*
WTSO - Madison, WI - *BrCabYB 84; NatRadPubDir Summer 83, Spring 84; TV&RadDir 84*
WTSP-TV - St. Petersburg, FL - *BrCabYB 84; LitMarPl 83, 84; TelAl 83, 84; TV&RadDir 84*
WTSP-TV - Tampa, FL - *DirUSTelSta 83; Tel&CabFB 84S*
WTSR-FM - Trenton, NJ - *BrCabYB 84; TV&RadDir 84*
WTSU-FM - Troy, AL - *BrCabYB 84; TV&RadDir 84*
WTSV - Claremont, NH - *BrCabYB 84; TV&RadDir 84*
WTTB - Vero Beach, FL - *BrCabYB 84; TV&RadDir 84*
WTTC - Towanda, PA - *BrCabYB 84; TV&RadDir 84*
WTTC-FM - Towanda, PA - *BrCabYB 84; TV&RadDir 84*
WTTE - Columbus, OH - *BrCabYB 84; Tel&CabFB 84S*
WTTF - Tiffin, OH - *BrCabYB 84; TV&RadDir 84*
WTTF-FM - Tiffin, OH - *BrCabYB 84; TV&RadDir 84*
WTTG-TV - Washington, DC - *BrCabYB 84; DirUSTelSta 83; TelAl 83, 84; Tel&CabFB 84S; TV&RadDir 84*
WTTI - Dalton, GA - *BrCabYB 84; TV&RadDir 84*
WTTL - Madisonville, KY - *BrCabYB 84; TV&RadDir 84*
WTTM - Trenton, NJ - *BrCabYB 84; NatRadPubDir Summer 83, Spring 84; TV&RadDir 84*
WTTN - Watertown, WI - *BrCabYB 84; TV&RadDir 84*
WTTO-TV - Birmingham, AL - *BrCabYB 84; DirUSTelSta 83; TelAl 84*
WTTO-TV - Homewood, AL - *Tel&CabFB 84S*
WTTP - Natick, MA - *BrCabYB 84*
WTTR - Westminster, MD - *BrCabYB 84; TV&RadDir 84*
WTTR-FM - Westminster, MD - *BrCabYB 84; TV&RadDir 84*
WTTS - Bloomington, IN - *BrCabYB 84; NatRadPubDir Spring 84; TV&RadDir 84*
WTTT - Amherst, MA - *BrCabYB 84; TV&RadDir 84*
WTTU-FM - Cookeville, TN - *BrCabYB 84; NatRadPubDir Summer 83, Spring 84; TV&RadDir 84*
WTTV-TV - Bloomington, IN - *BrCabYB 84; TelAl 83, 84; Tel&CabFB 84S*
WTTV-TV - Indianapolis, IN - *DirUSTelSta 83; TV&RadDir 84*
WTTW-TV - Chicago, IL - *BrCabYB 84; Tel&CabFB 84S; TV&RadDir 84*
WTTX - Appomattox, VA - *BrCabYB 84; TV&RadDir 84*
WTTX-FM - Appomattox, VA - *BrCabYB 84; TV&RadDir 84*
WTUC - Rock Hill, SC - *NatRadPubDir Spring 84*

WTUE-FM - Dayton, OH - *BrCabYB 84; NatRadPubDir Summer 83, Spring 84; TV&RadDir 84*
WTUF-FM - Thomasville, GA - *BrCabYB 84; TV&RadDir 84*
WTUG-FM - Tuscaloosa, AL - *BrCabYB 84; TV&RadDir 84*
WTUK - Florence, AL - *BrCabYB 84; Tel&CabFB 84S*
WTUL-FM - New Orleans, LA - *BrCabYB 84; NatRadPubDir Summer 83, Spring 84; TV&RadDir 84*
WTUN - Selma, AL - *BrCabYB 84; NatRadPubDir Summer 83*
WTUN-FM - Selma, AL - *TV&RadDir 84*
WTUP - Tupelo, MS - *BrCabYB 84; TV&RadDir 84*
WTUV - Utica, NY - *BrCabYB 84; Tel&CabFB 84S*
WTVA-TV - Tupelo, MS - *BrCabYB 84; DirUSTelSta 83; TelAl 83, 84; Tel&CabFB 84S; TV&RadDir 84*
WTVB - Coldwater, MI - *BrCabYB 84; TV&RadDir 84*
WTVC-TV - Chattanooga, TN - *BrCabYB 84; DirUSTelSta 83; TelAl 83, 84; Tel&CabFB 84S; TV&RadDir 84*
WTVD-TV - Durham, NC - *BrCabYB 84; LitMarPl 83, 84; TelAl 83, 84; Tel&CabFB 84S; TV&RadDir 84*
WTVD-TV - Raleigh, NC - *DirUSTelSta 83*
WTVE-TV - Harrisburg, PA - *DirUSTelSta 83*
WTVE-TV - Reading, PA - *BrCabYB 84; TelAl 83, 84; Tel&CabFB 84S; TV&RadDir 84*
WTVF-TV - Knoxville, TN - *TV&RadDir 84*
WTVF-TV - Nashville, TN - *BrCabYB 84; DirUSTelSta 83; LitMarPl 83, 84; TelAl 83, 84; Tel&CabFB 84S; TV&RadDir 84*
WTVG-TV - Toledo, OH - *BrCabYB 84; DirUSTelSta 83; LitMarPl 83, 84; TelAl 83, 84; Tel&CabFB 84S; TV&RadDir 84*
WTVH-TV - Syracuse, NY - *BrCabYB 84; DirUSTelSta 83; TelAl 83, 84; Tel&CabFB 84S*
WTVI-TV - Charlotte, NC - *BrCabYB 84; Tel&CabFB 84S; TV&RadDir 84*
WTVJ-TV - Miami, FL - *BrCabYB 84; DirUSTelSta 83; LitMarPl 83, 84; TelAl 83, 84; Tel&CabFB 84S; TV&RadDir 84*
WTVK - Knoxville, TN - *TelAl 84*
WTVK-TV - Knoxville, TN - *BrCabYB 84; DirUSTelSta 83; LitMarPl 83, 84; TelAl 83; Tel&CabFB 84S; TV&RadDir 84*
WTVL - Waterville, ME - *BrCabYB 84; TV&RadDir 84*
WTVL-FM - Waterville, ME - *BrCabYB 84; TV&RadDir 84*
WTVM-TV - Columbus, GA - *BrCabYB 84; DirUSTelSta 83; TelAl 83, 84; Tel&CabFB 84S; TV&RadDir 84*
WTVN - Columbus, OH - *BrCabYB 84; LitMarPl 83, 84; NatRadPubDir Summer 83, Spring 84; TV&RadDir 84*
WTVN-TV - Columbus, OH - *BrCabYB 84; DirUSTelSta 83; LitMarPl 83, 84; TelAl 83, 84; Tel&CabFB 84S; TV&RadDir 84*
WTVO-TV - Rockford, IL - *BrCabYB 84; DirUSTelSta 83; TelAl 83, 84; Tel&CabFB 84S; TV&RadDir 84*
WTVP-TV - Peoria, IL - *BrCabYB 84; Tel&CabFB 84S; TV&RadDir 84*
WTVQ-TV - Lexington, KY - *BrCabYB 84; DirUSTelSta 83; TelAl 83, 84; Tel&CabFB 84S; TV&RadDir 84*
WTVR - Richmond, VA - *BrCabYB 84; NatRadPubDir Summer 83, Spring 84; TV&RadDir 84*
WTVR-FM - Richmond, VA - *BrCabYB 84; TV&RadDir 84*
WTVR-TV - Richmond, VA - *BrCabYB 84; DirUSTelSta 83; LitMarPl 83, 84; TelAl 83, 84; Tel&CabFB 84S; TV&RadDir 84*
WTVS-TV - Detroit, MI - *BrCabYB 84; LitMarPl 83, 84; Tel&CabFB 84S; TV&RadDir 84*
WTVT-TV - Tampa, FL - *BrCabYB 84; DirUSTelSta 83; LitMarPl 83, 84; TelAl 83, 84; Tel&CabFB 84S; TV&RadDir 84*
WTVU-TV - New Haven, CT - *BrCabYB 84; Tel&CabFB 84S*
WTVW-TV - Evansville, IN - *BrCabYB 84; DirUSTelSta 83; TelAl 83, 84; Tel&CabFB 84S; TV&RadDir 84*
WTVX-TV - Ft. Pierce, FL - *BrCabYB 84; TelAl 83, 84; Tel&CabFB 84S; TV&RadDir 84*
WTVX-TV - West Palm Beach, FL - *DirUSTelSta 83*
WTVY-FM - Dothan, AL - *BrCabYB 84; TV&RadDir 84*
WTVY-TV - Dothan, AL - *BrCabYB 84; DirUSTelSta 83; TelAl 83, 84; Tel&CabFB 84S; TV&RadDir 84*
WTVZ-TV - Norfolk, VA - *BrCabYB 84; DirUSTelSta 83; TelAl 83, 84; Tel&CabFB 84S; TV&RadDir 84*
WTWA - Thomson, GA - *BrCabYB 84; TV&RadDir 84*
WTWB - Auburndale, FL - *BrCabYB 84; TV&RadDir 84*
WTWC - Tallahassee, FL - *BrCabYB 84; Tel&CabFB 84S*
WTWE-FM - Manning, SC - *BrCabYB 84; TV&RadDir 84*
WTWG - Birmingham, AL - *BrCabYB 84*
WTWN - Grand Rapids, MI - *BrCabYB 84; NatRadPubDir Summer 83, Spring 84; TV&RadDir 84*
WTWO-TV - Terre Haute, IN - *BrCabYB 84; DirUSTelSta 83; TelAl 83, 84; Tel&CabFB 84S; TV&RadDir 84*
WTWR-FM - Detroit, MI - *BrCabYB 84; NatRadPubDir Summer 83*
WTWR-FM - Monroe, MI - *NatRadPubDir Summer 83, Spring 84; TV&RadDir 84*
WTWV - Tupelo, MS - *Tel&CabFB 84S*
WTWX-FM - Guntersville, AL - *BrCabYB 84; TV&RadDir 84*
WTWZ - Clinton, MS - *BrCabYB 84*
WTXI-FM - Ripley, MS - *BrCabYB 84; TV&RadDir 84*
WTXI-TV - Pittsburgh, PA - *LitMarPl 84*
WTXN - Lafayette, AL - *BrCabYB 84; TV&RadDir 84*
WTXR-FM - Chillicothe, IL - *BrCabYB 84; TV&RadDir 84*
WTXX-TV - Waterbury, CT - *BrCabYB 84; DirUSTelSta 83; TelAl 84; Tel&CabFB 84S; TV&RadDir 84*
WTXY - Whiteville, NC - *BrCabYB 84; TV&RadDir 84*
WTYC - Rock Hill, SC - *BrCabYB 84; NatRadPubDir Summer 83; TV&RadDir 84*
WTYD-FM - New London, CT - *BrCabYB 84; NatRadPubDir Summer 83, Spring 84; TV&RadDir 84*
WTYJ - Fauette, MS - *BrCabYB 84*
WTYL - Tylertown, MS - *BrCabYB 84; TV&RadDir 84*
WTYL-FM - Tylertown, MS - *BrCabYB 84; TV&RadDir 84*
WTYM - Tampa, FL - *BrCabYB 84; TV&RadDir 84*
WTYN - Tryon, NC - *BrCabYB 84; TV&RadDir 84*
WTYO - Hammonton, NJ - *BrCabYB 84; TV&RadDir 84*
WTYS - Marianna, FL - *BrCabYB 84; TV&RadDir 84*
WTYX-FM - Jackson, MS - *BrCabYB 84; NatRadPubDir Summer 83, Spring 84; TV&RadDir 84*
WTZE - Tazewell, VA - *BrCabYB 84; TV&RadDir 84*
WTZE-FM - Tazewell, VA - *BrCabYB 84; TV&RadDir 84*
WTZX - Sparta, TN - *BrCabYB 84*
Wu, T. H. - Worthington, OH - *BoPubDir 4, 5*
WUAA - Jackson, TN - *BrCabYB 84; Tel&CabFB 84S*
WUAB-TV - Cleveland, OH - *DirUSTelSta 83; TV&RadDir 84*
WUAB-TV - Lorain, OH - *BrCabYB 84; TelAl 83, 84; Tel&CabFB 84S*
WUAG-FM - Greensboro, NC - *BrCabYB 84; NatRadPubDir Summer 83, Spring 84; TV&RadDir 84*
WUAL-FM - Stewart, AL - *TV&RadDir 84*
WUAL-FM - Tuscaloosa, AL - *BrCabYB 84; NatRadPubDir Summer 83, Spring 84*
WUAT - Pikeville, TN - *BrCabYB 84; TV&RadDir 84*
WUBE-FM - Cincinnati, OH - *BrCabYB 84; NatRadPubDir Summer 83, Spring 84; TV&RadDir 84*
WUCF-FM - Orlando, FL - *BrCabYB 84*
WUCF-FM - Fulton, MS - *TV&RadDir 84*
WUCM-TV - Bay City, MI - *Tel&CabFB 84S; TV&RadDir 84*
WUCM-TV - University Center, MI - *BrCabYB 84*
WUCO - Marysville, OH - *BrCabYB 84*
WUCR - Sparta, TN - *TV&RadDir 84*
WUDZ - Sweet Briar, VA - *BrCabYB 84*
WUEC-FM - Eau Claire, WI - *BrCabYB 84; NatRadPubDir Summer 83, Spring 84; TV&RadDir 84*
WUEV-FM - Evansville, IN - *BrCabYB 84; NatRadPubDir Summer 83, Spring 84; TV&RadDir 84*
WUEZ - Salem, VA - *BrCabYB 84; TV&RadDir 84*
WUFE - Baxley, GA - *BrCabYB 84; TV&RadDir 84*
WUFF - Eastman, GA - *BrCabYB 84; TV&RadDir 84*
WUFF-FM - Eastman, GA - *BrCabYB 84; TV&RadDir 84*
WUFK-FM - Ft. Kent, ME - *BrCabYB 84*
WUFK-FM - Orono, ME - *TV&RadDir 84*
WUFM-FM - Lebanon, PA - *BrCabYB 84; TV&RadDir 84*
WUFN-FM - Albion, MI - *BrCabYB 84; TV&RadDir 84*
WUFO - Amherst, NY - *BrCabYB 84*
WUFO - Buffalo, NY - *NatRadPubDir Summer 83, Spring 84; TV&RadDir 84*
WUFT-FM - Gainesville, FL - *BrCabYB 84*
WUFT-TV - Gainesville, FL - *BrCabYB 84; Tel&CabFB 84S; TV&RadDir 84*
WUGN-FM - Midland, MI - *BrCabYB 84; TV&RadDir 84*
WUGO-FM - Grayson, KY - *BrCabYB 84; TV&RadDir 84*
WUHF-TV - Rochester, NY - *BrCabYB 84; DirUSTelSta 83; TelAl 83; Tel&CabFB 84S; TV&RadDir 84*
WUHN - Pittsfield, MA - *BrCabYB 84; TV&RadDir 84*
WUHQ-TV - Battle Creek, MI - *BrCabYB 84; LitMarPl 83, 84; TelAl 83, 84; Tel&CabFB 84S; TV&RadDir 84*

WUHQ-TV - Grand Rapids, MI - *DirUSTelSta 83*
WUHS-FM - Urbana, OH - *BrCabYB 84; NatRadPubDir Summer 83, Spring 84; TV&RadDir 84*
WUHX-TV - Norfolk, VA - *BrCabYB 84; Tel&CabFB 84S*
WUHY-FM - Easton, PA - *NatRadPubDir Summer 83, Spring 84 p.315*
WUHY-FM - Philadelphia, PA - *TV&RadDir 84*
WUIA-TV - San German, PR - *BrCabYB 84; Tel&CabFB 84S*
WUIC-FM - Chicago, IL - *NatRadPubDir Summer 83, Spring 84*
WUIV - Icard Township, NC - *BrCabYB 84*
WUJA - Caguas, PR - *BrCabYB 84; Tel&CabFB 84S*
WUJC - University Heights, OH - *BrCabYB 84; NatRadPubDir Summer 83, Spring 84*
WUJC-FM - Cleveland, OH - *TV&RadDir 84*
WUJC-FM - University Heights, OH - *NatRadPubDir Summer 83, Spring 84*
WULA - Eufaula, AL - *BrCabYB 84; TV&RadDir 84*
WULA-FM - Eufaula, AL - *TV&RadDir 84*
WULF - Alma, GA - *BrCabYB 84; TV&RadDir 84*
WULT-TV - New Orleans, LA - *BrCabYB 84; Tel&CabFB 84S*
WUMB - Boston, MA - *BrCabYB 84*
WUME-FM - Paoli, IN - *BrCabYB 84; TV&RadDir 84*
WUMF-FM - Farmington, ME - *BrCabYB 84; NatRadPubDir Summer 83, Spring 84; TV&RadDir 84*
WUMP-FM - Ironwood, MI - *TV&RadDir 84*
WUNA - Aguadilla, PR - *BrCabYB 84*
WUNC-FM - Chapel Hill, NC - *BrCabYB 84; NatRadPubDir Summer 83, Spring 84; TV&RadDir 84*
WUNC-TV - Chapel Hill, NC - *BrCabYB 84; Tel&CabFB 84S; TV&RadDir 84*
WUND-TV - Chapel Hill, NC - *TV&RadDir 84*
WUND-TV - Columbia, NC - *BrCabYB 84; Tel&CabFB 84S*
Wunderman, Ricotta & Kline [Subs. of Young & Rubicam] - New York, NY - *AdAge 3-28-84; BrCabYB 84; DirMarMP 83; HBIndAd&MS 82-83; LitMarPl 83, 84; StaDirAdAg 2-84*
WUNE-TV - Chapel Hill, NC - *TV&RadDir 84*
WUNE-TV - Linville, NC - *BrCabYB 84; Tel&CabFB 84S*
WUNF-FM - Asheville, NC - *BrCabYB 84; NatRadPubDir Summer 83, Spring 84; TV&RadDir 84*
WUNF-TV - Asheville, NC - *BrCabYB 84; Tel&CabFB 84S*
WUNF-TV - Chapel Hill, NC - *TV&RadDir 84*
WUNG-TV - Chapel Hill, NC - *TV&RadDir 84*
WUNG-TV - Concord, NC - *BrCabYB 84; Tel&CabFB 84S*
WUNH-FM - Durham, NH - *BrCabYB 84; NatRadPubDir Summer 83, Spring 84; TV&RadDir 84*
WUNI - Mobile, AL - *BrCabYB 84; NatRadPubDir Summer 83, Spring 84; TV&RadDir 84*
WUNJ-TV - Chapel Hill, NC - *TV&RadDir 84*
WUNJ-TV - Wilmington, NC - *BrCabYB 84; Tel&CabFB 84S*
WUNK-TV - Greenville, NC - *BrCabYB 84; Tel&CabFB 84S*
WUNL-TV - Winston-Salem, NC - *BrCabYB 84; Tel&CabFB 84S*
WUNM-TV - Jacksonville, NC - *Tel&CabFB 84S*
WUNN - Mason, MI - *BrCabYB 84; TV&RadDir 84*
WUNO - San Juan, PR - *BrCabYB 84*
WUNR - Boston, MA - *TV&RadDir 84*
WUNR - Brookline, MA - *BrCabYB 84*
WUOA-FM - Tuscaloosa, AL - *BrCabYB 84; NatRadPubDir Summer 83, Spring 84; TV&RadDir 84*
WUOG-FM - Athens, GA - *BrCabYB 84; NatRadPubDir Summer 83, Spring 84; TV&RadDir 84*
WUOL-FM - Louisville, KY - *BrCabYB 84; NatRadPubDir Summer 83, Spring 84*
WUOM-FM - Ann Arbor, MI - *BrCabYB 84; NatRadPubDir Summer 83, Spring 84; TV&RadDir 84*
WUOT-FM - Knoxville, TN - *BrCabYB 84; NatRadPubDir Summer 83, Spring 84; TV&RadDir 84*
WUPE-FM - Pittsfield, MA - *BrCabYB 84; TV&RadDir 84*
WUPI-FM - Presque Isle, ME - *BrCabYB 84; NatRadPubDir Summer 83, Spring 84; TV&RadDir 84*
WUPM - Ironwood, MI - *BrCabYB 84*
WUPR - Utuado, PR - *BrCabYB 84*
WURD-FM - Georgetown, OH - *BrCabYB 84; TV&RadDir 84*
Wurf, Barbara - Los Angeles, CA - *FBInfSer 80*
Wurf/Indexpert Services, Barbara - Los Angeles, CA - *LitMarPl 83, 84*
Wurst Inc., Henry - North Kansas City, MO - *LitMarPl 83, 84; MagIndMarPl 82-83*
Wurtele Film Productions - Orlando, FL - *Tel&CabFB 84C*
WUSB-FM - Stony Brook, NY - *BrCabYB 84; NatRadPubDir Summer 83, Spring 84*
WUSB-FM - Wantagh, NY - *TV&RadDir 84*
WUSC-FM - Columbia, SC - *BrCabYB 84; NatRadPubDir Summer 83, Spring 84; TV&RadDir 84*
WUSF-FM - Tampa, FL - *BrCabYB 84; NatRadPubDir Summer 83, Spring 84; TV&RadDir 84*
WUSF-TV - Tampa, FL - *BrCabYB 84; Tel&CabFB 84S; TV&RadDir 84*
WUSI-TV - Olney, IL - *BrCabYB 84; Tel&CabFB 84S; TV&RadDir 84*
WUSL-FM - Philadelphia, PA - *BrCabYB 84; LitMarPl 84; NatRadPubDir Summer 83, Spring 84; TV&RadDir 84*
WUSM-FM - North Dartmouth, MA - *BrCabYB 84; NatRadPubDir Summer 83, Spring 84; TV&RadDir 84*
WUSN-FM - Chicago, IL - *BrCabYB 84; NatRadPubDir Summer 83, Spring 84; TV&RadDir 84*
WUSO-FM - Springfield, OH - *BrCabYB 84; NatRadPubDir Summer 83, Spring 84; TV&RadDir 84*
WUSQ-FM - Winchester, VA - *BrCabYB 84; TV&RadDir 84*
WUSS - Atlantic City, NJ - *BrCabYB 84; NatRadPubDir Summer 83, Spring 84; TV&RadDir 84*
WUST - Washington, DC - *BrCabYB 84; NatRadPubDir Summer 83, Spring 84; TV&RadDir 84*
WUSV - Schenectady, NY - *BrCabYB 84; Tel&CabFB 84S*
WUSY - Cleveland, TN - *BrCabYB 84*
WUTA-FM - Farmville, VA - *BrCabYB 84; TV&RadDir 84*
WUTC - Chattanooga, TN - *BrCabYB 84*
WUTK-FM - Knoxville, TN - *BrCabYB 84; TV&RadDir 84*
WUTM-FM - Martin, TN - *BrCabYB 84; NatRadPubDir Summer 83, Spring 84; TV&RadDir 84*
WUTQ - Utica, NY - *BrCabYB 84; NatRadPubDir Summer 83, Spring 84; TV&RadDir 84*
WUTR-FM - Roanoke, VA - *NatRadPubDir Summer 83, Spring 84*
WUTR-TV - Utica, NY - *BrCabYB 84; DirUSTelSta 83; TelAl 83, 84; Tel&CabFB 84S; TV&RadDir 84*
WUTS-FM - Sewanee, TN - *BrCabYB 84; NatRadPubDir Summer 83, Spring 84; TV&RadDir 84*
WUTV-TV - Buffalo, NY - *BrCabYB 84; DirUSTelSta 83; TelAl 83, 84; Tel&CabFB 84S*
WUTV-TV - Grand Island, NY - *TV&RadDir 84*
WUTZ-FM - Summertown, TN - *BrCabYB 84; TV&RadDir 84*
WUUN - Marquette, MI - *BrCabYB 84*
WUUU - Rome, NY - *BrCabYB 84*
WUVA-FM - Charlottesville, VA - *BrCabYB 84; NatRadPubDir Summer 83, Spring 84; TV&RadDir 84*
WUVT - Blacksburg, VA - *BrCabYB 84; TV&RadDir 84*
WUVT-FM - Blacksburg, VA - *NatRadPubDir Summer 83, Spring 84; TV&RadDir 84*
WUWF - Pensacola, FL - *BrCabYB 84*
WUWM-FM - Milwaukee, WI - *BrCabYB 84; NatRadPubDir Spring 84; TV&RadDir 84*
WUWU-FM - Newfield, NY - *TV&RadDir 84*
WUWU-FM - Wethersfield, NY - *BrCabYB 84*
WVAB - Norfolk, VA - *NatRadPubDir Summer 83 p.255, Spring 84 p.257*
WVAB - Virginia Beach, VA - *BrCabYB 84; TV&RadDir 84*
WVAC-FM - Adrian, MI - *BrCabYB 84; NatRadPubDir Summer 83, Spring 84; TV&RadDir 84*
WVAF-FM - Charleston, WV - *BrCabYB 84; NatRadPubDir Summer 83, Spring 84; TV&RadDir 84*
WVAH-TV - Charleston, WV - *BrCabYB 84; DirUSTelSta 83; TelAl 84; Tel&CabFB 84S*
WVAI - Winchester, VA - *BrCabYB 84; TV&RadDir 84*
WVAL - Sauk Rapids, MN - *BrCabYB 84*
WVAM - Altoona, PA - *BrCabYB 84; NatRadPubDir Summer 83, Spring 84; TV&RadDir 84*
WVAN-TV - Pembroke, GA - *TV&RadDir 84*
WVAN-TV - Savannah, GA - *BrCabYB 84; Tel&CabFB 84S*
WVAP - Langley, SC - *TV&RadDir 84*
WVAQ-FM - Morgantown, WV - *BrCabYB 84; NatRadPubDir Summer 83, Spring 84; TV&RadDir 84*
WVAR - Richwood, WV - *BrCabYB 84; TV&RadDir 84*

WVBC-FM - Bethany, WV - *BrCabYB 84; NatRadPubDir Summer 83, Spring 84; TV&RadDir 84*
WVBF-FM - Boston, MA - *NatRadPubDir Spring 84 p.121*
WVBF-FM - Framingham, MA - *BrCabYB 84; TV&RadDir 84*
WVBG - Beaufort, SC - *BrCabYB 84*
WVBK - Herndon, VA - *BrCabYB 84; TV&RadDir 84*
WVBR-FM - Ithaca, NY - *BrCabYB 84; TV&RadDir 84*
WVBS - Burgaw, NC - *BrCabYB 84; TV&RadDir 84*
WVBS-FM - Burgaw, NC - *BrCabYB 84; TV&RadDir 84*
WVBU - Lewisburg, PA - *NatRadPubDir Summer 83, Spring 84; TV&RadDir 84*
WVBU-FM - Lewisburg, PA - *BrCabYB 84; NatRadPubDir Summer 83, Spring 84; TV&RadDir 84*
WVCA-FM - Gloucester, MA - *BrCabYB 84; TV&RadDir 84*
WVCB - Shallotte, NC - *BrCabYB 84; TV&RadDir 84*
WVCC-FM - Linesville, PA - *BrCabYB 84; TV&RadDir 84*
WVCD-FM - Hazleton, PA - *BrCabYB 84*
WVCD-FM - Scranton, PA - *NatRadPubDir Summer 83, Spring 84 p.217*
WVCF - Ocoee, FL - *BrCabYB 84; TV&RadDir 84*
WVCF-FM - Orlando, FL - *TV&RadDir 84*
WVCG - Coral Gables, FL - *BrCabYB 84*
WVCG - Miami, FL - *NatRadPubDir Summer 83 p.62, Spring 84 p.62; TV&RadDir 84*
WVCH - Chester, PA - *BrCabYB 84; TV&RadDir 84*
WVCI - Bay City, MI - *BrCabYB 84; Tel&CabFB 84S*
WVCP-FM - Gallatin, TN - *BrCabYB 84; TV&RadDir 84*
WVCR-FM - Albany, NY - *TV&RadDir 84*
WVCR-FM - Loudonville, NY - *BrCabYB 84; NatRadPubDir Summer 83, Spring 84*
WVCS-FM - California, PA - *BrCabYB 84; NatRadPubDir Summer 83, Spring 84; TV&RadDir 84*
WVCY-FM - Milwaukee, WI - *BrCabYB 84; NatRadPubDir Spring 84*
WVCY-TV - Milwaukee, WI - *BrCabYB 84; Tel&CabFB 84S*
WVEC-TV - Hampton, VA - *BrCabYB 84; LitMarPl 83, 84; TelAl 83, 84; Tel&CabFB 84S; TV&RadDir 84*
WVEC-TV - Norfolk, VA - *DirUSTelSta 83*
WVEE-FM - Atlanta, GA - *BrCabYB 84; NatRadPubDir Summer 83, Spring 84; TV&RadDir 84*
WVEL - Pekin, IL - *BrCabYB 84; TV&RadDir 84*
WVEM-FM - Springfield, IL - *BrCabYB 84; NatRadPubDir Summer 83, Spring 84; TV&RadDir 84*
WVEN-FM - Franklin, PA - *BrCabYB 84; TV&RadDir 84*
WVEO - Aguadilla, PR - *BrCabYB 84; Tel&CabFB 84S*
WVEP-FM - Montpelier, VT - *BrCabYB 84; NatRadPubDir Summer 83, Spring 84*
WVER - Rutland, VT - *BrCabYB 84; Tel&CabFB 84S*
WVEU - Atlanta, GA - *BrCabYB 84; DirUSTelSta 83; TelAl 84; Tel&CabFB 84S*
WVEZ-FM - Louisville, KY - *BrCabYB 84; NatRadPubDir Summer 83, Spring 84; TV&RadDir 84*
WVFC - McConnellsburg, PA - *BrCabYB 84; TV&RadDir 84*
WVFJ-FM - Manchester, GA - *BrCabYB 84*
WVFK-FM - Key West, FL - *BrCabYB 84; TV&RadDir 84*
WVFM-FM - Lakeland, FL - *BrCabYB 84; NatRadPubDir Summer 83, Spring 84; TV&RadDir 84*
WVFR - Ridgefield, CT - *BrCabYB 84; TV&RadDir 84*
WVGA-TV - Tallahassee, FL - *DirUSTelSta 83*
WVGA-TV - Valdosta, GA - *BrCabYB 84; DirUSTelSta 83; TelAl 83, 84; Tel&CabFB 84S; TV&RadDir 84*
WVGB - Beaufort, SC - *TV&RadDir 84*
WVGO - Lansing, MI - *NatRadPubDir Summer 83, Spring 84; TV&RadDir 84*
WVGR-FM - Ann Arbor, MI - *NatRadPubDir Summer 83, Spring 84; TV&RadDir 84*
WVGR-FM - Grand Rapids, MI - *BrCabYB 84*
WVGS-FM - Statesboro, GA - *BrCabYB 84; TV&RadDir 84*
WVHC-FM - Hempstead, NY - *NatRadPubDir Summer 83, Spring 84; TV&RadDir 84*
WVHF-FM - Clarksburg, WV - *BrCabYB 84; TV&RadDir 84*
WVHG - La Belle, FL - *BrCabYB 84*
WVHI - Evansville, IN - *BrCabYB 84; NatRadPubDir Spring 84; TV&RadDir 84*
WVHI-FM - Evansville, IN - *NatRadPubDir Summer 83*
WVHP-FM - Highland Park, NJ - *BrCabYB 84; NatRadPubDir Summer 83, Spring 84*
WVHP-FM - Williamstown, NJ - *TV&RadDir 84*
WVIA-FM - Pittston, PA - *TV&RadDir 84*
WVIA-FM - Scranton, PA - *BrCabYB 84; NatRadPubDir Summer 83 p.314, Spring 84 p.316*
WVIA-TV - Pittston, PA - *TV&RadDir 84*
WVIA-TV - Scranton, PA - *BrCabYB 84; Tel&CabFB 84S*
WVIC-FM - East Lansing, MI - *BrCabYB 84*
WVIC-FM - Lansing, MI - *NatRadPubDir Summer 83, Spring 84; TV&RadDir 84*
WVID - Anasco, PR - *BrCabYB 84*
WVII-TV - Bangor, ME - *BrCabYB 84; DirUSTelSta 83; TelAl 83, 84; Tel&CabFB 84S; TV&RadDir 84*
WVIK-FM - Rock Island, IL - *BrCabYB 84; NatRadPubDir Summer 83, Spring 84; TV&RadDir 84*
WVIM-FM - Coldwater, MS - *BrCabYB 84; TV&RadDir 84*
WVIN - Bath, NY - *BrCabYB 84; TV&RadDir 84*
WVIN-FM - Bath, NY - *BrCabYB 84; TV&RadDir 84*
WVIN-FM - Hammondsport, NY - *BrCabYB 84*
WVIP - Mt. Kisco, NY - *BrCabYB 84; LitMarPl 83, 84; TV&RadDir 84*
WVIP - Westchester County, NY - *NatRadPubDir Summer 83 p.180, Spring 84 p.178*
WVIP-FM - Mt. Kisco, NY - *BrCabYB 84; LitMarPl 83; TV&RadDir 84*
WVIP-FM - Westchester County, NY - *NatRadPubDir Spring 84 p.178*
WVIR-TV - Charlottesville, VA - *BrCabYB 84; DirUSTelSta 83; TelAl 83, 84; Tel&CabFB 84S; TV&RadDir 84*
WVIS - Frederiksted, VI - *BrCabYB 84*
WVIT-TV - Elmwood, CT - *TV&RadDir 84*
WVIT-TV - Hartford, CT - *DirUSTelSta 83*
WVIT-TV - New Britain, CT - *BrCabYB 84; TelAl 83, 84; Tel&CabFB 84S*
WVIT-TV - West Hartford, CT - *LitMarPl 83, 84*
WVIZ-TV - Cleveland, OH - *BrCabYB 84; Tel&CabFB 84S; TV&RadDir 84*
WVJC-FM - Mt. Carmel, IL - *BrCabYB 84; TV&RadDir 84*
WVJP-FM - Caguas, PR - *BrCabYB 84*
WVJS - Owensboro, KY - *BrCabYB 84; TV&RadDir 84*
WVKC-FM - Galesburg, IL - *BrCabYB 84; NatRadPubDir Summer 83, Spring 84; TV&RadDir 84*
WVKO - Columbus, OH - *BrCabYB 84; NatRadPubDir Summer 83, Spring 84; TV&RadDir 84*
WVKR-FM - Poughkeepsie, NY - *BrCabYB 84; NatRadPubDir Summer 83, Spring 84; TV&RadDir 84*
WVKY - Louisa, KY - *BrCabYB 84; TV&RadDir 84*
WVLC - Orelans, MA - *BrCabYB 84*
WVLD - Valdosta, GA - *BrCabYB 84; TV&RadDir 84*
WVLE - Stillwater, MN - *BrCabYB 84*
WVLJ-FM - Monticello, IL - *BrCabYB 84; TV&RadDir 84*
WVLK - Lexington, KY - *BrCabYB 84; NatRadPubDir Summer 83, Spring 84; TV&RadDir 84*
WVLK-FM - Lexington, KY - *BrCabYB 84; NatRadPubDir Summer 83, Spring 84; TV&RadDir 84*
WVLN - Olney, IL - *BrCabYB 84; TV&RadDir 84*
WVLR-FM - Sauk City, WI - *TV&RadDir 84*
WVLS - Jackson, MS - *BrCabYB 84*
WVLV - Lebanon, PA - *BrCabYB 84; TV&RadDir 84*
WVLY - Water Valley, MS - *BrCabYB 84; TV&RadDir 84*
WVMC-FM - Mansfield, OH - *BrCabYB 84; TV&RadDir 84*
WVMG - Cochran, GA - *BrCabYB 84; TV&RadDir 84*
WVMG-FM - Cochran, GA - *BrCabYB 84; TV&RadDir 84*
WVMH-FM - Mars Hill, NC - *BrCabYB 84; NatRadPubDir Summer 83, Spring 84; TV&RadDir 84*
WVMI - Biloxi, MS - *BrCabYB 84; NatRadPubDir Summer 83, Spring 84; TV&RadDir 84*
WVMR - Frost, WV - *BrCabYB 84*
WVMS - Appleton, WI - *BrCabYB 84*
WVMS - Neenah, WI - *NatRadPubDir Summer 83, Spring 84; TV&RadDir 84*
WVMT - Burlington, VT - *BrCabYB 84; NatRadPubDir Summer 83*
WVMT - Colchester, VT - *NatRadPubDir Spring 84; TV&RadDir 84*
WVMW-FM - Pittston, PA - *TV&RadDir 84*
WVMW-FM - Scranton, PA - *BrCabYB 84*
WVNA - Tuscumbia, AL - *BrCabYB 84; TV&RadDir 84*

WVNA-FM - Tuscumbia, AL - *BrCabYB 84; TV&RadDir 84*
WVNH - Salem, NH - *BrCabYB 84; TV&RadDir 84*
WVNJ - Livingston, NJ - *TV&RadDir 84*
WVNJ - Newark/Jersey City, NJ - *NatRadPubDir Summer 83 p.159*
WVNJ-FM - Livingston, NJ - *TV&RadDir 84*
WVNJ-FM - Newark/Jersey City, NJ - *NatRadPubDir Summer 83 p.159*
WVNO-FM - Mansfield, OH - *BrCabYB 84; NatRadPubDir Summer 83, Spring 84; TV&RadDir 84*
WVNP - Wheeling, WV - *BrCabYB 84*
WVNR - Poultney, VT - *BrCabYB 84*
WVNY-TV - Burlington, VT - *BrCabYB 84; DirUSTelSta 83; TelAl 84; Tel&CabFB 84S*
WVOC - Columbus, GA - *NatRadPubDir Summer 83*
WVOC-FM - Columbus, GA - *BrCabYB 84; NatRadPubDir Spring 84; TV&RadDir 84*
WVOE - Chadbourn, NC - *BrCabYB 84*
WVOF - Fairfield, CT - *BrCabYB 84*
WVOG - New Orleans, LA - *BrCabYB 84; NatRadPubDir Summer 83, Spring 84; TV&RadDir 84*
WVOH - Hazlehurst, GA - *BrCabYB 84; TV&RadDir 84*
WVOH-FM - Hazlehurst, GA - *BrCabYB 84; TV&RadDir 84*
WVOI - Toledo, OH - *BrCabYB 84; NatRadPubDir Summer 83 p.199, Spring 84 p.197; TV&RadDir 84*
WVOJ - Jacksonville, FL - *NatRadPubDir Summer 83; TV&RadDir 84*
WVOK - Birmingham, AL - *BrCabYB 84; NatRadPubDir Summer 83, Spring 84; TV&RadDir 84*
WVOL - Berry Hill, TN - *BrCabYB 84*
WVOL - Nashville, TN - *TV&RadDir 84*
WVOL-FM - Columbus, GA - *NatRadPubDir Summer 83*
WVOM - Iuka, MS - *BrCabYB 84; TV&RadDir 84*
WVON - Chicago, IL - *NatRadPubDir Summer 83, Spring 84; TV&RadDir 84*
WVOP - Vidalia, GA - *BrCabYB 84; TV&RadDir 84*
WVOR-FM - Rochester, NY - *BrCabYB 84; NatRadPubDir Summer 83, Spring 84; TV&RadDir 84*
WVOS - Liberty, NY - *BrCabYB 84*
WVOS - Monticello, NY - *TV&RadDir 84*
WVOS-FM - Liberty, NY - *BrCabYB 84*
WVOS-FM - Monticello, NY - *TV&RadDir 84*
WVOT - Wilson, NC - *BrCabYB 84; TV&RadDir 84*
WVOV - Danville, VA - *BrCabYB 84; TV&RadDir 84*
WVOW - Logan, WV - *BrCabYB 84; TV&RadDir 84*
WVOW-FM - Logan, WV - *BrCabYB 84; TV&RadDir 84*
WVOX - New Rochelle, NY - *BrCabYB 84; LitMarPl 83, 84; TV&RadDir 84*
WVOX - Westchester County, NY - *NatRadPubDir Summer 83 p.180, Spring 84 p.178*
WVOX-FM - New Rochelle, NY - *BrCabYB 84*
WVOY - Charlevoix, MI - *BrCabYB 84; TV&RadDir 84*
WVOZ-FM - Carolina, PR - *BrCabYB 84*
WVOZ-FM - San Juan, PR - *BrCabYB 84*
WVPB-FM - Beckley, WV - *BrCabYB 84*
WVPB-FM - Charleston, WV - *NatRadPubDir Summer 83, Spring 84*
WVPE-FM - Elkhart, IN - *BrCabYB 84; TV&RadDir 84*
WVPH-FM - Piscataway, NJ - *BrCabYB 84; TV&RadDir 84*
WVPM-FM - Charleston, WV - *NatRadPubDir Summer 83, Spring 84*
WVPM-FM - Morgantown, WV - *BrCabYB 84*
WVPN-FM - Charleston, WV - *BrCabYB 84; NatRadPubDir Summer 83, Spring 84; TV&RadDir 84*
WVPO - Stroudsburg, PA - *BrCabYB 84; TV&RadDir 84*
WVPO-FM - Stroudsburg, PA - *BrCabYB 84; TV&RadDir 84*
WVPR-FM - Windsor, VT - *BrCabYB 84; TV&RadDir 84*
WVPS-FM - Burlington, VT - *BrCabYB 84*
WVPS-FM - Winooski, VT - *TV&RadDir 84*
WVPT-TV - Harrisonburg, VA - *TV&RadDir 84*
WVPT-TV - Staunton, VA - *BrCabYB 84; Tel&CabFB 84S*
WVPW-FM - Buckhannon, WV - *BrCabYB 84; TV&RadDir 84*
WVPW-FM - Charleston, WV - *NatRadPubDir Summer 83, Spring 84*
WVRC - Spencer, WV - *BrCabYB 84; TV&RadDir 84*
WVRM - Hazlet, NJ - *BrCabYB 84*
WVRT - Reform, AL - *BrCabYB 84*
WVRU - Radford, VA - *BrCabYB 84*
WVRY-FM - Waverly, TN - *BrCabYB 84; TV&RadDir 84*
WVSA - Vernon, AL - *BrCabYB 84; TV&RadDir 84*
WVSB-TV - West Point, MS - *BrCabYB 84; Tel&CabFB 84S*
WVSC - Somerset, PA - *BrCabYB 84; TV&RadDir 84*
WVSC-FM - Somerset, PA - *BrCabYB 84; TV&RadDir 84*
WVSH-FM - Huntington, IN - *BrCabYB 84; TV&RadDir 84*
WVSI - Jupiter, FL - *BrCabYB 84; TV&RadDir 84*
WVSI - West Palm Beach, FL - *NatRadPubDir Summer 83 p.66, Spring 84 p.67*
WVSI-FM - Jupiter, FL - *BrCabYB 84*
WVSI-FM - West Palm Beach, FL - *NatRadPubDir Summer 83 p.66, Spring 84 p.67*
WVSM - Rainsville, AL - *BrCabYB 84; TV&RadDir 84*
WVSP-FM - Warrenton, NC - *BrCabYB 84; TV&RadDir 84*
WVSR-FM - Charleston, WV - *BrCabYB 84; NatRadPubDir Summer 83, Spring 84; TV&RadDir 84*
WVSS-FM - Menomonie, WI - *BrCabYB 84; NatRadPubDir Spring 84; TV&RadDir 84*
WVST-FM - Bolivar, TN - *BrCabYB 84; TV&RadDir 84*
WVSU-FM - Birmingham, AL - *BrCabYB 84; NatRadPubDir Summer 83, Spring 84; TV&RadDir 84*
WVSV - Stevenson, AL - *BrCabYB 84*
WVTA - Windsor, VT - *BrCabYB 84; Tel&CabFB 84S*
WVTB - St. Johnsbury, VT - *BrCabYB 84; Tel&CabFB 84S*
WVTC-FM - Randolph Center, VT - *BrCabYB 84; NatRadPubDir Summer 83, Spring 84; TV&RadDir 84*
WVTF-FM - Roanoke, VA - *BrCabYB 84; TV&RadDir 84*
WVTH - Goodman, MS - *BrCabYB 84*
WVTL-FM - Monticello, IN - *TV&RadDir 84*
WVTM-TV - Birmingham, AL - *BrCabYB 84; DirUSTelSta 83; LitMarPl 83, 84; TelAl 83, 84; Tel&CabFB 84S; TV&RadDir 84*
WVTN - Gatlinburg, TN - *BrCabYB 84*
WVTS-FM - Terre Haute, IN - *BrCabYB 84; NatRadPubDir Summer 83, Spring 84*
WVTS-FM - West Terre Haute, IN - *TV&RadDir 84*
WVTV-TV - Milwaukee, WI - *BrCabYB 84; DirUSTelSta 83; TelAl 83, 84; Tel&CabFB 84S; TV&RadDir 84*
WVTY - Holiday, FL - *BrCabYB 84*
WVUA-FM - Tuscaloosa, AL - *BrCabYB 84; NatRadPubDir Summer 83, Spring 84*
WVUB-FM - Vincennes, IN - *BrCabYB 84; TV&RadDir 84*
WVUD-FM - Dayton, OH - *NatRadPubDir Summer 83, Spring 84; TV&RadDir 84*
WVUD-FM - Kettering, OH - *BrCabYB 84*
WVUE-TV - New Orleans, LA - *BrCabYB 84; DirUSTelSta 83; LitMarPl 83, 84; TelAl 83, 84; Tel&CabFB 84S; TV&RadDir 84*
WVUM-FM - Coral Gables, FL - *BrCabYB 84; NatRadPubDir Summer 83, Spring 84*
WVUM-FM - Miami, FL - *TV&RadDir 84*
WVUR-FM - Valparaiso, IN - *BrCabYB 84; NatRadPubDir Summer 83, Spring 84; TV&RadDir 84*
WVUS - Putney, VT - *BrCabYB 84*
WVUT-TV - Vincennes, IN - *BrCabYB 84; Tel&CabFB 84S; TV&RadDir 84*
WVVA-TV - Bluefield, WV - *BrCabYB 84; DirUSTelSta 83; TelAl 83, 84; Tel&CabFB 84S; TV&RadDir 84*
WVVS-FM - Valdosta, GA - *BrCabYB 84; NatRadPubDir Summer 83, Spring 84; TV&RadDir 84*
WVVV-FM - Blacksburg, VA - *BrCabYB 84; TV&RadDir 84*
WVVX - Highland Park, IL - *BrCabYB 84*
WVWC-FM - Buckhannon, WV - *BrCabYB 84; NatRadPubDir Summer 83, Spring 84; TV&RadDir 84*
WVWI - Charlotte Amalie, VI - *BrCabYB 84*
WVWV - Covington, IN - *BrCabYB 84*
WVXU-FM - Cincinnati, OH - *BrCabYB 84; NatRadPubDir Summer 83, Spring 84; TV&RadDir 84*
WVYC - York, PA - *BrCabYB 84*
W.W. Communications - Excelsior Springs, MO - *Tel&CabFB 84C p.1714*
WW Entertainment [Subs. of World Wide Holdings Corp.] - New York, NY - *AvMarPl 83*
WWAB - Lakeland, FL - *BrCabYB 84; NatRadPubDir Summer 83, Spring 84; TV&RadDir 84*

WWAC-TV - Atlantic City, NJ - *BrCabYB 84; TelAl 84; Tel&CabFB 84S*
WWAM - Macon, GA - *NatRadPubDir Summer 83 p.72*
WWAM - Milledgeville, GA - *TV&RadDir 84*
WWAS - Williamsport, PA - *BrCabYB 84*
WWAV-FM - Auburn, ME - *TV&RadDir 84*
WWAX - Mobile, AL - *BrCabYB 84; NatRadPubDir Summer 83, Spring 84; TV&RadDir 84*
WWAY-TV - Wilmington, NC - *BrCabYB 84; DirUSTelSta 83; TelAl 83, 84; Tel&CabFB 84S; TV&RadDir 84*
WWBA-FM - St. Petersburg, FL - *BrCabYB 84; TV&RadDir 84*
WWBA-FM - Tampa/St. Petersburg, FL - *NatRadPubDir Summer 83, Spring 84 p.66*
WWBB - Madison, WV - *BrCabYB 84; TV&RadDir 84*
WWBC - Cocoa, FL - *BrCabYB 84; TV&RadDir 84*
WWBD - Bamberg, SC - *BrCabYB 84; TV&RadDir 84*
WWBD-FM - Bamberg, SC - *BrCabYB 84; TV&RadDir 84*
WWBR - Johnstown, PA - *TV&RadDir 84*
WWBR - Winder, PA - *BrCabYB 84*
WWBT-TV - Richmond, VA - *BrCabYB 84; DirUSTelSta 83; LitMarPl 83, 84; TelAl 83, 84; Tel&CabFB 84S; TV&RadDir 84*
WWBZ - Vineland, NJ - *BrCabYB 84; TV&RadDir 84*
WWCA - Gary, IN - *BrCabYB 84; NatRadPubDir Summer 83, Spring 84; TV&RadDir 84*
WWCB - Corry, PA - *BrCabYB 84; TV&RadDir 84*
WWCG-FM - La Grange, GA - *TV&RadDir 84*
WWCH - Clarion, PA - *BrCabYB 84; TV&RadDir 84*
WWCJ - Jackson, MS - *BrCabYB 84*
WWCK-FM - Flint, MI - *BrCabYB 84; NatRadPubDir Summer 83, Spring 84; TV&RadDir 84*
WWCL-FM - Wesson, MS - *BrCabYB 84; NatRadPubDir Summer 83, Spring 84; TV&RadDir 84*
WWCM - Brazil, IN - *BrCabYB 84; TV&RadDir 84*
WWCN - Albany, NY - *BrCabYB 84; NatRadPubDir Spring 84 p.166*
WWCO - Waterbury, CT - *BrCabYB 84; NatRadPubDir Summer 83, Spring 84; TV&RadDir 84*
WWCS-FM - Hagerstown, MD - *NatRadPubDir Summer 83*
WWCT-FM - Peoria, IL - *BrCabYB 84; NatRadPubDir Summer 83, Spring 84; TV&RadDir 84*
WWCU-FM - Cullowhee, NC - *BrCabYB 84; NatRadPubDir Summer 83, Spring 84; TV&RadDir 84*
WWDB-FM - Philadelphia, PA - *BrCabYB 84; NatRadPubDir Summer 83, Spring 84; TV&RadDir 84*
WWDC - Washington, DC - *BrCabYB 84; NatRadPubDir Summer 83, Spring 84; TV&RadDir 84*
WWDC-FM - Washington, DC - *BrCabYB 84; NatRadPubDir Summer 83, Spring 84; TV&RadDir 84*
WWDE-FM - Hampton, VA - *BrCabYB 84; TV&RadDir 84*
WWDJ - Hackensack, NJ - *BrCabYB 84; NatRadPubDir Summer 83, Spring 84; TV&RadDir 84*
WWDL-FM - Scranton, PA - *BrCabYB 84; NatRadPubDir Summer 83, Spring 84; TV&RadDir 84*
WWDM-FM - Sumter, SC - *BrCabYB 84; TV&RadDir 84*
WWDR-FM - Murfreesboro, NC - *TV&RadDir 84*
WWDS-FM - Muncie, IN - *BrCabYB 84; TV&RadDir 84*
WWEB-FM - Wallingford, CT - *BrCabYB 84; TV&RadDir 84*
WWEE - Memphis, TN - *BrCabYB 84; NatRadPubDir Summer 83, Spring 84; TV&RadDir 84*
WWEL-FM - London, KY - *BrCabYB 84; TV&RadDir 84*
WWES - Hot Springs, VA - *BrCabYB 84*
WWET - Monticello, IN - *BrCabYB 84*
WWEV - Cumming, GA - *BrCabYB 84*
WWEZ-FM - Cincinnati, OH - *BrCabYB 84; TV&RadDir 84*
WWF Paper Corp. - Bala Cynwyd, PA - *LitMarPl 83, 84; MagIndMarPl 82-83*
WWFL - Clermont, FL - *BrCabYB 84; TV&RadDir 84*
WWFM - Trenton, NH - *BrCabYB 84*
WWGA-FM - Waynesboro, GA - *BrCabYB 84; TV&RadDir 84*
WWGC-FM - Carrollton, GA - *BrCabYB 84; TV&RadDir 84*
WWGM - Nashville, TN - *BrCabYB 84; NatRadPubDir Summer 83, Spring 84; TV&RadDir 84*
WWGP - Sanford, NC - *BrCabYB 84; TV&RadDir 84*
WWGR - Lafollette, TN - *BrCabYB 84*
WWGS - Tifton, GA - *BrCabYB 84; TV&RadDir 84*
WWH Press [Aff. of Women Working Home Inc.] - Scarsdale, NY - *BoPubDir 4, 5*
WWHB-FM - Hampton Bays, NY - *BrCabYB 84; TV&RadDir 84*
WWHC-FM - Hartford City, IN - *BrCabYB 84; TV&RadDir 84*
WWHI-FM - Muncie, IN - *BrCabYB 84; TV&RadDir 84*
WWHK - Mt. Clemens, MI - *BrCabYB 84; NatRadPubDir Summer 83, Spring 84*
WWHS-FM - Hampden Sydney, VA - *BrCabYB 84; NatRadPubDir Summer 83, Spring 84; TV&RadDir 84*
WWHT-TV - Newark, NJ - *BrCabYB 84; DirUSTelSta 83; TV&RadDir 84*
WWHT-TV - New York, NY - *DirUSTelSta 83; TelAl 83, 84; Tel&CabFB 84S*
WWHY - Huntington, WV - *BrCabYB 84; TV&RadDir 84*
WWIB-FM - Cornell, WI - *TV&RadDir 84*
WWIB-FM - Ladysmith, WI - *BrCabYB 84*
WWIC - Scottsboro, AL - *BrCabYB 84; TV&RadDir 84*
WWIC International Publishing Co. - Littleton, OH - *BoPubDir 4, 5*
WWID-FM - Gainesville, GA - *TV&RadDir 84*
WWIH-FM - High Point, NC - *BrCabYB 84; TV&RadDir 84*
WWIL - Wilmington, NC - *BrCabYB 84; TV&RadDir 84*
WWIN - Baltimore, MD - *BrCabYB 84; NatRadPubDir Summer 83, Spring 84; TV&RadDir 84*
WWIN-FM - Baltimore, MD - *NatRadPubDir Summer 83, Spring 84*
WWIN-FM - Glen Burnie, MD - *BrCabYB 84*
WWIS - Black River Falls, WI - *BrCabYB 84; TV&RadDir 84*
WWIT - Canton, NC - *BrCabYB 84; TV&RadDir 84*
WWIW - New Orleans, LA - *BrCabYB 84; NatRadPubDir Summer 83, Spring 84*
WWIZ-FM - Mercer, PA - *BrCabYB 84; TV&RadDir 84*
WWJ - Detroit, MI - *BrCabYB 84; NatRadPubDir Summer 83, Spring 84 p.127; TV&RadDir 84*
WWJB - Brooksville, FL - *BrCabYB 84; TV&RadDir 84*
WWJC - Duluth, MN - *BrCabYB 84; NatRadPubDir Summer 83, Spring 84; TV&RadDir 84*
WWJF-FM - Ft. Lauderdale, FL - *BrCabYB 84; NatRadPubDir Summer 83, Spring 84; TV&RadDir 84*
WWJL - Marion, KY - *TV&RadDir 84*
WWJM - New Lexington, OH - *BrCabYB 84*
WWJO-FM - St. Cloud, MN - *BrCabYB 84; NatRadPubDir Summer 83, Spring 84; TV&RadDir 84*
WWJQ - Holland, MI - *BrCabYB 84; TV&RadDir 84*
WWJR-FM - Sheboygan, WI - *BrCabYB 84; TV&RadDir 84*
WWJY-FM - Crown Point, IN - *BrCabYB 84; TV&RadDir 84*
WWJY-FM - South Bend, IN - *NatRadPubDir Summer 83*
WWJZ - Sanford, FL - *BrCabYB 84*
WWKA - Orlando, FL - *BrCabYB 84*
WWKC - Hazleton, PA - *TV&RadDir 84*
WWKE - Ocala, FL - *TV&RadDir 84*
WWKF-FM - Fulton, KY - *BrCabYB 84; TV&RadDir 84*
WWKI-FM - Kokomo, IN - *BrCabYB 84; TV&RadDir 84*
WWKK-FM - Ft. Knox, KY - *BrCabYB 84; TV&RadDir 84*
WWKO - Fair Bluff, NC - *BrCabYB 84; TV&RadDir 84*
WWKQ - Battle Creek, MI - *BrCabYB 84; NatRadPubDir Summer 83, Spring 84; TV&RadDir 84*
WWKS-FM - Beaver Falls, PA - *BrCabYB 84; TV&RadDir 84*
WWKT-FM - Kingstree, SC - *BrCabYB 84; TV&RadDir 84*
WWKX-FM - Gallatin, TN - *BrCabYB 84; TV&RadDir 84*
WWKY - Winchester, KY - *BrCabYB 84; TV&RadDir 84*
WWL - New Orleans, LA - *BrCabYB 84; NatRadPubDir Summer 83, Spring 84; TV&RadDir 84*
WWL-FM - New Orleans, LA - *NatRadPubDir Summer 83*
WWL-TV - New Orleans, LA - *BrCabYB 84; DirUSTelSta 83; LitMarPl 83, 84; TelAl 83, 84; Tel&CabFB 84S; TV&RadDir 84*
WWLF - St. Petersburg, FL - *NatRadPubDir Summer 83*
WWLH-FM - Pound, VA - *BrCabYB 84; TV&RadDir 84*
WWLP-TV - Springfield, MA - *BrCabYB 84; DirUSTelSta 83; TelAl 83, 84; Tel&CabFB 84S; TV&RadDir 84*
WWLR-FM - Lyndonville, VT - *BrCabYB 84; TV&RadDir 84*
WWLS - Norman, OK - *NatRadPubDir Summer 83, Spring 84; TV&RadDir 84*
WWLT - Gainesville, FL - *BrCabYB 84*
WWLV-FM - Daytona Beach, FL - *BrCabYB 84; NatRadPubDir Summer 83, Spring 84; TV&RadDir 84*
WWLX - Lexington, AL - *BrCabYB 84*
WWMA-TV - Grand Rapids, MI - *DirUSTelSta 83; TelAl 84*
WWMC-FM - Mifflinburg, PA - *BrCabYB 84; TV&RadDir 84*

WWMD-FM - Hagerstown, MD - *BrCabYB 84; NatRadPubDir Summer 83, Spring 84*
WWMG - New Bern, NC - *BrCabYB 84*
WWMH-FM - Minocqua, WI - *BrCabYB 84; TV&RadDir 84*
WWMJ-FM - Ellsworth, ME - *BrCabYB 84*
WWMJ-FM - New Lexington, OH - *TV&RadDir 84*
WWMN - Flint, MI - *BrCabYB 84; NatRadPubDir Spring 84; TV&RadDir 84*
WWMO-FM - Reidsville, NC - *BrCabYB 84; TV&RadDir 84*
WWMR-FM - Rumford, ME - *BrCabYB 84; TV&RadDir 84*
WWNC - Asheville, NC - *BrCabYB 84; NatRadPubDir Summer 83, Spring 84; TV&RadDir 84*
WWNH - Rochester, NH - *BrCabYB 84; TV&RadDir 84*
WWNH-FM - Rochester, NH - *BrCabYB 84; TV&RadDir 84*
WWNN - Dunedin, FL - *BrCabYB 84*
WWNO-FM - New Orleans, LA - *BrCabYB 84; NatRadPubDir Summer 83, Spring 84; TV&RadDir 84*
WWNR - Beckley, WV - *BrCabYB 84; TV&RadDir 84*
WWNS - Statesboro, GA - *BrCabYB 84; TV&RadDir 84*
WWNT - Dothan, AL - *BrCabYB 84; TV&RadDir 84*
WWNW-FM - New Wilmington, PA - *TV&RadDir 84*
WWNY-TV - Carthage, NY - *BrCabYB 84; TelAl 83, 84; Tel&CabFB 84S*
WWNY-TV - Watertown, NY - *DirUSTelSta 83; TV&RadDir 84*
WWOC-FM - Avalon, NJ - *BrCabYB 84; TV&RadDir 84*
WWOD - Lynchburg, VA - *BrCabYB 84; NatRadPubDir Summer 83, Spring 84; TV&RadDir 84*
WWOG - Boca Raton, FL - *BrCabYB 84*
WWOJ-FM - Avon Park, FL - *BrCabYB 84*
WWOK - Columbia, NC - *BrCabYB 84*
WWOL - Buffalo, NY - *NatRadPubDir Summer 83*
WWOM-FM - Albany, NY - *BrCabYB 84; NatRadPubDir Summer 83, Spring 84; TV&RadDir 84*
WWON - Woonsocket, RI - *BrCabYB 84; NatRadPubDir Summer 83, Spring 84; TV&RadDir 84*
WWON-FM - Woonsocket, RI - *BrCabYB 84; NatRadPubDir Summer 83, Spring 84; TV&RadDir 84*
WWOO-FM - Berryville, VA - *BrCabYB 84; TV&RadDir 84*
WWOW - Conneaut, OH - *BrCabYB 84; TV&RadDir 84*
WWPA - Williamsport, PA - *BrCabYB 84; NatRadPubDir Summer 83, Spring 84; TV&RadDir 84*
WWPB-TV - Clear Spring, MD - *TV&RadDir 84*
WWPB-TV - Hagerstown, MD - *BrCabYB 84; Tel&CabFB 84S*
WWPH-FM - Princeton Junction, NJ - *BrCabYB 84; NatRadPubDir Summer 83, Spring 84; TV&RadDir 84*
WWPT-FM - Westport, CT - *BrCabYB 84; TV&RadDir 84*
WWPV-FM - Colchester, VT - *BrCabYB 84*
WWPV-FM - Winooski, VT - *NatRadPubDir Summer 83, Spring 84; TV&RadDir 84*
WWPZ - Petoskey, MI - *BrCabYB 84; TV&RadDir 84*
WWQC-FM - Quincy, IL - *BrCabYB 84; TV&RadDir 84*
WWQI - La Crosse, WI - *BrCabYB 84; Tel&CabFB 84S*
WWQM-FM - Madison, WI - *NatRadPubDir Summer 83, Spring 84; TV&RadDir 84*
WWQM-FM - Middleton, WI - *BrCabYB 84*
WWQQ-FM - Wilmington, NC - *BrCabYB 84; TV&RadDir 84*
WWRK-FM - Elberton, GA - *BrCabYB 84; TV&RadDir 84*
WWRL - Flushing, NY - *TV&RadDir 84*
WWRL - New York, NY - *BrCabYB 84; NatRadPubDir Summer 83 p.176, Spring 84 p.173*
WWRM-FM - Gaylord, MI - *BrCabYB 84; TV&RadDir 84*
WWRT - Algood, TN - *BrCabYB 84*
WWRW-FM - Wisconsin Rapids, WI - *BrCabYB 84; TV&RadDir 84*
WWS/World Ports - Blauvelt, NY - *BaconPubCkMag 84*
WWSA - Savannah, GA - *BrCabYB 84; NatRadPubDir Summer 83, Spring 84; TV&RadDir 84*
WWSC - Glens Falls, NY - *BrCabYB 84; TV&RadDir 84*
WWSD-FM - Quincy, FL - *BrCabYB 84; TV&RadDir 84*
WWSE-FM - Jamestown, NY - *BrCabYB 84; NatRadPubDir Summer 83, Spring 84; TV&RadDir 84*
WWSG-TV - Philadelphia, PA - *BrCabYB 84; DirUSTelSta 83; TelAl 84; Tel&CabFB 84S*
WWSH-FM - Bala-Cynwyd, PA - *TV&RadDir 84*
WWSH-FM - Philadelphia, PA - *NatRadPubDir Summer 83 p.213, Spring 84 p.213*
WWSL-FM - Philadelphia, MS - *BrCabYB 84; TV&RadDir 84*
WWSM-FM - Bay Minette, AL - *BrCabYB 84; TV&RadDir 84*
WWSP-FM - Stevens Point, WI - *BrCabYB 84; NatRadPubDir Spring 84; TV&RadDir 84*
WWSR - St. Albans, VT - *BrCabYB 84; NatRadPubDir Summer 83, Spring 84; TV&RadDir 84*
WWST - Wooster, OH - *BrCabYB 84; TV&RadDir 84*
WWST-FM - Wooster, OH - *TV&RadDir 84*
WWSU-FM - Dayton, OH - *BrCabYB 84; TV&RadDir 84*
WWSW - Pittsburgh, PA - *BrCabYB 84; TV&RadDir 84*
WWSW-FM - Pittsburgh, PA - *BrCabYB 84; NatRadPubDir Summer 83, Spring 84; TV&RadDir 84*
WWTC - Minneapolis, MN - *BrCabYB 84; NatRadPubDir Summer 83, Spring 84; TV&RadDir 84*
WWTL - Marshfield, WI - *BrCabYB 84; Tel&CabFB 84S*
WWTO-TV - La Salle, IL - *BrCabYB 84*
WWTR-FM - Bethany Beach, DE - *BrCabYB 84; TV&RadDir 84*
WWTV-TV - Cadillac, MI - *BrCabYB 84; TelAl 83, 84; Tel&CabFB 84S; TV&RadDir 84*
WWTV/WWUP - Traverse City, MI - *DirUSTelSta 83*
WWUH-FM - Hartford, CT - *TV&RadDir 84*
WWUH-FM - West Hartford, CT - *BrCabYB 84*
WWUN - Batesville, MS - *BrCabYB 84; TV&RadDir 84*
WWUN-FM - Batesville, MS - *TV&RadDir 84*
WWUP-TV - Cadillac, MI - *TV&RadDir 84*
WWUP-TV - Sault Ste. Marie, MI - *BrCabYB 84; TelAl 83, 84; Tel&CabFB 84S*
WWUS-FM - Big Pine Key, FL - *BrCabYB 84; TV&RadDir 84*
WWUU-FM - Long Branch, NJ - *NatRadPubDir Summer 83*
WWVA - Wheeling, WV - *BrCabYB 84; LitMarPl 83, 84; NatRadPubDir Summer 83, Spring 84; TV&RadDir 84*
WWVR-FM - West Terre Haute, IN - *BrCabYB 84; TV&RadDir 84*
WWVU-FM - Morgantown, WV - *BrCabYB 84*
WWVU-TV - Morgantown, WV - *TV&RadDir 84*
WWWA-FM - Glenview, IL - *TV&RadDir 84*
WWWB - Jasper, AL - *BrCabYB 84; TV&RadDir 84*
WWWB-FM - Jasper, AL - *BrCabYB 84; TV&RadDir 84*
WWWC - Wilkesboro, NC - *BrCabYB 84; TV&RadDir 84*
WWWD - Schenectady, NY - *BrCabYB 84; TV&RadDir 84*
WWWE - Cleveland, OH - *BrCabYB 84; NatRadPubDir Summer 83, Spring 84; TV&RadDir 84*
WWWF - Fayette, AL - *BrCabYB 84; TV&RadDir 84*
WWWG - Rochester, NY - *BrCabYB 84; NatRadPubDir Summer 83, Spring 84; TV&RadDir 84*
WWWJ-FM - Johnstown, OH - *BrCabYB 84; TV&RadDir 84*
WWWK-FM - Warrenton, VA - *TV&RadDir 84*
WWWL - Miami Beach, FL - *BrCabYB 84; NatRadPubDir Spring 84*
WWWL-FM - Miami Beach, FL - *NatRadPubDir Summer 83; TV&RadDir 84*
WWWM-FM - Cleveland, OH - *BrCabYB 84*
WWWM-FM - Toledo, OH - *NatRadPubDir Spring 84*
WWWN - Vienna, GA - *BrCabYB 84; TV&RadDir 84*
WWWQ - Panama City, FL - *BrCabYB 84; TV&RadDir 84*
WWWR - Russellville, AL - *BrCabYB 84; TV&RadDir 84*
WWWS-FM - Saginaw, MI - *BrCabYB 84; NatRadPubDir Summer 83, Spring 84; TV&RadDir 84*
WWWT-FM - Oswego, NY - *BrCabYB 84; TV&RadDir 84*
WWWV-FM - Charlottesville, VA - *BrCabYB 84; TV&RadDir 84*
WWWW-FM - Detroit, MI - *BrCabYB 84; NatRadPubDir Summer 83, Spring 84; TV&RadDir 84*
WWWX - Albemarle, NC - *BrCabYB 84; TV&RadDir 84*
WWWY-FM - Columbus, IN - *BrCabYB 84; TV&RadDir 84*
WWWZ-FM - Summerville, SC - *BrCabYB 84; NatRadPubDir Summer 83 p.223, Spring 84; TV&RadDir 84*
WWXL-FM - Manchester, KY - *BrCabYB 84; TV&RadDir 84*
WWYD-FM - Westchester County, NY - *NatRadPubDir Summer 83 p.180*
WWYN-FM - Carthage, MS - *BrCabYB 84; TV&RadDir 84*
WWYO - Pineville, WV - *BrCabYB 84; TV&RadDir 84*
WWYZ-FM - Waterbury, CT - *BrCabYB 84; NatRadPubDir Summer 83, Spring 84; TV&RadDir 84*
WWZD-FM - Buena Vista, VA - *BrCabYB 84; TV&RadDir 84*
WWZE-FM - Central City, PA - *BrCabYB 84; TV&RadDir 84*
WWZZ - Sarasota, FL - *BrCabYB 84; TV&RadDir 84*

WXAC-FM - Reading, PA - *BrCabYB 84; NatRadPubDir Summer 83, Spring 84; TV&RadDir 84*
WXAG - Athens, GA - *BrCabYB 84*
WXAL - Demopolis, AL - *BrCabYB 84; TV&RadDir 84*
WXAM - Charlottesville, VA - *BrCabYB 84; NatRadPubDir Summer 83, Spring 84; TV&RadDir 84*
WXAN - Ava, IL - *BrCabYB 84*
WXAO-TV - Jacksonville, FL - *DirUSTelSta 83; TelAl 83, 84; TV&RadDir 84*
WXBA-FM - Brentwood, NY - *BrCabYB 84; NatRadPubDir Summer 83, Spring 84; TV&RadDir 84*
WXBK - Albertville, AL - *BrCabYB 84*
WXBM-FM - Milton, FL - *BrCabYB 84; TV&RadDir 84*
WXBQ-FM - Bristol, VA - *BrCabYB 84*
WXCC-FM - Williamson, WV - *BrCabYB 84; TV&RadDir 84*
WXCE - Amery, WI - *BrCabYB 84; NatRadPubDir Summer 83, Spring 84; TV&RadDir 84*
WXCF - Clifton Forge, VA - *BrCabYB 84; TV&RadDir 84*
WXCF-FM - Clifton Forge, VA - *BrCabYB 84*
WXCI - Danbury, CT - *BrCabYB 84*
WXCL - Peoria, IL - *BrCabYB 84; NatRadPubDir Summer 83, Spring 84; TV&RadDir 84*
WXCM - Jackson, MI - *BrCabYB 84; NatRadPubDir Summer 83, Spring 84*
WXCO - Wausau, WI - *BrCabYB 84; TV&RadDir 84*
WXCR - Safety Harbor, FL - *BrCabYB 84*
WXCS-FM - Hagerstown, MD - *BrCabYB 84; NatRadPubDir Spring 84*
WXCV - Homosassa Springs, FL - *BrCabYB 84*
WXDR-FM - Newark, DE - *BrCabYB 84; NatRadPubDir Summer 83, Spring 84*
WXDU - Durham, NC - *BrCabYB 84*
WXEE - Welch, WV - *BrCabYB 84; TV&RadDir 84*
WXEL-FM - New Orleans, LA - *NatRadPubDir Summer 83; TV&RadDir 84*
WXEW - Yabucoa, PR - *BrCabYB 84*
WXEX-TV - Petersburg, VA - *BrCabYB 84; Tel&CabFB 84S*
WXEX-TV - Richmond, VA - *DirUSTelSta 83; LitMarPl 83, 84; TelAl 83, 84; TV&RadDir 84*
WXEZ-FM - Toledo, OH - *NatRadPubDir Summer 83*
WXFL-TV - Tampa, FL - *BrCabYB 84; LitMarPl 84; Tel&CabFB 84S*
WXFM-FM - Chicago, IL - *NatRadPubDir Summer 83, Spring 84; TV&RadDir 84*
WXFM-FM - Elmwood Park, IL - *BrCabYB 84*
WXGA-TV - Waycross, GA - *BrCabYB 84; Tel&CabFB 84S; TV&RadDir 84*
WXGC-FM - Milledgeville, GA - *BrCabYB 84; TV&RadDir 84*
WXGI - Richmond, VA - *BrCabYB 84; NatRadPubDir Summer 83, Spring 84; TV&RadDir 84*
WXGR - Bay St. Louis, MS - *BrCabYB 84; TV&RadDir 84*
WXGT-FM - Columbus, OH - *BrCabYB 84; NatRadPubDir Summer 83, Spring 84; TV&RadDir 84*
WXIA-TV - Atlanta, GA - *BrCabYB 84; DirUSTelSta 83; LitMarPl 83, 84; TelAl 83, 84; Tel&CabFB 84S; TV&RadDir 84*
WXIC - Waverly, OH - *BrCabYB 84; TV&RadDir 84*
WXID-FM - Mayfield, KY - *BrCabYB 84; TV&RadDir 84*
WXIE - Oakland, MD - *BrCabYB 84*
WXII-TV - Greensboro, NC - *DirUSTelSta 83*
WXII-TV - Winston Salem, NC - *BrCabYB 84; LitMarPl 83, 84; TelAl 83, 84; Tel&CabFB 84S; TV&RadDir 84*
WXIK - Shelby, NC - *BrCabYB 84*
WXIL-FM - Parkersburg, WV - *BrCabYB 84; TV&RadDir 84*
WXIR-FM - Indianapolis, IN - *TV&RadDir 84*
WXIR-FM - Plainfield, IN - *BrCabYB 84*
WXIS-FM - Erwin, TN - *BrCabYB 84; TV&RadDir 84*
WXIT - Charleston, WV - *BrCabYB 84; NatRadPubDir Summer 83, Spring 84; TV&RadDir 84*
WXIX-FM - Shelby, NC - *TV&RadDir 84*
WXIX-TV - Cincinnati, OH - *BrCabYB 84; DirUSTelSta 83; TelAl 83, 84; Tel&CabFB 84S*
WXIY-FM - Bay Springs, MS - *BrCabYB 84; TV&RadDir 84*
WXIZ-FM - Waverly, OH - *BrCabYB 84; TV&RadDir 84*
WXJC-TV - Angola, IN - *BrCabYB 84; TelAl 84*
WXJY-FM - Menomonee Falls, WI - *TV&RadDir 84*
WXKE-FM - Ft. Wayne, IN - *BrCabYB 84; NatRadPubDir Summer 83, Spring 84; TV&RadDir 84*
WXKG-FM - Livingston, TN - *BrCabYB 84; TV&RadDir 84*
WXKO - Ft. Valley, GA - *BrCabYB 84; TV&RadDir 84*
WXKQ-FM - Whitesburg, KY - *BrCabYB 84; TV&RadDir 84*
WXKS - Medford, MA - *BrCabYB 84; TV&RadDir 84*
WXKS-FM - Medford, MA - *BrCabYB 84; TV&RadDir 84*
WXKW-FM - Allentown, PA - *BrCabYB 84; NatRadPubDir Summer 83 p.209, Spring 84 p.209*
WXKW-FM - Lehigh Valley, PA - *TV&RadDir 84*
WXKX-FM - Pittsburgh, PA - *TV&RadDir 84*
WXLC-FM - Waukegan, IL - *BrCabYB 84; NatRadPubDir Spring 84; TV&RadDir 84*
WXLD-FM - Davenport, IA - *NatRadPubDir Summer 83, Spring 84*
WXLE-FM - Abbeville, AL - *BrCabYB 84; TV&RadDir 84*
WXLI - Dublin, GA - *BrCabYB 84; TV&RadDir 84*
WXLK-FM - Roanoke, VA - *BrCabYB 84; TV&RadDir 84*
WXLL - Atlanta, GA - *TV&RadDir 84*
WXLL - Decatur, GA - *BrCabYB 84*
WXLN-FM - Louisville, KY - *BrCabYB 84; NatRadPubDir Summer 83, Spring 84; TV&RadDir 84*
WXLP-FM - Moline, IL - *BrCabYB 84*
WXLP-FM - Davenport, IA - *NatRadPubDir Summer 83, Spring 84; TV&RadDir 84*
WXLQ-FM - Berlin, NH - *TV&RadDir 84*
WXLR-FM - State College, PA - *BrCabYB 84; TV&RadDir 84*
WXLT-TV - Sarasota, FL - *BrCabYB 84; DirUSTelSta 83; LitMarPl 83, 84; TelAl 83, 84; Tel&CabFB 84S; TV&RadDir 84*
WXLV - Schnecksville, PA - *BrCabYB 84*
WXLW - Indianapolis, IN - *BrCabYB 84; NatRadPubDir Summer 83, Spring 84; TV&RadDir 84*
WXLY-FM - Jackson, MS - *NatRadPubDir Summer 83; TV&RadDir 84*
WXMC - Parsippany, NJ - *BrCabYB 84; TV&RadDir 84*
WXMG-FM - South Bend, IN - *NatRadPubDir Spring 84 p.92*
WXMI-TV - Grand Rapids, MI - *BrCabYB 84; Tel&CabFB 84S*
WXNE-TV - Boston, MA - *BrCabYB 84; DirUSTelSta 83; TelAl 83, 84; Tel&CabFB 84S*
WXNE-TV - Needham Heights, MA - *TV&RadDir 84*
WXOK - Baton Rouge, LA - *BrCabYB 84; NatRadPubDir Summer 83, Spring 84; TV&RadDir 84*
WXOL - Chicago, IL - *TV&RadDir 84*
WXOL - Cicero, IL - *BrCabYB 84*
WXON-TV - Detroit, MI - *BrCabYB 84; DirUSTelSta 83; Tel&CabFB 84S*
WXON-TV - Southfield, MI - *TV&RadDir 84*
WXOQ - Tupelo, MS - *TV&RadDir 84*
WXOR - Florence, AL - *BrCabYB 84; TV&RadDir 84*
WXOS-FM - Plantation Key, FL - *BrCabYB 84*
WXOS-FM - Tavernier, FL - *TV&RadDir 84*
WXOW-TV - La Crosse, WI - *BrCabYB 84; DirUSTelSta 83; TelAl 83, 84; Tel&CabFB 84S; TV&RadDir 84*
WXOX - Bay City, MI - *BrCabYB 84; NatRadPubDir Summer 83; TV&RadDir 84*
WXPN - Philadelphia, PA - *BrCabYB 84; TV&RadDir 84*
WXPN-FM - Easton, PA - *NatRadPubDir Summer 83, Spring 84 p.315*
WXPN-FM - Philadelphia, PA - *TV&RadDir 84*
WXPQ - Eatonton, GA - *BrCabYB 84; TV&RadDir 84*
WXPR - Rhinelander, WI - *BrCabYB 84*
WXPX - West Hazleton, PA - *BrCabYB 84*
WXQK - Spring City, TN - *BrCabYB 84*
WXQR-FM - Jacksonville, NC - *BrCabYB 84; TV&RadDir 84*
WXQT - Grand Rapids, MI - *BrCabYB 84; NatRadPubDir Spring 84; TV&RadDir 84*
WXRC-FM - Hickory, NC - *BrCabYB 84; TV&RadDir 84*
WXRD-FM - Crystal Lake, IL - *TV&RadDir 84*
WXRD-FM - Woodstock, IL - *BrCabYB 84*
WXRF - Guayama, PR - *BrCabYB 84*
WXRI-FM - Norfolk, VA - *BrCabYB 84; NatRadPubDir Summer 83, Spring 84 p.257*
WXRI-FM - Portsmouth, VA - *TV&RadDir 84*
WXRL - Lancaster, NY - *BrCabYB 84; TV&RadDir 84*
WXRO-FM - Beaver Dam, WI - *BrCabYB 84; TV&RadDir 84*
WXRQ - Mt. Pleasant, TN - *BrCabYB 84*
WXRS - Swainsboro, GA - *BrCabYB 84; TV&RadDir 84*

WXRS-FM - Swainsboro, GA - *BrCabYB 84*
WXRT-FM - Chicago, IL - *BrCabYB 84; LitMarPl 84; NatRadPubDir Summer 83, Spring 84; TV&RadDir 84*
WXRY-FM - Columbia, SC - *TV&RadDir 84*
WXTA - Rockford, IL - *BrCabYB 84; NatRadPubDir Summer 83, Spring 84; TV&RadDir 84*
WXTC-FM - Charleston, SC - *BrCabYB 84; NatRadPubDir Summer 83, Spring 84; TV&RadDir 84*
WXTN - Lexington, MS - *TV&RadDir 84*
WXTQ-FM - Athens, OH - *BrCabYB 84; TV&RadDir 84*
WXTR-FM - La Plata, MD - *BrCabYB 84*
WXTU-FM - Philadelphia, PA - *BrCabYB 84; NatRadPubDir Spring 84 p.214*
WXTV-TV - Paterson, NJ - *BrCabYB 84; Tel&CabFB 84S*
WXTV-TV - Secaucus, NJ - *TV&RadDir 84*
WXTV-TV - New York, NY - *DirUSTelSta 83; TelAl 83, 84*
WXTX - Columbus, GA - *BrCabYB 84; Tel&CabFB 84S*
WXTY - Ticonderoga, NY - *BrCabYB 84*
WXTZ-FM - Indianapolis, IN - *BrCabYB 84; NatRadPubDir Summer 83, Spring 84; TV&RadDir 84*
WXUS-FM - Lafayette, IN - *BrCabYB 84; NatRadPubDir Summer 83, Spring 84; TV&RadDir 84*
WXVA - Charles Town, WV - *BrCabYB 84; TV&RadDir 84*
WXVA-FM - Charles Town, WV - *BrCabYB 84; TV&RadDir 84*
WXVI - Montgomery, AL - *BrCabYB 84; NatRadPubDir Summer 83, Spring 84; TV&RadDir 84*
WXVL-FM - Crossville, TN - *TV&RadDir 84*
WXVQ - De Land, FL - *BrCabYB 84; TV&RadDir 84*
WXVT-TV - Greenville, MS - *BrCabYB 84; DirUSTelSta 83; TelAl 83, 84; Tel&CabFB 84S; TV&RadDir 84*
WXVW - Jeffersonville, IN - *BrCabYB 84; TV&RadDir 84*
WXVW - Louisville, KY - *NatRadPubDir Summer 83 p.105, Spring 84 p.104*
WXVY - Baltimore, MD - *BrCabYB 84*
WXXA-TV - Albany, NY - *BrCabYB 84; Tel&CabFB 84S*
WXXI-FM - Rochester, NY - *BrCabYB 84; NatRadPubDir Summer 83, Spring 84; TV&RadDir 84*
WXXI-TV - Rochester, NY - *BrCabYB 84; Tel&CabFB 84S; TV&RadDir 84*
WXXQ-FM - Freeport, IL - *BrCabYB 84; NatRadPubDir Summer 83, Spring 84*
WXXR - Cullman, AL - *BrCabYB 84; TV&RadDir 84*
WXXX - Hattiesburg, MS - *BrCabYB 84; NatRadPubDir Summer 83, Spring 84; TV&RadDir 84*
WXXY-FM - Montour Falls, NY - *TV&RadDir 84*
WXYC-FM - Chapel Hill, NC - *BrCabYB 84; NatRadPubDir Summer 83, Spring 84; TV&RadDir 84*
WXYL - Jeffersontown, KY - *BrCabYB 84*
WXYQ - Stevens Point, WI - *BrCabYB 84; TV&RadDir 84*
WXYV-FM - Baltimore, MD - *NatRadPubDir Summer 83, Spring 84; TV&RadDir 84*
WXYX - Bayamon, PR - *BrCabYB 84*
WXYY-FM - Wilson, NC - *BrCabYB 84; TV&RadDir 84*
WXYZ - Detroit, MI - *BrCabYB 84; NatRadPubDir Summer 83 p.127, Spring 84 p.127*
WXYZ - Southfield, MI - *TV&RadDir 84*
WXYZ-TV - Detroit, MI - *BrCabYB 84; DirUSTelSta 83; LitMarPl 83, 84; TelAl 84; Tel&CabFB 84S*
WXYZ-TV - Southfield, MI - *TelAl 83; TV&RadDir 84*
Wy-Dak Inc. - Edgemont, SD - *BrCabYB 84; Tel&CabFB 84C*
WYAH-TV - Portsmouth, VA - *BrCabYB 84; DirUSTelSta 83; TelAl 84; Tel&CabFB 84S; TV&RadDir 84*
WYAJ-FM - Sudbury, MA - *BrCabYB 84; TV&RadDir 84*
WYAK - Myrtle Beach, SC - *TV&RadDir 84*
WYAK - Surfside Beach, SC - *BrCabYB 84*
WYAK-FM - Myrtle Beach, SC - *TV&RadDir 84*
WYAK-FM - Surfside Beach, SC - *BrCabYB 84*
WYAL - Scotland Neck, NC - *BrCabYB 84; TV&RadDir 84*
Wyalusing Rocket-Courier - Wyalusing, PA - *BaconPubCkNews 84*
WYAN-FM - Upper Sandusky, OH - *BrCabYB 84; TV&RadDir 84*
Wyandotte Cablevision Inc. [of Communications Services Inc.] - Kansas City, KS - *BrCabYB 84; Tel&CabFB 84C*
Wyandotte County Shopper - Kansas City, KS - *AyerDirPub 83*
Wyandotte Echo - Kansas City, KS - *AyerDirPub 83*
Wyandotte Municipal Services - Wyandotte, MI - *Tel&CabFB 84C*
Wyandotte News-Herald - Wyandotte, MI - *AyerDirPub 83*
Wyandotte News Herald - *See* News-Herald Newspapers
Wyandotte Telephone Co. [Aff. of Century Telephone Enterprises Inc.] - Wyandotte, OK - *TelDir&BG 83-84*
Wyandotte West - Kansas City, KS - *AyerDirPub 83; Ed&PubIntYB 82; NewsDir 84*
Wyandotte Woodhaven News-Herald - Wyandotte, MI - *NewsDir 84*
WYAT - New Orleans, LA - *NatRadPubDir Spring 84*
Wyatt Advertising, Evans - Corpus Christi, TX - *ArtMar 84*
Wyatt Advertising Inc. - *See* Morris & Guthrie Marketing Communications
Wyatt & Associates, Kathy - Caldwell, NJ - *StaDirAdAg 2-84*
Wyatt, Oscar S. Jr. - Bridge City, TX - *Tel&CabFB 84C p.1714*
Wyatt Publishing Co. - Staten Island, NY - *BoPubDir 4, 5*
WYBC-FM - New Haven, CT - *BrCabYB 84; NatRadPubDir Summer 83, Spring 84; TV&RadDir 84*
Wybel Marketing Group Inc. - Barrington, IL - *LitMarPl 83, 84*
WYBG - Massena, NY - *BrCabYB 84; TV&RadDir 84*
Wyble Advertising - Millville, NJ - *AdAge 3-28-84; StaDirAdAg 2-84*
WYBR-FM - Belvidere, IL - *BrCabYB 84*
WYBR-FM - Rockford, IL - *NatRadPubDir Spring 84; TV&RadDir 84*
WYCA-FM - Hammond, IN - *BrCabYB 84; TV&RadDir 84*
WYCB - Washington, DC - *BrCabYB 84; NatRadPubDir Summer 83, Spring 84; TV&RadDir 84*
WYCC - Chicago, IL - *BrCabYB 84; Tel&CabFB 84S*
WYCE - Wyoming, MI - *BrCabYB 84*
Wyckoff News - Wyckoff, NJ - *BaconPubCkNews 84; Ed&PubIntYB 82; NewsDir 84*
Wycliffe Bible Translators [Aff. of Summer Institute of Linguistics] - Huntington Beach, CA - *BoPubDir 4 Sup, 5*
WYCM - Murfreesboro, NC - *BrCabYB 84*
WYCQ-FM - Shelbyville, TN - *BrCabYB 84; TV&RadDir 84*
WYCR-FM - Hanover, PA - *BrCabYB 84; TV&RadDir 84*
WYCS-FM - Yorktown, VA - *BrCabYB 84; TV&RadDir 84*
WYDD-FM - New Kensington, PA - *TV&RadDir 84*
WYDD-FM - Pittsburgh, PA - *BrCabYB 84; NatRadPubDir Summer 83 p.215, Spring 84 p.215*
WYDE - Birmingham, AL - *BrCabYB 84; NatRadPubDir Summer 83, Spring 84; TV&RadDir 84*
WYDK - Yadkinville, NC - *BrCabYB 84; TV&RadDir 84*
Wydro Consultants, Walter S. - Newtown, PA - *CabTVFinDB 83*
Wydro Consultants, Walter S. - Pineville, PA - *InterCabHB 3*
WYEA - Sylacauga, AL - *BrCabYB 84; TV&RadDir 84*
WYEA-TV - Columbus, GA - *TelAl 83, 84*
Wy'East Color Inc. - Portland, OR - *AvMarPl 83*
WYEN-FM - Des Plaines, IL - *BrCabYB 84; TV&RadDir 84*
WYEP-FM - Pittsburgh, PA - *BrCabYB 84; NatRadPubDir Summer 83, Spring 84; TV&RadDir 84*
WYER - Mt. Carmel, IL - *BrCabYB 84; TV&RadDir 84*
WYER-FM - Mt. Carmel, IL - *BrCabYB 84; TV&RadDir 84*
Wyer Music, Rolfe - *See* Fricon Entertainment Co. Inc.
WYES-TV - New Orleans, LA - *BrCabYB 84; Tel&CabFB 84S; TV&RadDir 84*
Wyeth Press [Aff. of ABC Leisure Magazines Inc.] - Great Barrington, MA - *BoPubDir 4, 5*
WYEZ-FM - Elkhart, IN - *BrCabYB 84; TV&RadDir 84*
WYFC - Ypsilanti, MI - *BrCabYB 84; NatRadPubDir Summer 83, Spring 84; TV&RadDir 84*
WYFE-FM - Rockford, IL - *NatRadPubDir Summer 83, Spring 84; TV&RadDir 84*
WYFE-FM - Winnebago, IL - *BrCabYB 84*
WYFF-TV - Greenville, SC - *BrCabYB 84; LitMarPl 84; TelAl 84; Tel&CabFB 84S*
WYFG - Gaffney, SC - *BrCabYB 84*
WYFI-FM - Norfolk, VA - *BrCabYB 84; NatRadPubDir Summer 83 p.255,p.321, Spring 84 p.257,p.324; TV&RadDir 84*
WYFJ - Ashland, VA - *BrCabYB 84*
WYFL-FM - Henderson, NC - *BrCabYB 84; TV&RadDir 84*
WYFM-FM - Sharon, PA - *BrCabYB 84; TV&RadDir 84*
WYFN - St. Petersburg, FL - *BrCabYB 84*
WYGO - Corbin, KY - *BrCabYB 84; TV&RadDir 84*
WYGO-FM - Corbin, KY - *BrCabYB 84; TV&RadDir 84*

WYGR - Grand Rapids, MI - *NatRadPubDir Summer 83 p.129, Spring 84; TV&RadDir 84*
WYGR - Wyoming, MI - *BrCabYB 84*
WYHY - Hendersonville, TN - *NatRadPubDir Summer 83*
WYHY - Lebanon, TN - *BrCabYB 84*
WYHY-FM - Hendersonville, TN - *NatRadPubDir Summer 83, Spring 84 p.228*
WYHY-FM - Lebanon, TN - *TV&RadDir 84*
WYII-FM - Hagerstown, MD - *NatRadPubDir Summer 83 p.117, Spring 84 p.117*
WYII-FM - Williamsport, MD - *BrCabYB 84; TV&RadDir 84*
WYIS - Phoenixville, PA - *BrCabYB 84; TV&RadDir 84*
WYKC - Grenada, MS - *BrCabYB 84; TV&RadDir 84*
WYKK - Quitman, MS - *BrCabYB 84*
WYKM - Rupert, WV - *BrCabYB 84; TV&RadDir 84*
Wykoff Telephone Co. - Grand Meadow, MN - *TelDir&BG 83-84*
WYKR - Wells River, VT - *BrCabYB 84; TV&RadDir 84*
WYKS-FM - Gainesville, FL - *BrCabYB 84; NatRadPubDir Summer 83, Spring 84; TV&RadDir 84*
WYKX - Escanaba, MI - *BrCabYB 84*
WYLD - New Orleans, LA - *BrCabYB 84; NatRadPubDir Summer 83, Spring 84; TV&RadDir 84*
WYLD-FM - New Orleans, LA - *BrCabYB 84; NatRadPubDir Summer 83, Spring 84; TV&RadDir 84*
Wyle Associates Inc. - New York, NY - *DirPRFirms 83*
Wyle Data Services [Div. of Wyle Laboratories] - Huntington Beach, CA - *DataDirOnSer 84*
WYLF-FM - Newfield, NY - *TV&RadDir 84*
WYLF-FM - South Bristol, NY - *BrCabYB 84*
Wylie Agency, Andrew - New York, NY - *LitMarPl 83, 84*
Wylie News - Wylie, TX - *BaconPubCkNews 84; Ed&PubIntYB 82*
Wylie Wilson & Munn Inc. - San Francisco, CA - *StaDirAdAg 2-84*
WYLO - Jackson, WI - *BrCabYB 84*
WYLO - Milwaukee, WI - *TV&RadDir 84*
WYLR-FM - Glens Falls, NY - *BrCabYB 84; TV&RadDir 84*
WYLS - York, AL - *BrCabYB 84; TV&RadDir 84*
Wyly Corp. - Dallas, TX - *DataDirSup 7-83; Datamation 6-83; Top100Al 83*
Wyman Associates - San Mateo, CA - *MicrocomMPl 83*
Wyman Co. Inc., The - Mill Valley, CA - *BrCabYB 84*
Wyman Marketing Inc. - New York, NY - *StaDirAdAg 2-84*
Wyman, Sherwood, Raymond & Otto - Mill Valley, CA - *StaDirAdAg 2-84*
WYMB - Manning, SC - *BrCabYB 84; TV&RadDir 84*
WYMC - Mayfield, KY - *BrCabYB 84; TV&RadDir 84*
WYMJ-FM - Beaver Creek, OH - *BrCabYB 84*
Wymore Arbor State - Wymore, NE - *BaconPubCkNews 84*
WYMS-FM - Milwaukee, WI - *BrCabYB 84; NatRadPubDir Spring 84; TV&RadDir 84*
WYMX-FM - Augusta, GA - *BrCabYB 84; NatRadPubDir Summer 83, Spring 84; TV&RadDir 84*
Wynaud Press - Las Cruces, NM - *BoPubDir 4, 5*
WYNC - Yanceyville, NC - *BrCabYB 84; TV&RadDir 84*
Wyndmere Missile, The - Wyndmere, ND - *Ed&PubIntYB 82*
WYNE - Appleton, WI - *NatRadPubDir Summer 83 p.265, Spring 84 p.267; TV&RadDir 84*
WYNE - Kimberly, WI - *BrCabYB 84*
WYNF-FM - St. Petersburg, FL - *TV&RadDir 84*
WYNF-FM - Tampa/St. Petersburg, FL - *NatRadPubDir Summer 83, Spring 84 p.66*
WYNG-FM - Evansville, IN - *BrCabYB 84; TV&RadDir 84*
WYNI - Mobile, AL - *BrCabYB 84*
WYNK - Baton Rouge, LA - *BrCabYB 84; NatRadPubDir Summer 83, Spring 84; TV&RadDir 84*
WYNK-FM - Baton Rouge, LA - *BrCabYB 84; NatRadPubDir Summer 83, Spring 84; TV&RadDir 84*
Wynkyn Press - Ganges, BC, Canada - *BoPubDir 4 Sup, 5*
WYNN - Florence, SC - *BrCabYB 84; TV&RadDir 84*
Wynne Progress - Wynne, AR - *BaconPubCkNews 84; Ed&PubIntYB 82; NewsDir 84*
Wynne Shoppers News, The - Wynne, AR - *Ed&PubIntYB 82*
Wynnehaven Publishing Co. - Beach Haven, NJ - *BoPubDir 4, 5*
Wynnewood Gazette - Wynnewood, OK - *BaconPubCkNews 84; Ed&PubIntYB 82*
WYNO - Nelsonville, OH - *BrCabYB 84; TV&RadDir 84*
WYNR - Brunswick, GA - *BrCabYB 84; TV&RadDir 84*
WYNS - Lehighton, PA - *BrCabYB 84; TV&RadDir 84*
WYNT - Colonial Heights, VA - *BrCabYB 84*
Wynwood Music Co. Inc. - Broad Run, VA - *BillIntBG 83-84*
WYNX - Smyrna, GA - *BrCabYB 84; TV&RadDir 84*
WYNY-FM - New York, NY - *BrCabYB 84; LitMarPl 84; NatRadPubDir Summer 83, Spring 84; TV&RadDir 84*
WYNZ - Portland, ME - *NatRadPubDir Summer 83, Spring 84; TV&RadDir 84*
WYNZ-FM - Portland, ME - *NatRadPubDir Summer 83, Spring 84; TV&RadDir 84*
Wyoming Beverage Analyst [of Bevan Inc.] - Denver, CO - *BaconPubCkMag 84; MagDir 84*
Wyoming Brand Music - Mt. Juliet, TN - *BillIntBG 83-84*
Wyoming Cable TV Inc. [of Bahakel Communications Ltd.] - Cyclone, WV - *Tel&CabFB 84C*
Wyoming Cable TV Inc. [of Bahakel Communications Ltd.] - Glen Rogers, WV - *Tel&CabFB 84C*
Wyoming Cable TV Inc. [of Bahakel Communications Ltd.] - Hotchkiss, WV - *Tel&CabFB 84C*
Wyoming Cable TV Inc. [of Bahakel Communications Ltd.] - Itmann, WV - *Tel&CabFB 84C*
Wyoming Cable TV Inc. [of Bahakel Communications Ltd.] - Kopperston, WV - *Tel&CabFB 84C*
Wyoming Cable TV Inc. [of Bahakel Communications Ltd.] - Maben, WV - *Tel&CabFB 84C*
Wyoming Cable TV Inc. [of Bahakel Communications Ltd.] - Pineville, WV - *BrCabYB 84; Tel&CabFB 84C*
Wyoming Cable TV Inc. [of Bahakel Communications Ltd.] - Saulsville, WV - *Tel&CabFB 84C*
Wyoming Cable TV Inc. [of Bahakel Communications Ltd.] - Wyoming County, WV - *BrCabYB 84*
Wyoming Catholic Register - Cheyenne, WY - *NewsDir 84*
Wyoming Color Comic Group - Cheyenne, WY - *Ed&PubIntYB 82*
Wyoming County Times & Attica News County Post - Geneseo, NY - *AyerDirPub 83*
Wyoming Dept. of Economic Planning & Development - Cheyenne, WY - *BoPubDir 4, 5*
Wyoming Eagle [of Cheyenne Newspapers Inc.] - Cheyenne, WY - *AyerDirPub 83; Ed&PubIntYB 82; LitMarPl 84; NewsDir 84*
Wyoming Education News - Cheyenne, WY - *MagDir 84*
Wyoming Information & Referral Services Inc. - Cheyenne, WY - *EISS 83*
Wyoming Midland Times - Wyoming, IA - *BaconPubCkNews 84*
Wyoming Mutual Telephone Co. - Wyoming, IA - *TelDir&BG 83-84*
Wyoming Natural Heritage Program [of Wyoming State Dept. of Environmental Quality] - Cheyenne, WY - *EISS 7-83 Sup*
Wyoming Newspaper Clipping Service - Laramie, WY - *ProGuPRSer 4*
Wyoming Plympton Gazette - Wyoming/Camlachie, ON, Canada - *Ed&PubIntYB 82*
Wyoming-Plympton Gazette, The - Sarnia, ON, Canada - *AyerDirPub 83*
Wyoming Post Herald - *See* News Publishing Co.
Wyoming Post-Herald, The - Wyoming, IL - *Ed&PubIntYB 82*
Wyoming Rural Electric News - Casper, WY - *BaconPubCkMag 84; MagDir 84; WritMar 84*
Wyoming Southkent News-Wyoming Advocate - Grand Rapids, MI - *NewsDir 84*
Wyoming State Archives (Museums & Historical Dept.) - Cheyenne, WY - *BoPubDir 5*
Wyoming State Journal - Lander, WY - *AyerDirPub 83; Ed&PubIntYB 82*
Wyoming State Tribune [of Cheyenne Newspapers Inc.] - Cheyenne, WY - *AyerDirPub 83; Ed&PubIntYB 82; LitMarPl 84; NewsDir 84*
Wyoming State Tribune - *See* Wyoming Eagle
Wyoming Stockman-Farmer - Cheyenne, WY - *BaconPubCkMag 84; MagDir 84*
Wyoming Telephone Co. Inc. - Pinedale, WY - *TelDir&BG 83-84*
Wyoming Televents Inc. - Gillette, WY - *BrCabYB 84; Tel&CabFB 84C*
Wyoming Tribune-Eagle - Cheyenne, WY - *AyerDirPub 83*

Wyoming Trucker - Casper, WY - *BaconPubCkMag 84; MagDir 84*
WYOR-FM - Coral Gables, FL - *BrCabYB 84*
WYOR-FM - Miami, FL - *NatRadPubDir Summer 83 p.62; TV&RadDir 84*
WYOU - Tampa, FL - *BrCabYB 84; NatRadPubDir Summer 83, Spring 84; TV&RadDir 84*
WYPC-FM - Gallipolis, OH - *BrCabYB 84; TV&RadDir 84*
Wyper, William W. - Palos Verdes, CA - *BoPubDir 4, 5*
Wyrd Magazine - Lakeport, CA - *LitMag&SmPr 83-84*
WYRE - Annapolis, MD - *BrCabYB 84; TV&RadDir 84*
WYRK-FM - Buffalo, NY - *BrCabYB 84; NatRadPubDir Summer 83, Spring 84; TV&RadDir 84*
WYRL-FM - Melbourne, FL - *BrCabYB 84; TV&RadDir 84*
WYRN - Louisburg, NC - *BrCabYB 84; TV&RadDir 84*
WYRQ-FM - Little Falls, MN - *BrCabYB 84; TV&RadDir 84*
WYRS-FM - Stamford, CT - *BrCabYB 84; NatRadPubDir Summer 83, Spring 84; TV&RadDir 84*
WYRU - Red Springs, NC - *BrCabYB 84; TV&RadDir 84*
WYSE - Inverness, FL - *BrCabYB 84; TV&RadDir 84*
Wyse Advertising - Cleveland, OH - *AdAge 3-28-84; BrCabYB 84; StaDirAdAg 2-84*
Wyse Technology Inc. - San Jose, CA - *DataDirSup 7-83*
WYSH - Clinton, TN - *BrCabYB 84; TV&RadDir 84*
WYSH-FM - Clinton, TN - *TV&RadDir 84*
WYSL - Buffalo, NY - *BrCabYB 84; NatRadPubDir Summer 83, Spring 84; TV&RadDir 84*
WYSO-FM - Yellow Springs, OH - *BrCabYB 84; NatRadPubDir Summer 83, Spring 84; TV&RadDir 84*
Wysong Quimby Lane & Jones - Kansas City, MO - *StaDirAdAg 2-84*
WYSP-FM - Bala-Cynwyd, PA - *TV&RadDir 84*
WYSP-FM - Philadelphia, PA - *BrCabYB 84; NatRadPubDir Summer 83 p.213, Spring 84 p.214*
WYSR - Franklin, VA - *BrCabYB 84; TV&RadDir 84*
WYST - Baltimore, MD - *BrCabYB 84; NatRadPubDir Summer 83, Spring 84; TV&RadDir 84*
WYST-FM - Baltimore, MD - *NatRadPubDir Summer 83, Spring 84; TV&RadDir 84*
WYSU-FM - Youngstown, OH - *BrCabYB 84; NatRadPubDir Summer 83, Spring 84; TV&RadDir 84*
WYTH - Madison, GA - *BrCabYB 84; TV&RadDir 84*
Wytheville Southwest Virginia Enterprise - Wytheville, VA - *BaconPubCkNews 84*
Wytheville TeleCable [of TeleCable Corp.] - Wytheville, VA - *BrCabYB 84; Tel&CabFB 84C*
WYTI - Rocky Mt., VA - *TV&RadDir 84*
WYTK-FM - Washington, PA - *BrCabYB 84; TV&RadDir 84*
WYTL - Oshkosh, WI - *BrCabYB 84; TV&RadDir 84*
WYTM-FM - Fayetteville, TN - *BrCabYB 84; TV&RadDir 84*
WYTV-TV - Youngstown, OH - *BrCabYB 84; DirUSTelSta 83; TelAl 83, 84; Tel&CabFB 84S; TV&RadDir 84*
WYUR-FM - Ripon, WI - *BrCabYB 84; TV&RadDir 84*
WYUS - Milford, DE - *BrCabYB 84*
WYUT-FM - Herkimer, NY - *BrCabYB 84; TV&RadDir 84*
WYVE - Wytheville, VA - *BrCabYB 84; TV&RadDir 84*
Wyvern House [Aff. of Riverside Reproductions] - Sarasota, FL - *BoPubDir 4, 5*
Wyvern Publications - Dumfries, VA - *BoPubDir 4, 5*
Wyvernwood Chronicle - Los Angeles, CA - *AyerDirPub 83*
Wyvernwood Chronicle - Wyvernwood, CA - *Ed&PubIntYB 82*
WYW - Philadelphia, PA - *TV&RadDir 84*
WYWY - Barbourville, KY - *BrCabYB 84; TV&RadDir 84*
WYWY-FM - Barbourville, KY - *BrCabYB 84; TV&RadDir 84*
WYXC - Cartersville, GA - *BrCabYB 84; TV&RadDir 84*
WYXI - Athens, TN - *BrCabYB 84; TV&RadDir 84*
WYXZ - Allendale, SC - *BrCabYB 84*
WYYD-FM - Raleigh, NC - *BrCabYB 84; NatRadPubDir Summer 83, Spring 84; TV&RadDir 84*
WYYN-FM - Jackson, MS - *BrCabYB 84; NatRadPubDir Spring 84*
WYYS-FM - Hamilton, OH - *TV&RadDir 84*
WYYY - Kalamazoo, MI - *NatRadPubDir Summer 83*
WYYY-FM - Syracuse, NY - *BrCabYB 84; NatRadPubDir Spring 84*
WYYZ - Jasper, GA - *BrCabYB 84; TV&RadDir 84*
WYZD - Dobson, NC - *BrCabYB 84*
WYZE - Atlanta, GA - *BrCabYB 84; NatRadPubDir Summer 83, Spring 84; TV&RadDir 84*
WYZZ-FM - Scranton, PA - *NatRadPubDir Summer 83, Spring 84 p.217*
WYZZ-FM - Wilkes Barre, PA - *BrCabYB 84; TV&RadDir 84*
WZA-TV - Bluefield, WV - *TV&RadDir 84*
WZAK-FM - Cleveland, OH - *BrCabYB 84; NatRadPubDir Summer 83, Spring 84; TV&RadDir 84*
WZAL - McDonough, GA - *BrCabYB 84; TV&RadDir 84*
WZAM - Norfolk, VA - *BrCabYB 84; NatRadPubDir Summer 83, Spring 84; TV&RadDir 84*
WZAP - Bristol, VA - *BrCabYB 84; NatRadPubDir Summer 83, Spring 84; TV&RadDir 84*
WZAR - Ponce, PR - *BrCabYB 84*
WZAT-FM - Savannah, GA - *BrCabYB 84; NatRadPubDir Summer 83, Spring 84; TV&RadDir 84*
WZBC-FM - Chestnut Hill, MA - *TV&RadDir 84*
WZBC-FM - Newton, MA - *BrCabYB 84*
WZBO - Edenton, NC - *BrCabYB 84*
WZBR - Amory, MS - *BrCabYB 84; TV&RadDir 84*
WZBS - Ponce, PR - *BrCabYB 84*
WZBT-FM - Gettysburg, PA - *BrCabYB 84; NatRadPubDir Summer 83, Spring 84; TV&RadDir 84*
WZDQ-FM - Humboldt, TN - *BrCabYB 84; TV&RadDir 84*
WZEE-FM - Madison, WI - *BrCabYB 84; NatRadPubDir Summer 83, Spring 84; TV&RadDir 84*
WZEL - Young Harris, GA - *BrCabYB 84*
WZEN-FM - Alton, IL - *BrCabYB 84*
WZEN-FM - St. Louis, MO - *TV&RadDir 84*
WZEP - De Funiak Springs, FL - *BrCabYB 84; TV&RadDir 84*
WZEW - Fairhope, AK - *BrCabYB 84*
WZEZ-FM - Nashville, TN - *BrCabYB 84; NatRadPubDir Summer 83, Spring 84; TV&RadDir 84*
WZFM-FM - Briarcliff Manor, NY - *BrCabYB 84*
WZFM-FM - Westchester County, NY - *NatRadPubDir Summer 83 p.180, Spring 84 p.178*
WZGC-FM - Atlanta, GA - *BrCabYB 84; LitMarPl 83, 84; NatRadPubDir Summer 83, Spring 84; TV&RadDir 84*
WZID-FM - Manchester, NH - *BrCabYB 84; NatRadPubDir Summer 83, Spring 84; TV&RadDir 84*
WZIP - Daytona Beach, FL - *NatRadPubDir Summer 83, Spring 84 p.57; TV&RadDir 84*
WZIP - South Daytona, FL - *BrCabYB 84*
WZIR-FM - Grand Island, NY - *TV&RadDir 84*
WZIR-FM - Niagara Falls, NY - *BrCabYB 84*
WZKB-FM - Wallace, NC - *BrCabYB 84; TV&RadDir 84*
WZKX-FM - Biloxi/Gulfport, MS - *NatRadPubDir Summer 83, Spring 84 p.137*
WZKX-FM - Gulfport, MS - *TV&RadDir 84*
WZKY - Albemarle, NC - *BrCabYB 84; TV&RadDir 84*
WZKZ-FM - Corning, NY - *BrCabYB 84; TV&RadDir 84*
WZLD-FM - Cayce, SC - *BrCabYB 84; TV&RadDir 84*
WZLE-FM - Lorain, OH - *BrCabYB 84; TV&RadDir 84*
WZLQ-FM - Tupelo, MS - *BrCabYB 84; NatRadPubDir Summer 83, Spring 84; TV&RadDir 84*
WZLT-FM - Lexington, TN - *BrCabYB 84; TV&RadDir 84*
WZLY-FM - Wellesley, MA - *BrCabYB 84; NatRadPubDir Summer 83, Spring 84; TV&RadDir 84*
WZMB-FM - Greenville, NC - *BrCabYB 84; NatRadPubDir Summer 83, Spring 84*
WZND-FM - Zeeland, MI - *BrCabYB 84; TV&RadDir 84*
WZNE-FM - Tampa/St. Petersburg, FL - *NatRadPubDir Spring 84 p.66*
WZNG - Lakeland/Winter Haven, FL - *NatRadPubDir Summer 83, Spring 84 p.60*
WZNG - Winter Haven, FL - *BrCabYB 84; TV&RadDir 84*
WZNT - San Juan, PR - *BrCabYB 84*
WZOB - Ft. Payne, AL - *BrCabYB 84; TV&RadDir 84*
WZOE - Princeton, IL - *BrCabYB 84; TV&RadDir 84*
WZOE-FM - Princeton, IL - *BrCabYB 84; TV&RadDir 84*
WZOK-FM - Rockford, IL - *BrCabYB 84; NatRadPubDir Summer 83, Spring 84; TV&RadDir 84*
WZOL - Luquillo, PR - *BrCabYB 84*
WZON - Bangor, ME - *NatRadPubDir Spring 84*
WZOO - Asheboro, NC - *BrCabYB 84; NatRadPubDir Summer 83, Spring 84; TV&RadDir 84*
WZOT-FM - Rockmart, GA - *BrCabYB 84; TV&RadDir 84*

WZOU-FM - Milwaukee, WI - *NatRadPubDir Spring 84*
WZOW-FM - Goshen, IN - *BrCabYB 84; TV&RadDir 84*
WZOZ - Oneonta, NY - *BrCabYB 84*
WZPL-FM - Greenfield, IN - *BrCabYB 84*
WZPL-FM - Indianapolis, IN - *NatRadPubDir Spring 84*
WZPR-FM - Meadville, PA - *BrCabYB 84; TV&RadDir 84*
WZRA - Chattanooga, TN - *BrCabYB 84*
WZRD-FM - Chicago, IL - *BrCabYB 84; TV&RadDir 84*
WZRK-FM - Hancock, MI - *BrCabYB 84; TV&RadDir 84*
WZRO - Farmer City, FL - *BrCabYB 84*
WZST - Leesburg, FL - *BrCabYB 84; TV&RadDir 84*
WZTA-FM - Tamaqua, PA - *BrCabYB 84; TV&RadDir 84*
WZTN - Montgomery, AL - *BrCabYB 84; NatRadPubDir Summer 83, Spring 84*
WZTQ - Hurricane, WV - *BrCabYB 84; TV&RadDir 84*
WZTV-TV - Nashville, TN - *BrCabYB 84; DirUSTelSta 83; TelAl 83, 84; Tel&CabFB 84S; TV&RadDir 84*
WZUE-FM - Carlisle, PA - *NatRadPubDir Summer 83*
WZUU - Milwaukee, WI - *BrCabYB 84; TV&RadDir 84*
WZUU-FM - Milwaukee, WI - *TV&RadDir 84*
WZVN-FM - Lowell, IN - *BrCabYB 84; TV&RadDir 84*
WZWZ-FM - Kokomo, IN - *BrCabYB 84; TV&RadDir 84*
WZXI-FM - Gastonia, NC - *BrCabYB 84; TV&RadDir 84*
WZXM - Gaylord, MI - *BrCabYB 84*
WZXQ - Gluckstadt, MS - *BrCabYB 84*
WZXR-FM - Memphis, TN - *BrCabYB 84; NatRadPubDir Summer 83, Spring 84; TV&RadDir 84*
WZXY - Kingsport, TN - *BrCabYB 84*
WZYC - Newport, NC - *BrCabYB 84*
WZYP-FM - Athens, AL - *BrCabYB 84; TV&RadDir 84*
WZYQ-FM - Braddock Heights, MD - *BrCabYB 84*
WZYQ-FM - Frederick, MD - *BrCabYB 84*
WZYX - Cowan, TN - *BrCabYB 84; TV&RadDir 84*
WZYX-FM - Gate City, VA - *TV&RadDir 84*
WZYZ-FM - Fairmont, NC - *BrCabYB 84; TV&RadDir 84*
WZZA - Tuscumbia, AL - *BrCabYB 84; TV&RadDir 84*
WZZB-FM - Centreville, MS - *BrCabYB 84; TV&RadDir 84*
WZZC-FM - East Moline, IL - *BrCabYB 84; TV&RadDir 84*
WZZC-FM - Easton, MD - *TV&RadDir 84*
WZZD - Lafayette Hill, PA - *LitMarPl 83, 84; TV&RadDir 84*
WZZD - Philadelphia, PA - *BrCabYB 84; NatRadPubDir Summer 83 p.213, Spring 84 p.214*
WZZE - Hockessin, DE - *BrCabYB 84*
WZZI - Madisonville, TN - *BrCabYB 84*
WZZK-FM - Birmingham, AL - *BrCabYB 84; NatRadPubDir Summer 83, Spring 84; TV&RadDir 84*
WZZM-TV - Grand Rapids, MI - *BrCabYB 84; DirUSTelSta 83; LitMarPl 83, 84; TelAl 83, 84; Tel&CabFB 84S; TV&RadDir 84*
WZZO-FM - Allentown, PA - *NatRadPubDir Summer 83, Spring 84 p.209*
WZZO-FM - Bethlehem, PA - *BrCabYB 84; TV&RadDir 84*
WZZP-FM - Cleveland, OH - *BrCabYB 84; TV&RadDir 84*
WZZQ-FM - Terre Haute, IN - *NatRadPubDir Spring 84*
WZZR-FM - Grand Rapids, MI - *BrCabYB 84; NatRadPubDir Summer 83 p.129, Spring 84 p.129; TV&RadDir 84*
WZZW-FM - Augusta, GA - *BrCabYB 84; NatRadPubDir Summer 83, Spring 84; TV&RadDir 84*
WZZX-FM - Louisville, KY - *TV&RadDir 84*
WZZY-FM - Winchester, IN - *BrCabYB 84; TV&RadDir 84*
WZZZ - West Point, GA - *BrCabYB 84*

X

X Mark Corp. - Costa Mesa, CA - *DirInfWP 82*
X/Market [of Economic Information Systems] - New York, NY - *DataDirOnSer 84; DBBus 82; DirOnDB Spring 84*
X-Press - Vancouver, BC, Canada - *BoPubDir 4 Sup, 5*
X/Profile [of Donnelley Marketing Information Services] - Stamford, CT - *DataDirOnSer 84; DirOnDB Spring 84*
X-Ray & Ionizing Radiation Data Center [of U.S. National Bureau of Standards] - Washington, DC - *EISS 83*
X-Ray & Ionizing Radiation Data Center - *See* Photon & Charged Particle Data Center
X/Region [of Control Data Corp.] - Greenwich, CT - *DataDirOnSer 84*
X/Region - *See* Evans Regional Economic Data Base
X-S Books Inc. - Carlstadt, NJ - *LitMarPl 83, 84*
X/Toll [of Control Data Corp.] - Greenwich, CT - *DataDirOnSer 84*
Xanadu - Huntington, NY - *WritMar 84*
Xanadu Records Ltd. - Bronx, NY - *BillIntBG 83-84*
Xanadu Records Ltd. - Kingsbridge, NY - *BillIntBG 83-84*
Xanthic Books - Citrus Heights, CA - *BoPubDir 4, 5*
Xavier Society for the Blind - New York, NY - *LitMarPl 83, 84*
XC Music Publishing - Worthington, OH - *BillIntBG 83-84*
Xcalibur Computers Ltd. - Northampton, England - *MicrocomSwDir 1*
XComp - San Diego, CA - *DataDirSup 7-83; MicrocomMPl 84; WhoWMicrocom 83*
XEBEC - Sunnyvale, CA - *DataDirSup 7-83*
Xedex Corp. - New York, NY - *MicrocomMPl 83*
Xedex Corp. - Suffern, NY - *MicrocomSwDir 1; WhoWMicrocom 83*
XEJ-TV - El Paso, TX - *TelAl 83, 84*
Xenia Daily Gazette [of Thomson Newspapers] - Xenia, OH - *BaconPubCkNews 84; NewsDir 84*
Xenos Books [Aff. of Potpourri Printers] - Gardena, CA - *BoPubDir 4, 5*
XEPM-TV - El Paso, TX - *TelAl 83, 84*
XEPRS - Glendale, CA - *TV&RadDir 84*
Xerographic Reproduction Center Inc. of New Jersey - Englewood Cliffs, NJ - *LitMarPl 83, 84*
Xerox College Publishing - Lexington, MA - *BoPubDir 4, 5*
Xerox Computer Services [Div. of Xerox Corp.] - Los Angeles, CA - *ADAPSOMemDir 83-84; DataDirOnSer 84; DataDirSup 7-83*
Xerox Corp. - Stamford, CT - *DataDirSup 7-83; Datamation 6-83; ElecNews 7-25-83; KnowInd 83; Top100Al 83*
Xerox Corp. (Office Products Div.) - Dallas, TX - *DirInfWP 82; WhoWMicrocom 83*
Xerox Education Publications [Div. of Xerox Publishing Group] - Middletown, CT - *LitMarPl 83, 84; MicrocomMPl 84*
Xerox Education Publications - Columbus, OH - *MagIndMarPl 82-83*
Xerox Education Publications (Commercial Printing Div.) - Columbus, OH - *MagIndMarPl 82-83*
Xerox Education Publications (Weekly Reader Mailing Lists) - Middletown, CT - *LitMarPl 83*
Xerox Library Services [of Xerox Corp.] - Webster, NY - *EISS 83*
Xerox Publishing Group - Greenwich, CT - *InfoS 83-84*
Xetron Corp. [SU Carbone Lorraine Industries Corp.] - Cedar Knolls, NJ - *AvMarPl 83*
XETV - San Diego, CA - *DirUSTelSta 83; TelAl 83, 84*
XETV-TV - San Diego, CA - *TV&RadDir 84*
XEWT-TV - San Diego, CA - *TelAl 83, 84*
XEWT-TV - San Pedro, CA - *TV&RadDir 84*
Xicom-Video Arts - Tuxedo, NY - *AvMarPl 83*
XIDAK Inc. - Menlo Park, CA - *WhoWMicrocom 83*
Xidex Corp. - Sunnyvale, CA - *DataDirSup 7-83*
Xitex Corp. - Dallas, TX - *MicrocomMPl 84*
XIV Music Co. Inc. - *See* Print Music Co. Inc.
XPS Inc. - Carlisle, PA - *MicrocomMPl 84*
XRT Inc. - Broomall, PA - *DataDirOnSer 84*
XTAL - Washington, DC - *DirOnDB Spring 84*
Xtra Soft Inc. - Sunnyville, CA - *MicrocomMPl 84*
Xtra Soft Inc. - Louisville, KY - *MicrocomMPl 83*
Xtras [of From Here Press] - Fanwood, NJ - *LitMag&SmPr 83-84*
XXCAL Inc. - Los Angeles, CA - *WhoWMicrocom 83*
Xybion Graphics Systems Corp. - Cedar Knolls, NJ - *MicrocomMPl 84*
XYCom - Saline, MI - *MicrocomMPl 83, 84*
Xylogics Inc. - Burlington, MA - *DataDirSup 7-83; WhoWMicrocom 83*
XyQuest Inc. - Bedford, MA - *MicrocomMPl 84; MicrocomSwDir 1*
XYZ Television Inc. - Grand Junction, CO - *BrCabYB 84*
XYZT Computer Dimensions Inc. - New York, NY - *MicrocomMPl 83, 84; MicrocomSwDir 1*
XYZZY - Boulder, CO - *MicrocomSwDir 1*

Y

Y Gwyddonydd [of University of Wales Press] - Cardiff, Wales - *LitMag&SmPr 83-84*
Y9 - Washington, DC - *DirOnDB Spring 84*
YABA World - Greendale, WI - *MagIndMarPl 82-83; WritMar 84*
Yacht Exchange Inc., The - Ft. Lauderdale, FL - *DirOnDB Spring 84*
Yacht Racing/Cruising [of North American Publishing Co.] - Darien, CT - *ArtMar 84; BaconPubCkMag 84; MagDir 84; MagIndMarPl 82-83; WritMar 84*
Yachting [of Ziff-Davis Publishing Co.] - Cos Cob, CT - *ArtMar 84; BaconPubCkMag 84; LitMarPl 83, 84; MagDir 84; WritMar 84*
Yachting - New York, NY - *MagIndMarPl 82-83*
Yachting Club of America - Pompano Beach, FL - *BoPubDir 4, 5*
Yachting News - Lakewood, CA - *BaconPubCkMag 84*
Yachting News - Long Beach, CA - *MagDir 84*
Yadkin Enterprise - Booneville, NC - *AyerDirPub 83*
Yadkin Enterprise [of Lindsay Publishing Co.] - Winston-Salem, NC - *NewsDir 84*
Yadkin Ripple - Yadkinville, NC - *AyerDirPub 83; Ed&PubIntYB 82*
Yadkin Valley Cablevision - Mt. Airy, NC - *BrCabYB 84*
Yadkin Valley Telephone Membership Corp. - Yadkinville, NC - *TelDir&BG 83-84*
Yadkinville Yadkin Ripple - Yadkinville, NC - *BaconPubCkNews 84; NewsDir 84*
Yaffe Berline - Southfield, MI - *AdAge 3-28-84; StaDirAdAg 2-84*
Yager, Ellen - New York, NY - *LitMarPl 83*
Yakima Herald-Republic - Yakima, WA - *BaconPubCkNews 84; Ed&PubIntYB 82; NewsDir 84*
Yakima Sun Press - Yakima, WA - *BaconPubCkNews 84*
Yakima Valley Genealogical Society - Yakima, WA - *BoPubDir 4, 5*
Yakima Valley Sun - Yakima, WA - *Ed&PubIntYB 82*
Yale Communications - New York, NY - *DirMarMP 83*
Yale Daily News - New Haven, CT - *NewsDir 84*
Yale Divinity School - New Haven, CT - *AvMarPl 83*
Yale Expositor - Yale, MI - *BaconPubCkNews 84; Ed&PubIntYB 82*
Yale Journal of Biology & Medicine, The - New Haven, CT - *MagDir 84*
Yale Laboratory Inc. - Hollywood, CA - *AvMarPl 83*
Yale Law Journal - New Haven, CT - *MagIndMarPl 82-83*
Yale News - Yale, OK - *BaconPubCkNews 84; Ed&PubIntYB 82*
Yale Review - New Haven, CT - *LitMag&SmPr 83-84; MagDir 84; MagIndMarPl 82-83; WritMar 84*
Yale Scientific Magazine - New Haven, CT - *BaconPubCkMag 84*
Yale Scientific Publications Inc. - New Haven, CT - *MagDir 84*
Yale University (Art Gallery) - New Haven, CT - *BoPubDir 4, 5*
Yale University (Far Eastern Publications) - New Haven, CT - *BoPubDir 4, 5*
Yale University (Observatory) - New Haven, CT - *BoPubDir 4, 5*
Yale University (Peabody Museum of Natural History) - New Haven, CT - *BoPubDir 4, 5*
Yale University (Publications in Anthropology) - New Haven, CT - *BoPubDir 4, 5*
Yale University (Southeast Asia Publications) - New Haven, CT - *BoPubDir 4, 5*
Yale University (Yale Center for British Art) - New Haven, CT - *BoPubDir 4, 5*
Yale University Library - New Haven, CT - *MicroMarPl 82-83*
Yale University Press - New Haven, CT - *LitMarPl 83, 84; WritMar 84*
Yam Songs - *See* Kenwon Music
Yamaha International Corp. - Buena Park, CA - *BillIntBG 83-84*
Yancey Journal - Burnsville, NC - *AyerDirPub 83; Ed&PubIntYB 82*
Yanceyville Caswell Messenger - Yanceyville, NC - *BaconPubCkNews 84; NewsDir 84*
Yaneff Gallery - Toronto, ON, Canada - *ArtMar 84*
Yaneff Ltd., Chris - Toronto, ON, Canada - *StaDirAdAg 2-84*
Yang, James - Chicago, IL - *LitMarPl 83, 84*
Yankee - Dublin, NH - *BaconPubCkMag 84; Folio 83; LitMarPl 83, 84; MagDir 84; MagIndMarPl 82-83; WritMar 84*
Yankee - Peterborough, NH - *MagIndMarPl 82-83*
Yankee Book Peddler Inc. - Contoocook, NH - *LitMarPl 83, 84; MagIndMarPl 82-83*
Yankee Books [Div. of Yankee Publishing Inc.] - Dublin, NH - *LitMarPl 83, 84; WritMar 84*
Yankee Food Service - South Weymouth, MA - *BaconPubCkMag 84*
Yankee Group, The - Boston, MA - *VideoDir 82-83*
Yankee Group, The - Cambridge, MA - *EISS 83*
Yankee Magazine's Travel Guide to New England - Dublin, NH - *ArtMar 84; MagDir 84; WritMar 84*
Yankee Oilman [of New England Fuel Institute] - Watertown, MA - *BaconPubCkMag 84; MagDir 84*
Yankee Peddler Book Co. [Aff. of Southampton Book Co.] - Southampton, NY - *BoPubDir 4, 5*
Yankee Peddler Bookshop - Pultneyville, NY - *BoPubDir 4, 5*
Yankee Photo Products Inc. - Culver City, CA - *AvMarPl 83*
Yankee Publishing Inc. - Dublin, NH - *DirMarMP 83*
Yankee Publishing Inc. (Book Div.) - Dublin, NH - *ArtMar 84*
Yankee Trader - Port Jefferson Station, NY - *AyerDirPub 83; BaconPubCkNews 84; NewsDir 84*
Yankelovich, Skelly & White [Subs. of Reliance Group] - New York, NY - *AdAge 5-17-84 p.33; EISS 83; IntDirMarRes 83; MagIndMarPl 82-83; ProGuPRSer 4*
Yankton Cable TV Ltd. - Yankton, SD - *BrCabYB 84; Tel&CabFB 84C*
Yankton Press & Dakotan - Yankton, SD - *BaconPubCkNews 84; Ed&PubIntYB 82; NewsDir 84*
Yan's Variety Co. Ltd. - Port Coquitlam, BC, Canada - *BoPubDir 4, 5*
Yaquina TV Cable [of Liberty Communications Inc.] - Newport, OR - *BrCabYB 84; Tel&CabFB 84C*
Yaquina TV Cable [of Liberty Communications Inc.] - Yachats, OR - *Tel&CabFB 84C*
Yara Press - Mendocino, CA - *BoPubDir 4, 5*

Yard & Garden Product News [of Johnson Hill Press Inc.] - Ft. Atkinson, WI - *BaconPubCkMag 84; MagDir 84; MagIndMarPl 82-83*
Yardang & Associates, Ed - San Antonio, TX - *AdAge 3-28-84; StaDirAdAg 2-84*
Yardis Advertising - Bryn Mawr, PA - *AdAge 3-28-84; DirPRFirms 83; StaDirAdAg 2-84*
Yardley Bucks County News - *See* Intercounty Newspaper Group
Yardley Group Inc., The - New York, NY - *DataDirSup 7-83*
Yardley News - Morrisville, PA - *NewsDir 84*
Yardley News [of Inter County Publishing Co.] - Philadelphia, PA - *NewsDir 84*
Yardley News - Yardley, PA - *AyerDirPub 83; Ed&PubIntYB 82*
Yards, A. - Mountain View, CA - *BoPubDir 4, 5*
Yarfitz/Photo Environments Inc., Joan - Los Angeles, CA - *LitMarPl 83, 84; MagIndMarPl 82-83*
Yarmouth Port Register - Yarmouth Port, MA - *BaconPubCkNews 84*
Yarmouth Sun - Yarmouth, MA - *Ed&PubIntYB 82*
Yarmouth Sun - *See* Orleans Hughes Newspapers Inc.
Yarmouth Sun, The - Orleans, MA - *NewsDir 84*
Yarn Market News - Ashville, NC - *BaconPubCkMag 84*
Yarrow - Kutztown, PA - *LitMag&SmPr 83-84*
Yarrow Inc. - Summit, NJ - *LitMarPl 83, 84*
Yatahey Records - Dallas, TX - *BillIntBG 83-84*
Yates Center News - Yates Center, KS - *BaconPubCkNews 84; Ed&PubIntYB 82*
Yates City Banner - Elmwood, IL - *AyerDirPub 83*
Yates City Banner - Yates City, IL - *Ed&PubIntYB 82*
Yates City Telephone Co. - Yates City, IL - *TelDir&BG 83-84*
Yates Enterprises Inc. - Harrodsburg, KY - *Tel&CabFB 84C*
Yates, Samuel - Delray Beach, FL - *BoPubDir 5*
Yazoo Answer Call Inc. of Rolling Fork - Rolling Fork, MS - *Tel&CabFB 84C*
Yazoo Herald [of Freeman Enterprises] - Yazoo City, MS - *BaconPubCkNews 84; Ed&PubIntYB 82; NewsDir 84*
Yazoo Records Inc. - New York, NY - *BillIntBG 83-84*
Ybarra Music - Lemon Grove, CA - *BillIntBG 83-84*
Ye Galleon Press - Fairfield, WA - *ArtMar 84; BoPubDir 4, 5*
Ye Olde Printery - Cincinnati, OH - *BoPubDir 4, 5*
Yeadon Times - Yeadon, PA - *BaconPubCkNews 84; Ed&PubIntYB 82*
Yeager Associates, Richard - Moorestown, NJ - *AdAge 3-28-84; StaDirAdAg 2-84*
Yeamans, George Thomas - Muncie, IN - *BoPubDir 4, 5*
Year Book Medical Publishers Inc. [Subs. of The Times Mirror Co.] - Chicago, IL - *LitMarPl 83, 84*
Years Press - East Lansing, MI - *BoPubDir 4 Sup, 5; LitMag&SmPr 83-84*
Yearwood Music Inc. - New York, NY - *BillIntBG 83-84*
Yeck & Yeck Inc. - Dayton, OH - *StaDirAdAg 2-84*
Yeck Brothers Co. - Dayton, OH - *DirMarMP 83*
Yelcot Telephone Co. Inc. - Mountain Home, AR - *TelDir&BG 83-84*
Yell County Telephone Co. - Danville, AR - *TelDir&BG 83-84*
Yellow Ball Workshop - Lexington, MA - *AvMarPl 83*
Yellow Bee Music [Div. of Yellow Bee Productions Inc.] - New York, NY - *BillIntBG 83-84*
Yellow Butterfly Press - Las Cruces, NM - *BoPubDir 4, 5*
Yellow Cat Productions - Silver Spring, MD - *AvMarPl 83*
Yellow Fox Press - Austin, TX - *BoPubDir 4 Sup, 5; LitMag&SmPr 83-84*
Yellow House Music - *See* Paragon/Benson Publishing Group
Yellow Moon Press - Brighton, MA - *LitMag&SmPr 83-84*
Yellow Moon Press - Cambridge, MA - *BoPubDir 4 Sup, 5*
Yellow Pages Marketing Services - Mequon, WI - *AdAge 3-28-84; StaDirAdAg 2-84*
Yellow Press - Chicago, IL - *BoPubDir 4, 5; LitMag&SmPr 83-84*
Yellow Silk [of Verygraphics] - Albany, CA - *LitMag&SmPr 83-84; WritMar 84*
Yellow Springs Computer Camp Inc. - Yellow Springs, OH - *LitMag&SmPr 83-84*
Yellow Springs News - Yellow Springs, OH - *BaconPubCkNews 84; Ed&PubIntYB 82*
Yellow Umbrella Press - Chatham, MA - *BoPubDir 5; LitMag&SmPr 83-84*
Yellow Umbrella Press - Lowell, MA - *BoPubDir 4*
Yellowhead Broadcasting - Edson, AB, Canada - *BrCabYB 84*
Yellowknifer - Yellowknife, NT, Canada - *AyerDirPub 83; Ed&PubIntYB 82*
Yellowstone Newspapers - Livingston, MT - *Ed&PubIntYB 82*
Yellowstone Records - Miles City, MT - *BillIntBG 83-84*
Yellville Mountain Echo - Yellville, AR - *BaconPubCkNews 84; NewsDir 84*
Yelm Nisqually Valley News - Yelm, WA - *BaconPubCkNews 84*
Yelm Telephone Co. - Yelm, WA - *TelDir&BG 83-84*
Yelvington Enterprises Inc., Rube - Mascoutah, IL - *BaconPubCkNews 84*
Yeoman Telephone Co. Inc. - Yeoman, IN - *TelDir&BG 83-84*
Yerington Fernley Leader - Yerington, NV - *BaconPubCkNews 84*
Yerington Mason Valley News - Yerington, NV - *BaconPubCkNews 84; NewsDir 84*
Yes! Inc. - Washington, DC - *BoPubDir 4, 5*
Yes You Can Kiss My Bare Feet...Our Children Are Always Saying [of The Bare Feet & Happy People Press] - Jemez Springs, NM - *LitMag&SmPr 83-84*
Yeshiva University Press - New York, NY - *BoPubDir 4, 5; LitMarPl 84*
Yesnaby Publishers - Danville, PA - *BoPubDir 4, 5*
Yesod Publishers - Brooklyn, NY - *BoPubDir 4, 5*
Yesteryear [of Yesteryear Publications] - Princeton, WI - *WritMar 84*
Yesteryear History Book Committee - Gull Lake, SK, Canada - *BoPubDir 4 Sup, 5*
Yevich Associates Inc., Richard - Cherry Hill, NJ - *WhoWMicrocom 83*
Yiddisher Kemfer - New York, NY - *Ed&PubIntYB 82; NewsDir 84*
Yith Press - Lawrence, KS - *LitMag&SmPr 83-84*
Yivo Institute for Jewish Research - New York, NY - *BoPubDir 4, 5*
Y'lolfa - Dyfed, Wales - *LitMag&SmPr 83-84*
Yoakum Features - Lakeville, CT - *Ed&PubIntYB 82*
Yoakum Herald-Times - Yoakum, TX - *BaconPubCkNews 84; NewsDir 84*
Yocum's Photo Center Inc. - Orange, TX - *AvMarPl 83*
Yoder Co., W. A. - Richmond, VA - *AvMarPl 83*
Yoga Journal, The [of California Yoga Teachers Association] - Berkeley, CA - *WritMar 84*
Yoga Publication Society - Jacksonville, FL - *BoPubDir 4, 5*
Yoga Research Foundation - Miami, FL - *BoPubDir 4, 5*
Yogi Gupta - Elmhurst, NY - *BoPubDir 4, 5*
Yoken & Co. - Briarcliff Manor, NY - *DirPRFirms 83*
Yoknapatawpha Press - Oxford, MS - *BoPubDir 4, 5; LitMag&SmPr 83-84*
Yokogawa Corp. of America - Shendoah, GA - *MicrocomMPl 84*
Yolla Bolly Press, The - Covelo, CA - *LitMag&SmPr 83-84*
Yolo County Shopper - Davis, CA - *AyerDirPub 83*
Yo'Mama's Music - *See* Hat Band Music
Yonkers Herald Statesman - White Plains, NY - *AyerDirPub 83; Ed&PubIntYB 82*
Yonkers Herald Statesman [of Westchester Rockland Newspapers Inc.] - Yonkers, NY - *NewsDir 84*
Yonkers Herald Statesman - *See* Westchester Rockland Newspapers Inc.
Yonkers Home News & Times - Yonkers, NY - *BaconPubCkNews 84; Ed&PubIntYB 82*
Yonkers Home News & Times/Eastchester Record - Yonkers, NY - *NewsDir 84*
Yonkers Record of Yonkers - Yonkers, NY - *NewsDir 84*
Yorba Linda Cable Television Co. [of Empire Cable TV Co. Inc.] - Yorba Linda, CA - *BrCabYB 84; Tel&CabFB 84C*
Yorba Linda Star - Yorba Linda, CA - *Ed&PubIntYB 82*
Yorba Linda Star - *See* Placentia News-Times Publishers
York Area Chamber of Commerce - York, PA - *BoPubDir 4, 5*
York Cable Corp. [of American Television & Communications Corp.] - Sanford, ME - *BrCabYB 84*
York Cablevision Inc. [of MetroVision Inc.] - York, NE - *Tel&CabFB 84C*
York Cablevision Inc. [of Rock Hill Telephone Co.] - York, SC - *BrCabYB 84; Tel&CabFB 84C*
York County Coast Star - Kennebunk, ME - *AyerDirPub 83*
York County Coast Star - York County, ME - *Ed&PubIntYB 82*

York Daily Record - York, PA - *BaconPubCkNews 84; Ed&PubIntYB 82; NewsDir 84*
York Dispatch - York, PA - *BaconPubCkNews 84; Ed&PubIntYB 82; NewsDir 84*
York Enterprises Inc. - New York, NY - *Tel&CabFB 84C*
York Graphic Services Inc. - York, PA - *LitMarPl 83, 84*
York News-Times [of Stauffer Communications Inc.] - York, NE - *BaconPubCkNews 84; Ed&PubIntYB 82; NewsDir 84*
York Press - Fredericton, NB, Canada - *BoPubDir 4, 5*
York Production Services [Div. of York Graphic Services Inc.] - York, PA - *LitMarPl 83, 84*
York Publishing & Printing - Toronto, ON, Canada - *BoPubDir 4, 5*
York Publishing Co. Ltd. - Toronto, ON, Canada - *BoPubDir 4, 5*
York Springs Cable [of American Tele-Systems Corp.] - York Springs, PA - *BrCabYB 84*
York Sumter County Journal - York, AL - *BaconPubCkNews 84; NewsDir 84*
York University (Centre for Research on Environmental Quality) - Downsview, ON, Canada - *BoPubDir 4, 5*
York University (Gerstein Lecture Series) - Downsview, ON, Canada - *BoPubDir 4, 5*
York University (Institute for Behavioural Research) - Downsview, ON, Canada - *BoPubDir 5; CompReadDB 82*
York Weekly - York, ME - *Ed&PubIntYB 82*
York Yorkville Enquirer - York, SC - *BaconPubCkNews 84*
Yorke Editors - *See* Galaxy Music Corp.
Yorke, Harvey - Novato, CA - *BoPubDir 5*
Yorke New England Surveys, Marcia S. - Cheshire, CT - *IntDirMarRes 83*
Yorker, The - Cooperstown, NY - *MagIndMarPl 82-83*
Yorkminster Publishing Ltd. - Willowdale, ON, Canada - *BoPubDir 4, 5*
Yorkton Enterprise - Yorkton, SK, Canada - *Ed&PubIntYB 82*
Yorkton This Week - Yorkton, SK, Canada - *Ed&PubIntYB 82*
Yorktown Advertising - Cleveland, OH - *StaDirAdAg 2-84*
Yorktown Cable Co. [of De-Cal Cable Inc.] - Yorktown, TX - *Tel&CabFB 84C*
Yorktown De Witt County View - Yorktown, TX - *BaconPubCkNews 84*
Yorktown Heights North County News - Yorktown Heights, NY - *BaconPubCkNews 84*
Yorktown Industries - Addison, IL - *DirInfWP 82*
Yorktown News - Yorktown, TX - *BaconPubCkNews 84; Ed&PubIntYB 82*
Yorktown-Somers Pennysaver - Yorktown Heights, NY - *AyerDirPub 83*
Yorkunas Advertising Agency, Al - Tampa, FL - *StaDirAdAg 2-84*
Yorkview Reporter - Toronto, ON, Canada - *Ed&PubIntYB 82*
Yorkville Enquirer - Yorkville, SC - *AyerDirPub 83; Ed&PubIntYB 82*
Yorkville Kendall County Record - Yorkville, IL - *BaconPubCkNews 84; NewsDir 84*
Yorkville Telephone Cooperative Inc. - Yorkville, TN - *TelDir&BG 83-84*
Yosemite Natural History Association - Yosemite, CA - *BoPubDir 4, 5*
Yost Advertising Agency, Charles E. - Pittsburgh, PA - *StaDirAdAg 2-84*
Yost Associates Inc., Mary - New York, NY - *LitMarPl 83, 84*
You Can Make It Enterprises - Novato, CA - *BoPubDir 4 Sup, 5*
Yough Television Co. Inc. [of Belisle Enterprises] - Friendsville, MD - *BrCabYB 84; Tel&CabFB 84C*
Young Agency, Katherine - New York, NY - *LitMarPl 83, 84; MagIndMarPl 82-83*
Young Ambassador [of The Good News Broadcasting Association Inc.] - Lincoln, NE - *ArtMar 84; MagIndMarPl 82-83; WritMar 84*
Young & Alive [of Christian Record Braille Foundation Inc.] - Lincoln, NE - *WritMar 84*
Young & Associates Inc. - Los Angeles, CA - *Tel&CabFB 84C*
Young & Associates Inc. - Rockville, MD - *DirPRFirms 83; InterCabHB 3*
Young & Co., Arthur - Milwaukee, WI - *DirInfWP 82*
Young & Roehr Inc. - Portland, OR - *StaDirAdAg 2-84*
Young & Rubicam - New York, NY - *AdAge 3-28-84, 6-25-84; ArtMar 84; Br 1-23-84; BrCabYB 84; HomeVid&CabYB 82-83; StaDirAdAg 2-84; TelAl 83, 84*
Young & Rubicam/Dentsu Inc. - New York, NY - *StaDirAdAg 2-84*
Young & Rubicam Ltd. - Montreal, PQ, Canada - *ArtMar 84*
Young & Rubicam/Los Angeles - Los Angeles, CA - *ArtMar 84*
Young & Rubicam/Zemp Inc. - St. Petersburg, FL - *BrCabYB 84; DirPRFirms 83; StaDirAdAg 2-84*
Young Beau Music - *See* Merit Music Corp.
Young Byrom Inc. - Hinsdale, IL - *DirPRFirms 83*
Young Children - Washington, DC - *MagIndMarPl 82-83*
Young China Daily News - San Francisco, CA - *Ed&PubIntYB 82; NewsDir 84*
Young Corp., Curtis - Pennsauken, NJ - *DirInfWP 82*
Young Crusader, The - Evanston, IL - *WritMar 84*
Young, Donald - New York, NY - *LitMarPl 83, 84*
Young Electronics Service - College Station, TX - *WhoWMicrocom 83*
Young, G. F. - Ft. Nelson, BC, Canada - *BoPubDir 4, 5*
Young, George - Halifax, NS, Canada - *BoPubDir 4, 5*
Young Inc., Adam - New York, NY - *TelAl 83, 84*
Young, Ione D. - Austin, TX - *BoPubDir 4, 5*
Young, Joy - Detroit, MI - *BoPubDir 4, 5*
Young Judaean [of Hadassah Zionist Youth Commission] - New York, NY - *ArtMar 84; WritMar 84*
Young, Laura S. - New York, NY - *LitMarPl 83, 84*
Young Miss [of Gruner & Jahr USA Inc.] - New York, NY - *BaconPubCkMag 84; Folio 83; MagDir 84; MagIndMarPl 82-83; WritMar 84*
Young Parents' Book Club [Div. of HBJ Communications & Services] - Stamford, CT - *LitMarPl 83*
Young Peoples' Logo Association - Richardson, TX - *MicrocomMPl 84*
Young Productions, Bill - Houston, TX - *AvMarPl 83*
Young Productions Inc. - Bellingham, WA - *Ed&PubIntYB 82*
Young Scientist - New York, NY - *BaconPubCkMag 84; MagIndMarPl 82-83*
Young Women's Christian Association of Canada [Aff. of World YWCA] - Toronto, ON, Canada - *BoPubDir 4, 5*
Young Women's Christian Organization - Baton Rouge, LA - *BoPubDir 4 Sup, 5*
Youngheart Records - Los Angeles, CA - *BillIntBG 83-84*
Younghusband Co. Inc. - Pasadena, CA - *BoPubDir 4, 5*
Youngjohn Publications - Santa Rosa, CA - *BoPubDir 5*
Youngreen, Gustav Russ - Winlaw, BC, Canada - *LitMarPl 83, 84*
Youngreen, Penny Emily - Winlaw, BC, Canada - *LitMarPl 84*
Young's Cable TV Corp. - Londonderry, VT - *BrCabYB 84; Tel&CabFB 84C*
Young's Cable TV Corp. - Springfield, VT - *BrCabYB 84 p.D-311*
Young's Cable TV Corp. - Windsor, VT - *Tel&CabFB 84C*
Young's Community Television Corp. - Winchendon, MA - *BrCabYB 84*
Young's Community Television Corp. - Springfield, VT - *BrCabYB 84; Tel&CabFB 84C p.1714*
Youngstar Productions - Hollywood, CA - *ArtMar 84*
Youngstown Buckeye Review [of Williams Publishing Co. Inc.] - Youngstown, OH - *BaconPubCkNews 84; NewsDir 84*
Youngstown Catholic Exponent - Youngstown, OH - *NewsDir 84*
Youngstown Graphics - Youngstown, OH - *LitMarPl 83, 84*
Youngstown MDS Inc. - New York, NY - *Tel&CabFB 84C*
Youngstown Vindicator - Youngstown, OH - *BaconPubCkNews 84; LitMarPl 83; NewsDir 84*
Youngsville TV Corp. - Youngsville, PA - *BrCabYB 84; Tel&CabFB 84C*
Youngsville TV Inc. - Youngsville, NY - *BrCabYB 84; Tel&CabFB 84C*
Your Church [of Religious Publishing Co.] - King of Prussia, PA - *BaconPubCkMag 84; MagIndMarPl 82-83; WritMar 84*
Your Church - Norristown, PA - *MagDir 84*
Your Family Shopper - Chippewa Falls, WI - *AyerDirPub 83*
Your Fashion Image - New York, NY - *Ed&PubIntYB 82*
Your Good Health Review & Digest - New Canaan, CT - *BaconPubCkMag 84*
Your Health [Div. of Our Baby's First Seven Years] - Chicago, IL - *AvMarPl 83*
Your Health & Fitness - Highland Park, IL - *ArtMar 84*

Your Home [of Meridian Publishing] - Ogden, UT - *ArtMar 84; WritMar 84*
Your Life & Health - Washington, DC - *MagDir 84*
Your Life & Health - Hagerstown, MD - *WritMar 84*
Your Patient & Cancer - Roslyn Heights, NY - *BaconPubCkMag 84; MagIndMarPl 82-83*
Your Virginia State Trooper Magazine - Springfield, VA - *ArtMar 84; WritMar 84*
Yourdon Press [Div. of Yourdon Inc.] - New York, NY - *BoPubDir 4, 5; LitMarPl 83, 84*
Youth Leader, The - Springfield, MO - *WritMar 84*
Youth Liberation Press Inc. - Brooklyn, NY - *BoPubDir 4, 5*
Youth Publications - Indianapolis, IN - *BoPubDir 4, 5*
Youth Research Institute - New York, NY - *Ed&PubIntYB 82*
Youth Research Institute - *See* Rand Youth Poll-Youth Research Institute
Ypsilanti Press [of Harte-Hanks Communications Inc.] - Ypsilanti, MI - *BaconPubCkNews 84; Ed&PubIntYB 82; NewsDir 84*
Yreka Siskiyou Daily News [of Thomson Newspapers Inc.] - Yreka, CA - *NewsDir 84*
Yreka TV Co. [of Cal-Nor Cableview Inc.] - Yreka, CA - *BrCabYB 84*
YU-TV - Spokane, WA - *BrCabYB 84*
Yucaipa & Calimesa News-Mirror [of Brehm Communications Inc.] - Yucaipa, CA - *AyerDirPub 83; BaconPubCkNews 84; Ed&PubIntYB 82; NewsDir 84*
Yucaipa Software - Yucaipa, CA - *MicrocomMPl 83, 84; WhoWMicrocom 83*
Yucca Valley Hi-Desert Star - Yucca Valley, CA - *BaconPubCkNews 84; NewsDir 84*
Yuchi Pines Institute - Seale, AL - *BoPubDir 4*
Yuchi Pines Institute/Thrash Publications - Seale, AL - *BoPubDir 5*
Yuggoth Music Co. - Beverly Hills, CA - *BillIntBG 83-84*
Yugoslav Center for Technical & Scientific Documentation - Belgrade, Yugoslavia - *EISS 83*
Yuguchi & Krogstad - Los Angeles, CA - *AdAge 3-28-84; StaDirAdAg 2-84*
Yuk, Yak Inc. - Harvard, MA - *BoPubDir 4, 5*
Yukon Bibliography [of University of Alberta] - Edmonton, AB, Canada - *CompReadDB 82; DataDirOnSer 84; DirOnDB Spring 84*
Yukon Cablevision Inc. [of Multimedia Cablevision Inc.] - Yukon, OK - *Tel&CabFB 84C*
Yukon News - Whitehorse, YT, Canada - *AyerDirPub 83; Ed&PubIntYB 82*
Yukon Review - Yukon, OK - *BaconPubCkNews 84; NewsDir 84*
Yukon Review & The Mustang Mirror - Yukon, OK - *Ed&PubIntYB 82*
Yukon Telephone Co. Inc. - Anchorage, AK - *TelDir&BG 83-84*
Yukon-Waltz Telephone Co. - Yukon, PA - *TelDir&BG 83-84*
Yulish Associates, Charles - New York, NY - *DirPRFirms 83*
Yuma Daily Sun [of Sun Printing Co.] - Yuma, AZ - *BaconPubCkNews 84; Ed&PubIntYB 82; NewsDir 84*
Yuma Pioneer - Yuma, CO - *BaconPubCkNews 84; Ed&PubIntYB 82; NewsDir 84*
Yuma Valley-Foothills News - Yuma, AZ - *BaconPubCkNews 84*
Yunak - Toronto, ON, Canada - *Ed&PubIntYB 82*
Yushodo Film Publications Ltd. - Tokyo, Japan - *MicroMarPl 82-83*
Yuste Publicidad [of the Univas Network] - Buenos Aires, Argentina - *StaDirAdAg 2-84*

Z

Z & W Public Relations/Public Affairs - Chicago, IL - *StaDirAdAg 2-84*
Z Channel - Los Angeles, CA - *CabTVPrDB 83; TelAl 83*
Z Press Inc. - Calais, VT - *BoPubDir 4, 5; LitMarPl 84*
ZA-TRO - New York, NY - *MicrocomMPl 83*
Zabin, James Barton - Baltimore, MD - *ArtMar 84*
Zachary & Front Inc. - New York, NY - *DirPRFirms 83*
Zachary & Sanders Inc. - New York, NY - *MagIndMarPl 82-83*
Zachary Plainsman - *See* Louisiana Suburban Press
Zachary Plainsman-News - Zachary, LA - *NewsDir 84*
Zachry Associates Inc. - Abilene, TX - *AvMarPl 83; Tel&CabFB 84C*
Zachry Publications - Abilene, TX - *BoPubDir 4, 5*
Zacks & Perrier - New York, NY - *AvMarPl 83*
Zacks Fundamentals - Chicago, IL - *DirOnDB Spring 84*
Zacks Investment Research - Chicago, IL - *DataDirOnSer 84*
Zadek & Associates Inc., B. - Bethesda, MD - *DirMarMP 83; StaDirAdAg 2-84*
Zadek & Associates Inc., Leonard - Washington, DC - *DirPRFirms 83*
Zagoren Group Inc. - Great Neck, NY - *StaDirAdAg 2-84*
Zahir - New Sharon, ME - *LitMag&SmPr 83-84*
Zahn & Associates Inc., Leonard - Great Neck, NY - *DirPRFirms 83*
Zajednicar - Pittsburgh, PA - *Ed&PubIntYB 82*
Zalo Publications & Services Inc. - Bloomington, IN - *BoPubDir 4, 5*
Zam & Kirshner & Geller Inc. - Great Neck, NY - *StaDirAdAg 2-84*
Zampelli TV - Lewistown, PA - *Tel&CabFB 84C p.1714*
Zampelli TV - McVeytown, PA - *BrCabYB 84*
Z.A.N. Press - Thornhill, ON, Canada - *BoPubDir 4, 5*
Zanel Publications - Tahoe Paradise, CA - *BoPubDir 4, 5*
Zaner-Bloser [Aff. of Highlights for Children] - Columbus, OH - *BoPubDir 4, 5; DirMarMP 83; LitMarPl 84; MicrocomMPl 84*
Zanes & Associates Inc. - Ft. Lee, NJ - *HBIndAd&MS 82-83; IntDirMarRes 83*
Zanesville Muskingum Advertiser - Zanesville, OH - *AyerDirPub 83*
Zanesville Times Recorder [of Thomson Newspapers] - Zanesville, OH - *BaconPubCkNews 84; NewsDir 84*
Zapata Microsystems - Garland, TX - *MicrocomMPl 83*
Zappa Music Inc., Frank - *See* Open End Music
Zaria Publications Inc. - London, ON, Canada - *BoPubDir 4, 5*
Zartscorp Inc. Books - New York, NY - *LitMag&SmPr 83-84*
Zatt & Co., Sol - New York, NY - *DirPRFirms 83*
Zauber Publishing - Dallas, TX - *BaconPubCkNews 84*
Zavala County Sentinel - Crystal City, TX - *AyerDirPub 83; Ed&PubIntYB 82*
Zavalla Herald - Huntington, TX - *Ed&PubIntYB 82*
Zawinul Music - *See* Gopam Enterprises Inc.
ZDDB [of Demographic Research Co. Inc.] - Santa Monica, CA - *DataDirOnSer 84*
ZDE - Frankfurt, West Germany - *DirOnDB Spring 84*
Ze Records - New York, NY - *BillIntBG 83-84*
Zearing Tri-County News - Zearing, IA - *BaconPubCkNews 84*
Zebra Books [Subs. of Norfolk Publishing Co.] - New York, NY - *LitMarPl 83, 84; WritMar 84*
Zebra Computer Products Inc. - Santa Monica, CA - *MicrocomMPl 84*
Zebulon Pike County Journal & Reporter - Zebulon, GA - *BaconPubCkNews 84*
Zebulon Record - Zebulon, NC - *AyerDirPub 83; BaconPubCkNews 84; Ed&PubIntYB 82*
Zechman & Associates Advertising Inc. - Chicago, IL - *AdAge 3-28-84; StaDirAdAg 2-84*
Zeckendorf Associates Inc., Susan - New York, NY - *LitMarPl 83, 84*
ZED Books [Div. of Zephyr Engineering Design] - Burbank, CA - *LitMarPl 83*
Zeda Computers International Ltd. - Provo, UT - *WhoWMicrocom 83*
Zeeland Flashes - Allegan, MI - *AyerDirPub 83*
Zeeland Record - Zeeland, MI - *BaconPubCkNews 84; Ed&PubIntYB 82*
Zeff Associates Inc., Roy - Skokie, IL - *StaDirAdAg 2-84*
Zeitgeist - Fresno, CO - *MicrocomMPl 84*
Zeitlin Periodicals Co. Inc. - Los Angeles, CA - *MagIndMarPl 82-83*
Zelienpole Butler County News - *See* News-Record Div. [of News Printing Co.]
Zell Publishers, Hans - Oxford, England - *LitMag&SmPr 83-84*
Zellan Enterprises Ltd. - New York, NY - *AvMarPl 83*
Zeller & Letica Inc. - New York, NY - *LitMarPl 83, 84; MagIndMarPl 82-83*
Zeller Inc., Alvin B. - New York, NY - *LitMarPl 83, 84; MagIndMarPl 82-83*
Zellerbach Paper Co. - South San Francisco, CA - *LitMarPl 83, 84*
Zelman Studios Ltd. - Brooklyn, NY - *ArtMar 84; AvMarPl 83; WritMar 84*
Zelot [of Bactrianus Enterprises] - Asker, Norway - *LitMag&SmPr 83-84*
Zelot Press, The - Vandergrift, PA - *LitMag&SmPr 83-84*
Zemp & Associates Inc. Public Relations, W. M. - *See* Young & Rubicam/Zemp Inc.
Zen-On - *See* European American Music Corp.
Zen Tek - Murray, UT - *MicrocomMPl 84*
Zena Micro Engineering Inc. - Puyallup, WA - *WhoWMicrocom 83*
Zenda Telephone Co. Inc. - Zenda, KS - *TelDir&BG 83-84*
Zendex Corp. - Dublin, CA - *WhoWMicrocom 83*
Zenger Productions - Culver City, CA - *AvMarPl 83*
Zenger Publishing Co. - Washington, DC - *BoPubDir 4, 5*
Zenith - Glenview, IL - *VideoDir 82-83*
Zenith CATV Group - Glenview, IL - *HomeVid&CabYB 82-83*
Zenith Data Systems [Subs. of Zenith Radio Corp.] - Glenview, IL - *DataDirSup 7-83; DirInfWP 82; InfIndMarPl 83; MicrocomMPl 83, 84; Top100Al 83; WhoWMicrocom 83*

Zenith/db Studios [Div. of Coken & Coken Inc.] - Chicago, IL - *AvMarPl 83*
Zenith Radio Corp. - Chicago, IL - *BillIntBG 83-84; HomeVid&CabYB 82-83*
Zenith Radio Corp. - Glenview, IL - *CabTVFinDB 83; ElecNews 7-25-83; TelAl 83, 84*
Zenovia House - Hamilton, ON, Canada - *BoPubDir 4, 5*
Zenrad Controls Co. - Santa Barbara, CA - *MicrocomMPl 84*
Zentec Corp. - Santa Clara, CA - *DataDirSup 7-83; InfIndMarPl 83; WhoWMicrocom 83*
Zentralarchiv fur Empirische Sozialforschung [of Universitat zu Koln] - Cologne, West Germany - *InfIndMarPl 83*
Zentralblatt fur Mathematik/Mathematics Abstracts [of Fachinformationszentrum Energie Physik Mathematik GmbH] - Berlin, West Germany - *OnBibDB 3*
Zentralstelle Dokumentation Elektrotechnik [of Fachinformationszentrum Technik eV] - Frankfurt, West Germany - *CompReadDB 82; InfIndMarPl 83*
Zentralstelle fur Agrardokumentation & Information - Bonn, West Germany - *InfIndMarPl 83*
Zephr Services - Pittsburgh, PA - *MicrocomMPl 84*
Zephyr [of Great South Bay Poetry Co-Op] - Central Islip, NY - *LitMag&SmPr 83-84*
Zephyr Communications Inc. - Westfield, NJ - *Tel&CabFB 84C*
Zephyr Media Productions - Ft. Thomas, KY - *LitMarPl 83, 84*
Zephyr Press [Aff. of Aspect Inc.] - Somerville, MA - *BoPubDir 4 Sup, 5; LitMag&SmPr 83-84*
Zephyr Publishers - Miami, FL - *BoPubDir 4, 5*
Zephyrhills News - Zephyrhills, FL - *BaconPubCkNews 84; Ed&PubIntYB 82; NewsDir 84*
Zephyrhills Sun - Zephyrhills, FL - *Ed&PubIntYB 82*
Zeplin Productions - New York, NY - *AvMarPl 83*
Zeppelin Publishing Co. [Aff. of Regent House Publishers] - Hollywood, CA - *BoPubDir 4*
Zeppelin Publishing Co. [Aff. of Regent House Publishers] - Baton Rouge, LA - *BoPubDir 5*
Zern, Gordon - Briarcliff Manor, NY - *HBIndAd&MS 82-83*
Zero One - London, England - *LitMag&SmPr 83-84*
Zeta Publishers Co. - Corona del Mar, CA - *BoPubDir 4, 5*
Zeta Software - Greenville, SC - *MicrocomMPl 83*
Zgoda - Chicago, IL - *Ed&PubIntYB 82*
Zhinochy Svit - Toronto, ON, Canada - *Ed&PubIntYB 82*
Zhivago Advertising & Public Relations - Palo Alto, CA - *StaDirAdAg 2-84*
Zia Cine Inc. - Santa FE, NM - *AvMarPl 83*
Zia Research Associates - Albuquerque, NM - *IntDirMarRes 83*
Ziatech Corp. - San Luis Obispo, CA - *MicrocomMPl 84*
Ziegler, Diskant Inc. - Los Angeles, CA - *LitMarPl 83, 84*
Ziegler, George - New York, NY - *LitMarPl 83, 84*
Ziegler Inc., John - New York, NY - *HBIndAd&MS 82-83*
Zielinski Productions - Huntington Beach, CA - *AvMarPl 83*
Ziesing Bros. Publishing Co. - Willimantic, CT - *LitMag&SmPr 83-84*
Ziff Corp. - New York, NY - *KnowInd 83*
Ziff-Davis Magazine Network, The - *Folio 83*
Ziff-Davis Publishing Co. [of Ziff Corp.] - New York, NY - *AdAge 6-28-84; DirMarMP 83; InfoS 83-84; MagIndMarPl 82-83*
Zigman-Joseph-Skeen - Milwaukee, WI - *ArtMar 84; DirPRFirms 83*
Zigner & Associates Inc., Gloria - Newport Beach, CA - *ArtMar 84; DirPRFirms 83; LitMarPl 83; MagIndMarPl 82-83*
Ziko & Associates, Atef - Houston, TX - *EISS 83*
Zilberstein, Georges J. - Waltham, MA - *MagIndMarPl 82-83*
Zilog Inc. [Aff. of Exxon Enterprises] - Campbell, CA - *DataDirSup 7-83; DirInfWP 82; WhoWMicrocom 83*
Zilog Inc. [Subs. of Exxon Enterprises] - Cupertino, CA - *WhoWMicrocom 83*
Zim Records - Jericho, NY - *BillIntBG 83-84*
Ziment Associates Inc. - New York, NY - *IntDirMarRes 83*
Zimmerman Advertising Agency - Omaha, NE - *StaDirAdAg 2-84*
Zimmerman Associates Inc., Walter J. - Rockville Centre, NY - *StaDirAdAg 2-84*
Zimmerman, Gary - Brooklyn, NY - *BoPubDir 4, 5*
Zimmerman, John D. - Six Mile Run, PA - *Tel&CabFB 84C p.1714*
Zimmerman Rights & Permissions, Barbara - New York, NY - *LitMarPl 83, 84; MagIndMarPl 82-83*
Zimmermann & Co., A. M. - San Francisco, CA - *BoPubDir 5*
Zimmermann & Sons Inc. - Burlington, WI - *BaconPubCkNews 84*
Zimmermann Marketing Inc. - New York, NY - *DirMarMP 83*
Zimmerman's Electronics - Broad Top, PA - *BrCabYB 84; Tel&CabFB 84C*
Zimmersmith/Radio Ranch - Dallas, TX - *HBIndAd&MS 82-83*
Zinc - New York, NY - *BaconPubCkMag 84*
Zinc Forecast - Bala Cynwyd, PA - *DirOnDB Spring 84*
Zinc Institute Inc. - New York, NY - *BoPubDir 5*
Zinc, Lead, & Cadmium Abstracts [of Pergamon International Information Corp.] - McLean, VA - *DataDirOnSer 84*
Zinc, Lead, & Cadmium Abstracts - London, England - *DirOnDB Spring 84*
Zinger & Associates Inc., Gloria - Newport Beach, CA - *LitMarPl 84*
Zink Inc., J. - Manhattan Beach, CA - *BoPubDir 5*
Zintz, Walter - Walnut Creek, CA - *BoPubDir 4, 5*
Zion-Benton News [of Northeastern Illinois Publishing Co.] - Zion, IL - *AyerDirPub 83; BaconPubCkNews 84; Ed&PubIntYB 82; NewsDir 84*
Zion Natural History Association [Aff. of Zion National Park] - Springdale, UT - *BoPubDir 4, 5*
Zion Television Cable Co. - Walker Township, PA - *BrCabYB 84; Tel&CabFB 84C*
Zionsville Eagle - Indianapolis, IN - *Ed&PubIntYB 82*
Zionsville Eagle - *See* Topic Newspapers Inc.
Zionsville Main Street - Zionsville, IN - *Ed&PubIntYB 82*
Zionsville Times - Zionsville, IN - *Ed&PubIntYB 82*
Zionsville Times & Main Street - Zionsville, IN - *BaconPubCkNews 84*
Ziontalis Book [Div. of Ziontalis Manufacturing Co. Inc.] - New York, NY - *LitMarPl 83, 84*
Zip Along Associates Inc. - Oceanside, NY - *LitMarPl 83, 84*
Zip-Call Inc. - Brighton, MA - *Tel&CabFB 84C*
Zip Code Demographic Data Base [of Demographic Research Co.] - Santa Monica, CA - *DBBus 82; DirOnDB Spring 84*
Zip Magazine [of North American Publishing Co.] - New York, NY - *DirMarMP 83; MagDir 84; MagIndMarPl 82-83; WritMar 84*
Zip Magazine - Philadelphia, PA - *ArtMar 84*
Zip/Target Marketing Magazine - New York, NY - *BaconPubCkMag 84*
Zipco Inc. - Denver, CO - *MicrocomMPl 84*
Zipp-Zapp Records Corp. - Joppatowne, MD - *BillIntBG 83-84*
Zipporah Films Inc. - Boston, MA - *AvMarPl 83*
ZIPSAN Systems Inc. - New York, NY - *LitMarPl 84*
ZIPWTHR [of Berkeley Solar Group] - Berkeley, CA - *DataDirOnSer 84; DirOnDB Spring 84*
Zircon International Inc. - Campbell, CA - *MicrocomMPl 84*
Zirker, Lorette - Sunspot, NM - *LitMarPl 83*
Zirzow, Delmore - Viroqua, WI - *Tel&CabFB 84C p.1714*
Zitel Corp. - San Jose, CA - *WhoWMicrocom 83*
Ziv International - Bel Air, CA - *BillIntBG 83-84; Tel&CabFB 84C*
Ziv International - Los Angeles, CA - *TelAl 84*
Zivi, Broitman & Kopelman Inc. - Chicago, IL - *StaDirAdAg 2-84*
Ziyad Inc. - Denville, NJ - *DirInfWP 82*
Zizi Press - New York, NY - *BoPubDir 4, 5*
ZM Squared - Cinnaminson, NJ - *ArtMar 84; AvMarPl 83*
Znarg Music - *See* Largo Music Inc.
Zoe Publications - Geneva, IL - *BoPubDir 4, 5*
Zoetrope Studios - Hollywood, CA - *TelAl 83, 84*
Zolnerzak, Robert - Brooklyn, NY - *LitMarPl 83, 84*
Zolotow Books, Charlotte - *See* Harper & Row (Junior Books Group)
Zomba Enterprises Inc. - *See* Participation Music Inc.
Zondervan Corp. - Grand Rapids, MI - *BillIntBG 83-84; DirMarMP 83; KnowInd 83; LitMarPl 83, 84; WritMar 84*
Zondervan Fiesta Corp. - *See* Zondervan Corp.
Zondervan Music Publishers - *See* Zondervan Corp.
Zondervan Records [Div. of Zondervan Corp.] - Grand Rapids, MI - *BillIntBG 83-84*
Zone - New York, NY - *BoPubDir 4, 5*
Zoological Record [of BioSciences Information Service] - Philadelphia, PA - *MagDir 84*

Zoological Record - Boston Spa, England - *OnBibDB 3*
Zoological Record [of BIOSIS U.K. Ltd.] - Wetherby, England - *EISS 83*
Zoological Record Online [of Biosciences Information Service] - Philadelphia, PA - *DataDirOnSer 84; DirOnDB Spring 84*
ZOOM Telephonics - Boston, MA - *DataDirSup 7-83*
Zoonooz - San Diego, CA - *MagIndMarPl 82-83*
Zornicka - Middletown, PA - *Ed&PubIntYB 82*
Zow Records - New York, NY - *BillIntBG 83-84*
Zozo Cable TV - Carrizozo, NM - *BrCabYB 84*
Zubal Inc., John T. - Cleveland, OH - *BoPubDir 5; MagIndMarPl 82-83*
Zubal, John T./Zubal & Dole - Cleveland, OH - *BoPubDir 4*
Zubi Advertising Services Inc. - Miami, FL - *StaDirAdAg 2-84*
Zucker, Irwin - Hollywood, CA - *DirPRFirms 83; LitMarPl 83, 84; MagIndMarPl 82-83*
Zucker, Marjorie B. - New York, NY - *BoPubDir 4, 5*
Zuckerman Public Relations/Advertising - Tustin, CA - *DirPRFirms 83*
Zuckerman Research Inc. - Trumbull, CT - *IntDirMarRes 83*
Zumbrota News - Zumbrota, MN - *BaconPubCkNews 84; Ed&PubIntYB 82*
Zumbrota Telephone Co. - Zumbrota, MN - *TelDir&BG 83-84*
Zwiazkowiec - Toronto, ON, Canada - *Ed&PubIntYB 82*
Zwiren & Wagner Advertising Inc. - Chicago, IL - *AdAge 3-28-84; StaDirAdAg 2-84*
Zyga Magazine Assemblage [of Zyga Multimedia Research] - Oakland, CA - *LitMag&SmPr 83-84*
Zyga Multimedia Research - Oakland, CA - *BoPubDir 5; LitMag&SmPr 83-84*
Zylke & Affiliates Inc. - Glenview, IL - *StaDirAdAg 2-84*
Zylke Public Relations [Div. of Zylke & Affiliates Inc.] - Glenview, IL - *DirPRFirms 83*
Zylstra Communications Corp. - Yankton, SD - *BrCabYB 84 p.D-311; Tel&CabFB 84C p.1714*
Zylstra Estate, Roger E. - Yankton, SD - *Tel&CabFB 84C p.1714*
Zylstra-United Cable TV Co. - Shakopee, MN - *Tel&CabFB 84C*
Zypcom - Boise, ID - *MicrocomMPl 84*
Zytron - Menlo Park, CA - *DataDirSup 7-83*
Zzyzx Records - Sun Valley, CA - *BillIntBG 83-84*